CHILTON'S AUTO REPAIR MANUAL 1982-1989

Editor-In-Chief	Kerry A. Freeman, S.A.E.
Managing Editor	Dean F. Morgantini, S.A.E.
Managing Editor	John H. Weise, S.A.E.
Assistant Managing Editor	David H. Lee, A.S.E., S.A.E.
Senior Editor	Richard J. Rivele, S.A.E.
Senior Editor	W. Calvin Settle, Jr., S.A.E.
Project Manager	Wayne A. Eiffes, A.S.E., S.A.E.
Editorial Staff	John M. Baxter, S.A.E.
	Lawrence C. Braun, S.A.E., A.S.C.
	Dennis Carroll
	Peter M. Conti, Jr.
	Nick D'Andrea
	Ken Grabowski, A.S.E.
	Martin J. Gunther
	Robert McAnally
	Michael J. Randazzo
	Richard T. Smith
	Larry E. Stiles
	Anthony Tortorici, A.S.E., S.A.E.
	Ron Webb
Production Manager	John J. Cantwell
Art & Production Coordinator	Robin S. Miller
Supervisor Mechanical Paste-up	Margaret A. Stoner
Mechanical Artist	Cynthia Fiore
	John A. Duncan

TL 152 C525 1989

OFFICERS

President	Lawrence A. Fornasieri
Vice President & General Manager	John P. Kushnerick

CHILTON BOOK COMPANY

ONE OF THE ABC PUBLISHING COMPANIES, A PART OF CAPITAL CITIES/ABC, INC.

Manufactured in USA
© 1988 Chilton Book Company
Chilton Way Radnor, Pa. 19089
ISBN 0-8019-7834-3
ISSN 0069-3634
Library of Congress Card Catalog No.76-648878

1234567890   7654321098

CAR MODELS

TABLE OF CONTENTS

Car Sections

Unit Repair Sections

INDEX

Section No. and Name	AMC./Jeep-Eagle	Chrysler FWD	Chrysler RWD	Ford FWD	Ford RWD	Ford Festiva	Taurus/Sable	Mercury Tracer	Buick RWD	Cadillac RWD	Corsica/Beretta	Chevrolet Corvette	Chevrolet Nova	Chevrolet RWD
	1	2	3	4	5	6	7	8	9	10	11	12	13	14
SERIAL NUMBER ID	1	1	1	1	1	1	1	1	1	1	1	1	1	1
SPECIFICATION CHARTS	2	2	2	2	2	1	1	2	2	2	1	2	2	2
FIRING ORDERS	3	4	4	4	5	2	3	3	6	3	2	3	2	4
TUNE-UP PROCEDURES	9	16	15	15	24	4	7	6	17	8	5	7	6	17
Ignition Timing	9	16	15	15	24	4	7	6	17	8	5	7	6	17
Valve Lash	9	17	15	16	25	4	8	6	18	9	5	7	6	18
Idle Speed & Mixture	10	19	15	17	25	5	8	6	18	9	5	7	7	18
ENGINE ELECTRICAL	13	22	16	23	27	5	10	7	19	10	5	9	10	21
Distributor	13	22	16	23	27	5	10	7	19	10	5	9	10	21
Alternator	13	23	17	24	28	6	10	7	20	10	5	9	11	21
Voltage Regulator	14	24	18	24	28	—	11	7	20	—	6	—	11	—
Starter	14	24	18	24	28	7	12	8	20	11	6	10	12	22
ENGINE MECHANICAL	14	25	18	25	30	7	12	8	21	11	6	11	12	22
Engine	14	25	18	25	30	7	12	8	21	11	6	11	12	22
Cylinder Head	17	27	19	27	31	8	13	10	21	12	7	11	13	23
Rocker Arms/Shafts	19	29	20	30	32	8	15	10	22	12	8	12	16	24
Intake Manifold	21	30	21	31	32	9	17	11	22	12	9	13	16	25
Exhaust Manifold	23	32	21	34	36	9	19	11	23	13	9	14	16	27
Combination Manifold	—	33	21	—	—	—	—	—	—	—	—	—	17	—
Turbocharger	—	33	—	36	36	—	—	—	23	—	—	—	—	—
Front Cover	24	34	21	36	38	10	21	12	25	14	10	15	171	27
Timing Chain & Sprocket	25	36	22	38	39	—	23	—	25	14	11	16	—	27
Timing Belt & Tensioner	26	38	—	40	40	10	—	12	—	—	—	—	19	—
Timing Sprockets	—	40	—	—	—	11	—	13	—	—	—	—	19	27
Camshaft	27	43	23	41	41	12	26	13	26	14	12	16	20	28
Piston & Connecting Rod	29	45	24	42	42	12	27	14	26	15	12	16	21	29
ENGINE LUBRICATION	29	45	24	47	46	13	28	14	26	15	12	17	21	29
Oil Pan	29	45	24	47	46	13	28	14	26	15	12	17	21	29
Rear Main Brg Oil Seal	30	45	25	48	49	13	29	14	27	15	13	17	21	29
Oil Pump	31	46	27	49	50	14	29	14	27	15	13	18	22	30
ENGINE COOLING	32	47	27	51	51	14	30	15	27	16	13	18	22	30
Radiator	32	47	27	51	51	14	30	15	27	16	13	18	22	30
Water Pump	32	47	27	51	51	14	30	15	27	16	13	18	22	30
Thermostat	34	48	27	52	52	15	31	15	28	17	14	19	23	30
FUEL SYSTEM	34	49	28	53	52	16	32	16	28	17	14	19	24	31
Fuel Filter	35	49	28	53	52	16	33	16	29	17	15	20	24	31
Fuel Pump	35	49	28	54	53	16	33	16	29	17	15	20	24	32
Carburetor	36	50	29	55	54	17	—	17	31	18	—	—	25	33
MANUAL TRANSMISSION	36	—	—	56	—	—	—	—	—	—	—	21	—	34
MANUAL TRANSAXLE	37	50	—	58	—	17	33	17	—	—	16	—	25	—
CLUTCH	38	52	—	60	57	18	34	18	—	—	17	22	26	34
Clutch Cable	39	54	—	60	57	20	36	19	—	—	—	—	—	—
Clutch Master Cylinder	40	—	—	58	—	—	—	—	—	—	17	23	26	—
Clutch Slave Cylinder	40	—	—	58	—	—	—	—	—	—	17	23	27	—
AUTO TRANSMISSION	40	—	29	—	59	—	—	—	33	20	—	24	—	35
AUTOMATIC TRANSAXLE	42	54	—	61	—	—	36	19	—	—	18	—	27	—
TRANSFER CASE	43	—	—	63	—	—	—	—	—	—	—	—	—	—

INDEX

Section No. and Name	AMC/Jeep-Eagle	Chrysler FWD	Chrysler RWD	Ford FWD	Ford RWD	Ford Festiva	Taurus/Sable	Mercury Tracer	Buick RWD	Cadillac RWD	Corsica/Beretta	Chevrolet Corvette	Chevrolet Nova	Chevrolet RWD
	1	2	3	4	5	6	7	8	9	10	11	12	13	14
DRIVE AXLE	19	24	27	35	16	21	26	34	22	15	43	54	30	63
Halfshaft	19	–	27	–	16	21	–	–	22	15	43	54	–	63
Driveshaft & U-Joints	–	24	–	35	–	–	26	34	–	–	44	–	30	64
Rear Axle Shaft	–	–	–	35	–	–	26	34	22	–	44	–	31	65
FWD Hub, Knuckle & Brg.	19	–	28	–	17	21	–	–	–	16	45	55	–	65
FRONT SUSPENSION	20	24	29	36	18	23	27	34	22	16	45	56	32	67
Shock Absorbers	–	24	–	36	–	–	27	34	22	–	45	–	32	–
MacPherson Strut	20	–	29	–	18	23	–	–	23	16	45	56	–	67
Springs	–	24	–	36	–	–	27	34	–	–	46	–	–	–
Torsion Bars	–	–	–	–	18	–	–	34	–	–	–	–	32	–
Ball Joints	20	26	30	37	18	23	28	35	24	17	46	56	33	69
Upper Control Arms	–	26	–	38	–	–	28	36	23	17	47	–	34	–
Lower Control Arms	21	26	30	38	18	23	28	34	23	17	47	57	34	69
Front Wheel Bearings	–	27	–	38	–	22	29	36	26	–	48	58	35	–
Front Wheel Alignment	21	27	30	39	19	23	29	36	26	17	49	58	35	70
REAR SUSPENSION	21	28	31	39	19	25	29	36	27	18	49	58	35	70
Shock Absorber	21	28	–	39	19	25	29	36	–	18	49	59	35	70
MacPherson Strut	–	–	31	–	–	–	–	–	27	–	–	59	–	–
Springs	21	28	–	39	19	25	29	36	–	18	49	59	35	71
Rear Control Arms	–	29	31	39	–	–	30	36	28	–	–	–	–	71
Rear Wheel Bearings	21	29	32	–	19	25	30	37	–	19	49	–	–	72
STEERING	22	30	32	40	20	26	30	37	28	19	50	59	36	72
Steering Wheel	22	30	32	40	20	26	30	37	28	19	50	59	36	72
Turn Signal Switch	–	30	–	40	–	26	–	37	28	20	50	59	–	–
Combination Switch	22	–	33	–	20	–	30	38	–	–	–	–	36	73
Ignition Lock/Switch	22	31	33	41	20	26	31	38	29	20	51	60	37	74
Manual Steering Gear	–	32	33	41	20	27	31	–	30	20	51	61	–	75
Power Steering Gear	23	32	34	42	20	–	31	38	30	21	52	61	37	76
Power Steering Pump	24	32	34	42	21	27	32	38	–	21	53	62	38	78
Tie Rod Ends	24	33	35	43	21	27	32	39	30	21	53	63	38	78
BRAKES	24	33	35	43	21	28	32	39	30	22	54	63	39	79
Master Cylinder	24	33	35	43	21	28	33	39	30	22	54	63	39	79
Proportioning Valve	25	33	36	43	21	–	33	39	30	22	–	63	39	81
Power Brake Booster	25	33	36	43	21	28	33	39	30	22	54	63	39	81
Wheel Cylinder	25	–	36	44	21	28	33	40	–	23	54	64	39	81
Parking Brake Cable	25	34	36	44	22	28	33	40	30	23	54	64	40	81
CHASSIS ELECTRICAL	26	34	37	44	23	29	34	40	31	24	55	64	40	82
Heater Blower	26	34	37	44	23	29	34	40	31	24	55	64	40	82
Heater Core	26	34	37	44	23	30	34	40	31	24	56	65	40	83
Radio	26	36	37	44	23	30	34	41	31	24	56	66	41	83
Wiper Switch	26	36	38	45	23	30	34	41	32	24	57	66	42	84
Wiper Motor	26	36	38	45	23	30	34	41	31	25	57	66	42	84
Instrument Cluster	26	36	38	45	23	30	34	42	32	25	57	67	42	85
Headlight Switch	26	36	38	46	24	30	35	42	32	25	58	68	42	85
Stoplight Switch	26	38	38	46	24	30	35	42	32	25	58	68	42	86
Fuses & Circuit Breakers	–	38	38	46	24	30	35	42	32	25	58	68	42	86

HOW TO USE THIS MANUAL

This manual is arranged in two sections:

Car Section

Car Sections are grouped by manufacturer and arranged in alphabetical order. The text and illustrations that comprise the service procedures in each Car Section are arranged in the following order of systems and components: Charging, Starting, Ignition, Fuel, and Cooling Systems; Emission Controls, Engine, Clutch, Manual Transmission, Automatic Transmission, Driveshaft and U-Joints, Rear Axle, Jacking and Hoisting, Front Suspension, Rear Suspension, Brakes, Steering, Instrument Panel, Windshield Wipers, Radio, and Heater. Specifications are always located at the front of each section. All illustrations are located as close as possible to the pertinent text. Procedures are for all models in the particular section unless specifically noted otherwise.

Unit Repair Section

The Unit Repair Section contains troubleshooting and overhaul procedures for the major components and systems of your car, and is intended to be used in conjunction with the Car Sections. For example, if your car's engine is misfiring and you do not know the cause, use the "Troubleshooting" portion of the Unit Repair Section to find the cause and its remedy. If the cause should prove to be defective piston rings which are allowing oil to foul the spark plugs, the remedy is to overhaul the engine. Turn to the proper Car Section to find the procedure for removing the engine from the car. After you have removed the engine, turn to "Engine Rebuilding" in the Unit Repair Section and follow the steps listed there to overhaul the engine.

Most Unit Repair Sections are arranged by brands, manufacturers, or types of components rather than models of cars, and all overhaul procedures begin with the component removed from the car. The reason for this division of material is economic. The steps involved in overhauling an engine, for example, are virtually the same for all engines, but the operation of removing the engine from the car varies greatly from model to model. By combining where possible and separating where necessary, we are able to publish the maximum amount of information.

Locating Information

The Table of Contents, at the front of the book, lists the beginning of each Car and Unit Repair Section in the manual. The Car Sections are grouped by manufacturer. There is also an alphabetical listing of names of cars, so that you can find the right section quickly, even if you are not sure of the manufacturer.

To find the page number for a particular Car Section, you need only look in the Table of Contents. Once you have found the proper section, you may wish to find where specific procedures are located in that section. Turn to the Index on the following page and read across the top of the grid until you reach the number that corresponds to the car section. When the proper column has been found, read down the side column to the procedure in question. The intersection of the two columns will provide the page number for the procedure.

Safety Notice

Proper service and repair procedures are vital to the safe, reliable operation of all motor vehicles, as well as the personal safety of those performing repairs. This manual outlines procedures for servicing and repairing vehicles using safe effective methods. The procedures contain many NOTES, CAUTIONS and WARNINGS which should be followed along with standard safety procedures to eliminate the possibility of personal injury or improper service which could damage the vehicle or compromise its safety.

It is important to note that repair procedures and techniques, tools and parts for servicing motor vehicles, as well as the skill and experience of the individual performing the work may vary widely. It is not possible to anticipate all of the conceivable ways or conditions under which vehicles may be serviced, or to provide cautions as to all of the possible hazards that may result. Standard and accepted safety precautions and equipment should be used when handling toxic or flammable fluids, and safety goggles or other protection should be used during cutting, grinding, chiseling, prying, or any other process that can cause material removal or projectiles.

Some procedures require the use of tools specially designed for a specific purpose. Before substituting another tool or procedure, you must be completely satisfied that neither your personal safety nor the performance of the vehicle will be endangered.

Part Numbers

Part numbers listed in this book are not recommendations by Chilton for any product by brand name. They are references that can be used with interchange manuals and aftermarket supplier catalogs to locate each brand supplier's discrete part number.

AMC/Jeep-Eagle

Concord, Eagle, Medallion, Premier, Spirit

SERIAL NUMBER IDENTIFICATION

VEHICLE IDENTIFICATION CHART

It is important for servicing and ordering parts to be certain of the vehicle and engine identification. The VIN (vehicle identification number) is a 17 digit number visible through the windshield on the driver's side of the dash and contains the vehicle and engine identification codes. The tenth digit indicates model year and the fourth digit indicates engine code. It can be interpreted as follows:

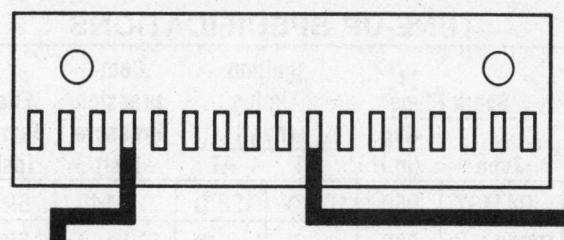

Engine Code						Model Year	
Code	Cu. In.	Liters	Cyl.	Fuel Sys.	Eng. Mfg.	Code	Year
B	151	2.5	4	2 bbl	Pontiac	C	1982
C	258	4.2	6	2 bbl	AMC	D	1983
U	150	2.5	4	1 bbl	AMC	E	1984
Z	150	2.5	4	TBI	AMC	F	1985
F	132	2.2	4	MPI	Renault	G	1986
J	182	3.0	6	MPI	Renault	H	1987
						J	1988
						K	1989

GENERAL ENGINE SPECIFICATIONS

Year	VIN	No. Cylinder Displacement cu. in. (liter)	Fuel System Type	Net Horsepower @ rpm	Net Torque @ rpm (ft.lbs.)	Bore × Stroke (in.)	Com- pression Ratio	Oil Pressure @ rpm
1982	B	4-151 (2.5)	2 bbl	110 @ 3200	134 @ 2400	4.000 × 3.000	8.3:1	36-41 @ 2000
	C	6-258 (4.2)	2 bbl	99 @ 4000	210 @ 1800	3.750 × 3.900	8.3:1	46 @ 2000
1983	B	4-151 (2.5)	2 bbl	99 @ 4000	134 @ 2400	4.000 × 3.000	8.3:1	36-41 @ 2000
	C	6-258 (4.2)	2 bbl	110 @ 3200	210 @ 1800	3.750 × 3.900	8.3:1	46 @ 2000
1984	U	4-150 (2.5)	1 bbl	83 @ 4200	116 @ 2600	3.876 × 3.188	9.2:1	40 @ 2000
	C	6-258 (4.2)	2 bbl	110 @ 3200	210 @ 1800	3.75 × 3.900	9.2:1	46 @ 2000
1985	C	6-258 (4.2)	2 bbl	110 @ 3200	210 @ 1800	3.75 × 3.900	9.2:1	46 @ 2000
1986	C	6-258 (4.2)	2 bbl	110 @ 3200	210 @ 1800	3.75 × 3.900	9.2:1	46 @ 2000
1987	C	6-258 (4.2)	2 bbl	110 @ 3200	210 @ 1800	3.75 × 3.900	9.2:1	46 @ 2000
1988–89	F	4-132 (2.2)	MPI	103 @ 5000	124 @ 2500	3.46 × 3.50	9.2:1	44 @ 3000
	Z	4-150 (2.5)	TBI	111 @ 4750	142 @ 2500	3.87 × 3.18	9.2:1	55 @ 3500
	J	6-182 (3.0)	MPI	150 @ 5000	171 @ 3750	3.66 × 2.87	9.3:1	60 @ 4000

TUNE-UP SPECIFICATIONS

Year	VIN	No. Cylinder Displacement cu. in. (liter)	Spark Plugs Type	Gap (in.)	Ignition Timing (deg.) MT	AT	Com- pression Pressure (psi)	Fuel Pump (psi)	Idle Speed (rpm) MT	AT	Valve Clearance In.	Ex.
1982	B	4-151 (2.5)	R44TSX	.060	10B①	12B②	140	6½-8	900	700	Hyd.	Hyd.
	C	6-258 (4.2)	RFN-14LY	.033	③	④	120-150	5-6½	700	600	Hyd.	Hyd.
1983	B	4-151 (2.5)	R44TSX	.060	10B①	12B②	140	6½-8	900	700	Hyd.	Hyd.
	C	6-258 (4.2)	RFN-14LY	.033	③	④	120-150	5-6½	700	600	Hyd.	Hyd.
1984	U	4-150 (2.5)	RFN14LY	.035	12B	12B	155-185	6½-8	750	750	Hyd.	Hyd.
	C	6-258 (4.2)	RFN14LY	.033	③	④	120-150	5-6½	700	600	Hyd.	Hyd.
1985	C	6-258 (4.2)	RFN14LY	.035	9B①	9B①	120-150	5-6½	900	800	Hyd.	Hyd.
1986	C	6-258 (4.2)	RFN14LY	.035	9B①	9B①	120-150	5-6½	900	800	Hyd.	Hyd.
1987	C	6-258 (4.2)	RFN14LY	.035	9B①	9B①	120-150	5-6½	900	800	Hyd.	Hyd.
1988	F	4-132 (2.2)	RS9YC	.035	⑥	⑥	⑤	34–36	800	700	.006	.008
	Z	4-150 (2.5)	RS9YC	.035	⑥	⑥	⑤	14–15	—	750	Hyd.	Hyd.
	J	6-182 (3.0)	RS9YC	.035	⑥	⑥	⑤	36–37	—	800	Hyd.	Hyd.
1989		SEE UNDERHOOD SPECIFICATIONS STICKER										

① Eagle exc. Calif.—11B
② Eagle Calif.—8B
③ Concord, Spirit—6B
   Eagle exc. Calif.—8B
   Eagle Calif.—4B
   Hi-Alt—15B
④ Concord, Spirit—6B
   Eagle exc. Calif.—8B
   Eagle Calif.—6B
   Hi-Alt—15B
⑤ The lowest reading should be no less than 75% of the highest reading.
⑥ Refer to Underhood Sticker

CAPACITIES

Year	VIN	No. Cylinder Displacement cu. in. (liter)	Engine Crankcase with Filter	without Filter	Transmission (pts.) MT	AT	Drive Axle (pts.)	Fuel Tank (gals.)	Cooling System (qts.)
1982	B①	4-151 (2.5)	4.0	3.0	4.0 ⑤	14.2	3	22	6.5
	B②	4-151 (2.5)	4.0	3.0	3.5	14.2	3 ③	22	6.5
	C①	6-258 (4.2)	5.0	4.0	4.0 ⑤	17	3	22	11 ④
	C②	6-258 (4.2)	5.0	4.0	3.5 ⑥	17	3 ③	22	14
1983	B①	4-151 (2.5)	4.0	3.0	4.0 ⑤	14.2	3	22	6.5
	B②	4-151 (2.5)	4.0	3.0	3.5 ⑥	14.2	3 ③	22	6.5
	C①	6-258 (4.2)	5.0	4.0	4.0 ⑤	17	3	22	11 ④
	C②	6-258 (4.2)	5.0	4.0	3.5 ⑥	17	3 ③	22	14
1984	U	4-150 (2.5)	5.0	4.0	3.5 ⑥	15.8	3 ③	22	10
	C	6-258 (4.2)	5.0	4.0	3.5 ⑥	17	3 ③	22	14
1985	C	6-258 (4.2)	5.0	4.0	3.5 ⑥	17	3 ③	22	14
1986	C	6-258 (4.2)	5.0	4.0	3.5 ⑥	17	3 ③	22	14
1987	C	6-258 (4.2)	5.0	4.0	3.5 ⑥	17	3 ③	22	14
1988-89	F	4-132 (2.2)	5.25	4.75	4.8	12.8	—	17	7
	Z	4-150 (2.5)	5.0	4.5	—	14.8	1.32 ⑦	17	8.6
	J	6-182 (3.0)	6.0	5.5	—	14.8	1.32 ⑦	17	8.6

① Spirit and Concord
② Eagle
③ Front axle—2.5
④ With A/C—14
⑤ 5 speed—4.5
⑥ 5 speed—4.0
⑦ Fluid change is not required for the life of the transaxle

FIRING ORDERS

NOTE: To avoid confusion, always replace spark plug wires one at a time.

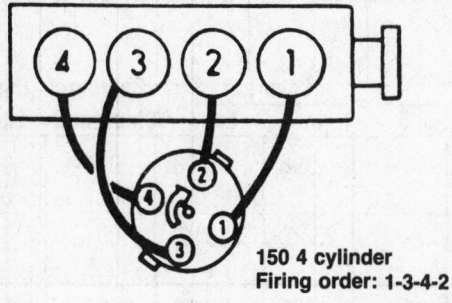

150 4 cylinder
Firing order: 1-3-4-2

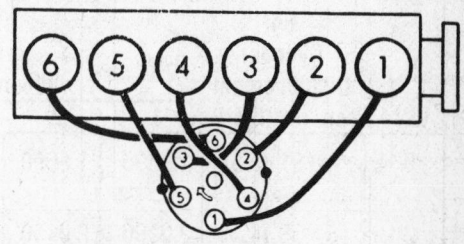

258 6 cylinder
Firing order: 1-5-3-6-2-4

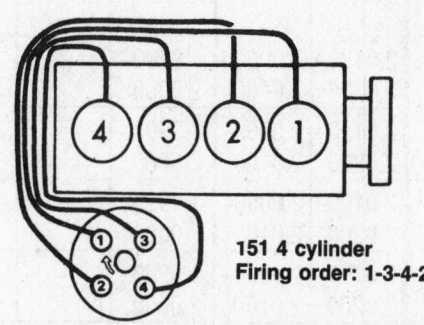

151 4 cylinder
Firing order: 1-3-4-2

FIRING ORDERS

NOTE: To avoid confusion, always replace spark plug wires one at a time.

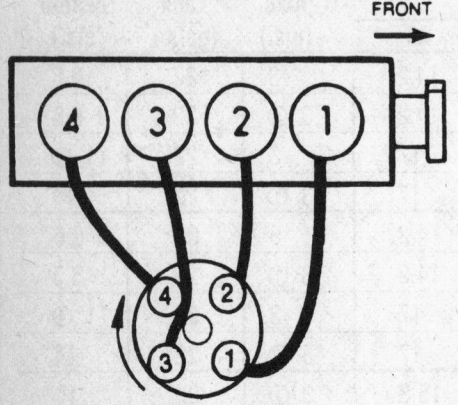

AMC 150 I4 (2.5L)
Engine firing order: 1–3–4–2
Distributor rotation: clockwise

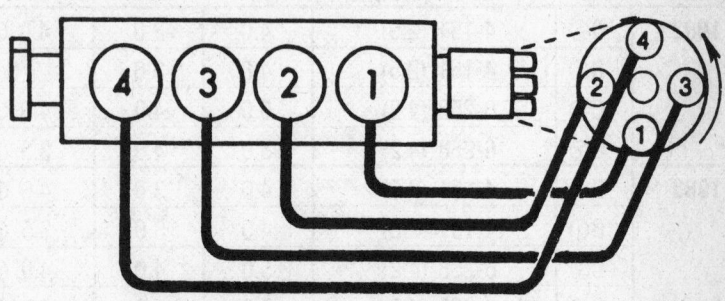

Renault 132 I4 (2.2L)
Engine firing order: 1–3–4–2
Distributor rotation: counterclockwise

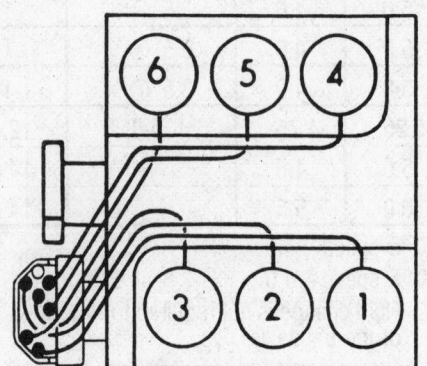

Renault 182 V6 (3.0L)
Engine firing order: 1–6–3–5–2–4
Distributor rotation: counterclockwise

CAMSHAFT SPECIFICATIONS
All measurements given in inches.

| Year | VIN | No. Cylinder Displacement cu. in. (liter) | Journal Diameter | | | | | Lobe Lift | | Bearing Clearance | Camshaft End Play |
			1	2	3	4	5	In.	Ex.		
1982	B	4-151 (2.5)	1.8690	1.8690	1.8690	–	–	.398	.398	.007–.0027	.0015–.0050
	C	6-258 (4.2)	2.0290–2.0300	2.0190–2.0200	2.0090–2.0100	1.9990–2.0000	–	.254①	.254①	.001–.003	0
1983	B	4-151 (2.5)	1.8690	1.8690	1.8690	–	–	.398	.398	.0007–.0027	.0015–.0050
	C	6-258 (4.2)	2.0290–2.0300	2.0190–2.0200	2.0090–2.0100	1.9990–2.0000	–	.254①	.254①	.001–.003	0
1984	U	4-150 (2.5)	2.0290–2.0300	2.0190–2.0200	2.0009–2.0100	1.9990–2.0000	–	.265	.265	.001–.003	0
	C	6-258 (4.2)	2.0290–2.0300	2.0190–2.0200	2.0090–2.0100	1.9990–2.0000	–	.254①	.254①	.001–.003	0
1985	C	6-258 (4.2)	2.0290–2.0300	2.0190–2.0200	2.0090–2.0100	1.9990–2.0000	–	.254①	.254①	.001–.003	0

CAMSHAFT SPECIFICATIONS
All measurements given in inches.

Year	VIN	No. Cylinder Displacement cu. in. (liter)	Journal Diameter 1	2	3	4	5	Lobe Lift In.	Ex.	Bearing Clearance	Camshaft End Play
1986	C	6-258 (4.2)	2.0290–2.0300	2.0190–2.0200	2.0090–2.0100	1.9990–2.0000	–	.254①	.254①	.001–.003	0
1987	C	6-258 (4.2)	2.0290–2.0300	2.0190–2.0200	2.0090–2.0100	1.9990–2.0000	–	.254①	.254①	.001–.003	0
1988–89	F	4-132 (2.2)	NA	NA	NA	NA	–	NA	NA	NA	.002–.005
	Z	4-150 (2.5)	2.0290–2.0300	2.0190–2.0200	2.0090–2.0100	1.9990–2.0000	–	.240	.250	.001–.003	0
	J	6-182 (3.0)	NA	NA	NA	NA	–	NA	NA	NA	.003–.0055

NA Not Available

① 2 bbl carb. – .248

CRANKSHAFT AND CONNECTING ROD SPECIFICATIONS
All measurements are given in inches.

Year	VIN	No. Cylinder Displacement cu. in. (liter)	Crankshaft Main Brg. Journal Dia.	Main Brg. Oil Clearance	Shaft End-play	Thrust on No.	Connecting Rod Journal Diameter	Oil Clearance	Side Clearance
1982	B	4-151 (2.5)	2.2988	.0005–.0022	.0035–.0085	5	2.000	.0005–.0026	.017
	C	6-258 (4.2)	2.4996–2.5001	.0010–.0025	.0015–.0065	3	2.0934–2.0955	.0010–.0030	.005–.014
1983	B	4-151 (2.5)	2.2988	.0005–.0022	.0035–.0085	5	2.000	.0005–.0026	.017
	C	60258 (4.2)	2.4998–2.5001	.0010–.0025	.0015–.0065	3	2.0934–2.0955	.0005–.0030	.005–.014
1984	V	4-150 (2.5)	2.4996–2.5001	.0005–.0022	.0015–.0060	2	2.0934–2.0955	.0010–.0030	.010–.019
	C	6-258 (4.2)	2.4996–2.5001	.0010–.0025	.0015–.0065	3	2.0934–2.0955	.0010–.0030	.005–.014
1985	C	6-258 (4.2)	2.4996–2.5001	.0010–.0025	.0015–.0065	3	2.0934–2.0955	.0010–.0030	.005–.014
1986	C	6-258 (4.2)	2.4996–2.5001	.0010–.0025	.0015–.0065	3	2.0934–2.0955	.0010–.0030	.005–.014
1987	C	6-258 (4.2)	2.4996–2.5001	.0010–.0025	.0015–.0065	3	2.0934–2.0955	.0010–.0030	.005–.014
1988–89	F	4-132 (2.2)	2.4660–2.4760	.0015–.0035	.002–.009	1	2.206–2.216	.0008–.0030	.012–.022
	Z	4-150 (2.5)	2.4996–2.5001	.0020	.0015–.0065	2	2.0934–2.0955	.0015–.0020	.010–.019
	J	6-182 (3.0)	2.7576–2.7583	.0015–.0035	.003–.010	1	2.3611–2.3618	.0008–.0030	.008–.015

VALVE SPECIFICATIONS

Year	VIN	No. Cylinder Displacement cu. in. (liter)	Seat Angle (deg.)	Face Angle (deg.)	Spring Test Pressure (lbs.)	Spring Installed Height (in.)	Stem-to-Guide Clearance (in.)		Stem Diameter (in.)	
							Intake	Exhaust	Intake	Exhaust
1982	B	4-151 (2.5)	46	45	176 @ 1.254	①	.0010–.0027	.0010–.0027	.3423	.3423
	C	6-258 (4.2)	44.5	44	195 @ 1.411	$1^{13}/_{16}$	.0010–.0030	.0010–.0030	.3720	.3720
1983	B	4-151 (2.5)	46	45	176 @ 1.254	①	.0010–.0027	.0010–.0027	.3423	.3423
	C	6-258 (4.2)	44.5	44	195 @ 1.411	$1^{13}/_{16}$	.0010–.0030	.0010–.0030	.3720	.3720
1984	U	4-150 (2.5)	44.5	44	212 @ 1.203	$1^{11}/_{32}$	.0010–.0030	.0010–.0030	.3115	.3115
	C	6-258 (4.2)	44.5	44	195 @ 1.411	$1^{13}/_{16}$	.0010–.0030	.0010–.0030	.3720	.3720
1985	C	6-258 (4.2)	44.5	44	195 @ 1.411	$1^{13}/_{16}$	.0010–.0030	.0010–.0030	.3720	.3720
1986	C	6-258 (4.2)	44.5	44	195 @ 1.411	$1^{13}/_{16}$	.0010–.0030	.0010–.0030	.3720	.3720
1987	C	6-258 (4.2)	44.5	44	195 @ 1.411	$1^{13}/_{16}$	.0010–.0030	.0010–.0030	.3720	.3720
1988–89	F	4-132 (2.2)	②	②	NA	NA	.0040	.0040	.3150	.3150
	Z	4-150 (2.5)	45	45	200 @ 1.216	$1^{11}/_{16}$	.001–.003	.001–.003	.312	.312
	J	6-182 (3.0)	45	45	155 @ 1.220	$1^{13}/_{16}$	NA	NA	.315	.315

NA Not available
① Intake–2.057 in.
   Exhaust–1.730 in.
② Intake–60 degrees
   Exhaust–45 degrees

PISTON AND RING SPECIFICATIONS
All measurments are given in inches.

Year	VIN	No. Cylinder Displacement 00002n. (liter)	Piston Clearance	Ring Gap			Ring Side Clearance		
				Top Compression	Bottom Compression	Oil Control	Top Compression	Bottom Compression	Oil Control
1982	B	4-151 (2.5)	.0025–.0035	.010–.022	.010–.028	.015–.055	.0030	.0030	.0010–.0080
	C	6-258 (4.2)	.0009–.0017	.010–.020	.010–.020	.010–.025	.0017–.0032	.0017–.0032	.0010–.0080
1983	B	4-151 (2.5)	.0025–.0035	.010–.022	.010–.028	.015–.055	.0030	.0030	.0010–.0080
	C	6-258 (4.2)	.0009–.0017	.010–.020	.010–.020	.010–.025	.0017–.0032	.0017–.0032	.0010–.0080
1984	U	4-150 (2.5)	.0009–.0017	.010–.020	.010–.020	.010–.025	.0017–.0032	.0017–.0032	.0010–.0080
	C	6-258 (4.2)	.0009–.0017	.010–.020	.010–.020	.010–.025	.0017–.0032	.0017–.0032	.0010–.0080

PISTON AND RING SPECIFICATIONS
All measurments are given in inches.

Year	VIN	No. Cylinder Displacement cu. in. (liter)	Piston Clearance	Ring Gap			Ring Side Clearance		
				Top Compression	Bottom Compression	Oil Control	Top Compression	Bottom Compression	Oil Control
1985	C	6-258 (4.2)	.0009–.0017	.010–.020	.010–.020	.010–.025	.0017–.0032	.0017–.0032	.0010–.0080
1986	C	6-258 (4.2)	.0009–.0017	.010–.020	.010–.020	.010–.025	.0017–.0032	.0017–.0032	.0010–.0080
1987	C	6-258 (4.2)	.0009–.0017	.010–.020	.010–.020	.010–.025	.0017–.0032	.0017–.0032	.0010–.0080
1988-89	F	4-132 (2.2)	NA	①	①	①	NA	NA	NA
	Z	4-150 (2.5)	.0013–.0021	.010–.020	.010–.020	.015–.055	.0010–.0032	.0010–.0032	.0010–.0095
	J	6-182 (3.0)	NA	.016–.022	.016–.022	—	.0010–.0020	.0010–.0020	.0015–.0035

NA—Not Available
① The factory specifies only 1 type of ring for this engine. The ring gap is pre-adjusted.

TORQUE SPECIFICATIONS
All readings in ft. lbs.

Year	VIN	No. Cylinder Displacement cu. in. (liter)	Cylinder Head Bolts	Main Bearing Bolts	Rod Bearing Bolts	Crankshaft Pulley Bolts	Flywheel Bolts	Manifold		Spark Plugs
								Intake	Exhaust	
1982	B	4-151 (2.5)	80-103	62-68	27-33	157-163	65-71	34-40	36-42	7-15
	C	6-258 (4.2)	80-90	75-85	30-35	70-90	95-115	18-28	18-28	7-15
1983	B	4-151 (2.5)	80-103	62-68	27-33	157-163	65-71	34-40	36-42	7-15
	C	6-258 (4.2)	80-90	75-85	30-35	70-90	95-115	18-28	18-28	7-15
1984	U	4-150 (2.5)	80-90	75-85	30-35	75-85	50-65	20-25	20-25	7-15
	C	6-258 (4.2)	80-90	75-85	30-35	70-90	95-115	18-28	18-28	7-15
1985	C	6-258 (4.2)	80-90	75-85	30-35	70-90	95-115	18-28	18-28	7-15
1986	C	6-258 (4.2)	80-90	75-85	30-35	70-90	95-115	18-28	18-28	7-15
1987	C	6-258 (4.2)	80-90	75-85	30-35	70-90	95-115	18-28	18-28	7-15
1988–89	F	4-132 (2.2)	①	69	46	96	44	11	13	11
	Z	4-150 (2.5)	100	80	33	80	48–54	23	23	28
	J	6-182 (3.0)	②	③	37	133	48–54	11	13	11

① Torque in 3 steps, in sequence:
1st — 37 ft. lbs.
2nd — 59 ft. lbs.
3rd — 69 ft. lbs.
Run engine for 15 minutes, shut off and allow to cool for 6 hours and re-check, should be 65–72 ft. lbs.

② Torque in 2 steps, in sequence:
1st — 45 ft. lbs.
2nd — Angular tighten to 106 degrees
Run engine for 15 minutes, shut off and allow to cool for 6 hours. Angular tighten to 45 degrees.

③ Tighten in 2 steps, in sequence:
1st — 20 ft. lbs.
2nd — Angular torque 75 degrees

BRAKE SPECIFICATIONS
All measurements in inches unless noted

Year	Model	Lug Nut Torque (ft. lbs.)	Master Cylinder Bore	Brake Disc		Standard Brake Drum Diameter	Minimum Lining Thickness	
				Minimum Thickness	Maximum Runout		Front	Rear
1982	Spirit	60-90	.945	.810	.003	9.000①	1/32	1/32
	Concord	60-90	.945	.810	.003	9.000①	1/32	1/32
	Eagle	60-90	.940	.810	.003	10.000	1/32	1/32
1983	Spirit	60-90	.945	.810	.003	9.000①	1/32	1/32
	Concord	60-90	.945	.810	.003	9.000①	1/32	1/32
	Eagle	60-90	.940	.810	.003	10.000	1/32	1/32
1984	Eagle	60-90	.940	.810	.003	10.000	1/32	1/32
1985	Eagle	60-90	.940	.810	.003	10.000	1/32	1/32
1986	Eagle	60-90	.940	.810	.003	10.000	1/32	1/32
1987	Eagle	60-90	.940	.810	.003	10.000	1/32	1/32
1988–89	Medallion	66	.810	.697②	.002	9.000	1/32	1/32
	Premier	63	.945	.807	.003	8.197	1/32	1/32

① Station wagon — 10.000

② Disc Rotor must not be machined. If excessive wear is evident, the rotor must be replaced.

WHEEL ALIGNMENT

Year	Model	Caster		Camber		Toe-in (in.)	Steering Axis Inclination (deg.)
		Range (deg.)	Preferred Setting (deg.)	Range (deg.)	Preferred Setting (deg.)		
1982	Spirit	3½–5P	5P	①	②	1/16–3/16	7¾
	Concord	3½–5P	5P	①	②	1/16–3/16	7¾
	Eagle	2P–3P	2½P	1/8N–5/8P	¾P	1/16–3/16③	11½
1983	Spirit	3½–5P	5P	①	②	1/16–3/16	7¾
	Concord	3½–5P	5P	①	②	1/16–3/16	7¾
	Eagle	2P–3P	2½P	1/8N–5/8P	¾P	1/16–3/16③	11½
1984	Eagle	2P–3P	2½P	1/8N–5/8P	¼P	1/16–3/16③	11½
1985	Eagle	2P–3P	2½P	1/8N–5/8P	¼P	1/16–3/16③	11½
1986	Eagle	2P–3P	2½P	1/8N–5/8P	¼P	1/16–3/16③	11½
1987	Eagle	2P–3P	2½P	1/8N–5/8P	¼P	1/16–3/16③	11½①
1988–89	Medallion	1½P–3½P	2½P	1/16P–13/16P	7/16P	5/64③	12¾
	Premier	1 5/16P–2 13/16P	2 1/8P	9/16N–1/16N	5/16N	1/8③	NA

P Positive
N Negative

① Left — ¾P-1/8P; Right — 1/8P
② Left — ¾P-1/8P; Right — ½P-1P
③ Toe-out

TUNE-UP PROCEDURES

Ignition Timing

ADJUSTMENT

Concord, Spirit and Eagle

A scale located on the timing chain cover and a notch milled into the vibration damper are used as references to set ignition timing. A magnetic timing probe socket is provided integral with the timing degree scale for use with a special magnetic timing probe. The probe socket is located at 9.5 degrees ATDC and the equipment used is calibrated to compensate for the location. Do not use the timing probe socket as a reference point to check the ignition timing when using a conventional timing light. Timing instructions are given on the underhood emission control sticker. Check the sticker instructions before adjusting the ignition timing and follow those directions if they differ from the procedures given below.

NOTE: Connect a tachometer to the SSI ignition system in the conventional way; to the negative (distributor) side of the coil and to a ground. HEI distributor caps have a "Tach" terminal. Some tachometers may not work with an SSI or HEI ignition system and there is a possibility that some could be damaged. Check with the manufacturer of the tachometer to make sure it can be used.

1982–83 2.5L ENGINE

1. Disconnect the vacuum hose, at the distributor vacuum unit. Plug the vacuum line to prevent leakage.

2. Connect a timing light and a tachometer in accordance with the manufacturer's instructions. If the timing light has an advance control, be sure it is **OFF**.

3. Start the engine. Adjust the carburetor curb idle screw so the engine idles at the specified curb idle speed at operating temperature. If there is a throttle stop solenoid, disconnect the electrical connector. Aim the timing light at the pointer marks.

4. Adjust the timing by loosening the distributor clamp nut and rotating the distributor. Set the timing to the specifications given in the Tune-Up chart or on the underhood emission sticker.

NOTE: On some models, a white paint mark is applied to the scale

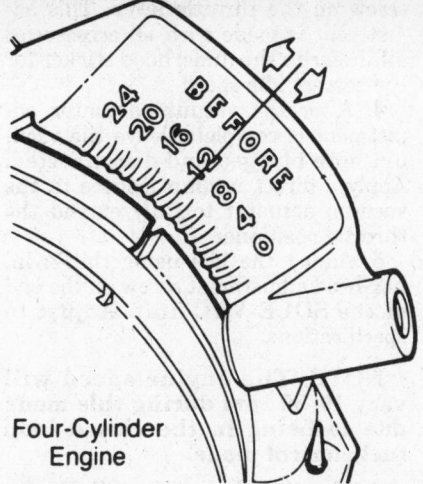

Four-Cylinder Engine

1984 2.5L timing degree scale and notch location

for the specified, initial timing setting. **Do not mistake this mark for TDC.**

5. Check the timing again after tightening the distributor clamp.

6. Connect the vacuum hose(s) and set the idle speed to specifications.

1984 2.5L AND 4.2L ENGINES

1. Start the engine and allow it to reach normal operating temperature, then switch the ignition off. Make sure the automatic transmission is in **PARK** or the manual transmission is in **NEUTRAL**.

2. On the 2.5L engines, disconnect the 3 wire connector to the vacuum input switch. On the 4.2L engines, disconnect the 2 wire connector (yellow and black wires) at the electronic ignition module. Install a jumper wire between the 2 wires at the module connector terminal.

3. Disconnect and plug the distributor vacuum advance hose.

4. Attach a timing light and tachometer to the engine according to the manufacturers instructions.

5. Start the engine and increase the engine speed to 1600 rpm while observing the timing marks with a timing light. If the timing light being used incorporates an advance control feature, make sure the control is in the **OFF** position.

6. Adjust the ignition timing to the specifications given in the Tune-Up chart or on the underhood emission sticker by loosening the distributor hold-down bolt and turning the distributor body. Exercise caution when working around a running engine; stay clear of all moving components, belts, etc. and do not wear loose clothing.

7. Once the timing has been set, re-

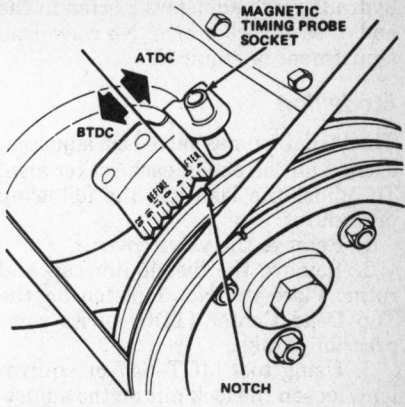

1982–83 2.5L timing degree scale and notch location

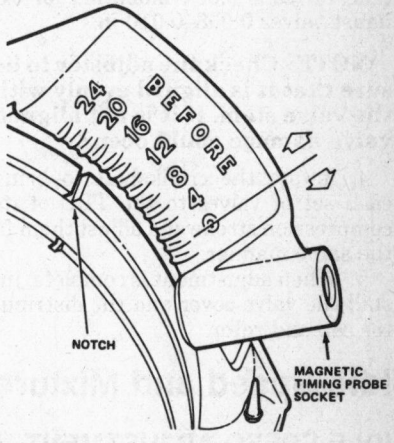

4.2L timing degree scale and notch location

connect the vacuum line and all electrical connectors.

Medallion and Premier

Ignition timing on the Eagle Premier and Medallion models is adjusted by the vehicles Electronic Control Unit (ECU). The ECU uses input from sensors in the engine to determine various conditions during operation such as, manifold pressure, engine speed, manifold air temperature and coolant temperature. These inputs allow the ECU to adjust the timing under a variety of engine conditions. Therefore no timing adjustment is needed for normal vehicle service.

Valve Lash

ADJUSTMENT

Concord, Spirit and Eagle

All the AMC engines covered by this section use hydraulic valve lifters which are not adjustable, even in connection with major repairs.

Premier

The Eagle Premier is equipped with

hydraulic lash adjusters loacted in the end of each rocker arm. No valve lash adjustment is required.

Medallion

The Medallion has valve lash adjusters located on the end of each rocker arm. To adjust the lash use the following procedures:

1. Remove the valve cover.
2. Remove the distributor cap and rotor. Place the No. 1 piston on the Top Dead Center (TDC) of its compression stroke.
3. Using tool MOT–647 or equivalent, loosen the lock nut on the adjuster and turn the adjuster to obtain the proper clearance. The clearance for intake valves is 0.004–0.006 in., for exhaust valves 0.008–0.010 in.

NOTE: Check the adjuster to be sure that it is aligned evenly with the valve stem. If it is not aligned valve damage could occur.

4. Rotate the crankshaft to bring each set of valves to the TDC of its compression stroke and adjust them in the same manner.
5. When adjustment is complete, install the valve cover and the distributor cap and rotor.

Idle Speed and Mixture

IDLE SPEED ADJUSTMENT

Carbureted Models

The engine and related systems must be operating normally before performing idle speed adjustments. The mixture adjustment should not have to be performed unless the mixture screw setting was altered during carburetor overhaul. Since automatic transmission vehicles are adjusted in **DRIVE**, set the parking brake firmly and do not accelerate the engine. Perform all procedures with the air cleaner installed or with the air cleaner removed and all vacuum hoses plugged. Make sure the ignition timing is correct before setting the idle speed.

MODEL YFA AND BBD CARBURETORS

1. Connect a tachometer according to the manufacturer instructions. Start the engine and allow it to reach normal operating temperature. The air cleaner should be installed, automatic transmissions in **DRIVE** and manual transmissions in **NEUTRAL**.
2. Remove the vacuum hose to the SOLE-VAC vacuum actuator unit and plug the hose. Disconnect the holding solenoid wire connector.
3. Adjust the curb idle speed by using the vacuum actuator adjustment

screw on the throttle lever. This adjustment is made with all accessories off. Refer to the underhood sticker for the correct idle speed.

4. After the vacuum actuator adjustment is complete, leave the vacuum hose plugged and disconnected. Apply a direct vacuum source to the vacuum actuator to fully extend the throttle positioner.
5. Adjust the idle using the ¼ in. hex-head adjustment screw on the end of the SOLE-VAC unit. Adjust to specifications.

NOTE: The engine speed will vary 10–30 rpm during this mode due to being in the closed loop fuel control mode.

6. If equipped, turn the A/C **ON**. Attach a jumper wire from the positive (+) battery cable to the holding solenoid terminal to energize it and hold the throttle open manually to allow the throttle positioner to fully extend.
7. If the holding solenoid is not within specifications, adjust the SOLE-VAC unit to obtain the correct idle rpm.
8. Disconnect the jumper wire, vacuum source and reconnect the hose to the vacuum actuator.

MODEL 2SE CARBURETOR

1. Start the engine and allow it to reach normal operating temperature. Set the parking brake firmly. Connect a tachometer to the ignition coil or the pigtail wire connector above the heater blower.
2. Disconnect the vacuum hose from the vacuum advance and plug the hose. Check and adjust the ignition timing if necessary and reconnect the vacuum advance.
3. Disconnect the decelerator valve hose and canister purge hose. Plug the hoses and remove the air cleaner assembly.
4. If equipped with A/C, turn it **ON** and open the throttle momentarily to make sure the solenoid arm is fully extended. Adjust the solenoid idle speed screw to obtain the rpm given on the underhood emission control sticker.
5. If not equipped with A/C, adjust the engine idle speed with the solenoid idle speed screw. Disconnect the solenoid and adjust the curb idle.
6. Install the air cleaner and reconnect all hoses.

MODEL E2SE CARBURETOR

1. Disconnect and plug the purge hose at the charcoal canister.
2. Connect a dwell meter to the single light blue wire which is taped to the mixture control solenoid wires at the carburetor. Set the meter on the 6 cylinder scale.

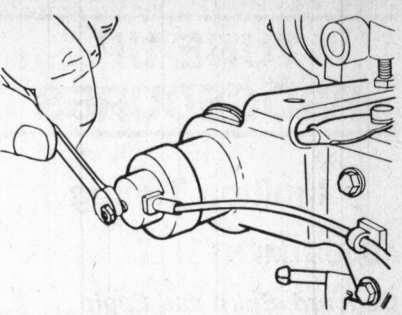

Curb idle speed adjustment

3. Connect a tachometer. There is a green wire above the heater fan motor for easy tachometer connection. Start the engine and allow it to reach normal operating temperature. On feedback models, the dwell meter should be fluctuating; the oscillation should be within 10–15 degrees of needle movement. If not, the feedback system is not operating correctly and must be repaired.
4. Set the parking brake, shift automatic transmissions to **DRIVE**; if equipped with air conditioning, turn it **ON**. Open the throttle to extend the solenoid plunger. Set idle speed by turning the solenoid idle screw. Turn **OFF** the A/C, if so equipped.
5. Disconnect the anti-dieseling solenoid wire. Use the curb idle screw to adjust idle to specifications. Connect the solenoid wire.

Fuel Injected Models

The idle speed on fuel injected models is controlled by the ECU through the use of an idle speed control motor (ISC). The ISC motor does not require periodic adjustment. If the ISC is removed or replaced, it must be adjusted to establish the intial position of the plunger. To adjust the ISC use the following procedure:

THROTTLE BODY INJECTION

1. Remove the air cleaner.
2. Start the engine and allow it to reach normal operating temperature. Make sure the A/C is turned **OFF**.
3. Locate the diagnostic terminals on the right side inner fender well. Connect a tachometer to terminals D1–1 and D1–3 of the diagnostic connector.
4. Turn the ignition **OFF**. The ISC plunger should move to the fully extended position.
5. Disconnect the ISC motor wire and start the engine. The engine idle should be 3300–3700 rpm. If not, turn the hex screw on the plunger to obtain a reading of 3500 rpm.
6. Connect the idle speed motor wire.
7. The idle speed should stay at

3500 rpm momentarily and then return to normal. Check the underhood sticker for the correct idle speed specification.

8. Disconnect the tachometer and install the air cleaner.

MULTI-PORT INJECTION

1. Disconnect the air inlet tube from the top of the throttle body.

2. Locate the diagnostic connectors on the right inner fender well. Connect a tachometer to terminals D1–1 and D1–3 of the diagnostic connector.

3. Disconnect the plug to the throttle body.

4. Locate the plug covering the idle stop screw on the side of the throttle body. Using an awl remove the plug.

5. Check the underhood sticker for the correct idle speed. If the idle speed does not fall within specification, turn the idle stop screw to adjust the rpm.

6. Once the idle speed has been adjusted to specification, reconnect the plug to the throttle body.

7. Cover the idle stop screw opening with RTV sealant or equivalent. Install the air inlet tube and disconnect the tachometer.

IDLE MIXTURE ADJUSTMENT

Carbureted Models

MODEL 2SE AND BBD CARBURETORS

NOTE: The idle mixture adjustment should only be performed if the idle mixture screw was removed or replaced during carburetor overhaul. Otherwise, the mixture is preset at the factory and requires no periodic adjustment. The carburetor may have to be removed to knock out the mixture screw tamper-proof plugs before any adjustment is attempted.

1. Connect a tachometer according to the manufacturer instructions, then start the engine and allow it to reach normal operating temperature.

2. Chock the wheels and set the parking brake firmly. Place automatic transmission in **DRIVE** or manual transmission in **NEUTRAL**.

3. Adjust the idle speed.

4. Using a suitable mixture adjusting tool, turn the mixture screw clockwise (lean) until a loss of engine rpm is noted.

5. Turn the mixture screw counterclockwise (rich) until the highest engine rpm is obtained. Do not turn the screw any further than the point at which the highest engine rpm is noted. This is referred to as the best lean idle. Engine speed will increase above curb idle speed an amount that approxi-

mately corresponds to the lean drop specifications.

6. As the final adjustment, turn the idle mixture screw clockwise in small increments until the specified speed drop is noted. Refer to the underhood emission control sticker for idle drop specifications.

NOTE: If the final engine rpm differs more than 30 rpm plus or minus the original set curb idle speed, adjust the curb idle speed again as required. Replace the idle mixture plugs when adjustment is complete.

MODEL YFA CARBURETOR

The mixture control (MC) solenoid dwell is used as a reference for the adjustment of the mixture and is indicated on a dwell meter set on the 6 cylinder scale. With the engine at idle, it is normal for the MC solenoid to increase or decrease dwell between 10–15 degrees. The mixture solenoid dwell is an indication of the ON/OFF time ratio between the energized and de-energized time of the solenoid.

1. Remove the carburetor.

2. To remove the mixture screw plug, center punch it then drill a ⅛ in. hole into the plug. Be careful not to damage the mixture screw while drilling. Install a self-tapping screw into the plug hole, then pull the screw out with pliers to remove the plug. Install the carburetor on the engine.

3. Connect a tachometer to the ignition coil TACH wire connector.

4. Connect a dwell meter to the MC solenoid test terminals in the diagnostic connector at terminals D2–14 and D2–7. Set the dwell meter on the 6 cylinder scale.

5. Place the automatic transmission in **PARK** or the manual transmission in **NEUTRAL** with the parking brake firmly set.

6. Disconnect and plug the canister purge vacuum hose at the canister.

7. Start the engine and operate it at fast idle speed for at least 3 minutes to allow the feedback system to enter closed loop operation. Allow the engine speed to stabilize at the specified idle rpm. Adjust the idle speed if necessary.

8. Adjust the idle mixture screw to obtain an average dwell reading of 30 degrees, within a span of 25–35 degrees. If the dwell is too low, slowly turn the mixture screw counterclockwise (out); if the dwell is too high, turn the mixture screw clockwise (in).

NOTE: Allow time for the system to react and stabilize after each movement of the adjustment screw. The system is very sensitive to adjustment.

9. If the dwell cannot be obtained by adjustment, check the carburetor idle circuit for air leaks or restrictions. Plug the idle mixture screws with RTV sealant when adjustments are complete.

MODEL E2SE CARBURETOR

Idle mixture is calibrated at the factory and should normally not need adjustment. Because the computer-controlled carburetor system is very complex, the procedure must be followed carefully. The mixture control (MC) solenoid dwell is used as a reference for the adjustment of the mixture and is indicated on a dwell meter set on the 6 cylinder scale. With the engine at idle, it is normal for the MC solenoid to increase or decrease dwell between 10–

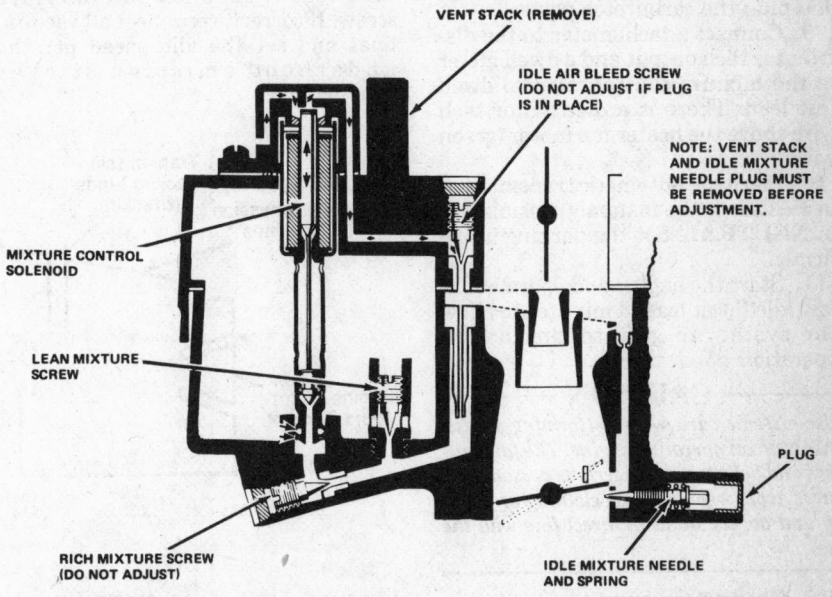

VENT STACK (REMOVE)

IDLE AIR BLEED SCREW
(DO NOT ADJUST IF PLUG IS IN PLACE)

NOTE: VENT STACK AND IDLE MIXTURE NEEDLE PLUG MUST BE REMOVED BEFORE ADJUSTMENT.

MIXTURE CONTROL SOLENOID

LEAN MIXTURE SCREW

RICH MIXTURE SCREW
(DO NOT ADJUST)

PLUG

IDLE MIXTURE NEEDLE AND SPRING

Cross section of typical E2SE carburetor, showing adjustment points

15 degrees. The mixture solenoid dwell is an indication of the ON/OFF time ratio between the energized and de-energized time of the solenoid.

1. Remove the carburetor and invert it in a suitable holding fixture.

2. Using a punch between the 2 locator points in the throttle body beneath the idle mixture screw plug (manifold side), break out the throttle body to gain access to the mixture screw plug. Drive out the hardened steel plug.

NOTE: The plug will probably shatter when removal is attempted. It is not necessary to remove the plug completely. Remove the loose pieces to allow the use of adjusting tool J–28706 or a $^3/_{16}$ in. thin wall deep socket wrench.

3. Lightly seat the mixture screw then back out 3 turns with automatic transmission, or 2½ turns on manual transmission for preliminary idle mixture adjustment.

4. If the plug in the air horn covering the idle air bleed screw has been removed, turn the bleed screw in until lightly seated, then back it out 1¼ turns. If the plug is in place, removal and adjustment is not required.

5. Remove the vent stack-screen assembly to gain access to lean mixture screw. Turn the lean mixture screw in until lightly bottomed and back out 3 turns.

6. Install the carburetor on the engine.

7. Disconnect the bowl vent line at the carburetor. Disconnect and plug the vacuum hose at the T-fitting n the bowl vent line, if used.

8. Disconnect the EGR valve and canister purge lines at the carburetor and plug the carburetor ports.

9. Connect a tachometer to the distributor tach output and a dwell meter to the mixture control solenoid dwell test lead. There is a distributor tach wire above the heater fan motor (green wire).

10. Place the automatic transmission in **PARK**, or the manual transmission in **NEUTRAL**. Set the parking brake firmly.

11. Start the engine and operate it at fast idle for at least 3 minutes to allow the system to go into closed loop operation.

—————— **CAUTION** ——————

Use extreme care when performing adjustments on an operating engine. The fan, pulleys and belts can cause serious personal injury. Avoid wearing loose clothing or jewelry and do not stand in direct line with the fan.

12. Operate the engine at 3000 rpm and adjust partial throttle lean mix-

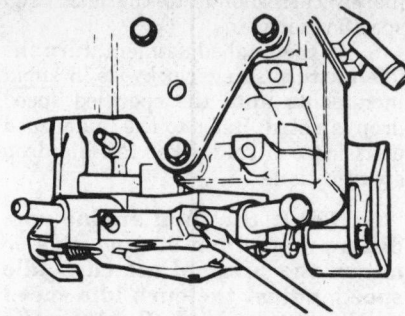

Idle mixture screw location on YFA carburetor

ture screw in increments to provide 25 degrees dwell. Allow time for the dwell to stabilize after each incremental adjustment. If the dwell is too low, back the screw out; if too high, turn the screw in.

13. Check and adjust the idle speed if necessary.

14. Adjust the idle mixture screw to obtain an average dwell of 25 degrees. Again, if too low back the screw out; if too high turn the screw in. Allow time for the dwell to stabilize after each adjustment and remove the tool when checking the dwell reading. The system is very sensitive to adjustment. If unable to adjust to specifications, check the idle system for leaks, restrictions, etc.

15. Disconnect the mixture control solenoid connector and check for an engine speed change of at least 50 rpm. If the rpm does not change enough, check the idle air bleed circuit for restrictions, leaks, etc. Connect the MC solenoid connector.

16. Repeat the 3000 rpm dwell check. If not correct, readjust the lean mixture screw, then the idle mixture screw. If correct, reconnect all vacuum lines and set the idle speed per the underhood emission sticker instructions.

Fuel Injected Models

The idle mixture on fuel injected engines is controlled by the ECU and is not adjustable for normal servicing.

FAST IDLE CAM BINDING

1985–87 Eagles built prior to Vehicle Identification Number 2CXXXXXXXHB701932 may suffer from fast idle cam binding and consequent racing of the engine. The fast idle cam linkage may bind because of contamination from road splash. The fast idle mechanism can be freed with ordinary solvent, but may require excessive attention unless a special splash shield, AMC Part No. 8983 100 047 or the equivalent is installed. Install the shield as follows:

1. Raise the vehicle and support it securely. Remove the skid plate.

2. Remove the left/front oil pan bolt; then, install the stud supplied with the kit in place of the bolt, torquing it to 7 ft. lbs.

3. Push the rear of the splash shield through the area between the transmission cooling lines and the pitman arm.

4. Then, locate the triangular section located between the 2 slots at the rear of the shield under the engine mount support bracket. Now, shift the shield so as to push the section to the right of the engine mount above the transmission cooler lines. At this point in the procedure, the section of the shield to the left of the engine mount should rest against the frame rail.

5. Push the front of the splash shield over the transmission cooling lines and then pull its front section forward and under the radiator. At this time, the front will rest between the coolant overflow hose and the radiator.

6. Shift the shield so the pre-drilled hole in the top will fit over the stud in-

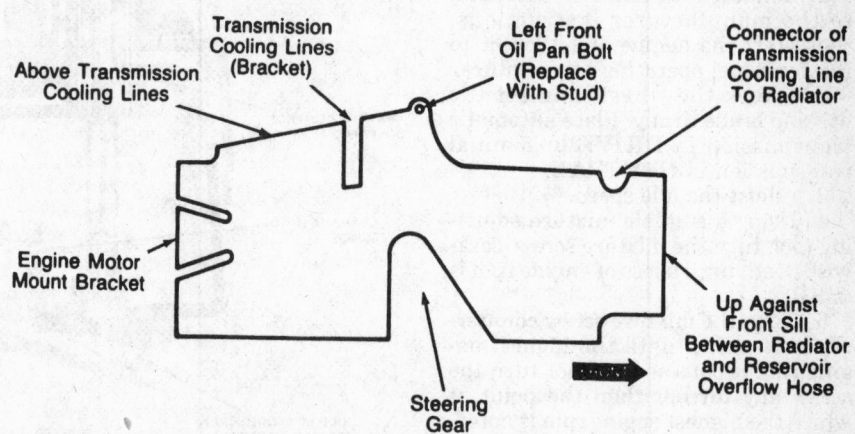

Install the splash shield (AMC Part No. 8983 100 047 or equivalent) fitting it into the engine compartment as shown

stalled in the oil pan in Step 2. Install the retaining nut and washer onto the stud.

7. Reinstall the skid plate and lower the vehicle.

ENGINE ELECTRICAL

Distributor

REMOVAL & INSTALLATION

For additional information on the ignition system, please refer to "Electronic Ignition Systems" in the Unit Repair section.

Timing Not Disturbed

ALL EXCEPT 3.0L ENGINE

1. Bring the engine's No. l piston to TDC on the compression stroke. Remove the distributor cap, mark the position of the rotor relative to the distributor body and mark the body relative to the block. Remove the air cleaner if necessary, then remove the distributor primary wire and the distributor vacuum lines. Tag any disconnected wires or hoses for installation.

NOTE: The primary connector contains a special conductive grease. Make sure not to disturb it. If the grease becomes dirty or contaminated, replace it with a conductive silicone grease designed for use with high energy ignition systems.

2. Remove the hold-down bolt and lift the distributor up out of the block.

3. The procedure for installation varies depending on whether or not the engine was turned while the distributor was out.

4. IF the timing was not disturbed, turn the rotor about ⅛ past the mark indicating its original position. This allows the helical gears to align properly.

5. Align the distributor locating marks on the distributor body and the block, and drop the unit into place. The rotor should turn back to the mark as the unit seats and the gear meshes. Wiggle the rotor slightly to start the gear in mesh as necessary.

6. Tighten the hold-down bolt and reconnect the primary wire and the vacuum line. Install the cap.

7. Check the ignition timing.

3.0L ENGINE

1. Remove the spark plug wires from the spark plugs.

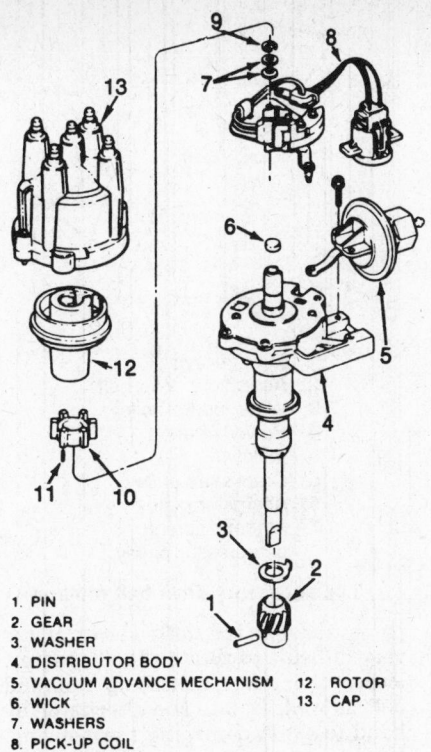

1. PIN
2. GEAR
3. WASHER
4. DISTRIBUTOR BODY
5. VACUUM ADVANCE MECHANISM
6. WICK
7. WASHERS
8. PICK-UP COIL
9. RETAINER
10. TRIGGER WHEEL
11. PIN
12. ROTOR
13. CAP

Typical HEI distributor and components

2. Remove the screws retaining the distributor cap.

3. Remove the screws that attach the distributor drive to the rotor and remove the rotor. Remove the dust shield from inside the housing.

4. To install, place the dust shield inside the distributor housing. Place the rotor on the the distributor drive shaft and install the retaining screws and tighten to 26 inch lbs.

5. Install the distributor cap and tighten the cap retaining bolts to 72 inch lbs. Attach the spark plug wires.

Timing Disturbed

2.2L, 1982–84 2.5L AND 4.2L ENGINES

1. Place the No. 1 cylinder in firing position by turning the engine with a finger held over the No. 1 spark plug hole. No. 1 spark plug is the front one on a 4 or 6 cylinder. When compression is felt, turn the engine to align the TDC mark on the timing pointer with the notch on the crankshaft pulley.

2. Align the metal end of the rotor with the No. 1 spark plug wire in the distributor cap.

3. Turn the distributor body counterclockwise about ⅛ turn and set it into place in the engine. Wiggle the rotor slightly to start the gear in mesh as necessary.

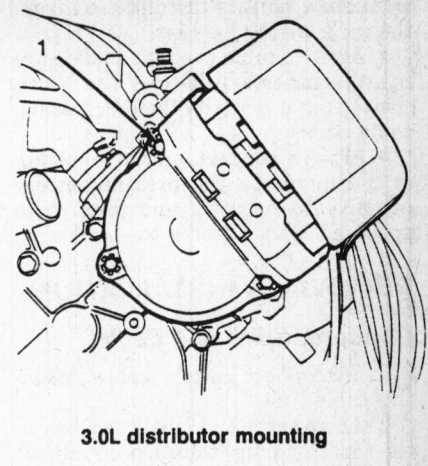

3.0L distributor mounting

4. The distributor should not be positioned so that the rotor is still pointing to the No. 1 wire location on the cap.

5. Tighten the hold-down bolt and reconnect the primary wire and the vacuum line. Replace the cap.

6. Check and adjust the ignition timing.

1988–89 2.5L ENGINE

1. Rotate the engine until the No. 1 piston is at TDC compression.

2. Using an appropriate tool inserted in the distributor hole, rotate the oil pump gear so that the slot in the oil pump shaft is slightly past the **3 O'CLOCK** position, relative to the length of the engine block.

3. With the distributor cap removed, install the distributor with the rotor at the **5 O'CLOCK** position, relative to the oil pump gear shaft slot. When the distributor is completely in place, the rotor should be at the **6 O'CLOCK** position. If not, remove the distributor and perform the entire procedure again.

4. Tighten the lockbolt.

Alternator

For information on alternator and regulator repair and troubleshooting, please refer to "Charging and Starting" in the Unit Repair section.

PRECAUTIONS

• Do not attempt to polarize the alternator, by running a hot wire from the battery to any of the alternator terminals.

• Never short circuit or cut across any of the terminals in the charging system unless a procedure specifically explains how to do so.

• Never allow the alternator to be driven by the engine when the output terminal circuit is disconnected from the car's wiring harness.

- Alway double check to make sure the alternator and battery use Negative Ground polarity before making connections.
- Always connect another battery or a charger to the present battery negative to negative and positive to positive (+ to + and – to –).

REMOVAL & INSTALLATION

Concord, Spirit and Eagle

1. Disconnect battery cables, negative cable first.
2. Disconnect and label the alternator wires or plug, then loosen adjusting bolt.
3. Remove the V-belt, mounting bolts and alternator.
4. To install, reverse the removal procedure.
5. The longest run of belt should deflect about ½ in. under moderate thumb pressure.

Medallion and Premier

1. Disconnect the negative battery cable.
2. Raise and safely support the vehicle. Remove the lower splash shield.
3. Disconnect the alternator electrical connector.
4. Relieve the belt tension on the alternator by turning the adjusting bolt. Remove the belt from the alternator.
5. Remove the mounting bolts and remove the alternator.
6. Install the alternator to the block and insert the retaining bolts.
7. Slide the belt over the pulley and adjust the belt tension. Torque the pivot bolt to 30 ft. lbs.

BELT TENSION ADJUSTMENT

The drive belts can be tensioned to a specific rating with the use of an appropriate belt tension gauge, placed midway between the pulleys. Make sure to install the gauge midway between the pulleys on the longest belt span. If the belt is notched on the inner surface, make sure the middle finger of the tensioner fits into one of the notches. Tension is 90–115 lbs. for standard belts and 140–160 lbs. for serpentine belts.

To test belt tension manually. Depress the belt with thumb pressure mid-way between the 2 top pulleys. It should be springy, not loose or with actual "play". Under moderate thumb pressure (about 15 lbs.), the belt should give approx.½–¾ in.

Adjust the belt by loosening the top alternator mounting jing bolt, which

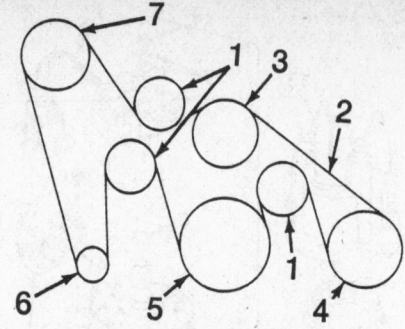

1. Idler pulleys
2. Accessory drive belt
3. Water pump pulley
4. Power steering pulley
5. Crankshaft pulley
6. Alternator pulley
7. Air conditioning compressor pulley

3.0L accessory drive belt routing

passes through the slotted lever. If it is very difficult to rotate the alternator, loosen the lower mounting nut and bolt as well. Rotate the alternator by hand to avoid damaging the housing. If it is necessary to pry with a bar, pry in the same plane as the alternator top bolt, if possible.

Regulator

REMOVAL & INSTALLATION

External Type

Disconnect the negative battery cable. Disconnect plug to the regulator. Remove the metal screws which hold the regulator in place, and lift off the regulator. Install in reverse order after cleaning the mounting surface around the screw holes.

Starter

For additional information on starters, please refer to "Charging and Starting" in the Unit Repair section.

REMOVAL & INSTALLATION

1. Disconnect the negative battery cable first, then the battery and solenoid lead at the starter (if used). Raise the car and support it safely.
2. Working underneath the car, remove the bolts which hold the starter to the bellhousing (and starter to engine brace on the 2.5L), remove the starter.

NOTE: When removing the starter, be careful to watch for and retain any shims which may have been used to align it with the ring gear. Be sure to watch for

and catch any shims that may be used behind the mounting bolts. Before installing the starter, make sure the mounting surfaces are free from burrs and dirt.

3. Install the starter onto the housing together with any shims, and tighten the bolts to 18 ft. lbs. on 4.2L engines. Tighten the bolts to 17 ft. lbs. on the 1982–83 2.5L engine and 33 ft. lbs. on the 1984 2.5L engine. Clean the battery and solenoid terminal(s), install the cable(s).

ENGINE MECHANICAL

Engine

REMOVAL & INSTALLATION

1982–84 2.5L Engines

1. Disconnect the battery cables.
2. Remove the air cleaner.
3. Remove the hood, after scribing the locations of the hinges.
4. Drain the radiator.
5. Remove the lower radiator hose.
6. Remove the upper radiator hose and coolant recovery hose.
7. Remove the fan shroud and disconnect the transmission fluid cooler tubing (automatic transmission).
8. Remove the radiator/condenser (if equipped with A/C).
9. Remove the fan assembly and install a $\frac{5}{16}$ x ½ in. capscrew through the fan pulley into the water pump flange, to maintain the pulley and water pump in alignment when the crankshaft is rotated.
10. Disconnect the heater hoses.
11. Disconnect the throttle linkages, cruise control cable (if so equipped) and throttle valve rod.
12. Disconnect the wires from the starter motor solenoid and disconnect CEC System wire harness connector. Tag all disconnected wires for reassembly.
13. Disconnect the fuel pipe from the fuel pump and plug the fuel line.
14. If equipped with air conditioning, remove the service valves and cap the compressor ports.
15. Disconnect the fuel return hose from the fuel filter.
16. Remove the power brake vacuum check valve from the booster, if so equipped.
17. If equipped with power steering:
   a. disconnect the power steering hoses from the fittings at the steering gear
   b. drain the pump reservoir
   c. cap the fittings on the hoses

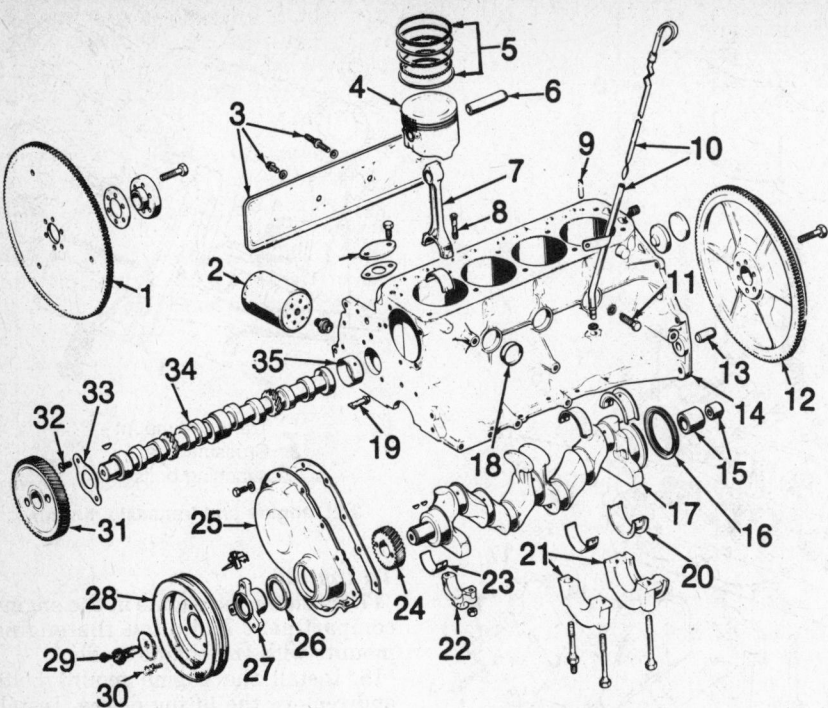

1. Drive plate and ring gear (automatic trans)
2. Oil filter
3. Push rod cover and bolts
4. Piston
5. Piston ring
6. Piston pin
7. Connecting rod
8. Connecting rod bolt
9. Dowel
10. Oil level indicator and tube
11. Block drain
12. Flywheel and ring gear (manual trans)
13. Dowel
14. Cylinder block
15. Pilot and/or converter bushing
16. Rear oil seal
17. Crankshaft
18. Block core plug
19. Timing gear oil nozzle
20. Main bearings
21. Main bearing caps
22. Connecting rod bearing cap
23. Connecting rod bearing
24. Crankshaft gear
25. Timing gear cover (front)
26. Timing gear cover oil seal
27. Crankshaft pulley hub
28. Crankshaft pulley
29. Crankshaft pulley hub bolt
30. Crankshaft pulley bolt
31. Crankshaft timing gear
32. Camshaft thrust plate screw
33. Camshaft thrust plate
34. Camshaft
35. Camshaft bearing
36. Oil pump driveshaft retainer plate, gasket and bolt

Exploded view of the 1982–83 2.5L engine

and steering gear to prevent foreign objects from entering the system.

18. Identify, tag and disconnect all necessary wire connectors and vacuum hoses.

19. Raise the vehicle and support it safely.

20. Remove the starter motor.

21. Disconnect the exhaust pipe from the manifold.

22. Remove the flywheel/converter housing access cover. On models with automatic transmission, mark the converter and flywheel location and remove the converter to drive plate bolts.

23. Remove the upper flywheel/converter housing bolts and loosen the bottom bolts. Remove the engine mount cushion to engine compartment bracket bolts.

24. Remove the engine mount cushion to engine compartment bracket bolts.

25. Attach a lifting device to the engine.

26. Raise the engine off the front supports.

27. Place a support stand under the converter (or flywheel) housing.

28. Remove the remaining converter (or flywheel) housing bolts.

29. Lift the engine out of the engine compartment.

30. Installation is in the reverse order of removal.

2.2L, 1988–89 2.5L and 3.0L Engines

All of the engines in the Eagle Medallion and Premier are removed with their transaxle assemblies attached.

1. Matchmark the hood to the hinges and remove the hood.

2. Disconnect the negative battery cable, the coil wire, all vacuum and fuel lines.

3. Disconnect the lower radiator hose and drain the coolant. Remove the air cleaner.

4. Remove the grille. Remove the screws retaining the front facia panel and radiator support and remove the panel and support.

5. Remove the radiator and cooling fan, if equipped with A/C remove the condensor and the radiator as an assembly.

NOTE: On models equipped with A/C, the system will have to be discharged before the engine can be removed.

6. Remove the ECU cover and disconnect the electrical leads to the unit.

7. Remove the accelerator cable from the brackets on the valve cover. Remove the throttle plate cover screws and remove the throttle plate.

8. Remove the bolts that attach the exhaust head pipes to the exhaust manifold. Remove the heater hoses and on automatic transmission equipped vehicles remove the cooler lines.

9. Raise the vehicle and safely support. Remove the underbody splash shield.

10. Remove the power steering pump mounting bolts and support the pump to the side. Remove the header pipe to converter bolts and remove the converter.

11. On models equipped with automatic transmissions disconnect the shifter linkages. On standard transmission vehicles disconnect the clutch cable at the transaxle.

12. Remove the wheel assemblies and remove the front stabilizer bar. Remove the brake calipers and support aside. Disconnect the ball joints from the steering knuckle. Remove the axle shaft retaining pin and remove the axle. Remove the strut to steering knuckle bolts.

13. Loosen the upper strut mounting bolts and swing the axle/strut assembly aside, support the axles safely.

14. Disconnect the speedometer cable. Disconnect the vapor canister and remove it.

15. Loosen the bolts attaching the transmission support to the engine cradle. Remove the bolts attaching the left and right halves of the crossmember to the transaxle. Lower the vehicle.

16. Attach a suitable lifting device to the engine lifting eyes and lift the engine slightly, remove the engine support bolts and remove the engine/transaxle assembly. Lift the engine out at an angle, make sure the transaxle clears the engine compartment.

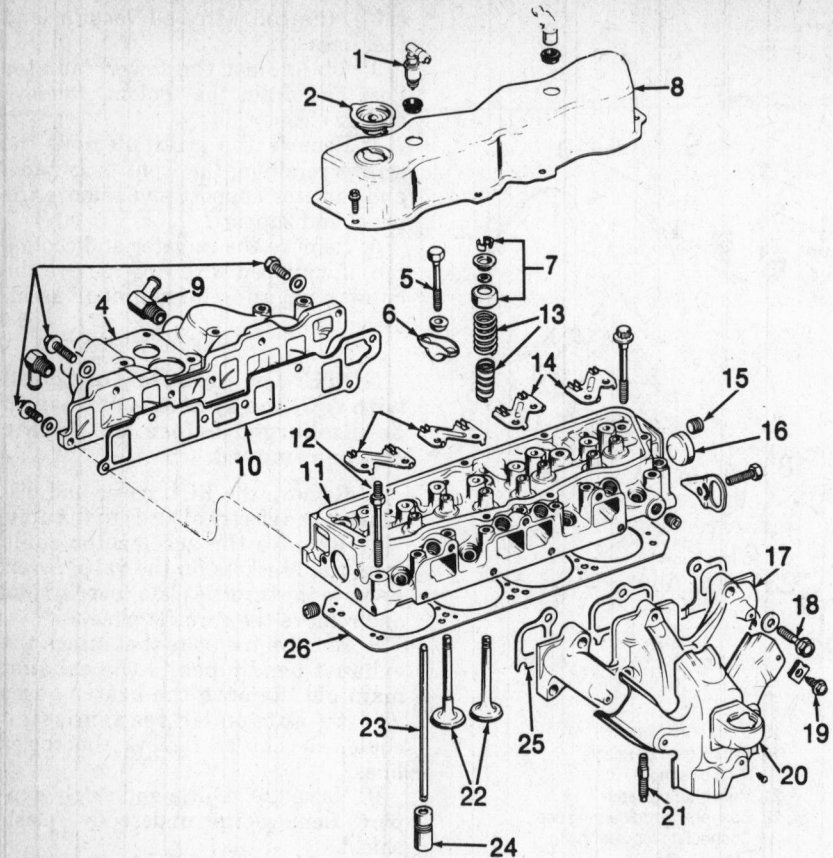

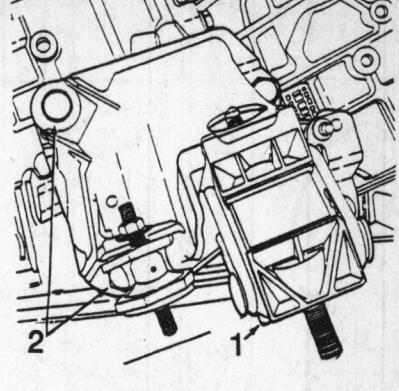

1. Transaxle mount
2. Crossmember attaching bolts

2.2L engine and transaxle mounts

1. PCV valve
2. Oil filler cap
3. Intake manifold attaching bolts
4. Intake manifold
5. Rocker arm capscrew
6. Rocker arm
7. Valve spring retainer assembly
8. Cylinder head cover (rocker cover)
9. Coolant hose fitting
10. Intake manifold gasket
11. Cylinder head
12. Cylinder head stud bolt
13. Valve spring
14. Push rod guide
15. Cylinder head plug
16. Cylinder head core plug
17. Exhaust manifold
18. Exhaust manifold bolt
19. Oil level indicator tube attaching screw
20. Exhaust manifold heat shroud (heat shield)
21. Exhaust manifold to exhaust pipe stud
22. Valves
23. Push rod
24. Tappet
25. Exhaust manifold gasket
26. Cylinder head gasket

Exploded view of the 1982–83 2.5L cylinder head assembly

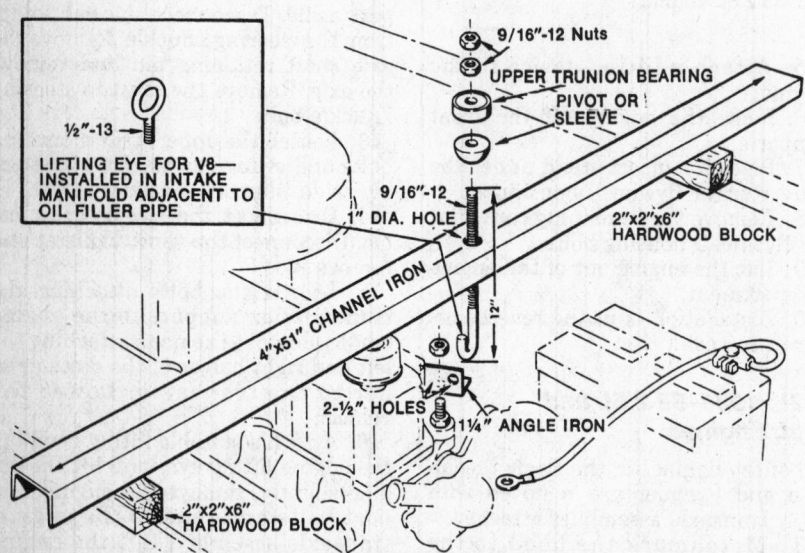

Lifting fixture can be fabricated as illustrated to facilitate oil pan and motor mount removal

To Install:

17. Position the engine in the engine compartment and align the engine mounts with the engine cradle.

18. Install the engine mount bolts and remove the lifting device. Install the left and right sections of the crossmember.

19. Position and install the axle shafts to the transaxle, use new axle shaft retaining pins. Install the shock absorber to steering knuckle bolts and attach the tie rod ends. Attach the front stabilizer bar.

20. Install the brake calipers on the rotors and tighten the retaining bolts to 73 ft. lbs. Install the front wheels.

21. Install the converter to the header pipe. Install the power steering pump and adjust the belt tension. Connect the shift linkage and throttle cables.

22. Reconnect all electrical and vacuum leads. Install the canister and the air cleaner assemblies. Reconnect the fuel lines and coolant hoses.

23. Install the radiator and fan assemblies. Attach the front facia and support assembly. Install the grill.

24. Attach the negtive battery cable and install the hood.

25. Check all fluid levels. Fill and bleed the cooling system.

4.2L Engine

1. Mark the hood hinge locations, disconnect the underhood light, if so equipped, and remove the hood.

2. Drain the coolant and engine oil.

3. Disconnect and remove the battery and air cleaner.

4. Disconnect and tag the alternator, ignition coil, distributor, temperature and oil sender wiring.

5. If equipped with transmission controlled spark (TCS), remove the switch bracket and vacuum solenoid wire harness.

6. Disconnect and plug the hose from the fuel pump.

7. Disconnect the engine ground strap at the block and the starter cable at the starter. Remove the right front engine support cushion to bracket bolt.

8. If equipped with air conditioning, the system must be bled, the hoses disconnected, and the compressor removed.

CAUTION

Compressed refrigerant will freeze any surface it contacts, including eyes. It also forms a poisonous gas in the presence of flame.

9. Bleed the refrigerant from the system. Remove the service valves, cap the compressor ports and the service valves, and disconnect the clutch wire.

10. Disconnect the return hose from the fuel filter, TAC hose from the manifold, carburetor vent hose, heater or A/C vacuum hose and/or power brake hose at intake manifold, and power brake vacuum check valve from booster, if so equipped. Tag all hoses for installation.

11. Disconnect the throttle cable and throttle valve rod, if so equipped.

12. Disconnect the radiator and heater hoses from the engine, automatic transmission cooler lines from the radiator, radiator shroud, fan, and spacer, and remove the radiator.

13. Install a $\frac{5}{16} \times \frac{1}{2}$ in. bolt through the fan pulley into the water pump flange to maintain alignment.

14. With power steering, disconnect the hoses, drain the reservoir, and cap the fittings. With power brakes, remove the vacuum check valve from the booster.

15. With automatic transmission, remove the filler tube.

16. Jack and support the front of the car. Remove the starter.

17. With automatic transmission remove the converter cover, converter bolts (rotate the crankshaft for access), and the exhaust pipe to transmission linkage support. With manual transmission, remove the clutch cover, bellcrank inner support bolts and springs, the bellcrank, outer bellcrank to strut retainer, and disconnect the back-up lamp wire harness at the firewall for access later.

18. Attach the lifting device and support the engine. Remove the engine mount bolts.

19. Disconnect the exhaust pipe from the manifold.

20. Remove the upper converter or clutch housing bolts and loosen the lower bolts. Raise the car and move the jackstands to the jack pad area. Remove the A/C idler pulley and bracket, if so equipped. Lift the engine off the front supports, support the transmission, remove the lower transmission cover attaching bolts, and lift the engine out of the car. Remove the transmission support, raise the front of the car so that the bottom of the bumper is 3 feet from the floor, and partially remove the engine/transmission assembly until the rear of the cylinder head clears the cowl. Lower the car and remove the engine.

21. On installations with manual transmission, insert the transmission shaft into the clutch spline and align the clutch housing to the engine. Install and tighten the lower housing bolts.

22. On installations with automatic transmission, align the converter housing to the engine and loosely install the bottom housing bolts. Then install the next higher bolts and tighten all 4 bolts. With both transmissions, next remove the transmission support, lower the engine onto the mounts, and install the mounting bolts.

23. The remainder of the installation is in the reverse order of removal. Lower the engine/transmission assembly into the compartment. Raise the transmission into position with a jack and install the rear crossmember. Install the front engine support cushions.

Cylinder Head

REMOVAL & INSTALLATION

If the head sticks, operate the starter to loosen it by compression or rap it upward with a soft hammer. Do not force anything between the head and the block. Cylinder head bolts should be retorqued after the first 500 miles or so, unless a special AMC gasket is used. The special gasket doesn't require retorquing. Make sure to blow any coolant out of the cylinder head bolt holes before reassembly to prevent inaccurate torque readings.

1982–83 2.5L Engine

1. Disconnect the negative battery cable. Drain the cooling system.

2. Disconnect the accelerator cable at the bellcrank, and the manifold vacuum and fuel lines at the carburetor.

3. Remove the intake and exhaust manifolds.

4. Remove the alternator and power steering pump. Unbolt the A/C compressor, if so equipped and move it aside without disconnecting any lines.

5. Disconnect all electrical connectors at the head.

6. Disconnect the radiator and heater hoses, and the battery ground strap.

7. Remove the spark plugs.

8. Remove the rocker arm cover,

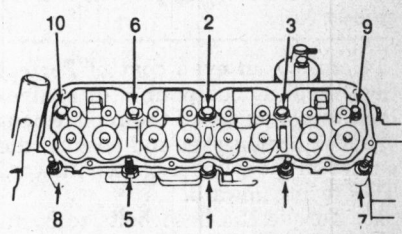

1982–83 2.5L cylinder head torque sequence

rocker arms, and pushrods. Keep all parts in order.

9. Unbolt and remove the cylinder head.

10. Clean the gasket surfaces thoroughly.

11. Install a new gasket over the dowels, and then position the cylinder head.

12. Coat the head bolt threads with sealer and install finger-tight.

13. Tighten the bolts in sequence, in 3 equal steps to the specified torque.

14. Install all parts in the reverse order of removal.

1984 2.5L Engine

CAUTION

Do not perform this procedure on a hot engine.

1. Disconnect the battery cables.

2. Drain the coolant and disconnect

1984 2.5L cylinder head torque sequence

the hoses at the thermostat housing.

3. Remove the air cleaner.

4. Remove the valve cover. The cover seal is RTV sealer. Break the seal with a clean putty knife or razor blade. Don't attempt to remove the cover until the seal is broken all around. To remove the cover, pry where indicated "PRY HERE" at the bolt holes.

5. Remove the rocker arms, bridge and pivot assemblies. Remove the pushrods.

NOTE: Retain the pushrods, bridge, pivot and rocker arms in the same order as removed to facilitate installation into their original positions.

6. Disconnect the power steering pump bracket. Set the pump and bracket aside. Do not disconnect the hoses.

7. Remove the intake and exhaust manifolds from the cylinder head.

8. If equipped with air conditioning, perform the following:

a. remove the air conditioner compressor drive belt

b. loosen the alternator drive belt

c. remove the A/C compressor/alternator bracket to cylinder head mounting screw.

d. remove the bolts from the A/C compressor (if so equipped) and alternator mounting bracket, and set the compressor aside.

NOTE: The serpentine drive belt tension is released by loosening the alternator.

9. Disconnect the ignition wires and remove the spark plugs.

10. Disconnect the temperature sending unit wire connector.

11. Remove the cylinder head bolts, cylinder head and gasket.

12. Thoroughly clean the machined surfaces of the cylinder head and block. Remove all gasket material and cement.

13. Installation is in the reverse order of removal, with the following recommendations.

— **CAUTION** —

Do not apply sealing compound to the cylinder head and block machined surfaces. Do not allow the sealing compound to enter the cylinder bores.

14. Apply an even coat of Perfect Seal® sealing compound, or equivalent, to both sides of the replacement cylinder head gasket and position the gasket on the cylinder block with word TOP facing upward.

15. Torque the head bolts to 85 ft. lbs. in the sequence.

16. Install the cylinder head cover with a ⅛ in. bead of RTV sealer along the sealing surface of the head. Make sure not to delay more than 10 minutes in installing the cover onto the bead of sealer.

4.2L Engine

1. Drain the cooling system. Disconnect throttle linkage, fuel lines, water hoses, spark plug wires and vacuum line. Remove the air cleaner, PCV hose, and the temperature sender.

2. Remove the valve cover and its gasket. The cover seal is RTV sealer. Break the seal with a clean putty knife or razor blade. Don't attempt to remove the cover until the seal is broken all around. To remove the cover, pry where indicated "PRY HERE" at the bolt holes. Remove the rocker arm assembly and the pushrods. With bridged pivots, loosen each bolt alternately, 1 turn at a time, to avoid damage.

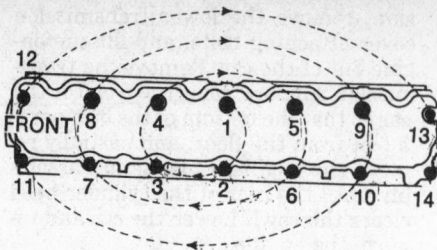

4.2L cylinder head torque sequence

age. Keep the pushrods in order. If equipped with power steering, remove the power steering pump bracket and Air Guard pump, and set them aside. Don't disconnect the hoses.

3. Remove the intake and exhaust manifold assemblies from the head.

4. Disconnect the spark plug wires, and remove the plugs.

5. Disconnect the battery ground cable, the coil, and the coil bracket from the head. Disconnect the temperature sending unit wire.

6. If the vehicle is equipped with air conditioning, remove the drive belt idler pulley bracket from the cylinder head. Loosen the alternator drive belt and remove the bolts from the compressor mounting bracket. Set the compressor aside, all hoses attached.

7. Remove the bolts and remove the cylinder head from the block.

8. Clean the gasket surfaces of both the head and the block. Remove the carbon deposits from the top of each piston, and from the combustion chambers.

9. Check the head for straightness. If the head (or the block) is 0.008 in. out of true over its entire length, 0.001 in. in 1 in. or 0.002 in. in 6 in., the head requires resurfacing.

10. Use a new head gasket, and coat both of its sides with sealer. The word TOP on the gasket faces upward.

11. Tighten the head bolts in 3 stages, in the proper sequence and to the proper torque specification.

12. Install the cylinder head cover with a ⅛ in. bead of RTV sealer along the sealing surface of the head. Make sure not to delay more than 10 minutes in installing the cover onto the bead of sealer.

13. Complete the installation in the reverse order of removal. Refill the cooling system.

2.2L Engine

1. Disconnect the negative battery cable.

2. Drain the cooling system. Remove the air inlet tube from the throttle body.

3. Remove the accessory drive belts. Remove the timing belt cover.

4. Loosen the bolts on the timing belt tensioner and remove the timing belt. Remove the spark plugs and wires.

5. Remove any hoses attached to the rocker cover and remove the rocker arm cover. Remove the distributor from the rear of the head.

6. Remove all of the cylinder head bolts except for the bolt at position No. 10 in the tightening sequence. Loosen the bolt at position No. 10 and pivot the cylinder head on that bolt. This can be done by tapping the opposite end of the head with an block of wood. This is necessary to free the cylinder head from the cylinder liners.

7. Once the head is free, remove the last bolt and remove the cylinder head.

To install:

8. Place the new cylinder head gasket on the block using the alignment dowel, on the block, to hold it in place.

9. Position the cylinder head on the block and insert the cylinder head bolts. Tighten the bolts in sequence and in 3 steps to specification.

10. Install the distributor to the head. Install the rocker arm cover, using a new gasket. Tighten the rocker cover bolts to 35 inch lbs.

11. Install the timing belt and adjust the belt tension. Install the timing belt cover. Install the spark plugs and wires.

12. Install the accessory drive belts and reconnect all hoses that were disconnected.

13. Install the air inlet tube. Fill the cooling system.

14. Reconnect the negative battery cable. Run the engine and bleed the cooling system. Check for leaks.

1988–89 2.5L Engine

1. Disconnect the negative battery cable.

2. Drain the cooling system.

3. Loosen the accessory drive belt and remove it.

4. Remove the bolts attaching the A/C compressor and without disconnecting the pressure lines, move the compressor aside.

5. Disconnect the upper radiator hose and the heater hoses.

6. Remove the rocker arm cover. Remove the rocker arms and assemblies, keep all of the valve train components in their original order, for installation.

7. Remove the intake and exhaust manifolds.

8. Remove the cylinder head bolts and remove the cylinder head.

To install:

9. Clean all gasket mating surfaces. Place the new cylinder had gasket on the block with the numbers facing **UP**.

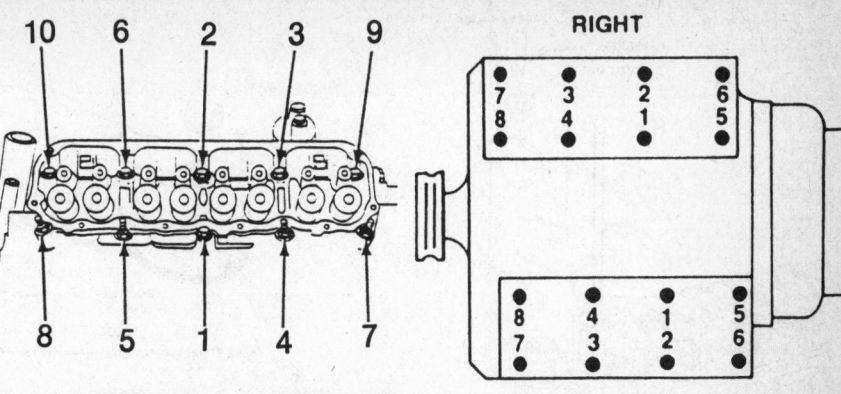

2.2L cylinder head bolt torque sequence

2.5L cylinder head bolt torque sequence

RIGHT

LEFT

3.0L cylinder head bolt torque sequence

NOTE: The cylinder head gasket used on this engine is a composite gasket and DOES NOT require the use of any sealing compound.

10. Place the cylinder head on the block and install the bolts. Tighten the bolts in 3 steps and in sequence to the correct torque.

11. Install the valve train components in their original sequence. Place a new gasket on the cylinder head and install the rocker cover.

12. Connect all of the hoses removed and install the A/C compressor, tighten the mounting bolts to 20 ft. lbs. Route the accessory drive belt and adjust the tension.

13. Connect the battery cable and fill the cooling system. Run the engine and bleed the cooling system, check for leaks.

3.0L Engine

1. Disconnect the negative battery cable.

2. Drain the cooling system.

3. Remove the accessory drive belt and remove the A/C compressor from the cylinder head cover.

4. Remove the intake and exhaust manifolds.

5. Remove the spark plug wires. Remove the rocker arm cover.

6. Remove the alternator mounting bracket and remove the top timing case bolts that thread into the cylinder head.

NOTE: The timing sprocket and chain must be supported in place and not allowed to drop into the timing case. If the chain and sprocket slip into the case the timing case will have to be removed.

7. Turn the engine over until the camshaft sprocket is straight up. Attach tool MOT–589 (timing chain support bracket) or equivalent, to the timing case cover. On the left cylinder head remove the distributor assembly.

8. Remove the threaded plug on the front of the timing case cover to gain access to the camshaft sprocket bolt.

9. Remove the cylinder head bolts. Remove the rocker shaft assembly.

10. Remove the rear camshaft cover and gasket at the rear of the cylinder head.

11. Loosen the camshaft thrust plate screw (located behind the timing sprocket) and move the thrust plate up. This will allow the camshaft to move in the head.

12. Loosen the camshaft sprocket bolt and pull the camshaft back until the bolt is free from the camshaft, the bolt will stay in the sprocket.

NOTE: DO NOT pull straight up on the cylinder head to remove it. This will cause the cylinder liners to come out of the block.

13. Position a block of wood on the intake manifold side of the head and strike it with a hammer, do the same on the exhaust manifold side of the head. Repeat this until the cylinder head is loose. Remove the cylinder head.

NOTE: When the cylinder head has been removed it is recommended by the manufacturer that the cylinder liners in the block, be supported with special tool MOT–588 liner hold down clamp or equivalent. This tool is designed to prevent the cylinder liners from be knocked out of position.

14. Remove the cylinder head gasket and clean all of the gasket mating surfaces.

To install:

15. At the back of the timing case cover, cut the gasket flush with the cylinder head gasket face and remove the pieces. Clean the back of the timing cover. Cut sections of new gasket to replace the pieces removed and attach them with adhesive.

16. Install a new cylinder head gasket over the alignment dowels on the head. Place a small bead of RTV or equivalent at the point where the head gasket meets the timing case cover.

17. Place the cylinder head on the block and install the top timing case cover to cylinder head bolts, only finger tighten the bolts.

18. Remove the timing sprocket support tool. Position the camshaft into

the sprocket and line up the dowel to the slot in the camshaft. Install the sprocket bolt and lightly tighten it. Slide the thrust plate into position and tighten the thrust plate bolt to 4 ft. lbs.

19. Install the rocker shaft assembly and install the head bolts. Tighten the cylinder head bolts in sequence and in 4 steps to specification.

20. Install the rocker covers, intake and exhaust manifold.

21. Install the timing case plug, spark plug wires and the A/C compressor. Reconnect all hoses and fill the cooling system.

22. Install the distributor assembly on the left cylinder head.

23. Install the accessory drive belt and adjust the tension. Connect the negative battery terminal. Start the engine and bleed the cooling system. Check for leaks.

OVERHAUL

For all cylinder head overhaul procedures, please refer to the "Engine Rebuilding" in the Unit Repair section.

Rocker Arms/Shafts

REMOVAL & INSTALLATION

1982–83 2.5L Engine

1. Remove the valve cover.

2. Remove the rocker arm nut and rocker arm ball.

3. Lift the rocker arm off the stud. Always keep the rocker arm assemblies together and assemble them on the same stud.

4. Remove the pushrod from its bore. Make sure the rods are returned to their original bores, with the same end in the block.

5. Reverse the removal procedure to install. Lubricate all parts before in-

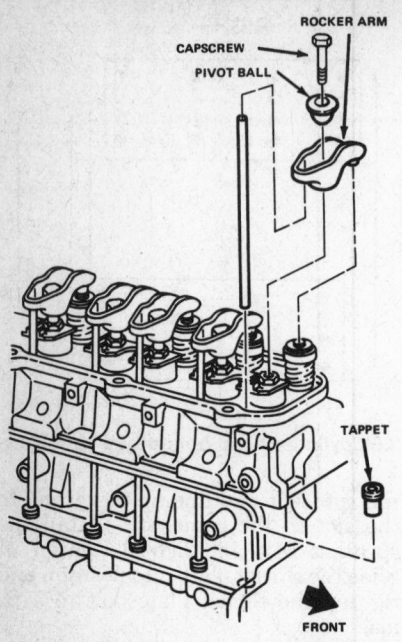

1982–83 2.5L rocker arm assembly

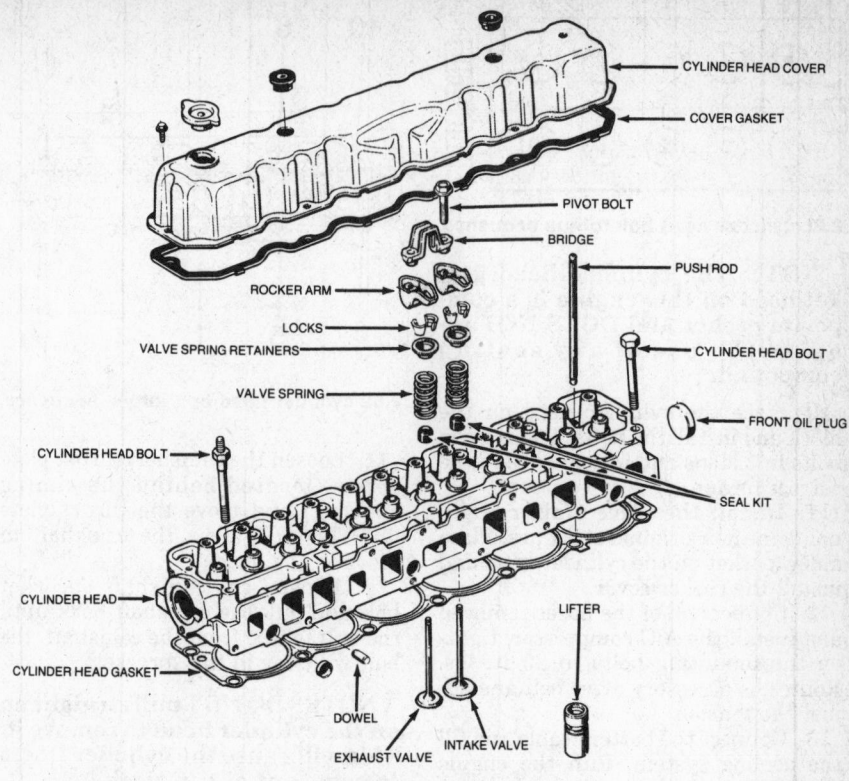

4.2L cylinder head assembly

stallation. Tighten the rocker arm ball retaining nut to 20 ft. lbs.

1984 2.5L Engines

1. Remove the valve cover. The cover seal on the 2.5L is RTV sealer. Break the seal with a clean putty knife or razor blade. Don't attempt to remove the cover until the seal is broken all around. To remove the cover, pry where indicated "PRY HERE" at the bolt holes.
2. Remove the capscrews at each bridge and pivot assembly.
3. Alternately loosen the capscrews 1 turn at a time to avoid damaging he bridge.
4. Remove the bridges, pivots and corresponding pair of rocker arms.
5. Installation is in the reverse order of removal. Tighten capscrews to 19 ft. lbs.

1988–89 2.5L and 4.2L Engine

The valve guides are integral with the head on all engines. The valve stem oil deflectors should be replaced whenever valve service is performed.

American Motors engines do not have replaceable valve guides. If stem to guide clearance is excessive, guides must be reamed to the proper oversize. 3 oversize valves are available with stems 0.003, 0.015 and 0.030 in. larger than standard diameter.

The intake and exhaust rocker arms for each cylinder pivot on a bridged pivot assembly bolted to the cylinder head. The pushrods are hollow to supply lubrication to the rocker arms. The pushrods act as guides to keep the rocker arms in alignment, so it is not

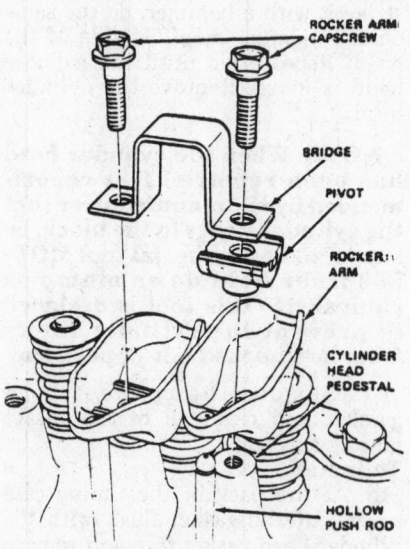

4.2L rocker arm assembly

abnormal for pushrods to rub slightly on the cylinder head.

1. Disconnect the negative battery cable. Remove the air cleaner and all related vacuum hoses. Remove the rocker cover retaining bolts and remove the rocker cover.
2. Unscrew the rocker arm capscrews evenly to avoid breaking the bridge.
3. Remove the pivot assemblies, rocker arms, and pushrods.

NOTE: Be sure to keep all parts in the same order in which they were removed.

4. Clean all parts in solvent. Blow all oil passages in the rocker arms and pushrods dry with compressed air. Replace any deeply pitted rocker arms and scuffed or worn pushrods. If the pushrod is worn from lack of oil, replace it, its valve lifter and rocker arm, as well.
5. Insert the pushrods in their bores. Be sure to center the bottom of each rod in the plunger cap of the hydraulic valve lifter.
6. Install the rocker arms, pivot assemblies and capscrews. Tighten the capscrews evenly 19 ft. lbs. on all engines.

NOTE: Be sure that the pushrods, pivot assemblies, and capscrews are returned to exactly the same places from which they were removed.

7. Wipe the gasket surface clean. If a silicone sealer is being used, wipe the surface with an oily rag and apply a 1/8 in. bead of silicone along the scaling surface. Before the silicone begins to harden, install the cover, being careful not to touch the silicone to the rocker arms. Apply a small amount of sealer to each screw hole and tighten the screws to specifications. When using a

gasket, cement the gasket in several places with a quick-drying adhesive.

8. Correctly position the cover and gasket on the engine and install the attaching screws.

9. Install the air cleaner and hoses. Connect the negative battery cable.

2.2L and 3.0L Engines

The rocker arms on these engine are mounted on a shaft, at the top of the head. All of the rocker arms come of at the same time with the shaft.

1. Disconnect the negative battery cable.

2. Remove the rocker arm cover retaining bolts and remove the rocker cover.

3. Remove the bolts retaining the rocker arm shaft to the cylinder head.

4. Install the rocker shaft assembly and tighten the rocker shaft retaining bolts to 66 inch lbs.

5. Install the rocker cover using a new gasket.

6. Connect the negative battery cable.

Intake Manifold

REMOVAL & INSTALLATION

1982–83 2.5L Engine

1. Remove the air cleaner. Drain the cooling system. Disconnect the heater hose from the intake manifold.

2. Disconnect and label the fuel line, all vacuum lines and electrical connectors from the carburetor, insulator and the intake manifold. Plug the fuel line.

3. Disconnect the throttle linkage.

4. Remove the carburetor and insulator.

5. Remove the alternator rear support bracket from the manifold.

6. Remove the A/C compressor, if so equipped.

——— **CAUTION** ———

Compressed refrigerant will freeze any surface it touches, including skin and eyes. It also forms a poisonous gas in the presence of an open flame.

7. Remove the intake manifold bolts and remove the manifold.

8. To install, place a new gasket against the cylinder head. Install the manifold in place by starting all bolts finger-tight.

9. Torque the intake manifold bolts to 25 ft. lbs. in 2 stages, using the torque sequence shown. The rest of the installation is in the reverse order of removal.

1984 2.5L Engine

NOTE: It is necessary to re-

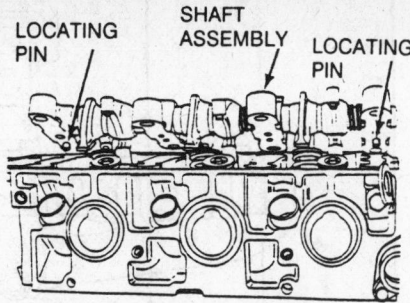

2.2L and 3.0L rocker arm shaft removal

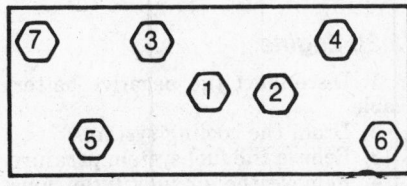

1982–83 2.5L intake manifold torque sequence

move the carburetor from the intake manifold before the manifold is removed. After removing the carburetor from the intake manifold, it may be set to one side with vacuum hoses still attached.

1. Disconnect the negative battery cable. Drain the cooling system.

2. Remove the air cleaner. Disconnect the fuel pipe, carburetor air horn vent hose, idle speed control vacuum hose, and wire connector. Disconnect the vacuum line from the EGR valve.

3. Disconnect the coolant hoses from the intake manifold.

4. Disconnect the throttle cable from the bellcrank.

5. Disconnect the PCV valve vacuum hose from the intake manifold and valve cover and remove it.

6. Remove the vacuum advance CTO valve vacuum hoses.

7. Disconnect the feedback system coolant temperature sender wire connector (located on the intake manifold).

8. Disconnect the vacuum hose from the EGR valve.

9. Disconnect the intake manifold electric heater wire connector.

10. Remove the power steering mounting bracket, if so equipped.

11. Detach the power steering pump and set aside, if so equipped.

12. Do not remove the pressure hoses.

13. Disconnect the throttle valve linkage, if equipped with automatic transmission.

14. Disconnect the EGR valve tube from the intake manifold.

NOTE: The intake and exhaust

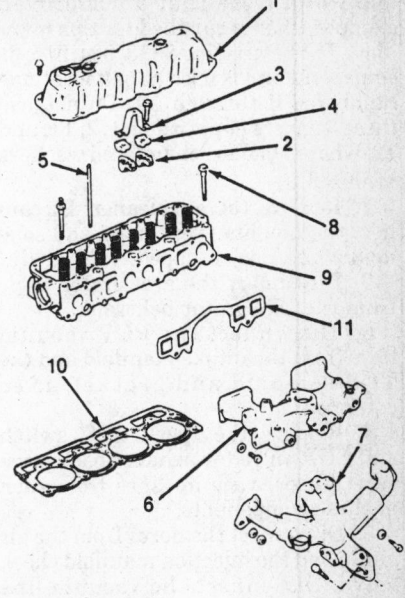

1 CYLINDER HEAD	7 EXHAUST MANIFOLD
2 ROCKER ARMS	8 CYL. HEAD BOLTS
3 BRIDGE	9 CYLINDER HEAD
4 PIVOT	10 CYL. HEAD GASKET
5 PUSHROD	11 INTAKE MANIF.
6 INTAKE MANIFOLD	GASKET

1984 2.5L cylinder head assembly

manifolds are 2 separate pieces, mounted on a common set of bolts, with a gasket for the intake manifold only.

15. Remove the intake and exhaust manifold retaining bolts and remove the manifold.

16. Clean the mating surfaces of the manifold and cylinder head.

NOTE: If the manifold is being replaced, ensure all fittings, etc. are transferred to the replacement manifold.

17. Install the exhaust manifold if it has been removed and finger tighten the center retaining bolt.

18. Position the intake gasket and install the intake manifold.

19. Tighten the intake and exhaust manifold bolts in the proper sequence to 23 ft. lbs. torque.

20. Install the EGR tube, the heat tube, electrical connectors, the carburetor, the fuel and vacuum lines and remaining components.

21. Start the engine and bring to normal operating temperature. Recheck torque on manifold retaining bolts.

22. Install the air cleaner assembly.

4.2L Engine

The intake manifold is mounted on the left-hand side of the engine and bolted to the cylinder head. A gasket is used between the intake manifold and the head; none is required for the exhaust manifold. Note that an improved clamp washer is supplied for this manifold. It is Part No. 8933 004 255 or equivalent and is used at bolt locations numbered 3 through 10. Do not use these washers at positions 1, 2, 11, and 12, where smaller, chamfered washers are used.

1. Remove the air cleaner. Disconnect the fuel line, vent hose, and solenoid wire, if so equipped.

2. Disconnect the accelerator cable from the accelerator bellcrank.

3. Disconnect the PCV vacuum hose from the intake manifold and the TCS solenoid and bracket, if so equipped.

4. Remove the spark CTO switch and EGR valve (or exhaust back pressure sensor) vacuum lines from each of these components.

5. Disconnect the hoses from the air pump and the injection manifold check valve. Disconnect the vacuum line from the diverter valve and remove the diverter valve with hoses, if so equipped.

6. Remove the air pump and power steering bracket (if so equipped) and remove the air pump. Move the power steering pump aside, out of the way, without disconnecting the hoses.

7. Remove the air conditioning drive belt idler assembly from the cylinder head, if so equipped. It is necessary on some models to remove the A/C compressor. Do not remove the refrigerant lines, support the A/C compressor aside.

8. Disconnect the throttle valve linkage if equipped with automatic transmission.

9. Disconnect the exhaust pipe from the manifold.

10. On some models, an oxygen sensor is screwed in the exhaust manifold just above the exhaust pipe connection. Disconnect the wire and remove the sensor, if so equipped.

11. Remove the manifold attaching bolts, nuts, and clamps and remove the intake and exhaust manifolds as an assembly. Discard the gasket. The 2 manifolds are separated at the heat riser.

12. Clean all the mating surfaces on the cylinder head and the manifolds.

13. Assemble the 2 manifolds and tighten the heat riser retaining nuts to 5 ft. lbs.

14. Position the manifold on the engine, together with a new intake manifold gasket, and tighten the manifold attaching bolts and nuts in the proper sequence to the specified torque.

15. Install the remaining components in the reverse order of removal. Adjust the automatic transmission throttle linkage, if so equipped. Adjust the drive belt tension.

Intake and exhaust manifold torque sequence— 6 cylinder

2.2L Engine

1. Disconnect the negative battery cable.

2. Drain the cooling system.

3. Relieve the fuel system pressure.

4. Remove the air inlet/filter housing and tube.

5. Disconnect the fuel lines at the injector rail. Disconnect the vacuum lines at the intake manifold.

6. Disconnect the throttle linkage at the throttle body. Remove the electrical connectors from the injectors.

7. Remove the intake manifold retaining bolts and remove the intake manifold.

8. Clean the gasket mating surfaces.

To install:

9. Position the intake manifold on the head using a new gasket and insert the bolts. Tighten the bolts to 11 ft. lbs.

10. Connect the electrical leads to the injectors and the fuel lines to the fuel rail.

11. Connect the vacuum lines at the manifold and the throttle linkage at the throttle body.

12. Attach the air inlet to the throttle body. Fill the cooling system and connect the negative battery cable.

13. Run the engine, bleed the cooling system and check for leaks.

1988–89 2.5L Engine

1. Disconnect the negative battery cable.

2. Remove the air inlet cover and hose from the throttle body.

3. Loosen the accessory drive belt and remove it. Remove the power steering pump and brackets. Support the pump to the side, do not disconnect the pressure lines.

4. Relieve the fuel system pressure.

5. Disconnect the fuel lines and the accelerator cable from the throttle body. Disconnect the electrical connectors for the idle speed sensor, throttle position sensor, coolant temperature sensor, air intake temperature sensor and the oxygen sensor.

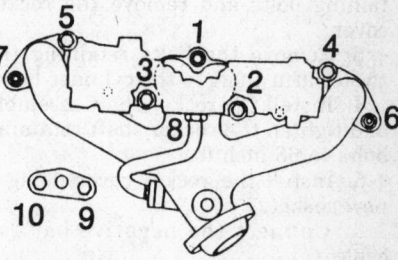

2.5L intake/exhaust manifold torque sequence

6. Disconnect the electrical plug from the fuel injector. Disconnect the vacuum lines at the intake manifold.

7. Remove the bolts supporting the EGR tube to the manifold. Remove the heater hoses from the intake manifold.

8. Remove the manifold mounting bolts and remove the manifold from the engine.

9. Clean all of the gasket mounting surfaces.

To install:

10. Install the new intake manifold gasket over the locating dowels and install the manifold to the head. Tighten the bolts in sequence and to the specified torque.

11. Install the EGR tube to the manifold. Connect the heater and vacuum hoses. Attach the fuel lines to the throttle body.

12. Reconnect all electrical connectors. Install the power steering pump and brackets.

13. Connect the acclerator cable. Install the accessory drive belt and adjust the tension. Install the air inlet tube and cover.

14. Connect the negative battery cable and fill the cooling system.

15. Run the engine and bleed the cooling system, check for leaks.

3.0L Engine

1. Disconnect the negative battery cable.

2. Remove the engine cover retaining bolts and remove the cover.

3. Remove the air inlet cover from the throttle body.

4. Disconnect the transmission kickdown cable, accelerator cable and cruise control cable from the throttle body. Remove the vacuum hoses from the intake manifold.

5. Remove the electrical connector from the throttle position sensor. Disconnect and tag the electrical connectors from the fuel injectors and lay the harness aside.

6. Remove the EGR tube. Remove the wire from the air temperature sensor.

7. Relieve the fuel system pressure and remove the fuel lines from the injector rails.

8. Remove the 4 bolts retaining the intake manifold and remove the manifold. Remove and discard the O-rings, from the cylinder heads.

NOTE: When the intake manifold has been removed the O-rings in the cylinder heads MUST be replaced.

9. Clean all gasket mating surfaces.
To install:
10. Install the new O-rings and install the intake manifold. Torque the retaining bolts to 11 ft. lbs., tighten in an "X" pattern.

11. Install the fuel lines to the fuel rail assembly. Connect the electrical connectors to the fuel injectors. Connect all of the elctrical connectors and vacuum hoses removed.

12. Connect the EGR tube. Connect the transmission kickdown cable, accelerator and cruise control cables. Connect the negative battery cable.

13. Install the air inlet to the throttle body. Install the engine cover.

14. Run the engine and check for leaks.

Exhaust Manifold

REMOVAL & INSTALLATION

1982–83 2.5L Engine

1. Remove the air cleaner and the hot air tube.

2. Remove the Pulsair system from the exhaust manifold.

3. Disconnect the exhaust pipe from the manifold at the flange. Spray the bolts first with penetrating oil, if necessary.

4. Remove the engine oil dipstick bracket bolt.

5. Remove the exhaust manifold bolts and remove the manifold from the head.

6. To install, place a new gasket against the cylinder head, then install the exhaust manifold over it. Start all the bolts into the head finger-tight.

7. Torque the exhaust manifold

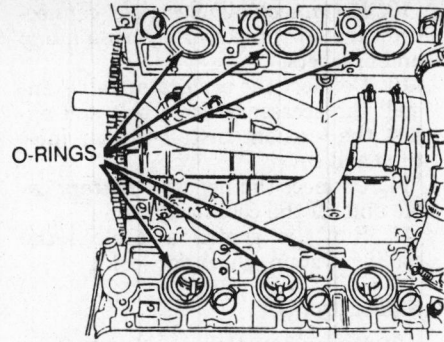

O-RINGS

Replace the O-rings before installing the manifold—3.0L

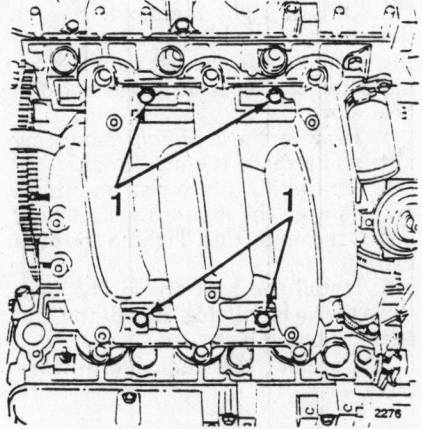

1. Retaining bolts

3.0L intake manifold mounting

bolts to 37 ft. lbs. in 2 stages, using the torque sequence illustrated.

8. Complete the installation in the reverse order of removal.

1984 2.5L Engine

1. Remove the intake manifold.

2. Disconnect the EGR valve tube.

3. Disconnect the exhaust pipe from the exhaust manifold.

4. Disconnect the oxygen sensor wire connector.

5. Remove the sensor from the manifold if a replacement manifold is to be installed.

6. Remove the nuts from the end studs. Remove the exhaust manifold.

7. Installation is in the reverse order of removal. Torque manifold nuts to 23 ft. lbs., oxygen sensor to 35 ft. lbs.

4.2L Engine

1. Remove the air cleaner. Disconnect the fuel line, vent hose, and solenoid wire, if so equipped.

2. Disconnect the accelerator cable from the accelerator bellcrank.

3. Disconnect the PCV vacuum

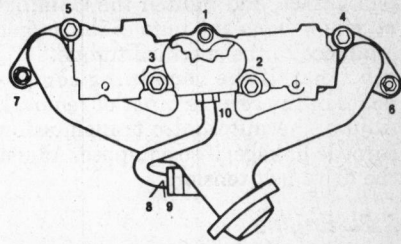

1984 2.5L intake manifold torque sequence

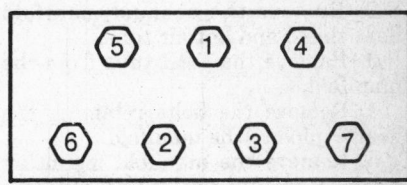

1982–83 2.5L exhaust manifold torque sequence

hose from the intake manifold and the TCS solenoid and bracket, if so equipped.

4. Remove the spark CTO switch and EGR valve (or exhaust back pressure sensor) vacuum lines from each of these components.

5. Disconnect the hoses from the air pump and the injection manifold check valve. Disconnect the vacuum line from the diverter valve and remove the diverter valve with hoses, if so equipped.

6. Remove the air pump and power steering bracket (if so equipped) and remove the air pump. Move the power steering pump aside, out of the way, without disconnecting the hoses.

7. Remove the air conditioning drive belt idler assembly from the cylinder head, if so equipped. It is necessary on some models to remove the A/C compressor. Do not remove the refrigerant lines, support the A/C compressor aside.

8. Disconnect the throttle valve linkage if equipped with automatic transmission.

9. Disconnect the exhaust pipe from the manifold.

10. On some models, an oxygen sensor is screwed in the exhaust manifold just above the exhaust pipe connection. Disconnect the wire and remove the sensor, if so equipped.

11. Remove the manifold attaching bolts, nuts, and clamps and remove the intake and exhaust manifolds as an assembly. Discard the gasket. The 2 manifolds are separated at the heat riser.

12. Clean all the mating surfaces on the cylinder head and the manifolds.

13. Assemble the 2 manifolds and tighten the heat riser retaining nuts to 5 ft. lbs.

14. Position the manifold on the engine, together with a new intake mani-

fold gasket, and tighten the manifold attaching bolts and nuts in the proper sequence to the specified torque.

15. Install the remaining components in the reverse order of removal. Adjust the automatic transmission throttle linkage, if so equipped. Adjust the drive belt tension.

2.2L Engine

1. Disconnect the negative battery cable.
2. Remove the exhaust manifold heat shield and hot air tube.
3. Remove the EGR tube from the manifold.
4. Remove the bolts retaining the header pipe to the manifold.
5. Remove the manifold mounting nuts. Remove the manifold and gaskets.
6. To install, place the manifold gaskets and the manifold on the block and tighten the mounting nuts to 13 ft. lbs.
7. Install the heat shield and the EGR tube.
8. Connect the negative battery cable.

1988–89 2.5L Engine

1. Disconnect the negative battery cable.
2. Remove the air inlet cover and hose from the throttle body.
3. Loosen the accessory drive belt and remove it. Remove the power steering pump and brackets. Support the pump to the side, do not disconnect the pressure lines.
4. Relieve the fuel system pressure.
5. Disconnect the fuel lines and the accelerator cable from the throttle body. Disconnect the electrical connectors for the idle speed sensor, throttle position sensor, coolant temperature sensor, air intake temperature sensor and the oxygen sensor.
6. Disconnect the electrical plug from the fuel injector. Disconnect the vacuum lines at the intake manifold.
7. Remove the bolts supporting the EGR tube to the exhaust manifold. Remove the heater hoses from the intake manifold.
8. Remove the intake/exhaust manifold mounting bolts and remove the manifolds from the engine.
9. Clean all of the gasket mounting surfaces.

To install:

10. Install the new intake manifold gasket and the new exhaust manifold spacers over the locating dowels and install the manifolds to the head. Tighten the bolts in sequence and to the specified torque.
11. Install the EGR tube to the exhaust manifold. Connect the heater and vacuum hoses. Attach the fuel lines to the throttle body.

12. Reconnect all electrical connectors. Install the power steering pump and brackets.
13. Connect the acclerator cable. Install the accessory drive belt and adjust the tension. Install the air inlet tube and cover.
14. Connect the negative battery cable and fill the cooling system.
15. Run the engine and bleed the cooling system, check for leaks.

3.0L Engine

1. Disconnect the negative battery cable.
2. Disconnect the EGR tube from the right manifold. Remove the nuts retaining the header pipe to the manifolds.
3. On the right manifold, remove the nuts securing the dipstick tube to the manifold. On the left manifold remove the starter heat shield and the heat stove.
4. Remove the manifold mounting nuts and remove the manifolds.
5. To install, place new manifold gaskets over the mounting studs and install the manifolds. Tighten the nuts to 13 ft. lbs.
6. Install the heat shield and heat stove to the manifolds. Install the dipstick retaining bolt.
7. Connect the negative battery cable.

Front Cover

REMOVAL & INSTALLATION

1982–83 2.5L Engine

1. Remove the crankshaft hub.
2. Remove the oil pan to front cover screws.
3. Remove the front cover to block screws.
4. Pull the cover slightly forward, just enough to allow cutting of the oil pan front seal flush with the block on both sides.
5. Remove the front cover and attached portion of the pan seal.
6. Clean the gasket surfaces thoroughly.
7. Cut the tabs from the new oil pan front seal.
8. Install the seal on the front cover, pressing the tips into the holes provided.
9. Coat the new gasket with sealer and position it on the front cover.
10. Apply a $\frac{1}{8}$ in. bead of silicone sealer to the joint formed at the oil pan and block.
11. Align the front cover seal with a centering tool and install the front cover. Tighten the screws to 7.5 ft. lbs. Install the crankshaft hub.

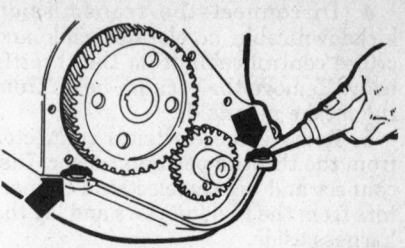

Sealer application prior to front cover installation – 1982–83 2.5L

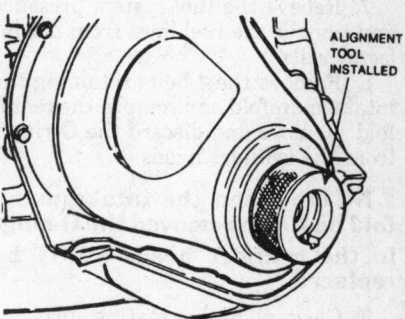

Typical 2.5L front cover alignment

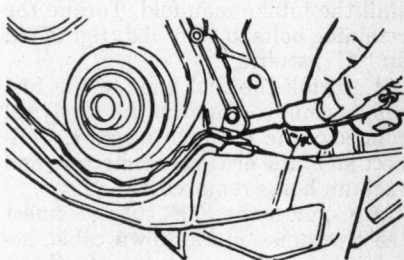

Trim the pan gasket edges before installing the front cover

1984 2.5L, 2.2L, 1988–89 2.5L and 4.2L Engines

1. Remove all V-belts, fan and pulley.
2. Remove vibration damper.
3. Remove oil pan to cover bolts and cover to block bolts.
4. Raise cover and pull oil pan front seal up far enough to extract the tabs from the holes in cover.

— **CAUTION** —

If this isn't done, the oil pan will have to be removed to get the seals into place.

5. Remove cover gasket from block; cut off seal tab flush with front face of block.
6. Clean all mating surfaces and remove oil seal.
7. Install a new front oil seal.
8. Install a new neoprene seal in front oil pan, cutting off protruding tabs to match original. Use sealer on the end tabs and the gasket surfaces.
9. Position cover on block and install bolts. Align the front cover with a centering tool. Tighten cover bolts to

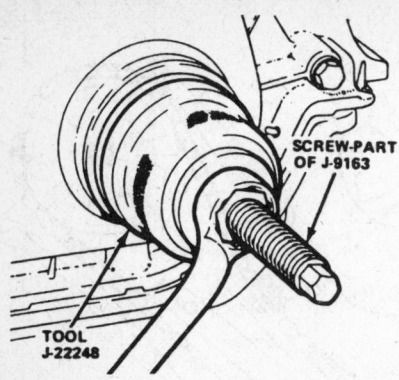

4.2L front cover seal Installation

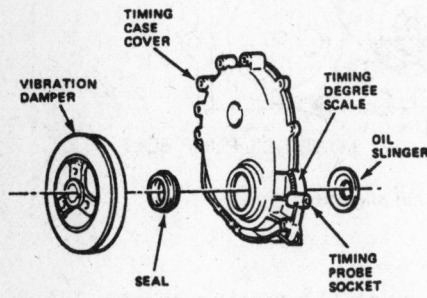

4.2L front cover assembly

4–6 ft. lbs.; 4 lower bolts to 10–12 ft. lbs. Remove the centering tool.

10. Install vibration damper, tightening the bolt to the specified torque. Install the accessory drive belt(s).

NOTE: Front oil seal can be installed with cover in place only if proper tool or equivalent is available.

3.0L Engine

1. Disconnect the negative battery cable.

2. Remove the rocker covers. Remove the distributor assembly.

3. Remove the accessory drive belt. Remove the nuts retaining the front engine vibration damper to the engine, move it toward the radiator.

4. Remove the crankshaft pulley nut and remove the crankshaft pulley.

NOTE: The cranshaft pulley nut is put on with a threaded lock installed with the nut. It may be necessary to strike the pulley nut with a brass hammer to loosen it.

5. Remove the cover retaining bolts and pry the cover away from the engine.

6. Using a drift, remove the oil seal from the cover.

7. Clean all of the gasket mating surfaces.
To install:

8. Using RTV sealer or equivalent,

apply a bead of sealer to the points where the cylinder heads meet the block and the lower case meets the block.

9. Install the cover with new gasket over the alignment dowels. Tighten the bolts to 9 ft. lbs.

10. Install the distributor assembly and install the rocker covers.

11. Install the crankshaft pulley, apply thread locking compound to the threads of the pulley nut and tighten to 133 ft. lbs.

12. Install the accessory drive belt and adjust the belt tension.

NOTE: It is very important the accessory drive belt is routed correctly. If it is incorrectly routed the water pump could be driven in the wrong direction causing the engine to overheat.

13. Install the engine vibration damper. Connect the negative battery cable.

Timing Chain and Sprockets

REMOVAL & INSTALLATION

1982–83 2.5L Engine

This engine uses timing gears instead of a chain and sprockets or a belt. The camshaft timing gear is pressed onto the camshaft. The camshaft must be removed to remove the gear, which must be pressed off the camshaft. The replacement cam gear must be pressed onto the camshaft. To replace the gear, first place the gear spacer ring and thrust plate over the end of the camshaft, then install the Woodruff key. Press the camshaft gear onto the cam until it bottoms against the gear spacer ring. End clearance of the thrust plate must be 0.0015–0.0050 in. If less than 0.0015 in., the spacer ring must be replaced. If more than 0.0050 in., the thrust plate must be replaced.

1984 2.5L and 1988–89 2.5L Engines

1. Disconnect the negative battery cable. Remove the front cover.

2. Rotate the crankshaft until the zero timing mark on the crankshaft sprocket is closest to and on center line with the mark on the cam sprocket.

3. Remove the oil slinger from the crankshaft.

4. Remove the camshaft retaining bolt and remove the sprockets and chain as an assembly.

5. Installation is in the reverse order of removal, with the following recommendations:

a. Turn the tensioner lever to the unlock (down) position.

b. Pull the tensioner block toward the tensioner lever to compress the spring. Hold the block and turn the tensioner lever to the **LOCK** position.

4.2L Engine

1. Remove the drive belt(s).

2. Remove the engine fan and hub assembly.

3. Remove the vibration damper pulley and remove the vibration damper.

4. Remove the timing case cover. Remove the seal from the timing case cover, the seal should be replaced every time the cover is removed from the engine.

5. Remove the camshaft sprocket retaining bolt and washer.

6. Turn the crankshaft until the 0 degree timing mark on the crankshaft sprocket is closest to and on a centerline with the timing pointer of the camshaft sprocket.

7. Remove the crankshaft sprocket, camshaft sprocket and timing chain as an assembly. Disassemble the chain and sprockets.

8. To install; assemble the timing chain, crankshaft sprocket, and camshaft sprocket with the timing marks aligned.

9. Install the assembly to the crankshaft and camshaft.

10. Install the camshaft sprocket retaining bolt and washer and tighten the bolt to 50 ft. lbs.

11. To ensure the correct installation of the timing chain, locate the timing mark of the camshaft sprocket at about the **1 O'CLOCK** position. This should place the timing mark on the crankshaft sprocket where the sprocket teeth mesh with the chain. There must be 15 timing chain pins between the timing marks of both sprockets.

3.0L Engine

1. Disconnect the negative battery cable.

2. Remove the front cover assembly.

3. Remove the oil pump sprocket retaining bolts and remove the sprocket/chain assembly.

4. Remove the bolt attaching the right side camshaft sprocket to the camshaft. Remove the right side tensioner and let the tensioner shoe hang down.

5. Remove the right side timing chain and sprocket. Remove the right side chain guide and tensioner shoe.

NOTE: Keep all of the components from each side together. This will aid in installation.

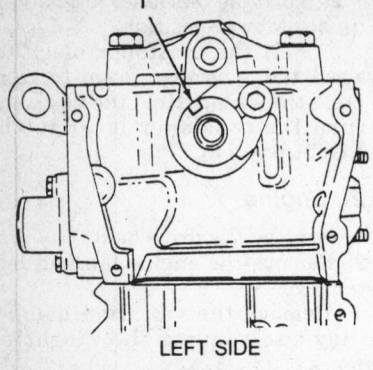

LEFT SIDE

1. Turn the left camshaft until the slot is positioned as shown
2. Turn the right camshaft until the slot is positioned as shown

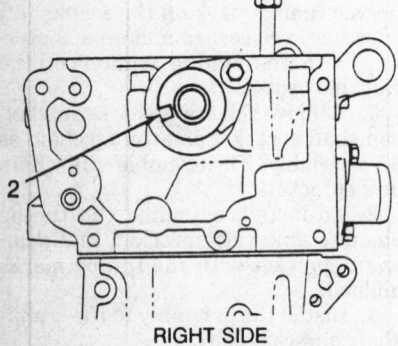

RIGHT SIDE

3.0L position the camshafts as shown before installing the timing chains

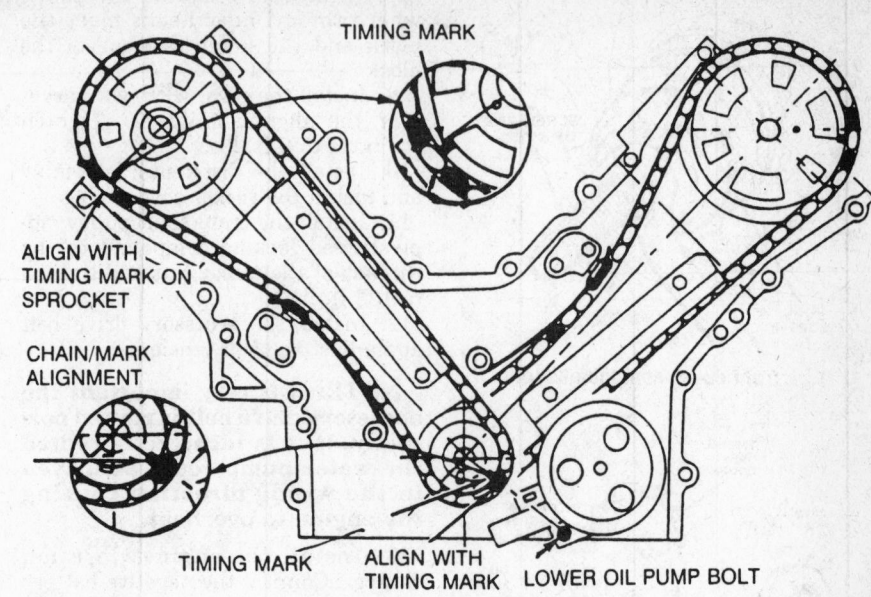

3.0L timing chain alignment

6. Remove the bolt attaching the left side camshaft sprocket to the camshaft. Remove the left side tensioner and let the tensioner shoe hang down.

7. Remove the left side timing chain and sprocket. Remove the left side chain guide and tensioner shoe.

To install:

8. Install the left and right chain guides, tighten the bolts to 48 inch lbs. Install the tensioner shoes and tighten the mounting bolts to 9 ft. lbs.

9. Turn the left camshaft until the keyway slot is in the **11 O'CLOCK** position. Turn the right camshaft so that the keyway is in the **8 O'CLOCK** position.

10. Turn the cranshaft until the keyway is aligned with the centerline of the left cylinder head.

NOTE: The crankshaft has 3 sprockets on it. A sprocket each for the left and right timing chains, 1 for the oil pump drive. The timing mark is located on the center sprocket.

11. Install the left camshaft sprocket. Install the left timing chain on the crankshaft. Position the single painted link of the timing chain, on the tooth of the rear sprocket, that is directly behind the timing mark of the center sprocket.

12. Install the left timing chain over the camshaft sprocket. The chain must be positioned with the unpainted link, that is between 2 painted links, aligned with the stamped timing mark on the camshaft sprocket.

13. Once the left chain is positioned, install the tensioner shoe and turn the tensioner arm in. Tighten the mounting bolts to 48 inch lbs.

14. Turn the crankshaft until the timing mark on the center sprocket is aligned with the lower oil pump mounting bolt.

15. Install the right camshaft sprocket. Install the right timing chain over the crankshaft sprocket. Position the single painted link over the timing mark on the crankshaft sprocket.

16. Position the right timing chain over the camshaft sprocket. The chain must be positioned with the unpainted link, that is between 2 painted links, aligned with the stamped timing mark on the camshaft sprocket.

17. Once the right chain is positioned, install the tensioner shoe and turn the tensioner arm in. Tighten the mounting bolts to 48 inch lbs.

18. Install the right camshaft sprocket bolt and tighten to 59 ft. lbs. Push both of the chain tensioner shoes in to release them, this will adjust the chain tension.

NOTE: Once the crankshaft has been rotated the painted marks on the chain will no longer align with the timing marks. When checking valve timing it is the relation of the timing marks to each other that is used, not the position of the paint marks on the chains.

19. Install the oil pump sprocket and chain, apply a suitable thread locking compound to the retaining bolts and tighten to 48 inch lbs.

20. Install the front cover assembly. Connect the negative battery cable.

Timing Belt and Tensioner

REMOVAL & INSTALLATION

2.2L Engine

1. Disconnect the negative battery cable.

2. Remove the timing belt cover.

3. Loosen the 2 bolts holding the timing belt tensioner in place and remove the timing belt.

To install:

4. Align the camshaft sprocket timing mark with the static timing mark on the cylinder cover.

5. Position the crankshaft so that the No. 1 cylinder is at the TDC of its compression stroke.

6. Push the timing belt tensioner pulley towards the water pump and tighten the bolts, this will make the timing belt installation easier.

7. Install the timing belt on the sprockets. Loosen the tensioner bolts and allow the tensioner to contact the

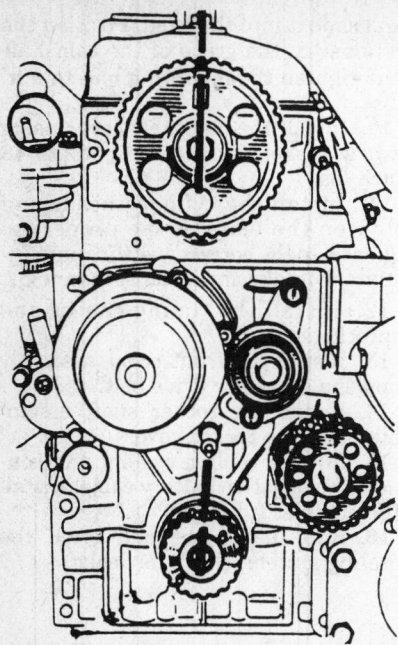

Align the camshaft sprocket and the crankshaft sprocket before installing the timing belt—2.2L

belt. This will automatically adjust the belt tension.

8. Tighten the tensioner bolts. Belt tension can be manually checked at this point.

9. Using belt tension gauge tool ELE-346 or equivalent, check the belt deflection. Correct belt deflection should be 0.216–0.276 in.

10. Install the timing belt cover.

11. Install the negative battery cable.

Camshaft

REMOVAL & INSTALLATION

1984 2.5L Engine

1. Drain and remove the radiator.

2. If so equipped, remove air conditioning condenser and receiver assembly as a charged unit.

3. Remove fuel pump, distributor and ignition wires.

4. Remove cylinder head cover and gasket.

5. Remove rocker arms, bridged pivot assemblies and pushrods. Be sure to replace these parts in the same order as removed.

6. Remove the cylinder head and gasket, remove the lifters.

7. Remove timing case cover.

8. Remove timing chain and sprockets as an assembly, being careful to rotate the crankshaft until the timing mark on the crankshaft sprocket is aligned with the timing pointer on the camshaft sprocket.

9. Remove the grille.

10. Carefully remove the camshaft from the engine.

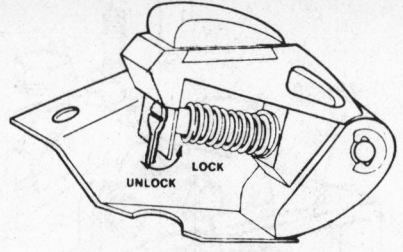

1984 2.5L timing chain tensioner

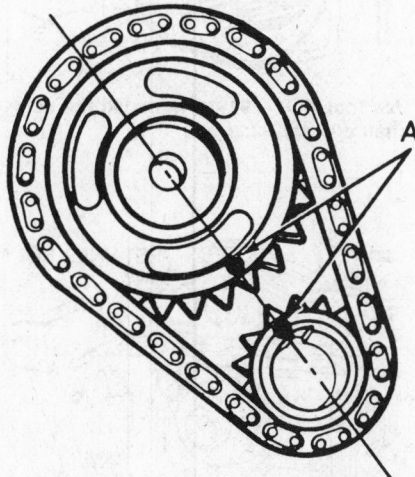

1984 2.5L timing mark (A) alignment

11. Installation is in the reverse order of removal.

1982–83 2.5L and 1988–89 2.5L Engines

1. Disconnect the negative battery cable. Drain the cooling system.

2. Remove the radiator.

3. Remove the fan and water pump pulley.

4. Remove the grille if necessary for clearance.

5. Remove the rocker cover, rocker arms, and pushrods.

6. Remove the distributor, spark plugs, and fuel pump.

7. Remove the lifters.

8. Remove the crankshaft hub and timing gear cover.

9. Remove the 2 camshaft thrust plate screws by working through the holes in the gear.

10. Remove the camshaft and gear assembly by pulling it through the front of the block. Take care not to damage the bearings.

To install:

11. Lubricate the camshaft with heavy oil and install it into the block.

12. Install the timing chain and sprockets. Install the timing case cover.

13. Install the valve lifters and related components. Install the rocker cover.

14. Install the crankshaft hub and the water pump pulley. Install the accessory drive belts.

15. Position the distributor and tighten the hold down bolt, install the spark plugs.

16. Install the grill. Connect the negative battery cable.

4.2L Engine

1. Drain the cooling system and remove the radiator.

2. If equipped with air conditioning, remove the condenser and the receiver unit as a charged assembly, only. Do not disconnect the pressure lines.

3. Remove the valve cover and gasket.

4. Remove the rocker arm assemblies and the cylinder head. Remove the pushrods and tappets.

NOTE: Pushrods and tappets should be kept in the proper order. They must be returned to their original places during assembly.

5. Remove the drive belt(s), fan assembly, accessory pulley(s), vibration damper, and the timing chain cover.

6. Remove the fuel pump. Remove the distributor assembly, including spark plug wires.

7. Turn the crankshaft until the **0** degree timing mark on the crankshaft sprocket is nearest to, on a centerline with, and aligns with the timing pointer on the camshaft sprocket.

8. Remove the sprockets and the timing chain as an assembly.

9. Remove the front bumper and/or grille as necessary. Withdraw the camshaft through the front of the vehicle.

10. Inspect the bearing journals, distributor drive, cam lobes, and tappets

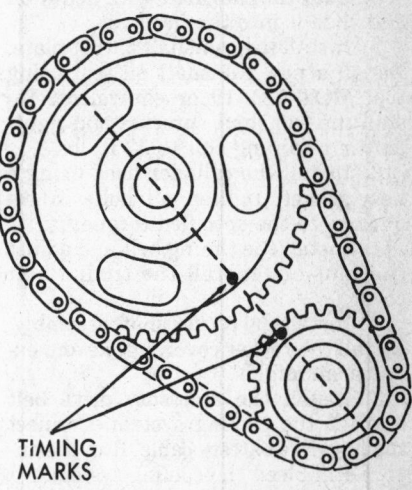

TIMING MARKS

4.2L timing mark alignment

for wear or damage. Replace worn parts, as required.

To install:

11. Use a generous amount of an engine oil supplement on the camshaft. Install it in the block, using care not to damage any surfaces.

12. Install the timing chain and sprocket assembly.

13. Install the timing chain cover and a new oil seal.

14. Install the vibration damper and the accessory drive pulley(s).

15. Install the engine fan assembly and the drive belt(s). Tighten the belts to the proper tension.

16. Install the fuel pump.

17. With the No. 1 piston at TDC of its compression stroke, fit the distributor so that the rotor is aligned with the No. 1 terminal on the cap (distributor fully seated on the block). Install the cap and the spark plug wires.

18. Install the tappets, cylinder head, its gasket, valve train (pushrods in the same order as removed), valve cover and its gasket.

2.2L Engine

1. Disconnect the negative battery cable. Drain the cooling system.

2. Remove the intake and exhaust manifolds.

3. Remove the rocker cover and remove the rocker shaft assembly.

4. Remove the accessory drive belt. Remove the timing belt cover.

5. Remove the timing belt. Remove the cylinder head retaining bolts and remove the cylinder head.

6. Remove the camshaft sprocket and the bolts retaining the camshaft thrust plate.

7. Pry the oil seal out from around the camshaft and slide the camshaft from the head. Use care not to damage the camshaft lobes or the bearings.

To install:

8. Coat the camshaft with heavy oil and slide it into the head.

9. Install the camshaft thrust plate. Install a new camshaft oil seal using tool MOT-791-10 or equivalent. Install the camshaft sprocket and tighten the retaining bolt to 37 ft. lbs.

10. Install the cylinder head using a new gasket, tighten all bolts in sequence, to the specified torque.

11. Install the timing belt and adjust the tension. Install the timing belt cover.

12. Install the rocker shaft assembly. Install the rocker cover, intake and exhaust manifolds.

13. Install the accessory drive belt and fill the cooling system. Connect the negative battery cable. Run the engine and bleed the cooling system.

3.0L Engine

The camshafts used in this engine are

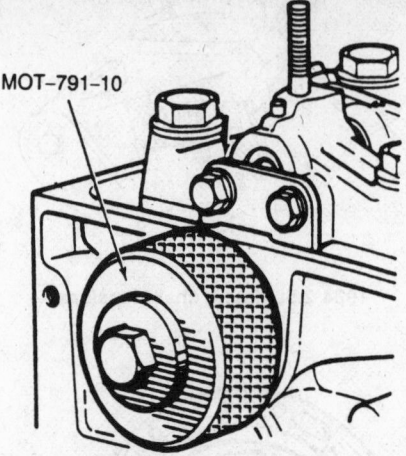

MOT-791-10

Use tool MOT-791-10 to install the camshaft oil seal—2.2L

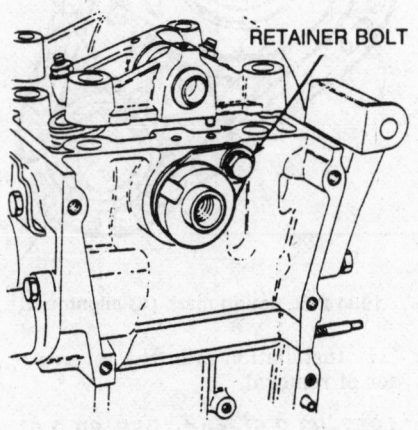

RETAINER BOLT

3.0L camshaft retainer

removed from the rear of the cylinder heads after the cylinder heads are removed.

1. Disconnect the negative battery cable.

2. Drain the cooling system.

3. Remove the accessory drive belt. Remove the air inlet tube from the throttle body.

4. Remove the intake and exhaust manifolds.

5. Remove the front cover and remove the timing chains and sprockets.

6. Remove the rocker covers and the rocker shaft assemblies. Remove the cylinder head(s).

7. Remove the camshaft cover at the rear of the cylinder head. Loosen the camshaft retainer bolt and slide the retainer away from the camshaft.

8. Slide the camshaft out of the head, use care not to damage the camshaft lobes or bearings.

To install:

9. Coat the camshaft with heavy oil

and slide it into the head. Position the retainer in the grove of the camshaft and tighten the mounting bolt to 9 ft. lbs.

10. Install the camshaft cover using a new gasket, tighten the bolts to 48 inch lbs.

11. Install the cylinder heads and tighten the bolts in the proper sequence, to the correct specification. Install the intake and exhaust manifolds.

12. Install the timing chains and sprockets.

13. Install the front cover assembly and the accessory drive belt.

14. Install the rocker shaft assemblies and the rocker covers.

15. Fill the cooling system and connect the negative battery cable. Install the air inlet tube.

16. Run the engine and bleed the cooling system, check for leaks.

Intermediate Shaft

REMOVAL & INSTALLATION

2.2L Engine

1. Disconnect the negative battery cable.

2. Remove the timing belt cover and the timing belt.

3. Remove the oil pump drive shaft cover (located on the side of the block).

4. Screw a piece of threaded rod into the top of oil pump drive shaft and remove it.

5. Remove the bolt retaining the intermediate shaft sprocket and remove the intermediate shaft sprocket.

6. Remove the bolts from the intermediate shaft cover. Remove the cover and gasket. Remove the bolt from the intermediate shaft retainer and pivot the retainer. Remove the intermediate shaft by pulling it from the block.

To Install:

7. Coat the shaft with heavy oil and slide it into the block. Pivot the retainer into position and tighten the bolt. Install the shaft cover and loosely install the retaining bolts.

8. Install the shaft oil seal and align the cover using tool MOT-790 or equivalent. Tighten the cover retaining bolts.

9. Install the sprocket and bolt, tighten the bolt to 37 ft. lbs.

10. Install the oil pump drive shaft and cover.

11. Install the timing belt and cover, check the belt tension.

12. Connect the negative battery cable.

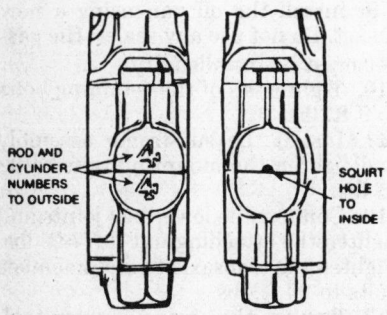

1. Bolt
2. Sprocket
3. Cover
4. Clamp plate
5. Intermediate shaft

2.2L intermediate shaft assembly

Pistons and Connecting Rods

POSITIONING

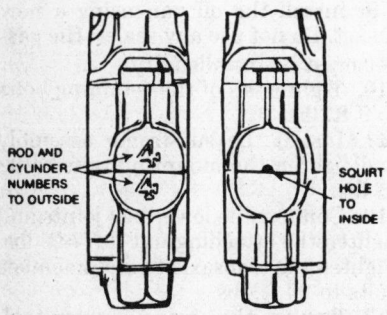

ROD AND CYLINDER NUMBERS TO OUTSIDE

SQUIRT HOLE TO INSIDE

1982–83 2.5L connecting rod positioning

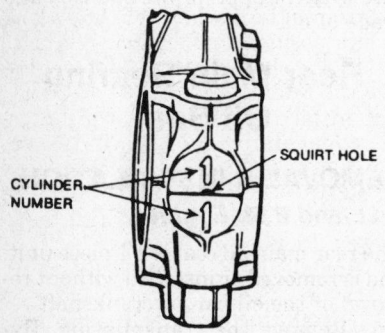

CYLINDER NUMBER

SQUIRT HOLE

4.2L Connecting rod positioning

NOTCH TO FRONT OF ENGINE

NUMBERS ON ROD & CAP TO CAMSHAFT SIDE OIL SPURT HOLE SAME SIDE

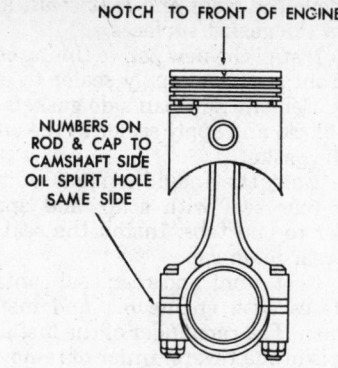

4.2L piston positioning

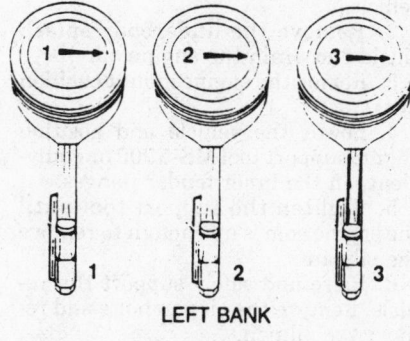

LEFT BANK

RIGHT BANK

3.0L piston positioning

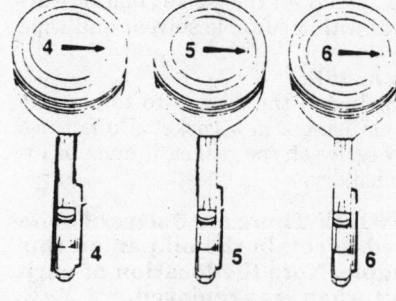

1. Oil hole must face the oil filter side of the engine

2.2L piston positioning

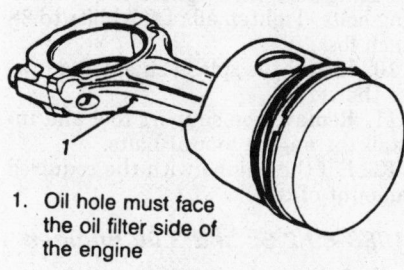

TOWARDS FRONT OF ENGINE

2.5L piston positioning

ENGINE LUBRICATION

Oil Pan

REMOVAL & INSTALLATION

1982–83 2.5L Engine

1. Raise and safely support the vehicle. Drain the oil.
2. Install an engine-lifting device and support the weight of the engine, while removing the engine bracket to mount cushion nuts. Loosen the strut and bracket screws.
3. Raise the engine approximately 2 in. and remove the crossmember to sill attaching parts.
4. Remove the steering gear idler bracket from the frame rail.
5. Pry the crossmember down and insert wooden blocks between the crossmember and the side sill on both sides.
6. Remove the oil pan and clean the gasket from the mating surfaces of the block and oil pan.
7. To install the pan, thoroughly clean all the gasket mating surfaces.
8. Install a new rear oil pan gasket in the rear main bearing cap. Apply a small quantity of RTV silicone sealer into the depressions where the rear pan gasket engages the block.
9. Install a new front oil pan gasket onto the timing gear cover. Press the tips into the holes in the cover.
10. Install the side gaskets onto the block, not the oil pan. Retain them with a thin film of grease. Apply a $\frac{1}{4}$ in. long bead of RTV silicone sealer to the split lines of the front and side gaskets; the bead should be $\frac{1}{8}$ in. wide.
11. Install the oil pan onto the engine. The timing cover bolts should be installed last. They are installed at an angle; the holes will line up after the rest of the pan bolts have been snugged down. The bolts should be tightened to 6 ft. lbs. all around. The remainder of the installation is in the reverse order of removal.

1984 2.5L Engine

1. Raise the vehicle and safely support it on jackstands. Disconnect the negative battery cable. Drain the engine oil.
2. Remove the starter motor.
3. If clearance is insufficient, place a jack under the transmission bell housing. Disconnect the engine right support cushion bracket from the block and raise the engine to allow sufficient clearance for oil pan removal. Remove the flywheel access cover.

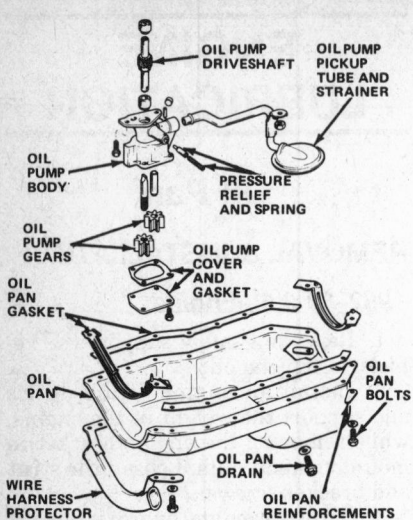

OIL PUMP DRIVESHAFT
OIL PUMP PICKUP TUBE AND STRAINER
OIL PUMP BODY
PRESSURE RELIEF AND SPRING
OIL PUMP GEARS
OIL PUMP COVER AND GASKET
OIL PAN GASKET
OIL PAN
OIL PAN BOLTS
OIL PAN DRAIN
WIRE HARNESS PROTECTOR
OIL PAN REINFORCEMENTS

1982–83 2.5L oil pan assembly

4. Remove the oil pan attaching bolts and remove the oil pan.

5. Remove the oil pan front and rear neoprene oil seals and the side gaskets. Thoroughly clean the gasket surfaces of the oil pan and the engine block. Remove all of the sludge and dirt from the oil pan sump.

6. Apply a generous amount of RTV silicone to the end tabs of a new oil pan front seal and install the seal onto the timing case cover.

7. Cement new oil pan side gaskets into position on the engine block and apply a generous amount of RTV silicone to the side gasket contacting surface of the seal end tabs.

8. Install the seal in the recess of the rear main bearing cap, making sure that it is fully sealed.

9. Coat the oil pan contacting surface of the front and rear oil pan seals with engine oil.

10. Install the oil pan and assemble the engine mount in the reverse order of removal.

4.2L Engine

1. Turn the steering wheel to full left lock. Support the engine with a hoist. Raise and safely support the vehicle. Disconnect the negative battery cable and engine ground strap cable.

2. Unbolt the steering idler arm at the side sill, and the engine cushions at the brackets.

3. Remove the sway bar, if so equipped. Remove the front crossmember to side sill bolts and pull the crossmember down. Remove the right engine bracket. Loosen but do not remove the strut rods at the lower control arm.

4. Drain the engine oil.

5. Remove the starter.

6. Remove the oil pan bolts and pan.

Remove the front and rear seals, and clean the gasket surfaces.

7. Install the new pan to timing cover front seal, and apply sealer to end tabs. Cement new pan side gaskets to the block, and apply sealer to the ends of the gasket.

8. Coat the inside surface of the new rear seal with soap, and apply sealer to end tabs. Install the seal in the rear main cap.

9. Coat front and rear seal contact surfaces with engine oil, and install the pan. The remainder of the installation is in the reverse order of removal.

2.2L Engine

1. Raise and safely support the vehicle.

2. Remove the underbody splash shield and drain the engine oil.

3. Remov the engine mount cushion nuts.

4. Lower the vehicle and position engine support tool MS–1900 or equivalent, on the inner fender flanges.

5. Tighten the support tool until the engine comes up enough to remove the oil pan.

6. Raise and safely support the vehicle. Remove the oil pan bolts and remove the oil pan.

7. Clean all the gasket mating surfaces with a suitable solvent and wipe dry.

To install:

8. Install the oil pan to the engine block using a new gasket. Do not use any sealer on the gasket, it must be installed dry.

NOTE: There are 3 sizes of bolts used to retain the oil pan on this engine. Note the location of each bolt when it is removed.

9. Tighten the oil pan bolts attaching the pan to the clutch/converter housing first, then tighten the remaining bolts. Tighten all of the bolts to 88 inch lbs.

10. Install the splash shield and lower the vehicle.

11. Remove the support tool and install the engine mount bolts.

12. Fill the engine with the required amount of oil.

1988–89 2.5L and 3.0L Engines

1. Raise and safely support the vehicle. Drain the oil.

2. Remove the front anti-sway bar retaining bolts and remove the sway bar.

3. Loosen the engine mount stud and nut assemblies. Remove the front tires.

4. Remove the lower ball joint retaining bolts and disengage the lower ball joints from the steering knuckles.

5. Remove the nuts at the center of

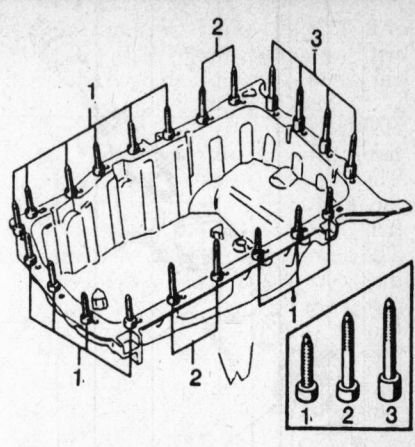

2.2L oil pan bolt positioning

the transaxle crossmember securing the rear of the transaxle to the crossmember.

6. Lower the vehicle and attach engine support tool MS–1900 to the engine.

7. With the vehicle down, loose the 4 sub-frame attaching nuts. Remove the front 2 first, allowing the sub-frame to pivot to the ground. Support the rear of the sub-frame and remove the 2 rear nuts. Lower the sub-frame away from the vehicle.

8. Raise and support the vehicle. Remove the oil pan retaining bolts and remove the oil pan. Clean all of the gasket mating surfaces.

To install:

9. Install the oil pan using a new gasket. Do not use any sealer, the gasket must be installed dry.

10. Tighten all of the retaining bolts to 9 ft. lbs.

11. Install the sub-frame assembly and tighten the mounting nuts to 92 ft. lbs.

12. Connect the lower ball joints and tighten the attaching nut to 77 ft. lbs. Tighten the transaxle to crossmember bolts to 20 ft. lbs.

13. Remove the engine support tool. Attach the anti-sway bar and install the front wheels.

14. Lower the vehicle. Fill the crankcase with the appropriate quantity and grade of oil.

Rear Main Bearing Oil Seal

REMOVAL & INSTALLATION
2.2L and 2.5L Engines

The rear main oil seal is a 1 piece unit, and is removed or installed without removal of the oil pan or crankshaft.

1. Remove the transmission, flywheel or torque converter bellhousing, and the flywheel or flex plate.

2. Remove the rear main oil seal with a small prying tool. Be extremely careful not to scratch the crankshaft.

3. Oil the lips of the new seal with clean engine oil. Install the new seal by hand onto the rear crankshaft flange. The helical lip side of the seal should face the engine. Make sure the seal is firmly and evenly installed.

The new seal is installed with a special installer. Use the tool as follows:

a. Back the plastic wing nut off until it contacts the capnut on the end of the shaft.

b. Lightly lubricate both the inside and outside edges of the seal.

c. Install the seal on the tool with the dust shield facing toward the plastic wing nut.

d. Fit the tool pilot in the center of the front surface of the installer into the pilot hole in the back of the crankshaft; the small dowel at the top of the front surface of the tool must fit into the corresponding small hole in the crankshaft at the same time. Hold the tool in this position and thread the 2 attaching screws into the crankshaft.

e. Turn the plastic wingnut in until it bottoms out to fully seat the seal. Unscrew the attaching nuts and remove the seal installer.

f. Inspect the dust shield all around to make sure it is not curled under. If it is, gently to pull the lip out.

4. Replace the flywheel or flexplate, bellhousing and transmission.

4.2L Engine

1. Remove oil pan as previously described.

2. Scrape clean all gasket surfaces, then remove rear main cap.

3. Discard lower portion of seal. Clean the main bearing cap thoroughly and loosen all remaining bearing capscrews.

4. Using a brass drift and a hammer, tap the upper seal out until it can be grasped by pliers and pulled out completely.

5. Coat the lip of the new upper seal with SAE 40 engine oil.

6. Install upper seal portion with the lip facing the front.

7. Coat both sides of the lower seal end tabs with sealant.

NOTE: Do not apply sealer to the cylinder block mating surfaces of the cap.

8. Coat the back surface of new lower seal with soap, coat the lip with engine oil. Install lower seal firmly into main cap.

9. Coat both chamfered edges of rear main cap with sealant, install bearing inserts (if removed) and tight-

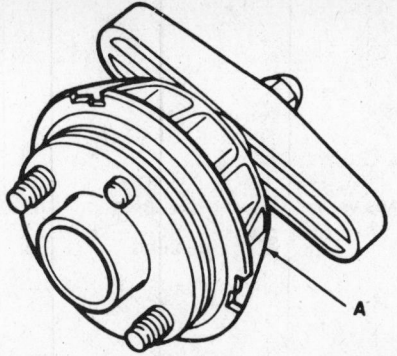

Special sela installer used for 1 piece rear main seal installation

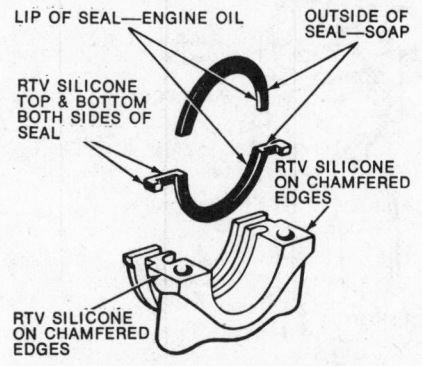

4.2L rear main seal installation

en all cap bolts to 100 ft. lbs. on 4 and 8 cylinder engines and to 80 ft. lbs. on 6 cylinder engines.

10. Install the oil pan.

3.0L Engine

1. Disconnect the negative battery cable.

2. Remove the transaxle assembly.

3. Remove the bolts from the lower rear main seal housing.

4. Remove the rear main seal housing bolts and remove the housing.

5. Push the old rear main seal from the housing.

6. Clean the gasket mating surfaces.

7. Install the rear main seal housing on the block. Use a new housing gasket.

8. Tighten the seal housing to block bolts first, then tighten the lower bolts. Torque all bolts to 9 ft. lbs.

9. Install the new rear seal to tool MOT–259–01 or equivalent, lightly coat the inner edges of the seal with oil. Install the seal to the seal housing by lightly tapping on the installation tool.

10. Remove the installation tool. Install the transaxle assembly.

11. Connect the negative battery cable. Start the vehicle and check for leaks.

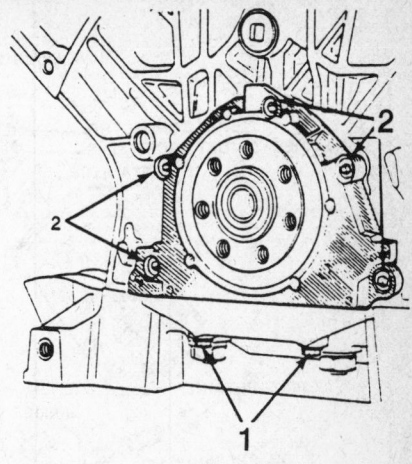

1. Lower casing bolts
2. Housin bolts

3.0L rear main seal housing mounting

Oil Pump

REMOVAL & INSTALLATION

CAUTION

Whenever the oil pump cover is removed or the pump diassembled, the pump must be primed by filling the spaces around the gears with petroleum jelly. Do not use grease.

2.5L and 4.2L Engines

1. Remove engine oil pan.

2. Remove the bolts and nut securing the oil pump, and carefully lower the pump.

3. Reinstall in reverse order. To ensure immediate oil pressure on start-up, the oil pump gear cavity can be packed with petroleum jelly. Torque the mounting bolts to 30 ft. lbs.

2.2L Engine

1. Remove the oil pump drive cover plate bolts and remove the cover.

2. Using a threaded rod, thread it into the top of the pump drive shaft. Remove the pump drive shaft by pulling it out of the block.

3. Raise and safely support the vehicle. Drain the oil.

4. Remove the oil pan. Remove the oil pump mounting bolts and remove the pump.

5. Install the oil pump using a new gasket. Tighten the mounting bolts to 33 ft. lbs.

6. Install the oil pan. Fill the crankcase with the correct grade and quantity of oil.

7. Install the oil pump drive shaft and cover.

8. Start the vehicle and check for leaks.

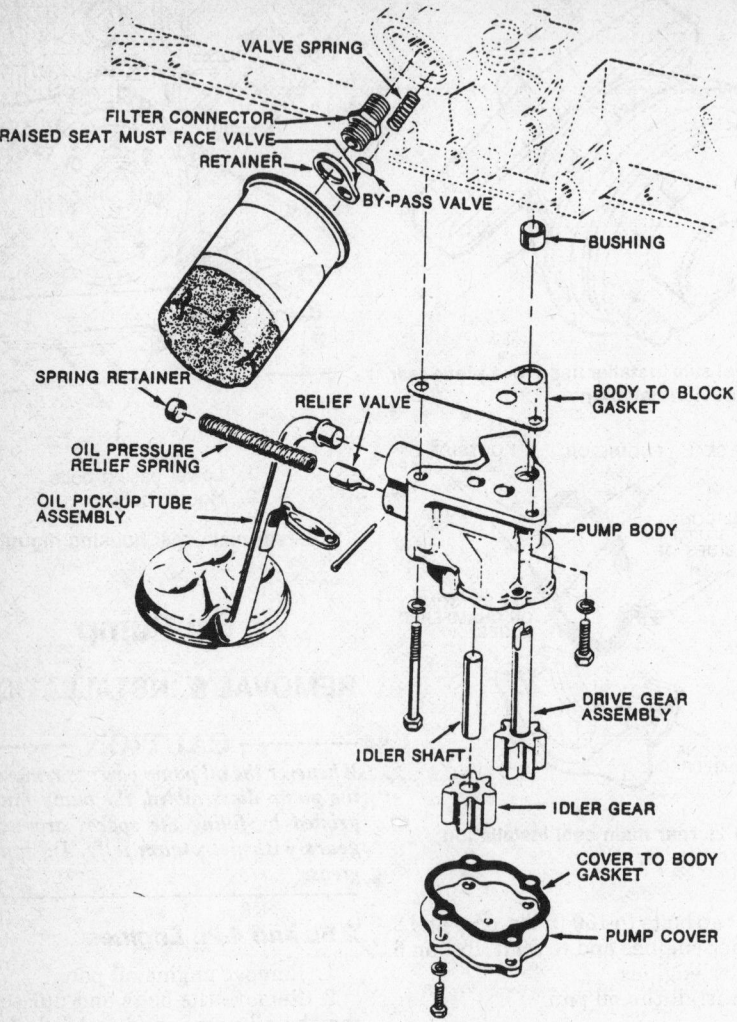

4.2L oil pump assembly

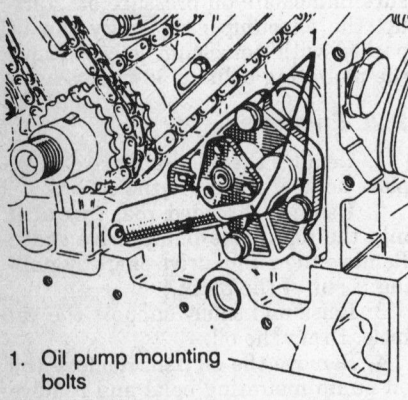

1. Oil pump mounting bolts

3.0L oil pump mounting

3.0L Engine

1. Remove the timing chain cover assembly.
2. Remove the bolts retaining the oil pump drive sprocket. Remove the sprocket and the oil pump drive chain.
3. Remove the oil pump mounting bolts and remove the oil pump.

4. Install the oil pump to the block using a new gasket. Tighten the bolts to 9 ft. lbs.
5. Install the oil pump drive sprocket and chain. Coat the threads of the sprocket bolts with a thread locking compound and torque them to 48 inch lbs.
6. Install the timing chain cover.

ENGINE COOLING

Radiator

REMOVAL & INSTALLATION

Concord, Spirit and Eagle

1. Raise the hood and remove the radiator cap. Be sure the engine is cold.

2. Drain the radiator.
3. Remove the upper and lower radiator hoses. Disconnect the coolant recovery hose, if so equipped.
4. On 4 cylinder models, remove the ambient air intake from the radiator support.
5. On 4 cylinder air conditioned models, remove the charcoal canister and the bracket.
6. Remove the fan shroud, if so equipped. On models equipped with an electric cooling fan; disconnect the motor and sensor wiring harnesses, remove the motor, fan and support; or remove as an assembly with the radiator.
7. On automatic transmission models, disconnect and plug the fluid cooler lines.
8. Remove the radiator attaching screws and bolts and lift out the radiator.
9. To install radiator, reverse the removal procedure.

Medallion and Premier

1. Disconnect the negative battery cable.
2. Remove the screws retaining the grill and remove the grill.
3. Remove the screws attaching the radiator support and front facia panel. Remove the support and the facia panel.
4. Disconnect the cooling fan electrical connectors. Disconnect the upper and lower radiator hoses.
5. Remove the radiator mounting bolts, seperate the A/C condensor from the radiator and place it aside. Remove the radiator and fan assembly.
6. Install the radiator into the vehicle and attach the A/C condensor.
7. Connect the electrical wires and the radiator hoses.
8. Install the support bracket and the front facia panel.
9. Install the grill. Fill and bleed cooling system.

Water Pump

REMOVAL & INSTALLATION

1982–83 2.5L Engine

1. Drain the cooling system. Make sure the engine is cold.
2. Remove all drive belts.
3. Remove the fan and pump pulley.
4. Unbolt and remove the pump from the engine.
5. Clean the gasket surfaces, coat the new gasket with non-hardening type sealer and position the gasket on the block.
6. Coat the threaded areas of the bolts with waterproof sealer and in-

stall the pump. Torque the bolts to 25 ft. lbs.

7. Install the pulley and fan.

8. Install the drive belts. The belts should be adjusted so that a ½ in. deflection is present when they are depressed mid-point along their longest straight run.

1984 2.5L Engine

NOTE: Some engines with air conditioning are equipped with a serpentine drive belt and have a reverse rotating water pump coupled with a viscous fan drive assembly. The components are identified by the words REVERSE stamped on the cover of the viscous drive and on the inner side of the fan. The word REV is also cast into the body of the water pump.

1. Disconnect all hoses at the pump.
2. Remove the drive belts.
3. Remove the fan shroud attaching screws.
4. Unbolt the fan and fan drive assembly, and remove along with the shroud. On some models it may be easier to turn the shroud ½ turn, to remove it.
5. Unbolt and remove the pump.

――――― CAUTION ―――――

Engines built for sale in California having a single, serpentine drive belt and viscous fan drive, use a reverse rotating pump and drive. These components are identified by the word REVERSE stamped on the drive cover and inner side of the fan, and REV cast into the water pump body. Never interchange standard rotating parts with these.

6. Installation is in the reverse order of removal. Always use a new gasket coated with sealer. Torque the water pump bolts to 13 ft. lbs., the fan bolts to 18 ft. lbs.

4.2L Engine

1. Drain the cooling system. Disconnect the negative cable from the battery.
2. Unfasten the radiator and the heater hoses at the pump.
3. Loosen the adjustment bolts from the alternator and the power steering pump, if so equipped. Remove the V-belts.
4. Unfasten the fan ring securing bolts. Remove the fan and pump pulley assembly. Withdraw the fan ring (or shroud).
5. Remove the securing bolts from the water pump. Withdraw the pump along with its gasket.

NOTE: Engines built for sale in California having a single, serpentine drive belt and viscous fan drive, have a reverse rotating

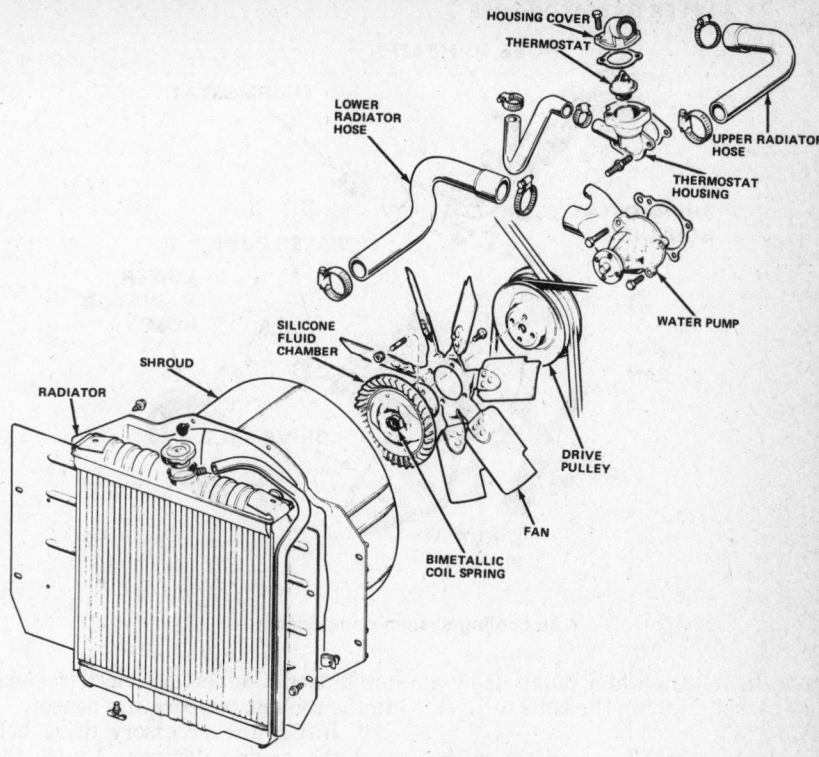

1982–83 cooling system components

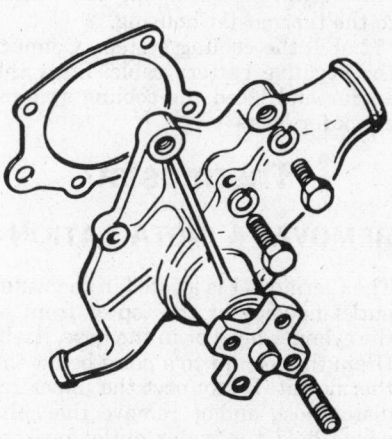

1984 2.5L water pump

pump and drive. These components are identified by the word REVERSE stamped on the drive cover and inner side of the fan, and REV cast into the water pump body. Never interchange standard rotating parts with these.

6. Installation is in the reverse order of removal. Always clean all mating surfaces and use a new pump gasket. The water pump mounting bolts should be tightened to 10–15 ft. lbs. and the fan bolts to 18 ft. lbs.

2.2L Engine

1. Disconnect the negative battery cable.

2. Drain the cooling system.
3. Remove the accessory drive belts.
4. Remove the timing belt cover.
5. Remove the water pump pulley bolt and remove the pulley.
6. Remove the timing belt and tensioner. Remove the hoses from the pump.
7. Remove the water pump attaching bolts and remove the water pump.
8. Clean the gasket mating surfaces.

To install:

9. Using a new gasket install the pump to the engine block. Tighten the bolts to 20 ft. lbs.
10. Install the timing belt and tensioner. Adjust the timing belt tension.
11. Install the timing belt cover. Install the water pump pulley and the accessory drive belts. Install the hoses.
12. Fill the cooling system and connect the negative battery cable. Bleed the cooling system.

1988–89 2.5L Engine

1. Disconnect the negative battery cable.
2. Drain the cooling system. Remove the serpentine drive belt.
3. Disconnect the hoses from the engine. Remove the water pump pulley mounting bolts and remove the pulley.
4. Remove the water pump mounting bolts and remove the pump.
5. Clean the gasket mating sur-

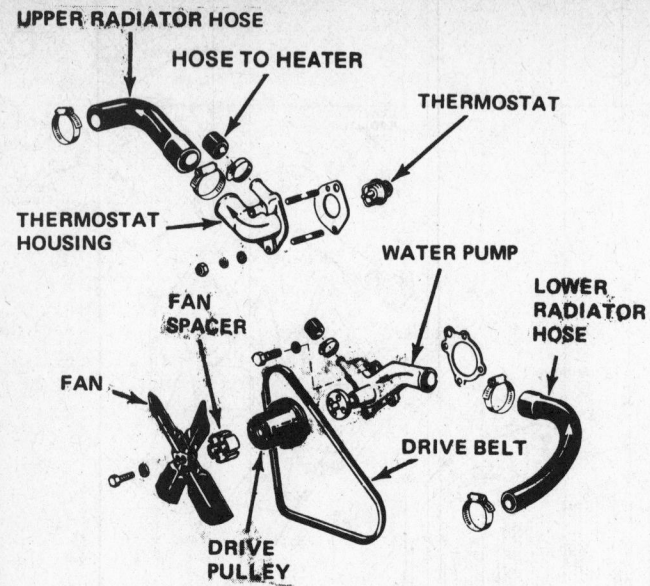

UPPER RADIATOR HOSE

HOSE TO HEATER

THERMOSTAT

THERMOSTAT HOUSING

WATER PUMP

FAN SPACER

LOWER RADIATOR HOSE

FAN

DRIVE BELT

DRIVE PULLEY

4.2L cooling system components

faces. Install the water pump using a new gasket. Tighten the bolts to 13 ft. lbs.

6. Install the hoses and the water pump pulley. Tighten the pulley retaining bolts to 20 ft. lbs.

7. Install the accessory drive belt.

CAUTION

It is important that the serpentine belt is installed correctly. If it is incorrectly routed the water pump could be rotated in the wrong direction, causing the engine to overheat.

8. Fill the cooling system. Connect the negative battery cable. Start the engine and bleed the cooling system.

3.0L Engine

1. Disconnect the negative battery cable.

2. Drain the cooling system.

3. Remove the spark plug wire holder from the top of the thermostat housing. Remove the nuts holding the engine damper to the engine.

4. Remove the accessory drive belt. Remove the upper and lower radiator hoses from the radiator.

5. Disconnect the electrical lead to the coolant temperature sensor.

6. At the back of the water pump disconnect the hoses to the cylinder heads and the heater hoses.

7. Remove the water pump mounting bolts and remove the water pump.

To install:

8. Install the water pump to the block and tighten the mounting bolts to 13 ft. lbs.

9. Connect all of the hoses to the water pump, making sure that they

are kinked. Connect the electrical lead to the coolant temperature sensor.

10. Install the accessory drive belt and the engine damper. Adjust the drive belt tension.

11. Install the spark plug wire holder to the thermostat housing.

12. Fill the cooling system. Connect the negative battery cable. Start the engine and bleed the cooling system, check for leaks.

Thermostat

REMOVAL & INSTALLATION

The thermostat is located in the water outlet housing at the top or front of the cylinder head or in the hose, itself. Drain the coolant to a point below the thermostat. Disconnect the upper radiator hose and/or remove the bolts which hold the water outlet neck to the engine. Remove the thermostat.

When installing the thermostat, make certain the pellet or coil spring is facing the engine. Thermostats are marked on the outer flange with the proper installing direction. Replace the gasket between the thermostat and the housing cover. The bleed hole on the thermostats used on 6 cylinder engines must be installed up (at 12 o'clock), to prevent "burping" caused by trapped air. Refill the cooling system, and run the engine for a while with the heater on to bleed the system of air. Recheck the coolant level.

CAUTION

Tightening the housing bolts unevenly, or with the thermostat cocked in its recess, will cause the housing to crack.

COOLING SYSTEM BLEEDING

After working on the cooling system, even to replace the thermostat, it must be bled. Air trapped in the system will, otherwise, prevent proper filling, leaving the radiator coolant level low and causing risk of overheating.

To bleed the system, start with the system cool, the radiator cap off, and the radiator filled to about an inch below the filler neck. Start the engine and run it at slightly above normal idle speed, to ensure adequate circulation. If air bubbles appear and the coolant level drops, fill the system with anti-freeze/water mix to bring the level back to the proper level. Run the engine this way until the thermostat opens. When this happens, coolant will move abruptly across the top of the radiator and the temperature of the radiator will suddenly rise. At this point, air is often expelled, and the level may drop quite a bit. Keep refilling the system until the level is near the top of the radiator and remains constant. If the car has an overflow tank, fill the radiator right up to the filler neck. Replace the radiator cap.

EMISSION CONTROLS

Please refer to "Emission Control" in the Unit Repair section for system maintenance procedures. Due to the complex nature of modern electronic engine control systems, comprehensive diagnosis and testing procedures fall outside the confines of this repair manual. For complete information on diagnosis, testing and repair procedures concerning all modern engine and emission control systems, please refer to *Chilton's Guide To Electronic Engine Controls.*

FUEL SYSTEM

Fuel System Service Precaution

When working with the fuel system certain precautions should be taken;

• Always work in a well ventilated area

- Keep a dry chemical (Class B) fire extinguisher near the work area
- Always disconnect the negative battery cable and do not make any repairs to the fuel system until all the necessary steps for repair have been reviewed

FUEL SYSTEM PRESSURE RELIEF

Modern fuel injection systems operate under high pressure, this makes it necessary to first relieve the system of pressure before servicing. The pressurized fuel when released may ignite or cause personal injury. the following outlined steps may be used for most fuel systems:

- Remove the fuel pump fuse from the fuse block
- Crank the engine and let it run until the remaining fuel in the lines is consumed
- Crank engine again to make sure any fuel in the lines has been removed
- With the ignition **OFF** replace the fuel pump fuse

Fuel Filter

REMOVAL & INSTALLATION

Concord, Spirit and Eagle

American Motors uses an in-line fuel filter in the line from the carburetor to the fuel pump on all engines except the 1982–83 2.5L engine. All models (except the 1982–83 2.5L engine) also have a vapor return line from the filter to the tank.

1. Remove the air cleaner as necessary.
2. Put an absorbent rag under the filter to catch spillage.
3. Remove the hose clamps.
4. Remove the filter and short attaching hoses.
5. Assemble the new filter and hoses. If the filter has a return line, position the line at the top.

NOTE: The original equipment type hose clamps can't be reused with much success. It is much better to replace them with screw type clamps. If there is an arrow on the new filter, it must point toward the carburetor.

6. Fit the filter in place, tighten the clamps, start the engine and check for leaks. Discard the gas-soaked rag safely.

1982–83 2.5L ENGINE

This engine uses a replaceable filter located within the carburetor body at the fuel inlet fitting.

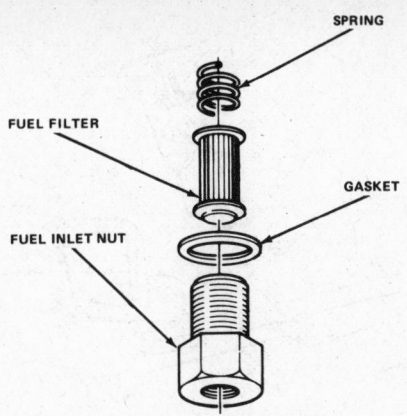

1982–83 2.5L fuel filter assembly

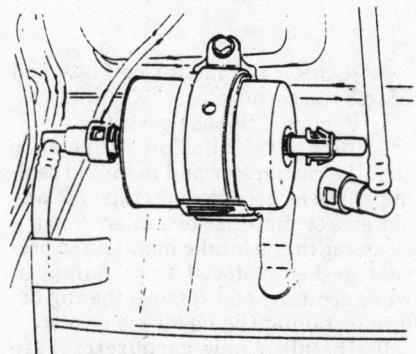

Medallion and Premier fuel filter

1. Place an absorbent cloth under the inlet fitting at the carburetor.
2. Using a suitable line wrench on the fuel line fitting and a backup wrench on the fuel inlet nut, loosen the fuel line and pull it out of the inlet nut. Unscrew the fuel inlet nut.
3. The filter will be pushed out part way by a spring located behind the filter. Remove the filter.
4. Install the new filter with the hole in the filter facing the inlet fitting. Install a new gasket on the fitting. Tighten to 18 ft. lbs.

Medallion and Premier

The fuel filter on these vehicles is located under the rear of the vehicle. It is attached to the frame near the fuel tank.

1. Relieve the fuel system pressure.
2. Disconnect the fuel lines from the fuel filter.
3. Remove the retaining bolt and remove the filter cartridge.
4. Install the new filter in place and tighten the retaining bolt.
5. Connect the fuel lines.

Mechanical Fuel Pump

PRESSURE TESTING

To pressure test the fuel pump, dis-

connect the discharge line at the inlet to the fuel filter and connect a gauge to the open end. Start the engine and idle it on the fuel in the carburetor until the pressure reading on the gauge stabilizes. The reading should be 5.0–6.5 psi. If the pressure is outside the range, replace the pump.

REMOVAL & INSTALLATION

1. Disconnect the inlet and outlet fuel lines, and any vacuum lines.
2. Remove the 2 fuel pump body attaching nuts and lockwashers.
3. Pull the pump and gasket free of the engine. Make sure the mating surfaces of the fuel pump and the engine are clean. Scrape off any old gasket material and sealer before installation.
4. Cement a new gasket to the mounting flange of the fuel pump.
5. Position the fuel pump on the engine block so that the lever of the fuel pump rests on the fuel pump cam of the camshaft.
6. Secure the fuel pump to the block with the 2 capscrews and lockwashers.
7. Connect the intake and outlet fuel lines to the fuel pump, and any vacuum lines.

Electric Fuel Pump

The fuel pump on Medallion and Premier models is located in the fuel tank, attached to the fuel sending unit. All of the fuel lines and the fuel tank are made of plastic. When working with them care should be taken not to puncture or kink the lines.

PRESSURE TESTING

1. Relieve the fuel system pressure.
2. Disconnect the black fuel supply line from the fuel injector rail.

NOTE: The fuel line connectors are of the quick-connect type. Whenever they are disconnected the clip retainer remains on the tube. The lines should never be connected unless the retainer is in place. After a line has been connected it should be checked to see that the retainer has locked, this can be done by pulling on the lines.

3. Attach tool MS–1976 (fuel line adaptor) or equivalent, connect a 0–60 psi. fuel pressure gauge.
4. Start the engine and check the fuel pressure, it should be 36–37 psi.
5. Remove the fuel pressure gauge and the fuel line adaptor. Reconnect the fuel line to the fuel rail.

REMOVAL & INSTALLATION

1. Relieve the fuel system pressure.

2. Disconnect the negative battery cable.

3. Drain the fuel from the fuel tank and store it in an appropriate container.

4. Raise and safely support the vehicle. Remove the right rear wheel and inner fender spalsh shield.

5. Disconnect the fuel lines at the fuel filter and the electrical connectors from the tank. Disconnect the fuel tank vent tube from the filler neck. Disconnect the ground wire from the body.

6. Place a suitable support under the tank and remove the retaining straps. Lower the tank from the vehicle.

7. Remove the bolts holding the tank sending unit to the tank. Pull the sending unit/pump from the tank, note the position of the gasket.

8. Install the sending unit/pump into the fuel tank, position the gasket properly. Install the retaining bolts.

9. Install the fuel tank into the vehicle, tighten the retaining strap bolts to 12 ft. lbs. Connect all of the fuel lines securely. Connect the electrical connectors to the tank unit and reconnect the ground strap.

10. Install the inner fender shield and the right wheel. Lower the vehicle.

11. Refill the tank and connect the negative battery cable.

Carburetor

Depending on the engine, 4 types of carburetors are used on the Concord, Spirit and Eagle models. The 1982–83 2.5L engine, uses a Rochester 2SE on Federal models, or a Rochester E2SE on California models. The 1984 2.5L engine, uses a Carter YFA feedback carburetor and the 4.2L engine, uses a Carter BBD feedback carburetor.

For further information on feedback carburetors, please refer to *Chilton's Guide To Fuel Injection And Feedback Carburetors.*

REMOVAL & INSTALLATION

—————— CAUTION ——————
Take precautions to avoid the risk of fire as some fuel will remain in the carburetor float bowl.

1. Remove the air cleaner.

2. Disconnect and tag the fuel and vacuum lines, along with any electrical connectors.

3. Disconnect the choke rod.

4. Disconnect the accelerator linkage.

5. Disconnect the automatic transmission linkage.

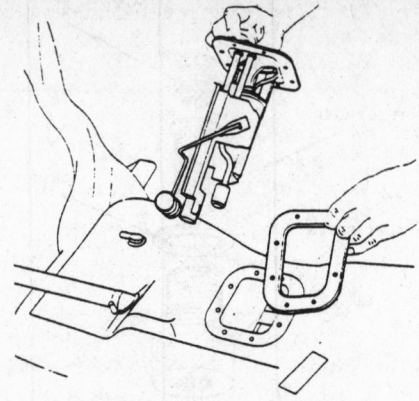

Removing the in tank fuel pump on Medallion and Premier models

6. Remove the mounting bolts and lift off the carburetor.

7. Remove the base gasket.

8. Before installation, make sure that the carburetor and manifold sealing surfaces are clean. Scrape off any old gasket material or sealer. Place a clean rag in the intake manifold to prevent gasket material from falling in while scraping and remove the rag before installing the new base gasket.

9. Install a new carburetor base gasket.

10. Install the carburetor and loosely install the fuel and vacuum lines.

11. Bolt down the carburetor evenly, using an ''X'' pattern when tightening.

12. Tighten the fuel and vacuum lines.

13. Connect the accelerator and automatic transmission linkage. If the transmission linkage was disturbed, refer to the Unit Repair section on Automatic Transmissions.

14. Connect the choke rod.

15. Install the air cleaner. Adjust the idle speed.

OVERHAUL

For all carburetor overhaul and adjustment procedures, refer to "Carburetor Service" in the Unit Repair section.

Fuel Injection

Due to the complex nature of modern fuel injection systems, comprehensive diagnosis and testing procedures fall outside the confines of this repair manual. For complete information on fuel injection diagnosis, testing and repair procedures refer to *Chilton's Guide To Fuel Injection And Feedback Carburetors.*

MANUAL TRANSMISSION

REMOVAL & INSTALLATION
Concord and Spirit

NOTE: Open the hood to avoid damage when the rear crossmember is removed. If the overdrive and transmission are to be separated, first engage then disengage the overdrive with the clutch pedal depressed and the engine running.

1. Matchmark the driveshaft and rear axle yoke for correct installation. Split the gear universal joint and slide the driveshaft off the back of the transmission. Support the transmission with a jack.

2. Detach the column shift mechanism linkage to the transmission, and disconnect the clutch linkage and speedometer cable; disconnect the reverse light switch wiring and TCS switch wiring. On a floorshift, remove the shift lever. Remove the boot and unbolt the lever. Detach the column reverse lockup rod. Pull the lever and gauge out together. Support the engine.

3. Disconnect the overdrive wiring. Remove the rear transmission support cushion bolts. Also remove the starter on 4 cylinder models.

4. Remove the transmission support crossmember. Remove the 2 lower studs which hold the transmission to the bell housing and replace these 2 studs.

5. Remove the 2 top studs and slide the transmission assembly along the pilot studs and out of the car.

To install:

6. Fill the slots in the inner groove of the throwout bearing with high temperature grease and soak the crankshaft pilot bushing wick in engine oil. Fit the throwout bearing and the sleeve assembly into the clutch fork. Center the bearing over the clutch lever.

7. Carefully slide the transmission into place. Be careful not to damage the clutch driven plate splines while mating them with the transmission input shaft.

8. Install the upper screws, which attach the case to the housing. Remove the 2 pilot studs and install the 2 lower cap screws.

9. If the vehicle is equipped with a floor shift, install the shift lever retainer and shift rods, if removed.

10. Attach the speedometer cable, connect the back-up light switch wires and the transmission controlled spark

(TCS) wire, if so equipped. Connect the clutch cable and adjust as necessary. Also install the inspection cover and the catalytic converter bracket bolts.

11. Raise the transmission. Attach the rear crossmember and support to the transmission. Fasten the crossmember to the side sills and finger-tighten the bolts. Install and tighten the crossmember to support bolts. Tighten the crossmember stud nuts.

12. Install the front U-joint yoke on the transmission. Do the same for the rear U-joint at the differential. Be sure the alignment marks made earlier line up.

13. Connect the shift rods on the column shift transmissions and the reverse lockup rod on the floorshift transmission. Check the transmission oil level and add lubricant as needed.

14. Remove the supports and lower the vehicle.

15. If the vehicle has a floorshift transmission, install the shift lever.

16. Adjust the shift linkage, if it was disturbed.

Eagle

1. Shift transmission into **NEUTRAL.**

2. Remove screws attaching gearshift lever bezel and boot to floorpan.

3. Slide bezel and boot upward on gearshift lever to provide access to lever attaching bolts.

4. Remove bolts attaching gearshift lever to lever mounting cover on transmission adapter housing and remove gearshift lever.

5. Remove bolts attaching gearshift lever mounting cover to transmission adapter and remove mounting cover to provide access to transfer case upper mounting stud nut in transmission adapter housing.

6. Remove nut from transfer case upper mounting stud located inside transmission adapter housing.

7. Raise the vehicle.

8. Remove the skid plate.

9. Remove speedometer adapter retainer bolt and remove retainer, adapter, and cable. Discard adapter O-ring and plug adapter opening in transfer case to prevent excessive oil spillage.

NOTE: Matchmark the position of the speedometer adapter for assembly alignment, before removing it.

10. Matchmark propeller shafts and axle yokes for assembly alignment, and disconnect propeller shafts at transfer case.

11. Disconnect backup lamp switch wire.

12. Place support stand under the engine.

13. Support transmission and transfer case using suitable transmission jack.

14. Remove rear crossmember.

15. Remove catalytic converter bracket from transfer case, and brace rod from racket.

16. Remove bolts attaching transmission to clutch housing.

17. Remove transmission and transfer case as an assembly.

18. Remove nuts from transfer case mounting studs and remove transmission from transfer case.

To Install:

19. Install transmission on transfer case. Install and tighten all transfer case mounting stud nuts to 26 ft. lbs. torque.

20. Support transmission-transfer case assembly on suitable transmission jack.

21. Align transmission clutch shaft without throwout bearing and clutch disc splines and seat transmission against clutch housing.

22. Install and tighten transmission to clutch housing attaching bolts to 55 ft. lbs. torque.

23. Connect propeller shafts to transfer case yokes. Tighten clamp strap bolts to 15 ft. lbs. torque.

24. Install brace rod and rear crossmember. Tighten attaching bolts to 30 ft. lbs. torque.

25. Connect backup lamp switch wire.

26. Install replacement O-ring on speedometer adapter and install adapter and cable, and retainer. Tighten retainer bolt to 100 inch lbs.

CAUTION

Do not attempt to reuse the original adapter O-ring. The ring is designed to swell in service to improve its sealing qualities and could be cut or torn during installation if reuse is attempted.

27. Attach catalytic converter bracket to transfer case. Tighten skid plate attaching bolts to 30 ft. lbs. torque.

28. Check and correct lubricant levels in transmission and transfer case, if necessary.

29. Install skid plate. Tighten skid plate attaching bolts to 30 ft. lbs. torque.

30. Remove stand used to support engine, and remove transmission jack, if not removed previously.

31. Lower the vehicle.

32. Clean mating surfaces of gearshift lever mounting cover and of transmission adapter housing.

33. Apply RTV-type sealant to gearshift lever mounting cover, install cover bolts and torque to 13 ft. lbs. torque.

34. Install gearshift lever on mount-

ing cover. Before tightening lever attaching bolts make certain lever is engaged with shift rail. Tighten lever attaching bolts to 18 ft. lbs. torque.

35. Position gearshift lever boot and bezel in floorpan and install bezel attaching screws.

MANUAL TRANSAXLE

REMOVAL & INSTALLATION

Medallion

1. Disconnect the negative battery cable.

2. Disconnect and remove the flexible heat tube from the engine.

3. Remove the TDC sensor retaining bolt and remove the sensor.

4. Remove the bolts retaining the steering bracket and remove the bracket.

5. Remove the bolts attaching the crossmember to the side sill and body.

6. Raise and safely support the vehicle.

7. Remove the front wheels. Disconnect and remove the passenger side tie rod.

8. Loosen the bolt retaining the coolant expansion tank and move the tank aside.

9. Attach engine support tool MS–1900 or equivalent, to the engine and tighten the adjuster nut until there is no slack in the chain.

10. Remove the bolts attaching the exhaust head pipe to the manifold. Remove the bolts attaching the exhaust head pipe to the converter and remove the head pipe.

11. Remove the crossmember by turning it and taking out through the passenger side wheel well.

12. Disengage the clutch cable. Remove the upper steering knuckle mounting bolt and loosen the lower bolt.

13. Remove the drive shaft retaining pin. Swing each rotor and steering knuckle outward and slide the driveshafts from the transaxle.

14. Disconnect the reverse lockout cable and disconnect the shift rod from the lever. Disconnect the speedometer cable. Disconnect the ground strap at the transaxle.

15. Support the transaxle. Remove the transaxle support cushion nuts. Remove the bolts that attach the 2

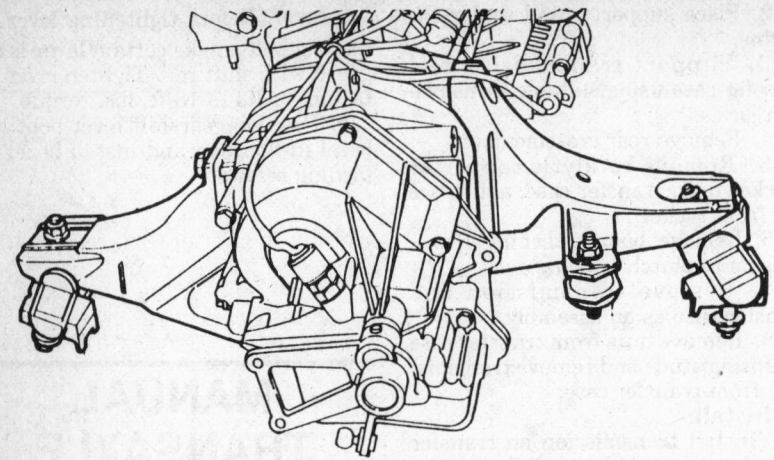

Medallion and Premier transaxle rear mounts

transaxle mounting brackets to the transaxle.

16. Disconnect the wiring harness connector and remove the starter. Remove the bolts attaching the clutch housing to the engine.

17. Pull the transaxle straight back until the clutch shaft is clear of the engine and lower the transaxle.

To install:

18. Raise and position the transaxle into the vehicle. Align the release bearing and the release fork.

19. Install the transaxle to engine mounting bolts. Tighten to 37 ft. lbs.

20. Install the starter and connect the electrical connectors. Slightly raise the transaxle and install the mounting brackets. Align the transaxle support cushion bolts and install the retaining nuts.

21. Connect the speedometer cable and the shift rods. Connect the clutch cable.

22. Install the axleshafts by tilting the steering knuckle in, install the upper bolt and tighten both bolts to 148 ft. lbs.

23. Install the axle retaining pins. Connect the ground strap to the case.

24. Install the crossmember through the wheel well opening and position it on the side sills. Install and tighten the bolts.

25. Connect the tie rods to the steering bracket and tighten the mounting bolts to 25 ft. lbs. Connect the steering gear bracket to the steering rack and tighten the bolts to 30 ft. lbs.

26. Install the front wheels. Install the TDC sensor and the heat tube. Connect the exhaust header pipe to the converter and manifold.

27. Check and fill the transaxle fluid. Remove the engine support tool and connect the battery.

28. Check the operation of the shift mechanism.

CLUTCH

REMOVAL & INSTALLATION

1982–83 2.5L Engine

1. Remove the starter, disconnect the slave cylinder spring at the throwout lever, and remove the transmission.

2. Remove the clutch housing to engine bolts. Remove the housing.

3. Remove the throwout bearing.

4. Matchmark the clutch cover and flywheel for installation. Loosen the clutch cover bolts alternately and evenly, to avoid distortion, and remove the clutch cover and disc.

5. Inspect the parts for signs of overheating (blue color), scoring, or abnormal wear. Overheated parts should be replaced. Deep scoring or wear may require replacement of the disc and cover, and refacing or replacement of the flywheel.

6. If the same cover is being used, place the disc and cover on the flywheel, aligning the marks made previously. Be sure the cover is engaged with the dowel pins. Install the cover bolts finger-tight.

7. Align the disc with an alignment tool.

8. Tighten the cover bolts alternately and evenly to 23 ft. lbs. Remove the alignment tool.

9. Install the throwout bearing, clutch housing, and transmission. The housing to engine bolts and transmission to housing bolts should be tightened to 54 ft. lbs.

1984 2.5L Engine

1. Remove the transmission transfer case assembly.

2. Mark the position of the clutch pressure plate in relation to the flywheel, for installation.

3. Loosen the pressure plate bolts evenly, a little at a time each! Failure to loosen the bolts evenly, in rotation, will cause warping of the pressure plate.

4. When all spring tension is relieved from the pressure plate, back out the bolts and remove the pressure plate and driven plate.

5. If the pilot bushing is equipped with a lubricating wick, remove it and soak it in clean engine oil.

6. Installation is in the reverse order of removal. Tighten the pressure plate bolts evenly, in rotation, in 3 or 4 different steps, to 23 ft. lbs.

4.2L Engine

1. Remove the transmission, starter motor and throwout bearing.

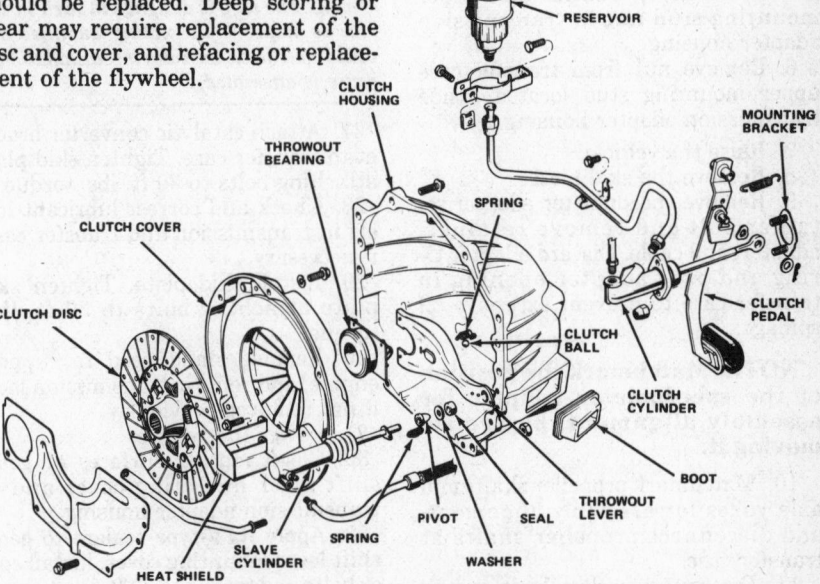

1982–83 2.5L clutch assembly

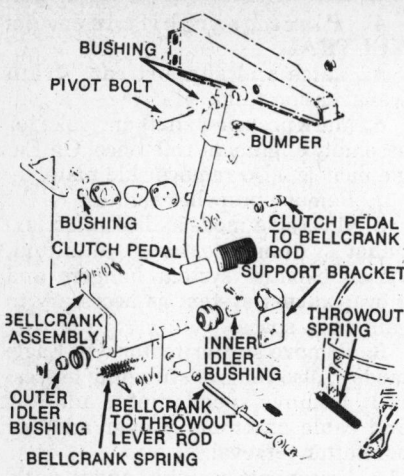

Typical clutch linkage

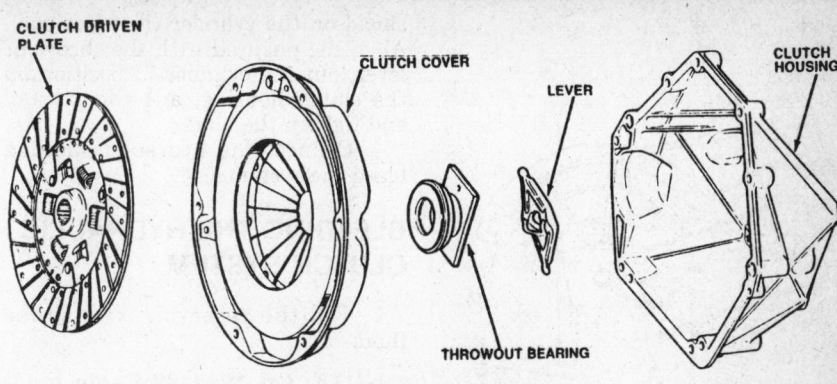

1984 2.5L clutch assembly

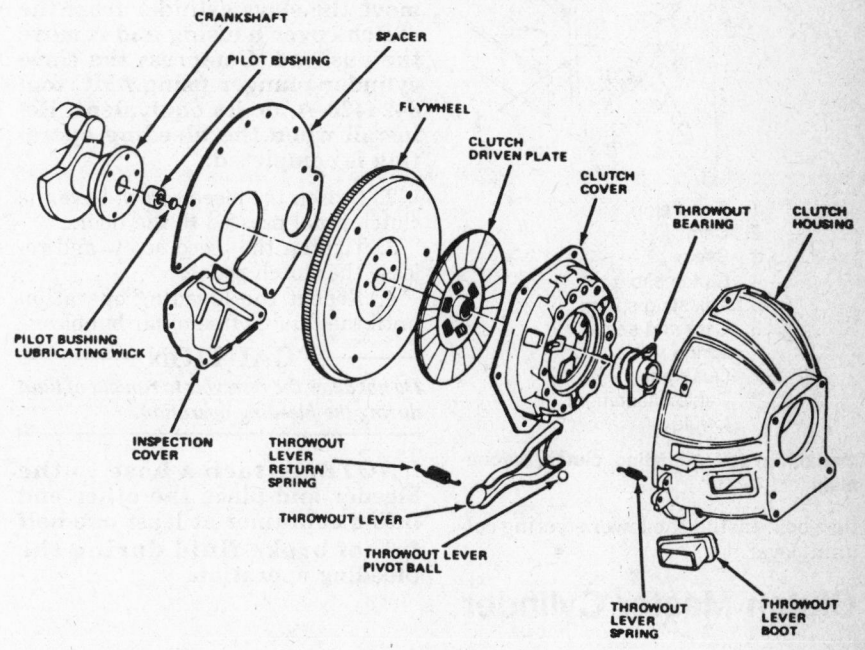

4.2L clutch assembly

2. Disconnect the clutch linkage at the housing and remove the housing.

3. Mark the clutch cover and flywheel for reassembly.

4. Remove the clutch cover and the driven plate by loosening the bolts alternately and in several stages.

5. Remove the pilot bushing lubricating wick and soak the wick in engine oil.

6. Inspect the parts for signs of overheating (blue color), distortion, scoring, or wear. Overheated or deeply scored or worn parts should be replaced. Light wear may be cleaned up by sanding or refacing.

7. Installation is in the reverse order of removal. Use an alignment tool to position the driven plate on the flywheel. Tighten the cover bolts alternately and in several stages.

2.2L Engine

1. Remove the transaxle assembly from the vehicle.

2. Remove the pressure plate attaching bolts.

3. Remove the pressure plate release bearing assembly and the clutch disc.

4. Inspect the condition of the clutch components and replace any worn parts.

NOTE: The release bearing and pressure plate are not serviced seperately. The bearing is permanently attached to the pressure plate diaphragm fingers. The pressure plate and bearing must be serviced as an assembly.

5. Inspect the flywheel for heat damage or cracks. Replace it if necessary.

6. Install the clutch disc to the flywheel. Install alignment tool EMB-786-01 orequivalent. Install the pressure plate assembly and tighten the pressure plate bolts evenly to 18 ft. lbs. Remove the alignment tool.

7. Install the transaxle assembly and check the clutch operation.

PEDAL FREE-PLAY ADJUSTMENT

Concord, Spirit and Eagle

All Concord, Spirit and Eagle models have hydraulically actuated clutch systems with no provision for adjustment.

Medallion

The Medallion uses an cable operated, self adjusting clutch mechanism. The adjustment is automatically set during operation by a quadrant mechanism on the clutch pedal assembly.

Clutch Cable

REMOVAL & INSTALLATION

Medallion

1. Remove the lower steering column cover. Open the fuse box door and slide the fuse box out of the door and move it the side.

2. Disconnect the heater ducts located just in front of the clutch and brake pedals.

3. On the clutch pedal assembly, disconnect the cam and sector spring.

4. In the engine compartment, disconnect the clutch cable from the release lever.

5. In the vehicle, depress the clutch pedal all the way to extend the cable. Release the pedal and remove the cable from the quadrant. Push the cable through the fire wall and remove through the engine compartment.

6. Feed the cable through the fire wall and connect the cable to the quadrant.

7. Connect the opposite end to the release lever on the transaxle.

8. In the vehicle, connect the sector spring. Adjust the cable by pulling up on the pedal until it contacts the stop.

9. Install the heater ducts and the

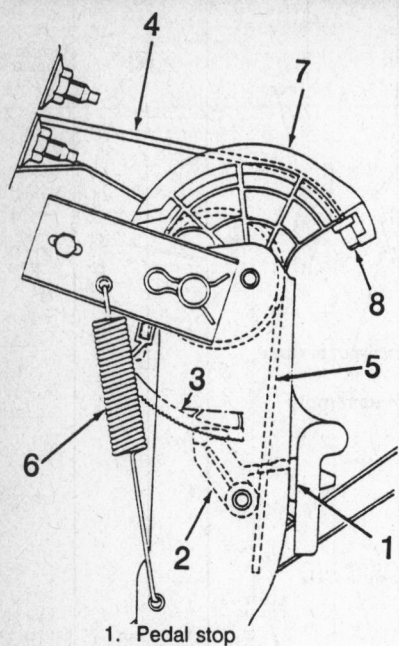

1. Pedal stop
2. Cam
3. Sector
4. Clutch cable
5. Adjusting spring
6. Cam and sector spring
7. Quadrant
8. Cable attachment ferrule

Medallion self adjusting clutch mechanism

fuse box. Install the lower steering column cover.

Clutch Master Cylinder

REMOVAL & INSTALLATION

Concord, Spirit and Eagle

1. Disconnect the hydraulic lines at the cylinder.
2. Disconnect the cylinder pushrod at the clutch pedal.
3. Remove the mounting nuts attaching the cylinder to both the dash panel and mounting bracket, and remove it.
4. Installation is the reverse of removal. Bleed the system.

Clutch Slave Cylinder

REMOVAL & INSTALLATION

Concord, Spirit and Eagle

1. Raise the vehicle and support it securely. Disconnect the hydraulic line at the cylinder.
2. Remove the bolts that attach both the cylinder and the heat shield (if there is one) to the clutch housing and remove the cylinder.
3. To install, position the heat shield on the cylinder (if it has one). Align the pushrod with the throwout lever, put the cylinder in position on the clutch housing, and then install and tighten the bolts.
4. Connect the hydraulic line and bleed the system.

BLEEDING THE HYDRAULIC CLUTCH SYSTEM

1. Fill the reservoir with brake fluid.

NOTE: On 1984–88 Eagle models with the 4 cylinder engines, remove the slave cylinder from the clutch cover housing and remove the pushrod. Compress the slave cylinder plunger using AMC tool J–24420–A, or its equivalent. Reinstall when the bleeding operation is completed.

2. Loosen the bleed screw, have the clutch pedal pressed to the floor.
3. Tighten the bleed screw and release the clutch pedal.
4. Repeat the bleeding operation until the fluid is free of air bubbles.

—————— **CAUTION** ——————
Do not allow the reservoir to run out of fluid during the bleeding operation.

NOTE: Attach a hose to the bleeder and place the other end into a container at least one-half full of brake fluid during the bleeding operation.

AUTOMATIC TRANSMISSION

For further information on automatic transmission, please refer to "Automatic Transmissions" in the Unit Repair section.

REMOVAL & INSTALLATION

Concord, Spirit and Eagle

2.5L ENGINES

1. Disconnect the negative battery cable.

—————— **CAUTION** ——————
The hood must remain open to avoid damaging the hood and air cleaner when the rear crossmember is removed.

2. Disconnect fan shroud.
3. Remove bolt attaching transmission fill tube to engine.
4. Place gearshift lever in **NEUTRAL**.
5. Raise and support car. Drain transmission fluid.
6. Mark propeller shaft and yoke for assembly alignment reference. On Eagle models, also remove skid plate.
7. Remove propeller shafts.
8. On Eagle models, disconnect exhaust system at exhaust manifold, loosen exhaust system hangers and move exhaust system as necessary to gain work space.
9. Remove starter motor. On Eagle models, also remove stiffening braces.
10. Remove speedometer adapter and cable assembly. Cover adapter bore after removal.
11. Disconnect gearshift and throttle linkage. On models with column shift, remove bolt that mounts the linkage bellcrank bracket on the converter housing.
12. Remove cover at front of converter housing.
13. Mark converter drive plate and converter for assembly alignment reference.
14. To gain excess to and remove the bolts attaching the drive plate to the converter, rotate the crankshaft and drive plate.

NOTE: The crankshaft pulley bolt is a metric size bolt.

15. Support transmission using transmission jack. Retain transmission on jack using safety chain.

—————— **CAUTION** ——————
On Eagle models, both the transmission and transfer case must be properly supported on the transmission jack and retained with a safety chain.

16. Disconnect oil cooler lines at transmission.
17. Remove bolt attaching rear support cushion to rear support cushion bracket (bracket is attached to transmission extension housing).
18. Remove rear crossmember attaching nuts and remove crossmember and support cushion as an assembly.
19. Place support stand under front of engine.
20. Remove bolts attaching catalytic converter support bracket to transmission, if so equipped.
21. Remove fill tube.
22. Remove bolts attaching transmission to engine.

NOTE: The transmission to engine block bolts are metric size bolts.

23. Move transmission (and transfer case, if so equipped) and converter back until clear of crankshaft.
24. Hold converter in position and

lower transmission until transmission converter housing clears engine.

To install:

25. If torque converter was removed, insert Pump Aligning Tool J–24033 into pump rotor and engage tool slots with pump rotor drive lugs.

26. Rotate aligning tool until hole in tool is vertical, then remove tool.

27. Rotate converter until pump drive slots in converter hub are vertical.

28. Carefully insert converter hub into oil pump. Be sure the drive lugs of pump inner rotor are completely engaged with the drive slots in converter hub.

29. Raise transmission and align converter with the drive plate. Refer to alignment marks made during removal.

────── **CAUTION** ──────

On Eagle models, both the transmission and transfer case must be supported on a transmission jack and retained with safety chain.

30. Move transmission forward and raise, lower, or tilt transmission to align transmission converter housing dowel holes with dowels in engine block.

NOTE: If the downward angle at the rear of the engine is not sufficient to permit transmission installation, raise the front of the engine to increase the downward angle.

31. Install 2 transmission to engine lower attaching bolts and tighten bolts evenly to pull transmission to engine.

32. Install drive plate to converter attaching bolts. Tighten bolts to 40 ft. lbs. torque.

NOTE: Coat threads of drive plate to converter attaching bolts with Loctite® 271 or equivalent.

33. Install remaining transmission to engine attaching bolts. Tighten bolts to 54 ft. lbs. torque.

34. Connect oil cooler lines.

35. Install propeller shaft using reference marks made during assembly.

36. Install rear crossmember and support cushion. Tighten attaching nuts to 30 ft. lbs. torque.

37. Install rear support cushion to support bracket bolt. Tighten bolt to 48 ft. lbs. torque.

38. Remove safety chain and transmission jack.

39. Install converter housing inspection cover.

40. Install starter motor. On Eagle models also install stiffening brace and skid plater.

41. Connect the neutral start switch wires to switch terminal.

42. Connect gearshift and throttle linkage. On models with column shift, position linkage bellcrank bracket on converter housing and install bracket attaching bolt.

43. Install speedometer cable and adapter assembly. Be sure adapter is correctly indexed.

44. Connect catalytic converter, if so equipped. On Eagle models, add correct quantity of transfer case lubricant.

45. Lower the vehicle.

46. Fill transmission to correct fluid level.

47. Check and adjust gearshift lever and throttle linkage if necessary.

NOTE: The gearshift lever adjusting trunnion is located at the lower end of the steering column.

48. Road test to check transmission operation.

4.2L ENGINE

1. Disconnect fan shroud, if so equipped.

2. Disconnect transmission fill tube at upper bracket.

3. Open hood.

────── **CAUTION** ──────

It is necessary that the hood be open to avoid damaging the hood and air cleaner when the rear crossmember is removed.

4. Raise and support car. Drain transmission fluid.

5. Remove inspection cover from converter housing.

6. On Spirit and Concord, remove screw attaching exhaust pipe clamp to exhaust pipe support bracket and slide clamp off bracket.

7. Remove transmission fill tube.

8. Remove starter. On Eagle models, also remove stiffening braces.

9. Mark propeller shaft(s) and yoke(s) for assembly alignment reference.

10. Remove propeller shaft(s).

11. On Eagle models, disconnect exhaust pipe and move it aside for working clearance.

12. Remove speedometer adapter and cable assembly. Discard adapter and cable seals, they are not reuseable. Cover adapter bore after removal.

13. Disconnect gearshift and throttle linkage.

14. Disconnect wires at the neutral start switch.

15. Mark converter drive plate and converter for assembly alignment reference.

16. To gain access to and remove the bolts attaching the drive plate to the converter, rotate the crankshaft and drive plate.

17. On Eagle models, remove skid plate and stiffening brace.

18. Support transmission (and transfer case on Eagle models) using a suitable transmission jack. Retain transmission on jack using safety chain.

19. Disconnect oil cooler lines at transmission.

20. Remove bolts attaching rear support cushion to transmission.

21. Remove rear crossmember.

22. Remove bolts attaching transmission to engine.

23. Move transmission and converter back to clear crankshaft.

24. Hold converter in position and lower transmission until converter housing clears engine.

To install:

25. If torque converter was removed, insert Pump Aligning Tool J–24033 in pump rotor until rotor drive lugs engage slots in tool.

26. Rotate tool until drilled hole in tool is vertical and remove tool.

27. Rotate converter until pump drive slots in converter hub into pump. Be sure drive lugs of pump inner rotor are properly engaged in drive slots of converter hub.

28. Raise transmission (and transfer case on Eagle models) and align converter with drive plate. Refer to assembly alignment marks.

29. Move transmission forward.

30. Raise, lower, or tilt transmission to align converter housing pilot holes with dowels in engine.

31. Install 2 transmission lower attaching bolts and tighten bolts evenly to pull transmission to engine.

32. Install drive plate to converter attaching bolts.

33. Install remaining transmission attaching bolts and tighten all bolts to 28 ft. lbs. torque.

34. Connect oil cooler lines.

35. Install rear support cushion on transmission, if removed.

36. Install rear crossmember.

37. Remove safety chain and transmission jack.

38. Install inspection cover.

39. On Spirit and Concord, install exhaust pipe clamp on support bracket.

40. Install starter. On Eagle models, also install stiffening braces.

41. Connect wires to the neutral start switch.

42. Connect gearshift and throttle linkage.

43. Install speedometer cable and adapter assembly. Be sure adapter is correctly indexed.

44. On Eagle models, connect exhaust pipes, attach stiffening brace and install skid plate.

45. Install propeller shaft(s). Refer to alignment marks made during removal. On Eagle models, add correct quantity of transfer case lubricant.

46. Lower automobile.

47. Fill transmission to correct level.

48. Check and adjust gearshift and throttle linkage, if necessary.
49. Road-test the vehicle to check transmission operation.

AUTOMATIC TRANSAXLE

For further information on automatic transaxles, please refer to "Automatic Transmissions" in the Unit Repair section.

REMOVAL & INSTALLATION

Medallion

1. Disconnect the negative battery cable.
2. Disconnect and remove the flexible heat tube from the engine.
3. Remove the TDC sensor retaining bolt and remove the sensor.
4. Remove the bolts retaining the steering bracket and remove the bracket.
5. Remove the bolts attaching the crossmember to the side sill and body.
6. Raise and safely support the vehicle.
7. Remove the front wheels. Disconnect and remove the passenger side tie rod.
8. Loosen the bolt retaining the coolant expansion tank and move the tank aside.
9. Attach engine support tool MS–1900 or equivalent, to the engine and tighten the adjuster nut until there is no slack in the chain.
10. Remove the bolts attaching the exhaust head pipe to the manifold. Remove the bolts attaching the exhaust head pipe to the converter and remove the head pipe. Disconnect the coolant lines to the heat exchanger.
11. Remove the crossmember by turning it and taking out through the passenger side wheel well.
12. Disengage the shift cable and support it to the side. Remove the upper steering knuckle mounting bolt and loosen the lower bolt.
13. Remove the drive shaft retaining pin. Swing each rotor and steering knuckle outward and slide the driveshafts from the transaxle.
14. Disconnect the speedometer cable. Disconnect the ground strap at the transaxle. Disconnect the BVA module harness.
15. Support the transaxle. Remove the transaxle support cushion nuts. Remove the bolts that attach the 2 transaxle mounting brackets to the transaxle.

16. Disconnect the wiring harness connector and remove the starter. Remove the converter to flywheel bolts. Remove the transaxle to engine bolts.
17. Pull the transaxle straight back until the converter is clear of the engine and lower the transaxle. Install converter retainer BVI–465 or equivalent, to keep the converter from falling out.

To install:
18. Raise and position the transaxle into the vehicle. Apply a small amount of grease to the torque converter pilot. Align the painted marks on the converter with the painted marks on the flywheel. Install the converter to flywheel bolts, tighten to 34 ft. lbs.
19. Install the transaxle to engine mounting bolts. Tighten to 37 ft. lbs.
20. Install the starter and connect the electrical connectors. Slightly raise the transaxle and install the mounting brackets. Align the transaxle support cushion bolts and install the retaining nuts.
21. Connect the speedometer cable and the shift cable.
22. Install the axleshafts by tilting the steering knuckle in, install the upper bolt and tighten both bolts to 148 ft. lbs.
23. Install the axle retaining pins. Connect the ground strap to the case.
24. Install the crossmember through the wheel well opening and position it on the side sills. Install and tighten the bolts.
25. Connect the tie rods to the steering bracket and tighten the mounting bolts to 25 ft. lbs. Connect the steering gear bracket to the steering rack and tighten the bolts to 30 ft. lbs. Connect the cooling lines.
26. Install the front wheels. Install the TDC sensor and the heat tube. Connect the exhaust header pipe to the converter and manifold. Connect the BVA wiring.
27. Check and fill the transaxle fluid. Remove the engine support tool and connect the battery.

Premier

1. Disconnect the negative battery cable.
2. Loosen the throttle valve cable adjusting nut and remove the cable from the engine bracket.
3. Disengage the shift cable and support it to the side. Remove the upper steering knuckle mounting bolt and loosen the lower bolt.
4. Remove the drive shaft retaining pin. Swing each rotor and steering knuckle outward and slide the driveshafts from the transaxle.
5. Remove the underbody splash shield.
6. Remove the converter housing

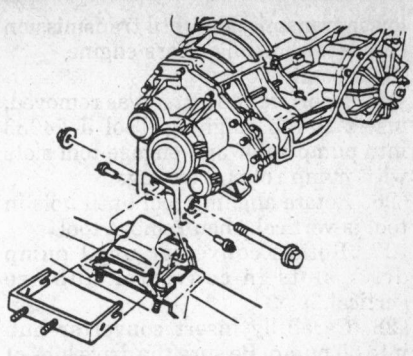

Automatic transaxle mounting Medallion and Premier

covers. Remove the converter to driveplate bolts. Support the transaxle.
7. Remove the nuts attaching the crossmember to the side sills. Remove the large bolt and nut that attach the rear cushion to the support bracket.
8. Remove the support bracket and rear cushion.
9. Disconnect the header pipes from the exhaust manifolds and the catalytic converter.
10. Loosen the engine cradle bolts. Remove the starter, plate and dowel. Disconnect the shift cable from the transmission lever. Remove the cable bracket bolts and seperate the bracket from the case.
11. Disconnect and remove the TDC sensor, disconnect the speedometer sensor. Disconnect the transaxle cooling lines.
12. Remove the transaxle to engine bolts, pull the transaxle back and away from the engine.

To install:
13. Position the transaxle to the engine. Install the transaxle to engine bolts ans tighten to 31 ft. lbs.
14. Connect all electrical leads, install the TDC sensor. Connect the speedometer. Install the transaxle cooler lines.
15. Attach the shift bracket to the case and tighten the bolts to 125 inch lbs. Install the shift cable into the bracket.
16. Install the starter. Connect the exhaust head pipes to the manifolds and he converter.
17. Install the rear support and cushion, install the mounting bolts and tighten to 49 ft. lbs.
18. Tighten the engine cradle bolts to 92 ft. lbs. Connect the driveshafts.
19. Install the converter to driveplate bolts and tighten to 24 ft. lbs. Install the converter housing covers.
20. Tilt the steering knuckles in and install the top bolts, tighten all to 148 ft. lbs.
21. Install the front wheels. Install

the under body splash shield. Attach the throttle valve cable.

22. Connect the negative battery cable. Check the fluid level.

Transfer Case

REMOVAL & INSTALLATION

Manual Transmission

1. Raise and support the vehicle safely.
2. Remove skid plate and rear brace rod at transfer case.
3. Remove speedometer adapter retainer attaching bolt and remove retainer, adapter, and cable. Plug adapter opening in transfer case to prevent excessive oil spillage.

NOTE: Mark the position of the speedometer adapter for assembly reference before removing it.

4. Mark propeller shafts and axle yokes for assembly alignment reference and disconnect propeller shafts at transfer case.
5. On models so equipped, remove transfer case shift motor vacuum harness.
6. Support transfer case with a suitable transmission jack.
7. Remove nuts from transfer case mounting studs and remove transfer case.
8. Align transmission output and transfer case input shafts and install transfer case on transmission adapter housing.
9. Install and tighten transfer case mounting stud nuts to 33 ft. lbs. torque.
10. Remove jack used to support transfer case.
11. Align and connect propeller shafts to axle yokes. Tighten clamp strap bolts to 15 ft. lbs. torque.
12. Install replacement O-ring on speedometer adapter and install adapter and cable and retainer. Tighten retainer bolt to 100 inch lbs. torque.

── CAUTION ──

Do not attempt to reuse the original adapter O-ring. The O-ring is designed to "swell" in service to improve its sealing qualities and it could be cut or torn during installation if reuse is attempted.

13. Install skid plate and rear brace rod. Torque retaining bolts to 30 ft. lbs. torque.
14. On models so equipped, install transfer case shift motor vacuum harness.
15. Check and correct lubricant levels in transmission and transfer case, if necessary.
16. Lower the vehicle.
17. Install nut on transfer case

mounting stud located inside transmission adapter housing. Tighten nut to 33 ft. lbs. torque.

18. Install gearshift lever mounting cover on transmission adapter housing.
19. Install gearshift lever on mounting cover. Be sure lever is engaged with shift rail before tightening lever attaching bolts.
20. Position gearshift lever boot and bezel on floorpan or console, if so equipped, and install bezel attaching screws.

Automatic Transmission

1. Raise the vehicle and support it safely.
2. Support engine and transmission with support stand or transmission jack.
3. Disconnect catalytic converter support bracket at adapter housing.
4. Remove skid plate and rear brace rod at transfer case.
5. Remove speedometer cable and adapter from transfer case. Discard adapter O-ring, it is not reusable.
6. Matchmark propeller shafts and transfer case yokes for assembly reference.
7. Disconnect propeller shafts at yokes. Secure shafts to underside of vehicle.
8. Disconnect gearshift and throttle linkage at transmission.
9. Lower the rear crossmember.
10. Remove all transfer case to adapter housing stud nuts and remove transfer case.
11. Install transfer case on adapter housing. Be careful not to damage output shaft splines during installation.
12. Install transfer case to adapter housing stud nuts. Tighten nuts to 33 ft. lbs. torque.
13. Install rear crossmember and tighten the attaching nuts to 30 ft. lbs.
14. Install the rear brace rod.
15. Remove transmission jack or support stand.
16. Connect gearshift and throttle linkage to transmission.
17. Connect propeller shafts. Tighten clamp strap bolts to 15 ft. lbs. torque.
18. Install new O-ring on speedometer adapter and install adapter and cable in transfer case.

NOTE: Do not attempt to reuse the old adapter O-ring. O-ring is designed to swell in service to provide improved sealing qualities and could be cut or torn if reinstallation is attempted.

19. Install skid plate and stiffening brace, if so equipped. Tighten retaining bolts to 30 ft. lbs.

20. Connect catalytic converter support bracket to adapter housing.
21. Check transfer case lubricant level and transmission linkage adjustments to make certain they are correct.
22. Lower the vehicle.

DRIVE AXLE

Halfshafts

REMOVAL & INSTALLATION

Medallion and Premier

1. Raise and safely support the vehicle. Remove the wheel and tire assembly.
2. Remove the disc brake caliper and support it aside. Do not support the caliper by the brake line.
3. Remove the axle to hub retaining nut and loosen the axle in the hub.
4. At the transaxle, remove the axle retaining pin (roll pin) using a drift to drive it from the axle shaft.
5. Remove the tie rod end attaching nut and disconnect the tie rod. Remove the 2 bolts that attach the steering knuckle to the strut.
6. Tilt the steering knuckle away from the strut and remove the axleshaft.

To install:

7. Install the axle to the transaxle and install the retaining pin, using a hammer and a drift.
8. Insert the end of the axle into the front hub and bearing. Connect the steering knuckle to the strut, tighten the bolts to 148 ft. lbs.
9. Connect the tie rod end to the steering knuckle. Install and tighten the axleshaft to hub retaining nut and tighten to 181 ft. lbs.
10. Install the brake caliper. Install the wheel and tire assembly.
11. Lower the vehicle and check the fluid level.

CV JOINT OVERHAUL

For all CV-joint overhaul procedures, refer to "Universal Joint/CV Joint Overhaul" in the Unit Repair section.

Front Drive Axle Shaft, Shaft Seal and Bearing

REMOVAL & INSTALLATION

Eagle with 4 Wheel Drive

The procedure for replacing the axle

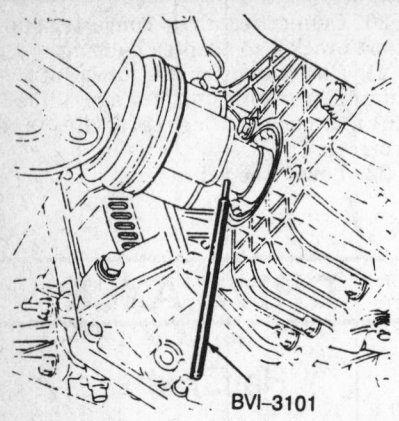

Removing the axle retaining pin.

BVI-3101

shafts and seals on 4 wheel drive models calls for removal of the axle first.

1. Raise and support the front of the car. Install protectors over the halfshaft boots. Remove the halfshaft to axle flange bolts, and tie the halfshafts out of the way.

2. Matchmark the driveshaft and the axle yoke. Remove the driveshaft.

3. Support the axle on stands. Remove the 5 axle to engine mounting bolts.

4. Lower the axle part way and remove the vent hose. Remove the axle.

5. Remove the differential cover and drain the oil. Remove the axle shaft C-clips.

6. Remove the axle shafts.

7. Carefully remove the shaft seal.

8. Two different bearings are used; the left side uses a ball bearing, and the right side uses a needle bearing. The ball bearing should be removed using a brass drift and a hammer; the needle bearing should be removed using a needle bearing removal tool.

NOTE: If the proper bearing removal tool is not available, remove the differential and remove the needle bearing using a $^{15}/_{16}$ inch socket and a 3 foot ratchet extension.

9. Install the bearings, using drivers of the appropriate type and size.

10. Oil the lips of the new seal and install into the housing using a driver of the correct size.

11. Install the axle shafts and C-clips.

12. Apply a bead of silicone seal to the differential cover and install the cover.

13. Fill the axle with 2.5 pints of 85W–90 GL–5 gear oil.

14. Move the axle into place under the car. Raise it sufficiently to connect the vent hose, then raise it fully into place and install the mounting bolts. Tighten to 50 ft. lbs.

15. Install the driveshaft, aligning

the marks made during removal. Install the halfshaft to axle flange bolts, and tighten to 45 ft. lbs.

Driveshaft and U-Joints

A one-piece tubular driveshaft is used with a yoke at each end, to position the cross-and-roller tube universal joints.

NOTE: The driveshaft is a balanced unit; care must be used in handling. Do not bend or distort the tube or yokes, or vibration will result.

REMOVAL & INSTALLATION

Concord and Spirit

1. Matchmark and disassemble rear U-joint by removing nuts. Retention is by U-bolts or straps, depending on model.

2. Drop rear of driveshaft and slide front yoke out of transmission.

3. To install, reverse removal procedure, tightening U-joint nuts to 15 ft. lbs.

Eagle

Both driveshafts are secured at the transfer case end and the axle yoke end by straps. The straps are retained by Torx® head bolts.

1. Shift into **NEUTRAL**. Raise and support the car.

2. Matchmark the driveshaft(s) at the transfer case and axle yoke for alignment reference.

3. Remove the retaining straps with a Torx® bit tool of the proper size. Remove the driveshaft(s).

4. To install, align the matchmarks made during removal to assure proper balance. Seat the universal joints in the yokes and install the straps, tightening to 17 ft. lbs.

UNIVERSAL JOINT OVERHAUL

For all U-Joint overhaul procedures, please refer to "U-Joint/CV-Joint Overhaul" in the Unit Repair section.

Rear Axle Shaft, Bearing and Seal

REMOVAL & INSTALLATION

Concord, Spirit and Eagle

1. The hub and drum are separate units and are removed after the wheel is removed. The hub and axle shaft are

serrated together on the taper. An axle shaft key assures proper alignment during assembly.

2. With the wheel on the ground and the parking brake applied, remove and discard the axle shaft nut cotter pin and remove the nut. Raise the car and remove the wheel. Release the parking brakes and remove the drum.

3. Attach a puller to the rear hub and remove the hub. The use of a "knock-out" puller should be discouraged, since it may result in damage to the axle shaft or wheel bearings.

4. Disconnect the parking brake cable at the equalizer.

5. Disconnect the brake tube at the wheel cylinder and remove the brake support plate assembly, oil seal, and axle shims. Note that the axle shims are located on the left side only.

6. Using a screw type puller, remove the axle shaft and bearings from the axle housing.

7. Remove the axle shaft inner oil seal and install new seals at assembly.

8. The bearing is a press fit and should be removed with an arbor press.

9. The axle shaft bearings have no provision for lubrication after assembly. Before installing the bearings, they should be packed with a good quality wheel bearing lubricant.

10. Press the axle shaft bearings onto the axle shaft with the small diameter of the cone toward the outer (tapered) end of the shaft.

11. Soak the inner axle shaft seal in light lubricating oil. Coat the outer surface of the seal retainer with sealant.

12. Install the inner oil seal.

13. Install the axle shafts, indexing the splined end with the differential side gears.

14. Install the outer bearing cup.

15. Install the brake support plate. Sealant should be applied to the axle housing flange and to the brake support mounting plate.

16. Install the original shims, oil seal and brake support plate. Torque the nuts to 30–35 ft. lbs.

NOTE: The oil seal and retainer go between the axle housing flange and the brake support plate on 9 in. brakes. On 10 in. brakes, they go on the outside of the brake support plate.

17. To adjust the axle shaft end-play, strike the axle shafts with a lead mallet to seat the bearings. Install a dial indicator on the brake support plate and check the play while pushing and pulling the axle shaft. End-play should be 0.004–0.008 in., with 0.006 in. desirable. Add shims to the left side only

to decrease the play and remove shims to increase the play.

18. Slide the hub onto the axle shafts by aligning the serrations and the keyway on the hub with the axle shaft key.

19. Replace the hub and drum, install the wheel, lower the car onto the floor and tighten the axle shaft nut to 250 ft. lbs. If the cotter pin hole is not aligned with a castellation on the nut, tighten the nut to the next castellation.

NOTE: A new hub must be installed whenever a new axle shaft is installed. Install 2 thrust washers on the shaft. Tighten the new hub onto the shaft until the hub is 1.19 in. from the end of the shaft. Remove the nut and remove 1 thrust washer. Install the nut and torque to 250 ft. lbs. New hubs do not have serrations on the axle shaft mating surface. The serrations are cut when the hub is installed onto the axle shaft.

20. Connect the parking brake cable at the equalizer.

21. Connect the brake tube at the wheel cylinder and bleed the brakes.

Front Wheel Drive Hub, Knuckle and Bearings

REMOVAL & INSTALLATION

Medallion and Premier

1. Raise and safely support the vehicle.

2. Remove the wheel.

3. Remove the brake caliper and support it to the side. Do not disconnect the brake lines or support the caliper by the brake lines.

4. Push the axleshaft out of the hub, if it does not push out easily use tool TAV-1050 or equivalent, on the hub.

5. Remove the brake rotor. Working through the access hole in the hub, remove the bolts that retain the bearing assembly. Remove the hub and wheel bearing as an assembly using tool TAV-1050 or equivalent, to pull the hub off the knuckle.

6. If the wheel bearing is being replaced, remove it from the hub by pulling on it. Discard the bearing race.

7. Remove the ball joint key bolt and disconnect the ball joint from the knuckle. Remove the 2 bolts that attach the strut to the steering knuckle.

8. Remove the steering knuckle.

To install:

9. Insert the ball joint into the steering knuckle and install the ball joint key bolt, tighten to 77 ft. lbs. Po-

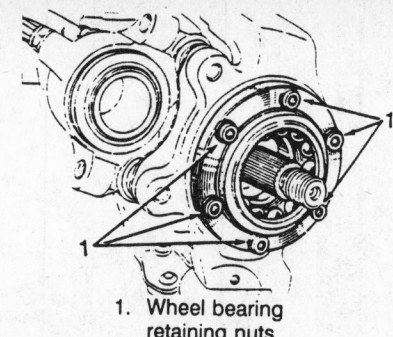

1. Wheel bearing retaining nuts

Medallion and Premier—front wheel bearing removal

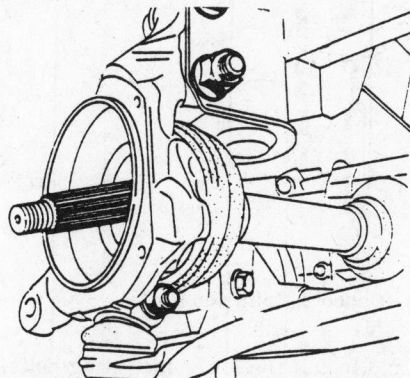

Medallion and Premier—front hub removal

sition the steering knuckle to the strut and install the retaining bolts, tighten to 123 ft. lbs.

10. Install the wheel bearing over the rear of the hub and install the hub/bearing assembly over the axleshaft.

11. Working through the access hole in the hub, install the bearing retaining bolts, tighten to 11 ft. lbs.

12. Install the axle retaining nut and tighten it to 181 ft. lbs.

NOTE: It is essential that the axle retaining nut be tightened to the specified torque. The nut sets the wheel bearing preload besides retaining the axle.

13. Install the brake rotor and the caliper.

14. Install the wheel and lower the vehicle.

FRONT SUSPENSION

Shock Absorber

REMOVAL & INSTALLATION

NOTE: When installing new shock absorbers, purge them of

air by extending them in their normal position and compressing them while inverted. Do this several times. It is normal for new shock absorbers to be more resistant to extension than to compression.

Concord, Spirit and Eagle

1. Remove the 2 lower shock absorber attaching nuts. Remove the washers and the grommets.

2. Remove the upper mounting bracket nuts and bolts.

3. Remove the bracket, complete with shock.

4. Remove the upper attaching nut and separate the shock from the mounting bracket.

5. For adjustable shocks: To adjust the shock, compress the piston completely. Holding the upper part of the shock, turn the shock until the lower arrow is aligned with the desired setting. A click will be heard when the desired setting is reached.

6. To install, fit the grommets, washers, upper mounting bracket and nut on the shock in the reverse order of removal. Tighten the nut to 8 ft. lbs.

7. Fully extend the shock and install 2 grommets on the lower mounting stud.

8. Lower the shock through the hole in the wheel well. Fit the lower attachment studs through the lower spring seat.

9. Install the grommets, washers, and nuts. Tighten the nuts to 15 ft. lbs.

10. Secure the upper mounting bracket with its attachment nuts and bolts. Tighten them to 20 ft. lbs.

MacPherson Strut

REMOVAL & INSTALLATION

Medallion and Premier

1. Raise and safely support the vehicle, allowing the front wheels to hang.

2. Remove the wheel. Remove the outer tie rod securing nut and remove the tie rod.

3. Remove the 3 upper strut retaining bolts.

— **CAUTION** —

DO NOT remove the center strut retaining nut. The coil spring is under very high pressure. Removal of this nut could allow the coil spring to release possibly causing serious injury.

4. Remove the nuts securing the strut to the steering knuckle. Remove the strut and spring assembly.

5. To install the assembly, first guide the strut assembly into place

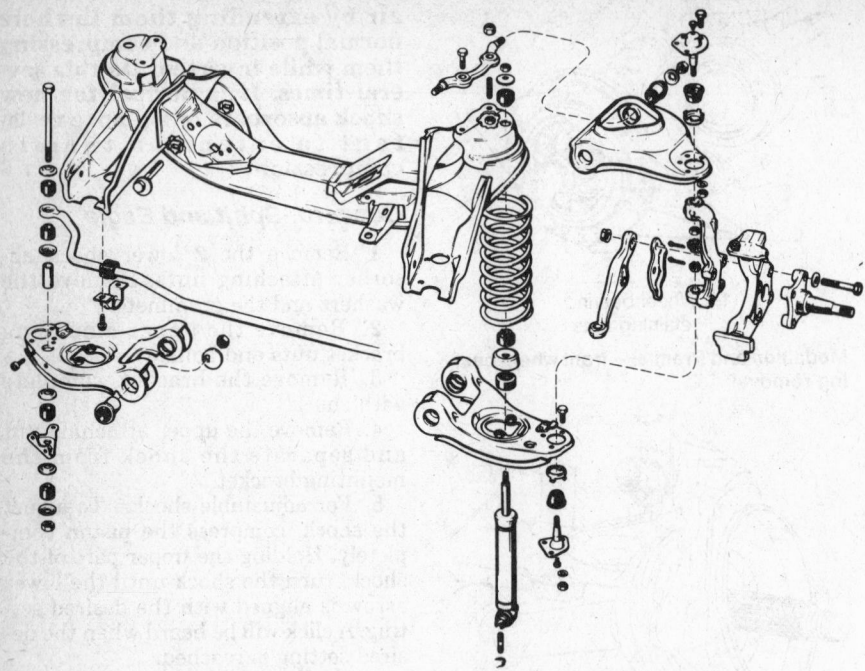

Front suspension components—Concord, Spirit and Eagle

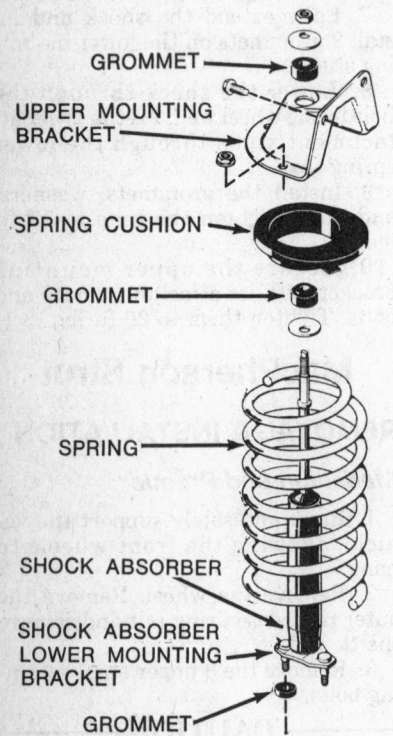

GROMMET

UPPER MOUNTING BRACKET

SPRING CUSHION

GROMMET

SPRING

SHOCK ABSORBER

SHOCK ABSORBER LOWER MOUNTING BRACKET

GROMMET

IDENTIFICATION

THE COIL SPRING IS IDENTIFIED BY THE LAST THREE NUMBERS ON THE TAG ATTACHED TO THE SPRING

Concord, Spirit and Eagle—shock and spring assembly

and install the lower mounting bolts, tighten to 123 ft. lbs.

6. Install the upper strut plate retaining bolts and tighten to 17 ft. lbs.

7. Install the tie rod and retaining bolt, tighten it to 27 ft. lbs. Install the wheel and lower the vehicle.

OVERHAUL

For all spring and shock absorber removal and installation procedures and all strut overhaul procedures, refer to "Strut Overhaul" in the Unit Repair section.

Springs

REMOVAL & INSTALLATION

Concord, Spirit and Eagle

1. Remove the shock absorber.

2. Install a spring compressor through the upper spring seat opening and bolt it to the lower spring seat using the lower shock absorber mounting holes.

3. Remove the lower spring seat pivot retaining nuts, then tighten the compressor tool to compress the spring about 1 in.

4. Raise and safely support the front of the vehicle allowing the front wheels to hang freely.

5. Remove the front wheel and pull the lower spring seat out and away from the car, then slowly release the spring tension and remove the coil spring and lower spring seat.

6. To install, place the spring compressor through the coil spring and tape the rubber spring cushion to the small-diameter end of the spring (upper).

7. Place the lower spring seat against the spring with the end of the coil against the formed shoulder in the seat. The shoulder and coil end face inward, toward the engine, when the spring is installed.

8. Place the spring up against the upper seat, then align the lower spring seat pivot so the retaining studs will enter the holes in the upper control arm.

9. Compress the coil spring and install the spring, then install the wheel and tire and lower the car to the floor to place weight on suspension.

10. Install and tighten lower spring seat spindle retaining nuts and tighten them to 35 ft. lbs. Remove the spring compressor and install the shock absorber.

Ball Joints

INSPECTION

Concord, Spirit and Eagle

NOTE: Before checking the upper ball joint, make certain the front wheel bearings are adjusted to specifications.

1. Raise and safely support the front of the vehicle. The control arms must hang free if an accurate reading is to be obtained.

2. Check the lower ball joints by grasping the lower portion of the wheel and pulling it in and out.

3. If there is noticeable lateral freeplay, the lower ball joint is worn and must be replaced.

NOTE: On Eagle, the lower ball joints and control arms must be replaced as assemblies.

4. To check the condition of the upper ball joint, place a dial indicator with its plunger against the tie scrub bead (just outside the whitewall).

5. Move the upper portion of the wheel and tire toward the car's center, while watching the dial indicator.

6. Move the wheel and tire back out while watching the indicator.

7. The upper ball joint should be replaced if its total movement is greater than 0.160 in.

NOTE: On Eagle, the upper ball joints are replaceable separately.

REMOVAL & INSTALLATION
Concord, Spirit and Eagle
LOWER BALL JOINT

1. Place a 2 × 4 × 5 in. block of

wood on the side sill so that it supports the control arm.

2. Raise and safely support the front of the vehicle allowing the wheels to hang freely.

3. Remove the wheel, the caliper and rotor.

4. Disconnect the lower control arm strut rod. Disconnect the stabilizer bar, if so equipped.

5. Separate the steering arm from the steering knuckle.

6. Remove the ball stud retaining nut, after removing its cotter pin.

7. Install a ball joint removal tool, then loosen the ball stud in the knuckle pin. Leave the tool in place on the stud.

8. Place a jackstand under the lower control arm.

9. Chisel the heads off the rivets which secure the ball joint to the control arm. Use a punch to remove the rivets.

10. Remove the tool from the ball stud.

11. Remove the ball stud from the knuckle pin and remove the joint from the control arm.

12. Position the new ball joint so that its securing holes align with the rivet holes in the control arm.

13. Loosely install the special ⁵⁄₁₆ in. bolts used to secure the ball joint.

CAUTION

Use only the hardened ⁵⁄₁₆ in. bolts supplied with the ball joint replacement kit; standard bolts are not strong enough.

14. Install the steering strut and stop on the lower control arm. Tighten their bolts to 75 ft. lbs.

15. Apply chassis grease to the steering stops and fit the knuckle pin and retaining nut on the ball stud; tighten the nut to 75 ft. lbs. Install a new cotter pin.

16. Complete the installation procedure in the reverse order of removal, then check front end alignment.

UPPER BALL JOINT

1. Place a 2 × 4 × 5 in. block of wood on the side sill so that it supports the control arm.

2. Raise and safely support the front of the vehicle allowing the wheels to hang freely.

3. Remove the wheel, the caliper and rotor.

NOTE: On Eagle models temporarily reinstall 2 lugnuts to retain each brake rotor. This eliminates repositioning rotors and calipers prior to reassembly.

4. Remove the ball stud retaining nut, after removing its cotter pin.

5. Install a ball joint removal tool, then loosen the ball stud in the knuck-

le pin. Leave the tool in place on the stud.

6. Place a jackstand under the lower control arm.

7. Chisel the heads off the rivets which secure the ball joint to the control arm. Use a punch to remove the rivets.

8. Separate the upper ball joint from the control arm.

9. Remove the ball joint puller from the knuckle pin.

10. Remove the ball stud from the knuckle pin and remove the joint from the control arm.

11. Position the new ball joint so that its securing holes align with the rivet holes in the control arm.

12. Loosely install the special ⁵⁄₁₆ in. bolts used to secure the ball joint.

CAUTION

Use only the hardened ⁵⁄₁₆ in. bolts supplied with the ball joint replacement kit; standard bolts are not strong enough.

13. Install the steering strut and stop on the lower control arm. Tighten their bolts to 75 ft. lbs.

14. Apply chassis grease to the steering stops and fit the knuckle pin and retaining nut on the ball stud; tighten the nut to 75 ft. lbs. Install a new cotter pin.

15. Complete the installation in the reverse order of removal and check front end alignment.

Medallion and Premier

LOWER BALL JOINT

1. Raise and safely support the vehicle. Remove the wheel.

2. Loosen the inner stabilizer bar bracket bolts.

3. Remove the nuts from the outer stabilizer bar bracket and slide the bracket off the bolts.

4. Move the stabilizer bar away from the lower control arm. Remove the ball joint key bolt.

5. Loosen the lower control arm bolts. Remove the ball joint by tapping it with a brass hammer in an upward direction.

6. Install the ball joint in the lower control arm and install but do not tighten the retaining bolts.

7. Insert the ball joint stud in the steering knuckle and install the key bolt, tighten the key bolt to 77 ft. lbs.

8. Connect the stabilizer bar brackets to the control arm, but do not tighten the bolts. Install the wheel and lower the vehicle.

9. Tighten the lower control arm bolts to 103 ft. lbs. Tighten the ball joint bolts to 60 ft. lbs. and tighten the stabilizer bar bolts to 29 ft. lbs.

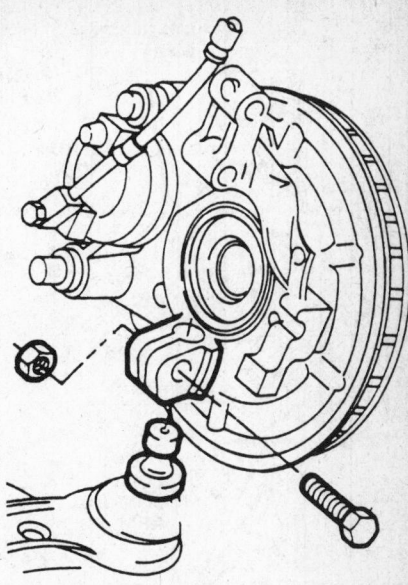

Medallion and Premier—ball joint to hub mounting

Upper Control Arms

REMOVAL & INSTALLATION

Concord, Spirit and Eagle

1. Remove the shock absorber and compress the coil spring approximately 2 in.

2. Raise and safely support the front of the vehicle, allowing the control arms to hang freely.

3. Remove the wheel and the upper ball joint cotter pin and retaining nut.

4. Separate the ball joint stud from the steering knuckle using a ball joint removal tool.

5. Remove the inner pivot bolts, then remove the control arm.

6. To install, reverse the removal procedure. Do not tighten the pivot bolt nuts until the full weight of the car is on the wheels. The ball joint stud nut must be tightened to 75 ft. lbs., the lower spring seat pivot retaining nuts to 35 ft. lbs., and the control arm inner pivot bolts to 80 ft. lbs.

Lower Control Arm

REMOVAL & INSTALLATION

Concord and Spirit

The inner end of the lower control arm is attached to a removable crossmember. The outer end is attached to the steering knuckle pin and ball joint assembly.

1. Raise and safely support the front of the vehicle, allowing the front suspension to hang.

2. Remove the caliper and rotor

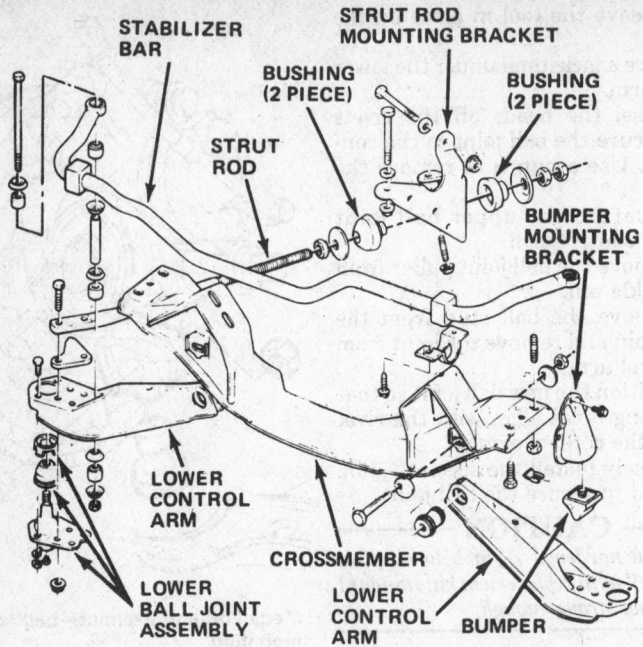

STABILIZER BAR

STRUT ROD MOUNTING BRACKET

BUSHING (2 PIECE)

BUSHING (2 PIECE)

STRUT ROD

BUMPER MOUNTING BRACKET

LOWER CONTROL ARM

LOWER BALL JOINT ASSEMBLY

CROSSMEMBER

LOWER CONTROL ARM

BUMPER

Lower control arm and components—Concord, Spirit and Eagle

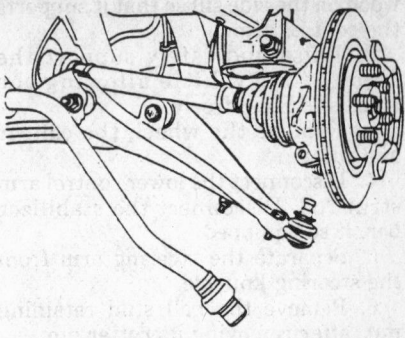

Lower control arm removal—Medallion and Premier

from the spindle, then disconnect the steering arm from the knuckle pin.

3. Remove the lower ball joint stud cotter pin and nut. Separate the ball joint from the knuckle pin using a ball joint removal tool.

4. Disconnect the sway bar from the control arm, unbolt the strut rod. Remove the inner pivot bolt and the control arm.

5. To install, reverse the removal procedure; do not tighten the inner pivot bolt until the car weight is on the wheels. Tighten the ball joint retaining nut to 75 ft. lbs; strut rod bolts to 75 ft. lbs.; sway bar bolts to 8 ft. lbs.; steering arm bolts to 55 ft. lbs. and control arm inner pivot bolt to 110 ft. lbs.

Eagle

1. Remove the wheel cover. Remove and discard the cotter pin. Remove the nut lock and the hub pin.

2. Raise and safely support the front of the vehicle. Remove the wheel. Remove the brake caliper from the knuckle and suspend it from the body by a length of wire; do not allow it to hang by the hose. Remove the rotor.

3. Remove the lower ball joint cotter pin and retaining nut. Discard the cotter pin.

4. Separate the ball joint stud from the steering knuckle using a ball joint removal tool.

5. Remove the halfshaft flange bolts and remove the halfshaft.

6. Remove the strut rod to control arm bolts. Disconnect the stabilizer bar from the arm.

7. Remove the inner pivot bolt and remove the control arm.

8. To install, place the control arm into position and install the inner pivot bolt, but do not tighten the pivot bolt yet.

9. Install the ball joint stud into the steering knuckle. Install the nut and tighten to 75 ft. lbs. Continue to tighten until the holes align, and install a new cotter pin.

10. Connect the stabilizer bar to the arm; tighten the bolts to 7 ft. lbs. Install the strut rod; tighten the bolts to 75 ft. lbs.

11. Install the halfshaft to axle flange bolts; tighten to 45 ft. lbs.

12. Place a jack under the lower control arm. Raise the jack carefully to compress the spring slightly. Tighten the control arm pivot bolt to 110 ft. lbs.

13. Install the rotor, caliper, and hub nut. Tighten the hub nut to 180 ft. lbs. Install the nut lock and a new cotter pin.

14. Install the wheel. Check and adjust the front end alignment as necessary.

Medallion and Premier

1. Raise and safely support the front of the vehicle, allowing the front wheels to hang freely.

2. Remove the wheel.

3. Loosen the inner stabilizer bar bracket bolts, remove the the outer stabilizer bracket bolts and move the stabilizer bar away from the control arm.

4. Remove the ball joint key bolt

and remove the ball joint from the knuckle.

5. Remove the bolts and nuts attaching the control arm and remove the control arm. Replace any worn components.

6. Position the lower control arm to the cradle and install the mounting bolts, do not tighten the mounting bolts.

7. Install the ball joint to the steering knuckle. Insert the key bolt and tighten it to 77 ft. lbs.

8. Connect the stabilizer bar brackets to the control arm, do not tighten the bolts. Install the wheel and lower the vehicle.

9. With the weight of the vehicle now on the suspension tighten the lower control arm bolts to 103 ft. lbs. and the stabilizer bar bolts to 29 ft. lbs.

Front Wheel Bearings

Four wheel drive models have sealed, non-adjustable front hubs and bearings. Refer to the "Drive Axle" procedures in this section for removal and installation procedures.

ADJUSTMENT

Concord, Spirit and Eagle

1. Raise and safely support the vehicle. Remove the wheel and remove the dust cover from the spindle.

2. Remove the cotter pin and nut retainer.

3. Rotate the wheel while tightening the spindle nut to 20–25 ft. lbs.

4. Loosen the spindle nut ⅓ of a turn.

5. Rotate the wheel while tightening the spindle nut to 6 inch lbs.

6. Fit the nut retainer over the spindle and align the slots in it with the cotter pin hole. Insert the cotter pin.

7. Install the dust cover.

Medallion and Eagle

Refer to "Drive Axle" in this section for front wheel bearing removal and installation.

Front Wheel Alignment

Caster

Caster is the tilting of the steering axis either forward or backward from the vertical, when viewed from the side of the vehicle. A backward tilt is said to be positive and a forward tilt is said to be negative.

Camber

Camber is the tilting of the wheels from the vertical when viewed from the front of the vehicle. When the wheels tilt outward from the top, the camber is said to be positive. When the wheels tilt inward from the top the camber is said to be negative. The amount of tilt is measured in degrees from the vertical. This measurement is called camber angle.

Toe-In

Toe-in is the turning in of the wheels. The actual amount of toe-in is normally only a fraction of an inch. The purpose of toe-in specification is to ensure parallel rolling of the wheels. Toe-in also serves to offset the small deflections of the steering support system which occur when the vehicle is rolling forward.

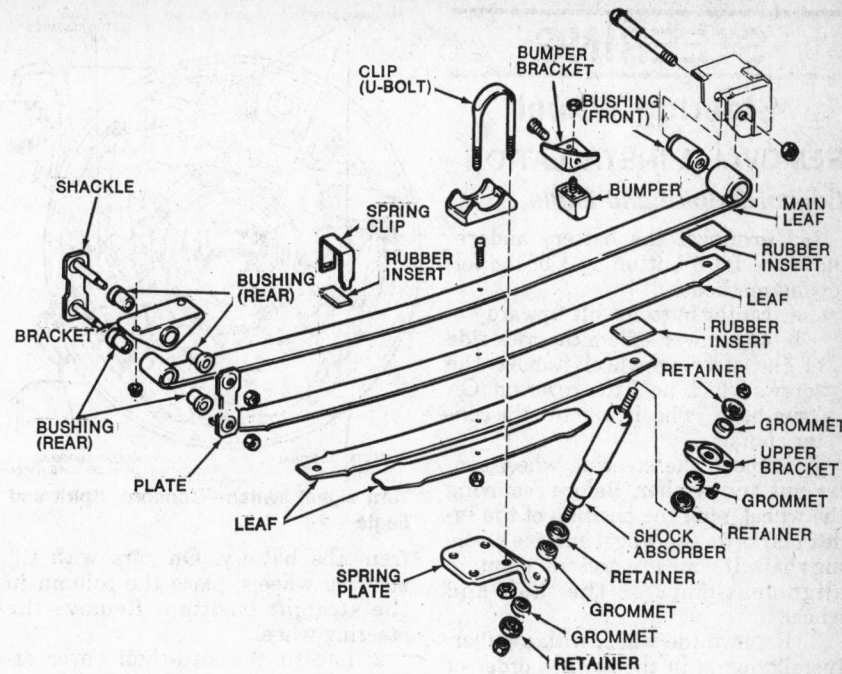

Typical leaf spring rear suspension

REAR SUSPENSION

Shock Absorber

REMOVAL & INSTALLATION

Concord, Spirit and Eagle

NOTE: When installing new shocks purge them of air by repeatedly extending them in their normal position and compressing them while inverted. It is normal for new shocks to be more resistant to extension than to compression.

1. Raise and safely support the rear of the vehicle.
2. Remove the lower shock attachment.
3. Remove the access plate on the rear underbody panel, and remove the upper securing nut. It may be necessary to hold the top of the shock while unfastening the nut.

NOTE: Some models do not have an access plate. On these cars, remove the upper attachment plate complete as an assembly, from under the car.

4. Remove the shock from under the car.
5. Installation is in the reverse order of removal.

Medallion and Premier

1. Raise and safely support the rear of the vehicle.

— CAUTION —
Never raise the rear of the vehicle by lifting it under the "V" shaped channel of the rear axle. Serious damage to the torsion bars can occur.

2. Remove the bolts securing the top and bottom of the shock absorber and remove the shock.
3. Install the shock absorber and install the retaining bolts. Tighten the upper shock bolt to 60 ft. lbs. and the lower to 85 ft. lbs.
4. Lower the vehicle.

Springs

REMOVAL & INSTALLATION

Concord, Spirit and Eagle

1. Raise and safely support the rear of the vehicle.

2. Disconnect the rear shock from the lower mounting stud.
3. Disconnect the axle U-bolts.
4. Remove the nut from the bolt which attaches the eye of the spring to the front mount. Remove the bolt.
5. Remove the nuts from the rear shackle. Remove the shackle.
6. Installation is in the reverse order of removal.

Rear Wheel Bearing and Hub Assembly

REMOVAL & INSTALLATION

Medallion and Premier

The rear wheel bearings and hubs are replaced as assemblies only. They are non-adjustable. The maximum allowable bearing end play is 0.001 in. If the end play exceeds this the bearing/hub assembly must be replaced.

1. Raise and safely support the rear of the vehicle. Remove the wheel.
2. Remove the brake drum from the axle shaft hub.
3. Remove the axle shaft hub nut and remove the hub/bearing assembly.
4. Lightly oil the axle shaft before installing the hub/bearing assembly. Install the hub to the axle shaft using a NEW nut. Tighten the nut to 123 ft. lbs.
5. Install the brake drum. Install the wheel and lower the vehicle.

STEERING

Steering Wheel

REMOVAL & INSTALLATION
Concord, Spirit and Eagle

1. Disconnect the battery and remove the horn button by 1 of the following methods:

 a. center button—lift upward

 b. trim cover—from the back side of the steering wheel remove the screws which hold the cover on. On "rim-blow" wheels, remove the center contact.

2. Remove the steering wheel center nut and washer. Before removing the wheel, note the position of the index marks on the wheel and the steering shaft. If none are present, paint an alignment mark on the shaft and wheel.

3. Remove the wheel with a puller. Installation is in the reverse order of removal. Tighten the steering wheel nut to 20 ft. lbs.

NOTE: Some shafts have metric threads. These can be identified by a groove in the shaft splines. Metric nuts are coded blue.

――――――― CAUTION ―――――――

Do not hammer on the end of the steering shaft; hammering could shear the plastic retainers which maintain the rigidity of the energy-absorbing steering column.

Medallion and Premler

1. Disconnect the negative battery cable.

2. Unsnap the horn button and disconnect the wires. Remove the horn button.

3. Note the position of the reference mark on the end of the steering shaft. Remove the nut and slide the wheel off the shaft.

4. Install the electrical connector. Align the pin on the turn signal cam with the pin bore in the steering wheel and slide the wheel into place.

5. Align the wheel with the reference mark on the steering shaft and install the nut. Tighten the nut to 52 ft. lbs.

6. Connect the negative battery cable.

Turn Signal Switch, Hazard Signal and Lock Cylinder

REMOVAL & INSTALLATION
Concord, Spirit and Eagle

1. Disconnect the ground cable

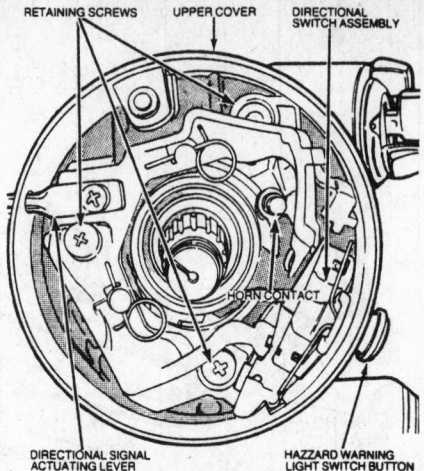

Turn signal switch—Concord, Spirit and Eagle

from the battery. On cars with tilt steering wheels, place the column in the straight position. Remove the steering wheel.

2. Loosen the anti-theft cover attaching screws and remove the cover from the column. Do not hammer on the shaft. Do not remove the screws from the cover; they are attached to it with plastic retainers.

3. To remove the lockplate, a special compressing tool is required. This tool is an inverted U-shape with a hole for the shaft. The shaft nut is used to force it down. Depress the lockplate and pry the snap-ring from the groove in the steering shaft. Remove the tool, snap-ring, plate turn signal cam, upper bearing preload spring, and the thrust washer from the shaft.

4. Place the turn signal lever in the Right turn position and remove it.

5. Depress the hazard warning switch button and remove it by rotating it counterclockwise. Remove the package tray (if so equipped) and the lower trim panel.

6. Disconnect the wire harness connector block at its mounting bracket, which is located on the right side of the lower column. Remove the steering column mounting bracket attaching bolts. Remove the turn signal switch wiring harness protector from the bottom of the column.

NOTE: To ease the removal and replacement of the directional switch harness, tape the harness connector to the wire harness. This will prevent snagging while removing the wiring harness assembly through the steering column. Prepare the new turn signal switch harness in the same manner to ease installation.

7. On late model vehicles, it is necessary to perform the following 3 steps to get the harness out of the column:

 a. Remove the steering tube cover.

 b. Remove the steering column bracket bolts and then just loosen the column bracket nuts.

 c. Fold the wire harness connector over the harness itself and then wrap it with tape to prevent snagging when it is removed.

8. If the car (Concord and Spirit only) is equipped with a column-mounted automatic transmission selector, use a paper clip to depress the locktab that holds the shift quadrant light wire in the connector block.

9. Remove the switch attaching screws. Withdraw the switch and wire harness from the column. On those late model vehicles requiring that Step 7 be done, lift the column and pull the switch and harness out. If the vehicle has a tilt column, remove the plastic harness protector.

10. Insert the key into the lock cylinder and turn the key to the **ON** position. Remove the warning buzzer switch and the contacts as an assembly using needlenose pliers. Take care not to let the contacts fall into the column.

11. Turn the key to the **LOCK** position and compress the lock cylinder retaining tab. Remove the lock cylinder. If the tab is not visible through the slot, knock the casting flash out of the slot.

To install:

12. Hold the lock cylinder sleeve and turn the lock cylinder counterclockwise until it contacts the stop.

13. Align the lock cylinder key with the keyway in the housing and slip the cylinder into the housing.

14. Lightly depress the cylinder against the sector, while turning it counterclockwise, until the cylinder and sector are engaged.

15. Depress the cylinder until the retaining tab engages, and the lock cylinder is secured.

16. When installing the turn signal switch, don't screw it in place until the actuating lever pivot is properly seated and aligned in the top of the housing boss.

17. Install the turn signal lever and check the operation of the switch.

18. Install the thrust washer, spring and turn-signal cancelling cam on the steering shaft.

19. Align the lockplate and steering shaft splines, and position the lockplate so the turn signal camshaft protrudes from the "dogleg" opening in the lockplate.

20. Use snap-ring pliers to install the snap-ring on the end of the steering shaft.

21. Secure the anti-theft cover with its screws.

22. Install the button on the hazard warning switch. Install the steering

wheel as detailed above. If the column nuts and bolts have been loosened, retorque the bolts to 15 ft. lbs. and the nuts to 10 ft. lbs.

Medallion

1. Disconnect the negative battery cable.
2. Remove the screws from the lower steering column cover and remove the cover.
3. On vehicles equipped with cruise control, pull down on the piece of wire at the forward edge of the cover. This will pull the spring loaded cruise control commutator into its housing.
4. Remove the upper and lower steering column covers.
5. Remove the 2 screws attaching the wiper switch and remove the switch.
6. Disconnect the wire connectors.
7. Install the switch to the column and install the retaining screws. Install the steering column covers.
8. Install the lower steering column cover. Connect the negative battery cable.

Premier

The turn signal switch in the premier is locate in a pod on the left side of the steering column. The switch is removed with the pod assembly.
1. Disconnect the negative battery cable.
2. Remove the instrument panel lower cover. Remove the lower instrument panel support bar.
3. Pull the air duct out of the way. Seperate the steering column electrical connector.
4. Remove the screws that retain the pod to the column and pull the pod part way out. Remove the 2 screws retaining the electrical connector to the pod casing.
5. Pull the harness out and through the pod.
6. Install the pod wiring connector and install the pod to the column. Connect the steering column connector and install the lower support. Connect the air duct.
7. Connect the negative battery cable.

Ignition Switch

REMOVAL & INSTALLATION

Concord, Spirit and Eagle

The ignition switch on all models is mounted on the lower steering column tube and is connected to the lock cylinder via a lock rod.
1. Place the key in **OFF-LOCK** position.
2. Remove switch mounting screws.

3. Disconnect the lock rod, remove harness connector and switch.
4. To install on the standard column, move the switch slide as far as it will go to the left (toward the wheel). On the tilt-column, push the slide to the extreme right.
5. Position the lock rod into the hole on the switch slide.
6. Install the switch on the steering column. Be sure that the slide stays in its detent.
7. On the tilt-column, do not tighten the mounting screws. Instead, push the switch down the column, away from the steering wheel. This will remove any slack from the lock rod.
8. Tighten the switch mounting screws.

Medallion

1. Disconnect the negative battery cable.
2. Remove the screws from the lower steering column cover and remove the cover.
3. On vehicles equipped with cruise control, pull down on the piece of wire at the forward edge of the cover. This will pull the spring loaded cruise control commutator into its housing.
4. Remove the upper and lower steering column covers. Remove the screws retaining the lower instrument panel and remove the panel.
5. Remove the ignition switch cover. Remove the ignition switch mounting screw.
6. Insert the key into the ignition and turn it to the unmarked arrow on the switch. Push in the locking tabs on the side of the housing, with a punch and remove the switch. Seperate the switch from the wires by removing the screw retaining the connector.
7. Install the switch into the lock cylinder, push the wires through the cylinder hole. Push the locking tabs in and lock the switch in position.
8. Connect the electrical leads. Install the ignition switch cover. Install the trim covers.
9. Connect the negative battery cable.

Premier

1. Disconnect the negative battery cable. Remove the steering wheel.
2. Remove the turn signal cancelling cam, unlock the tabs and slide the canceler off the steering shaft.
3. If equipped with a tilt wheel remove the tilt control lever.
4. Remove the screws retaining the right and left switch pods. Remove the ignition switch trim ring.
5. Remove the screws from the pod housing/column cover. Remove the pod housing/column cover by pulling it

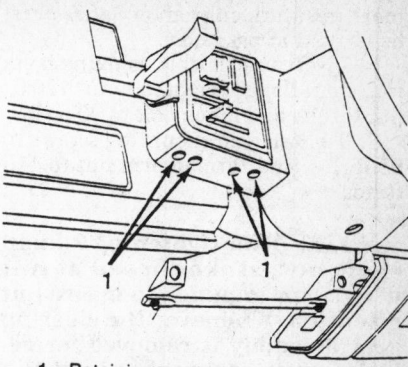

1. Retaining screws

Control pod removal — Medallion and Premier

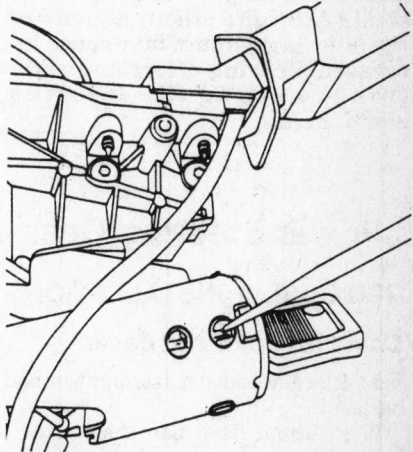

Ignition lock/switch removal — Medallion and Premier

up, guide the pods through the cover and remove the cover.
6. Insert the key into the ignition and turn it to the unmarked arrow on the switch. Push in the locking tab on the bottom of the housing, with a punch and remove the switch. Seperate the switch from the wires by removing the screw retaining the connector.
7. Insert the switch into the housing. Install the pod housing/column cover and install the pods. Install the ignition switch trim ring.
8. Install the tilt lever, on models equipped. Install the turn signal canceler and connect the electrical plug.
9. Install the steering wheel. Connect the negative battery cable.

Manual Steering Gear

REMOVAL & INSTALLATION

Concord, Spirit and Eagle

1. Remove flexible coupling bolts.
2. Remove Pitman arm, using puller J-5566-04 or equivalent.
3. Remove steering gear mounting screws and lower the steering gear.
4. Center steering gear with index

mark up. Mark on shaft of flange must be aligned at assembly.

5. Insert the flexible coupling bolts into shaft flange. Tighten nuts to 20 ft. lbs. torque and pinch bolt to 30 ft. lbs.

6. Tighten gear mounting screws to 65 ft. lbs. and Pitman arm nut to 115 ft. lbs.

NOTE: After tightening Pitman shaft nut, stake thread at nut with a center punch to insure nut retention. Whenever the steering gear assembly is removed for replacement or overhaul, or the mounting bolts are loosened for any reason, the steering column MUST be realigned to the gear assembly. Slight misalignment of the steering column may cause increased steering effort and additional wear to the steering components.

Power Steering Gear

REMOVAL & INSTALLATION

Concord, Spirit and Eagle

1. Place wheels in straight-ahead position.

2. Position drain pan under steering gear.

3. Disconnect hoses at gear. Raise and secure hoses above pump fluid level to prevent excessive oil spillage and cap ends of hoses to keep out dirt.

4. Remove flexible coupling to intermediate shaft attaching nuts.

5. Raise the car and support it safely. On Eagle models, remove the skid plate, if so equipped; the left side crossmember to still support brace; and the stabilizer bar brackets from the frame.

6. Paint alignment marks on pitman arm and pitman shaft for assembly reference.

7. Remove pitman arm using puller tool J-5566-04 or equivalent.

8. Remove steering gear mounting bolts and remove steering gear.

9. Center steering gear. Turn stub shaft (using flexible coupling) from stop to stop and count total number of turns; then turn back from either stop one-half total number of turns to center gear. At this point, flat on stub shaft should be facing upward.

10. Align flexible coupling and intermediate shaft flange.

11. Install gear mounting bolts in gear, install spacer on gear, and mount gear on frame side-sill. Tighten gear mounting bolts to 65 ft. lbs. torque.

12. Install and tighten flexible coupling nuts to 25 ft. lbs. torque.

13. Install pitman arm. Index arm to the shaft using alignment marks made during removal.

14. Install pitman arm nut. Tighten nut to 115 ft. lbs. torque and stake the nut to the pitman shaft.

———— CAUTION ————

The pitman arm nut must be staked to the shaft to retain it properly.

15. On Eagle models, install the stabilizer bar brackets, left side crossmember to sill support brace and skid plate, if so equipped. Lower the vehicle.

16. Align flexible coupling, if necessary.

17. Connect hoses to gear and tighten fittings to 25 ft. lbs. torque.

18. Fill pump reservoir with power steering fluid and bleed air from system.

Medallion and Premier

1. Disconnect the negative battery cable. Raise and safely support the vehicle, remove the left wheel.

2. Unsnap the steering shaft boot flange from the dash panel opening and slide the boot upward.

3. Remove the intermediate steering shaft bolt. Reference mark the intermediate shaft and the steering gear shaft, seperate the shafts.

4. In the engine compartment, remove the splash shield from the steering gear. Disconnect the pressure lines.

5. Fold back the lock tabs on the inner tie rod retaining bolts. Disconnect the tie rods from the steering knuckles. Remove the 3 bolts that hold the steering gear to the body and remove the steering gear through the left fender well.

To install:

6. Position the steering gear and install the mounting nuts. Connect the tie rods to the steering knuckles.

7. Tighten the steering gear mounting bolts to 35 ft. lbs.

8. Connect the power steering lines. Tighten the bolts attaching the tie rods to the steering gear to 55 ft. lbs. and bend the lock tabs over the bolts.

9. Install the splash shield over the steering gear.

10. Inside the vehicle, align the intermediate shaft with the steering shaft and connect the shafts. Install the retaining bolt, tighten it to 25 ft. lbs.

11. Reposition the shaft boot. Connect the negative battery cable.

12. Fill and bleed the power steering system.

ADJUSTMENT

Concord, Spirit and Eagle

———— CAUTION ————

Perform these adjusting procedures exactly as described below, and in the sequence described there. Worm bearing preload must be adjusted before overcenter drag torque, or the steering box will be severely damaged.

Worm bearing preload is controlled by the amount of compression force the adjuster plug exerts on the conical worm bearing races. Pitman shaft overcenter torque is controlled by the adjustment of the pitman shaft adjuster screw. The position of this screw determines the clearance between the rack piston and pitman shaft sector teeth.

1. Remove the steering gear from the vehicle. Mount the steering gear in a vise, using the unmachined housing boss as a mounting pad. The pitman shaft bore should be facing downward.

2. Remove the adjuster plug locknut. Seat the adjuster plug firmly in the housing using a spanner tool, AMC part number J-7624 or equivalent. About 20 ft. lbs. of torque is required.

3. Scribe an index mark onto the gear housing opposite either of the holes in the adjuster plug. Then, measure backward (counterclockwise) $3/16$–$1/4$ in. from the index mark and scribe another mark on the housing. Now, turn the adjuster plug counterclockwise in the housing until the hole in the plug is aligned with the second mark on the housing.

4. Install the adjuster plug locknut. Torque it to 85 ft. lbs., watching to make sure the the adjuster plug does not turn.

5. Turn the stub shaft clockwise until it touches the stop; then, turn it back $1/4$ turn. Use an inch pound torque wrench with a maximum capacity of 50 inch lbs. and a twelve point deep well socket to measure the torque required to turn the stub shaft. Turn the stub shaft at an even rate, watch the scale and take the reading as the beam of the torque wrench passes the the vertical position. Record the torque for use later. The torque reading must be 4–10 inch lbs. Incorrect torque can be caused by an improperly positioned adjuster plug, incorrectly assembled steering gear or defective thrust bearings and races.

6. Turn the pitman shaft adjuster screw counterclockwise until it is fully extended; then turn it back $1/2$ turn. Rotate the stub shaft from stop to stop, counting the number of turns. Then, turn the shaft back $1/2$ the total number of turns to center it. At this point, the flat on the stub shaft should

face upward and be parallel with the side cover and the master spline on the pitman shafts should be in line with the adjuster screw.

7. Install the same torque wrench and socket used to turn the stub shaft, with the handle of the wrench in the vertical position. Slowly rotate the wrench 45 degrees either side of center, watching the gauge. Record the highest reading measured at or near the center of travel. The drag torque should be 4–8 inch lbs. above the worm bearing preload torque not to exceed 18 inch lbs. on new steering gears and 4–5 inch lbs. above worm bearing preload torque not to exceed 14 inch lbs. on used steering gears. If necessary, adjust overcenter drag torque by turning the pitman shaft adjusting screw clockwise.

8. When the correct torque has been obtained, torque the pitman shaft adjusting screw locknut to 35 ft. lbs.

9. Install the steering gear. Fill the reservoir and bleed the system.

Medallion and Premier

The power steering gear used in the Medallion and Premier is not adjustable.

Power Steering Pump

REMOVAL & INSTALLATION

Concord, Spirit and Eagle

1. Remove the fan belt.
2. Place a container under the pump to catch fluid. Remove the fuel vapor storage canister and 6 cylinder air cleaner, if necessary.
3. Disconnect the hoses and cap the outlets, so the power steering unit does not lose fluid. Remove the air pump belt.
4. On the 4.2L engines, equipped with air conditioning, loosen the idler pulley adjusting bolt and idler pulley, air pump adjusting strap mounting bolt and remove the compressor drive belt from the idler pulley. Loosen the 2 nuts that attach the upper leg of the aluminum idler pulley mounting bracket to the cylinder head and remove the bolt that attaches the lower leg of the mounting bracket to the engine front cover.
5. On the 4.2L engine, remove the nut from the air pump mounting stud, remove the power steering pump to engine front cover front adapter plate (do not unbolt the adapter plate from the pump), remove the long adjusting bolt that passes through the adapter plate, and remove the bolt hidden behind the flange in the rear adapter plate. Remove the pump, adapter plate and mounting bracket together.

On 2.5L engines, remove the adjuster locknuts and washers which retain the pump and pivot bracket on the mounting bracket. All of the pump mounting bolts are metric, except for the $^9/_{16}$ in. adjuster locknuts. Move the pump and remove the belt. Remove the bolts which connect the front bracket to the rear bracket and engine block, and remove the pump complete with the pivot and front brackets.

6. Fill the system with Dextron® II power steering fluid or equivalent. Bleed the system.

Medallion and Eagle

1. Raise and safely support the vehicle.
2. Remove the underbody splash shield. Loosen the accessory drive belt.
3. Disconnect and plug the pressure lines.
4. Remove the pump mounting bolts and remove the pump. On the 3.0L engine remove the pump with the mounting brackets attached.
5. Install the pump to the engine and connect the pressure lines. Install the accessory drive belt and adjust the tension.
6. Lower the vehicle. Fill and bleed the cooling system.

BELT ADJUSTMENT

Concord, Spirit and Eagle

The power steering pump belt must be properly tensioned, or it may slip and may cause noise and excess wear. To tension the belt, first loosen the pump hinge bolts just slightly and then loosen the bolt that passes through the slotted pump bracket. The belt is to be tensioned to 120 lbs. This means it must be tightened until it is snug and it requires a significant amount of pressure to depress it ½ in. Do not pry on the pump to move it. Tighten the mounting bolt that runs through the slot and, when tension is correct, tighten the other mounting bolts/nuts.

Medallion and Premier

The Medallion and Premier use a serpentine belt to drive all of the accessories. To adjust the belt tension, loosen the power steering pump bolts and turn the adjusting bolt until the correct tension is achieved. Proper tension for a new belt is 180 lbs. and 140 lbs. for a used belt.

SYSTEM BLEEDING

All Models

1. With the wheels turned all the way to the left, add power steering fluid to the **COLD** mark on the fluid level indicator.

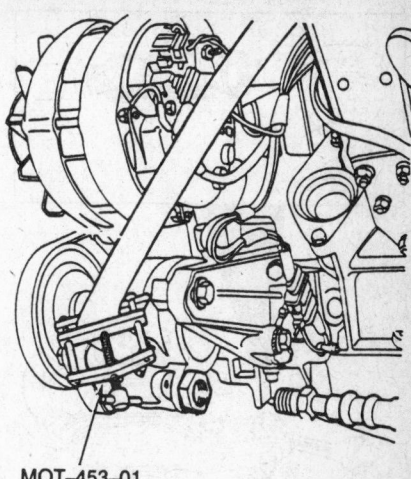

MOT–453–01

2.2L power steering pump mounting

2. Start the engine and run at fast idle momentarily, shut engine **OFF** and recheck fluid level. If necessary add fluid to to bring level to the **COLD** mark.
3. Start the engine and bleed the system by turning the wheels from side to side without hitting the stops.

NOTE: Fluid with air in it has a light tan or red appearance.

4. Return the wheels to the center position and keep the engine running for 2 or 3 minutes.
5. Road test the car and recheck the fluid level making sure it is at the **HOT** mark.

Tie Rod Ends

REMOVAL & INSTALLATION

Concord, Spirit and Eagle

1. Raise and safely support the front of the vehicle.
2. Remove the cotter pin and retaining nut from the tie rod end stud.
3. Mark the position of the tie rod end adjuster tube and inner tie rod, for reference.
4. Loosen the adjuster tube clamps.
5. Disconnect the tie rod end from the steering arm with a puller.
6. Remove the tie rod end from the adjuster tube. Count the number of turns so that the replacement part may be installed in the same position.
7. Install the replacement tie rod end in the adjuster tube, and insert the end stud in the steering arm. Tighten the nut to 35 ft. lbs. and install a new cotter pin. Do not loosen the nuts to align. Adjust the toe-in and tighten the clamps.

Medallion and Premier

1. Raise and safely support the vehicle.

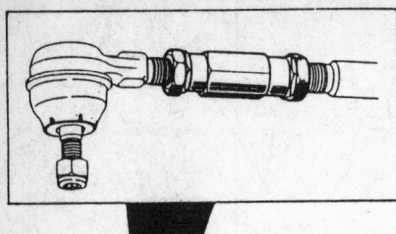

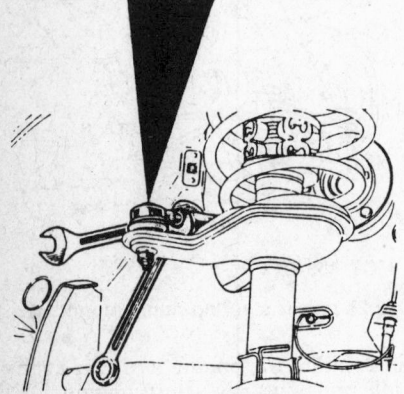

Tie rod removal—Medallion and Premier

2. Remove the wheel.

3. Loosen the adjusting sleeve lock-nuts on the rod end.

4. Remove the retaining nut from the tie rod ball stud.

5. Disconnect the tie rod from the steering knuckle using tool TAV–476 or equivalent. Back off the tie rod lock-nuts as far as possible.

6. Turn the adjusting sleeve completely off the tie rod end. Slide the rod end off the tie rod.

7. Insert the tie rod end into the tie rod, thread the adjusting sleeve on to the tie rod end.

8. Connect the tie rod end to the steering knuckle and tighten the nut to 35 ft. lbs.

9. Install the wheel and lower the vehicle, check the toe-out specifications.

BRAKES

For all brake system repair and service procedures not detailed below, please refer to "Brakes" in the Unit Repair section.

Master Cylinder

REMOVAL & INSTALLATION

1. Disconnect the front and rear brake lines from the master cylinder. Both outlets must be plugged, to prevent fluid loss.

2. Remove the nuts which attached the master cylinder to the firewall or

the power brake booster, if so equipped.

3. On cars without power brakes, disconnect the pedal push-rod at the brake pedal.

4. Remove the master cylinder from the car.

5. Installation is in the reverse order of removal. Bleed the brake system once the master cylinder has been installed.

Combination Valve

REMOVAL & INSTALLATION

Concord, Spirit and Eagle

A combination proportioning and differential valve is mounted on the right side fender panel near the heater blower motor. The valve can be removed and installed by simply disconnecting the electrical connector and removing the pipe fittings. Keep all fittings extremely clean. Torque these fittings on installation, to 160–175 inch lbs. Bleed the system thoroughly.

Medallion and Premier

The combination valve on the Medallion and Premier is located to the left of the master cylinder. It is removed by disconnecting the brake lines from the valve and removing the retaining bolt. Bleed the brake system after the valve has been installed.

Power Brake Booster

REMOVAL & INSTALLATION

Concord, Spirit and Eagle

1. Disconnect the power brake clevis pin from the power unit operating rod at the linkage under the hood, or from the brake pedal inside the car, depending on which type is being serviced.

2. Remove the vacuum hose from the check valve.

3. Separate the master cylinder from the power unit. Do not disconnect the hydraulic lines from the master cylinder.

4. Remove the power unit mounting bolts, and lift the unit from the car.

5. Installation is in the reverse order of removal.

Medallion and Premier

1. Disconnect the negative battery cable.

2. Disconnect the vacuum line from the booster.

3. Remove the clip retaining the throttle cables to the bracket on the booster. Remove the master cylinder.

4. Inside the vehicle, disconnect the

connector from the brake light switch. Remove the push rod from the brake pedal.

5. Remove the booster retaining nuts and remove the booster.

6. Install the booster to the firewall and connect the pushrod to the brake pedal. Connect the brakelight switch.

7. Install the master cylinder and clip the throttle cables in place.

8. Connect the negtive battery cable and bleed the brake system.

Wheel Cylinder

REMOVAL & INSTALLATION

All Models

1. Raise and safely support the vehicle. Remove the rear wheel and brake drum.

2. Remove the brake shoes. Disconnect the brake line fitting at the wheel cylinder.

3. Remove the 2 attaching bolts from behind the backing plate and remove the wheel cylinder.

4. To install, first clean the pipe fitting and the female fitting in the wheel cylinder. Then, put the wheel cylinder into position and connect the pipe fitting loosely. Then, install the wheel cylinder mounting bolts, torquing them to 15 ft. lbs. Torque the brake line fitting to 10–12 ft. lbs.

5. Complete the installation in reverse of removal. Bleed the system thoroughly.

Parking Brake Cable

ADJUSTMENT

All Models

1. To adjust the drum brakes, apply the brakes several times while backing up. Make 1 forward application for each reverse application to equalize the adjustment. Fully apply the parking brake about 10 times. Set the pedal on the first notch from the released position.

2. Block the front wheels and raise the rear wheels.

3. Tighten the cable at the equalizer so the wheels can just barely be turned forward. Be sure to hold the end of the cable screw to prevent the cable from turning.

4. Release the parking brake and check for rear brake drag. The wheels should rotate freely with the parking brake off.

REMOVAL & INSTALLATION

Front Cable

CONCORD, SPIRIT AND EAGLE

1. Disconnect the return spring at

the parking brake pedal lever. Raise and support the vehicle securely and disconnect the cable adjuster nut at the equalizer (where the front cable actuates the 2 rear cables).

2. Remove the retaining clip the retains the cable to the frame. Working inside the car, remove the cable to floorpan mounting clips.

3. Remove the left side cowl trim panel and scuff plate. Then remove the front cable retaining clip at the lever.

4. Roll back the carpet and disengage the front cable at the lever assembly. Pull the grommet out of the floorpan and remove the front cable.

5. Install in reverse order. Adjust the parking brake.

MEDALLION AND PREMIER

1. Raise and safely support the vehicle.

2. Remove the brake cable adjusting nut. Remove the cable retaining clip and push the cable into the vehicle.

3. Lower the vehicle. Inside the vehicle, remove the trim panel under the steering column.

4. Disconnect the cable from the parking brake assembly. Remove the plastic trim along the door sill on the drivers side of the vehicle. Fold back the carpeting in front of the drivers seat and remove the plastic cover from the brake cable.

5. Unbolt and remove the drivers seat.

6. Remove the trim covering the hood release lever. Remove the rear seat cushion and fold back the carpeting to gain access to the cable.

7. Pull the cable from the access holes and remove it from the vehicle.

To install:

8. Raise and support the vehicle. Route the parking brake cable through the access holes from below the vehicle.

9. Attach the cable to all of the retainers and connect the end to the parking brake pedal assembly. Lower the vehicle.

10. Return the carpet to its original position. Install the drivers seat and

the rear seat cushion. Install all of the trim panels removed.

11. Raise and support the vehicle. Install the brake cable retainer clip and install the adjuster nut. Adjust the parking brake and lower the vehicle.

Rear Cable

ALL MODELS

There are 2 parking brake cables, 1 for each side. The procedure below applies to the replacement of either cable unless noted.

1. Raise the car and support it securely. Loosen the cable adjusting nut at the equalizer.

2. Remove the cotter pin for the cable to be replaced from the equalizer. Then, remove the retaining clip attaching the cable to be removed at the frame.

3. Disconnect the cable at the frame bracket. Only if replacing the right cable: remove the bolts attaching the cable to the rear axle housing.

4. Remove the rear wheel and brake drum. Remove the shoes. Compress the locking tabs at the backing plate, with a worm drive type hose clamp and remove the cable.

5. Install in reverse order, using a new cotter pin for the connection to the equalizer. Adjust the brake mechanism.

Heater Blower

REMOVAL & INSTALLATION

Concord, Spirit and Eagle

1. Drain about 2 quarts of coolant from the radiator.

2. Disconnect the heater hoses from the heater core tubes and plug the core tubes.

3. Disconnect blower wires.

4. Remove retaining nut from cover and remove motor and fan assembly.

5. To remove the blower fan from the motor shaft, squeeze and remove the blower retainer clip. Then, slide the blower hub off the motor shaft. This will give access to the nuts attaching the motor to the mounting plate. Remove them and unbolt and re-

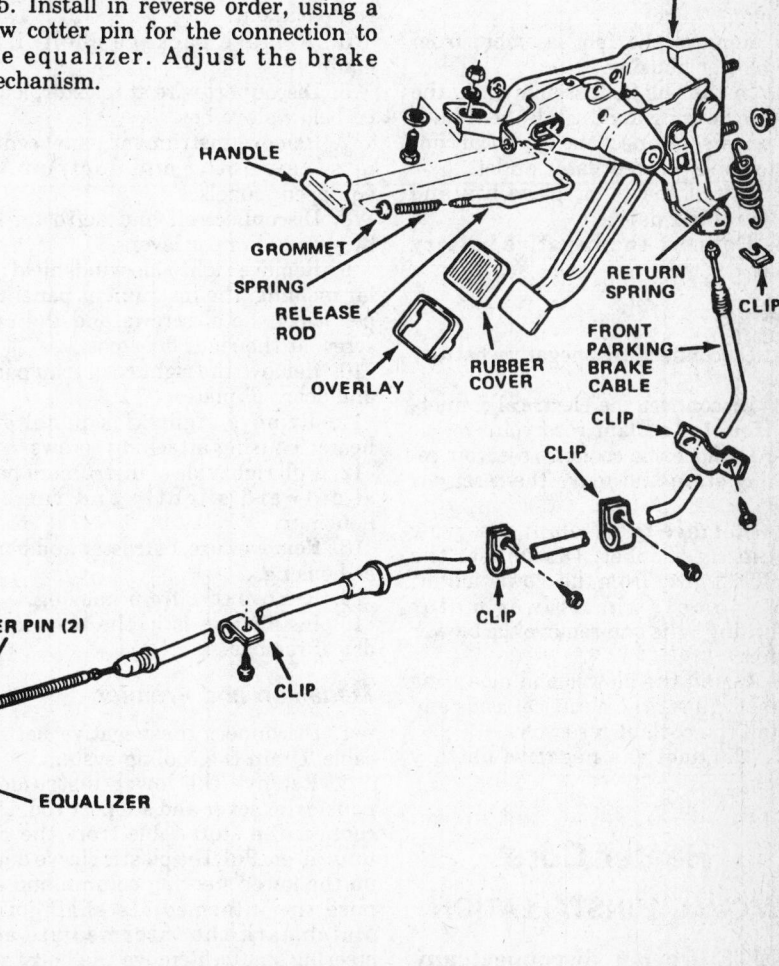

Typical front brake cable – Spirit, Concord, and Eagle

move the motor from the mounting plate.

6. Install the blower motor onto the mounting plate. Install the fan onto the motor shaft. Position the fan so that a 0.350 in. clearance exists between the mounting plate of the motor and the end of the blower fan.

7. Position the ears of the spring clip retainer over the flat surface of the motor shaft. The edge of the clip must be flush with the edge of the fan hub.

8. Install the blower motor into the housing and install the retaining bolts or nuts.

9. Connect the wiring to the motor and check operation of the motor and fan assembly.

Medallion

1. Disconnect the negative battery cable.

2. Remove the glove box door straps and remove the glove box door. Remove the inner glove box.

3. Unclip the ventilator outlet from the right side of the blower housing. Disconnect the electrical connector from the blower motor.

4. Remove the blower housing retaining screws and remove the housing.

5. Remove the fan assembly from the blower housing.

6. Install the fan assembly into the blower housing and install the retaining screws. Connect the electrical connector and the ventilator outlet.

7. Install the inner glove box and the glove box door.

8. Connect the negative battery cable.

Premier

1. Disconnect the negative battery cable.

2. Disconnect the electrical connector from the coolant reservoir.

3. Remove the coolant reservoir retaining strap and move the reservoir aside.

4. Remove the coolant reservoir mounting bracket. Disconnect the electrical wires from the blower motor.

5. Remove the blower motor mounting bolts and remove the blower motor.

6. Install the blower and mounting bolts. Connect the electrical leads and install the coolant reservoir.

7. Connect the negative battery cable.

Heater Core

REMOVAL & INSTALLATION

NOTE: Do not disconnect any of the air conditioning refriger-

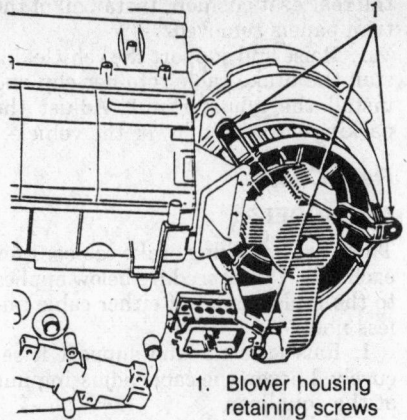

1. Blower housing retaining screws

Blower motor mounting—Medallion

ant lines when removing the heater core.

Concord, Spirit, and Eagle

1. Disconnect the negative battery cable and drain 1 qt. of coolant.

2. Disconnect and plug the heater hoses and cover the fittings.

3. Disconnect blower wires and remove motor and fan assembly.

4. Remove the housing attaching nut from the stud in the engine compartment.

5. Remove package shelf, if so equipped.

6. Disconnect wire at resistor, located below glove box.

7. Remove instrument panel center bezel, air outlet and duct, on A/C equipped models.

8. Disconnect air and defroster cables from damper levers.

9. Remove right-side windshield pillar molding, the instrument panel upper sheet metal screws and the capscrew at the right door post.

10. Remove the right cowl trim panel and door sill plate.

11. Remove right kick panel and heater housing attaching screws.

12. Pull right side of instrument panel outward slightly and remove housing.

13. Remove core, defroster and blower housing.

14. Remove core from housing.

15. Installation is in the reverse order of removal.

Medallion and Premier

1. Disconnect the negative battery cable. Drain the cooling system.

2. Remove the lower instrument panel trim cover and support rod. Disconnect the shift cable from the column lever. Pull the plastic sleeve down on the lower steering column and expose the intermediate shaft joint. Matchmark the intermediate and steering shafts. Remove the bolt from the intermediate shaft.

3. Remove the bolts that hold the steering column to the instrument panel and lower the column. Disconnect the column electrical connector. Remove the column from the vehicle.

4. Remove the windshield defroster grill. Remove the parking brake assembly mounting screws and lower the assembly. Remove the ashtray and cigarette lighter.

5. Disconnect all of the electrical connectors behind the instrument panel. Remove the bolts that hold the instrument panel to the center floor bracket.

6. Lift up and rearward on the instrument panel and remove it from the vehicle.

7. Disconnect the coolant, refrigerant lines and all electrical connectors to the heater housing. Disconnect all of the air ducts from the case.

CAUTION

The A/C system MUST be discharged before disconnecting the refrigerant lines. The refrigerant will freeze anything it contacts including skin and eyes.

---

8. Remove the nuts retaining the heater case to the firewall and remove the case from the vehicle.

9. Remove the plastic tabs retaining the heater core and remove the heater core from the case.

To install:

10. Install the heater core in the heater housing and install the heater housing in the vehicle.

11. Connect the coolant and refrigerant lines. Connect all the electrical wires to the case. Connect the air ducts.

12. Position the instrument panel in the vehicle and install the mounting bolts. Connect the electrical connectors to the instrument panel. Install the ashtray.

13. Install the parking brake assembly. Install the defroster grill. Align the matchmarks made on the intermediate and steering shafts and install the steering column, tighten the column mounting bolts to 35 ft. lbs. Tighten the intermediate shaft bolt.

14. Attach the shift cable and the steering column electrical connector. Install the instrument panel lower support bar and the lower panel trim cover.

15. Connect the negative battery cable and fill the cooling system. Recharge the A/C system.

Radio

REMOVAL & INSTALLATION
Concord, Spirit and Eagle

1. Disconnect the battery ground cable.

2. Pull off the radio knobs and remove shaft retaining nuts.

3. Remove the bezel retaining screws and remove the bezel. On models with A/C, remove the center housing of the instrument panel.

4. Disconnect the speaker, antenna, and power leads, and remove the radio.

5. Installation is the reverse of the removal procedure.

Medallion

1. Disconnect the negative battery cable.

2. Remove the 4 screws retaining the radio housing to the lower instrument panel and remove the radio housing.

3. Remove the screws retaining the radio to the radio mounting bracket and pull it from the instrument panel. Disconnect the speaker, antenna and power leads.

4. Connect the speaker, antenna and power leads to the radio and install it into the radio mounting bracket.

5. Install the radio housing. Connect the negative battery cable.

Premier

1. Disconnect the negative battery cable.

2. Remove the screws retaining the instrument cluster bezel and remove the bezel.

3. Remove the radio mounting screws and slide the radio from the instrument panel. Disconnect the plugs from the rear of the radio.

4. Install the plugs at the rear of the radio and slide the radio into position.

5. Install the radio retaining screws. Install the instrument cluster bezel.

6. Connect the negative battery cable.

Windshield Wiper Switch

REMOVAL & INSTALLATION

Concord, Spirit and Eagle

1. Disconnect the negative battery cable. Locate the small notch at the base of the switch knob. Insert a small screwdriver into the notch and hold it there to apply pressure to the release spring. Pull the knob off the shaft.

2. Remove the slotted trim nut from the front of the switch. Push the switch through the instrument panel. Disconnect the wiring and remove it.

3. Install in reverse order, aligning the control knob carefully before pushing it onto the shaft.

Medallion

1. Disconnect the negative battery cable.

2. Remove the screws from the lower steering column cover and remove the cover.

3. On vehicles equipped with cruise control, pull down on the piece of wire at the forward edge of the cover. This will pull the spring loaded cruise control commutator into its housing.

4. Remove the upper and lower steering column covers.

5. Remove the 2 screws attaching the wiper switch and remove the switch.

6. Disconnect the wire connectors.

7. Install the switch to the column and install the retaining screws. Install the steering column covers.

8. Install the lower steering column cover. Connect the negative battery cable.

Premier

The windshield wiper switch in the premier is locate in a pod on the left side of the steering column. The switch is removed with the pod assembly.

1. Disconnect the negative battery cable.

2. Remove the instrument panel lower cover. Remove the lower instrument panel support bar.

3. Pull the air duct out of the way. Seperate the steering column electrical connector.

4. Remove the screws that retain the pod to the column and pull the pod part way out. Remove the 2 screws retaining the electrical connector to the pod casing.

5. Pull the harness out and through the pod.

6. Install the pod wiring connector and install the pod to the column. Connect the steering column connector and install the lower support. Connect the air duct.

7. Connect the negative battery cable.

Windshield Wiper Motor

REMOVAL & INSTALLATION

Concord, Spirit and Eagle

1. Remove the wiper arms and blades.

2. Remove the screws holding the motor adapter plate on the dash panel.

3. Separate the wiper wiring harness connector at the motor.

4. Pull the motor and linkage out of the opening to expose the drive link to crank stud retaining clip. Raise up the lock tab of the clip with a screwdriver

and slide the clip off the stud. Remove the wiper motor assembly.

5. Install the windshield wiper motor in the reverse order of removal.

Medallion

1. Disconnect the negative battery cable.

2. Remove the wiper arms. Remove the screws retaining the cowl in front of the windhield and remove the cowl.

3. Disconnect the electrical plug at the wiper motor. Remove the screws retaining the wiper motor and transmission and remove the assembly.

4. Install the wiper and transmission assembly. Connect the electrical plug to the wiper motor.

5. Install the cowl and the wiper arms.

6. Connect the negative battery cable.

Premier

1. Disconnect the negative battery cable.

2. Remove the wiper arms. Remove the screws retaining the left and right cowl screenc and remove both screens.

3. Remove the wiper motor center shaft locknut. Remove the motor mounting screws.

4. Disconnect the electrical connector and remove the motor.

5. Install the motor and connect the electrical lead. Attach the linkage and install the center shaft locknut, tighten it to 9 ft. lbs.

6. Install the cowl screens and the wiper arms. Connect the negative battery cable.

Instrument Cluster

REMOVAL & INSTALLATION

Concord, Spirit and Eagle

1. Disconnect the battery cable.

2. On certain models, the lower steering column cover must be removed, while on other models, the gear selector cable must be disconnected from the steering column shift shroud. Protect the steering column from scratching with a rag or piece of cardboard.Remove the package tray, if equipped.

3. Remove the bezel retaining screws across top, over radio and behind the glove box door. Disconnect wire to box light. Tip bezel outward at top and disengage bottom tabs.

4. Disconnect the speedometer cable and push down on the 3 illumination lamp housings above the bezel to clear the instrument panel.

5. Disconnect the headlamp switch, the wiper control connectors and the switch lamp. The headlamp switch is

disconnected by lifting the 2 locking tabs to disconnect its electrical connector.

6. Remove the cluster illumination sockets and the instrument cluster wire connectors.

7. If equipped with clock or tachometer, remove their attaching screws. Disconnect the wiring harness from the printed circuit board.

8. Remove the cluster housing and circuit board to bezel attaching screws and remove the assembly from the bezel.

9. The installation is the reverse of the removal procedure. Make sure that the clock ground and feed wire terminals contact the foil beneath the circuit board mounting screws.

Medallion

1. Disconnect the negative battery cable.

2. Remove the instrument glare shield retaining screws. Press the holding tabs in and remove the glare shield.

3. Open the fuse panel access door, reach through the fuse panel door and remove the speedometer cable from the rear of the instrument cluster.

4. Remove the instrument cluster mounting screws and pull the cluster forward. Disconnect the electrical wiring and remove the cluster from the vehicle.

5. Install the cluster and connect the electrical wiring. Install the glare shield. Connect the speedometer cable and connect the negative battery cable.

Premier

1. Disconnect the negative battery cable.

2. Remove the screws retaining the instrument cluster bezel and remove the bezel.

3. Remove the cluster retaining screws and tilt the cluster forward. Disconnect the electrical connectors.

4. Remove the lower instrument panel cover and remove the cluster.

5. Install the cluster and lower trim cover. Connect the electrical leads to the cluster.

6. Install the instrument panel bezel. Connect the negative battery cable.

Headlight Switch

REMOVAL & INSTALLATION

Concord, Spirit and Eagle

Light switches are similar in all mod-

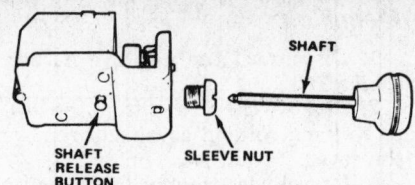

SHAFT
SHAFT RELEASE BUTTON
SLEEVE NUT

Concord, Spirit and Eagle—headlight switch

els. Some variation occurs in the shape and position of the nut mounting the switch on the dash.

1. Disconnect battery and remove the switch overlay cover attaching screws so the cover can be pulled forward.

2. With the switch in the ON position, press the release button on the switch and remove the knob and shaft.

3. Remove screws that attach switch or bracket to panel.

4. Reverse the above procedure for installation, positioning switch so that the shaft is lined up properly before tightening the bracket screws.

Medallion

The headlight switch in the Medallion is removed with the turn signal and wiper switch assembly.

Premier

The headlight switch in the Premier is located in a pod assembly on the steering column. The switch is removed with the turn signal and windshield wiper switches.

Stoplight Switch

REMOVAL & INSTALLATION

Concord, Spirit and Eagle

NOTE: Before performing this operation, get a new stamped nut and locknut for the brake pedal bolt, as they must be replaced each time the operation is performed.

1. Disconnect the negative battery cable. Remove the package tray, if the car has one.

2. Disconnect the brake lamp switch wiring. (The switch is located behind the pedal shaft).

3. Remove both the stamped nut and locknut from the brake pedal bolt and discard them.

4. Remove the stoplight switch mounting bolt and spacers from the pedal shaft.

5. Push the brakelamp switch bushing out of the master cylinder pushrod bushing and remove the switch.

6. Remove the bushing from the eye of the master cylinder pushrod, noting its direction of installation.

7. Inspect all parts and replace worn or cracked bushings or the bolt if the threads are damaged.

8. To install, first install the bushing in the eye of the master cylinder pushrod. Install the stoplight switch on the pushrod and insert the switch bushing through the switch and pushrod bushing.

9. Install the spacers on the ends of the switch bushing. Position the assembled switch and pushrod onto the brake pedal and install the mounting bolt. If the car has power brakes, there will be 2 holes. Install the bolt into the lower hole.

10. Install a replacement brake pedal bolt locknut and a replacement stamped nut. Torque the locknut to 25 ft. lbs. and the stamped nut to 75 inch lbs. (just over 6 ft. lbs.).

11. Connect the wiring and check the operation of the switch.

Medallion and Eagle

1. Disconnect the negative battery cable.

2. Remove the bolt retaining the master cylinder pushrod to the brake pedal.

3. Disconnect the electrical wires from the stoplight switch and remove the switch.

4. Install the switch and the master cylinder pushrod to the brake pedal and install the retaining bolt.

5. Connect the electrical wires to the switch. Connect the negative battery cable and check the operation of the brake lights.

Fuses and Circuit Breakers

LOCATION

Concord, Spirit and Eagle

The fuse box is located, on all models, on the kick panel at the left side of the car. It is right behind the parking brake mechanism.

Medallion

The fuse panel in the Medallion is located below the steering column on the left side of the instrument panel.

Premier

The fuse panel in the premier is located below the instrument panel on the left side, above the parking brake release handle.

Chrysler Corp.
Front Wheel Drive
Chrysler — E-Class, Laser, LeBaron, New Yorker, Town & Country
Dodge — Aries, Charger, Daytona, Dynasty, Lancer, Omni, Shadow, 400, 600
Plymouth — Caravelle, Horizon, Reliant, Sundance, Turismo

SERIAL NUMBER IDENTIFICATION

VEHICLE IDENTIFICATION CHART

It is important for servicing and ordering parts to be certain of the vehicle and engine identification. The VIN (vehicle identification number) is a 17 digit number visible through the windshield on the driver's side of the dash and contains the vehicle and engine identification codes. The tenth digit indicates model year and the eighth digit indicates engine code. It can be interpreted as follows:

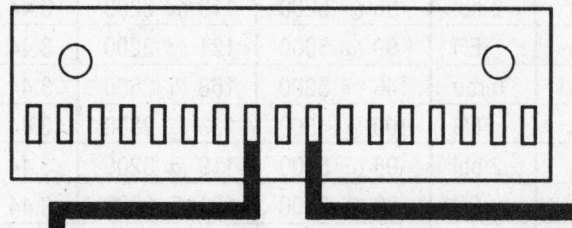

Engine Code						Model Year	
Code	Cu. In.	Liters	Cyl.	Fuel Sys.	Eng. Mfg.	Code	Year
A ('84–'86)	98	1.6	4	Carb.	Peugeot	C	1982
A ('82–'86)	105	1.7	4	Carb.	VW	D	1983
B ('83)	105	1.7	4	Carb.	VW	E	1984
B ('82–'82)	135	2.2	4	Carb.	Chrysler	F	1985
C ('83–'89)	135	2.2	4	Carb.	Chrysler	G	1986
D ('83–'89)	135	2.2	4	EFI	Chrysler	H	1987
E ('84–'89)	135	2.2	4	Turbo	Chrysler	J	1988
K ('86–'89)	153	2.5	4	EFI	Chrysler	K	1989
D ('82)	156	2.6	4	Carb.	Mitsubishi		
G ('83–'85)	156	2.6	4	Carb.	Mitsubishi		
3 ('87–89)	181	3.0	6	EFI	Mitsubishi		

GENERAL ENGINE SPECIFICATIONS

Year	VIN	No. Cylinder Displacement cu. in. (liter)	Fuel System Type	Net Horsepower @ rpm	Net Torque @ rpm (ft.lbs.)	Bore × Stroke (in.)	Compression Ratio	Oil Pressure @ rpm
1982	A	4-105 (1.7)	2 bbl	63 @ 4800	83 @ 3200	3.13 × 3.40	8.2:1	75 @ 2000
	B	4-135 (2.2)	2 bbl	84 @ 4800	111 @ 2800	3.44 × 3.62	8.5:1	50 @ 2000
	D	4-156 (2.6)	2 bbl	92 @ 4500	131 @ 2500	3.59 × 3.86	8.2:1	58 @ 2500
1983	A	4-98 (1.6)	2 bbl	64 @ 4800	87 @ 2800	3.17 × 3.07	8.8:1	65 @ 3000
	B	4-105 (1.7)	2 bbl	63 @ 4800	83 @ 2400	3.13 × 3.40	8.2:1	75 @ 2000
	C	4-135 (2.2)	2 bbl	94 @ 5200	117 @ 3200	3.44 × 3.62	9.0:1	50 @ 2000
	D	4-135 (2.2)	EFI	99 @ 5600	121 @ 3200	3.44 × 3.62	9.5:1	50 @ 2000
	G	4-156 (2.6)	2 bbl	93 @ 5600	132 @ 2800	3.59 × 3.86	8.2:1	58 @ 2500
1984	A	4-98 (1.6)	2 bbl	64 @ 4800	87 @ 2800	3.17 × 3.07	8.8:1	65 @ 3000
	C	4-135 (2.2)	2 bbl	96 @ 5200	119 @ 3200	3.44 × 3.62	9.5:1	50 @ 2000
	D	4-135 (2.2)	EFI	99 @ 5600	121 @ 3200	3.44 × 3.62	9.5:1①	50 @ 2000
	E	4-135 (2.2)	Turbo	146 @ 5200	168 @ 3600	3.44 × 3.62	8.5:1	50 @ 2000
	G	4-156 (2.6)	2 bbl	101 @ 5600	140 @ 2800	3.59 × 3.86	8.7:1	85 @ 2500
1985	A	4-98 (1.6)	2 bbl	64 @ 4800	87 @ 2800	3.17 × 3.07	8.8:1	65 @ 3000
	C	4-135 (2.2)	2 bbl	96 @ 5200	119 @ 3200	3.44 × 3.62	9.5:1	50 @ 2000
	D	4-135 (2.2)	EFI	99 @ 5600	121 @ 3200	3.44 × 3.62	9.5:1①	50 @ 2000
	E	4-135 (2.2)	Turbo	146 @ 5200	168 @ 3600	3.44 × 3.62	8.5:1	50 @ 2000
	G	4-156 (2.6)	2 bbl	101 @ 5600	140 @ 2800	3.59 × 3.86	8.7:1	85 @ 2500
1986	A	4-98 (1.6)	2 bbl	64 @ 4800	87 @ 2800	3.17 × 3.07	8.8:1	65 @ 3000
	C	4-135 (2.2)	2 bbl	96 @ 5200	119 @ 3200	3.44 × 3.62	9.5:1	50 @ 2000
	D	4-135 (2.2)	EFI	99 @ 5600	121 @ 3200	3.44 × 3.62	9.5:1①	50 @ 2000
	E	4-135 (2.2)	Turbo	146 @ 5200	168 @ 3600	3.44 × 3.62	8.5:1	50 @ 2000
	K	4-153 (2.5)	EFI	100 @ 4800	133 @ 2800	3.44 × 4.09	9.0:1	80 @ 3000
1987	C	4-135 (2.2)	2 bbl	96 @ 5200	119 @ 3200	3.44 × 3.62	9.5:1	50 @ 2000
	D	4-135 (2.2)	EFI	99 @ 5600	121 @ 3200	3.44 × 3.62	9.5:1①	50 @ 2000
	E	4-135 (2.2)	Turbo	146 @ 5200	170 @ 3600	3.44 × 3.62	8.0:1	50 @ 2000
	K	4-153 (2.5)	EFI	100 @ 4800	133 @ 2800	3.44 × 4.09	9.0:1	80 @ 3000
1988-89	C	4-135 (2.2)	2 bbl	96 @ 5200	119 @ 3200	3.44 × 3.62	9.5:1	50 @ 2000
	D	4-135 (2.2)	EFI	99 @ 5600	121 @ 3200	3.44 × 3.62	9.5:1①	50 @ 2000
	E	4-135 (2.2)	Turbo	146 @ 5200	170 @ 3600	3.44 × 3.62	8.0:1	50 @ 2000
	K	4-153 (2.5)	EFI	100 @ 4800	133 @ 2800	3.44 × 4.09	9.0:1	80 @ 3000
	3	6-181 (3.0)	EFI	136 @ 4800	168 @ 2800	3.59 × 2.99	8.85:1	80 @ 3000

① 10:1 – Shelby and Hi-Performance Models

GASOLINE ENGINE TUNE-UP SPECIFICATIONS

Year	VIN	No. Cylinder Displacement cu. in. (liter)	Spark Plugs Type	Gap (in.)	Ignition Timing (deg.) MT	AT	Compression Pressure (psi)	Fuel Pump (psi)	Idle Speed (rpm) MT	AT	Valve Clearance In.	Ex.
1982	A	4-105 (1.7)	P65-PR4	.048 ②	20B	10B	100⑥	4.5–6.0	900	900	.010H	.018H
	B	4-135 (2.2)	P65-PR4	.035	10B	10B	130–150	4.5–6.0	900	900	Hyd.	Hyd.
	D	4-156 (2.6)	P65-PR4	.040 ③	7B	7B	149 ⑦	4.5–6.0	800①	800①	.006H	.010H
1983	A	4-98 (1.6)	RN-12Y	.035	⑤	⑤	100⑥	4.5–6.0	850	850	.012C	.014C
	B	4-105 (1.7)	65PR	.035	20B	12B	100⑥	4.4–5.8	900	900	.010H	.018H
	C	4-135 (2.2)	RN12YC	.035	⑤	⑤	130–150	4.5–6.0	800④	900	Hyd.	Hyd.
	D	4-135 (2.2)	RN-12Y	.035	⑤	⑤	130–150	15	900	800	Hyd.	Hyd.
	G	4-156 (2.6)	RN-12Y	.040 ③	⑤	⑤	149 ⑦	4.5–6.0	800①	800①	.006H	.010H
1984	A	4-98 (1.6)	RN-12Y	.035	⑤	⑤	100⑥	4.5–6.0	850	850	.012C	.014C
	C	4-135 (2.2)	RN12YC	.035	⑤	⑤	130–150	4.5–6.0	800④	900	Hyd.	Hyd.
	D	4-135 (2.2)	RN-12Y	.035	⑤	⑤	130–150	15	900	800	Hyd.	Hyd.
	E	4-135 (2.2)	RN12YC	.035	⑤	⑤	130–150	55	900	800	Hyd.	Hyd.
	G	4-156 (2.6)	RN-12Y	.040 ③	⑤	⑤	149 ⑦	4.5–6.0	800①	800①	.006H	.010H
1985	A	4-98 (1.6)	RN-12Y	.035	⑤	⑤	100⑥	4.5–6.0	850	850	.012C	.014C
	C	4-135 (2.2)	RN12YC	.035	⑤	⑤	130–150	4.5–6.0	800④	900	Hyd.	Hyd.
	D	4-135 (2.2)	RN-12Y	.035	⑤	⑤	130–150	15	900	800	Hyd.	Hyd.
	E	4-135 (2.2)	RN12YC	.035	⑤	⑤	130–150	55	900	800	Hyd.	Hyd.
	G	4-156 (2.6)	RN-12Y	.040 ③	⑤	⑤	149 ⑦	4.5–6.0	800①	800①	.006H	.010H
1986	A	4-98 (1.6)	RN-12Y	.035	⑤	⑤	100⑥	4.5–6.0	850	850	.012C	.014C
	C	4-135 (2.2)	RN12YC	.035	⑤	⑤	100⑥	4.5–6.0	800④	900	Hyd.	Hyd.
	D	4-135 (2.2)	RN-12Y	.035	⑤	⑤	100⑥	15	900	800	Hyd.	Hyd.
	E	4-135 (2.2)	RN12YC	.035	⑤	⑤	100⑥	55	900	800	Hyd.	Hyd.
	K	4-153 (2.5)	RN12YC	.035	⑤	⑤	100⑥	15	800	700	Hyd.	Hyd.
1987	C	4-135 (2.2)	RN12YC	.035	10B	10B	100⑥	4.5–6.0	800④	900	Hyd.	Hyd.
	D	4-135 (2.2)	RN12YC	.035	12B	12B	100⑥	15	900	700	Hyd.	Hyd.
	E	4-135 (2.2)	RN12YC	.035	12B	12B	100⑥	55	900	800	Hyd.	Hyd.
	K	4-153 (2.5)	RN12YC	.035	12B	12B	100⑥	15	900	900	Hyd.	Hyd.
1988	C	4-135 (2.2)	RN12YC	.035	10B	10B	100⑥	4.5–6.0	800④	900	Hyd.	Hyd.
	D	4-135 (2.2)	RN12YC	.035	12B	12B	100⑥	15	900	700	Hyd.	Hyd.
	E	4-135 (2.2)	RN12YC	.035	12B	12B	100⑥	55	900	800	Hyd.	Hyd.
	K	4-153 (2.5)	RN12YC	.035	12B	12B	100⑥	15	900	900	Hyd.	Hyd.
	3	6-181 (3.0)	RN11YC4	.039	—	12B	178⑦	48	—	⑧	Hyd.	Hyd.
1989					SEE UNDERHOOD SPECIFICATIONS STICKER							

NOTE: The underhood specifications sticker often reflects tune-up specification changes made in production. Sticker figures must be used if they disagree with those in this chart. Part numbers in this chart are not recommendations by Chilton for any product by brand name

Hyd. Hydraulic
H Hot
C Cold
① 750 rpm — Canada
② .035 — Canada
③ .030 — Canada

④ 900 rpm — Canada
⑤ Refer to emission control label on vehicle
⑥ Minimum
⑦ @ 250 rpm

⑧ 700 rpm in Drive
800 rpm in Neutral

FIRING ORDERS

NOTE: To avoid confusion, always replace spark plug wires one at a time.

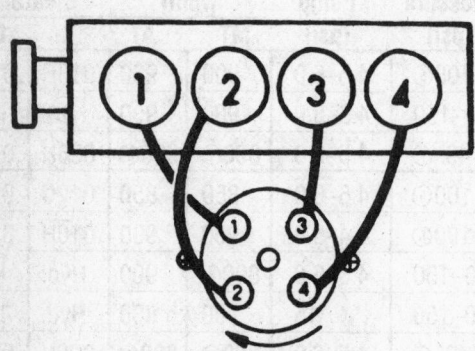

**Chrysler Corp. 2.2L and 2.5L
Engine Firing Order: 1–3–4–2
Distributor Rotation: Clockwise**

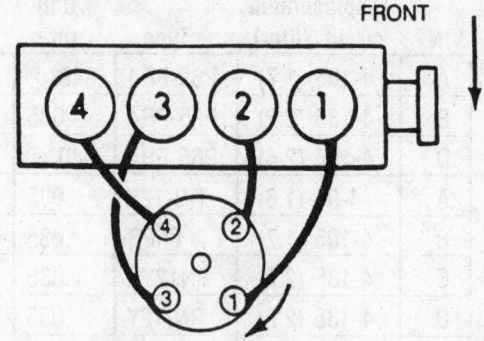

FRONT

**Chrysler Corp. 1.6L engine
Firing order: 1–3–4–2
Distributor rotation: Clockwise**

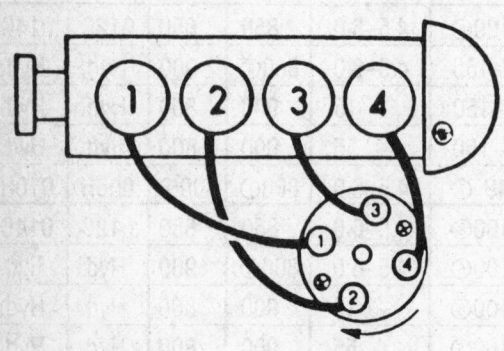

**Chrysler Corp. 1.7L engine
Firing order: 1–3–4–2
Distributor rotation: Clockwise**

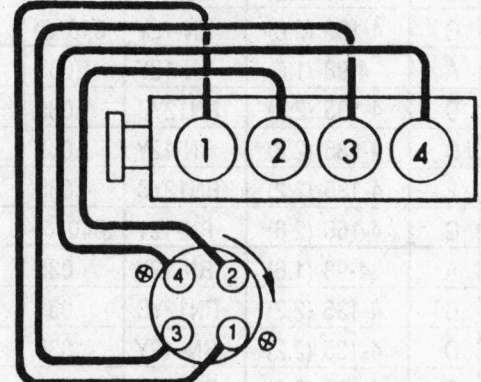

**Chrysler Corp. (Mitsubishi) 2.6L engine
Firing order: 1–3–4–2
Distributor rotation: Clockwise**

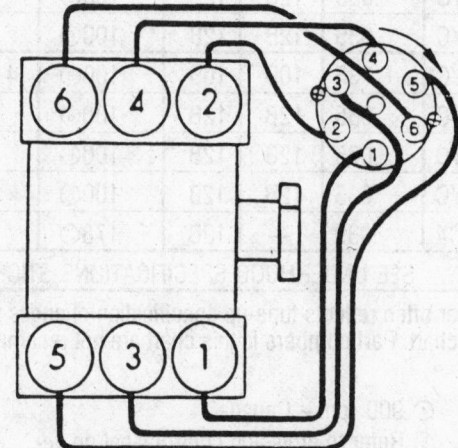

**Chrysler Corp. 3.0L V6 engine
Firing order: 1–2–3–4–5–6
Distributor rotation: Clockwise**

CAPACITIES

Year	VIN	No. Cylinder Displacement cu. in. (liter)	Engine Crankcase with Filter	Engine Crankcase without Filter	Transmission (pts.) MT	Transmission (pts.) AT	Drive Axle (pts.)	Fuel Tank (gals.)	Cooling System (qts.)
1982	A	4-105 (1.7)	4	4	2.6	14.5①	—	13	6.0
	B	4-135 (2.2)	4	4	2.6	15.0①	—	13	7.5
	D	4-156 (2.6)	5	4.5	3.75	15.0①	—	13	8.5
1983	A	4-98 (1.6)	3.5	3	②③	16①	—	13	6.8
	B	4-105 (1.7)	4	4	②③	16.75①	—	13	6.0
	C	4-135 (2.2)	4	4	②③	17.75①	—	13	9.0
	D	4-135 (2.2)	4	4	②③	17.75①	—	13	9.0
	G	4-156 (2.6)	5	4.5	—	17.75①	—	13	9.0
1984	A	4-98 (1.6)	3.5	3	②③	16①	—	14④	6.8
	C	4-135 (2.2)	4	4	②③	17.75①	—	14④	9.0
	D	4-135 (2.2)	4	4	②③	17.75①	—	14④	9.0
	E	4-135 (2.2)	5	5	②③	17.75①	—	14④	9.0
	G	4-156 (2.6)	5	4.5	②③	17.75①	—	14④	9.0
1985	A	4-98 (1.6)	3.5	3	②③	16①	—	14④	6.8
	C	4-135 (2.2)	4	4	②③	17.75①	—	14④	9.0
	D	4-135 (2.2)	4	4	②③	17.75①	—	14④	9.0
	E	4-135 (2.2)	5	5	②③	17.75①	—	14④	9.0
	G	4-156 (2.6)	5	4.5	②③	17.75①	—	14④	9.0
1986	A	4-98 (1.6)	3.5	3	②③	16①	—	14④	6.8
	C	4-135 (2.2)	4	4	②③	17.75①	—	14④	9.0
	D	4-135 (2.2)	4	4	②③	17.75①	—	14④	9.0
	E	4-135 (2.2)	5	5	②③	17.75①	—	14④	9.0
	K	4-153 (2.5)	4	4	②③	17.75①	—	14④	9.0
1987	C	4-135 (2.2)	4	4	②③	17.75①	—	14④	9.0
	D	4-135 (2.2)	4	4	②③	17.75①	—	14④	9.0
	E	4-135 (2.2)	5	5	②③	17.75①	—	14④	9.0
	K	4-153 (2.5)	4	4	②③	17.75①	—	14④	9.0
1988-89	C	4-135 (2.2)	4	4	②③	17.75①	—	14④	9.0
	D	4-135 (2.2)	4	4	②③	17.75①	—	14④	9.0
	E	4-135 (2.2)	5	5	②③	17.75①	—	14④	9.0
	K	4-153 (2.5)	4	4	②③	17.75①	—	14④	9.0
	3	6-181 (3.0)	4	4	—	17.75①	—	16	9.5

NOTE: If the starter motor is located on the radiator side of the engine, the car is equipped with an A–412 manual transaxle; use GL–4 Hypoid lubricant. Use only Dexron®II in the A–460, A465 and A–525 transaxles

① Includes torque converter. Approx. 6 pts. without draining converter

② 4-speed: 3.75 — use Dexron®II lubricant

③ 5-speed
    A465: 4.5 — use Dexron®II lubricant
    A520: 4.9 — use SAE 5W-30
    A525: 4.5 — use Dexron®II lubricant
    A555: 4.9 — use SAE 5W-30

④ 13 gal. — Charger, Horizon, Omni, Turismo

CAMSHAFT SPECIFICATIONS
All measurements given in inches.

Year	VIN	No. Cylinder Displacement cu. in. (liter)	Journal Diameter 1	2	3	4	5	Lobe Lift In.	Ex.	Bearing Clearance	Camshaft End Play
1982	A	4-105 (1.7)	1.021–1.023	1.021–1.023	1.021–1.023	1.021–1.023	1.021–1.023	0.406	0.406	0.0016–0.0030	0.006
	B	4-135 (2.2)	1.375–1.376	1.375–1.376	1.375–1.376	1.372–1.376	1.375–1.376	0.430	0.430	0.010 Max	0.006
1983	B	4-105 (1.7)	1.021–1.023	1.021–1.023	1.021–1.023	1.021–1.023	1.021–1.023	0.406	0.406	0.0016–0.0030	0.006
	C	4-135 (2.2)	1.375–1.376	1.375–1.376	1.375–1.376	1.375–1.376	1.375–1.376	0.430	0.430	0.010 Max	0.006
	D	4-135 (2.2)	1.375–1.376	1.375–1.376	1.375–1.376	1.375–1.376	1.375–1.376	0.430	0.430	0.010 Max	0.006
1984	C	4-135 (2.2)	1.375–1.376	1.375–1.376	1.375–1.376	1.375–1.376	1.375–1.376	0.430	0.430	0.010 Max	0.006
	D	4-135 (2.2)	1.375–1.376	1.375–1.376	1.375–1.376	1.375–1.376	1.375–1.376	0.430	0.430	0.010 Max	0.006
	E	4-135 (2.2)	1.375–1.376	1.375–1.376	1.375–1.376	1.375–1.376	1.375–1.376	0.430	0.430	0.010 Max	0.006
1985	C	4-135 (2.2)	1.375–1.376	1.375–1.376	1.375–1.376	1.375–1.376	1.375–1.376	0.430	0.430	0.010 Max	0.006
	D	4-135 (2.2)	1.375–1.376	1.375–1.376	1.375–1.376	1.375–1.376	1.375–1.376	0.430	0.430	0.010 Max	0.006
	E	4-135 (2.2)	1.375–1.376	1.375–1.376	1.375–1.376	1.375–1.376	1.375–1.376	0.430	0.430	0.010 Max	0.006
1986	C	4-135 (2.2)	1.375–1.376	1.375–1.376	1.375–1.376	1.375–1.376	1.375–1.376	0.430	0.430	0.010 Max	0.006
	D	4-135 (2.2)	1.375–1.376	1.375–1.376	1.375–1.376	1.375–1.376	1.375–1.376	0.430	0.430	0.010 Max	0.006
	E	4-135 (2.2)	1.375–1.376	1.375–1.376	1.375–1.376	1.375–1.376	1.375–1.376	0.430	0.430	0.010 Max	0.006
	K	4-153 (2.5)	1.375–1.376	1.375–1.376	1.375–1.376	1.375–1.376	1.375–1.376	0.430	0.430	0.010 Max	0.006
1987	C	4-135 (2.2)	1.375–1.376	1.375–1.376	1.375–1.376	1.375–1.376	1.375–1.376	0.430	0.430	0.010 Max	0.006
	D	4-135 (2.2)	1.375–1.376	1.375–1.376	1.375–1.376	1.375–1.376	1.375–1.376	0.430	0.430	0.010 Max	0.006
	E	4-135 (2.2)	1.375–1.376	1.375–1.376	1.375–1.376	1.375–1.376	1.375–1.376	0.430	0.430	0.010 Max	0.006
	K	4-153 (2.5)	1.375–1.376	1.375–1.376	1.375–1.376	1.375–1.376	1.375–1.376	0.430	0.430	0.010 Max	0.006

CAMSHAFT SPECIFICATIONS
All measurements given in inches.

Year	VIN	No. Cylinder Displacement cu. in. (liter)	Journal Diameter					Lobe Lift		Bearing Clearance	Camshaft End Play
			1	2	3	4	5	In.	Ex.		
1988-89	C	4-135 (2.2)	1.375–1.376	1.375–1.376	1.375–1.376	1.375–1.376	1.375–1.376	0.430	0.430	0.010 Max	0.006
	D	4-135 (2.2)	1.375–1.376	1.375–1.376	1.375–1.376	1.375–1.376	1.375–1.376	0.430	0.430	0.010 Max	0.006
	E	4-135 (2.2)	1.375–1.376	1.375–1.376	1.375–1.376	1.375–1.376	1.375–1.376	0.430	0.430	0.010 Max	0.006
	K	4-153 (2.5)	1.375–1.376	1.375–1.376	1.375–1.376	1.375–1.376	1.375–1.376	0.430	0.430	0.010 Max	0.006
	3	6-181 (3.0)	NA	NA	NA	NA	NA	NA	NA	NA	NA

NOTE: Specifications for the 1.6L and 2.6L engines are not available.
NA Not available

CRANKSHAFT AND CONNECTING ROD SPECIFICATIONS
All measurements are given in inches.

Year	VIN	No. Cylinder Displacement cu. in. (liter)	Crankshaft				Connecting Rod		
			Main Brg. Journal Dia.	Main Brg. Oil Clearance	Shaft End-play	Thrust on No.	Journal Diameter	Oil Clearance	Side Clearance
1982	A	4-105 (1.7)	2.124–2.128	.0009–.0031	.003–.007	3	1.809–1.813	.0011–.0034	.015
	B	4-135 (2.2)	2.362–2.363	.0004–.0026	.002–.007	3	1.968–1.969	.0004–.0026	.005–.013
	D	4-156 (2.6)	2.3622	.0008–.0028	.002–.007	3	2.0866	.0008–.0028	.004–.010
1983	A	4-98 (1.6)	2.046	.0009–.0031	.0035–.0110	3	1.612	.0010–.0025	.006–.009
	B	4-105 (1.7)	2.1236–2.1244	.0008–.0030	.003–.007	3	1.809–1.813	.0011–.0034	.0140
	C	4-135 (2.2)	2.362–2.363	.0003–.0031	.002–.007	3	1.968–1.969	.0008–.0034	.005–.013
	D	4-135 (2.2)	2.362–2.363	.0003–.0031	.002–.007	3	1.968–1.969	.0008–.0034	.005–.013
	G	4-156 (2.6)	2.3622	.0008–.0028	.002–.007	3	2.0866	.0008–.0028	.004–.010
1984	A	4-98 (1.6)	2.046	.0009–.0031	.0035–.0110	3	1.612	.0010–.0025	.006–.009
	C	4-135 (2.2)	2.362–2.363	.0003–.0031	.002–.007	3	1.968–1.969	.0008–.0034	.005–.013
	D	4-135 (2.2)	2.362–2.363	.0003–.0031	.002–.007	3	1.968–1.969	.0008–.0034	.005–.013
	E	4-135 (2.2)	2.362–2.363	.0004–.0023	.002–.007	3	1.968–1.969	.0008–.0031	.005–.013
	G	4-156 (2.6)	2.3622	.0008–.0028	.002–.007	3	2.0866	.0008–.0028	.004–.010

CRANKSHAFT AND CONNECTING ROD SPECIFICATIONS
All measurements are given in inches.

Year	VIN	No. Cylinder Displacement cu. in. (liter)	Crankshaft				Connecting Rod		
			Main Brg. Journal Dia.	Main Brg. Oil Clearance	Shaft End-play	Thrust on No.	Journal Diameter	Oil Clearance	Side Clearance
1985	A	4-98 (1.6)	2.046	.0009–.0031	.0035–.0110	3	1.612	.0010–.0025	.006–.009
	C	4-135 (2.2)	2.362–2.363	.0003–.0031	.002–.007	3	1.968–1.969	.0008–.0034	.005–.013
	D	4-135 (2.2)	2.362–2.363	.0003–.0031	.002–.007	3	1.968–1.969	.0008–.0034	.005–.013
	E	4-135 (2.2)	2.362–2.363	.0004–.0023	.002–.007	3	1.968–1.969	.0008–.0031	.005–.013
	G	4-156 (2.6)	2.3622	.0008–.0028	.002–.007	3	2.0866	.0008–.0028	.004–.010
1986	A	4-98 (1.6)	2.046	.0009–.0031	.0035–.0110	3	1.612	.0010–.0025	.006–.009
	C	4-135 (2.2)	2.362–2.363	.0003–.0031	.002–.007	3	1.968–1.969	.0008–.0031	.005–.013
	D	4-135 (2.2)	2.362–2.363	.0003–.0031	.002–.007	3	1.968–1.969	.0008–.0034	.005–.013
	E	4-135 (2.2)	2.362–2.363	.0004–.0023	.002–.007	3	1.968–1.969	.0008–.0031	.005–.013
	K	4-153 (2.5)	2.362–2.363	.0003–.0031	.002–.007	3	1.968–1.969	.0008–.0034	.005–.013
1987	C	4-135 (2.2)	2.362–2.363	.0003–.0031	.002–.007	3	1.968–1.969	.0008–.0031	.005–.013
	D	4-135 (2.2)	2.362–2.363	.0003–.0031	.002–.007	3	1.968–1.969	.0008–.0034	.005–.013
	E	4-135 (2.2)	2.362–2.363	.0004–.0023	.002–.007	3	1.968–1.969	.0008–.0031	.005–.013
	K	4-153 (2.5)	2.362–2.363	.0003–.0031	.002–.007	3	1.968–1.969	.0008–.0034	.005–.013
1988-89	C	4-135 (2.2)	2.362–2.363	.0003–.0031	.002–.007	3	1.968–1.969	.0008–.0031	.005–.013
	D	4-135 (2.2)	2.362–2.363	.0003–.0031	.002–.007	3	1.968–1.969	.0008–.0034	.005–.013
	E	4-135 (2.2)	2.362–2.363	.0004–.0023	.002–.007	3	1.968–1.969	.0008–.0031	.005–.013
	K	4-153 (2.5)	2.362–2.363	.0003–.0031	.002–.007	3	1.968–1.969	.0008–.0034	.005–.013
	3	6-181 (3.0)	2.361–2.363	.0006–.0020	.002–.010	3	NA	NA	NA

NA Not available

VALVE SPECIFICATIONS

Year	VIN	No. Cylinder Displacement cu. in. (liter)	Seat Angle (deg.)	Face Angle (deg.)	Spring Test Pressure (lbs.)	Spring Installed Height (in.)	Stem-to-Guide Clearance (in.) Intake	Exhaust	Stem Diameter (in.) Intake	Exhaust
1982	A	4-105 (1.7)	45	45	①	③	.0028	.0035	.314	.313
	B	4-135 (2.2)	45	45.5	175 @ 1.22	1.65	.001–.003	.002–.003	.312–.313	.311–.312
	D	4-156 (2.6)	43.75	45.25	61 @ 1.59	1.59	.001–.002	.002–.003	.315	.315
1983	A	4-98 (1.6)	45	45	—	1.65	.0005–.0018	.0013–.0026	.3140–.3146	.3132–.3138
	B	4-105 (1.7)	45	45	①	③	.0028	.0035	.314	.313
	C	4-135 (2.2)	45	45	135 @ 1.22 ②	1.65	.0009–.0026	.0030–.0047	.3124	.3103
	D	4-135 (2.2)	45	45	135 @ 1.22 ②	1.65	.0009–.0026	.0030–.0047	.3124	.3103
	G	4-156 (2.6)	45	45	61 @ 1.59	1.59	.0012–.0024	.0020–.0035	.315	.315
1984	A	4-98 (1.6)	45	45	—	1.65	.0005–.0018	.0013–.0026	.3140–.3146	.3132–.3138
	C	4-135 (2.2)	45	45	135 @ 1.22 ②	1.65	.0009–.0026	.0030–.0047	.3124	.3103
	D	4-135 (2.2)	45	45	135 @ 1.22 ②	1.65	.0009–.0026	.0030–.0047	.3124	.3103
	E	4-135 (2.2)	45	45	175 @ 1.22	1.65	.0009–.0026	.0030–.0047	.3124	.3103
	G	4-156 (2.6)	45	45	61 @ 1.59	1.59	.0012–.0024	.0020–.0035	.315	.315
1985	A	4-98 (1.6)	45	45	—	1.65	.0005–.0018	.0013–.0026	.3140–.3146	.3132–.3138
	C	4-135 (2.2)	45	45	150 @ 1.22 ②	1.65	.0009–.0026	.0030–.0047	.3124	.3103
	D	4-135 (2.2)	45	45	150 @ 1.22 ②	1.65	.0009–.0026	.0030–.0047	.3124	.3103
	E	4-135 (2.2)	45	45	175 @ 1.22	1.65	.0009–.0026	.0030–.0047	.3124	.3103
	G	4-156 (2.6)	45	45	61 @ 1.59	1.59	.0012–.0024	.0020–.0035	.315	.315
1986	A	4-98 (1.6)	45	45	—	1.65	.0005–.0018	.0013–.0026	.3140–.3146	.3132–.3138
	C	4-135 (2.2)	45	45	150 @ 1.22	1.65	.0009–.0026	.0030–.0047	.3124	.3103
	D	4-135 (2.2)	45	45	150 @ 1.22	1.65	.0009–.0026	.0030–.0047	.3124	.3103
	E	4-135 (2.2)	45	45	175 @ 1.22	1.65	.0009–.0026	.0030–.0047	.3124	.3103
	K	4-153 (2.5)	45	45	150 @ 1.22	1.65	.0009–.0026	.0030–.0047	.3124	.3103

VALVE SPECIFICATIONS

Year	VIN	No. Cylinder Displacement cu. in. (liter)	Seat Angle (deg.)	Face Angle (deg.)	Spring Test Pressure (lbs.)	Spring Installed Height (in.)	Stem-to-Guide Clearance (in.)		Stem Diameter (in.)	
							Intake	Exhaust	Intake	Exhaust
1987	C	4-135 (2.2)	45	45	150 @ 1.22	1.65	.0009–.0026	.0030–.0047	.3124	.3103
	D	4-135 (2.2)	45	45	150 @ 1.22	1.65	.0009–.0026	.0030–.0047	.3124	.3103
	E	4-135 (2.2)	45	45	175 @ 1.22	1.65	.0009–.0026	.0030–.0047	.3124	.3103
	K	4-153 (2.5)	45	45	150 @ 1.22	1.65	.0009–.0026	.0030–.0047	.3124	.3103
1988-89	C	4-135 (2.2)	45	45	150 @ 1.22	1.65	.0009–.0026	.0030–.0047	.3124	.3103
	D	4-135 (2.2)	45	45	150 @ 1.22	1.65	.0009–.0026	.0030–.0047	.3124	.3103
	E	4-135 (2.2)	45	45	175 @ 1.22	1.65	.0009–.0026	.0030–.0047	.3124	.3103
	K	4-153 (2.5)	45	45	150 @ 1.22	1.65	.0009–.0026	.0030–.0047	.3124	.3103
	3	6-181 (3.0)	44	45	73 @ 1.59	1.988	.0010–.0020	.0019–.0030	.3140	.3125

① Outer—101 @ .878
Inner—49 @ .720
② Hi-Performance—175 @ 1.22
③ Outer—1.28
Inner—1.13

PISTON AND RING SPECIFICATIONS
All measurments are given in inches.

Year	VIN	No. Cylinder Displacement cu. in. (liter)	Piston Clearance	Ring Gap			Ring Side Clearance		
				Top Compression	Bottom Compression	Oil Control	Top Compression	Bottom Compression	Oil Control
1982	A	4-105 (1.7)	.0005–.0015	.012–.018	.012–.018	.016–.055	.0016–.0028	.0008–.0020	.008 Max
	B	4-135 (2.2)	.0005–.0015	.011–.021	.011–.021	.015–.055	.0015–.0031	.0015–.0037	.008 Max
	D	4-156 (2.6)	.0008–.0016	.011–.018	.011–.018	.0078–.035	.0024–.0039	.0008–.0024	①
1983	A	4-98 (1.6)	.0016–.0020	.012–.018	.012–.018	.010–.016	.0018–.0028	.0018–.0020	.008 Max
	B	4-105 (1.7)	.0005–.0015	.012–.018	.012–.018	.016–.055	.0016–.0028	.0008–.0020	.008 Max
	C	4-134 (2.2)	.0005–.0015	.011–.021	.011–.021	.015–.055	.0015–.0031	.0015–.0037	.008 Max
	D	4-134 (2.2)	.0005–.0015	.011–.021	.011–.021	.015–.055	.0015–.0031	.0015–.0037	.008 Max
	G	4-156 (2.6)	.0008–.0016	.011–.018	.011–.018	.0078–.035	.0024–.0039	.0008–.0024	①

PISTON AND RING SPECIFICATIONS
All measurments are given in inches.

Year	VIN	No. Cylinder Displacement cu. in. (liter)	Piston Clearance	Ring Gap Top Compression	Ring Gap Bottom Compression	Ring Gap Oil Control	Ring Side Clearance Top Compression	Ring Side Clearance Bottom Compression	Ring Side Clearance Oil Control
1984	A	4-98 (1.6)	.0016– .0020	.012– .018	.012– .018	.010– .016	.0018– .0028	.0018 .0020	.008 Max
	C	4-134 (2.2)	.0005– .0015	.011– .021	.011– .021	.015– .055	.0015– .0031	.0015– .0037	.008 Max
	D	4-134 (2.2)	.0005– .0015	.011– .021	.011– .021	.015– .055	.0015– .0031	.0015– .0037	.008 Max
	E	4-135 (2.2)	.0015– .0025	.010– .020	.009– .018	.015– .055	.0015– .0031	.0015– .0037	.008 Max
	G	4-156 (2.6)	.0008– .0016	.011– .018	.011– .018	.0078– .035	.0024– .0039	.0008– .0024	①
1985	A	4-98 (1.6)	.0016– .0020	.012– .018	.012– .018	.010– .016	.0018– .0028	.0018 .0020	.008 Max
	C	4-134 (2.2)	.0005– .0015	.011– .021	.011– .021	.015– .055	.0015– .0031	.0015– .0037	.008 Max
	D	4-134 (2.2)	.0005– .0015	.011– .021	.011– .021	.015– .055	.0015– .0031	.0015– .0037	.008 Max
	E	4-135 (2.2)	.0015– .0025	.010– .020	.009– .018	.015– .055	.0015– .0031	.0015– .0037	.008 Max
	G	4-156 (2.6)	.0008– .0016	.011– .018	.011– .018	.0078– .035	.0024– .0039	.0008– .0024	①
1986	A	4-98 (1.6)	.0016– .0020	.012– .018	.012– .018	.010– .016	.0018– .0028	.0018 .0020	.008 Max
	C	4-134 (2.2)	.0005– .0015	.011– .021	.011– .021	.015– .055	.0015– .0031	.0015– .0037	.008 Max
	D	4-134 (2.2)	.0005– .0015	.011– .021	.011– .021	.015– .055	.0015– .0031	.0015– .0037	.008 Max
	E	4-135 (2.2)	.0015– .0025	.010– .020	.009– .018	.015– .055	.0015– .0031	.0015– .0037	.008 Max
	K	4-153 (2.5)	.0005– .0015	.011– .021	.011– .021	.015– .055	.0015– .0031	.0015– .0037	.008 Max
1987	C	4-134 (2.2)	.0005– .0015	.011– .021	.011– .021	.015– .055	.0015– .0031	.0015– .0037	.008 Max
	D	4-134 (2.2)	.0005– .0015	.011– .021	.011– .021	.015– .055	.0015– .0031	.0015– .0037	.008 Max
	E	4-135 (2.2)	.0015– .0025	.010– .020	.009– .018	.015– .055	.0015– .0031	.0015– .0037	.008 Max
	K	4-153 (2.5)	.0005– .0015	.011– .021	.011– .021	.015– .055	.0015– .0031	.0015– .0037	.008 Max

PISTON AND RING SPECIFICATIONS
All measurments are given in inches.

Year	VIN	No. Cylinder Displacement cu. in. (liter)	Piston Clearance	Ring Gap			Ring Side Clearance		
				Top Compression	Bottom Compression	Oil Control	Top Compression	Bottom Compression	Oil Control
1988-89	C	4-134 (2.2)	.0005–.0015	.011–.021	.011–.021	.015–.055	.0015–.0031	.0015–.0037	.008 Max
	D	4-134 (2.2)	.0005–.0015	.011–.021	.011–.021	.015–.055	.0015–.0031	.0015–.0037	.008 Max
	E	4-135 (2.2)	.0015–.0025	.010–.020	.009–.018	.015–.055	.0015–.0031	.0015–.0037	.008 Max
	K	4-153 (2.5)	.0005–.0015	.011–.021	.011–.021	.015–.055	.0015–.0031	.0015–.0037	.008 Max
	3	6-181 (3.0)	.0008–.0015	.012–.018	.010–.016	.012–.035	.0020–.0035	.0008–.0020	—

① Must be free to rotate after assembly

TORQUE SPECIFICATIONS
All readings in ft. lbs.

Year	VIN	No. Cylinder Displacement cu. in. (liter)	Cylinder Head Bolts	Main Bearing Bolts	Rod Bearing Bolts	Crankshaft Pulley Bolts	Flywheel Bolts	Manifold		Spark Plugs
								Intake	Exhaust	
1982	A	4-105 (1.7)	60①	47	35	58	60②	200④	200④	20
	B	4-135 (2.2)	③	30①	40①	50	65	200④	200④	26
	D	4-156 (2.6)	69⑤	58	34	87	70	150④	150④	18
1983	A	4-98 (1.6)	52	48	28	110	70	133④	180④	22
	B	4-105 (1.7)	60①	47	35	58	60②	200④	200④	20
	C	4-135 (2.2)	③	30①	40①	50	65	200④	200④	26
	D	4-135 (2.2)	③	30①	40①	50	65	200④	200④	26
	G	4-156 (2.6)	69⑤	58	34	87	70	150④	150④	18
1984	A	4-98 (1.6)	52	48	28	110	70	133④	180④	22
	C	4-135 (2.2)	③	30①	40①	50	65	200④	200④	26
	D	4-135 (2.2)	③	30①	40①	50	65	200④	200④	26
	E	4-135 (2.2)	③	30①	40①	50	65	200④	200④	26
	G	4-156 (2.6)	69⑤	58	34	87	70	150④	150④	18
1985	A	4-98 (1.6)	52	48	28	110	70	133④	180④	22
	C	4-135 (2.2)	③	30①	40①	50	65	200④	200④	26
	D	4-135 (2.2)	③	30①	40①	50	65	200④	200④	26
	E	4-135 (2.2)	③	30①	40①	50	65	200④	200④	26
	G	4-156 (2.6)	69⑤	58	34	87	70	150④	150④	18
1986	A	4-98 (1.6)	52	48	28	110	70	133④	180④	22
	C	4-135 (2.2)	⑥	30①	40①	50	70	200④	200④	26
	D	4-135 (2.2)	⑥	30①	40①	50	70	200④	200④	26
	E	4-135 (2.2)	⑥	30①	40①	50	70	200④	200④	26
	K	4-153 (2.5)	⑥	30①	40①	50	70	200④	200④	26

TORQUE SPECIFICATIONS
All readings in ft. lbs.

Year	VIN	No. Cylinder Displacement cu. in. (liter)	Cylinder Head Bolts	Main Bearing Bolts	Rod Bearing Bolts	Crankshaft Pulley Bolts	Flywheel Bolts	Manifold Intake	Manifold Exhaust	Spark Plugs
1987	C	4-135 (2.2)	⑥	30①	40①	50	70	200④	200④	26
	D	4-135 (2.2)	⑥	30①	40①	50	70	200④	200④	26
	E	4-135 (2.2)	⑥	30①	40①	50	70	200④	200④	26
	K	4-153 (2.5)	⑥	30①	40①	50	70	200④	200④	26
1988-89	C	4-135 (2.2)	⑥	30①	40①	50	70	200④	200④	26
	D	4-135 (2.2)	⑥	30①	40①	50	70	200④	200④	26
	E	4-135 (2.2)	⑥	30①	40①	50	70	200④	200④	26
	K	4-153 (2.5)	⑥	30①	40①	50	70	200④	200④	26
	3	6-181 (3.0)	70	60	38	110	70	200④	200④	20

① Plus ¼ turn more
② 50 with auto. trans.
③ 4 step torque sequence — 30, 45, 45 plus ¼ turn more
④ Inch lbs.
⑤ Cold
⑥ 4 step torque sequence — 45, 65, 65 plus ¼ turn more

BRAKE SPECIFICATIONS
All measurements in inches unless noted

Year	Model	Lug Nut Torque (ft. lbs.)	Master Cylinder Bore	Brake Disc Minimum Thickness	Brake Disc Maximum Runout	Standard Brake Drum Diameter	Minimum Lining Thickness Front	Minimum Lining Thickness Rear
1982	Omni, Horizon	85	.875	.431	.005	7.87 ①	.300	.300
	Aries, Reliant 400, LeBaron	85	.875	.882	.005	7.87 ①	.300	.300
1983	Omni, Horizon, Turismo, Charger	85	.875	.431	.005	8.98 ①	.300	.300
	Aries, Reliant, 400, 600, E-Class, New Yorker, LeBaron	85	.875	.882	.005	①②	.300	.300
1984	Omni, Horizon, Turismo, Charger	95	.827	.431	.005	8.98 ①	.300	.300
	Aries, Reliant, 400, 600, E-Class, New Yorker, LeBaron, Daytona, Laser	95	.827	.882	.005	①②	.300	.300

BRAKE SPECIFICATIONS
All measurements in inches unless noted

Year	Model	Lug Nut Torque (ft. lbs.)	Master Cylinder Bore	Brake Disc Minimum Thickness	Brake Disc Maximum Runout	Standard Brake Drum Diameter	Minimum Lining Thickness Front	Minimum Lining Thickness Rear
1985	Omni, Horizon, Turismo, Charger	95	.827	.431	.005	8.98 ①	.300	.300
	Aries, Reliant, 400, 600, E-Class, GTS, New Yorker, LeBaron, Daytona, Laser, Lancer	95	.875	.882	.005	①②	.300	.300
1986	Omni, Horizon, Turismo, Charger	95	.827	.431	.005	8.98 ①	.300	.300
	Aries, Reliant, 600, E-Class, New Yorker, LeBaron, GTS, Laser, Daytona, Lancer	95	.875	.882	.005	①②	.300	.300
1987	Omni, Horizon, Aries, Turismo, Charger	95	.827	.431	.005	8.98 ①	.300	.300
	Reliant, 600, E-Class, New Yorker, LeBaron, Daytona, Lancer, Shadow, Sundance, LeBaron GTS	95	.875	.882	.005	①②③	.300	.300
	Daytona (Rear Disc)	95	.827	.291	.005	—	.300	.300
1988-89	Omni, Horizon	95	.827	.431	.005	8.98 ①	.300	.300
	Reliant, 600, Caravelle, Sundance, Lancer, Shadow, LeBaron GTS, New Yorker Turbo, Daytona, Dynasty	95	.875	.882	.005	①②③	.300	.300
	Dynasty, Daytona, New Yorker (Rear Disc)	95	.827	.291	.005	—	.300	.300

① Maximum allowable diameter stamped on drum
② Aries and Reliant—9.45; all other models—10.24
③ Shadow and Sundance—9.45

WHEEL ALIGNMENT

Year	Model		Caster Range (deg.)	Caster Preferred Setting (deg.)	Camber Range (deg.)	Camber Preferred Setting (deg.)	Toe-in (in.)	Steering Axis Inclination (deg.)
1982	Omni, Horizon	Front	—	$1\frac{7}{8}$P ①	¼N–¾P	$\frac{5}{16}$P	$\frac{1}{16}$ ③	$13\frac{3}{8}$
		Rear	—	—	1¼N–¼N	¾N	$\frac{3}{32}$	—
	Aries, Reliant	Front	—	$1\frac{3}{16}$P ②	¼N–¾P	$\frac{5}{16}$P	$\frac{1}{16}$ ③	$13\frac{5}{16}$P
	400, 600, LeBaron	Rear	—	—	1N–0	½N	0	—
1983	Omni, Horizon	Front	—	$1\frac{7}{8}$P ①	¼N–¾P	$\frac{5}{16}$P	$\frac{1}{16}$ ③	$13\frac{3}{8}$P
	Turismo, Charger	Rear	—	—	1¼N–¼N	¾N	$\frac{3}{32}$	—
	Aries, Reliant	Front	—	$1\frac{3}{16}$P ②	¼N–¾P	$\frac{5}{16}$P	$\frac{1}{16}$ ③	$13\frac{5}{16}$P
	400, 600, E-Class, New Yorker, LeBaron	Rear	—	—	1N–0	½N	0	—
1984	Omni, Horizon	Front	—	$1\frac{7}{8}$P ①	¼N–¾P	$\frac{5}{16}$P	$\frac{1}{16}$ ③	$13\frac{3}{8}$P
	Turismo, Charger	Rear	—	—	1¼N–¼N	¾N	$\frac{3}{32}$	—
	Aries, Reliant	Front	—	$1\frac{3}{16}$P ②	¼N–¾P	$\frac{5}{16}$P	$\frac{1}{16}$ ③	$13\frac{5}{16}$P
	400, 600, E-Class, New Yorker, LeBaron, Daytona, Laser	Rear	—	—	1N–0	½N	0	—
1985	Omni, Horizon	Front	—	$1\frac{7}{8}$P ①	¼N–¾P	$\frac{5}{16}$P	$\frac{1}{16}$ ③	$13\frac{3}{8}$
	Turismo, Charger	Rear	—	—	1¼N–¼N	¾N	$\frac{3}{32}$	—
	Aries, Reliant	Front	—	$1\frac{3}{16}$P ②	¼N–¾P	$\frac{5}{16}$P	$\frac{1}{16}$ ③	$13\frac{5}{16}$P
	400, 600, E-Class, New Yorker, LeBaron, Daytona, Laser, LeBaron GTS, Lancer	Rear	—	—	1¼N–¼N	½N	0	—
1986	Omni, Horizon	Front	—	$1\frac{7}{8}$P ①	¼N–¾P	$\frac{5}{16}$P	$\frac{1}{16}$ ③	$13\frac{3}{8}$
	Turismo, Charger	Rear	—	—	1¼N–¼N	¾N	$\frac{3}{32}$	—
	Aries, Reliant	Front	—	$1\frac{3}{16}$P ②	¼N–¾P	$\frac{5}{16}$P	$\frac{1}{16}$ ③	$13\frac{5}{16}$P
	400, 600, E-Class, New Yorker, LeBaron, Daytona, Laser, LeBaron GTS, Lancer	Rear	—	—	1¼N–¼N	½N	0	—
1987	Omni, Horizon	Front	—	$1\frac{7}{8}$P ①	¼N–¾P	$\frac{5}{16}$P	$\frac{1}{16}$ ③	$13\frac{3}{8}$
	Turismo, Charger	Rear	—	—	1¼N–¼N	¾N	$\frac{3}{32}$	—
	Aries, Reliant	Front	—	$1\frac{3}{16}$P ②	¼N–¾P	$\frac{5}{16}$P	$\frac{1}{16}$ ③	$13\frac{5}{16}$P
	400, 600, E-Class, New Yorker, LeBaron, Daytona, Laser, LeBaron GTS, Lancer, Shadow, Sundance	Rear	—	—	1¼N–¼N	½N	0	—

WHEEL ALIGNMENT

Year	Model		Caster Range (deg.)	Caster Preferred Setting (deg.)	Camber Range (deg.)	Camber Preferred Setting (deg.)	Toe-in (in.)	Steering Axis Inclination (deg.)
1988-89	Omni, Horizon	Front	—	$1\frac{7}{8}$P ①	$\frac{1}{4}$N–$\frac{3}{4}$P	$\frac{5}{16}$P	$\frac{1}{16}$ ③	$13\frac{3}{8}$
		Rear	—	—	$1\frac{1}{4}$N–$\frac{1}{4}$N	$\frac{3}{4}$N	$\frac{3}{32}$	—
	Reliant, 600, Caravelle,	Front	—	$1\frac{3}{16}$P ②	$\frac{1}{4}$N–$\frac{3}{4}$P	$\frac{5}{16}$P	$\frac{1}{16}$ ③	$13\frac{5}{16}$P
	Sundance, Lancer,	Rear	—	—	$1\frac{1}{4}$N–$\frac{1}{4}$N	$\frac{1}{2}$N	0	—
	Shadow, LeBaron,							
	New Yorker, Daytona,							
	Dynasty							

① 4 Door — $1\frac{3}{8}$P
② Wagon — $\frac{7}{8}$P
③ Toe-out

TUNE-UP PROCEDURES

Ignition Timing

On all engines except the 1.6L and 3.0L, the ignition is timed using the No. 1 cylinder at the left side of the engine, facing the vehicle. The 1.6L engine, the No. 1 cylinder is on the right (flywheel) side. The 3.0L engine has the No. 1 cylinder at the left rear, when facing the vehicle.

NOTE: 1986-87 vehicles equipped with 2.2L (EFI) and automatic transmission, may exhibit erratic idle when the A/C compressor is engaged. On these vehicles equipped with one of the logic module part numbers listed below, it will be necessary to retard the ignition timing 4°; from 12° BTDC to 8° BTDC.

Logic Module
Product P/N.....................Service P/N

'86 FED.5227505....5227505,5227893
'86 CAL.5227508...................5227510
'87 FED.5227579...................5227880
'87 CAL.5227581...................5227882

ADJUSTMENT

All Engines

1. Connect a timing light according to the manufacturer's instructions.

Connect the red lead of a tachometer to the negative coil terminal and the black lead to ground. Place the cylinder selector switch in the appropriate position for the engine tested.
2. Start and run the engine until it reaches normal operating temperature.
3. Momentarily open the throttle and release it. Make sure that there is no binding of the throttle linkage and that the idle speed screw (on carburetor models) is against the stop.

NOTE: On EFI models, disconnect and reconnect the water temperature sensor connector on the thermostat housing. The loss of power lamp on the dash should turn on and stay on.

4. On carburetor models (equipped with a carburetor switch), connect a jumper wire between the carburetor switch and ground. At the Spark Control Computer (SCC), disconnect and plug the vacuum line.
5. Using the 1000 rpm scale, read the curb idle speed. If the rpm is higher than the specification, adjust the idle speed screw (on carburetor models) on top of the solenoid.
6. Loosen the distributor holddown bolt so the distributor can be rotated.

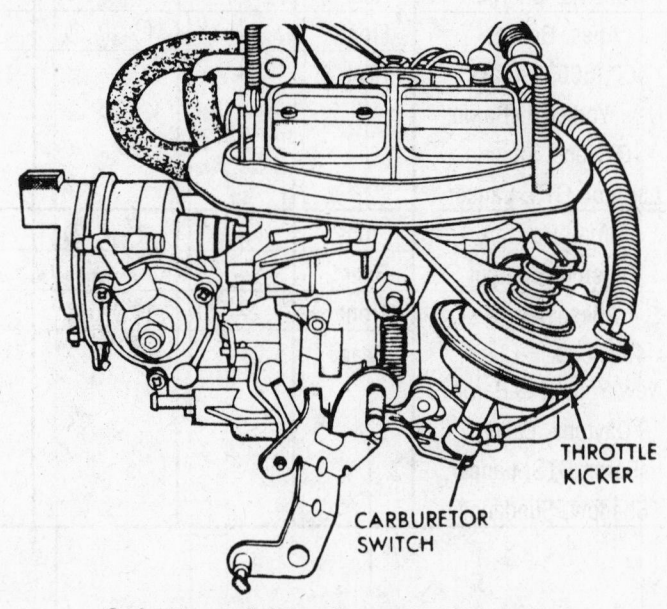

THROTTLE KICKER

CARBURETOR SWITCH

Carburetor switch location on the 2.2L engine

7. Aim the timing light or read the magnetic timing unit. For the 1.7L, 2.2L and 2.5L engines, remove the timing hole access cover on the bell housing or read the magnetic timing unit. The timing marks, for the 1.6L, 2.6L and 3.0L engines, are on the crankshaft pulley and front cover. Carefully rotate the distributor until the timing marks are aligned.

8. Tighten the distributor hold down bolt and recheck the timing. Check and adjust the idle speed, if necessary.

9. Unplug and reconnect the vacuum hose to the Spark Control Computer.

Valve Lash

ADJUSTMENT

1.6L Engine

NOTE: Valve clearance must be set with the piston at TDC on the compression stroke and the engine cold.

1. Remove the valve cover. Rotate the crankshaft and watch movement of exhaust valves. When one is closing, (moving upward) continue rotating the crankshaft slowly, until the inlet valve on the same cylinder just starts to open. This is the "valve rocking" position. The piston in the opposite cylinder is now at TDC on it's compression stroke and the valve lash can be checked and adjusted.

2. Example: To check valve clearances on No. 1 cylinder, position the valves on the companion cylinder No. 4, in the "rocking" position as follows:

a. Observe rockers on companion cylinder number four. Turn crankshaft until exhaust valve rocker is moving upward (valve closing)—keep turning slowly until intake valve rocker just starts to move down (valve opening)—stop.

b. Check both valve clearances on No. 1 cylinder.

3. After checking both valve clearances, rotate the crankshaft one half turn, the next cylinder in the firing order should have its valves "rocking" and the companion cylinder can be adjusted.

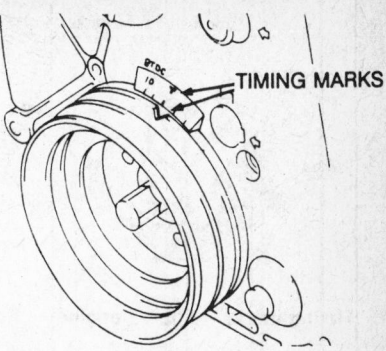

Timing marks—2.6L engine

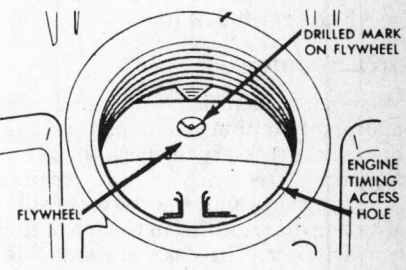

Drilled mark on 1.7L engine flywheel

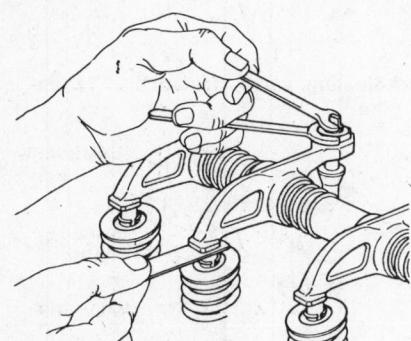

1.6L engine—adjusting valve clearance

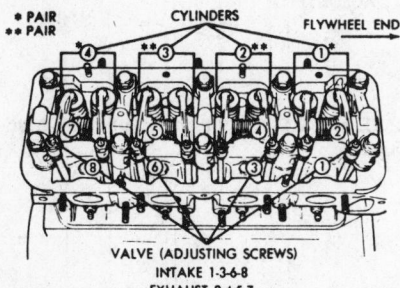

VALVE (ADJUSTING SCREWS)
INTAKE 1-3-6-8
EXHAUST 2-4-5-7

Adjusting valve clearance—1.6L engine

Valves 'Rocking' on Cylinder Number	Adjust Valves on Cylinder Number
4	1
2	3
1	4
3	2

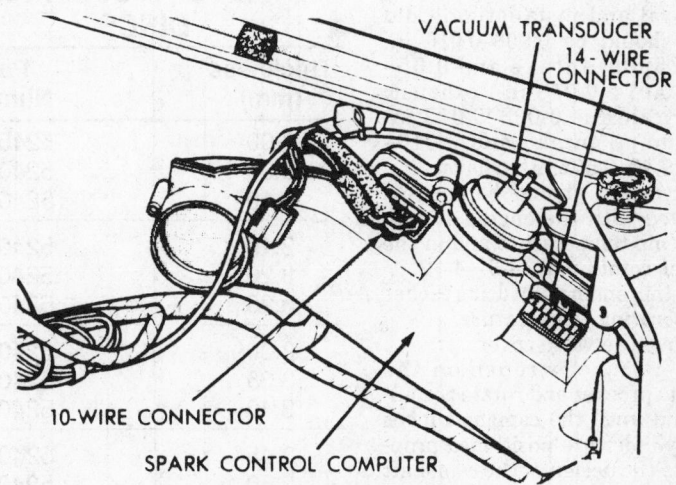

Spark Control Computer

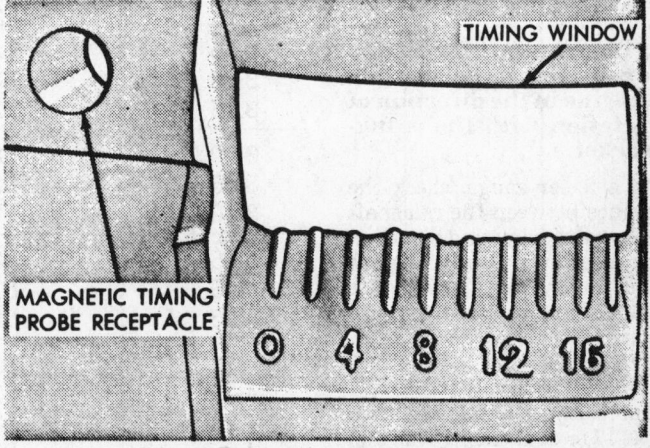

Timing mark—2.2L and 2.5L engines

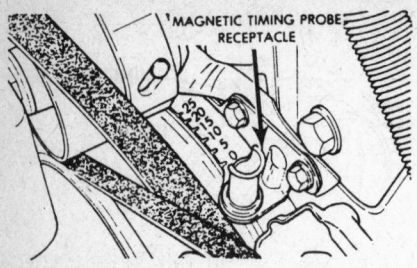

Timing marks—3.0L V6 engine

4. Adjust the valves to obtain the following specifications:

Intake 0.010 in.
Exhaust 0.012 in.

1.7L Engine

Valve adjustment is not required as a matter of routine maintenance. It is however, necessary to check the valve clearance after cylinder head repairs. Adjusting clearance is a matter of substituting discs located in the top of the cam follower. The discs are available in 0.05mm increments from 3.0mm to 4.24mm. One disc is located in each follower. A special tool is required for disc removal and installation. Cold clearance should be 0.006–0.010 in. (0.15–0.25mm) intake and 0.35–0.45mm (0.014–0.018 in.) exhaust; warm clearance is 0.008–0.012 in. (0.20–0.30mm) intake and 0.016–0.020 in. (0.40–0.50mm) exhaust.

The valve lash should be checked and adjusted with the engine at normal operating temperature and in the firing order rotation of 1–3–4–2.

1. Run the engine until it reaches normal operating temperature.

2. Remove the valve cover.

3. Use a socket wrench on the crankshaft sprocket and rotate the engine around until the camshaft lobes of No. 1 cylinder are positioned properly. Due to the design of the camshaft lobes, it is not necessary that the lobes be pointing directly away (perpendicular) from the adjusting disc.

NOTE: Do not rotate the engine using the camshaft sprocket. Only turn the engine in the direction of normal rotation with the crankshaft sprocket.

4. Using a feeler gauge, check the valve clearance between the camshaft lobe and the valve adjusting disc.

5. If the measured clearance is not as specified, the valve adjusting disc can be removed and replaced with another of the proper size to give the correct valve clearance.

6. To remove the disc:

a. Depress the cam follower with Tool L-4417 or equivalent. This tool is necessary to remove the disc without damaging the camshaft or cylinder head.

b. Remove the valve adjusting disc with a magnet.

c. Calculate the thickness of a new disc and install one of the proper size. Be sure the number indicating the thickness (measured in mm) of the disc faces down when installed.

d. Recheck the valve clearance.

7. Recheck or adjust all other valves using the same procedure.

NOTE: When the camshaft is in position to check the valves of No. 1 cylinder, cylinders No. 3 and 4 can also be checked or adjusted. It is only necessary to rotate the engine one time to position the camshaft to check No. 2 cylinder.

8. Reinstall the valve cover using a new gasket.

2.2L, 2.5L, and 3.0L Engines

The 2.2L, 2.5L and 3.0L engines use hydraulic lash adjusters. No routine adjustments are necessary.

VALVE ADJUSTING DISCS

Thickness (mm)	Part Number
3.00	5240946
3.05	5240945
3.10	5240944
3.15	5240943
3.20	5240942
3.25	5240941
3.30	5240573
3.35	5240574
3.40	5240575
3.45	5240576
3.50	5240577
3.55	5240578
3.60	5240579
3.65	5240580
3.70	5240581
3.75	5240582
3.80	5240583
3.85	5240584
3.90	5240585
3.95	5240586
4.00	5240587
4.05	5240588
4.10	5240589
4.15	5240590
4.20	5240591
4.25	5240592

2.6L Engine

The 2.6L engine has a jet valve located beside the intake valve of each cylinder.

NOTE: When adjusting valve clearances, the jet valve must be adjusted before the intake valve.

1. Start and run the engine until it reaches normal operating temperature.

2. Stop the engine and remove the air cleaner. Disconnect and tag any cables, hoses, wires, etc., which are attached to the valve cover. Remove the valve cover.

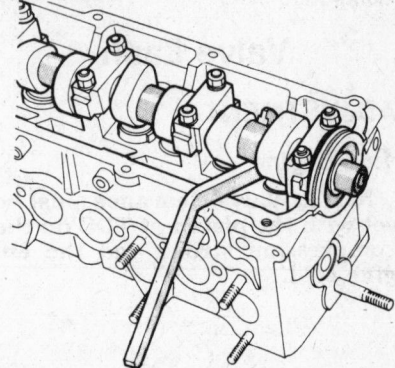

Adjusting valve clearance—1.7L engine

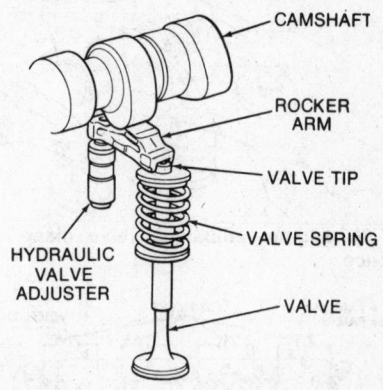

2.2L and 2.5L engine hydraulic valve adjuster

Exhaust Valve Closing	Adjust
No. 1 Cylinder	No. 4 Cylinder Valves
No. 2 Cylinder	No. 3 Cylinder Valves
No. 3 Cylinder	No. 2 Cylinder Valves
No. 4 Cylinder	No. 1 Cylinder Valves

3. Disconnect the high tension coil wire at the coil.

4. Watch the rocker arms for No. 1 cylinder and rotate the crankshaft until the exhaust valve is closing and the intake valve has just started to open. At this point, No. 4 cylinder will be at Top Dead Center (TDC), starting it's firing stroke.

5. Loosen the locknut on the No. 4 intake valve and back off the intake valve adjusting screw 2 or more turns.

6. Loosen the locknut on the jet valve adjusting screw.

7. Turn the jet valve adjusting screw counterclockwise and insert a 0.006 in. feeler gauge between the jet valve stem and the adjusting screw.

8. Tighten the adjusting screw until it touches the feeler gauge. Take care not to press down on the valve while adjusting. The jet valve spring is very weak.

NOTE: If the adjusting screw is tight, special care must be taken to avoid pressing down on the jet valve when adjusting the clearance or a false reading will result.

9. Tighten the locknut securely while holding the rocker arm adjusting screw with a suitable tool, to prevent it from turning.

10. Make sure that a 0.006 in. feeler gauge can be easily inserted between the jet valve and rocker arm.

11. Adjust the No. 4 cylinder intake valve to 0.006 in. and the exhaust valve to 0.010 in. Tighten the adjusting screw locknuts and recheck each clearance.

12. Perform Step 4 in conjunction with the chart to adjust the remaining three cylinders.

13. Install the valve cover and connect all other components. Run the engine and check for oil leaks when finished.

Idle Speed and Mixture

ADJUSTMENT

Carbureted Models

HOLLEY 5220/6520

1. Set the parking brake and place the transaxle in Neutral.

2. Turn off the headlights, all accessories and the air conditioning.

3. Connect a tachometer to the engine following the manufacturer's instructions.

4. If equipped with a Spark Control Computer (SCC), connect a jumper wire from the carburetor switch to ground.

5. Start the engine and allow it to reach normal operating temperature.

6. Refer to the emission control label in the engine compartment. Check and/or adjust the ignition timing, if necessary.

7. Unplug the connector at the radiator fan and install a jumper wire so the fan will run continuously. Pull the PCV valve from the cylinder head cover and the $\frac{3}{16}$ in. diameter control hose at the canister and allow both to draw fresh air.

8. On 1982 models, disconnect and plug the vacuum hoses to the EGR valve and the $\frac{3}{16}$ in. dia. control hose at the canister. If it is equipped with A/C, turn on the A/C and open the throttle to energize the solenoid. If it is equipped with an automatic transaxle, place the transaxle in Drive. Remove the adjusting screw and spring from the top of the A/C solenoid. Insert a $\frac{1}{8}$ in. Allen wrench into the solenoid and adjust the idle speed (check emission control label for specifications) with the compressor clutch engaged. Place the automatic transaxle in Park. Reinstall the A/C solenoid spring and screw. Proceed to Step 11.

9. On 1983 models, disconnect and plug the vacuum connector at the CCEGR/CVSCC. Proceed to Step 11.

Adjusting valve lash—2.6L engine

10. On 1984–89 models, disconnect and plug the vacuum connector at the CVSCC. With the Holley 6520, disconnect the O₂ sensor test connector on the left fender shield.

NOTE: If equipped with A/C (1983–89), check the A/C kicker operation and the kicker vacuum system for leaks. Service is by replacement of the kicker or vacuum lines only.

11. Wait one minute. If the idle speed does not meet the curb idle rpm specifications, adjust the idle speed screw on top of the solenoid.

12. After the idle speed has been set, remove the test equipment and reinstall the wiring and hoses.

MIKUNI

1. Set the parking brake and place the transaxle in Neutral.

2. Turn off all lights and accessories. Disconnect the cooling fan.

3. Connect a tachometer to the engine, following the manufacturer's instructions.

4. Start the engine, allow it to reach normal operating temperature and refer to the emission control label in the engine compartment.

5. Install a timing light; check the timing and adjust (if necessary). Remove the timing light.

6. Open the throttle, run the engine at 2500 rpm for 10 seconds. Return to idle, wait two minutes and read the idle rpm. If it is not the same as the curb idle specified on the emission control label, adjust the idle speed adjusting screw. The screw is accessible through the hole in the choke cover plate and is at a 45 degree angle inward.

NOTE: On 1984–89 models, remove the idle switch connector.

7. If equipped with A/C, set the temperature control lever to the coldest position and turn on the A/C. With the compressor running, set the engine speed to 900 rpm by turning the idle up adjusting screw.

8. Turn the engine off, disconnect the tachometer, reconnect the cooling fan and idle switch connector (if equipped).

PROPANE ASSISTED IDLE SPEED AND AIR/FUEL MIXTURE ADJUSTMENT

HOLLEY 5220/6520

NOTE: Remove the air/fuel mixture concealment plug, by referring to "Carburetors" in the Unit Repair section.

ADJUSTING SCREW

JET VALVE

JET VALVE CLEARANCE

Adjusting the jet valve—2.6L engine

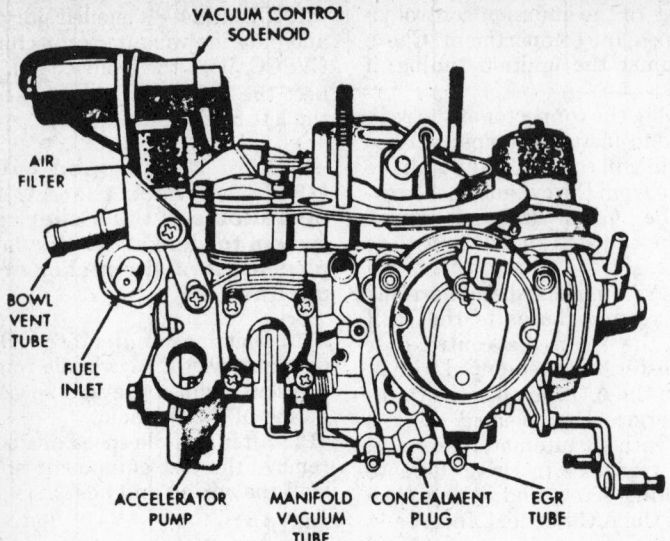

Model 5220 Carburetor

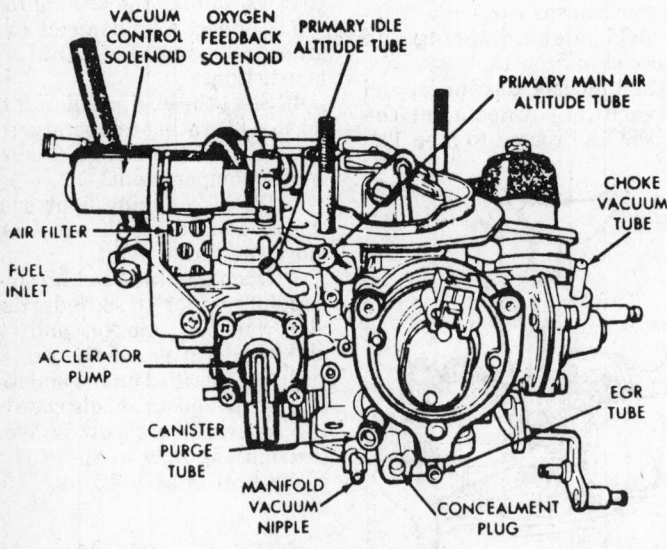

Model 6520 Carburetor

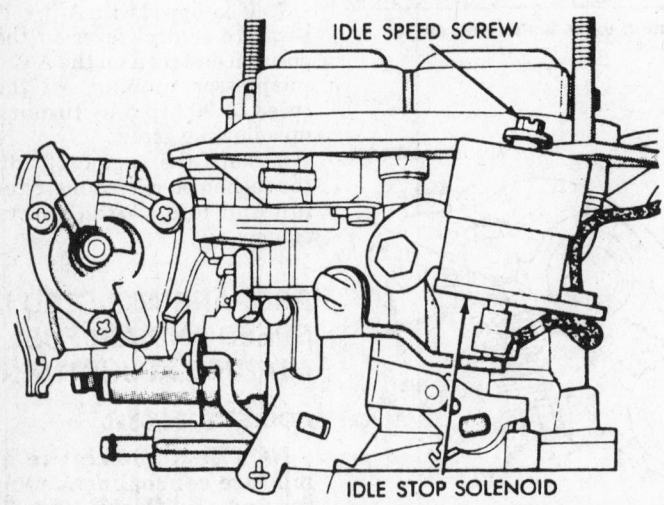

Adjusting the idle speed with the solenoid idle stop screw

1. Set the parking brake and place the transaxle in Neutral.

2. Turn off the headlights, all accessories and the A/C compressor.

3. Connect a tachometer to the engine following the manufacturer's instructions.

4. If equipped with a Spark Control Computer (SCC), connect a jumper wire from the carburetor switch to ground.

5. Start the engine and allow it to reach normal operating temperature.

6. Refer to the emission control label in the engine compartment, then check and adjust the timing, if necessary.

7. Unplug the connector at the radiator fan and install a jumper so the fan will run continuously. Pull the PCV valve from the cylinder head cover and the $3/16$ in. dia. control hose at the canister, allow them to draw fresh air.

8. Using a propane tank with a main and metering valve (make sure the valves are closed and the tank is an upright and safe location), install the supply hose to the carburetor.

9. On 1982 models, disconnect and plug the vacuum hoses to the EGR valve and the $3/16$ in. dia. control hose at the canister. Disconnect the vacuum hose of the heated door sensor at the 3-way connector and replace it with the propane supply hose. If equipped with A/C, turn on the A/C and open the throttle to energize the solenoid. Remove the adjusting screw and spring from the top of the A/C solenoid. Insert a $1/8$ in. Allen wrench into the solenoid and adjust the idle speed (check emission control label for specifications) with the compressor clutch engaged. After adjustment, place the automatic transaxle in Park. Reinstall the A/C solenoid spring and screw. Proceed to Step 11.

10. On 1983 models, disconnect and plug the vacuum connector at the Coolant Controlled Exhaust Gas Recirculation/Coolant Vacuum Switch Cold Closed (CCEGR/CVSCC). Disconnect the vacuum hose of the heated door sensor at the 3-way connector and replace it with the propane supply hose. Proceed to Step 12.

11. On 1984–89 models, disconnect and plug the vacuum connector at the Coolant Vacuum Switch Cold Closed (CVSCC). If equipped with a Holley 6520, disconnect the O_2 sensor test connector on the left fender shield. Disconnect the vacuum hose of the heated door sensor at the 3-way connector and replace it with the propane supply hose.

NOTE: If equipped with A/C (1983–86), check the A/C kicker operation and the kicker vacuum

system for leaks, service is by replacement of the kicker or vacuum lines ONLY.

12. Open the main valve of the propane tank, then slowly open the metering valve until the highest rpm is reached (excessive propane will decrease the engine rpm). Fine tune the metering valve to get the highest engine rpm. With the propane still flowing, adjust the idle speed screw (on top of the solenoid) to meet the propane rpm specified on the emission control label.

13. Again, fine tune the propane metering valve to get the highest rpm. If the engine speed changed, readjust the idle speed screw to meet the propane rpm specified on the emission control label.

14. Turn off the main valve of the propane tank, allow the engine to stabilize and adjust the air/fuel mixture screw, with an Allen wrench, to achieve the specified idle rpm. After adjustment, allow the engine to stabilize.

15. Turn On the main valve of the propane tank and fine tune the metering valve to achieve the highest engine rpm. If the highest rpm is 25 rpm or higher than the specified propane rpm, repeat the propane assisted adjustment steps; if the highest rpm is 25 rpm or less than the specified propane rpm, turn off the valves and remove the propane tank.

16. After the air/fuel mixture and idle speed have been set, remove the test equipment. Reinstall the concealment plugs, the wiring and hoses.

MIKUNI

NOTE: Remove the air/fuel mixture concealment plug, by referring to "Carburetors" in the Unit Repair section.

1. Set the parking brake and place the transaxle in Neutral.
2. Turn off all lights and accessories. Disconnect the cooling fan.
3. Connect a tachometer to the engine, following the manufacturer's instructions.
4. Start the engine, allow it to reach normal operating temperature and stop the engine.
5. Disconnect the negative battery cable, wait three seconds and reconnect it.
6. Start the engine, open the throttle, run the engine at 2500 rpm for 10 seconds, return to idle and wait two minutes. Refer to the emission control label in the engine compartment.

NOTE: On 1984–89 models, remove the idle switch connector and the bullet connector at the O$_2$ sensor.

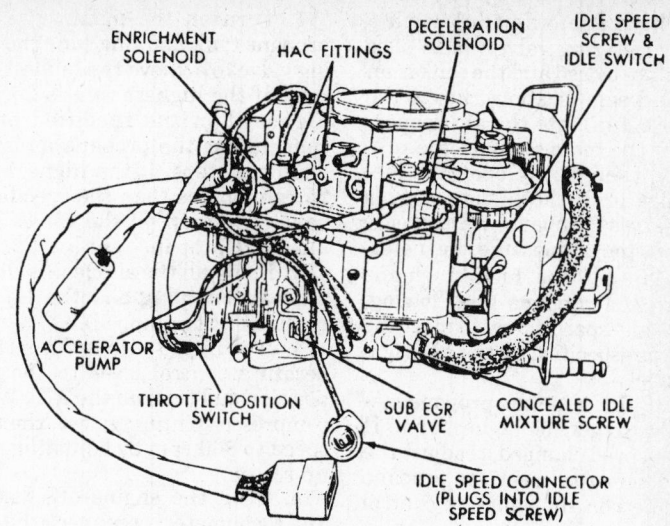

Mikuni Carburetor

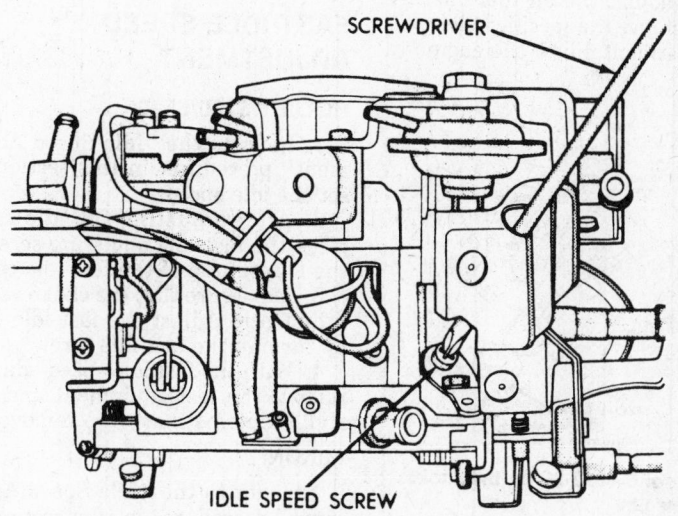

Adjusting the idle speed screw

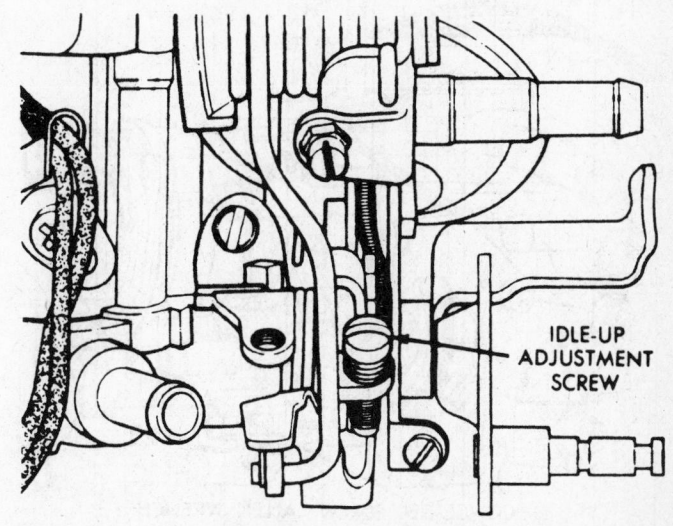

Adjusting the idle-up screw

7. Using a propane tank with a main and metering valve (make sure the valves are closed and the tank is an upright and safe location), insert the supply hose 4 in. into the air cleaner.

8. Open the main valve of the propane tank, then slowly open the metering valve until the highest rpm is reached (excess propane will decrease the engine rpm). Fine tune the metering valve to get the highest engine rpm. With the propane still flowing, adjust the idle speed screw to meet the propane rpm specified on the emission control label.

9. Again, fine tune the propane metering valve to get the highest rpm. If the engine speed changed, readjust the idle speed screw to meet the propane rpm specified on the emission control label.

10. Turn off the main valve of the propane tank, allow the engine to stabilize and adjust the air/fuel mixture screw to achieve the specified idle rpm. After adjustment, allow the engine to stabilize.

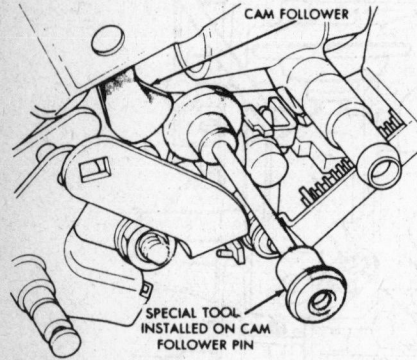

Installing tool C-4812-2C on the choke cam follower pin

11. Turn on the main valve of the propane tank and fine tune the metering valve to achieve the highest engine rpm. If the highest rpm is 25 rpm or higher than the specified propane rpm, repeat the propane assisted adjustment steps; if the highest rpm is 25 rpm or less than the specified propane rpm, turn off the valves and remove the propane tank.

12. Reinstall the air cleaner duct, the concealment plug and the O_2 sensor connector (if equipped).

13. If equipped with A/C, set the temperature control lever to the coldest position and turn on the A/C. With the compressor running, set the engine speed to 900 rpm by adjusting the idle up screw.

14. Turn the engine off, disconnect the tachometer, reconnect the cooling fan and idle switch connector (if equipped).

FAST IDLE SPEED ADJUSTMENT

HOLLEY 5220/6520

1. Refer to the "Idle Speed Adjustment" procedures in this section and set the idle speed.

2. After adjusting the idle speed, place the fast idle adjusting screw on the lowest step of the fast idle cam.

3. Make sure that the choke valve is fully Open. Adjust the fast idle speed by turning the fast idle screw.

4. With the fast idle speed adjusted, remove the test equipment and reinstall the items that were removed.

MIKUNI

1. Refer to the "Idle Speed Adjustment" procedures in this section and set the idle speed.

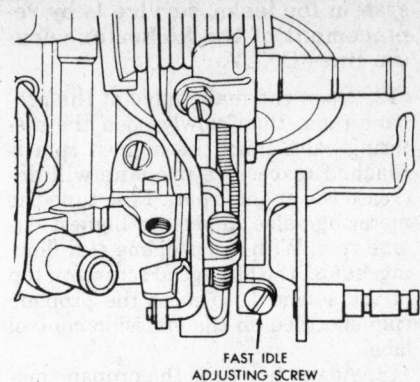

FAST IDLE
ADJUSTING SCREW

Adjusting the fast idle speed screw

2. After adjusting the idle speed, open the throttle slightly and install the tool No. C-4812-2C or equivalent, onto the choke cam follower pin.

3. Release the throttle and adjust the fast idle screw to the specified fast idle rpm.

4. With the fast idle speed adjusted, remove the adjusting tool and test equipment; then reinstall the items that were removed.

Fuel Injected Models

The idle speed is controlled by the automatic idle speed (AIS) motor which is controlled by the logic module. The logic module gathers data from various sensors and switches in the system and adjusts the engine idle to a pre-determined speed. Idle speed specifications can be found on the vehicle emission control information (VECI) label located in the engine compartment.

ENGINE ELECTRICAL

Distributor

All engine except the 2.6L, are equipped with a computer controlled Hall Effect ignition system and use a three-pronged spark control computer connector at the distributor. The 2.2L Turbocharged engine uses the same type system, but it has two three-pronge connectors at the distributor. The 2.6L engine electronic ignition system is slightly different from that used on the other models. To remove the spark plug cables from the distributor cap, remove the distributor cap and squeeze the inside retaining prongs together to remove the cables.

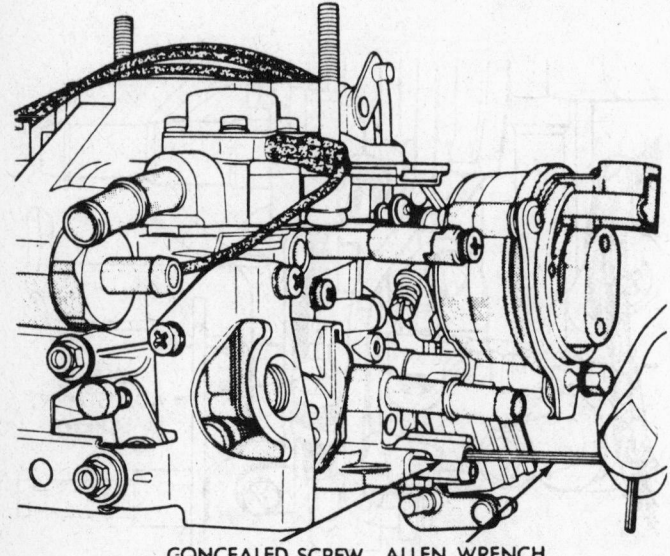

CONCEALED SCREW   ALLEN WRENCH
Adjusting the Air/Fuel mixture screw

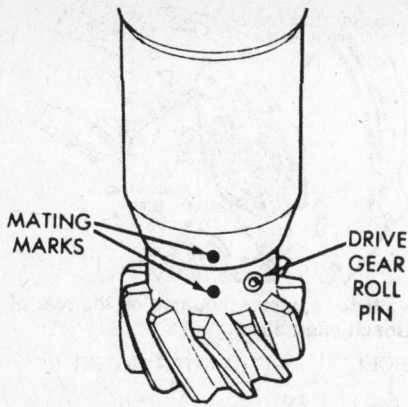

Mating the distributor timing marks

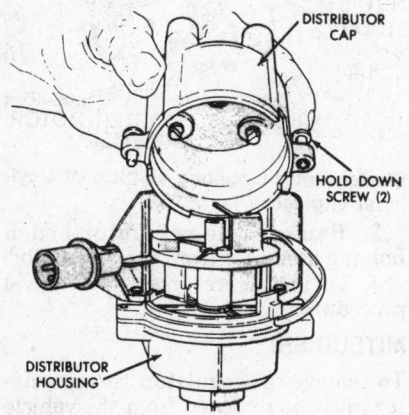

Typical distributor used on all 1982–87 engines

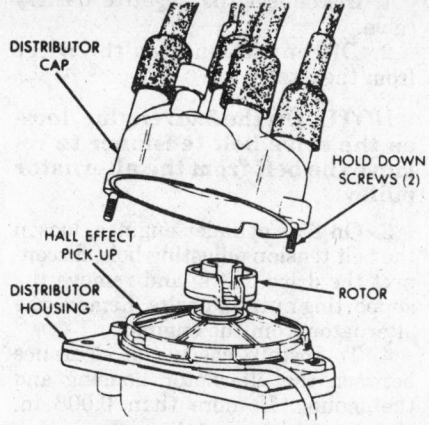

Typical distributor used on all 1987–89 engines

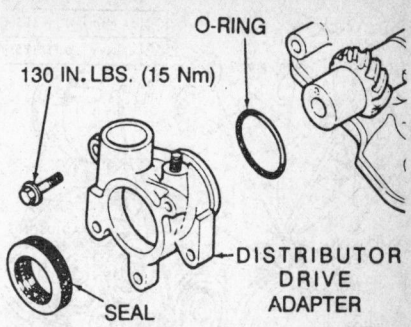

Distributor drive adapter—3.0L V6 engine

REMOVAL & INSTALLATION

2.6L Engine

1. Disconnect the negative battery cable and the distributor pickup lead wire at the harness connector. Remove the spark plug cables from the distributor cap.
2. Remove the vacuum hose from the the vacuum control unit.
3. Remove the hold-down nut and the distributor assembly.
4. To install the distributor:
   a. Rotate the crankshaft until the No. 1 piston is at TDC on the compression stroke. Align the crankshaft pulley timing mark to the TDC mark on the timing plate.
   b. Align the mating mark (line) with the mating punch mark on the distributor gear.
   c. Install the distributor to the cylinder head. Align the distributor flange mating mark with the center of the distributor hold-down stud.
5. To complete the installation, reverse the removal procedures. Start the engine. Check and adjust the timing, if necessary.

All Other Engines

1. Disconnect the distributor pick-up lead wire at the harness connector. If equipped, remove the the splash shield.
2. Remove the retaining screws and the distributor cap.
3. Rotate the engine crankshaft (in the direction of normal rotation) until No. 1 cylinder is at TDC on the compression stroke. Make a mark on the block and the distributor housing where the rotor points for installation reference.
4. Remove the hold-down bolt and clamp.
5. Carefully lift the distributor from the engine. The shaft on some engines may rotate slightly as the distributor is removed.
6. If the engine has been rotated while the distributor was removed, perform the following procedures:
   a. Rotate the crankshaft until the No. 1 piston is at TDC on the compression stroke. This will be indicated by the timing mark on the flywheel or crank pulley aligning with the 0 degree mark on the bell housing or engine front cover.
   b. Position the rotor just ahead of the No. 1 terminal of the cap and lower the distributor into the engine.
   c. With the distributor fully seated (make sure that the O-ring is seated), the rotor should be directly under the No. 1 terminal.
7. If the engine was not disturbed while the distributor was removed, lower the distributor into the engine, engaging the gears and making sure that the O-ring is properly seated in the block. The rotor should align with the marks made before removal.
8. Tighten the hold-down bolt and connect the wires (make sure they snap into place).

9. To complete the installation, reverse the removal procedures. Start the engine. Check and adjust the ignition timing, if necessary.

Alternator

For further information on the charging system, please refer to "Charging And Starting" in the Unit Repair Section.

The following alternators may be found on the various vehicle models:
   a. Chrysler 60/70 amp alternator with external electronic voltage regulator.
   b. Chrysler 40/90 amp alternator with voltage regulator in the engine electronics.
   c. Chrysler 60 and 78 amp alternator with voltage regulator in the engine electronics.
   d. Bosch 65 amp alternator and Chrysler electronic voltage regulator.
   e. Bosch 40/90 and 40/100 amp alternators with voltage regulators in the engine electronics.
   f. Bosch alternator and internal (integral) electronic voltage regulator.
   g. Mitsubishi alternator and internal (integral) electric voltage regulator.

PRECAUTIONS

To prevent serious damage to the alternator and the rest of the charging system, the following precautions must be observed:
- When installing a battery, make sure that the positive cable is connected to the positive terminal and the negative to the negative
- When jump-starting the vehicle with another battery, make sure that like terminals are connected and the ignition switch is turned off when making the connections. This also applies when using a battery charger

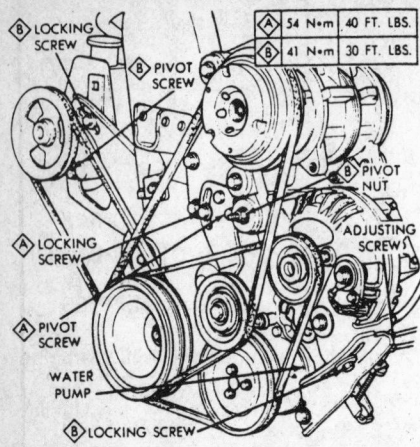

| A | 54 N•m | 40 FT. LBS. |
| B | 41 N•m | 30 FT. LBS. |

Adjustment of accessory drive belts—typical of 4 cylinder engines

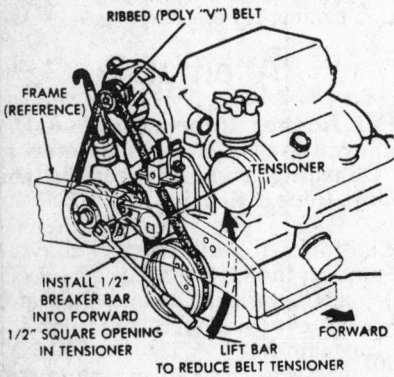

Adjusting drive belt tension—3.0L V6 engine

- Never operate the alternator with the battery disconnected or otherwise on an uncontrolled open circuit. Double-check to see that all connections are tight
- Do not short across or ground any alternator or regulator terminals
- Do not try to polarize the alternator
- Do not apply full battery voltage to the field connector
- Always disconnect the battery ground cable before disconnecting the alternator lead.

BELT TENSION ADJUSTMENT

For the belt tension adjustments, please refer to the alternator removal and installation procedures.

REMOVAL & INSTALLATION

All Engines

NOTE: To perform the alternator adjustment on some models, it may be necessary to raise the vehicle and remove the splash shield.

1. Disconnect the negative battery cable.
2. Disconnect and tag the wires from the alternator.

NOTE: On the 3.0L engine, loosen the drive belt tensioner to remove the belt from the alternator pulley.

3. On four cylinder engines, loosen the belt tension adjusting bolt, disconnect the drive belt(s) and remove the supporting nuts and bolts. Remove the alternator from the engine.
4. To install, check the clearance between the alternator housing and the mount. If more than 0.008 in. clearance exists, install shims.
5. On four cylinder engines, adjust the belt tension to ¼–⅜ in. deflection between the longest span between two pulleys, using moderate thumb pressure.
6. On the 3.0L engine, adjust the belt tension with the belt tensioner.

Voltage Regulator

Neither the internal nor external voltage regulators have any moving parts. They require no adjustments. If service is required, the regulator must be replaced as a unit.

REMOVAL & INSTALLATION

NOTE: Several types of voltage regulators are used; external, internal and in-circuit (contained within the power/logic modules). The external and in-circuit types are used with Chrysler and Bosch alternators. The internal type is used with Bosch and Mitsubishi alternators.

External Type

1. Disconnect the negative battery cable.
2. Disconnect the connector from the regulator.
3. Remove the sheet metal screws and the regulator.
4. To install, reverse the removal procedures. Make sure regulator has a clean mounting contact.

In-Circuit Type

The in-circuit type can only be serviced by replacing the power/logic module.

Internal Type

BOSCH

1. Disconnect the negative battery cable.
2. At the rear of the alternator, remove the two regulator mounting screws.

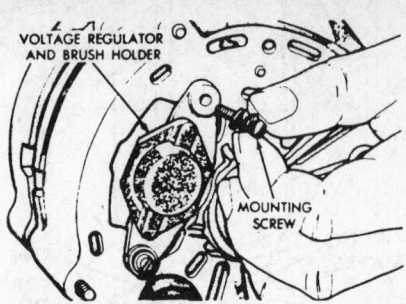

Voltage regulator mounted on the rear of Bosch alternators

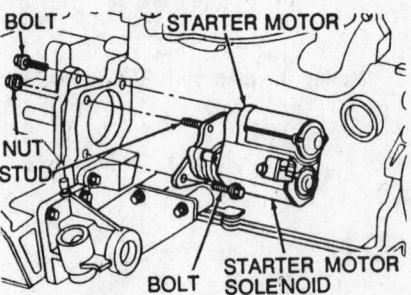

Starter motor mounting—typical of 4 cylinder engines

3. Remove the regulator/brush holding assembly from the alternator.
4. To install, reverse the removal procedures.

MITSUBISHI

To remove the regulator, the alternator must be removed from the vehicle and disassembled. For disassembly procedures, please refer to "Charging and Starting" in the Unit Repair section.

Starter

For further information on the starter system, please refer to "Charging and Starting" in the Unit Repair Section.

NOTE: Three makes of starters are used; Bosch, Mitsubishi and Nippondenso. Removal and installation procedures are the same for all units. The starter solenoid is mounted on the starter motor.

REMOVAL & INSTALLATION

All Engines

1. Disconnect the negative battery cable. Raise and support the vehicle safely.
2. Remove the starter motor heat shield, if equipped.
3. With the 2.2L or 2.5L engine, loosen the air pump tube at the exhaust manifold and swivel the tube bracket away from the starter.
4. Disconnect and tag the starter motor wiring.

5. Support the starter and remove the mounting bolts. Remove the starter from the flywheel housing and transaxle support bracket.

6. To install, reverse the removal procedures.

ENGINE MECHANICAL

Engine

REMOVAL & INSTALLATION

1.7L Engine with Manual Transaxle

NOTE: **The engine and manual transaxle must be removed as an assembly.**

1. Disconnect the battery cables, negative first.
2. Matchmark and remove hood.
3. Drain the cooling system.
4. Remove and tag all coolant hoses from the radiator and engine.
5. Remove the radiator and shroud assembly.
6. Remove the air cleaner with hoses.
7. If equipped with A/C, remove the A/C compressor mounting bolts and secure the compressor aside.
8. Disconnect and tag all electrical connections at the alternator, carburetor and engine.
9. Disconnect the fuel line, heater hoses and accelerator cable.
10. Remove the air diverter valve and lines from the air pump, if equipped.
11. Remove the alternator belt and alternator.
12. Raise and support the vehicle safely.
13. Disconnect the axleshafts from the transaxle and secure them to the vehicle and out of the way.

NOTE: **The inner stub axleshafts are retained by constant spring tension. With the outer shaft removed from the hub, the driveshaft can be removed by pulling the assembly from the transaxle; except with the right shaft, which must first have the speedometer gear removed.**

14. Disconnect the exhaust pipe from exhaust manifold.
15. Remove the air pump hoses and lines, if equipped.
16. Remove air pump belt and air pump, if equipped.

17. Disconnect the transaxle linkage.
18. Lower the vehicle.
19. Attach an engine lifting fixture to engine/transaxle assembly.
20. Raise the assembly slightly and remove the front engine mounting bolt.
21. Remove the right engine mounting bolt.
22. Remove the left engine mounting bolt.
23. Lift engine/transaxle assembly from the vehicle.
24. Align the dimple on the flywheel to the indicator before removing transaxle from the engine.
25. Remove transaxle to engine mounting bolts. Remove the transaxle from the engine.

To install:

1. Install the transaxle to the engine. Make sure that the flywheel recess is lined up. The transaxle must be installed to the engine in this position.
2. Install the engine lifting fixture to the engine/transaxle assembly and lower it into the engine compartment.
3. Align the engine mounts and install the mounting bolts. Do not tighten until all three bolts have been loosely installed. Tighten to 40 ft. lbs. with the engine weight on the mounts.
4. Remove the engine lifting fixture.
5. Raise and support the vehicle safely.
6. Install the axleshafts to the transaxle.
7. Connect the transaxle linkage.
8. Install the air pump and pump belt.
9. Connect air pump hoses and lines.
10. Connect the exhaust pipe to the exhaust manifold.
11. Lower the vehicle.
12. Connect the clutch and speedometer cable at the transaxle.
13. Install the alternator and drive belt.
14. Connect the diverter valve and lines to the air pump.
15. Connect the fuel line, heater hose and accelerator cable at the engine.
16. Connect all electrical connections to the engine, carburetor and alternator.
17. Install the air conditioning compressor in the mounts. Tighten the mounting bolts.
18. Install the air cleaner and vacuum hoses.
19. Install radiator and shroud assembly.
20. Fill the cooling system.
21. Install a new oil filter and refill the crankcase with the proper oil to correct level.
22. Align the matchmarks and install the hood.
23. Connect the battery cables.

24. Start and run the engine until it reaches normal operating temperature.
25. Check and/or adjust the ignition timing, carburetor and transaxle linkage, if necessary.

1.7L Engine with Automatic Transaxle

NOTE: **The engine can be removed without removing the automatic transaxle.**

1. Disconnect battery cables, negative first.
2. Matchmark and remove the hood.
3. Drain the cooling system.
4. Remove the coolant hoses from the radiator and engine.
5. Disconnect and plug the transaxle cooling lines.
6. Remove radiator and shroud assembly.
7. Remove the air cleaner with vacuum hoses. Tag the hoses for installation.
8. If equipped with A/C, remove the A/C compressor mounting bolts and support the compressor out of the way.
9. Disconnect and tag all electrical connections at the alternator, carburetor and engine.
10. Disconnect fuel line, heater hose and accelerator cable at the engine.
11. Remove the air diverter valve and lines from the air pump, if equipped.
12. Remove the alternator drive belt and remove the alternator.
13. Remove the upper bell housing bolts.
14. Raise and support the vehicle safely.
15. Remove the left side splash shield.
16. Remove both front wheel assemblies.
17. Remove the right side splash shield.
18. Remove the power steering pump belt and pump from the engine. Support the pump out of the way, without disconnecting the fluid lines.
19. Remove the lower radiator hose from the water pump.
20. Remove the water pump and crankshaft pulleys from the engine.
21. Remove the front engine mounting bolt.
22. Remove the inspection cover from the transaxle. Remove the flywheel bolts.
23. Disconnect and tag the starter motor wiring and remove the starter.
24. Remove all remaining lower bell housing bolts.
25. Lower the vehicle and place an adjustable jack under the transaxle with the vehicle on the ground.

26. Attach an engine lifting fixture to the engine.

27. Remove the oil filter.

28. Remove the right engine mount.

29. Lift and remove the engine from the vehicle.

To install:

1. Lower the engine into the engine compartment.

2. Install, but do not tighten the upper bell housing bolts.

3. Install the right side engine mount.

4. Remove engine lifting fixture. Tighten all mounting bolts.

5. Remove the jack from under the transaxle.

6. Raise and support the vehicle safely. Install the center engine mount.

7. Install flywheel mounting bolts and inspection cover.

8. Install the starter motor and connect the wiring.

9. Install a new oil filter. Refill the engine crankcase with proper oil to correct level.

10. Install the crankshaft and water pump pulleys.

11. Install the power steering pump and drive belt.

12. Lower the vehicle.

13. Install the alternator, connect the wiring and install the drive belt.

14. Install the lower radiator hose.

15. Install the A/C compressor and drive belt, if equipped.

16. Install the upper radiator hose.

17. Connect the fuel line, heater hose and accelerator cable.

18. Connect the hoses to the thermostat housing. Fill the cooling system.

19. Connect the booster vacuum hose to the intake manifold.

20. Connect the carburetor linkage and all electrical connections to the carburetor and engine.

21. Raise and support the vehicle safely. Connect the exhaust pipe to the exhaust manifold.

22. Lower the vehicle and install the air cleaner.

23. Connect the vacuum hoses to the air cleaner.

24. Connect the battery.

25. Align the matchmarks and install the hood.

26. Start and run the engine until it reaches normal operating temperature.

27. Check and/or adjust the ignition timing. Adjust the carburetor, if necessary.

1.6L, 2.2L, 2.5L and 2.6L Engines

1. Disconnect the negative battery cable and all engine ground straps.

2. Mark the hood hinge outline on the hood and remove the hood.

3. Drain the cooling system. Remove the radiator hoses, fan assembly, radiator shroud and radiator.

4. Remove the air cleaner, duct hoses and oil filter.

5. If equipped, remove the A/C compressor and position it out of the way.

6. If equipped, remove the power steering pump mounting bolts and set the pump aside, without disconnecting any fluid lines.

7. Disconnect and tag the electrical connectors from the engine, alternator and carburetor or fuel injection system.

NOTE: If equipped with a fuel injection system, it will be necessary to relieve the pressure in the fuel system before disconnecting the fuel lines.

8. Disconnect the fuel line, heater hoses and accelerator linkage.

9. If equipped, disconnect the air pump lines and remove the pump.

10. Remove the alternator from the engine.

11. Disconnect the shift linkage(s), clutch (M/T only) and speedometer cables.

12. Raise and support the front of the vehicle safely.

13. If equipped with a manual transaxle, perform the following procedures:

 a. Disconnect the clutch cable.

 b. Remove the lower cover from the transaxle case.

 c. Remove the exhaust pipe to exhaust manifold bolts. Separate the pipe from the manifold.

 d. Remove the starter and support it out of the way.

 e. Using a transmission holding tool, secure it to the transaxle.

 f. If equipped, remove the anti-roll strut or damper (turbocharged) from the transaxle.

14. If equipped with an automatic transaxle, perform the following procedures:

 a. Remove the lower cover from the transaxle case.

 b. Remove the exhaust pipe to exhaust manifold bolts. Separate the pipe from the manifold.

 c. Remove the starter and set it aside.

 d. Mark the flex plate to the torque converter, for installation purposes.

 e. Remove the torque converter to flex plate bolts. Separate the converter from the flex plate.

 f. Using a C-clamp, secure the bottom of the torque converter to the transaxle so that it will not fall out.

 g. Using a transmission holding tool, secure it to the transaxle.

15. Attach an engine lifting fixture and vertical lift to the engine.

16. To lower the engine, separate the right side engine bracket from the yoke bracket. To raise the engine, remove the yoke/insulator long bolt.

NOTE: If removing the insulator-to-rail screws, first mark the position of the insulator on the side rail to insure proper alignment during reinstallation.

17. Remove the transaxle to engine bolts, front engine mount nut/bolt and the left insulator through bolt (from inside the wheelhouse) or the insulator bracket-to-transaxle bolts.

18. Lift the engine from the vehicle.

19. To install, reverse the removal procedures. Loosely install all of the mounting bolts. With all bolts installed, tighten the engine-to-mount bolts to 40 ft. lbs.; the engine-to-transaxle bolts to 70 ft. lbs. and the torque converter-to-flex plate bolts to 40 ft. lbs.

20. Refill the cooling system. Start the engine, allow it to reach normal operating temperature. Check for leaks. Check the ignition timing and adjust if necessary. Adjust the idle speed/mixture (if possible) and the transaxle linkage.

3.0L V6 Engine

1. Disconnect the battery cable, negative first.

2. Matchmark and remove the hood.

3. Drain the cooling system.

4. Disconnect and tag all engine electrical connections.

5. Remove the coolant hoses from the radiator and engine.

6. Remove the radiator and cooling fan assembly.

7. Relieve the fuel pressure and disconnect the fuel lines from the engine.

8. Disconnect the accelerator cable from the engine.

9. Remove the air cleaner assembly.

10. Raise and support the vehicle safely. Drain the engine oil.

11. Remove the A/C compressor mounting bolts, remove the drive belt and support the compressor out of the way.

12. Remove the transaxle inspection cover, matchmark the converter to the flexplate and remove the converter bolts. Attach a C-clamp on the bottom of the converter to prevent the converter from falling out.

13. Disconnect the exhaust pipe at the exhaust manifold.

14. Remove the power steering pump mounting bolts and set the pump aside upright, with the fluid lines attached.

15. Remove the lower transaxle to engine mounting bolts.

16. Disconnect and tag the starter motor wiring and remove the starter motor from the engine.

17. Lower the vehicle. Remove and tag the vacuum hoses and engine ground straps.

18. Install a transmission holding fixture.

19. Attach an engine lifting fixture to the engine. Support the engine.

20. Remove the upper transaxle to engine mounting bolts.

21. Separate the engine mounts from the insulators as follows:

    a. Mark the right insulator to the right frame support. Remove the mounting bolts.

    b. Remove the front engine mount through bolt.

    c. Remove the left insulator through bolt, from inside the wheel housing.

    d. Remove the insulator bracket to transaxle bolts.

22. Lift and remove the engine from the vehicle.

To install:

1. Lower the engine into the engine compartment.

2. Align the engine mounts and install the bolts. Do not tighten the bolts until all bolts have been installed. Tighten the through bolts to 75 ft. lbs.

3. Install the upper transaxle to engine mounting bolts and tighten the bolts to 75 ft. lbs.

4. With all mounting bolts tightened, remove the engine lifting fixture from the engine.

5. Raise and support the vehicle safely. Remove the C-clamp from the converter housing.

6. Align the converter marks and install the flex plate to converter bolts. Tighten the bolts to 55 ft. lbs.

7. Install the transaxle inspection cover.

8. Connect the exhaust pipe at the exhaust manifold.

9. Install the starter motor and connect the wiring.

10. Install the power steering pump and A/C compressor. Install and adjust the drive belt tension.

11. Lower the vehicle. Reconnect all vacuum hoses and electrical connections to the engine.

12. Connect the fuel lines and accelerator cable.

13. Install the radiator and fan assembly. Connect the fan motor wiring.

14. Install the radiator hoses and fill the cooling system.

15. Refill the engine with the proper oil to the correct level.

16. Connect the engine ground straps.

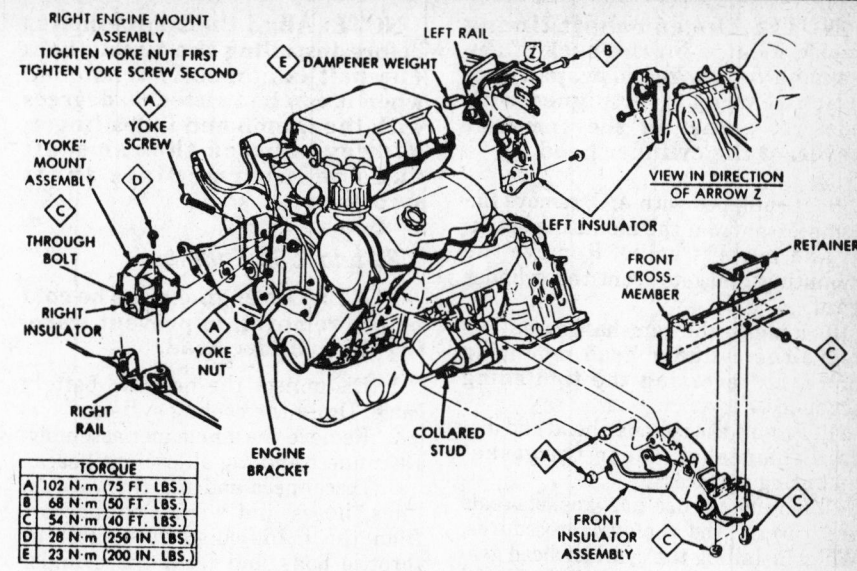

Engine mounting – 3.0L V6 engine

TORQUE	
A	102 N·m (75 FT. LBS.)
B	68 N·m (50 FT. LBS.)
C	54 N·m (40 FT. LBS.)
D	28 N·m (250 IN. LBS.)
E	23 N·m (200 IN. LBS.)

17. Install the hood, aligning the matchmarks.

18. Connect the battery.

19. Start and run the engine until it reaches normal operating temperature.

20. Check for leaks. Adjust the transaxle linkage, if necessary.

Cylinder Head

REMOVAL & INSTALLATION

1.6L Engine

NOTE: The engine must be cold before cylinder head removal, to prevent warping the cylinder head.

1. Remove the valve cover and all necessary vacuum lines. Drain the cooling system.

2. Remove the cylinder head bolts evenly, starting at the ends and working toward the center. The brackets supporting the rocker assembly are located on dowels and are retained by the cylinder head bolts. Only brackets No. 2 and 4 are pinned to the rocker arm shafts.

3. Move and support the end brackets and remove the rocker assembly.

4. Remove the pushrods, noting their position so they can be installed in the same position.

5. Remove the cylinder head from the engine.

6. Clean the cylinder head and engine block gasket surfaces.

NOTE: When installing the head gasket, the word "DESSUS" or "TOP" must be facing upward.

7. To install, use new gaskets and reverse the removal procedures. When installing the cylinder head, tighten the bolts in three steps to 52 ft. lbs.

8. Refill the cooling system.

9. Run the engine until it reaches normal operating temperature. Check for leaks.

10. Allow the engine to cool to normal air temperature. Retorque the cylinder head bolts, as needed.

1.7L Engine

NOTE: The engine must be cold before removal, to prevent warping the cylinder head.

1. Disconnect the negative battery cable. Drain the cooling system.

2. Remove the air cleaner assembly.

3. Disconnect and tag all vacuum lines, hoses and wires from the cylinder head, intake manifold and carburetor. Disconnect the accelerator linkage.

4. Remove the distributor cap.

5. Disconnect the exhaust pipe from the exhaust manifold.

6. Remove the carburetor, intake/exhaust manifolds and the upper portion of the front timing belt cover.

7. Rotate the engine by hand, until the timing sprocket marks are aligned.

8. Loosen the timing belt tensioner and slip the belt off the camshaft sprocket.

FRONT

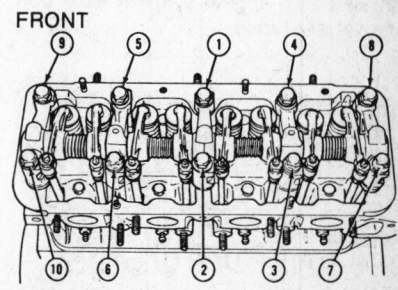

1.6L engine cylinder head bolt torque sequence

NOTE: The camshaft timing mark, located on the back of the camshaft sprocket, is properly positioned when it is aligned with the left corner of the camshaft cover, at the cylinder head.

9. If equipped with A/C, remove the compressor from the mounting bracket and move it aside. Remove the mounting brackets from the cylinder head.

10. Remove the camshaft cover. Remove the cylinder head mounting bolts, by reversing the tightening sequence.

11. Lift off the cylinder head and discard the gasket. Clean the gasket mounting surfaces.

12. To install, use new gaskets/seals and reverse the removal procedures. When installing the cylinder head gasket, make sure the word "OBEN" (top) faces up.

13. When positioning the cylinder head on the engine block, insert bolts No. 8 and 10 to align the cylinder head. Torque the cylinder head bolts in sequence to 30 ft. lbs. Again torque the bolts to 60 ft. lbs. Add another ¼ (90 degree) turn. Refill the cooling system. Start the engine and check for leaks.

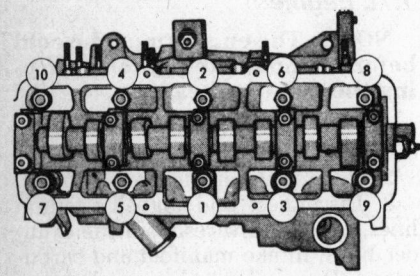

1.7L engine cylinder head bolt torque sequence

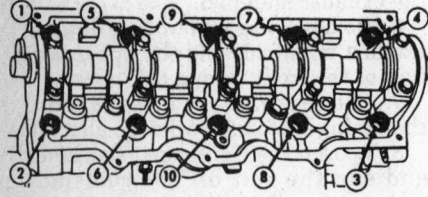

2.2L and 2.5L engine cylinder head bolt removal sequence

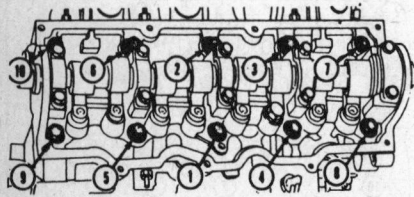

2.2L and 2.5L engine cylinder head bolt torque sequence

NOTE: Align the timing marks before installing the timing belt. The belt is correctly tensioned when it can be twisted 90 degrees with the thumb and index finger, midway between the camshaft and the intermediate shaft sprockets.

2.2L and 2.5L Engines

NOTE: The engine must be cold before removal, to prevent warping the cylinder head.

1. Disconnect the negative battery cable. Drain the cooling system.

2. Remove the air cleaner assembly. Disconnect and tag all coolant hoses.

3. Disconnect and tag the vacuum lines, hoses and wiring connectors from the manifold(s), carburetor or throttle body and from the cylinder head.

4. Disconnect the accelerator linkage, the converter and the exhaust pipe. Remove the intake and exhaust manifolds with the carburetor or throttle body.

5. Remove the upper part of the front timing case cover.

6. Rotate the engine by hand, until the timing marks align (No. 1 piston at TDC).

7. With timing marks aligned, loosen the timing belt tensioner and remove the belt from the camshaft sprocket.

8. If equipped with A/C, remove the compressor mounting brackets and move the compressor aside, with the hoses attached.

9. Remove the valve cover. Remove the cylinder head bolts in the reverse sequence of installation.

10. Remove the cylinder head from the engine block.

11. Clean the cylinder head gasket mounting surfaces.

12. To install, use new gaskets/seals and reverse the removal procedures. Torque the cylinder head bolts, in the sequence to 30 ft. lbs. Again to 45 ft. lbs. With the bolts at 45 ft. lbs., add another ¼ turn (90 degrees).

13. Refill the cooling system. Start the engine and check for leaks.

NOTE: Align the timing marks before installing the timing belt. The belt is correctly tensioned when it can be twisted 90 degrees with the thumb and index finger, midway between the cam and intermediate shaft sprockets.

2.6L Engine

NOTE: The engine must be cold before removal, to prevent warping the cylinder head. In order to

remove the engine front cover, support the engine and remove the motor mount.

1. Disconnect the negative battery cable. Drain the cooling system. Remove the upper radiator and heater hoses.

2. Tag and disconnect the spark plug cables. Remove the carburetor-to-cylinder head cover bracket.

3. Remove the air cleaner, fuel lines, fuel pump and the cylinder head cover.

4. Remove and tag the vacuum hoses and the electrical connectors. Separate the carburetor linkage.

5. Remove the distributor. Remove the water pump belt and the pump pulley.

6. Rotate the crankshaft until the No. 1 piston is at TDC of the compression stroke.

7. Mark the timing chain, in line with the timing mark of the camshaft sprocket.

8. Remove the camshaft sprocket bolt, sprocket, distributor drive gear and air feeder hoses (from under the vehicle).

9. Remove the power steering pump from the mounts and set it aside. Remove the ground wire and dipstick tube.

10. Remove the exhaust manifold heat shield. Separate the manifold from the converter.

11. Remove the cylinder head bolts, by reversing the torquing sequence. The head bolts should be loosened in 2-3 steps, to prevent head warpage.

12. Remove the cylinder head and gasket from the engine.

13. Clean the gasket mating surfaces.

14. To install, use new gaskets and seals and reverse the removal procedures.

15. Install the ten cylinder head bolts. Tighten the cylinder head bolts, in sequence, to 35 ft. lbs. Retighten the bolts to 69 ft. lbs. Tighten the two front (chain case cover) bolts to 11–15 ft. lbs.

16. Align the timing marks and install the timing chain/camshaft sprocket. Torque the camshaft sprocket bolt to 40 ft. lbs.

17. Very slowly, rotate the engine over two times, to make sure the valve timing is correct.

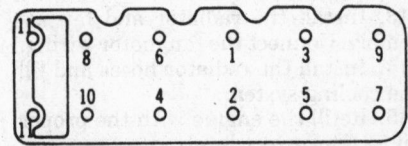

2.6L engine cylinder head bolt torque sequence

18. Fill the cooling system. Start the engine and check for leaks.

3.0L V6 Engine

1. Disconnect the negative battery cable. Drain the cooling system.

2. Remove the A/C compressor or power steering pump, from the mounts and support them out of the way. Remove the serpentine drive belt tensioner.

3. Remove the upper timing belt cover(s) mounting bolts and remove the cover(s).

4. Mark the direction of the timing belt rotation. Mark the relationship between the timing belt and the camshaft sprocket.

5. Loosen the timing belt tensioner enough to slip the timing belt off of the camshaft sprocket.

NOTE: When removing the timing belt from the one camshaft sprocket, make sure that the belt does not come off of the other camshaft sprocket. Support the belt so that the belt can not slip off of the crankshaft sprocket and opposite side camshaft sprocket.

6. Remove the air cleaner assembly. Tag and disconnect the spark plug wire for the right side.

7. Remove the camshaft cover.

8. Install auto lash adjuster retainers (PN MD998443) on the rocker arms.

9. On the right side cylinder head, remove the distributor extension.

10. Remove the rocker arms, rocker shafts and bearing caps as an assembly from the cylinder head.

11. Remove the camshaft from the cylinder head.

12. Remove the upper intake manifold assembly from the engine.

13. On the right side cylinder head, remove the distributor from the engine.

14. Remove the exhaust manifold and cross-over pipe from the cylinder head.

15. Remove the cylinder head mounting bolts in the reverse sequence of tightening.

16. Remove the cylinder head from the engine.

17. Clean the gasket mating surfaces on the engine block and cylinder head.

To install:

1. Install the cylinder head gasket over the dowels on the engine block.

2. Install the cylinder head on the engine.

3. Using the proper sequence, install and tighten the cylinder head bolts gradually, until a final torque of 70 ft. lbs. is reached.

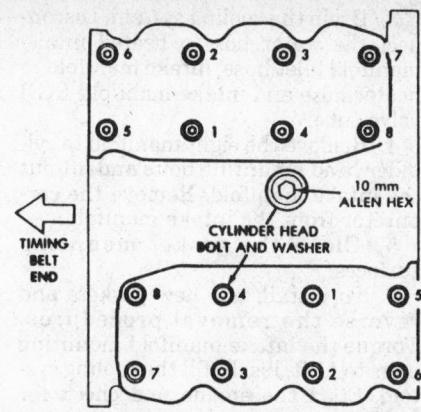

Cylinder head bolt torque sequence—3.0L V6 engine

4. The remainder of the installation is the reverse of the removal procedure.

5. When installing the timing belt over the camshaft sprocket, use care not to allow the belt to slip off of the opposite camshaft sprocket.

6. Check to make sure that the timing belt is installed on the camshaft sprocket in the same position as when removed.

NOTE: If the engine is rotated, or the timing belt is removed from the other sprockets, refer to "Timing Belt, Removal & Installation" to install the timing belt.

OVERHAUL

For all cylinder head overhaul procedures, please refer to "Engine Rebuilding" in the Unit Repair section.

Rocker Arms/Shafts

REMOVAL & INSTALLATION

1.6L Engine

1. Refer to the "Cylinder Head Removal & Installation" procedures in this section, to remove the rocker arm assembly.

2. With the rocker arm assemblies removed from the engine, slide the end brackets, rocker arms and springs from the rocker arm shafts.

NOTE: Store all parts in the order of removal. The rocker arms are assembled in pairs.

3. Inspect all items for wear and/or distortion. Make sure the oil holes are clear.

4. To install, use new gaskets, lubricate the parts and reverse the removal procedures.

1.7L Engine

The 1.7L engine is an OHC design and uses no rocker arms or rocker arm shaft. The camshaft lobes make direct contact with the valve mechanism.

2.2L and 2.5L Engines

1. Remove the PCV module from the rocker cover by turning it counterclockwise.

2. Remove the rocker cover retaining bolts and remove the cover.

3. Rotate the crankshaft until the base circle of the camshaft journal is in contact with the rocker arm.

4. Using the valve spring compression tool No. 4682 or equivalent, depress the valve spring and slide out the rocker arm.

NOTE: Be careful not to dislodge the valve spring retainer locks, when compressing the valve springs.

5. To install, use new gaskets and reverse the removal procedures.

2.6L Engine

1. Remove the carburetor to rocker cover bracket.

2. Remove the rocker cover bolts and remove the cover.

3. Remove the camshaft bearing caps, but do not remove the bolts from the bearing caps.

4. Remove the camshaft bearing/rocker arm assembly from the cylinder head.

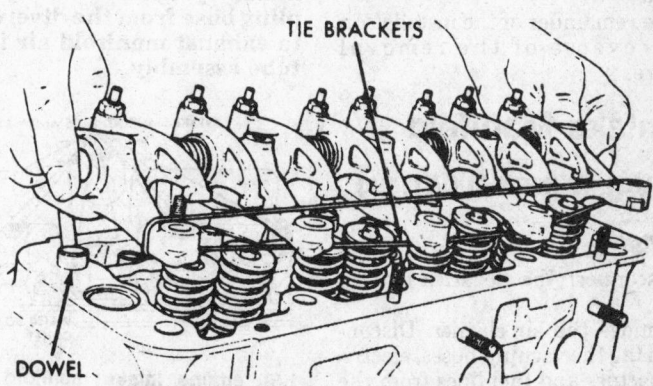

1.6L engine rocker arm and shaft removal

5. Remove the camshaft bearing bolts from the bearing caps. Slide the bearing caps, rocker arms and springs from the rocker arm shafts.

NOTE: Store the rocker arm assembly parts in the correct order of removal. The rocker arms and bearing caps must be installed in the same direction. The left rocker arm shaft has two oil holes at the bottom; the right shaft has four oil holes at the bottom.

6. Check for wear and/or distortion, replace the damaged parts.

7. To install, lubricate the parts, use a new cover gasket and reverse the removal procedures. Starting with the center bearing cap and working toward both ends, tighten the bearing caps to 7 ft. lbs. Retighten the caps to 14 ft. lbs.

3.0L V6 Engine

1. Disconnect the negative battery cable. Remove the air cleaner assembly and valve cover.

2. Install auto lash adjuster retainers (PN MD998443) on the rocker arms.

3. On the right side cylinder head, remove the distributor extension.

4. Remove the camshaft bearing caps, but do not remove the bolts from the caps.

5. Remove the rocker arms, rocker shafts and bearing caps, as an assembly.

6. To install, apply sealant to the ends of the bearing caps.

7. Install the rocker arm/shaft assembly, making sure that the arrow mark on the cap and the arrow mark on the cylinder head are aligned.

8. Tighten the cap bolts to 85 inch lbs. in the following pattern:

    a. No. 3 first, No. 2 second, No. 1 third and No. 4 fourth.

9. Repeat Step 8 and 8a, but increase the torque to 180 inch lbs.

10. Install the distributor adapter on the right side cylinder head, if removed.

11. The remainder of the installation is the reverse of the removal procedure.

Intake Manifold

REMOVAL & INSTALLATION

1.6L Engine

1. Disconnect the negative battery cable.

2. Remove the air cleaner. Disconnect and tag the vacuum hoses, electrical connectors and fuel lines from the carburetor.

3. Drain the cooling system. Disconnect the water box to heated intake manifold inlet hose, intake manifold to heater hose and intake manifold EGR valve tube.

4. Remove the eight manifold to cylinder head mounting bolts and lift out the intake manifold. Remove the carburetor from the intake manifold.

5. Clean the gasket mounting surfaces.

6. To install, use new gaskets and reverse the removal procedures. Torque the intake manifold mounting bolts to 11 ft. lbs. Refill the cooling system. Start the engine and check for leaks.

NOTE: When tightening the intake manifold to cylinder head bolts, start in the center of the manifold and work outward.

2.2L and 2.5L Engines

NOTE: On turbocharged engines, refer to "Turbocharger, Removal & Installation" procedures in this section and remove the turbocharger. After the turbocharger has been removed, remove the intake manifold-to-cylinder head bolts and the intake manifold.

1. Disconnect the negative battery cable. Drain the cooling system.

2. Remove the air cleaner. Disconnect and tag the vacuum lines, electrical connectors. Disconnect the fuel lines from the carburetor, or fuel injection system.

NOTE: If equipped with fuel injection, it will be necessary to relieve the pressure in the fuel system before disconnecting the fuel lines.

3. Disconnect the throttle linkage.

4. Loosen the power steering pump and remove the belt.

5. Remove the power brake vacuum hose from the intake manifold.

NOTE: If equipped with an A.I.R. system, remove the coupling hose from the diverter valve to exhaust manifold air injection tube assembly.

6. Remove the water crossover hoses.

7. Raise and support the vehicle safely. Remove the exhaust pipe to exhaust manifold bolts. Separate the pipe from the manifold.

8. Remove the power steering pump assembly and set it aside in an upright position.

9. Remove the intake manifold support bracket and EGR tube.

NOTE: If equipped with an A.I.R. system, remove the four injection tube bolts and air injection assembly.

10. Remove the intake manifold to cylinder head mounting bolts. Lower the vehicle and remove the intake manifold from the engine.

11. Clean the gasket mating surfaces.

12. To install, use new gaskets and reverse the removal procedures. Torque the intake manifold to cylinder head bolts to 17 ft. lbs. Refill the cooling system. Start the engine and check for leaks.

NOTE: When tightening the intake manifold to cylinder head bolts, start in the center of the manifold and work outward.

2.6L Engine

1. Disconnect the negative battery cable.

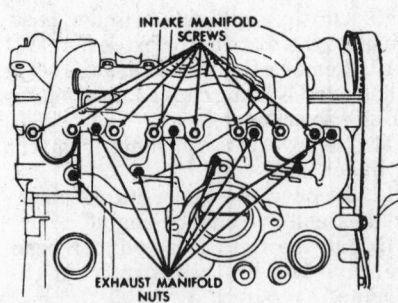

2.2L and 2.5L non-turbo engine intake/exhaust manifold mounting

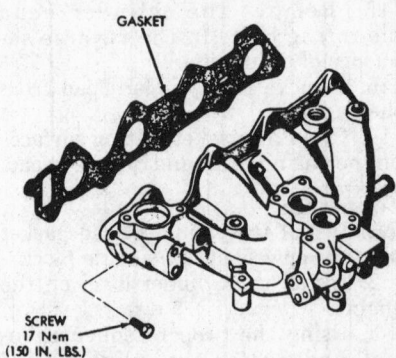

2.6L engine intake manifold mounting

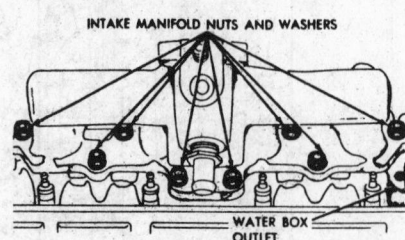

1.6L engine intake manifold mounting bolts

2. Drain the cooling system. Disconnect the water pump to intake manifold hoses.

3. Disconnect the carburetor air horn and set it aside.

4. Disconnect and tag the vacuum hoses and throttle linkage from the carburetor and intake manifold.

5. Disconnect the fuel inlet line at the fuel filter.

6. Remove the fuel filter and fuel pump. Position them out of the way.

7. Remove the intake manifold retaining nuts and remove the manifold. Remove the carburetor from the intake manifold.

8. Clean the gasket mounting surfaces.

9. To install, use new gaskets and reverse the removal procedures. Torque the intake manifold retaining nuts to 12 ft. lbs. Refill the cooling system. Start the engine and check for leaks.

NOTE: When torquing the intake manifold to cylinder head bolts, start in the center of the manifold and work outward.

3.0L V6 Engine

1. Disconnect the negative battery cable. Relieve the fuel system pressure.

2. Drain the cooling system.

3. Remove the throttle body to air cleaner hose.

4. Remove the throttle body and transaxle kickdown linkage.

5. Remove the automatic idle speed (AIS) motor and throttle position sensor (TPS) wiring connectors from the throttle body.

6. Remove and tag the vacuum hose harness from the throttle body.

7. Remove the EGR tube flange from the plenum.

8. Disconnect and tag the charge and temperature sensor wiring at the intake manifold.

9. Remove the vacuum connections from the air intake plenum vacuum connector.

10. Remove the fuel hoses from the fuel rail.

11. Remove the air intake to plenum mounting bolts and remove the plenum.

NOTE: When servicing the engine with the air intake plenum removed, cover the intake manifold holes with a clean cloth when servicing.

12. Remove the vacuum hoses from the fuel rail and pressure regulator.

13. Disconnect the fuel injector wiring harness from the engine wiring harness.

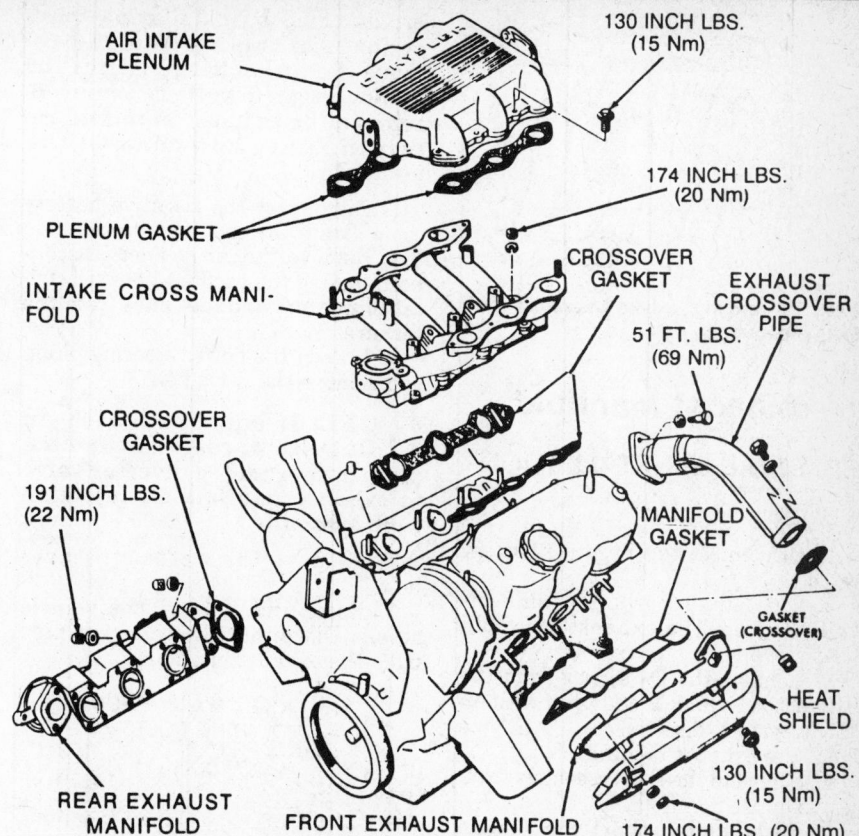

3.0L V6 engine intake and exhaust manifold mounting

14. Remove the fuel pressure regulator mounting bolts and remove the regulator from the fuel rail.

15. Remove the fuel rail mounting bolts and remove the fuel rail from the intake manifold.

16. Separate the radiator hose from the thermostat housing and heater hoses from the heater pipe.

17. Remove the intake manifold mounting bolts and remove the manifold from the engine.

18. Clean the gasket mounting surfaces on the engine and intake manifold.

To install:

1. Using new gaskets, position the intake manifold on the engine and install the mounting nuts and washers.

2. Tighten the nuts in sequence, to 174 inch lbs. (20 Nm).

3. Make sure that the injector holes are clean. Lubricate the injector O-rings with a drop of clean engine oil and install the injector assembly onto the engine.

4. Install and tighten the fuel rail mounting bolts to 115 inch lbs.

5. Install the fuel pressure regulator onto the fuel rail. Tighten the mounting bolts to 95 inch lbs.

6. Install the fuel supply and return tube and the vacuum crossover hold down bolt. Tighten the bolt to 95 inch lbs.

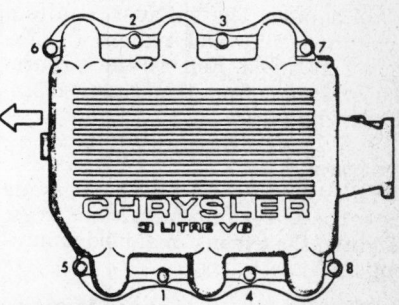

3.0L V6 engine intake plenum bolt torque sequence

7. Connect the fuel injection wiring harness to the engine wiring harness.

8. Connect the vacuum harness to the fuel pressure regulator and fuel rail assembly.

9. Remove the cover from the lower intake manifold and clean the mating surface.

10. Place the intake manifold gasket with the beaded sealant side up, on the intake manifold. Install the air intake plenum and tighten the mounting bolts to 115 inch lbs.

11. The remainder of the installation is the reverse of the removal procedure.

12. When finished, fill the cooling system, connect the negative battery cable, run the engine and check for leaks.

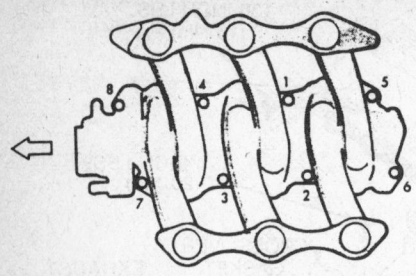

3.0L V6 engine intake manifold bolt torque sequence

Exhaust Manifold

REMOVAL & INSTALLATION

1.6L Engine

1. Disconnect the negative battery cable.

2. Separate the carburetor air heater tube from the exhaust manifold heat stove.

3. Remove the O_2 sensor from the exhaust manifold. If equipped with an A.I.R. system, disconnect the AIR pipe from the exhaust manifold.

4. Separate the EGR assembly from the exhaust manifold.

5. Raise and support the vehicle safely. Remove the exhaust pipe-to-exhaust manifold nuts and separate the pipe from the manifold.

6. Remove the exhaust manifold mounting nuts and remove the exhaust manifold. Remove the carburetor air heater from the exhaust manifold, if necessary.

7. Clean the gasket mating surfaces.

8. To install, use new gaskets and reverse the removal procedures. Tighten the exhaust manifold mounting bolts to 15 ft. lbs.

NOTE: When tightening the manifold bolts, start with the center bolt and work outwards.

2.2L and 2.5L Engines

NOTE: If equipped with a turbocharger, refer to "Turbocharg-

er, Removal & Installation" procedures in this section and remove the turbocharger. After the turbocharger has been removed, remove the exhaust manifold retaining nuts and remove the manifold.

1. Disconnect the negative battery cable. Drain the cooling system.

2. Remove the air cleaner. Disconnect and tag the vacuum lines, electrical connectors and fuel lines from the carburetor.

3. Loosen the power steering pump and remove the drive belt.

NOTE: If equipped with an A.I.R. system, remove the coupling hose from the diverter valve to exhaust manifold air injection tube assembly.

4. Remove the water crossover hoses.

5. Raise and support the vehicle safely. Disconnect the exhaust pipe from the exhaust manifold.

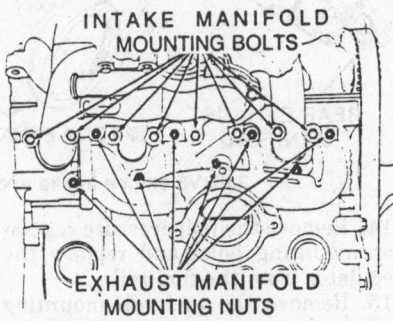

2.2L and 2.5L engine intake and exhaust manifold mounting

6. Remove the power steering pump assembly and set it aside, upright.

7. Remove the intake manifold support bracket and EGR tube.

NOTE: If equipped with an A.I.R. system, remove the four injection tube bolts and air injection assembly.

8. Lower the vehicle. Remove the exhaust manifold nuts and remove the manifold.

9. Clean the gasket mating surfaces.

10. To install, use new gaskets and reverse the removal procedures. Torque the exhaust manifold to 17 ft. lbs. Refill the cooling system. Start the engine and check for leaks.

NOTE: When tightening the exhaust manifold bolts, start with the center bolt and work outwards.

2.6L Engine

1. Disconnect the negative battery cable. Drain the cooling system.

2. Remove the air cleaner.

3. Remove the drive belt from the power steering pump.

4. Raise and support the vehicle safely. Remove the exhaust pipe from the manifold.

5. Disconnect the air injection tube assembly from the exhaust manifold and lower the vehicle.

6. Disconnect the air injection tube assembly from the air pump and move it aside.

7. Remove the power steering pump assembly and move it aside.

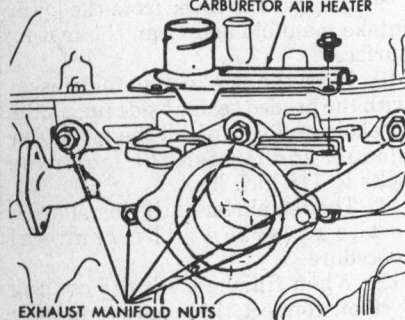

1.6L engine exhaust manifold mounting

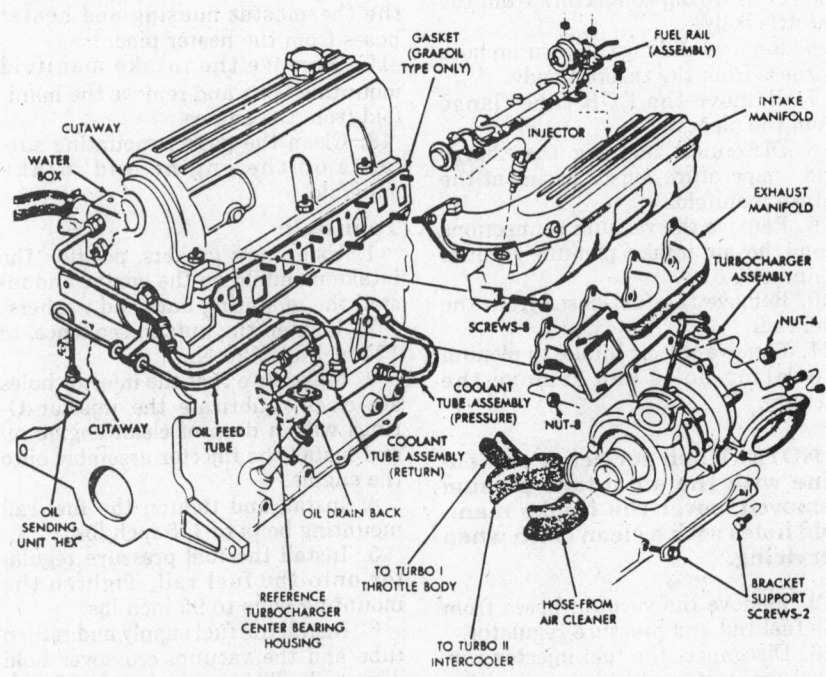

2.2L Turbocharged engine intake and exhaust manifold mounting

8. Remove the heat cowl from the exhaust manifold.

9. Remove the exhaust manifold mounting nuts and remove the manifold assembly.

10. Remove the carburetor air heater from the manifold.

11. Separate the exhaust manifold from the catalytic converter by removing the mounting bolts.

12. Clean the gasket mating surfaces.

13. To install, use a new gasket (coat the cylinder head side lightly with sealer) and reverse the removal procedures. Tighten the exhaust manifold to converter mounting bolts to 24 ft. lbs. and the exhaust manifold mounting nuts to 12 ft. lbs. Refill the cooling system. Start the engine and check for leaks.

NOTE: When tightening the exhaust manifold mounting bolts, start with the center bolt and work outward.

3.0L V6 Engine

1. Disconnect the negative battery cable. Raise and support the vehicle safely.

2. Disconnect the exhaust pipe from the rear exhaust manifold, at the articulated joint.

3. Disconnect the EGR tube from the rear manifold. Disconnect the oxygen sensor wire.

4. Remove the bolts retaining the cross-over pipe to the manifolds.

5. To remove the rear manifold, remove the rear manifold mounting nuts and remove the manifold.

6. To remove the front manifold, lower the vehicle and remove the heat shield from the manifold.

7. Remove the manifold mounting nuts and remove the manifold.

8. To install, clean the gasket mating surfaces, use new gaskets and reverse the removal procedures.

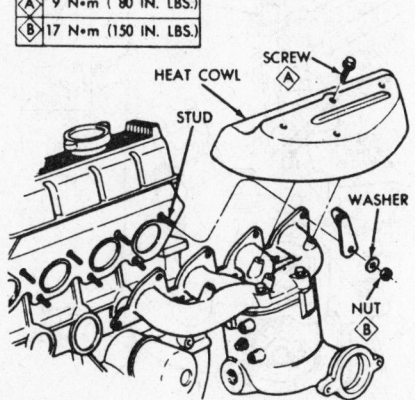

2.6L engine exhaust manifold mounting

NOTE: When installing, the numbers 1-3-5 on the gaskets are used with the rear cylinders and 2-4-6 are on the gasket for the front cylinders.

9. Install the manifold(s) and tighten the mounting nuts to 175 inch lbs.

10. Tighten the exhaust cross-over nuts to 51 ft. lbs. and the exhaust manifold to pipe nuts to 250 inch lbs.

11. When finished, run the engine and check for exhaust leaks.

Combination Manifold

REMOVAL & INSTALLATION

1.7L Engine

1. Disconnect the negative battery cable.

2. Remove the air cleaner. Disconnect and tag the vacuum lines, electrical connectors and fuel line from the carburetor.

3. Remove the throttle linkage.

4. Remove the power brake hose from the intake manifold.

5. Raise and support the vehicle safely. Remove the exhaust pipe from the exhaust manifold.

6. Remove the power steering pump and set it out of the way, upright.

7. Remove the intake/exhaust manifold mounting nuts.

8. Lower the vehicle. Remove the carburetor and intake/exhaust manifold assembly.

9. Remove the carburetor and separate the intake and exhaust manifolds.

10. Clean the gasket mounting surfaces.

11. To install, use new gaskets and reverse the removal procedures. Install a new gasket between the manifolds, assemble but DO NOT tighten the fasteners. Coat the manifold-to-cylinder head gaskets with sealer, assemble and torque the nuts/screws to 10–15 inch lbs. Torque the inboard manifold nuts to 12 ft. lbs. and the outboard nuts to 17 ft. lbs. Torque the manifolds-to-cylinder head nuts and screws to 17 ft. lbs.

NOTE: When tightening the exhaust manifold to cylinder head nuts, start with the center nut and work outward.

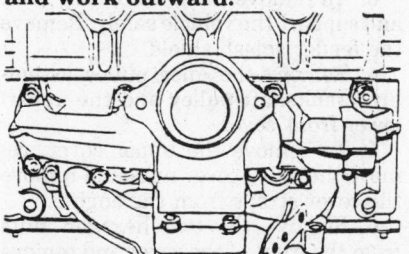

1.7L engine intake and exhaust manifold mounting

Turbocharger

Turbochargers are only available on the 1984–89 2.2L engine.

REMOVAL & INSTALLATION

2.2L Turbocharged Engines

1. Disconnect the negative battery cable. Drain the cooling system.

2. Disconnect the exhaust pipe from the turbocharger and the oxygen sensor electrical connector.

3. Remove the turbocharger to engine support bracket.

4. Loosen the oil drain back hose clamps and slide the hose down on the engine nipple.

5. Disconnect the turbocharger coolant tube nut at the engine outlet (below the power steering pump bracket) and the support bracket.

6. Remove the air cleaner assembly, throttle body adaptor, hose, air cleaner box and bracket.

7. Disconnect the accelerator linkage. Disconnect and tag the throttle body electrical connector and vacuum hoses.

8. Loosen the throttle body to turbocharger inlet hose clamps.

9. Remove the three throttle body to intake manifold screws and remove the throttle body.

10. Loosen the turbocharger discharge hose end clamp ONLY. The center band retains the deswirler and must not be removed.

11. At the fuel rail, remove the hose retainer bracket screw, four intake bracket screws from the intake manifold and the two bracket to heat shield bracket clips. Lift the fuel rail (with the injectors, wiring harness and fuel lines intact) up and secure out of the way.

12. Disconnect the oil feed line from the turbocharger bearing housing.

13. Remove the three heat shield-to-intake manifold screws and the heat shield.

14. Disconnect the coolant return tube and hose assembly from the turbocharger and the water box. Remove the tube support bracket from the cylinder head and the assembly.

15. Remove the four turbocharger to exhaust manifold nuts. Lift the turbocharger off the studs, push down towards the passenger side, lift up and out of the engine compartment.

16. Clean the gasket mounting surfaces.

17. To install, use new gaskets and reverse the removal procedures.

NOTE: Before installing the turbocharger assembly, be sure that it is first charged with oil.

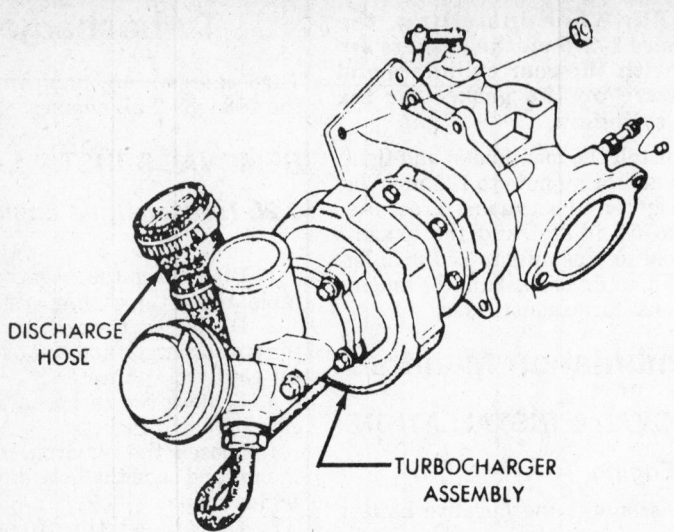

Turbocharger assembly used with 1984– 89 2.2L turbo engines

Failure to do this may cause damage to the turbocharger assembly.

TROUBLESHOOTING

For more information on Turbocharging, please refer to "Turbocharging" in the Unit Repair Section.

Front Cover

REMOVAL & INSTALLATION

1.6L Engine

1. Remove the air pump and alternator drive belts. Remove the air pump mounting bracket.
2. Raise and support the vehicle safely. Remove the right inner splash shield.
3. Remove the crankshaft pulley bolt and washer. Remove the pulley.
4. Drain the cooling system through the water pump drain plug. Remove the water pump to front cover hose.

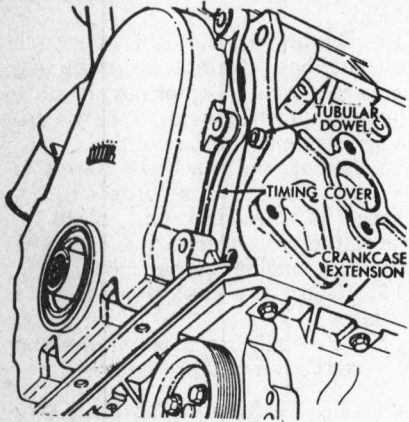

1.6L engine timing chain cover

5. Slightly raise and carefully support the front cover end of the engine.
6. Remove the bolts securing the engine mount bracket to the front cover and engine block.
7. Remove the two crankcase extension to front cover and front cover to engine block screws. Remove the front cover.

NOTE: When removing the front cover, make sure that the two front cover to engine screws, passing through the tubular locating dowels, do not fall into the crankcase extension.

8. Clean the gasket mating surfaces.
9. To install, use a new gasket and reverse the removal procedures. Torque the front cover to engine bolts to 9 ft. lbs. (6mm) or to 15 ft. lbs. (8mm). Torque the crankshaft pulley bolt to 110 ft. lbs.

1.7L Engine

1. Disconnect the negative battery cable.
2. Without disconnecting any hoses, remove the A/C compressor, alternator, power steering pump and the drive belts. Support them out of the way.
3. To remove the lower cover, raise and support the vehicle safely. Remove the fender splash shield.
4. Remove the idler pulley assembly, crankshaft pulley and the upper/lower front cover.
5. To remove the upper cover, remove the valve cover nuts and remove the cover straps from the engine.
6. Remove the two hexagon nuts from the front of the cover and remove the cover.

NOTE: After removing the upper cover, note the position of the spacers between the cover and the engine. Install in the same position.

7. To install, reverse the removal procedures.

2.2L and 2.5L Engine

1. If equipped with A/C, remove the mounting bracket bolts and move the compressor aside. Remove the water pump and power steering pump drive belts.

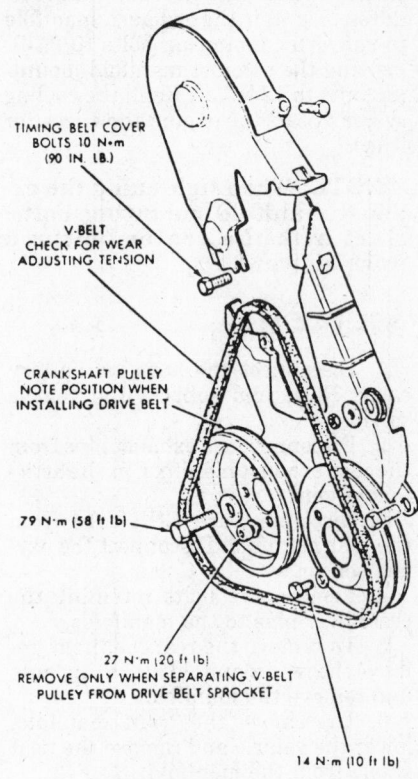

1.7L engine timing belt covers

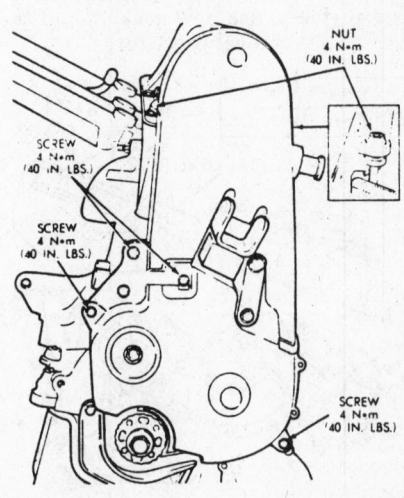

2.2L and 2.5L engine timing belt covers

2. Remove the crankshaft pulley bolt and remove the pulley.

3. Remove the upper and lower timing belt covers.

4. Installation is the reverse of the removal procedures. Tighten the front cover to engine bolts to 40 inch lbs. and the crankshaft pulley bolt to 21 ft. lbs.

2.6L Engine

1. Disconnect the negative battery cable.

2. Remove the alternator, alternator bracket and drive belt.

3. If equipped with A/C, remove the compressor bracket and move it aside.

4. Remove the power steering pump bracket and move the pump aside.

5. Remove the distributor retaining nut, remove the distributor and move it aside.

6. Raise and support the vehicle safely. Remove the right inner splash shield. Remove the crankshaft pulley bolt and remove the pulley.

7. Lower the vehicle and support the engine. Remove the right side engine mounting bolt and raise the engine slightly.

8. Remove the dip stick tube. Drain the engine oil. Remove the oil pan screws, oil pan and screen.

9. Remove the air cleaner. Disconnect and tag the spark plug wires and cylinder head vacuum hose connections.

10. Remove the valve cover screws and remove the cover.

11. At the front of the engine, remove the timing indicator plate and engine mounting plate screws.

12. Remove the front cover screws and remove the cover.

13. Clean the gasket mating surfaces.

14. To install, use a new gaskets and reverse the removal procedures. Torque the front cover to engine bolts to 13 ft. lbs. and the crankshaft pulley bolt to 87 ft. lbs.

15. Fill the engine oil to the correct level.

3.0L V6 Engine

1. Disconnect the negative battery cable.

2. Remove the serpentine drive belt(s) from all engine accessories.

3. Remove the A/C compressor, power steering pump and alternator from the mounts. Support them out of the way.

4. Raise and support the vehicle safely. Remove the right inner fender splash shield.

5. Remove the crankshaft pulley bolt and remove the pulley and damper from the crankshaft.

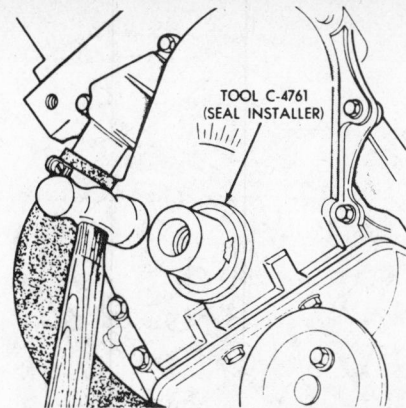

1.6L engine front crankshaft oil seal installation

6. Lower the vehicle and place and adjustable support under the engine.

7. Separate the front engine mount insulator from the bracket. Raise the engine slightly and remove the mount bracket.

8. Remove the outer cover bolts and remove the front and rear covers from the engine.

9. To install, reverse the removal procedures. Tighten the front cover mounting bolts to 115 inch lbs., the engine mount to engine block bolts to 35 ft. lbs., the insulator to frame bolts to 250 inch lbs. and the engine mount through bolt to 75 ft. lbs.

NOTE: The engine mount through bolt must be tightened to 75 ft. lbs. with the engine support removed and the engine's weight on the mount.

OIL SEAL REPLACEMENT

1.6L Engine

1. Remove the air pump and alternator drive belts. Remove the air pump mounting bracket.

2. Raise and support the vehicle safely. Remove the right inner splash shield.

3. Remove the crankshaft pulley bolt and washer. Remove the pulley.

4. Install the seal remover tool C–748 or equivalent, over the crankshaft nose and turn, tightly into the seal.

5. Tighten the thrust screw to remove the seal.

NOTE: If the front cover is removed from the engine, tap the side of the thrust screw to remove the seal.

6. Using the oil seal installation tool No. C-4761 or equivalent, drive the new seal into the front cover.

7. To complete the installation, reverse the removal procedures. Tighten the crankshaft pulley bolt to 110 ft. lbs.

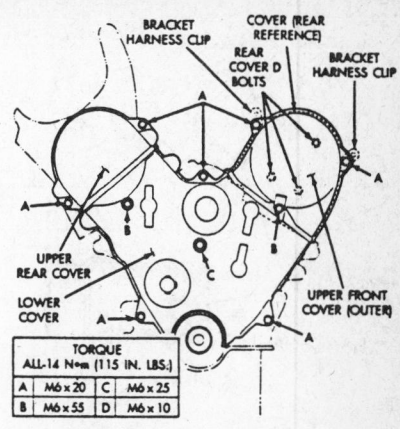

3.0L V6 engine timing belt covers

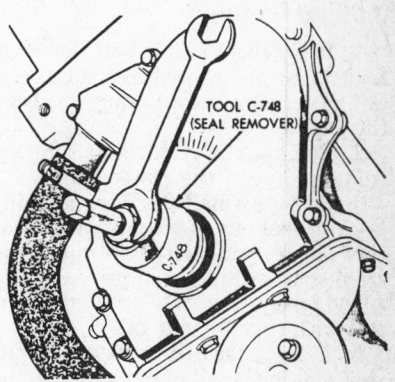

1.6L engine crankshaft oil seal removal

2.6L Engine
COVER INSTALLED

1. Refer to the ''Front Cover, Removal and Installation'' procedures in this section and remove the crankshaft pulley.

2. Using a small pry bar, pry the oil seal from the front cover. Use care not to damage the crankshaft sealing surface.

3. To install, lubricate the seal lips with clean engine oil. Drive the seal into the front cover with a seal driver tool, until it seats in the cover.

4. To complete the installation, reverse the removal procedures. Tighten the crankshaft pulley bolt to 87 ft. lbs.

COVER REMOVED

1. Using a drift punch, remove the oil seal from the front cover.

2. To install, lubricate the seal lips with clean engine oil. Drive the seal into the front cover using a seal driver tool, until it seats in the cover.

3. To complete the installation, use a new gasket and reverse the removal procedures.

4. Tighten the front cover bolts to 13 ft. lbs. and the crankshaft pulley bolt to 87 ft. lbs.

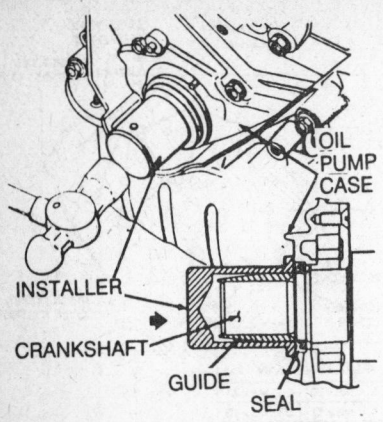

3.0L V6 engine front crankshaft oil seal installation

3.0L V6 Engine

1. Refer to "Timing Belt, Removal & Installation" procedures in this section and remove the timing belt from the engine.
2. Remove the crankshaft sprocket from the end of the crankshaft.
3. Using a small pry bar, carefully pry the seal out of the oil pump. Use care not to damage the oil pump and crankshaft sealing surfaces.
4. Lightly coat the lip of the new seal with clean engine oil.
5. Using a seal driver, install the new seal in the oil pump, with the lip facing the engine.
6. Install the crankshaft sprocket on the engine.
7. Refer to "Timing Belt, Removal & Installation" procedures and install the timing belt, front covers and engine accessories on the engine.
8. The remainder of the installation is the reverse of the removal procedure.

Timing Chain and Sprockets

CHECKING

1.6L Engine

1. Refer to the "Front Cover, Removal & Installation" procedures in this section and remove the front cover and discard the gasket.
2. Hold a ruler with the edge of a chain link.
3. Using a torque wrench and socket (installed on the top bolt), apply torque in the direction of the crankshaft rotation to take up the slack, to 30 ft. lbs. with the cylinder head installed or 15 ft. lbs. with the cylinder head removed. Do not allow the crankshaft to rotate during this procedures.
4. Clean the gasket mating surfaces.

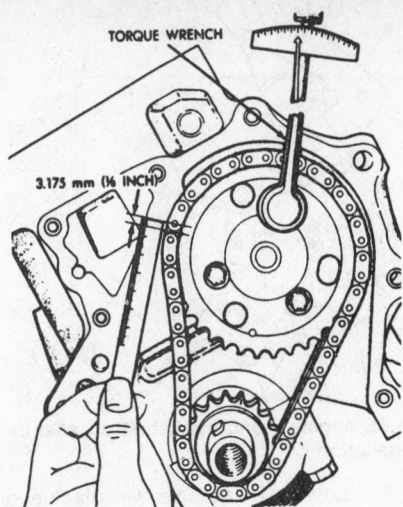

On 1.6L engines, measure the timing chain stretch and wear

5. Apply the same torque as specified above, in the reverse direction and note the amount of chain movement. If the chain movement exceeds 1/8 in., a new chain should be installed.

REMOVAL & INSTALLATION

1.6L Engine

1. Refer to the "Front Cover, Removal and Installation" procedures in this section and remove the front cover.
2. Rotate the camshaft sprocket so that one of the three bolt heads is located at the top of a centerline drawn through the camshaft and crankshaft sprockets.
3. Check the timing chain for excessive wear and/or stretch. Replace, if necessary.
4. Remove the timing gear bolts, timing gear and chain. Clean the gasket mating surfaces.
5. To install the camshaft sprocket and the timing chain, align the mark(s) on the crankshaft sprocket with the hole in the camshaft sprocket. Align the camshaft sprocket to the camshaft and install the bolts. Tighten the camshaft sprocket bolts to 9 ft. lbs.

NOTE: If the crankshaft sprocket has two marks (side by side), align the camshaft sprocket between the two marks.

6. To complete the installation, apply sealer to the new front cover gasket and reverse the removal procedures. Tighten the front cover bolts to 9 ft. lbs. (6mm) and 15 ft. lbs. (8mm). Tighten the crankshaft pulley bolt to 110 ft. lbs.

2.6L Engine

NOTE: The 2.6L engine is equipped with two balance shafts which cancel the vertical vibrating force of the engine and the secondary vibrating forces, which include the sideways rocking of the engine due to the turning direction of the crankshaft and other rolling parts. The timing sprockets are linked by a duplex chain. The balance shaft chain assembly is mounted in the front of the timing chain assembly. The balance chain assembly must be removed to service the timing chain assembly.

1. Refer to the "Front Cover, Removal and Installation" procedures in this section and remove the front cover.
2. From the "Balance Shaft" chain system, remove the three chain guides: side (A), top (B) and bottom (C).
3. Remove the two sprocket screws, crankshaft sprocket, silent shaft sprockets and drive chain.
4. Remove the camshaft sprocket and the distributor drive gear. Remove the camshaft sprocket holder and the right/left chain guides.
5. Depress the tensioner and remove the drive chain, crankshaft and camshaft sprockets.
6. Clean the gasket mating surfaces. Inspect the parts for damage or wear and replace, if necessary.

To install:

1. Position the dowel pin of the camshaft sprocket end, at the top.
2. Install the camshaft sprocket holder and the right and left chain guides.
3. Rotate the crankshaft until the No. 1 piston is at TDC of the compression stroke.
4. Install the tensioner spring and shoe to the oil pump body.
5. Install the timing chain on the camshaft and the crankshaft sprockets.

NOTE: Align the punch marks of the sprockets with the plated links of the timing chain.

6. With timing marks aligned, slide the camshaft sprocket onto the camshaft dowel pin and the crankshaft sprocket onto the crankshaft keyway.
7. At the camshaft sprocket, install the distributor gear dowel pin, distributor gear, washer and camshaft bolt. Tighten the camshaft sprocket bolt to 40 ft. lbs.
8. Install the balance shaft chain drive pulley on the crankshaft.
9. Install the balance chain to the oil pump and the balance shaft sprock-

ets. Align the crankshaft sprocket to the balance chain.

NOTE: Align the punch marks of the sprockets with the plated links of the balance chain.

10. Tighten the screws of the oil pump and balance shaft sprockets to 25 ft. lbs. Loosely install the three balance chain guides.

11. Tighten the bolts of the balance chain guides (A) and (C), to 13 ft. lbs. Shake the oil pump and balance shaft sprockets to gain the chain slack at point "P" (midway between the two sprockets).

12. Adjust the balance chain guide B so that 0.040–0.140 in. of clearance exists between the center of the chain guide and the chain. Tighten the bolt to 13 ft. lbs.

13. To complete the installation, apply sealant to the new gaskets and reverse the removal procedures. Tighten the oil pan bolts to 4 ft. lbs. and the two cylinder head and front cover bolts to 13 ft. lbs.

Silent Shafts and Sprockets

2.6L Engine

NOTE: 2.6L engines are equipped with two "Silent Shafts" which cancel the vertical vibrating force of the engine and the secondary vibrating forces, which include the sideways rocking of the engine due to the turning direction of the crankshaft and other rolling parts. The shafts are driven by a duplex chain and are turned by the crankshaft. The silent shaft chain assembly is mounted in front of the timing chain assembly and must be removed to service the timing chain.

1. Disconnect the negative battery cable.

2. Drain the cooling system and remove the radiator from the vehicle.

3. Refer to "Cylinder Head, Removal & Installation" and remove the cylinder head.

4. Remove the cooling fan, spacer, water pump pulley and belt.

5. Remove the alternator and water pump.

6. Raise and support the vehicle safely.

7. Remove the oil pan and screen. Remove the crankshaft pulley.

8. Remove the timing case cover.

9. Remove the chain guides, side (A), top (B), bottom (C), from the "B" chain (outer).

10. Remove the locking bolts from the "B" chain sprockets.

11. Remove the crankshaft sprocket, silent shaft sprocket and the outer chain.

12. Remove the crankshaft and camshaft sprockets and the timing chain.

13. Remove the camshaft sprocket holder and the chain guides, both left and right.

14. Remove the tensioner.

15. Remove the sleeve from the oil pump. Remove the oil pump by first removing the bolt locking the oil pump driven gear and the right silent shaft, then remove the oil pump mounting bolts. Remove the silent shaft from the engine block.

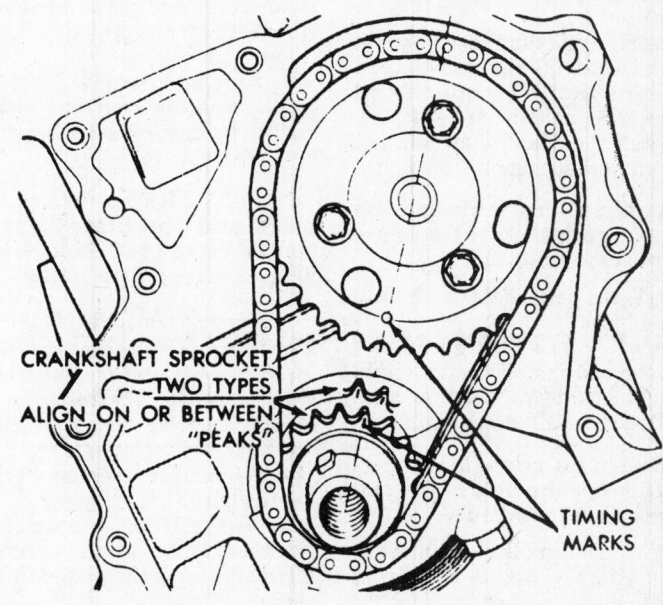

CRANKSHAFT SPROCKET TWO TYPES ALIGN ON OR BETWEEN "PEAKS"

TIMING MARKS

1.6L engine timing chain and sprocket alignment marks

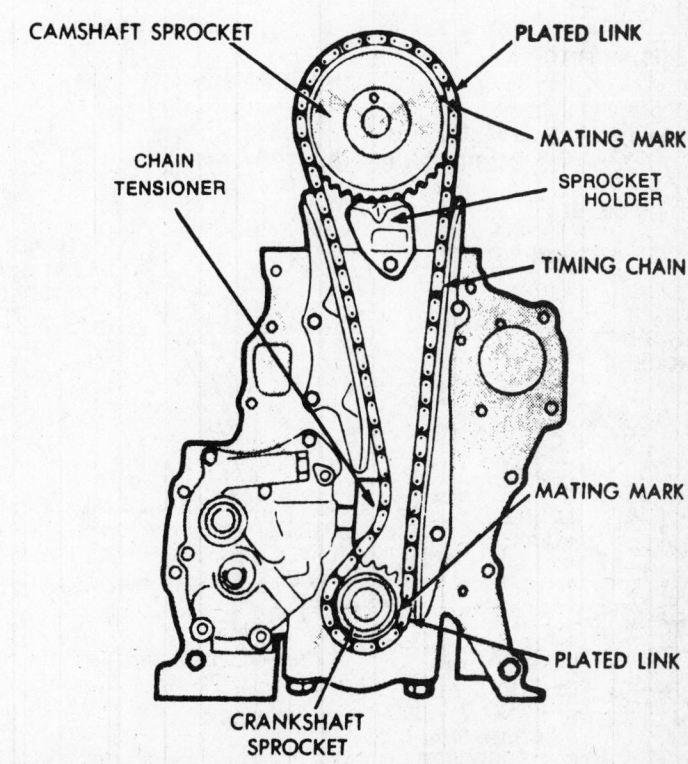

CAMSHAFT SPROCKET

CHAIN TENSIONER

PLATED LINK

MATING MARK

SPROCKET HOLDER

TIMING CHAIN

MATING MARK

PLATED LINK

CRANKSHAFT SPROCKET

2.6L engine timing chain installation. Align the plated links on the timing chain with the mating marks on the camshaft and crankshaft sprockets

NOTE: If the bolt locking the oil pump and the silent shaft is hard to loosen, remove the oil pump and the shaft as a unit.

16. Remove the left silent shaft thrust washer and take the shaft from the engine block.

To install:

1. Install the right silent shaft into the engine block.

2. Install the oil pump assembly. Do not lose the woodruff key from the end of the silent shaft. Torque the oil pump mounting bolts from 6–7 ft. lbs.

3. Tighten the silent shaft and the oil pump driven gear mounting bolt.

NOTE: The silent shaft and the oil pump can be installed as a unit, if necessary.

4. Install the left silent shaft into the engine block.

5. Install a new O-ring on the thrust plate and install the unit into the engine block, using a pair of bolts without heads, as alignment guides.

NOTE: If the thrust plate is turned to align the bolt holes, the O-ring may be damaged.

6. Remove the guide bolts and install the regular bolts into the thrust plate and tighten securely.

7. Rotate the crankshaft to bring No. 1 piston to TDC.

8. Install the cylinder head.

9. Install the sprocket holder and the right and left chain guides.

10. Install the tensioner spring and sleeve on the oil pump body.

11. Install the camshaft and crankshaft sprockets on the timing chain, aligning the sprocket punch marks to the plated chain links.

12. While holding the sprocket and chain as a unit, install the crankshaft sprocket over the crankshaft and align it with the keyway.

13. Keeping the dowel pin hole on the camshaft in a vertical position, install the camshaft sprocket and chain on the camshaft.

NOTE: The sprocket timing mark and the plated chain link should be at 2 to 3 o'clock position when correctly installed.

————— CAUTION —————

The chain must be aligned in the right and left chain guides with the tensioner pushing against the chain. The tension for the inner chain is determined by spring tension.

14. Install the crankshaft sprocket for the outer or "B" chain.

15. Install the two silent shaft sprockets and align the punched mating marks with the plated links of the chain.

16. Holding the two shaft sprockets and chain, install the outer chain in alignment with the mark on the crank-

shaft sprocket. Install the shaft sprockets on the silent shaft and the oil pump driver gear. Install the lock bolts and recheck the alignment of the punch marks and the plated links.

17. Temporarily install the chain guides, Side (A), Top (B) and Bottom (C).

18. Tighten Side (A) chain guide securely.

19. Tighten Bottom (B) chain guide securely.

20. Adjust the position of the Top (B) chain guide, after shaking the right and left sprockets to collect any chain slack, so that when the chain is moved toward the center, the clearance between the chain guide and the chain links will be approximately $9/64$ in. Tighten the Top (B) chain guide bolts.

21. Install the timing chain cover using a new gasket, being careful not to damage the front seal.

22. Install the oil screen and the oil pan, using a new gasket. Torque the bolts to 4.5–5.5 ft. lbs.

23. Install the crankshaft pulley, alternator and accessory belts, and the distributor.

24. Install the oil pressure switch, if removed, and install the battery ground cable.

25. Install the fan blades, radiator, fill the system with coolant and start the engine.

Timing Belt and Tensioner

ADJUSTMENT

1.7L Engine

1. Refer to the "Front Cover, Removal and Installation" procedures in this section and remove the front cover.

2. Remove the spark plugs and rotate the crankshaft until the No. 1 piston is at the TDC position.

3. Place belt tensioning tool No. L–4502 or equivalent, horizontally on

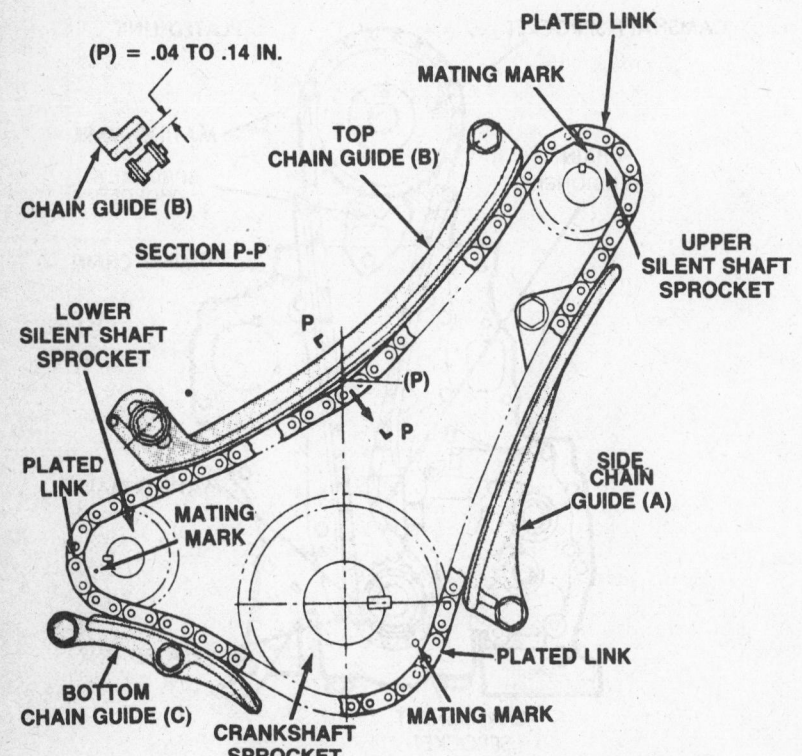

2.6L engine silent shaft chain and sprockets alignment marks

1.7L engine timing belt tension adjustment

the large hex of the timing belt tensioner pulley. Loosen the tensioner lock nut.

4. Reset the belt tensioning tool No. L–4502 or equivalent. Index if necessary, to have the axis within 15 degrees of horizontal.

5. Turn the engine crankshaft clockwise from TDC, two revolutions to TDC.

6. Tighten the locknut to 32 ft. lbs.

7. To complete the installation, reverse the removal procedures.

2.2L and 2.5L Engine

1. Refer to the "Front Cover, Removal and Installation" procedures in this section and remove the front covers.

2. While holding the large hex wrench on the tension pulley, loosen the pulley nut.

3. Adjust the tensioner by turning the large tensioner hex to the right.

NOTE: The tension is correct when the belt can be twisted 90 degrees with the thumb and finger midway between the camshaft and the intermediate pulleys.

4. Tighten the tensioner locknut to 32 ft. lbs.

5. To complete the installation, reverse the removal procedures. Torque the front cover bolts to 40 inch lbs. and the crankshaft pulley bolt to 21 ft. lbs.

3.0L V6 Engine

NOTE: The 3.0L V6 engine is equipped with a spring-loaded timing belt tensioner. The tensioner will compensate in either direction as necessary. No adjustments are possible. If the timing belt is loose and the tensioner is out of it's travel range, check the condition of the belt, tensioner and/or tensioner spring.

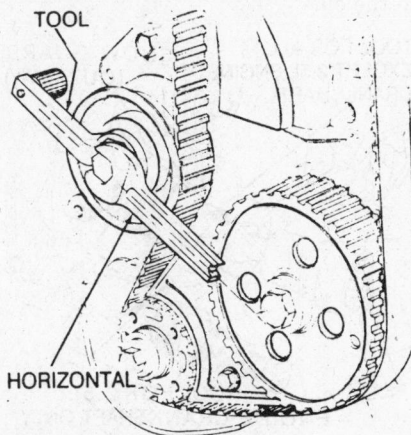

2.2L and 2.5L engine timing belt tension adjustment

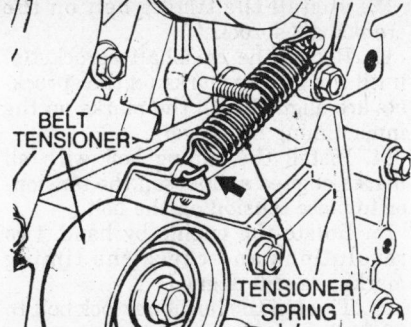

3.0L V6 engine timing belt tensioner and spring installation

REMOVAL & INSTALLATION

1.7L Engine

1. Refer to the "Front Cover, Removal and Installation" procedures in this section and remove the upper and lower covers.

2. Lower the vehicle and place a support under the engine.

3. Remove the right side engine mounting bolt and raise the engine slightly.

4. Loosen the timing belt tensioner and remove the timing belt.

NOTE: If reinstalling the timing belt, be sure to install it in the same direction of rotation.

5. To install, turn the crankshaft and intermediate sprockets until both markings on the sprockets are aligned.

6. Turn the camshaft sprocket until the mark on the sprocket is aligned with the valve cover.

7. Install the timing belt and adjust the tension.

8. To complete the installation, reverse the removal procedures. Adjust the timing belt tension.

NOTE: If a whirring noise is heard from the timing belt with the engine running, the belt is too tight.

2.2L and 2.5L Engine

1. Refer to the "Front Cover, Removal & Installation" procedures in this section and remove the front covers.

2. While holding the large hex wrench on the tension pulley, loosen the pulley nut.

3. Remove the timing belt from the tensioner.

4. Slide the belt off the three toothed sprockets.

5. Using the larger bolt on the crankshaft pulley, turn the engine until the No. 1 cylinder is at TDC of the compression stroke. At this point the valves for the No. 1 cylinder will be closed and the timing mark will be

aligned with the pointer on the flywheel housing. Make sure the arrows on the camshaft sprocket are aligned with the camshaft cap/cylinder head line.

6. Verify that the dot mark on the crankshaft pulley aligns with the line mark on the intermediate shaft.

7. Install the timing belt on the toothed sprockets.

8. Adjust the timing belt tension.

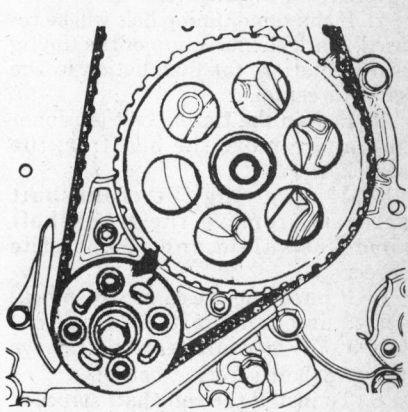

1.7L engine crankshaft and intermediate shaft sprockets alignment marks

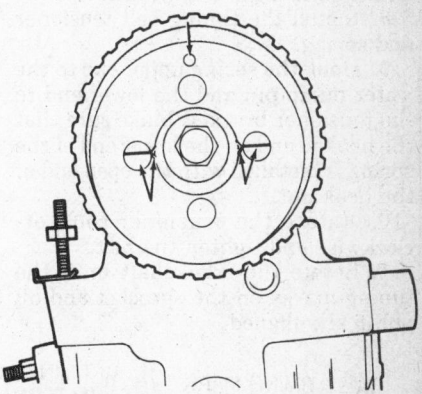

2.2L and 2.5L engines camshaft timing marks alignment

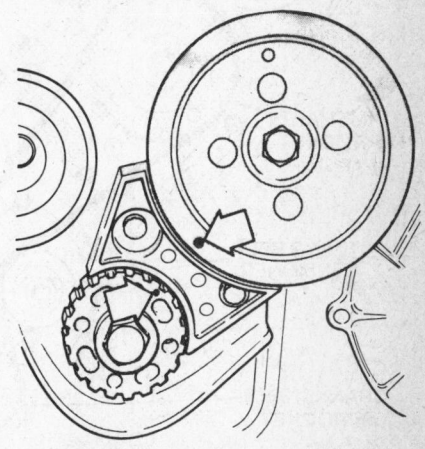

2.2L and 2.5L engines crankshaft and intermediate shaft timing mark alignment

9. To complete the installation, reverse the removal procedures. Tighten the tensioner locknut to 32 ft. lbs., the front cover-to-engine bolts to 40 inch lbs. and the crankshaft pulley bolt to 21 ft. lbs. Check the ignition timing.

3.0L V6 Engine

1. Refer to "Front Cover, Removal & Installation" and remove the front covers from the engine.

2. If the same timing belt will be reused, mark the direction of the timing belt's rotation, for installation in the same direction.

3. Loosen the timing belt tensioner bolt and remove the belt from the sprockets.

4. If removing the crankshaft sprocket, remove the crankshaft sprocket shield and remove the sprocket.

5. If removing the camshaft sprocket(s), use camshaft holding tool MB990775 or equivalent and remove the camshaft sprocket bolt(s).

6. To install the camshaft sprocket, hold the camshaft with tool MB990775 or equivalent and tighten the bolt to 70 ft. lbs.

7. Install the crankshaft sprocket and shield on the crankshaft.

8. Install the timing belt tensioner and spring.

9. Hook the spring upper end to the water pump pin and the lower end to the tensioner bracket. Make sure that the hooked end on the lower end of the spring is installed with the open end of the hook out.

10. Rotate the tensioner counterclockwise and tighten the bolt.

11. Rotate the crankshaft until the timing marks on the sprocket and oil pump are aligned.

12. Install the timing belt on the crankshaft sprocket.

13. Rotate the camshaft sprocket(s) until the timing marks on the sprockets are aligned with the marks on the inner timing belt covers.

14. Install the timing belt with all marks aligned and loosen the tensioner to place tension on the belt.

15. Rotate the engine by hand, two revolutions and check the timing marks are still aligned.

16. Tighten the tensioner lock bolt to 23 ft. lbs.

17. Install the timing belt covers, engine bracket, insulator, crankshaft pulley, accessories and drive belt.

Timing Sprockets

REMOVAL & INSTALLATION

1.7L Engine

The camshaft, intermediate shaft and crankshaft sprockets are located by keys on their respective shafts. Each sprocket is retained by a bolt. Remove the center bolts and pull the sprockets off of the shafts.

1. Refer to the "Front Cover and Belt Removal & Installation" procedures in this section and remove the timing belt.

2. Remove the crankshaft sprocket bolt. Using tool No. L–4524 or equivalent, on the crankshaft sprocket, pull the sprocket from the crankshaft.

3. Remove the crankshaft key. Using the oil seal removal tool No. L–4424 or equivalent, pry the oil seal from the crankshaft.

4. Using the seal installer tool No. L–4422 or equivalent, drive the new oil seal into the crankshaft housing.

5. To complete the installation, use new gaskets and reverse the removal procedures. Tighten the crankshaft center bolt to 58 ft. lbs. Check the ignition timing.

2.2L and 2.5L Engines

1. Refer to the "Timing Belt, Removal and Installation" procedures in this section and remove the timing belt.

2. Remove the crankshaft sprocket bolt. Using the puller tool No. C–4685 or equivalent and the button from tool No. L–4524 or equivalent, remove the crankshaft sprocket.

3. Using the tool No. C–4687 or equivalent, hold the camshaft and/or intermediate sprocket, remove the center bolt(s) and the sprocket(s).

4. To install, use new gaskets and reverse the removal procedures. Torque the camshaft and intermediate sprocket bolts to 65 ft. lbs. and the crankshaft sprocket bolt to 50 ft. lbs. Adjust the timing belt tension.

2.5L Engine

The 2.5L engine is equipped with a pair of dual counter-rotating balance shafts, below and on both sides of the crankshaft, at almost a center position.

The two counter-rotating eccentric balance shafts, interconnected by gears, are driven by a short chain from the crankshaft. They turn at two times the engine speed to offset the reciprocating mass of the pistons and connecting rods. This achieves the desired balancing effect. The balance shafts are enclosed in an aluminum housing, mounted beneath the crankshaft. The housing is bolted to the bottom of the main bearing webs of the engine block and rests in the oil supply of an enlarged oil pan. When the engine is running, the balance shafts pump oil out of the housing to minimize the drag which would occur if the shafts spun in the oil.

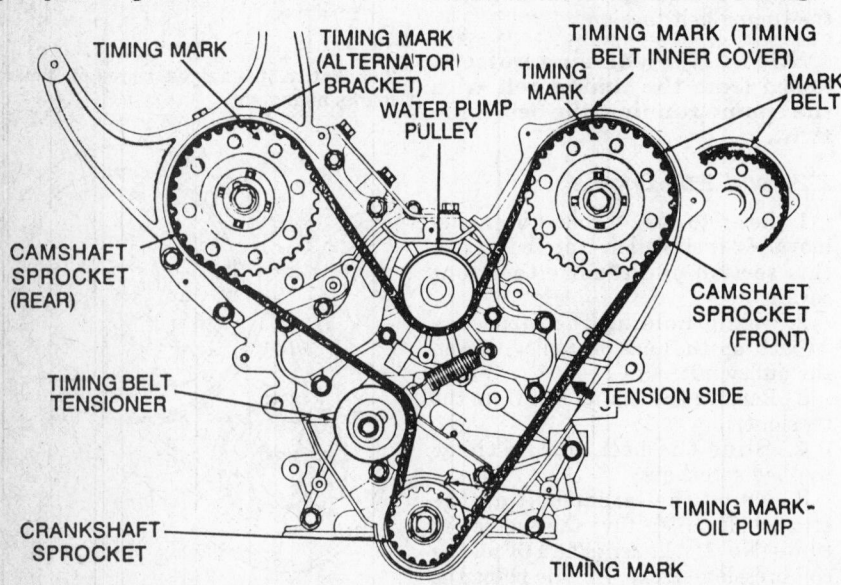

3.0L V6 engine timing belt and engine timing mark alignment

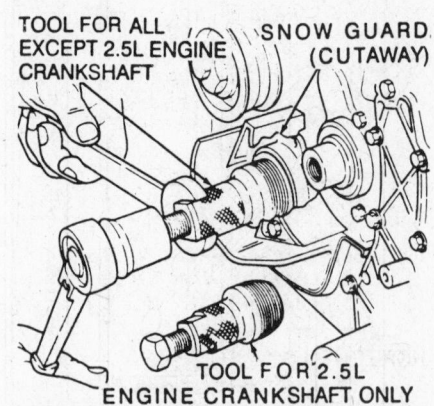

2.2L and 2.5L engine crankshaft, intermediate shaft or camshaft oil seal removal

NOTE: The oil pan, oil pickup, timing cover, belt, crankshaft belt sprocket and front crankshaft oil seal retainer must be first removed to gain access to the drive chain and sprockets.

1. Remove the necessary components, such as the alternator and the air conditioning compressor. Remove the timing belt cover retaining bolts in both timing cover sections. Remove both halves of the cover and lay aside.

2. Remove the right inner fender panel. Place a jack under the engine and raise the engine slightly. Remove the right engine mounting bolt.

3. While holding the large hex on the tension pulley, loosen the pulley nut. Remove the belt from the tensioner.

4. Slide the belt off the three toothed pulleys.

NOTE: The crankshaft sprocket gear may be removed at this time with special puller tools. The crankshaft intermediate shaft and camshaft oil seals may also be removed at this time.

5. With the crankshaft pulley back on the crankshaft, turn the crankshaft and the intermediate shaft until the markings on the sprockets are in line. (bisecting an imaginary line between the bolt head of the crankshaft gear and the bolt head of the intermediate shaft gear).

— CAUTION —

If the timing marks are not perfectly aligned, poor engine performance and engine damage will result.

6. Turn the camshaft until the arrows on the hub are in line with No. 1 camshaft cap to the cylinder head line. The small hole must be in the center line of the engine.

NOTE: The center line of the engine will be canted to the left of vertical, when looking at the crankshaft/camshaft gear end of the engine.

7. Install the belt on the pulleys. If a weighted wrench is available, its axis must be within 15 degrees of horizontal during the adjustment of the timing belt.

8. If a weighted wrench is not available, adjust the tensioner by turning the large tensioner hex to the right. Tension is correct when the belt can be twisted 90 degrees with the thumb and forefinger, midway between the camshaft and intermediate pulleys.

9. Tighten the tensioner locknut.

10. Rotate the crankshaft two full revolutions and recheck the timing.

11. Install the timing belt cover.

NOTE: To check the timing with the timing belt cover installed, have the number one cylinder at the TDC position. Remove the cover timing hole plug. The small hole in the sprocket must be centered in the timing belt cover hole.

12. Install the remaining components and check the ignition timing.

3.0L V6 Engine

Refer to "Timing Belt, Removal & Installation" to remove the timing sprockets.

OIL SEAL REPLACEMENT

1.7L Engine

The camshaft, intermediate shaft and crankshaft sprockets are located by keys on their respective shafts and each is retained by a bolt. Remove the center bolts and pull the sprockets from the shafts.

1. Refer to the "Timing Belt Removal & Installation" procedures in this section and remove the timing belt.

2. Remove the crankshaft sprocket bolt. Connect the removal tool No. L–4524 or equivalent, to the crankshaft sprocket and pull the sprocket from the crankshaft.

3. Remove the crankshaft key. Using the oil seal removal tool No. L–4424 or equivalent, pry the oil seal from the crankshaft.

4. Using the seal installer tool No. L–4422 or equivalent, drive the new crankshaft seal (lubricate the seal lips with oil) into the crankshaft housing until it seats.

5. To complete the installation, use new gaskets and reverse the removal procedures. Torque the crankshaft center bolt to 58 ft. lbs. Check the ignition timing.

2.2L and 2.5L Engines

1. Refer to the "Timing Sprocket, Removal & Installation" procedures in this section and remove the timing sprockets.

2. Using the tool No. C–4679 or equivalent, remove the crankshaft, the camshaft and/or intermediate seal(s).

3. To install the oil seals, polish the shafts with 400 grit emery paper, use the oil seal installation tool No. C–4680 or equivalent and drive the seal into its seat.

NOTE: If the seal has a steel case, lightly coat the seal with Loctite Stud N' Bearing Mount® or its equivalent. If the seal case is rubber coated, apply soap and water to facilitate the installation.

4. To complete the installation, use new gaskets and reverse the removal procedures. Torque the camshaft and intermediate sprocket bolts to 65 ft. lbs. and the crankshaft sprocket bolt to 50 ft. lbs. Adjust the timing belt tension.

Balance Shafts

The 2.5L and 2.6L engines are equipped with two "Balance Shafts" which cancel the vertical vibrating force of the engine and the secondary vibrating forces, which include the sideways rocking of the engine due to the turning direction of the crankshaft and other rolling parts. The timing sprockets are linked by a duplex chain.

FASTENER TORQUE

Letter Code	Nm	Inch Lbs.	Ft. Lbs.
A	12	105	9
B	28	250	21
C	54	480	40
D①	41①	360①	30①
E	95	840	70
F	Plug—Loctite®		277
G	15	130	11

① Specified torque plus ¼ turn

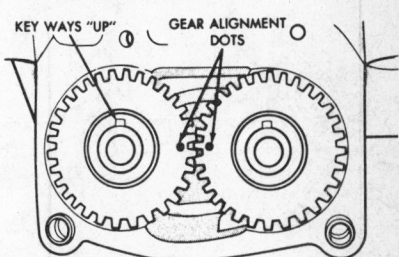

2.5L engine balance shaft gears alignment marks

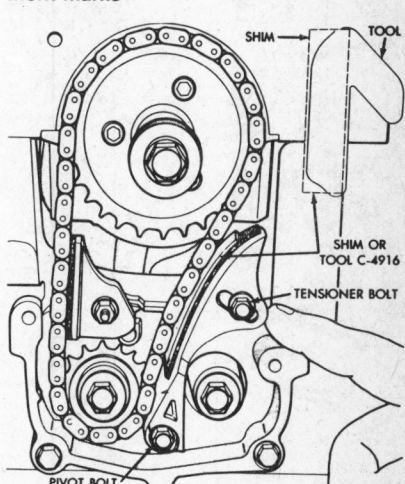

2.5L engine balance shaft chain tensioning

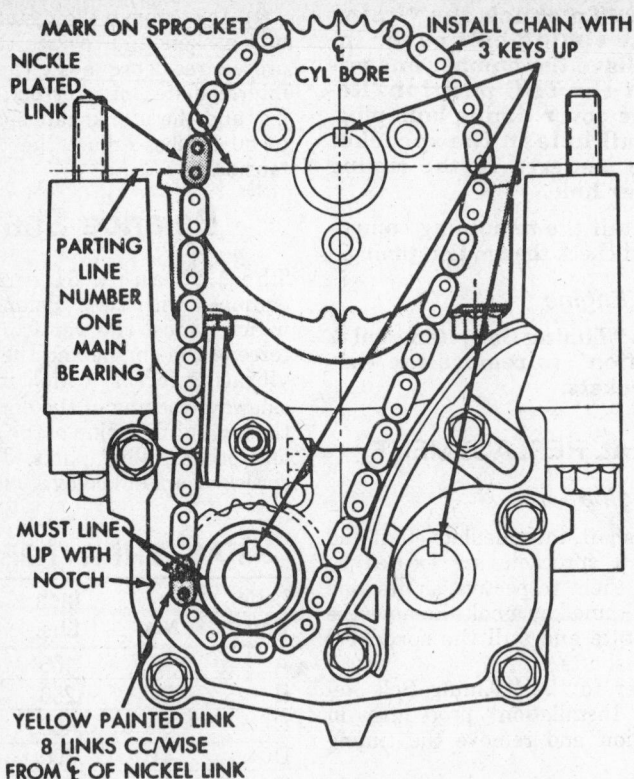

2.5L engine balance shaft and chain alignment marks

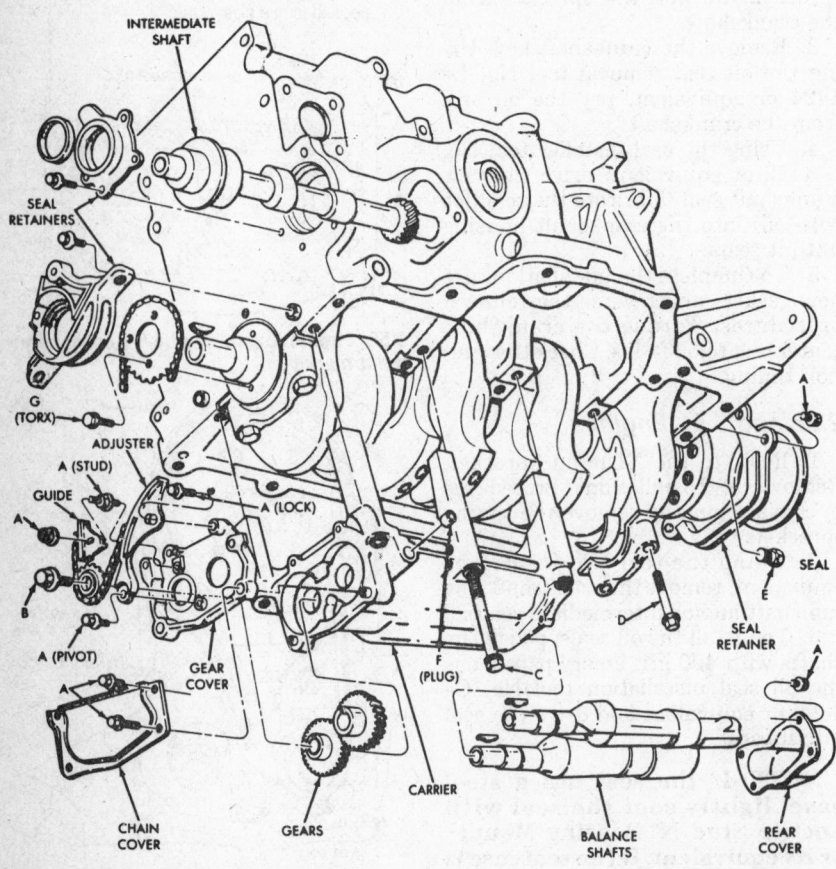

2.5L engine crankshaft, intermediate shaft and balance shaft assemblies—exploded view

REMOVAL & INSTALLATION

1986–89 2.5L Engine

The balance shaft chain assembly is installed in a carrier attached to the lower crankcase. The balance shaft chain assembly is located behind the timing belt assembly. The timing belt must be removed before removing the balance chain assembly.

1. Refer to the "Timing Belt Removal & Installation" procedures in this section and remove the timing belt.

2. Raise and support the vehicle safely. Remove the oil pan, the oil pick-up, the crankshaft belt sprocket and the front crankshaft oil seal retainer.

3. Remove the balance shaft chain cover, the guide and the tensioner.

4. Remove the balance shaft sprocket-to-shaft bolt, the gear cover-to-balance shaft bolt and the crankshaft sprocket-to-crankshaft bolts, then the sprockets with the balance chain.

5. Remove the front gear cover-to-carrier housing stud, the gear cover and the balance shaft drive gears.

6. Remove the rear gear cover-to-carrier housing bolts, the rear cover and the balance from the rear of the carrier.

7. If necessary, remove the carrier housing-to-crankcase bolts and the housing.

8. To install the balance shaft/carrier assembly, perform the following procedures:

   a. If the carrier housing is being installed, torque the carrier housing-to-crankcase bolts to 40 ft. lbs. (54 Nm).

   b. Rotate the balance shafts until the keyways are facing upward (parallel to the vertical centerline of the engine).

   c. Install the short hub gear on the sprocket driven shaft and the long hub gear on the gear driven shaft; make sure that the gear timing marks are aligned (facing each other).

   d. Install the front gear cover and torque the front gear cover-to-carrier housing stud bolt to 8.5 ft. lbs. (12 Nm).

   e. Install the balance chain sprocket and torque the sprocket-to-crankshaft bolts to 11 ft. lbs. (13 Nm).

   f. Rotate the crankshaft to position the No. 1 cylinder on the TDC of the compression stroke; the timing marks on the chain sprocket should align with the parting line on the left side of the No. 1 main bearing cap.

   g. Position the balance shaft sprocket into the balance chain so that the sprocket (yellow dot) timing mark mates with the chain (yellow) link.

h. Install the balance chain/sprocket assembly onto the crankshaft and the balance shaft. Torque the sprocket-to-shaft bolts to 21 ft. lbs. (28 Nm).

NOTE: If necessary to secure the crankshaft while tightening the bolts, place a block of wood between the crankcase and the crankshaft counterbalance.

i. Loosely install the chain tensioners and place a shim (0.039 in. x 2.75 in.) between the chain and the tensioner. Apply firm pressure (to reduce the chain slack) to the tensioner shoe. Torque the tensioner-to-front gear cover bolts to 8.5 ft. lbs. (12 Nm).

j. Install the chain cover and the rear cover to the carrier housing and torque the bolts to 8.5 ft. lbs. (12 Nm).

9. To complete the installation, use new gasket, sealant and reverse the removal procedures. Refill the crankcase. Adjust the timing belt tension. Check and/or adjust the engine timing.

2.6L Engine

The silent shaft chain assembly is mounted in the front of the timing chain assembly; the assembly must be removed to service the timing chain assembly.

RIGHT SIDE (LOWER)

1. Refer to the "Oil Pump Removal & Installation" procedures in this section and remove the oil pump.
2. Remove the oil pump adapter plate.
3. Pull the balance shaft through the front of the engine.
4. To install, reverse the removal procedures.

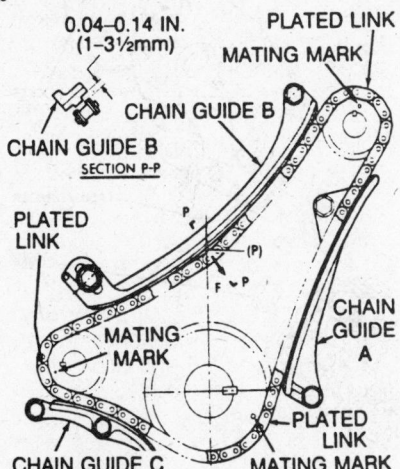

2.6L engine silent shaft sprocket alignment marks

LEFT SIDE (UPPER)

1. Refer to the "Oil Pump Removal & Installation" procedures in this section. Remove the balance chain sprocket bolt, the sprocket, the chain and the spacer.
2. Remove the two balance shaft thrust plate bolts and pull the thrust plate from the engine.
3. Pull the balance shaft through the front of the engine.
4. To install, reverse the removal procedures. Torque the sprocket bolt to 25 ft. lbs.

Camshaft

REMOVAL & INSTALLATION

1.6L Engine

NOTE: Refer to the "Engine Removal & Installation" procedures in this section and remove the engine.

1. With the engine removed from the vehicle and supported safely, remove the front cover, timing chain and camshaft sprocket.
2. Remove the cylinder head, pushrods and valve tappets. Identify the tappets to ensure installation in their original positions.
3. Remove the fuel pump, oil pump, distributor and the distributor drive housing. Mark the engine in relation to the drive slot.
4. Using a magnet, remove the distributor drive from halfshaft spindle.
5. Remove shaft drive gear circlip.

NOTE: Insert a shop towel in the drive gear cavity to insure that the circlip does not fall into the crankcase during removal or installation.

6. Tap the halfshaft toward the pump side of crankcase until shaft drive gear is free from the spline and remove the gear/washer.
7. Remove the halfshaft from the pump side of the crankcase.
8. Remove the two camshaft thrust plate bolts and the thrust plate.
9. Carefully remove the camshaft from the front of the engine. Check for wear and/or damage, then replace the parts, as necessary.
10. To install, use new gaskets and reverse the removal procedures. Torque the thrust plate bolts to 11 ft. lbs. Install a dial indicator to the engine and check the camshaft end play (0.004–0.008 in.).

NOTE: When installing a new camshaft or tappets, add one pint of Chrysler Crankcase Conditioner, Part Number 3419130 or equivalent, to the engine oil. Retain oil mixture for a minimum of 500 miles. When replacing the camshaft, use a straight edge to check all tappet faces for wear. Replace tappets with negative crown or dishing.

1.7L Engine

1. Remove the timing belt covers and rotate the engine until No. 1 cylinder is at the TDC of the compression stroke.

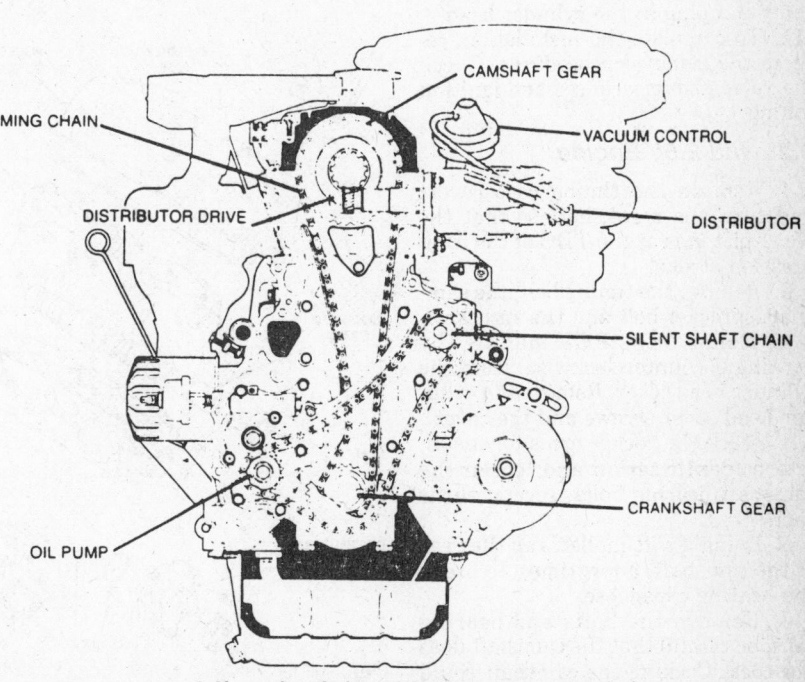

2.6L engine timing and silent shaft chains

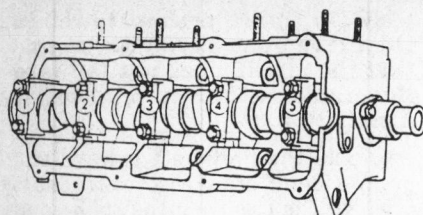

1.7L engine camshaft bearing cap identification numbers

2. Remove the timing belt, camshaft sprocket bolt and camshaft sprocket.

3. Remove the air cleaner assembly and the valve cover.

4. Remove the No. 1, 3 and 5 camshaft bearing caps.

5. Loosen caps No. 2 and 4 diagonally and remove the caps.

6. Carefully, lift out the camshaft. Check for wear and/or damage, replace the parts, if necessary.

7. Clean the gasket mating surfaces.

8. To install, lubricate the camshaft journals and lobes, position the camshaft in the cylinder head and install a new oil seal and gaskets. Tighten the camshaft bearing cap bolts to 14 ft. lbs., in the reverse order of removal.

—— CAUTION ——

All of the bearing caps are slightly offset. They should be installed so the numbers on the caps read right side up from the driver's seat.

9. Position a dial indicator to the front of the engine and check the camshaft end play. Play should not exceed 0.006 in.

10. If necessary, replace the camshaft end plug in the cylinder head.

11. To complete the installation, reverse the removal procedures. Check the valve lash clearances and ignition timing.

2.2L and 2.5L Engine

1. Remove the timing case covers and turn the crankshaft so that the No. 1 piston is at the TDC of the compression stroke.

2. Remove the timing belt, the camshaft sprocket bolt and the sprocket.

3. Remove the PCV module (by turning it counterclockwise) from the cylinder head cover. Remove the cylinder head cover screws and the cover.

4. Mark the rocker arms for installation identification and loosen the camshaft bearing bolts, several turns each.

5. Using a soft mallet, rap the rear of the camshaft, a few times, to break the bearing caps loose.

6. Remove the bolts and bearing caps, be careful that the camshaft does not cock. Cocking the camshaft could cause damage to the bearings.

7. Check the oil holes for blockages and the parts for wear and/or damage, replace the parts, if necessary. Clean the gasket mounting surfaces.

8. To install, lubricate the camshaft, place the bearing caps with No. 1 at the timing belt end and No. 5 at the transaxle end. The camshaft bearing caps are numbered and have arrows facing forward. Torque the camshaft bearing bolts to 18 ft. lbs.

NOTE: Apply RTV silicone gasket material to the No. 1 and 5 bearing caps. Install the bearing caps before the seals are installed.

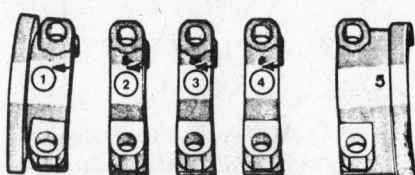

2.2L and 2.5L engines camshaft bearing caps installation position

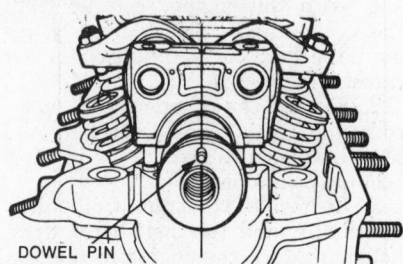

Install the camshaft on 2.6L engine by aligning the dowel pin with the notch in the top of the front bearing cap

9. Mount a dial indicator to the front of the engine and check the camshaft endplay. Play should not exceed 0.006 in.

10. To complete the installation, use new gaskets/seals and reverse the removal procedures. Check the valve lash clearances and the ignition timing.

2.6L Engines

1. Refer to the "Timing Chain Removal & Installation" procedures in this section. Remove the timing chain cover, the timing chain, the camshaft sprocket and the cylinder head cover.

2. At the rear side of the camshaft, remove the water pump, the camshaft pulley bolt and the pulley.

3. Loosen the camshaft bearing bolts but DO NOT remove the bolts. Lift the camshaft bearing and the rocker arm assembly from the cylinder head.

4. Remove the camshaft from the cylinder head.

5. Check the parts for wear and/or damage, replace the parts, if necessary. Clean the gasket mounting surfaces.

6. To install, lubricate the parts, install new camshaft seals, the camshaft, the camshaft bearing and rocker arm assembly. Torque the camshaft bearing bolts to 7 ft. lbs. and then to 14 ft. lbs. in the following order: Bearing caps No. 3, 2, 4, front and rear.

7. To complete the installation, use new gaskets and reverse the removal procedures. Check the valve lash clearances and ignition timing.

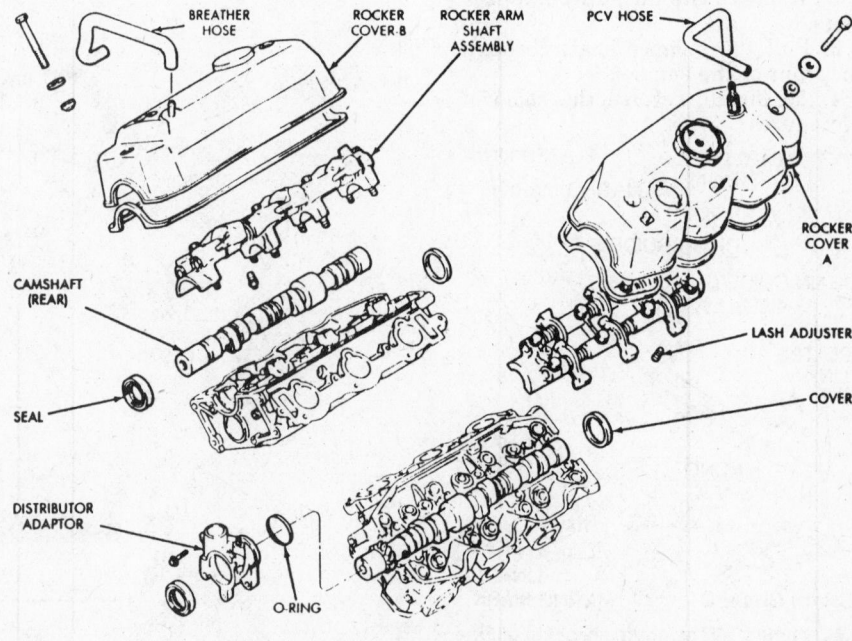

3.0L V6 engine rocker shafts and camshafts—exploded view

3.0L V6 Engine

1. Disconnect the negative battery cable. Remove the air cleaner assembly and valve cover.

2. Install auto lash adjuster retainers (PN MD998443) on the rocker arms.

3. On the right side cylinder head, remove the distributor extension.

4. Remove the camshaft bearing caps, but do not remove the bolts from the caps.

5. Remove the rocker arms, rocker shafts and bearing caps, as an assembly.

6. Remove the camshaft from the cylinder head.

7. Inspect the bearing journals on the camshaft, cylinder head and bearing caps.

8. To install, lubricate the camshaft journals and camshaft with clean engine oil and install the camshaft in the cylinder head.

9. Align the camshaft bearing caps with the arrow mark (depending on cylinder numbers) and in numerical order.

10. Apply sealer at the ends of the bearing caps and install the assembly.

11. Tighten the bearing cap bolts in the following sequence to 85 inch lbs.
   - a. First, No. 3.
   - b. Second, No. 2.
   - c. Third, No. 1.
   - d. Fourth, No. 4

12. Repeat Steps 11a–11d, but increase the tightening torque to 180 inch lbs.

13. Install the distributor drive assembly, if removed.

14. The remainder of the installation is the reverse of the removal procedure.

Pistons And Connecting Rod

POSITIONING

All Engines

On all the engines except the 1.6L and 3.0L engines, the piston crown is marked with an arrow or an indent, which must point toward the timing belt/chain end of the engine. On the 1.6L engine, the pistons are notched at the bottom of the piston skirt. Install the No. 1 and 3 pistons with the notch facing the flywheel and the No. 2 and 4 pistons with the notch facing the front cover. The connecting rod's crankshaft bearing oil hole must face the camshaft.

On the 1.7L engine, the connecting rod and cap are marked with rectangular forge marks which must face the intermediate shaft side of the engine.

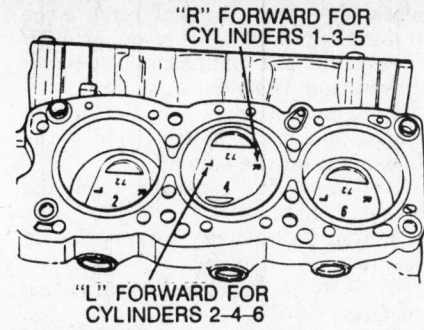

"R" FORWARD FOR CYLINDERS 1–3–5

"L" FORWARD FOR CYLINDERS 2–4–6

3.0L V6 engine piston marking and cylinder numbers

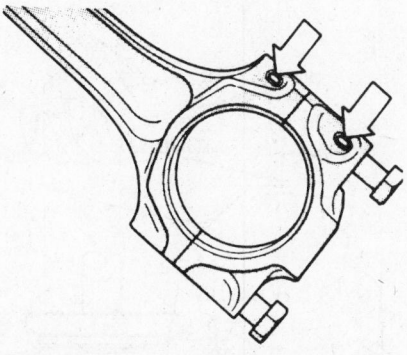

1.7L engine connecting rod and cap matchmarks

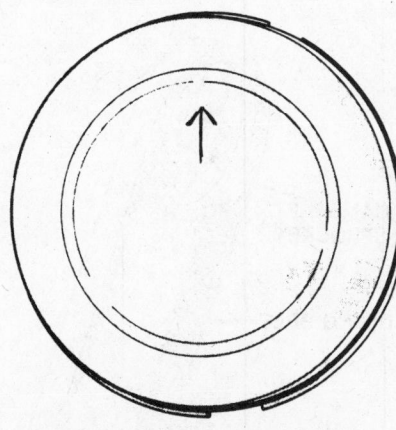

1.6L, 1.7L, 2.2L and 2.5L engines all have an arrow showing the piston installation position in the engine

On the 2.2L and 2.5L engines, the connecting rod and bearing cap are match marked, the oil hole must face the timing end of the engine. On the 2.6L engine, the connecting rod and bearing cap are match marked, which must face the right side of the engine.

On the 3.0L V6 engine, the pistons are marked with an "R" for cylinders 1, 3 and 5 and with an "L" for cylinders 2, 4 and 6. The connecting rod must be numbered when removed.

Mark both halves of the cap for proper installation.

For all piston and connecting rod overhaul procedures, please refer to "Engine Rebuilding" in the Unit Repair Section.

ENGINE LUBRICATION

Oil Pan

REMOVAL & INSTALLATION

All Engines

1. Raise and support the vehicle safely. Drain the engine oil.

2. Support the oil pan and remove the mounting bolts.

3. Remove the oil pan and discard the gaskets.

4. Clean the oil pan and gasket mating surfaces.

5. To install, use a new pan gasket with sealer and reverse the removal procedures. Refill the engine oil, run the engine and check for leaks.

NOTE: Oil pan bolt torque is 7 ft. lbs. (1.6L); 6 ft. lbs. (1.7L); 17 ft. lbs. (2.2L and 2.5L); 5 ft. lbs. (2.6L) and 51 inch lbs. (3.0L).

Rear Main Bearing Oil Seal

REMOVAL & INSTALLATION

1.6L Engine

NOTE: The rear main seal removal is easier to accomplish if the engine is removed first.

1. Refer to the "Engine, Removal & Installation" procedures in this section and remove the engine from the vehicle. Remove the flywheel or drive plate from the crankshaft.

2. Remove the rear oil seal housing mounting bolts and remove the housing.

3. Place the housing inner surface on two blocks of wood, allowing clearance for the seal removal.

4. Using the seal removal/installation tool No. C–4759 or equivalent, drive the seal from the housing.

5. To install, invert the seal housing and place it on a smooth surface. Using the seal removal/installation tool No. C–4759 or equivalent, drive the new seal into the housing until it seats.

6. To complete the installation, use a new gasket, lubricate the seal lips and reverse the removal procedures. Tighten the seal housing mounting bolts to 9 ft. lbs.

1.7L, 2.2L and 2.5L Engines

The rear main seal is located in a housing on the rear of the block. To replace the seal the engine must be removed.

1. Refer to the "Engine Removal & Installation" procedures in this section and remove the engine from the vehicle. Remove the flywheel or the drive plate from the crankshaft.

NOTE: Before removing the transaxle, align the dimple on the flywheel with the pointer on the flywheel housing. The transaxle will not mate with the engine during installation, unless this alignment is observed.

2. Using a small pry bar, carefully pry the old seal out of the oil seal housing.

3. Coat the new seal with Loctite® Stud N' Bearing Mount (4057987) or equivalent and drive it into place, using the installation tool No. L–4425-1 or equivalent, (1.7L engine) or No. L–4681 or equivalent, (2.2L and 2.5L engines). Take care not to scratch the seal or the crankshaft.

4. To install, reverse the removal procedures.

2.6L Engine

The rear main bearing oil seal is located in a housing on the rear of the

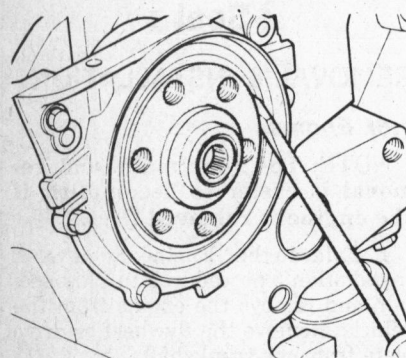

1.7L, 2.2L and 2.5L engines rear main bearing oil seal removal

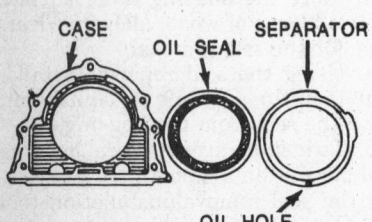

2.6L engine rear main bearing oil seal and seal housing

block. To replace the seal, remove the transaxle and work from underneath the vehicle. The engine can also be removed from the vehicle.

1. Remove the oil seal housing to engine mounting bolts. Remove the housing from the engine.

2. Remove the separator from the oil seal housing.

3. Using a small pry bar, pry the old seal from the housing.

4. Clean the gasket mating surfaces.

5. To install, use new gaskets/seals, lubricate the new oil seal and seat it in the housing. Install the separator with the oil hole facing down.

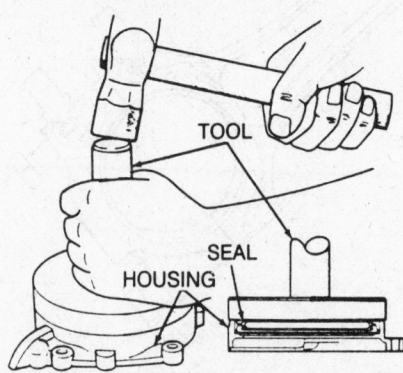

3.0L V6 engine rear main bearing oil seal installation

6. To complete the installation, reverse the removal procedures.

3.0L V6 Engine

1. Refer to "Transaxle, Removal & Installation" and remove the transaxle from the vehicle.

2. Remove the rear oil seal retainer from the rear of the engine.

3. Using a seal driver, place the retainer on two blocks of wood and drive the seal from the retainer.

4. Clean and inspect the retainer for damage. Clean the gasket mating surfaces.

5. Using seal driver tool MB998718 or equivalent, drive the new seal into the retainer, with the lip facing inward, until it bottoms out.

6. Apply RTV sealer to the retainer mating surface and lightly coat the seal lip with clean engine oil.

7. Install the seal retainer on the engine. Tighten the mounting bolts to 104 inch lbs.

8. Install the transaxle in the vehicle.

9. When finished, run the engine and check for leaks.

Oil Pump

The conventional lubrication system uses a gear type oil pump, with a pressure relief valve to prevent extreme pressure build up.

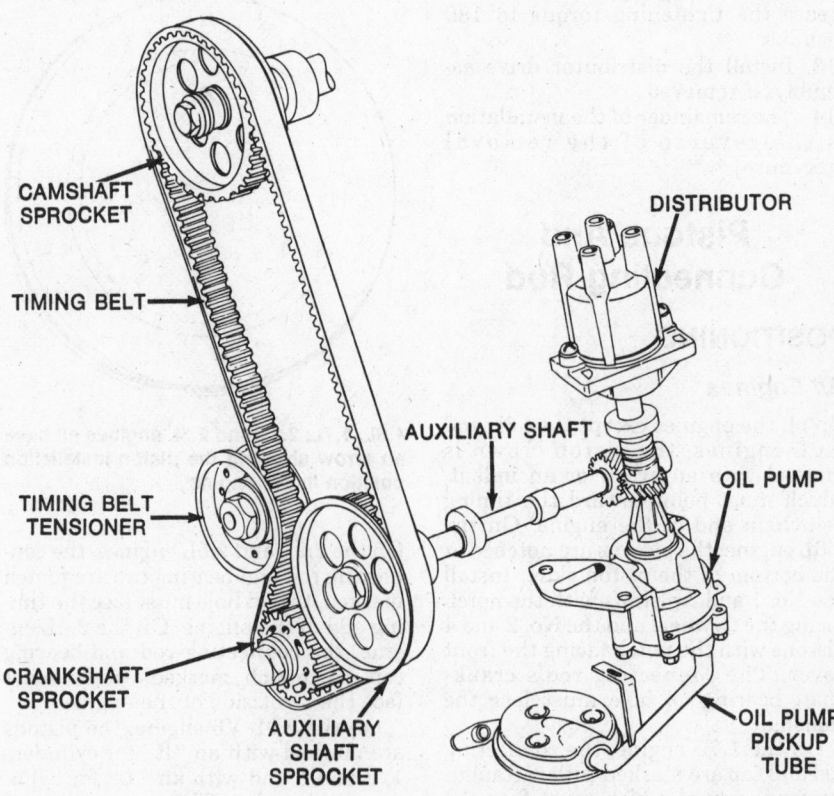

2.2L and 2.5L engines timing belt, intermediate shaft, oil pump and distributor drives

REMOVAL & INSTALLATION

1.6L Engine

The oil pump is located on the right side of the engine block.

1. Remove the oil filter.
2. Holding the oil pump cover and housing together, remove the seven mounting bolts and pull the assembly away from the engine.
3. Remove the gaskets. Clean the gasket mating surfaces.
4. To install; prime the pump body with petroleum jelly. Use new gaskets and place sealer on the mounting bolt threads.
5. Insert the two bolts to align the pump body with the housing. Align the pump with the engine (engage the driving shaft gear tongue with the slot in the halfshaft) and tighten the mounting bolts to 9 ft. lbs.
6. Run the engine and check for leaks.

1.7L, 2.2L and 2.5L Engines

1. Raise and support the vehicle safely. Drain the engine oil and remove the oil pan.
2. On 2.2L and 2.5L engines, remove the No. 3 bearing cap bolt (holding the pickup tube) and remove the tube.
3. Remove the oil pump mounting bolts. Pull the pump down and out of the engine.
4. To install, use new gaskets, prime the pump with petroleum jelly, align the pump with the distributor drive gear tongue and reverse the removal procedures.
5. Tighten the pump mounting bolts to 14 ft. lbs. (1.7L engine) or to 17 ft. lbs. (2.2L and 2.5L engines).

2.6L Engine

1. Refer to the "Front Cover and Belt Removal & Installation" procedures in this section. Remove the timing belt cover, the silent chain guides, the silent chain/oil pump sprocket, the silent chain and the timing chain tensioner (if necessary).
2. Remove the silent shaft bolt (the bolt directly above the silent chain sprocket).
3. Remove the oil pump bolts and pull the pump housing straight forward. Remove the gaskets and the oil pump backing plate. Clean the gasket mounting surfaces.
4. To install the oil pump, use new gaskets/seals, align the mating marks of the oil pump gears, refill the pump with oil, install the pump and reverse the removal procedures. Torque the oil pump mounting bolts to 6 ft. lbs., the balance chain guide and sprocket bolts to 13 ft. lbs.

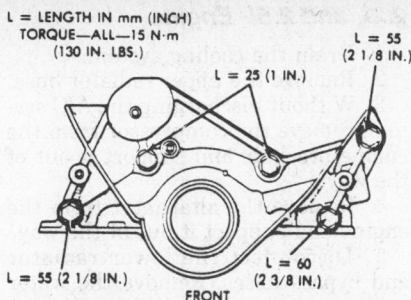

L = LENGTH IN mm (INCH)
TORQUE—ALL—15 N·m
(130 IN. LBS.)
L = 25 (1 IN.)
L = 55 (2 1/8 IN.)
L = 55 (2 1/8 IN.)
L = 60 (2 3/8 IN.)
FRONT

3.0L V6 engine oil pump mounting—note different bolt lengths

3.0L V6 Engine

1. Refer to "Timing Belt, Removal & Installation" procedures and remove the timing belt from the engine.
2. Remove the balancer and crankshaft sprocket from the end of the crankshaft.
3. Remove the oil pump mounting bolts and remove the pump from the front of the engine. Not the different length bolts and their position in the pump, for installation.
4. Clean the gasket mating surfaces of the pump and engine block.
5. Using a new gasket, install the oil pump on the engine and tighten all bolts to 130 inch lbs.
6. Install the crankshaft sprocket and balancer on the engine.
7. Refer to "Timing Belt, Removal & Installation" procedures and install the timing belt and related components on the engine.
8. When finished, run the engine at idle until oil pressure is obtained.
9. Check for leaks.

ENGINE COOLING

Radiator

REMOVAL & INSTALLATION

All Models

1. Disconnect the negative battery cable. Drain the cooling system.
2. Remove the hoses from the radiator.
3. Remove the coolant reserve tank to filler neck tube.
4. Disconnect the fan motor wiring. Remove the upper shroud attachment screws.
5. Lift the shroud upwards and out of the bottom mounting clips.
6. Remove the fan support and fan motor as an assembly, from the vehicle.

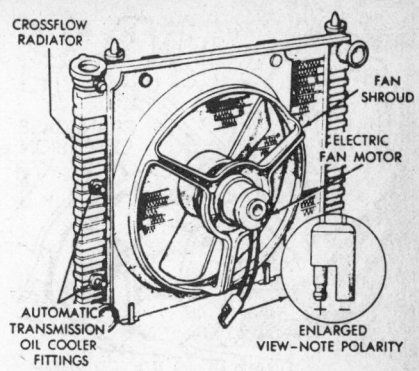

CROSSFLOW RADIATOR
FAN SHROUD
ELECTRIC FAN MOTOR
AUTOMATIC TRANSMISSION OIL COOLER FITTINGS
ENLARGED VIEW—NOTE POLARITY

Radiator and cooling fan—typical of all models

7. Remove the upper radiator mounting screws.
8. Disconnect the engine block heater and transaxle cooler lines, if equipped.
9. Remove the radiator from the vehicle.
10. To install, reverse the removal procedures and add coolant until it meets the radiator cap seat.
11. On the 1.6L, 2.2L and 2.5L engines, add coolant until it rises to the top of the hole in the thermostat housing. Install the vacuum valve or plug and continue adding fluid until it meets the radiator cap seat.
12. On all vehicles, after the radiator cap is installed, fill the reserve tank to the "MAX" line with the engine cold.

Water Pump

REMOVAL & INSTALLATION

1.6L Engine

1. Remove the radiator cap and drain the cooling system through the water pump drain plug.
2. Disconnect the coolant hose at the pump.
3. Loosen the water pump drive belt. Remove the retaining screws and remove the water pump pulley.
4. Remove the four pump to engine extension screws and remove the water pump assembly.
5. To install, use a new gasket and reverse the removal procedures. Tighten the pump extension bolts to 9 ft. lbs. and the pump drain plug to 13 ft. lbs.
6. Adjust the belt tension, so that it can be depressed ¼ in., under light thumb pressure, on the longest span between the two pulleys.

1.7L Engine

1. Drain the cooling system.
2. Without disconnecting the refrigerant lines, remove the A/C compressor from the engine brackets and support it out of the way.

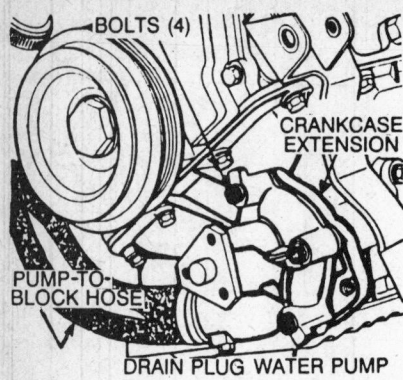

Water pump mounting—1.6L, 2.2L and 2.5L engines

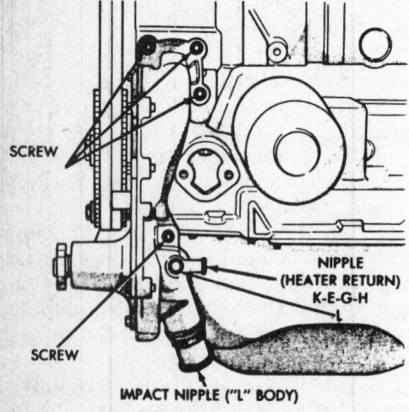

2.2L and 2.5L engines water pump mounting and location

3. Remove the alternator and the water pump pulleys.

4. Disconnect the diverter valve hose at the diverter valve. Remove the front and rear A.I.R. pump brackets.

5. Remove the alternator bracket from the water pump.

6. Disconnect the lower radiator and bypass hoses.

7. Loosen the timing belt cover bolt. Remove the water pump bolts and remove the water pump.

8. To install, use a new rubber O-ring seal and reverse the removal procedures. When tightening the bolts, follow this sequence:

a. Tighten the two upper water pump attaching bolts to 20 ft. lbs.

b. Tighten the two front air pump bracket to water pump bolts (one to 20 ft. lbs. and the other to 40 ft. lbs.).

c. Tighten the two air pump bolts to 24 ft. lbs.

d. Tighten the two air pump rear brackets and the lower water pump-to-engine bolts to 20 ft. lbs.

9. Adjust the belt tension, so that the belt can be depressed ¼ in., under light thumb pressure, on the longest span between the pulleys.

2.2L and 2.5L Engine

1. Drain the cooling system.
2. Remove the upper radiator hose.
3. Without discharging the A/C system, remove the compressor from the engine brackets and support it out of the way.
4. Remove the alternator from the engine and support it out of the way.
5. Disconnect the lower radiator and bypass hoses. Remove the water pump mounting bolts and remove the water pump.
6. To install, reverse the removal procedures. Tighten the top three retaining screws to 20 ft. lbs. and the lower screw to 50 ft. lbs.
7. Adjust the belt tension, so that the belt can be depressed ¼ in., under light thumb pressure, on the longest span between the two pulleys.

2.6L Engine

1. Drain the cooling system.
2. Remove the radiator, bypass and heater hoses from the water pump.
3. Remove the drive pulley shield.
4. Remove the locking and pivot screws.
5. Remove the water pump drive belt and remove the pump from the engine.

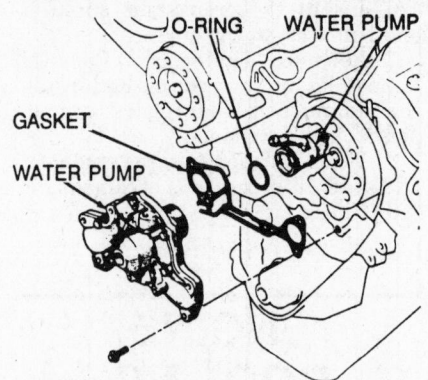

Water pump mounting—3.0L V6 engine

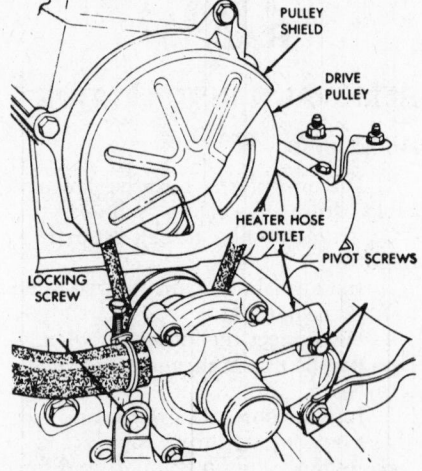

2.6L engine water pump mounting and location

6. To install, use a new gasket and O-ring and reverse the removal procedures.
7. Tighten the locking and pivot screws to 17 ft. lbs. and the drive pulley shield to 9 ft. lbs.
8. Adjust the belt tension, so that the belt can be depressed ¼ in., under light thumb pressure, on the longest span between the two pulleys.

3.0L V6 Engine

1. Refer to "Timing Belt, Removal & Installation" procedures and remove the timing belt from the water pump pulley.
2. Drain the cooling system.
3. Remove the water pump mounting bolts, separate the pump from the water inlet pipe and remove the pump from the engine.
4. Clean the gasket mating surfaces of the pump, engine and water inlet pipe.
5. To install, place a new O-ring on the water inlet pipe. Wet the O-ring with water to aid with installation.

NOTE: Do not use oil or grease on the O-ring. Either may cause the O-ring to slip out of the groove on the pipe and cause leakage.

6. Install a new gasket on the water pump. Install the inlet opening over the water pipe and press on the assembly to insert the pipe into the pump body.
7. Install the water pump mounting bolts. Tighten the bolts to 20 ft. lbs.
8. Refer to "Timing Belt, Removal & Installation" procedures to install the timing belt and related components.
9. When finished, fill the cooling system, run the engine and check for leaks.

Thermostat

REMOVAL & INSTALLATION

All Engines

1. Drain the cooling system to a level below the thermostat.
2. Remove the thermostat housing mounting bolts and remove the housing.
3. Remove the thermostat and discard the gasket.
4. Clean the gasket mating surfaces.
5. To install, use a new gasket, position the thermostat in the housing and reverse the removal procedures.
6. On all engines except the 3.0L V6, tighten the housing bolts to 200 inch lbs.
7. On the 3.0L V6 engine, tighten the bolts to 133 inch lbs.

COOLING SYSTEM BLEEDING

After working on the cooling system, even to replace the thermostat, it must be bled. Air trapped in the system will prevent proper filling and leave the radiator coolant level low, causing a risk of overheating.

1. To bleed the system, start with the system cool, radiator cap off and radiator filled to about an inch below the filler neck.

2. Start the engine and run it at slightly above normal idle speed. This will insure adequate circulation. If air bubbles appear and the coolant level drops, fill the system with an antifreeze/water mixture to bring the level back to the proper level.

3. Run the engine until the thermostat opens. When this happens, coolant will move abruptly across the top of the radiator and the temperature of the radiator will suddenly rise.

4. At this point, air is often expelled and the level may drop quite a bit. Keep refilling the system until the level is near the top of the radiator and remains constant.

5. If the vehicle has an overflow tank, fill the radiator right up to the filler neck. Replace the radiator filler cap.

EMISSION CONTROLS

NOTE: Please refer to "Emission Control" in the Unit Repair section for system maintenance

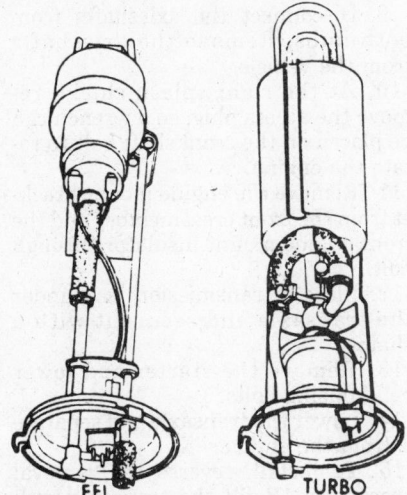

Electric fuel pumps used with EFI and Turbocharged engines

procedures. Due to the complex nature of modern electronic engine control systems, comprehensive diagnosis and testing procedures fall outside the confines of this repair manual. For complete information on diagnosis, testing and repair procedures concerning all modern engine and emission control systems, please refer to *"Chilton's Guide to Electronic Engine Controls"*.

FUEL SYSTEM

Fuel System Service Precaution

RELIEVING FUEL SYSTEM PRESSURE

———— CAUTION ————
Whenever working on or around any part of the fuel system, take precautions to avoid the risk of fire. The fuel system is under constant pressure which must be relieved before attempting any service procedures.

1. To release the pressure, remove the fuel tank cap and the wiring connector from the fuel injector (SFI) or any fuel injector (MFI).

2. Connect a jumper wire from one fuel injector terminal to ground and a second jumper wire from the other injector terminal to the positive battery terminal for 10 seconds.

3. With the fuel pressure reduced, remove the jumper wires and continue with the fuel system service.

Fuel Filter

Several types of fuel filters are used. One is located in the fuel tank of all the vehicles and is part of the fuel gauge unit assembly. Second is a sealed paper element, in-line unit; mechanical system—located on the engine (above the fuel pump) or electrical system—located in front of the fuel tank. Third is a paper element, in-line fuel filter/vapor separator, housed in a fuel reservoir. Normally, the in-tank filter does not require changing. If it does, the fuel tank must be drained and removed from the vehicle.

REMOVAL & INSTALLATION

NOTE: If removing the filter on a EFI or an MFI system, release the pressure in the fuel system before any service to the system.

1. Place a rag around the fuel filter hose(s)/tube(s) to catch the excess fuel.

2. Remove the clamps, the fuel hose(s)/tube(s) and the fuel filter (discard it).

3. To install a new filter, note the direction of fuel flow (usually indicated by an arrow) and reverse the removal procedures.

Mechanical Fuel Pump

PRESSURE TESTING

1. Insert a "T" fitting in fuel line at carburetor.

2. Connect a six inch piece of hose between "T" fitting and gauge.

3. Vent the pump for a few seconds to relieve air trapped in fuel chamber. If this is not done, the pump will not operate at full capacity and a low pressure reading will result.

4. Connect a tachometer, start engine and run at idle. The reading should be as shown in specifications (depending on pump) and remain constant.

NOTE: The mechanical fuel pump is not adjustable. If found to be defective, it must be replaced. A return to zero indicates a leaky outlet valve. If pressure is too low, a weak diaphragm main spring, or improper assembly of diaphragm may be the cause. If pressure is to high, the main spring is too strong or the air vent is plugged.

REMOVAL & INSTALLATION

1. Disconnect and plug the fuel lines at the fuel pump, located on the left side of the engine.

2. Remove the fuel pump to engine mounting bolts.

3. Clean the gasket mating surfaces.

4. To install, use new gaskets and reverse the removal procedures.

NOTE: On 2.6L engines, coat both sides of the insulator and gasket with sealer.

Electric Fuel Pump

PRESSURE TESTING

1. Relieve the fuel system pressure.

2. On engines with SPI, disconnect $5/16$ in. fuel supply line from throttle body. On engines with MPI, remove protective cover from service valve on the fuel rail.

3. Connect pressure tester C-3292 and C-4749 or equivalent, between the fuel supply hose and throttle body

on SPI or to the fuel rail service valve on MPI.

4. Using ATM tester C–4805 or equivalent, with the ignition in run position, depress the ATM button. This will activate the fuel pump and pressurize the system. Reading should be 14.5 psi (100 Kpa) on SPI and 55 psi (380 kpa) on MPI.

REMOVAL & INSTALLATION

NOTE: Refer to the "Relieving Fuel System Pressure" procedures in this section and relieve the fuel pressure. The electric fuel pump is located in the fuel tank.

1. Release the pressure in the fuel system. Raise and support the vehicle safely.
2. Disconnect the negative battery terminal.
3. Remove the fuel tank cap and the fuel tube to quarter panel screws.
4. Remove the draft tube cap from the sending unit, connect a siphon hose to the draft tube and siphon the fuel from the tank.
5. Disconnect the fuel pump wiring connector from the lock ring cap. Wrap a cloth around the fuel hose and remove the hose from the lock ring cap.
6. Disconnect and lower the fuel tank from the vehicle.
7. Using a non-metallic drift and a hammer, remove the lock ring by driving it counterclockwise.
8. Remove the fuel pump and O-ring seal from the tank. Check the in-tank filter and replace, if necessary.
9. To install, use a new O-ring seal and reverse the removal procedures. Start the engine and check for leaks. If necessary, check the fuel pressure: EFI–14.5 psi or Turbo–55 psi.

Carburetor

REMOVAL & INSTALLATION

1. Disconnect the negative battery cable.
2. Remove the air cleaner and the fuel tank cap.

NOTE: On the 2.6L engine, remove the air intake housing and the carburetor protector. Drain the radiator and remove the coolant hoses from the carburetor.

3. At the carburetor, place a container under the the fuel inlet hose and disconnect the fuel line.
4. Disconnect the vacuum hoses and wiring connectors after marking their locations with tape for installation.
5. Disconnect the throttle linkage.

6. Remove the mounting bolts or nuts and the carburetor.
7. Clean the gasket mounting surfaces with a suitable scraper.
8. To install, use a new gasket and reverse the removal procedures.

OVERHAUL

For all carburetor overhaul and adjustment procedures, please refer to "Carburetor Service" in the Unit Repair section.

Fuel Injection

NOTE: Due to the complex nature of modern fuel injection systems, comprehensive testing and diagnosis procedures fall outside the confines of this repair manual. For complete information on diagnosis, testing and repair procedures concerning all modern fuel injection systems, please refer to *Chilton's Guide To Fuel Injection and Feedback Carburetors*.

MANUAL TRANSAXLE

REMOVAL & INSTALLATION

NOTE: Whenever the differential cover is removed, a new gasket should be formed, using RTV sealant.

A-412 Transaxle

1. Disconnect the negative battery cable. Disconnect and tag the starter wires and backup light switch wire.
2. Remove the starter mounting bolts and remove the starter.
3. Disconnect the shift linkage rods and clutch cable.
4. Remove the speedometer cable retaining bolt and remove the cable from the transaxle.
5. Using a vertical hoist or fabricated support fixture, support the engine from above. Loosen the left wheel hub

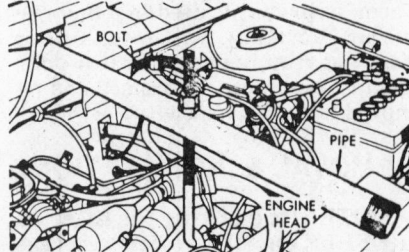

Engine support fixture installed while removing and installing the transaxle

nut. Raise and support the front of the vehicle safely.

6. Disconnect the right axleshaft and support it out of the way. Remove the left axleshaft and t it aside.
7. Remove the left splash shield. Remove the large and small dust cover bolts at the bell housing.
8. Drain the transaxle. Place a transmission jack under the transaxle and chain the transaxle in place.
9. Unbolt the left engine mount and remove the transaxle to engine bolts.
10. Slide the transaxle to the left until the mainshaft clears and lower it from the vehicle.
11. To install, reverse the removal procedures. Adjust the clutch cable and the shift linkage with the transaxle installed. Refill the transaxle and road test.

A-460, A-465, A-520, A-525 and A-555 Transaxles

1. Disconnect the negative battery cable.
2. Install an engine lifting "eye" fixture on the No. 4 cylinder exhaust manifold bolt and support the engine.
3. Disconnect the shift and the throttle linkages.
4. Remove the hub castle lock nut and cotter pin from both front wheels. Raise and support the front of the vehicle safely. Remove both front wheels.
5. Remove the left front splash shield and left engine/transaxle mount.
6. Remove the two upper bell housing bolts.
7. Remove the speedometer cable bolt and disconnect the cable from the transaxle.
8. Disconnect the sway bar. Remove the right and left lower ball joint bolts. Using a pry bar, separate the lower ball joints from the steering knuckles.
9. Disconnect the axleshafts from both hubs. Remove the axleshafts from the vehicle.
10. At the right splash shield, remove the access plug, so a wrench can be placed on the crankshaft bolt to rotate the engine.
11. Remove the engine mount bracket from the front crossmember and the front engine mount insulator through bolt.
12. Place a transmission jack under the transaxle and secure it with a chain.
13. Remove the starter and lower bell housing bolts.
14. Lower the transaxle and separate it from the engine.
15. To install, reverse the removal procedures. Refill the transaxle with SAE 5W–30 engine oil. Adjust the shift and throttle linkages.

SHIFT LINKAGE ADJUSTMENT

A-412 Transaxle Only

1. Place the transaxle in Neutral at the 3–4 position.
2. Loosen the shift tube clamp.
3. Place a ¾ in. spacer between the shift tube flange and the yoke at the shift base.
4. Tighten the shift tube clamp and remove the spacer.

NOTE: While tightening the shift tube clamp nut, no force should be exerted upward. No adjustments are possible on other transaxles.

LOCKUP ADJUSTMENT

A-412 Transaxle Only

NOTE: It is possible for the A-412 transaxle to become locked in two gears at once. This will occur if the interlock blocker on the gearshift selector lever has spread apart. The result of operating with this condition may result in clutch or driveline failure. To correctly diagnose the problem, the interlock should be checked using the following procedures:

1. Disconnect the shift linkage operating lever from the transaxle selector shaft.
2. Remove the transaxle detent spring assembly and selector shaft boot.
3. Remove the aluminum selector shaft plug.
4. Place the transaxle in Neutral and pull the selector shaft assembly out of the case.
5. Measure the interlock blocker gap "A", if the gap exceeds 0.330 in. replace the gearshift selector shaft assembly.
6. Apply a thick coating of chassis grease to the selector shaft shoulder at the threaded end and carefully insert the shaft through the selector shaft oil seal.
7. To install, reverse the removal procedures. Adjust the shift linkage.

A-460, A-465, A-520, A-525 and A-555 Transaxles

ROD OPERATED TYPE

1. Working over the left front fender, remove the lock pin from the transaxle selector shaft housing.
2. Reverse the lock pin (so the long end is down) and insert the lock pin into same threaded hole while pushing the selector shaft into the selector housing.

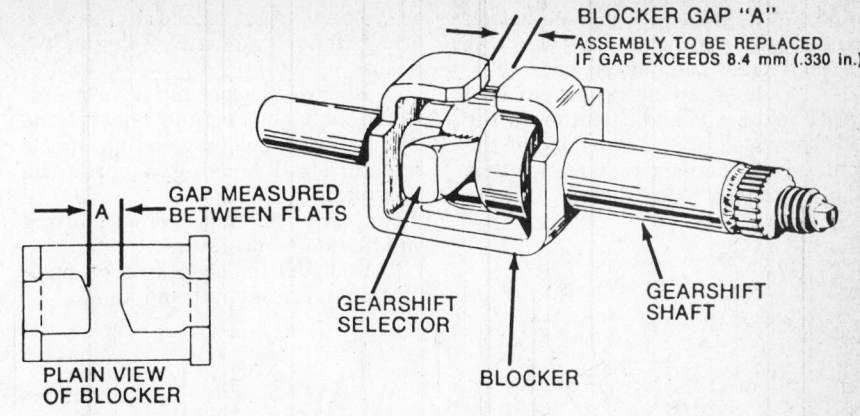

Checking the interlock blocker for failure on A-412 manual transaxles

3. A hole in the selector shaft will align with the lock pin, allowing the lock pin to be screwed into the housing. This operation locks the selector shaft in the 1-2 neutral position.
3. Raise and support the vehicle safely.
4. Loosen the clamp bolt that secures the gearshift tube to the gearshift connector.
5. Check that the gearshift connector slides and turns freely in the gearshift tube.
6. Position the shifter mechanism connector assembly so that the isolator is contacting the upstanding flange and that the rib on the isolater is aligned in both directions with the hole in the blockout bracket. Hold the connector isolator in this position while tightening the clamp bolt on the gearshift tube to 14 ft. lbs. No significant force should be exerted on the linkage during this operation.
7. Lower the vehicle.
8. Remove the lock pin from the selector shaft housing and reinstall the lock pin (with the long end up) in the selector shaft housing. Tighten the lock pin to 9 ft. lbs.
9. Check the first/reverse shifting and the blockout into reverse.

CABLE OPERATED TYPE

1. Working over the left front fender, remove the lock pin from the transaxle selector shaft housing.
2. Reverse the lock pin (so the long end is down) and insert lock pin into same threaded hole while pushing the selector shaft into the selector housing. A hole in the selector shaft will align with the lock pin, allowing the lock pin to be screwed into the housing. This operation locks the selector shaft in the 1-2 neutral position.
3. Remove the gearshift knob, the retaining nut and the pull-up ring from the gearshift lever.
4. If necessary, remove the shift lever boot and console to expose the gearshift linkage.

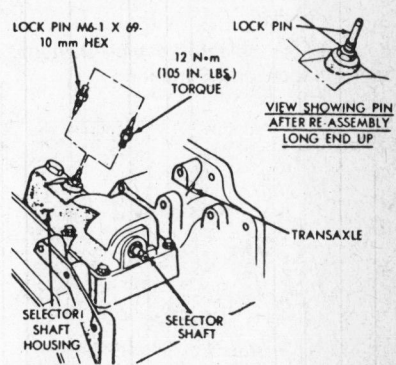

Transaxle pinned in the 1-2 neutral position to adjust gearshift linkage (rod or cable operated)

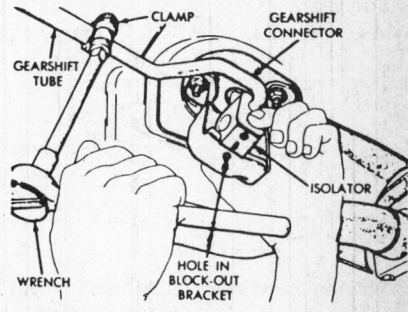

Adjusting gearshift linkage (rod operated)

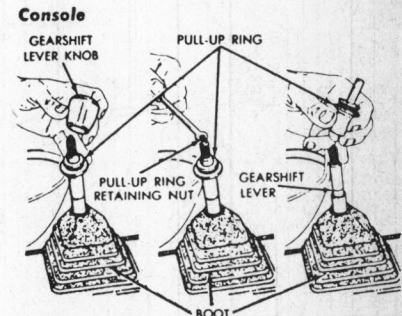

Gearshift knob, retaining nut and pull-up ring (Cable operated linkage)

5. Fabricate two cable adjusting pins: $\frac{3}{16}$ in. dia. x 5 in. long with a $\frac{1}{2}$ in. 90 degrees bend at one end.

6. Place one pin in the hole provided at the right side and the other in the hole provided at the rear side of the shifting mechanism (make sure that the alignment holes match). Torque

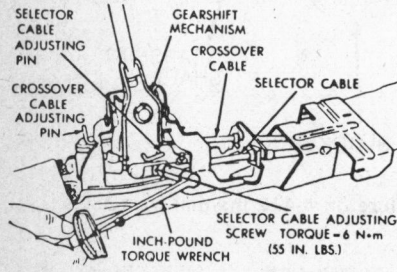

Adjusting the selector cable—Daytona, Laser, Shadow and Sundance

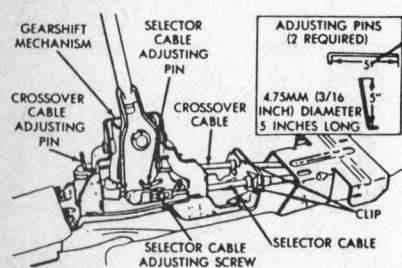

Fabricate (2) cable adjusting pins—Daytona, Laser, Shadow and Sundance

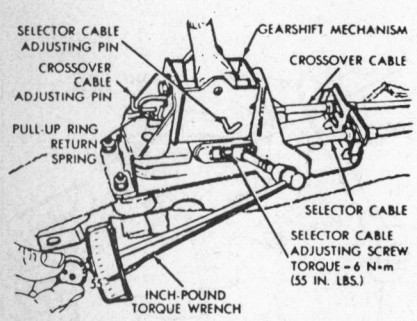

Adjusting the selector cable for all except Daytona, Laser, Shadow and Sundance

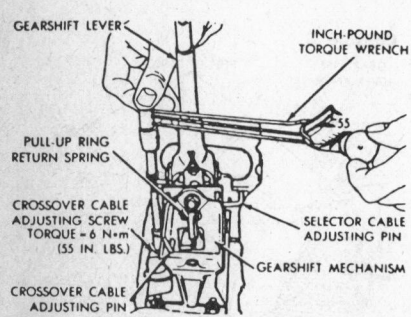

Adjusting the crossover cable for all except Daytona, Laser, Shadow and Sundance

the selector (right side) and the crossover (left side) adjusting bolts, to 4–5 ft. lbs.

7. Remove the lock pin from the selector shaft housing and reinstall the lock pin (with the long end up) in the selector shaft housing. Tighten the lock pin to 9 ft. lbs.

8. Check the first/reverse shifting and blockout into reverse.

9. Reinstall the console, boot, pull-up ring, retaining nut and knob.

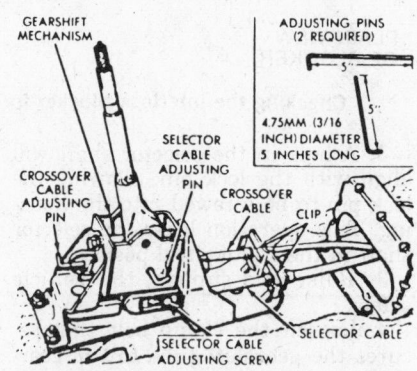

Fabricate (2) cable adjusting pins—all except Daytona, Laser, Shadow and Sundance

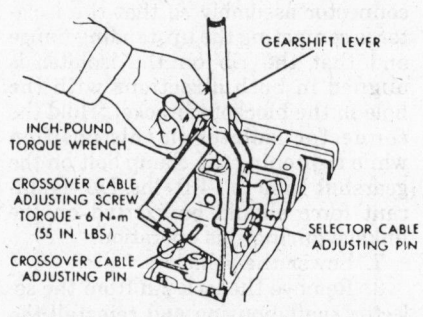

Adjusting the crossover cable—Daytona, Laser, Shadow and Sundance

CLUTCH

— CAUTION —

When servicing the clutch assembly, DO NOT create dust by sanding or cleaning the clutch parts (a water dampened cloth should be used). The clutch disc may contain asbestos fibers, which can create a health hazard by breathing during service operations.

REMOVAL & INSTALLATION

A-412 Transaxle

1. Refer to the "Manual Transaxle Removal & Installation" procedures in this section and remove the transaxle.

2. Diagonally loosen the flywheel-to-pressure plate bolts, 1–2 turns at a time to avoid warpage.

3. Remove the flywheel and clutch disc from the pressure plate.

4. Remove the retaining ring and the release plate.

5. Diagonally loosen the pressure plate-to-crankshaft bolts. Mark all of the parts for reassembly.

6. Remove the mounting bolts, the backing plate and pressure plate.

7. The flywheel and pressure plate surfaces should be cleaned thoroughly with a water dampened cloth.

8. To install, align the marks of the pressure plate, the backing plate and bolts. Coat the bolts with thread compound and torque them to 55 ft. lbs.

9. Install the release plate and the retaining ring.

10. Using the clutch disc installation tool No. L–4533 or equivalent, install the clutch disc and the flywheel on the pressure plate.

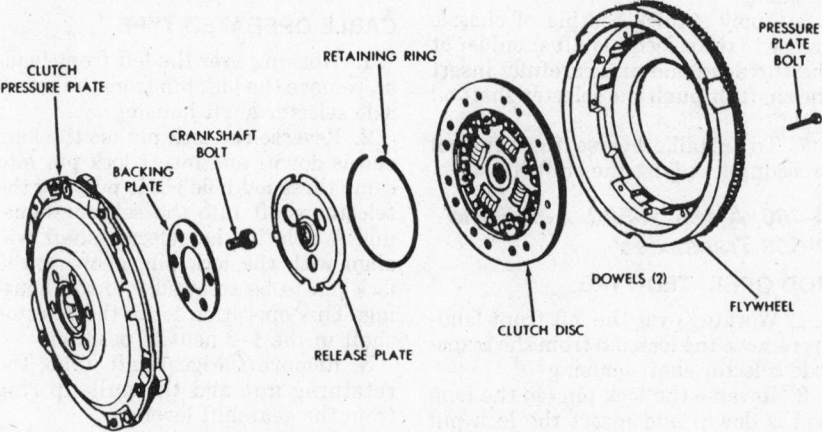

A-412 transaxle clutch assembly—exploded view

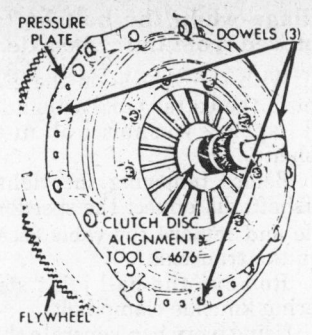

Clutch assembly and alignment tool

NOTE: Make certain the drilled mark on the flywheel is at the top, so that the two dowels on the flywheel align with the proper holes of the pressure plate.

11. To complete the installation, torque the six flywheel bolts to 15 ft. lbs. and reverse the removal procedures.

A-460, A-465, A-520, A-525 and A-555 Transaxles

1. Refer to the "Manual Transaxle Removal & Installation" procedures in this section and remove the transaxle.

2. Match mark the clutch/pressure plate cover and flywheel. Insert the clutch plate alignment tool No. C–4676 or equivalent, into the clutch disc hub.

3. Loosen the flywheel-to-pressure plate bolts diagonally, 1–2 turns at a time to avoid warpage.

4. Remove the pressure plate/clutch assembly from the flywheel.

5. To install, use clutch disc alignment tool No. C–4676 or equivalent, (to hold the clutch) and reverse the re-

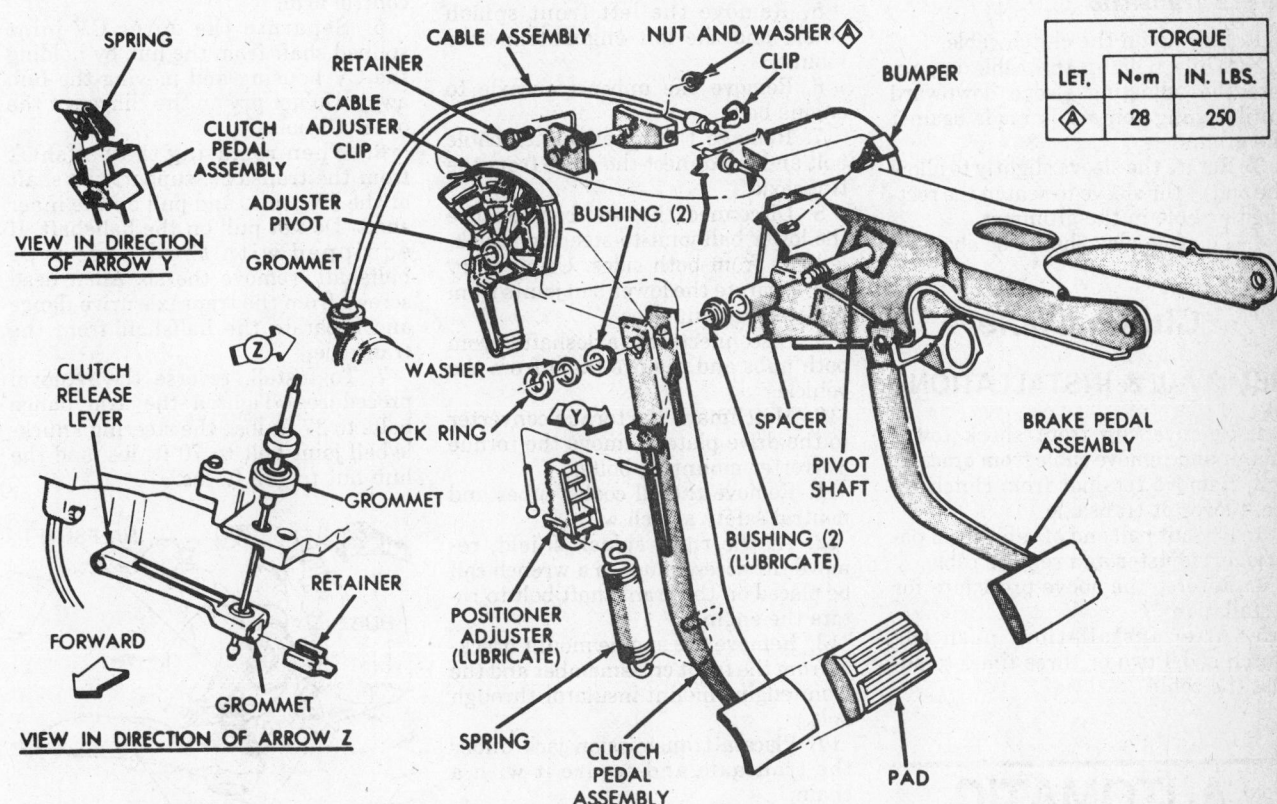

TORQUE		
LET.	N•m	IN. LBS.
△	28	250

Manual transaxle self-adjusting clutch release mechanism—for all except A-412 model

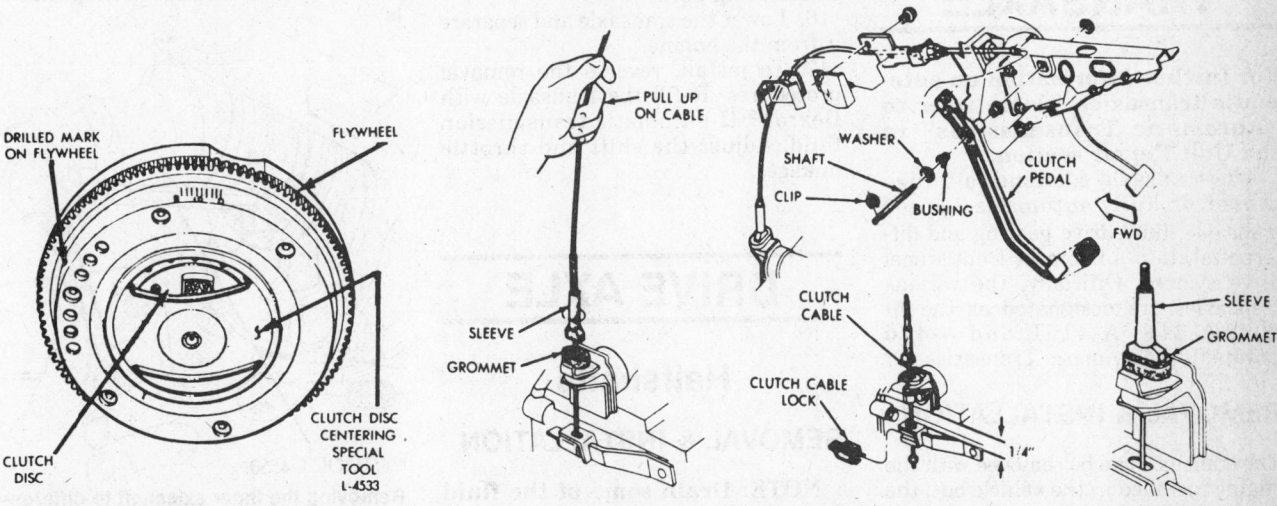

Using the special aligning tool

Adjusting the clutch pedal free-play—A-412 manual transaxle

moval procedures. Torque the pressure plate/clutch assembly mounting bolts to the flywheel, a few turns at a time (diagonally), to 21 ft. lbs. After installation, adjust the clutch freeplay.

PEDAL HEIGHT/FREE-PLAY ADJUSTMENT

NOTE: The A-460, A-465, A-520, A-525 and A-555 transaxles are equipped with a self-adjusting clutch release mechanism. No adjustment is necessary.

A-412 Transaxle

1. Pull up on the clutch cable.
2. While holding the cable up, rotate the adjusting sleeve downward until a snug contact is made against the grommet.
3. Rotate the sleeve slightly to allow the end of the sleeve to seat in the rectangular hole in the grommet.
4. The free-play should be about ¼ in.

Clutch Cable

REMOVAL & INSTALLATION

1. Remove clip from shock tower mount and remove cable from bracket.
2. Remove retainer from clutch release lever at transaxle.
3. Pry out ball end of cable from positioner adjuster and remove cable.
4. Reverse the above procedure for installation.
5. After installation, push the clutch pedal two or three times to adjust the cable.

AUTOMATIC TRANSAXLE

For further information on automatic transaxles, please refer to "Automatic Transmissions" in the Unit Repair section.

The transaxle combines a torque converter, fully automatic 3-speed transaxle, final drive gearing and differential, into a compact front wheel drive system. Officially, the various transaxles are designated as the A-404, A-413, A-415L and A-470 Torqueflite Automatic Transaxles.

REMOVAL & INSTALLATION

The transaxle can be removed with the engine installed in the vehicle but, the transaxle and torque converter must be removed as an assembly. Otherwise the drive plate, pump bushing or oil seal could be damaged. The drive plate will not support a load. No weight should be allowed on the drive plate.

1. Disconnect the negative battery cable.
2. Install an engine lifting eye fixture on the No. 4 cylinder exhaust manifold bolt and support the engine.
3. Disconnect the shift and the throttle linkages.
4. Remove the hub castle lock nut and the cotter pin from both front wheels. Raise and support the vehicle safely. Remove both front wheels.
5. Remove the left front splash shield and the left engine/transaxle mount.
6. Remove the upper transaxle to engine bolts.
7. Remove the speedometer cable bolt and disconnect the cable from the transaxle.
8. Disconnect the sway bar. Remove the lower ball joint-to-steering knuckle bolts from both sides. Using a pry bar, separate the lower ball joints from the steering knuckles.
9. Disconnect the axleshafts from both hubs and remove them from the vehicle.
10. Matchmark the torque converter to the drive plate. Remove the torque converter mounting bolts.
11. Remove the oil cooler tubes and neutral safety switch wire.
12. At the right splash shield, remove the access plug, so a wrench can be placed on the crankshaft bolt to rotate the engine.
13. Remove the engine mount bracket from the front crossmember and the front engine mount insulator through bolt.
14. Place a transmission jack under the transaxle and secure it with a chain.
15. Remove the starter and the lower bell housing bolts.
16. Lower the transaxle and separate it from the engine.
17. To install, reverse the removal procedures. Refill the transaxle with Dexron® II automatic transmission fluid. Adjust the shift and throttle linkages.

DRIVE AXLE

Halfshafts

REMOVAL & INSTALLATION

NOTE: Drain some of the fluid from the transaxle to prevent oil spillage when the halfshafts are removed from the transaxle.

1. With the vehicle on the ground, remove the cotter pin, castle hub nut lock, spring washer, hub nut and washer.
2. Before removing the right side halfshaft, disconnect the speedometer cable and remove the cable assembly from the transaxle.
3. Remove the ball joint stud to steering knuckle clamp bolt.
4. Using a pry bar, separate the ball joint stud from the steering knuckle, by prying against the knuckle leg and control arm.
5. Separate the outer CV-joint splined shaft from the hub by holding the CV housing and moving the hub away. Do not pry on the slinger or the outer CV-joint.
6. When removing the halfshaft from the transaxle, support the shaft at the CV-joints and pull on the inner shaft. Do not pull on the halfshaft. If equipped with the flange type halfshaft, remove the six Allen head screws from the transaxle drive flange and separate the halfshaft from the transaxle.
7. To install, reverse the removal procedures. Tighten the axle flange bolts to 37 ft. lbs., the steering knuckle/ball joint bolt to 70 ft. lbs. and the hub nut to 180 ft. lbs.

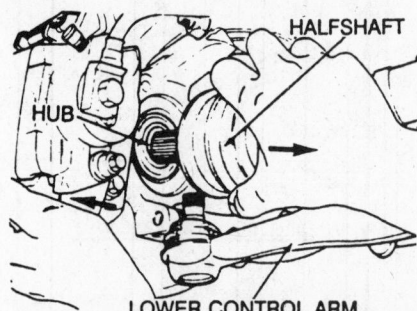

Removing halfshaft from steering knuckle

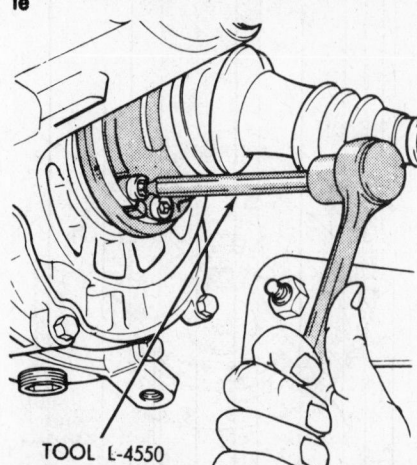

Removing the inner axleshaft to differential flange Allen head bolts

CV-JOINT OVERHAUL

For all CV-Joint overhaul procedures, please refer to "U/CV-Joint Overhaul" in the Unit Repair section.

Front Wheel Drive Hub, Knuckle and Bearings

ADJUSTMENT

1. Raise and support the vehicle safely.
2. Remove the grease cap, cotter pin, lock nut and spring washer. Loosen the hub nut.
3. Apply pressure to the brakes.
4. Tighten the hub nut to 180 ft. lbs.
5. To install, reverse the removal procedures. Lower the vehicle.

REMOVAL & INSTALLATION

Steering Knuckle

1. Remove the grease cap, cotter pin, lock nut and spring washer. Loosen the hub nut with the vehicle on the floor and with the brakes applied.
2. Raise and support the vehicle safely. Remove the wheel assembly, hub nut and washer.
3. Using a ball joint removal tool No. C–3894–A or equivalent, separate the tie rod end from the steering knuckle.
4. Disconnect the brake hose retainer from the MacPherson strut.
5. Remove the ball joint to steering knuckle bolt. Using pry bar, separate the control arm from the steering knuckle.

NOTE: Do not pull outwards on the steering knuckle. The inner CV-joint may separate from the transaxle.

6. Remove the brake caliper adaptor bolt and washer assemblies. Support the caliper on a wire, not on the brake hose.
7. Remove the brake rotor. Using a soft mallet, pull the steering knuckle assembly outward and tap the halfshaft out of the hub. Support the halfshaft on a wire.
8. Mark the location of the strut to steering knuckle bolts. Remove the bolts and remove the steering knuckle assembly.
9. To install, reverse the removal procedures. Tighten the tie rod to steering knuckle nut to 35 ft. lbs., the control arm to steering knuckle bolt to 70 ft. lbs., the hub nut bolt to 180 ft. lbs., the brake caliper to steering

knuckle bolts to 160 ft. lbs. and the strut to steering knuckle bolts to 45 ft. lbs. (Omni and Horizon) or 75 ft. lbs., plus a $\frac{1}{4}$ turn (all other models).

Hub and Bearings

1982–83

1. Using the hub removal tool No. C–4539 or equivalent, and the triangular adapter, attach the tools to the three rear threaded holes of the steering knuckle housing with the thrust button and the fabricated washer ($\frac{15}{16}$ in. dia. x $1\frac{1}{2}$ in. dia.), inside the hub bore.
2. Tighten the center bolt of the tool to press the hub from the steering knuckle. Remove the tools.
3. Using the thrust button from tool No. C–4539 or equivalent, and a wheel puller, remove the bearing outer race from the hub.
4. Remove the three bolts and bearing retainer from the outside of the steering knuckle.
5. Carefully pry the bearing seal from the machined recess of the steering knuckle and clean the recess.
6. Using an arbor press, place the steering knuckle face down on two supports, place a 1⅝ in. socket on the hub bearing. Press the bearing from the steering knuckle. Discard the bearing.
7. To install, place the steering knuckle (face up) on two wooden blocks, under an arbor press. Place the new bearing in the steering knuckle and the installation tool No. L–4463 or equivalent, on the bearing. Press the bearing into the steering knuckle.
8. Install the bearing retainer and the three bolts to the steering knuckle. Torque the bearing retainer bolts to 20 ft. lbs.

9. Using an arbor press, place the hub (face down) on a wooden support, position the steering knuckle on the hub, a 1⅝ in. socket on the hub bearing and press the assembly together.
10. Place a new seal on the rear of the steering knuckle. Using the bearing installation tool No. C–4698 or equivalent, and a mallet, drive the new dust seal into the steering knuckle. Lubricate the wear sleeve with multipurpose grease and install on the new seal.

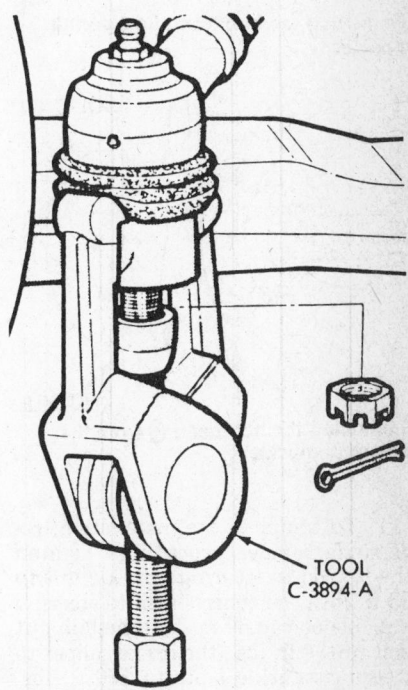

Disconnecting the tie rod from the steering knuckle

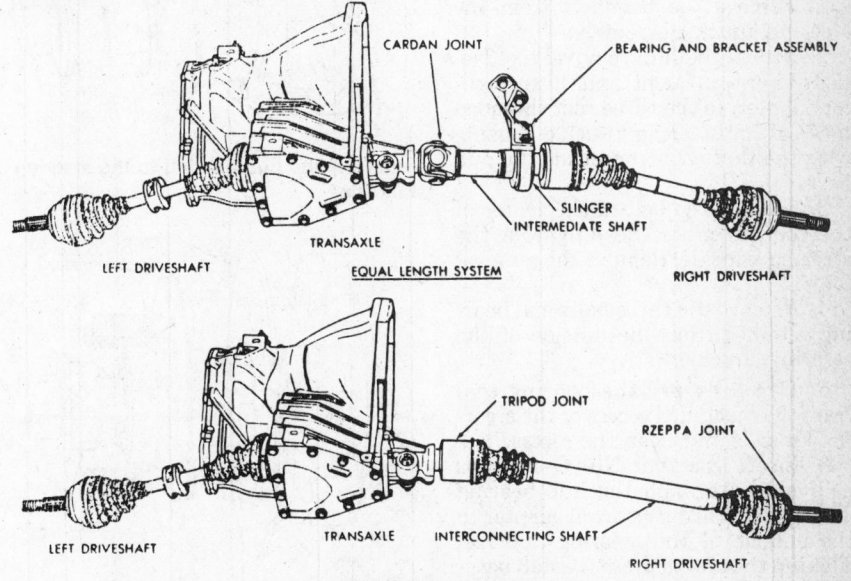

Identifying the equal and unequal length axleshaft systems

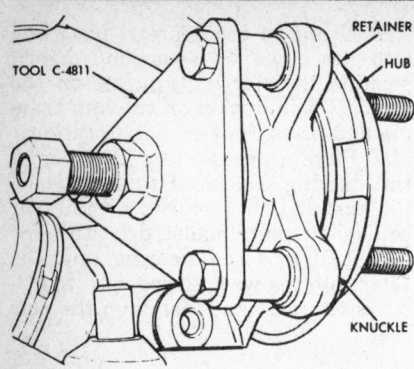

Removing the hub from the steering knuckle

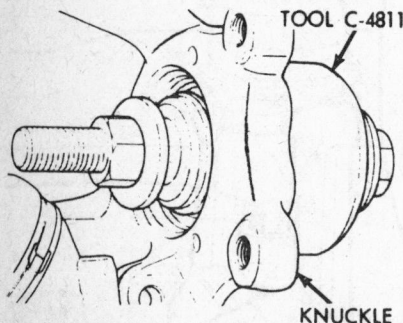

Removing the hub bearing from the steering knuckle

11. To complete the installation, reverse the removal procedures. Tighten the tie rod to steering knuckle nut to 35 ft. lbs., the control arm to steering knuckle bolt to 50 ft. lbs., the hub nut bolt to 180 ft. lbs., the brake caliper to steering knuckle bolts to 160 ft. lbs. and strut to steering knuckle bolts to 45 ft. lbs., plus a ¼ turn.

1984–89

1. Remove the halfshaft from the steering knuckle assembly.
2. Attach the hub removal tool No. C–4811 or equivalent, and the triangular adapter, to the three rear threaded holes of the steering knuckle housing with the thrust button inside the hub bore.
3. Tighten the bolt in the center of the tool, to press the hub from the steering knuckle. Remove the removal tools.
4. Remove the three bolts and bearing retainer from the outside of the steering knuckle.
5. Carefully pry the bearing seal from the machined recess of the steering knuckle and clean the recess.
6. Insert the tool No. C–4811 or equivalent, through the hub bearing and install bearing removal adapter to the outside of the steering knuckle. Tighten the tool to press the hub bearing from the steering knuckle. Discard the bearing and the seal.

7. To install, use tool No. C–4811 or equivalent, and the bearing installation adapter to press in the hub bearing into the steering knuckle.
8. Install a new seal, the bearing retainer and the three bolts to the steering knuckle. Tighten the bearing retainer bolts to 20 ft. lbs.
9. Use the tool No. C–4811 or equivalent, and the hub installation adapter, to press the hub into the hub bearing.
10. Using the bearing installation tool No. C–4698 or equivalent, drive the new dust seal into the rear of the steering knuckle.
11. To complete the installation, reverse the removal procedures. Tighten the tie rod to steering knuckle nut to 35 ft. lbs., the control arm to steering knuckle bolt to 70 ft. lbs., the hub nut bolt to 180 ft. lbs. and the brake caliper to steering knuckle bolts to 160 ft. lbs.

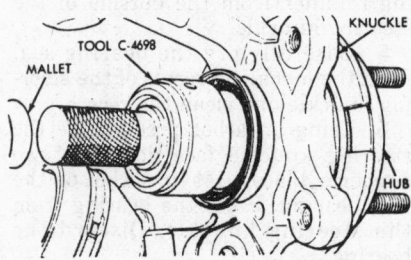

Installing the seal to the steering knuckle

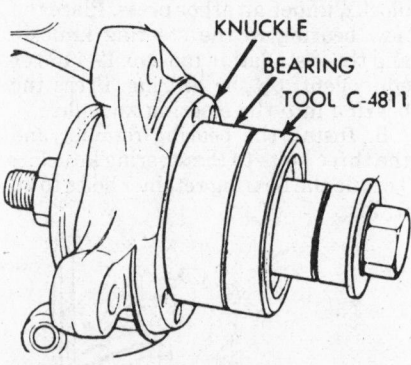

Installing the hub bearing to the steering knuckle

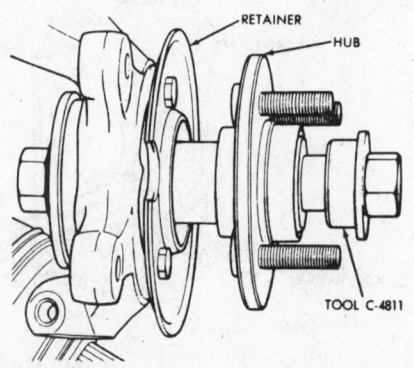

Installing the hub to the steering knuckle

FRONT SUSPENSION

A MacPherson front suspension is used along with vertical shock absorbers attached to the upper fender reinforcement and steering knuckle. The lower control arms are attached inboard, to a cross-member and outboard, to the steering knuckle through a ball joint, provided at the lower steering knuckle position.

MacPherson Strut

REMOVAL & INSTALLATION

1. Raise and support the vehicle safely. Remove the wheel assembly.
2. If the original strut is being assembled to the original knuckle, mark the cam adjusting bolt. Remove the cam adjusting bolt, steering knuckle bolt and brake hose bracket retaining screw.
3. Support the strut from below, remove the strut to body mounting nuts and remove the strut assembly from the vehicle.
4. To install, reverse the removal procedures. Position the steering knuckle in the strut and install the upper (cam) bolt. Index the cam bolt with the matchmarks. Tighten the strut to body nuts to 20 ft. lbs., the wheel nuts to 80–95 ft. lbs., the brake hose bracket screw to 10 ft. lbs., the cam/steering knuckle bolts to 45 ft. lbs. (Omni and Horizon) or 75 ft. lbs. (all other models), plus a ¼ turn.

OVERHAUL

For all spring and shock absorber removal and installation procedures, and all strut overhaul procedures, please refer to "Strut Overhaul" in the Unit Repair Section.

Ball Joints

INSPECTION

The lower ball joint is checked at the lube fitting. Shake the lube fitting, if it moves, the ball joint is worn and should be replaced.

REMOVAL & INSTALLATION

NOTE: On some models the ball joints are welded to the control arms and can not be pressed out. To service this type of ball joint, remove and replace the ball joint and control arm as an assembly.

1. Raise and support the vehicle safely.

2. Remove the clamp bolt and separate the ball joint from the steering knuckle. Remove the control arm pivot bolt and control arm.

3. Pry the dust seal from the ball joint.

4. Using an arbor press, position a receiving cup tool No. C–4699–2 or equivalent, to support the lower control arm. Install a 1 1/16 in. deep socket over/against the stud joint upper housing. Press the ball joint from the control arm.

5. To install, position a new ball joint housing into the control arm cavity.

6. Position the ball joint and the control arm in the press, with an installer tool No. C–4699–1 or equivalent, (under the ball joint) and the receiver cup tool No. C–4699–2 or equivalent, (over the ball joint stud). Align the assembly and press it together, until the housing ledge stops against the control arm cavity down flange.

7. Place a new seal over the ball joint stud, followed by a 1½ in. socket, support the ball joint housing with installer tool No. C–4699–1 or equivalent, and press the seal onto the ball joint housing, until it seats against the control arm.

8. To complete the installation, reverse the removal procedures. Tighten the control arm pivot bolt to 105 ft. lbs. and the ball joint to steering knuckle bolt to 70 ft. lbs.

Lower Control Arm

REMOVAL & INSTALLATION

1. Raise and support the vehicle safely.

If the grease nipple (arrow) in the ball joint wobbles or turns, the ball joint is worn and should be replaced.

2. Remove the front inner pivot through bolt, stub strut nut, retainer and ball joint to steering knuckle clamp bolt.

3. Separate the ball joint stud from the steering knuckle by prying between the steering knuckle and the control arm.

NOTE: Pulling the steering knuckle out from the vehicle, after releasing it from the ball joint, can separate the inner CV-joint.

4. Remove the sway bar to control arm nut and rotate the control arm over the sway bar. Remove the control arm from the stub strut bushing assembly.

NOTE: The substitution of fasteners with other than those of the grade originally used is not recommended.

5. To install, reverse the removal procedures. Tighten ball joint stud to

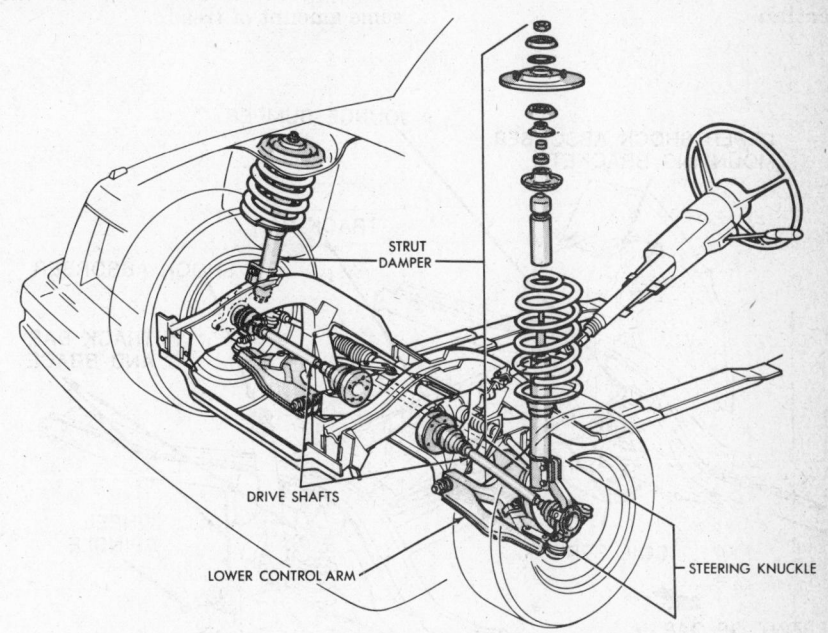

Front suspension—Omni and Horizon shown; other models similar

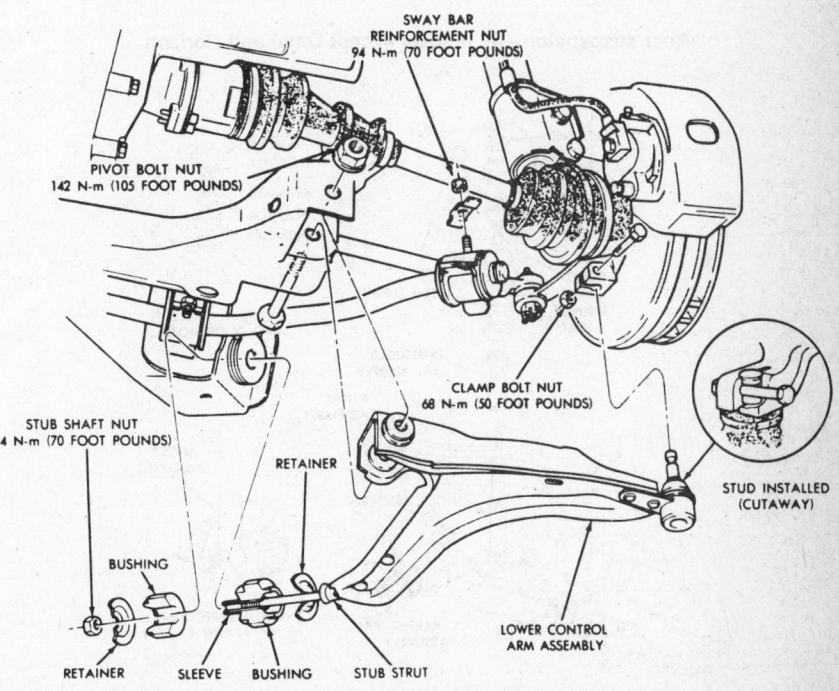

Lower control arm mounting—all models similar

steering knuckle bolt to 70 ft. lbs. and the sway bar bracket nuts to 25 ft. lbs.

6. Lower the vehicle.

7. Tighten the front pivot bolt to 105 ft. lbs. and stub strut nut to 70 ft. lbs.

Front Wheel Bearings

Refer to the "Front Wheel Drive Hub, Knuckle, and Bearings" procedures in the "Drive Axle" section.

Front Wheel Alignment

PRE-ALIGNMENT CHECKING

Before attempting to align the vehicle, the following checks should be performed and any necessary corrections made.

1. Check the air pressure in the tires. Set the pressure to the recommended pressure.

2. All tires should be of the same size, in good condition and with the same amount of tread.

3. Inspect the lower ball joint and steering linkage for play.

4. Check for broken or sagging, front and rear springs.

CAMBER

Camber is adjusted by loosening the cam and knuckle bolts and rotating the cam bolt until the proper specification is obtained.

CASTER

Caster is not adjustable. If the caster is out of specifications, check for worn, loose or broken suspension and/or steering components.

TOE

Toe is adjusted by changing the tie rod length. Loosen the right and left tie rod end lock nuts first and then turn left and right tie rods by the same amount to align toe to specification.

NOTE: Before turning the tie rods, apply grease between tie rods and rack boots so that the boots won't be twisted. After adjustment, tighten lock nuts to specified torque and make sure that the rack boots are not twisted.

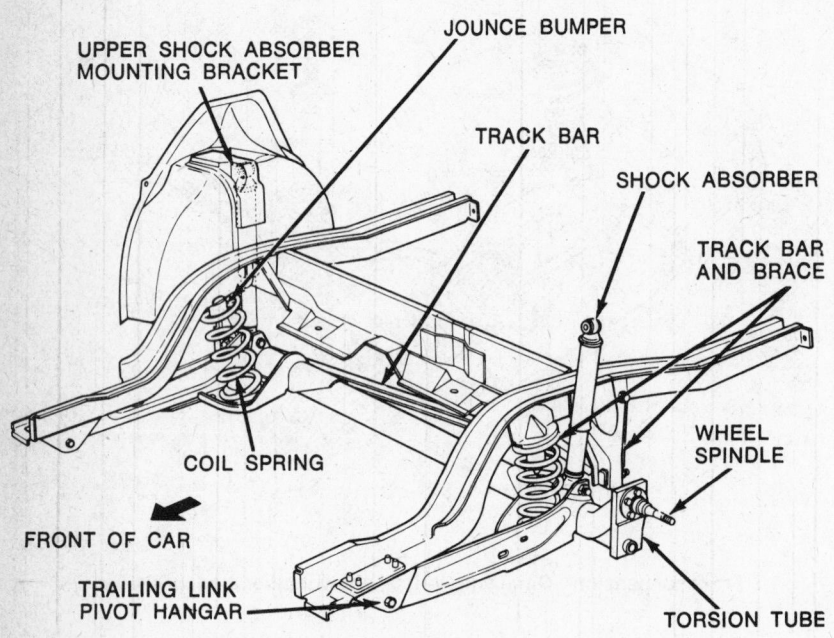

Rear suspension—All models except Omni and Horizon

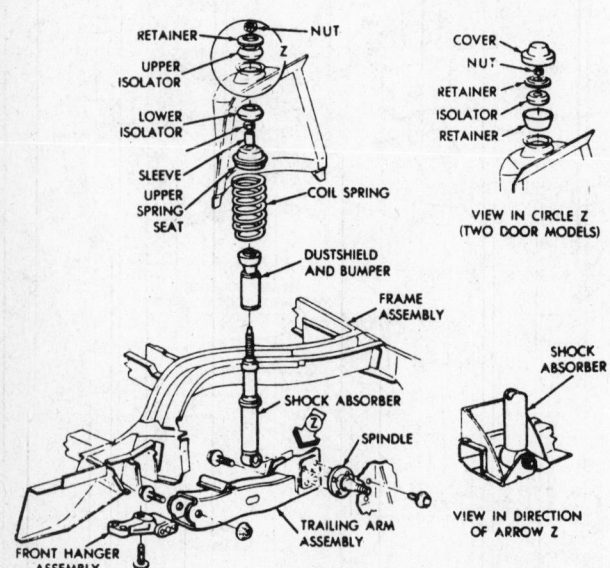

Rear suspension—Omni and Horizon models only

REAR SUSPENSION

Omni, Horizon, Charger, Turismo, TC3 and 024

These vehicles use an independent trailing arm assembly, with an integral sway bar. Each wheel spindle is attached to a MacPherson type shock absorber and a trailing arm, that extends rearward from the body mounting point. A crossmember is welded to the trailing arms, which provides lateral location and anti-roll bar type stabilizing.

All Other Models

On these models, a flexible beam axle with trailing links and coil springs is used. A shock absorber, mounted near each coil spring, is attached to the body and to the beam axle. Each wheel spindle is bolted to the outer end of the beam axle.

Shock Absorber

REMOVAL & INSTALLATION

All Models Without MacPherson Strut

1. Raise and support the vehicle safely. If equipped with air shocks, disconnect the air lines at the shocks.
2. Support the axle assembly and disconnect the upper and lower shock absorber mounting bolts.
3. Remove the shock absorber from the vehicle.
4. Purge the new shocks of air, by compressing them while inverted and extending them in their normal position, several times.
5. To install, reverse the removal procedures. Tighten the upper bolt to 45 ft. lbs. and the lower bolt to 40 ft. lbs.

MacPherson Strut

REMOVAL & INSTALLATION

1. Remove the protective cap from the upper mounting nut. On two door models, remove the lower rear quarter panel trim.
2. Remove the upper mounting nut, isolator retainer and isolator.
3. Raise and support the vehicle safely.
4. Remove the lower strut to trailing arm bolt.
5. Remove the strut from the vehicle.
6. To install, reverse the removal procedures. Tighten the lower strut to trailing bolt to 40 ft. lbs. and the upper strut to body nut to 20 ft. lbs.

OVERHAUL

For all strut overhaul procedures, please refer to "Strut Overhaul" in the Unit Repair section.

Springs

REMOVAL & INSTALLATION

All Models Without MacPherson Strut

1. Raise and support the vehicle safely. Position a floor jack under the axle assembly.
2. Remove the shock absorber to axle mounting bolts.
3. Lower the axle assembly to remove the spring and insulator.
4. To install, reverse the removal procedures. Tighten the lower bolts to 40 ft. lbs.

Rear Wheel Bearings

ADJUSTMENT

1. Raise and support the vehicle safely.
2. Remove the grease cap, cotter pin and lock nut.
3. Tighten the hub nut until it is snug and it back off slightly.
4. Install lock nut and a new cotter pin.
5. Rotate the wheel assembly to make sure that it rotates freely.

REMOVAL & INSTALLATION

Models With Rear Drum Brakes

1. Raise and support the vehicle safely.
2. Remove the grease cap, cotter pin, lock nut, hub nut, washer and outer wheel bearing.
3. Pull the brake drum and wheel assembly off of the axle spindle.
4. From inside the brake drum, remove the dust seal and inner wheel bearing.
5. If necessary, remove the wheel bearing races, by using a brass drift and a hammer to drive the races from the opposite side of the drum.
6. Clean and inspect the bearings and races for damage. Replace, if necessary.
7. Repack the bearings with clean wheel bearing grease. Drive the races into the hub until seated, coat the inside of the drum with grease, install the inner bearing and a new dust seal (flush with the drum).
8. To install, reverse the removal procedures.
9. Adjust the wheel bearings when finshed.

Models With Rear Disc Brakes

1. Raise and support the vehicle safely. Remove the brake caliper from the mount and remove the brake rotor.
2. Remove the grease cap, cotter pin, lock nut, hub nut, washer and outer wheel bearing.
3. Pull the hub assembly off of the spindle.
4. From inside the hub assembly, remove the dust seal and inner wheel bearing.
5. If necessary, remove the wheel bearing races, by using a brass drift and a hammer to drive the races from the opposite side of the hub.
6. Clean and inspect the bearings and races for damage. Replace, if necessary.
7. Repack the bearings with clean wheel bearing grease. Drive the races into the hub until seated, coat the inside of the hub with grease, install the inner bearing and a new dust seal (flush with the hub).
8. To install, reverse the removal procedures.
9. Adjust the wheel bearings when finshed.

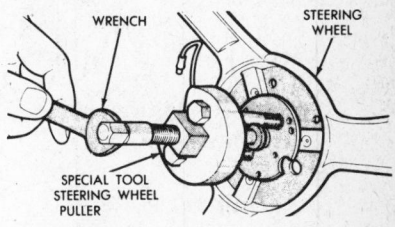

Steering wheel removal

STEERING

Steering Wheel

REMOVAL & INSTALLATION

1. Disconnect the negative battery cable and the wiring connector at the steering column.
2. Remove the horn button or the pad and the horn switch.
3. Remove the steering wheel nut.
4. Using a steering wheel puller tool No. C–3428B or equivalent, remove the steering wheel.
5. To install, align the master serration in the wheel hub with the missing tooth on the shaft. Tighten the shaft nut to 45 ft. lbs.

NOTE: To avoid possible damage, do not tighten the nut against the steering column lock.

6. Replace the horn switch and button.

Turn Signal Switch

REMOVAL & INSTALLATION

Omni, Horizon, Charger, Turismo, TC3 and 024

1. Disconnect the electrical connector at the column.
2. Remove the steering wheel and the lower column cover.
3. Remove the wash/wipe switch.
4. Remove the wiring clip, the three turn signal switch screws and the switch from the steering column.
5. To install, reverse the removal procedures.

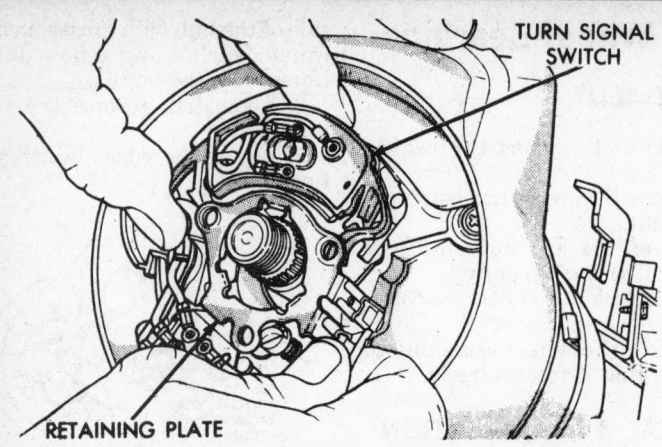

Turn signal switch removal—Aries and Reliant

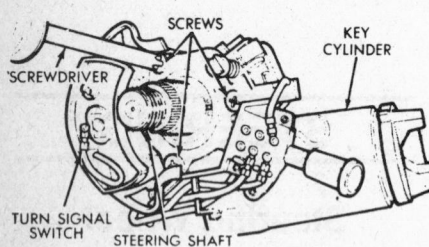

Turn signal switch removal—Omni and Horizon

All Other Models

TILT WHEEL

1. Disconnect the negative battery cable.

2. Remove the steering wheel, the column under cover and the lower instrument panel bezel.

3. Pry out the wiring trough plastic retainers and lift out the trough.

4. Position the gearshift lever to the full clockwise position.

5. Disconnect the turn signal wiring connectors at the steering column.

6. If equipped, remove the plastic cover from the lock plate. Using tool No. C–4156 or equivalent, depress the lock plate and pry out the retaining ring.

7. Remove the lock plate, the cancelling cam and the upper bearing spring.

8. Place the turn signal switch in the right turn position and remove the turn signal-to-wash/wiper switch pivot screw.

9. Remove the hazard warning switch knob screw and the three turn signal switch-to-steering column screws.

10. Remove the turn signal/hazard warning switch assembly by pulling the switch up the column, while straightening and guiding the wires up through the column opening.

11. To install, reverse the removal procedures. Lubricate the switch pivot with light grease. Place the switch in the right turn position, when installing. Use tool No. C–4156 or equivalent, to install the upper bearing spring, the cancelling cam and the lock plate.

WITHOUT TILT WHEEL

1. Disconnect the negative battery cable.

2. Remove the steering wheel, the column under cover and the lower instrument panel bezel.

3. Pry out the wiring trough plastic retainers and lift out the trough.

4. Position the gearshift lever to the full clockwise position.

5. Disconnect the turn signal wiring connectors at the steering column.

6. Remove the wash/wipe switch-to-turn signal switch pivot screw.

NOTE: Leave the turn signal lever in the installed position.

7. Remove the three turn signal switch-to-upper bearing housing screws.

8. Remove the turn signal/hazard warning switch assembly by pulling the switch up the column, while straightening and guiding the wires up through the column opening.

9. To install, reverse the removal procedures. Lubricate the switch pivot with light grease.

Ignition and Steering Lock

REMOVAL & INSTALLATION

Omni, Horizon, Charger, Turismo, TC3 and 024

1. Place the cylinder in the LOCK position and remove the key.

2. Remove the steering wheel, the four column cover screws, the covers, the sound deadener panel and the turn signal switch.

3. Using a hacksaw blade, cut the upper ¼ in. from the key cylinder retainer pin boss.

4. Using a drift punch, drive the roll pin from the housing and remove the key cylinder.

5. To install, insert the cylinder into the housing, make sure it engages the lug on the ignition switch driver, install the roll pin and reverse the removal procedures. Check the cylinder for free operation.

All Other Models

TILT WHEEL

1. Disconnect the negative battery cable. Remove the column covers and the wiring connectors.

2. Place the cylinder in the LOCK position and remove the key.

3. Remove the tilt lever. Push the hazard warning in and unscrew the knob.

4. Remove the steering wheel and the ignition key lamp assembly.

5. Using the lock plate depressing tool No. C–4156 or equivalent, remove the lock plate, the cancelling arm and the upper bearing spring.

6. Remove the three turn signal switch assembly screws, place the shift bowl in the low (1) position, wrap tape around the wiring connector and pull the switch/wiring connector from the steering column.

7. Insert a small tool into the slot, next to the cylinder lock mounting boss, depress the tool and pull the lock assembly from the steering column.

8. To install, insert the cylinder lock (moving it up and down to align the parts) and reverse the removal procedures. Check the operation of the cylinder lock.

WITHOUT TILT WHEEL

1. Disconnect the negative battery cable and remove the column covers.

2. Place the cylinder in the LOCK position and remove the key.

3. Remove the steering wheel, the turn signal/wash/wipe switch assembly, the upper bearing retaining plate, the lock plate spring and the lock plate from the steering column.

4. Remove the buzzer/chime switch screw and the switch.

5. Remove the two ignition switch-to-column screws and the switch, slide off the actuating rod.

6. Remove the two dimmer switch screws and disengage from the actuating rod.

7. Remove the two bellcrank screws and slide it up the in the lock housing to disengage it from the ignition actuator rod.

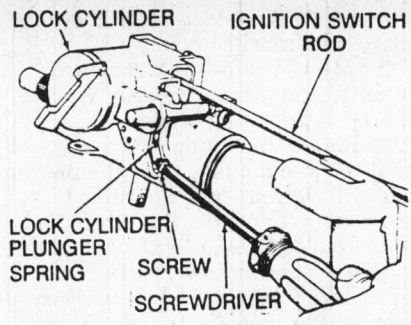

Removing lock cylinder plunger spring

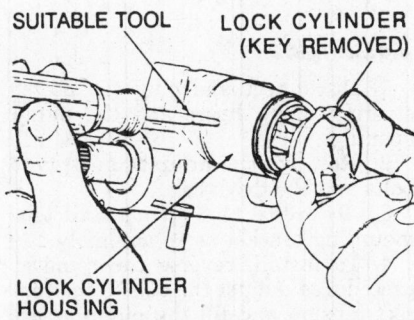

Depressing retainer to remove lock cylinder

8. Insert a small diameter tool into both cylinder lock release holes, push in on the tools and pull the lock cylinder out of the housing.

9. To install, reverse the removal procedures. Check the operation of the cylinder lock.

Ignition Switch

REMOVAL & INSTALLATION

1. Disconnect the negative battery cable. Place the ignition cylinder in the LOCK position and remove the key.

2. Remove the four column cover screws, the covers and the sound deadener panel.

3. Loosen the two ignition switch mounting plate screws and push the switch up to take up the rod system slack.

4. Remove the clutch speed control switch.

5. Remove the mounting bolts and drop the steering column for the switch replacement.

6. Remove the two ignition switch-to-column screws.

7. Rotate the switch 90 degrees and pull up to disengage the switch from the switch rod.

8. To install, push-up on the switch to take up the rod slack, tighten the lock screws and reverse the removal procedures. Check the switch for proper operation.

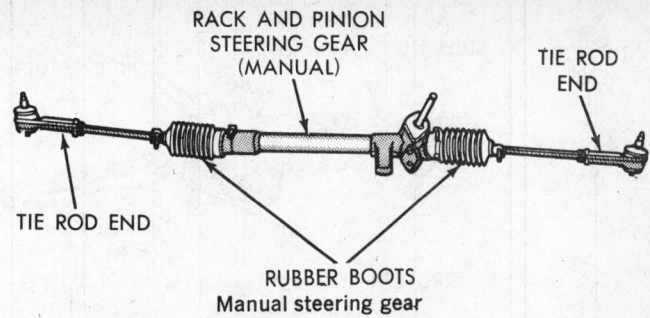

Manual steering gear

Manual Steering Gear

REMOVAL & INSTALLATION

NOTE: On some models, except Omni, Horizon, Charger, Shadow, Sundance, Turismo, TC3 and 024, the steering column must be removed.

1. Raise and support the vehicle safely. Remove front wheel assemblies.

2. Remove the cotter pins, castle nuts and tie rod ends (using a ball joint puller) from the steering knuckles.

3. Except for the Omni, Horizon, Charger, Shadow, Sundance, Turismo, TC3 and 024 models, remove the steering column-to-steering gear coupling pin; follow the procedures in Step 6, this will expose the coupling pin so that it can be driven out. If equipped, remove the anti-rotational link from the crossmember and the air diverter valve bracket, from the left side of the crossmember.

NOTE: The lower universal joint is removed with the steering gear.

4. On the Omni, Horizon, Charger, Shadow, Sundance, Turismo, TC3 and 024 models, drive out the lower roll pin attaching the pinion shaft to the lower universal joint. Use a back-up, to protect the universal joint, while driving the roll pin.

5. On the Omni, Horizon, Charger, Shadow, Sundance, Turismo, TC3 and 024 models, support the front suspension crossmember with a hydraulic jack. Remove the two rear nuts attaching the crossmember to the frame. Loosen the two front bolts attaching the crossmember to the frame and lower the crossmember slightly for access to the boot seal shields.

6. Except for the Omni, Horizon, Charger, Shadow, Sundance, Turismo, TC3 and 024 models, remove the four front suspension crossmember attaching bolts and the lower front suspension crossmember, using a transaxle jack, so that the steering gear can be removed from the crossmember.

7. Remove the splash and the boot seal shields.

8. Remove the steering gear bolts from the front suspension crossmember.

10. Remove the steering gear from the left side of the vehicle.

11. To install, reverse the removal procedures. The right rear crossmember bolt is a pilot bolt that correctly locates the crossmember, tighten it first. Torque the four crossmember bolts to 90 ft. lbs. and the steering gear attaching bolts to 21 ft. lbs.

ADJUSTMENT

1. Loosen the adjuster plug lock nut on the steering gear.

2. Turn the adjuster plug clockwise until it bottoms, then back it off 40–60 degrees.

3. While holding the adjuster plug stationary, torque the lock nut to 50 ft. lbs.

Power Steering Gear

REMOVAL & INSTALLATION

NOTE: On some models, except Omni, Horizon, Charger, Shadow, Sundance, Turismo, TC3 and 024, the steering column must be removed.

1. Raise and support the vehicle safely. Remove front wheel assemblies.

2. Remove the cotter pins, castle nuts and tie-rod ends (using a ball joint puller) from the steering knuckles.

3. Except for the Omni, Horizon, Charger, Shadow, Sundance, Turismo, TC3 and 024 models, remove the steering column-to-steering gear coupling pin; follow the procedures in Step 6, this will expose the coupling pin so that it can be driven out. If equipped, remove the anti-rotational link from the crossmember and the air diverter valve bracket, from the left side of the crossmember.

NOTE: The lower universal joint is removed with the steering gear.

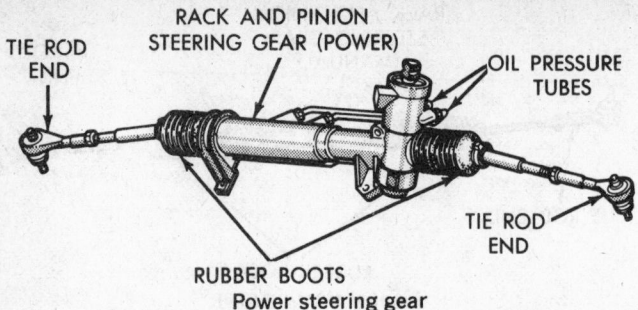

TIE ROD
END

RACK AND PINION
STEERING GEAR (POWER)

OIL PRESSURE
TUBES

TIE ROD
END

RUBBER BOOTS
Power steering gear

4. Disconnect and plug the oil pressure lines from the power steering pump.

5. On the Omni, Horizon, Charger, Shadow, Sundance, Turismo, TC3 and 024 models, drive out the lower roll pin attaching the pinion shaft to the lower universal joint. Use a back-up, to protect the universal joint, while driving the roll pin.

6. On the Omni, Horizon, Charger, Shadow, Sundance, Turismo, TC3 and 024 models, support the front suspension crossmember with a hydraulic jack. Remove the two rear nuts attaching the crossmember to the frame. Loosen the two front bolts attaching the crossmember to the frame and lower the crossmember slightly for access to the boot seal shields.

7. Except for the Omni, Horizon, Charger, Shadow, Sundance, Turismo, TC3 and 024 models, remove the four front suspension crossmember attaching bolts and the lower front suspension crossmember, using a transaxle jack, so that the steering gear can be removed from the crossmember.

8. Remove the splash and the boot seal shields.

9. Remove the steering gear bolts from the front suspension crossmember.

10. Remove the steering gear from the left side of the vehicle.

11. To install, reverse the removal procedures. The right rear crossmember bolt is a pilot bolt that correctly locates the crossmember, tighten it first. Torque the four crossmember bolts to 90 ft. lbs. and the steering gear attaching bolts to 21 ft. lbs. Refill the power steering pump. Bleed the power steering system.

ADJUSTMENT

1. Loosen the adjuster plug lock nut on the steering gear.

2. Turn the adjuster plug clockwise until it bottoms, then back it off 40–60 degrees.

3. While holding the adjuster plug stationary, torque the lock nut to 50 ft. lbs.

Power Steering Pump

REMOVAL & INSTALLATION

1.6L Engine

1. Loosen, but do not remove, the power steering pump pressure hose.

2. Remove the belt adjustment nut and loosen the three locking nuts from the rear pump studs.

3. Place a container on the radiator yoke to catch the power steering fluid.

4. Remove the drive belt and three locking nuts. Lift the pump, bracket and rubber isolator (as an assembly) from the engine.

5. Remove the pump reservoir cap and pour the fluid into the container.

6. Remove and plug the hoses and pump openings.

7. To install, reverse the removal procedures. Adjust the drive belt tension, refill the reservoir with power steering fluid and tighten the locking nuts to 21 ft. lbs. Bleed the power steering system.

1.7L, 2.2L, 2.5L and 3.0L Engines

NOTE: The power steering pump mounting nuts and bolts are metric.

1. Disconnect the vapor separator hose from the carburetor or throttle body and the two wires from the air conditioning clutch cycling switch, if equipped.

2. Loosen the drive belt adjustment bolt and the hose bracket nut, if equipped. Remove the belt from the pump pulley.

3. Raise and support the vehicle safely.

4. Disconnect the return hose from the gear tube and drain the oil from the pump through the end of the hose.

5. Remove the right side splash shield that protects the drive belts.

6. Disconnect both hoses from the pump. Cap the hoses and the pump openings.

7. Remove the lower stud nut and the pivot bolt from the pump.

8. Lower the vehicle and remove the drive belt from the pulley.

9. Move the pump rearward, to clear the mounting bracket and remove the adjusting bracket.

10. Rotate the pump clockwise, so that the pump pulley faces the rear of the vehicle and pull upwards to remove the pump from the vehicle.

11. To install, use new O-rings on the pressure hose and reverse the removal procedures. Adjust the belt to the correct tension and fill the pump reservoir to the proper level with power steering fluid. Torque the adjustment bolt to 30 ft. lbs., the lower stud nut and the pivot bolt to 40 ft. lbs. Bleed the power steering system.

2.6L Engine

1. Disconnect and plug the power steering pump hoses and the pump openings.

2. Remove the adjustment/pivot bolts and the drive belt.

3. Remove the pump and the mounting bracket as an assembly.

4. To install, reverse the removal procedures. Adjust the belt to the correct tension and fill the pump reservoir to the proper level with power steering fluid. Torque the adjustment/pivot bolts to 40 ft. lbs. Bleed the power steering system.

BELT ADJUSTMENT

V-Belts

1. Working on top of the vehicle, loosen the top power steering pump-to-bracket bolt. Working under the vehicle, loosen the bottom power steering pump-to-bracket bolt.

2. Using a 1/2 in. breaker bar, place it into the square hole on the adjusting bracket and turn the adjusting bracket to apply pressure to the belt.

3. Using a straight edge and thumb pressure, at the center of the belt, establish a belt deflection of 1/4 in. (new) or 7/16 in. (used).

4. When the correct deflection is established, torque the top (first) and the bottom (second) power steering pump to bracket bolt to 40 ft. lbs.

SYSTEM BLEEDING

1. Check and/or refill the power steering pump reservoir.

2. Raise and support the vehicle safely.

3. Start the engine and turn the steering wheel from side-to-side (lock-to-lock) several times, to bleed the air from the system.

4. Check and/or refill the power steering pump reservoir.

NOTE: If air bubbles are still present in the oil, repeat the bleeding procedure until the system is free of air bubbles.

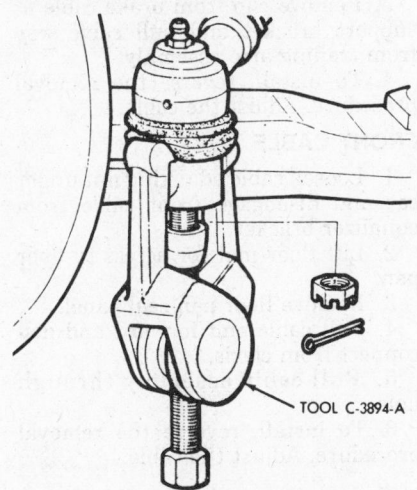

Tie rod end removal—typical

Tie Rod End

REMOVAL & INSTALLATION

All Models

1. Loosen the jam nut which connects the outer tie rod end to the inner tie rod. Mark the tie rod position on the threads.
2. At the steering knuckle, remove the cotter pin, castle nut and tie rod end. Using a ball joint puller tool, separate the ball joint from the steering knuckle.
3. Remove the outer tie rod from the inner tie rod threads, count the number of turns need to remove the tie rod.
4. To install, reverse the removal procedures. Install the new tie rod the same number of turns in as the old one was removed. Check the front wheel alignment.

BRAKES

For all brake system repair and service procedures not detailed below, please refer to "Brakes" in the Unit Repair Section.

Master Cylinder

REMOVAL & INSTALLATION

Power Brakes

1. Disconnect the primary and secondary brake tubes from the master cylinder. Plug the tubes and the cylinder openings.

2. Remove the master cylinder to power brake booster nuts.
3. Slide the master cylinder straight out, away from the booster.
4. To install, reverse the removal procedures. Align the pushrod with the master cylinder piston and tighten the nuts to 16 ft. lbs. Connect the brake tubes and bleed the brakes.

Without Power Brakes

1. Disconnect the primary and secondary brake tubes from the master cylinder. Plug the tubes and the cylinder openings.
2. Disconnect the stoplight switch mounting bracket from under the instrument panel.
3. Pull the brake pedal backward to disengage the pushrod from the master cylinder piston.

NOTE: This will destroy the grommet.

4. Remove the master cylinder-to-firewall nuts.
5. Slide the master cylinder out and away from the firewall. Remove the pieces of the broken grommet.
6. Install the boot on the pushrod.
7. Install a new grommet on the pushrod.
8. Apply a soap and water solution to the grommet and slide it firmly into position in the primary piston socket. Move the pushrod side-to-side to seat the grommet.
9. From the engine side, press the pushrod through the master cylinder mounting plate and align the mounting studs with the holes in the cylinder.
10. Install the nuts and torque them to 16 ft. lbs.
11. From under the instrument panel, place the pushrod on the pin on the pedal and install a new retaining clip. Lubricate the pin.
12. Install the brake tubes on the master cylinder and bleed the brake system.

Combination Valve

The combination valve combines a pressure warning switch and a dual proportioning valve. The systems are diagonally balanced, that is, the front left and right rear are on one system and the front right and left rear on the other. The valve is located below the master cylinder and attached to the frame rail.

REMOVAL & INSTALLATION

1. Disconnect the elecrical connector from the brake warning switch.
2. Disconnect and plug the brake lines from the combination valve.

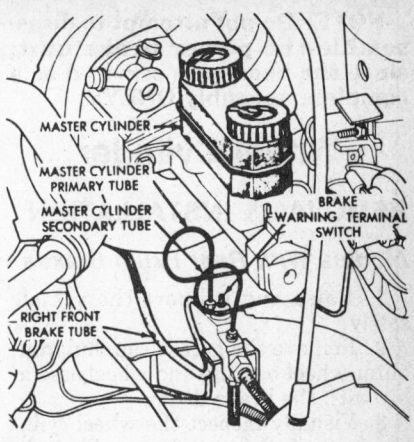

Master cylinder, power booster and combination valve—typical

3. Remove the combination valve-to-frame rail bolts and the valve from the vehicle.
4. To install, reverse the removal procedures. Bleed the brake system.

Power Brake Booster

REMOVAL & INSTALLATION

1. Remove the master cylinder-to-power brake booster nuts and pull the cylinder away from the booster without disconnecting the brake lines.

NOTE: If equipped with a manual transaxle, remove the clutch cable mounting bracket. Pull the wiring harness away and up from the strut tower.

2. Disconnect the vacuum hose from the booster.
3. Under the instrument panel, pry the retainer clip center tang over the end of the brake pedal pin and pull the retainer clip from the pin. Discard the clip.

NOTE: Except for the Omni, Horizon, Charger, Turismo, TC3 and 024 models, remove the stop lamp switch and the striker plate.

4. Remove the booster-to-firewall nuts and the booster from the vehicle.
5. To install, position the booster on the firewall and reverse the removal procedures. Torque the booster-to-firewall and the master cylinder-to-booster mounting nuts to 21 ft. lbs. Lubricate the bearing surface of the pedal pin. Install a new pushrod-to-pedal pin clip. Check the stoplight operation. With vacuum applied to the power brake unit and pressure applied to the pedal, the master cylinder should vent (force a jet of fluid through the front chamber vent port).

NOTE: Do not attempt to disassemble the power brake unit, since the booster is serviced as a complete assembly ONLY.

Wheel Cylinder

REMOVAL & INSTALLATION

Models With Rear Drum Brakes

1. Raise and support the vehicle safely.
2. Remove the grease cap, hub nut, outer wheel bearing and wheel assembly with the brake drum.
3. Visually inspect the wheel cylinder boots for signs of excessive leakage. Replace any boots that are torn or broken.

NOTE: A slight amount of fluid on the boots may not be a leak. The fluid may be preservative fluid.

4. If a leak is detected, remove the brake shoes and check for contamination. Replace the linings if they are soaked with grease or brake fluid.
5. Disconnect the brake line from the wheel cylinder.
6. Remove the wheel cylinder attaching bolts, then pull the wheel cylinder out of its support.
7. To install, reverse the removal procedures. Tighten the wheel cylinder to backing plate bolts to 6 ft. lbs. Bleed the brake system.

Parking Brake Cable

ADJUSTMENT

With Rear Drum Brakes

NOTE: The service brakes must be properly adjusted before adjusting the parking brakes.

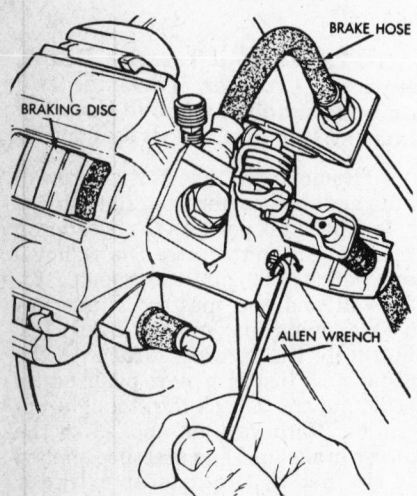

Brake adjustment—rear disc brakes

1. Raise and support the vehicle safely. Fully release the parking brake.
2. Clean the threads of the adjusting nut with a wire brush and lubricate with grease.
3. Loosen the adjusting nut until there is slack in the cable.
4. Check service brakes for proper adjustment. Adjust if necessary.
5. Tighten the adjusting nut until a slight drag in the brakes are felt while rotating the wheels.
6. Loosen the cable adjusting nut until both rear wheels turn freely, then back-off the nut two full turns.
7. Apply and release the parking brake several times to make sure the wheels rotate freely.

REMOVAL & INSTALLATION

Omni, Turismo, Charger, TC3, 024 and Horizon

REAR CABLE

NOTE: Raise and support the vehicle safely. Remove wheel assembly. Back off cable adjusting nut to provide slack and disconnect rear brake cable from connector.

1. Remove retaining clip from brake cable bracket.
2. Remove the brake drum from spindle.
3. Disconnect the cable from brake shoe level.
4. Compress the retainers on end of the cable housing and start the housing out of the support plate.
5. Remove the clamp when the retainer is free.
6. Pull out the brake cable assembly from the trailing arm.
7. To install, reverse the removal procedure. Adjust the cable.

FRONT CABLE

1. Remove cable adjusting nut under car and disengage front cable from connectors.
2. Remove cable housing to floor pan bracket and clips. Loosen heat shield for access to front clip.
3. Remove brake lever housing inside car and lift floor mat for access to floor pan.
4. Pull cable end forward and disconnect from clevis.
5. Remove floor pan seal panel.
6. Compress cable housing retainer and push cable out of floor pan.
7. To install, reverse the removal procedure. Adjust the cable

All Other Models With Drum Brakes

REAR CABLE

1. Disconnect cable from brake shoe level.

2. Using a suitable hose clamp, compress the retainers on end of cable housing and start housing out of support plate.
3. Remove clip from brake cable at support bracket and pull cable way from trailing arm assembly.
4. To install, reverse the removal procedure. Adjust the cable.

FRONT CABLE

1. Loosen cable adjusting nut under car and disengage front cable from equalizer bracket.
2. Lift floor mat for access to floor pan.
3. Remove floor pan seal panel.
4. Pull cable end forward and disconnect from clevis.
5. Pull cable assembly through hole.
6. To install, reverse the removal procedure. Adjust the cable.

All Other Models With Disc

REAR CABLE

1. Remove brake cable retaining clips from hanger bracket and caliper.
2. Disconnect cable from parking brake lever on caliper.
3. Remove wire form cable guide from trailing arm.
4. Pull brake cables assembly out from hanger bracket and caliper.
5. To install, reverse the removal procedure. Adjust the cable.

FRONT CABLE

1. Loosen cable adjusting nut under car and disengage front cable from equalizer bracket.
2. Lift floor mat for access to floor pan.
3. Remove floor pan seal panel.
4. Pull cable end forward and disconnect from clevis.
5. Pull cable assembly through hole.
6. To install, reverse the removal procedure. Adjust the cable.

CHASSIS ELECTRICAL

Heater Blower

REMOVAL & INSTALLATION

NOTE: On A/C equipped vehicles, the blower motor is located inside the Heater/Evaporator Unit. The unit must be removed from the vehicle and disassembled to remove the blower motor.

Blower motor assembly – typical

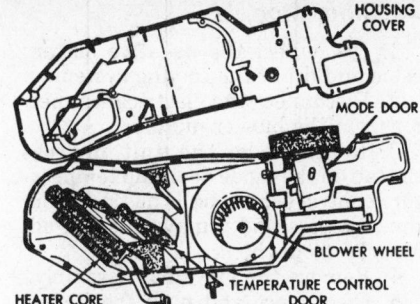

Heater core without A/C location – typical

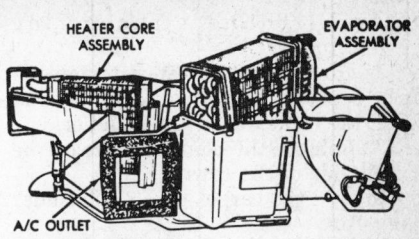

Heater core with A/C location – typical

Omni, Horizon, Charger, Turismo, TC3 and 024

The blower motor is located behind the instrument panel on the left side of the heater assembly.

1. Disconnect the motor electrical connector.
2. Remove the left outlet duct on some models.
3. Remove the motor retaining screws and the motor.
4. To install, reverse the removal procedures.

All Others Models

The blower motor is located under the instrument panel on the left side of the heater assembly.

1. Disconnect the negative battery cable.
2. Disconnect the motor electrical connector.
3. Remove the motor retaining screws and the motor.
4. To install, reverse the removal procedures.

Heater Core (Without A/C)

REMOVAL & INSTALLATION

Omni, Horizon, Charger, Turismo, TC3 and 024

1. Drain the cooling system and remove the heater assembly.
2. Remove the left outlet duct.
3. Remove the blower motor mounting screws and the motor.
4. Remove the outside air and defroster door cover.
5. Remove the defroster door.
6. Remove the defroster door control rod.
7. Remove the core cover.
8. Lift the core out of the unit.
9. To install, reverse the removal procedures.

All Other Models

1. Drain the cooling system and remove the heater assembly.

2. Remove the padding from around the heater core outlets and the upper core mounting screws.
3. Pry loose the retaining snaps from around the outer edge of the housing cover.

NOTE: If a retaining snap should break, the housing cover has provisions for mounting screws.

4. Remove the housing top cover.
5. Remove the bottom heater core mounting screw.
6. Slide the heater core out of the housing.
7. To install, reverse the removal procedures.

Heater Core (With A/C)

REMOVAL & INSTALLATION

Removal of the Heater/Evaporator Unit is required for the core removal. Two people will be required to perform the operation. Discharge, evacuation, recharge and leak testing of the refrigerant system is necessary and should only be performed by someone familiar with and qualified to work on air conditioning systems. During installation, a small can of refrigerant oil will be necessary.

Omni, Horizon, Charger, Turismo, TC3 and 024

1. Disconnect the negative battery cable, discharge the A/C system and drain the cooling system.
2. Disconnect and plug the heater hoses at the heater core and the A/C lines, at the dash.
3. Disconnect the blend air door cable and disengage from the heated air duct clip.
4. Remove the glove box, the center bezel and the bezel.
5. Remove the center distribution duct and the defroster duct adapter.
6. Disconnect the vacuum lines at the engine and the water valve.

7. Remove the assembly retaining nuts at the dash.
8. Remove the right side cowl trim panel.
9. Remove the right instrument panel pivot screw and the steering column-to-panel screws.
10. Remove the top panel cover.
11. Remove all of the panel screws, except the left fenceline screw.
12. Pull the carpet back from under the A/C unit.
13. Remove the hanger strap nut, the blower motor ground cable and the plenum strap nut.
14. Lift the unit rearward, to clear the studs and pull the instrument panel rearward to provide clearance for the unit removal. Drop the unit down and slide it rearward. Remove the assembly from the vehicle and place it on a bench.
15. Remove the 1/4 in. nut from the top of the mode actuator. Remove the two retaining clips from the front edge of the cover and the actuator door.
16. Remove the assembly cover attaching screws and the cover. Remove the heater core tube retaining bracket screw and lift the core from the unit.
17. To install, reverse the removal procedures. Refill the cooling system and charge the A/C system.

All Other Models

1. Disconnect the negative battery cable, discharge the A/C system and drain the cooling system.
2. Disconnect and plug the heater hoses at the heater core.
3. Disconnect the vacuum lines at the engine intake manifold and the water valve.
4. Remove the right scuff plate and the cowl side trim.
5. Remove the glove box and the A/C control.
6. Remove the console and the forward console mounting bracket (if equipped).
7. Remove the center distribution duct and the demister adapter (if equipped).
8. From under the panel, pull out the defroster duct.
9. Remove the clamp and the condensate drain tube.

10. Disconnect the wiring connectors.

11. On the heater/evaporator assembly, depress the control cable flag and pull the cable out of the retainer.

12. Remove the plenum brace on the right side of the cowl.

13. Pull the carpet back from under the unit.

14. Remove the hanger strap-to-assembly screw.

15. Remove the A/C-to-dash panel mounting nuts from the engine compartment.

16. Pull the unit rearward, to clear the studs, drop it down to the converter tunnel, rotate and slide it to one side. Remove the assembly from the vehicle.

17. Remove the actuator arm by squeezing it off the shaft. Remove the two retaining clips from the front edge of the cover and the actuator door.

18. Remove the assembly cover attaching screws and the cover. Remove the heater core tube retaining bracket screw and lift the core from the unit.

19. To install, reverse the removal procedures. Refill the cooling system and charge the A/C system.

Heater Assembly Without A/C

REMOVAL & INSTALLATION

Omni, Horizon, Charger, Turismo, TC3 and 024

1. Disconnect the negative battery cable and drain the cooling system.

2. Disconnect the blower motor wiring connector.

3. Remove the ash tray.

4. Depress the temperature control cable tab and pull the cable out of the receiver (on the heater assembly).

5. Remove the glove box and the door assembly.

6. Disconnect and plug the heater hoses and the heater core tube openings.

7. Remove the heater assembly-to-dash mounting nuts.

8. Remove the wire connector at the blower motor heater block.

9. Remove the heater support bracket-to-instrument panel screw and nut.

10. Under the instrument panel, disconnect the plenum stud/heater assembly strap.

11. On the heater assembly, depress the mode door control cable tab and pull the cable out of the receiver.

12. Move the heater assembly to the right side and remove it from the vehicle.

13. To install, reverse the removal procedures.

All Other Models

1. Disconnect the negative battery cable and drain the cooling system.

2. Disconnect the electrical connector from the blower motor.

3. Reach under the unit, depress the tab on the mode door and temperature control cables, pull the flags from the receivers and remove the self-adjust clip from the crank arm.

4. Remove the glove box assembly.

5. Disconnect and plug the heater hoses and the heater core tube openings.

6. Through the glove box opening, remove the screw attaching the hanger strap to the heater assembly.

7. Remove the nut attaching the hanger strap to the dash panel and remove the hanger strap.

8. Remove the two heater assembly-to-dash panel nuts; the nuts are on the engine side.

9. Pull out the bottom of the instrument panel and slide out the heater assembly.

10. To install, reverse the removal procedures.

Radio

REMOVAL & INSTALLATION

Omni, Horizon, Charger, Turismo, Lancer, LeBaron, TC3 and 024

1. Remove the bezel-to-dash screws and the bezel.

2. Disconnect the radio ground strap. Remove the radio mounting screws.

3. Pull the radio from the panel.

4. Disconnect the wiring and the antenna lead.

5. To install, reverse the removal procedures.

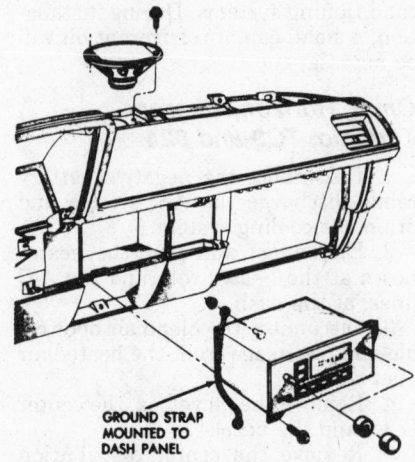

Radio Installation—Omni and Horizon shown, others similar

GROUND STRAP MOUNTED TO DASH PANEL

Daytona and Laser

1. Remove the mounting screws from the bottom of the console trim bezel.

2. Remove the bezel from the console.

3. Remove the radio-to-console mounting screws.

4. Pull the radio out and disconnect the wiring connector, the antenna lead and the ground strap.

5. To install, reverse the removal procedures.

Shadow and Sundance

1. Remove the radio bezel from the center of the dash.

2. If equipped with a base console, remove the lower center module cover.

3. If equipped with a full console assembly, remove the right console sidewall.

4. Remove the radio-to-dash screws and pull the radio out of the dash.

5. Disconnect the wiring, the antenna cable and the ground strap from the radio. Remove the radio from the vehicle.

6. To install, reverse the removal procedures.

All Other Models

1. Remove the left instrument cluster bezel, (if necessary) and the radio bezel(s).

2. Remove the two screws attaching the radio to the base panel.

3. Pull the radio out and disconnect the wiring connector, the antenna lead and the ground strap.

5. To install, reverse the removal procedures.

Windshield Wiper Switch

The wiper switch is located on the end of the turn signal switch lever.

REMOVAL & INSTALLATION

Refer to the "Turn Signal Switch, Removal & Installation" procedures in this section and remove the turn signal/windshield wiper switch from the steering column.

Windshield Wiper Motor

REMOVAL & INSTALLATION

Front Motor

1. Disconnect the linkage from the motor crank arm.

2. Remove the wiper motor plastic cover.

3. Disconnect the wiring harness from the motor.

4. Remove the three mounting bolts and the motor from the motor bracket.

5. To install, reverse the removal procedures.

Rear Motor

OMNI, HORIZON, CHARGER, TURISMO, TC3 AND 024

1. Open the tailgate.

2. Remove the wiper motor plastic cover.

3. Remove the wiper arm assembly.

4. Remove the nut, the ring and the seal from the pivot shaft.

5. From inside the tailgate, disconnect the wiring connector.

6. Remove the motor mounting screws and the motor.

7. To install, reverse the removal procedures.

ALL OTHER MODELS

1. Remove the arm and blade assembly.

2. Open the tailgate.

3. Remove the motor cover (if equipped) and disconnect the wiring connector.

4. Remove the grommet from the glass.

5. Remove the bracket retaining screws and the motor from the tailgate.

6. To install, reverse the removal procedures.

Instrument Cluster

REMOVAL & INSTALLATION

NOTE: On certain models, after the bezel, mask/lens assemblies have been removed, the gauges are accessible for replacement as required. Extreme care must be exercised to avoid damage to the instrument panel components.

Omni, Horizon, TC3, 024, Turismo and Charger

1. Disconnect the negative battery cable.

2. Remove the cluster bezel. Remove the two mask/lens lower attaching screws, allow the mask/lens to drop slightly and remove, as required.

3. If the cluster is to be removed, the mask/lens would be removed with the cluster, as outlined in the following steps.

4. Remove the four screws retaining the cluster to the instrument panel.

5. Pull cluster away from the panel, disconnect the speedometer and the wiring connector.

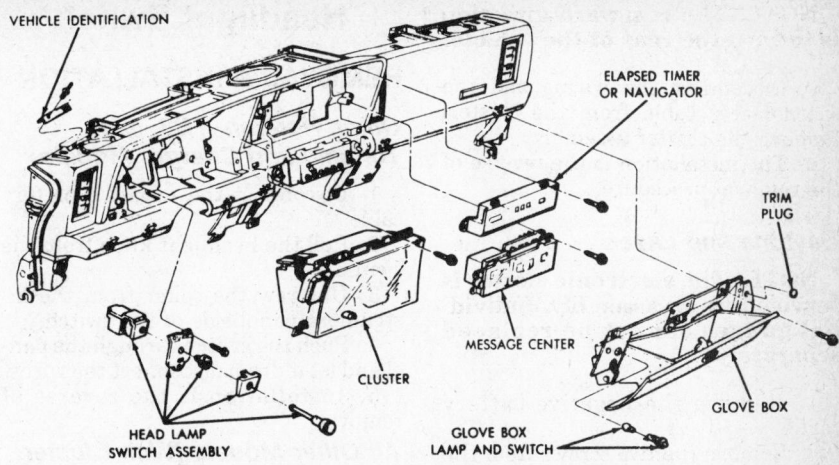

Instrument panel assembly—typical

6. Remove the cluster assembly from the instrument panel.

7. The installation is the reverse of the removal procedure.

Aries, Reliant, Dodge 400 and LeBaron

1. Remove the negative battery cable.

2. Place the shift lever in the position "1".

3. Remove the upper left and lower cluster bezel screws.

4. Remove the instrument cluster bezel by snapping the bezel off the five retaining clips.

5. Remove the instrument panel cluster mask by snapping the mask off the four retaining clips.

6. Remove the instrument panel top cover mounting screws and lift the edge of the top panel to remove the two screws attaching the cluster housing to the base panel.

7. Lift the rearward edge of the top panel and slide the cluster housing rearward.

NOTE: Rearward direction is toward the rear of the vehicle.

8. Reach behind the cluster assembly and disconnect the right and left printed circuit board connector.

9. Disconnect the speedometer cable and remove the cluster assembly.

10. The installation is the reverse of the removal procedure.

Caravelle, Lancer, LeBaron GTS, LeBaron, Dynasty, 600 and E Class/New Yorker

NOTE: The electronic cluster is serviced as an assembly. The individual gauges cannot be serviced separately.

1. Disconnect the negative battery cable.

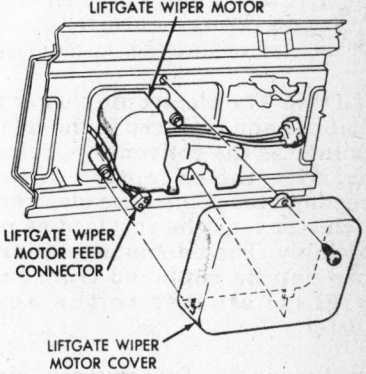

Rear wiper assembly—Omni, Horizon, Turismo and 024 shown, others similar

2. Place the shift lever in the position "1".

3. Remove the radio knobs and the six screws from the cluster bezel.

4. Remove the bezel by snapping the bezel off of the five retaining clips.

5. Remove the cluster mask by snapping the mask off the four retaining clips.

NOTE: The electronic cluster is removed and installed in the same manner as the conventional cluster, except for the speedometer cable. When replacing the electronic cluster, the odometer memory chip can be installed into another electronic cluster.

6. Remove the rearward screws from the instrument panel upper pad assembly.

7. Lift the rearward edge of the instrument panel upper pad and remove the two screws from the top of the cluster.

8. Remove the two screws from the bottom of the cluster and lift the rearward edge of the upper pad and pull the cluster rearward.

NOTE: The rearward direction is toward the rear of the vehicle.

9. Disconnect the wiring and the speedometer cable from the cluster. Remove the cluster assembly.

10. The installation is the reverse of the removal procedure.

Daytona and Laser

NOTE: The electronic cluster is serviced as an assembly. Individual gauges cannot be replaced separately.

1. Remove the negative battery cable.

2. Remove the five screws from the top of the cluster bezel, pull the bezel rearward to disengage the three clips on the bottom of the bezel and remove.

3. Remove the five bayonet clips holding the cluster mask to the cluster housing and remove the cluster mask.

NOTE: The electronic cluster is removed and replaced in the same manner as the conventional cluster, with the exception of the speedometer cable. The electronic cluster must be serviced as an assembly. The odometer memory chip can be replaced from the original cluster to the new cluster.

4. Remove the four screws retaining the cluster to the base panel.

5. Pull the cluster rearward, reach behind the cluster and disconnect the speedometer cable and the wiring harness. Remove the cluster assembly.

6. The installation of the cluster is the reverse of the removal procedure.

Shadow and Sundance

1. Remove the instrument cluster bezel.

2. Remove the instrument cluster retaining screws

3. Move the cluster assembly rearward for access to the speedometer cable and cluster wiring connectors.

4. Pull the cluster rearward and towards the center of the vehicle to remove it from the dash.

NOTE: It is not necessary to remove the instrument cluster from the vehicle for gauge removal. The cluster bezel, mask and lens must be removed to expose the gauges. The gauges must be pulled straight out from the cluster to avoid damage to the gauge pins.

5. The installation of the cluster is the reverse of its removal procedure.

Headlight Switch

REMOVAL & INSTALLATION

Omni, Horizon, TC3, 024, Turismo and Charger Models

1. Disconnect the negative battery cable.

2. Pull the headlight knob from the switch.

3. Unscrew the collar from the instrument panel side of the switch.

4. Push the switch through the panel and let it drop; disconnect the wires.

5. Installation is the reverse of removal.

All Other Models (With Cluster Bezel Removed)

1. Snap out headlight switch bezel out of instrument panel.

2. Remove the three screws securing the headlight switch mounting plate to the base panel.

3. Push the switch and plate rearward and disconnect the wiring connector.

4. Depress the button on the switch and remove the knob and stem.

5. Snap out the mounting plate cover, then remove the nut that attaches the switch to the mounting plate.

6. Installation is the reverse of removal.

Stoplight Switch

REMOVAL & INSTALLATION

1. Lower the steering column.

2. Remove the nut located on the inboard side of the brake support bracket which fastens the switch to the bracket.

3. Remove the wiring from the dash and disconnect the wiring connector.

4. Remove the switch.

5. The installation is the reverse procedure of the removal.

ADJUSTMENT

Omni, Horizon, Turismo, TC3, 024 and Charger

1. Loosen the switch to pedal bracket attaching screw and slide the assembly away from the pedal blade.

2. Push the brake pedal down and allow to return on its own. Do not pull the pedal back.

3. Place a 0.130 in. spacer gauge on the pedal blade and slide the switch toward the pedal blade until the switch plunger is fully depressed against the spacer gauge.

4. Tighten the switch bracket screw to 75 inch lbs. torque and remove the spacer.

5. Operate the brake pedal and be sure the brake stop light switch does not prevent full pedal return.

All Other Models

The stop lamp switch is self-adjusting during the installation.

1. Install the switch in the retaining bracket and push the switch forward as far as it will go.

2. The brake pedal will move forward slightly. Pull the pedal back, bringing the striker back towards the switch until the pedal will go no further.

3. This movement of the pedal will cause the switch to ratchet backwards to the correct position. Very little movement is required and no further adjustment is necessary.

Fuses and Circuit Breakers

LOCATION

Circuit Breakers

Circuit breakers are used along with the fusible links to protect electrical system components such as headlamps, windshield wipers, electric windows, tailgate front and rear switches. The circuit breakers are located either in the switch, in the fuse panel or mounted on/near the lower lip of the instrument panel, to the right or left side of the steering column.

Fuse Panels

The fuse panel is used to house the fuses that protect the individual or combined electrical circuits within the vehicle. The turn signal flasher, the hazard warning flasher and the seat belt warning buzzer/timer are located on the fuse panel for quick identification and replacement. The fuses are usually identified by abbreviated circuit names or number, with the number of the rated fuse needed to protect the circuit printed below the fuse holder.

Fusible Links

Fusible links are used to prevent major wire harness damage in the event of a short circuit or an overload condition in electrical circuits. Each fusible link is of a fixed value for a specific electrical load. Should a link fail, the cause of the failure must be determined and repaired prior to installing a new link of the same value. The fusible links are located in the left front fender, below the starter relay.

Chrysler Corp. 3
Rear Wheel Drive
Cordoba, Diplomat, Fifth Avenue, Gran Fury,
Imperial, LeBaron, Mirada, New Yorker

VEHICLE IDENTIFICATION CHART

It is important for servicing and ordering parts to be certain of the vehicle and engine identification. The VIN (vehicle identification number) is a 17 digit number visible through the windshield on the driver's side of the dash and contains the vehicle and engine identification codes. The tenth digit indicates model year and the eighth digit indicates engine code. It can be interpreted as follows:

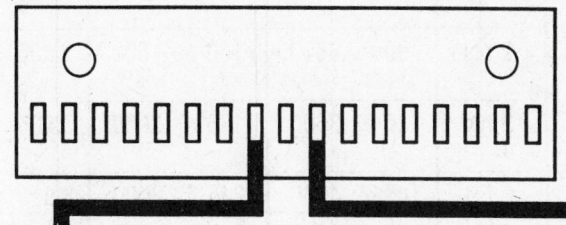

Engine Code						Model Year	
Code	Cu. In.	Liters	Cyl.	Fuel Sys.	Eng. Mfg.	Code	Year
E	225	3.7	6	1 bbl	Chrysler	C	1982
H	225	3.7	6	1 bbl	Chrysler	D	1983
F	225 H.D.	3.7	6	1 bbl	Chrysler	E	1984
J	225 H.D.	3.7	6	1 bbl	Chrysler	F	1985
G	225	3.7	6	2 bbl ①	Chrysler	G	1986
K	225	3.7	6	2 bbl ①	Chrysler	H	1987
H	225 H.D.	3.7	6	2 bbl①	Chrysler	J	1988
L	225 H.D.	3.7	6	2 bbl①	Chrysler	K	1989
K	318	5.2	8	2 bbl	Chrysler		
P	318	5.2	8	2 bbl	Chrysler		
L	318 H.D.	5.2	8	2 bbl	Chrysler		
J	318	5.2	8	EFI	Chrysler		
N	318	5.2	8	EFI	Chrysler		
R	318	5.2	8	4 bbl	Chrysler		
M	318	5.2	8	4 bbl	Chrysler		
N	318 H.D.	5.2	8	4 bbl	Chrysler		
S	318 H.D.	5.2	8	4 bbl	Chrysler		
4	318	5.2	8	4 bbl	Chrysler		

H.D.   Heavy Duty
EFI   Electronic Fuel Injection
① Canada Only

GENERAL ENGINE SPECIFICATIONS

Year	VIN	No. Cylinder Displacement cu. in. (liter)	Fuel System Type	Net Horsepower @ rpm	Net Torque @ rpm (ft.lbs.)	Bore × Stroke (in.)	Compression Ratio	Oil Pressure @ rpm
1982	E	6-225 (3.7)	1 bbl	85 @ 3600	165 @ 1600	3.406 × 4.125	8.4:1	55 @ 2000
	F	6-225 (3.7) H.D.	1 bbl	NA	NA	3.406 × 4.125	8.4:1	55 @ 2000
	G	6-225 (3.7)	2 bbl	NA	NA	3.406 × 4.125	8.4:1	55 @ 2000
	H	6-225 (3.7) H.D.	2 bbl	NA	NA	3.406 × 4.125	8.4:1	55 @ 2000
	J	8-318 (5.2)	EFI	140 @ 4000	245 @ 2000	3.910 × 3.310	8.5:1	55 @ 2000
	K	8-318 (5.2)	2 bbl	130 @ 4000	235 @ 1600	3.910 × 3.310	8.6:1	55 @ 2000
	L	8-318 (5.2) H.D.	2 bbl	NA	NA	3.910 × 3.310	8.6:1	55 @ 2000
	M	8-318 (5.2)	4 bbl	165 @ 4000	240 @ 2000	3.910 × 3.310	8.5:1	55 @ 2000
	N	8-318 (5.2) H.D.	4 bbl	NA	NA	3.910 × 3.310	8.5:1	55 @ 2000
1983	H	6-225 (3.7)	1 bbl	85 @ 3600	165 @ 1600	3.406 × 4.125	8.4:1	55 @ 2000
	J	6-225 (3.7) H.D.	1 bbl	NA	NA	3.406 × 4.125	8.4:1	55 @ 2000
	K	6-225 (3.7)	2 bbl	90 @ 3600	160 @ 1600	3.406 × 4.125	8.4:1	55 @ 2000
	L	6-225 (3.7) H.D.	2 bbl	110 @ 3600	180 @ 2000	3.406 × 4.125	8.4:1	55 @ 2000
	N	8-318 (5.2)	EFI	140 @ 4000	245 @ 2000	3.910 × 3.310	8.5:1	55 @ 2000
	P	8-318 (5.2)	2 bbl	140 @ 3600	265 @ 1600	3.910 × 3.310	8.6:1	55 @ 2000
	R	8-318 (5.2)	4 bbl	165 @ 4000	240 @ 2000	3.910 × 3.310	8.6:1	55 @ 2000
	S	8-318 (5.2) H.D.	4 bbl	165 @ 4000	240 @ 2000	3.910 × 3.310	8.4:1	55 @ 2000
1984	P	8-318 (5.2)	2 bbl	130 @ 4000	235 @ 1600	3.910 × 3.310	8.6:1	55 @ 2000
	R	8-318 (5.2)	4 bbl	165 @ 4000	240 @ 2000	3.910 × 3.310	8.6:1	55 @ 2000
	S	8-318 (5.2) H.D.	4 bbl	165 @ 4000	240 @ 2000	3.910 × 3.310	8.4:1	55 @ 2000
1985	P	8-318 (5.2)	2 bbl	130 @ 4000	235 @ 1600	3.910 × 3.310	9.0:1	55 @ 2000
	R	8-318 (5.2)	4 bbl	165 @ 4000	240 @ 2000	3.910 × 3.310	9.0:1	55 @ 2000
	S	8-318 (5.2) H.D.	4 bbl	165 @ 4000	240 @ 2000	3.910 × 3.310	8.4:1	55 @ 2000
1986	P	8-318 (5.2)	2 bbl	140 @ 3600	265 @ 1600	3.910 × 3.310	9.0:1	55 @ 2000
	R	8-318 (5.2)	4 bbl	165 @ 4000	240 @ 2000	3.910 × 3.310	8.6:1	55 @ 2000
	S	8-318 (5.2) H.D.	4 bbl	175 @ 4000	250 @ 3200	3.910 × 3.310	8.0:1	55 @ 2000
1987	P	8-318 (5.2)	2 bbl	140 @ 3600	265 @ 1600	3.910 × 3.310	9.0:1	55 @ 2000
	R	8-318 (5.2)	4 bbl	165 @ 4000	240 @ 2000	3.910 × 3.310	8.6:1	55 @ 2000
	S	8-318 (5.2) H.D.	4 bbl	175 @ 4000	250 @ 3200	3.910 × 3.310	8.0:1	55 @ 2000

GENERAL ENGINE SPECIFICATIONS

Year	VIN	No. Cylinder Displacement cu. in. (liter)	Fuel System Type	Net Horsepower @ rpm	Net Torque @ rpm (ft.lbs.)	Bore × Stroke (in.)	Compression Ratio	Oil Pressure @ rpm
1988-89	P	8-318 (5.2)	2 bbl	140 @ 3600	265 @ 1600	3.910 × 3.310	9.0:1	55 @ 2000
	4	8-318 (5.2)	4 bbl	165 @ 4000	240 @ 2000	3.910 × 3.310	8.6:1	55 @ 2000
	S	8-318 (5.2) H.D.	4 bbl	175 @ 4000	250 @ 3200	3.910 × 3.310	8.0:1	55 @ 2000

H.D. Heavy Duty

TUNE-UP SPECIFICATIONS

Year	VIN	No. Cylinder Displacement cu. in. (liter)	Spark Plugs Type	Gap (in.)	Ignition Timing (deg.) MT	AT	Compression Pressure (psi)	Fuel Pump (psi)	Idle Speed (rpm) MT	AT	Valve Clearance In.	Ex.
1982	E	6-225 (3.7)	560PR	.035	—	12B	100	4-5.5	—	625	Hyd.	Hyd.
	F	6-225 (3.7)	560PR	.035	—	12B	100	4-5.5	—	725	Hyd.	Hyd.
	G	6-225 (3.7)	560PR	.035	—	12B	100	4-5.5	—	750	Hyd.	Hyd.
	H	6-225 (3.7)	560PR	.035	—	12B	100	4-5.5	—	750	Hyd.	Hyd.
	J	8-318 (5.2)	68ER	.048	—	12B	100	7.5-11.5	—	580	Hyd.	Hyd.
	K	8-318 (5.2)	65PR	.035	—	16B	100	5.75-7.25	—	600	Hyd.	Hyd.
	L	8-318 (5.2)	65PR	.035	—	16B	100	5.75-7.25	—	600	Hyd.	Hyd.
	M	8-318 (5.2)	65PR	.035	—	16B	100	5.75-7.25	—	650	Hyd.	Hyd.
	N	8-318 (5.2)	65PR	.035	—	16B	100	5.75-7.25	—	650	Hyd.	Hyd.
1983	H	6-225 (3.7)	RBL16Y	.035	—	16B	100	4-5.5	—	750	Hyd.	Hyd.
	J	6-225 (3.7)	RBL16Y	.035	—	16B	100	4-5.5	—	750	Hyd.	Hyd.
	K	6-225 (3.7)	RBL16Y	.035	—	12B	100	4-5.5	—	750	Hyd.	Hyd.
	L	6-225 (3.7)	RBL16Y	.035	—	12B	100	4-5.5	—	750	Hyd.	Hyd.
	N	8-318 (5.2)	RN12YC	.035	—	12B	100	7.5-11.5	—	580	Hyd.	Hyd.
	P	8-318 (5.2)	RN12YC	.035	—	16B	100	5.75-7.25	—	700	Hyd.	Hyd.
	R	8-318 (5.2)	RN12YC	.035	—	16B	100	5.75-7.25	—	700	Hyd.	Hyd.
	S	8-318 (5.2)	RN12YC	.035	—	16B	100	5.75-7.25	—	700	Hyd.	Hyd.
1984	P	8-318 (5.2)	RN12YC	.035	—	16B	100	5.75-7.25	—	700	Hyd.	Hyd.
	R	8-318 (5.2)	RN12YC	.035	—	16B	100	5.75-7.25	—	700	Hyd.	Hyd.
	S	8-318 (5.2)	RN12YC	.035	—	16B	100	5.75-7.25	—	700	Hyd.	Hyd.
1985	P	8-318 (5.2)	RN12YC	.035	—	7B	100	5.75-7.25	—	680	Hyd.	Hyd.
	R	8-318 (5.2)	RN12YC	.035	—	16B	100	5.75-7.25	—	750	Hyd.	Hyd.
	S	8-318 (5.2)	RN12YC	.035	—	16B	100	5.75-7.25	—	750	Hyd.	Hyd.
1986	P	8-318 (5.2)	RN12YC	.035	—	7B	100	5.75-7.25	—	680	Hyd.	Hyd.
	R	8-318 (5.2)	RN12YC	.035	—	16B	100	5.75-7.25	—	750	Hyd.	Hyd.
	S	8-318 (5.2)	RN12YC	.035	—	16B	100	5.75-7.25	—	750	Hyd.	Hyd.
1987	P	8-318 (5.2)	RN12YC	.035	—	7B	100	5.75-7.25	—	680	Hyd.	Hyd.
	R	8-318 (5.2)	RN12YC	.035	—	16B	100	5.75-7.25	—	750	Hyd.	Hyd.
	S	8-318 (5.2)	RN12YC	.035	—	16B	100	5.75-7.25	—	750	Hyd.	Hyd.

TUNE-UP SPECIFICATIONS

Year	VIN	No. Cylinder Displacement cu. in. (liter)	Spark Plugs Type	Gap (in.)	Ignition Timing (deg.) MT	AT	Compression Pressure (psi)	Fuel Pump (psi)	Idle Speed (rpm) MT	AT	Valve Clearance In.	Ex.
1988	P	8-318 (5.2)	RN12YC	.035	—	7B	100	5.75-7.25	—	680	Hyd.	Hyd.
	4	8-318 (5.2)	RN12YC	.035	—	16B	100	5.75-7.25	—	750	Hyd.	Hyd.
	S	8-318 (5.2)	RN12YC	.035	—	16B	100	5.75-7.25	—	750	Hyd.	Hyd.
1989			SEE UNDERHOOD SPECIFICATIONS STICKER									

NOTE: The underhood specifications sticker often reflects tune-up specification changes made in production. Sticker figures must be used if they disagree with those in this chart.

Part numbers in this chart are not recommendations by Chilton for any product by brand name.

FIRING ORDERS

NOTE: To avoid confusion, always replace spark plug wires one at a time.

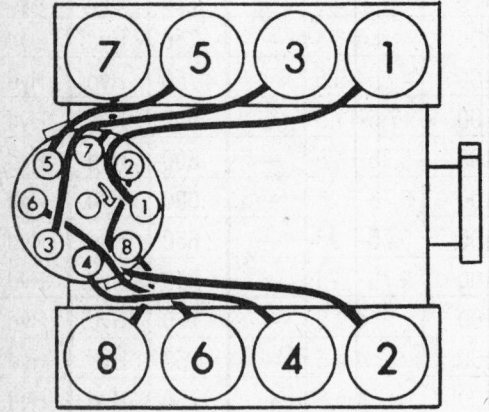

CHRYSLER CORP. 318 V8 Engine
Engine firing order: 1–8–4–3–6–5–7–2
Distributor rotation: clockwise

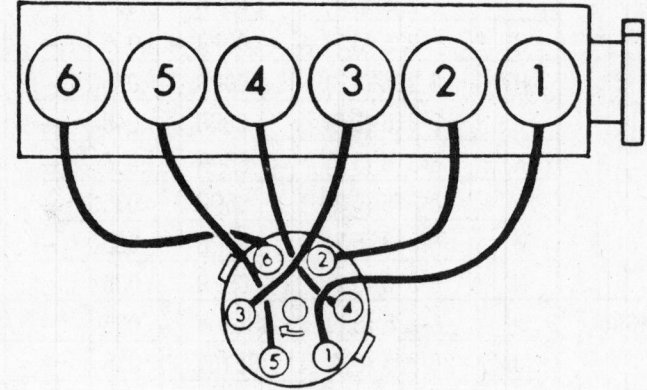

CHRYSLER CORP. 6-cyl.
Engine firing order: 1-5-3-6-2-4
Distributor rotation: clockwise

CAPACITIES

Year	VIN	No. Cylinder Displacement cu. in. (liter)	Engine Crankcase with Filter	without Filter	Transmission (pts.) MT	AT	Drive Axle (pts.)	Fuel Tank (gals.)	Cooling System (qts.)
1982	E	6-225 (3.7)	5	4	—	16.3	①	18	11.5 ⑤
	F	6-225 (3.7)	5	4	—	16.3	①	18	11.5 ⑤
	G	6-225 (3.7)	5	4	—	16.3	①	18	11.5③
	H	6-225 (3.7)	5	4	—	16.3	①	18	11.5③
	J	8-318 (5.2)	5	4	—	②	①	18④	15③
	K	8-318 (5.2)	5	4	—	②	①	18④	15③
	L	8-318 (5.2)	5	4	—	②	①	18	15③

CAPACITIES

Year	VIN	No. Cylinder Displacement cu. in. (liter)	Engine Crankcase with Filter	Engine Crankcase without Filter	Transmission (pts.) MT	Transmission (pts.) AT	Drive Axle (pts.)	Fuel Tank (gals.)	Cooling System (qts.)
	M	8-318 (5.2)	5	4	—	②	①	18④	15③
	N	8-318 (5.2)	5	4	—	②	①	18	15③
1983	H	6-225 (3.7)	5	4	—	②	①	18	11.5③
	J	6-225 (3.7)	5	4	—	②	①	18	11.5③
	K	6-225 (3.7)	5	4	—	②	①	18	11.5③
	L	6-225 (3.7)	5	4	—	②	①	18	11.5③
	N	8-318 (5.2)	5	4	—	②	①	18	15③
	P	8-318 (5.2)	5	4	—	②	①	18	15③
	R	8-318 (5.2)	5	4	—	②	①	18	15③
	S	8-318 (5.2)	5	4	—	②	①	18	15③
1984	P	8-318 (5.2)	5	4	—	②	①	18	15.5③
	R	8-318 (5.2)	5	4	—	②	①	18	15.5③
	S	8-318 (5.2)	5	4	—	②	①	18	15.5③
1985	P	8-318 (5.2)	5	4	—	16.3	①	18	15.5③
	R	8-318 (5.2)	5	4	—	16.3	①	18	15.5③
	S	8-318 (5.2)	5	4	—	16.3	①	18	15.5③
1986	P	8-318 (5.2)	5	4	—	16.3	①	18	15.5③
	R	8-318 (5.2)	5	4	—	16.3	①	18	15.5③
	S	8-318 (5.2)	5	4	—	16.3	①	18	15.5③
1987	P	8-318 (5.2)	5	4	—	16.3	①	18	15.5③
	R	8-318 (5.2)	5	4	—	16.3	①	18	15.5③
	S	8-318 (5.2)	5	4	—	16.3	①	18	15.5③
1988-89	P	8-318 (5.2)	5	4	—	16.3	①	18	15.5③
	4	8-318 (5.2)	5	4	—	16.3	①	18	15.5③
	S	8-318 (5.2)	5	4	—	16.3	①	18	15.5③

① 7¼ in. axle—2.5 pts.,
　 8¼ in. axle—4.4 pts.,
　 9¼ in axle—4.5 pts.
② 904 transmissions—16.3 pts.,
　 727 transmissions—15.9 pts.
③ Add 1 qt. for models equipped with A/C
④ St. Regis, Gran Fury, Newport and New Yorker—21 gal.

CAMSHAFT SPECIFICATIONS
All measurements given in inches.

Year	VIN	No. Cylinder Displacement cu. in. (liter)	Journal Diameter 1	Journal Diameter 2	Journal Diameter 3	Journal Diameter 4	Journal Diameter 5	Lobe Lift In.	Lobe Lift Ex.	Bearing Clearance	Camshaft End Play
1982	E	6–225 (3.7)	1.998–1.999	1.982–1.983	1.967–1.968	1.951–1.952	—	0.406	0.414	0.001–0.003	0.002–0.010
	F	6–225 (3.7)	1.998–1.999	1.982–1.983	1.967–1.968	1.951–1.952	—	0.406	0.414	0.001–0.003	0.002–0.010

CAMSHAFT SPECIFICATIONS
All measurements given in inches.

| Year | VIN | No. Cylinder Displacement cu. in. (liter) | Journal Diameter | | | | | Lobe Lift | | Bearing Clearance | Camshaft End Play |
			1	2	3	4	5	In.	Ex.		
1982	G	6–225 (3.7)	1.998–1.999	1.982–1.983	1.967–1.968	1.951–1.952	—	0.406	0.414	0.001–0.003	0.002–0.010
	H	6–225 (3.7)	1.998–1.999	1.982–1.983	1.967–1.968	1.951–1.952	—	0.406	0.414	0.001–0.003	0.002–0.010
	J	6–318 (5.2)	1.998–1.999	1.982–1.983	1.967–1.968	1.951–1.952	1.5605–1.5615	0.373	0.400	0.001–0.003	0.002–0.010
	K	6–318 (5.2)	1.998–1.999	1.982–1.983	1.967–1.968	1.951–1.952	1.5605–1.5615	0.373	0.400	0.001–0.003	0.002–0.010
	L	6–318 (5.2)	1.998–1.999	1.982–1.983	1.967–1.968	1.951–1.952	1.5605–1.5615	0.373	0.400	0.001–0.003	0.002–0.010
	M	6–318 (5.2)	1.998–1.999	1.982–1.983	1.967–1.968	1.951–1.952	1.5605–1.5615	0.373	0.400	0.001–0.003	0.002–0.010
	N	6–318 (5.2)	1.998–1.999	1.982–1.983	1.967–1.968	1.951–1.952	1.5605–1.5615	0.373	0.400	0.001–0.003	0.002–0.010
1983	H	6–225 (3.7)	1.998–1.999	1.982–1.983	1.967–1.968	1.951–1.952	—	0.406	0.414	0.001–0.003	0.002–0.010
	J	6–225 (3.7)	1.998–1.999	1.982–1.983	1.967–1.968	1.951–1.952	—	0.406	0.414	0.001–0.003	0.002–0.010
	K	6–225 (3.7)	1.998–1.999	1.982–1.983	1.967–1.968	1.951–1.952	—	0.406	0.414	0.001–0.003	0.002–0.010
	L	6–225 (3.7)	1.998–1.999	1.982–1.983	1.967–1.968	1.951–1.952	—	0.406	0.414	0.001–0.003	0.002–0.010
	N	6–318 (5.2)	1.998–1.999	1.982–1.983	1.967–1.968	1.951–1.952	1.5605–1.5615	0.373	0.400	0.001–0.003	0.002–0.010
	P	6–318 (5.2)	1.998–1.999	1.982–1.983	1.967–1.968	1.951–1.952	1.5605–1.5615	0.373	0.400	0.001–0.003	0.002–0.010
	R	6–318 (5.2)	1.998–1.999	1.982–1.983	1.967–1.968	1.951–1.952	1.5605–1.5615	0.373	0.400	0.001–0.003	0.002–0.010
	S	6–318 (5.2)	1.998–1.999	1.982–1.983	1.967–1.968	1.951–1.952	1.5605–1.5615	0.373	0.400	0.001–0.003	0.002–0.010
1984	P	8–318 (5.2)	1.998–1.999	1.982–1.983	1.967–1.968	1.951–1.952	1.5605–1.5615	0.373	0.400	0.001–0.003	0.002–0.010
	R	8–318 (5.2)	1.998–1.999	1.982–1.983	1.967–1.968	1.951–1.952	1.5605–1.5615	0.373	0.400	0.001–0.003	0.002–0.010
	S	8–318 (5.2)	1.998–1.999	1.982–1.983	1.967–1.968	1.951–1.952	1.5605–1.5615	0.373	0.400	0.001–0.003	0.002–0.010
1985	P	8–318 (5.2)	1.998–1.999	1.982–1.983	1.967–1.968	1.951–1.952	1.5605–1.5615	0.373	0.400	0.001–0.003	0.002–0.010
	R	8–318 (5.2)	1.998–1.999	1.982–1.983	1.967–1.968	1.951–1.952	1.5605–1.5615	0.373	0.400	0.001–0.003	0.002–0.010
	S	8–318 (5.2)	1.998–1.999	1.982–1.983	1.967–1.968	1.951–1.952	1.5605–1.5615	0.373	0.400	0.001–0.003	0.002–0.010

CAMSHAFT SPECIFICATIONS
All measurements given in inches.

Year	VIN	No. Cylinder Displacement cu. in. (liter)	Journal Diameter 1	2	3	4	5	Lobe Lift In.	Ex.	Bearing Clearance	Camshaft End Play
1986	P	8–318 (5.2)	1.998–1.999	1.982–1.983	1.967–1.968	1.951–1.952	1.5605–1.5615	0.373	0.400	0.001–0.003	0.002–0.010
	R	8–318 (5.2)	1.998–1.999	1.982–1.983	1.967–1.968	1.951–1.952	1.5605–1.5615	0.373	0.400	0.001–0.003	0.002–0.010
	S	8–318 (5.2)	1.998–1.999	1.982–1.983	1.967–1.968	1.951–1.952	1.5605–1.5615	0.373	0.400	0.001–0.003	0.002–0.010
1987	P	8–318 (5.2)	1.998–1.999	1.982–1.983	1.967–1.968	1.951–1.952	1.5605–1.5615	0.373	0.400	0.001–0.003	0.002–0.010
	R	8–318 (5.2)	1.998–1.999	1.982–1.983	1.967–1.968	1.951–1.952	1.5605–1.5615	0.373	0.400	0.001–0.003	0.002–0.010
	S	8–318 (5.2)	1.998–1.999	1.982–1.983	1.967–1.968	1.951–1.952	1.5605–1.5615	0.373	0.400	0.001–0.003	0.002–0.010
1987-88	P	8–318 (5.2)	1.998–1.999	1.982–1.983	1.967–1.968	1.951–1.952	1.5605–1.5615	0.373	0.400	0.001–0.003	0.002–0.010
	4	8–318 (5.2)	1.998–1.999	1.982–1.983	1.967–1.968	1.951–1.952	1.5605–1.5615	0.373	0.400	0.001–0.003	0.002–0.010
	S	8–318 (5.2)	1.998–1.999	1.982–1.983	1.967–1.968	1.951–1.952	1.5605–1.5615	0.373	0.400	0.001–0.003	0.002–0.010

CRANKSHAFT AND CONNECTING ROD SPECIFICATIONS
All measurements are given in inches.

Year	VIN	No. Cylinder Displacement cu. in. (liter)	Crankshaft Main Brg. Journal Dia.	Main Brg. Oil Clearance	Shaft End-play	Thrust on No.	Connecting Rod Journal Diameter	Oil Clearance	Side Clearance
1982	E	6–225 (3.7)	2.7495–2.7505	.0010–.0025	.0035–.0095	3	2.1865–2.1875	.0010–.0025	.007–.013
	F	6–225 (3.7)	2.7495–2.7505	.0010–.0025	.0035–.0095	3	2.1865–2.1875	.0010–.0025	.007–.013
	G	6–225 (3.7)	2.7495–2.7505	.0010–.0025	.0035–.0095	3	2.1865–2.1875	.0010–.0025	.007–.013
	H	6–225 (3.7)	2.7495–2.7505	.0010–.0025	.0035–.0095	3	2.1865–2.1875	.0010–.0025	.007–.013
	J	8–318 (5.2)	2.4995–2.5005	①	.002–.010	3	2.1240–2.1250	.0005–.0022	.006–.014
	K	8–318 (5.2)	2.4995–2.5005	①	.002–.010	3	2.1240–2.1250	.0005–.0022	.006–.014
	L	8–318 (5.2)	2.4995–2.5005	①	.002–.010	3	2.1240–2.1250	.0005–.0022	.006–.014
	M	8–318 (5.2)	2.4995–2.5005	①	.002–.010	3	2.1240–2.1250	.0005–.0022	.006–.014
	N	8–318 (5.2)	2.4995–2.5005	①	.002–.010	3	2.1240–2.1250	.0005–.0022	.006–.014

CRANKSHAFT AND CONNECTING ROD SPECIFICATIONS

All measurements are given in inches.

Year	VIN	No. Cylinder Displacement cu. in. (liter)	Crankshaft				Connecting Rod		
			Main Brg. Journal Dia.	Main Brg. Oil Clearance	Shaft End-play	Thrust on No.	Journal Diameter	Oil Clearance	Side Clearance
1983	H	6–225 (3.7)	2.7495–2.7505	.0010–.0025	.0035–.0095	3	2.1865–2.1875	.0010–.0025	.007–.013
	J	6–225 (3.7)	2.7495–2.7505	.0010–.0025	.0035–.0095	3	2.1865–2.1875	.0010–.0025	.007–.013
	K	6–225 (3.7)	2.7495–2.7505	.0010–.0025	.0035–.0095	3	2.1865–2.1875	.0010–.0025	.007–.013
	L	6–225 (3.7)	2.7495–2.7505	.0010–.0025	.0035–.0095	3	2.1865–2.1875	.0010–.0025	.007–.013
	N	8–318 (5.2)	2.4995–2.5005	①	.002–.010	3	2.1240–2.1250	.0005–.0022	.006–.014
	P	8–318 (5.2)	2.4995–2.5005	①	.002–.010	3	2.1240–2.1250	.0005–.0022	.006–.014
	R	8–318 (5.2)	2.4995–2.5005	①	.002–.010	3	2.1240–2.1250	.0005–.0022	.006–.014
	S	8–318 (5.2)	2.4995–2.5005	①	.002–.010	3	2.1240–2.1250	.0005–.0022	.006–.014
1984	P	8–318 (5.2)	2.4995–2.5005	①	.002–.010	3	2.1240–2.1250	.0005–.0022	.006–.014
	R	8–318 (5.2)	2.4995–2.5005	①	.002–.010	3	2.1240–2.1250	.0005–.0022	.006–.014
	S	8–318 (5.2)	2.4995–2.5005	①	.002–.010	3	2.1240–2.1250	.0005–.0022	.006–.014
1985	P	8–318 (5.2)	2.4995–2.5005	①	.002–.010	3	2.1240–2.1250	.0005–.0022	.006–.014
	R	8–318 (5.2)	2.4995–2.5005	①	.002–.010	3	2.1240–2.1250	.0005–.0022	.006–.014
	S	8–318 (5.2)	2.4995–2.5005	①	.002–.010	3	2.1240–2.1250	.0005–.0022	.006–.014
1986	P	8–318 (5.2)	2.4995–2.5005	①	.002–.010	3	2.1240–2.1250	.0005–.0022	.006–.014
	R	8–318 (5.2)	2.4995–2.5005	①	.002–.010	3	2.1240–2.1250	.0005–.0022	.006–.014
	S	8–318 (5.2)	2.4995–2.5005	①	.002–.010	3	2.1240–2.1250	.0005–.0022	.006–.014
1987	P	8–318 (5.2)	2.4995–2.5005	①	.002–.010	3	2.1240–2.1250	.0005–.0022	.006–.014
	R	8–318 (5.2)	2.4995–2.5005	①	.002–.010	3	2.1240–2.1250	.0005–.0022	.006–.014
	S	8–318 (5.2)	2.4995–2.5005	①	.002–.010	3	2.1240–2.1250	.0005–.0022	.006–.014
1988-89	P	8–318 (5.2)	2.4995–2.5005	①	.002–.010	3	2.1240–2.1250	.0005–.0022	.006–.014
	4	8–318 (5.2)	2.4995–2.5005	①	.002–.010	3	2.1240–2.1250	.0005–.0022	.006–.014

CRANKSHAFT AND CONNECTING ROD SPECIFICATIONS
All measurements are given in inches.

Year	VIN	No. Cylinder Displacement cu. in. (liter)	Crankshaft				Connecting Rod		
			Main Brg. Journal Dia.	Main Brg. Oil Clearance	Shaft End-play	Thrust on No.	Journal Diameter	Oil Clearance	Side Clearance
1988-89	S	8–318 (5.2)	2.4995–2.5005	①	.002–.010	3	2.1240–2.1250	.0005–.0022	.006–.014

① No. 1 — .0005-.0015; No. 2–5 — .0005-.0020

VALVE SPECIFICATIONS

Year	VIN	No. Cylinder Displacement cu. in. (liter)	Seat Angle (deg.)	Face Angle (deg.)	Spring Test Pressure (lbs. @ inch)	Spring Installed Height (in.)	Stem-to-Guide Clearance (in.)		Stem Diameter (in.)	
							Intake	Exhaust	Intake	Exhaust
1982	E	6–225 (3.7)	45	①	143 @ 1.31	$1\frac{11}{16}$	.0010–.0030	.0020–.0040	.3725	.3715
	F	6–225 (3.7)	45	①	143 @ 1.31	$1\frac{11}{16}$	.0010–.0030	.0020–.0040	.3725	.3715
	G	6–225 (3.7)	45	①	143 @ 1.31	$1\frac{11}{16}$	.0010–.0030	.0020–.0040	.3725	.3715
	H	6–225 (3.7)	45	①	143 @ 1.31	$1\frac{11}{16}$	.0010–.0030	.0020–.0040	.3725	.3715
	J	8–318 (5.2)	45	45	193 @ 1.25	$1\frac{21}{32}$	.0015–.0035	.0025–.0045	.3720	.3710
	K	8–318 (5.2)	45	45	177 @ 1.31	$1\frac{21}{32}$	.0010–.0030	.0020–.0040	.3725	.3715
	L	8–318 (5.2)	45	45	177 @ 1.31	$1\frac{21}{32}$	.0010–.0030	.0020–.0040	.3725	.3715
	M	8–318 (5.2)	45	45	177 @ 1.31	$1\frac{21}{32}$	.0010–.0030	.0020–.0040	.3725	.3715
	N	8–318 (5.2)	45	45	177 @ 1.31	$1\frac{21}{32}$	.0010–.0030	.0020–.0040	.3725	.3715
1983	H	6–225 (3.7)	45	①	143 @ 1.31	$1\frac{21}{32}$	.0010–.0030	.0020–.0040	.3725	.3715
	J	6–225 (3.7)	45	①	143 @ 1.31	$1\frac{21}{32}$	.0010–.0030	.0020–.0040	.3725	.3715
	K	6–225 (3.7)	45	①	143 @ 1.31	$1\frac{21}{32}$	.0010–.0030	.0020–.0040	.3725	.3715
	L	6–225 (3.7)	45	①	143 @ 1.31	$1\frac{21}{32}$	.0010–.0030	.0020–.0040	.3725	.3715
	N	8–318 (5.2)	45	45	193 @ 1.25	$1\frac{21}{32}$	.0015–.0035	.0025–.0045	.3720	.3710
	P	8–318 (5.2)	45	45	177 @ 1.31	$1\frac{21}{32}$	.0010–.0030	.0020–.0040	.3725	.3715
	R	8–318 (5.2)	45	45	177 @ 1.31	$1\frac{21}{32}$	.0010–.0030	.0020–.0040	.3725	.3715
	S	8–318 (5.2)	45	45	177 @ 1.31	$1\frac{21}{32}$	.0010–.0030	.0020–.0040	.3725	.3715

VALVE SPECIFICATIONS

Year	VIN	No. Cylinder Displacement cu. in. (liter)	Seat Angle (deg.)	Face Angle (deg.)	Spring Test Pressure (lbs. @ inch)	Spring Installed Height (in.)	Stem-to-Guide Clearance (in.)		Stem Diameter (in.)	
							Intake	Exhaust	Intake	Exhaust
1984	P	8–318 (5.2)	45	45	177 @ 1.31	$1^{21}/_{32}$	.0010–.0030	.0020–.0040	.3725	.3715
	R	8–318 (5.2)	45	45	177 @ 1.31	$1^{21}/_{32}$	.0010–.0030	.0020–.0040	.3725	.3715
	S	8–318 (5.2)	45	45	193 @ 1.25	$1^{21}/_{32}$	.0015–.0035	.0025–.0045	.3720	.3710
1985	P	8–318 (5.2)	45	45	177 @ 1.31	$1^{21}/_{32}$	.0010–.0030	.0020–.0040	.3725	.3715
	R	8–318 (5.2)	45	45	177 @ 1.31	$1^{21}/_{32}$	.0010–.0030	.0020–.0040	.3725	.3715
	S	8–318 (5.2)	45	45	193 @ 1.25	$1^{21}/_{32}$	.0015–.0035	.0025–.0045	.3720	.3710
1986	P	8–318 (5.2)	45	45	177 @ 1.31	$1^{21}/_{32}$	.0010–.0030	.0020–.0040	.3725	.3715
	R	8–318 (5.2)	45	45	177 @ 1.31	$1^{21}/_{32}$	.0010–.0030	.0020–.0040	.3725	.3715
	S	8–318 (5.2)	45	45	193 @ 1.25	$1^{21}/_{32}$	.0015–.0035	.0025–.0045	.3720	.3710
1987	P	8–318 (5.2)	45	45	177 @ 1.31	$1^{21}/_{32}$	.0010–.0030	.0020–.0040	.3725	.3715
	R	8–318 (5.2)	45	45	177 @ 1.31	$1^{21}/_{32}$	.0010–.0030	.0020–.0040	.3725	.3715
	S	8–318 (5.2)	45	45	193 @ 1.25	$1^{21}/_{32}$	.0015–.0035	.0025–.0045	.3720	.3710
1988-89	P	8–318 (5.2)	45	45	177 @ 1.31	$1^{21}/_{32}$	.0010–.0030	.0020–.0040	.3725	.3715
	4	8–318 (5.2)	45	45	177 @ 1.31	$1^{21}/_{32}$	.0010–.0030	.0020–.0040	.3725	.3715
	S	8–318 (5.2)	45	45	193 @ 1.25	$1^{21}/_{32}$	.0015–.0035	.0025–.0045	.3720	.3710

① Intake 45°; exhaust 43°

PISTON AND RING SPECIFICATIONS
All measurments are given in inches.

Year	VIN	No. Cylinder Displacement cu. in. (liter)	Piston Clearance	Ring Gap			Ring Side Clearance		
				Top Compression	Bottom Compression	Oil Control	Top Compression	Bottom Compression	Oil Control
1982	E	6–225 (3.7)	.0005–.0015	.010–.020	.010–.020	.015–.055	.0015–.0030	.0015–.0030	.0002–.0050
	F	6–225 (3.7)	.0005–.0015	.010–.020	.010–.020	.015–.055	.0015–.0030	.0015–.0030	.0002–.0050
	G	6–225 (3.7)	.0005–.0015	.010–.020	.010–.020	.015–.055	.0015–.0030	.0015–.0030	.0002–.0050

PISTON AND RING SPECIFICATIONS
All measurments are given in inches.

Year	VIN	No. Cylinder Displacement cu. in. (liter)	Piston Clearance	Ring Gap			Ring Side Clearance		
				Top Compression	Bottom Compression	Oil Control	Top Compression	Bottom Compression	Oil Control
1982	H	6–225 (3.7)	.0005–.0015	.010–.020	.010–.020	.015–.055	.0015–.0030	.0015–.0030	.0002–.0050
	J	8–318 (5.2)	.0005–.0015 ①	.010–.020	.010–.020	.015–.055	.0015–.0030	.0015–.0030	.0002–.0050
	K	8–318 (5.2)	.0005–.0015 ①	.010–.020	.010–.020	.015–.055	.0015–.0030	.0015–.0030	.0002–.0050
	L	8–318 (5.2)	.0005–.0015 ①	.010–.020	.010–.020	.015–.055	.0015–.0030	.0015–.0030	.0002–.0050
	M	8–318 (5.2)	.0005–.0015 ①	.010–.020	.010–.020	.015–.055	.0015–.0030	.0015–.0030	.0002–.0050
	N	8–318 (5.2)	.0005–.0015 ①	.010–.020	.010–.020	.015–.055	.0015–.0030	.0015–.0030	.0002–.0050
1983	H	6–225 (3.7)	.0005–.0015	.010–.020	.010–.020	.015–.055	.0015–.0030	.0015–.0030	.0002–.0050
	J	6–225 (3.7)	.0005–.0015	.010–.020	.010–.020	.015–.055	.0015–.0030	.0015–.0030	.0002–.0050
	K	6–225 (3.7)	.0005–.0015	.010–.020	.010–.020	.015–.055	.0015–.0030	.0015–.0030	.0002–.0050
	L	6–225 (3.7)	.0005–.0015	.010–.020	.010–.020	.015–.055	.0015–.0030	.0015–.0030	.0002–.0050
	N	8–318 (5.2)	.0005–.0015 ①	.010–.020	.010–.020	.015–.055	.0015–.0030	.0015–.0030	.0002–.0050
	P	8–318 (5.2)	.0005–.0015 ①	.010–.020	.010–.020	.015–.055	.0015–.0030	.0015–.0030	.0002–.0050
	R	8–318 (5.2)	.0005–.0015 ①	.010–.020	.010–.020	.015–.055	.0015–.0030	.0015–.0030	.0002–.0050
	S	8–318 (5.2)	.0005–.0015 ①	.010–.020	.010–.020	.015–.055	.0015–.0030	.0015–.0030	.0002–.0050
1984	P	8–318 (5.2)	.0005–.0015 ①	.010–.020	.010–.020	.015–.055	.0015–.0030	.0015–.0030	.0002–.0050
	R	8–318 (5.2)	.0005–.0015 ①	.010–.020	.010–.020	.015–.055	.0015–.0030	.0015–.0030	.0002–.0050
	S	8–318 (5.2)	.0005–.0015 ①	.010–.020	.010–.020	.015–.055	.0015–.0030	.0015–.0030	.0002–.0050

PISTON AND RING SPECIFICATIONS
All measurments are given in inches.

Year	VIN	No. Cylinder Displacement cu. in. (liter)	Piston Clearance	Ring Gap			Ring Side Clearance		
				Top Compression	Bottom Compression	Oil Control	Top Compression	Bottom Compression	Oil Control
1985	P	8–318 (5.2)	.0005–.0015 ①	.010–.020	.010–.020	.015–.055	.0015–.0030	.0015–.0030	.0002–.0050
	R	8–318 (5.2)	.0005–.0015 ①	.010–.020	.010–.020	.015–.055	.0015–.0030	.0015–.0030	.0002–.0050
	S	8–318 (5.2)	.0005–.0015 ①	.010–.020	.010–.020	.015–.055	.0015–.0030	.0015–.0030	.0002–.0050
1986	P	8–318 (5.2)	.0005–.0015 ①	.010–.020	.010–.020	.015–.055	.0015–.0030	.0015–.0030	.0002–.0050
	R	8–318 (5.2)	.0005–.0015 ①	.010–.020	.010–.020	.015–.055	.0015–.0030	.0015–.0030	.0002–.0050
	S	8–318 (5.2)	.0005–.0015 ①	.010–.020	.010–.020	.015–.055	.0015–.0030	.0015–.0030	.0002–.0050
1987	P	8–318 (5.2)	.0005–.0015 ①	.010–.020	.010–.020	.015–.055	.0015–.0030	.0015–.0030	.0002–.0050
	R	8–318 (5.2)	.0005–.0015 ①	.010–.020	.010–.020	.015–.055	.0015–.0030	.0015–.0030	.0002–.0050
	S	8–318 (5.2)	.0005–.0015 ①	.010–.020	.010–.020	.015–.055	.0015–.0030	.0015–.0030	.0002–.0050
1988-89	P	8–318 (5.2)	.0005–.0015 ①	.010–.020	.010–.020	.015–.055	.0015–.0030	.0015–.0030	.0002–.0050
	4	8–318 (5.2)	.0005–.0015 ①	.010–.020	.010–.020	.015–.055	.0015–.0030	.0015–.0030	.0002–.0050
	S	8–318 (5.2)	.0005–.0015 ①	.010–.020	.010–.020	.015–.055	.0015–.0030	.0015–.0030	.0002–.0050

① High Performance engines — .001–.002

BRAKE SPECIFICATIONS
All measurements in inches unless noted

Year	Model	Lug Nut Torque (ft. lbs.)	Master Cylinder Bore	Brake Disc		Standard Brake Drum Diameter	Minimum Lining Thickness	
				Minimum Thickness	Maximum Runout		Front	Rear
1982	All Models	85	0.827 ①	0.940	.004	10.000 ②	1/8	1/8
1983	All Models	85	0.827 ①	0.940	.004	10.000 ②	1/8	1/8
1984	All Models	85	0.827 ①	0.940	.004	10.000 ②	1/8	1/8
1985	All Models	85	0.827 ①	0.940	.004	10.000 ②	1/8	1/8
1986	All Models	85	0.827 ①	0.940	.004	10.000 ②	1/8	1/8
1987	All Models	85	0.827 ①	0.940	.004	10.000 ②	1/8	1/8
1988-89	All Models	85	0.827 ①	0.940	.004	10.000 ②	1/8	1/8

① Heavy Duty — 1.03
② Heavy Duty — 11.000

TORQUE SPECIFICATIONS
All readings in ft. lbs.

Year	VIN	No. Cylinder Displacement cu. in. (liter)	Cylinder Head Bolts	Main Bearing Bolts	Rod Bearing Bolts	Crankshaft Pulley Bolts	Flywheel Bolts	Manifold		Spark Plugs
								Intake	Exhaust	
1982	E	6-225 (3.7)	70	85	45	Press fit	55	①	10	10
	F	6-225 (3.7)	70	85	45	Press fit	55	①	10	10
	G	6-225 (3.7)	70	85	45	Press fit	55	①	10	10
	H	6-225 (3.7)	70	85	45	Press fit	55	①	10	10
	J	8-318 (5.2)	95	85	45	100	55	45	②	30
	K	8-318 (5.2)	95	85	45	100	55	45	②	30
	H	8-318 (5.2)	95	85	45	100	55	45	②	30
	L	8-318 (5.2)	95	85	45	100	55	45	②	30
	M	8-318 (5.2)	95	85	45	100	55	45	②	30
1983	H	6-225 (3.7)	70	85	45	Press fit	55	①	10	10
	J	6-225 (3.7)	70	85	45	Press fit	55	①	10	10
	K	6-225 (3.7)	70	85	45	Press fit	55	①	10	10
	L	6-225 (3.7)	70	85	45	Press fit	55	①	10	10
	N	8-318 (5.2)	95	85	45	100	55	45	②	30
	P	8-318 (5.2)	95	85	45	100	55	45	②	30
	R	8-318 (5.2)	95	85	45	100	55	45	②	30
	S	8-318 (5.2)	95	85	45	100	55	45	②	30
1984	P	8-318 (5.2)	95	85	45	100	55	45	②	30
	R	8-318 (5.2)	95	85	45	100	55	45	②	30
	S	8-318 (5.2)	95	85	45	100	55	45	②	30
1985	P	8-318 (5.2)	105	85	45	100	55	45	②	30
	R	8-318 (5.2)	105	85	45	100	55	45	②	30
	S	8-318 (5.2)	105	85	45	100	55	45	②	30

TORQUE SPECIFICATIONS
All readings in ft. lbs.

Year	VIN	No. Cylinder Displacement cu. in. (liter)	Cylinder Head Bolts	Main Bearing Bolts	Rod Bearing Bolts	Crankshaft Pulley Bolts	Flywheel Bolts	Manifold Intake	Manifold Exhaust	Spark Plugs
1986	P	8-318 (5.2)	105	85	45	100	55	45	②	30
	R	8-318 (5.2)	105	85	45	100	55	45	②	30
	S	8-318 (5.2)	105	85	45	100	55	45	②	30
1987	P	8-318 (5.2)	105	85	45	100	55	45	②	30
	R	8-318 (5.2)	105	85	45	100	55	45	②	30
	S	8-318 (5.2)	105	85	45	100	55	45	②	30
1987-89	P	8-318 (5.2)	105	85	45	100	55	45	②	30
	4	8-318 (5.2)	105	85	45	100	55	45	②	30
	S	8-318 (5.2)	105	85	45	100	55	45	②	30

① Intake to exhaust manifold bolts—17 ft. lbs.; studs—20 ft. lbs.
② Nuts—15 ft. lbs., bolts—20 ft.lb

WHEEL ALIGNMENT

Year	Model	Caster Range (deg.)	Caster Preferred Setting (deg.)	Camber Range (deg.)	Camber Preferred Setting (deg.)	Toe-in (in.)	Steering Axis Inclination (deg.)
1982	Diplomat, Mirada, Cordoba, Gran Fury, Imperial, New Yorker	1¼P-3¾P	2½P	¼N-1¼P	½P	⅛	8
1983	New Yorker, Fifth Avenue Diplomat, Mirada, Cordoba, Gran Fury, Imperial	1¼P-3¾P	2½P	¼N-1¼P	½P	⅛	8
1984	Fifth Avenue, Gran Fury, Diplomat, Newport	1¼P-3¾P	2½P	¼N-1¼P	½P	⅛	8
1985	Fifth Avenue, Gran Fury, Diplomat, Newport	1¼P-3¾P	2½P	¼N-1¼P	½P	⅛	8
1986	Fifth Avenue, Gran Fury, Diplomat, Newport	1¼P-3¾P	2½P	¼N-1¼P	½P	⅛	8
1987	Fifth Avenue, Gran Fury, Diplomat, Newport	1¼P-3¾P	2½P	¼N-1¼P	½P	⅛	8
1988-89	Fifth Avenue, Gran Fury, Diplomat, Newport	1¼P-3¾P	2½P	¼N-1¼P	½P	⅛	8

TUNE-UP PROCEDURES

Ignition Timing

ADJUSTMENT

NOTE: When installing the timing light, do not puncture the cables, boots or nipples with test probes – always use the proper adaptors. Ignition timing must be checked ONLY when the engine is at normal operating temperature and correct idle speed.

1. Connect an adjustable timing light or magnetic timing unit (use a 10 degrees offset unit, when required) according to the manufacturer's instructions. Check the underhood sticker for any further instructions.
2. Connect a tachometer to the engine; the red lead to the negative primary terminal of the coil and the black lead to a solid ground. Set the selector switch on the appropriate cylinder position.
3. Set the parking brake, place the transmission in **NEUTRAL** or **PARK** and start the engine.
4. If not equipped with Electronic Spark Advance (ESA), disconnect and plug the vacuum line at the distributor. If equipped with ESA, install a jumper wire from the carburetor switch connector-to-ground and leave the vacuum line attached to the ESA.
5. When the engine has reached normal operating temperature, check and/or set the idle speed (See the under hood sticker for specifications).
6. Loosen the distributor hold-down screw so the housing can be rotated.

NOTE: Do not use the distributor vacuum advance chamber as a handle when turning the distributor.

7. If a timing light is used, aim it at the timing plate located at the timing case cover; if a magnetic unit is used, read the unit (it must be within ± 2 degrees of the specified value). Check and, if necessary, set the timing.

NOTE: If the timing is ahead of the mark, turn the distributor housing in the direction of rotor rotation to retard the timing. If it is past the mark, rotate the distributor against its direction of rotation to advance the timing.

8. When the timing is adjusted to specifications, tighten the distributor lock clamp.

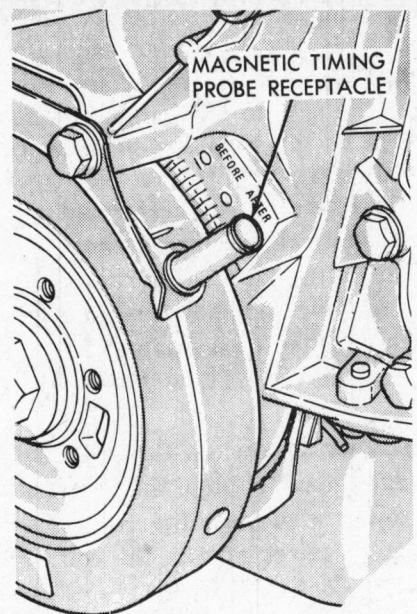

Magnetic timing probe provision for V8. Six-cylinder similiar

9. If the engine idle speed has changed, readjust the idle speed. Do not reset the timing.
10. Turn off the engine, unplug/reconnect the vacuum line, disconnect the timing equipment and jumper wire.

Valve Lash

All 6 and 8 cylinder engines use hydraulic lifters and non-adjustable rocker arms. The lifters take up lash automatically and no adjustment is possible. After engine re-assembly, these lifters adjust themselves shortly after oil pressure builds up.

Idle Speed and Mixture

NOTE: The factory recommended procedures for the idle mixture adjustment requires the addition of propane to the air mixture. Before checking or adjusting any idle speed, check ignition timing and adjust if necessary. Only the Idle Set RPM adjustments are given.

IDLE SET RPM ADJUSTMENT

Holley 6145, Carter BBD and Thermo-Quad® Electronic Feedback Carburetors

1. Disconnect and plug the vacuum hose at the EGR valve.
2. Connect a jumper wire between the carburetor ground switch and a good ground. The air cleaner cannot be removed but may be propped up to provide access to the carburetor.
3. Disconnect and plug the $3/16$ in. diameter control hose at the canister.
4. Remove the PCV valve from the cylinder head cover and allow the valve to draw fresh air.
5. Connect a tachometer to the engine, start engine and let run to normal operating temperature is reached.
6. Remove and plug the vacuum hose from the computer. Connect an auxiliary vacuum supply to computer and apply 16 in. of vacuum.
7. Disconnect the engine harness lead from the O_2 sensor and ground the engine harness lead with a jumper wire.

NOTE: Care should be exercised so that no pulling force is put on the wire attached to the O_2 sensor. The "bullet" connector to be disconnected is approximately 4 in. from the sensor. Use care in working around the sensor as the exhaust manifold is extremely hot.

8. Allow the engine to run for four minutes to allow the effect of disconnecting the O_2 sensor to take place.
9. If the idle rpm is not correct, turn the screw on the solenoid to obtain the correct rpm as shown on the Emission label.
10. Reconnect O_2 sensor wire, hose to computer, PCV valve and canister hose.
11. Remove ground wire from carburetor switch and reconnect hose to EGR valve.
12. Turn off engine and remove tachometer.

NOTE: Idle speed with the engine in normal operating condition, all hoses and wires connected, may vary from set speeds. Do not readjust.

Holley 6280 Electronic Feedback Carburetor

1. Turn off all lights and accessories.
2. Place transmission in **NEUTRAL** or **PARK** and set parking brake.
3. Start engine and run until operating temperature is reached.
4. Ground the carburetor ground switch with a jumper wire.
5. Disconnect and plug computer, EGR valve and $3/16$ in. diameter canister vacuum hoses.
6. Remove PCV valve from the valve cover and allow it to draw underhood air.
7. Disconnect wire from the O_2 sensor and ground it with a jumper wire.

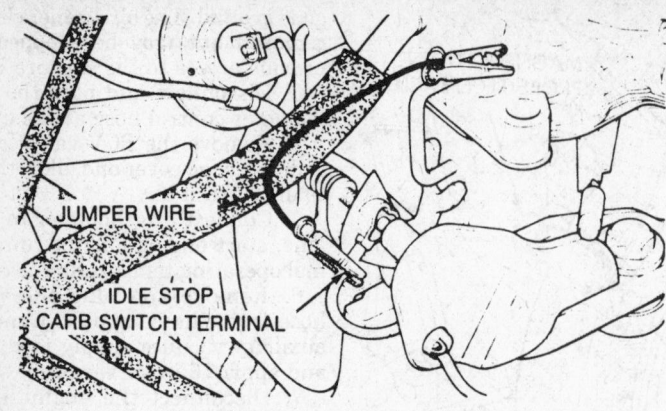

Grounding carburetor switch

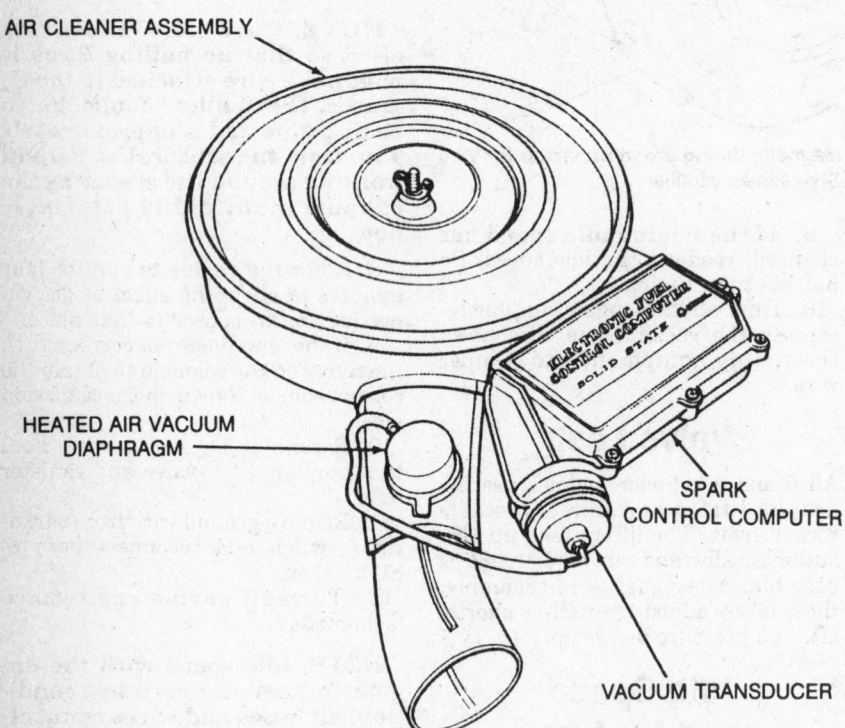

Spark control computer

Let the engine run for four minutes before making adjustment.

8. Connect a tachometer to engine.

9. Turn the screw on the solenoid and adjust engine speed to specified rpm as shown on the emission label.

10. Remove jumper wire from O_2 sensor harness connector and reconnect to O_2 sensor.

11. Reinstall PCV into valve cover.

12. Reconnect all vacuum hoses.

13. Remove jumper wire from carburetor switch.

14. Turn off engine and remove tachometer.

NOTE: Idle speed with the engine in normal operating condition, all hoses and wires connected, may vary from set speeds. Do not readjust.

Rochester Quadrajet Electronic Feedback Carburetor

1. Disconnect and plug the vacuum hose at the EGR valve.

2. Disconnect and plug the hose from carburetor at the heated air temperature sensor.

3. Disconnect carburetor electrical connector. Attach a jumper wire between the ground switch terminal of the wiring harness connector and a good ground.

4. Remove air cleaner and disconnect and plug the canister purge hose at the canister.

5. Remove the PCV valve from the cylinder head cover and allow the valve to draw fresh air.

6. Connect a tachometer to the engine, run engine to normal operating temperature is reached.

7. Disconnect the engine harness lead from the O_2 sensor and ground the engine harness lead with a jumper wire.

NOTE: Care should be exercised so that no pulling force is put on the wire attached to the O_2 sensor. The "bullet" connector to be disconnected is approximately 4 in. from the sensor. Use care in working around the sensor as the exhaust manifold is extremely hot.

8. Allow the engine to run for four minutes to allow the effect of disconnecting the O_2 sensor to take place.

9. If the idle rpm is not correct, turn the screw on the solenoid to obtain the correct rpm as shown on the Emission label.

10. Reconnect O_2 sensor wire, PCV valve and canister hose.

11. Remove ground wire from carburetor switch and reconnect hose to EGR valve.

12. Turn off engine and remove tachometer.

NOTE: Idle speed with the engine in normal operating condition, all hoses and wires connected, may vary from set speeds. Do not readjust.

ENGINE ELECTRICAL

Distributor

NOTE: The tachometer hookup with electronic ignition is the same as with conventional point-type systems. The red lead connects to the negative primary coil terminal and the black lead to a good ground. Some meters will not work with this system.

REMOVAL

1. Disconnect the negative battery cable.

2. Disconnect the vacuum advance line at the distributor and the lead wire(s) at the harness connector.

3. Unfasten the distributor cap retaining clips and lift off the cap.

4. Rotate the engine until the dis-

tributor rotor is pointing toward the No. 1 spark plug wire. Matchmark the distributor body and the engine block to indicate the position of the distributor to the block.

5. Place a mark on the edge of the distributor housing to indicate the position of the rotor to the distributor.

6. Remove the distributor hold-down clamp screw and clamp.

7. Carefully lift the distributor from of the block; the shaft will rotate slightly as the distributor is removed.

INSTALLATION

NOTE: Use the reference marks that were made to correctly position the distributor in the block.

Engine Undisturbed

1. On the 6 cylinder engine, position the rotor just ahead of the No. 1 distributor cap terminal. Lower the distributor into the engine block opening. Mesh the distributor gear with the camshaft drive gear. Be certain that the rubber O-ring seal is in the groove of the distributor shank.

2. On the V8 engine, clean the top of the engine block around the distributor opening and position the rotor even with the No. 1 distributor cap terminal position. Lower the distributor into the engine block opening and engage the tongue of the distributor shaft with the slot in the distributor oil pump drive gear.

NOTE: When the distributor is properly seated, the rotor should be directly under the No. 1 distributor cap terminal.

3. Install the distributor hold-down clamp and tighten the retaining screw finger tight.

4. Install the distributor cap. Connect the primary lead wire(s) to the harness connector.

5. Start the engine. Check and adjust the ignition timing.

6. Connect the vacuum advance line to the distributor.

Engine Disturbed

1. Remove the No. 1 spark plug, cover spark plug hole with finger and rotate the engine until the No. 1 piston reaches TDC of the compression stroke (compression pressure can be felt as the No. 1 piston approaches TDC). The 0 degree mark on the crankshaft vibration damper should now be aligned with the indicator on the timing cover.

2. If installing the distributor on a 6 cylinder engine, position the rotor just ahead of the No. 1 distributor cap terminal. Lower the distributor into the

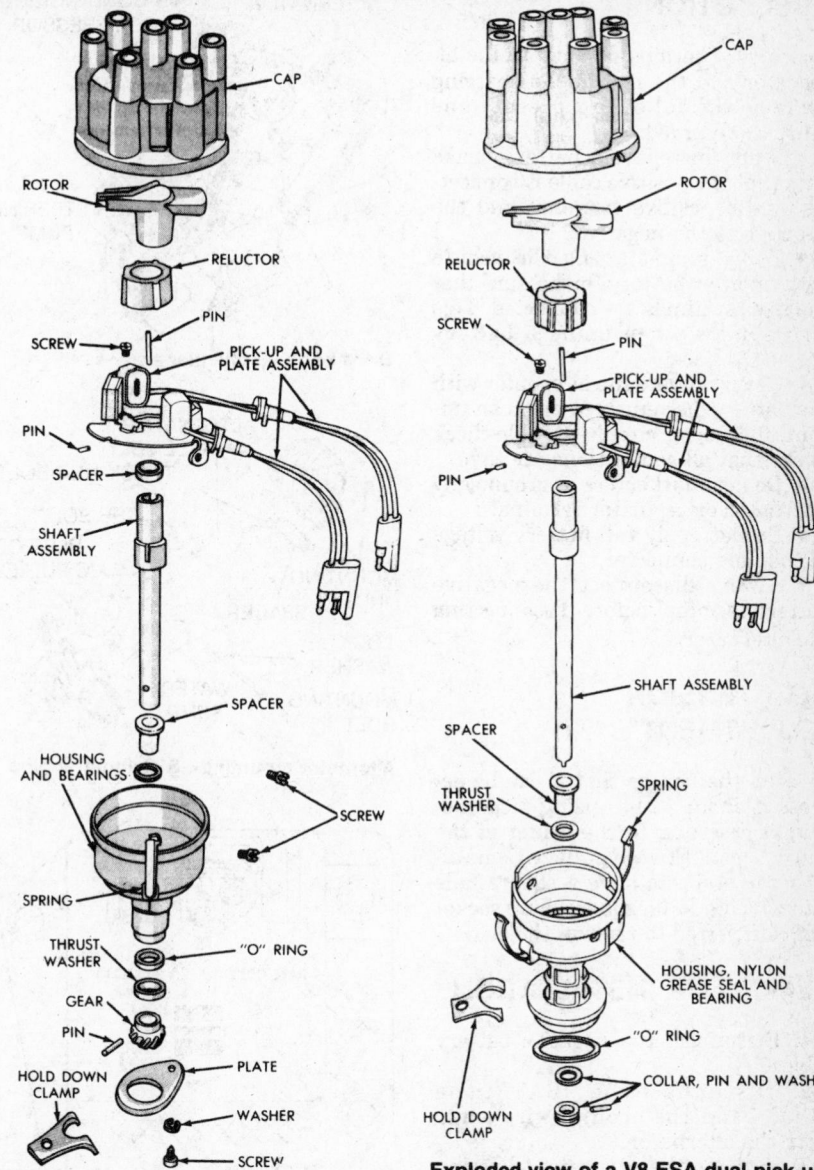

Exploded view of a 6-cyl. ESA dual pick-up distributor. Earlier models use single pick-up

Exploded view of a V8 ESA dual pick-up distributor. Earlier models use single pick-up

engine block opening. Mesh the distributor gear with the camshaft drive gear. Be certain that the rubber O-ring seal is in the groove of the distributor shank.

3. If installing the distributor on a V8 engine, clean the top of the engine block around the distributor opening and position the rotor even with the No. 1 distributor cap terminal position. Lower the distributor into the engine block opening and engage the tongue of the distributor shaft with the slot in the distributor oil pump drive gear.

NOTE: When the distributor is properly seated, the rotor should

be directly under the No. 1 distributor cap terminal.

4. Install the distributor hold-down clamp and tighten the retaining screw finger tight.

5. Install the distributor cap. Connect the primary lead wire(s) to the harness connector.

6. Start the engine. Check and adjust the ignition timing.

7. Connect the vacuum advance line to the distributor.

Alternator

For further information on the charging system, please refer to the Charging and Starting Unit Repair section.

PRECAUTIONS

To prevent serious damage to the alternator and the rest of the charging system, the following precautions must be observed:

• When installing a battery, make sure that the positive cable is connected to the positive terminal and the negative to the negative.

• When jump-starting the vehicle with another battery, make sure that the like terminals are connected. This also applies when using a battery charger.

• Never operate the alternator with the battery disconnected or on an uncontrolled open circuit. Double-check to see that all connections are tight.

• Do not short across or ground any alternator or regulator terminals.

• Do not apply full battery voltage to the field connector.

• Always disconnect the negative battery terminal before disconnecting the alternator.

BELT TENSION ADJUSTMENT

Tighten the belt so that it can be depressed about ½ in., using moderate thumb pressure, in the center of the longest span between pulleys. Some alternator brackets have a square hole into which a ½ in. square drive socket can be inserted to tension the belt.

REMOVAL & INSTALLATION

1. Disconnect the negative battery cable.
2. Disconnect the "BAT", the "FLD" and the ground wire leads from the alternator.
3. Back out the alternator adjusting bolt, push the alternator down and remove the drive belt.

NOTE: If equipped with A/C, remove the alternator pivot bolt.

4. Remove the alternator by removing the mounting bolts and the belt tensioner bracket bolt.
5. To install, reverse the removal procedures. Using a voltmeter, check the current output.

Regulator

For all information on the regulator testing procedures, please refer to the "Charging and Starting" Unit Repair section.

ADJUSTMENT

All models use a solid-state (silicone transistor) voltage regulator which is

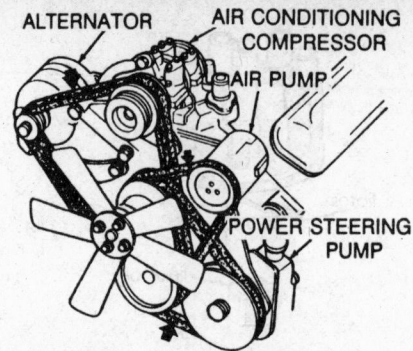

Drive belts—8 clyinder engine

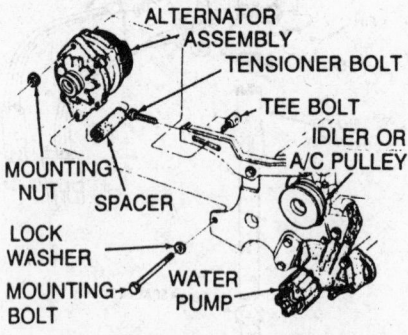

Alternator mounting—8 clyinder engine

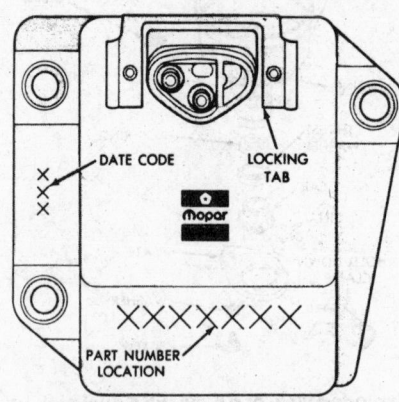

View of the voltage regulator

nonadjustable. The regulator is mounted in the engine compartment and clearly labeled.

REMOVAL & INSTALLATION

1. Release the spring clips and pull off the regulator wiring plug.
2. Remove the retaining bolts and regulator.
3. To install, reverse the removal procedures. Be sure that the spring clips engage the wiring plug and that the unit has a good ground.

Starter

For further information on the starter system, please refer to the

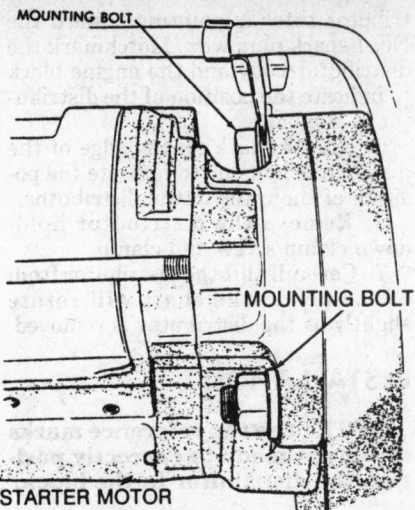

Starter mounting

charging and starting in the Unit Repair section.

REMOVAL & INSTALLATION

1. Disconnect the negative battery cable.
2. Remove the battery cable from the starter.
3. On 1984–89 models, remove the nut and bolt retaining the heat shield to the starter, then remove the heat shield.
4. Disconnect the electrical leads from the solenoid terminals.
5. Remove the starter securing nut/bolt and remove the starter from the flywheel housing. If equipped with an automatic transmission, remove the starter securing nut/bolt, slide the cooler tube bracket off the stud and remove the starter.

NOTE: When removing the starter, be careful not to damage the flywheel housing seal.

6. To install, reverse the removal procedures. Be sure that the starter and flywheel housing mating surfaces are free of dirt and oil. Position the starter to the flywheel housing seal. When tightening the bolt and nut, hold the starter away from the engine to ensure proper alignment.

ENGINE MECHANICAL

Engine

REMOVAL & INSTALLATION
6 Cylinder Engine

1. Scribe the hood hinge outlines on

the underside of the hood, then remove the hood.

2. Drain the cooling system. Remove the negative battery cable and the air cleaner.

3. Remove the radiator hoses, heater hoses, transmission oil cooler lines and the radiator. Remove the PCV and the evaporative control system from the cylinder head cover.

4. Disconnect the fuel lines, carburetor linkage and wiring from the engine. Disconnect the exhaust pipe at the exhaust manifold and raise the vehicle on a hoist.

5. Drain the transmission/converter fluid. Remove the fluid cooler lines, the filler tube and the shift linkage.

6. Remove the speedometer cable. Disconnect the driveshaft and tie out of the way.

7. Install an engine support fixture to the rear of the engine. Remove the engine rear support crossmember.

8. Matchmark the converter and drive plate for reassembly. Unbolt the drive plate from the torque converter.

9. Lower the vehicle. Fasten an engine lifting fixture to the engine and attach a vertical hoist to the fixture eyebolt. Remove the bolts from the front engine mounts.

10. Lift the engine out of the engine compartment and attach it to an engine stand.

11. To install, reverse the removal procedures. Replace the transmission and the coolant fluids. Start the engine, allow it to reach operating temperatures and check for fluid leaks.

V8 Engines

1. Scribe the outline of the hood hinge brackets on the hood and remove the hood. Remove the negative battery cable.

2. Drain the cooling system. Remove the radiator hoses, the fan shroud, the transmission oil cooler lines and the radiator.

3. Remove the fuel line(s), the air cleaner, the accelerator linkage and the carburetor. Remove all of the wires attach to the engine.

4. Attach an engine lifting fixture to the engine. A special tool is available that attaches to the carburetor mounting studs.

5. Raise the vehicle and install an engine support fixture tool No. C-3487A to the rear of the engine. Drain the transmission and the convertor.

6. If equipped with air conditioning and/or power steering, remove the unit(s) from the engine and position it out of the way without disconnecting the lines.

7. Disconnect the exhaust pipe(s) from the exhaust manifold(s). Remove the driveshaft, wires, linkage, speed-

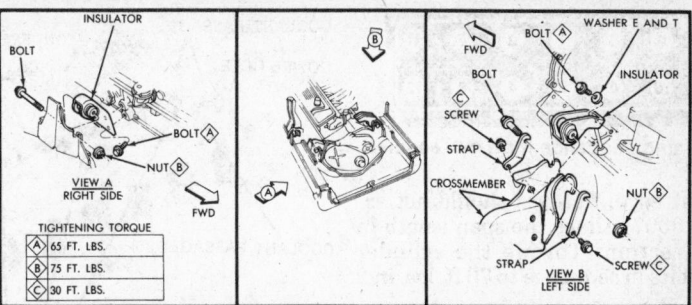

Engine front mounts, Slant Six, all models

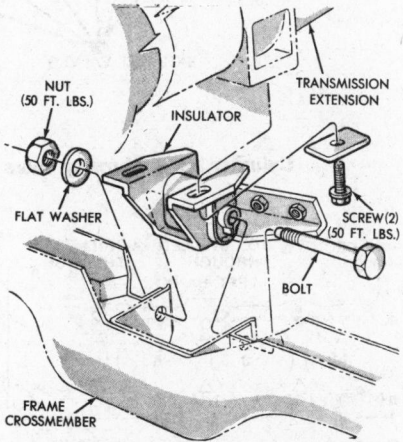

Typical V8 rear engine mount

ometer cable and oil cooler lines that are attached to the transmission.

8. Matchmark the converter and drive plate for reassembly. Remove the torque converter-to-drive plate bolts. Remove the engine rear support crossmember, the transmission-to-engine bolts and the transmission.

9. Lower the vehicle. Attach a vertical hoist to the engine lifting fixture, lift the engine slightly and remove the motor mount bolts.

10. Raise the engine, carefully remove it from the engine compartment and mount it onto an engine stand.

11. To install, reverse the removal procedures. Fill the transmission and cooling system with fluid. Start the engine, allow it to reach operating temperatures and check for leaks.

Cylinder Head

REMOVAL & INSTALLATION

NOTE: Do not loosen the head bolts until the engine is thoroughly cool, to prevent warping the head. If the head sticks to the block, operate the starter to loosen it with compression or tap it upward with a soft rubber hammer. Do not force anything between the head and the block. The

cylinder head bolts should be retorqued after the first 500 miles, unless a special gasket is used.

6 Cylinder Engines

1. Drain the cooling system and disconnect the negative battery cable.

2. Remove the carburetor air cleaner and the fuel lines. Disconnect the accelerator linkage.

3. Remove the vacuum lines from the carburetor and the distributor. Disconnect the spark plug wires from the spark plugs.

4. Disconnect the heater hose and the clamp holding the by-pass hose. Disconnect the heat indicator sending unit wire.

5. Disconnect the exhaust pipe at the exhaust manifold flange. If equipped, disconnect the diverter valve vacuum line from the intake manifold; also remove the air injection assembly (if applicable) from the cylinder head cover.

6. Remove the PCV tube, evaporative control system and cylinder head cover.

7. Remove the rocker arm/shaft assembly. Remove the pushrods and keep them in order.

NOTE: It is a good idea to set the pushrods in order (as they are removed from the engine) in a piece of lumber that has been drilled. The twelve pushrods can be labeled by writing the cylinder number and "In" and "Ex" under each hole in the lumber.

8. Remove the 14 head bolts in reverse of the torque sequence and lift off the cylinder head. The cylinder head is removed with the intake and exhaust manifold assembly. Clean the machined mounting surfaces.

NOTE: To ease the installation procedures, remove the intake/exhaust manifold assembly from the cylinder head.

9. To install, use new gaskets and reverse the removal procedures. Check all of the mounting surfaces with a

Tightening sequence for 6 cyl. engines

straight edge, flatness should not exceed 0.00075 times the span length in any direction. Torque the cylinder head bolts in sequence to 70 ft. lbs. in 2 steps.

10. Refill the cooling system. Start the engine and operate it (at idle) until the normal operating temperatures have been reached.

V8 Engines

1. Drain the cooling system and disconnect negative battery cable.

2. Remove the alternator, the air cleaner and fuel line(s). Disconnect the accelerator linkage.

3. Remove the vacuum hose(s) from the carburetor/throttle body and the distributor. Remove the distributor cap and wires and the spark plugs.

4. Disconnect the coil wires, the temperature sending wire, the heater and by-pass hoses.

5. Remove the PCV valve, the evaporative control system and the valve covers.

6. Remove the intake manifold, the ignition coil and the carburetor/throttle body as an assembly. Remove the tappet chamber cover, if equipped.

7. Disconnect the exhaust pipes and remove the exhaust manifolds.

8. Remove the rocker arm/shaft assemblies. Remove the pushrods and identify to insure installation in the original locations.

9. Remove the 10 head bolts from each cylinder head and lift off the heads. Clean all of the machine mounting surfaces.

NOTE: If there is any reason to suspect leakage between the cylinder block and head, inspect all surfaces with a straight edge. The out of flatness should not exceed 0.00075 times the span length in any direction.

10. To install, use new head gaskets and reverse the removal procedures. Torque the cylinder head bolts to 105 ft. lbs. in 3 steps.

11. Refill the cooling system. Start the engine and operate it (at idle) until the normal operating temperatures have been reached.

OVERHAUL

For all cylinder head overhaul procedures, please refer to engine rebuilding in the Unit Repair section.

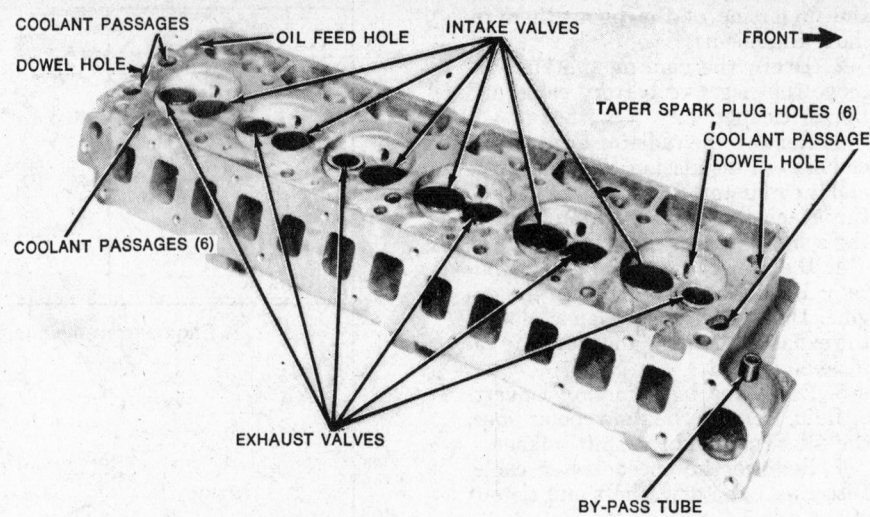

Cylinder head, showing valve sequence—six cylinder engines

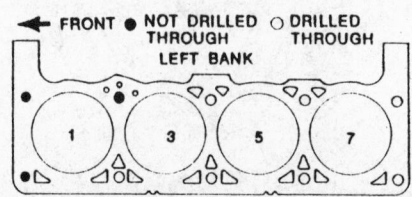
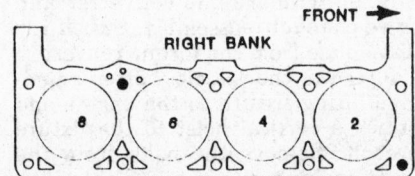

Sealant must be applied to the drilled through head bolt threads on the V8 engines

Tightening sequence for V8 engines

Rocker Arm/Shaft

REMOVAL & INSTALLATION

6 Cylinder Engines

1. Remove the PCV hose, distributor advance hose, vapor canister hose, temperature gauge wire, electric choke wire and the alternator wiring harness clips.

2. Disconnect the fender support bracket. Remove the valve cover with its gasket. If equipped with A/C, hold the A/C hoses up out of the way and then remove the valve cover.

3. Take out the rocker arm/shaft assembly securing bolts and remove the rocker arm/shaft assembly.

4. To install, use a new gasket, reverse the removal procedures.

NOTE: The shaft oil holes must be installed facing the bottom to provide proper lubrication to the rocker arms. A special bolt goes to the rear of the shaft. Torque the rocker arm bolts to 25 ft. lbs.

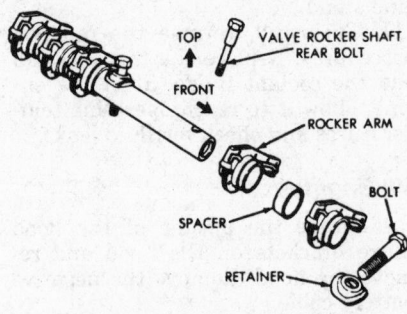

Slant Six rocker shaft details

V8 Engines

The stamped steel rocker arms are arranged on one rocker arm shaft per cylinder head. To remove the rocker arms and shaft:

1. Disconnect the spark plug wires.

2. Disconnect the closed ventilation and evaporative control system from the cylinder head covers.

3. Remove the cylinder head covers with their gaskets.

4. Remove the 5 rocker shaft bolts and retainers, then lift off the rocker arm and shaft assembly.

5. Clean the gasket mounting surfaces.

6. To install, use new gaskets and reverse the removal procedures.

NOTE: The notch on the end of both rocker shafts should point to

the engine centerline and toward the front of the engine on the left cylinder head or toward the rear on the right cylinder head. Torque the rocker shaft bolts to 17 ft. lbs. and the cylinder head covers to 7 ft. lbs. If removing the rocker arms from the shaft, be sure to install them in their correct order of removal (right and left directions).

Intake Manifold

REMOVAL & INSTALLATION

V8 Engines

1. Drain the cooling system. Disconnect the negative battery cable.
2. Remove the alternator, the air cleaner and disconnect the fuel lines(s) from the carburetor or throttle body.
3. Disconnect all vacuum lines and the throttle linkage that attach to the carburetor/throttle body and intake manifold.
4. Disconnect the spark plug wires from the plugs. Remove the distributor cap and wires as an assembly.
5. Disconnect the wires from the coil and the temperature sending unit.
6. Disconnect the heater and bypass hose from the intake manifold.
7. Remove the intake manifold attaching bolts. Remove the manifold, carburetor/throttle body and coil from the engine as an assembly.
8. Clean all gasket mounting surfaces and firmly cement new gaskets to the engine.

NOTE: Do not use sealer on the composition side gasket.

9. To install, reverse the removal procedures. Torque the bolts to 45 ft. lbs. in 3 steps, in the sequence shown.

Exhaust Manifold

REMOVAL & INSTALLATION

V8 Engines

1. Disconnect the exhaust manifold at the exhaust pipe flange. Access to these bolts is from underneath the vehicle. If equipped, disconnect the air injection nozzles and the carburetor heated air stove. Disconnect any components of the EGR system which are in the way.
2. Remove the exhaust manifold by removing the securing bolts and washers. To reach these bolts, it may be necessary to jack the engine slightly off its front mounts.

NOTE: When the exhaust manifold is removed, sometimes the securing studs will come out with

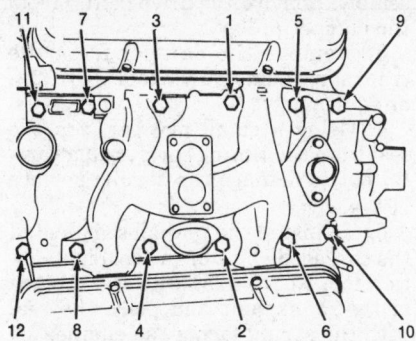

Intake manifold tightening sequence for V8 engines

the nuts. If this occurs, studs must be replaced with the aid of sealing compound on the coarse thread ends. If this is not done, water leaks may develop at the studs.

3. To install the exhaust manifold, reverse the removal procedures. On the center branch of the V8's manifold, no conical washers are used. Torque the exhaust manifold bolts to 20 ft. lbs. and the nuts to 15 ft. lbs.

Combination Manifold

REMOVAL & INSTALLATION

6 Cylinder Engine

1. Disconnect the air cleaner vacuum control tube from the carburetor. Disconnect the flexible connector between the carburetor and the air cleaner.
2. Disconnect the breather cap from the air cleaner line and remove the air cleaner.
3. Disconnect the crankcase ventilation tube, the carburetor bowl vent line and the vacuum lines. Remove the carburetor air heater.
4. Disconnect the automatic choke rod, the fuel line, the throttle linkage and remove the carburetor.
5. Disconnect the exhaust pipe at the exhaust manifold.
6. Remove the nuts and washers securing the manifold assembly to the cylinder head. Remove the manifold from the cylinder head.

NOTE: Make note of the location of the different types of washers for installation.

7. Remove the 3 screws securing the intake manifold to the exhaust manifold. Separate the manifolds and discard the gasket.
8. Clean all the gasket surfaces. Check the mating surfaces of the manifolds with a straightedge. Surfaces should be flat within 0.006 in. per foot of length.

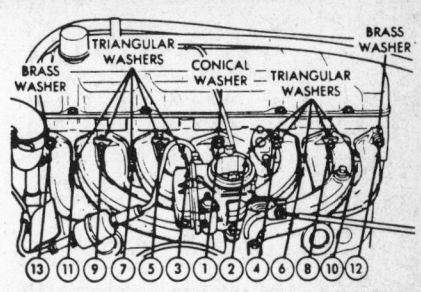

Nut and washer location/torquing sequence-6 cylinder engine

9. To install, place a new gasket between the 2 manifolds. Install the stud nut and the 2 long screws securing the manifolds, DO NOT tighten the screws. Using a new gasket, position the manifold assembly on the cylinder head.
10. Install the triangular washers/nuts on the upper studs and on the 4 lower studs opposite No. 2 and 5 cylinders. The 8 triangular washers should be positioned squarely on the machined surfaces of both manifold retaining pads. These washers must be installed with the cup side against the manifold. Install the nuts and washers only when the engine is cold.
11. Install the steel conical washers with the cup (concave) side to the manifold, 1 on the center upper stud and 2 on the center lower studs. Install a brass washer on each end, with the flat side to the manifold. Install the nuts with the flat side away from the washers. Snug up the nuts.
12. Tighten the 3 intake-to-exhaust manifold screws to 12 ft. lbs., starting with the inner stud. Tighten the manifold-to-head nuts to 10 ft. lbs.
13. Attach the exhaust pipe-to-manifold, using a new gasket and tighten the nuts to 35 ft. lbs. To complete the installation, reverse the removal procedures.

Front Cover

REMOVAL & INSTALLATION

6 Cylinder Engines

1. Drain the cooling system and disconnect the negative battery cable.
2. Remove the radiator and cooling fan. Remove the alternator, the power steering and the A/C drive belts, if equipped.
3. Remove the damper pulley bolt. Using a suitable puller tool (C–3732A, or equivalent), remove the damper pulley.
4. Remove the front oil pan bolts and the timing cover bolts. Remove the timing cover and gasket.
5. Clean the gasket mounting surfaces.

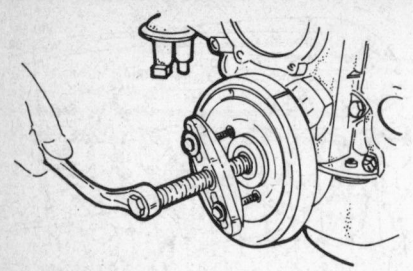

Removing vibration damper assembly, 318 V8. Slant Six similar

6. To install, apply an 1/8 in. bead of sealer to the new gasket and reverse the removal procedures. Torque the oil pan and timing cover bolts to 17 ft. lbs. Refill the cooling system.

V8 Engines

1. Disconnect the negative battery cable and drain the cooling system. Remove the fan shroud bolts.

2. Disconnect the top radiator hose from the radiator and tie it back over the engine. Remove the alternator and the power steering pump (if equipped) belts.

3. Remove the fan, fan shroud, fan spacer, fan drive and the water pump pulley. Disconnect the alternator bracket and it set aside. Remove the air compressor and the power steering pump (if equipped); then, set aside.

4. Disconnect the lower radiator and bypass hose from the water pump. Remove the water pump bolts and the pump.

5. Remove the damper pulley bolt and washer from the crankshaft. Install the bar from the tool set No. C-3688 and the screw from the tool set No. C-3732A or its equivalent then pull the damper from the crankshaft.

6. Remove the fuel line(s) and fuel pump (carburated engines). Loosen the oil pan bolts and remove the front bolt from each side.

7. Remove the timing gear cover.

8. Clean the gasket mounting surfaces.

9. To install, use a new gasket, oil seal (lubricate the seal lips with oil) and reverse the removal procedures. Torque the damper pulley bolt to 100 ft. lbs., the timing chain cover to 30 ft. lbs. and the damper pulley to 17 ft. lbs.

NOTE: Use tool No. C-3688 or equivalent to install the damper pulley onto the crankshaft.

OIL SEAL REPLACEMENT

6 Cylinder Engine

1. Disconnect the negative battery cable and drain the cooling system.

2. Remove the radiator and fan as-

sembly. Remove the drive belt(s) from the damper pulley.

3. Remove the damper from the crankshaft using puller tool C-3732A, or equivalent.

4. Using a small pry bar, pry the seal from the timing cover, being careful not to damage the sealing surface of the cover.

5. To install the new oil seal, install the threaded shaft of the seal installation tool No. C-4251 into the threads of the crankshaft and place the seal with the spring facing the engine.

6. Using an installation adapter tool No. C-4251-2, place the thrust bearing/nut on the shaft and tighten until the tool is flush with the timing chain cover.

7. Lubricate the seal lip with Lubriplate®, then install the damper using tool No. C-3732A.

8. To complete the installation, reverse the removal procedures.

V8 Engines

1. Disconnect the negative battery cable and drain the cooling system. Remove the fan shroud bolts.

2. Remove the alternator and the power steering pump (if equipped) belts. Remove the fan and the fan shroud.

3. Remove the damper pulley bolt and washer from the crankshaft. Install the bar from tool set No. C-3688 and the screw from tool set No. C-3732A, then pull the vibration damper from the end of the crankshaft.

4. Using a small pry bar, carefully pry the seal from the timing cover without scratching the sealing surface of the cover.

5. To install the seal, lubricate the seal lip with Lubriplate®, place it on the crankshaft with the spring side facing the engine. Mount the threaded shaft of the seal installation tool No. C-4251 into the threads of the crankshaft.

6. Using an installation adapter tool No. C-4251-3, place the thrust bearing and nut on the shaft and tighten until the tool is flush with the timing chain cover.

7. To complete the installation, reverse the removal procedures. Torque the damper bolt to 135 ft. lbs. and the pulley bolts to 17 ft. lbs.

Timing Chain and Sprockets

REMOVAL & INSTALLATION

6 Cylinder Engines

1. Remove the front cover.

2. Turn the crankshaft to align (facing each other on the center line of the

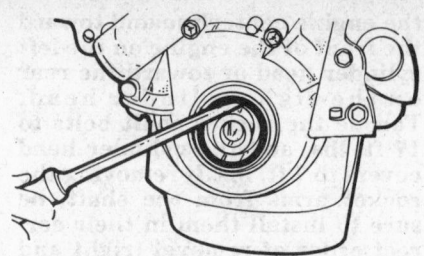

Oil seal removal for V8. 6 cyl. similar

sprockets) the timing marks, the crankshaft sprocket with the timing mark on the camshaft sprocket.

3. Remove the camshaft sprocket bolt, the camshaft sprocket and crankshaft sprocket with the timing chain.

4. To install the timing chain, place the camshaft and crankshaft sprockets on a flat surface, with the timing indicators (facing each other) on an imaginary centerline through both sprocket bores. Place the timing chain around both sprockets. Be sure the timing marks are in alignment.

5. Align the sprockets with the keyway location in the crankshaft sprocket and the keyway or dowel hole in the camshaft sprocket.

6. Slide both sprockets evenly onto their respective shafts, while keeping the sprockets tight against the chain in the correct position.

NOTE: Using a straightedge, measure the alignment of the sprocket timing marks; they must be perfectly aligned.

7. To complete the installation, reverse the removal procedures. Use tool No. C-3732A to press the damper pulley onto the crankshaft. Torque the camshaft sprocket bolt to 35 ft. lbs. Apply an 1/8 in. bead of sealer to the new gasket. Torque the oil pan and timing cover bolts to 17 ft. lbs. Refill the cooling system.

V8 Engines

1. Remove the front cover.

NOTE: Before removing the timing chain, rotate the engine to align the timing mark of the camshaft sprocket with the timing mark of the crankshaft sprocket. The timing marks must face each other on the center line between the two sprockets.

2. Remove the camshaft sprocket lockbolt, cup washer and fuel pump eccentric. Remove the timing chain with both sprockets.

3. To install the timing chain, place the camshaft and crankshaft sprockets on a flat surface, with the timing indicators (facing each other) on an

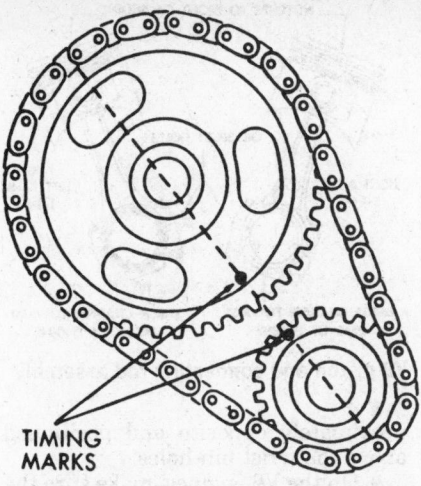

Alignment of timing marks—6 cylinder

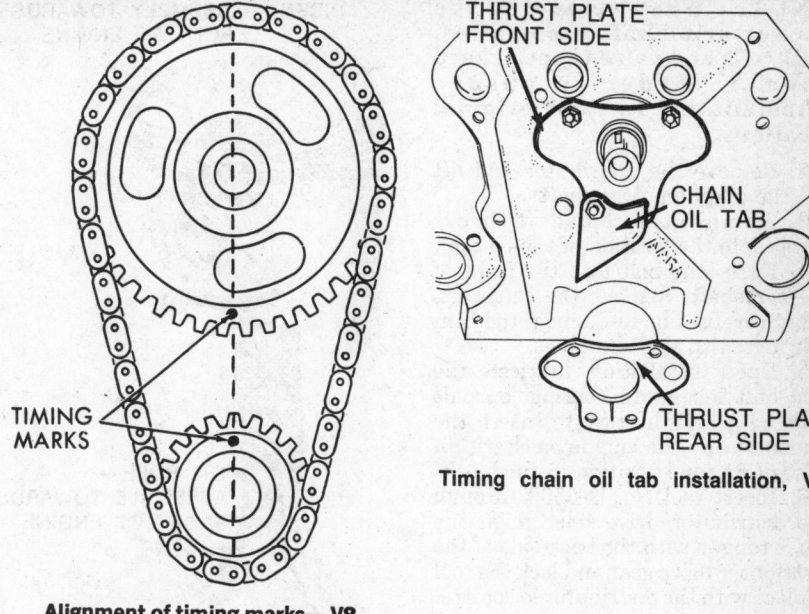

Alignment of timing marks—V8

Timing chain oil tab installation, V8s

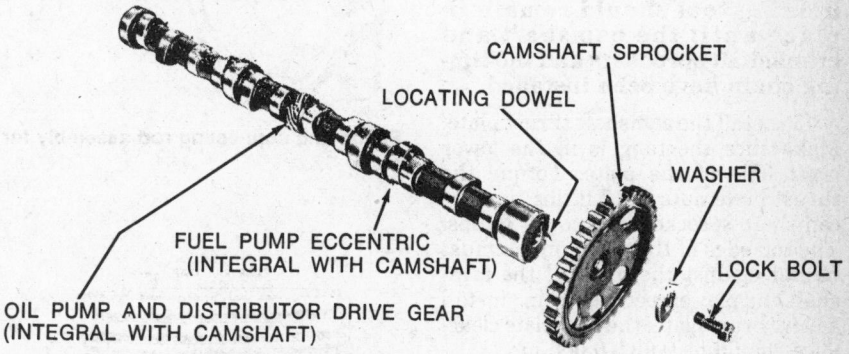

Camshaft and sprocket assembly—six cylinder

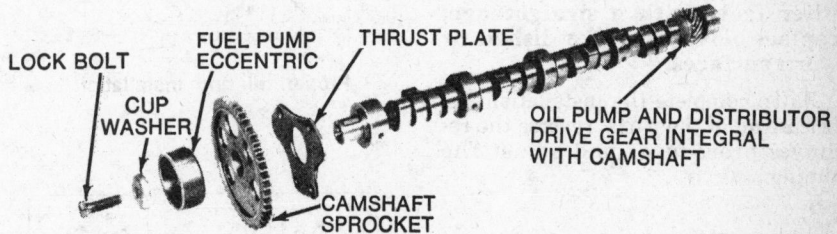

Camshaft and sprocket assembly—V8

imaginary centerline through both sprocket bores. Place the timing chain around both sprockets. Be sure the timing marks are in alignment.

4. Align the sprockets with the keyway location in the crankshaft sprocket and the keyway or dowel hole in the camshaft sprocket.

5. Slide both sprockets evenly onto their respective shafts, while keeping the sprockets tight against the chain in the correct position.

NOTE: Using a straightedge, measure the alignment of the sprocket timing marks; they must be perfectly aligned.

6. To complete the installation, reverse the removal procedures. To install the damper pulley, use tool No. C–3688. Torque the camshaft bolt to 35 ft. lbs., the damper pulley bolt to 135 ft. lbs., the timing chain cover to 30 ft. lbs. and the damper pulley bolts to 17 ft. lbs.

NOTE: If the camshaft end play exceeds 0.010 in., install a new thrust plate, it should be 0.002–0.006 in. with the new plate.

Camshaft

REMOVAL & INSTALLATION

NOTE: Whenever a new camshaft and/or new tappets are installed, the manufacturer recommends that 1 qt. of crankcase conditioner should be added to the engine oil to aid break-in. This oil mixture should be left in the engine for a minimum of 500 miles. Chrysler recommends that the engine be removed from the vehicle before removing the camshaft. However, in some cases it may be

possible to remove the camshaft from the engine, with the engine still in the vehicle, by removing the radiator and grille, then sliding the camshaft out through the front of the vehicle.

6 Cylinder Engines

1. Remove tappets and push rods, keeping them in order to insure installation in their original locations.

2. Remove the fuel pump.

3. Remove the distributor and the oil pump.

4. Fit a long bolt into the front of

the camshaft to facilitate the camshaft removal. Remove the camshaft, being careful not to damage the cam bearings with the cam lobes.

5. Before installation, lubricate the camshaft lobes and bearing journals. Inspect the crowns of all the tappet faces with a straightedge. Replace any tappets that have dished or worn surfaces.

6. To complete the installation, reverse the removal procedures.

V8 Engines

1. Remove rocker arm and shaft assemblies.

NOTE: When removing the rocker arm/shaft assemblies, pushrods and valve tappets, keep them in order to ensure reinstallation in their original locations.

2. Remove the distributor and lift out the oil pump driveshaft.

3. Remove the camshaft thrust plate (note the location of the oil tab).

4. Fit a long bolt into the front of the camshaft. Remove the camshaft, being careful not to damage the cam bearings with the cam lobes.

5. Upon installation, lubricate the camshaft lobes and bearing journals with camshaft lubricant. Insert the camshaft into the engine block within 2 in. of its final position in the block.

6. Insert tool No. C–3509 through the distributor drive hole, align the tool's tongue with the back side of the distributor drive gear and lock the tool in place with the distributor lock plate.

NOTE: The distributor drive holding tool should remain in place until the camshaft and crankshaft sprockets and the timing chain have been installed.

7. Install the camshaft thrust plate. Make sure the tang is in the lower right hole of the plate. Torque the thrust plate nuts to 17 ft. lbs. and the camshaft sprocket bolt to 35 ft. lbs. The top edge of the chain oil tab must be flat against the plate. If the camshaft end play exceeds 0.010 in., install a new thrust plate; the new plate clearance should be 0.002–0.006 in.

NOTE: Before installing the lifters, inspect the crowns of the lifter faces with a straightedge; replace any that have dished or worn surfaces.

8. To complete the installation, lubricate all of the parts, reverse the removal procedures and adjust the timing.

Piston and Connecting Rod

POSITIONING

For all piston and connecting rod overhaul procedures, refer to engine rebuilding in the Unit Repair section.

Upon installation of the piston assemblies, stagger the compression ring gaps, so that they do not line up with the oil ring gaps, as follows:

- On the 6 cylinder engines, rotate the oil ring expander so that the ends are at the right-side of the engine. Rotate the steel rails so the gaps are ap-

Piston and connecting rod assembly for 6 cyl.

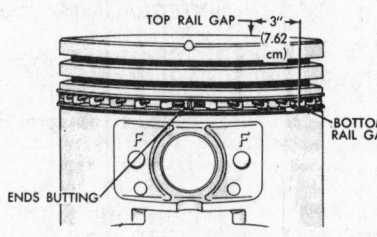

Proper oil ring installation

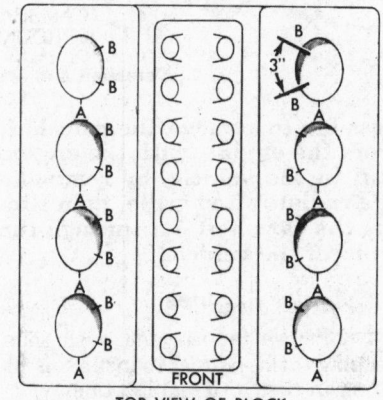

Correct piston ring arrangement in cylinder bores, V8s. Slant Six similar

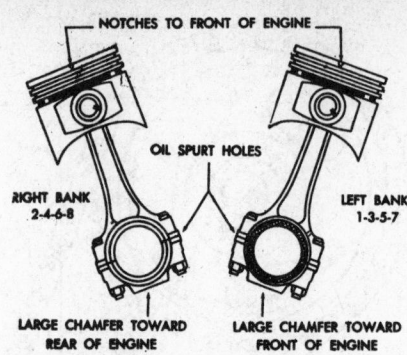

V8 piston and connecting rod assembly

proximately opposite and positioned above the wrist pin holes.

- On the V8 engines, make sure the oil ring expander ends are butted and the rail gap ends are located as shown in the illustration.

- On all 6 cylinder engines, the squirt hole in the connecting rod should face forward.

- On the V8 engines, a "V" groove is cut into the parting bearing face. When installing, make sure that the groove in the rod aligns with the groove in the cap (the groove provides for lubrication of the cylinder wall in the opposite bank).

ENGINE LUBRICATION

Oil Pan

REMOVAL & INSTALLATION

6 Cylinder Engines

1. Disconnect the negative battery cable. Remove the engine dipstick.

2. Remove the radiator shroud attaching screws and move the shroud rearward on the engine.

3. Jack up the vehicle and drain the oil. Remove the engine-to-transmission bracket, the exhaust pipe and the torque converter inspection shield, if equipped with an automatic transmission.

4. Remove the steering center link from the steering and idler arm ball joints.

5. Position a jack stand at the right-front corner of the engine oil pan. Be sure not to support the engine at the crankshaft pulley or damper.

6. Remove the front engine mount bolts. Raise the engine about 1½–2 in.

7. Remove the oil pan bolts, rotate the engine crankshaft to clear the counterweights and remove the oil pan.

8. To install, use a new pan gasket set, apply sealer to the 4 junctions of the gaskets, install the oil pan and torque it to 17 ft. lbs. Make sure the pickup screen contacts the bottom of the pan.

9. To complete the installation, reverse the removal procedures. Torque engine mounts to 75 ft. lbs. and the steering/idler arms to 175 ft. lbs.; be sure to install new cotter pins. Replace the oil, then start and run the vehicle for 5 minutes and check for leaks.

V8 Engines

1. Disconnect the negative battery cable and remove the dipstick.

2. Raise and support the front of the vehicle on jackstands, then drain the oil. Remove the torque converter-to-engine left housing strut, if equipped.

3. Disconnect the steering center link from the steering and idler arms on all models if necessary to gain added clearance to remove oil pan.

4. Disconnect the exhaust pipes from the manifolds and secure them out of the way. Remove the starter, starter mounting stud and the torque converter inspection plate if necessary to gain added clearance to remove oil pan.

5. Check to see if there is sufficient clearance to reach all of the oil pan bolts; if not, it will be necessary to raise the engine about 1½–2 in. To do this, remove the motor mounts and raise the engine only until the bolts become accessible. Do not raise engine to high which will cause cooling fan to hit shroud and damage shroud also it may be necessary to remove distributor cap for clearance.

6. Remove the oil pan bolts, rotate the engine crankshaft to clear the counterweights and remove the oil pan with a twisting motion.

NOTE: On some models, you may have to unbolt the transmission until the pan clears.

7. When installing the oil pan, be sure the oil strainer is parallel to and in contact with the oil pan bottom. Apply sealer to the corner junctions of the cork and rubber gaskets. The side gaskets should overlap the rear seal. Torque the oil pan bolts to 17 ft. lbs.

8. To complete the installation, reverse the removal procedures. Torque the engine mount bolts to 75 ft. lbs. Install the engine-to-converter housing strut (if equipped).

Rear Main Oil Seal

REMOVAL & INSTALLATION

Split Type

Service replacement seals are of split,

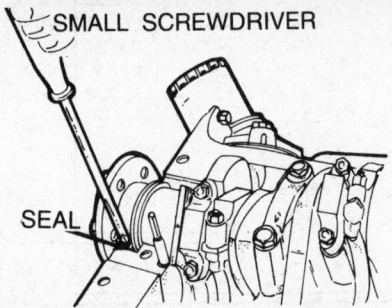

Removing upper main bearing oil seal with screwdriver. View showed with engine out of car.

rubber-type composition. This type of seal makes it possible to replace the upper half of the rear main oil seal without removing the engine from the vehicle or the crankshaft from the engine. When installing rubber seals, they must be replaced as a set and cannot be combined with the rope type rear main seal. The following procedure is for removing the rope type seal and replacing it with the rubber type seal.

1. Remove the oil pan.

2. Remove the rear seal retainer and the rear main bearing cap.

3. Remove the lower rope seal by carefully prying from the side with a small screwdriver.

4. To remove the upper rope seal, drive the exposed end of the seal with a 6 in. piece of $^3/_{16}$ in. diameter brazing rod. When the opposite end of the seal starts to protrude from the block, grasp it with pliers and gently pull it from the block while the opposite end is being driven. Be very careful not to damage the crankshaft. There are also screw type extractor tools available.

5. Before installing the seal, clean and lightly oil the crankshaft and new seal.

6. To ease the installation, loosen all the main bearing caps slightly to lower the crankshaft.

DO NOT allow the crankshaft to drop enough to let the main bearings become displaced on the crankshaft.

7. Hold the seal tightly against the crankshaft with thumb pressure (with paint stripe to the rear) and install the seal in the block groove. Rotate the crankshaft (if necessary) while installing the seal in the groove. Make sure the sharp edges on the block groove do not cut or nick the rear of the seal.

8. Install the lower half of the seal (with paint stripe to the rear) into the lower seal retainer. On the 5.2L engine, insert the cap seals into the slots in the bearing cap; the one with the yellow paint goes on the right side. Be

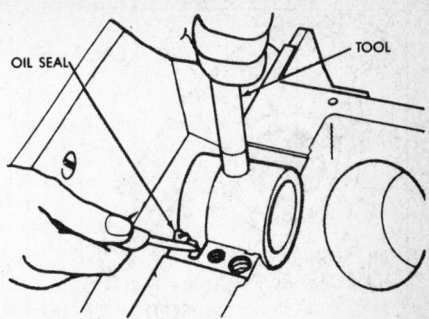

Installing the seal to the rear main bearing

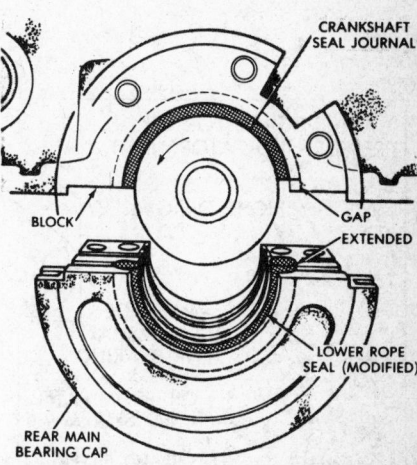

Exploded view of the rear main bearing oil seal

sure the narrow edge is facing up. Pull outward on the small end of the seal until its edge lines up with the shoulder. On all engines, lightly oil the seal lips before installation.

9. To complete the installation, install the rear main bearing cap, torque the main bearing caps to 85 ft. lbs. and reverse the removal procedures.

NOTE: Before tightening the main bearing caps, make sure all the main bearings are located in their proper positions.

Rope Type

To perform this procedure, the crankshaft must be removed from the engine with the exception of 1987–89 models. On these models, the crankshaft can remain in the vehicle and an oil seal remover and installer tool KD-492 or equivalent is used for upper seal replacement.

UPPER SEAL

1. Install the new oil seal in the cylinder block so that the ends of the seal protrude.

2. Using the Seal Installation tool No. C–3511, tap the new seal into position until the tool is seated in the bearing bore.

3. While holding this tool in posi-

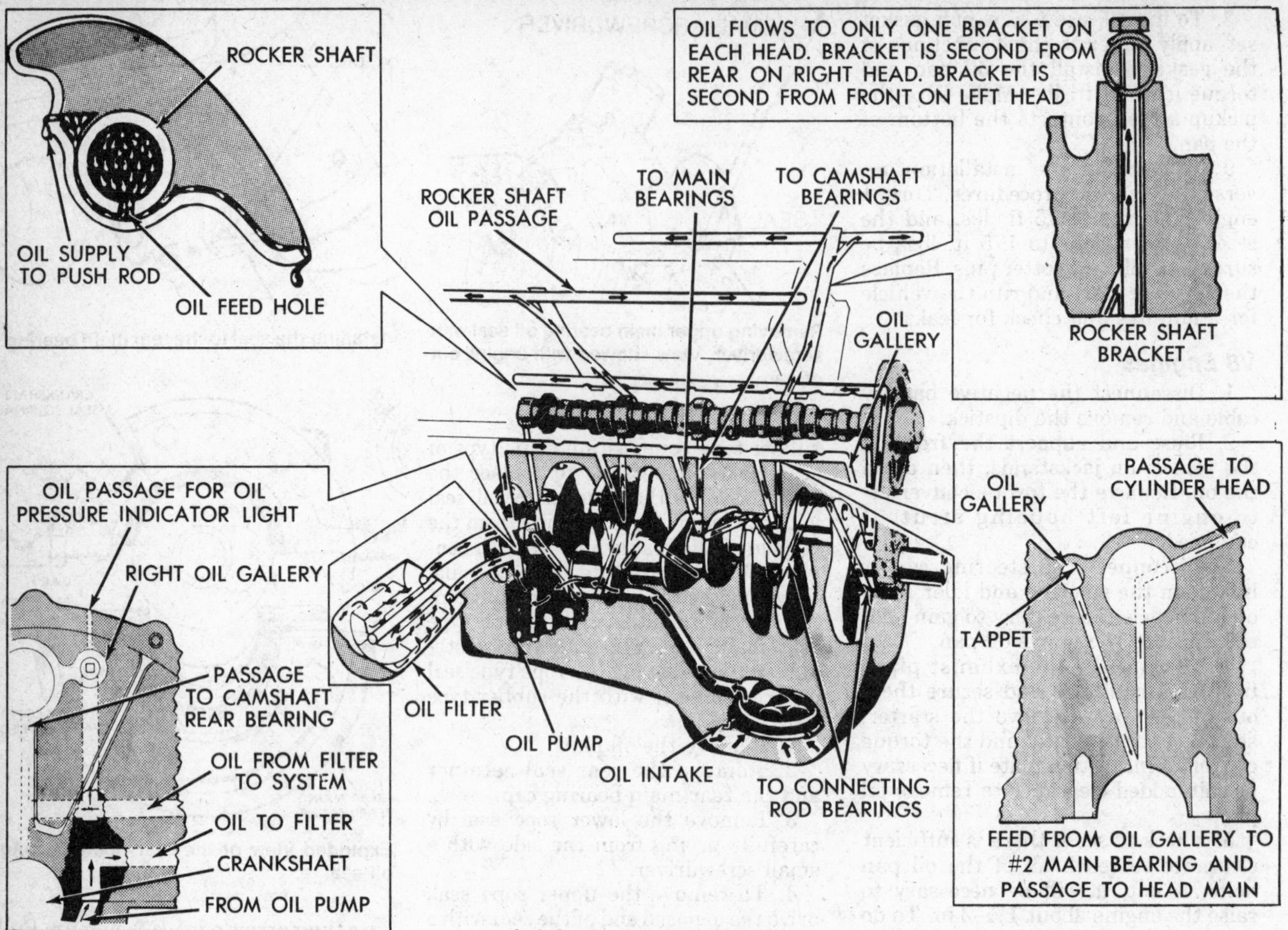

ROCKER SHAFT

OIL SUPPLY TO PUSH ROD

OIL FEED HOLE

OIL FLOWS TO ONLY ONE BRACKET ON EACH HEAD. BRACKET IS SECOND FROM REAR ON RIGHT HEAD. BRACKET IS SECOND FROM FRONT ON LEFT HEAD

ROCKER SHAFT OIL PASSAGE

TO MAIN BEARINGS

TO CAMSHAFT BEARINGS

OIL GALLERY

ROCKER SHAFT BRACKET

OIL PASSAGE FOR OIL PRESSURE INDICATOR LIGHT

RIGHT OIL GALLERY

PASSAGE TO CAMSHAFT REAR BEARING

OIL FROM FILTER TO SYSTEM

OIL TO FILTER

CRANKSHAFT

FROM OIL PUMP

OIL FILTER

OIL PUMP

OIL INTAKE

TO CONNECTING ROD BEARINGS

OIL GALLERY

PASSAGE TO CYLINDER HEAD

TAPPET

FEED FROM OIL GALLERY TO #2 MAIN BEARING AND PASSAGE TO HEAD MAIN

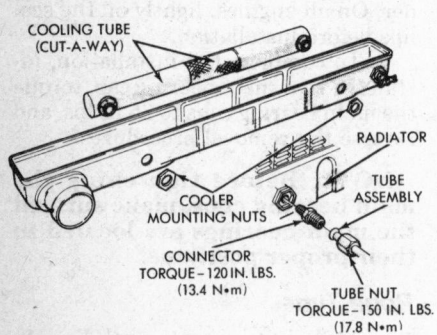

COOLING TUBE (CUT-A-WAY)

RADIATOR

TUBE ASSEMBLY

COOLER MOUNTING NUTS

CONNECTOR TORQUE – 120 IN. LBS. (13.4 N·m)

TUBE NUT TORQUE – 150 IN. LBS. (17.8 N·m)

Internal details of the in-radiator transmission fluid cooler

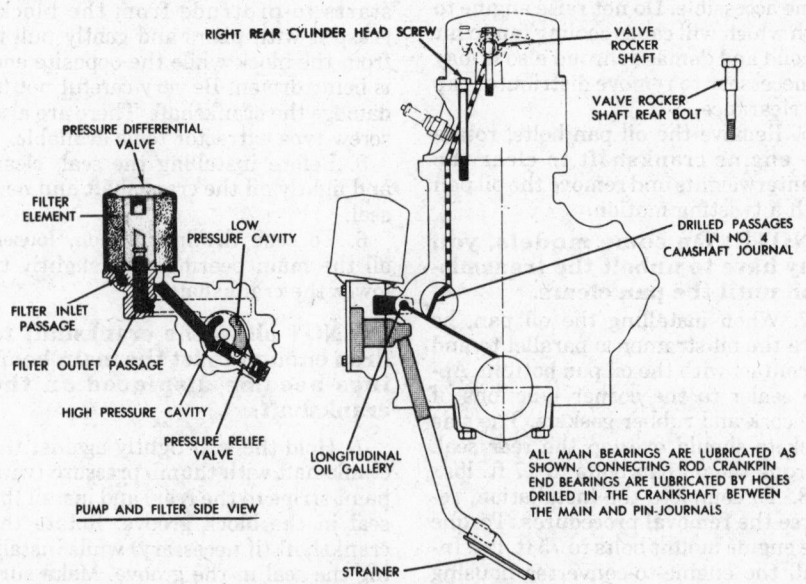

Lubrication system for V8

RIGHT REAR CYLINDER HEAD SCREW

VALVE ROCKER SHAFT

VALVE ROCKER SHAFT REAR BOLT

PRESSURE DIFFERENTIAL VALVE

FILTER ELEMENT

LOW PRESSURE CAVITY

FILTER INLET PASSAGE

FILTER OUTLET PASSAGE

HIGH PRESSURE CAVITY

PRESSURE RELIEF VALVE

LONGITUDINAL OIL GALLERY

DRILLED PASSAGES IN NO. 4 CAMSHAFT JOURNAL

ALL MAIN BEARINGS ARE LUBRICATED AS SHOWN. CONNECTING ROD CRANKPIN END BEARINGS ARE LUBRICATED BY HOLES DRILLED IN THE CRANKSHAFT BETWEEN THE MAIN AND PIN-JOURNALS

PUMP AND FILTER SIDE VIEW

STRAINER

Six-cylinder lubrication system

tion, cut off the portion of the seal that extends below the block (on both sides).

LOWER SEAL

1. Install the new oil seal in the bearing cap so that the ends of the seal protrude.
2. Using the Seal Installation tool No. C–3511, tap the seal into position until the tool is seated in the bearing cap.
3. While holding this tool in posi-

tion, cut off the portion of the seal that extends above the cap (on both sides).

NOTE: If this procedure is not done, oil leakage will occur.

4. Assemble the bearing cap to the

cylinder block. Torque the bearing cap bolts to 85 ft. lbs.

5. Apply sealer to the bearing cap-to-engine block joints.

6. To complete the installation, reverse the removal procedures.

Oil Pump

REMOVAL & INSTALLATION

6 Cylinder Engines

1. Remove the negative battery cable, the fan shroud screws and the fan shroud, push the fan shroud rearward.
2. Raise vehicle on hoist, support front of engine with jackstand placed under right-front corner of the engine and remove engine mount bolts. Do not support engine at crankshaft pulley or damper.
3. Raise the engine approximately 1½–2 in.
4. Remove the oil filter, oil pump mounting bolts, oil pump assembly and the gaskets from the mounting surfaces.
5. To install, prime the oil pump and reverse the removal procedures. Torque the oil pump bolts to 17 ft. lbs.

V8 Engines

1. Remove the oil pan.
2. Remove oil pump mounting bolts and the oil pump from the rear main bearing cap.
3. To install, prime the pump with engine oil and reverse the removal procedures. Torque the oil pump bolts to 30 ft. lbs.

ENGINE COOLING

NOTE: Chrysler recommends that 50/50 mixture of ethylene glycol type anti-freeze mixed with water be used in cooling system.

Radiator

REMOVAL & INSTALLATION

1. Place the heater temperature selector to **"Full On"**. Drain the cooling system by opening the drain cock at the bottom of the radiator. When the reserve tank is empty, remove the pressure cap.
2. Remove the oil cooler lines from the radiator.
3. Remove the upper and lower hose clamps and hoses. Remove the coolant reserve tank tube.
4. Remove the screws and position the shroud rearward to provide maximum clearance.
5. Loosen the retaining screws at the bottom of the radiator and remove the screws at the top.

6. Lift the radiator out of the engine compartment.

Extreme care should be taken during removal not to damage the radiator cooling fins or water tubes.

7. To install, reverse the removal procedures. Fill the radiator to the top of neck and the reserve tank to the **"MAX"** level. Warm up the engine with the heater on and check the coolant level. Check the transmission fluid level after warm-up and add fluid as required.

Water Pump

REMOVAL & INSTALLATION

NOTE: When replacing water pump because of a bearing shaft failure, the cooling fan should be checked for fatigue cracks

1. Drain the cooling system. Disconnect the negative battery cable.
2. Remove the fan shroud screws and move the shroud out of the way.
3. Remove the upper radiator hose and tie it back over the engine. Remove the lower radiator hose, bypass hose and heater hose from the water pump.
4. Loosen the alternator, power steering pump and air pump (if equipped). Remove all of the accessory belts.
5. Remove the fan, fan shroud, fan spacer, fluid drive and the water pump pulley.

NOTE: With fluid-coupled fan drives, to prevent silicone fluid from leaking, do not set the drive unit with its shaft pointing downward.

6. On the 6 cylinder engines, remove the air pump pulley. Remove the front bracket of the air compressor, air pump and power steering pump (if equipped). Set aside the air and the power steering pumps.
7. On the V8 engines, remove and set aside the alternator/brackets, air compressor and the power steering pump.
8. Remove the water pump bolts and the water pump. Discard the gasket and clean the mounting surfaces.
9. To install, use a new gasket and reverse the removal procedures. Torque the water pump bolts to 30 ft. lbs. Fill the radiator to the neck and the reserve tank to the **"MAX"** level. Warm up the engine with the heater on and inspect the water pump for any

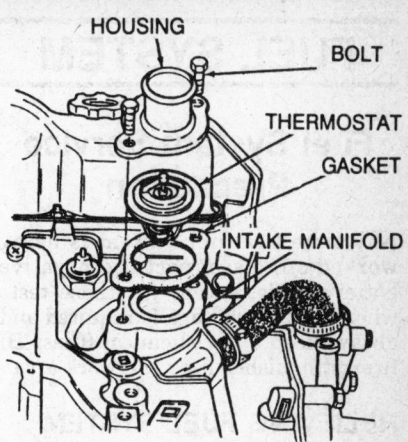

Thermostat and housing—8 cylinder engine

leaks. Check the coolant level and add as required.

Thermostat

REMOVAL & INSTALLATION

1. Drain the cooling system to below the level of the thermostat.
2. Remove the housing bolts and the thermostat housing and thermostat. Clean the gasket surfaces.
3. To install, use a new gasket (dipped in water) or sealant and reverse the removal procedures. On the V8, be sure that the pellet end is facing the engine. On the 6 cylinder the vent hole must face upwards.
4. Refill the system, allow the engine to warm up with the heater on and check for leaks.

EMISSION CONTROLS

Please refer to emission control in the Unit Repair section for system maintenance procedures. Due to the complex nature of modern electronic engine control systems, comprehensive diagnosis and testing procedures fall outside the confines of this repair manual. For complete information on diagnosis, testing and repair procedures concerning all modern engine and emission control systems, please refer to *Chilton's Guide To Electronic Engine Controls.*

FUEL SYSTEM

Fuel System Service Precaution

Any time the fuel system is being worked on, disconnect the negative battery cable, except for those tests where battery voltage is required and always keep a dry chemical (Class B) fire extinguisher near the work area.

RELIEVING FUEL SYSTEM PRESSURE

The fuel tank is sealed with a pressure–vacuum relief filler cap. The relief valves in the cap operate only to prevent excessive pressure or vacuum in the tank caused by a malfunction in the system or damage to the vent lines. The cap has a threaded configuration which allows the seal to be broken and pressure to be relieved. Before starting any repair to fuel system always slowly remove gas cap to relieved any excessive pressure.

Fuel Filter

There are 2 fuel filters in the fuel system. One is part of the gauge unit assembly located inside the fuel tank on the end of the fuel suction tube. The filter does not normally need servicing, but can be replaced, if necessary. The second filter is a sealed paper element , located in the fuel line in the engine compartment.

REMOVAL & INSTALLATION

Carbureted Engines

Locate the filter in the fuel line between the fuel pump and the carburetor. Using hose clamp pliers, remove the retaining clamps and pull off the filter. Reverse this procedure for installation. Be sure the arrow on the filter is pointing toward the carburetor (direction of fuel flow).

NOTE: Some filters have a third line, to prevent vapor lock by allowing fuel vapors to return to the tank.

Fuel Injected Engines

The 5.2L V8 (EFI) engine is equipped with parallel fuel filters mounted in the delivery line between the fuel tank and the throttle body. The filters are mounted side by side on a common bracket. Replace both filters when servicing.

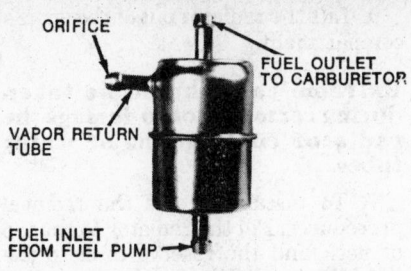

The combination filter and vapor separator found on some models

1. Disconnect and plug the fuel lines at the fuel filters.
2. Remove the fuel filter bracket from the vehicle.
3. Remove the fuel filters from the bracket.
4. To install, use new fuel filters and reverse the removal procedures.

NOTE: When installing the fuel filters, be sure to install them in the correct direction of the fuel flow.

Mechanical Fuel Pump

PRESSURE TESTING

1. Insert a "T" fitting in fuel line at the carburetor.
2. Connect a 6 in. piece of hose between "T" fitting and gauge C–3411–A or equivalent.

NOTE: The hose should not exceed 6 in. The longer hose may collect fuel and additional weight of fuel would be added to pressure of pump and result in an inaccurate reading.

3. Vent pump for a few seconds to relieve air trapped in fuel chamber. If this is not done, pump will not operate at full capacity and low pressure reading will result.
4. Connect a tachometer, then start engine and run at idle. The reading should be as shown in specifications (depending on pump) and remain constant or return to 0 slowly, when engine is stopped. An instant drop to 0 indicates a leaky outlet valve. If pressure is too low, a weak diaphragm main spring, or improper assembly of diaphragm may be the cause. If pressure is too high, main spring is too strong or the air vent is plugged.

REMOVAL & INSTALLATION

Mechanical fuel pumps are used on carbureted engines. On the 3.7L 6 cylinder engine, the pump is driven by a small cam eccentric cast into the main camshaft. On the V8 engines, the

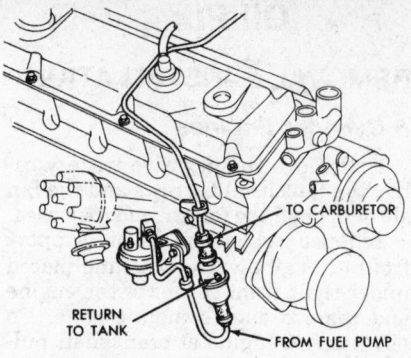

Fuel pump and filter location, six cylinder

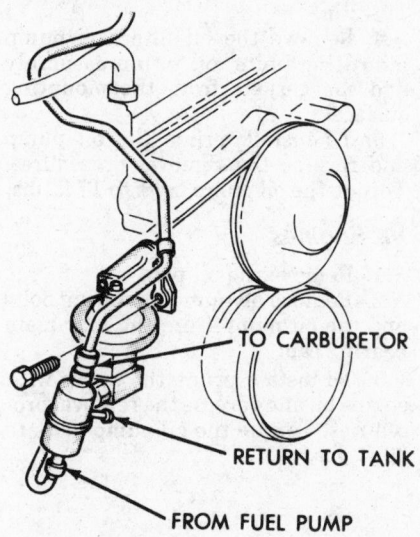

Fuel pump and filter location for V8

pump is driven by a steel eccentric cam pressed on the camshaft gear end. On all engines, the pump is driven directly by the pump rocker arm riding on the cam eccentric.

1. Remove the dirt/oil from the pump exterior and remove the fuel lines.
2. Remove the pump-to-block bolts and the pump.
3. Using a putty knife, clean the gasket mounting surfaces.
4. To install, coat both sides of the pump gasket with sealer and reverse the removal procedures.

NOTE: The pump rocker arm must be installed correctly on the cam eccentric or damage to fuel pump will occur. If the pump is difficult to engage with the eccentric, rotate the engine slightly never force the pump in.

5. Connect the fuel lines and tighten the pump bolts. Start the engine and check for leaks.

Electric Fuel Pump

The 5.2L V8 (EFI) engine is equipped

with an electric fuel pump (with check valve) in the fuel tank, dual fuel filters and a fuel control check valve mounted near the throttle body. Fuel pressure is automatically relieved from the system when the engine is not in operation.

PRESSURE TESTING

1. Connect a fuel pressure gauges to fuel supply line "T" fitting on the hydraulic support plate.
2. Crank the engine. Fuel pressure should be at least 8 psi. If fuel pressure is less than 8 psi, check for fuel restrictions. If pressure is 0 psi, check voltage and pump.

REMOVAL & INSTALLATION

1. Open the trunk and pull back the carpet. Remove the fuel line clamps/hoses from the delivery and return tubes.
2. Disconnect the 4 terminal electrical connector. Using a mallet and a non-metallic drift, drive the sealing ring nut (loosen it) from the fuel tank.
3. Remove the fuel pickup unit from the fuel tank, being careful not to get dirt in the tank. Separate the fuel pump from the in-tank filter and pick-up assembly.
4. To install, reverse the removal procedures. Make sure that the sealing ring gasket is secure.

Carburetor

REMOVAL & INSTALLATION

1. Disconnect the negative battery terminal.
2. Remove the air cleaner.
3. Remove the filler cap from the fuel tank.
4. Place a small fuel container under the fuel inlet fitting.
5. Using 2 wrenches, to avoid twisting the line, disconnect the fuel inlet line and drain the excess fuel into the container.
6. Disconnect all of the vacuum lines, electrical connectors (if equipped), the throttle and choke linkage.
7. Remove the carburetor mounting bolts/nuts and the carburetor from the engine. To avoid spillage of the fuel, hold the carburetor level.
8. To install, reverse the removal procedures. Check to be certain that the choke plate opens/closes fully (when operated) and that full throttle travel is obtained.
NOTE: To prime the carburetor after installation, crank the engine and depress the accelerator several times.

OVERHAUL

For all carburetor overhaul and adjustment procedures, please refer to the carburetor service in the Unit Repair section.

Fuel Injection

Due to the complex nature of modern fuel injection systems, comprehensive diagnosis and testing procedures fall outside the confines of this repair manual. For complete information on diagnosis, testing and repair procedures concerning all fuel injection systems, please refer to *Chilton's Guide To Fuel Injection And Feedback Carburetors.*

AUTOMATIC TRANSMISSION

For further information on automatic transmission, please refer to automatic transmission in the Unit Repair section.

REMOVAL

NOTE: **The transmission and converter must be removed as an assembly; otherwise, the converter drive plate, pump bushing and/or oil seal may be damaged. The drive plate will not support a load; do not allow the weight of the transmission to rest on the plate during removal. Also, removal and installation will vary slightly from this procedure by vehicle and model.**

1. Disconnect the negative battery cable. Raise and support the vehicle on jackstands. A hydraulic floor jack should be used for removal of the transmission unit.
2. Some models may require that the exhaust system be dropped. If necessary, disconnect the exhaust pipe from the exhaust manifold and all of the exhaust system hangers from the vehicle.
3. If equipped, remove the engine-to-transmission struts. Remove and plug the oil cooler lines at the transmission.
4. Remove the starter motor, oil cooler line bracket and the converter access cover.
5. Using a socket wrench on the damper bolt, rotate the engine clockwise to bring the converter drain plug to the bottom. Drain the converter, loosen the pan (break it loose), drain the transmission and reinstall the pan.
6. Matchmark the converter and drive plate to aid in later installation. The crankshaft flange bolt circle, the inner/outer circle of holes in the drive plate and the 4 tapped holes in the front face of the converter all have 1 hole offset, so that these parts will be installed in their original positions. This maintains the balance of the engine and converter.
7. Rotate the engine clockwise with the socket wrench on the damper bolt (to position the bolts) and remove the torque converter-to-drive plate bolts.
8. Matchmark the drive shaft at the rear universal joint for reassembly purposes and disconnect it. Carefully pull the shaft assembly out of the extension housing.
9. Disconnect the wire connector from the back-up light and neutral starting switch.
10. Disconnect the gearshift rod and torque shaft assembly from the transmission

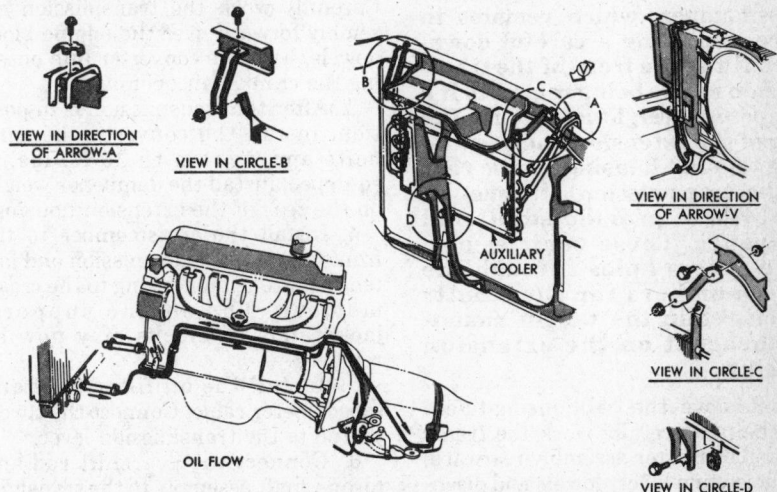

Oil flow—transmission oil coolers, Slant Six engine

Converter and drive plate markings

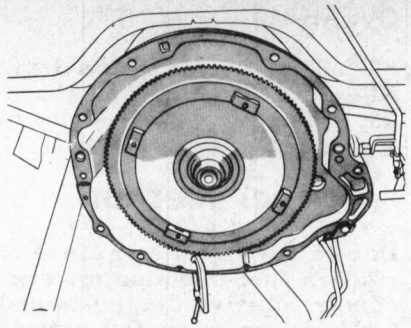

Attach a C-clamp to automatic transmission bell housing to keep torque converter in place when removing engine

NOTE: When disassembling the linkage rods from the levers, equipped with plastic grommets as retainers, replace the grommets. Use a small pry bar to pry the rod from the grommet; then, cut away the old grommet. Use pliers to snap the new grommet into the lever and the rod into the grommet.

11. Disconnect the throttle rod from the lever at the left side of the transmission. If equipped, remove the linkage bellcrank from the transmission.

12. Remove the oil filer tube and the speedometer cable. Support the rear of the engine with an engine support fixture tool No. C-3487-A, wooden blocks or jackstands.

13. Using a floor jack, raise the transmission slightly to relieve the load on the support.

14. Remove the transmission-to-crossmember and the crossmember-to-frame bolts, then remove the crossmember.

NOTE: Vehicles with longitudinal torsion bars (in line with the chassis) have a torsion bar anchor crossmember, which remains in place, requiring a careful downward tilt of the front of the transmission as it is being removed. If a dampening weight is bolted to the rear of the extension housing (the long tapered housing on the rear of the transmission), it must be removed to provide additional clearance. These vehicles also have access holes through the crossmembers for the 3 bolts which retain the weight mounting bracket on the extension housing.

15. Remove the bellhousing-to-engine bolts. Carefully work the transmission/converter assembly rearward, off the engine block dowels and disengage the converter hub from the

crankshaft. Attach a small C-clamp to the edge of the bellhousing to hold converter in place during transmission removal.

16. Lower the transmission and remove it from under the vehicle.

INSTALLATION

NOTE: The transmission and converter must be installed as an assembly; otherwise the converter drive plate, pump bushing, and oil seal will be damaged. The drive plate will not support a load, so none of the transmission weight should be allowed to rest on the plate during installation.

1. Coat the crankshaft converter hub hole with multi-purpose grease. Place the transmission/converter assembly on the floor jack and position the assembly under the vehicle. Raise or tilt as necessary until the transmission is aligned with the engine.

2. Rotate the converter so that the mark on the converter (made during removal) will align with the mark on the drive plate. The offset holes in the plate are located next to the 1/8 in. hole in the inner circle of the drive plate. Carefully work the transmission assembly forward over the engine block dowels, with the converter hub entering the crankshaft opening.

3. After the transmission is in position, install the converter housing bolts and tighten to 30 ft. lbs. If equipped, install the dampener weight on the rear of the extension housing.

4. Install the crossmember to the frame, lower the transmission and fasten the extension housing to the crossmember. The engine support, jackstands or blocks may now be removed.

5. Install the oil filter tube and speedometer cable. Connect the throttle rod to the transmission lever.

6. Connect the gearshift rod and torque shaft assembly to the transmission lever and frame.

7. Place the wire connector on the combination back-up light and Neutral/Park starter switch.

8. Carefully guide the sliding yoke onto the extension housing, output splines. Align the marks made at removal, then connect the driveshaft to the rear axle pinion shaft yoke.

9. Rotate the engine clockwise to install the converter-to-drive plate bolts, matching the marks made at removal. Torque to 22 ft. lbs.

10. Install the converter access cover, the starter motor and the cooler line bracket. Tighten the oil cooler lines to the transmission fittings.

11. Install the engine-to-transmission struts (if equipped) and replace the exhaust system (if it was disturbed).

12. Adjust the shift and throttle linkages. Refill the transmission with Dexron® II type automatic transmission fluid.

DRIVE AXLE

Driveshaft And U-Joints

The driveshaft is a one-piece tubular shaft with 2 universal joints, one at each end. The front joint yoke serves as a slip yoke on the transmission output shaft. The rear universal joint is of the type that must be unbolted to be removed.

REMOVAL & INSTALLATION

Lubricant loss from the rear of the transmission can be avoided by raising the rear of the vehicle before removing the driveshaft. Keep a clean rag handy to plug the end of the extension housing when the driveshaft is removed.

1. Match-mark the driveshaft, U-joint and pinion flange before disassembly. These marks must be re-aligned during reassembly to maintain the balance of the driveline. Failure to align them may result in excessive vibration.

2. Remove both clamps from the differential pinion yoke and slide the driveshaft forward slightly to disengage the U-joint from the pinion yoke. Tape the two loose U-joint bearings together to prevent them from falling off.

NOTE: Do not disturb the bearing assembly retaining strap. Never allow the driveshaft to hang from either of the U-joints. Al-

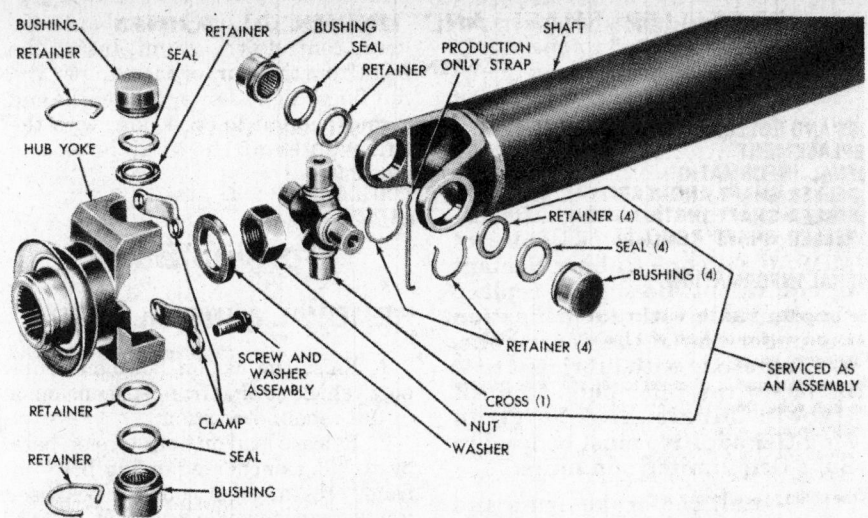

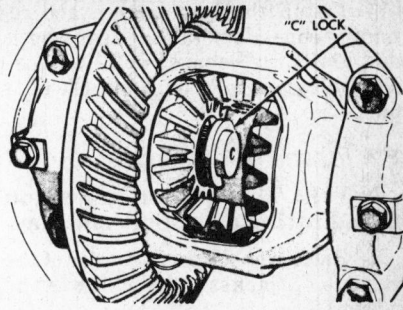

Removing and installing the "C" lock on the axle shaft

Rear driveshaft universal joint assembly—remove the two clamps to remove driveshaft

Removal of differential pinion shaft lock screw on the 8¼ in. rear axle

ways support the unattached end of the shaft to prevent damage to the joints.

3. Lower the rear end of the driveshaft, gently slide the front yoke/driveshaft assembly rearward and disengage the assembly from the transmission output shaft. Be careful not to damage the splines or the surface on which the output shaft seal rides.

4. Check the transmission output shaft seal for signs of leakage.

5. To install, reverse the removal procedures; be sure to align the matchmarks. Torque the U-joint bolts to 14 ft. lbs.

Rear Axle Shafts

3 different (ring gear diameter) rear axle assemblies are used. These axles can be visually identified as follows:

a. The 7¼ in. has 9 bolts and an oval shape.

b. The 8¼ in. has a 10 bolt rear cover without a filler plug.

c. The 9¼ in. has a 12 bolt cover.

Some vehicles are equipped with the Sure-Trip limited slip differential. Identification of the Sure-Grip rear axle can be made easily by lifting both rear wheels off the ground and turning them. If both rear wheels turn in the same direction simultaneously, the vehicle has the Sure-Grip axle. All axles have a ratio identification tag under one of the cover or carrier bolts.

REMOVAL & INSTALLATION

Because the axle shafts are slightly different from one rear axle assembly to another, individual service procedures are required for each axle shaft assembly. Two very important points to re-

member when servicing any rear axle assembly are:

1. Always elevate both rear wheels when performing any rear axle service, when using the engine or other means to rotate the axle.

2. On vehicles equipped with a Sure-Grip differential, NEVER rotate one axle shaft without rotating the other. If it is necessary to rotate one of the axle shafts, both shafts must be in position and both must be rotated. Otherwise, alignment of the axle shafts will be very difficult.

7¼ in. Axle

NOTE: Whenever this axle assembly is serviced, both the brake support plate gaskets and the inner axle shaft oil seal must be renewed. There is no provision for adjusting the axle shaft end-play.

1. Raise and support the rear of the vehicle on jackstands. Remove the rear wheels.

2. Detach the clips securing the brake drum to the axle shaft studs and remove the brake drum.

3. Disconnect and plug the brake lines at the wheel cylinders.

4. Through the access hole in the axle shaft flange, remove the axle shaft retaining nuts.

5. Attach a puller or slide hammer to the axle shaft flange and remove the axle shaft.

6. Remove the brake assembly from the axle housing.

7. Remove the axle shaft oil seal from the axle housing.

Never use a torch or other heat source as an aid in removing any axle shaft components as this will result in serious damage to the axle assembly.

8. Place the axle shaft collar in a vise or on a anvil. Using a chisel, cut deeply into the retaining collar at 90 degree intervals. This will loosen it enough so it can be removed. Using an arbor press, press the bearing from the axle shaft.

9. To assemble, replace the retainer plate, bearing and bearing retainer collar on the axle shaft, use an arbor press to install the bearing retainer on the axle shaft.

10. Lightly grease the outside diameter of a new oil seal and insert it into the axle housing. Using the seal installation tool No. C–3734, or equivalent, seat the seal in the axle housing.

11. Install a new inner gasket on the studs of the axle housing and replace the brake support plate assembly. Refit a new outer gasket onto the axle housing studs.

12. Very carefully slide the axle shaft assembly through the oil seal and engage the splines of the differential side gear. Using a non-metallic hammer, lightly tap the end of the axle shaft to position the axle shaft bearing in the recess of the axle housing. Install the retainer plate over the axle housing studs and torque the securing nuts to 35 ft. lbs.

13. Reconnect the brake lines to the wheel cylinders and bleed the rear brake system.

14. Install the brake drum and retaining clips. Reinstall the rear wheels and lower the vehicle. Refill the axle with lubricant to ⅜ in. below the filler plug.

8¼ in. and 9¼ in. Axles

NOTE: There is no provision for adjusting axle shaft end play.

1. Raise and support the rear of the vehicle on jackstands. Remove the wheels.

2. Clean all dirt from the housing cover and remove the cover to drain the lubricant.

3. Remove the brake drum.

4. Rotate the differential case until the differential pinion shaft lockscrew can be removed. Remove the lockscrew and pinion shaft.

5. Push the axle shaft toward the center of the vehicle and remove the C-lock from the groove on the axle shaft.

6. Pull the axle shaft from the housing, being careful not to damage the bearing which remains in the housing.

NOTE: During Sure-Grip axle shaft removal and installation, do not rotate an axle shaft unless both are in position. Rotation of one shaft without the other in place may result in misalignment of the two spline segments with which the axle shaft spline engages and will mean difficult re-alignment procedures when the shaft is installed.

7. Inspect the axle shaft bearings and replace any doubtful parts. Whenever the axle shaft is replaced, the bearings should also be replaced.

8. Remove the axle shaft seal from the bore in the housing.

9. Using a slide hammer, remove the axle shaft bearing from the housing. DO NOT reuse the seal; always install a new axle shaft seal.

10. Check the bearing shoulder in the axle housing for imperfections. These should be smoothed out with a fine file or polish.

11. Clean the axle shaft bearing cavity.

12. Install the axle shaft bearing in the axle housing. Be sure that the bearing is seated firmly against the shoulder.

13. Install a new axle shaft bearing seal, seat it against the housing flange face.

14. Insert the axle shaft, make sure the splines do not damage the seal. Be sure the splines are properly engaged with the differential side gear splines.

15. Install the C-lock in the grooves on the axle shafts. Pull the shafts outward so the C-locks seat in the counterbore of the differential side gears.

16. Install the differential pinion shaft through the case and pinions. Install the lockscrew and torque to 8 ft. lbs.

17. Clean the housing and gasket surfaces. Install the cover and a new gasket.

NOTE: Replacement gaskets may not be available for differential covers. In this case, use of MOPAR Silicone Rubber Sealant or equivalent. Be sure to replace the rear axle ratio identification tag under one of the cover bolts. Refill the axle with lubricant to ½ in. below the filler plug. MOPAR Hypoid Lubricant & Friction Modifier additive must be used in Sure-Grip limited slip units.

18. Install the brake drum and wheel. Lower the vehicle.

FRONT SUSPENSION

Shock Absorber

REMOVAL & INSTALLATION

1. Raise the front of the vehicle (until the wheels clear the ground) and support it on jackstands. Remove the front wheels. Remove the nut and retainer from shock absorber upper end.

2. Grip the shock absorber base, remove the lower attaching nut, retainer and bushing.

3. Fully compress the shock absorber by pushing it upward, disengaging it from the lower control arm. Pull the shock absorber down, firmly and remove it from the vehicle.

4. Check the shock absorber bushings, if they are worn, cracked or scored, replace them. Remove and install the busings with a press or using a drift and a hammer. To ease installation, lubricate with soapy water.

NOTE: Do not use oil to ease the installation.

5. Purge the new shock absorber by repeatedly extending it in the upright position and compressing it in the inverted position. It is normal to have more resistance to extend than to compress.

6. To install, fully compress the new shock absorber, insert the top end through the upper bushing, then install the retainer and nut. Torque the nut to 25 ft. lbs.

NOTE: Be sure all the retainers are installed with the concave side in contact with rubber.

7. Install the shock absorber to the lower control arm mount. Install the bolt (from the rear) or the retainer and nut finger tight. Lower the vehicle and torque the nut to 35 ft. lbs., with the full weight of the vehicle on the wheels.

Torsion Bars

REMOVAL & INSTALLATION

1. Raise the car on hoist and support vehicle so that front suspension is in full rebound position.

2. Release load on both torsion bars by turning anchor adjusting bolts in frame crossmember counterclockwise. Remove anchor adjusting bolt on torsion bar to be removed.

3. Raise lower control arms until clearance between crossmember ledge (at jounce bumper) and torsion bar end bushing is 2⅛ in. (63.0 mm). Support lower control arms at this design height (equal to three passenger position with vehicle on ground). This is necessary to align sway bar and lower control arm attaching points for disassembly and component re-alignment and attachment during reassembly.

4. Remove sway bar to control arm attaching bolt and retainers.

5. Remove 2 bolts attaching torsion bar end bushing to lower control arm.

6. Remove 2 bolts attaching torsion bar pivot cushion bushing to crossmember, and remove torsion bar and anchor assembly from crossmember.

7. Carefully separate anchor from torsion bar.

8. To install carefully slide balloon seal over end of torsion bar (cupped end toward hex).

9. Coat hex end of torsion bar with waterproof grease.

10. Install torsion bar hex end into anchor bracket. With torsion bar in a horizontal position, the ears of the anchor bracket should be positioned nearly straight up. Position swivel into anchor bracket ears.

11. Place bushing end of bar into position on top of lower control arm. Then install anchor bracket assembly into crossmember anchor retainer and install anchor adjusting bearing and bolt.

12. Attach pivot cushion bushing to crossmember with two bolt and washer assemblies. Leave bolt and washer assemblies loose enough to install friction plates.

13. With lower control arms at design height install two bolt and nut assemblies attaching torsion bar bushing to lower control arm. Torque to 70 ft. lbs. (95 Nm.).

14. Ensure that torsion bar anchor

Ball Joints

INSPECTION

NOTE: Before making the inspection, verify that the wheel bearings are adjusted correctly and that the control arm bushings are in good condition.

1. Place a jack under the lower control arm as close to the wheel as possible.
2. Raise the vehicle until there is 1–2 in. of clearance under the wheel.
3. Insert a bar under the wheel and pry upward. If the wheel raises noticeably the ball joints are worn. While prying on the wheel, visually check to determine if the upper or lower ball joint is worn.
4. You can make a more accurate measurement by clamping a dial indicator to the lower control arm and measuring the lower ball joint stud movement.

NOTE: Due to the distribution of forces in the suspension, the lower ball joint is usually the one that needs replacing. The manufacturer's limit for lower ball joint play, measured at the joint, is 0.030 in. (0.76mm) for all models.

5. Lower the jack enough to let the tire lightly contact the floor. Tighten the wheel bearing adjusting nut enough to remove all play. Have an assistant try to move the top of the tire in and out while you observe the upper ball joint. If there is any noticeable side play, replace the upper ball joint.
6. Correct the wheel bearing adjustment.

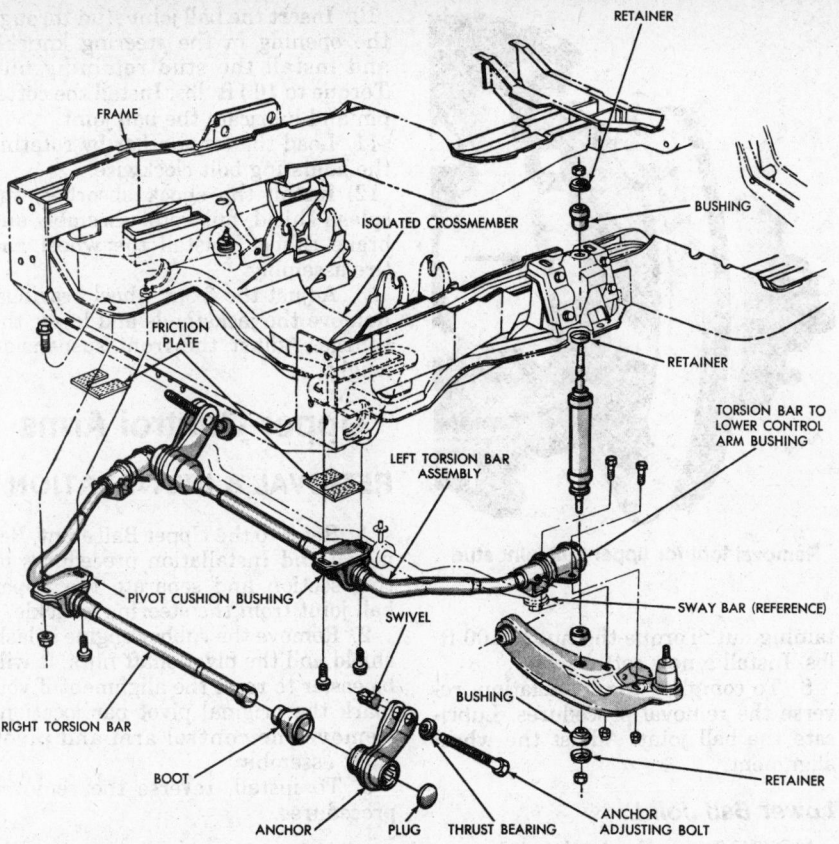

Transverse torsion bar isolated front suspension system

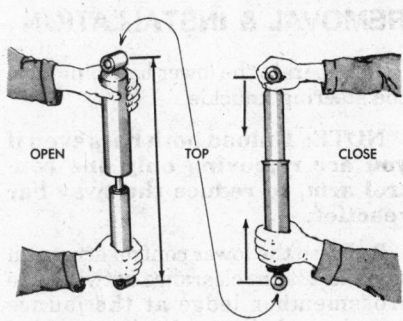

Purging new shock absorbers of air

bracket is fully seated in crossmember. Then install friction plates between crossmember and pivot cushion bushing with open end of slot to rear and bottomed out on mounting bolts. Tighten cushion bushing bolts to 85 ft. lbs. (115 Nm.).
15. Position balloon seal over anchor bracket.
16. Reinstall bolt, through sway bar, retainer cushions and sleeve and attach to lower control arm end bushing. Torque bolt to 50 ft. lbs. (68 Nm.).
17. Load torsion bar by turning anchor adjusting bolt clockwise.
18. Lower vehicle and adjust torsion bar height to specifications.
19. Road test vehicle make sure vehicle tracks straight. Set front end alignment adjustments if necessary.

NOTE: Front car height is measured from the head of the the front suspension front crossmember isolator bolt to the ground. To adjust turn torsion bar adjusting bolt clockwise to increase height and counterclockwise to reduce height.

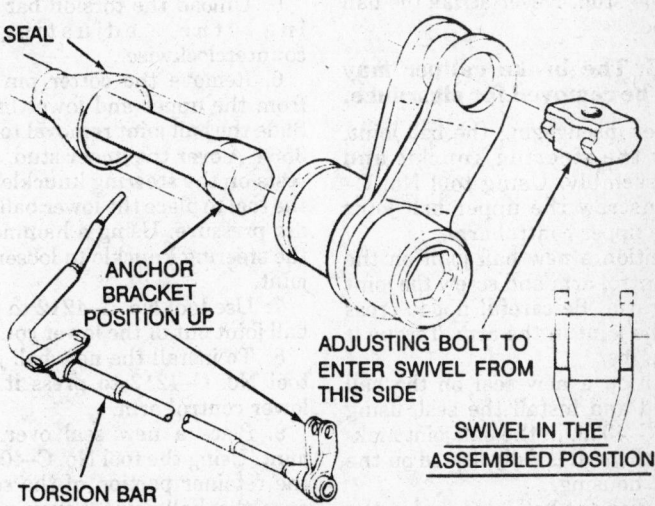

Torsion bar anchor and swivel

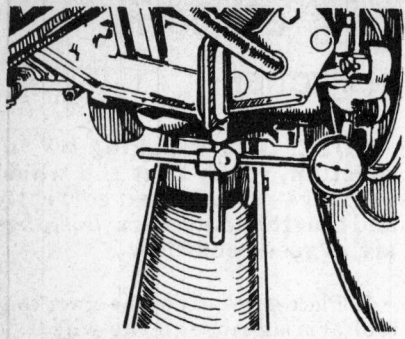

Measuring lower ball joint play;
see text for specifications

REMOVAL & INSTALLATION

Upper Ball Joint

———— CAUTION ————
The torsion bar remains under tension during this procedure.

NOTE: Turn the ignition key to the OFF or UNLOCKED position.

1. Raise and support the front of the vehicle. Place a jackstand under the lower control arm as close to the wheel as possible. Remove the wheel. The jackstand should not contact the brake splash shield and the rubber rebound bumper must not contact the frame.

2. Remove the cotter pin and nut that attaches the upper ball joint to the steering knuckle. Remove the cotter pin and nut from the lower ball joint, to enable the removal tool to be used.

3. Slide the ball joint removal tool No. C–3564–A onto the lower ball joint stud, allowing the tool to rest on the knuckle arm. Set the tool securely against the upper stud. Apply pressure to the upper stud by tightening the tool and strike the knuckle sharply to loosen the stud. Never strike the ball joint stud.

NOTE: The brake caliper may have to be removed for clearance.

4. After disengaging the ball joint, support the steering knuckle and brake assembly. Using tool No. C–3560, unscrew the upper ball joint from the upper control arm.

5. Position a new ball joint on the upper control arm and screw the joint into the arm. Be careful not to cross thread the joint in the arm. Torque it to 125 ft. lbs.

6. Position a new seal on the ball joint stud and install the seal, using tool No. C–4039, in the ball joint making sure the seal is fully seated on the ball joint housing.

7. Position the ball joint stud in the steering knuckle and install the re-

Removal tool for upper ball joint stud

taining nut. Torque the nut to 100 ft. lbs. Install a new cotter pin.

8. To complete the installation, reverse the removal procedures. Lubricate the ball joint. Adjust the wheel alignment.

Lower Ball Joint

NOTE: Turn the ignition key to the OFF or UNLOCKED position.

1. Raise the vehicle so that the front suspension drops to the downward limit of its travel. Position jackstands beneath the front frame for extra support.

2. Remove the wheel and tire assembly.

3. Remove the brake caliper and tie it up out of the way, so that there is no strain on the flexible brake hose.

4. Remove the hub/rotor assembly and splash shield. Disconnect shock absorber from the lower control arm.

5. Unload the torsion bar by rotating the adjusting bolt counterclockwise.

6. Remove the cotter pin and nut from the upper and lower ball joints. Slide the ball joint removal tool No. C–3564–A over the upper stud, so that it rests on the steering knuckle. Tighten the tool to place the lower ball joint under pressure. Using a hammer, strike the steering knuckle to loosen the ball joint.

7. Use tool No. C–4212 to press the ball joint out of the lower control arm.

8. To install the new ball joint, use tool No. C–4212 to press it into the lower control arm.

9. Place a new seal over the ball joint. Using the tool No. C–4039, press the retainer portion of the seal down over the ball joint housing, until it locks into position.

10. Insert the ball joint stud through the opening in the steering knuckle and install the stud retaining nut. Torque to 100 ft. lbs. Install the cotter pin and lubricate the ball joint.

11. Load the torsion bar by rotating the adjusting bolt clockwise.

12. Install the shock absorber, the splash shield, hub/rotor assembly and brake caliper. Install the wheel and tire assembly.

13. Adjust the front wheel bearings. Remove the jackstands and lower the vehicle. Adjust the front suspension height.

Upper Control Arms

REMOVAL & INSTALLATION

1. Refer to the Upper Ball Joint, Removal and Installation procedures in this section and separate the upper ball joint from the steering knuckle.

2. Remove the rubber engine splash shield and the pivot shaft nuts. It will be easier to reset the alignment if you mark the original pivot bar location. Remove the control arm and pivot shaft assembly.

3. To install, reverse the removal procedures.

Lower Control Arms

REMOVAL & INSTALLATION

1. Separate the lower ball joint from the steering knuckle.

NOTE: Unload both bars even if you are removing only one control arm, to reduce the sway bar reaction.

2. Raise the lower control arm until there is 2⅞ in. clearance between the crossmember ledge at the jounce bumper and the torsion bar bushing on the lower control arm. Unbolt the torsion bar busing from the control arm.

3. Remove the lower control arm pivot bolt and the control arm.

NOTE: If the control arm shaft bushings indicates wear or deterioration, replace them.

4. To install, reverse the removal procedures. Torque the control arm pivot bolt to 75 ft. lbs. and the torsion bar end bushing-to-lower control arm to 50 ft. lbs.

Sway Bar

REMOVAL & INSTALLATION

1. Raise and support the front of the vehicle on jackstands.

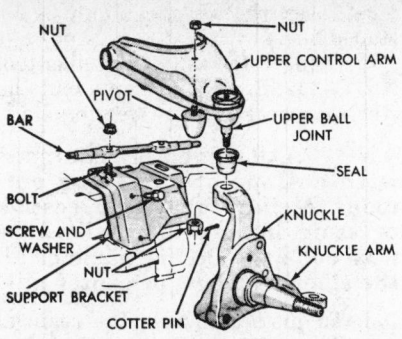

Typical upper control arm and steering knuckle

2. Release the load on both torsion bars by turning the anchor adjusting bolts counterclockwise.

3. Raise the lower control arms until there is $2\frac{7}{8}$ in. clearance between the crossmember ledge, at the jounce bumper and the torsion bar bushing, on the lower control arm.

4. Support the lower control arms with a jackstands. Remove the sway bar-to-torsion bar bushing bolts, retainers, cushions and sleeves. Remove the retainer assembly strap and retainer bolts. Remove the sway bar.

NOTE: Inspect the cushions/ bushings for wear or deterioration and replace, if necessary.

5. To install, reverse the removal procedures. Torque the sway bar-to-torsion bar to 50 ft. lbs. and the sway bar retainer/strap bolts to 30 ft. lbs. Load the torsion bar by turning the crossmember adjusting bolt clockwise. Lower the vehicle and adjust the torsion bar height.

Front Wheel Bearing

ADJUSTMENT

1. Raise and support the front of the vehicle so that the front wheels are off the ground.

2. Remove the hub caps, grease cut, cotter pin and nut lock.

3. Back off on the adjusting nut. Check for free wheel rotation.

4. While rotating the wheel, tighten the wheel bearing adjustment nut to 20–25 ft. lbs.

5. Loosen the adjusting nut, then retighten to finger-tight while rotating the wheel.

6. Position the nut lock so that one pair of slots is in line with the cotter pin hole and install the cotter pin. This adjustment should give 0.001–0.003 in. end play.

7. To complete the installation, reverse the removal procedures. Repeat the procedures for the other wheel and lower the vehicle.

REMOVAL & INSTALLATION

1. Raise the vehicle and support it safely.

2. Remove tire and wheel assembly.

3. Remove brake caliper assembly (do not disconnect the brake line) and move to the side.

NOTE: Avoid strain on the flexible brake hose.

4. Remove the grease cup, cotter pin and locknut.

5. Remove the adjusting nut and washer.

6. Remove the outer bearing and remove brake disc from spindle.

7. Remove the inner bearing by removing the bearing seal with a suitable tool.

8. For installation, reverse the removal procedure.

9. Adjust wheel bearing and use a new cotter pin.

Front Wheel Alignment

ADJUSTMENT

Caster and Camber

1. Determine initial caster and camber readings.

2. Remove foreign material from exposed threads of pivot bar bolts and loosen nuts slightly holding pivot bar. (Slightly loosening the pivot bar nuts will allow the upper control arm to be repositioned without slipping to end of adjustment slots.)

3. Position claw of tool C–4576 or equivalent on pivot bar and pin of tool into holes provided in tower or bracket. Make adjustments by moving pivot bar in or out.

NOTE: Front wheel alignment settings must be held to specifications to hold tire wear to a minimum and to maintain steering ease and handling of vehicle. Any parts of the front suspension system should be replaced if they are found to be bent. Do not attempt to straighten any bent part.

Toe-In

1. Secure the steering wheel in the straight ahead position. If the vehicle is equipped with power steering, start engine and center wheel. (Toe should be set with engine running.)

2. Loosen tie rod clamp bolts.

3. Adjust toe by turning tie rod sleeves. Turn both tie rod ends in the same direction during adjustment.

4. After adjustments have been made, position sleeve clamps so ends do not locate in the sleeve slot, then tighten clamp bolts.

REAR SUSPENSION

Shock Absorber

REMOVAL & INSTALLATION

1. Raise and support the rear of the vehicle under the axle assembly with jackstands, so as to relieve load from the shock absorbers.

2. Remove the nut, retainer and bushing, attaching the shock to the spring mounting plate. To avoid damage to the shock, grip the base of the shock below the base-to-reservoir weld while loosening the retaining nut.

3. At the upper mount, remove the shock attaching bolt/nut and the shock.

4. Purge the new shock of air by repeatedly extending it in its upright position and compressing it, in an inverted position. It is normal to have more resistance to extend than compress.

5. To install the shock, position it so the upper bolt or nut may be replaced, hand-tighten only. Align the shock with the spring mounting plate and install the bolt or nut, hand-tighten only.

6. Lower the vehicle and tighten the shock absorber mounting bolts. Torque the bottom bolt to 35 ft. lbs. and the top bolt to 70 ft. lbs.

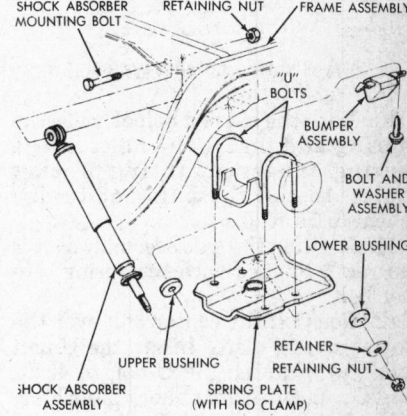

Typical rear shock mounting

Springs

REMOVAL & INSTALLATION

1. Raise and support the rear of the vehicle on jackstands; placed the jackstands under the axle so as to relieve weight from the rear springs. Remove the wheels.

2. Disconnect the rear shock ab-

sorbers at the bottom. Lower the axle assembly to allow the rear springs to hang free. Disconnect the rear sway bar links, if equipped.

3. Remove the U-bolt nuts, bolts and spring plates. Remove the nuts securing the front spring hanger to the body mounting bracket.

4. Remove the rear spring hanger bolts and allow the spring to drop enough to allow the front spring hanger bolts to be removed.

5. Remove the front pivot bolt from the front spring hanger.

6. Remove the shackle nuts and shackle from the rear of the spring.

7. To install, assemble the shackle/bushings in the rear of the spring and hanger. Start the shackle bolt nut. Do not lubricate rubber bushings to ease installation or tighten the bolt nut.

8. Align the front spring hanger with the front spring eye and insert the pivot bolt and nut. Do not tighten.

9. Install the rear spring hanger-to-body bracket and torque the bolts to 35 ft. lbs.

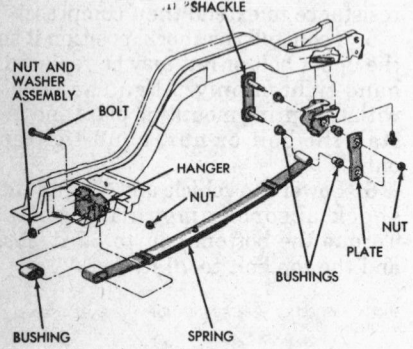

Rear spring details, typical

10. With the aid of a helper, raise the spring and insert the bolts in the spring hanger mounting bracket holes. Install the nuts and torque them to 35 ft. lbs.

11. Position the axle assembly so it is correctly aligned with the spring center bolt.

12. Position the center bolt over the lower spring plate. Insert the U-bolt and nut. Tighten the U-bolt to 45 ft. lbs. Connect the rear shock absorbers.

13. Lower the vehicle. Torque the pivot bolts to 105 ft. lbs. and the shackle nuts to 35 ft. lbs.

NOTE: Drive the vehicle, then remeasure the front suspension heights and correct, if necessary.

Sway Bar

REMOVAL & INSTALLATION

1. Raise and support the rear of the vehicle on jackstands.

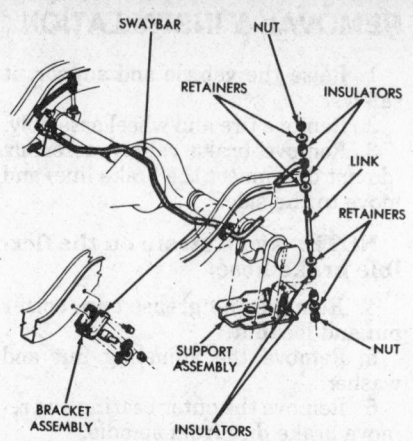

Rear sway bar mounting

2. Remove the two sway bar link retaining nuts, retainers and insulators from the support.

3. Remove the nuts and retainer from each bracket fastened to each rail.

4. Remove the sway bar.

5. To install, reverse the removal procedures. Torque the retainer-to-bracket bolts to 17 ft. lbs. and the link nuts to 8 ft. lbs.

STEERING

Steering Wheel

REMOVAL & INSTALLATION

— CAUTION —

The 1988 and later rear wheel drive Chrysler Corporation models are equipped with a Supplemental Restraint System (SRS) or Inflatable Restraint System (IRS) as a option. Improper maintenance, including incorrect removal and installation of related components, can lead to personal injury caused by unintentional activation of the Airbag. Related components on these models should be serviced only by authorized service technicians.

1. Disconnect the negative battery cable.

2. Remove the padded center assembly. This center assembly is often held on only by spring clips. There are usually holes in the back of the wheel so the pad can be pushed off. However, on some deluxe interiors it is held on by screws behind the arms of the wheel. Remove the horn wire.

3. Remove the large center nut. Matchmark the steering wheel and steering shaft so that the wheel may be replaced in its original position. In most cases, the wheel can only be installed one way.

4. Using a steering wheel puller tool No. C–3428B or equivalent, pull the steering wheel from the steering shaft.

NOTE: All models are equipped with collapsible steering columns. A sharp blow or excessive pressure on the column will cause it to collapse. Do not hammer on the steering wheel or center nut

5. To install, reverse the removal procedures. When placing the wheel on the shaft, make sure the tires are straight ahead and the matchmarks are aligned. Torque the nut to 45 ft. lbs.

Combination Switch

REMOVAL & INSTALLATION

1. Disconnect the negative battery cable. Remove the steering wheel center cover and the steering wheel.

2. Remove the steering column cover and the lower instrument panel bezel. Loosen the gearshift housing Allen screw and remove the gearshift indicator.

3. If equipped with a tilt steering wheel, place the steering wheel at its mid-point position. Remove the steering column-to-lower panel reinforcement nuts and the 4 mounting bracket-to-steering column bolts.

Support the steering column to prevent damage.

4. Pry out the plastic buttons holding the wiring trough to the column and remove the trough. Disconnect the turn signal wiring connector and wrap it with a piece of tape.

5. On the standard column, remove the screws holding the turn signal lever assembly to the turn signal switch pivot and the screws/retainers holding the turn signal switch to the upper bearing housing.

6. On the tilt column, remove the plastic cover (if equipped) from the lock plate. Using the lock plate depression tool No. C–4156, depress the lock plate and pry the ring out of the groove with a small pry bar.

7. Remove the lock plate, the canceling cam and the canceling cam spring. Place the turn signal switch in the right position. Remove the screw holding the hazard warning switch knob and the screws holding the turn signal switch to the steering column.

8. Pull the switch gently from the column while guiding the wires through the column opening.

9. To install, reverse the removal procedures. Tighten the mounting bracket-to-steering column bolts and

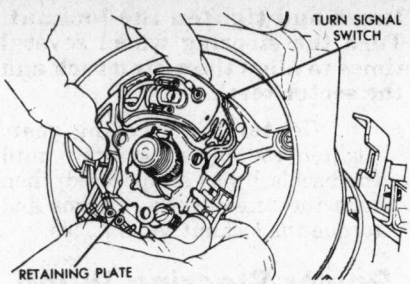

Removing turn signal switch from steering column

the lower reinforcement nuts to 9 ft. lbs.

Ignition Lock Cylinder

REMOVAL & INSTALLATION

Standard Steering Column

1. Remove the steering wheel.
2. Remove the housing cover-to-lock housing screws and the cover.
3. Remove the wash/wipe switch assembly. Pull the hider up the control stalk and remove the control stalk sleeve-to-wash/wipe switch assembly screws. Turn the control stalk shaft clockwise 1 revolution and pull it straight out of the switch.
4. Remove the turn signal/upper bearing retainer screws and retainer. Lift the switch and move out of the way.
5. Disconnect the horn and key light ground wires. Remove the key light assembly screw and lift the assembly out of the way.
6. Remove the 4 bearing housing-to-lock housing screws, the snap ring from the upper end of the steering shaft and the bearing housing.
7. Remove the lock plate and spring from the steering shaft.
8. Remove the ignition key, the buzzer/chime screw and switch.
9. On the steering column housing, remove the ignition switch screws, twist the switch 90 degrees and slide off the actuator rod. Remove the dimmer switch mounting screws and disconnect the switch from the actuator rod.
10. Remove the bellcrank screws and slide it up into the lock housing until it can be disconnected from the ignition actuator rod.
11. Place the ignition cylinder in the **LOCK** position and remove the key. Install a small screwdriver in both lock cylinder release holes, push inward to release the retaining spring and pull the lock cylinder out of the housing.
12. To install, insert the lock cylinder, insert the key, press inward, rotate the cylinder (this will align the

parts), snap the cylinder into place and reverse the removal procedures.

Tilt Steering Column

1. Remove the steering wheel.
2. Remove the tilt lever. Push in and unscrew the hazard knob. Remove the key lamp assembly.
3. Pull off the wash/wipe switch knob. Pull up the control stalk hider, remove the 2 sleeve-to-wash/wipe switch screws and the sleeve.
4. Turn the control stalk shaft clockwise, 1 revolution and pull it straight out of the switch.
5. Remove the plastic cover (if equipped) from the lock plate. Using the lock plate depression tool No. C–4156, depress the lock plate and pry the ring out of the groove with a small pry bar. Remove the lock plate, the canceling cam and the canceling cam spring.
6. Place the shift bowl in the **LOW** position. Remove the turn signal switch screws, the switch actuator screw, the actuator arm and the key lamp.
7. Place the ignition cylinder in the **LOCK** position. Install a small screwdriver in the lock cylinder (right hand slot) release hole, push inward to release the retaining spring and pull the lock cylinder out of the housing.
8. To install, press the cylinder lock inward (make contact with the drive shaft), move the actuator rod up and down (to align the parts), snap the cylinder into place and reverse the removal procedures.

Ignition Switch

REMOVAL & INSTALLATION

1. Remove the screws that attach the upper steering column housing to

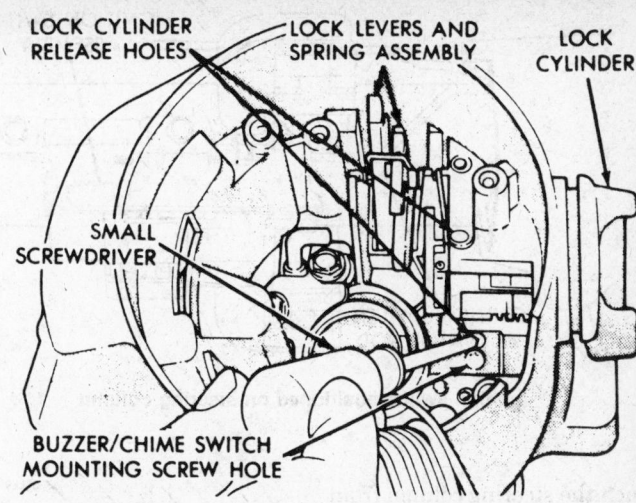

Removal of lock cylinder from steering wheel

the steering column and remove the housing.
2. Move the column to the **FULL UP** position.
3. Insert a screwdriver into the slot in the spring retainer and press in on the retainer, approximately $3/16$ in. Turn the retainer approximately $1/8$ turn to the left until the ears align with the grooves in the housing. Remove the spring retainer, spring and guide.
4. Make sure the ignition switch is in the **ACCESSORY** position, then remove the wire connector from the ignition switch and remove the screws that attach the ignition switch to the outside of the steering column.
5. Lift the ignition switch from the column, twisting it to disengage the switch actuating rod from the rack. Remove the switch.
6. To install, place the ignition switch in the **ACCESSORY** position, insert the actuating rod into the steering column.
7. Twist the switch and rod assembly 90 degrees to engage the actuating rod with the rack. Make sure the ignition lock cylinder is in the correct position.
8. Loosely install the ignition switch and mounting screws. Move the ignition switch downward, away from the steering wheel and tighten the mounting screws. Make sure the ignition switch has not moved out of the lock detent.
9. To complete the installation, reverse the removal procedures.

Power Steering Gear

REMOVAL & INSTALLATION

1. Disconnect the negative battery cable.

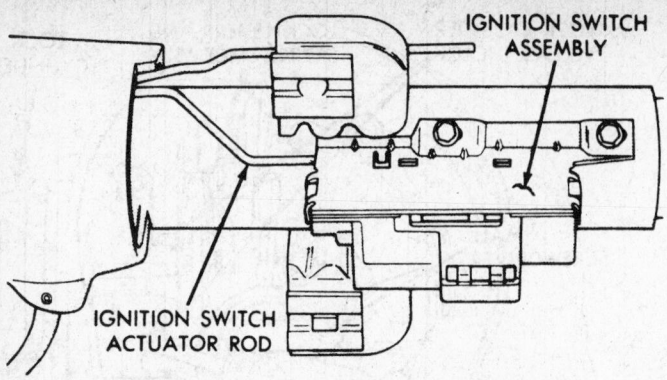

Ignition switch positioned on steering column

2. Detach the steering column from the instrument panel and the floor.

3. Disconnect the power steering pressure/return hoses from the steering gear and tie the free ends above the power steering pump to avoid fluid loss. Cap the steering gear fittings.

4. Remove the steering arm nut and lock washer from under the vehicle. Using the steering arm removal tool No. C–4150 or equivalent, remove the steering arm from the steering gear.

5. Disconnect and drop the exhaust system.

6. Remove the starter heat shield, the steering gear bolts and the steering gear.

7. To install, reverse the removal procedures. Torque the steering gear bolts to 100 ft. lbs. Rotate the worm shaft (by hand) and center the sector shaft at mid-point of its travel. Install the steering arm and torque it to 175 ft. lbs. Fill the power steering pump with fluid. Start the engine and turn the wheels to the extreme opposite sides (several times) to bleed the system.

ADJUSTMENT

1. Position the steering wheel in the centered and straight ahead position, then start the engine. If the steering wheel rotates (self-steering), stop the engine and adjust the steering gear.

2. To adjust the steering gear, perform the following procedures:

a. Loosen the valve assembly mounting bolts, then tighten to 7 ft. lbs. to prevent oil leakage during the centering operation.

b. Position the steering wheel in the centered and straight ahead position, then start the engine. If the steering wheel rotates to the left, stop the engine and tap the valve assembly toward the rear of the vehicle.

c. If the steering wheel rotates to the right, stop the engine and tap

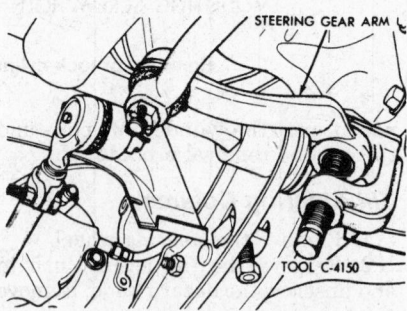

Steering gear arm removal

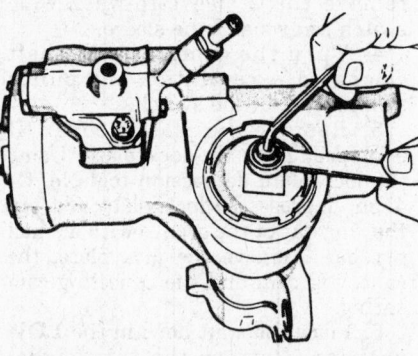

Removing the backlash from the steering gear

the valve assembly toward the front of the vehicle.

d. Repeat the alignment procedures until the steering wheel does not rotate when the engine is started. Retorque the valve assembly to 15–20 ft. lbs.

3. If backlash is noticed the steering gear, perform the following procedures to remove it:

a. Using a box-end wrench and an Allen wrench, loosen the sector shaft adjusting screw locknut and turn the adjusting screw to remove the backlash.

NOTE: If the power train has been removed from the vehicle, tighten the adjusting screw 1¼

turns and tighten the locknut. Turn the steering wheel several times to align the piston rack and the sector teeth.

b. Center the steering gear. Tighten the adjusting screw until the backlash has disappeared, then turn the screw in ⅜–½ turns and torque the locknut to 28 ft. lbs.

Power Steering Pump

REMOVAL & INSTALLATION

1. Back off the pump mounting adjusting bolts and remove the pump drive belt.

2. Disconnect the pump hoses at the pump.

3. Remove the pump bolts and pump with the bracket.

4. To install, reverse the removal procedures. Torque the pump mounting bolts to 30 ft. lbs. When installing the pump hoses, lubricate with power steering fluid and replace the O-rings. Adjust the drive belt and bleed the system.

BELT ADJUSTMENT

1. Install the pump drive belt and adjust.

2. There should be no more than ½ in. of play, under moderate thumb pressure, on the longest span of belt.

3. If equipped with a ½ in. square hole on the adjusting bracket, use a ½ in. breaker bar to adjust the belt tension or torque wrench and adjust to specifications.

SYSTEM BLEEDING

1. Fill the pump with power steering fluid.

2. Start the engine and rotate the steering wheel from stop to stop several times, to bleed the system.

3. Make sure that there are no air bubbles in the fluid.

4. Check the pump fluid level and fill as required.

Tie Rod End

REMOVAL & INSTALLATION

1. Loosen the tie rod adjuster sleeve clamp nuts.

2. Remove the tie rod end stud nut and cotter pin.

3. If the outer tie rod end is being removed, remove the stud from the steering knuckle. If the inner tie rod end is being removed, remove the stud from the center link. The studs on all the tie rod ends fit in a tapered hole.

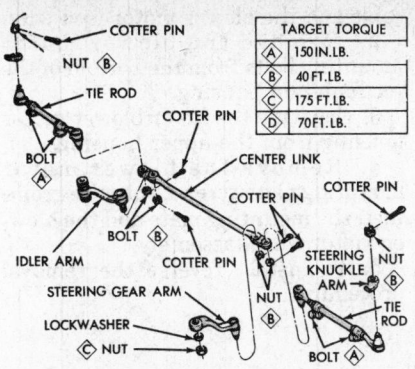

TARGET TORQUE	
Ⓐ	150 IN. LB.
Ⓑ	40 FT. LB.
Ⓒ	175 FT. LB.
Ⓓ	70 FT. LB.

Steering linkage, all models similar

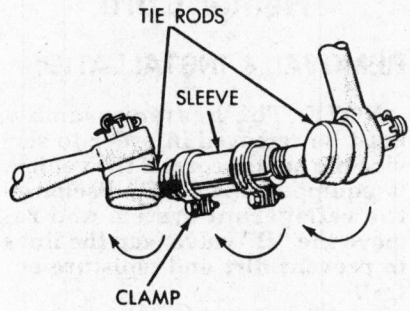

Tie Rod adjustment

They can be removed with the ball joint removal tool No. C–3894–A.

NOTE: Use extreme care not to damage the rubber grease seals at the tie rod ends. If the seals become damaged they must be removed and the tie rod ends inspected.

4. Unscrew the tie rod end from the threaded sleeve and record the number of turns required to remove it. The threads may be left or right hand threads.

5. To install, grease the tie rod threads and reverse the removal procedures. Screw in the tie rod end as many turns as were needed to remove it. This will give approximately correct toe-in. Torque the stud nuts to 40 ft. lbs. and install new cotter pins. Adjust the toe.

BRAKES

For all brake system repair and service procedures not detailed below, please refer to brakes in the Unit Repair section.

Master Cylinder

REMOVAL & INSTALLATION

1. Disconnect the brake lines from the master cylinder. Plug the brake line outlets to prevent fluid loss.

2. Remove the nuts that attach the master cylinder to the cowl panel or the power brake booster.

3. On non-power brakes models, disconnect the pushrod from the brake pedal and the stop light switch bracket. Pull the brake pedal back hard enough to separate the push rod from the master cylinder piston; the pushrod grommet will be destroyed, replaced it. Upon installation, lubricate the new grommet with a drop of water.

4. Slide the master cylinder straight out and off the cowl panel or power brake booster.

5. To install, reverse the removal procedures. Torque the mounting nuts to 17 ft. lbs. Bleed the brake system.

Combination Valve

The combination valve is located below the master cylinder and attached to the fender splash shield. The valve assembly contains a warning switch (with a hold off valve) and a proportioning valve.

REMOVAL & INSTALLATION

1. Disconnect the electrical connector from the combination valve.
2. Disconnect and plug the brake tubes at the combination valve.
3. Remove the valve-to-fender splash shield bolts and the combination valve from the vehicle.
4. To install, reverse the removal procedures. Bleed the brake system.

Power Brake Booster

REMOVAL & INSTALLATION

1. Remove the master cylinder retaining nuts from the power brake booster and position the master cylinder out of the way without disconnecting the brake lines. Use care not to kink the brake lines.
2. Disconnect the vacuum hose from the power brake booster.
3. Working under the dash, remove the nut and bolt that attaches the power brake booster pushrod to the brake pedal. Use a small screwdriver to expand the retainer clip and remove it from the brake pedal pin. Discard the clip. Unbolt and remove the lower pivot bolt/nut.
4. Remove the 4 power brake booster attaching nuts/washers and the booster assembly from the vehicle.
5. To install, reverse the removal procedures. Use a new retainer clip. Torque the mounting bolts/nuts to 17 ft. lbs.

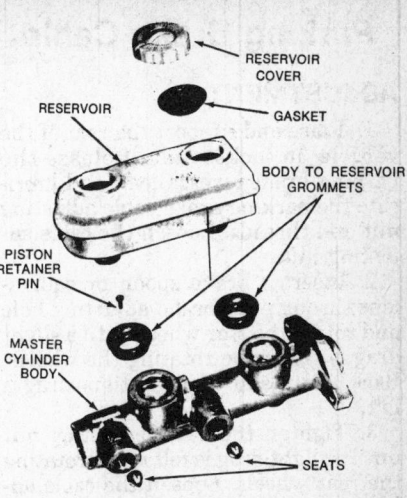

Aluminum master cylinder—primary and secondary system components similar to cast iron cylinder

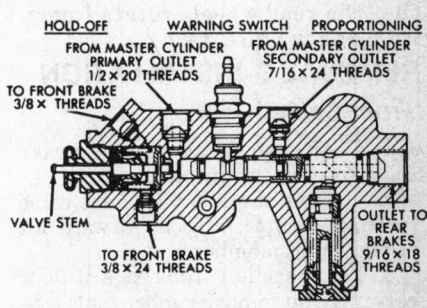

Exploded view of the combination valve

Wheel Cylinder

REMOVAL & INSTALLATION

1. Raise and support the rear of the vehicle on jackstands.
2. Remove the wheel assembly and the brake drum.
3. Inspect the wheel cylinder for signs of leakage.

NOTE: If signs of leakage are present, the wheel cylinder must be replaced.

4. Remove the brake shoe assembly from the backing plate.
5. Disconnect and plug the brake line at the wheel cylinder.
6. Remove the wheel cylinder-to-backing plate bolts and separate the wheel cylinder from the backing plate.

NOTE: It is recommended to replace the wheel cylinder instead of rebuilding it.

7. To install, use a new wheel cylinder and reverse the removal procedures. Torque the wheel cylinder-to-backing plate bolts to 6 ft. lbs. Bleed the brake system.

Parking Brake Cable

ADJUSTMENT

1. Raise and support the rear of the vehicle on jackstands. Release the parking brake lever. Clean and lubricate the parking brake cable adjusting nut and threads. Loosen the cable adjusting nut.

2. Insert a brake spoon or equivalent through the brake adjusting hole and rotate the star wheel until a slight drag is felt while rotating the wheels. Back off the star wheel until no drag is felt.

3. Tighten the cable adjusting nut until a slight drag is felt when rotating the rear wheels. Loosen the cable adjusting nut until the rear wheels can be rotated freely. Back off the cable adjusting nut two additional turns.

4. Apply and release the parking brake several times. Check, to verify that the rear wheels rotate freely, without any brake drag.

REMOVAL & INSTALLATION

Front Cable

1. Disengage front parking brake cable from left connector.

2. Using a suitable tool, force cable housing and attaching clip forward out of body crossmember.

3. Fold back left front edge of floor covering and remove rubber cable cover from floor pan.

4. Engage parking brake and work brake cable up and out of clevis linkage.

5. Using a suitable tool, force upper end of cable housing and clip down out of pedal assembly bracket.

6. Work cable and housing assembly up through floor pan.

To install:

7. Insert parking brake cable through floor pan.

8. Insert retainer into hole in the bottom of the parking brake pedal assembly bracket. Insert cable through hole and insert cable end fitting into linkage clevis. Force upper cable housing into retainer until firmly seated against pedal assembly bracket.

9. Insert retainer into hole in crossmember. Insert cable through hole in crossmember and force cable housing into retainer until firmly seated.

10. Install rubber cable cover and floor pan clip.

11. Attach cable to connector.

12. Adjust service brakes and parking brake system.

13. Apply brakes several times and test for free wheel rotation.

Rear Cable

1. With vehicle jacked up or on a suitable hoist, remove rear wheels.

2. Disconnect brake cable from connector.

3. Remove retaining clip from brake cable bracket.

4. Remove brake drum from rear axle.

5. Remove brake shoe return springs and adjuster mechanism.

6. Remove brake shoe retaining springs.

7. Remove brake shoe strut and spring and disconnect brake cable from operating arm.

8. Compress retainers on end of brake cable housing and remove cable from support place.

To install:

9. Insert brake cable and housing into brake support plate making certain that housing retainers lock the housing firmly into place.

10. Holding brake shoes in place on support plate, engage brake cable into brake shoe operating lever. Install parking brake strut and spring.

11. Install brake shoe retaining springs, adjuster mechanism and brake shoe return springs.

12. Install brake drum and wheel.

13. Insert brake cable and housing into cable bracket and install retaining clip.

14. Insert brake cable into equalizer.

15. Adjust service brakes and then parking brake cable.

CHASSIS ELECTRICAL

Heater Blower

REMOVAL & INSTALLATION

NOTE: All service to the blower motor is made under the right-side of the instrument panel.

Without Air Conditioning

1. Disconnect the negative battery cable.

2. Remove the glove box assembly if necessary to gain access.

3. Disconnect motor electrical connections.

4. Remove the heater assembly-to-plenum mounting brace.

5. Remove screws fastening blower motor assembly-to-heater housing and remove motor.

6. To install, reverse the removal procedures.

With Air Conditioning

1. Disconnect the negative battery cable and the blower motor feed wire.

2. Remove the blower motor mounting bolts from the bottom of the recirculation housing.

3. Separate the lower blower motor housing from the upper housing.

4. Remove the blower motor mounting plate screws, the wire grommet, the mounting plate and the blower motor/wheel assembly.

5. To install, reverse the removal procedures.

Heater Core

REMOVAL & INSTALLATION

NOTE: The heater assembly must be removed in order to service the heater core. If the vehicle is equipped with A/C, discharge the refrigerant system and remove the "H" valve (cap the lines to prevent dirt and moisture entry).

──────── CAUTION ────────

Extreme care must be taken to prevent any liquid refrigerant from contacting the skin and especially the eyes. Always work in a well-ventilated room.

──────────────────────────

1. Disconnect the negative battery cable. Drain the cooling system.

2. Disconnect the heater hoses at the firewall and plug the heater core tubes.

3. Disconnect the vacuum lines from the water valve and the manifold vacuum tree and push the rubber grommet and vacuum lines through the dash panel.

4. Remove the 4 heater assembly-to-dash panel nuts.

5. Slide the passenger seat all the way back to provide good clearance for removing the heater assembly. If equipped with a floor console, remove it.

NOTE: For the Mirada, 1982–83 Cordoba and 1982–83 Imperial, remove the glove box, ash tray and housing assembly. Remove the right lower trim panel, the right cowl trim panel and the top panel (if necessary). Then go to Step 10. For the 1982 New Yorker, 1983 New Yorker Fifth Avenue/ Gran Fury, remove the glove box, ash tray and housing assembly. Disconnect the right side lap cooler tube from the lap cooler, the right trim bezel and the right cowl trim. Then go to Step 10.

6. Remove the cluster bezel assem-

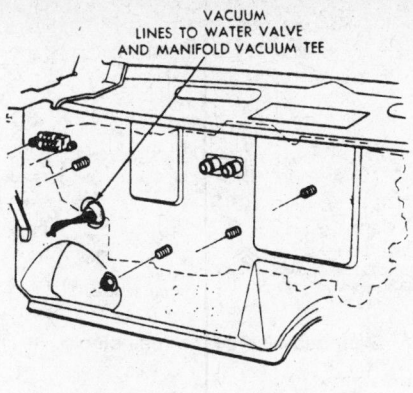

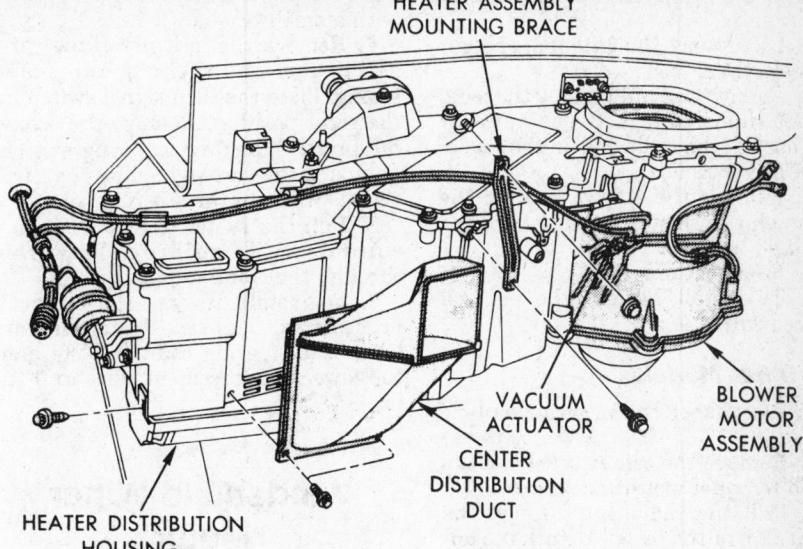

1983 Cordoba and Mirada heater assembly. Other models similar

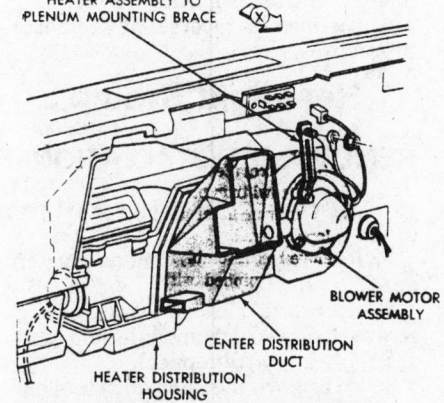

Heater assembly—air conditioned
vehicles; 1981–83

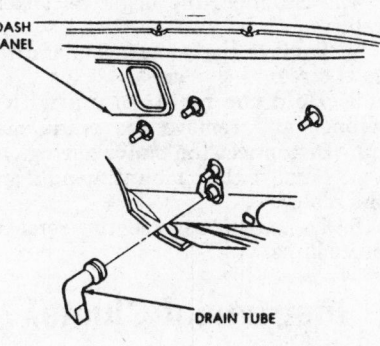

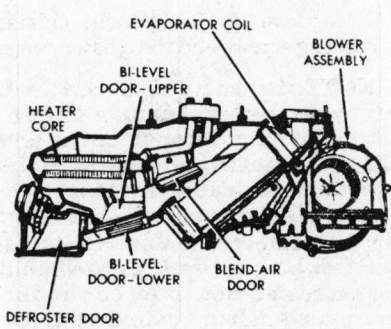

Evaporator/heater assembly, typical

bly and the upper instrument panel
cover.

7. Remove the steering column cover and the right side intermediate cowl
trim panel.

8. Remove the lower instrument
panel and the center-to-lower
reinforcement.

9. Remove the right center air distribution duct.

10. Disconnect the locking tab or defroster duct, the blower feed and
ground wires.

11. Depress the flag tab at the temperature control cable and remove the
heat distribution housing from the
heater housing receiver.

12. While holding up the assembly,
remove the heater assembly-to-plenum mounting brace.

13. Pull the assembly out, rotate it to
the right and remove it from under the
instrument panel. If equipped with A/
C, remove the blend air door from the
shaft.

14. Remove the servo motor from the
shaft, the screws from the top of the
unit and lift off the cover.

15. Remove the mounting flange
screws (if equipped) from behind the
core seal on the unit face and lift out
the heater core.

16. To install, reverse the removal

procedures and refill the cooling
system.

17. Start engine and check for proper
operation.

**NOTE: Water which accumulates on the bottom of the evaporator housing is expelled through
a single molded rubber drain
tube. This tube or hose must be
kept open or a water leak will appear on the floor in the passenger
compartment.**

Radio

REMOVAL & INSTALLATION

*Diplomat, 1982–83 Imperial,
1982 New Yorker, 1983 New
Yorker Fifth Avenue/Gran Fury*

1. Disconnect the negative battery
cable.

**NOTE: On the Diplomat and
1982 New Yorker/Gran Fury remove the instrument cluster bezel by removing the 4 screws
along the lower edge. Place the
automatic transmission selector
in No. 1 position and pull out to detach the top edge clips. Remove
the center bezel on 1982–83 Mirada and 1982–83 Imperial.**

2. Remove the radio mounting
screws.

3. On monaural radios, remove the
lamp assembly from the front of the
radio.

4. Remove the radio-to-panel
mounting screws.

5. Remove the instrument panel
upper cover. Work through the access
hole in the top of the instrument panel
to disconnect the antenna and speaker
leads. Remove the bracket mounting
nut.

6. Remove the radio and disconnect
the electrical lead.

7. To install, reverse the removal
procedures.

Cordoba

1. Disconnect the negative battery
cable.

2. Remove the instrument cluster lower bezel.

3. Disconnect the antenna, speaker and electrical leads.

4. Remove the nut holding the radio to the support bracket. The nut is at the back of the radio and on the side of tape player/radios.

5. Remove the screws holding the radio on the cluster housing from the front.

6. Remove the radio.

7. To install, reverse the removal procedures.

All Other Models

1. Disconnect the negative battery cable.

2. Remove the center bezel and the radio-to-panel mounting screws.

3. Pull the radio out through the front face of the panel. Detach the antenna lead, ground strap, power wire and speaker leads.

4. To install, reverse the removal procedures.

Windshield Wiper Switch

REMOVAL & INSTALLATION

1. Disconnect the negative battery cable. Remove the steering wheel center cover and the steering wheel.

2. Remove the steering column cover and the lower instrument panel bezel. Loosen the gearshift housing Allen screw and remove the gearshift indicator.

3. If equipped with a tilt steering wheel, place the steering wheel at its mid-point position. Remove the steering column-to-lower panel reinforcement nuts and the 4 mounting bracket-to-steering column bolts.

Support the steering column to prevent damage.

4. Pry out the plastic buttons holding the wiring trough to the column and remove the trough. Disconnect the turn signal wiring connector and wrap it with a piece of tape.

5. On the standard column, remove the screws holding the turn signal lever assembly to the turn signal switch pivot and the screws/retainers holding the turn signal switch to the upper bearing housing.

6. On the tilt column, remove the plastic cover (if equipped) from the lock plate. Using the lock plate depression tool No. C–4156, depress the lock plate and pry the ring out of the groove with a small pry bar.

7. Remove the lock plate, the canceling cam and the canceling cam spring. Place the turn signal switch in the right position. Remove the screw holding the hazard warning switch knob and the screws holding the turn signal switch to the steering column.

8. Pull the switch gently from the column while guiding the wires through the column opening.

9. To install, reverse the removal procedures. Tighten the mounting bracket-to-steering column bolts and the lower reinforcement nuts to 9 ft. lbs.

Windshield Wiper Motor

REMOVAL & INSTALLATION

1. Disconnect the negative battery cable.

2. Remove the wiper arms and the cowl screen.

3. Hold the motor crank with a wrench and remove the crank arm nut. Disconnect the motor wiring.

4. Remove the 3 mounting nuts and the motor.

5. To install, reverse the removal procedures.

Instrument Cluster

REMOVAL & INSTALLATION

1. Remove the instrument cluster mounting screws and the cluster bezel.

NOTE: On some models, it will be necessary to remove the instrument panel upper cover and the sub-bezel to gain access to the speedometer cable and the electrical wire connectors that must be disconnected before the cluster can be removed. Care should be exercised not to force the finish panels when removing or installing, for breakage can occur.

2. Place the gearshift indicator on the No. 1 position.

3. The speedometer cable is attached to the speedometer housing by a spring clip, which locks into a groove on the speedometer housing. To release the cable, depress the spring clip arm to disengage it from the groove and pull the cable away from the speedometer housing.

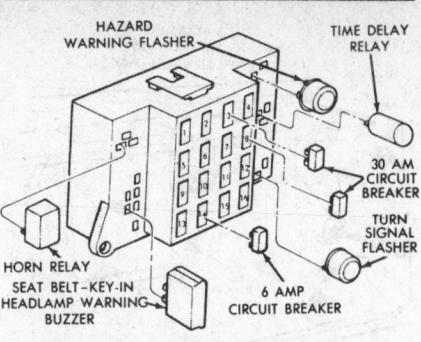

Exploded view of the fuse block

4. Disconnect the wiring connectors and the cluster from the vehicle.

5. To install, reverse the removal procedures.

Headlight Switch

REMOVAL & INSTALLATION

1. Disconnect negative battery cable.

2. Remove the instrument cluster bezel.

3. Remove the two mounting screws from switch module and pull assembly away from panel.

4. To remove the knob and stem assembly, depress the headlight switch stem release button and pull assembly from switch.

5. Disconnect electrical wiring.

6. Remove the switch from the vehicle.

7. Installation is the reverse of the removal procedure.

Stoplight Switch

The stoplight switch and its mounting bracket are attached to the brake pedal bracket. Adjustment is correct when stoplights illuminate after ½ in. brake pedal travel.

Fuses and Circuit Breakers

LOCATION

The fuses, relays and circuit breakers are located on the fuse panel. The fuse panel is located on the left side of the passenger compartment, either mounted to the underside of the dash panel or to the inner side of the firewall panel. When replacing the fuses or circuit breakers, be sure to replace them with ones of the same amperage.

Ford Motor Co.
Front Wheel Drive
Escort, EXP, Lincoln Continental, LN7, Lynx, Tempo, Topaz

SERIAL NUMBER IDENTIFICATION

VEHICLE IDENTIFICATION CHART

It is important for servicing and ordering parts to be certain of the vehicle and engine identification. The VIN (vehicle identification number) is a 17 digit number visible through the windshield on the driver's side of the dash and contains the vehicle and engine identification codes. The tenth digit indicates model year, and the eighth digit indicates engine code. It can be interpreted as follows:

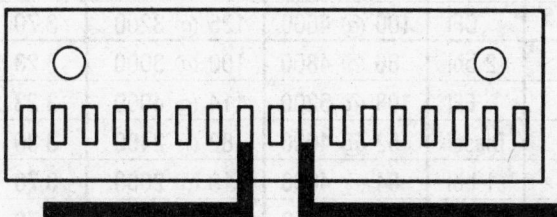

Engine Code						Model Year	
Code	Cu. In.	Liters	Cyl.	Fuel Sys.	Eng. Mfg.	Code	Year
2	98	1.6	4	2 bbl	Ford	C	1982
5	98	1.6	4	EFI	Ford	D	1983
4 ('84–'85)	98	1.6 HO	4	2 bbl	Ford	E	1984
7	98	1.6 MHO	4	2 bbl	Ford	F	1985
8	98	1.6 Turbo	4	EFI	Ford	G	1986
J	98	1.6	4	EFI	Ford	H	1987
9 ('82–'87)	116	1.9	4	2 bbl	Ford	J	1988
9 ('88–'89)	116	1.9	4	CFI	Ford	K	1989
J	116	1.9 HO	4	EFI	Ford		
H	122	2.0	4	Diesel	Toyo Kogyo		
R	140	2.3 HSC	4	1/EFI	Ford		
X	140	2.3	4	CFI	Ford		
S	140	2.3 HO	4	CFI	Ford		
4 ('88–'89)	232	3.8	6	EFI	Ford		

GENERAL ENGINE SPECIFICATIONS

Year	VIN	No. Cylinder Displacement cu. in. (liter)	Fuel System Type	Net Horsepower @ rpm	Net Torque @ rpm (ft.lbs.)	Bore × Stroke (in.)	Com- pression Ratio	Oil Pressure @ rpm
1982	2	4-98 (1.6)	2 bbl	70 @ 4600	89 @ 3000	3.15 × 3.13	8.8:1	35-65 @ 2000
1983	2	4-98 (1.6)	2 bbl	70 @ 4600	89 @ 3000	3.15 × 3.13	8.8:1	35-65 @ 2000
1984	2	4-98 (1.6)	2 bbl	70 @ 4600	88 @ 2600	3.15 × 3.13	9.0:1	35-65 @ 2000
	4	4-98 (1.6)	2 bbl	80 @ 5400	88 @ 3000	3.15 × 3.13	9.0:1	35-65 @ 2000
	5	4-98 (1.6)	EFI	120 @ 5200	120 @ 3400	3.15 × 3.13	8.0:1	35-65 @ 2000
	H	4-122 (2.0)	Diesel	52 @ 4000	82 @ 2400	3.39 × 3.39	22.7:1	55-60 @ 2000
	R	4-140 (2.3)	1/EFI	84 @ 4600	118 @ 2600	3.70 × 3.30	9.0:1	55-70 @ 2000
1985	2	4-98 (1.6)	2 bbl	70 @ 4600	88 @ 2600	3.15 × 3.13	9.0:1	35-65 @ 2000
	4	4-98 (1.6)	2 bbl	80 @ 5400	88 @ 3000	3.15 × 3.13	9.0:1	35-65 @ 2000
	5	4-98 (1.6)	EFI	120 @ 5200	120 @ 3400	3.15 × 3.13	8.0:1	35-65 @ 2000
	8	4-98 (1.6)	EFI	84 @ 5200	90 @ 2800	3.15 × 3.13	9.0:1	35-65 @ 2000
	7	4-98 (1.6)	2 bbl	80 @ 5400	88 @ 3000	3.15 × 3.13	9.0:1	35-65 @ 2000
	H	4-122 (2.0)	Diesel	52 @ 4000	82 @ 2400	3.39 × 3.39	22.7:1	55-60 @ 2000
	R	4-140 (2.3)	1 bbl	84 @ 4600	118 @ 2600	3.70 × 3.30	9.0:1	55-70 @ 2000
	X	4-140 (2.3)	CFI	100 @ 4600	125 @ 3200	3.70 × 3.30	9.0:1	55-70 @ 2000
	S	4-140 (2.3)	CFI	100 @ 4600	125 @ 3200	3.70 × 3.30	9.0:1	55-70 @ 2000
1986	9	4-116 (1.9)	2 bbl	86 @ 4800	100 @ 3000	3.23 × 3.46	9.0:1	35-65 @ 2000
	J	4-116 (1.9)	EFI	108 @ 5200	114 @ 4000	3.23 × 3.46	9.0:1	35-65 @ 2000
	H	4-122 (2.0)	Diesel	52 @ 4000	82 @ 2400	3.39 × 3.39	22.7:1	55-60 @ 2000
	R	4-140 (2.3)	1 bbl	84 @ 4600	118 @ 2600	3.70 × 3.30	9.0:1	35-65 @ 2000
	X	4-140 (2.3)	CFI	100 @ 4600	125 @ 3200	3.70 × 3.30	9.0:1	55-10 @ 2000
1987	9	4-116 (1.9)	2 bbl	86 @ 4800	100 @ 3000	3.23 × 3.46	9.0:1	35-65 @ 2000
	J	4-116 (1.9)	EFI	108 @ 5200	114 @ 4000	3.23 × 3.46	9.0:1	35-65 @ 2000
	H	4-122 (2.0)	Diesel	52 @ 4000	82 @ 2400	3.39 × 3.39	22.7:1	55-60 @ 2000
	R	4-140 (2.3)	1 bbl	84 @ 4600	118 @ 2600	3.70 × 3.30	9.0:1	35-65 @ 2000
	X	4-140 (2.3)	CFI	100 @ 4600	125 @ 3200	3.70 × 3.30	9.0:1	55-70 @ 2000
1988-89	9	4-116 (1.9)	C.F.I	90 @ 4600	106 @ 3400	3.23 × 3.46	9.0:1	35-65 @ 2000
	J	4-116 (1.9)	EFI	110 @ 5400	115 @ 4200	3.23 × 3.46	9.0:1	35-65 @ 2000
	X	4-140 (2.3)	EFI	98 @ 4400	124 @ 2200	3.70 × 3.30	9.0:1	55-70 @ 2000
	S	4-140 (2.3)	EFI	100 @ 4400	130 @ 2600	3.70 × 3.30	9.0:1	55-70 @ 2000
	4	6-232 (3.8)	EFI	140 @ 3800	215 @ 2200	3.81 × 3.39	9.0:1	40-60 @ 2000

GASOLINE ENGINE TUNE-UP SPECIFICATIONS

Year	VIN	No. Cylinder Displacement cu. in. (liter)	Spark Plugs Type	Spark Plugs Gap (in.)	Ignition Timing (deg.) MT	Ignition Timing (deg.) AT	Com- pression Pressure (psi)	Fuel Pump (psi)	Idle Speed (rpm) MT	Idle Speed (rpm) AT	Valve Clearance In.	Valve Clearance Ex.
1982	2	4-98 (1.6)	AGSP-32④	.044	10B	10B	—	4-6	800	800	Hyd.	Hyd.
1983	2	4-98 (1.6)	AWSF-34	.044	8B②	10B	—	③	800	750	Hyd.	Hyd.

GASOLINE ENGINE TUNE-UP SPECIFICATIONS

Year	VIN	No. Cylinder Displacement cu. in. (liter)	Spark Plugs Type	Gap (in.)	Ignition Timing (deg.) MT	AT	Compression Pressure (psi)	Fuel Pump (psi)	Idle Speed (rpm) MT	AT	Valve Clearance In.	Ex.
1984	2	4-98 (1.6)	AWSF-34	.044	8B	8B	—	4-6	700	700	Hyd.	Hyd.
	4	4-98 (1.6)	AWSF-34	.044	12B	14B	—	4-6	800	800	Hyd.	Hyd.
	5	4-98 (1.6)	AWSF-22	.034	10B	10B	—	35-45	800	750	Hyd.	Hyd.
	R	4-140 (2.3)	AWSF-52	.044	15B	15B⑤	—	4-6	800	700	Hyd.	Hyd.
1985	2	4-98 (1.6)	AWSF-34	.044	8B	8B	—	4-6	700	700	Hyd.	Hyd.
	4	4-98 (1.6)	AWSF-34	.044	12B	14B	—	4-6	800	800	Hyd.	Hyd.
	5	4-98 (1.6)	AWSF-24	.044	10B	10B	—	35-45	800	750	Hyd.	Hyd.
	8	4-98 (1.6)	AWSF-22C	.044	8B	8B	—	35-45	800	750	Hyd.	Hyd.
	7	4-98 (1.6)	AWSF-34	.044	12B	14B	—	4-6	800	800	Hyd.	Hyd.
	R	4-140 (2.3)	AWSF-52C	.044	10B	10B	—	4-6	800	750	Hyd.	Hyd.
	X	4-140 (2.3)	AWSF-52C	.044	10B	10B	—	35-45	725	570	Hyd.	Hyd.
	S	4-140 (2.3)	AWSF-52C	.044	10B	10B	—	35-45	725	570	Hyd.	Hyd.
1986	9	4-116 (1.9)	AWSF-34C	.044	10B	10B	—	4-6	750	750	Hyd.	Hyd.
	J	4-116 (1.9)	AWSF-24C	.044	10B	10B	—	35-45	900	800	Hyd.	Hyd.
	R	4-140 (2.3)	AWSF-44C	.044	10B	10B	—	4-6	800	750	Hyd.	Hyd.
	X	4-140 (2.3)	AWSF-52	.044	10B	10B	—	35-46	750	650	Hyd.	Hyd.
1987	9	4-116 (1.9)	AWSF-34C	.044	10B	10B	—	4-6	750	750	Hyd.	Hyd.
	J	4-116 (1.9)	AWSF-24C	.044	10B	10B	—	35-45	800	750	Hyd.	Hyd.
	R	4-140 (2.3)	AWSF-44C	.044	10B	10B	—	4-6	800	750	Hyd.	Hyd.
	X	4-140 (2.3)	AWSF-52	.044	10B	10B	—	35-45	750	650	Hyd.	Hyd.
1988	9	4-116 (1.9)	AGSF-34C	.044	①	①	—	30-45	900–1000	900–1000	Hyd.	Hyd.
	J	4-116 (1.9)	AGSF-24C	.044	①	①	—	13-17	900–1000	900–1000	Hyd.	Hyd.
	X	4-140 (2.3)	AWSF-52C	.044	①	①	—	45-60	⑥	⑦	Hyd.	Hyd.
	S	4-140 (2.3)	AWSF-42C	.044	①	①	—	45-60	⑥	⑦	Hyd.	Hyd.
	4	6-232 (3.8)	AWSF-44C	.052	—	①	—	30-45	—	①	Hyd.	Hyd.
1989		SEE UNDERHOOD SPECIFICATIONS STICKER										

B Before Top Dead Center

① Refer to the Vehicle Emission Control label
② EFI models—10B
③ Carbureted models 4-6 psi. Fuel injected models 35-45 psi.
④ There are two different plug designs used on the 1.6L engine. All 1982 EXP/LN7 models built before 9/4/81 use gasket equipped plugs. All 1982 and later Escort/Lynx and EXP/LN7 models built after 9/4/81 are equipped with tappered seat plugs. Do not interchange types.
⑤ 1 bbl models—10B
⑥ 2.3L w/MTX—1500–1600
⑦ 2.3L w/ATX—975–1075

DIESEL ENGINE TUNE-UP SPECIFICATIONS

Year	VIN	No. Engine Displacement cu. in. (liter)	Valve Clearance		Intake Valve Opens (deg.)	Injection Pump Setting (deg.)	Injection Nozzle Pressure (psi)		Idle Speed (rpm)	Cranking Compression Pressure (psi)
			Intake (in.)	Exhaust (in.)			New	Used		
1984	H	4-122 (2.0)	.010	.014 ①	13	TDC Hot	1990–2105	1849–1990	725 ± 50	390-435 @ 2000
1985	H	4-122 (2.0)	.010	.014	13	TDC Hot	1990–2105	1849–1990	725 ± 50	390-435 @ 2000
1986	H	4-122 (2.0)	.010	.014	13	TDC Hot	1990–2105	1849–2105	725 ± 50	390-435 @ 2000
1987	H	4-122 (2.0)	.010	.014	13	TDC Hot	1990–2105	1849–2105	725 ± 50	390-435 @ 2000

NOTE: See the Diesel Injection Timing Procedure text in this section.
TDC Top Dead Center
① The valve clearance specifications are set Cold.

FIRING ORDERS

NOTE: To avoid confusion, always replace spark plug wires one at a time.

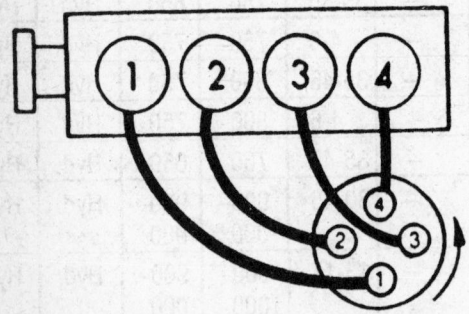

Escort/Lynx, EXP/LN7 1.6L and 1.9L engines
Firing order: 1—3—4—2
Distributor rotation: counterclockwise

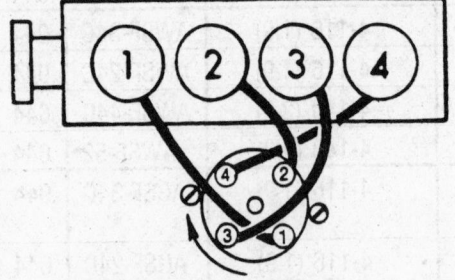

Tempo/Topaz 2.3L HSC and HSO engines
Firing Order: 1—3—4—2
Distributor Rotation: Clockwise

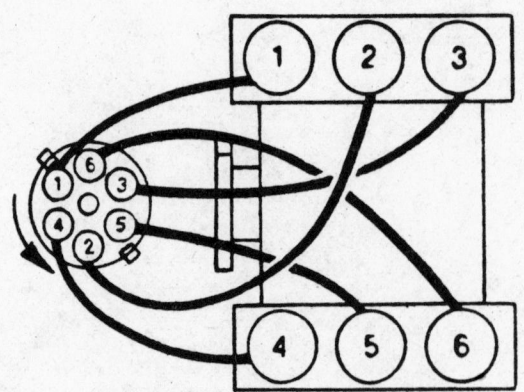

Lincoln Continental 3.8L engine
Firing Order: 1—4—2—5—3—6
Distributor rotation: counterclockwise

CAPACITIES

Year	VIN	No. Cylinder Displacement cu. in. (liter)	Engine Crankcase with Filter	Engine Crankcase without Filter	Transmission (pts.) MT	Transmission (pts.) AT	Drive Axle (pts.)	Fuel Tank (gals.)	Cooling System (qts.)
1982	2	4-98 (1.6)	4.0	3.5	5.0	①	②	10.0	6.4
1983	2	4-98 (1.6)	4.0	3.5	⑦	①	②	③	6.4
1984	2	4-98 (1.6)	4.0	3.5	⑦	①	②	③	8.1
	4	4-98 (1.6)	4.0	3.5	⑦	①	②	③	8.1
	5	4-98 (1.6)	4.0	3.5	⑦	①	②	③	8.1
	H	4-122 (2.0) Diesel	7.2	7.0	6.1	①	②	④	8.1
	R	4-140 (2.3)	4.5	4.0	6.1	①	②	④	8.1
1985	2	4-98 (1.6)	4.0	3.5	⑦	①	②	③	8.1
	4	4-98 (1.6)	4.0	3.5	⑦	①	②	③	8.1
	5	4-98 (1.6)	4.0	3.5	⑦	①	②	③	8.1
	8	4-98 (1.6)	4.0	3.5	⑦	①	②	③	8.1
	7	4-98 (1.6)	4.0	3.5	⑦	①	②	③	8.1
	H	4-122 (2.0) Diesel	7.2	7.0	6.1	①	②	④	8.1
	R	4-140 (2.3)	4.5	4.0	6.1	①	②	④	8.1
	X	4-140 (2.3) CFI	4.5	4.0	⑦	①	②	④	8.1
	S	4-140 (2.3)	4.5	4.0	⑦	①	②	④	8.1
1986	9	4-116 (1.9)	5.0	4.5	⑦	⑤	②	⑥	8.3
	J	4-116 (1.9)	5.0	4.5	⑦	⑤	②	⑥	8.3
	H	4-122 (2.0) Diesel	7.2	7.0	6.1	①	②	③	8.1
	R	4-140 (2.3)	4.5	4.0	6.1	①	②	④	8.1
	X	4-140 (2.3)	4.5	4.0	⑦	①	②	④	8.1
1987	9	4-116 (1.9)	5.0	4.5	⑦	⑤	②	⑥	8.3
	J	4-116 (1.9)	5.0	4.5	⑦	⑤	②	⑥	8.3
	H	4-122 (2.0) Diesel	7.2	7.0	6.1	①	②	③	8.1
	R	4-140 (2.3)	4.5	4.0	6.1	①	②	④	8.1
	X	4-140 (2.3)	4.5	4.0	⑦	①	②	④	8.1
1988-89	9	4-116 (1.9)	3.5	4.0	⑦	⑤	②	⑥	7.9
	J	4-116 (1.9)	3.5	4.0	⑦	⑤	②	③	7.9
	X	4-140 (2.3)	4.5	4.0	⑦	⑧	②	⑥	8.3
	S	4-140 (2.3)	4.5	4.0	6.1	⑧	②	⑥	8.3
	4	6-232 (3.8)	4.5	4.0	26.2	–	②	18.6	12.1

① Total dry capacity—converter, cooler and sump drained.
   1982—19.6 pints
   1983-88—16.6 pints
② Included in transmission capacity
③ 1983-88—10 gallons, FE & LX models
   13 gallons—Standard models
   13 gallons—EXP/LN7 models
④ 1984-85: 14 gallons
   1986-88: 15.2 gallons
⑤ All automatic transaxle models except the all wheel drive models are 8.3 pts. The all wheel drive models are 10.0 pts.

⑥ Standard fuel tank is 15.4 gallons. All wheel drive model fuel tank is 14.2 gallons
⑦ 4 speed—5.0 pts
   5 speed—6.1 pts.
⑧ ATX—16.1
   All wheel drive—19.3

CAMSHAFT SPECIFICATIONS
All measurements given in inches.

Year	VIN	No. Cylinder Displacement cu. in. (liter)	Journal Diameter 1	2	3	4	5	Lobe Lift	Bearing Clearance	Camshaft End Play
1982	2	4-98 (1.6)	1.761–1.762	1.771–1.772	1.781–1.782	1.791–1.792	1.801–1.802	0.229	0.0008–0.0028	0.0018–0.0060
1983	2	4-98 (1.6)	1.761–1.762	1.771–1.772	1.781–1.782	1.791–1.792	1.801–1.802	0.229	0.0008–0.0028–	0.0018–0.0060–
1984	2	4-98 (1.6)	1.761–1.762	1.771–1.772	1.781–1.782	1.791–1.792	1.801–1.802	0.229	0.0008–0.0028	0.0018–0.0060
	4	4-98 (1.6)	1.761–1.762	1.771–1.772	1.781–1.782	1.791–1.792	1.801–1.802	0.240	0.0008–0.0028	0.0018–0.0060
	5	4-98 (1.6)	1.761–1.762	1.771–1.772	1.781–1.782	1.791–1.792	1.801–1.802	0.240	0.0008–0.0028	0.0018–0.0060
	H	4-122 (2.0) Diesel	1.2582–1.2589	1.2582–1.2589	1.2582–1.2589	1.2582–1.2589	1.2582–1.2589	NA	0.0010–0.0026	0.0008–0.0059
	R	4-140 (2.3)	2.006–2.008	2.006–2.008	2.006–2.008	2.006–2.008	2.006–2.008	①	0.001–0.003	0.009
1985	2	4-98 (1.6)	1.761–1.762	1.771–1.772	1.781–1.782	1.791–1.792	1.801–1.802	0.229	0.0008–0.0028	0.0018–0.0060
	4	4-98 (1.6)	1.761–1.762	1.771–1.772	1.781–1.782	1.791–1.792	1.801–1.802	0.240	0.0008–0.0028	0.0018–0.0060
	5	4-98 (1.6)	1.761–1.762	1.771–1.772	1.781–1.782	1.791–1.792	1.801–1.802	0.240	0.0008–0.0028	0.0018–0.0060
	8	4-98 (1.6)	1.761–1.762	1.771–1.772	1.781–1.782	1.791–1.792	1.801–1.801	0.240	0.0008–0.0028	0.0018–0.0060
	7	4-98 (1.6)	1.761–1.762	1.771–1.772	1.781–1.782	1.791–1.792	1.801–1.802	0.240	0.0008–0.0028	0.0018–0.0060
	H	4-122 (2.0) Diesel	1.2582–1.2589	1.2582–1.2589	1.2582–1.2589	1.2582–1.2589	1.2582–1.2589	NA	0.001–0.0026	0.0008–0.0059
	R	4-140 (2.3)	2.006–2.008	2.006–2.008	2.006–2.008	2.006–2.008	2.006–2.008	①	0.001–0.003	0.009
	X	4-140 (2.3)	2.006–2.008	2.006–2.008	2.006–2.008	2.006–2.008	2.006–2.008	①	0.001–0.003	0.009
	S	4-140 (2.3)	2.006–2.008	2.006–2.008	2.006–2.008	2.006–2.008	2.006–2.008	①	0.001–0.003	0.009
1986	9	4-116 (1.9)	1.8017–1.8007	1.8017–1.8007	1.8017–1.8007	1.8017–1.8007	1.8017–1.8007	0.240	0.0013–0.0033	0.0018–0.0060
	J	4-116 (1.9)	1.8017–1.8007	1.8017–1.8007	1.8017–1.8007	1.8017–1.8007	1.8017–1.8007	0.240	0.0013–0.0033	0.018–0.0060
	H	4-122 (2.0) Diesel	1.2582–1.2589	1.2852–1.2589	1.2582–1.2589	1.2582–1.2589	1.2582–1.2589	NA	0.001–0.0026	0.0008–0.0059
	R	4-140 (2.3)	2.006–2.008	2.006–2.008	2.006–2.008	2.006–2.008	2.006–2.008	①	0.001–0.003	0.009
	X	4-140 (2.3)	2.006–2.008	2.006–2.008	2.006–2.008	2.006–2.008	2.006–2.008	①②	0.001–0.003	0.009

CAMSHAFT SPECIFICATIONS
All measurements given in inches.

Year	VIN	No. Cylinder Displacement cu. in. (liter)	Journal Diameter					Lobe Lift	Bearing Clearance	Camshaft End Play
			1	2	3	4	5			
1987	9	4-116 (1.9)	1.8017–1.8007	1.8017–1.8007	1.8017–1.8007	1.8017–1.8007	1.8017–1.8007	0.240	0.0013–0.0033	0.0018–0.0060
	J	4-116 (1.9)	1.8017–1.8007	1.8017–1.8007	1.8017–1.8007	1.8017–1.8007	1.8017–1.8007	0.240	0.0013–0.0013	0.0018–0.0060
	H	4-122 (2.0) Diesel	1.2582–1.2589	1.2582–1.2589	1.2582–1.2589	1.2582–1.2589	1.2582–1.2589	NA	0.001–0.0026	0.0008–0.0059
	R	4-140 (2.3)	2.006–2.008	2.006–2.008	2.006–2.008	2.006–2.008	2.006–2.008	①	0.001–0.003	0.009
	X	4-140 (2.3)	2.006–2.008	2.006–2.008	2.006–2.008	2.006–2.008	2.006–2.008	①②	0.001–0.003	0.009
1988-89	9	4-116 (1.9)	1.8017–1.8007	1.8017–1.8007	1.8017–1.8007	1.8017–1.8007	1.8017–1.8007	0.240	0.0013–0.0033	0.0018–0.0060
	J	4-116 (1.9)	1.8017–1.8007	1.8017–1.8007	1.8017–1.8007	1.8017–1.8007	1.8017–1.8007	0.240	0.0013–0.0013	0.006–0.0018
	X	4-140 (2.3)	2.010–2.009	2.010–2.019	2.010–2.009	2.010–2.009	2.010–2.009	①②	0.0010–0.0030	0.009
	S	4-140 (2.3)	2.010–2.009	2.010–2.019	2.010–2.009	2.010–2.009	2.010–2.009	①②	0.0010–0.0030	0.009
	4	6-232 (3.8)	2.0515–2.0505	2.0515–2.0505	2.0515–2.0505	2.0515–2.0505	—	③	0.0010–0.0030	NA

NA Not available
① Intake — .249 in.
   Exhaust — .239 in.
② 2.3L HO engine .2625 in.
③ Intake — 0.240
   Exhaust — 0.241

CRANKSHAFT AND CONNECTING ROD SPECIFICATIONS
All measurements are given in inches.

Year	VIN	No. Cylinder Displacement cu. in. (liter)	Crankshaft				Connecting Rod		
			Main Brg. Journal Dia.	Main Brg. Oil Clearance	Shaft End-play	Thrust on No.	Journal Diameter	Oil Clearance	Side Clearance
1982	2	4-98 (1.6)	2.2826–2.2834	0.0008–0.0015	0.004–0.008	3	1.885–1.886	0.0002–0.0003	0.004–0.011
1983	2	4-98 (1.6)	2.2826–2.2834	0.0008–0.0015	0.004–0.008	3	1.885–1.886	0.0002–0.0003	0.004–0.011
1984	2	4-98 (1.6)	2.2826–2.2834	0.0008–0.0015	0.004–0.008	3	1.885–1.886	0.0002–0.0003	0.004–0.011
	4	4-98 (1.6)	2.2826–2.2834	0.0008–0.0015	0.004–0.008	3	1.885–1.886	0.0002–0.0003	0.004–0.011
	5	4-98 (1.6)	2.2826–2.2834	0.0008–0.0015	0.004–0.008	3	1.885–1.886	0.0002–0.0003	0.004–0.011
	H	4-122 (2.0) Diesel	2.3598–2.3605	0.0012–0.0020	0.0016–0.0011	3	2.0055–2.0061	0.0010–0.0022	0.0043–0.0103
	R	4-140 (2.3)	2.2489–2.2490	0.0008–0.0015	0.004–0.008	3	2.1232–2.1240	0.0008–0.0015	0.0035–0.0105

CRANKSHAFT AND CONNECTING ROD SPECIFICATIONS
All measurements are given in inches.

Year	VIN	No. Cylinder Displacement cu. in. (liter)	Crankshaft				Connecting Rod		
			Main Brg. Journal Dia.	Main Brg. Oil Clearance	Shaft End-play	Thrust on No.	Journal Diameter	Oil Clearance	Side Clearance
1985	2	4-98 (1.6)	2.2826–2.2834	0.0008–0.0015	0.004–0.008	3	1.885–1.886	0.0002–0.0003	0.004–0.011
	4	4-98 (1.6)	2.2826–2.2834	0.0008–0.0015	0.004–0.008	3	1.885–1.886	0.0002–0.0003	0.004–0.011
	5	4-98 (1.6)	2.2826–2.2834	0.0008–0.0015	0.004–0.008	3	1.885–1.886	0.0002–0.0003	0.004–0.011
	7	4-98 (1.6)	2.2826–2.2834	0.0008–0.0015	0.004–0.008	3	1.885–1.886	0.0002–0.0003	0.004–0.011
	8	4-98 (1.6)	2.2826–2.2834	0.0008–0.0015	0.004–0.008	3	1.885–1.886	0.0002–0.0003	0.004–0.011
	H	4-122 (2.0) Diesel	2.3598–2.3605	0.0012–0.0020	0.0016–0.0011	3	2.0055–2.0061	0.0010–0.0020	0.0043–0.0103
	R	4-140 (2.3)	2.2489–2.2490	0.0008–0.0015	0.004–0.008	3	2.1232–2.1240	0.0008–0.0015	0.0035–0.0105
	S	4-140 (2.3)	2.2489–2.2490	0.0008–0.0015	0.004–0.008	3	2.1232–2.1240	0.0008–0.0015	0.0055–0.0105
1986	9	4-116 (1.9)	2.2827–2.2835	0.0008–0.0015	0.004–0.008	3	1.8854–1.8862	0.0008–0.0015	0.004–0.011
	J	4-116 (1.9)	2.2827–2.2835	0.0008–0.0015	0.004–0.008	3	1.8854–1.8862	0.0008–0.0015	0.004–0.011
	H	4-122 (2.0) Diesel	2.3598–2.3605	0.0012–0.0020	0.0016–0.0011	3	2.0055–2.0061	0.0010–0.0020	0.0043–0.0103
	R	4-140 (2.3)	2.2489–2.2490	0.0008–0.0015	0.004–0.008	3	2.1232–2.1240	0.0008–0.0015	0.0035–0.0105
	X	4-140 (2.3)	2.2489–2.2490	0.0008–0.0015	0.004–0.008	3	2.1232–2.1240	0.0008–0.0015	0.0035–0.0105
1987	9	4-116 (1.9)	2.2821–2.2835	0.0008–0.0015	0.004–0.008	3	1.8854–1.8862	0.0008–0.0015	0.004–0.011
	J	4-116 (1.9)	2.2827–2.2835	0.0008–0.0015	0.004–0.008	3	1.8854–1.8862	0.0008–0.0015	0.004–0.011
	H	4-122 (2.0) Diesel	2.3598–2.3605	0.0012–0.0020	0.0016–0.0011	3	2.0055–2.0061	0.0010–0.0020	0.0043–0.0103
	R	4-140 (2.3)	2.2489–2.2490	0.0008–0.0015	0.004–0.008	3	2.1232–2.1240	0.0008–0.0015	0.0035–0.0105
	X	4-140 (2.3)	2.2489–2.2490	0.0008–0.0015	0.004–0.008	3	2.1232–2.1240	0.0008–0.0015	0.0035–0.0105
1988-89	9	4-116 (1.9)	2.2827–2.2835	0.0008–0.0015	0.004–0.008	3	1.7257–1.7279	0.0008–0.0015	0.004–0.011
	J	4-116 (1.9)	2.2827–2.2835	0.0008–0.0015	0.004–0.008	3	1.7257–1.7279	0.0008–0.0015	0.004–0.011
	X	4-140 (2.3)	2.2489–2.2490	0.0008–0.0015	0.004–0.008	3	2.1232–2.1240	0.0008–0.0015	0.0035–0.0105

CRANKSHAFT AND CONNECTING ROD SPECIFICATIONS
All measurements are given in inches.

Year	VIN	No. Cylinder Displacement cu. in. (liter)	Main Brg. Journal Dia.	Crankshaft Main Brg. Oil Clearance	Shaft End-play	Thrust on No.	Connecting Rod Journal Diameter	Oil Clearance	Side Clearance
1988-89	S	4-140 (2.3)	2.2489–2.2490	0.0008–0.0015	0.004–0.008	3	2.1232–2.1240	0.0008–0.0015	0.0035–0.0105
	4	6-232 (3.8)	2.5190–2.5198	0.0010–0.0014	0.004–0.008	3	2.3103–2.3111	0.0010–0.0014	0.0047–0.0114

VALVE SPECIFICATIONS

Year	VIN	No. Cylinder Displacement cu. in. (liter)	Seat Angle (deg.)	Face Angle (deg.)	Spring Test Pressure (lbs.)	Spring Installed Height (in.)	Stem-to-Guide Clearance (in.) Intake	Exhaust	Stem Diameter (in.) Intake	Exhaust
1982	2	4-98 (1.6)	45	45.5	200 @ 1.09	1.480	0.0008–0.0027	0.0018–0.0037	0.316	0.315
1983	2	4-98 (1.6)	45	45.5	200 @ 1.09	1.480	0.0008–0.0027	0.0008–0.0037	0.316	0.315
1984	2	4-98 (1.6)	45	45.5	200 @ 1.09	1.480	0.0008–0.0027	0.0008–0.0037	0.316	0.315
	4	4-98 (1.6)	45	45.5	216 @ 1.016	1.450–1.480	0.0008–0.0027	0.0008–0.0037	0.316	0.315
	5	4-98 (1.6)	45	45.5	216 @ 1.016	1.450–1.480	0.0008–0.0027	0.0008–0.0037	0.316	0.315
	H	4-122 (2.0) Diesel	45	45.5	NA	1.7760	0.0016–0.0029	0.0018–0.0031	0.3138	0.3138
	R	4-140 (2.3)	45	45.5	182 @ 1.10	1.490	0.0018	0.0023	0.3415	0.3411
1985	2	4-98 (1.6)	45	45.5	200 @ 1.09	1.480	0.0008–0.0027	0.0018–0.0037	0.316	0.315
	4	4-98 (1.6)	45	45.5	216 @ 1.016	1.450–1.480	0.0008–0.0027	0.0008–0.0037	0.316	0.315
	5	4-98 (1.6)	45	45.5	216 @ 1.016	1.450–1.480	0.0008–0.0027	0.0008–0.0037	0.316	0.315
	7	4-98 (1.6)	45	45.5	200 @ 1.09	1.480	0.0008–0.0027	0.0008–0.0037	0.316	0.315
	8	4-98 (1.6)	45	45.5	216 @ 1.016	1.450–1.480	0.0008–0.0027	0.0008–0.0037	0.316	0.315
	H	4-122 (2.0) Diesel	45	45	NA	1.7760	0.0016–0.0029	0.0018–0.0031	0.3138	0.3138
	R	4-140 (2.3)	45	45.5	182 @ 1.10	1.490	0.0018	0.0023	0.3415	0.3411
	X	4-140 (2.3)	45	45.5	182 @ 1.10	1.490	0.0018	0.0023	0.3415	0.3411
	S	4-140 (2.3)	45	45.5	182 @ 1.10	1.490	0.0018	0.0023	0.3415	0.3411
1986	9	4-116 (1.9)	45	45	200 @ 1.09	1.440–1.480	0.0008–0.0027	0.0018–0.0037	0.316	0.315
	J	4-116 (1.9)	45	45	216 @ 1.016	1.440–1.480	0.0008–0.0027	0.0018–0.0037	0.316	0.315

VALVE SPECIFICATIONS

Year	VIN	No. Cylinder Displacement cu. in. (liter)	Seat Angle (deg.)	Face Angle (deg.)	Spring Test Pressure (lbs.)	Spring Installed Height (in.)	Stem-to-Guide Clearance (in.)		Stem Diameter (in.)	
							Intake	Exhaust	Intake	Exhaust
1986	H	4-122 (2.0) Diesel	45	45	NA	1.7760	0.0016–0.0029	0.0018–0.0031	0.3138	0.3138
	R	4-140 (2.3)	45	45.5	182 @ 1.10	1.40	0.0018	0.0023	0.316	0.315
	X	4-140 (2.3)	45	45.5	182 @ 1.10	1.40	0.018	0.0023	0.316	0.315
1987	9	4-116 (1.9)	45	45	200 @ 1.09	1.44–1.48	0.0008–0.0027	0.0018–0.0037	0.316	0.315
	J	4-116 (1.9)	45	45	216 @ 1.016	1.44–1.48	0.0008–0.0027	0.0018–0.0037	0.316	0.315
	H	4-122 (2.0) Diesel	45	45	NA	1.7760	0.0016–0.0029	0.0018–0.0031	0.3138	0.3138
	R	4-140 (2.3)	45	45.5	182 @ 1.10	1.49	0.0018	0.0023	0.316	0.315
	X	4-140 (2.3)	45	45.5	182 @ 1.10	1.49	0.0018	0.0023	0.316	0.315
1988-89	9	4-116 (1.9)	45	46	200 @ 1.09	1.44–1.48	0.0008–0.0027	0.0018–0.0037	0.317	0.315
	J	4-116 (1.9)	45	46	216 @ 1.016	1.44–1.48	0.0008–0.0027	0.0018–0.0037	0.317	0.315
	X	4-140 (2.3)	44.5	44.5	181 @ 1.07	1.49	0.0018	0.0023	0.3415–0.3422	0.3411–0.3418
	S	4-140 (2.3)	44.5	44.5	181 @ 1.07	1.49	0.0018	0.0023	0.3415–0.3422	0.3411–0.3418
	4	6-232 (3.8)	46	46		2.02	0.0010–0.0028	0.0015–0.0033	0.3423–0.3415	0.3118–0.3410

PISTON AND RING SPECIFICATIONS
All measurments are given in inches.

Year	VIN	No. Cylinder Displacement cu. in. (liter)	Piston Clearance	Ring Gap			Ring Side Clearance		
				Top Compression	Bottom Compression	Oil Control	Top Compression	Bottom Compression	Oil Control
1982	2	4-98 (1.6)	.0012–.0020	0.012–0.020	0.021–0.020	0.016–0.055	0.001–0.003	0.002–0.003	Snug
1983	2	4-98 (1.6)	.0018–.0026	0.012–0.020	0.021–0.020	0.016–0.055	0.001–0.003	0.002–0.003	Snug
1984	2	4-98 (1.6)	.0018–.0026	0.012–0.020	0.012–0.020	0.016–0.055	0.001–0.003	0.002–0.003	Snug
	4	4-98 (1.6)	.0018–.0026	0.012–0.020	0.012–0.020	0.016–0.055	0.001–0.003	0.002–0.003	Snug
	5	4-98 (1.6)	.0018–.0026	0.012–0.020	0.012–0.020	0.016–0.055	0.001–0.003	0.002–0.003	Snug
	H	4-122 (2.0) Diesel	.0013–.0020	0.0079–0.0157	0.0079–0.0157	0.0079–0.0157	0.0020–0.0035	0.0016–0.0031	Snug
	R	4-140 (2.3)	.0013–.0021	0.008–0.016	0.008–0.016	0.015–0.055	0.002–0.004	0.002–0.004	Snug

PISTON AND RING SPECIFICATIONS
All measurments are given in inches.

Year	VIN	No. Cylinder Displacement cu. in. (liter)	Piston Clearance	Ring Gap Top Compression	Ring Gap Bottom Compression	Ring Gap Oil Control	Ring Side Clearance Top Compression	Ring Side Clearance Bottom Compression	Oil Control
1985	2	4-98 (1.6)	.0018–.0026	0.012–0.020	0.012–0.020	0.016–0.055	0.001–0.003	0.002–0.003	Snug
	4	4-98 (1.6)	.0018–.0026	0.012–0.020	0.012–0.020	0.016–0.055	0.001–0.003	0.002–0.003	Snug
	5	4-98 (1.6)	.0018–.0026	0.012–0.020	0.012–0.020	0.016–0.055	0.001–0.003	0.002–0.003	Snug
	7	4-98 (1.6)	.0018–.0026	0.012–0.020	0.012–0.020	0.016–0.055	0.001–0.003	0.002–0.003	Snug
	8	4-98 (1.6)	.0018–.0026	0.012–0.020	0.012–0.020	0.016–0.055	0.001–0.003	0.002–0.003	Snug
	H	4-122 (2.0) Diesel	.0013–.0020	0.0079–0.0157	0.0079–0.0157	0.0079–0.0157	0.0020–0.0035	0.0016–0.0031	Snug
	R	4-140 (2.3)	.0013–.0021	0.008–0.016	0.008–0.016	0.015–0.055	0.002–0.004	0.002–0.004	Snug
	X	4-140 (2.3)	.0013–.0021	0.008–0.016	0.008–0.016	0.015–0.055	0.002–0.004	0.002–0.004	Snug
	S	4-140 (2.3)	.0013–.0021	0.008–0.016	0.008–0.016	0.015–0.055	0.002–0.004	0.002–0.004	Snug
1986	9	4-116 (1.9)	.0016–.0024	0.010–0.020	0.010–0.020	0.016–0.055	0.0015–0.0032	0.0015–0.0035	Snug
	J	4-116 (1.9)	.0016–.0024	0.010–0.020	0.010–0.020	0.016–0.055	0.0015–0.0032	0.0015–0.0035	Snug
	H	4-122 (2.0) Diesel	.0012–.0020	0.0079–0.0157	0.0079–0.0157	0.0079–0.0157	0.0020–0.0035	0.0016–0.0031	Snug
	R	4-140 (2.3)	.0013–.0021	0.008–0.016	0.008–0.016	0.0015–0.055	0.002–0.004	0.002–0.004	Snug
	X	4-140 (2.3)	.0013–.0021	0.008–0.016	0.008–0.016	0.015–0.055	0.002–0.004	0.002–0.004	Snug
1987	9	4-116 (1.9)	.0016–.0024	0.010–0.020	0.010–0.020	0.016–0.055	0.0015–0.0032	0.0015–0.0035	Snug
	J	4-116 (1.9)	.0016–.0024	0.010–0.020	0.010–0.020	0.016–0.055	0.0015–0.0032	0.0015–0.0035	Snug
	H	4-122 (2.0) Diesel	.0013–.0020	0.0079–0.0157	0.0079–0.0157	0.0079–0.0157	0.0020–0.0035	0.0016–0.0031	Snug
	R	4-140 (2.3)	.0013–.0021	0.008–0.016	0.008–0.016	0.015–0.055	0.002–0.004	0.002–0.004	Snug
	X	4-140 (2.3)	.0013–.0021	0.008–0.016	0.008–0.016	0.015–0.055	0.002–0.004	0.002–0.004	Snug
1988-89	9	4-116 (1.9)	0.0016–0.0024	0.010–0.020	0.010–0.020	0.016–0.055	0.0015–0.0032	0.0015–0.0035	Snug
	J	4-116 (1.9)	0.0016–0.0024	0.010–0.020	0.010–0.020	0.016–0.055	0.0015–0.0032	0.0015–0.0035	Snug
	X	4-140 (2.3)	0.0012–0.0022	0.008–0.016	0.008–0.016	0.015–0.055	0.002–0.004	0.002–0.004	Snug

PISTON AND RING SPECIFICATIONS
All measurments are given in inches.

Year	VIN	No. Cylinder Displacement cu. in. (liter)	Piston Clearance	Ring Gap			Ring Side Clearance		
				Top Compression	Bottom Compression	Oil Control	Top Compression	Bottom Compression	Oil Control
1988–89	S	4-140 (2.3)	0.0012–0.0022	0.008–0.016	0.008–0.016	0.015–0.055	0.002–0.004	0.002–0.004	Snug
	4	6-232 (3.8)	0.0014–0.0032	0.010–0.020	0.010–0.020	0.015–0.055	0.0016–0.0037	0.0016–0.0037	Snug

TORQUE SPECIFICATIONS
All readings in ft. lbs.

Year	VIN	No. Cylinder Displacement cu. in. (liter)	Cylinder Head Bolts	Main Bearing Bolts	Rod Bearing Bolts	Crankshaft Pulley Bolts	Flywheel Bolts	Manifold		Spark Plugs
								Intake	Exhaust	
1982	2	4-98 (1.6)	①	67–80	19–25	74–90	59–69	12–15②	15–20	17–22
1983	2	4-98 (1.6)	①	67–80	19–25	74–90	59–69	12–15②	15–20	8–15
1984	2	4-98 (1.6)	①	67–80	19–25	74–90	59–69	12–15②	15–20	8–15
	4	4-98 (1.6)	①	67–80	19–25	74–90	59–69	12–15②	15–20	8–15
	5	4-98 (1.6)	①	67–80	19–25	74–90	59–69	12–15②	15–20	8–15
	H	4-122 (2.0) Diesel	①	61–65	51–54	115–123	130–137	12–16	16–19③	—
	R	4-140 (2.3)	④	51–66	21–26	140–170	54–64	15–23	20–30③	5–10
1985	2	4-98 (1.6)	①	67–80	19–25	74–90	59–69	12–15②	15–20	8–15
	4	4-98 (1.6)	①	67–80	19–25	74–90	59–69	12–15②	15–20	8–15
	5	4-98 (1.6)	①	67–80	19–25	74–90	59–69	12–15②	15–20	8–15
	8	4-98 (1.6)	①	67–80	19–25	74–90	59–69	12–15②	15–20	8–15
	7	4-98 (1.6)	①	67–80	19–25	74–90	59–69	12–15②	15–20	8–15
	H	4-122 (2.0) Diesel	①	61–65	51–54	115–123	130–137	12–16	16–19③	
	R	4-140 (2.3)	④	51–66	21–26	140–170	54–64	15–23	20–30③	5–10
	X	4-140 (2.3)	④	51–66	21–26	140–170	54–64	15–23	20–30③	5–10
	S	4-140 (2.3)	④	51–66	21–26	140–170	54–64	15–23	20–30③	5–10
1986	9	4-166 (1.9)	①	67–80	19–25	74–90	59–69	12–15	15–20	8–15
	J	4-116 (1.9)	①	67–80	19–25	74–90	59–69	12–15	15–20	8–15
	H H	4-122 (2.0) Diesel	①	61–65	51–54	115–123	130–137	12–16	16–19③	5–10
	R	4-140 (2.3)	④	51–56	21–26	140–170	54–64	15–23	20–30③	5–10
	X	4-140 (2.3)	④	51–66	21–26	140–170	54–64	15–23	20–30③	5–10
1987	9	4-116 (1.9)	①	67–80	19–25	74–90	59–69	12–15	15–20	8–15
	J	4-116 (1.9)	①	67–80	19–25	74–90	59–69	12–15	15–20	8–15
	H	4-122 (2.0) Diesel	①	61–65	51–54	115–123	130–137	12–16	16–19③	5–10
	R	4-140 (2.3)	④	51–66	21–26	140–170	54–64	15–23	20–30③	5–10
	X	4-140 (2.3)	④	51–66	21–26	140–170	54–64	15–23	20–30③	5–10

TORQUE SPECIFICATIONS
All readings in ft. lbs.

Year	VIN	No. Cylinder Displacement cu. in. (liter)	Cylinder Head Bolts	Main Bearing Bolts	Rod Bearing Bolts	Crankshaft Pulley Bolts	Flywheel Bolts	Manifold Intake	Manifold Exhaust	Spark Plugs
1988-89	9	4-116 (1.9)	①	67–80	19–25	74–90	59–69	12–15	15–20	8–15
	J	4-116 (1.9)	①	67–80	19–25	74–90	59–69	12–15	15–20	8–15
	X	4-140 (2.3)	④	51–66	21–26	140–170	54–64	15–23	③	5–10
	S	4-140 (2.3)	④	51–66	21–26	140–170	54–64	15–23	③	5–10
	4	6-232 (3.8)	①	65–81	31–36	93–121	54–64	⑤	16–24	5–11

① Please refer to "Cylinder Head" procedure in text for instructions
② Manifold stud nuts: 12–13 ft. lbs.
③ Tighten in two stages: 5–7 ft. lbs., then 20–30 ft. lbs.
④ Tighten in two steps: 52–59 ft. lbs. and then the final torque of 70–76 ft. lbs.
⑤ Tighten in three steps:
   Step 1: 7 ft. lbs.
   Step 2: 15 ft. lbs.
   Step 3: 24 ft. lbs.

BRAKE SPECIFICATIONS
All measurements in inches unless noted

Year	Model	Lug Nut Torque (ft. lbs.)	Master Cylinder Bore	Brake Disc Minimum Thickness	Brake Disc Maximum Runout	Standard Brake Drum Diameter	Minimum Lining Thickness Front	Minimum Lining Thickness Rear
1982	Escort, Lynx	80-105	.828	.940	.003	7.090①	0.48	1.26②
	EXP, LN7	80-105	.828	.940	.003	8.000	0.48	1.34
1983	Escort, Lynx	80-105	.828	.940	.003	7.090①	0.48	1.26②
	EXP, LN7	80-105	.828	.940	.003	8.000	0.48	1.34
1984	Escort, Lynx	80-105	.828	.940	.003	7.090①	0.48	1.26②
	EXP, LN7	80-105	.828	.940	.003	8.000	0.48	1.34
	Tempo, Topaz	80-105	.828	.882	.003	8.000	0.48	1.34
1985	Escort, Lynx	80-105	.828	.940	.003	7.090①	0.48	1.26②
	EXP	80-105	.828	.940	.003	8.000①	0.48	1.34
	Tempo, Topaz	80-105	.828	.882	.003	8.000	0.48	1.34
1986	Escort, Lynx	80-105	.828	.940	.003	7.090①	0.48	1.26②
	Tempo, Topaz	80-105	.828	.882	.003	8.000	0.48	1.34
1987	Escort, Lynx	80-105	.828	.940	.003	7.090①	0.48	1.26②
	Tempo, Topaz	80-105	.828	.882	.003	8.000	0.48	1.34
1988-89	Escort	80-105	.828	.940	.003	7.090①	0.48	1.26②
	Tempo, Topaz	80-105	.828	.882	.003	8.000	0.48	1.34
	Continental	80-105	—	.974	.002	—	0.25	1.23

① 4/5–door models—8.000
② 4/5–door models—1.34

WHEEL ALIGNMENT

Year	Model	Caster Range (deg.)	Caster Preferred Setting (deg.)	Camber Range (deg.)	Camber Preferred Setting (deg.)	Toe-in (in.)	Wheel Turning Angle (deg.)
1982	Escort, Lynx, EXP, LN7	35/64P-2 1/20P	1 1/3①	②	③	1/50N-11/50P	Left 20.0 Right 17.0
1983	Escort, Lynx, EXP, LN7	35/64P-2 1/20P	1 1/3①	②	③	1/50N-11/50P	Left 20.0 Right 17.0
1984	Escort, Lynx, EXP	21/32P-2 5/32P	1 2/5①	②	③	1/64N-7/32P	Left 20.0 Right 18.2
	Tempo, Topaz EXP	35/64P-2 1/20P	1 1/3①	④	⑤	1/32N-7/32P	Left 20.0 Right 18.2
1985	Escort, Lynx, EXP	1 11/16P-3 3/16P	2 7/16①	⑥	⑦	7/32N-1/64P	Left 20.0 Right 18.2
	Tempo/Topaz Sport Coupe	1 5/8P-3 1/8P	2 3/8①	⑧	⑨	7/32N-1/64P	Left 20.0 Right 18.2
	Tempo/Topaz exc. Sport Coupe	1 11/16P-3 3/16P	2 7/16①	⑩	⑪	7/32N-1/64P	Left 20.0 Right 18.4
1986	Escort, Lynx, EXP	1 11/16P-3 3/16P	2 7/16①	⑥	⑦	7/32N-1/64P	Left 20.0 Right 18.2
	Tempo/Topaz Sport Coupe	1 5/8P-3 1/8P	2 3/8①	⑧	⑨	7/32N-1/64P	Left 20.0 Right 18.2
	Tempo/Topaz exc. Sport Coupe	1 11/16P-3 3/16P	2 7/16①	⑩	⑪	7/32N-1/64P	Left 20.0 Right 18.4
1987	Escort, Lynx, EXP	1 5/8P-3 1/8P	2 3/8①	⑫	⑬	0-1/4P	Left 20.0 Right 18.2
	Tempo, Topaz Sport Coupe	1 11/16P-3 3/16P	2 7/16①	⑭	⑮	0-1/4P	Left 20.0 Right 18.2
1988-89	Escort, EXP	1 5/8P-3 1/8P	2 3/8	⑯	⑰	1/2N-0	15 3/8
	Tempo, Topaz	1 11/16P-3 3/16P	2 7/16	⑱	⑲	1/2N-0	⑳
	Continental	4-5 5/8	4 13/16	㉑	㉒	㉓	15 1/2

① Caster and camber are not adjustable. Measurements must be made by turning the wheel left and right through their respective sweep angles.

② Left: 1 2/5P-2 9/10P
Right: 61/64P-2 29/64P

③ Left: 2 5/32P
Right: 1 11/16P

④ Left: 1 1/8P-2 5/8P
Right: 11/16P-2 1/5

⑤ Left: 1 29/32P
Right: 1 1/2P

⑥ Left: 5/8P-2 1/8P
Right: 3/16P-1 11/16P

⑦ Left: 1 3/8P
Right: 15/16P

⑧ Left: 7/16P-1 15/16P
Right: 0-1 1/2P

⑨ Left: 1 3/16P
Right: 3/4P

⑩ Left: 13/32P-1 29/32P
Right: 1/32N-1 15/32P

⑪ Left: 1 5/32P
Right: 23/32P

⑫ Left: 5/16P-1 13/16P
Right: 0-1 1/2P

⑬ Left: 1 1/16P
Right: 3/4P

⑭ Left: 21/32P-2 5/32P
Right: 7/32P-1 23/32P

⑮ Left: 1 13/32P
Right: 31/32P

⑯ Left: 3/8P-1 7/8P
Right: 0-1 1/2P

⑰ Left: 1 1/8P
Right: 3/4P

⑱ Left: 21/32P
Right: 1 21/32P

⑲ Left: 1 13/32
Right: 31/32

⑳ Left: 14 21/32
Right: 15 3/32

㉑ Front: 1 1/2N-5/16N
Rear: 2N-5/8N

㉒ Front: 7/8N
Rear: 1 15/16

㉓ Front: 21/32N-1/16P
Rear: 1/16N-7/16

TUNE-UP PROCEDURES

Ignition Timing

ADJUSTMENT

NOTE: If the vehicle (1.6L or 1.9L engines) is equipped with a barometric pressure switch (12A243), disconnect it from the ignition module and place a jumper wire across the pins at the ignition module connector (yellow and black wires). On 1.6L models equipped with EFI (electronic fuel injection), disconnect the single wire connector near the distributor prior to timing operation.

1. Timing marks on 1.6L and 1.9L engines consist of a notch on the crankshaft pulley and a graduated scale molded into the camshaft drive belt cover. The number of degrees before or after TDC (top dead center) represented by each mark can be interpreted according to the decal affixed to the top of the belt cover (emission decal).

2. Timing marks on 2.3L engines are located on the flywheel edge (manual transaxle) or flywheel face (automatic transaxle) and are visible through a slot in the transaxle case at the back of the engine. A cover plate retained by 2 screws must be removed to view the timing marks on manual cars. Each mark (small graduation) equals 2 degrees. Early automatic cars have timing marks punched on the fly-

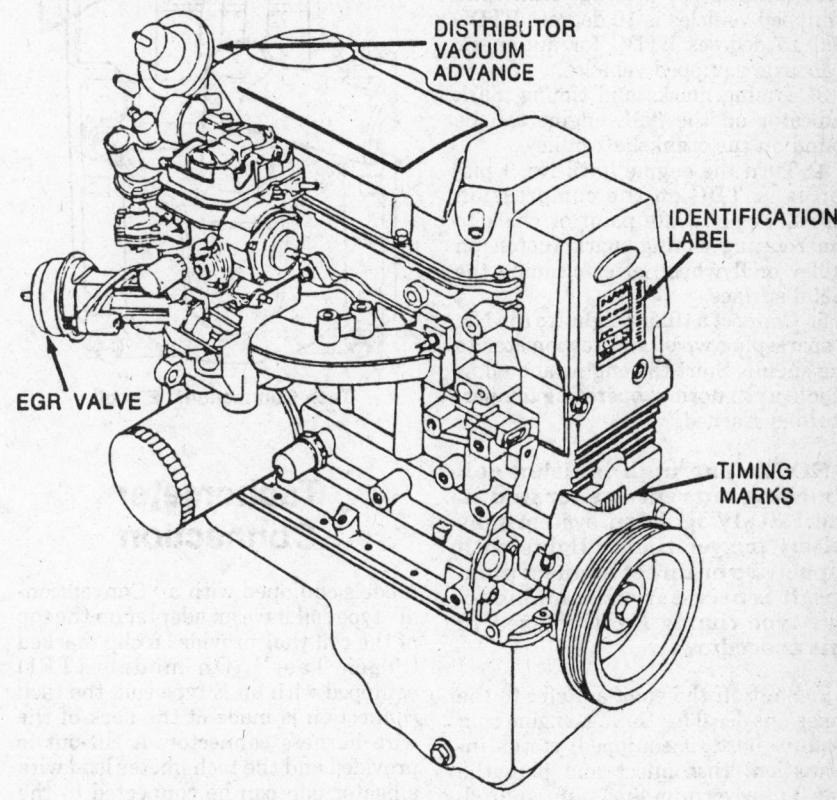

1.6L and 1.9L engine timing marks are located on the front cover

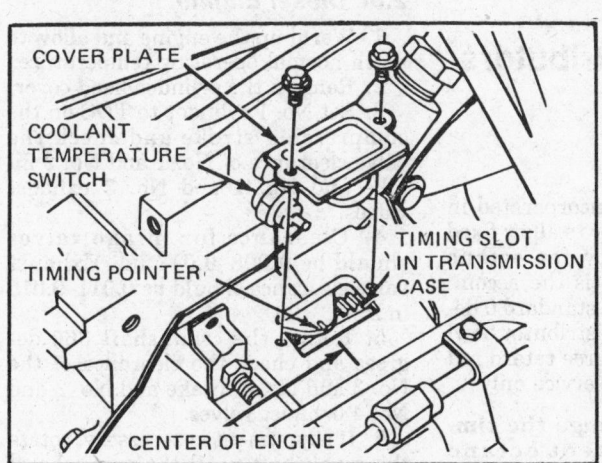

TIMING LOCATION FOR MTX

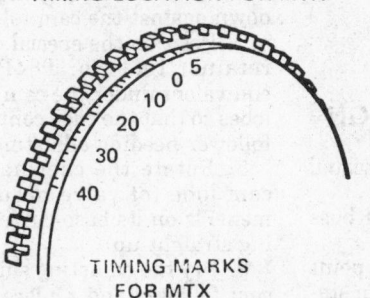

TIMING MARKS FOR MTX

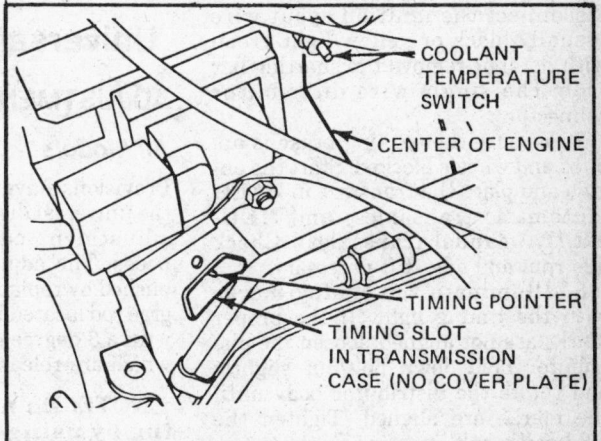

TIMING LOCATION FOR ATX

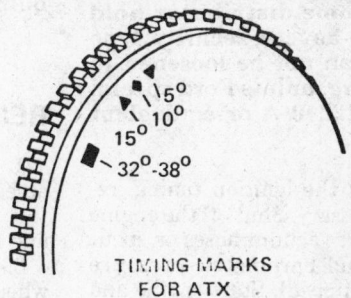

TIMING MARKS FOR ATX

Tempo/Topaz timing marks

wheel, the marks are 5 degrees apart. The required degree mark should align with the timing slot pointer. Unless the emission decal specifies otherwise, timing for manual transaxle equipped vehicles is 10 degrees BTDC and 15 degrees BTDC for automatic transaxle equipped vehicles.

3. Timing marks and timing mark indicator on the 3.8L engine can be found on the crankshaft pulley.

4. Turn the engine until No. 1 piston is at TDC on the compression stroke. Apply white paint or chalk to the rotating timing mark (notch on pulley or flywheel) after cleaning the metal surface.

5. Connect a timing light (to the No. 1 spark plug wire) and tachometer to the engine. Start the engine and allow to idle until normal operating temperature is reached.

NOTE: The high ignition coil charging currents generated in the EEC-IV ignition system may falsely trigger timing lights with capacitive or direct connect pickups. It is necessary that an inductive type timing light be used in this procedure.

6. Shut off the engine. Refer to the emissions decal for timing, engine rpm vacuum hose (if equipped) status information. Disconnect and plug the distributor vacuum line(s) if required. On vehicles equipped with 1.6L EFI, 1.9L, 2.3L and 3.8L engines (EEC-IV), disconnect the ignition spout wire (usually black or yellow/light green with dots) or remove the shorting bar from the single wire distributor connector.

7. Be sure the parking brake is applied and wheels blocked. Start the engine and place the transaxle in **PARK** (automatic transaxles) and **NEUTRAL** (manual transaxles). Check idle rpm and adjust if necessary.

8. Illuminate the timing marks with the timing light. If the proper marks are not aligned, loosen the distributor hold down bolt/nut slightly and rotate the distributor body until the marks are aligned. Tighten the hold down bolt.

NOTE: Some distributor hold down bolts have a security type head and can not be loosened to adjust timing, unless Ford special tool T82L–12270–A or equivalent is available.

9. Recheck the ignition timing, readjust if necessary. Shut off the engine and reconnect vacuum hoses or spout connector and barometric pressure switch (if equipped). Start engine and readjust idle rpm if necessary.

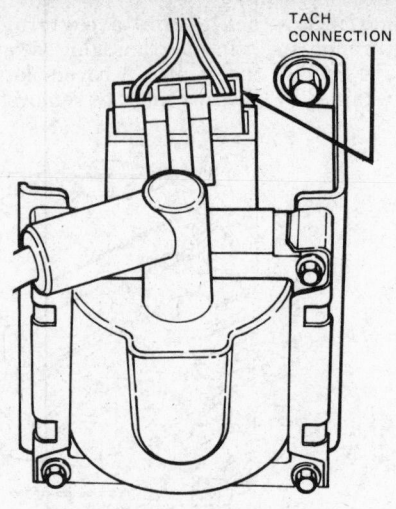

Tach Connection, "E" coil

Tachometer Connection

Models equipped with a "Conventional" type coil have an adapter on the top of the coil that provides a clip marked "Tach Test". On models (TFI) equipped with an E type coil, the tach connection is made at the back of the wire harness connector. A cut-out is provided and the tachometer lead wire alligator clip can be connected to the dark green/yellow dotted wire of the electrical harness plug.

Universal Distributors

ADJUSTMENTS

All Models

Provisions have been incorporated in the universal distributor to allow fixed adjustment capability for octane needs. The adjustment is the accomplished by replacing the standard 0 degree rod located in the distributor bowl with a 3 degree or 6 degree retard rod which are released for service only.

NOTE: Do not change the timing by using different octane rods, as Federal Emission Requirements will be affected.

Octane Rod

REMOVAL & INSTALLATION

1. Remove cap and rotor for visual access.
2. Locate octane adjustments boss and remove retaining screw.
3. Slide rod/grommet out to a point where rod can be disengaged from stator retaining post.

NOTE: Retain grommet for use with new rod.

4. Install grommet on new service rod and reinstall in the distributor, making sure to capture the stator post.
5. Install retaining screw and tighten to 15–35 inch lbs.
6. Replace cap and rotor. Tighten caps screws to 33–43 inch lbs. and rotor to 25–35 inch lbs.

NOTE: Except for the cap, rotor, TFI-IV module, O-ring and octane rod, no other distributor assembly parts are replaceable. There is no calibration required with the universal distributor.

Valve Lash

The intake and exhaust valves are driven by the camshaft, working through hydraulic lash adjusters and stamped rocker arms (1.6L and 1.9L engines) or through hydraulic lifters, tappets, pushrods and rocker arms (2.3L and 3.8L engines). The hydraulic lash adjusters or lifters eliminate the need for periodic valve lash adjustments or maintenance. Hydraulic valve components can be best maintained through regular and scheduled oil and filter changes.

ADJUSTMENT

2.0L Diesel Engine

1. Warm up the engine and allow to reach normal operating temperature.
2. Remove the cylinder head cover.
3. Set No. 1 cylinder to TDC on the compression stroke and check the valve clearance of No. 1 and No. 2 intake and No. 1 and No. 3 exhaust valves.
4. Clearance for intake valves should be 0.008–0.011 in.. Exhaust valve clearance should be 0.011–0.015 in..
5. Rotate the crankshaft 360 degrees and check the clearance of the No. 3 and No. 4 intake and No. 2 and No. 4 exhaust valves.
6. If adjustment is necessary, rotate the crankshaft until the cam lobe of the valve requiring adjustment is down against the cam follower.
7. Position the special cam follower retainer tool No. T84P-6513-B or equivalent under the cam between the lobes so that the edge contacts the cam follower needing adjustment.
8. Rotate the camshaft until the cam lobe (of valve needing adjustment) is on its base circle (lobe pointing straight up).
9. Pry the adjusting shim out of the cam follower and replace with a new shim.

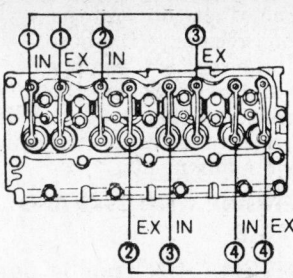

Diesel engine valve adjustment sequence

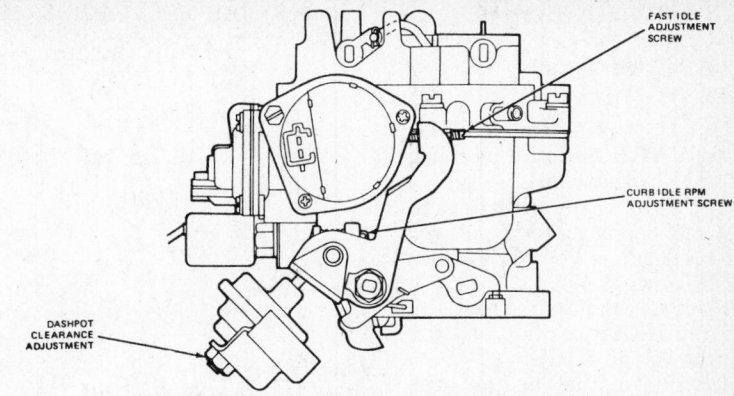

1.6L fast idle and curb idle adjustment points

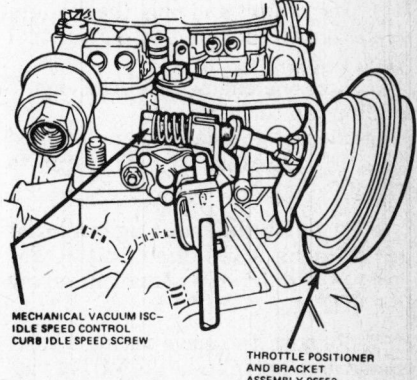

Fast idle and throttle stop adjustment points

NOTE: Valve shims are available in thicknesses ranging from 3.40mm to 4.60mm. If the valve was too tight or loose, install a shim of the appropriate size. Shim thickness is stamped on the valve shim. Install the shim with the numbers down to avoid wearing the numbers off.

10. Rotate the camshaft until the lobe is down and remove the retainer tool.

11. Recheck the valve clearance by repeating the previous steps.

12. Install the engine cover using a new gasket. Tighten the retaining bolts to 5–7 ft. lbs.

Idle Speed and Mixture Gasoline Engines

CURB IDLE ADJUSTMENT

Carbureted Engines

NOTE: Most carburetor mixture adjustments are factory set and are designed to reduce engine emissions. Mixture adjustments should be made only if absolutely necessary and should be checked on a machine as soon as possible to see if the emission level is satisfactory. A tachometer must be used while making any idle rpm adjustments. Refer to the proceeding section for tachometer connecting instructions. Refer to emissions decal for idle speed and specific instructions.

1.6L ENGINE WITH 740–2V
Without Idle Speed Control

1. Place the transaxle in **NEUTRAL** or **PARK**, firmly set the parking brake and block the wheels.
2. Start the engine and allow to reach normal operating temperature.
3. Disconnect and plug the vacuum hose at the thermactor air control valve bypass section.
4. Place the fast idle adjustment screw on the second highest step of the fast idle cam. Run engine until cooling fan comes on.

5. Slightly depress the throttle to allow the fast idle cam to rotate. Place the transaxle in the gear specified on the Vehicle Emission Control Label, and check/adjust the curb idle rpm to specification.

NOTE: Engine cooling fan must be running when checking curb idle rpm. Use a jumper wire if necessary.

6. Return the transaxle to **NEUTRAL** or **PARK**. Rev the engine momentarily. Place transaxle in specified position and recheck curb idle rpm. Readjust if required.
7. If the vehicle is equipped with a dashpot, check/adjust clearance to specification.
8. Remove the plug from the hose at the thermactor air control valve bypass section and reconnect.
9. If the vehicle is equipped with an automatic transaxle and curb idle adjustment is more than 50 rpm, an automatic transaxle linkage adjustment may be necessary.

1.6L ENGINE WITH 740–2V
With Mechanical Vacuum Idle
Speed ControL (ISC)

1. Place the transaxle in **NEUTRAL** or **PARK**, firmly set the parking brake and block the wheels.
2. Start the engine and allow to reach normal operating temperature.
3. Disconnect and plug the vacuum hose at the thermactor air control valve bypass section.
4. Place the fast idle adjustment screw on the second highest step of the fast idle cam. Run the engine until cooling fan comes on.
5. Slightly depress the throttle to allow fast idle cam to rotate. Place the transaxle in **DRIVE** if equipped with automatic transaxle (fan on) and check curb idle rpm to specification.

NOTE: Engine cooling fan must be running when checking curb idle rpm.

6. If adjustment is required, perform the folllowing:

a. Place the transaxle in **PARK** or **NEUTRAL** and deactivate the ISC by removing the vacuum hose at the ISC and plugging the hose.

b. Turn ISC adjusting screw until ISC plunger is clear of the throttle lever.

c. Place the transaxle in **DRIVE**, and if rpm is not at the ISC retracted speed (fan on), adjust rpm by turning the throttle stop adjusting screw.

d. Place the transaxle in **PARK** remove plug from the ISC vacuum line and reconnect to ISC.

e. Place the transaxle in **DRIVE** if rpm is not at the curb idle speed (fan on), adjust by turning the ISC adjustment screw.

7. Place transaxle in **NEUTRAL** or **PARK**. Rev the engine momentarily. Place the transaxle in specified position and recheck curb idle rpm. Readjust if required.

8. Remove the plug from the thermactor air control valve bypass section hose and reconnect.

9. If the vehicle is equipped with an automatic transaxle and curb idle adjustment is more than 50 rpm, an automatic transaxle linkage adjustment may be necessary.

1.6L AND 1.9L ENGINES WITH 740–2V

Vacuum Operated Throttle Modulator (VOTM)

1. Place the transaxle in **NEUTRAL** or **PARK**, set the parking brake and block the wheels.
2. Start the engine and allow to reach normal operating temperature.
3. To check/adjust VOTM rpm, perform the following:
   a. Place air conditioning heat sector in the **HEAT** position and the blower switch on **HIGH**.
   b. Disconnect the vacuum hose from VOTM and plug, install a slave vacuum hose from the intake manifold vacuum to the VOTM.
4. Disconnect and plug the vacuum hose at the thermactor air control valve bypass section.
5. Run the engine until the engine cooling fan comes on.
6. Place the transaxle in specified gear, and check/adjust VOTM rpm to specification.

NOTE: Engine cooling fan must be running when checking VOTM rpm. Adjust rpm by turning screw on VOTM.

7. Remove the slave vacuum hose. Remove the plug from the VOTM vacuum hose and reconnect the hose to the VOTM.
8. Return the intake manifold vacuum supply source to original location.
9. Remove the plug from the vacuum hose at the thermactor air control valve bypass section and reconnect.

1.9L ENGINES WITH 740–2V AND 5740–2V

Mechanical Vacuum Idle Speed Control (ISC)

1. Connect a tachometer and timing light to the engine. Place the transaxle in **NEUTRAL** or **PARK**, and the Air Conditioner-Heater selector in the **OFF** position. Set the parking brake and block the wheels.
2. Run the engine until normal operating temperature is reached.
3. Check the engine ignition timing. Adjust as necessary.
4. Disconnect and plug the vacuum hose at the thermactor air control bypass.
5. Place the fast idle adjusting screw on the second step of the fast idle cam. Run the engine until the cooling fan comes on.
6. Depress the throttle slightly. The engine cooling fan must be on to allow the fast idle cam to rotate. Place the transaxle in **DRIVE**. Check idle rpm, adjust if necessary.
7. If adjustment is required; place the transaxle in **PARK** or **NEU-**

FAST IDLE ADJUSTMENT SCREW

THROTTLE STOP
ADJUSTMENT SCREW

1.6L with idle speed control (ISC) adjustment points

TRAL. Deactivate the ISC (idle speed control) by removing the vacuum hose at the ISC and plugging the hose.
8. If the full stroke rpm is not within specifications, adjust the rpm by turning the full stroke speed adjusting screw.
9. Connect a suitable hand vacuum pump to the ISC and supply enough vacuum to retract the ISC plunger clear of the full stroke adjusting screw.
10. Place the transaxle in **DRIVE** or **NEUTRAL.** If the throttle stop rpm is not to specification, adjust by turning the throttle stop adjusting screw.
11. Adjust the dashpot, if necessary at this point; turn the engine off and make sure the ISC plunger is retracted.
12. Depress the dashpot plunger into the dashpot assembly. Measure the distance between the throttle lever pad and the dashpot plunger. Adjust to specification by loosening the dashpot lock nut and turning the dashpot assembly. When adjustment is completed, tighten the locknut. Restart the engine and allow it to reach normal operating temperature with the cooling fan on.
13. Place the transaxle in **PARK** or **NEUTRAL**, and remove the vacuum hand pump from the ISC. Remove the plug from the vacuum line and reconnect the ISC.
14. Place the transaxle in **DRIVE** or **NEUTRAL** and check idle rpm. If rpm is not within specification (cooling fan on), adjust by turning the ISC curb idle adjusting screw. The plug must be removed from the back of the unit during adjustment. Reinstall plug after adjustment is completed.
15. Place the transaxle in **PARK** or **NEUTRAL** and increase the engine speed momentarily. Place the transaxle in **DRIVE** or **NEUTRAL** if manual and recheck idle rpm. Readjust if necessary.
16. Remove the plug from the

thermactor air control bypass section hose and reconnect the hose.
17. If the vehicle is equipped with an automatic transaxle and the curb idle requires more than a 50 rpm adjustment, refer to the Automatic transaxle Linkage Adjustment.

2.3L ENGINE WITH 1949 AND 6149 FB

NOTE: A/C-ON rpm is non-adjustable. TSP-OFF rpm is not required. Verify that TSP plunger extends with ignition key in the ON position.

1. Place the transaxle in **NEUTRAL** or **PARK**, set the parking brake and block the wheels.
2. Disconnect the throttle kicker vacuum line and plug.
3. Bring the engine to normal operating temperature (cooling fan should cycle).
4. Place the air conditioner selector in the **OFF** position.
5. Place gear selector in specified position.
6. Activate the cooling fan by grounding the control wire with a jumper wire.
7. Check/adjust curb idle rpm as required. If adjustment is required, turn curb idle adjusting screw.
8. Place the transaxle in **NEUTRAL** or **PARK**. Increase the engine speed momentarily. Place the transaxle in specified position and recheck curb idle rpm. Readjust if required.
9. Reconnect the cooling fan wiring.
10. Turn the ignition key to the **OFF** position.
11. Reconnect the vacuum line to the throttle kicker.
12. If the vehicle is equipped with an automatic transaxle and curb idle adjustment exceeds 50 rpm, an automatic transaxle linkagae adjustment may be necessary.
13. Remove all test equipment and reinstall the air cleaner assembly.

2.3L ENGINE WITH 1949 AND 6149 FB

TSP Off RPM

NOTE: This adjustment is not required as part of a normal engine idle RPM check/adjustment. If engine continues to run after ignition key is turned to OFF position.

1. Place the transaxle in **NEUTRAL** or **PARK**, set the parking brake and block the wheels.
2. Start the engine and allow to reach normal operating temperature.
3. Disconnect the throttle kicker vacuum line and plug.
4. Place the air conditioner selector to **OFF** position.

5. Disconnect the electrical lead to the TSP and verify that plunger collapses. Check/adjust engine rpm to specification (600 rpm).

6. Adjust the TSP Off rpm to specification.

7. Shut the engine off, reconnect TSP electrical lead and throttle kicker vacuum line.

2.3L HSC ENGINE WITH 1949
Curb Idle RPM

NOTE: Verify that the TSP plunger extends with the ignition key in the ON position. The idle specifications can be found on the calibration sticker located under the hood.

1. Apply the parking brake, block the drive wheels and place the vehicle in **NEUTRAL**. Remove the air cleaner assembly, disconnect and plug the throttle kicker vacuum line.

2. Start the engine and let it run until it reaches normal operating temperature, then turn the engine off. Connect a suitable tachometer.

3. Place the air conditioner selector in the **OFF** position and activate the cooling fan by grounding the control wire with a jumper wire.

4. Check and adjust the curb idle rpm. If adjustment is required, turn the curb idle adjusting screw. Rev the engine for a minute and recheck the curb idle rpm. readjust the curb idle if necessary.

5. Reconnect the cooling fan wiring. Turn the ignition key to the **OFF** position. Reconnect the vacuum line to the throttle kicker and remove all test equipment.

NOTE: If the vehicle is equipped with an automatic transaxle and the curb idle adjustment still exceeds 50 rpm, the transaxle linkage must be adjusted.

2.3L HSC ENGINE WIH YFA-IV AND YFA-IV FB
Curb Idle RPM

NOTE: A/C-ON rpm is non-adjustable TSP-OFF rpm is not required.

1. Place the transaxle in **NEUTRAL or PARK**.

2. Start the engine and allow to reach normal operating temperature.

3. Place air conditioner selector in the **OFF** position.

4. Place the transaxle in specified position.

5. Check/adjust curb idle rpm. if adjustment is required, turn the hex head adjustment at the rear of the TSP or VOTM/TSP housing.

6. Place the transaxle in **NEU-**

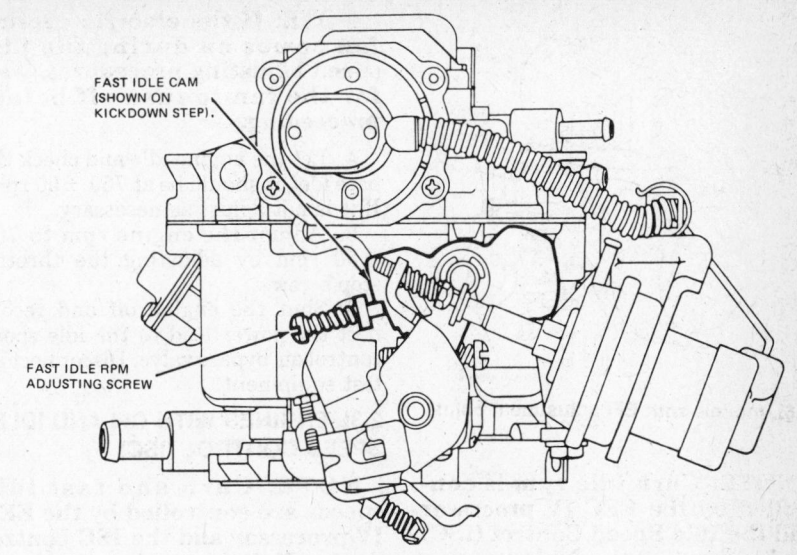

2.3L HSC curb idle adjustment

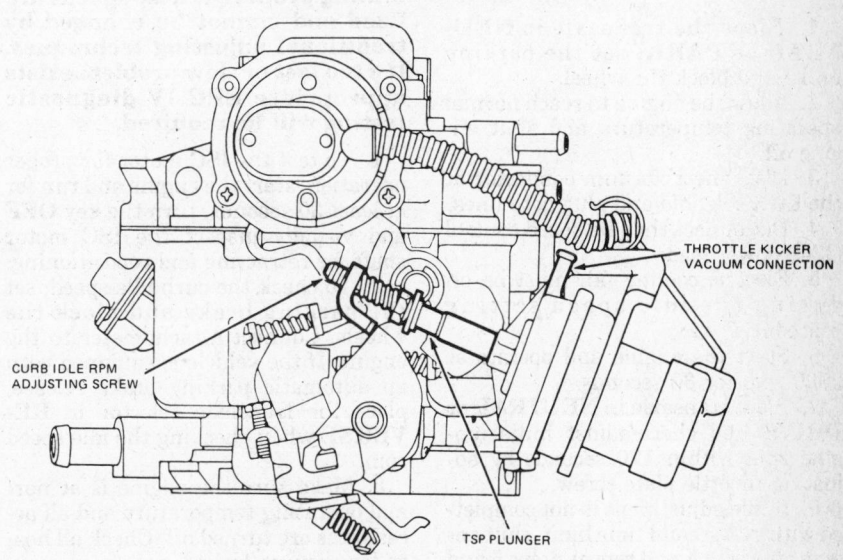

2.3L HSC fast idle adjustment

TRAL or **PARK**. Increase the engine speed momentarily. Place transaxle in specified position and recheck curb idle rpm. Readjust if required.

7. Turn the ignition key to the **OFF** position.

8. Check/adjust the bowl vent setting as follows:

a. Turn ignition key to the **ON** position to activate the TSP (engine not running). Open throttle so that the TSP plunger extends.

b. Secure the choke plate in the wide open position.

c. Open throttle so that the throttle vent lever does not touch the bowl vent rod. Close the throttle to the idle set position and measure the travel of the fuel bowl vent rod from the open throttle position.

d. Travel of the bowl vent rod should be within specification (0.100–0.150 in.).

e. If out of specification, bend the throttle vent lever at notch, to obtain required travel.

9. Remove all test equipment and reinstall air cleaner assembly. Properly tighten the hold down bolt.

Fuel Injected Vehicles

1.6L AND 1.9L ENGINE WITHELECTRONIC FUEL INJECTION (EFI)
Initial Engine RPM Adjustment (ISC DISCONNECTED)

The purpose of this procedure is to provide a means of verifying the initial engine rpm setting with the ISC disconnected. If engine idle rpm is not within specification after performing this procedure, it will be necessary to have 1.6L/1.9L EFI EEC IV diagnostics performed.

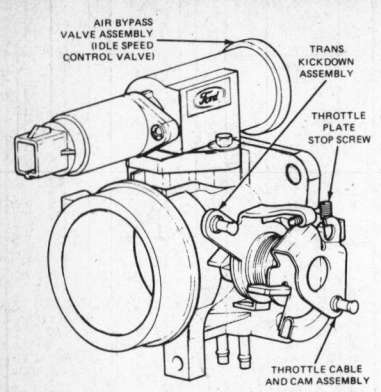

1.6L models with EFI adjustment point

NOTE: Curb idle rpm is controlled by the EEC IV processor and the Idle Speed Control (ISC) device (part of the fuel charging assembly).

1. Place the transaxle in **NEUTRAL** or **PARK**, set the parking brake and block the wheel.

2. Allow the engine to reach normal operating temperature and shut engine off.

3. Disconnect vacuum connector at the EGR solenoid and plug both lines.

4. Disconnect the idle speed control (ISC) power lead.

5. Electric cooling fan must be on during the idle speed setting procedure.

6. Start the engine and operate at 2000 rpm for 60 seconds.

7. Place transaxle in **NEUTRAL** or **DRIVE** and check/adjust initial engine rpm within 120 seconds by adjusting throttle plate screw.

8. If idle adjustment is not completed with 120 second time limit, shut engine off, restart and repeat Steps 6 and 7.

9. If the vehicle is equipped with an automatic transaxle and initial engine rpm adjustment increases or decreases by more than 50 rpm, an automatic transaxle linkage adjustment may be necessary.

10. Turn the engine off and remove the plugs from the EGR vacuum lines at the EGR solenoid and reconnect.

11. Reconnect the idle speed control (ISC) power lead.

2.3L EFI TURBO

1. Apply the parking brake, block the drive wheels and place the vehicle in **NEUTRAL**.

2. Start the engine and let it run until it reaches normal operating temperature, then turn the engine off. Connect a suitable tachometer.

3. Disconnect the idle speed control air bypass valve power lead. Start the engine and run the engine at 2000 rpm for 120 seconds.

NOTE: If the electric cooling fan comes on during the idle speed adjusting procedures, wait for the fan to turn off before proceeding.

4. Let the engine idle and check the base idel, it should be at 750 ± 50 rpm. If it is not adjust as necessary.

5. Adjust the engine rpm to 700 ± 50 rpm by adjusting the throttle stop screw.

6. Shut the engine off and reconnect the power lead to the idle speed control air bypass valve. Disconnect all test equipment.

2.3L ENGINES WITH CFI AND IDLE SPEED CONTROL (ISC)

NOTE: Curb and fast idle speeds are controlled by the EEC IV processor and the ISC control device. If the control system is operating properly, these speeds are fixed and cannot be changed by traditional adjusting techniques. If a too fast or slow problem exists appropriate EEC IV diagnostic testing will be required.

1. To test the ISC motor for proper operation, start the engine and run for at least 30 seconds, turn the key **OFF** and visually inspect the ISC motor shaft for retracting and repositioning.

2. To check the curb idle speed; set the parking brake and block the wheels. Connect a tachometer to the engine. If the vehicle is equipped with an automatic parking brake release, place the transaxle selector in **REVERSE** when checking the idle speed rpm.

3. Make sure the engine is at normal operating temperature and all accessories are turned off. Check all hoses for vacuum leaks.

4. Idle engine for about 120 seconds and check rpm with the transaxle in the proper gear, **DRIVE** or **REVERSE** for automatic, **NEUTRAL** for manual. Place the transaxle back into **NEUTRAL** or **PARK**, engine rpm should increase by approximately 100 rpm.

5. Lightly step on and off the accelerator. The engine rpm should return to specification. If the idle rpm remains high, repeat the sequence. It may take at least 120 seconds for the system to "learn". If correct idle specifications are not present EEC IV system check is required.

1.9L AND 2.3L ENGINES WITH CFI AND DC MOTOR IDLE SPEED CONTROL (ISC)

NOTE: If for any reason the battery is disconnected or the vehicle has to be jump started, it may be necessary to perform this following procedure.

1. Apply the parking brake, block the drive wheels and place the vehicle in **PARK** or **NEUTRAL**.

2. Start the engine and let it run until it reaches normal operating temperature, then turn the engine off. Connect a suitable tachometer.

3. Start the engine and place the transmission in **DRIVE** on automatic transaxle vehicles and **NEUTRAL** on manual transaxle vehicles, let the engine run at idle for 120 seconds. The idle rpm should now return to the specified idle speed (The idle specifications can be found on the calibration sticker located under the hood).

4. Place the transmission in **NEUTRAL** or **PARK** and the engine rpm should increase by approximately 100 rpm. Now lightly step on and off the accelerator. The engine rpm should return to the specified idle speed. If the rpm remains high, repeat the sequence. Remember it may take the the system approximately 2 minutes to adjust. If the vehicle does not respond as previously described, perform the following adjustment. On the 1.9L CFI engine, removal of the CFI assembly is not required to adjust the idle speed at this point in the procedure. On these engines proceed directly to Step 5.

 a. Shut the engine off and remove the air cleaner. Locate the self-test connector and self-test input connector in the engine compartment.

 b. Connect a jumper wire between the self-test input connector and the signal return pin (is the top right terminal) on the self-test connector.

 c. Place the ignition key in the run position and be careful not to start the engine. The ISC plunger will retract, so wait approximately 10 – 15 seconds until the ISC plunger is fully retracted. Turn the ignition key to the off position and wait 10–15 seconds.

 d. Remove the jumper wire and unplug the ISC motor from the wire harness. Now perform the throttle stop adjustment as follows:

 e. Remove the Central Fuel Injection (CFI) assembly from the vehicle.

 f. Use a small punch or equivalent to punch through and remove the aluminum plug which covers the throttle stop adjusting screw.

 g. Remove and replace the throttle stop screw. Reinstall the CFI assembly onto the vehicle.

5. Start the engine and allow to the idle to stabilize. Set the idle rpm to the specifications (listed on the calibration decal located under the hood) on the throttle stop adjusting screw.

6. Shut off the engine. Reconnect the ISC motor wire harness, remove

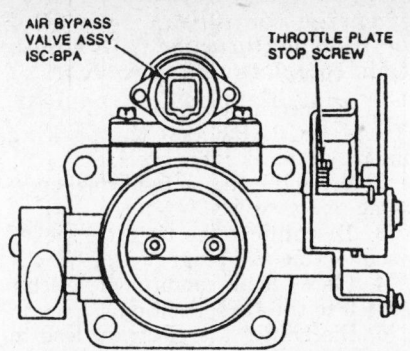

Location of the throttle plate stop screw −3.8L engine

all test equipment and reinstall the air cleaner assembly.

3.8L ENGINE

1. Apply the parking brake, block the drive wheels and place the vehicle in **DRIVE** or **NEUTRAL**.
2. Start the engine and let it run until it reaches normal operating temperature, then turn the engine off. Connect a suitable tachometer.
3. Start the engine and run the engine at 2500 rpm for 30 seconds.
4. Let the engine idle to stabilize.
5. Adjust the engine idle rpm to the specification shown on the vehicle emission control label by adjusting the throttle stop screw.
6. After the idle speed is within specification, repeat Steps 3–5 to ensure that the adjustment is correct.
7. Stop the engine and reconnect the power lead to the idle speed control air bypass valve. Disconnect all test equipment.

DASHPOT CLEARANCE ADJUSTMENT

Carbureted Engines

1.3L AND 1.6L ENGINES

NOTE: If the carburetor is equipped with a dashpot, it must be adjusted if the curb idle speed is adjusted.

1. With the engine **OFF**, push the dashpot plunger in as far as possible and check the clearance between the plunger and the throttle lever pad.

NOTE: Refer to the emissions decal for proper dashpot clearance. If not available, set clearance to 0.138 ± 0.020 in.

2. Adjust the dashpot clearance by loosening the mounting locknut and rotating the dashpot.

—————— **CAUTION** ——————
If the locknut is very tight, remove the mounting bracket, hold it in a suitable device, so that it will not bend, and loosen the locknut. Reinstall bracket and dashpot.

3. After gaining the required clearance, tighten the locknut and recheck adjustment.

FAST IDLE RPM ADJUSTMENTS

Carbureted Engines

1.6L and 1.9L ENGINES

NOTE: Refer to the emissions decal for the specified fast idle speed specification.

1. Place the transaxle in **NEU-TRAL** or **PARK**, set the parking brake and block the wheels.
2. Bring the engine to the normal operating temperature.
3. Disconnect the vacuum hose at the EGR and plug.
4. Place the fast idle adjustment screw on the second highest step of the fast idle cam. Run engine until cooling fan comes on.

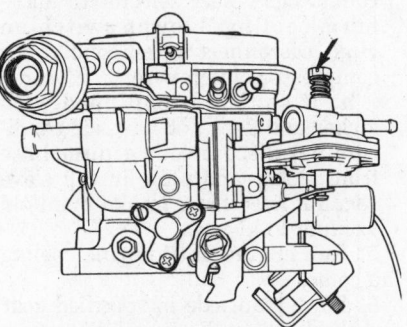

1.6L VOTM idle adjustment point

5. Check/adjust fast idle rpm to specification. If adjustment is required, loosen locknut, adjust and retighten.

NOTE: Engine cooling fan must be running when checking fast idle rpm. Use a jumper wire if necessary.

6. Remove the plug from the EGR hose and reconnect.

2.3L ENGINE WITH 1949 AND 6149 FB

1. Place the transaxle in **NEU-TRAL** or **PARK**, set the parking brake and block the wheels.
2. Bring the engine to normal operating temperature with the carburetor set on second step of fast idle cam.
3. Return the throttle to normal idle position.
4. Place the air conditioer selector switch in the **OFF** position.
5. Disconnect the vacuum hose at the EGR valve and plug.
6. Place the fast idle adjusting screw on the specified step of the fast idle cam.
7. Check/adjust the fast idle rpm to specification.
8. Increase the engine speed momentarily, allowing engine to return to idle and turn ignition key to **OFF** position.
9. Remove the plug from the EGR vacuum hose and reconnect.

2.3L HSC ENGINE WITH YFA-IV AND YFA/IV FB

1. Place transaxle in **NEUTRAL** or **PARK**.

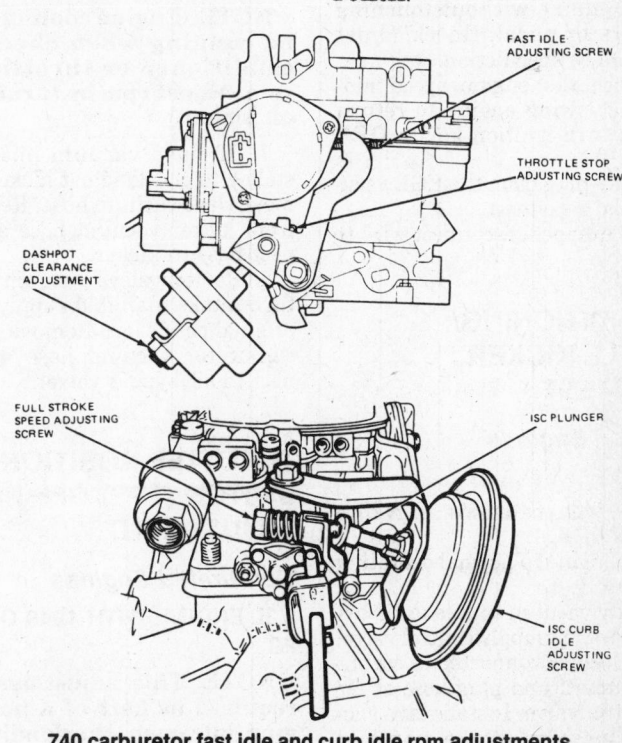

740 carburetor fast idle and curb idle rpm adjustments

2. Bring engine to normal operating temperature.

3. Turn the ignition key to the **OFF** position.

4. Put air conditioner selector switch in the **OFF** position.

5. Disconnect vacuum hose at the EGR valve and plug.

6. If equipped, disconnect wire to electric PVS.

7. Place the fast idle adjusting screw on the specified step of the fast idle cam.

8. Start engine without touching the accelerator pedal: Check/adjust fast idle rpm to specification.

9. Increase the engine speed, allowing engine to return to idle and turn ignition key to **OFF** position.

10. Remove plug from the EGR vacuum hose and reconnect.

11. If equipped, reconnect wire to electric PVS.

2.3L ENGINE W/YFA-IV AND YFA/IV FB

1. Place transaxle in **NEUTRAL** or **PARK**.

2. Bring engine to normal operating temperature.

3. Turn the ignition key to the **OFF** position.

4. Place the air conditioning selector switch in the **OFF** position.

5. Disconnect vacuum hose at the EGR valve and plug.

6. If equipped, disconnect wire to electric PVS.

7. Place the fast idle adjusting screw on the specified step of the fast idle cam.

8. Start engine without touching the accelerator pedal: Check/adjust fast idle rpm to specification.

9. Increase the engine speed momentarily, allowing engine to return to idle and turn ignition key to **OFF** position.

10. Remove plug from the EGR vacuum hose and reconnect.

11. If so equipped, reconnect wire to electric PVS.

AIR CONDITIONING/ THROTTLE KICKER ADJUSTMENT

Carbureted Engines

1.6L ENGINE

1. Place the transaxle in **NEUTRAL** or **PARK**.

2. Bring engine to normal operating temperature.

3. Identify vacuum source to air bypass section of air supply control valve. If vacuum hose is connected to carburetor, disconnect and plug hose at air supply control valve. Install slave vacuum hose between intake manifold

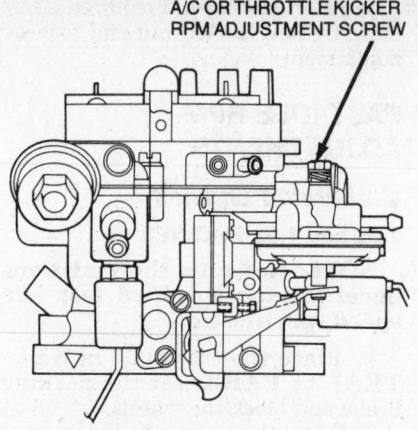

A/C OR THROTTLE KICKER RPM ADJUSTMENT SCREW

A/C or Throttle Kicker adjustment

and air bypass connection on air supply control valve.

4. To check/adjust air conditioner or throttle kicker rpm, perform the following:

   a. If vehicle is equipped with air conditioner, place selector to maximum cooling, blower switch on High. Disconnect the air conditioner compressor clutch wire.

   b. If vehicle is equipped with kicker and does not have air conditioning, disconnect vacuum hose from kicker and plug, install slave vacuum hose from intake manifold vacuum to kicker.

5. Run engine until engine cooling fan comes on.

6. Place transaxle in specified gear and check/adjust the air conditioner or throttle kicker rpm to specification.

NOTE: Engine cooling fan must be running when checking air conditioner or throttle kicker rpm. Adjust rpm by turning screw on kicker.

7. If slave vacuum hose was installed to check/adjust kicker rpm, remove slave vacuum hose. Remove plug from kicker vacuum hose and reconnect hose to kicker.

8. Remove slave vacuum hose. Return intake manifold supply source to original condition. Remove plug from carburetor vacuum hose and reconnect to air bypass valve.

THROTTLE POSITIONER SWITCH (TPS) OFF RPM ADJUSTMENT

Carbureted Engines

2.3L ENGINE WITH 1949 OR 6149 FB

NOTE: This adjustment is not required as part of a normal engine idle rpm check/adjustment.

If engine continues to run after ignition key is turned to OFF position, complete this procedure.

1. Place the transaxle in **NEUTRAL** or **PARK**, set the parking brake and block the wheels.

2. Bring the engine to normal operating temperature.

3. Disconnect the throttle kicker vacuum line and plug.

4. Place the air conditioner selector switch to the **OFF** position.

5. Disconnect the electrical lead to the TPS and verify that plunger collapses. Check/adjust engine rpm to specification (600 rpm).

6. Adjust the TPS Off rpm to specification.

7. Shut the engine off, reconnect TPS electrical lead and throttle kicker vacuum line.

Idle Speed Diesel Engine

ADJUSTMENT

1. Place the transaxle in **NEUTRAL**.

2. Bring the engine up to normal operating temperature. Stop engine.

3. Remove the timing hole cover. Clean the flywheel surface and install reflective tape.

4. Idle speed is measured with manual transaxle in **NEUTRAL**.

5. Check curb idle speed, using Rotunda hand-held tachometer No. 99–0001 or equivalent. Curb idle speed is specified on the vehicle emissions control information decal (VECI). Adjust to specification by loosening the lock-

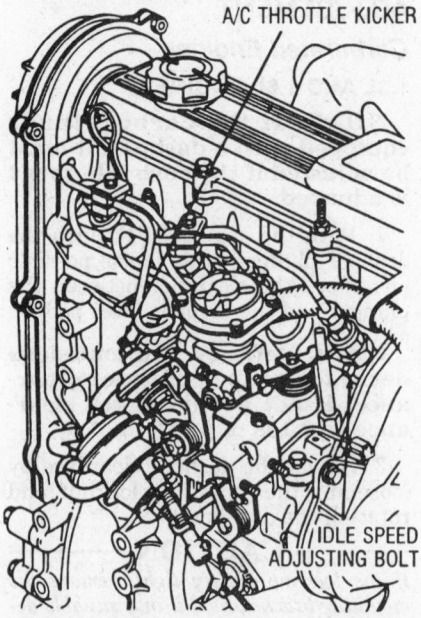

A/C THROTTLE KICKER

IDLE SPEED ADJUSTING BOLT

Adjusting the idle speed on the 2.0L diesel engine

nut on the idle speed adjusting bolt. Turn te idle speed adjusting bolt clockwe to increase, or counterclockwise to decrease engine idle speed. Tighten the locknut.

6. Place transaxle in **NEUTRAL**. Increase the engine speed momentarily and check the curb idle rpm. Readjust if necessary.

7. Turn air conditioner **ON**. Check the idle speed. Adjust to specification by loosening nut on the air conditioner throttle kicker and rotating screw.

ENGINE ELECTRICAL

Distributor

REMOVAL & INSTALLATION

1.6L and 1.9L Engine

The camshaft-driven distributor is located at the top left end of the cylinder head. It is retained by 2 hold down bolts at the base of the distributor shaft housing.

1. Turn engine to No. 1 piston at TDC of the compression stroke. Disconnect negative battery cable. Disconnect the vacuum hose(s), if equipped, from the advance unit. Disconnect the wiring harness at the distributor.

2. Remove the capscrews and remove the distributor cap. Position the distributor cap with attached wires aside so as not to interfere with distributor removal.

3. Scribe a mark on the distributor body, showing the position of the ignition rotor. Scribe another mark on the distributor body and cylinder head, showing the position of the body in relation to the head. These marks can be used for reference when installing the distributor, as long as the engine remains undisturbed (turned).

4. Remove the 2 distributor holddown bolts. Pull the distributor out of the head.

NOTE: Some engines are equipped with a security type distributor hold-down bolt and special tool No. T82L-12270-A or equivalent must be used to remove this hold down bolt. The 1.9L engine uses 2 hold-down bolts of this type.

5. To install the distributor with the engine undisturbed, place the distributor in the cylinder head, seating the off-set tang of the drive coupling into the groove on the end of the cam-

shaft. Install the 2 distributor holddown screws and tighten them so that the distributor can just barely be moved. Install the rotor (if removed), the distributor cap and all wiring. Make certain that the ignition wires are properly seated in the distributor cap. Set the ignition timing.

6. If the crankshaft was rotated while the distributor was removed for any reason, the engine must be brought to TDC on the compression stroke of the No. 1 cylinder. Remove the No. 1 spark plug. Place a finger over the hole and rotate the crankshaft slowly (use a wrench on the crankshaft pulley bolt) in the direction of normal engine rotation, until engine compression is felt.

— CAUTION —

Turn the engine only in the direction of normal rotation. Backward rotation will cause the cam belt to slip or lose teeth, altering engine timing.

7. When engine compression is felt at the spark plug hole, indicating that the piston is approaching TDC, continue to turn the crankshaft until the timing mark on the pulley is aligned with the **0** mark (timing marking) on the engine front cover. Turn the distributor shaft until the ignition rotor is at the No. 1 firing position. Install the distributor into the cylinder head, as outlined in Step 5 of this procedure.

2.3L and 3.8L Engines

The TFI-IV distributor is mounted on the side of the engine block. Some engines may be equipped with a "security" type distributor hold down bolt which requires a special wrench for removal. The TFI-IV distributor incorporates a "Hall Effect" vane switch stator assembly and an integrally mounted thickfilm module. When the "Hall Effect" device is turned on and a pulse is produced, the EEC-IV electronics computes crankshaft position and engine demand to calibrate spark advance. Initial ignition timing adjustment/checking is necessary when the distributor has been removed. Repairs to the distributor are accomplished by a distributor replacement.

1. Turn engine to No. 1 piston at TDC of the compression stroke. Disconnect the negative battery cable.

2. Disconnect the wiring harness at the distributor. Mark No. 1 spark plug wire cap terminal location on the distributor body. Remove the coil wire from cap.

3. Remove the distributor cap with plug wires attached and position out of the way. Remove the rotor.

4. Remove the distributor base hold down bolt and clamp. Slowly withdraw the distributor from the engine. Be

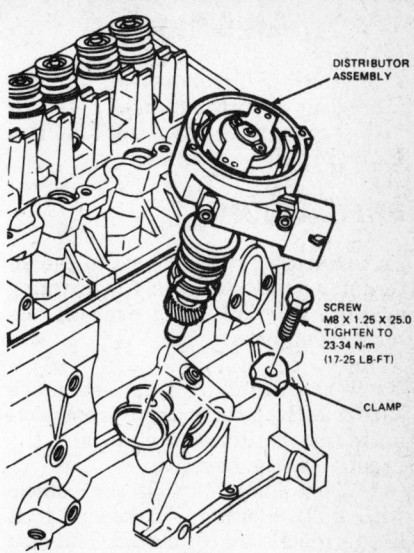

SCREW M8 X 1.25 X 25.0 TIGHTEN TO 23-34 N·m (17-25 LB-FT)

DISTRIBUTOR ASSEMBLY

CLAMP

Distributor Installation on 2.3L HSC Engine

careful not to disturb the intermediate driveshaft.

5. Rotate the engine until No. 1 position is on compression stroke.

a. Align timing marks for correct initial timing.

b. Rotate distributor shaft so that center rod on multi-point rotor is pointing toward mark previously made on distributor base.

c. Continue rotating slightly so that leading edge of vane is centered in the vane switch stator assembly.

d. Rotate distributor in block to align leading edge and the vane switch stator assembly and verify that the rotor is pointing at No. 1 cap terminal.

e. Install distributor hold down bolt and clamp. Do not tighten at this time.

6. If the vane and vane switch stator cannot be aligned by rotating the distributor in the block, pull distributor out of block enough to disengage distributor gear and rotate distributor shaft to engage a different distributor gear tooth. Repeat Step 1 as necessary.

7. Connect distributor to wiring harness.

8. Install distributor cap, rotor and ignition wires. Check that ignition wires are securely connected to the distributor cap and spark plugs. Tighten distributor cap screws to 18–25 inch lbs.

9. Set initial timing with a suitable timing light. Refer to the Vehicle Emission Control Information Decal.

10. Tighten distributor hold down bolt to 17–35 ft. lbs. On 3.8L engines torque the bolt to 40 ft. lbs.

11. Recheck initial timing. Readjust if necessary.

Alternator

For further information on the charging system, please refer to "Charging and Starting" in the Unit Repair section.

PRECAUTIONS

To prevent serious damage to the alternator and the rest of the charging system, the following precautions must be observed:

- When installing a battery, make sure that the positive cable is connected to the positive terminal and the negative to the negative.
- When jump-starting the vehicle with another battery, make sure that like terminals are connected. This also applies when using a battery charger.
- Never operate the alternator with the battery disconnected or otherwise on an uncontrolled open circuit. Double-check to see that all connections are tight.
- Do not short across or ground any alternator or regulator terminals.
- Do not try to polarize the alternator.
- Do not apply full battery voltage to the field connector.
- Always disconnect the battery ground cable before disconnecting the alternator lead.

BELT TENSION ADJUSTMENT

All Except V-Ribbed Belts

1. Loosen the accessory adjustment and pivot bolts.
2. On the 2.0L diesel engine, loosen the shake brace nut and bolt.
3. Pry the proper accessory (using the belt adjusting hole in the accessory bracket) and use care not to damage the accessory housing.
4. Tighten the adjustment bolts to specifications. Release the pressure and tighten the pivot bolt to specifications.
5. On the 2.0L diesel engine, tighten the shake brace nut and bolt.
6. Check the belt tension and readjust if necessary.

V-Ribbed Belts

1. Loosen the idler pulley bracket bolts. Turn the adjusting bolt until the belt is adjusted to specifications.

NOTE: Turning the wrench to the right tightens the belt adjustment and turning the wrench to the left loosens the belt tension.

2. Tighten the 2 idler pulley bracket bolts to specifications. Check the belt tension.
3. Recheck the belt tension and adjust if necessary.

REMOVAL & INSTALLATION

1. Disconnect the negative battery cable.
2. If the alternator is equipped with a pulley cover shield, remove the shield at this time.
3. Loosen the alternator pivot bolt. Remove the adjustment bracket to alternator bolt (and nut, if equipped). Pivot the alternator to gain slack in the drive belt and remove the belt.
4. Disconnect and label (for correct installation) the alternator wiring.

NOTE: Some vehicles use a push-on wiring connector on the field and stator connections. Pull or push straight off or on, or damage to the connectors may occur.

5. Remove the pivot bolt and the alternator.
6. Install in the reverse order of removal. Torque the pivot bolt to 45–55 ft. lbs. Adjust the drive belt tension so that there is approximately ¼–½ in. deflection on the longest belt span between the pulleys. Reinstall the pulley shield, if equipped and connect the negative battery cable.

Voltage Regulator

NOTE: Three different types of regulators are used, depending on model, engine, alternator output and type of dash mounted charging indicator used (light or ammeter). The regulators are 100 percent solid state and are calibrated and preset by the manufacturer. No readjustment is required or possible on these regulators.

SERVICE

Whenever system components are being replaced the following precautions should be followed so that the charging system will work properly and the components will not be damaged.
1. Always use the proper alternator.
2. The electronic regulators are color coded for identification. Never install a different coded regulator for the 1 being replaced. General coding identification follows, if the regulator removed does not have the color mentioned, identify the output of the alternator and method of charging indication, then consult a parts department to obtain the correct regulator. A black coded regulator is used in systems which use a signal lamp for charging indication. Gray coded regu-

lators are used with an ammeter gauge. Neutral coded regulars are used on models equipped with diesel engine. The special regulator must be used on vehicles equipped with diesel engine to prevent glow plug flure.
3. Models using a charging lamp indicator are equipped with a 90 ohm resistor on the back of the instrument panel.

REMOVAL & INSTALLATION

1. Disconnect the negative battery cable.
2. Unplug the wiring harnss from the regulator.
3. Remove the regulator mounting bolts.
4. Install in the reverse order of removal.
5. Test the system for proer voltage regulation.

Starter

For all starter overhaul procedures, please refer to "Charging and Starting" in the Unit Repair section.

REMOVAL & INSTALLATION

Except 3.8L Engine

1. Disconnect the negative battery cable.
2. Raise and safely support the front of the vehicle on jackstads. Disconnect the starter cable fom the starter motor.
3. On vehicles equipped with a manual transaxle, remove the 3 nuts that attach the roll resistor brace to the starter mounting studs at the transaxle. Remove the brace (On Tempo/Topaz, remove the cable support from the top of the brace). On models that are equipped with an automatic transaxle, remove the hose bracket mounted on the starter studs.
4. Remove the 2 bolts attaching the rear starter support bracket, remove the retaining nut from the rear of the starter motor and remove the support bracket.
5. On vehicles equipped with a manual transaxle, remove the 3 starter mounting studs and the starter motor. On vehicles equipped with an automatic transaxle, remove the 2 starter mounting studs, mounting bolt and the starter motor.
6. Position the starter motor on the transaxle housing and install in the reverse order of removal. Tighten the mounting bolts or studs to 30–40 ft. lbs.

3.8L Engine

1. Disconnect the negative battery

cable and the cable connection at the starter.

2. Raise and support the front of the vehicle safely and block the rear wheels.

3. Remove the cable support and ground cable connection from the upper starter stud bolt.

4. Remove the starter brace from the cylinder block and the starter.

5. Support the starter by hand. Remove the starter between the subframe and the radiator.

6. Complete the installation of the starter by reversing the removal procedure. Torque the starter mounting bolts to 30–40 ft. lbs.

2.0L Diesel Engine

1. Remove the battery cover and disconnect the negative battery cable.

2. Disconnect the starter cable assembly from the starter relay and starter solenoid, located on the fender apron.

3. Remove the upper starter mounting stud bolt. Raise and support the vehicle safely.

4. Disconnect the vacuum hose from the vacuum pump.

5. Remove the 3 starter support bracket screws and bracket. Remove the power steering hose bracket.

6. Remove the ground wire assembly and cable support on the starter bolt studs.

7. Remove the 2 starter mounting studs and position the them out of the way of the starter.

8. Remove the vacuum pump bracket. Remove the starter from the vehicle.

9. Installation is the reverse order of the removal procedure.

Diesel Glow Plugs

REMOVAL & INSTALLATION

1. Disconnect the battery ground cable from the battery, located in the luggage compartment.

2. Disconnect the glow plug harness from the glow plugs.

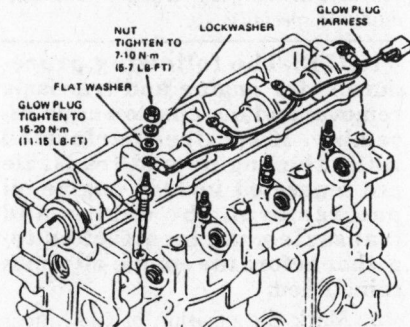

Glow plugs—2.0L diesel engine

3. Using a 12mm deepwell socket, remove the glow plugs.

4. Install the glow plugs, using a 12mm deepwell socket. Tighten the glow plugs to 11–15 ft. lbs.

5. Connect the glow plug harness to the glow plugs. Tighten the nuts to 5–7 ft. lbs.

6. Connect the battery ground cable to the battery.

7. Check the glow plug system operation.

GASOLINE ENGINE MECHANICAL

Engine

REMOVAL & INSTALLATION

1.6L Engine

NON-TURBOCHARGED

1. Mark the position of the hinges on the hood underside and remove the hood.

2. Remove the air cleaner assembly. Remove the air feed duct and the heat tube. Remove the air duct to the alternator.

3. Disconnect the battery cables from the battery. Remove the battery. If equipped with air conditioning, remove compressor with line still connected and position out of the way.

---— **CAUTION** ---—

Never loosen refrigerant lines, as the escaping refrigerant and can freeze exposed skin instantly.

4. Position a suitable drain pan under the radiator and drain the cooling system. Remove the drive belts from the alternator and thermactor pump. Disconnect the thermactor air supply hose. Disconnect the wiring harness at the alternator. Remove alternator and thermactor.

5. Disconnect and remove the upper and lower radiator hoses. If equipped with an automatic transaxle, disconnect and plug the fluid cooler lines at the radiator.

6. Disconnect the heater hoses from the engine. Unplug the electric cooling fan wiring harness. Remove the fan and radiator shroud as an assembly.

7. Remove the radiator. Label and disconnect all vacuum lines, including power brake booster, from the engine. Label and disconnect all linkage, including kickdown linkage if automatic,

and wiring harness connectors from the engine.

8. If equipped with fuel injection, discharge the system pressure. Remove supply and return fuel lines to the fuel pump. Plug the line from the gas tank.

9. Raise and safely support the car on jackstands. Remove the clamp from the heater supply and return tubes, remove the tubes.

10. Disconnect the battery cable from the starter motor. Remove brace or bracket from the back of the starter and remove the starter.

11. Disconnect the exhaust system from the exhaust manifold. Drain the engine oil.

12. Remove the brace in front of the bell housing (flywheel or converter) inspection cover. Remove the inspection cover.

13. Remove the crankshaft pulley. If equipped with a manual transaxle, remove the timing belt cover lower attaching bolts.

14. If equipped with an automatic transaxle, remove the torque converter to flywheel mounting nuts.

15. Remove the lower engine to transaxle attaching bolts.

16. Loosen the hose clamps on the bypass hose and remove the hose from the intake manifold.

17. Remove the bolt and nut attaching the right front mount insulator to the engine bracket.

18. Lower the car from the jackstands.

19. Attach an engine lifting sling to the engine. Connect a chain hoist to the lifting sling and remove all slack. Remove the through bolt from the right front engine mount and remove the insulator.

20. If the car is equipped with a manual transaxle, remove the timing belt cover upper mounting bolts and remove the cover.

21. Remove the right front insulator attaching bracket from the engine.

22. Position a floor jack under the transaxle. Raise the jack just enough to take the weight of the transaxle.

23. Remove the upper bolts connecting the engine and transaxle.

24. Slowly raise the engine and separate from the transaxle. Be sure the torque converter stays on the transaxle. Remove the engine from the car. On models equipped with manual transaxles, the engine must be separated from the input shaft of the transaxle before raising.

25. Install the engine in the reverse order of removal. On manual transaxle vehicles take care when engaging the clutch disc splines. On automatic transaxle vehicles be sure the converter mounting studs engage the fly-

wheel. Be sure the alignment dowels on the back of the engine engage the transaxle and the engine and transaxle mate together flush.

TURBOCHARGED

1. Mark the position of the hood hinges and remove the hood.
2. Disconnect the negative battery cable and drain the cooling system.
3. Remove the air cleaner and vane meter assembly including the air intake tube assembly.
4. Disconnect the secondary wire from the ignition coil. Remove the alternator drive belt, remove the alternator mounting bolts and position the alternator out of the way.
5. Disconnect the radiator hoses at the engine. Remove the radiator guard, fan assembly and the radiator.
6. Disconnect the heater at the metal tube. Label and disconnect all electrical connectors and vacuum lines.
7. Disconnect the fuel supply and return lines at the intake manifold. Disconnect the power brake booster vacuum line (if equipped). Disconnect the throttle cable and bracket at the air horn assembly. Disconnect the carbon canister tube. Disconnect the purge hose at the canister purge solenoid.
8. Raise and support the front of the vehicle on jackstands. Drain the engine oil. Remove the oil cooler.
9. Remove the heater supply and return tubes. Disconnect the battery cable from the starter motor.
10. Remove the knee brace from the front of the starter motor and remove the starter motor.
11. Disconnect the exhaust pipe from the turbocharger. Remove the support bracket located in the front of the bell housing inspection cover and remove the inspection cover. Remove the exhaust pipe support bracket.
12. Remove the crankshaft pulley. Remove the timing cover lower attaching bolts.
13. Remove the flywheel housing lower mounting bolts. Remove the bracket bolt that attaches the negative battery cable to the engine block. Remove the nut and bolt attaching the mounting insulator bracket to the engine bracket located at the front of the engine.
14. Disconnect the EGR tube at the intake manifold. Disconnect the pulse air hose at the check valve and air cleaner assembly.
15. Lower the vehicle from the jackstands.
16. Install suitable lifting brackets on the engine. Attach a chain hoist to the lifting device and apply slight upward tension.
17. Remove the nuts that attach the casting of the front engine insulator

and remove the casting. Remove the remaining timing cover attaching bolts and remove the cover.
18. Position a jack underneath the transaxle and raise the jack enough to support the weight of the transaxle.
19. Remove the flywheel housing upper mounting bolts.
20. Remove the engine from the vehicle. Install the engine in the reverse order of removal.

1.9L Engine

1. Mark position of hood hinges and remove hood.
2. Remove air cleaner, air intake duct and heat tube.
3. Disconnect negative battery cable.
4. Drain the cooling system. Remove the secondary wire from the ignition coil.
5. Remove the alternator drive belt. Remove alternator mounting bolts and position the alternator to the side.
6. Disconnect and remove thermactor air pump, if equipped.
7. Disconnect radiator hoses and oil cooler lines if equipped with ATX.
8. Disconnect the radiator cooling fan electrical connector. Remove radiator cooling fan and shroud as an assembly.
9. Remove the transaxle cooler line routing clip located at the radiator, if equipped with ATX. Remove the radiator and disconnect the heater at the metal tube.
10. Indentify, tag and disconnect heater hoses, electrical connections and vacuum hoses as necessary. Disconnect the fuel pump supply and return lines. If equipped with power assist brakes, disconnect the power boost vacuum hose at the engine.
11. Disconnect kickdown rod at the fuel charging assembly, ATX only.
12. Disconnect accelerator cable at the fuel charging assembly and remove the cable routing bracket attaching screws. Disconnect the vapor hose at the carbon canister tube.
13. Raise the vehicle and support safely.
14. Remove the clamp from the heater supply and return hose. Remove knee brace at front of starter motor and remove battery cable from starter.
15. Disconnect exhaust inlet pipe at manifold.
16. Remove support bracket in front of converter cover if equipped with ATX (inspection cover for MTX), and remove cover.
17. Remove cranskshaft pulley and damper.
18. Remove torque converter to flywheel nuts, if equipped with ATX.
19. Remove timing belt cover lower attaching bolts, if equipped with MTX.
20. Remove converter housing (ATX)

or flywheel housing (MTX) lower attaching bolts.
21. Remove 2 oil pan-to-transaxle attaching bolts. Disconnect coolant bypass hose from intake manifold. If equipped, remove the bolt attaching the battery negative cable to the cylinder block.
22. Remove nut and bolt attaching insulator bracket to the engine bracket at front of engine.
23. Lower vehicle.
24. Install suitable lifting brackets on engine.

NOTE: The top rear bolt attaching the thermactor pump bracket to the engine can be removed and used as a lifting bracket attaching point.

25. Use a suitable lifting device connected to the engine lifting brackets and raise engine just enough to remove the through bolt from the front engine insulator and remove insulator.
26. Remove the remaining timing belt cover bolts and remove the cover, MTX only.
27. Remove insulator attaching bracket from engine.
28. Position a jack under the transaxle. Raise jack just enough to support the weight of the transaxle.
29. Remove the converter housing, flywheel housing upper attaching bolts.
30. Remove engine assembly from vehicle.
31. Complete the installation of the engine by reversing the removal procedure.

2.3L Engine

——— CAUTION ———
The engine and transaxle assembly are removed together as a unit from underneath the car. Provision must be made to safely raise and support the car for powertrain removal and installation. The air conditioning system (if equipped) must be discharged prior to engine removal. The refrigerant is contained under high pressure and is very dangerous when released. The system should be discharged by a qualified air conditioning specialist.

NOTE: The following procedure is for engine and transaxle removal and installation as an assembly. If services performed while the engine and transaxle are separated include engine oil pan removal, the engine and transaxle must be attached together before the engine oil pan is reinstalled.

1. Mark the position of the hinges on the underside of the hood and remove the hood.

2. Disconnect the battery cables from the battery, negative cable first. Remove the air cleaner assembly.

3. Remove the radiator cap and position a suitable drain pan under the radiator. Disconnect the lower radiator hose from the radiator to drain the cooling system. Drain the engine oil and transaxle lubricant into a suitable drain pan.

4. Remove the upper and lower radiator hoses. On models equipped with an automatic transaxle, disconnect and plug the oil cooler lines from the rubber connectors in the radiator.

5. Disconnect and remove the coil from the cylinder head. Disconnect the cooling fan wiring harness. Remove the radiator shroud and electric fan as an assembly. Remove the radiator.

6. Be sure the air conditioning system is properly and safely discharged. Remove the hoses from the compressor. Label and disconnect all electrical harness connections, linkage and vacuum lines from the engine.

7. On automatic transaxle equipped vehicles, disconnect the T.V. (throttle valve) linkage at the transaxle. On manual transaxle equipped vehicles disconnect the clutch cable from the lever at the transaxle.

8. Disconnect the fuel supply and return lines. Plug the fuel line from the gas tank. Disconnect the thermactor pump discharge hose at the pump, if equipped.

9. If equipped with power steering, disconnect the pressure and return lines lines at the pump. Remove the hose support bracket from the cylinder head. Remove the coil and bracket assembly.

10. Install an 2 lifting eyes and engine support sling (Ford Tool T79L-5000A, or equivalent) and support the weight of the engine/transaxle assembly.

11. Raise and safely support the vehicle on jackstands.

12. Remove the starter cable from the starter motor terminal.

13. Disconnect the hose from the catalytic converter. Remove the bolts retaining the exhaust pipe bracket to the oil pan.

14. Remove the exhaust pipe to exhaust manifold mounting nuts. Remove the pipes from the mounting bracket insulators and position out of the way.

15. Disconnect the speedometer cable from the transaxle. Position a drain pan under the heater hoses and remove the heater hoses from the water pump inlet and intake manifold connector.

16. Remove the water intake tube bracket from the engine block. Remove the 2 clamp attaching bolts from

the bottom of the oil pan. Remove the water pump inlet tube.

17. Remove the bolts attaching the control arms to the body. Remove the stabilizer bar bracket retaining bolts and remove the brackets.

18. Remove the half shafts (drive-axles) from the transaxle.

19. On vehicles equipped with a manual transaxle, remove the roll restrictor nuts from the transaxle and pull the roll restrictor from mounting bracket.

20. On vehicles equipped with a manual transaxle, remove the shift stabilizer bar to transaxle attaching bolts. Remove the shift mechanism to shift shaft attaching nut and bolt at the transaxle.

21. On vehicles equipped with an automatic transaxle, disconnect the shift cable clip from the transaxle lever. Remove the manual shift linkage bracket bolts from the transaxle and remove the bracket.

22. Remove the left rear No. 4 insulator mount bracket from the body by removing the retaining nuts.

23. Remove the left front No. 1 insulator to transaxle mounting bolts.

24. Lower the vehicle and support with stands so that the front wheels are just above the ground. Do not allow the wheels to touch the ground.

25. Connect an engine sling to the lifting brackets provided. Connect a hoist to the sling and apply slight tension. Remove the support sling (Step 10).

26. Remove the right hand insulator No. 3 intermediate bracket to engine bracket bolts, intermediate bracket to insulator attaching nuts and the nut on the bottom of the double ended stud which attaches the intermediate bracket and engine bracket. Remove the bracket.

27. Lower the engine and transaxle assembly to the ground.

28. Raise and support the car at a height suitable from assembly to be removed.

29. Installation is the reverse of removal procedure.

Cylinder Head

REMOVAL & INSTALLATION

1.6L and 1.9L Engine

NOTE: The engine must be "overnight" cold before removing the cylinder head, to reduce the possibility of warpage or distortion.

--- **CAUTION** ---
Do not reuse the cylinder head retaining bolts. Use new bolts when installing head.

1. Disconnect the negative battery cable.

2. On non-turbocharged engines, drain the cooling system and disconnect the heater hose at the fitting located under the intake manifold and the upper radiator hose at the engine.

3. Disconnect the wiring terminal from the cooling fan switch.

4. On turbocharged engines, drain the cooling system and disconnect the upper radiator hose at the engine.

5. On non-turbocharged engines, remove the air cleaner assembly, remove the PCV hose, and disconnect all interfering vacuum hoses after marking them for reassembly. On turbocharged engines, remove the air supply hose at the throttle body assembly and remove the PCV oil separator system.

6. Turn the engine until No. 1 piston is at TDC (top dead center) on the compression stroke and the timing marks are aligned.

7. Remove the valve cover and disconnect all accessory drive belts. Remove the crankshaft pulley. (Use crankshaft pulley wrench No. T81P-6312-A and crankshaft bolt wrench No. YA-826 or equivalents). Remove the timing belt cover.

8. Remove the distributor cap and spark plug wires as an assembly.

9. Loosen both belt tensioner attaching bolts using tool No. T81P-6254-A or the equivalent. Secure the belt tensioner as far left as possible. Remove the timing belt.

10. Disconnect the tube at the EGR valve, then remove the PVS hose connectors using tool No. T81P-8564-A or equivalent. Label the connectors and set aside.

11. Disconnect the choke wire, the fuel supply and return lines located on the right side of the engine, the accelerator cable and speed control cable (if equipped). Disconnect the altitude compensator, if equipped, from the dash panel and place on the heater/air conditioner air intake.

12. Disconnect and remove the alternator and alternator bracket.

13. If equipped with power steering, remove the thermactor pump drive belt, the pump and its bracket. Disconnect the turbocharger inlet hose (if equipped). Disconnect the turbocharger oil supply tube at the turbocharger coolant outlet and the engine block. Remove the supply line.

14. Raise the vehicle and and support on jackstands. Disconnect the exhaust pipe from the manifold or turbocharger. Disconnect the oil return line from the turbocharger.

15. Lower the vehicle and remove the cylinder head bolts and washers. Discard the bolts, they cannot be used again.

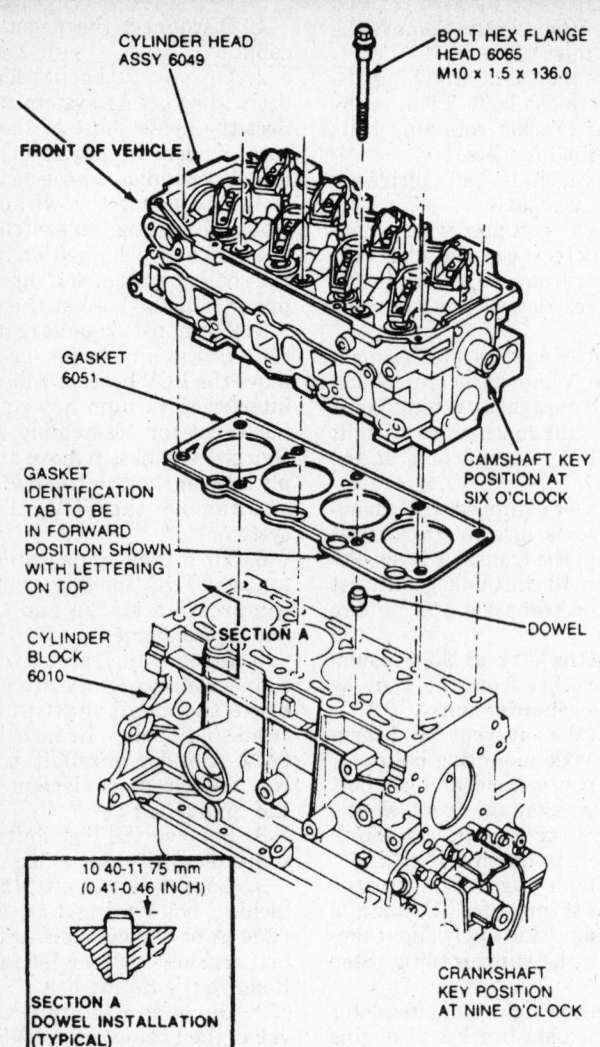

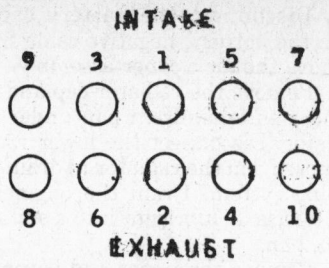

CYLINDER HEAD
ASSY 6049

BOLT HEX FLANGE
HEAD 6065
M10 x 1.5 x 136.0

FRONT OF VEHICLE

GASKET
6051

GASKET
IDENTIFICATION
TAB TO BE
IN FORWARD
POSITION SHOWN
WITH LETTERING
ON TOP

CAMSHAFT KEY
POSITION AT
SIX O'CLOCK

SECTION A

CYLINDER
BLOCK
6010

DOWEL

10 40-11 75 mm
(0.41-0.46 INCH)

SECTION A
DOWEL INSTALLATION
(TYPICAL)

CRANKSHAFT
KEY POSITION
AT NINE O'CLOCK

View of the cylinder head assembly—1.9L engine

INTAKE

9   3   1   5   7

8   6   2   4   10

EXHAUST

Cylinder head bolt torque sequence—1.6L and 1.9L engines

proper level. Start the engine, check the ignition timing and check for fluid leaks.

CHECKING PISTON SQUISH HEIGHT

NOTE: If no other service or parts other than just cylinder head gasket replacement has been done on the engine, the piston squish should be within specification. If the cylinder head surface has be reworked or replacement parts such as a crankshaft, connecting rod or piston installed the height clearance between the piston head and cylinder head combustion chamber must be checked.

1. Clean all gasket surfaces, piston head and combustion chamber.
2. Place a small amount of soft lead solder a various points on the high part of the piston head.
3. Rotate the crankshaft to lower the piston in the bore. Install the cylinder head with a used head gasket (a used gasket is perferred since it has already been compressed, however a new gasket can be used) between the cylinder head and block.
4. Install the used head bolts and tighten them to 44 ft. lbs in the proper torque sequence.
5. Rotate the crankshaft to move the piston through its TDC position. Remove the cylinder head and measure the thickness of the solder. Proper clearance is 0.039–0.070 in.

2.3L Engine

1. Disconnect the negative battery cable. Drain the cooling system by disconnecting the lower radiator hose.
2. Disconnect the heater hose at the fitting under the intake manifold. Disconnect the upper radiator hose at the cylinder head connector.
3. Disconnect the electric cooling fan switch at the plastic connector. Remove the air cleaner assembly. Label and disconnect any vacuum lines that will interfere with cylinder head removal.
4. Disconnect all drive belts. Remove rocker arm cover. Remove the

16. Remove the cylinder head with the manifolds (and turbocharger) attached. Remove and discard the head gasket. Do not place the cylinder head with combustion chambers down or damage to the spark plugs or gasket surfaces may result.

--- **CAUTION** ---

Before installing the cylinder head on both the turbocharged and non-turbocharged engines, check the piston squish height.

17. To install, clean all gasket material from both the block face and the cylinder head. Prior to installing the cylinder head rotate the crankshaft so that the No. 1 piston is 90 degrees BTDC (before top dead center). Turn the crankshaft back until the crankshaft pulley keyway is at 9 o'clock (this is the 90 degrees BTDC position). This will prevent damage to the valves and pistons. To time the valve train to this piston position, turn the camshaft until the keyway is at the 6 o'clock position. The camshaft and crankshaft

must not be turned until after the installation of the timing gears and belt.

18. Position the cylinder head gasket on the engine block. The gasket for the turbocharged engine is different than the non-turbo. Be sure the correct head gasket is installed. Position the cylinder head on the engine block. Lightly oil the threads of the new head bolts and install them. (Do not reuse the cylinder head bolts. ALWAYS install new ones.). Tighten the bolts in sequence to 44 ft. lbs. Loosen all bolts approximately 2 turns, then retighten in sequence to 44 ft. lbs. After tightening all bolts the second time, turn all bolts an additional 90 degrees in sequence. When the first 90 degree sequence is completed, repeat an additional 90 degree turn, once again in sequence.

19. Complete the installation of the cylinder head by reversing the removal procedure. Recheck engine timing at No. 1 piston on TDC.

20. Fill the cooling system to the

distributor cap and spark plug wires as an assembly.

5. Disconnect the EGR tube at EGR valve. Disconnect the choke wire from the choke.

6. Discharge the fuel system pressure if equipped with CFI (central fuel injection). Disconnect the fuel supply and return lines. Disconnect the accelerator cable and speed control cable, if equipped. Loosen the bolts retaining the thermactor pump pulley.

7. Raise and safely support the front of the car. Disconnect the exhaust pipe from the exhaust manifold. Lower the car.

8. Loosen the rocker arm bolts until the arms can pivot for pushrod removal. Remove the pushrods, keep the pushrods in order for installation in original position.

9. Remove the cylinder head bolts. Remove the cylinder head, gasket, thermactor pump, intake and exhaust manifolds as an assembly. Do not lay the cylinder head down flat before removing the spark plugs; take care not to damage the gasket surface.

10. Clean all gasket material from the head and block surfaces.

11. Position a new head gasket on the block surface, use sealer to retain the gasket.

12. Prior to installing the cylinder head, thread 2 cylinder head alignment studs No. T84P-6065-A or equivalent at opposite corners of the block.

NOTE: Cylinder head alignment studs may be fabricated by purchasing 2 head bolts and cutting off the heads.

13. Position the cylinder head over the guide bolts and lower onto the engine block.

14. Install head bolts, remove the guides and replace with regular bolts.

15. Torque the head bolts in sequence in 2 steps:
    a. Step 1 – 52–59 ft. lbs.
    b. Step 2 – 70–76 ft. lbs.

16. Complete the installation of the remaining cylinder head components by reversing the removal procedure.

3.8L Engine

1. Remove the radiator cap, open the drain cock and drain the cooling system into a suitable drain pan. Disconnect the negative battery cable.

2. Remove the air cleaner assembly including air intake duct and heat tube.

3. Loosen the accessory drive belt idler and remove the drive belt.

4. If the right head is being removed, disregard this step and proceed to Step 5. If the left side cylinder head

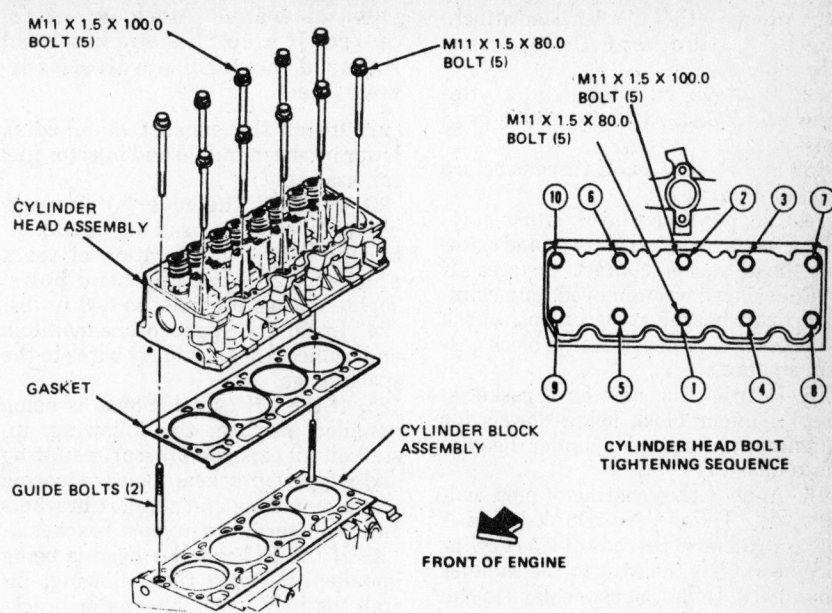

Cylinder head torque sequence—2.3L HSC

is being removed, perform the following to gain access to the upper intake manifold:
    a. Remove the oil fill cap.
    b. Remove power steering pump. Leave the hoses connected and place the pump/bracket assembly aside in a position to prevent fluid from leaking out.
    c. If equipped with air conditioning, remove mounting bracket attaching bolts. Leaving the hoses connected, position compressor aside.
    d. Remove the alternator and mounting bracket.

5. If the right side cylinder head is being removed, perform the following to gain access to the upper intake manifold:
    a. Disconnect the thermactor air control valve or bypass valve hose assembly at the air pump.
    b. Disconnect the thermactor

tube support bracket from the rear of cylinder head.
    c. Remove accessory drive idler.
    d. Remove the thermactor pump pulley and thermactor pump.
    e. Remove the PCV valve.

6. Remove the upper intake manifold.

7. Remove the valve rocker arm cover attaching screws and lift the rocker arm cover and cover gasket away from the cylinder head.

8. Remove the injector fuel rail assembly.

9. Remove the lower intake manifold and remove the exhaust manifold(s).

10. Loosen rocker arm fulcrum attaching bolts enough to allow rocker arm to be lifted off the push rod and rotate to 1 side. Remove the push rods. Identify and label the position of each rod. Rods should be installed in their original position during assembly.

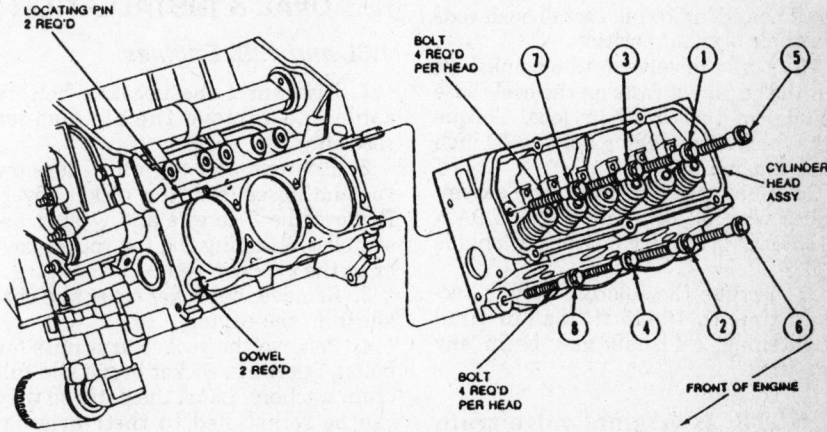

View of the cylinder head assembly with bolt torque sequence – 3.8L engine

11. Remove the cylinder head attaching bolts and discard. Do not re-use the old bolts.

12. Remove cylinder head(s). Remove and discard old cylinder head gasket(s).

13. Lightly oil all bolt threads before installation.

14. Clean cylinder head, intake manifold, valve rocker arm cover and cylinder head gasket contact surfaces. If cylinder head was removed for a cylinder head gasket replacement, check flatness of cylinder head and block gasket surfaces.

15. Position the new head gasket(s) onto cylinder block using dowels for alignment. Position cylinder head(s) onto block.

16. Apply a thin coating of pipe sealant with Teflon® No. D8AZ-19554-A or equivalent to threads of short cylinder head bolts (nearest to the exhaust manifold). Do not apply sealant to the long bolts. Install cylinder head bolts (8 each side).

———— CAUTION ————

Always use new cylinder head bolts to ensure a leak-tight assembly. Torque retention with used bolts can vary, which may result in coolant or compression leakage at the cylinder head mating surface area.

17. Torque the cylinder head attaching bolts in sequence as follows:
   a. 37 ft. lbs.
   b. 45 ft. lbs.
   c. 52 ft. lbs.
   d. 59 ft. lbs.
   e. Back-off each attaching bolt 2 to 3 turns.
   f. Repeat steps a–d.

NOTE: When cylinder head attaching bolts have been tightened using the above procedure, it is not necessary to retighten bolts after extended engine operation. However, bolts can be checked for tightness if desired.

18. Dip each push rod end in oil conditioner No. D9AZ-19579-C or equivalent heavy engine oil. Install push rods in their original position.

19. For each valve, rotate crankshaft until the tappet rests on the heel (base circle) of the camshaft lobe. Torque the fulcrum attaching bolts to 43 inch lbs. maximum.

20. Lubricate all rocker arm assemblies with oil conditioner No. D9AZ-19579-C or equivalent heavy engine oil.

21. Torque the fulcrum bolts a second time to 19–25 ft. lbs. For final tightening, camshaft may be in any position.

NOTE: If original valve train components are being installed, a valve clearance check is not required. If a component has been replaced, perform a valve clearance check.

22. Install the exhaust manifold(s), lower intake manifold and injector fuel rail assembly.

23. Position the cover(s) and new gasket on cylinder head and install attaching bolts. Note location of spark plug wire routing clip stud bolts. Tighten attaching bolts to 6–8 ft. lbs.

24. Install the upper intake manifold and connect the secondary wires to the spark plugs.

25. If the LH cylinder head is being installed, perform the following: install oil fill cap, compressor mounting and support brackets, power steering pump mounting and support brackets and the alternator/support bracket.

26. If the RH cylinder head is being installed, perform the following: install the PCV valve, alternator bracket, thermactor pump and pump pulley, accessory drive idler, thermactor air control valve or air bypass valve hose.

27. Install the accessory drive belt. Attach the thermactor tube(s) support bracket to the rear of the cylinder head. Torque the attaching bolts to 30–40 ft. lbs.

28. Connect the negative battery cable and fill the cooling system.

29. Start the engine and check for leaks.

30. Check and, if necessary, adjust curb idle speed.

31. Install the air cleaner assembly including air intake duct and heat tube.

OVERHAUL

For all cylinder head overhaul procedures, refer to "Engine Rebuilding" in the Unit Repair Section.

Rocker Arm/Shafts

REMOVAL & INSTALLATION

1.6L and 1.9L Engines

1. Disconnect the negative battery cable and remove the air cleaner assembly.

2. Remove and tag all necessary vacuum hoses from the rocker cover. Remove the 7 screws and washer assemblies retaining the the rocker cover to the cylinder head.

3. Remove the rocker cover and gasket from the engine.

4. Remove the rocker arm nuts (or bolts), fulcrums, rocker arms, and fulcrum washers. Label the parts so they can be reinstalled to their original positions.

5. Before installation, coat the valve tips, rocker arm and fulcrum contact areas with Lubriplate® or equivalent.

6. Rotate the engine until the lifter is on the base circle of the cam (valve closed).

NOTE: Be sure to turn the engine only in the normal rotation. Backward rotation will cause the camshaft belt to slip or lose teeth, altering the valve timing and causing serious engine damage.

7. Install the rocker arm and components in reverse order of removal. Torque the rocker arm nuts to 15–19 ft. lbs. and bolts (if installed) to 17–22 ft. lbs. Be sure the lifter is on the base circle of the cam for each rocker arm as it is installed. Adjust the valves as previously outlined.

8. Install guide pins into the cylinder head and guide the gasket and rocker arm cover over the pins. Install the retaining screws and washer and torque the screws to 6–8 ft. lbs.

NOTE: Do not use any glue or sealant compound with the silcone gasket.

2.3L and 3.8L Engines

1. Disconnect the negative battery cable and remove the air cleaner assembly.

2. Remove and tag all necessary vacuum hoses from the rocker cover. Remove the oil fill cap and set it aside. Disconnect the PCV hose and set it aside.

3. Disconnect the throttle linkage cable from the top of the rocker arm cover. Disconnect the speed control cable from the top of the rocker arm if so equipped.

4. Remove the nine rocker arm cover bolts. Remove the rocker cover and gasket from the engine. Inspect the gasket for damage and replace as required.

5. Remove the rocker arm bolts, fulcrums, rocker arms, and fulcrum washers. Label and keep all parts in order so they can be reinstalled to their original positions.

6. Before installation, coat the valve tips, rocker arm and fulcrum contact areas with Lubriplate® or equivalent.

7. Rotate the engine until the lifter is on the base circle of the cam (valve closed).

8. Install the rocker arm and components and torque the rocker arm bolts in 2 steps the first to 6–8 ft. lbs and the second torque to 20–26 ft. lbs. Be sure the lifter is on the base circle of the cam for each rocker arm as it is installed. Adjust the valves as previously outlined.

9. Install guide pins into the cylin-

der head and quide the gasket and rocker arm cover over the pins. Install the retaining screws and washer and torque the screws to 7–10 ft. lbs.

NOTE: Do not use any glue with the silcone gasket.

Intake Manifold

REMOVAL & INSTALLATION

1.6L and 1.9L EFI Engines

1. Raise and secure the hood in the open position.
2. Install protective fender covers.
3. Disconnect the negative battery cable.
4. Partially drain the cooling system and disconnect the heater hose at the fitting located under the intake manifold into a suitable drain pan.
5. Remove air cleaner assembly.
6. Label and disconnect the vacuum hoses.
7. Label and disconnect wiring connectors at the following points:
   a. Choke cap wire
   b. Bowl vent
   c. Idle fuel solenoid
   d. Coolant temperature sensor
   e. Air charge temperature sensor
8. Remove EGR supply tube.
9. Raise the vehicle and support safely.
10. Remove the PVS hose connectors. Label the connecters and set aside.
11. Remove 4 of the 7 lower intake manifold retaining nuts.
12. Lower the vehicle.
13. Disconnect fuel lines at the fuel filter (and or the throttle body) and the return line at the carburetor.
14. Disconnect accelerator and, if equipped, the speed control cable.
15. Disconnect the throttle valve linkage at the carburetor and remove the cable bracket attaching bolts (ATX only).
16. If equipped with power steering, remove the thermactor pump drive belt, the pump, the pump mounting bracket and the thermactor bypass hose.
17. Remove the fuel pump.
18. Remove the remaining 3 intake manifold attaching nuts, intake manifold and gasket.

NOTE: Do not lay the intake manifold flat as the gasket surfaces may be damaged.

19. Make sure the mating surfaces on the intake manifold and the cylinder head are clean and free of gasket material.
20. Install a new intake manifold gasket.
21. Position the intake manifold on

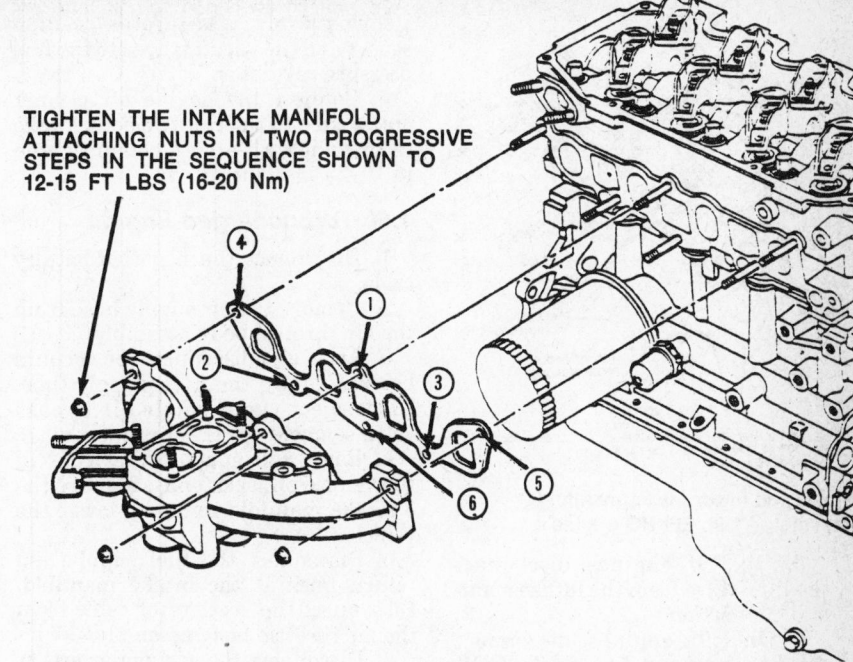

TIGHTEN THE INTAKE MANIFOLD ATTACHING NUTS IN TWO PROGRESSIVE STEPS IN THE SEQUENCE SHOWN TO 12-15 FT LBS (16-20 Nm)

Intake manifold bolt torque sequence – 1.6L and 1.9L engines

the engine and install the attaching nuts. Tighten the nuts to 12–15 ft. lbs.
22. Complete the installation of the remaining intake manifold components by reversing the removal procedure.

1.6L and 1.9L EFI HO Engines

NOTE: The air intake manifold used on these engine is a 2-piece (upper intake and lower intake manifold) aluminum casting. If the upper and lower sub-assemblies are to be serviced and/or removed, with the fuel charging assembly mounted to the engine, perform the following steps.

1. Open hood and install protective covers.
2. Make certain that ignition switch is in **OFF** position.
3. Drain the cooling system into a suitable drain pan.
4. Disconnect the negative battery cable and set aisde.
5. Remove fuel cap to relieve fuel tank pressure.
6. With tool No. T80L–9974–A or equivalent, release pressure from the fuel system at the fuel pressure relief valve on the fuel injector manifold assembly. To gain access to the fuel pressure relief valve, the valve cap must first be removed.
7. Disconnect the push connect fuel supply line. With a suitable prying tool inserted under the hairpin clip tab, "pop" the clip free from the push connect tube fitting and disconnect the push connect tube fitting and discon-

nect the tube. Save the hairpin clip for use in reassembly.
8. Identify and disconnect the fuel return lines and vacuum connections. Have a shop towel on hand to absorb any excess fuel.
9. Disconnect the injector wiring harness by disconnecting the ECT sensor in the heater supply tube under lower intake manifold and the electronic engine control harness.
10. Disconnect air bypass connector from EEC harness.

NOTE: Not all assemblies may be serviceable while on the engine. In some cases, removal of the fuel charging assembly may facilitate service of the various sub-assemblies. Remove the fuel charging assembly as required and proceed with the following steps:

   a. Disonnect the engine air cleaner outlet tube between the vane air meter and air throttle body.
   b. Unplug the throttle position sensor from the wiring harness. On 1.9L engines, disconnect and remove the accelerator and speed control cables, if equipped, from the accelerator mounting bracket and throttle lever.
   c. Unplug the air bypass valve connector. On 1.9L engines, disconnect the top manifold vacuum fitting connections by disconnecting the rear vacuum line to dash panel vacuum tree and vacuum line at the intake manifold tee.

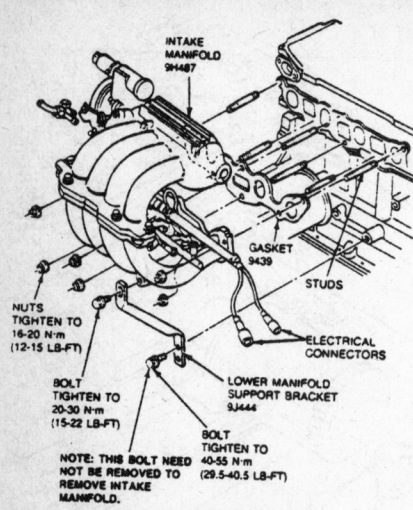

Upper and lower intake manifold assembly—1.9L EFI HO engine

d. On 1.9L engines, disconnect the PCV valve from the intake manifold connection.

e. On 1.9L engines, disconnect the EGR vacuum line at the EGR valve, and disconnect the EGR tube from the intake manifold.

f. On 1.9L engines, disconnect the upper support bracket by removing the top bolt only (leave the bottom bolts attached), and disconnect the main harness and ETC electrical connectors.

g. Remove the fuel supply and return lines. Remove the upper manifold retaining bolts. On 1.9L engines, remove the 6 manifold retaining nuts and disconnect the lower support manifold bracket.

h. Remove upper manifold assembly with wiring harness and set aside.

i. Remove and discard the gasket from the lower manifold assembly.

NOTE: If scraping is necessary, be careful not to damage the gasket surfaces of the upper and lower manifold assemblies, or allow material to drop into lower manifold. Insert a clean rag into the lower intake manifold opening to prevent the entry of gasket scrapings.

11. Ensure that the gasket surfaces of the upper and lower intake manifolds are clean. Clean the intake manifold studs and coat the threads with clean engine oil.

12. Place a new service gasket on the lower manifold assembly and mount the upper intake manifold to the lower, securing it with the retaining nuts and bolts. Torque the bolts to 15–22 ft. lbs. On the 1.9L engine, torque the attaching nuts to 12–15 ft. lbs.

13. Ensure the wiring harness in properly installed.

14. Connect electrical connectors to air bypass valve and throttle position sensor and the vacuum hose to the fuel pressure regulator.

15. Connect the engine air cleaner outlet tube to the throttle body intake securing it with a hose clamp tighten to 15–25 inch lbs.

1.6L Turbocharged Engine

1. Disconnect the negative battery cable.

2. Remove the air supply hose from the air throttle body assembly.

3. Label and disconnect the vacuum hoses. Remove the EGR supply tube. Disconnect the throttle air bypass valve solenoid electrical connector.

4. Raise and support the front of the vehicle on jackstands. Remove the 3 intake manifold nuts and lower the vehicle.

5. Disconnect the fuel supply and return lines at the intake manifold. Disconnect the accelerator cable from the air throttle body assembly.

6. Disconnect the wiring harness at the shock tower. Disconnect the PCV hose at the rocker arm cover and intake manifold. Remove the PCV valve.

7. Remove the 3 remaining mounting nuts. The center nut may need tool T81P-9425-A for removal and installation purposes.

8. Install the intake manifold in the reverse order of removal using a new gasket. Tighten the mounting nuts to 12–15 ft. lbs.

2.3L Engine

1. Open and secure the hood.

2. Disconnect the negative battery cable.

3. Position a suitable drain pan under the radiator and drain the cooling system.

4. Remove accelerator cable.

5. Remove air cleaner assembly and heat stove tube at heat shield.

6. Remove required vacuum lines.

7. Remove thermactor belt from pulley. Remove hose below thermactor pump. Remove thermactor pump.

8. Disconnect the 3 exhaust pipe-to-exhaust manifold retaining nuts.

9. Remove exhaust manifold heat shield. Disconnect the oxygen sensor wire at the connector.

10. Disconnect EGO sensor wire at connector.

11. Disconnect thermactor check valve hose at tube assembly. Remove bracket-to-EGR valve attaching nuts.

12. Disconnect the water inlet tube at the intake manifold.

13. Disconnect EGR tube at EGR valve.

14. Remove intake manifold. Remove the gasket and clean the gasket contact surfaces.

15. Install intake manifold with gasket and retaining bolts. Torque the retaining bolts to 15–22 ft. lbs.

16. Complete the installation of the remaining components by reversing the removal procedure.

17. Connect the negative battery cable and fill the cooling system to the proper level.

18. Start engine and check for leaks.

3.8L Engine

The air intake manifold used on these engines is a two-piece design that consists of upper and lower intake manifold assemblies. The manifold provides mounting flanges for the air throttle body assembly, fuel supply manifold, accelerator control bracketry and EGR valve.

1. Drain the cooling system into a suitable drain pan.

2. Remove the air cleaner assembly including air intake duct and heat tube.

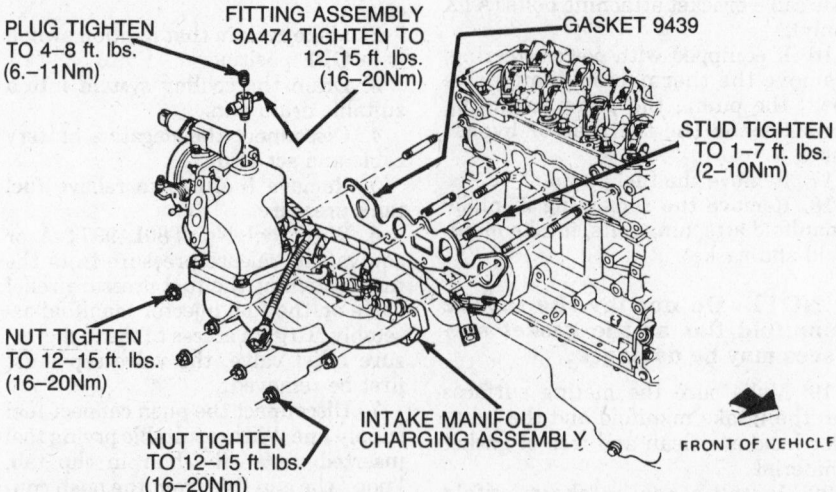

Install the intake manifold and tighten the retaining bolts in the sequence shown on 1.6L engine

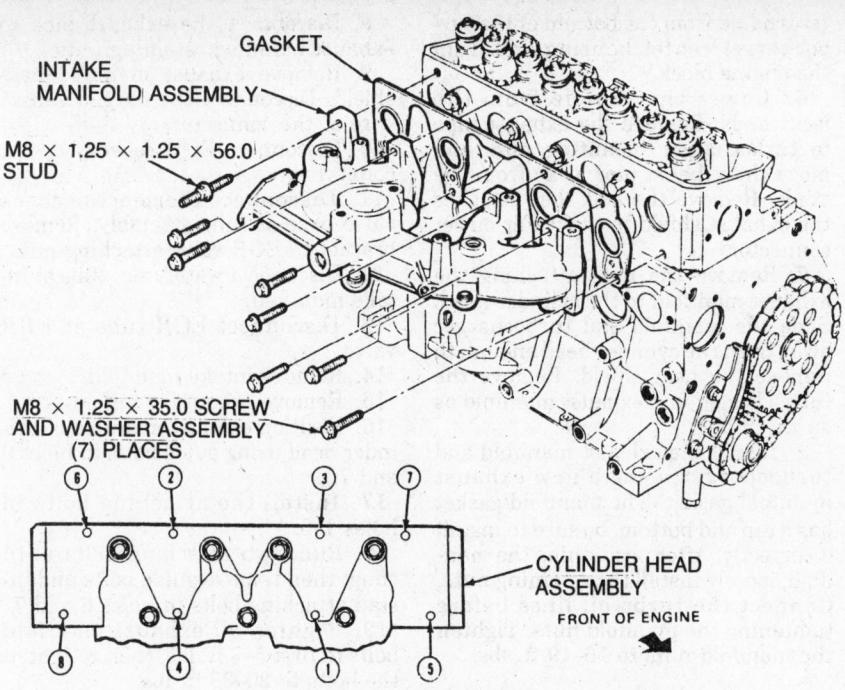

GASKET

INTAKE
MANIFOLD ASSEMBLY

M8 × 1.25 × 1.25 × 56.0
STUD

M8 × 1.25 × 35.0 SCREW
AND WASHER ASSEMBLY
(7) PLACES

CYLINDER HEAD
ASSEMBLY

FRONT OF ENGINE

Intake manifold installation—2.3L HSC engine

block mating surfaces should be clean and free of oil, grease and gasketing material. Use a suitable solvent to clean these surfaces.

23. Apply a bead of contact adhesive No. D7AZ-19B508-A or equivalent to each cylinder head mating surface. Press the new intake manifold gaskets into place, using locating pins as necessary to aid in assembly alignment.

24. Apply a 1/8 in. bead of silicone sealer No. D6AZ-19562-B or equivalent at each corner where the cylinder head joins the cylinder block.

25. Install the front and rear intake manifold end seals.

26. Carefully lower the intake manifold into position on cylinder block and cylinder heads. Use locating pins as necessary to guide the manifold.

27. Install the retaining bolts and stud bolts in their original locations. Torque the retaining bolts in numerical sequence to the following specifications in 3 steps.

 a. Step 1 – 8 ft. lbs.
 b. Step 2 – 15 ft. lbs.
 c. Step 3 – 24 ft. lbs.

28. Connect the rear PCV line to upper intake tube and install the front PCV tube so the mounting bracket sits over the lower intake stud.

29. Install the injectors and fuel rail assembly.

30. Position the upper intake gasket and manifold on top of the lower intake manifold. Use locating pins to secure position of gasket between manifolds.

31. Install bolts and studs in their original locations. Tighten the 4 center bolts, then tighten the end bolts. Torque the lower intake manifold bolts using the procedure described in Step 27.

32. Install the EGR valve assembly on the manifold. Tighten the attaching bolt to 15–22 ft. lbs.

33. Install the throttle body. Cross-tighten hold-down nuts to 15–22 ft. lbs.

34. Connect the rear PCV line at PCV valve and upper intake manifold connections. If equipped with air conditioning, install the compressor support bracket. Tighten attaching fasteners to 15–22 ft. lbs.

35. Connect all electrical connectors and vacuum hoses.

36. Connect the heater tube hose to the heater elbow. Position the heater tube support bracket and tighten attaching nut to 15–22 ft. lbs. Connect the heater hose to the rear of the heater tube and tighten hose clamp.

37. Connect coolant bypass and upper radiator hoses and secure with hose clamps.

38. Connect the fuel line(s) at injec-

3. Disconnect the accelerator cable at throttle body assembly and position off to the side. Disconnect speed control cable, if equipped.

4. Disconnect the transaxle linkage at the upper intake manifold.

5. Remove the attaching bolts from accelerator cable mounting bracket and position cables aside.

6. Disconnect the thermactor air supply hose at the check valve.

7. Disconnect the flexible fuel lines from steel lines over rocker arm cover.

8. Disconnect the fuel lines at injector fuel rail assembly.

9. Disconnect the radiator hose at thermostat housing connection.

10. Disconnect the coolant bypass hose at manifold connection.

11. Disconnect the heater tube at the intake manifold. Remove the heater tube support bracket attaching nut. Remove the heater hose at rear of heater tube. Loosen hose clamp at heater elbow and remove heater tube with hose attached. Remove heater tube with fuel lines attached and set the assembly aside.

12. Disconnect vacuum lines at fuel rail assembly and intake manifold.

13. Label and disconnect all necessary electrical connectors.

14. If equipped with air conditioning, remove the air compressor support bracket.

15. Disconnect the PCV lines. One is located on upper intake manifold. The second is located at the left rocker cover and the lower intake stud.

16. Remove the throttle body assem-

bly and remove the EGR valve assembly from the upper manifold.

17. Remove the attaching nut and remove wiring retainer bracket located at the left front of the intake manifold and set aside with the spark plug wires.

18. Remove the upper intake manifold attaching bolts/studs. Remove the upper intake manifold.

19. Remove the injectors with fuel rail assembly.

20. Remove the heater water outlet hose.

21. Remove the lower intake manifold attaching bolts/stud and remove the lower intake manifold. Remove the manifold side gaskets and end seals. Discard and replace with new.

NOTE: The manifold is sealed at each end with RTV-type sealer. To break the seal, it may be necessary to pry on the front of the manifold with a small or medium pry bar. If it is necessary to pry on the manifold, use care to prevent damage to the machined surfaces.

22. Lightly oil all attaching bolt and stud threads with clean engine oil before installation.

NOTE: When using silicone rubber sealer, assembly must occur within 15 minutes after sealer application. After this time, the sealer may start to set-up and its sealing effectiveness may be reduced. The lower intake manifold, cylinder head and cylinder

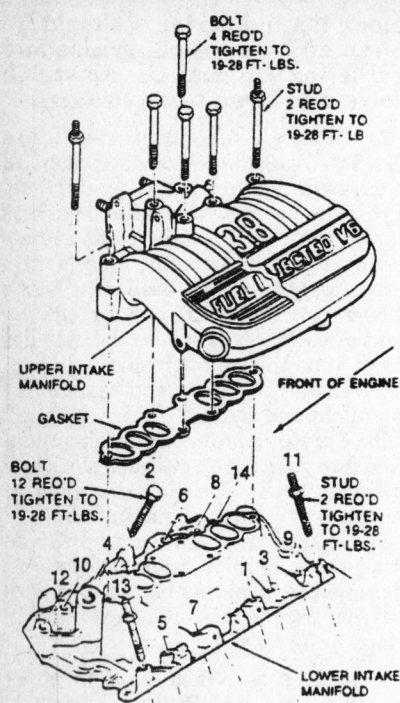

Upper and lower intake manifold assembly—3.8L engine

tor fuel rail assembly and connect the flexible fuel lines to steel lines.

39. Position the accelerator cable mounting bracket and install and tighten attaching bolts to 15–22 ft. lbs.

40. Connect the speed control cable, if equipped. Connect the transaxle linkage at upper intake manifold.

41. Fill the cooling system to the proper level.

42. Start the engine and check for coolant or fuel leaks.

43. Check and, if necessary, adjust engine idle speed, transaxle throttle linkage and speed control.

44. Install the air cleaner assembly and air intake duct.

Exhaust Manifold

REMOVAL & INSTALLATION

Turbocharged Engines

1. Disconnect the negative battery cable. Remove the guard from the radiator.

2. Loosen the turbo outlet hose clamp at the throttle housing. Remove the hose from the turbo housing and rotate the hose up out of the way.

3. Disconnect the inlet hose to the turbocharger.

4. Remove the alternator and bracket. Disconnect the EGO sensor electrical harness connector.

5. Raise and support the front of the vehicle safely. Disconnect the oil supply line at the coolant outlet and at the turbocharger. Disconnect the oil

return line from the bottom of the turbocharger center housing and from the engine block.

6. Lower the vehicle from the jackstands. Remove the exhaust pipe to turbocharger mounting nuts and move the exhaust pipe away from the studs. Remove the bolt that attaches the exhaust shield to the water outlet connector.

7. Remove the nuts attaching the exhaust manifold to the cylinder head. Slide the manifold and turbocharger away from the cylinder head enough to remove the heat shield. Remove the turbocharger and exhaust manifold as an assembly.

8. Install the exhaust manifold and turbocharger using a new exhaust manifold gasket. The manifold gasket has a top and bottom, be sure to install it correctly. After positioning the manifold, loosely install the retaining nuts. Connect the turbo oil lines before tightening the manifold nuts. Tighten the manifold nuts to 16–19 ft. lbs.

1.6L and 1.9L Engines with HO and EFI

1. Disconnect battery cable.
2. Remove air cleaner tray.
3. Disconnect electric fan wire.
4. Remove radiator shroud bolts and radiator shroud.
5. Disconnect EGR tube at the exhaust manifold.
6. Disconnect thermactor tube at the exhaust manifold. Remove the air condtioning hose bracket.
7. Remove exhaust manifold heat stove. Remove the oxygen sensor from the exhaust manifold.
8. Remove exhaust manifold retaining nuts.
9. Raise the vehicle and support safely.
10. Remove anti-roll brace.
11. Disconnect water tube brackets.
12. Disconnect exhaust pipe at the catalyst.
13. Remove exhaust manifold.
14. Clean gasket areas.
15. Position gasket and exhaust manifold (EFI HO engines only).
16. Installation is the reverse order of removal.

2.3L Engine

1. Open and secure the hood.
2. Disconnect negative ground cable at battery.
3. Drain cooling system.
4. Remove accelerator cable.
5. Remove air cleaner assembly and heat stove tube at heat shield.
6. Remove required vacuum lines.
7. Remove thermactor belt from pulley. Remove hose below thermactor pump. Remove thermactor pump.

8. Disconnect the exhaust pipe to exhaust manifold retaining nuts.
9. Remove exhaust manifold heat shield. Disconnect the oxygen sensor wire at the connector.
10. Disconnect EGR sensor wire at connector.
11. Disconnect thermactor check valve hose at tube assembly. Remove bracket to EGR valve attaching nuts.
12. Disconnect water inlet tube at intake manifold.
13. Disconnect EGR tube at EGR valve.
14. Remove intake manifold.
15. Remove exhaust manifold.
16. Position exhaust manifold to cylinder head using guide bolts in holes 6 and 7.
17. Install the attaching bolts in holes 1–5.
18. Rundown attaching bolts until snug, then remove guide bolts and install attaching bolts in holes 6 and 7.
19. Tighten all exhaust manifold bolts to first 5–7 ft. lbs. then retighten the bolts to 20–30 ft. lbs.
20. Install intake manifold gasket and bolts and tighten to specification.
21. Connect water inlet tube at intake manifold.
22. Connect thermactor check valve hose at tube assembly. Install bracket to EGR valve attaching nuts.
23. Connect EGR sensor wire and the oxygen sensor wire at their proper connector.
24. Connect EGR tube to EGR valve.
25. Install exhaust manifold studs.
26. Connect exhaust pipe to exhaust manifold.
27. Install thermactor pump hose to pump. Install thermactor pump and thermactor pump drive belt.
28. Install vacuum lines.
29. Install air cleaner assembly and heat stove tube.
30. Install acclerator cable.
31. Connect negative battery cable.
32. Fill cooling system to the proper level.
33. Start engine and check for leaks.

3.8L Engine

LEFT EXHAUST MANIFOLD

1. Remove the oil level dipstick tube support bracket.
2. Tag and disconnect the spark plug wires.
3. Raise the vehicle and support safely.
4. Remove the manifold-to-exhuast pipe attaching nuts.
5. Lower the vehicle.
6. Remove the exhuast manifold retaining bolts and remove the manifold from vehicle. Discard the gasket and replace with new.
7. Lightly oil all bolt and stud threads before installation. Clean the

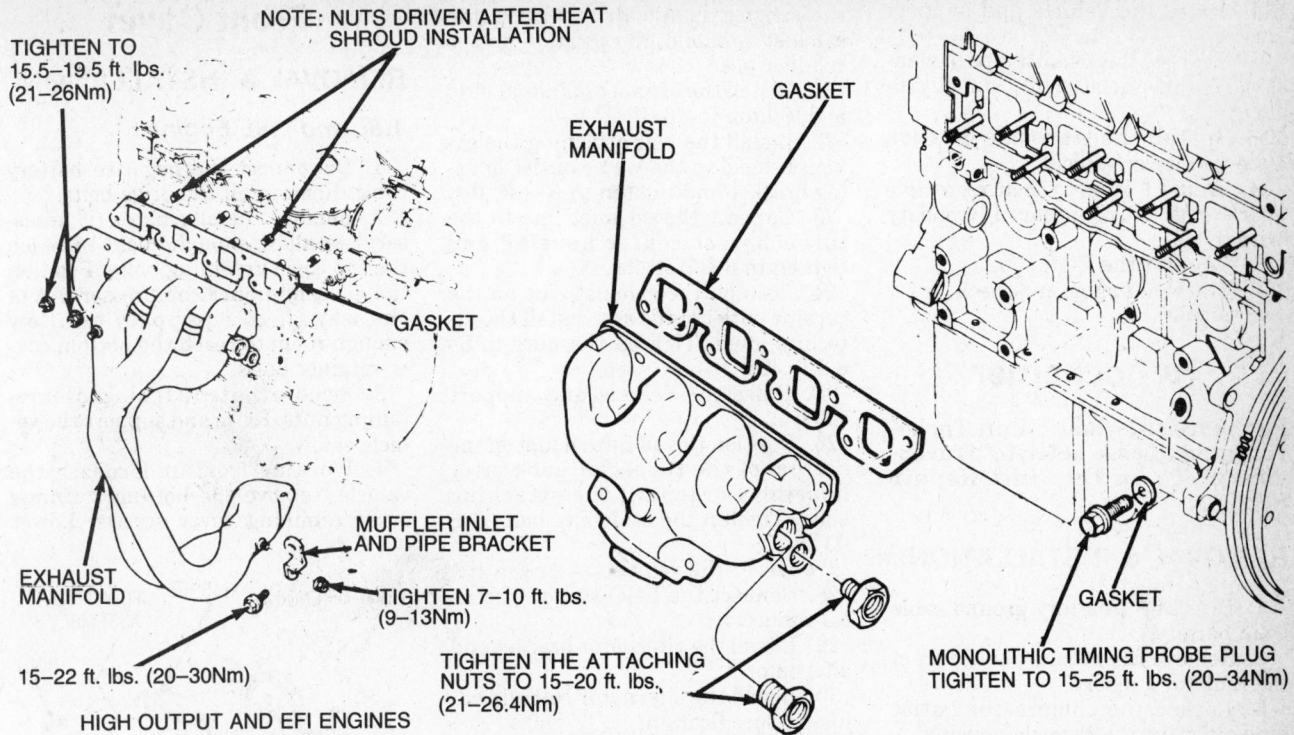

NOTE: NUTS DRIVEN AFTER HEAT SHROUD INSTALLATION

TIGHTEN TO 15.5–19.5 ft. lbs. (21–26Nm)

GASKET

EXHAUST MANIFOLD

GASKET

EXHAUST MANIFOLD

MUFFLER INLET AND PIPE BRACKET

TIGHTEN 7–10 ft. lbs. (9–13Nm)

EXHAUST MANIFOLD

15–22 ft. lbs. (20–30Nm)

TIGHTEN THE ATTACHING NUTS TO 15–20 ft. lbs., (21–26.4Nm)

GASKET

MONOLITHIC TIMING PROBE PLUG TIGHTEN TO 15–25 ft. lbs. (20–34Nm)

HIGH OUTPUT AND EFI ENGINES

Install the exhaust manifold and tighten the remaining bolts in the sequence shown on 1.6L engine

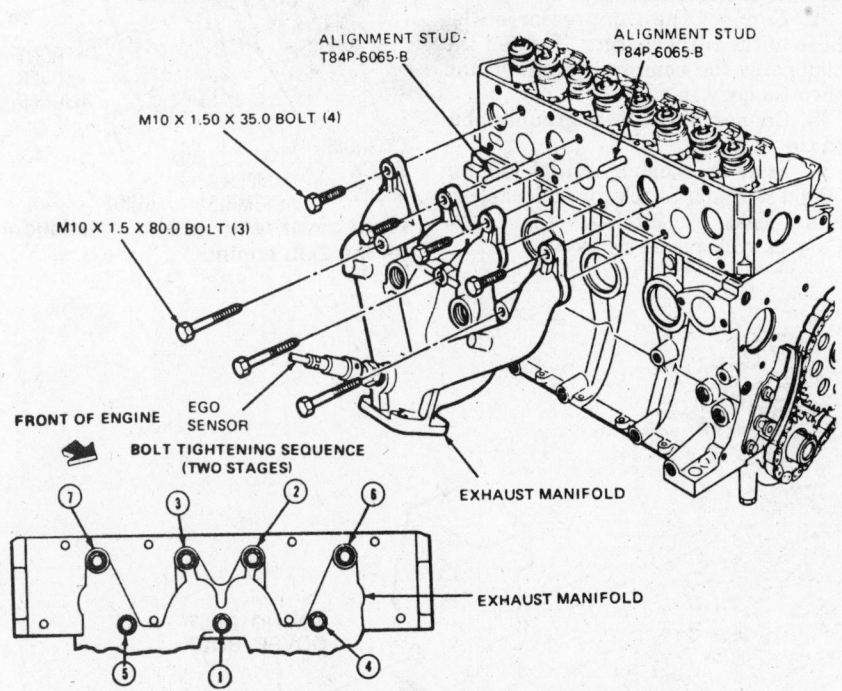

ALIGNMENT STUD T84P-6065-B

ALIGNMENT STUD T84P-6065-B

M10 X 1.50 X 35.0 BOLT (4)

M10 X 1.5 X 80.0 BOLT (3)

FRONT OF ENGINE

EGO SENSOR

EXHAUST MANIFOLD

BOLT TIGHTENING SEQUENCE (TWO STAGES)

EXHAUST MANIFOLD

Exhaust manifold installation—2.3L HSC engine

mating surfaces on the exhaust manifold, cylinder head and exhaust pipe so that they are free of grease and old gasket material.

8. Position the gasket and exhaust manifold on the cylinder head. Install pilot bolt (lower front bolt hole on No. 5 cylinder).

9. Install the remaining manifold retaining bolts. Torque the bolts 15–22 ft. lbs.

NOTE: A slight warpage in the exhaust manifold may cause a misalignment between the bolt holes in the head and the manifold. Elongate the holes in the exhaust manifold as necessary to correct the misalignment, if apparent. Do not elongate the pilot hole (lower front bolt on No. 5 cylinder).

10. Raise the vehicle and support safely.

11. Connect the exhaust pipe to the manifold. Torque the attaching nuts to 16–24 ft. lbs.

12. Lower the vehicle.

13. Connect the spark plug wires. Install dipstick tube support bracket attaching nut.

14. Start the engine and check for exhaust leaks.

RIGHT EXHAUST MANIFOLD

1. Remove the air cleaner outlet tube assembly.

2. Tag and disconnect the coil secondary wire from coil and the wires from spark plugs.

3. Disconnect the EGR tube.

4. Raise the vehicle and support safely.

5. Remove the transaxle dipstick tube.

6. Remove the manifold-to-exhaust pipe attaching nuts.

7. Lower the vehicle.

8. Remove the exhaust manifold retaining bolts.

9. Lightly oil all bolt and stud threads before installation. Clean the mating surfaces on exhaust manifold cylinder head and exhaust pipe so that they are free of grease and old gasket material.

10. Position the gasket and exhaust manifold on cylinder head. Start 2 attaching bolts to align the manifold with the cylinder head. Install the remaining retaining bolts and torque to 15–22 ft. lbs.

11. Raise the vehicle and support safely.

12. Connect the exhaust pipe to manifold. Torque the attaching nuts to 16-24 ft. lbs.

13. Install the transaxle dipstick tube and lower vehicle.

14. Connect wires to their respective spark plugs and connect coil secondary wire to coil.

15. Connect the EGR tube.

16. Start the engine and check for exhaust leaks.

Turbocharger

For more information on Turbocharging, please refer to "Turbocharging" in the Unit Repair Secion.

REMOVAL & INSTALLATION

1. Disconnect battery ground cable from battery.

2. Remove the radiator shield from the radiator support.

3. Loosen the compressor outlet hose clamp at the throttle housing.

4. Remove the hose from the turbocharger compressor outlet, and rotate the hose up and out of the way.

5. Disconnect the compressor inlet hose from the turbocharger.

6. Remove the alternator and bracket.

7. Disconnect the EGR sensor electrical connector.

8. Raise the vehicle on a hoist.

9. Disconnect the oil return line from the bottom of the turbocharger center housing.

10. Lower the vehicle.

11. Remove the exhaust pipe-to-turbocharger attaching nuts.

12. Remove the bolt attaching the exhaust shield to the water outlet connector.

13. Disconnect the oil feed line at the top of the turbocharger center housing.

14. Remove the nuts attaching the exhaust manifold to the cylinder head. Slide the exhaust manifold and turbocharger away from the cylinder head enough to remove the exhaust shield.

15. Remove the turbocharger and exhaust manifold as an assembly.

16. Remove the 4 nuts attaching the turbocharger to the exhaust manifold and remove the turbocharger.

17. Position the turbocharger on the exhaust manifold and tighten the nuts to 16-19 ft. lbs.

18. Install a new exhaust gasket on the cylinder head.

19. Position the exhaust manifold and turbocharger assembly on the cylinder head studs.

20. Position the exhaust shield on the exhaust manifold, and move the exhaust manifold into position on the cylinder head.

21. Install the exhaust manifold nuts and tighten to 16-19 ft. lbs.

22. Install the bolt attaching the exhaust shield to the water outlet housing bracket and tighten to 6-8 ft. lbs.

23. Connect the oil inlet line to the turbocharger center housing and tighten to 6-8.8 ft. lbs.

24. Position the exhaust pipe on the turbine outlet studs and install the attaching nuts. Tighten the nuts to 6-8.8 ft. lbs.

25. Raise the vehicle and support safely.

26. Position the oil return line on the bottom of the turbocharger center housing and install the attaching bolts. Tighten the attaching bolts 6-8 ft. lbs.

27. Lower the vehicle.

28. Connect the EGO sensor electrical connector.

29. Install the alternator bracket and alternator.

30. Install the alternator belt and adjust to specification.

31. Connect the compressor inlet hose to the turbocharger.

32. Connect the compressor outlet hose to the turbocharger. Tighten the clamps at the compressor outlet and throttle body inlet.

33. Connect the battery ground cable to the battery.

34. Start the engine and let idle for 30-60 seconds. Check for oil leaks, exhaust leaks and intake system leaks. Correct all leaks as necessary.

Front Cover

REMOVAL & INSTALLATION

1.6L and 1.9L Engines

1. Disconnect the negative battery cable. Remove all the drive belts.

2. Remove the alternator (if necessary) to allow enough room to reach the top cover retaining bolts. Position the air conditioner compressor out of the way (if so equipped) to allow enough room to reach the bottom cover retainer bolts.

3. Remove the top 2 timing cover retaining nuts. Raise and support the vehicle safely.

4. Working from underneath the vehicle, remove the bottom 2 timing cover retaining cover screws. Lower

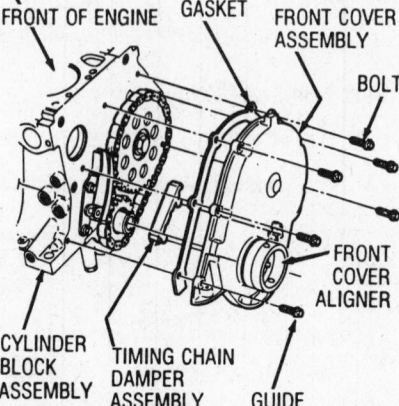

Front cover removal and installation on the 2.3L engine

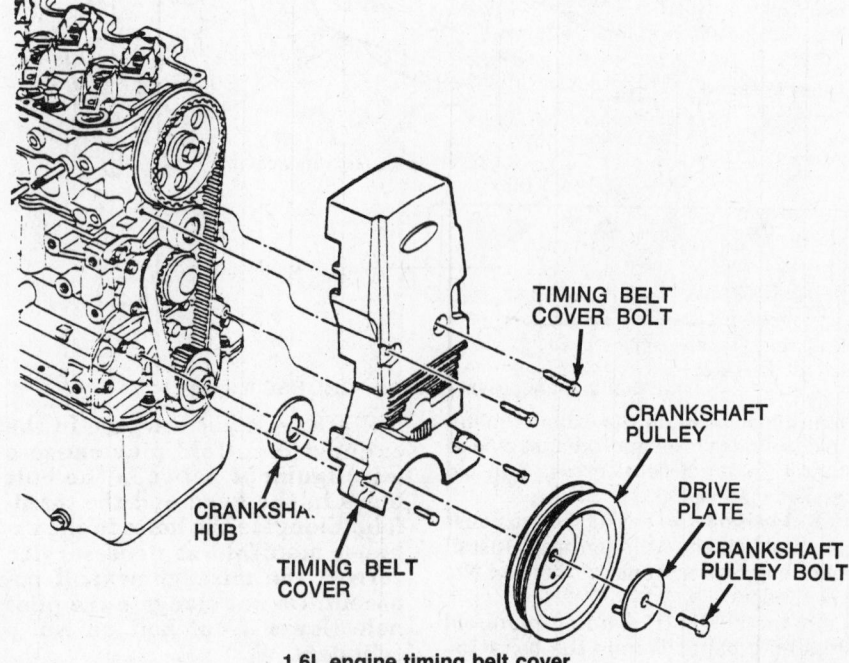

1.6L engine timing belt cover

the vehicle and remove the timing cover by prying it loose from the engine block and lifting it straight out.

5. Installation is the reverse order of the removal procedure.

2.3L Engine

NOTE: The engine must be removed from the vehicle to remove the front cover.

1. Remove the bolt and washer retaining the drive pulley. Use a suitable puller (damper removal tool No. T77F–4220B1 or equivalent) and remove the crankshaft pulley.

2. Remove the front cover retaining bolts, pry the top of the cover away from the engine block and remove the cover.

3. Installation is the reverse order of removal.

3.8L Engine

1. Disconnect the negative battery cable. Drain the cooling system and crankcase.

2. Loosen the accessory drive belt idler. Remove the drive belt and water pump pulley.

3. Remove the power steering pump mounting bracket attaching bolts. Leaving the hoses connected, place the pump/bracket assembly in a position that will prevent the loss of power steering fluid.

4. If equipped with air conditioning, remove the compressor front support bracket. Leave the compressor with hoses in place.

5. Disconnect coolant bypass and heater hoses at the water pump. Disconnect radiator upper hose at thermostat housing.

6. Disconnect the coil wire from distributor cap and remove cap with secondary wires attached. Remove the distributor hold-down clamp and lift distributor out of the front cover.

7. Raise the vehicle and support safely.

8. Remove the crankshaft damper and pulley.

NOTE: If the crankshaft pulley and vibration damper have to be separated, mark the damper and pulley so that they may be reassembled in the same relative position. This is important as the damper and pulley are initially balanced as a unit. If the crankshaft damper is being replaced, check if the original damper has balance pins installed. If so, new balance pins (E0SZ-6A328-A or equivalent) must be installed on the new damper in the same position as the original damper. The crankshaft pulley (new or orignial) must also be installed in original installation position.

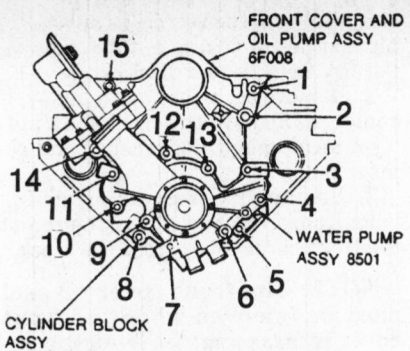

FRONT COVER AND OIL PUMP ASSY 6F008

WATER PUMP ASSY 8501

CYLINDER BLOCK ASSY

View of the front cover assembly— 3.8L engine

9. Remove the oil filter, disconnect the radiator lower hose at the water pump.

10. Remove the oil pan.

11. Lower the vehicle.

12. Remove the front cover attaching bolts.

CAUTION

Do not overlook the cover attaching bolt located behind the oil filter adapter. The front cover will break if pried upon if all attaching bolts are not removed.

13. Remove the ignition timing indicator.

14. Remove the front cover and water pump as an assembly. Remove the cover gasket and discard.

NOTE: The front cover houses the oil pump. If a new front cover is to be installed, remove the water pump and oil pump from the old front cover.

15. Lightly oil all bolt and stud threads before installation. Clean all gasket surfaces on the front cover, cylinder block and fuel pump. If reusing the front cover, replace crankshaft front oil seal.

16. If a new front cover is to be installed, complete the following:

   a. Install the oil pump gears.

   b. Clean the water pump gasket surface thoroughly. Position a new water pump gasket on the front cover and install water pump. Install the pump attaching bolts and torque 15-22 ft. lbs.

17. Lubricate the crankshaft front oil seal with clean engine oil.

18. Position a new cover gasket on the cylinder block and install the front cover/water pump assembly using dowels for proper alignment. A suitable contact adhesive (No. D7AZ-19B508-A or equivalent) is recommended to hold the gasket in position while the front cover is installed.

19. Position the ignition timing indicator.

20. Install the front cover attaching bolts. Apply Loctite® or equivalent to the threads of the bolt installed below

the oil filter housing prior to installation. This bolt is to be installed and tightened last. Tighten all bolts to 15–22 ft. lbs.

21. Raise the vehicle and support safely.

22. Install the oil pan an torque the retaining bolts 7–9 ft. lbs. Connect the radiator lower hose. Install a new oil filter.

23. Coat the crankshaft damper sealing surface with clean engine oil.

24. Position the crankshaft pulley key in the crankshaft keyway.

25. Install the damper with damper washer and attaching bolt. Torque bolt to 104–132 ft. lbs.

26. Install the crankshaft pulley and torque the attaching bolts 19-28 ft. lbs.

27. Lower the vehicle.

28. Connect the coolant bypass hose.

29. Install the distributor with rotor pointing at No. 1 distributor cap tower. Install the distributor cap and coil wire.

30. Connect the radiator upper hose at thermostat housing.

31. Connect the heater hose.

32. If equipped with air conditioning, install compressor and mounting brackets.

33. Install the power steering pump and mounting brackets.

34. Position the accessory drive belt over the pulleys.

35. Install the water pump pulley. Position the accessory drive belt over water pump pulley and tighten the belt.

36. Connect battery ground cable. Fill the crankcase and cooling system to the proper level.

37. Start the engine and check for leaks.

38. Check the ignition timing and curb idle speed, adjust as required.

CRANKSHAFT SEAL REPLACEMENT

1.6L and 1.9L Engines

1. Remove timing belt.

2. Remove crankshaft pulley/damper.

3. Remove the crankshaft front seal. Coat the new seal with clean engine oil.

4. Install the crankshaft front seal using a suitable seal installer tool (No. T81P–6700-A or equivalent).

5. Complete the installation of the crankshaft damper and timing belt by reversing the removal procedure. Tighten the crankshaft damper attaching bolt to 74–90 ft. lbs.

6. Adjust the drive belt tension and connect the negative battery cable.

2.3L Engine

NOTE: The front cover oil seal can only be replaced with the engine removed from the vehicle.

1. Remove bolt and washer at crankshaft pulley.
2. Using damper removal tool No. T77F-4220B-1 or equivalent, remove the crankshaft pulley.
3. Using front seal remover tool T74P-6700-A or equivalent, remove the front cover oil seal.
4. Coat a new seal with grease. Using front seal replacer tool, install seal into cover. Drive seal in until it is fully seated. Check the seal after installation to be sure the spring is properly positioned in the seal.
5. Install crankshaft pulley, attaching bolt and washer. Tighten to specification.

3.8L Engine

1. Disconnect the negative battery cable.
2. Loosen the accessory drive belt idler.
3. Raise the vehicle and support safely.
4. Disengage the accessory drive belt and remove crankshaft pulley.
5. Remove the crankshaft damper.
6. Remove the seal from the front cover with a suitable prying tool. Use care to prevent damage to front cover and crankshaft.

NOTE: Inspect the front cover and crankshaft damper for damage, nicks, burrs or other imperfections which may cause the seal to fail. Service or replace components as necessary.

7. Lubricate the seal lip with clean engine oil and install the seal using seal installers No. T82L-6316-A and T70P-6B070-A or equivalents.
8. Lubricate the seal surface on the damper with clean engine oil. Install damper and pulley assembly. Install the damper attaching bolt and torque to 103–132 ft. lbs.9. Position accessory drive belt over crankshaft pulley.
10. Lower the vehicle.
11. Check accessory drive belt for proper routing and engagement in the pulleys. Adjust the drive belt tension.
12. Connect the negative battery cable. Start the engine and check for leaks.

Timing Chain and Sprockets

REMOVAL & INSTALLATION

2.3L Engine

1. Remove the engine and transaxle

removed from the vehicle as an assembly and position in a suitable holding fixture. Remove the dipstick.
2. Remove accessory drive pulley, if equipped, Remove the crankshaft pulley attaching bolt and washer and remove pulley.
3. Remove front cover attaching bolts from front cover. Pry the top of the front cover away from the block.

NOTE: The front cover oil seal must be removed when the front cover is disassembles from the engine in order to use front cover aligner tool No. T84P-6019-C or equivalent, for proper installation of the front cover.

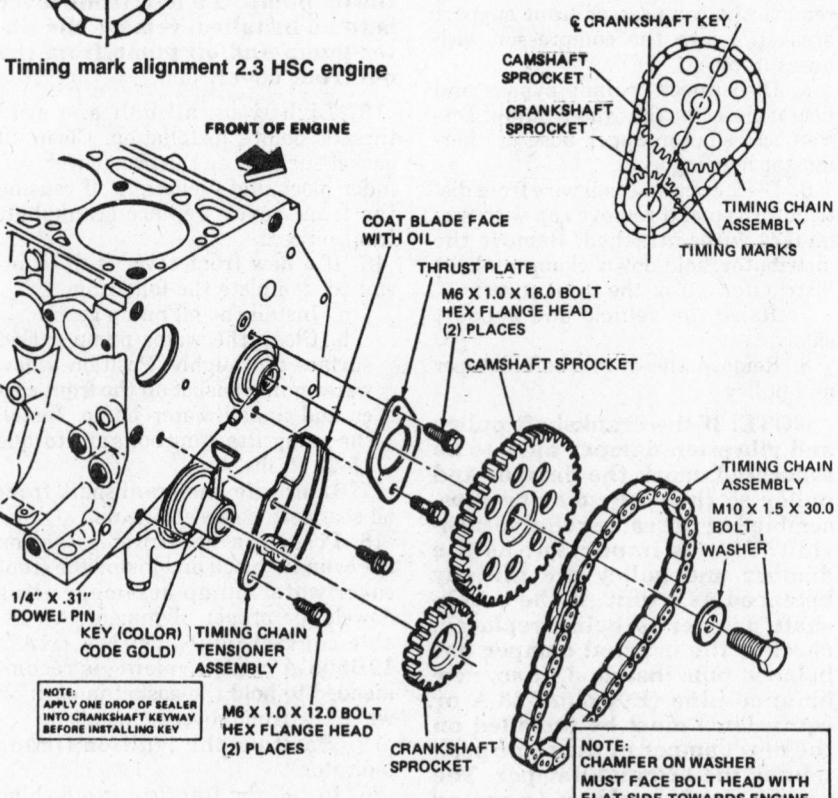

Timing mark alignment 2.3 HSC engine

2.3 HSC engine timing chain and gear assembly

4. Clean any gasket material from the surfaces.
5. Check timing chain deflection. If the deflection exceeds specification, replace the timing chain and sprockets.
6. Check timing chain tensioner blade for wear depth. If the wear depth exceeds specification, replace tensioner.
7. Turn engine over until the timing marks are aligned. Remove camshaft sprocket attaching bolt and washer. Slide both sprockets and timing chain forward and remove as an assembly.
8. Check timing chain vibration damper for excessive wear. Replace if necessary (the damper is located inside the front cover).
9. Remove oil pan.
10. Clean and inspect all parts before installation. Clean oil pan, cylinder block, and front cover gasket contact surfaces of gasket material and dirt.
11. Slide both sprockets and timing chain onto the camshaft and crankshaft with timing marks aligned. Install camshaft bolt and washer and tighten to specification. Oil timing chain, sprockets, and tensioner after installation.
12. Apply oil resistant sealer to a new front cover gasket and position gasket into front cover.
13. Cut 2 front cover attaching bolt

heads off. Install these guide bolts into cylinder block.

14. Position front cover aligner tool T84P–6019–C or equivalent onto the end of the crankshaft, ensuring the crank key is aligned with the keyway in the tool. Bolt the front cover to the engine. Remove guide bolts and install 2 new bolts. Tighten all attaching bolts to specification. Remove the front cover aligner tool.

15. Lubricate the hub of the crankshaft pulley with Polyethylene Grease to prevent damage to the seal during installation and initial engine start. Install crankshaft pulley.

16. Install oil pan.

17. Install the accsssory drive pulley, if equipped.

18. Install crankshaft pulley attaching bolt and washer. Tighten to specification.

19. Remove engine from work stand and install in vehicle.

3.8L Engine

1. Disconnect the negative battery cable. Drain the cooling system and crankcase.

2. Loosen the accessory drive belt idler. Remove the drive belt and water pump pulley.

3. Remove the power steering pump mounting bracket attaching bolts. Leaving the hoses connected, place the pump/bracket assembly in a position that will prevent the loss of power steering fluid.

4. If equipped with air conditioning, remove the compressor front support bracket. Leave the compressor in place with hoses connected.

5. Disconnect coolant bypass and heater hoses at the water pump. Disconnect radiator upper hose at thermostat housing.

6. Disconnect the coil wire from distributor cap and remove cap with secondary wires attached. Remove the distributor hold-down clamp and lift distributor out of the front cover.

7. Raise the vehicle and support safely.

8. Remove the crankshaft damper and pulley.

NOTE: If the crankshaft pulley and vibration damper have to be separated, mark the damper and pulley so that they may be reassembled in the same relative position. This is important as the damper and pulley are initially balanced as a unit. If the crankshaft damper is being replaced, check if the original damper has balance pins installed. If so, new balance pins (E0SZ-6A328-A or equivalent) must be installed on the new damper in the same posi-

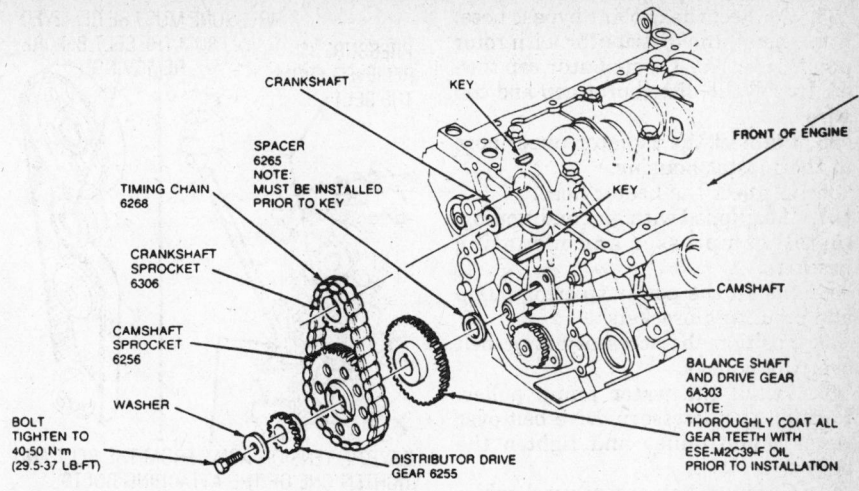

Timing chain and sprockets – 3.8L engine

tion as the original damper. The crankshaft pulley (new or orignial) must also be installed in original installation position.

9. Remove the oil filter, disconnect the radiator lower hose at the water pump.

10. Remove the oil pan and lower the vehicle.

11. Remove the front cover attaching bolts.

—— CAUTION ——
Do not overlook the cover attaching bolt located behind the oil filter adapter. The front cover will break if pried upon if all attaching bolts are not removed.

12. Remove the ignition timing indicator.

13. Remove the front cover and water pump as an assembly. Remove the cover gasket and discard.

14. Remove the camshaft bolt and washer from end of the camshaft. Remove the distributor drive gear.

15. Remove the camshaft sprocket, crankshaft sprocket and timing chain.

NOTE: The front cover houses the oil pump. If a new front cover is to be installed, remove the water pump and oil pump from the old front cover.

16. Lightly oil all bolt and stud threads before installation. Clean all gasket surfaces on the front cover, cylinder block and fuel pump. If reusing the front cover, replace crankshaft front oil seal.

17. If a new front cover is to be installed, complete the following:

　a. Install the oil pump gears.

　b. Clean the water pump gasket surface. Position a new water pump gasket on the front cover and install water pump. Install the pump attaching bolts and torque 15-22 ft. lbs.

18. Rotate the crankshaft as necessary to position piston No. 1 at TDC.

19. Lubricate timing chain with clean engine oil. Install the camshaft sprocket, crankshaft sprocket and timing chain. Make certain the timing marks are positioned across from each other.

20. Install the distributor drive gear.

21. Install the washer and bolt at end of camshaft and torque to 54–67 ft. lbs.

22. Lubricate the crankshaft front oil seal with clean engine oil.

23. Position a new cover gasket on the cylinder block and install the front cover/water pump assembly using dowels for proper alignment. A suitable contact adhesive (No. D7AZ-19B508-A or equivalent) is recommended to hold the gasket in position while the front cover is installed.

24. Position the ignition timing indicator.

25. Install the front cover attaching bolts. Apply Loctite® or equivalent to the threads of the bolt installed below the oil filter housing prior to installation. This bolt is to be installed and tightened last. Tighten all bolts to 15-22 ft. lbs.

26. Raise the vehicle and support safely.

27. Install the oil pan and torque the retaining bolts to 7–9 ft. lbs. Connect the radiator lower hose. Install a new oil filter.

28. Lubricate the crankshaft damper sealing surface with clean engine oil.

29. Position the crankshaft pulley key in the crankshaft keyway.

30. Install the damper with damper washer and attaching bolt. Torque bolt to 104–132 ft. lbs.

31. Install the crankshaft pulley and torque the attaching bolts 19-28 ft. lbs.

32. Lower the vehicle.

33. Connect the coolant bypass hose.

34. Install the distributor with rotor pointing at No. 1 distributor cap tower. Install the distributor cap and coil wire.

35. Connect the radiator upper hose at thermostat housing.

36. Connect the heater hose.

37. If equipped with air conditioning, install compressor and mounting brackets.

38. Install the power steering pump and mounting brackets.

39. Position the accessory drive belt over the pulleys.

40. Install the water pump pulley. Position the accessory drive belt over water pump pulley and tighten the belt.

41. Connect battery ground cable. Fill the crankcase and cooling system to the proper level.

42. Start the engine and check for leaks.

43. Check the ignition timing and curb idle speed, adjust as required.

Timing Belt

REMOVAL & INSTALLATION

1.6L and 1.9L Engines

NOTE: With the timing belt removed and pistons at TDC, do not rotate the camshaft for fear of bending the valves. If the camshaft must be rotated, align the crankshaft pulley 90 degrees BTDC (crankshaft keyway at 9 o'clock).

1. Disconnect the negative battery cable. Remove all accessory drive belts and remove the timing belt cover.

NOTE: Align the timing mark on the camshaft sprocket with the timing mark on the cylinder head.

2. After aligning the camshaft timing marks, reinstall the timing belt cover and verify that the timing mark on the crankshaft pulley aligns with the TDC mark on the front cover. Remove the timing belt cover.

3. Loosen both timing belt attaching bolts using tool T81P-6254-A or equivalent. Pry the tensioner away from the belt as far as possible and hold it in that position by tightening 1 of the tensioner attaching bolts.

4. Remove the crankshaft pulley. Remove and discard the timing belt.

NOTE: Due to limited working space, special tools are required to remove the crankshaft pulley. Crankbelt wrench (Ford) tool number YA826 (to hold the pulley stationary) and a Crankshaft Pulley wrench (Ford) tool number

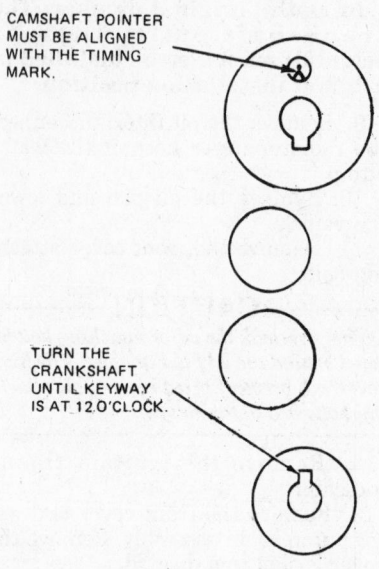

PRESSURE IS RELIEVED FROM THE BELT

PRESSURE MUST BE RELIEVED FROM THE BELT BEFORE REMOVING

PRY THE TENSION AWAY FROM THE BELT AND TIGHTEN ONE OF THE ATTACHING BOLTS

Adjusting the timing belt tension on 1.6L and 1.9L engines

CAMSHAFT POINTER MUST BE ALIGNED WITH THE TIMING MARK.

TURN THE CRANKSHAFT UNTIL KEYWAY IS AT 12 O'CLOCK.

Aligning the timing marks on 1.6 and 1.9L engines

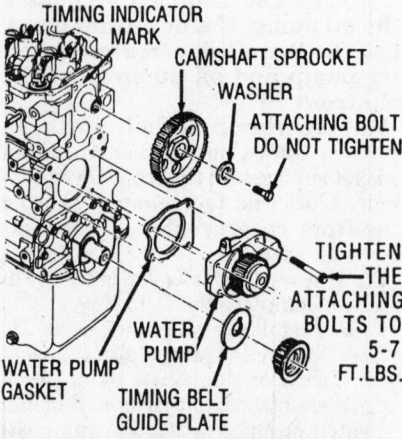

TIMING INDICATOR MARK

CAMSHAFT SPROCKET

WASHER

ATTACHING BOLT DO NOT TIGHTEN

TIGHTEN THE ATTACHING BOLTS TO 5-7 FT.LBS.

WATER PUMP

WATER PUMP GASKET

TIMING BELT GUIDE PLATE

View of the timing sprockets and water pump assembly—1.6L engine

T81P-6312-A or equivalent tools will make the job easier.

5. Install timing belt over the sprockets in a counterclockwise direction starting at the crankshaft. Keep the belt span from the crankshaft to the camshaft tight as the belt is installed over the remaining sprocket.

6. Loosen belt tensioner attaching bolts and allow the tensioner to snap against the belt.

7. Tighten 1 of the tensioner attaching bolts.

8. If timing belt was replaced, install crankshaft pulley, drive plate and pulley attaching bolt. Hold the crankshaft pulley stationary, and tighten the pulley attaching bolt to 74–90 ft. lbs.

9. To seat the belt on the sprocket teeth:

   a. Connect cable to the battery negative terminal.

   b. Crank engine for 30 seconds.

   c. Disconnect cable from the battery negative terminal.

   d. Turn camshaft, as necessary, to align the timing pointer on the cam sprocket with the timing mark on the cylinder head.

   e. Position the timing belt cover on the engine and check to see that the timing mark on the crankshaft aligns with the TDC pointer on the cover. If the timing marks do not align, remove the belt, align the timing marks and return to Step 5.

10. Loosen the belt tensioner attaching bolt tightened in Step 7.

11. To prevent rotation of the crankshaft, have an assistant hold the crankshaft. In Step 12 a specified amount of torque will be applied to the camshaft sprocket. While the torque is applied, the crankshaft must not be allowed to turn.

12. With the crankshaft held, turn the cam sprocket counterclockwise. Tighten the belt tensioner attaching bolt when the torque wrench reads as follows:

   a. New Belt: 27–32 ft. lbs.

   b. Used Belt: 10 ft. lbs. (30 days or more in service).

NOTE: The engine must be at ambient temperature when the torque is applied to the cam sprocket. Do not set torque on a hot engine. Do not apply torque to the camshaft sprocket attaching bolt. Apply it to the hex on the sprocket.

13. Intall timing belt cover.

14. Install accessory drive belts and adjust to specification.

15. Connect negative cable at the battery.

Camshaft

REMOVAL & INSTALLATION

1.6L and 1.9L Engines

NOTE: The camshaft can be removed with the engine in the vehicle.

1. Disconnect negative battery cable.
2. Remove air cleaner, and PCV hose.
3. Remove accessory drive belts, and crankshaft pulley.
4. Remove timing belt cover, and valve cover.
5. Set the engine number 1 cylinder at TDC prior to removing timing belt.

── **CAUTION** ──

Make sure the crankshaft is positioned at TDC and do not turn the crankshaft until the timing belt is installed.

6. Remove rocker arms and tappets as follows:
   a. Remove hex flange nuts.
   b. Remove fulcurms.
   c. Remove rocker arms.
   d. Remove fulcrum washer.
   e. Remove tappets.
7. Remove distributor assembly.
8. Loosen both timing belt tensioner attaching bolts using torque wrench adapter.
9. Remove timing belt.
10. Remove camshaft sprocket, key and thrust plate.
11. Remove fuel pump.
12. Remove ignition coil and coil bracket.
13. Remove camshaft through the back of the head toward the transaxle.
14. Inspect camshaft seal. Replace the seal if it shows any signs of wear or damage.
15. Thoroughly coat the camshaft bearing journals, cam lobe surfaces, and thrust plate groove with clean engine oil.
16. Install camshaft through the rear of the cylinder head. Rotate camshaft during installation.
17. Install camshaft thrust plate. Tighten attaching bolts to 7–11 ft. lbs.
18. Align and install the cam sprocket over the cam key. Install attaching washer and bolt. While holding camshaft, tighten bolt to 37–46 ft. lbs.
19. Install timing belt. Install timing belt cover.
20. Install fuel pump.
21. Install rocker arm assembly as follows:

NOTE: Replace used hex flange nuts with new ones. Lubricate all the parts with a heavy engine oil before installation.

   a. Install the tappets.
   b. Install the fulcrum washers.
   c. Install the rocker arms.
   d. Install the fulcrums.
   e. Install new rocker arm stud hex flange nuts. Tighten to 15–19 ft. lbs.
22. Install the distributor assembly.
23. Apply a $^3/_{16}$ in. (4.75mm) bead of sealer to the valve cover flange.

NOTE: Make sure the surfaces on the cylinder head and valve cover are clean and free of sealant material.

24. Install rocker arm cover attaching bolts and studs. Tighten bolts and studs to 6–8 ft. lbs.
25. Install PCV hose.
26. Install air cleaner assembly.
27. Start engine and set ignition timing to specification.

2.3L Engine

1. With the engine removed from the vehicle and placed on an engine work stand, remove oil dipstick.
2. Drain the cooling system, fuel system and crankcase.
3. Remove necessary drive belts and pulleys.
4. Remove cylinder head.
5. Using a magnet, remove the hydraulic tappets and keep them in order so that they can be installed in their original positions. If the tappets are stuck in the bores by excessive varnish, etc., use hydraulic tappet puller No. T70L–6500–A or equivalent to remove tappets.
6. Loosen and remove the drive belt, fan and pulley, and crankshaft pulley.
7. Remove oil pan.
8. Remove cylinder front cover and gasket.
9. Check the camshaft end play as follows:
   a. Push the camshaft toward the rear of the engine and install dial indicator tool 4201–C or equivalent, so that the indicator point is on the camshaft sprocket attaching screw.
   b. Zero the dial indicator. Position a large screwdriver between the camshaft sprocket or gear and block.
   c. Pull the camshaft forward and release it. Compare the dial indicator reading with the camshaft end play specification of 0.009 in.
   d. If the camshaft end play is over

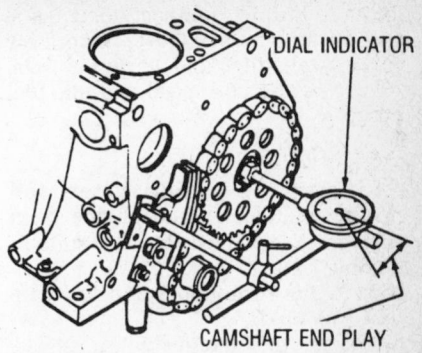

Checking the camshaft endplay

the amount specified, replace the thrust plate.
10. Remove fuel pump, gasket, and fuel pump pushrod.
11. Remove timing chain, sprockets and timing chain tensioner.
12. Remove camshaft thrust plate. Carefully remove the camshaft by pulling it toward the front of the engine. Use caution to avoid damaging bearings, journals, and lobes.
13. Clean and inspect all parts before installation.
14. Lubricate camshaft lobes and journals with heavy engine oil. Carefully slide the camshaft through the bearings in the cylinder block.
15. Instal thrust plate. Tighten attaching bolts to specification.
16. Install timing chain, sprockets, and timing chain tensioner.
17. Install cylinder front cover and crankshaft pulley.
18. Clean oil pump inlet tube screen, oil pan, and cylinder block gasket surfaces. Prime oil pump by filling the inlet opening with oil and rotate the pump shaft until oil emerges from the outlet tube. Install oil pump, oil pump inlet tube screen, and oil pan.
19. Install accessory drive belts and pulleys.
20. Lubricate tappets and tappet bores with heavy engine oil. Install tappets into their original bores.
21. Install cylinder head.
22. Using a new gasket, install fuel pump pushrod and fuel pump. Tighten attaching bolts to specification.
23. Install engine as outlined.
24. Position No. 1 piston at TDC after the compression stroke. Position distributor in the block with the rotor at the No. 1 firing position. Install distributor hold down clamp.
25. Connect engine temperature sending unit wire. Connect coil primary wire. Install distributor cap. Connect spark plug wires and the coil high tension lead.
26. Fill the cooling system. Fill crankcase with the correct viscosity and amount of engine oil.
27. Start engine. Check and adjust

ignition timing. Connect distributor vacuum line to distributor. Check for coolant, oil, fuel and vacuum leaks. Adjust engine idle speed and idle fuel mixture.

3.8L Engine

1. Drain the cooling system and crankcase. Remove the engine from the vehicle and position in a suitable holding fixture.
2. Remove the upper and lower intake manifolds.
3. Remove the tappets.
4. Remove the front cover and timing chain.
5. Remove the oil pan.
6. Remove the camshaft through the front of the engine, being careful not to damage bearing surfaces.
7. Lightly oil all attaching bolts and stud threads before installation. Lubricate the cam lobes, thrust plate and bearing surfaces with a suitable heavy engine oil.
8. Install the camshaft being careful not to damage bearing surfaces while sliding into position.
9. Install the front cover and timing chain.
10. Install the oil pan.
11. Install the tappets.
12. Install the intake upper and lower intake manifolds.
13. Complete the installation of the engine by reversing the removal procedure.
14. Fill the cooling system and crankcase to the proper level. Connect the negative battery cable.
15. Start the engine. Check and adjust the ignition timing and engine idle speed as necessary. Check for leaks of any kind.

Piston and Connecting Rod

POSITIONING

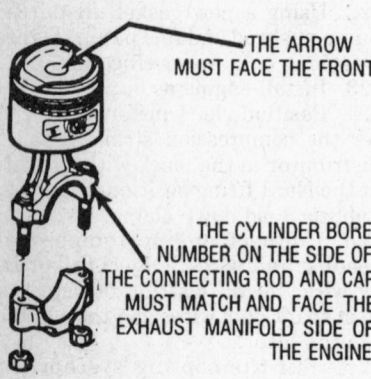

THE ARROW MUST FACE THE FRONT

THE CYLINDER BORE NUMBER ON THE SIDE OF THE CONNECTING ROD AND CAP MUST MATCH AND FACE THE EXHAUST MANIFOLD SIDE OF THE ENGINE

Piston and rod assembly—1.6L engine

NOTE: PISTON TO DECK CLEARANCE TO BE 0.27 BELOW DECK TO 0.25 ABOVE DECK WHEN MEASURED AT PISTON T.D.C. PARALLEL TO CRANKSHAFT ON TRUE CENTERLINE OF PISTON. (AVERAGE OF TWO READINGS)

NOTE: DOME AND BUTTON IDENTIFICATION MUST BE ON SAME SIDE AND TOWARDS FRONT OF ENGINE (AS SHOWN)

PISTON AND ROD ASSY 6100

OIL SQUIRT HOLE

VIEW A

VIEW A

Piston positioning—3.8L engine

ARROW POINTING TOWARD FRONT OF ENGINE

OIL SQUIRT HOLE

NUMBER ON LEFT SIDE OF ROD

2.3L engine piston and rod assembly

PISTON RING SPACING

OIL RING SPACER
(A)

OIL RING SEGMENT
(B)

OIL RING SEGMENT
(B)

PISTON

150 DEGREES

150 DEGREES

PIN BORE

COMPRESSION RING
(C)

COMPRESSION RING
(C)

FRONT OF VEHICLE

Piston ring positioning—1.9L engine

NOTE: STAMP CORRESPONDING BORE NUMBERS ON CAP AND ROD IN THESE AREAS FOR NUMBER SIZE REFER TO 6100 PISTON AND ROD ASSY

1.5 MIN. NO DISTORTION OF PARTING SURFACE PERMITTED

CONNECTING ROD TO CRANKSHAFT SIDE CLEARANCE 0.11-0.29

VIEW A

For all piston and connecting rod overhaul procedures, refer to "Engine Rebuilding" in the Unit Repair Section.

DIESEL ENGINE MECHANICAL

Engine

REMOVAL & INSTALLATION

2.0L Diesel Engine

NOTE: Suitable jackstands or hoisting equipment are necessary to remove the engine and transaxle assembly, as the assembly is removed from underneath the vehicle.

— **CAUTION** —

The air conditioning system contains refrigerant (R-12) under high pressure. Use extreme care when discharging system. If the tools and qualified personnel are not available, have the system discharged prior to start of engine removal.

1. Mark the position of the hood hinges and remove the hood.
2. Remove the negative ground cable from battery that is located in luggage compartment.
3. Remove the air cleaner assembly.
4. Position a drain pan under the lower radiator hose. Remove the hose and drain the engine coolant.

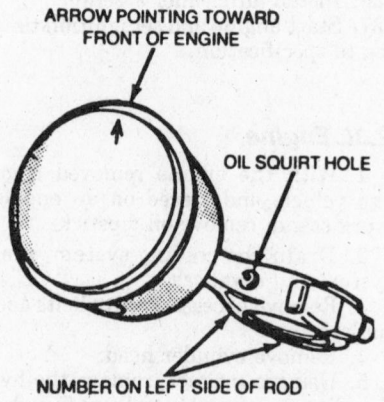

5. Remove the upper radiator hose from the engine.

6. Disconnect the cooling fan at the electrical connector.

7. Remove the radiator shroud and cooling fan as an assembly. Remove the radiator.

8. Remove the starter cable from the starter.

9. Discharge air conditioning system, if equipped. Remove the pressure and suction lines from the air conditioning compressor. Cover or plug the line openings to prevent the entry of moisture and dirt.

10. Identify and disconnect all vacuum lines as necessary.

11. Disconnect the engine harness connectors (2) at the dash panel. Disconnect the glow plug relay connectors at the dash panel.

NOTE: Connectors are located under the plastic shield on the dash panel. Remove and save plastic retainer pins. Disconnect the alternator wiring connector on right hand fender apron.

12. Disconnect the clutch cable from the shift lever on transaxle.

13. Disconnect the injection pump throttle linkage.

14. Disconnect the fuel supply and return hoses on the engine.

15. Disconnect the power steering pressure and return lines at the power steering pump, if equipped. Remove the power steering lines bracket at the cylinder head.

16. Install Engine Support Tool D79P-8000-A or equivalent to existing engine lifting eye.

17. Raise vehicle and safely support on jackstands.

18. Remove the bolt attaching the exhaust pipe bracket to the oil pan.

19. Remove the 2 exhaust pipes to exhaust manifold attaching nuts.

20. Pull the exhaust system out of rubber insulating grommets and set aside.

21. Remove the speedometer cable from the transaxle.

22. Position a drain pan under the heater hoses. Remove 1 heater hose from the water pump inlet tube. Remove the other heater hose from the oil cooler.

23. Remove the bolts attaching the control arms to the body. Remove the stabilizer bar bracket retaining bolts and remove the brackets.

24. Halfshaft assemblies must be removed from the transaxle at this time.

25. On MTX models, remove the shift stabilizer bar-to-transaxle attaching bolts. Remove the shift mechanism to shift shaft attaching nut and bolt at the transaxle.

26. Remove the LH rear insulator

mount bracket from body bracket by removing the 2 nuts.

27. Remove the LH front insulator to transaxle mounting bolts.

28. Lower the vehicle. Install lifting equipment to the 2 existing lifting eyes on engine.

— **CAUTION** —
Do not allow front wheels to touch floor.

29. Remove Engine Support Tool D79L-8000-A or equivalent.

30. Remove RH insulator intermediate bracket to engine bracket bolts, intermediate bracket to insulator attaching nuts and the nut on the bottom of the double ended stud attaching the intermediate bracket to engine bracket. Remove the bracket.

31. Carefully lower the engine and transaxle assembly to the floor.

32. Raise the vehicle support safely.

33. Position the engine and transaxle assembly directly below the engine compartment.

34. Slowly lower the vehicle over the engine and transaxle assembly.

— **CAUTION** —
Do not allow the front wheels to touch floor.

35. Install the lifting equipment to both existing engine lifting eyes on engine.

36. Raise the engine and transaxle assembly up through engine compartment and position accordingly.

37. Install RH insulator intermediate attaching nuts and intermediate bracket to engine bracket bolts. Install nut on bottom of double ended stud attaching intermediate bracket to engine bracket. Tighten to 75–100 ft. lbs.

38. Install Engine Support Tool D79L-8000-A or equivalent to the engine lifting eye.

39. Remove the lifting equipment.

40. Raise the vehicle.

41. Position a suitable floor or transaxle jack under engine. Raise the engine and transaxle assembly into mounted position.

42. Install insulator to bracket nut and tighten to 75–100 lbs.

43. Tighten the LH rear insulator bracket to body bracket nuts to 75–100 ft. lbs.

44. Install the lower radiator hose and install retaining bracket and bolt.

45. Install the shift stabilizer bar to transaxle attaching bolt. Tighten to 23–35 ft. lbs.

46. Install the shift mechanism to input shift shaft (on transaxle) bolt and nut. Tighten to 7–10 ft. lbs.

47. Install the lower radiator hose to the radiator.

48. Install the speedometer cable to the transaxle.

49. Connect the heater hoses to the water pump and oil cooler.

50. Position the exhaust system up and into insulating rubber grommets located at the rear of the vehicle.

51. Install the exhaust pipe to exhaust manifold bolts.

52. Install the exhaust pipe bracket to the oil pan bolt.

53. Place the stabilizer bar and control arm assembly into position. Install control arm to body attaching bolts. Install the stabilizer bar brackets and tighten all fasteners.

54. Halfshaft assemblies must be installed at this time.

55. Lower the vehicle.

56. Remove the Engine Support Tool D79L-6000-A or equivalent.

57. Connect the alternator wiring at RH fender apron.

58. Connect the engine harness to main harness and glow plug relays at dash panel. Reinstall the plastic shield.

59. Connect the vacuum lines.

60. Install the air conditioning discharge and suction lines to air conditioning compressor, if so equipped. Do not charge system at this time.

61. Connect the fuel supply and return lines to the injection pump.

62. Connect the injection pump throttle cable.

63. Install the power steering pressure and return lines. Install bracket.

64. Connect the clutch cable to shift lever on transaxle.

65. Connect the battery cable to starter.

66. Install the radiator shroud and coolant fan assembly. Tighten attaching bolts.

67. Connect the coolant fan electrical connector.

68. Install the upper radiator hose to engine.

69. Fill and bleed the cooling system.

70. Install the negative ground battery cable to battery.

71. Install the air cleaner assembly.

72. Install the hood.

73. Charge air conditioning system, if so equipped. System can be changed at a later time if outside source is used.

74. Check and refill all fluid levels, (power steering, engine, MTX).

75. Start the vehicle. Check for leaks.

Cylinder Head

REMOVAL & INSTALLATION

2.0L Diesel Engine

1. Disconnect the battery ground cable from the battery, which is located in the luggage compartment.

2. Drain the cooling system into a suitable drain pan.

3. Remove the camshaft cover, front and rear timing belt covers, and front and rear timing belts.

4. Raise the vehicle and safely support on jackstands.

5. Disconnect the muffler inlet pipe at the exhaust manifold. Lower the vehicle.

6. Disconnect the air inlet duct at the air cleaner and intake manifold. Install a protective cover.

7. Disconnect the electrical connectors and vacuum hoses to the temperature sensors located in the thermostat housing.

8. Disconnect the upper and lower coolant hoses, and the upper radiator hose at the thermostat housing.

9. Disconnect and remove the injection lines at the injection pump and nozzles. Cap all lines and fittings with Cap Protective Set T84P-9395-A or equivalent.

10. Disconnect the glow plug harness from the main engine harness.

11. Remove the cylinder head bolts in the sequence shown. Remove the cylinder head.

12. Remove the glow plugs. Then remove pre-chamber cups from the cylinder head using a brass drift.

13. Clean the pre-chamber cups, pre-chambers in the cylinder heads and all gasket mounting surfaces on the cylinder head and engine block.

14. Install the pre-chambers in the cylinder heads making sure the locating pins are aligned with the slots provided.

15. Install the glow plugs and tighten to 11–15 ft. lbs. Connect glow plug harness to the glow plugs. Tighten the nuts to 5–7 ft. lbs.

CAUTION

Carefully blow out the head bolt threads in the crankcase with compressed air. Failure to thoroughly clean the thread bores can result in incorrect cylinder head torque or possible cracking of the crankcase.

---

16. Position a new cylinder head gasket on the crankcase making sure the cylinder head oil feed hole is not blocked.

17. Measure each cylinder head bolt dimension A. If the measurement is more than 114.5mm (4.51 in.), replace the head bolt. Rotate the camshaft in the cylinder head until the cam lobes for No. 1 cylinder are at the base circle (both valves closed). Then, rotate the crankshaft clockwise until No. 1 piston is halfway up in the cylinder bore toward TDC. This is to prevent contact between the pistons and valves.

18. Install the cylinder head on the crankcase.

NOTE: Before installing the cylinder head bolts, paint a white reference dot on each one, and apply a light coat of engine oil on the bolt threads.

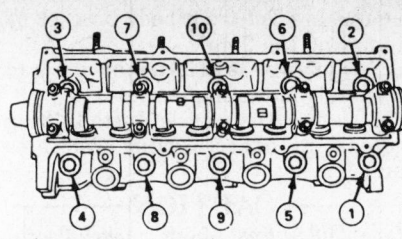

2.0L diesel cylinder head bolt removal

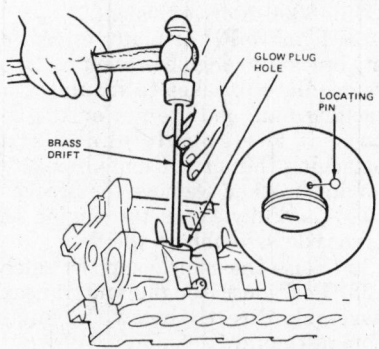

2.0L diesel pre-chamber removal

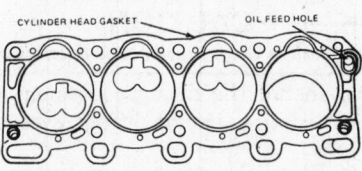

2.0L diesel head gasket identification

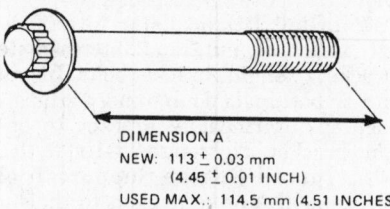

DIMENSION A
NEW: 113 ± 0.03 mm
(4.45 ± 0.01 INCH)
USED MAX.: 114.5 mm (4.51 INCHES)

2.0L diesel head bolt measurement

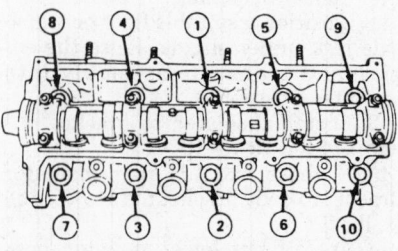

2.0L diesel head bolt tightening sequence

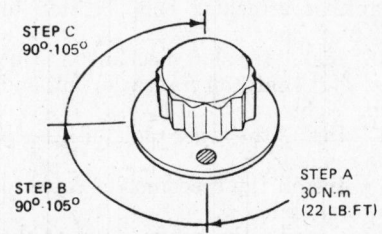

STEP C 90°-105°
STEP B 90°-105°
STEP A 30 N·m (22 LB·FT)

2.0L diesel head bolt tightening steps

19. Tighten cylinder head bolts as follows:

   a. Tighten bolts in sequence to 22 ft. lbs.

   b. Using the painted reference marks, tighten each bolt in sequence another 90 degrees to 105 degrees.

   c. Repeat Step b by turning the bolts another 90–105 degrees.

20. Connect the glow plug harness to main engine harness.

21. Remove the protective caps and install injection lines to the injection pump and nozzles. Tighten capnuts to 18–20 ft. lbs.

22. Air bleed the system.

23. Connect the upper and lower coolant hoses, and the upper radiator hose to the thermostat housing. Use a new gasket with the upper hose. Tighten upper coolant hose bolts to 5–7 ft. lbs.

24. Connect the electrical connectors and the vacuum hoses to the temperature sensors in the thermostat housing.

25. Remove the protective cover and install the air inlet duct to the intake manifold and air cleaner.

26. Raise vehicle and support on jackstands. Connect the muffler inlet pipe to the exhaust manifold. Tighten nuts to 25–35 ft. lbs.

27. Lower the vehicle.

28. Install and adjust the front timing belt.

29. Install and adjust the rear timing belt.

30. Install the front upper timing belt cover and rear timing belt cover. Tighten the bolts to 5–7 ft. lbs.

31. Check and adjust the valves as outlined. Install the valve cover and tighten the bolts to 5–7 ft. lbs.

32. Fill and bleed the cooling system.

33. Check and adjust the injection pump timing.

34. Connect battery ground cable to battery. Run engine and check for oil, fuel and coolant leaks.

OVERHAUL

For all cylinder head overhaul procedures, refer to "Engine Rebuilding" in the Unit Repair Section.

Intake Manifold

REMOVAL & INSTALLATION

2.0L Diesel Engine

1. Disconnect the air inlet duct from the intake manifold and install the protective cap in the intake manifold, (part or Protective Cap Set T84P-9395-A or equivalent).

2. Disconnect the glow plug resistor electrical connector.

3. Disconnect the breather hose.

4. Drain the cooling system into a suitable drain pan.

5. Disconnect the upper radiator hose at the thermostat housing.

6. Disconnect the two-coolant hoses at the thermostat housing.

7. Disconnect the connectors to the temperature sensors in the thermostat housing.

8. Remove the bolts attaching the intake manifold to the cylinder head and remove the intake manifold.

9. Clean the intake manifold and cylinder head gasket mating surfaces.

10. Install the intake manifold, using a new gasket, and tighten the bolts to 12–16 ft. lbs.

11. Connect the temperature sensor connectors.

12. Connect the lower coolant hose to the thermostat housing and tighten the hose clamp.

13. Connect the upper coolant tube, using a new gasket and tighten bolts to 5–7 ft. lbs.

14. Connect the upper radiator hose to the thermostat housing.

15. Connect the breather hose.

16. Connect the glow plug resistor electrical connector.

17. Remove the protective cap and install the air inlet duct.

18. Fill and bleed the cooling system.

19. Run the engine and check for intake air leaks and coolant leaks.

Exhaust Manifold

REMOVAL & INSTALLATION

2.0L Diesel Engine

1. Remove the nuts attaching the muffler inlet pipe to the exhaust manifold.

2. Remove the bolts attaching the heat shield to the exhaust manifold.

3. Remove the nuts attaching the exhaust manifold to cylinder head and remove the exhaust manifold.

4. Install the exhaust manifold, using new gaskets, and tighten nuts to 16–20 ft. lbs.

5. Install the exhaust shield and tighten bolts to 12–16 ft. lbs.

6. Connect the muffler inlet pipe to the exhaust manifold and tighten the nuts to 25–35 ft. lbs.

7. Run the engine and check for exhaust leaks.

Timing Belt

ON CAR SERVICE

2.0L Diesel Engine

NOTE: Use the following procedure for in-vehicle service of the water pump, camshaft or cylinder

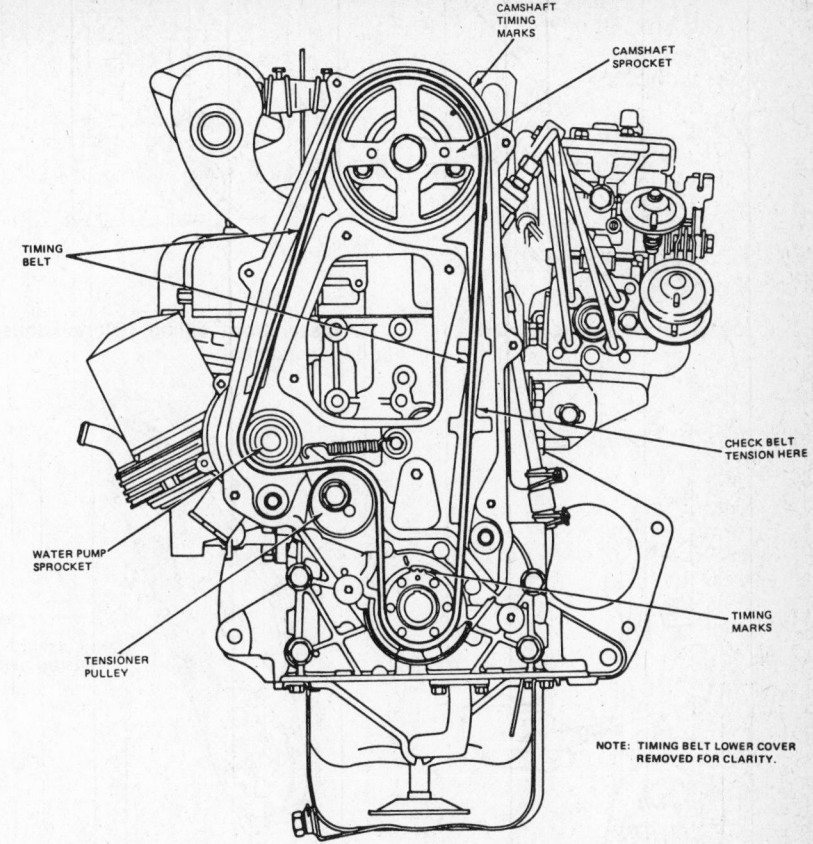

2.0L diesel timing belt installation

head. The timing belt cannot be replaced with the engine installed in the vehicle.

1. Remove the front timing belt upper cover and the flywheel timing mark cover.

2. Rotate engine clockwise until the timing marks on the flywheel and the front camshaft sprocket are aligned with their pointers.

3. Loosen tensioner pulley lockbolt and slide the timing belt off the water pump and camshaft sprockets.

4. The water pump and/or camshaft can now be serviced.

——————— CAUTION ———————

Unless the camshaft is being removed, DO NOT rotate the crankshaft with the front timing belt removed.

ADJUSTMENTS

Front Belt

1. Remove the flywheel timing mark cover.

2. Remove the front timing belt upper cover.

3. Remove the belt tension spring from the storage pocket in the front cover.

4. Install the tensioner spring in the belt tensioner lever and over the stud mounted on the front of the crankcase.

5. Loosen the tensioner pulley lockbolt.

6. Rotate the crankshaft pulley 2 revolutions clockwise until the flywheel TDC timing mark aligns with the pointer on the rear cover plate.

7. Check the front camshaft sprocket to see that it is aligned with its timing mark.

8. Tighten the tensioner lockbolt to 23–34 ft. lbs.

9. Check the bolt tension using Rotunda Belt Tension Gauge Model 21-0028 or equivalent. Belt tension should be 33–44 lbs.

10. Remove the tensioner spring and install it in the storage pocket in the front cover.

11. Install the front cover and tighten the attaching bolts to 5–7 ft. lbs.

12. Install the flywheel timing mark cover.

Rear Belt

1. Remove the flywheel timing mark cover.

2. Remove the rear timing belt cover.

3. Loosen the tensioner pulley locknut.

4. Rotate the crankshaft 2 revolutions until the flywheel TDC timing mark aligns with the pointer on the rear cover plate.

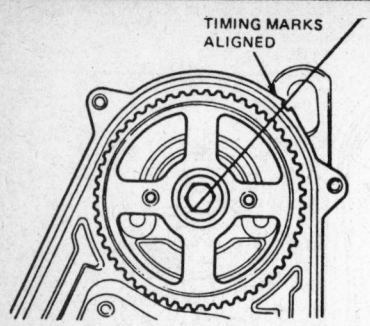

2.0L diesel camshaft timing mark

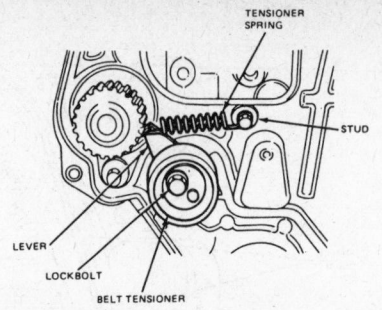

2.0L diesel front timing belt tensioner spring installation

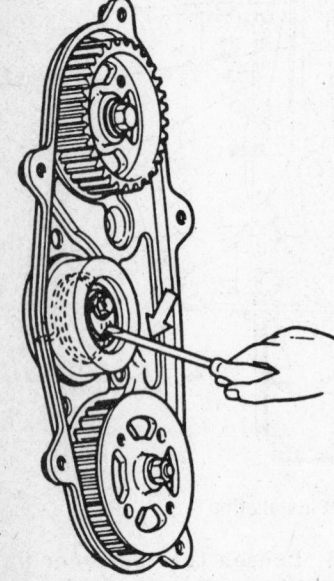

Loosening tensioner pulley on 2.0L diesel

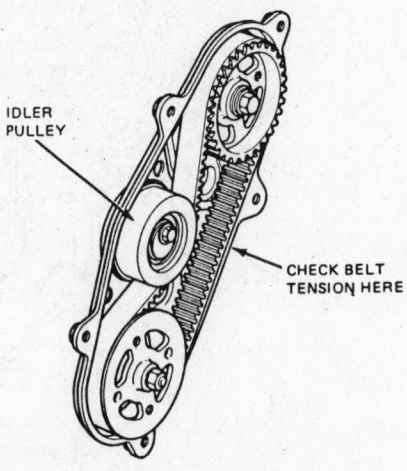

2.0L diesel timing belt tensioner rear belt

7. Align the camshaft sprocket with the timing mark.

NOTE: Check the crankshaft sprocket to see that the timing marks are aligned.

8. Remove the tensioner spring from the pocket in the front timing belt upper cover and install it in the slot in the tensioner lever and over the stud in the crankcase.

9. Push the tensioner lever toward the water pump as far as it will travel and tighten lockbolt snug.

10. Install timing belt.

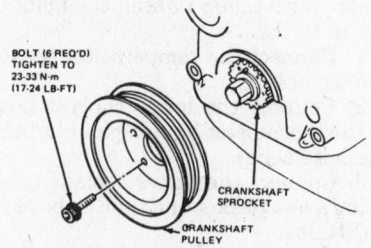

2.0L diesel crankshaft pulley removal

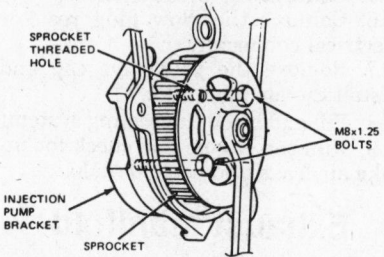

2.0L diesel injector pump sprocket removal

5. Check that the camshaft sprocket and injection pump sprocket are aligned with their timing marks.

6. Tighten tensioner locknut to 15–20 ft. lbs.

7. Check belt tension using Rotunda Belt Tension Gauge Model 21–0028 or equivalent. Belt tension should be 22–33 lbs.

8. Install the rear timing belt cover. Tighten the 6mm bolts to 5–7 ft. lbs. and the 8mm bolt to 12–16 ft. lbs.

9. Install the flywheel timing mark cover.

REMOVAL & INSTALLATION

Rear Belt

1. Remove the rear timing belt cover.

2. Remove the flywheel timing mark cover from clutch housing.

3. Rotate the crankshaft until the flywheel timing mark is at TDC on No. 1 cylinder.

4. Check that the injection pump and camshaft sprocket timing marks are aligned.

5. Loosen the tensioner locknut. With a suitable tool inserted in the slot

provided, rotate the tensioner clockwise to relieve belt tension. Tighten locknut snug.

6. Remove the timing belt.

7. Install the belt.

8. Loosen the tensioner locknut and adjust timing belt as outlined in previous section.

9. Install rear timing belt cover and tighten bolts to 5–7 ft. lbs.

Front Belt

NOTE: The engine must be removed from the vehicle to replace the front timing belt.

1. With engine removed from the vehicle and installed on an engine stand, remove from timing belt upper cover.

2. Install a Flywheel Holding Tool No. T84P6375A or equivalent.

3. Remove the 6 bolts attaching the crankshaft pulley to the crankshaft sprocket.

4. Install a crankshaft pulley remover No. T58P-6316-D or equivalent using adapter No. T74P-6700-B or equivalent, and remove crankshaft pulley.

5. Remove the front timing belt lower cover.

6. Loosen the tensioning pulley and remove the timing belt.

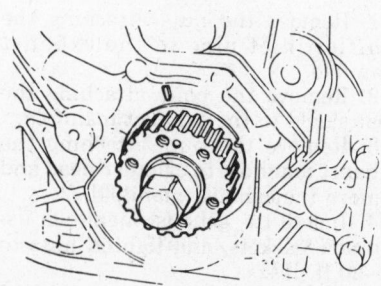

2.0L diesel crankshaft pulley timing marks

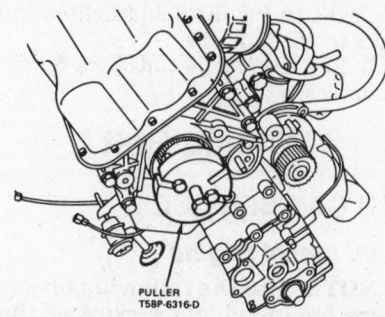

2.0L diesel crankshaft sprocket removal

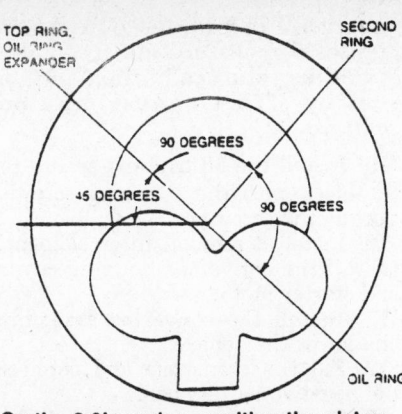

On the 2.0L engine, position the piston rings approximately 90 degrees apart

11. Adjust the timing belt tension as outlined in previous section.

12. Install the front timing belt lower cover and tighten bolts to 5–7 ft. lbs.

13. Install the crankshaft pulley and tighten bolts to 17–24 ft. lbs.

14. Install the front timing belt upper cover and tighten bolts to 5–7 ft. lbs.

Piston and Connecting Rod

POSITIONING

For all piston and connecting rod overhaul procedures, refer to "Engine Rebuilding" in the Unit Repair Section.

Diesel Engine

1. When installing rings, make sure that the side with the stamped mark faces upward.

2. Assemble the compression and oil rings. The gap of the top ring and second ring should be positioned on the opposite side from the turbulent flow chamber.

3. The gap of the ring should not be directed toward the thrust side or counter-thrust side and the gap of the top ring should be set opposite (180 degrees) to that of the oil ring.

4. When assembling the connecting rod and bearing cap, make sure the weight marks of the rod and cap are matched correctly.

ENGINE LUBRICATION

Oil Pan

REMOVAL & INSTALLATION

NOTE: The oil pan can be re- moved with the engine in the car. No suspension or chassis components need be removed.

1.6L and 1.9L Engines

1. Disconnect negative cable at the battery.
2. Raise the vehicle on a hoist.
3. Drain crankcase.
4. Disconnect cable at the starter.
5. Remove knee-brace located at the front of the starter.
6. Remove starter attaching bolts and starter.
7. Remove knee-braces at the transaxle.
8. Disconnect the exhaust inlet pipe at the manifold and converter. Remove pipe.
9. Remove oil pan retaining bolts and oil pan.
10. Remove oil pan front seal, if installed.
11. Remove oil pan rear seal, if installed.
12. Remove 2 oil pan side gaskets, if installed.

NOTE: 1987–89 vehicles use a 1-piece oil pan gasket with press fit tabs. After the gasket is removed, discard and replace with new.

13. Clean the oil pan gasket surface and the mating surface on the cylinder block.
14. Remove the clean the oil pump pick up tube and screen assembly. Install tube and screen assembly with a new gasket.
15. Apply sealer approximately 3.0mm wide at the corner of the oil pan front and rear seals and at the seating point of the oil pump to the block retainer joint.

NOTE: If a 1-piece gasket is used, install the gasket in the oil pan making sure that the press fit tabs are fully engaged in the oil pan gasket channel.

16. Install the front oil pan seal by pressing firmly into the oil pump slot cut into the bottom of the oil pump (if equipped).
17. Install the oil pan rear seal by pressing firmly into the slot cut into the rear retainer assembly (if equipped).

NOTE: Install the seals before the sealer has cured (within 10 minutes of application).

18. Apply adhesive evenly to the oil pan flange and to the pan side of the gaskets. Allow the adhesive to dry past the "wet" stage and then install the gaskets on the oil pan.
19. Install the oil pan on the cylinder block.
20. Install the oil pan attaching bolts. Tighten the bolts in the sequence to 6–8 ft lbs.

21. Position the transaxle inspection plate and the rear section of the knee-brace on the transaxle and install 2 attaching bolts. Tighten bolts to specification.

NOTE: On 1987–89 vehicles, torque the 2 "M–10" oil pan-to-transaxle bolts to 29–40 ft. lbs. (40–54 Nm) then back off ½ turn, torque the "M–8" oil pan-to-cylinder block bolts in sequence to 15–22 ft. lbs. (20–30 Nm) and retorque the "M–10" bolts to 30–40 ft. lbs. (40–54 Nm).

22. Position the transaxle inspection plate and the rear section of the knee-brace on the transaxle and install 2 attaching bolts (1985 vehicles only). Install the starter.
23. Install knee-brace at the starter.
24. Connect starter cable.
25. Install exhaust inlet pipe.
26. Lower vehicle and fill the crankcase with oil.
27. Connect negative cable at the battery.
28. Start engine and check for oil leaks.

2.3L Engine

NOTE: 1984–85 vehicles do not use a gasket to seal the oil pan.

1. Disconnect negative ground cable at battery.
2. Raise vehicle.
3. Drain crankcase.
4. Drain coolant by removing lower radiator hose.
5. Remove roll restrictor (MTX only).
6. Disconnect starter cable.
7. Remove starter.
8. Disconnect exhaust pipe from oil pan.
9. Remove engine coolant tube located at the lower radiator hose, at the water pump and at the tabs on the oil pan., Position air conditioner line off to the side. Remove oil pan. On 1986–89 vehicles, remove the oil pan gasket and replace with new.
10. Clean both mating surfaces of oil pan, front cover and cylinder block rails making certain that all traces of the old RTV sealant are completely removed.
11. Remove and clean oil pump pickup tube and screen assembly. After cleaning, install tube and screen assembly.

NOTE: Before proceeding to install the oil pan on 1984–85 vehicles, a trial installation of the pan to cylinder block must be performed to insure smooth pan installation, thus preventing smear-

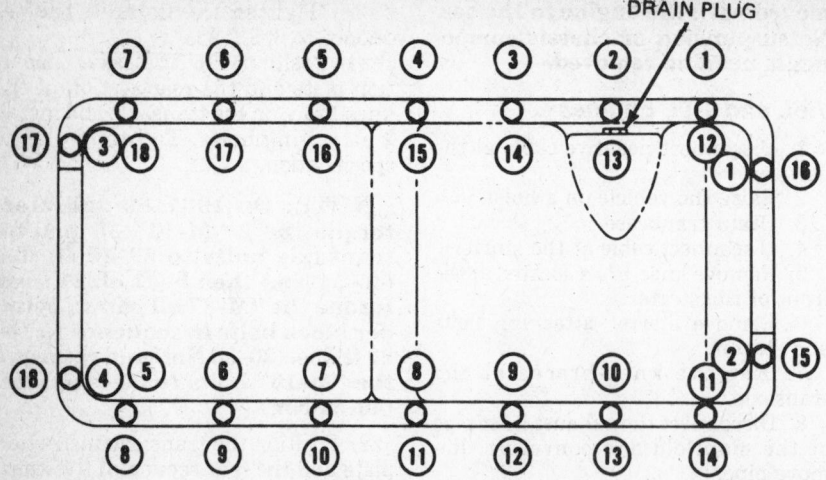

DRAIN PLUG

1.6L engine oil pan. Torque the bolts using the inside sequence first, the retorque the bolts using the outside sequence

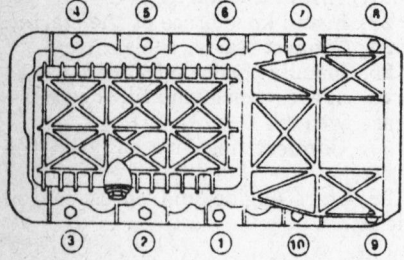

Oil pan bolt torque sequence—
1.9L engine

ing of sealant. Check again for any residual oil that may have leaked down (particularly the rear of the engine) and re-clean as necessary.

12. On 1984–85 vehicles, apply a continuous 3/16 in. diameter bead of Silicone Gasket Sealant to groove in oil pan flange. Immediately place the oil pan against the block and transaxle before the sealant "skins" over, approximately 2 minutes.

13. On 1986–89 vehicles, insert the oil pan gasket into the groove in the pan and place a bead of sealant onto the rear joint cylinder block, rear oil seal retainer assembly/front joint cylinder block and front cover assembly. Once the sealant is applied, immediately raise the pan to the block and install the attaching bolts finger tight until the 2 pan-to-transaxle bolts can be installed.14. Install oil pan flange bolts tight enough to compress sealant to the point that the 2 oil pan transaxle hoses are aligned with the 2 tapped holes in transaxle but loose enough to allow the pan to move relative to the block.

14. Install 2 oil pan to transaxle bolts. Tighten to 30–39 ft. lbs. to align oil pan with transaxle, then loosen bolts ½ turn.

15. Tighten all oil pan flange bolts to 6–9 ft. lbs.

16. Tighten 2 oil pan to transaxle bolts to 30–39 ft. lbs.

17. Install exhaust pipe bracket to oil pan. Rework the bracket as necessary to fit to the oil pan.

18. Install engine coolant tube (with a new O-ring) and air conditioning line.

19. Install starter and cable.

20. Install roll restrictor (MTX only).

21. Lower vehicle.

22. Install engine oil and coolant.

23. Connect negative ground cable at battery.

24. Start engine and check for leaks.

3.8L Engine

1. Disconnect the negative battery cable.

2. Raise the vehicle and support safely.

3. Drain the crankcase and remove the oil filter element.

4. Remove the converter assembly, starter motor and converter housing cover.

5. Remove the attaching bolts and lower the oil pan from the cylinder block.

6. Clean the gasket surfaces on cylinder block, oil pan and oil pickup tube.

7. Trial fit oil pan to cylinder block. Ensure enough clearance has been provided to allow oil pan to be installed without sealant being scraped off when pan is positioned under engine.

8. Apply a bead of silicone rubber sealer No. D6AZ-19562-A or equivalent to the oil pan flange. Also apply a zig-zag bead of sealer to the front cover/cylinder block joint and fill the grooves on both sides of the rear main seal cap.

NOTE: When using silicone rubber sealer, assembly must oc-

cur within 15 minutes after sealer application. After this time, the sealer may start to harden and its sealing effectiveness may be reduced.

9. Install the oil pan and secure to the block with the attaching screws. Torque the screws to 7–9 ft. lbs.

10. Install a new oil filter element. Install the converter housing cover and starter motor.

11. Install the converter assembly and lower the vehicle.

12. Fill the crankcase and connect the negative battery cable.

13. Start the engine and check for leaks.

2.0L Diesel Engine

1. Disconnect the negative battery cable.

2. Raise and safely support the vehicle on jackstands. Drain the engine oil.

3. Remove the bolts that attach the oil pan to the engine and remove the oil pan.

4. Clean all gasket mounting surfaces.

5. Apply a ⅛ in. bead of Silicone Sealer on the oil pan mounting surface.

6. Install the oil pan and tighten the bolts to 5–7 ft. lbs.

Rear Main Bearing Oil Seal

REMOVAL & INSTALLATION

All Except 2.0L and 3.8L Engines

NOTE: A 1-piece ring-type rear main oil seal is used.

1. Remove the transaxle.

2. Remove the rear cover plate.

3. Remove the flywheel or flexplate, if equipped.

4. With a sharp awl, punch a hole into the seal metal surface between the lip and block. Screw in the threaded end of slide hammer tool No. T77L–9533–B or equivalent and use the slide hammer to remove the seal.

NOTE: Use caution to avoid damaging the oil seal surface.

5. Inspect the crankshaft seal area for any damage which may cause the seal to leak. If damage is evident service or replace the crankshaft as necessary.

6. Coat the crankshaft seal area and the seal lip with clean engine oil.

7. Using seal installer tool No. T82L–6701–A or equivalent to install the seal. Tighten the 2 bolts of the seal

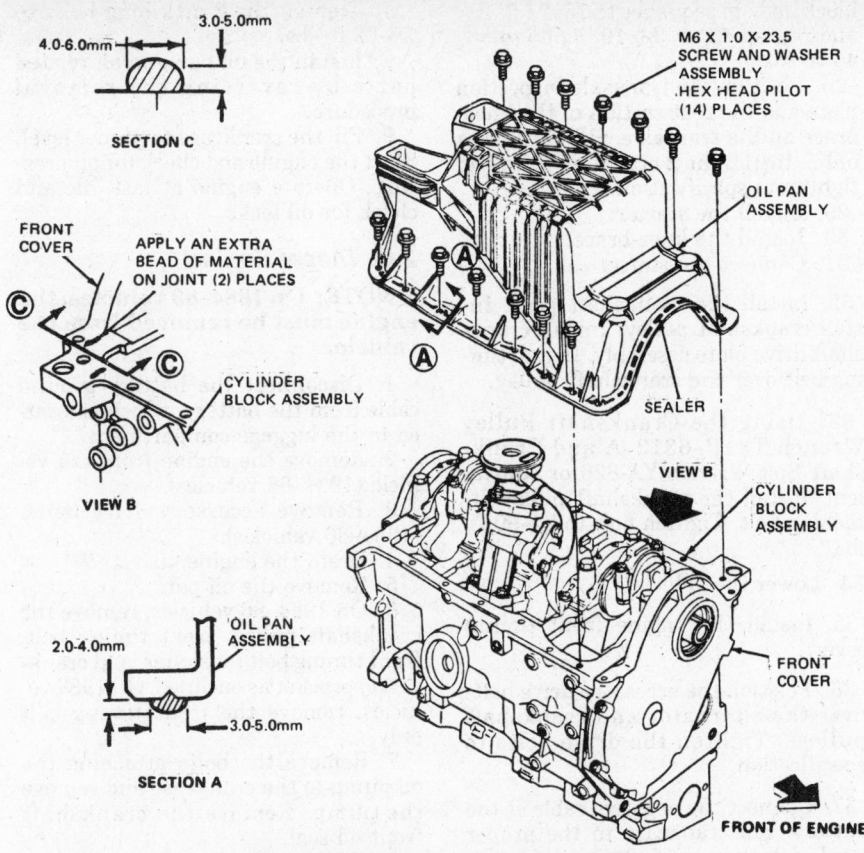

Oil pan installation on 2.3L HSC engine

installer tool evenly so that the seal is straight and seats without misalignment.

8. Install the flywheel. Tighten attaching bolts to 54–64 ft. lbs.

9. Install rear cover plate. Install transaxle.

2.0L Diesel Engine

1. Disconnect the negative battery cable.

2. Raise and safely support the vehicle on jackstands. Drain the engine oil.

3. Remove the bolts that attach the oil pan to the engine and remove the oil pan.

4. Clean all gasket mounting surfaces.

5. Apply a ⅛ in. bead of Silicone Sealer on the oil pan mounting surface.

6. Install the oil pan and tighten the bolts to 5–7 ft. lbs.

3.8L Engine

NOTE: A 1-piece crankshaft rear main oil seal is used on this engine.

1. With a suitable tool, punch a hole into the seal metal surface between lip and block. Screw in the threaded end of jet plug remover No. T77L–9553–B or equivalent. Remove the seal and re-

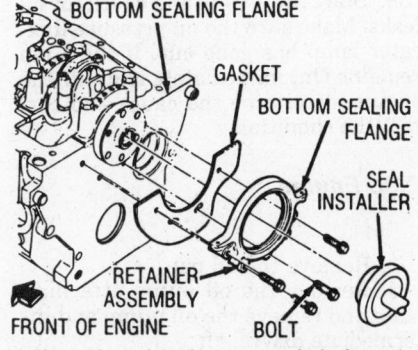

1.6L, 1.9L and 2.3L rear crankshaft seal installation

place with new. Use caution to avoid scratching or damaging oil seal surface.

2. Apply the new seal to mating edges.

3. Position the seal on a rear main seal installer No. T82L–6701–A or equivalent. Position tool and seal to rear of engine. Alternate bolt tightening to seat the seal properly. Engine flywheel bolts may be used if necessary.

Oil Pump

REMOVAL & INSTALLATION

1.6L and 1.9L Engines

1. Disconnect the negative cable at the battery.

2. Loosen the alternator bolt on the alternator adjusting arm. Lower the alternator to remove the accessory drivebelt from the crankshaft pulley.

3. Remove the timing belt cover.

NOTE: Set No. 1 cylinder at TDC prior to timing belt removal.

4. Loosen both belt tensioner attaching bolts using Tool T81P6254A or equivalent on the left bolt. Using a pry bar or other suitable tool pry the tensioner away from the belt. While holding the tensioner away from the belt, tighten 1 of the tensioner attaching bolts.

5. Disengage the timing belt from the camshaft sprocket, water pump sprocket and crankshaft sprocket.

6. Raise the vehicle and safely support on jackstands. Drain the crankcase.

7. Using a Crankshaft Pulley Wrench No. T81P–6312–A and Crankshaft Bolt Wrench No. YA–826 or equivalents, remove the crankshaft pulley attaching bolt.

8. Remove the timing belt.

9. Remove the crankshaft drive

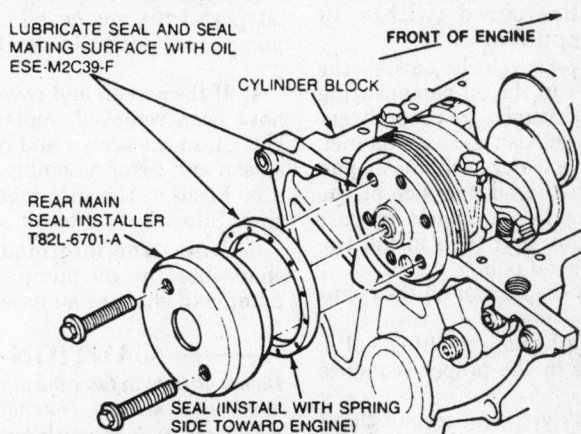

NOTE: REAR FACE OF SEAL MUST BE WITHIN 0.127mm (0.005 INCH) OF THE REAR FACE OF THE BLOCK

Installation of the rear main seal on 3.8L engines

plate assembly. Remove the crankshaft pulley. Remove the crankshaft sprocket.

10. Disconnect the starter cable at the starter.

11. Remove the knee-brace from the engine.

12. Remove the starter.

13. Remove the rear section of the kneebrace and inspection plate at the transaxle (1985 vehicles only).

14. Remove the oil pan retaining bolts and oil pan. Remove the front and rear oil pan seals. Remove the oil pan side gaskets. Remove the oil pump attaching bolts, oil pump and gasket. Remove the oil pump seal. On 1987–89 vehicles a 1 piece oil pan gasket is used.p

15. Make sure the mating surfaces on the cylinder block and the oil pump are clean and free of gasket material.

16. Remove the oil pick-up tube and screen assembly from the pump for cleaning.

17. Lubricate the outside diameter of the oil pump seal with clean engine oil.

18. Install the oil pump seal using Seal Installer T81P-6700-A or equivalent.

19. Install the pick-up tube and screen assembly on the oil pump. Tighten attaching bolts to 6–9 ft. lbs.

20. Lubricate the oil pump seal lip with light engine oil.

21. Position the oil pump gasket over the locating dowels. Install attaching bolts and tighten to 5–7 ft. lbs.

22. Apply a bead of silicone sealer approximately 3.0mm wide at the corner of the front and rear oil pan seals or and at the seating point of the oil pump to the block retainer joint.

23. Install the front oil pan seal by pressing firmly into the slot cut into the bottom of the pump.

24. Install the rear oil seal by pressing firmly into the slot cut into rear retainer assembly.

NOTE: Install the seal before the sealer has cured (within 10 minutes of application).

25. On 1987–89 vehicles, install the 1-piece gasket in the oil pan ensuring that the press fit tabs are proprely engaged in the oil pan gasket channel. Apply adhesive sealer evenly to oil pan flange and to the oil pan side of the gaskets. Allow the adhesive to dry past the "wet" stage and then install the gaskets on the oil pan.

26. Position the oil pan on the cylinder block.

27. Install oil pan attaching bolts. Tighten bolts in the proper sequence 6–8 ft. lbs.

On 1987–89 vehicles, torque the 2 "M-10" oil pan-to-transaxle bolts to 30–40 ft. lbs. then back off ½ turn, torque the "M-8" oil pan-to-cylinder

block bolts in sequence to 15–22 ft. lbs. and retorque the "M-10" bolts to 30–40 ft. lbs.

28. Position the transaxle inspection plate and the rear section of the kneebrace on the transaxle. (1985 vehicles only). Install the 2 attaching bolts and tighten to specification.

29. Install the starter.

30. Install the knee-brace.

31. Connect the starter cable.

32. Install the crankshaft gear. Install crankshaft pulley. Install crankshaft drive plate assembly. Install timing belt over the crankshaft pulley.

33. Using the Crankshaft Pulley Wrench T81P-6312-A and Crankshaft Bolt Wrench YA-826 or equivalent, install the crankshaft pulley attaching bolt. Tighten bolt to 74–90 ft. lbs.

34. Lower the vehicle.

35. Install the engine front timing cover.

36. Position the accessory drive belts over the alternator and crankshaft pulleys. Tighten the drive belts to specification.

37. Connect the negative cable at the battery. Fill crankcase to the proper level with the specified oil.

38. Start the engine and check for oil leaks. Make sure the oil pressure indicator lamp has gone out. If the lamp remains On, immediately shut off the engine, determine the cause and correct the condition.

2.3L Engine

1. Remove the oil pan.

2. Remove the oil pump attaching bolts and remove the oil pump and intermediate driveshaft.

3. Prime the oil pump by filling inlet port with engine oil. Rotate the pump shaft until oil flows from outlet port.

4. If the screen and cover assembly have been removed, replace the gasket. Clean the screen and reinstall the screen and cover assembly.

5. Position the intermediate driveshaft into the distributor socket.

6. Insert the intermediate driveshaft into the oil pump. Install the pump and shaft as an assembly.

─────── **CAUTION** ───────

Do not attempt to force the pump into position if it will not seat. The shaft hex may be misaligned with the distributor shaft. To align, remove the oil pump and rotate the intermediate driveshaft into a new position.

7. Tighten the 2 attaching bolts to 15–22 ft. lbs.

8. Install the oil pan and all related parts by reversing the removal procedure.

9. Fill the crankcase to proper level. Start the engine and check for oil pressure. Operate engine at fast idle and check for oil leaks.

2.0L Diesel Engine

NOTE: On 1984–86 vehicles, the engine must be removed from the vehicle.

1. Disconnect the battery ground cable from the battery, which is located in the luggage compartment.

2. Remove the engine from the vehicle (1984–86 vehicles).

3. Remove accessory drive belts. (1984–86 vehicles).

4. Drain the engine oil.

5. Remove the oil pan.

6. On 1984–86 vehicles, remove the crankshaft pulley, front timing belt, front timing belt tensioner, and crankshaft sprocket as outlined. On 1987 vehicles, remove the front timing belt only.

7. Remove the bolts attaching the oil pump to the crankcase and remove the pump. Remove the crankshaft front oil seal.

8. Clean the oil pump and the crankcase gasket mating surfaces.

9. Apply a ⅛ in. bead of silicone sealer on the oil pump-to-crankcase mating surface.

10. Install a new O-ring.

11. Install the oil pump, making sure the oil pump inner gear engages with the splines on the crankshaft. Tighten the 10mm bolts to 23–34 ft. lbs. and the 8mm bolts to 12–16 ft. lbs.

12. Install a new crankshaft front oil seal.

13. Clean the oil pan-to-crankcase mating surfaces.

14. Apply a in. in. bead of silicone sealer on the oil-pan-to-crankcase mating surface.

15. Install the oil pan and tighten the bolts to 5–7 ft. lbs.

16. Install and adjust as necessary the crankshaft sprocket, front timing belt tensioner and front timing belt.

17. Install and adjust the accessory drive belts, if removed.

18. Install engine in the vehicle, if removed.

19. Fill and bleed the cooling system.

20. Fill the crankcase with the specified quantity and quality of oil.

21. Run the engine and check for oil, fuel and coolant leaks.

3.8L Engine

The oil pump is located in the front cover assembly.

1. Disconnect the negative battery cable. Drain the cooling system and crankcase.

2. Remove the front cover.

3. Remove the oil pump cover attaching bolts and remove the cover. Lift the pump gears off the front cover pocket. Remove the cover gasket and replace with new.

4. Clean the front cover gasket contact surface. Place a straight edge across the front cover mounting surface and check for wear or warpage using a feeler gauge. If the surface is out of flat by more than 0.0016 in., replace the cover.

5. Lightly pack the gear pocket with petroleum jelly or coat all pump gear surfaces with oil conditioner No. D9AZ-19579-C or equivalent.

6. Install the gears in the pocket. Make certain that the petroleum jelly fills the gap between the gears and the pocket. Position the cover gasket and install the front cover. Torque the cover retaining bolts to 15-22 ft. lbs.

7. Complete the installation of the front cover by reversing the removal procedure. Torque the camshaft retaining bolt to 54-67 ft. lbs., oil pan retaining bolts to 7-9 ft. lbs., crankshaft damper bolt to 104-132 ft. lbs. and crankshaft pulley attaching bolts to 19-28 ft. lbs.

8. Connect the negative battery cable. Fill the cooling system and crankcase to the proper levels.

9. Start the engine and allow to reach normal operating temperature. Check for leaks.

ENGINE COOLING

Radiator

REMOVAL & INSTALLATION

All Except 3.8L Engine

1. Disconnect the negative battery cable. Position a suitable drain pan under the radiator and drain the cooling system.

2. If equipped, remove the carburetor air intake tube and alternator air tube from the radiator support. If installed, remove the 2 fasteners that attach the upper end of the fan shroud to the radiator and sight shield.

NOTE: On vehicles equipped with air conditioning, remove the nut and screw attaching the upper end of the fan shroud to the radiator at the cross support frame.

3. Remove the upper shroud mountings, disconnect the wire harness to the electric fan motor and remove the shroud and fan as an assembly.

4. Remove the upper and lower radiator hoses. Disconnect the coolant recovery reservoir.

5. On vehicles equipped with an automatic transaxle, disconnect and plug the transaxle cooler lines at the radiator.

6. Remove radiator mountings, tilt radiator toward engine and lift from engine compartment. make certain that the isomounts do not stick to the lower mounting brackets.

7. Install the radiator in the reverse order. Be sure the lower radiator mounts are positioned correctly on the radiator support.

3.8L Engine

1. Disconnect the negative battery cable.

2. Position a suitable drain pan under the radiator. Remove the radiator cap. Open the draincock located at the lower rear corner of the radiator tank and drain the cooling system.

3. Disconnect the rubber overflow tube from the coolant recovery bottle and detach it from the radiator.

4. Remove the 2 upper shroud attachng screws and lift the shroud from the lower retaining clips.

5. Disconnect the electric cooling fan motor wires and remove the fan and shroud assembly.

6. Loosen the hose clamps and remove the upper and lower hoses from the raditor.

7. With cooler line disconnect tool No. T82l-9500-AH or equivalent, disconnect the 2 transmission oil cooling lines from the fittings on the radiator.

8. Remove the attaching hardware from the left and right radiator support brackets. Remove the brackets.

9. Tilt the radiator back approximately 1 in. and lift straight up to clear the radiator support.

10. Inspect the upper and lower radiator hoses for wear and damage. Replace the hoses as required. Remove the lower rubber support pads and inspect for damage. Replace with new as required.

11. Complete the installation of the radiator by reversing the removal procedure. During installation observe the following:

a. When installing the upper and lower hoses, postion the hose on the radiator connector so that the index arrow on the hose is aligned with the index mark on the conenctor.

b. Fill the cooling system with a 50/50 mixture of anti-freeze and water to the proper level. Add 2 Cooling

System Protector Pellets No. C9AZ-19558-a or equivalent to the mixture.

c. Start the engine and operate for 15 minutes. Check for leaks

Water Pump

REMOVAL & INSTALLATION

1.6L and 1.9L Engines

1. Disconnect the negative battery cable. Drain the cooling system.

2. Remove the alternator drive belt. If equipped with an air conditioning or power steering, remove the drive belts.

3. Use a wrench on the crankshaft pulley to rotate the engine so No. 1 piston is on TDC of the compression stroke.

— CAUTION —

Turn the engine only in the direction of normal rotation. Backward rotation will cause the camshaft belt to slip or lose teeth.

4. Remove the cam belt (timing) cover.

5. Loosen the belt tensioner attaching bolts, then secure the tensioner over as far as possible.

6. Pull the belt from the camshaft tensioner, and water pump sprockets. Do not remove it from, or allow it to change its position on, the crankshaft sprocket.

NOTE: Do not rotate the engine with the camshaft belt removed.

7. Remove the camshaft sprocket.

8. Remove the rear timing cover stud. Remove the heater return tube hose connection at the water pump inlet tube.

9. Remove the water pump inlet tube fasteners and the inlet tube and gasket.

10. Remove the water pump to cylinder block bolts and remove the water pump and its gasket.

11. To install, make sure the mating surfaces on the pump and the block are clean.

12. Using a new gasket and sealer, install the water pump and tighten the bolts to 5-7 ft. lbs. on 1982 vehicles. On 1983-87 vehicles, torque the water pump retaining bolts to 30-40 ft. lbs. On 1988-89 vehicles, torque the retaining bolts to 6-9 ft. lbs. Rotate the pump by hand to ensure the pump impeller turns freely.

13. Install remaining parts in the reverse order of removal. Use new gaskets and sealer. Install the camshaft sprocket over the cam key. Install the timing belt and adjust tension.

2.0L Diesel Engine

1. Remove the front timing belt upper cover.

2. Loosen and remove the front timing belt, refer to timing belt in-vehicle services.

3. Drain the cooling system.

4. Raise the vehicle and support safely on jackstands.

5. Disconnect the lower radiator hose and heater hose from the water pump.

6. Disconnect the coolant tube from the thermostat housing and discard gasket.

7. Remove the 3 bolts attaching the water pump to the crankcase. Remove the water pump. Discard gasket.

8. Clean the water pump and crankshaft gasket mating surfaces.

9. Install the water pump, using a new gasket. Tighten bolts to 23–34 ft. lbs.

10. Connect the coolant tube from the thermostat housing on the water pump using a new gasket. Tighten bolts to 5–7 ft. lbs.

11. Connect the heater hose and lower radiator hose to the water pump.

12. Lower vehicle.

13. Fill and bleed the cooling system.

14. Install and adjust the front timing belt.

15. Run the engine and check for coolant leaks.

16. Install the front timing belt upper cover.

2.3L Engine

1. Disconnect the negative battery cable. Drain the cooling system.

2. Loosen the thermactor pump mounting and remove the drive belt. Disconnect and remove the hose clamp below the pump. Remove the 3 thermactor pump bracket mounting bolts and remove the thermactor and bracket as an assembly.

3. Loosen the water pump drive belt idler pulley and remove the drive belt.

4. Disconnect the heater hose from the water pump.

5. Remove the 3 water pump mounting bolts and the pump.

6. Clean the engine mounting surface. Apply gasket cement to both sides of the mounting gasket and position the gasket on the engine.

7. Install the pump in reverse order of removal. Torque the mounting bolts to 15–22 ft. lbs.

8. Add the proper coolant mixture, start the engine and check for leaks.

3.8L Engine

NOTE: This engine uses an aluminum cylinder head and requires special corrosion inhibiting coolant to avoid radiator damage.

1. Remove the radiator cap, open the radiator drain cock and drain the cooling system.

2. Remove the lower nut on both right hand engine mounts. Raise and safely support the engine.

3. Loosen the accessory drive belt idler and remove the drive belt. Remove the water pump pulley-to-hub bolts and lift the pulley from the vehicle.

4. Remove the air suspension pump.

5. Remove the power steering pump mounting bracket attaching bolts. Leaving hoses connected, place pump/bracket assembly aside in a position to prevent the loss of fluid.

6. If equipped with air conditioning, remove the compressor front support bracket. Leave the compressor in place with hoses connected.

7. Disconnect coolant bypass and heater hoses at the water pump.

8. Remove the water pump-to-front cover attaching bolts. Separate and remove the pump from the vehicle. Discard the gasket and replace with new.

NOTE: If using a prying tool to separate the water pump from the front cover, take care no to damage the mating susrfaces.

9. Lightly oil all bolt and stud threads before installation. Thoroughly clean the water pump and front cover gasket contact surfaces.

10. Apply a coating of contact adhesive No. D7AZ-19B508-A or equivalent to both surfaces of the new gasket. Position the new gasket on water pump sealing surface.

11. Position water pump on the front cover and install attaching bolts.

12. Torque the attaching bolts to 15–22 ft. lbs.

13. Connect the cooling bypass hose, heater hose and radiator lower hose to water pump and tighten the clamps.

14. If equipped with air conditioning, install compressor front support bracket.

15. Install the air suspension pump.

16. Position the accessory drive belt over the pulleys.

17. Install the water pump pulley, fan/clutch assembly and fan shroud.

Cross-tighten fan/clutch assembly attaching bolts to 12–18 ft. lbs.

18. Position accessory drive belt over pump pulley and adjust drive belt tension.

19. Lower the engine.

20. Install and tighten the lower right hand engine mount nuts.

21. Fill cooling system to the proper level with a 50/50 mixture of antifreeze and water to the proper level. Add 2 Cooling System Protector Pellets No. C9AZ-19558–A or equivalent to the mixture.

22. Start engine and check for coolant leaks.

Thermostat

REMOVAL & INSTALLATION

All Engines

1. Disconnect the negative battery cable. Drain the radiator until the coolant level is below the thermostat.

2. Disconnect the wire connector at the thermostat housing thermoswitch.

3. Loosen the top radiator hose clamp. Remove the thermostat housing mounting bolts and lift up the housing.

4. Remove the thermostat by turning counterclockwise.

5. Clean the thermostat housing and engine gasket mounting surfaces. Install new mounting gasket and fully insert the thermostat to compress the mounting gasket. Turn the thermostat clockwise to secure in housing.

NOTE: Some engines use silicone sealant instead of a mounting gasket.

6. Position the housing onto the engine. Install the mounting bolts and torque to 6–8 ft. lbs. on 1.6L & 1.9L engines, 12–18 ft. lbs. on 2.3L engines and 18–22 ft. lbs. on 3.8L engines.

7. Complete the installation by reversing the removal procedure. Fill the cooling system to the proper level. Start the engine and check for leaks.

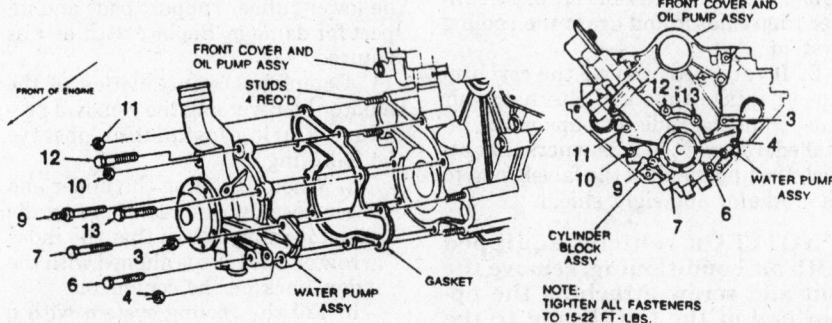

3.8L engine water pump/front cover assembly. Water pump fastener locations shown

EMISSION CONTROLS

Refer to "Emission Control" in the Unit Repair section for system maintenance procedures. Due to the complex nature of modern electronic engine control systems, comprehensive diagnosis and testing procedures fall outside the confines of this repair manual. For complete information on diagnosis, testing and repair procedures concerning all modern engine and emission control systems, please refer to *Chilton's Guide To Electronic Engine Controls.*

GASOLINE FUEL SYSTEM

Fuel System Service Precaution

Safety is the most important factor to adhere to when preforming fuel system maintenance. Failure to conduct fuel system maintenance and repairs in a safe manner may result in serious personal injury or death. Maintenance and testing of the vehicle's fuel system components can be accomplished safely and effectively by adhering to the following rules and guidelines.

• To avoid the possibility of fire and personal injury, always disconnect the negative battery cable unless the repair or test procedure specifically requires that battery voltage be applied.

• Always relieve the fuel system pressure prior to disconnecting any fuel system component (injector, fuel rail, pressure regulator, ect...), fitting or fuel line connection. Exercise extreme caution whenever relieving fuel system pressure to avoid exposing skin, face and eyes to fuel spray. Please be advised that fuel under pressure may penetrate the skin or any part of the body that it comes in contact with.

• Always place a shop towel or cloth around the fitting or connection prior to loosening to absorb any excess fuel due to spillage. Ensure that all fuel spillage (should it occur) is quickly removed from engine surfaces. Ensure that all fuel soaked cloths or towels are deposited into a suitable waste container.

• Always have a properly charged fire extinguisher in the vincinity of the work area and always ensure work areas are adequatley ventilated.

• Do not allow fuel spray or fuel vapors to come in contact with spark or open flame.

• Always use a backup wrench when loosening and tightening fuel line connection fittings. This will prevent unnecessary stress and torsion to fuel line piping. Always follow the proper torque specifications.

• Always replace worn fuel fitting O-rings with new. Do not substitute fuel hose or equivalent where fuel pipe is installed.

• Use common sense.

RELIEVING FUEL SYSTEM PRESSURE

On all engines with fuel injection, the pressure in the fuel system must be released before attempting to remove the fuel pump. A special valve is incorporated in the fuel rail assembly for the purpose of relieving the pressure in the fuel system. Remove the air cleaner and attach pressure gauge tool No. T80L–9974–A or equivalent to the fuel pressure valve on the fuel rail assembly and release the pressure from the system. On the models not equipped with a relieve valve, disconnect the inertia switch and crank the engine for 15 seconds to relieve the fuel pressure in the fuel system.

Fuel Filter

REMOVAL & INSTALLATION

Carbureted Engines

1. If the fuel filter is located in the carburetor inlet and connected with rubber hose, remove clamps and inlet rubber hose. Unscrew the filter from the carburetor.

2. If the fuel filter is mounted in the carburetor inlet and connected with steel line, hold the filter nut with the proper size wrench and unscrew the inverted fitting nut on the steel line using a flare or suitable wrench. Remove the line and unscrew the filter.

3. If the fuel filter is connected to the carburetor with steel lines, hold the filter nuts with proper wrench and disconnect the steel lines with a flare or suitable wrench.

4. Install the fuel filter in the reverse order of removal.

Fuel Injected Engines

1. Relieve the fuel pressure in the fuel system.

2. Remove the push connect fittings at both ends of the fuel filter.

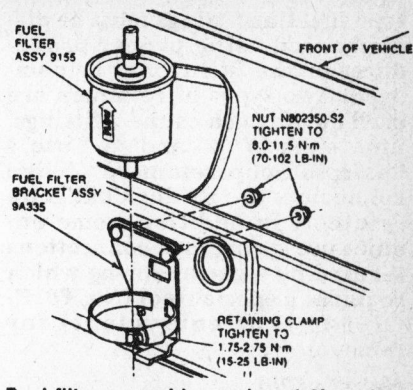

Fuel filter assembly used on 1.6L and 1.9L engines with fuel injection

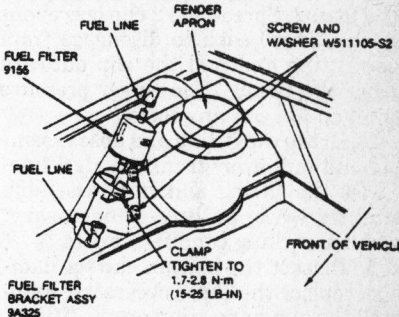

Location of the fuel filter on Tempo/Topaz

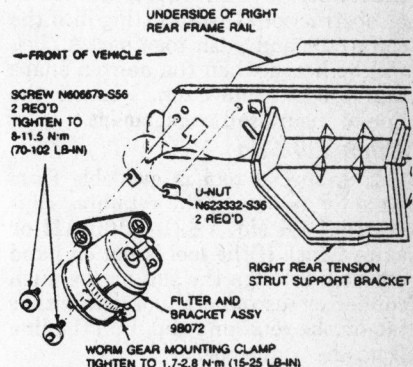

Location of the fuel filter on Continental

NOTE: The flow arrow direction should be positioned as installed in the bracket to ensure the proper flow of fuel through the replacement filter.

3. Remove the filter from the bracket, by loosening the filter retaining clamp enough to allow the filter to pass through.

4. Installation is the reverse order of the removal procedure, ensuring the proper direction of flow as noted earlier.

Quick Connect Fuel Line Fittings

REMOVAL & INSTALLATION

NOTE: Quick Connect (push)

type fuel line fittings must be disconnected using proper procedures or the fitting may be damaged. Two types of retainers are used on the push connect fittings. Line sizes of ⅜" and 5/16" use a "hairpin" clip retainer. ¼" line connectors use a "duck bill" clip retainer. In addition, some engines use spring lock connections secured by a garter spring which requires a special tool (No. T81P-L19623-G or equivalent) for removal.

Hairpin Clip

1. Clean all dirt and/or grease from the fitting. Spread the 2 clip legs about ⅛ in. (3mm) each to disengage from the fitting and pull the clip outward from the fitting. Use finger pressure only, do not use any tools.
2. Grasp the fitting and hose assembly and pull away from the steel line. Twist the fitting and hose assembly slightly while pulling, if necessary, when a sticking condition exists.
3. Inspect the hairpin clip for damage, replace the clip if necessary. Reinstall the clip in position on the fitting.
4. Inspect the fitting and inside of the connector to insure freedom of dirt or obstruction. Install fitting into the connector and push together. A click will be heard when the hairpin snaps into proper connection. Pull on the line to insure full engagement.

Duck Bill Clip

1. A special tool is available from Ford for removing the retaining clips (Ford Tool No. T82L-9500-AH or equivalent). If the tool is not on hand see Step 2. Align the slot on the push connector disconnect tool with either tab on the retaining clip. Pull the line from the connector.
2. If the special clip tool is not available, use a pair of narrow 6 in. (152mm) channel lock pliers with a jaw width of 0.2 in. (5mm) or less. Align the jaws of the pliers with the openings of the fitting case and compress the part of the retaining clip that engages the case. Compressing the retaining clip will release the fitting which may be pulled from the connector. Both sides of the clip must be compressed at the same time to disengage.
3. Inspect the retaining clip, fitting end and connector. Replace the clip if any damage is apparent.
4. Push the line into the steel connector until a click is heard, indicting the clip is in place. Pull on the line to check engagement.

Mechanical Fuel Pump

PRESSURE TESTING

1. Disconnect the negative battery

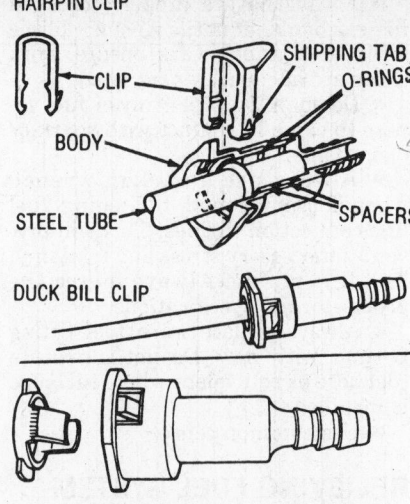

Typical push connections

cable and remove the air cleaner assembly (as required).
2. Connect a calibrated 0–15 psi pressure gauge (Rotunda pressure tester No. 059–00008 or equivalent) to the fuel filter end of the fuel line.
3. Connect the negative battery cable.
4. Start the engine. The engine will be able to run for 30 seconds with the fuel left in the carbureteor bowl. Observe the reading on the gauge after 10 seconds. The fuel pump pressure should be within 4.5–6.5 psi.
5. If the fuel pressure is not within specification, first verify that the length of the fuel pump pushrod is correct. The length of the push rod should be as follows:

    a. 1.6L and 1.9L engines – 3.88 in. minimum.
    b. 2.3L engines – 2.34 in. minimum

6. If the pushrod length is within specification, replace the pump.
7. Disconnect the pressure gauge from the fuel filter line. Place a backup wrench on the fuel filter hex nut and connect the fuel filter line. Properly tighten the connection. Install air cleaner assembly, if removed.
8. Start the engine and check for leaks.

REMOVAL & INSTALLATION

All Carbureted Engines

1. Loosen the threaded fuel line connection(s) with the proper size wrench (flare nut wrench preferred) and retighten snugly. Do not remove lines at this time.
2. Loosen mounting bolts 2 turns. Apply force with hand to loosen fuel pump if gasket is stuck. Rotate the engine, by "bumping" the starter, until the fuel pump cam lobe is near its low

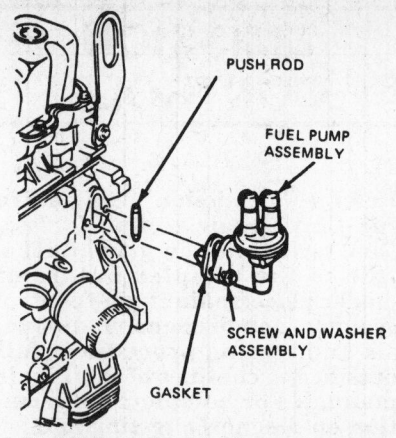

2.3L HSC engine, fuel pump removal and installation

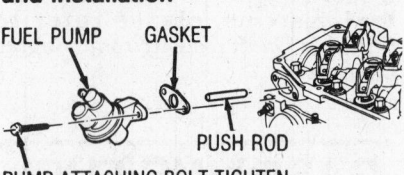

Fuel pump installation on 1.3L engines

position. The tension on the fuel pump will be greatly reduced at the low cam position.
3. Outlet line is pressurized. Disconnect the fuel pump inlet and outlet lines. Use care to prevent combustion from any fuel spillage. Place a rag or shop towel under the line to absorb any excess fuel.
4. Remove the fuel pump attaching bolts and remove the pump and gasket. Discard the old gasket.
5. Measure the fuel pump pushrod length. It should be 3.88 in. (98.6mm) minimum on the 1.6L and the 1.9L engines. On the 2.3L engine it should be 2.34 in. (61.7mm) minimum. Replace if worn or out of specification. Reinstall fuel pump and repeat pressure test.
6. To install, remove all fuel pump gasket material from the engine and the fuel pump if installing the original pump.
7. Install the attaching bolts into the fuel pump and install a new gasket on the bolts. Position the fuel pump to the mounting pad. Turn the attaching bolts alternately and evenly and tighten to 11–19 ft. lbs.
8. Install fuel lines to fuel pump. Start the threaded fitting by hand to avoid cross threading. Tighten outlet nut to 15–18 ft. lb.
9. Start engine and observe for fuel leaks for 2 minutes.
10. Stop engine and check all fuel pump fuel line connections for fuel leaks by running a finger under the connections. Check for oil leaks at the fuel pump mounting gasket.

Electric Fuel Pump

PRESSURE TESTING

1. Install a suitable fuel pressure gauge (No. T80L9974–A or equivalent) on the fuel rail pressure fitting.
2. Turn the ignition on and off for 3 second intervals, (5–10 times) until the pressure gauge reads 13 psi on the CFI models and 35 psi on the EFI models.
3. Remove the pressure gauge, start the engine and check for fuel leaks.

REMOVAL & INSTALLATION

1984–86 Escort/EXP, Lynx/LN7 with Fuel Injection

1. Position the vehicle so it is ready to be raised, depressurized the fuel system and raise and support the vehicle safely.
2. Locate the fuel pump at the right rear, near the fuel tank and remove the assembly from the vehicle by loosening the mounting bolt until the assembly can slide off of the mounting bracket.
3. Remove the parking brake cable from the clip on the pump and disconnect the electrical connector and fuel pump outlet fitting.
4. Disconnect the fuel pump inlet line and remove the pump from under the vehicle. Be sure to either drain the fuel tank or raise the end of the fuel pump inlet line above the level in the tank to prevent siphon action.
5. Installation is the reverse order of the removal procedure.

Tempo/Topaz with Fuel Injection, Continental and 1987–89 Escort

NOTE: The fuel pump is mounted inside the fuel tank with the fuel sender assembly.

1. Position the vehicle so it is ready to be raised and relieve the fuel system pressure.
2. In a well ventilated area, remove the fuel from the fuel tank by pumping it out through the filler neck into a suitable waste container. Use care to prevent combustion from any fuel spillage.
3. Raise and support the vehicle safely and remove the fuel filler tube (neck).
4. Support the fuel tank and remove the fuel tank straps, lower the fuel tank enough to be able to remove the fuel lines, electrical connectors and vent lines from the tank.
5. Remove the fuel tank from under the vehicle and place it on a suitable

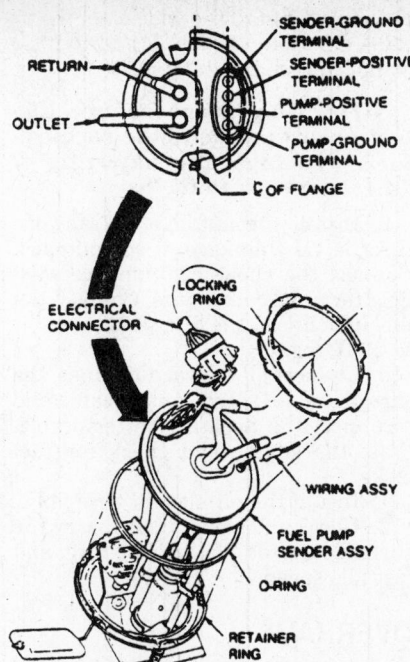

In-tank mounted electric fuel pump with terminal connections

work bench. Remove any dirt around the fuel pump attaching flange.
6. Turn the fuel pump locking ring counterclockwise and remove the lock ring.
7. Remove the fuel pump from the fuel tank and discard the flange gasket.
8. Installation is the reverse order of the removal procedure.

Carburetor

REMOVAL & INSTALLATION

Motorcraft Model 740

1. Remove the air cleaner assembly.
2. Disconnect the throttle cable and speed control cable, if so equipped.
3. Identify and disconnect the following components: bowl vent tube, altitude compensator tubes (idle, primary and secondary if so equipped), air conditioning and/or power steering vacuum kicker (if so equipped).
4. Identify and disconnect: EGR vacuum tube, venturi vacuum tube, distributor vacuum tube, ISC vacuum tube (if so equipped), choke pulldown motor vacuum tube, and fuel inlet lie at filter.
5. Disconnect the idle solenoid wire an choke cap terminal connectors.
6. Remove the automatic transaxle throttle valve (T.V.) linkage, if so equipped.
7. Remove the 4 carburetor flange nuts. If so equipped, remove WOT A/C cut out switch.
8. Remove the carburetor from the manifold.

9. Clean all gasket surfaces. Replace any gasket(s) as necessary.
10. Position the carburetor on the spacer and install the WOT A/C cut out switch, if so equipped and the attaching nuts.
11. Install the automatic transaxle throttle valve (TV) linkage, if so equipped.
12. Connect the choke cap and the idle solenoid terminal connectors.
13. Connect the fuel inlet line at the filter and tighten the 22 ft. lbs.
14. Connect the distributor vacuum line, venturi vacuum line, EGR vacuum line, choke pulldown motor line, and ISC vacuum line, if so equipped.
15. Connect the air conditioning and/or power steering kicker vacuum line (if so equipped).
16. Connect the altitude compensator vacuum lines: idle, primary and secondary, if so equipped.
17. Connect the bowl vent line.
18. Connect the throttle cable. Connect the speed control cable.
19. Start the engine and check for leaks.
20. Install the air cleaner assembly.
21. Check and/or adjust the curb idle and fast idle speed as necessary.

Model 1949 Non-Feedback and 6149 Feedback

1. Remove the air cleaner assembly.
2. Dsconnect the throttle cable from the throttle lever.
3. Disconnect the ATX (automatic transaxle) T.V. rod from the throttle lever, if so equipped.
4. Disconnect the distributor vacuum line, if so equipped, EGR vacuum line, if so equipped, venturi vacuum line, if so equipped, purge vacuum lines, PCV vacuum line, solenoid kicker vacuum line, and fuel line. Use a back-up wrench on the fuel inlet fitting when removing the fuel line to avoid changing the float level.

NOTE: Identify and label all vacuum lines before removing to aid in installation.

5. Disconnect the TSP electrical connection at the connector. Disconnect the electric choke wire at the connector.
6. Disconnect the canister vent hose at the bowl vent tube.
7. Disconnect the throttle position sensor electrical lead at the connector, Model 6949 carburetor.
8. Disconnect the WOT A/C cut-off switch electrical lead at the connector, Model 1949, if equipped.
9. Remove EGR sensor wire from clip on pulldown diaphragm assembly mounting screw, Model 6149.
10. Remove 2 carburetor attaching nuts and remove the carburetor from

the intake manifold. Remove carburetor mounting gasket.

11. Clean the gasket mounting surfaces of the intake manifold and the carburetor. Place a new gasket on the intake manifold. Position the carburetor on the gasket and install the attaching nuts. To prevent leakage, distortion, or damage to the carburetor body flange, snug the nuts and then tighten each nut to 20 ft. lbs.

12. Install EGO sensor wire into clip on pulldown diaphragm assembly mounting screw. Model 6149.

13. Connect WOT A/C cut-off switch electrical lead at the connector, Model 6149.

14. Connect the canister vent hose at the bowl vent tube.

15. Connect the TSP electrical connection and the electric choke wire at the connector.

16. Connect the distributor vacuum line, if equipped, EGR vacuum line, if so equipped, venturi vacuum line, if so equipped, purge vacuum line, solenoid kicker vacuum line, and fuel line. Use a back-up wrench on the fuel inlet fitting when installing the fuel line to avoid changing the float level.

17. Connect the ATX (automatic transaxle) T.V. rod to the throttle lever.

18. Connect the throttle cable to the throttle lever.

19. Install the air cleaner assembly.

20. Check and adjust if necessary the curb idle speed, idle fuel mixture, and fast idle speed.

Motorcraft Mode 5740 Carburetor

1. Disconnect the negative battery cable and remove the air cleaner assembly.

2. Disconnect the throttle cable and speed control cable, if so equipped.

3. Disconnect and tag the bowl vent tube and altitude compensator tubes (idle, primary and secondary if equipped).

4. Disconnect and tag the EGR vacuum line, distributor vacuum line, ISC vacuum line, choke pulldown motor vacuum line and fuel inlet line at the filter.

5. Disconnect the idle solenoid wire and choke cap terminal connectors. Remove the automatic transaxle throttle valve linkage, if so equipped.

6. Remove the 4 carburetor flange nuts using carburetor wrench T74P-9510-A or equivalent. Remove the wide open throttle A/C cutout switch bracket, if so equipped.

7. Remove the carburetor from the intake manifold. Clean all gasket surfaces. Replace any gaskets as necessary.

8. Position the carburetor on the

spacer and install the wide open throttle A/C cutout switch bracket, if so equipped and attaching nuts.

NOTE: To prevent leakage, distortion or damage to the carburetor body flange, alternately tighten each nut to 14 ft. lbs.

9. Install the autom,atic transaxle throttle valve linkage, if so equipped. Connect the choke cap and idle solenoid terminal connectors. Connect the fuel inlet line at the filter and torque it to 22 ft. lbs.

10. Connect all the vacuum lines, the throttle cable, speed control cable and reconnect the negative battery cable. Start the engine and check for fuel leaks.

11. Install the air cleaner assembly.

12. Check and adjust if necessary the curb idle speed, idle fuel mixture, and fast idle speed.

OVERHAUL

For all carburetor overhaul and adjustment procedures, please refer to "Carburetor Service" In the Unit Repair section.

Fuel Injection

Due to the complex nature of modern fuel injection systems, comprehensive diagnosis and testing procedures fall outside the confines of this repair manual. For complete information on diagnosis, testing and repair procedures concerning all modern feedback carburetors, please refer to *Chilton's Guide To Fuel Injection And Feedback Carburetors.*

DIESEL FUEL SYSTEM

Fuel Filter

REMOVAL & INSTALLATION

1. Make sure the engine and ignition switch are off.

2. Disconnect the module connector from the water level sensor probe pigtail located on the bottom of the fuel filter element.

NOTE: Failure to disconnect the water sensor connector/module will damage the water sensor probe.

3. Disconnect the heater power lead at the fuel heater connector.

4. The following procedure applies to 1984–86 vehicles:

a. Use a suitable filter wrench and remove the filter element from the filter adapter.

b. Remove the water drain/valve sensor probe assembly from the bottom of the filter element by unscrewing the probe. Wipe the probe with a clean dry cloth.

c. Unsnap the sensor probe pigtail connector from the bottom of the filter element and wipe clean with a clean dry cloth.

5. The following procedure applies to 1987 vehicles:

a. Disconnect the the fuel line connections from the fuel inlet and outlet fittings of the fuel filler adapter.

b. Drain the fuel from the fuel condtioner assembly.

c. Remove the 2 bolts securing the filter adapter to the filter bracket and withdraw the fuel conditioner assembly (filler adapter and filter element).

d. Secure the filter adapter into a suitable vise. Using a suitable filter wrench, remove the filter element from the filter adapter.

NOTE: Position the filter adapter in the vise to prevent rotation during element disassembly. Do not position the filter adapter in such a manner as to cause stress to the fuel filter fittings or filter adapter flange, as damage to the filter adapter casting mat occur.

e. Remove the water drain/valve sensor probe assembly from the bottom of the filter element by unscrewing the probe. Wipe the probe with a clean dry cloth.

f. Unsnap the sensor probe pigtail connector from the botom of the filter element and wipe clean with a clean dry cloth.

6. Installation is the reverse order of the removal procedure. On 1987 vehicles, torque the 2 filter adapter to filter bracket bolts to 13–16 ft. lbs.

7. Clean the filter mounting surfaces. Coat the gasket of the new filter with clean diesel fuel.

8. Tighten the filter until the gasket touches the filter header, then tighten an additional ½ turn.

9. Air-Bleed the fuel system using the following procedure:

a. Open the water drain valve on the bottom of the fuel filter conditioner (2–3 turns).

b. Press in the fuel bypass button and hold it down tightly. Pump the priming pump on the top of the filter adapter. Continue pumping until clear fuel, free from air bubbles, flows from the water drain valve.

c. Depress the priming pump and hold down while closing the water drain valve.

10. Start the engine and check for fuel leaks.

NOTE: To avoid fuel contamination do not add fuel directly to the new filter.

AIR-BLEEDING THE FUEL SYSTEM

NOTE: Whenever the fuel filter is replaced, or system service performed, the filter must be air-bled as follows.

1. Open the water drain valve.
2. Pump the priming pump on the head of the filter.
3. Continue to pump until the fuel flows from the water vent valve in a steady stream free of air bubbles.
4. Depress the head of the priming pump and close the water vent valve.
5. If the engine should run out of fuel during operation or the system is opened allowing air to enter, bleed the air from the fuel filter first.
6. Pump the priming pump on the head of the filter repeatedly until it becomes hard to pump (about 15 times) to force air from the system.

Diesel Injection Pump

REMOVAL & INSTALLATION

1. Disconnect battery ground cable from the battery, located in the luggage compartment.
2. Disconnect the air inlet duct from the air cleaner and intake manifold. Install protective cap in intake manifold.
3. Remove rear timing belt cover and flywheel timing mark cover.
4. Remove rear timing belt as follows:
   a. Remove rear timing belt cover.
   b. Remove flywheel timing mark cover from clutch housing.
   c. Rotate crankshaft until the flywheel timing mark is at TDC on No. 1 cylinder.
   d. Check that the injection pump and camshaft sprocket timing marks are aligned.
   e. Loosen tensioner locknut. With a prybar, or equivalent tool, inserted in the slot provided, rotate the tensioner clockwise to relieve belt tension. Tighten locknut snug.
   f. Remove timing belt.
5. Disconnect throttle cable and speed cable, if so equipped.
6. Disconnect vacuum hoses at the altitude compensator and cold start diaphragm.

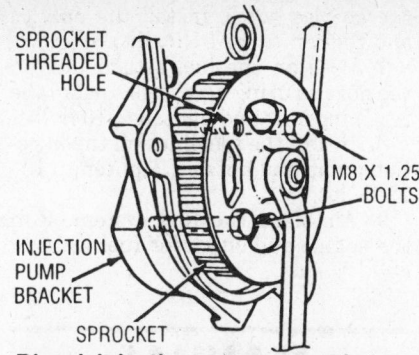

Diesel injection pump sprocket removal and installation

7. Disconnect fuel cut-off solenoid connector.
8. Disconnect fuel supply and fuel return hoses at injection pump.
9. Remove injection lines at the injection pump and nozzles. Cap all lines and fittings.
10. Rotate injection pump sprocket until timing marks are aligned. Install 2 bolts in the holes to hold the injection pump sprocket. Remove sprocket retaining nut.
11. Remove injection pump sprocket using a suitable gear puller with 2 bolts installed in the threaded holes in the sprocket.
12. Remove bolt attaching the injection pump to the pump front bracket.
13. Remove the 2 bolts attaching the injection pump to the pump rear bracket and remove the pump.
14. Install injection pump in position on the pump brackets.
15. Install 2 nuts attaching the pump to the rear bracket and tighten to 23–34 ft. lbs.
16. Install bolt attaching the pump to the front bracket and tighten to 12–16 ft. lbs.
17. Install injection pump sprocket. Hold the sprocket in place using the procedure described in Step 10. Install the sprocket retaining nut and tighten to 51–58 ft. lbs.
18. Remove protective caps and install the fuel lines at the injection pump and nozzles. Tighten the fuel line capnuts to 18–22 ft. lbs.
19. Connect fuel supply and fuel return hoses at the injection pump.
20. Connect fuel cut-off solenoid connector.
21. Connect vacuum lines to the cold start diaphragm and altitude compensator.
22. Connect throttle cable and speed control cable, if so equipped.
23. Install the rear timing belt. Loosen tensioner locknut and adjust timing belt. Install rear timing belt cover and tighten bolts to 5–7 ft. lbs.
24. Remove protective cap and install the air inlet duct to the intake manifold and air cleaner.

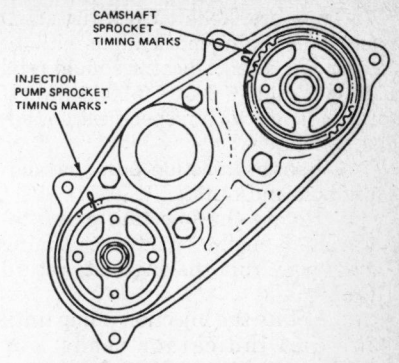

2.0L diesel camshaft and injector pump timing marks

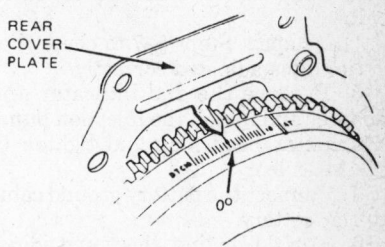

2.0L diesel flywheel timing mark

25. Connect battery ground cable to battery.
26. Air bleed fuel system.
27. Check and adjust the injection pump timing.
28. Run engine and check for fuel leaks.
29. Check and adjust engine idle.

Injection Timing

ADJUSTMENT

NOTE: Engine coolant temperature must be above 176°F (80°C) before the injection timing can be checked and/or adjusted.

1. Disconnect the battery ground cable from the battery located in luggage compartment.
2. Remove the injection pump distributor head plug bolt and sealing washer.
3. Install static timing gauge adapter, Rotunda No. 14-0303 or equivalent with Metric Dial Indicator, so that indicator pointer is in contact with injection pump plunger.
4. Remove timing mark cover from transaxle housing. Align timing mark (TDC) with pointer on the rear engine cover plate.
5. Rotate the crankshaft pulley slowly, counterclockwise until the dial indicator pointer stops moving (approximately 30–50 degrees BTDC).
6. Adjust dial indicator to zero.

NOTE: Confirm that dial indicator pointer does not move from zero by slightly rotating crankshaft left and right.

7. Turn crankshaft clockwise until crankshaft timing mark aligns with indicator pin. Dial indicator should read 1 ± 0.02mm (0.04 ± 0.0008 in.). If reading is not within specification, adjust as follows:

   a. Loosen injection pump attaching bolt and nuts.

   b. Rotate the injection pump toward the engine to advance timing and away from the engine to retard timing.

   c. Rotate the injection pump until the dial indicataor reads 1 ± 0.02mm (0.04 ± 0.0008 in..

   d. Tighten the injection pump attaching nuts and bolt to 13–20 ft. lbs.

   e. Repeat Steps 5–7 to check that timing is adjusted correctly.

8. Remove the dial indicator and adapter and install the injection pump distributor head plug and tighten to 10–14 ft. lbs.

9. Connect the battery ground cable to the battery.

10. Run the engine, check and adjust idle rpm, if necessary. Check for fuel leaks.

Injection Nozzle

REMOVAL & INSTALLATION

1. Disconnect and remove the injection lines from the injection pump and nozzles. Cap all lines and fitting to prevent dirt contamination.

2. Remove the nuts attaching the fuel return line to the nozzles and remove the return line and seals.

3. Remove the injector nozzles using a 27mm socket. Remove the nozzle gaskets and washers from the nozzle seats using an O-ring pick tool T71P-19703-C or the equivalent.

4. Clean the outside of the nozzles with safety solvent and dry them thoroughly.

5. Position new sealing gaskets in the nozzle seats with the red painted surface facing up.

6. Position new copper gaskets in

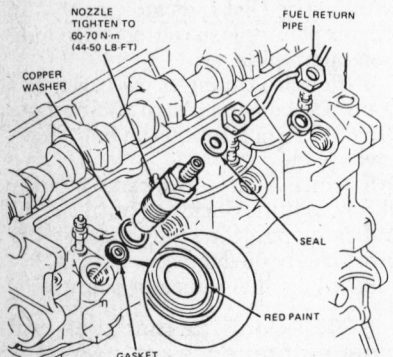

NOZZLE TIGHTEN TO 60–70 N·m (44–50 LB-FT)

FUEL RETURN PIPE

COPPER WASHER

SEAL

RED PAINT

GASKET

2.0L diesel injection nozzle installation

the nozzles bores. Install the nozzles and tighten to 44–51 ft. lbs.

7. Position the fuel return line on the nozzles using new seals. Install the retaining nuts and tighten to 10 ft. lbs.

8. Install the fuel lines on the injection pump and nozzles. Tignten to 18–22 ft. lbs.

9. Air bleed the fuel system. Run the engine and check for fuel leaks.

MANUAL TRANSAXLE

REMOVAL & INSTALLATION

1982–85 Escort/EXP and Lynx/LN7

1. Remove the 2 transaxle to engine top mounting bolts.

2. Grasp the clutch cable and pull forward, disconnecting it from the clutch release lever. Remove the clutch cable casing from the rib on the top surface of the transaxle case.

3. Raise the vehicle on a hoist and remove the bolt attaching brake hose routing clip to the suspension strut bracket at both front wheels.

4. Remove the bolt that secures the lower control arm ball joint to the steering knuckle assembly. Pry the lower control arm away from the knuckle.

NOTE: The plastic shield installed behind the rotor contains a molded pocket into which the lower control arm ball joint fits. When disengaging the control arm from the knuckle, clearance for the ball joint can be provided by bending the shield back toward the rotor. Failure to provide clearance for the ball joint can result in damage to the shield.

——— **CAUTION** ———
The nut and bolt must be discarded.

NOTE: Exercise care not to damage or cut ball joint boot. The pry bar must not contact lower arm.

5. Using a pry bar or equivalent, pry the right inboard CV-joint assembly from the transaxle. Remove the inner CV-joint from the transaxle by grasping the right hand steering knuckle and swinging the knuckle and shaft outward from the transaxle.

NOTE: Lubricant will drain from the seal at this time. Install shipping plug T81p-1177-B2 or

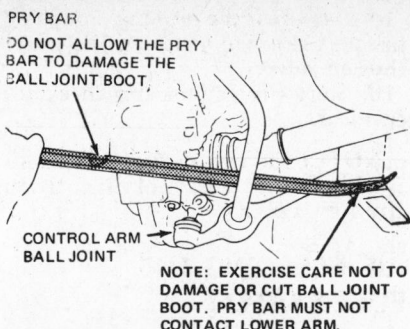

PRY BAR

DO NOT ALLOW THE PRY BAR TO DAMAGE THE BALL JOINT BOOT

CONTROL ARM BALL JOINT

NOTE: EXERCISE CARE NOT TO DAMAGE OR CUT BALL JOINT BOOT. PRY BAR MUST NOT CONTACT LOWER ARM.

Separating the steering knuckle from the ball joint

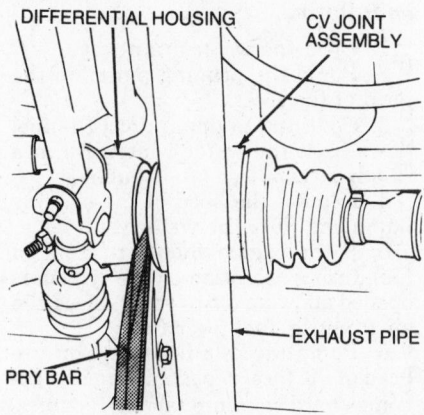

DIFFERENTIAL HOUSING

CV JOINT ASSEMBLY

EXHAUST PIPE

PRY BAR

Halfshaft removal

equivalent to prevent the dislocation of the differential side gears. Use caution during the use of the pry bar and removal of the join assembly to prevent damage to the oil seal.

6. Wire the joint assembly in a near level position to prevent over-extending the assembly during the remaining operations.

7. Repeat Step 5 on the left inboard CV-joint assembly. If it cannot be pried from the transaxle, insert service tool T81P-4026-A or equivalent through the right side and tap the joint out. Remove in the same manner as the right side. Wire the joint assembly as in Step 6.

8. Disconnect the front stabilizer bar at both control arms. Discard the nuts.

9. Remove the 2 front stabilizer bar mounting brackets. Remove the stabilizer bar. Discard the bolts.

10. Disconnect the speedometer cable from the transaxle.

11. Disconnect the backup lamp switch connector from the transaxle switch.

12. Remove the 3 nuts from the starter mounting studs which hold the engine roll restrictor bracket.

13. Remove the engine roll restrictor. Remove the starter stud bolts.

14. Remove the 2 stiffener brace attaching bolts from the lower portion of the clutch housing.

15. Remove the shift mechanism crossover spring.

16. Remove the shift mechanism stabilizer bar to transaxle attaching bolt.

17. Remove the shift mechanism to shift shaft attaching bolt. Remove the shift mechanism from the shift shaft.

18. Position a transaxle jack under the transaxle.

19. Loosen the nut on the rear mount stud.

20. Remove the attaching bolt from the bottom of the rear mount and loosen the 2 bolts at the top of the mount.

21. Remove the 3 bolts holding the front mount to the transaxle case.

22. Lower the MTX support jack until the transaxle clears the rear mount. Support the engine with a screw-type jack stand underneath the oil pan.

23. Remove the remaining 4 engine to transaxle attaching bolts.

24. Remove the transaxle from the rear face of the engine and lower from the vehicle.

NOTE: The transaxle case casting may have sharp edges. Wear protective gloves when handling the transaxle assembly.

25. Using a suitable transmission jack, raise the transaxle into position. Engage the input shaft spline into the clutch disc and work the transaxle onto the dowel sleeves.

NOTE: Make sure the transaxle assembly is flush with the rear face of the engine prior to installation of the attaching bolts.

26. Install the 4 attaching bolts and tighten to specification.

────── **CAUTION** ──────

Do not attempt to start the vehicle prior to installing the CV-joints. Doing so will result in differential side gear dislocation and damage.

27. Connect the speedometer cable.

28. Position the managed air valve bracket and rear mount over the rear mount bolt locations in the case.

29. Install the attaching bolts and tighten to 40–50 ft. lbs.

30. Position the transaxle to tighten the nut on the mount stud. Tighten the nut to 38–41 ft. lbs.

31. Position the transaxle to align with the front mount bracket. Install the 3 bracket-to-transaxle case attaching bolts and tighten to 40–50 ft. lbs.

32. Connect the back-up lamp switch harness. Push the connector on until the locking tabs engage. Remove the transaxle jack.

33. Install the 2 stiffener brace attaching bolts and tighten to 15–21 ft. lbs.

34. Position the starter motor against the engine rear cover plate, insuring that it is correctly piloted in the alignment bore. Install the 3 starter attaching stud bolts and tighten to 30–40 ft. lbs.

35. Install the engine roll restrictor.

36. Install the 3 roll restrictor attaching nuts and tighten to 25–30 ft. lbs.

37. Install the shift mechanism stabilizer attaching bolt and tighten to 23–32 ft. lbs.

38. Install the shift mechanism to the input shift rail and tighten the attaching bolt to 7–10 ft. lbs.

39. Install the shift mechanism crossover spring.

40. Remove the seal plugs and install the inner CV-joints into transaxle.

────── **CAUTION** ──────

To insure proper installation, the following points must be observed.

a. New circlips are required on both inner joints prior to installation.

b. Exercise caution while inserting the shaft into the transaxle to avoid damage to the oil seals.

c. Check to insure that both joints are fully seated in the transaxle. Lightly pry outward to confirm that the retaining rigs are seated. If rings are not seated, the joint will move out of the transaxle.

41. Attach the lower ball joint to the steering knuckle, taking care not to damage or cut the ball joint boot. Install a new pinch bolt and nut. Torque the nut to 37–44 ft. lbs. DO NOT TIGHTEN THE BOLT.

────── **CAUTION** ──────

A new nut and bolt must be installed.

42. Position the right brake line routing clip. Install the attaching bolt and tighten to 8 ft. lbs. Repeat the procedure for the left-hand wheel.

43. Install the new attaching nuts and washers. Do not tighten the nuts.

44. Install both stabilizer mounting brackets. Tighten the new attaching bolts to 40–44 ft. lbs. Tighten the stabilizer to control arm nuts 59–73 ft. lbs.

45. Fill the transaxle with lubricant ESW-M2C33-F (automatic transmission fluid) or equivalent. Tighten the fill plug to 9–15 ft. lbs.

46. Lower the vehicle.

47. Connect the clutch cable.

Tempo/Topaz and 1986–89 Escort/EXP and Lynx

1. Wedge a wood block approximately 7 in. ong under the clutch pedal to hold the pedal up slightly beyond its normal position. Grasp the clutch cable and pull forward, disconnecting it from the clutch release shaft assembly. Remove the clutch casing from the rib on the top surface of the transaxle case.

2. Using a 13mm socket, remove the 2 top transaxle-to-engine mounting bolts. Using a 10mm socket, remove the air cleaner. On Escort, EXP and Lynx models, remove the top bolt that secures the air management valve bracket to the transaxle.

3. Raise and safely support the vehicle. Remove the front stabilizer bar to control arm attaching nut and washer (drivers side). Discard the attaching nut. Remove the 2 front stabilizer bar mounting brackets. Discard the bolts.

4. Using a 15mm socket, remove the nut and bolt that secures the lower control arm ball joint to the steering knuckle assembly. Discard the nut and bolt. Repeat this procedure on the opposite side.

5. Using a large pry bar, pry the lower control arm away from the knuckle.

────── **CAUTION** ──────

Exercise care not to damage or cut the ball joint boot. Pry bar must not contract the lower arm. Repeat this procedure n the opposite side.

6. Using a large pry bar, pry the left inboard CV-joint assembly from the transaxle.

NOTE: Lubricant will drain from the seal at this time. Install shipping plugs (T81P-1177-B or equivalent). 2 plugs are required (1 for each seal). Remove the inboard CV-joint from the transaxle by grasping the left-hand steering knuckle and swinging the knuckle and halfshaft outward from the transaxle.

────── **CAUTION** ──────

Exercise care when using a pry bar to remove the CV joint assembly, If not careful, damage to the differential oil seal may result.

7. If the CV-joint assembly cannot be pried from the transaxle, insert differential rotater tool (T81P-4026-A or equivalent), through the left side and tap the joint out. Tool can be used from either side of transaxle.

8. Wire the halfshaft assembly in a rear level position to prevent damage to the assembly during the remaining operations. Repeat this procedure on the opposite side.

9. Remove the backup lamp switch connector from the transaxle backup lamp switch.

10. Using a suitable socket, remove

the 3 nuts from the starter mounting studs which hold the engine roll restrictor bracket. Remove the engine roll restrictor.

11. Using a suitable deep well socket, remove the 3 starter bolts.

12. Using a suitable socket, remove the shift mechanism to shift shaft attaching nut and bolt and control selector indicator switch arm. Remove the shift shaft.

13. Using a 15mm socket, remove the shift mechanism stabilizer bar to transaxle attaching bolt. Remove the $\frac{7}{32}$ in. sheet metal screw and the control selector indicator switch and bracket assembly.

14. Using a 22mm ($\frac{7}{8}$ in.) crows foot wrench, remove the speedometer cable from the transaxle.

15. Using a 13mm universal socket, remove the 2 stiffener brace attaching bolts from the oil pan to clutch housing.

16. Position a suitable jack under the transaxle. Using an 18mm socket, remove the 2 nuts that secure the left hand rear No. 4 insulator to the body bracket.

17. Using a suitable socket, remove the bolts that secure the left hand front No.1 insulator to the body bracket. Lower the transaxle jack until the transaxle clears the rear insulator. Support the engine with a screw jack stand under the oil pan. Use a 2x4 in. piece of wood top of the screw jack.

18. Using a 13mm socket, remove the 4 engine to transaxle attaching bolts. One of these bolts holding the ground strap and wiring loom stand off bracket.

19. Remove the transaxle from the rear face of the engine and lower transaxle from the vehicle.

20. Complete the installation of the transaxle assembly by reversing the removal procedure. Torque the engine-to-transaxle bolts to 28–31 ft. lbs., front mount-to-transaxle bolts to 25–35 ft. lbs., bottom bracket bolt to 28–31 ft. lbs., rear mount-to-floorpan brace bolts to 40–50 ft. lbs., stabilizer bar and transaxle control selector indicator bolt to 23–35 ft. lbs., starter bolts 30–40 ft. lbs. and lower ball joint nut to 37–44 ft. lbs.

CLUTCH

REMOVAL & INSTALLATION

1. Remove the transaxle.
2. Mark the pressure plate assembly and the flywheel so that they can be assembled in the same position.
3. Loosen the attaching bolts 1 turn

at a time, in sequence, until spring tension is relieved.

4. Support the pressure plate and remove the bolts. Remove the pressure plate and clutch disc.

5. Inspect the flywheel, clutch disc, pressure plate, throwout bearing, and the clutch fork for wear. Replace parts as required. If the flywheel shows any signs of overheating (blue discoloration) or if it is badly grooved or scored, it should be refaced or replaced.

6. Clean the pressure plate and flywheel surfaces thoroughly. Position the clutch disc and pressure plate into the installed position, aligning the marks made previously. Support them with a dummy shaft or clutch aligning tool.

7. Install the pressure plate-to-flywheel bolts. Tighten them gradually in a criss-cross pattern to 12–24 ft. lbs. Remove the alignment tool.

8. Lubricate the release bearing and install it in the fork.

9. Install the transaxle.

NOTE: Since the release bearing in this system is constant-running, transaxle neutral rollover noise can be detected as such only by disengaging the release bearing from the clutch release fingers. This is best accomplished by disconnecting the cable from the release lever and moving the lever away from the cable. If neutral noise is evident under this condition, it is emanating from the transaxle. Be sure to lift the clutch pedal to the upmost position when connecting or disconnecting the clutch cable.

Noise associated with the release bearing/clutch system will be evident during all or some portion of pedal travel. During engagement and disengagement of the pawl and sector a "clicking" noise may be heard. This is normal and is in fact assurance that the adjusting mechanism is operating normally.

CLUTCH LINKAGE FREE-PLAY ADJUSTMENT

The free-play in the clutch is adjusted by a built in mechanism that allows the clutch controls to be self-adjusted during normal operation. The self-adjusting feature should be checked every 5000 miles. This is accomplished by insuring that the clutch pedal travels to the top of its upward position. Grasp the clutch pedal with hand or put foot under the clutch pedal, pull up on the pedal until it stops. Very little effort is required (about 10 lbs.). During the application of upward pres-

sure, a click may be heard which means an adjustment was necessary and has been accomplished.

Clutch Cable

REMOVAL & INSTALLATION

1. Prop up the clutch pedal to lift the pawl free of the quadrant which is part of the self adjuster mechanism.

2. Remove the air cleaner assembly to gain access to the clutch cable.

3. Grasp the extended end of the clutch cable with a pair of pliers, and unhook the clutch cable from the clutch bearing release lever.

NOTE: Do not grasp wire strand portion of inner cable since this may cut wires and result in cable failure.

4. Disconnect the cable from the insulator that is located on the rib of the transaxle.

5. Remove the panel above the clutch pedal pad (Tempo/Topaz).

6. Position the clutch shield away from the brake pedal support bracket by removing the rear retaining screw (located nearest the instrument panel). Loosen the front retaining screw and rotate the shield out of the way. Secure the shield by snugging up the front screw.

7. With the clutch pedal lifted up to release the pawl, rotate the gear quadrant forward. Unhook the clutch cable from the gear quadrant. Allow the quadrant to swing rearward. DO NOT ALLOW THE QUADRANT TO SNAP BACK.

8. Pull the cable out through the recess between the clutch pedal and the gear quadrant, and from the insulator on the pedal assembly.

9. Withdraw the cable from the engine compartment.

10. Insert the clutch cable assembly from the engine or passenger compartment through the dash panel and pash panel groummet.

NOTE: If the clutch pedal assembly was removed, the cable may be installed through the passenger compartment. Make sure that the cable is routed under the brake lines and not trapped at the spring tower by the brake lines. If the vehicle is equipped with power steering, the clutch cable is to be routed inboard of the power steering hose.

11. Push the clutch cable through insulator on the stop bracket, and through recess between the pedal and gear quadrant.

12. With the clutch pedal lifted up to release the pawl, rotate the gear

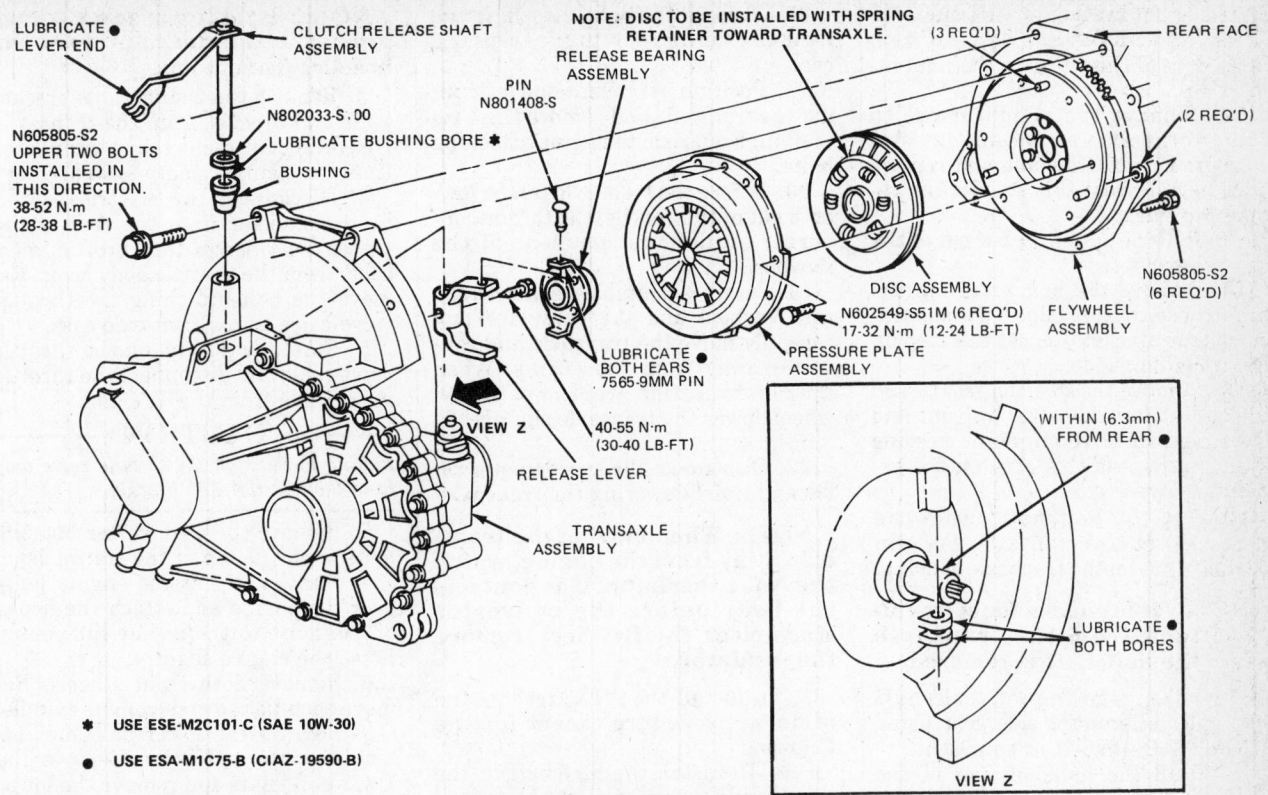

Typical clutch assembly installation

Within the illustration:

LUBRICATE LEVER END ●

CLUTCH RELEASE SHAFT ASSEMBLY

NOTE: DISC TO BE INSTALLED WITH SPRING RETAINER TOWARD TRANSAXLE.

RELEASE BEARING ASSEMBLY

PIN N801408-S

(3 REQ'D)

REAR FACE

N605805-S2 UPPER TWO BOLTS INSTALLED IN THIS DIRECTION. 38-52 N·m (28-38 LB-FT)

N802033-S .00

LUBRICATE BUSHING BORE ✱

BUSHING

(2 REQ'D)

N605805-S2 (6 REQ'D)

DISC ASSEMBLY

N602549-S51M (6 REQ'D) 17-32 N·m (12-24 LB-FT)

FLYWHEEL ASSEMBLY

VIEW Z

LUBRICATE BOTH EARS 7565-9MM PIN

PRESSURE PLATE ASSEMBLY

40-55 N·m (30-40 LB-FT)

RELEASE LEVER

TRANSAXLE ASSEMBLY

WITHIN (6.3mm) FROM REAR ●

LUBRICATE BOTH BORES ●

VIEW Z

✱ USE ESE-M2C101-C (SAE 10W-30)

● USE ESA-M1C75-B (CIAZ-19590-B)

quardrant forward. Hook the cable into the gear quardrant.

13. Install the clutch shield on the brake pedal support bracket.

14. Install the panel above the clutch pedal.

15. Secure the pedal in the upmost position using a piece of wire, cord or tape.

16. Hook the cable into the clutch release lever in the engine compartment.

17. Remove the device used to temporarily secure the pedal.

18. Adjust the clutch by depressing the pedal several times.

19. Install the air cleaner.

AUTOMATIC TRANSAXLE

For all automatic transaxle adjustment procedures, please refer to "Automatic Transmissions" in the Unit Repair section.

REMOVAL & INSTALLATION

All Except 3.8L Engine and Tempo/Topaz with 2.3L HSC Engine

1. Disconnect the cable from the battery negative terminal.

NOTE: Due to ATX case configuration, the right-hand halfshaft assembly must be removed first. The differential service tool T81P–4026–A or equivalent is then inserted into the transaxle to drive the left hand inboard CV joint assembly from the transaxle.

2. Remove the bolts attaching the managed air valve to the ATX valve body cover.

3. Disconnect the wiring harness connector from the neutral safety switch.

4. Disconnect the throttle valve linkage and the manual lever cable at their respective levers.

NOTE: Failure to disconnect the linkage during transaxle removal and allowing the transaxle to hang will fracture the throttle valve cam shaft joint (which is located under the transaxle cover).

5. Cover up the timing window in the converter housing to prevent contamination. Remove the bolts retaining the thermactor hoses, if equipped.

6. Remove the ground strap located above the upper engine mount, if so equipped. Remove the coil and bracket assembly, if equipped.

7. Remove the 2 transaxle-to-engine upper attaching bolts. The bolts are located below and on either side of the distributor. Loosen the wheel

nuts. Raise and support the vehicle safely and remove the wheels.

8. Remove the nut from the control arm to steering knuckle attaching bolt (at the ball joint).

9. Drive the bolt out of the knuckle using a punch and hammer. Repeat this step on the remaining side.

—— **CAUTION** ——
The nut and bolt must be discarded.

NOTE: Exercise care not to damage or cut ball joint boot. The pry bar must not contact lower arm.

10. Disengage the control arm from the steering knuckle using a pry bar. Repeat this step on the remaining side.

—— **CAUTION** ——
Do not use a hammer on the knuckle to remove the ball joints.

NOTE: The plastic shield installed behind the rotor contains a molded pocket into which the lower control arm ball joint fits. When disengaging the control arm from the knuckle, clearance for the ball joint can be provided by bending the shield back toward to rotor. Failure to provide clearance for the ball joint can result in damage to the shield.

11. Remove the bolts attaching the

stabilizer bar bracket to the frame rail. Discard the bolts and replace with new. Repeat this step on the remaining side.

12. Remove the stabilizer bar to control the arm attaching nut and washer. Discard the nut and replace with new. Repeat this step on the remaining side.

13. Pull the stabilizer bar out of the control arms.

14. Remove the bolt attaching the brake hose routing clip to the suspension strut bracket. Repeat this step on the remaining side.

15. Remove the steering gear tie rod to steering knuckle attaching nut and disengage the tie rod from the steering knuckle. Repeat this step on the remaining side.

16. Pry the halfshaft out of the right side of the transaxle. Position the halfshaft on the transaxle housing.

NOTE: It is normal for some fluid to leak from the transaxle when the halfshaft is removed.

17. Disengage the left halfshaft from the differential side gear using driver T81P-4026-A or equivalent.

a. Pull the halfshaft out of the transaxle.

b. Support the end of the shaft by suspending if from a convenient underbody component with a length of wire.

NOTE: Do not allow the shaft to hand unsupported, as damage to the outboard CV-joint may result.

18. Install seal plugs T81P-1177-B or equivalent into the differential seals.

19. Remove the starter support bracket and disconnect the starter cable.

20. Remove the starter attaching bolts and the starter. On the throttle body equipped vehicles, remove the 2 hose and bracket bolts on the starter and 1 bolt attached to the converter and disconnect the hoses.

21. Remove the transaxle support bracket.

22. Remove the dust cover from the torque converter housing.

23. Remove the torque converter to flywheel attaching nuts. Turn the crankshaft pulley bolt to bring the attaching nuts into an accessible position.

24. Remove the nuts attaching the left front insulator to the body bracket.

25. Remove the bracket to body attaching bolts and remove the bracket.

26. Remove the left rear insulator bracket attaching nut.

27. Disconnect the transaxle cooler lines.

28. Remove the bolts attaching the manual lever bracket to the transaxle case.

29. Position a transmission jack under the transaxle and remove the 4 remaining transaxle to engine attaching bolts.

30. Before the transaxle can be lowered out of the vehicle, the torque converter studs must be clear of the flywheel.

31. Insert a suitable tool between the flywheel and the converter and carefully move the transaxle and converter away from the engine. When the converter studs are clear of the flywheel, lower the transaxle slightly (2–3 in.).

32. Disconnect the speedometer cable and finish lowering the transaxle.

NOTE: When moving the transaxle away from the engine, watch the No. 1 insulator. If it contacts the body before the converter studs clear the flywheel, remove the insulator.

33. To install the ATX, reverse the removal procedure except for the following:

a. To install the halfshaft in the transaxle, carefully align the splines of the CV-joint with the splines in the differential.

b. Exerting some force, push the CV-joint into the differential until the circlip is felt to seat in the differential side gear.

NOTE: Use care to prevent damage to the differential oil seal.

c. Attach the lower ball joint to the steering knuckle, taking care not to damage or cut the ball joint boot. Insert new service pinch bolt N780305-S100 and attach new nut N801308.

d. Torque the nut to 37–44 ft. lbs. DO NOT TIGHTEN THE BOLT.

Tempo/Topaz with 2.3L Engine

The automatic transaxle and the 2.3L HSC engine on the Tempo/Topaz models must be removed and installed as an assembly. If any attempt is made to remove either component separately, it will cause damage to the transaxle or the lower engine compartment metal structure.

3.8L Engine

1. Disconnect the negative battery cable. Raise and support the vehicle safely. Remove the air cleaner assembly.

2. Remove the bolt retaining the shift cable and bracket assembly to the transaxle.

NOTE: Hold the bracket with a pry bar in the slot to prevent the bracket from moving.

3. Remove the 2 shift cable bracket bolts and bracket from the transaxle. Disconnect the electrical connector from the neutral safety switch.

4. Disconnect the electrical bulkhead connector from the rear of the transaxle. Unsnap the throttle valve cable from the throttle body lever. Remove the bolt attaching the throttle valve cable to the transaxle case.

5. Carefully pull up on the throttle valve cable and disconnect the throttle valve cable from the T.V. link.

——— CAUTION ———

Pulling to hard on the throttle valve may bend the internal T.V. bracket.

6. Remove the 4 converter housing bolts from the top of the transaxle.

7. Position a suitable engine hoist over the engine and attach the hooks of the hoist to the engine lift points. Raise the engine slightly.

8. Remove both front wheels. Remove each tie rod end from its spindle.

9. Remove the lower ball joint attaching nuts and bolts. Remove the lower ball joints and remove the lower control arms from each spindle. Remove the stabilizer bar nuts.

10. Remove the rack and pinion from the sub frame. Support the steering gear with a piece of wire from the tie rod end to the coil spring. Secure the housing of the gear to a suitable support to hold it in position.

11. Remove the nuts from the engine mounts. Disconnect the oxygen sensor electrical connection. Remove the exhaust Y-pipe from the engine and rear portion of the exhaust system.

12. Remove the sub frame.

13. Remove the bolts from the subframe ataching points. Remove the bolts from the LH engine support mount and lower the sub-frame.

14. Position a suitable transaxle jack under the oil pan of the transaxle. Remove the vehicle speed sensor from the transaxle.

NOTE: Vehicles equipped with electronic instrument clusters do not use a speedometer cable.

15. Remove the 2 bolts from the transaxle mount. Remove the LH engine support by removing the 4 bolts. Unbolt the separator plate.

16. Remove the starter ataching bolts and position the starter out of the way. Remove the separator plate.

17. With a ½ in. drive ratchet and ⅞ in. deep well socket, rotate the crankshaft pulley bolt to align the torque converter bolts with the starter drive hole. Then remove the torque converter-to-flywheel attaching nuts.

18. Disconnect the transmision cooler lines. Remove the halfshafts.

19. Remove the remaining torque converter housing bolts. Separate the transaxle from the engine and carefully lower the transaxle out of the vehicle.

20. Complete the installation of the transaxle by reversing the removal procedure.

Transfer Case

REMOVAL & INSTALLATION

All Wheel Drive Tempo/Topaz

1. Drain the oil by removing the drive housing lower left hand retaining bolt.

2. Remove the vacuum line retaining bracket bolt. Remove the driveshaft front retaining bolts and caps. Disengage the front driveshaft from the drive yoke.

3. If the transfer case is to be disassembled, check the backlash before removal in order to reset to existing backlash at installation. The backlash should be 0.012–0.024 in. on a 3 in. radius as measured through the cup plug opening to the input gear.

4. Remove the 3 bolts retaining the vacuum motor shield and remove the shield.

5. Remove the vacuum lines from the vacuum servo. Remove the 13 bolts retaining the transfer case to the transaxle. Note the length and locations of the bolts.

6. Remove the the transfer case from the vehicle.

7. Position the transfer case to the transaxle.

8. Install the transfer case bolts in the proper positions. Torque the bolts to 23–38 ft. lbs. On 1988–89 vehicles, torque the bolts to 15–19 ft. lbs.

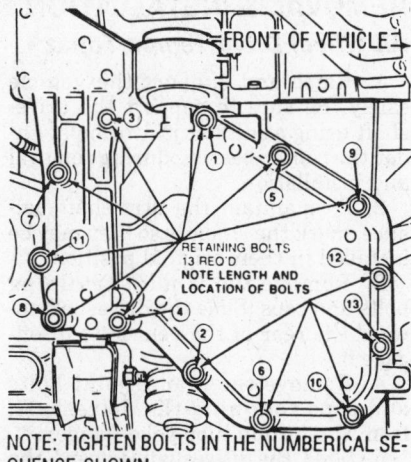

FRONT OF VEHICLE

RETAINING BOLTS
13 REQ'D
NOTE LENGTH AND
LOCATION OF BOLTS

NOTE: TIGHTEN BOLTS IN THE NUMBERICAL SEQUENCE SHOWN

Transfer case retaining bolts - installation and torque sequence

9. Install the vacuum motor supply hose connector. Position the vacuum motor shield and install the 3 retaining bolts. Torque the bolts to 7–12 ft. lbs.

10. Position the driveshaft to the drive yoke. Install the retaining bolts and torque the bolts to 15–17 ft. lbs. Install the vacuum line retaining bracket and bolt and torque it to 7–12 ft. lbs.

11. Fill the transaxle and lower the vehicle. Road test the vehicle and check the performance of the transfer case.

DRIVE AXLE

Halfshaft

REMOVAL & INSTALLATION

When removing both the left and right halfshafts on the MTX and the ATX equipped vehicles, shipping plugs T81P-1177-B or equivalent must be installed. Failure to use these tools can reult in dislocation of the differential side gears. Should the gears become misaligned, the differential will have to be removed from the transaxle to realign the side gears.

NOTE: Due to the ATX case configuration, the right-hand halfshaft assembly must be removed first. Differential Rotator T81P-4026-A or equivalent is then inserted into the transaxle to drive the left-hand inboard CV-joint assembly from the transaxle. If only the left-hand halfshaft assembly is to be removed for service, remove only the right-hand halfshaft assembly from the transaxle. After removal, support it with a length of wire. Then drive the left-hand halfshaft assembly from the transaxle.

1. Remove the cap from the hub and loosen the hub nut. Set the parking brake to prevent the car from rolling while the nut is loosened. The nut must be loosened without unstaking. The use of a chisel or similar tool may damage the spindle thread.

2. After raising the vehicle and removing the wheel and tire assembly, remove the hub nut and washer.

--- CAUTION ---
The retainer nut must be discarded after it is removed.
---

3. Remove the bolt attaching the brake hose routing clip to the suspension strut (all engines except the 3.8L).

4. Remove the nut from the ball joint to steering knuckle attaching bolt. Drive the bolt out of the steering knuckle using a punch and hammer.

--- CAUTION ---
Discard the bolt and nut. They are of a torque prevailing design and cannot be reused.
---

5. On the 3.8L engine: remove the anti-lock brake sensor from the steering knuckle, remove the height sensor from the lower arm ball stud attachment, and remove the stabilizer bar link at the stabilizer.

6. Separate the ball joint from the steering knuckle using a pry bar. Position the end of the pry bar outside of the bushing pocket to avoid damage to the bushing. Use care to prevent damage to the ball joint boot.

NOTE: The lower control arm ball joint fits into a pocket formed in the plastic disc brake rotor shield. This shield must be bent back away from the ball joint while prying the ball joint out of the steering knuckle.

7. Remove the halfshaft from the differential housing using a pry bar. Position the pry bar between the case and the shaft, but be careful not to damage the dust deflector location between the shaft and the case.

NOTE: If extreme resistance is encountered when using a pry bar to remove the haftshafts from the differential, then do not use the pry bar to remove them. Avoid damage to the transaxle case and oil pan; remove the oil pan and use a large prying tool to dislodge the circlip from between the pinion shaft and the inboard CV-joint. This will free the haftshaft from the differential.

--- CAUTION ---
Extreme care must be taken not to damage the differential oil seal, the CV-joint boot or the CV-joint dust deflector.
---

8. On the 3.8L engine, perform the following to disconnect the left and right inboard CV-joints:

a. Install the CV-joint puller T86P-3514-A1 or equivalent between CV-joint and transaxle case. Turn the steering hub and or wire strut assembly out of the way.

b. Screw Extension T86P-3514-A2 or equivalent, into the CV-Joint puller and hand tighten. Screw Impact Slide Hammer D79-100-A or equivalent onto the extension and remove the CV-joint.

9. Support the end of the shaft by suspending it from a convenient un-

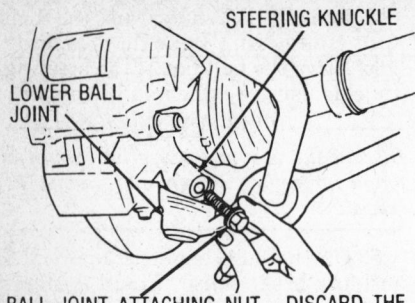

Removing the lower ball joint pinch bolt

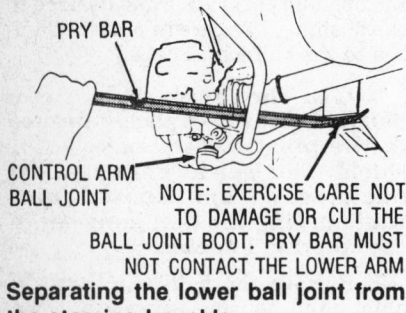

Separating the lower ball joint from the steering knuckle

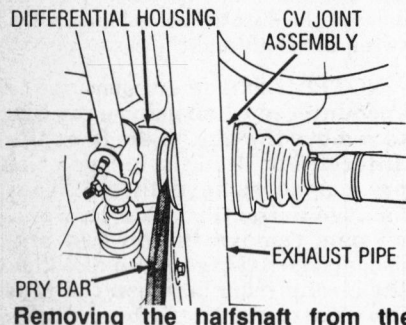

Removing the halfshaft from the transaxle assembly

derbody component with a length of wire.

NOTE: Do not allow the shaft to hang unsupported, as damage to the outboard CV-joint may result.

10. Separate the outboard CV-joint from the hub using puller T81P-1104-C or equivalent, and metric adapters T81P-1104-B and T81P-1104-A or equivalent. Remove the halfshaft from the vehicle.

--- CAUTION ---

Never use a hammer or separate the outboard CV-joint stub shaft from the hub. Damage to the CV-joint internal components may result.

11. Install a new circlip on the inboard CV-joint stub shaft. The outboard CV-joint stub shaft does not have a circlip.

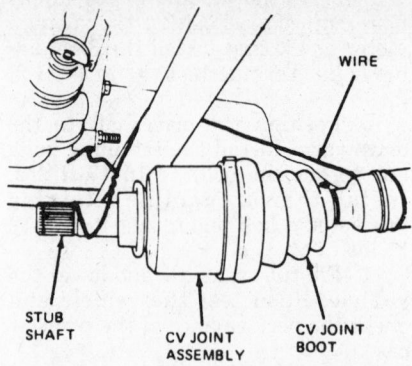

Support the halfshaft by wiring it to the body

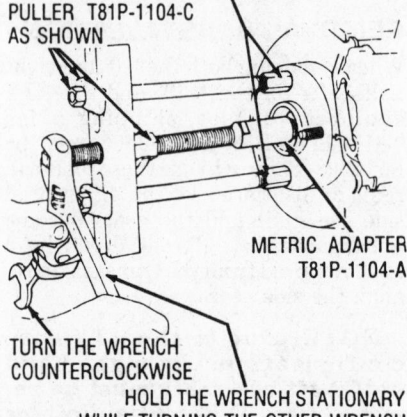

Removing the hub from the shaft assembly

NOTE: To install the circlip properly, start one end in the groove and work the circlip over the stub shaft end and into the groove. This will avoid over expanding the circlip.

12. Carefully align the splines of the inboard CV-joint stub shaft with the splines in the differential. Exerting some force, push the CV-joint into the differential until the circlip is felt to seat in the differential side gear. Use care to prevent damage to the differential oil seal.

NOTE: A non-metallic mallet may be used to aid in seating the circlip into the differential side gear groove. if a mallet is necessary, tap only on the outboard CV-joint stub shaft.

13. Carefully align the splines of the outboard CV-joint stub shaft with the splines in the hub and push the shaft into the hub as far as possible. Use

puller T81P-1104-C or equivalent and metric adapters T81P-1104-A and T81P-1104-B or equivalent to complete the installation.

14. On the 3.8L engine, temporarily fasten the rotor to the hub with washers and 2 wheel lug nuts. Insert a steel rod into the rotor and rotate clockwise to contact the knuckle to prevent the rotor from turning when the CV-joints are installed.

15. On the 3.8L engine, install the hub nut washer and new hub retainer nut. Manually thread the retainer onto the CV-joint shaft as far as possible.

16. Connect the control arm to the steering knuckle and install a new nut and bolt. Torque the nut to 40–54 ft. lbs.

17. On the 3.8L engine, connect the stabilizer bar link to the stabilizer bar with the retaining nut. Torque the retaining nut to 35–48 ft. lbs. Connect the ride height sensor link and connect the anti-lock sensor link in the control arm and tighten the retaining bolt.

18. On the 3.8L engine, torque the hub retainer nut to 180–200 ft. lbs.

19. Position the brake hose routing clip on the suspension strut and install the attaching bolts. Install the hub nut washer and a new hub nut (all engines except the 3.8L).

20. Install the wheel and tire assembly and lower the vehicle.

21. Tighten the wheel nuts 80–105 ft. lbs.

CV-JOINT OVERHAUL

For disassembly and inspection procedures, please refer to "CV-Joint Overhaul" in the Unit Repair Section.

Driveshaft

REMOVAL & INSTALLATION
All Wheel Drive Tempo/Topaz

1. Raise and support the vehicle safely. Be sure to support the driveshaft using a suitable jack or hoist under the center bearing during removal and installation.

2. To maintain the driveshaft balance, mark the U-joints so they may be installed in their original position.

3. Remove the U-joint retaining bolts and caps. Slide the driveshaft toward the rear of the vehicle to disengage it.

4. Remove the rear U-joint bolts and caps retaining the driveshaft, from the torque tube yoke flange.

5. Slide the driveshaft toward the front of the vehicle to disengage. Do not allow the splined shafts to contact with excessive force.

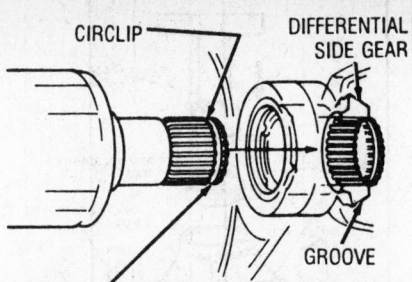

SHAFT IS FULLY INSTALLED WHEN THE CIRCLIP IS FELT TO SEAT IN THE DIFFERENTIAL SIDE GEAR

Seating the circlip in the transaxle differential side gear

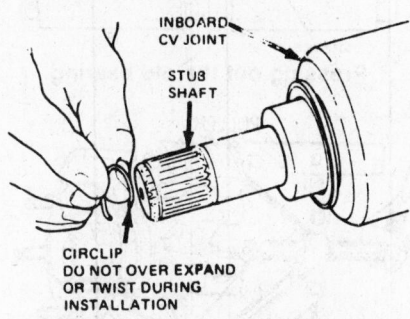

CIRCLIP
DO NOT OVER EXPAND OR TWIST DURING INSTALLATION

Stub shaft circlip installation

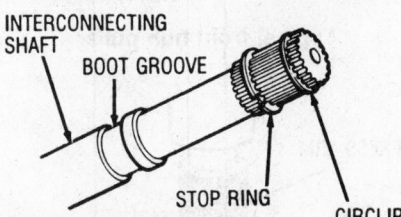

Circlip and stop ring used on the inter connecting shafts

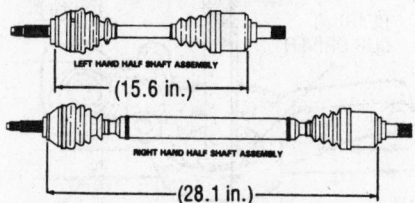

Dimensions for the left and right halfshaft assembled lengths

6. Remove the center bearing retaining bolts. Remove the driveshaft and retain the bearing cups with tape, if necessary.

7. Inspect the U-joint assemblies for wear and or damage, replace the U-joint if necessary.

8. Install the driveshaft at the rear torque yoke flange. Ensure that the U-joint is in its original position.

9. Install the U-joint retaining bolts and caps. Torque them to 15–17 ft. lbs. Position the front U-joint. Install the

U-joint retaining caps and bolts. Torque them to 15–17 ft. lbs.

10. Install the center bearing and retaining bolts. Torque them to 23–30 ft. lbs. Do not drop the assemble driveshafts as the impact may cause damage to the U-joint bearing cups.

Rear Axle Shafts

REMOVAL & INSTALLATION

All Wheel Drive Tempo/Topaz

1. Raise the vehicle on a hoist and support it safely. Position a hoist or a suitable transaxle jack under the rear axle housing.

2. Remove the muffler and exhaust system from the catalytic converter back.

3. Remove the rear U-joint bolts and caps retaining the driveshaft, from the torque tube yoke flange. Lower the and support the driveshaft.

4. Remove the 4 retaining bolts from the torque tube support bracket. Remove the axle retaining bolt from the left hand differential support bracket.

5. Remove the axle retaining bolt from the center differential support bracket.

6. Lower the axle assembly and remove the inboard U-joint retaining bolts and caps from each of the halfshaft. Remove and wire the halfshaft assemblies out of the way.

7. Lower the jack and remove the rear axle from the vehicle.

8. Position the rear axle assembly under the vehicle. Raise the rear axle far enough for the U-joint and halfshaft assembies to be installed.

9. Position each inboard U-joint to the rear axle. Install the U-joint caps and retaining bolts. Using a T-30 Torx® bit or equivalent, torque the bolts to 15–17 ft. lbs. to each halfshaft.

10. Raise the rear axle into position and install the bolts attaching the differential housing to the left hand center differential support bracket. Torque to 70–80 ft. lbs.

11. Position the torque tube and mounting bracket to the crossmember. Install the 4 attaching bolts and torque them to 28–35 ft. lbs. Install the driveshaft and retaining to the torque tube yoke flange. Using a T-30 Torx® bit or equivalent, torque the bolts to 15–17 ft. lbs.

12. Install the exhaust system from the catalytic converter back. Install the muffler.

13. Check the lubricant level in the rear axle and add if necessary. Lower the vehicle and roadtest to check the rear axle for proper operation.

Front Wheel Hub, Knuckle and Bearings

Front wheel bearings are located in the front knuckle, not the rotor. The bearings are protected by inner and outer grease seals and an additional inner grease shield immediately inboard of the inner grease seal. The wheel hub is installed with an interference fit to the constant velocity universal joint outer race shaft. The hub nut and washer are installed and tightened to 180–200 ft. lbs. The rotor fits loosely on the hub assembly and is secured when the wheel and wheel nuts are installed.

The front wheel bearings have a set-right design that requires no scheduled maintenance. The bearing design relies on component stack-up and deformation/torque at assembly to determine bearing setting. Therefore, bearings cannot be adjusted. In addition to maintaining bearing adjustment, the hub nut torque of 180–200 ft. lbs. restricts bearing/hub relative movement and maintains axial position of the hub.

REMOVAL & INSTALLATION

1. Remove the wheelcover/hub cover from the wheel and tire assembly and loosen the lug nuts.

2. Remove the hub retaining nut and washer by applying sufficient torque to the nut to overcome the prevailing torque feature of the crimp in the nut collar. Do not use an impact type tool to remove the hub nut. The hub nut must be discarded after removal.

NOTE: On the later models, remove the hub retainer assembly and washer by applying a sufficient torque (counterclockwise) to the nut to break the locking tab and remove the retainer. Do not use tools such as a screwdriver or chisel to remove the locking tab. The retainer must be discarded after removal.

3. On 3.8L engine vehicles, remove the 2 top strut-to-fender apron nuts.

4. Raise and support the vehicle safely. Remove the wheel and tire assembly.

5. Remove the brake caliper by removing the caliper locating pins and rotoating the caliper off of the rotor, starting from the lower end of the caliper and lifting upward. Lift the caliper off the rotor and hang it free of the rotor. Do not allow the caliper assembly to hang from the brake hose. Support the caliper assembly with a length of wire.

6. Remove the rotor from the hun by pulling it off the hub bolts. If the rotor is difficult to remove from the hub, strike the rotor sharply between the studs with a rubber or plastic hammer.

NOTE: If the rotor will not pull off apply a suitable penetrating fluid to the inboard and outboard rotor hub mating surfaces. Install a 3 jaw puller and remove thr rotor by pulling on the rotor outside diameter and pushing on the hub center. If excessive force is required, check the rotor for lateral runout prior to installation.

7. The lateral runout must be checked with the nuts clamping the stamped hat section of the rotor.

8. Disconnect the lower control arm and tie rod from the steering knuckle. Loosen the strut pinch bolt, but do not remove the strut. On 3.8L engines, remove the rotor splash shield.

9. Install hub remover/installer T81P-1104-A with T81P-1104-C and hub knucle adapters T83P-1104-BH1 and T86P-1104-A1 or equivalent.

10. Remove the hub, bearing and knuckle assembly by pushing out the constant velocity joint outer shaft until it is free of assembly. Wire the halfshaft to the body to maintain a level position.

11. Remove the strut bolt and slide the hub/bearings/knuckle assembly off the strut using spindle carrier lever T85M-3206-A or equivalent. Carefully remove the support wire and carry the hub/bearing /knuckle assembly to a suitable workbench.

12. On the bench, install front hub puller D80L-1002-L and shaft protector D80L-625-1 or equivalent, with the jaws of the puller on the knuckle bosses and remove the hub.

NOTE: Be sure the shaft protector is centered, clears the bearing ID and rests on the end face of the hub journal.

13. Remove the snapring, which retains the bearing in the knuckle assembly, with the snapring pliers and discard.

14. Using a suitable hydraulic press, place the front bearing spacer T86P-1104-A2 or equivalent step side up on the press plate and position the knuckle (outboard side up) on the spacer.

15. Install bearing remover T83P-1104-AH2 or equivalent centered on the bearing inner race and press the bearing out of the knuckle. Discard the old bearing.

16. Remove the halfshaft and place it in a suitable vise.

17. Remove the bearing dust seal by

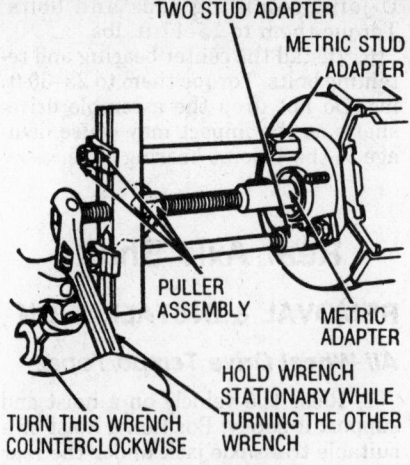

Removing the hub

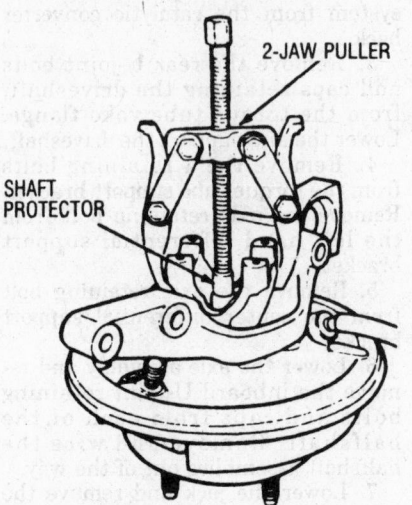

Removing the stub shaft yoke

equally tapping on the outer edge with a light duty hammer and a suitable tool. Discard the dust seal.

18. Remove all forgien material from the knuckle bearing bore and hub bearing journal to ensure trhe correct seating of a new bearing.

NOTE: If the hub bearing journal is scored or damaged, replace the hub. Do not attaempt to service a bad hub. The front wheel bearings are of a cartridge design and are pre-greased, sealed and require no schedule maintenance. The bearings are preset and cannot be adjusted. If a bearing is disassembled for any reason, it must be replaced as a unit. No individual service seals, roller or races are available.

19. Place the front bearing spacer T86P-1104-A or equivalent step side down on a press plate and position the knuckle (outboard side down) on a spacer. Position a new bearing in the inboard side of the knuckle.

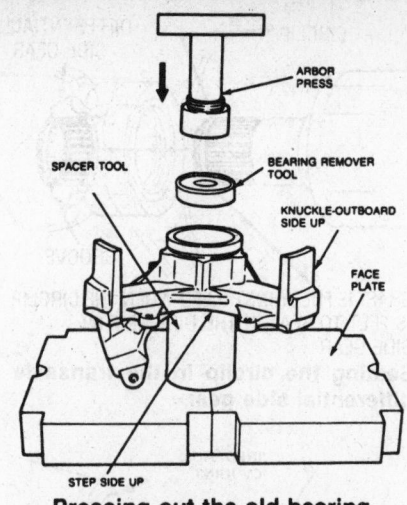

Pressing out the old bearing

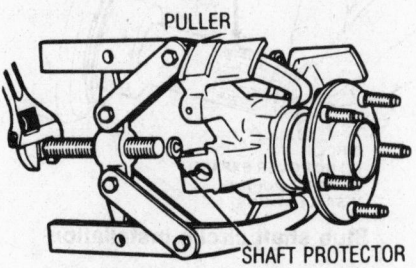

Typical front hub puller

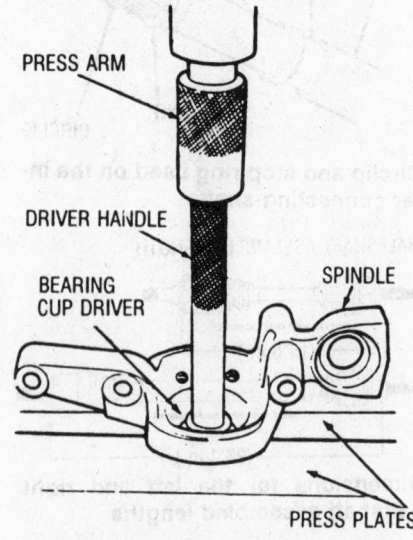

Removing the wheel bearing

20. Install the bearing installer T86P-1104-A3 or equivalent (under-cut side facing the bearing) on the bearing outer race and press bearing into the knuckle.

21. Check that the bearing seats completely against the shoulder of the knuckle bore. The bearing installer must be installed as indicated above to prevent bearing damage during installation.

22. Install a new snapring in the

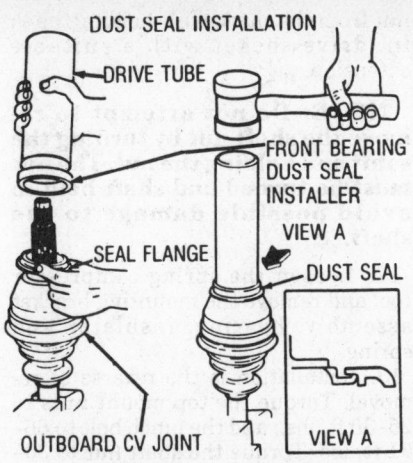

DUST SEAL INSTALLATION

DRIVE TUBE

FRONT BEARING DUST SEAL INSTALLER

VIEW A

SEAL FLANGE

DUST SEAL

VIEW A

OUTBOARD CV JOINT

Installing the dust seal

knuckle groove with a suitable pair of snaping pliers. Place the front bearing spacer T86P-1104-A2 or equivalent on the arbor press plate and position the hub on the tool with the lugs facing downward. Position the knuckle assembly (outboard side down) on the hub barrel.

23. Place bearing remover T83P-1104-AH2 or equivalent flat side down, centered on the inner race of the bearing and press down on the tool until the bearing is fully seated onto the hub. Check that the hub rotates freely in the kunuckle after installation.

24. Prior to the hub/bearing/knuckle installation, replace the bearing dust seal on the outboard CV/joint with a new seal from the bearing kit.

25. Install the dust seal, ensuring the seal flange faces outboard toward the bearing. Use drive tube T83P-3132-A1 and front bearing dust seal installer T86P-1104-A4 or equivalent.

26. Suspend the hub/bearing/knuckle assembly on the vehicle with a wire and attach the strut loosely to the knuckle. Lubricate the CV/joint stub shaft splines with a SAE 30 weight motor oil and insert the shaft onto the hub spilnes as far as possible using hand pressure only. Check that the splines are properly engaged.

27. On 1.6L, 1.9L and 2.3L engines, install hub/knuckle tools Nos. T81P-1104-C, T81P-1104-A and T83P-1104-BH or equivalents to the hub and stub shaft. Tighten the tool assembly to 120 ft. lbs to ensure hub is properly seated. On 3.8L engines, temporarily fasten the rotor to hub with washers and 2 wheel lugnuts. Insert a steel rod into the rotor diameter and rotate it clockwise to contact the knuckle.

28. On 3.8L engines, install the hub nut washer and new hub nut. Rotate the nut clokwise to seat the CV/joint. Tighten the nut to 180–200 ft. lbs. Do not use power or impact tools to install the hub nut. Remove the steel rod,

washers and lug nuts (3.8L engines only).

29. Complete installation of the front suspension components by reversing the removal procedure. On 3.8L engines, install the rotor splash shield.

30. Install the disc brake caliper over the rotor. Be sure the outer brake shoe spring hook is seated under the upper arm of the knuckle.

31. Install the wheel and tire assembly, tighten the lug nuts finger tight. Lower the vehicle and block the wheels to prevent the vehicle from moving. Tighten the lug nuts to 80–105 ft. lbs.

NOTE: Replacement lug nuts or studs must be of the same type and size as those being replaced.

32. On 1.6L, 1.9L and 2.3L engines, manually thread the hub retainer assembly onto the CV output shaft as far as possible. Torque the retainer assembly to 180–200 ft. lbs. Never use power tool to tighten the hub nut and do not move the vehicle before the retainer is tightened. During the tightening, an audible click should will indicate a proper ratchet of the retainer. As the retainer tightens, be sure that 1 of the 3 locking tabs is in the slot of the CV-joint shaft. If the hub retainer assembly is damaged or more than 1 locking tab is broken, replace the retainer.

NOTE: On the later models, when installing the retainer, if a locking tab does not engage in a shaft slot, or a tab breaks during installation, service the retainer as follows: Using a suitable pair of needle nose pliers, place the plier tips between the rachet tabs and rotate in a counterclockwise direction until the next locking tab falls into slot. If 2 or more locking tabs are broken during installation, replace the retainer.

33. Install the wheel cover or hub cover. Lower the vehicle completely to the ground and remove wheel blocks. Road test the vehicle and check to see if the vehicle is operating properly.

FRONT SUSPENSION

All models are equipped with a MacPherson strut front suspension with cast steering knuckles. The shock absorber strut assembly includes a rubber top mount and a coil spring insulator, mounted on the shock strut.

The entire strut assembly is at-

tached to the top by 2 bolts. The lower end of the assembly is attached to the steering knuckle. A pinch joint is designed into the knuckle. The forged lower arm assembly is attached to the underbody side apron and steering knuckle. A stabilizer bar connects the outer end of the lower arm to the engine mount bracket. Caster and camber are preset and non-adjustable. The suspension fittings are lubricated for the life of the component; no grease fittings are provided.

MacPherson Strut

REMOVAL & INSTALLATION

1982–84 Vehicles

1. Raise the vehicle and support it with jack stands.
2. Remove the front wheels. Remove caliper and rotor.
3. Remove the brake line flex hose clip from the strut.
4. Jack up the lower control arm and raise the strut as far as possible without lifting the vehicle from the jack stands.
5. Install a suitable spring compressor on the spring. Install the spring compressor by placing the top jaw on the fifth or sixth coil from the bottom.
6. Tighten the spring until there is approximately ⅛ in. between any 2 coils (or compress the spring a minimum of 3½ in.).

--- **CAUTION** ---

The spring must be compressed before the strut is removed to insure that excessive force is not applied to the constant velocity joints. Be sure not to use the Escort/Lynx spring compressor tool T81P-5310-A when servicing the Tempo/Topaz vehicles.

7. Remove the pinch bolt from the steering knuckle.
8. Loosen the 2 top mounting bolts, but do not remove them.
9. Lower the jack away from the control arm.
10. Use a suitable tool to spread the pinch joint.
11. Place a piece of 2 × 4 wood about 7½ in. long against the shoulder of the knuckle.
12. Insert a pry bar between the wooden block and the strut base, or apron. Separate the strut from the knuckle.
13. Remove the top mounting nuts.
14. Remove the strut and spring assembly.
15. Place an 18mm deep docket on the strut shaft nut. Insert a 8mm hex deep socket with ¼ in. drive wrench and clamp the strut into a vise.

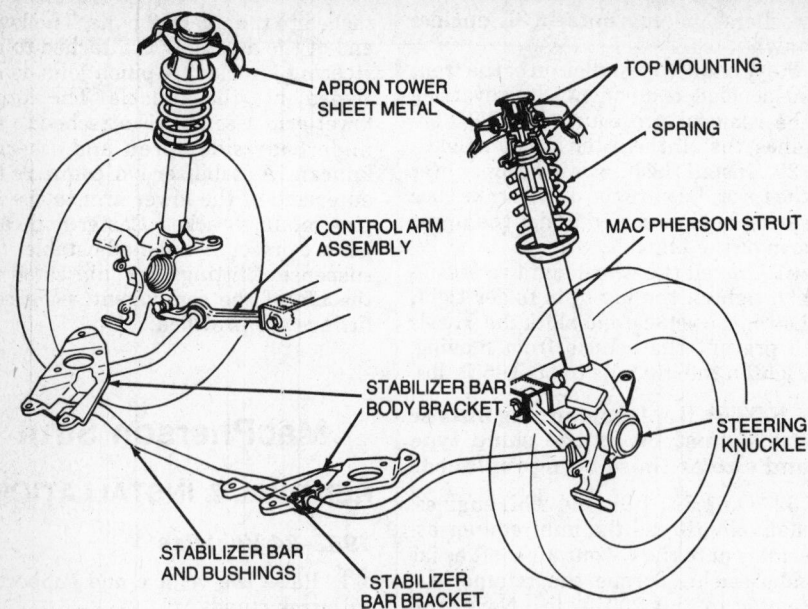

APRON TOWER
SHEET METAL

TOP MOUNTING

SPRING

CONTROL ARM
ASSEMBLY

MAC PHERSON STRUT

STABILIZER BAR
BODY BRACKET

STEERING
KNUCKLE

STABILIZER BAR
AND BUSHINGS

STABILIZER
BAR BRACKET

Front suspension components

NOTE: Do not clamp directly on a strut with a vise. Damage to the strut may occur. It is important that the mounting nut be turned and the rod held still to prevent fracture of the rod at the base of the hex. Wood blocks may be used as outlined at the begining of the procedure.

16. Remove the top shaft mounting nut from the shaft while holding the ¼ in. drive socket with a suitable extension.

NOTE: When servicing the strut assembly, it is necessary to prevent the piston rod (or strut rod) from turning. The end of the strut rod incorporates a 8mm hexagon to allow the rod to be held using an 8mm deep socket with a ¼ in. drive.

17. Remove the strut top mounting components. When servicing the Tempo/Topaz models, be sure to check the spring insulator for damage. Replace if necessary.

18. Remove the spring compressor from the strut and remove the spring.

19. Installation is the reverse of removal. Torque the top mount bolts to 20–30 ft. lbs., and the pinch bolt to 66–81 ft. lbs. Torque the shaft nut to 30–50 ft. lbs.

1985–89 Vehicles except Continental

NOTE: Never attempt to disassemble the spring or top mounted without the first compressing the spring using coil spring compressor 086-00002 or equivalent. Be sure to check the spring insulator

for damage before assembly. If the outer metal splash shield is deformed, it must be bent carefully so that it does not touch the locator tabs on the bearing and seal assembly.

——— CAUTION ———

All vehicles except the Tempo/Topaz with base suspension are equipped with gas pressurized shock absorbers which will extend unassisted. Do not apply heat or flame to the shock strut tube during removal.

1. Loosen the 2 top shock tower mounting nuts, but do not remove them.

2. Jack up the vehicle and support it with jack stands.

3. Remove the front wheels. Remove caliper and rotor.

4. Remove the brake line flex hose clip from the strut.

5. Remove the pinch bolt from the steering knuckle.

6. Use a suitable tool to spread the pinch joint.

7. Using a suitable tool, place the top of the tool under the fender apron and pry down on the knuckle until the strut separtes from the knuckle. Be careful not to pinch the brake flex line.

8. Remove the top mount to shock tower nuts and remove the strut from the vehicle.

9. Install the spring compressor in a bench mount. Compress the spring with Universal MacPherson Strut Spring Compressor No. 086-00029 or equivalent.

10. Place an 18mm deep docket on the strut shaft nut. Insert a 8 mm hex deep socket with ¼ in. drive wrench.

11. Remove the top shaft mounting

nut from the shaft while holding the ¼ in. drive socket with a suitable extension.

NOTE: Do not attempt to remove the shaft nut by turning the sahft and holding the nut. The nut must be turned and shaft held to avoid possible damage to the shaft.

12. Loosen the spring compressor tool and remove the mounting bracket assembly, bearing, insulator and spring.

13. Installation is the reverse of removal. Torque the top mount nuts to 25–30 ft. lbs., and the pinch bolt to 66–81 ft. lbs. Torque the shaft nut to 30–50 ft. lbs.

Continental

The front suspension utilizes MacPherson struts with integral air springs and dual dampening mechanisms. The front struts are mounted to the body by means of a high percision ball bearing and rubber mount system.

1. Turn off the air suspension switch located in the left side luggage compartment. Loosen the wheel nuts.

2. Turn the ignition switch to the **OFF** position to unlock the steering wheel.

3. Remove the plastic cover from the shock tower to expose the upper mounting nuts and dual dampening actuator.

4. Remove the actuator retaining screws. Lift the actuator off the shock mount and set aside.

5. Remove the wheel/hub cover. Remove the wheel hub retainer nut by applying sufficient torque to overcome the prevailing torque of the crimp in the nut collar. Discard the nut and replace with new.

6. Loosen the 3 top mount-to-shock tower mounting nuts, but do not remove at this time.

7. Raise the vehicle and support safely.

NOTE: DO NOT raise the vehicle by the lower control arms.

8. Remove the wheel and tire assembly.

9. Remove the brake line bracket from the strut assembly.

10. Disconnect the height sensor link from the ball stud pin at the lower controm arm.

11. Disconnect the air line from the spring solenoid valve. The line is released from the valve by pushing and holding the plastic retaining ring on the valve down and withdrawing the nylon tube.

12. Disconnect the electrical connector at the solenoid valve.

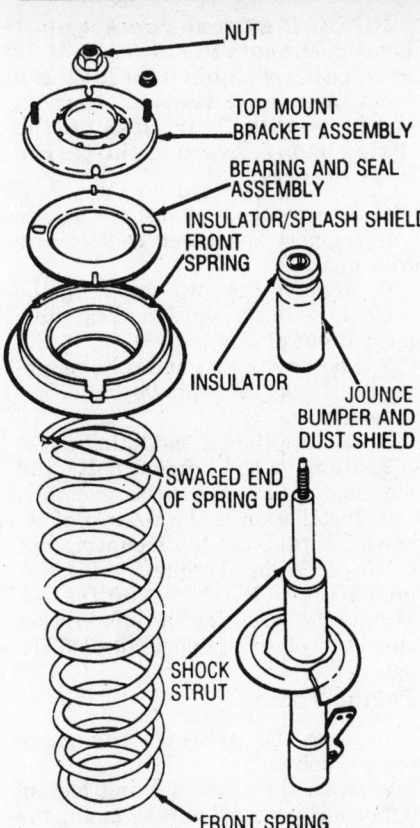

NUT

TOP MOUNT
BRACKET ASSEMBLY

BEARING AND SEAL
ASSEMBLY

INSULATOR/SPLASH SHIELD
FRONT
SPRING

INSULATOR

JOUNCE
BUMPER AND
DUST SHIELD

SWAGED END
OF SPRING UP

SHOCK
STRUT

FRONT SPRING

Exploded view of the strut assembly

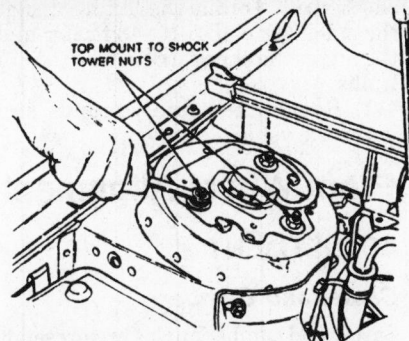

TOP MOUNT TO SHOCK
TOWER NUTS

**Upper shock tower mounting hardware
—Continental**

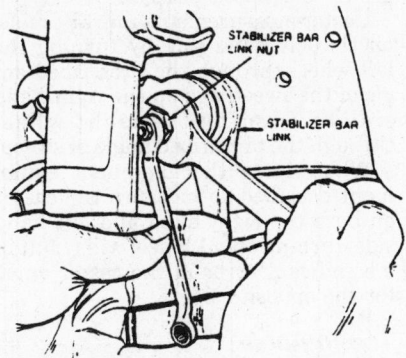

STABILIZER BAR
LINK NUT

STABILIZER BAR
LINK

**Stabilizer link removal and installation
—Continental**

13. Move the brake caliper and suspend with a piece of wire from a convenient body component.

14. Remove the brake rotor.

15. Remove the cotter pin from the tie rod end stud and remove the slotted nut. Discard the cotter pin and nut and replace with new.

16. With tie rod end remover No. 3290-D and tie rod end remover adapter No. T81P-3504-W or equivalents, separate the tie rod end from the knuckle.

17. Remove the stabilizer bar link nut and remove the link from the strut.

18. Remove the lower arm-to-steering knuckle pinch bolt and nut. A drift punch may be used to remove the bolt. With a suitable prying tool, slightly spread the knuckle-to-lower arm pinch bolt joint and remove the lower arm from the steering knuckle. Discard the bolt and replace with new.

19. Press the halfshaft from the hub and wire the halfshaft to the body in a level position.

20. Remove the shock absorber-to-steering knuckle pinch bolt. Spread the knuckle-to-strut pinch joint as required to assist in the removal of the bolt.

21. Remove the steering knuckle and hub assembly from the shick absorber strut.

22. Remove the 3 top mount-to-shock tower nuts and remove the strut and spring assembly from the vehicle.

23. Complete the installation of the strut and spring assembly by reversing the removal procedure. Torque the tie rod end nut to 23-35 ft. lbs., top mount-to-shock tower nuts to 22-32 ft. lbs. and hub nut to 180-200 ft. lbs.

OVERHAUL

For all spring and shock absorber removal & installation procedures, and all strut overhaul procedures, please refer to "Strut Overhaul" in the unit repair section.

Lower Control Arms and Ball Joints

REMOVAL & INSTALLATION

All Vehicles Except Continental

1. Loosen the wheel nuts, raise and support the vehicle, and remove the wheel and tire.

2. Remove the nut from the stabilizer bar. Pull of the large dished washer.

3. Remove the control arm inner mounting pivot nut and bolt.

4. Remove the lower control arm

ball joint stud pinch bolt from the steering knuckle.

5. Pull the control arm and ball joint down and away from the steering knuckle. Slightly separate the pinch ears with a small pry bar if necessary.

6. Remove the stabilizer bar spacer from the arm bushings. Remove the control arm.

NOTE: Be sure the steering column is in the unlock position. Do not use a hammer to separate the ball joint from the steering knuckle.

7. Installation is the reverse of the removal procedure. Tighten the pinch bolt to 38-45 ft. lbs., inner control arm mounting bolt and nut to 48-55 ft. lbs. and stabilizer bar nut to 98-115 ft. lbs.

Continental

1. Turn off the air suspension switch located in the left side of the luggage compartment. Loosen the wheel nuts. Place the steering wheel in the unlocked position.

2. Raise the vehicle and support safely. Remove the wheel and tire assembly.

3. Disconnect the height sensor link from the ball stud pin.

4. Remove the nut and dished washer from the tension strut. Discard the nut and replace with new.

5. Remove the lower control arm pinch bolt. With a suitable prying tool, spread the knuckle pinch joint and separate the control arm from the steering knuckle. A drift punch may be used to remove the bolt. Take care not to damage the bolt seal.

— **CAUTION** —

Do not allow the steering knuckle/halfshaft to move outward. Over-extension of the tripod CV-joint may cause separation of the internal parts which may result in failure of the joint.

6. Remove the lower control arm assembly from the tension strut.

7. Complete the installation of the lower control arm by reversing the removal procedure. Torque the pinch bolt to 40-55 ft. lbs., tension strut nut to 70-95 ft. lbs. and wheel nuts to 80-105 ft. lbs. Ensure all threaded surfaces are free from dirt and grease.

Stabilizer Bar

REMOVAL & INSTALLATION

All Vehicles Except Continental

1. Raise and support the vehicle safely.

2. Remove the nut from the stabilizer bar at each lower control arm and

pull off the large dished washer. Discard the nuts and replace with new.

3. Remove the stabilizer bar insulator U-bracket bolts and U-brackets and remove the stabilizer bar assembly. Discard the bolts and replace with new.

NOTE: Stabilizer bar U-bracket insulators can be serviced without removing the stabilizer bar assembly.

4. Remove the worn insulators from the stabilizer bar and replace with new.

5. Installation is the reverse order of the removal procedure.

6. Tighten all bolts halfway, then tighten bolts 59–68 ft. lbs. on the Tempo/Topaz and 85–100 ft. lbs. on the Escort/Exp, Lynx/LN7.

7. Using the new nuts and the original dished washers (dished away from bushing), attach the stabilizer bar to the lower control arm. Tighten the nuts to 98–115 ft. lbs.

Continental

1. Raise the vehicle and support with jackstands positioned behind the subframe.

2. Disconnect the stabilizer bar from the shock strut by removing the attaching nuts.

3. Remove the nuts retaining the steering gear to the sub-frame. Move the gear off the sub-frame.

4. Position another set of jack stands under the sub-frame and remove the 2 rear sub-frame mounting bolts. After the bolts are removed, lower the rear of the sub-frame to gain access to the stabilizer mounting brackets.

5. Remove the stabilizer bar U-bracket bolts. Remove the U-brackets and/or stabilizer bar as required. Discard the insulators and bolts and replace with new.

6. Remove all dirt and grease from the stabilizer bar insulator mounting areas. Lubricate the inside of the new insulators with No. E25Y-19553–A or equivalent lubricant. DO NOT use mineral oil or similar petroleum based lubricants as they will deteriorate the rubber insulators.

7. Install the new insulators on the stabilizer bar and place in the approximate installation positions.

8. Install the U-brackets on the insulators with new retaining bolts. Torque the bolts to 21–32 ft. lbs.

9. Raise the sub-frame and install the sub-frame-to-body attaching bolts. Position the steering gear onto the sub-frame and install the retaining nuts. Torque the retaining nuts to 85–100 ft. lbs.

10. Install new nuts and secure the link assembly to the stabilizer bar and

shock strut. Torque the nut located at the stabilizer end to 35–48 ft. lbs. and the nut at the shock strut end to 55–75 ft. lbs.

11. Remove the safety stands and lower the vehicle.

Front Wheel Alignment

ADJUSTMENT

Caster and Camber

Caster and camber angles are preset at the factory and cannot be adjusted. Measurement procedures that follow are for diagnostic purposes.

Caster measurements must be made on the left hand side by turning the left wheel through the prescribed angle of the sweep and on the right hand side by turning the right wheel through the prescribed angle of sweep.

When using the alignment equipment designed to measure the caster on both the right hand and left hand side, turning only 1 wheel will result in a significant error in the caster angle for the opposite side.

Toe-In Angle

The toe-in is controlled by adjusting the tie rod ends. To adjust the toe-in seeting, loosen the tie-rod jam nuts. Rotate the tie rod as required to adjust the toe-in into specifications. Once the toe-in is set, re-tighten the tie rod jam nuts.

REAR SUSPENSION

Shock Absorber

REMOVAL & INSTALLATION

Escort/EXP and Lynx/LN7

1. Remove the rear compartment access panels. Four door models require the removal of the quarter panel trim.

NOTE: Do not attempt to remove the shaft nut by turning shaft and holding nut. The nut must be turned and the shaft held to avoid possible damage to the shaft.

2. Loosen, but do not remove the top strut nut. If the shock absorber is to be re-used do not grip the shock absorber shaft with pliers, as this will damage the shaft.

3. Jack up the vehicle and support it with jackstands.

NOTE: If a frame contact hoist is used, support the lower control arm with a suitable floor jack. If a twin post hoist is used, support the body with floor jacks on the lifting pads forward of the tie rod body bracket.

4. Remove the rear tire.

5. Support the lower control arm with a jack.

6. Remove the clip retaining the brake hose to the shock and carefully move it out of the way.

7. Loosen the nuts and bolts retaining the shock to the spindle, but do not remove them.

8. Remove the top mounting nut.

9. Remove the bottom bolts and nuts and remove the shock assembly.

10. Installation is the reverse of removal. Torque the top mounting nut to 35–55 ft. lbs. Torque the 2 lower mounting bolts to 70–100 ft. lbs. Torque the stabilizer bar link bracket on shock bolt (if equipped) to 40–55 ft. lbs.

Tempo/Topaz

1. Raise the jack only enough to contact body.

2. Open the trunk lid and loosen, but do not remove 2 nuts retaining the upper strut mount to body.

3. Raise the vehicle. Remove the wheel and tire.

4. Place a jackstand under the control arms to support the suspension.

——— **CAUTION** ———

Care should be taken when removing the strut that the rear brake flex hose is not stretched or the steel brake tube is not bent.

5. Remove the bolt attaching the brake hose bracket to the strut and carefully move it out of the way.

6. Remove the 2 bolts retaining the jounce bumper bracket and strut to the spindle.

7. Remove the jounce bumper bracket from the vehicle.

8. Remove the shock strut from the spindle.

9. Remove the 2 upper mount-to-body nuts.

10. Remove the strut from vehicle.

11. Place the strut, spring and upper mount assembly into a suitable spring compressor.

NOTE: Do not attempt to remove the spring from the strut without first compressing the spring with a tool designed for that purpose.

——— **CAUTION** ———

Do not attempt to remove the shaft nut by turning the shaft and holding the nut. The nut must be turned and the shaft held to avoid a possible fracture of the shaft at the base of the hex.

12. With the spring compressed, remove the strut shaft-to-mount nut and then remove the spring, strut and mount from the compressor tool.

13. Install in reverse order. Torque the top mount to body bolts 20–30 ft. lbs. and strut to spindle bolts 70–96 ft. lbs. Always install new strut to spindle bolts.

Continental

1. Turn off the air suspension switch located in the luggage compartment.

2. From inside the luggage compartment, disconnect the electrical connector from the dual dampening actuator.

3. Loosen, but DO NOT remove the 3 retaining the strut to the upper body.

4. Raise and suppot the vehicle safely.

5. Disconect the air line and electrical connector from the solenoid valve.

6. Remove the brake hose retainer at the strut bracket.

7. Disconnect the parking brake cable from the brake caliper. Remove all the wire retainers and parking brake cable retainers from the lower suspension arm.

8. Disconnect the height sensor link from the ball stud pin on the lower arm.

9. Remove the caliper asembly from the spindle and position off ot the side with a piece of wire. DO NOT kink or place a load on the brake hose.

10. Bleed the air spring by performing the following:

   a. Remove the solenoid clip.

   b. Rotate the solenoid counterclockwise to the first stop.

   c. Slowly pull the solenoid straight out to the second stop and bleed the air from the system.

———— CAUTION ————
Do not fully release the solenoid until the air is fully bled from the spring.

   d. After the air is fully bled from the system, rotate the solenoid to the third stop and remove the solenoid from the housing.

   e. Mark the position of the notch on the toe adjustment cam.

11. Remove the nut from the inboard bushing on the suspension arm.

12. Install torsion spring remover No. T88P–5310–A or equivalent on the suspension arm. Pry up on the tool and arm using a ¾ in. drive ratchet to relieve the pressure on the pivot bolt. An assistant may be required to pull outboard on the spindle simultaneously to fully relieve the tension on the bolt. Remove the bolt and lower arm. Repeat this procedure for the opposite arm.

13. Remove the torsion spring from the arms.

14. Remove the stabilizer U-bracket from the body.

15. Remove the nut, washer and insulator attaching the stabilizer bar to the link. Separate the stabilizer bar from the link.

16. Remove the nut washer and insulator retaining the tension strut to the spindle. Move the spindle rearward enough to separate it from the tension strut.

17. Remove and discard the shock strut-to-spindle pinch bolt. With a suitable prying tool, spread the strut-to-spindle pinch joint as required to assist in removing the bolt.

18. Separate the spindle from the strut. Remove the spindle as an assembly with the arms attached.

19. From inside the luggage compartment area, support the shock strut by hand remove and discard the 3 upper mount-to-body nuts. Care should be taken not to drop the shock strut when removing the upper nuts. Guide the electric actuator wire through the opening to prevent snagging and damage while removing the strut assembly.

20. Complete the installation of the shock strut assembly by reversing the removal procedure. Torque the 3 retaining nuts 19–26 ft. lbs.

21. Turn on the air suspension switch.

22. Fill the air spring and check and/or adjust the toe as required.

OVERHAUL

For all spring and shock absorber removal and installation procedures, and all strut overhaul procedures, please refer to the "Strut Overhaul" in the Unit Repair section.

Springs

REMOVAL & INSTALLATION
Escort/Lynx

1. Jack up the vehicle and support it with jackstands.

2. Place a jack under the control arm and raise the control arm enough to put tension on the spring.

NOTE: Be careful not to raise the car off the jackstands. If a twin post hoist is used, support the body with floor jacks on the lifting pads forward of the tie rod body bracket.

3. Remove the tire and wheel assembly. Remove and discard the nut, bolt and washers retaining the lower control arm to the spindle.

4. Slowly lower the control arm until the spring can be removed.

5. Installation is the reverse of removal. Torque the lower control arm-to-spindle bolt to 70–96 ft. lbs.

Rear Control Arms

REMOVAL & INSTALLATION

Escort/EXP and Lynx/LN7

1. Raise and support the vehicle safely.

NOTE: If a twin post hoist is used, support the body with floor jacks on the lifting pads forward of the tie rod body bracket.

2. Remove tire and wheel assembly.

3. Place a floor jack under the lower control arm between the spring and the spindle end mounting. The rear suspension should be at ful rebound and the shock strut fully extended.

4. Remove the nuts from the control arm to body mounting and control arm spindle mounting. Do not remove the bolts at this time.

5. Remove and discard the spindle end mounting bolt. Slowly lower the floor jack until the spring insulator can be removed.

6. Remove and discard the bolt from the body end and remove the control arm from the vehicle.

7. Installation is the reverse order of the removal procedure. Torque the control arm to spindle bolt to 70–96 ft. lbs. and the control arm to body bolt to 52–74 ft. lbs.

Tempo/Topaz

1. Raise and safely support vehicle.

2. Remove tire and wheel assembly.

3. Remove the arm-to-spindle bolts and nut.

4. Remove the center mounting bolt and nut.

5. Remove the arm from vehicle.

6. Install in reverse order. Torque arm to body bolt 40–55 ft. lbs. and arm to spindle bolt 60–86 ft. lbs.

NOTE: When installing the the new control arms, the bushing with the 0.39 in. (10mm) hole is installed to the center of the vehicle and the bushing with the 0.48 in. (12mm) is to the spindle. Also, the offset on the arm must face up on the right hand side of the vehicle and down on the left hand side of the vehicle. The flange edge of the arm stamping also must face the rear of the vehicle.

Continental

1. Turn off the air suspension switch located in the luggage compartment.

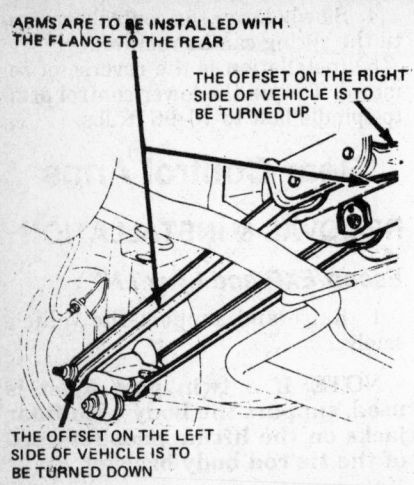

ARMS ARE TO BE INSTALLED WITH THE FLANGE TO THE REAR

THE OFFSET ON THE RIGHT SIDE OF VEHICLE IS TO BE TURNED UP

THE OFFSET ON THE LEFT SIDE OF VEHICLE IS TO BE TURNED DOWN

Tempo/Topaz rear control arm mounting

2. Raise the vehicle and support safely.

3. Remove all wire andf parking brake cable retainers from the front lower suspension arm only. Disconect the height link sensor from the ball stud pin on the right lower arm.

4. Mark the position of the notch on the toe adjustment cam (rear arm only).

5. Remove the nut from the inboard bushing on the suspension arm.

6. Install torsion spring remover No. T88P–5310–A or equivalent on the suspension arm. Pry up on the tool and arm using a ¾ in. drive ratchet to relieve the pressure on the pivot bolt. An assistant may be required to pull outboard on the spindle simultaneously to fully relieve the tension on the bolt. Remove the bolt and lower arm.

7. Remove the nut retaing the torsion spring to the arm. Separate the spring from the arm.

8. Remove the outboard attaching bolt at the spindle.

9. Repeat the procedure for the remaining arm(s).

NOTE: When installing the new control arms, the offset must face up. The arms are stamped "BOTTOM" on the lower edge. The rear control arms have adjustment cams that fit inside the bushings at the arm-to-body attachment. These cams are installed from the front of both arms.

10. Complete the installation by reversing the removal procedure. Check and adjust the rear toe as necessary.

Rear Wheel Bearings

REMOVAL & INSTALLATION

All Vehicles Except Tempo/ Topaz All Wheel Drive

The rear wheel bearings are located in

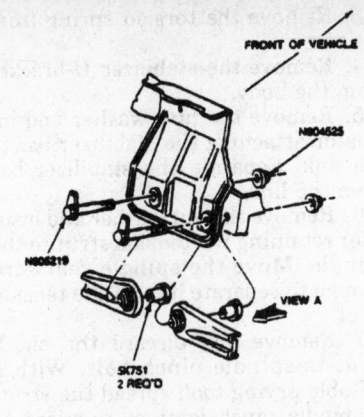

FRONT OF VEHICLE

VIEW A

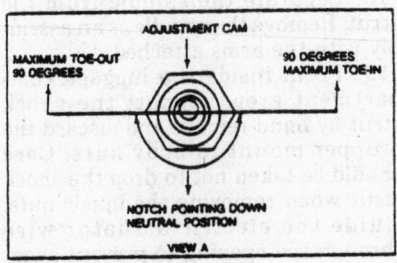

ADJUSTMENT CAM

MAXIMUM TOE-OUT 90 DEGREES

90 DEGREES MAXIMUM TOE-IN

NOTCH POINTING DOWN NEUTRAL POSITION

VIEW A

Rear control arm adjustment cam used on the Continental

the brake drum hub. The inner wheel bearing is protected by a grease seal. A washer and spindle nut retain the hub/drum assembly and control the bearing end play.

NOTE: For rear axle shaft bearing remove and installation on the Tempo/Topaz all wheel drive vehicles, refer to the rear axle removal and installation procedure in this section.

1. Raise and support the rear of the vehicle and remove the wheel from the hub.

2. On the Continental, remove the brake caliper by removing the bolts that attach the caliper support to the cast iron brake adapter. Lift the caliper from the rotor and support with a piece of wire. Do not allow the caliper to hang by the brake hose.

3. Remove the dust cover, cotter pin nut retainer, adjusting nut and keyed flatwasher from the spindle.

4. Pull the hub and drum assembly off the spindle being careful not to drop the outer bearing assembly.

5. Remove the outer bearing assembly. Using seal remover tool No. 1175–AC or equivalent, remove the grease seal. Remove the inner bearing assembly from the hub.

6. Wipe all lubricant from the spindle and the inside of the hub. Cover the spindle with a clean cloth and vac-

uum all the loose dust and dirt from the brake assembly. Carefully remove the cloth to prevent dirt from falling onto the spindle.

7. Clean both bearing assemblies and cups using a suitable solvent. Inspect the bearing assemblies and cups for excessive wear, scratches, pits or other damage. Replace all worn and damaged parts as necessary.

NOTE: Be sure to let the solvent dry before repacking the bearings. Do not spin dry the bearings with air pressure.

8. If the cups are to be replaced, remove them with a slide hammer No. D79P-100-A and bearing cup puller No. T77F, 1102-A or equivalent.

9. Pack the bearings with a multi-purpose grease.

10. Coat the cups with a thin film of grease. Install the inner bearings and a new grease seal.

11. Coat the bearing surfaces of the spindle with a thin film of grease. Slowly and carefully slide the drum and hub over the spindle and brake shoes. Install the outer bearing over the spindle and into the hub.

12. Install the keyed flat washer and adjusting nut on the spindle.

13. Tighten the adjusting nut to between 17–25 ft. lbs.

14. Back-off the adjusting nut ½ turn. Then retighten it to between 10–15 ft. lbs. On the Continental, rotate the hub ¼ turn then torque the adjusting nut to 24–28 inch lbs.

15. Position the nut retainer on the nut and install the cotter pin. Do not tighten the nut to install the cotter pin.

16. Spread the ends of the cotter pin and bend then around the nut retainer. Install the center grease cap.

17. On the Continental, install the disc brake rotor to the hub and install the disc brake caliper to the rotor.

18. Install the tire and wheel assembly. Lower the car and tighten the wheel lugs to 80–105 ft. lbs.

STEERING

CAUTION

If the vehicle is equipped with a driver airbag restraint system, any required service should be performed by personnel trained on servicing the system so that accidental firing of the airbag will not occur.

Steering Wheel

REMOVAL & INSTALLATION

All Vehicles Except Continental

1. Disconnect the negative battery cable. Remove the steering wheel center horn pad cover, by removing the the retaining screws from the steering wheel assembly.

NOTE: The emblem assembly is removed after the horn pad cover is removed, by pushing it out from the backside of the emblem.

2. Remove the energy absorbing foam from the wheel assembly if so equipped. Remember the energy absorbing foam must be installed when the steering wheel is assembled. Disconnect the horn pad wiring conector.
3. On the 1985–89 vehicles equipped with Air Bag Restraint System, remove the 4 nuts holding the air bag module to the steering wheel (the nuts are located on the back of the steering wheel).
4. Lift the air bag module from the wheel and disconnect the air bag module to slip-ring clock spring connector.
5. On all vehicles loosen and remove the center mounting nut, and on the models equipped with speed control system remove the electrical connectors.
6. Remove the steering wheel with a crowsfoot type of puller or equivalent. Do not use a knock-off type puller, because it will cause damage to the collapsible steering column.
7. Position the steering wheel on the end of the steering wheel shaft. Align the mark on the steering wheel with the mark on the shaft to assure the straight-ahead steering wheel position corresponds to the straight-ahead steering wheel position corresponds to the straight-ahead position of the front wheels.
8. Install a new service wheel locknut and torque it to 23–33 ft. lbs., also reconnect all the electrical connectors on the models equipped with speed control.
9. On the air bag models, connect the air bag module wire to slip ring connector and place the module on the steering wheel with the 4 attaching nuts, torque the nuts to 35–33 inch lbs.
10. On the other vehicles install the steering wheel hub cover and torque the nuts to 13–20 inch lbs.
11. Reconnect the negative battery cable and check out the operation of the steering wheel.

Continental

1. Disconnect the negative battery cable.

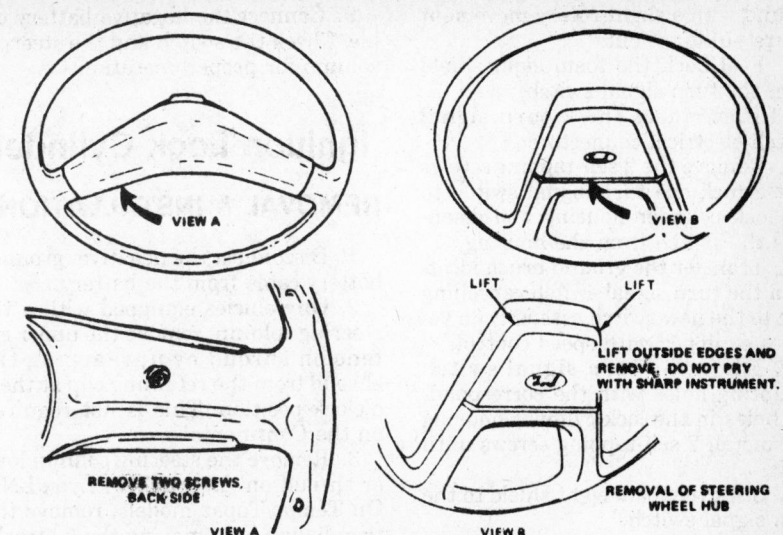

Steering wheel cover removal

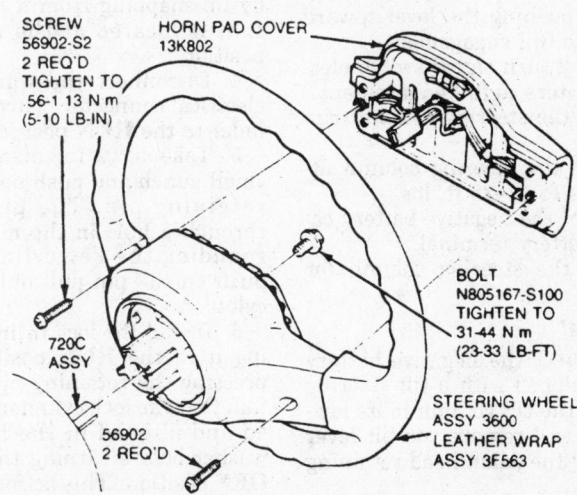

Steering wheel and horn pad assembly—Continental

2. Remove the steering wheel horn pad cover by removing the 2 screws at the back of the steering wheel.
3. Remove and discard the steering wheel bolt.
4. Remove the sateering wheel from the upper shaft by grasping the rim of the steering wheel and pulling off. DO NOT use a steering wheel puller.

NOTE: The multi-switch lever switch must be in the NEUTRAL position before installing the steering wheel or damage to the switch cam may result.

5. Position the steering wheel on the end of the steering wheel shaft. Align the mark on the steering wheel with the mark on the shaft to assure the straight-ahead steering wheel position corresponds to the straight-ahead position of the front wheels.
6. Install a new service wheel bolt. Torque the bolt to 23–33 ft. lbs.

7. Install the steering wheel horn pad with the 2 screws.
8. Connect the negative battery cable and check the steering column for proper operation.

Combination Switch

REMOVAL & INSTALLATION

All Vehicles Except Continental

1. Disconnect the negative battery cable from the battery terminal.
2. Remove the 5 shroud screws and remove the lower shroud.
3. Loosen the 4 steering column attaching nuts enough to allow the removal of the upper trim shroud.
4. Remove the upper shroud.
5. Remove the turn signal switch lever by pulling the lever straight out from the switch. To make removal easier, work the outer end of the lever

around with a slight rotary movement before pulling it out.

6. Peel back the foam sight shield from the turn signal switch.

7. Disconnect the 2 turn signal switch electrical connectors.

8. Remove the 2 self-tapping screws that attach the turn signal switch to the lock cylinder housing and disengage the switch from the housing.

9. Transfer the ground brush located in the turn signal switch cancelling cam to the new switch assembly on vehicles equipped with speed control.

10. Align the turn signal switch mounting holes with the corresponding holes in the lock cylinder housing and install 2 self-tapping screws until tight.

11. Stick the foam sight shield to the turn signal switch.

12. Install the turn signal switch lever into the switch by aligning the key on the lever with the keyway in the switch and pushing the lever toward the switch to full engagement.

13. Install 2 turn signal switch electrical connectors to full engagement.

14. Install the steering column trim shrouds.

15. Torque the steering column attaching nuts to 17–25 ft. lbs.

16. Connect the negative battery cable to the battery terminal.

17. Check the steering column for proper operation.

Continental

1. Disconnect the negative battery cable. If equipped with a tilt steering column, set the tilt column to its lowest position and remove the tilt lever by removing the Allen head retaining screw.

2. Remove the ignition lock cylinder. Remove the steering column shroud screws and remove the upper and lower shrouds.

3. Remove the wiring harness retainer and disconnect the 3 electrical connectors.

4. Remove the 2 self tapping screws attaching the switch to the steering column and disengage the switch from the steering column casting.

5. Align the turn signal switch mounting holes with the corresponding holes in the steering column and install self-tapping screws. Torque the screws to 18–27 inch lbs.

6. Install the electrical connectors and install the wiring harness retainer.

7. Install the upper and lower steering column shroud and shroud retaining screws, torque the screws to 6–9 inch lbs.

8. Install the ignition lock cylinder. Attach the tilt lever (if removed) and torque the tilt lever Allen head retaining screw to 6–9 inch lbs.

9. Connect the negative battery cable. Check the switch and the steering column for proper operation.

Ignition Lock Cylinder

REMOVAL & INSTALLATION

1. Disconnect the negative (ground) battery cable from the battery.

2. On vehicles equipped with a tilt steering column, remove the upper extension shroud by unsnapping the shroud from the retaining clip at the 9 o'clock position. This is not required on the Continental.

3. Remove the steering column lower shroud on Escort/EXP, Lynx/LN7. On Tempo/Topaz models, remove the trim halves by removing the 5 attaching screws. On models with tilt wheel, Remove the upper extension shroud by un-snapping from a retaining clip that is located at the nine o'clock position.

4. Disconnect the warning buzzer electrical connector. Turn the key cylinder to the RUN position.

5. Take a ⅛ in. diameter pin or small punch and push on the cylinder retaining pin. The pin is visible through a hole in the mounting surrounding the key cylinder. As you push on the pin pull out on the lock cylinder.

6. Install the lock cylinder by turning it to the RUN position and depressing the retaining pin. Make certain that the lock cylinder is fully seated and aligned in the interlocking washer before turning the key to the OFF position. This action will permit the cylinder retaining pin to extend into the cylinder housing hole.

7. Rotate the lock cylinder, using the lock cylinder key, to ensure correct mechanical operation in all positions.

8. Install the electrical connector for the key warning buzzer.

9. Install the lower steering column shroud.

10. Connect the negative (ground) battery cable to battery terminal.

11. Check for proper start in PARK or NEUTRAL. Also, make certain that that the start circuit cannot be actuated in the DRIVE and REVERSE positions and that the column is locked in the LOCK position.

Ignition Switch

The ignition switch has blade type terminals with 1 multiple connector. The switch is attached to the steering column with break-off head bolts. The bolts must be removed with an easy-out tool or other means.

REMOVAL & INSTALLATION

All Vehicles Except Continental

1. Disconnect the negative battery cable from the battery terminal.

2. Remove the steering column upper and lower trim shroud by removing 5 self-tapping screws. The 4 steering column attaching nuts may have to be loosened enough to allow removal of the upper shroud.

3. On the 1987–89 vehicles, remove the steering column lower cover from the instrument panel by removing the 2 screws from the bottom. Disengage the snap-in retainers at the top.

4. Disconnect the ignition switch electrical connector.

5. Rotate ignition key lock cylinder to ON position.

6. Drill out the break-off head bolts that connect the switch to the lock cylinder housing using an ⅛ in. drill. On the 1987–89 vehicles, the 2 retaining screws on the ignition switch do not have to be drilled out.

7. Remove the 2 bolts using an suitable easy-out tool.

8. Disengage the ignition switch from the actuator pin.

NOTE: If reinstalling the old switch, it must be adjusted to the LOCK or RUN (depending on year and vehicle) position. Slide the carrier of the switch to the required position and insert a ¹⁄₁₆ in. drill bit or pin through the switch housing into the carrier. This keeps the carrier from moving when the switch in connected to the actuator. It may be necessary to wiggle the carrier back and forth to line up the holes when installing the drill or pin. New switches come with a pin in place.

9. Adjust the ignition switch by sliding the carrier to the switch Run position. Insert a ¹⁄₁₆ in. Drill bit or smaller tool through the switch housing and into the carrier, thereby preventing movement of the carrier with respect to the switch housing. It may be necessary to move the carrier slightly back and forth to align the carrier and housing adjustment holes.

NOTE: A new replacement switch assembly will be set in the RUN position when purchased.

10. Check to be sure the ignition key lock cylinder is in approximately the RUN position. The RUN position is achieved by rotating the key lock cylinder approximately 90 degrees from the LOCK position.

11. Install the ignition switch onto the actuator pin. It may be necessary to move the switch slightly back and fourth to align the switch mounting

holes with the cloumn lock housing threaded holes.

12. Install the new break-off head bolts (or attaching bolts) and hand tighten.

13. Move the ignition switch up the steering column until all the travel in the screw slots in used. Hold the switch in this position and tighten the break-off head bolts until the heads break off.

14. Remove the adjustment drill bit or pin, if used.

15. Connect the electrical connector to the ignition switch. Connect the negative battery cable and check the ignition switch for proper function including **START** and **ACC** positions. Also make certain that the steering cloumn is in the **LOCK** position.

16. Align the steering column mounting holes with the support bracket and install the 2 bolts and nuts. Install the steering column trim shrouds.

17. Install the steering column lower cover on the instrument panel, if so equipped.

18. Check the ignition switch for proper starting in **PARK** or **NEUTRAL**. Also make certain that the start circuit can not be actuated in the **DRIVE** or **DRIVE** position and that the column is locked in the **LOCK** position.

Continental

1. Disconnect the negative battery cable.

2. Rotate the ignition lock cylinder to the **RUN** position and depress the lock cylinder retaining pin through the access hole in the shroud with a ⅛ in. drift punch or wire pin. Push on the pin and pull out on the lock cylinder.

3. Remove the tilt release lever by removing the Allen head cap screw that holds the tilt lever to the steering column.

4. Remove the lower steering column/instrument panel cover by removing the 4 Torx® head sheet metal screws.

5. Remove the steering column shroud.

6. Remove the bolts and nuts that attach the steering column to support bracket and lower column. Disconnect the ignition switch electrical connector.

7. Remove the lock actuator cover plate by removing the tamper resistant Torx® head bolt.

NOTE: The lock actuator assembly will slide freely out of the lock cylinder housing when the ignition switch is removed.

8. Remove the ignition switch and cover by removing the 2 tamper-resistant Torx® head bolts.

9. Ensure ignition switch is in the **RUN** position by rotating the steering column shaft fully clockwise to the **START** position and releasing it.

10. Install the lock actuator assembly into the ignition switch housing to a depth of 0.46–0.54 in. from the bottom of the actuator assembly top the bottom of the lock cylinder housing.

11. While holding the actuator assembly at the proper depth, install the ignition switch.

12. Install the ignition switch and cover. Torque the cover retaining screws to 30–48 inch lbs.

13. Install the lock cylinder. Rotate the ignition switch to the **LOCK** position and measure the depth of the actuator assembly. The actuator must be 0.92–1.00 in. inside the lock cylinder housing. If the actuator depth does not meet specifications, it must be removed and reinstalled.

14. Install the lock actuator cover plate with the Torx® head screw and torque the screw to 30–48 inch lbs. Install the ignition switch electrical connector.

15. Connect the negative battery cable to the battery terminal. Check the ignition switch for proper starting in all positions including **START** and **ACC**.

16. Check the column function as follows:

a. With the column shift lever in the **PARK** position or with the floor shift key release button depressed and with the ignition lock cylinder in the **LOCK** position, make certain that the steering column locks.

b. Position the column shift lever in the **DRIVE** position or the floor shift key release button fully extended and rotate the cylinder lock to the **RUN** position. Continue to rotate the cylinder toward the **LOCK** position until it stops. In this position make certain that engine electrical off has been acheived and that the steering shaft DOES NOT lock.

c. Turn the radio power button on. Rotate the cylinder counter-clockwise to the **ACC** position to verify that the radio is energized.

d. Place the shift lever in **PARK** and rotate the cylinder clockwise to the **START** position to verify that the starter energizes.

17. Remove the ignition lock cylinder.

18. Align the steering column mounting holes with the support bracket and center the column in the instrument panel opening. Install and tighten the 4 retaining nuts to 15–25 ft. lbs.

19. Install the 3 self-tapping screws and install the column trim shrouds. Install the instrument panel lower

cover with 4 Torx® head sheet metal screws.

20. Install the tilt release lever and socket head screw. Install the lock cylinder.

21. Check column travel through the entire range to ensure that there is no interference between the column and the instrument panel.

Manual Steering Gear

REMOVAL & INSTALLATION

1. Disconnect the negative battery cable.

2. Turn the ignition key to the **RUN** position.

3. Remove the access trim panel from below the steering column.

4. Remove the intermediate shaft bolts at the rack and pinion input shaft and the steering column shaft.

5. Spread the slots enough to loosen the intermediate shaft at both ends. They cannot be separated at this time.

6. Working from underneath the vehicle, separate the tie rod ends from the steering knuckles, using tool 3290-C or equivalent. Turn the steering wheel a full left turn so that the tie rod will clear the shift linkage for removal.

7. Separate the tie rod ends from the steering knuckles. Turn the right wheel to the full left turn position.

8. Remove the left tie rod end from the left tie rod and disconnect the speedometer cable at the transaxle on automatic transaxles only.

9. Disconnect the secondary air tube at the check valve. Disconnect the exhaust system at the manifold and support the exhaust system to allow clearance for the gear removal.

--- **CAUTION** ---

Do not allow the exhaust system to hang by the rear support hangers. The system could fall to the floor.

10. Remove the exhaust hanger bracket from below the steering gear.

11. Remove the gear mounting brackets and insulators. Keep separated as they are not interchangeable.

12. Separate the gear assembly from the intermediate shaft, with an assistant pulling upward on the shaft from the inside of the vehicle.

NOTE: Care should be taken during steering gear removal and installation to prevent tearing or damaging the steering gear bellows.

13. Rotate the gear forward and down to clear the input shaft through the dash panel opening.

14. With the gear in the full left turn position, move the gear through the right (passenger side) apron opening

until the left tie rod clears the shift linkage and other parts so it may be lowered.

15. Lower the left side of the gear assembly and remove from the vehicle.

16. If some strux nuts should break loose from the body sheet metal during steering gear removal or installation on the Escort/Lynx, use the following service procedure:

  a. Hold the strux nuts with a suitable wrench and remove the bolt.

  b. Use a flanged nut with an M10 × 1.5 thread or a flanged nut and retainer in place of the strux nut which broke loose.

17. If the strux nuts threads should become crossed or stripped on the Escort/Lynx, remove the strux nut by striking sharply (the sharp impact can be applied by a chisel from the side of the body bracket) on the strux nut, toward the rear of the vehicle, until the strux nut breaks loose.

  a. Use a flanged nut with an M10 × 1.5 thread or a flanged nut and retainer in place of the strux nut which broke loose.

18. Rotate the input shaft to a full left turn stop. Position the right road wheel to a full left turn.

19. Start the right side of the gear through the opening in the right apron. Move the gear in until the left tie rod clears all parts so that it may be raised up to the left apron opening.

20. Raise the gear and insert the left hand side through the apron opening. Rotate the gear so that the joint shaft enters the dash panel opening.

21. With an assistant guiding the intermediate shaft from the inside of the vehicle, insert the input shaft into the intermediate shaft coupling. Insert the intermediate shaft clamp bolts finger tight. Do not tighten to specifications at this time.

22. Install the gear mounting insulators and brackets in their proper places. Ensure the flat in the left mounting area is parallel to the dash panel. Tighten the bracket bolts in the sequence as described below:

  a. Tighten the left (driver's side) upper bolt halfway.

  b. Tighten the left hand lower bolt to specifications.

  c. Tighten the left hand upper bolt to specifications.

  d. Tighten the right hand bolts to specifications.

  e. Do not forget that the right hand and left hand insulators and brackets are not interchangeable side to side.

23. Attach the tie rod ends to the steering knuckles. Tighten the castellated nuts to minimum specifications, then tighten the nuts until the slot aligns with the cotter pin hole. Insert a new cotter pin.

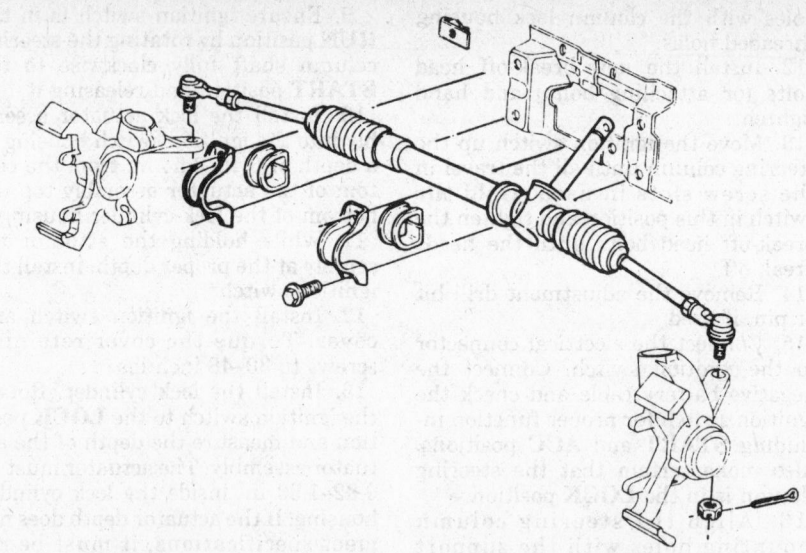

Tempo/Topaz manual rack and pinion steering mounting

24. Install the exhaust system. Install the speedometer cable, if removed.

25. Tighten the gear input shaft to intermediate shaft coupling clamp bolt first. Then, tighten the upper intermediate shaft clamp bolt.

26. Install the access panel below the steering column. Turn the ignition key **OFF**.

27. Check and adjust the toe. Tighten the tie rod end jam nuts, check for twisted bellows.

Power Steering Gear

REMOVAL & INSTALLATION

All Vehicles Except Continental

1. Disconnect negative battery cable from battery.

2. Turn the ignition key to the **RUN** position.

3. Remove access panel from dash below the steering column.

4. Remove 4 screws from steering column boot at the dash panel and slide boot up intermediate shaft.

5. Remove intermediate shaft bolt at gear input shaft and loosen the bolt at the steering column shaft joint.

6. With a suitable tool, spread the slots enough to loosen intermediate shaft at both ends. The intermediate shaft and gear input shaft cannot be separated at this time.

7. Remove air cleaner.

8. On Escort/EXP, Lynx/LN7 with air conditioning, wire the air conditioner liquid line above the dash panel opening. Doing so provides clearance for gear input shaft removal and installation.

9. Separate pressure and return lines at intermediate connections and drain fluid.

10. On Tempo/Topaz non-diesel vehicles, remove pressure switch.

11. Disconnect exhaust secondary air tube at check valve. Disconnect exhaust system at exhaust manifold and remove exhaust systems.

12. Separate tie rod ends from steering knuckles, using tool No. 3290–C and adapter T81P–3504–W or equivalents.

13. Remove left tie rod end from tie rod on manual transaxle vehicles. This will allow tie rod to clear the shift linkage.

NOTE: Mark location of rod end prior to removal.

14. Disconnect speedometer cable and transmission cable at transaxle (automatic transaxle only). Remove the vehicle speed sensor.

15. Remove transaxle shift cable assembly at transaxle (automatic transaxle only).

16. Turn steering wheel to full left turn stop for easier gear removal.

17. On Escort/EXP, Lynx/LN7, remove 2 screws holding heater water tube to shake brace below the oil pan.

18. On Escort/EXP, Lynx/LN7, move nut from the lower of 2 bolts holding engine mount support bracket to transaxle housing. Tap bolt out as far as it will go.

19. Remove gear mounting brackets and insulators.

20. Drape cloth towel over both apron opening edges to protect bellows during gear removal.

21. Separate gear from intermediate shaft by either pushing up on shaft with a bar from underneath the vehicle while pulling the gear down, or with a assistant removing the shaft from inside the vehicle.

22. Rotate gear forward and down to

clear the input shaft through the dash panel opening.

23. Make sure input shaft is in full left turn position. Move gear through the right (passenger) side apron opening until left tie rod clears left apron opening and other parts so it may be lowered. Guide the power steering hoses around the nearby componenst as the gear is being removed.

24. Lower the left hand side of the gear and remove the gear out of the vehicle. Use care not to tear the bellows.

25. Rotate the input shaft to a full left turn stop. Position the right road wheel to a full left turn.

26. Start the right side of the gear through the opening in the right apron. Move the gear in until the left tie rod clears all parts so that it may be raised up to the left apron opening.

27. Raise the gear and insert the left hand side through the apron opening. Move the power steering hoses into their proper position at the same time. Rotate the gear so that the joint shaft enters the dash panel opening.

28. With an assisant guiding the intermediate shaft from the inside of the vehicle, insert the input shaft into the intermediate shaft coupling. Insert the intermediate shaft clamp bolts finger tight. Do not tighten to specifications at this time.

29. Install the gear mounting insulators and brackets in their proper places. Ensure the flat in the left mounting area is parallel to the dah panel. Tighten the bracket bolts in the sequence as described below:

   a. Tighten the left (driver's side) upper bolt halfway.
   b. Tighten the left hand lower bolt to specifications.
   c. Tighten the left hand upper bolt to specifications.
   d. Tighten the right hand bolts to specifications.

30. Attach the tie rod ends to the steering knuckles. Tighten the castellated nuts to 27 ft. lbs. minimum, then tighten the nuts until the slot aligns with the cotter pin hole. Insert a new cotter pin.

31. On the Escort/EXP, Lynx/LN7 install the engine mount nut and tighten to specifications.

32. On the Escort/EXP, Lynx/LN7 install the heater water tube to the shake brace.

33. Install the exhaust system. Install the speedometer cable and transmission shift cable, if removed. Install the vehicle speed sensor and the transaxle shift cable.

34. Connect the secondary air tube at the check valve. Connect the pressure and return lines at the steering gear. Install the pressure switch, if removed.

35. Tighten the gear input shaft to

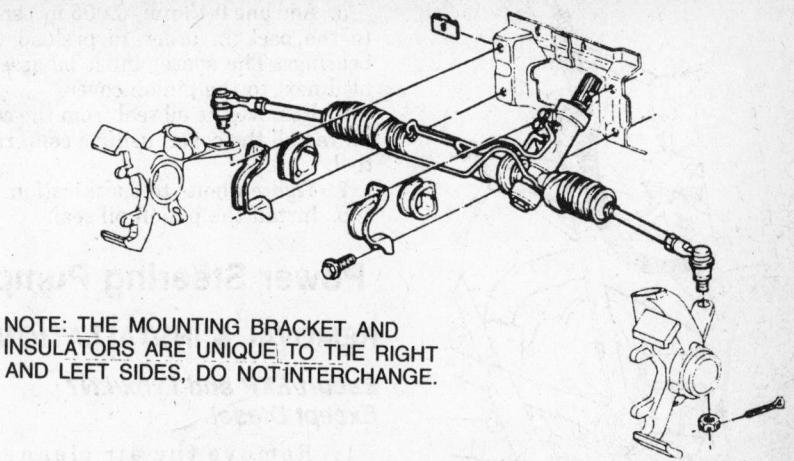

NOTE: THE MOUNTING BRACKET AND INSULATORS ARE UNIQUE TO THE RIGHT AND LEFT SIDES, DO NOT INTERCHANGE.

Tempo/Topaz power rack and pinion steering assembly

intermediate shaft coupling clamp bolt first. Then, tighten the upper intermediate shaft clamp bolt.

36. Install the access panel below the steering column. Turn the ignition key OFF.

37. Fill the system. Check and adjust the toe. Tighten the tie rod end jam nuts, check for twisted bellows.

Continental

The Variable Assist Power Steering System (VAPS) used on the 1988–89 Continental consists of a microprocessor based module, a power rack and pinion steering gear, an actuator valve assembly, hose assemblies and a high efficiency power steering pump.

1. Remove the primary steering column attachments.

2. Remove the intermediate shaft retaining bolts and remove the intermediate shaft.

3. From inside the passenger compartment, remove the secondary steering column boot.

4. Raise the vehicle and support safely. Remove the front wheels. Support the vehicle under the rear edge of the sub-frame.

5. Remove the tie rod cotter pins and nuts. Remove the tie rod ends from the spindle.

6. Remove the tie rod ends from the shaft. Mark the position of the jam nut to maintain the alignment.

7. Remove the nuts from the gear-to-sub-frame attaching bolts.

8. Remove both height sensor attachments.

9. Remove the rear sub-frame-to-attaching bolts.

10. Remove the exhaust pipe-to-catalytic converter attachment.

11. Lower the vehicle approximately 4 in. or until the sub-frame separates from the body.

12. Remove the heat shield band and fold the shield down.

13. Disconnect the VAPS electrical

connector from the actuator assembly.

14. Rotate the gear to clear the bolts from the sub-frame and pull to the left to facilitate line fitting removal.

15. Position a drain pan under the vehicle and remove the line fittings. Remove the o-rings from the fiting connections and replace with new.

16. Remove the left side sway bar.

17. Remove the steering gear assembly through the left side wheel well.

18. Install new o-rings into the line fittings.

19. Place the gear attachment bolts in the gear housing.

20. Install the steering gear assembly through the left side wheel well.

21. Connect and tighten the line fittings to the steering gear assembly.

22. Connect the VAPS electrical connector.

23. Position the steering gear into the sub-frame.

24. Install the tie rod ends onto the shaft.

25. Install the heat shield band.

26. Attach the tie rod ends onto the spindle. Install the nuts and secure with new cotter pins.

27. Attach the sway bar links.

28. Raise the vehicle until the sub-frame contacts the body. Install the sub-frame attaching bolts.

29. Install the gear-to-sub-frame nuts and torque to 85–100 ft. lbs.

30. Attach the exhaust pipe to the catalytic converter.

31. Attach the height sensors, install the wheels and lower the vehicle.

32. Fill the power steering system.

33. Install the secondary steering column boot and attach the intermediate shaft to the steering column.

34. Bleed the system and align the front end.

STEERING GEAR ADJUSTMENT

The power rack and pinion steering

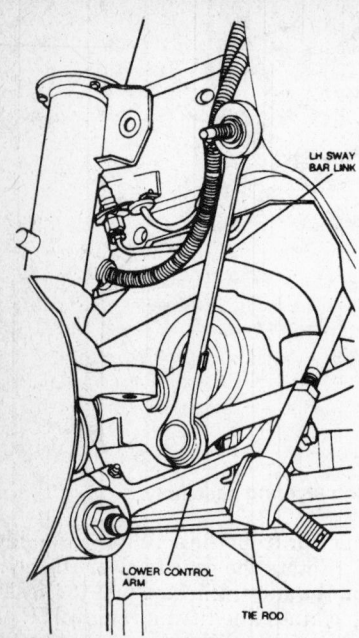

Left side sway bar removal and installation – Continental

gear provides for only 1 service adjustment. The gear must be removed from the vehicle in order to make this adjustment. No adjustment is required on the Continental.

1. Clean the exterior of the gear in the yoke plug area and mount the gear in a suitable vise, gripping it near the center of the tube. Do not over tighten.

2. Loosen and remove the yoke plug locknut. Back off the yoke plug 1 turn.

3. Tighten the yoke plug to 45 inch lbs. using yoke plug adapter T81P-3504-U or equivalent and an inch pound torque wrench with a full scale reading to 100 inch lbs. maximum.

4. Scribe the gear housing in line with an **0** mark on the yoke plug adapter tool.

5. Back off the yoke plug so that the second mark on the yoke plug adapter tool aligns with the scribe mark on the gear housing.

6. Hold the plug, install and tighten the locknut to specifications using yoke locknut wrench T81P-3504-G or equivalent.

PINION BEARING PRELOAD

Assembly Removed

1. Loosen the bolts of the yoke cover to relieve spring pressure on the rack.

2. Remove the pinion cover and gasket. Clean the cover flange area thoroughly.

3. Remove the spacer and shims.

4. Install a new gasket and fit the shims between the upper bearing and spacer until the top of the spacer is flush with the gasket. Check with a straightedge, using light pressure.

5. Add one 0.13mm (0.005 in.) shim to the pack in order to preload the bearings. The spacer must be assembled next to the pinion cover.

6. Remove the oil seal from the cover. Install the cover, using a centering tool.

7. Tighten bolts to specification.

8. Install the pinion oil seal.

Power Steering Pump

REMOVAL & INSTALLATION

Escort/EXP and Lynx/LN7 Except Diesel

1. Remove the air cleaner, thermactor air pump and belt. Remove the reservoir filler extension and cover the hole to prevent dirt from entering.

2. On vehicles equipped with EFI and remote reservoir, remove the reservoir supply hose at the pump, drain the fluid and plug or cap the opening at the pump to prevent entry of contaminants during removal.

3. From under the vehicle, loosen 1 pump adjusting bolt. Remove 1 pump to bracket mounting bolt and disconnect the fluid return line.

4. From above the vehicle, loosen 1 adjusting bolt and the pivot bolt. Remove the drive belt and the 2 remaining pump to bracket mountning bolts.

5. Remove the pump by passing the pulley through the adjusting bracket pening. Remove the pressure hose from the pump assembly.

6. Reverse the removal procedure to install the pump assembly. Fill the pump with fluid and bleed the system.

Tempo/Topaz Except Diesel

1. Loosen the alternator and remove the drive belt. Pivot the alternator to it most upright position or remove the alternator as required.

2. Remove the radiator overflow bottle. Loosen and remove the power steering pump drive belt. Mark the pulley and pump drive hub with paint or grease pencil for location reference.

3. Remove the pulley retaining bolts and the 2 pulleys from the pump shaft hubs.

4. Remove the return line from the pump. Be prepared to catch any spilled fluid in a suitable container.

5. Back off the pressure line attaching nut completely. The line will separate from the pump connection when the pump is removed.

6. Remove the 3 pump mounting bolts and remove the pump.

7. Place the pump in position and connect the pressure line loosely. Install the pump in the reverse order. Fill the pump with fluid and check for proper operation.

Diesel Engine Vehicles

1. Remove the drive belts.

2. On air condition models, remove the alternator.

3. Remove both braces from the support bracket on air conditioned models.

4. Disconnect the power steering fluid lines and drain the fluid into a suitable container.

5. Remove the 4 bracket mounting bolts and remove the pump and bracket assembly.

6. The pulley must be removed before the pump can be separated from the mounting bracket. Tool No. T65P-3A733-C or equivalent is required to remove and install the drive pulley.

7. Install the pump and mounting bracket in the reverse order of removal. Fill the pump with fluid and check for proper operation.

Continental

1. Disconnect the negative battery cable. Loosen the tensioner pulley attaching bolts and using the ½ in. drive hole provided in the tensioner pulley, rotate the tensioner pulley clockwise and remove the belt from the alternator and power steering pulley.

2. Position a drain pan under the power steering pump from underneath the vehicle. Disconnect the hydraulic pressure and return lines.

3. Remove the pulley from the pump shaft using hub puller T69L-10300-B or equivalent. Remove the 3 bolts retaining pump to bracket and remove the power steering pump.

4. Complete the installation of the pump assembly by reversing the removal procedure. Fill the pump with fluid and check the system for proper operation.

NOTE: To install the power steering pump pulley, use steering pump pulley replacer T65P-3A733-C or equivalent. When using this tool, the small diameter threads must be fully engaged in the pump shaft before pressing on the pulley. Hold the head screw and turn the nut to install the pulley. Install the pulley face flush with the pump shaft within ± 0.100 in.

Tie Rod End

REMOVAL & INSTALLATION

1. Raise and support the vehicle safely.

2. Remove the cotter pin from the tie rod end strut and remove the slotted nut. Discard the cotter pin and nut.

3. Using the tie rod end remover tool 3290-D and tie rod remover adapter T81P-3504-W or equivalent, remove the tie rod end from the steering knuckle spindle.

4. Matchmark the position of the locknut with paint on the tie rod if the tie rod end is to be reused. Hold the tie rod end with a wrench and loosen the locknut. Grip the tie rod hex flats and unscrew the tie rod end from the rack arm, counting the number of turns required to remove it.

5. Clean the tie rod threads. Apply a coating of grease to the threads. Install the new tie rod end, screwing it on the same number of turns counted in Step 3. Attach the tie rod end to the steering knuckle. Install a new slotted nut and torque the nut to 28–32 ft. lbs. Continue tightening the nut until the next castellation aligns with the cotter pin hole in the stud. Install a new cotter pin.

6. Check and adjust the toe as necessary. Tighten the tie rod end locknut.

BRAKES

For all brake system repair and service procedures not detailed below, please refer to "Brakes" in the Unit Repair section.

Master Cylinder

REMOVAL & INSTALLATION

Standard Brakes

1. Disconnect the negative battery terminal.
2. Working under the instrument panel, disconnect the master cylinder pushrod from the brake pedal.
3. Disconnect the stoplight switch and remove it.
4. Inside the engine compartment, disconnect the brake lines from the master cylinder.
5. Unbolt the master cylinder from the firewall and remove it. Be careful not to damage the firewall grommet.
6. To install, reverse the removal process, leaving the brake tubes slightly loose at the master cylinder fittings.
7. Fill the master cylinder with fresh brake fluid. Use the foot pedal to bleed the master cylinder. Tighten the brake line fittings.

Power Brakes

1. Disconnect the brake lines from the primary and secondary outlet ports of the master cylinder and the pressure control valve.
2. Remove the 2 nuts attaching the master cylinder to the brake booster assembly. Disconnect the brake warning lamp wire.
3. Slide the master cylinder forward and upward from the vehicle.
4. To install, mount the master cylinder on the booster. Attach the brake fluid lines to the master cylinder, but leave the fittings slightly loose. Install the brake warning lamp wire.
5. Fill the reservoirs with fresh brake fluid. Use the foot pedal to bleed the master cylinder. Tighten the brake line fittings. Bleed the system.

Anti-Lock Brake System (ABS)

The Continental is equipped with a 4 wheel anti-lock brake system (ABS). The ABS consists of the following major components: hydraulic actuation unit, electric pump assembly, solenoid valve block assembly, electric controller, brake control valve and pressure switch, proportioning valve and brake fluid reservoir/level indicator assembly. The hydraulic actuation unit contains the master cylinder and brake booster sections arranged in fore and aft sequence.

CAUTION

Before the actuation assembly is removed, the hydraulic pressure must be discharged from the system. To discharge the hydraulic pressure from the system, turn the ignition switch to the OFF position and pump the brake pedal a minimum of 20 times until an increase in pedal pressure is felt.

---

1. Disconnect the negative battery cable.
2. Remove the air cleaner housing and duct assembly.
3. Disconnect and label the following component electrical connectors: fluid level indicator, main valve, solenoid valve block, pressure waring switch, hydraulic pump motor and ground connector from the master cylinder portion of the actuation assembly.
4. Disconnect the 3 brake tube fittings from the solenoid block valve connections. Cover or plug the openings immediately to prevent the loss of fluid and contamination.

CAUTION

Do not allow brake fluid to come in contact with any of the electrical connectors.

---

5. Remove the trim panel under the steering column.
6. Disconnect the actuation rod from the brake pedal by removing the hairpin connector adjacent to the

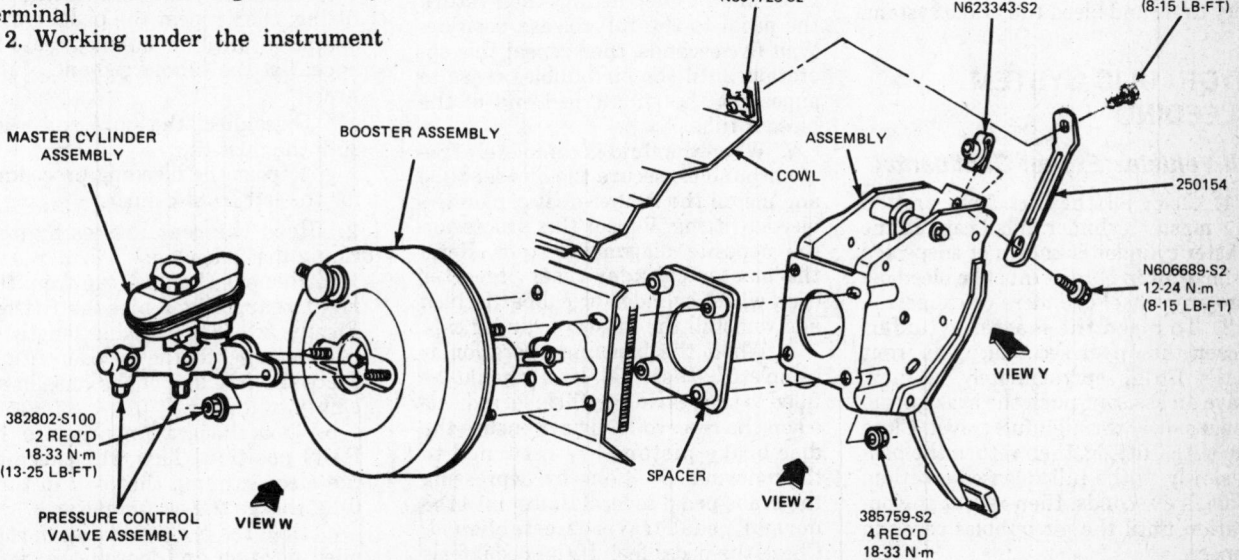

Typical master cylinder and power brake booster mounting

stoplamp switch. Slide the switch, push rod and plastic bushings off the pedal pin.

7. Remove the retaining nuts that fasten the actuation assembly to the brake pedal support bracket. Remove the actuation assembly from the vehicle.

8. Inspect the foam gasket and rubber boot for damage and replace with new as required.

9. Position the actuation assembly with foam gasket and rubber boot onto the engine side of the dash panel by aligning the mounting studs and push-rod with the proper dash panel holes.

10. From inside the passenger compartment, attach the actuation assembly to the pedal support bracket with the retaining nuts and make finger tight.

11. Connect the push rod, flanged plastic bushing and washer to the brake pedal pin. Position the stoplamp switch so that the slot on the switch bracket straddles the brake pedal pin (with the hole on the opposite leg of the switch bracket just clearing the pin). Slide the switch until it bottoms on the pin then install the outer nylon bushing. Secure the assembly with the hairpin retainer.

12. Tighten the actuating/support bracket retaining nuts to 13–25 ft. lbs.

13. From inside the engine compartment, connect the solenoid block brake tubes 1 at a time. Tighten the brake tube locknuts to 13–25 ft. lbs.

14. Make certain that all electrical connectors are clean an all connector seals are properly in place. Connnect all electrical connectors to the respective components and secure the ground wire to the master cylinder portion of the actuation assembly.

15. Install the air cleaner and duct assembly. Connect the negative battery cable and bleed the brake system.

HYDRAULIC SYSTEM BLEEDING

All Vehicles Except Continental

1. Clean all the dirt from around the master cylinder filler cap. If the master cylinder is known or suspected to have air in bore, it must be bleed before any wheel cylinders or calipers.

2. To bleed the master cylinder, loosen the upper secondary left front outlet fitting aprroximately ¾ turn. Have an assisant push the brake pedal down slowly through full travel. Close the outlet fitting, then return the pedal slowly to the full released position. Wait five seconds, then repeat the operation until the air bubbles cease to appear.

3. Loosen the upper primary right

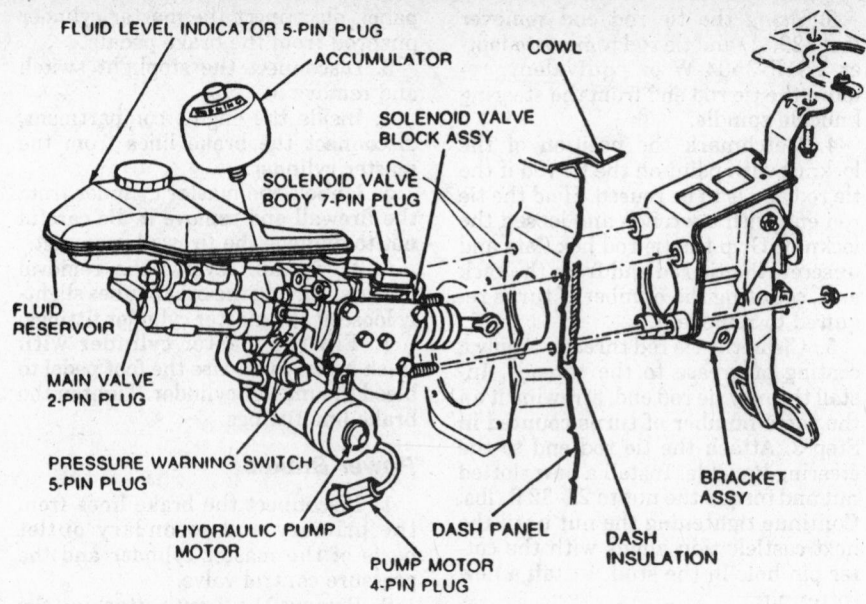

Hydraulic actuation unit used on the Continental

[Diagram labels: FLUID LEVEL INDICATOR 5-PIN PLUG, ACCUMULATOR, COWL, SOLENOID VALVE BLOCK ASSY, SOLENOID VALVE BODY 7-PIN PLUG, FLUID RESERVOIR, MAIN VALVE 2-PIN PLUG, PRESSURE WARNING SWITCH 5-PIN PLUG, HYDRAULIC PUMP MOTOR, PUMP MOTOR 4-PIN PLUG, DASH PANEL, DASH INSULATION, BRACKET ASSY]

front outlet fitting approximately ¾ turn. and repeat Step 3.

4. To continue to bleed the system, remove the rubber cap dust cap from the wheel cylinder bleeder fitting or caliper fitting. Check to make sure the bleeder fitting is positioned at the upper half on the front of the caliper, if not the caliper is located on the wrong side.

5. Place a suitable box wrench on the bleeder fitting and attach the rubber drain tube to the fitting. Submerge the free end of the tube in a container partially filled with clean brake fluid and loosen the bleeder fitting approitmately ¾ of a turn.

6. Have the assisant push brake pedal down slowly through full travel. Close the bleeder fitting, then return the pedal to the full release position. Wait five seconds, then repeat this operation until the air bubbles cease to appear at the submerged end of the bleeder tube.

7. When the fluid is completely free of air bubbles, secure the bleeder tube and install the rubber dust cap on the bleeder fitting. Repeat this process on the opposite diagonal system. Refill the master cylinder reservoir after each wheel cylinder or caliper id bled and reinstall the master cylinder cap.

8. When the bleeding operation is completed, the fluid level should be filled to the maximum fill level indicated on the reservoir. Always ensure the disc brake pistons are returned to their normal positions by depressing the brake pedal several times until the normal pedal travel is established. Check the pedal feel. If the pedal feels spongy repeat the bleed procedure.

Continental

1. Bleed the front brakes by performing the following:

a. Remove the dust cap from the right front caliper bleeder fitting. Firmly attach a suitable length of rubber hose to the bleeder fitting.

b. Submerge the free end of the tube in a container partially filled with clean brake fluid and loosen the bleeder fitting approximately ¾ turn.

c. Depress the brake pedal slowly through its full length of travel and hold at that position.

d. Tighten the bleeder fitting and return the brake pedal to the full release position.

e. Wait 5 seconds after closing the fitting, then repeat the pedal travel operation until air bubbles cease to appear at the submerged end of the hose.

f. Disconnect the hose and reinstall the dust cap.

g. Repeat the bleeding procedure for the left front caliper.

2. Bleed the rear brakes by performing the following:

a. Remove the dust cap from the right rear caliper bleeder fitting. Firmly attach a suitable length of rubber hose to the bleeder fiting. Place the free end of the hose in an empty container.

b. Turn the ignition switch to the **RUN** position. This will energize the electric pump that will in turn fully charge the accumulator.

c. Hold the brake pedal in the applied position and loosen the right caliper bleeder fitting for 10 seconds at a time until an air-free stream of brake fluid is observed.

--- **CAUTION** ---

Care must be exercised when opening the bleeder fitting due the high pressure generated by a fully charged accumulator.

d. Repeat the bleeding procedure for the left rear caliper.

NOTE: If the pump motor is allowed to run continuously for approximately 20 minutes, a thermal safety switch inside the motor will shut the motor off to prevent overheating. If that happens, a 2–10 minute cool down period is required until normal pump operation can resume.

Proportioning Valve

The proportioning valve regulates the rear brake system hydraulic pressure. It is located between the rear brake system inlet and outlet ports. There are no adjustments possible on this valve. If found to be defective it must be replaced.

Power Brake Booster

REMOVAL & INSTALLATION

All Vehicles Except Continental

1. Disconnect the battery and remove the tubes from the primary and the secondary outlet ports of the master cylinder.
2. Remove the 2 nuts attaching the master cylinder to the brake booster assembly and remove the master cylinder.
3. Working inside the vehicle below the instrument panel, remove the wiring connector from the stop lamp switch. Remove the push rod retainer and the outer nylon washer from the pedal pin. Slide the stop lamp switch along the brake pedal pin just far enough for the outer hole to clear the pin. Remove the switch by sliding it upward, being careful not to damage the switch during removal.
4. Remove the booster-to-dash panel attaching nuts. Slide the booster push rod and push rod bushing off the brake pedal pin.
5. Inside the engine compartment, disconnect the manifold vacuum hose from the booster check valve. Move the booster forward until the booster studs clear the dash panel and remove the booster.
6. Align the pedal support and support spacer inside the vehicle and place the booster in position on the dash panel. Hand start the attaching nuts.
7. Working inside the vehicle, install the pushrod and pushrod bushing on the brake pedal pin. Tighten the booster-to-dash panel adjusting nuts to 13–25 ft. lbs.
8. Position the stop lamp switch so that it straddles the booster push rod with the switch slot toward the pedal blade and the hole just clearing the pin. Slide switch down onto pin. Slide the assembly toward the pedal arm, being careful not to damage the switch. Install the nylon washer on pin and secure all parts to pin with hairpin retainer. Make sure that the retainer is fully installed and locked over the pedal pin. Install the stop lamp switch wiring connector on the stop lamp.
9. Connect the manifold vacuum hose to the booster check valve using a hose clamp.
10. Position the master cylinder assembly on the booster assembly studs. Tighten the nuts 13–25 ft. lbs.
11. Install the brake tube fittings into the master cylinder ports and tighten 10–18 ft. lbs.
12. Bleed the brake system.
13. Connect the battery and start the engine. Check to make sure the power brake system is functioning properly.
14. On vehicles equipped with speed control, the vacuum dump valve must be adjusted if the brake booster has been removed. To adjust the vacuum dump valve, perform the following:
   a. Firmly depress and hold the brake pedal.
   b. Push in the dump valve until the valve collar bottoms against the retaining clip.
   c. Place a 0.050–0.100 in. shim between the white button of the valve and the pad on the brake pedal.
   d. Firmly pull the brake pedal rearward to its normal position, allowing the dump valve to ratchet backward in the retaining clip.

Continental

The power booster and the master cylinder are contained in the hydraulic actuation unit. To remove the power booster/master cylinder assembly, refer to "Master Cylinder, Anti-Lock Brake System, Removal and Installation".

Wheel Cylinder

REMOVAL & INSTALLATION

1. Remove the wheel/tire and hub/drum assemblies.
2. Remove the brake shoe assembly.
3. Disconnect the brake tube from the wheel cylinder.
4. Remove the wheel cylinder attaching bolts and remove the wheel cylinder.

NOTE: Use caution to prevent brake fluid from contacting brake linings or they must be replaced.

5. Installation is in the reverse order of the removal procedure.
6. Adjust the brakes and bleed the brake system.

Parking Brake Cable

ADJUSTMENT

All Vehicles Except Continental

1. Apply approximately 100 lbs. pedal effort to the hydraulic service brake 3 times (with the engine running, on vehicles equipped with power brakes) before adjusting the parking brake.
2. Place the parking brake control assembly in the 12th notch position (two notches from full application). Tighten the adjusting nut until the rear wheel brakes drag slightly when the control assembly is fully released. Repeat as necessary.
3. Reposition the control assembly in the 12th notch. Loosen the adjusting nut just enough to eliminate rear brake drag when the control assembly is fully released.

Continental

1. Make sure the parking brake is fully released. Place the transaxle in the **NEUTRAL** position.
2. Raise the vehicle and support safely. Tighten the adjusting nut against the cable adjuster bracket until there is a slight (less than $1/16$ in.) movement of either parking brake lever at the caliper. If the brake cables were replaced, stroke the parking brake several times, then release control and repeat this step.
3. Lower the vehicle and check the operation of the parking brake..

REMOVAL & INSTALLATION

All Vehicles Except Continental

1. Place control assembly in the seventh notch position and loosen adjusting nut. Completely release control assembly.
2. Raise vehicle and remove the rear parking brake cable from equalizer.
3. Remove the hairpin clip holding cable to floor pan tunnel bracket.
4. Remove wire retainer holding cable to fuel tank mounting bracket. Remove cable from wire retainer.
5. Remove screw (Tempo/Topaz) or drill out pop rivet (Escort/EXP, Lynx/LN7), holding cable retaining clip at rear tie rod attaching bracket. Remove cable from clip.
6. Remove wheel and tire assembly, and rear brake drum.

7. Disengage cable end from brake assembly parking brake lever. Depress cable prongs holding cable to backing plate and remove cable through the hole in the backing plate.

8. Insert cable through the hole in backing plate. Attach cable end to rear brake assembly parking brake lever.

9. Insert conduit end fitting into backing plate. Make sure retention prongs are locked into place.

10. Insert cable into rear attaching clip and attach clip to rear tie rod attaching bracket with screw (Tempo/Topaz) or a new pop rivet (Escort/EXP, Lynx/LN7).

11. Route cable through bracket in floor pan tunnel and install hairpin retaining clip.

12. Install cable end into the equalizer.

13. Insert cable into wire retainer and snap retainer into hole in fuel tank mounting bracket.

Continental

FRONT

1. Raise the vehicle and support safely.

2. Loosen the adjuster nut on the cable adjuster bracket.

3. Lower the vehicle.

4. Disconnect the cable from the control assembly at the clevis, using a 13mm wrench to depress the retaining prongs. Remove the cable end pronged fitting from the parking brake control.

5. Raise the vehicle and support safely.

6. Disconnect the front cable from the rear cable at the cable connector.

7. Remove the cable and push-in prong retainer from the cable bracket, using a 13mm wrench to depress the retaining prongs.

8. Pull the grommet down from the floorpan.

9. Complete the installation of the front cable by reversing the removal procedure. Make certain that all retaining prongs are securely locked in place. Adjust the parking brake and check for proper operation.

REAR LEFT SIDE

1. Raise the vehicle and support safely.

2. Remove the parking brake cable adjusting nut.

3. Remove the rear cable end fitting from the rear cable connector.

4. Disconnect the brake cable end from the parking brake actuating lever by removing the E clip from the conduit end of the caliper fitting. Remove the cable from the caliper.

5. Push the plastic snap-in grommet rearward to disconnect it from the side rail bracket.

6. Remove the pronged connector

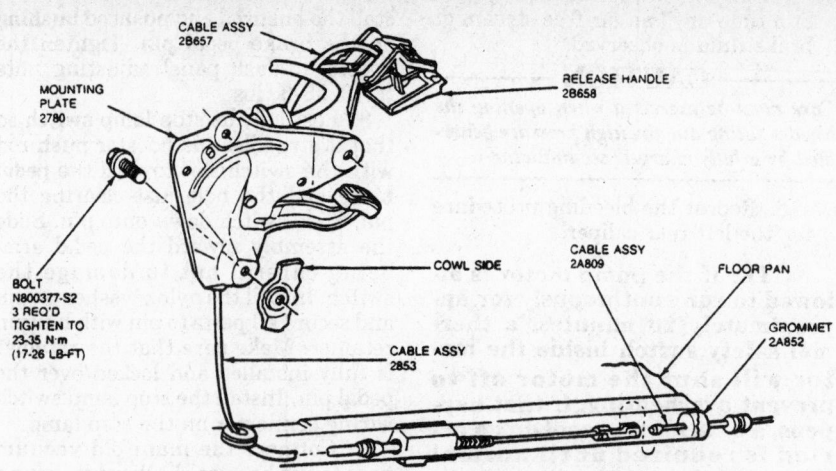

Front parking brake cable assembly – Continental

from the parking brake adjuster bracket. Remove the cvable assembly.

7. Insert the cable through the side rail and adjuster brackets. Ensure the pronged connector is securely attached to the brake adjuster bracket.

8. Seat the plastic snap-in grommet inside the rail bracket.

9. Insert the cable end into the caliper and install the E clip.

NOTE: The cable must be located over the right cable.

10. Attach the cable end to the parking brake actuating lever.

11. Install the brake cable attaching nut.

12. Adjust the parking brake and lower the vehicle.

13. Check the parking brake for proper operation.

REAR RIGHT SIDE

1. Raise the vehicle and support safely.

2. Remove the parking brake cable adjusting nut.

3. With a 13mm box end wrench, remove the conduit retainer prongs from the side rail bracket.

4. Disconnect the brake cable end from the parking brake actuating lever by removing the E clip from the conduit end of the caliper fitting. Remove the cable from the caliper.

5. Cut and remove the tie-strap that encircles the cable and the left tension strut. Discard the tie strap and replace with new.

6. Remove the cable retaining and clip from the lower suspension arm. Remove the screw from the cable bracket at the crossmember. Remove the cable assembly.

7. Complete the installation of the cable assebly by reversing the removal procedure. Adjust the parking brake and check for proper operation.

CHASSIS ELECTRICAL

Heater Blower

REMOVAL & INSTALLATION

All Vehicles without Air Conditioning Except Continental

1. On the Escort/EXP, Lynx/LN7 remove the air inlet duct assembly. On the Tempo/Topaz, remove the right ventilator assembly.

2. Remove the hub clamp spring from the blower wheel hub.

3. Pull the blower wheel from the blower motor shaft.

4. Remove the 3 blower motor flange attaching screws located inside the blower housing.

5. Pull the blower motor out from the blower housing (heater case) and disconnect the blower motor wires from the motor.

6. Connect the wires to the blower motor and position the motor in the blower housing.

7. Install the 3 blower motor attaching screws.

8. Position the blower wheel on the motor shaft and install the hub clamp spring.

9. Install the air inlet duct assembly and the right ventilator assembly.

10. Check the system for proper operation.

All Vehicles with Air Conditioning Except Continental

1. Empty out the contents of the glove compartment. Remove the glove compartment door.

2. Disconnect the blower motor

wires from the blower motor resistor. Loosen the instrument panel at the lower right hand side prior to removing the motor through the glove compartment opening.

3. Remove the 4 screws attaching the blower motor and mounting to the evaporator case.

4. Rotate the motor until the mounting plate flat clears the edge of the clove compartment opening and remove the motor.

5. Remove the hub clamp spring from the blower wheel hub. Then, remove the blower wheel from the motor shaft.

6. Installation is the reverse order of the removal procedure.

Continental

1. Open the glove compartment door, release the door retainers and lower the door.

2. Remove the screw attaching the recirculation duct support bracket to the instrumnent panel cowl.

3. Remove the vacuum connection to the recirculation door vacuum motor. Remove the screws attaching the recirculation duct to the heater assembly.

4. Remove the recirculation duct from the heater assembly, lowering the duct from between the instrument panel and the heater case.

5. Disconnect the blower motor electrical lead. Remove the blower motor wheel clip and remove the blower motor wheel.

6. Remove the 4 blower motor mounting plate screws and remove the blower motor from the evaporator case.

7. Complete the installation of the blower motor by reversing the removal procedure.

Heater Core

REMOVAL & INSTALLATION

NOTE: In some cases removal of the instrument panel may be necessary.

All Vehicles without Air Conditioning Except Continental

1. Drain the cooling system.

2. Loosen the heater hose clamps at the heater core tubes and disconnect the heater hoses from the heater core tubes.

3. Cap the heater core tubes to prevent spilling coolant into the passenger compartment.

4. Remove the glove compartment door, liner and lower reinforcement.

5. Move the temperature control lever to the **WARM** position.

6. Remove the 4 screws attaching the heater core cover to the heater assembly and remove the cover.

7. Working in the engine compartment, loosen the 2 nuts attaching the heater case assembly to the dash panel.

8. Push the heater core tubes toward the passenger compartment to loosen the heater core from the heater case assembly.

9. Pull the heater core from the heater case assembly and remove the heater core through the glove compartment opening.

10. To install, reverse the removal procedure.

All Vehicles With Air Conditioning Except Continental

1. Drain the coolant from the radiator.

2. Disconnect the heater hoses from the heater core.

3. Working inside the vehicle, remove the floor duct from the plenum (2 screws) and the instrument panel (1 or 2 screws) and the evaporator assembly (1 screw).

NOTE: Most vehicles are equipped with a removable heater core cover to provide access for servicing.

4. Remove the screws attaching the heater core cover to the evaporator case.

5. Remove the heater core and cover from the plenum.

6. Installation is the reverse of removal.

Continental

1. Remove the instrument panel assembly and lay it on the front seat.

2. Remove the evaporator case.

3. Remove the vacuum source line from the heater core tube seal.

4. Remove the 4 screws attaching the blend door actuator to the door shaft on the evaporator case. Relieve the spring tension and remove the actuator and cold engine lock out (CELO) switch from the evaporator case.

5. Remove the heater core access cover and foam seal from the evaporator case.

6. Lift the heater core with 3 foam seals from the evaporator case. Transfer the foam seals to the new heater core.

7. Complete the installation of the heater core by reversing the removal procedure.

Radio

REMOVAL & INSTALLATION

1982–83 Vehicles Except Continental

1. Disconnect the negative battery cable.

NOTE: Remove the air conditioning floor duct if equipped.

2. Remove the ash tray and bracket.

3. Pull the knobs from the shafts.

4. Working under the instrument panel, remove the support bracket nut from the radio chassis.

5. Remove the shaft nuts and washers.

6. Drop the radio down from behind the instrument panel. Disconnect the power lead, antenna, and speaker wires. Remove the radio.

7. Installation is the reverse.

1984–89 Vehicles Except Continental

1. Disconnect the negative battery cable.

2. Remove the center instrument panel trim panel.

3. Remove the 4 screws retaining the radio and mounting bracket to the instrument panel.

4. Pull the radio to the front and raise the back end of the radio slightly so the rear support bracket clears the clip in the instrument panel.

5. Pull the radio out of the instrument panel slowly. Disconnect the wiring connectors and antenna cable.

6. Installation is the reverse order of the removal procedures. Transfer the mounting brackets to the new radio, if necessary.

Continental

1. Disconnect the negative battery cable.

2. Remove the center instrument trim panel.

3. Remove the 4 screws retaining the radio to the instrument panel.

4. Push the radio to the front and raise the back of the radio enough so that the rear support bracket clears the rear support panel. Slowly withdraw the radio from the instrument panel.

5. Disconnect the wiring connectors and antenna cable.

6. Complete the installation of the radio by reversing the removal procedure. Test the radio and/or tape player for proper operation.

Wiper Switch

REMOVAL & INSTALLATION

Escort/EXP and Lynx/LN7
NON-TILT STEERING WHEEL

NOTE: **The switch handle is an integral part of the switch and can not be removed separately.**

1. Disconnect the negative (ground) battery cable from the battery terminal.
2. Loosen the steering column attaching nuts enough to remove the upper trim shroud.
3. Remove the trim shrouds.
4. Disconnect the quick connect electrical connector.
5. Peel back the foam sight shield remove the 2 hex-head screws holding the switch and remove the wash/wipe switch.
6. Position the switch on the column and install the 2 hex-head screws. Replace the foam sight shield over the switch.
7. connect the quick connect electrical connector.
8. Install the upper and lower trim shrouds.
9. Tighten the steering column attaching nuts to 17–25 ft. lbs.
10. Connect the negative (ground) battery cable to the battery terminal.
11. Check the steering column for proper operation.

TILT STEERING WHEEL

1. Disconnect the negative (ground) battery cable from the battery terminal.
2. Remove the steering column shroud.
3. Peel back the side shield and disconnect the switch wiring connector.
4. Remove the screw attaching the wiring retainer to the steering column.
5. Grasp the switch handle and pull straight out to disengage the wiper switch from the turn signal switch.
6. Complete the installation of the switch by reversing the removal procedure.

Tempo/Topaz

The standard and interval front wiper and washer systems on 1988–89 Tempo/Topaz vehicles feature an instrument panel-mounted rotary switch for wiper and washer control, whereas the switch on earlier vehicles was integral with the column mounted switch handle.

COLUMN MOUNTED

1. Remove the instrument panel finish panel.
2. Remove the wiper switch housing retaining screws and remove the switch housing from the instrument panel.
3. Remove (pull off) the wiper switch knob. Disconnect the electrical connectors from the switch assembly.
4. Remove the 2 screws holding the wiper switch in the switch housing plate and remove the switch.
5. Installation is the reverse order of the removal procedure.

INSTRUMENT PANEL MOUNTED

1. Disconnect the negative battery cable.
2. Insert a suitable prying tool into the small slot on top of the switch bezel.
3. Push down on the tool to work the top of the switch away from the instrument panel.
4. Work the bottom portion of the switch from the panel and completely remove the switch from the panel opening. Hold the switch and pull the wiring at the rear of the switch until the switch connector can be easily disconnected. Disconnect the connector and allow the wiring to hang from the switch mounting opening.
5. Connect the wiring connector to the new switch and route the wiring back into the mounting opening. Insert the switch into the opening so that the graphics are properly aligned.
6. Push on the switch until the bezel seats against the instrument panel and the clips lock the switch into place.

Continental

The standard and interval wiper systems used on the Continental feature a rotary actuated switch which is part of the turn signal lever of the multifunction switch. To replace the wiper switch, refer to "Combination Switch, Removal and Installation".

Rear Wiper Switch

REMOVAL & INSTALLATION

1. Remove the 2 or 4 cluster opening finish panel retaining screws and remove the finish panel by rocking the upper edge toward the driver.
2. Disconnect the wiring connector from the rear washer switch.
3. Remove the washer switch from the instrument panel.
4. Install the cluster opening finish panel and the retaining screws.
5. Connect the wiring connector.
6. Push the rear washer switch into the cluster finish panel until it snaps into place.

Windshield Wiper Front Motor

NOTE: **The internal permanent**

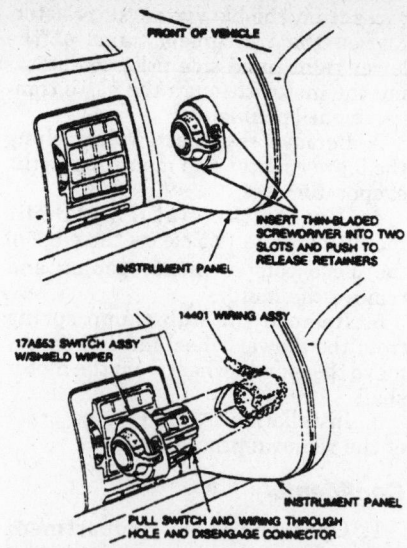

Instrument panel mounted rotary washer/wiper switch used on the 1988–89 Tempo.

magnets used in the wiper motor are a ceramic (glass-like) material. Care must be exercised in handling the motor to avoid damaging the magnets. The motor must not be struck or tapped with a hammer or other object.

REMOVAL & INSTALLATION

All Models

1. Disconnect the battery cables. On the Continental, remove the left wiper arm.
2. Lift the water shield cover from the cowl on the passenger side.
3. Disconnect the power lead from the motor.
4. Remove the linkage retaining clip from the operating arm on the motor.
5. Remove 3 attaching screws from the motor and bracket assembly and remove.
6. Remove the operating arm from the motor. Unscrew the 3 bolts and separate the motor form the mounting bracket.
7. To install, reverse the removal procedures.

Windshield Wiper Rear Motor

REMOVAL & INSTALLATION

All Hatchback Vehicles

1. Remove the wiper arm and blade from the wiper motor.
2. Remove the pivot shaft attaching nut and spacers.
3. Remove the liftgate inner trim panel. Disconnect the electrical connector to the wiper motor.

4. Remove the 3 screws holding the bracket to the inner door skin and remove the motor assembly, braket and linkage assembly.

5. Installation is the reverse order of the removal procedure.

All Station Wagon Vehicles

1. Remove the wiper arm and blade from the wiper motor.

2. Remove the pivot shaft attaching nut and spacers.

3. Remove the screws attaching the license plate housing. Disconnect the license plate light and remove the housing. Remove the wiper motor and bracket assembly retaining screws, disconnect the electrical connector to the wiper motor and remove the motor.

4. Installation is the reverse order of the removal procedure.

Instrument Cluster

REMOVAL & INSTALLATION

All Vehicles Except Continental

1. Disconnect the negative battery cable and remove the 2 retaining screws at the bottom of the steering column and snap the steering column cover out. On 1988–89 Tempo/Topaz vehicles, remove the steering column trim shroud and snap-in lower cluster fininsh panels.

NOTE: On vehicles equipped with speed control disconnect the wires from the amplifier assembly.

2. On the Tempo/Topaz models, remove the 8 instrument panel finish screws, radio knobs and remove the finish panel. On the 1988–89 Tempo/ Topaz vehicles, remove the 4 cluster opening finish panel retaining screws and pull the panel rearward. On these same vehicles, disconnect the speedometer cable from the transaxle at this time.

3. On the Escort/EXP, Lynx/LN7 vehicles remove the 4 (10 on the later vehicles) cluster opening finish panel retainer screws and remove the finish panel.

4. Remove the 2 upper and lower screws, and retaining cluster to remove the instrument panel. On the 1988–89 Tempo/Topaz vehicles, carefully pull the instrument panel rearward enough to disengage the speedometer cable.

5. From under the instrument panel, disconnect the speedometer cable by pressing the flat surface of the plastic quick connector.

6. Pull the cluster away from the instrument panel and disconnect the

electrical feed plug to the cluster from its receptacle in the printed circuit.

7. To install, reverse the removal procedure.

Continental

1. Position the vehicle on a flat surface to prevent movement when the gear shift selector is out of position. Apply the parking brake and block the wheels.

2. Rotate the ignition switch to unlock the the shift lever and move the lever from the front of the cluster. Tilt the steering wheel as far as possible.

3. Gently pry the strip of trim mounted below the instrument panel applique. Remove the 5 Torx® screws that secure the applique below the instrument panel. Unsnap the applique along the top and pull away from the panel.

4. Disconnect the switch assembly connector from the instrument cluster. Disconnect the warning lamp and clock connector. Set the applique aside.

5. Remove the 2 Torx® screws (below the instrument cluster) that secure the reinforcement strip (metal support) to the substructure. Set the metal support aside.

6. Remove the screws from the bottom of the steering column shroud. Remove the tilt lever.

7. Raise the top section of the shroud to release a clip located on the left hand side of the steering wheel. Separate the upper section of the shroud from the side section near the ignition switch. Remove the upper section from the shift lever.

8. Gently pull the gap cover from below the instrument cluster.

9. Remove the 4 Torx® screws attaching the instrument cluster to the substructure.

10. Tilt the bottom of the instrument cluster slightly toward the rear of the vehicle. Disconnect the **PRNDL** assembly from the cluster by undoing the 2 snaps located beneath the cluster. Pull the **PRNDL** assembly down and to the right and position off to the side.

11. Place a clean, soft cloth on the steering column to prevent scratching the surface of the steering column as the instrument cluster is removed.

12. Push the bottom of the instrument cluster into the instrument panel cavity. Tilt the top of the instrument cluster toward the rear of the vehicle. Push the cluster up and out of the cavity.

13. Reach around the back of the instrument cluster to disconnect the 4 connectors (1 on the right side, 2 in the middle and 1 on the left). The connectors have locking tabs that must be pressed in to release.

14. Complete the installation of the instrument cluster by reversing the removal procedure.

Headlight Switch

REMOVAL & INSTALLATION

1982–83 Vehicles

1. Disconnect the negative battery terminal.

2. Remove the left hand air vent control cable, and drop the cable and bracket down out of the way (cars without air conditioning only).

3. Remove the fuse panel bracket retaining screws and move the fuse panel assembly out of the way.

4. Pull the headlight knob out, to the on position.

5. Reach behind the dashboard and depress the release button on the switch housing, while at the same time pulling the knob and shaft from the switch.

6. Remove the retaining nut from the dashboard.

7. Pull the switch from the dash and remove the electrical connections.

8. Installation is the reverse of removal.

1984–85 Vehicles

1. Disconnect batttery ground cable.

2. Insert a thin flat blade under flange at side of switch, to depress spring retaining clip. Twist blade to remove switch on 1 side.

3. Repeat Step 2 on other side of switch.

4. Pull switch and connector out from instrument panel.

5. Disconnect electrical connector.

6. Install connector on switch.

7. Insert headlamp switch into instrument panel. Push on front face of switch until switch is retained by the spring clips.

8. Connect battery ground cable and test headlamp switch operation.

1986-89 Vehicles Except Continental

1. Disconnect the neagtive battery cable.

2. On vehicles without air conditioning, remove the left hand side air vent control cable retaining screws and drop the cable to the floor.

3. Remove the fuse panel bracket retaining screws. Move the fuse panel assembly aside to gain access to the headlamp switch.

4. Pull the headlamp knob out to the **ON** position. Depress the headlamp knob and shaft retainer button, which is located on the bottom of the

headlight switch. Remove the knob and the shaft assembly from the switch.

5. Remove the headlamp switch retaining bezel. Disconnect the multiple connector plug and remove the switch from the instrument panel.

6. Install the headlamp switch into the instrument panel. Connect the multiple connector and install the headlamp switch retaining bezel.

7. Install the knob and shaft assembly by inserting the shaft into the headlamp switch gently pushing until the shaft is in the lock position.

8. Move the fuse panel back into position and install the fuse panel bracket with the 2 retaining screws.

9. On vehicles without air conditioning, install the left hand side air vent control cable and bracket. Install the negative battery cable and check the headlamp switch for the proper operation.

Continental

1. Disconnect the negative battery cable. Remove the headlight switch knob.

2. Remove the lower left finish panel from the instrument panel and remove the moulding above the finish panel.

3. Remove the 2 screws retaining the headlight switch to the finish panel, disconnect the electrical connector and remove the switch from the vehicle.

4. Complete the installation of the headlight switch by reversing the removal procedure.

Stoplight Switch

REMOVAL & INSTALLATION

Without Power Brakes and Continental

1. Disconnect the wire harness at the connector from the switch.

NOTE: The locking tab must be lifted before the connector can be removed.

2. Remove the hairpin retainer. Slide the stop lamp switch, the push rod and the white nylon washer and black busing away from the pedal. Remove the switch by sliding the switch up/down.

NOTE: Since the switch side plate nearest the brake pedal is

slotted, it is not necessary to remove the brake master cylinder push rod black busing and 1 white spacer washer nearest the pedal arm from the brake pedal pin.

3. Position the switch so that the U-shaped side is nearest the pedal and directly over/under the pin. The black bushing must be in position in the push rod eyelet with the washer face on the side closest to the retaining pin.

4. Then slide the switch up/down, trapping the master cylinder push rod and black bushing between the switch side plates. Push the switch and push rod assembly firmly towards the brake pedal arm. Assembly outside the white plastic washer to pin and install the hairpin retainer to trap the whole assembly.

CAUTION

Do not substitute other types of pin retainer. Replace only with production hairpin retainer.

---

5. Assembly the wire harness connector to the switch.

6. Check the stop lamp switch for proper operation. stoplights should illuminate with less than 6 lbs. applied to the brake pedal at the pad.

NOTE: The stoplamp switch wire harness must have sufficient length to travel with the switch during full stroke at the pedal.

With Power Brakes

1. Disconnect the negative battery cable.

2. Disconnect the stoplamp switch wire connector from the switch.

3. Remove the hairpin retainer and outer white nylon washer from the pedal pin. Slide the stoplamp switch off the brake pedal pin just far enough for the outer side plate of the switch to clear the pin. Then remove the switch.

4. Position the new stoplamp switch so that it straddles the push rod, with the slot on the pedal pin and the switch outer frame hole just clearing the pin. Slide the switch downward onto the pin and push rod. Slide the assembly inboard toward the brake pedal arm.

5. Install the outer white nylon washer and the hairpin retainer.

6. Connect the stoplamp switch wire connector to the switch. Connect the negative battery cable.

7. Check the stoplights for proper operation with the engine running. stoplights should illuminate with less than 6 pounds applied to the brake pedal at the pad.

Fuses, Fusible Links and Circuit Breakers

LOCATION

Fusible links are used on all vehicles except the Continental to prevent major wire harness damage in the event of a short circuit or an overload condition in the wiring circuits that are normally not fused, due to carrying high amperage loads or because of their locations within the wiring harness. Each fusible link is of a fixed value for a specific electrical load and should a fusible link fail, the cause of the failure must be determine and repaired prior to installing a new fusible link of the same value.

Production fuse links are color-coded.

- 12 gauge: Grey.
- 14 gauge: Dark Greeen.
- 16 gauge: Black.
- 18 gauge: Brown.
- 20 gauge: Dark Blue.

NOTE: Replacement fuse link color coding may vary from production fuse link color coding.

When heavy current flows, such as when a booster battery is connected incorrectly or when a short to ground occurs in the wiring harness, the fuse link burns out and protects the alternator or wiring.

The Continental does not use fusible links. Circuit protection is provided by a high-current fuse panel located in the engine compartment on the left fender apron. Whenever servicing the high-current fuse panel, ALWAYS disconnect the negative battery cable first.

Turn Signal, Fuse Block And Hazard Warning Flasher

LOCATION

The turn signal flasher is plugged directly into the fuse block.

The fuse block panel is located on the driver's side of the dash panel, adjacent to the parking brake mechanism.

On all vehicles except the 1982–1983 Escort/Lynx vehicles, the hazard flasher is mounted on the instrument panel and located between the steering column and the fuse block. On the 1982–1983 Escort/Lynx models, the hazard flasher is located in the rear of the fuse block.

Ford Motor Co.
Rear Wheel Drive
Ford — Crown Victoria, Country Squire,
LTD, Mustang, Thunderbird
Lincoln — Continental, Mark VII, Town Car
Mercury — Capri, Colony Park, Grand Marquis, Marquis

SERIAL NUMBER IDENTIFICATION

VEHICLE IDENTIFICATION CHART

It is important for servicing and ordering parts to be certain of the vehicle and engine identification. The VIN (vehicle identification number) is a 17 digit number visible through the windshield on the driver's side of the dash and contains the vehicle and engine identification codes. The tenth digit indicates model year and the eighth digit indicates engine code. It can be interpreted as follows:

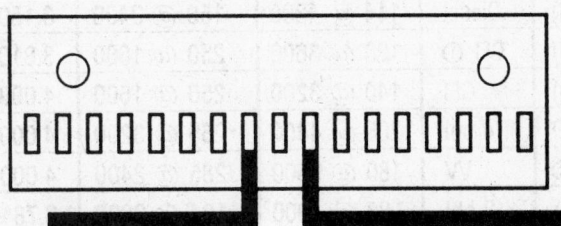

Engine Code						Model Year	
Code	Cu. In.	Liters	Cyl.	Fuel Sys.	Eng. Mfg.	Code	Year
A	140	2.3	4	1 bbl	Ford	C	1982
A	140	2.3	4	EFI	Ford	D	1983
T	140	2.3	4 (Turbo)	EFI	Ford	E	1984
W	140	2.3	4 (Turbo)	EFI	Ford	F	1985
L	149	2.4	6	Diesel	BMW	G	1986
B	200	3.3	6	1 bbl	Ford	H	1987
C	232	3.8	6	2 bbl	Ford	J	1988
3	232	3.8	6	CFI	Ford	K	1989
3	232	3.8	6	EFI	Ford		
4	232	3.8	6	EFI	Ford		
D	255	4.2	8	2 bbl	Ford		
F	302	5.0	8	V	Ford		
F	302	5.0	8	CFI	Ford		
F	302	5.0	8	EFI	Ford		
M	302 (HO)	5.0	8	CFI	Ford		
M	302 (HO)	5.0	8	EFI	Ford		
E	302 (HO)	5.0	8	EFI	Ford		
G	351	5.8	8	V	Ford		
G	351 (HO)	5.8	8	V	Ford		

GENERAL ENGINE SPECIFICATIONS

Year	VIN	No. Cylinder Displacement cu. in. (liter)	Fuel System Type	Net Horsepower @ rpm	Net Torque @ rpm (ft.lbs.)	Bore × Stroke (in.)	Compression Ratio	Oil Pressure @ 2000 rpm
1982	A	4-140 (2.3)	2 bbl	86 @ 4600	117 @ 2600	3.781 × 3.126	9.0:1	40-60
	B	6-200 (3.3)	1 bbl	87 @ 3800	154 @ 1400	3.680 × 3.130	8.6:1	30-50
	3	6-232 (3.8)	2 bbl	112 @ 4000	175 @ 2600	3.810 × 3.390	8.8:1	54-59
	D	8-255 (4.2)	2 bbl	122 @ 3400	209 @ 2400	3.680 × 3.000	8.2:1	40-60
	D	8-255 (4.2)	W	120 @ 3400	205 @ 2600	3.680 × 3.000	8.2:1	40-60
	F	8-302 (5.0)	W	132 @ 3400	236 @ 1800	4.000 × 3.000	8.4:1	40-60
	F	8-302 (5.0)	EFI	143 @ 3400	232 @ 3200	4.000 × 3.000	8.4:1	40-60
	G	8-351 (5.8)HO④	2 bbl	140 @ 3400	265 @ 2000	4.000 × 3.500	8.3:1	40-60
1983	A	4-140 (2.3)	2 bbl	88 @ 4800	118 @ 2800	3.781 × 3.126	9.0:1	40-60
	X	6-200 (3.3)	1 bbl①	88 @ 3800	154 @ 1400	3.680 × 3.130	8.6:1	30-50
	3	6-232 (3.8)	2 bbl	120 @ 3600	250 @ 1600	3.810 × 3.390	8.7:1	40-60
	F	8-302 (5.0)	EFI ②	130 @ 3200	240 @ 2000	4.000 × 3.000	8.4:1	40-60
	G	8-351 (5.8)HO④	2 bbl	140 @ 3400	265 @ 2000	4.000 × 3.500	8.3:1	40-60
1984	A	4-140 (2.3)	2 bbl	88 @ 4000	122 @ 2400	3.781 × 3.126	9.0:1	40-60
	W	4-140 (2.3)T	EFI	145 @ 4600	180 @ 3600	3.781 × 3.126	8.0:1	40-60
	L	6-149 (2.4)	Diesel	114 @ 4800	150 @ 2400	3.150 × 3.189	23:1	57-85
	3	6-232 (3.8)	CFI ①	120 @ 3600	250 @ 1600	3.810 × 3.390	8.7:1	40-60
	F	8-302 (5.0)	CFI	140 @ 3200	250 @ 1600	4.000 × 3.000	8.4:1	40-60
	M	8-302 (5.0)HO	4 bbl	205 @ 4400	265 @ 3200	4.000 × 3.000	8.3:1	40-60
	G	8-351 (5.8)HO④	W	180 @ 3600	285 @ 2400	4.000 × 3.500	8.3:1	40-60
1985	A	4-140 (2.3)	2 bbl	88 @ 4000	124 @ 2800	3.781 × 3.126	9.0:1	40-60
	W	4-140 (2.3)T	EFI	145 @ 4600	180 @ 3600	3.781 × 3.126	8.0:1	40-60
	T	4-140 (2.3)T③	EFI	175 @ 4400	210 @ 3000	3.781 × 3.126	8.0:1	40-60
	L	6-149 (2.4)	Diesel	114 @ 4800	150 @ 2400	3.150 × 3.189	23:1	57-85
	3	6-232 (3.8)	2 bbl	120 @ 3600	250 @ 1600	3.810 × 3.390	8.7:1	40-60
	F	8-302 (5.0)	CFI	165 @ 3200	250 @ 1600	4.000 × 3.000	8.4:1	40-60
	M	8-302 (5.0)HO	4 bbl	210 @ 4400	265 @ 3200	4.000 × 3.000	8.3:1	40-60
	G	8-351 (5.8)④	2 bbl	180 @ 3600	285 @ 2400	4.000 × 3.500	8.3:1	40-60
1986	A	4-140 (2.3)	2 bbl	88 @ 4200	122 @ 2600	3.781 × 3.126	9.0:1	40-60
	T	4-140 (2.3)T③	EFI	145 @ 4400	180 @ 3000	3.781 × 3.126	8.0:1	40-60
	W	4-140 (2.3)T	EFI	155 @ 4600	190 @ 2800	3.781 × 3.126	8.0:1	40-60
	3	6-232 (3.8)	CFI ①	120 @ 3600	205 @ 1600	3.810 × 3.390	8.7:1	40-60
	F	8-302 (5.0)	SEFI	150 @ 3200	270 @ 2000	4.000 × 3.000	8.9:1	40-60
	M	8-302 (5.0)HO	4 bbl	210 @ 4400	265 @ 3200	4.000 × 3.000	8.3:1	40-60
	G	8-351 (5.8)	W	180 @ 3600	285 @ 2400	4.000 × 3.500	8.3:1	40-60
1987	A	4-140 (2.3)OHC	EFI	88 @ 4200	122 @ 2600	3.781 × 3.126	9.0:1	40-60
	W	4-140 (2.3)T	EFI	155 @ 4600	190 @ 2800	3.781 × 3.126	8.0:1	40-60
	3	6-232 (3.8)	EFI	120 @ 3600	205 @ 1600	3.810 × 3.390	8.7:1	40-60
	E	8-302 (5.0)	EFI	150 @ 3200	270 @ 2000	4.000 × 3.000	8.9:1	40-60
	F	8-302 (5.0)	EFI	150 @ 3200	270 @ 2000	4.000 × 3.000	8.9:1	40-60

GENERAL ENGINE SPECIFICATIONS

Year	VIN	No. Cylinder Displacement cu. in. (liter)	Fuel System Type	Net Horsepower @ rpm	Net Torque @ rpm (ft.lbs.)	Bore × Stroke (in.)	Compression Ratio	Oil Pressure @ 2000 rpm
1987	M	8-302 (5.0)HO	EFI	210 @ 4400	265 @ 3200	4.000 × 3.000	8.3:1	40-60
	G	8-351 (5.8)HO④	VV	180 @ 3600	285 @ 2400	4.000 × 3.500	8.3:1	40-60
1988-89	A	4-140 (2.3)	EFI	88 @ 4200	122 @ 2600	3.780 × 3.126	9.0:1	40-60
	T	4-140 (2.3)T	EFI	155 @ 4600	190 @ 2800	3.780 × 3.126	8.0:1	40-60
	4	6-232 (3.8)	EFI	120 @ 3600	205 @ 1600	3.810 × 3.390	8.7:1	40-60
	F	8-302 (5.0)	EFI	150 @ 3200	270 @ 2000	4.000 × 3.000	8.9:1	40-60
	E	8-302 (5.0)HO	EFI	220 @ 4400	265 @ 3200	4.000 × 3.000	8.3:1	40-60
	G	8-351 (5.8)HO	VV	180 @ 3600	285 @ 2400	4.000 × 3.500	8.3:1	40-60

■Horsepower and torque are SAE net figures. They are measured at the rear of the transmission with all accessories installed and operating. Since the figures vary when a given engine is installed in different models, some are representative rather than exact.
T Turbocharger
EFI Electronic fuel injection
SEFI Sequential electronic fuel injection
HO High output
HSC High Swirl Combustion
CFI Central fuel injection
VV Variable Venturi carburetor

① Canadian models are equipped with a 2-bbl carburetor
② Some Mustang/Capri models are equipped with a 4-bbl carburetor
③ SVO
④ Canada and police only

GASOLINE ENGINE TUNE-UP SPECIFICATIONS

Year	VIN	No. Cylinder Displacement cu. in. (liter)	Spark Plugs Type	Gap (in.)	Ignition Timing (deg.) MT	Ignition Timing (deg.) AT	Compression Pressure (psi)	Fuel Pump (psi)	Idle Speed (rpm) MT	Idle Speed (rpm) AT	Valve Clearance In.	Valve Clearance Ex.
1982	A	4-140 (2.3)	AWSF-42	.034	①	①	NA	5½-6½	850	750	Hyd.	Hyd.
	B	6-200 (3.3)	BSF-92	.050	①	①	NA	6-8	700①	600	Hyd.	Hyd.
	D	8-255 (4.2)	ASF-52	.050	10B	10B	NA	5½-6½	900	700	Hyd.	Hyd.
	3	6-232 (3.8)	AGSP-52	.044	①	①	NA	6-8	①	①	Hyd.	Hyd.
	F	8-302 (5.0)	ASF-52	.050	—	①④	NA	6-8	①	①	Hyd.	Hyd.
	G	8-351 (5.8)	ASF-52	.050	—	①④	NA	6½-8	—	600	Hyd.	Hyd.
1983	A	4-140 (2.3)	AWSF-44	.044	①	①	NA	5½-6½	850	800	Hyd.	Hyd.
	X	6-200 (3.3)	BSF-92	.050	①	①	NA	6-8	600	600	Hyd.	Hyd.
	3	6-232 (3.8)	AWSF-52	.044	①	①	NA	39	550	550	Hyd.	Hyd.
	F	8-302 (5.0)	ASF-52②	.050	①	①	NA	6-8 ③	—	550	Hyd.	Hyd.
	G	8-351 (5.8)	ASF-42	.044	①	①	NA	6-8	—	700	Hyd.	Hyd.
1984	A	4-140 (2.3)	AWSF-44	.044	①	①	NA	5-7	850	750	Hyd.	Hyd.
	W	4-140 (2.3)T	AWSF-32	.034	①	①	NA	39	①	①	Hyd.	Hyd.
	3	8-232 (3.8)	AWSF-54	.044	①	①	NA	39	—	550	Hyd.	Hyd.
	F	8-302 (5.0)	ASF-52	.050	①	①	NA	39	550	550	Hyd.	Hyd.
	M	8-302 (5.0) HO	ASF-42	.044	①	①	NA	6-8	700	700	Hyd.	Hyd.
	G	8-351 (5.8)	ASF-42	.044	①	①	NA	6-8	—	600	Hyd.	Hyd.

GASOLINE ENGINE TUNE-UP SPECIFICATIONS

Year	VIN	No. Cylinder Displacement cu. in. (liter)	Spark Plugs Type	Gap (in.)	Ignition Timing (deg.) MT	AT	Compression Pressure (psi)	Fuel Pump (psi)	Idle Speed (rpm) MT	AT	Valve Clearance In.	Ex.
1985	A	4-140 (2.3)	AWSF-44	.044	①	①	NA	6-8	850	750	Hyd.	Hyd.
	W	4-140 (2.3)T	AWSF-32	.034	①	①	NA	39	750	750	Hyd.	Hyd.
	T	4-140 (2.3)T	AWSF-32	.034	①	①	NA	39	①	①	Hyd.	Hyd.
	3	6-232 (3.8)	AGSP-52	.044	①	①	NA	6-8	600	600	Hyd.	Hyd.
	F	8-302 (5.0)	ASF-52	.050	①	①	NA	39	—	550	Hyd.	Hyd.
	M	8-302 (5.0) HO	ASF-42	.044	①	①	NA	6-8	700	700	Hyd.	Hyd.
	G	8-351 (5.8)	ASF-42	.044	①	①	NA	6-8	—	600	Hyd.	Hyd.
1986	A	4-140 (2.3)	AWSF-44C	.044	①	①	NA	6-8	750	750	Hyd.	Hyd.
	T	4-140 (2.3)T	AWSF-32C	.034	①	①	NA	39	825-975	825	Hyd.	Hyd.
	W	4-140 (2.3)T	AWSF-32C	.034	①	①	NA	39	825-975	825	Hyd.	Hyd.
	3	6-232 (3.8)	AWSF-54	.044	①	①	NA	39	—	550	Hyd.	Hyd.
	F	8-302 (5.0)	ASF-32C	.044	①	①	NA	39	①	①	Hyd.	Hyd.
	M	8-302 (5.0) HO	ASF-42	.044	①	①	NA	6-8	700	700	Hyd.	Hyd.
	G	8-351 (5.8)	ASF-32C	.044	①	①	NA	6-8	650	650	Hyd.	Hyd.
1987	A	4-140 (2.3)	AWSF-44C	.044	①	①	NA	35	750	750	Hyd.	Hyd.
	W	4-140 (2.3)T	AWSF-320	.034	①	①	NA	35	825-975	825-975	Hyd.	Hyd.
	3	6-232 (3.8)	AWSF-54	.044	①	①	NA	35	—	550	Hyd.	Hyd.
	E	8-302 (5.0)	ASF-32C	.044	①	①	NA	39	①②	①②	Hyd.	Hyd.
	F	8-302 (5.0)	ASF-32C	.044	①	①	NA	35	①	①	Hyd.	Hyd.
	M	8-302 (5.0) HO	ASF42	.044	①	①	NA	35	700	700	Hyd.	Hyd.
	G	8-351 (5.8)	ASF-32C	.044	①	①	NA	6-8	650	650	Hyd.	Hyd.
1988	A	4-140 (2.3)	AWSF-44C	.044	①	①	NA	35	750	750	Hyd.	Hyd.
	T	4-140 (2.3)	AWSF-32C	.034	①	①	NA	35	825-975	825-975	Hyd.	Hyd.
	4	6-232 (3.8)	AWSF-54	.044	①	①	NA	39	—	550	Hyd.	Hyd.
	F	8-302 (5.0)	ASF-32C	.044	①	①	NA	39	①	①	Hyd.	Hyd.
	E	8-302 (5.0)HO	ASF42	.044	①	①	NA	39	700	700	Hyd.	Hyd.
	G	8-351 (5.8)	ASF-32C	.044	①	①	NA	6-8	650	650	Hyd.	Hyd.
1989						SEE UNDERHOOD SPECIFICATIONS STICKER						

NOTE: The underhood specifications sticker often reflects tune-up specifications changes made in production. Sticker figures must be used if they disagree with those in this chart.

T Turbocharger
B Before top dead center
HO High output
— Not applicable
HSC High Swirl Combustion
① Calibrations vary depending upon the model; refer to the underhood sticker

② The carbureted models use spark plug ASF-42 (.044) and the idle speed is 700 rpm
③ On fuel injected models the pressure is 39 psi

④ Electronic engine control models. The ignition timing, idle speed and idle mixture are not adjustable

DIESEL ENGINE TUNE-UP SPECIFICATIONS

Year	VIN	No. Engine Displacement cu. in. (liter)	Valve Clearance Intake (in.)	Valve Clearance Exhaust (in.)	Intake Valve Opens (deg.)	Injection Pump Setting (deg.)	Injection Nozzle Pressure (psi) New	Injection Nozzle Pressure (psi) Used	Idle Speed (rpm)	Cranking Compression Pressure (psi)
1984	L	6-149 (2.4)	0.010	0.010	6	2.5	2133	NA	750 ±50	348
1985	L	6-149 (2.4)	0.010	0.010	6	2.5	2133	NA	750 ±50	348

FIRING ORDERS

NOTE: To avoid confusion, always replace spark plug wires one at a time.

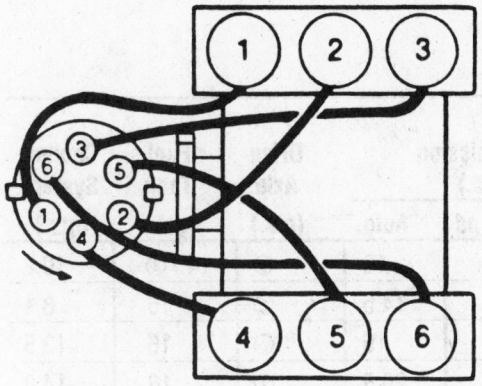

FORD MOTOR CO. 232 V6
Engine firing order: 1-4-2-5-3-6
Distributor rotation: counterclockwise

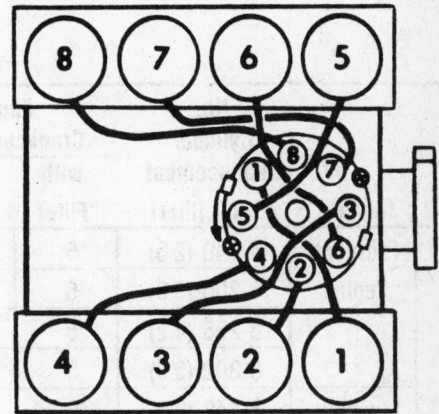

Ford Motor Co. 255 and 302 engines
Firing order: 1-5-4-2-6-3-7-8
Distributor rotation: clockwise

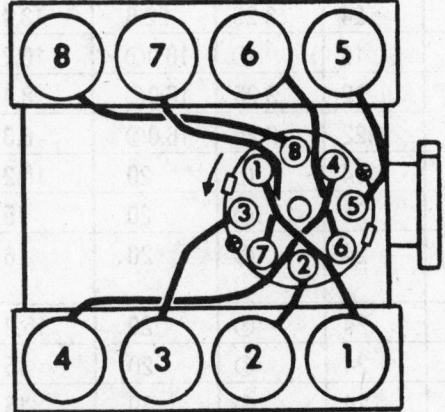

FORD MOTOR CO. 351 engines
Firing Order: 1-3-7-2-6-5-4-8
Distributor rotation: counterclockwise

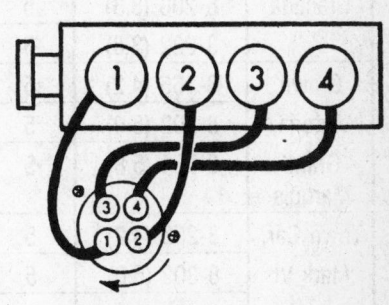

FORD MOTOR CO. 2300 cc 4-cyl.
Engine firing order: 1-3-4-2
Distributor rotation: clockwise

FIRING ORDERS

NOTE: To avoid confusion, always replace spark plug wires one at a time.

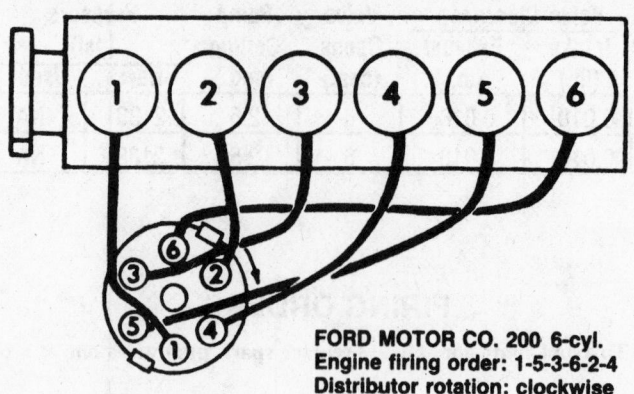

FORD MOTOR CO. 200 6-cyl.
Engine firing order: 1-5-3-6-2-4
Distributor rotation: clockwise

CAPACITIES

Year	Model	No. Cylinder Displacement cu. in. (liter)	Engine Crankcase (qts.) with Filter	Engine Crankcase (qts.) without Filter	Transmission (pts.) 4-Spd	Transmission (pts.) 5-Spd	Transmission (pts.) Auto.	Drive Axle (pts.)	Fuel Tank (gal.)	Cooling System (qts.)
1982	Fairmont,	4-140 (2.3)	5	4	2.8①	—	16	②	14.7③	10.2
	Zephyr	6-200 (3.3)	5	4	2.8①	—	14.5	②	16	8.1
		8-255 (4.2)	5	4	—	—	19	②	16	13.5
		8-302 (5.0)	5	4	—	—	20.5	②	16	14.0
	Mustang,	4-140 (2.3)	5	4	2.8	—		②	15.4	9
	Capri	4-140 (2.3)T	5	4.5	3.5	—	④	②	15.4	10.2
		6-200 (3.3)	5	4	2.8	—	12	②	15.4	8.1
		8-255 (4.2)	5	4	4.5	4.5	19	②	15.4	15
		8-302 (5.0)	5	4	4.5	4.5	19	②	15.4	14.2
	T-bird, XR7	6-200 (3.3)	5	4	—	—	22	3.25	21	8.4
	Continental	8-255 (4.2)	5	4	—	—	24	3.25	21	15
		8-302 (5.0)	5	4	—	—	24	3.25	22.6	13.4
	Cougar,	4-140 (2.3)	5	4	—	—	16	②	16.0③	10.2
	Granada	6-200 (3.3)	5	4	—	—	22	3.25	16.0③	8.4
		3-232 (3.8)	5	4	—	—	22	3.25	16.0③	8.3
	Crown	8-255 (4.2)	5	4	—	—	24	②	20	15.2
	Victoria,	8-302 (5.0)	5	4	—	—	24	⑥	20	15
	Grand Marquis	8-351 (5.8)	5	4	—	—	24	⑥	20	16
	Town Car,	8-255 (4.2)	5	4	—	—	24	⑥	20	15.2
	Mark VI	8-302 (5.0)	5	4	—	—	24	⑥	20	15
		8-351 (5.8)	5	4	—	—	24	⑥	20	16
1983	Fairmont,	4-140 (2.3)	5	4	2.8	—	16	3.25⑥	16	10.2
	Zephyr	6-200 (3.3)	5	4	—	—	22	3.25⑥	16	8.4

CAPACITIES

Year	Model	No. Cylinder Displacement cu. in. (liter)	Engine Crankcase (qts.) with Filter	without Filter	Transmission (pts.) 4-Spd	5-Spd	Auto.	Drive Axle (pts.)	Fuel Tank (gal.)	Cooling System (qts.)
1983	Mustang,	4-140 (2.3)	5	4⑦	2.8	4.75	16	3.25⑥	15.4	9.4
	Capri	3-232 (3.8)	5	4	—	—	22	3.25⑥	15.4	8.4
		8-302 (5.0)	5	4	4.5	4.5	—	3.55	15.4	13.4
	LTD,	4-140 (2.3)	5	4	2.8	—	16	3.25⑥	16	9.4
	Marquis	6-200 (3.3)	5	4	—	—	22	3.25⑥	16	8.5
		6-232 (3.8)	5	4	—	—	22⑤	3.25⑥	16	10.8
	T-bird,	4-140 (2.3)	5	4.5	4.75	4.75	—	3.25⑥	18	8.7
	Cougar	3-232 (3.8)	5	4	—	—	22⑤	3.25⑥	21	10.7
	Continental	8-302 (5.0)	5	4	—	—	22⑤	3.25⑥	20.7⑧	13.4
	Crown	8-302 (5.0)	5	4	—	—	24	②	20	15
	Victoria, Grand Marquis	8-351 (5.8)	5	4	—	—	24	②	20	16
	Town Car,	8-302 (5.0)	5	4	—	—	24	②	20	15
	Mark VI	8-351 (5.8)	5	4	—	—	24	②	20	16
1984	Mustang,	4-140 (2.3)	5	4⑦	2.8	4.75	16	3.25⑥	15.4	9.4
	Capri	6-232 (3.8)	5	4	—	—	22	3.25⑥	15.4	8.4
		8-302 (5.0)	5	4	4.5	4.5	—	3.55	15.4	13.4
	LTD,	4-140 (2.3)	5	4	2.8	—	16	3.25	16	9.4
	Marquis	6-200 (3.3)	5	4	—	—	22	3.25⑥	16	8.5
		6-232 (3.8)	5	4	—	—	22⑤	3.25⑥	16	10.8
	T-bird,	4-140 (2.3)	5	4⑦	4.75	4.75	—	3.25⑥	18	8.7
	Cougar	6-232 (3.8)	5	4	—	—	22	3.25⑥	21	10.7
		8-302 (5.0)	5	4	—	—	22	3.25⑥	20.7	13.4
	Mark VII,	6-149 (2.4)	7.9	6.9	—	—	15	②	21	11.8
	Continental	8-302 (5.0)	5	4	—	—	22	3.25⑥	20.7⑧	13.4
	Crown Victoria, Grand Marquis	8-302 (5.0)	5	4	—	—	24	②	20	15
	Town Car	8-302 (5.0)	5	4	—	—	24	②	20	16
1985	Mustang,	4-140 (2.3)	5	4⑦	2.8	4.75	16	3.25⑥	15.4	9.4
	Capri	6-232 (3.8)	5	4	—	—	22	3.25⑥	15.4	13.4
		8-302 (5.0)	5	4	4.5	4.5	—	3.25	15.4	13.4
	LTD,	4-140 (2.3)	5	4	2.8	—	16	3.25	16	9.4
	Marquis	6-232 (3.8)	5	4	—	—	22	3.25⑥	16	10.8
	T-bird,	4-140 (2.3)	5	4.5	4.75	4.75	—	3.25⑥	18	8.7
	Cougar	6-232 (3.8)	5	4	—	—	22	3.25⑥	21	10.7
		8-302 (5.0)	5	4	—	—	22	3.25	20	13.4
	Mark VII,	6-149 (2.4)	7.9	6.9	—	—	15	②	21	11.8
	Continental	8-302 (5.0)	5	4	—	—	22	3.25⑥	20.7⑧	13.4

CAPACITIES

Year	Model	No. Cylinder Displacement cu. in. (liter)	Engine Crankcase (qts.) with Filter	without Filter	Transmission (pts.) 4-Spd	5-Spd	Auto.	Drive Axle (pts.)	Fuel Tank (gal.)	Cooling System (qts.)
1985	Crown Victoria, Grand Marquis	8-302 (5.0)	5	4	—	—	24	②	20	15
	Town Car	8-302 (5.0)	5	4	—	—	24	②	20	16
1986	Mustang, Capri	4-140 (2.3)	5	4⑦	2.8	4.75	16	3.25⑥	15.4	9.4
		6-232 (3.8)	5	4	—	—	22	3.25⑥	15.4	13.4
		8-302 (5.0)	5	4	4.5	4.5	—	3.25	15.4	13.4
	LTD, Marquis	4-140 (2.3)	5	4	2.8	—	16	3.25	16	9.4
		6-232 (3.8)	5	4	—	—	22	3.25⑥	16	10.8
	T-bird, Cougar	4-140 (2.3)	5	4.5⑦	4.75	4.75	—	3.25⑥	18	8.7
		6-232 (3.8)	5	4	—	—	22	3.25⑥	21	10.7
		8-302 (5.0)	5	4	—	—	22	3.25	20	13.4
	Mark VII, Continental	8-302 (5.0)	5	4	—	—	22	3.25⑥	20.7	13.4
	Crown Victoria, Grand Marquis,	8-302 (5.0)	5	4	—	—	24	②	20	15
	Town Car	8-302 (5.0)	5	4	—	—	24	②	20	10
1987	Mustang	4-140 (2.3)	5	4	3.7	3.7	22	4.5	15.4	10
		8-302 (5.0)	5	4	3.7	3.7	22	3.25	15.4	14.1
	T-bird, Cougar	4-140 (2.3)	5	4.5⑦	4.75	4.75	16	3.25⑥	18	10
		6-232 (3.8)	5	4	—	—	22	3.25⑥	21	11.8
		8-302 (5.0)	5	4	—	—	22	3.25⑥	20.7	14.1
	Mark VII, Continental	8-302 (5.0)	5	4	—	—	22	3.25	20.7⑧	14.1
	Crown Victoria, Grand Marquis	8-302 (5.0)	5	4	—	—	24	②	20	15
	Town Car	8-302 (5.0)	5	4	—	—	24	②	20	16
1988-89	Mustang	4-140 (2.3)	5	4	3.7	3.7	22	4.5	15.4	10
		8-302 (5.0)	5	4	3.7	3.7	22	3.25	15.4	14.1
	T-bird, Cougar	4-140 (2.3)	5	4.5⑦	4.75	4.75	16	3.25⑥	18	10
		6-232 (3.8)	5	4	—	—	22	3.25⑥	21	11.8
		8-302 (5.0)	5	4	—	—	22	3.25⑥	20.7	14.1
	Mark VII	8-302 (5.0)	5	4	—	—	22	3.25	20.7⑧	14.1

CAPACITIES

Year	Model	No. Cylinder Displacement cu. in. (liter)	Engine Crankcase (qts.) with Filter	Engine Crankcase (qts.) without Filter	Transmission (pts.) 4-Spd	Transmission (pts.) 5-Spd	Transmission (pts.) Auto.	Drive Axle (pts.)	Fuel Tank (gal.)	Cooling System (qts.)
1988-89	Crown Victoria, Grand Marquis	8-302 (5.0)	5	4	—	—	24	②	20	15
	Town Car	8-302 (5.0)	5	4	—	—	24	②	20	16

① 4-speed overdrive — 4.5 pts.
② 6.75 in. axle, 2.5 pts.
  7.5 in. axle, 3.5 pts.
  8.5 in axle, 4.0 pts.
③ 20 gals. optional

④ C3, 16 pts, — C4, 14 pts.
⑤ AOD Trans. — 24 pts.
⑥ Traction-lok — 3.55 pts.
⑦ Turbo 4.5, add .5 w/filter
⑧ Continental — 22.3

CAMSHAFT SPECIFICATIONS
All measurements given in inches.

Year	VIN	No. Cylinder Displacement cu. in. (liter)	Journal Diameter 1	Journal Diameter 2	Journal Diameter 3	Journal Diameter 4	Journal Diameter 5	Lobe Lift In.	Lobe Lift Ex.	Bearing Clearance	Camshaft End Play
1982	A	4-140 (2.3)	1.7713–1.7720	1.7713–1.7720	1.7713–1.7720	1.7713–1.7720	—	.2437	.2437	.001–.003	.001–.007
	B	6-200 (3.3)	1.8095–1.8105	1.8095–1.8105	1.8095–1.8105	1.8095–1.8105	—	.245	.245	.001–.003	.001–.007
	3	6-232 (3.8)	2.0515–2.0505	2.0515–2.0505	2.0515–2.0505	2.0515–2.0505	—	.240	.241	.001–.003	①
	D	8-255 (4.2)	2.0805–2.0815	2.0655–2.0665	2.0505–2.0515	2.0355–2.0365	2.0205–2.0215	.2375	.2375	.001–.003	.001–.007
	F	8-302 (5.0)	2.0805–2.0815	2.0655–2.0665	2.0505–2.0515	2.0355–2.0365	2.0205–2.0215	.2375	.2474	.001–.003	.001–.007
	G	8-351 (5.8)	2.0805–2.0815	2.0655–2.0665	2.0505–2.0515	2.0355–2.0365	2.0205–2.0215	.2780	.2830	.001–.003	.001–.007
1983	A	4-140 (2.3)	1.7713–1.7720	1.7713–1.7720	1.7713–1.7720	1.7713–1.7720	—	.2437	.2437	.001–.003	.001–.007
	X	6-200 (3.3)	1.8095–1.8105	1.8095–1.8105	1.8095–1.8105	1.8095–1.8105	—	.245	.245	.001–.003	.001–.007
	3	6-232 (3.8)	2.0515–2.0505	2.0515–2.0505	2.0515–2.0505	2.0515–2.0505	—	.240	.241	.001–.003	①
	F	8-302 (5.0)	2.0805–2.0815	2.065–2.0665	2.0505–2.0515	2.0355–2.0365	2.0205–2.0215	.2375 ②	.2474 ②	.001–.003	.001–.007
	G	8-351 (5.8)	2.0805–2.0815	2.0655–2.0665	2.0505–2.0515	2.0355–2.0365	2.0205–2.0215	.2780	.2830	.001–.003	.001–.007

CAMSHAFT SPECIFICATIONS
All measurements given in inches.

Year	VIN	No. Cylinder Displacement cu. in. (liter)	Journal Diameter					Lobe Lift		Bearing Clearance	Camshaft End Play
			1	2	3	4	5	In.	Ex.		
1984	A	4-140 (2.3)	1.7713–1.7720	1.7713–1.7720	1.7713–1.7720	1.7713–1.7720	—	.2381	.2381	.001–.003	.001–.007
	T	4-140 (2.3)	1.7713–1.7720	1.7713–1.7720	1.7713–1.7720	1.7713–1.7720	—	.2381	.2381	.001–.003	.001–.007
	W	4-140 (2.3)	1.7713–1.7720	1.7713–1.7720	1.7713–1.7720	1.7713–1.7720	—	.2381	.2381	.001–.003	.001–.007
	L	6-149 (2.4)	1.2582–1.2589	1.2582–1.2589	1.2582–1.2589	1.2582–1.2589	1.2582–1.2589	.374	.376	.0039	
	3	6-232 (3.8)	2.0515–2.0505	2.0515–2.0505	2.0515–2.0505	2.0515–2.0505	—	.240	.241	.001–.003	①
	F	8-302 (5.0)	2.0805–2.0815	2.0655–2.0665	2.0505–2.0515	2.0355–2.0365	2.0205–2.0215	.2375 ②	.2474 ②	.001–.003	.001–.007
	M	8-302 (5.0)	2.0805–2.0815	2.0655–2.0665	2.0505–2.0515	2.0355–2.0365	2.0205–2.0215	.2375 ②	.2474 ②	.001–.003	.001–.007
	G	8-351 (5.8)	2.0805–2.0815	2.0655–2.0665	2.0505–2.0515	2.0355–2.0365	2.0205–2.0215	.2780	.2830	.001–.003	.001–.007
1985	A	4-140 (2.3)	1.7713–1.7720	1.7713–1.7720	1.7713–1.7720	1.7713–1.7720	—	.400	.400	.001–.003	.001–.007
	W	4-140 (2.3)	1.7713–1.7720	1.7713–1.7720	1.7713–1.7720	1.7713–1.7720	—	.400	.400	.001–.003	.001–.007
	L	6-149 (2.4)	1.2582–1.2589	1.2582–1.2589	1.2582–1.2589	1.2582–1.2589	1.2582–1.2589	.374	.376	.0039	—
	3	6-232 (3.8)	2.0515–2.0505	2.0515–2.0505	2.0515–2.0505	2.0515–2.0505	—	.240	.241	.001–.003	①
	F	8-302 (5.0)	2.0805–2.0815	2.0655–2.0665	2.0505–2.0515	2.0355–2.0365	2.0205–2.0215	.2375 ②	.2474 ②	.001–.003	.001–.007
	M	8-302 (5.0)	2.0805–2.0815	2.0655–2.0665	2.0505–2.0515	2.0355–2.0365	2.0205–2.0215	.2375 ②	.2474 ②	.001–.003	.001–.007
	G	8-351 (5.8)	2.0805–2.0815	2.0655–2.0665	2.0505–2.0515	2.0355–2.0365	2.0505–2.0215	.2780	.2830	.001–.003	.001–.007
1986	A	4-140 (2.3)	1.7713–1.7720	1.7713–1.7720	1.7713–1.7720	1.7713–1.7720	—	.400	.400	.001–.003	.001–.007
	T	4-140 (2.3)	1.7713–1.7720	1.7713–1.7720	1.7713–1.7720	1.7713–1.7720	—	.400	.400	.001–.003	.001–.007
	W	4-140 (2.3)	1.7713–1.7720	1.7713–1.7720	1.7713–1.7720	1.7713–1.7720	—	.400	.400	.001–.003	.001–.007
	3	6-232 (3.8)	2.0515–2.0505	2.0515–2.0505	2.0515–2.0505	2.0515–2.0505	—	.240	.241	.001–.003	①

CAMSHAFT SPECIFICATIONS
All measurements given in inches.

Year	VIN	No. Cylinder Displacement cu. in. (liter)	Journal Diameter 1	2	3	4	5	Lobe Lift In.	Ex.	Bearing Clearance	Camshaft End Play
1986	F	8-302 (5.0)	2.0805–2.0815	2.0655–2.0665	2.0505–2.0515	2.0355–2.0365	2.0205–2.0515	.2375 ②	.2474 ②	.001–.003	.001–.007
	M	8-302 (5.0)	2.0805–2.0815	2.0655–2.0665	2.0505–2.0515	2.0355–2.0365	2.0205–2.0515	.2375 ②	.2474 ②	.001–.003	.001–.007
	G	8-351 (5.8)	2.0805–2.0815	2.0655–2.0665	2.0505–2.0515	2.0355–2.0365	2.0505–2.0515	.2780	.2830	.001–.003	.001–.007
1987	A	4-140 (2.3)	1.7713–1.7720	1.7713–1.7720	1.7713–1.7720	1.7713–1.7720	—	.400	.400	.001–.003	.001–.007
	W	4-140 (2.3)	1.7713–1.7720	1.7713–1.7720	1.7713–1.7720	1.7713–1.7720	—	.400	.400	.001–.003	.001–.007
	3	6-232 (3.8)	2.0515–2.0505	2.0515–2.0505	2.0515–2.0505	2.0515–2.0505	—	.240	.241	.001–.003	①
	E	8-302 (5.0)	2.0805–2.0815	2.0655–2.0665	2.0505–2.0515	2.0355–2.0365	2.0205–2.0215	.2375 ②	.2474 ②	.001–.003	.001–.007
	F	8-302 (5.0)	2.0805–2.0815	2.0655–2.0665	2.0505–2.0515	2.0355–2.0365	2.0205–2.0215	.2375 ②	.2474 ②	.001–.003	.001–.007
	M	8-302 (5.0)	2.0805–2.0815	2.0655–2.0665	2.0505–2.0515	2.0355–2.0365	2.0205–2.0215	.2375 ②	.2474 ②	.001–.003	.001–.007
	G	8-351 (5.8)	2.0805–2.0815	2.0655–2.0665	2.0505–2.0515	2.0355–2.0365	2.0205–2.0215	.2780	.2830	.001–.003	.001–.007
1988-89	A	4-140 (2.3)	1.7713–1.7720	1.7713–1.7720	1.7713–1.7720	1.7713–1.7720	—	.400	.400	.001–.003	.001–.007
	T	4-140 (2.3)	1.7713–1.7720	1.7713–1.7720	1.7713–1.7720	1.7713–1.7720	—	.400	.400	.001–.003	.001–.007
	4	6-232 (3.8)	2.0515–2.0505	2.0515–2.0505	2.0515–2.0505	2.0515–2.0505	—	.240	.241	.001–.003	①
	F	8-302 (5.0)	2.0805–2.0815	2.0655–2.0665	2.0505–2.0515	2.0355–2.0365	2.0205–2.0215	.2375 ②	.2474 ②	.001–.003	.001–.007
	E	8-302 (5.0)	2.0805–2.0815	2.0655–2.0665	2.0505–2.0515	2.0355–2.0365	2.0205–2.0215	.2375 ②	.2474 ②	.001–.003	.001–.007
	G	8-351 (5.8)	2.0805–2.0815	2.0655–2.0665	2.0505–2.0515	2.0355–2.0365	2.0205–2.0215	.2375 ②	.2474 ②	.001–.003	.001–.007

① The end play is controlled by the button and spring on the camshaft end

② On the 1983–85 H.O. engine, intake lobe lift is .2600, exhaust is .2780
On the 1986–89 H.O. engine, intake lobe lift is .2780, exhaust is .2780

CRANKSHAFT AND CONNECTING ROD SPECIFICATIONS
All measurements are given in inches.

Year	VIN	No. Cylinder Displacement cu. in. (liter)	Crankshaft Main Brg. Journal Dia.	Crankshaft Main Brg. Oil Clearance	Crankshaft Shaft End-play	Crankshaft Thrust on No.	Connecting Rod Journal Diameter	Connecting Rod Oil Clearance	Connecting Rod Side Clearance
1982	A	4-140 (2.3)	2.3990– 2.3982	0.0008– 0.0015	0.004– 0.008	3	2.0464– 2.0472	0.0008– 0.0015	0.0035– 0.0105
	B	6-200 (3.3)	2.2482– 2.2490	0.0008– 0.0015	0.004– 0.008	5	2.1232– 2.1240	0.0008– 0.0015	0.0035– 0.0105
	3	6-232 (3.8)	2.5190	0.0001– 0.0010	0.004– 0.008	3	2.3103– 2.3111	0.0008– 0.0026	0.0047– 0.0114
	D	8-255 (4.2)	2.2482– 2.2490	0.0004– 0.0025	0.004– 0.008	3	2.1228– 2.1236	0.0008– 0.0026	0.010– 0.020
	F	8-302 (5.0)	2.2482– 2.2490	0.0004– 0.0025	0.004– 0.008	3	2.1228– 2.1236	0.0008– 0.0015	0.010– 0.020
	G	8-351 (5.8)	2.2994– 3.0002	0.0008– 0.0015 ③	0.004– 0.008	3	2.3103– 2.3111	0.0008– 0.0015	0.010– 0.020
1983	A	4-140 (2.3)	2.3990– 2.3982	0.0008– 0.0015	0.004– 0.008	3	2.0464– 2.0472	0.0008– 0.0015	0.0035– 0.0105
	X	6-200 (3.3)	2.2482– 2.2490	0.0008– 0.0015	0.004– 0.008	5	2.1232– 2.1240	0.0008– 0.0015	0.0035– 0.0105
	3	6-232 (3.8)	2.5190	0.0001– 0.0010	0.004– 0.008	3	2.3103– 2.3111	0.0008– 0.0026	0.0047– 0.0114
	F	8-302 (5.0)	2.2482– 2.2490	0.0004– 0.0025	0.004– 0.008	3	2.1228– 2.1236	0.0008– 0.0015	0.010– 0.020
	G	8-351 (5.8)	2.2994– 3.0002	0.0008– 0.0015 ③	0.004– 0.008	3	2.3103– 2.3111	0.0008– 0.0015	0.010– 0.020
1984	A	4-140 (2.3)	2.3990– 2.3982	0.0008– 0.0015	0.004– 0.008	3	2.0464– 2.0472	0.0008– 0.0015	0.0035– 0.0105
	T	4-140 (2.3)	2.3990– 2.3982	0.0008– 0.0015	0.004– 0.008	3	2.0464– 2.0472	0.0008– 0.0015	0.0035– 0.0105
	W	4-140 (2.3)	2.3990– 2.3982	0.0008– 0.0015	0.004– 0.008	3	2.0464– 2.0472	0.0008– 0.0015	0.0035– 0.0105
	3	6-232 (3.8)	2.5190	0.0001– 0.0010	0.004– 0.008	3	2.3103– 2.3111	0.0008– 0.0026	0.0047– 0.0114
	F	8-302 (5.0)	2.2482– 2.2490	0.0004– 0.0025	0.004	3	2.1228– 2.1236	0.0008– 0.0015	0.010– 0.020
	M	8-302 (5.0)	2.2482– 2.2490	0.0004– 0.0025	0.004	3	2.1228– 2.1236	0.0008– 0.0015	0.010– 0.020
	G	8-351 (5.8)	2.2994– 3.0002	0.0008– 0.0015 ③	0.004– 0.008	3	2.3103– 2.3111	0.0008– 0.0015	0.010– 0.020
	L	6-149 (2.4)	①	0.0008– 0.0018	0.003– 0.006	6	②	0.0008– 0.0016	0.0016

CRANKSHAFT AND CONNECTING ROD SPECIFICATIONS
All measurements are given in inches.

Year	VIN	No. Cylinder Displacement cu. in. (liter)	Crankshaft				Connecting Rod		
			Main Brg. Journal Dia.	Main Brg. Oil Clearance	Shaft End-play	Thrust on No.	Journal Diameter	Oil Clearance	Side Clearance
1985	A	4-140 (2.3)	2.3990–2.3982	0.0008–0.0015	0.004–0.008	3	2.0464–2.0472	0.0008–0.0015	0.0035–0.0105
	T	4-140 (2.3)	2.3990–2.3982	0.0008–0.0015	0.004–0.008	3	2.0464–2.0472	0.0008–0.0015	0.0035–0.0105
	W	4-140 (2.3)	2.3990–2.3982	0.0008–0.0015	0.004–0.008	3	2.0464–2.0472	0.0008–0.0015	0.0035–0.0105
	3	6-232 (3.8)	2.5190	0.0001–0.0010	0.004–0.008	3	2.3103–2.3111	0.0008–0.0026	0.0047–0.0114
	F	8-302 (5.0)	2.2482–2.2490	0.0004–0.0015 ③	0.004–0.015	3	2.1228–2.1236	0.0008–0.0015	0.010–0.020
	M	8-302 (5.0)	2.2482–2.2490	0.0004–0.0015 ③	0.004–0.015	3	2.1228–2.1236	0.0008–0.0015	0.010–0.020
	G	8-351 (5.8)	2.2994–3.0002 3.0002	0.0008–0.0015 ③	0.004–0.008	3	2.3103–2.3111	0.0008–0.0015	0.010–0.020
	L	6-149 (2.4)	①	0.0008–0.0018	0.003–0.006	6	②	0.0008–0.0060	0.0016
1986	A	4-140 (2.3)	2.3990–2.3982	0.0008–0.0015	0.004–0.008	3	2.0464–2.0472	0.0008–0.0015	0.0035–0.0105
	T	4-140 (2.3)	2.3990–2.3982	0.0008–0.0015	0.004–0.008	3	2.0464–2.0472	0.0008–0.0015	0.0035–0.0105
	W	4-140 (2.3)	2.3990–2.3982	0.0008–0.0015	0.004–0.008	3	2.0464–2.0472	0.0008–0.0015	0.0035–0.0105
	3	6-232 (3.8)	2.5190	0.0001–0.0010	0.004–0.008	3	2.3103–2.3111	0.0008–0.0026	0.0047–0.0114
	F	8-302 (5.0)	2.2482–2.2490	0.0004–0.0015	0.004–0.008	3	2.1228–2.1236	0.0008–0.0015	0.010–0.020
	M	8-302 (5.0)	2.2482–2.2490	0.0004–0.0015	0.004–0.008	3	2.1228–2.1236	0.0008–0.0015	0.010–0.020
	G	8-351 (5.8)	2.2994–3.0002	0.0008–0.0015 ③	0.004–0.008	3	2.3103–2.3111	0.0008–0.0015	0.010–0.020
1987	A	4-140 (2.3)	2.3990–2.3982	0.0008–0.0015	0.004–0.008	3	2.0464–2.0472	0.0008–0.0015	0.0035–0.0105
	W	4-140 (2.3)	2.3990–2.3982	0.0008–0.0015	0.004–0.008	3	2.0464–2.0472	0.0008–0.0015	0.0035–0.0105
	3	6-232 (3.8)	2.5190	0.0001–0.0010	0.004–0.008	3	2.3103–2.3111	0.0008–0.0026	0.0047–0.0114
	F	8-302 (5.0)	2.2482–2.2490	0.0004–0.0015	0.004–0.008	3	2.1228–2.1236	0.0008–0.0015	0.010–0.020
	M	8-302 (5.0)	2.2482–2.2490	0.0004–0.0015	0.004–0.008	3	2.1228–2.1236	0.0008–0.0015	0.010–0.020

CRANKSHAFT AND CONNECTING ROD SPECIFICATIONS

All measurements are given in inches.

Year	VIN	No. Cylinder Displacement cu. in. (liter)	Crankshaft				Connecting Rod		
			Main Brg. Journal Dia.	Main Brg. Oil Clearance	Shaft End-play	Thrust on No.	Journal Diameter	Oil Clearance	Side Clearance
1987	E	8-302 (5.0)	2.2482–2.2490	0.0004–0.0015	0.004–0.008	3	2.1228–2.1236	0.0008–0.0015	0.010–0.020
	G	8-351 (5.8)	2.2994–3.0002	0.0008–0.0015 ③	0.004–0.008	3	2.3103–2.3111	0.0008–0.0015	0.010–0.020
1988-89	A	4-140 (2.3)	2.3990–2.3982	0.0008–0.0015	0.004–0.008	3	2.0464–2.0472	0.0008–0.0015	0.0035–0.0105
	T	4-140 (2.3)	2.3990–2.3982	0.0008–0.0015	0.004–0.008	3	2.0464–2.0472	0.0008–0.0015	0.0035–0.0105
	4	6-232 (3.8)	2.5190	0.0001–0.0010	0.004–0.008	3	2.3103–2.3111	0.0008–0.0026	0.0047–0.0114
	F	8-302 (5.0)	2.2482–2.2490	0.0004–0.0015	0.004–0.008	3	2.1228–2.1236	0.0008–0.0015	0.010–0.020
	E	8-302 (5.0)HO	2.2482–2.2490	0.0004–0.0015	0.004–0.008	3	2.1228–2.1236	0.0008–0.0015	0.010–0.020
	G	8-351 (5.8)	2.2994–3.0002	0.0008–0.0015	0.004–0.008	3	2.3103–2.3111	0.0008–0.0015	0.010–0.020

NA Not available
① Yellow mark—2.3615–2.3618
 Green mark—2.3613–2.3615
 White mark—2.3610–2.3612
② Red mark—1.8885–1.8887
 Blue mark—1.8888–1.8903
③ No. 1—0.0001–0.0005

VALVE SPECIFICATIONS

Year	VIN	No. Cylinder Displacement cu. in. (liter)	Seat Angle (deg.)	Face Angle (deg.)	Spring Test Pressure (lbs. @ in.)	Spring Installed Height (in.)	Stem-to-Guide Clearance (in.)		Stem Diameter (in.)	
							Intake	Exhaust	Intake	Exhaust
1982	A	4-140 (2.3)	45	44	167 @ 1.16	1 9/16	0.0010–0.0027	0.0015–0.0032	0.3420	0.3415
	B	6-200 (3.3)	45	44	55 @ 1.59	1 19/32	0.0008–0.0025	0.0010–0.0027	0.3104	0.3102
	D	8-255 (4.2)	①	①	1.92 @ 1.40 ②	—	0.0010–0.0027	0.0015–0.0032	0.3420	0.3420
	F	8-302 (5.0)	45	45	205 @ 1.36	1 3/4	0.0010–0.0027	0.0015–0.0032	0.3420	0.3420
	G	8-351 (5.8)	45	45	204 @ 1.33	1 49/64 ③	0.0010–0.0027	0.0015–0.0027	0.3416–0.3423	0.3411–0.3418
1983	A	4-140 (2.3)	45	44	149 @ 1.12	1 9/16	0.0010–0.0027	0.0015–0.0032	0.3420	0.3415
	X	6-200 (3.3)	45	44	55 @ 1.59	1 19/32	0.0008–0.0025	0.0010–0.0027	0.3104	0.3102

VALVE SPECIFICATIONS

Year	VIN	No. Cylinder Displacement cu. in. (liter)	Seat Angle (deg.)	Face Angle (deg.)	Spring Test Pressure (lbs. @ in.)	Spring Installed Height (in.)	Stem-to-Guide Clearance (in.)		Stem Diameter (in.)	
							Intake	Exhaust	Intake	Exhaust
1983	F	8-302 (5.0)	45	45	205 @ 1.36	1¾	0.0010–0.0027	0.0015–0.0032	0.3420	0.3420
	G	8-351 (5.8)	45	45	204 @ 1.33	1⁴⁹⁄₆₄③	0.0010–0.0027	0.0015–0.0027	0.3416–0.3423	0.3411–0.3418
1984	A	4-140 (2.3)	45	44	154 @ 1.12	1⁹⁄₁₆	0.0010–0.0027	0.0015–0.0032	0.3420	0.3415
	T	4-140 (2.3)	45	44	154 @ 1.12	1⁹⁄₁₆	0.0010–0.0027	0.0015–0.0032	0.3420	0.3415
	W	4-140 (2.3)	45	44	154 @ 1.12	1⁹⁄₁₆	0.0010–0.0027	0.0015–0.0032	0.3420	0.3415
	3	6-232 (3.8)	44.5	45.8	215 @ 1.79	1¾	0.0010–0.0027	0.0015–0.0032	0.3420	0.3415
	F	8-302 (5.0)	45	45	205 @ 1.36	1¾	0.0010–0.0027	0.0015–0.0032	0.3420	0.3420
	M	8-302 (5.0)	45	45	205 @ 1.36	1¾	0.0010–0.0027	0.0015–0.0032	0.3420	0.3420
	L	6-149 (2.4)	45	45	④	–	0.0008–0.0010	0.0008–0.0010	–	–
	G	8-351 (5.8)	45	45	204 @ 1.33	1⁴⁹⁄₆₄③	0.0010–0.0027	0.0015–0.0027	0.3416–0.3423	0.3411–0.3418
1985	A	4-140 (2.3)	45	44	154 @ 1.12	1⁹⁄₁₆	0.0010–0.0027	0.0015–0.0032	0.3420	0.3415
	T	4-140 (2.3)	45	44	154 @ 1.12	1⁹⁄₁₆	0.0010–0.0027	0.0015–0.0032	0.3420	0.3415
	W	4-140 (2.3)	45	44	154 @ 1.12	1⁹⁄₁₆	0.0010–0.0027	0.0015–0.0032	0.3420	0.3415
	3	6-232 (3.8)	44.5	45.8	215 @ 1.79	1¾	0.0010–0.0027	0.0015–0.0032	0.3420	0.3415
	F	8-302 (5.0)	45	45	205 @ 1.36	1¾	0.0010–0.0027	0.0015–0.0032	0.3420	0.3420
	M	8-302 (5.0)	45	45	205 @ 1.36	1¾	0.0010–0.0027	0.0015–0.0032	0.3420	0.3420
	L	6-149 (2.4)	45	45	④	–	0.0008–0.0010	0.0008–0.0010	–	–
	G	8-351 (5.8)	45	45	204 @ 1.33	1⁴⁹⁄₆₄③	0.0010–0.0027	0.0015–0.0027	0.3416–0.3423	0.3411–0.3418
1986	A	4-140 (2.3)	45	44	154 @ 1.12	1⁹⁄₁₆	0.0010–0.0027	0.0015–0.0032	0.3420	0.3415
	T	4-140 (2.3)	45	44	154 @ 1.12	1⁹⁄₁₆	0.0010–0.0027	0.0015–0.0032	0.3420	0.3415
	W	4-140 (2.3)	45	44	154 @ 1.12	1⁹⁄₁₆	0.0010–0.0027	0.0015–0.0032	0.3420	0.3415
	3	6-232 (3.8)	44.5	45.8	215 @ 1.79	1¾	0.0010–0.0027	0.0015–0.0032	0.3420	0.3415

VALVE SPECIFICATIONS

Year	VIN	No. Cylinder Displacement cu. in. (liter)	Seat Angle (deg.)	Face Angle (deg.)	Spring Test Pressure (lbs. @ in.)	Spring Installed Height (in.)	Stem-to-Guide Clearance (in.)		Stem Diameter (in.)	
							Intake	Exhaust	Intake	Exhaust
1986	F	8-302 (5.0)	45	45	205 @ 1.36	1¾	0.0010–0.0027	0.0015–0.0032	0.3420	0.3420
	M	8-302 (5.0)	45	45	205 @ 1.36	1¾	0.0010–0.0027	0.0015–0.0032	0.3420	0.3420
	G	8-351 (5.8)	45	45	204 @ 1.33	1 49/64 ③	0.0010–0.0027	0.0015–0.0027	0.3416–0.3423	0.3411–0.3418
1987	A	4-140 (2.3)	45	44	154 @ 1.12	1 9/16	0.0010–0.0027	0.0015–0.0032	0.3420	0.3415
	T	4-140 (2.3)	45	44	154 @ 1.12	1 9/16	0.0010–0.0027	0.0015–0.0032	0.3420	0.3415
	3	6-232 (3.8)	44.5	45.8	215 @ 1.79	1¾	0.0010–0.0027	0.0015–0.0032	0.3420	0.3415
	E	8-302 (5.0)	45	45	205 @ 1.36	1¾	0.0010–0.0027	0.0015–0.0032	0.3420	0.3420
	F	8-302 (5.0)	45	45	205 @ 1.36	1¾	0.0010–0.0027	0.0015–0.0032	0.3420	0.3420
	M	8-302 (5.0)	45	45	205 @ 1.36	1¾	0.0010–0.0027	0.0015–0.0032	0.3420	0.3420
	G	8-351 (5.8)	45	45	204 @ 1.33	1 49/64 ③	0.0010–0.0027	0.0015–0.0027	0.3416–0.3423	0.3411–0.3418
1988-89	A	4-140 (2.3)	45	44	154 @ 1.12	1 9/16	0.0010–0.0027	0.0015–0.0032	0.3420	0.3415
	T	4-140 (2.3)	45	44	154 @ 1.12	1 9/16	0.0010–0.0027	0.0015–0.0032	0.3420	0.3415
	4	6-232 (3.8)	44.5	45.8	215 @ 1.79	1¾	0.0010–0.0027	0.0015–0.0032	0.3420	0.3415
	F	8-302 (5.0)	45	45	205 @ 1.36	1¾	0.0010–0.0027	0.0015–0.0032	0.3420	0.3420
	E	8-302 (5.0)HO	45	45	205 @ 1.36	1¾	0.0010–0.0027	0.0015–0.0032	0.3420	0.3420
	G	8-351 (5.8)	45	45	204 @ 1.33	1 49/64 ③	0.0010–0.0027	0.0015–0.0027	0.3416–0.3423	0.3411–0.3418

① Exhaust: 45° 30'–45° 45'

② Intake: 192 @ 1.40
Exhaust: 191 @ 1.23

③ Exhaust: 1 37/64

④ Install spring in tool No.6513-00. Apply torque until a click is heard and multiply the torque reading by 2

PISTON AND RING SPECIFICATIONS
All measurments are given in inches.

Year	VIN	No. Cylinder Displacement cu. in. (liter)	Piston Clearance	Ring Gap			Ring Side Clearance		
				Top Compression	Bottom Compression	Oil Control	Top Compression	Bottom Compression	Oil Control
1982	A	4-140 (2.3)	0.0014–0.0022	0.010–0.020	0.010–0.020	0.015–0.055	0.002–0.004	0.002–0.004	Snug
	3	6-232 (3.8)	0.0014–0.0022	0.010–0.022	0.010–0.022	0.015–0.055	0.002–0.004	0.002–0.004	Snug
	B	6-200 (3.3)	0.0013–0.0021	0.008–0.016	0.008–0.016	0.015–0.055	0.002–0.004	0.002–0.004	Snug
	D	8-255 (4.2)	0.0014–0.0026	0.010	0.010	0.015	0.002	0.002	Snug
	F	8-302 (5.0)	0.0018–0.0026	0.020	0.020	0.055	0.004	0.004	Snug
	G	8-351 (5.8)	0.0022–0.0030	0.020	0.020	0.055	0.004	0.004	Snug
1983	A	4-140 (2.3)	0.0014–0.0022	0.010–0.020	0.010–0.020	0.015–0.055	0.002–0.004	0.002–0.004	Snug
	3	6-232 (3.8)	0.0014–0.0022	0.010–0.022	0.010–0.022	0.015–0.055	0.002–0.004	0.002–0.004	Snug
	X	6-200 (3.3)	0.0013–0.0021	0.008–0.016	0.008–0.016	0.015–0.055	0.002–0.004	0.002–0.004	Snug
	F	8-302 (5.0)	0.0018–0.0026	0.020	0.020	0.055	0.004	0.004	Snug
	G	8-351 (5.8)	0.0022–0.0030	0.020	0.020	0.055	0.004	0.004	Snug
1984	A	4-140 (2.3)	0.0030–0.0038	0.010–0.020	0.010–0.020	0.015–0.055	0.002–0.004	0.002–0.004	Snug
	T	4-140 (2.3)	0.0030–0.0038	0.010–0.020	0.010–0.020	0.015–0.055	0.002–0.004	0.002–0.004	Snug
	W	4-140 (2.3)	0.0030–0.0038	0.010–0.020	0.010–0.020	0.015–0.055	0.002–0.004	0.002–0.004	Snug
	3	6-232 (3.8)	0.0014–0.0032	0.010–0.022	0.010–0.022	0.015–0.055	0.002–0.004	0.002–0.004	Snug
	F	8-302 (5.0)	0.0018–0.0026	0.020	0.020	0.055	0.004	0.004	Snug
	M	8-302 (5.0)	0.0018–0.0026	0.020	0.020	0.055	0.004	0.004	Snug
	G	8-351 (5.8)	0.0022–0.0030–	0.020	0.020	0.055	0.004	0.004	Snug
	L	6-149 (2.4)	①	0.008–0.016	0.008–0.016	0.010–0.020	0.024–0.055	0.002–0.003	0.0012–0.0024
1985	A	4-140 (2.3)	0.0030–0.0038	0.010–0.020	0.010–0.020	0.015–0.055	0.002–0.004	0.002–0.004	Snug
	T	4-140 (2.3)	0.0030–0.0038	0.010–0.020	0.010–0.020	0.015–0.055	0.002–0.004	0.002–0.004	Snug
	W	4-140 (2.3)	0.0030–0.0038	0.010–0.020	0.010–0.020	0.015–0.055	0.002–0.004	0.002–0.004	Snug

PISTON AND RING SPECIFICATIONS
All measurments are given in inches.

Year	VIN	No. Cylinder Displacement cu. in. (liter)	Piston Clearance	Ring Gap			Ring Side Clearance		
				Top Compression	Bottom Compression	Oil Control	Top Compression	Bottom Compression	Oil Control
1985	3	6-232 (3.8)	0.0014–0.0032	0.010–0.022	0.010–0.022	0.015–0.055	0.002–0.004	0.002–0.004	Snug
	F	8-302 (5.0)	0.0018–0.0026	0.020	0.020	0.055	0.004	0.004	Snug
	M	8-302 (5.0)	0.0018–0.0026	0.020	0.020	0.055	0.004	0.004	Snug
	G	8-351 (5.8)	0.0022–0.0030	0.020	0.020	0.055	0.004	0.004	Snug
	L	6-149 (2.4)	①	0.008–0.016	0.008–0.016	0.010–0.020	0.024–0.055	0.002–0.003	0.0012–0.0024
1986	A	4-140 (2.3)	0.0030–0.0038	0.010–0.020	0.010–0.020	0.015–0.055	0.002–0.004	0.002–0.004	Snug
	T	4-140 (2.3)	0.0030–0.0038	0.010–0.020	0.010–0.020	0.015–0.055	0.002–0.004	0.002–0.004	Snug
	W	4-140 (2.3)	0.0030–0.0038	0.010–0.020	0.010–0.020	0.015–0.055	0.002–0.004	0.002–0.004	Snug
	3	6-232 (3.8)	0.0014–0.0032	0.010–0.022	0.010–0.022	0.015–0.055	0.002–0.004	0.002–0.004	Snug
	F	8-302 (5.0)	0.0018–0.0026	0.020	0.020	0.055	0.004	0.004	Snug
	M	8-302 (5.0)	0.0018–0.0026	0.020	0.020	0.055	0.004	0.004	Snug
	G	8-351 (5.8)	0.0022–0.0030	0.020	0.020	0.055	0.004	0.004	Snug
1987	A	4-140 (2.3)	0.0030–0.0038	0.010–0.020	0.010–0.020	0.015–0.055	0.002–0.004	0.002–0.004	Snug
	W	4-140 (2.3)	0.0030–0.0038	0.010–0.020	0.010–0.020	0.015–0.055	0.002–0.004	0.002–0.004	Snug
	3	6-232 (3.8)	0.0014–0.0032	0.010–0.022	0.010–0.022	0.015–0.055	0.002–0.004	0.002–0.004	Snug
	F	8-302 (5.0)	0.0018–0.0026	0.020	0.020	0.055	0.004	0.004	Snug
	E	8-302 (5.0)	0.0018–0.0026	0.020	0.020	0.055	0.004	0.004	Snug
	M	8-302 (5.0)	0.0018–0.0026	0.020	0.020	0.055	0.004	0.004	Snug
	G	8-351 (5.8)	0.0022–0.0030	0.020	0.020	0.055	0.004	0.004	Snug
1988-89	A	4-140 (2.3)	0.0030–0.0038	0.010–0.020	0.010–0.020	0.015–0.055	0.002–0.004	0.002–0.004	Snug
	T	4-140 (2.3)	0.0030–0.0038	0.010–0.020	0.010–0.020	0.015–0.055	0.002–0.004	0.002–0.004	Snug
	4	6-232 (3.8)	0.0014–0.0032	0.010–0.022	0.010–0.022	0.015–0.055	0.002–0.004	0.002–0.004	Snug

PISTON AND RING SPECIFICATIONS
All measurments are given in inches.

Year	VIN	No. Cylinder Displacement cu. in. (liter)	Piston Clearance	Ring Gap			Ring Side Clearance		
				Top Compression	Bottom Compression	Oil Control	Top Compression	Bottom Compression	Oil Control
1988-89	F	8-302 (5.0)	0.0018–0.0026	0.020	0.020	0.055	0.004	0.004	Snug
	E	8-302 (5.0)HO	0.0018–0.0026	0.020	0.020	0.055	0.004	0.004	Snug
	G	8-351 (5.8)	0.0022–0.0030	0.020	0.020	0.055	0.004	0.004	Snug

① Alcan pistons: 0.0010–0.0021
KS pistons: 0.0016–0.0027
Mahle pistons: 0.0018–0.0029

TORQUE SPECIFICATIONS
All readings in ft. lbs.

Year	VIN	No. Cylinder Displacement cu. in. (liter)	Cylinder Head Bolts	Main Bearing Bolts	Rod Bearing Bolts	Crankshaft Pulley Bolts	Flywheel Bolts	Manifold		Spark Plugs
								Intake	Exhaust	
1982	A	4-140 (2.3)	④	⑧	⑨	100–120	54–64	14–21	16–23	5–10
	3	6-232 (3.8)	②	65–81	31–36	85–100	75–85	⑤	15–22	5–11
	B	6-200 (3.3)	70–75	60–70	21–26	85–100	75–85	—	18–24	10–15
	D	8-255 (4.2)	65–72	60–70	19–24	70–90	75–85	18–20①	18–24	10–15
	F	8-302 (5.0)	65–72	60–70	19–24	70–90	75–85	23–25①	18–24	10–15
	G	8-351 (5.8)	105–112	95–105	40–45	70–90	75–85	23–25①	18–24	10–15
1983	A	4-140 (2.3)	④	⑧	⑨	100–120	54–64	14–21③	16–23	5–10
	3	6-232 (3.8)	②	65–81	31–36	85–100	75–85	⑤	15–22	5–11
	B	6-200 (3.3)	70–75	60–70	21–26	85–100	75–85	—	18–24	10–15
	D	8-255 (4.2)	65–72	60–70	19–24	70–90	75–85	18–20①	18–24	10–15
	F	8-302 (5.0)	65–72	60–70	19–24	70–90	75–85	23–25①	18–24	10–15
	G	8-351 (5.8)	105–112	95–105	40–45	70–90	75–85	23–25①	18–24	10–15
1984	A	4-140 (2.3)	④	⑧	⑨	100–120	54–64	14–21③	16–23	5–10
	T	4-140 (2.3)	④	⑧	⑨	100–120	54–64	14–21③	16–23	5–10
	3	6-232 (3.8)	②	65–81	31–36	85–100	75–85	⑤	15–22	5–11
	F	8-305 (5.0)	65–72	60–70	19–24	70–90	75–85	23–25①	18–24	10–15
	G	8-351 (5.8)	105–112	95–105	40–45	70–90	75–85	23–25①	18–24	10–15
	L	6-149 (2.4)	⑥	43–48	⑦	16–17	71–81	14–17	14–17	14–22
1985	A	4-140 (2.3)	④	⑧	⑨	100–120	54–64	14–21③	16–23	5–10
	T	4-140 (2.3)	④	⑧	⑨	100–120	54–64	14–21	16–23	5–10
	3	6-232 (3.8)	②	65–81	31–36	85–100	75–85	⑤	15–22	5–11
	F	8-302 (5.0)	65–72	60–70	19–24	70–90	75–85	23–25①	18–24	10–15
	G	8-351 (5.8)	105–112	95–105	40–45	70–90	75–85	23–25①	18–24	10–15
	L	6-149 (2.4)	⑥	43–48	⑦	16–17	71–81	14–17	14–17	14–22

TORQUE SPECIFICATIONS
All readings in ft. lbs.

Year	VIN	No. Cylinder Displacement cu. in. (liter)	Cylinder Head Bolts	Main Bearing Bolts	Rod Bearing Bolts	Crankshaft Pulley Bolts	Flywheel Bolts	Manifold Intake	Manifold Exhaust	Spark Plugs
1986	A	4-140 (2.3)	④	⑧	⑨	100–120	54–64	14–21③	16-23	5-10
	T	4-140 (2.3)	④	⑧	⑨	100–120	54–64	14–21	16-23	5-10
	3	6-232 (3.8)	②	65–81	31–36	85–100	75–85	⑤	15–22	5–11
	F	8-302 (5.0)	65–72	60–70	19–24	70–90	75–85	23–25①	18–24	10–15
	G	8-351 (5.8)	105–112	95–105	40–45	70–90	75–85	23–25①	18–24	10–15
1987	A	4-140 (2.3)	④	⑧	⑨	103–133	54–64	14–21③	20-30	5-10
	3	6-232 (3.8)	②	65–81	31–36	20–28	54–64	⑤	15–22	5–11
	E	8-302 (5.0)	65–72	60–70	19–24	70–90	75–85	23–25①	18–24	10–15
	F	8-302 (5.0)	65–72	60–70	19–24	70–90	75–85	23–25①	18–24	10–15
	G	8-351 (5.8)	105–112	95–105	40–45	70–90	75–85	23–25①	18–24	10–15
1988-89	A	4-140 (2.3)	④	⑧	⑨	103–133	54–64	14–21③	20-30	5-10
	T	4-140 (2.3)	④	⑧	⑨	103–133	54–64	13–18	20-30	5-10
	4	6-232 (3.8)	②	65–81	31–36	20–28	54–64	⑤	15–22	5–11
	F	8-302 (5.0)	65–72	60–70	19–24	70–90	75–85	23–25①	18–24	10–15
	E	8-302 (5.0)HO	65–72	60–70	19–24	70–90	75–85	23–25①	18–24	10–15
	G	8-351 (5.8)	105–112	95–105	40–45	70–90	75–85	23–25①	18–24	10–15

① Retorque with engine hot
② a. Tighten in 4 steps:
   37 ft. lbs. (50 Nm)
   45 ft. lbs. (60 Nm)
   52 ft. lbs. (70 Nm)
   59 ft. lbs. (80 Nm)
   b. Back-off all bolts 2–3 revolutions
   c. Repeat Step a (above)
③ Turbo: 5–7 ft. lbs., then 13–18 ft. lbs.
④ Tighten in 2 steps: 50–60 ft. lbs. and then 80–90 ft. lbs.
⑤ Tighten in 3 steps:
   7 ft. lbs. (10 Nm)
   15 ft. lbs. (20 Nm)
   24 ft. lbs. (32 Nm)

⑥ Tighten in 3 steps:
   36–43 ft. lbs.
   65–69 ft. lbs.
   90 ft. lbs. plus 5 degrees
⑦ Tighten in 2 steps:
   14 ft. lbs.
   70 degrees
⑧ Tighten in 2 steps: 50–60 ft. lbs. and then 75–85 ft. lbs.
⑨ Tighten in 2 steps: 25–30 ft. lbs. and then 30–36 ft. lbs.

BRAKE SPECIFICATIONS
All measurements in inches unless noted

Year	Model	Lug Nut Torque (ft. lbs.)	Master Cylinder Bore	Brake Disc Minimum Thickness	Brake Disc Maximum Runout	Standard Brake Drum Diameter	Minimum Lining Thickness Front	Minimum Lining Thickness Rear
1982	Fairmont Zephyr	80–105	$\frac{7}{8}$	0.810	0.003	9.00①	0.125	0.030
	Mustang Capri	80–105	$\frac{7}{8}$	0.810	0.003	9.00①	0.125	0.030
	Thunderbird XR-7	80–105	$\frac{7}{8}$	0.810	0.003	9.00①	0.125	0.030
	Cougar Granada	80–105	$\frac{7}{8}$	0.810	0.003	9.00①	0.125	0.030

BRAKE SPECIFICATIONS
All measurements in inches unless noted

Year	Model	Lug Nut Torque (ft. lbs.)	Master Cylinder Bore	Brake Disc		Standard Brake Drum Diameter	Minimum Lining Thickness	
				Minimum Thickness	Maximum Runout		Front	Rear
1982	Crown Victoria, Grand Marquis	80–105	1	0.972	0.003	10.00②	0.125	0.030
	Town Car Mark VI	80–105	1	0.972	0.003	10.00②	0.125	0.030
	Continental	80–105	1	0.972	0.003	10.00②	0.125	0.030
1983	Fairmont Zephyr	80–105	$\frac{7}{8}$	0.810	0.003	9.00①	0.125	0.030
	Mustang Capri	80–105	$\frac{7}{8}$	0.810	0.003	9.00①	0.125	0.030
	Thunderbird Cougar	80–105	$\frac{7}{8}$	0.810	0.003	9.00①	0.125	0.030
	LTD Marquis	80–105	$\frac{7}{8}$	0.810	0.003	9.90①	0.125	0.030
	Crown Victoria, Grand Marquis	80–105	1	0.972	0.003	10.00②	0.125	0.030
	Town Car Mark VI	80–105	1	0.972	0.003	10.00②	0.125	0.030
	Continental	80–105	$1\frac{1}{8}$	0.972③	0.003④	–	0.125	0.125
1984	Mustang Capri	80–105	$\frac{7}{8}$	0.810	0.003	9.00①	0.125	0.030
	Thunderbird Cougar	80–105	$\frac{7}{8}$	0.810	0.003	9.00①	0.125	0.030
	LTD Marquis	80–105	$\frac{7}{8}$	0.810	0.003	9.90①	0.125	0.030
	Crown Victoria, Grand Marquis	80–105	1	0.972	0.003	10.00②	0.125	0.030
	Town Car	80–105	1	0.972	0.003	10.00②	0.125	0.030
	Continental Mark VII	80–105	$1\frac{1}{8}$	0.972③	0.003④	–	0.125	0.125
1985	Mustang Capri	80–105	$\frac{7}{8}$	0.810	0.003	9.00①	0.125	0.030
	Thunderbird Cougar	80–105	$\frac{7}{8}$	0.810	0.003	9.00①	0.125	0.030
	LTD Marquis	80–105	$\frac{7}{8}$	0.810	0.003	9.90①	0.125	0.030
	Crown Victoria, Grand Marquis	80–105	1	0.972	0.003	10.00②	0.125	0.030

BRAKE SPECIFICATIONS
All measurements in inches unless noted

| Year | Model | Lug Nut Torque (ft. lbs.) | Master Cylinder Bore | Brake Disc | | Standard Brake Drum Diameter | Minimum Lining Thickness | |
				Minimum Thickness	Maximum Runout		Front	Rear
1985	Town Car	80–105	1	0.972	0.003	10.00②	0.125	0.030
	Continental Mark VII	80–105	1⅛	0.972③	0.003④	–	0.125	0.125
1986	Mustang Capri	80–105	⅞	0.810	0.003④	9.00①	0.125	0.030
	Thunderbird Cougar	80–105	⅞	0.810	0.003④	9.00①	0.125	0.030
	LTD Marquis	80–105	⅞	0.810	0.003	9.90①	0.125	0.030
	Crown Victoria, Grand Marquis	80–105	1	0.972	0.003	10.00②	0.125	0.030
	Town Car	80–105	1	0.972	0.003	10.00②	0.125	0.030
	Continental Mark VII	80–105	1⅛	0.972③	0.003④	–	0.125	0.125
1987	Mustang	80–105	⅞	.972③	0.003④	9.00①	0.125	0.030⑤
	Thunderbird Cougar	80–105	⅞	.972③	0.003④	9.00①	0.125	0.030⑤
	Crown Victoria, Grand Marquis	80–105	1	0.972	0.003	10.00②	0.125	0.030
	Town Car	80–105	1	0.972	0.003	10.00②	0.125	0.030
	Continental Mark VII	80–105	1⅛	0.972③	0.003④	–	0.125	0.125
1988-89	Mustang	80–105	⅞	.972③	0.003④	9.00①	0.125	0.030⑤
	Thunderbird Cougar	80–105	⅞	.972③	0.003④	9.00①	0.125	0.030⑤
	Crown Victoria, Grand Marquis	80–105	1	0.972	0.003	10.00②	0.125	0.030
	Town Car	80–105	1	0.972	0.003	10.00②	0.125	0.030
	Mark VII	80–105	1⅛	0.972③	0.003④	–	0.125	0.125

① 10.00 optional
② 11.00 optional
③ 0.945 with rear disc brake
④ 0.004 with rear disc brake
⑤ 0.125 with rear disc brake

WHEEL ALIGNMENT

Year	Model	Caster Range (deg.)	Caster Preferred Setting (deg.)	Camber Range (deg.)	Camber Preferred Setting (deg.)	Toe-in (in.)	Steering Axis Inclination (deg.)
1982	Fairmont/Zepher	$\frac{1}{8}$P–1$\frac{7}{8}$P	1P	$\frac{5}{16}$N–1$\frac{3}{16}$P	$\frac{7}{16}$P	$\frac{1}{16}$–$\frac{5}{16}$	15$\frac{1}{4}$
	Mustang/Capri	$\frac{1}{4}$P–1$\frac{3}{4}$P	1P	$\frac{1}{2}$N–1P	$\frac{1}{4}$P	$\frac{1}{16}$–$\frac{5}{16}$	15$\frac{1}{4}$
	Thunderbird XR-7	$\frac{1}{8}$P–1$\frac{7}{8}$P	1P	$\frac{1}{2}$N–1$\frac{1}{4}$P	$\frac{3}{8}$P	$\frac{1}{16}$–$\frac{5}{16}$	15$\frac{1}{3}$
	Cougar/Granada	$\frac{1}{8}$P–1$\frac{7}{8}$P	1P	$\frac{5}{16}$N–1$\frac{3}{16}$	$\frac{7}{16}$P	$\frac{1}{16}$–$\frac{5}{16}$	15$\frac{1}{4}$
	Crown Victoria Grand Marquis	2$\frac{1}{4}$P–3$\frac{3}{4}$P	3P	$\frac{1}{4}$N–1$\frac{1}{4}$P	$\frac{1}{2}$P	$\frac{1}{16}$–$\frac{3}{16}$	10$\frac{31}{32}$
	Town Car Mark VI	2$\frac{1}{4}$P–3$\frac{3}{4}$P	3P	$\frac{1}{4}$N–1$\frac{1}{4}$P	$\frac{1}{2}$P	$\frac{1}{16}$–$\frac{3}{16}$	11
	Continental	1$\frac{3}{8}$P–2$\frac{1}{8}$P	1$\frac{1}{4}$P	$\frac{1}{2}$N–1$\frac{1}{4}$P	$\frac{3}{8}$P	0–$\frac{1}{4}$	—
1983	Fairmont/Zepher	$\frac{1}{8}$P–1$\frac{7}{8}$P	1P	$\frac{5}{16}$N–1$\frac{3}{16}$P	$\frac{7}{16}$P	$\frac{1}{16}$–$\frac{5}{16}$	15$\frac{1}{4}$
	Mustang/Capri	$\frac{1}{2}$P–2P	1$\frac{1}{4}$P	$\frac{3}{4}$N–$\frac{3}{4}$P	0	$\frac{1}{16}$–$\frac{5}{16}$	—
	Thunderbird Cougar	$\frac{1}{2}$P–2	1$\frac{1}{4}$P	$\frac{1}{2}$N–1P	$\frac{1}{4}$P	$\frac{1}{16}$–$\frac{5}{16}$	—
	LTD/Marquis (Sedan)	1$\frac{1}{8}$P–2$\frac{1}{8}$P	1$\frac{5}{8}$P	$\frac{5}{16}$N–1$\frac{3}{16}$	$\frac{7}{16}$P	$\frac{1}{16}$–$\frac{5}{16}$	—
	(Wagon)	$\frac{1}{8}$N–1$\frac{7}{8}$P	$\frac{7}{8}$P	$\frac{1}{4}$N–1$\frac{1}{4}$P	$\frac{1}{2}$P	$\frac{1}{16}$–$\frac{5}{16}$	—
	Crown Victoria Grand Marquis	2$\frac{1}{4}$P–3$\frac{3}{4}$P	3P	$\frac{1}{4}$N–1$\frac{1}{4}$P	$\frac{1}{2}$P	$\frac{1}{16}$–$\frac{3}{16}$	10$\frac{31}{32}$
	Town Car Mark VI	2$\frac{1}{4}$P–3$\frac{3}{4}$P	3P	$\frac{1}{4}$N–1$\frac{1}{4}$P	$\frac{1}{2}$P	$\frac{1}{16}$–$\frac{3}{16}$	11
	Continental	1$\frac{3}{8}$P–2$\frac{1}{8}$P	1$\frac{1}{4}$P	$\frac{1}{2}$N–1$\frac{1}{4}$P	$\frac{3}{8}$P	0–$\frac{1}{4}$	—
1984	Mustang/Capri	$\frac{1}{2}$P–2P	1$\frac{1}{4}$P	$\frac{3}{4}$N–$\frac{3}{4}$P	0	$\frac{1}{16}$–$\frac{5}{16}$	—
	Thunderbird Cougar	$\frac{1}{2}$P–2	1$\frac{1}{4}$P	$\frac{1}{2}$N–1P	$\frac{1}{4}$P	$\frac{1}{16}$–$\frac{5}{16}$	—
	LTD/Marquis (Sedan)	1$\frac{1}{8}$P–2$\frac{1}{8}$P	1$\frac{5}{8}$P	$\frac{5}{16}$N–1$\frac{3}{16}$	$\frac{7}{16}$P	$\frac{1}{16}$–$\frac{5}{16}$	—
	(Wagon)	$\frac{1}{8}$N–1$\frac{7}{8}$P	$\frac{7}{8}$P	$\frac{1}{4}$N–1$\frac{1}{4}$P	$\frac{1}{2}$P	$\frac{1}{16}$–$\frac{5}{16}$	—
	Crown Victoria Grand Marquis	2$\frac{1}{4}$P–3$\frac{3}{4}$P	3P	$\frac{1}{4}$N–1$\frac{1}{4}$P	$\frac{1}{2}$P	$\frac{1}{16}$–$\frac{3}{16}$	10$\frac{31}{32}$
	Town Car	2$\frac{3}{8}$P–4$\frac{1}{8}$P	3$\frac{1}{8}$P	$\frac{1}{4}$N–1$\frac{1}{4}$P	$\frac{1}{2}$P	$\frac{1}{16}$–$\frac{3}{16}$	11
	Continental Mark VII	$\frac{7}{8}$P–2$\frac{15}{16}$P	1$\frac{3}{4}$P	$\frac{7}{8}$N–$\frac{7}{8}$P	0	0–$\frac{1}{4}$	11
1985	Mustang/Capri	$\frac{1}{2}$P–2P	1$\frac{1}{4}$P	$\frac{3}{4}$N–$\frac{3}{4}$P	0	$\frac{1}{16}$–$\frac{5}{16}$	—
	Thunderbird Cougar	$\frac{1}{2}$P–2	1$\frac{1}{4}$P	$\frac{1}{2}$N–1P	$\frac{1}{4}$P	$\frac{1}{16}$–$\frac{5}{16}$	—
	LTD/Marquis (Sedan)	1$\frac{1}{8}$P–2$\frac{1}{8}$P	1$\frac{5}{8}$P	$\frac{5}{16}$N–1$\frac{3}{16}$	$\frac{7}{16}$P	$\frac{1}{16}$–$\frac{5}{16}$	—
	(Wagon)	$\frac{1}{8}$N–1$\frac{7}{8}$P	$\frac{7}{8}$P	$\frac{1}{4}$N–1$\frac{1}{4}$P	$\frac{1}{2}$P	$\frac{1}{16}$–$\frac{5}{16}$	—
	Crown Victoria Grand Marquis	2$\frac{1}{4}$P–3$\frac{3}{4}$P	3P	$\frac{1}{4}$N–1$\frac{1}{4}$P	$\frac{1}{2}$P	$\frac{1}{16}$–$\frac{3}{16}$	10$\frac{31}{32}$
	Town Car	2$\frac{1}{4}$P–4P	3P	$\frac{1}{4}$N–1$\frac{1}{4}$P	$\frac{1}{2}$P	$\frac{1}{16}$–$\frac{3}{16}$	11
	Continental Mark VII	$\frac{5}{8}$P–2$\frac{3}{4}$P	1$\frac{1}{2}$P	$\frac{3}{4}$N–$\frac{3}{4}$P	0	0–$\frac{1}{4}$	11

WHEEL ALIGNMENT

Year	Model	Caster		Camber		Toe-in (in.)	Steering Axis Inclination (deg.)
		Range (deg.)	Preferred Setting (deg.)	Range (deg.)	Preferred Setting (deg.)		
1986	Mustang/Capri	½P–2P	1¼P	¾N–¾P	0	1/16–5/16	—
	Thunderbird Mark VII	½P–2	1¼P	½N–1P	¼P	1/16–5/16	—
	LTD/Marquis (Sedan)	1⅛P–2⅛P	1⅝P	5/16N–1³/16	7/16P	1/16–5/16	—
	(Wagon)	⅛N–1⅞P	⅞P	¼N–1¼P	½P	1/16–5/16	—
	Crown Victoria Grand Marquis	2¼P–3¾P	3P	¼N–1¼P	½P	1/16–3/16	10³¹/32
	Town Car	2¼P–4P	3P	¼N–1¼P	½P	1/16–3/16	11
	Continental Mark VII	⅝P–2¾P	1½P	¾N–¾P	0	0–¼	11
1987	Mustang	½P–2P	1¼P	¾N–¾P	0	1/16–5/16	—
	Thunderbird Cougar	½P–2	1¼P	½N–1P	¼P	1/16–5/16	—
	Crown Victoria Grand Marquis	2¼P–3¾P	3P	¼N–1¼P	½P	1/16–3/16	10³¹/32
	Town Car	2¼P–4P	3P	¼N–1¼P	½P	1/16–3/16	11
	Continental Mark VII	⅝P–2¾P	1½P	¾N–¾P	0	0–¼	11
	Thunderbird Turbo	¹³/32P–1²⁹/32P	1⁵/32P	9/16N–³¹/32P	1⁵/32P	3/16	—
1988-89	Mustang	½P–2P	1¼P	¾N–¾P	0	1/16–5/16	—
	Thunderbird Cougar	½P–2	1¼P	½N–1P	¼P	1/16–5/16	—
	Crown Victoria Grand Marquis	2¼P–3¾P	3P	¼N–1¼P	½P	1/16–3/16	10³¹/32
	Town Car	2¼P–4P	3P	¼N–1¼P	½P	1/16–3/16	11
	Mark VII	⅝P–2¾P	1½P	¾N–¾P	0	0–¼	11
	Thunderbird Turbo	¹³/32P–1²⁹/32P	1⁵/32P	9/16N–³¹/32P	1⁵/32P	3/16	—

P Positive
N Negative

TUNE-UP PROCEDURES

Ignition Timing

ADJUSTMENT

NOTE: Some engines have monolithic timing set at the factory. The monolithic system uses a timing receptacle on the front of the engine which can be connected to digital read-out equipment, which electronically determines timing. Timing can also be adjusted in the conventional way. Initial ignition timing is not adjustable and no attempt at adjustment should be made on EEC III or EEC IV models. Requirements vary from model to model. Always refer to the emissions specification sticker for exact timing procedures. If the specifications shown on the sticker differ from those in the charts in this manual, follow the sticker procedures and specifications as they reflect production changes and calibrations.

1. To check and/or adjust the ignition timing; locate the timing marks and pointer on the crankshaft (lower) pulley and the engine front cover.
2. Clean the marks and apply chalk or bright-colored paint to the pointer and correct timimg scale mark. This will aid in setting the timing correctly.

3. If the vehicle is equipped with a barometric pressure switch (12A243), disconnect it (two wire harness connector) from the ignition module and place a jumper wire across the pins at the ignition module connector (yellow and black wires). On engines equipped with the EEC IV system, disconnect the single wire in line spout connector near the distributor.

4. Attach a timing light and tachometer according to manufacturer's specifications.

5. On non-EEC IV equipped vehicles, disconnect and plug all vacuum lines leading to the distributor.

6. Start the engine, allow it to warm to normal operating temperature, then set the idle to the specifications given on the underhood sticker.

7. Aim the timing light at the timing mark and pointer on the front of the engine. If the timing marks do not align, turn the engine off and loosen the distributor holddown clamp slightly.

8. Start the engine again and observe the alignment of the timing marks. Turn the distributor counterclockwise or clockwise until the marks are aligned. When the timing marks are aligned, turn the engine off and tighten the distributor hold-down clamp. Remove the test equipment, reconnect the vacuum hoses, single wire connector (EEC IV) and the barometric pressure switch (on vehicles so equipped).

Valve Lash

ADJUSTMENT

All Engines Except Diesel

Hydraulic valve lifters are used on these engines. This eliminates the need for periodic valve adjustment. The hydraulic lifters compensate for any minor changes in the valve system. However, if excessive play is evident in the valve train, a thorough inspection of all componenets should be performed.

2.4L Diesel Engine

NOTE: Valve lash adjustment on the 2.4L diesel engine should only be performed with the engine cold.

1. Remove the valve cover.

2. Position the camshaft so that base circle of the lobe of the valve to be adjusted is facing the rocker arm.

3. Loosen the adjusting eccentric locknut using a valve clearance adjusting wrench, Tool T84P-6575-A, or equivalent and a 12mm open end wrench.

4. Rotate the eccentric using a small

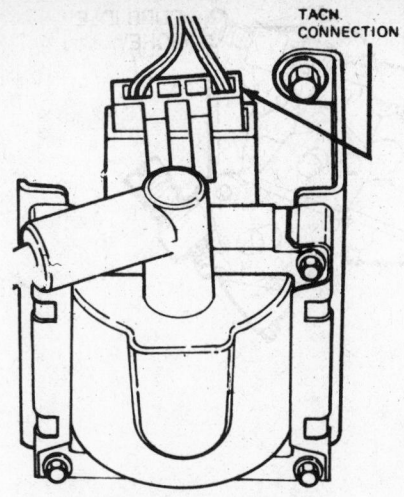
Tach connection, "E" coil

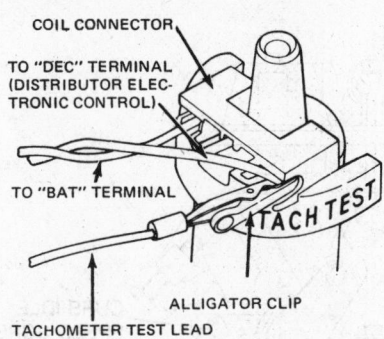
Electronic ignition test tachometer hookup

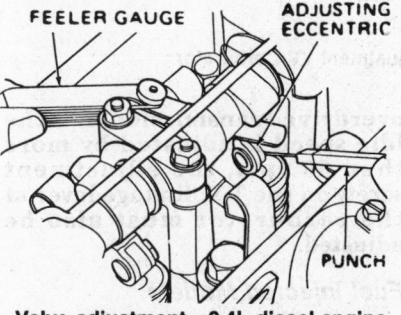
Valve adjustment—2.4L diesel engine

punch until the valve clearance is adjusted to specification: Intake: 0.012 in.; Exhaust: 0.016 in. Tighten the eccentric locknut.

5. Position the camshaft with the base of the lobe towards the valve to be adjusted and adjust the valve clearance. Repeat this procedure for each valve.

6. Install the valve cover.

7. Start the engine and check for oil leaks.

Idle Speed and Mixture Gasoline Engines

NOTE: Vehicles equipped with

EEC-IV, curb idle speed (rpm) is controlled by the EEC-IV processor and the idle speed control device. If the control system is operating properly, these speeds are self compensating and cannot be changed by traditional adjustment techniques.

ADJUSTMENT

Carbureted Models

ALL EXCEPT 7200VV

1. Place the transmission in **PARK**. Apply the emergency brake and block the wheels.

2. Bring the engine to normal operating temperature. Turn off all accessories and connect a tachometer.

3. Disconnect and plug the vacuum hose at the EGR valve. Place the fast idle adjustment on the specified step of the fast idle cam, (Check the underhood sticker). Check/adjust fast idle rpm to specification. Rev engine momentarily, place fast idle adjustment on the specified step and recheck fast idle rpm. Remove plug and reconnect EGR vacuum hose.

4. Place A/C-heat selector in the **OFF** position. Place the transmission in the specified position. Check the curb idle rpm, if adjustment is required loosen TSP/dashpot mounting bracket hold down screw. Adjust the rpm by turning the curb idle adjustment screw. Tighten the mounting bracket holddown screw and recheck the idle speed.

7200VV CARBURETOR

1. Place the transmission in **NEUTRAL** (manual transmission) or **PARK** (automatic transmission). Apply the emergency brake and block the wheels. Bring the engine to normal operating temperature. Disconnect the vacuum hose at the EGR valve and plug.

2. Place the fast idle adjustment on the second step of the fast idle cam. Check the fast idle rpm to verify that it is to specification. Rev the engine momentarily and recheck. Remove the plug from EGR vacuum hose and reconnect.

3. Place the A/C selector in the **OFF** position. Disconnect and plug the vacuum hose at the throttle kicker and place the transmission in the specified position (check the underhood sticker). If adjustment is required turn the curb idle speed screw, clockwise to increase speed and counter-clockwise to decrease speed. Put the transmission in **NEUTRAL**, rev the engine and recheck the idle speed.

4. Apply a slight pressure on the top of the nylon nut located on the acceler-

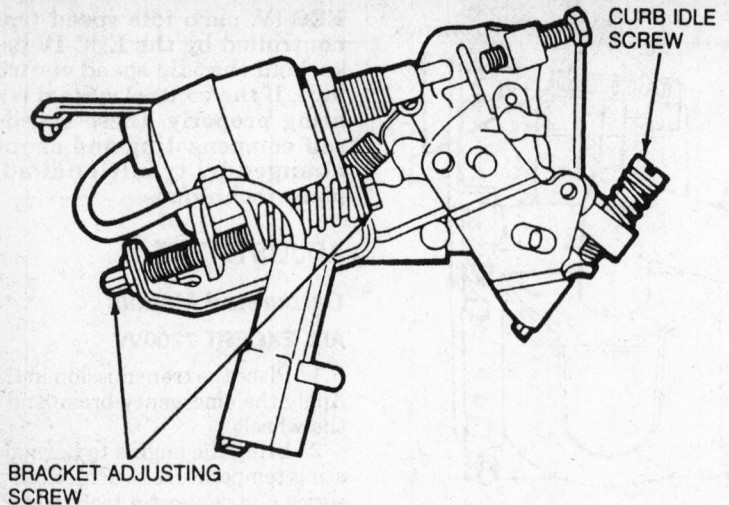

CURB IDLE SCREW

BRACKET ADJUSTING SCREW

Curb idle speed adjustment

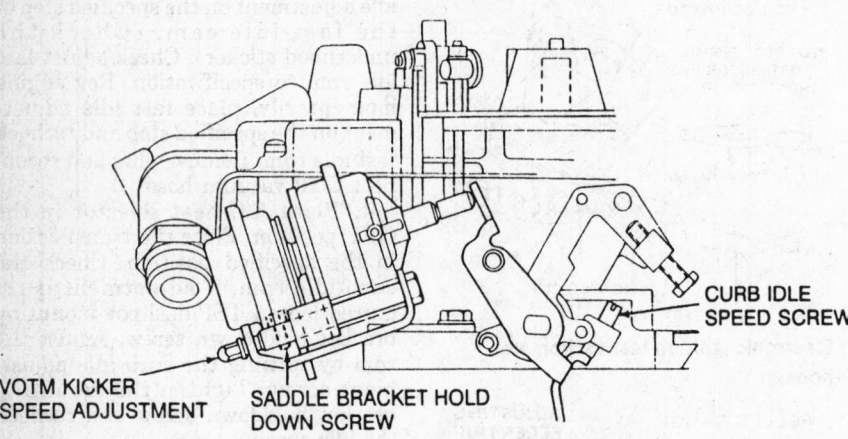

CURB IDLE SPEED SCREW

VOTM KICKER SPEED ADJUSTMENT

SADDLE BRACKET HOLD DOWN SCREW

Idle speed an dashpot adjustment VV Carburetor

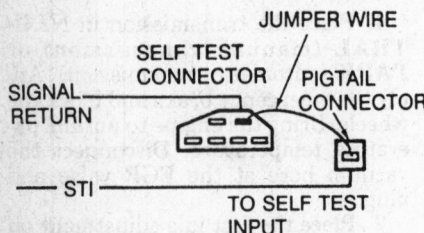

JUMPER WIRE

SELF TEST CONNECTOR

PIGTAIL CONNECTOR

SIGNAL RETURN

STI

TO SELF TEST INPUT

Jumping the self test connector on EEC-IV vehicles

ator pump, to take up the linkage clearance. Turn the nut on the accelerator pump rod clockwise until a clearance of 0.010–0.005 in. is obtained between the top of the accelerator pump and the pump lever.

5. Turn the accelerator pump rod 1 turn counterclockwise to set the lever lash preload.

6. Remove the plug from the throttle kicker vacuum hose and reconnect it.

NOTE: If the vehicle is equipped with Ford's automatic overdrive transmission and the idle speed is adjusted by more than 50 rpm, the adjustment screw on the T.V. linkage lever at the carburetor must also be adjusted.

Fuel Injected Models

2.3L AND 3.8L ENGINES WITH CENTRAL FUEL INJECTION

1. Remove the air cleaner.
2. Locate the self-test connector and self-test input connector in the engine compartment.
3. Connect a jumper wire between the self-test input connector and the signal return pin (the top right terminal) on the self-test connector.
7. Place the ignition key in the **RUN** position and be careful not to start the engine. Wait approxitmately 10–15 seconds until the ISC plunger is fully retracted. Turn the ignition key to the off position and wait an additional 10–15 seconds.
8. Remove the jumper wire from the diagnostic connector and discon-

nect the electrical connector from the ISC motor. Now perform the throttle stop adjustment as follows:

   a. Remove the Central Fuel Injection (CFI) assembly from the vehicle.

   b. Use a small punch or equivalent to punch through and remove the aluminum plug which covers the throttle stop adjusting screw.

   c. Remove the throttle stop screw and install a new one.
9. Reinstall the CFI assembly on the vehicle, start engine and allow to stabilize. Check and adjust the idle speed, to specification, by turning the throttle stop screw. Cover throttle stop screw hole with a new cover.
10. Shut off the engine and reconnect the electrical connnector to the ISC motor. Remove all test equipment and reinstall the air cleaner assembly.

2.3L OHC/TURBO WITH ELECTRONIC FUEL INJECTION

1. Apply the parking brake and block the drive wheels. Place the transmission in **NEUTRAL**.
2. Start the engine and let it run until it reaches normal operating temperature. Once the engine is hot, connect a suitable tachometer.
3. Disconnect the electrical connector to the air bypass valve/idle speed control motor. Start the engine and run it at 1500 rpm for 20 seconds.

NOTE: If the electric cooling fan comes on during the idle speed adjusting procedures, wait for the fan to turn off before proceeding.

4. Let the engine return to idle and check the base idle speed.
5. The idle speed should be 700–800 rpm. If adjustment is necessary, turn the throttle stop adjusting screw to reach the specified rpm.
6. Shut the engine off and reconnect the power lead to the idle speed control air bypass valve. Disconnect all test equipment.

5.0L ENGINES WITH ELECTRONIC FUEL INJECTION

1. Apply the parking brake, block the drive wheels and place the vehicle in **NEUTRAL**.
2. Start the engine and let it run until it reaches normal operating temperature, then turn the engine off. Connect a tachometer to the engine.
3. Turn off all accessories and place the transmission in **PARK** (automatic transmission) or **NEUTRAL** (manual transmission).
4. Run the engine at 1800 rpm for at least 30 seconds.
5. Place the transmission in

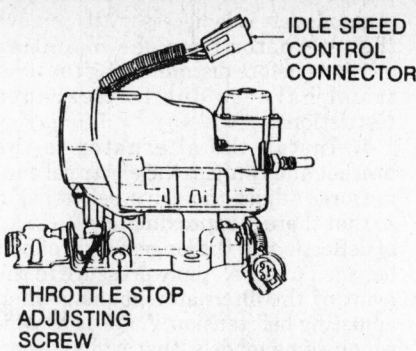

2.3L CFI engine – idle speed adjusting

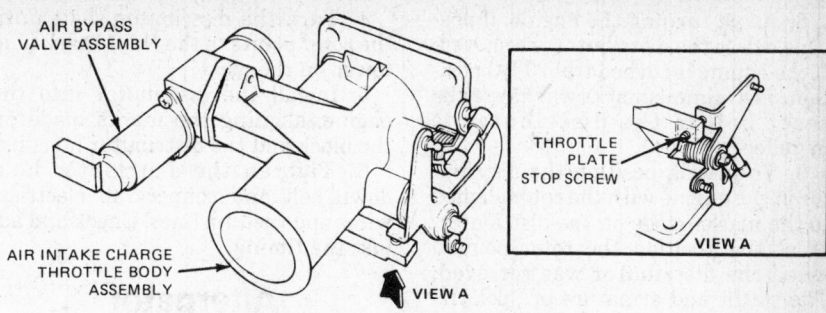

Multi-point injection adjustment

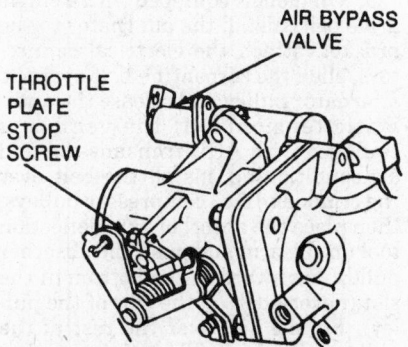

2.3L EFI engine – idle speed adjusting

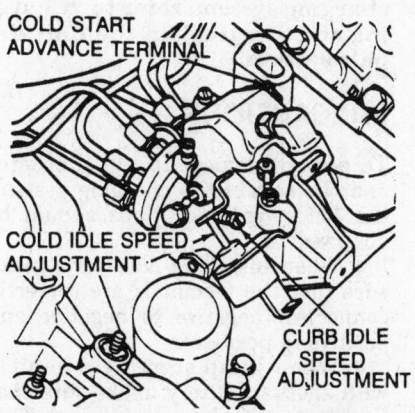

Diesel engine – idle speed adjusting

DRIVE (automatic) or **NEUTRAL** (manual). Check the idle speed.

6. The idle speed specifications should be, 575 ± 20 rpm (base 5.0L A/T), 625 ± 20 rpm (5.0L H.O. A/T), 700 ± 20 rpm (5.0L H.O. M/T).

7. If the idle speed is not within specifications adjust it by turning the throttle plate stop screw.

8. After the correct rpm is reached, turn the throttle plate stop screw out an additional 1 turn to bring the ISC motor into its operating range.

9. Shut off the engine and remove all test equipment.

Idle Speed Diesel Engine

ADJUSTMENT

1. Place the transmission in **NEUTRAL** and apply the parking brake.

2. Bring the engine up to normal operating temperature. Stop the engine.

NOTE: Idle speed is measured with manual transmission in neutral.

3. Remove the timing hole cover. Clean the flywheel surface and install reflective tape.

4. Check the curb idle speed using Rotunda 099–00001 or equvalent. Curb idle speed is specified on the Vehicle Emissions Control Information (VECI) decal. Adjust the engine to specification by loosening the lock nut on the idle speed bolt. Turn the idle speed adjusting bolt clockwise to increase, or counterclockwise to decrease engine idle speed. Tighten the lock nut.

5. Place the transmission in **NEUTRAL**. Rev the engine momentarily and recheck the curb idle rpm. Readjust if necessary.

6. Turn A/C **ON**. Check the idle speed. Adjust to specification by loosening the nut on the A/C throttle kicker and rotating the screw.

ENGINE ELECTRICAL

Distributor

REMOVAL & INSTALLATION

1. Remove the air cleaner on V6 and V8 engines. On 4 and 6 cylinder in-line engines, removal of a thermactor (air) pump mounting bolt and drive belt will allow the pump to be moved to the side and permit access to the distributor. If necessary, disconnect the thermactor air filter and lines as well.

2. Remove the distributor cap and position the cap and ignition wires to the side.

3. Disconnect the wiring harness plug from the distributor connector. Disconnect and plug the vacuum hoses from the vacuum diaphragm assembly (if equipped).

4. Rotate the engine (in normal direction of rotation) until No. 1 piston is on TDC (Top Dead Center) of the compression stroke. The TDC mark on the crankshaft pulley and the pointer should align. Rotor tip pointing at the No. 1 spark plug wire position on the distributor cap.

5. On DuraSpark I or II equipped engines, turn the engine slightly past the No. 1 spark plug position to align the stator (pick-up coil) assembly pole with an armature pole (the closest one). On DuraSpark III, the distributor sleeve groove (when looking down from the top) and the cap adaptor alignment slot should align. On models equipped with EEC IV (1984–89), remove the rotor (2 screws) and note the position of the "polarizing square" and shaft plate for reinstallation reference.

6. Scribe a mark on the distributor body and the engine block to indicate the position of the rotor tip and the position of the distributor in the engine. DuraSpark III and some EEC IV system distributors are equipped with a notched base and will only locate at one position on the engine.

7. Remove the holddown bolt and clamp located at the base of the distributor. Some DuraSpark III and EEC IV system distributors are equipped with a special holddown bolt that requires a Torx head wrench for removal. Remove the distributor from the engine. Pay attention to the direction the rotor tip points if it moves from the No. 1 position when the drive gear disengages. For reinstallation purposes, the rotor should be at this point to insure proper gear mesh and timing.

8. Avoid turning the engine, if possible, while the distributor is removed. If the engine is turned from TDC position, TDC timing marks will have to be reset before the distributor is installed.

9. To install, position the distributor in the engine with the rotor aligned to the marks made on the distributor, or at the position the rotor pointed when the distributor was removed. The stator and armature or "polarizing square" and shaft plate should also be aligned. Engage the oil pump intermediate shaft and insert the distributor until fully seated on the engine, if the distributor does not fully seat, turn the engine slightly to fully engage the intermediate shaft.

10. On models equipped with an indexed distributor base, make sure when positioning the distributor that the slot in the distributor base will engage the block tab and the sleeve/adaptor slots are aligned.

11. After the distributor has been fully seated onto he block, recheck the timing mark and rotor alignment. Install the holddown bracket and bolt. On models equipped with an indexed base, tighten the mounting bolt. On other models, snug the mounting bolt so the distributor can be turned for ignition timing purposes.

12. On 4 and 6 cylinder models reinstall the thermactor pump belt and adjust the tension. On V6 and V8 models install the air cleaner assembly. Connect all electrical and vacuum leads. Check and reset the ignition timing.

NOTE: A silicone compound is used on rotor tips, distributor cap contacts and on the inside of the connectors on the spark plugs cable and module couplers. Always apply Silicone Dielectric Compound after servicing any component of the ignition system. Various models use a multi-point rotor which does not require the application of the dielectric compound.

DISTRIBUTOR INSTALLATION— ENGINE CRANKED

If the engine was cranked with the distributor removed, it will have to be put into its compression stroke with the No. 1 cylinder at TDC. The following procedure will enable the proper setting of the timing.

1. Remove the No. 1 spark plug.
2. Place a finger over the spark plug hole and crank the engine slowly untl compressin is felt.
3. align the timing mark on the crankshaft pulley with the **0** degree mark on the timing scale. This places the No. 1 cylinder at the TDC of its compression stroke.

4. Turn the distributor shaft until the rotor points to the No. 1 spark plug tower on the cap.
5. Install the distributor into the engine, aligning the marks made on the block and the distributor housing.
6. Tighten the distributor hold down bolt and connect all electrical wires and vacuum lines. **Check and adjust the timing.**

Alternator

For further information on the charging system, refer to "Charging and Starting" in the Unit Repair section.

PRECAUTIONS

To prevent damage to the alternator and the rest of the charging system, the following precautions should be observed:

• When installing a battery, make sure that the terminals are correctly connected (negative to negative and positive to positive).
• When jump starting a vehicle with another battery, make sure that the like terminals are connected. This also applies when using a battery charger.
• Never operate the alternator with the battery disconnected or on an uncontrolled open circuit. Double-check to see that all connections are tight.
• Do not short across or ground any alternator or regulator terminals.
• Do not apply full battery voltage to the field connector.
• Always disconnect the negative battery terminal before disconnecting the alternator.

REMOVAL, INSTALLATION AND BELT TENSION ADJUSTMENT

1. Disconnect the negative battery ground cable.
2. Loosen the adjustment tensioner bolt (if equipped) and (or) the alternator slotted adjustment and mounting bolt. Remove the drive belt(s). Models equipped with a single drive belt (serpentine): lever the tensioner away from the belt and remove belt from alternator pulley.

NOTE: Various models are equipped with a 5-rib or 6-rib K-section (V-ribbed) belt and an automatic absorber tensioner, these belts do not need adjustment.

3. Disconnect the electrical harness connectors from the alternator. Remove the adjustment and mounting bolts and remove the alternator. On

some models it is necessary to remove the alternator from the mounting brackets before disconnecting the electrical harness due to clearance restrictions.

4. Install the alternator to the bracket and connect the electrical connectors. Adjust the drive belt tension so that there is approximately 1/4–1/2 in. of deflection on the longest span of belt between pulleys. Apply pressure to the front of the alternator housing when adjusting belt tension. A flat is provided, on some models, that will allow an open end wrench to be used for applying tension to the belt.

5. On models equipped with a single drive belt, install the alternator to the bracket, attach the electrical connectors, slide the serpentine belt over the alternator pulley and release the automatic tensioner. If the vehicle is equipped with AOD transmission and air conditioning, install the belt over the crank and A/C compressor pulleys, then place the absorber arm deflection tool on the arm and push the absorber pulley downward to the bottom of the slot (never push on the ribs of the pulley). Fit the belt over the rest of the pulleys. While holding the absorber pulley down, adjust the idler pulley by hand until it is snug and tighten the adjustment bolt and pivot bolt on the idler pulley assembly. Release the deflection tool; the proper tension will be set automatically.

Voltage Regulator

REMOVAL & INSTALLATION

1. Disconnect the negative battery cable.
2. Disconnect the wire harness connector. Remove the mounting screws and the regulator.
3. Mount the regulator in position and tighten the attaching screws. If equipped with a radio suppression capacitor, mount the capacitor in position.
4. Connect the wiring harness. Connect the negative battery cable.

For removal and installation procedures of integral voltage regulators, please refer to "Charging and Starting" in the Unit Repair Section.

Starter

For further information on the starter system, refer to "Charging and Starting" in the Unit Repair Section.

REMOVAL & INSTALLATION
Gasoline Engines

1. Disconnect the negative battery cable.

2. Raise the vehicle and support it safely.

3. Disconnect the starter cable from the starter.

NOTE: If clearance is a problem, it may be necessary to remove an engine mount and raise the engine.

4. On some models with the 5.0L engine it may be necessary to remove the right engine mount and raise the engine. On some models with the 3.8L engine it may be necessary to remove the wish-bone brace. Mustang, remove the crossmember from under the bell housing and remove the steering gear assembly from the side rail. On Thunderbirds/Cougars, LTDs/Marquis and 1982–87 Continentals remove the cross brace.

5. Disconnect and tag the electrical wiring. Remove the starter housing bolts and crossmember from under the engine. Remove the heat shield, if equipped.

6. Manipulate the starter so that it can be lowered through the steering linkage. On some engine/chassis combinations, this can be accomplished by turning the front wheels either right or left, or by removing the idler arm bracket attaching bolts and lowering the steering linkage away from the engine.

7. Install the starter by sliding it into position on the block, tighten the mounting bolts to 15–20 ft. lbs. Reconnect the electrical leads.

Diesel Engine

1. Disconnect the battery ground (negative) cable.

2. Remove the bolt holding the dipstick tube to the intake manifold.

3. Remove the wires from the starter solenoid. Remove the front starter support bracket.

4. Remove the 2 starter to torque converter housing mounting bolts.

5. Pull the dipstick tube outward slightly allowing clearance for starter motor removal. Remove the starter motor.

6. Position the starter to torque converter housing and install the 2 bolts. Tighten to 30–40 ft. lbs.

7. Install the starter support bracket and tighten the attaching bolts to 14–20 ft. lbs.

8. Connect the cables to the starter solenoid. Tighten the red wire to 80–120 inch lbs. Tighten the black wire to 25 inch lbs.

9. Reposition the dipstick to the intake manifold, install the bolt and tighten to 6–7 ft. lbs.

10. Install the battery ground cable.

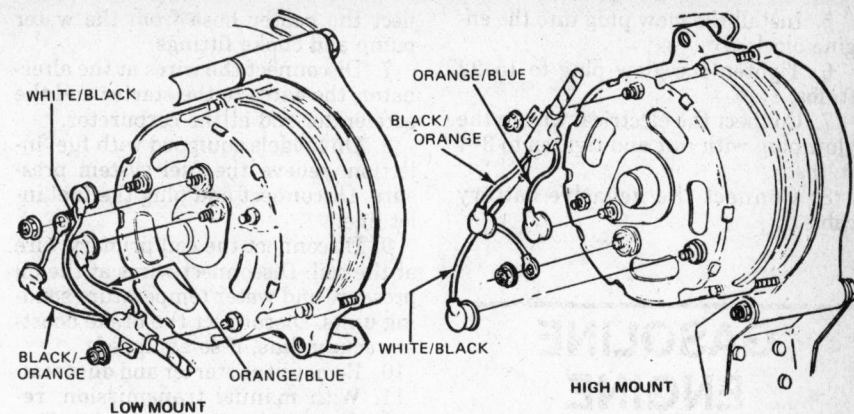

Typical connector details for the rear terminal alternator

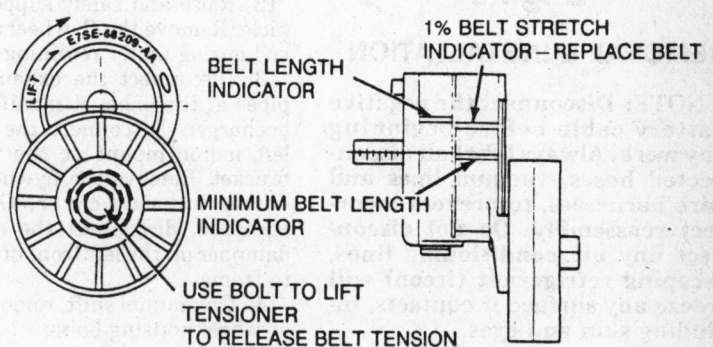

2.3L belt tension indicator—automatic tensioner

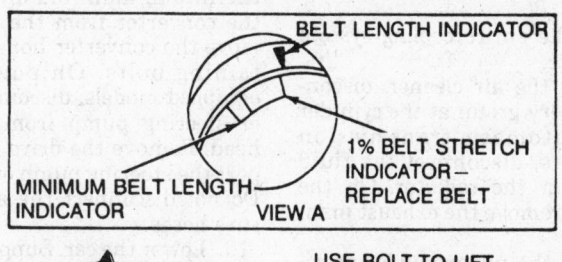

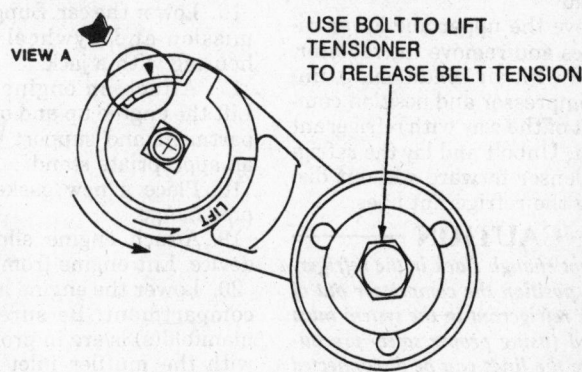

3.8L and 5.0L belt tensioner

Diesel Glow Plugs

REMOVAL & INSTALLATION

1. Disconnect the negative battery cable.

2. Unscrew the glow plug electrical connector and remove the wire.

3. Remove the glow plug using a 12mm deepwell socket.

4. Coat the glow plug threads with a copper based, anti-sieze compound.

5. Install the glow plug into the engine block.

6. Tighten the glow plug to 15–22 ft. lbs.

7. Connect the electrical wire to the glow plug with nut and tighten to 3–4 ft. lbs.

8. Connect the negative battery cable.

GASOLINE ENGINE MECHANICAL

Engine

REMOVAL & INSTALLATION

NOTE: **Disconnect the negative battery cable before beginning any work. Always label all disconnected hoses, vacuum lines and wire harnesses, to prevent incorrect reassembly. Do not disconnect any air conditioning lines, escaping refrigerant (freon) will freeze any surface it contacts, including skin and eyes.**

1. Mark the relationship of the hood to the hinges. Disconnect the hood and remove it.

2. Drain the entire cooling system and crankcase.

3. Remove the air cleaner, disconnect the battery groun at the cylinder head. On automatic transmission equipped cars, disconnect the fluid cooler lines at the radiator. On the 2.3L engine, remove the exhaust manifold shroud.

4. Remove the upper and lower radiator hoses and remove the radiator. If equipped with air conditioning, unbolt the compressor and position compressor out of the way with refrigerant lines intact. Unbolt and lay the refrigerant condenser forward without disconnecting the refrigerant lines.

—————— CAUTION ——————

If there is not enough slack in the refrigerant lines to position the compressor out of the way, the refrigerant in the system must be evacuated (using proper safety precautions) before the lines can be disconnected from the compressor.

5. Remove the fan, fan belt and upper pulley. On models equipped with an electric cooling fan, disconnect the power lead and remove the fan and shroud as an assembly.

6. Disconnect the heater hoses from the engine. On 2.3L engines, disconnect the heater hose from the water pump and choke fittings.

7. Disconnect the wires at the alternator, the wires to the starter and the accelerator rod at the carburetor.

8. On models equipped with fuel injection, relieve the fuel system pressure. Disconnect and plug the fuel inlet line.

9. Disconnect the coil primary wire at the coil. Disconnect wires at the oil pressure and water temperature sending units. Disconnect the brake booster vacuum line, if so equipped.

10. Remove the starter and dust seal.

11. With manual transmission, remove the clutch retracting spring. Disconnect the clutch equalizer shaft and arm bracket at the underbody rail and remove the arm bracket and equalizer shaft.

12. Raise and safely support the vehicle. Remove the flywheel or converter housing upper retaining bolts.

13. Disconnect the exhaust pipe or pipes at the exhaust manifold or turbocharger. Disconnect the right and left motor mount at the underbody bracket. Remove the flywheel or converter housing cover. On models equipped, disconnect the engine roll dampner on the left front of the engine to frame.

14. On manual shift, remove the lower wheel housing bolts.

15. On automatic transmission, disconnect throttle valve vacuum line at the intake manifold and disconnect the converter from the flywheel. Remove the converter housing lower retaining bolts. On power steering equipped models, disconnect the power steering pump from the cylinder head. Remove the drive belt and support the steering pump out of the way. Do not disconnect the steering pressure hoses.

16. Lower the car. Support the transmission and flywheel or converter housing with a jack.

17. Attach an engine lifting hook. Lift the engine up and out of the compartment and support the engine on an appropriate stand.

18. Place a new gasket on exhaust pipe flange.

19. Attach engine sling and lifting device. Lift engine from workstand.

20. Lower the engine into the engine compartment. Be sure the exhaust manifold(s) is/are in proper alignment with the muffler inlet pipe(s). Align the dowels in the block with the holes in the flywheel housing. On vehicles equipped with an automatic transmission, start the converter pilot into the crankshaft make sure the converter studs align with the flexplate holes. On vehicles equipped with manual transmissions, start the transmission main drive gear into the clutch disc. If

the engine hangs up after the shaft enters, rotate the crankshaft slowly (with transmission in gear) until the shaft and clutch disc splines mesh. Rotate 4 cylinder engines clockwise only (when viewed from the front).

21. Install the flywheel or converter housing upper bolts, torque to 28–38 ft. lbs.

22. Install the engine support insulator to bracket retaining nuts, tighten to 33 ft. lbs. Disconnect the engine lifting sling and remove lifting brackets.

23. Raise the front of car and safely support. Connect the exhaust pipes to the manifold, tighten to 16–24 ft. lbs.

24. Install the starter, tighten the starter mounting bolts to 15–20 ft. lbs.

25. On vehicles equipped with manual transmissions, install the remaining fywheel housing to engine bolts. Connect the clutch release rod. Position the clutch equalizer bar and bracket and install retaining bolts. Install the clutch pedal retracting spring.

26. On vehicles equipped with automatic transmissions, remove the retainer holding the converter in the housing. Attach the converter to the flywheel, tighten the bolts to 20–34 ft. lbs. Install the converter housing inspection cover, tighten the bolts to 12–16 ft. lbs. and the remaining converter housing retaining bolts.

27. Remove the support from the transmission and lower the car.

28. Connect the engine ground strap and coil primary wire.

29. Connect the water temperature gauge wire and the heater hose at coolant outlet housing. Connect the accelerator rod at the bellcrank.

30. On vehicles equipped with automatic transmissions, connect the transmission filler tube bracket. Connect the throttle valve vacuum line.

31. On vehicles with power steering, install the drive belt and power steering pump bracket. Install the bracket retaining bolts and adjust the drive belt tension.

32. Remove the plug from the fuel tank line. Connect the flexible fuel line and the oil pressure sending unit wire.

33. Install the water pump pulley anf fan assembly. Adjust belt tension.

34. Tighten the alternator adjusting bolts. Connect the wires and the battery ground cable. On 4 cylinder engines, install the exhaust manifold shroud.

35. Install the radiator. Connect the radiator hoses. On air conditioned cars, install the compressor and condensor. On vehicles equipped with electric cooling fans, install the fan and shroud assembly.

36. On automatic transmission, connect fluid cooler lines. On cars with power brakes, connect the brake booster line.

37. Install the oil filter. Connect the heater hose at the water pump and carburetor choke (4 cyl).

38. Bring the crankcase to the full level with engine oil. Run the engine at fast idle and check for leaks. Install the air cleaner and make any final engine adjustments.

39. Install and adjust the hood.

3.3L cylinder head bolt torque sequence

Cylinder Head

REMOVAL & INSTALLATION

NOTE: The engine should be "overnight" cold before removing the cylinder head(s), to prevent warpage or distortion. Always label all disconnected hoses and wires to assure proper assembly.

2.3L Engines

1. Drain the cooling system.
2. Remove the air cleaner and the valve rocker cover. On turbo equipped models remove the inlet tube between the turbocharger and the throttle body.
3. Remove the intake and exhaust manifolds. The intake manifold, installed valves and sensors (if equipped) and carburetor can be removed as an assembly.
4. Remove the camshaft drive belt cover.
5. Loosen the drive belt tensioner and remove the drive belt.
6. Remove the water outlet from the cylinder head.
7. Remove the cylinder head bolts evenly and remove the cylinder head.
8. Position a new cylinder head gasket on the block. Rotate the camshaft so that the locating pin is at the 5 o'clock position, to avoid valve damage.
9. Position the cylinder head on the block. Install the bolts finger tight and torque in sequence, to specifications in 2 stages.

NOTE: If difficulty in positioning the head on the block is encountered, guide pins may be fabricated by cutting the heads off 2 extra cylinder head bolts.

10. Set the crankshaft at TDC and be sure that the camshaft drive gear and distributor are positioned correctly.
11. Install the camshaft drive belt and release the tensioner. Rotate the crankshaft 2 full turns clockwise (facing the engine) to remove all slack from the belt. The timing marks should again be aligned. Tighten the tensioner lockbolt and pivot bolts.
12. Install the camshaft drive belt cover.

2.3L Head bolt tightening sequence

13. Apply sealer to the water outlet and new gasket and install.
14. Install the intake and exhaust manifolds.
15. Adjust the valve clearance.
16. Install a new valve cover gasket and install the valve cover.
17. Install the air cleaner and crankcase ventilation hose. On turbo models install the inlet tube between the turbocharger and the throttle body.
18. Refill the cooling system. Run the engine and check for leaks.

3.3L Engine

1. Drain the cooling system, remove the air cleaner and disconnect the battery ground cable at the cylinder head.
2. Disconnect the exhaust pipe at the manifold end, swing the exhaust pipe down and remove the flange gasket.
3. Disconnect the fuel and vacuum lines from the carburetor. Disconnect the intake manifold line at the intake manifold.
4. Disconnect the accelerator linkage and retracting spring at the carburetor. Disconnect the transmission kick-down linkage, if equipped.
5. Disconnect the carburetor spacer outlet line at the spacer. Disconnect the radiator upper hose and the heater hose at the water outlet elbow. Disconnect the radiator lower hose and the heater hose at the water pump.
6. Disconnect the distributor vacuum control line(s) at the distributor. Disconnect the gas filter line on the inlet side of the filter.
7. Disconnect and label the spark plug wires and remove the plugs. Disconnect the temperature sending unit wire.
8. Remove the rocker arm cover.
9. Loosen the rocker arm shaft attaching bolts and remove the rocker arm and shaft assembly. Remove the

valve pushrods, in order, for installation in their original positions.
10. Remove 1 cylinder head bolt from each end of the head (at opposite corners) and install cylinder head guide studs for lifting the head. Remove the remaining cylinder head bolts and lift off the cylinder head. Do not pry under the cylinder head as damage to the mating surfaces can easily occur.

NOTE: To help in removal and installation of cylinder head, two 6 in. $^7/_{16}$ x 14 bolts with heads cut off, will reduce the possibility of damage during head replacement.

11. Clean the cylinder head and block surfaces. Check for warpage and surface damage.
12. Apply cylinder head gasket sealer to both sides of the new gasket and slide the gasket down over the 2 guide studs in the cylinder block.

NOTE: Apply gasket sealer only to steel shim head gaskets. Steel/asbestos composite head gaskets are to be installed without any sealer.

13. Carefully lower the cylinder head over the guide studs. Place the exhaust pipe flange on the manifold studs (new gasket).
14. Coat the threads of the end bolts for the right side of the cylinder head with a small amount of water-resistant sealer. Install, but do not tighten, 2 head bolts at opposite ends to hold the head gasket in place. Remove the guide studs and install the remaining bolts.
15. Cylinder head torquing should proceed in 3 steps and in prescribed order. Tighten to 55 ft. lbs., then tighten to 65 ft. lbs. The final step is to 75 ft. lbs., at which they should remain undisturbed.
16. Lubricate both ends of the pushrods and install them in their original locations.
17. Apply lubricant to the rocker arm pads and the valve stem tips and position the rocker arm shaft assembly on the head. Be sure the oil holes in the shaft are in a down position.
18. Tighten all the rocker shaft retaining bolts to 30–35 ft. lbs. Start

tightening in the middle and work evenly end to end.

19. Hook up the exhaust pipe.
20. Reconnect the heater and radiator hoses.
21. Connect the distributor vacuum line, the carburetor gas line and the intake manifold vacuum line on the engine.
22. Connect the accelerator rod and retracting spring. Connect the choke wire. Connect the transmission kickdown linkage.
23. Lightly lubricate the spark plug threads and install them. Connect spark plug wires and be sure the wires are all the way down in their sockets. Connect the temperature sending unit wire. Connect the negative battery cable.
24. Coat a side of the new rocker cover gasket with oil-resistant sealer. Lay the treated side of the gasket on the cover and install the cover. Be sure the gasket seals evenly all around the cylinder head.
25. Fill the cooling system. Install the PCV system and air cleaner. Start the engine and check for leaks.

3.8L, 4.2L/5.0L and 5.8L Engines

1. Disconnect the negative battery cable.
2. Remove the valve covers. Remove the intake manifold and carburetor assembly. On port fuel injected models, remove the upper intake manifold and throttle body as an assembly. Remove the lower intake manifold.
3. On cars equipped with air conditioning, remove the compressor from the engine and position it aside, without disconnecting the refrigerant lines.
4. If removing the left cylinder head, on cars equipped with power steering, remove the pump, bracket and drive belt and position to one side without disconnecting the lines. On cars with Thermactor emission control system, disconnect the hose from the air manifold on the left cylinder head.
5. If removing the right cylinder head, remove the alternator mounting bracket bolt and spacer, ignition coil and air cleaner inlet duct. On cars equipped with Thermactor emission control, remove the air pump and bracket. Disconnect the hose from the right cylinder head.
6. Disconnect the exhaust pipe(s) from the exhaust manifold.
7. Loosen the rocker arm stud nuts or bridge bolts so that the arms can be rotated to the side to clear the pushrods. Remove the pushrods. Keep them in order for installation in their original positions.
8. Remove the cylinder head bolts and lift off the cylinder head. On some

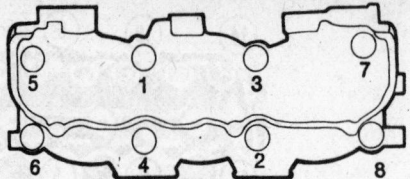

V6 cylinder head bolt torque sequence

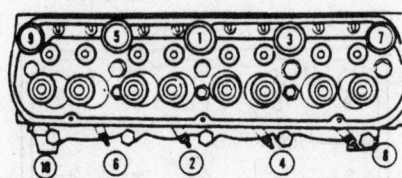

5.0L and 5.8L cylinder head bolt torque sequence

5.8L engines, it may be necessary to remove the exhaust manifold to gain access to the lower cylinder head bolts.

9. To install, reverse the removal procedure. Tighten all head bolts in sequence and to the specified torque. Run engine and check for fluid leaks.

OVERHAUL

For all cylinder head overhaul procedures, refer to "Engine Rebuilding" in the Unit Repair section.

Rocker Arms/Shafts

REMOVAL & INSTALLATION

2.3L Engines

CAMSHAFT FOLLOWER

1. Remove the valve cover and associated parts as required.
2. Rotate the camshaft so that the base circle of the cam is against the cam follower you intend to remove.
3. Remove the retaining spring from the cam follower, if so equipped.
4. Using a valve spring compressor tool, collapse the lash adjuster and/or depress the valve spring, as necessary and slide the cam follower over the lash adjuster and out from under the camshaft.
5. Install the cam follower in the reverse order of removal. Make sure that the lash adjuster is collapsed and released before rotating the camshaft.

3.3L Engine

1. Remove the air cleaner and PCV line. Remove the accelerator control cable bracket.
2. Remove the rocker arm cover and gasket.
3. Remove the rocker shaft bolts, 2 turns at a time each, working from the ends toward the center.
4. Lift off the rocker shaft assem-

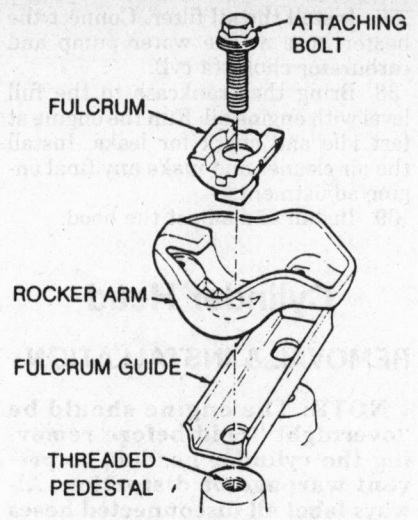

V8 rocker arm assembly

bly. Keep the pushrods in order, if removed, for installation in their original positions.
5. Installation is the revers of removal. Torque the rocker shaft bolts, 2 turns at a time, working from the center toward the ends, to 30–35 ft. lbs.

3.8L, 4.2L/5.0L and 5.8L Engines

1. Right side: Disconnect the automatic choke heat chamber air inlet hose. Remove the air cleaner and duct. Remove the automatic choke heat tube (3.8L and 5.0L). Remove the PCV fresh air tube from the rocker cover and disconnect the EGR vacuum amplifier hoses.
2. Remove the Thermactor by-pass valve and air supply hoses.
3. Disconnect the spark plug wires.
4. On the left side: Remove the wiring harness from the clips. Remove the rocker arm cover.
5. Remove the rocker arm stud nut or bolt, fulcrum seat and rocker arm.
6. Lubricate all parts with heavy SE oil before installation. When installing, rotate the crankshaft until the lifter is on the base of the cam circle (low point, no lift) and assemble the rocker arm. Torque the nut or bolt to 17–23 ft. lbs.

NOTE: Some later engines are using RTV sealant instead of valve cover gaskets. Always apply an even ⅛ in. bead of sealant along the channel of the valve cover after cleaning.

Intake Manifold
REMOVAL & INSTALLATION

2.3L Engine with Carburetor

1. Drain the cooling system and remove the air cleaner.

2. Disconnect the accelerator cable.

3. Disconnect and label the vacuum hoses at the carburetor.

4. Remove the engine oil dipstick.

5. Disconnect the heat tube at the EGR valve.

6. Disconnect and plug the fuel line at the carburetor.

7. Remove the bolt attaching the dipstick to the manifold.

8. Remove the PCV valve from the manifold.

9. Remove the 2 distributor cap screws and the distributor cap.

10. Remove the intake manifold attaching bolts and remove the manifold.

11. Clean all dirt and gasket material from the surfaces on the cylinder head and intake manifold.

12. Position a new gasket and the manifold on the studs. Torque the bolts and nuts to the specified torque in 2 stages.

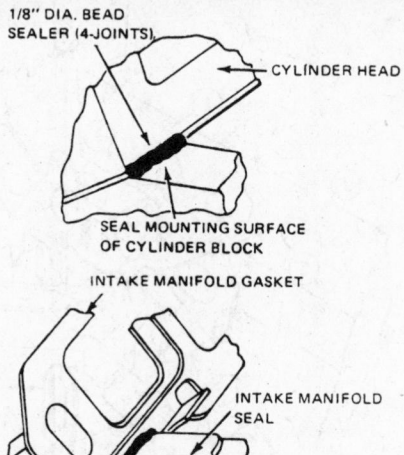

Intake manifold sealer application

13. Connect the crankcase ventilation hose to the manifold. Connect the heater hoses to the choke cover and manifold, if equipped.

14. Replace the heat tube, accelerator cable and dipstick assembly.

15. Connect the distributor vacuum lines to the manifold.

16. Connect the fuel line to the carburetor.

17. Install the air cleaner assembly. Fill the cooling system, if draine and check for leaks.

2.3L Engine with Fuel Injection

1. Disconnect the negative battery cable. Disconnect and label the electrical connectors at:

   a. the air bypass valve

   b. the throttle positioning sensor

   c. injector wiring harness

   d. knock sensor

   e. fan temperature sensor and coolant temperature sensor

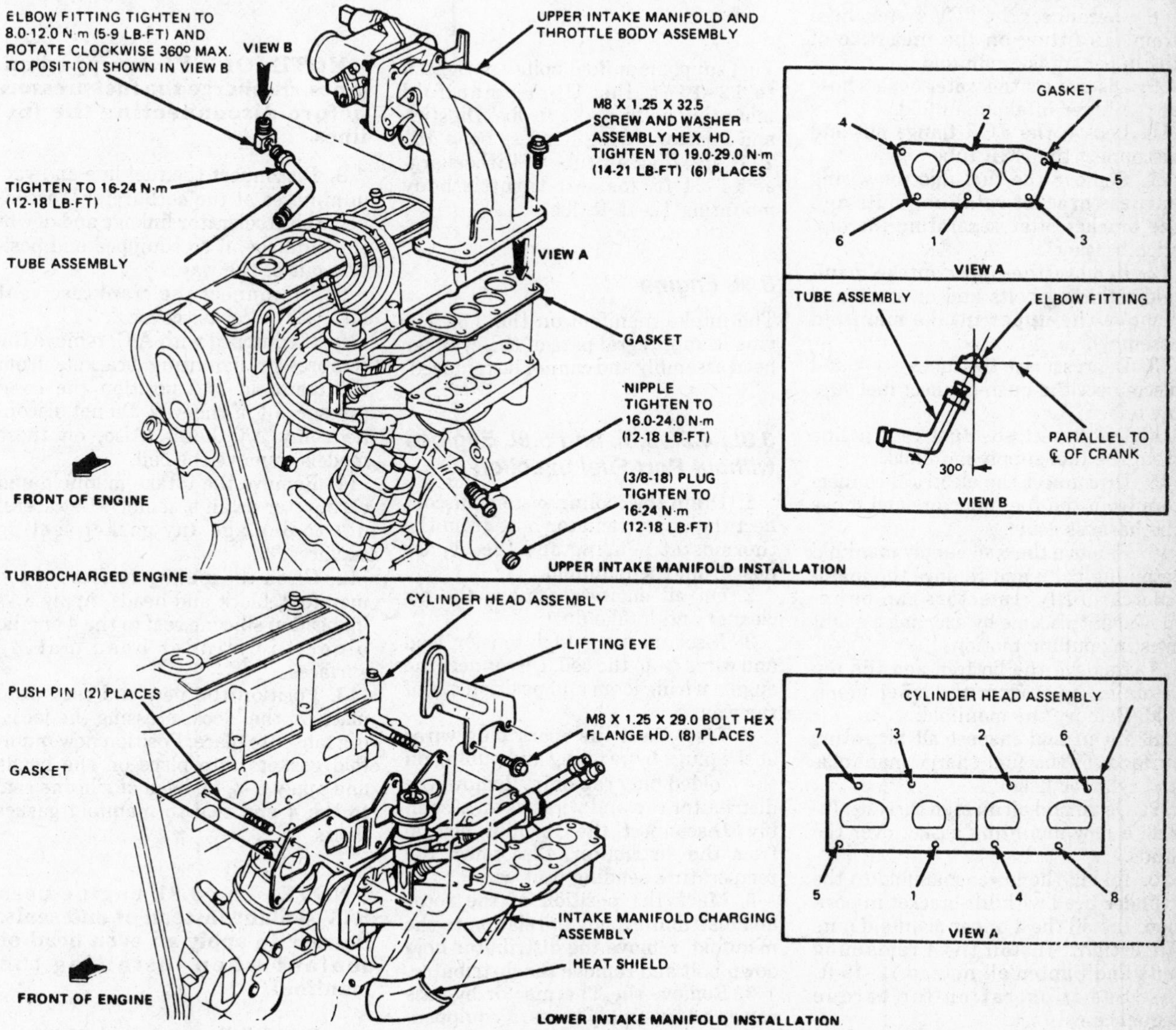

Multi-point injection, 2.3L (140) engine-upper and lower intake manifold removal and installation

2. Disconnect the upper intake manifold vacuum fitting connections by disconnecting the vacuum line fitting at the cast air tube. Disconnect the rear vacuum line at the dash panel tree. Remove the vacuum line to the EGR valve and the vacuum line to the fuel pressure regulator. Label all lines for reinstallation identification.

3. Disconnect the throttle linkage. Unbolt the accelerator cable from the bracket and position the cable out of the way.

4. Remove the bolts that attach the cast air tube/intercooler assembly to the turbocharger.

5. Remove the nuts that attach the air throttle body to the fuel charging assembly.

6. Separate the cast air tube/intercooler from the turbocharger.

7. Remove and discard the mounting gasket between the cast tube and the turbocharger. Remove the throttle body and cast tube.

8. Disconnect the PCV system hose from the fitting on the underside of the upper intake manifold.

9. Disconnect the water bypass hose at the lower intake manifold.

10. Loosen the EGR flange nut and disconnect the EGR tube.

11. Remove the fuel injector wiring harness bracket retaining nuts and the bracket after separating the dipstick bracket.

12. Remove the upper intake manifold retaining bolts and or studs and remove the upper intake manifold assembly.

13. Depressurize the fuel system and disconnect the push-connect fuel supply line.

14. Disconnect the fuel return line from the fuel supply manifold.

15. Disconnect the electrical connectors from the fuel injectors and move the harness aside.

16. Remove the fuel supply manifold retaining bolts and remove the manifold carefully. Injectors can be removed at this time by exerting a slight twisting/pulling motion.

17. Remove the bottom and the top retaining bolts from the lower manifold. Remove the manifold.

18. Clean and inspect all mounting surfaces of the fuel charge manifolds and cylinder head.

19. Clean and oil all stud threads. Install a new mounting gasket over the studs.

20. Install the lower manifold to the cylinder head with lift bracket in position. Install the 4 upper manifold nuts fingertight. Install the 4 remaining nuts and tighten all nuts to 12–15 ft. lbs. See illustration for torque sequence.

21. Install the remaining components in the reverse order of removal.

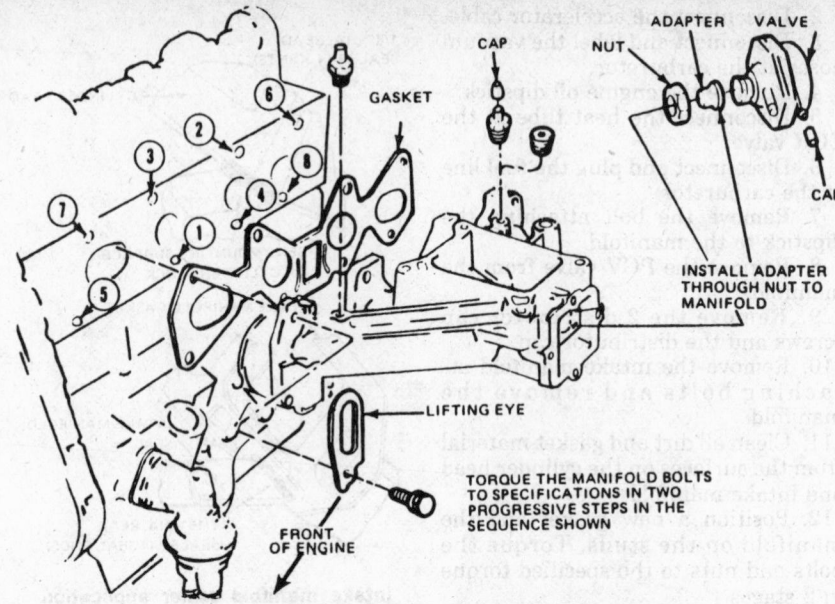

2.3L Engine intake manifold tightening sequence

TORQUE THE MANIFOLD BOLTS TO SPECIFICATIONS IN TWO PROGRESSIVE STEPS IN THE SEQUENCE SHOWN

INSTALL ADAPTER THROUGH NUT TO MANIFOLD

Fuel supply manifold bolts are tighten to 12–15 ft. lbs. Upper manifold mounting bolts 15–22 ft. lbs. Dipstick and injector wiring harness bolts 15–22 ft. lbs. Cast air tube to turbocharger 14–21 ft. lbs. Air throttle body mounting 12–15 ft. lbs.

3.3L Engine

The intake manifold on the 3.3L engine is an integral part of the cylinder head assembly and cannot be removed.

3.8L, 4.2L/5.0L and 5.8L Engines without Port Fuel Injection

1. Drain the cooling system, disconnect the upper radiator hose from the thermostat housing and the bypass hose from the manifold.

2. On all engines, remove the air cleaner and intake duct.

3. Disconnect the high tension lead and wires from the coil. Disconnect the engine wiring loom and position out of the way.

4. Disconnect the spark plug wires at the plugs by twisting and pulling on the molded plug cap only. Remove the distributor cap and wires as an assembly. Disconnect the vacuum hose(s) from the distributor. Disconnect temperature sending unit wire.

5. Mark the position of the rotor and distributor body in relation to the manifold, remove the distributor hold down bolt and remove the distributor.

6. Remove the Thermactor by-pass valve and air supply hoses, if equipped.

7. Remove all vacuum lines from the manifold.

NOTE: On CFI equipped engines, discharge the fuel pressure before disconnecting the fuel lines.

8. Disconnect the fuel line and vacuum hoses at the carburetor. Disconnect the accelerator linkage and downshift linkage, if so equipped and position out of the way.

9. Disconnect the crankcase vent hose at the rocker cover.

10. If equipped with A/C, remove the compressor mounting brackets from the manifold and position the compressor out of the way. Do not disconnect any A/C hoses. Also, on these models, remove the coil.

11. Remove the intake manifold and carburetor as an assembly. Be careful not to damage any gasket sealing surfaces.

12. Clean the mating surfaces of the manifold, block and heads. Apply a 1/8 in. bead of silicone seal to the 4 engine block to cylinder head mating surfaces.

13. Position the new end seals into place on the block, pressing the locating tabs into place. Position new manifold gaskets into place on the heads and apply a 1/8 in. bead of silicone seal to the 4 end seal to manifold gasket joints.

NOTE: The 3.8L engine uses RTV sealant instead of end seals. Be sure to apply an even bead of sealant when installing the manifold.

14. Carefully lower the manifold into place. After it is positioned, check the

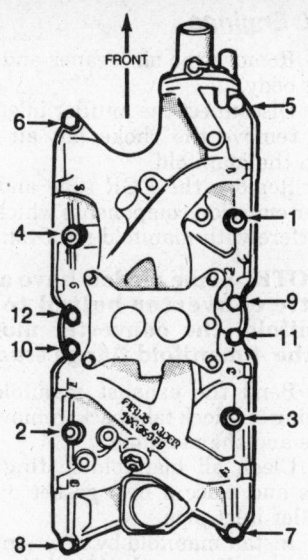

Intake manifold torque sequence 5.0L and 5.8L engines

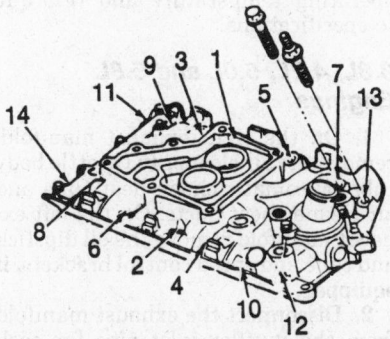

3.8L intake manifold torque sequence— CFI

seal area to be sure the seals are properly positioned. If they are not, remove the manifold and reposition the seals.

15. Torque the manifold to specification and in sequence in 3 stages. The rest of installation is the reverse of removal. After installation, run the engine to operating temperature and retorque the manifold bolts.

3.8L and 5.0L with Port Fuel Injection
UPPER

1. Disconnect the negative battery cable.
2. Relieve the fuel system pressure.
3. Disconnect the electrical connectors at the air bypass valve, throttle position sensor and EGR position sensor.
4. Disconnect the throttle linkage at the throttle ball and the transmission linkage from the throttle body. Remove the 2 bolts securing the cable

bracket to the intake manifold and position out of the way.

5. Disconnect and tag the upper intake manifold vacuum lines. Disconnect the vacuum line to the EGR valve and the fuel pressure regulator.
6. Disconnect the vacuum connection to the canister purge line.
7. Remove the PCV vent closure tube at the throttle body and disconnect the hose at the rear of the manifold.
8. Remove the EGR coolant lines from the fittings on the EGR spacer.
9. Remove the 6 upper intake manifold retaining bolts. Remove the manifold and the throttle body as an assembly.
10. To install, clean and inspect the mounting surfaces.
11. Install the upper manifold and throttle body assembly and install the 6 mounting bolts. Torque the mounting bolts to 12–18 ft. lbs.
12. Reconnect all vacuum lines and electrical connections.
13. Connect the throttle linkage and bracket to the manifold.

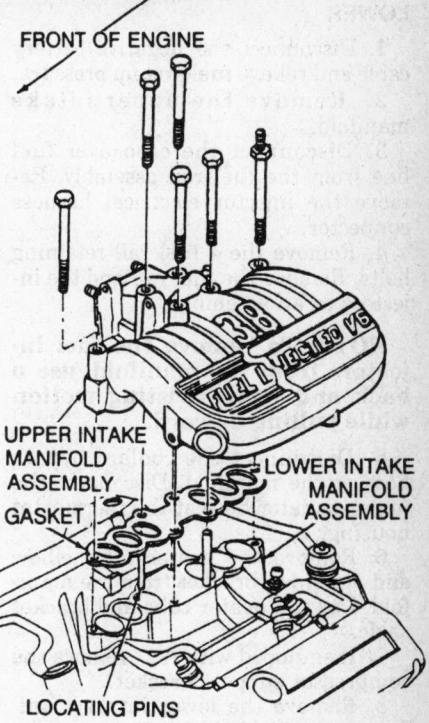

3.8L upper intake manifold removal

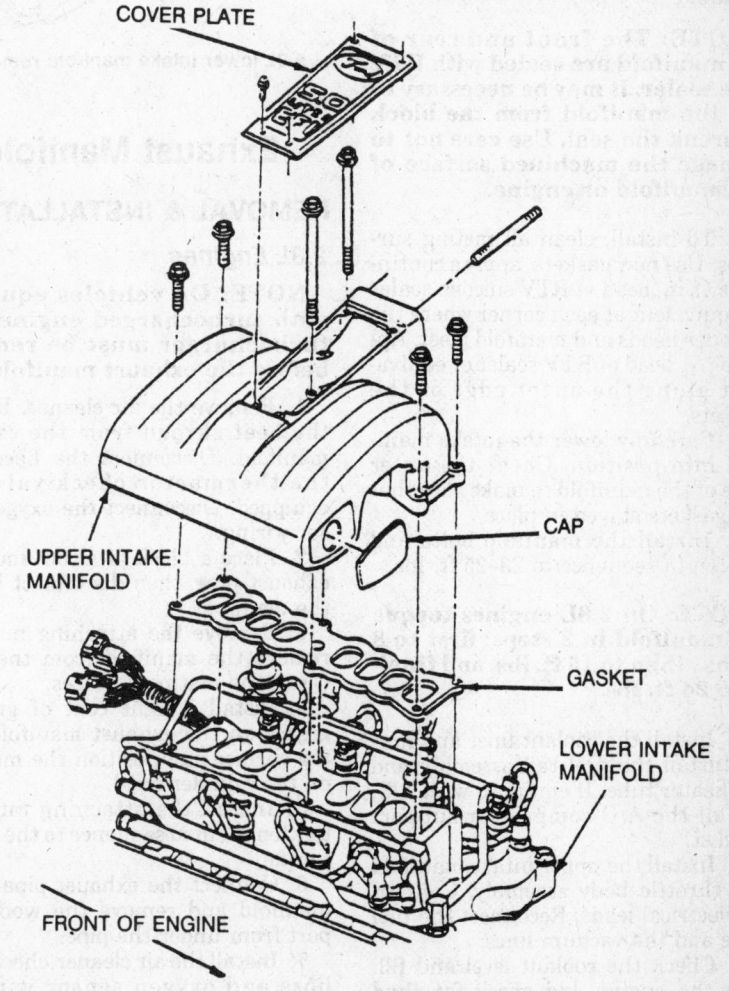

5.0L upper intake manifold removal

LOWER

1. Disconnect the negative battery cable and relieve fuel system pressure.
2. Remove the upper intake manifold.
3. Disconnect the croosover fuel line from the fuel rail assembly. Remove the injector electrical harness connector.
4. Remove the 4 fuel rail retaining bolts. Remove the fuel rail and the injectors as an assembly.

NOTE: To remove the fuel injectors from the manifold, use a back and forth twisting motion while pulling upward.

5. Disconnect the coolant bypass hose at the manifold. Disconnect the upper radiator hose at the thermostat housing.
6. Remove the heater tube, elbow and attaching bracket from the manifold. Lay the heater tube and bracket aside.
7. If equipped with A/C, remove the compressor support bracket.
8. Remove the lower intake manifold mounting bolts and remove the manifold.

NOTE: The front and rear of the manifold are sealed with RTV type sealer. It may be necessary to pry the manifold from the block to break the seal. Use care not to damage the machined surface of the manifold or engine.

9. To install, clean all mating surfaces. Use new gaskets, apply a continuous 1/8 in. bead of RTV silicone sealer or equivalent at each corner where the cylinder heads and manifold meet. Apply a 1/16 bead of RTV sealer or equivalent along the outer edge of the gaskets.
10. Carefully lower the intake manifold into position. Check the outer edge of the manifold to make sure that the gaskets stayed in place.
11. Install the manifold bolts and tighten in sequence to 23–25 ft. lbs.

NOTE: On 3.8L engines torque the manifold in 3 steps: first to 8 ft. lbs., then to 15 ft. lbs. and finally to 24 ft. lbs.

12. Install the coolant lines and hoses. Install the fuel rail assembly and the heater tube. If equipped with A/C, install the A/C compressor support bracket.
13. Install the upper intake manifold and throttle body assembly. Connect all electrical leads. Reconnect the fuel lines and the vacuum lines.
14. Check the coolant level and fill. Run the engine and check for fluid leaks.

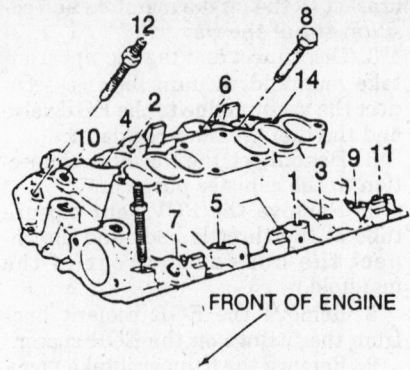

3.8L lower intake manifold removal

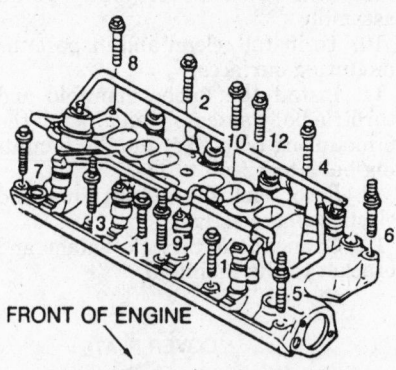

5.0L lower intake manifold removal

Exhaust Manifold

REMOVAL & INSTALLATION

2.3L Engines

NOTE: On vehicles equipped with turbocharged engines, the turbocharger must be removed before the exhaust manifold.

1. Remove the air cleaner. Remove the heat shroud from the exhaust manifold. Disconnect the hose from the thermactor check valves, if equipped. Disconnect the oxygen sensor wiring.
2. Place a block of wood under the exhaust pipe, then disconnect it from the manifold.
3. Remove the attaching nuts and remove the manifold from the head. Clean the mating surfaces.
4. Install a light coat of graphite grease on the exhaust manifold mating surface and position the manifold on the cylinder head.
5. Install the attaching nuts and tighten them in sequence to the proper torque.
6. Connect the exhaust pipe to the manifold and remove the wood support from under the pipe.
7. Install the air cleaner, check valve hose and oxygen sensor wiring if present.

3.3L Engines

1. Remove the air cleaner and heat duct body.
2. Disconnect the muffler inlet pipe and remove the choke hot air tube from the manifold.
3. Remove the EGR tube and any other emission components which will interfere with manifold removal.

NOTE: Some models have a catalytic converter bolted to the manifold; the converter mounts on the 4 manifold flange studs.

4. Bend the exhaust manifold attaching bolt lock tabs back, remove the bolts and the manifold.
5. Clean all manifold mating surfaces and place a new gasket on the muffler inlet pipe.
6. Install manifold by reversing the procedure. Torque the attaching bolts in sequence to specification. After installation, warm the engine to normal operating temperature and retorque to specifications.

3.8L, 4.2L, 5.0L and 5.8L Engines

1. On the right exhaust manifold, remove the air cleaner to throttle body tube, automatic choke heat tube and air cleaner heat ducts. On the left exhaust manifold remove the oil dipstick and tube and speed control brackets, if equipped.
2. Disconnect the exhaust manifold from the muffler inlet pipe for each side.
3. Remove the spark plug wires, spark plugs and heat shields. Disconnect the exhaust gas oxygen sensor, if so equipped. Label all wires before removal if they are not already marked.
4. Remove the manifold attaching bolts and remove the manifold.
5. Reverse the procedure to reinstall, using new inlet pipe gaskets. Torque the manifold bolts in sequence (from the center bolts outwards to the end bolts) to 18–24 ft. lbs. on 8 cylinder engines and 15–22 ft. lbs. on 6 cylinder engines.

Turbocharger

REMOVAL & INSTALLATION

NOTE: The turbocharger, wastegate and exhaust elbow assemblies are serviced by replacement only.

1. Remove negative cable from the battery.
2. Drain coolant from radiator. Loosen upper and lower clamps securing hoses to intercooler.
3. Disconnect aspirator hoses at in-

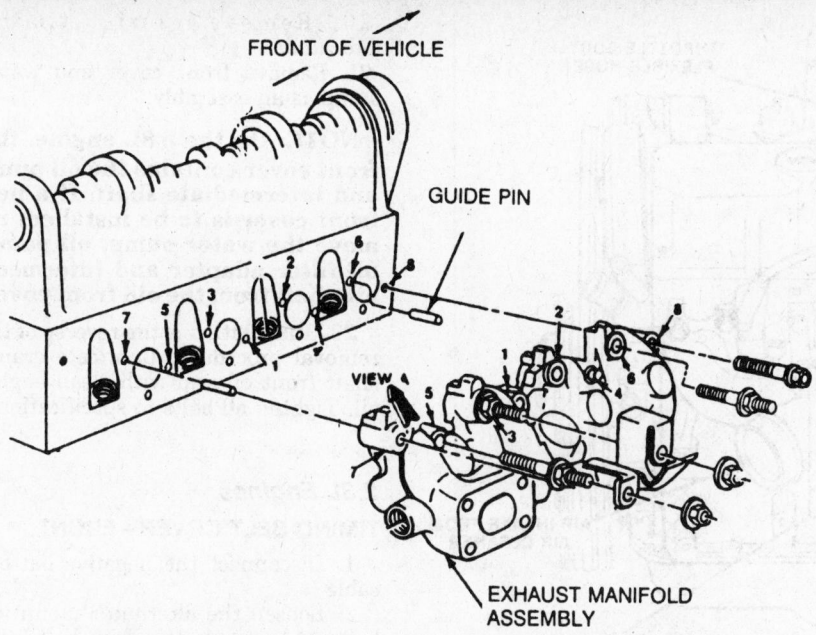

FRONT OF VEHICLE

GUIDE PIN

VIEW 4

EXHAUST MANIFOLD ASSEMBLY

2.3L OHC/TURBO exhaust manifold removal and torque sequence

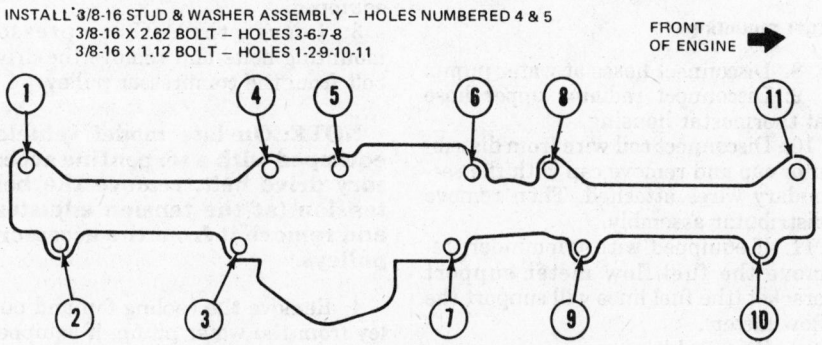

INSTALL 3/8-16 STUD & WASHER ASSEMBLY — HOLES NUMBERED 4 & 5
3/8-16 X 2.62 BOLT — HOLES 3-6-7-8
3/8-16 X 1.12 BOLT — HOLES 1-2-9-10-11

FRONT OF ENGINE ➡

3.3L exhaust manifold torque sequence

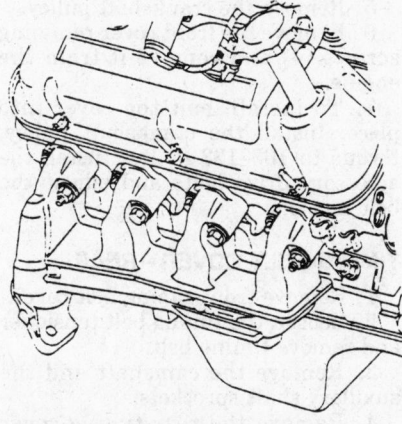

5.0L and 5.8L exhaust manifold mounting

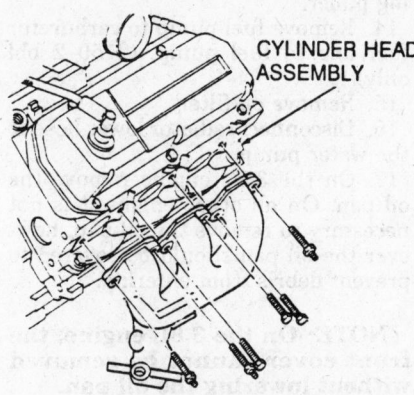

CYLINDER HEAD ASSEMBLY

3.8L exhaust manifold mounting

tercooler and loosen nut securing bracket to engine. Remove intercooler by first lifting and then pulling out.

4. Remove 2 hex head bolt retaining throttle body discharge tube to the turbocharger. Also, loosen upper clamp on inlet hose.

5. Identify and disconnect vacuum hose tubes.

6. Disconnect PCV tube from the turbocharger air inlet elbow.

7. Remove throttle body discharge tube and hose as a assembly.

8. Disconnect electrical ground wire from turbocharger air inlet elbow.

9. Remove turbocharger oil supply line.

10. Disconnect oxygen sensor connector at turbocharger.

11. Raise vehicle on hoist.

12. Disconnect exhaust pipe by removing the 2 exhaust pipe to turbocharger bolts.

13. Remove the 2 bolts from oil return line located below turbocharger. Do not kink or damage line as it is removed.

14. Remove lower turbocharger bracket to block bolt.

15. Lower the vehicle.

16. Remove front lower turbocharger retaining bolt.

17. Simultaneously, remove the 3 remaining nuts as turbocharger is slid off studs.

18. Remove turbocharger assembly from vehicle.

19. Position a new turbocharger gasket on mounting studs. Be sure the bead faces outward.

20. Install turbocharger assembly on the 4 mounting studs.

21. Install turbocharger bracket on 2 lower studs. Start 2 lower retaining nuts followed by 2 upper retaining nuts.

22. Raise vehicle on hoist.

23. Install lower bracket to block bolt and tighten to 28–40 ft. lbs. (38–54 Nm).

24. Install a new oil return line gasket. Bolt oil return line to turbocharger. Tighten bolts to 12–21 ft. lbs. (19–29 Nm).

25. Install exhaust pipe. Tighten retaining nuts to 25–35 ft. lbs. (34–47 Nm).

26. Lower vehicle.

27. Using 4 new nuts, tighten turbocharger to exhaust manifold nuts to 28–40 ft. lbs. (38–54 Nm).

28. Install air inlet tube to turbocharger inlet elbow. Tighten bolts to 15–22 ft. lbs. (20–30 Nm). Tighten hose clamp to 15–22 inch lbs. (1.7–2.5 Nm).

29. Install PCV tube fitting and tighten clamp to 15–22 inch lbs. (1.7–2.5 Nm).

30. Connect all vacuum lines.

31. Connect oxygen sensor.

32. Connect electrical ground wire to air inlet elbow.

33. Install turbocharger oil supply lie. Tighten fitting to 9–16 ft. lbs. (12–22 Nm).

34. Install air intake tube and clamp between turbocharger outlet and air intake throttle body. Tighten clamp to 15–20 ft. lbs. (20–27 Nm).

35. Connect ground cable to battery.

36. Start engine and check for leaks.

37. Install hood. Check for proper operation and alignment.

NOTE: When installing the tur-

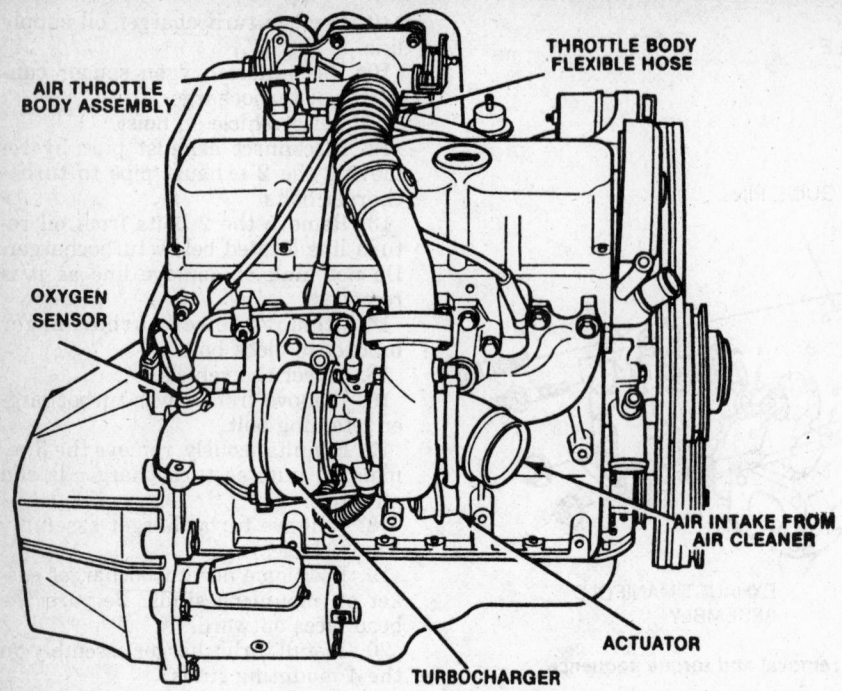

AIR THROTTLE
BODY ASSEMBLY

THROTTLE BODY
FLEXIBLE HOSE

OXYGEN
SENSOR

AIR INTAKE FROM
AIR CLEANER

ACTUATOR

TURBOCHARGER

Typical turbocharger mounting

bocharger, or after an oil and filter change, disconnect the distributor feed harness and crank the engine with the starter motor until the oil pressure light on the dash goes out. Oil pressure must be up before starting the engine.

TROUBLESHOOTING

NOTE: For more information on Turbocharging, please refer to "Turbocharging" in the Unit Repair Section

Front Cover

REMOVAL & INSTALLATION

All Except 2.3L Engines

1. Drain cooling system.
2. Disconnect cable from battery negative terminal.
3. Remove air cleaner assembly and air intake duct.
4. Remove fan/clutch assembly and shroud.
5. Loosen accessory drive belt idler. Remove drive belt and water pump pulley.
6. If equipped with power steering, remove pump mounting brackets' attaching bolts. Leaving the hoses connected, place the pump/bracket assembly aside in a position to prevent the fluid from leaking out.
7. If equipped with air conditioning, remove compressor front support bracket. Leave compressor in place.

8. Disconnect hoses at water pump.
9. Disconnect radiator upper hose at thermostat housing.
10. Disconnect coil wire from distributor cap and remove cap with the secondary wires attached. Then remove distributor assembly.
11. If equipped with tripminder, remove the fuel flow meter support bracket (the fuel lines will support the flow meter).
12. Raise vehicle.
13. Remove crankshaft damper using puller.
14. Remove fuel pump to carburetor fuel line to fuel pump, (2150–2 bbl only).
15. Remove oil filter.
16. Disconnect radiator lower hose at the water pump.
17. On the 3.8L engine remove the oil pan. On all other engine it is not necessary to remove the oil pan, however the oil pan should be covered to prevent debris from entering.

NOTE: On the 3.8L engine, the front cover cannot be removed without lowering the oil pan.

18. Lower vehicle.
19. Remove front cover attaching bolts. It is not necessary to remove water pump.

─────── **CAUTION** ───────
Do not overlook the cover attaching bolt located behind the oil filter adapter. the front cover will break if pried upon and all attaching bolts are not removed.

20. Remove ignition timing indicator.
21. Remove front cover and water pump as an assembly.

NOTE: On the 3.8L engine, the front cover contains the oil pump and intermediate shaft. If a new front cover is to be installed, remove the water pump, oil pump, oil filter adapter and intermediate shaft from the old front cover.

22. Installation is the reverse of the removal procedure. Lubricate crankshaft front oil seal with clean engine oil. Tighten all bolts to specifications.

2.3L Engines

TIMING BELT COVER—FRONT

1. Disconnect the negative battery cable.
2. Loosen the alternator mounting bolts and remove the drive belt from the alternator pulley. Remove the belt from the power steering pump, if equipped.
3. Loosen the A/C compressor mounting bolts and remove the drive belt from the compressor pulley.

NOTE: On late model vehicles equipped with a serpentine accessory drive belt, remove the belt tension (at the tension adjuster) and remove it from the accessory pulleys.

4. Remove the cooling fan and pulley from the water pump, if equipped with an electric cooling fan remove the water pump pulley.
5. Remove the crankshaft pulley.
6. Remove the front cover retaining screws (4) and remove it from the engine.
7. To install, bolt the cover into place. Install the crankshaft pulley, torque to 103–133 ft. lbs. Install the accessory drive belts and adjust the belt tensions.

TIMING BELT COVER—REAR

1. Remove front timing belt cover.
2. Loosen the timing belt tensioner and remove timing belt.
3. Remove the camshaft and the auxillary shaft sprockets.
4. Remove the rear timing cover bolts (1 panhead screw and 1 stud) and remove the cover.
5. To install, position on engine block and torque the retaining screw to 15 inch lbs. and the retaining stud to 21 ft. lbs. Install the camshaft and auxillary shaft sprockets, tighten both to 34 ft. lbs. Slide timing belt over the sprockets and adjust tension to specification. Install front cover.

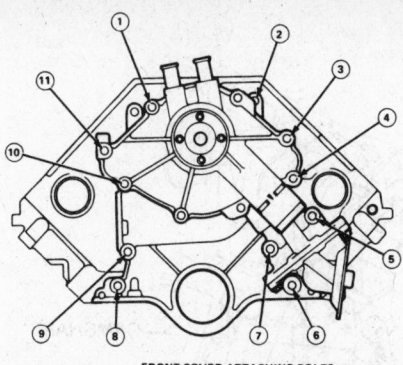

FRONT COVER ATTACHING BOLTS

Front cover attaching bolts—3.8L engine

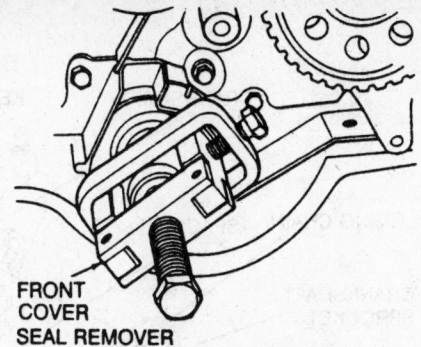

FRONT COVER SEAL REMOVER

2.3L front cover seal removal

OIL SEAL REPLACEMENT

All Except 2.3L Engines

1. Disconnect the negative battery cable.

2. Remove the fan shroud assembly. Remove the cooling fan and pulley.

3. Remove the accessory drive belts.

4. Remove the crankshaft pulley, install puller on crankshaft damper and remove the damper.

5. Place front cover seal remover T70P–6B070–B or equivalent on to the front cover plate over the front seal. Tighten the 2 through bolts to force the puller under the seal flange. Alternately tighten the puller bolts one turn at a time to remove the seal.

6. To install, use a new oil seal and coat with oil. Install the seal into tool T70P–6B070–A or equivalent. Install the tool on the front of the crankshaft and tighten adjuster screw to force the seal into the front cover.

7. Coat the outside of the seal and install the damper and pulley to the crankshaft.

8. Install the cooling fan and pulley. Install the accessory drive belts and adjust the belt tension. Attach the fan shroud to the radiator and run the engine to check for leaks.

2.3L Engines

1. Remove the front timing belt cover.

2. Relieve the tension on the timing belt and remove it.

3. Remove the crankshaft sprocket using tool T74P–6306–A crankshaft sprocket remover or equivalent.

4. Using front seal removing tool T74P–6700–B or equivalent, place the jaws of the tool on the thin edge of the seal and remove the seal.

5. To install, lubricate the outer edge of the seal with light grease. Using front seal installer T74P–6150–A, place the seal on to the tool and install the seal/tool into place.

6. Install the crankshaft sprocket and install the timing belt on to the timing gear.

7. Install the front cover. Run the engine and check for leaks.

Timing Chain and Sprockets

REMOVAL & INSTALLATION

All Except 2.3L Engine

1. Drain cooling system, remove air cleaner and disconnect the battery.

2. Disconnect the radiator hoses and remove the radiator.

3. Disconnect heater hose at water pump. Slide water pump by-pass hose clamp toward the pump.

4. Loosen alternator mounting bolts at the alternator. Remove the alternator support bolt at the water pump. Remove Thermactor (air) pump on all engines so equipped. If equipped with power steering or air conditioning. unbolt the component, remove the belt and lay the pump aside with the lines attached.

5. Remove the fan, spacer, pulley and drive belt.

6. Drain the crankcase.

7. Remove pulley from crankshaft pulley adapter. Remove cap screw and washer from front end of crankshaft. Remove crankshaft pulley adapter with a puller.

8. On models equipped with fuel injection, relieve the fuel system pressure. Disconnect fuel pump outlet line at the pump. Remove fuel pump retaining bolts and lay the pump to the side. Remove the engine oil dipstick. Remove the distributor on 3.8L engines.

NOTE: On the 3.8L engine, it is necessary to drop the oil pan before the front cover cam be removed.

9. Remove the front cover attaching bolts. On the 3.8L engine, remove the water pump and front cover as an assembly.

10. Remove the crankshaft oil slinger if so equipped. On 1982–87 3.8L engines, remove the camshaft thrust button and spring.

NOTE: 1988–89 3.8L engines are equipped with an internal balance shaft. The balance shaft is driven off of the camshaft, by a gear positioned behind the camshaft timing sprocket. When removing the timing chain and sprockets, care should be taken to keep this gear in its proper position.

11. Check the timing chain deflection.

12. Crank engine until the timing sprocket timing marks are aligned at their closest together position.

13. Remove crankshaft sprocket cap screw, washers and fuel pump eccentric. Slide both sprockets and chain forward and off as an assembly.

14. Position sprockets and chain on the camshaft and crankshaft with both of the timing marks aligned at their closest together position. Install the fuel pump eccentric, washers and sprocket attaching bolt. Torque the sprocket attaching bolt to 40–45 ft. lbs.

15. Install the crankshaft front oil slinger.

NOTE: When replacing the front cover on the 1982–1987 3.8L

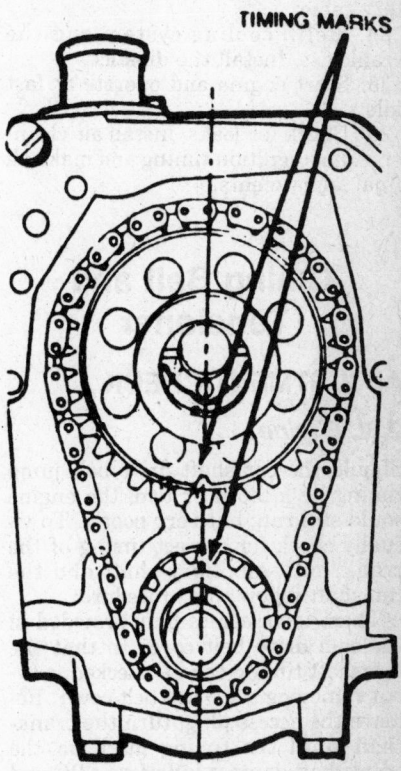

TIMING MARKS

5.0L and 5.8L timing mark alignment

engine, RTV sealer is used. Apply an even $\frac{1}{8}$ in. bead on the cover mating surface. 1988–89 3.8L engines use a gasket.

16. Clean all gasket mating surfaces and install a new front cover seal.

17. Coat a new cover gasket with sealer and position it on the block.

NOTE: On all engines, trim away the exposed portion of the oil pan gasket flush with the cylinder block. Cut and position the required portion of a new gasket to the oil pan, applying sealer to both sides of it. On 3.8L engines, after installing the cylinder front cover, install the oil pan using a new gasket.

18. Install front cover, using a crankshaft to cover alignment tool. Coat the threads of the attaching bolts with sealer. Torque attaching bolts to 12–15 ft. lbs.

19. Install the fuel pump, connect fuel pump outlet tube.

20. Install the crankshaft pulley adapter and torque attaching bolt. Install crankshaft pulley.

21. Install the water pump pulley, drive belt, spacer and fan.

22. Install the alternator support bolt at the water pump. Tighten the alternator mounting bolts. Adjust drive belt tension. Install Thermactor pump is so equipped.

23. Install radiator and connect all coolant and heater hoses. Connect battery cables.

24. Refill cooling system and the crankcase. Install the dipstick.

25. Start engine and operate at fast idle.

26. Check for leaks, install air cleaner. Adjust ignition timing and make all final adjustments.

Timing Belt and Tensioner

ADJUSTMENT CHECK

2.3L Engine

Should the camshaft drive belt jump timing by a tooth or two, the engine could still run; but very poorly. To visually check for correct timing of the crankshaft, auxiliary shaft and the camshaft follow this procedure:

There is an access plug provided in the cam drive belt cover so that the camshaft timing can be checked without removing the drive belt cover. Remove the access plug, turn the crankshaft until the timing mark on the crankshaft damper indicates TDC and observe that the timing mark on the

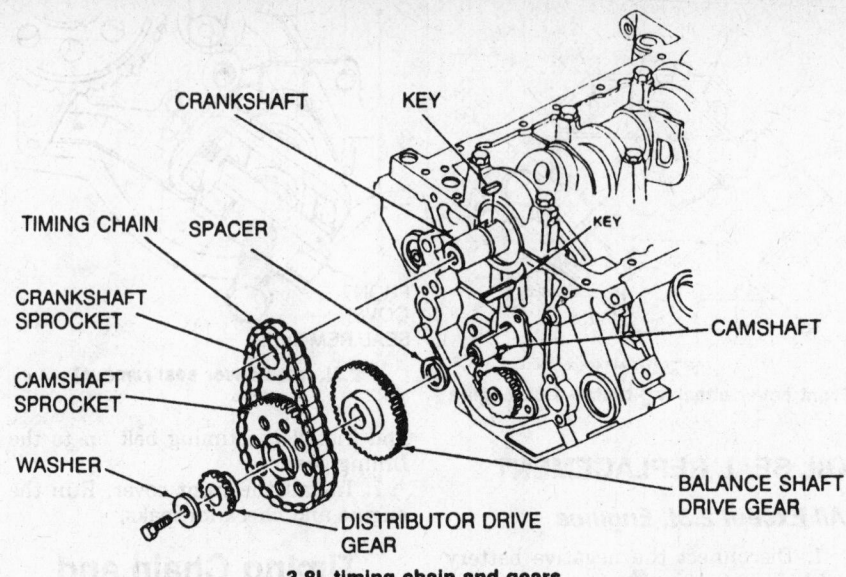

3.8L timing chain and gears

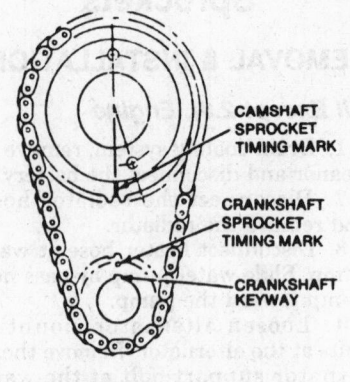

3.8L timing mark alignment

camshaft drive sprocket is aligned with the pointer on the inner belt cover. Also, the rotor of the distributor must align with the No. 1 cylinder firing position.

REMOVAL & INSTALLATION

2.3L Engine

1. Set the engine with the No. 1 cylinder at TDC. The crankshaft and camshaft timing marks should align with their respective pointers and the distributor rotor should point to the No. 1 plug tower.

2. Loosen the adjustment bolts on the alternator and accessories and remove the drive belts. To provide clearance for removing the camshaft belt, remove the fan and pulley.

3. Remove the timing belt front cover.

4. Remove the distributor cap from the distributor and position it out of the way.

5. Loosen the belt tensioner adjustment and pivot bolts. Lever the ten-

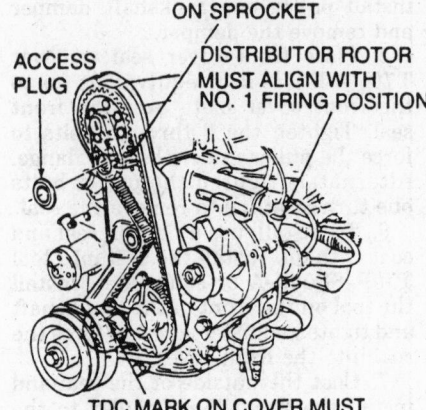

2.3L timing belt alignment check

sioner away from the belt and retighten the adjustment bolt to hold it away.

6. Remove the crankshaft bolt and pulley. Remove the belt guide behind the pulley.

7. Remove the timing belt, by sliding it off the camshaft pulley and off of the engine.

8. Install the new belt over the crankshaft pulley first, then counterclockwise over the auxiliary shaft sprocket and the camshaft sprocket. Adjust the belt fore and aft so that it is centered on the sprockets.

9. Loosen the tensioner adjustment bolt, allowing it to spring back against the belt.

10. Rotate the crankshaft 2 complete turns in the normal rotation direction to remove any belt slack. Turn the crankshaft until the timing check marks are lined up. If the timing has

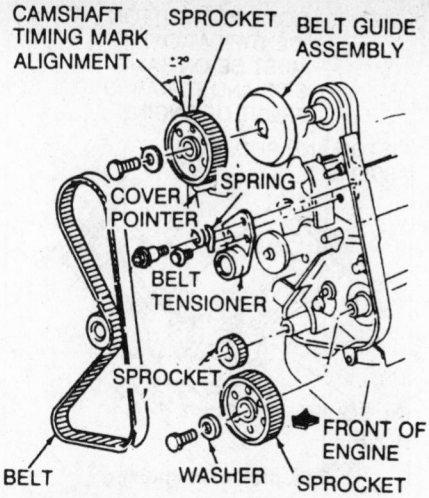

2.3L timing belt and sprockets

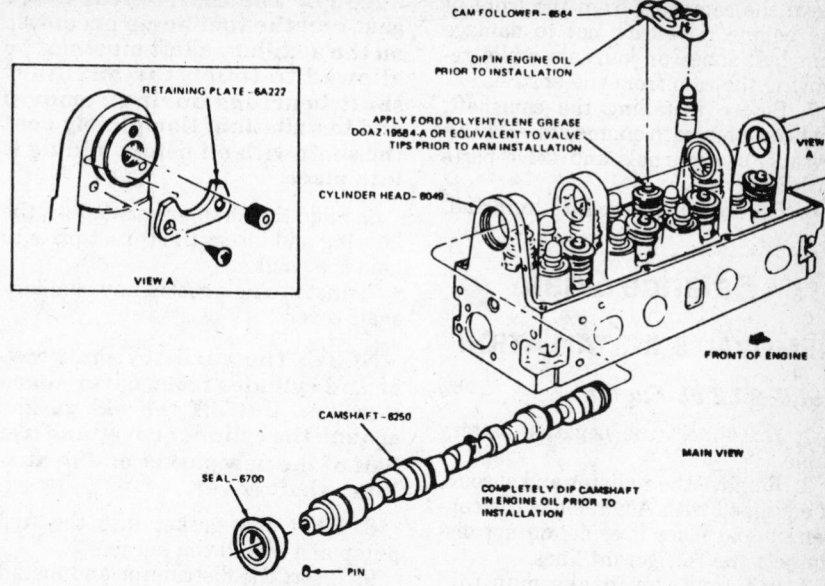

Camshaft installation—2.3L (140) engine

slipped, remove the belt and repeat the procedure.

11. Tighten the tensioner adjustment bolt to 14–21 ft. lbs. and the pivot bolt to 28–40 ft. lbs.

12. Replace the belt guide and crankshaft pulley, distributor cap, belt outer cover, fan and pulley, drive belts and accessories. Adjust the accessory drive belt tension. Start the engine and check the ignition timing.

NOTE: Never turn the crankshaft in the opposite direction of normal rotation. Backward rotation of the crankshaft may cause the timing belt to slip and alter the timing.

Camshaft

REMOVAL & INSTALLATION

2.3L Engine

NOTE: The camshaft can be replaced with the cylinder head still mounted on the engine in the vehicle, or with the cylinder head removed from the vehicle.

1. Disconnect the negative battery cable. Drain the cooling system. Remove the air cleaner assembly. On turbocharged models remove the intercooler to throttle body tube and the intercooler inlet tube. Remove the intercooler mounting bolts and remove the intercooler.

2. Label and remove all wires, electrical harnesses, vacuum lines and cables that will interfere with valve cover removal.

3. On fuel injected models, relieve the fuel system pressure.

4. Remove the alternator and mounting brackets as an assembly and position to the side.

5. Remove the upper and lower radiator hoses. Remove the fan, motor and mounting shroud as an assembly.

6. Remove the valve cover.

7. Set the engine at No. 1 cylinder TDC on the compression stroke. Remove the timing belt.

8. Raise and safely support the front of the vehicle. Remove the right and left engine mount thru-bolts and joint to bracket retaining bolts.

9. Place a block of wood on a floor jack and raise the engine, carefully, as high as it will go. Place blocks of wood between the engine mounts. Lower the jack and lower the vehicle to the ground.

10. Remove the rocker arms.

11. Remove the camshaft drive gear attaching bolt and washer and remove the gear and belt guide plate.

12. The camshaft is removed through the front of the cylinder head after removing the front cam bearing seal. Use a new seal during assembly.

13. Reverse the removal procedure to install the camshaft and cylinder head (if removed).

NOTE: Liberally coat the camshaft with oil before sliding it into the cylinder head. Apply a coat of sealer or Teflon® tape to the cam drive gear bolt before installation.

—— CAUTION ——

After any procedure requiring removal of the rocker arms, each lash adjuster must be fully collapsed after assembly, then released. This must be done before the camshaft is turned.

3.3L Engine

1. Remove the cylinder head.

2. Remove the front cover and remove the timing chain and gears.

3. Disconnect and remove the grille. Remove the radiator. If equipped with air conditioning, unbolt the condenser and move it aside without disconnecting any lines.

4. Remove the valve lifters and keep them in order so that they can be installed in their original positions.

5. Remove the camshaft thrust plate and remove the camshaft by pulling it from the front of the engine. Use care not to damage the camshaft or bearings while removing the cam from the engine.

6. Before installing the camshaft, coat the lobes with engine assembly lubricant, the journals and all valve parts with heavy oil. Clean the oil passage at the rear of the cylinder block with compressed air.

7. Reverse the procedure to install, following recommended torque settings and tightening sequences.

3.8L, 4.2L, 5.0L and 5.8L Engines

1. Disconnect the negative battery cable. Remove the intake manifold.

2. Remove the cylinder front cover, timing chain and sprockets.

3. Remove the grille and radiator. On models with air conditioning, remove the condenser retaining bolts and position it out of the way. Do not disconnect refrigerant lines.

4. Remove the rocker arm covers.

5. Remove the pushrods and lifters and keep them in order so that they can be installed in their original positions.

6. Remove the camshaft thrust plate and washer if so equipped. Re-

move the camshaft from the front of the engine. Use care not to damage camshaft lobes or journals while removing the cam from the engine.

7. Before installing the camshaft, coat the lobes with engine assembly lubricant, the journals and valve parts with heavy oil.

8. Reverse the procedure to install.

Balance Shaft

REMOVAL & INSTALLATION

1988–89 3.8L Engine

1. Disconnect the negative battery cable.

2. Remove the radiator and shroud. If equipped with A/C remove the condenser and place it aside, do not disconnect the refrigerant lines.

3. Remove the intake manifold assembly.

4. Remove the cylinder front cover assembly.

5. Remove the camshaft timing sprocket and the timing chain. Remove the balance shaft drive gear from the camshaft end. Mark the relationship of the balance shaft with the driven gear.

6. Remove the balance shaft gear from the end of the balance shaft. Remove the balance shaft thrust plate and remove the shaft.

7. To install, lubricate the bearing lobes of the balance shaft with assembly lubricant and install the balance shaft into the block. Install the shaft thrust plate and the driven gear.

8. Install the balance shaft drive gear, aligning the keyway, on the end of the camshaft.

9. Install the timing belt and gear, the front cover assembly and the intake manifold. Install the radiator and A/C condensor. Install the grill.

10. Fill all fluids and run the engine to check for leaks.

Auxiliary Shaft

REMOVAL & INSTALLATION

2.3L Engine

1. Remove the front timing belt cover.

2. Remove the drive belt. Remove the auxiliary shaft sprocket. A puller may be necessary to remove the sprocket.

3. Remove the distributor and fuel pump.

4. Remove the auxiliary shaft cover and thrust plate.

5. Withdraw the auxiliary shaft from the block.

NOTE: The distributor drive gear and the fuel pump eccentric on the auxiliary shaft must not be allowed to touch the auxiliary shaft bearings during removal and installation. Completely coat the shaft with oil before sliding it into place.

6. Slide the auxiliary shaft into the housing and insert the thrust plate to hold the shaft.

7. Install a new gasket and auxiliary shaft cover.

NOTE: The auxiliary shaft cover and cylinder front cover share a gasket. Cut off the old gasket around the cylinder cover and use half of the new gasket on the auxiliary shaft cover.

8. Fit a new gasket into the fuel pump and install the pump.

9. Insert the distributor and install the auxiliary shaft sprocket.

10. Align the timing marks and install the timing belt.

11. Install the timing belt cover.

12. Check the ignition timing.

Piston and Connecting Rod

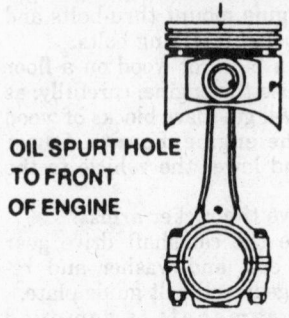

NOTCH TO FRONT OF ENGINE

OIL SPURT HOLE TO FRONT OF ENGINE

V6 piston and rod assembly

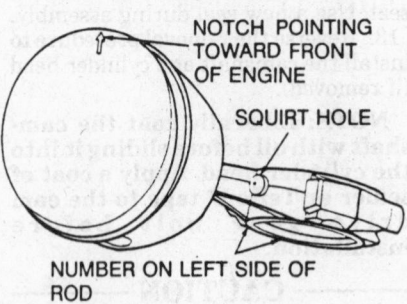

NOTCH POINTING TOWARD FRONT OF ENGINE

SQUIRT HOLE

NUMBER ON LEFT SIDE OF ROD

2.3L piston positioning

POSITIONING

For all piston and connecting rod overhaul procedures, please refer to "Engine Rebuilding" in the unit repair section.

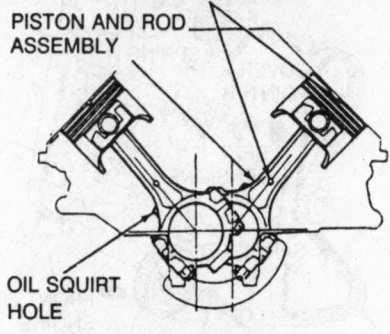

DOME AND BUTTON IDENTIFICATION MUST BE ON SAME SIDE AND TOWARDS FRONT OF ENGINE

PISTON AND ROD ASSEMBLY

OIL SQUIRT HOLE

3.8L piston positioning

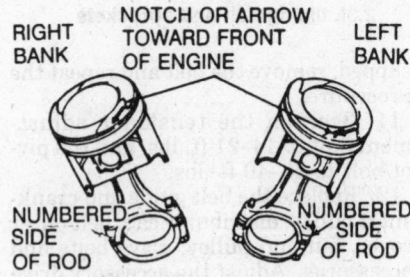

RIGHT BANK

NOTCH OR ARROW TOWARD FRONT OF ENGINE

LEFT BANK

NUMBERED SIDE OF ROD

NUMBERED SIDE OF ROD

5.0L and 5.8L piston positioning

DIESEL ENGINE MECHANICAL

Engine

REMOVAL & INSTALLATION

1. Disconnect the negative battery cable.

2. Disconnect the wiring assembly for the engine underhood light.

3. Scribe hinge mark locations and remove the hood.

4. Drain the cooling system. Drain the engine oil.

5. Remove the air cleaner assembly.

6. Remove the fan shroud attaching bolts and remove the fan shroud. Remove the engine cooling fan assembly.

7. Remove upper and lower radiator hoses.

8. Disconnect the transmission oil cooler tubes from the radiator fittings.

9. Disconnect the muffler inlet pipe.

10. Label and disconnect the vacuum hoses and wiring harnesses.

11. Disconnect the engine oil cooler hoses.

12. Disconnect the accelerator cable at the fuel injection pump.

13. Disconnect the fuel line from the tank to fuel injection pump.
14. Disconnect the transmission gear shift linkage.
15. Disconnect the battery ground cable at engine.
16. Remove the coolant expansion bottle and position it out of the way.
17. Disconnect the heater hoses at the dash panel (firewall).
18. Disconnect the wire to A/C compressor clutch.
19. Disconnect the power steering pump hose(s).
20. Disconnect the fuel line to the injectors.
21. Disconnect the wiring harness to instrument panel. Disconnect engine the ground leads.
22. Install an engine support Tool D79F–6000–A or equivalent (bar and "J" hook or chain).
23. Raise the vehicle and safely support on jackstands.
24. Remove the muffler inlet pipe.
25. Remove the lower engine oil cooler bracket and brace.
26. Remove the stabilizer bar, bracket retaining bolts and position forward.
27. Remove the left hand front fender splash shield.
28. Disconnect the steering gear input shaft to steering column shaft coupling.
29. Remove the retainer nuts to the engine insulator supports.
30. Position a jack under the engine. Raise the engine assembly. Position the steering gear out of the way.
31. Lower the engine assembly.
32. Remove the converter housing access cover.
33. Remove the converter assembly retainer nuts.
34. Insert a pair of locking pliers in the converter housing to hold the converter in place during engine removal.

NOTE: Make sure that the upper jaw of the locking pliers contacts the converter while clamped to the converter housing. This will apply adequate pressure on the converter to prevent separation during engine movements and removal.

35. Remove the crossmember retainer nuts.
36. Remove the transmission gear shift lever bellcrank.
37. Raise the transmission.
38. Remove the crossmember retainer bolts. Lower the transmission.
39. Remove engine to transmission converter housing retainer bolts.
40. Install crossmember retainer bolts.
41. Lower the vehicle.
42. Install engine lifting equipment.

43. Remove the engine support Tool D79T–6000–A or equivalent.
44. Remove the engine assembly.
45. Position engine and install on engine work stand and service as necessary.
46. Install engine lifting equipment. Raise the engine and install in vehicle.
47. Install engine support Tool D79T–6000–A or equivalent.
48. Remove the engine lifting equipment. Raise vehicle and safely support on jackstands.
49. The remainder of the installation procedure is in reverse order of removal.

Cylinder Head

REMOVAL & INSTALLATION

1. Disconnect the battery ground cable.
2. Drain the cooling system. Disconnect the heater hose(s).
3. Loosen and remove accessory drive belts.
4. Remove the valve cover.
5. Disconnect the diagnostic connectors.
6. Disconnect the coolant temperature switch and glow plug connector.
7. Disconnect the breaker hose and bracket.
8. Remove the clamp attaching the oil dipstick tube to the intake manifold and position out of the way.
9. Disconnect the boost pressure switch connector.
10. Disconnect the temperature controlled idle boost coolant hose.
11. Remove the vacuum pump from cylinder head.
12. Disconnect No. 1 nozzle to the injection pump leak hose.
13. Disconnect the injection lines from the nozzles and injection pump.

—— **CAUTION** ——

Cap the nozzles and lines to prevent dirt from contaminating the fuel system.

14. Disconnect the turbocharger oil lines.
15. Rotate the crankshaft until No. 1 cylinder is at TDC of compression stroke (intake and exhaust valves on base circle). Install TDC Aligning Pin, T84P–6400–A or equivalent.
16. Loosen the camshaft drive sprocket retaining bolt.
17. Loosen the camshaft drive belt tensioning roller nut and bolt and remove drive belt.
18. Loosen the cylinder head bolts in sequence and remove cylinder head.
19. Clean gasket sealing surfaces on the cylinder head and crankcase.
20. Check for cylinder head warpage.

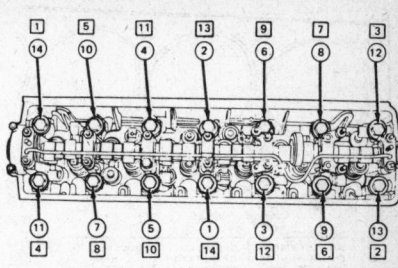

2.4L diesel engine cylinder head torque sequence

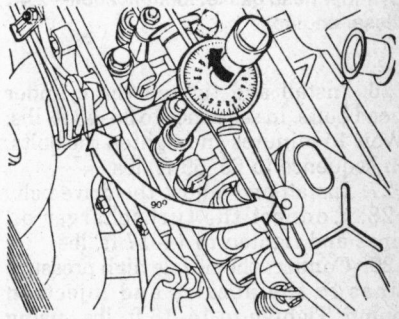

Cylinder head bolt tightening—2.4L diesel engine

—— **CAUTION** ——

Use care when cleaning gasket surfaces. Slight scoring of these surfaces can cause leakage due to high compression pressures.

21. Clean the top of each piston.
22. Using a dial indicator D82L–4201–A and Piston Height Gauge D84P–6100–A or equivalent, measure the amount the piston top extends above crankcase gasket surface as follows: Mount the dial indicator and bracket with dial indicator tip on the piston. Rotate the crankshaft to position piston at TDC, using the dial indictor. Zero the dial indicator with the tip on crankcase. Move the tip to the front of the piston. Record the measurement. Move the tip to the rear of the piston. Record the measurement. Repeat this procedure for each cylinder. Average the 2 readings for each cylinder. Using the measurement of highest piston, select the correct cylinder head gasket. Clean carbon and oil deposits from the cylinder head bolts.

—— **CAUTION** ——

Keep oil and/or antifreeze from entering cylinder head bolt holes. If either enters bolt holes, carefully blow out with compressed air. The presence of oil and/or antifreeze in bolt holes could result in insufficient cylinder head bolt tightening, or a cracked crankcase.

24. Position the correct cylinder head gasket on the crankcase.
25. Carefully lower the cylinder head onto the crankcase, using care not to damage the gasket.

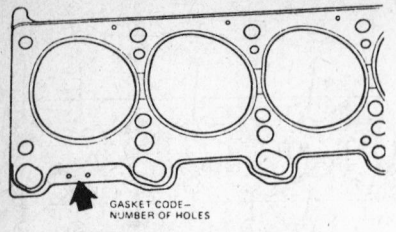

HIGHEST PISTON PROTRUSION OF ALL 6 PISTONS mm	CYL. HEAD GASKET CODE NO. OF HOLES	THICKNESS OF CYL. HEAD GASKET mm
0.60 – 0.70	1	1.4
0.70 – 0.85	2	1.5
0.85 – 1.00	3	1.6

Cylinder head gasket identification—2.4L diesel engine

26. Install and tighten the cylinder head bolts, in sequence to 36–43 ft. lbs. Wait 15 minutes and tighten the bolts, in sequence to 65–69 ft. lbs.
27. Install and adjust the drive belt.
28. Connect the turbocharger oil lines and tighten to 14–17 ft. lbs.
29. Connect the nozzle high pressure lines to the nozzles and injection pump. Tighten to 14–18 ft. lbs., using fuel line wrench.
30. Connect No. 1 nozzle to the injection pump leak hose.
31. Install the vacuum pump on the cylinder head and tighten to 6–7 ft. lbs.
32. Connect the temperature controlled, idle boost coolant hose.
33. Connect the radiator hoses to the cylinder head.
34. Connect the oil pressure switch connector.
35. Install the oil dipstick tube.
36. Install the breather hose and bracket.
37. Connect the coolant temperature switch and glow plug connectors.
38. Connect the diagnostic connectors.
39. Install the valve cover.
40. Install and adjust accessory drive belts.
41. Connect the heater hose(s).
42. Fill and bleed coolant system. Connect the battery ground cable.

OVERHAUL

For all cylinder head overhaul procedures, please refer to "Engine Rebuilding" in the unit repair section.

Rocker Arms

REMOVAL & INSTALLATION

1. Remove valve cover and vacuum pump.
2. Rotate engine until cam lobe for cylinder of rocker arm to be removed is on base circle.
3. Remove rocker arm retaining clip.

4. Compress spring assembly using proper tool and remove rocker arm.

— CAUTION —
Be sure that valve spring retainers remain locked in valve stem.

5. Remove rocker arm pivot ball pin if necessary, using proper tool.
6. Reverse procedure for installation. Coat the barrel of the pivot ball pin with loctite or equivalent. Adjust the valve clearance.

Intake Manifold

REMOVAL & INSTALLATION

1. Disconnect the battery ground cable.
2. Remove the diagnostic plug bracket and position out of the way.
3. Disconnect the turbo boost pressure indicator connector.
4. Disconnect the oil dipstick tube clamp from intake manifold and position out of the way.
5. Loosen the clamp at the turbo crossover pipe boot.
6. Remove the bolts attaching the intake manifold to the cylinder head and remove the intake manifold.
7. Clean the intake manifold and cylinder head gasket mating surfaces.
8. Install the intake manifold on the cylinder head, with a new gasket, making sure the inlet port is installed in the turbo crossover pipe boot.
9. Tighten the intake manifold bolts to 14–17 ft. lbs. and tighten the crossover pipe boot clamp.
10. Connect the turbo boost pressure indicator switch connector.
11. Install the diagnostic plug bracket and tighten the bolts to 14–17 ft. lbs.
12. Connect the battery ground cable. Start the engine and check for intake leaks.

Exhaust Manifold

REMOVAL & INSTALLATION

1. Disconnect the battery ground cable.
2. Disconnect the muffler inlet pipe at the turbo outlet and cap turbo outlet.
3. Disconnect the EGR valve vacuum line.
4. Disconnect the inlet duct at turbo and cap turbo inlet.
5. Loosen the clamp at the turbo crossover pipe boot.
6. Remove the clamp attaching the turbo oil feed tube to the oil return tube.
7. Remove the bolts attaching the oil feed tube to the turbo.

— CAUTION —
Cap the oil feed tube and oil feed inlet port on the turbo, to prevent contamination of the turbo oiling system.

8. Disconnect the oil return line from the turbo oil drain port.

— CAUTION —
Cap the oil return line and the oil return port on the turbo, to prevent contamination of the turbo oiling system.

9. Remove the bolts attaching the exhaust manifold to the cylinder head and remove the exhaust manifold and turbo as an assembly. Cap turbo outlet to crossover pipe.
10. Clean the exhaust manifold and cylinder head gasket mating surfaces.
11. Install the exhaust manifold, with a new gasket, making sure the turbo outlet is installed in crossover pipe boot. Tighten bolts to 14–17 ft. lbs. and tighten the crossover pipe boot clamp.
12. Remove the caps and install the oil feed line, with a new gasket, on the turbo oil inlet port. Tighten bolts to 14–17 ft. lbs.
13. Remove the caps and connect the oil return line to the turbo oil return port. Tighten fitting to 29–36 ft. lbs.
14. Install the oil feed tube to the exhaust manifold clamp and tighten to 6.5–7 ft. lbs.
15. Remove the cap and connect the inlet duct to the turbo inlet.
16. Remove the cap and connect the muffler inlet pipe to the turbo exhaust outlet. Tighten bolts to 31–35 ft. lbs.
17. Connect the EGR valve vacuum line.
18. Connect the battery ground cable.
19. Run the engine and check for intake, exhaust and oil leaks.

Turbocharger

REMOVAL & INSTALLATION

— CAUTION —
Do not accelerate the engine before engine oil pressure has been built up. Also, do not switch off the engine while it is running at high speed; the turbocharger will continue to spin for a long time without oil pressure. These conditions can damage the engine and/or turbocharger.

1. Remove the 2 bolts attaching the exhaust pipe to the turbocharger.
2. Remove the EGR tube and clamps.
3. Loosen the 4 hose clamps on the crossover tube and then remove tube.
4. Remove the air cleaner assembly and bellows. Cap turbocharger openings.

5. Remove the 2 oil supply line bolts on top of the turbocharger center housing.

6. Remove the clamp from oil lines.

7. Remove the oil return line.

8. Remove the bolt and sealing washers attaching the oil supply line to oil filter housing.

9. Disconnect and remove the EGR valve.

10. Remove the 4 bolts attaching the turbocharger to the exhaust manifold and remove the turbocharger.

11. Clean the mating surfaces of the turbocharger and exhaust manifold.

12. Position the turbocharger on the exhaust manifold and install the 4 mounting bolts. Tighten to 17–20 ft. lbs.

13. Install the EGR valve. Tighten to 18 ft. lbs.

14. Install the oil supply line using new seals. Tighten the bolt to 26–33 ft. lbs.

15. Install the clamp retaining the oil lines.

16. Install the oil supply line bolts to the turbocharger housing and tighten to 15–18 ft. lbs.

17. Remove the protective caps from the turbocharger and install the air cleaner assembly and bellows.

18. Install the crossover tube. Tighten the hose clamps snug.

19. Install the EGR tube clamp.

20. Install the 2 bolts attaching the exhaust pipe to the turbocharger and tighten to 17–20 ft. lbs.

21. Run the engine and check for oil and air leaks.

TROUBLESHOOTING

For further information on turbocharging, please refer to "Turbocharging" in the Unit Repair section.

Front Cover

REMOVAL & INSTALLATION

1. Disconnect the battery ground cable.

2. Loosen and remove the engine accessory drive belts.

3. Drain the cooling system and remove engine cooling fan and clutch assembly.

4. Remove the vibration damper.

5. Disconnect heater hose from the thermostat housing.

6. Remove the camshaft drive belt cover from crankcase. Remove drive belt.

7. Remove bolts attaching the intermediate shaft sprocket.

8. Remove the vibration damper flange and sprocket using proper pulling tool.

9. Remove 3 oil pan to front cover attaching bolts. Loosen but do not remove, remaining oil pan bolts.

10. Remove 6 bolts attaching the front cover to crankcase and remove cover.

11. Reverse the removal procedure for installation. Tighten all bolts to specifications.

NOTE: Coat areas where the front cover meets the oil pan gasket with RTV sealant. Sealant should be applied immediately prior to front cover installation.

OIL SEAL REPLACEMENT

NOTE: It is recommended to replace the front cover oil seal any time the front cover is removed.

1. With the cover removed from the car, drive the old seal from the rear of cover with a pinpunch. Clean out the recess in the cover.

2. Coat the new seal with grease and drive it into the cover until it is fully seated. Check the seal after installation to be sure the spring is properly positioned in the seal.

Timing Belt

REMOVAL & INSTALLATION

1. Disconnect the battery ground cable.

2. Drain the cooling system.

3. Remove the accessory drive belts.

4. Remove the fan assembly and water pump assembly.

5. Remove the vibration damper and pulley.

6. Disconnect the heater hose from the thermostat housing.

7. Remove the 4 bolts attaching the camshaft drive belt cover to crankcase and remove the cover.

8. Remove the rocker cover.

9. Rotate the engine until No. 1 cylinder is at TDC on compression stroke (intake and exhaust valves on base circle).

10. Install TDC Aligning Pin T84P–6256–A or equivalent.

NOTE: Flat side of nut or cam position tool should be facing down.

11. Loosen the camshaft sprocket bolt.

12. Using a piece of chalk, or similar marker, mark the direction of engine rotation on drive belt, unless a new belt is to be installed.

13. Loosen the 2 bolts on the belt tensioner.

14. Remove the camshaft drive belt.

15. Insert a 0.098 in. (2.5mm) thick

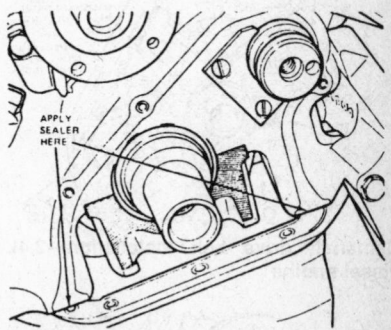

Crankshaft flange removal—2.4L diesel engine

Front cover gasket sealing areas—2.4L diesel engine

feeler gauge blade between Cam Positioning Tool T84P–6256–A or equivalent, at the right front corner of the gasket mating surface of the cylinder head if using a new drive belt or a drive belt used with less than 10,000 miles.

16. Install Injection Pump Aligning Pin T84P–9000–A or equivalent, through injection pump sprocket.

17. Rotate the cam sprocket clockwise against pin.

18. Install the camshaft drive belt. Starting at the crankshaft, route the belt around the intermediate shaft sprocket, injection pump sprocket, camshaft sprocket and then tension roller, keeping slack to a minimum.

19. Hand tighten belt with the belt tensioner until all slack is gone.

20. Remove Injection Pump Aligning Pin T84P–9000–A or equivalent, from the injection pump sprocket.

21. Adjust the belt tension by tightening the belt tensioner. Tighten belt tensioner to 34–36 ft. lbs. on belts with less than 10,000 miles and 23–25 ft. lbs. for belts with more than 10,000 miles.

22. Tighten the 2 belt tensioner holding bolts to 15–18 ft. lbs.

23. Tighten the camshaft sprocket to 41–47 ft. lbs.

24. Remove the Cam Positioning Tool, T84P–6265–A or equivalent.

25. Install the camshaft drive belt cover and tighten bolts to 6–7 ft. lbs.

26. Connect the heater hose to the thermostat housing.

27. Install the vibration damper.
28. Install fan and water pump pulley assembly.
29. Install and adjust the accessory drive belts.
30. Fill and bleed the cooling system.
31. Connect the battery ground cable.
32. Run the engine and check for oil and coolant leaks.
33. Check the injection pump timing.

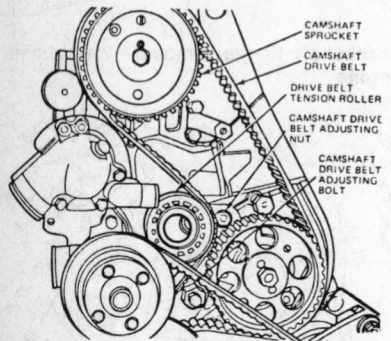

Camshaft drive belt installation—2.4L diesel engine

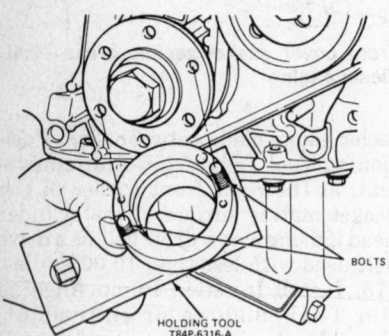

Alignment of bolts in the vibration damper—2.4L diesel engine

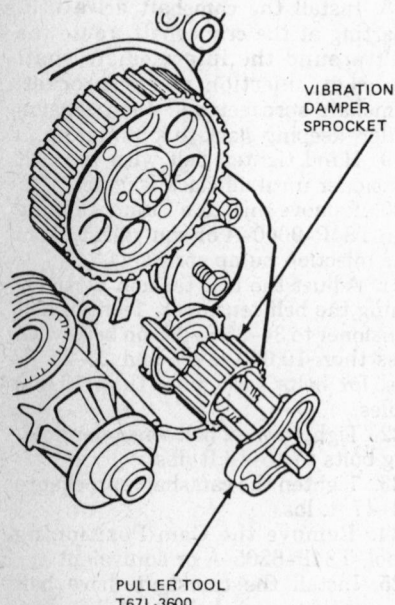

Vibration damper sprocket removal—2.4L diesel engine

Camshaft

REMOVAL & INSTALLATION

1. Disconnect the battery ground cable.
2. Remove the valve cover.
3. Remove the vacuum pump.
4. Remove the fan assembly.
5. Remove the camshaft drive belt cover.
6. Remove the rocker arms.
7. Rotate the engine until No. 1 cylinder is at TDC of compression stroke. Install TDC Aligning Pin, T84–P–6400–A, or equivalent.
8. Loosen the camshaft sprocket bolt.
9. Loosen the drive belt tension roller nut and bolt.
10. Remove the camshaft sprocket.
11. Remove the camshaft bearing caps, mark the caps so that they can be reinstalled in their original position and remove the camshaft.
12. To install, position the camshaft in the cylinder head.
13. Install the camshaft bearing caps, making sure that they are installed in the correct position. Tighten 6mm nuts to 6–7 ft. lbs. and 8mm nuts to 14–17 ft. lbs.
14. Install the camshaft sprocket but do not tighten at this time.
15. Install and adjust the camshaft drive belt.
16. Adjust the cam and pump timing.
17. Remove the TDC Aligning Pin Tool T84P-6400–A or equivalent.
18. Install the rocker arms.

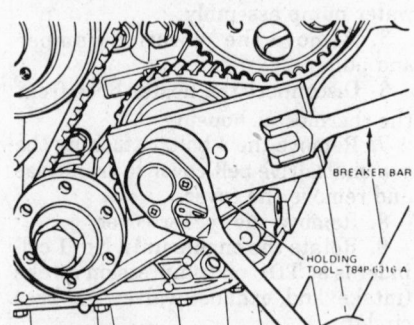

Intermediate shaft sprocket removal—2.4L diesel engine

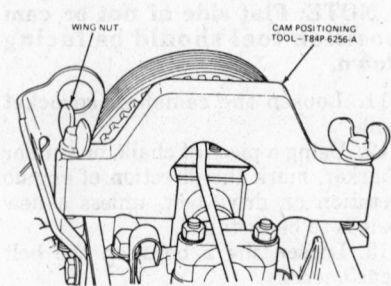

Cam positioning tool—2.4L diesel engine

19. Install the camshaft drive belt cover and tighten the bolts to 6–7 ft. lbs.
20. Install the fan assembly and install the vacuum pump.
21. Install the rocker arm cover.
22. Connect the battery ground cable.
23. Run the engine and check for oil, intake air and coolant leaks.

Piston and Connecting Rod

POSITIONING

For all piston and connecting rod overhaul procedures, please refer to "Engine Rebuilding" in the Unit Repair section.

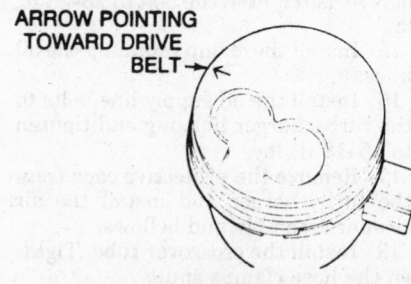

Arrow on piston head

ENGINE LUBRICATION

Oil Pan

REMOVAL & INSTALLATION

NOTE: On certain engine-chassis combinations, interference will be encountered between the oil pan and oil pump while attempting to remove the oil pan. If interference occurs, lower the oil pan as far as possible, reach inside and remove the bolts mounting the oil pump or pickup tube. Lower the pump and/or pickup tube into the oil pan. Remove the oil pan. Interference may also occur between the pan and the rear counter balance weight of the crankshaft. Turn the crank to position the weight in an upward position if necessary.

2.3L Engines

1. Disconnect the negative battery cable.

2. Remove the fan shroud or fan shroud and electric fan assembly.

3. Drain the crankcase.

4. Remove the right and left engine support bolts and nuts.

5. Using a jack with a piece of wood between the raising point and jack contact points, raise the engine as high as it will go. Place blocks of wood between the mounts and chassis brackets. Remove the jack. Remove shake brace.

6. Remove the sway bar retaining bolts and lower the sway bar.

7. Remove the starter motor.

8. Remove steering gear retaining bolts and lower the gear.

9. Remove the oil pan retaining bolts. Pivot the oil pan forward over the crossmember and remove.

10. Install new oil pan gasket and end seals.

11. Position the oil pan to the cylinder block and install retaining bolts and tighten to 20 inch lbs..

12. Reposition the steering gear and install bolts and nuts.

13. Install starter.

14. Raise the engine enough to remove the wood blocks, lower the engine and remove jack. Install shake brace.

15. Install the right and left engine mount bolts and nuts, tighten to 33–45 ft. lbs..

16. Install the sway bar.

17. Install the fan shroud.

18. Fill the crankcase with oil.

19. Connect battery cable, run engine and check for leaks.

3.3L Engine

1. Disconnect 2 oil cooler lines at radiator.

2. Remove radiator top support bolts. Remove or position fan shroud back over fan.

3. Remove oil level dipstick and drain crankcase.

4. Remove 4 bolts and nuts attaching sway bar to chassis and allow sway bar to hang down.

5. Remove K brace.

6. Lower front steering rack and pinion, or center link and linkage, if necessary for clearance.

7. Remove starter.

8. Remove 2 nuts attaching engine mounts to support brackets.

9. Loosen 2 rear insulator to crossmember attaching bolts.

10. Raise engine and place a 1¼ in. spacer between engine support insulator and chassis brackets.

11. Position a jack under the transmission and raise slightly.

12. Remove the oil pan attaching bolts and lower the pan to the crossmember. Position transmission cooler lines out of the way and remove the oil pan (rotating crankshaft if required).

13. The oil pan has a 2 piece gasket. Coat the block surface and the oil pan gasket surfaces with oil resistant sealer and position gaskets to cylinder block.

14. Position the oil pan seals in the cylinder front cover and rear bearing cap.

15. Insert gasket tabs under front and rear seals.

16. Position the oil pan to the cylinder block and install attaching bolts, torque to 7–9 ft. lbs.

17. Position transmission cooler lines.

18. Lower jack under transmission.

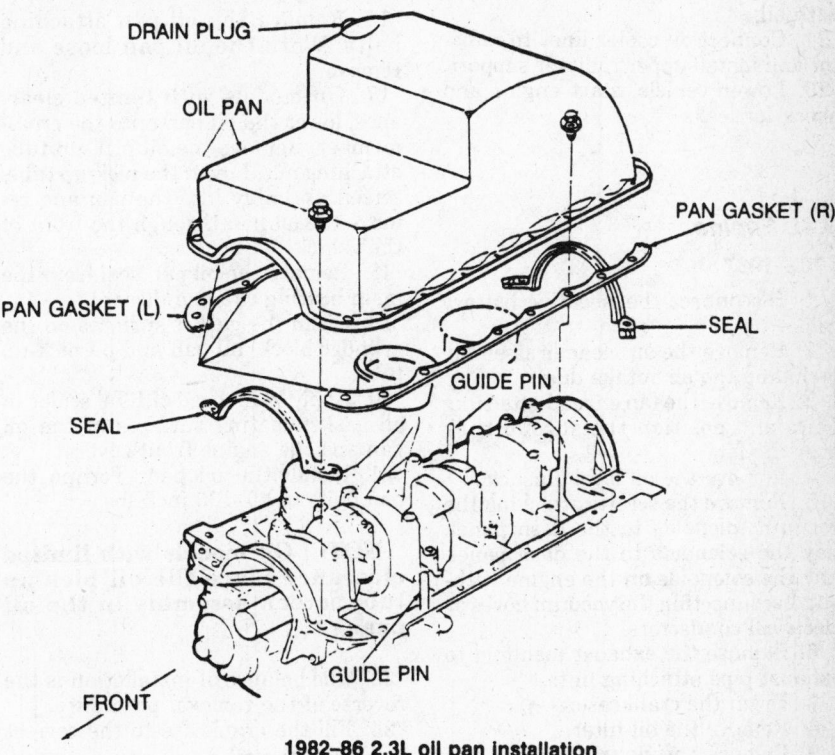

1982–86 2.3L oil pan installation

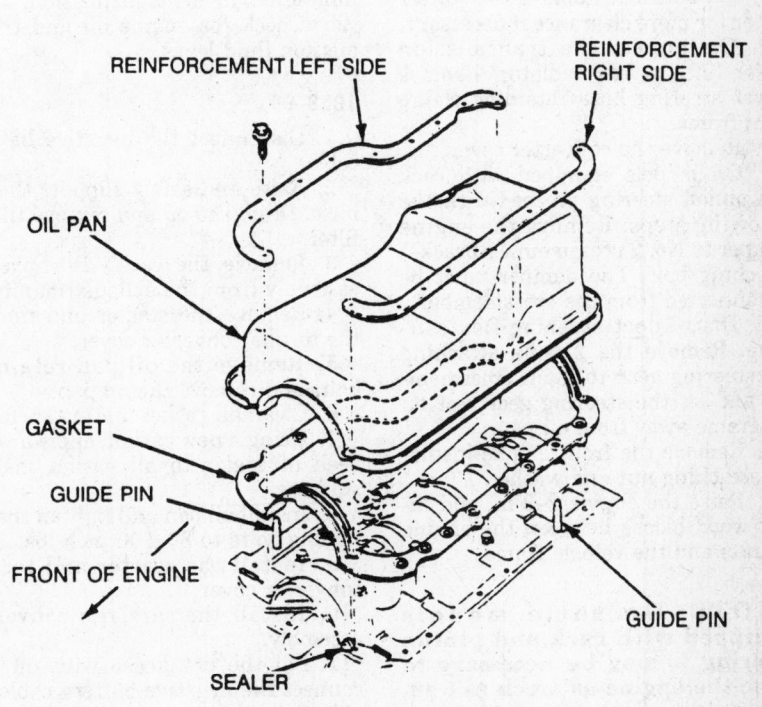

1987–89 2.3L oil pan installation

19. Raise the engine to remove the spacers and lower engine to chassis.

20. Tighten 2 nuts attaching rear support insulator to crossmember.

21. Install 2 engine support to chassis thru-bolts and nuts.

22. Install starter motor and sway bar.

23. Install "K" brace, fill crankcase with oil.

24. Connect oil cooler lines to radiator and install upper radiator support.

25. Lower vehicle, start engine and check for leaks.

3.8L Engine

1982–1987

1. Disconnect the negative battery cable.

2. Remove the air cleaner assembly including the air intake duct.

3. Remove the fan shroud attaching bolts and position the shroud back over the fan.

4. Remove the oil level dipstick.

5. Remove the screws attaching the vacuum solenoids to the dash panel. Lay the solenoids on the dash panel. Lay the solenoids on the engine without disconnecting the vacuum hoses or electrical connectors.

6. Remove the exhaust manifold to exhaust pipe attaching nuts.

7. Drain the crankcase.

8. Remove the oil filter.

9. Remove the bolts attaching the shift linkage bracket to the transmission bell housing. Remove the starter motor for more clearance if necessary.

10. Disconnect the transmission cooler lines at the radiator. Remove power steering hose retaining clamp from frame.

11. Remove the converter cover.

12. On models equipped with rack and pinion steering proceed with the following steps: Remove the engine damper to No. 2 crossmember bracket attaching bolt. The damper must be disconnected from the crossmember.

13. Disconnect steering flex coupling. Remove the 2 bolts attaching the steering gear to main crossmember and let the steering gear rest on the frame away from oil pan.

14. Remove the front engine insulator attaching nut and washer.

15. Raise the engine 2–3 in. and insert wood blocks between the engine mounts and the vehicle frame.

NOTE: On some models equipped with rack and pinion steering it may be necessary to raise the engine as much as 5 in. to provide adequate pan to crossmember clearance.

CAUTION

Watch the clearance between the transmission dipstick tube and the thermactor downstream air tube. If the tubes contact before adequate pan to crossmember clearance is provided, lower the engine and remove the transmission dipstick tube and the downstream air tube.

---

16. Remove the oil pan attaching bolts. Work the oil pan loose and remove.

17. On models with limited clearance, lower the oil pan onto the crossmember. Remove the oil pick-up tube attaching nut. Lower the pick-up tube/screen assembly into the pan and remove the oil pan through the front of the vehicle.

18. Remove the oil pan seal from the main bearing cap and discard.

19. Clean the gasket surfaces on the cylinder block, oil pan and oil pick-up tube.

20. Apply ⅛ in. bead of RTV sealer to all gasket mating surfaces of the oil pan and the engine front cover.

21. Install the oil pan. Torque the pan bolts to 80–106 inch lbs.

NOTE: On models with limited clearance place the oil pick-up tube/screen assembly in the oil pan.

22. The balance of installation is the reverse of the removal procedure.

23. Fill the crankcase to the correct level with the oil.

24. Start the engine and check the fluid levels in the transmission.

25. Check for engine oil and transmission fluid leaks.

1988–89

1. Disconnect the negative battery cable.

2. Raise and safely support the vehicle. Drain the oil and remove the oil filter.

3. Remove the catalytic converter assembly from the exhaust manifold.

4. Remove the starter and remove the torque converter cover.

5. Remove the oil pan retaining bolts and remove the oil pan.

6. Clean all gasket mating surfaces.

7. Using a new gasket, apply a ⅛ in. bead of sealer to all gasket mating surfaces.

8. Install oil pan and tighten the retaining bolts to 80–106 inch lbs.

9. Install the starter and torque converter cover.

10. Install the catalytic converter assembly.

11. Fill the crankcase with oil and connect the negative battery cable.

12. Run the engine and check for leaks.

4.2L, 5.0L and 5.8L Engines

NOTE: On vehicles equipped with a dual sump oil pan, both drain plugs must be removed to thoroughly drain the crankcase. When raising the engine for oil pan removal clearance; drain cooling system, disconnect hoses, check fan to radiator clearance when jacking. Remove the radiator if clearance is inadequate.

1. Remove the fan shroud attaching bolts, positioning the fan shroud back over the fan. Remove the dipstick and tube assembly. Disconnect negative battery cable.

2. Drain the crankcase.

3. Remove the stabilizer bar from the chassis. Disconnect the engine stabilizer on models equipped.

4. On rack and pinion models disconnect steering flex coupling. Remove 2 bolts attaching steering gear to main crossmember and let steering gear rest on frame away from oil pan. Disconnect power steering hose retaining clamp from frame. Remove the starter motor.

5. Remove the idler arm bracket retaining bolts (if equipped) and pull the linkage down and out of the way.

6. Disconnect and plug the fuel line from the gas tank at the fuel pump. Disconnect and lower the exhaust pipe/converter assemblies if they will interfere with pan removal/installation. Raise the engine and place 2 wood blocks between the engine mounts and the vehicle frame. Remove converter inspection cover.

NOTE: On fuel injected models, relieve the fuel system pressure.

8. Remove the K braces (four bolts).

9. Remove the oil pan attaching bolts and lower oil pan to the frame.

10. Remove oil pump attaching bolts and the inset tube attaching nut from the No. 3 main bearing cap stud and lower the oil pump into the oil pan.

11. Remove the oil pan, rotating the crankshaft as necessary to clear the counterweights.

12. Clean the gasket mounting surfaces thoroughly. Coat the surfaces on the block and pan with sealer. Position the pan side gaskets on the engine block. Install the rear main cap seal with the tabs over the pan side gaskets.

13. Position oil pump and inlet tube into the oil pan. Slide the oil pan into position under the engine. With the oil pump intermediate shaft in position in the oil pump, position the oil pump to the cylinder block and the inlet tube to the stud on the No. 3 main bearing cap attaching bolt. Install the attaching bolts and tighten to specification. Position the oil pan on the engine and in-

stall the attaching bolts. Tighten the bolts (working from the center toward the ends) 9–11 ft. lbs. for $5/16$ in. bolts and 7–9 ft. lbs. for $1/4$ in. bolts.

14. Position the steering gear to the main crossmember. Install the 2 attaching bolts and tighten to specification. Connect the steering flex coupling to the steering gear.

15. Position the rear K braces and install the 4 attaching bolts.

16. Raise the engine and remove the wood blocks.

17. Install the stabilizer bar.

18. Lower the engine and install the engine mount attaching bolts. Tighten to 33–46 ft. lbs.. Install the torque converter inspection cover.

19. Install the oil dipstick, tube assembly and fill crankcase with the specified engine oil. Install the idler arm.

20. Connect the transmission oil cooler lines. Connect the battery cable.

21. Position the shroud to the radiator and install the 2 attaching bolts. Start the engine and check for leaks.

Rear Main Bearing Oil Seal

REMOVAL & INSTALLATION

Split-Type Seal — Gasoline Engines

1. Remove the oil pan and on all engines except the 2.3L, remove the oil pump.

2. Loosen all the main bearing caps allowing the crankshaft to lower slightly.

NOTE: The crankshaft should not be allowed to drop more than $1/32$ in.

3. Remove the rear main bearing cap and remove the seal from the cap and block.

NOTE: Be very careful not to scratch the sealing surface. Remove the oil seal retaining pin from the cap, if equipped. It is not used with the replacement seal.

4. Carefully clean the seal grooves in the cap and block with solvent.

5. Soak the new seal halves in clean engine oil.

6. Install the upper half of the seal in the block with the undercut side of the seal toward the front of the engine. Slide the seal around the crankshaft journal until $3/8$ in. protrudes beyond the base of the block.

7. Tighten all the main bearing caps (except the rear main) to specifications.

8. Install the lower seal into the

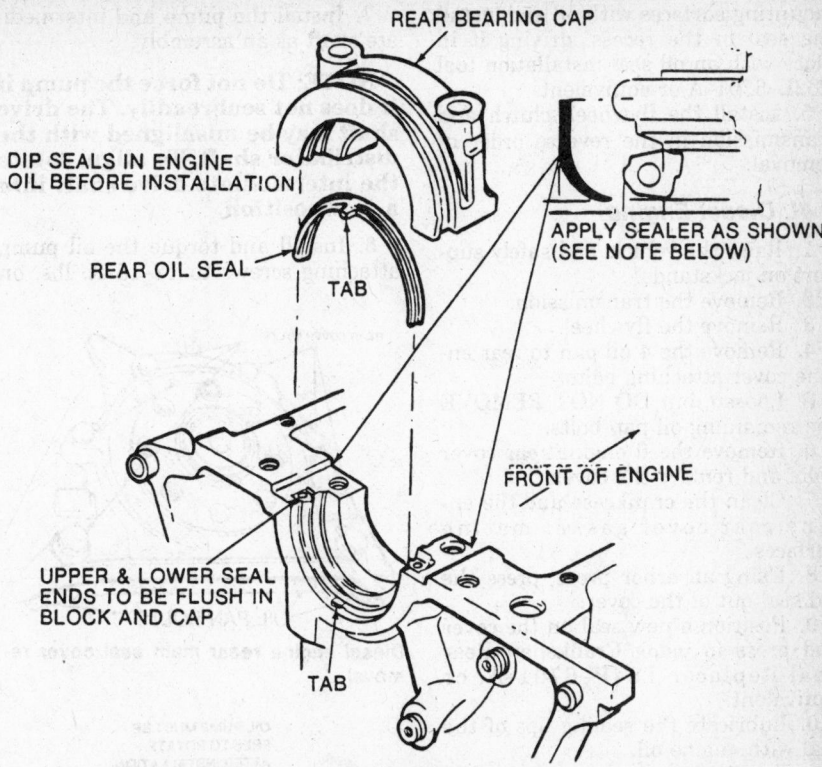

NOTE: CLEAN THE AREA WHERE SEALER IS TO BE APPLIED BEFORE INSTALLING THE SEALS. AFTER THE SEALS ARE IN PLACE, APPLY A 1/16 INCH BEAD OF SEALER AS SHOWN. *SEALER MUST NOT TOUCH SEALS*

Replacement of the rear main bearing oil seal—2.3L (140) engine with split seal

rear cap, with the undercut side facing the front of the engine. Allow $3/8$ in. of the seal to protrude above the surface, at the opposite end from the block seal.

9. Squeeze a $1/16$ in. bead of silicone sealant onto the outer center edges of the bearing cap.

10. Install the rear cap and torque to specifications.

11. Install the oil pump and pan. Fill the crankcase with oil, start the engine and check for leaks.

One-Piece Seal — Gasoline Engines

1. Remove the transmission and the clutch and flywheel (manual transmission).

2. Punch 2 holes in the crankshaft rear oil seal on opposite sides of the crankshaft, just above the bearing cap to cylinder block split line. Install a sheet metal screw in each of the holes or use a small slide hammer and pry the crankshaft rear main oil seal from the block.

NOTE: Use extreme caution not to scratch the crankshaft oil seal surface.

3. Clean the oil seal recess in the cylinder block and main bearing cap.

4. Coat the seal and all of the seal

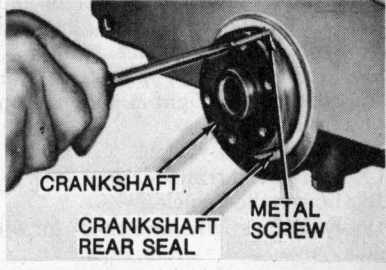

Typical one piece rear main bearing seal removal

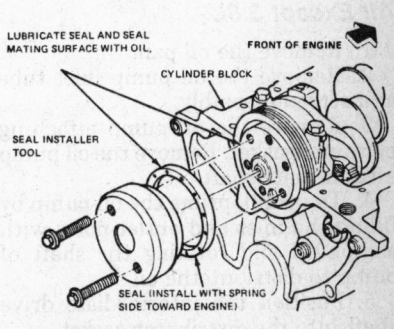

One piece rear main bearing oil seal installation

mounting surfaces with oil and install the seal in the recess, driving it in place with an oil seal installation tool T82L–6701–A or equivalent.

5. Install the flywheel, clutch and transmission in the reverse order of removal.

2.4L Diesel Engine

1. Raise the vehicle and safely support on jackstands.
2. Remove the transmission.
3. Remove the flywheel.
4. Remove the 4 oil pan to rear engine cover attaching bolts.
5. Loosen, but DO NOT REMOVE the remaining oil pan bolts.
6. Remove the 6 engine rear cover bolts and remove the cover.
7. Clean the crankcase and the engine rear cover gasket mating surfaces.
8. Using an arbor press, press the old seal out of the cover.
9. Position a new seal on the cover and press in using Crankshaft Rear Seal Replacer T84P–6701–A, or equivalent.
10. Lubricate the sealing lips of the seal with engine oil.
11. Position a new rear cover gasket on the crankcase.
12. Apply gasket sealer at points where the rear cover gasket meets the oil pan gasket.
13. Position the rear cover on the crankshaft.
14. Install the rear cover bolts and tighten 6mm bolts to 6–7 ft. lbs. and 8mm bolts to 14–17 ft. lbs.
15. Install the 4 oil pan to rear cover attaching bolts. Tighten all oil pan bolts to 6.5–7 ft. lbs.
16. Install the flywheel.
17. Install the transmission.
18. Lower the vehicle.
19. Run the engine and check for oil leaks.

Oil Pump

REMOVAL & INSTALLATION

All Except 3.8L

1. Remove the oil pan.
2. Remove the oil pump inlet tube and screen assembly.
3. Remove the oil pump attaching bolts and gasket. Remove the oil pump intermediate shaft.
4. To install, prime the oil pump by filling the inlet and outlet ports with engine oil and rotating the shaft of pump to distribute the oil.
5. Position the intermediate drive shaft into the distributor socket.
6. Position a new gasket on the pump body and insert the intermediate drive shaft into pump body.

7. Install the pump and intermediate shaft as an assembly.

NOTE: Do not force the pump if it does not seal readily. The drive shaft may be misaligned with the distributor shaft. To align, rotate the intermediate drive shaft into a new position.

8. Install and torque the oil pump attaching screws to 12–15 ft. lbs. on

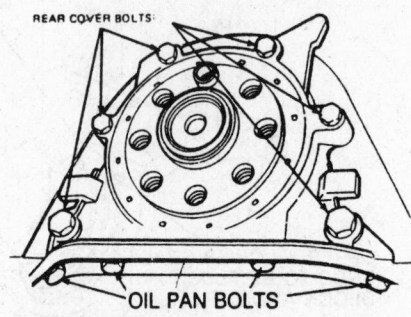

Diesel engine reear main seal cover removal

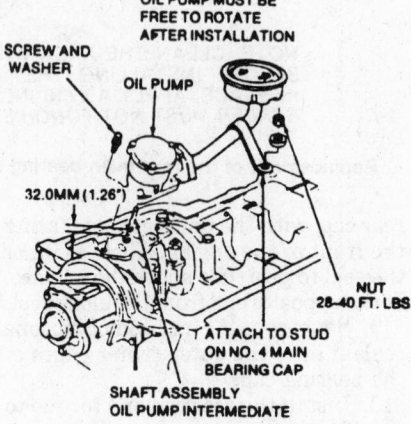

4 Cyl oil pump installation

the 2.3L and 3.3L engine, 20–25 ft. lbs. on 4.2L, 5.0L and 5.8L engines.
9. Install oil pan.

3.8L ENGINE

NOTE: The oil pump is mounted in the front cover assembly. Oil pan removal is necessary for pick-up tube/screen replacement or service only.

1. Raise and safely support the vehicle on jackstands.
2. Remove the oil filter.
3. Remove the cover/filter mount assembly.
4. Lift the 2 pump gears from their mounting pocket in the front cover.
5. Clean all gasket mounting surfaces.
6. Inspect the mounting pocket for wear. If excessive wear is present, complete timing cover assembly replacement is necessary.
7. Inspect the cover/filter mount gasket to timing cover surface for flatness. Place a straight edge across the flat and check clearance with a feeler gauge. If the measured clearance exceeds 0.004 in., replace the cover/filter mount.
8. Replace the pump gears if wear is excessive.
9. Remove the plug from the end of the pressure relief valve passage using a small drill and slide hammer. Use caution when drilling.
10. Remove the spring and valve from the bore. Clean all dirt, gum and metal chips from the bore and valve. Inspect all parts for wear. Replace as necessary.

NOTE: It is necessary to prime the oil pump after it has been disassembled to prevent it from failing on initial startup. this can be done by lightly packing the oil pump gear cavity with petroleum jelly before final assembly.

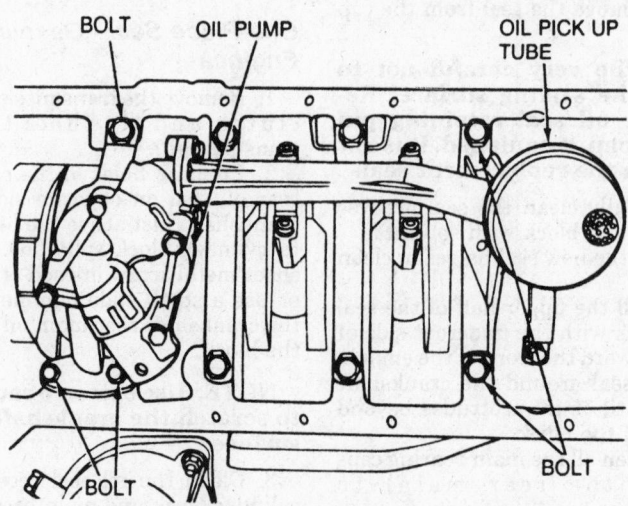

Diesel engine oil pump and screen mounting

11. Install the valve and spring after lubricating them with engine oil. Install cover/filter mount using a new mounting gasket. Tighten the mounting bolts to 18–22 ft. lbs. Install the oil filter, add necessary oil for correct level.

Oil Pan and Pump

REMOVAL & INSTALLATION

Diesel Engine

1. With the engine removed from vehicle and placed on an engine stand, remove the bolts attaching the oil pan to the crankcase.

2. Remove the 2 bolts attaching the oil pump pick-up to the crankcase.

3. Remove the 3 bolts attaching the oil pump to the crankcase and remove the oil pump.

4. Remove the oil pump driveshaft, if necessary.

5. To install, install the oil pump driveshaft, if removed, making sure it is fully engaged with intermediate shaft.

6. Install the oil pump on the crankcase, making sure driveshaft is fully engaged in the oil pump. Tighten the oil pump and oil pick-up bolts to 16–17 ft. lbs.

ENGINE COOLING

Radiator

REMOVAL & INSTALLATION

1. Drain the cooling system.

2. Disconnect the upper, lower and overflow hoses at the radiator.

3. On automatic transmission equipped cars, disconnect the fluid cooler lines at radiator.

4. Depending on model; remove the 2 top mounting bolts and remove radiator and shroud assembly, or remove the shroud mounting bolts and position the shroud out of the way. If the air conditioner condenser is attached to the radiator, remove the retaining bolts and position the condenser out of the way. DO NOT disconnect the refrigerant lines.

5. Remove the radiator attaching bolts or top brackets and lift out the radiator.

6. If a new radiator is to be installed, transfer the petcock from the old radiator to the new one. On cars equipped with automatic transmissions, transfer the fluid cooler line fittings from the old radiator.

7. Position the radiator and install, do not tighten the radiator support bolts. On cars equipped with automatic transmissions, connect the fluid cooler lines. Then tighten the radiator support bolts or shroud and mounting bolts.

8. Connect the radiator hoses. Close the radiator petcock. Fill and bleed the cooling system.

9. Start the engine and bring to operating temperature. Check for leaks.

10. On cars equipped with automatic transmission, check the cooler lines for leaks and interference. Check the transmission fluid level.

Water Pump

REMOVAL & INSTALLATION

Gasoline Engine

1. Drain the cooling system.

2. Disconnect the negative battery cable.

3. On cars with power steering, remove the drive belt.

4. If the vehicle is equipped with air conditioning, remove the idler pulley bracket and air conditioner drive belt.

5. On engines with Thermactor, remove the belt.

6. Disconnect the lower radiator hose and heater hose from the water pump.

7. On cars equipped with a fan shroud, remove the retaining screws and position the shroud rearward.

8. Remove the fan, fan clutch and spacer from the engine. On vehicles equipped with an electric cooling fan, remove the fan as an assembly for working clearance.

9. On the 2.3L engines, remove the timing belt outer cover.

10. On cars equipped with water pump mounted alternators, loosen the alternator mounting bolts, remove the alternator belt and remove the alternator adjusting arm bracket from the water pump. If interference is encountered, remove the air pump pulley and pivot bolt. Remove the air pump adjusting bracket and swing the upper bracket aside. Detach the air conditioner compressor and lay it aside. Do not disconnect any of the A/C lines. Remove any accessory mounting brackets from the water pump.

11. Loosen the bypass hose clamp at the water pump, if equipped.

12. Remove the water pump mounting bolts and remove the pump from the engine.

13. Clean any gasket material from the pump mounting surface. On engines equipped with a water pump backing plate; remove the plate, clean

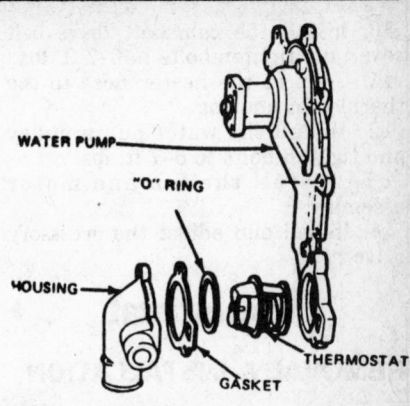

Water pump and thermostat installation 3.8L engine

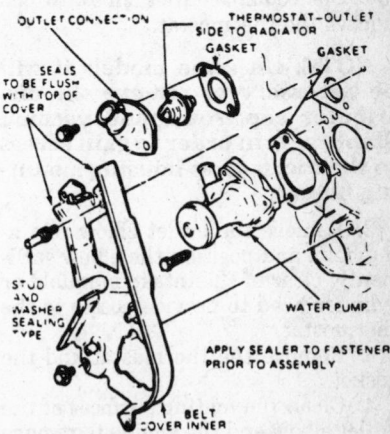

Water pump and thermostat installation 2.3L engine

the gasket surfaces, install a new gasket and plate on the water pump.

14. Remove the heater hose fitting from the old pump and install it on the new pump.

15. Coat both sides of the new gasket with a water-resistant sealer, then install the pump by reversing the removal procedure.

Diesel Engine

1. Drain the cooling system.

2. Loosen and remove the accessory drive belts.

3. Remove the fan and motor assembly.

4. Remove the water pump pulley.

5. Disconnect the heater hose from the thermostat housing.

6. Remove the camshaft drive belt cover.

7. Remove the 3 bolts attaching the water pump to the crankcase and remove the water pump.

NOTE: Do not loosen the timing belt.

8. Clean the gasket mating surfaces of the water pump and crankcase.

9. Install the water pump with a new gasket, on the crankcase and tighten bolts to 14–17 ft. lbs.

10. Install the camshaft drive belt cover and tighten bolts to 6–7 ft. lbs.

11. Connect the heater hose to the thermostat housing.

12. Install the water pump pulley and tighten bolts to 6–7 ft. lbs.

13. Install the fan and motor assembly.

14. Install and adjust the accessory drive belts.

Thermostat

REMOVAL & INSTALLATION

1. Open the drain cock and drain the radiator so the coolant level is below the coolant outlet elbow which houses the thermostat.

NOTE: On some models it will be necessary to remove the distributor cap, rotor and vacuum diaphragm in order to gain access to the thermostat housing mounting bolts.

2. Remove the outlet elbow retaining bolts and position the elbow sufficiently clear of the intake manifold or cylinder head to provide access to the thermostat.

3. Remove the thermostat and the gasket.

4. Clean the mating surfaces of the outlet elbow and the engine to remove all old gasket material and sealer. Coat the new gasket with water-resistant sealer. Install the thermostat in the coolant elbow. The thermostat must be rotated clockwise to lock it in position on all 8 cylinder engines. On 4 cylinder engines, be sure the full width of the heater outlet tube is visible within the thermostat port.

5. Install the outlet elbow and retaining bolts on the engine. Torque the bolts to 12–15 ft. lbs.

6. Refill the radiator. Run the engine at operating temperature and

check for leaks. Recheck the coolant level.

EMISSION CONTROLS

Please refer to "Emission Control" in the unit repair section for all system maintenance procedures. Due to the complex nature of modern electronic engine control systems, comprehensive diagnosis and testing procedures fall outside the confines of this repair manual. For complete information on diagnosis, testing and repair procedures concerning all modern engine and emission control systems, please refer to *"Chilton's Guide to Electronic Engine Controls".*

GASOLINE FUEL SYSTEM

Fuel System Service Precaution

When working with the fuel system certain precautions should be taken:
- Always work in a well ventilated area
- Keep a dry chemical (Class B) fire extinguisher near the work area
- Always disconnect the negative battery cable
- Do not make any repairs to the fuel system until all the necessary steps for repair have been reviewed

RELIEVING FUEL SYSTEM PRESSURE

1. If the fuel charging assembly is mounted to the engine, remove the fuel tank cap then using fuel pressure gauge T80L–9974–A, install it to the relief valve and release the pressure from the system by opening the pressure relief valve.

NOTE: The cap on the relief valve must be removed in order to install the fuel pressure gauge.

2. Once the pressure has been relieved, using an open-end wrench, remove the pressure relief valve from the fuel line.

3. Install the pressure relief valve

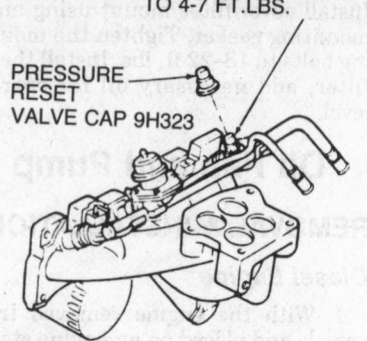

Fuel pressure relief valve removal and installation

and cap. Tighten the valve to 48–84 inch lbs. Tighten the cap to 4–6 inch lbs.

Fuel Filter

REMOVAL & INSTALLATION

Carbureted Engines

IN-LINE HOSE CONNECTED FILTERS

1. Remove the air cleaner.
2. Loosen the hose clamps.
3. Unscrew the filter from the carburetor.
4. Disconnect the filter from the hose and discard the filter, hose and clamps. Replacement filters usually come with a length of hose and new clamps, always use the new parts when filter replacement is necessary.
5. Reverse the procedure to install the fuel filter. After installation, start the engine and check for fuel leakage.

INVERTED NUT (STEEL LINE) CONNECTED FILTERS

1. Remove the air cleaner assembly.
2. Position an $^{11}/_{16}$ in. open end wrench on the filter hex nut to hold the filler in position and remove the steel fuel line from the filter using a suitable wrench.
3. Unscrew the filter from the carburetor.
4. Install the new filter in reverse order of removal.

IN CARBURETOR FILTERS (VV CARBS)

1. Remove the air cleaner.
2. Disconnect the fuel line from the carburetor inlet fitting, while holding the inlet fitting with a suitable wrench.
3. Remove inlet fitting and fuel filter.
4. Install the spring, filter, gasket and fitting.

V8 engine thermostat installation

RECESS

BRIDGE

FLATS

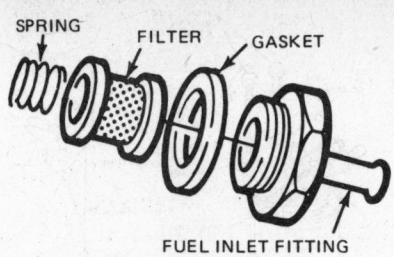

VV carburetor fuel filter

5. Connect the fuel line, start engine and check for leaks.

Fuel Injected Engines

NOTE: Models equipped with fuel injection actually have 4 fuel filters; a nylon mesh "sock" at the fuel pump inlet in the fuel tank; a large paper element filter mounted in the fuel line under the car; a small canister filter mounted in the engine compartment; and individual mesh filters at each injector fuel inlet. Of these, only the undercar paper element filter is scheduled for regular replacement (at 50,000 mile intervals). Filter replacement requires discharging of the fuel injection system pressure prior to filter change. Discharge pressure, disconnect the fuel lines and remove filter retainer. Note the direction of the fuel flow arrow on filter. Install new filter in reverse order.

Mechanical Fuel Pump

PRESSURE TESTING

1. Connect a suitable pressure guage to the carburetor end of the fuel line.
2. Start the engine and read the pressure after 10 seconds. (It should be able to run for over 30 seconds on the fuel in the carburetor bowl.)
3. Fuel pump pressure should be 6–8 psi. for 6 and 8 cylinder carbureted engines, 5–7 psi for 4 cylinder carbureted engines. If pump pressure is too low or too high, install a new fuel pump.

REMOVAL & INSTALLATION

NOTE: Before removing the pump, rotate the engine so that the low point of the cam lobe is against the pump arm. This can be determined by rotating the engine with a fuel pump mounting bolts loosened slightly; when tension (resistance) is removed from the arm, proceed with removal.

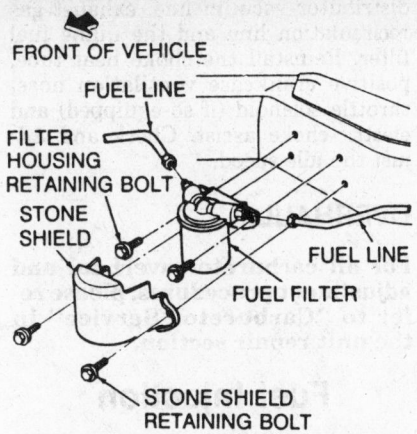

In-line fuel filter mounting and removal

1. Remove the inlet, outlet and return vapor (if equipped) lines from the pump.
2. Remove the fuel pump mounting bolts and remove the pump and gasket. Remove the fuel pump pushrod on 3.8L engines.
3. Clean all gasket material from the pump mounting surface on the engine and apply a coat of oil-resistant sealer to the new gasket.
4. Reinstall the pushrod on models equipped. Position pump on engine and install retaining screws.
5. Reinstall lines, start engine and check for leaks.

NOTE: If resistance is felt while positioning the fuel pump on the block, the camshaft eccentric is in the high position. To ease installation, rotate the engine until the camshaft eccentric is in the low position.

Electric Fuel Pump

REMOVAL & INSTALLATION

NOTE: A single internally fuel tank mounted pump is used on fuel injected models from 1982–89. Other 1984–89 models equipped with a high output injected or turbocharged injected engine are equipped with 2 electric pumps. A low-pressure pump is mounted in the tank and a high pressure pump is externally mounted.

1. Disconnect the negative battery cable.
2. Relieve the fuel system pressure and drain as much gas as possible from the tank by pumping out through the filler neck.
3. Raise and safely support the rear of the vehicle.
4. Disconnect the fuel supply, re-

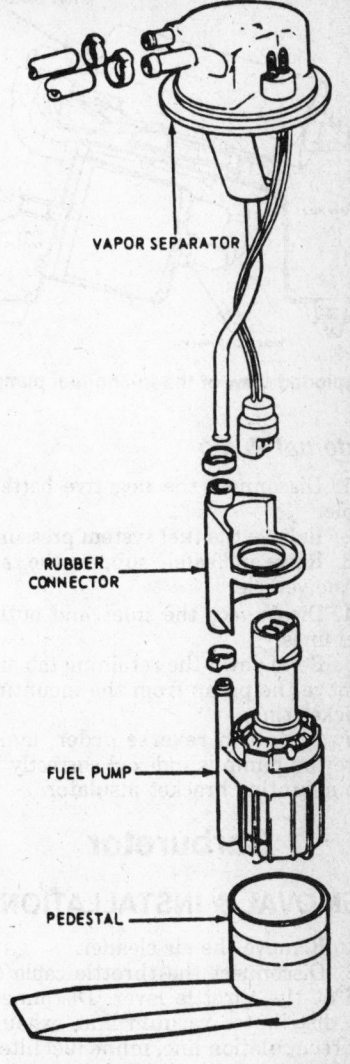

Tank mounted electric fuel pump

turn and vent lines at the right and left side of the frame.
5. Disconnect the wiring harness to the fuel pump.
6. Support the gas tank, loosen and remove the mounting straps. Remove the gas tank.
7. Disconnect the lines and harness at the pump flange.
8. Clean the outside of the mounting flange and retaining ring. Turn the fuel pump lock ring counterclockwise and remove.
9. Remove the fuel pump.
10. Clean the mounting surfaces. Put a light coat of grease on the mounting sufaces and on the new sealing ring. Install the new fuel pump.
11. Installation is in the reverse order of removal. If single high pressure pump system, fill the tank with at least 10 gals. of gas. Turn the ignition key **ON** for 3 seconds. Repeat 6 or 7 times until the fuel system is pressurized. Check for any fitting leaks. Start the engine and check for leaks.

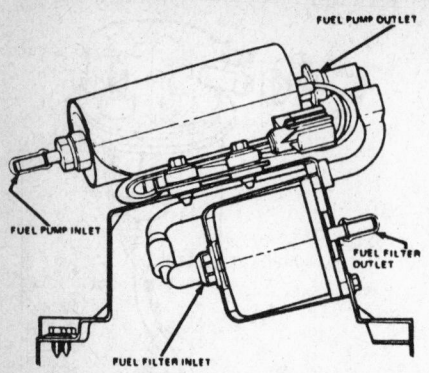

Exploded view of the in-line fuel pump

External Pump

1. Disconnect the negative battery cable.
2. Relieve the fuel system pressure.
3. Raise and safely support the rear of the vehicle.
4. Disconnect the inlet and outlet fuel lines.
5. Bend down the retaining tab and remove the pump from the mounting bracket ring.
7. Install in reverse order, make sure the pump is indexed correctly in the mounting bracket insulator.

Carburetor

REMOVAL & INSTALLATION

1. Remove the air cleaner.
2. Disconnect the throttle cable or rod at the throttle lever. Disconnect the distributor vacuum line, exhaust gas recirculation line, inline fuel filter, choke heat tube and the positive crankcase ventilation hose at the carburetor.
3. Disconnect the throttle solenoid (if so equipped) and electric choke assist at their connectors.
4. Remove the carburetor retaining nuts. Lift off the carburetor carefully and remove the carburetor mounting gasket and discard it. Remove the carburetor mounting spacer, if so equipped, from the intake manifold.
5. Prior to installation, clean the gasket mounting surfaces of the intake manifold, spacer (if so equipped) and carburetor. When using a spacer, use 2 new gaskets. sandwiching the spacer between the gaskets. If a spacer is not used, only 1 new carburetor mounting gasket is required.
6. Place the new gasket(s) and spacer (if so equipped) on the carburetor mounting studs. Position the carburetor on top of the gasket and hand tighten the retaining nuts. Then tighten the nuts in a crisscross pattern to 10-15 ft. lbs.
7. Connect the throttle linkage and

distributor vacuum line, exhaust gas recirculation line and the inline fuel filter. Reinstall the choke heat tube, positive crankcase ventilation hose, throttle solenoid (if so equipped) and electric-choke assist. Check and Adjust the idle speed.

OVERHAUL

For all carburetor overhaul and adjustment procedures, please refer to "Carburetor Service" in the unit repair section.

Fuel Injection

Due to the complex nature of modern fuel injection systems, comprehensive diagnosis and testing procedures fall outside the confines of this repair manual. For complete information on fuel injection diagnosis, testing and repair procedures please refer to *"Chilton's Guide to Fuel Injection and Feedback Carburetors"*.

DIESEL FUEL SYSTEM

Fuel Filter

REPLACEMENT

1. Drain the fuel from the fuel filter by opening the vent screw on the top of the filter and then depressing the drain valve on the bottom of the filter.
2. Disconnect the Water-in-Fuel sensor connector.
3. Remove the filter cartridge using a standard oil filter wrench, if necessary.
4. Remove the protective cover.
5. Remove the drain valve from the old filter and install on the new filter.
6. Install the protective cover.
7. Coat the surface of the sealing gasket with engine oil and install the filter on the adapter. Turn the filter until the gasket contacts the sealing surface of the filter adapter.
8. Turn the filter an additional one-half turn.
9. Close the vent screw.
10. Start the engine and check for fuel leaks, tightening the filter further, if necessary.

DRAINING WATER FROM THE SYSTEM

The diesel engine uses a spin-on car-

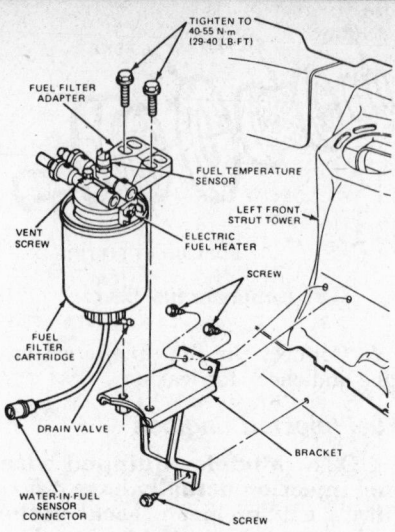

Diesel fuel filter assembly

tridge-type fuel filter. The filter is used to provide a clean supply of fuel to the injection pump and to seperate water from the fuel. When the water level in the filter reaches a certain point, a sensor in the filter turns on the Water-in-Fuel indicator on the instrument panel. The water must be drained as soon as possible. This is accomplished by opening the vent screw on top of the filter and then depressing the drain valve on the bottom of the filter cartridge. Hold the drain valve open until all of the water drains from the filter.

Injection Pump

REMOVAL & INSTALLATION

1. Disconnect the battery ground cable. Drain the cooling system.
2. Remove the accessory drive belts.
3. Remove the fan and clutch assembly or electric motor and fan assembly.
4. Remove the camshaft drive belt.
5. Install Injection Pump Sprocket Aligning Pin T84P-9000-A or equivalent and remove nut and washer attaching sprocket to the injection pump.
6. Install puller T67L-3600-A or equivalent and remove the sprocket. Remove the Woodruff key from pump shaft.
7. Disconnect the clamp attaching the oil dipstick tube to the intake manifold and position out of the way.
8. Disconnect the turbo pressure indicator switch connector. Remove the diagnostic plug bracket and position out of the way.
9. Loosen the clamp attaching the turbo crossover pipe boot to the intake manifold.

10. Remove the nuts attaching the intake manifold to cylinder head and remove the intake manifold.

NOTE: To prevent fuel system contamination, cap all fuel lines and fittings.

11. Disconnect and cap the nozzle fuel lines at nozzles.

12. Remove the injection nozzle lines from injection pump using Fuel Line Nut Wrench T84P–9396–A or equivalent. Install caps on each end of each fuel line and pump fitting as it is removed and identify each fuel line accordingly.

13. Disconnect the coolant hoses from the idle speed boost housing.

14. Disconnect the electrical connectors to the fuel shut-off and cold start accelerator valves, micro-switch and fuel pressure switch.

15. Disconnect the nozzle return line at the injection pump.

16. Disconnect the fuel return hose from the fuel return line on the left fender apron.

17. Disconnect the fuel inlet hose from the fuel inlet line on the left fender apron.

18. Disconnect the vacuum hoses at the altitude compensation valve. Note position of hoses, so they may be returned to the original position.

19. Disconnect the throttle cable and speed control cable, if equipped, from the injection pump.

20. Remove the 3 nuts attaching the injection pump to mounting bracket.

21. Remove the 2 nuts attaching the injection pump to the engine front cover and remove the injection pump.

To install:

22. Install the injection pump in position. Line up the mark on the front cover with the mark on the injection pump mounting boss. Install attaching nuts and bolts. Tighten to 14–17 ft. lbs.

23. Connect the throttle cable and speed control cable, if so equipped.

24. Remove the protective caps and install the fuel inlet hose to the fuel inlet line on left fender apron. Connect the fuel return hose to the fuel return line on the left fender apron.

25. Connect the vacuum hoes to the altitude compensation valve. Refer to the Vehicle Emissions Information decal for exact positioning.

26. Connect the nozzle return line to the injection pump.

27. Connect the electrical connectors to the fuel pressure sensor, micro-switch, cold start accelerator valve and fuel shut-off valve.

28. Connect the coolant hoses to the idle speed boost housing.

29. Install the fuel lines on injection pump, using Tool T84P–9396–A or equivalent and tighten to 14–17 ft. lbs.

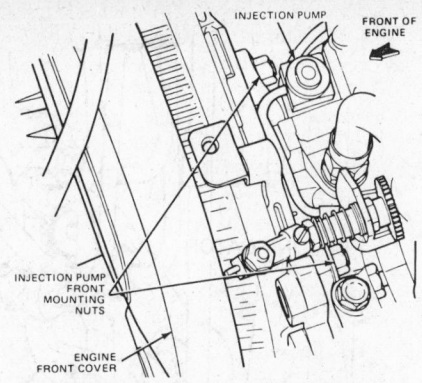

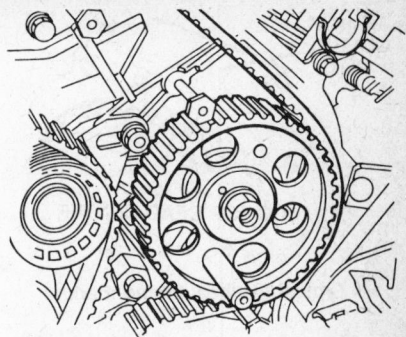

Injection pump front mounting bolts—2.4L diesel engine

Injector pump aligning tool—2.4L diesel engine

30. Connect the fuel lines to the nozzles and tighten to 14–17 ft. lbs.

31. Clean the intake manifold and cylinder head gasket mating surfaces. Position a new intake manifold gasket on the cylinder head and install the intake manifold. Be sure the intake manifold inlet port is inserted into the turbo crossover pipe boot. Tighten attaching bolts to 14–17 ft. lbs. Tighten the clamp at the crossover pipe boot.

32. Install the diagnostic plug bracket on the cylinder head and tighten to 14–17 ft. lbs.

33. Connect the turbo pressure indicator switch connector.

34. Position the oil dipstick tube to the intake manifold and install clamp.

35. Install the Woodruff key in injection pump shaft.

36. Install the sprocket on injection pump. Install injection Pump Aligning Pin T84P–9000–A or equivalent, in sprocket. Install the sprocket attaching washer and nut and tighten to 33–36 ft. lbs.

37. Install and adjust camshaft drive belt.

38. Install the camshaft drive belt cover and tighten to 6–7 ft. lbs.

39. Install fan and clutch assembly or electric motor and fan assembly.

40. Install and adjust the accessory drive belts.

41. Fill and bleed the cooling system.

42. Air bleed the fuel system.

43. Adjust the injection pump timing.

44. Connect the battery ground cable.

45. Start the engine and check for fuel, coolant and oil leaks.

46. Adjust the curb idle, fast idle and injection pump timing.

Injection Timing

NOTE: This procedure requires the use of special tools.

ADJUSTMENT

NOTE: Engine coolant temperature must be above 176°F before injection timing can be checked and/or adjusted.

1. Disconnect the negative battery cable, located in the luggage compartment.

2. Remove the injection pump distributor head plug bolt and sealing washer.

3. Install Static Timing Gauge Adapter, Rotunda 014–00303, with Metric Dial Indicator, D82L–4201–A or equvalent so that indicator pointer is in contact with injection pump plunger.

4. Remove the timing mark cover from the transmission housing. Align timing mark (TDC) with pointer on rear engine cover plate.

5. Rotate the crankshaft pulley slowly, counterclockwise until the dial indicator pointer stops moving (approximately 30–50 degrees BTDC).

NOTE: There is a 40 degrees BTDC timing mark on the flywheel.

6. Adjust the dial indicator to zero.

NOTE: Confirm that the dial indicator pointer does not move from zero by slightly rotating the crankshaft left to right.

7. Turn the crankshaft clockwise until the crankshaft timing mark aligns with the indicator pin. Dial indicator should read 0.04 ± 0.0008 in. If reading is not within specification, adjust as follows:

   a. Loosen injection pump bolts and nuts.

   b. Rotate the injection pump toward the engine to advance timing and away from the engine to retard timing. Rotate the injection pump until the dial indicator reads 0.04 ± 0.0008 in.

   c. Tighten the injection pump attaching nuts and bolts to 13–20 ft. lbs.

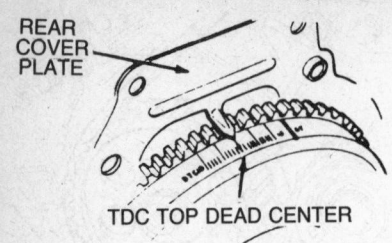

Typical flywheel timing mark

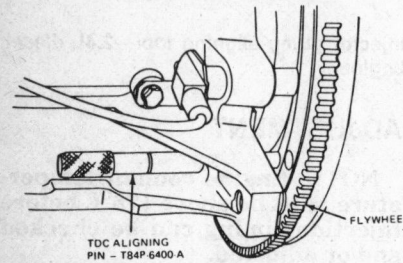

TDC aligning tool installation—2.4L diesel engine

d. Repeat Steps 5–7 to check that the timing is adjusted properly.

8. Remove the dial indicator and adapter and install the injection pump distributor head plug and tighten to 10–15 ft. lbs.

9. Connect the negative battery cable.

10. Run the engine and check and adjust idle rpm, if necessary. Check for fuel leaks.

Injection Nozzle

REMOVAL & INSTALLATION

1. Pull off the leak oil lines from the injector nozzles.

NOTE: Make sure area around injector is clean.

2. Remove the fuel lines at the injectors and at the fuel injection pump with Fuel Line Wrench T84P-9527-A or equivalent. Cap all fuel lines and openings as the fuel lines are removed.

3. Unscrew the fuel injectors with Injector Nozzle Socket T84P-9527-A or equivalent. Note injector order for installation.

NOTE: On injectors with sensors, disconnect the sensor plug wires and guide sensor wires through Injector Nozzle Socket T84P-9527-A or equivalent, while installing tool on the injector.

4. Plug the cylinder block injector nozzle opening.

5. Clean the injector nozzle opening in the cylinder block.

6. Install new heat shields into the injection nozzle openings.

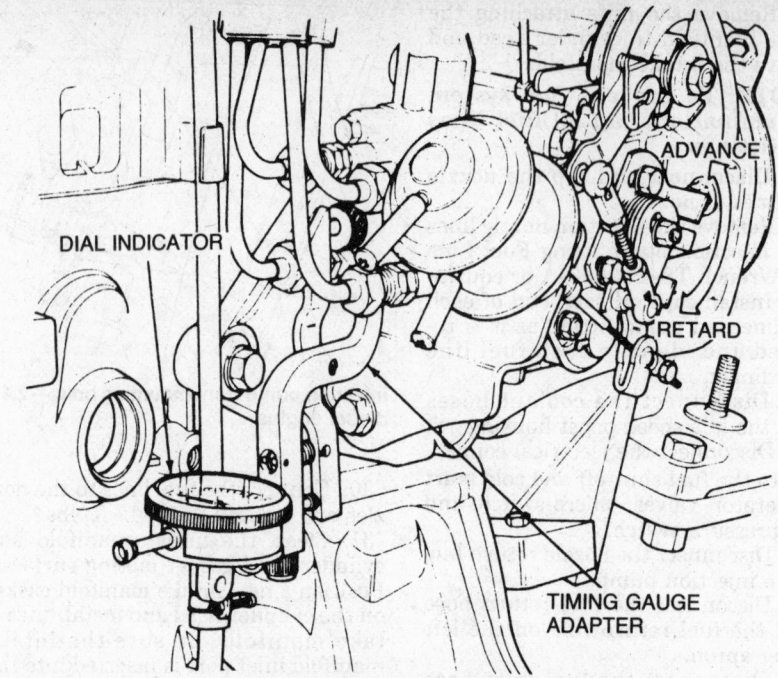

Installing timing gauge on diesel engine

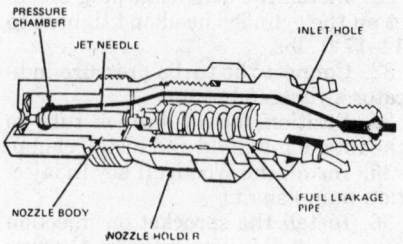

Injector nozzle

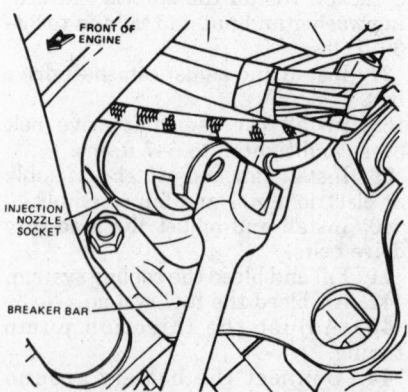

Injector nozzle removal and installation

7. Apply a copper based, anti-sieze compound to the injector nozzle threads. Remove the protective plug in the cylinder block and install injector nozzles in original positions with Injector Nozzle Socket T84P-9527-A or equivalent. Tighten to 30–33 ft. lbs.

NOTE: On injectors with sensors, guide the sensor plug wire

through socket before installing the injector nozzle. Reconnect the sensor wire after nozzle installation.

8. Remove the protective caps from the fuel lines, injector pump and injector nozzles and install fuel lines using Fuel Line Wrench T84P-9396-A or equivalent. Tighten to 15–18 ft. lbs.

MANUAL TRANSMISSION

REMOVAL & INSTALLATION

1. Disconnect and remove the starter and dust ring, if the clutch is to be removed. On floor shift models, remove the boot retainer and shifter lever.

2. On models with the 83ET, 84ET and 85ET 4 speed transmission: working under the hood, remove the upper clutch housing to engine bolts.

3. Raise the car.

4. Matchmark the driveshaft and axle flange for reassembly. Disconnect the driveshaft at the rear universal joint and remove the driveshaft. Plug the extension housing.

5. Disconnect the speedometer cable at the transmission extension. Disconnect the seat belt sensor wires and the back-up lamp switch wires. Re-

move the clutch lever boot and cable on Mustang and Capri if so equipped.

6. Disconnect the gear shift rods from the transmission shift levers. If the car is equipped with a 4 speed, remove the bolts that secure shift control bracket to extension housing. Support the engine with a jack.

7. Remove the bolt holding the extension housing to the rear support and remove the muffler inlet pipe bracket to housing bolt.

8. Remove the 2 rear support bracket insulator nuts from the underside of the crossmember. Remove the crossmember.

9. Place a jack (equipped with a protective piece of wood) under the rear of the engine oil pan. Raise or lower the engine slightly as necessary to provide access to the bolts.

10. Remove transmission to flywheel housing bolts.

11. Slide the transmission back and out of the car. It may be necessary to slide the catalytic converter bracket forward to provide clearance on some models.

To install:

12. To install, move the transmission back just far enough for the pilot shaft to clear the clutch housing, move it upward and into position on the flywheel housing. It may be necessary to put the transmission in gear and rotate the output shaft to align the input shaft and clutch splines.

13. Move the transmission forward and into place against the flywheel housing and install the transmission attaching bolts finger-tight.

14. Tighten the transmission bolts to 37–42 ft. lbs. on all cars.

15. Install the crossmember and torque the mounting bolts to 20–30 ft. lbs. Slowly lower the engine onto the crossmember.

16. Torque the rear mount to 30–50 ft. lbs.

17. Connect gear shift rods and the speedometer cable.

18. Remove the plug from the extension housing and install the driveshaft, aligning the marks made previously.

19. Refill transmission to proper level. On floorshift models, install the boot retainer and shift lever.

LINKAGE ADJUSTMENT

1. Loosen 3 shift linkage adjustment nuts.

2. Install a ¼ in. diameter alignment pin through control bracket and levers.

3. Tighten 3 shift linkage adjustment nuts and remove alignment pin.

4. Check gear lever for smooth crossover.

CLUTCH

REMOVAL & INSTALLATION

1. Remove the transmission from the vehicle.

2. Remove release lever retracting spring. Disconnect the clutch pedal at the equalizer bar, or the clutch cable from the housing, as applicable.

3. Remove bolts that secure engine rear plate to front lower part of bellhousing.

4. Remove the bolts that attach the bell housing to the cylinder block and remove the bellhousing and release lever as a unit. Remove the clutch release lever by pulling it through the window in the housing until the retainer spring disengages from the pivot.

5. Loosen the 6 pressure plate cover attaching bolts evenly to release spring pressure. Mark the cover and flywheel to facilitate reassembly in same position.

6. Remove the 6 pressure plate attaching bolts while holding the pressure plate cover. Remove pressure plate and clutch disc.

--------- CAUTION ---------
Do not depress the clutch pedal while the transmission is removed.

To install:

7. Before installing the clutch, clean the flywheel surface. Inspect the flywheel and pressure plate for wear, scoring, or burn marks (blue color). Light scoring and wear may require refacing of the flywheel or replacement of the damaged parts.

8. Attach the clutch disc and pressure plate assembly to the flywheel. The 3 dowel pins on the flywheel, if so equipped, must be properly aligned. Damaged pins must be replaced. Avoid touching the clutch plate surface. Tighten the bolts finger tight.

9. Align the clutch disc with the pilot bushing. Torque cover bolts to 12–24 ft. lbs. with the 2.3L engine, 12–20 ft. lbs. for all others.

10. Lightly lubricate the release lever fulcrum ends. Install the release lever in the flywheel housing and install the dust shield.

11. Apply very little lubricant on the release bearing retainer journal. Fill the groove in the release bearing hub with grease. Clean all excess grease from the inside bore of the hub to prevent clutch disc contamination. Attach the release bearing and hub on the release lever.

12. Make sure the flywheel housing and engine block are clean. Any missing or damaged mounting dowels must

be replaced. Install the flywheel housing and torque the attaching bolts to 38–61 ft. lbs. on 4.2L, 5.0L and 5.8L engines, 28–38 ft. lbs. on 2.3L engines. Install the dust cover and torque the bolts to 17–20 ft. lbs.

13. Connect the release rod or cable and the retracting spring. Connect the pedal to equalizer rod at the equalizer bar.

14. Install starter and dust ring.

15. After moving the transmission back just far enough for the pilot shaft to clear the clutch housing, move it upward and into position on the flywheel housing. It may be necessary to put the transmission in gear and rotate the output shaft to align the input shaft and clutch splines.

16. Move the transmission forward and into place against the flywheel housing and install the transmission attaching bolts finger-tight.

17. Tighten the transmission bolts to 37–42 ft. lbs. on all cars.

NOTE: All models have self-adjusting clutches. No adjustments are necessary.

SELF-ADJUSTING CLUTCH

The free play in the clutch is adjusted by a built in mechanism that allows the clutch controls to be self-adjusted during normal operation. The self-adjusting feature should be checked every 5000 miles. This is accomplished by insuring that the clutch pedal travels to the top of its upward position. Grasp the clutch pedal and pull up on the pedal until it stops. Very little effort is required (about 10 lbs.). During the application of upward pressure, a click may be heard which means an adjustment was necessary and has been accomplished.

Clutch Cable

REMOVAL & INSTALLATION

1. Lift the clutch pedal to its upward most position to disengage the pawl and quadrant. Push the quadrant forward, unhook the cable from the quadrant and allow it to swing rearward.

2. Remove the screw that holds the cable insulator to the dash panel and pull the cable through the dash panel and into the engine compartment.

3. On 2.3L EFI and 5.0L engines, remove the cable bracket from the fender apron. Raise the vehicle and remove the dust cover from the bell housing.

4. Remove the clip retainer holding the cable to the bell housing.

5. Slide the ball on the end of the ca-

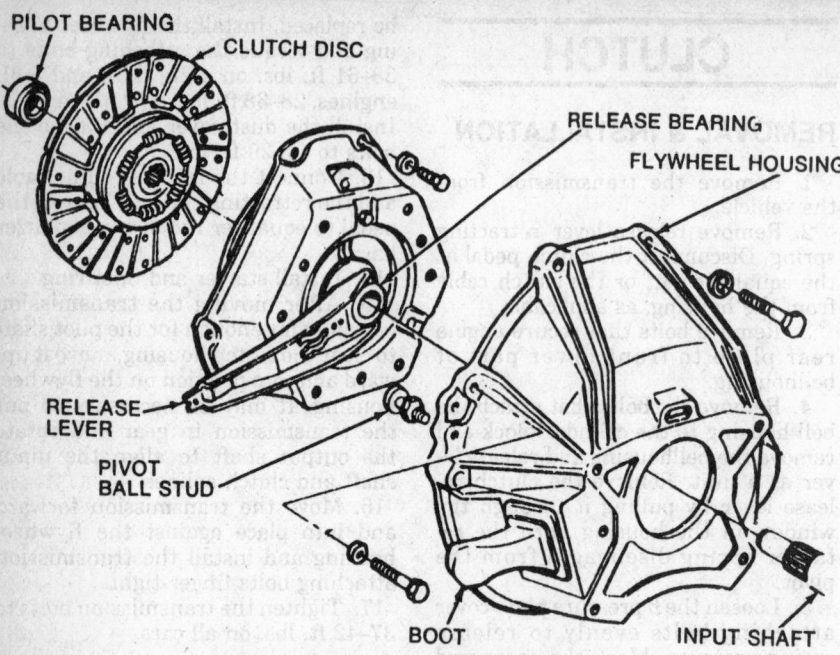

Exploded view of clutch and related parts

Labels: PILOT BEARING, CLUTCH DISC, RELEASE BEARING, FLYWHEEL HOUSING, RELEASE LEVER, PIVOT BALL STUD, BOOT, INPUT SHAFT

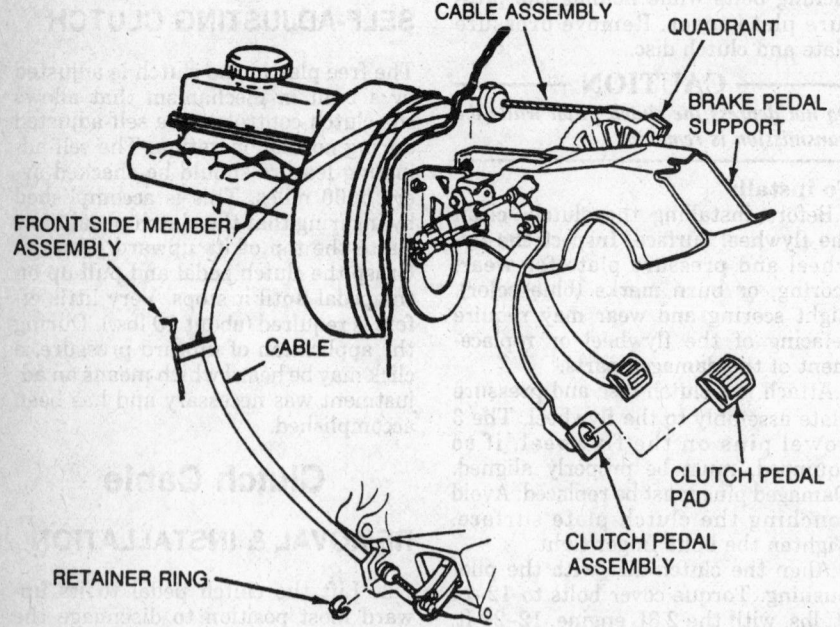

Clutch cable routing—most models

Labels: CABLE ASSEMBLY, QUADRANT, BRAKE PEDAL SUPPORT, FRONT SIDE MEMBER ASSEMBLY, CABLE, CLUTCH PEDAL PAD, CLUTCH PEDAL ASSEMBLY, RETAINER RING

ble through the hole in the clutch release lever and remove the cable.

Clutch Master Cylinder

REMOVAL & INSTALLATION

1987–89 Thunderbird/Cougar

1. Remove the clutch slave cylinder.
2. Remove master cylinder reser-voir by removing 2 self-tapping screws.
3. Remove the clutch pedal push rod from the clutch master cylinder.
3. Remove master cylinder by turn-ing it 45 degrees clockwise, pull the master cylinder out from the pedal mounting bracket, through the firewall.
4. Remove the pressure line.
5. To install, connect the pressure line and slide the clutch master cylin-der into place.
6. Insert the clutch pedal push rod and attach the fluid reservoir.

Clutch Slave Cylinder

REMOVAL & INSTALLATION

1987–89 Thunderbird/Cougar

1. Remove dust cover by removing self tapping screw.
2. Unlatch slave cylinder from the transmission housing bracket.
3. Remove pressure line if neces-sary. Reverse procedure for installation.

BLEEDING THE HYDRAULIC CLUTCH SYSTEM

1987–89 Thunderbird/Cougar

1. Clean all dirt and grease from the cap to make sure that no foreign subtances enter the system.
2. Remove the cap and diaphragm and fill the reservoir to the top with the approved DOT 3 brake fluid. Fully loosen the bleed screw which is in the slave cylinder body next to the inlet connection.
3. At this point bubbles of air will appear at the bleed screw outlet. When the slave cylinder is full and a steady stream of fluid comes out of the slave cylinder bleeder, tighten the bleed screw.
4. Assemble the diaphragm and cap to the reservoir, fluid in the reservoir should be level with the step. Exert a light load of about 20 lbs. to the slave cylinder piston by pushing the release lever towards the cylinder and loosen the bleed screw. Maintain a constant light load, fluid and any air that is left will be expelled through the bleed port. Tighten the bleed screw when a steady flow of fluid and no air is being expelled.
5. Fill the reservoir fluid level back to normal capacity and if necessary re-peat Step 4.
6. Exert a light load to the release lever, but do not open the bleeder screw as the piston in the slave cylin-der will move slowly down the bore. Repeat this operation 2–3 times, the fluid movement will force any air left in the system into the reservoir. The hydraulic system should now be fully bled.
7. Check the the operation of the clutch hydraulic system and repeat this procedure if necesary. Check the push rod travel at the slave cylinder to insure the minimum travel 0.57 in.

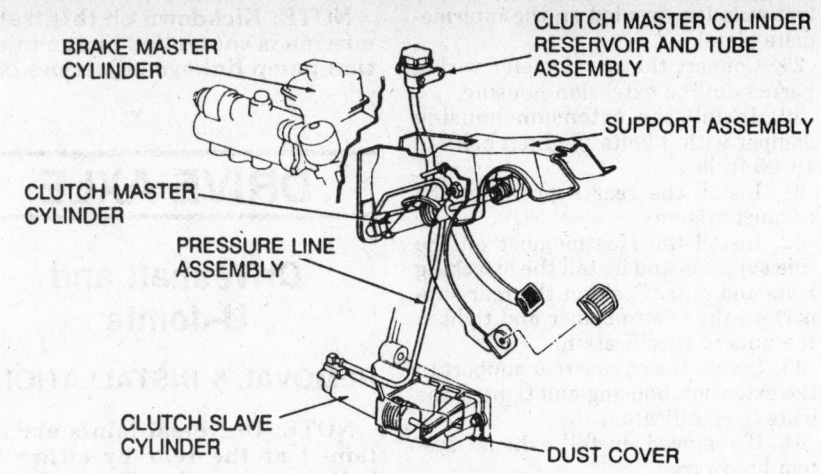

BRAKE MASTER CYLINDER

CLUTCH MASTER CYLINDER RESERVOIR AND TUBE ASSEMBLY

SUPPORT ASSEMBLY

CLUTCH MASTER CYLINDER

PRESSURE LINE ASSEMBLY

CLUTCH SLAVE CYLINDER

DUST COVER

Hydraulic clutch system components

AUTOMATIC TRANSMISSION

For further information on automatic transmissions, please refer to "Automatic Transmissions" in the unit repair section.

REMOVAL & INSTALLATION

Except ZF Transmission

1. Disconnect the negative battery cable. Raise and safely support the vehicle.

2. Place the drain pan under the transmission fluid pan. Remove the fluid filler tube, if pan mounted and drain the transmission fluid. On models that do not have a pan mounted filler tube, loosen the pan attaching bolts and allow the fluid to drain. Start loosening the bolts at the rear of the pan and work toward the front. Finally remove all of the pan attaching bolts except 2 at the front, to allow the fluid to further drain. After the fluid has drained, install 2 bolts on the rear side of the pan to temporarily hold in place.

3. Remove the converter drain plug access cover from the lower end of the converter housing.

4. Remove the converter to flywheel attaching nuts. Place a wrench on the crankshaft pulley attaching bolt to turn the engine to gain access to the nuts. DO NOT turn OHC (overhead cam) engines opposite the normal direction or damage to the timing belt may occur.

5. With the wrench on the crankshaft pulley attaching bolt, turn the engine to gain access to the converter drain plug and remove the plug. Place a drain pan under the converter to catch the fluid. After the fluid has been drained from the converter, reinstall the plug. Tighten to 20–25 ft. lbs.

6. Remove the drive shaft and plug the back of the transmission extension housing to prevent dirt from entering.

7. Label and remove all vacuum lines and wiring harnesses connected to the transmission. Remove the filler tube from the transmission after removing the engine mounting bolt. Disconnect the speedometer cable. Disconnect the shift linkage and kickdown cable.

8. Remove the transmission support to crossmember bolts or nuts. Disconnect the starter cable and remove the starter motor. Remove any exhaust system parts (pipes, converters, brackets etc.) that will interfere with transmission removal.

9. Disconnect the oil cooler lines from the transmission case.

10. Position a suitable transmission jack to support the transmission and secure the transmission to the jack with a safety chain. Raise the transmission slightly and remove the crossmember attaching bolts and remove the crossmember.

CAUTION

The engine will lower slightly when the transmission is removed. Check clearance between the front of the engine and radiator shroud. Remove the shroud and position it over the fan if necessary. Remove the air cleaner assembly. Check the upper radiator hose, do not permit it to be stretched, or damage to the radiator connection may occur.

11. Remove the converter housing to engine attaching bolts. Pull the transmission back and away from the engine after prying the converter away from the drive plate. After the transmission is separated from the engine, attach a small C-clamp on the housing in a position that will not permit the converter from falling out of the housing. Lower the transmission slowly and remove it from under the vehicle.

12. Apply white grease to the converter hub. Install the transmission in the reverse order of removal. Make sure the converter holes are aligned correctly with the drive plate and the converter pilot is flat against the crank pilot. Torque the converter to drive plate; 25–30 ft. lbs. Transmission to engine; 23–28 ft. lbs. on 2.3L engines and the 3.3L engine. 40–50 ft. lbs. On 3.8L and 4.2L/5.0L and 5.8L engines except with the AOD transmission. AOD transmission; 35–40 ft. lbs.

13. If the converter has been completely drained, add 4 quarts of the proper transmission fluid, start the engine and move the selector through the gears. Recheck and add fluid as necessary until the correct level is reached.

NOTE: Dextron®II fluid is used in all transmissions except FMX models which use Type F and C5 models which require Type H.

ZF Transmission

1. Remove the kickdown (TV) cable and insert from the injection pump side lever and cable bracket in the engine compartment.

2. Place the transmission selector lever in **Neutral**. Raise the vehicle on a hoist.

3. Remove the outer manual lever and nut from the transmission selector shaft.

4. Remove position sensor from converter housing.

5. Remove the engine brace from the lower end of the converter housing.

6. Place a transmission jack under the transmission.

7. Place a wrench on the crankshaft pulley attaching bolt and turn the converter to gain access to the converter to flywheel attaching nuts. Remove the converter to flywheel attaching nuts.

NOTE: The converter studs are installed in the converter with Loctite®. During disassembly the nuts may override the Loctite® and the nut and stud come out as a "bolt". This poses no concern. The stud and converter threads should be cleaned, Loctite® applied and the "bolt" reinstalled and tightened to specification.

8. Disconnect the driveshaft from the rear axle and slide the shaft rearward from the transmission.

NOTE: To maintain driveshaft balance, mark the rear driveshaft

yoke and axle companion flange so the driveshaft can be installed in its original position. Install a seal installation tool in the extension housing to prevent fluid leakage.

9. Disconnect the neutral start switch electrical connector.

10. Remove the extension housing damper.

11. Remove the rear support to crossmember attaching nuts and the 2 crossmember to side support attaching bolts.

12. Remove the 2 engine rear support to extension housing attaching bolts and remove the rear mount from the exhaust system.

13. On 1982–87 Continentals with column shift, remove the 2 bolts securing the bellcrank bracket to the engine.

14. Disconnect each oil line from the fittings on the transmission using push connect service Tool T82L-9500–AH or equivalent.

15. Disconnect the speedometer wiring harness from the extension housing.

16. Remove the 2 converter housing to starter motor bolts.

17. Secure the transmission to the jack with a safety chain and lower the jack slightly.

18. Remove the 4 converter housing to cylinder block attaching bolts.

19. Remove the filler tube and dipstick.

20. Carefully move the transmission and converter assembly away from the engine and, at the same time, lower the jack to clear the underside of the vehicle.

21. Mount the transmission in a holding fixture.

To install:

22. To install, place the transmission on the jack. Secure the transmission to the jack with a safety chain.

23. Rotate the converter until the studs are in alignment with the holes in the flywheel and flexplate.

24. Move the converter and transmission assembly forward into position, using care not to damage the flywheel, flexplate and the converter pilot. The converter face must seat squarely against the flexplate (This indicates that the converter pilot is not binding in the engine crankshaft).

25. Install the filler tube and dipstick, position bracket over the upper right housing to engine bolt holes.

26. Install and tighten the 4 converter housing to engine attaching bolts to 38–48 ft. lbs.

27. Remove the safety chain from around the transmission.

28. Connect the oil cooler lines by pushing them into the fittings on the transmission (located on the intermediate plate).

29. Connect the speedometer wiring harness to the extension housing.

30. Install the extension housing damper with 3 bolts. Tighten bolts to 18–25 ft. lbs.

31. Install the rear support on the exhaust system.

32. Install the crossmember on the side supports and install the attaching bolts and nuts. Position the rear support on the crossmember and tighten the nuts to specification.

33. Secure the engine rear support to the extension housing and tighten the bolts to specification.

34. If removed, install exhaust system hardware.

35. Lower the transmission and remove the jack.

36. On the 1982–87 Continentals equipped with column shift, position the bellcrank to the transmission brace and install the 2 attaching bolts. Tighten the bolts to 10–20 ft. lbs.

37. Guide the kickdown (TV) cable up into the engine compartment.

38. Install the outer manual lever on the transmission selector shaft. Tighten the attaching nut to 10–20 ft. lbs.

39. Install the converter to flywheel attaching nuts (or bolts) and tighten to 20–34 ft. lbs.

40. Install the engine brace on the lower end of the converter housing and engine block. Tighten the bolts to 15–18 ft. lbs.

41. Connect the neutral start switch harness at the transmission.

42. Install position sensor to converter housing.

43. Connect the driveshaft to the rear axle. Install the driveshaft so the index marks, made during removal, are correctly aligned. Lubricate the yoke splines with C1AZ–19590–B or equivalent.

44. Lower the vehicle and adjust the kickdown (TV) cable.

45. Fill the transmission to the correct level with the specified fluid. Start the engine and shift the transmission to all positions, then recheck the fluid level.

TV CABLE ADJUSTMENT

1. Set the injection pump lever at the full throttle position.

2. Tighten the rear adjusting nut on the threaded barrel until a gap of 1.54–1.57 in. exists between the edge of the crimped bead on the cable closest to the barrel and the end of the threaded barrel.

3. Tighten the forward adjusting nut to lock the cable assembly to the bracket to 80–106 inch lbs.

4. Recheck the gap and readjust as necessary.

NOTE: Kickdown on this transmission is controlled by the injection pump linkage adjustments.

DRIVE AXLE

Driveshaft and U-Joints

REMOVAL & INSTALLATION

NOTE: Universal joints are retained at the rear by either U-bolts or a coupling flange that is bolted to the pinion (differential) flange. Various models are equipped with a double Cardan-type universal joint at the rear. Service for the front U-joint on these models is the same as for other models.

1. Matchmark the rear driveshaft yoke and the companion flange so that the parts may be reassembled in the same way to maintain balance.

2. Remove the U-bolts and straps or coupling flange nuts and bolts at the rear of the driveshaft and tape the loose bearing caps to the yoke.

3. Allow the rear of the driveshaft to drop down slightly. Pull the driveshaft and slip yoke out of the transmission extension housing.

4. Plug the transmission to prevent fluid leakage.

5. To install, lubricate the yoke splines and install the yoke into the transmission extension housing, aligning the splines. Be careful not to bottom the slip yoke hard against the transmission seal.

6. Rotate the pinion flange as necessary to align the matchmarks made earlier. Install the U-bolts and tighten to 8–15 ft. lbs. Various models use special wax-dipped coupling to pinion flange bolts which may not be reused. They must be replaced with special new bolts, torqued to 71–96 ft. lbs.

Rear Axle Shaft, Bearing and Seal

NOTE: Both integral and removable carrier type axles are used. Traction-Lok (limited slip) axles are available only as removable carrier types. The axle type and ratio are stamped on a plate attached to a rear housing cover bolt. Axle types also indicate whether the axle shafts are retained by C-locks. To properly identify a C-lock axle, drain the

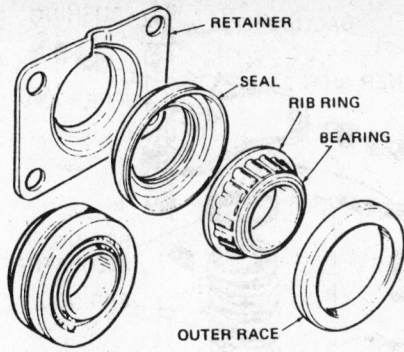

Tapered bearing and retainer–removable carrier axle

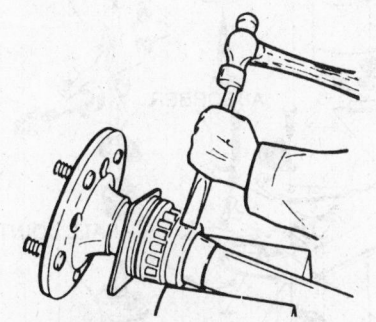

Axle shaft bearing retainer removal—removable carrier axle

lubricant, remove the rear cover and look for the C-lock on the end of the axle shaft in the differential side gear bore. If the second letter of the axle model code is F, it is a Traction-Loc axle.

REMOVAL & INSTALLATION

Except C-Lock Type

NOTE: Bearings must be pressed on and off of the axle shaft.

1. Remove the wheel assembly and brake drum. With disc brakes, remove the caliper, retaining nuts and rotor. New anchor plate bolts will be needed for reassembly.

2. Remove the nuts holding the retainer plate to the backing plate, or remove the axle shaft retainer bolts from the housing. Disconnect the brake line with drum brakes.

3. Remove the retainer and install nuts, finger tight, to prevent the brake backing plate from being dislodged.

4. Pull out the axle shaft and bearing assembly, using a slide hammer. On models with a tapered roller bearing, the tapered cup will normally remain in the axle housing when the shaft is removed. The cup must be removed from the housing to prevent seal damage when the shaft is reinstalled. The cup can be removed with a slide hammer and an expander puller.

5. Using a chisel, nick the bearing retainer in 3 or 4 places. The retainer does not have to be cut, but merely collapsed sufficiently to allow the bearing retainer to be slid from the shaft.

6. Press off the bearing and install the new one by pressing it into position. With tapered bearings, place the lubricated seal and bearing on the axle shaft (cup rib ring facing the flange). Make sure that the seal is the correct length. Disc brake seal rims are black, drum brake seal rims are grey. Press the bearing and seal onto the shaft.

7. Press on the new retainer.

NOTE: Do not attempt to press the bearing and the retainer on at the same time.

8. Install the tapered cup on the bearing and lubricate the outer diameter of the cup and the seal with axle lube. Install the shaft and bearing assembly into the housing.

9. Install the retainer, drum or rotor and caliper, wheel and tire. Bleed the brake system.

C-Lock Type

1. Raise and safely support the rear of the vehicle.

2. Remove the wheel assemblies.

3. Place a drain pan under the housing and drain the lubricant by loosening the housing cover.

4. Remove the locks securing the brake drums to the axle shaft flanges and remove the drums.

5. Remove the housing cover and gasket, if used.

6. Working through the opening in the differential case, remove the side gear pinion shaft lockbolt and the side gear pinion shaft.

7. Push the axle shafts inward and remove the C-lock clips from the inner ends of the axle shafts. Temporarily replace the shaft and lockbolt to retain the differential gears in position.

8. Remove the axle shafts with a slide hammer. Be sure the seal is not damaged by the splines on the axle shaft.

9. Remove the bearing and oil seal from the housing. Both the seal and bearing can be removed with a slide hammer. 2 types of bearings are used on some axles, one requiring a press fit and the other a loose fit. A loose fitting bearing does not necessarily indicate excessive wear.

10. Inspect the axle shaft housing and axle shafts for burrs or other irregularities. Replace any worn or damaged parts. A light yellow color on the bearing journal of the axle shaft is normal and does not require replacement of the axle shaft. Slight pitting and wear is also normal.

To install

11. Lightly coat the wheel bearing rollers with axle lubricant. Install the bearings in the axle housing until the bearing seats firmly against the shoulder.

12. Wipe all lubricant from the oil seal bore, before installing the seal.

13. Inspect the original seals for wear. If necessary, these may be replaced with new seals, which are prepacked with lubricant and do not require soaking.

14. Install the oil seal.

CAUTION

Installation of the seal without the proper tool can cause distortion and seal leakage. Seals may be colored coded for side indentification. Do not interchange seals from side to side, if they are coded.

---

15. Remove the lockbolt and pinion shaft. Carefully slide the axle shafts into place. Be careful not to damage the seal with the splined end of the axle shaft. Engage the splined end of the shaft with the differential side gears.

16. Install the axle shaft C-locks on the inner end of the axle shafts and seat the C-locks in the counterbore of the differential side gears.

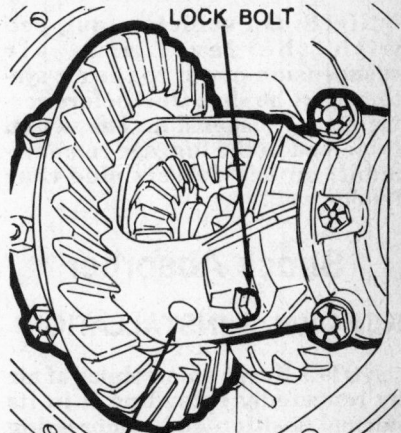

Removing the differential pinion shaft lockbolt

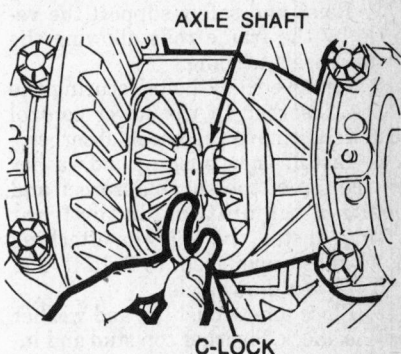

Removing the axle shaft C-locks

17. Rotate the differential pinion gears until the differential pinion shaft can be installed. Install the differential pinion shaft lockbolt. Tighten to 15–22 ft. lbs.

18. Install the brake drum on the axle shaft flange.

19. Install the wheel and tire on the brake drum and tighten the attaching nuts.

20. Clean the gasket surface of the rear housing and install a new cover gasket and the housing cover. Some models do not use a "paper" gasket. On these models, apply a bead of silicone sealer on the gasket surface. The bead should run inside of the bolt holes.

21. Raise the rear axle so that it is in the running position. Add the amount of specified lubricant to bring the lubricant level to ½ in. below the filler hole.

FRONT SUSPENSION

NOTE: On vehicles equipped with the level ride air susupension power to the air system must be shut OFF before servicing the suspension. The switch is located in the luggage compartment, on the drivers side rear fender well.

Shock Absorber

REMOVAL & INSTALLATION

NOTE: Purge a new shock of air by repeatedly extending it in its normal position and compressing it while inverted.

1. Remove the nut, washer and bushing from the upper end of the shock absorber.

2. Raise and safely support the vehicle by the frame rails allowing the front wheels to hang.

3. Remove the 2 bolts securing the shock absorber to the lower control arm and remove the shock absorber.

4. Install a new bushing and washer on the top of the shock absorber and position the unit inside the front spring. Install the 2 lower attaching bolts and torque them to 8–15 ft. lbs.

5. Lower the vehicle.

6. Place a new bushing and washer on the shock absorber top stud and install a new attaching nut. Torque to 22–30 ft. lbs.

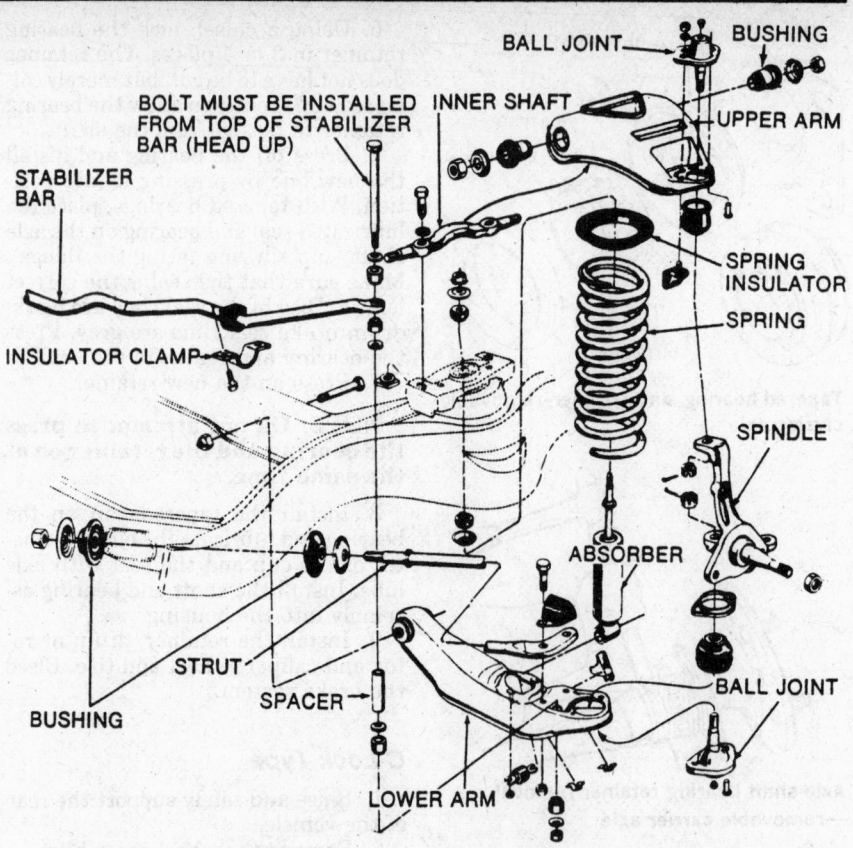

Front suspension—spring on lower arm

MacPherson Strut

REMOVAL & INSTALLATION

1. Raise and safely support the front of the vehicle allowing the suspension to hang freely.

2. Remove the wheel and tire. Remove the brake caliper and position out of the way, do not allow the caliper to hang from the brake hose. Raise the lower control arm with a floor jack to compress the spring.

3. Remove the 3 upper strut mounting nuts from the top of the shock tower. (if the upper mount is to be replaced on Thunderbird/Cougar models, loosen the 16mm strut rod nut at this time.)

4. Remove the 2 lower strut nuts that attach the strut to the spindle bracket. Leave the bolts in place.

5. Compress the strut to clear the upper mount. With the strut compressed, remove the lower strut thrubolts. Push the mounting bracket free of the spindle and remove the strut.

NOTE: On models equipped with gas pressurized struts, the strut will remain fully extended. Carefully remove both lower strut to spindle bolts, push the bracket free of the spindle and remove the strut.

6. To install, place the upper mount in position on the shock tower. Loosely install new upper mounting nuts. Extend the strut and position in the spindle bracket. Install the 2 lower mounting bolts and nuts. Tighten the nuts to 140–170 ft. lbs.

7. Raise the control arm with a floorjack and tighten the upper mount nuts to 50–70 ft. lbs.

8. Install the remaining parts in the reverse order of removal.

OVERHAUL

For all spring and shock absorber removal and installation procedures and all strut overhaul procedures, please refer to "Strut Overhaul" in the unit repair section.

Coil Spring

REMOVAL & INSTALLATION

1. Raise and safely support the vehicle. Remove the tire and wheel.

2. Disconnect the stabilizer link from the lower arm.

3. Remove the lower shock absorber attaching bolts.

4. Remove the shock absorber upper nut and remove the shock.

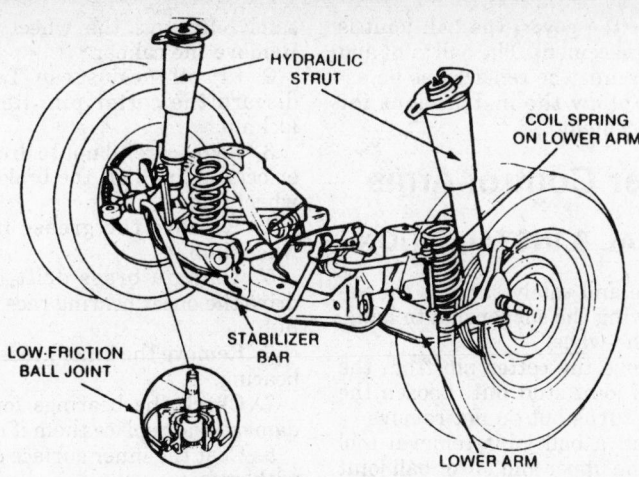

Typical strut suspension

5. Remove the steering center link from the pitman arm.

6. Install a spring compressor tool. Insert the securing pin through the upper ball nut and the compression rod. This pin can only be inserted 1 way. With the upper ball nut secured, turn the upper plate so it walks up the coil and contacts the upper spring seat. Back the nut off ½ turn.

7. Install the lower ball nut and the thrust washer on the compression rod and tighten the forcing nut until the spring is free in the seat.

8. Remove the 2 lower control arm pivot bolts.

9. Disengage the arm from the frame and remove the spring assembly.

10. If a new spring is being installed, mark the position of the upper and lower plates on the old spring. Also, measure the length of the spring and the amount of curvature in order to simplify the compressing and installation of the new spring.

11. Loosen the forcing nut and remove the spring from the tool.

12. Assemble the spring compressor tool on the new spring in the same position as the old spring was removed.

13. Position the spring in the lower arm.

14. Reverse the removal procedure to reinstall.

Lower Control Arm

REMOVAL & INSTALLATION

1. Raise and safely support the front of the vehicle. Remove the wheel and brake caliper. Suspend the caliper with hose connected, out of the way.

2. Disconnect the tie rod end from the steering spindle.

3. Disconnect the stabilizer bar from the arm. Remove the steering gear bolts and lower the gear out of the

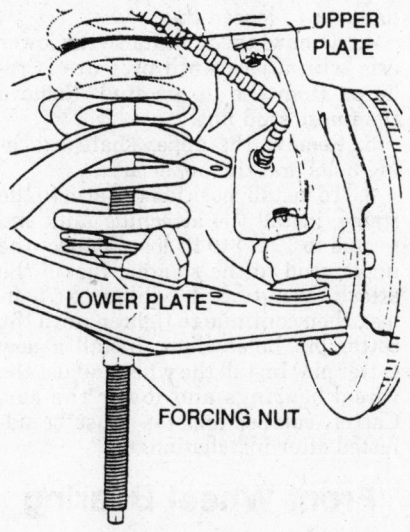

Front spring removal

way to provide clearance (if necessary) for suspension arm bolt removal.

4. Install a spring compressor. Turn the tightening nut on the tool so the spring is free in the seat.

5. Remove the 2 lower control arm pivot bolts and disengage the arm from the frame. Remove the spring.

6. Reverse to install. Be sure the lower end of the spring is properly positioned between the 2 holes in the lower arm spring pocket.

Torsion Bars

REMOVAL & INSTALLATION

1. Turn the air suspension switch **OFF**.

2. Raise the vehicle and safely support.

3. Disconnect the stabilizer bar from each link and bushing U-clamps. Remove the stabilizer bar assembly.

4. Remove the adapter brackets and U-clamps.

5. Cut the worn bushings from the stabilizer bar.

6. Coat the necessary parts of the stabilizer bar with Ford Rubber Suspension Insulator Lubricant, E25Y-19533-A or equivalent and slide bushings onto the stabilizer bar. Reinstall the U-clamps.

7. Reinstall the adapter brackets on the U-clamps.

8. Using a new nut and bolt, secure each end of the stabilizer bar to the lower suspension arm.

9. Using new bolts, clamp the stabilizer bar to the attaching brackets on the side rail.

10. Lower the vehicle. Turn air suspension switch **ON**.

Ball Joints

INSPECTION

1. Support the vehicle in normal driving position with ball joints loaded.

2. Wipe the wear indicator and ball joint cover checking surface clean.

3. The checking surface should project outside the cover. If the checking surface is inside the cover, replace the lower arm assembly.

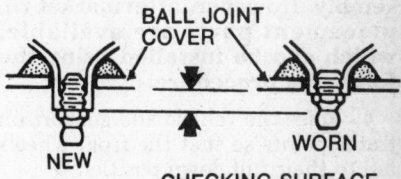

Ball joint wear indicator

REMOVAL & INSTALLATION

Except Strut Suspension
LOWER BALL JOINT

1. Raise and safely support the front of the vehicle allowing the front wheels to hang.

2. Have an assistant grasp the wheel top and bottom and apply alternate in and out pressure to the top and bottom of the wheel.

3. Radial play of ¼ in. is acceptable measured at the inside of the wheel adjacent to the lower arm.

4. Drill a ⅛ in. hole completely through each ball joint attaching rivet.

5. Using a large chisel, cut off the head of each rivet and drive them from the arm.

6. Place a jack under the lower arm and raise it to compress the coil spring.

7. Remove the cotter pin and attaching nut from the ball joint stud.

8. Using a ball joint removal tool, loosen the ball joint stud from the spindle and remove the ball joint from the arm.

9. Clean all metal burrs from the arm and install the new ball joint, using the service part nuts and bolts to attach the ball joint. Do not attempt to rivet the ball joint once it has been removed.

10. Check the front end alignment.

Upper Ball Joint

1. Raise and safely support the vehicle allowing the front wheels to hang.

2. Have an assistant grasp the bottom of the tire and move the wheel in and out.

3. As the wheel is being moved, observe the upper control arm where the spindle attaches to it. Any movement between the upper part of the spindle and the upper ball joint indicates a bad ball joint which must be replaced.

NOTE: During this check the lower ball joint will be unloaded and may move; this is normal and not an indiction of a bad ball joint. Also, do not mistake a loose wheel bearing for a defective ball joint. Ford Motor Company recommends replacement of the control arm and ball joint as an assembly. However, aftermarket replacement parts are available, which can be installed using the following procedure.

4. Raise the vehicle and support on frame points so that the front wheels fall to their full down position.

5. Drill a $1/8$ in. hole completely through each ball joint attaching rivet.

6. Using a large chisel, cut off the head of each rivet and drive them from the arm.

7. Place a jack under the lower arm and raise to compress the coil spring.

8. Remove the cotter pin and attaching nut from the ball joint stud.

9. Using a ball joint removal tool, loosen the ball joint stud from the spindle and remove the ball joint from the arm.

10. Clean all metal burrs from the arm and install the new ball joint, using the service part nuts and bolts to attach the ball joint. Do not attempt to rerivet the ball joint once it has been removed.

11. Check front end alignment.

Strut suspension

A single ball joint is used on each side, located in the lower arm. It is provided with a grease fitting, which projects beyond the ball joint cover. When the checking surface (the round boss into which the grease fitting is threaded) is flush with the cover, the ball joint is due for replacement. The ball joint and lower arm must be replaced as an assembly. Follow the instructions for arm replacement.

Upper Control Arms

REMOVAL & INSTALLATION

1. Raise and safely support the vehicle allowing the suspension to hang. Remove the wheel.

2. Remove the cotter pin from the upper ball joint stud nut. Loosen the nut a few turns but do not remove.

3. Install a ball joint removal tool between the upper and lower ball joint studs. Expand the tool until it places the upper stud under compression. Tap the spindle near the stud with a hammer to loosen the stud.

4. Remove the tool. Raise the lower arm with a jack until pressure is relieved from the upper stud. Remove the upper stud nut.

5. Remove the upper shaft attaching bolts and the upper arm.

6. To install, position the arm to the frame, install the attaching nuts and torque to 120–140 ft. lbs. Connect the upper stud to the spindle. Install the attaching nuts and tighten to 75 ft. lbs., then continue to tighten until the cotter pin holes align. Install a new cotter pin. Install the wheel, adjust the wheel bearings and lower the car. Caster, camber and toe must be adjusted after installation.

Front Wheel Bearing

ADJUSTMENT

1. Raise and safely support the front of the vehicle.

2. Remove the wheel cover and grease cap.

3. Remove the cotter pin and nut lock.

4. Loosen the adjusting nut 3 turns and rock the wheel back and forth a few times to release the brake pads from the rotor.

5. While rotating the wheel and hub assembly, tighten the adjusting nut to 17–25 ft. lbs. (23–34 Nm).

6. Back off the adjusting nut ½ turn, then retighten to 10–12 inch lbs. (1.1–1.7 Nm).

7. Install the locknut and a new cotter pin. Check the wheel rotation. If it is noisy or rough, the bearings either need to be cleaned or repacked, or readjusted. After adjustments are complete, replace the grease cap.

REMOVAL & INSTALLATION

1. Raise and support the vehicle

safely. Remove the wheel assembly. Remove the caliper.

2. Pry off the dust cap. Tap out and discard the cotter pin. Remove the locknut.

3. Being careful not to drop the outer bearing, pull off the brake disc and wheel hub.

4. Remove the grease inside the wheel hub.

5. Using a brass drift, carefully drive the outer bearing race out of the hub.

6. Remove the inner grease seal and bearing.

7. Check the bearings for wear or damage and replace them if necessary.

8. Coat the inner surface of the hub with grease.

9. Grease the outer surface of the bearing race and drift it into place in the hub.

10. Pack the inner and outer wheel bearings with grease. If the brake disc has been removed and/or replaced, tighten the retaining bolts to specification.

11. Install the inner bearing in the hub. Being careful not to distort it, install the oil seal with its lip facing the bearing. Drive the seal on until its outer edge is even with the edge of the hub.

12. Install the hub/disc assembly on the spindle, being careful not to damage the oil seal.

13. Install the outer bearing, washer and spindle nut. Adjust the bearing.

Front Wheel Alignment

ADJUSTMENT

Except Crown Victoria, Grand Marquis and Town Car

NOTE: The caster is set at the factory and cannot be changed. Toe and camber is adjustable. After front wheel alignment factors have been checked, make the necessary adjustment. Do not attempt to adjust front wheel alignment by bending the suspension or steering parts.

Camber

Remove the pop-rivet in the camber plate and loosen the 3 nuts which hold the strut mount to the body apron. Adjustment is made by moving the top of the shock strut to the desired position. Tighten nuts to specification. It is not necessary to replace the pop-rivet.

Toe

Start the engine and move the steering back and forth several times until it is

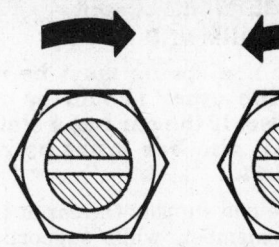

WITH WHEEL ROTATING, TORQUE ADJUSTING NUT, TO 17-25 FT. LBS.

BACK ADJUSTING NUT OFF 1/2 TURN

TIGHTEN ADJUSTING NUT TO 10-15 IN.-LBS.

INSTALL THE LOCK AND A NEW COTTER PIN

Front wheel bearing adjustment

in the straight ahead position, so that the power steering control valve will be in the center position. Lock the steering wheel in place using a steering wheel holder. Adjust the left and right tie rod lengths until each wheel has ½ of the desired total toe specification.

NOTE: Whenever the lam nuts are loosened for toe adjustment, the nut and tie rod threads must be cleaned and lubricated and the lam nut tightened to 43–50 ft. lbs. (58–67 Nm).

Crown Victoria, Grand Marquis and Town Car

Special caster and camber adjusting tools T97P-3000-A are used in order to accurately adjust the caster and camber. Using these tools and 3 alignment charts allows the inter-related caster/camber adjustment as a single operation. Both angles are set at 1 time.

The front suspension ride height is adjusted by moving the front right or left level sensor. To adjust the ride height locate the level sensor and loosen the attaching bolt, adjust up or down as needed.

The rear suspension ride height is adjusted by moving the rear level sensor attaching bracket up or down relative to the right upper arm. Loosen the attaching nut and move the sensor to obtain the ride height needed.

REAR SUSPENSION

Shock Absorbers

REMOVAL & INSTALLATION

NOTE: Purge a new shock of air by repeatedly extending it in its normal position and compressing

it while inverted. Models equipped with axle dampers are serviced by supporting the rear of the vehicle, removing the wheel and disconnecting the front and rear mounting nuts and removing the damper.

1. Remove the lower end of the shock absorber from the spring plate.
2. Remove the nut retaining the upper end of the shock absorber to the mounting bracket underneath the car.
3. Compress and remove the shock absorber. Discard the nuts.
4. Transfer the washers and bushings to the new shock absorber. Insert the upper stud through the mounting bracket and install a new attaching nut finger-tight.
5. Compress and install the shock absorber to the spring plate. Install the washer, bushings and attaching nuts.
6. Tighten the upper and lower attaching nuts.

SPRING BETWEEN AXLE HOUSING AND FRAME

1. Raise the vehicle and install jackstands.
2. Remove the shock absorber outer attaching nut, washer and insulator from the stud at the top side of the spring upper seat. Compress the shock

sufficiently to clear the spring seat hole and remove the inner insulator and washer from the upper attaching stud.
3. Remove the locknut and disconnect the shock absorber lower stud at the mounting bracket on the axle housing. Remove the shock absorber.
4. Position a new inner washer and insulator on the upper spring seat. While maintaining the shock in this position, install a new outer insulator, washer and nut on the stud from the top side of the spring upper seat.
5. Extend the shock absorber. Locate the lower stud in the mounting bracket hole on the axle housing and install the locknut.

SPRING BETWEEN LOWER CONTROL ARM AND FRAME

1. Remove the upper attaching nut, washer and insulator. Access is through the trunk on sedans or side panel trim covers on station wagons and hatchbacks. Sedan studs have rubber caps.
2. Raise the car. Compress the shock to clear the upper tower. Remove the lower nut and washer; remove the shock.
3. Purge the shock of air and compress. Place the lower mounting eye over the lower stud and install the washer and a new locking nut. Do not tighten the nut yet.
4. Place the insulator and washer on the upper stud. Extend the shock, installing the stud through the upper mounting hole.
5. Torque the lower mounting nut to 40–55 ft. lbs.
6. Lower the car. Install the outer insulator and washer on the upper stud and install a new nut. Tighten to 14–26 ft. lbs. Install the trim panel on station wagons and hatchbacks or the rubber cap on sedans.

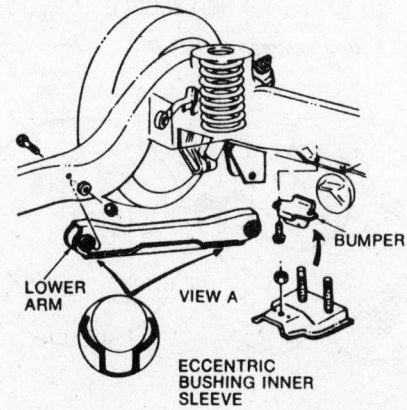

LOWER ARM

VIEW A

BUMPER

ECCENTRIC BUSHING INNER SLEEVE

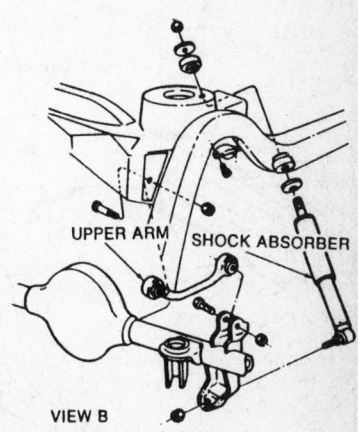

UPPER ARM

SHOCK ABSORBER

VIEW B

Coil spring rear suspension

Springs

REMOVAL & INSTALLATION

Coil Spring Suspension
SPRING BETWEEN AXLE HOUSING AND FRAME.

1. Raise and safely support the rear of the vehicle. Place a floor jack under the rear axle and lift the rear axle enough to take the tension off the springs.

2. Disconnect the lower studs of the shock absorbers from the mounting brackets on the axle housing.

3. Lower the axle housing until the springs are fully released.

4. Remove the springs and insulators from the vehicle.

5. Place the insulators in each upper seat and position the springs between the upper and lower seats.

6. With the springs in position, raise the axle housing until the lower studs of the rear shock absorbers reach the mounting brackets on the axle housing. Connect the lower studs and install the attaching nuts.

7. Remove the jack and lower the vehicle.

SPRING BETWEEN LOWER CONTROL ARM AND FRAME

NOTE: If a spring must be replaced, the other should be replaced also. If the car has a stabilizer bar, the bar must be removed first.

1. Raise and support the car at the rear crossmember, while supporting the axle with a jack.

2. Lower the axle until the shocks are fully extended.

3. Place a jack under the lower control arm pivot bolt. Remove the pivot bolt and nut. Carefully and slowly lower the arm until the spring load is relieved.

4. Remove the spring and insulators.

5. To install, tape the insulator in place in the frame and place the lower insulator in place on the arm. Install the internal damper in the spring.

6. Position the spring in place and slowly raise the jack under the lower arm. Install the pivot bolt and nut, with the nut facing outwards. Do not tighten the nut.

7. Raise the axle to curb height and tighten the lower pivot bolt to 70–100 ft. lbs. Remove the crossmember stands and lower the car.

Rear Control Arms

REMOVAL & INSTALLATION

1. Raise and safely support the vehicle.

2. Position a floor jack under the rear axle and raise slightly. Position jackstands at both ends of the axle to support the axle weight.

3. Position a jack under the lower arm pivot bolt and raise to support. Remove the pivot bolt and nut.

4. Lower the jack slowly and remove the coil spring. Remove the control arm.

5. Install the control arm in the reverse order of removal.

Rear Wheel Bearings

Refer to the rear axle removal and installation section for rear wheel bearing removal, packing and installation procedures.

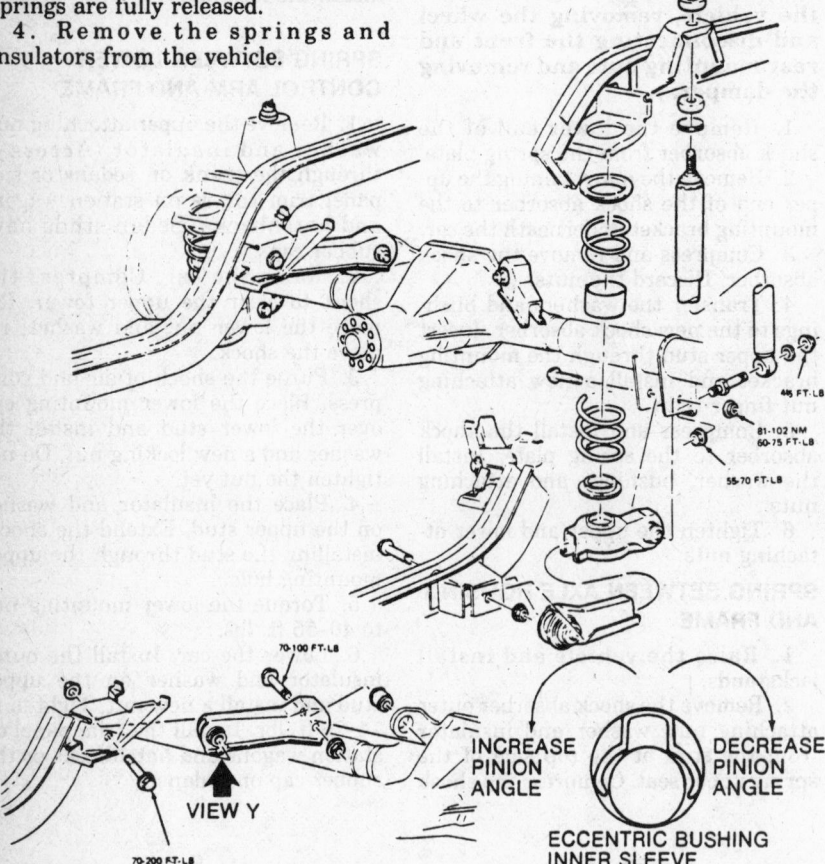

Four-bar link coil spring suspension

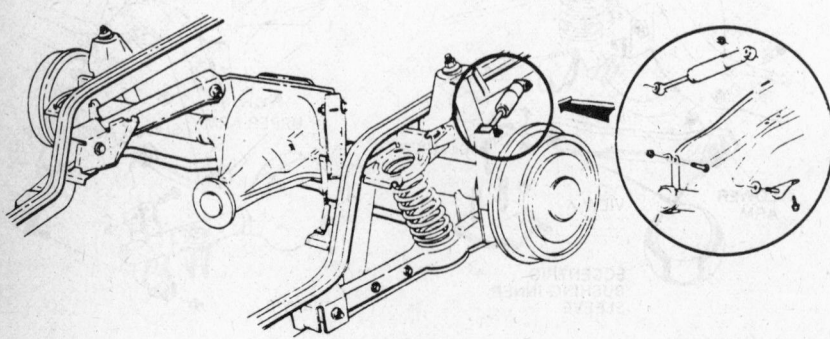

Hydra–trac rear suspension showing dampers

STEERING

Steering Wheel

REMOVAL & INSTALLATION

1. Disconnect the negative battery cable.

2. If the vehicle is equipped with a horn ring, remove it by rotating it clockwise. If equipped with a steering wheel crash pad, remove the retaining screws from the underside of the steering wheel and then remove the crash pad.

3. Disconnect the horn and speed control (if so equipped) wires from the inside of the steering wheel center. Remove the steering wheel hub cover by pushing the cover retaining posts out with a rod through the 2 holes provided on the back side of the hub.

4. Remove and discard the steering wheel nut, install a steering wheel puller on the end of the shaft and remove the steering wheel.

5. With the front wheels positioned straight ahead, line up the marks on the steering wheel and column and install the steering wheel and a new locknut. Tighten the nut to 30–40 ft. lbs.

6. Connect the horn and speed control wires and install the horn ring and the crash pad and retaining screws. Locate the hub cover posts in the holes and push the cover into place.

7. Connect the negative battery cable.

Turn Signal Switch

REMOVAL & INSTALLATION

1. On standard steering columns, remove the upper extension shroud (below the steering wheel) by snapping the shroud from the retaining clip. On tilt columns, remove the trim shroud by removing the 5 self-tapping screws.

2. Use a pulling and twisting motion, while pulling straight out, to remove the turn signal switch lever.

3. Peel back the piece of foam rubber from around the switch.

4. Disconnect the 2 switch electrical connectors.

5. Remove the 2 self-tapping screws which secure the switch to the lock cylinder housing and disengage the switch from the housing.

6. To install, align the switch mounting holes with the corresponding holes in the lock cylinder housing. Install the 2 screws.

7. Stick the foam back into place.

8. Align the key on the turn signal lever with the keyway in the switch and push the lever into place.

9. Install the 2 electrical connectors and the trim shrouds.

Ignition Lock/Switch

REMOVAL & INSTALLATION

1. Disconnect the negative battery cable.

2. Remove the upper shroud below the steering wheel by unsnapping the retaining clips. On the tilt column it will be necessary to remove the 5 attaching screws.

3. Disconnect the electrical connector from the ignition switch.

4. Remove the bolts holding the switch to the lock cylinder.

NOTE: On 1982–84 model vehicles it will be necessary to drill out the screws retaining the ignition switch. This can accomplished with an ⅛ in. drill bit. Also it will be necessary to use new break off head bolts to install the switch.

5. Disengage the switch from the actuator pin.

6. Adjust the new ignition switch by sliding the carrier to the **LOCK** position. Insert a small drill bit through the switch housing and into the carrier to restrict movement of the carrier with respect to the switch housing. A replacement comes with an adjusting pin already installed.

7. Turn the ignition key to the **LOCK** position.

8. Install the ignition switch on the actuator pin.

9. Install the retaining bolts and tighten evenly.

10. Remove the drill bit or adjusting pin.

11. ReConnect all electrical connections and the negative battery cable.

12. Start the car and check for proper operation of the switch.

13. Install the steering column shroud.

Manual Steering Gear

REMOVAL & INSTALLATION

1. Disconnect the battery negative cable.

2. Remove the retaining bolt from the flexible coupling to the steering shaft.

3. Place the ignition switch in the ON position and raise the vehicle and support safely.

4. Remove the right and left tie rod end retaining nuts and separate the studs from the spindle arms, using a separator tool.

5. Support the steering rack and pinion assembly and remove the retaining nuts, bolts and washers insulators.

NOTE: On certain models it is necessary to remove the crossmember to allow clearance for the removal of the rack and pinion.

6. Remove the rack and pinion from the vehicle.

7. The installation is the reverse of the removal procedure.

ADJUSTMENTS

The manual rack and pinion gear provides 2 means of service adjustment. The gear must be removed from the vehicle to perform both adjustments.

SUPPORT YOKE TO RACK

1. Mount the steering gear on a bench mounted holding fixture, tool T57L–500–B or equivalent. Rotate the pinion to set gear on center.

2. Remove yoke cover, gasket, shims and yoke spring. Clean cover and housing flange areas thoroughly. Reinstall the cover, omitting the gasket, shims and the spring.

3. Tighten the bolts lightly until the cover just touches the yoke. Measure the gap between the cover and the housing flange. With the gasket, add selected shims to give a combined pack thickness 0.005–0.006 in. (0.13–0.15mm) greater than the measured gap.

4. Remove the cover. Assemble the gasket next to the housing flange. Then add the selected shims, spring and cover. Tighten cover bolts to 15–21 ft. lb. (21–29 Nm).

PINION BEARING PRELOAD

1. Mount the steering gear on a

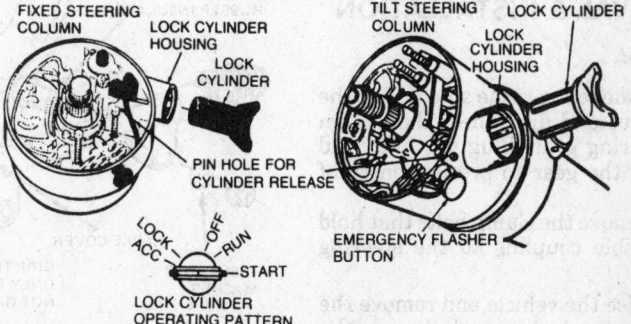

Lock cylinder replacement with locking column

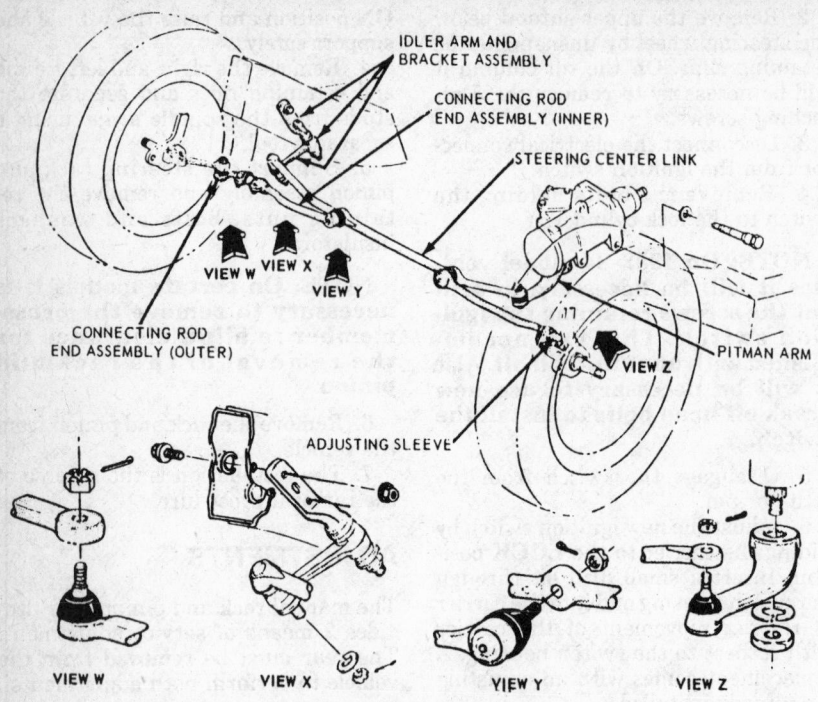

IDLER ARM AND BRACKET ASSEMBLY

CONNECTING ROD END ASSEMBLY (INNER)

STEERING CENTER LINK

CONNECTING ROD END ASSEMBLY (OUTER)

VIEW W   VIEW X   VIEW Y

PITMAN ARM

VIEW Z

ADJUSTING SLEEVE

VIEW W   VIEW X   VIEW Y   VIEW Z

Typical steering linkage

bench mounted holding fixture, tool T57L–500–B or equivalent. Loosen the bolts of the yoke cover to relieve spring pressure on the rack.

2. Remove pinion cover and gasket. Remove the spacer and shims. Install a new gasket.

3. Fit shims between the upper bearing and the spacer until the top of the spacer is flush with the gasket. Check with a straight edge using light pressure.

4. Add one 0.0025 in. (0.06mm) shim to the pack in order to preload the bearings. The spacer must be assembled next to the pinion cover.

5. Remove oil seal from cover using centering tool T81P–3504–Y or equivalent. Tighten bolts to 15–21 ft. lbs. (21–29 Nm). Install pinion shaft oil seal.

Power Steering Gear

REMOVAL & INSTALLATION

Integral

1. Remove the stone shield. Tag the fluid lines and disconnect them from the steering gear. Plug the lines and ports in the gear to prevent entry of dirt.

2. Remove the clamp bolts that hold the flexible coupling to the steering gear.

3. Raise the vehicle and remove the sector shaft attaching nut. Remove the pitman arm with a special pulling tool.

4. Support the steering gear and remove the attaching bolts.

5. Work the gear free of the flex coupling. Remove the gear and flex coupling.

6. Installation is the reverse of the removal procedure. Fill with fluid and bleed the system.

Rack and Pinion

1. Disconnect the negative battery cable.

2. Remove the bolt retaining the flexible coupling to the steering input shaft.

3. Place the ignition key in the **ON** position and raise the vehicle and support safely.

4. Remove the 2 tie rod end retaining nuts and cotter pins. Separate the tie rod stud from the spindle arms with the use of a separator tool.

5. Support the rack and pinion and remove the retaining nuts, washers and bolts from the rack and pinion to the crossmember.

6. Lower the gear assembly slightly to gain access to the pressure and return line fittings. Disconnect the fittings and plug the openings to prevent the entry of dirt.

7. Remove the rack and pinion gear assembly from the vehicle.

8. The installation of the rack and pinion assembly is the reverse of the removal procedure. Fill with fluid and bleed the system.

1985–88 MARK VII/1982–87 CONTINENTAL

1. Turn off the air suspension switch, which is located in the left fenderwell, in the trunk of the vehicle.

2. Disconnect the negative battery cable and turn the ignition switch to the **RUN** position.

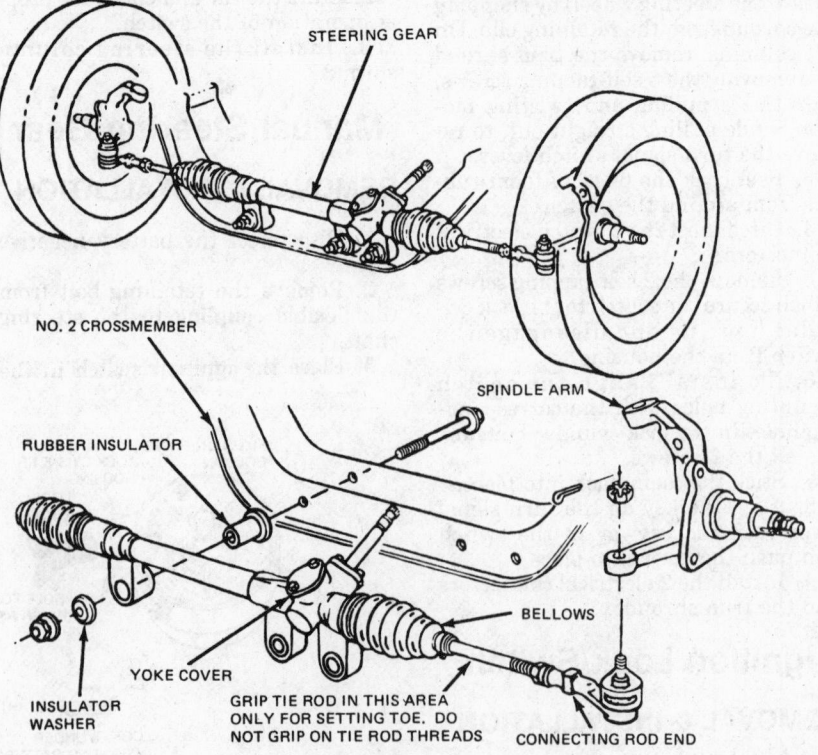

STEERING GEAR

NO. 2 CROSSMEMBER

RUBBER INSULATOR

SPINDLE ARM

BELLOWS

YOKE COVER

INSULATOR WASHER

GRIP TIE ROD IN THIS AREA ONLY FOR SETTING TOE. DO NOT GRIP ON TIE ROD THREADS

CONNECTING ROD END

Rack and pinion steering linkage

3. Raise and support the vehicle safely, position a drain pan under the power steering lines in order to catch the fluid when the lines are removed.

4. Remove 1 bolt retaining the flexible coupling to the intake shaft.

5. Remove the 2 tie rod end retaining cotter pins and nuts. Separate the studs from the spindle arms, using ball joint spindle press T57P–3006–B or equivalent.

6. Remove the 2 nuts, insulator washers and bolts retaining the steering gear to the No. 2 crossmember.

7. Remove the front rubber insulators and move the gear assembly forward so as to be able to remove the rear rubber insulators.

8. Position the gear to allow access to the hydraulic lines and disconnect the lines.

9. Pull the left hand side of the steering gear forward to clear the mounting spike and allow it to drop as far as possible without forcing it. Rotate the top of the gear assembly forward to clear the engine oil filter and remove the steering gear.

10. Installation is the reverse order of the removal procedure. Be sure to install a new rubber insulators and also new plastic seals on the hydraulic line fittings, torque the lines to 10–15 ft. lbs. (14–20 Nm).

11. Refill the system with power steering fluid and bleed the system.

ADJUSTMENT

There is a normal service adjustment on the Integral Power Steering Gear. It is the mesh load adjustment with the gear in the vehicle.

1. Disconnect the pitman arm from the sector shaft.

2. Disconnect the fluid return line at the reservoir and cap the reservoir return line pipe.

3. Turn the steering wheel from left stop to right stop several times to discharge the fluid from the gear.

4. Turn the steering wheel to 45 degrees from the left stop. If vehicle is equipped with a tilt column, place the steering wheel in the center tilt position.

5. Using a torque wrench on the steering wheel nut, determine the torque required to rotate the shaft slowly approximately ¼ turn from the 45 degree position.

6. Turn the steering wheel back to center and determine the torque required to rotate the shaft back and forth across the center position. If the reading is not to specification (14–29 inch lbs.), loosen the nut, and turn the adjuster screw until the reading is to specification. Tighten the nut while holding the screw in place.

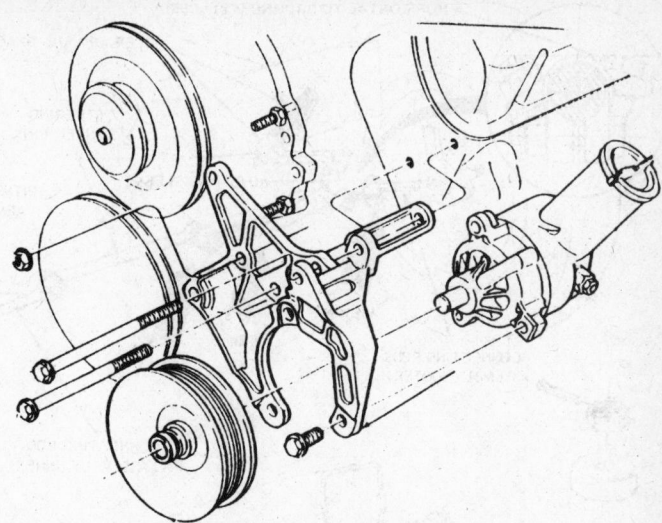

Power steering pump mounting V8 engines

Power Steering Pump

REMOVAL & INSTALLATION

1. Drain the fluid from the pump reservoir by disconnecting the fluid return hose at the pump. Disconnect the pressure hose from the pump.

2. Remove the drive belt. Remove the mounting bolts from the mounting bracket(s) and remove the pump. In some cases, depending on model, it is necessary to remove the pulley (using a special puller) before the pump can be removed from the mounting bracket.

3. To reinstall the pump, position on mounting bracket and loosely install the mounting bolts and nuts. Put the drive belt over the pulley and move the pump outward against the belt until the proper belt tension is obtained. Do not pry against the pump body. Measure the belt tension with a belt tension gauge for the proper adjustment. Only in cases where a belt tension gauge is not available should the belt deflection method be used.

4. Tighten the mounting bolts and nuts.

BELT ADJUSTMENT

Pivot System

Loosen the pivot bolts and insert a tool into the square hole in the pivot bracket. Lift the pivot bracket up to obtain the proper belt tension and tighten the pivot bolts. Tighten all bolts to 30–45 ft. lbs. (40–62 Nm).

Fixed Pump System

Belt tension is adjusted by pivoting the alternator.

NOTE: **Do not pry against the reservoir to obtain proper belt tension. Pressure on the fiberglass reservoir may crack the reservoir.**

On engines that have serpentine drive belts, tension is adjusted with the idler pulley.

Tie Rod Ends

REMOVAL & INSTALLATION

Except Rack and Pinion

1. Raise and support the front end.

2. Remove the cotter pin and nut from the rod end ball stud.

3. Loosen the sleeve clamp bolts and remove the rod end from the spindle arm center link using a ball joint separator.

4. Remove the rod end from the sleeve, counting the exact number of turns required.

5. Install the new end using the exact number of turns it took to remove the old one.

6. Install all parts. Torque the stud to 40–43 ft. lbs. and the clamp to 20–22 ft. lbs.

7. Check the toe-in.

Rack and Pinion Models

1. Remove the cotter pin and nut at the spindle. Separate the tie rod end stud from the spindle with a puller.

2. Matchmark the position of the locknut with paint on the tie rod. Unscrew the locknut. Unscrew the tie rod end, counting the number of turns required to remove.

3. Install the new end the same number of turns. Attach the tie rod end stud to the spindle. Install the nut

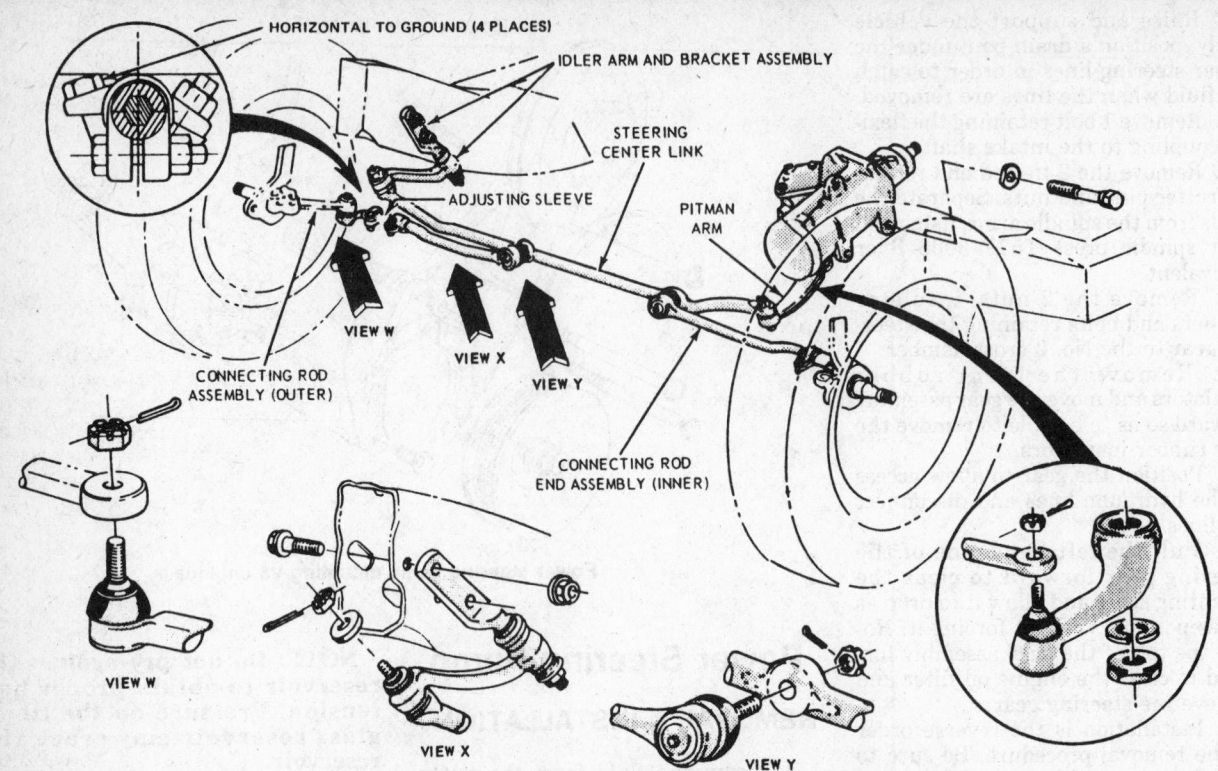

Typical manual or power steering linkage and gear assembly

and torque to 35 ft. lbs., then continue to tighten until the cotter pin holes align. Install a new cotter pin. Check the toe and adjust if necessary, then torque the tie rod end locknut to 35 ft. lbs.

BRAKES

For all brake system repair and service procedures not detailed below, please refer to "Brakes" in the unit repair section.

Master Cylinder

REMOVAL & INSTALLATION

NOTE: On vehicles equipped with the anti-lock braking system, it is necessary to remove the brake system pressure before performing any type of service. The pressure can be removed by, placing the key in the OFF position and pumping the brake pedal at least 20 times or until increased pedal effort is felt.

1. Disconnect the negative battery cable.
2. Remove the brake tubes from the primary and secondary outlet ports of the master cylinder and pressure control valves.
3. Remove 2 nuts attaching master cylinder to the brake booster assembly. Disconnect brake warning lamp connector.
4. Slide the master cylinder forward and upward from vehicle.
5. Installation is the reverse of the removal procedure. Fill master cylinder to **MAX** line on side of reservoir with heavy duty brake fluid. Bleed brake system.

Proportioning Valve

REMOVAL & INSTALLATION

1. Disconnect the brake warning lamp switch wire harness connector from the warning lamp switch.
2. Disconnect the front brake system inlet tube and rear system inlet tube from the brake control valve assembly.
3. Disconnect the left and right front brake outlet tubes from the brake control valve assembly.
4. Disconnect the rear system outlet tube from the brake control valve assembly.
5. Remove the screw that retains the brake control valve assembly on the frame. Remove the assembly from the vehicle.

NOTE: The brake control valve assembly is serviced only as an assembly.

6. Position the brake valve assembly on the frame. Install the mounting screw for frame mounting and tighten to 7–11 ft. lbs.
7. Install the inlet and outlet tubes in the reverse order of the removal procedure and torque tube nuts to 10–18 ft. lbs.
8. Connect the brake warning lamp switch wiring harness connector to the brake warning lamp switch. Verify the connection by turning the ignition switch to the **ON** position; lamp must go on. Also confirm that the 2 locking fingers on the connector are locked into the switch.
9. Bleed the brake system and centralize the the pressure differential valve by:
   a. Turn the ignition switch to the **ON** or **ACC** position.
   b. Depress the brake pedal and the piston will center itself, causing the brake warning lamp to go out (if it was illuminated).
   c. Turn the ignition switch to the **OFF** position.
   d. Before driving the vehicle, check the operation of the brakes and be sure that a firm pedal is obtained.

NOTE: During the brake system bleeding operation on vehicles equipped with a metering valve, the metering valve bleeder rod must be pushed in (pressure bleeding).

Power Brake Booster

REMOVAL & INSTALLATION

1. Working inside the car below the instrument panel, disconnect booster valve operating rod from the brake pedal assembly. To do this, disconnect the stop light switch wires at the connector. Remove the hairpin retainer and nylon washer from the pedal pin. Slide the switch off just enough for the outer arm to clear the pin. Remove the switch. Slide the boost push rod, bushing and inner nylon washer off the pedal pin.

2. Remove the air cleaner for working clearance if necessary. On models equipped with the 2.3L engine, disconnect the accelerator cable at the carburetor. Remove the securing screw from the accelerator shaft bracket and remove the cable from the bracket. Remove the 2 screws attaching the bracket to the manifold; rotate the bracket toward the engine.

3. Disconnect the brake lines at the master cylinder outlet fittings.

4. Disconnect manifold vacuum hose from the booster unit. On cars equipped with speed control, remove the left cowl screen in the engine com-

partment. Remove the 3 nuts retaining the speed control servo to the firewall and move the servo out of the way.

5. Remove the 4 bracket to firewall attaching bolts.

6. Remove the booster and bracket assembly from the firewall, sliding the valve operating rod out from the engine side.

7. Installation is the reverse of removal. Bleed the brakes after installation is complete.

Hydro-Boost Power Unit

REMOVAL & INSTALLATION

1. Open the hood and remove the 2 nuts attaching the master cylinder to the brake booster.

2. Remove the master cylinder from the Hydro-Boost accumulator.

3. Set the master cylinder aside without disturbing the hydraulic lines.

4. Disconnect the pressure, steering and return lines from the accumulator.

5. Plug the lines and ports.

6. Working below the instrument panel, disconnect the Hydro-Boost pushrod from the brake pedal. To do this, disconnect the stoplight switch at the connector. Remove the hairpin retainer. Slide the stoplight switch from the brake pedal pin far enough to clear

the switch outer pin hole. Remove the switch from the pin.

7. Loosen the Hydro-Boost attaching nuts and remove the pushrod, washers and bushings from the brake pedal pin.

8. Remove the accumulator.

9. Installation is the reverse of removal. Leave the Hydro-Boost mounting nuts loose until the pushrod and stoplight switch are connected to the brake pedal. After installation, remove the coil wire from the distributor. Fill the power steering reservoir and while cranking the engine, pump the brake pedal. Do not move the steering wheel until all the air has been pumped out of the system. Check the power steering fluid level, install the coil wire, start the engine and pump the brakes while steering from lock to lock. Check for leaks.

Wheel Cylinder

REMOVAL & INSTALLATION

1. Remove the wheel and brake drum.

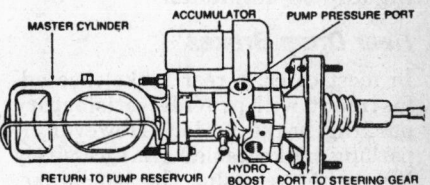

Hydro—boost brake unit

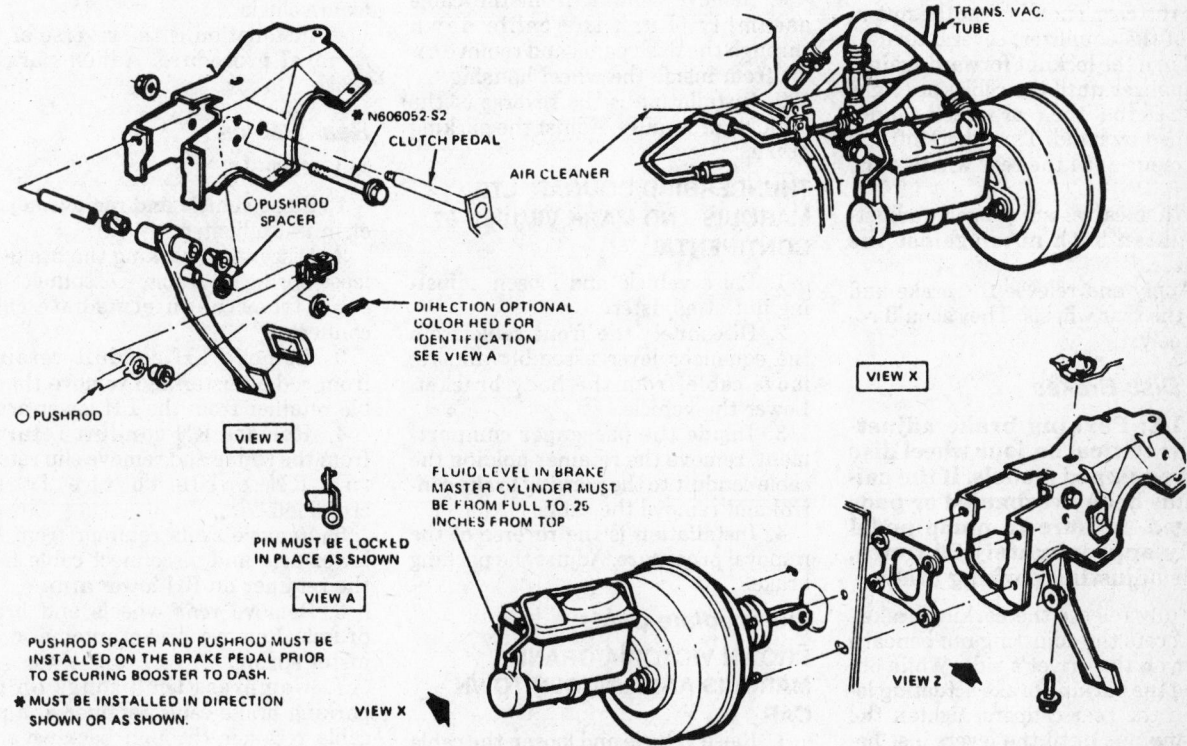

Typical power brake vacuum unit

2. Remove the brake shoe assemblies.

3. Disconnect the brake tube from the brake cylinder at the backing plate.

4. Remove the wheel cylinder attaching bolts and remove the wheel cylinder.

5. Installation is in the reverse order of the removal procedure.

6. Torque the wheel cylinder attaching bolts to 10–20 ft. lbs. Torque the brake tube fitting nut to 10–18 ft. lbs. using a tube nut wrench.

7. Install the links in the ends of the wheel cylinder and install the shoes and adjuster assemblies.

8. Adjust the brakes. Install the brake drum and wheel. Bleed the brakes.

Parking Brake Cable

ADJUSTMENT

NOTE: If a new cable is installed, prestretch it by applying and releasing 5 times before making any adjustments.

Rear Drum Brakes

In most cases, a rear brake shoe adjustment will provide satisfactory parking brake action. However, if parking brake cables are excessively loose after releasing the handbrake, proceed as follows:

1. Fully release the parking brake.

2. Loosen locknut on equalizer rod under the car. Then loosen the nut in front of the equalizer, several turns.

3. Turn the locknut forward against the equalizer until the cables are tight enough so that the rear wheels cannot be turned by hand. Then, back off the adjustment until the rear wheels turn freely.

4. When cables are properly adjusted, tighten both nuts against the equalizer.

5. Apply and release the brake and check the rear wheels. They should rotate freely.

Rear Disc Brakes

NOTE: Parking brake adjustment is critical on four wheel disc brake equipped models. If the caliper has been overhauled or pads changed, be sure to pump pedal lightly approximately 30 times, before adjusting parking brake.

1. Fully release the parking brake.

2. Locate the adjusting nut beneath the car on the driver's side. While observing the parking brake actuating levers on the rear calipers, tighten the adjusting nut until the levers just begin to move.

3. Apply and release parking brake control. Check the parking brake levers on the calipers to determine if they are fully returned to the stop position by attempting to pull them rearward.

4. If lever does not contact caliper lever stop, the cable adjustment is to tight. Repeat adjustment procedure.

REMOVAL & INSTALLATION

Front Cable

CROWN VICTORIA/GRAND MARQUIS AND LINCOLN TOWN CAR

1. Raise vehicle and loosen adjusting nut at adjuster.

2. Disconnect cable from intermediate cable connector located along LH frame side rail.

3. Remove conduit retainer from frame. Remove screw holding the plastic inner fender apron to the frame, at the rear of the fender panel.

4. Pull back the fender apron and remove the spring clip retainer that holds the parking brake cable to the frame.

5. Pull the cable through the frame and let it hang in wheel housing. Lower the vehicle.

6. Inside the passenger compartment, remove the sound deadener cover from the cable at the dash panel.

7. Remove the spring retainer and cable end from the clevis at the parking brake control.

8. Remove conduit from the cable assembly. Push the cable down through the dash panel and remove cable from inside the wheel housing.

9. Installation is the reverse of the removal procedure. Adjust the parking brake.

THUNDERBIRD/COUGAR, LTD/ MARQUIS AND MARK VII/1982–87 CONTINENTAL

1. Raise vehicle and loosen adjusting nut at adjuster.

2. Disconnect the front cable from the equalizer lever assembly and remove cable from the body bracket. Lower the vehicle.

3. Inside the passenger compartment, remove the retainer holding the cable conduit to the parking brake control and remove the cable.

4. Installation is the reverse of the removal procedure. Adjust the parking brake.

Intermediate Cable

CROWN VICTORIA/GRAND MARQUIS AND LINCOLN TOWN CAR

1. Raise vehicle and loosen the cable adjusting nut.

2. Disconnect parking brake release spring at frame.

3. Disconnect the cable from the cable connectors and remove it from the vehicle.

4. Installation is the reverse of the removal procedure. Adjust the parking brake.

THUNDERBIRD/COUGAR, LTD/ MARQUIS AND MARK VII/1982–87 CONTINENTAL

1. Raise vehicle and remove cable adjusting nut.

2. Disconnect the cable ends from the LH rear and the transverse cable.

3. Remove the cotter pin, washer and spring from the pin protruding through the equalizer lever assembly and remove the lever.

4. Installation is the reverse of the removal procedure. Adjust the parking brake.

NOTE: The intermediate cable cannot be seperated from the lever assembly.

Transverse Cable

THUNDERBIRD/COUGAR, LTD/ MARQUIS AND MARK VII/1982–87 CONTINENTAL

1. Raise vehicle and loosen the adjusting nut on the rod until it is off rod.

2. Remove the cable ends from the RH rear and intermediate cables.

3. Remove hairpin clips, or conduit bracket as required to remove cable from vehicle.

4. Installation is the reverse of the removal procedure. Adjust parking brake.

Rear Cables

ALL MODELS

1. Raise vehicle and remove adjuster nut at adjuster.

2. Disconnect parking the brake release spring at frame. Disconnect LH cable from the intermediate cable connector.

3. Remove LH conduit retainer from rod adjuster and remove the cable retainer from the LH lower arm.

4. Release RH conduit retainer from the frame and remove clip retaining RH cable to the frame crossmember.

5. Remove cable retainer from RH lower arm and disconnect cable from the retainer on RH lower arm.

6. Remove rear wheels and brake drums. Remove brake automatic adjuster spring.

7. Compress the prongs on the parking brake cable retainer and pull cable retainer through backing plate hole.

8. With the tension off the cable spring at the parking brake lever, lift the cable end out of the slot in the lever. Remove the cable through backing plate hole.

9. Installation is the reverse of the removal procedure. Adjust the parking brake.

CHASSIS ELECTRICAL

Heater Blower

REMOVAL & INSTALLATION

With or Without Air Conditioning

CROWN VICTORIA/GRAND MARQUIS AND LINCOLN TOWN CAR

1. Disconnect the ground cable from the battery.

2. Disconnect the blower motor lead connector from the wiring harness connector.

3. Remove the blower motor cooling tube from the blower motor.

4. Remove the 4 blower motor retaining screws.

5. Turn the motor and wheel assembly slightly to the right so that the bottom edge of the mounting plate follows the contour of the wheel well splash panel. Lift up on the blower and remove it from the blower housing.

6. Installation is the reverse or removal.

With Air Conditioning

1982–87 CONTINENTAL, MARK VII, THUNDERBIRD, COUGAR, LTD, MARQUIS AND 1982–86 CAPRI/MUSTANG

1. Disconnect the ground cable from the battery.

2. Remove the air inlet duct and blower housing assembly from the vehicle.

3. Remove the 4 blower housing retaining screws.

4. Turn the motor and wheel assembly slightly to the right so that the bottom edge of the mounting plate follows the contour of the wheel well splash panel. Lift up on the blower and remove it from the blower housing.

5. Installation is the reverse of removal.

Without Air Conditioning

1982–86 MUSTANG/CAPRI

1. Remove right ventilator assem-

bly and remove the hub clamp spring from the blower wheel hub.

2. Pull the blower wheel off the blower motor shaft and remove the 3 blower flange attaching screws located inside the blower housing.

3. Pull the blower motor out of the housing and disconnect the blower motor wires from the motor.

4. Installation is the reverse of the removal procedure.

NOTE: DO NOT remove the mounting plate from the blower motor.

1987–89 MUSTANG

1. Loosen glove compartment assembly by squeezing the sides together to disengage the retainer tabs.

2. Let the glove compartment and door hang down in front of instrument panel and remove blower motor cooling hose.

3. Disconnect electrical wiring harness. Remove the 4 screws attaching motor to housing. Pull the motor and wheel out of the housing.

Heater Core

REMOVAL & INSTALLATION

Without Air Conditioning

CROWN VICTORIA/GRAND MARQUIS AND TOWN CAR

1. Drain the coolant and save for reuse.

2. Disconnect the negative cable from the battery.

3. Remove the heater hoses from the heater core.

4. Plug the heater core tubes to prevent coolant from spilling under the dash during plenum removal.

5. Remove the plenum to dash bolt, located under the windshield wiper motor at the left end of the plenum chamber.

6. Remove the 1 nut from the heater case (engine side).

7. Disconnect the vacuum supply hose from the vacuum fitting and push the grommet and hose into the pasenger compartment.

8. Remove the glove box assembly.

9. Loosen the right door sillplate and remove the right side cowl trim panel.

10. Remove the lower right instrument panel to side cowl bolt.

11. Remove the instrument panel pad.

12. Remove the temperature control cable from the top of the plenum. Disconnect the temperature control cable from the blend door crank arm.

13. Remove the push clip attaching the center register duct bracket to the

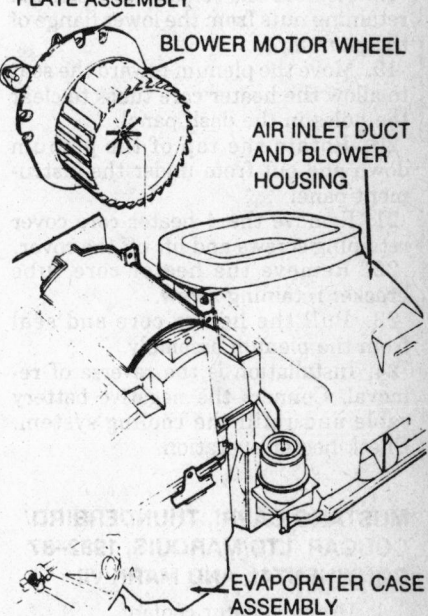

Air inlet and blower motor housing assembly 1987–88 Mustang

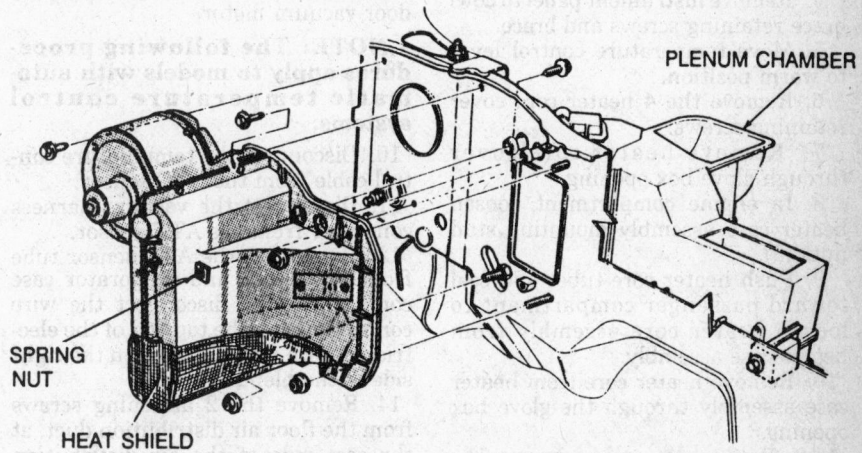

Typical heater core and blower housing mounting

plenum and rotate the bracket up to the right.

14. Disconnect the vacuum jumper harness at the multiple vacuum connector near the floor air distribution duct.

15. Disconnect the white vacuum hose from the outside air door vacuum motor.

16. Remove the 2 screws attaching the seat side of the floor air distribution duct to the plenum.

NOTE: It may be necessary to remove the 2 screws attaching the lower panel door vacuum motor to the mounting bracket to gain access to the floor air distribution duct screw.

17. Remove the plastic push-pin fastener from the floor air distribution duct and remove the duct.

18. Remove the remaining 2 plenum retaining nuts from the lower flange of the plenum.

19. Move the plenum toward the seat to allow the heater core tubes to clear the holes in the dash panel.

20. Rotate the top of the plenum down and out from under the instrument panel.

21. Remove the 4 heater core cover retaining screws and lift off the cover.

22. Remove the heater core tube bracket retaining screw.

23. Pull the heater core and seal from the plenum assembly.

24. Installation is the reverse of removal. Connect the negative battery cable and refill the cooling system. Check heater operation.

MUSTANG/CAPRI, THUNDERBIRD/COUGAR, LTD/MARQUIS, 1982–87 CONTINENTAL AND MARK VII

1. Drain radiator coolant.

2. Disconnect heater hoses at core connections.

3. Remove glove box.

4. Remove instrument panel to cowl brace retaining screws and brace.

5. Move temperature control lever to warm position.

6. Remove the 4 heater core cover retaining screws.

7. Remove heater core cover through glove box opening.

8. In engine compartment, loosen heater case assembly mounting stud nuts (3).

9. Push heater core tubes and seal toward passenger compartment to loosen heater core assembly from heater case assembly.

10. Remove heater core from heater case assembly through the glove box opening.

11. Reverse procedure for installation.

With Air Conditioning—Including Automatic Temperature Control

CROWN VICTORIA/GRAND MARQUIS AND TOWN CAR

1. Disconnect the negative battery cable.

2. Remove the heater hoses from the core tubes and plug the ends to prevent coolant loss.

3. Plug the heater core tubes to prevent coolant loss during plenum and core removal.

4. In the engine compartment, remove the bolt located under the windshield wiper motor. Remove the nut at the upper left corner (engine side) of the evaporator case.

5. Disconnect the control system vacuum supply hose from the vacuum source and push the grommet and vacuum supply hose in the passenger compartment.

6. Remove the glove box assembly.

7. Loosen the right door sill plate and remove the right side cowl trim panel.

8. Remove the lower right instrument panel to side cowl bolt.

9. Remove the instrument panel.

NOTE: The following procedures apply to models without automatic temperature control systems.

10. Remove the bracket from the temperature control cable housing at the top of the plenum assembly. Disconnect the temperature control cable from the blend door crank arm.

11. Remove the push clip attaching the center register duct bracket to the plenum and rotate the bracket up to the right.

12. Disconnect the vacuum jumper harness at the multiple vacuum connector near the floor air distribution duct.

13. Disconnect the white vacuum hose from the outside recirculating door vacuum motor.

NOTE: The following procedures apply to models with automatic temperature control systems.

10. Disconnect the temperature control cable from the ATC sensor.

11. Disconnect the vacuum harness connector from the ATC sensor.

12. Disconnect the ATC sensor tube from the sensor and evaporator case connector. Also, disconnect the wire connector from the top end of the electric-vacuum relay, located on the right side of the plenum case.

14. Remove the 2 attaching screws from the floor air distribution duct, at the seat side of the air distribution duct.

15. Remove the plastic push fastener, holding the air distribution duct to the left of the plenum and remove the air distribution duct.

16. Remove the final 2 retaining nuts from the lower flange of the plenum assembly.

17. Move the plenum assembly toward the seat to allow the heater core tubes to clear the holes in the dash panel. Rotate the plenum assembly down and out from under the dash panel.

18. Installation is the reverse of removal. Refill the cooling system and check the heater operation.

THUNDERBIRD/COUGAR/XR-7, LTD/MARQUIS AND MUSTANG/CAPRI

1. Remove the instrument panel and lay it on the front seat.

2. Drain the coolant from the cooling system. Disconnect the heater hoses from the core tubes and plug the tubes to prevent spillage.

3. From the engine compartment side remove the 2 nuts attaching the evaporator case to the dash panel.

4. Under the dash area remove the screws attaching the evaporator case support bracket and the air inlet duct support bracket to the cowl top panel.

5. Remove the retaining nut from the bracket at the left end of the evaporator case and the nut attaching the heater core access cover to the evaporator case.

6. Carefully pull the evaporator case assembly away from the dash panel to gain access to the screws retaining the heater core access cover to the evaporator case.

7. Remove the heater core cover attaching screws and remove the cover.

8. Lift the heater core and seals from the evaporator case. Remove the 2 seals from the core tubes.

9. Installation is the reverse of removal. Refill the cooling system and check heater operation.

1982–87 CONTINENTAL AND MARK VII

NOTE: The instrument panel must be removed for access to the heater core. The A/C system must be evacuated in order to remove the dash panel and gain access to the heater core. It is advisable to remove and replace the A/C receiver drier when the system has been evacuated.

1. Disconnect the negative battery cable.

2. Remove the instrument panel pad:

a. Remove the screws attaching the instrument cluster trim panel to the pad.

b. Remove the screw attaching the pad to the panel at each defroster opening.

c. Remove the screws attaching the edge of the pad to the panel.

3. **Remove the steering column** opening cover.

4. **Remove the nut and bracket** holding the steering column to the instrument panel and lay the column across the seat.

5. Remove the instrument panel to brake pedal support screw at the column opening.

6. Remove the screws attaching the lower brace to the panel below the radio and below the glove compartment.

7. Disconnect the temperature cable from the door and case bracket.

8. Unplug the 7 port vacuum hose connectors at the evaporator case.

9. Disconnect the resistor wire connector and the blower motor feed wire.

10. Remove the screws attaching the top of the panel to the cowl and support the panel while removing the screws.

11. Remove the 1 screw at each end attaching the panel to the cowl panels.

12. Move the panel rearward and disconnect the speedometer cable and any wires preventing the panel from laying flat on the seat.

13. Drain the coolant and disconnect the heater hoses from the heater core, plug the heater core tubes.

14. Remove the nuts retaining the evaporator case to the firewall in the engine compartment.

15. Remove the case support bracket screws and air inlet duct support bracket.

16. Remove the nut retaining the bracket to the dash panel at the left side of the evaporator case and the nut retaining the bracket below the case to dash panel.

17. Pull the case assembly away from the panel to get to the screws retaining the heater core cover to the case.

18. Remove the cover screws and cover, lift the hater core and seals out of the case assembly.

19. Installation is the reverse order of the removal procedure.

Radio

REMOVAL & INSTALLATION

Lincoln

1. Disconnect the negative battery cable.

2. Remove the 4 radio plate to panel screws. Pull the radio with the front plate attached rearward until the rear bracket is clear.

3. Disconnect the wires from the

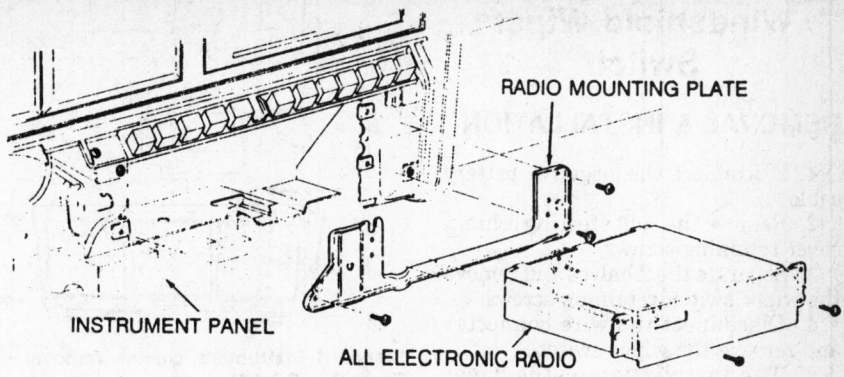

Radio removal – Town Car, Ford/Mercury

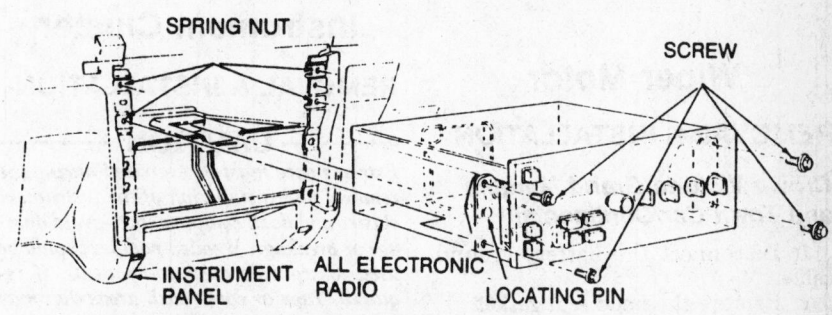

Radio removal – Cougar/Thunderbird, Continental, Mustang/Capri

chassis. If equipped with premium sound, remove the control assembly attaching nut and washer, remove the switch and remove the illumination lamp socket from the front bracket.

4. Remove the radio with the front plate attached. Remove the 4 screws and remove the plate. Installation is the reverse of removal.

Crown Victoria/Grand Marquis

1. Disconnect the battery ground cable.

2. On all electronic radios, remove the radio to mounting plate screws and remove the mounting plate.

3. Remove the radio knobs, the screws that attach the bezel to the instrument panel and remove the bezel.

4. Remove the radio mounting plate attaching screws (standard radios) and disengage the radio by pulling it from the lower rear support bracket.

5. Disconnect all the leads from the radio.

6. Remove the radio mounting plate and the rear upper support; remove the radio from the instrument panel.

7. Reverse the procedure to install.

Fairmont, Mustang, Capri, Granada and Cougar

1. Disconnect the negative battery cable.

2. Disconnect the electrical, speaker and antenna leads from the radio.

3. Remove the knobs, discs and control shaft nuts and washers from the radio shafts.

4. Remove the ash tray receptacle and bracket.

5. Remove the rear support nut from the radio.

6. Remove the instrument panel lower reinforcement and the heater or air conditioning floor ducts.

7. Remove the radio from the rear support and drop the radio down and out from behind the instrument panel.

8. To install, reverse the removal procedure.

Thunderbird/Cougar/XR-7 and LTD/Marquis

1. Disconnect the negative battery cable.

2. Remove the radio knobs (pull off). Remove the center trim panel.

3. Remove the radio mounting plate screws. Pull the radio towards the front seat to disengage it from the lower bracket.

4. Disconnect the radio and antenna connections.

5. Remove the radio. Remove the nuts and washers (conventional radios) as necessary.

6. On electronic radios, install the mounting plates before installing the retaining nuts and washers or screws. The rest of installation is the reverse of removal.

Windshield Wiper Switch

REMOVAL & INSTALLATION

1. Disconnect the negative battery cable.
2. Remove the split steering column cover retaining screws.
3. Separate the 2 halves and remove the wiper switch retaining screws.
4. Disconnect the wire connector and remove the wiper switch.
5. The installation of the wiper switch is the reverse of the removal procedure.

Wiper Motor

REMOVAL & INSTALLATION

Crown Victoria/Grand Marquis and Town Car/Continental

1. Disconnect the battery ground cable.
2. Remove the hood seal gasket.
3. Disconnect the right washer nozzle hose and remove the right wiper arm and blade assembly from the pivot shaft.
4. Remove the windshield wiper motor and linkage cover by removing the 2 attaching screws.
5. Disconnect the linkage drive arm from the motor output arm crankpin by removing the retaining clip.
6. Disconnect the 2 push-on wire connectors from the motor.
7. Remove the 3 bolts that retain the motor to the dash panel extension and remove the motor.
8. To install, be sure the output arm is in the park position and reverse the removal procedure.

All Others

1. Disconnect the battery ground cable.
2. Remove the right wiper and blade assembly.

NOTE: On Fairmont, Granada and Cougar models, also remove the left wiper arm and blade.

3. Remove the grille on the top of the cowl.
4. Disconnect the linkage drive arm from the motor crankpin after removing the clip.
5. Disconnect the wiper motor electrical connector and remove the 3 attaching screws from the motor. Pull the motor from the opening.
6. Be sure the motor crank arm is in the park position and reverse the removal procedure to install.

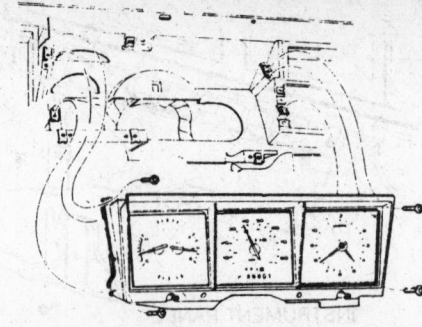

Standard instrument cluster removal— Town Car, Ford/Mercury

Instrument Cluster

REMOVAL & INSTALLATION

—— CAUTION ——

Extreme care must be exercised during the removal and installation of the instrument cluster and dash components to avoid damage or breakage. Wooden paddles should be used to separate dash components, if required. Tape or cover dash areas that may be damaged by the removal and installation of the dash components.

NOTE: During the removal and installation procedures, slight variations may be required from the general outline, to facilitate the removal and installation of the instrument panel and cluster components, due to production changes from model year to model year.

Crown Victoria/Grand Marquis and Town Car

1. Disconnect the battery ground cable.
2. Remove the lower steering column cover.
3. Remove the instrument cluster trim cover and the bottom half of the steering column shroud.
4. Reach behind the cluster and disconnect the cluster electrical feed plug and the speedometer cable.
5. Unsnap and remove the steering column shroud cover, if not previously done. Disconnect the transmission indictor cable from the tab in the shroud retainer.
6. Remove the attaching screw for the transmission indicator cable bracket to steering column. Disconnect the cable loop from the pin on the steering column.
7. Remove the cluster retaining screws and remove the cluster assembly.
8. The installation is the reverse of the removal procedure.

Thunderbird/Cougar/XR-7 and 1982–87 Continental

1. Disconnect the negative battery cable.
2. Disconnect the speedometer cable (Standard cluster).
3. Remove the instrument panel trim cover and steering column lower shroud.
4. Remove the cluster retaining screws (Electronic cluster).
5. Remove the attaching screw from the transmission indictor quadrant cable bracket to the steering column. Disconnect the cable loop from the pin on the steering column.
6. Remove the cluster retaining screws (Standard cluster).
7. Pull the cluster away from the instrument panel and disconnect the speedometer cable (Electronic cluster).
9. Remove the cluster from the instrument panel.
10. Reverse the removal procedure to install.

Fairmont, Granada and Cougar

1. Disconnect the battery negative cable.
2. Remove the steering column shroud and the cluster trim cover.
3. Remove 1 screw from the shift quadrant control cable bracket to steering column and disconnect the cable loop from the pin n the shift cane lever. Remove the plastic clamp from around the steering column.
4. Remove the retaining screws holding the cluster to the instrument panel.
5. Pull the cluster away from the instrument panel and disconnect the speedometer cable. disconnect the electrical connectors and remove the cluster from the dash.
6. To install the cluster, reverse the removal procedure.

Mustang/Capri

1. Disconnect the battery ground cable.
2. Remove the instrument trim cover.
3. From under the dash, reach up and disconnect the speedometer cable.
4. Remove the cluster retaining screws and pull the cluster away from the dash. Disconnect the tachometer and wiring connectors. Remove the cluster assembly.
5. The installation is the reverse of the removal procedure.

1982–86 LTD, Marquis

STANDARD CLUSTER

1. Disconnect the negative battery cable.
2. Disconnect the speedometer ca-

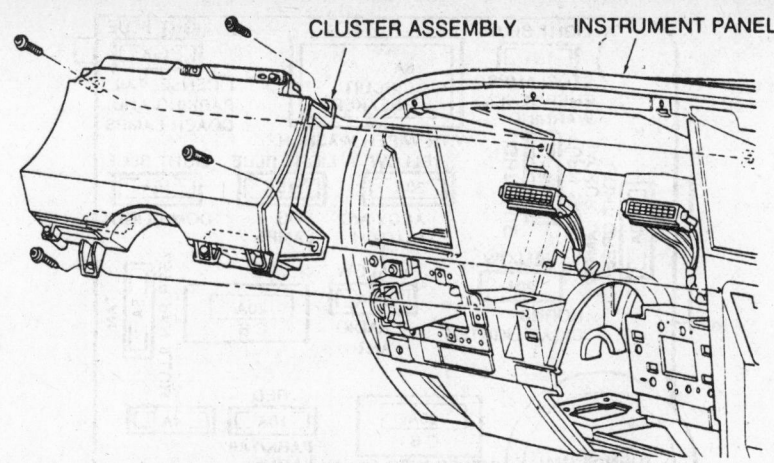

Cougar/Thunderbird instrument cluster removal

ble. Remove the screws retaining the cluster trim panel and remove the panel.

3. Remove the steering wheel shroud. Remove the screw retaining the shift indictor control cable to the steering column. Disconnect the indicator cable loop from the shift lever pin. Remove the plastic clamp from the steering column.

4. Remove the cluster retaining screws. Disconnect the cluster feed plug from the printed circuit. Disconnect the engine warning lamp.

5. Remove the instrument cluster.

6. Install the cluster in the reverse order of removal.

ELECTRONIC CLUSTER

1. Disconnect the negative battery cable.

2. Remove the screws retaining the lower instrument cluster trim panel. Remove the steering column cover.

3. Remove the screws retaining the instrument cluster to the instrument panel.

4. Remove the screw attaching the transmission indictor cable bracket to the steering column. Disconnect the cable loop from the pin on the steering column.

5. Carefully pull the instrument cluster away from the panel and disconnect the speedometer cable. Disconnect the cluster feed plug and ground receptacle from the cluster back plate.

6. Remove the cluster assembly.

7. Install the cluster in the reverse order of removal.

Headlight Switch

REMOVAL & INSTALLATION

Crown Victoria/Grand Marquis, LTD/Marquis and Mustang/Capri

1. Disconnect the negative battery cable.

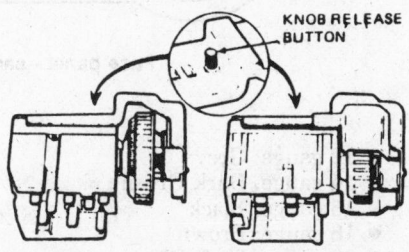

Headlight switch and release button location

2. Underneath the instrument panel, depress the shaft retaining knob and pull the knob straight out.

3. Unscrew the trim bezel and remove the locknut.

4. Underneath the instrument panel, move the switch toward the front of the car while tilting it downward.

5. Disconnect the wiring from the switch and remove the switch from the car.

6. Installation is the reverse of removal.

Town Car

1. Disconnect the ground cable from the battery.

2. Remove the headlamp switch knob.

3. Remove the auto dimmer bezel and the autolamp delay bezel, if so equipped.

4. Remove the steering column lower shroud.

5. Remove lower LH instrument panel trim bezel.

6. Remove the 5 screws that retain the headlamp switch mounting bracket to the instrument panel.

7. Carefully pull the switch and bracket from the instrument panel and disconnect the wiring connector(s) from the headlamp switch.

8. Remove the locknut and 1 screw

that retain the headlamp switch to the switch bracket.

9. Installation is the reverse order of the removal procedure.

Mark VII/1982–87 Continental and Thunderbird/Cougar

1. Remove the lens assembly attaching screws and then the lens assembly.

2. Remove the screws securing the switch to the instrument panel and pull the switch out from the panel.

3. Disconnect the electrical connector and remove the switch from the vehicle.

4. Installation is the reverse order of the removal procedure.

Stoplight Switch

REMOVAL & INSTALLATION

Except With Vacuum Powered Brakes

1. Disconnect the wire harness at the connector from the switch.

2. Remove the hairpin retainer, slide the stop lamp switch, the push rod and the nylon washers and bushings away from the pedal and remove the switch.

NOTE: Since the switch side plate nearest the brake pedal is slotted, it is not necessary to remove the brake master cylinder pushrod and 1 washer from the brake pedal pin.

3. Position the switch, push rod, bushing and washers on the brake pedal pin. Install the hairpin retainer.

4. Assemble the wire harness connector to the switch and install the wires in the retaining clip.

Vacuum Powered Brakes

1. Disconnect the negative battery cable.

2. Disconnect the stop lamp switch wire connector from the switch.

3. Loosen the brake booster nuts at the pedal support approximately ¼ in., so that the booster is free to move eliminating binding during switch removal.

4. Remove the hairpin retainer and outer nylon washer from the pedal pin. Slide the stoplamp switch off the brake pedal pin just far enough for the outer arm to clear the pin, remove the switch.

NOTE: Since the switch side plate nearest the brake pedal is slotted it is not necessary to remove the brake master cylinder pushrod and 1 spacer washer from the brake pedal pin.

5. Position the new stop lamp switch so that it straddles the push rod, with the slot on the pedal pin and the switch outer frame hole just clearing the pin. Slide the switch upward onto the pin and pushrod. Slide the assembly inboard toward the brake pedal arm.

6. Install the outer nylon washer and the hairpin retainer.

7. Tighten the booster attaching nuts to specification.

8. Connect the stoplamp switch wire connector to the switch. Connect the negative battery cable.

NOTE: The stoplamp switch wire harness must have sufficient length to travel with switch during full stroke of pedal. If wire length is insufficient, reroute harness or service as required.

9. Check the stoplamps for proper operation.

Fuses, Fusible Links and Circuit Breakers

LOCATION

A fusible link is a short length of insulated wire, integral with the engine compartment wiring harness. It is several wire gauges smaller than the circuit it protects and is located in-line directly from the positive terminal of the battery.

When heavy current flows or when a short to ground occurs in the wiring harness, the fusible link burns out and protects the alternator or wiring. Production fusible links are color coded:

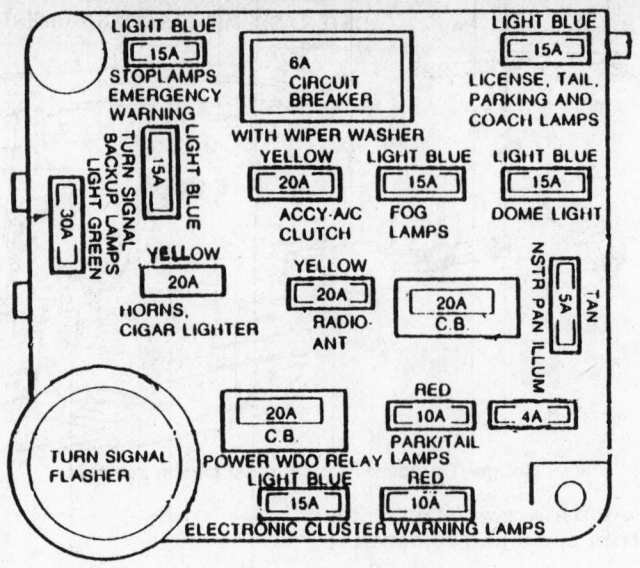

Fuse panel—same for most models

- 12 gauge: Grey
- 14 gauge: Dark Green
- 16 gauge: Black
- 18 gauge: Brown
- 20 gauge: Dark Blue

NOTE: Replacement fusible link color coding may vary from production fusible link color coding.

Circuit breakers are used on certain electrical components requiring high amperage, such as the headlamp circuit, electrical seats and/or windows. The advantage of the circuit breaker is its ability to open and close the electrical circuit as the load demands. Most circuit breakers are located on the fuse panel.

A fuse panel is used to house the numerous fuses protecting the various branches of the electrical system and is normally the most accessible. the mounting of the fuse panel is usually on the left side of the passenger compartment, under the dash, either on the side kick panel or on the firewall to the left of the steering column. Certain models will have the fuse panel exposed while other models will have it covered with a removable trim cover.

Ford Motor Co. 6
Front Wheel Drive
Ford Festiva

SERIAL NUMBER IDENTIFICATION

VEHICLE IDENTIFICATION CHART

It is important for servicing and ordering parts to be certain of the vehicle and engine identification. The VIN (vehicle identification number) is a 20 digit number visible through the windshield on the driver's side of the dash and contains the vehicle and engine identification codes. The tenth digit indicates model year and the eighth digit indicates engine code. It can be interpreted as follows:

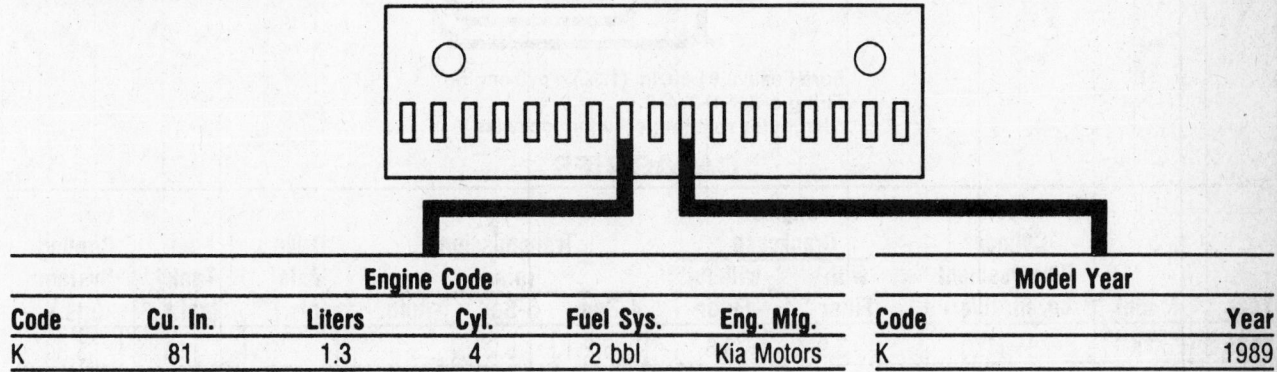

Engine Code						Model Year	
Code	Cu. In.	Liters	Cyl.	Fuel Sys.	Eng. Mfg.	Code	Year
K	81	1.3	4	2 bbl	Kia Motors	K	1989

GENERAL ENGINE SPECIFICATIONS

Year	VIN	No. Cylinder Displacement cu. in. (liter)	Fuel System Type	Net Horsepower @ rpm	Net Torque @ rpm (ft.lbs.)	Bore × Stroke (in.)	Compression Ratio	Oil Pressure @ rpm
1988-89	K	81 (1.3)	2 bbl	58 @ 5000	73 @ 3500	2.78 × 3.29	9.7:1	50–64 @ 3000

GASOLINE ENGINE TUNE-UP SPECIFICATIONS

Year	VIN	No. Cylinder Displacement cu. in. (liter)	Spark Plugs Type	Spark Plugs Gap (in.)	Ignition Timing (deg.) MT	Ignition Timing (deg.) AT	Com-pression Pressure (psi)	Fuel Pump (psi)	Idle Speed (rpm) MT	Idle Speed (rpm) AT	Valve Clearance In.	Valve Clearance Ex.
1988	K	81 (1.3)	AGS32C	.040	TDC	—	①	3–6	700–750	—	.012	.012
1989		SEE UNDERHOOD SPECIFICATIONS										

① The lowest cylinder pressure should be within 75% of the highest cylinder pressure reading. For example, if the highest cylinder is 134 psi, the lowest cylinder should be 101 psi. Engine should be at normal operating temperature with throttle body valve in the wide open position

FIRING ORDERS

NOTE: To avoid confusion, always replace spark plug wires one at a time.

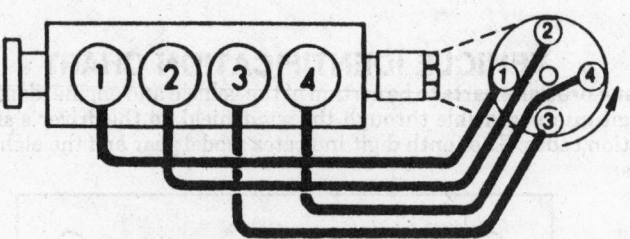

Ford Festiva 81 cu. in. (1.3L) 4 cyl. engine
Firing order 1–3–4–2
Distributor rotation: counterclockwise

CAPACITIES

Year	Model	No. Cylinder Displacement cu. in. (liter)	Engine Crankcase with Filter	Engine Crankcase without Filter	Transmission (pts.) 4-Spd	Transmission (pts.) 5-Spd	Transmission (pts.) Auto.	Drive Axle (pts.)	Fuel Tank (gal.)	Cooling System (qts.)
1988-89	K	81 (1.3)	3.9	3.6	5.2	5.2	—	—	10	5.3

CAMSHAFT SPECIFICATIONS
All measurements given in inches.

Year	VIN	No. Cylinder Displacement cu. in. (liter)	Journal Diameter 1	Journal Diameter 2	Journal Diameter 3	Journal Diameter 4	Journal Diameter 5	Lobe Lift In.	Lobe Lift Ex.	Bearing Clearance	Camshaft End Play
1988-89	K	81 (1.3)	1.7103–1.7112	1.7091–1.7100	1.7103–1.7112	—	—	1.4188–1.4224	1.4185–1.4224	.0026–.0045 ①	.002–.007 ②

① Center bearing oil clearance shown. Front and rear bearing oil clearance — .0014–.0033

② In service limit — .008

CRANKSHAFT AND CONNECTING ROD SPECIFICATIONS

All measurements are given in inches.

Year	VIN	No. Cylinder Displacement cu. in. (liter)	Crankshaft				Connecting Rod		
			Main Brg. Journal Dia.	Main Brg. Oil Clearance	Shaft End-play	Thrust on No.	Journal Diameter	Oil Clearance	Side Clearance
1988-89	K	81 (1.3)	1.9661–1.9668	0009–.0017	.0031–.0111	–	1.5724–1.5731	.0009–.0017	.012

VALVE SPECIFICATIONS

Year	VIN	No. Cylinder Displacement cu. in. (liter)	Seat Angle (deg.)	Face Angle (deg.)	Spring Test Pressure (lbs.)	Spring Installed Height (in.)	Stem-to-Guide Clearance (in.)		Stem Diameter (in.)	
							Intake	Exhaust	Intake	Exhaust
1988-89	K	81 (1.3)	45	45	–	1.717	.008	.008	.2744–.2750	.2742–.2748

PISTON AND RING SPECIFICATIONS

All measurments are given in inches.

Year	VIN	No. Cylinder Displacement cu. in. (liter)	Piston Clearance	Ring Gap			Ring Side Clearance		
				Top Compression	Bottom Compression	Oil Control	Top Compression	Bottom Compression	Oil Control
1988-89	K	81 (1.3)	.006	.006–.012	.006–.012	.008–.028	.0602–.0608	.0598–.0604	.1583–.1591

TORQUE SPECIFICATIONS

All readings in ft. lbs.

Year	VIN	No. Cylinder Displacement cu. in. (liter)	Cylinder Head Bolts	Main Bearing Bolts	Rod Bearing Bolts	Crankshaft Pulley Bolts	Flywheel Bolts	Manifold		Spark Plugs
								Intake	Exhaust	
1988-89	K	81 (1.3)	①	②	③	11–15	71–76	14–19	④	11–17

① Torque cylinder head bolts in sequence as follows:
    Step 1 – 35–40 ft. lbs.
    Step 2 – 56–60 ft. lbs.

② Torque main bearing cup bolts in sequence as follows:
    Step 1 – 22–27 ft. lbs.
    Step 2 – 40–43 ft. lbs.

③ Torque rod bearing nuts in sequence as follows:
    Step 1 – 11–13 ft. lbs.
    Step 2 – 22–25 ft. lbs.

④ Torque exhaust manifold in sequence as follows:
    Step 1 – 5–7 ft. lbs.
    Step 2 – 37–41 ft. lbs.

BRAKE SPECIFICATIONS

All measurements in inches unless noted

Year	Model	Lug Nut Torque (ft. lbs.)	Master Cylinder Bore	Brake Disc		Standard Brake Drum Diameter	Minimum Lining Thickness	
				Minimum Thickness	Maximum Runout		Front	Rear
1988-89	Festiva	65–87	–	.463	.003	6.69	.120	.040

WHEEL ALIGNMENT

Year	Model	Caster Range (deg.)	Caster Preferred Setting (deg.)	Camber Range (deg.)	Camber Preferred Setting (deg.)	Toe-in (in.)	Steering Axis Inclination (deg.)
1988-89	Festiva	$1\frac{5}{16}P-1\frac{11}{16}P$	$1\frac{9}{16}$	$\frac{1}{4}N-1\frac{9}{16}P$	$\frac{11}{16}P$	$\frac{1}{32}-\frac{1}{2}①$	$14\frac{3}{16}P$

P Positive
N Negative
① Prefered setting — $\frac{5}{16}$

TUNE-UP PROCEDURES

Ignition Timing

ADJUSTMENT

1. Connect a tachometer to the engine, start the engine and allow to reach normal operating temperature.
2. Check the curb idle speed. Normal curb idle speed is 700–750 rpm. Adjust the idle speed if necessary.
3. Secure the engine. Disconnect the vacuum hose connecting from the carburetor spark port to the lower chamber nipple on the vacuum advance and the hose from the intake manifold to the upper chamber nipple. Plug the hose openings.
4. Turn off all electrical accessories. At high altitudes, disconnect the barometric pressure switch (mounted high on the firewall on the right side of the engine).
5. Connect a suitable timing light and start the engine.
6. With the timing light, observe the timing marks on the crankshaft pulley and timing case. Correct ignition timing is top dead center (TDC) at idle with no vacuum advance.
7. If the timing is not as specified, loosen the distributor mounting bolts and grasp the distributor by hand. Rotate the distributor clockwise to advance the timing and counterclockwise to retard the timing.
8. When the timing is adjusted to specification, tighten the distributor mounting bolts.
9. Secure the engine and disconnect the timing light. Unplug the vacuum hoses and connect them to the vacuum advance unit. Connect the barometric pressure switch (if removed).
10. Start the engine and check the idle speed. Adjust the idle speed as required.

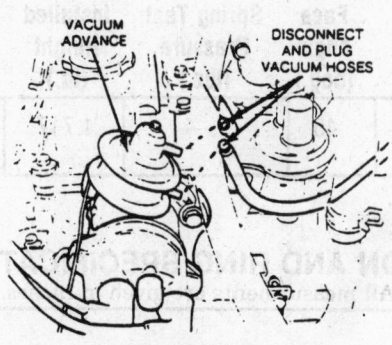

Vacuum advance unit hose connections

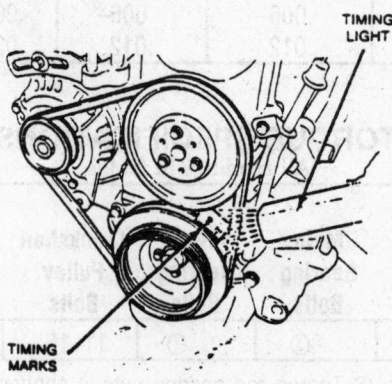

Ignition timing mark location

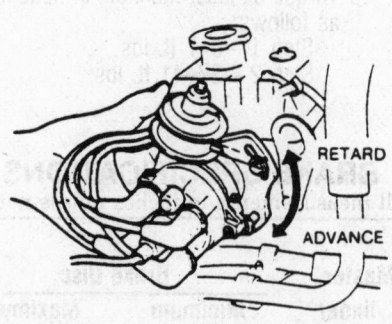

Rotating distributor to adjust ignition timing.

Valve Lash

ADJUSTMENT

1. Start the engine and allow to reach normal operating temperature. Secure the engine. Set the No.1 piston to TDC by rotating the crankshaft pulley bolt until the **TC** mark on the belt cover aligns with the notch on the crankshaft pulley.
2. Loosen the air conditioning compressor drive belt idler pulley adjusting screw and remove the belt.
3. Loosen the alternator adjusting bolt and push the alternator towards the engine. Remove the drive belt from the alternator pulley and set aside.
4. Hold the water pump pulley stationary with a suitable pry bar or equivalent holding tool and remove the 3 bolts attaching the water pump pulley to water pump hub. Remove the pulley from the hub.
5. Remove the right inner fender panel by removing the 3 attaching screws.
6. Remove the 4 bolts attaching the outer crankshaft pulley to the inner crankshaft pulley. Remove the outer crankshaft pulley with the outer stiffener/spacer.
7. Remove the inner stiffener/spacer. Remove the inner crankshaft pulley and baffle by loosening the the 2 attaching screws.
8. Remove the upper timing cover by removing the the 4 retaining bolts.
9. Identify and tag all vacuum hoses connected to the air cleaner assembly. Disconnect the hoses and remove the air cleaner assembly.
10. Remove the rocker arm cover as follows:
   a. Separate the EGO (Exhaust Gas Oxygen) sensor connector from its routing clip.
   b. Locate the carburetor throttle lever and disconnect the throttle cable from the lever. Remove the cable routing bracket from the rocker arm cover by removing the 2 attaching

Ford Motor Co.
Front Wheel Drive
Ford Taurus, Mercury Sable

SERIAL NUMBER IDENTIFICATION

VEHICLE IDENTIFICATION CHART

It is important for servicing and ordering parts to be certain of the vehicle and engine identification. The VIN (vehicle identification number) is a 17 digit number visible through the windshield on the driver's side of the dash and contains the vehicle and engine identification codes. The tenth digit indicates model year and the eighth digit indicates engine code. It can be interpreted as follows:

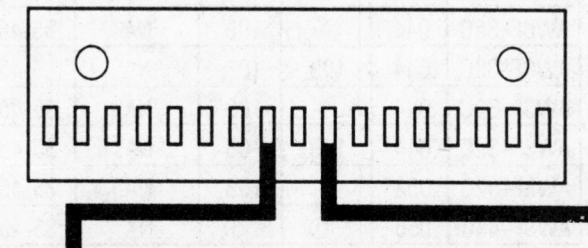

Engine Code						Model Year	
Code	Cu. In.	Liters	Cyl.	Fuel Sys.	Eng. Mfg.	Code	Year
D	153	2.5	4	CFI	Ford	G	1986
U	182	3.0	6	EFI	Ford	H	1987
4	232	3.8	6	EFI	Ford	J	1988
						K	1989

CFI Central Fuel Injection
EFI Electronic Fuel Injection

GENERAL ENGINE SPECIFICATIONS

Year	VIN	No. Cylinder Displacement cu. in. (liter)	Fuel System Type	Net Horsepower @ rpm	Net Torque @ rpm (ft.lbs.)	Bore × Stroke (in.)	Compression Ratio	Oil Pressure @ rpm
1986	D	4-153 (2.5)	CFI	88 @ 4600	130 @ 2800	3.70 × 3.60	9.7:1	55-70 @ 2000
	U	6-182 (3.0)	EFI	140 @ 4800	160 @ 3000	3.50 × 3.10	9.3:1	55-70 @ 2000

GENERAL ENGINE SPECIFICATIONS

Year	VIN	No. Cylinder Displacement cu. in. (liter)	Fuel System Type	Net Horsepower @ rpm	Net Torque @ rpm (ft.lbs.)	Bore × Stroke (in.)	Com-pression Ratio	Oil Pressure @ rpm
1987	D	4-153 (2.5)	CFI	88 @ 4600	130 @ 2800	3.70 × 3.60	9.7:1	55-70 @ 2000
	U	6-182 (3.0)	EFI	140 @ 4800	160 @ 3000	3.50 × 3.10	9.3:1	55-70 @ 2000
1988-89	D	4-153 (2.5)	CFI	88 @ 4600	130 @ 2800	3.70 × 3.60	9.7:1	55-70 @ 2000
	U	6-182 (3.0)	EFI	140 @ 4800	160 @ 3000	3.50 × 3.10	9.3:1	55-70 @ 2000
	4	6-232 (3.8)	EFI	140 @ 3800	215 @ 2200	3.81 × 3.39	9.0:1	40-60 @ 2000

CFI—Central Fuel Injection
EFI—Electronic Fuel Injection

ENGINE TUNE-UP SPECIFICATIONS

Year	VIN	No. Cylinder Displacement cu. in. (liter)	Spark Plugs Type	Gap (in.)	Ignition Timing (deg.) MT	Ignition Timing (deg.) AT	Com-pression Pressure (psi)	Fuel Pump (psi)	Idle Speed (rpm) ① MT	Idle Speed (rpm) ① AT	Valve Clearance In.	Valve Clearance Ex.
1986	D	4-153 (2.5)	AWSF–32C	.044	10B	10B	NA	35-45	725	650	Hyd.	Hyd.
	U	6-182 (3.0)	AWSF–32C	.044	—	10B	NA	35-45	—	625	Hyd.	Hyd.
1987	D	4-153(2.5)	AWSF–32C	.044	10B	10B	NA	35-45	725	650	Hyd.	Hyd.
	U	6-182 (3.0)	AWSF–32C	.044	—	10B	NA	35-45	—	625	Hyd.	Hyd.
1988	D	4-153(2.5)	AWSF–32C	.044	10B	10B	NA	35-45	725	650	Hyd.	Hyd.
	U	6-182 (3.0)	AWSF–32C	.052	—	10B	NA	35-45	—	625	Hyd.	Hyd.
	4	6-232 (3.8)	AWSF–44C	.056	①	①	NA	35-45	①	①	Hyd.	Hyd.
1989			SEE UNDERHOOD SPECIFICATIONS STICKER									

NA Not available
B Before Top Dead Center
Hyd. Hydraulic valve lash lifters.
① The Calibration levels vary from vehicle to vehicle. Refer to the Vehicle Emission Control Information label for ignition timing and idle speed specifications

FIRING ORDERS

NOTE: To avoid confusion, always replace spark plug wires one at a time.

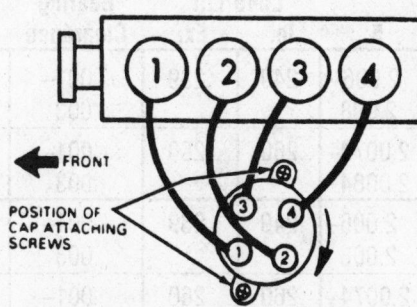

Ford 2500 cc 4 cyl (2.5L)
Firing order: 1–3–4–2
Distributor rotation: clockwise

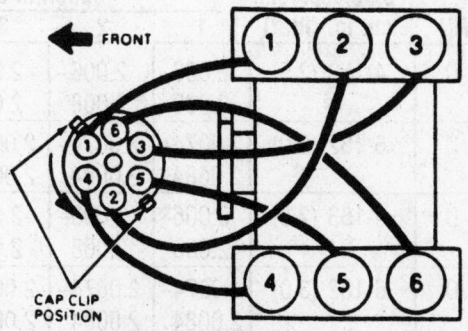

Ford 3800 cc (3.8L)
Firing order:1–4–2–5–3–6
Distributor rotation: counterclockwise

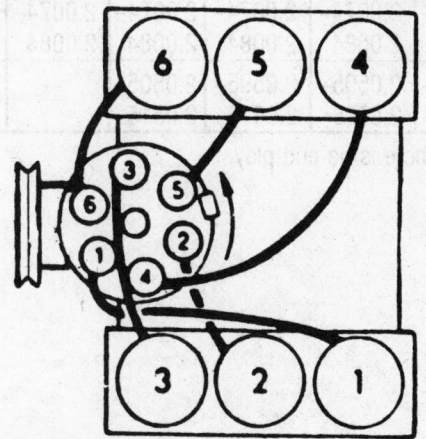

Ford 3000cc 6 cylinderl (3.0L)
Firing order:1–4–2–5–3–6
Distributor rotation: counterclockwise

CAPACITIES

Year	VIN	No. Cylinder Displacement cu. in. (liter)	Engine Crankcase with Filter	Engine Crankcase without Filter	Transmission (pts.) MT	Transmission (pts.) AT	Drive Axle (pts.)	Fuel Tank (gals.)	Cooling System (qts.)
1986	D	4-153 (2.5)	5.0	4.5	④	①	②	③	8.3
	U	6-182 (3.0)	4.5	4.0	—	①	②	③	11.0
1987	D	4-153 (2.5)	5.0	4.5	④	①	②	③	8.3
	U	6-182 (3.0)	4.5	4.0	—	①	②	③	11.0
1988-89	D	4-153 (2.5)	5.0	4.5	④	①	②	③	8.3
	U	6-182 (3.0)	4.5	4.0	—	①	②	③	11.0
	4	6-232 (3.8)	4.5	4.0	—	⑤	②	③	12.1

① Automatic transaxles with overdrive—
   10.0 pts.
   Standard automatic transaxle—8.3 pts.
② Included in the transmission capacity
③ Standard fuel tank is 16.0 gallons.
   Optional extended range fuel tank is 18.6
   gallons

④ 4 speed transaxle—5.0 pts.
   5 speed transaxle—6.1 pts.
⑤ 26.2 pts.

CAMSHAFT SPECIFICATIONS
All measurements given in inches.

Year	VIN	No. Cylinder Displacement cu. in. (liter)	Journal Diameter 1	2	3	4	5	Lobe Lift In.	Ex.	Bearing Clearance	Camshaft End Play
1986	D	4-153 (2.5)	2.006–2.008	2.006–2.008	2.006–2.008	2.006–2.008	2.006–2.008	.249	.239	.001–.003	.009
	U	6-182 (3.0)	2.0074–2.0084	2.0074–2.0084	2.0074–2.0084	2.0074–2.0084	2.0074–2.0084	.260	.260	.001–.003	①
1987	D	4-153 (2.5)	2.006–2.008	2.006–2.008	2.006–2.008	2.006–2.008	2.006–2.008	.249	.239	.001–.003	.009
	U	6-182 (3.0)	2.0074–2.0084	2.0074–2.0084	2.0074–2.0084	2.0074–2.0084	2.0074–2.0084	.260	.260	.001–.003	①
1988-89	D	4-153 (2.5)	2.006–2.008	2.006–2.008	2.006–2.008	2.006–2.008	2.006–2.008	.249	.239	.001–.003	.009
	U	6-182 (3.0)	2.0074–2.0084	2.0074–2.0084	2.0074–2.0084	2.0074–2.0084	2.0074–2.0084	.260	.260	.001–.003	①
	4	6-232 (3.8)	2.0505–2.0515	2.0505–2.0515	2.0505–2.0515	2.0505–2.0515	—	.240	.241	.001–.003	①

① The camshaft is retained by a spring; there is no end play.

CRANKSHAFT AND CONNECTING ROD SPECIFICATIONS
All measurements are given in inches.

Year	VIN	No. Cylinder Displacement cu. in. (liter)	Crankshaft Main Brg. Journal Dia.	Main Brg. Oil Clearance	Shaft End-play	Thrust on No.	Connecting Rod Journal Diameter	Oil Clearance	Side Clearance
1986	D	4-153 (2.5)	2.2489–2.2490	.0008–.0015–	.004–.008–	3	2.1232–2.1261	.0008–.0014–	.0035–.0105
	U	6-182 (3.0)	2.5190–2.5189	.001–.0014	.004–.008	3	2.1253–2.1240	.001–.0014	.006–.014
1987	D	4-153 (2.5)	2.2489–2.2490	.0008–.0015–	.004–.008–	3	2.1232–2.1261	.0008–.0014–	.0035–.0105
	U	6-182 (3.0)	2.5190–2.5189	.001–.0014	.004–.008	3	2.1253–2.1240	.001–.0014	.006–.014
1988-89	D	4-153 (2.5)	2.2489–2.2490	.0008–.0015–	.004–.008–	3	2.1232–2.1261	.0008–.0014–	.0035–.0105
	U	6-182 (3.0)	2.5190–2.5189	.001–.0014	.004–.008	3	2.1253–2.1240	.001–.0014	.006–.014
	4	6-232 (3.8)	2.5190–2.5189	.001–.0014	.004–.008	3	2.3103–2.3111	.001–.0014	.0047–.0114

VALVE SPECIFICATIONS

Year	VIN	No. Cylinder Displacement cu. in. (liter)	Seat Angle (deg.)	Face Angle (deg.)	Spring Test Pressure (lbs.)	Spring Installed Height (in.)	Stem-to-Guide Clearance (in.) Intake	Stem-to-Guide Clearance (in.) Exhaust	Stem Diameter (in.) Intake	Stem Diameter (in.) Exhaust
1986	D	4-153 (2.5)	90	45	182 @ 1.13	1.49	.0018	.0023	.3422	.3418
	U	6-182 (3.0)	45	44	185 @ 1.11	1.85	.0001–.0027	.0015–.0032	.3126	.3121
1987	D	4-153 (2.5)	90	45	182 @ 1.13	1.49	.0018	.0023	.3422	.3418
	U	6-182 (3.0)	45	44	185 @ 1.11	1.85	.0001–.0027	.0015–.0032	.3126	.3121
1988-89	D	4-153 (2.5)	90	45	182 @ 1.13	1.49	.0018	.0023	.3422	.3418
	U	6-182 (3.0)	45	44	185 @ 1.11	1.85	.0001–.0027	.0015–.0032	.3126	.3121
	4	6-232 (3.8)	46	46	190 @ 1.28	2.02	.0010–.0028	.0015–.0033	.3423–.0033	.3418–.3410

PISTON AND RING SPECIFICATIONS
All measurments are given in inches.

Year	VIN	No. Cylinder Displacement cu. in. (liter)	Piston Clearance	Ring Gap Top Compression	Ring Gap Bottom Compression	Ring Gap Oil Control	Ring Side Clearance Top Compression	Ring Side Clearance Bottom Compression	Ring Side Clearance Oil Control
1986	D	4-153 (2.5)	.0012–.0022	.008–.016	.008–.016	.015–.055	.002–.004	.002–.004	Snug
	U	6-182 (3.0)	.0012–.0023	.010–.020	.010–.020	.010–.049	.0016–.0037	.0016–.0037	Snug
1987	D	4-153 (2.5)	.0012–.0022	.008–.016	.008–.016	.015–.055	.002–.004	.002–.004	Snug
	U	6-182 (3.0)	.0012–.0023	.010–.020	.010–.020	.010–.049	.0016–.0037	.0016–.0037	Snug
1988-89	D	4-153 (2.5)	.0012–.0022	.008–.016	.008–.016	.015–.055	.002–.004	.002–.004	Snug
	U	6-182 (3.0)	.0014–.0022	.010–.020	.010–.020	.010–.049	.0016–.0037	.0016–.0037	Snug
	4	6-232 (3.8)	.0014–.0032	.010–.020	.010–.020	.0150–.0583	.0016–.0037	.0016–.0037	Snug

TORQUE SPECIFICATIONS
All readings in ft. lbs.

Year	VIN	No. Cylinder Displacement cu. in. (liter)	Cylinder Head Bolts	Main Bearing Bolts	Rod Bearing Bolts	Crankshaft Pulley Bolts	Flywheel Bolts	Manifold Intake	Manifold Exhaust	Spark Plugs
1986	D	4-153 (2.5)	①	51-66	21-26	140-170	54-64	15-23	②	5-10
	U	6-182 (3.0)	③	65-81	④	141-169	54-64	⑤	②	5-10

TORQUE SPECIFICATIONS
All readings in ft. lbs.

Year	VIN	No. Cylinder Displacement cu. in. (liter)	Cylinder Head Bolts	Main Bearing Bolts	Rod Bearing Bolts	Crankshaft Pulley Bolts	Flywheel Bolts	Manifold Intake	Manifold Exhaust	Spark Plugs
1987	D	4-153 (2.5)	①	51-66	21-26	140-170	54-64	15-23	③	5-10
	U	6-182 (3.0)	③	65-81	④	141-169	54-64	⑤	②	5-10
1988-89	D	4-153 (2.5)	①	51-66	21-26	140-170	54-64	15-23	③	5-10
	U	6-182 (3.0)	③	65-81	④	141-169	54-64	⑤	②	5-10
	4	6-232 (3.0)	⑥	65-81	31-36	93-121	54-64	⑦	16-24	5-11

① Tighten in 2 steps: 52-59 ft. lbs. and then the final torque of 70-76 ft. lbs.
② Tighten in 2 steps
Step 1 – 5-7 ft. lbs.
Step 2 – 20-30 ft. lbs.
③ Tighten in 2 steps: 48-54 ft. lbs. and then the final torque of 63-80 ft. lbs.
④ Tighten to 20-28 ft. lbs. and then back off the nuts a minimum of 2 revolutions; then apply the final torque of 20-25 ft. lbs.
⑤ Tighten in 3 steps: 11, 18 and the final torque of 24 ft. lbs.
⑥ Tighten in 4 steps:
Step 1 – 37 ft. lbs.
Step 2 – 45 ft. lbs.
Step 3 – 52 ft. lbs.
Step 4 – 59 ft. lbs.
⑦ Tighten in 3 steps:
Step 1 – 7 ft. lbs.
Step 2 – 15 ft. lbs.
Step 3 – 24 ft. lbs.

BRAKE SPECIFICATIONS
All measurements in inches unless noted

Year	Model	Lug Nut Torque (ft. lbs.)	Master Cylinder Bore	Brake Disc Minimum Thickness	Brake Disc Maximum Runout	Standard Brake Drum Diameter	Minimum Lining Thickness Front	Minimum Lining Thickness Rear
1986	Sedan	80-105	.828	.896	.005	8.85	.125	1.49
	Wagon	80-105	.828	.896	.005	9.84	.125	1.49
1987	Sedan	80-105	.828	.896	.005	8.85	.125	1.49
	Wagon	80-105	.828	.896	.005	9.84	.125	1.49
1988-89	Sedan	80-105	.828	.896	.005	8.85	.125	1.49
	Wagon	80-105	.828	.896	.005	9.84	.125	1.49

WHEEL ALIGNMENT

Year	Model		Caster Range (deg.)	Caster Preferred Setting (deg.)	Camber Range (deg.)	Camber Preferred Setting (deg.)	Toe-in (in.)	Steerig Axis Inclination (deg.)
1986	Taurus	Front	3P-6P ①	4P	$1\frac{3}{32}$N-$\frac{3}{32}$P	½N	$\frac{7}{32}$-$\frac{1}{64}$	$15\frac{3}{8}$
		Rear	—	—	$1\frac{5}{8}$N-$\frac{1}{4}$N	—	$\frac{13}{64}$N-$\frac{19}{64}$P②	—
	Sable	Front	3P-6P ①	4P	$1\frac{3}{32}$N-$\frac{3}{32}$P	½N	$\frac{7}{32}$-$\frac{1}{64}$	$15\frac{3}{8}$
		Rear	—	—	$1\frac{5}{8}$N-$\frac{1}{4}$N	—	$\frac{13}{64}$N-$\frac{19}{64}$P②	—
1987	Taurus	Front	3P-6P ①	4P	$1\frac{3}{32}$N-$\frac{3}{32}$P	½N	$\frac{7}{32}$-$\frac{1}{64}$	$15\frac{3}{8}$
		Rear	—	—	$1\frac{5}{8}$N-$\frac{1}{4}$N	—	$\frac{13}{64}$N-$\frac{19}{64}$P②	—
	Sable	Front	3P-6P ①	4P	$1\frac{3}{32}$N-$\frac{3}{32}$P	½N	$\frac{7}{32}$-$\frac{1}{64}$	$15\frac{3}{8}$
		Rear	—	—	$1\frac{5}{8}$N-$\frac{1}{4}$N	—	$\frac{13}{64}$N-$\frac{19}{64}$P②	—

WHEEL ALIGNMENT

Year	Model		Caster		Camber		Toe-in (in.)	Steerig Axis Inclination (deg.)
			Range (deg.)	Preferred Setting (deg.)	Range (deg.)	Preferred Setting (deg.)		
1988-89	Taurus	Front	3P-6P ①	4P	1³/₃₂N-³/₃₂P	½N	⁷/₃₂-¹/₆₄	15³/₈
		Rear	—	—	1⁵/₈N-¼N	—	¹³/₆₄N-¹⁹/₆₄P②	—
	Sable	Front	3P-6P ①	4P	1³/₃₂N-³/₃₂P	½N	⁷/₃₂-¹/₆₄	15³/₈
		Rear	—	—	1⁵/₈N-¼N	—	¹³/₆₄N-¹⁹/₆₄P②	—

① The caster measurements are made by turning each individual wheel through the prescribed angle of sweep

② Individual sides

TUNE-UP PROCEDURES

Ignition Timing

ADJUSTMENT

The locations of the timing marks on the 2.5L engine are as follows:

a. Manual transaxles—the timing marks are located on the flywheel and visible through a hole in the top of the transaxle case. To view the timing marks, a cover plate on top of the transaxle must be removed.

b. Automatic transaxles—the timing marks are visible through a hole in the transmission case. There is no cover plate.

The 3.0L and 3.8L engines employ timing marks on the crankshaft pulley and a timing pointer near the pulley.

1. Place the transaxle in the **PARK (ATX)** or **NEUTRAL (MTX)** position.

2. Open the hood and clean the timing marks with a stiff brush or solvent. On the 2.5L, MTX models, it will be necessary to remove the transaxle cover plate which allows access to the timing marks.

3. Using a white chalk or paint mark, mark the specified timing mark and pointer.

4. Near the distributor, disconnect the in-line spout connector. The spout connector is the center wire between the Electronic Control Assembly (ECA) connector and the Thick Film Ignition (TFI) module.

5. Connect an inductive type timing light (Rotunda tool No. 059-00006 or equivalent) to the No. 1 spark plug wire. DO NOT puncture the ignition wire with any type of probing device.

NOTE: The high ignition coil currents generated in the EEC-IV ignition system may falsely trigger the timing lights with capacitive or direct connect pick-ups. It is necessary that an inductive type timing light be used in this procedure.

6. Connect a tachometer (Rotunda tool No. 099-00003 or equivalent) to the ignition coil.

NOTE: The ignition coil electrical connector allows a test lead with an alligator clip to be connected to it's dark green/yellow dotted wire terminal without removing the connector. Be careful not to ground the alligator clip, for permanent damage will result to the coil.

7. Start the engine and allow it run

until the normal operating temperature is reached.

8. Check the engine idle rpm, if it is not within specifications, adjust as necessary. After the rpm has been adjusted or checked, aim the timing light at the timing marks. If they are not aligned, loosen the distributor clamp bolts slightly and rotate the distributor body until the marks are aligned under the timing light illumination.

9. Tighten the distributor clamp bolts and recheck the ignition timing. Re-adjust the idle speed (if necessary).

10. Turn the engine off, remove the

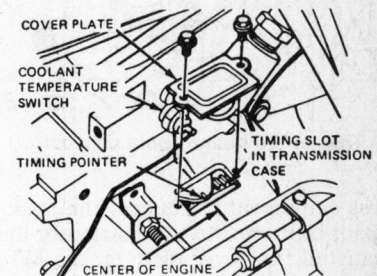

Location of the timing marks—2.5L engine with M/T

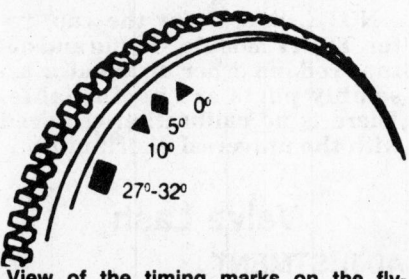

View of the timing marks on the flywheel—2.5L engine with M/T

View of the timing marks on the flywheel—2.5L engine with A/T

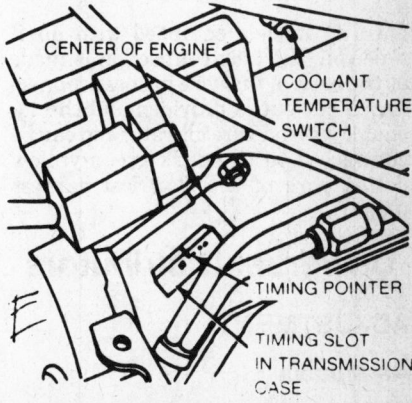

Location of the timing marks—2.5L engine with A/T

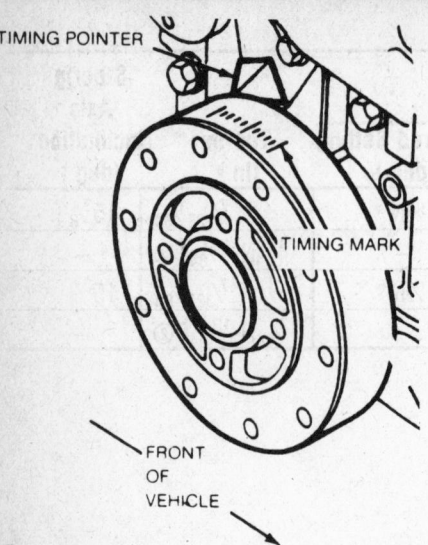

View of the timing marks on the 3.0L and 3.8L engines

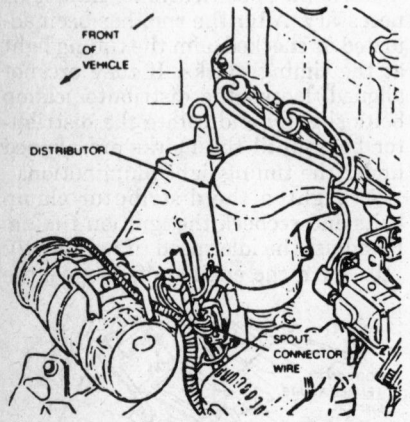

View of the in-line spout connector

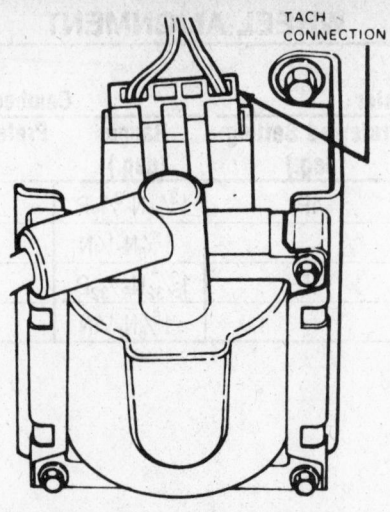

View of the tachometer connecting point of the "E" coil

test equipment, reconnect the in-line spout connector to the distributor and reinstall the cover plate on the MTX models.

CONNECTING THE TACHOMETER

On TFI models equipped with an E type coil, the tach connection is made at the back of the wire harness connector. A cut-out is provided and the tachometer lead wire alligator clip can be connected to the dark green/yellow dotted wire of the electrical harness plug.

Universal Distributors

ADJUSTMENT

All Models

Provisions have been incorporated in the universal distributor to allow fixed

adjustment capability for octane needs. The adjustment is the accomplished by replacing the standard 0 degree rod located in the distributor bowl with a 3 degree or 6 degree retard rod which are released for service only.

--- CAUTION ---
Do not change the timing by using different octane rods, as Federal Emission Requirements will be affected.

Octane Rod
REMOVAL & INSTALLATION

1. Remove cap and rotor for visual access.
2. Locate octane adjustments boss and remove retaining screw.
3. Slide rod/grommet out to a point where rod can be disengaged from stator retaining post.

NOTE: Retain grommet for use with new rod.

4. Install grommet on new service rod and reinstall in the distributor, making sure to capture the stator post.
5. Install retaining screw and tighten to 15–35 inch lbs. (1.8–4.3 Nm).
6. Replace cap and rotor. Tighten caps screws to 33–43 inch lbs. (2.0–2.6 Nm) and rotor to 25–35 inch lbs. (2.8–3.9 Nm).

NOTE: Except for the cap, rotor, TFI-IV module, O-ring and octane rod, no other distributor assembly parts are replaceable. There is no calibration required with the universal distributor.

Valve Lash
ADJUSTMENT

All engines are equipped with hydrau-

lic tappets and do not require adjustment.

Idle Speed and Mixture

ADJUSTMENT

2.5L CFI Engine

The curb idle and fast idle speeds are controlled by the EEC-IV computer and the idle speed control (ISC) device. If the control system is operating correctly, the speeds are fixed and should not be changed.

1. Apply the parking brake and block the wheels.

NOTE: If equipped with an ATX and an automatic parking brake, ALWAYS place the transaxle in REVERSE (not DRIVE) when checking the idle speed in gear.

2. Start the engine and allow it run until normal operating temperatures are reached; make sure that all of the accessories are turned off. Connect a tachometer to the ignition coil connector.
3. Check the vacuum lines for leaks.
4. Place the transaxle in **DRIVE** (or **REVERSE**) for ATX or **NEUTRAL** for MTX and allow the engine to operate for 2 minutes. The idle speed should be within specifications listed on the underhood decal.

NOTE: If the electric cooling fan comes on during this procedure, wait for it to turn itself off before proceeding.

5. If equipped with an ATX, place the transaxle in **NEUTRAL**, the idle speed should increase about 100 rpm.
6. Lightly step on and off the accelerator, the engine speed should return to the specifications on the decal.
7. If the engine speed remains high, repeat the checking sequence.
8. If the curb idle speed remains above the underhood specifications, perform the following procedures:

   a. Verify that the throttle linkage is free and unobstructed. If equipped with cruise control, make sure that it is not holding the throttle open.

NOTE: If the throttle lever is not in contact with the idle speed control (ISC) motor, while the engine is running, but is being held open by the throttle stop adjusting screw (TSAS), this screw must be adjusted.

   b. Stop the engine and remove the air cleaner. Locate the self-test and the self-test input (STI) connectors in the engine compartment.

c. Using a jumper wire, connect it between the self-test input (STI) connector and the signal return pin on the self-test connector.

d. Turn the ignition switch to the **ON** position but do not start the engine.

e. Wait for 10–15 seconds, the idle speed control (ISC) plunger will fully contract; if not, inspect the ISC.

f. Turn the ignition switch **OFF** and wait for 10–15 seconds, then remove the jumper wire and disconnect the ISC electrical connector from the electrical harness.

g. Remove the throttle body from the engine and position in a suitable holding fixture. With the proper tool, puncture and remove the throttle stop adjusting screw cover plug, then replace the screw.

h. Reinstall the throttle body to the engine. Start and stabilize the engine, then set idle speed according to the underhood decal by adjusting the throttle stop screw.

i. Reconnect the ISC electrical harness.

9. Turn the engine **OFF** and disconnect the tachometer.

3.0L EFI Engine

NOTE: The curb idle speed rpm is controlled by the EEC-IV computer (ECM) and the idle speed control (ISC) air bypass valve assembly. The throttle stop screw is factory set and does not directly control the idle speed. Adjustment to this setting should be performed only as part of a full EEC-IV diagnosis of irregular idle conditions or idle speeds. Failure to accurately set the throttle plate stop position as described in the following procedure could result in false idle speed control.

1. Apply the parking brake, turn the A/C control selector **OFF** and block the wheels.

2. Connect a tachometer and an inductive timing light to the engine. Start the engine and allow it to reach normal operating temperatures.

3. Unplug the spout line (at the distributor), the check and/or adjust the ignition timing to 8–12 degrees BTDC.

4. Stop the engine and disconnect the electrical connector from the air bypass valve assembly. Remove the PCV entry line from the PCV valve.

5. Using the orifice (0.200 in. dia.) tool No. T86P-9600-A or equivalent, install it the PCV entry line.

6. Start the engine. Place the transaxle in **DRIVE** (ATX) or **NEUTRAL** (MTX). Disconnect the electrical connector from the electric cooling fan.

7. Check and/or adjust (if necessary) the idle speed to 595–655 rpm by turning the throttle plate stop screw.

8. After adjusting the idle speed, stop the engine and wait for 3–5 minutes.

9. Start the engine and confirm that the idle speed is now adjusted to specifications, if not, readjust as necessary.

10. Stop the engine and remove the orifice. Reconnect the PCV entry line, the spout line, the ISC motor and the electric cooling fan.

11. Make sure that the throttle plate is not stuck in the bore and that the throttle plate stop screw is setting on the rest pad with the throttle closed.

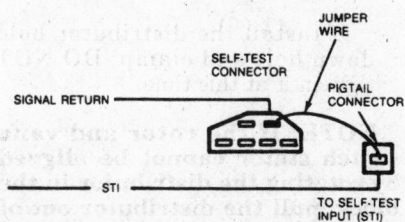

Connecting a jumper wire between the self-test and the self-test input connectors

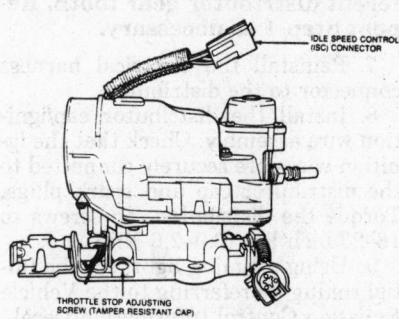

View of the throttle body—2.5L CFI engine

Correct any condition that will not allow the throttle to close to the stop set position.

12. Restart the engine. After 3–5 minutes of operation, the engine idle speed should be at specifications.

3.8L EFI Engine

1. Apply the parking brake, block the drive wheels and place the vehicle in **DRIVE** or **NEUTRAL**.

2. Start the engine and let it run until it reaches normal operating temperature, then turn the engine off. Connect a suitable tachometer.

3. Start the engine and run the engine at 2500 rpm for 30 seconds.

4. Allow the engine idle to stabilize.

5. Adjust the engine idle rpm to the specification shown on the vehicle emission control label by rotating the throttle stop screw.

6. After the idle speed is within specification, repeat Steps 3–5 to ensure that the adjustment is correct.

7. Stop the engine and reconnect the power lead to the idle speed control air bypass valve. Disconnect all test equipment.

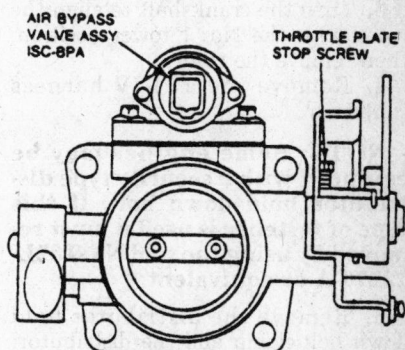

View of the throttle body—3.8L EFI engine

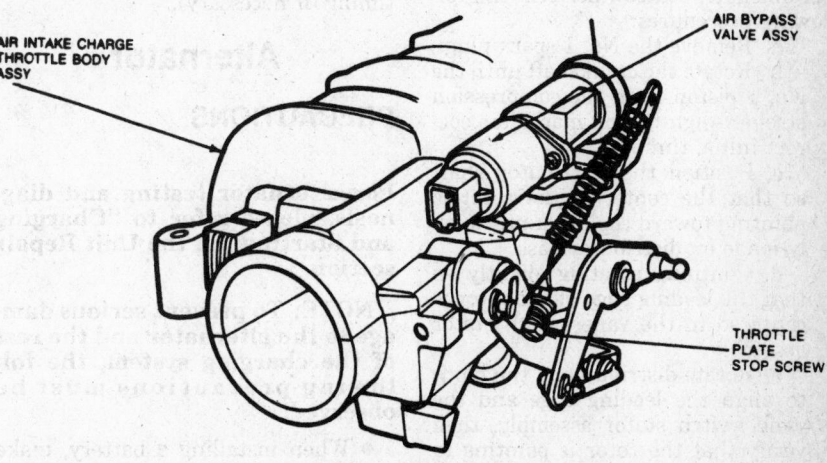

View of the throttle body—3.0L EFI engine

ENGINE ELECTRICAL

Distributor

The distributor is a universal gear driven design with a die cast base that incorporates an integrally mounted TFI-IV (Thick Film Ignition) ignition module, a "Hall Effect" vane switch stator assembly and provision for a fixed octane adjustment. The design deletes conventional centrifugal and vacuum advance mechanisms.

NOTE: No distributor calibration is required; initial timing is the normal adjustment.

REMOVAL & INSTALLATION

1. Disconnect the primary wiring connector from distributor.

NOTE: Before removing the distributor cap, mark the relationship of the No. 1 wire tower on the distributor base.

2. Remove distributor cap (with the wires attached) and position it aside.
3. Turn the crankshaft to align the rotor with the No. 1 tower position, then remove the rotor.
4. Remove the TFI-IV harness connector.

NOTE: Some engines may be equipped with a security type distributor hold down bolt. If this type of fastener is used it must removed by using the tool No. T82L-12270-A or equivalent.

5. Remove the distributor hold down bolt/clamp and the distributor; be careful not to disturb the intermediate driveshaft.
6. If the engine has been disturbed (crankshaft rotated), perform the following procedures:

  a. Remove the No. 1 spark plug.

  b. Rotate the crankshaft until the No. 1 piston is on the compression stroke. Align timing marks for correct initial timing.

  c. Position the distributor shaft so that the center of the rotor is pointing toward the mark previously made on distributor base.

  d. Continue rotating slightly so that the leading edge of the rotor is centered in the vane switch stator assembly.

  e. Rotate distributor in the block to align the leading edge and the vane switch stator assembly, then verify that the rotor is pointing to the No. 1 cap terminal.

  f. Install the distributor hold down bolt and clamp; DO NOT tighten it at this time.

NOTE: If the rotor and vane switch stator cannot be aligned by rotating the distributor in the block, pull the distributor out of block enough to disengage the distributor gear and rotate the distributor shaft to engage a different distributor gear tooth. Repeat Step 1 as necessary.

7. Reinstall the electrical harness connector to the distributor.
8. Install the distributor cap/ignition wire assembly. Check that the ignition wires are securely connected to the distributor cap and spark plugs. Torque the distributor cap screws to 18–23 inch lbs. (2.0–2.6 Nm).
9. Using a timing light, set the initial timing by referring to the Vehicle Emission Control Information Decal.
10. Torque the distributor hold down bolt to 17–25 ft. lbs. (23–34 Nm).
11. Check and/or adjust the initial timing (if necessary).

Alternator

PRECAUTIONS

For alternator testing and diagnosis, please refer to "Charging and Starting" in the Unit Repair section.

NOTE: To prevent serious damage to the alternator and the rest of the charging system, the following precautions must be observed:

• When installing a battery, make sure that the positive cable is connected to the positive terminal and the negative to the negative.

• When jump-starting the vehicle with another battery, make sure that like terminals are connected. This also applies when using a battery charger.

• Never operate the alternator with the battery disconnected or otherwise on an uncontrolled open circuit. Double-check to see that all connections are tight.

• Do not short across or ground any alternator or regulator terminals.

• Do not try to polarize the alternator.

• Do not apply full battery voltage to the field connector.

• Always disconnect the battery ground cable before disconnecting the alternator lead.

BELT TENSION ADJUSTMENT

2.5L & 3.8L Engines

The V-ribbed belts used on the 2.5L and 3.8L engines utilize an automatic belt tensioner whose function is to maintain the proper belt tension for the life of the belt. Adjustment of the automatic tensioner is not required.

The automatic belt tensioners incorporate wear indicator **MINIMUM** and **MAXIMUM** marks that can be inspected with the engine off (not running). If the indicator mark is not within the two marks, the belt is worn or an improper belt is installed. A loose or improper belt will result in slippage which will in turn cause a noise complaint or improper accessory operation. Automatic tensioners do not require removal when making a drive belt replacement. When removing a drive belt, simply rotate the tensioner away from the belt.

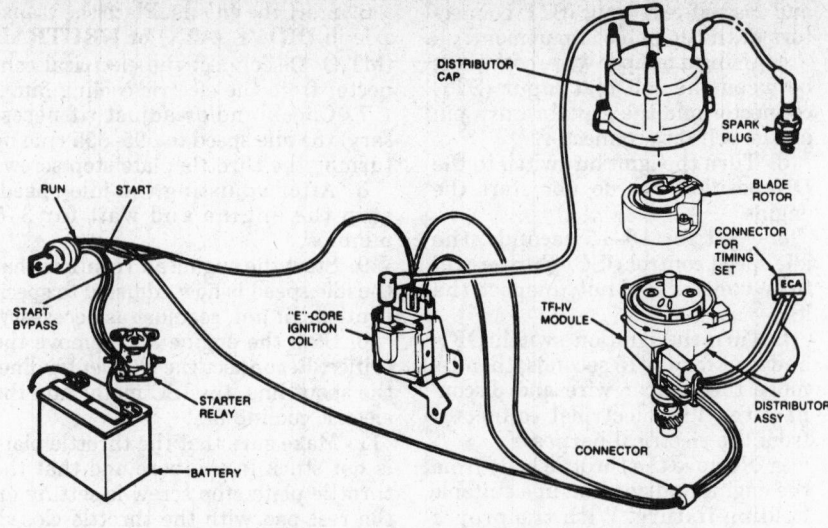

Exploded view of the distributor and ignition system

3.0L Engine

1. Loosen the alternator adjusting arm bolt.

2. Adjust the drive belt tension using one of the following methods:

   a. Using the Belt Tension Gauge tool No. 021-00028, install it onto the drive belt, on the longest belt span between the pulleys and adjust the drive belt tension to 100–140 lbs. (new) or 80–100 lbs. (used).

   b. Apply thumb pressure on the longest belt span between the pulleys so that there is approximately $\frac{1}{4}$–$\frac{1}{2}$ in. of deflection.

3. Torque the adjusting arm bolt 22–32 ft. lbs. and recheck the belt tension.

REMOVAL & INSTALLATION

All engines are equipped with V-ribbed type belts. To increase the belt life, make sure that the V-grooves make proper contact on the pulleys.

2.5L Engine

1. Place a $\frac{1}{2}$ in. flex handle in the square hole of the belt tensioner or an 18mm socket on the tensioner pulley nut.

2. Turn the tensioner counterclockwise and remove the drive belt.

3. At the back of the alternator, label and disconnect the electrical connectors.

NOTE: The alternator uses a push-on wiring connector on the field and stator connections. Depress the locking tab when removing the electrical connector from the alternator.

4. Remove the mounting bolts and the alternator from the vehicle.

5. To install, reverse the removal procedures. Torque the alternator-to-engine bolts to 45–57 ft. lbs.

6. To install the drive belt, place it on the pulleys (except the alternator), turn the tensioner counterclockwise and position the belt on the alternator pulley so that the V-grooves are aligned correctly.

3.0L & 3.8L Engines

1. Disconnect the negative battery cable.

2. Remove the alternator adjusting arm bolt and the drive belt.

3. At the back of the alternator, label and disconnect the electrical connectors.

NOTE: The alternator uses a push-on wiring connector on the field and stator connections. Depress the locking tab when removing the electrical connector from the alternator.

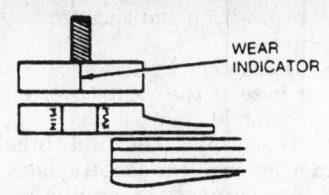

Automatic tensioner drive belt wear indicator used on some 3.0L engines and all 2.5 and 3.8L engines

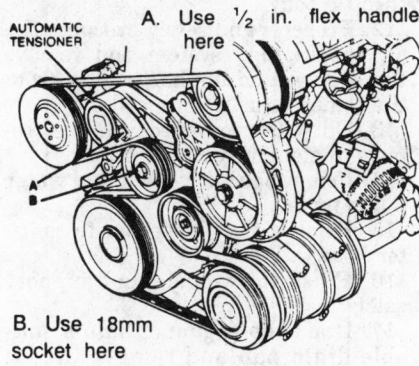

A. Use $\frac{1}{2}$ in. flex handle here

B. Use 18mm socket here

View of the drive belts—2.5L engine.

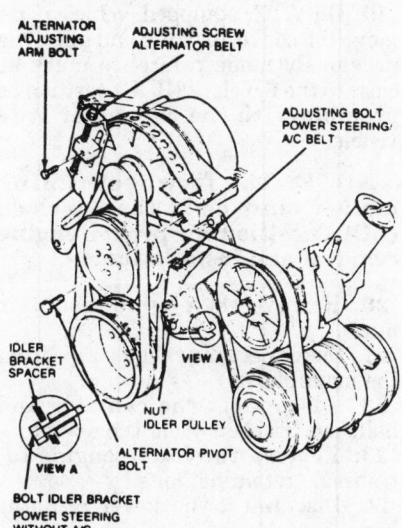

View of the drive belts—3.0L engine

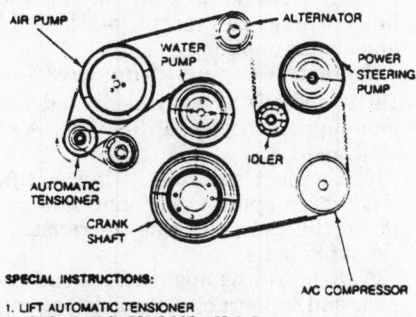

SPECIAL INSTRUCTIONS:

1. LIFT AUTOMATIC TENSIONER USING A 1/2-INCH DRIVE BREAKER BAR IN DIRECTION OF ARROW
2. INSTALL DRIVE BELT OVER PULLEYS PER APPROPRIATE BELT ROUTING

Drive belt arrangement–3.8L engines

4. Remove the pivot bolt and the alternator from the vehicle.

5. Place a $\frac{1}{2}$ in. flex handle in the square hole of the belt tensioner or an 18mm socket on the tensioner pulley nut. Rotate the tensioner counterclockwise and remove the drive belt.

6. To install, reverse the removal procedures. Adjust the drive belt tension. Torque the pivot bolt to 45–57 ft. lbs. and the adjusting arm bolt to 22–32 ft. lbs.

Voltage Regulator

NOTE: Two types of regulators are used, depending on the engine, the alternator output and type of dash mounted charging indicator used (light or ammeter). The regulators are 100% solid state, calibrated and preset by the manufacturer. No readjustments are required or possible.

REMOVAL & INSTALLATION

External

1. Remove the negative battery cable.

2. Label and disconnect the electrical connectors from the regulator.

3. Remove the regulator mounting screws and the regulator.

4. To install, reverse the removal procedures.

5. Test the system for proper voltage regulation.

Internal

1. Disconnect the negative battery cable.

2. At the rear of the alternator, disconnect the electrical connector from the regulator.

3. Remove the regulator-to-alternator screws and the regulator. If necessary, remove the brush holder-to-regulator screws and the brush holder from the regulator.

4. If the brush holder was removed from the regulator, install it using the following procedure:

   a. Push the brushes into the brush holder and install a stiff wire (in the brush holder pin hole) to hold the brushes in place.

   b. Align the brush holder with the regulator and torque the screws to 20–30 inch lbs.

   c. When the regulator/brush holder assembly is installed on the alternator, remove the wire retainer from the brush holder.

NOTE: If the wire is not removed from the brush holder, a short circuit will result and destroy the regulator.

5. To install, reverse the removal procedures. Torque the regulator-to-alternator screws to 25–35 inch lbs.

Starter

REMOVAL & INSTALLATION

1. Disconnect the negative battery cable and the cable from the starter.
2. Raise and support the front of the vehicle safely and block the rear wheels.
3. From the upper starter stud bolt, remove the cable support and ground cable connection.
4. Remove the starter brace and the starter.
5. Remove the 3 starter-to-bell housing bolts (2.5L engine) or the 2 starter-to-bell housing bolts (3.0L and 3.8L engines).
6. If equipped with an ATX, remove the starter between the sub-frame and radiator. If equipped with a MTX, remove the starter between the sub-frame and the engine.
7. To install, reverse the removal procedures. Torque the starter bolts to 30–40 ft. lbs.

ENGINE MECHANICAL

Engine

REMOVAL & INSTALLATION

2.5L Engine

1. Relieve the fuel system pressure by disconnecting the electrical connector at the inertia switch and cranking the engine for 15 seconds.
2. On vehicles equipped with ATX, remove the transaxle timing window cover and rotate the engine until the flywheeel timing marker is aligned with the timing pointer.
3. Place a reference mark on the crankshaft pulley at the 12 o'clock position (TDC) then rotate the crankshaft pulley mark to the 6 o'clock position (BDC).
4. Disconnect the negative battery cable. With a machinists scribe or equivalent, mark the position of the hood hinges and remove the hood.
5. Remove the air cleaner assembly. Position a suitible drain pan under the radiator, open the radiator drain cock and drain the cooling system.
6. Disconnect the upper radiator hose at the engine.
7. Identify, tag and disconnect all

electrical wiring and vacuum hoses as required.
8. Disconnect the crankcase ventilation hose at the valve cover and intake manifold.
9. Disconnect the fuel lines and heater hoses at the throttle body.
10. Disconnect the engine ground wire.
11. Disconnect the accelerator and throttle valve control cables at the throttle body.
12. Properly and safely evacuate the air conditioning system and remove the suction and discharge lines from the compressor (if equipped).
13. On MTX equipped vehicles, remove the engine damper brace.
14. Remove the drive belt and water pump pulley.
15. Remove the air cleaner-to-canister hose.
16. Raise the vehicle and support safely.
17. Drain the engine oil into a suitable drain pan and remove the oil filter.
18. Disconnect the starter cable and remove the starter motor.
19. On ATX equipped vehicles, remove the converter nuts and align the previously made reference mark as close to the 6 o'clock (BDC) position as possible with the converter stud visible.

NOTE: The flywheel timing marker must be in the 6 o'clock (BDC) position for proper engine removal and installation.

20. Remove the engine insulator nuts.
21. Disconnect the exhaust pipe from the manifold.
22. Disconnect the canister and halfshaft brackets from the engine.
23. Remove the lower engine-to-transaxle retaining bolts.
24. Disconnect the lower radiator hose.
25. Lower the vehicle and position a suitable floor jack under the transaxle.
26. Disconnect the power steering lines from the pump. Cover or plug the line openings to prevent loss of fluid and contamination.
27. Install engine lifting eyes No. D81L–6001–D or equivalent and engine support tool No. T79P–6000–A or equivalent.
28. Connect suitable lifting equipment to support the engine and remove the upper engine-to-transaxle retaining bolts.
29. Remove the engine from the vehicle and support on a suitable holding fixture.
30. Complete the installation of the engine assembly by reversing the removal procedure. Refill the cooling

system. Check and/or refill the engine oil and the transaxle fluid. Start the engine and check for leaks.

3.0L Engine

1. Disconnect the battery cables from the battery. Place a drain pan under the radiator and drain the cooling system. Using a scribing tool, mark the hood hinge location and remove the hood. Properly and safely evacuate the air conditioning system, if equipped.
2. If equipped with A/C, remove the compressor and move it aside.
3. Remove the air cleaner assembly, the battery and the battery tray.
4. Remove the integrated relay controller, the cooling fan and the radiator with fan shroud. Remove the engine bounce damper bracket from the shock tower.
5. Remove the evaporative emission line, the upper/lower radiator hose and the starter brace.
6. Remove the exhaust pipes from both exhaust manifolds. Remove and plug the power steering pump lines to prevent loss of fluid and contamination.
7. Bleed the pressure from the fuel system and remove the fuel lines. Remove and tag all of the necessary vacuum lines.
8. Disconnect the ground strap, the heater hoses, the accelerator cable linkage, the throttle valve linkage and the speed control cable (if equipped).
9. Disconnect and label the electrical cable connectors from the following items: the alternator, the air conditioner clutch, the oxygen sensor, the ignition coil, the radio frequency suppressor, the cooling fan voltage resistor, the engine coolant temperature sensor, the thick film ignition module, the fuel injectors, the ISC motor wire, the throttle position sensor, the oil pressure sending switch, the ground wire, the block heater (if equipped), the knock sensor, the EGR sensor and the oil level sensor.
10. Remove the engine mounting bolts and engine mounts. Remove the transaxle-to-engine mounting bolts and the transaxle brace assembly.
11. Connect an engine lifting plate and a vertical hoist to the engine, then remove the engine from the vehicle. Remove the main wire harness from the engine.
12. To install, reverse the removal procedures. Torque the transaxle brace assembly bolts to 40–55 ft. lbs., the engine mount nuts to 55–75 ft. lbs. and the engine mount bolts to 40–55 ft. lbs. Refill the cooling system. Check and/or refill the crankcase and the transaxle. Start the engine and check for leaks.

NOTE: On the engine mount assembly 6F063 and 6F065, torque the engine mount nuts and engine mount bolts to 70–96 ft. lbs.

3.8L Engine

1. Disconnect the negative battery cable. Position a suitable drain pan under the radiator and drain the cooling system.

2. Disconnect the underhood lamp wiring connector. Mark position of hood hinges with a machinists scribe and remove hood.

3. Remove the oil level indicator tube.

4. Disconnect alternator to voltage regulator wiring assembly.

5. Remove the radiator upper sight shield. Remove the engine cooling fan motor relay retaining bolts and position cooling fan motor·relay out of the way.

6. Remove the air cleaner assembly. Identify, tag and disconnect all vacuum lines as necessary.

7. Disconnect the radiator electric fan and motor assembly. Remove fan shroud.

8. Remove upper radiator hose.

9. Disconnect the transaxle oil cooler inlet and outlet tubes and cover the openings to prevent the entry of dirt and grease. Disconnect the heater hoses.

10. Disconnect the power steering pressure hose assembly.

11. Disconnect the air conditioner compressor clutch wire assembly. Discharge the air conditioning system and disconnect the compressor-to-condenser line.

12. Remove the radiator coolant recovery reservoir assembly. Remove the wiring shield.

13. Remove accelerator cable mounting bracket.

14. Disconnect fuel inlet and return hoses. Make certain that a enough absorbent material is available to collect any excess fuel.

15. Disconnect power steering pump pressure and return tube brackets.

16. Disconnect the engine control sensor wiring assembly.

17. Identify, tag and disconnect all necessary vacuum hoses.

18. Disconnect the ground wire assembly. Remove the duct assembly.

19. Disconnect one end of the throttle control valve cable. Disconnect the bulkhead electrical connector and transaxle pressure switches.

20. Remove transaxle support assembly retaining bolts and remove transaxle and support assembly from vehicle.

21. Loosen the front wheel lug nuts. Raise the vehicle and support safely.

Drain the engine oil into a suitable drain pan and remove the filter.

22. Disconnect the heated exhaust gas oxygen (HEGO) sensor assembly.

23. Loosen and remove drive belt assembly. Remove the crankshaft pulley and drive belt tensioner assemblies.

24. Remove the starter motor assembly. Remove the converter housing assembly and remove the inlet pipe converter assembly.

25. Remove the engine LH and RH front support insulator retaining nuts.

26. Remove the converter-to-flywheel nuts.

27. Disconnect the oil level indicator sensor. Remove crankshaft pulley assembly.

28. Disconnect the lower radiator hose.

29. Remove the engine-to-transaxle bolts and partially lower engine. Remove the wheel assemblies.

30. Remove the water pump pulley retaining bolts and remove water pump from the vehicle.

31. Remove the distributor cap and position out of the way. Remove distributor rotor.

32. Remove the exhaust manifold bolt lock retaining bolts. Remove the thermactor air pump retaining bolts and remove the thermactor air pump.

33. Disconnect the oil pressure engine unit gauge assembly.

34. Install engine lifting eyes and connect suitable lifting equipment to the lifting eyes.

35. Position a suitable jack under the transaxle and raise the transaxle a small amount.

36. Remove the engine from the vehicle and position in a suitable holding fixture.

37. To install, reverse the removal procedure.

Cylinder Head

REMOVAL & INSTALLATION

2.5L Engine

1. Disconnect the negative battery cable. Remove the air cleaner assembly.

2. Place a drain pan under the radiator and drain the cooling system.

3. Disconnect the heater hose from under the intake manifold and the upper radiator hose from the cylinder head.

4. Disconnect the electrical harness connector from the cooling fan.

5. Label and disconnect the necessary vacuum hoses.

6. Remove the rocker arm cover, the rocker arms and the pushrods.

7. Loosen and remove the accessory drive belts.

8. Label and disconnect the spark plug wires, then remove the distributor from the engine.

9. Disconnect the EGR tube from the EGR valve, the choke cap wire from the throttle body, the accelerator cable and the speed control cable (if equipped).

10. Reduce the pressure in the fuel system and remove the fuel lines.

11. Loosen the Thermactor pump belt pulley, then raise and support the front of the vehicle on jackstands.

12. Disconnect the exhaust pipe from the exhaust manifold and the hose from the tube. Lower the vehicle.

NOTE: DO NOT remove the intake and/or exhaust manifolds from the cylinder head unless absolutely necessary.

13. Remove the cylinder head-to-engine bolts, the cylinder head (with the intake/exhaust manifolds and the Thermactor pump attached) and the gasket (discard it).

NOTE: If removing the cylinder head with the components attached, be sure not to lay the cylinder head flat as physical damage may occur to the gasket surface or spark plugs.

14. Using a putty knife, clean the gasket mounting surfaces.

15. To install, use new gaskets, sealant (to hold the head gasket onto the engine block) and reverse the removal procedures. Torque the cylinder head-to-engine bolts in 2 steps to: 52–59 ft. lbs. (70–80 Nm) on the first step, then 70–76 ft. lbs. (95–103 Nm) on the second step. Refill the cooling system. Start the engine and check for leaks.

NOTE: When installing the cylinder head, use two Alignment Stud tools No. T84P-6065-A to guide the head into place.

3.0L Engine

1. Remove the intake manifold.

2. Loosen the accessory drive belt idler pulley and remove the drive belt.

3. On the left cylinder head, remove the alternator adjusting arm, the coil bracket and dipstick tube.

4. On the right cylinder head, remove the accessory drive belt idler pulley and the grounding strap throttle cable support bracket.

5. If equipped with power steering, remove the pump mounting bracket-to-engine bolts. Leave the pump hoses connected and position the pump out of the way.

6. From both sides of the engine, remove the exhaust pipe-to-exhaust manifold bolts, the exhaust manifolds-to-cylinder head bolts and the exhaust manifolds from the engine.

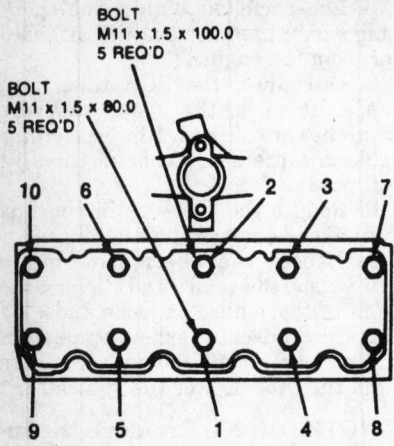

Cylinder head bolt torquing sequence— 2.5L engine

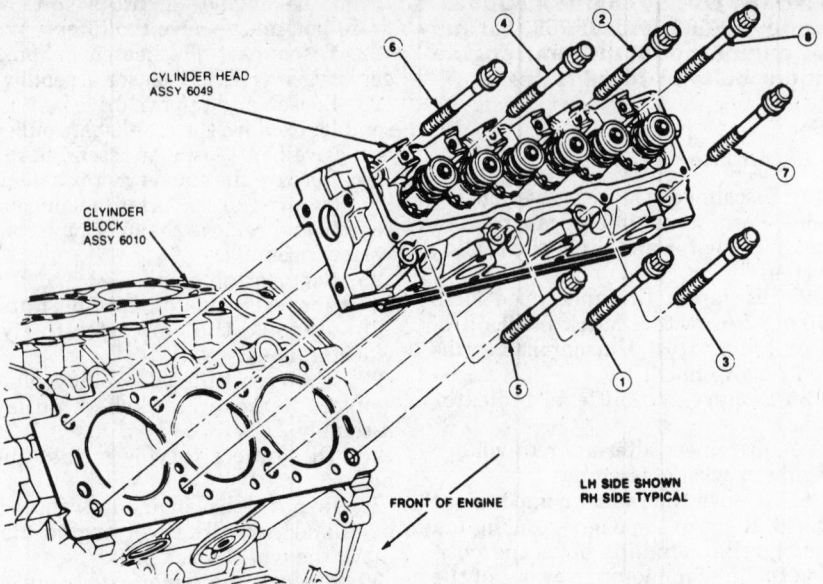

Cylinder head bolt torquing sequence— 3.0L engine

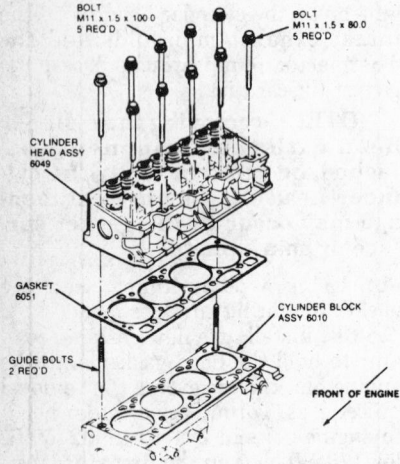

Installing the cylinder head—2.5L engine

7. Remove the PCV valve and the rocker arm covers. Loosen the rocker arm fulcrum bolts enough to allow the rocker arm to be lifted from the pushrod and rotated to one side.

8. Remove the pushrods, keeping them in order for installation purposes.

9. Remove the cylinder head-to-engine bolts and the cylinder heads from the engine. Discard the cylinder head gaskets.

10. Using a putty knife, clean and inspect the gasket mounting surfaces.

11. To install, use new gaskets and reverse the removal procedures. Torque the cylinder head-to-engine bolts (in 2 steps) to 48–54 ft. lbs. (1st step) and to 63–80 ft. lbs. (2nd step), the rocker arm fulcrum bolts to 19–29 ft. lbs. Start the engine and check for coolant, fuel, oil and exhaust leaks. Check and/or adjust the transmission throttle linkage and the speed control.

NOTE: Before installation, lightly oil the bolt and stud

threads except for those specifying that a special sealant be applied. If the flat surface of the cylinder head is warped, do not plane or grind off more than 0.010 in. (0.254mm). If the head is machined past the resurface limit, it will have to be replaced with a new one.

3.8L Engine

1. Position a suitable drain pan under the radiator and drain the cooling system. Disconnect the negative battery cable.

2. Remove the air cleaner assembly including air intake duct and heat tube.

3. Loosen the accessory drive belt idler and remove the drive belt.

4. If the right side head is being removed, proceed to Step 5. If the left side cylinder head is being removed, perform the following to gain access to the upper intake manifold:

a. Remove the oil fill cap.

b. Remove the power steering pump. Leave the hoses connected and place the pump/bracket assembly aside in a position to prevent fluid from leaking out.

c. If equipped with air conditioning, remove mounting bracket attaching bolts. Leaving the hoses connected, position compressor aside.

d. Remove the alternator and bracket.

5. To remove the right side cylinder head, perform the following to gain access to the upper intake manifold:

a. Disconnect the thermactor air

control valve or bypass valve hose assembly at the air pump.

b. Disconnect the thermactor tube support bracket from the rear of cylinder head.

c. Remove the accessory drive idler.

d. Remove the thermactor pump pulley and thermactor pump.

e. Remove the PCV valve.

6. Remove the upper intake manifold.

7. Remove the valve rocker arm cover attaching screws.

8. Remove the injector fuel rail assembly.

9. Remove the lower intake manifold and remove the exhaust manifold(s).

10. Loosen rocker arm fulcrum attaching bolts a sufficient amount to allow rocker arm to be lifted off the push rod and rotate to one side. Remove the push rods. Identify and label the position of each rod as each one is removed. Rods should be installed in their original position during assembly to ensure proper operation.

11. Remove the cylinder head attaching bolts and discard. Do not re-use the old bolts.

12. Remove cylinder head(s) from the engine block surface. Remove and discard old cylinder head gasket(s).

To install:

13. Lightly oil all bolt threads before installation.

14. Clean cylinder head, intake manifold, valve rocker arm cover and cylinder head gasket contact surfaces with a gasket scraper or equivalent. If cylinder head was removed for a cylinder head gasket replacement, check flat-

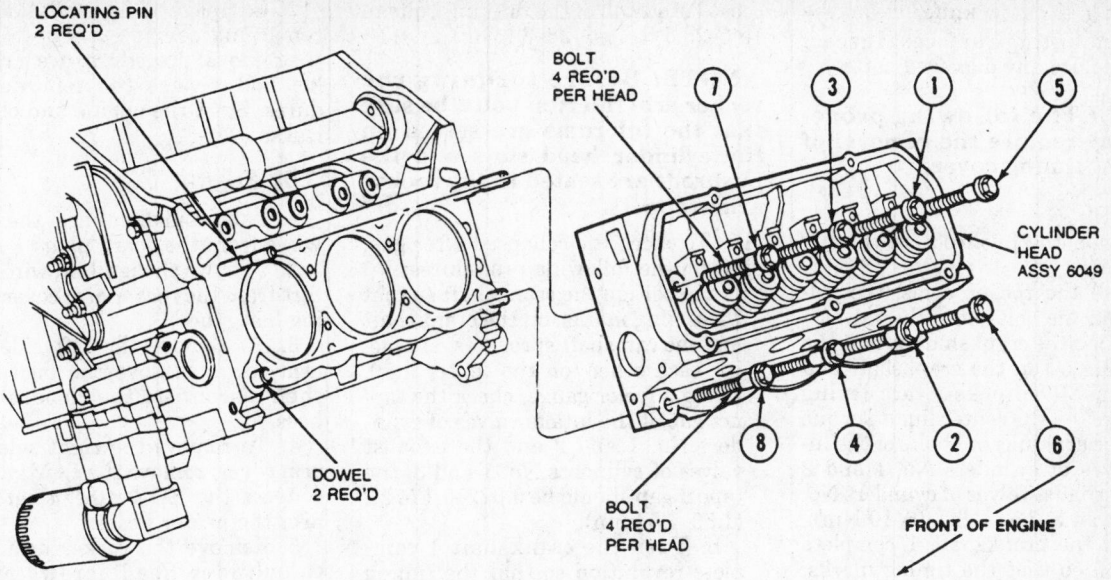

LOCATING PIN
2 REQ'D

BOLT
4 REQ'D
PER HEAD

CYLINDER
HEAD
ASSY 6049

DOWEL
2 REQ'D

BOLT
4 REQ'D
PER HEAD

FRONT OF ENGINE

Cylinder head with bolt torque sequence—3.8L engines

ness of cylinder head and block gasket surfaces.

15. Position the new head gasket(s) onto cylinder block using dowels for alignment. Position cylinder head(s) onto block.

16. Apply a thin coating of pipe sealant with Teflon® No. D8AZ-19554-A or equivalent to threads of short cylinder head bolts (nearest to the exhaust manifold). Do not apply sealant to the long bolts. Install cylinder head bolts (eight each side).

—————— **CAUTION** ——————

Always use new cylinder head bolts to ensure a leak-tight assembly. Torque retention with used bolts can vary, which may result in coolant or compression leakage at the cylinder head mating surface area.

17. Tighten cylinder head attaching bolts by performing the following 6 step sequence:
   a. Step 1: 37 ft. lbs.
   b. Step 2: 45 ft. lbs.
   c. Step 3: 52 ft. lbs.
   d. Step 4: 59 ft. lbs.
   e. Step 5: Back-off each cylinder head bolt 2–3 turns.
   f. Step 6: Repeat Steps 1–4.

NOTE: When cylinder head attaching bolts have been tightened using the above procedure, it is not necessary to retighten bolts after extended engine operation. However, bolts can be checked for tightness if desired.

18. Dip each push rod end in oil conditioner D9AZ-19579-C or equivalent heavy engine oil. Install push rods in their original positions.

19. For each valve, rotate crankshaft until the tappet rests on the heel (base

circle) of the camshaft lobe. Torque the fulcrum attaching bolts to 43 inch lbs. maximum.

20. Lubricate all rocker arm assemblies with oil conditioner No. D9AZ-19579-C or equivalent heavy engine oil.

21. Torque the fulcrum bolts a second time to 19–25 ft. lbs. For final tightening, camshaft may be in any position.

NOTE: If original valve train components are being installed, a valve clearance check is not required. If a component has been replaced, perform a valve clearance check.

22. Install the exhaust manifold(s), lower intake manifold and injector fuel rail assembly.

23. Position the cover(s) and new gasket on cylinder head and install attaching bolts. Note location of spark plug wire routing clip stud bolts. Tighten attaching bolts to 6–8 ft. lbs.

24. Install the upper intake manifold and connect the secondary wires to the spark plugs.

25. If the left side cylinder head is being installed, perform the following: install oil fill cap, compressor mounting and support brackets, power steering pump mounting and support brackets and the alternator/support bracket.

26. If the right side cylinder head is being installed, perform the following: install the PCV valve, alternator bracket, thermactor pump and pump pulley, accessory drive idler, thermactor air control valve or air bypass valve hose.

27. Install the accessory drive belt.

Attach the thermactor tube(s) support bracket to the rear of the cylinder head. Torque the attaching bolts to 30-40 ft. lbs.

28. Connect the negative battery cable and fill the cooling system.

29. Start the engine and check for leaks.

30. Check and, if necessary, adjust curb idle speed.

31. Install the air cleaner with air intake duct and heat tube.

OVERHAUL

For all cylinder head overhaul procedures, please refer to "Engine Rebuilding" in the Unit Repair section.

Rocker Arms

REMOVAL & INSTALLATION

2.5L & 3.8L Engines

1. Raise the hood and place protective aprons on the fenders.

2. Remove the oil filler cap. Disconnect the PCV hose, the throttle linkage and the speed control cable from the top of the rocker arm cover (if equipped).

3. Remove the rocker arm cover-to-cylinder head bolts and the cover.

4. Remove the rocker arm fulcrum bolts, the fulcrums and the rocker arms. If necessary, remove the pushrods.

NOTE: When removing the rocker arm assemblies, be sure to keep all of the parts in order for installation purposes.

5. Using a putty knife, clean the gasket mounting surfaces. Inspect and/or replace any damaged parts.

NOTE: The following procedure may require the removal of the front timing cover.

To install:

6. Position the pushrods in the hydraulic lifter.

7. Install the rocker arms, the fulcrums and the bolts onto the valves.

8. Position the crankshaft so that the timing marks, on the crankshaft and the camshaft sprockets, are facing each other (on the center line). Torque the rocker arm fulcrum bolts of the intake valves of cylinders No. 1 and 2 and the exhaust valves of cylinders No. 1 and 3 to 4.5–7.5 ft. lbs. (6–10 Nm).

9. Turn the crankshaft 1 complete revolution so that the timing marks, on the crankshaft and the camshaft sprockets, are facing opposite each other (on the center line). Torque the rocker arm fulcrum bolts of the intake valves of cylinders No. 3 and 4 and the exhaust valves of cylinders No. 2 and 4 to 4.5–7.5 ft. lbs. (6–10 Nm).

10. Apply SAE 50 oil to all of the fulcrums, the rocker arms and the pushrods. Torque all of the fulcrum bolts to 19.5–26.5 ft. lbs. (26–38 Nm).

NOTE: Before torquing the rocker arm fulcrum bolts, be sure that the fulcrums are seated on the cylinder head slots and the pushrods are seated in the rocker arms/tappets.

11. To check the collapsed lifter gap, perform the following procedures:

a. Position the crankshaft so that the timing marks, on the crankshaft and the camshaft sprockets, are facing each other (on the center line). Using a feeler gauge, check the tappet gap of the intake valves of cylinders No. 1 and 2 and the exhaust valves of cylinders No. 1 and 3; the tappet gap should be 0.072–0.174 in. (1.80–4.34mm).

b. Turn the crankshaft 1 complete revolution so that the timing marks, on the crankshaft and the camshaft sprockets, are facing opposite each other (on the center line). Using a feeler gauge, check the tappet gap of the intake valves of cylinders No. 3 and 4 and the exhaust valves of cylinders No. 2 and 4; the tappet gap should be 0.072–0.174 in. (1.80–4.34mm).

12. Complete the installation of the remaining components by reversing the removal procedure, use a new gasket and reverse the removal procedures. Start the engine and check for leaks.

3.0L Engine

1. Label and disconnect the ignition wires from the spark plugs.

2. Remove the ignition wire separators from the rocker arm cover mounting bolt studs.

3. To remove the left side rocker arm cover: remove the oil filler cap then disconnect the closure system hose.

4. To remove the right side rocker arm cover: remove the PCV valve, disconnect the EGR tube, then disconnect the heater hoses.

5. Remove the rocker arm covers-to-cylinder head screws and the covers.

6. Remove the rocker arm fulcrum bolts, the fulcrums and the rocker arms. If necessary, remove the pushrods.

NOTE: When removing the rocker arm assemblies, be sure to keep all of the parts in order for installation purposes.

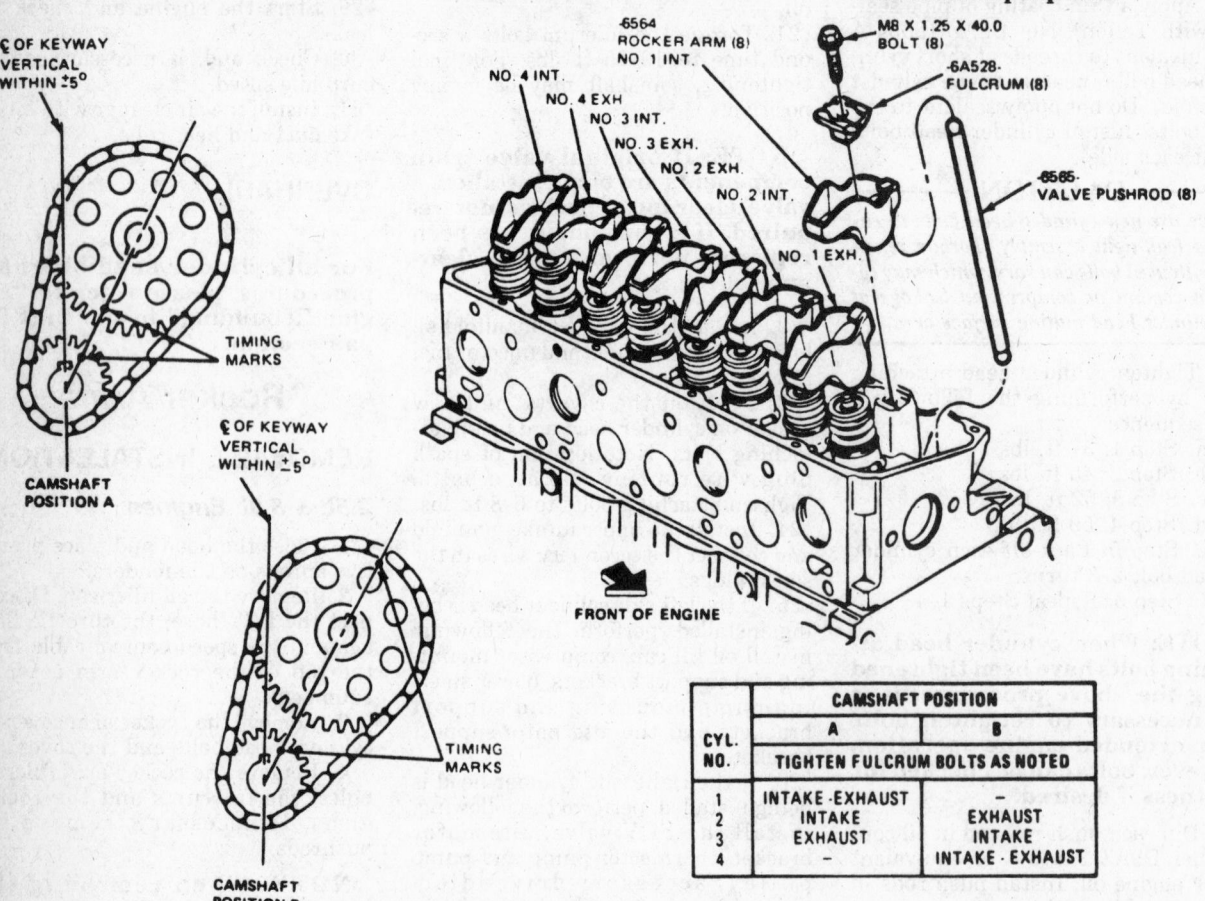

CYL. NO.	CAMSHAFT POSITION	
	A	B
	TIGHTEN FULCRUM BOLTS AS NOTED	
1	INTAKE · EXHAUST	–
2	INTAKE	EXHAUST
3	EXHAUST	INTAKE
4	–	INTAKE · EXHAUST

Exploded view of the rocker arm assemblies and valve procedures—2.5L engine

7. Using a putty knife, clean the gasket mounting surfaces. Inspect and/or replace any damaged parts.

8. To install the rocker arm components, first position the pushrods on the tappets. Install the rocker arms, the fulcrums and the bolts onto the valves, but DO NOT tighten the bolts. Using SAE 50 oil, apply it to all of the fulcrums, the rocker arms and the pushrods.

NOTE: Before torquing the rocker arm fulcrum bolts, be sure that the fulcrums are seated in the cylinder head slots and the pushrods are seated in the rocker arms/tappets.

9. For each valve, rotate the crankshaft until the tappet rests on the heel (base circle) of the camshaft lobe. Torque the rocker arm fulcrum bolts to 19–25 ft. lbs. (25–35 Nm).

NOTE: If the original valve components are being installed, a valve clearance check is not required. Valve Clearance: 0.088–0.189 in. (2.23–4.77mm).

10. Rotate the crankshaft to place the No. 1 cylinder on TDC of the compression stroke, then allow the lifters to bleed down.

11. Using a feeler gauge, check that the valve clearances of cylinders No. 1, 3 & 6 (intake) and No. 1, 2 & 4 (exhaust) are 0.088–0.189 in. (2.23–4.77mm).

12. Rotate the crankshaft one com-plete revolution, positioning the No. 2 cylinder on TDC of the compression stroke, then allow the lifters to bleed down.

13. Using a feeler gauge, check that the valve clearances of cylinders No. 2, 4 & 5 (intake) and No. 3, 5 & 6 (exhaust) are 0.088–0.189 in. (2.23–4.77mm).

14. To complete the installation, use a new gasket and reverse the removal procedures. Start the engine and check for leaks.

Intake Manifold

REMOVAL & INSTALLATION

2.5L Engine

1. Raise and secure the hood. Disconnect the negative battery cable.

2. Place a drain pan under the radiator, remove the radiator cap, open the draincock and drain the cooling system.

3. Remove the accelerator cable, the air cleaner assembly and the heat stove tube from the heat shield.

4. Label and remove the necessary vacuum lines. Remove the 3 exhaust pipe-to-exhaust manifold retaining nuts.

5. Remove the thermactor belt, the hose below thermactor pump and the thermactor pump, as required.

6. Remove the heat shield from the exhaust manifold.

7. Disconnect the thermactor check valve hose from the tube assembly. Remove the bracket-to-EGR valve nuts.

8. Disconnect the water inlet tube from the intake manifold.

9. Disconnect the EGR tube from the EGR valve.

10. Remove the intake manifold-to-engine bolts and the manifold.

11. Using a putty knife or equivalent, clean the gasket mounting surfaces.

12. Complete the installation of the intake manifold by reversing the removal procedure. Use a new gasket to ensure proper sealing. Torque the intake manifold-to-engine bolts in sequence to 15–23 ft. lbs. (20–30 Nm). Refill the cooling system. Start engine and check for leaks.

3.0L Engine

1. Disconnect the negative battery cable. Drain the cooling system to a level below the intake manifold.

2. Refer to the "Throttle Body, Removal & Installation" procedures in this section to remove the throttle body from the engine.

3. Reduce the pressure in the fuel system and disconnect the fuel lines.

4. Disconnect and remove the fuel injector electrical harness from the engine.

5. Label and disconnect the spark plug wires (for easy installation). Mark and remove the distributor from the engine.

6. Disconnect the upper radiator hose, the water outlet heater hose and

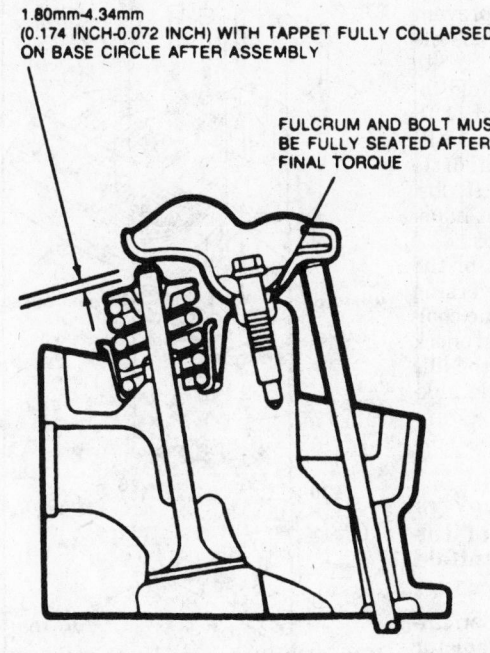

1.80mm-4.34mm
(0.174 INCH-0.072 INCH) WITH TAPPET FULLY COLLAPSED ON BASE CIRCLE AFTER ASSEMBLY

FULCRUM AND BOLT MUST BE FULLY SEATED AFTER FINAL TORQUE

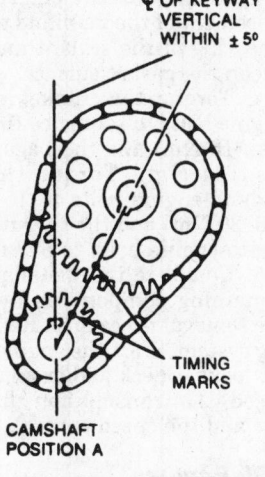

₵ OF KEYWAY VERTICAL WITHIN ± 5°

TIMING MARKS

CAMSHAFT POSITION A

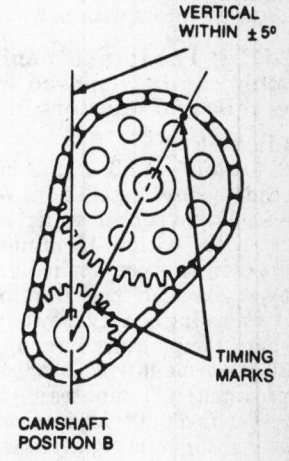

₵ OF KEYWAY VERTICAL WITHIN ± 5°

TIMING MARKS

CAMSHAFT POSITION B

CYL. NO.	CAMSHAFT POSITION	
	A	B
	TIGHTEN FULCRUM BOLTS AS NOTED	
1	INTAKE-EXHAUST	—
2	INTAKE	EXHAUST
3	EXHAUST	INTAKE
4	—	INTAKE-EXHAUST

Checking the tappet gap—2.5L engine

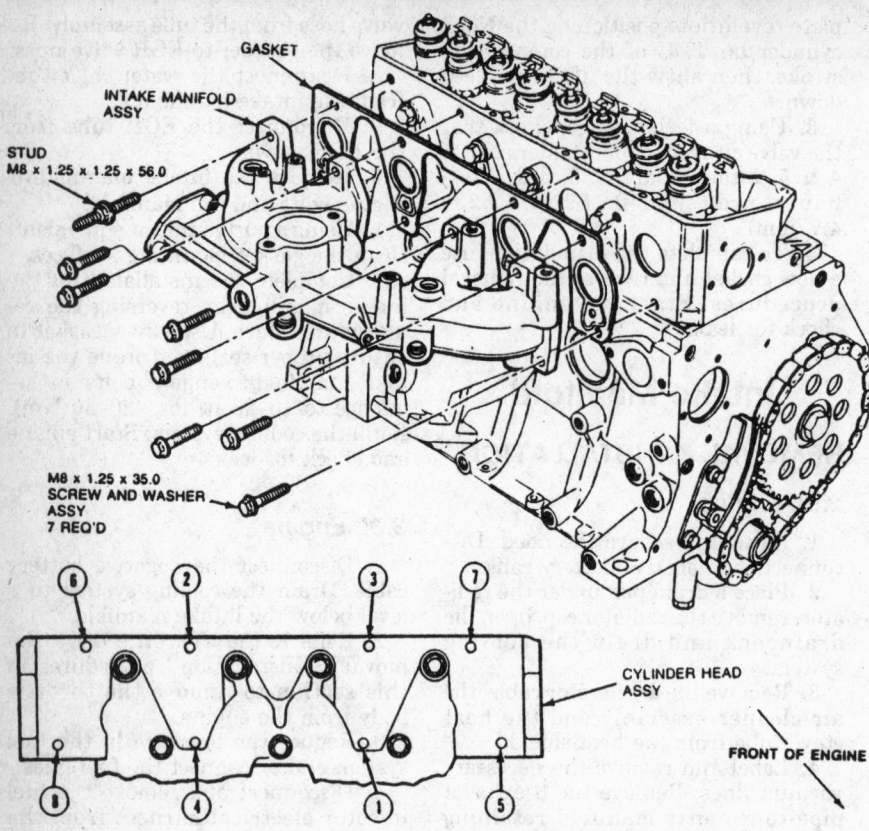

View of the intake manifold. Torque bolts in sequence as shown

including air intake duct and heat tube.

3. Disconnect the accelerator cable at throttle body assembly. Disconnect speed control cable, if equipped.

4. Disconnect the transaxle linkage at the upper intake manifold.

5. Remove the attaching bolts from accelerator cable mounting bracket and position cables aside.

6. Disconnect the thermactor air supply hose at the check valve.

7. Disconnect the flexible fuel lines from steel lines over rocker arm cover.

8. Disconnect the fuel lines at injector fuel rail assembly.

9. Disconnect the radiator hose at thermostat housing connection.

10. Disconnect the coolant bypass hose at manifold connection.

11. Disconnect the heater tube at the intake manifold. Remove the heater tube support bracket attaching nut. Remove the heater hose at rear of heater tube. Loosen hose clamp at heater elbow and remove heater tube with hose attached. Remove heater tube with fuel lines attached and set the assembly aside.

12. Disconnect vacuum lines at fuel the rail assembly and intake manifold.

13. Identify, tag and disconnect all necessary electrical connectors.

14. If equipped with air conditioning, remove the air compressor support bracket.

15. Disconnect the PCV lines. One is located on upper intake manifold. The second is located at the left side rocker cover and the lower intake stud.

the thermostat housing from the engine.

7. Remove the intake manifold-to-engine bolts/studs, the intake manifold; discard the side gaskets and end seals and replace with new.

NOTE: The intake manifold assembly can be removed with the fuel rails and injectors in place.

To install:

8. Lightly oil all of the bolts/stud threads before installation. When using a silicone rubber sealer, assembly must occur within 15 minutes after the sealer has been applied. After this time, the sealer may start to set-up and its sealing quality may be reduced. In high temperature/humidity conditions the sealant will start to set up in approximately 5 minutes.

9. Using a putty knife, clean all the gasket/seal mounting surfaces. All the old silicone rubber sealant must be completely removed to ensure effective sealing.

10. Apply a suitable silicone rubber sealant to the intersection of the cylinder block and cylinder head assemblies.

11. Install the front and rear intake manifold seals and secure with the seal retainers.

12. Position the intake manifold gaskets in place and insert the locking tabs over the cylinder head tabs.

13. Carefully lower the intake manifold onto the cylinder block and cylinder heads. Careful positioning and placement of the manifold will prevent smearing of the sealant and voids between the gasket surface.

14. Torque the intake manifold-to-engine bolts in sequence first to 11 ft. lbs. (15 Nm) and then again to 18 ft. lbs. (24 Nm). Torque the throttle body-to-engine bolts to 15–22 ft. lbs. (20–30 Nm) and the thermostat housing-to-engine bolts to 6–8 ft. lbs.

15. Complete the installation of the remaining components by reversing the removal procedure. Refill the cooling system. Start the engine and check for leaks. Check and/or adjust the idle speed, the transmission throttle linkage and the speed control.

3.8L Engine

NOTE: This procedure covers removal and installation of the upper and lower intake manifold assemblies.

1. Position a suitable drain pan under the radiator, remove the radiator cap, open the draincock and drain the cooling system.

2. Remove the air cleaner assembly

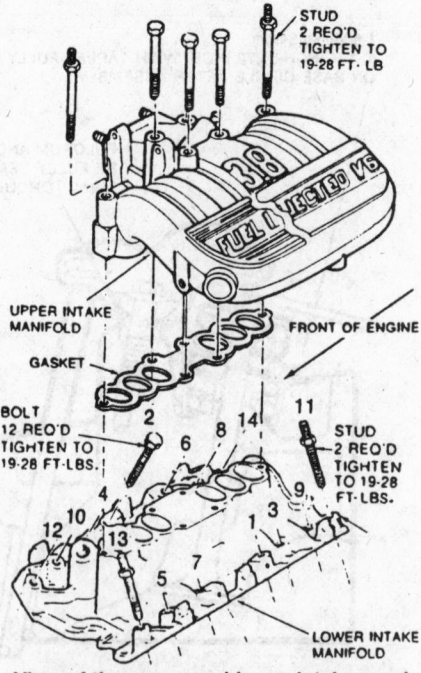

View of the upper and lower intake manifold used on 3.8L engines. Torque lower intake manifold bolts in sequence as shown

b. Step 2: 15 ft. lbs (20 Nm).

c. Step 3: 24 ft. lbs (24 Nm).

28. Connect the rear PCV line to upper intake tube and install the front PCV tube so the mounting bracket sits over the lower intake stud.

29. Install the injectors and fuel rail assembly.

30. Position the upper intake gasket and manifold on top of the lower intake. Use locating pins to secure position of gasket between manifolds.

31. Install bolts and studs in their original locations. Tighten the 4 center bolts, then tighten the end bolts. Use the same sequence that was described in Step 27.

32. Install the EGR valve assembly on the manifold. Tighten the attaching bolt to 15-22 ft. lbs.

33. Install the throttle body. Cross-tighten hold-down nuts to 15-22 ft. lbs.

34. Connect the rear PCV line at PCV valve and upper intake manifold connections. If equipped with air conditioning, install the compressor support bracket. Tighten attaching fasteners to 15-22 ft. lbs. (20–30) ft. lbs.

35. Connect all electrical connectors and vacuum hoses.

36. Connect the heater tube hose to the heater elbow. Position the heater tube support bracket and tighten attaching nut to 15–22 ft. lbs. Connect the heater hose to the rear of the heater tube and tighten hose clamp.

37. Connect coolant bypass and upper radiator hoses and secure with hose cplamps.

38. Connect the fuel line(s) at injector fuel rail assembly and connect the flexible fuel lines to steel lines.

39. Position the accelerator cable mounting bracket and install and tighten attaching bolts to 15–22 ft. lbs.

40. Connect the speed control cable, if equipped. Connect the transaxle linkage at upper intake manifold.

41. Fill the cooling system to the proper level.

42. Start the engine and check for coolant or fuel leaks.

43. Check and, if necessary, adjust engine idle speed, transaxle throttle linkage and speed control.

44. Install the air cleaner assembly and air intake duct.

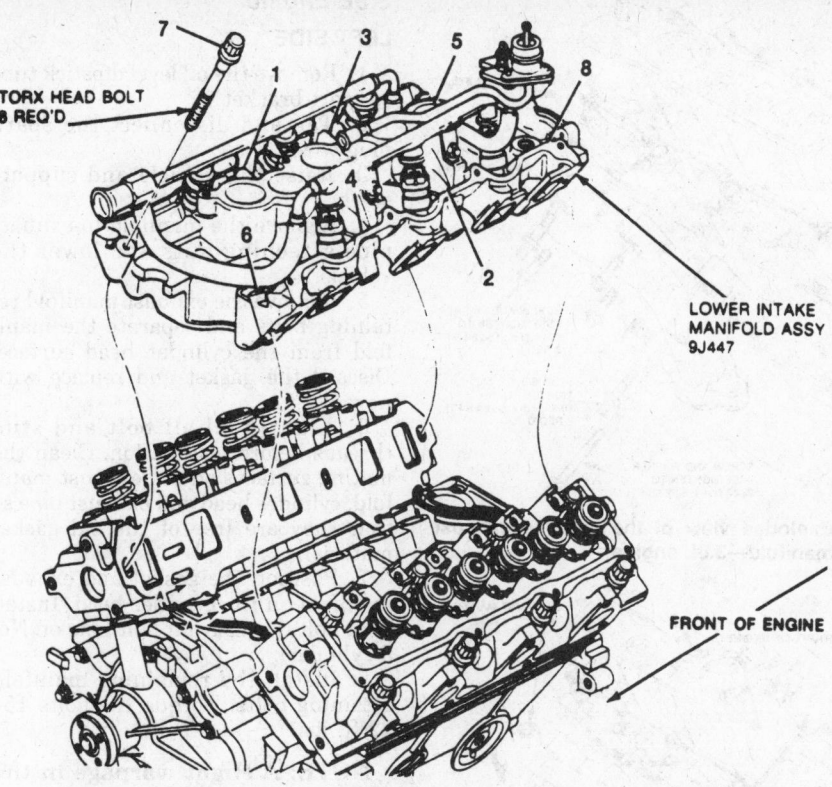

TORX HEAD BOLT 8 REQ'D

LOWER INTAKE MANIFOLD ASSY 9J447

FRONT OF ENGINE

Exploded view and torque sequence of the intake manifold—3.0L engine

16. Remove the throttle body assembly and remove the EGR valve assembly from the upper manifold.

17. Remove the attaching nut and remove wiring retainer bracket located at the left side front of the intake manifold and set aside with the spark plug wires.

18. Remove the upper intake manifold attaching bolts/studs. Remove the upper intake manifold from the surface of the lower intake manifold.

19. Remove the injectors with fuel rail assembly.

20. Remove the heater water outlet hose.

21. Remove the lower intake manifold attaching bolts/stud and remove the lower intake manifold. Remove the manifold side gaskets and end seals. Discard and replace with new.

NOTE: The manifold is sealed at each end with RTV-type sealer. To break the seal, it may be necessary to pry on the front of the manifold with a small or medium pry bar. If it is necessary to pry on the manifold, use care to prevent damage to the machined surfaces. To install:

22. Lightly oil all attaching bolt and stud threads before installation.

NOTE: When using silicone rubber sealer, assembly must oc- cur within 15 minutes after sealer application. After this time, the sealer may start to set-up, and its sealing effectiveness may be reduced. The lower intake manifold, cylinder head, and cylinder block mating surfaces should be clean and free of oil residue and all existing gasket material to ensure maximum sealing effectiveness. Use a suitable solvent or a gasket scraper to clean these surfaces.

23. Apply a bead of contact adhesive No. D7AZ-19B508-A or equivalent to each cylinder head mating surface. Press the new intake manifold gaskets into place, using locating pins as necessary to aid in assembly alignment.

24. Apply a 1/8 inch bead of silicone sealer No. D6AZ-19562-B or equivalent at each corner where the cylinder head joins the cylinder block.

25. Install the front and rear intake manifold end seals.

26. Carefully position the lower intake manifold on the cylinder block and cylinder head surface. Use locating pins as necessary to guide the manifold into place.

27. Install the retaining bolts and stud bolts in their original locations. Torque the retaining bolts in numerical sequence in 3 steps as follows:

a. Step 1: 8 ft. lbs (10 Nm).

Exhaust Manifold

REMOVAL & INSTALLATION

2.5L Engine

1. Disconnect the negative battery cable and drain the cooling system.

2. Remove the accelerator cable.

3. Remove the air cleaner assembly and heat stove at heat shield.

4. Disconnect and label all required vacuum lines.

5. Remove the 3 exhaust pipe-to-exhaust manifold retaining nuts. On the 1986–87 vehicles, disconnect the EGO sensor electrical wiring connector at this time.

6. Disconnect the thermactor check valve hose from the tube assembly. Remove the bracket-to-EGR valve nuts.

7. Disconnect the water tube at the intake manifold. Disconnect the EGR tube from the EGR valve.

8. Remove the intake manifold.

9. Remove the exhaust manifold-to-engine bolts and the manifold from the vehicle.

10. Using a putty knife or suitable gasket scraper, clean the gasket mounting surfaces.

NOTE: When installing the exhaust manifold, use the Alignment Stud tools No. T84P-6065-B to align the manifold with the block.

11. Complete the installation the exhaust and intake manifolds and related components by reversing the removal procedure. Use new gaskets during installation. Torque the exhaust manifold-to-engine bolts (in 2 steps) to 20–30 ft. lbs. (27–41 Nm), the exhaust manifold-to-exhaust pipe nuts to 25–34 ft. lbs. (34–47 Nm) and the intake manifold-to-engine bolts to 15–23 ft. lbs. (20–30 Nm). Refill the cooling system. Start engine and check for leaks.

3.0L Engine

LEFT SIDE

1. Disconnect the negative battery cable. Remove the oil level indicator support bracket.

2. Disconnect and plug the power steering hoses at the power steering pump.

3. Remove the exhaust manifold-to-exhaust pipe nuts and separate the exhaust pipe from the exhaust manifold.

4. Remove the exhaust manifold-to-cylinder head bolts and the exhaust manifold from the engine.

5. Using a putty knife, clean gasket mounting surfaces. Lightly oil all of the bolt/stud threads prior to installation.

6. To install, use new gaskets and reverse the removal procedures. Torque the exhaust manifold-to-engine bolts to 15–22 ft. lbs. (20–30 Nm) and the exhaust manifold-to-exhaust pipe nuts to 16–24 ft. lbs. (21–32 Nm). Refill and bleed the power steering system.

RIGHT SIDE

1. Disconnect the negative battery

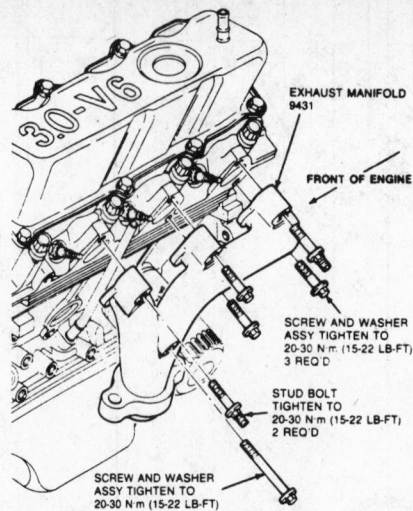

Exploded view of the left-side exhaust manifold—3.0L engine

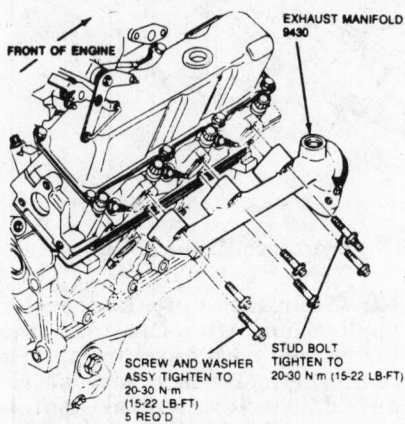

Exploded view of the right-side exhaust manifold—3.0L engine

cable. Remove the heater hose support bracket.

2. Disconnect and plug the heater hoses. Remove the EGR tube from the exhaust manifold; use a back-up wrench on the lower adapter.

3. Remove the exhaust manifold-to-exhaust pipe nuts and separate the pipe from the manifold.

4. Remove the exhaust manifold-to-engine bolts and the exhaust manifold from the engine.

5. Using a putty knife, clean the gasket mounting surfaces.

NOTE: Lightly oil all of the bolt and stud threads prior to installation.

6. To install, use new gaskets and reverse the removal procedure. Torque the exhaust manifold-to-engine bolts to 15–22 ft. lbs. (20–30 Nm), the exhaust pipe-to-exhaust manifold nuts to 16–24 ft. lbs. (21–32 Nm) and the EGR tube-to-exhaust manifold to 25–36 ft. lbs. (35–50 Nm).

3.8L Engine

LEFT SIDE

1. Remove the oil level dipstick tube support bracket.

2. Tag and disconnect the spark plug wires.

3. Raise the vehicle and support safely.

4. Remove the manifold-to-exhaust pipe attaching nuts and lower the vehicle.

5. Remove the exhaust manifold retaining bolts and separate the manifold from the cylinder head surface. Discard the gasket and replace with new.

6. Lightly oil all bolt and stud threads before installation. Clean the mating surfaces on the exhaust manifold, cylinder head and exhaust pipe so that they are free of the old gasket material.

7. Position the gasket and exhaust manifold on the cylinder head. Install pilot bolt (lower front bolt hole on No. 5 cylinder).

8. Install the remaining manifold retaining bolts. Torque the bolts 15–22 ft. lbs.

NOTE: A slight warpage in the exhaust manifold may cause a misalignment between the bolt holes in the head and the manifold. Elongate the holes in the exhaust manifold as necessary to correct the misalignment, if apparent. Do not elongate the pilot hole (lower front bolt on No. 5 cylinder).

9. Raise the vehicle and support safely.

10. Connect the exhaust pipe to the manifold. Torque the attaching nuts to 16–24 ft. lbs and lower the vehicle.

11. Connect the spark plug wires. Install dipstick tube support bracket attaching nut. Tighten to 15–22 ft. lbs.

12. Start the engine and check for exhaust leaks.

RIGHT SIDE

1. Remove the air cleaner outlet tube assembly. Disconnect the thermactor hose from the downstream air tube check valve.

2. Tag and disconnect the coil secondary wire from the coil and the wires from spark plugs.

3. Disconnect the EGR tube.

4. Raise the vehicle and support safely.

5. Remove the transaxle dipstick tube. Remove the thermactor air tube by cutting the tube clamp at the underbody catalyst fitting with a suitable cutting tool.

6. Remove the manifold-to-exhaust pipe attaching nuts.

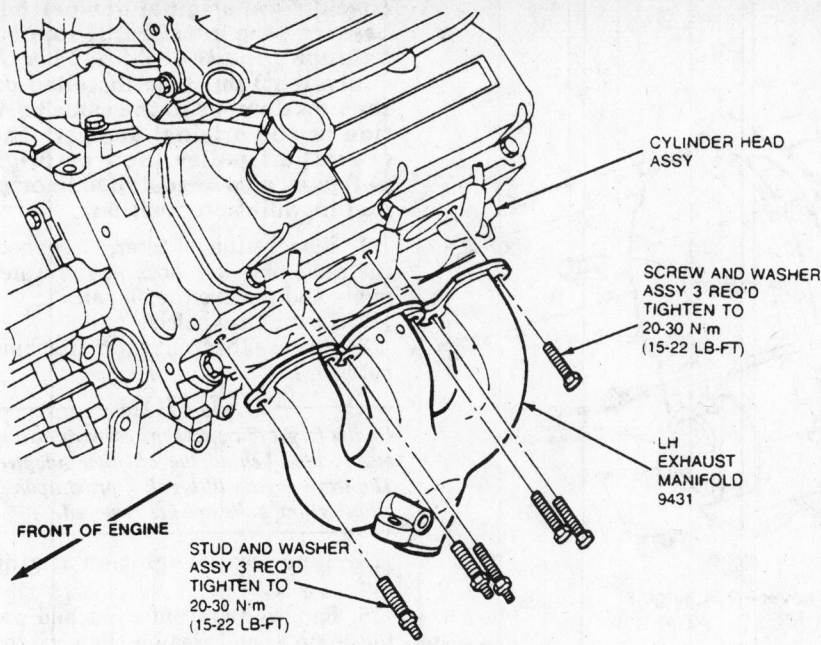

CYLINDER HEAD ASSY

SCREW AND WASHER ASSY 3 REQ'D TIGHTEN TO 20-30 N·m (15-22 LB-FT)

LH EXHAUST MANIFOLD 9431

FRONT OF ENGINE

STUD AND WASHER ASSY 3 REQ'D TIGHTEN TO 20-30 N·m (15-22 LB-FT)

Left side exhaust manifold assembly — 3.8L engine

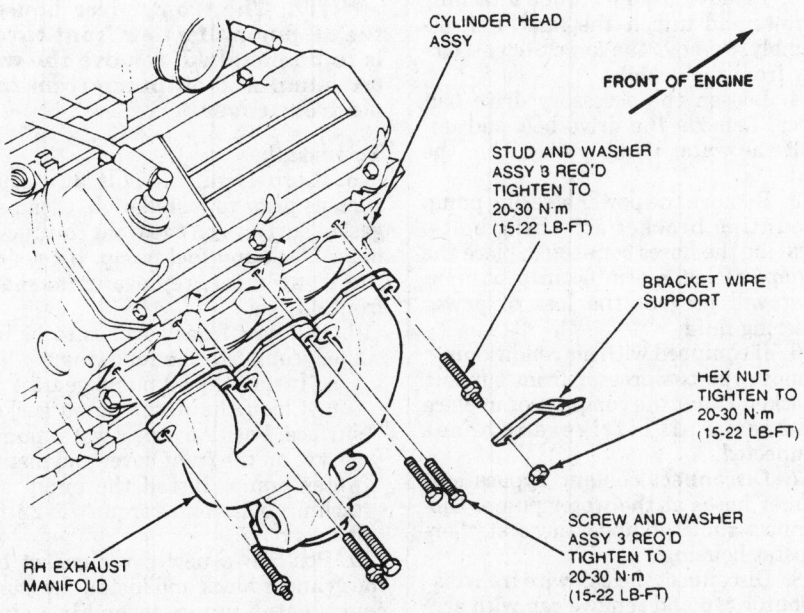

CYLINDER HEAD ASSY

FRONT OF ENGINE

STUD AND WASHER ASSY 3 REQ'D TIGHTEN TO 20-30 N·m (15-22 LB-FT)

BRACKET WIRE SUPPORT

HEX NUT TIGHTEN TO 20-30 N·m (15-22 LB-FT)

SCREW AND WASHER ASSY 3 REQ'D TIGHTEN TO 20-30 N·m (15-22 LB-FT)

RH EXHAUST MANIFOLD

Right side exhaust manifold assembly — 3.8L engine

7. Lower the vehicle.

8. Remove the exhaust manifold retaining bolts. Remove the manifold and heat shroud and gasket from the vehicle. Discard the gasket and replace with new.

9. Lightly oil all bolt and stud threads before installation. Clean the mating surfaces on exhaust manifold cylinder head and exhaust pipe so that they are free of the old gasket material.

10. Position the gasket, inner half of the heat shroud and exhaust manifold on cylinder head. Start two attaching bolts to align the manifold with the cylinder head. Install the remaining retaining bolts and torque to 15–22 ft. lbs.

11. Raise the vehicle and support safely.

12. Connect the exhaust pipe to manifold. Torque the attaching nuts to 16-24 ft. lbs. Position the thermactor hose to the downstream air tube and clamp tube to the underbody catalyst fitting.

13. Install the transaxle dipstick tube and lower vehicle.

14. Connect ignition wires to their respective spark plugs and connect coil secondary wire to the coil.

15. Connect the EGR tube. Connect the thermactor hose to the downstream air tube and secure with clamp. Install the air cleaner outlet tube assembly.

16. Start the engine and check for exhaust leaks.

Front Cover

REMOVAL & INSTALLATION

2.5L Engine

1. Remove the engine and the transmission from the vehicle as an assembly.

2. Remove the dipstick and the accessory drive pulley (if equipped). Remove the crankshaft pulley-to-crankshaft bolt, the washer and the pulley.

3. Remove front cover-to-engine bolts and pry the top of the front cover away from the block.

NOTE: The front cover oil seal must be removed in order to use the Front Cover Aligner tool No. T84P-6019-C to install the front cover.

4. Using a putty knife, clean the gasket contact surfaces.

5. To install, use a new gasket, sealant, a new oil seal and reverse the removal procedures. Torque the front cover-to-engine bolts to 6–9 ft. lbs. and the crankshaft pulley bolt to 140–170 ft. lbs.

3.0L Engine

1. Remove the idler pulley and bracket assembly. Remove the drive and accessory belts. Unbolt the water pump pulley from the hub and allow to remain suspended on the hub.

2. Remove the crankshaft pulley and the damper from the crankshaft.

3. Remove the lower radiator hose from the front cover.

4. Remove the oil pan. Unbolt the front cover and water pump assembly from the cylinder block. Remove the loose pulley from the hub.

NOTE: Do not cut the oil pan gasket and attempt to reseal. Either reuse the gasket or replace with new.

5. Using a putty knife, clean the gasket mounting surfaces. Apply sealant to the threads of the bolts that are installed in the cylinder block water jacket.

NOTE: When the front cover is removed, the oil seal should be replaced.

6. To install, use new gaskets, seal-

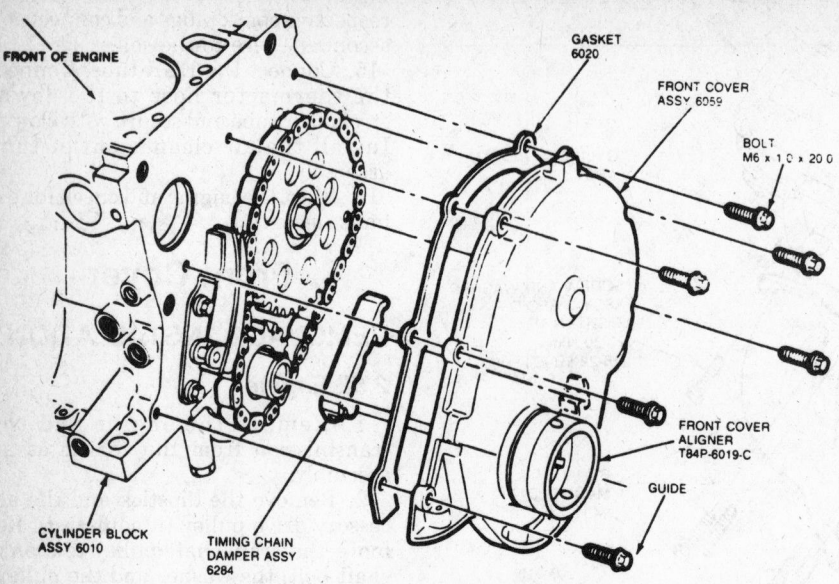

Exploded view of the front cover—2.5L engine

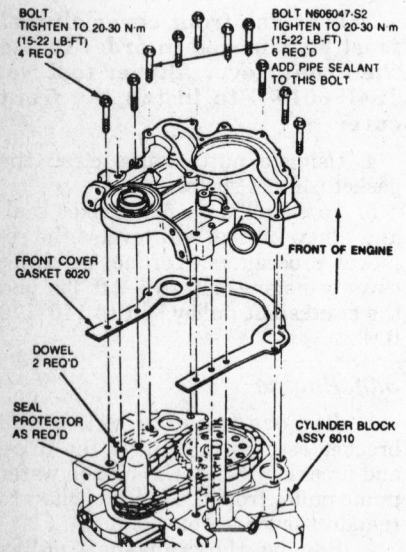

Exploded view of the front cover assembly—3.0L engine

ant and reverse the removal procedures. Torque the front cover-to-engine bolts to 15–22 ft. lbs. (20–30 Nm), the front cover-to-oil pan bolts to 80–106 inch lbs. (9–12 Nm), the water pump-to-front cover bolts to 6–8 ft. lbs. (8–12 Nm), the crankshaft damper-to-crankshaft bolt to 141–169 ft. lbs. (190–230 Nm), the crankshaft pulley-to-crankshaft damper bolts to 20–28 ft. lbs. (26–38 Nm), the water pump pulley-to-water pump bolts to 15–22 ft. lbs. (20–30 Nm).

3.8L Engine

1. Disconnect the negative battery cable. Drain the cooling system and crankcase.

2. Remove the air cleaner assembly and air intake duct.
3. Remove the fan shroud attaching screws and unbolt the fan/clutch assembly. Remove the fan/clutch assembly from the vehicle.
4. Loosen the accessory drive belt idler. Remove the drive belt and unbolt the water pump pulley from the hub.
5. Remove the power steering pump mounting bracket attaching bolts. Leaving the hoses connected, place the pump/bracket assembly in a position that will prevent the loss of power steering fluid.
6. If equipped with air conditioning, remove the compressor front support bracket. Leave the compressor in place and leave all refrigerant hoses connected.
7. Disconnect coolant bypass and heater hoses at the water pump. Disconnect radiator upper hose at thermostat housing.
8. Disconnect the coil wire from distributor cap and remove cap with secondary wires attached. Remove the distributor hold-down clamp and lift distributor out of the front cover.
9. Raise the vehicle and support safely.
10. Remove the crankshaft damper and pulley.

NOTE: If the crankshaft pulley and vibration damper have to be separated, mark the damper and pulley so that they may be reassembled in the same relative position. This is important as the damper and pulley are initially balanced as a unit. If the crankshaft damper is being replaced,

check if the original damper has balance pins installed. If so, new balance pins (E0SZ-6A328-A or equivalent) must be installed on the new damper in the same position as the original damper. The crankshaft pulley (new or original) must also be installed in original installation position.

11. Remove the oil filter, disconnect the radiator lower hose at the water pump and remove the oil pan.
12. Lower the vehicle.
13. Remove the front cover attaching bolts.

CAUTION

Do not forget to remove the cover attaching bolt located behind the oil filter adapter. The front cover will break if pried upon if all attaching bolts are not removed.

14. Remove the ignition timing indicator.
15. Remove the front cover and water pump as an assembly. Remove the cover gasket. Discard the gasket and replace with new.

NOTE: The front cover houses the oil pump. If a new front cover is to be installed, remove the water pump and oil pump from the old front cover.

To install:

16. Lightly oil all bolt and stud threads prior to installation. Clean all gasket surfaces on the front cover, cylinder block and fuel pump. If reusing the front cover, replace crankshaft front oil seal.
19. If a new front cover is to be installed, complete the following:
   a. Install the oil pump gears.
   b. Clean the water pump gasket surface. Position a new water pump gasket on the front cover and install water pump. Install the pump attaching bolts and torque 15–22 ft. lbs.
20. Position a new cover gasket on the cylinder block and install the front cover/water pump assembly using dowels for proper alignment. A suitable contact adhesive (No. D7AZ-19B508-A or equivalent) is recommended to hold the gasket in position while the front cover is installed.
26. Position the ignition timing indicator.
27. Install the front cover attaching bolts. Apply Loctite® or equivalent to the threads of the bolt installed below the oil filter housing prior to installation. This bolt is to be installed and tightened last. Tighten all bolts to 15–22 ft. lbs.
28. Raise the vehicle and support safely.
29. Thoroughly clean the oil pan sur-

face and install the oil pan. Torque the oil pan retaining bolts to 6–9 ft. lbs. (9–12 Nm). Connect the radiator lower hose. Install a new oil filter.

30. Coat the crankshaft damper sealing surface with clean engine oil.

31. Position the crankshaft pulley key in the crankshaft keyway.

32. Install the damper with damper washer and attaching bolt. Torque bolt to 104–132 ft. lbs.

33. Install the crankshaft pulley and torque the attaching bolts 19–28 ft. lbs.

34. Lower the vehicle.

35. Connect the coolant bypass hose.

36. Install the distributor with rotor pointing at No. 1 distributor cap tower. Install the distributor cap and coil wire.

37. Connect the radiator upper hose at thermostat housing.

38. Connect the heater hose.

39. If equipped with air conditioning, install compressor and mounting brackets.

40. Install the power steering pump and mounting brackets.

41. Position the accessory drive belt over the pulleys. Install the fan/clutch assembly and fan shroud. Cross tighten the attaching bolts to 12–18 ft. lbs.

42. Install the water pump pulley. Position the accessory drive belt over water pump pulley and tighten the belt.

43. Connect battery ground cable. Fill the crankcase and cooling system to the proper level.

44. Start the engine and check for leaks.

45. Check the ignition timing and curb idle speed, adjust as required.

46. Install the air cleaner assembly and air intake duct.

OIL SEAL REPLACEMENT

2.5L Engine

1. Remove the engine from the vehicle and place it on a workstand.

2. Remove the drive belt(s), the crankshaft pulley bolt/washer and the crankshaft pulley.

3. Using the Damper Removal tool No. T77F-4220-B1, remove the crankshaft pulley.

4. Using the Front Seal Removal tool No. T74P-6700-A, remove the front cover oil seal.

5. Coat the new seal with grease. Using the Front Seal Replacer tool No. T83T-4676-A, install the seal into the cover; drive the seal in until it is fully seated. Check the seal after installation to ensure that the seal spring is properly positioned.

6. To complete the installation, reverse the removal procedures. Torque the crankshaft pulley-to-crankshaft bolt to 140–230 ft. lbs. (190–230 Nm).

3.0L Engine

1. Disconnect the negative battery cable and loosen the accessory drive belts.

2. Raise and support the front of the vehicle on jackstands, then remove the right side front wheel.

3. Remove the crankshaft pulley-to-damper bolts. Disengage the accessory drive belts and remove the crankshaft pulley.

4. Using the Crankshaft Damper Removal tool No. T58P-6316-D and the Vibration Damper Removal Adapter tool No. T82L-6316-B, remove the crankshaft damper from the crankshaft.

5. Using a small pry bar, pry the oil seal from the front cover; be careful not to damage the front cover and the crankshaft.

NOTE: Before installation; inspect the front cover and shaft seal surface of the crankshaft damper for damage, nicks, burrs or other roughness which may cause the new seal to fail. Service or replace the components as necessary.

6. To install, lubricate the new seal lip with clean engine oil, then install the seal using the seal installer tool No. T82L-6316-A and the front cover seal replacer tool No. T70P-6B070-A, or equivalents.

7. Coat the crankshaft damper sealing surface with clean engine oil. Apply RTV to the keyway of the damper prior to installation. Install the damper using the vibration damper seal installer tool No. T82L-6316-A.

8. Complete the installation by reversing the removal procedure. Torque the crankshaft damper-to-crankshaft bolt to 141–169 ft. lbs. (190–230 Nm), the crankshaft pulley-to-damper bolts to 20–28 ft. lbs. (26–38 Nm).

3.8L Engine

1. Disconnect the negative battery cable.

2. Remove the fan shroud attaching screws and position the shroud back over the fan.

3. Unbolt the fan clutch assembly and remove.

4. Loosen the accessory drive belt idler.

5. Raise the vehicle and support safely.

6. Disengage the accessory drive belt and remove crankshaft pulley.

7. Remove the crankshaft damper.

8. Remove the seal from the front cover with a suitable prying tool. Use care to prevent gouging or scoring the front cover and crankshaft.

NOTE: Inspect the front cover and crankshaft damper for damage, nicks, burrs or other roughness which may attribute to the failure of the seal. Service or replace components as necessary.

9. Lubricate the seal lip with clean engine oil and install the seal using suitable seal installer.

10. Lubricate the seal surface on the damper with clean engine oil. Install damper and pulley assembly. Install the damper attaching bolt and torque to 103–132 ft. lbs.

11. Position accessory drive belt over crankshaft pulley.

12. Lower the vehicle.

13. Check accessory drive belt for proper routing and engagement in the pulleys. Adjust the drive belt tension.

14. Install the fan/clutch assembly and reposition the fan shroud with the attaching screws.

15. Connect the negative battery cable. Start the engine and check for leaks.

Timing Chain and Sprockets

REMOVAL & INSTALLATION

2.5L Engine

1. Remove the engine and secure it to a workstand.

2. Remove the front cover.

3. Rotate the crankshaft until the timing marks of the crankshaft and the camshaft sprockets are aligned.

4. Remove the camshaft sprocket bolt and washer, then slide the camshaft sprocket, the timing chain and the crankshaft sprocket off as an assembly.

5. Inspect and/or replace the parts as necessary.

6. To install, slide the sprocket/timing chain assembly onto the camshaft and crankshaft with timing marks aligned. Oil the timing chain, the sprocket teeth and the tensioner after installation.

7. Apply oil resistant sealer to a new front cover gasket and position gasket onto the front cover.

8. Using the Front Cover Aligner tool No. T84P-6019-C, position it onto the end of the crankshaft, ensuring that the crank key is aligned with the keyway in the tool. Bolt the front cover to the engine. Tighten all the attaching bolts to specification. Remove the front cover aligner tool.

9. Lubricate the hub of the crankshaft pulley with Polyethylene Grease to prevent damage to the seal during installation and initial engine start. Install crankshaft pulley.

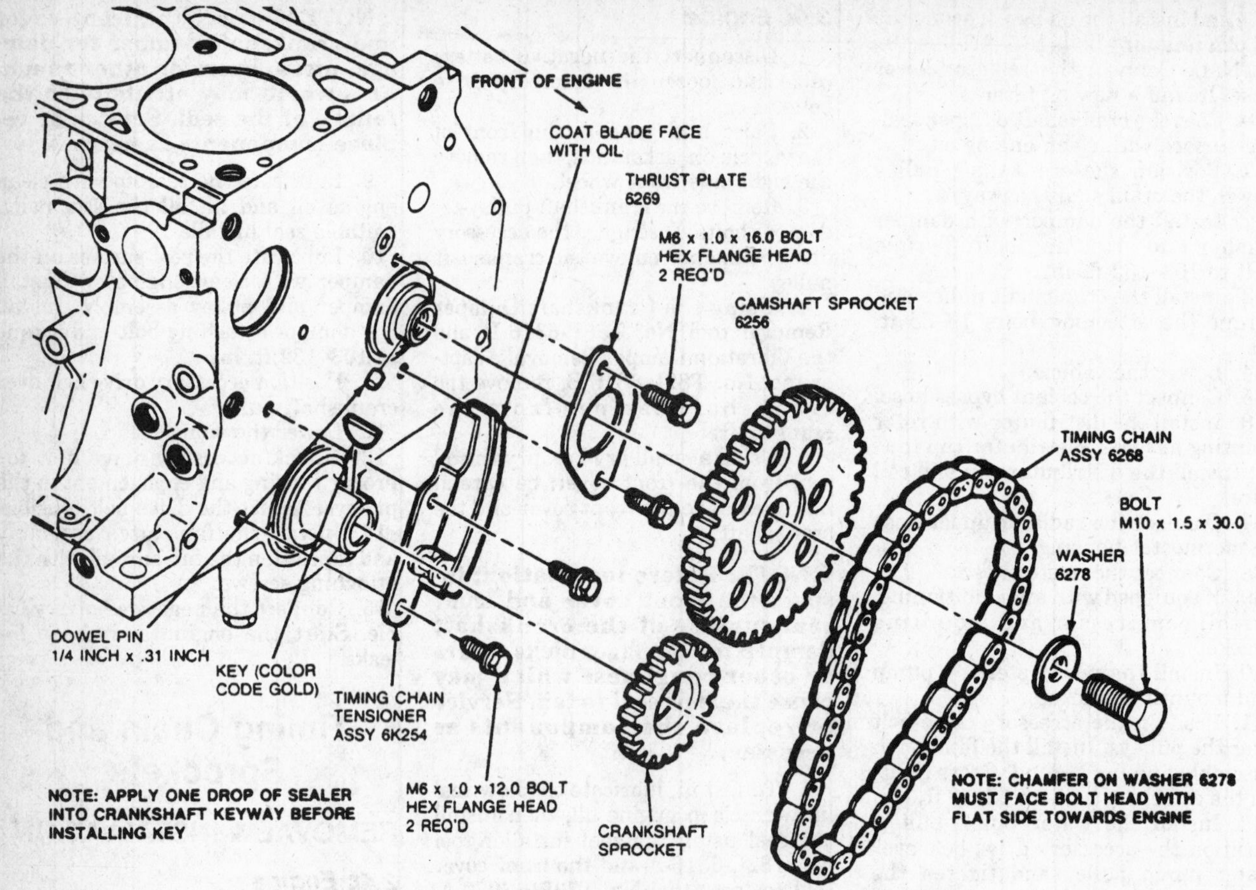

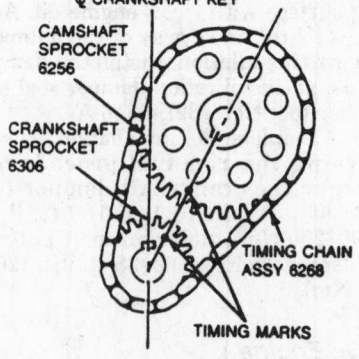

FRONT OF ENGINE

COAT BLADE FACE
WITH OIL

THRUST PLATE
6269

M6 x 1.0 x 16.0 BOLT
HEX FLANGE HEAD
2 REQ'D

CAMSHAFT SPROCKET
6256

TIMING CHAIN
ASSY 6268

BOLT
M10 x 1.5 x 30.0

WASHER
6278

DOWEL PIN
1/4 INCH x .31 INCH

KEY (COLOR
CODE GOLD)

TIMING CHAIN
TENSIONER
ASSY 6K254

M6 x 1.0 x 12.0 BOLT
HEX FLANGE HEAD
2 REQ'D

CRANKSHAFT
SPROCKET

NOTE: APPLY ONE DROP OF SEALER
INTO CRANKSHAFT KEYWAY BEFORE
INSTALLING KEY

NOTE: CHAMFER ON WASHER 6278
MUST FACE BOLT HEAD WITH
FLAT SIDE TOWARDS ENGINE

View of the timing chain and timing sprockets—2.5L engine

10. To complete the installation, reverse the removal procedures. Torque the camshaft sprocket-to-camshaft bolt to 41–56 ft. lbs. (55–75 Nm), the front cover-to-engine bolts to 6–9 ft. lbs. (8–12 Nm), the crankshaft pulley bolt to 140–170 ft. lbs. (190–230 Nm). Refill the cooling system. Start the engine and check for leaks.

3.0L Engine

1. Remove the crankshaft pulley/damper/front cover assemblies.

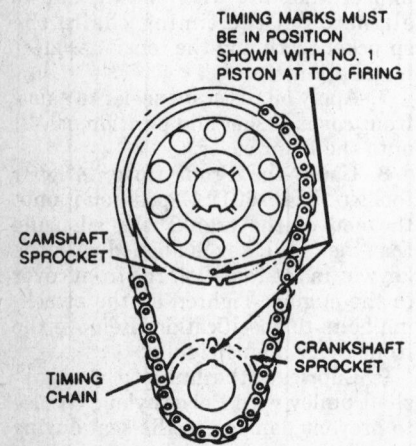

TIMING MARKS MUST
BE IN POSITION
SHOWN WITH NO. 1
PISTON AT TDC FIRING

CAMSHAFT
SPROCKET

TIMING
CHAIN

CRANKSHAFT
SPROCKET

Timing mark alignment—3.0L engines

Ç CRANKSHAFT KEY

CAMSHAFT
SPROCKET
6256

CRANKSHAFT
SPROCKET
6306

TIMING CHAIN
ASSY 6268

TIMING MARKS

Timing mark alignment—2.5L engine

2. Cover the oil pan opening to prevent the entry of dirt and grease.
3. Rotate the crankshaft until the No. 1 piston is at the TDC of the compression stroke and the timing marks are aligned.
4. Remove the camshaft sprocket-to-camshaft bolt and washer, then slide the sprockets and timing chain forward to remove them as an assembly.
5. Inspect the timing chain and sprockets for excessive wear; replace them, if necessary.
6. Using a putty knife, clean the gasket mounting surfaces.

7. Apply oil to the timing chain and sprockets after installation.

NOTE: The camshaft bolt has a drilled oil passage in it for timing chain lubrication. If the bolt is damaged do not replace it with a standard bolt.

8. Apply a bead of RTV sealant on the gap at the cylinder block.
9. Apply an oil resistant sealer No. B5A-19554-A, or equivalent, to a new front gasket and position the gasket onto the front cover.
10. Position the front cover on the engine taking care not to damage the front seal. Make sure the cover is installed over the alignment dowels.

NOTE: When installing the front cover onto the engine, make sure that the oil pan seal is not dislodged.

11. If necessary, replace the front cover seal using the Seal Installation tool No. T70P-6B070-A.
12. To complete the installation, reverse the removal procedures. Torque the camshaft sprocket-to-camshaft bolt to 40–51 ft. lbs. (55–70 Nm), the front cover-to-engine bolts to 15–22 ft. lbs. (20–30 Nm), the water pump-to-front cover bolts to 6–8 ft. lbs. (8–12 Nm), the damper-to-crankshaft bolt to

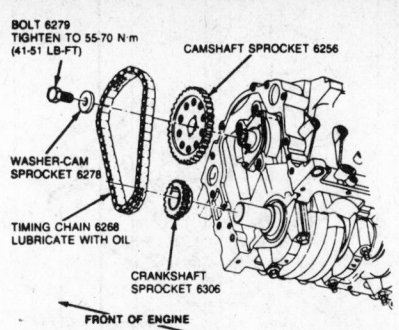

Exploded view of the timing chain and sprockets—3.0L engine

141–169 ft. lbs. (190–230 Nm) and the damper pulley-to-damper bolts to 20–28 ft. lbs. (26–38 Nm). Refill the crankcase and the cooling system. Start the engine and check for leaks.

3.8L Engine

1. Disconnect the negative battery cable. Drain the cooling system and crankcase.

2. Remove the air cleaner assembly and air intake duct.

3. Remove the fan shroud attaching screws and unbolt the fan/clutch assembly. Remove the fan/clutch assembly from the vehicle.

4. Loosen the accessory drive belt idler. Remove the belt and water pump pulley.

5. Remove the power steering pump mounting bracket attaching bolts. Leaving the hoses connected, place the pump/bracket assembly in a position that will prevent the loss of power steering fluid.

6. If equipped with air conditioning, remove the compressor front support bracket. Leave the compressor in place with all refrigerant hoses connected.

7. Disconnect coolant bypass and heater hoses at the water pump. Disconnect radiator upper hose at thermostat housing.

8. Disconnect the coil wire from distributor cap and remove cap with secondary wires attached. Remove the distributor hold-down clamp and lift distributor out of the front cover.

9. Raise the vehicle and support safely.

10. Remove the crankshaft damper and pulley.

NOTE: If the crankshaft pulley and vibration damper have to be separated, mark the damper and pulley so that they may be reassembled in the same relative position. This is important as the damper and pulley are initially balanced as a unit. If the crankshaft damper is being replaced, check if the original damper has

balance pins installed. If so, new balance pins (E0SZ-6A328-A or equivalent) must be installed on the new damper in the same position as the original damper. The crankshaft pulley (new or original) must also be installed in original installation position.

11. Remove the oil filter, disconnect the radiator lower hose at the water pump and remove the oil pan.

12. Lower the vehicle.

13. Remove the front cover attaching bolts.

———————— CAUTION ————————

Do not forget to remove the cover attaching bolt located behind the oil filter adapter. The front cover will break if pried upon if all attaching bolts are not removed.

—————————————————————————

14. Remove the ignition timing indicator.

15. Remove the front cover and water pump as an assembly. Remove the cover gasket and discard.

16. Remove the camshaft bolt and washer from end of the camshaft. Remove the distributor drive gear.

17. Remove the camshaft sprocket, crankshaft sprocket and timing chain.

NOTE: If the crankshaft is difficult to remove, the sprocket may be pryed from the shaft by using 2 suitable prying tools on both sides of the sprocket.

To install:

18. Lightly oil all bolt and stud threads before installation. Clean all gasket surfaces on the front cover, cylinder block and fuel pump. If reusing the front cover, replace crankshaft front oil seal.

19. Rotate the crankshaft as necessary to position piston No. 1 at TDC.

20. Lubricate timing chain with clean engine oil. Install the camshaft sprocket, crankshaft sprocket and timing chain. Make certain the timing marks are positioned across from each other.

21. Install the distributor drive gear.

22. Install the washer and bolt at end of camshaft and torque to 54–67 ft. lbs.

23. Lubricate the crankshaft front oil seal with clean engine oil.

24. Position a new cover gasket on the cylinder block and install the front cover/water pump assembly using dowels for proper alignment. A suitable contact adhesive (No. D7AZ-19B508-A or equivalent) is recommended to hold the gasket in position while the front cover is installed.

25. Complete the installation of the remaining components by reversing the removal procedure. Torque the front cover retaining bolts to 15–22 ft.

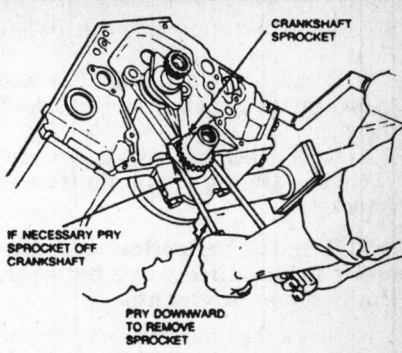

Removing the crankshaft sprocket (typical)

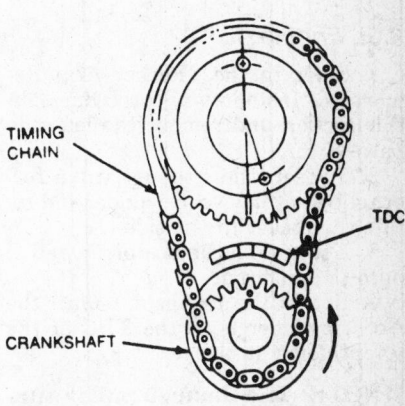

Checking the slack of the timing chain

lbs. (20–30 Nm), crankshaft damper bolt to 104–132 ft. lbs. (140–180 Nm), crankshaft pulley to 19–28 ft. lbs. (26–28 Nm) and the fan/clutch assembly attaching bolts to 19–28 ft. lbs. (26–28 Nm).

26. Connect battery ground cable. Fill the crankcase and cooling system to the proper level.

27. Start the engine and check for leaks.

28. Check the ignition timing and curb idle speed, adjust as required.

29. Install the air cleaner assembly and air intake duct.

ADJUSTMENT

NOTE: No adjustments of the timing chain are necessary or possible. The ONLY check to be make is the deflection measurement. If the deflection is beyond specifications, replace the timing chain, the sprockets and/or the tensioners.

2.5L Engine

1. To check the timing chain deflection, first rotate the crankshaft in the counterclockwise direction (view from the front) to take up the slack.

2. Mark a reference point on the block, then measure the mid-section

distance to the timing chain on the left side.

3. Rotate the crankshaft clockwise to take up the slack on the right side of the chain.

4. If the deflection exceeds 1/2 in., replace the timing chain and/or the sprockets.

NOTE: The deflection measurement is the difference between the two measurements.

5. Check the timing chain tensioner blade for wear depth. If the wear depth exceeds specification, replace the tensioner.

3.0L Engine

1. Refer to the "Rocker Arm Removal & Installation" procedures in this section and remove the left side valve cover.

2. Loosen the exhaust valve fulcrum bolt of the No. 5 cylinder and rotate the rocker to one side.

3. Using a dial indicator, install it onto the pushrod.

4. Rotate the crankshaft until the No. 1 cylinder is at the TDC of the compression stroke.

NOTE: The damper pulley timing mark should be on the TDC of the timing plate. This operation will take the slack from the right side of the timing chain.

5. Using the dial indicator, set the dial on zero.

6. Slowly turn the crankshaft counterclockwise until the slightest movement on the dial indicator is observed, then inspect the position of the damper pulley with the timing plate.

7. If the reading on the timing plate exceeds 6 degrees, replace the timing chain and the sprockets.

3.8L Engine

1. Remove the right side rocker arm cover by performing the following:

a. Disconnect and label the spark plug wires.

b. Remove the spark plug routing clips from the rocker arm cover mounting studs.

c. Position the air cleaner assembly to the side and remove the PCV valve.

d. Remove the rocker arm cover attaching screws and the cover with cover gasket from the cylinder head.

2. Loosen the No. 3 exhaust rocker arm and push to the side.

3. Install a dial indicator on the end of the push rod.

4. Turn the crankshaft clockwise until, the No. 1 piston is at TDC. The damper pulley timing mark should be on the TDC of the timing plate. This

will remove the slack from the right side of the timing chain.

5. Zero the dial indicator.

6. Slowly turn the crankshaft counterclockwise until the slightest movement on the dial indicator is observed, then inspect the position of the damper pulley with the timing plate.

7. If the reading on the timing plate exceeds 6 degrees, replace the timing chain and the sprockets.

Camshaft

REMOVAL & INSTALLATION

2.5L Engine

1. Remove the engine and place it on a workstand.

2. Remove the timing chain with the camshaft sprocket.

3. Remove the cylinder head.

4. Using a magnet, remove the hydraulic tappets and keep them in order so that they can be installed in their original positions. If the tappets are stuck in the bores by excessive varnish, etc., use a suitable claw type puller to remove the tappets.

5. Loosen and remove the drive belt. Remove the fan and pulley with a suitable puller (No. T77F–4220–B1 or equivalent).

6. Remove the oil pan. Remove the cylinder front cover and gasket.

7. To check the camshaft end play, install the camshaft sprocket to the camshaft and perform the following procedures:

a. Push the camshaft toward the rear of the engine and install a dial indicator tool No. 4201-C, so that the indicator point is on the camshaft sprocket mounting bolt.

b. Zero the dial indicator. Position a a small pry bar between the camshaft sprocket and the block.

c. Pull the camshaft forward and release it. Compare the dial indicator reading with the camshaft end play specification of 0.009 in. (0.229mm).

d. If the camshaft end play is over the amount specified, replace the thrust plate.

8. Remove the camshaft sprocket and the camshaft thrust plate.

9. Carefully remove the camshaft by pulling it toward the front of the engine. Use caution to avoid damaging the bearings, journals and lobes.

10. Using a putty knife, clean the gasket mounting surfaces.

11. Clean the oil pump inlet tube screen, the oil pan and the cylinder block gasket surfaces. Prime the oil pump by filling the inlet opening with oil and rotate the pump shaft until oil emerges from the outlet tube. Install

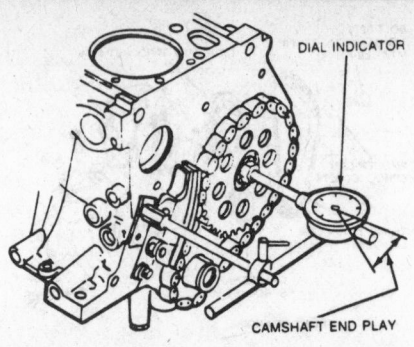

Using a dial micrometer to check the camshaft end play

the oil pump, the oil pump inlet tube screen and the oil pan.

12. To install, use new gaskets, sealant, lubricate the internal parts with SAE 50 weight oil and reverse the removal procedures. Torque the camshaft thrust plate bolts to 6–9 ft. lbs. (8–12 Nm), the camshaft sprocket-to-camshaft bolt to 41–56 ft. lbs. (55–75 Nm), the front cover-to-engine bolts to 6–9 ft. lbs. (8–12 Nm), the damper pulley-to-crankshaft bolt to 140–170 ft. lbs. (190–230 Nm), the cylinder head bolts-to-engine bolts (in 2 steps) to 70–76 ft. lbs. (95–103 Nm) and the oil pan-to-engine bolts to 15–23 ft. lbs. (20–30 Nm). Adjust the valves. Refill the cooling system and the crankcase. Start the engine and check for leaks. Check and/or adjust the ignition timing and the engine idle speed.

3.0L Engine

1. Remove the engine and place it on a workstand.

2. Ensure the cooling system, the fuel system and the crankcase have been drained.

3. Remove the idler pulley and bracket assembly. Remove the drive and accessory belts. Remove the water pump.

4. Remove the crankshaft pulley and damper. Remove the lower radiator hose. Remove the oil pan-to-front cover bolts, the front cover-to-engine bolts and the front cover from the engine.

5. Label and remove the spark plug wires and the rocker arm covers. Loosen the rocker arm fulcrum nuts and turn them to the side to expose the pushrods. Remove the pushrods and keep them in their original position.

6. Using a magnet, remove the hydraulic tappets and keep them in order so that they can be installed in their original positions. If the tappets are stuck in the bores by excessive varnish, use the Hydraulic Tappet Puller tool No. T70L-6500-A, to remove the tappets.

7. To check the camshaft end play, perform the following procedures:

a. Push the camshaft toward the rear of the engine and install a Dial Indicator tool No. 4201-C, so that the indicator point is on the camshaft sprocket bolt. Zero the dial indicator.

b. Using a medium pry bar, position it between the camshaft sprocket and the block.

NOTE: When applying pressure to the camshaft sprocket, be careful not to break the powdered metal camshaft sprocket.

c. Pry the camshaft forward and release it. Compare the dial indicator reading with the camshaft end play specification of 0.009 in.

d. If the camshaft end play is over the amount specified, replace the thrust plate.

8. Remove the timing chain and sprockets.

9. Remove the camshaft thrust plate. Carefully remove the camshaft by pulling it toward the front of the engine. Remove it slowly to avoid damaging the bearings, journals and lobes.

10. Using a putty knife, clean the gasket mounting surfaces.

11. To install, use new gaskets, sealant, lubricate the internal parts with SAE 50 weight oil and reverse the removal procedures. Torque the camshaft thrust plate-to-engine bolts to 6–8 ft. lbs. (8–12 Nm), the front cover-to-engine bolts to 15–22 ft. lbs. (20–30 Nm), the water pump-to-front cover bolts to 6–8 ft. lbs. (8–12 Nm), the crankshaft damper-to-crankshaft bolt to 141–169 ft. lbs. (190–230 Nm) and the crankshaft pulley-to-damper bolts to 20–28 ft. lbs. (26–38 Nm). Refill the cooling system and the crankcase. Start the engine and check for leaks. Check and/or adjust the ignition timing and the engine idle speed.

3.8L Engine

NOTE: The camshaft on these vehicles can be removed through the front of the engine with the engine in place.

1. Disconnect the negative battery cable. Drain the cooling system and crankcase.

2. Remove the radiator by performing the following:

a. Remove the overflow tube and detach the coolant recovery bottle from the radiator.

b. Remove the 2 shroud upper attaching screws and lift the shroud from the retaining clips.

c. Disconnect the cooling fan wires and remove the fan and shroud assembly from the vehicle.

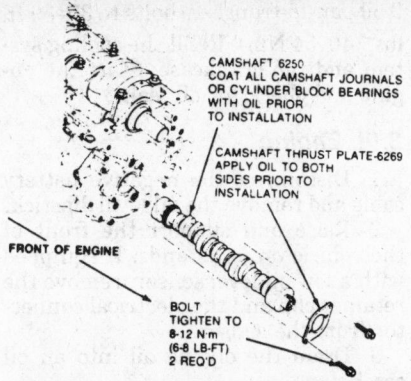

CAMSHAFT 6250 COAT ALL CAMSHAFT JOURNALS OR CYLINDER BLOCK BEARINGS WITH OIL PRIOR TO INSTALLATION

CAMSHAFT THRUST PLATE-6269 APPLY OIL TO BOTH SIDES PRIOR TO INSTALLATION

FRONT OF ENGINE

BOLT TIGHTEN TO 8-12 N·m (6-8 LB-FT) 2 REQ'D

Exploded view of the camshaft—3.0L engine

d. On vehicles with automatic transaxles, disconnect the transaxle oil cooling lines with cooler line disconnect tool No. T82L–9500–AH or equivalent.

e. Remove the radiator upper attaching screws. Tilt the radiator towards the rear of the engine about an inch and lift upward to clear the radiator support.

3. On vehicles equipped with air conditioning, carefully and properly evacuate the the air conditioning system. Disconnect the refrgerant lines from the right hand side of the radiator by undoing the spring lock couplings. Unbolt and remove the condenser from the radiator support.

4. Remove the grill.

5. Remove the upper and lower intake manifolds.

6. Remove the tappets.

7. Remove the front timing cover and timing chain.

8. Withdraw the camshaft through the front of the engine being careful

not to damage the the bearing surfaces.

To install:

9. Lubricate the cam lobes, thrust plate and bearing surfaces with a suitable heavy engine oil prior to installation.

10. Insert the camshaft into the front of the engine being careful not to damage the bearing surfaces.

11. Install the front cover and timing chain.

12. Install the oil pan.

12. Install the tappets.

13. Install the intake manifolds.

15. Install the grille.

16. Complete the installation of the condenser (if removed) and radiator by reversing the removal procedure.

17. Fill the cooling system and crankcase to the proper level and connect the negative battery cable.

18. Start the engine. Check and adjust the ignition timing and engine idle speed as necessary. Check for leaks of any kind.

Piston And Connecting Rod

POSITIONING

For all piston and connecting rod overhaul procedures, please refer to "Engine Rebuilding" in the Unit Repair section.

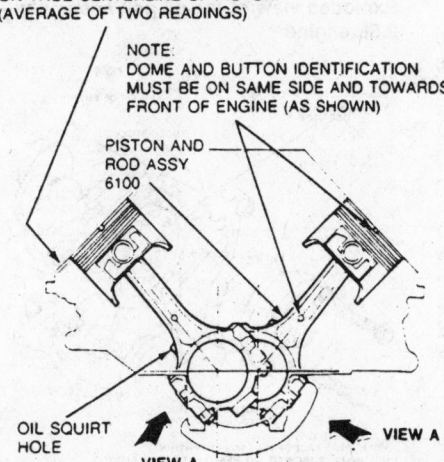

NOTE: PISTON TO DECK CLEARANCE TO BE 0.27 BELOW DECK TO 0.25 ABOVE DECK WHEN MEASURED AT PISTON T.D.C. PARALLEL TO CRANKSHAFT ON TRUE CENTERLINE OF PISTON. (AVERAGE OF TWO READINGS)

NOTE: DOME AND BUTTON IDENTIFICATION MUST BE ON SAME SIDE AND TOWARDS FRONT OF ENGINE (AS SHOWN)

PISTON AND ROD ASSY 6100

OIL SQUIRT HOLE

VIEW A

VIEW A

3.8L engine piston and rod assembly

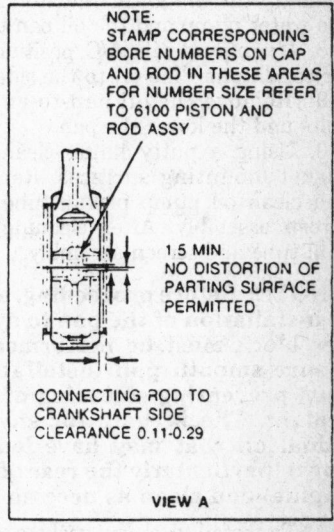

NOTE: STAMP CORRESPONDING BORE NUMBERS ON CAP AND ROD IN THESE AREAS FOR NUMBER SIZE REFER TO 6100 PISTON AND ROD ASSY

1.5 MIN. NO DISTORTION OF PARTING SURFACE PERMITTED

CONNECTING ROD TO CRANKSHAFT SIDE CLEARANCE 0.11-0.29

VIEW A

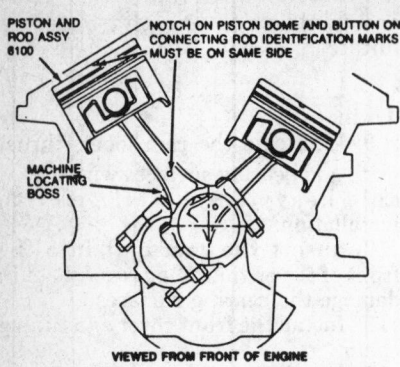

3.0L engine piston and rod assembly

ENGINE LUBRICATION

Oil Pan

REMOVAL & INSTALLATION

2.5L Engine

1. Disconnect negative ground cable at battery.
2. Raise and support the front of the vehicle of jackstands.
3. Remove the crankcase oil plug and drain the fluid. Remove the lower radiator hose and drain the cooling system.
4. If equipped with a manual transaxle, remove the roll restrictor.
5. Disconnect the starter electrical connectors and the starter.
6. Disconnect the exhaust pipe from the oil pan.
7. Remove the engine coolant tube located near the lower radiator hose, the water pump and the oil pan tabs.
8. If equipped with A/C, position the air conditioner line off to the side.
9. Remove the oil pan-to-engine bolts and the lower the pan.
10. Using a putty knife, clean the gasket mounting surfaces. Remove and clean oil pump pickup tube and screen assembly. After cleaning, install tube and screen assembly.

NOTE: Before proceeding, a trial installation of the pan to cylinder block must be performed to insure smooth pan installation, thus preventing smearing of the sealant. Check again for any residual oil that may have leaked down (particularly the rear of the engine) and clean as necessary.

11. To install, use new gaskets, sealant and reverse the removal procedures. Torque the oil pan-to-engine bolts to 6–9 ft. lbs. (8–12 Nm) and the

2 oil pan-to-transaxle bolts to 30–39 ft. lbs. (40–54 Nm). Refill the cooling system and the crankcase. Start the engine and check for oil leaks.

3.0L Engine

1. Disconnect the negative battery cable and remove the oil level dipstick.
2. Raise and support the front of the vehicle on jackstands. If equipped with a low oil level sensor, remove the retainer clip and the electrical connector from the sensor.
3. Drain the engine oil into an oil catch pan.
4. Disconnect the electrical connectors from the starter and remove the starter.

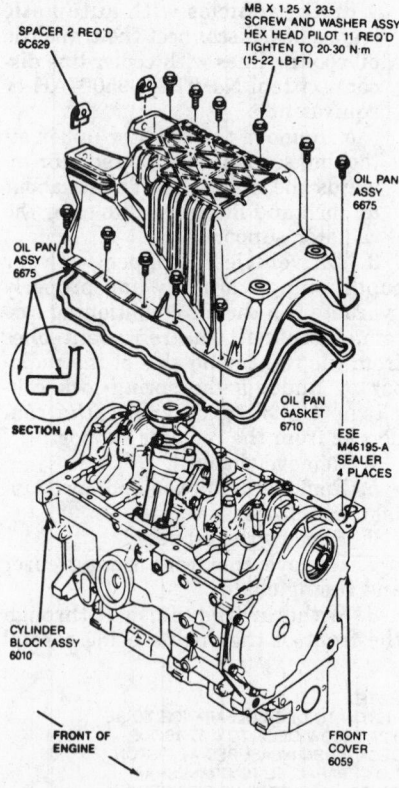

Exploded view of the oil pan assembly— 2.5L engine

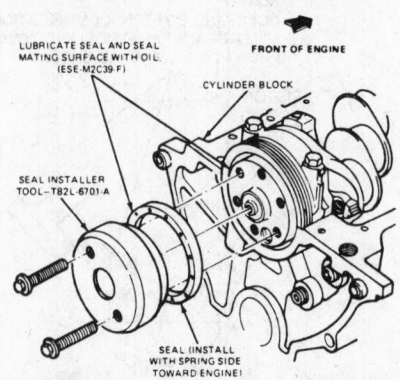

Installing the rear main oil seal—typical

5. In the exhaust manifold, disconnect the electrical connector from the oxygen sensor.
6. Remove the catalytic converter and the exhaust pipe assembly.
7. From the torque converter housing, remove the lower engine/flywheel dust cover.
8. Remove the oil pan-to-engine mounting bolts and lower the pan from the engine.
9. Using a putty knife, clean the gasket mounting surfaces.
10. To install, use new gaskets, sealant and reverse the removal procedures. Torque the oil pan-to-engine bolts to 6–8 ft. lbs. (8–12 Nm). Refill the cooling system and the crankcase. Start the engine and check for leaks.

3.8L Engine

1. Disconnect the negative battery cable.
2. Raise the vehicle and support safely.
3. Drain the crankcase into a suitable drain pan and remove the oil filter element.
4. Remove the converter assembly, starter motor and converter housing cover.
5. Remove the pan flange bolts and lower the oil pan.
6. Thoroughly clean the gasket surfaces on cylinder block, oil pan and oil pickup tube.

NOTE: Due to the number of locations that sealant is applied, a trial installation of the oil pan to cylinder block must be performed. Ensure enough clearance has been provided to allow oil pan to be installed without sealant being scraped off when pan is positioned under engine.

8. Apply a bead of silicone rubber sealer No. D6AZ–19562–A or equivalent to the oil pan flange. Also apply a bead of sealer to the front cover/cylinder block joint and fill the grooves on both sides of the rear main seal cap.

NOTE: When using silicone rubber sealer, assembly must occur within 15 minutes after sealer application. After this time, the sealer may start to harden and its sealing effectiveness may be reduced.

9. Install the oil pan and secure to the block with the attaching screws. Torque the screws to 7–9 ft. lbs.
10. Install a new oil filter element. Install the converter housing cover and starter motor.
11. Install the converter assembly and lower the vehicle.
12. Fill the crankcase and connect the negative battery cable.

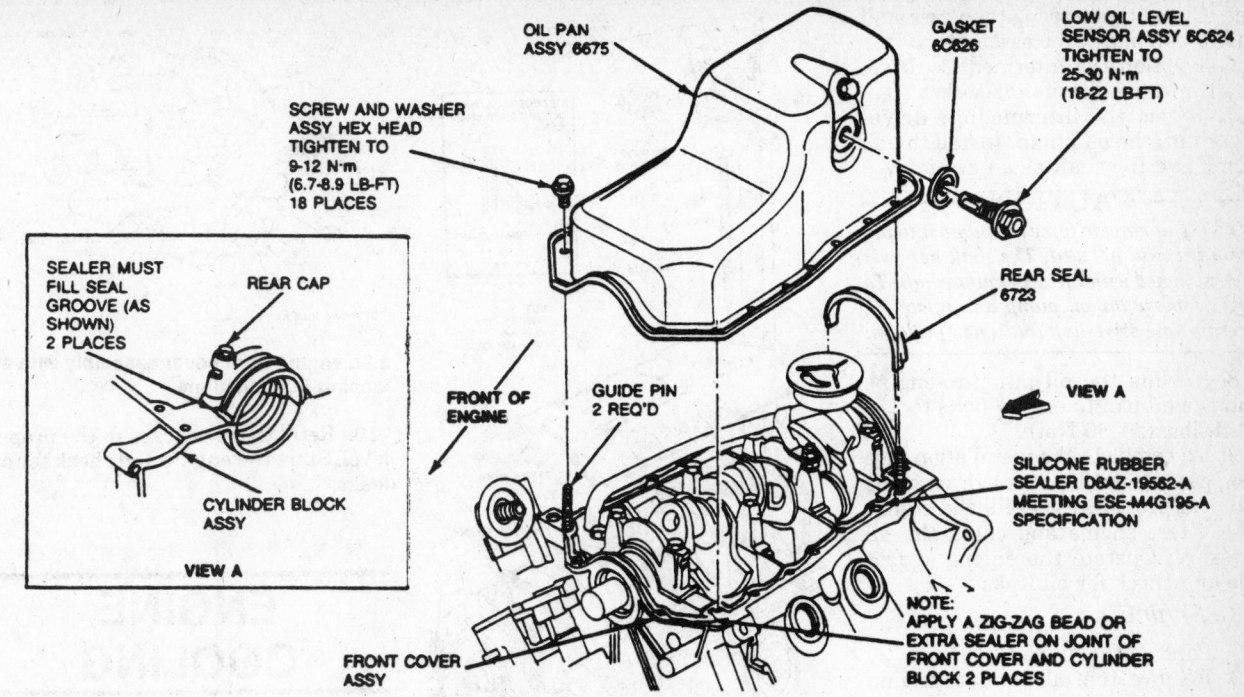

View of the oil pan assembly—3.8L engine

13. Start the engine and check for leaks.

Rear Main Bearing Oil Seal

REMOVAL & INSTALLATION

2.5L and 3.0L Engine

1. Remove the transaxle from the vehicle.

2. If equipped with a MTX, remove the pressure plate, the clutch and the flywheel. If equipped with an ATX, remove the flexplate.

3. With a suitable puncturing tool, punch a hole into the seal metal surface between the seal lip and the block.

4. Using the threaded end of slide hammer tool No. T77L-9533-B, screw it into the hole in the seal. Using a slide hammer, pull the seal from the block.

NOTE: Use caution to avoid damaging the oil seal surface.

5. Inspect the crankshaft seal area for damage which may cause the seal to leak. If damage is evident, service or replace the crankshaft as necessary.

6. Coat the crankshaft seal area and the seal lip with engine oil.

7. Using the seal installer tool No. T82L-6701-A, or equivalent, press the new seal into the block.

NOTE: When using the installer tool, tighten the bolts evenly so that the seal is straight and seats without misalignment.

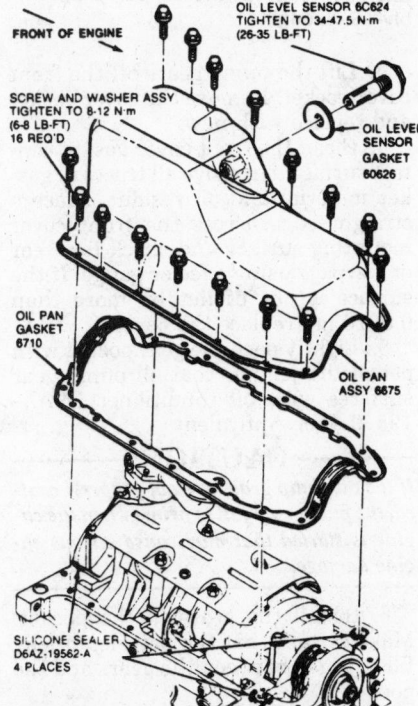

Exploded view of the oil pan assembly—3.0L engine

8. To complete the installation, reverse the removal procedures. Torque the flywheel-to-crankshaft bolts to 54–64 ft. lbs. (73–87 Nm); the pressure plate-to-flywheel bolts to 12–24 ft. lbs. (17–32 Nm); the torque convertor-to-flexplate bolts to 23–39 ft. lbs. (31–53 Nm); the transaxle-to-engine bolts to 25–33 ft. lbs. (34–45 Nm).

3.8L Engine

NOTE: A one-piece crankshaft rear main oil seal is used on this engine.

1. With a suitable puncturing tool, punch one hole into the seal metal surface between lip and block. Screw in the threaded end of jet plug remover No. T77L-9553-B or equivalent. Remove the seal and replace with new. Use caution to avoid scratching or damaging oil seal surface.

2. Apply the new seal to mating edges.

3. Position the seal on a rear main seal installer No. T82L-6701-A or equivalent. Position tool and seal to rear of engine. Alternate bolt tightening to seat the seal properly. Engine flywheel bolts may be used if necessary.

Oil Pump

REMOVAL & INSTALLATION

2.5L Engine

1. Remove the oil pan.

2. Remove oil pump-to-engine bolts, the oil pump and the intermediate driveshaft.

3. Using a putty knife, clean the gasket mounting surfaces.

4. Prime the oil pump by filling the inlet port with engine oil. Rotate the pump shaft until oil flows from the outlet port.

5. If the screen and cover assembly have been removed, replace the gas-

ket. Clean the screen, then reinstall the screen and cover assembly.

6. Position the intermediate driveshaft into the distributor socket.

7. Insert the intermediate driveshaft into the oil pump. Install the oil pump and the shaft as an assembly.

— CAUTION —

DO NOT attempt to force the pump into position if it will not seat. The shaft hex may be misaligned with the distributor shaft. To align, remove the oil pump and rotate the intermediate driveshaft into a new position.

8. Torque the oil pump-to-engine and the oil pan-to-engine bolts to 15–23 ft. lbs. (20–30 Nm).

9. To complete the installation, use new gaskets, sealant and reverse the removal procedures. Refill the crankcase. Start engine and check the oil pressure. Operate the engine at fast idle and check for oil leaks.

3.0L Engine

1. Remove the oil pan.

2. Remove the oil pump-to-engine bolts, then lift the pump from the engine and withdraw the oil pump driveshaft.

3. Using a putty knife, clean the gasket mounting surfaces.

4. Prime the oil pump by filling either the inlet or the outlet port with engine oil. Rotate the pump shaft to distribute the oil within the oil pump body.

5. Insert the oil pump driveshaft into the pump with the retainer end facing inward. Place the oil pump in the proper position with a new gasket and install the mounting bolts.

6. Torque the oil pump-to-engine bolts to 30–40 ft. lbs. (40–55 Nm). Clean and install the oil pump inlet tube and screen assembly with a new gasket.

7. To complete the installation, use new gaskets, sealant and reverse the removal procedures. Torque the oil pan-to-engine bolts to 6–8 ft. lbs. (8–12 Nm). Refill the crankcase to the proper level with recommended engine oil. Start the engine and check the oil pressure. Operate the engine at fast idle and check for oil leaks.

3.8L Engine

NOTE: The oil pump, oil pressure relief valve and drive intermediate shaft are contained in the front cover assembly.

1. Remove the front cover.

— CAUTION —

When removing the front cover attaching bolts, do not overlook the cover attaching bolt located behind the oil filter adapter. The front cover will break when pried upon if all attaching bolts are not removed.

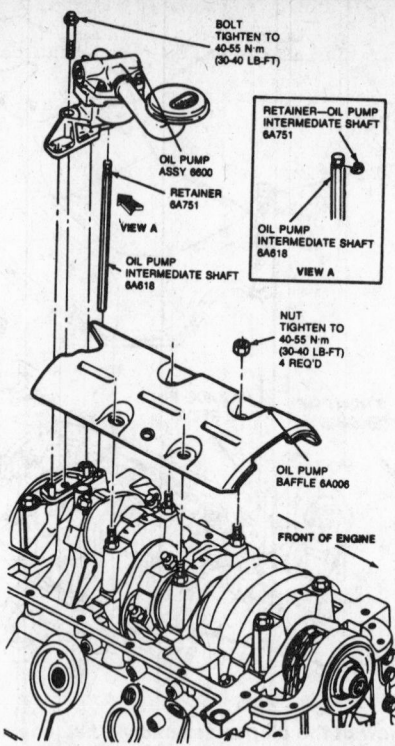

Exploded view of the oil pump assembly—3.0L engine

3. Lift the pump gears off the front cover pocket. Remove the cover gasket and replace with new.

4. Clean the front cover gasket contact surface to remove all traces of gasket material and oil residue. Place a straight edge across the front cover mounting surface and check for wear or warpage using a feeler gauge. If the surface is out of flat by more than 0.0016 in., replace the cover.

5. Lightly pack the gear pocket with petroleum jelly or coat all pump gear surfaces with oil conditioner D9AZ–19579–C or equivalent.

— CAUTION —

If the oil pump gears are not properly coated, the pump may fail to prime when the engine is started that may cause serious engine damage.

6. Install the gears in the pocket. Make certain that the petroleum jelly fills the gap between the gears and the pocket.

7. Position the cover gasket and install the front cover. Torque the cover retaining bolts to 18–22 ft. lbs.

8. Replace the crankshaft oil seal. Coat the new seal with clean engine oil prior to installation.

9. Complete the installation of the front cover by reversing the removal procedure using new gaskets and sealer where required. Torque the front cover mounting bolts to 15–22 ft. lbs. (20–30 Nm) and the oil pan flange bolts to 7–9 ft. lbs. (9–12 Nm).

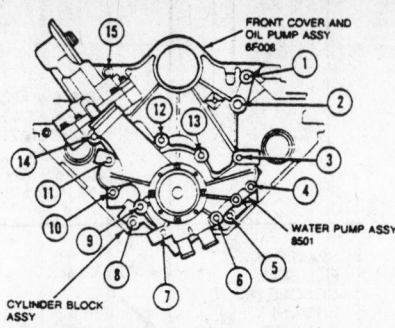

3.8L engine front cover assembly with attaching bolt locations.

10. Refill the crankcase to the proper level. Start the engine and check for oil leaks.

ENGINE COOLING

NOTE: These vehicles use aluminum components that require a special corrosion inhibitor coolant formulation to avoid radiator damage. The cooling system should be filled with a 50/50 mix of water and antifreeze, with the addition of 2 Cooling System Protector Pellets No. D9AZ-19558-A.

Radiator

REMOVAL & INSTALLATION

1. Disconnect the negative battery cable. Place a fluid catch pan under the radiator. Open the radiator draincock and remove the radiator cap, then drain the cooling system.

NOTE: If reusing the cooling fluid, be sure to keep it dirt free.

2. Remove the overflow hose from the radiator and the coolant tank and detach it from the radiator.

3. Remove the upper shroud screws, lift the shroud from the lower retaining clips and position it over the fan.

4. Disconnect the electric cooling fan motor wires and remove the fan and shroud assembly from the vehicle.

5. Loosen the upper/lower radiator hose clamps, then using a twisting motion, remove the hoses from the radiator.

5. If equipped with an ATX, use the Cooler Line Disconnect tool No. T82L-9500-AH to disconnect the oil cooling lines from the radiator. Be sure to plug the cooling lines to prevent fluid draining from the transaxle.

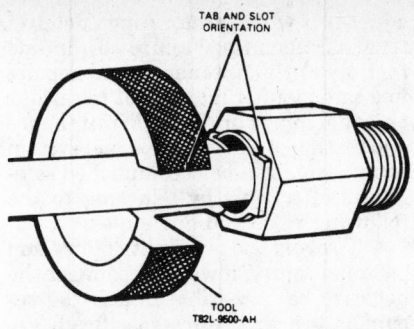

Using tool to remove and replace the transaxle oil cooler lines at the radiator

6. Remove the upper radiator-to-vehicle screws, then tilt the radiator rearward (approx. 1 inch), lift it upward (clearing the support and the fan).

7. Remove the radiator lower support rubber pads. If the pads are damaged, replace with new.

8. To install, reverse the removal procedures. Torque the upper radiator-to-support bolts to 13–20 ft. lbs. (17–27 Nm), the upper shroud-to-radiator screws to 4–6 ft. lbs. (5.5–8 Nm) and the hose clamps to 20–30 inch lbs. (2.25–3.38 Nm).

NOTE: When installing the radiator, position the molded pins (at the bottom of nylon end tanks) in the slotted holes of the lower support rubber pads.

9. Refill the cooling system (to a level of 1½ in. below the radiator filler neck). Connect the negative battery cable, start the engine, operate for 15 minutes and check for leaks. Check the coolant level and add as required.

NOTE: If replacing the cooling fluid, use a 50/50 mixture of water and anti-freeze. Be sure to add 2 Cooling System Protector Pellets No. D9AZ-19558-A to the radiator.

Water Pump

REMOVAL & INSTALLATION

2.5L ENGINE

1. Open the hood, place protection aprons on the fenders and disconnect the negative battery cable.

2. Remove the radiator cap and position a drain pan under the radiator.

3. Raise and support the front of the vehicle on jackstands. Remove the lower radiator hose from the radiator and drain the coolant into the drain pan.

4. Remove the water pump inlet tube. Loosen the belt tensioner by inserting a ½ inch flex handle in the square hole of the tensioner, then ro-

tate the tensioner counterclockwise and remove the drive belt from the vehicle.

5. Disconnect the heater hose from the water pump. Remove the 3 water pump-to-engine block bolts and separate the pump from the engine.

6. Using a putty knife, clean the gasket mounting surfaces.

7. To install, use a new gasket, sealant and reverse the removal procedures. Torque the water pump-to-engine bolts to 15–22 ft. lbs. (20–30 Nm). Check and/or adjust the drive belt tension. Refill the cooling system, start the engine and allow to reach normal operating temperature. Check for leaks and check the coolant level. Add coolant as required.

3.0L and 3.8L Engines

1. Disconnect the negative battery cable and place a suitable drain pan under the radiator draincock.

NOTE: Drain the system with the engine cool and the heater temperature control set at the maximum heat position. Attach a ⅜ in. hose to the drain cock so as to direct the coolant into the drain pan.

2. Remove the radiator cap, open the drain cock on the radiator and drain the cooling system.

3. Loosen the accessory drive belt idler pulley and remove the drive belts.

4. Remove the idler pulley bracket-to-engine nuts/bolt. Disconnect the heater hose from the water pump.

5. Remove the 4 pulley-to-pump hub bolts. The pulley will remain loose on the hub due to the insufficient clearance between the inner fender and the water pump.

6. Remove the water pump-to-engine bolts (there are 11 bolts in total),

then lift the water pump and pulley out of the vehicle.

7. Using a putty knife, clean the water pump and front cover gasket contact surfaces.

8. To install, use a new gasket, sealant and reverse the removal procedures. Torque the water pump-to-engine bolts to 15–22 ft. lbs. (20–30 Nm) for 8mm and to 6–8 ft. lbs. (8–12 Nm) for 6mm and the water pump pulley-to-water pump bolts to 15–22 ft. lbs. (20–30 Nm); be sure to apply a suitable thread sealer to the bolts before installing them. Check and/or adjust the drive belt tension. Refill the cooling system, start the engine and check for leaks.

Thermostat

The thermostat is located in the water outlet housing at the top rear of the engine.

REMOVAL & INSTALLATION

1. Raise the hood and place protective aprons on the fenders.

2. Disconnect the negative battery cable.

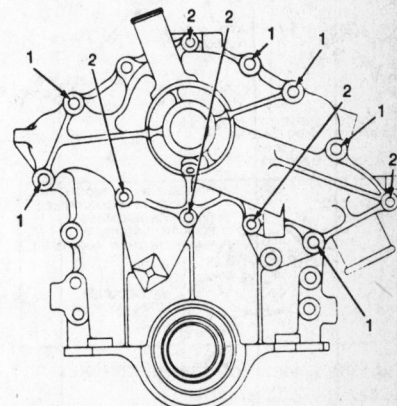

Position of the water pump bolts on the 3.0L engine—one M8 and two M6

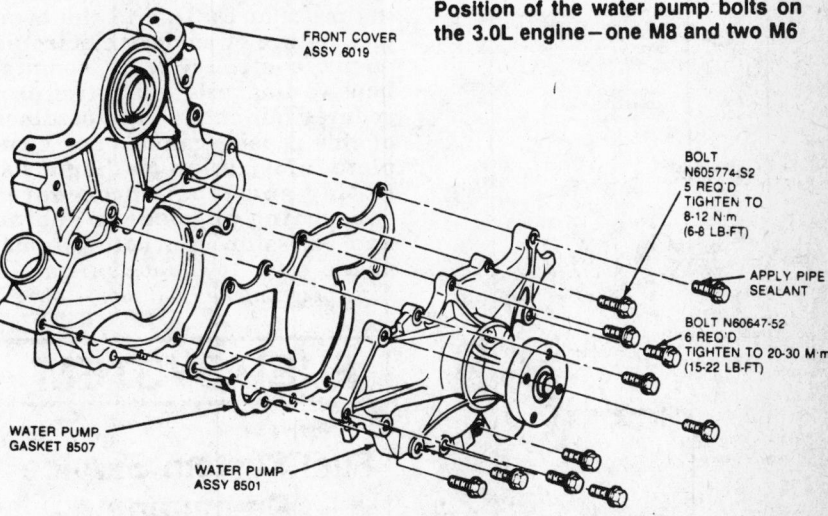

Exploded view of the water pump assembly—3.0L engine

3. Position a drain pan under the radiator and remove the radiator cap. Attach a suitable length of hose to the drain tube and open the draincock. Drain the radiator to a level below the water outlet connection.

4. On the 2.5L engine, remove the vent plug from the water outlet housing.

5. Loosen the upper hose clamp at the radiator. Remove the water outlet housing-to-engine bolts, lift the outlet clear of the engine and remove the thermostat from the housing. Do not pry on the housing to separate.

6. Using a putty knife, clean the gasket mounting surfaces. Ensure the water oultlet connection pocket and air vent passage are free from rust. On

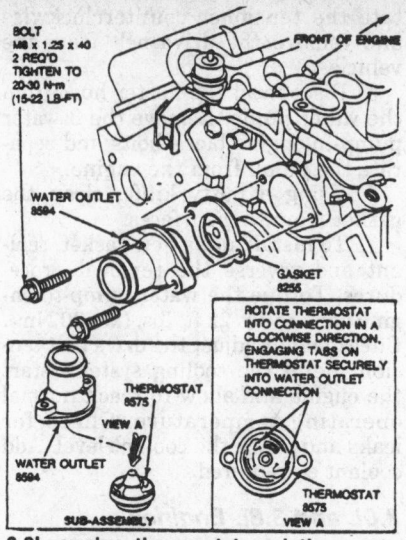

3.8L engine thermostat and thermostat housing assembly

the 2.5L engine, clean the vent plug and gasket.

7. To install, use a new gasket, sealant, thermostat and reverse the removal procedures. Torque the water outlet housing-to-engine bolts to 12–18 ft. lbs. (16–24 Nm) for 2.5L engine and 6–8 ft. lbs. (8–12 Nm) for 3.0L engine and 15–22 ft. lbs (20–30 Nm) on 3.8L engine.

NOTE: When installing the thermostat, rotate it clockwise into the water outlet housing. On the 3.0L engine, position the thermostat ball check valve at the top.

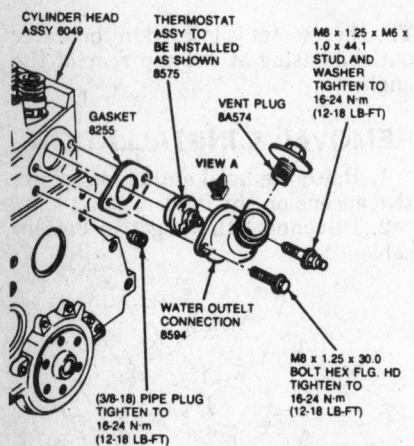

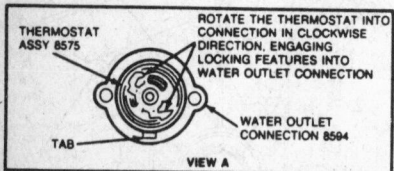

Exploded view of the thermostat and housing—2.5L engine

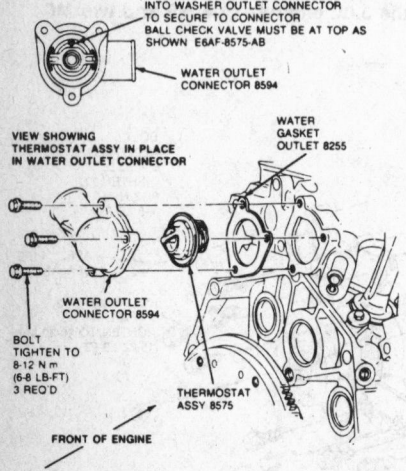

Exploded view of the thermostat and housing—3.0L engine

EMISSION CONTROLS

Please refer to the "Emission Control" Unit Repair section for system maintenance and servicing procedures. Due to the complex nature of modern electronic engine control systems, comprehensive diagnosis and testing procedures fall outside the confines of this repair manual. For complete information on diagnosis, testing and repair procedures concerning all modern engine and emission control systems, please refer to *Chilton's Guide To Electronic Engine Controls*.

FUEL SYSTEM

Fuel System Service Precaution

Safety is the most important factor to adhere to when preforming fuel system maintenance. Failure to conduct fuel system maintenance and repairs in a safe manner may result in serious personal injury or death. Maintenance and testing of the vehicle's fuel system components can be accomplished safely and effectively by adhering to the following rules and guidelines.

• To avoid the possibility of fire and personal injury, always disconnect the negative battery cable unless the repair or test procedure specifically requires that battery voltage be applied.

• Always relieve the fuel system pressure prior to disconnecting any fuel system component (injector, fuel rail, pressure regulator, ect...), fitting or fuel line connection. Exercise extreme caution whenever relieving fuel system pressure to avoid exposing skin, face and eyes to fuel spray. Please be advised that fuel under pressure may penetrate the skin or any part of the body that it comes in contact with.

• Always place a shop towel or cloth around the fitting or connection prior to loosening to absorb any excess fuel due to spillage. Ensure that all fuel spillage (should it occur) is quickly removed from engine surfaces. Ensure that all fuel soaked cloths or towels are deposited into a suitable waste container.

• Always have a properly charged fire extinguisher in the vincinity of the work area and always ensure work areas are adequately ventilated.

• Do not allow fuel spray or fuel vapors to come in contact with spark or open flame.

• Always use a backup wrench when loosening and tightening fuel line connection fittings. This will prevent unnecessary stress and torsion to fuel line piping. Always follow the proper torque specifications.

• Always replace worn fuel fitting O-rings with new. Do not substitute fuel hose or equivalent where fuel pipe is installed.

• Always use common sense.

RELIEVING FUEL SYSTEM PRESSURE

Central Fuel Injection (CFI) – 2.5L Engine

1. On the left side of the luggage compartment, disconnect the electrical connector from the inertia switch.

2. Using the ignition switch, crank the engine for 15 seconds to reduce the pressure in the fuel system.

3. To pressurize the fuel system, perform the following procedures:

  a. Reconnect the electrical connector to the inertia switch.

b. Start the engine and check for leaks.

Electronic Fuel Injection (EFI) – 3.0L and 3.8L Engines

1. Remove the fuel tank cap and the air filter.

2. Disconnect the negative battery cable.

3. Using the Fuel Pressure Gauge tool No. T80L-9974-A, connect it to the pressure relief valve (remove the valve cap) on the fuel injection manifold.

4. Open the pressure relief valve and reduce the fuel pressure.

5. To pressurize the fuel system, perform the following:

   a. Tighten the pressure relief valve and remove the pressure gauge.

   b. Reinstall the negative battery cable.

   c. Start the engine and check for fuel leaks. Correct all fuel leaks immediately.

Fuel Filter

The fuel filter is mounted under the vehicle, next to the right front corner of the fuel tank.

REMOVAL & INSTALLATION

1. Relieve the pressure in the fuel system.

2. At the fuel filter bracket, loosen the worm gear clamp.

3. Using a pair of soft face vise-grips or equivalent, clamp or crimp the fuel line to prevent fuel from siphoning from the fuel tank.

4. Remove the clamps and the fuel lines from the fuel filter.

5. Slide the fuel filter from the bracket retaining clamp.

6. To install, use a new filter (position it with the arrow facing forward and downward to ensure proper flow) and reverse the removal procedures. Torque the fuel filter clamp to 15–25 inch lbs. (1.7–2.8 Nm).

Electric Fuel Pump

The electric fuel pump is located in the fuel tank and is a part of the fuel gauge sending unit.

REMOVAL & INSTALLATION

1. Position the vehicle on a level surface.

2. Relieve the pressure in the fuel system.

3. Remove the fuel from the fuel tank by pumping it out through the filler neck. Take all necessary precau-

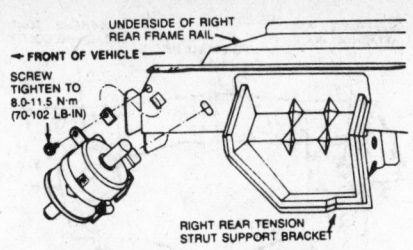

Exploded view of the fuel filter

tions to avoid the risk of fire when handling gasoline.

4. Raise and support the rear of the vehicle on jackstands. Remove the fuel filler tube (neck).

5. Support the fuel tank and remove the fuel tank straps. Lower the fuel tank slightly, then remove the fuel lines, the electrical connectors and the vent lines.

6. Remove the fuel tank and place it on a workbench. Clean any dirt from around the fuel pump attaching flange.

7. Using a brass drift and a hammer, turn the fuel pump locking ring counterclockwise and remove it.

8. Remove the fuel pump assembly from the fuel tank and discard the flange gasket.

To install:

9. Using Multipurpose Long Life Lubricant C1AZ-19590 or equivalent, coat the new O-ring and install it in the fuel ring groove.

10. Carefully install the fuel pump and sender assembly to prevent damage to the filter. Ensure that the locating keys are in the keyways and the seal ring remains in place.

11. Hold the assembly in place and install the locking ring finger-tight.

12. Secure the unit with the locking ring by rotating the ring clockwise until the the ring stops against the stops.

13. Remove the fuel tank from the bench and support the tank by hand under the vehicle. Connect and secure all fuel lines, vent line and electrical connection to their respective connections.

14. Install the tank in the vehicle and secure with the straps.

15. Lower the vehicle.

16. Install the filler tube and attaching screws.

17. Add a minimum of 10 gallons of fuel to the tank and check for leaks.

18. Install a fuel pressure gauge and turn the ignition switch **ON** and **OFF**, 5–10 times, for 3 second intervals, until the pressure gauge reads 13 psi (CFI) or 30 psi (EFI).

19. Remove the pressure gauge, start the engine and check for fuel leaks.

Fuel Injection

Due to the complex nature of

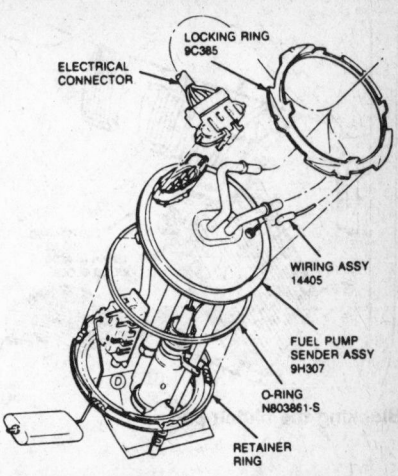

Exploded view of the fuel sender assembly

modern fuel injection systems, comprehensive diagnosis, testing and repair procedures fall outside the confines of this repair manual. For complete information on diagnosis, testing and repair procedures concerning all modern fuel injection systems, please refer to *Chilton's Guide To Fuel Injection And Feedback Carburetors.*

MANUAL TRANSAXLE

REMOVAL & INSTALLATION

1. Using a wood block approximately 7 in. long, wedge it under the clutch pedal to hold the pedal up slightly beyond its normal position. Grasp the clutch cable and pull it forward, disconnecting it from the clutch release bearing assembly. Remove the clutch casing from the rib on the top surface of the transaxle case.

2. Using a 13mm socket, remove the two top transaxle-to-engine bolts.

3. Raise and support the front of the vehicle on jackstands.

4. If equipped, remove the front stabilizer bar-to-control arm nut and washer (driver's side); discard the nut and replace with new . Remove the front stabilizer bar-to-chassis brackets; discard the bolts and replace with new.

5. Using a 15mm socket, remove the lower control arm ball joint-to-steering knuckle nut and bolt; discard the nut and bolt. Repeat this procedure on the opposite side.

6. Using a large pry bar, separate the lower control arm from the steer-

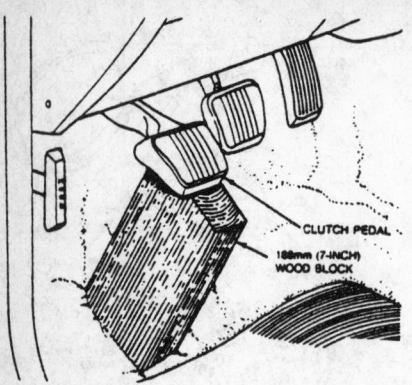

Blocking the clutch pedal

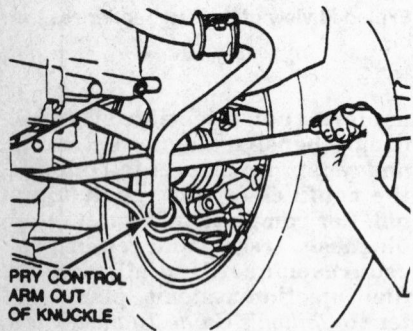

Releasing the control arm from the steering knuckle

ing knuckle. Repeat this procedure for the opposite side.

—— **CAUTION** ——

Exercise care not to damage or cut the ball joint boot. The pry bar must not contact the lower arm.

7. Using a large pry bar, pry the left inboard CV-joint assembly from the transaxle.

NOTE: With the halfshaft removed from the transaxle, the lubricant will drain from the seal. To prevent fluid loss, install the shipping plugs No. T81P-1177-B; two plugs are required (one for each seal).

8. To remove the inboard CV-joint from the transaxle, grasp the left-hand steering knuckle, then swing the knuckle and halfshaft outward from the transaxle. Repeat this procedure for the right side.

—— **CAUTION** ——

Exercise care when using a pry bar to remove the CV-joint assembly, or damage may occur to the differential oil seal.

9. If the CV-joint assembly cannot be pried from the transaxle, insert the differential rotator tool No. T81P-4026-A, or equivalent, through the left side and tap the joint out. The tool can be used from either side of transaxle.

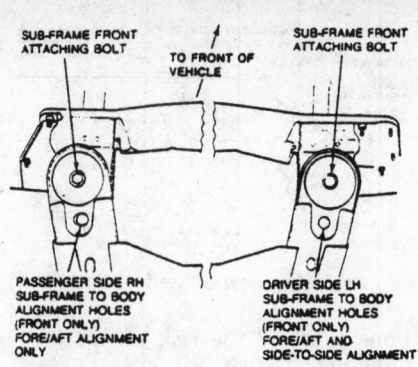

Sub-frame assembly with view of attaching bolts and alignment holes

10. With a piece of wire, support the halfshaft assembly in a rear level position to prevent damage to the assembly during the remaining operations; repeat this procedure on the opposite side.

11. With a suitable prying tool, remove the backup lamp switch connector from the transaxle backup lamp switch.

12. Using a 13mm deep well socket, remove the starter-to-engine stud bolts.

13. Remove the 6M shift mechanism-to-shift shaft nut/bolt, the control selector indicator switch arm and the shift shaft.

14. Using a 22mm crows foot wrench, remove the speedometer cable from the transaxle.

15. Using a 13mm socket, remove the stiffener brace-to-clutch housing bolts from the lower position of the clutch housing.

16. Remove the sub-frame and position a transaxle jack under the transaxle.

17. Using a 13mm wrench, remove the lower engine-to-transaxle bolts. Lower the transaxle jack until the transaxle clears the rear insulator. Support the engine with a screw jack stand under the oil pan; use a 2 x 4 in. piece of wood on top of the screw jack.

18. Remove the transaxle from the rear face of the engine and lower it from the vehicle.

19. To install, reverse the removal procedures. Torque the transaxle-to-engine bolts to 28–31 ft. lbs. (38–42 Nm), the shift cable/bracket-to-transaxle bolts to 16–22 ft. lbs. (22–30 Nm) for 10mm or 22–35 ft. lbs. (31–47 Nm) for 12mm; the shift mechanism-to-shift shaft bolt to 7–10 ft. lbs. (9–13 Nm); the stiffener brace-to-clutch housing bolts to 15–21 ft. lbs. (21–28 Nm); the starter-to-engine stud bolts to 30–40 ft. lbs. (41–54 Nm); the lower ball joint-to-steering knuckle nut/bolt to 37–44 ft. lbs. (50–60 Nm) and the top transaxle-to-engine bolts to 28–31 ft. lbs. (38–42 Nm). Check the transax-

le fluid level; if adding fluid, use Dextron® II automatic transmission fluid. Set the hand brake, pump the clutch pedal several times to adjust the clutch.

—— **CAUTION** ——

The transaxle case casting may have sharp edges. Wear protective gloves when handling the transaxle assembly.

NOTE: NEVER attempt to start the engine with the CV-joints disconnected from the transaxle or side gear dislocation may occur.

CLUTCH

REMOVAL & INSTALLATION

1. Remove the transaxle.
2. Make alignment marks on the pressure plate assembly and the flywheel for reassembly purposes.
3. Loosen the pressure plate-to-flywheel bolts one turn at a time, in sequence, until spring tension is relieved. Loosening the bolts in this manner will prevent distortion of the pressure plate cover.
4. Support the pressure plate/clutch disc assembly and remove the bolts. Remove the pressure plate and the clutch disc.
5. Inspect the flywheel, the clutch disc, the pressure plate, the throwout bearing and the clutch fork for wear; replace the parts as necessary. If the flywheel shows signs of overheating (blue discoloration) or is badly grooved/scored, it should be refaced or replaced.
6. Clean the pressure plate and flywheel surfaces thoroughly. Position the clutch disc and pressure plate into the assembled position, aligning the match-marks. Support the assembly with the clutch arbor tool No. T81P-7550-A, or equivalent.
7. Install the pressure plate-to-flywheel bolts and torque them gradually in a criss-cross pattern to 20–24 ft. lbs. (17–32 Nm). Remove the alignment tool.
8. Lubricate the release bearing and install it onto the fork.
9. To complete the installation, reverse the removal procedures. Torque the transaxle-to-engine bolts to 28–38 ft. lbs. (38–52 Nm).

NOTE: Since the release bearing in this system is constant-running, transaxle Neutral rollover noise can be detected as such only by disengaging the release bearing from the clutch release fin-

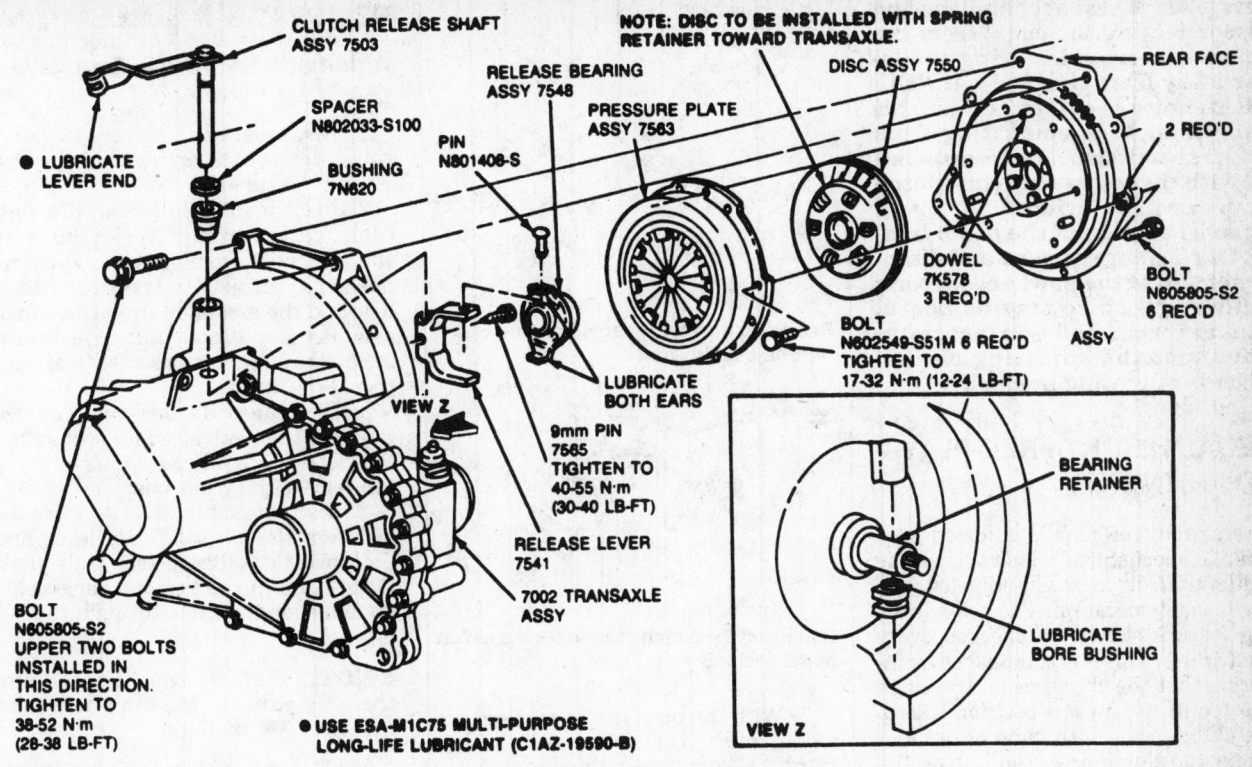

Exploded view of the clutch assembly

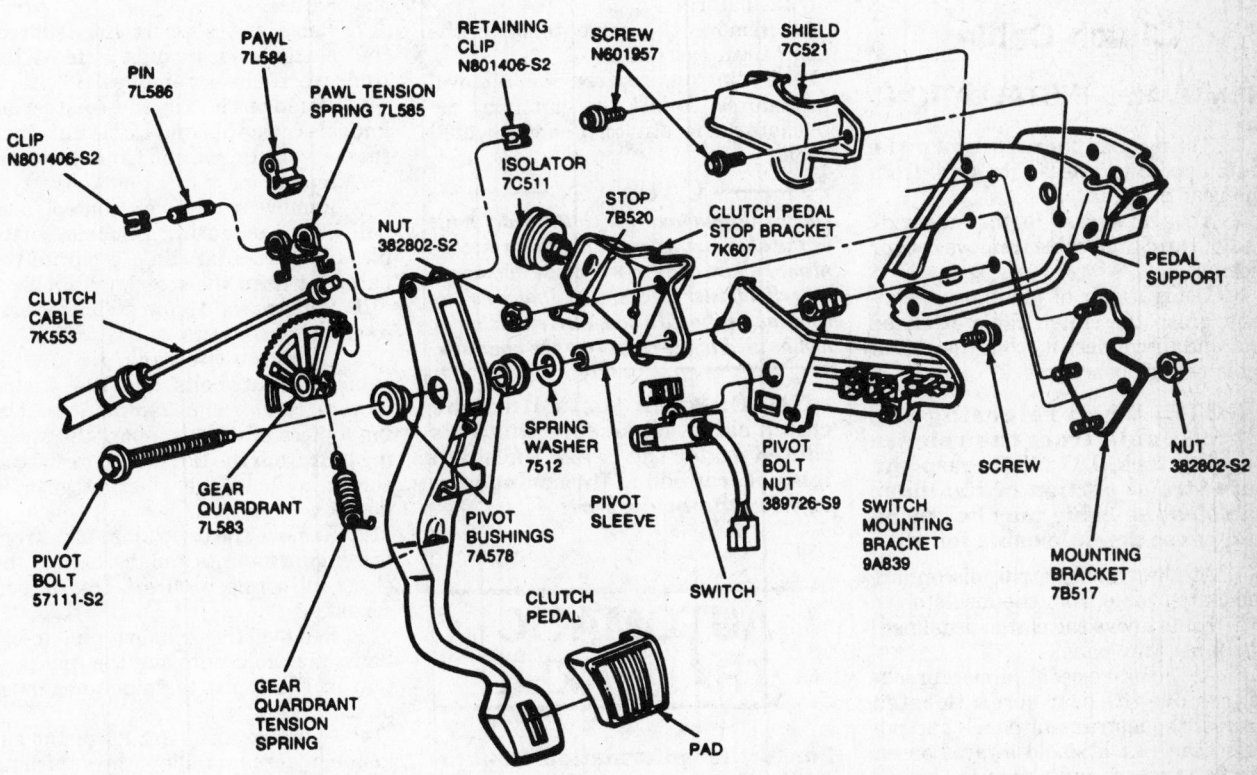

Exploded view of the clutch pedal assembly

gers. This is best accomplished by disconnecting the cable from the release lever and moving the lever away from the cable. If NEUTRAL noise is evident under this condition, it is emanating from the transmission. Noise associated with the release bearing/clutch system will be evident during all or some portion of the pedal travel. During engagement and disengagement of the pawl and sector a "clicking" noise may be heard. This is normal and is in fact assurance that the adjusting mechanism is operating normally.

PEDAL HEIGHT/FREE-PLAY ADJUSTMENT

The clutch free play is adjusted by a built in mechanism which allows the clutch controls to be self-adjusted during normal operation. The self-adjusting feature should be checked every 5000 miles. This is accomplished by insuring that the clutch pedal travels to the top of its upward position. Grasp the clutch pedal with hand or put foot under the clutch pedal, pull up on the pedal until it stops. Very little effort is required (about 10 lbs.). During the application of upward pressure, a click may be heard which means an adjustment was necessary and has been accomplished.

Clutch Cable

REMOVAL & INSTALLATION

1. Using a support, prop up the clutch pedal to release the pawl from the gear quadrant.
2. To gain access to the transaxle end of the clutch cable, remove the air cleaner.
3. Using a pair of pliers or equivalent, grasp the clutch cable extended end and disconnect it from the clutch cable release bearing fork.

NOTE: When releasing the clutch cable from the release bearing fork, DO NOT grasp the wire strand portion of the inner cable as the cable may be cut by and cause possible cable failure.

4. At the transaxle rib, disconnect the clutch cable from the insulator.
5. From above the clutch pedal pad, disconnect the panel.
6. At the brake pedal support bracket, remove the rear screw (located nearest the instrument panel) and position the clutch shield away. Loosen the front screw and rotate the shield out of the way, then secure the front screw.

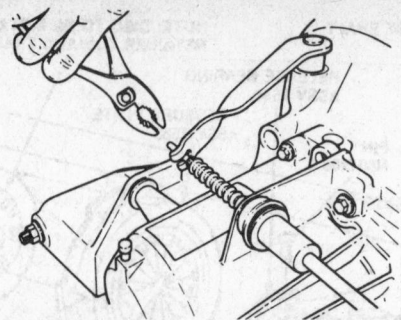

Removing the clutch cable from the clutch release bearing fork

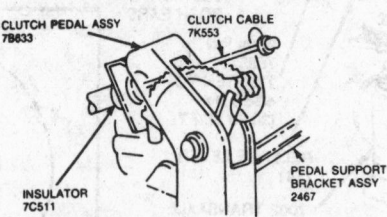

Removing the clutch cable from the clutch pedal assembly

7. With the pawl in the released position, rotate the gear quadrant forward and disconnect the clutch cable from the gear quadrant. DO NOT allow the gear quadrant to swing rearward or snap back.
8. Pull the cable through the recess between the clutch pedal and the gear quadrant, then from the pedal assembly insulator.
9. Remove the cable through the engine compartment.
10. To install, reverse the removal procedures. Adjust the clutch by depressing the clutch pedal several times.

─── CAUTION ───

During installation, the clutch pedal must be raised to disengage the adjusting mechanism. Failure to do so will cause damage to the self-adjuster mechanism. Under no circumstances should a screwdriver or similar tool be used to the cable into the quadrant.

NOTE: When installing the clutch cable, make sure that it is routed under the brake lines and it is not trapped at the spring tower near the brake lines.

AUTOMATIC TRANSAXLE

For further information on automatic transaxles, please refer to "Automatic Transmissions" in the Unit Repair section.

REMOVAL & INSTALLATION

Automatic Overdrive Transaxle (AXOD)

1. Disconnect the battery negative cable. Remove the air cleaner, the hoses and the tubes.
2. Place a suitable tool in the shift cable/bracket assembly slot, to keep the assembly from moving, then remove the assembly-to-transaxle 13mm bolt and the assembly from the transaxle. Remove 10mm shift cable bracket bolts and bracket from the transaxle.
3. Disconnect the electrical connector from the neutral safety switch and the electrical bulkhead connector from the rear of the transaxle.
4. Disconnect the throttle valve cable from the throttle body lever and the throttle valve-to-transaxle bolt. Carefully pull the throttle valve cable up and slide the cable through the TV link.

NOTE: Pulling too hard on the throttle valve cable may bend the internal TV bracket.

5. On the left side, remove the engine support-to-strut nut/bolt. Remove the four 15mm top torque converter housing-to-engine bolts.
6. Attach the engine support (3-bar system) hooks to the engine lifting points, tighten the hooks to slowly lift the engine.
7. Raise and support the front of the vehicle on jackstands. Remove the front wheel/tire assemblies.
8. Remove the tie rod-to-steering knuckle cotter pin and castle nut, then separate the tie rod end from the steering knuckle.
9. Remove the lower control arm ball joint-to-steering knuckle cotter pin and castle nut, then separate the ball joint from the steering knuckle.
10. Remove the 18mm stabilizer bar-to-control arm nuts.
11. Remove the rack/pinion-to-subframe nuts/bolts and the engine mount-to-subframe 24mm nuts. Using a piece of wire, support the steering gear from the tie rod end to the coil spring to hold the steering gear in position.
12. Remove the two 22mm nuts from the engine mounts and disconnect the electrical connector from the oxygen sensor.
13. Remove the exhaust pipe-to-exhaust manifold nuts and the rear portion of the convertor pipe-to-exhaust pipe.
14. Using an assistant, lower the adjustable jacks and allow the subframe to lower. Rotate the front of the subframe down and pick up the rear of the subframe off the exhaust pipe.

Work the subframe rearward until it can be lowered past the exhaust pipe.

15. Remove the subframe-to-chassis bolts. Remove the left side engine support mount-to-subframe nuts/bolts and lower the subframe.

16. Position a transmission jack under the transaxle oil pan. Remove the vehicle speed sensor from the transaxle.

NOTE: Vehicles equipped with electronic instrument clusters do not use a speedometer cable.

17. On the left side, remove the engine support-to-transaxle 15mm bolts. Remove the engine support-to-chassis 15mm bolts and the support.

18. Remove the separator plate-to-transaxle 8mm bolt and the starter-to-transaxle bolts, then position the starter out of the way. Remove the separator plate.

19. Using a $\frac{1}{2}$ in. drive ratchet and a $\frac{7}{8}$ in. deep socket on the crankshaft pulley bolt, rotate the crankshaft to align the torque converter bolts with the starter drive hole. As the torque converter-to-flywheel 15mm nuts are exposed, remove them.

20. Disconnect and plug the oil cooler lines from the transaxle.

21. To remove the halfshafts perform the following procedures:

  a. Screw the extension tool No. T86P-3514-A2, or equivalent, into the CV-Joint puller tool No. T86P-3514-A1 and install the slide hammer tool No. D79P-100-A onto the extension.

  b. Position the puller behind the inboard CV-joint and pull the CV-joint from the transaxle; DO NOT pry against the case.

22. Remove the remaining 15mm lower torque converter housing-to-engine bolts. Separate the transmission from the engine and carefully lower it out of the vehicle.

24. To install, reverse the removal procedures. Torque the transaxle-to-engine bolts to 41–50 ft. lbs. (55–68 Nm); the control arm ball joint-to-steering knuckle nut to 36–44 ft. lbs. (50–60 Nm); the tie rod end-to-steering knuckle nut to 23–35 ft. lbs. (31–47 Nm); the starter-to-transaxle bolts to 30–40 ft. lbs. (41–54 Nm); the engine support-to-transaxle bolts to 25–33 ft. lbs. (34–45 Nm); the engine mount-to-subframe bolts to 55–70 ft. lbs. (75–90 Nm); the subframe-to-chassis bolts to 40–50 ft. lbs. (55–70 Nm); the stabilizer bar-to-control arm nuts to 98–125 ft. lbs. (133–169 Nm) and the stabilizer U-clamp-to-chassis

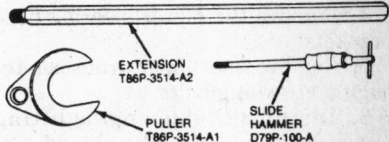

View of the tools necessary to remove the halfshafts

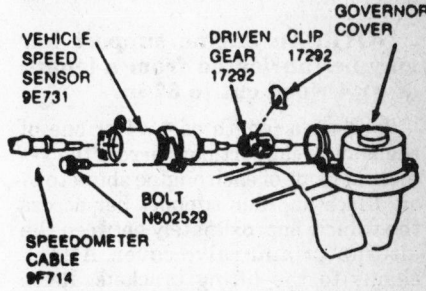

Exploded view of the engine stabilizer—automatic overdrive

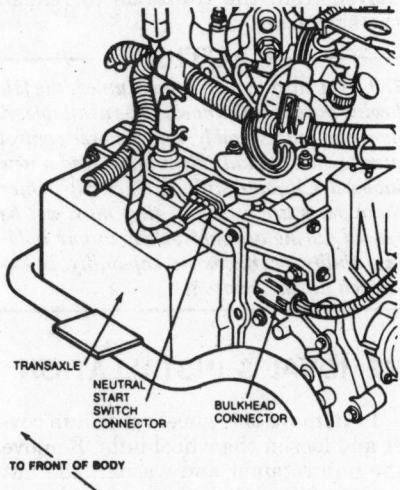

View of the transaxle electrical connectors—automatic overdrive

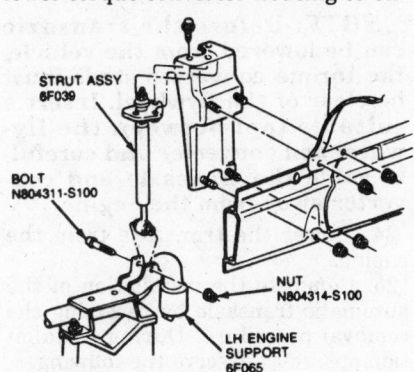

Exploded view of the vehicle speed sensor—automatic overdrive

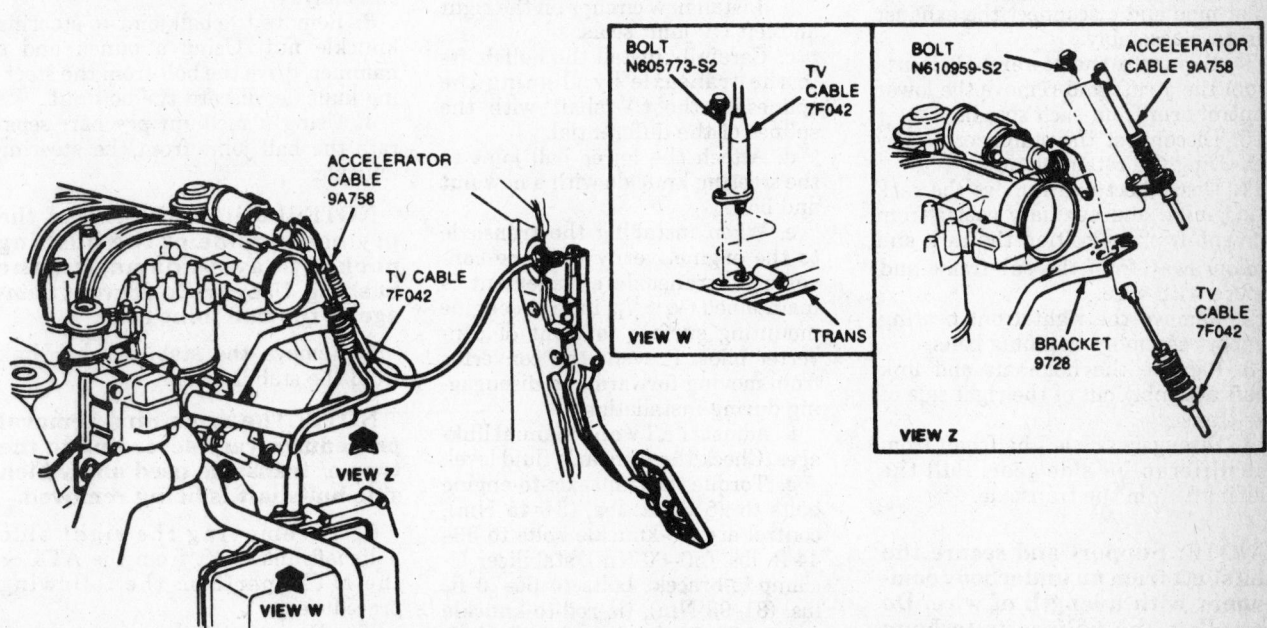

Exploded view of the TV cable assembly—automatic overdrive

bolts to 60–70 ft. lbs. (81–95 Nm). Check and add fluid to the transaxle.

Automatic Transaxle (ATX)

1. Disconnect the negative battery cable and remove the air cleaner assembly.

2. Position the engine control wiring harness away from the transaxle converter housing.

3. Disconnect the TV linkage and manual lever cable at the respective levers.

———— CAUTION ————

Failure to disconnect the linkage during transaxle removal and allowing the transaxle to hang will fracture the throttle valve cam shaft joint (which is located under the transaxle cover).

4. Remove the power steering hose brackets.

5. Remove the upper transaxle-to-engine attaching bolts.

6. Install suitable engine lifting brackets to the left and right sides of the cylinder head and attach with bolts. Install 2 suitable engine support bars.

NOTE: An engine support bar may be fabricated from a length of 4×4 wood cut to 57 in.

7. Place a length of 4×4 or one of the engine support bars across the vehicle in front of each engine shock tower. Place another support bar across the vehicle approximately between the alternator and valve cover. Attach chains to the lifting brackets. Raise the vehicle and support safely. Remove the wheels.

8. Remove the catalytic converter inlet pipe and disconnect the exhaust air hose assembly.

9. Separate the lower ball joints from the struts and remove the lower control arm from each spindle.

10. Disconnect the stabilizer bar by removing the retaining nuts.

11. Disconnect and remove the rack and pinion and auxiliary cooler from the sub-frame. Position the rack and pinion away from the sub-frame and secure with wire.

12. Remove the right front bearing support assembly retaining bolts.

13. Remove the halfshaft and link shaft assembly out of the right side of the transaxle.

14. Disengage the left halfshaft from the differential side gear. Pull the halfshaft from the transaxle.

NOTE: Support and secure the halfshaft from an underbody component with a length of wire. Do not allow the halfshafts to hang unsupported.

15. Install transaxle differntial shipping plugs No. T81P-1177B or equivalent.

16. Remove the front support insulator and position the left front spalsh shield aside.

17. Properly support the sub-frame and lower the vehicle onto the sub-frame support. Remove the sub-frame and disconnect the neutral start switch wire assembly.

18. Raise the vehicle after the sub-frame is removed. Disconnect the speedometer cable.

19. Disconnect and remove the shift cable from the transaxle.

20. Disconnect the oil cooler lines and remove the starter.

21. Remove the dust cover from the torque converter housing and remove the torque converter-to-flywheel housing nuts.

22. Position a suitable transaxle jack under the transaxle.

23. Remove the remaining transaxle-to-engine attaching bolts.

NOTE: Before the transaxle can be lowered from the vehicle, the torque converter studs must be clear of the flywheel. Insert a suitable tool between the flywheel and converter and carefully guide the transaxle and converter away from the engine.

24. Lower the transaxle from the engine.

25. Complete the installation of the automatic transaxle by reversing the removal procedure. During installation ensure to observe the follwing:

a. Clean the oil cooler lines with a suitable cleaning compound. (No. 014–00028 or equivalent.

b. Install new circlips on the right and left CV-joint seals.

c. Carefully install the halfshafts in the transaxle by aligning the splines of the CV shaft with the splines of the differential.

d. Attach the lower ball joint to the steering knuckle with a new nut and bolt.

e. When installing the transaxle to the engine, verify that the converter-to-transaxle engagement is maintained ($\frac{1}{2} \pm \frac{1}{16}$ in. from engine mounting surface to front of converter pilot. Prevent the converter from moving forward and disengaging during installation.

f. Adjust the TV and manual linkages. Check the transaxle fluid level.

g. Torque the transaxle-to-engine bolts to 25–33 ft. lbs. (34–45 Nm), control arm-to-knuckle bolts to 36–44 ft. lbs. (50–60 Nm), stabilizer U-clamp-to-bracekt bolts to 60–70 ft. lbs. (81–95 Nm), tie rod-to-knuckle nut to 23–35 ft. lbs. (31–47 Nm), starter-to-transaxle bolts to 30–40

ft. lbs. (41–54 Nm), torque converter-to-flywheel bolts to 23–39 ft. lbs. (31–53 Nm) and insulator-to-bracket bolts to 55–70 ft. lbs. (75–90 Nm).

DRIVE AXLE

Halfshafts

When removing both the left and right halfshafts, shipping plug tools No. T81P-1177-B must be installed. Failure to use these tools can result in dislocation of the differential side gears. Should the gears become misaligned, the differential will have to be removed from the transaxle to realign the side gears.

———— CAUTION ————

DO NOT start this procedure unless the following parts are to known to be available: A new hub nut assembly, a new lower control arm-to-steering knuckle nut/bolt and a new inboard CV-joint stub shaft circlip. Once these parts are removed, they must not be reused during assembly; their torque holding ability or retension capability is destroyed during removal.

REMOVAL & INSTALLATION

1. Remove the wheel cover/hub cover and loosen the wheel nuts. Remove the hub retainer and washer; the nut must be discarded after removal.

2. Raise and support the vehicle on jackstands, then remove the wheel/tire assembly.

3. Remove the ball joint-to-steering knuckle nut. Using a punch and a hammer, drive the bolt from the steering knuckle; discard the bolt/nut.

4. Using a medium pry bar, separate the ball joint from the steering knuckle.

NOTE: Position the end of the pry bar outside of the bushing pocket to avoid damaging the bushing. Use care to prevent damage to the ball joint boot.

5. Remove the stabilizer bar link from the stabilizer bar.

NOTE: The remaining removal procedures vary according to the type of transaxle used and which side halfshaft is being removed.

6. If removing the right side halfshaft/link shaft from the ATX or the MTX, perform the following procedures:

a. Remove the bearing support-to-bracket bolts, then slide the shaft out of the transaxle. Using a piece of wire, support the end of the shaft from a convenient underbody component.

NOTE: DO NOT allow the shaft to hang unsupported, as damage to the outboard CV-joint may occur.

b. Separate the outboard CV-joint from the hub using the front hub remover tool No. T81P-1104-C, the metric adapters tools No. T83-P-1104-BH, T86P-1104-Al and T81P-1104-A.

NOTE: NEVER use a hammer to separate the outboard CV-joint stub shaft from the hub; damage to the CV-joint threads and internal components may result. The right side link shaft and halfshaft assembly is removed as a complete unit.

7. If removing the right side and left side halfshafts from the AXOD (over-drive) or the left side halfshaft from the MTX, perform the following procedures:

a. Position the CV-joint puller tool No. T86P-3514-A1 between the CV-joint and transaxle case. Turn

the steering hub and/or wire the strut assembly out of the way.

b. Assemble the screw extension tool No. T86P-3514-A2 into the CV-Joint puller and hand tighten. Assemble the screw impact slide ham-

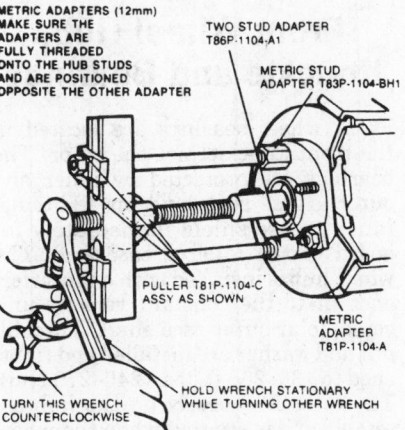

Removing the halfshaft from the hub

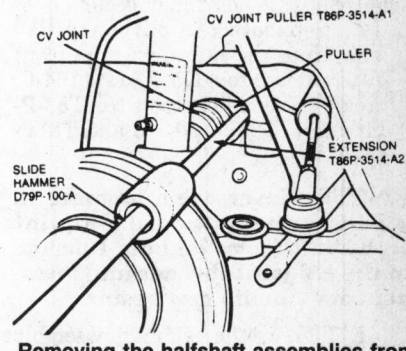

Removing the halfshaft assemblies from AXOD (right-side) or MTX (left-side)

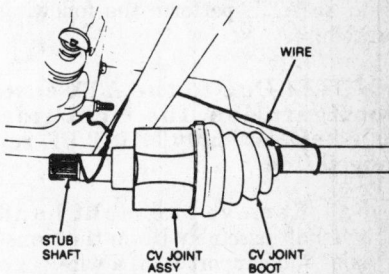

Supporting the halfshaft with a wire

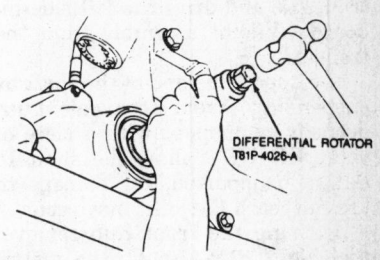

Removing the left-side halfshaft from the transaxle—ATX

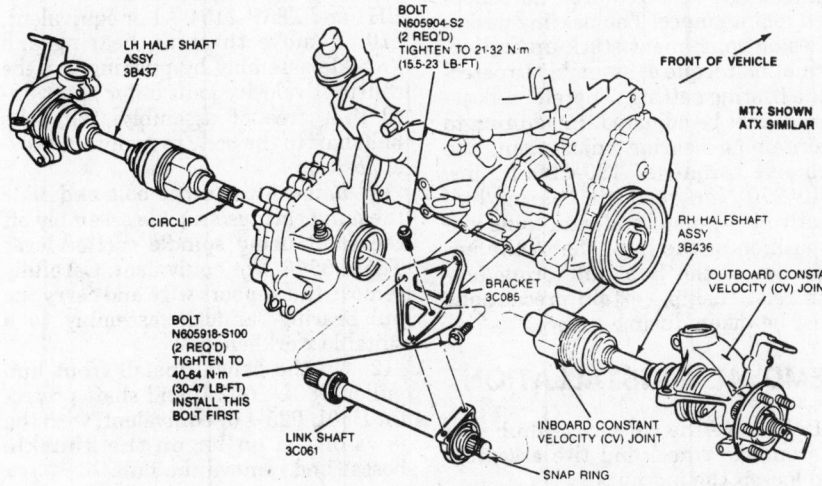

Exploded view of the halfshaft assembly—used with the MTX and ATX

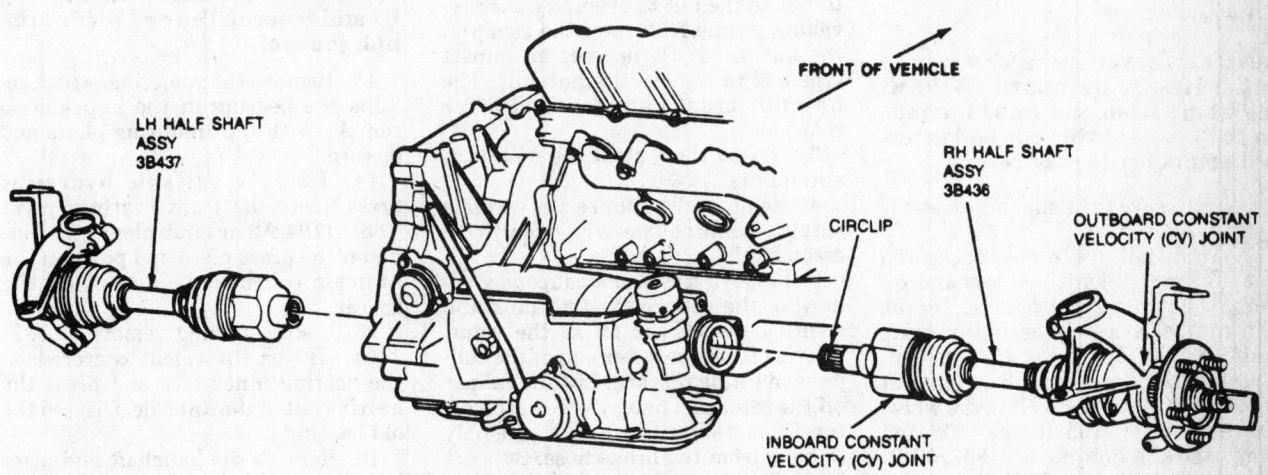

Exploded view of the halfshaft assembly—AXOD

mer tool No. D79-100-A onto the extension and remove the CV-joint.

c. Support the end of the shaft by suspending it from a convenient underbody component with a piece of wire. DO NOT allow the shaft to hang unsupported, damage to the outboard CV-joint may occur.

d. Separate the outboard CV-joint from the hub using the front hub remover tool No. T81P-1104-C, the metric adapters tools No. T83-P-1104-BH, T86P-1104-Al and T81P-1104-A.

NOTE: Never use a hammer to separate the outboard CV-joint stub shaft from the hub. Damage to the CV-joint threads and internal components may result.

e. Remove the halfshaft assembly from the vehicle.

8. To remove the left side halfshaft from an ATX, perform the following procedures:

NOTE: Due to the ATX case configuration, the right side halfshaft assembly MUST BE removed first.

a. Remove the right hand halfshaft assembly (from the transaxle) and support it on a wire.

b. Insert the differential rotator tool No. T81P-4026-A into the transaxle and drive the left side inboard CV-joint assembly from the transaxle.

c. Support the end of the shaft by suspending it from a convenient underbody component with a piece of wire. DO NOT allow the shaft to hang unsupported, for damage to the outboard CV-joint may occur.

d. Using the front hub removal tool No. T81P-1104-C, the metric adapter tools No. T83-P-1104-BH, T86P-1104-Al and T81P-1104-A, separate the outboard CV-joint from the hub.

NOTE: Never use a hammer to separate the outboard CV-joint halfshaft from the hub. Damage to the CV-joint threads and internal components may result.

e. Remove the halfshaft assembly from the vehicle.

9. To install, use a new circlip (on the inboard CV-joint), oil seal and reverse the removal procedures. Torque the control arm-to-steering knuckle nut/bolt to 40–55 ft. lbs. (54–74 Nm); the stabilizer bar-to-stabilizer link nut to 35–50 ft. lbs. (47–65 Nm); the wheel lug nuts to 80–105 ft. lbs (108–144 Nm). and the hub nut to 180–200 ft. lbs. Refill the transaxle to the proper level with the specified fluid.

CV-JOINT OVERHAUL

For all CV-joint overhaul procedures, please refer to "CV-Joint Overhaul" in the Unit Repair section.

Front Wheel Hub, Knuckle and Bearings

Front wheel bearings are located in the front knuckle, not the rotor. The bearings are protected by inner and outer grease seals and an additional inner grease shield immediately inboard of the inner grease seal. The wheel hub is installed with an interference fit to the constant velocity universal joint outer race shaft. The hub nut and washer are installed and tightened to 180–200 ft. lbs. (240–270 Nm). The rotor fits loosely on the hub assembly and is secured when the wheel and wheel nuts are installed.

The front wheel bearings have a set-right design that requires no scheduled maintenance. The bearing design relies on component stack-up and deformation/torque at assembly to determine bearing setting. Therefore, bearings cannot be adjusted. In addition to maintaining bearing adjustment, the hub nut torque of 180–200 ft. lbs. (240–270 Nm) restricts bearing/hub relative movement and maintains axial position of the hub. Die to the importance of the hub nut torque/tension relationship, certain precautions must be taken during service.

REMOVAL & INSTALLATION

1. Remove the wheelcover/hub cover from the wheel and tire assembly and loosen the lug nuts.

2. Remove the hub retaining nut and washer by applying sufficient torque to the nut to overcome the prevailing torque feature of the crimp in the nut collar. Do not use an impact type tool to remove the hub nut. The hub nut must be discarded after removal.

3. Loosen the 3 strut top mount to apron nuts.

4. Raise and support the vehicle safely. Remove the wheel and tire assembly.

5. Remove the brake caliper by removing the caliper locating pins and rotating the caliper off of the rotor, starting from the lower end of the caliper and lifting upward. Lift the caliper off the rotor and hang it free of the rotor. Do not allow the caliper assembly to hang from the brake hose. Support the caliper assembly with a length of wire.

6. Remove the rotor from the hub by pulling it off the hub bolts. If the rotor is difficult to remove from the hub, strike the rotor sharply between the studs with a rubber or plastic hammer.

NOTE: If the rotor will not pull off, apply a suitable penetrating fluid to the inboard and outboard rotor hub mating surfaces. Install a 3 jaw puller and remove the rotor by pulling on the rotor outside diameter and pushing on the hub center. If excessive force is required, check the rotor for lateral runout prior to installation.

7. The lateral runout must be checked with the nuts clamping the stamped section of the rotor. Remove the rotor splash shield.

8. Disconnect the lower control arm and tie rod from the steering knuckle. Loosen the strut pinch bolt, but do not remove the strut.

9. Install hub remover/installer T81P-1104-A with T81P-1104-C and hub knuckle adapters T83P-1104-BH1 and T86P-1104-A1 or equivalent.

10. Remove the hub, bearing and knuckle assembly by pushing out the constant velocity joint outer shaft until it is free of assembly. Wire the halfshaft to the body to maintain a level position.

11. Remove the strut bolt and slide the hub/bearings/knuckle assembly off the strut using spindle carrier lever T85M-3206-A or equivalent. Carefully remove the support wire and carry the hub/bearing /knuckle assembly to a suitable workbench.

12. On the bench, install front hub puller D80L-1002-L and shaft protector D80L-625-1 or equivalent, with the jaws of the puller on the knuckle bosses and remove the hub.

NOTE: Be sure the shaft protector is centered, clears the bearing ID and rests on the end face of the hub journal.

13. Remove the snap ring, which retains the bearing in the knuckle assembly, with the snap ring pliers and discard.

14. Using a suitable hydraulic press, place the front bearing spacer T86P-1104-A2 or equivalent step side up on the press plate and position the knuckle (outboard side up) on the spacer.

15. Install bearing remover T83P-1104-AH2 or equivalent centered on the bearing inner race and press the bearing out of the knuckle. Discard the old bearing.

16. Remove the halfshaft and place it in a suitable vise with protective jaws.

17. Remove the bearing dust seal by equally tapping on the outer edge with a light duty hammer and a suitable tool. Discard the dust seal.

To install:

18. Remove all foreign material from the knuckle bearing bore and hub bearing journal to ensure the correct seating of a new bearing.

NOTE: If the hub bearing journal is scored or damaged, replace the hub. Do not attempt to service a bad hub. The front wheel bearings are of a cartridge design and are pre-greased, sealed and require no schedule maintenance. The bearings are preset and cannot be adjusted. If a bearing is disassembled for any reason, it must be replaced as a unit. No individual service seals, roller or races are available.

19. Place the front bearing spacer T86P-1104-A or equivalent step side down on a press plate and position the knuckle (outboard side down) on a spacer. Position a new bearing in the inboard side of the knuckle.

20. Install the bearing installer T86P-1104-A3 or equivalent (undercut side facing the bearing) on the bearing outer race and press bearing into the knuckle.

21. Check that the bearing seats completely against the shoulder of the knuckle bore. The bearing installer must be installed as indicated above to prevent bearing damage during installation.

22. Install a new snap ring in the knuckle groove with a suitable pair of snap ring pliers. Place the front bearing spacer T86P-1104-A2 or equivalent on the arbor press plate and position the hub on the tool with the lugs facing downward. Position the knuck-

le assembly (outboard side down) on the hub barrel.

23. Place bearing remover T83P-1104-AH2 or equivalent flat side down, centered on the inner race of the bearing and press down on the tool until the bearing is fully seated onto the hub. Check that the hub rotates freely in the knuckle after installation.

24. Prior to the hub/bearing/knuckle installation, replace the bearing dust seal on the outboard CV-joint with a new seal from the bearing kit.

25. Install the dust seal, ensuring

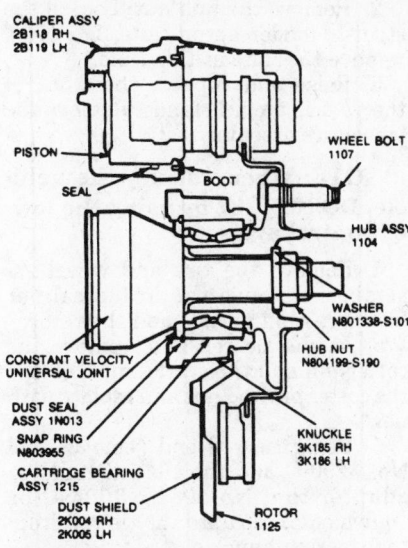

Cross-sectional view of the front hub/bearing assembly

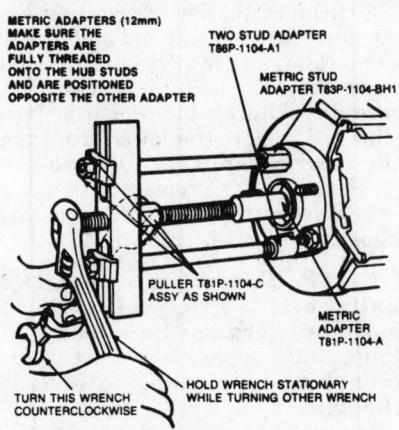

Pressing the halfshaft from the front hub assembly

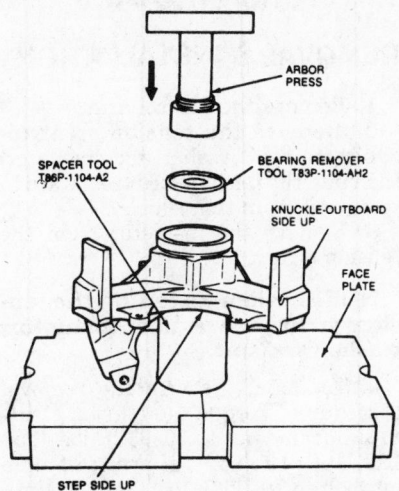

Removing the bearing from the steering knuckle

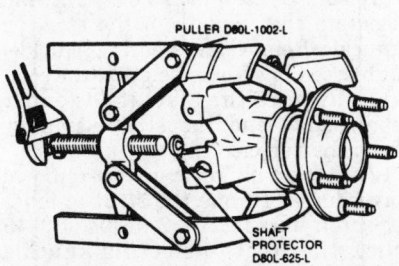

Separating the hub from the steering knuckle

the seal flange faces outboard toward the bearing. Use drive tube T83P-3132-A1 and front bearing dust seal installer T86P-1104-A4 or equivalent.

26. Suspend the hub/bearing/knuckle assembly on the vehicle with a wire and attach the strut loosely to the knuckle. Lubricate the CV-joint stub shaft splines with a SAE 30 weight motor oil and insert the shaft onto the hub splines as far as possible using hand pressure only. Check that the splines are properly engaged.

27. Temporarily fasten the rotor to hub with washers and 2 wheel lugnuts. Insert a steel rod into the rotor diameter and rotate it clockwise to contact the knuckle.

28. Install the hub nut washer and new hub nut. Rotate the nut clockwise to seat the CV-joint. Tighten the nut

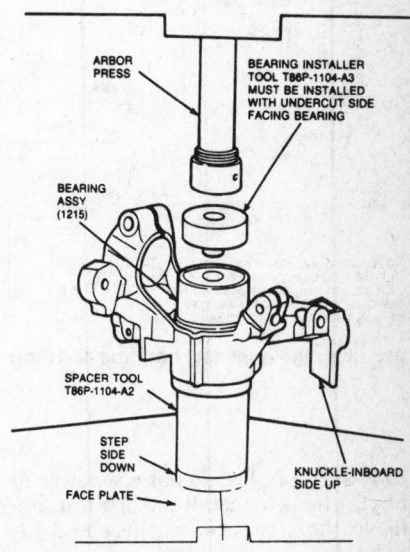

Installing the new bearing into the steering knuckle

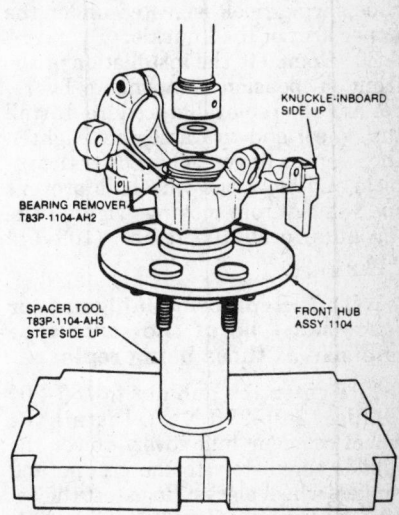

Pressing the hub into the steering knuckle

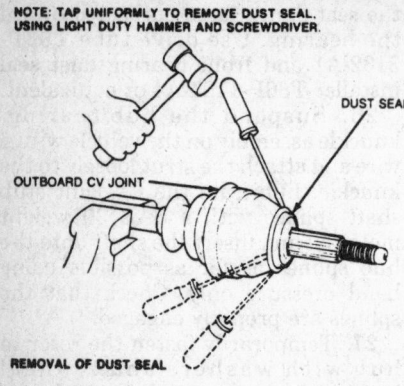

NOTE: TAP UNIFORMLY TO REMOVE DUST SEAL. USING LIGHT DUTY HAMMER AND SCREWDRIVER.

Removing the dust seal from the halfshaft

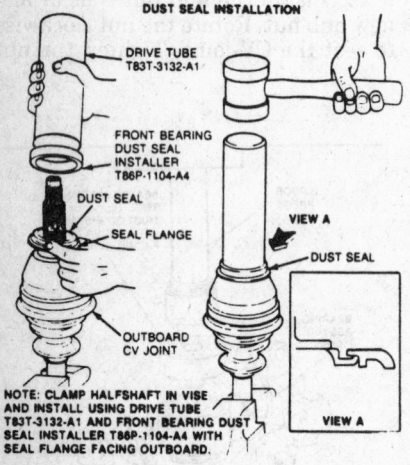

NOTE: CLAMP HALFSHAFT IN VISE AND INSTALL USING DRIVE TUBE T83T-3132-A1 AND FRONT BEARING DUST SEAL INSTALLER T86P-1104-A4 WITH SEAL FLANGE FACING OUTBOARD.

Installing the dust seal onto the halfshaft

to 180–200 ft. lbs. do not use power or impact tools to install the hub nut. Remove the steel rod, washers and lug nuts.

29. Install the disc brake caliper over the rotor. Be sure the outer brake shoe spring hook is seated under the upper arm of the knuckle.

30. Complete the installation of the front suspension components by reversing the removal procedure. Install the wheel and tire assembly, tighten the lug nuts finger tight. Lower the vehicle and block the wheels to prevent the vehicle from moving. Tighten the lug nuts to 80–105 ft. lbs. (109–142 Nm).

NOTE: Replacement lug nuts or studs must be of the same type and size as those being replaced.

31. Tighten the hub nut to 180–200 ft. lbs. (240–270 Nm). Install the wheel cover or hub cover. Lower the vehicle completely to the ground and remove wheel blocks. Road test the vehicle and check to see if the vehicle is operating properly.

FRONT SUSPENSION

MacPherson Strut

REMOVAL & INSTALLATION

1. Place the ignition switch to the **OFF** position and the steering column in the unlocked position.
2. Remove the hub nut. Loosen the strut-to-fender apron nuts; DO NOT remove the nuts at this time.
3. Raise and support the front of the vehicle on jackstands. Remove the wheel/tire assembly.

NOTE: When raising the vehicle, DO NOT lift by using the lower control arms.

4. Remove the tire and wheel assembly. Remove the brake caliper (support it on a wire) and the rotor.
5. At the tie rod end, remove the cotter pin and the castle nut. Discard the cotter pin and nut and replace with new.
6. Using tie rod end remover tool No. 3290-C and the tie rod remover adapter tool No. T81P-3504-C or equivalents, separate the tie rod from the steering knuckle.
7. Remove the stabilizer bar link nut and the link from the strut.
8. Remove the lower arm-to-steering knuckle pinch bolt and nut; it may be necessary to use a drift punch to remove the bolt. Using a screwdriver, spread the knuckle-to-lower arm pinch joint and remove the lower arm from the steering knuckle. Discard the pinch nut/bolt and replace with new.
9. Remove the halfshaft from the hub and support it on a wire.

NOTE: When removing the halfshaft, DO NOT allow it to move outward as the tripod CV-joint could separate from the internal parts, causing failure of the joint.

10. Remove the strut-to-steering knuckle pinch bolt. Using a small pry bar, spread the pinch bolt joint and separate the strut from the steering knuckle. Remove the steering knuckle/hub assembly from the strut tower.
11. Remove the 3 strut-to-fender apron nuts and the strut assembly from the vehicle.
12. To install, reverse the removal procedures. Torque the strut-to-fender apron nuts to 22–32 ft. lbs. (30–40 Nm); the strut-to-steering knuckle bolt to 70–95 ft. lbs. (95–129 Nm); the control arm-to-steering knuckle bolt

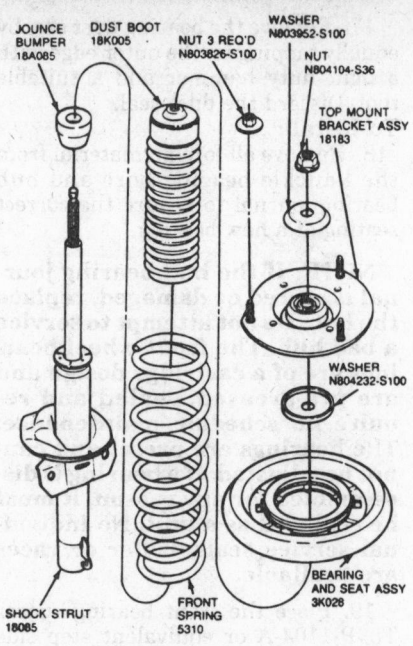

Exploded view of the strut assembly

to 40–55 ft. lbs. (54–74 Nm); the stabilizer bar-to-link assembly nut to 35–48 ft. lbs. (47–65 Nm); the tie rod end-to-steering knuckle nut to 23–25 ft. lbs. (31–47 Nm) and the hub nut to 180–200 ft. lbs. (244–271 Nm). Check the front end alignment.

OVERHAUL

For all spring and shock absorber removal and installation procedures, and all strut overhaul procedures, please refer to "Strut Overhaul" in the Unit Repair section.

Tension Struts

REMOVAL & INSTALLATION

1. Remove the control arm.
2. Remove the tension strut-to-subframe nut, washer and insulator, then pull the tension strut rearward to remove it from the vehicle.
3. Remove the insulator from the tension strut.

NOTE: When installing the tension strut, use a new insulator, washer and nut.

4. To install, reverse the removal procedures. Torque the tension strut-to-sub-frame nut to 70–95 ft. lbs. (95–129 Nm); the control arm-to-frame nut/bolt to 70–95 ft. lbs. (95–129 Nm); the control arm-to-steering knuckle nut/bolt to 40–55 ft. lbs. (54–74 Nm); the tension strut-to-control arm nut to

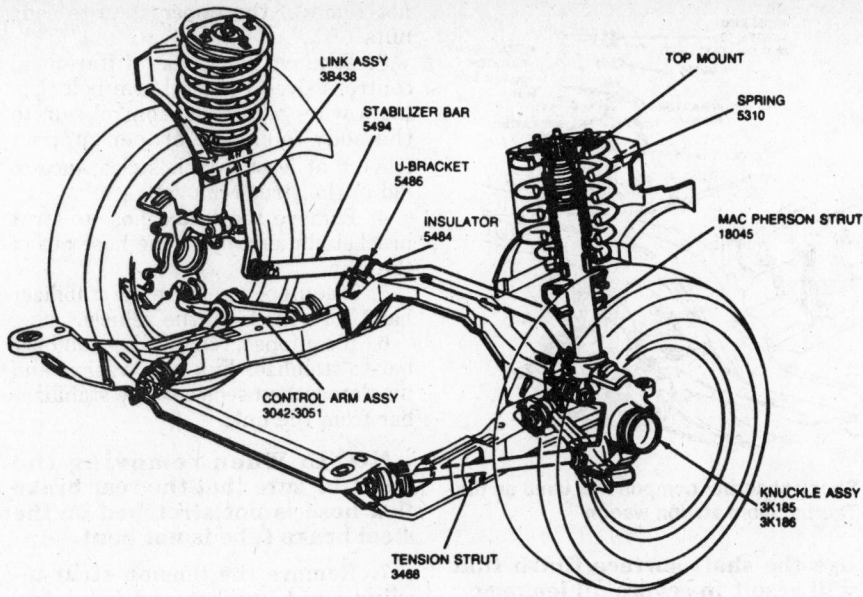

View of the front suspension system

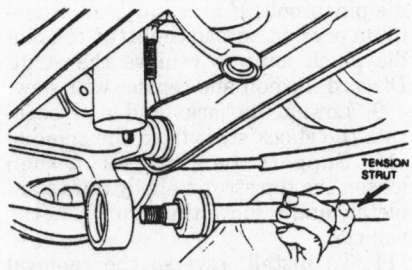

Positioning the tension strut

70–95 ft. lbs. (95–129 Nm) and the wheel lug nuts to 80–105 ft. lbs. (109–142 Nm). Check and/or adjust the front wheel alignment.

Ball Joints

The ball joint is a part of the front control arm and cannot be replaced. If the ball joint is worn, the control arm must be replaced.

INSPECTION

1. Raise the vehicle until the front wheels fall to the full down position.

NOTE: DO NOT raise or support the vehicle on the front control arms.

2. Have an assistant grasp the lower edge of the wheel/tire assembly and move the assembly in and out.

3. As the wheel is being moved, observe the control arm-to-steering knuckle ball joint for movement; movement indicates a worn out ball joint.

4. If ball joint movement is present, replace the lower control arm.

REMOVAL & INSTALLATION

Ball joints are integral parts of the lower control arms. If an inspection reveals an unsatisfactory ball joint, the entire lower control arm assembly must be replaced.

Lower Control Arms

REMOVAL & INSTALLATION

1. Raise and support the front of the vehicle on jackstands. Remove the tire assembly. Position the steering column in the unlocked position.

2. Remove the tension strut-to-control arm nut and the dished washer.

3. Remove and discard the control arm-to-steering knuckle pinch bolt. Using a small pry bar, spread the pinch joint and separate the control arm from the steering knuckle.

NOTE: When separating the control arm from the steering knuckle, DO NOT use a hammer. Be careful not to damage the bolt seal.

4. Remove the control arm-to-frame nut/bolt, then the control arm from the frame and the tension strut.

NOTE: DO NOT allow the halfshaft to move outward or the tripod CV-joint could separate from the internal parts, causing failure of the joint.

5. To install, use a new pinch nut/bolt and reverse the removal procedures. Torque the control arm-to-frame nut/bolt to 70–95 ft. lbs. (95–

129 Nm); the control arm-to-steering knuckle nut/bolt to 40–55 ft. lbs. (54–74 Nm); the tension strut-to-control arm nut to 70–95 ft. lbs. (95–129 Nm) and the wheel lug nuts to 80–105 ft. lbs. (109–142 Nm). Check the front end alignment.

NOTE: When installing a new control arm, be sure to saturate the new bushing with vegetable oil; DO NOT use brake fluid, petroleum-based oil or mineral oil as these fluids will cause deterioration and failure of the bushing.

Stabilizer Bar

REMOVAL & INSTALLATION

1. Raise and support the front of the vehicle on jackstands behind the subframe.

NOTE: DO NOT raise or support the vehicle on the front control arms.

2. Remove and discard the stabilizer bar link-to-stabilizer bar nut, the stabilizer bar link-to-strut nut and the link from the vehicle.

3. Remove the steering gear-to-subframe nuts and the gear from the sub-frame.

4. Position another set of jackstands under the subframe and remove the rear subframe-to-frame bolts. Lower the subframe rear to gain access to the stabilizer bar brackets.

5. Remove the stabilizer bar U-bracket bolts and the stabilizer bar from the vehicle.

NOTE: When removing the stabilizer bar, replace the insulators and the U-bracket bolts with new ones.

6. To install, reverse the removal procedures. Torque the U-bracket-to-subframe bolts to 21–32 ft. lbs. (28–43 Nm); the subframe-to-steering gear bolts to 85–100 ft. lbs. (115–135 Nm); the stabilizer bar-to-stabilizer bar link nut to 35–48 ft. lbs. (47–65 Nm) and the stabilizer bar-to-strut nut to 35–48 ft. lbs. (47–65 Nm). Coat the inside diameter of the new insulators with No. E25Y-19553–A or equivalent lubricant. Do not use any mineral or petroleum base lubricants as they will cause deterioration of the rubber insulators.

Front Wheel Alignment

ADJUSTMENT

Caster and Camber

Caster and camber angles are preset at the factory and cannot be adjusted.

Measurement procedures that follow are for diagnostic purposes.

Caster measurements must be made on the left hand side by turning the left wheel through the prescribed angle of the sweep and on the right hand side by turning the right wheel through the prescribed angle of sweep.

When using the alignment equipment designed to measure the caster on both the right hand and left hand side, turning only one wheel will result in a significant error in the caster angle for the opposite side.

Toe-In

The toe-in is controlled by adjusting the tie rod ends. To adjust the toe-in setting, loosen the tie rod jam nuts. Rotate the tie rod as required to adjust the toe-in into specifications. Once the toe-in is set, re-tighten the tie rod jam nuts.

REAR SUSPENSION

Shock Absorbers

The rear suspension system used on the station wagon models features shock absorber assemblies attached to the body side panels. The shock absorbers are mounted by a rubber insulated top mount assembly and attaching nut and are attached to the lower suspension arm by two studs pressed into a bar pin mounted in a rubber bushing.

REMOVAL & INSTALLATION

Wagon

1. Raise and support the rear of the vehicle safely.
2. Remove the wheel and tire assembly.
3. Position a jack stand under the lower suspension arm. Remove the 2 nuts retaininng the shock absorber to the lower suspension arm.
4. From inside the vehicle, remove the rear compartment access panels.
5. Remove and discard the top shock absorber attaching nut using a suitable crow's foot wrench and rachet while holding the shock absorber shaft stationary with an open end wrench.

NOTE: If the shock absorber is to reused, do not grip the shaft with pliers or vise grips. Gripping the shaft in this manner will dam-

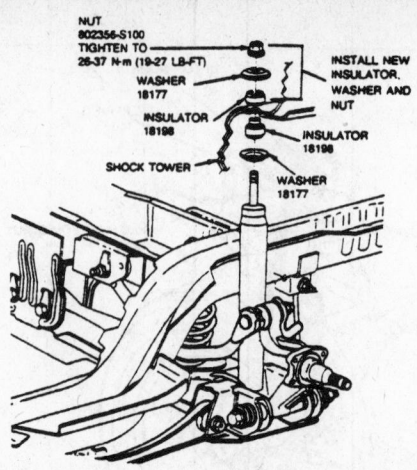

Shock absorber components used on the Taurus/Sable station wagon

age the shaft surface finish that will result in severe oil leakage.

6. Remove the rubber insulator from the shock and remove the shock from the vehicle.

NOTE: The shocks are gas filled. It will require an effort to remove the shock from the lower arm.

7. Install a new washer and insulator on the upper shock absorber rod.
8. Maneuver the upper part of the shock absorber into the shock tower opening in the body. Push slowly on the lower part of the shock absorber until the mounting studs are aligned with the mounting holes in the lower suspension arm.
9. Install new lower attaching nuts but do not tighten at this time.
10. Install a new insulator, washer and nut on top of the shock absorber. Torque the nut to 19–27 ft. lbs. (26–37 Nm.).
11. Install the rear compartment access panel.
12. Torque the 2 lower attaching nuts to 13–20 ft. lbs. (17–27 Nm).
13. Install the wheel and tire assembly. Remove the safety stand supporting the lower suspension arm and lower the vehicle.

MacPherson Strut

REMOVAL & INSTALLATION

Sedan

1. Raise and support the rear of the vehicle on jackstands. Remove the rear tires.

NOTE: DO NOT raise or support the vehicle using the tension struts.

2. Raise the rear lid and loosen (do

not remove) the upper strut-to-body nuts.
3. Remove the brake differential control valve-to-control arm bolt. Using a wire, secure the control arm to the body to ensure proper support leaving at least 6 inches clearance to aid in the strut removal.
4. Remove the brake hose-to-strut bracket clip and move the hose out of the way.
5. If equipped, remove the stabilizer bar U-bracket from the vehicle.
6. If equipped, remove the stabilizer bar-to-stabilizer link nut, washer and insulator, then separate the stabilizer bar from the link.

NOTE: When removing the strut, be sure that the rear brake flex hose is not stretched or the steel brake tube is not bent.

7. Remove the tension strut-to-spindle nut, washer and insulator. Move the spindle rearward to separate it from the tension strut.
8. Remove the shock strut-to-spindle pinch bolt. If necessary, use a medium pry bar, spread the strut-to-spindle pinch joint to remove the strut. Discard the bolt and replace with new.
9. Lower the jackstand and separate the shock strut from the spindle.
10. Support the shock strut, then loosen the top strut-to-body nuts completely and remove the strut from the vehicle.
11. To install, reverse the removal procedures. Torque the shock strut-to-body nuts to 19–26 ft. lbs. (26–35 Nm); the shock strut-to-spindle bolt to 55–81 ft. lbs. (75–110 Nm); the control arm-to-spindle bolt to 52–74 ft. lbs. (70–100 Nm); the control arm-to-body bolt to 52–74 ft. lbs. (70–100 Nm); the tension strut-to-spindle nut to 52–74 ft. lbs. (70–100 Nm); the stabilizer bar link-to-stabilizer bar nut to 6–12 ft. lbs. (8–16 Nm) and the stabilizer U-bracket-to-body bolts to 15–25 ft. lbs. (20–34 Nm).

OVERHAUL

For all spring and shock absorber removal and installation procedures, and all strut overhaul procedures, please refer to "Strut Overhaul" in the Unit Repair section.

Springs

REMOVAL & INSTALLATION

Sedan and Wagon

1. Raise the rear of the vehicle and support safely. Position a floor jack

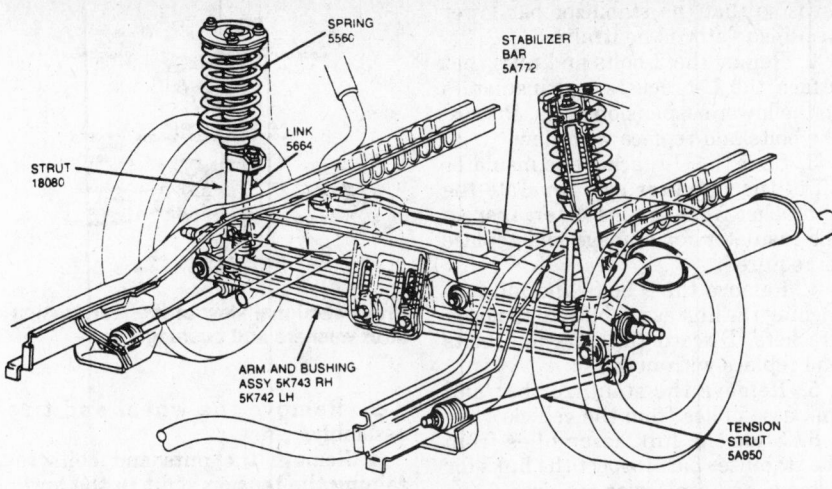

View of the rear suspension components—Taurus/Sable sedan

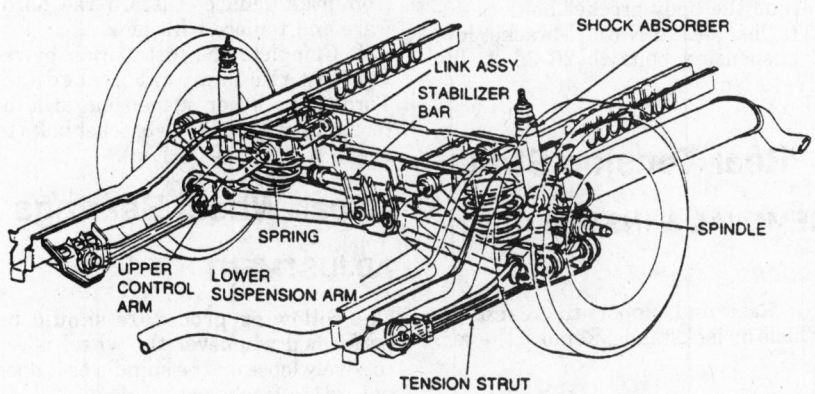

Rear suspension components—Taurus/Sable station wagon

and clip to the lower suspension arm.

18. Position the shock absorber on the lower suspension arm and install 2 new nuts. Torque the nuts to 13–20 ft. lbs. (17–27 Nm).

19. Attach the stabilizer U-bracket to the lower suspension arm using a new bolt. Torque the bolt to 20–30 ft. lbs. (27–40 Nm).

20. Attach the flexible brake hose to the body and tighten the bolt to 8–12 ft. lbs. (11–16 Nm).

21. With the floor jack, raise the lower suspension to normal curb height. Torque the lower suspension arm to 60–86 ft. lbs. (81–115 Nm). Torque the bolt that attaches the tension strut to the body bracket to 40–55 ft. lbs. (54–74 Nm).

22. Install the wheel and tire assembly. Remove the floor jack and lower the vehicle.

23. Check the rear wheel alignment and adjust if necessary.

Rear Control Arms

REMOVAL & INSTALLATION

Sedan

1. Raise and support the rear of the vehicle on jackstands. Remove the rear tires.

NOTE: **DO NOT** raise or support the vehicle using the tension struts.

2. From the left side of the front control arm, disconnect the brake proportioning valve.

3. From the front of the control arms, disconnect the parking brake cable.

4. Remove the control arm-to-spindle bolt, washer and nut.

5. Remove and discard the control arm-to-body nut/bolt and the arm from the vehicle.

NOTE: **When installing new control arms, be sure that the offset is facing upwards; the arms are stamped with "Bottom" on the lower edge. The flange edge of the right side rear arm stamping MUST face the front of the vehicle; the other three MUST face the rear of the vehicle.**

6. To install, position the arm and cam where required at the center of the vehicle (insert the bolts but do not tighten) and complete the installation of the remaining components by reversing the removal procedures. Torque the control arm-to-spindle bolts to 42–57 ft. lbs. (57–77 Nm) and the control arm-to-body nuts to 45–65

under the lower suspension arm and raise the lower arm to normal curb height.

2. Remove the wheel and tire assembly.

3. Locate the bracket retaining the flexible hose to the body. Remove the bracket retaining bolt and bracket from the body.

4. Remove the stabilzer bar U-bracket from the lower suspension arm.

5. Remove and discard the nuts attaching the shock absorber to the lower suspension arm.

6. Disconnect and remove the parking brake cable and clip from the lower suspension arm.

7. Remove and discard the bolt and nut attaching the tension strut to the lower suspension arm.

8. Suspend the spindle and upper suspension arms from the body with a piece of wire to prevent them from dropping.

9. Remove the nut, bolt, washer and adjusting cam that retain the lower suspension arm to the spindle. Discard the nut, bolt and washer and replace with new. Set the cam aside.

10. With the floor jack, slowly lower the suspension arm until the spring, lower and upper insulators can be removed. Replace the spring and insulators as required.

11. Position the lower insulator on the lower suspension arm and press the insulator downward into place. Make certain that the insulator is properly seated.

12. Position the upper insulator on top of the spring. Install the spring on the lower suspension arm. Make certain that the spring is properly seated.

13. With the floor jack, slowly raise the suspension arm. Guide the upper spring insultor onto the upper spring underbody seat.

14. Position the spindle in the lower suspension arm with a new bolt, nut washer, and the existing cam. Install the bolt with the head of the bolt toward the front of the vehicle. DO NOT tighten the bolt at this time.

15. Remove the wire supporting the spindle and suspension arms.

16. Install the tension strut in the lower suspension arm using a new nut and bolt. DO NOT tighten at this time.

17. Attach the parking brake cable

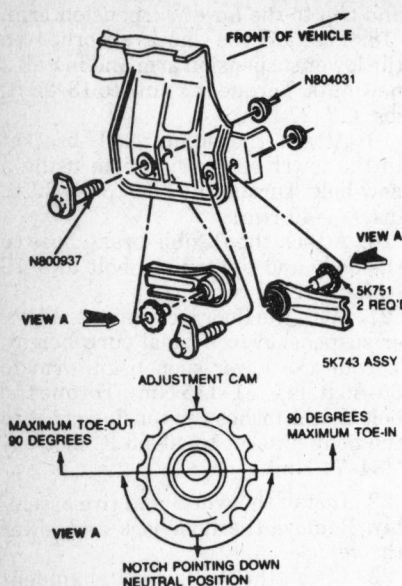

Exploded view of the rear control arm adjusting cam

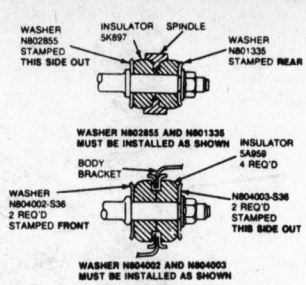

Cross-sectional view of the rear tension strut washers and bushings

ft. lbs. (62–88 Nm). Check the rear wheel alignment and adjust as required.

StabilizerBar/Link

REMOVAL & INSTALLATION

Sedan

1. Raise and support the rear of vehicle on jackstands. Remove the rear tires.

NOTE: DO NOT raise or support the vehicle using the tension struts.

2. Remove the stabilizer bar-to-link (both sides) nuts, washers and insulators. Discard the nuts and replace with new.

3. Remove the stabilizer bar U-bracket-to-body bolts and the stabilizer bar from the vehicle. Discard the bolts and replace with new.

4. Remove the stabilizer link-to-shock strut bracket nut, washer and insulator; inspect the condition of the insulators and replace them if necessary.

5. To install, reverse the removal procedures. Torque the stabilizer link-to-shock strut bracket nut to 6–12 ft. lbs. (8–16 Nm); the stabilizer bar U-bracket-to-body bolts to 15–25 ft. lbs. (20–34 Nm) and the stabilizer bar-to-link nuts to 6–12 ft. lbs. (8–16 Nm).

Wagon

1. Raise and support the vehicle with jackstands. Position the jackstands under the lower control arms so that the stabilizer bar lower arm insulator is neutralized.

2. Remov the 2 bolts and nuts that attach the U-brackets and insulators to the lower suspension arms. Discard the bolts and replace with new.

3. Slide the U-bracket and insulator off of the stabilizer bar. Separate the U-bracket from the insulator. Inspect the insulator for damage and replace as required.

4. Remove the 2 bolts and nuts attaching the link assemblies to the body brackets. Discard the nuts and bolts and replace with new.

5. Remove the stabilizer bar and link assemblies from the vehicle.

6. Slide the link assemblies from the stabilizer bar. Inspect the links for damage and replace as required.

7. Complete the installation by reversing the removal procedure. Torque the body bracket bolts to 40–55 ft. lbs. (54–74 Nm), U-bracket lower suspension bolts to 20–30 ft. lbs. (27–40 Nm).

Rear Tension Strut

REMOVAL & INSTALLATION

Sedan

1. Raise and support the rear of the vehicle on jackstands. Remove the rear tires.

NOTE: DO NOT raise or support the vehicle using the tension struts.

2. From inside the luggage compartment, loosen but DO NOT remove the 3 shock strut-to-body nuts.

3. Remove the tension strut-to-spindle nut and the tension strut-to-body nut. Discard the nuts and replace with new.

4. Move the spindle rearward and remove the tension strut from the vehicle.

NOTE: The tension strut bushings at the front and the rear are different; the rear bushings have indentations in them.

5. To install, use new tension strut washers/bushings and reverse the removal procedures. Torque the tension strut-to-spindle nut to 52–74 ft. lbs. (70–100 Nm) and the tension strut-to-body bracket nut 52–74 ft. lbs. (70–100 Nm). Check the rear wheel alignment.

Wagon

1. Loosen the rear wheel nuts. Raise the vehicle and position a floorjack with a block of wood under the rear lower suspension arm. Raise the arm to normal curb height.

2. Remove the wheel and tire assembly.

3. Remove the nuts and bolts retaining the tension strut to the lower suspension arm and body bracket. Remove the tension strut assembly frommthe vehicle. Discard the hardware and replace with new.

4. Complete the installation by reversing the removal procedure. Torque the lower suspension arm-to-tension strut and body bracket bolts to 40–55 ft. lbs. (54–74 Nm).

Rear Wheel Bearings

ADJUSTMENT

The following procedure should be performed whenever the wheel is excessively loose on the spindle or it does not rotate freely.

NOTE: The rear wheel uses a tapered roller bearing which may feel loose when properly adjusted; this condition should be considered normal.

1. Raise and support the rear of vehicle until tires clear the floor.

2. Remove the wheelcover or the ornament and nut covers. Remove the hub grease cap.

NOTE: If the vehicle is equipped with styled steel or aluminum wheels, the wheel/tire assembly must be removed to remove the dust cover.

3. Remove the cotter pin and the nut retainer.

4. Back off the hub nut one full turn.

5. While rotating the hub/drum assembly, tighten the adjusting nut to 17–25 ft. lbs. (23–24 Nm). Back off the adjusting nut ½ turn, then retighten it to 10–15 inch lbs. (1.1–1.7 Nm).

6. Position the nut retainer over the adjusting nut so that the slots are in line with cotter pin hole (without rotating the adjusting nut).

7. Install the cotter pin and bend the ends around the retainer flange.

8. To complete the installation, reverse the removal procedures.

REMOVAL & INSTALLATION

1. Raise the vehicle and support it safely. Remove the wheel from the hub and drum.

2. Remove the grease cap from the hub, making sure not to damage the cap. Remove the cotter pin, nut retainer, adjusting nut and keyed flat washer from the spindle. Discard the cotter pin.

3. Pull the hub and drum assembly off the spindle being careful not to drop the outer bearing assembly. Remove the outer bearing assembly.

4. Using a suitable seal remover, remove and discard the grease seal. Remove the inner bearing assembly from the hub.

5. Installation is the reverse order of the removal procedure. Be sure to use a new grease seal and new cotter pin at the installation.

STEERING

Steering Wheel
REMOVAL & INSTALLATION

1. Disconnect the negative battery cable. Position the steering wheel so that the wheels are in the straight-forward position.

2. From the rear of the steering wheel, remove the steering wheel-to-horn pad screws.

3. Disconnect the horn pad electrical connectors. If equipped with cruise control, disconnect the electrical connector from the slip ring terminal.

4. Remove and discard the steering wheel-to-steering column nut. The nut has been replaced with a bolt on later vehicles. If a bolt is used, discard the bolt and replace with new.

5. Firmly grasp the steering wheel and pull it from the steering column; a wheel puller is not required.

6. Place the multi-function switch lever in the **NEUTRAL** position and install the steering wheel on the end of the steering shaft. Align the mark on the steering wheel with the mark on the shaft to ensure that the straight-ahead steering position corresponds to the straight ahead position of the front wheels.

—— CAUTION ——
The multi-function switch lever must be in the NEUTRAL position prior to installing the steering wheel or damage to the switch cam may result.

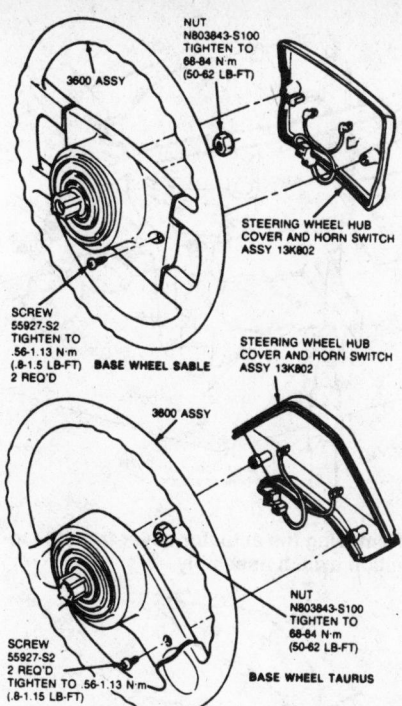

Exploded view of the steering wheel assembly

7. Torque the steering wheel-to-steering column nut to 50–62 ft. lbs. (68–84 ft. lbs.). Torque the bolt, if removed, to 22–33 ft. lbs. (31–45 Nm).

8. Install the wheel horn pad cover with attaching screws. Torque the screws to 5–10 inch lbs. (0.5–1.0 Nm).

9. Connect the negative battery cable and check the steering wheel for proper operation.

Combination Switch

The combination switch is mounted on the steering column and consists of the following switches: turn signal, cornering lights, hazard warning, headlight dimmer, headlight flash-to-pass, windshield washer and windshield wiper.

REMOVAL & INSTALLATION

1. Disconnect the negative battery cable.

2. If equipped with a tilt-steering column, position the steering wheel in the lowest position and remove the tilt lever.

3. Remove the ignition lock cylinder from the steering column.

4. Remove the upper/lower shroud-to-steering column screws and the shrouds from the steering column.

5. Remove the electrical harness-to-

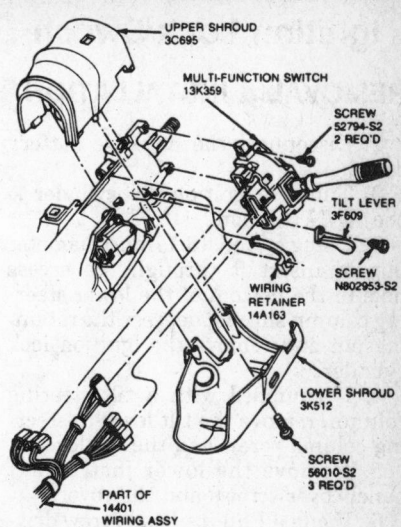

Exploded view of the upper steering column—combination switch

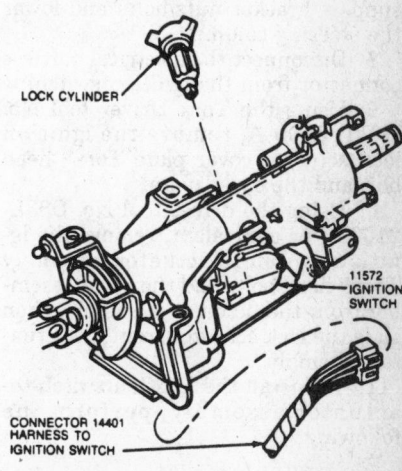

Removing the lock cylinder from the ignition switch assembly

steering column retainer and disconnect the 3 electrical connectors from the steering column.

6. Remove the combination switch-to-steering column self-tapping screws and the disengage the switch from the steering column casting.

7. To install, reverse the removal procedures. Torque the combination switch-to-steering column screws to 18–27 inch lbs. (2–3 Nm), the shroud-to-steering column screws to 6–10 inch lbs. (0.7–1.0 Nm), the steering wheel-to-steering column nut to 50–62 ft. lbs. (68–84 Nm) and the tilt lever-to-steering column screw to 6–8.5 inch lbs. (0.7–1.0 Nm).

NOTE: During installation, align the multi-function switch with the corresponding holes in the steering column casting. Make certain to start the self-tapping screws in the existing holes.

Ignition Lock/Switch

REMOVAL & INSTALLATION

1. Disconnect the negative battery cable.

2. Turn the ignition lock cylinder to the **RUN** position.

3. Using a ⅛ in. (3.17mm) diameter punch, insert it through the access hole in the bottom of the lower steering column shroud, depress the retaining pin and remove the ignition lock cylinder.

4. If equipped with a tilt steering column, remove the tilt lever-to-steering column screw and the tilt lever.

5. Remove the lower instrument panel cover screws and the cover.

6. Using a Phillips head screwdriver, remove the upper/lower steering column shrouds.

7. Remove the steering column-to-support bracket nuts/bolts and lower the steering column.

8. Disconnect the electrical harness connector from the ignition switch.

9. Using the Torx Driver tool No. D83L-2100-A, remove the ignition lock actuator cover plate Torx® head bolt and the cover plate.

10. Using the driver tool No. D83L-2100-A, or equivalent, remove the ignition switch-to-actuator assembly Torx® head bolts and the cover assembly from the actuator assembly, then slide the lock actuator from the actuator assembly.

11. To install the ignition switch-to-actuator assembly, perform the following:

   a. Position the ignition switch in the **RUN** position by turning the switch drive shaft fully clockwise to the **START** position and release it.

   b. Using a small ruler, insert the lock actuator into the actuator assembly to a depth of 0.46–0.54 in. (11.75–13.25mm).

   c. While holding the lock actuator at the proper depth, install the ignition switch.

   d. Using new tamper-resistant Torx® head bolts, torque the ignition switch-to-actuator assembly bolts to 30–48 inch lbs. (3.4–5.4 Nm).

12. To install the lock cylinder, perform the following procedures:

   a. While measuring the lock actuator, turn the ignition switch to the Lock position and install it, the depth should be 0.92–1.0 in. (23.5–25.5mm); if this specification is not met, repeat the lock actuator installation.

   b. Using a new tamper-resistant Torx® head bolt, torque the cover-

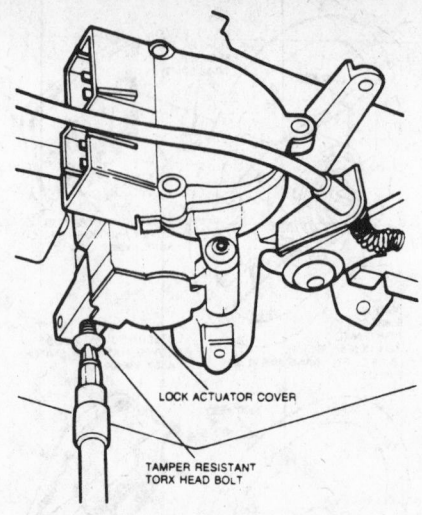

Removing the actuator cover from the ignition switch assembly

LOCK ACTUATOR COVER

TAMPER RESISTANT TORX HEAD BOLT

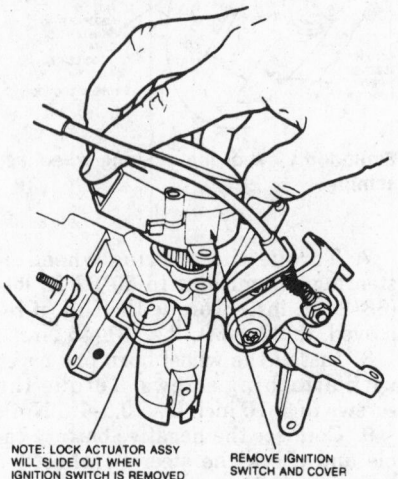

NOTE: LOCK ACTUATOR ASSY WILL SLIDE OUT WHEN IGNITION SWITCH IS REMOVED

REMOVE IGNITION SWITCH AND COVER

Removing the ignition switch from the lock actuator assembly

to-lock actuator assembly bolt to 30–48 in. lbs. (3.4–5.4 Nm).

13. Check the operation of the ignition lock cylinder; if the operation is satisfactory, remove the ignition lock cylinder.

14. To complete the installation, reverse the removal procedures and reinstall the ignition lock cylinder. Torque the steering column support bracket-to-instrument panel nuts/bolts to 15–25 ft. lbs. (20–34 Nm), the shroud-to-steering column screws to 6–10 inch lbs. (0.7–1.1 Nm) and the tilt release lever-to-steering column screw to 6.5–8.5 ft. lbs. (9–11 Nm).

Power Steering Gear

REMOVAL & INSTALLATION

1. From inside the vehicle, remove the steering shaft weather boot-to-dash panel nuts.

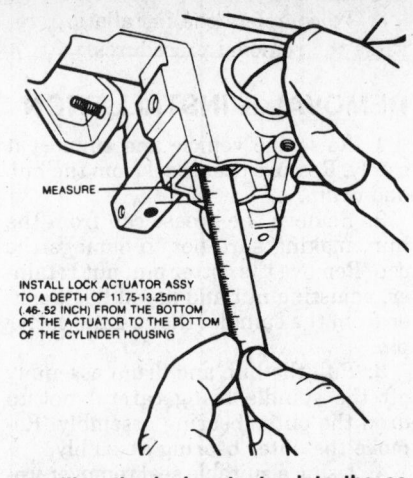

MEASURE

INSTALL LOCK ACTUATOR ASSY TO A DEPTH OF 11.75-13.25mm (.46-.52 INCH) FROM THE BOTTOM OF THE ACTUATOR TO THE BOTTOM OF THE CYLINDER HOUSING

Installing the lock actuator into the actuator housing

ROTATE SHAFT CLOCKWISE UNTIL IT STOPS AND SLOWLY RELEASE TO POSITION SWITCH IN RUN

Positioning the ignition switch drive shaft

2. Remove the intermediate shaft-to-steering column shaft bolts and set the weather boot aside. Remove the steering gear input shaft pinch bolt and the intermediate shaft.

3. Raise and support the front of the vehicle on jackstands.

4. Remove the left front wheel and the heat shield, then cut the bundling strap lines from the steering gear.

5. Remove the tie rod ends from the steering knuckles.

6. Position a drain pan under the vehicle, then disconnect the pressure and return hoses from the steering gear and drain the fluid.

NOTE: The pressure and return hoses are located on the front of the valve housing. Do not confuse them with the transfer lines on the side of the valve.

7. Remove the steering gear-to-chassis nuts.

NOTE: The steering gear bolts are pressed into the housing; no attempt should be made to remove them.

8. While pushing the weather boot into the vehicle, lift the steering gear from the mounting holes, rotate the gear (so that the input shaft will pass between the brake booster and the floorpan) and work it through the left fender apron opening.

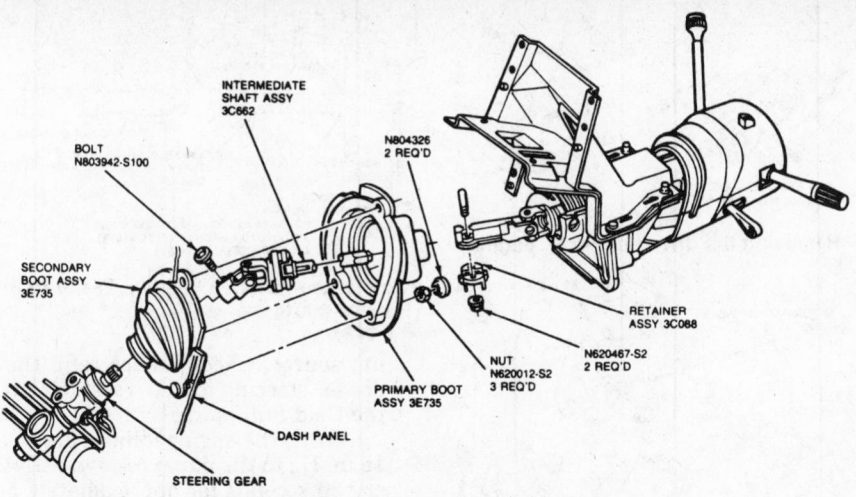

Exploded view of the steering column assembly

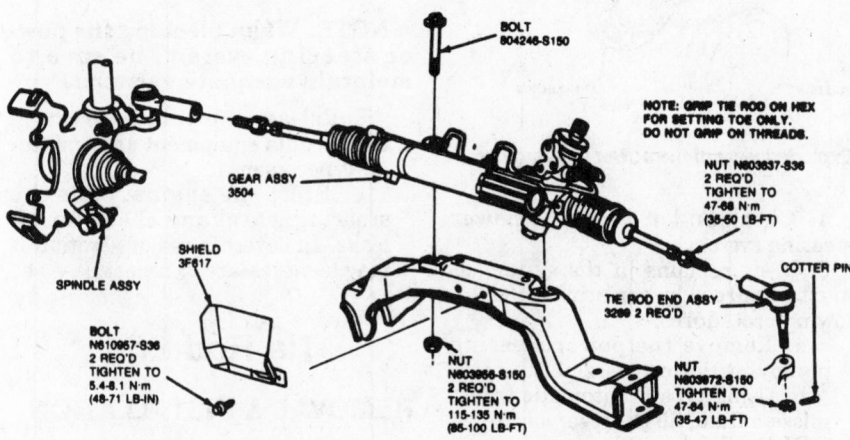

Exploded view of the power steering gear assembly

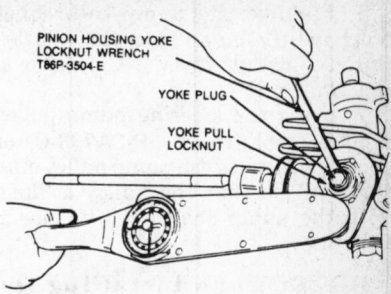

Adjusting the yoke plug of the power steering gear

View of the power steering gear adjuster disc

Nm); be sure to clean the yoke plug threads before torquing.

7. Mark the position of the 0 degrees mark on the steering gear housing. Using the disc-yoke preload adjuster tool (No. T86P-3504-H), back off the adjuster to align the 48 degrees mark with the 0 degree mark.

8. Using the pinion housing yoke locknut wrench to hold the yoke plug, torque the yoke plug locknut to 40–50 ft. lbs. (54–68 Nm).

NOTE: When torquing the yoke plug locknut, DO NOT allow the yoke plug to move.

9. To install the steering gear, reverse the removal procedures. Refill the power steering reservoir, bleed the system and check for leaks.

Power Steering Pump

REMOVAL & INSTALLATION

2.5L Engine

1. Disconnect the negative battery cable.

2. Using a ½ in. drive ratchet, insert it into the square hole of the drive belt tensioner pulley, rotate the pulley clockwise and remove the drive belt.

3. Position a drain pan under the vehicle, disconnect the power steering pump fluid lines and drain the fluid into the pan.

4. Using the hub puller tool No. T69L-10300-B, or equivalent, remove the pulley from the power steering pump.

NOTE: If the steering gear appears to be stuck, check the right side tie rod to ensure that it is not caught on anything.

9. To install, use new plastic seals on the hydraulic line fittings and reverse the removal procedures. Torque the steering gear-to-chassis nuts to 85–100 ft. lbs. (115–135 Nm); the tie rod end-to-steering knuckle nuts to 35–50 ft. lbs. (48–68 Nm); the intermediate shaft-to-steering gear bolt to 30–38 ft. lbs. (41–51 Nm). Refill the power steering pump reservoir and bleed the system. Check the system for leaks and proper operation. Adjust the toe setting.

ADJUSTMENT

The power steering gear preload adjustment must be performed with the steering gear removed from the vehicle.

1. Remove the power steering gear from the vehicle.

2. Mount the steering gear in a holding fixture (tool No. T57L-500-B, or equivalent).

NOTE: If the steering gear mounting holes in the holding fixture are too small, drill the holes larger using a ⁹⁄₁₆ in. drill bit.

3. DO NOT remove the external pressure lines from the steering gear unless they are leaking or damaged. If they are removed, they must be replaced with new ones.

4. Using the pinion shaft torque adjuster tool No. T86P-3504-K, or equivalent, position it on the input shaft and rotate the shaft (twice), from lock-to-lock, to drain the power steering fluid.

5. Using the pinion housing yoke locknut wrench (tool No. T86P-3504-E, or equivalent), loosen the yoke plug locknut and the yoke plug.

6. Position the steering gear in the center of it's travel and torque the yoke plug to 45–50 inch lbs. (5–5.6

5. Remove the pump-to-bracket bolts and the pump from the vehicle.

6. To install, reverse the removal procedures.

7. Using the steering pump pulley replacer tool No. T65P-3A733-C, or equivalent, press the pump pulley onto the shaft so that the pulley is flush with the pump shaft ± 0.10 in. (± 0.25mm).

NOTE: When installing the pump pulley, the small diameter tool threads must be fully engaged in the pump shaft.

8. Fill the pump reservoir with power steering fluid, bleed the system and check for leaks.

3.0L Engine

1. Disconnect the negative battery cable.

2. Loosen the idler pulley and remove the power steering belt.

3. Remove the pulley from the pump hub and the return line from the pump.

4. Back off the pressure line nut until the line separates from the pump.

5. Remove the 3 pump-to-bracket bolts and the pump from the vehicle.

6. To install, reverse the removal procedures. Torque the pump-to-bracket bolts to 30–45 ft. lbs. (40–62 Nm). Refill the power steering pump reservoir, bleed the system and check for leaks.

BELT ADJUSTMENT

NOTE: Belt adjustment applies only to 3.0L engines that use idler pulleys. Engines that use automatic belt tension adjusters do not require adjustment. When adjusting the belt tension on the 3.0L engine, use Rotunda Offset Belt Tension Gauge No. 021–00028 or equivalent.

3.0L Engine

1. Loosen the idler pulley nut and turn the adjusting screw until the belt is properly adjusted. Turning the wrench to the right tightens the belt.

2. Torque the idler pulley nut to 50–65 ft. lbs. (68–88 Nm).

SYSTEM BLEEDING

1. Fill the power steering pump reservoir to the **COLD FULL** fill line.

2. Run the engine until it reaches normal operating temperature.

3. Turn the steering wheel from the left-to-right (all the way) several times.

NOTE: When turning the steering wheel, do not hold it in the far left or right positions too long.

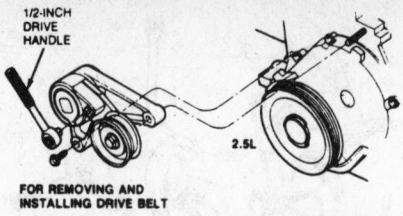

FOR REMOVING AND INSTALLING DRIVE BELT

Removing the drive belt—2.5L engine

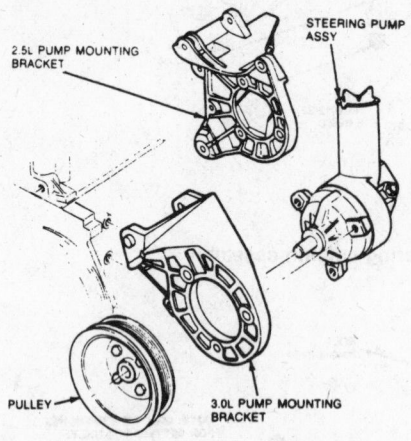

Exploded view of the power steering pump

4. Check and/or refill the power steering system.

5. If air remains in the system, it must be purged by performing the following procedures:

a. Remove the power steering pump dipstick cap assembly.

b. Using type F automatic transmission fluid, fill the reservoir to the **COLD FULL** mark on the pump dipstick.

c. Disconnect the ignition coil wire. Raise and support the front of the vehicle on jackstands.

d. Using the starter motor, crank the engine, then check the fluid level; do not turn the steering wheel at this time.

e. Check and/or refill the pump reservoir to the **COLD FULL**. Using the starter motor, crank the engine and cycle the steering wheel from lock-to-lock, then recheck the fluid level.

f. Using the vacuum tester tool No. 021-00014, or equivalent, press the rubber stopper into the pump reservoir. Install the coil wire and start the engine.

g. Apply 15 in. Hg to the pump reservoir for at least 3 minutes (engine idling).

NOTE: As the air is being purged from the system, the vacuum will fall off; be sure to maintain adequate vacuum with the vacuum source.

h. Release and remove the vacu-

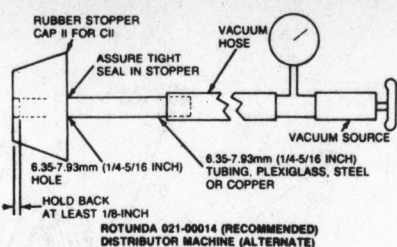

View of the Rotunda Vacuum Tester tool No. 021-00014

um source. Check and/or refill the power steering pump reservoir to the Cold Full mark.

i. With the engine idling, connect 15 in. Hg to the pump reservoir. Every 30 seconds for approximately 5 min., turn the steering wheel from lock-to-lock; DO NOT hold the steering wheel in the lock position.

NOTE: When bleeding the power steering system, be sure to maintain adequate vacuum.

j. Release the vacuum, remove the vacuum equipment and add fluid, if necessary.

k. Start the engine, cycle the steering wheel and check for oil leaks. In severe cases of aeration it may be necessary to repeat Steps e–j.

Tie Rod End

REMOVAL & INSTALLATION

1. Raise and support the front of the vehicle on jackstands.

2. Remove the discard the cotter pin and the nut from the tie rod end ball stud.

3. Using the tie rod remover tool No. TOOL-3290-C, or equivalent, separate the tie rod end from the steering knuckle.

4. While holding the tie rod end, loosen the tie rod jam nut.

5. Note the depth of the tie rod end-to-tie rod, then remove the tie rod end from the tie rod.

6. To install, reverse the removal procedures. Torque the tie rod-to-steering knuckle nut to 36 ft. lbs. (48 Nm) and the tie rod end-to-tie rod nut to 35–50 ft. lbs. (47–68 Nm). Check and/or adjust the toe-in.

BRAKES

For all brake system repair and service procedures not detailed below, please refer to "Brakes" in the Unit Repair section.

Master Cylinder

REMOVAL & INSTALLATION

1. Disconnect and plug the brake lines from the primary and secondary outlet ports of the master cylinder and pressure control valves.

2. Disconnect the electrical connector (brake warning lamp) from the master cylinder.

3. Remove the 2 master cylinder-to-power booster nuts. Slide the master cylinder forward and upward from the vehicle.

4. To install, reverse the removal procedures. Torque the master cylinder-to-power booster nuts to 13–25 ft. lbs. (18–33 Nm). Fill the master cylinder to the **MAX** line on the side of the reservoir and bleed the brake system.

5. Operate the brakes several times and check for fluid leaks.

Control Valve

REMOVAL & INSTALLATION

Sedan

The control valve is mounted to the floorpan near the left-rear wheel. It utilizes a mechanical linkage to the lower suspension arm to vary the valve performance based on the rear weight of the vehicle.

1. Raise and support the rear of the vehicle on jackstands.

NOTE: DO NOT raise or support the vehicle by the tension struts.

2. Label and disconnect the 4 brake tubes from the control valve assembly.

3. Remove the screw attaching the valve bracket to the lower suspension arm. Remove the valve bracket-to-underbody screws and the control valve assembly from the vehicle.

NOTE: The service replacement control valve will have a red plastic gauge clip on it, which MUST NOT BE removed until installation.

4. To install, make sure that the rear suspension is in the full rebound position and the control valve operating screw is loose, then reverse the removal procedures. Torque the control valve-to-underbody screws to 8–10 ft. lbs. (11–13 Nm). Perform the control valve assembly adjustment procedures. Bleed the rear brake system.

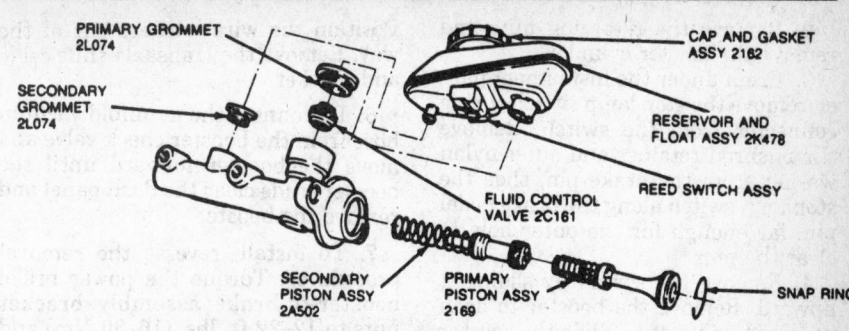

Exploded view of the master cylinder—sedan model

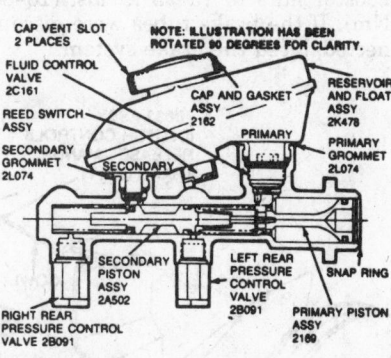

Cross-sectional view of the master cylinder—station wagon model

Station Wagon

The control valves are screwed into the bottom of the master cylinder. They control the braking pressure to the rear wheels to minimize rear wheel skidding during hard braking.

1. Disconnect and plug the primary and/or secondary brake tube from the master cylinder.

2. Loosen and remove the pressure control valve(s) from the master cylinder housing port.

3. To install, reverse the removal procedures. Torque the control valve-to-master cylinder to 10–18 ft. lbs. (13–24 Nm). Bleed the brake system and fill as required .

ADJUSTMENT

Sedan

1. Place the vehicle on a hoist or an alignment machine, so that the vehicle is at the curb load level and the wheels are on a flat surface.

2. At the control valve, loosen the adjuster screw.

3. Using a piece of rubber or plastic tubing $5/8$–$21/64$ in. (16–16.5mm), $3/8$ in. (OD) x $1/4$ in. (ID), slice it lengthwise (on one edge), then install it on the operating rod.

4. Make sure that the adjuster is resting on the lower mounting bracket; tighten the set screw.

NOTE: DO NOT change the position of the upper nut on the

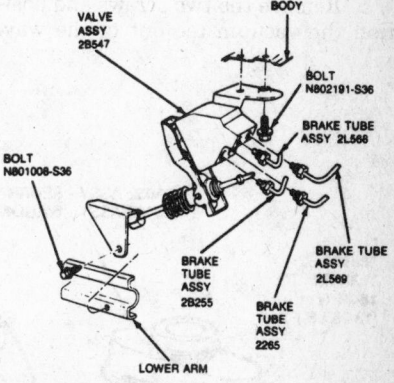

Exploded view of the control valve—sedan model

valve operating rod; the dimension will position the valve for normal operation.

5. To decrease the rear brake pressure, perform the following procedures:

   a. Make sure that the vehicle is at curb height.

   b. Loosen the control valve set screw.

   c. Move the piston DOWN the operating rod 1mm for each 60 psi pressure decrease.

   d. Tighten the set screw in the desired position.

6. To increase the rear brake pressure, perform the following procedures:

   a. Make sure that the vehicle is at curb height.

   b. Loosen the control valve set screw.

   c. Move the piston UP the operating rod 1mm for each 60 psi pressure increase.

   d. Tighten the set screw in the desired position.

Power Brake Booster

REMOVAL & INSTALLATION

1. Disconnect the battery ground cable and remove the brake lines from the master cylinder.

2. Remove the retaining nuts and remove the master cylinder.

3. From under the instrument panel, remove the stop lamp switch wiring connector from the switch. Remove the pushrod retainer and outer nylon washer from the brake pin, slide the stoplamp switch along the brake pedal pin, far enough for the outer hole to clear the pin.

4. Remove the switch by sliding it upward. Remove the booster to dash panel retaining nuts. Slide the booster pushrod and pushrod bushing off the brake pedal pin.

5. Remove the two screws and position the vacuum tee out of the way.

Position the wire harness out of the way. Remove the transaxle shift cable and bracket.

6. Disconnect the manifold vacuum hose from the booster check valve and move the booster forward until the booster studs clear the dash panel and remove the booster.

7. To install, reverse the removal procedures. Torque the power brake booster-to-brake assembly bracket nuts to 12–22 ft. lbs. (16–30 Nm) and the master cylinder-to-power brake booster nuts to 13–25 ft. lbs. (18–34 Nm). If the brake tubes were disconnected, bleed the brake system.

Wheel Cylinder

REMOVAL & INSTALLATION

1. Raise and support the rear of the vehicle on jackstands.

NOTE: DO NOT raise or support the vehicle using the tension struts.

2. Remove the wheelcover or the ornament and nut covers. Remove the hub grease cap.

NOTE: If the vehicle is equipped with styled steel or alu-

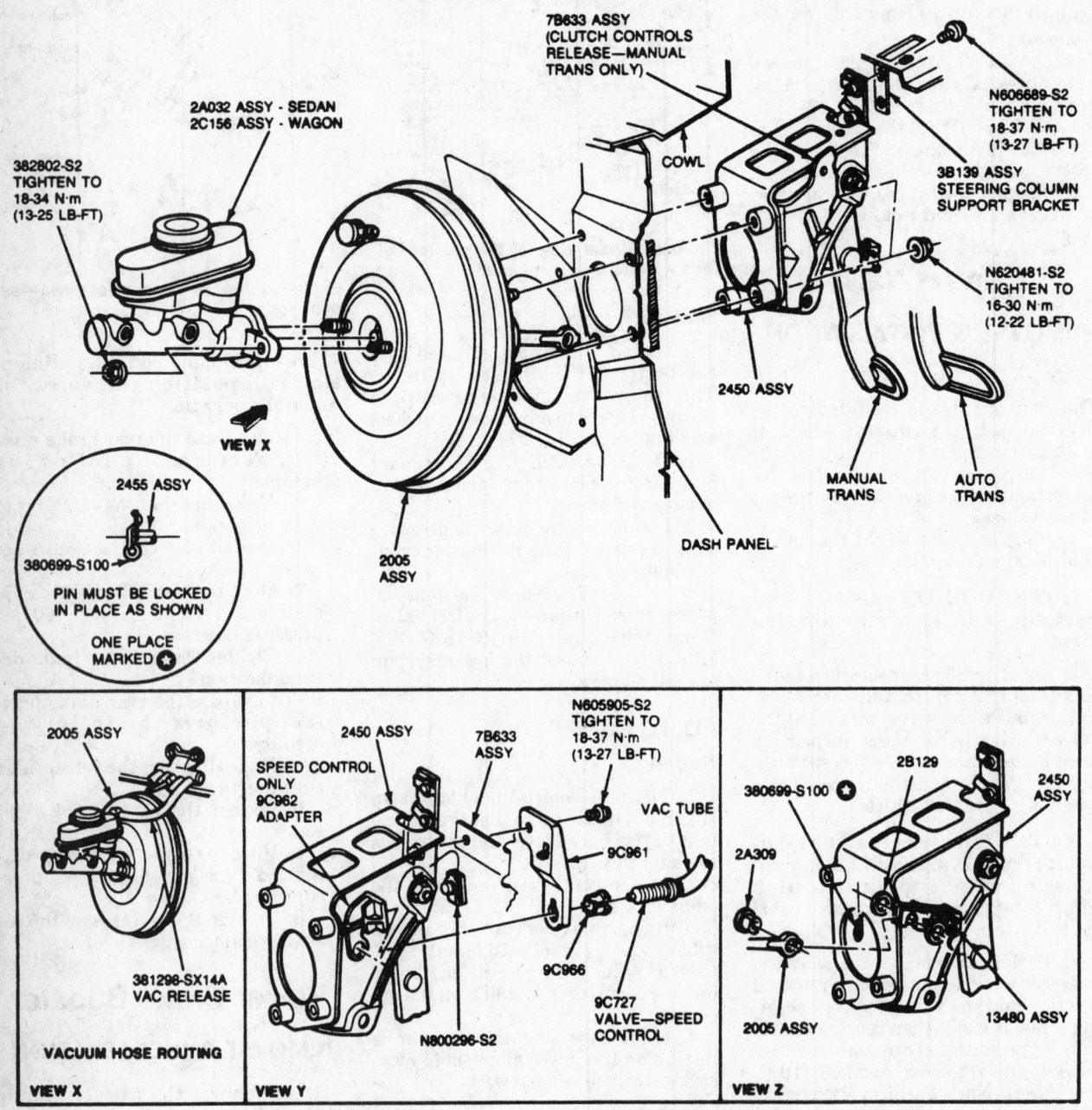

Exploded view of the power brake booster/master cylinder

minum wheels, the wheel/tire assembly must be removed to remove the dust cover.

3. Remove the cotter pin and the nut retainer.

4. Remove the hub nut, the thrust washer, the outer bearing and the brake drum assembly.

5. Remove the brake shoes, the retainers and the springs from the backing plate.

6. Disconnect and plug the brake tube at the rear-side of the wheel cylinder.

7. Remove the wheel cylinder-to-backing plate bolts and the wheel cylinder from the vehicle.

8. To install, reverse the removal procedures. Torque the wheel cylinder-to-backing plate bolts to 7.5–10 ft. lbs. (10–14 Nm). Adjust the rear wheel bearing. Bleed the rear brake system.

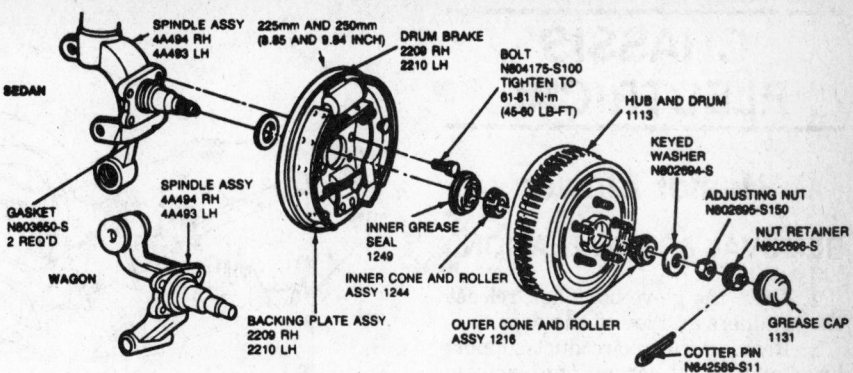

Exploded view of the rear wheel assembly

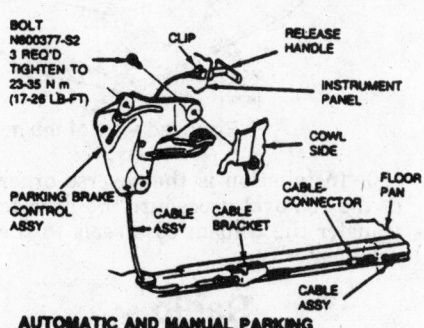

AUTOMATIC AND MANUAL PARKING BRAKE RELEASE HANDLE

Front parking brake cable asembly

Parking Brake Cable

ADJUSTMENT

1. Raise and support the rear of the vehicle on jackstands.

NOTE: DO NOT raise or support the vehicle using the tension struts.

2. Make sure that the parking brake is fully released and the transaxle is in **NEUTRAL**.

3. At the parking brake cable equalizer, turn the adjusting nut until drag is felt at the rear wheel.

4. Loosen the adjusting nut until no brake drag is felt.

NOTE: If the parking brake cables have been replaced, in a foot-operated control assembly, set the parking brake lever with approximately 100 lbs. of pressure, then release the control and repeat the procedure.

5. Lower the vehicle and check the operation of the parking brake.

REMOVAL & INSTALLATION

Front Cable

1. Raise the front of the vehicle and support safely.

2. Loosen the adjuster nut at the cable adjuster bracket.

3. Lower the vehicle.

4. Disconnect the cable from the control assembly at the clevis.

5. Raise the vehicle and support safely.

6. At the cable connector, disconnect the front cable from the rear cable.

7. Remove the cable and push-in prong retainer from the cable bracket, using a 13mm box end wrench to depress the retaining prongs. Allow the cable to hang.

8. Push the grommet up through the floor pan and lower the vehicle.

9. Remove the left hand cowl side panel.

10. From inside the vehicle, remove the cable end from the clevis and remove the conduit retainer from the control assembly.

11. Complete the installation of the front cable by reversing the removal procedure. Adjust the parking brake and check the brake for proper operation.

Rear Cable

LEFT SIDE

1. Raise the vehicle and support safely.

2. Remove the parking brake cable adjusting nut.

3. Remove the rear cable end fitting from the front cable connector.

4. Disconnect the brake cable from the parking brake actuating lever. With a 13mm box end wrench, depress the conduit retaining prongs and remove the cable end pronged fitting from the backing plate.

5. Push the plastic snap-in grommet rearward to disconnect it from the side rail bracket.

6. Remove the pronged connector from the parking park adjuster bracket. Remove the cable assembly.

7. Complete the installation of the cable by reversing the removal procedure. Ensure that the all pronged connectors are locked in place.

Rear Cable

RIGHT SIDE

1. Raise the vehicle and support safely.

2. Remove the parking brake cable adjuster nut.

3. Use a 13mm box wrench to remove the conduit retainer prongs and remoev the cable from the frame side rail bracket.

4. Remove the rear wheel and drum assembly.

5. Disconnect the brake cable from the parking brake actuating lever. With a 13mm box end wrench, depress the conduit retaining prongs and remove the cable end pronged fitting from the backing plate.

6. On sedan vehicles, perform the follwoing:

a. Remove the brake pressure control valve bracket at the control arm.

b. Remove the cable retaining screw and clip from the lower suspension arm.

c. Remove one screw from the cable bracket at the crossmember.

d. Remove the entire right hand cable assembly.

7. On station wagon vehicles, perform the following:

a. Remove the cable retaining clip and screw from each lower suspension arm.

b. Remove the cable clip retaining screw from lower suspension arm inner mounting bracket.

8. Complete the installation of the cable by reversing the removal procedure. Ensure the pronged fitting is securely locked in place.

CHASSIS ELECTRICAL

Heater Blower

REMOVAL & INSTALLATION

1. Open the glove box door, release the retainers and lower the door.
2. Remove the recirc duct support bracket-to-cowl screw, the vacuum line-to-vacuum motor hose and the recirc duct-to-heater assembly screws.
3. Remove the recirc duct-to-heater assembly duct, then lower the recirc duct from between the instrument panel and the heater case.
4. Disconnect the heater motor electrical connector.
5. Remove the heater motor wheel clip and the heater wheel.
6. Remove the heater motor-to-mounting plate screws and heater motor from the evaporator case.
7. To install, reverse the removal procedures.

Heater Core

REMOVAL & INSTALLATION

1. Disconnect the negative battery cable and drain the coolant into a suitable drain pan.
2. Remove the instrument as previously outlined in this section and lay it on the front seat.
3. Disconnect and cap the heater hose from the heater core. Disconnect the vacuum supply hose from the in-line vacuum check valve in the engine compartment.
4. Remove the screw holding the instrument panel shake brace to heater case and remove the instrument panel shake brace.
5. Remove the floor register (or the rear seat adapter) attached by 2 screws at the bottom of the heater case.
6. Remove the 3 nuts attaching the heater case to the dash panel in the engine compartment.
7. Remove the 2 screws attaching the brackets to the cowl top panel. Carefully pull the heater assembly away from the dash panel and remove the heater case assembly from the vehicle.
8. Remove the vacuum source line from the heater core tube seal. Remove the seal from the heater core tubes.
9. Remove the 4 heater core access cover attaching screws and remove the access cover from the heater case. Lift the heater core and seal from the heater case.

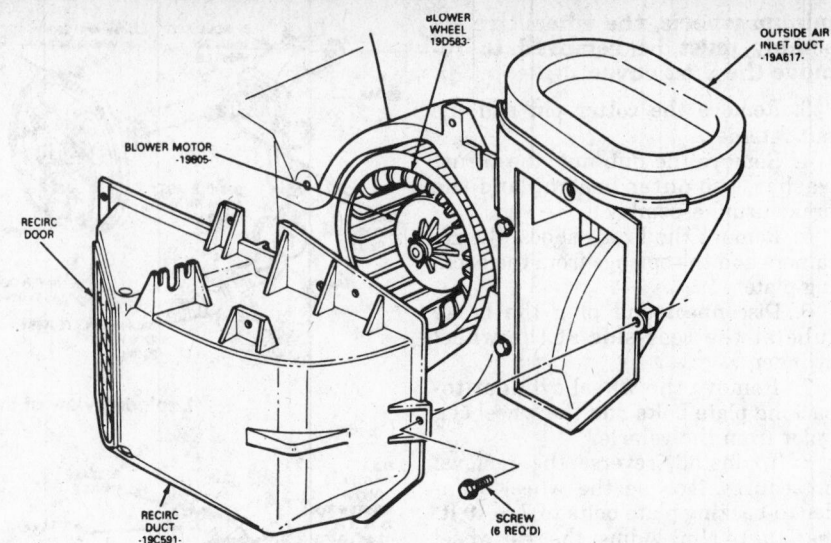

Exploded view of the heater motor and duct assembly

10. Installation is the reverse order of the removal procedure. Be sure to transfer the 3 foam core seals to the new heater core.

Radio

REMOVAL & INSTALLATION

1. Disconnect the negative battery cable.
2. Remove the center instrument trim panel.
3. Remove the 4 radio/bracket-to-instrument panel screws.
4. Push the radio toward the front, then raise the rear of the radio slightly so that the rear support bracket clears the clip in the instrument panel. Slowly withdraw the radio from the instrument panel.
5. Disconnect the electrical connectors and the antenna cable from the radio.
6. To install, reverse the removal procedures. Torque the radio/bracket-to-instrument panel screws to 14–16 in. lbs. (1.5–1.9 Nm). Test the radio and/or tape player for proper operation.

Windshield Wiper Switch

REMOVAL & INSTALLATION

Front — Sedan and Station Wagon

The front windshield wiper switch is a part of the combination switch, which is mounted to the steering column. Refer to the "Combination Switch Removal & Installation" procedures in this section and remove the combination switch from the steering column.

To install, reverse the removal procedures.

Rear — Station Wagon

1. Disconnect the negative battery cable.
2. Remove the 4 finish panel-to-instrument panel screws, then rock the upper edge toward the driver seat.
3. Disconnect the electrical connector from the rear washer switch.
4. Remove the washer switch from the instrument panel.

NOTE: On the Sable model, the switch is retained by 2 screws.

5. To install, reverse the removal procedures.

Windshield Wiper Motor

REMOVAL & INSTALLATION

Front — Sedan and Station Wagon

1. Disconnect the negative battery cable.
2. Disconnect the electrical connector from the motor.
3. Remove the left side wiper arm.
4. On the passenger side, lift the water shield cover (leaf screen) from the cowl.
5. Remove the linkage-to-operating arm clip.

NOTE: When removing the retaining clip, lift up the locking tab and pull the clip away from the pin.

6. Remove the motor/bracket-to-cowl bolts and the assembly from the vehicle.
7. To install, reverse the removal

procedures. Torque the motor/bracket-to-cowl bolts to 60–85 inch lbs. (7–9 Nm). Check wiper motor operation through all modes.

Rear – Station Wagon

1. Disconnect the negative battery cable.
2. Remove the wiper arm/blade assembly from the rear wiper motor.
3. Remove the rear motor pivot shaft-to-glass nut/spacers.
4. Disconnect the electrical connector from the rear wiper motor.

NOTE: When removing the electrical connector, pull on the connector and not the wire.

5. Remove the motor-to-handle nut and the motor from the vehicle.
6. To install, reverse the removal

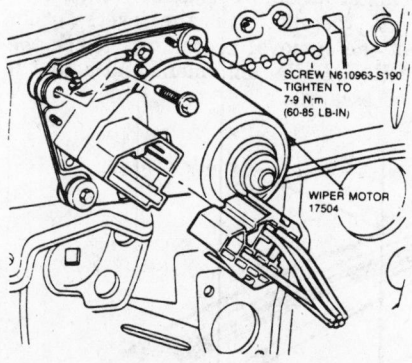

View of the front wiper motor assembly

procedures. Torque the motor-to-handle nut to 4–6 ft. lbs. (5–8 Nm) and the wiper motor-to-glass nut to 11–14 ft. lbs. (15–20 Nm).

Instrument Cluster

REMOVAL & INSTALLATION
Conventional Instrument Cluster
1986

1. Disconnect the negative battery cable.

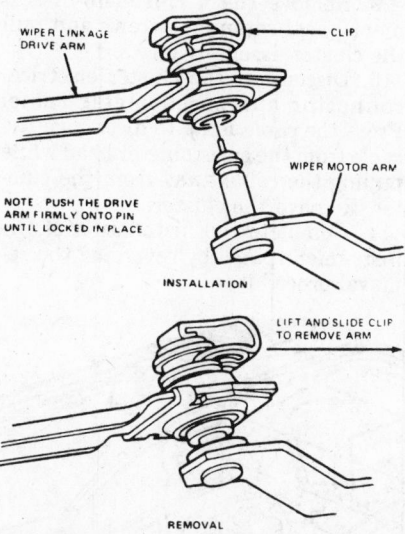

Separating the wiper linkage from the motor linkage

2. Drop the fuse panel (on its hinges), to provide access to the speedometer cable latch attachment. Disconnect the speedometer cable by disengaging the cable latch from the speedometer head and pulling the cable away from the speedometer.
3. Remove the instrument panel finish screws and the instrument finish panel.
4. Remove the steering column shroud.

NOTE: On Sable models equipped with a tachometer cluster, remove the lower trim panel screws and the trim panel from the vehicle.

5. Remove the mask/lens-to-instrument panel screws and the mask/lens from the vehicle.

NOTE: On Sable models equipped with a tachometer cluster, remove the lower floodlight bulb and socket assemblies from the vehicle.

6. Lift the main dial assembly from the backing plate.

NOTE: The speedometer, tachometer and gauges are mounted to the main dial and some effort may be required to pull the quick-connect electrical terminals from the clip.

7. On column shift vehicles, remove the transmission selector indicator-to-

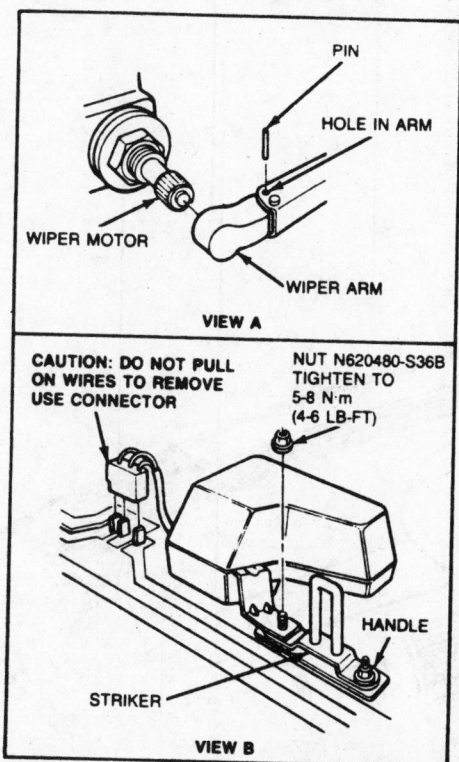

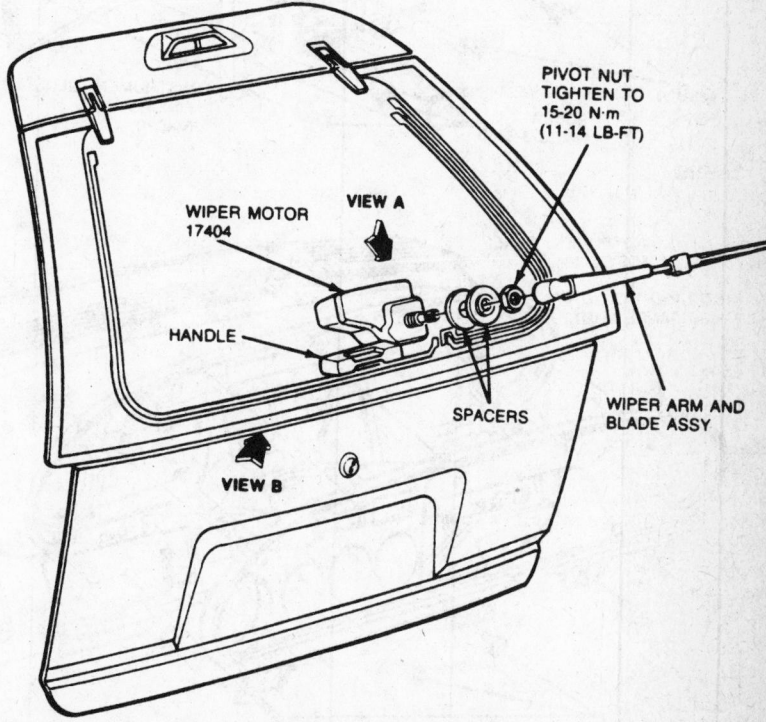

Exploded view of the rear wiper motor assembly—Station Wagon model

main dial (**PRNDL** or **PRNDD1**) screws and the indicator from the vehicle.

8. Remove the instrument cluster-to-instrument panel screws and the instrument cluster from the vehicle.

9. To install, reverse the removal procedures.

Conventional Instrument Cluster

1987–89

1. Disconnect the negative battery cable.

2. Remove the ignition lock cylinder to allow removal of the steering column shrouds. Refer to "Ignition Lock/Switch, Removal and Installation".

3. Remove the steering column trim shrouds.

4. Remove the lower left hand and radio finish panel screws and snap the panels out.

5. On Taurus, remove the clock assembly (or clock cover) to gain access to the finish panel screw behind the clock.

6. Remove the 7 cluster opening finish panel retaining screws and jam nut behind the headlamp switch. Remove the finish panel by rocking the edge upward and outward.

7. On column shift vehicles, remove the transmission selector indicator-to-main dial (**PRNDL** or **PRNDD1**) screws and the indicator from the column.

8. Disconnect the speedometer cable at the transaxle.

9. Remove the 4 cluster-to-instrument panel retaining screws and pull the cluster assembly forward.

10. Disconnect the cluster electrical connector and speedometer cable. Press the cable latch to disengage the cable from the speedometer head while pulling the cable away from the cluster. Remove the cluster.

11. Complete the installation of the instrument panel by reversing the removal procedure.

Electronic Instrument Cluster

ALL YEARS

1. Disconnect the negative battery cable. Remove the two lower panel trim covers.

2. Remove the steering column cover and disconnect the transmission **PRNDL** selector indicator cable from the steering column.

3. Remove the cluster trim panel and disconnect the electrical connector to the switch module.

4. Remove the 4 cluster mounting screws and pull the bottom of the cluster out towards the steering wheel.

5. Disconnect the 3 cluster connectors, from behind the cluster assembly.

6. Swing the bottom of the cluster out to clear the top of the cluster from the crash pad and then remove the cluster assembly from the vehicle.

7. Installation is the reverse order of the removal procedure. Check the **PRNDL** dial alignment and adjust if necessary.

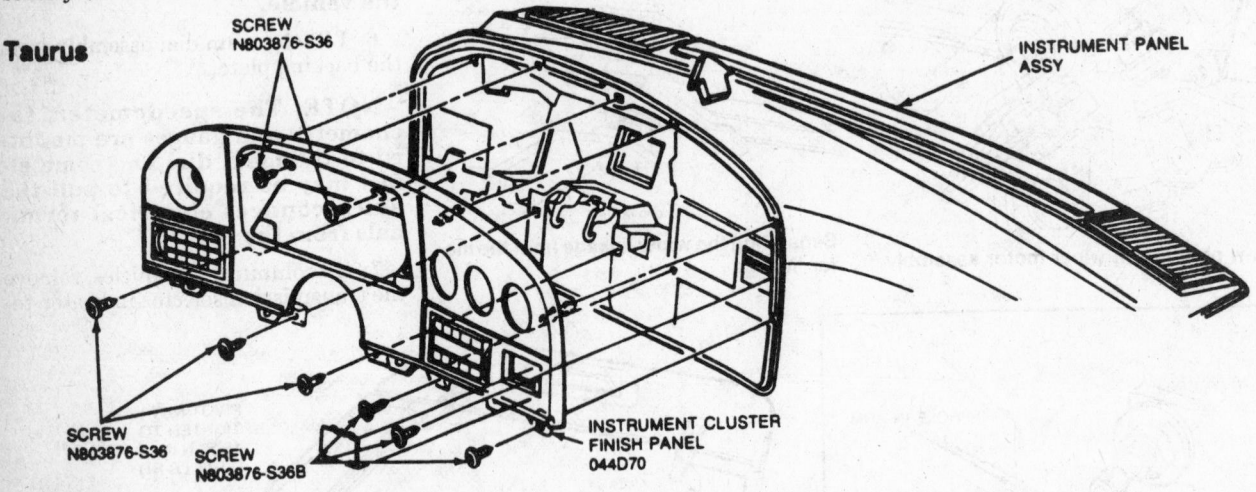

Taurus

SCREW
N803876-S36

SCREW
N803876-S36

SCREW
N803876-S36B

INSTRUMENT PANEL
ASSY

INSTRUMENT CLUSTER
FINISH PANEL
044D70

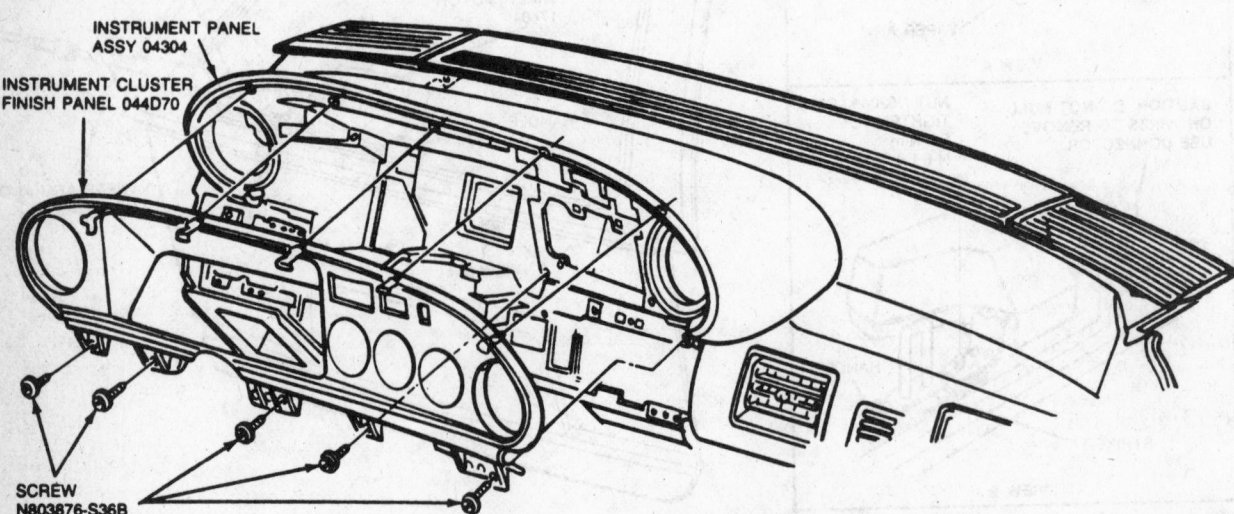

Sable

INSTRUMENT PANEL
ASSY 04304

INSTRUMENT CLUSTER
FINISH PANEL 044D70

SCREW
N803876-S36B

Exploded view of the instrument clusters

Headlight Switch

REMOVAL & INSTALLATION

1. Disconnect the negative battery cable. On the Taurus models, remove the headlight switch knob.
2. On the Taurus models, remove the bezel retaining nut and remove the bezel. On the Sable models, remove the lower left finish panel from the instrument panel.
3. On the Taurus models, remove the instrumnet cluster finish panel and remove the 2 screws retaining the headlamp switch to the instrument panel. Pull the switch out of the instrument panel and disconnect the electrical connector. Remove the switch from the vehicle.
4. On the Sable models, remove the 2 screws retaining the headlight switch to the finish panel, disconnect the electrical connector and remove the switch from the vehicle.
5. Installation is the reverse order of the removal procedure.

Stop Lamp Switch

The mechanical stop lamp switch assembly is mounted on the pin of the brake pedal arm so that ot straddles the master cylinder push rod.

REMOVAL & INSTALLATION

1. Disconnect the wire harness at the connector from the switch.

NOTE: The locking tab must be lifted before the connector can be removed.

2. Remove the hairpin retainer. Slide the stop lamp switch, the push rod and the white nylon washer and black bushing away from the pedal. Remove the switch by sliding the switch up/down.

NOTE: Since the switch side plate nearest the brake pedal is slotted, it is not necessary to remove the brake master cylinder push rod black bushing and one white spacer washer nearest the pedal arm from the brake pedal pin.

3. Position the switch so that the U-shaped side is nearest the pedal and directly over/under the pin. The black bushing must be in position in the push rod eyelet with the washer face on the side closest to the retaining pin.
4. Slide the switch up/down, trap-

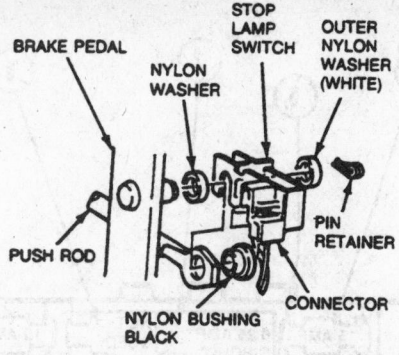

View of the stoplamp switch assembly

ping the master cylinder push rod and black bushing between the switch side plates. Push the switch and push rod assembly firmly towards the brake pedal arm. Assemble the outside white plastic washer to pin and install the hairpin retainer to trap the whole assembly.

——————— **CAUTION** ———————

Do not substitute other types of pin retainer. Replace only with production hairpin retainer.

5. Connect the wire harness connector to the switch.
6. Check the stop lamp switch for proper operation. stoplights should illuminate with less than 6 lbs. applied to the brake pedal at the pad.

NOTE: The stoplamp switch wire harness must have sufficient length to travel with the switch during full stroke at the pedal.

Fuses and Fusible Links

LOCATION

Fuses

The fuses are installed on the fuse panel which is located to the left side of the steering column and is hung from the instrument panel. To expose the fuse panel, pull the release bar up with the right hand and the panel down with the left hand.

Fusible Links

Fusible links are used to prevent major wire harness damage in the event of a short circuit or an overload condition in the wiring circuits that are normally not fused, due to carrying high

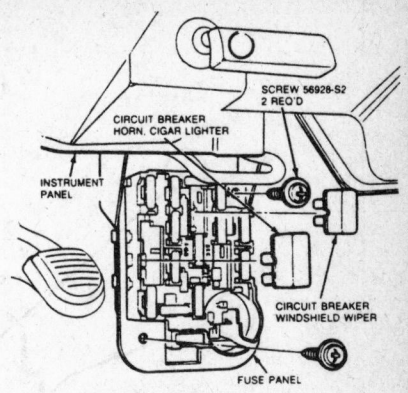

Location of the fuse panel

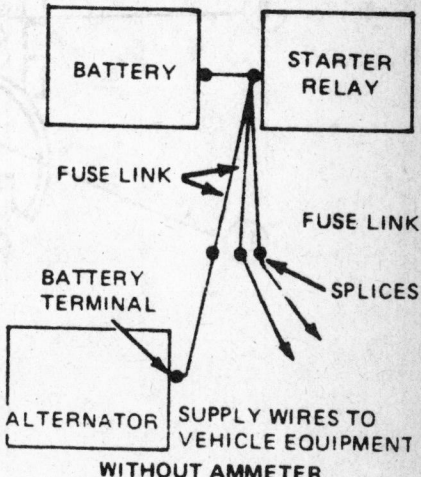

Location of the fusible links

amperage loads or because of their locations within the wiring harness. Each fusible link is of a fixed value for a specific electrical load and should a fusible link fail, the cause of the failure must be determine and repaired prior to installing a new fusible link of the same value.

Circuit Breakers

Circuit breakers are used to protect the various components of the electrical system, such as headlights and windshield wipers. The circuit breakers are located either in the control switch or mounted on or near the fuse panel.

The Taurus and Sable have 3 circuit breakers all located in the fuse block. The 6 amp circuit breaker is used for the windshield wiper circuit and one 20 amp circuit breaker is used for the instrument illumination. There is also an in-line 30 amp circuit breaker for the power windows.

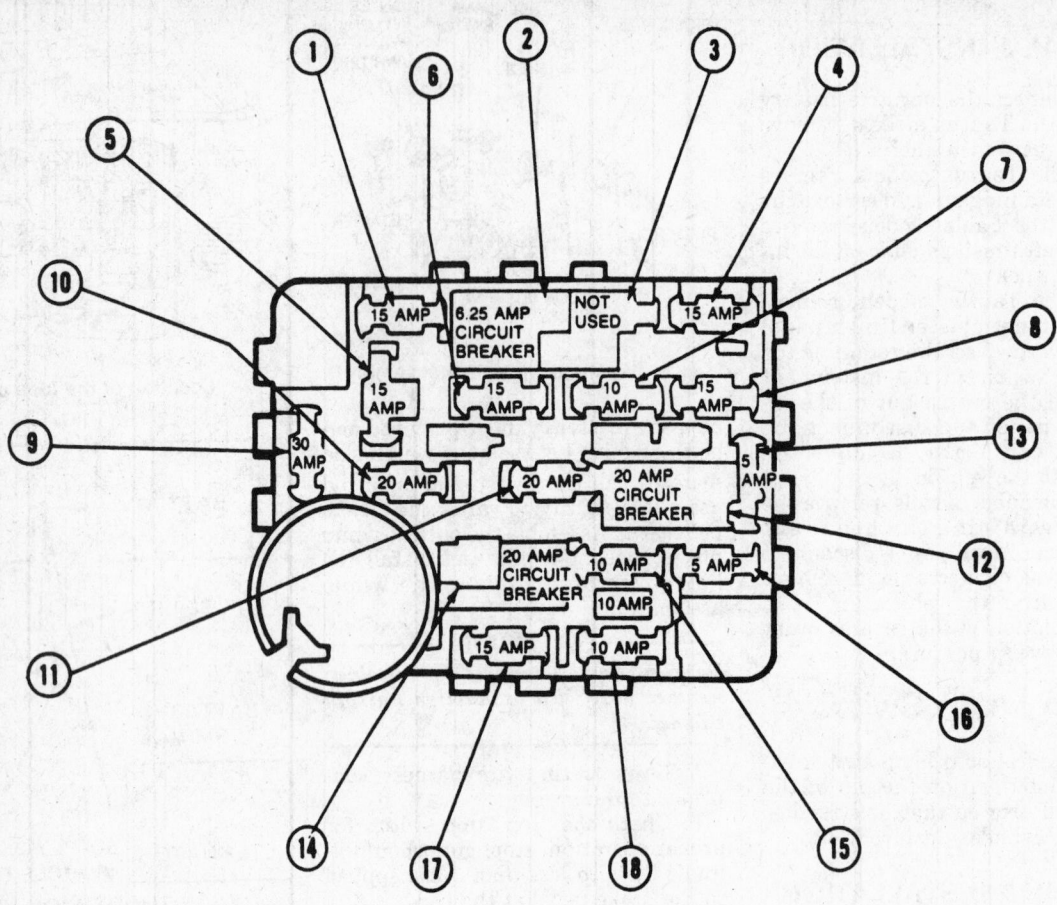

CAVITY NUMBER	CIRCUIT PROTECTED
1	HIGH MOUNT STOPLAMP, STOPLAMPS, FRONT AND REAR TURN SIGNALS, INSTRUMENT PANEL TURN INDICATOR LAMPS.
2	WINDSHIELD WIPER MOTOR, INTERMITTENT WIPER MODULE, WINDSHIELD WASHER MOTOR.
3	NOT USED
4	FRONT PARK, SIDE MARKER AND TAILLAMPS, "HEADLAMPS-ON" WARNING BUZZER/CHIME, FRONT LASER LAMP (SABLE).
5	ELECTRONIC CLUSTER, HEATED BACKLIGHT SWITCH, ELECTRONIC FLASHER, BACKUP LAMPS, HEATED E.G.O., ILLUMINATED/KEYLESS ENTRY MODULE.
6	REAR WINDOW WIPER AND WASHER MOTORS (WAGONS), DIAGNOSTIC WARNING LAMP MODULE, WARNING CHIME, HEADLAMP SWITCH ILLUMINATION (SABLE), CLOCK ILLUMINATION, RADIO ILLUMINATION, EATC CONTROL ILLUMINATION, POWER WINDOW RELAY.
7	NOT USED
8	CLOCK, RADIO MEMORY, GLOVE COMPT. LAMP, LUGGAGE COMPT. LAMP, INST. PANEL COURTESY LAMPS, INTERIOR LAMPS, ILLUMINATED/KEYLESS ENTRY MODULE.

CAVITY NUMBER	CIRCUIT PROTECTED
9	BLOWER MOTOR, BLOWER SPEED CONTROLLER (EATC).
10	FLASH-TO-PASS, HIGH BEAM HEADLAMPS AND INDICATOR LAMP.
11	RADIO, PREMIUM SOUND AMPLIFIER, POWER ANTENNA MOTOR.
12	FRONT AND REAR CIGAR LIGHTERS, HORN RELAY, HORNS.
13	CLUSTER ILLUMINATION, RADIO DISPLAY, ASH TRAY ILLUM., EATC CONTROL DISPLAY, HEATED BACKLIGHT SWITCH ILLUM., HEATED WINDSHIELD SWITCH ILLUM., REAR WIPER SWITCH ILLUM., HEADLAMP SWITCH ILLUM., CLOCK DISPLAY, P.R.N.D.L. ILLUMINATION.
14	NOT USED
15	LICENSE LAMPS, SIDE MARKER AND TAILLAMPS, "HEADLAMPS-ON" WARNING BUZZER/CHIME.
16	ELECTRONIC CLUSTER EATC CONTROL SWITCH.
17	EATC COMPRESSOR CLUTCH, EATC BLEND DOOR ACTUATOR, A/C COMPRESSOR CLUTCH.
18	AUTOLAMP MODULE, CLUSTER WARNING LAMPS, LOW OIL LEVEL RELAY, BUZZER/CHIME.

Taurus/Sable fuse box

Ford Motor Co. 8
Front Wheel Drive
Mercury Tracer

SERIAL NUMBER IDENTIFICATION

Vehicle Identification Number

The vehicle identification number is stamped on a plate which is attached to the left side of the instrument panel; the plate is visible through the windshield.

The VIN is also stamped on a plate in the engine compartment which is usually located on the firewall and a third VIN plate is attached to the driver's door jam.

The serial number is a 17 digit format. The first 3 digits are the World Manufacturer Identification number. The next 5 digits are the Vehicle Description Section. The remaining 9 numbers are the production numbers.

VEHICLE IDENTIFICATION CHART

It is important for servicing and ordering parts to be certain of the vehicle and engine identification. The VIN (vehicle identification number) is a 17 digit number visible through the windshield on the driver's side of the dash and contains the vehicle and engine identification codes. The tenth digit indicates model year and the eighth digit indicates engine code. It can be interpreted as follows:

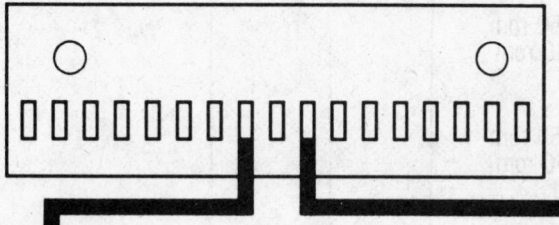

Engine Code						Model Year	
Code	Cu. In.	Liters	Cyl.	Fuel Sys.	Eng. Mfg.	Code	Year
7	98	1.6	4	2 bbl	Ford①	H	1987
5	98	1.6	4	EFI	Ford①	J	1988
① Mexico						K	1989

GENERAL ENGINE SPECIFICATIONS

Year	VIN	No. Cylinder Displacement cu. in. (liter)	Fuel System Type	Net Horsepower @ rpm	Net Torque @ rpm (ft.lbs.)	Bore × Stroke (in.)	Compression Ratio	Oil Pressure @ rpm
1987	5	4-98 (1.6)	EFI	61 @ 5000	125 @ 2500	3.07 × 3.29	9.3:1	50–64①
	7	4-98 (1.6)	2 bbl	NA	NA	3.07 × 3.29	9.3:1	50–64①
1988-89	5	4-98 (1.6)	EFI	61 @ 5000	125 @ 2500	3.07 × 3.29	9.3:1	50–64①
	7	4-98 (1.6)	2 bbl	NA	NA	3.07 × 3.29	9.3:1	50–64①

NA Not available
① 3000 rpm — hot

GASOLINE ENGINE TUNE-UP SPECIFICATIONS

Year	VIN	No. Cylinder Displacement cu. in. (liter)	Spark Plugs Type	Gap (in.)	Ignition Timing (deg.) MT	AT	Compression Pressure (psi)	Fuel Pump (psi)	Idle Speed (rpm) MT	AT	Valve Clearance (in.) In.	Ex.
1987	5	4-98 (1.6)	AGS32C	0.044	7B③	7B③	134–250⑤	64–85	800–900 ①	950–1050 ②	.012H	.012H
	7	4-98 (1.6)	AGS32C	0.044	1–3B④	1–3B④	134–250⑤	4–5	800–900	950–1050	.012H	.012H
1988	5	4-98 (1.6)	AGS32C	0.044	7B③	7B③	134–250⑤	64–85	800–900	800–900	.012H	.012H
	7	4-98 (1.6)	AGS32C	0.044	1–3B④	1–3B④	134–250⑤	4–5	800–900	950–1050	.012H	.012H
1989					SEE UNDERHOOD SPECIFICATIONS STICKER							

H Hot
① Idle-up; Pre Nov. '87
    Air conditioning — 1250–1350 rpm
    Power steering — 1000–1100 rpm
    Electrical load — 900–950
② Idle-up; Pre Nov. '87
    Air conditioning — 1250–1550 rpm
    Power steering — 1150–1250 rpm
    Electrical load — 1050–1100
③ Vacuum hose connected
④ Vacuum hose disconnected
⑤ All cylinders must be within 75% of each other

FIRING ORDERS

NOTE: To avoid confusion, always replace spark plug wires one at a time.

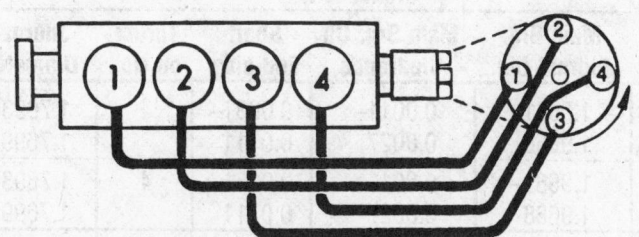

Ford 98 cu. in. (1.6L)
Firing order: 1–3–4–2
Distributor rotation: Counterclockwise

CAPACITIES

Year	Model	No. Cylinder Displacement cu. in. (liter)	Engine Crankcase with Filter	Engine Crankcase without Filter	Transmission (pts.) 4-Spd	Transmission (pts.) 5-Spd	Transmission (pts.) Auto.	Drive Axle (pts.)	Fuel Tank (gal.)	Cooling System (qts.)
1987	Tracer	4-98 (1.6)	3.5	3.2	NA	3.4	6.0	NA	11.9	①
1988-89	Tracer	4-98 (1.6)	3.5	3.2	NA	3.4	6.0	NA	11.9	①

NA Not available

① Manual transaxle—5.3 qts.
　Automatic transaxle—6.3 qts.

CAMSHAFT SPECIFICATIONS
All measurements given in inches.

Year	VIN	No. Cylinder Displacement cu. in. (liter)	Journal Diameter 1	Journal Diameter 2	Journal Diameter 3	Journal Diameter 4	Journal Diameter 5	Lobe Lift In.	Lobe Lift Ex.	Bearing Clearance	Camshaft End Play
1987	5	4-98 (1.6)	1.7103–1.7112	1.6870–1.7091	1.7103–1.7112	–	–	NA	NA	0.006	0.002–0.007
	7	4-98 (1.6)	1.7103–1.7112	1.6870–1.7091	1.7103–1.7112	–	–	NA	NA	0.006	0.002–0.007
1988-89	5	4-98 (1.6)	1.7103–1.7112	1.6870–1.7091	1.7103–1.7112	–	–	NA	NA	0.006	0.002–0.007
	7	4-98 (1.6)	1.7103–1.7112	1.6870–1.7091	1.7103–1.7112	–	–	NA	NA	0.006	0.002–0.007

CRANKSHAFT AND CONNECTING ROD SPECIFICATIONS

All measurements are given in inches.

Year	VIN	No. Cylinder Displacement cu. in. (liter)	Crankshaft				Connecting Rod		
			Main Brg. Journal Dia.	Main Brg. Oil Clearance	Shaft End-play	Thrust on No.	Journal Diameter	Oil Clearance	Side Clearance
1987	5	4-98 (1.6)	1.9661–1.9668	0.0011–0.0027	0.0031–0.0111	4	1.7693–1.7699	0.0009–0.0017	0.012
	7	4-98 (1.6)	1.9661–1.9668	0.0011–0.0027	0.0031–0.0111	4	1.7693–1.7699	0.0009–0.0017	0.012
1988-89	5	4-98 (1.6)	1.9661–1.9668	0.0011–0.0027	0.0031–0.0111	4	1.7693–1.7699	0.0009–0.0017	0.012
	7	4-98 (1.6)	1.9661–1.9668	0.0011–0.0027	0.0031–0.0111	4	1.7693–1.7699	0.0009–0.0017	0.012

VALVE SPECIFICATIONS

Year	VIN	No. Cylinder Displacement cu. in. (liter)	Seat Angle (deg.)	Face Angle (deg.)	Spring Test Pressure (lbs.)	Spring Installed Height (in.)	Stem-to-Guide Clearance (in.)		Stem Diameter (in.)	
							Intake	Exhaust	Intake	Exhaust
1987	5	4-98 (1.6)	45	45	NA	NA	0.008	0.008	0.2744–0.2750	0.2742–0.2748
	7	4-98 (1.6)	45	45	NA	NA	0.008	0.008	0.2744–0.2750	0.2742–0.2748
1988-89	5	4-98 (1.6)	45	45	NA	NA	0.008	0.008	0.2744–0.2750	0.2742–0.2748
	7	4-98 (1.6)	45	45	NA	NA	0.008	0.008	0.2744–0.2750	0.2742–0.2748

NA Not available

PISTON AND RING SPECIFICATIONS

All measurments are given in inches.

Year	VIN	No. Cylinder Displacement cu. in. (liter)	Piston Clearance	Ring Gap			Ring Side Clearance		
				Top Compression	Bottom Compression	Oil Control	Top Compression	Bottom Compression	Oil Control
1987	5	4-98 (1.6)	0.006	0.006–0.012	0.006–0.012	0.008–0.028	0.001–0.003	0.001–0.003	Snug
	7	4-98 (1.6)	0.006	0.006–0.012	0.006–0.012	0.008–0.028	0.001–0.003	0.001–0.003	Snug
1988-89	5	4-98 (1.6)	0.006	0.006–0.012	0.006–0.012	0.008–0.028	0.001–0.003	0.001–0.003	Snug
	7	4-98 (1.6)	0.006	0.006–0.012	0.006–0.012	0.008–0.028	0.001–0.003	0.001–0.003	Snug

TORQUE SPECIFICATIONS
All readings in ft. lbs.

Year	VIN	No. Cylinder Displacement cu. in. (liter)	Cylinder Head Bolts①	Main Bearing Bolts①	Rod Bearing Nuts	Crankshaft Pulley Bolts	Flywheel Bolts	Manifold Intake	Manifold Exhaust	Spark Plugs
1987	5	4-98 (1.6)	56–60	40–43	37–41	71–76	71–76	14–19	12–20	11–17
	7	4-98 (1.6)	56–60	40–43	37–41	71–76	71–76	14–19	12–20	11–17
1988-89	5	4-98 (1.6)	56–60	40–43	37–41	71–76	71–76	14–19	12–20	11–17
	7	4-98 (1.6)	56–60	40–43	37–41	71–76	71–76	14–19	12–20	11–17

① Using 2 steps

BRAKE SPECIFICATIONS
All measurements in inches unless noted

Year	Model	Lug Nut Torque (ft. lbs.)	Master Cylinder Bore	Brake Disc Minimum Thickness	Brake Disc Maximum Runout	Standard Brake Drum Diameter	Minimum Lining Thickness Front	Minimum Lining Thickness Rear
1987	Hatchback	65–87	0.875	0.630	0.003	7.870	0.120	0.040
	Sedan	65–87	0.875	0.630	0.003	7.870	0.120	0.040
1988-89	Hatchback	65–87	0.875	0.630	0.003	7.870	0.120	0.040
	Sedan	65–87	0.875	0.630	0.003	7.870	0.120	0.040

WHEEL ALIGNMENT

Year	Model		Caster Range (deg.)	Caster Preferred Setting (deg.)	Camber Range (deg.)	Camber Preferred Setting (deg.)	Toe-in (in.)	Steering Axis Inclination (deg.)
1987	Tracer	Front	$\frac{5}{6}$P–2$\frac{2}{3}$P	1$\frac{7}{12}$P	$\frac{1}{20}$P–1$\frac{11}{20}$P	$\frac{12}{15}$P	0.04N–0.20P	—
		Rear	—	—	¾N–¾P①	0	0–0.16	—
1988-89	Tracer	Front	$\frac{5}{6}$P–2$\frac{2}{3}$P	1$\frac{7}{12}$P	$\frac{1}{20}$P–1$\frac{11}{20}$P	$\frac{12}{15}$P	0.04N–0.20P	—
		Rear	—	—	¾N–¾P①	0	0–0.16	—

① Not adjustable

TUNE-UP PROCEDURES

Ignition Timing

ADJUSTMENT

1. Operate the engine until normal operating temperatures are reached.
2. Check and/or adjust the idle speed.
3. Turn **OFF** all of the accessories.
4. Disconnect and plug the vacuum line (carbureted) or lines (EFI).

NOTE: If using 2 vacuum lines, be sure to mark them for installation purposes.

5. If equipped with EFI, disconnect the black electrical connector at the distributor.
6. Using a Rotunda® Timing Light tool No. 059–00005 or equivalent, connect it to the engine.
7. Aim the timing light at the crankshaft pulley/timing plate location; the crankshaft pulley notch should align with the 1–3 degree BTDC mark on the timing plate.
8. If necessary to adjust the ignition timing, perform the following procedures:

a. Loosen the distributor hold-down bolts, just enough so the distributor can be turned.

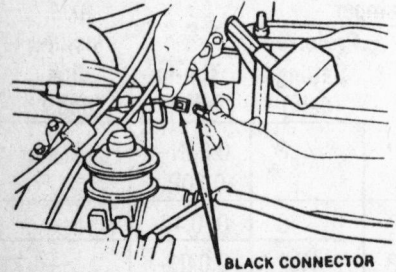

Disconnect the black electrical connector near the distributor—EFI models

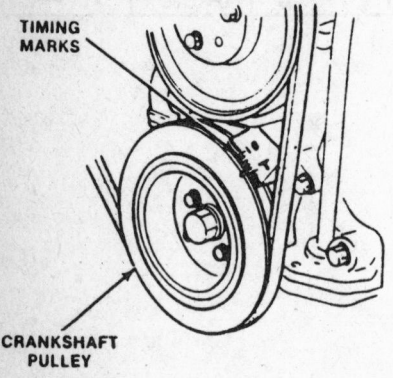

View of the ignition timing marks

b. Rotate the distributor clockwise (to advance) or counterclockwise (to retard) the timing.
c. With the timing corrected, tighten the distributor hold-down bolts.
d. Recheck the timing.
9. To complete the operation, reverse the removal procedures. Check and/or adjust the idle speed.

Valve Lash

The engine uses hydraulic lifters which operates with zero clearance in the valve train. The rocker arms are non-adjustable. The lifter will compensate for slack in the system but if there is excessive play, the entire system should be checked.

If the valve guides are found to be worn past allowable limits, new ones can be installed.

Idle Speed and Mixture

ADJUSTMENT

Carbureted Models

NOTE: The idle mixture and timing must be adjusted before the idle speed is adjusted; adjustment must be done with cooling inoperative.

IDLE MIXTURE

The carburetor is equipped with a non-tamperable feature: A roll pin blocks the entry to the idle mixture screw and cannot be driven downward.

1. To remove the roll pin from the carburetor's idle mixture screw, perform the following procedures.

a. Remove the carburetor.
b. Invert the carburetor.
c. Using a pin punch and a hammer, drive the roll pin toward the top of the carburetor.
d. Using new gaskets, reinstall the carburetor and the air filter (secure the wing nut).
2. At the air filter housing, disconnect air injection hoses; plug the front air injection hose. Using an Exhaust Gas Analyzer tool, install and seal the probe into the rear air injection hose to prevent leakage.
3. Start the engine and allow it to reach normal operating temperatures.
4. Turn the idle mixture screw to obtain a carbon monoxide (CO) reading of 1.5–2.5 percent.
5. Adjust the idle speed.
6. When the idle speed and idle mixture are balanced, perform the following procedures:

a. Remove the air cleaner housing.

b. Using a hammer and a punch, install the roll pin to block the idle mixture screw.
7. To complete the installation, reverse the removal procedures. Check for leaks.

IDLE SPEED

1. Place the transaxle in **NEUTRAL** (manual) or **PARK** (automatic).
2. Start the engine and allow it to reach normal operating temperatures.
3. Turn **OFF** all light and accessories.
4. Using a Rotunda® Tachometer tool No. 059–00001 or equivalent, install it to the engine.
5. Check the idle speed; if necessary, to adjust the idle speed, turn the idle speed screw at the base of the carburetor.
6. If equipped with a manual transaxle, adjust the dashpot.

DASHPOT—MANAUL TRANSAXLE

1. Operate the engine until normal operating temperatures are reached.
2. Using a Rotunda® Tachometer tool No. 059–00001 or equivalent, install it to the engine.
3. Loosen the dashpot jam nut.
4. Increase the engine speed to 3000 rpm and slowly reduce the engine speed to 2400–2600 rpm.
5. Screw in the dashpot until contact is made with the carburetor linkage and tighten the jam nut.

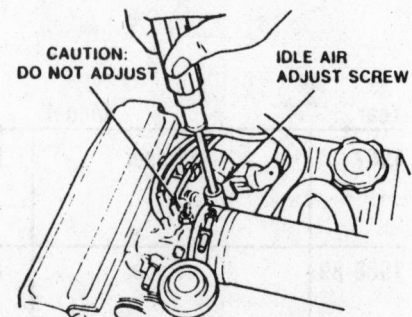

Adjusting the idle speed by turning the idle air adjusting screw—EFI engines

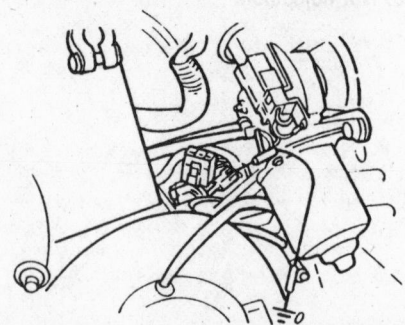

View of the jumper wire connected to the test connector—EFI engines

Fuel Injected Models

NOTE: The timing must be adjusted before the idle speed is adjusted; adjustment must be done with cooling inoperative. The idle mixture screw is preset/sealed at the factory and must not be adjusted.

1. Operate the engine until normal operating temperatures are reached.
2. Using a Rotunda® Tachometer tool No. 059–00001 or equivalent, connect it to Pin 1 (white) of the test connector and check the idle speed.
3. If necessary to adjust the idle speed, connect a jumper wire between Pin 1 (green) of the test connector and ground and turn the air adjustment screw to obtain the correct idle speed.

NOTE: DO NOT turn the adjustment screw located to the right of the idle adjustment screw, for it will affect the driveability and may damage the throttle body.

4. After adjustment, remove the jumper wire and the test equipment.

ENGINE ELECTRICAL

Distributor

REMOVAL & INSTALLATION

Engine Undisturbed

1. Disconnect the negative terminal from the battery.
2. Remove the distributor cap-to-distributor screws and move the cap (wires attached) aside. Remove the gasket.
3. Disconnect the vacuum hose (carbureted) or hoses (EFI) from the distributor vacuum advance.

NOTE: On the EFI models, label the hoses for reinstallation purposes.

4. Disconnect the electrical connector(s) from the distributor; note the wire locations for reinstallation purposes.
5. Mark the relationship of the distributor-to-engine and the rotor-to-distributor housing for reinstallation purposes.
6. Remove the distributor-to-engine hold-down bolts and the distributor from the engine. Remove and discard the O-ring from the distributor.
7. To install, use a new O-ring (lubricate with clean engine oil), align the

matchmarks and reverse the removal procedures; be sure to align the distributor with the camshaft dog. Check and/or adjust the engine timing.

Engine Disturbed

1. Remove the No. 1 spark plug.
2. Rotate the crankshaft to position the No. 1 piston on the TDC of its compression stroke.

NOTE: To locate the TDC of the compression stroke of the No. 1 piston, hold a finger or stuff a clean shop rag in the spark plug hole. Rotate the crankshaft until compression is noticed and adjust the crankshaft pulley notch to align the with the 1–3 degree mark on the timing plate.

3. Rotate the rotor to position it with the No. 1 spark plug wire on the distributor cap and reinstall the distributor; be sure to align the distributor with the camshaft dog.
4. To complete the installation, reverse the removal procedures. Check and/or adjust the timing.

Alternator

For further information on the charging system, please refer to "Charging and Starting" in the Unit Repair section.

PRECAUTIONS

Several precautions must be observed with alternator equipped vehicles to avoid damage to the unit.

- If the battery is removed for any reason, make sure it is reconnected with the correct polarity. Reversing the battery connections may result in damage to the one-way rectifiers.
- When utilizing a booster battery as a starting aid, always connect the positive to positive terminals, and the negative terminal from the booster battery to a good engine ground on the vehicle being started.
- Never use a fast charger as a booster to start vehicles with alternating-current (AC) circuits.
- Disconnect the battery cables when charging the battery with a fast charger.
- Never attempt to polarize an alternator.
- Avoid long soldering times when making alternator repairs. Prolonged head will damage the alternator.
- Do not use test lamps of more than 12V when checking diode continuity.
- Do not short across or ground any of the alternator terminals.

- The polarity of the battery, alternator and regulator must be matched and considered before making any electrical connections within the system.
- Never separate the alternator on an open circuit. Make sure all connections within the circuit are clean and tight.
- Disconnect the battery ground terminal when performing any service on electrical components.
- Disconnect the battery if arc welding is to be done on the vehicle.

BELT TENSION ADJUSTMENT

The belt tension on most components is adjusted by moving the component (alternator) within the range of the slotted bracket. Check the belt tension every 12 months or 10,000 miles. Push in on the drive belt about midway between the water pulley and the alternator. Belt deflection should be 0.31–0.35 in. (new) or 0.35–0.39 in. (used).

1. Loosen the adjustment nut and bolt in the slotted bracket. Slightly loosen the pivot bolt.
2. Pull (don't pry) the component outward to increase tension. Push inward to reduce tension. Tighten the adjusting nut/bolt and the pivot bolt.
3. Recheck the drive belt tension and readjust (if necessary). Torque the alternator mounting bolt to 27–38 ft. lbs. and the alternator pivot bolt to 14–19 ft. lbs.

REMOVAL & INSTALLATION

1. Disconnect the negative terminal from the battery.
2. Label and disconnect each alternator wiring connector.
3. Remove the alternator-to-adjusting bracket bolt. Loosen the alternator through bolt and allow it to pivot. Shift the alternator toward the block and remove the drive belt.
4. Remove the through bolt and the alternator.
5. To install, reverse the removal procedures. Torque the alternator through bolt to 27–38 ft. lbs. and the adjusting bracket bolt to 35–45 ft. lbs. Start the engine and check the operation.

Voltage Regulator

ADJUSTMENT

The voltage regulator is built into the alternator and cannot be adjusted. If the voltage regulator becomes faulty, it must be replaced.

REMOVAL & INSTALLATION

1. Remove the alternator.
2. Remove the nut and terminal insulator.
3. Remove the 3 nuts and the end cover.
4. Remove the 5 screws, brush holder and IC regulator.
5. Using a soldering iron, separate the stator leads from the brush holder/regulator assembly.
6. To install, solder the leads onto the brush holder/regulator assembly and reverse the removal procedures.

Starter

For further information on the starter system, please refer to "Charging and Starting" in the Unit Repair section.

REMOVAL & INSTALLATION

1. Disconnect the negative terminal from the battery.
2. Disconnect the electrical connectors from the starter terminals.
3. Remove the starter-to-bracket bolts, the support bracket bolts and the brackets.
4. Remove the starter-to-transaxle bolts and the starter from the vehicle.
5. To install, reverse the removal procedures. Torque the starter-to-engine bolts to 23–30 ft. lbs. and the support bracket thru bolt to 54–71 inch lbs.

ENGINE MECHANICAL

Engine

REMOVAL & INSTALLATION

1. Using a scratch awl, matchmark the hood hinges to the hood. Remove the hood-to-hinge bolts and the hood.
2. If equipped with EFI, relieve the fuel pressure by performing the following procedures:
  a. Remove the back seat cushion.
  b. While the engine is operating, disconnect the electrical harness connector from the fuel pump.
  c. When the engine stalls, the fuel pressure will be relieved.
3. Disconnect the terminals from the battery; negative terminal first. Remove the battery-to-vehicle bolts and the tray.
4. Using a clean drain pan, place it

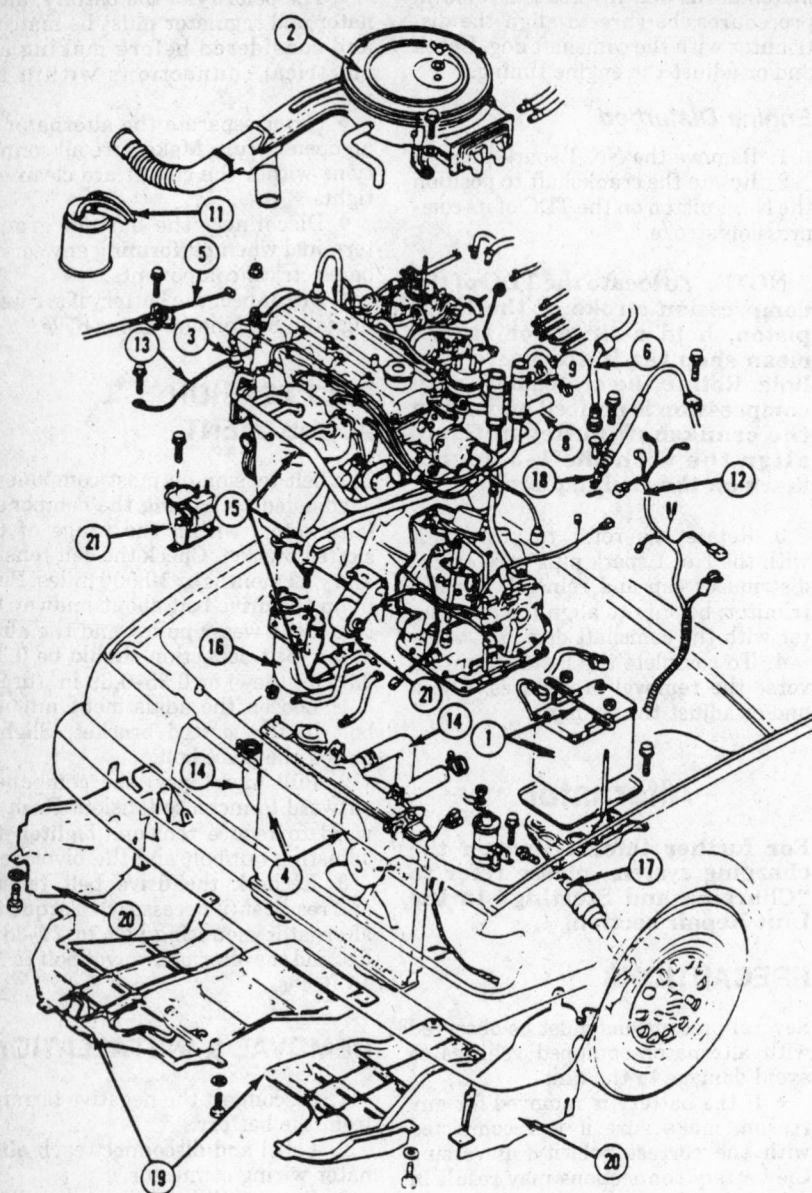

1. Battery and carrier
2. Air cleaner assembly
3. Dipstick
4. Cooling fan and radiator cowling
5. Accelerator cable and cruise control cable (if equipped)
6. Speedometer cable
7. Fuel hoses
8. Heater hoses
9. Brake vacuum hose
10. 3-way solenoid valve hoses
11. Canister hoses
12. Engine harness connectors
13. Engine ground
14. Upper and lower radiator hose
15. Secondary air pipe
16. Exhaust pipe
17. Halfshafts
18. Shift control cable or rod
19. Engine splash shield
20. Inner fender panel
21. Engine mounts

Exploded view of the engine/transaxle assembly removal and installation – carbureted

under the radiator. Remove the cooling system expansion tank cap, open the drain cock and drain the cooling system.

5. Drain the engine crankcase and the transaxle; discard the fluids.

6. Remove the air cleaner assembly and the dipstick.

7. Disconnect the electrical connector from the fan. Remove the fan shroud-to-radiator bolts, the fan and the shroud.

8. Disconnect the accelerator cable, the speedometer cable and the speed control cable (if equipped).

9. If equipped with a mechanical fuel pump (carburetor), place a shop rag under fuel pump to catch the excess fuel. Disconnect and plug the fuel lines.

10. Disconnect the heater hoses and the radiator hoses from the engine.

11. From the power brake booster, disconnect the vacuum hose.

12. Disconnect the idle-up solenoid hoses and the carbon canister hoses.

13. Disconnect the engine ground wire and the electrical harness connectors which will interfere with the engine removal.

14. If equipped with a carburetor, remove the secondary air pipe.

15. Remove the exhaust pipe-to-exhaust manifold bolts and separate the pipe from the manifold.

16. If equipped with air conditioning, remove the compressor from the engine bracket and move it aside.

17. If equipped with power steering, remove the pump from the engine bracket and move it aside; DO NOT disconnect pressure hoses.

18. If equipped with a manual transaxle, disconnect the clutch control cable. Disconnect the shift control cable (automatic) or rod (manual).

19. Raise and support the front of the vehicle on jackstands.

20. Remove the engine splash shield-to-vehicle bolts and the shield. Remove the inner fender panel.

21. To remove the halfshafts from the transaxle, perform the following procedures:

    a. Remove the lower ball joint-to-steering knuckle assembly nut and bolt. Using a medium pry bar, pry the lower ball joint (downward) to separate it from the steering knuckle assembly.

    b. Turn the steering knuckle assembly and pull the halfshaft from the transaxle. If necessary, separate the tie rod end from the steering knuckle.

NOTE: If difficulty is experienced, place a pry bar between the halfshaft/transaxle assembly and pry the halfshaft from the transaxle.

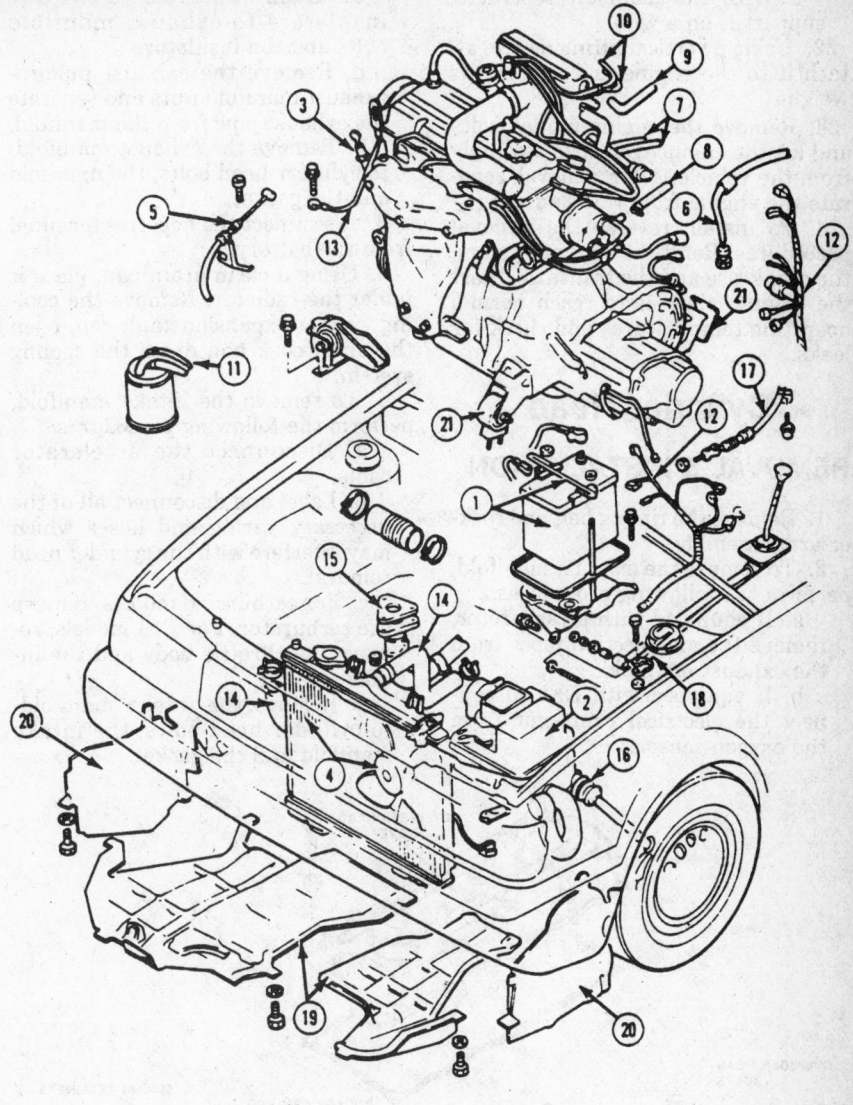

1. Battery and carrier
2. Air cleaner assembly
3. Dipstick
4. Cooling fan and radiator cowling
5. Accelerator cable and cruise control cable (if equipped)
6. Speedometer cable
7. Fuel hoses
8. Heater hoses
9. Brake vacuum hose
10. Idle-up solenoid valve hoses
11. Canister hoses
12. Engine harness connectors
13. Engine ground
14. Upper and lower radiator hose
15. Exhaust pipe
16. Halfshafts
17. Clutch control cable (manual transaxle)
18. Shift control rod
19. Engine splash shield
20. Inner fender panel
21. Engine mounts

Exploded view of the engine/transaxle assembly removal and installation—EFI

c. With the halfshaft separated, support it on a wire.

22. Using a vertical lifting device, attach it to the engine and support its weight.

23. Remove the engine mount bolts and lift the engine/transaxle assembly from the vehicle. After removal, separate the engine from the transaxle.

24. To install, reverse the removal procedures. Refill the cooling system, the crankcase and the transaxle. Start the engine, allow it to reach normal operating temperatures and check for leaks.

Cylinder Head

REMOVAL & INSTALLATION

1. Remove the timing belt and rocker arm assembly.

2. To remove the exhaust manifold, perform the following procedures:

   a. If equipped with a carburetor, remove the air injection pipes from the exhaust manifold.

   b. If equipped with EFI, disconnect the electrical connector from the oxygen sensor.

   c. Remove the exhaust insulators-to-exhaust manifold bolts and the insulators.

   d. Remove the exhaust pipe-to-exhaust manifold nuts and separate the exhaust pipe from the manifold.

   e. Remove the exhaust manifold-to-cylinder head bolts, the manifold and the gasket.

3. Disconnect the negative terminal from the battery.

4. Using a clean drain pan, place it under the radiator. Remove the cooling system expansion tank cap, open the drain cock and drain the cooling system.

5. To remove the intake manifold, perform the following procedures:

   a. Disconnect the accelerator cable.

   b. Label and disconnect all of the necessary wiring and hoses which may interfere with the cylinder head removal.

   c. For carbureted models, remove the carburetor. For EFI models, remove the throttle body and the intake plenum.

   d. Remove the intake manifold-to-cylinder head bolts, the intake manifold and the gasket.

6. Remove the spark plug wires and the spark plugs.

7. Remove the distributor-to-cylinder head bolts and the distributor from the engine.

8. From the front/rear of the engine, remove the engine lifting eyes. Disconnect the ground wire from the engine.

9. Disconnect the electrical harness connectors which may interfere with the cylinder head removal.

10. Remove the upper radiator hose, the water by-pass hose and bracket.

11. Remove the cylinder head-to-engine bolts and the cylinder head.

12. Using a putty knife, clean the gasket mounting surfaces. Check and/or replace the damaged or worn parts.

13. To install, use new gaskets, sealant (if necessary) and reverse the removal procedures. Torque the cylinder head-to-engine bolts (in sequence) to 25–30 ft. lbs. (1st) and 37–40 ft. lbs. (2nd), the intake manifold-to-cylinder head bolts to 14–19 ft. lbs., the exhaust manifold-to-cylinder head bolts to 23–34 ft. lbs. and the air injection pipes-to-exhaust manifold bolts to 12–20 ft. lbs. Refill the cooling system. Start the engine, allow it to reach normal operating temperatures and check for leaks.

OVERHAUL

For all cylinder head overhaul procedures, please refer to the "Engine Rebuilding" in the Unit Repair section.

Rocker Arms/Shafts

REMOVAL & INSTALLATION

1. Remove the upper front cover.

2. Remove the air cleaner (carbureted) or air duct (EFI).

3. Remove the accelerator and cruise control cables (if equipped) from the rocker arm cover.

4. Disconnect the vent hose from the rocker arm cover and the spark plug wires from their clips.

5. Remove the rocker arm cover-to-cylinder head bolts, the cover and the gasket (discard it).

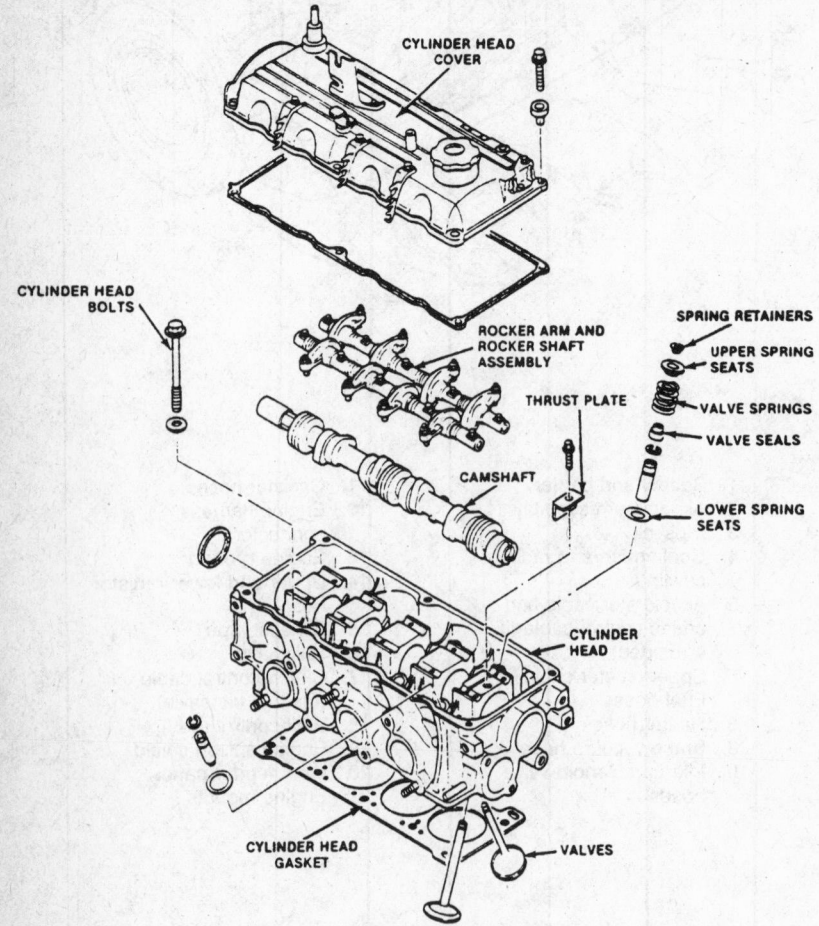

Exploded view of the cylinder head assembly

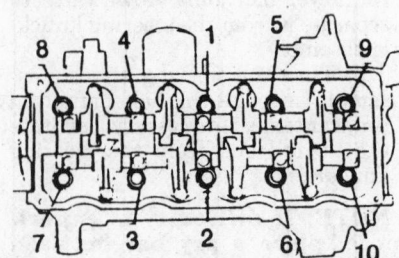

View of the cylinder head torque sequence

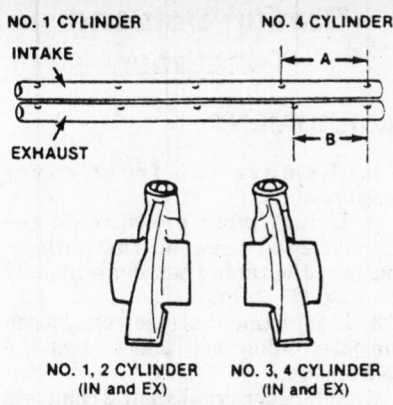

NO. 1 CYLINDER NO. 4 CYLINDER

INTAKE

EXHAUST

NO. 1, 2 CYLINDER NO. 3, 4 CYLINDER
(IN and EX) (IN and EX)

View of the rocker arm shafts and rocker arms

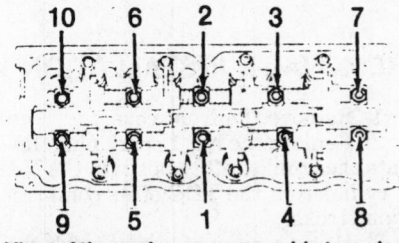

View of the rocker arm assembly torquing sequence

6. Remove the rocker arm shaft(s)-to-cylinder head bolts and the rocker arm shaft assemblies.

7. If necessary to separate the rocker arms from the rocker arm shafts, perform the following procedures:

a. Remove the bolts from the rocker arm(s).

b. Slide the rocker arm and springs from the shafts.

NOTE: Be sure to keep all the parts in order of disassembly for reinstallation purposes. The rocker arm shafts can only be installed in 1 position.

8. Using a putty knife, clean the gasket mounting surfaces. Check and/or replace the parts if worn or damaged.

NOTE: To prevent damage to the O-ring on the Hydraulic Lash Adjuster (HLA) of the rocker arm, DO NOT tamper with it unless replacement is necessary.

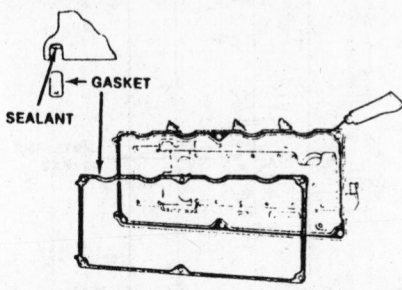

GASKET

SEALANT

Preparing the valve cover for Installation

9. To install, use new gasket, sealant (if necessary) and reverse the removal procedures. Torque the rocker arm shaft(s)-to-cylinder head (oil holes facing downward) bolts to 16–21 ft. lbs. and the rocker arm cover-to-cylinder head bolts to 44–79 inch lbs.

NOTE: When torquing the rocker arm shaft(s)-to-cylinder head bolts, start in the center and move outwards in both directions.

10. To complete the installation, reverse the removal procedures. Start the engine and check for leaks.

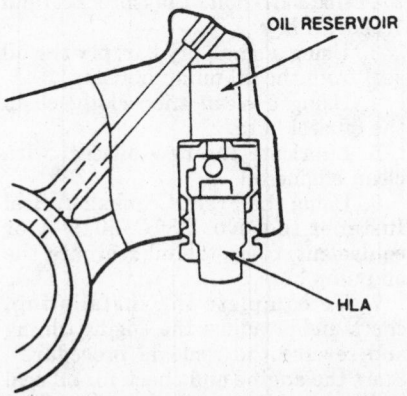

OIL RESERVOIR

HLA

Cross-sectional view of the rocker arm, showing the Hydraulic Lash adjuster (HLA)

Intake Manifold

REMOVAL & INSTALLATION

1. Disconnect the negative terminal from the battery.

2. Using a clean drain pan, place it under the radiator. Remove the cooling system expansion tank cap, open the drain cock and drain the cooling system.

3. Disconnect the accelerator cable.

4. Label and disconnect all of the necessary wiring and hoses which may interfere with the cylinder head removal.

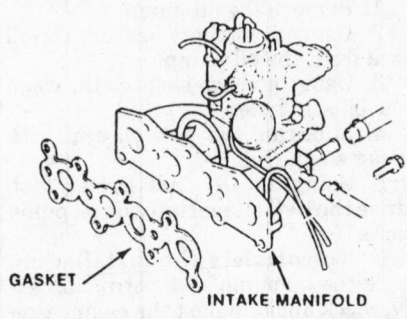

GASKET

INTAKE MANIFOLD

View of the intake manifold—carbureted engines

5. For carbureted models, remove the carburetor. For EFI models, remove the throttle body and the intake plenum.

6. Remove the intake manifold-to-cylinder head bolts, the intake manifold and the gasket.

7. Using a putty knife, clean the gasket mounting surfaces. Clean and inspect the parts for damage and/or wear; replace the parts, if necessary.

8. To install, use new gaskets and reverse the removal procedures. Torque the intake manifold-to-cylinder head bolts to 14–19 ft. lbs. Refill the cooling system. Start the engine, allow it to reach normal operating temperatures and check for leaks.

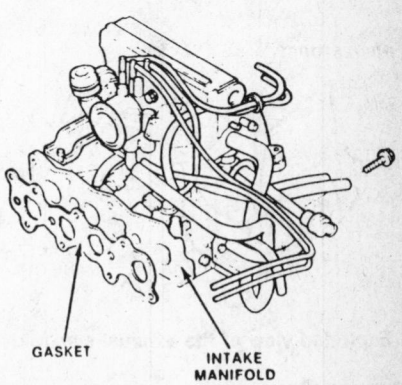

GASKET INTAKE MANIFOLD

View of the intake manifold—EFI engines

Exhaust Manifold

REMOVAL & INSTALLATION

1. If equipped with a carburetor, remove air cleaner and the air injection pipes from the exhaust manifold.

2. If equipped with EFI, disconnect the electrical connector from the oxygen sensor.

3. Remove the exhaust insulators-to-exhaust manifold bolts and the insulators.

4. Remove the exhaust pipe-to-exhaust manifold nuts and separate the exhaust pipe from the manifold.

5. Remove the exhaust manifold-to-cylinder head bolts, the manifold and the gasket.

6. Using a putty knife, clean the gasket mounting surfaces. Inspect the parts for damage and replace them if necessary.

7. To install, use new gaskets and reverse the removal procedures. Torque the exhaust manifold-to-cylinder head bolts to 23–34 ft. lbs. and the air injection pipes-to-exhaust manifold bolts to 12–20 ft. lbs. Start the engine and check for exhaust leaks.

Front Cover

REMOVAL & INSTALLATION

Upper Cover

1. Disconnect the negative terminal from the battery.
2. Remove the drive belt(s) from the front of the engine.
3. Remove the water pump pulley-to-water pump bolts and the pulley.
4. Remove the upper front cover-to-engine bolts and the cover.
5. Using a putty knife, clean the gasket mounting surfaces.
6. To install, use a new gasket (if necessary) and reverse the removal procedures. Torque the front cover-to-engine bolts to 69–95 inch lbs.

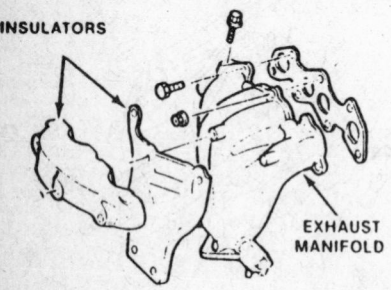

Exploded view of the exhaust manifold

Lower Cover

1. Disconnect the negative terminal from the battery.
2. Remove the drive belt(s) from the front of the engine.
3. Remove the water pump pulley-to-water pump bolts and the pulley.
4. To remove the crankshaft pulley, perform the following procedures:
   a. Remove the right inner fender panel.
   b. Remove the crankshaft pulley-to-crankshaft bolts, outer spacer, outer pulley, inner spacer, inner pulley and baffle.
5. Remove the upper/lower front cover-to-engine bolts and the covers.
6. Using a putty knife, clean the gasket mounting surfaces.

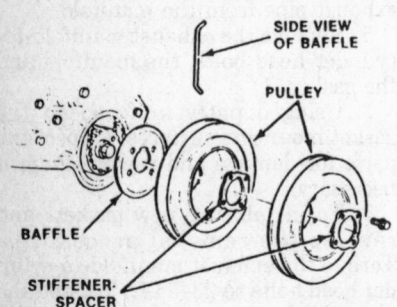

Exploded view of the crankshaft pulley assembly

7. To install, use a new gasket (if necessary) and reverse the removal procedures. Torque the front cover-to-engine bolts to 69–95 inch lbs., the crankshaft pulley-to-crankshaft bolts to 36–45 ft. lbs. and the water pump pulley-to-water pump bolts to 36–45 ft. lbs.

OIL SEAL REPLACEMENT

The front oil seal is actually the front seal of the oil pump.

Oil Pump Installed

1. Remove the timing belt.
2. Remove the crankshaft sprocket-to-crankshaft bolt, the sprocket and Woodruff key.
3. Using a small pry bar, pry the oil seal from the oil pump housing.
4. Using a clean shop cloth, clean the oil seal bore.
5. Lubricate the new oil seal with clean engine oil.
6. Using the Front Crankshaft Seal Installer tool No. T87C–6019–A or equivalent, press the oil seal into the oil pump bore.
7. To complete the installation, check and/or adjust the engine timing and reverse the removal procedures. Start the engine and check for oil seal leaks.

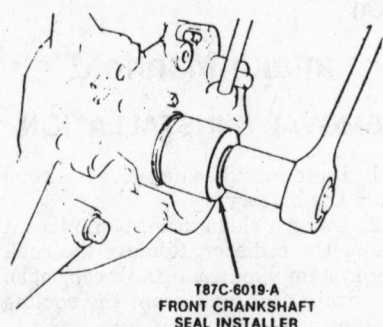

Pressing the new front oil seal into the oil pump

Oil Pump Removed

1. Remove the oil pump.
2. Using a small pry bar, pry the oil seal from the oil pump.
3. Using a clean shop cloth, clean the oil seal bore.
4. Lubricate the new oil seal with clean engine oil.
5. Using an Oil Seal Driver tool, drive the new oil seal into the oil pump bore.
6. To complete the installation, pack the oil pump with petroleum jelly, check and/or adjust the engine timing and reverse the removal procedures. Start the engine and check for oil seal leaks.

Timing Belt and Tensioner

ADJUSTMENT

1. Remove the front cover assembly.
2. Using finger pressure on the longest span between the pulleys, measure the timing belt deflection; 22 lbs. @ 0.35–39 in.
3. If adjustment is incorrect, loosen the idler pulley bolt and correct the belt tension.
4. Rotate the crankshaft 2 complete revolutions and recheck the deflection.
5. To install, the front covers, reverse the removal procedures.

REMOVAL & INSTALLATION

1. Remove the front covers.
2. Remove the No. 1 spark plug. Rotate the crankshaft to position the No. 1 cylinder on the TDC of its compression stroke.
3. Using a piece of chalk, mark the rotation direction on the timing belt.
4. Remove the timing belt tensioner spring, mounting bolt and tensioner.
5. Remove the timing belt.
6. Inspect the timing belt tensioner and sprockets for signs are clean and not worn; if necessary, clean or replace the parts.
7. Check and/or align the camshaft and crankshaft sprockets with the cylinder head and oil pump alignment marks.

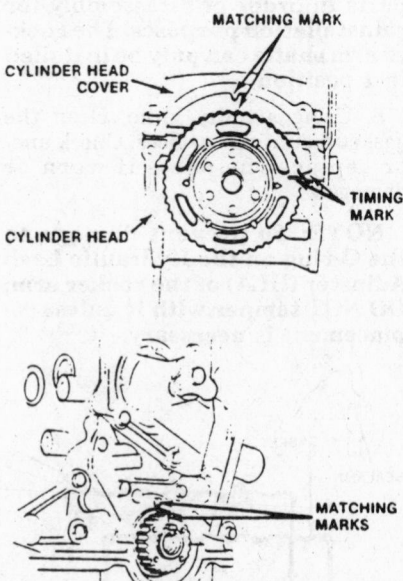

View of the camshaft and crankshaft sprocket alignment marks

NOTE: If the No. 1 cylinder is not on the TDC of its compression stroke, rotate the crankshaft 1 complete revolution and realign the timing mark on the oil pump housing.

8. If reusing the timing belt, install it in the direction of the rotation mark.

9. Install the timing belt tensioner and spring; tighten the timing belt tensioner finger tight.

10. Rotate the crankshaft 2 complete revolutions and realign the timing marks. Reaffirm that the timing marks are aligned, if not, repeat the alignment procedures.

11. Torque the tensioner bolt to 14–19 ft. lbs. and check the timing belt deflection; the timing belt deflection should be 22 lbs. @ 0.35–0.39 in.

12. To complete the installation, reverse the removal procedures. Torque the front cover-to-engine bolts to 69–95 inch lbs., the crankshaft pulley-to-crankshaft bolts to 36–45 ft. lbs. and the water pump pulley-to-water pump bolts to 36–45 ft. lbs. Start the engine and allow it to reach normal operating temperatures. Check and/or adjust the ignition timing.

Timing Sprockets

REMOVAL & INSTALLATION

Camshaft

1. Remove the timing belt.
2. Using a medium pry bar or a metal dowel, lock the camshaft sprocket from turning and remove the camshaft sprocket-to-camshaft bolt.
3. Pull the camshaft sprocket from the camshaft; be sure not to loose the Woodruff key.
4. If necessary, replace the camshaft oil seal.
5. To install, reverse the removal procedures. Torque the camshaft sprocket-to-camshaft bolt to 36–45 ft. lbs. Start the engine and inspect the ignition timing.

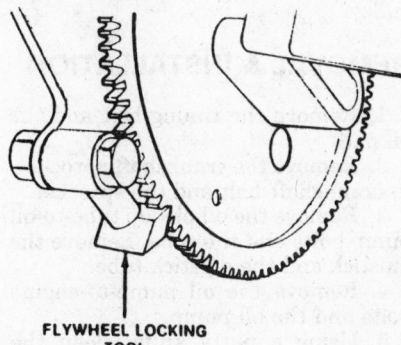

FLYWHEEL LOCKING TOOL

Using the Flywheel Locking tool to secure the flywheel

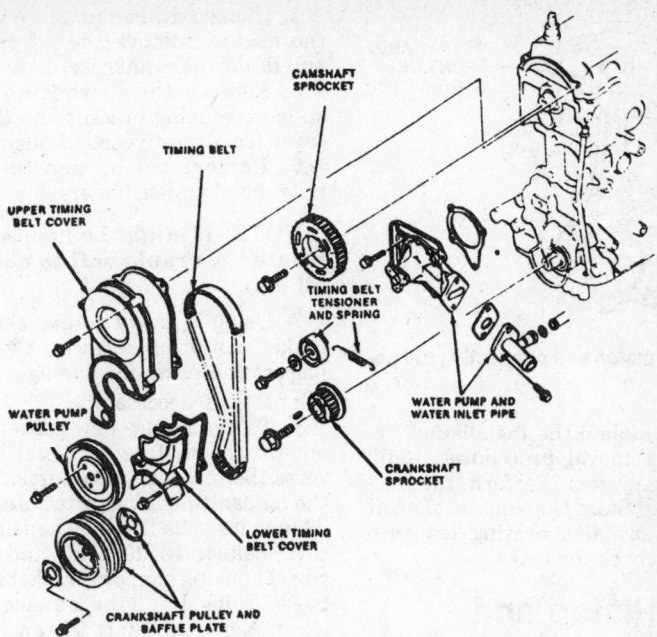

Exploded view of the timing belt assembly

Crankshaft

1. Remove the timing belt.
2. If equipped with a manual transaxle, place the shift control lever in 4th gear and apply the parking brake.
3. If equipped with an automatic transaxle, remove the flywheel dust cover. Using the Flywheel Locking tool No. T84P–6375–A or equivalent, secure the flywheel.
4. With the crankshaft secured, remove the crankshaft sprocket-to-crankshaft bolt and the sprocket; be sure not to loose the woodruff key.
5. If necessary, replace the crankshaft oil seal.
6. To install, reverse the removal procedures. Torque the crankshaft sprocket-to-crankshaft bolt to 80–94 ft. lbs. Start the engine and inspect the ignition timing.

CAMSHAFT OIL SEAL REPLACEMENT

1. Remove the camshaft sprocket.
2. Using a small pry bar, pry the camshaft oil seal from the cylinder head.
3. Using a clean shop rag, clean the camshaft oil seal bore.
4. To install the oil seal, perform the following procedures:
   a. Using a new oil seal, lubricate it with clean engine oil.
   b. Using the Front Seal Replacer tool No. T87C–6019–A or equivalent, and the Drive Handle tool No. T80T–4000–W or equivalent, drive the new oil seal into the cylinder head bore until it seats.

5. To complete the installation, reverse the removal procedures.

Camshaft

REMOVAL & INSTALLATION

1. Remove the timing belt and rocker arm assembly.
2. Matchmark the distributor housing-to-cylinder head and rotor-to-distributor housing. Remove the distributor hold-down bolts and the distributor from the rear end of the camshaft.
3. Using a medium pry bar (to prevent the camshaft from turning), remove the camshaft sprocket-to-camshaft bolt and the sprocket.
4. Using a small pry bar, pry the camshaft oil seal from the cylinder.
5. From the rear camshaft bearing journal, remove the thrust plate-to-cylinder head bolt and the thrust plate.
6. Slide the camshaft forward and from the cylinder head; be careful not to damage the journals and/or the lobes.
7. Using a putty knife, clean the gasket mounting surfaces. Clean and inspect the parts for damage and/or wear; replace the parts, if necessary.
8. To install, lubricate the parts with clean engine oil, use new gaskets, sealant (if necessary) and reverse the removal procedures. Torque the camshaft thrust plate bolt to 6–9 ft. lbs., the camshaft sprocket-to-camshaft bolt to 36–45 ft. lbs., the distributor hold-down bolt to 14–22 ft. lbs.

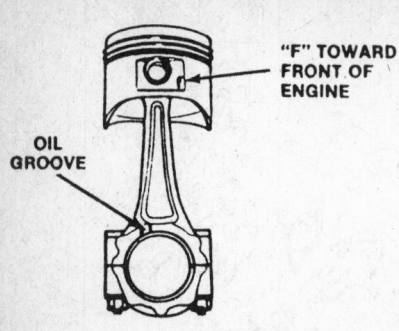

"F" TOWARD FRONT OF ENGINE

OIL GROOVE

View of the piston and connecting rod positioning

9. To complete the installation, reverse the removal procedures. Refill the cooling system. Perform the ignition timing. Start the engine, allow it to reach normal operating temperatures and check for leaks.

Piston and Connecting Rod

POSITIONING

For all piston and connecting rod overhaul procedures, please refer to "Engine, Rebuilding" in the Unit Repair section.

ENGINE LUBRICATION

Oil Pan

REMOVAL & INSTALLATION

1. Disconnect the negative terminal from the battery.
2. Raise and support the front of the vehicle on jackstands.
3. Remove the under engine splash shields and the right front inner fender panel.

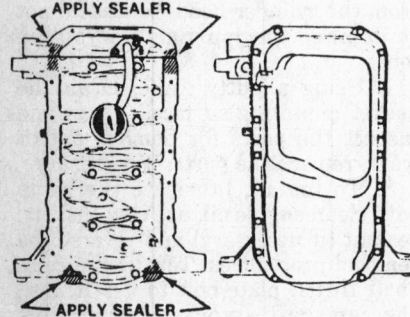

APPLY SEALER

APPLY SEALER

Apply sealant to oil pan-to-engine mating surfaces

4. Using a drain pan, place it under the engine, remove the oil pan plug and drain the crankcase.
5. Remove the flywheel-to-engine support housing bracket and the dust cover from the flywheel housing.
6. Remove the oil pan-to-engine nuts, bolts and stiffeners.

NOTE: If might be necessary to rotate the crankshaft to clear the oil pan.

7. Using a putty knife, clean the gasket mounting surfaces. Clean and inspect the parts for damage; replace the parts, it necessary.
8. To install, use new gaskets, sealant (at the mating surfaces) and reverse the removal procedures. Torque the oil pan-to-engine nuts/bolts to 69–79 inch lbs., the flywheel housing dust cover bolts to 13–20 ft. lbs. and the flywheel housing support bracket bolts to 69–86 ft. lbs. Refill the crankcase with clean engine oil. Start the engine and check for leaks.

Rear Main Bearing Oil Seal

REMOVAL & INSTALLATION

Retainer Removed

1. Remove the transaxle.
2. If equipped with a manual transaxle, perform the following procedures:
    a. Matchmark the clutch assembly-to-flywheel.
    b. Remove the pressure plate-to-flywheel bolts (evenly) a little at a time and the clutch assembly.
3. Remove the flywheel-to-crankshaft bolts, the flywheel and the spacer plates (automatic transaxle).
4. If necessary, remove the rear engine plate-to-engine bolts and the plate.
5. Remove the rear oil seal retainer-to-engine bolts, the oil pan-to-rear oil seal retainer bolts and the retainer.
6. Using a pry bar, press the oil seal from the rear oil seal retainer.
7. Using a putty knife the gasket mounting surfaces. Using a clean shop cloth, clean the oil seal bore.
8. Using a new oil seal, lubricate it with clean engine oil and press it into the retainer until seats.
9. To install, use new gaskets, sealant and reverse the remove procedures. Torque the flywheel-to-crankshaft bolts to 71–76 ft. lbs. and the transaxle-to-engine bolts to 16–40 ft. lbs. (manual) or 47–66 ft. lbs.

Retainer Installed

1. Remove the transaxle.

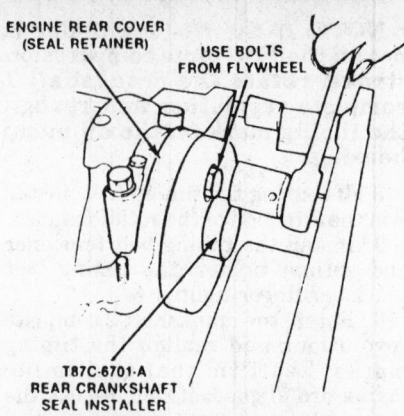

ENGINE REAR COVER (SEAL RETAINER)

USE BOLTS FROM FLYWHEEL

T87C-6701-A
REAR CRANKSHAFT SEAL INSTALLER

Using the oil seal installation tool to install the rear main oil seal.

2. If equipped with a manual transaxle, perform the following procedures:
    a. Matchmark the clutch assembly-to-flywheel.
    b. Remove the pressure plate-to-flywheel bolts (evenly) a little at a time and the clutch assembly.
3. Remove the flywheel-to-crankshaft bolts, the flywheel and the spacer plates (automatic transaxle).
4. If necessary, remove the rear engine plate-to-engine bolts and the plate.
5. Using a pry bar, pry the oil seal from the rear oil seal retainer.
6. Using a clean shop cloth, clean the oil seal bore.
7. Lubricate the new seal with clean engine.
8. Using the Rear Main Seal Installer tool No. T87C–6701–A or equivalent, press the new oil seal into the retainer until it seats.
9. To complete the installation, reverse the removal procedures. Torque the flywheel-to-crankshaft bolts to 71–76 ft. lbs. and the transaxle-to-engine bolts to 16–40 ft. lbs. (manual) or 47–66 ft. lbs. (automatic).

Oil Pump

The oil pump is located at the front of the engine behind the crankshaft pulley.

REMOVAL & INSTALLATION

1. Remove the timing belt and the oil pan.
2. Remove the crankshaft sprocket-to-crankshaft bolt and the sprocket.
3. Remove the oil pickup tube-to-oil pump bolts and the tube. Remove the dipstick and the dipstick tube.
4. Remove the oil pump-to-engine bolts and the oil pump.
5. Using a putty knife, clean the gasket mounting surfaces. Clean and inspect the parts for wear and/or damage, replace the parts (if necessary).

NOTE: When the oil pump is removed, it is recommended to replace the oil seal.

6. Using petroleum jelly, pack the pump cavity.

7. To install, use new gaskets, sealant and reverse the removal procedures. Torque the oil pump-to-engine bolts to 14–19 ft. lbs. Refill the crankcase with clean engine oil. Start the engine and check for leaks.

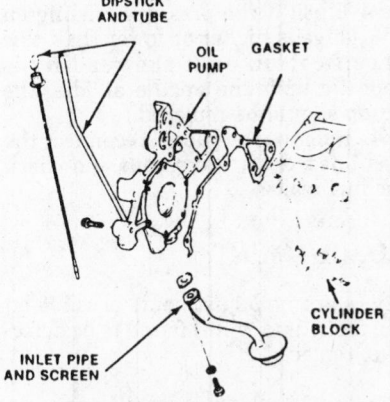

Exploded view of the oil pump assembly

ENGINE COOLING

CAUTION

Never open the cooling system with the engine hot, scalding could occur.

Radiator

REMOVAL & INSTALLATION

NOTE: Be certain the engine is cool before attempting any work on the cooling system.

1. Disconnect the electrical connector from the cooling fan.
2. Remove the radiator cap.
3. Place a clean drain pan under the radiator, open the drain valve and drain the cooling system.
4. Disconnect the upper and lower hoses from the radiator. From the radiator filler neck, disconnect the overflow tube.
5. From the outer edges of the cooling fan shroud, disconnect the wiring harness from the retaining clips.
6. From the lower radiator tank, disconnect the coolant temperature sensor wires.
7. If equipped with an automatic transaxle, disconnect and plug the oil cooler lines.

8. Remove the upper radiator assembly-to-support bolts and the radiator assembly. Remove the cooling fan shroud-to-radiator bolts and the fan/shroud assembly.
9. Inspect the parts for damage and/or wear, replace the parts (if necessary).
10. To install, reverse the removal procedures. Refill the cooling system. Start the engine, allow it to reach normal operating temperatures and check for leaks.

Water Pump

REMOVAL & INSTALLATION

1. Remove the timing belt.
2. Place a clean drain pan under the radiator. Remove the radiator drain plug and the radiator cap; drain the cooling system to a level below the water pump.
3. Remove the coolant inlet pipe-to-water pump bolts and the inlet pipe.
4. Remove the water pump-to-engine bolts and the water pump.
5. Using a putty knife, clean the gasket mounting surfaces. Inspect the parts for wear and/or damage, if necessary, replace the parts.
6. To install, use new gaskets, sealant and reverse the removal procedures. Torque the water pump-to-engine bolts to 14–19 ft. lbs., the water inlet pipe-to-water pump bolts to 14–19 ft. lbs. and the water pump pulley-to-water pump bolts to 11–13 ft. lbs. Refill the cooling system. Start the engine, allow it to reach normal operating temperatures and check for leaks.

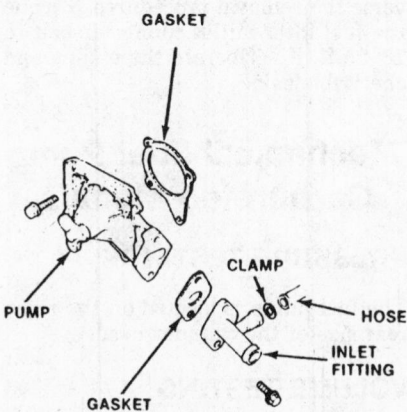

Exploded view of the water pump

Thermostat

The thermostat is located at the rear of the cylinder head.

REMOVAL & INSTALLATION

1. Disconnect the electrical connector from the cooling fan switch, located on the thermostat housing.
2. Place a clean drain pan under the radiator. Remove the radiator drain plug and the radiator cap; drain the cooling system to a level below the thermostat housing.
3. Disconnect the upper radiator hose from the thermostat housing.
4. Remove the thermostat housing-to-cylinder head bolts, the housing, the thermostat and the gasket (discard it).
5. Using a putty knife, clean the gasket mounting surfaces. Inspect the parts for damage and/or wear; replace the parts (if necessary).

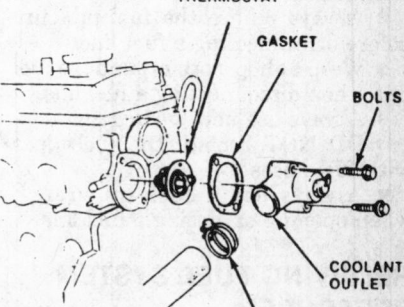

Exploded view of the thermostat housing and the thermostat

NOTE: When installing the thermostat, be sure to position the jiggle valve at the top.

6. To install, use a new gasket, sealant (if necessary) and reverse the removal procedures. Torque the thermostat housing-to-cylinder head bolts to 14–22 ft. lbs. Refill the cooling system. Start the engine, allow it to reach normal operating temperatures and check for leaks.

EMISSION CONTROLS

Please refer to "Emission Control" in the Unit Repair section for system maintenance procedures. Due to the complex nature of modern electronic engine control systems, comprehensive diagnosis and testing procedures fall outside the confines of this repair manual. For complete information on diagnosis, testing and re-

pair procedures concerning all modern engine and emission control systems, please refer to *"Chilton's Guide to Electronic Engine Controls"*.

GASOLINE FUEL SYSTEM

Fuel System Service Precautions

- Disconnect the negative battery terminal.
- Keep a Class B dry chemical fire extinguisher available.
- Always relieve the fuel pressure before disconnecting a fuel line.
- Wrap a shop cloth around the fuel line when disconnecting a fuel line.
- Always use new O-rings.
- DO NOT replace the fuel pipes with fuel hoses.
- Always use a back-up wrench when opening or closing a fuel line.

RELIEVING FUEL SYSTEM PRESSURE

EFI Engines

The fuel system remains under high pressure, even when the engine is not running.

VANE FLOW AIR METER METHOD

1. Start the engine and disconnect the vane air flow meter.
2. When the engine stalls, turn the ignition switch OFF.
3. Reconnect the vane air flow meter.

FUEL PUMP CONNECTOR METHOD

1. Remove the back seat cushion.
2. Operate the engine.
3. Disconnect the fuel pump electrical connector.
4. Operate the engine until it stalls.

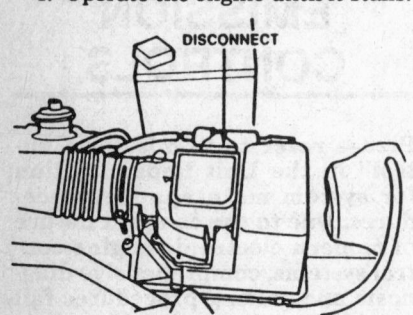

View of the vane air flow meter with electrical connector—EFI system

5. Turn the ignition switch OFF and reconnect the electrical connector.

Fuel Filter

REMOVAL & INSTALLATION

Carbureted

An inline fuel filter is located in the engine compartment.

1. Disconnect the negative terminal from the battery.
2. Using a shop cloth, place it under the fuel filter to catch the excess fuel.
3. Disconnect and plug the fuel hoses from the fuel filter.
4. Remove the fuel filter brace-to-engine bolt(s) and the filter from the vehicle.

NOTE: The fuel filter is equipped with a directional arrow, indicating fuel flow direction, be sure to install it in the proper direction.

5. To install, use a new filter and reverse the removal procedures.

Fuel Injected

An inline fuel filter is located in the engine compartment.

1. Relieve the fuel pressure.
2. Using a shop cloth, place it under the fuel filter to catch the excess fuel.
3. From the inlet of the fuel filter, remove the clamp and the hose; plug the line.
4. From the fuel filter outlet, remove the bolt, the 2 washers and the outlet line.
5. Remove the fuel filter-to-chassis bolts and the filter.
6. To install, use a new filter and reverse the removal procedures. Torque the fuel filter outlet connector bolt to 18–25 ft. lbs. Operate the engine and check for leaks.

Mechanical Fuel Pump Carbureted Models

PRESSURE TESTING

The fuel pump is located on the right rear side of the cylinder head.

VOLUME TESTING

1. Disconnect the fuel line from the carburetor. Run the fuel line into a suitable container.
2. Run the engine at idle until there is 1 pint of fuel in the container; 1 pint should be pumped in 30 seconds or less.
3. If the flow is below minimum, check for a restriction in the fuel line.

4. Tighten any loose line connections and look for any kinks or restrictions.

PRESSURE TESTING

1. Using a fuel pressure gauge, connect it between the fuel pump and carburetor; using a pair of vise grips, squeeze off the return hose.
2. Operate the engine at idle and note the reading on the gauge.
3. The fuel pump pressure should be 4–5 psi; if the pressure reading on the gauge is higher or lower than this specification or if the reading is sporatic with the engine at idle, the pump should be replaced.
4. Remove the gauge, reconnect the fuel lines. Start the engine and check for fuel leaks.

ADJUSTMENT

There are no adjustments possible on the fuel pump; if it is found to be defective, replaced it.

REMOVAL & INSTALLATION

1. Place a shop cloth under the fuel pump to catch the excess fuel.
2. Label, disconnect and plug the fuel inlet, the discharge and return lines.
3. Remove the fuel pump-to-cylinder head bolts, the fuel pump, gaskets (discard them) and spacer.
4. Using a putty knife, clean the gasket mounting surfaces. Inspect the pump for damage and/or wear; replace it (if necessary).
5. To install, use new gaskets and reverse the removal procedures. Torque the fuel pump-to-cylinder head bolts to 17–22 ft. lbs.

Electric Fuel Pump

The electric fuel pump is located in the fuel tank.

A fuel pump shut-off switch (inertia switch) is connected in series with the fuel pump switch circuit; the fuel pump will cease operation in the event of the roll-over or a major collision. The switch must be pushed to activate the fuel pump.

On the 3 or 5 door models, the inertia switch is located on the left side of the spare tire well. On the station wagon models, the inertia switch is located inside the axle jack storage compartment at the right rear side.

REMOVAL & INSTALLATION

1. Relieve the fuel pressure.

2. Disconnect the fuel lines from the fuel sending unit at the fuel tank.

3. Remove the fuel sending unit-to-fuel tank bolts and the sending unit.

4. Remove the fuel filter from the fuel pump.

5. Disconnect the electrical connectors from the fuel pump.

6. Remove the retaining clamp screw, the outlet hose clamp and the fuel pump.

7. To install, use a new sending unit-to-fuel tank gasket and reverse the removal procedures.

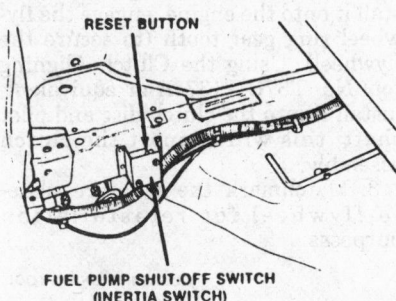

View of the fuel pump inertia switch—EFI equipped 3/5 door models

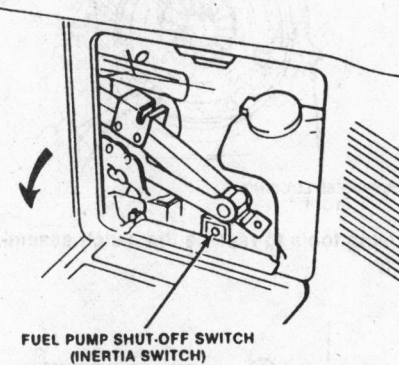

View of the fuel pump inertia switch—EFI equipped station wagon models

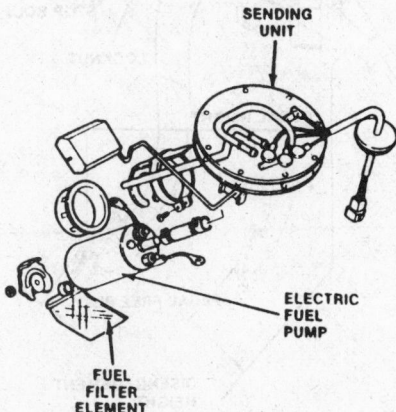

Exploded view of the electric fuel pump—EFI models

Carburetor

REMOVAL & INSTALLATION

1. Disconnect the negative terminal from the battery.
2. Remove the air cleaner assembly.
3. Disconnect and plug the fuel line to prevent leakage.
4. Label and disconnect the vacuum lines from the carburetor.
5. Disconnect the electrical harness connector from the carburetor.
6. Frm the rear of the alternator, disconnect the choke heater wire.
7. Fully open the throttle and disconnect the throttle cable.
8. Remove the carburetor-to-intake manifold nuts. Lift the carburetor and remove the idle-up diaphragm link from the carburetor linkage.

NOTE: If the PTC heater sticks to the carburetor, carefully remove it.

9. Using a putty knife, clean the gasket mounting surfaces.
10. To install, use new gaskets and reverse the removal procedures. Start the engine. Check and/or adjust the idle mixture and idle speed. Check the fuel float level.

OVERHAUL

For all carburetor overhaul and adjustment procedures, please refer to "Carburetor Service" in the Unit Repair section.

Fuel Injection

Due to the complex nature of modern fuel injection systems, comprehensive diagnosis and testing procedures fall outside the confines of this repair manual. For complete information on Fuel injection diagnosis, testing and repair procedures please refer to Chilton's Guide to Fuel Injection And Feedback Carburetors.

MANUAL TRANSAXLE

REMOVAL & INSTALLATION

1. Disconnect the negative terminal from the battery.
2. Remove the air cleaner. Loosen the front wheel lug nuts.
3. From the transaxle, disconnect the speedometer cable.

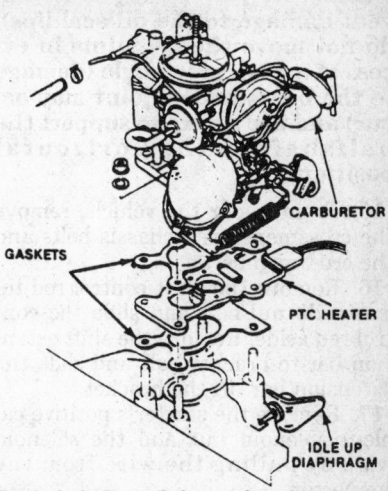

Exploded view of the carburetor assembly

4. From the clutch release lever, remove the adjusting nut, pin and the clutch cable. Remove the clutch cable bracket-to-transaxle bolts and the bracket. Remove the ground wire bolt and ground wire.
5. Remove the coolant pipe bracket bolt and the bracket.
6. Remove the secondary air pipe, the EGR pipe bracket and the electrical harness clip.
7. Disconnect the neutral switch/back-up light switch coupler and the body ground connector.
8. Remove the upper 2 transaxle-to-engine bolts.
9. Using the Engine Support Bar tool No. D79P–6000–B or equivalent, attach it to the rear engine lifting hook and support the engine's weight.
10. Raise and support the front of the vehicle with jackstands positioned under the frame.
11. Place a drain pan under the transaxle, remove the drain plug and drain the transaxle.
12. Remove the front wheel lug nuts and the wheels. Remove the engine undercover and side covers.
13. Remove the front stabilizer bar. From both sides, remove the lower control arm ball joint-to-steering knuckle nut/bolt, pull the control arm downward and separate the lower control arm from the steering knuckle.

NOTE: When separating the ball joint, be careful not to damage the ball joint dust boot.

14. Using both hands, grasp the steering knuckle/hub assembly, apply even pressure (gradually increasing), pull both halfshafts from the transaxle.

NOTE: When removing the halfshafts, withdraw them completely from the transaxle (to pre-

vent damage to the oil seal lips), do not move the CV-joints in excess of a 20 degree angle (damage to the boots and/or joint may occur) and use a wire to support the halfshaft in the horizontal position.

15. From under the vehicle, remove the crossmember-to-chassis bolts and the crossmember.

16. Remove the shift control rod-to-transaxle nut/bolt and slide the control rod aside. Remove the shift extension bar-to-bracket bolt and slide the extension bar off the bracket.

17. Remove the starter's positive cable-to-solenoid nut and the solenoid wire by pulling the wire from the connector.

18. Remove the starter-to-engine bolts and the starter. Remove the dust cover-to-clutch housing bolts and the cover.

19. Loosen the bracket bar on the engine support tool to lower the transaxle. Using a floor jack, support the transaxle.

20. Remove the No. 2 engine mount-to-transaxle nut/bolt, the transaxle-to-engine bolts and lower the transaxle from the vehicle.

21. To install the transaxle, perform the following procedures:

a. Apply a small amount of clutch grease to the input shaft spline and reverse the removal procedures.

b. Torque the transaxle-to-engine bolts to 47–66 ft. lbs., the No. 2 engine mount-to-transaxle nut/bolt to 27–38 ft. lbs., the starter to engine bolts to 23–34 ft. lbs., the extension bar-to-transaxle bracket bolt to 23–34 ft. lbs., the control rod-to-transaxle nut/bolt to 12–17 ft. lbs., the crossmember-to-chassis bolts to 47–66 ft. lbs., the rear engine mount-to-crossmember nut to 20–34 ft. lbs.

c. Refill the transaxle with Dexron® II or equivalent.

22. To install the halfshaft into the transaxle, perform the following procedures:

a. Install a new locking clip on the halfshaft spline; be sure the gap in the clip is at the top of the clip groove.

b. Slide the halfshafts into the transaxle bore; be careful not to damage the oil seal lip.

c. Push firmly on the hub assembly, making sure the circlip snaps into place.

d. After installation, pull the front hub outward to confirm that the circlips are engaged.

23. To complete the installation, reverse the removal procedures. Torque the lower control arm ball joint-to-steering knuckle nut/bolt to 32–40 ft. lbs., the stabilizer bar-to-chassis nuts/bolts to 23–33 ft. lbs., stabilizer bar-to-lower control arm nuts to 9–13 ft. lbs. Adjust the clutch pedal free-play. Test the vehicle performance.

LINKAGE ADJUSTMENT

No adjustment to the linkage is necessary or possible.

CLUTCH

REMOVAL & INSTALLATION

1. Remove the transaxle.

2. Using the Flywheel Locking tool No. T84P–6375–A or equivalent, install it onto the engine, engage the flywheel ring gear tooth (to secure the flywheel). Using the Clutch Aligning tool No. T87C–7137–A or equivalent, install it into the clutch disc and pilot shaft; this will support the clutch assembly.

3. Matchmark the pressure plate-to-flywheel for reinstallation purposes.

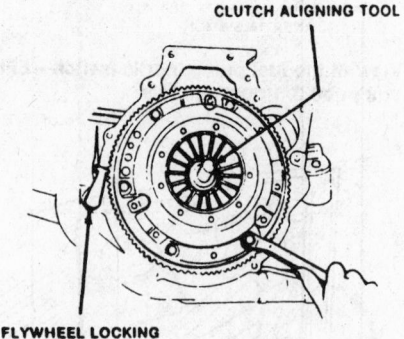

CLUTCH ALIGNING TOOL

FLYWHEEL LOCKING TOOL

Using tools to replace the clutch assembly

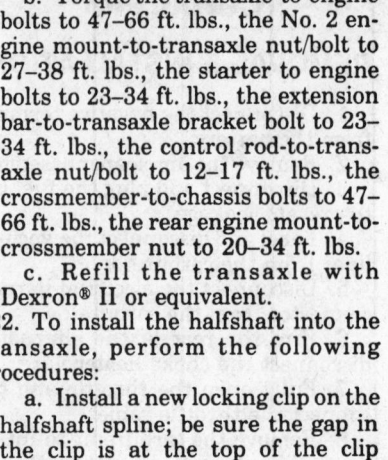

STABILIZER BAR

SHIFT CONTROL ROD

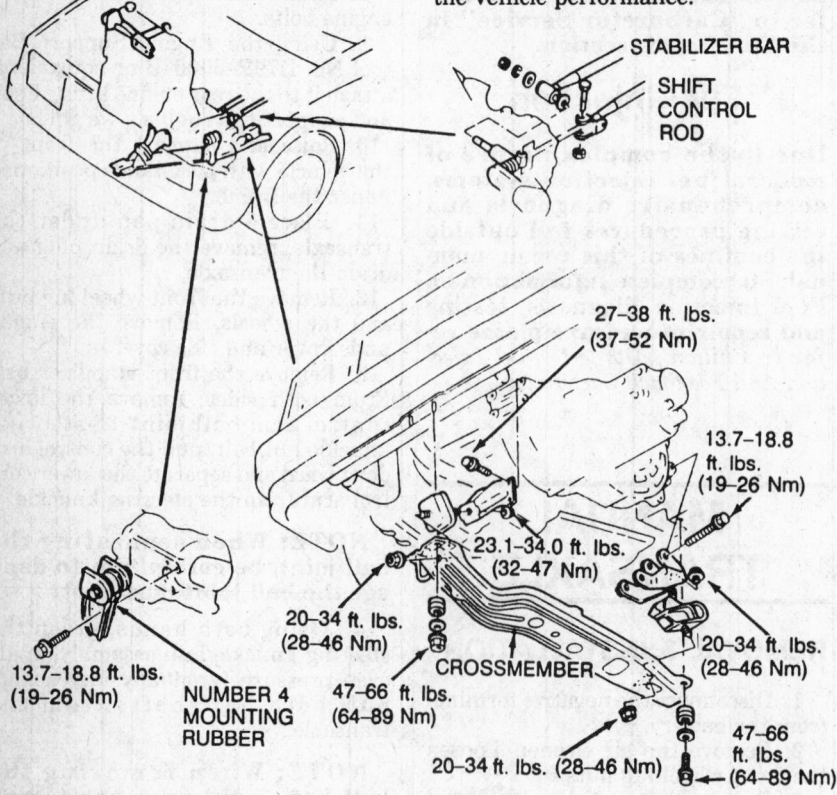

27–38 ft. lbs. (37–52 Nm)

13.7–18.8 ft. lbs. (19–26 Nm)

23.1–34.0 ft. lbs. (32–47 Nm)

20–34 ft. lbs. (28–46 Nm)

CROSSMEMBER

20–34 ft. lbs. (28–46 Nm)

13.7–18.8 ft. lbs. (19–26 Nm)

NUMBER 4 MOUNTING RUBBER

47–66 ft. lbs. (64–89 Nm)

20–34 ft. lbs. (28–46 Nm)

47–66 ft. lbs. (64–89 Nm)

Exploded view of the crossmember and bracket assemblies

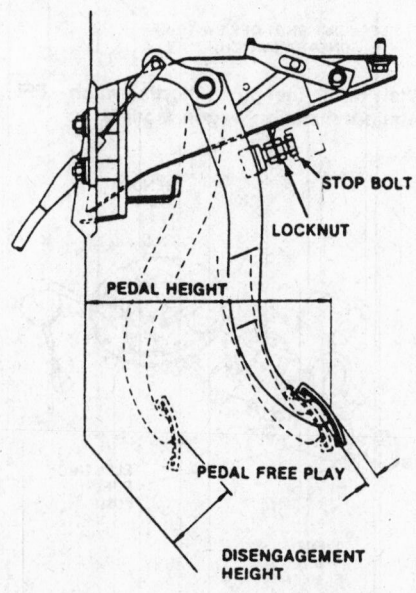

STOP BOLT

LOCKNUT

PEDAL HEIGHT

PEDAL FREE PLAY

DISENGAGEMENT HEIGHT

Adjusting the clutch pedal height and free-play

4. Remove the pressure plate-to-fly-wheel bolts, evenly, a little at a time.

5. Remove the pressure plate and clutch disc.

6. Inspect the pilot bearing, the fly-wheel, the pressure plate and clutch disc for wear and/or damage; replace the parts, if necessary.

7. To install, reverse the removal procedures. Torque the flywheel-to-crankshaft bolts to 71–75 ft. lbs., the pressure plate-to-flywheel bolts to 13–20 ft. lbs. Adjust the clutch pedal free-play.

PEDAL HEIGHT/FREE-PLAY ADJUSTMENT

Pedal Height

Pedal height is the distance from the cowl to the center of the clutch pedal pad.

1. Remove the necessary instrument panel components which block access to the clutch pedal.

2. Loosen the clutch pedal locknut.

3. Turn the stop bolt to obtain the correct pedal height of 8.4–8.6 inch and tighten the locknut.

4. If components from the instrument panel were removed, replace them.

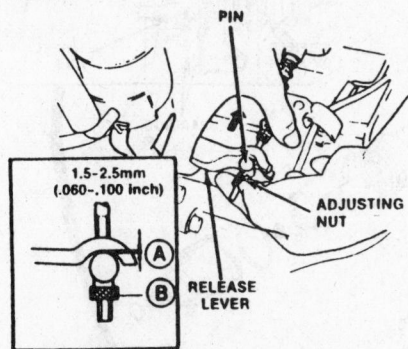

Adjusting the clutch pedal free-play

3. Depress the pedal and check the disengagement height of 3.3 or more inches; the distance from the floor and the center of the clutch pedal pad.

Free-Play

Free-play is the distance the clutch pedal moves without engaging it.

1. Depress the clutch pedal and pull the pin away from the clutch lever (at the transaxle).

2. Turn the cable locknut to adjust the clutch pedal free-play of 0.35–0.59 inch.

Clutch Cable

REMOVAL & INSTALLATION

1. At the transaxle, remove the clutch cable adjusting nut and pin;

separate the cable from the fork.

2. Remove the clutch cable bracket-to-cowl nuts and the bracket.

3. From under the instrument panel, separate the clutch cable from the top of the clutch pedal.

4. Pull the cable through the cowl and remove the cable assembly from the engine side.

5. Inspect the clutch cable housing for frayed wire, cracked or worn housing and the cable for smooth operation; replace the cable assembly, if necessary.

6. To install, lubricate the cable with multi-purpose grease and reverse the removal procedures. Adjust the clutch pedal free-play.

AUTOMATIC TRANSAXLE

For further information on automatic transaxles, please refer to "Automatic Transmissions" in the Unit Repair section.

REMOVAL & INSTALLATION

1. Disconnect the negative terminal from the battery.

2. Remove the air cleaner. Loosen the front wheel lug nuts.

3. From the transaxle, disconnect the speedometer cable.

4. Disconnect the shift control cable-to-transaxle clip and 2 bracket bolts. Remove the ground wire from the cylinder head.

5. Remove the water pipe bracket bolt and the bracket.

6. Remove the secondary air pipe, the EGR pipe bracket and the electrical harness clip.

7. Disconnect the electrical connectors from the inhibitor switch, the neutral switch and the kick-down solenoid. Disconnect the body ground connector.

8. Remove the upper 2 transaxle-to-engine bolts.

9. Remove the vacuum hose from the vacuum diaphragm line. Disconnect and plug the oil cooler line at the transaxle.

10. Using the Engine Support Bar tool No. D79P–6000–B or equivalent, attach it to the rear engine lifting hook and support the engine's weight.

11. Raise and support the front of the vehicle with jackstands positioned under the frame.

12. Place a drain pan under the transaxle, remove the drain plug and drain the transaxle.

13. Remove the front wheel lug nuts and the wheels. Remove the engine undercover and side covers.

14. Remove the front stabilizer bar. From both sides, remove the lower control arm ball joint-to-steering knuckle nut/bolt, pull the control arm downward and separate the lower control arm from the steering knuckle.

NOTE: When separating the ball joint, be careful not to damage the ball joint dust boot.

15. Using a medium pry bar, insert it between the halfshaft and the transaxle (a notch is provided), pry both halfshafts from the transaxle.

NOTE: When removing the halfshafts, withdraw them completely from the transaxle (to prevent damage to the oil seal lips), do not move the CV-joints in excess of a 20 degree angle (damage to the boots and/or joint may occur) and use a wire to support the halfshaft in the horizontal position.

16. From under the vehicle, remove the crossmember-to-chassis bolts and the crossmember.

17. Remove the starter's positive cable-to-solenoid nut and the solenoid wire by pulling the wire from the connector.

18. Remove the starter-to-engine bolts and the starter. Remove the dust cover-to-clutch housing bolts and the cover.

19. Matchmark the torque converter-to-flexplate location. Remove the torque converter-to-flexplate bolts and slide the torque converter back into the transaxle.

20. Loosen the bracket bar on the engine support tool to lower the transaxle. Using a floor jack, support the transaxle.

21. Remove the No. 2 engine mount-to-transaxle nut/bolt, the transaxle-to-engine bolts and lower the transaxle from the vehicle.

22. To install the transaxle, reverse the removal procedures. Torque the transaxle-to-engine bolts to 47–66 ft. lbs., the No. 2 engine mount-to-transaxle nut/bolt to 27–38 ft. lbs., the starter to engine bolts to 23–34 ft. lbs., the crossmember-to-chassis bolts to 47–66 ft. lbs., the rear engine mount-to-crossmember nut to 20–34 ft. lbs. Refill the transaxle with Dexron® II or equivalent.

23. To install the halfshaft into the transaxle, perform the following procedures:

    a. Install a new locking clip on the halfshaft spline; be sure the gap in the clip is at the top of the clip groove.

b. Slide the halfshafts into the transaxle bore; be careful not to damage the oil seal lip.

c. Push firmly on the hub assembly, making sure the circlip snaps into place.

d. After installation, pull the front hub outward to confirm that the circlips are engaged.

24. To complete the installation, reverse the removal procedures. Torque the lower control arm ball joint-to-steering knuckle nut/bolt to 32–40 ft. lbs., the stabilizer bar-to-chassis nuts/bolts to 23–33 ft. lbs., stabilizer bar-to-lower control arm nuts to 9–13 ft. lbs. Test the vehicle performance.

DRIVE AXLE

Halfshaft

REMOVAL & INSTALLATION

1. Raise and support the front of the vehicle on jackstands.

2. Remove the necessary splash covers from under the vehicle.

3. Remove the stabilizer bar-to-lower control arm nuts, bolt, washers and bushing.

4. Remove the wheel/tire assembly and the hub grease cap.

5. Using a stake chisel and a hammer, raise the staked portion of the hub nut.

6. Using an assistant to apply the brakes, loosen the hub nut.

7. Remove the lower control arm ball joint-to-steering knuckle clamp bolt, pull the lower control arm downward to separate the ball joint from the steering knuckle.

NOTE: When separating the ball joint, be careful not to damage the ball joint dust boot.

8. If equipped with a manual transaxle, use both hands, grasp the steering knuckle/hub assembly, apply even pressure (gradually increasing), pull both halfshafts from the transaxle. If equipped with an automatic transaxle, insert a medium pry bar between the halfshaft and the transaxle (a notch is provided), pry both halfshafts from the transaxle.

NOTE: When removing the halfshafts, withdraw them completely from the transaxle (to prevent damage to the oil seal lips), do not move the CV-joints in excess of a 20 degree angle (damage to the boots and/or joint may occur) and use a wire to support the

halfshaft in the horizontal position.

9. Remove the hub nut (discard it) and washer. Pull the halfshaft from the steering knuckle assembly.

NOTE: If the wheel hub binds on the halfshaft splines, use the Puller tool No. D80L–1002–L or equivalent, to press the halfshaft from the wheel hub. Never use a hammer to separate the halfshaft from the wheel hub, for damage to the CV-joint may occur.

10. Using the Differential Plug tool(s) No. T87C–7025–C or equivalent, plug the transaxle bore(s) to prevent oil leakage.

11. Check the halfshaft for damage, wear and/or good working order; replace the halfshaft, if necessary.

12. To install the halfshaft into the transaxle, perform the following procedures:

a. Install a new locking clip on the halfshaft spline; be sure the gap in the clip is at the top of the clip groove.

b. Slide the halfshafts into the transaxle bore; be careful not to damage the oil seal lip.

c. Push firmly on the hub assembly, making sure the circlip snaps into place.

d. After installation, pull the front hub outward to confirm that the circlips are engaged.

13. Using multi-purpose grease, lubricate the halfshaft splines, lightly.

14. To complete the installation, reverse the removal procedures. Torque the lower control arm ball joint-to-steering knuckle bolt to 32–40 ft. lbs. and the halfshaft nut to 157–235 ft. lbs. Using a cold chisel (with the cutting edge rounded), stake the hub nut.

NOTE: Replace the hub nut if it splits after staking.

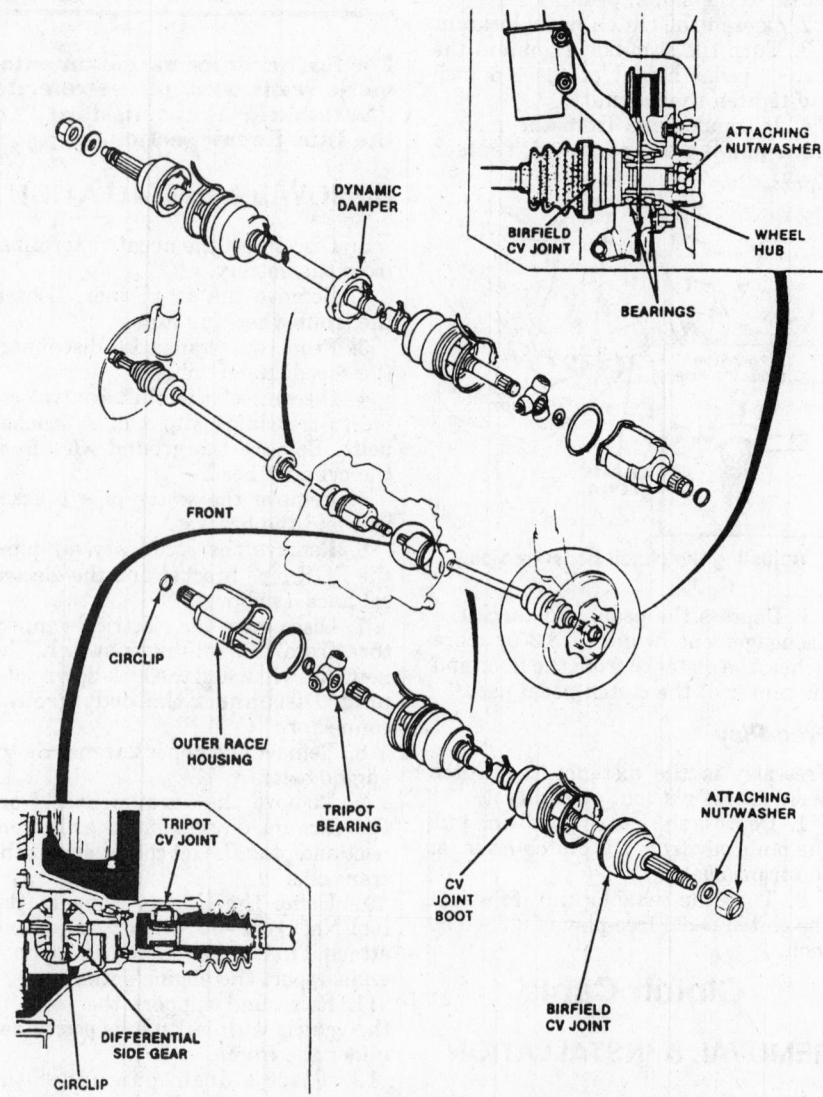

Exploded view of the halfshaft assemblies

CV-JOINT OVERHAUL

NOTE: For all CV-joint overhaul procedures, please refer to "U/CV-Joint Overhaul" in the Unit Repair section.

Front Wheel Drive Hub, Knuckle and Bearings

The front wheel hub, steering knuckle and wheel bearings are all integral of each other and must be removed as an assembly.

REMOVAL & INSTALLATION

Steering Knuckle

1. Remove the halfshaft.
2. Disconnect the U-shaped clip from the center section of the caliper hose; DO NOT disconnect the hose from the caliper. Remove the brake caliper-to-steering knuckle bolts and support the caliper on a length of wire; DO NOT allow the caliper to hang by the brake hose.
3. Remove the tie rod-to-steering knuckle ball joint cotter pin and nut. Using a hammer and the Tie Rod Separator tool No. T85M-3395-A or equivalent, separate the tie rod end from the steering knuckle.
4. Using a scratch awl, mark the camber alignment cam bolt for reassembly. Remove the cam bolt and the upper attaching bolt from the strut and spindle.

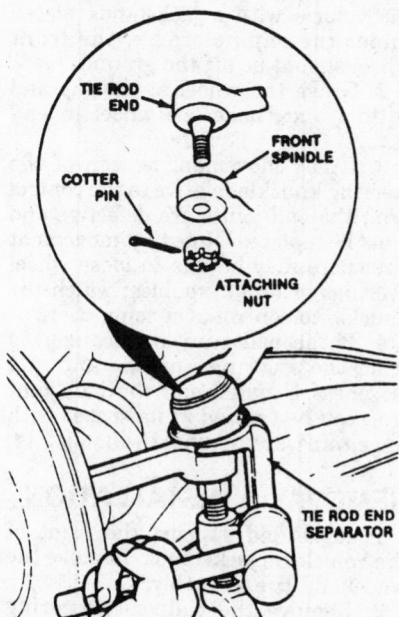

Separating the tie rod end from the steering knuckle

5. Pull the steering knuckle assembly from the strut bracket.
6. To remove the rotor or the wheel bearings the steering knuckle assembly must be disassembled.
7. To install, use a new cotter pin (tie rod end) and reverse the removal procedures. Torque the steering knuckle-to-strut bolts to 69–86 ft. lbs., the lower control arm-to-steering knuckle clamp bolt to 32–40 ft. lbs., the tie rod-to-steering knuckle nut to 22–33 ft. lbs. and the caliper-to-steering knuckle bolts to 29–36 ft. lbs.
8. Lower the vehicle to the ground and torque the hub nut to 116–174 ft. lbs.; stake the hub nut. Check and/or adjust the front wheel alignment.

Wheel Bearings

1. Remove the steering knuckle.
2. Using the Hub Removal tool No. T87C-1104-A or equivalent, separate the steering knuckle from the hub assembly.
3. From the rear of the hub assembly, remove the bearing preload spacer.

NOTE: The bearing spacer, located between the bearings, determines the bearing preload; DO NOT discard it.

4. Using paint or chalk, matchmark the rotor-to-hub alignment for reassembly purposes.
5. Unless the brake disc is damaged, it should remain attached to the hub. Remove the rotor-to-hub bolts and the rotor.
6. Using the Bearing Puller Attachment tool No. D-1123-A or equivalent, and the Puller tool No. D80L-927-A or equivalent, or a Bearing Splitter tool, press the wheel bearing from the hub. A socket may have to be used to complete the bearing removal. Remove the outer grease seal from the hub and discard it.
7. Using a small pry bar at the inner side of the steering knuckle, pry the grease seal from the knuckle and discard it. Lift the inner wheel bearing from the steering knuckle.

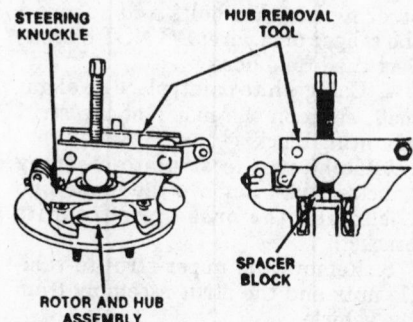

Separating the hub from the steering knuckle

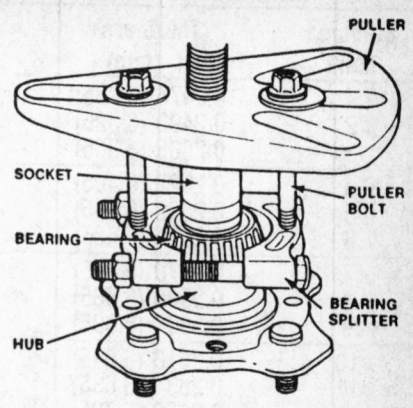

Pressing the wheel bearing from the hub

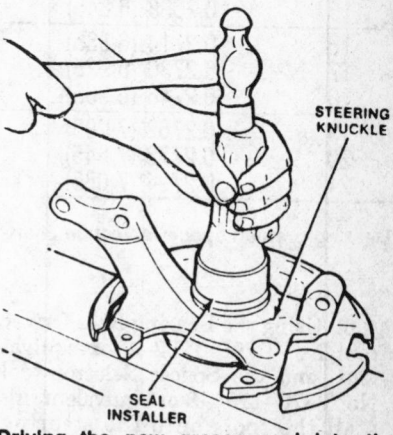

Driving the new grease seal into the steering knuckle

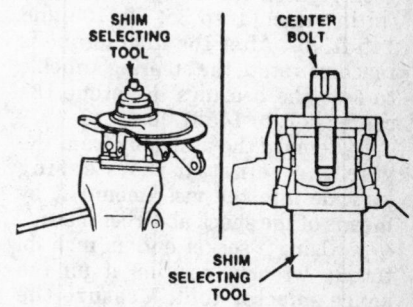

Installing wheel bearing races and adjusting the rotating torque

8. If necessary to replace the bearing races in the steering knuckle, perform the following procedures:
   a. Using a brass drift and a hammer, drive the bearing races from the steering knuckle.
   b. Clean and inspect the steering knuckle for wear and/or damage, replace the steering knuckle, if necessary.
   c. To install, new or used bearing races, lubricate them with wheel bearing grease. Assemble the parts into the steering knuckle.

Stamped Mark	Thickness in. (mm)
1	0.2474 (6.285)
2	0.2490 (6.325)
3	0.2506 (6.365)
4	0.2522 (6.405)
5	0.2538 (6.445)
6	0.2554 (6.485)
7	0.2570 (6.525)
8	0.2586 (6.565)
9	0.2602 (6.605)
10	0.2618 (6.645)
11	0.2634 (6.685)
12	0.2650 (6.725)
13	0.2666 (6.765)
14	0.2682 (6.805)
15	0.2698 (6.845)
16	0.2714 (6.885)
17	0.2730 (6.925)
18	0.2746 (6.965)
19	0.2762 (7.005)
20	0.2778 (7.045)
21	0.2794 (7.085)

Bearing preload spacer selection chart

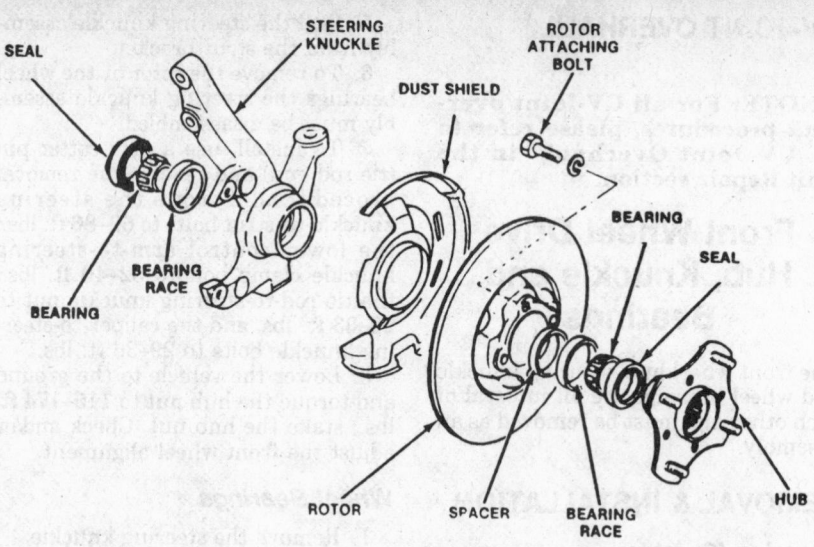

Exploded view of the steering knuckle/hub/wheel bearing assembly

d. Using the Bearing Race Driver tool No. D79P-1202-A or equivalent, and the Spacer Selector tool No. T87C-1104-B or equivalent, install the tools onto the steering knuckle assembly and the assembly onto a vise.

e. Tighten the tool's center bolt (in increments) to 36, 72, 108 and 145 ft. lbs. After the final torque is reached, rotate the steering knuckle to seat the bearings. Retorque the center bolt to 145 ft. lbs.

f. Remove the assembly from the vise and reinstall the steering knuckle into the vise; mount it by means of the shock absorber mount.

g. Using a socket and an inch lb. torque wrench, position it on the space selector tool. Measure the torque required to just move the assembly. The torque should be 2.21–10.44 inch lbs. If the torque is less than 2.21 inch lbs., a thinner spacer should be used; if the torque is more than 10.44 inch lbs., a thicker spacer should be used.

9. Clean and inspect all of the parts for wear and/or damage; replace the parts (if necessary). Using new wheel bearing grease, pack the inside of the steering knuckle.

10. Install a greased inner bearing into the steering knuckle. Using a new inner grease seal, lubricate with wheel bearing grease and drive it into the steering knuckle using the Seal Installer tool No. T87C-1175-A or equivalent.

11. Lubricate and position the bearing preload spacer and the outer wheel bearing in the steering knuckle.

12. If the rotor was removed from the hub, align the match-marks and install the hub-to-rotor bolts. Torque the hub-to-rotor bolts to 33–40 ft. lbs.

13. Position the hub/rotor assembly onto the steering knuckle. Using a hydraulic press, press the assembly together until the parts seat.

14. To complete the installation, reverse the removal procedures.

FRONT SUSPENSION

MacPherson Strut

REMOVAL & INSTALLATION

1. Raise and support the front of the vehicle on jackstands.

2. Remove the wheel and tire assembly.

3. Remove the brake caliper-to-steering knuckle bolts and suspend the caliper on a wire; DO NOT disconnect the brake hose.

4. Using white paint, place an alignment strip on the inside of the strut mounting block.

5. Remove the strut-to-steering knuckle bolts. Remove the brake line U-clip and the brake line from its bracket.

6. Remove the upper strut-to-vehicle nuts and the strut assembly from the vehicle.

7. To install, align the match-marks and reverse the removal procedures.

Torque the strut-to-steering knuckle bolts to 69–72 ft. lbs. Check and/or adjust the front wheel alignment.

OVERHAUL

For all spring and shock absorber removal and installation procedures, and all strut overhaul procedures, please refer to "Strut Overhaul" in the Unit Repair section.

Ball Joints

INSPECTION

1. Raise and support the front of the vehicle with a jackstands placed under the engine cradle; the front wheel should be off the ground.

2. Grasp the wheel at the top and bottom and shake the wheel in and out.

3. If any movement is seen of the steering knuckle relative to the control arm, the ball joints are defective and must be replaced. Note that movement elsewhere may be due to loose wheel bearings or other troubles; watch the knuckle-to-control arm connection.

4. If the ball stud is disconnected from the steering knuckle and any looseness is noted and the ball joint stud can be twisted in its socket with finger pressure, replace the ball joints.

REMOVAL & INSTALLATION

1. Raise and support the front of the vehicle on jackstands. Remove the wheel and tire assembly.

2. Remove the caliper-to-steering knuckle bolts and the caliper; suspend the caliper on a wire.

3. Remove the stabilizer bar-to-low-

er control arm nuts/bolts and separate the stabilizer bar.

4. Remove the tie rod end cotter pin and nut. Using the Tie Rod Remover tool No. T85M-3395-A or equivalent, separate the tie rod from the steering knuckle.

5. Remove the ball joint-to-steering knuckle clamp bolt. Using a small pry bar, pry the lower control arm from the steering knuckle.

6. Remove the ball joint-to-steering knuckle nuts and the ball joint. It may be necessary the pry the ball joint assembly from the lower control arm.

7. To install, reverse the removal procedures. Torque the ball joint-to-steering knuckle clamp bolt to 32-40 ft. lbs., the tie rod end-to-steering knuckle nut to 22-33 ft. lbs. and the caliper-to-steering knuckle bolts to 29-36 ft. lbs.

Lower Control Arms

REMOVAL & INSTALLATION

1. Raise and support the front of the vehicle on jackstands. Remove the wheel and tire assembly.

2. Remove the caliper-to-steering knuckle bolts and the caliper; suspend the caliper on a wire.

3. Remove the stabilizer bar-to-lower control arm nuts/bolts and separate the stabilizer bar.

4. Using white paint, match-mark the rear control arm bushing-to-mounting bracket and the rear control arm bushing-to-control arm.

5. Remove the ball joint-to-steering knuckle clamp bolt. Using a small pry bar, pry the lower control arm from the steering knuckle.

6. Loosen the lower control arm front bushing and rear bushing nuts.

7. Remove the lower control arm rear bushing bracket-to-chassis bolts. Remove the lower control arm front bushing bracket-to-chassis bolts.

8. Remove the lower control arm rear bushing bolt and the lower control arm.

9. Remove the lower control arm front bushing nut and the front bushing.

10. If necessary to remove the ball joint from the lower control arm, perform the following procedures:

   a. Remove the ball joint-to-steering knuckle nuts and the ball joint.

   b. If necessary, pry the ball joint assembly from the lower control arm.

11. To install, reverse the removal procedures. Torque the ball joint-to-steering knuckle clamp bolt to 32-40 ft. lbs. and the caliper-to-steering knuckle bolts to 29-36 ft. lbs.

REAR SUSPENSION

MacPherson Strut

REMOVAL & INSTALLATION

1. Raise and support the rear of the vehicle on jackstands.

2. Remove the wheel and tire assembly.

3. If equipped with a drum brakes, remove the brake drum and the backing plate assembly. If equipped with disc brakes, remove the disc brake caliper and the rotor.

4. Remove the trailing arm bolt and the spindle-to-shock absorber bolts.

5. Using white paint, match-mark the upper strut rubber-to-chassis location. Remove the upper strut-to-chassis nuts and the strut.

6. To install, align the match-marks and reverse the removal procedures. Torque the spindle-to-strut bolts to 69-86 ft. lbs.

OVERHAUL

For all spring and shock absorber removal and installation procedures, and all strut overhaul procedures, please refer to "Strut Overhaul" in the Unit Repair section.

Rear Control and Trailing Arms

REMOVAL & INSTALLATION

1. Raise and support the rear of the vehicle on jackstands.

2. Remove the wheel and tire assembly.

3. If equipped with a drum brakes, remove the brake drum and the backing plate assembly. If equipped with disc brakes, remove the disc brake caliper and the rotor.

4. Using white paint, match-mark the rear toe adjusting cam/control arm, the control arms, the control arm bushings and the trailing arm-to-crossmember locations. Remove the upper strut-to-chassis nuts and the strut.

5. Remove the stabilizer link-to-spindle nuts/bolts, the stabilizer bar, bushings and stabilizer. Loosen both trailing arm-to-spindle bolts and the spindle-to-shock absorber bolts.

6. Remove the parking brake attachment-to-trailing arm bolt. Re-

move all the loosened bolts, the control arms and the trailing arms.

7. Inspect the parts for damage and/or wear; replace the parts, if necessary.

NOTE: Final torquing of the suspension system is done with vehicle fully loaded and the wheels resting on the ground.

8. To install, align the match-marks and reverse the removal procedures. Torque the spindle-to-control arm bolts to 69-86 ft. lbs., the control arm-to-crossmember bolts to 69-86 ft. lbs., the stabilizer bar nuts/bolts to 32-40 ft. lbs.

Rear Wheel Bearings

ADJUSTMENT

1. Raise and support the rear of the vehicle on jackstands.

2. Remove the wheel and tire assembly.

3. Remove the grease cup from the rear wheel hub.

4. Rotate the brake drum to make sure there is no brake drag; if there is drag, adjust the brake shoes.

5. Using a small cape chisel and a hammer, carefully raise the staked portion of locknut; remove the discard the locknut.

NOTE: The locknuts are threaded for left and right hand applications; be sure to acquire the right one.

6. Install the new locknut, rotate the drum and torque it to 18-21 ft. lbs.; loosen the locknut (slightly) until it can be turned by hand.

NOTE: Before the bearing preload can be set, the amount of seal drag must be measured and added to the preload torque.

7. Using an inch lb. torque wrench, position it (12 o'clock position) on 1 of the lug nuts and measure the torque necessary to start the wheel hub to turn.

8. To calculate the new torque, perform the following procedures:

   a. The required preload torque is 1.3-4.3 inch lbs.

   b. If the measure (seal drag) turning torque is 2.2 inch lbs., add it to the lowest and highest preload torque.

   c. The newly calculated preload torque is 3.5-6.5 inch lbs.

9. Torque the wheel bearing locknut slightly and recheck the wheel hub turning torque. When the wheel bearing torque falls within the newly calculated torque range, the torquing sequence is complete. Using a rounded

cold chisel, stake the wheel locknut and reverse the removal procedures.

REMOVAL & INSTALLATION

1. Raise and support the rear of the vehicle on jackstands.
2. Remove the wheel and tire assembly.
3. Remove the grease cup from the rear wheel hub.
4. Using a small cape chisel and a hammer, carefully raise the staked portion of locknut; remove the discard the locknut.

NOTE: The locknuts are threaded for left and right hand applications; be sure to acquire the right one.

5. Remove the outer wheel bearing from the hub and the brake drum/bearing hub assembly.
6. Using a small pry bar, pry the grease seal from the rear of the drum. Remove the inner wheel bearing from the hub.
7. To replace the bearing races, perform the following procedures:
   a. Using a brass drift and a hammer, drive the races from the drum.
   b. Clean and inspect the parts for wear and/or damage; replace the parts, if necessary.
   c. To install the races, use a brass drift and a hammer, lubricate the races with wheel bearing grease and drive the races into the hub until they seat.
8. Using wheel bearing grease, pack the inside of the hub and the wheel bearings. Install the inner bearing into the hub.
9. To install the new grease seal, lubricate it with wheel bearing grease. Using a Seal Installation tool, drive the seal into the rear of the wheel hub.
10. To complete the installation, reverse the removal procedures and adjust the bearing preload.

STEERING

Steering Wheel

REMOVAL & INSTALLATION

1. Disconnect the negative terminal from the battery.
2. From the rear of the steering wheel, remove the cover pad-to-steering wheel screws and the pad.
3. Remove the steering wheel-to-steering column nut.

Exploded view of the steering column assembly

4. Remove the steering wheel cover pad bracket-to-steering wheel screws and the bracket.
5. Using white paint, matchmark the steering wheel-to-steering column position.
6. Using the Steering Wheel Puller tool No. T67L–3600–A or equivalent, press the steering wheel from the steering column.
7. To install, align the matchmarks and reverse the removal procedures.

Combination Switch

The combination switch consists of the turn signal, hazard flasher, wiper/washer and headlight switches and is mounted on the steering column.

REMOVAL & INSTALLATION

1. Disconnect the negative terminal from the battery and remove the steering wheel.
2. Remove the steering column covers-to-steering column screws and the covers.
3. Depress the small tang on the electrical harness clip and disconnect the clip; move the electrical harness aside.

4. Loosen the combination switch-to-steering column clamp, slide the switch slightly forward and disconnect the electrical connector from the rear of the combination switch.
5. Remove the combination switch from the steering column.
6. To install, reverse the removal procedures. Check the switch operations.

Ignition Lock/Switch

REMOVAL & INSTALLATION

1. Disconnect the negative terminal from the battery.
2. Grasp the black trim ring around the ignition lock switch and pull it straight out.
3. From the driver's side, remove the sound deadening panel and the lap duct cover.
4. If equipped with air conditioning, remove the air conditioning duct assembly-to-access panel support bracket center screw, the access panel support bracket screws and the bracket.
5. From under the steering column, grasp the side window defogger duct ends, pull it outward, while twisting it slightly. From the ignition switch, lo-

cated under the steering column, disengage the plastic strap connector locking tang and remove the plastic strap.

6. Remove the steering column-to-instrument panel bolts and lower the column.

7. Lift the upper steering column shroud and remove it from the steering column.

8. Remove the ignition switch-to-ignition switch housing screw, grasp the ignition switch body and pull it straight outward.

9. To disengage the electrical connectors from the ignition switch, perform the following procedures:

a. Disengage the electrical connector locking tang.

b. Grasp an electrical body in each hand and pull them straight apart.

NOTE: Be aware of the electrical connector cavity position for reassembly purposes.

10. Using a straightened paper clip, disengage the 2 in-key buzzer wires from the 4-terminal connector; the wire colors are red and red wire/orange tracer.

11. To install, wires and connector, perform the following procedures:

a. Align the wire end flat sides with the grooved portion of the connector and push the wire inward until the locking tang engages wire end.

b. Push the 4-terminal connector into the housing connector until the locking tangs are in place.

c. Using electrical tape, wrap it around the ignition switch wires.

12. Install the ignition switch-to-ignition switch housing screw and the plastic snap connector around the ignition switch wiring. Attach the connector peg to the steering column mounting bracket.

13. Using electrical tape, wrap it around the ignition switch wiring and steering column.

14. To complete the installation, reverse the removal procedures. Check the ignition switch operation.

Manual Steering Gear

REMOVAL & INSTALLATION

1. Disconnect the terminals from the battery and remove the battery from the vehicle.

2. Raise and support the front of the vehicle on jackstands. Remove the front wheel assemblies.

3. Remove the tie rod end-to-steering knuckle cotter pins and nuts. Using the Tie Rod Separator tool No. T85M–3395–A or equivalent, separate

the tie rod end from the steering knuckle.

4. From the right side lower inner fender, remove the plastic dust shield.

5. Using a pair of diagonal cutters, cut the steering column dust boot-to-steering gear plastic wire tie clamp. Pull the dust boot back. Have an assistant turn the steering wheel until the steering column shaft bolt is accessible and lock the steering column.

6. Using white paint, matchmark the steering gear pinion shaft-to-intermediate lower shaft universal joint.

7. Remove the steering gear pinion shaft-to-intermediate lower shaft universal joint clamp bolt.

8. Remove the steering gear-to-chassis bolts, lower the steering gear to disengage it from the intermediate shaft universal joint. Carefully slide the steering gear out through the right side fender well.

9. To install, align the match marks and reverse the removal procedures. Torque the tie rod end-to-steering knuckle nut to 25–30 ft. lbs. Install a plastic strap over the steering column dust boot. Inspect the steering operation.

ADJUSTMENT

1. Remove the steering gear from the vehicle and place it in a vise.

2. Using an inch lb. wrench and a Pinion Torque Adapter tool T87C–3504–C or equivalent, place the assembly on the pinion and measure the pinion torque; the torque should be 8–11 inch lbs.

3. To adjust the pinion torque, perform the following procedures:

a. Loosen the adjusting bolt lock nut.

b. Make sure the rack is centered in the housing.

c. Move the adjusting bolt slightly and recheck the pinion torque.

d. When the pinion torque of 8–11 inch lbs. is reached, retorque the adjusting bolt lock nut to 7–11 ft. lbs.

4. To install the steering gear, reverse the removal procedures. Check the steering operation.

Power Steering Gear

REMOVAL & INSTALLATION

1. Disconnect the terminals from the battery and remove the battery from the vehicle.

2. Raise and support the front of the vehicle on jackstands. Remove the front wheel assemblies.

3. Remove the tie rod end-to-steering knuckle cotter pins and nuts. Using the Tie Rod Separator tool No.

T85M–3395–A or equivalent, separate the tie rod end from the steering knuckle.

4. From the right side lower inner fender, remove the plastic dust shield.

5. Using a pair of diagonal cutters, cut the steering column dust boot-to-steering gear plastic wire tie clamp. Pull the dust boot back. Have an assistant turn the steering wheel until the steering column shaft bolt is accessible and lock the steering column.

6. Using white paint, matchmark the steering gear pinion shaft-to-intermediate lower shaft universal joint.

7. Remove the steering gear pinion shaft-to-intermediate lower shaft universal joint clamp bolt.

8. Using a 17mm crowfoot tubing wrench, disconnect and plug the fluid return line from the power steering gear.

9. Using a 14mm socket, remove the banjo bolt from the pressure line at the power steering gear and discard the copper washers.

NOTE: Be sure to position the pressure lines out of the way.

10. Remove the steering gear-to-chassis bolts, lower the steering gear to disengage it from the intermediate shaft universal joint. Carefully slide the steering gear out through the right side fender well.

11. To install, align the match marks, use 2 new washers at the banjo fitting and reverse the removal procedures. Torque the tie rod end-to-steering knuckle nut to 22–33 ft. lbs. Install a plastic strap over the steering column dust boot. Refill the power steering reservoir. Bleed the power steering system. Inspect the steering operation.

ADJUSTMENT

1. Remove the power steering gear from the vehicle and place it in a vise.

2. Using an inch lb. wrench and a Pinion Torque Adapter tool T87C–3504–C or equivalent, place the assembly on the pinion and measure the pinion torque; the torque should be 0.52–1.3 inch lbs.

3. To adjust the pinion torque, perform the following procedures:

a. Loosen the adjusting bolt lock nut.

b. Make sure the rack is centered in the housing.

c. Move the adjusting bolt slightly and recheck the pinion torque.

d. When the pinion torque of 0.52–1.3 inch lbs. is reached, retorque the adjusting bolt lock nut to 29–36 ft. lbs.

4. To install the steering gear, re-

verse the removal procedures. Check the steering operation.

Power Steering Pump

REMOVAL & INSTALLATION

1. At the power steering pump, loosen the lock nut and adjuster bolt. Move the pump toward the engine and remove the drive belt.

2. From the engine lifting eye, remove the ground wire.

3. Disconnect and plug the hoses from the power steering pump. Disconnect the electrical connector from the pump's pressure switch.

4. Remove the adjusting screw, nut, block, pivot bolt and pump; if necessary, remove the pump pulley.

5. To install, reverse the removal procedures. Adjust the drive belt tension. Using Dexron® II automatic transmission fluid, fill the power steering pump reservoir. Bleed the power steering system.

BELT ADJUSTMENT

1. Inspect the condition of the drive belt; replace it, if necessary.

2. At the power steering pump, loosen the lock nut and adjuster bolt.

3. Using a Drive Belt Tension Gauge tool No. T63L-8620-A or equivalent, position it between the power steering pump pulley and the crankshaft pulley. The drive belt deflection should be 0.31–0.35 in. (new belt) or 0.35–0.39 in. (used belt) @ 22 lbs. pressure.

NOTE: A used belt is one that has at least 10 minutes run time.

4. If the power steering pump locknut was loosened, torque it to 32–45 ft. lbs.

SYSTEM BLEEDING

1. Raise and support the front of the vehicle on jackstands.

2. Using Dexron® II automatic transmission fluid, fill the power steering reservoir to the **L** mark on the dipstick.

3. Start the engine and allow it to reach normal operating temperatures.

4. Slowly turn the steering wheel (back and forth) lock-to-lock about 10 times, until all of the air is bled from the system and the reservoir is maintaining a full level.

NOTE: When bleeding the system, be sure to refill the reservoir several times.

5. Position the wheels in the straight ahead position and turn the engine **OFF**.

6. Refill the power steering reservoir until the fluid level is between the **L** and the **H** marks on the dipstick.

7. Lower the vehicle, start the engine, check for leaks and road test the vehicle.

Tie Rod Ends

REMOVAL & INSTALLATION

1. Raise and support the front of the vehicle on jackstands.

2. Remove the tie rod-to-steering knuckle cotter pin and nut.

3. Using the Tie Rod Puller tool No. T85M-3395-A or equivalent, separate the tie rod from the steering knuckle.

NOTE: If the tie rod does not separate from the steering knuckle, give it a sharp blow with a brass hammer.

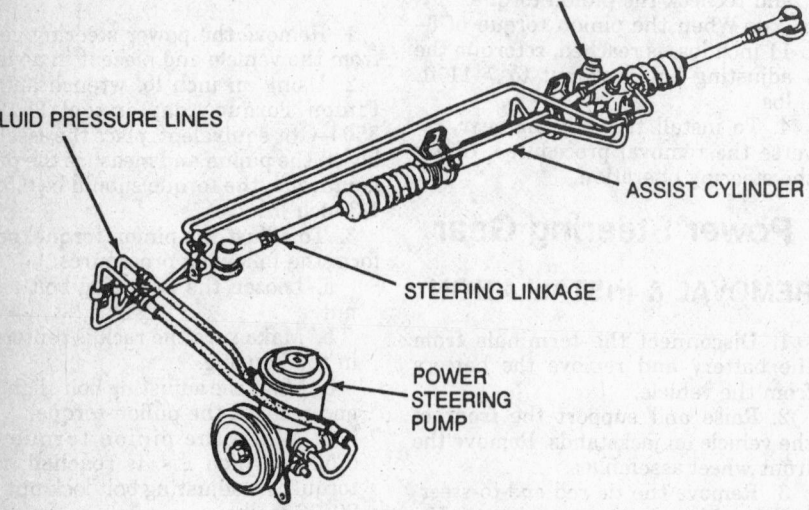

View of the power steering system

4. Using white paint, matchmark the tie rod end-to-tie rod.

5. Loosen the tie rod end jamb nut. Remove the tie rod end by counting the number of rotations necessary to remove it.

6. To install, rotate the tie rod end the same number of turns necessary to remove it, align the matchmarks and reverse the removal procedures. Torque the tie rod end-to-steering knuckle to 22–33 ft. lbs. Install a new cotter pin.

NOTE: If the tie rod end-to-steering knuckle nut slot does not align with the hole in the ball joint, tighten it until it does; never loosen the nut.

BRAKES

For all brake system repair service procedures not detailed below, please refer to "Brakes" in the Unit Repair section.

Master Cylinder

REMOVAL & INSTALLATION

1. Using a small pry bar, disconnect the low fluid level sensor wiring connector.

2. Disconnect and plug the brake tubes from the master cylinder. Cap the master cylinder tube openings.

3. Remove the master cylinder-to-cowl (manual brakes) or master cylinder-to-power booster (power brakes) nuts and the master cylinder from the vehicle.

4. To install, reverse the removal procedures. Torque the master cylinder mounting nuts to 15–25 ft. lbs. Using DOT 3 brake fluid, fill the master cylinder reservoir. Bleed the brake system.

Proportioning Valve

The dual proportioning valve is mounted to the cowl on the right side of the master cylinder. No adjustment is necessary or possible.

REMOVAL & INSTALLATION

1. Remove all of the brake lines from the proportioning valve.

2. Remove the proportioning valve-to-cowl bolts and the valve from the vehicle.

3. To install, reverse the removal procedures. Bleed the brake system.

Power Brake Booster

REMOVAL & INSTALLATION

1. Remove the terminals from the battery and the battery.
2. Remove the master cylinder.
3. Remove the vacuum hose from the brake booster.
4. From under the instrument panel, remove the spring clip and the clevis pin from the brake pedal.
5. Remove the brake booster-to-cowl nuts and the brake booster.
6. To install, reverse the removal procedures. If necessary, adjust the master cylinder push rod. Check the brake operation.

Wheel Cylinder

REMOVAL & INSTALLATION

1. Raise and support the rear of the vehicle on jackstands. Remove the wheel assembly.
2. To remove the brake drum assembly, perform the following procedures:
   a. Remove the hub grease cup.
   b. Using a cape chisel and a hammer, raise the staked portion of the hub nut.

NOTE: The hub nuts are of the left and right thread designes; the left-threaded nut is on the right side and the right-threaded nut is on the left side.

   c. Remove the hub nut (discard it), the thrust washer and the outer wheel bearing.
   d. Remove the brake drum/hub bearing assembly.

NOTE: When the brake drum is removed, it is a good idea to inspect and repack the wheel bearing; it may be necessary to replace the grease seal.

3. Remove the brake shoe assembly from the backing plate.

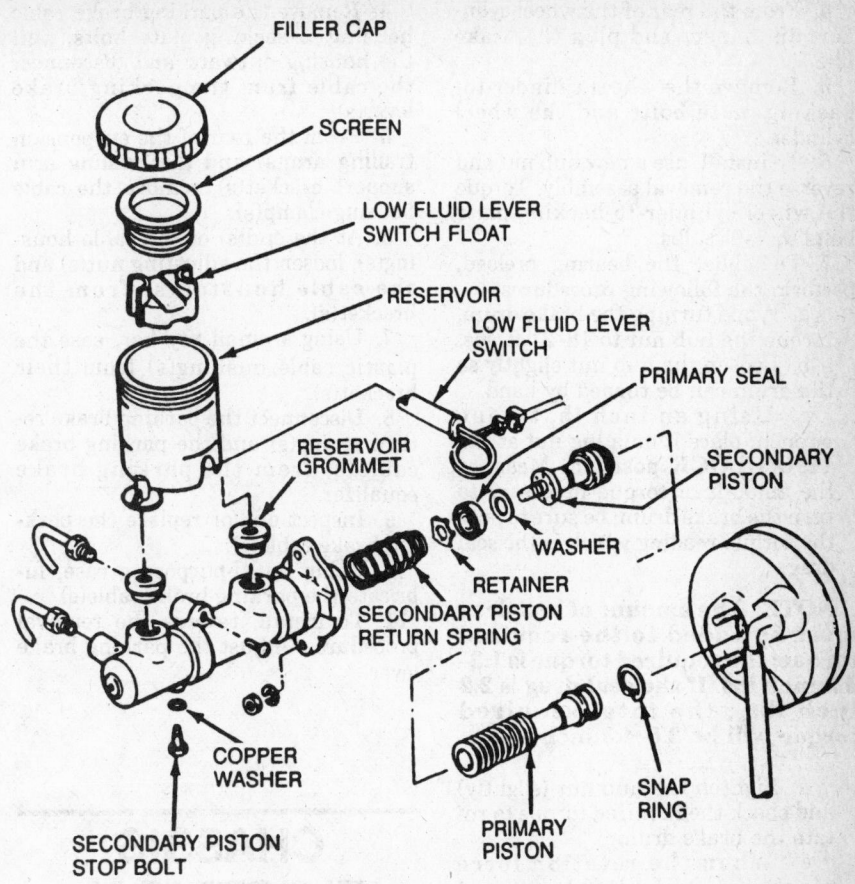

Exploded view of the master cylinder

Labels: FILLER CAP, SCREEN, LOW FLUID LEVER SWITCH FLOAT, RESERVOIR, LOW FLUID LEVER SWITCH, PRIMARY SEAL, SECONDARY PISTON, WASHER, RETAINER, SECONDARY PISTON RETURN SPRING, RESERVOIR GROMMET, COPPER WASHER, SECONDARY PISTON STOP BOLT, PRIMARY PISTON, SNAP RING

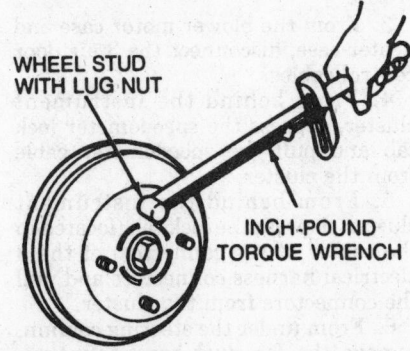

Measuring the grease seal drag and the bearing preload

Labels: WHEEL STUD WITH LUG NUT, INCH-POUND TORQUE WRENCH

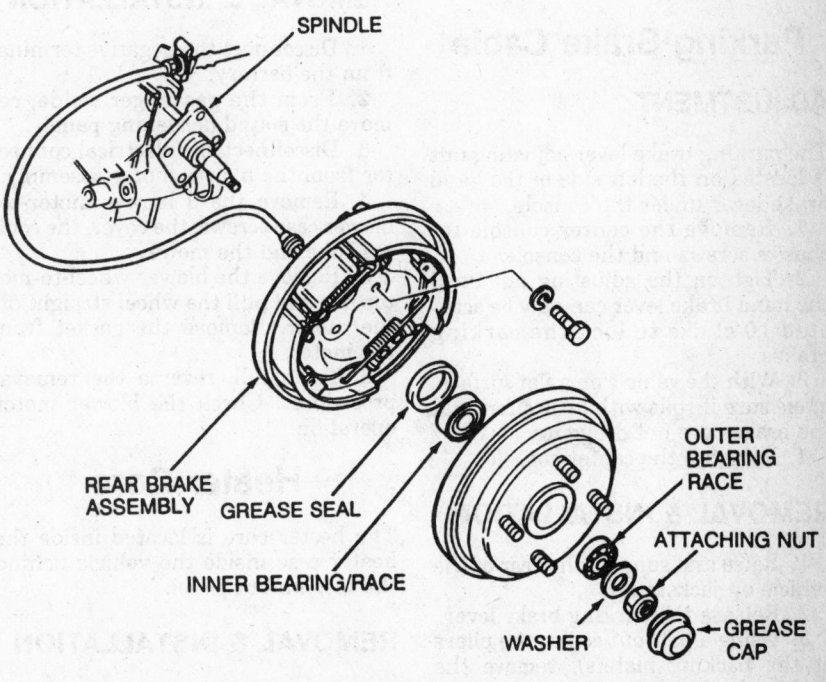

Exploded view of the rear wheel assembly—drum brakes

Labels: SPINDLE, REAR BRAKE ASSEMBLY, GREASE SEAL, INNER BEARING/RACE, WASHER, OUTER BEARING RACE, ATTACHING NUT, GREASE CAP

4. From the rear of the wheel cylinder, disconnect and plug the brake line.

5. Remove the wheel cylinder-to-backing plate bolts and the wheel cylinder.

6. To install, use a new hub nut and reverse the removal assembly. Torque the wheel cylinder-to-backing plate bolts to 7–9 ft. lbs.

7. To adjust the bearing preload, perform the following procedures:

   a. While turning the brake drum, torque the hub nut to 18–21 ft. lbs.

   b. Loosen the hub nut slightly so the drum can be turned by hand.

   c. Using an inch lb. torque wrench, place it on a lug nut at the **12 O'CLOCK** position. Measure the amount of torque necessary to turn the brake drum; be sure to note the torque reading which is the seal drag.

NOTE: The amount of seal drag must be added to the required torque; the required torque is 1.3–4.3 inch lbs. If the seal drag is 2.2 inch lbs., the total required torque will be 3.5–4.3 inch lbs.

   d. Tighten the hub nut (slightly) and check the required torque to rotate the brake drum.

   e. When the rotation force reaches the calculated required torque, stake the hub nut, using a rounded cold chisel and a hammer.

8. To complete the installation, reverse the removal procedures. Torque the wheel lug nuts to 65–87 ft. lbs. Road test the vehicle.

Parking Brake Cable

ADJUSTMENT

The parking brake lever adjusting nut is located on the left side of the hand brake lever under the console.

1. Remove the center console-to-chassis screws and the console.

2. Tighten the adjusting nut until the hand brake lever can only be actuated 10 clicks to lock the parking brakes.

3. With the vehicle on a flat surface, make sure it rolls with little effort and the brakes are not dragging.

4. Reinstall the center console.

REMOVAL & INSTALLATION

1. Raise and support the rear of the vehicle on jackstands.

2. Release the parking brake lever.

3. Using a pair of needle nose pliers at the backing plate(s), remove the parking brake return spring; be careful not to overextend the spring.

4. Remove the parking brake cable housing-to-backing plate bolts, pull the housing outward and disconnect the cable from the parking brake lever(s).

5. From the rear of the suspension trailing arm(s) and the trailing arm support bracket(s), remove the cable housing clamp(s).

6. At the end(s) of the cable housing(s), loosen the adjusting nut(s) and the cable housing(s) from the bracket(s).

7. Using a small pry bar, ease the plastic cable bushing(s) from their bracket(s).

8. Disconnect the parking brake return spring(s) and the parking brake cable(s) from the parking brake equalizer.

9. Inspect and/or replace the parking brake cable(s).

10. Using multi-purpose grease, lubricate the parking brake cable(s).

11. To install, reverse the removal procedures. Adjust the parking brake lever.

CHASSIS ELECTRICAL

Heater Blower

REMOVAL & INSTALLATION

1. Disconnect the negative terminal from the battery.

2. From the passenger's side, remove the sound deadening panel.

3. Disconnect the electrical connector from the blower motor assembly.

4. Remove the 3 blower motor-to-blower case screws, the cover, the cooling tube and the motor.

5. Remove the blower wheel-to-motor nut and pull the wheel straight off the motor. Remove the gasket from the motor.

6. To install, reverse the removal procedures. Check the blower motor operation.

Heater Core

The heater core is located inside the heater case inside the vehicle behind the instrument panel.

REMOVAL & INSTALLATION

1. Disconnect the negative terminal from the brattery.

2. From under the instrument panel, remove both sound deadening panels and the lap duct register panel.

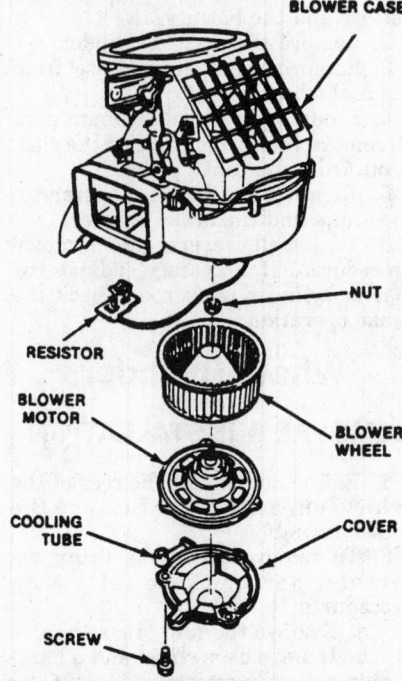

Exploded view of the heater blower motor assembly

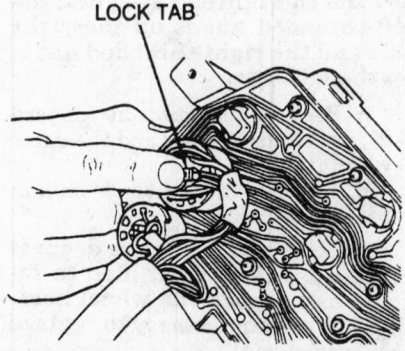

Depressing the electrical connector lock tab located at the rear of the instrument

3. From the blower motor case and heater case, disconnect the 3 air door control cables.

4. From behind the instrument cluster, depress the speedometer lock tab and pull the speedometer cable from the cluster.

5. From behind the instrument cluster, depress the lock tab (located in the center of the connector) of the 3 electrical harness connectors and pull the connectors from the cluster.

6. From under the steering column, remove the lap duct brace-to-instrument panel screws, the brace, the lap duct and the driver's deminster tube.

7. Remove the lower cover-to-steering column screws and the lower cover.

8. Remove the steering column-to-instrument panel bolts and lower the steering column.

9. Remove the glove box-to-instrument panel screws and the glove box.

10. Remove the hood release-to-instrument panel nut and move the release cable aside.

11. Remove the center floor console-to-chassis screws and the cover.

12. From below the radio, remove the lower trim panel-to-instrument panel screws and the lower panel.

13. Using a small pry bar, pry the 5 instrument panel-to-chassis bolt covers from the perimeter of the instrument panel. Remove the instrument panel-to-chassis nuts/bolts. Lift and pull the panel out slightly.

14. Disconnect the electrical connector from the blower motor assembly.

15. From the rear of the radio, disconnect the antenna cable.

16. From the left corner of the instrument panel, disconnect the 3 instrument panel harness connectors and remove the instrument panel.

17. Using a clean drain pan, place it under the radiator, open the radiator drain cock, remove the radiator cap and drain the cooling system to a level below the heater case.

18. Disconnect and plug the heater hoses from the heater case.

19. Remove the defroster tubes-to-heater case push pins and the defroster tubes from the heater case. Remove the main air duct-to-heater case push pins and the main air duct.

20. From under the heater case, remove the lower carpet panel push pins, screw and the panel.

21. From the heater case, disconnect the electrical harness braces and remove the lower brace screws and brace.

22. Remove the heater case-to-chassis nut and bolts. Remove the lower duct-to-heater case push pins and lower duct. Remove the heater case by pulling it straight out; be careful not to damage the extension tubes.

23. Remove the heater core cover-to-heater case screws and the cover. Remove the tube braces and pull the heater core straight out.

24. Remove the outlet extension tube clip and tube. Loosen the inlet extension tube clamp and the extension tube.

25. To install, use a new O-ring (outlet extension tube) and reverse the removal procedures. Refill the cooling system. Start the engine, allow it to reach normal operating temperatures and turn the heater control to **FULL**

HEAT. Inspect the system for leakage and operations.

Radio

REMOVAL & INSTALLATION

1. Disconnect the negative battery terminal from the battery.

2. Remove the radio facia from the instrument panel.

3. Remove the radio-to-instrument panel screws and pull the radio from the instrument panel.

4. From the rear of the radio, disconnect the 4 electrical harness connectors, the antenna cable and the ground cable.

5. To install, reverse the removal procedures. Inspect the radio operations.

Windshield Wiper Switch

REMOVAL & INSTALLATION

Front

The windshield wiper switch is a part of the combination switch.

1. Remove the combination switch from the steering column and place it on a work table.

2. Remove the turn signal/headlight switch lever-to-combination switch screws and carefully lift the lever from the combination switch; be careful not to loose the detent balls and springs.

3. Remove the turn signal/headlight switch from the combination switch.

4. Remove the windshield wiper switch-to-combination switch screws and the wiper switch.

5. If removing the windshield wiper switch lever from the combination switch, be careful not to loose the retaining pin, the O-ring, the detent plunger and the spring.

Rear—Station Wagon

The rear windshield wiper switch is located on the left side of the instrument panel.

1. Disconnect the negative terminal from the battery.

2. Using a small pry bar, gently pry the switch from the instrument panel and pull it outward.

3. Disconnect the electrical harness connector(s) from the rear of the switch.

4. To install, reverse the removal procedures. Inspect the operation of the rear wiper system.

Windshield Wiper Motor

Removal & Installation

Front

1. Disconnect the negative terminal from the battery.

2. From the top left side of the cowl, remove the windshield wiper motor shield-to-chassis plastic retainers and the shield.

3. From the windshield wiper motor shaft, remove the drive link nut and split washer.

4. Disconnect the electrical connector from the windshield wiper motor.

5. Remove the windshield wiper motor-to-cowl bolts, the motor and rubber insulators.

6. To install, make sure the windshield wiper motor is in the **PARK** position and reverse the removal procedures. Inspect the operation of the windshield wiper system.

Rear—Station Wagon

1. Disconnect the negative terminal from the battery.

2. From the liftgate, remove the wiper arm/blade assembly and pull the luggage compartment end trim from inside.

3. Remove the seal cap, nut, outer bushings, packings and inner bushings.

4. Disconnect the electrical connector and the ground wire from the windshield wiper motor.

5. Remove the windshield wiper motor-to-liftgate bolts, the motor and rubber insulators.

6. To install, make sure the windshield wiper motor is in the **PARK** position and reverse the removal procedures. Inspect the operation of the windshield wiper system.

Instrument Cluster

REMOVAL & INSTALLATION

1. Disconnect the negative terminal from the battery.

2. Remove the steering wheel.

3. Remove the instrument cluster bezel-to-instrument panel screws and bezel.

4. Remove the instrument cluster-to-instrument panel screws.

5. From under the dash, depress the speedometer lock tab and pull the speedometer cable from the instrument cluster.

6. Pull the instrument cluster outward, depress the lock tab (located in

the center of the connector) of the 3 electrical harness connectors and pull the connectors from the cluster.

7. To install, reverse the removal procedures. Inspect the operation of the instruments.

Headlight Switch

REMOVAL & INSTALLATION

1. Disconnect the negative terminal from the battery.

2. Remove the combination switch from the steering column and place it on a work table.

3. Remove the turn signal/headlight switch lever-to-combination switch screws and carefully lift the lever from the combination switch; be careful not to loose the detent balls and springs.

4. To install, reverse the removal procedures. Inspect the headlight operation.

Stoplight Switch

The stoplight switch is attached to the top of the brake pedal and controls the brake pedal height.

REMOVAL & INSTALLATION

1. Disconnect the electrical connector from the stoplight switch.

2. Remove the stoplight switch-to-bracket nut and unscrew the switch from the bracket.

3. To install, screw the stoplight into the bracket until the brake pedal height is 8.62–8.82 in.

NOTE: Brake pedal height is the distance from the cowl to the front center of the brake pedal.

4. Tighten the switch locknut and install the electrical connector.

Fuses and Circuit Breakers

LOCATION

The main fuse panel is located on the right side of the engine compartment.

An electrical equipment panel is located on under the left side of the instrument panel; it is part of the fuse panel and incorporates plug-in relays, a flasher, a buzzer and a circuit breaker.

SERIAL NUMBER IDENTIFICATION

VEHICLE IDENTIFICATION CHART

It is important for servicing and ordering parts to be certain of the vehicle and engine identification. The VIN (vehicle identification number) is a 17 digit number visible through the windshield on the driver's side of the dash and contains the vehicle and engine identification codes. The tenth digit indicates model year and the eighth digit indicates engine code. It can be interpreted as follows:

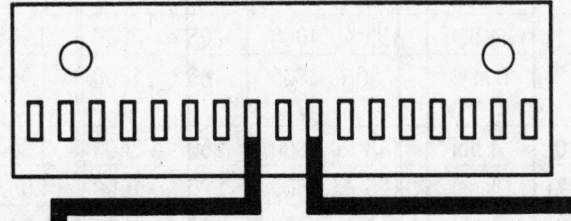

| Engine Code | | | | | | Model Year | |
Code	Cu. In.	Liters	Cyl.	Fuel Sys.	Eng. Mfg.	Code	Year
A	231	3.8	V6	2 bbl	Buick	C	1982
3	231	3.8	V6	2 bbl/Turbo	Buick	D	1983
7	231	3.8	V6	SFI/Turbo	Buick	E	1984
8	231	3.8	V6	4 bbl/Turbo	Buick	F	1985
9	231	3.8	V6	SFI/Turbo	Buick	G	1986
4	252	4.1	V6	4 bbl	Buick	H	1987
V	263	4.3	V6	Diesel	Oldsmobile	J	1988
J	267	4.3	V8	2 bbl	Chevrolet	K	1989
H	305	5.0	V8	4 bbl	Chevrolet		
Y	307	5.0	V8	4 bbl	Oldsmobile		
N	350	5.7	V8	Diesel	Oldsmobile		

GENERAL ENGINE SPECIFICATIONS

Year	VIN	No. Cylinder Displacement cu. in. (liter)	Fuel System Type	Net Horsepower @ rpm	Net Torque @ rpm (ft.lbs.)	Bore × Stroke (in.)	Compression Ratio	Oil Pressure @ rpm
1982	A	6-231 (3.8)	2 bbl	110 @ 3800	190 @ 1600	3.800 × 3.400	8.0:1	37 @ 2400
	3	6-231 (3.8) ①	2 bbl	170 @ 4000	275 @ 2400	3.800 × 3.400	8.0:1	37 @ 2400
	4	6-252 (4.1)	4 bbl	125 @ 4000	205 @ 2000	3.965 × 3.400	8.0:1	37 @ 2400
	V	6-263 (4.3)	Diesel	85 @3600	165 @ 1600	4.057 × 3.385	21.6:1	35-45 @ 1500
	J	8-267 (4.3)	2 bbl	115 @ 4000	200 @ 2400	3.500 × 3.480	8.3:1	45 @ 2000
	H	8-305 (5.0)	4 bbl	140 @ 3600	240 @ 1600	3.736 × 3.480	8.0:1	35-40 @ 2600
	Y	8-307 (5.0)	4 bbl	148 @ 3800	250 @ 2400	3.800 × 3.385	8.0:1	40 @ 1500
	N	8-350 (5.7)	Diesel	125 @ 3600	225 @ 1600	4.057 × 3.385	22.5:1	40 @ 1500
1983	A	6-231 (3.8)	2 bbl	110 @ 3800	190 @ 1600	3.800 × 3.400	8.0:1	37 @ 2400
	8	6-231 (3.8) ①	2 bbl	170 @ 3800	275 @ 2600	3.800 × 3.400	8.0:1	37 @ 2400
	4	6-252 (4.1)	4 bbl	125 @ 4000	205 @ 2000	3.965 × 3.400	8.0:1	37 @ 2400
	V	6-263 (4.3)	Diesel	85 @3600	165 @ 1600	4.057 × 3.385	21.6:1	35-45 @ 1500
	Y	8-307 (5.0)	4 bbl	148 @ 3800	250 @ 2400	3.800 × 3.385	8.0:1	40 @ 1500
	N	8-350 (5.7)	Diesel	125 @ 3600	225 @ 1600	4.057 × 3.385	22.5:1	40 @ 1500
1984	A	6-231 (3.8)	2 bbl	110 @ 3800	190 @ 1600	3.800 × 3.400	8.0:1	37 @ 2400
	9	6-231 (3.8)	SFI/ Turbo	190 @ 4000	300 @ 2480	3.800 × 3.400	8.0:1	37 @ 2400
	4	6-252 (4.1)	4 bbl	125 @ 4000	205 @ 2000	3.965 × 3.400	8.0:1	37 @ 2400
	V	6-263 (4.3)	Diesel	85 @3600	165 @ 1600	4.057 × 3.385	21.6:1	35-45 @ 1500
	Y	8-307 (5.0)	4 bbl	148 @ 3800	250 @ 2400	3.800 × 3.385	8.0:1	40 @ 1500
	N	8-350 (5.7)	Diesel	125 @ 3600	225 @ 1600	4.057 × 3.385	22.5:1	40 @ 1500
1985	A	6-231 (3.8)	2 bbl	110 @ 3800	190 @ 1600	3.800 × 3.400	8.0:1	37 @ 2400
	9	6-231 (3.8)	SFI/ Turbo	190 @ 4000	300 @ 2480	3.800 × 3.400	8.0:1	37 @ 2400
	Y	8-307 (5.0)	4 bbl	148 @ 3800	250 @ 2400	3.800 × 3.385	8.0:1	40 @ 1500
	N	8-350 (5.7)	Diesel	125 @ 3600	225 @ 1600	4.057 × 3.385	22.5:1	40 @ 1500
1986	A	6-231 (3.8)	2 bbl	110 @ 3800	190 @ 1600	3.800 × 3.400	8.0:1	37 @ 2400
	7	6-231 (3.8)	SFI/ Turbo	235 @ 4400	330 @ 2800	3.800 × 3.400	8.0:1	37 @ 2400
	Y	8-307 (5.0)	4 bbl	148 @ 3800	250 @ 2400	3.800 × 3.385	8.0:1	40 @ 1500
1987	A	6-231 (3.8)	2 bbl	110 @ 3800	190 @ 1600	3.800 × 3.400	8.0:1	37 @ 2400
	7	6-231 (3.8)	SFI/ Turbo	235 @ 4400	330 @ 2800	3.800 × 3.400	8.0:1	37 @ 2400
	Y	8-307 (5.0)	4 bbl	148 @ 3800	250 @ 2400	3.800 × 3.385	8.0:1	40 @ 1500
1988-89	Y	8-307 (5.0)	4 bbl	148 @ 3800	250 @ 2400	3.800 × 3.385	8.0:1	40 @ 1500

SFI—Sequential Fuel Injection
① Turbocharged engines

GASOLINE ENGINE TUNE-UP SPECIFICATIONS

Year	VIN	No. Cylinder Displacement cu. in. (liter)	Spark Plugs Type	Gap (in.)	Ignition Timing (deg.) MT	AT	Compression Pressure (psi)	Fuel Pump (psi)	Idle Speed (rpm) MT	AT	Valve Clearance In.	Ex.
1982	A	6-231 (3.8)	R45TS8	0.080	—	15	②	5½-6½	—	900	Hyd.	Hyd.
	3	6-231 (3.8)	R45TSX	0.060	—	15	②	5½-6½	—	900	Hyd.	Hyd.
	S	6-252 (4.1)	R45TS8	0.080	—	15	②	5½-6½	—	900	Hyd.	Hyd.
	J	8-267 (4.3)	R45TS	0.045	—	12	②	5½-6½	—	900	Hyd.	Hyd.
	H	8-305 (5.0)	R45TS	0.045	—	6	②	5½-6½	—	800	Hyd.	Hyd.
	Y	8-307 (5.0)	R46SX	0.080	—	15	②	5½-6½	—	850	Hyd.	Hyd.
1983	A	6-231 (3.8)	R45TS8	0.080	—	15	②	5½-6½	—	900	Hyd.	Hyd.
	8	6-231 (3.8)	R45TSX	0.060	—	15	②	5½-6½	—	900	Hyd.	Hyd.
	4	6-252 (4.1)	R45TS8	0.080	—	15	②	5½-6½	—	900	Hyd.	Hyd.
	Y	8-307 (5.0)	R46SX	0.080	—	15	②	5½-6½	—	850	Hyd.	Hyd.
1984	A	6-231 (3.8)	R45TSX	0.060	—	15	②	5½-6½	—	700	Hyd.	Hyd.
	9	6-231 (3.8)	R44TS	0.045	—	①	②	26-51	—	700	Hyd.	Hyd.
	4	6-252 (4.1)	R45TSX	0.060	—	15	②	5½-6½	—	900	Hyd.	Hyd.
	Y	8-307 (5.0)	R46SX	0.080	—	20	②	5½-6½	—	900	Hyd.	Hyd.
1985	A	6-231 (3.8)	R45TSX	0.060	—	15	②	5½-6½	—	700	Hyd.	Hyd.
	9	6-231 (3.8)	R44TS	0.045	—	①	②	26-51	—	700	Hyd.	Hyd.
	Y	8-307 (5.0)	R45TS	0.060	—	20	②	5½-6½	—	900	Hyd.	Hyd.
1986	A	6-231 (3.8)	R45TSX	0.060	—	15	②	5½-6½	—	700	Hyd.	Hyd.
	7	6-231 (3.8)	R44TS	0.045	—	15	②	26-51	—	700	Hyd.	Hyd.
	Y	8-307 (5.0)	R45TS	0.060	—	20	②	5½-6½	—	900	Hyd.	Hyd.
1987	A	6-231 (3.8)	R45TSX	0.060	—	15	②	5½-6½	—	700	Hyd.	Hyd.
	7	6-231 (3.8)	R44TS	0.035	—	①	②	26-51	—	700	Hyd.	Hyd.
	Y	8-307 (5.0)	FR3LS6	0.060	—	20	②	5½-6½	—	900	Hyd.	Hyd.
1988	Y	8-307 (5.0)	FR3LS6	0.060	—	20	②	5½-6½	—	900	Hyd.	Hyd.
1989	All	SEE UNDERHOOD SPECIFICATIONS STICKER										

① See the Emission Control Label for timing setting procedures

② The lowest cylinder compression reading should not be less than 70% of the highest reading, and no cylinder should be less than 100 PSI

DIESEL ENGINE TUNE-UP SPECIFICATIONS

Year	VIN	No. Engine Displacement cu. in. (liter)	Valve Clearance Intake (in.)	Valve Clearance Exhaust (in.)	Intake Valve Opens (deg.)	Injection Pump Setting (deg.)	Injection Nozzle Pressure (psi) New	Injection Nozzle Pressure (psi) Used	Idle Speed (rpm)	Cranking Compression Pressure (psi)
1982	V	6-263 (4.3)	Hyd.	Hyd.	16B	6A	①	②	1300	③
	N	8-350 (5.7)	Hyd.	Hyd.	16B	4A	1225	1000	1250	③
1983	V	6-263 (4.3)	Hyd.	Hyd.	16B	6A	①	②	1300	③
	N	8-350 (5.7)	Hyd.	Hyd.	16B	4A	1225	1000	1250	③
1984	V	6-263 (4.3)	Hyd.	Hyd.	16B	6A	①	②	1300	③
	N	8-350 (5.7)	Hyd.	Hyd.	16B	4A	1225	1000	1250	③
1985	N	8-350 (5.7)	Hyd.	Hyd.	16B	4A	1225	1000	1250	③

Hyd. — Hydraulic lifters
B — BTDC
A — ATDC
① Green band — 1000 psi,
  Red band — 800 psi
② Nozzle pressure 200 psi less than new
③ The lowest cylinder compression reading should not be less than 80% of the highest reading, and no reading should be less than 300 psi

CAPACITIES

Year	VIN	No. Cylinder Displacement cu. in. (liter)	Engine Crankcase with Filter	Engine Crankcase without Filter	Transmission (pts.) MT	Transmission (pts.) AT	Drive Axle (pts.)	Fuel Tank (gals.)	Cooling System (qts.)
1982	A	6-231 (3.8)	①	4	—	②③	④	18.1⑥	13.0
	3	6-231 (3.8)	①	5	—	②③	②③	18.1⑦	13.0
	4	6-252 (4.1)	①	4	—	②③	④	18.1⑦	13.0
	V	6-263 (4.3)	①	6	—	②③	④	18.1⑦	21.0
	J	8-267 (4.3)	①	4	—	②③	④	18.1⑦	21.0
	H	8-305 (5.0)	①	4	—	②③	④	18.1⑦	16.3
	Y	8-307 (5.0)	①	4	—	②③	④	25.0⑥	16.3
	N	8-350 (5.7)	①	6	—	②③	④	23.0⑥	17.5
1983	A	6-231 (3.8)	①	4	—	②③	④	18.1⑥	13.0
	8	6-231 (3.8)	①	5	—	②③	④	19.0⑦	13.1
	4	6-252 (4.1)	①	4	—	②③	④	19.0⑦	13.1
	V	6-263 (4.3)	①	6	—	②③	④	19.0⑦	14.8
	Y	8-307 (5.0)	①	4	—	②③	④	25.0	16.2
	N	8-350 (5.7)	①	6½	—	②③	④	25.0	17.9
1984	A	6-231 (3.8)	①	4	—	②③	④	⑤	13.0
	9	6-231 (3.8)	①	5	—	②③	④	⑤	13.0
	4	6-252 (4.1)	①	4	—	②③	④	⑤	13.0
	V	6-263 (4.3)	①	6	—	②③	④	⑤	14.4
	Y	8-307 (5.0)	①	4	—	②③	④	⑤	16.0
	N	8-350 (5.7)	①	6½	—	②③	④	⑤	17.9

CAPACITIES

Year	VIN	No. Cylinder Displacement cu. in. (liter)	Engine Crankcase with Filter	without Filter	Transmission (pts.) MT	AT	Drive Axle (pts.)	Fuel Tank (gals.)	Cooling System (qts.)
1985	A	6-231 (3.8)	①	4	–	②③	④	⑤	13.0
	9	6-231 (3.8)	①	5	–	②③	④	⑤	13.0
	Y	8-307 (5.0)	①	4	–	②③	④	⑤	16.0
	N	8-350 (5.7)	①	6½	–	②③	④	⑤	17.9
1986	A	6-231 (3.8)	①	4	–	②③	④	⑤	13.0
	7	6-231 (3.8)	①	5	–	②③	④	⑤	13.0
	Y	8-307 (5.0)	①	4	–	②③	④	⑤	16.0
1987	A	6-231 (3.8)	①	4	–	②③	④	⑤	13.0
	7	6-231 (3.8)	①	5	–	②③	④	⑤	13.0
	Y	8-307 (5.0)	①	4	–	②③	④	⑤	15.8
1988-89	Y	8-307 (5.0)	①	4	–	②③	④	⑤	15.8

① 0.5-1 qt. of engine oil may be required to bring oil level to full mark

② Additional transmission fluid may be required to bring level to full mark if overhauled or torque converter drained

③ Normal service
   THM 200C – 7.0 pts.
   THM 200-4R – 7.0 pts.
   THM 250C – 8.0 pts.
  Overhaul refill
   THM 200C – 19 pts.
   THM 200-4R – 22 pts.
   THM 250C – 20 pts.

④ 7½ in. ring gear – 3.5 pts.
  8½ in. ring gear – 4.25 pts.
  8¾ in. ring gear – 5.4 pts.

⑤ Coupe – 18 gal.
  Wagon – 22 gal.

⑥ Electra & LeSabre only
  Station Wagon – 27.0 gallons

⑦ Electra & LeSabre – 25.0 gallons

FIRING ORDERS

NOTE: To avoid confusion, always replace spark plug wires one at a time.

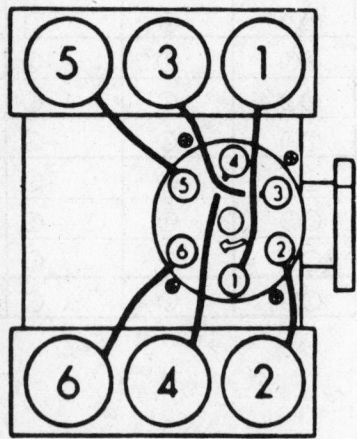

GM (Buick) 231, 252 V6
Engine firing order: 1-6-5-4-3-2
Distributor rotation: clockwise

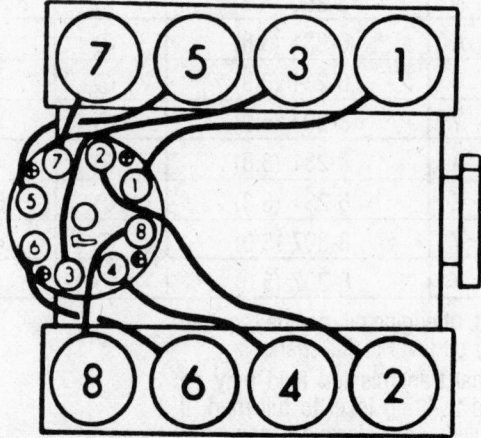

Chevrolet-manufactured V8 engines
Engine firing order: 1-8-4-3-6-5-7-2
Distributor rotation: clockwise

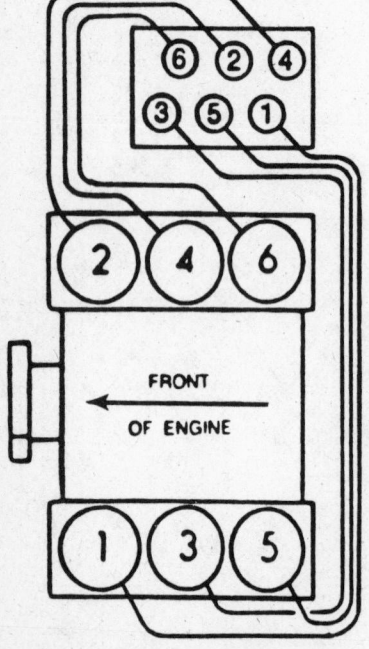

Buick V6 with C3I ignition system
Engine firing order: 1-6-5-4-3-2

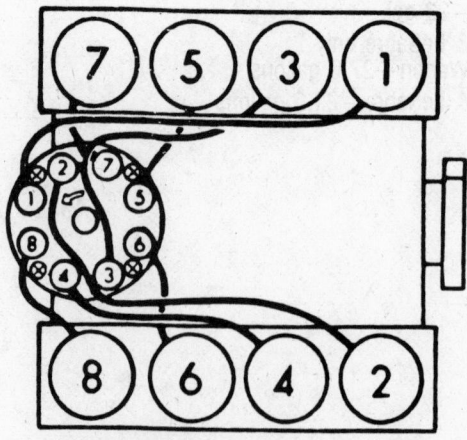

Oldsmobile 5.0L V8 engine
Firing order: 1–8–4–3–6–5–7–2
Distributor rotation: counterclockwise

CAMSHAFT SPECIFICATIONS
All measurements given in inches.

Year	VIN	No. Cylinder Displacement cu. in. (liter)	Journal Diameter 1	2	3	4	5	Lobe Lift In.	Ex.	Bearing Clearance	Camshaft End Play
1982	A	6-231 (3.8)	1.785–1.786	1.785–1.786	1.785–1.786	1.785–1.786	1.785–1.786	NA	NA	①	NA
	3	6-231 (3.8)	1.785–1.786	1.785–1.786	1.785–1.786	1.785–1.786	1.785–1.786	NA	NA	①	NA
	4	6-252 (4.1)	1.785–1.786	1.785–1.786	1.785–1.786	1.785–1.786	1.785–1.786	NA	NA	①	NA
	V	6-263 (4.3)	—	2.185–2.224	2.165–2.204	2.145–2.185	—	NA	NA	0.002–0.005	0.008–0.022
	J	8-267 (4.3)	1.868–1.869	1.868–1.869	1.868–1.869	1.868–1.869	1.868–1.869	0.357	0.390	NA	0.004–0.012
	H	8-305 (5.0)	1.868–1.869	1.868–1.869	1.868–1.869	1.868–1.869	1.868–1.869	0.248	0.266	NA	0.004–0.012
	Y	8-307 (5.0)	2.035–2.036	2.015–2.016	1.995–1.996	1.975–1.976	1.955–1.956	NA	NA	NA	0.011–0.077
	N	8-350 (5.7)	2.035–2.036	2.015–2.016	1.995–1.996	1.975–1.976	1.955–1.956	0.252	0.279	0.002–0.006	Spring Load
1983	A	6-231 (3.8)	1.785–1.786	1.785–1.786	1.785–1.786	1.785–1.786	1.785–1.786	NA	NA	①	NA
	8	6-231 (3.8)	1.785–1.786	1.785–1.786	1.785–1.786	1.785–1.786	1.785–1.786	NA	NA	①	NA
	4	6-252 (4.1)	1.785–1.786	1.785–1.786	1.785–1.786	1.785–1.786	1.785–1.786	NA	NA	①	NA
	V	6-263 (4.3)	—	2.185–2.224	2.165–2.205	2.145–2.185	—	0.252	0.279	0.002–0.006	0.001–0.003
	Y	8-307 (5.0)	2.036–2.037	2.016–2.017	1.995–1.996	1.975–1.976	1.955–1.956	0.400	0.400	0.002–0.006	0.011–0.077
	N	8-350 (5.7)	2.035–2.036	2.015–2.016	1.995–1.996	1.975–1.976	1.955–1.956	0.252	0.279	0.002–0.006	0.011–0.077
1984	A	6-231 (3.8)	1.785–1.786	1.785–1.786	1.785–1.786	1.785–1.786	1.785–1.786	NA	NA	0.001–0.003	NA
	9	6-231 (3.8)	1.785–1.786	1.785–1.786	1.785–1.786	1.785–1.786	1.785–1.786	NA	NA	0.001–0.003	NA
	4	6-252 (4.2)	1.785–1.786	1.785–1.786	1.785–1.786	1.785–1.786	1.785–1.786	NA	NA	0.001–0.003	NA
	V	6-263 (4.3)	—	2.015–2.016	1.995–1.996	1.975–1.976	—	0.252	0.279	0.002–0.006	0.001–0.023
	Y	8-307 (5.0)	2.036–2.037	2.016–2.017	1.999–2.000	1.976–1.977	1.956–1.977	0.400	0.400	0.002–0.006	0.011–0.077
	N	8-350 (5.7)	2.035–2.037	2.015–2.016	1.995–1.996	1.975–2.976	1.955–1.956	0.252	0.279	0.002–0.006	Spring Load

CAMSHAFT SPECIFICATIONS
All measurements given in inches.

Year	VIN	No. Cylinder Displacement cu. in. (liter)	Journal Diameter 1	2	3	4	5	Lobe Lift In.	Ex.	Bearing Clearance	Camshaft End Play
1985	A	6-231 (3.8)	1.785–1.786	1.785–1.786	1.785–1.786	1.785–1.786	1.785–1.786	NA	NA	0.001–0.003	NA
	9	6-231 (3.8)	1.785–1.786	1.785–1.786	1.785–1.786	1.785–1.786	1.785–1.786	NA	NA	0.001–0.003	NA
	Y	8-307 (5.0)	2.035–2.037	2.015–2.017	1.995–1.997	1.975–1.977	1.955–1.957	0.400	0.400	0.002–0.006	0.006–0.022
	N	8-350 (5.7)	2.035–2.037	2.015–2.016	1.995–1.996	1.975–1.976	1.955–1.956	0.252	0.279	0.002–0.006	Spring Load
1986	A	6-231 (3.8)	1.785–1.786	1.785–1.786	1.785–1.786	1.785–1.786	1.785–1.786	NA	NA	0.001–0.003	NA
	7	6-231 (3.8)	1.785–1.786	1.785–1.786	1.785–1.786	1.785–1.786	1.785–1.786	NA	NA	0.001–0.003	NA
	Y	8-307 (5.0)	2.035–2.037	2.015–2.017	1.995–1.997	1.975–1.977	1.955–1.957	0.247	0.251	0.002–0.006	0.006–0.022
1987	A	6-231 (3.8)	1.785–1.786	1.785–1.786	1.785–1.786	1.785–1.786	1.785–1.786	NA	NA	0.001–0.003	NA
	7	6-231 (3.8)	1.785–1.786	1.785–1.786	1.785–1.786	1.785–1.786	1.785–1.786	NA	NA	0.001–0.003	NA
	Y	8-305 (5.0)	2.035–2.037	3.015–2.017	1.995–1.997	1.975–1.977	1.955–1.957	0.247	0.251	0.002–0.006	0.006–0.022
1988-89	Y	8-305 (5.0)	2.035–2.037	3.015–2.017	1.995–1.997	1.975–1.977	1.955–1.957	0.247	0.251	0.002–0.006	0.006–0.022

NA-Not available

① 0.0005-0.0025 (No. 1)
 0.0005-0.0035 (Nos. 2, 3 and 4)

CRANKSHAFT AND CONNECTING ROD SPECIFICATIONS
All measurements are given in inches.

Year	VIN	No. Cylinder Displacement cu. in. (liter)	Crankshaft Main Brg. Journal Dia.	Main Brg. Oil Clearance	Shaft End-play	Thrust on No.	Connecting Rod Journal Diameter	Oil Clearance	Side Clearance
1982	A	6-231 (3.8)	2.4995	0.0003–0.0018	0.003–0.011	2	2.2487–2.2495	0.0005–0.0026	0.006–0.023
	3	6-231 (3.8)	2.4995	0.0003–0.0018	0.003–0.011	2	2.2487–2.2495	0.0005–0.0026	0.006–0.023
	4	6-252 (4.1)	2.4995	0.0003–0.0018	0.003–0.011	2	2.2487–2.2495	0.0005–0.0026	0.006–0.023
	V	6-263 (4.3)	2.9993–3.0003	0.0005–0.0021	0.0035–0.0135	3	2.1238–2.1248	0.0005–0.0026	0.006–0.023
	J	8-267 (4.3)	⑦ ⑨	0.0008–0.0020	0.002–0.006	5	2.0986–2.0998	0.0013–0.0035	0.006–0.014

CRANKSHAFT AND CONNECTING ROD SPECIFICATIONS
All measurements are given in inches.

Year	VIN	No. Cylinder Displacement cu. in. (liter)	Crankshaft				Connecting Rod		
			Main Brg. Journal Dia.	Main Brg. Oil Clearance	Shaft End-play	Thrust on No.	Journal Diameter	Oil Clearance	Side Clearance
1982	H	8-305 (5.0)	⑦	0.0008–0.0020	0.002–0.006	5	2.0986–2.0998	0.0013–0.0035	0.006–0.014
	Y	8-307 (5.0)	2.4973–2.4998 ⑧	0.0005–0.0021 ③	0.0035–0.0135	3	2.1238–2.1248	0.0004–0.0033	0.006–0.020
	N	8-350 (5.7)	2.9993–3.0003	0.0005–0.0021	0.0035–0.0135	3	2.2495–2.2500	0.0005–0.0026	0.006–0.020
1983	A	6-231 (3.8)	2.4995	0.0003–0.0018	0.003–0.011	2	2.2487–2.2495	0.0005–0.0026	0.006–0.023
	8	6-231 (3.8)	2.4995	0.0003–0.0018	0.003–0.011	2	2.2487–2.2495	0.0005–0.0026	0.006–0.023
	4	6-252 (4.1)	2.4995	0.0003–0.0018	0.003–0.011	2	2.2487–2.2495	0.0005–0.0026	0.006–0.023
	V	6-263 (4.3)	2.9993–3.0003	0.0005–0.0021	0.0035–0.0135	3	2.1238–2.1248	0.0005–0.0026	0.006–0.020
	Y	8-307 (5.0)	2.4973–2.4998 ⑧	0.0005–0.0021 ③	0.0035–0.0135	3	2.1238–2.1248	0.0004–0.0033	0.006–0.020
	N	6-350 (5.7)	2.9993–3.0003 ⑤	0.0005–0.0021	0.0035–0.0135	3	2.2495–2.2500	0.0005–0.0026	0.020–0.020
1984	A	6-231 (3.8)	2.4995	0.0003–0.0018	0.003–0.011	2	2.2487–2.2495	0.0005–0.0026	0.006–0.023
	9	6-231 (3.8)	2.4995	0.0003–0.0018	0.003–0.011	2	2.2487–2.2495	0.0005–0.0026	0.006–0.023
	4	6-252 (4.1)	2.4995	0.0003–0.0018	0.003–0.011	2	2.2487–2.2495	0.0005–0.0026	0.006–0.023
	V	6-263 (4.3)	2.9993–3.0003	0.0005–0.0020 ⑤	0.0035–0.0135	3	2.2490–2.2500	0.0005–0.0026	0.006–0.020
	Y	8-307 (5.0)	2.4990–2.4995 ①	0.0005–0.0021 ③	0.0035–0.0135	3	2.1238–2.1248	0.0004–0.0033	0.006–0.020
	N	8-350 (5.7)	2.9993–3.0003	0.0005–0.0021 ⑥	0.0035–0.0135	3	2.2495–2.2500	0.0005–0.0026	0.006–0.020

CRANKSHAFT AND CONNECTING ROD SPECIFICATIONS
All measurements are given in inches.

Year	VIN	No. Cylinder Displacement cu. in. (liter)	Crankshaft				Connecting Rod		
			Main Brg. Journal Dia.	Main Brg. Oil Clearance	Shaft End-play	Thrust on No.	Journal Diameter	Oil Clearance	Side Clearance
1985	A	6-231 (3.8)	2.4995	0.0003–0.0018	0.003–0.011	2	2.2487–2.2495	0.0005–0.0026	0.006–0.023
	9	6-231 (3.8)	2.4995	0.0003–0.0018	0.003–0.011	2	2.2487–2.2495	0.0005–0.0026	0.006–0.023
	Y	8-307 (5.0)	2.4985–2.4995 ②	0.0005–0.0021 ④	0.0035–0.0135	3	2.1238–2.1248	0.0004–0.0033	0.006–0.020
	N	8-350 (5.7)	2.9993–3.0003	0.0005–0.0021 ⑥	0.0035–0.0085	3	2.1238–2.1248	0.0005–0.0026	0.006–0.020
1986	A	6-231 (3.8)	2.4995	0.0003–0.0018	0.003–0.011	2	2.2487–2.2495	0.0005–0.0026	0.003–0.015
	7	6-231 (3.8)	2.4995	0.0003–0.0018	0.003–0.011	2	2.2487–2.2495	0.0005–0.0026	0.003–0.015
	Y	8-307 (5.0)	2.4985–2.4995 ②	0.0005–0.0021 ④	0.0035–0.0135	3	2.1238–2.1248	0.0004–0.0033	0.006–0.020
1987	A	6-231 (3.8)	2.4995	0.0003–0.0018	0.003–0.011	2	2.2487–2.2495	0.0005–0.0026	0.003–0.015
	7	6-231 (3.8)	2.4995	0.0003–0.0018	0.003–0.011	2	2.2487–2.2495	0.0005–0.0026	0.003–0.015
	Y	8-307 (5.0)	2.4985–2.4995 ②	0.0005–0.0021 ④	0.0035–0.0135	3	2.1238–2.1248	0.0004–0.0033	0.006–0.020
1988-89	Y	8-307 (5.0)	2.4985–2.4995 ②	0.0005–0.0021 ④	0.0035–0.0135	3	2.1238–2.1248	0.0004–0.0033	0.006–0.020

① No.1: 2.4973-2.4998 in.
② No.1: 2.4988-2.4998 in.
③ No.5: 0.0015-0.0031 in.
④ No.5: 0.0016-0.0032 in.
⑤ No.4: 0.0020-0.0034 in.
⑥ No.5: 0.0020-0.0034 in.
⑦ No.1: 2.4484-2.4493
  Nos. 2,3,4: 2.4481-2.4490
  No.5: 2.4479-2.4488
⑧ Nos. 2, 3, 4, 5: 2.4990-2.4995
⑨ Intermediate — 0.0011-0.0023
  Rear — 0.0017-0.0033

VALVE SPECIFICATIONS

Year	VIN	No. Cylinder Displacement cu. in. (liter)	Seat Angle (deg.)	Face Angle (deg.)	Spring Test Pressure (lbs.)	Spring Installed Height (in.)	Stem-to-Guide Clearance (in.) Intake	Exhaust	Stem Diameter (in.) Intake	Exhaust
1982	A	6-231 (3.8)	45	45	182	$1^{47}/_{64}$	0.0015–0.0035	0.0015–0.0032	0.3407	0.3409
	3	6-231 (3.8)	45	45	182	$1^{47}/_{64}$	0.0015–0.0035	0.0015–0.0032	0.3407	0.3409
	4	6-252 (4.1)	45	45	164	$1^{47}/_{64}$	0.0015–0.0035	0.0015–0.0032	0.3401–0.3412	0.3405–0.3412
	V	6-263 (4.3)	45[1]	44[1]	217	$1^{47}/_{64}$	0.0010–0.0027	0.0015–0.0032	0.3425–0.3432	0.3420–0.3427
	J	8-267 (4.3)	46	45	180	$1^{22}/_{32}$	0.0010–0.0027	0.0010–0.0027	0.3414	0.3414
	H	8-305 (5.0)	46	45	180	$1^{22}/_{32}$[2]	0.0010–0.0027	0.0010–0.0027	0.3414	0.3414
	Y	8-307 (5.0)	45[1]	44[1]	187	$1^{47}/_{64}$	0.0010–0.0027	0.0015–0.0032	0.3425–0.3432	0.3400–0.3427
	N	8-350 (5.7)	45[1]	44[1]	210	$1^{47}/_{64}$	0.0010–0.0027	0.0015–0.0032	0.3425–0.3432	0.3400–0.3427
1983	A	6-231 (3.8)	45	45	182	$1^{47}/_{64}$	0.0015–0.0035	0.0015–0.0032	0.3401–0.3412	0.3405–0.3412
	8	6-231 (3.8)	45	45	185	$1^{47}/_{64}$	0.0015–0.0035	0.0015–0.0032	0.3401–0.3412	0.3405–0.3412
	4	6-252 (4.1)	45	45	182	$1^{47}/_{64}$	0.0015–0.0035	0.0015–0.0032	0.3401–0.3412	0.3405–0.3412
	V	6-263 (4.3)	45[1]	44[1]	209	$1^{47}/_{64}$	0.0010–0.0027	0.0015–0.0032	0.3425–0.3432	0.3420–0.3427
	Y	8-307 (5.0)	45[1]	44[1]	187	$1^{47}/_{64}$	0.0010–0.0027	0.0015–0.0032	0.3425–0.3432	0.3420–0.3427
	N	8-350 (5.7)	45[1]	44[1]	209	$1^{47}/_{64}$	0.0010–0.0027	0.0015–0.0032	0.3425–0.3432	0.3420–0.3427
1984	A	6-231 (3.8)	45	45	182	$1^{47}/_{64}$	0.0015–0.0035	0.0015–0.0032	0.3401–0.3412	0.3405–0.3412
	9	6-231 (3.8)	45	45	220	$1^{47}/_{64}$	0.0015–0.0035	0.0015–0.0032	0.3401–0.3412	0.3405–0.3412
	4	6-252 (4.1)	45	45	182	$1^{47}/_{64}$	0.0015–0.0035	0.0015–0.0032	0.3401–0.3412	0.3405–0.3412
	V	6-263 (4.3)	45[1]	44[1]	209	$1^{47}/_{64}$	0.0010–0.0027	0.0015–0.0032	0.3425–0.3432	0.3420–0.3427
	Y	8-307 (5.0)	45[1]	44[1]	187	$1^{47}/_{64}$	0.0010–0.0027	0.0015–0.0032	0.3425–0.3432	0.3420–0.3427
	N	8-350 (5.7)	45[1]	44[1]	209	$1^{47}/_{64}$	0.0010–0.0027	0.0015–0.0032	0.3425–0.3432	0.3420–0.3427

VALVE SPECIFICATIONS

Year	VIN	No. Cylinder Displacement cu. in. (liter)	Seat Angle (deg.)	Face Angle (deg.)	Spring Test Pressure (lbs.)	Spring Installed Height (in.)	Stem-to-Guide Clearance (in.) Intake	Exhaust	Stem Diameter (in.) Intake	Exhaust
1985	A	6-231 (3.8)	45	45	182	$1^{47}/_{64}$	0.0015–0.0035	0.0015–0.0032	0.3401–0.3412	0.3405–0.3412
	9	6-231 (3.8)	45	45	185	$1^{47}/_{64}$	0.0015–0.0035	0.0015–0.0032	0.3401–0.3412	0.3405–0.3412
	Y	8-307 (5.0)	45①	44①	187	$1^{47}/_{64}$	0.0010–0.0027	0.0015–0.0032	0.3425–0.3432	0.3420–0.3427
	N	8-350 (5.7)	45①	44①	209	$1^{47}/_{64}$	0.0010–0.0027	0.0015–0.0032	0.3425–0.3432	0.3420–0.3420
1986	A	6-231 (3.8)	45	45	182	$1^{47}/_{64}$	0.0015–0.0035	0.0015–0.0032	0.3401–0.3412	0.3405–0.3412
	7	6-231 (3.8)	45	45	185	$1^{47}/_{64}$	0.0015–0.0035	0.0015–0.0032	0.3401–0.3412	0.3405–0.3412
	Y	8-307 (5.0)	45①	44①	187	$1^{47}/_{64}$	0.0010–0.0027	0.0015–0.0032	0.3425–0.3432	0.3420–0.3427
1987	A	6-231 (3.8)	45	45	182	$1^{47}/_{64}$	0.0015–0.0035	0.0015–0.0032	0.3401–0.3412	0.3405–0.3412
	7	6-231 (3.8)	45	45	185	$1^{47}/_{64}$	0.0015–0.0035	0.0015–0.0032	0.3401–0.3412	0.3405–0.3412
	Y	8-307 (5.0)	45①	45①	187	$1^{47}/_{64}$	0.0010–0.0027	0.0015–0.0032	0.3425–0.3432	0.3420–0.3427
1988-89	A	6-231 (3.8)	45	45	182	$1^{47}/_{64}$	0.0015–0.0035	0.0015–0.0032	0.3401–0.3412	0.3405–0.3412
	7	6-231 (3.8)	45	45	185	$1^{47}/_{64}$	0.0015–0.0035	0.0015–0.0032	0.3401–0.3412	0.3405–0.3412
	Y	8-307 (5.0)	45①	45①	187	$1^{47}/_{64}$	0.0010–0.0027	0.0015–0.0032	0.3425–0.3432	0.3420–0.3427

① Exhaust valve seat angle – 31 degrees
  Exhaust valve face angle – 30 degrees
② Exhaust – $1^{19}/_{32}$

PISTON AND RING SPECIFICATIONS
All measurments are given in inches.

Year	VIN	No. Cylinder Displacement cu. in. (liter)	Piston Clearance	Ring Gap Top Compression	Bottom Compression	Oil Control	Ring Side Clearance Top Compression	Bottom Compression	Oil Control
1982	A	6-231 (3.8)	0.0008–0.0020	0.010–0.020	0.010–0.020	0.015–0.055	0.0030–0.0050	0.0030–0.0050	0.0035 Max
	3	6-231 (3.8)	0.0008–0.0020	0.010–0.020	0.010–0.020	0.015–0.055	0.0030–0.0050	0.0030–0.0050	0.0035 Max
	4	6-252 (4.1)	0.0008–0.0020	0.010–0.020	0.010–0.020	0.015–0.055	0.0030–0.0050	0.0030–0.0050	0.0035 Max

PISTON AND RING SPECIFICATIONS
All measurments are given in inches.

Year	VIN	No. Cylinder Displacement cu. in. (liter)	Piston Clearance	Ring Gap Top Compression	Ring Gap Bottom Compression	Ring Gap Oil Control	Ring Side Clearance Top Compression	Ring Side Clearance Bottom Compression	Ring Side Clearance Oil Control
	V	6-263 (4.3)	0.0035– 0.0045	0.019– 0.027	0.013– 0.021	0.015– 0.055	0.0050– 0.0070	0.0030– 0.0050	0.0010– 0.0050
	J	8-267 (4.3)	0.0025– 0.0033	0.010– 0.020	0.010– 0.025	0.015– 0.055	0.0012– 0.0032	0.0012– 0.0032	0.0020– 0.0080
	H	8-305 (5.0)	0.0027 Max	0.010– 0.030	0.010– 0.035	0.015– 0.065	0.0012– 0.0032	0.0012– 0.0032	0.0020– 0.0080
	Y	8-307 (5.0)	0.0008– 0.0018	0.009– 0.019 ②	0.009– 0.019 ②	0.015– 0.055	0.0020– 0.0040	0.0020– 0.0040	0.0010– 0.0050
	N	8-350 (5.7)	0.0035– 0.0045	0.015– 0.025	0.015– 0.025	0.015– 0.055	0.0050– 0.0070	0.0030– 0.0050	0010– 0.0050
1983	A	6-231 (3.8)	0.0008– 0.0020	0.010– 0.020	0.010– 0.020	0.015– 0.055	0.0030– 0.0050	0.0030– 0.0050	0.0035 Max
	8	6-231 (3.8)	0.0008– 0.0020	0.010– 0.020	0.010– 0.020	0.015– 0.055	0.0030– 0.0050	0.0030– 0.0050	0.0035 Max
	4	6-252 (4.1)	0.0008– 0.0020	0.010– 0.020	0.010– 0.020	0.015– 0.055	0.0030– 0.0050	0.0030– 0.0050	0.0035 Max
	V	6-263 (4.3)	0.0035– 0.0045	0.019– 0.027	0.013– 0.021	0.015– 0.055	0.0050– 0.0070	0.0030– 0.0050	0.0010– 0.0050
	Y	8-307 (5.0)	0.0008– 0.0018	0.009– 0.019 ②	0.009– 0.019 ②	0.015– 0.055	0.0020– 0.0040	0.0020– 0.0040	0.0010– 0.0050
	N	8-350 (5.7)	0.0035– 0.0045	0.015– 0.025	0.015– 0.025	0.015– 0.055	0.0050– 0.0070	0.0030– 0.0050	0.0010– 0.0050
1984	A	6-231 (3.8)	0.0008– 0.0020	0.010– 0.020	0.010– 0.020	0.015– 0.055	0.0030– 0.0050	0.0030– 0.0050	0.0035 Max
	9	6-231 (3.8)	0.0008– 0.0026	0.010– 0.020	0.010– 0.020	0.015– 0.055	0.0030– 0.0050	0.0030– 0.0050	0.0035 Max
	4	6-252 (4.1)	0.0008– 0.0026	0.010– 0.020	0.010– 0.020	015– 0.055	0.0030– 0.0050	0.0030– 0.0050	0.0035 Max
	V	6-263 (4.3)	0.0035– 0.0045	0.019– 0.027	0.013– 0.021	0.010– 0.022	0.0050– 0.0070	0.0030– 0.0050	0.0010– 0.0050
	Y	8-307 (5.0)	0.0008– 0.0018	0.009– 0.019 ①	0.009– 0.019 ①	0.015– 0.055 ②	0.0020– 0.0040	0.0020– 0.0040	0.0010– 0.0050
	N	8-350 (5.7)	0.0004– 0.0005	0.019– 0.027	0.013– 0.021	0.010– 0.022	0.0050– 0.0070	0.003– 0.005	0.0010– 0.0050

PISTON AND RING SPECIFICATIONS
All measurments are given in inches.

Year	VIN	No. Cylinder Displacement cu. in. (liter)	Piston Clearance	Ring Gap Top Compression	Ring Gap Bottom Compression	Ring Gap Oil Control	Ring Side Clearance Top Compression	Ring Side Clearance Bottom Compression	Ring Side Clearance Oil Control
1985	A	6-231 (3.8)	0.0008–0.0020	0.010–0.020	0.010–0.020	0.015–0.055	0.0030–0.0050	0.0030–0.0050	0.0035 Max
	9	6-231 (3.8)	0.0008–0.0026	0.010–0.020	0.010–0.020	0.015–0.055	0.0030–0.0050	0.0030–0.0050	0.0035 Max
	Y	8-307 (5.0)	0.0008–0.0018	0.009–0.019	0.009–0.019	0.015–0.055	0.0018–0.0038	0.0018–0.0038	0.0010–0.0050
	N	8-350 (5.7)	0.0035–0.0045	0.015–0.025	0.015–0.025	0.015–0.055	0.0050–0.0070	0.003–0.005	0.0010–0.0050
1986	A	6-231 (3.8)	0.0008–0.0020	0.010–0.020	0.010–0.020	0.015–0.055	0.0030–0.0050	0.0030–0.0050	0.0035 Max
	7	6-231 (3.8)	0.0008–0.0020	0.010–0.020	0.010–0.020	0.015–0.055	0.0030–0.0050	0.0030–0.0050	0.0035 Max
	Y	8-307 (5.0)	0.0008–0.0018	0.009–0.019	0.009–0.019	0.015–0.055	0.0018–0.0038	0.0018–0.0038	0.0010–0.0050
1987	A	6-231 (3.8)	0.0008–0.0020	0.010–0.020	0.010–0.020	0.015–0.055	0.0030–0.0050	0.0030–0.0050	0.0035 Max
	7	6-231 (3.8)	0.0008–0.0020	0.010–0.020	0.010–0.020	0.015–0.055	0.0030–0.0050	0.0030–0.0050	0.0035 Max
	Y	8-307 (5.0)	0.0008–0.0018	0.009–0.019	0.009–0.019	0.015–0.055	0.0018–0.0038	0.0018–0.0038	0.0010–0.0050
1988–89	Y	8-307 (5.0)	0.0008–0.0018	0.009–0.019	0.009–0.019	0.015–0.055	0.0018–0.0038	0.0018–0.0038	0.0010–0.0050

① TRW® rings – 0.010-0.020 in.
② TRW® rings – 0.010-0.025 in.

TORQUE SPECIFICATIONS
All readings in ft. lbs.

Year	VIN	No. Cylinder Displacement cu. in. (liter)	Cylinder Head Bolts	Main Bearing Bolts	Rod Bearing Bolts	Crankshaft Pulley Bolts	Flywheel Bolts	Manifold Intake	Manifold Exhaust	Spark Plugs
1982	A	6-231 (3.8)	80	100	40	225	60	45	25	15
	3	6-231 (3.8)	80	100	40	225	60	45	25	15
	4	6-252 (4.1)	80	100	40	225⑤	60	45	25	15
	V	6-263 (4.3)	142④	107	42	160-350	48	41	29	—
	J	8-267 (4.3)	65	70	45	60	60	30	20	15
	H	8-305 (5.0)	65	70	45	60	60	30	20	25
	Y	8-307 (5.0)	130	80②	42	255⑤	60⑦	40	25	25
	N	8-350 (5.7)	130	120	42	200-300 ⑤	60	40	25	—

TORQUE SPECIFICATIONS
All readings in ft. lbs.

Year	VIN	No. Cylinder Displacement cu. in. (liter)	Cylinder Head Bolts	Main Bearing Bolts	Rod Bearing Bolts	Crankshaft Pulley Bolts	Flywheel Bolts	Manifold Intake	Manifold Exhaust	Spark Plugs
1983	A	6-231 (3.8)	80	100	40	200	60	47	25	15
	8	6-231 (3.8)	80	100	40	200	60	47	25	15
	4	6-252 (4.1)	80	100	40	225	60	45	25	15
	V	6-263 (4.3)	142④	89⑥	42	203-350	48	41	28	—
	Y	8-307 (5.0)	125	80②	42	200-310	60	40	25	25
	N	8-350 (5.7)	130	120	42	200-310	60	40	25	—
1984	A	6-231 (3.8)	80	100	40	225	60	45	25	15
	9	6-231 (3.8)	80	100	40	225	60	45	25	15
	4	6-252 (4.1)	80	100	40	225	60	45	25	15
	V	6-263 (4.3)	142④	105	42	203-350	57	41	31	—
	Y	8-307 (5.0)	125①	80②	42	200-310	60	40①	25	25
	N	8-350 (5.7)	130①	120	42	200-310	60	40①	25	25
1985	A	6-231 (3.8)	80	100	40	200	60	47	25	15
	9	6-231 (3.8)	80	100	40	200	60	40①	25	15
	Y	8-307 (5.0)	125①	80②	42	200-310	60	40①	25	25
	N	8-350 (5.7)	130①	120	42	200-310	60	40①	25	25
1986	A	6-231 (3.8)	③	100	40	200	60	45	20	20
	7	6-231 (3.8)	③	100	40	200	60	45	20	20
	Y	8-307 (5.0)	125①	80②	42	200-310	60	40①	20	25
1987	A	6-231 (3.8)	③	100	40	219	60	45	37	20
	7	6-231 (3.8)	③	100	40	219	60	45	37	20
	Y	8-307 (5.0)	130①	80②	48	200-310	60	40①	25	25
1988-89	Y	8-307 (5.0)	130①	80②	48	200-310	60	40①	25	25

NOTE: Verify correct original equipment engine is in vehicle by referring to the VIN engine code before torquing any bolts.

① Clean and dip entire bolt in engine oil before tightening to obtain a correct torque reading.

② Rear main bearing cap bolts—120 ft.lbs.

③ Torque cylinder head bolts to 25 ft.lbs. in tightening sequence. Continue the torquing sequence, tightening each bolt ¼ turn (90 degrees) until 60 ft.lbs. is read on any one cylinder head bolt. Do not continue sequence at this point.

④ Nos. 5, 6, 11, 12, 13 & 14 cylinder head bolts—59 ft.lbs.

⑤ Fan pulley to balancer—20 ft.lbs.

⑥ Manual Transmission—90 ft.lbs.

⑦ No. 2 and 3 Outer—52 ft.lbs.

BRAKE SPECIFICATIONS
All measurements in inches unless noted

Year	Model	Lug Nut Torque (ft. lbs.)	Master Cylinder Bore	Brake Disc Minimum Thickness	Brake Disc Maximum Runout	Standard Brake Drum Diameter	Minimum Lining Thickness Front	Minimum Lining Thickness Rear
1982	Regal	③	1⅛	0.980	0.004	9.50 ②	⅛	⅛
	Electra	③	1⅛	0.980	0.004	11.00	⅛	⅛
	LeSabre	③	1⅛	0.980	0.004	9.50	⅛	⅛
1983	Regal	③	1⅛	0.956	0.004	9.50 ②	⅛	⅛
	Electra	③	1⅛	0.980	0.004	11.00	⅛	⅛
	LeSabre	③	1⅛	0.980	0.004	11.00	⅛	⅛
1984	Electra	100	1⅛ ①	0.965	0.004	11.00	⅛	⅛
	LeSabre	③	1⅛	0.965	0.004	9.50	⅛	⅛
	Regal	⑤	1⅛	0.965	0.004	9.50	⅛	⅛
1985	Electra	③	1¼	0.965	0.004	11.00	⅛	⅛
	LeSabre	③	1¼	0.965	0.004	9.50	⅛	⅛
	Estate	③	1¼	0.965	0.004	11.00	⅛	⅛
	Regal	80	1¼ ④	0.965	0.004	9.50	⅛	⅛
1986	Estate Wagon	③	1⅛⑤	0.965	0.004	11.00	⅛	⅛
	Regal	100	¹⁵⁄₁₆⑤	0.965	0.004	9.50	⅛	⅛
1987	Estate Wagon	③	1⅛	0.965	0.004	11.00	⅛	⅛
	Regal	100	¹⁵⁄₁₆⑤	0.965	0.004	9.50	⅛	⅛
1988-89	Estate Wagon	③	1⅛	0.965	0.004	11.00	⅛	⅛

① Hydroboost—1³⁄₁₆ in.
② Optional 11.00 in. brakes were available.
③ Wheel lug type: ½ × 20—100 ft.lbs.
　⁷⁄₁₆ × 20 Steel—80 ft.lbs.
　⁷⁄₁₆ × 20 Aluminum—90 ft.lbs.
④ Quick take-up—¹⁵⁄₁₆ in.
⑤ Power master—1¼ in.

WHEEL ALIGNMENT

Year	Model	Caster Range (deg.)	Caster Preferred Setting (deg.)	Camber Range (deg.)	Camber Preferred Setting (deg.)	Toe-in (in.)	Steering Axis Inclination (deg.)
1982	Regal	2½P-3½P	3P	0-1P	½P	$\frac{1}{16}$-$\frac{3}{16}$	NA
	Electra, LeSabre	2P-4P	3P	0-1⅝P	$\frac{3}{16}$P	$\frac{1}{16}$-$\frac{1}{4}$	NA
1983	Regal			⅓N-1⅓P	NA	$\frac{1}{16}$-$\frac{1}{4}$	NA
	Electra, LeSabre	2P-4P	3P	0-1⅝P	$\frac{3}{16}$P	$\frac{1}{16}$-$\frac{1}{4}$	NA
1984	Electra, LeSabre	2P-4P	3P	0-1⅝P	$\frac{13}{16}$P	⅛	NA
	Regal	2P-4P	3P	$\frac{5}{16}$N-1$\frac{5}{16}$P	½P	⅛	8
1985	Electra, LeSabre, Estate	2P-4P	3P	0-1⅝P	$\frac{13}{16}$P	⅛	NA
	Regal	2P-4P	3P	$\frac{5}{16}$N-1$\frac{5}{16}$P	½P	⅛	8
1986	Estate Wagon	2P-4P	3P	0-1⅝P	$\frac{13}{16}$P	⅛	NA
	Regal	2P-4P	3P	$\frac{5}{16}$N-1$\frac{5}{16}$P	½P	⅛	8
1987	Estate Wagon	2P-4P	3P	0-1⅝P	$\frac{13}{16}$P	⅛	NA
	Regal	2P-4P	3P	$\frac{5}{16}$N-1$\frac{5}{16}$P	½P	⅛	8
1988-89	Estate Wagon	2P-4P	3P	0-1⅝P	$\frac{13}{16}$P	⅛	NA

N—Negative
P—Positive
NA-Not available

TUNE–UP PROCEDURES

Ignition Timing

ADJUSTMENT

1984–87 Turbocharged 3.8L V6 engines are equipped with computer controlled coil ignition (C^3I). These engines do not use a distributor. All ignition timing adjustments are controlled by the electronic control module (ECM).

All other gasoline engines without the C^3I ignition, refer to the specific timing instructions on the emission control sticker under the hood. All timing marks are located on the front engine covers and harmonic balancers, or crankshaft pulley.

Some engines have a magnetic timing probe hole in the timing tab for the use of electronic timing equipment. Consult the manufacture's instructions for the proper use of the equipment.

Carbureted Engines Only

1. With engine at operating temperature, air cleaner installed and air conditioning in OFF position, connect timing light or meter and verify "Check Engine" light is not on.
2. Disconnect distributor four wire electrical connector. The "Check Engine" light will come on.

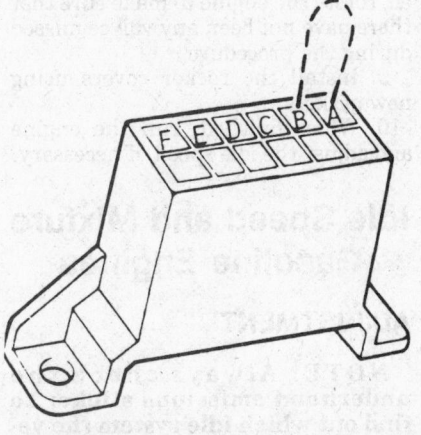

Ground the diagnostic lead with a jumper wire as shown, if necessary.

3. Set ignition timing to specification shown on Vehicle Emission Control Information (VECI) Label by loosening the distributor clamp bolt and rotating the distributor until the correct specification is obtained.
4. Tighten the distributor clamp bolt and recheck timing to make sure distributor has not moved.
5. Reconnect the distributor electrical connector.
6. With the engine off, momentarily disconnect battery to cancel any stored trouble codes.

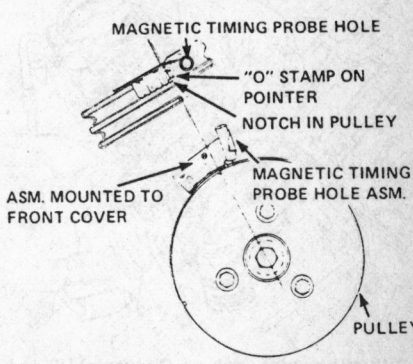

Location of hole for magnetic timing probe

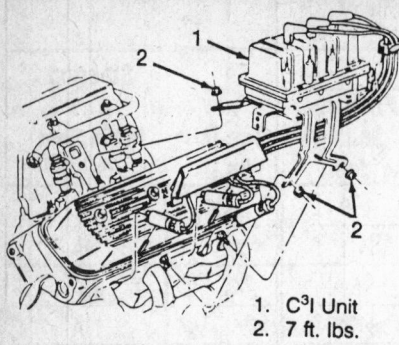

1. C³I Unit
2. 7 ft. lbs.

3.8L V6 engine with C³I Ignition

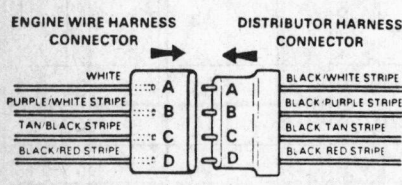

4 terminal distributor wiring harness connector

Valve Lash

ADJUSTMENT

Buick and Oldsmobile Engines

The valve lash on Buick and Oldsmobile engines is not adjustable. If there is excess play in the valve train, check for worn pushrods, rocker arms, valve springs and/or collapsed lifters.

Chevrolet Engines

NOTE: Chevrolet engines do not require any routine valve lash adjustments. Whenever the rocker arms are removed, the initial valve lash must be adjusted before the engine is started.

1. With the rocker covers removed and the rocker arms loosely installed on the engine, rotate the engine slowly

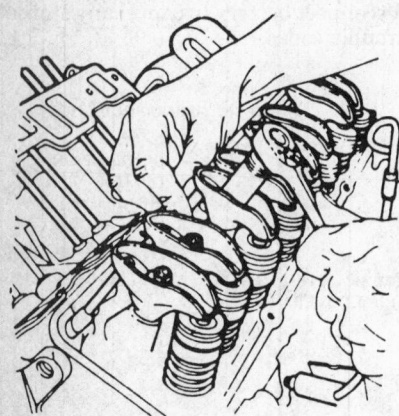

Adjusting valve lash on Chevrolet V8 engine

while tightening the rocker arm nuts until all of the lash is removed. This can be determined by rotating the pushrods while tightening the rocker arm nuts.

2. The valves are adjusted while the lifter is on the base circle, or lower part of the camshaft.

3. After all the lash is removed, rotate the engine until the timing marks at the front of the engine are aligned.

4. If the valves are open on No. 1 cylinder, (rocker arm depressing the valve spring), rotate the engine one complete revolution and align the timing marks again. This is No.1 cylinder's firing position.

NOTE: When adjusting the valve lash, it may be a good idea to mark the rocker arms to be sure that all valves were adjusted during the procedure.

5. With the engine in the No.1 firing position, the following valves can be adjusted:
V6 Engine:
- Exhaust 1, 5, 6
- Intake 1, 2, 3

V8 Engine:
- Exhaust 1, 3, 4, 8
- Intake 1, 2, 5, 7

6. To adjust the valves, turn the adjusting nut outwards until lash is felt at the pushrod. When lash is felt, turn the nut inwards just until there is no lash. Then turn the nut one complete revolution more. This will apply the proper load on the lifter.

7. Rotate the engine one complete revolution and align the timing marks again. With the engine in this position the following valves can be adjusted:
V6 Engine:
- Exhaust 2, 3, 4
- Intake 4, 5, 6

V8 Engine:
- Exhaust 2, 3, 4
- Intake 4, 5, 6

8. When all valves have been adjusted, rotate the engine to make sure that there have not been any valves missed during the procedure.

9. Install the rocker covers using new gaskets.

10. When finished, run the engine and adjust the idle speed, if necessary.

Idle Speed and Mixture Gasoline Engines

ADJUSTMENT

NOTE: Always check the underhood emissions sticker to find out which idle system the vehicle is equipped with prior to any adjustment.

Carbureted Models

WITH IDLE SPEED SOLENOID

1. Run the engine until it reaches normal operating temperature.

2. Make sure the choke is fully opened, turn the A/C off, set the parking brake and block the wheels.

3. Connect a tachometer to the engine.

4. Disconnect the purge hose from the vapor canister. Do not plug the purge hose.

5. Disconnect and plug the EGR vacuum hose at the valve. Disconnect and plug the vacuum advance hose at the distributor.

6. With the parking brake on and the wheels blocked, place the transmission in PARK.

7. Check and adjust the timing, if necessary.

8. Reconnect the vacuum advance hose at the distributor.

9. Place the transmission in Drive.

NOTE: If the instructions on the underhood sticker differ from these, follow the procedure on the underhood sticker.

10. On models without A/C, turn the idle speed screw to obtain the specified rpm. On models with A/C, turn the idle speed screw to set the specified curb idle speed. Turn the A/C on and disconnect the compressor clutch wire. Open the throttle momentarily to extend the solenoid plunger. Adjust the solenoid screw to obtain the solenoid idle speed shown on the underhood sticker. Reconnect the compressor clutch and turn the A/C off.

11. Reconnect all hoses and remove the tachometer.

WITHOUT IDLE SPEED SOLENOID

Most models are equipped with an Idle Speed Control (ISC) mounted on the float bowl. Idle speeds are computer controlled and the ICS should not be adjusted.

On some V8 models an Idle Load Compensator (ILC) is mounted on the float bowl to control the curb idle speed. The ILC is adjusted at the factory and capped to prevent readjustment.

On models that are not equipped with either an ISC or ILC, but are quipped with air conditioning, an idle speed solenoid is used to maintain idle speed. For adjustment of these models, refer to the previous adjustment procedures.

Fuel Injected Models

The fuel mixture is controlled by the electronic control module (ECM). No adjustments are possible.

IDLE MIXTURE ADJUSTMENT

Carbureted and Fuel Injected Models

The idle mixture on both carbureted and fuel injected models is controlled by the ECM. No adjustments are possible.

Idle Speed Diesel Engines

ADJUSTMENT

Slow Idle

1. Run the engine until it reaches normal operating temperature.
2. Insert the probe of a magnetic pickup timer into the timing indicator hole.
3. Set the parking brake and block the drive wheels.
4. Place the transmission in Drive and turn off the a/c (if equipped).
5. Turn the slow idle adjustment screw on the injection pump to obtain the idle speed specified on the emissions control label.

Fast Idle

1. Set the parking brake and block the drive wheels.
2. Run the engine until it reaches normal operating temperature.
3. Place the transmission in Drive and disconnect the two lead connectors at the alternator.
4. Disconnect the connector from thr EGR–TVS and install a jumper wire between the terminal of the connector.
5. Adjust the fast idle solenoid plunger to obtain the specified RPM.
6. Reconnect the wiring connectors when finished.

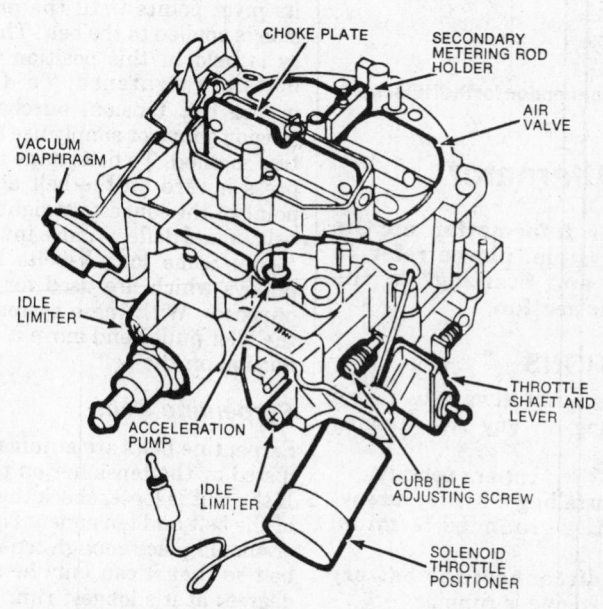

③ SOLENOID ENERGIZED – A/C COMPRESSOR LEAD DISCONNECTED AT A/C COMPRESSOR , A/C ON, A/T TRANSMISSION IN DRIVE, M/T IN NEUTRAL

ELECTRICAL CONNECTION

① PREPARE VEHICLE FOR ADJUSTMENTS – SEE EMISSION LABEL ON VEHICLE. NOTE: IGNITION TIMING SET PER LABEL.

⑤ TURN SOLENOID SCREW TO ADJUST TO SPECIFIED RPM. (RECONNECT A/C COMPRESSOR LEAD AFTER ADJUSTMENT)

④ OPEN THROTTLE SLIGHTLY TO ALLOW SOLENOID PLUNGER TO FULLY EXTEND

② TURN IDLE SPEED SCREW TO SET CURB IDLE SPEED TO SPECIFICATIONS - A/C OFF (SEE EMISSION LABEL)

Idle speed solenoid adjustment

CHOKE PLATE

SECONDARY METERING ROD HOLDER

AIR VALVE

VACUUM DIAPHRAGM

IDLE LIMITER

THROTTLE SHAFT AND LEVER

ACCELERATION PUMP

IDLE LIMITER

CURB IDLE ADJUSTING SCREW

SOLENOID THROTTLE POSITIONER

4 bbl carburetor

ENGINE ELECTRICAL

Distributor

REMOVAL & INSTALLATION

1. Remove the distributor cap, primary wire and vacuum line at the distributor. Unplug the V6 and V8 distributor cap HEI connectors.
2. Scribe a mark on the distributor body, to locate the position of the rotor. Scribe another mark on the engine block to show the position of the distributor body in the engine.
3. Remove the hold-down clamp. Mark the position of the rotor, then lift the distributor out of the block until the rotor stops turning. Mark the position of the rotor again and remove the distributor from the engine.

NOTE: For firing order and cylinder numbering, see the specifications at the beginning of this section.

4. If the engine has not been disturbed with the distributor removed, insert the distributor into the engine, making sure the tip of the rotor is aligned with the marks that were scribed on the distributor housing and engine block.

5. If the engine has been disturbed with the distributor removed, remove the No.1 spark plug and place a finger over the hole. Slowly turn the engine until compression is felt. Align the timing marks so No.1 cylinder is in firing position. Position the distributor in the engine with the rotor at No. 1 firing position. Make sure the oil pump intermediate driveshaft is properly seated in the oil pump and distributor.
6. Install but do not tighten the distributor lock.
7. Rotate the distributor body clockwise. Tighten the retaining screw.
8. Connect the primary wire and vacuum line to the distributor. Install distributor cap.
9. Start the engine and adjust the ignition timing.

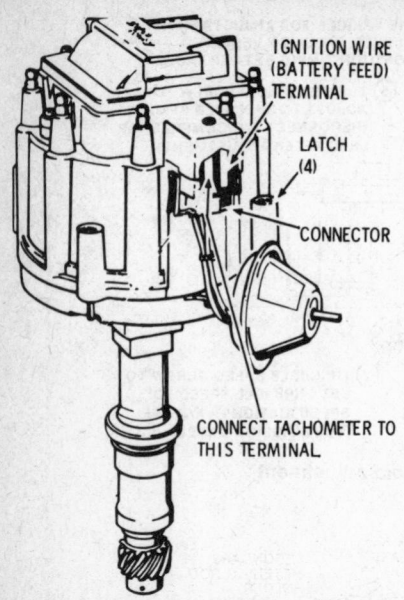

Tachometer connection for the HEI system

IGNITION WIRE
(BATTERY FEED)
TERMINAL

LATCH
(4)

CONNECTOR

CONNECT TACHOMETER TO
THIS TERMINAL

Alternator

For further information on the charging system, please refer to "Charging and Starting" in the Unit Repair section.

PRECAUTIONS

Precautions must always be taken when working on any AC charging system.
● Never switch battery polarity.
● When installing a battery, always connect the grounded terminal first.
● Never disconnect the battery while the engine is running.

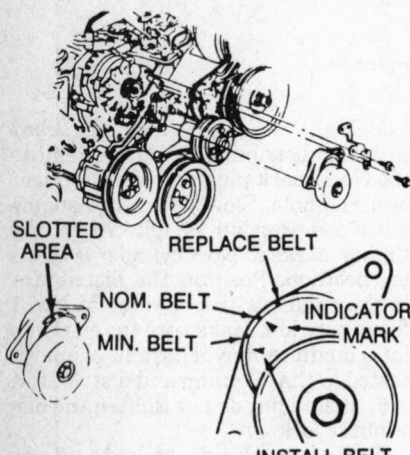

SLOTTED AREA

REPLACE BELT

NOM. BELT

MIN. BELT

INDICATOR MARK

INSTALL BELT

THE INDICATOR MARK ON THE MOVEABLE PORTION OF THE TENSIONER MUST BE WITHIN THE LIMITS OF THE SLOTTED AREA ON THE STATIONARY PORTION OF THE TENSIONER. ANY READING OUTSIDE THESE LIMITS INDICATES EITHER A DEFECTIVE BELT OR TENSIONER.

Serpentine belt and tensioner—3.8L V6 engine

● If the molded connector is disconnected from the alternator, never ground the hot wire.
● Never run the alternator with the main output cable disconnected.
● Never electric weld around the vehicle without disconnecting the alternator.
● Never apply any voltage in excess of battery voltage while testing.
● Never jump a battery for starting purposes with more than 12v.

BELT TENSION ADJUSTMENT

V-Belts

V-Belts are normally adjusted by loosening the bolts of the accessory being driven and moving that accessory on its pivot points until the proper tension is applied to the belt. The accessory is held in this position while the bolts are tightened. To determine proper belt tension, purchase a belt tension gauge or simply use the deflection method. To determine deflection, press inward on the belt at the midpoint of the longest straight run. The belt should deflect (move inward) $3/8$ to $1/2$ in. Some long V-belts have idler pulleys which are used for adjusting purposes. With these systems, loosen the idler pulley and move it to take up tension on the belt.

Serpentine Belts

Serpentine belts are automatically adjusted by the tensioner on the engine. If the belt is loose, check the condition of the belt and tensioner. The tensioner should place enough tension on the belt so that it can only be twisted 90 degrees at it's longest run.

REMOVAL & INSTALLATION

1. Disconnect the negative battery cable.
2. Disconnect and tag the electrical connections.
3. With V-Belts, remove the bolt holding the slotted adjusting bracket to the alternator and remove the belt.
4. With serpentine belts, loosen and rotate the tensioner to release the drive belt.
5. Remove the thru-bolt to release the alternator from the engine.
6. When reinstalling, adjust the drive belt to allow $1/2$ in. play on the longest run between pulleys.

NOTE: On some models, it may be necessary to loosen and rotate the fan shroud. On models with air conditioning, it may be necessary to remove the compressor bracket. Do not discharge the A/C system.

Voltage Regulator

REMOVAL & INSTALLATION

NOTE: All models are equipped with an internal voltage regulator. The alternator must be disassembled to replace the regulator. Refer to "Charging and Starting" in the Unit Repair section for the procedure.

Starter

For further information on starting system, please refer to "Charging and Starting" in the Unit Repair section.

REMOVAL & INSTALLATION

1. Disconnect the negative battery cable.
2. Raise and support the vehicle safely. Remove the starter brace and heat shield(s).

NOTE: On some automatic transmission models, it may be necessary to remove the exhaust crossover pipe. On manual transmission models, loosen the engine crossmember by removing the six crossmember bolts and two stabilizer shaft bolts from the passenger's side. Then loosen the four crossmember bolts on the driver's side.

3. Disconnect and tag the wires at the starter solenoid.
4. Support the starter and remove the mounting bolts, taking note of any shims and their placement.
5. Remove the starter from the engine.
6. Installation is the reverse of the removal procedure.
7. Reinstall any shims that were removed in there original location.

Diesel Glow Plugs

NOTE: A burned out FAST GLOW glow plug tip may bulge then break off and drop into the pre-chamber when removed. When this occurs, the cylinder head must be removed and the pre-chamber removed from the head to remove the the broken tip.

REMOVAL & INSTALLATION

V6 and V8 Engine

1. Disconnect the negative battery cable(s).
2. Remove the wire from the end of the glow plug.

3. Using a six point socket, remove the glow plugs one at a time.

4. Installation is the reverse of the removal procedure.

5. Lightly coat the threads of the glow plug with an anti-sieze compound and torque it to 15 ft. lbs.

TESTING

To test each individual glow plug, disconnect the busbar and/or wire connector from the glow plug and connect a test light between the glow plug terminal and the positive battery terminal. If the test light lights, the glow plug is functioning properly.

NOTE: GM V8 diesel engines are equipped with either "slow glow" or "fast glow" glow plugs. Refer to the "Oldsmobile Rear Wheel Drive" section for information on these two systems. Do not attempt to interchange any parts between these two systems. The GM V6 diesel uses the "fast glow" style glow plugs exclusively.

To test the glow plug circuit, connect a test light to the terminal of one of the glow plugs with the wiring still attached. Turn the ignition to the preheat position. The "WAIT" lamp should come on at the dashboard. The test light should light for a short while when the "WAIT" lamp is on. If not, the glow plug circuit is malfunctioning and must be diagnosed and repaired.

ENGINE MECHANICAL

NOTE: Refer to the charts in the beginning of this section to determine the type and manufacturer of the engine used in the vehicle. Engine mechanical information, for engines other than those manufactured by Buick, will be found in the section of the engine manufacturer. The Chevrolet 4.3L and 5.0L engines will be found in "Chevrolet Rear Wheel Drive" section of this manual). The Oldsmobile 5.0L and 5.7L engine will be found in the "Oldsmobile Rear Wheel Drive" section.

Engine

REMOVAL & INSTALLATION

V6 Engine

1. Matchmark and remove the hood.

2. Disconnect the battery cables and remove the battery from the vehicle.

3. Drain the coolant into a suitable container.

4. Remove the air cleaner.

5. Disconnect the A/C compressor ground wire from the mounting bracket. Remove the electrical connector from the compressor clutch, remove the compressor to mounting bracket attaching bolts and position the compressor out of the way.

— CAUTION —

If the compressor refrigerant lines do not have enough slack to position the compressor out of the way without disconnecting the refrigerant lines, the air conditioning system will have to be discharged. Do not attempt to bleed the system unless familiar with air conditioning systems. Compressed refrigerant will freeze any surface it contacts (including skin and eyes) and forms a poisonous gas in the presence of flame.

6. Remove fan blade, pulleys and belts.

7. Disconnect the radiator and heater hoses from engine.

8. Remove the fan shroud assembly.

9. Remove the power steering pump to mounting bracket bolts and position pump assembly out of the way.

10. Disconnect and plug the fuel hoses.

— CAUTION —

On engines equipped with fuel injection, the fuel system must be depressurized before removing any fuel lines. To depressurize the fuel system, remove the fuel pump fuse and run the engine until it stalls. Crank the engine for three seconds after it stalls to make sure all fuel is exhausted from the fuel lines, then replace the fuel pump fuse with the key OFF.

11. Disconnect the battery ground cable from engine.

12. Disconnect the vacuum supply hose from carburetor to the vacuum manifold. On vehicles so equipped, the vacuum modulator, load leveler and power brake vacuum hoses should all be disconnected at the engine.

13. Disconnect accelerator cable at carburetor or throttle body.

14. Disconnect alternator, oil and coolant sending unit switch connections at the engine. Remove the alternator from the engine.

15. Disconnect engine to body ground strap(s) at engine.

16. Raise and support the vehicle safely. Disconnect the cable shield from the engine.

17. Disconnect the exhaust pipes from the exhaust manifolds.

18. Remove the lower torque converter cover.

19. Remove flywheel to torque converter attaching bolts. Scribe a chalk mark on the flywheel and converter for proper reassembly alignment.

20. Remove transmission to engine bolts.

21. Remove the left side engine mount through bolt and cruise control bracket, if equipped.

22. Lower the vehicle and support the transmission.

23. Attach a lifting device to the engine and raise the engine enough so right side mounting through bolt can be removed. Make certain wiring harness, vacuum hoses and other parts are free and clear before lifting engine out of the vehicle.

24. Raise engine far enough to clear engine mount, raise transmission support accordingly until the engine can be disengaged from the transmission and removed.

25. Installation is the reverse of the removal procedure.

Cylinder Head

REMOVAL & INSTALLATION

1982–85 V6 Engine

1. Disconnect the negative battery cable.

2. Remove the intake manifold.

3. Loosen and remove the drive belts.

4. When removing the left side cylinder head:

   a. Remove the oil dipstick.

   b. Remove the air pump with the mounting bracket and move it out of the way with the hoses attached.

5. When removing the right cylinder head:

   a. Remove the alternator.

   b. Disconnect the power steering pump and the brackets attaching to the cylinder head.

6. Disconnect the spark plug wires at the plugs. Remove the spark plug wire clips from the rocker arm cover studs.

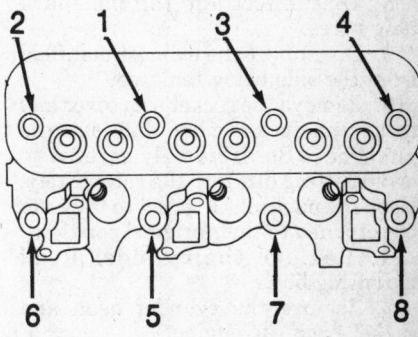

Buick V6 cylinder head bolt torque sequence

7. Remove the exhaust manifold bolts from the cylinder head being removed.

8. With an air hose and cloth, clean the dirt off the cylinder head and adjacent area to avoid getting dirt into the engine.

9. Remove the rocker arm cover and then the rocker arm and shaft assembly from the cylinder head. Lift out the push rods. Keep the pushrods in order for installation.

10. Loosen all the cylinder head bolts, then remove the bolts and lift off the cylinder head from the engine.

11. Installation is the reverse of the removal procedure. Refer to Torque Specification Chart for correct bolt torque. For 1986–89 engines, torque all cylinder head bolts, in tightening sequence, to 25 ft. lbs. (34 Nm). Continue the torquing sequence, tightening each bolt ¼ turn (90 degrees) UNTIL 60 ft. lbs.(81 Nm) is read on any one cylinder head bolt. Do not continue the torquing sequence when this point is reached.

1986–89 V6 Engine

1. Disconnect the battery cables, negative first and remove the battery from the vehicle.

2. Drain the cooling system into a suitable container.

3. Remove the air cleaner.

4. Remove the air conditioning compressor, but do not disconnect any lines. Disconnect the AIR hose at the check valve. Remove the turbocharger assembly, if equipped. Depressurize the fuel system before removing any fuel lines or components.

5. Remove the intake manifold.

6. When removing the right cylinder head, loosen the alternator belt, disconnect the wiring and remove the alternator. Remove the A/C compressor from the mounting bracket and position it out of the way. Do not disconnect any of the hoses.

7. When removing the left cylinder head, remove the dipstick, power steering pump and air pump.

8. Disconnect and tag the spark plug wires.

9. Disconnect the exhaust manifold from the side being removed.

10. Remove the rocker arm cover and rocker shaft assembly. Lift out the pushrods. Be extremely careful to avoid getting dirt into the valve lifters. Keep the pushrods in order so they can be returned to their original positions.

11. Remove the cylinder head mounting bolts.

12. Remove the cylinder head and gasket from the engine.

13. Reverse the above steps to install. Torque the head bolts to specifications in three steps. On the 1986–89

3.8L V6 engines, torque the head bolts in the following manner:

    a. Use a heavy duty thread sealer on the head bolts.

    b. Torque the head bolts to 25 ft. lbs. in the sequence shown.

NOTE: If 60 ft. lbs. is reached at any time in the next two steps, stop at this point. Do not complete the remainder of the 90 degree turn.

    c. Tighten each bolt ¼ turn (90 degrees) in sequence.

    d. Tighten each bolt an additional ¼ turn (90 degrees) in sequence.

OVERHAUL

NOTE: For all cylinder head overhaul procedures, please refer to "Engine Rebuilding" in the Unit Repair section.

Rocker Arms/Shafts

REMOVAL & INSTALLATION

1. Remove the rocker arm cover.

2. Remove the rocker arm shaft assembly bolts and the assembly.

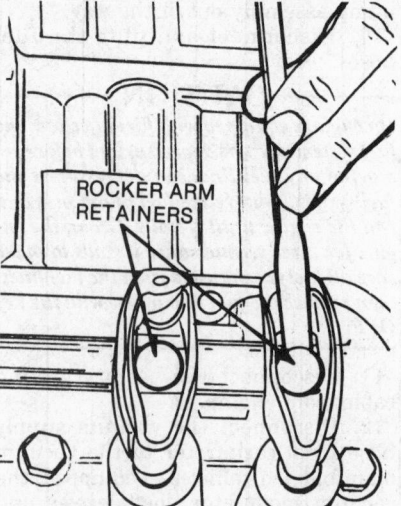

Removing nylon rocker arm retainer

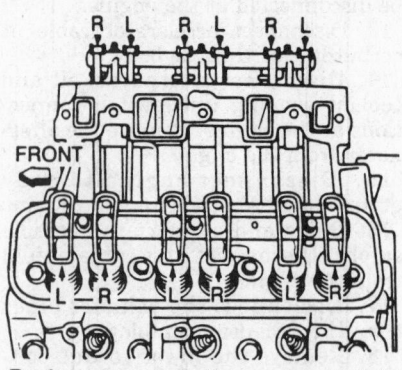

Rocker arm and shaft assembly – 3.8L V6 engine

3. Wear eye protection and remove the nylon arm retainers by prying them out.

4. Remove the rocker arms.

5. Install the rocker arms on the shaft and lubricate them with oil.

6. Center each arm on the ¼ in. hole in the shaft. Install new nylon rocker arm retainers in the holes using a ½ in. drift.

7. Locate the pushrods in the rocker arms and insert the shaft-to-cylinder head bolts. Tighten each bolt a little at a time until they are tightened to 30 ft. lbs.

8. Install the rocker cover using a new gasket.

Intake Manifold

REMOVAL & INSTALLATION

V6 Engines

1. Disconnect the negative battery cable and drain the radiator.

2. Remove the air cleaner. Remove the mass air flow sensor on fuel injected engines.

3. Disconnect the upper radiator hose and heater hose at the manifold. Remove the serpentine drive belt, if equipped.

4. Disconnect the accelerator linkage and linkage bracket at the manifold. Remove the cruise control chain, if equipped.

5. Remove the fuel line from the carburetor and the booster vacuum pipe from the manifold. Remove turbocharger, if equipped.

NOTE: On fuel injected models, the fuel system must be depressurized before disconnecting any fuel lines.

6. Disconnect and tag the transmission vacuum modulator line, idle stop solenoid wire (if equipped), distributor wires and temperature sending unit wire.

7. Disconnect and tag the vacuum hoses at the distributor and carburetor.

8. Disconnect the coolant bypass hose at the manifold.

9. Remove the distributor cap and wires to gain access to the Torx® head bolt. Remove the bolt. On fuel injected engines, remove the C3I ignition coil assembly.

10. Remove the throttle linkage springs.

11. Remove the A/C compressor top mounting bracket.

12. Remove the intake manifold from the engine.

13. When installing, always use new gaskets. Use sealer on the ends of the rubber gasket seals. Carefully guide

the manifold onto the engine block dowel pin. Observe "Turbocharger Precautions" given with the Turbocharger information. Tighten the bolts in the proper order.

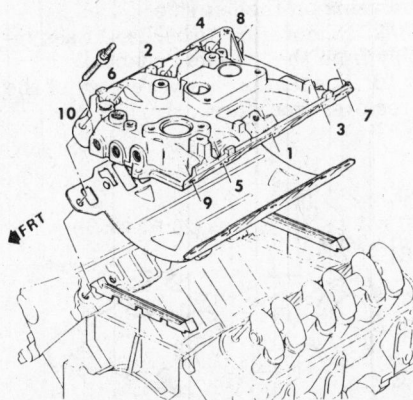

Intake manifold bolt tightening sequence—Buick built V6 engines with carburetor

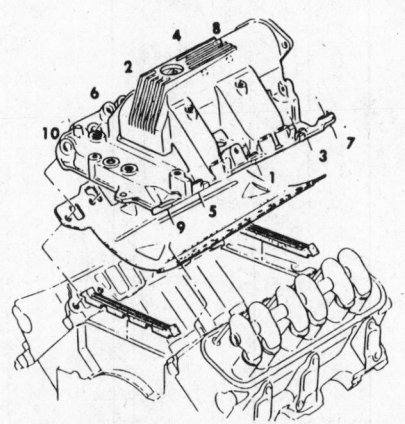

Intake manifold bolt tightening sequence-V6 engine with fuel injection.

Exhaust Manifold

REMOVAL & INSTALLATION

1. Raise the vehicle and support on jackstands. Disconnect and tag the spark plug wires.
2. Disconnect the exhaust crossover pipe from the manifolds on both sides of the engine and lower it. Disconnect the choke pipe if working on the right side, the Early Fuel Evaporation (EFE) line if working on the left side. Disconnect the oxygen sensor wire. Remove the heat shield, if equipped.
3. Disconnect the turbocharger, if so equipped.
4. Remove the exhaust manifold-to-cylinder head bolts.
5. Remove the manifold from beneath the vehicle.

6. Installation is the reverse of the removal procedure. Always use new bolt locks on the exhaust manifold mounting bolts.

Turbocharger Assembly

REMOVAL & INSTALLATION

1982–83

1. Disconnect the exhaust inlet and outlet pipes from the turbocharger.
2. Disconnect the oil feed pipe from the center housing.
3. Remove the nut attaching the air intake elbow to the carburetor and remove the elbow and the flex tube from the carburetor.
4. Disconnect the accelerator, cruise and detent linkages from the carburetor. Disconnect the plenum linkage bracket.
5. Remove the two bolts attaching the plenum to the side bracket.
6. Disconnect the fuel line and all vacuum lines from the carburetor.
7. Drain the cooling system.
8. Disconnect the coolant lines from the front and rear of the plenum.
9. Disconnect the power brake vacuum line from the plenum.
10. Remove the two bolts attaching the turbine housing to the intake manifold bracket.
11. Remove the two bolts attaching the EGR valve manifold to the plenum. Loosen the two bolts attaching the EGR valve to the intake manifold.
12. Remove the A.I.R. bypass hose from the check valve.

13. Remove the three bolts attaching the compressor housing to the intake manifold.
14. Remove the turbocharger, actuator, carburetor and plenum from the engine.
15. Remove the six bolts attaching the carburetor and plenum to the turbocharger and actuator.
16. Remove the oil drain from the center housing.

To install:

1. Install the oil drain on the center housing. Torque the bolts to 15 ft. lbs.
2. Install the six turbocharger actuator to plenum bolts.
3. Place the assembly on the engine and connect all vacuum hoses.
4. Install the three bolts attaching the compressor housing to the intake manifold. Torque the bolts to 35 ft. lbs.
5. Install the A.I.R. bypass hose.
6. Loosely install the two bolts attaching the EGR valve to the plenum. Tighten the two bolts attaching the EGR valve to 15 ft. lbs. Tighten the EGR manifold to plenum bolts to 15 ft. lbs.
7. Install the two bolts attaching the turbine housing to the intake manifold bracket. Torque the bolts to 20 ft. lbs.
8. Connect the power brake vacuum line at the plenum. Torque the bolts to 10 ft. lbs.
9. Connect the plenum front bracket and install one bolt attaching the bracket to the manifold. Torque the bolt to 20 ft. lbs.
10. Connect the coolant hoses to the plenum.
11. Refill the cooling system.

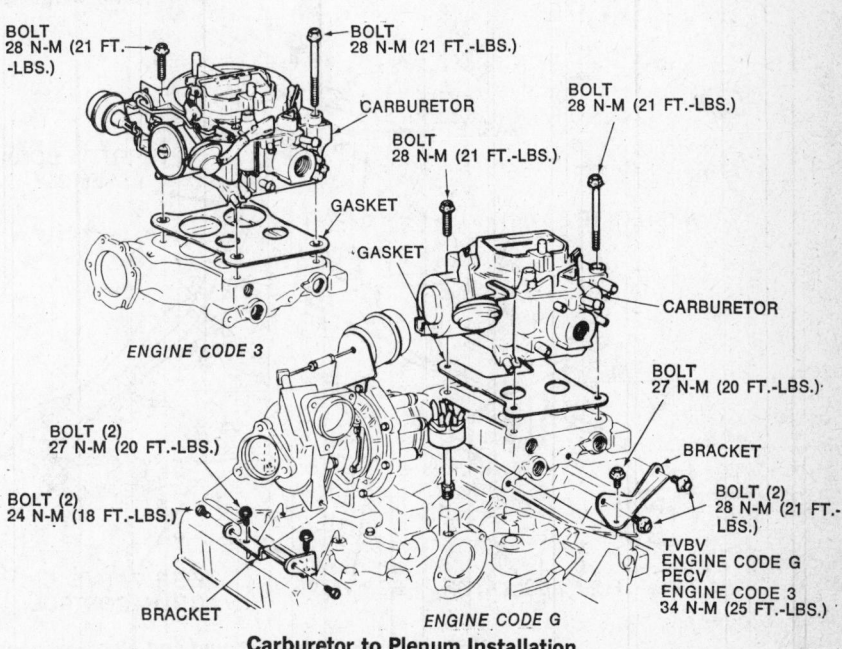

Carburetor to Plenum Installation

12. Connect the fuel line and remaining vacuum hoses.

13. Install the two bolts attaching the plenum to the side bracket. Torque the bolts to 20 ft. lbs.

14. Connect the linkage bracket to the plenum. Torque the bolts to 20 ft. lbs.

15. Connect the accelerator, detent and cruise control linkages.

16. Install the nut attaching the air intake elbow to the carburetor. Torque the bolts to 15 ft. lbs.

17. Connect the oil feed pipe to the center housing. Torque the bolts to 7 ft. lbs.

18. Connect the inlet and outlet pipes to the turbocharger. Torque the bolts to 14 ft. lbs.

1984–85

1. Disconnect the negative battery cable. Remove the air inlet tube at the throttle body.

2. Disconnect the throttle body vacuum harness connector.

3. Disconnect the water lines at the throttle body. Plug the lines in order to prevent coolant loss.

4. Remove the throttle body retaining bolts. Remove the throttle body assembly.

5. Disconnect and plug the oil pressure feed line at the turbocharger assembly.

6. Disconnect the exhaust inlet pipe at the exhaust manifold and at the turbocharger. Disconnect the outlet pipe at the turbocharger.

7. Remove the turbocharger mounting bracket nuts that attach the upper to lower bracket on the right side of the assembly.

8. Remove the turbocharger stabilizer bracket bolt at the compressor housing on the left side.

9. Remove the turbocharger assembly from the manifold adapter.

10. Installation is the reverse of the removal procedure.

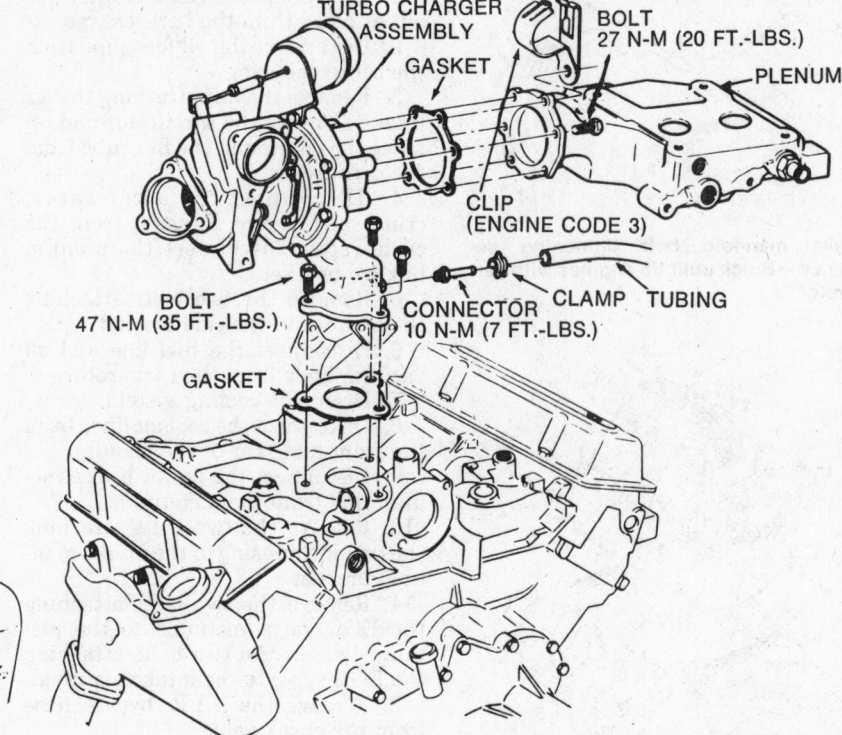

Turbocharger and Plenum Assembly

1986–87 turbocharger assembly with intercooler

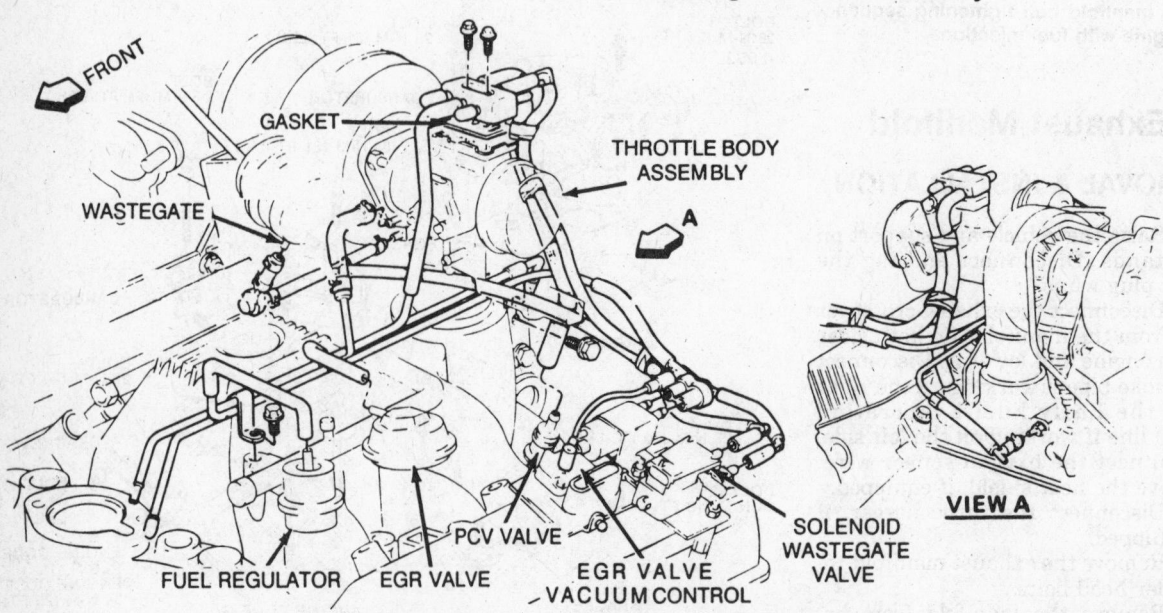

1984–85 turbocharger vacuum and electrical connections

NOTE: Before installing the turbocharger assembly be sure that it is first charged with oil. Failure to do this may cause damage to the assembly.

1986–87

1. Disconnect the negative battery cable. Remove the air inlet hose from the compressor section of the turbocharger.
2. Disconnect the compressor outlet pipe from the compressor.
3. Disconnect the oil breather and turbocharger heat shields.
4. Remove the exhaust pipe from the turbine outlet.
5. Remove the oil breather vent from the valve cover. Disconnect and plug the oil pressure feed line at the turbocharger assembly.
6. Remove the turbocharger mounting bracket nuts. Disconnect the turbine inlet pipe from the exhaust manifold.
7. Disconnect the oil return line from turbocharger.
8. Remove the vacuum line from the turbocharger wastegate actuator.
9. Disconnect the intercooler outlet to throttle body pipe.
10. Remove the turbocharger assembly from the manifold adapter.
11. Installation is the reverse of the removal procedure. Always use new gaskets during installation.

TROUBLESHOOTING

For more information on turbocharging, please refer to "Turbocharging" in the Unit Repair section.

Front Cover and Oil Seal

REMOVAL & INSTALLATION

V6 Engine

1. Disconnect the negative battery cable. Drain the radiator.
2. Disconnect the radiator hoses and the heater return hose at the water pump.
3. Remove the fan assembly and pulleys. Remove the crankshaft vibration damper.
4. Remove the fuel pump, if carbureted . Remove the alternator.
5. Remove the distributor, if equipped. If timing chain and sprockets are not going to be disturbed, note position of distributor rotor for reinstallation in same position.
6. Loosen and slide front clamp on thermostat bypass hose rearward.

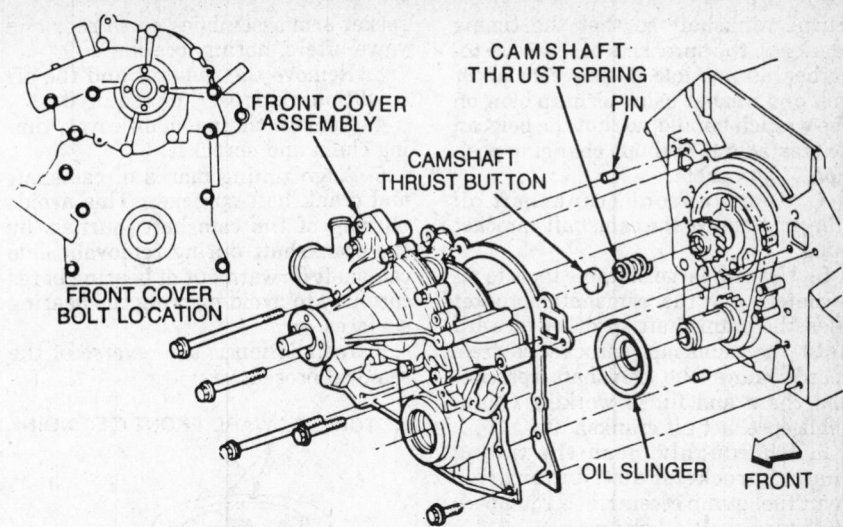

Timing chain cover installation—3.8L V6 engine

7. Remove bolts attaching timing chain cover to cylinder block. Remove two oil pan to timing chain cover bolts. Remove timing chain cover assembly and gasket.
8. Thoroughly clean the cover, taking care to avoid damage to the gasket surface.
9. Installation is the reverse of the removal procedure.
10. Remove oil pump cover and pack the space around the oil pump gears completely full of petroleum jelly. There must be no air space left inside the pump. Reinstall cover using new gasket.
11. To replace the front oil seal, use a punch and drive out the old seal and shedder. Drive the seal out from the front toward the rear of the timing chain cover.
12. Coil new packing around opening so ends of packing are at top. Drive in shedder using suitable punch. Stake the shedder in place in at least 3 places.
13. Size the packing by rotating a hammer handle or similar tool around the packing until the balancer hub can be inserted through the opening.
14. Torque the front cover retaining bolts to 28 ft. lbs. (39 Nm).

Timing Chain and Sprockets

REMOVAL & INSTALLATION

V6 Engine

1. Disconnect the negative battery cable.
2. Drain the cooling system. Remove the engine front cover.
3. With timing chain cover removed, temporarily install balancer bolt and washer in end of crankshaft.

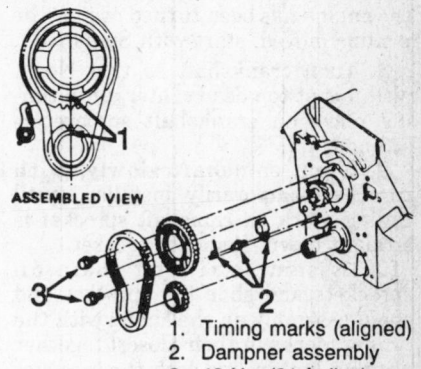

1. Timing marks (aligned)
2. Dampner assembly
3. 42 Nm.(31 ft. lbs.)

V6 engine timing marks

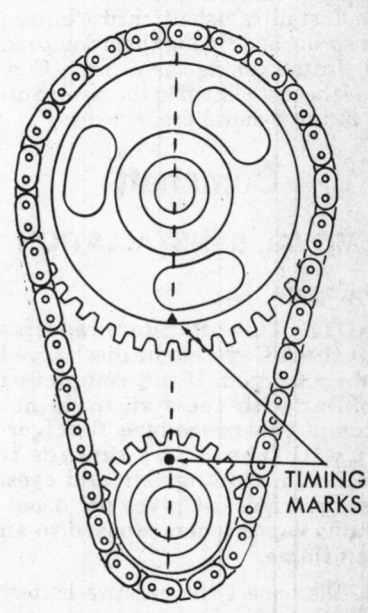

Timing mark alignment—V6 engine

Turn crankshaft so that the timing marks on the sprockets are as close together as possible. Remove balancer bolt and washer using a sharp blow on the wrench handle, so that the bolt can be started out without changing position of sprockets.

4. Remove front crankshaft oil slinger. Remove the camshaft sprocket bolts.

5. Use two large suitable tools to alternately pry the camshaft sprocket then the crankshaft sprocket forward until the camshaft sprocket is free, then remove the camshaft sprocket and chain and finish working crankshaft sprocket off crankshaft.

6. Thoroughly clean the timing chain, sprockets, distributor drive gear, fuel pump eccentric (if equipped) and crankshaft oil slinger.

7. If the pistons have not been moved in the engine, go to Step 10. If the engine has been turned over or the pistons moved, start with Step 8.

8. Turn crankshaft so that No. 1 piston is at top dead center, until timing mark on crankshaft sprocket is straight up.

9. Turn camshaft slowly, with sprocket temporarily installed, until timing mark on camshaft sprocket is straight down. Remove sprocket.

10. Assemble timing chain on sprockets and slide the sprocket and chain assembly on the shafts with the timing marks in their closest together position and in line with the sprocket hubs.

11. Assemble slinger on crankshaft with large part of cone to front of engine.

12. Install camshaft sprocket bolts. Torque to specification.

13. Install camshaft thrust button and spring and timing chain dampers.

14. Install timing chain cover. Continue the installation in the reverse order of the removal procedure.

Camshaft

REMOVAL & INSTALLATION

V6 Engine

NOTE: This procedure requires that the A/C system be discharged and recharged. If not completely familiar with the system, do not attempt this procedure. Refrigerant will freeze any surface it touches, including skin and eyes. Also, refrigerant gives off a poisonous vapor when exposed to an open flame.

1. Disconnect the negative battery cable. Drain the radiator.

2. Remove the intake manifold. Remove the rocker covers. Remove the

rocker arm assemblies, push rods and valve lifters, noting location.

3. Remove the radiator and the air condition condenser, as required.

4. Remove timing chain cover, timing chain and sprocket.

5. Align timing marks of camshaft and crankshaft sprocket. This avoids burring of the camshaft journals by the crankshaft during removal. Slide camshaft forward out of bearing bores carefully to avoid marring the bearing surfaces.

6. Installation is the reverse of the removal procedure.

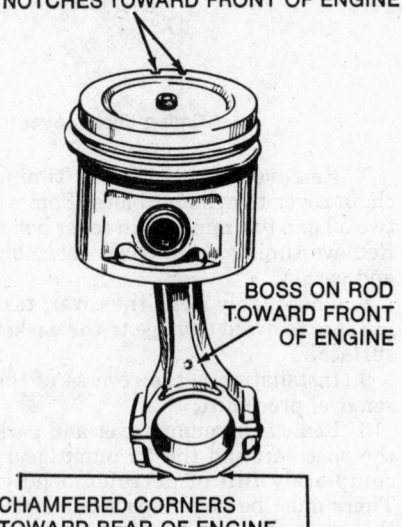

NOTCHES TOWARD FRONT OF ENGINE

BOSS ON ROD TOWARD FRONT OF ENGINE

CHAMFERED CORNERS TOWARD REAR OF ENGINE

RIGHT NO. 2-4-6

Right bank piston and rod positioning—231 and 252

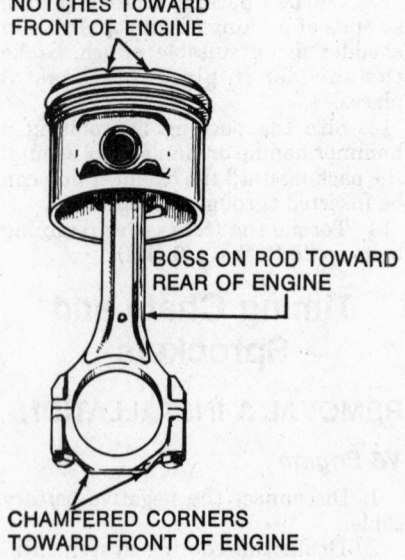

NOTCHES TOWARD FRONT OF ENGINE

BOSS ON ROD TOWARD REAR OF ENGINE

CHAMFERED CORNERS TOWARD FRONT OF ENGINE

LEFT NO. 1-3-5

Left bank piston and rod positioning—231 and 252

7. Before installing the camshaft and the lifters, be sure to coat them with clean engine oil.

8. Be sure to use new gaskets and seals as required.

Pistons and Connecting Rods

POSITIONING

NOTE: For all piston and connecting rod overhaul procedures, please refer to "Engine Rebuilding" in the Unit Repair Section.

ENGINE LUBRICATION

Oil Pan

REMOVAL & INSTALLATION

V6 Engine

1. Disconnect the negative battery cable.

2. Raise the vehicle and support it safely. Drain the engine oil.

3. Remove the flywheel cover and the engine crossover pipe.

4. Remove the engine mounts from frame brackets.

5. Raise engine and support it safely.

6. Remove the oil pan bolts. Remove the oil pan from the engine assembly.

7. Installation is the reverse of removal.

V8 Engine

1. Disconnect the negative battery cable. Remove the engine oil dipstick.

2. Remove the fan shroud attaching screws. Raise and support the vehicle safely. Remove distributor cap and align rotor in the No. 1 firing position. This positions the crankshaft counter weights and connecting rods for the least amount of interference with the oil pan.

3. Drain the engine oil from the oil pan into a suitable drain pan. Remove the flywheel cover and crossover pipe.

4. Remove the starter. Using a jack, with a block of wood on top, place it under the crankshaft hub to support the engine. Remove the engine mounts at the cylinder block.

5. Raise the front of engine as high as possible. Remove the oil pan retaining bolts and remove the oil pan from the engine.

CAUTION

Use care when removing oil pan gasket which has a steel core that when it is exposed, can cause injury.

6. Clean all the gasket material from the pan and the block mating surfaces. Use a new gasket kit and sealer. Make sure the seals are firmly positioned on the flange surfaces with each seal properly located in the cutout notches of the pan gasket.

7. Installation is the reverse of the removal procedure.

Rear Main Bearing Oil Seal

REMOVAL & INSTALLATION

NOTE: Braided fabric seals are used on all Buick engines. The upper seal half cannot be replaced without removing the crankshaft.

1. Remove the oil pan and rear main bearing cap.

2. Remove the old seal from the bearing cap and place a new seal in the groove with both ends projecting above the mating surface of the cap.

3. Force the seal into the groove by rubbing down with a smooth tool, until the seal projects above the groove not more than $\frac{1}{16}$ in. Cut the ends off flush with the surface of the cap with a sharp tool.

4. On the 231 and 252 engines, place new neoprene seals in the grooves in the sides of the bearing cap after soaking the seals in kerosene for a minute or two.

NOTE: The neoprene composition seals will swell up once exposed to the oil and heat. It is normal for the seals to leak for a short time, until they become properly seated. The seals must NOT be cut to fit.

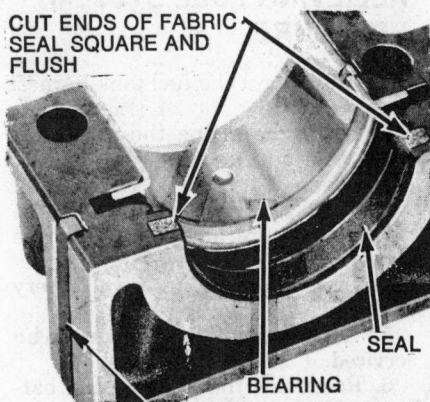

Rear main bearing cap

5. When installing, use a small amount of sealer on the bearing cap mating surface.

6. Install the bearing cap on the engine and refer to the torque specification chart for the proper tightening torque for the vehicle's engine.

NOTE: Unless the crankshaft has been removed, do not torque any other main bearing cap bolts other than the rear main.

7. When finished, operate the engine at low rpm when first started. This will give the seal time to seat in the cap and against the crankshaft.

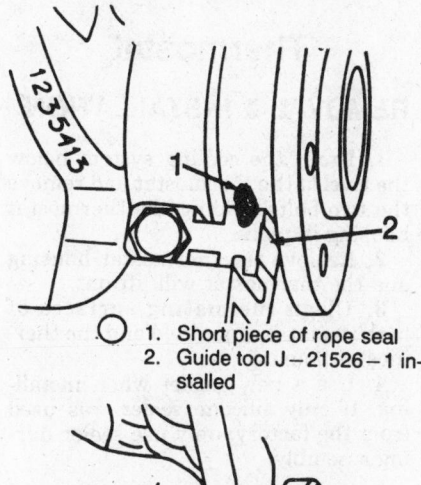

1. Short piece of rope seal
2. Guide tool J–21526–1 installed

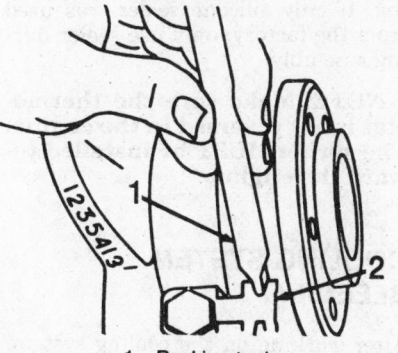

1. Packing tool
2. Guide tool

Rear main oil seal installation – V6 engine

Oil Pump

REMOVAL & INSTALLATION

NOTE: On Buick V6 engines, the oil pump is located on the left side of the timing chain cover. It is connected by a drilled passage in the cylinder crankcase, to an oil screen housing and standpipe assembly.

1. Remove the oil filter.

2. Unbolt the pump cover assembly from the timing chain cover.

3. Remove the cover assembly and slide out the pump gears.

4. Remove the oil pressure relief valve cap, spring and valve. Do not remove the oil filter by-pass valve and spring.

5. Check that the relief valve spring is not worn on the side, or collapsed.

6. Check that the relief valve is no more than an easy "slip-fit" in the bore in the cover.

NOTE: If there is any perceptible sideplay in the relief valve, replace the valve. If there is still sideplay, replace the cover also.

8. Check the filter by-pass valve for wear. Replace if necessary.

To assemble the pump:

9. Lubricate and install the pressure relief valve and spring in the cover bore. Install the gasket and cap, torquing the cap to 35 ft. lbs.

10. Install the gears and check that gear-to-cover end clearance is between 0.002–0.006 in. If the clearance is less, check the timing cover gear pocket for wear.

11. Remove the gears and pack the gear pocket full of petroleum jelly. Don't use grease.

CAUTION

Unless the pump is primed this way, it won't produce any oil pressure when the engine is started.

12. Install the gears. Install a new gasket and the cover. Torque the bolts evenly to 10 ft. lbs. Replace the oil filter when finshed.

ENGINE COOLING

Radiator

REMOVAL & INSTALLATION

1982–85 LeSabre and Electra
1982–89 Estate Wagon

1. Drain the radiator and disconnect the upper and lower radiator hoses. Disconnect the transmission fluid cooling lines at the radiator. Plug the cooling lines to prevent fluid loss.

2. Disconnect the coolant recovery tank hose.

3. Remove the fan shroud to radiator screws. Lift the shroud out of the bottom clips and hang the shroud over the fan.

4. Remove the radiator upper cover panel.

5. Remove the radiator.

6. Before installation, check the condition of the lower radiator hose and clamps. It's easier to replace the hose while there is working room.

7. Installation is the reverse of the removal procedure. Fill the cooling system and check for leaks when finished.

1982–87 Regal

1. Drain the radiator and disconnect the radiator hoses and coolant recovery tank hose. Disconnect the transmission fluid cooling lines at the radiator. Plug the cooling lines to prevent fluid loss.

2. Remove the fan with the fan clutch. Support the fan in an upright position after removal.

3. Remove the fan housing attaching screws and lift out the shroud. On models which have the fan shroud stapled together, remove the staples and remove the upper shroud half. During assembly, the shroud halves must be drilled and bolted or riveted together.

4. Remove the radiator. Installation is the reverse of removal.

NOTE: Some air conditioned models have a high-pressure A/C line which runs across the top of the upper radiator shroud. It is not necessary to remove the line in order to remove the shroud. If the A/C line is clamped to the shroud, disconnect the clamp. Carefully slide the upper shroud half out from under the A/C line, toward the passenger side of the vehicle with the fan removed.

Water Pump

REMOVAL & INSTALLATION

1. Drain the cooling system. Remove the fan shroud.

2. Loosen the drive belt(s) and remove the fan blade and pulley(s) from the hub on the water pump. Remove the drive belt(s).

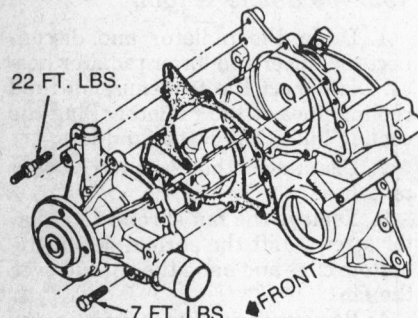

22 FT. LBS.

7 FT. LBS. ◄FRONT

Water pump mounting–V6 engine

3. Disconnect the hose from the water pump inlet and heater hose from the nipple. Remove the water pump mounting bolts and remove the pump and gasket from the timing case cover.

4. Clean the mounting surfaces and install the pump with a new gasket. Bolts and lock washers must be torqued evenly.

5. Connect the radiator hose to the pump inlet and the heater hose to the nipple. Fill the cooling system and check all points of possible coolant leaks.

6. Install the fan pulley or pulleys and the fan blade. Install the drive belt(s) and adjust the tension.

Thermostat

REMOVAL & INSTALLATION

1. Drain the cooling system below the level of the thermostat and remove the two bolts holding the thermostat housing in place.

2. Remove the thermostat housing and the thermostat will lift out.

3. Clean the mating surfaces of both the intake manifold and the thermostat housing.

4. Use a new gasket when installing. If only silicone sealer was used from the factory, only use sealer during assembly.

NOTE: Make sure the thermostat is not reversed in the engine. The spring MUST be installed toward the engine.

COOLING SYSTEM BLEEDING

After working on the cooling system, even to replace the thermostat, it must be bled. Air trapped in the system will prevent proper filling and leave the radiator coolant level low, causing a risk of overheating.

1. To bleed the system, start with the system cool, the radiator cap off and the radiator filled to about an inch below the filler neck.

2. Start the engine and run it at slightly above normal idle speed. This will insure adequate circulation. If air bubbles appear and the coolant level drops, fill the system with an antifreeze/water mixture to bring the level back to the proper level.

3. Run the engine this way until the thermostat opens. When this happens, coolant will move abruptly across the top of the radiator and the temperature of the radiator will suddenly rise.

4. At this point, air is often expelled and the level may drop quite a bit.

Keep refilling the system until the level is near the top of the radiator and remains constant.

5. If the vehicle has an overflow tank, fill the radiator right up to the filler neck. Replace the radiator filler cap.

EMISSION CONTROLS

NOTE: Please refer to "Emission Controls" in the Unit Repair section for system maintanence. Due to the complex nature of modern electronic engine control systems, comprehensive diagnosis and testing procedures fall outside the confines of this repair manual. For complete information on diagnosis, testing and repair procedures concerning all modern engine and emission control systems, refer to *"Chilton's Guide To Electronic Engine Controls"*

GASOLINE FUEL SYSTEM

Fuel System Service Precaution

Whenever working on fuel injected engines, always relieve the fuel before opening the fuel system for service.

RELIEVING FUEL SYSTEM PRESSURE

1. Disconnect the fuel tank harness connector.

2. Crank the engine, the engine will start and run until all the fuel is consumed.

3. Crank the starter for three seconds to be sure all fuel pressure is relieved.

4. Disconnect the negative battery cable.

5. The fuel system can now be serviced.

6. Reconnect the harness and battery cable only after all work is completed on the system and the system is completely together.

NOTE: An additional precaution can be taken by wrapping a shop towel around the fuel line being opened in case there is any remaining pressure in the system. However, this should NEVER be substitited for relieving the pressure.

Fuel Filter

REMOVAL & INSTALLATION

Carbureted Models

1. Disconnect the fuel line connection at the inlet of the carburetor.
2. Remove the inlet fuel filter nut from the carburetor.
3. Remove the filter element and spring.
4. If the filter is a bronze element, blow through the cone end; the element should allow air to pass freely.
5. Install the spring and a new element into the carburetor. Bronze elements are installed with the small section of the cone facing outward.
6. Install a new gasket on the fitting nut and install the nut.
7. Install the fuel line and tighten it securely. Start the engine and check for leaks.

Fuel Injection Models

——— **CAUTION** ———

The fuel system is under pressure. Refer to "Releiving Fuel System Pressure" before attempting to open or remove any fuel lines.

The fuel injection system uses an inline filter located in the fuel feed line under the hood, attached to the frame rail, or on the rear crossmember of the vehicle. Always use a backup wrench on the fittings any time a fuel filter is removed or installed, and never replace a metal fuel line with a rubber insert. The high pressure fuel system used with all fuel injection systems requires metal fuel lines to contain the pressure. Replace the O-ring at the connection and torque the fuel fitting to 22 ft. lbs.

Fuel Pump

All air conditioned cars with carbureted V8 engines have a special fuel pump. This pump has a vapor return line which returns hot fuel and fuel vapor to the fuel tank. The possibility of vapor lock is thus greatly reduced by keeping cool fuel circulating through the pump.

The fuel pump used on engines equipped with fuel injection is an electric, high-pressure unit that maintains a constant fuel pressure of 28–50 psi.

It is attached to the fuel sending unit located in the fuel tank.

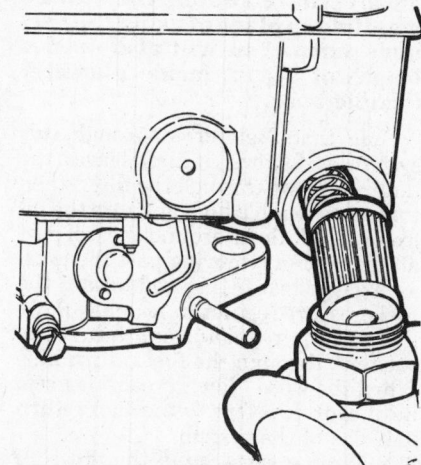

Fuel filter installation–carbureted models

REMOVAL & INSTALLATION

Mechanical Fuel Pump

1. Disconnect the fuel inlet hose from the pump. Disconnect the vapor return hose, if equipped. Disconnect the inlet hose.
2. Remove the two mounting bolts.
3. Remove the fuel pump.
4. Clean the mating surfaces and install a new gasket.
5. Install the fuel pump and tighten the bolts.
6. Reconnect the hoses, start the engine and check for leaks.

Electric Fuel Pump

——— **CAUTION** ———

The fuel injection system is constantly under pressure. Fuel pressure must be relieved before disconnecting any fuel lines. To relieve the fuel pressure, disconnect the fuel pump wiring harness and start the engine. Allow the engine to run until it stalls, then crank the engine an additional three seconds to make sure all fuel is exhausted from the lines. Reconnect the harness after all service is completed.

1. Relieve the fuel system pressure as described above.
2. Disconnect the negative battery cable.
3. Raise and support the vehicle safely.
4. Remove the fuel tank as outlined under "Fuel Tank Removal".
5. Remove the fuel tank sending unit and pump assembly by turning the cam lock ring counterclockwise. Lift the assembly from the fuel tank and remove the fuel pump from the sending unit.

6. Pull the fuel pump up into the attaching hose while pulling outward away from the bottom support. Take care to prevent damage to the rubber insulator and strainer during removal. After the pump assembly is clear of the bottom support, pull the pump assembly out of the rubber connector for removal.
7. Inspect the pump attaching hose for any signs of deterioration and replace if necessary. Check the rubber sound insulator at the bottom of the pump and replace as required.
8. Push the fuel pump into the attaching hose.
9. Install the tank sending unit and pump assembly into the fuel tank. Use a new O-ring during assembly.
10. Install the cam lock over the assembly and lock into place by turning clockwise.
11. Install the fuel tank.

PRESSURE TESTING

Electric Fuel Pump

When the ignition switch is turned ON, the intank fuel pump is energized for as long as the engine is cranking or running and the control unit is receiving signals from the HEI distributor. If there are no reference pulses, the control unit will shut off the fuel pump within two seconds. The pump will deliver fuel to the fuel rail and injectors, then the pressure regulator where the system pressure is controlled to maintain 24-46 psi. The pressure is regulated down in direct relation to the manifold vacuum so that fuel metering will be directly proportional to time under all operating conditions. Thus, reading fuel pressure under various engine operating conditions can help find the source of fuel system problems.

1984–85 Models

1. Wrap a rag around the pressure tap to absorb any leakage that may occur when installing the gauge and then connect pressure gauge J–34730–1, or equivalent, to the fuel pressure test point on the fuel rail.
2. Turn the ignition ON and check that pump pressure is 34–40 psi. This pressure is controlled by spring pressure within the regulator assembly.
3. Start the engine and allow it to idle. The fuel pressure should drop to 28–32 psi due to the lower manifold pressure.

NOTE: The fuel pressure at idle will vary somewhat depending on barometric presure. Check for a drop in pressure indicating regulator control, rather than specific values.

4. Use a low pressure air pump to apply air pressure to the regulator to simulate turbocharger boost pressure. Boost pressure should increase fuel pressure one pound for every pound of boost. Again, look for consistent changes rather than specific pressures. The maximum fuel pressure should not exceed 46 psi.

5. If the fuel pressure drops, check the operation of the check valve, the pump coupling connection, fuel pressure regulator valve and the injectors. A restricted fuel line or filter may also cause a pressure drop. To check the fuel pump output, restrict the fuel return line and run 12 volts to the pump. The fuel pressure should rise to approximately 75 psi with the return line restricted.

1986–87 Models

—————— CAUTION ——————

In many of the steps in the procedure below, it is necessary for you to disconnect fuel lines. Note that you must always depressurize the system as described above, before disconnecting these lines. Failure to do this will result in a high pressure spray of fuel which could ignite and cause a fire.

NOTE: To perform all of the steps of this test, it will be necessary to supply a source of 12–14 in. Hg. of vacuum to the fuel pressure regulator. A hand vacuum pump of some sort is useful in doing this; an accurate gauge and fittings needed to tee it into the vacuum line are required. You may be able to rig a vacuum line from an alternate tap on the intake manifold in place of using the vacuum pump. You will also need a length of ⁵⁄₁₆ in. inside diameter flexible hose.

Note that fuel flows through this system as follows: It first leaves the tank and flows through the filter, then through a flexible hose and into the injector rail. It flows around the rail past all six injectors, moving past the pressure gauge test fitting and toward the fuel pressure regulator. It finally flows through the regulator and returns to the tank through the fuel return line. When the word "downstream" is used, it, of course, refers to the fuel return line side of the system.

1. Wrap a rag around the pressure tap to absorb any leakage that may occur when installing the gauge and then connect pressure gauge J–34730–1, or equivalent, to the fuel pressure test point on the fuel rail. This is located between the No. 6 injector and the pressure regulator on the injector fuel rail.

2. Make sure the ignition switch has been off for at least 10 seconds and that the air conditioning is off, if the car has it. Then, turn the ignition switch on, noting the sound of the fuel pump.

3. Verify that the pump runs for about two seconds. Then, check fuel pressure. It should be 25–35 psi. If there is some pressure but it is outside of specification, go to Step 6. If there is no pressure at all, see the procedure below for checking the fuel system wiring. Turn off the ignition switch. Note whether or not the pressure holds by watching the gauge for more than 10 seconds. If it does, proceed with the next step; if the pressure is correct but does not hold, proceed with the rest of this step:

a. Pinch the fuel supply hose closed tightly at the flex hose on the downstream (pressure regulator) side of the fuel pressure gauge test fitting.

b. Turn on (or have an assistant turn on) the ignition switch *just* until the pressure rises to specification. Then, turn it back off. Watch the pressure to see if it holds. If it drops off, check for a leaking flex coupling at the pump. Otherwise, check and, if necessary, replace the in-tank fuel pump. If the pressure does not hold, proceed with "c".

c. Move the pinching device (or your fingers) to the flex hose on the downstream side of the fuel pressure regulator. Then, repeat the application of power to the fuel pump by turning on the ignition switch for a few seconds, and then turning it back off after the pump stops.

d. If the pressure holds now, replace the pressure regulator assembly. If not, remove the spark plugs to check for a flooded cylinder. If the cylinder is flooding, the plugs will show evidence of dry, soft, black soot in most cases. If the engine has been cranked a great deal recently, there may actually be a smell of raw fuel on the plug. If the cylinder has been flooding, this will be due to a leaking injector. Replace that cylinder's injector unit.

e. If the problem is not due to a leaking injector, check for small but visible leaks in the injector pipe, connections, or flexible hoses and repair as necessary.

4. Start the engine and allow it to idle. If necessary, run it until it warms up; this test must be done with the engine at normal operating temperature. With the engine idling and at operating temperature (so that warm coolant is flowing through the radiator), read the fuel pressure. It should be 25–35 psi. If the system meets this specification, search for trouble in areas other than fuel pump and pressure regulator performance.

5. If the pressure is outside this range, continue running the test and disconnect the vacuum hose from the fuel pressure regulator. Supply a vacuum of 12–14 in. Hg to the vacuum connection on the regulator. The fuel pressure should be 24–35 psi. If it is now within the specified range, locate and correct the cause of insufficient

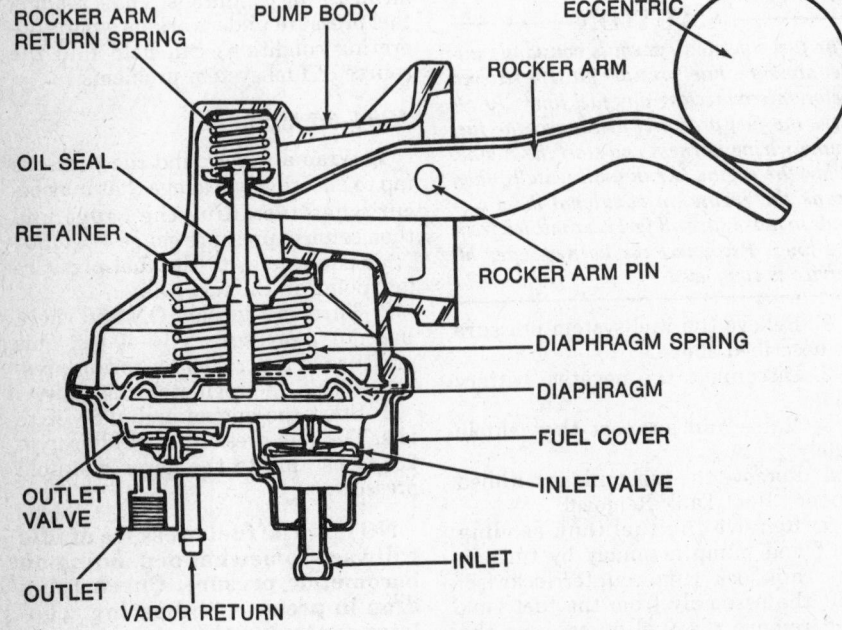

Cut away view of mechanical fuel pump

ROCKER ARM RETURN SPRING
PUMP BODY
ECCENTRIC
ROCKER ARM
OIL SEAL
RETAINER
ROCKER ARM PIN
DIAPHRAGM SPRING
DIAPHRAGM
FUEL COVER
INLET VALVE
OUTLET VALVE
OUTLET
VAPOR RETURN
INLET

vacuum to the regulator. This might be a broken connection, cracked or soft line that pinches closed under high vacuum, or a clogged line or connection. If the fuel pressure is still incorrect, replace the pressure regulator.

6. This Step is for fuel pressure that is too low; if pressure is too high, go to Step 8. Depressurize the system, remove the fuel filter and tilt it to drain the intake (tank) side into a metal container. Check for the presence of water and dirt. If there is evidence of more than a minimal amount of either, install a new filter and recheck the pressures.

7. Pinch the fuel return line downstream of the pressure regulator to close it off tightly. Then, turn on the ignition switch until the pressure stabilizes and read the pressure gauge. Pressure should be above 75 psi. If it is, check for a restricted pressure line or flexible hose in the line somewhere between the tank and the test gauge. If all the lines are okay, replace the pressure regulator. If the pressure is below 75 psi, check the hose coupling the tank to the pressure line and, if that's okay, replace the pump, which must be faulty or of incorrect specification.

8. Depressurize the system and then disconnect the flexible hose from the return line. Attach the $^5/_{16}$ in. inside diameter flexible hose to the return line connection on the pressure regulator. Insert the downstream end into a metal container. Turn the ignition switch on for just two seconds and read the fuel pressure. It should be 37–43 psi. If it is, you will have to clean or repair the return line to the tank to remove an obstruction. If it is not, replace the fuel pressure regulator.

Carburetor

REMOVAL & INSTALLATION

1. Remove the air cleaner. Disconnect the throttle linkage.
2. Disconnect and plug the fuel line.
3. Disconnect and tag all vacuum lines and electrical connectors to the carburetor.
4. Remove the carburetor mounting bolts.
5. Remove the carburetor.
6. Installation is the reverse of the removal procedure

OVERHAUL

For all carburetor overhaul procedures, please refer to "Carburetor Service" in the Unit Repair section.

Fuel Injection

Due to the complex nature of modern fuel injection systems, comprehensive diagnosis and testing procedures fall outside the confines of this repair manual. For complete information on fuel injection diagnosis, repair and testing procedures, please refer to *"Chilton's Guide To Fuel Injection And Feedback Carburetors".*

DIESEL FUEL SYSTEM

Fuel Filter

The fuel filter is located on the back of the engine above the intake manifold.

REPLACEMENT

1. Disconnect the negative battery cable. Relieve the fuel system pressure.
2. Disconnect the fuel lines from the filter. Plug the lines to prevent dirt from entering the system.
3. Remove the filter retaining bolts
4. Remove the filter.
5. Install the lines to the new filter. Start the engine and check for leaks.

DRAINING WATER FROM THE SYSTEM

NOTE: If the "WATER IN FUEL" light does come on, and the fuel system is not purged of water, engine fuel injection system damage could result.

1. Vehicles that have a "WATER IN FUEL" light may have the water removed from the tank by a pump or siphon.

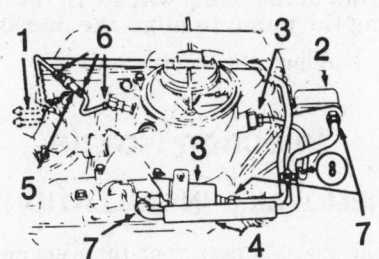

1. Return line
2. Fuel filter
3. Fuel pump
4. Fuel line heater (optional)
5. Housing pressure altitude advance
6. 10 ft. lbs.
7. 19 ft. lbs.
8. 11 ft. lbs.

Fuel lines—V6 diesel engine

2. The pump or siphon hose should be hooked up to the 1/4 in. fuel return hose (smaller of the two) above the rear axle or under the hood near the fuel pump. Siphoning should continue until all water is removed from the fuel tank.

3. Use a clear plastic hose to determine when clear fuel begins to flow. Be sure to remove the cap on the fuel tank during this procedure. Be sure two replace the cap when finished.

4. Use the same precautions with diesel fuel as with gasoline.

Diesel Injection Pump

REMOVAL & INSTALLATION

1. Disconnect the negative battery cable. Remove the air cleaner.
2. Remove the filters and pipes from the valve covers and air crossover.

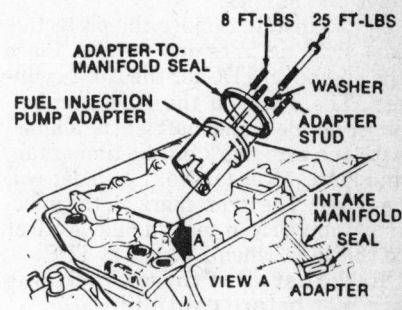

Injection pump adapter bolts

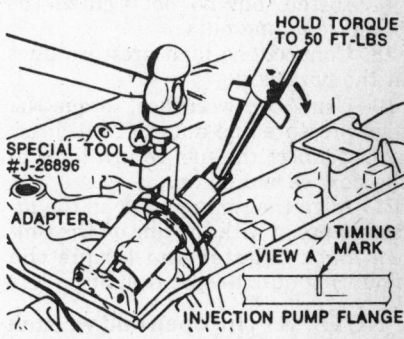

Marking injection pump adapter

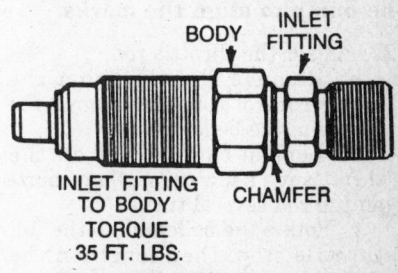

Fuel injector—V6 diesel engine

3. Remove the air crossover and cap the intake manifold with screened covers or tape.

4. Disconnect the throttle rod and return spring.

5. Remove the bellcrank.

6. Remove the throttle and transmission cables from the intake manifold brackets.

7. Disconnect the fuel lines from the filter and remove the filter.

8. Disconnect the fuel inlet line at the pump.

9. Remove the rear air conditioner compressor brace and remove the fuel line.

10. Disconnect the fuel return line from the injection pump.

11. Remove the clamps and pull the fuel return lines from each injection nozzle.

12. Using two wrenches, disconnect the high pressure lines at the nozzles.

13. Remove the three injection pump retaining nuts with tool J-26987 or its equivalent.

14. Remove the pump and cap all lines and nozzles.

15. To install, remove the protective caps from all lines and nozzles. Place the engine on TDC for the No. 1 cylinder. The mark on the harmonic balancer on the crankshaft will be aligned with the zero mark on the timing tab, and both valves for No. 1 cylinder will be closed. The index mark on the injection pump driven gear should be offset to the right when No. 1 is at TDC. **Check that all of these conditions are met before continuing.**

16. Line up the offset tang on the pump driveshaft with the pump driven gear and install the pump.

17. Install, but do not tighten the pump retaining nuts.

18. Connect the high pressure lines at the nozzles.

19. Using two wrenches, torque the high pressure line nuts to 25 ft. lbs.

20. Connect the fuel return lines to the nozzles and pump.

21. Align the timing mark on the injection pump with the line on the timing mark adapter and torque the mounting nuts to specification.

NOTE: A ¾ in. open end wrench on the boss at the front of the injection pump will aid in rotating the pump to align the marks.

22. Adjust the throttle rod:

a. Remove the clip from the cruise control rod and remove the rod from the bellcrank.

b. Loosen the locknut on the throttle rod a few turns, then shorten the rod several turns.

c. Rotate the bellcrank to the full throttle stop, then lengthen the throttle rod until the injection pump

lever contacts the injection pump full throttle stop, then release the bellcrank.

d. Tighten the throttle rod locknut.

23. Install the fuel inlet line between the transfer pump and the filter.

24. Install the rear air conditioner compressor brace.

25. Install the bellcrank and clip.

26. Connect the throttle rod and return spring.

27. Adjust the transmission cable:

a. Push the snaplock to the disengaged position.

b. Rotate the injection pump lever to the full throttle stop and hold it there.

c. Push in the snaplock until it is flush.

d. Release the injection pump lever.

28. Remove the screened covers or tape and install the air crossover.

29. Install the tubes in the air flow control valve in the air crossover and install the ventilation filters in the valve covers. Install the air cleaner.

30. Start the engine and allow it to run for two minutes. Stop the engine, let it stand for two minutes, then restart. This permits the air to bleed off within the pump.

INJECTION TIMING

For the engine to be properly timed, the lines on the top of the injection pump adapter and the flange of the injection pump must be aligned.

1. The engine must be off for resetting the timing.

2. Loosen the three pump retaining nuts with tool J-26987 or equivalent, which is an injection pump intake manifold wrench.

3. Align the timing marks and torque the pump retaining nuts to specification.

NOTE: The use of a ¾ inch open end wrench on the boss at the front of the pump will aid in rotating the pump to align the marks.

4. Adjust the throttle rod.

Injection Nozzle

REMOVAL & INSTALLATION

The injection nozzles on these engines are simply unbolted from the cylinder head, after the fuel lines are removed, in similar fashion to a spark plug. Be careful not to damage the nozzle end and make sure you remove the copper nozzle gasket from the cylinder head if it does not come off with the nozzle.

Clean the carbon off the tip of the nozzle with a soft brass wire brush and install the nozzles, with gaskets.

NOTE: Some vehicles use two types of injectors, CAV Lucas and Diesel Equipment. When installing the inlet fittings, torque the Diesel Equipment injector fitting to 45 ft. lbs. and the CAV Lucas to 25 ft. lbs.

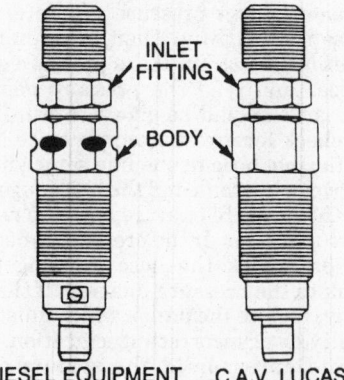

INLET FITTING TO BODY TORQUE – DIESEL EQUIPMENT 45 FT. LBS. – C.A.V. LUCAS 25 FT. LBS.

INLET FITTING

BODY

DIESEL EQUIPMENT   C.A.V. LUCAS

Fuel injector identification – V8 diesel engine

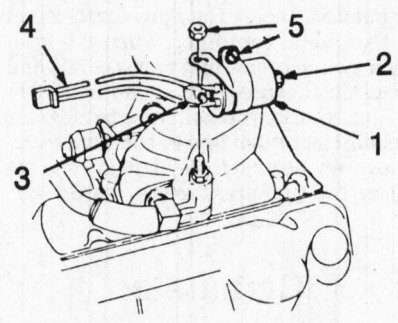

1. Fuel pump 4. Lead
2. Inlet   5. 18 ft. lbs.
3. Outlet

Fuel pump – V6 diesel engine

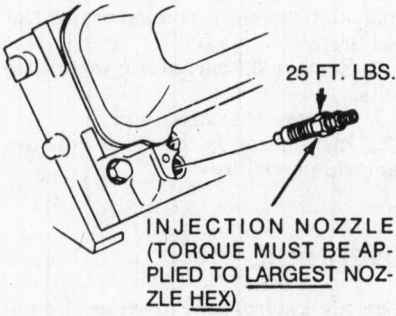

25 FT. LBS.

INJECTION NOZZLE (TORQUE MUST BE APPLIED TO LARGEST NOZZLE HEX)

Injector installation – V8 diesel engine

AUTOMATIC TRANSMISSION

For further information on automatic transmissions, please refer to "Automatic Transmissions" in the Unit Repair section.

REMOVAL & INSTALLATION

NOTE: Due to the various transmissions available in these vehicles, removal and installation procedures are general. Some of the Steps will have to rearranged to fit the model being serviced.

1. Disconnect the negative battery cable at the battery.
2. If so equipped, disconnect the detent/downshift cable at its upper end (accelerator pedal or carburetor).
3. Raise the vehicle and support it safely. The the vehicle must be raised enough to provide adequate clearance for transmission removal.
4. Disconnect the exhaust crossover pipe at the manifolds, if exhaust system-to-transmission interference is obvious. It may be necessary to remove the catalytic converter, exhaust pipe or just the brackets in order to clear the transmission.
5. Remove the torque converter inspection cover.
6. Remove the torque converter to flywheel bolts. The relationship between the flywheel and converter must be marked so that proper balance is maintained after installation.
7. Matchmark the driveshaft and rear yoke for reinstallation. With a drain pan positioned under the front yoke, unbolt and remove the driveshaft.
8. Tag and disconnect the vacuum lines, wiring and speedometer cable from the transmission.
9. Place a transmission jack up to the transmission oil pan and secure the transmission to the jack.
10. Remove the transmission mounting pad bolt(s). Carefully raise the transmission just enough to take the weight of the transmission off of the supporting crossmember.

— **CAUTION** —
Exercise extreme care to avoid damage to underhood components while raising or lowering the transmission.

11. Unbolt and remove the transmission crossmember, complete with the mount. It may be necessary to raise or lower the transmission a small amount to remove the crossmember.
12. Remove the transmission dipstick, then unbolt and remove the filler tube.
13. Disconnect the shift linkage (or cable on floor shift models) and oil cooler lines from the transmission.
14. Support the engine under the oil pan. Be sure to put a block of wood between the support and oil pan to prevent damage to the pan.
15. Secure the torque converter to the transmission case.
16. Remove the transmission-to-engine mounting bolts, then carefully move the transmission rearward, downward and out from beneath the vehicle.

— **CAUTION** —
If interference is encountered with the cable(s), cooler lines, etc., remove the component(s) before finally lowering the transmission. Refer to the Automatic Transmission segment of the Unit Repair section for further information.

To Install:

1. Install the transmission against the engine and tighten the transmission-to-engine mounting bolts to 30–40 ft. lbs. Install the cross member and tighten the bolts to 40 ft. lbs. Remove the jack.
2. Align the matchmarks on the driveshaft with the marks on the rear yoke before installing the joint straps and bolts.
3. Align the converter and flywheel markings before installing the converter bolts.
4. Add the proper quantity of Dexron II® transmission fluid. If the converter was replaced, an additional 4 pints (approx.) should be added. NEVER overfill the transmission.
5. Adjust the shift linkage (or cable) and the detent/downshift cable.
6. Make sure that all vacuum lines, electrical connections and oil cooler line connections are secure before starting the vehicle.
7. Check for fluid leakage. After the transmission is hot, recheck the fluid level.

DRIVE AXLE

Driveshaft and U-Joints

REMOVAL & INSTALLATION

1. Raise and support the vehicle safely. Matchmark and remove the driveshaft.
2. If the front yoke is to be disassembled, matchmark the driveshaft and sliding splined yoke so that driveline balance is preserved upon reassembly. Remove the snap rings that retain the bearing caps.
3. Select two press components, with one small enough to pass through the yoke holes for the bearing caps and the other large enough to receive the bearing cap.
4. Use a vise or a press and position the small and large press components on either side of the U-joint. Press in on the smaller press component so that it presses the opposite bearing cap out of the yoke and into the larger press component. If the cap does not come all the way out, grasp it with a pair of pliers and work it out.
5. Reverse the position of the press components so that the smaller press component presses on the cross. Press the other bearing cap out of the yoke.
6. Repeat the procedure on the other bearings.
7. To install, grease the bearing caps and needles thoroughly if they are not pregreased. Start a new bearing cap into one side of the yoke. Position the cross in the yoke.

NOTE: Some U-joints have a grease fitting that must be installed in the joint before assembly. When installing the fitting, make sure that once the driveshaft is installed in the vehicle that the fitting is accessible to be greased at a later date.

8. Select two press components small enough to pass through the yoke holes. Put the press components against the cross and the cap and press the bearing cap ¼ in. below the surface of the yoke. If there is a sudden increase in the force needed to press the cap into place, or if the cross starts to bind, the bearings are cocked. They must be removed and restarted in the yoke. Failure to do so will cause premature bearing failure.
9. Install a new snap-ring.
10. Start the new bearing into the opposite side. Place a press component on it and press in until the opposite bearing contacts the snap ring.
11. Install a new snap ring. It may be necessary to grind the facing surface of the snap ring slightly to permit easier installation.
12. Install the other bearings in the same manner.
13. Check the joint for free movement. If binding exists, smack the yoke ears with a brass or plastic faced hammer to seat the bearing needles. If binding still exists, disassemble the joint and check to see if the needles are in place. Do not strike the bearings unless the shaft is supported firmly. Do

not install the driveshaft until free movement exists at all joints.

14. Installation of the driveshaft is the reverse of the removal procedure.

15. Align the matchmarks made during the removal.

16. If any transmission fluid was lost when the driveshaft was removed, check the fluid level.

Axle Shaft, Bearing and Seal

REMOVAL & INSTALLATION

Before attempting any service to the drive axle or axle shafts, remove the carrier cover and visually determine the ring gear size.

1. Raise and support the vehicle safely. Remove the wheel assembly on the side being serviced.

2. With the differential cover already removed, remove the differential pinion shaft lockscrew and slide out the differential pinion shaft.

3. Push the wheel end of the axle shaft toward the carrier and remove the C-lock from the end of the axle shaft.

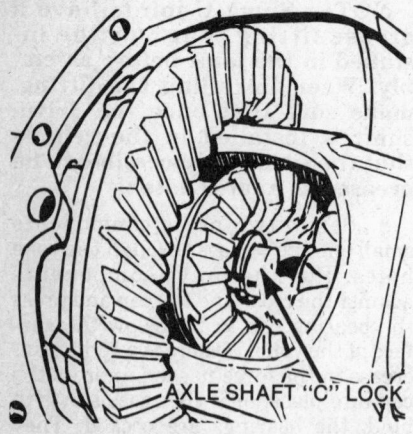

Removing the axle shaft C lock

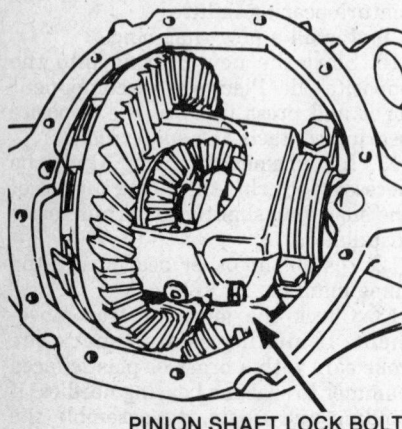

PINION SHAFT LOCK BOLT

Removing pinion shaft lock bolt from differential

4. Slide the axle shaft out of the housing, being careful not to damage the oil seal.

5. Remove the oil seal by inserting the carrier end of the axle shaft behind the steel case of the oil seal. Pry the seal loose from the bore in the housing. Use care not to damage the axle shaft or housing.

6. Using a slide hammer type bearing puller, place the legs of a bearing puller behind the bearing. Seat a washer against the bearing and hold it in place with a nut. Use a slide hammer to remove the bearing from the housing.

7. Pack the cavity between the seal lips with a wheel bearing lubricant and lubricate the new bearing with the same.

8. Use a suitable driver and install the bearing until it bottoms against the housing tube. Install the oil seal using a seal driver.

9. Slide the axle shaft into place. Be sure that the splines on the shaft do not damage the oil seal. Make sure that the splines engage the carrier side gear and the axle shaft is in far enough to install the C-lock.

10. Install the C-lock on the inner end of the axle shaft and push the shaft outward so that the C-lock seats in the differential side gear counterbore.

11. Position the differential pinion shaft through the case and pinions, aligning the hole in the case with the hole for the lockscrew.

12. Install and tighten the pinion shaft lockscrew.

13. Use a new gasket and install the carrier cover. Be sure that the gasket surfaces are clean before installing the gasket and cover.

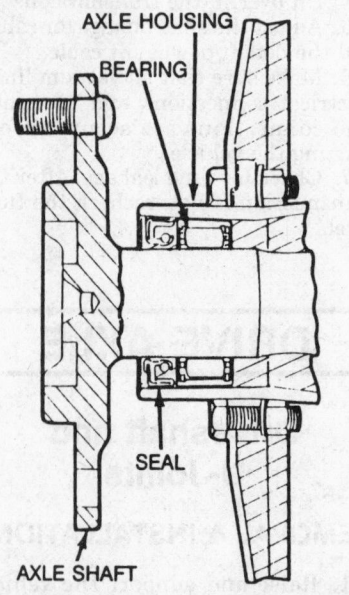

AXLE HOUSING

BEARING

SEAL

AXLE SHAFT

Axle shaft, bearing and seal—cutaway view

14. Fill the axle with Hypoid gear lubricant to the bottom of the filler hole.

15. Install the brake drum and wheel assembly.

FRONT SUSPENSION

Shock Absorbers

REMOVAL & INSTALLATION

All Models

1. Before raising the vehicle, remove the upper shock absorber attaching nut, grommet retainer and grommet. Raise and support the vehicle safely.

2. Remove the lower retaining bolt. Lower the shock through the hole in the lower control arm.

NOTE: Before installation, purge the new shocks of air by repeatedly extending them in from their normal position and then compressing them while holding the shock upside down.

3. When installing, tighten the upper nut to 8 ft. lbs. and the lower bolts to 20 ft. lbs.

Ball Joints

INSPECTION

Lower Ball Joint

All lower ball joints have visual wear indicators on the ball joints. The lower ball joint grease plug screws into the wear indicator, which protrudes from the bottom of the ball joint housing. As long as the wear indicator extends out of the ball joint housing, the ball joint is not worn. If the tip of the wear indi-

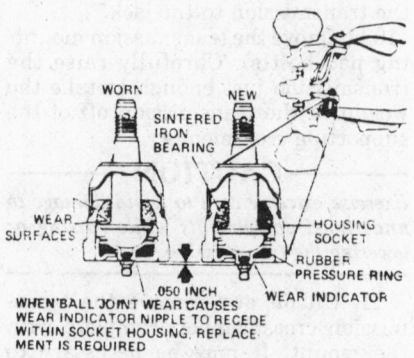

WORN

NEW

SINTERED IRON BEARING

WEAR SURFACES

HOUSING SOCKET

RUBBER PRESSURE RING

WEAR INDICATOR

.050 INCH

WHEN BALL JOINT WEAR CAUSES WEAR INDICATOR NIPPLE TO RECEDE WITHIN SOCKET HOUSING, REPLACEMENT IS REQUIRED

Lower ball joint wear indicator

cator is parallel with, or recessed into the ball joint housing, the ball joint is defective.

Upper Ball Joint

Place a jack under each lower control arm between the suspension sprint pocket and the ball joint and raise the vehicle. Grasp the tire at the top and bottom and shake it in and out. Observe the steering knuckle for any movement relative to the control arm. If the ball joint is loose, it must be replaced.

Upper Control Arm and Ball Joint

REMOVAL & INSTALLATION

All Models

1. Raise and support the verhicle under the frame. Remove the wheel and tire.
2. Using a jack, support the vehicle weight under the outer edge of the lower control arm. Raise the jack enough to free the upper control arm for the upper ball stud.
3. Remove the cotter pin from the upper ball joint stud.
4. Loosen, but do not remove, the ball joint nut.

— CAUTION —

If the ball joint nut is removed, the full force of the coil spring could be released and cause injury. Use a ball joint removal tool to free the stud from the knuckle.

5. Wire the brake caliper and steering knuckle in place to prevent brake hose damage, then lift the upper arm from the knuckle.

NOTE: If only the ball joint is being replaced, stop at this point. Center punch and drill out the four rivets, then chisel off the heads. Remove the old ball joint. The new joint comes with four specially hardened bolts which must be torqued to 8 ft. lbs. The nut must always go on top.

6. Remove the upper control arm shaft-to-bracket nuts and lock washers. Carefully note the number, thickness and location of the shims. Remove the control arm assembly.
7. Observe the following torque figures during assembly. Upper control arm-to-frame nuts: 46 ft. lbs.; Ball joint stud nut: 60–65 ft. lbs.; Upper control arm bushing nuts: 85 ft. lbs.
8. The upper control arm bushing nuts must be torqued with the weight of the vehicle on the wheels.

When installing the cotter pin, never loosen the nut to align the cotter pin holes. Always tighten the nut to the next slot that lines up with the hole.

Lower Control Arm and Coil Spring

REMOVAL & INSTALLATION

All Models

1. Raise the front of the vehicle and remove the wheel.
2. Remove the shock absorber.

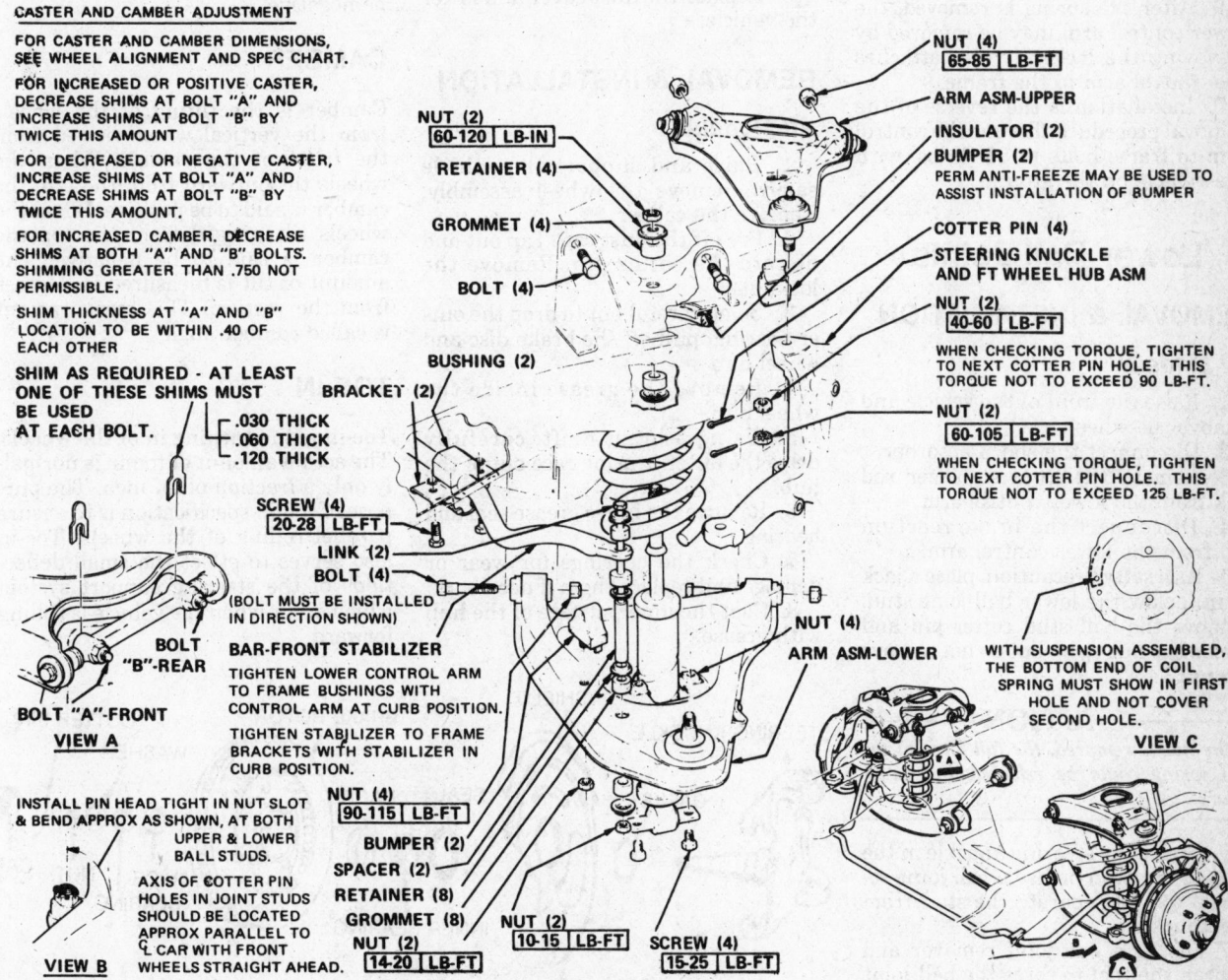

CASTER AND CAMBER ADJUSTMENT

FOR CASTER AND CAMBER DIMENSIONS, SEE WHEEL ALIGNMENT AND SPEC CHART.

FOR INCREASED OR POSITIVE CASTER, DECREASE SHIMS AT BOLT "A" AND INCREASE SHIMS AT BOLT "B" BY TWICE THIS AMOUNT

FOR DECREASED OR NEGATIVE CASTER, INCREASE SHIMS AT BOLT "A" AND DECREASE SHIMS AT BOLT "B" BY TWICE THIS AMOUNT

FOR INCREASED CAMBER, DECREASE SHIMS AT BOTH "A" AND "B" BOLTS. SHIMMING GREATER THAN .750 NOT PERMISSIBLE.

SHIM THICKNESS AT "A" AND "B" LOCATION TO BE WITHIN .40 OF EACH OTHER

SHIM AS REQUIRED - AT LEAST ONE OF THESE SHIMS MUST BE USED AT EACH BOLT.
.030 THICK
.060 THICK
.120 THICK

BRACKET (2)

SCREW (4)
20-28 LB-FT

LINK (2)
BOLT (4)
(BOLT MUST BE INSTALLED IN DIRECTION SHOWN)

BAR-FRONT STABILIZER
TIGHTEN LOWER CONTROL ARM TO FRAME BUSHINGS WITH CONTROL ARM AT CURB POSITION.

TIGHTEN STABILIZER TO FRAME BRACKETS WITH STABILIZER IN CURB POSITION.

BOLT "B"-REAR
BOLT "A"-FRONT
VIEW A

INSTALL PIN HEAD TIGHT IN NUT SLOT & BEND APPROX AS SHOWN, AT BOTH UPPER & LOWER BALL STUDS.

AXIS OF COTTER PIN HOLES IN JOINT STUDS SHOULD BE LOCATED APPROX PARALLEL TO ₵ CAR WITH FRONT WHEELS STRAIGHT AHEAD.

VIEW B

NUT (2)
60-120 LB-IN
RETAINER (4)
GROMMET (4)
BOLT (4)

BUSHING (2)

NUT (4)
90-115 LB-FT
BUMPER (2)
SPACER (2)
RETAINER (8)
GROMMET (8)
NUT (2)
14-20 LB-FT

NUT (2)
10-15 LB-FT

NUT (4)

ARM ASM-LOWER

SCREW (4)
15-25 LB-FT

NUT (4)
65-85 LB-FT
ARM ASM-UPPER
INSULATOR (2)
BUMPER (2)
PERM ANTI-FREEZE MAY BE USED TO ASSIST INSTALLATION OF BUMPER
COTTER PIN (4)
STEERING KNUCKLE AND FT WHEEL HUB ASM
NUT (2)
40-60 LB-FT
WHEN CHECKING TORQUE, TIGHTEN TO NEXT COTTER PIN HOLE. THIS TORQUE NOT TO EXCEED 90 LB-FT.
NUT (2)
60-105 LB-FT
WHEN CHECKING TORQUE, TIGHTEN TO NEXT COTTER PIN HOLE. THIS TORQUE NOT TO EXCEED 125 LB-FT.

WITH SUSPENSION ASSEMBLED, THE BOTTOM END OF COIL SPRING MUST SHOW IN FIRST HOLE AND NOT COVER SECOND HOLE.
VIEW C

Typical front suspension

3. Remove the front stabilizer rod link from the lower control arm.

4. Disconnect the brake reaction rod from the lower control arm.

5. As a safety precaution and to gain maximum leverage, place a jack about $\frac{1}{2}$ in. below the lower ball joint stud. Remove the cotter pin and loosen the nut about $\frac{1}{8}$ in. but do not remove the nut.

―――――― **CAUTION** ――――――

If the nut is removed, the full force of the coil spring could be released and cause injury.

6. Strike the steering knuckle in the area of the stud or use a ball joint removal tool to separate the stud from the knuckle.

7. After the stud has broken loose from the knuckle, raise the jack against the control arm. Remove the nut and separate the steering knuckle from the tapered stud.

8. Carefully lower the jack under the control arm and release the spring. With the jack entirely lowered, it may be necessary to pry the spring off its seat on the lower control arm.

9. After the spring is removed, the lower control arm may be removed by removing the lock nut that attaches the control arm to the frame.

10. Installation is the reverse of the removal procedure. Torque the control arm to frame bolts to 85 ft. lbs. with the vehicle on the ground.

Lower Ball Joints

REMOVAL & INSTALLATION

All Models

1. Raise the front of the vehicle and remove the wheel.

2. Disconnect the shock absorber.

3. Remove the front stabilizer rod link from the lower control arm.

4. Disconnect the brake reaction rod from the lower control arm.

5. As a safty precaution, place a jack $\frac{1}{2}$ in. below the lower ball joint stud. Remove the ball stud cotter pin and loosen the nut $\frac{1}{8}$ in. but do not remove the nut.

―――――― **CAUTION** ――――――

If the nut is removed, the full force of the coil spring could be released and cause injury.

6. Strike the steering knuckle in the area of the stud or use a ball joint removal tool to separate the stud from the knuckle.

7. Install a ball joint remover and tighten the tool to force the ball joint out of the lower control arm.

8. Installation is the reverse of the removal procedure. Tighten the nut to 85–90 ft. lbs. Always tighten the nut to the next slot if necessary to align the cotter pin.

Front Wheel Bearings

ADJUSTMENT

All Models

1. Raise and support the vehicle safely.

2. Remove the dust cap from the hub.

3. Remove the cotter pin.

4. Tighten the spindle nut to 12 ft. lbs. while turning the wheel. Then back off the nut $\frac{1}{4}$–$\frac{1}{2}$ turn.

5. Retighten the nut by hand until it is finger-tight.

6. Loosen the nut no more than $\frac{1}{6}$ of a turn until the nearest hole in the spindle lines up with the slot in the spindle nut. Insert a new cotter pin.

7. Check for looseness in the hub assembly. There should be 0.001–0.005 in. end-play.

8. Replace the dust cover and lower the vehicle.

REMOVAL & INSTALLATION

All Models

1. Raise and support the vehicle safely. Remove the wheel assembly. Remove the caliper.

2. Pry off the dust cap. Tap out and discard the cotter pin. Remove the locknut.

3. Being careful not to drop the outer bearing, pull off the brake disc and wheel hub.

4. Remove the grease inside the wheel hub.

5. Using a brass drift, carefully drive the outer bearing race out of the hub.

6. Remove the inner grease seal and bearing.

7. Check the bearings for wear or damage and replace them if necessary.

8. Coat the inner surface of the hub with grease.

9. Grease the outer surface of the bearing race and drift it into place in the hub.

10. Pack the inner and outer wheel bearings with grease. If the brake disc has been removed and/or replaced, tighten the retaining bolts to specification.

11. Install the inner bearing in the hub. Being careful not to distort it, install the oil seal with its lip facing the bearing. Drive the seal on until its outer edge is even with the edge of the hub.

12. Install the hub/disc assembly on the spindle, being careful not to damage the oil seal.

13. Install the outer bearing, washer and spindle nut. Adjust the bearing.

Front Wheel Alignment

CASTER

Caster is the tilting of the steering axis either forward or backward from the vertical, when viewed from the side of the vehicle. A backward tilt is said to be positive and a forward tilt is said to be negative.

CAMBER

Camber is the tilting of the wheels from the vertical when viewed from the front of the vehicle. When the wheels tilt outward from the top, the camber is said to be positive. When the wheels tilt inward from the top the camber is said to be negative. The amount of tilt is measured in degrees from the vertical. This measurement is called camber angle.

TOE-IN

Toe-in is the turning in of the wheels. The actual amount of toe-in is normally only a fraction of an inch. The purpose of toe-in specification is to ensure parallel rolling of the wheels. Toe-in also serves to offset the small deflections of the steering support system which occur when the vehicle is rolling forward.

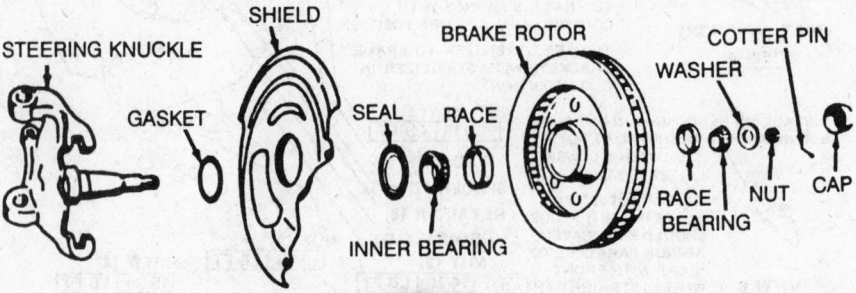

Front wheel hub and bearings—exploded view

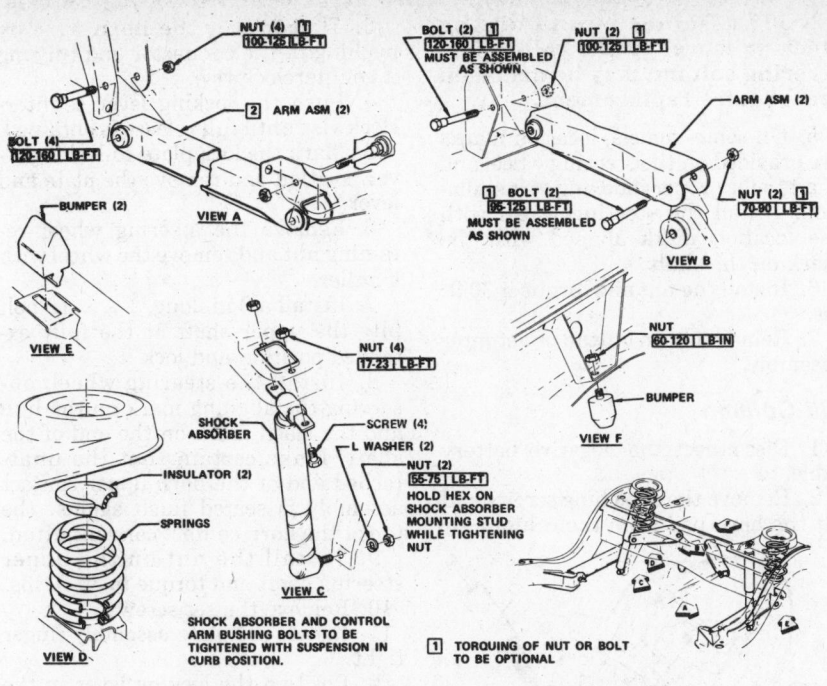

BOLT (4) 1
120-160 LB-FT

NUT (4) 1
100-125 LB-FT

BOLT (2) 1
120-160 LB-FT
MUST BE ASSEMBLED
AS SHOWN

NUT (2) 1
100-125 LB-FT

ARM ASM (2)

2 ARM ASM (2)

BUMPER (2)

VIEW A

VIEW E

1 BOLT (2)
95-125 LB-FT
MUST BE ASSEMBLED
AS SHOWN

ARM ASM (2)

NUT (2) 1
70-90 LB-FT

VIEW B

NUT
60-120 LB-IN

BUMPER

VIEW F

SHOCK ABSORBER

SCREW (4)

L WASHER (2)

NUT (2)
55-75 LB-FT
HOLD HEX ON
SHOCK ABSORBER
MOUNTING STUD
WHILE TIGHTENING
NUT

INSULATOR (2)

SPRINGS

VIEW C

VIEW D

SHOCK ABSORBER AND CONTROL
ARM BUSHING BOLTS TO BE
TIGHTENED WITH SUSPENSION IN
CURB POSITION.

1 TORQUING OF NUT OR BOLT
TO BE OPTIONAL

Rear suspension details—typical with coil springs

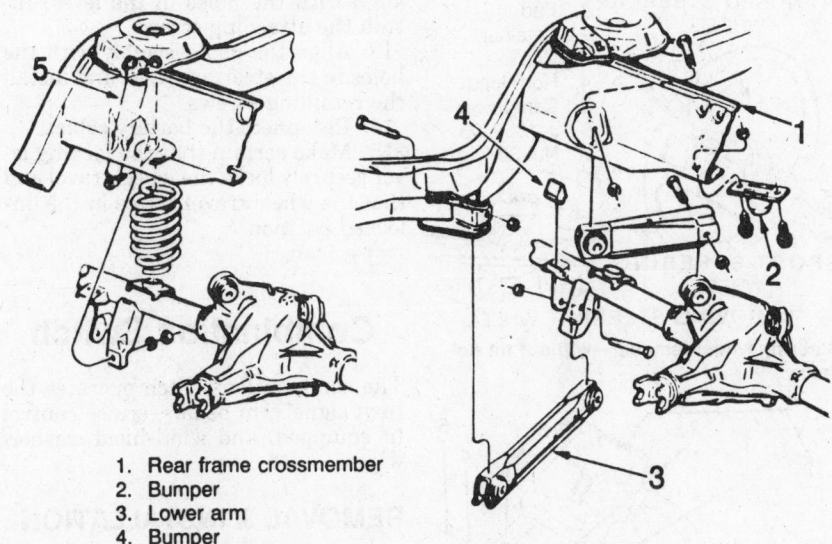

1. Rear frame crossmember
2. Bumper
3. Lower arm
4. Bumper
5. Shock absorber

Rear axle mounting – typical

REAR SUSPENSION

Shock Absorbers

REMOVAL & INSTALLATION

NOTE: Purge new shocks of air by repeatedly extending them in their normal position and compressing them while inverted.

1. Raise and support the vehicle at the axle housing.

2. Remove the nut, retainer and grommet or lockwasher that attaches the lower end of the shock absorber to the mounting.

3. Remove the two upper attaching screws and remove the shock absorber.

4. When installing, tighten the upper bolts to 18–20 ft. lbs. The nuts that lock the upper bolts on some models are torqued to 12 ft. lbs. Tighten the lower nut to 65 ft. lbs.

Coil Springs

REMOVAL & INSTALLATION

All Models

1. Raise and support the vehicle so the rear axle hangs freely. Support the rear axle with an adjustable lifting device. Disconnect the shock absorber.

2. Detach the upper control arm at the housing.

3. Disconnect the stabilizer bar, if equipped.

4. Remove any brake hose supports but do not disconnect the brake hose, if necessary.

5. Carefully lower the axle until the tension is released from the coil spring. Be careful not to stretch the brake hose. Remove the spring. Note the direction in which the end of the last coil is pointing. Install the spring in the same position.

6. When installing a new coil spring, make certain that the bottom of the coil is properly inserted into the socket in the frame and into the form plate on the trailing arm.

7. Raise the housing into place and reinstall the control arm bolt. Tighten the bolts with the vehicle weight on the springs.

Rear Lower Control Arm

REMOVAL & INSTALLATION

All Models

NOTE: Remove and install one lower control arm at a time. If both arms are removed at the same time, the axle could roll or slip sideways, making installation very difficult.

1. Raise and support the rear of the vehicle safely under the rear axle. If equipped with a stabilizer bar, remove it.

2. Remove the control arm attaching bolts and remove the control arm.

3. To install, reverse the removal procedures. Torque the control arm-to-frame nut to 92 ft. lbs. (LeSabre and Electra) or 70 ft. lbs. (Regal), the control arm-to-axle bolt to 125 ft. lbs. (LeSabre and Electra) or 79 ft. lbs. (Regal). If equipped with a stabilizer bar, torque the mounting fasteners to 52 ft. lbs. (LeSabre and Electra) or 35 ft. lbs. (Regal).

NOTE: Before torquing the fasteners, the weight of the vehicle must be resting on the wheels.

Rear Upper Control Arm

REMOVAL & INSTALLATION

All Models

NOTE: Remove and install one lower control arm at a time. If both arms are removed at the same time, the axle could roll or slip sideways, making the installation of the arms difficult.

1. Raise and support the rear of the vehicle safely under the axle.
2. Remove the upper control arm nut at the axle. To remove the mounting bolt from the axle, it may be necessary to rock the axle. On some models, it may be necessary to remove the lower shock absorber stud to provide clearance for the upper control arm removal.
3. Remove the upper control arm-to-frame nut and bolt, then the control arm.
4. To install, reverse the removal procedures. Torque the upper control arm-to-axle nut to 70 ft. lbs., the upper control arm-to-axle bolt to 79 ft. lbs. and the upper control arm-to-frame bolt to 92 ft. lbs. (LeSabre and Electra) or 70 ft. lbs. (Regal).

Rear Wheel Bearings

For rear wheel bearing removal and installation, please refer to the "Drive Axle" section.

STEERING

Steering Wheel

REMOVAL & INSTALLATION

Except Tilt Column

1. Disconnect the negative battery cable and unplug the horn wire connector from the steering column.
2. Pull off the cap, remove the three screws, and remove the contact, insulator and spring. On models with the bar-type horn actuator, remove the screws securing the actuator from the underside of the steering wheel, unhook the lead connector plug and remove the actuator assembly.
3. Mark the steering wheel to shaft position for installation and loosen the steering wheel nut.
4. Using a steering wheel puller, remove the steering wheel.

NOTE: Do not pound on the steering wheel or the collapsible steering column may be damaged and require replacement.

5. On some models, location marks are provided on the steering wheel and shaft to for proper indexing at installation. Install the steering wheel with the location mark aligned with the mark on the shaft.
6. Install the nut and torque it 30 ft. lbs.
7. Reinstall horn button or actuator assembly.

Tilt Column

1. Disconnect the negative battery cable.
2. Remove the attaching screws and lift the horn pad from the column.

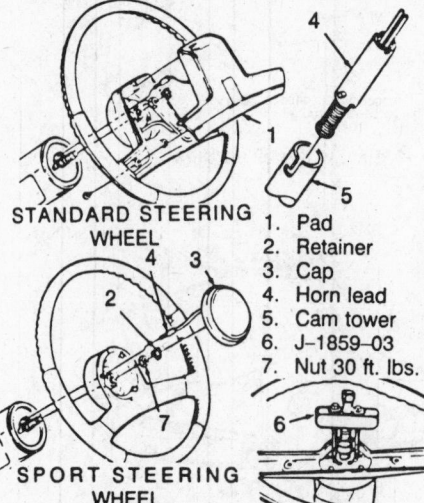

STANDARD STEERING WHEEL

SPORT STEERING WHEEL

REMOVING STEERING WHEEL

1. Pad
2. Retainer
3. Cap
4. Horn lead
5. Cam tower
6. J–1859–03
7. Nut 30 ft. lbs.

Steering wheel removal—without tilt column

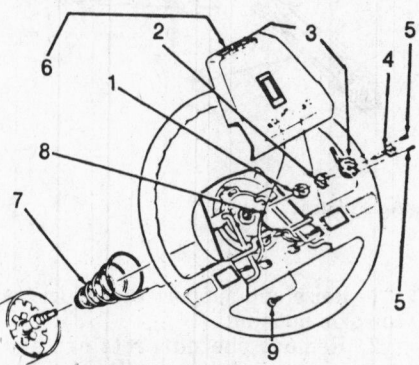

1. Steering wheel nut 30 ft. lbs.
2. Steering wheel nut retainer
3. Telescoping adjusting lever
4. Steering shaft lock knob bolt
5. Steering shaft lock knob bolt positioning screw (2)
6. Steering wheel pad
7. Horn contact spring
8. Horn lead
9. Fully driven, seated and not stripped

Steering wheel removal—with tilt column

3. Disconnect the horn wire by pushing in the connector and turning it counterclockwise.
4. Push the locking lever counterclockwise until full release is obtained.
5. Mark the lock plate-to-locking lever position and remove the plate and lever.
6. Remove the steering wheel retaining nut and remove the wheel with a puller.
7. Install a 3 in. long, $5/16 \times 18$ bolt into the upper shaft at the fully extended position and lock it.
8. Install the steering wheel, observing the aligning mark on the hub and the slash mark on the end of the shaft. Make certain that the unattached end of the horn upper contact assembly is seated flush against the top of the horn contact carrier button.
9. Install the nut on the upper steering shaft and torque to 30 ft. lbs.
10. Remove the set screw.
11. Install the plate assembly finger tight.
12. Position the locking lever in the vertical position and move it counterclockwise until the holes in the plate align with the holes in the lever. Install the attaching screws.
13. Align the pad assembly with the holes in the steering wheel and install the retaining screws.
14. Reconnect the battery cables.
15. Make certain that the locking lever securely locks the wheel travel and that the wheel travel is free in the unlocked position.

Combination Switch

The combination switch operates the turn signals, hi beams, cruise control (if equipped) and windshield washer/wipers.

REMOVAL & INSTALLATION

All Models

1. Disconnect the negative battery cable. Remove the steering wheel. Remove the turn signal switch.
2. It may be necessary to loosen the two column mounting nuts and remove the four bracket-to-mast jacket screws, then separate the bracket from the mast jacket to allow the connector clip on the ignition switch to be pulled out of the column assembly.
3. Disconnect the washer/wiper switch lower connector.
4. Remove the screws attaching the column housing to the mast jacket. Be sure to note the position of the dimmer switch actuator rod for reassembly in the same position. Remove the column housing and switch as an assembly.

NOTE: The tilt and travel columns have a removable plastic cover on the column housing. This provides access to the wiper switch without removing the entire column housing.

5. Turn the switch upside down and use a drift to remove the pivot pin from the washer/wiper switch. Remove the switch.

6. Place the switch into position in the housing, then install the pivot pin.

7. Position the housing onto the mast jacket and attach by installing the screws. Install the dimmer switch actuator rod in the same position as noted earlier. Check switch operation.

8. Reconnect lower end of switch assembly.

9. Install remaining components in reverse order of removal. Be sure to attach column mounting bracket in original position.

Ignition Lock/Switch

REMOVAL & INSTALLATION

Standard Column

1. Follow Steps 1–6 under "Combination Switch, Removal and Installation".

2. Disconnect the turn signal connector from the harness and pull out the turn signal switch. Allow it to hang.

3. With the lock cylinder in the RUN position, insert a small screwdriver into the slot next to the turn signal switch mounting screw boss (right-hand slot), depress the spring latch and remove the key lock.

4. Pull the buzzer switch straight out, depressing the switch clip with pliers.

5. Place the ignition switch in the OFF-UNLOCKED position by pulling up on the connecting rod until there is a definite stop or detent felt.

6. Remove the two attaching screws and the ignition switch.

7. Assembly is the reverse of the removal. Note the following steps before proceeding with the reassembly.

8. To install the steering lock, hold the lock cylinder sleeve and rotate the knob clockwise against the stop. Insert the cylinder into the cover bore with the key on the cylinder sleeve aligned with the keyway in the housing. Then push the cylinder until it bottoms. Maintaining a light inward pressure, rotate the knob counterclockwise until the drive section of the cylinder mates with the driveshaft. Push in until the snapring pops into the groove and the lock cylinder is secured in the cover. Check for free rotation.

9. Move the switch slider to the extreme left position (ACC), then two detents to the right, to the OFF-UNLOCKED position. Fit the actuator rod into the hole and attach the switch to the column.

10. The neutral start switch is adjusted with the shift lever in the Drive position.

Tilt Column

1. Follow Steps 1–6 under "Combination Switch, Removal and Installation".

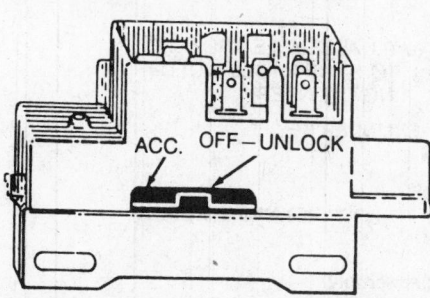

Ignition switch assembly in installation position

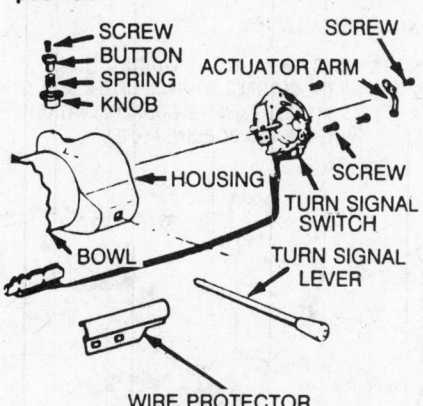

Turn signal switch mounting

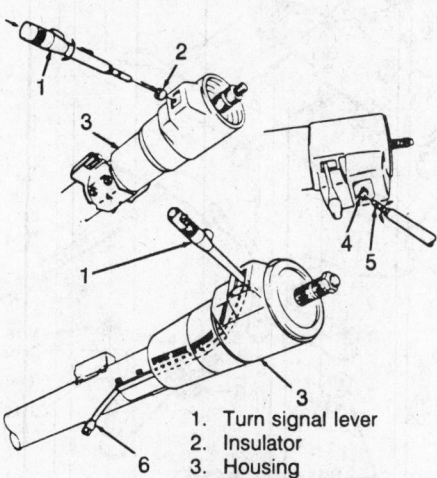

1. Turn signal lever
2. Insulator
3. Housing
4. Switch notch
5. Tang
6. Cruise control wiring

Multi function switch lever removal

2. Position the tilt column in the center position and remove the three turn signal switch screws. Tape the wires to the wire connector at the upper end and place the shift bowl in Low. Pull the switch straight up and out, allowing it to hang.

3. Insert a small tool into the slot next to the turn signal switch mounting screw boss (right-hand slot), depress the spring latch and remove the key lock. Remove the retaining screw and the lock cylinder.

4. Remove the buzzer switch straight out, depressing the switch clip with pliers.

5. Remove the three housing cover screws and cover.

6. Install the tilt release lever and place column in full UP position.

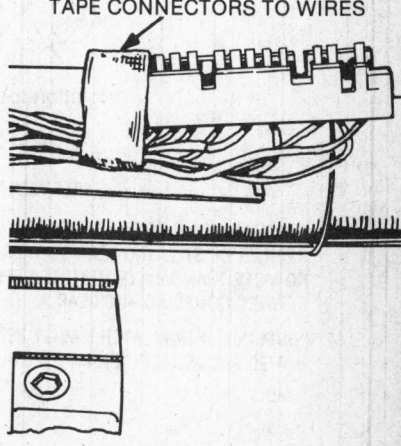

Tape the connector to the wires so that it will slip easily up the steering column

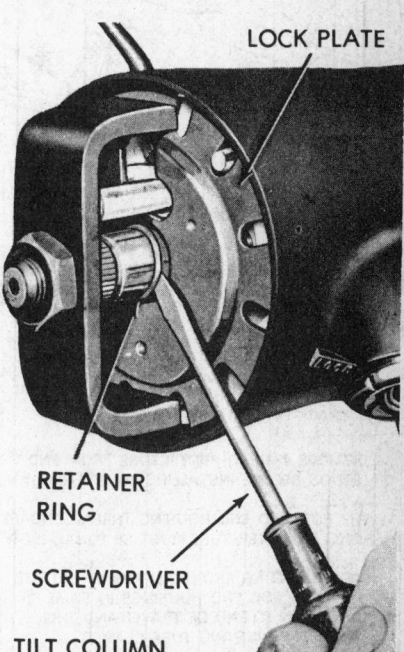

Removing lock plate

7. Place a screwdriver in the slot of the tilt spring retainer, press in about $^3/_{16}$ in. and turn counterclockwise. Remove the spring and guide.

NOTE: The spring is very strong; use care.

8. Place the column in neutral position, push in on the upper steering shaft, remove the inner race seat and race.

9. Remove the upper flange pinch bolt, place the ignition switch in the accessory position, remove the two switch mounting screws and switch.

NOTE: The neutral start switch can be removed at this time, if necessary.

10. Assembly is the reverse of the removal. Note the following steps before proceeding with the reassembly.

11. To install the steering lock, hold the lock cylinder sleeve and rotate the knob clockwise against the stop. Insert the cylinder into the cover bore with the key on the cylinder sleeve aligned with the keyway in the housing. Push the cylinder in until it bottoms. Maintaining a light inward pressure, rotate the knob counterclockwise until the drive section of the cylinder mates with the driveshaft. Push in until the snap-ring pops into the groove and the lock cylinder is secured in the cover. Check for free rotation.

12. When installing the ignition switch, be sure the lock cylinder is in the LOCK position. Put the shift bowl or shroud in the PARK position. Make sure the ignition switch is in the LOCK position. Insert the actuator rod into the switch and assemble the switch to the column.

13. The neutral-start switch is adjusted with the shift lever in the DRIVE position.

Power Steering Gear

REMOVAL & INSTALLATION

All Models

— **CAUTION** —

Failure to disconnect the flexible coupling from the steering gear stub shaft can result in damage to the steering gear and/or intermediate shaft. This damage can cause loss of steering control which could result in loss of vehicle control.

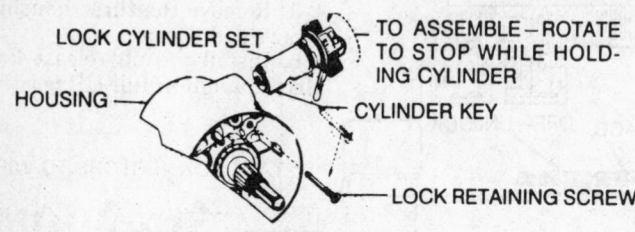

Ignition lock assembly

INTERMEDIATE SHAFT INSTALLATION

1. COUPLING MUST BE FULLY ENGAGED WITH SPLINES OF STEERING GEAR SO THERE IS NO MORE THAN 3mm OF VISIBLE SPLINES BETWEEN COUPLING AND GEAR A.

2. COUPLING SHIELD LATCH B MUST BE SEATED AROUND THE RETURN PIPE NUT.

3. AFTER THE SHIELD IS LATCHED, IF ANY OF THE COLORED PORTION OF THE SEAL C IS VISIBLE THEN THE COUPLING ATTACHMENT SHOULD BE REINSPECTED.

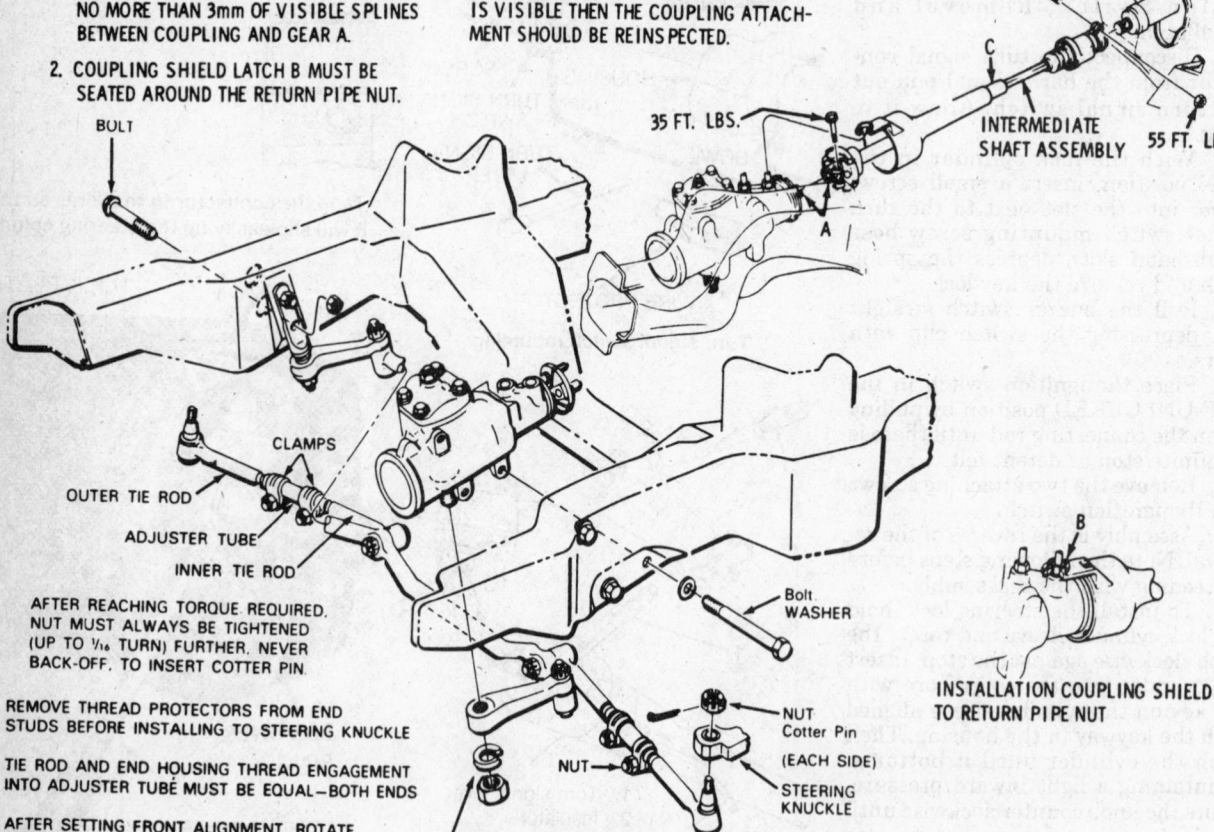

AFTER REACHING TORQUE REQUIRED. NUT MUST ALWAYS BE TIGHTENED (UP TO $^1/_{16}$ TURN) FURTHER. NEVER BACK-OFF. TO INSERT COTTER PIN.

REMOVE THREAD PROTECTORS FROM END STUDS BEFORE INSTALLING TO STEERING KNUCKLE

TIE ROD AND END HOUSING THREAD ENGAGEMENT INTO ADJUSTER TUBE MUST BE EQUAL—BOTH ENDS

AFTER SETTING FRONT ALIGNMENT, ROTATE BOTH TIE ROD END HOUSINGS IN SAME DIRECTION TO END OF TRAVEL AND THEN TIGHTEN ADJUSTING TUBE CLAMPS.

INSTALLATION COUPLING SHIELD TO RETURN PIPE NUT

Steering linkage and gear mounting—typical

1. Remove the flexible coupling shield.

2. Disconnect the hoses from the gear and cap the hose fittings.

3. Raise and support the vehicle safely.

4. Remove the Pitman shaft nut, then disconnect the Pitman arm from the pitman shaft using a puller.

5. Remove the three bolts attaching the gear to the frame side rail and remove the gear with the hoses attached.

NOTE: If the mounting threads are stripped, do not repair. Replace the housing.

6. Installation is the reverse of removal. Tighten the steering gear to frame bolts 80 ft. lbs. and the Pitman shaft nut 180 ft. lbs.

Power Steering Pump

REMOVAL & INSTALLATION

All Models

1. Disconnect and plug the hoses at the pump. Plug the openings in the pump also to prevent contamination.

2. Remove the pump drive belt.

3. Remove the pump retaining bolts and braces and remove the pump.

4. Install the pump on the engine with the retaining bolts hand-tight.

5. Connect and tighten the hoses.

6. Refill the pump with fluid and bleed the system by turning the pulley by hand. Adjust the belt tension, run the engine and refill the pump to the proper level.

Tie Rod Ends

REMOVAL & INSTALLATION

All Models

1. Raise and support the vehicle safely. Loosen the tie rod adjuster sleeve clamp nuts.

2. Remove the cotter pin and nut from the tie rod end.

3. Remove the tie rod stud from the steering arm or intermediate rod. This is a taper fit. Removal is accomplished using a ball joint removal tool or by hitting the steering arm sharply, while using a heavy instrument as a backup.

4. Unscrew the tie rod from the adjusted sleeve. Outer tie rods have right-hand threads and inner tie rods have left-hand threads. Count the number of turns the tie rod must be rotated to remove it from the adjusting sleeve. This will allow a reasonably accurate realignment upon reassembly.

5. Installation is the reverse of the removal procedure. Clean any rust and dirt from the threads. Observe the fol-

lowing torque specifications: steering arm-to-tie rod end nut, 35 ft. lbs.; tie rod clamp nuts, 11–14 ft. lbs.; tie rod-to-intermediate nut, 40 ft. lbs. Check the alignment and adjust as necessary.

BRAKES

For information of the brake system not detailed below, please refer to "Brakes" in the Unit Repair section.

Master Cylinder

REMOVAL & INSTALLATION

All Models

1. Disconnect and plug the brake lines at the master cylinder.

2. Disconnect the fluid level sensor wiring at the master cylinder, if equipped.

3. Remove the master cylinder-to-booster mounting nuts. Remove the master cylinder. Be careful not to spill any brake fluid on the paint.

4. Install the master cylinder on the booster and torque the mounting nuts to 28 ft. lbs. Tighten the hydraulic line nuts, fill the master cylinder and bleed the hydraulic system.

Combination Valve

REMOVAL & INSTALLATION

All Models

NOTE: The combination valve is not repairable and must be replaced if found to be defective. It may be necessary to raise some models for access to the valve.

1. Disconnect the electrical connector at the pressure differential switch by squeezing the eliptical shaped plastic locking ring and pulling upwards. This will move the locking tangs away from the switch.

2. Disconnect and plug the hydraulic lines at the combination valve then remove the valve.

3. Installation is the reverse of the removal procedure.

4. Bleed the entire brake system when finished.

NOTE: Do not move the vehicle until a firm brake pedal is obtained.

Power Brake Booster

REMOVAL & INSTALLATION

1. Remove the master cylinder to power brake booster mounting nuts. Using care not to kink or bend the brake lines, pull the master cylinder away from the power unit without disconnecting the brake lines.

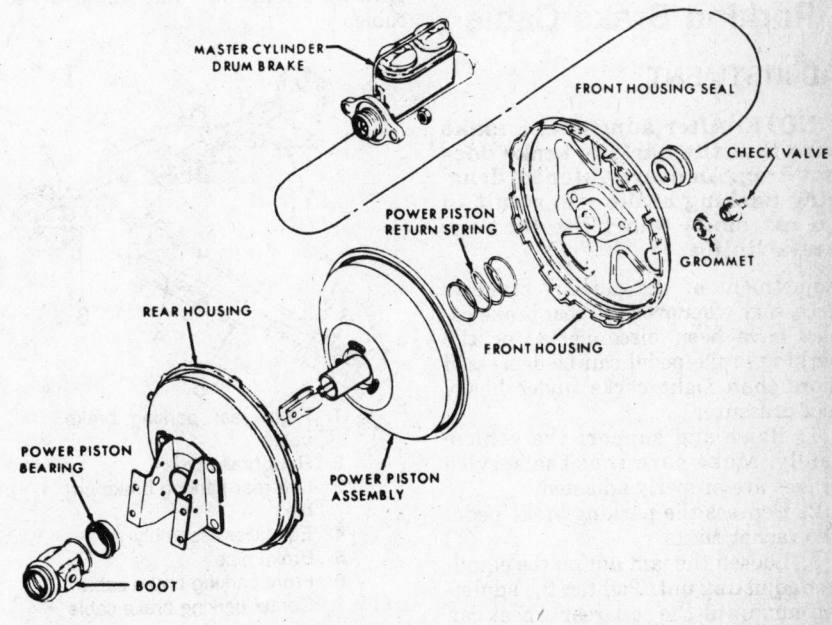

Power brake unit and master cylinder

2. Disconnect the vacuum hose on the booster.

3. Disconnect the brake pushrod from the brake pedal.

4. Remove the booster from the vehicle.

5. To install, mount the booster on the firewall and tighten the nuts.

6. Install the master cylinder to the booster and tighten the nuts to 15 ft. lbs. on the Regal and 25 ft. lbs. on the others.

7. Connect the vacuum hose to the booster.

8. Connect the power brake pushrod to the brake pedal.

9. Start the engine and allow vacuum to build up before moving the vehicle.

Wheel Cylinder

REMOVAL & INSTALLATION

All Models

1. Raise and safely support the vehicle.

2. Remove the wheel, brake drum and brake shoes.

3. Clean all dirt from around the wheel cylinder. Disconnect and plug the brake line.

4. Remove the wheel cylinder from the backing plate.

5. Installation is the reverse of the removal procedure. Torque the brake line to 12 ft. lbs.

6. Bleed the wheel cylinder and check the fluid level in the master cylinder.

Parking Brake Cable

ADJUSTMENT

NOTE: After adjustment, make sure that the parking brake does not drag. An overtightened, dragging parking brake will result in an extremely short life for rear brake linings.

Adjustment of the parking brake is necessary whenever the rear brake cables have been disconnected or the parking brake pedal can be depressed more than eight clicks under heavy foot pressure.

1. Raise and support the vehicle safely. Make sure that the service brakes are properly adjusted.

2. Depress the parking brake pedal two rachet clicks.

3. Loosen the jam nut on the equalizer adjusting nut. Tighten the adjusting nut until the left rear wheel can just be turned rearward by hand, but not forward.

4. Release the rachet one click; the rear wheel should rotate rearward freely and forward with a slight drag.

5. Release the rachet fully; the rear wheel should turn freely in either direction.

REMOVAL & INSTALLATION

Left Rear

1. Raise and support the vehicle safely. Remove the wheel and tire.

2. Loosen the adjuster nut and compress the retainer fingers at the equalizer.

3. Disconnect the cable from the connector and remove from equalizer.

4. Remove the brake drum.

5. Remove the primary shoe return spring and parking brake strut.

6. Compress the retainer and loosen the cable from the backing plate.

7. Installation is the reverse of the removal. Adjust the cable after installation.

Right Rear

1. Raise and support the vehicle safely. Remove the wheel and tire.

2. Remove the adjuster nut at the equalizer and compress the retainer fingers to loosen the cable from the retainers at the frame and from axle housing clip.

3. Remove the brake drum.

4. Remove the primary shoe return spring, parking brake strut and secondary shoe hold down spring.

5. Compress the retainer fingers and loosen the cable from the backing plate.

6. Disconnect the cable from the parking brake lever and remove the cable.

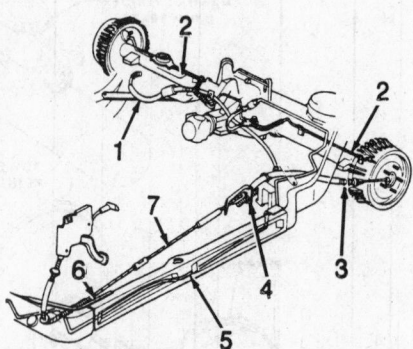

1. Right rear parking brake cable
2. Rear brake pipe
3. Left rear parking brake cable
4. Equalizer assembly
5. Brake pipe
6. Front parking brake cable
7. Center parking brake cable

Parking brake cable – Regal shown, Electra and LeSabre similar

7. Installation is the reverse of the removal. Adjust the cable after installation.

CHASSIS ELECTRICAL

Heater Blower

NOTE: Vacuum hose routing clips, electrical wires and relays, weather seals, and other items, may be attached to the heater housing and will have to be re-located during removal and replacement of the heater core and/or the blower motor. Always tag any disconnected hoses or wires for installation.

REMOVAL & INSTALLATION

All Models

1. Disconnect the negative battery cable and the blower motor wiring.

2. Remove the blower motor attaching screws and remove the motor.

3. Transfer the fan cage from the old motor to the new motor. The open end of the fan cage faces away from the motor.

4. Installation is the reverse of the removal procedure.

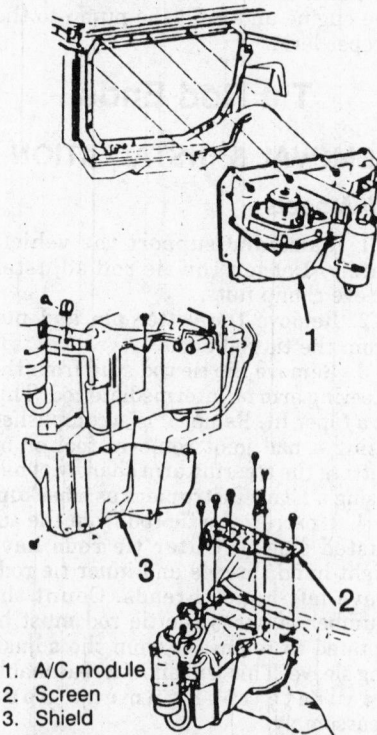

1. A/C module
2. Screen
3. Shield

Removing blower module assembly – Regal shown, others similar

Heater Core

REMOVAL & INSTALLATION

1982–87 Regal

1. Disconnect the negative battery cable.

2. Disconnect all electrical connections from the heating unit. Disconnect the heater core ground strap.

3. Remove the right hood seal and the air inlet screens. Remove the case to dash bolts, upper to lower case screws around the flange and the case screws inside the air intake plenum.

4. Disconnect the heater hoses, after draining the radiator. Remove the upper cover case.

5. Remove the heater core assembly by lifting it straight up and out of the case.

6. Installation is the reverse of the removal procedure.

1982–85 LeSabre and Electra
1982–89 Estate Wagon

1. Disconnect the negative battery cable. Drain the cooling system.

2. Remove the right side insulator, the center instrument panel trim plate and the lower instrument panel trim plate.

3. Remove the right speaker grille and speaker. Remove the electrical connections, wires and hoses from the programmer.

4. Remove the programmer linkage cover and linkage. Remove the programmer.

5. Remove the heater core cover retaining screws and then the heater core cover.

6. Remove the splash cover to gain access to the heater core hoses. Remove the heater core hoses and remove the heater core.

7. Installation is the reverse order of the removal procedure.

8. Reseal the module cover during installation.

Radio

REMOVAL & INSTALLATION

NOTE: Removal and installation procedures are for factory installed radios. Consult the radio manufacturer if equipped with an aftermarket radio.

Regal

1. Disconnect the negative battery cable and remove the radio knobs.

2. Remove the center trim plate.

3. Remove the glove box to gain access to the radio.

4. Disconnect the radio mounting bracket.

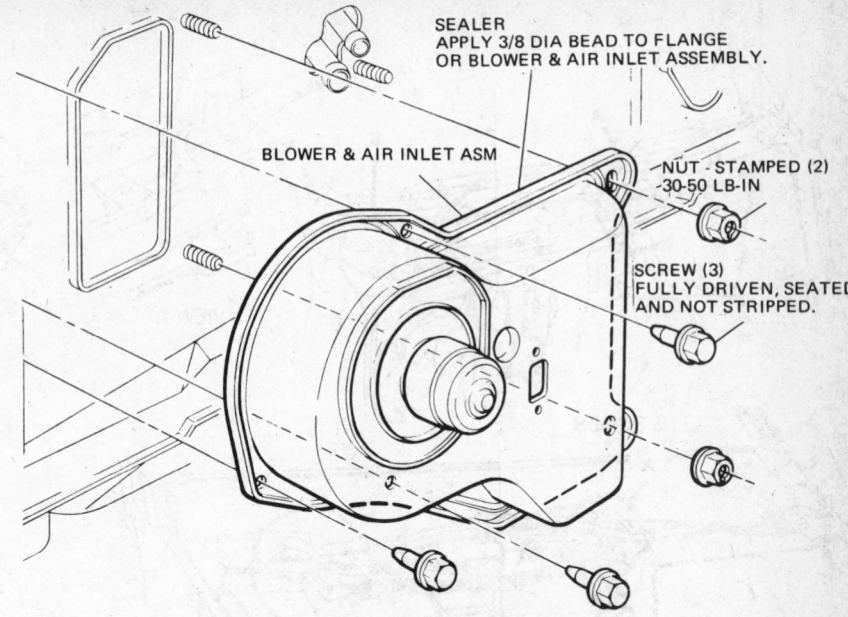

Blower motor and air inlet assembly—Regal

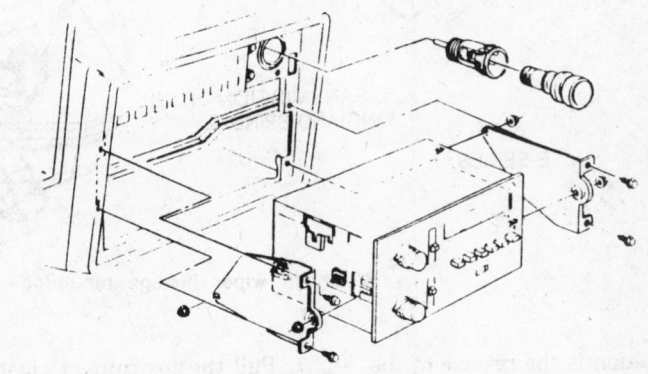

Typical radio mounting

5. Disconnect the radio wiring.

6. Remove the radio with the bracket attached.

7. Installation is the reverse of the removal procedure.

1982–85 Electra and LeSabre
1982–89 Estate Wagon

1. Disconnect the negative battery cable.

2. Remove the ashtray and mounting bracket bracket.

3. Pull off the radio knobs and trim washers.

4. Remove the lower left air duct.

5. Remove the two retaining nuts from the control shafts.

6. Disconnect the power lead, speaker wire and antenna lead.

7. Remove the rear radio mounting nut and slide the radio out.

8. Installation is the reverse of the removal procedure.

Windshield Wiper Motor

REMOVAL & INSTALLATION

All Models

1. Disconnect the negative battery cable.

2. Raise the hood and remove the cowl screen.

3. Loosen the transmission drive link to crank arm retaining bolts. Remove the drive link from the motor crank arm.

4. Disconnect the electrical wiring and the washer hoses from the motor assembly.

5. Remove the motor retaining screws. Remove the windshield wiper motor while guiding the crank arm through the hole.

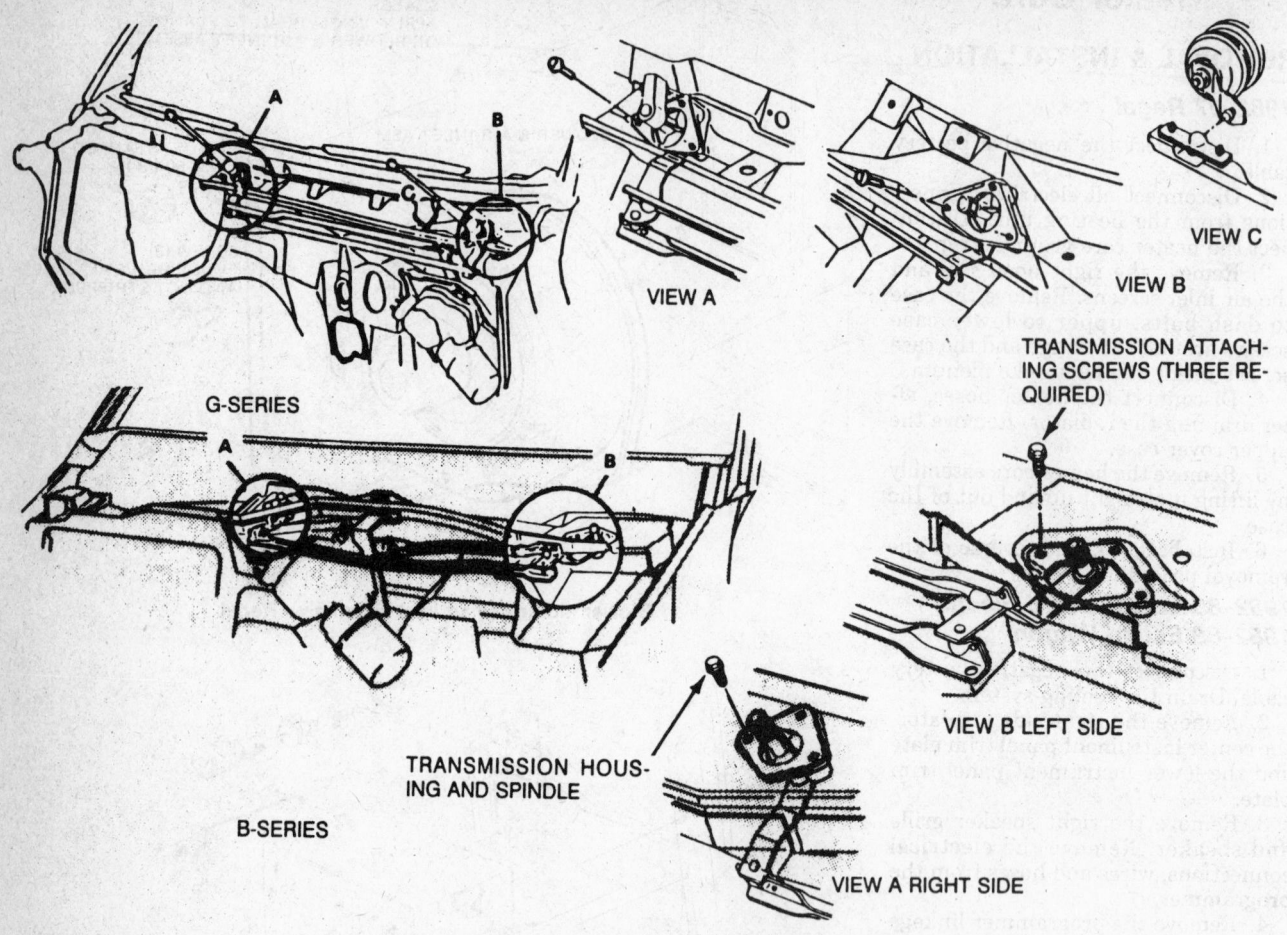

VIEW A

VIEW B

VIEW C

G-SERIES

TRANSMISSION ATTACH-
ING SCREWS (THREE RE-
QUIRED)

VIEW B LEFT SIDE

TRANSMISSION HOUS-
ING AND SPINDLE

B-SERIES

VIEW A RIGHT SIDE

Winshield wiper linkage mounting—all models

6. Installation is the reverse of the removal procedure. The motor must be in the PARK position before assembling the crank arm to the drive link.

Instrument Cluster

REMOVAL & INSTALLATION

1982–87 Regal (Standard Cluster)

1. Disconnect the negative battery cable. Remove the left side trim cover.
2. Remove the retaining screws holding the cluster carrier to the instrument panel.
3. Disconnect the speedometer cable from the split in the engine compartment, if a two piece cable is used.
4. Remove the steering column trim cover.
5. Disconnect the shift indicator clip.
6. Lower the steering column. If the vehicle is equipped with a tilt wheel it will be necessary to lower the wheel as far as possible and then unscrew the tilt lever.

7. Pull the instrument cluster forward enough to disconnect the speedometer cable from the rear of the cluster. Disconnect the wiring for I/P lighting.
8. Pull the gear selector lever down into the LOW position.
9. Pull the cluster out far enough to remove the screw retaining the Vehicle Speed Sensor (VSS) to the head of the speedometer.
10. Remove the cluster.
11. The installation of the cluster assembly is the reverse of the removal procedure.

1982–87 Regal (Digital Cluster)

1. Disconnect the negative battery cable. Remove the left hand trim panel.
2. Remove the instrument cluster housing as previously outlined. Pull the cluster out far enough to remove the screw retaining the Vehicle Speed Sensor (VSS) to the head of the speedometer.
3. Disconnect the two edgeboard connectors on the printed circuit from the tube and circuit board assembly.

Remove the four screws from the face of the cluster and remove the lense and bezel. All pushbuttons must be removed first, by pulling them straight out.
4. Remove the six screws holding the tube and circuit board to the cluster carrier. Remove the tube and circuit board.
5. Remove the two regular screws to remove the mechanical odometer from the tube and circuit board.
6. Remove the two telltale lenses and pads from the face plate. The shift indicator needle, spring and cable stay with the tube and circuit board. Do not remove.
7. Installation is the reverse order of the removal procedure.

1982–85 Electra and LeSabre 1982–89 Estate Wagon

1. Disconnect the negative battery cable. Remove the defroster grille.
2. Remove the 10 screws retaining the instrument panel top cover to the instrument panel.

3. If the vehicle is equipped with a twilight sentinel, pop up the photocell retainer and turn the photocell counterclockwise in the retainer and pull it down and out.

4. Slide the instrument panel top cover out far enough to disconnect the aspirator hose, electrical connector to the in-car sensor and the electrical connector to the electroluminescent inverter.

5. Remove the instrument panel top cover from the instrument panel. On models equipped with Quartz Electronic Speedometer clusters, remove the steering column trim cover, so that the shift indicator can be removed.

6. Remove the 5 screws from the instrument cluster to the instrument panel carrier. Pull the cluster housing assembly straight out, this will also separate the electrical connectors to the cluster.

NOTE: It may be helpful to tilt the wheel all the way down and pull the gear select lever to LOW, when removing the cluster.

7. Installation is the reverse order of the removal procedure.

Headlight Switch

REMOVAL & INSTALLATION

Rocker Switch

1. Disconnect the negative battery cable.
2. Remove the left hand trim cover.
3. Remove the left side switch trim cover.
4. Remove three screw, center screw shares the top of the switch and the bottom of the interior light rheostat.
5. Pull the switch and rheostat straight outwards, disconnect the wiring and remove the switch.
6. Installation is the reverse of the removal procedure.

Knob Switch

1. Disconnect the negative battery cable.
2. Pull the headlamp switch to the "ON" position.
3. Depending upon the switch mechanism, pull the trim knob from the switch by either reaching under the dash and depressing the switch shaft release button while pulling the knob and shaft from the light switch or by using a suitable tool and pushing the tang under the trim knob while pulling the knob from the shaft.
4. Remove the ferrule nut retaining the switch to the dash panel. Disconnect the electrical connector and remove the switch.

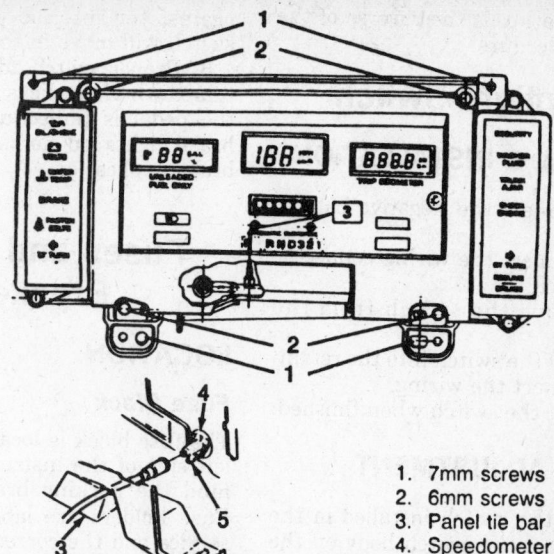

1. 7mm screws
2. 6mm screws
3. Panel tie bar
4. Speedometer head
5. Push down to release

Digital instrument cluster removal

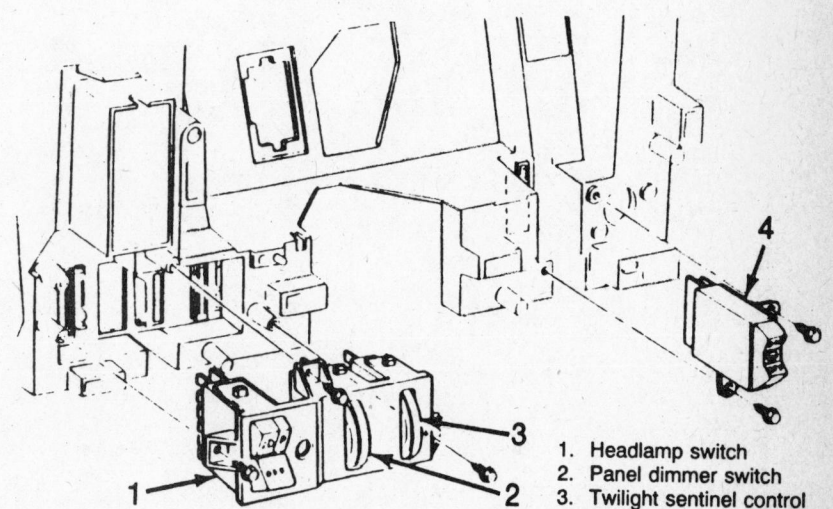

1. Headlamp switch
2. Panel dimmer switch
3. Twilight sentinel control
4. Rear defogger switch

Headlight switch mounting – rocker type

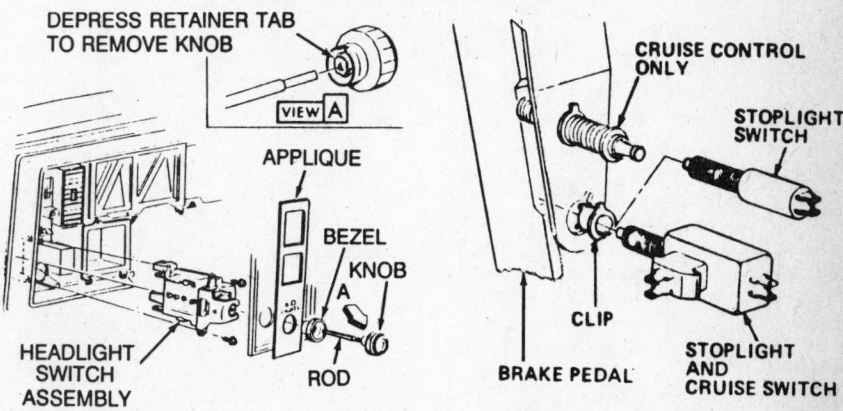

Headlight switch removal – knob type

Stoplight switch – typical

5. Installation is the reverse of the removal procedure.

Stoplight Switch

REMOVAL & INSTALLATION

1. Disconnect the negative battery cable.

2. Disconnect the wiring connector at the switch.

3. Remove the switch from the retainer.

4. Install the switch into the retainer and connect the wiring.

5. Adjust the switch when finished.

SWITCH ADJUSTMENT

1. With the switch installed in the retainer, seat the switch body on the tubular clip.

2. Pull the brake pedal rearward against the internal pedal stop. The switch will move in the tubular clip.

3. Proper switch adjustment is obtained when no clicks are heard when the pedal is pulled upward and the brake lights do not stay on without brake application.

Fuses and Circuit Breakers

LOCATION

Fuse Block

The fuse block is located beneath the left side of the instrument panel, behind the parking brake mechanism. Fuse holders are labeled as to their service and the correct amperage. Always replace blown fuses with new ones of the correct amperage.

Circuit Breakers

Circuit breakers are used along with the fusible links to protect the various components of the electrical system, such as the headlamps, power seats, electric windows, automatic door locks, etc.. The circuit breakers are located either in the switch or mounted on the fuse panel.

TURN SIGNAL FLASHER

All Models

Turn signal flasher is located at the base of steering column.

HAZARD FLASHER

All Models

Hazard flasher is located at the upper lefthand corner of the fuse block.

Cadillac
Rear Wheel Drive
Brougham, DeVille, Fleetwood

10

SERIAL NUMBER IDENTIFICATION

VEHICLE IDENTIFICATION CHART

It is important for servicing and ordering parts to be certain of the vehicle and engine identification. The VIN (vehicle identification number) is a 17 digit number visible through the windshield on the driver's side of the dash and contains the vehicle and engine identification codes. The tenth digit indicates model year, and the eighth digit indicates engine code. It can be interpreted as follows:

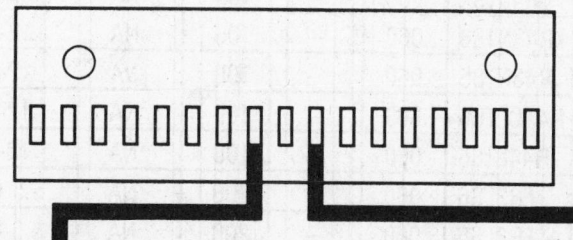

	Engine Code						Model Year	
Code	Cu. In.	Liters	Cyl.	Fuel Sys.	Eng. Mfg.	Code		Year
4	252	4.1	6	4 bbl	Buick	C		1982
N	350	5.7	8	Diesel	Oldsmobile	D		1983
8	250	4.1	8	DFI	Cadillac	E		1984
Y	307	5.0	8	Carburetor	Oldsmobile	F		1985
						G		1986
						H		1987
						J		1988
						K		1989

DFI — Digital Fuel Injection

GENERAL ENGINE SPECIFICATIONS

Year	VIN	No. Cylinder Displacement cu. in. (liter)	Fuel System Type	Net Horsepower @ rpm	Net Torque @ rpm (ft.lbs.)	Bore × Stroke (in.)	Compression Ratio	Oil Pressure @ rpm
1982	4	6-252 (4.1)	4 bbl	125 @ 3800	210 @ 2000	3.965 × 3.400	8.0:1	35①
	N	8-350 (5.7)	Diesel	105 @ 3200	205 @ 1600	4.057 × 3.385	22.5:1	40①
	8	8-250 (4.1)	DFI	135 @ 4200	190 @ 2000	3.465 × 3.307	8.5:1	30①
1983	N	8-350 (5.7)	Diesel	105 @ 3200	205 @ 1600	4.057 × 3.385	22.5:1	40①
	8	8-250 (4.1)	DFI	135 @ 4200	190 @ 2000	3.465 × 3.307	8.5:1	30①
1984	N	8-350 (5.7)	Diesel	105 @ 3200	205 @ 1600	4.057 × 3.385	22.5:1	40①
	8	8-250 (4.1)	DFI	135 @ 4200	190 @ 2000	3.465 × 3.307	8.5:1	30①
1985	N	8-350 (5.7)	Diesel	105 @ 3200	205 @ 1600	4.057 × 3.385	22.5:1	40①
	8	8-250 (4.1)	DFI	135 @ 4200	190 @ 2000	3.465 × 3.307	8.5:1	30①
1986	Y	8-307 (5.0)	4 bbl	140 @ 3200	255 @ 2000	3.800 × 3.390	8.0:1	30②
1987	Y	8-307 (5.0)	4 bbl	140 @ 3200	255 @ 2000	3.800 × 3.390	8.0:1	30②
1988-89	Y	8-307 (5.0)	4 bbl	140 @ 3200	255 @ 2000	3.800 × 3.390	8.0:1	30-45②

DFI—Digital Fuel Injection   ① @ 2000 rpm   ② @ 1500 rpm

GASOLINE ENGINE TUNE-UP SPECIFICATIONS

Year	VIN	No. Cylinder Displacement cu. in. (liter)	Spark Plugs Type	Gap (in.)	Ignition Timing (deg.) MT	Ignition Timing (deg.) AT	Compression Pressure (psi)	Fuel Pump (psi)	Speed (rpm) MT	Speed (rpm) AT	Valve Clearance In.	Valve Clearance Ex.
1982	4	6-252 (4.1)	R45TSX	.060	—	15B	NA	4.25-5.75	—	550	Hyd.	Hyd.
	8	8-250 (4.1)	R43NTS6	.060	—	10B	NA	12-14	—	450	Hyd.	Hyd.
1983	8	8-250 (4.1)	R43NTS6	.060	—	10B	NA	12-14	—	450	Hyd.	Hyd.
1984	8	8-250 (4.1)	R42CLTS6	.060	—	10B	NA	12-14	—	450	Hyd.	Hyd.
1985	8	8-250 (4.1)	R44LTS6	.060	—	10B	NA	12-14	—	450	Hyd.	Hyd.
1986	Y	8-307 (5.0)	FR3LS6	.060	—	20B	NA	5.5-6.5	—	475	Hyd.	Hyd.
1987	Y	8-307 (5.0)	FR3LS6	.060	—	20B	NA	5.5-6.5	—	475	Hyd.	Hyd.
1988	Y	8-307 (5.0)	FR3LS6	.060	—	20B	NA	6.0-7.5	—	450	Hyd.	Hyd.
1989		SEE UNDERHOOD SPECIFICATIONS STICKER										

DIESEL ENGINE TUNE-UP SPECIFICATIONS

Year	VIN	No. Engine Displacement cu. in. (liter)	Valve Clearance Intake (in.)	Valve Clearance Exhaust (in.)	Intake Valve Opens (deg.)	Injection Pump Setting (deg.)	Injection Nozzle Pressure (psi) New	Injection Nozzle Pressure (psi) Used	Idle Speed (rpm)	Cranking Compression Pressure (psi)
1982	N	8-350 (5.7)	Hyd.	Hyd.	16	NA	870	NA	600 ①	275
1983	N	8-350 (5.7)	Hyd.	Hyd.	16	NA	1225	1025	600 ①	275
1984	N	8-350 (5.7)	Hyd.	Hyd.	16	NA	1000	850	600 ①	300
1985	N	8-350 (5.7)	Hyd.	Hyd.	16	NA	1000	NA	600 ①	300

① Fast Idle 750 rpm
Hyd.—Hydraulic Valve Adjusters—zero lash

CAPACITIES

Year	VIN	No. Cylinder Displacement cu. in. (liter)	Engine Crankcase with Filter	Engine Crankcase without Filter	Transmission (pts.) AT	Transmission (pts.) (pts.)	Drive Axle (gals.)	Fuel Tank (qts.)	Cooling System
1982	4	6-252 (4.1)	5	4	–	8.0	4.25	25.0	18.2
	N	8-350 (5.7)	7	6	–	10.6	3.50	26.0	23.7
	8	8-250 (4.1)	5	4	–	10.0	3.50	24.5	11
1983	N	8-350 (5.7)	7	6	–	10.6	3.50	26.0	23.7
	8	8-250 (4.1)	5	4	–	10.0	3.50	24.5	11
1984	N	8-350 (5.7)	7	6	–	10.6	3.50	26.0	23.7
	8	8-250 (4.1)	5	4	–	10.0	3.50	24.5	11
1985	N	8-350 (5.7)	7	6	–	10.6	3.50	26.0	23.7
	8	8-250 (4.1)	5	4	–	10.0	3.50	24.5	11
1986	Y	8-307 (5.0)	5	4	–	10.6	3.50	24.5	15.3
1987	Y	8-307 (5.0)	5	4	–	10.6	3.50	20.7	15.3
1988-89	Y	8-307 (5.0)	5	4	–	10.6	4.25	25.0	15.3

FIRING ORDERS

NOTE: To avoid confusion, always replace spark plugs and wires one at a time.

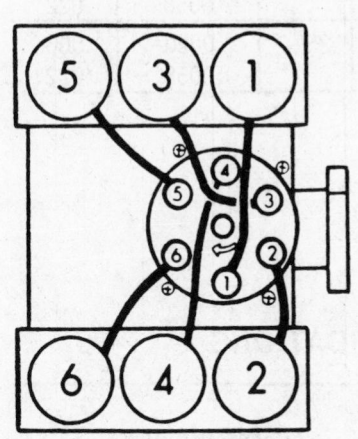

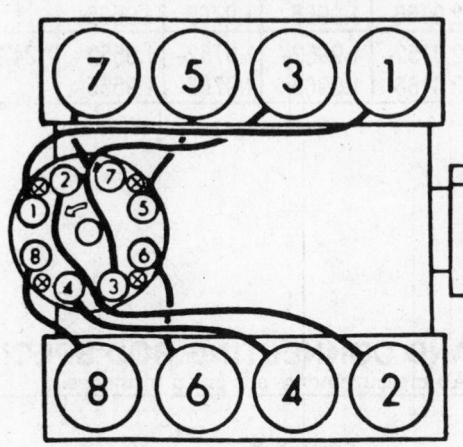

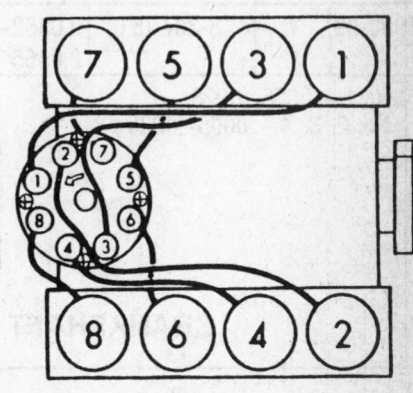

GM (Buick) 252 (4.1 L) V6
Engine firing order: 1-6-5-4-3-2
Distributor rotation: clockwise

GM (Oldsmobile) 8–307 (5.0L)
Engine firing order: 1–8–4–3–6–5–7–2
Distributor rotation: counterclockwise

GM (Cadillac) 8–250 (4.1L)
Engine firing order: 1–8–4–3–6–5–7–2
Distributor rotation: counterclockwise

CAMSHAFT SPECIFICATIONS
All measurements given in inches.

Year	VIN	No. Cylinder Displacement cu. in. (liter)	Journal Diameter 1	Journal Diameter 2	Journal Diameter 3	Journal Diameter 4	Journal Diameter 5	Lobe Lift In.	Lobe Lift Ex.	Bearing Clearance	Camshaft End Play
1982	4	6-252 (4.1)	1.7850–1.7860	1.7850–1.7860	1.7850–1.7860	1.7850–1.7160	–	NA	NA	①	NA
	N	8-350 (5.7)	2.0357–2.0365	2.0157–2.0165	1.9957–1.9965	1.9757–1.9765	1.9557–1.9565	.252	.279	.0020–.0058	.011–.077

CAMSHAFT SPECIFICATIONS
All measurements given in inches.

Year	VIN	No. Cylinder Displacement cu. in. (liter)	Journal Diameter 1	2	3	4	5	Lobe Lift In.	Ex.	Bearing Clearance	Camshaft End Play
1982	8	8-250 (4.1)	NA	NA	NA	NA	NA	.384	.396	.0018–.0037	NA
1983	N	8-350 (5.7)	2.0357–2.0365	2.0157–2.0165	1.9957–1.9965	1.9757–1.9765	1.9557–1.9565	.252	.279	.0020–.0058	.011–.077
	8	8-250 (4.1)	NA	NA	NA	NA	NA	.384	.396	.0018–.0037	NA
1984	N	8-350 (5.7)	2.0357–2.0365	2.0157–2.0165	1.9957–1.9965	1.9757–1.9765	1.9557–1.9565	.252	.279	.0020–.0058	.011–.077
	8	8-250 (4.1)	NA	NA	NA	NA	NA	.384	.396	.0018–.0037	NA
1985	N	8-350 (5.7)	2.0357–2.0365	2.0157–2.0165	1.9957–1.9965	1.9757–1.9765	1.9557–1.9565	.252	.279	.0020–.0058	.011–.077
	8	8-250 (4.1)	NA	NA	NA	NA	NA	.384	.396	.0018–.0037	NA
1986	Y	8-307 (5.0)	2.0352–2.0365	2.0152–2.0166	1.9952–1.9965	1.9752–1.9765	1.9552–1.9565	.247	.251	.0020–.0058	.006–.022
1987	Y	8-307 (5.0)	2.0352–2.0365	2.0152–2.0166	1.9952–1.9965	1.9752–1.9765	1.9552–1.9565	.247	.251	.0020–.0058	.006–.022
1988-89	Y	8-307 (5.0)	2.0352–2.0365	2.0152–2.0166	1.9952–1.9965	1.9752–1.9765	1.9552–1.9565	.247	.251	.0020–.0058	.006–.022

① No.1 – .0005–.0025
No. 2, 3, 4 – .0005–.0035

CRANKSHAFT AND CONNECTING ROD SPECIFICATIONS
All measurements are given in inches.

Year	VIN	No. Cylinder Displacement cu. in. (liter)	Crankshaft Main Brg. Journal Dia.	Main Brg. Oil Clearance	Shaft End-play	Thrust on No.	Connecting Rod Journal Diameter	Oil Clearance	Side Clearance
1982	4	6-252 (4.1)	2.4995	.0003–.0018	.003 .009	2	2.2487–2.2495	.0005–.0026	.006–.023
	N	8-350 (5.7)	2.9993–3.0003	.0005–.0021 ①	.004–.014	3	2.1238–2.1248	.0005–.0026	.006–.020
	8	8-250 (4.1)	2.640	.0008–.0039	.001–.007	3	2.052–2.054	.0005–.0028	.006–.020
1983	N	8-350 (5.7)	2.9993–3.0003	.0005–.0021 ①	.004–.014	3	2.1238–2.1248	.0005–.0026	.006–.020
	8	8-250 (4.1)	2.640	.0008–.0039	.001–.007	3	2.052–2.054	.0005–.0028	.006–.020

CRANKSHAFT AND CONNECTING ROD SPECIFICATIONS
All measurements are given in inches.

Year	VIN	No. Cylinder Displacement cu. in. (liter)	Crankshaft				Connecting Rod		
			Main Brg. Journal Dia.	Main Brg. Oil Clearance	Shaft End-play	Thrust on No.	Journal Diameter	Oil Clearance	Side Clearance
1984	N	8-350 (5.7)	2.9993–3.0003 ①	.0005–.0021 ①	.004–.014	3	2.1238–2.1248	.0005–.0026	.006–.020
	8	8-250 (4.1)	2.640	.0008–.0039	.001–.007	3	2.052–2.054	.0005–.0028	.006–.020
1985	N	8-350 (5.7)	2.9993–3.0003 ①	.0005–.0021 ①	.004–.014	3	2.1238–2.1248	.0005–.0026	.006–.020
	8	8-250 (4.1)	2.640	.0008–.0039	.001–.007	3	2.052–2.054	.0005–.0028	.006–.020
1986	Y	8-307 (5.0)	2.4985–2.4995 ②	.0005–.0021 ①	.0035–.0135	3	2.1238–2.1248	.0004–.0033	.006–.020
1987	Y	8-307 (5.0)	2.4985–2.4995 ②	.0005–.0021 ①	.0035–.0135	3	2.1238–2.1248	.0004–.0033	.006–.020
1988-89	Y	8-307 (5.0)	2.4985–2.4995 ②	.0005–.0021 ①	.0035–.0135	3	2.1238–2.1248	.0004–.0033	.006–.020

① No. 5 — .0015–.0031
② No. 1 — 2.4988–2.4998

VALVE SPECIFICATIONS
All measurements are given in inches.

Year	VIN	No. Cylinder Displacement cu. in. (liter)	Seat Angle (deg.)	Face Angle (deg.)	Spring Test Pressure (lbs.)	Spring Installed Height (in.)	Stem-to-Guide Clearance (in.)		Stem Diameter (in.)	
							Intake	Exhaust	Intake	Exhaust
1982	4	6-252 (4.1)	45①	45①	210-230 @ 1.34	$1\frac{47}{64}$	.0015–.0035	.0015–.0032	.3401–.3412	.3405–.3412
	N	8-350 (5.7)	45②	44②	203-217 @ 1.22	$1\frac{43}{64}$	.0010–.0027	.0015–.0032	.3425–.3432	.3420–.3427
	8	8-250 (4.1)	45③	44③	175-189 @ 1.28	$1\frac{47}{64}$	.0010–.0030	.0010–.0030	.3413–.3420	.3411–.3418
1983	N	8-350 (5.7)	45②	44②	203-217 @ 1.22	$1\frac{43}{64}$	.0010–.0027	.0015–.0032	.3425–.3432	.3420–.3427
	8	8-250 (4.1)	45③	44③	175-189 @ 1.28	$1\frac{47}{64}$	.0010–.0030	.0010–.0030	.3413–.3420	.3411–.3418
1984	N	8-350 (5.7)	45②	44②	203-217 @ 1.22	$1\frac{43}{64}$	.0010–.0027	.0015–.0032	.3425–.3432	.3420–.3427
	8	8-250 (4.1)	45③	44③	175-189 @ 1.28	$1\frac{47}{64}$	.0010–.0030	.0010–.0030	.3413–.3420	.3411–.3418

VALVE SPECIFICATIONS

Year	VIN	No. Cylinder Displacement cu. in. (liter)	Seat Angle (deg.)	Face Angle (deg.)	Spring Test Pressure (lbs.)	Spring Installed Height (in.)	Stem-to-Guide Clearance (in.)		Stem Diameter (in.)	
							Intake	Exhaust	Intake	Exhaust
1985	N	8-350 (5.7)	45②	44②	203-217 @ 1.22	1$^{43}/_{64}$	.0010–.0027	.0015–.0032	.3425–.3432	.3420–.3427
	8	8-250 (4.1)	45③	44③	175-189 @ 1.28	1$^{47}/_{64}$	.0010–.0030	.0010–.0030	.3413–.3420	.3411–.3418
1986	Y	8-307 (5.0)	45②	44②	180–194 @ 1.27	1$^{43}/_{64}$	.0010–.0027	.0015–.0032	.3425–.3432	.3420–.3427
1987	Y	8-307 (5.0)	45②	44②	180–194 @ 1.27	1$^{43}/_{64}$	.0010–.0027	.0015–.0032	.3425–.3432	.3420–.3427
1988-89	Y	8-307 (5.0)	45②	44②	180–194 @ 1.27	1$^{43}/_{64}$	.0010–.0027	.0015–.0032	.3425–.3432	.3420–.3427

① Exhaust Valve—45° Seat, 45° Face
② Exhaust Valve—31° Seat, 30° Face
③ Exhaust Valve—45° Seat, 44° Face

PISTON AND RING SPECIFICATIONS
All measurments are given in inches.

Year	VIN	No. Cylinder Displacement cu. in. (liter)	Piston Clearance	Ring Gap			Ring Side Clearance		
				Top Compression	Bottom Compression	Oil Control	Top Compression	Bottom Compression	Oil Control
1982	4	6-252 (4.1)	.0013–.0035 ②	.013–.023	.013–.023	.015–.035	.0030–.0050	.0030–.0050	.0035 Max
	N	8-350 (5.7)	.0030–.0040 ③	.015–.025	.015–.025	.015–.055	.050–.007	.0030–.0050	.0010–.0050
	8	8-250 (4.1)	.0010–.0018 ④	.009–.020	.009–.020	.010–.050	.0016–.0037	.0016–.0037	None ①
1983	N	8-350 (5.7)	.0030–.0040 ③	.015–.025	.015–.025	.015–.055	.050–.007	.0030–.0050	.0010–.0050
	8	8-250 (4.1)	.0010–.0018 ④	.009–.020	.009–.020	.010–.050	.0016–.0037	.0016–.0037	None ①
1984	N	8-350 (5.7)	.0030–.0040 ③	.015–.025	.015–.025	.015–.055	.050–.007	.0030–.0050	.0010–.0050
	8	8-250 (4.1)	.0010–.0018 ④	.009–.020	.009–.020	.010–.050	.0016–.0037	.0016–.0037	None ①

PISTON AND RING SPECIFICATIONS
All measurments are given in inches.

Year	VIN	No. Cylinder Displacement cu. in. (liter)	Piston Clearance	Ring Gap			Ring Side Clearance		
				Top Compression	Bottom Compression	Oil Control	Top Compression	Bottom Compression	Oil Control
1985	N	8-350 (5.7)	.0030– .0040 ③	.015– .025	.015– .025	.015– .055	.050– .007	.0030– .0050	.0010– .0050
	8	8-250 (4.1)	.0010– .0018 ④	.009– .020	.009– .020	.010– .050	.0016– .0037	.0016– .0037	None ①
1986	Y	8-307 (5.0)	.00075– .00175 ③	.009– .019	.009– .019	.015– .055	.0018– .0038	.0018– .0038	.001– .005
1987	Y	8-307 (5.0)	.00075– .00175 ③	.009– .019	.009– .019	.015– .055	.0018– .0038	.0018– .0038	.001– .005
1988-89	Y	8-307 (5.0)	.00075– .00175 ③	.009– .019	.009– .019	.015– .055	.0018– .0038	.0018– .0038	.001– .005

① Side sealing
② Measurement taken at skirt bottom
③ Clearance to bore (selective)
④ Piston skirt top clearance

TORQUE SPECIFICATIONS
All readings in ft. lbs.

Year	VIN	No. Cylinder Displacement cu. in. (liter)	Cylinder Head Bolts	Main Bearing Bolts	Rod Bearing Bolts	Crankshaft Pulley Bolts	Flywheel Bolts	Manifold		Spark Plugs
								Intake	Exhaust	
1982	4	6-252 (4.1)	80	100	40	225	60	45	25	15
	N	8-350 (5.7)	130②	120	42	200-310	60	40①	25	NA
	8	8-250 (4.1)	90 ③	85	22	Press fit	37⑤	⑥	18	10
1983	N	8-350 (5.7)	130②	120	42	200-310	60	40①	25	NA
	8	8-250 (4.1)	90③	85	22	Press fit	37⑤	⑥	18	10
1984	N	8-350 (5.7)	130②	120	42	200-310	60	40①	25	NA
	8	8-250 (4.1)	90③	85	22	Press fit	37⑤	⑥	18	10
1985	N	8-350 (5.7)	130②	120	42	200-310	60	40①	25	NA
	8	8-250 (4.1)	90 ③	85	22	Press fit	37⑤	⑥	18	10
1986	Y	8-307 (5.0)	125①	80 ④	42	200-310	60	40 ①	25	25
1987	Y	8-307 (5.0)	130①	80 ④	48	200-310	60	40 ①	25	25
1988-89	Y	8-307 (5.0)	130①	80 ④	48	200-310	60	40 ①	25	25

① Dip bolt in oil before installation
② Tighten first to 45 ft. lbs., then go to 90 ft. lbs., then to specification
③ Tighten first to 45 ft. lbs., then to specification
④ Rear main bearing torque 120 ft. lbs.
⑤ 17 mm bolt head—63 ft. lbs.
⑥ Tighten bolts 1, 2, 3, 4 in sequence to 11-15 ft. lbs.; tighten bolts 5 thru 16 to 18-22 ft. lbs.; retighten all bolts in sequence to 18-22 ft. lbs.

BRAKE SPECIFICATIONS
All measurements in inches unless noted

Year	Model	Lug Nut Torque (ft. lbs.)	Master Cylinder Bore	Brake Disc Minimum Thickness	Brake Disc Maximum Runout	Standard Brake Drum Diameter	Minimum Lining Thickness Front	Minimum Lining Thickness Rear
1982	All	100	NA	.980	.965	11.000	.030	.030①
1983	All	100	NA	.980	.965	11.000	.030	.030①
1984	All	100	NA	.980	.965	11.000	.030	.030①
1985	All	100	NA	.980	.965	11.000	.030	.030①
1986	All	100	NA	.980	.965	11.000	.030	.030①
1987	All	100	NA	.980	.965	11.000	.030	.030①
1988-89	All	100	NA	.980	.965	11.000	.030	.030①

① Bonded lining .062

WHEEL ALIGNMENT

Year	Model	Caster Range (deg.)	Caster Preferred Setting (deg.)	Camber Range (deg.)	Camber Preferred Setting (deg.)	Toe-in (in.)	Steering Axis Inclination (deg.)
1982	All	2P–4P	3P	$\frac{5}{16}$N – 1$\frac{5}{16}$P	$\frac{1}{2}$P	$\frac{1}{8}$	10$\frac{14}{32}$
1983	All	2P–4P	3P	$\frac{5}{16}$N – 1$\frac{5}{16}$P	$\frac{1}{2}$P	$\frac{1}{8}$	10$\frac{14}{32}$
1984	All	2P–4P	3P	$\frac{5}{16}$N – 1$\frac{5}{16}$P	$\frac{1}{2}$P	$\frac{1}{8}$	10$\frac{14}{32}$
1985	All	2P–4P	3P	$\frac{5}{16}$N – 1$\frac{5}{16}$P	$\frac{1}{2}$P	$\frac{1}{8}$	10$\frac{14}{32}$
1986	All	2P–4P	3P	$\frac{5}{16}$N – 1$\frac{5}{16}$P	$\frac{1}{2}$P	$\frac{1}{8}$	10$\frac{14}{32}$
1987	All	2P–4P	3P	$\frac{3}{16}$P – $\frac{13}{16}$P	$\frac{5}{16}$P	$\frac{3}{64}$	10$\frac{19}{32}$
1988-89	All	2P–4P	3P	$\frac{3}{16}$P – $\frac{13}{16}$P	$\frac{5}{16}$P	$\frac{3}{64}$	10$\frac{19}{32}$

TUNE-UP PROCEDURES

Ignition Timing

ADJUSTMENT

NOTE: Always follow the tune-up procedures (timing, idle speed) listed on the Emission Control Information Label if they disagree with the following data.

1. If the vehicle is equipped with EST, disconnect the four terminal connector from the wiring harness. On 1985 vehicles equipped with the HT 4100 (250 V8) engine, disconnect the green reference signal connectors on the engine wire assembly at the rear of the engine near the distributor assembly. On the 1986–89 vehicles, ground the assembly line diagnostic lead connector.

2. Make sure the timing marks are clean and readable. Timing marks are located on the front engine cover and one the harmonic balancer or pulley.

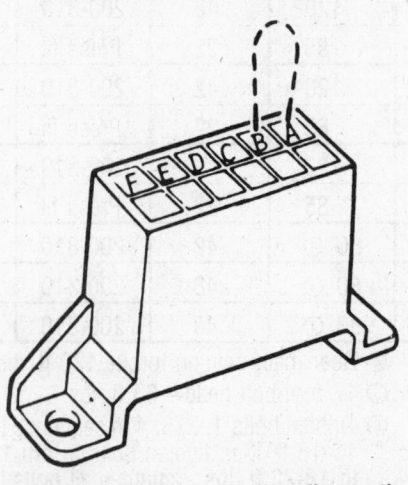

Grounding the assembly line diagnostic connector

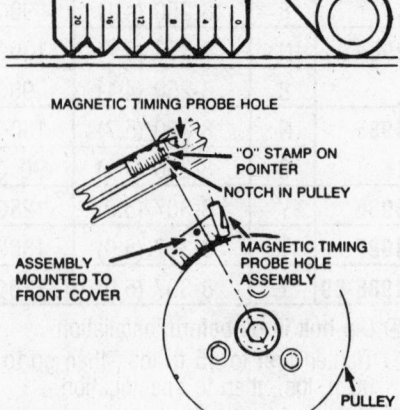

Magnetic timing probe hole location—250 V8

Start the engine and let it run until it reaches normal operating temperature.

3. Stop the engine and connect a timing light to No.1 cylinder. Connect a suitable tachometer.

4. Loosen the distributor clamp.

5. Start the engine. Rotate the distributor until the correct marks line up. Tighten the distributor clamp and recheck the timing. As required, unground the the assembly line diagnostic lead connector while the engine is still running.

6. Adjust the engine idle rpm if necessary.

Valve Lash

ADJUSTMENT

All engines use hydraulic valve lifters which require no periodic maintenance or adjustment.

Idle Speed and Mixture Gasoline Engines

ADJUSTMENT

Carbureted Models

NOTE: All carburetors have mixture needles concealed under staked in plugs. Mixture adjustments are possible only during carburetor overhaul or extreme circumstances. Vehicles equipped with the computer command control system can not use the propane enrichment or lean drop methods of idle mixture adjustment.

1. Place the transmission in the park position, set the parking brake and block the drive wheels. Connect a suitable tachometer to the engine. Remove the air cleaner assembly and plug the vacuum hose to the Thermal Vacuum Valve (TVV).

2. Disconnect and plug the vacuum hose to the EGR valve and the vacuum hose to the canister purge port.

3. Disconnect and plug the vacuum hose to the idle load compensator (ILC). Back out the idle stop screw on the carburetor three turns.

4. Turn the air condition control switch to the OFF position. With the engine running and at normal operating temperature, place the transmission in the drive position. Fully extend the idle load compensator plunger (no vacuum applied).

5. Using tool J-29607, Bt-8022 or equivalent, adjust the ILC plunger to obtain a 725 ± 50 rpm. The jam nut on the plunger must be held with a

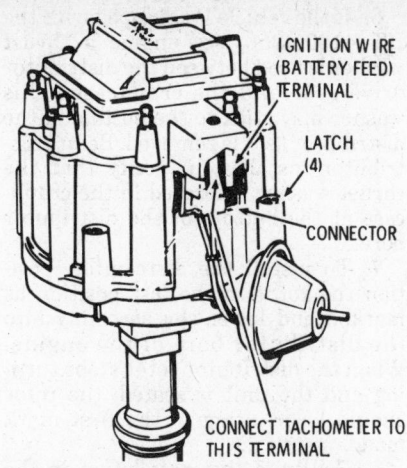

IGNITION WIRE (BATTERY FEED) TERMINAL

LATCH (4)

CONNECTOR

CONNECT TACHOMETER TO THIS TERMINAL

HEI tachometer hookup without EST

suitable wrench to prevent damage to the guide tabs.

6. Measure the distance from the jam nut to the tip of the plunger. The dimension must not exceed 1 in. If the dimension does exceed 1 in., check for a low idle condition. Remove the plug from the ILC vacuum hose and plug the hose back into the ILC. Adjust the idle speed to specification in the drive position.

7. If the idle speed is correct then the adjustment is over. If the idle speed does not meet specifications perform the following.

8. Stop the engine and remove the idle load compensator. It will not be necessary to remove the idle load compensator if a hex wrench is modified to clear the obstructions.

9. Remove the rubber cap from the center outlet tube. Using a $\frac{3}{32}$ in. hex key wrench, insert it through the open center tube to engage the idle speed adjusting screw inside the tube.

10. If the idle speed was low, turn the adjusting screw counterclockwise one turn for every 75–100 rpm low. If the idle was too high, turn the adjusting screw clockwise one turn for every 75–100 rpm high. Reinstall the plug on the center of the outlet tube.

11. Reinstall the idle load compensator on the carburetor and attach the the throttle return spring and other related parts removed. Recheck the idle speed in the drive position and closed loop mode. If the idle speed is still not within specification, repeat the procedure.

12. Disconnect the power feed (fuse) to the ECM with the ignition off, for ten seconds. This will allow the ECM to reset the throttle position sensor valve.

13. Disconnect and plug the vacuum source to the ILC. Apply a vacuum source using a hand held vacuum pump or equivalent to the ILC vacuum inlet tube to fully retract the plunger.

14. Adjust the idle stop screw on the carburetor float bowl to obtain a 450 rpm in the drive position. Place the transmission in park and stop the engine.

15. Remove the plug from the vacuum hose and install the hose on the ILC vacuum inlet tube. Remove all the plugs from the disconnected vacuum lines and reconnect the vacuum lines to their proper ports.

16. Install the air cleaner and gasket, remove the blocks from the drive wheels and road test the vehicle.

Fuel Injected Models

NOTE: The HT 4100 (250 V8) engine idle speed is controlled by the electronic control module. The idle adjustment is only necessary when the idle speed control motor or the throttle body has been replaced. Before making this idle speed adjustment, record, repair and clear all trouble codes in the electronic control module memory.

1. Remove the air cleaner assembly. Connect a suitable tachometer and timing light. Start the engine and let it run until it reaches normal operating temperature.

2. Turn all the accessories off. Check and adjust the ignition timing.

3. Place the steering wheel in the center position and the transmission selector in the park position.

4. Retract the idle speed control motor (ISC) plunger. To do this, unlock the ISC motor connector, but do not disconnect the motor. Open the throttle and hold it at approximately 1500 rpm.

5. Using the same hand close the throttle switch by depressing the ISC plunger. When the plunger is fully retracted, continue to hold the throttle open and the throttle switch closed, while disconnecting the ISC motor.

6. Return the throttle to idle. Be sure not to power the ISC motor in the fully retracted position for more than four seconds or damage to the electronic control module may occur.

7. The ISC plunger should now be retracted. If the plunger still contacts the throttle lever, turn the plunger in so it is not touching. With the ISC plunger fully retracted and not touching the throttle lever, the idle speed should be 450 rpm.

8. Check the throttle position sensor adjustment. With the ISC motor fully retracted and the throttle against the stop screw. Turn the ISC plunger adjustment screw to obtain a 0.160 in. gap between the throttle lever and the plunger.

9. Shut the engine off, disconnect all the test equipment and plug in all

harness connectors. Turn the ignition off for a least ten seconds. Start the engine and check the ISC motor for proper operation.

NOTE: This procedure could have recorded intermittent trouble codes in the DFI computer. After all the connections have been made and the system is restored to normal operations, these codes must be cleared.

Idle Speed Diesel Engine

ADJUSTMENT

1. Run the engine until normal operating temperature is reached.
2. Insert the probe of the magnetic pickup tachometer into the timing indicator hole. Set the parking brake and block the drive wheels.
3. Turn all accessories off. Position the transmission selector lever in the drive position.
4. Turn the slow idle screw on the injection pump to obtain the idle speed specified on the emission control label.

ENGINE ELECTRICAL

Distributor

REMOVAL & INSTALLATION

NOTE: If required, malfunction trouble codes must be cleared after the removal or adjustment of the distributor. For complete information refer to *"Chilton's Guide to Electronic Engine Controls".*

Timing Not Disturbed

1. Disconnect the negative battery cable. Disconnect the electrical wires from the distributor cap. Disconnect the coil locking tab connectors.
2. Remove the distributor cap retaining screws. Remove the distributor cap and position it to the side.
3. Disconnect the four terminal ECM harness from the distributor.
4. Remove the distributor assembly retaining bolt.
5. Note and mark the position of the rotor. Pull the distributor upward until the rotor stops turning and again note the position of the rotor. Remove the distributor assembly from the vehicle.

6. If the vehicle is equipped with the HT 4100 (250 V8) engine a thrust washer is used between the distributor drive gear and the crankcase. This washer may stick to the bottom of the distributor as it is removed. Before distributor installation, verify that the thrust washer is located in the crankcase at the bottom of the distributor bore.
7. To install the distributor, position the rotor in the last position as marked and lower the assembly into the distributor bore of the engine. When the distributor rotor stops turning and the unit is seated, the rotor should be pointing to the first mark made.
8. Continue the installation in the reverse order of the removal procedure.
9. If required, malfunction trouble codes must be cleared after the removal or adjustment of the distributor.

Timing Disturbed

1. Disconnect the negative battery cable. Disconnect the electrical wires from the distributor cap. Disconnect the coil locking tab connectors.
2. Remove the distributor cap retaining screws. Remove the distributor cap and position it to the side.
3. Disconnect the four terminal ECM harness from the distributor.
4. Remove the distributor assembly retaining bolt.
5. Note and mark the position of the rotor. Pull the distributor upward until the rotor stops turning and again note the position of the rotor. Remove the distributor assembly from the vehicle.
6. If the engine has been accidently cranked with the distributor out, remove the number one spark plug. Place your finger over the number one spark plug hole and crank the engine slowly until a compression build up can be felt in that cylinder.
7. Carefully align the timing mark on the crankshaft pulley to the "O" mark on the timing indicator of the engine. Turn the distributor rotor to point between the No. 1 and No. 8 spark plug towers on the distributor cap.
8. If the vehicle is equipped with the HT 4100 (250 V8) engine a thrust washer is used between the distributor drive gear and the crankcase. This washer may stick to the bottom of the distributor as it is removed. Before distributor installation, verify that the thrust washer is located in the crankcase at the bottom of the distributor bore.
9. To install the distributor, position it as indicated and lower the assembly into the distributor bore of the

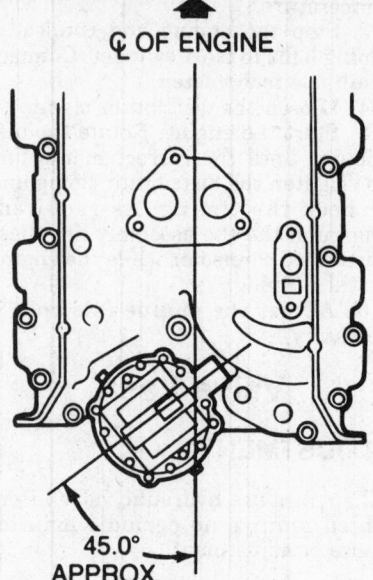

FRONT OF ENGINE

℄ OF ENGINE

45.0° APPROX.

Distributor positioning—250 V8

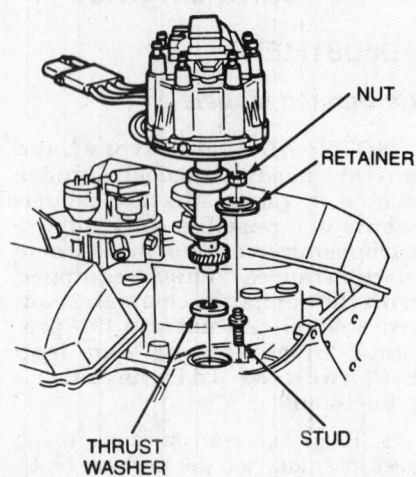

NUT

RETAINER

THRUST WASHER

STUD

Thrust washer location on distributor shaft—250 V8

engine. When the distributor rotor stops turning and the unit is seated, the rotor should be pointing as indicated above.
10. Continue the installation in the reverse order of the removal procedure.
11. If required, malfunction trouble codes must be cleared after the removal or adjustment of the distributor.

Alternator

For further information on the charging system, please refer to "Charging and Starting" in the Unit Repair section.

PRECAUTIONS

Several precautions must be observed with alternator equipped vehicles to avoid damage to the unit.

• If the battery is removed for any reason, make sure it is reconnected with the correct polarity. Reversing the battery connections may result in damage to the one-way rectifiers.

• When utilizing a booster battery as a starting aid, always connect the positive to positive terminals, and the negative terminal from the booster battery to a good engine ground on the car being started.

• Never use a fast charger as a booster to start vehicles with alternating-current (AC) circuits.

• Disconnect the battery cables when charging the battery with a fast charger.

• Never attempt to polarize an alternator.

• Avoid long soldering times when making alternator repairs. Prolonged heat will damage the alternator.

• Do not use test lamps of more than 12 volts when checking diode continuity.

• Do not short across or ground any of the alternator terminals.

• The polarity of the battery, alternator and regulator must be matched and considered before making any electrical connections within the system.

• Never separate the alternator on an open circuit. Make sure all connections within the circuit are clean and tight.

• Disconnect the battery ground terminal when performing any service on electrical components.

• Disconnect the battery if arc welding is to be done on the vehicle.

BELT TENSION ADJUSTMENT

Using belt tension gauge J–23600 or equivalent adjust the alternator belt if the tension is below 300N, as indicated on the gauge. If the belt is used the correct belt tension is 600N, as indicated on the gauge. If the belt is new the correct tension is 900N, as indicated on the gauge.

REMOVAL & INSTALLATION

1. Disconnect the negative battery cable.
2. Disconnect the electrical leads from the alternator.
3. Remove the screw from the alternator adjusting bracket.
4. Remove the screw from the rear of the alternator. If equipped with shims save them for reinstallation.

5. Loosen the alternator pivot bolt and remove the drive belt.
6. Loosen the two screws securing the front bracket to the engine.
7. Remove the alternator along with the spacer and lower through bolt.
8. Installation is the reverse of the removal procedure.

Starter

For further information on the starter system, please refer to "Charging and Starting" in the Unit Repair section.

REMOVAL & INSTALLATION

1. Disconnect the negative battery terminal. Raise and support the vehicle safely.
2. Disconnect and tag the battery lead and the wires from the solenoid. Disconnect the exhaust system, as required.
3. If equipped, remove the bolt holding the support bracket to the starter.
4. Remove the starter retaining bolts. Remove the starter by pulling it forward and down.
5. Installation is the reverse of the removal procedure.

Diesel Glow Plugs

REMOVAL & INSTALLATION

1. Disconnect both negative battery cables.
2. Remove all necessary components in order to gain access to the glow plugs.
3. Disconnect the glow plug electrical wire. Using the proper tool remove the glow plug from its mounting.

NOTE: A burned out glow plug tip may bulge then break off and drop into the pre chamber when the glow plug is removed from the engine. When this occurs the cylinder head must be removed and the pre chamber removed from the head in order to remove the broken tip.

4. Installation is the reverse of the removal procedure.

ENGINE MECHANICAL

NOTE: The 350 V8 diesel engine and the 307 V8 gas engine are pro- duced by General Motors Oldsmobile division. For all engine mechanical service procedures, please refer to the "Oldsmobile Rear Wheel Drive" car section. The 252 V6 gas engine is produced by the Buick division. Service procedures are contained in the "Buick Rear Wheel Drive" car section.

Engine

REMOVAL & INSTALLATION

250 V8

1. Disconnect the negative battery cable.
2. Remove the hood, after scribing hood hinge outline for proper alignment.
3. Remove the air cleaner and heat shroud. Disconnect and plug the automatic transmission fluid lines. Disconnect and plug the oil cooler lines, if equipped.
4. Drain the cooling system. Disconnect the heater hoses from the engine. Unfasten the fender struts from the radiator shroud. Remove the radiator hose bracket, radiator cover and fan. Remove the radiator hoses. Remove the radiator.
5. If equipped, disconnect the throttle and cruise control linkage at the carburetor.
6. Disconnect the brake vacuum hose from the vacuum pipe. Remove the cruise control power unit, if equipped.
7. Disconnect the power steering pump bracket and position the pump out of the way with the hoses still connected. If equipped, position the power steering fluid cooler out of the way.
8. Remove the air condition compressor bracket bolts and position the compressor out of the way with the hoses still connected. Do not discharge the system.
9. Disconnect all electrical wires and vacuum lines that will interfere with the removal of the engine. If the vehicle is equipped with the HT 4100 (250 V8) engine, disconnect the EFI manifold harness and all the necessary wires.
10. Disconnect the automatic level control line, if equipped. Remove the alternator. Remove the air pump, if equipped.
11. Disconnect the strut rods connecting the engine mounts to the flywheel inspection cover.
12. Raise and support the vehicle safely. Remove the engine to transmission bolts. Remove each engine mount through bolt.
13. Properly relieve the fuel pressure.

14. Remove the starter. Disconnect the exhaust pipes from the exhaust manifolds.

15. Remove the four bolts attaching the flywheel inspection cover to the transmission. Remove the cover. Remove the bolts attaching the flywheel to the converter.

16. Disconnect and plug the fuel line and the vapor return line.

17. Lower the vehicle. Install a lifting bracket to the engine. Support the transmission properly. Raise the engine slightly and pull it forward to disengage it from the transmission. Remove the engine from the vehicle.

18. Installation is the reverse of the removal procedure.

Cylinder Head

REMOVAL & INSTALLATION

250 V8

1. Disconnect the negative battery cable. Drain the engine coolant.

2. Remove the intake and exhaust manifolds.

3. Disconnect all electrical and ground connections from the cylinder head.

4. When removing the left cylinder head, partially remove the power steering pump.

5. When removing the right cylinder head, remove the alternator and the heater hose from the rear of the head.

6. Remove the air pump, if so equipped.

7. Remove bolts holding the rocker arm cover to the heads and remove the cover.

8. Remove nuts holding the rocker arm support to cylinder head, then remove the support and rocker arm assemblies. Store these assemblies so that they may be reinstalled in their correct locations.

9. Remove pushrods and store them with their respective rocker arm assemblies.

10. Remove the cylinder head bolts.

11. Lift the cylinder head off of the block.

NOTE: Install cylinder liner holders to prevent loss of the bottom seal.

12. Remove all gasket material from the cylinder head and block mating surfaces.

13. Install by reversing removal procedures.

14. When torquing the head bolts, use the three step method. Torque the bolts to $\frac{1}{3}$ of the total torque listed in the sequence shown. Once this is done,

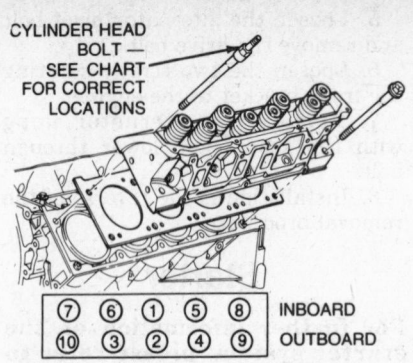

Cylinder head bolt torque sequence—250 V8

repeat the same procedure, this time torquing all the bolts to $\frac{2}{3}$ of the total listed torque. Finally torque the bolts to the recommended torque of 90 ft. lbs.

OVERHAUL

For all cylinder head overhaul procedures, please refer to "Engine Rebuilding" in the Unit Repair section.

Rocker Arms/Shafts

REMOVAL & INSTALLATION

250 V8

1. Disconnect the negative battery cable. Remove the necessary components in order to gain access to the rocker arm cover retaining bolts. Remove the rocker arm covers.

2. Remove the valve train support by removing the nuts from the stud headed cylinder head bolts, a little at a time until pressure is relieved from the assembly. Remove the valve train support with the rocker arms and pivots attached as an assembly.

NOTE: This method of removal is preferred as the pivot assemblies may be damaged if the pivot bolt torque is not removed evenly against the valve spring tension.

3. Secure the support assembly in a vise and individually remove the rocker arms and pivots.

4. When installing new components, thoroughly lubricate all parts.

5. With the valve train support secured in a vise, position the rocker arms and pivots to the valve train support. Loosely install the pivot bolts on all studs and torque each to 20 ft. lbs.

6. Position the pushrod into the seat of each rocker arm and loosely install the retaining nuts.

7. Recheck the pushrods for being seated correctly. Tighten the nuts al-

ternately and evenly, checking the position of the pushrods while tightening.

8. When the nuts have been seated and the pushrods are correct, tighten the nuts to 35 ft. lbs. torque.

9. Continue the installation in the reverse order of the removal procedure.

Intake Manifold

REMOVAL & INSTALLATION

250 V8

NOTE: Some vehicles equipped with the HT 4100 (250 V8) engine have been experiencing oil leakage at the intake manifold to block seal, due to a split intake manifold seal. When repairing this leak, replace the old seal with a new silicone seal (Part No. 3634619) The new seal is easily identified by its gray color.

1. Disconnect the negative battery cable. Drain the coolant. Disconnect the upper radiator hose from the thermostat housing.

2. Disconnect the following electrical connections and position the wiring harness out of the way, coolant sensor, mass airflow temperature sensor, throttle position sensor, four way connector at the distributor, idle speed control motor and fuel injectors.

3. Disconnect the heater hose from the nipple at the rear of the intake manifold. Disconnect the fuel inlet and return lines from the throttle body.

4. Remove the distributor. Remove both rocker arm covers. Remove the rocker arm support with the rocker arms intact by first alternately and evenly removing the four bolts followed by the five nuts. Keep the pushrods in sequence so they may be reassembled in their original positions.

5. Partially remove the air condition compressor and do not discharge the system. Remove the vacuum harness connections from the TVS at the rear of the intake manifold.

6. Remove the intake manifold bolts and remove the two bolts securing the lower thermostat housing to the front cover. Remove the engine lift brackets or bend them out of the way.

7. Remove the intake manifold and lower the thermostat housing as an assembly by lifting it straight up off of the dowels.

8. Installation is the reverse order of the removal procedure. Apply a suitable RTV sealant to the four corners where the end seals will meet the side gaskets, place the end seals into position, then again apply the RTV sealant to the four corners. Apply a suitable

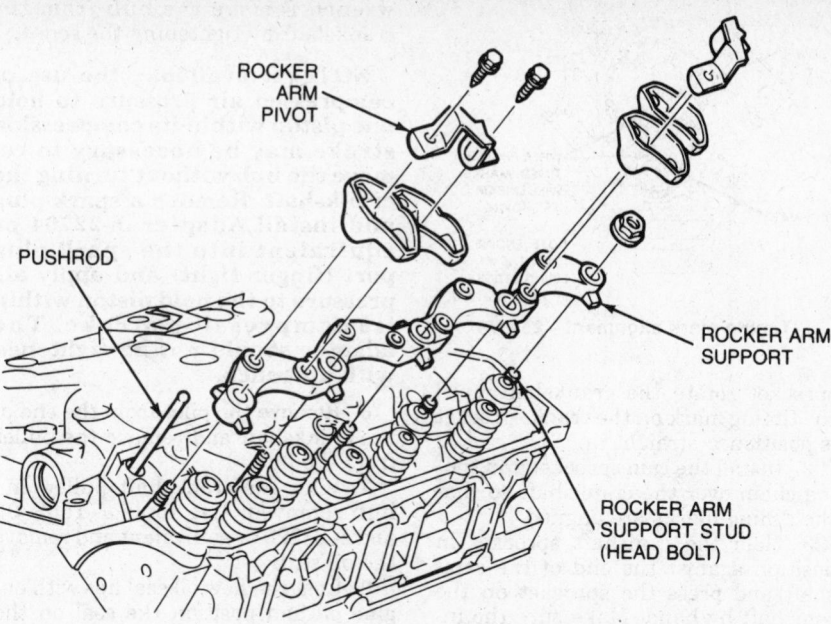

Rocker arm assembly—250 V8 engine

thread sealer to the manifold retaining bolts.

NOTE: The right intake manifold gasket for 1985 vehicles, contains a restrictor which controls the flow of the exhaust gas into the intake manifold. The gaskets that do not have this restrictor are identified by a tab which protrudes from between the cylinder head and the intake manifold. On the left side of the engine the tab will protrude from the rear of the engine. If a gasket without a restrictor is used on the right side of the engine the tab will protrude from the front of the engine. The manifold gasket with the restrictor has "Right Bank" printed on it to aid identification when the gasket is out of the vehicle.

Exhaust Manifold

REMOVAL & INSTALLATION

250 V8

LEFT SIDE

1. Disconnect the negative battery cable. Remove the air cleaner and tube assembly from the air preheat stove.

2. Remove the screw securing the oil dipstick tube to the air preheat stove. Remove the screws securing the air preheat stove to the exhaust manifold and remove the air preheat stove.

3. Remove the nut from the two stud/bolts securing the transmission linkage support to the manifold. Disconnect the "Y" pipe from the exhaust manifold.

4. Remove the oxygen sensor using a suitable box end wrench. Special tools such as J–29533 are available to perform this operation.

5. Remove the bolts securing the exhaust manifold to the cylinder head. Remove the manifold from the engine compartment.

6. Installation is the reverse order of the removal procedure. Be sure to install new gaskets.

RIGHT SIDE

1. Remove the nut from the stud/bolt securing the transmission cooler line bracket to the exhaust manifold.

2. Remove the two nuts securing the air valve bracket to the exhaust manifold. Remove the upper exhaust manifold to head bolts.

3. Raise and support the vehicle safely. Remove the lower exhaust manifold to head bolts.

4. Disconnect the "Y" pipe from the exhaust manifold. Remove the exhaust manifold from the engine compartment.

5. Installation is the reverse order of the removal procedure. Be sure to install new gaskets.

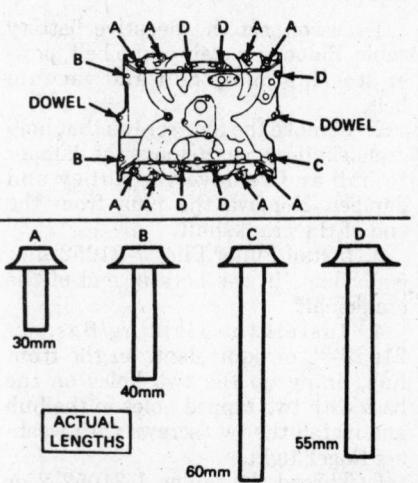

Intake manifold bolt size and location 1982-84 250 V8

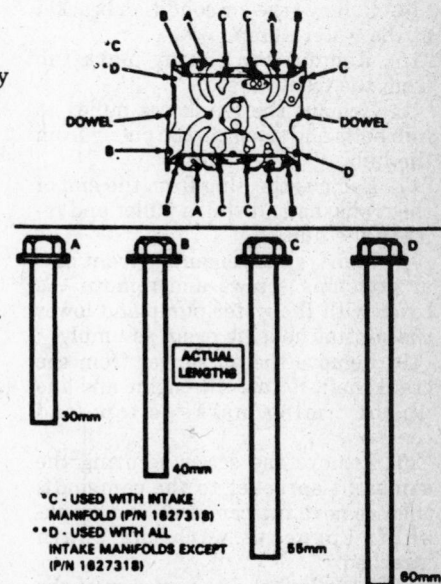

Intake manifold bolt size and location 1985 250 V8

BOLT TIGHTENING SEQUENCE

1. TIGHTEN BOLTS 1, 2, 3, & 4 IN SEQUENCE TO 20.0 N·m (15 FT-LBS).

2. TIGHTEN BOLTS 5 THRU 16 IN SEQUENCE TO 30.0 N·m (22 FT-LBS).

3. RETIGHTEN ALL BOLTS IN SEQUENCE TO 30.0 N·m (22 FT-LBS).

4. REPEAT STEP 3.

Intake manifold torque sequence—250 V8

Front Cover, Timing Chain, and Sprockets

REMOVAL & INSTALLATION

250 V8

1. Disconnect the negative battery cable. Drain the radiator.
2. Remove the screws on each side of the radiator securing the support rod. Move the support rods out of the way.
3. Remove the wiring harness from the upper fan shroud clamps.
4. Remove the power steering pump reservoir from the upper radiator shroud.
5. Remove the upper fan shroud from the lower fan shroud by removing the staples.
6. Remove the clutch fan assembly.
7. Remove the alternator, air pump, vacuum pump, and air condition compressor drive belts.
8. Partially remove the air condition compressor from the engine mounting brackets without discharging the system.
9. Remove the alternator and support bracket from the engine.
10. Loosen the clamp and disconnect the coolant reservoir to water pump hose at the pump.
11. Disconnect the inlet and outlet hoses at the water pump.
12. Drain the crankcase by either removing the crankcase plugs (one on each side) or by elevating the rear wheels. This will prevent coolant from draining into the oil pan as the front cover is removed.
13. Remove the water pump and crankcase pulleys.
14. Remove the air condition bracket at the water pump.
15. Remove the timing mark tab from the front cover.
16. Remove the crankcase pulley to hub bolts and separate the pulley from the hub.
17. Remove the plug from the end of the crankshaft. Install a puller and remove the hub.
18. Remove the remaining front cover attaching screws and remove the cover with the water pump and lower thermostat housing as an assembly.
19. Remove the oil slinger from the crankshaft. Rotate the engine and line up the timing marks to top dead center.
20. Remove the screw securing the camshaft sprocket to the camshaft, then remove the camshaft and crankshaft sprocket with the chain attached.
21. Installation is the reverse of the removal procedure. After installing the timing chain over the camshaft

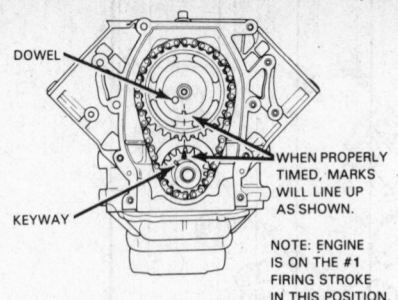

Timing mark alignment—250 V8

sprocket rotate the crankshaft until the timing mark on the crank sprocket is positioned straight up.
22. Install the cam sprocket and timing chain over the crankshaft so that the timing marks are aligned.
23. Hold the camshaft sprocket in position against the end of the camshaft and press the sprocket on the camshaft by hand. Make sure the index pin in the camshaft is lined up with the index hole in the sprocket.
24. If necessary, keep the engine from rotating while torquing the camshaft sprocket screw to 35 ft. lbs.

NOTE: Engine timing has been set so that the No. 1 cylinder is in the TDC firing position. If for some reason the distributor was removed make sure the rotor is set so that cylinder No. 1 is in the firing position.

25. Install the oil slinger on the crankshaft with the smaller end of the slinger against the crankshaft sprocket. Install the engine front cover.
26. Continue the installation in the reverse order of the removal procedure.

OIL SEAL REPLACEMENT

250 V8

1. Disconnect the negative battery cable. Remove the air pump belt, power steering pump belt and vacuum belt.
2. Remove the four screws that hold crankshaft pulley. Remove the damper to hub and remove the pulley and damper. Remove the plug from the end of the crankshaft.
3. Install Puller Pilot J–21052–4 or equivalent, in the bore in end of the crankshaft.
4. Install the Holding Base J–21052–02 or equivalent, on the front hub, lining up the two holes on the base with two tapped holes in the hub and install the two screws with washers finger tight.
5. Thread the puller J–21052–2 or equivalent into the base until the screw contact point. Using a suitable

wrench remove the hub from the crankshaft by tightening the screw.

NOTE: If available, the use of compressed air pressure to hold one piston within its compression stroke may be necessary to remove the hub without turning the crankshaft. Remove a spark plug and install Adapter J–22794 or equivalent into the spark plug port (finger tight) and apply air pressure to the hold piston within its compression stroke. The adapter should not be tightened with a wrench.

6. Remove the pilot from the end of the crankshaft and remove the puller from the hub.
7. With the crankshaft pulley and hub removed. Use tools J–1859–03 and J–23129 or equivalent and remove the oil seal.
8. Coat the new oil seal lips with engine oil and position the seal on the end of the crankshaft with the garter spring side toward the engine.
9. Using seal installer J–29662 or equivalent, use a hammer and drive the seal into the front cover until the tool bottoms out against the front cover.

NOTE: The tool J–29662 is designed is such a way that the front cover seal can also be pressed on by using the balancer hub installer J–29774 or equivalent.

10. Lubricate the bore of the hub and seal with extreme pressure lubricant to prevent seizure to the crankshaft and provide lubrication of the oil seal lip. Position the hub on the crankshaft, lining up the key slot in the hub with the key on the crankshaft.
11. Install Thread Installer Screw J–29774 or equivalent into the end of the crankshaft. Position the thrust bearing with the inner race forward, washer next and Installer Nut last. Using a suitable wrench install the hub on the crankshaft by tightening the installer nut.
12. To finish the installation reverse the removal procedure. Torque the crankshaft pulley to damper screws to 20 ft. lbs.

Camshaft

REMOVAL & INSTALLATION

250 V8

1. Disconnect the negative battery cable. Drain the cooling system. Remove the radiator. Remove the distributor.
2. Remove the engine front cover. Remove the oil pump and the oil slinger from the crankshaft.

3. Remove the fuel pump and the fuel pump eccentric from the camshaft.

4. Remove the camshaft sprocket and the timing chain.

NOTE: Make certain that the marks on the sprockets are correctly aligned before removing the timing chain.

5. Remove the intake manifold. Remove the valve lifters. Carefully slide the camshaft out of the engine block. Do not allow the camshaft lobes to scratch the camshaft bearings.

6. Installation is the reverse of the removal procedure. Before installation, the camshaft should be lubricated with clean engine oil.

7. The camshaft sprocket screws should be torqued to 18 ft. lbs. while the fuel pump eccentric screw is tightened to 35 ft. lbs.

Piston and Connecting Rod

POSITIONING

NOTE: For all piston and connection rod overhaul procedures, please refer to "Engine Rebuilding" in the Unit Repair section.

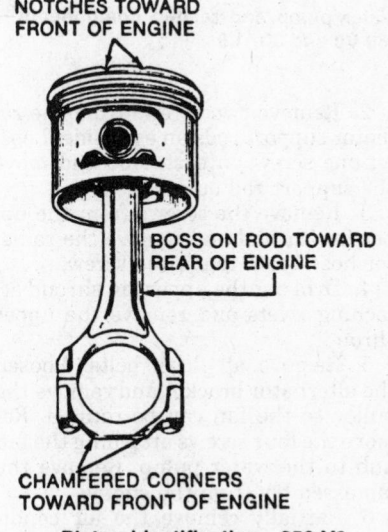

Piston identification—250 V8

ENGINE LUBRICATION

Oil Pan

REMOVAL & INSTALLATION
250 V8

1. Disconnect the negative battery cable. Raise and support the vehicle safely.

2. Drain the engine oil and remove the oil filter. Remove the flywheel inspection cover and the support struts.

3. Disconnect the exhaust "Y" pipe at the exhaust manifolds and remove the bolt at the catalytic converter bracket. Lower the exhaust pipe.

4. Remove the oil pan bolts. Remove the oil pan. If the pan is difficult to remove lightly tap the edges of the pan with a plastic hammer.

5. Installation is the reverse of the removal procedure. Seal the oil pan to the block with RTV sealant. Tighten the oil pan retaining bolts to 11 ft. lbs.

Rear Main Bearing Oil Seal

REMOVAL & INSTALLATION
250 V8

1. Remove the oil pan.

2. Remove the rear main bearing cap and loosen the bolts holding the other four bearings about three turns each. Remove the old rear main bearing seals.

3. Clean the groove in the cap and in the block. Lubricate seals with engine oil.

4. Make an installation tool.

5. Start the upper half into the groove in the block with the lip facing forward and rotate it into position, using the tool as a guide. Press firmly on both ends to be sure it is protruding uniformly on each side.

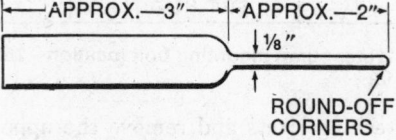

Rear main bearing oil seal installation tool

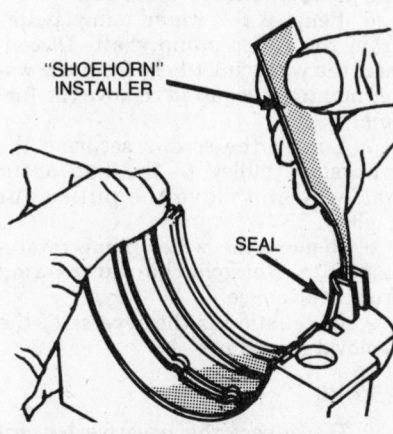

Installing rear main bearing oil seal

6. Install the lower half of the seal into the bearing cap with the lip facing forward and one end of the seal over the ridge and flush with the split line. Hold one finger over this end to prevent it from slipping, and push the seal into seated position by applying pressure to the other end. Be sure the seal is firmly seated and protrudes evenly on each side. Do not apply pressure to the lip. This may damage the effectiveness of the seal.

NOTE: On vehicles equipped with neoprene type seals, make sure that the seal is flush at the split line to avoid leaks.

7. Apply rubber cement to the mating surfaces of the block and cap being careful not to get any cement on the bearing, the crankshaft or the seal. The cement coating should be about 0.010 in. thick.

8. Tighten the bearing bolts to 89 ft. lbs. Be sure to tighten the bolts of the other four bearings also. Rotate the crankshaft one full turn to check for binding.

9. Reinstall the oil pan.

Oil Pump

REMOVAL & INSTALLATION
250 V8

1. Disconnect the negative battery cable. Raise and support the vehicle safely.

2. Drain the engine oil. Remove the oil pan. Remove the screws and nut securing the oil pump to the engine. Remove the oil pump from the engine.

3. To disassemble, remove the screws holding the oil pump cover to the the housing, then slide the drive shaft, drive gear and driven gear out of the pump housing.

4. Remove the oil pressure regulator valve and spring from the bore in the housing assembly.

5. Remove the oil pressure regulator valve and spring from the bore in the housing assembly.

6. Inspect the oil pressure regulator valve for nicks and burrs.

7. Measure the free length of the regulator valve spring. It should be 2.57–2.69 in.

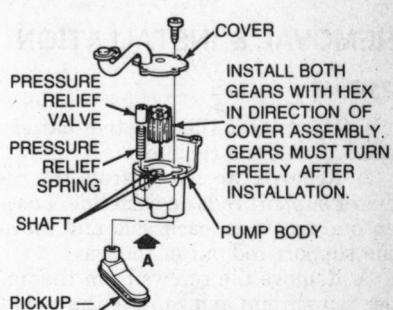

Oil pump disassembled—250 V8 engine

8. Inspect the drive gear and driven gear for nicks and burrs.

9. Assemble the pump drive gear over the driveshaft so that the retaining ring is inside the gear. Position the drive gear over the pump housing shaft closest to the pressure regulator bore.

10. Slide the driven gear over the remaining shaft in the pump housing, meshing the driven gear with the drive gear.

11. Install the oil pressure regulator spring and valve in the bore of the pump housing assembly.

12. Install the pump cover and four retaining screws.

13. Install the oil pump assembly to the block, engaging the driveshaft to the distributor gear. Tighten the nut to 22 ft. lbs. and the screws to 15 ft. lbs.

14. Install the oil pan and lower the vehicle..

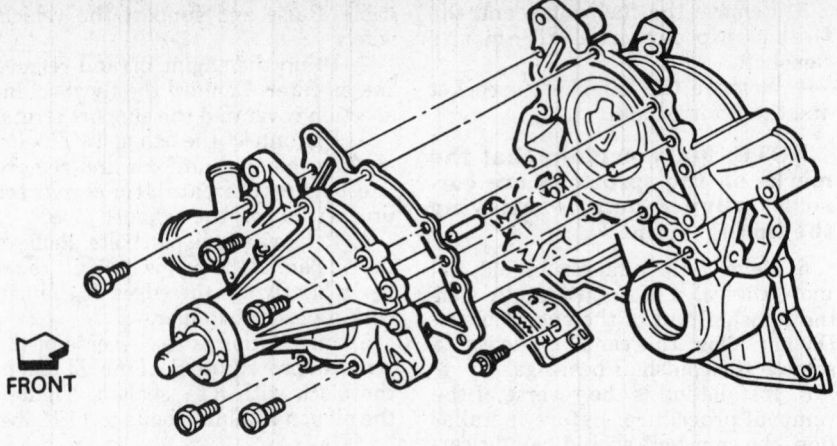

Water pump and related components—252 V6

ENGINE COOLING

Radiator

REMOVAL & INSTALLATION

1. Disconnect the negative battery cable.

2. Drain the cooling system. Disconnect and remove the radiator hoses.

3. Disconnect and plug the automatic transmission lines. if equipped, disconnect and plug the oil cooler lines.

4. Remove the upper radiator shroud. Remove the radiator retaining bolts, as required.

5. Remove the radiator assembly from the vehicle.

6. Installation is the reverse of the removal procedure.

Water Pump

REMOVAL & INSTALLATION

252 V6

1. Disconnect the negative battery cable. Drain the radiator.

2. Remove two screws from the radiator support rods on each side. Loosen one screw on each side and move the support rod out of the way.

3. Remove the screws from the upper fan shroud and remove the radiator hose brace to shroud screw.

4. Drill out the upper fan shroud at-

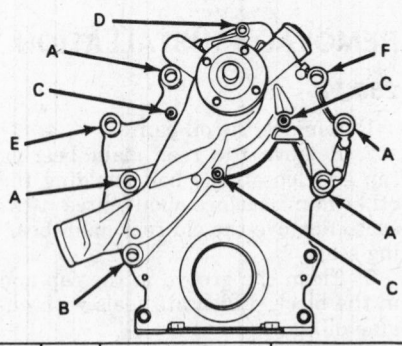

KEY	NO.	SIZE	TORQUE	
			N·M	FT. LBS.
A	4	M10 X 1.50 X 45	40	30
B	1	M8 X 1.25 X 35	20	15
C	3	M6 X 1.0 (NUT)	7	5
D	1	(1620262)	10	7
E	1	M10 X 1.50 (NUT)	40	30
F	1	M10 X 1.50 X 50 (STUD HEAD)	40	30

Water pump mounting bolt location—250 V8

taching rivets and remove the upper shroud.

5. Loosen the alternator and remove the belt. Loosen the power steering pump and remove the belt.

6. Remove the water pump pulley from the water pump shaft. Disconnect the water inlet hose from the water pump. As required remove the fuel line.

7. Loosen the screws securing the crankshaft pulley to the hub about half way and move the pulley out slightly.

8. Remove the water pump retaining bolts. Remove the water pump from the vehicle.

9. Installation is the reverse of the removal procedure.

250 V8

1. Disconnect the negative battery cable. Drain the radiator.

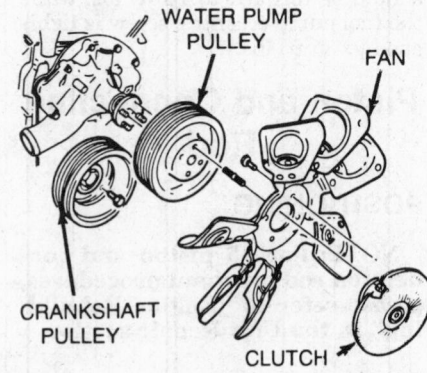

Water pump and related components—350 V8 and 307 V8

2. Remove two screws from the radiator support rods on each side. Loosen one screw on each side and move the support rod out of the way.

3. Remove the screws from the upper fan shroud and remove the radiator hose brace to shroud screw.

4. Drill out the upper fan shroud attaching rivets and remove the upper shroud.

5. Remove all drive belts. Loosen the alternator bracket and remove the pulley so the fan can be rotated. Remove the four screws attaching the fan hub to the water pump. Remove the fan assembly from the engine.

6. Partially remove the air condition compressor unit from the engine mounting brackets. Do not remove the high and low pressure lines from the compressor head.

7. Remove the alternator and support bracket from the engine. Remove the power steering pump pulley with tool J–25034 or equivalent.

8. Loosen the clamps and disconnect the water pump inlet and outlet hoses at the pump. Disconnect the bypass hose at the water pump. Remove the air condition compressor bracket at the water pump.

9. Remove the timing mark tab from the front cover. Remove the water pump mounting bolts and remove the water pump. Remove all old gasket material.

10. Installation is the reverse of the removal procedure. Use a new gasket and apply a RTV sealant on the gasket. Install the drive belts and tighten them to the proper tension. Refill the cooling system with the correct mixture of antifreeze and water. Start the engine and check for leaks.

350 and 307 V8

1. Disconnect the negative battery cable. On diesel engines disconnect both negative battery cables.
2. Drain the radiator. Disconnect the lower radiator hose at the water pump. Remove the drive belts. Remove the radiator fan and water pump pulley.
3. Remove the front air condition compressor bracket. Remove the front alternator bracket. Remove the power steering pump adjusting bracket. Remove the air pump mounting bracket.
4. Remove the water pump retaining bolts. Remove the water pump from the engine.
5. Installation is the reverse of the removal procedure. Use a new gasket and apply a RTV sealant on the gasket. Install the drive belts and tighten them to the proper tension. Refill the cooling system with the correct mixture of antifreeze and water. Start the engine and check for leaks.

Thermostat

REMOVAL & INSTALLATION

1. Disconnect the negative battery cable. Drain the cooling system until the coolant level is below the thermostat housing.
2. Remove the upper radiator hose at the thermostat housing. Remove the thermostat housing retaining bolts.
3. Remove the thermostat from the engine.
4. Installation is the reverse of the removal procedure. Be sure to use a new gasket or RTV sealant as required.

EMISSION CONTROLS

Please refer to "Emission Control" in the Unit Repair section for system maintenance procedures. Due to the complex nature of modern electronic engine control systems, comprehensive diagnosis and testing procedures fall outside the confines of this repair manual. For complete information on diagnosis, testing and repair procedures concerning all modern engine and emission control systems, please refer to *"Chilton's Guide To Electronic Engine Controls"*.

GASOLINE FUEL SYSTEM

Fuel System Service Precaution

Any time the fuel system is being worked on, disconnect the negative battery cable, execept for those tests where battery voltage is required and always keep a dry chemical (Class B) fire extinguisher near the work area.

RELIEVING FUEL SYSTEM PRESSURE

1. Remove the fuel pump fuse from the fuse block or disconnect the harness connector at the tank.
2. Start the engine. It should run and then stall when the fuel in the lines is exhausted. When the engine stops, crank the starter for about three seconds to make sure all pressure in the fuel lines is released.
3. Install the fuel pump fuse after repair is made.

Fuel Filter

REMOVAL & INSTALLATION

Carbureted Engine

1. Disconnect the negative battery cable. Disconnect the fuel line at the carburetor inlet.
2. Remove the fuel inlet nut from the carburetor using a box wrench.
3. Remove the fuel filter element and spring.
4. Install the filter spring and new fuel filter element into the carburetor.
5. Install a new gasket on the fuel inlet nut and install the nut.
6. Connect the fuel line to the fuel inlet nut and tighten securely. Start the engine and check for leaks.

Fuel Injected Engine

NOTE: The fuel filter element can be replaced by unscrewing the bottom cover and removing it.

1. Bleed the pressure from the fuel delivery system. Disconnect the negative battery cable. Remove the fuel inlet and outlet hoses from the fuel filter.
2. Remove the two screws retaining the fuel filter to the bracket and remove the filter from the engine or frame.
3. Remove the inlet and outlet fittings from the filter assembly if they are needed for the new filter.
4. Install the fittings to the new filter, using a sealer on the threads.
5. Attach the filter to the bracket and tighten the retaining screws to 12 ft. lbs.
6. Connect the inlet and outlet line, using new clamps.

NOTE: It may require considerable cranking before the engine starts, due to the drained fuel lines.

Mechanical Fuel Pump

PRESSURE TESTING

1. Disconnect the fuel line at the carburetor. Install a rubber hose about 10 inches long. Attach a low reading pressure gauge.
2. Hold the gauge at least 16 inches above the fuel pump. If equipped, pinch the fuel return line.
3. Start the engine and run at slow idle, using the fuel that is left in the carburetor.
4. If the fuel pump is operating properly the pressure on the gauge should read a constant 5.5–6.5 psi.
5. If the pressure is too low, too high or significantly different at various engine speeds the pump should be replaced.

REMOVAL & INSTALLATION

1. Disconnect the negative battery cable. Remove the air condition compressor drive belt.
2. If equipped with an air pump, loosen the air pump pulley bolts and remove the air pump hoses and electrical leads to the air pump. Remove the air pump pulley and the air pump from the engine.
3. Remove the compressor front bracket. Remove the fuel inlet hose from the fuel pump. Disconnect the vapor return hose, if so equipped.
4. Remove the fuel outlet pipe. Remove the nuts securing the fuel pump to the engine. Remove the fuel pump from the engine.

5. Installation is the reverse order of the removal procedure.

Electric Fuel Pump

PRESSURE TESTING

The only way to check fuel pump pressure is by connecting a fuel pressure gage J-25400–300 or its equivalent at the fuel line service fitting. Measure the fuel pressure while cranking the engine. The correct pressure range is 9–12 psi. If the fuel pressure is less than 9 psi or greater than 12 psi a problem exists in the fuel injection system.

REMOVAL & INSTALLATION

NOTE: Fuel is under high pressure, if the following steps are not followed the fuel could spray out and result in a fire hazard or possible injury. The fuel pump is located inside the gas tank.

1. Relieve fuel pump pressure and disconnect the negative battery cable. Siphon the fuel from the fuel tank.
2. Raise the rear of the vehicle and remove the screw securing the ground wire to the crossmember.
3. Disconnect the fuel line, evaporative emission lines and the fuel return lines at the front of the tank.
4. Support the tank and remove the screw on each side of the tank that retains the fuel tank support straps to the body at the front of the tank.
5. Lower the tank enough so that the fuel pump electrical lead can be disconnected. Disconnect the wire.
6. Remove the fuel tank from the vehicle.
7. Remove the locknuts securing the fuel gauge tank unit and fuel pump feed wires to the tank unit.
8. Turn the cam locking ring counterclockwise with a soft nonferrous punch and hammer. When the lock ring is disengaged, remove it and lift the gauge/pump unit from the tank.
9. Installation is the reverse of the removal procedure. Tighten the fuel retaining strap screws to 25 ft. lbs.

Carburetor

REMOVAL & INSTALLATION

1. Disconnect the negative battery cable. Remove the air cleaner assembly and disconnect the accelerator linkage.
2. Disconnect the transmission detent cable, if so equipped. Disconnect the cruise control linkage, if so equipped.
3. Remove and tag all vacuum and electrical lines to the carburetor. Disconnect the choke heat pipe.
4. Remove the fuel line at the carburetor inlet. Remove the carburetor mounting bolts. Remove the carburetor from the manifold.
5. Installation is the reverse order of the removal procedure. Be sure to install a new carburetor base gasket.

OVERHAUL

For all carburetor overhaul and adjustment procedures, please refer to "Carburetor Service" in the Unit Repair section.

Fuel Injection

Due to the complex nature of modern fuel injection systems, comprehensive diagnosis and testing procedures fall outside the confines of this repair manual. For complete information on fuel injection diagnosis, testing and repair procedures please refer to *"Chilton's Guide To Fuel Injection and Feedback Carburetors"*.

DIESEL FUEL SYSTEM

Fuel Filter

REPLACEMENT

The fuel filter is a square assembly located at the back of the engine above the intake manifold. Disconnect the fuel lines. Remove the filter retaining bolts. Remove the filter. Install the lines to the new filter. Start the engine and check for leaks.

DRAINING WATER FROM THE SYSTEM

Cars which have a "Water in Fuel" light may have the water removed from the fuel tank with a pump or by siphoning. The pump or siphon hose should be hooked up to the 1/4 in. fuel return hose (smaller of the two fuel hoses) above the rear axle or under the hood near the fuel pump. Siphoning should continue until all water is removed from the fuel tank. Use a clear plastic line or observe filter bowl on draining equipment to determine when clear fuel begins to flow. Besure to remove the cap on fuel tank while using this purge procedure. Re-place the cap when finished. The same precautions for handling gasoline should be observed when purging diesel fuel tanks.

Diesel Injection Pump

REMOVAL & INSTALLATION

NOTE: This procedure contains throttle rod and transmission cable adjustments.

1. Disconnect the negative battery cable. Remove the air cleaner.
2. Remove the filters and pipes from the valve covers and air crossover.
3. Remove the air crossover and cap the intake manifold with screened covers or tape.
4. Disconnect the throttle rod and return spring.
5. Remove the bellcrank.

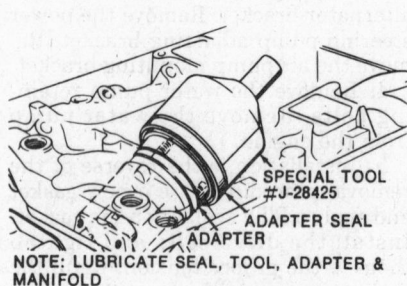

NOTE: LUBRICATE SEAL, TOOL, ADAPTER & MANIFOLD

Installing adapter seal

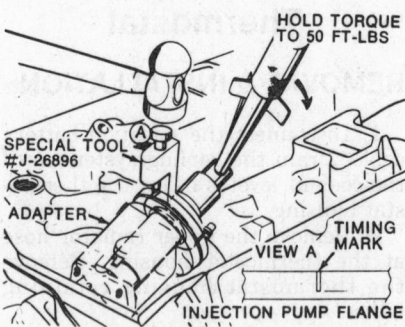

Marking injection pump adapter

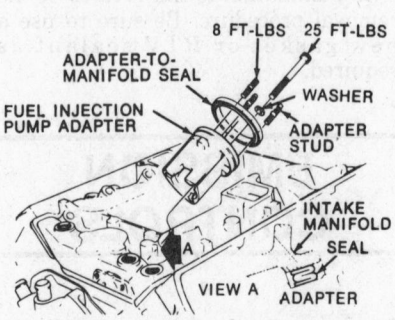

Injector pump adapter bolts

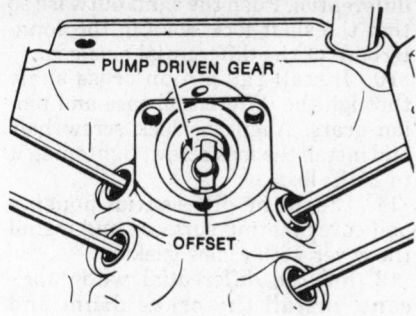

Offset on pump driven gear

6. Remove the throttle and transmission cables from the intake manifold brackets.

7. Disconnect the fuel lines from the filter and remove the filter.

8. Disconnect the fuel inlet line at the pump.

9. Remove the rear air conditioner compressor brace and remove the fuel line.

10. Disconnect the fuel return line from the injection pump.

11. Remove the clamps and pull the fuel return lines from each injection nozzle.

12. Using two wrenches, disconnect the high pressure lines at the nozzles.

13. Remove the three injection pump retaining nuts with tool J–26987 or its equivalent.

14. Remove the pump and cap all lines and nozzles.

15. To install, remove the protective caps from all lines and nozzles. Place the engine on TDC for the No. 1 cylinder. The mark on the harmonic balancer on the crankshaft will be aligned with the zero mark on the timing tab, and both valves for No. 1 cylinder will be closed. The index mark on the injection pump driven gear should be offset to the right when No. 1 is at TDC. Check that all of these conditions are met before continuing.

16. Line up the offset tang on the pump driveshaft with the pump driven gear and install the pump.

17. Install, but do not tighten the pump retaining nuts.

18. Connect the high pressure lines at the nozzles.

19. Using two wrenches, torque the high pressure line nuts to 25 ft. lbs.

20. Connect the fuel return lines to the nozzles and pump.

21. Align the timing mark on the injection pump with the line on the timing mark adapter and torque the mounting nuts to 18 ft. lbs.

NOTE: A ¾ in. open end wrench on the boss at the front of the injection pump will aid in rotating the pump to align the marks.

22. Adjust the throttle rod:

a. remove the clip from the cruise control rod and remove the rod from the bellcrank.

b. loosen the locknut on the throttle rod a few turns, then shorten the rod several turns.

c. rotate the bellcrank to the full throttle stop, then lengthen the throttle rod until the injection pump lever contacts the injection pump full throttle stop, then release the bellcrank.

d. tighten the throttle rod locknut.

23. Install the fuel inlet line between the transfer pump and the filter.

24. Install the rear air conditioner compressor brace.

25. Install the bellcrank and clip.

26. Connect the throttle rod and return spring.

27. Adjust the transmission cable:

a. push the snaplock to the disengaged position.

b. rotate the injection pump lever to the full throttle stop and hold it there.

c. push in the snaplock until it is flush.

d. release the injection pump lever.

28. Remove the screened covers or tape and install the air crossover.

29. Install the tubes in the air flow control valve in the air crossover and install the ventilation filters in the valve covers. Install the air cleaner.

30. Start the engine and allow it to run for two minutes. Stop the engine, let it stand for two minutes, then restart. This permits the air to bleed off within the pump.

INJECTION TIMING ADJUSTMENT

For the engine to be properly timed, the lines on the top of the injection pump adapter and the flange of the injection pump must be aligned.

1. The engine must be off for resetting the timing.

2. Loosen the three pump retaining nuts with tool J–26987 or equivalent, which is an injection pump intake manifold wrench.

3. Align the timing marks and torque the pump retaining nuts to 18 ft. lbs.

NOTE: The use of a ¾ in. open end wrench on the boss at the front of the pump will aid in rotating the pump to align the marks.

4. Adjust the throttle rod.

Injection Nozzle

REMOVAL & INSTALLATION

The injection nozzles on these engines are simply unbolted from the cylinder head, after the fuel lines are removed, in similar fashion to a spark plug. Be careful not to damage the nozzle end and make sure you remove the copper nozzle gasket from the cylinder head if it does not come off with the nozzle.

Clean the carbon off the tip of the nozzle with a soft brass wire brush and install the nozzles, with gaskets.

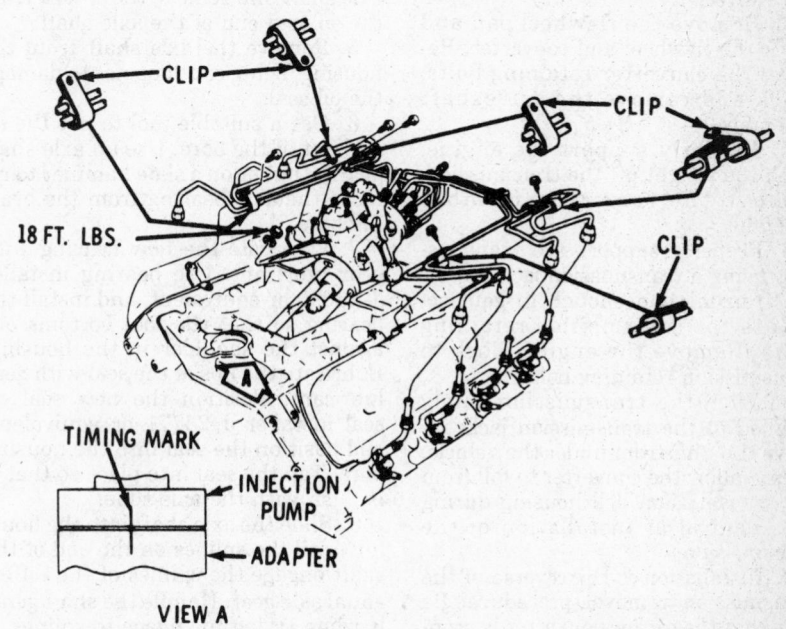

V8 diesel engine injection pump timing marks

NOTE: Some vehicles use two types of injectors, CAV Lucas and Diesel Equipment. When installing the inlet fittings, torque the Diesel Equipment injector fitting to 45 ft. lbs. and the CAV Lucas to 25 ft. lbs.

AUTOMATIC TRANSMISSION

For further information on automatic transmissions, please refer to "Automatic Transmissions" in the Unit Repair section.

REMOVAL & INSTALLATION

1. Disconnect the negative battery cable. Place the shift selector lever in the neutral position. If necessary, remove the dipstick and the upper bolt on the dipstick tube.
2. Raise the vehicle and support it safely. Drain the transmission fluid.
3. Remove the shift linkage from the transmission shift lever, the bolt retaining the TV cable or the vacuum hose to the transmission modulator.
4. Disconnect the speedometer cable and electrical connection at the detent solenoid, if equipped.
5. Disconnect the oil cooler lines and any exhaust/converter brackets or pipes as required. If required remove the starter.
6. Remove the flywheel pan and mark the flywheel and converter. Remove the converter retaining bolts. Mark and remove the driveshaft assembly.
7. Properly support the engine. With the weight off the transmission, remove the rear crossmember assembly.
8. Properly support the transmission using a transmission jack. Lower the transmission enough to gain access to the transmission retaining bolts. Remove the engine block to transmission retaining bolts.
9. With the transmission safely chained to the transmission jack, remove the unit from under the vehicle. Do not allow the converter to fall from the transmission bell housing during the removal or installation of the transmission.
10. Installation is the reverse of the transmission removal procedure. Be sure that the torque converter is properly installed in the transmission housing.

DRIVE AXLE

Driveshaft and U-Joints

REMOVAL & INSTALLATION

1. Disconnect the negative battery cable. Position the selector lever in neutral. Raise and support the vehicle safely.
2. Remove the rear driveshaft flange capscrews. Never let the full weight of the driveshaft be supported only by the front universal joint.
3. Push shaft forward to clear pinion flange, then pull the driveshaft rearward to disengage the slip yoke from the transmission. Plug the transmission to prevent oil leakage or the entry of dirt.
4. Installation is the reverse of the removal procedure.

Rear Axle Shafts

REMOVAL & INSTALLATION

1. Raise and support the vehicle safely. Remove the wheel and brake drum.
2. Clean any dirt from the differential cover and loosen the cover attaching bolts. Allow the lubricant to drain out into a drain container.
3. Remove the pinion crossshaft lockscrew and remove the cross shaft.
4. Push in on the flanged end of the axle shaft and remove the C-lock from the splined end of the axle shaft.
5. Remove the axle shaft from the housing, being cautious not to damage the oil seal.
6. Use a suitable tool to pry the oil seal out of the bore. Use an axle shaft bearing puller on a slide hammer to remove the axle bearing from the bearing bore.
7. Lubricate the new bearing with gear lubricant. Use bearing installer J–23690 or equivalent, and install the bearing so that the tool bottoms out against the shoulder in the housing. Lubricate the lips of the seal with gear lubricant. Position the new seal on seal installer J–23771 or equivalent, and position the seal into the housing bore. Tap the seal into place so that it is flush with the axle tube.
8. Slide the axle shaft into the housing until the splines on the end of the shaft engage the splines of the differential side gear. Handle the shaft gently when trying to engage to splines.
9. Install the axle shaft C-lock on the splined end of the axle shaft in the

differential. Push the shaft outward so that the shaft lock seats in the counterbore of the differential side gear.
10. Install the pinion cross shaft through the differential case and pinion gears. Align the lock screw hole and install the lock screw, tightening it to 25 ft. lbs.
11. Clean the differential housing and cover mating surfaces and install the cover with a new gasket.
12. Fill the differential with lubricant, install the brake drum and wheel, and lower the vehicle.

FRONT SUSPENSION

Shock Absorber

REMOVAL & INSTALLATION

NOTE: Purge a new shock of air by repeatedly extending it in its normal position and compressing it while inverted.

1. Disconnect the negative battery cable. Open the hood. Remove the retaining nut from the frame spring tower. Use a pair of locking type pliers, to prevent the shock stem from turning while the nut is being unfastened.
2. Raise the vehicle as required. Remove the bottom shock absorber bolts.
3. Remove the shock through the bottom of the lower arm.
4. Install the retainer and the lower grommet.
5. Extend the shock rod as far as it will go.
6. Install the shock up through the coil spring and install the top grommet, retainer and nut.
7. Position the lower end of the shock on the lower control arm. Install the bolt, lockwasher, and nut. Tighten the bolt to 22 ft. lbs.
8. Tighten the retaining nut on the upper stem to 15 ft. lbs., while holding the stem with a pair of locking type pliers keep it from turning.

NOTE: Hold the shock absorber on the square tip with locking pliers to prevent damaging the threads when removing or installing the top nut.

Springs

REMOVAL & INSTALLATION

1. Raise and support the vehicle safely.
2. Remove the lower shock absorber

screws. Push the shock absorber up through the suspension arm and into the spring.

3. With the vehicle supported so that the suspension arms hang free position tool number J–23028–01 so that it cradles the inner lower control arm bushings.

NOTE: Be sure that the special tool J–23028–01 is properly secured to a suitable jack, or personal injury could occur.

4. Remove the stabilizer to lower suspension arm attachment.

5. Raise the jack and relieve the tension on the lower control arm pivot bolts. Install a chain around the spring and through the lower control arm.

6. Remove the nuts and bolts, remove the rear bolt first. Lower the control arm by slowly lowering the jack.

7. When all tension is removed from the spring remove the chain and the spring from the vehicle.

NOTE: Do not use force on the lower control arm and ball joint to remove the spring. Proper maneuvering of the spring will allow for easy removal

8. Installation is the reverse of the removal procedure. The lower end of the coil must cover all or part of one inspection hole in the lower control arm. The second hole must be partly or completely uncovered.

9. Check and adjust the front end alignment as required.

Ball Joints

INSPECTION

NOTE: Before performing this inspection, make sure the wheel bearings are adjusted correctly and that the control arm bushings are in good condition.

1. Jack the vehicle up under the front lower control arm at the spring seat.

2. Raise the vehicle until there is 1–2 in. of clearance under the wheel.

3. Insert a bar under the wheel and pry upward. If the wheel rises more than $\frac{1}{8}$ in., the ball joints are worn. Determine if the upper or lower ball joint is worn by visual inspection while prying on the wheel.

NOTE: Due to the distribution of forces in the suspension, the lower ball joint is usually the defective joint. Cadillacs are equipped with wear indicators on the lower ball joint. As long as the wear indicator neck extends be-

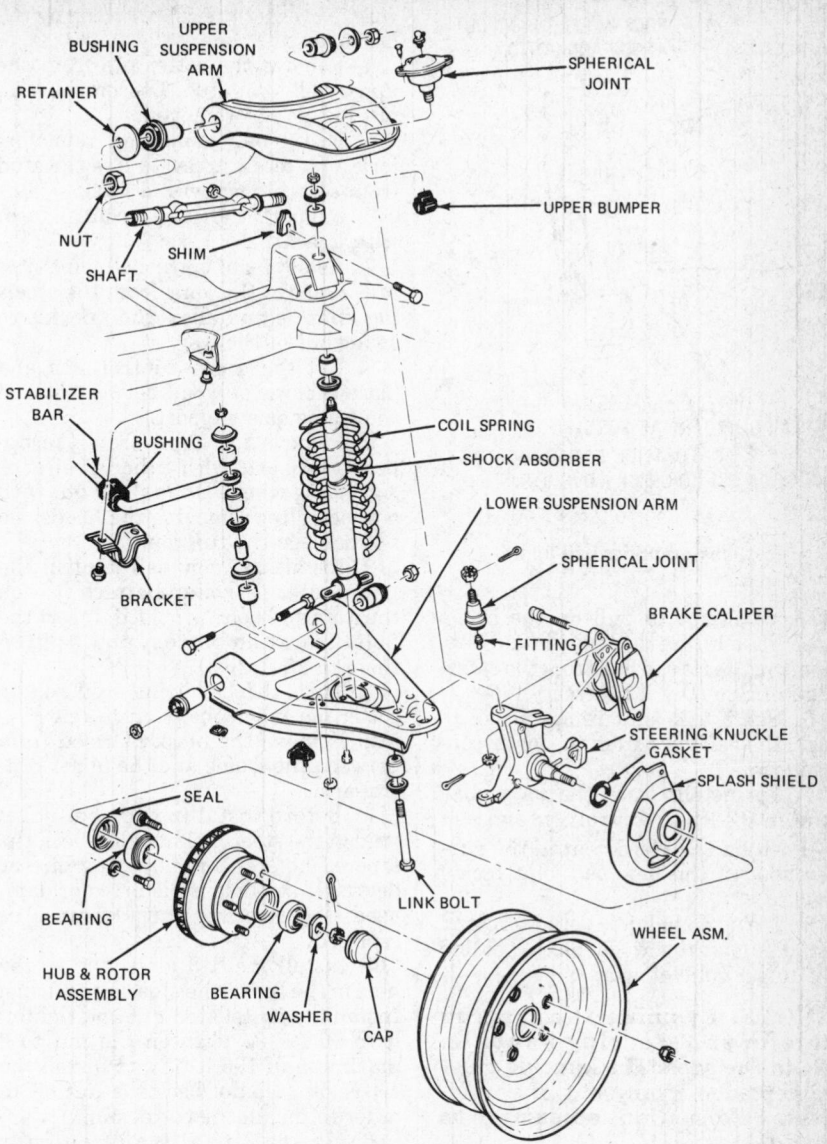

Front suspension

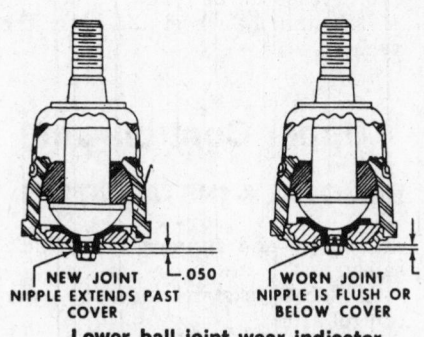

Lower ball joint wear indicator

low the ball stud seat, replacement is unnecessary.

REMOVAL & INSTALLATION

Lower Ball Joint

1. Raise and support the vehicle safely. Remove the tire and wheel.

2. Remove the lower ball joint stud cotter pin. Loosen (not more than one turn), but do not remove, the stud nut.

3. Install a ball joint removal tool between the studs and turn the threaded end of the tool until the stud is free of the steering knuckle.

NOTE: The lower control arm must be supported so that the spring cannot force the arm down.

4. Remove the lower stud nut. Pull out on bottom of the brake disc and simultaneously push up to free the steering knuckle from the ball joint stud. If additional leverage is needed, it may be necessary to reinstall the tire for the above procedure.

5. Lift up on the upper control arm (with the steering knuckle and hub attached), and place a block of wood between the frame and the upper arm.

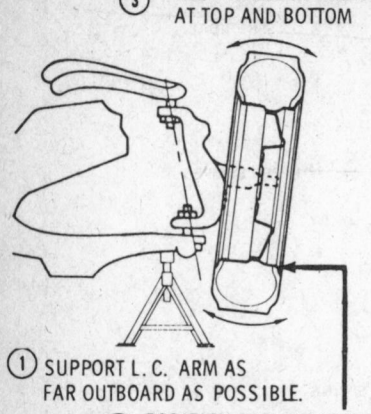

③ ROCK WHEEL IN AND OUT AT TOP AND BOTTOM

① SUPPORT L.C. ARM AS FAR OUTBOARD AS POSSIBLE.

② POSITION DIAL INDICATOR TO CHECK MOVEMENT AT THIS POINT

Checking upper ball joint

Be careful not to pull on the brake hose when lifting the knuckle and hub. Remove the tie rod end from the steering knuckle only if necessary.

6. Use a ball joint removal tool to push the ball joint from the lower control arm.

7. To install, place the lower ball joint in the lower control arm and seat it. Position the bleed vent in the rubber boot of the new ball joint facing inward.

8. Turn the ball joint stud fore and aft. Remove the wood block holding the upper control arm.

NOTE: Examine the tapered hole in the steering knuckle. Clean the area. The knuckle must be replaced if any out of roundness, deformation, or damage is found.

9. Attach the ball joint stud to the steering knuckle and install the stud nut. Torque the nut to 80 ft. lbs. and install a new cotter pin.

NOTE: 125 ft. lbs. or ⅛ turn maximum is allowed to align the cotter pin slot. Do not back off the nut to install the cotter pin.

10. Lubricate the ball joint. If removed, install the tie rod end and torque the nut to 35 ft. lbs. Install the cotter pin.

11. Install the wheel and tire and lower the car. Have the front wheel alignment checked and adjusted as necessary.

Upper Ball Joint

1. Raise and support the vehicle safely.

2. Remove the wheel and tire.

3. Remove the disc brake caliper assembly and support it with a length of wire. Never let the caliper hang by the brake hose.

4. Remove the cotter pin from the upper ball joint stud. Loosen the stud nut but do not remove it.

5. Use a ball joint stud removing fork, or a screw press, to free the stud from control arm with a jack.

6. Support the lower control arm with a jack.

7. Remove the upper ball joint stud nut. Remove the joint from the steering knuckle and allow the knuckle to swing out of the way.

8. Lift the upper control arm and place a block of wood between it and the frame as a support.

9. Remove the rivets from the upper control arm with either a chisel or a grinding wheel. Drive them out with a punch after removing the heads. Do not damage the ball joint seat.

10. Install the new ball joint in the upper control arm and attach it with the nuts and bolts provided. Insert the bolts from the bottom and tighten them to 25 ft. lbs.

11. Turn the ball joint stud so the cotter pin hole runs front to rear.

12. Remove the block of wood from between the frame and the upper control arm.

13. Before installing the ball joint stud in the steering knuckle, check the tapered hole and remove any dirt or debris. If the hole is distorted or damaged, the steering knuckle must be replaced.

14. Install the ball joint stud in the hole in the top of the steering knuckle. Install the castellated nut and tighten it to 60 ft. lbs. Tighten the nut to a maximum of 100 ft. lbs. to install the cotter pin. Do not back the nut off in order to install the cotter pin.

15. Install the brake caliper assembly.

16. Grease the ball joint.

17. Install the wheel and lower the vehicle.

Upper Control Arm

REMOVAL & INSTALLATION

1. Raise and support the vehicle safely.

2. Place a jackstand under the lower control arm.

3. Remove the tire and wheel.

4. Remove the upper ball joint stud from the steering knuckle. Separate the upper arm spherical joint stud from the steering knuckle using the proper tools.

5. Remove the two nuts securing the upper arm shaft to the frame bracket. Note the number and positioning of the shims for reassembly.

6. It may be necessary to support the caliper and rotor assembly before removing the upper control arm assembly. Remove the control arm from the vehicle.

7. Install the suspension arm cross shaft on the attaching bolts.

8. Using a free running nut instead of a locknut, tighten both nuts until the serrated bolts are reseated.

9. Remove the free running nuts and install the locknuts. Install the shims as removed.

10. Torque the mounting nuts to 75 ft. lbs. Tighten the nut on the thinner shim pack first.

11. Install the ball joint stud through the knuckle and tighten the nut to 60 ft. lbs. Install the cotter pin.

12. Install the wheel and torque the lug nuts to 100 ft. lbs.

Lower Control Arm

REMOVAL & INSTALLATION

1. Raise and support the vehicle by the frame so the control arms hang freely.

2. Remove the lower shock absorber mounting bolts.

3. Attach a special supporting tool (No. J–23028–01) to a floor jack. Position the tool and the jack so as to cradle the inner bushings.

4. Remove the stabilizer to lower control arm attaching bolt.

5. Raise the jack to relieve the tension on the lower control arm pivot bolts. As a safety measure, install a chain around the spring and through the lower control arm.

6. Lower the jack slowly.

7. When all the spring pressure is relieved, remove the safety chain and the spring.

8. Remove the lower ball joint stud cotter pin.

9. Loosen, but do not remove, the ball joint nut.

10. Install a ball stud remover between the studs and screw the threaded end of the tool until the stud is freed.

11. Remove the lower stud nut.

12. Pull outward on the bottom of the tire while at the same time pushing the tire upward to free the steering knuckle from the ball joint stud.

13. Remove the lower control arm from the vehicle.

14. Installation is the reverse of removal. Tighten the attaching bolts to the following values. Lower control arm ball joint stud to steering knuckle boss, 80 ft. lbs. (tighten to align the cotter pin hole). Control arm pivot bolts, 90 ft. lbs.

Front Wheel Bearings

ADJUSTMENT

1. Raise and support the vehicle safely. Remove the dust cap from the wheel bearing and remove the cotter pin.
2. While spinning the wheel, tighten the adjusting nut to 12 ft. lbs. Stop spinning the wheel.
3. Back off the nut until it is free and then tighten it finger tight.
4. Insert the cotter pin. If the pin cannot be installed in this position, back off the nut until the holes align. Make certain that the pin fits tightly. There will be 0.001–0.005 in. end play when the wheel bearings are properly adjusted.

REMOVAL & INSTALLATION

1. Raise and support the vehicle safely. Remove the tire and wheel assembly.
2. Remove the dust cap. Remove the cotter pin. Remove the locknut.
3. Remove the outer wheel bearing from its mounting.
4. Remove the rotor. Remove the inner wheel bearing from its mounting.
5. Installation is the reverse of the removal procedure.

Front Wheel Alignment

CASTER

Caster is the tilting of the steering axis either forward or backward from the vertical, when viewed from the side of the vehicle. A backward tilt is said to be positive and a forward tilt is said to be negative.

CAMBER

Camber is the tilting of the wheels from the vertical when viewed from the front of the vehicle. When the wheels tilt outward from the top, the camber is said to be positive. When the wheels tilt inward from the top the camber is said to be negative. The amount of tilt is measured in degrees from the vertical. This measurement is called camber angle.

TOE IN

Toe in is the turning in of the wheels. The actual amount of toe in is normally only a fraction of an inch. The purpose of toe in specification is to ensure parallel rolling of the wheels. Toe in also serves to offset the small deflections of the steering support system

which occur when the vehicle is rolling forward.

REAR SUSPENSION

Shock Absorber

REMOVAL & INSTALLATION

NOTE: Purge a new shock of air by repeatedly extending it in its normal position and compressing it while inverted.

1. Raise and support the vehicle safely. Preoperly support the rear axle.
2. If the vehicle is equipped with electronic level control, remove the air lines at the shocks.

NOTE: The shocks act as rebound stops for the rear suspension and under no circumstances should the rear end be raised excessively high while disconnecting the shocks, unless both the rear axle and the frame are supported.

3. Remove the upper shock absorber retaining bolts and nuts.
4. Remove the lower retaining nut while holding the stem by the grommet to keep the stem from turning.
5. Remove the shock absorber from the vehicle.
6. Installation is the reverse of the removal procedure.

Springs

REMOVAL & INSTALLATION

1. Raise and support the vehicle safely.
2. Place a jack under the differential housing.
3. Remove the tires and wheels.
4. If the vehicle has electronic level control, disconnect the link at the overtravel lever and position it in its center location.
5. Remove the shock absorber lower retaining nuts and washers.

NOTE: The shock absorbers act as stops for the suspension. Make certain that both the axle and the frame are supported before continuing.

6. Disconnect the brake line retaining clip from the axle and frame, but do not disconnect the brake line. This should allow enough slack, as the axle

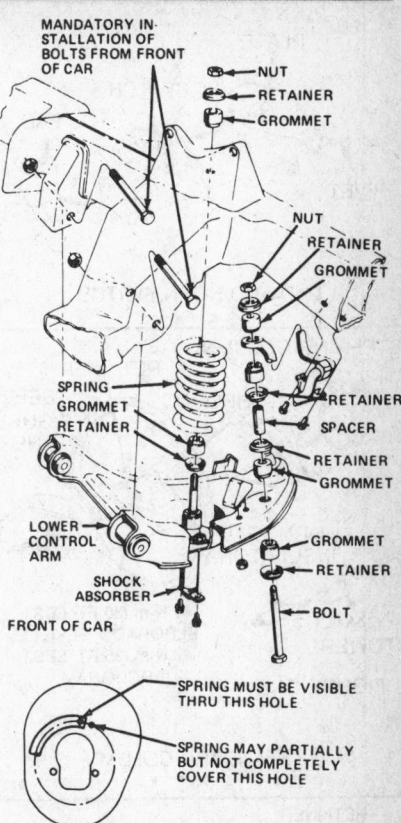

Shock, spring and related components

is lowered, to eliminate the need for disconnecting and reconnecting the brake line. If enough slack cannot be obtained, disconnect the brake line from the hose and plug both openings. Be sure to bleed the brakes after installation.

7. As required, disconnect the rear U-joint and wire the driveshaft out of the way. Do not allow the driveshaft to hang unsupported.
8. Remove nuts and bolts that secure both upper control arms to the axle brackets.
9. Lower rear axle assembly slowly until the springs are free and remove the springs. Do not allow the differential to wind up as it is lowered as the spring may fly out.
10. To install, reverse the removal procedure. Tighten the upper and lower control arm bolts to 75 ft. lbs.

STEERING

Steering Wheel

REMOVAL & INSTALLATION

1. Disconnect the negative battery cable.

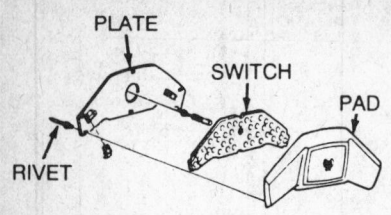

PAD AND HORN SWITCH

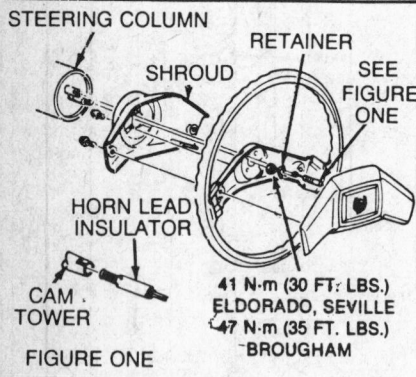

STANDARD COLUMN

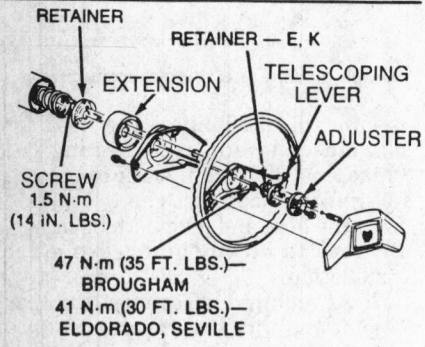

TILT AND TELESCOPING COLUMN

Steering wheel and related components

2. Remove the horn trim pad. Remove the horn contact wire from the plastic tower by pushing in on the wire and turning counterclockwise. The wire will spring out of the tower. It may be necessary to turn the ignition to the on position in order to facilitate removal.

3. If the vehicle is equipped with tilt and telescoping steering wheel remove the three screws that secure the telescope locking lever assembly to the adjuster. Unscrew and remove the adjuster from the steering shaft.

4. Remove the locking lever assembly. Scribe an alignment mark on the steering wheel hub in line with the slash mark on the steering shaft.

5. Loosen the locknut on the steering shaft and position it flush with the end of the shaft. Using the proper steering wheel removal tool remove the wheel from its mounting on the steering shaft.

6. Remove the steering wheel removal tool from the steering wheel. Remove the locknut from the steering shaft. Remove the steering wheel from the vehicle.

7. Installation is the reverse of the removal procedure. When installing the steering wheel it should not be driven on the steering shaft as damage to the steering column and its components could occur.

Turn Signal Switch

REMOVAL & INSTALLATION

Standard Steering Column

1. Disconnect the negative battery cable.

2. Remove the steering wheel.

3. Insert a suitable tool into the lockplate and remove the lockplate cover assembly.

4. Install a spring compressor onto the steering shaft. Tighten the tool to compress the lockplate and the spring. Remove the snapring from the groove in the shaft.

5. Remove the lockplate and slide the turn signal cam and the upper bearing preload spring and the thrust washer off the upper steering shaft.

6. Remove the steering column lower cover.

7. Remove the turn signal lever from the column.

8. On vehicles equipped with cruise control disconnect the cruise control wire from the harness near the bottom of the column. Remove the harness protector from the cruise control wire. Remove the turn signal lever. Do not remove the wire from the column.

9. Remove the vertical bolts at the steering column upper support. Remove the shim packs. Keep the shims in order for reinstallation.

10. Remove the screws securing the column upper mounting bracket to the column. Remove the bracket.

11. Disconnect the turn signal wiring and remove the wires from the plastic protector.

12. Remove the turn signal switch mounting screws.

13. Slide the switch connector out of the bracket on the steering column.

14. If the switch is known to be bad, cut the wires and discard the switch. Tape the connector of the new switch to the old wires, and pull the new harness down through the steering column while removing the old wires.

15. If the original switch is to be reused, wrap tape around the wire and

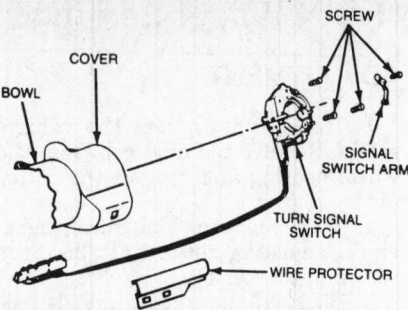

Standard steering column turnsignal switch assembly

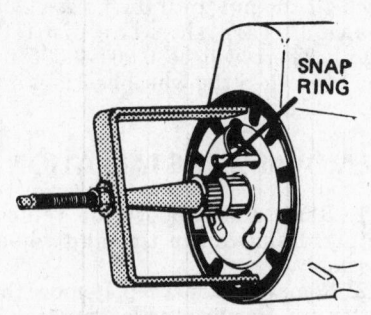

Lock plate removal tool

connector and pull the harness up through the column. It may be helpful to attach a length of wire to the harness connector before pulling it up through the column to facilitate installation.

16. After freeing the switch wiring protector from its mounting, pull the turn signal switch straight up and remove the switch, switch harness, and the connector from the column.

17. Installation is the reverse of the removal procedure.

Tilt and Telescoping Steering Column

1. Disconnect the battery and remove the steering wheel.

2. Remove the rubber sleeve bumper from the steering shaft.

3. Remove the plastic retainer and disengage the tabs on the retainer from the C-ring.

4. Compress the upper steering shaft preload spring with a spring compressor and remove the C-ring. When installing the spring compressor, pull the upper shaft up about 1 in. and turn the ignition to the lock position to hold the shaft in place.

5. Remove the spring compressor and remove the upper steering shaft lock plate, horn contact carrier and the preload spring.

6. Remove the steering column lower cover. Unscrew and remove the turn signal lever.

7. If equipped with cruise control disconnect the cruise control wire

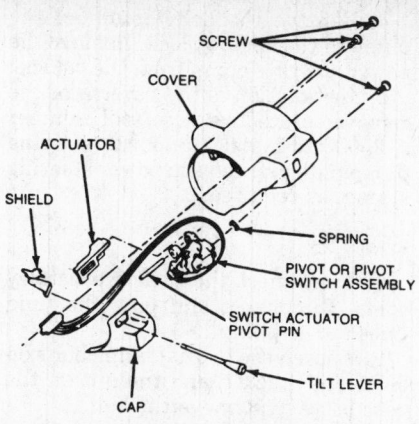

Tilt and telescoping steering column turnsignal switch assembly

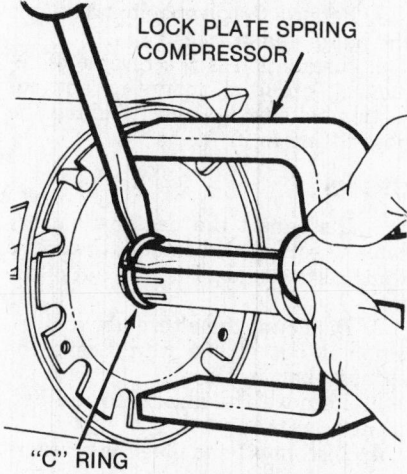

LOCK PLATE SPRING COMPRESSOR

"C" RING

Removing the C-ring

from the harness near the bottom of the steering column. Slide the protector off the cruise control wire. Remove the lever attaching screw and carefully pull the lever out enough to allow the removal of the turn signal switch.

8. Remove the nuts and shim packs from the upper column support. Keep the shims together as a unit for reinstallation.

9. Remove the bracket from the steering column by removing the two attaching screws from each side.

10. Disconnect the turn signal wiring harness and remove the wires from the plastic protector.

11. Remove the turn signal switch retaining screws and pull the switch up out of the steering column.

12. If the switch is to be replaced, cut the wires from the switch and tape the new switch connector to the old wires. Carefully pull the new harness down through the column as the old wires are removed.

13. If the old switch is to be reused, tape the connector to the wires and

carefully pull the harness up out of the column.

14. Feed the wiring harness down through the steering column to replace the old switch.

15. Secure the switch in the steering column.

16. Install the upper shaft preload spring.

17. Install the lock plate and carrier assembly. Make sure that the flat on the lower end of the steering shaft is pointing up and that the small plastic tab on the carrier is up or nearest the top of the column. The flat surface of the lock plate must be installed facing down against the turn signal switch.

18. Install the spring compressor, compress the preload spring and lock plate and install the C-ring with the wide side toward the keyway.

19. Remove the spring compressor and install the plastic retainer on the C-ring.

20. Install the rubber sleeve bumper over the steering shaft and install the steering wheel.

21. Install the turn signal lever. If the vehicle is equipped with cruise control, secure the lever to the switch with the retaining screw and install the wiring harness.

22. Remove the tape from the end of the harness and connect the switch and cruise control, if so equipped, to the wire harness.

23. Cover both harnesses with the plastic protector and position it to the column. The turn signal connector slides on the tabs of the column.

24. Position the steering column upper bracket over the turn signal switch harness plastic protector.

25. Install the mounting bracket nuts and shims in their original positions.

26. Install the steering column lower cover.

Ignition Lock

REMOVAL & INSTALLATION

Standard Steering Column

1. Disconnect the negative battery cable. Remove the steering wheel.

2. Remove the lockplate cover assembly.

3. After compressing the lockplate spring, remove the snapring from the groove in the shaft.

4. Remove the lockplate and slide the turn signal cam and the upper bearing preload spring off the upper steering shaft.

5. Remove the thrust washer from the shaft.

6. Remove the hazard warning

switch knob from the column along with the turn signal lever.

7. If the vehicle is equipped with cruise control attach a piece of wire to the connector on the cruise control switch harness. Gently pull the harness up and out of the column.

8. Remove the turn signal switch mounting screws.

9. Slide the switch connector out of the bracket on the steering column.

10. As required free the turn signal switch wiring protector from its mounting after disconnecting the turn signal switch electrical connectors, then pull the turn signal switch straight up and out of the steering column along with the switch harness and the connector from the steering column.

11. Turn the ignition switch to the on or run position. Insert a small drift pin into the slot next to the switch mounting screw boss. Push the lock cylinder tab and remove the lock cylinder.

12. Installation is the reverse of the removal procedure.

Tilt and Telescoping Steering Column

1. Disconnect the negative battery cable. Remove the steering wheel.

2. Remove the rubber sleeve bumper from the steering shaft.

3. Using an appropriate tool, remove the plastic retainer.

4. Using a spring compressor, compress the upper steering shaft spring and remove the C-ring. Release the steering shaft lockplate, the horn contact carrier, and the upper steering shaft preload spring.

5. Remove the four screws which hold the upper mounting bracket and then remove the bracket.

6. Slide the harness connector out of the bracket on the steering column. Tape the upper part of the harness and connector.

7. Disconnect the hazard button and position the shift bowl in park. Remove the turn signal lever from the column.

8. If the vehicle is equipped with cruise control remove the harness protector from the harness. Attach a piece of wire to the switch harness connector. Before removing the turn signal lever, loop a piece of wire and insert it into the turn signal lever opening. Use the wire to pull the cruise control harness out through the opening. Pull the rest of the harness up through and out of the column. Remove the guide wire from the connector and secure the wire to the column. Remove the turn signal lever.

9. Pull the turn signal switch up until the end connector is within the shift

bowl. Remove the hazard flasher lever. Allow the switch to hang.

10. Place the ignition key in the run position.

11. Depress the center of the lock cylinder retaining tab with a suitable tool and then remove the lock cylinder.

12. Installation is the reverse of the removal procedure.

Ignition Switch

REMOVAL & INSTALLATION

1. Disconnect the negative battery terminal.

2. Position lock cylinder in lock position.

3. Remove steering column lower cover.

4. Loosen the nuts on the upper steering column, allowing column to drop and support on the seat.

5. Disconnect the ignition switch connector at switch.

6. Remove the screws securing the dimmer switch and ignition switch to the steering column. Position the dimmer switch out of the way and remove the screw securing the ignition switch to the steering column. Remove the ignition switch from the vehicle.

7. To install, assemble the ignition switch on the actuator rod and adjust it to the lock position as follows.

8. If the vehicle is equipped with a standard column hold the switch actuating rod stationary with one hand while moving the switch toward the bottom of the column until it reaches the end of its travel (Acc. position). Back off two detents to the right (Off/Unlock position), then with the key also in the Off/Unlock position, tighten the switch mounting screws to 35 in. lbs.

9. If the vehicle is equipped with a tilt wheel hold the switch actuating rod stationary with one hand while moving the switch toward the upper end of column until it reaches the end of its travel (Acc. position). Back off one detent and with the key in lock position, tighten the switch mounting screws to 35 in. lbs.

10. Continue the installation in the reverse order of the removal procedure. Test the starting system to start in Park and Neutral only.

Power Steering Gear

REMOVAL & INSTALLATION

1. Disconnect the negative battery cable. Position a drain pan under the steering gear. Disconnect the pressure and return lines from the steering gear assembly. Plug the opening to prevent the entrance of dirt.

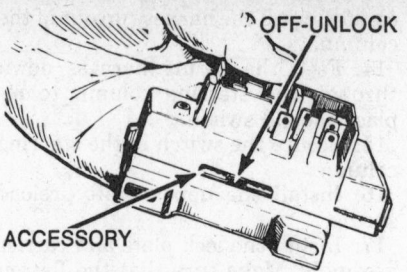

MOVE SWITCH SLIDER TO EXTREME LEFT (ACCESSORY) POSITION THEN MOVE SLIDER TO DETENTS TO THE RIGHT OF "OFF-UNLOCK"

Ignition switch in Off-Unlocked position

2. If equipped, disconnect the stone shield from the return pipe.

3. Remove the pinch bolt from the flex coupling, and disconnect the coupling from the gear.

NOTE: Failure to disconnect the flexible coupling from the steering gear stub shaft can result in damage to the steering gear and or the intermediate shaft. This damage can cause the loss of steering control which could result in a vehicle crash and bodily injuries.

4. Raise the vehicle and support it safely.

5. Remove the pitman arm nut and washer. Remove the pitman arm from the sector shaft with a pitman arm puller tool.

6. Remove the retaining bolts and washers holding the steering gear to the side rail. Lower the gear assembly from the vehicle.

7. The installation is the reverse of the removal procedure. Tighten the pitman arm nut to 185 ft. lbs., the mounting bolts to 70 ft. lbs. and the flex coupling pinch bolt to 30 ft. lbs.

Power Steering Pump

REMOVAL & INSTALLATION

250 V8

1. Disconnect the negative battery cable. Disconnect and plug the fluid lines at the pump.

2. Loosen the air condition compressor mounting bracket and the vacuum pump bracket. Remove the vacuum pump as required. Remove the belts from the power steering pump pulley.

3. Disconnect and plug the power steering pump lines. Remove the power steering pump pulley using tool number J–25034 or equivalent. It is not necessary to remove the radiator fan shroud.

4. Remove the bolts retaining the pump to the engine block. Remove the power steering pump from the vehicle.

5. Installation is the reverse of the removal procedure. Use tool number J–25033 to install the power steering pump pulley. Bleed the power steering system as required.

252 V6

1. Disconnect the neagtive battery cable. Disconnect and plug the fluid lines at the pump.

2. Loosen the two adjusting bolts on the front bracket, and the nut on the rear bracket. Remove the belt.

3. Remove the two front mounting bracket bolts.

4. Remove the nut securing the pump to the rear bracket.

5. Remove the pivot bolt and lift out the pump and bracket.

6. Installation is the reverse of removal. Torque all mounting and adjusting bolts to 34 ft. lbs. Tighten the hose fitting to 21 ft. lbs.

350 V8

1. Disconnect the negative battery cable. If equipped, dismount the cruise control servo and position it out of the way.

2. Dismount the alternator and position it out of the way. Leave the through bolt in place.

3. Remove the alternator adjustment bracket.

4. Disconnect and plug the pressure and return lines.

5. Loosen the pump adjusting bolt, pivot bolt and pivot nut. Remove the belt.

6. Remove the two nuts and spacer securing the pump mounting bracket to the water pump and timing chain cover.

7. Remove the pump bracket bolt and lift out the pump and bracket.

8. Installation is the reverse of removal. Torque the lower nut at the spacer to 30 ft. lbs.; the upper nut and bracket bolt to 20 ft. lbs., each; the adjusting bolt to 30 ft. lbs.; the hose connections to 35 ft. lbs.

307 V8

1. Disconnect the negative battery cable. Disconnect and relocate the air cleaner inlet tube and the upper radiator hose to gain access to the pump.

2. Loosen the alternator mounting bolts except for the long bolt. Rotate the unit upward to gain access by pivoting the long bolt.

3. Remove and plug the pressure and return hoses from the pump. Remove the front pump bracket mounting bolts and spacer. Remove the rear pump mounting nut.

4. Remove the pump and bracket from the engine as an assembly.

5. Installation is the reverse order of the removal procedure. Be sure to bleed the air from the system.

BELT ADJUSTMENT

1. Disconnect the negative battery cable.

2. Loosen the power steering pump mounting bolts.

3. Adjust the power steering pump by carefully prying the pump away from the engine using the proper tool.

4. Tighten the power steering pump retaining bolts.

5. Check the adjustment using tool J–23600–B or equivalent. A new belt should be adjusted too 170 lb. max. and a used belt should be adjusted too 90 lb. max.

SYSTEM BLEEDING

1. Raise and support the front of the vehicle safely.

2. With the wheels turned all the way to the left add power steering fluid to the "cold" mark on the dipstick.

3. Start the engine. Check the fluid level. Add fluid as necessary to bring the level to the "cold" mark on the dipstick.

4. Bleed the system by turning the steering wheel from side to side without hitting the stops.

5. Be sure to maintain the fluid level at the "hot/cold" mark on the dipstick. Fluid with air in it will have a light tan appearance. This air must be expelled from the system before normal steering action can be obtained.

6. Return the wheels to the center position. Allow the engine to run for about two minutes and then shut it off.

7. Road test the vehicle and make sure that the steering performs properly and there is no noise from the power steering pump. Correct problems as required.

8. Recheck the power steering level. Be sure that the fluid level is at the "hot" mark on the dipstick after the system has stabilized at its normal operating temperature.

Tie Rod Ends

REMOVAL & INSTALLATION

1. Raise and support the vehicle safely.

2. Remove the cotter pin and castellated nut from the outer tie rod end. If the torque required to remove the nut is in excess of 80 ft. lbs. it is recommended that new bolts and nuts be

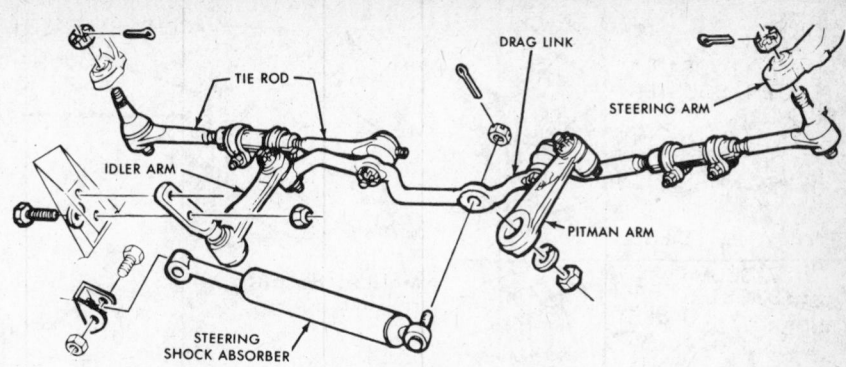

Cadillac steering linkage

used. Be sure that the new parts are the same quality as the old ones.

3. Disconnect the tie rod end from the steering knuckle using tool number J–24319–01 or equivalent.

4. Remove the inner ball stud from the intermediate rod using tool number J–24319–01 or equivalent.

NOTE: When disconnecting a linkage joint no attempt should be made to disengage the joint by driving a wedge between the joint and the attached part as damage to the seal may occur.

5. Remove the tie rod from the adjuster tube by loosening the clamp bolts and unscrewing the end assembly.

6. Installation is the reverse of the removal procedure. Coat the threaded rod ends with chassis lube before installation.

BRAKES

For all brake system repair and service procedures not detailed below, please refer to "Brakes" in the Unit Repair section.

Master Cylinder

REMOVAL & INSTALLATION

1. Disconnect the negative battery cable. Disconnect and plug the brake lines at the master cylinder.

2. Remove the nuts securing the master cylinder to the power booster.

3. Remove the master cylinder from the vehicle.

4. Installation is the reverse of the removal procedure. As required, bleed the system.

Proportioning Valve

REMOVAL & INSTALLATION

The valve is non serviceable and is located on the frame extension on the left side of the vehicle. To remove it, disconnect the brake lines at the valve. Unbolt and remove the valve. Installation is the reverse of removal. Bleed the brakes.

Power Brake Booster

REMOVAL & INSTALLATION

Gasoline Engine

1. Disconnect the negative battery cable. Remove the master cylinder retaining nuts and position the assembly out of the way.

2. Disconnect vacuum line from vacuum check valve on unit.

3. Remove steering column lower cover.

4. Remove cotter pin, washer and spring spacer that secures power unit pushrod to brake pedal arm.

5. Remove the nuts that secure the power unit to the firewall. Remove the power unit.

6. Installation is the reverse of the removal procedure.

Diesel Engine

1. Disconnect the negative battery cable. With the engine off, pump the brake pedal four or five times to empty the accumulator of pressurized fluid.

2. Disconnect the brake lines from the master cylinder and cap the lines.

3. Remove and plug the three hydraulic lines from the booster. Remove the washer and retainer that secures the booster pedal rod to the brake pedal arm.

NOTE: To avoid booster damage, do not pry the pedal rod off the pedal arm.

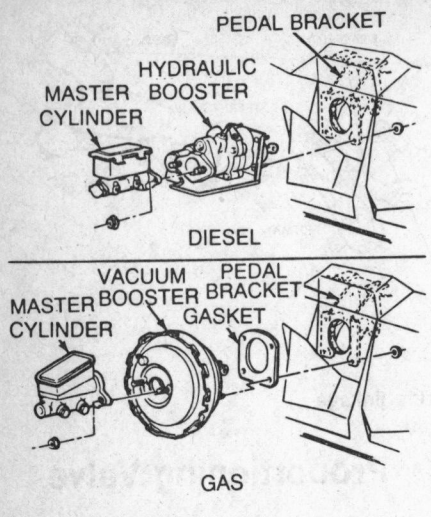

Power brake booster mounting

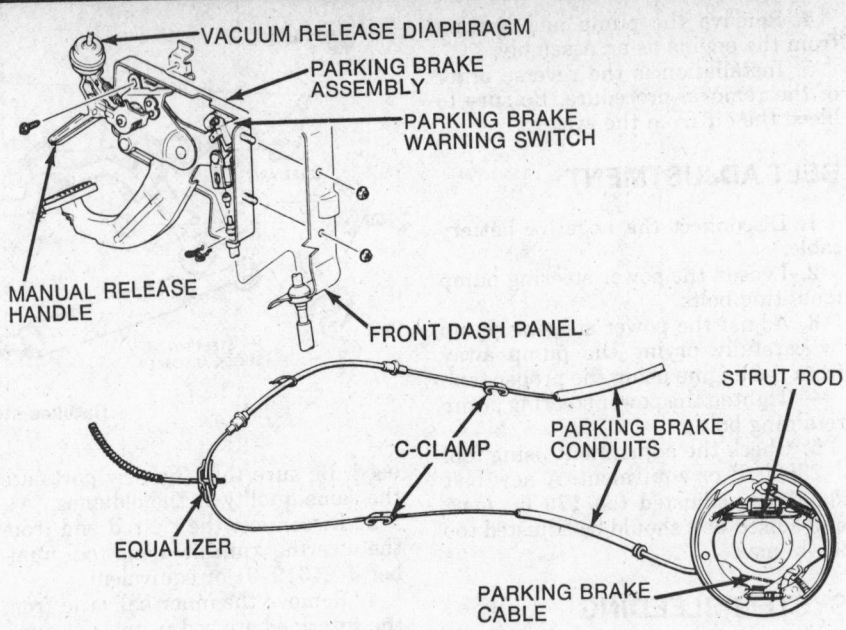

Parking brake system

4. Remove the four nuts holding the booster to the firewall.

5. Loosen the booster from the firewall and move the booster pedal rod inboard until it disconnects from the brake pedal arm. Remove the spring washer from the brake pedal arm and remove the booster.

6. Installation is the reverse of the removal procedure.

Wheel Cylinder

REMOVAL & INSTALLATION

1. Raise and support the vehicle safely. Remove the tire and wheel.

2. Remove the brake drum. Remove the brake shoes.

3. Disconnect the brake line from the wheel cylinder assembly.

4. Remove the wheel cylinder retaining bolts. Remove the wheel cylinder from the vehicle.

5. Installation is the reverse of the removal procedure. Be sure to bleed the system.

Parking Brake Cable

ADJUSTMENT

1. Be sure that the rear brakes are properly adjusted before adjusting the parking brake. Check the parking brake linkage for the free movement of all the cables. Lubricate, if necessary.

2. Depress the parking brake pedal 1½ in.

3. Raise and support the vehicle safely.

4. Holding the cable stud to keep it from turning, tighten the equalizer nut until a light drag is felt on either wheel when they are spun in the forward direction.

5. When the parking brake is released there should be no brake shoe drag.

REMOVAL & INSTALLATION

Front Cable

1. Release the parking brake.

2. Raise the vehicle and support it safely.

3. Disconnect the cable stud at the equalizer by removing the equalizer nut and separating the cable stud from the equalizer.

4. Remove the front cable from the cable connector.

5. Loosen the adjuster nut and disconnect the front cable from the connector. Compress the retainer fingers and loosen the assembly at the frame.

6. Remove the cable at the pedal assembly.

7. Remove the cable end from the parking brake assembly clevis.

8. Pull the cable through the hole in the frame and remove it from the vehicle.

9. Installation is the reverse of the removal procedure.

Rear Cable

1. Release the parking brake.

2. Raise and support the vehicle safely.

3. Remove the rear wheel and drum on same side of the vehicle as the parking brake cable being replaced.

4. Remove the equalizer nut and retainer. Separate the equalizer from the right rear cable stud.

5. Remove the end of the left rear cable from the cable connector and equalizer.

6. Remove the clip securing the right rear cable to control arm bracket. Remove the cable from the bracket by pulling it rearward.

7. Remove the cable from the brake backing plate. Removal can be assisted by compressing the multiple prong retainer.

8. Remove the pawl spring and the pawl lever from the actuating lever. Remove the cable end from the operating lever and remove the cable from backing plate.

9. Installation is the reverse of the removal procedure.

CHASSIS ELECTRICAL

Heater Blower

REMOVAL & INSTALLATION

1. Disconnect the negative battery cable.

2. Remove the rubber cooling hose from the nipple and blower motor.

3. Disconnect the electrical connections from the motor assembly.

4. Remove the screws that secure the heater motor to the heater case. Remove the heater motor from the vehicle.

5. Installation is the reverse of the removal procedure.

Heater Core

REMOVAL & INSTALLATION

1. Disconnect the negative battery cable. Disconnect wiring from the blower, power module, resistors, compressor cycling switch and the power antenna connections. Position the wiring harness out of the way.

2. Remove the right windshield washer nozzle.

3. Remove the right air inlet screen from the plenum. Partially remove the rubber molding above the plenum (one screw on the right hand side). Drain the radiator.

4. Remove the remaining screws and remove the primary inlet screen. Remove the blower motor.

5. Remove the two screws holding the compressor cycling switch to the module and carefully reposition the switch off of the module cover.

6. Remove the screws retaining the case module cover. Remove the cover. Remove and plug the heater hoses from the heater core nipples.

7. Remove the screw and the retainer holding the heater core to the frame at the top of the assembly.

8. With the temperature door in the max/hot position, reach through the temperature housing and push the lower forward corner of the heater core away from the housing.

9. Rotate the core parallel to the housing. This will cause the core to snap out of the lower clamp. The core can now be removed in a vertical direction due to the configuration of the component.

10. Installation is the reverse order of the removal procedure. Be sure to install a new module cover seal as required.

Radio

REMOVAL & INSTALLATION

1. Disconnect the negative battery cable. Remove the radio knobs and antirattle springs.

2. Remove the two hex nuts securing the bezel to the radio.

3. Remove the two center air conditioning outlet grilles. Remove the one screw in each outlet.

4. Remove the the center panel insert. retaining screws. Remove the panel.

5. Unbolt and remove the radio from its mounting.

6. Disconnect the electrical wiring. Disconnect the antenna lead in wire.

7. Installation is the reverse of the removal procedure.

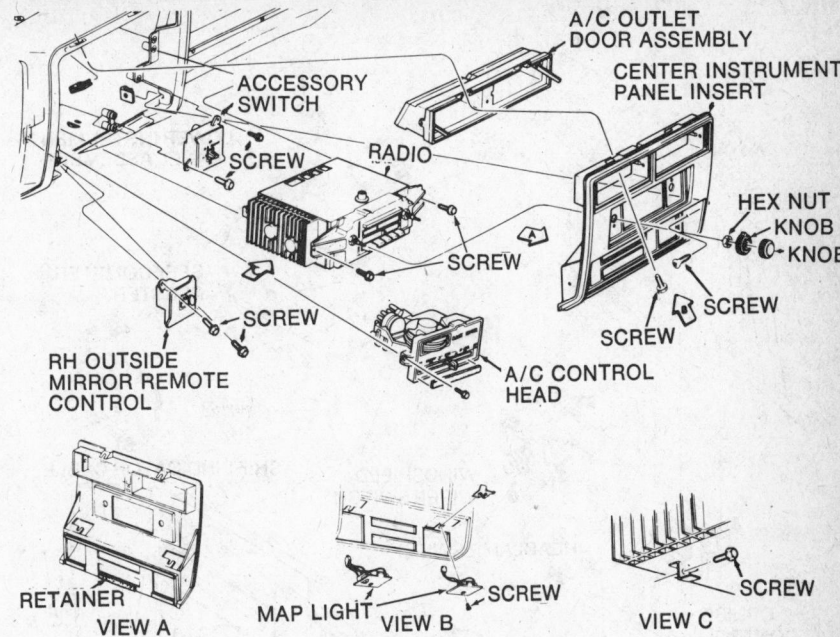

Typical radio installation

Windshield Wiper Switch

REMOVAL & INSTALLATION

1. Disconnect the negative battery cable.

2. Remove the instrument panel insert.

3. Remove the screws securing the switch to the instrument panel.

4. Pull the switch forward and disconnect the electrical connections. Remove the switch from the vehicle.

5. Installation is the reverse of the removal procedure.

Windshield Wiper Motor

REMOVAL & INSTALLATION

1. Disconnect the negative battery cable.

2. Remove the cowl screen.

3. Reach through the opening and disengage the transmission drive link from the wiper crank arm by loosening the nuts.

4. Disconnect the electrical wiring and washer hoses.

5. Remove the bolts that secure the wiper/washer unit to the firewall.

6. Remove the entire assembly.

7. Installation is the reverse of the removal procedure. Be sure that the wiper crank arm is in the Park position.

Instrument Cluster

REMOVAL & INSTALLATION

1. Disconnect the negative battery cable.

2. Remove the instrument panel insert.

3. With the shift lever in the Park position, remove the shift indicator cable and clip retaining screw from the steering column.

4. Remove the upper and lower cluster assembly retaining screws. Remove the screw directly above the steering column which retains the cluster to the speedometer mounting plate.

5. Pull the cluster outward and disengage the speedometer cable and the electrical connections.

6. If equipped, disconnect the speed control sensor from the cluster assembly. Disconnect other connectors as required.

7. Place the shift lever in the Low position, and if equipped with tilt wheel, place the wheel in its lowest position. Remove the cluster assembly from the dash.

8. Installation is the reverse of the removal procedure. Set the shift, indicator cable in the Neutral position and adjust the cable accordingly.

Headlight Switch

REMOVAL & INSTALLATION

1. Disconnect the negative battery cable.

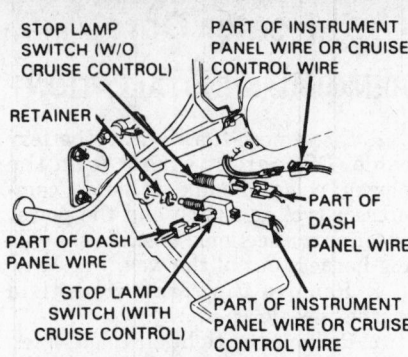

Stoplight switch location

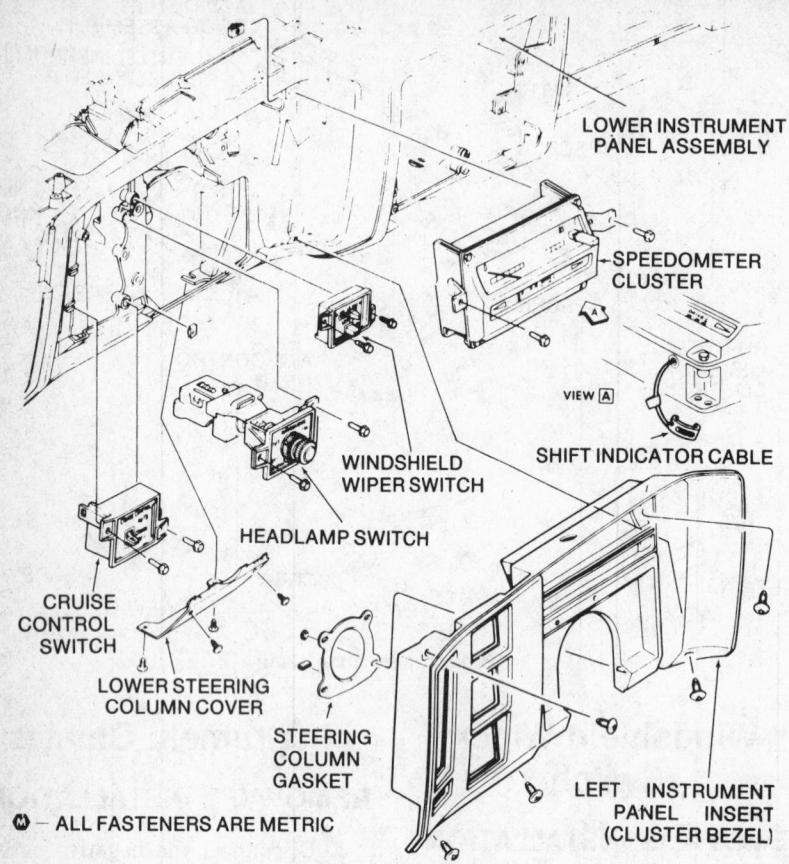

Instrument panel and related components

Ⓜ — ALL FASTENERS ARE METRIC

2. Remove the instrument panel insert.

3. Remove the screws securing the switch to the instrument panel.

4. On vehicles equipped with cruise control and twilight sentinel remove the screws securing the cruise control switch to the instrument panel.

5. Slide the cruise control switch forward to remove the light switch. If equipped, disconnect the two piece connector from the headlight switch. Disconnect the guidematic and twilight sentinel electrical connectors from under the instrument panel.

6. Remove the headlight switch retaining screws. Remove the switch assembly from the vehicle.

7. Installation is the reverse of the removal procedure.

Stoplight Switch

REMOVAL & INSTALLATION

NOTE: The cruise control release switch and the stoplight switch are adjusted or replaced in the same manner.

1. Disconnect the negative battery

cable. Disconnect the wire harness connector from the switch.

2. Remove the switch from the clip and then remove the clip from the bracket.

3. To install, place the clip in its bore on the bracket.

4. With the brake pedal depressed, insert the switch into the clip and depress the switch body. Clicks can be heard as the threaded portion of the switch is pushed through the clip towards the brake pedal.

5. Pull the brake pedal fully rearward against the pedal stop until the clicking sounds cannot be heard. The switch can be moved in the clip to correct the adjustment.

6. Release the brake pedal and repeat Step 5 to assure that no clicking sounds remain. The switch is now correctly adjusted.

7. Install the harness connector and verify the stoplights operate correctly.

Fuses and Circuit Breakers

FUSIBLE LINKS

Fusible links are used to prevent ma-

jor wire harness damage in the event of a short circuit or an overload condition in the wiring circuits which are normally not fused, due to carrying high amperage loads or because of their locations within the wiring harness. Each fusible link is of a fixed value for a specific electrical load and should a link fail, the cause of the failure must be determined and repaired prior to installing a new fusible link of the same value.

CIRCUIT BREAKERS

Various circuit breakers are located under the instrument panel. In order to gain access to these components it may be necessary to first remove the under dash padding.

FUSE PANEL

The fuse panel is located on the left side of the vehicle. It is under the instrument panel assembly. In order to gain access to the fuse panel it may be necessary to first remove the under dash padding.

TURN SIGNAL FLASHER

The turn signal flasher is located behind the instrument panel bracket to the right of the steering column. In order to gain access to the turn signal flasher it may be necessary to first remove the under dash padding.

HAZARD FLASHER

The hazard flasher is located in the fuse block. It is positioned on the lower right hand corner of the fuse block assembly. In order to gain access to the turn signal flasher it may be necessary to first remove the under dash padding.

Chevrolet
Front Wheel Drive
Beretta, Corsica

SERIAL NUMBER IDENTIFICATION

VEHICLE IDENTIFICATION CHART

It is important for servicing and ordering parts to be certain of the vehicle and engine identification. The VIN (vehicle identification number) is a 17 digit number visible through the windshield on the driver's side of the dash and contains the vehicle and engine identification codes. The tenth digit indicates model year, and the eighth digit indicates engine code. It can be interpreted as follows:

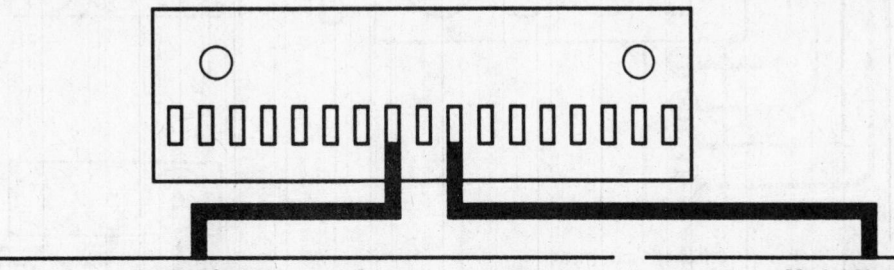

Engine Code							Model Year	
Code	Cu. In.	Liters	Cyl.	Fuel Sys.	Eng. Mfg.		Code	Year
1	121	2.0	4	TBI	Chevrolet		H	1987
W	173	2.8	V6	MFI	Chevrolet		J	1988
							K	1989

GENERAL ENGINE SPECIFICATIONS

Year	VIN	No. Cylinder Displacement cu. in. (liter)	Fuel System Type	Net Horsepower @ rpm	Net Torque @ rpm (ft.lbs.)	Bore × Stroke (in.)	Compression Ratio	Oil Pressure @ rpm
1987	1	4-121 (2.0)	TBI	90 @ 5600	108 @ 3200	3.500 × 3.150	9.0:1	63-77 @ 1200
	W	6-173 (2.8)	MFI	125 @ 4500	160 @ 3600	3.500 × 2.990	8.9:1	50-65 @ 1200
1988-89	1	4-121 (2.0)	TBI	90 @ 5600	108 @ 3200	3.500 × 3.150	9.0:1	63-77 @ 1200
	W	6-173 (2.8)	MFI	125 @ 4500	160 @ 3600	3.500 × 2.990	8.9:1	50-65 @ 1200

GASOLINE ENGINE TUNE-UP SPECIFICATIONS

Year	VIN	No. Cylinder Displacement cu. in. (liter)	Spark Plugs Type	Gap (in.)	Ignition Timing (deg.) MT	AT	Com-pression Pressure (psi)	Fuel Pump (psi)	Idle Speed (rpm) MT	AT	Valve Clearance In.	Ex.
1987	1	4-121 (2.0)	FR3LM	0.035	①	①	②	10-12	①	①	Hyd.	Hyd.
	W	6-173 (2.8)	R43CTLSE	0.045	①	①	②	10-12	①	①	Hyd.	Hyd.
1988-89	1	4-121 (2.0)	FR3LM	0.035	①	①	②	10-12	①	①	Hyd.	Hyd.
	W	6-173 (2.8)	R43CTLSE	0.045	①	①	②	10-12	①	①	Hyd.	Hyd.

① Ignition timing and idle speed is controlled by the electronic control module. No adjustments are possible

② When analyzing compression test results, look for uniformity among cylinders rather than specific pressures

FIRING ORDER

NOTE: To avoid confusion, always replace spark plug wires one at a time.

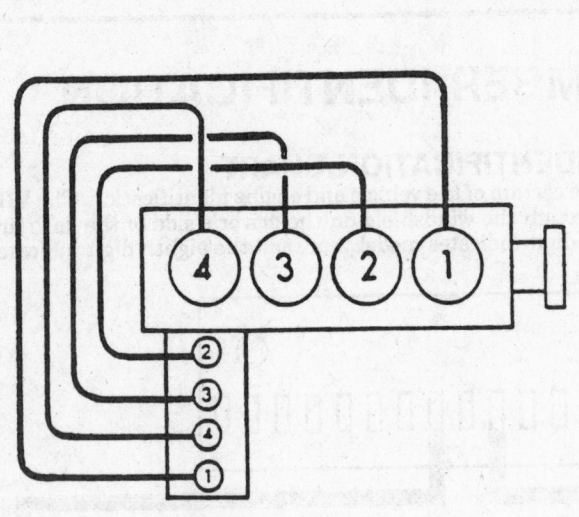

2.0L, 121 cu. in.
Firing order: 1–3–4–2

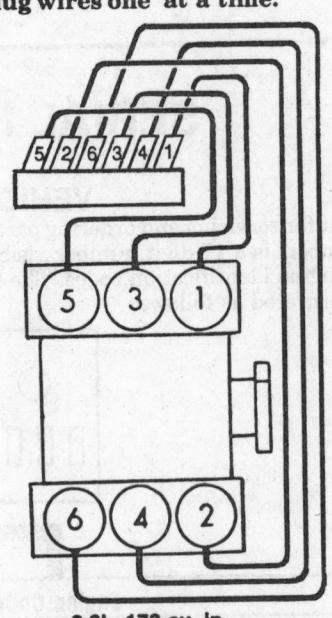

2.8L, 173 cu. in.
Firing order: 1-2-3-4-5-6

CAPACITIES

Year	Model	No. Cylinder Displacement cu. in. (liter)	Engine Crankcase with Filter	without Filter	Transmission (pts.) 4-Spd	5-Spd	Auto.	Drive Axle (pts.)	Fuel Tank (gal.)	Cooling System (qts.)
1987	Beretta	4-121 (2.0)	4.5	4.0	NA	5.36①	8.0②	NA	13.6	8.8
		6-173 (2.8)	4.5	4.0	NA	5.36①	8.0②	NA	13.6	11.4
	Corsica	4-121 (2.0)	4.5	4.0	NA	5.36①	8.0②	NA	13.6	8.8
		6-173 (2.8)	4.5	4.0	NA	5.36①	8.0②	NA	13.6	11.4
1988-89	Beretta	4-121 (2.0)	4.0	4.0	NA	5.4①	8.0②	NA	14	9.6③
		6-173 (2.8)	4.0	4.0	NA	5.4①	8.0②	NA	14	11④
	Corsica	4-121 (2.0)	4.0	4.0	NA	5.4①	8.0②	NA	14	9.6③
		6-173 (2.8)	4.0	4.0	NA	5.4①	8.0②	NA	14	11④

NA—Not Applicable

① 5 speed (GETRAG): 4 pts.

② This figure is for drain and refill. After a complete overhaul, use 16.0 pts. If the torque converter is replaced, use 18.0 pts.

③ With A/C: 9.8 qts.

④ With A/C: 11.1 qts.

CAMSHAFT SPECIFICATIONS
All measurements given in inches.

Year	VIN	No. Cylinder Displacement cu. in. (liter)	Journal Diameter					Lobe Lift		Bearing Clearance	Camshaft End Play
			1	2	3	4	5	In.	Ex.		
1987	1	4-121 (2.0)	1.867–1.869	1.867–1.869	1.867–1.869	1.867–1.869	1.867–1.869	0.260	0.260	0.001–0.004	NA
	W	6-173 (2.8)	1.867–1.881	1.867–1.881	1.867–1.881	1.867–1.881	— —	0.262	0.273	0.001–0.004	NA
1988-89	1	4-121 (2.0)	1.867–1.869	1.867–1.869	1.867–1.869	1.867–1.869	1.867–1.869	0.260	0.260	0.001–0.004	NA
	W	6-173 (2.8)	1.867–1.881	1.867–1.881	1.867–1.881	1.867–1.881	— —	0.262	0.273	0.001–0.004	NA

NA—Not Available

CRANKSHAFT AND CONNECTING ROD SPECIFICATIONS
All measurements are given in inches.

Year	VIN	No. Cylinder Displacement cu. in. (liter)	Crankshaft				Connecting Rod		
			Main Brg. Journal Dia.	Main Brg. Oil Clearance	Shaft End-play	Thrust on No.	Journal Diameter	Oil Clearance	Side Clearance
1987	1	4-121 (2.0)	2.4945–2.4954	0.0006–0.0019	0.002–0.008	1	1.9983–1.9994	0.001–0.003	0.004–0.015
	W	6-173 (2.8)	2.6473–2.6483	0.0016–0.0033	0.0024–0.0083	4	1.9983–1.9993	0.0013–0.0026	0.006–0.017
1988-89	1	4-121 (2.0)	2.4945–2.4954	0.0006–0.0019	0.002–0.008	1	1.9983–1.9994	0.001–0.003	0.004–0.015
	W	6-173 (2.8)	2.6473–2.6483	0.0016–0.0033	0.0024–0.0083	4	1.9983–1.9993	0.0013–0.0026	0.006–0.017

VALVE SPECIFICATIONS

Year	VIN	No. Cylinder Displacement cu. in. (liter)	Seat Angle (deg.)	Face Angle (deg.)	Spring Test Pressure (lbs.)	Spring Installed Height (in.)	Stem-to-Guide Clearance (in.)		Stem Diameter (in.)	
							Intake	Exhaust	Intake	Exhaust
1987	1	4-121 (2.0)	46	45	73-81①	1.60	0.0011–0.0023	0.0014–0.0028	NA	NA
	W	6-173 (2.8)	46	45	90①	1.70	0.0010–0.0027	0.0010–0.0027	NA	NA
1988-89	1	4-121 (2.0)	46	45	73-81①	1.60	0.0011–0.0023	0.0014–0.0028	NA	NA
	W	6-173 (2.8)	46	45	90①	1.70	0.0010–0.0027	0.0010–0.0027	NA	NA

NA—Not Available
① With valve closed

PISTON AND RING SPECIFICATIONS
All measurments are given in inches.

Year	VIN	No. Cylinder Displacement cu. in. (liter)	Piston Clearance	Ring Gap			Ring Side Clearance		
				Top Compression	Bottom Compression	Oil Control	Top Compression	Bottom Compression	Oil Control
1987	1	4-121 (2.0)	0.0010–0.0022	0.010–0.020	0.010–0.020	0.010–0.050	0.001–0.003	0.001–0.003	0.0080
	W	6-173 (2.8)	0.0020–0.0030	0.010–0.020	0.010–0.020	0.020–0.055	0.001–0.003	0.001–0.003	0.0080
1988-89	1	4-121 (2.0)	0.0010–0.0022	0.010–0.020	0.010–0.020	0.010–0.050	0.001–0.003	0.001–0.003	0.0080
	W	6-173 (2.8)	0.0020–0.0030	0.010–0.020	0.010–0.020	0.020–0.055	0.001–0.003	0.001–0.003	0.0080

TORQUE SPECIFICATIONS
All readings in ft. lbs.

Year	VIN	No. Cylinder Displacement cu. in. (liter)	Cylinder Head Bolts	Main Bearing Bolts	Rod Bearing Bolts	Crankshaft Pulley Bolts	Flywheel Bolts	Manifold		Spark Plugs
								Intake	Exhaust	
1987	1	4-121 (2.0)	62-70 ①	63-77	34-43	66-89	45-59②	15-22	6-13	7-20
	W	6-173 (2.8)	③	63-83	34-44	67-85	45-59②	18	15-23	10-25
1987-88	1	4-121 (2.0)	62-70 ①	63-77	34-43	66-89	45-59②	15-22	6-13	7-20
	W	6-173 (2.8)	③	63-83	34-44	67-85	45-59②	18	15-23	10-25

① Specification is for the shorter bolts. Torque the longer bolts to 73-83 ft.lbs.

② Specification is for automatic transaxle. Torque the manual transaxle bolts to 47-63 ft.lbs.

③ 2.8L engine cylinder head bolts should first be torqued to 33 ft.lbs. Then tighten the bolts by rotating the torque wrench an additional 90 degrees

BRAKE SPECIFICATIONS
All measurements in inches unless noted

Year	Model	Lug Nut Torque (ft. lbs.)	Master Cylinder Bore	Brake Disc		Standard Brake Drum Diameter	Minimum Lining Thickness	
				Minimum Thickness	Maximum Runout		Front	Rear
1987	Beretta	100	0.945	0.830	0.004	7.879	$3/32$	$3/32$
	Corsica	100	0.945	0.830	0.004	7.879	$3/32$	$3/32$
1988-89	Beretta	100	0.945	0.830	0.004	7.879	$3/32$	$3/32$
	Corsica	100	0.945	0.830	0.004	7.879	$3/32$	$3/32$

WHEEL ALIGNMENT

Year	Model	Caster Range (deg.)	Caster Preferred Setting (deg.)	Camber Range (deg.)	Camber Preferred Setting (deg.)	Toe-in (in.)	Steering Axis Inclination (deg.)
1987	Beretta, Corsica	$^{11}/_{16}$P-2$^{11}/_{16}$P	1$^{11}/_{16}$P①	$^{1}/_{2}$P-$^{13}/_{16}$P	$^{13}/_{16}$P	$^{1}/_{16}$N-$^{1}/_{16}$P	14
1988-89	Beretta, Corsica	$^{11}/_{16}$P-2$^{11}/_{16}$P	1$^{11}/_{16}$P①	$^{5}/_{16}$P-1$^{5}/_{16}$P	$^{13}/_{16}$P	$^{1}/_{16}$N-$^{1}/_{16}$P	14

① Not Adjustable

TUNE-UP PROCEDURES

Ignition Timing

ADJUSTMENT

Ignition timing is controlled by the Electronic Control Module (ECM). No adjustments are possible.

Valve Lash

ADJUSTMENT

Hydraulic valve lifters used in the 2.0L and 2.8L engines are not adjustable. If valve system noise is present, check the torque on the rocker arm nuts. The correct torque should be 7–11 ft. lbs. (2.0L) or 14–20 ft. lbs. (2.8L). If noise is still present, check the condition of the camshaft, lifters, push rods and valves.

Idle Speed and Mixture

ADJUSTMENT

Idle speed and mixture are controlled by the Electronic Control Module (ECM). No adjustments are possible.

ENGINE ELECTRICAL

Distibutor

All engines use a distributor-less ignition. Distributor-less ignition systems use a "Waste-Spark" method of spark distribution. Each cylinder is paired with its opposing cylinder in the firing order. This makes one cylinder that is on the compression stroke fire with the opposing cylinder that is on the exhaust stroke. The cylinder that is on the exhaust stroke uses very little spark allowing most of the spark to go to the cylinder on the compression stroke. This process reverses when the cylinder roles reverse. There are two coils for the 2.0L engine (Direct Ignition System-DIS) and three coils for the 2.8L engine (Computer Command Controlled Ignition-C³I).

Alternator

NOTE: For further information on the charging system, please refer to "Charging and Starting" in the Unit Repair section.

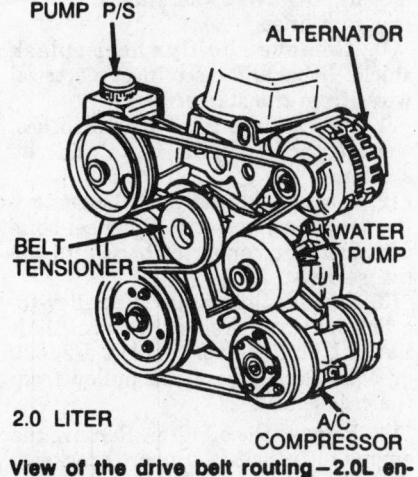

View of the drive belt routing – 2.0L engine with A/C

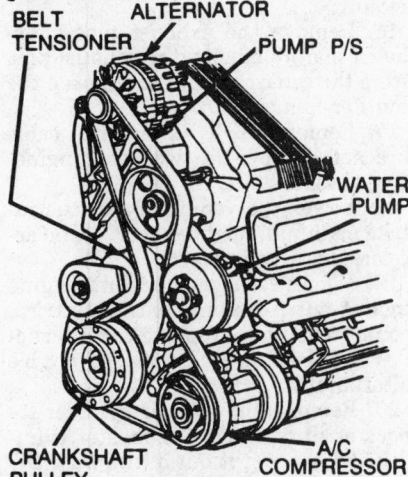

Drive belt routing-2.0 and 2.8 Liter engines with A/C

PRECAUTIONS

- Observe the proper polarity of the battery connections by making sure that the positive (+) and negative (−) terminal connections are not reversed. Misconnection will allow current to flow in the reverse direction, resulting in damaged diodes and an overheated wire harness.
- Never ground or short out any alternator or alternator regulator terminals.
- Never operate the alternator with any of its or the battery's leads disconnected.
- Always remove the battery or disconnect its output lead while charging it.
- Always disconnect the ground cable when replacing any electrical components.
- Never subject the alternator to excessive heat or dampness.
- Never use arc-welding equipment with the alternator connected.

REMOVAL & INSTALLATION

1. Disconnect the negative battery terminal from the battery.
2. Label and disconnect the electrical connectors from the back of the alternator.
3. Loosen the alternator mounting bolts.
4. Remove the serpentine drive belt.
5. Remove the alternator-to-bracket bolts and the alternator.
6. To install, reverse the removal procedures.

BELT TENSION ADJUSTMENT

A single (serpentine) belt is used to drive all engine mounted components. Drive belt tension is maintained by a spring loaded tensioner.

NOTE: The drive belt tensioner can control belt tension over a wide range of belt lengths; however, there are limits to the tensioner's ability to compensate for various belt lengths. Installing the wrong size belt and using the

tensioner outside its operating range can result in poor tension control and/or damage to the tensioner, belt and driven components.

REMOVAL & INSTALLATION

To remove or install the drive belt, rotate the tensioner with a 15mm socket (2.0L) or a ¾ in. open end wrench (2.8L). This will eliminate the belt tension and allow the belt to be removed or installed.

Voltage Regulator

An alternator with an integral voltage regulator is standard equipment. There are no adjustments possible with this unit. Testing procedures can be found in "Charging and Starting" in the Unit Repair Section.

Starter

NOTE: For further information on the starter system, please refer to "Charging and Starting" in the Unit Repair section.

REMOVAL & INSTALLATION

1. Disconnect the negative battery terminal from the battery.
2. Raise and support the front of the vehicle on jackstands.
3. Label and disconnect the electrical connectors from the starter.
4. On the 2.0L engine, remove the rear starter motor support bracket and A/C compressor support rod.
5. Remove the starter-to-engine bolts and the starter.
6. To install, reverse the removal procedures; reinstall any shims that were removed.

ENGINE MECHANICAL

Engine

REMOVAL & INSTALLATION

2.0L Engine

1. Disconnect the battery terminals (negative terminal first) from the battery. Remove the battery from the vehicle.
2. Position a clean drain pan under the radiator, open the drain cock and drain the cooling system. Remove the air intake hose.
3. From the throttle body, disconnect the T.V. and accelerator cables. Disconnect the ECM electrical harness connector from the engine.
4. Remove all vacuum hoses (not a part of the engine assembly), the upper/lower radiator hoses and the heater hoses from the engine.
5. Remove the heat shield from the exhaust manifold. Disconnect and tag the engine wiring harness at the firewall.
6. Disconnect the hoses and remove the windshield washer bottle. Rotate the tensioner pulley (to reduce the belt tension) and remove the serpentine belt.
7. Disconnect and plug the fuel hoses. Raise and support front of the vehicle on jackstands.
8. Remove the right-side inner fender splash shield.
9. Remove the A/C compressor-to-bracket bolts and move it aside (so it will not interfere with the engine removal); DO NOT disconnect the refrigerant lines.
10. Remove the flywheel splash shield. Label and disconnect electrical wires from the starter.
11. Remove the front starter brace, the starter-to-engine bolts and the starter.
12. If equipped with an ATX, remove the torque converter-to-flywheel bolts and push the converter back into the transaxle.
13. Remove the crankshaft pulley-to-crankshaft bolt. Using the Crankshaft Pulley Hub Remover tool No. J-24420 or equivalent, press the pulley from the crankshaft.
14. Remove the oil filter. Remove the engine-to-transaxle support bracket.
15. Disconnect the right-rear engine mount.
16. Remove the exhaust pipe-to-exhaust manifold bolts, the exhaust pipe from the center hanger and loosen the muffler hanger.
17. Remove the T.V. and shift cable bracket. Remove the two lower engine-to-transaxle bolts.
18. Lower the vehicle. From the intake manifold, remove the T.V. and accelerator cable bracket.
19. Remove the right-front engine mount nuts. Disconnect the electrical connectors, then, remove the alternator-to-bracket bolts and the alternator.
20. Remove the master cylinder-to-booster nuts, move the master cylinder and support it out of the way; DO NOT disconnect the brake lines.
21. Using a vertical lifting device, install to the engine and lift it slightly.
22. Remove the right-front engine mount bracket. Remove the remaining engine-to-transaxle bolts.
23. Remove the power steering pump-to-engine bolts and move it aside; DO NOT disconnect the high pressure hoses.
24. Carefully lift and remove the engine from the vehicle.
25. To install, reverse the removal procedures. Install the power steering pump while lowering the engine into the vehicle.
26. To insure proper engine alignment, loosely install the engine mounts and raise the engine slightly. Then, torque the engine to engine mount bolts to 40 ft. lbs. and the mount nuts to 20 ft. lbs. Torque the engine-to-transaxle bolts to 55 ft. lbs. Refill the cooling system. Start the engine, allow it to reach normal operating temperatures and check for leaks.

2.8L Engine

1. Disconnect the battery cables (the negative terminal first). Remove the battery from the vehicle.
2. Remove the air cleaner, the air inlet hose and the mass air flow sensor.
3. Position a clean drain pan under the radiator, open the drain cock and drain the cooling system. Remove the exhaust manifold crossover assembly bolts and separate the assembly from the exhaust manifolds.
4. Remove the serpentine belt tensioner and the drive belt. Remove the power steering pump-to-bracket bolts and support the pump out or the way.
5. Disconnect the radiator hose from the engine.
6. Disconnect the T.V. and accelerator cables from the throttle valve bracket on the plenum.
7. Disconnect the electrical connectors, then, remove the alternator-to-bracket bolts and the alternator. Label and disconnect the electrical wiring harness from the engine.
8. Disconnect and plug the fuel hoses. Remove the coolant overflow and bypass hoses from the engine.
9. From the charcoal canister, disconnect the purge hose. Label and disconnect all the necessary vacuum hoses.
10. Using the Engine Holding Fixture tool No. J-28467 or equivalent, support the engine.
11. Raise and support the front of the vehicle on jackstands.
12. Remove the right-inner fender splash shield. Remove the crankshaft pulley-to-crankshaft bolt. Using the Wheel Puller tool No. J-24420 or equivalent, press the crankshaft pulley from the crankshaft.
13. Remove the flywheel cover. Label and disconnect the starter wires, then,

remove the starter-to-engine bolts and the starter.

14. Disconnect the wires at the oil pressure sending unit.

15. Remove the A/C compressor-to-bracket bolts and the bracket-to-engine bolts, then, support the compressor so it will not interfere with the engine; DO NOT disconnect the refrigerant lines.

16. Disconnect the exhaust pipe from the rear of the exhaust manifold.

17. If equipped with an ATX, remove the torque converter-to-flywheel bolts and push the converter into the transaxle.

18. Remove the front and rear engine mount bolts, then, the mount brackets.

19. Remove the intermediate shaft bracket from the engine.

20. Disconnect the shifter cable from the transaxle.

21. Remove the lower engine-to-transaxle bolts and lower the vehicle.

22. Disconnect the heater hoses from the engine.

23. Using an vertical engine lift, install it to the engine and lift it. Remove the engine holding fixture. Using a floor jack, support the transaxle.

24. Remove the upper engine-to-transaxle bolts. Remove the front engine mount bolts and transaxle mounting bracket.

25. Remove the engine from the vehicle.

26. To install, reverse the removal procedures.

27. To insure proper engine alignment, loosely install the engine mounts and raise the engine slightly. Then, torque the engine mounting bolts to 65 ft. lbs. Torque the engine-to-transaxle bolts to 55 ft. lbs. Refill the cooling system. Start the engine, allow it to reach normal operating temperatures and check for leaks.

Cylinder Head

REMOVAL & INSTALLATION

2.0L Engine

1. Disconnect the negative battery terminal from the battery.

2. Drain the cooling system. Remove the TBI cover.

3. Raise and support the front of the vehicle on jackstands.

4. Disconnect the exhaust pipe-to-exhaust manifold bolts and separate the exhaust pipe from the manifold.

5. Lower the vehicle. Disconnect the heater hose from the intake manifold.

6. Disconnect the T.V. and accelerator cable bracket.

7. Label and disconnect the vacuum

lines from the intake manifold and thermostat.

8. Disconnect the accelerator linkage from the TBI unit.

9. Label and disconnect the electrical wiring from the engine.

10. Disconnect the upper radiator hose from the thermostat. Remove the serpentine belt.

11. Remove the power steering pump-to-bracket bolts and support it out of the way; DO NOT disconnect the high pressure hoses from the pump.

12. Disconnect and plug the fuel lines. Remove the alternator-to-bracket bolts and the alternator, then, position it out of the way (with electrical connectors attached).

13. Remove the alternator rear brace.

14. Remove the rocker arm cover-to-cylinder head bolts and the cover. Remove the rocker arm bolts, the rocker arms and push rods; be sure to keep valve train components in the order that they were removed.

15. Starting with the outer bolts, remove the cylinder head-to-engine bolts.

16. Using a putty knife, clean and inspect the gasket mounting surfaces. Make sure the threads on the cylinder head bolts and in the block are clean.

17. Using GM Gasket Sealant No. 1050026 or equivalent, coat both sides of the new head gasket and install the gasket on the dowel pins on the block.

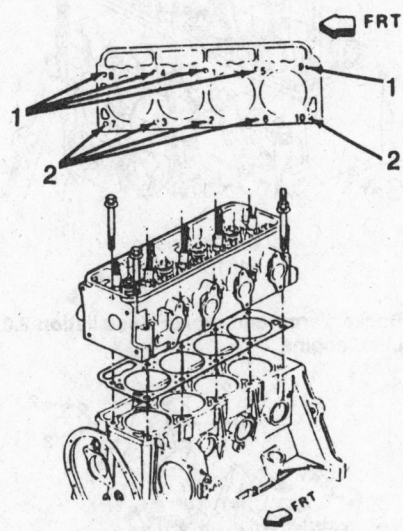

1. 73–83 ft. lbs.
2. 62–70 ft. lbs.

Cylinder head bolt torque sequence-2.0 Liter engine

18. Install the cylinder head and tighten the head bolts hand tight.

19. Following the torquing sequence, torque the head bolts (in three steps) to 73–83 ft. lbs. (intake-side) or 62–70 ft. lbs. (exhaust-side).

20. Install the push rods and rocker arms in the same order they were removed. Torque the rocker arm nuts to 7–11 ft. lbs.

21. To complete the installation, reverse the removal procedures. Refill the cooling system. Start the engine, allow it to reach normal operating temperatures and check for leaks.

2.8L Engine

LEFT-SIDE

1. Drain the cooling system. Remove the rocker cover.

2. Remove the intake manifold-to-cylinder head bolts and the intake manifold. Disconnect the exhaust crossover from the right exhaust manifold.

3. Disconnect the oil level indicator tube bracket.

4. Loosen the rocker arms nuts, turn the rocker arms and remove the push rods.

NOTE: Be sure to keep the parts in order for installation purposes.

5. Remove the cylinder head-to-engine bolts; start with the outer bolts and work toward the center. Remove the cylinder head with the exhaust manifold.

6. Using a putty knife, clean the gasket mounting surfaces. Inspect the surfaces of the cylinder head, block and intake manifold damage and/or warpage. Clean the threaded holes in the block and the cylinder head bolt threads.

7. To install, use new gaskets, align the new cylinder head gasket over the dowels on the block with the note "This Side Up" facing the cylinder head.

HEAD TORQUE SEQUENCE

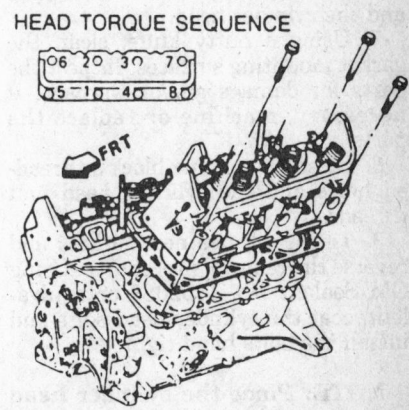

Cylinder head bolt torque sequence-2.8 Liter engine

8. Install the cylinder head and exhaust manifold crossover assembly on the engine.

9. Using GM Sealant No. 1052080 or equivalent, coat the cylinder head bolts and install the bolts hand tight.

10. Using the torquing sequence, torque the bolts to 33 ft. lbs. After all bolts are torqued to 33 ft. lbs., rotate the torque wrench another 90° or ¼ turn. This will apply the correct torque to the bolts.

11. Install the push rods in the same order that they were removed. Torque the rocker arm nuts to 14–20 ft. lbs.

12. Install the intake manifold using a new gasket and following the correct sequence, torque the bolts to the correct specification.

13. To complete the installation, reverse the removal procedures. Refill the cooling system. Operate the engine until normal operating temperatures are reached and check for leaks.

RIGHT-SIDE

1. Disconnect the negative battery terminal from the battery. Drain the cooling system.

2. Raise and support the front of the vehicle on jackstands. Remove the exhaust manifold-to-exhaust pipe bolts and separate the pipe from the manifold.

3. Lower the vehicle. Remove the exhaust manifold-to-cylinder head bolts and the manifold.

4. Remove the rocker arm cover. Remove the intake manifold-to-cylinder head bolts and the intake manifold.

5. Loosen the rocker arms nuts, turn the rocker arms and remove the push rods.

NOTE: Be sure to keep the components in order for reassembly purposes.

6. Remove the cylinder head-to-engine bolts (starting with the outer bolts and working toward the center) and the cylinder head.

7. Using a putty knife, clean the gasket mounting surfaces. Inspect the parts for damage and/or warpage; if necessary, machine or replace the parts.

8. Clean the engine block's threaded holes and the cylinder head bolt threads.

9. To install, use new gaskets and reverse the removal procedures. Using GM Sealant No. 1052080 or equivalent, coat the cylinder head bolts and install the bolts hand tight.

NOTE: Place the cylinder head gasket on the engine block dowels with the note "This Side Up" facing the cylinder head.

10. Using the torquing sequence, torque the bolts to 33 ft. lbs. After all bolts are torqued to 33 ft. lbs., rotate the torque wrench another 90° or ¼ turn. This will apply the correct torque to the bolts.

11. Install the push rods in the same order as they were removed. Torque the rocker arm nuts to 14–20 ft. lbs.

12. Follow the torquing sequence, use a new gasket and install the intake manifold.

13. To complete the installation, reverse the removal procedures. Refill the cooling system. Start the engine, allow it to reach normal operating temperatures and check for leaks.

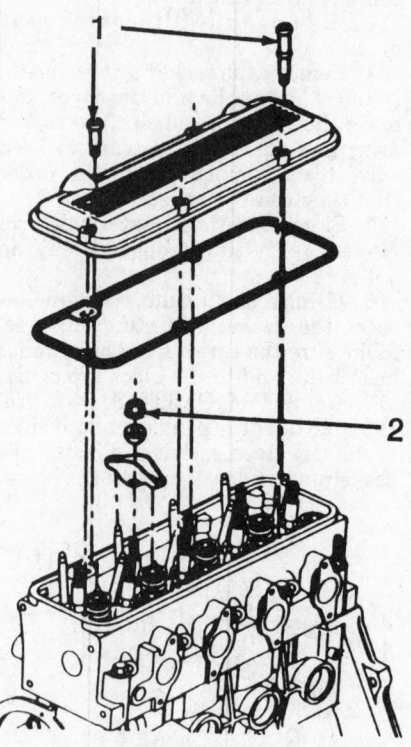

1. 6–9 ft. lbs.
2. 11–18 ft. lbs.

Rocker arm and cover installation-2.0 Liter engine

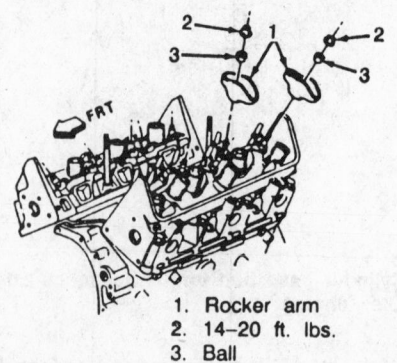

1. Rocker arm
2. 14–20 ft. lbs.
3. Ball

Rocker arm installation-2.8 Liter engine

OVERHAUL

NOTE: For all cylinder head overhaul procedures, please refer to the "Engine Rebuilding" in the Unit Repair section.

Rocker Arms

REMOVAL & INSTALLATION

2.0L Engine

1. Disconnect the negative battery terminal. Remove the air hose from the TBI unit and the air cleaner.

2. Remove the intake manifold-to-rocker cover hose.

3. Remove the rocker arm cover bolts and the cover.

4. Remove the rocker arm nuts and remove the rocker arms.

NOTE: Be sure to keep the components in order for installation purposes.

5. To install, use new gaskets, sealant (if necessary) and reverse the removal procedures. Torque the rocker arm nuts to 7–11 ft. lbs.

6. To complete the installation, reverse the removal procedures.

2.8L Engine

LEFT-SIDE

1. Disconnect the negative terminal from the battery . Disconnect the bracket tube from the rocker cover.

2. Remove the spark plug wire cover. Drain the cooling system and remove the heater hose from the filler neck.

3. Remove the rocker arm cover-to-cylinder head bolts and the rocker cover.

NOTE: If the rocker arm cover will not lift off the cylinder head easily, strike the end with the palm of the hand or a rubber mallet.

4. Remove the rocker arm nuts and remove the rocker arms; be sure to keep the components in order for installation purposes.

5. Using a putty knife, clean the gasket mounting surfaces.

6. To install, use new gaskets, sealant (GM No. 1052917 or equivalent) and reverse the removal procedures. Torque the rocker arm nuts to 14–20 ft. lbs. Start the engine and check for leaks.

RIGHT-SIDE

1. Disconnect the negative terminal from the battery. Disconnect the brake booster vacuum line from the bracket.

2. Disconnect the cable bracket

from the plenum.

3. Disconnect the vacuum line bracket from the cable bracket.

4. Disconnect the lines from the alternator brace stud.

5. Remove the rear alternator brace and the serpentine drive belt.

6. Remove the alternator and support it out of the way.

7. Remove the PCV valve.

8. Loosen the alternator bracket.

9. Disconnect the spark plug wires from the spark plugs. Remove the rocker cover-to-cylinder head bolts and the rocker cover.

NOTE: If the rocker arm cover will not lift off the cylinder head easily, strike the end with the palm of the hand or a rubber mallet.

10. Remove the rocker arm nuts and the rocker arms; be sure to keep the components in order for installation purposes.

11. Using a putty knife, clean the gasket mounting surfaces.

12. To install, use new gaskets, sealant (GM No. 1052917 or equivalent) and reverse the removal procedures. Torque the rocker arm nuts to 14–20 ft. lbs.

Intake Manifold

REMOVAL & INSTALLATION

2.0L Engine

1. Disconnect the negative terminal from the battery. Remove the TBI cover.

2. Drain the cooling system. Label and disconnect the vacuum lines and electrical connectors from the intake manifold.

3. Disconnect and plug the fuel line.

4. Disconnect the TBI linkage. Remove the throttle body-to-intake manifold bolts and the throttle body.

5. Disconnect the serpentine drive belt. Remove the power steering pump-to-bracket bolts and support the pump out of the way; DO NOT disconnect the pressure hoses.

6. Raise and support the front of the vehicle on jackstands.

7. Disconnect the T.V. and accelerator cables and brackets.

8. Remove the heater hose from the bottom of the intake manifold. Lower the vehicle.

9. Remove the intake manifold-to-cylinder head nuts/bolts and the manifold.

10. Using a putty knife, clean the gasket mounting surfaces.

11. To install, use new gaskets and reverse the removal procedures. Torque the intake manifold-to-cylin-

der heads bolts (in the proper sequence) to 15–22 ft. lbs. Refill the cooling system. Start the engine, allow it to reach normal operating temperatures and check for leaks.

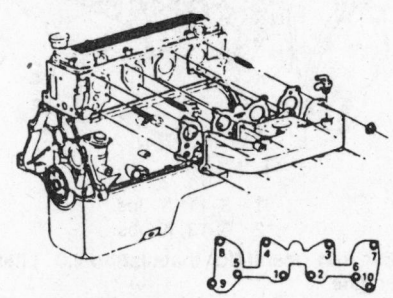

1. 15–22 ft. lbs.

Intake manifold bolt torque sequence-2.0 Liter engine

2.8L Engine

1. Disconnect the negative terminal from the battery. Drain the cooling system.

2. Disconnect the T.V. and accelerator cables from the plenum.

3. Remove the throttle body-to-plenum bolts and the throttle body. Remove the EGR valve.

4. Remove the plenum-to-intake manifold bolts and the plenum. Disconnect and plug the fuel lines and return pipes at the fuel rail.

5. Remove the serpentine drive belt. Remove the power steering pump-to-bracket bolts and support the pump out of the way; DO NOT disconnect the pressure hoses.

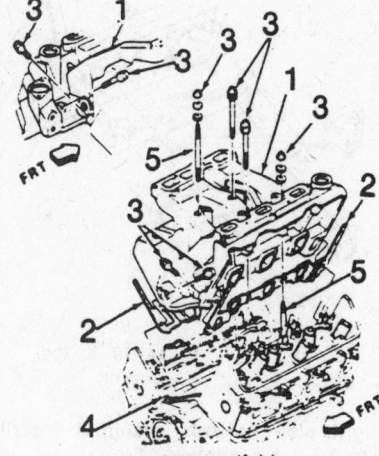

1. Intake manifold
2. Gasket
3. 18 ft. lbs.
4. Sealer
5. 24 ft. lbs

Intake manifold installation-2.8 Liter engine

6. Remove the alternator-to-bracket bolts and support the alternator out of the way.

7. Loosen the alternator bracket. From the throttle body, disconnect the idle air vacuum hose.

8. Label and disconnect the electrical connectors from the fuel injectors. Remove the fuel rail.

9. Remove the breather tube. Disconnect the runners.

10. Remove both rocker arm cover-to-cylinder head bolts and the covers. Remove the radiator hose from the thermostat housing.

11. Label and disconnect the electrical connectors from the coolant temperature sensor and oil pressure sending unit. Remove the coolant sensor.

12. Remove the bypass hose from the filler neck and cylinder head.

13. Remove the intake manifold-to-cylinder head bolts and the manifold.

14. Loosen the rocker arm nuts, turn them 90° and remove the push rods; be sure to keep the components in order for installation purposes.

15. Using a putty knife and degreaser, clean all gasket mounting surfaces.

16. To install, use new gaskets, RTV sealant (place a $\frac{3}{16}$ in. bead of sealant on the ridges of the manifold) and reverse the removal procedures. Torque (following the torquing sequence) the intake manifold-to-cylinder head bolts to 24 ft. lbs. and the nuts to 18 ft. lbs. Refill the cooling system. Start the engine, allow it to reach normal operating temperatures and check for leaks.

Exhaust Manifold

REMOVAL & INSTALLATION

2.0L Engine

1. Disconnect the negative terminal from the battery.

2. Disconnect the oxygen sensor wire.

3. Remove the serpentine belt.

4. Remove the alternator-to-bracket bolts and support the alternator (with the wires attached) out of the way.

5. Raise and support the front of the vehicle on jackstands.

6. Disconnect the exhaust pipe-to-exhaust manifold bolts and lower the vehicle.

7. Remove the exhaust manifold-to-cylinder head bolts.

8. Remove the exhaust manifold from the exhaust pipe flange and the manifold from the vehicle.

9. Using a putty knife, clean the gasket mounting surfaces.

10. To install, use new gaskets and reverse the removal procedures. Torque the exhaust manifold-to-cylin-

der head nuts to 3–11 ft. lbs. and the bolts to 6–13 ft. lbs. Start the engine and check for leaks.

2.8L Engine

LEFT-SIDE

1. Disconnect the negative terminal from the battery. Drain the cooling system.
2. Remove the air cleaner, air inlet hose and the mass air flow sensor.
3. Remove the coolant bypass pipe. Remove the manifold heat shield.
4. Disconnect the exhaust manifold crossover assembly at the right manifold.
5. Remove the exhaust manifold to cylinder head attaching bolts.
6. From the right manifold, remove the exhaust manifold with the crossover assembly.
7. Using a putty knife, clean the gasket mounting surfaces.
8. To install, use new gaskets and reverse the removal procedures. Torque the exhaust manifold-to-cylinder head bolts to 19 ft. lbs. and the crossover bolts to 25 ft. lbs. Start the engine and check for exhaust leaks.

RIGHT-SIDE

1. Disconnect the negative terminal from the battery.
2. Raise and support the front of the vehicle on jackstands.
3. Remove the heat shield.
4. Remove the exhaust pipe-to-exhaust manifold bolts and the crossover pipe-to-exhaust manifold bolts.
5. Remove the EGR pipe-to-exhaust manifold bolts and the pipe.
6. Disconnect the oxygen sensor wire.
7. Remove the exhaust manifold-to-cylinder head bolts and the exhaust manifold from the vehicle.
8. Using a putty knife, clean the gasket mounting surfaces.
9. To install, use new gaskets and reverse the removal procedures. Torque the exhaust manifold-to-cylinder head bolts to 19 ft. lbs. and the crossover pipe bolts to 25 ft. lbs. Start the engine and check for leaks.

Front Cover

REMOVAL & INSTALLATION

2.0L Engine

1. Disconnect the negative terminal from the battery.
2. Raise and support the vehicle on jackstands.
3. Drain the engine oil and remove the oil pan.

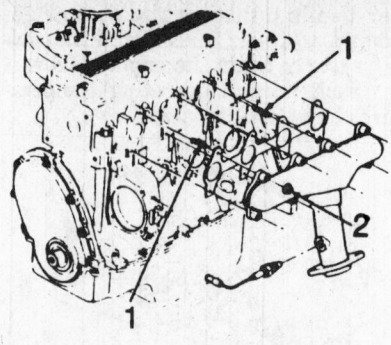

1. 3–11 ft. lbs.
2. 6–13 ft. lbs.

Exhaust manifold installation-2.0 Liter engine

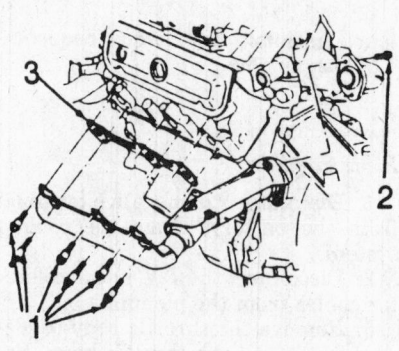

1. 14–22 ft. lbs.
2. 22–30 ft. lbs.
3. Gasket

Left side exhaust manifold installation-2.8 Liter engine

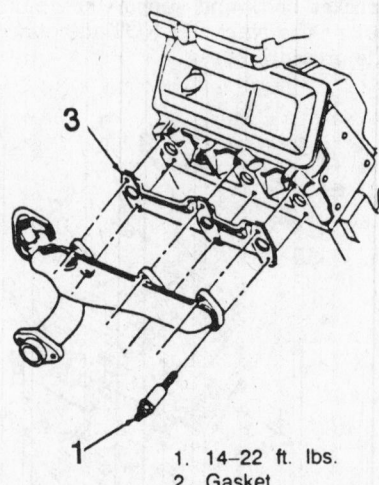

1. 14–22 ft. lbs.
2. Gasket

Right side exhaust manifold installation-2.8 Liter engine

4. Lower the vehicle.
5. Remove the serpentine belt and the belt tensioner.
6. Remove the crankshaft pulley retaining bolt. Using the Crankshaft

Pulley Puller tool No. J-24420 or equivalent, remove the crankshaft pulley.
7. Remove the front cover bolts. Tap the cover with a rubber mallet and remove the cover.
8. Using a putty knife, clean gasket mounting surfaces.

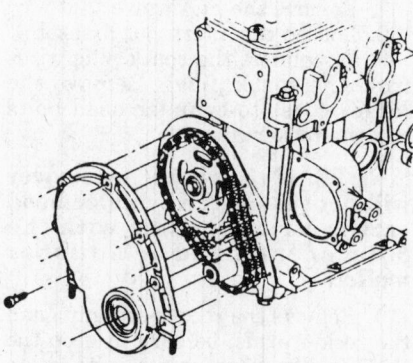

Front cover installation-2.0 Liter engine

9. To install, use new gaskets (install the front cover over the dowels on the block) and reverse the removal procedures. Torque the front cover-to-engine bolts to 6–9 ft. lbs.
10. Using the Crankshaft Pulley Installer tool No. J-29113 or equivalent, press the pulley onto the crankshaft. Torque the crankshaft pulley bolt to 66–88 ft. lbs.
11. To complete the installation, reverse the removal procedures. Start the engine and check for leaks.

2.8L Engine

1. Disconnect the negative terminal from the battery. Drain the cooling system.
2. Remove the serpentine belt and the belt tensioner.
3. Remove the alternator-to-bracket bolts, then, with the wires attached, support it out of the way.
4. Remove the power steering pump-to-bracket bolts and support it out of the way; DO NOT disconnect the pressure hoses.
5. Raise and support the vehicle on jackstands.
6. Remove the right-side inner fender splash shield. Remove the flywheel dust cover.
7. Using the Crankshaft Pulley Puller tool No. J-24420 or equivalent, remove the crankshaft damper.
8. Label and disconnect the starter wires, then, remove the starter.
9. Loosen the front five oil pan bolts (on both sides) enough to lower the oil pan ½ in.
10. Lower the vehicle. Disconnect the radiator hose from the water pump.

11. Disconnect the heater coolant hose from the cooling system filler pipe.

12. Remove the bypass and overflow hoses.

13. Remove the water pump pulley. Disconnect the canister purge hose.

14. Remove the spark plug wire shield from the water pump.

15. Remove the upper front cover-to-engine bolts and the front cover.

16. Using a putty knife, clean gasket mounting surfaces.

17. Apply a thin bead of silicone sealant on the front cover mating surface and using a new gasket, install the front cover on the engine. Apply silicone sealant to the sections of the oil pan rails that were lowered and install the mounting bolts.

18. Using the Crankshaft Pulley Installer tool No. J-29113 or equivalent, press the damper pulley onto the crankshaft.

19. To complete the installation, reverse the removal procedures. Start the engine and check for oil leaks.

OIL SEAL REPLACEMENT

2.0L Engine

1. Disconnect the negative terminal from the battery. Remove the serpentine belt.

2. Raise and support the vehicle on jackstands. Remove the wheel and tire assembly.

3. Remove the inner fender splash shield.

4. Remove the crankshaft pulley bolt.

5. Using the Crankshaft Pulley Puller tool No. J-24420 or equivalent, remove the crankshaft pulley.

6. Using a small pry bar, pry the oil seal from the front cover.

NOTE: Use care not to damage the seal seat or the crankshaft while removing or installing the seal. Inspect the sealing surface of the crankshaft for grooves or other wear.

7. Using the Oil Seal Centering tool No. J-35468 or equivalent, drive the new seal into the cover with the lip facing towards the engine.

8. Install the Crankshaft Pulley Installer tool No. J-29113 or equivalent, onto the crankshaft pulley and press the pulley onto the crankshaft.

9. To complete the installation, reverse the removal procedures. Torque the pulley bolt to 66–88 ft. lbs.

2.8L Engine

1. Disconnect the negative terminal from the battery. Remove the serpentine belt.

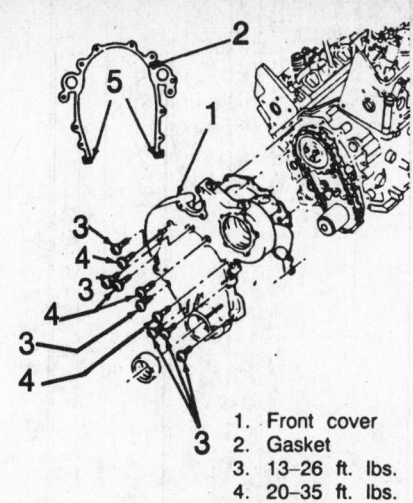

1. Front cover
2. Gasket
3. 13–26 ft. lbs.
4. 20–35 ft. lbs.
5. Sealer

Front cover installation-2.8 Liter engine

2. Raise and support the vehicle on jackstands. Remove the right-side inner fender splash shield.

3. Remove the damper retaining bolt.

4. Using the Crankshaft Pulley Puller tool No. J-24420 or equivalent, press the damper pulley from the crankshaft.

5. Using a small pry bar, pry out the seal in the front cover.

NOTE: Use care not to damage the seal seat or the crankshaft while removing or installing the seal. Inspect the crankshaft seal surface for signs of grooves or wear.

6. Using a Seal Installer tool No. J-35468 or equivalent, drive the new seal in the cover with the lip facing towards the engine.

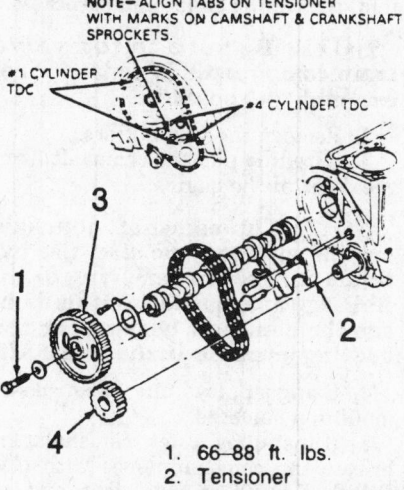

NOTE—ALIGN TABS ON TENSIONER WITH MARKS ON CAMSHAFT & CRANKSHAFT SPROCKETS.

#1 CYLINDER TDC

#4 CYLINDER TDC

1. 66–88 ft. lbs.
2. Tensioner
3. Camshaft sprocket
4. Crankshaft sprocket

Timing chain and sprockets installation-2.0 Liter engine

7. Crankshaft Pulley Installer tool No. J-29113 or equivalent, press the crankshaft pulley onto the crankshaft. Torque the damper bolt to 67–85 ft. lbs.

8. To complete the installation, reverse the removal procedures.

Timing Chain and Sprockets

REMOVAL & INSTALLATION

2.0L Engine

1. Refer to the "Front Cover, Removal and installation" procedures, remove the front cover.

2. Rotate the crankshaft to until the marks on the crankshaft and camshaft sprockets are aligned.

3. Remove the timing chain tensioner upper bolt.

4. Loosen the timing chain tensioner nut as far as possible but do not remove the nut.

5. Remove the timing chain and sprocket.

6. Using a Gear Puller tool No. J-22888 or equivalent, remove the crankshaft sprocket.

7. Before installing the sprocket, lubricate the thrust side with Molykote®. Using the Sprocket Installer tool No. J-5590 or equivalent, install the crankshaft sprocket.

8. Align the camshaft sprocket with the crankshaft sprocket marks, then, install the timing chain and camshaft sprocket.

9. Press the camshaft sprocket onto the camshaft using the camshaft sprocket bolt. Torque the camshaft sprocket bolt to 66–88 ft. lbs.

10. Align the tabs on the tensioner with the marks on the camshaft and crankshaft sprockets and tighten the tensioner.

11. To complete the installation, reverse the removal procedures.

2.8L Engine

1. Refer to the "Front Cover, Removal and Installation" procedures, remove the front cover.

2. Rotate the crankshaft to position the No. 1 piston at TDC with the crankshaft and camshaft sprockets aligned.

NOTE: When the camshaft and crankshaft marks are aligned, the No. 4 piston is on the TDC of its compression stroke.

3. Remove the camshaft sprocket bolts, the sprocket and the timing chain.

4. Remove the crankshaft sprocket.

5. Before installing the sprocket(s), apply Molykote® or equivalent, to the thrust face of the sprocket(s).

6. Install the sprocket on the crankshaft.

7. Hold the camshaft sprocket with the chain hanging down. Align the marks on the camshaft and crankshaft sprockets.

8. Align the dowel in the camshaft with the sprocket, then, install the sprocket and timing chain using a camshaft bolt to pull the sprocket into position.

9. Torque the camshaft bolts to 15–20 ft. lbs.

10. Lubricate the new timing chain with clean engine oil.

11. To complete the installation, reverse the removal procedures. Start the engine and check for leaks.

Camshaft

NOTE: To perform the following procedures, the engine must be removed from the vehicle.

REMOVAL & INSTALLATION

2.0L Engine

1. Refer to the "Timing Chain and Sprocket, Removal and Installation" procedures, remove the timing chain and sprocket from the engine.

2. Drain the engine oil. Remove the oil filter.

3. Remove the rocker cover. Loosen the rocker arms and turn the rocker arms 90°, then, remove the pushrods and lifters; note the position of the valve train components for reassembly purposes.

4. Remove the oil pump drive.

5. Remove the camshaft thrust plate-to-engine bolts, then, carefully pull the camshaft from the front of the engine.

NOTE: Use care when removing and installing the camshaft. Do not damage the camshaft bearings or the bearing surfaces on the camshaft.

7. Using a putty knife, clean gasket mounting surfaces.

8. To install, lubricate the lobes of the new camshaft with GM E.O.S. 1051396 or equivalent, and insert the camshaft into the engine.

NOTE: If a new camshaft is being used replace all of the lifters. Used lifters can only be used on the camshaft that they were originally installed with; provided that they are replaced in the exact same position that they were removed.

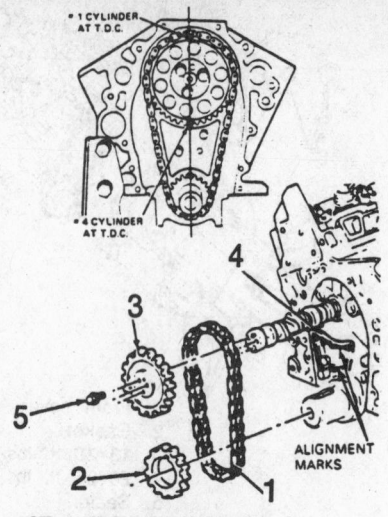

NOTE—ALIGN TIMING MARKS ON CAM & CRANK SPROCKETS USING ALIGNMENT MARKS ON DAMPER STAMPING OR CAST ALIGNMENT MARKS ON CYL & CASE.

1. Timing chain
2. Crankshaft sprocket
3. Camshaft sprocket
4. Damper
5. 15–20 ft. lbs.

Timing chain and sprockets installation-2.8 Liter engine

9. Align the marks on the camshaft and crankshaft sprockets, then, install the timing chain and sprocket.

10. To complete the installation, use new gaskets and reverse the removal procedures. Torque the rocker arm nuts to 11–18 ft. lbs.

2.8L Engine

1. Refer to the "Intake Manifold, Removal and Installation" and the "Timing Chain and Sprocket, Removal and Installation" procedures in this section and remove the intake manifold, the timing chain and sprockets.

NOTE: Be sure to the valve train components in order for reassembly purposes.

2. Remove the valve lifters.

3. Carefully pull the camshaft from the front of the engine.

NOTE: The camshaft journals are the all the same size. Use extreme care when removing or installing the camshaft not to damage the camshaft bearings or the bearing journals on the camshaft.

4. Using a putty knife, clean gasket mounting surfaces.

5. If installing a new camshaft, lubricate the camshaft lobes with GM E.O.S. 1051396 or equivalent, and insert the camshaft in the engine.

NOTE: If a new camshaft is being used replace all of the lifters.

Used lifters can only be used on the camshaft that they were originally installed with; provided that they are replaced in the exact same position that they were removed.

6. Align the camshaft and crankshaft sprocket marks, then, install the timing chain and sprocket.

7. Install the front cover and valve train components. Torque the rocker arm nuts to 14–20 ft. lbs.

8. To complete the installation, reverse the removal procedures. Start the engine, allow it to reach normal operating temperatures and check for leaks.

Piston and Connecting Rod

POSITIONING

NOTE: For all piston and connecting rod overhaul procedures, please refer to "Engine, Rebuilding" in the Unit Repair section.

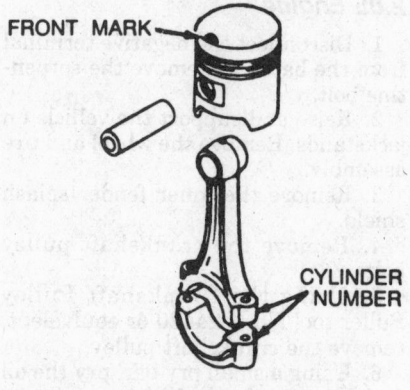

Piston and connecting rod position-2.0 and 2.8 Liter engine

ENGINE LUBRICATION

Oil Pan

REMOVAL & INSTALLATION

2.0L Engine

1. Disconnect the negative terminal from the battery. Remove the exhaust pipe shield.

2. Raise and support the vehicle on jackstands. Drain the engine oil.

3. Disconnect the A/C brace from the starter and the A/C bracket.

4. Disconnect the starter brace from the block. Label and disconnect the starter wires, then, remove the starter.

5. Remove the flywheel dust cover.

6. Remove the four (4) right support bolts and lower the support for clearance to remove the oil pan. If equipped with an ATX, remove the oil filter and extension.

7. Remove the oil pan-to-engine bolts and the oil pan.

8. Using a putty knife, clean gasket mounting surfaces.

9. To install, use new gaskets, sealant and reverse the removal procedures. Torque the oil pan-to-engine bolts to 6 ft. lbs.

NOTE: Place a small bead of RTV sealant on the oil pan-to-engine block sealing surface. Apply a thin layer of RTV sealant on the ends of the oil pan rear seal.

10. To complete the installation, reverse the removal procedures. Install a new oil filter. Refill the engine with the clean engine oil. Start the engine and check for leaks.

2.8L Engine

1. Disconnect the negative terminal from the battery.

2. Raise and support the vehicle on jackstands. Drain the engine oil.

3. Remove the flywheel dust cover.

4. Label and disconnect the starter wires, then, remove the starter.

5. Remove the oil pan-to-engine nuts/bolts and the oil pan.

6. Using a putty knife, clean gasket mounting surfaces.

7. To install, use new gasket(s), sealant and reverse the removal procedures. Torque the oil pan nuts to 6–9 ft. lbs. or bolts to 15–22 ft. lbs. Install a new oil filter. Refill the engine with the correct engine oil. Start the engine and check for leaks.

Rear Main Bearing Oil Seal

REMOVAL & INSTALLATION

NOTE: This procedure should only be performed if tool No. J-34686 or equivalent, is available. This is a special tool designed for this application.

1. Refer to the "Transaxle, Removal and Installation" procedures in this section, then, support the engine and remove the transaxle.

2. If equipped with a MTX, matchmark and remove the clutch as-

sembly and flywheel. If equipped with an ATX, remove the flywheel.

3. Using a small pry bar, pry the rear main seal from the engine.

NOTE: Use care when removing or installing the seal to avoid damage to the crankshaft sealing surface. If equipped with a MTX, inspect the condition of the clutch to insure that the clutch was not damaged by oil loss from the rear main seal.

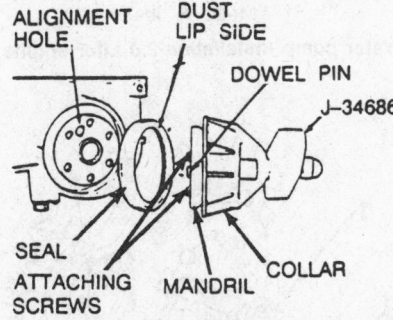

Rear main bearing oil seal installation-2.0 and 2.8 Liter engine

4. To install the rear main oil seal, perform the following procedures:

    a. Lubricate the seal bore and seal surface with engine oil.

    b. Using the Seal Installation tool No. J-34686 or equivalent, press the new rear oil seal into the engine. The seal must fit squarely against the back of the tool.

    c. Align the dowel pin of the tool with the dowel pin in the crankshaft and tighten the attaching screws on the tool to 2–5 ft. lbs.

    d. Tighten the "T" handle of the tool to push the seal into the seal bore.

    e. Loosen the "T" handle and remove the attaching screws and tool.

    f. Check the seal to make sure it is seated squarely in the bore.

5. To complete the installation, reverse the removal procedures. Torque the flywheel-to-crankshaft bolts to 45–59 ft. lbs. (ATX) or 47–63 ft. lbs. (MTX). Start the engine and check for leaks.

Oil Pump

REMOVAL & INSTALLATION

1. Raise and support the vehicle on jackstands. Drain the engine oil.

2. Remove the oil pan-to-engine bolts and the oil pan.

3. Remove the oil pump-to-rear main bearing cap bolt, the oil pump and extension shaft.

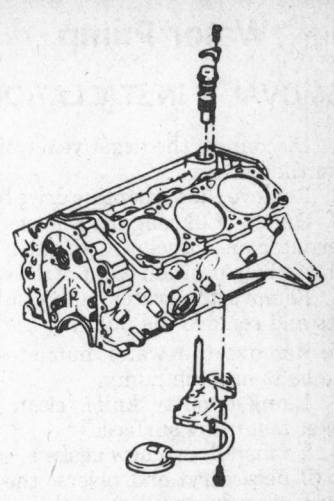

Oil pump installation-2.8 Liter engine shown-2.0 Liter engine similar

4. To install, use new gaskets, sealant and reverse the removal procedures. Torque the oil pump-to-bearing cap bolt to 25–38 ft. lbs., the upper oil pump drive bolt to 14–22 ft. lbs. (2.0L) or 25–38 ft. lbs. (2.8L). Refill the engine with clean engine oil. Start the engine and check for oil pressure and leaks.

ENGINE COOLING

Radiator

REMOVAL & INSTALLATION

1. Disconnect the negative terminal from the battery.

2. Drain the cooling system. Remove the air cleaner housing and the bracket.

3. Remove the upper radiator air baffle. On some models, remove the right and left air baffles.

4. Remove the air intake duct. Disconnect the cooling fan wire.

5. Remove the cooling fan.

6. Disconnect the radiator hoses from the radiator.

7. Disconnect the upper radiator retainers.

8. Remove the headlight attaching bolts and retainers, then, position them out of the way.

9. Remove the radiator-to-vehicle bolts and the radiator from the vehicle.

10. To install, reverse the removal procedures. Refill and bleed the cooling system.

Water Pump

REMOVAL & INSTALLATION

1. Disconnect the negative terminal from the battery.
2. Remove the serpentine drive belt.
3. On the 2.0L engine, remove the alternator and bracket with wires attached, then, position it out of the way.
4. Remove the water pump pulley bolts and remove the pulley.
5. Remove the water pump-to-engine bolts and the pump.
6. Using a putty knife, clean the gasket mounting surfaces.
7. To install, use new gaskets, sealant (if necessary) and reverse the removal procedures. Torque the water pump-to-engine bolts to 14–22 ft. lbs. (2.0L) or 6–9 ft. lbs. (2.8L). Refill and bleed the cooling system.
8. To complete the installation, reverse the removal procedures. Start the engine, allow it to reach normal operating temperatures and check for leaks.

Thermostat

REMOVAL & INSTALLATION

1. Drain the cooling system to a level below the thermostat.
2. Remove the thermostat housing-to-engine bolts and the housing.
3. Using a putty knife, clean the gasket mounting surfaces.
4. To install, use new gaskets, sealant (if necessary) and reverse the removal procedures. Torque the thermostat housing-to-engine bolts to 6–9 ft. lbs. (2.0L) or 15–22 ft. lbs. (2.8L). Refill and bleed the cooling system. Start the engine, allow it to reach normal operating temperatures and check for leaks.

COOLING SYSTEM BLEEDING

After working on the cooling system, even to replace the thermostat, it must be bleed. Air trapped in the system will, otherwise, prevent proper filling, leaving the radiator coolant level low and causing risk of overheating.

To bleed the system, start with the system cool, the radiator cap off and the radiator filled to about 1 in. below the filler neck. Start the engine and run it at slightly above normal idle speed, to ensure adequate circulation. If air bubbles appear and the coolant level drops, fill the system with a 50% antifreeze/water mixture to bring the level up to the proper level. Run the engine until the thermostat opens.

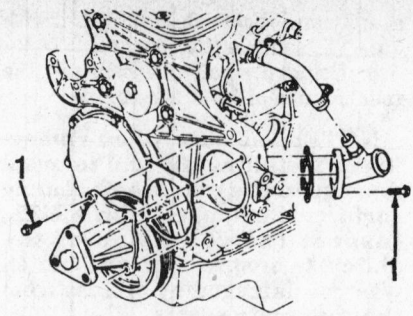

1. 14–22 ft. lbs.

Water pump installation-2.0 Liter engine

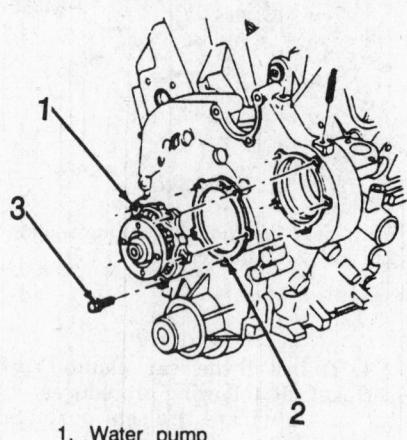

1. Water pump
2. Gasket
3. 6–9 ft. lbs.

Water pump installation-2.8 Liter engine

When this happens, coolant will move abruptly across the top of the radiator and the temperature of the radiator will suddenly rise. At this point, air is often expelled and the level may drop quite a bit. Keep refilling the system until the level is near the top of the radiator and remains constant. If the vehicle has an overflow tank, fill the radiator up to the filler neck. Replace the radiator filler cap.

EMISSION CONTROLS

NOTE: Please refer to "Emission Control" in the Unit Repair section for system maintenance procedures. Due to the complex nature of modern electronic engine control systems, comprehensive diagnosis and testing procedures fall outside the confines of this repair manual. For complete information on diagnosis, testing and repair procedures concerning all modern engine and emission control systems, please refer to "Chilton's Guide to Electronic Engine Controls".

FUEL SYSTEM

Fuel System Service Precaution

• Disconnect the negative battery terminal
• Keep a Class B dry chemical fire extinguisher available
• Always relieve the fuel pressure before disconnecting a fuel line
• Wrap a shop cloth around the fuel line when disconnecting a fuel line
• Always use new O-rings
• DO NOT replace the fuel pipes with fuel hoses
• Always use a back-up wrench when opening or closing a fuel line

RELIEVING FUEL SYSTEM PRESSURE

NOTE: Make sure the engine is Cold before disconnecting any portion of the fuel system.

TBI

1. Using a shop rag, wrap it around the fuel line fitting.
2. Open the fuel line and absorb any excess fuel remaining in the line.
3. To install, use a new O-ring and reverse the removal procedures.

PFI

1. Using the Fuel Gauge tool No. J-34730-1 or equivalent, connect it to the fuel pressure connector.

NOTE: Be sure to wrap a shop cloth around the fuel line fitting when connecting the fuel gauge tool to the fuel pressure connector.

2. Place the bleeder hose and shop cloth in an approved container, then, open the pressure valve to bleed the fuel from the system.

3. After the fuel is bleed, retighten the fuel pressure valve.

Fuel Filter

REMOVAL & INSTALLATION

The fuel filter is mounted on the rear crossmember of the vehicle directly behind the fuel tank.

CAUTION

The fuel pressure must be relieved before working on any part of the fuel system. Fuel systems that are under constant pressure will spray a small amount of fuel when opened. On the TBI injection, cover all fuel fittings with a shop towel while loosening them to collect the excess fuel. Place the shop towel in an approved container and discard it properly. On the PFI injection, install the Pressure Gauge tool No. J-34730-1 or equivalent, on the pressure fitting located on the front of the fuel rail. Place a shop towel around the fitting to collect the excess fuel. Dispose of the shop towel correctly. Place a bleed hose into an approved container and bleed off the system pressure. Dispose of the fuel properly. After servicing either system, check all connections, run the engine and check for leaks.

1. Refer to the "Relieving Fuel System Pressure" and relieve the fuel pressure.

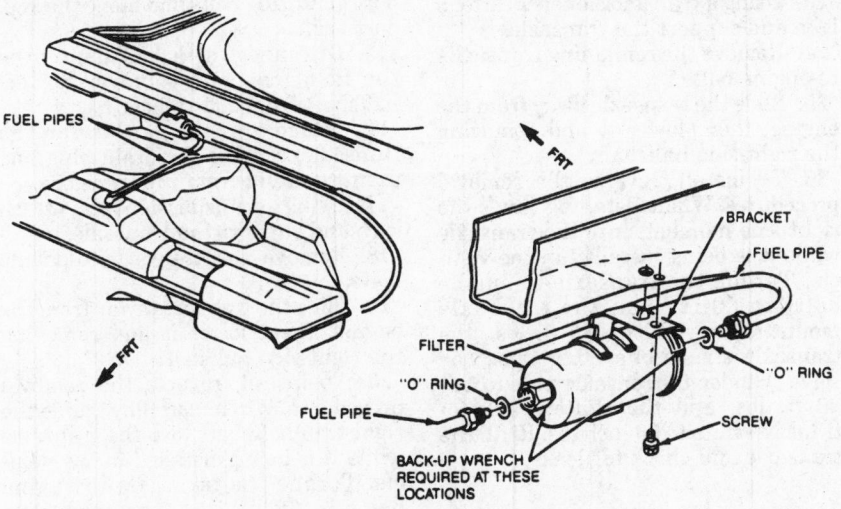

Fuel filter location and mounting

2. Using a back-up wrench to hold the fuel filter fitting and loosen the fuel line fitting.
3. Remove the fuel lines from the filter.
4. Remove the filter from the mounting clamp.
5. To install, use a new filter, O-rings and reverse the removal procedures. Torque the fuel line-to-fuel filter fittings to 22 ft. lbs. Operate the engine and check for leaks.

Electric Fuel Pump

PRESSURE TESTING

TBI Injection

1. Turn the engine OFF and allow the system to bleed down.
2. Remove the cover bonnet and gasket from the TBI unit.
3. Wrap a shop cloth around the fuel line connection and disconnect the fuel line in the engine compartment. Using a Fuel Pressure Gauge, install it between the steel line and the flexible hose.

NOTE: When installing the pressure gauge, be sure to tighten the connections to ensure there are no fuel leaks.

4. Start the engine and check the fuel pressure reading; it should be 62–90 kPa.
5. Turn the engine OFF, allow the fuel pressure to bleed-down and remove the pressure gauge from the system.
6. To install, use new O-rings and reverse the removal procedures. Start the engine and check for leaks.

PFI

1. Refer to the "Relieving Fuel System Pressure" and relieve the fuel pressure.
2. Place a shop cloth under the fuel pressure connector on the fuel rail. Using the Fuel Pressure Gauge tool No. J-34730-1 or equivalent, connect it to the fuel rail pressure connector.
3. Turn the ignition switch ON; the fuel pressure should be 40–47 psi (280–325 kPa).
4. Start the engine and allow it to idle; the fuel pressure will be lower.

NOTE: The manifold pressure (being lower) operates the fuel pressure regulator.

5. Stop the engine, relieve the fuel pressure and remove the fuel pressure gauge.

ADJUSTMENT

No adjustments are possible on either system. If the pressure is not within specifications, problems could be caused by a faulty fuel pump, clogged fuel filter, a leaking coupling or hose, a faulty regulator or an injector sticking open.

REMOVAL & INSTALLATION

The fuel pump is located in the fuel tank. Removal and installation procedures require the fuel tank to be removed from the vehicle.

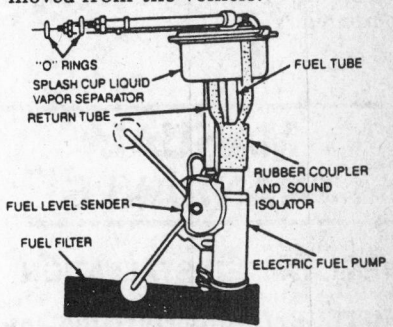

View of the in-tank fuel pump—2.0L engine

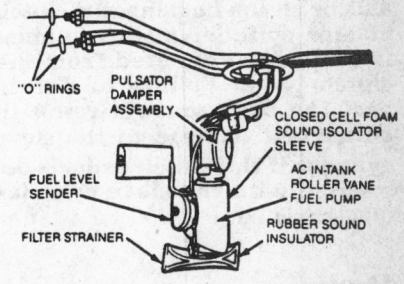

Fuel pump and sending unit assemblies

1. Refer to the "Relieving Fuel System Pressure" and relieve the fuel pressure.
2. Disconnect the negative terminal from the battery.
3. Using a siphon hose, drain the fuel from the fuel tank.
4. Raise and support the rear of the vehicle on jackstands.
5. Support the fuel tank and disconnect the retaining straps.
6. Lower the tank some, then, disconnect the sending unit wire, the hoses and the ground strap. Remove the fuel tank from the vehicle.
7. Using the Locking Cam tool No. J-24187 or equivalent, remove the sending unit retaining cam from the fuel tank.

8. Remove the sending unit and the O-ring gasket from the fuel tank.

9. To install, use a new O-ring gasket and reverse the removal procedures; be sure to reinstall the antisqueak pieces on top of the fuel tank. Torque the retaining straps to 26 ft. lbs. Refill the fuel tank, start the engine and check for leaks.

Fuel Injection

NOTE: Due to the complex nature of modern fuel injection systems, comprehensive diagnosis and testing procedures fall outside the confines of this repair manual. For complete information on Fuel injection diagnosis, testing and repair procedures please refer to *Chilton's Guide to Fuel Injection And Feedback Carburetors.*

MANUAL TRANSAXLE

REMOVAL & INSTALLATION

NOTE: Before performing any maintenance that requires the removal of the slave cylinder, transaxle or clutch housing, the clutch master cylinder push rod must first be disconnected from the clutch pedal. Failure to disconnect the push rod will result in permanent damage to the slave cylinder if the clutch pedal is depressed with the slave cylinder disconnected.

Muncie

1. Disconnect the negative terminal from the battery.

2. Using the Engine Support Fixture tool No. J-28467 or equivalent, and Adapter tool No. J-35953 or equivalent, install them on the engine, then, raise the engine enough to take the engine weight off of the engine mounts.

3. Remove the left-side sound insulator.

4. Disconnect the clutch master cylinder push rod from the clutch pedal.

5. Remove the air cleaner and duct assembly.

6. Disconnect the clutch slave cylinder-to-transaxle support bolts and position the cylinder aside.

7. Remove the transaxle-to-mount thru bolt.

8. Raise and support the front of the vehicle on jackstands.

9. If equipped with a 2.8L engine, remove the two (2) exhaust crossover bolts at the right-side manifold.

10. Lower the vehicle. If equipped with a 2.8L engine, remove the left-side exhaust manifold.

11. Disconnect the transaxle mounting bracket.

12. Disconnect the shifter cables.

13. Remove the upper transaxle-to-engine bolts.

14. Raise and support the front of the vehicle on jackstands.

15. Remove the left-front wheel/tire assembly and the left-side inner splash shield.

16. Remove the transaxle strut and bracket.

17. Place a drain pan under the transaxle, remove the drain plug and drain the fluid from the transaxle.

18. Remove the clutch housing cover bolts.

19. Disconnect the speedometer wire.

20. From the left suspension support and control arm, disconnect the stabilizer shaft.

21. Remove the left suspension support mounting bolts and move the support aside.

22. Disconnect both halfshafts from the transaxle and remove the left halfshaft from the vehicle.

23. Using a transmission jack, attach it to and support the transaxle.

24. Remove the remaining transaxle-to-engine bolts.

25. Slide the transaxle away from the engine, then, lower it and removing the right-side halfshaft.

26. To install, reverse the removal procedures. When installing, guide the right-side halfshaft into the transaxle while it is being installed in the vehicle. Torque the transaxle-to-engine bolts to 60 ft. lbs., the transaxle mount-to-body bolt to 80 ft. lbs., the transaxle strut bolts 50 ft. lbs., the slave cylinder-to-transaxle nuts to 14–20 ft. lbs. and the shifter cable-to-transaxle nuts to 90 inch lbs. Refill the transaxle and check for leaks.

NOTE: The clutch lever must not be moved towards the flywheel until the transaxle is bolted to the engine. Damage to the transaxle, release bearing and clutch fork could occur if this is not followed.

Isuzu

1. Disconnect the negative terminal from the battery.

2. Using the Engine Support Fixture tool No. J-28467 or equivalent, and Adapter tool No. J-35953 or equiv-alent, install them on the engine, then, raise the engine enough to take the engine weight off of the engine mounts.

3. Remove the left-side sound insulator.

4. Disconnect the clutch master cylinder push rod from the clutch pedal.

5. Disconnect the clutch slave cylinder-to-transaxle support bolts and position the cylinder aside.

6. Remove the wiring harness from the transaxle mount bracket and the shift wire electrical connector.

7. Remove the transaxle-to-mount bolts and the transaxle mount bracket-to-chassis nuts/bolts.

8. Disconnect the shift cables and remove the retaining clamp from the transaxle. Remove the ground cables from the transaxle mounting studs.

9. Raise and support the front of the vehicle on jackstands.

10. Remove the left-front wheel/tire assembly and the left-side inner splash shield.

11. Remove the transaxle front strut and bracket.

12. Remove the clutch housing cover bolts. Disconnect the speedometer wire connector.

13. From the left suspension support and control arm, disconnect the stabilizer shaft.

14. Remove the left suspension support mounting bolts and move the support aside.

15. Disconnect both halfshafts from the transaxle and remove the left halfshaft from the vehicle.

16. Place a drain pan under the transaxle, remove the drain plug and drain the fluid from the transaxle.

17. Using a transmission jack, attach it to and support the transaxle.

18. Remove the transaxle-to-engine bolts.

19. Slide the transaxle away from the engine, then, lower it and removing the right-side halfshaft.

20. To install, reverse the removal procedures. When installing, guide the right-side halfshaft into the transaxle while it is being installed in the vehicle. Torque the transaxle-to-engine bolts to 60 ft. lbs., the transaxle mount-to-body bolt to 80 ft. lbs., the transaxle strut bolts 50 ft. lbs., the slave cylinder-to-transaxle nuts to 14–20 ft. lbs. and the shifter cable-to-transaxle nuts to 90 inch lbs. Refill the transaxle and check for leaks.

NOTE: The clutch lever must not be moved towards the flywheel until the transaxle is bolted to the engine. Damage to the transaxle, release bearing and clutch fork could occur if this is not followed.

LINKAGE ADJUSTMENT

No adjustments are possible on the manual transaxle shifting cables or linkage. If the transaxle is not engaging completely, check for stretched cables or broken shifter components or a faulty transaxle.

CLUTCH

A hydraulic clutch mechanism is used on all vehicles. This mechanism uses a clutch master cylinder with a remote reservoir and a slave cylinder connected to the master cylinder. Whenever the system is disconnected for repair or replacement, the clutch system must be bleed to insure proper operation.

REMOVAL & INSTALLATION

1. Disconnect the negative terminal from the battery.
2. From inside the vehicle, remove the hush panel.
3. Disconnect the clutch master cylinder push rod from the clutch pedal.
4. Refer to the "Transaxle, Removal and Installation" procedures in this section and remove the transaxle.
5. With the transaxle removed, matchmark the pressure plate and flywheel assembly to insure proper balance during reassembly.
6. Loosen the pressure plate-to-flywheel bolts (one turn at a time) until the spring pressure is removed.
7. Support the pressure plate and remove the bolts.
8. Remove the pressure plate and disc assembly; be sure to note the flywheel side of the clutch disc.

9. Clean and inspect the clutch assembly, flywheel, release bearing, clutch fork and pivot shaft for signs of wear. Replace any necessary parts.
10. To install, position the clutch disc and pressure plate in the appropriate position, support the assembly with Alignment tool No. J-29074, J-35822 or equivalent.

NOTE: Make sure the clutch disc is facing the same direction it was removed. If the same pressure plate is being reused, align the marks made during removal and install, install the pressure plate retaining bolts and tighten them gradually and evenly.

11. Remove the alignment tool and torque the pressure plate-to-flywheel bolts to 15 ft. lbs. Lightly lubricate the clutch fork ends. Fill the recess ends of the release bearing with grease. Lubricate the input shaft with a light coat of grease.
12. To complete the installation, reverse the removal procedures.

NOTE: The clutch lever must not be moved towards the flywheel until the transaxle is bolted to the engine. Damage to the transaxle, release bearing and clutch fork could occur if this is not followed.

13. Bleed the clutch system and check the clutch operation when finished.

PEDAL HEIGHT/FREE-PLAY ADJUSTMENT

Push the clutch pedal all the way to the floor; the distance of travel should be 7.4 in.

Clutch Master and Slave Cylinder Assembly

The clutch master and slave cylinder assembly must be serviced as an assembly.

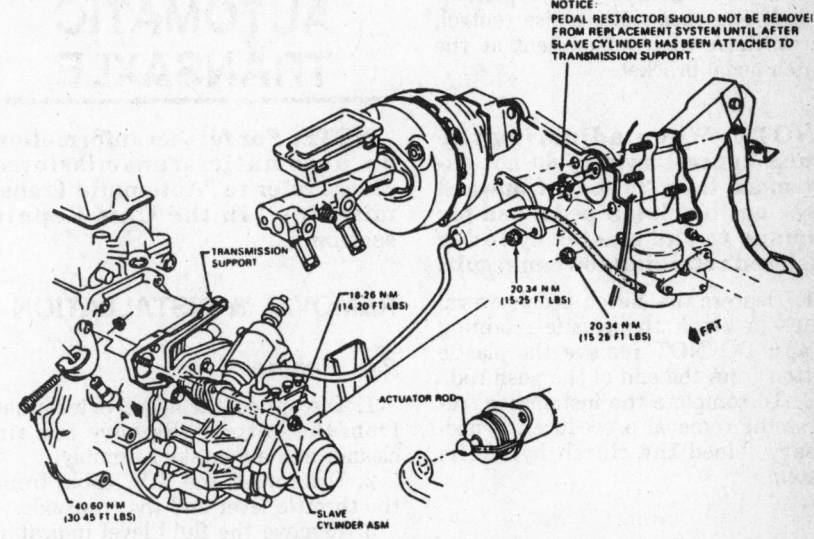

Clutch master and slave cylinder installation

REMOVAL & INSTALLATION

1. Disconnect the negative terminal from the battery.
2. From inside the vehicle, remove the hush panel.

NOTE: If equipped with a 2.8L engine, remove the air cleaner, the mass air flow sensor and the air intake duct as an assembly.

3. Disconnect the clutch master cylinder push rod from the clutch master cylinder.
4. From the front of the dash, remove the trim cover.

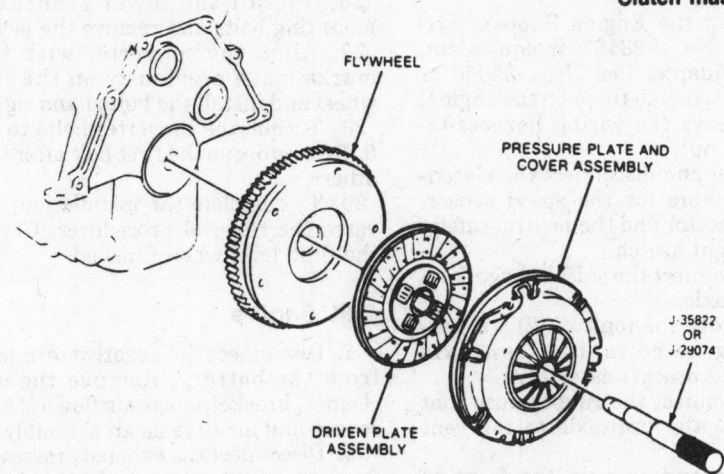

Typical clutch assembly installation

5. Remove the clutch master cylinder-to-clutch pedal bracket nuts and the remote reservoir-to-chassis screws.

6. Remove the slave cylinder-to-transaxle nuts and the slave cylinder.

7. Remove the hydraulic system (as a unit) from the vehicle.

8. Install the slave cylinder-to-transaxle support, align the push rod to the clutch fork outer lever pocket. Torque the slave cylinder-to-transaxle support nuts to 14–20 ft. lbs.

NOTE: If installing a new clutch hydraulic system, DO NOT break the push rod plastic retainer; the straps will break on the first pedal application.

9. Install the master cylinder-to-clutch pedal bracket, then, torque the nuts evenly (to prevent damaging the master cylinder) to 15–20 ft. lbs. and reverse the removal procedures. Remove the pedal restrictor from the push rod. Lubricate the push rod bushing on the clutch pedal; if the bushing is cracked or worn, replace it.

10. If equipped with cruise control, check the switch adjustment at the clutch pedal bracket.

NOTE: When adjusting the cruise control switch, do not exert more than 20 lbs. of upward force on the clutch pedal pad for damage to the master cylinder push rod retaining rod can result.

11. Depress the clutch pedal several times to break the plastic retaining straps; DO NOT remove the plastic button from the end of the push rod.

12. To complete the installation, reverse the removal procedures. If necessary, bleed the clutch hydraulic system.

ADJUSTMENT

No adjustments are possible on the hydraulic clutch system. If the clutch is not engaging correctly, bleed and check the system.

BLEEDING THE HYDRAULIC CLUTCH SYSTEM

1. Remove any dirt or grease around the reservoir cap so that dirt cannot enter the system.

2. Fill the reservoir with an approved DOT 3 brake fluid.

3. Loosen, but do not remove, the bleeder screw on the slave cylinder.

4. Fluid will now flow from the master cylinder to the slave cylinder.

NOTE: It is important that the reservoir remain filled throughout the procedure.

5. Air bubbles should now appear at the bleeder screw.

6. Continue this procedure until a steady stream of fluid without any air bubbles is present.

7. Tighten the bleeder screw. Check the fluid level in the reservoir and fill to the proper mark.

8. The system is now fully bled. Check the clutch operation by starting the engine, pushing the clutch pedal to the floor and placing the transmission in reverse.

9. If any grinding of the gears is noted, repeat the entire procedure.

NOTE: Never under any circumstances reuse fluid that has been in the system. The fluid may be contaminated with dirt and moisture.

AUTOMATIC TRANSAXLE

NOTE: For further information on automatic transmissions, please refer to "Automatic Transmissions" in the Unit Repair section.

REMOVAL & INSTALLATION

2.0L Engine

1. Disconnect the negative terminal from the battery. Remove the air cleaner and air intake assembly.

2. Disconnect the T.V. cable from the throttle lever and the transaxle.

3. Remove the fluid level indicator and the filler tube.

4. Using the Engine Support Fixture tool No. J-28467 or equivalent, and the Adapter tool No. J-35953 or equivalent, install them on the engine.

5. Remove the wiring harness-to-transaxle nut.

6. Label and disconnect the electrical connectors for the speed sensor, TCC connector and the neutral safety/backup light switch.

7. Disconnect the shift linkage from the transaxle.

8. Remove the top two (2) transaxle-to-engine bolts, the transaxle mount and bracket assembly.

9. Disconnect the rubber hose that runs from the transaxle to the vent pipe.

10. Raise and support the front of the vehicle on jackstands.

11. Remove the front wheels and tire assemblies.

12. Disconnect the shift linkage and bracket from the transaxle.

13. Remove the left-side splash shield.

14. Using a modified Drive Axle Seal Protector tool No. J-34754 or equivalent, install one on each drive axle to protect the seal from damage and the joint from possible failure.

15. Using care not to damage the halfshaft boots, disconnect the halfshafts from the transaxle.

16. Remove the transaxle strut. Remove the left-side stabilizer link pin bolt and bushing clamp nuts from the support.

17. Remove the left frame support bolts and move it out of the way.

18. Disconnect the speedometer wire from the transaxle.

19. Remove the transaxle converter cover and matchmark the converter to the flywheel for assembly.

20. Disconnect and plug the transaxle cooler pipes.

21. Remove the transaxle to engine support.

22. Using a transmission jack, position and secure the jack to the transaxle, then, remove the remaining transaxle-to-engine bolts.

23. Making sure the torque converter does not fall out, remove the transaxle from the vehicle.

NOTE: The transaxle cooler and lines should be flushed any time the transaxle is removed for overhaul or replacing the pump, case or converter.

24. To install, put a small amount of grease on the pilot hub of the converter and make sure that the converter is properly engaged with the pump.

25. Raise the transaxle to the engine while guiding the right-side halfshaft into the transaxle.

26. Install the lower transaxle mounting bolts and remove the jack.

27. Align the converter with the marks made previously on the flywheel and install the bolts hand tight.

28. Torque the converter bolts to 46 ft. lbs.; retorque the first bolt after the others.

29. To complete the installation, reverse the removal procedures. Check the fluid level when finished.

2.8L Engine

1. Disconnect the negative terminal from the battery. Remove the air cleaner, bracket, mass air flow (MAF) sensor and air tube as an assembly.

2. Disconnect the exhaust crossover from the right-side manifold and remove the left-side exhaust manifold,

then, raise and support the manifold/crossover assembly.

3. Disconnect the T.V. cable from the throttle lever and the transaxle.

4. Remove the vent hose and the shift cable from the transaxle.

5. Remove the fluid level indicator and the filler tube.

6. Using the Engine Support Fixture tool No. J-28467 or equivalent, and the Adapter tool No. J-35953 or equivalent, install them on the engine.

7. Remove the wiring harness-to-transaxle nut.

8. Label and disconnect the wires for the speed sensor, TCC connector and the neutral safety/backup light switch.

9. Remove the upper transaxle-to-engine bolts.

10. Remove the transaxle-to-mount thru bolt, the transaxle mount bracket and the mount.

11. Raise and support the vehicle on jackstands.

12. Remove the front wheel and tire assemblies.

13. Disconnect the shift cable bracket from the transaxle.

14. Remove the left-side splash shield.

15. Using a modified Drive Axle Seal Protector tool No. J-34754 or equivalent, install one on each drive axle to protect the seal from damage and the joint from possible failure.

16. Using care not to damage the halfshaft boots, disconnect the halfshafts from the transaxle.

17. Remove the torsional and lateral strut from the transaxle. Remove the left-side stabilizer link pin bolt.

18. Remove the left frame support bolts and move it out of the way.

19. Disconnect the speedometer wire from the transaxle.

20. Remove the transaxle converter cover and matchmark the converter to the flywheel for assembly.

21. Disconnect and plug the transaxle cooler pipes.

22. Remove the transaxle-to-engine support.

23. Using a transmission jack, position and secure it to the transaxle and remove the remaining transaxle to engine bolts.

24. Make sure that the torque converter does not fall out and remove the transaxle from the vehicle.

NOTE: The transaxle cooler and lines should be flushed any time the transaxle is removed for overhaul, or to replace the pump, case or converter.

25. To install, put a small amount of grease on the pilot hub of the converter and make sure that the converter is properly engaged with the pump.

26. Raise the transaxle to the engine while guiding the right-side halfshaft into the transaxle.

27. Install the lower transaxle mounting bolts and remove the jack.

28. Align the converter with the marks made previously on the flywheel and install the bolts hand tight.

29. Torque the converter bolts to 46 ft. lbs.; retorque the first bolt after the others.

30. To complete the installation, reverse the removal procedures. Check the fluid level when finished.

DRIVE AXLE

Halfshaft

REMOVAL & INSTALLATION

The inner joint on the right-side halfshaft uses a male spline that lock on the transaxle gears. The left-side halfshaft uses a female spline that is installed over the stub shaft on the transaxle.

1. With the weight of the vehicle on the tires, loosen the hub nut.

2. Raise and support the vehicle on jackstands.

3. Remove the hub nut.

4. Install boot protectors on the boots.

5. Remove the brake caliper with the line attached and safely support it

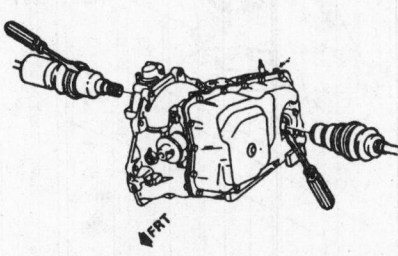

Removing halfshafts from transaxle-automatic shown-manual similar

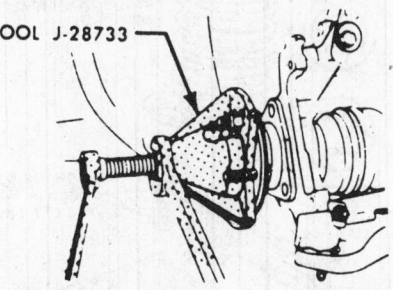

Removing halfshaft from steering knuckle bearing

out of the way; DO NOT allow the caliper to hang from the line.

6. Remove the brake rotor and caliper mounting bracket.

7. Remove the strut to steering knuckle bolts. Pull the steering knuckle out of the strut bracket.

8. Using the Halfshaft Removal tool J-33008 or equivalent and the Extention tool No. J-29794 or equivalent, remove the halfshafts from the transaxle and support them safely.

9. Using a Spindle Remover tool No. J-28733 or equivalent, remove the halfshaft from the hub and bearing.

10. To install, loosely place the halfshaft on the transaxle and in the hub and bearing.

11. Properly position the steering knuckle to the strut bracket and install the bolt. Torque the bolts to 133 ft. lbs.

12. Install the brake rotor, caliper bracket and caliper. Place a holding device in the rotor to prevent it from turning.

13. Install the hub nut and washer. Torque the nut to 71 ft. lbs.

14. Seat the halfshafts into the transaxle using a screwdriver on the groove on the inner retainer.

15. Verify that the shafts are seated by grasping the CV joint and pulling outwards. DO NOT grasp the shaft. If the snap ring is seated, the halfshaft will remain in place.

16. To complete the installation, reverse the removal procedures. When the vehicle is lowered with the weight on the wheels, final torque the hub nut to 191 ft. lbs.

CV JOINT OVERHAUL

NOTE: For all CV-joint overhaul procedures, please refer to "U/CV-Joint Overhaul" in the Unit Repair section.

Front Wheel Drive Hub, Knuckle and Bearing

REMOVAL & INSTALLATION

The hub and bearing are replaced as an assembly only.

1. With the vehicle weight on the tires, loosen the hub nut.

2. Raise and support the vehicle on jackstands. Remove the wheel and tire assembly.

3. Install a boot cover over the outer CV joint boot.

4. Remove the hub nut. Remove the brake caliper and support it out of the way; DO NOT allow the caliper to hang on the brake line.

5. Remove the three (3) hub and bearing mounting bolts.

6. Remove the brake rotor splash shield.

7. Install the Hub Puller tool No. J-28733 or equivalent, and press the hub and bearing from the halfshaft.

8. Disconnect the stabalizer link from the lower control arm.

9. Using the Ball Joint Puller tool No. J-29330 or equivalent, separate the ball joint from the steering knuckle.

10. Remove the halfshaft from the knuckle and support it out of the way.

11. Using a brass drift, remove the inner knuckle seal.

12. Clean and inspect the steering knuckle bore and the bearing mating surfaces.

13. Install a new O-ring between the bearing and knuckle assembly.

14. Install the hub and bearing assembly and torque the nuts to 90 ft. lbs.

15. Using a Seal Driver tool No. J-34658 or equivalent, install it into the steering knuckle; be sure to lubricate the new seal and the bearing with a high temperature wheel bearing grease.

16. Reconnect the lower ball joint.

17. Install the hub, bearing nut and washer on the halfshaft, then, torque the nut to 71 ft. lbs.

18. Install the brake rotor and caliper. Install the wheel and tire.

19. Lower the vehicle and torque the hub nut to 191 ft. lbs.

FRONT SUSPENSION

MacPherson Strut

REMOVAL & INSTALLATION

1. From inside the engine compartment, remove the upper strut-to-body bolts.

2. Raise and support the vehicle on jackstands allowing the suspension to hang freely.

3. Remove the wheel and tire assembly.

4. Remove the tie rod nut. Using the Ball Joint Remover tool No. J-29330 or equivalent, press the tie rod from the steering knuckle.

5. Support the steering knuckle to prevent the brake hose from being torn.

6. Support the strut assembly and remove the strut-to-steering knuckle bolts.

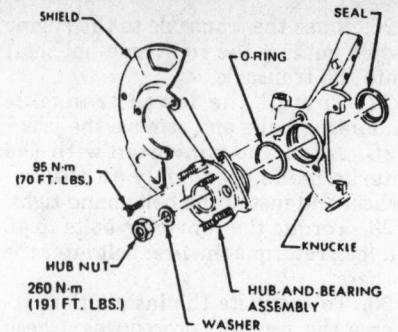

Hub, knuckle and bearing-exploded view

7. Remove the strut from the vehicle.

8. To install, reverse the removal procedures. Torque the strut-to-knuckle bolts to 133 ft. lbs. and the strut-to-body nuts/bolts to 18 ft. lbs.

OVERHAUL

NOTE: For all spring and shock absorber removal and installation procedures, and all strut overhaul procedures, please refer to "Strut Overhaul" in the Unit Repair section.

Lower Ball Joints

INSPECTION

1. Raise and support the vehicle on jackstands, so the front suspension is hanging freely.

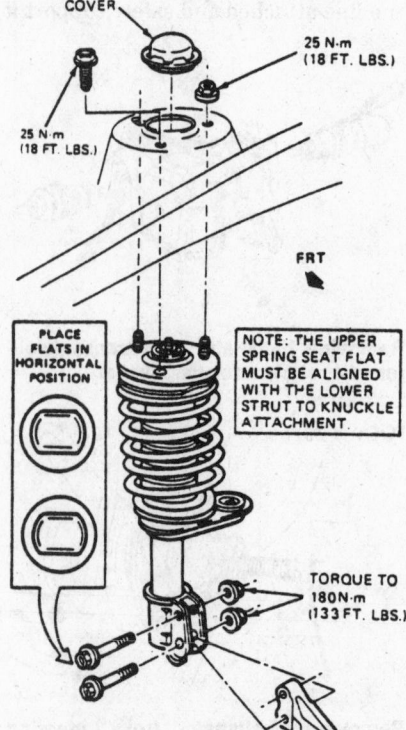

Front strut mounting

2. Grasp and shake the wheel at the top and bottom to feel if there is any in and out movement.

3. Replace the ball joint if any movement is detected.

4. When the ball joint is disconnected from the knuckle, check for any looseness or if the ball joint can be twisted freely in the socket by hand.

REMOVAL & INSTALLATION

1. Raise and support the vehicle on jackstands. Remove the wheel and tire assembly.

2. Using a center punch and a hammer, countersink the center of the mounting rivets.

3. Using a drill and an 1/8 in. bit, drill a pilot hole through the rivet.

4. Using a 1/2 in. drill bit, drill completely through the rivet.

5. Using Ball Joint Remover tool No. J-29330 or equivalent, separate the ball joint from the steering knuckle.

6. Remove the ball joint from the lower control arm. Clean any debris from the ball joint rivet.

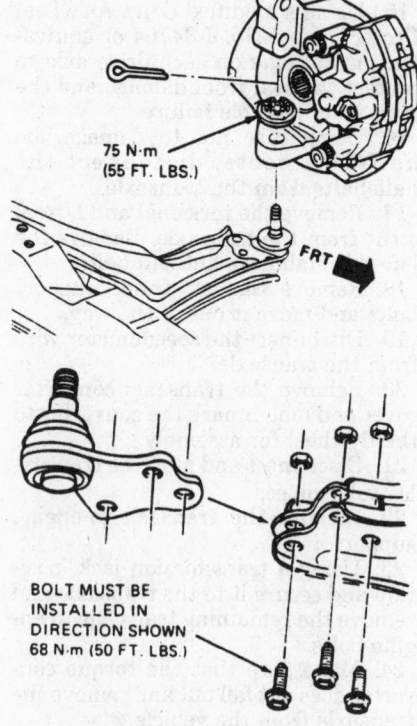

Lower ball joint installation

7. To install, position a new ball joint on the control arm and install the three (3) mounting bolts with the nuts on the top. Torque the nuts to 50 ft. lbs.

8. To complete the installation, reverse the removal procedures. Torque the ball joint stud to 55 ft. lbs.

Lower Control Arm

REMOVAL & INSTALLATION

1. Raise and support the vehicle on jackstands. Remove the wheel and tire assembly.

2. Disconnect the stabilizer bar from the control arm.

3. Using the Ball Joint Remover tool No. J-29330 or equivalent, separate the ball joint from the steering knuckle.

4. Remove the control arm-to-subframe bolts and the control arm.

5. To install, reverse the removal procedures. Torque the control arm-to-subframe bolts to 63 ft. lbs. and the ball joint stud nut to 55 ft. lbs.

Front Wheel Alignment

ADJUSTMENT

Caster and camber are preset at the factory and are not adjustable. Toe can be adjusted by loosening the clamps on the outer tie rods and rotating the tie rods to obtain the proper specification. Torque the tie rod clamp to 33 ft. lbs.

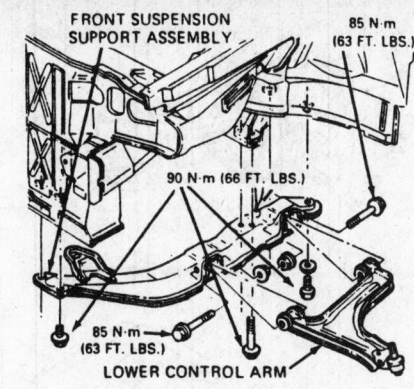

FRONT SUSPENSION SUPPORT ASSEMBLY

85 N·m (63 FT. LBS.)

90 N·m (66 FT. LBS.)

85 N·m (63 FT. LBS.)

LOWER CONTROL ARM

Lower control arm mounting

REAR SUSPENSION

Shock Absorbers

REMOVAL & INSTALLATION

1. With the deck lid or trunk open, remove the trim cover and the upper shock-to-chassis nuts.

2. Raise and support the rear of the vehicle on jackstands. Using a floor jack, support the rear axle.

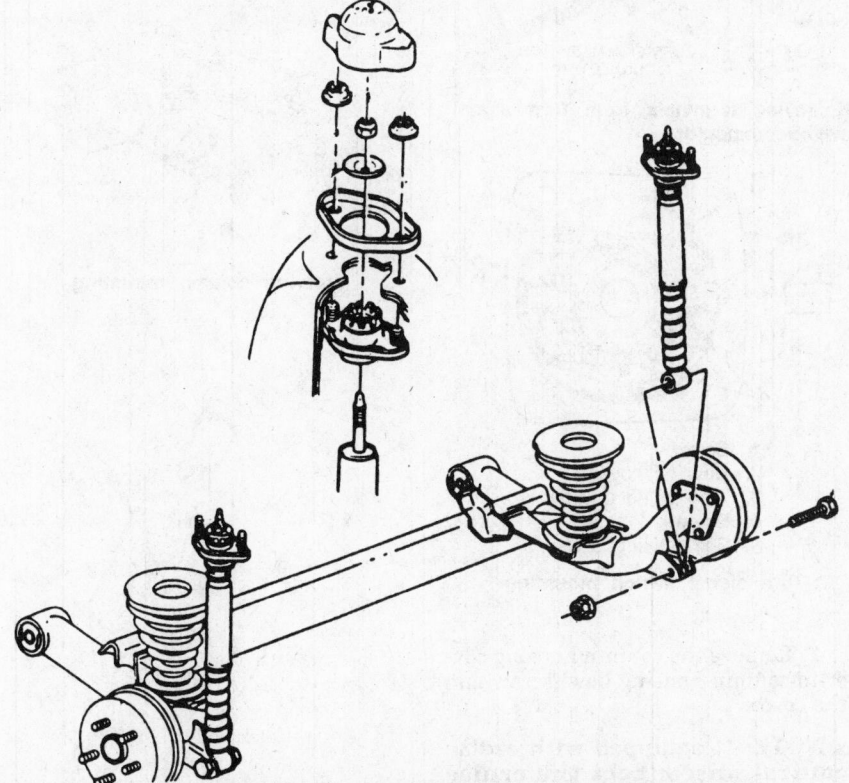

Rear shock absorber mounting-Corsica shown-Beretta similar

3. Remove the lower shock absorber-to-axle nut/bolt, lower the rear axle assembly and remove the shock absorber.

4. To install, reverse the removal procedures. Torque the lower shock absorber-to-axle nut/bolt to 43 ft. lbs. (Beretta) or 35 ft. lbs. (Corsica) and the shock absorber-to-chassis nuts to 22 ft. lbs. Check and/or adjust the vehicle ride height.

OVERHAUL

NOTE: For all spring and shock absorber removal and installation procedures, and all strut overhaul procedures, please refer to "Strut Overhaul" in the Unit Repair section.

Springs

REMOVAL & INSTALLATION

————— CAUTION —————
DO NOT use a twin-post type lift when removing the rear springs. This type of lift may cause the rear axle to slip when certain bolts are removed because the rear axle must swing down to remove the springs.

1. Raise and support the rear of the vehicle on jackstands (located under the frame).

2. Remove the wheel and tire assembly. Using a floor jack, support the rear axle assembly.

3. Disconnect the right and left brake line brackets from the body and allow the lines to hang freely.

4. Remove the lower shock absorber-to-axle nuts and bolts.

5. Lower the rear axle and remove the springs.

6. To install, reverse the removal procedures. Torque the lower shock absorber-to-axle nuts/bolts to 43 ft. lbs. (Beretta) or 35 ft. lbs. (Corsica).

Rear Wheel Bearings

REMOVAL & INSTALLATION

The rear wheel hub and bearing are replaced as an assembly only.

1. Raise and support the rear of the vehicle on jackstands.

2. Remove the wheel and tire assembly. Remove the brake drum.

3. Remove the hub/bearing assembly-to-rear axle nuts/bolts.

NOTE: The top mounting bolt will not clear the brake shoe when removing the hub and bearing. The hub and bearing must be partially removed while the top bolts is being turned out.

4. To install, insert and turn the top bolt in while installing the hub and bearing. Then install the other three bolts.

5. Torque the hub/bearing assembly-to-rear axle nuts/bolts to 38 ft. lbs.

6. Install the brake drum and wheel/tire assembly.

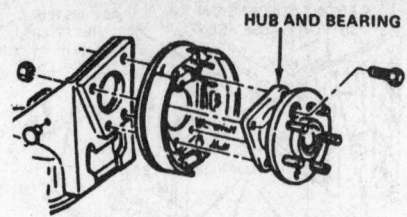

Rear wheel hub and bearing mounting

STEERING

Steering Wheel

REMOVAL & INSTALLATION

1. Disconnect the negative terminal from the battery. Turn the steering wheel so the wheels are in the straight ahead position.

2. From the rear of the steering wheel, remove the horn cover-to-steering wheel screws. Disconnect the horn electrical connector from the steering wheel.

3. Remove the steering wheel-to-column retainer, nut, washer (if equipped) and damper assembly.

4. Using a marking tool, mark the steering wheel alignment with the steering shaft for realignment purposes.

5. Using the Steering Wheel Puller tool No. J-1859-03 or equivalent, press the steering wheel from the steering column.

6. To install, reverse the removal procedures. Torque the steering wheel nut to 30 ft. lbs.

Combination Switch

The combination switch consists of the turn signal assembly and cruise control lever.

REMOVAL & INSTALLATION

NOTE: Tool No. J-35689-A or equivalent, is required to remove the terminals from the connector on the turn signal switch.

1. Refer to the "Steering Wheel, Removal and Installation" in this section and remove the steering wheel.

2. Pull the turn signal cancelling cam assembly from the steering shaft.

3. Remove the hazard warning knob-to-steering column screw and the knob.

NOTE: Before removing the turn signal assembly, position the turn signal lever so the turn turn signal assembly-to-steering column screws can all be removed.

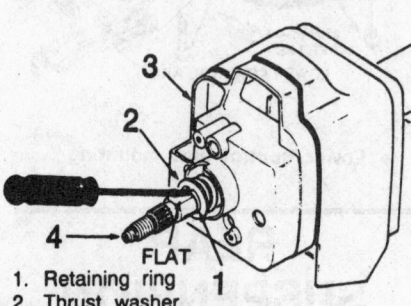

1. Retaining ring
2. Thrust washer
3. Turn signal switch housing
4. Steering shaft assembly

Removing turn signal switch housing

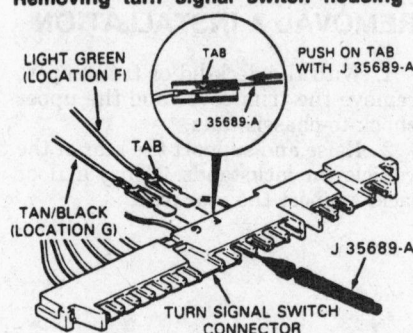

LIGHT GREEN (LOCATION F)

TAB

PUSH ON TAB WITH J 35689-A

J 35689-A

TAB

TAN/BLACK (LOCATION G)

J 35689-A

TURN SIGNAL SWITCH CONNECTOR

Removing terminals from turn signal switch connector

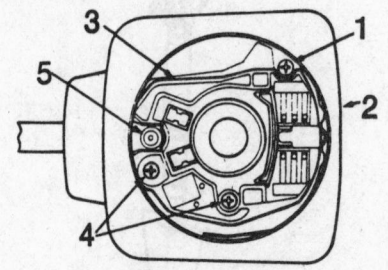

1. Screw
2. Housing cover
3. Turn signal switch
4. Screw
5. Self tapping screw

Turn signal switch mounting

4. Remove the column housing cover-to-column housing bowl screw and the cover.

NOTE: If equipped with cruise control, disconnect the cruise control electrical connector.

5. Remove the turn signal lever-to-pivot assembly screw and the lever; one screw is in the front and one is in the rear.

6. Using the Terminal Remover tool No. J-35689-A or equivalent, disconnect and label the wires "F" and "G" on the connector at the buzzer switch assembly from the turn signal switch electrical harness connector.

7. Remove the turn signal switch-to-steering column screws and the switch.

8. To install, reverse the removal procedures. Torque the turn signal switch-to-steering column screws to 35 inch lbs. and the steering wheel nut to 30 ft. lbs.

Ignition Lock/Switch

REMOVAL & INSTALLATION

1. Disconnect the negative terminal from the battery. Remove the left-side lower trim panel.

2. Remove the steering column-to-support screws and lower the steering column.

3. Disconnect the dimmer switch and turn signal switch connectors.

4. Remove the wiring harness-to-firewall nuts and steering column.

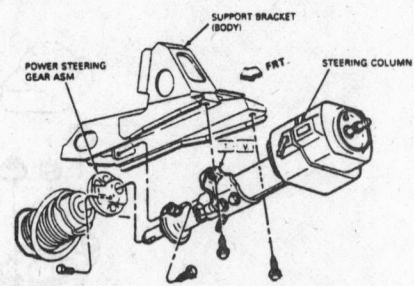

SUPPORT BRACKET (BODY)

POWER STEERING GEAR ASM

FRT

STEERING COLUMN

Steering column mounting

Ignition lock cylinder removal

5. Remove the steering column-to-steering gear bolt and the steering column from the vehicle.

6. Refer to the "Combination Switch, Removal and Installation" procedures in this section and remove the combination switch.

7. Place the lock cylinder in the Run position.

8. Remove the steering shaft assembly and turn signal switch housing as an assembly.

9. Using the Terminal Remover tool No. J-35689-A or equivalent, disconnect and label the wires "F" and "G" on the connector at the buzzer switch assembly from the turn signal switch electrical harness connector.

10. Place the lock cylinder in the Run position and remove the buzzer switch.

11. Place the lock cylinder in the Accessory position, then, remove the lock cylinder retaining screw and the lock cylinder.

12. Remove the dimmer switch nut/bolt, the dimmer switch and actuator rod.

13. Remove the dimmer switch mounting stud (the mounting nut was mounted to it).

14. Remove the ignition switch-to-steering column screws and the ignition switch.

15. Remove the lock bolt screws and the lock bolt.

16. Remove the switch actuator rack and ignition switch.

17. Remove the steering shaft lock and spring.

18. To install, reverse the removal procedures. Torque the steering Lock screw 27 inch lbs., the dimmer Switch stud to 35 inch lbs., the turn signal switch housing screws to 88 inch lbs., the turn signal switch screws to 35 inch lbs. and the steering wheel lock nut to 30 ft. lbs.

19. To install the lock bolt, lubricate it with lithium grease and install the lock bolt, spring and retaining plate.

20. Lubricate the teeth on the switch actuator rack, then, install the rack and the ignition switch through the opening in the steering bolt until it rests on the retaining plate.

21. Install the steering column lock cylinder set by holding the barrel of the lock cylinder, insert the key and turning the key to the Accessory position.

22. Install the lock set in the steering column while holding the rack against the lock plate.

23. Install the lock retaining screw. Insert the key in the lock cylinder and turn the lock cylinder to the Start position and the rack will extend.

24. Center the slotted holes on the ignition switch mounting plate and install the ignition switch mounting screw and nut.

25. Install the dimmer switch and actuator rod into the center slot on the switch mounting plate.

26. Install the buzzer switch and turn the lock cylinder to the Run position. Push the switch in until it is bottomed out with the plastic tab that covers the lock retaining screw.

27. Install the steering shaft and turn signal housing as an assembly.

28. Install the turn signal switch. To complete the installation, reverse the removal procedures.

Power Steering Gear

REMOVAL & INSTALLATION

1. From inside the vehicle, remove the left-side lower sound insulator.

2. Remove the upper steering shaft-to-steering rack coupling pinch bolt.

3. Place a drain pan under the steering gear and disconnect the pressure lines from the steering gear.

4. Raise and support the front of the vehicle on jackstands.

5. Remove both front wheel and tire assemblies.

6. Using the Ball Joint Remover tool No. J-24319-01 or equivalent, disconnect the tie rod ends from the steering knuckles.

7. Lower the vehicle.

8. Remove both steering gear-to-chassis clamps.

9. Slide the steering gear forward and remove the lower steering shaft-to-steering rack coupling pinch bolt.

10. From the firewall, disconnect the coupling and seal from the steering gear.

11. Raise and support the front of the vehicle on jackstands.

12. Through the left-wheel opening, remove the steering gear with the tie rods.

13. To install, reverse the removal procedures. Torque the steering gear-to-chassis clamp bolts to 28 ft. lbs., the tie rod nut to 44 ft. lbs. and the fluid lines to 18 ft. lbs. Bleed the power steering system after installation.

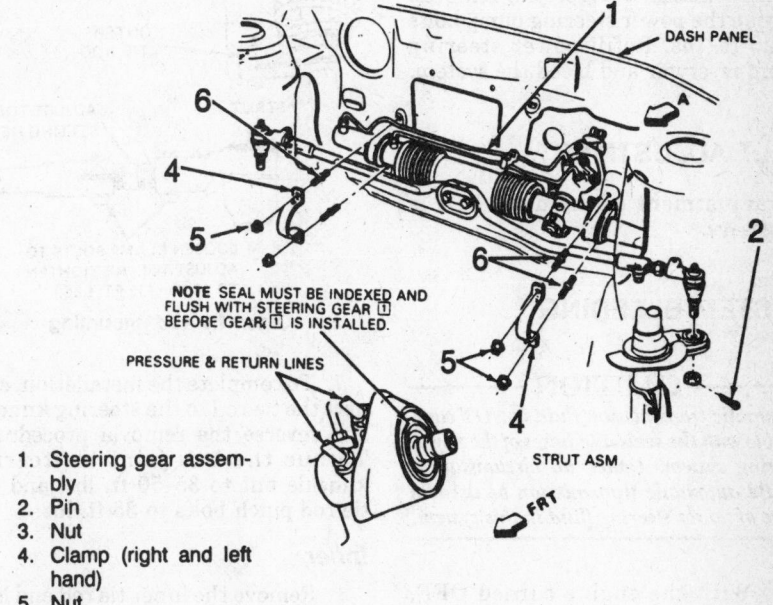

NOTE SEAL MUST BE INDEXED AND FLUSH WITH STEERING GEAR ① BEFORE GEAR ① IS INSTALLED.

PRESSURE & RETURN LINES

1. Steering gear assembly
2. Pin
3. Nut
4. Clamp (right and left hand)
5. Nut
6. Stud

DASH PANEL

STRUT ASM

FRT

Power steering gear mounting

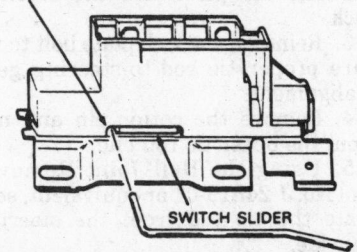

PLACE SWITCH SLIDER IN FAR LEFT POSITION

SWITCH SLIDER

Ignition switch installation position

ADJUSTMENT

1. Raise and support the front of the vehicle.

2. With the front tires off the ground, loosen the lock nut on the bottom of the steering rack.

3. Turn the adjuster plug clockwise until it bottoms out in the housing.

4. Turn the adjuster plug in the opposite direction 50–70°.

5. Torque the lock nut to 50 ft. lbs. while holding the adjuster plug.

NOTE: If the adjuster plug is not held, damage to the pinion teeth on the steering rack will occur.

6. Check to make sure that the steering wheel returns to center.

Power Steering Pump

REMOVAL & INSTALLATION

1. Disconnect the negative terminal from the battery.
2. Remove the pressure and return hoses from the pump and drain the system into a suitable container.
3. Cap the fittings at the pump.
4. Remove the serpentine belt.
5. Locate the pump attaching bolts through the pulley and remove the bolts.
6. Remove the pump assembly.
7. To install, reverse the removal. Torque the power steering pump bolts to 20 ft. lbs. Refill power steering pump reservoir and bleed the system.

BELT ADJUSTMENT

No adjustment of the drive belt is necessary.

SYSTEM BLEEDING

──── **CAUTION** ────

Automatic transmission fluid is NOT compatible with the seals and hoses of the power steering system. Under no circumstances should automatic transmission be used in place of power steering fluid in this system.

1. With the engine turned OFF, turn the wheels all the way to the left.
2. Fill the reservoir with power steering fluid until the level is at the Cold mark on the reservoir.
3. Start and Run the engine at fast idle for 15 seconds. Turn the engine OFF.
4. Recheck the fluid level and fill it to the Cold mark.
5. Start the engine and bleed the system by turning the wheels in both directions slowly to the stops.
6. Stop the engine and check the fluid. Fluid that still has air in it will be a light tan color.
7. Repeat this procedure until all of the air is removed from the system.

Tie Rod Ends

REMOVAL & INSTALLATION

Outer

1. Raise and support the front of the vehicle on jackstands. Remove the wheel and tire assembly.
2. Remove the cotter pin and nut from the outer tie rod end.
3. Loosen the outer tie rod pinch bolts.
4. Using the Ball Joint Remover tool No. J-24319-01 or equivalent, separate the tie rod from the steering knuckle.
5. Remove the outer tie rod from the adjuster by counting the exact number of turns required to remove it. This will allow proper installation without having to reset the toe in.
6. Install the new tie rod end by turning it in the same amount of turns as during the removal.

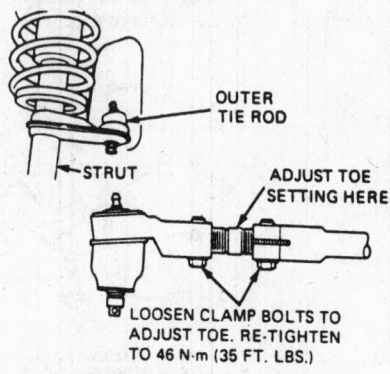

Outer tie rod mounting

7. To complete the installation, connect the tie rod to the steering knuckle and reverse the removal procedures. Torque the ball joint-to-steering knuckle nut to 35–50 ft. lbs. and the tie rod pinch bolts to 35 ft. lbs.

Inner

1. Remove the inner tie rod end lock plate bolt. If both inner tie rods are being replaced, discard the used lock plate.
2. Slide the inner tie rod out from between the plate and the steering rack.
3. Reinstall the lock plate bolt to insure proper tie rod-to-steering gear realignment.
4. Remove the cotter pin and nut from the outer tie rod end.
5. Using the Ball Joint Remover tool No. J-24319-01 or equivalent, separate the tie rod from the steering knuckle.
6. Remove the inner and outer tie rod assembly from the vehicle.

7. Note the position of the inner and outer tie rods in relation to each other. Place the assembly in a vise and loosen the adjuster pinch bolts.
8. Remove the outer tie rod from the adjuster by counting the exact number of turns required to remove it. This will allow proper installation without having to reset the toe in.
9. To install, place the new inner tie rod in the vise and install the outer tie rod end and adjuster the same amount of turns as when removing it.
10. Check the alignment between the inner and outer tie rods is the same as during removal.
11. To complete the installation, use a new lock plate and reverse the removal procedures. Torque the inner tie rod-to-lock plate bolts to 65 ft. lbs., the pinch bolts to 35 ft. lbs. and the outer tie rod nut to 35–50 ft. lbs.

BRAKES

NOTE: For all brake system repair service procedures not detailed below, please refer to "Brakes" in the Unit Repair section.

Master Cylinder

REMOVAL & INSTALLATION

1. Disconnect the electrical connector from the fluid level sensor.
2. Disconnect and cap the four (4) brake lines on the master cylinder.

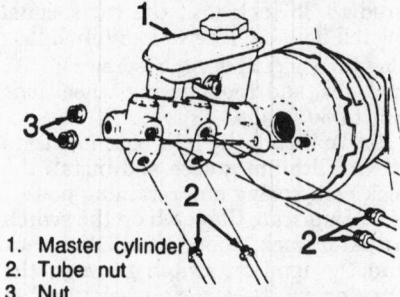

1. Master cylinder
2. Tube nut
3. Nut

Master cylinder mounting

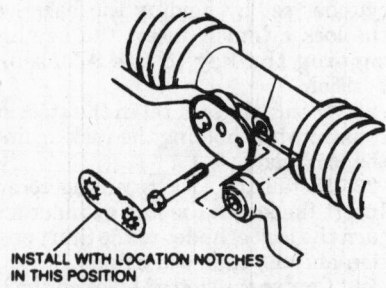

INSTALL WITH LOCATION NOTCHES IN THIS POSITION

Inner tie rod mounting

3. Remove the master cylinder-to-power booster nuts and the master cylinder with the reservoir attached.

4. To install, bench bleed the new master cylinder and reverse the removal procedures. Torque the master cylinder-to-power booster nuts to 20 ft. lbs. and the brake lines-to-master cylinder to 13 ft. lbs. Connect the fluid level electrical sensor wires. Refill the reservoir with an approved DOT 3 brake fluid and bleed the brake system.

Proportioning Valve

REMOVAL & INSTALLATION

NOTE: It may be necessary to remove the reservoir in order to remove the proportioning valve. If the reservoir is removed, bleed the brake system when finished.

1. Remove the proportioning valve cap on the master cylinder.
2. Remove and discard the O-rings.
3. Remove the springs, the proportioning valve pistons and the seals from the valves.
4. Inspect the valves for corrosion or abnormal wear; to replace, if necessary.

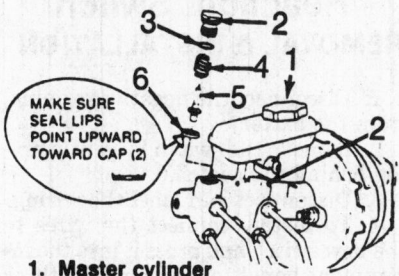

MAKE SURE SEAL LIPS POINT UPWARD TOWARD CAP (2)

1. **Master cylinder**
2. **Proportioning valve cap**
3. **O-ring**
4. **Spring**
5. **Proportioning valve piston**
6. **Proportioning valve seal**

Proportioning valve Installation

5. Clean all parts in denatured alcohol and dry them with air before reassembling.
6. To install, use new O-rings (coated with silicone grease) and reverse the removal procedures. Install the new seals on the pistons with the lip facing the cap. Torque the caps to 20 ft. lbs. Refill the reservoir and bleed the brake system.

Wheel Cylinder

REMOVAL & INSTALLATION

1. Raise and support the rear of the vehicle on jackstands. Remove the wheel/tire assembly and brake drum. Remove the brake shoes and attaching hardware.

2. Clean any dirt from around the wheel cylinder.
3. Disconnect and plug the brake line from the wheel cylinder.
4. Remove the wheel cylinder-to-backing plate bolt and lockwasher.
5. Remove the wheel cylinder.
6. To install, apply a liquid gasket to the shoulder of the wheel cylinder that faces the backing plate and reverse the removal procedures. Torque the wheel cylinder-to-backing plate bolt to 106 inch lbs. and the brake line-to-wheel cylinder to 13 ft. lbs. Bleed the brake system. Inspect the brake operation.

Power Brake Booster

REMOVAL & INSTALLATION

1. Refer to the "Master Cylinder, Removal and Installation" procedures in this section and remove the master cylinder.

NOTE: Place the master cylinder in an upright position to prevent fluid loss.

2. Remove the left lower trim panel inside the vehicle and disconnect the brake pedal-to-booster push rod from the brake pedal.
3. Disconnect the vacuum line from the booster.
4. Remove the brake booster mounting nuts and the booster.
5. To install, reverse the removal procedures. Torque the master cylinder-to-power booster to 20 ft. lbs. and the power booster mounting nuts to 20 ft. lbs. Bleed the brake system.

Parking Brake Cable

ADJUSTMENT

1. Apply and release the parking brake lever (10 clicks) at least 6 times. Apply the parking brake lever four (4) clicks.
2. Raise and support the rear of vehicle on jackstands.

3. Locate the access hole in the backing plate and adjust the parking brake cable until a ⅛ in. drill bit can be inserted between the the brake shoe webbing and the parking brake lever.
4. Check to make sure that a ¼ in. drill bit will NOT fit in the same position.
5. Release the parking brake and check to see if both wheels turn freely by hand.
6. Lower the vehicle.

REMOVAL & INSTALLATION

Front Cable

1. Raise and support the vehicle on jackstands.
2. Loosen, but do not remove, the equalizer nut to remove the cable.
3. Disconnect the cable from the equalizer and right-side cable.
4. Remove the hand grip from the parking brake lever inside the vehicle.
5. Remove the console.
6. Disconnect the cable from the parking brake lever.
7. Remove the nut holding the cable to the floor.
8. Remove the exhaust hanger bracket mounting nuts.
9. Remove the catalytic converter shield.
10. Remove the cable.
11. To install, Lubricate the cable and reverse the removal procedures. Adjust the parking brake.

Rear Cable

1. Raise and support the vehicle on jackstands.
2. Loosen the equalizer nut until the cable tension is released.
3. Disconnect the right-side cable button from the connector.
4. Disconnect the conduit end of the cable from the bracket on the axle.
5. Remove the wheel/tire assembly and the brake drum.
6. Disconnect the cable from the parking brake lever attached to the brake shoes.

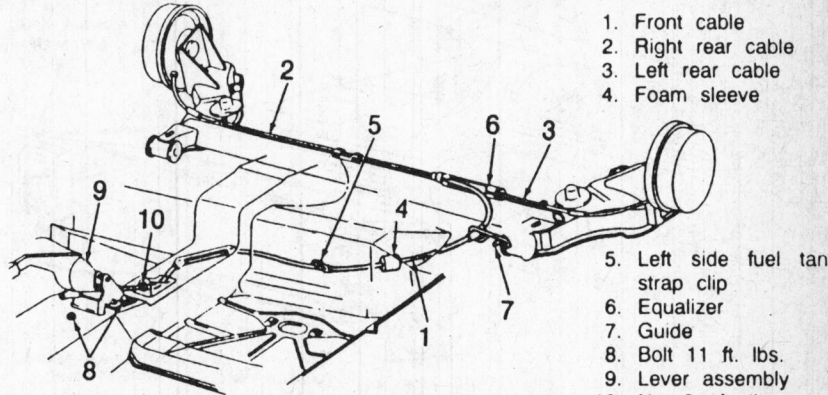

1. Front cable
2. Right rear cable
3. Left rear cable
4. Foam sleeve
5. Left side fuel tank strap clip
6. Equalizer
7. Guide
8. Bolt 11 ft. lbs.
9. Lever assembly
10. Nut 24 ft. lbs.

View of the parking brake cables—Beretta shown—Corsica similar

7. Remove the conduit end from the brake shoe backing plate.

8. To install, lubricate the cable and reverse the removal procedures. Adjust the parking brake.

CHASSIS ELECTRICAL

Heater Blower
REMOVAL & INSTALLATION

1. Disconnect the negative terminal from the battery.

2. Disconnect the electrical connections from the blower motor and resistor.

3. Remove the plastic water shield from the right-side of the cowl.

4. Remove the blower motor-to-chassis screws and the blower motor.

5. Remove the cage retaining nut and the cage.

6. Install the cage on the new blower motor with the opening facing away from the motor.

7. To complete the installation, reverse the removal procedures.

Heater Core

REMOVAL & INSTALLATION

1. Drain the cooling system.

2. Disconnect the heater hoses from the heater core.

3. Remove the heater air outlet deflector.

4. Remove the heater core cover, the heater core and retaining straps.

5. To install, reverse the removal procedures. Refill and bleed the cooling system. Start the engine, allow it to reach normal operating temperatures and check for leaks.

Radio
REMOVAL & INSTALLATION

1. Remove the trim panel from the radio.

NOTE: The Corsica trim panel is attached by clips and pulls off. The Beretta trim panel is attached by two screws from under the panel.

2. With the trim panel removed, the radio will pull outwards.

3. Disconnect and label the radio wiring, then, remove the radio.

4. To install, reverse the removal procedures.

Windshield Wiper Switch
REMOVAL & INSTALLATION

1. Disconnect the negative terminal from the battery.

2. Remove the switch by gently prying behind the switch.

3. Disconnect and label the wiring.

4. Connect the wires to the new switch and press it into the instrument panel to the same depth as the old switch.

5. Reconnect the negative battery cable and check the wiper operation.

Windshield Wiper Motor
REMOVAL & INSTALLATION

1. Disconnect the negative terminal from the battery.

2. Remove the left-side wiper arm.

3. Disconnect the wiper motor drive link from the crank arm.

4. Disconnect the electrical connectors and washer hoses.

5. Remove the wiper motor-to-chassis bolts and the wiper motor by guiding the crank arm through the hole.

6. To install, reverse the removal procedures.

Instrument Cluster
REMOVAL & INSTALLATION

1. Disconnect the negative terminal from the battery.

2. Remove the screw in the upper center of the instrument cluster trim plate.

3. Slide the steering column seal out and remove the trim plate by pulling it straight outwards.

4. Remove the two (2) upper instrument cluster-to-dash screws and pull the instrument cluster straight outwards, then, disconnect and label the electrical connectors.

5. To install, position the instrument cluster close to the wiring harness and connect the harness.

6. Slide the instrument cluster into the mounting clips and install the mounting screws.

7. Install the cluster trim plate, slide the steering column seal in place and connect the negative battery cable.

Headlight Switch
REMOVAL & INSTALLATION

1. Disconnect the negative terminal from the battery.

2. Remove the switch by gently prying behind the switch.

3. Disconnect and label the wiring.

4. To install, connect the wires to the new switch and press it into the instrument panel to the same depth as the old switch and reverse the removal procedures.

Stoplight Switch

REMOVAL & INSTALLATION

1. Disconnect the negative terminal from the battery.

2. Remove the lower-left trim panel. Locate the stoplight switch on the brake pedal support.

3. Disconnect the plug on the switch and remove the switch by twisting it out of the tubular retaining clip.

4. Install the new switch using a new retaining clip and connect the wire.

5. Adjust the switch by pulling back on the brake pedal noting the "clicks" as the switch is pushed through the retaining clip.

6. Repeat the procedure until no "clicks" can be heard.

7. Connect the negative battery cable and check the switch operation.

Exploded view of the instrument panel—Corsica shown—Beretta similar

Chevrolet
Rear Wheel Drive
Corvette

12

SERIAL NUMBER IDENTIFICATION

VEHICLE IDENTIFICATION CHART

It is important for servicing and ordering parts to be certain of the vehicle and engine identification. The VIN (vehicle identification number) is a 17 digit number visible through the windshield on the driver's side of the dash and contains the vehicle and engine identification codes. The tenth digit indicates model year, and the eighth digit indicates engine code. It can be interpreted as follows:

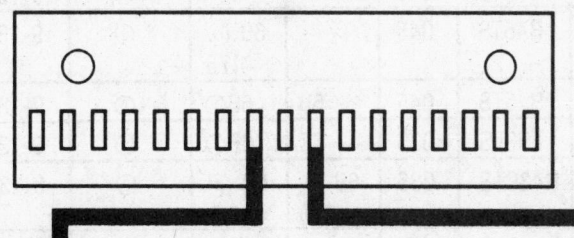

Engine Code						Model Year	
Code	Cu. In.	Liters	Cyl.	Fuel Sys.	Eng. Mfg.	Code	Year
8 ('82)	350	5.7	8	TBI	Chevy	C	1982
8 ('84)	350	5.7	8	CFI	Chevy	D	1983
8 ('85)	350	5.7	8	TPI	Chevy	E	1984
8 ('86)	350	5.7	8	TPI	Chevy	F	1985
8 ('87)	350	5.7	8	TPI	Chevy	G	1986
8 ('88-'89)	350	5.7	8	TPI	Chevy	H	1987
						J	1988
						K	1989

GENERAL ENGINE SPECIFICATIONS

Year	VIN	No. Cylinder Displacement cu. in. (liter)	Fuel System Type	Net Horsepower @ rpm	Net Torque @ rpm (ft.lbs.)	Bore × Stroke (in.)	Compression Ratio	Oil Pressure @ rpm
1982	8	8-350 (5.7)	TBI	200 @ 4200	285 @ 2800	4.000 × 3.480	9.0:1	45 @ 2000
1984	8	8-350 (5.7)	CFI	205 @ 4300	290 @ 2800	4.000 × 3.480	9.0:1	50-65 @ 2000
1985	8	8-350 (5.7)	TPI	205 @ 4300	290 @ 2800	4.000 × 3.480	9.0:1	50-65 @ 2000
1986	8	8-350 (5.7)	TPI	230 @ 4000	330 @ 3200	4.000 × 3.480	9.0:1	50-65 @ 2000
1987	8	8-350 (5.7)	TPI	230 @ 4000	330 @ 3200	4.000 × 3.480	9.5:1	50-65 @ 2000
1988-89	8	8-350 (5.7)	TPI	245 @ 4300 ①	340 @ 3200 ②	4.000 × 3.480	9.5:1	50-65 @ 2000

TBI — Throttle Body Injection
CFI — Cross Fire Injection
TPI — Tuned Port Injection
① Convertible: 240 @ 4000
② Convertible: 335 @ 3200

GASOLINE ENGINE TUNE-UP SPECIFICATIONS

Year	VIN	No. Cylinder Displacement cu. in. (liter)	Spark Plugs Type	Spark Plugs Gap (in.)	Ignition Timing (deg.) MT	Ignition Timing (deg.) AT	Compression Pressure (psi)	Fuel Pump (psi)	Idle Speed (rpm) MT	Idle Speed (rpm) AT	Valve Clearance In.	Valve Clearance Ex.
1982	8	8-350 (5.7)	R45TS	.045	—	—	②	9-13	—	—	Hyd.	Hyd.
1984	8	8-350 (5.7)	R45TS	.045	—	6B @ 475	②	9-13	—	475	Hyd.	Hyd.
1985	8	8-350 (5.7)	R45TS	.045	6B	6B①	②	9-13	450	400①	Hyd.	Hyd.
1986	8	8-350 (5.7)	FR3LS	.035	6B	6B①	②	9-13	450	400①	Hyd.	Hyd.
1987	8	8-350 (5.7)	R43CTS	.035	6B @ 450	6B @ 400①	②	9-13	450	400①	Hyd.	Hyd.
1988	8	8-350 (5.7)	FR3CLS	.035	④	④	②	3-10	450③	450③	Hyd.	Hyd.
1989				SEE UNDERHOOD SPECIFICATIONS STICKER								

① In Drive
② When checking cylinder compression pressures, the throttle should be open, all spark plugs should be removed and the battery should be near or at full charge. The lowest reading cylinder should not be less than 70% of the highest cylinder. No individual cylinder reading should be less than 100 lbs.
③ Minimum idle speed specification shown. Idle speed is usually a non-adjustable specification controlled by the ECM
④ Refer to VEHICLE EMISSION CONTROL INFORMATION label for ignition timing specifications. If no specifications are shown, no adjustment is required

CAPACITIES

Year	VIN	No. Cylinder Displacement cu. in. (liter)	Engine Crankcase with Filter	Engine Crankcase without Filter	Transmission (pts.) MT	Transmission (pts.) AT	Drive Axle (pts.)	Fuel Tank (gals.)	Cooling System (qts.)
1982	8	8-350 (5.7)	5	4	—	10	4	24	22
1984	8	8-350 (5.7)	5	4	3.5 ①	10	3.75	20	14
1985	8	8-350 (5.7)	5	4	3.5 ①	10	3.75	20	14
1986	8	8-350 (5.7)	5	4	3.5 ①	10	3.75	20	14
1987	8	8-350 (5.7)	5	4	3.5 ①	10	3.75	20	14
1988-89	8	8-350 (5.7)	5	4	3.5①	10	3.75	20	14

① Four speed overdrive uses Dexron II in the overdrive section and 80WGL5 in the transmission section

FIRING ORDERS

NOTE: To avoid confusion, always replace spark plug wires one at a time.

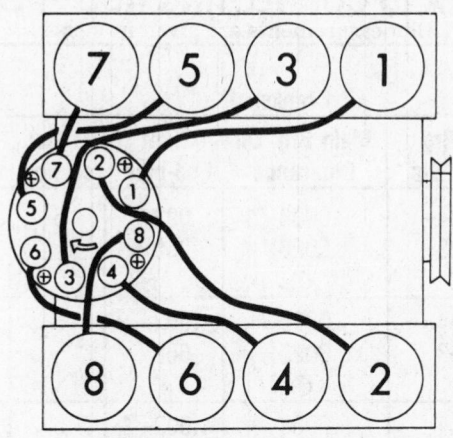

GM (Chevrolet) V8
Engine firing order: 1-8-4-3-6-5-7-2
Distributor rotation: clockwise

CAMSHAFT SPECIFICATIONS
All measurements given in inches.

Year	VIN	No. Cylinder Displacement cu. in. (liter)	Journal Diameter 1	2	3	4	5	Lobe Lift In.	Ex.	Bearing Clearance	Camshaft End Play
1982	8	8-350 (5.7)	1.8682–1.8692	1.8682–1.8692	1.8682–1.8692	1.8682–1.8692	1.8682–1.8692	.2733①	.2820①	—	.004–.012
1984	8	8-350 (5.7)	1.8682–1.8692	1.8682–1.8692	1.8682–1.8692	1.8682–1.8692	1.8682–1.8692	.2733①	.2820①	—	.004–.012
1985	8	8-350 (5.7)	1.8682–1.8692	1.8682–1.8692	1.8682–1.8692	1.8682–1.8692	1.8682–1.8692	.2733①	.2820①	—	.004–.012
1986	8	8-350 (5.7)	1.8682–1.8692	1.8682–1.8692	1.8682–1.8692	1.8682–1.8692	1.8682–1.8692	.2733①	.2820①	—	.004–.012
1987	8	8-350 (5.7)	1.8682–1.8692	1.8682–1.8692	1.8682–1.8692	1.8682–1.8692	1.8682–1.8692	.2733①	.2820①	—	.004–.012
1988-89	8	8-350 (5.7)	1.8682–1.8692	1.8682–1.8692	1.8682–1.8692	1.8682–1.8692	1.8682–1.8692	.2733①	.2820①	—	.004–.012

① ± .002

CRANKSHAFT AND CONNECTING ROD SPECIFICATIONS
All measurements are given in inches.

Year	VIN	No. Cylinder Displacement cu. in. (liter)	Crankshaft Main Brg. Journal Dia.	Main Brg. Oil Clearance	Shaft End-play	Thrust on No.	Connecting Rod Journal Diameter	Oil Clearance	Side Clearance
1982	8	8-350 (5.7)	2.4484–2.4493 ①	.0008–.0020 ②	.002–.006	5	2.0988–2.0998	.0013–.0035	.008–.014
1984	8	8-350 (5.7)	2.4484–2.4493 ①	.0008–.0020 ②	.002–.006	5	2.0988–2.0998	.0013–.0035	.008–.014
1985	8	8-350 (5.7)	2.4484–2.4493 ①	.0008–.0020 ②	.002–.006	5	2.0988–2.0998	.0013–.0035	.008–.014
1986	8	8-350 (5.7)	2.4484–2.4493 ①	.0008–.0020 ②	.002–.006	5	2.0988–2.0998	.0013–.0035	.006–.014
1987	8	8-350 (5.7)	2.4484–2.4493 ①	.0008–.0020 ②	.002–.006	5	2.0988–2.0998	.0013–.0035	.006–.014
1988-89	8	8-350 (5.7)	2.4484–2.4493 ①	.0008–.0020 ②	.002–.006	5	2.0988–2.0998	.0013–.0035	.006–.014

① Specification applies to the No. 1 bearing.
Nos. 2, 3, 4 — 2.4481-2.4490
No. 5 — 2.4479-2.4488

② Specification applies to the No. 1 bearing.
Nos. 2, 3, 4 — .0011-.0023
No. 5 — .0017-.0032
Specifications shown apply to new components

VALVE SPECIFICATIONS

Year	VIN	No. Cylinder Displacement cu. in. (liter)	Seat Angle (deg.)	Face Angle (deg.)	Spring Test Pressure (lbs.)	Spring Installed Height (in.)	Stem-to-Guide Clearance (in.)		Stem Diameter (in.)	
							Intake	Exhaust	Intake	Exhaust
1982	8	8-350 (5.7)	46	45	194-206 @ 1.25①	$1^{23}/_{32}$②	.0010–.0027	.0010–.0027	.3410–.3417	.3410–.3417
1984	8	8-350 (5.7)	46	45	194-206 @ 1.25①	$1^{23}/_{32}$②	.0010–.0027	.0010–.0027	.3410–.3417	.3410–.3417
1985	8	8-350 (5.7)	46	45	194-206 @ 1.25①	$1^{23}/_{32}$②	.0010–.0027	.0010–.0027	.3410–.3417	.3410–.3417
1986	8	8-350 (5.7)	46	45	194-206 @ 1.25①	$1^{23}/_{32}$②	.0010–.0027	.0010–.0027	.3410–.3417	.3410–.3417
1987	8	8-350 (5.7)	46	45	194-206 @ 1.25①	$1^{23}/_{32}$②	.0010–.0027	.0010–.0027	.3410–.3417	.3410–.3417
1988-89	8	8-350 (5.7)	46	45	194-206 @ 1.25①	$1^{23}/_{32}$②	.0010–.0027	.0010–.0027	.3410–.3417	.3410–.3417

① 1.16: exhaust valve
② $1^{19}/_{32}$: exhaust

PISTON AND RING SPECIFICATIONS
All measurments are given in inches.

Year	VIN	No. Cylinder Displacement cu. in. (liter)	Piston Clearance	Ring Gap			Ring Side Clearance		
				Top Compression	Bottom Compression	Oil Control	Top Compression	Bottom Compression	Oil Control
1982	6	8-350 (5.7)	.0046–.0061	.010–.020	.010–.023	.015–.065	.0012–.0032	.0012–.0032	.002–.007
1984	8	8-350 (5.7)	.0025–.0035	.010–.020	.010–.025	.015–.055	.0012–.0032	.0012–.0032	.002–.007
1985	8	8-350 (5.7)	.0025–.0035	.010–.020	.010–.025	.015–.055	.0012–.0032	.0012–.0032	.002–.007
1986	8	8-350 (5.7)	.0025–.0035	.010–.020	.010–.025	.015–.055	.0012–.0032	.0012–.0032	.002–.007
1987	8	8-350 (5.7)	.0007–.0017 ①	.010–.020	.013–.025	.015–.055	.0012–.0032	.0012–.0029	.002–.008
1988-89	8	8-350 (5.7)	.0007–.0017 ①	.010–.020	.013–.025	.015–.055	.0012–.0029	.0012–.0029	.002–.008

① .0025 Max.

TORQUE SPECIFICATIONS
All readings in ft. lbs.

Year	VIN	No. Cylinder Displacement cu. in. (liter)	Cylinder Head Bolts	Main Bearing Bolts	Rod Bearing Bolts	Crankshaft Pulley Bolts	Flywheel Bolts	Manifold Intake	Manifold Exhaust	Spark Plugs
1982	8	8-350 (5.7)	65	80	45	60	60	30	20①	17-27
1984	8	8-350 (5.7)	65	80	45	60	60	30	20	22
1985	8	8-350 (5.7)	65	80	45	60	60	30	20	22
1986	8	8-350 (5.7)	65 ②	80	45	60	60	30	20	22
1987	8	8-350 (5.7)	65 ②	80	45	60	60	30	20	22
1988-89	8	8-350 (5.7)	60-75	80	45	59-81	60	35	20	22

① Inboard bolts: 30 ft. lbs.
② Long and medium; short 60 ft.lbs.

BRAKE SPECIFICATIONS
All measurements in inches unless noted

Year	Model	Lug Nut Torque (ft. lbs.)	Master Cylinder Bore	Brake Disc Minimum Thickness	Brake Disc Maximum Runout	Standard Brake Drum Diameter	Minimum Lining Thickness Front	Minimum Lining Thickness Rear
1982	Corvette	70②	—	1.230	.005	—	.030①	.030①
1984	Corvette	100②	—	.724	.006	—	.062	.062
1985	Corvette	100②	—	.724	.006	—	.062	.062
1986	Corvette	100②	—	.724	.006	—	.062	.062
1987	Corvette	100②	—	.724	.006	—	.062	.062
1988-89	Corvette	100	—	.724	.006	—	.062	.062

① Rivit—.062 bonded
② Aluminum wheels—80

WHEEL ALIGNMENT

Year	Model		Caster Range (deg.)	Caster Preferred Setting (deg.)	Camber Range (deg.)	Camber Preferred Setting (deg.)	Toe-in (in.)	Steering Axis Inclination (deg.)
1982	Corvette	Front	1¼-3¼	2¼	0-1½	¾	¼	7¹¹⁄₁₆
		Rear	—	—	½N-½P	0	¹⁄₁₆	—
1984	Corvette	Front	2½-3½	3	⁵⁄₁₆-1⁵⁄₁₆	¹³⁄₁₆	⁵⁄₃₂	8¾
		Rear	—	—	½N-½P	0	⁵⁄₃₂	—
1985	Corvette	Front	2½-3½	3	⁵⁄₁₆-1⁵⁄₁₆	¹³⁄₁₆	⁵⁄₃₂	8¾
		Rear	—	—	½N-½P	0	⁵⁄₃₂	—
1986	Corvette	Front	5½-6½	6	⁵⁄₁₆-1⁵⁄₁₆	¹³⁄₁₆	⁵⁄₃₂	8¾
		Rear	—	—	¹⁄₃₂N-²⁹⁄₃₂P	¹³⁄₃₂	⁵⁄₃₂	—
1987	Corvette	Front	4¹¹⁄₁₆-6⁵⁄₁₆	5½	⁵⁄₁₆-1⁵⁄₁₆	¹³⁄₁₆	³⁄₃₂	8¾
		Rear	—	—	¹⁄₁₆N-²⁹⁄₃₂P	¹³⁄₃₂	³⁄₃₂	—
1988	Corvette	Front	4¹¹⁄₁₆-6⁵⁄₁₆	5½	⁵⁄₁₆-1⁵⁄₁₆	¹³⁄₁₆	³⁄₃₂	8¾
		Rear	—	—	¹⁄₁₆N-²⁹⁄₃₂P	¹³⁄₃₂	³⁄₃₂	—

N—Negative
P—Positive

TUNE-UP PROCEDURES

Ignition Timing

ADJUSTMENT

The Electronic Spark Timing (EST) bypass wire from the distributor must be disconnected prior to the timing adjustment. Trace the four wires from the distributor housing which join at a common multi- connector, close to the distributor. Follow the tan wire with a black stripe (EST bypass wire) from the multiconnector. Past the multiconnector, the EST bypass wire has its own, single connector. Separate this connector before.adjusting the timing. While the EST bypass wire is disconnected, the CHECK ENGINE light on the instrument panel will illuminate. After adjusting the timing, reconnect the EST bypass connector; the CHECK ENGINE light will go out.

1984–89 vehicles incorporate an Electronic Spark Control (ESC) into the distributor which retards the spark advance when engine detonation occurs. If the controller fails, the result could be no ignition, no retard or full retard. Some engines will also have a magnetic timing probe hole for use with electronic timing equipment. Consult the manufacturer's instructions for the use of this equipment.

The use of an inductive pick-up timing light is recommended. Follow the timing light manufacturers instructions to attach the timing light. Due to the battery location of Corvettes, 12 volt DC timing lights may be connected as follows: positive lead—alternator BAT terminal; negative lead—ground on engine.

Do not use an older style timing light which requires piercing of the spark plug lead.

NOTE: It is not necessary to adjust the idle speed on 1982–89 vehicles prior to the timing adjustment, though the engine must be at normal operating temperature.

1. Disconnect the distributor spark advance hose and plug the vacuum opening.
2. Start the engine and run it at idle speed. Aim the timing light at the degree scale just over the harmonic balancer. The line on the balancer or pulley will align with the the timing mark.
3. If required, adjust the timing by loosening the securing clamp hold-down bolt and rotating the distributor until the desired ignition advance is achieved, then tighten the bolt.
4. To advance the timing, rotate the distributor opposite to the normal direction of rotor rotation. Retard the timing by rotating the distributor in the normal direction of rotor rotation. On vehicles with computer controlled emissions systems, follow the information on the underhood decal to set the timing.

Valve Lash

ADJUSTMENT

NOTE: The 350 V8 engine utilizes hydraulic lifters that normally require VERY little maintenance or adjustment. These components are simple in design and are best maintained through regular, scheduled engine oil changes. If the engine is running well and no audible "clicking" sounds are heard from the valve train, DO NOT attempt to remove or disassemble the valve lifters.

1. Remove the valve covers.
2. Tighten the rocker arm nuts until all lash is eliminated.

← FRONT

Intake and exhaust valve arrangement for the 350 engine

3. Adjust the valves when the lifter is on the base circle of the camshaft lobe by cranking the engine until the mark on the vibration damper lines up with the center or "0" mark on the timing tab fastened to the crankcase front cover and the engine is in the No.1 firing position.

NOTE: This may be determined by placing your fingers on the No. 1 valve as the mark on the damper comes near the "0" mark on the crankcase front cover. If the valves move as the mark comes up to the timing tab, the engine is in the No. 6 firing position and should be turned over one more time to reach to No. 1 firing position.

4. With the engine in the No. 1 firing position, adjust the following valves:
   a. Exhaust—1, 3, 4, 8.
   b. Intake—1, 2, 5, 7.
5. Back out adjusting nut until lash is felt at the push rod then turn in adjusting nut until all lash is removed. This can be determined by rotating push rod while turning adjusting nut. When play has been removed, turn adjusting nut in one full additional turn.
6. Crank the engine one revolution until the pointer "0" mark and the vibration damper mark are again in alignment. This is the No. 6 firing position.
7. With the engine in this position, adjust the following valves:
   a. Exhaust—2, 5, 6, 7.
   b. Intake—3, 4, 6, 8.
8. Install the rocker arm covers.
9. Start the engine and adjust the idle speed as required.

Idle Speed and Mixture

ADJUSTMENT

Fuel Injected Models

Vehicles manufactured from 1982 to 1985 are equipped with TBI fuel injection. The Model 400 Throttle Body Injection System (TBI) includes a pair of throttle body injection units, connected by a throttle rod, mounted in front and rear positions on a single manifold cover. This arrangement allows each

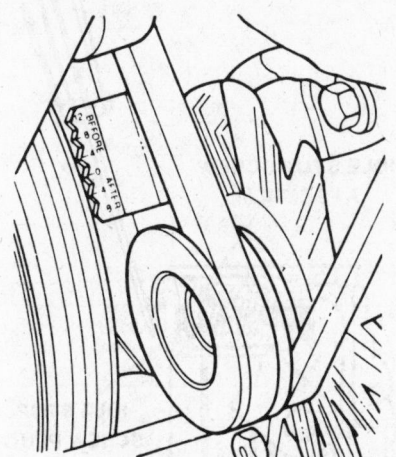

Timing mark–typical

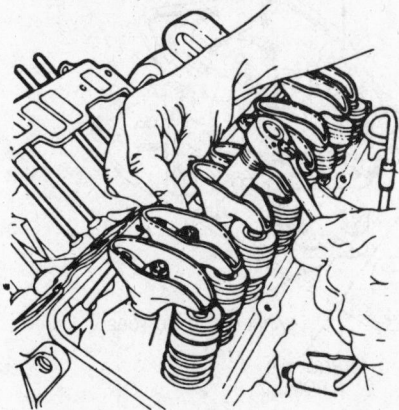

Valve adjustment procedure

TBI unit to supply the correct air/fuel mixture through a tuned crossover runner in the intake manifold to the bank of cylinders on the opposite side of the engine, thus the name "Crossfire Injection" or "CFI". In addition, a throttle bore tube or "Swirl plate" is located under the manifold cover, below each throttle valve, to aid in mixture distribution.

Another type of fuel injection is tune port injection (TPI). The introduction of this new TPI system has improved the torque and power of the V8 engine. The induction system for the TPI is made up of large forward mounted air cleaners, a new mass air flow sensor, a cast aluminum throttle body assembly with dual throttle blades, a large extended cast aluminum plenum, individual aluminum tuned runners and a protruding dual fuel rail assembly with computer controlled injectors. The base plate is cast aluminum and incorporates the crossover portion of the tuned runners. The base plate also serves as a mounting for the fuel injectors. The individual aluminum runners are designed to provide the best tuning or frequency of air pulses within the runners and for the optimum throttle response throughout the driving range, thus the name Tuned Port Injection. The runners are selected by length and size so to take advantage of the air pulses set up by the opening and closing of the intake valves. The high pressure pulses result in denser air at each intake valve, and timing the pressure pulses to occur during the valve open period forces more air into the combustion chamber, which results in a more efficient cylinder charging and improved volumetric efficiency.

Idle Speed Adjustment

TBI (THROTTLE BODY INJECTION)

1. Remove the air cleaner and the gasket.

2. Disconnect and plug the THERMAC vacuum port at the rear TBI unit.

3. If necessary, remove the plug covering the minimum air adjusting screw.

4. Block the wheels, set the parking brake, connect a tachometer to the engine, start the engine and allow the engine speed to stabilize.

5. Place the automatic transmission in Drive.

6. Using 2 tools J–33047, plug the idle air passages of each throttle body. Make sure that the tools are seated and no air leaks exist.

NOTE: When the plugs are installed, the rpm should drop below the curb idle speed. If the speed does not drop, check for an air leak.

7. At the rear TBI unit, remove the cap from the ported tube and connect a water manometer J–23951 or equivalent.

8. Adjust the minimum air adjustment screw to obtain 6 in. of water on the manometer. Remove the manometer and install the cap on the ported tube.

9. At the front TBI unit, remove the cap from the ported tube and connect the water manometer J–23951 or equivalent. The reading should be 6 in. of water on the manometer.

10. If the manometer reading is not correct, locate the idle balance screw on the throttle linkage. If the screw is welded, break the weld and install a new screw with thread sealing compound. Adjust the screw to obtain 6 in. of water on the manometer.

11. Remove the manometer and install the cap on the ported tube.

12. At the rear TBI unit, adjust the minimum air adjustment screw to obtain 475 rpm.

13. Stop the engine and remove the idle air passage plugs.

14. Place the transmission in Neutral and start the engine.

NOTE: The engine will run at a high rpm but will decrease when the IAC motors close the air passages. When the rpm drops, stop the engine.

15. Check the Throttle Position Sensor (TPS) voltage and adjust, if necessary.

NOTE: To reset the IAC motors, drive the vehicle at 30 mph or if equipped with cruise control, disconnect the speedometer cable at the transducer, turn the key ON and rotate the cable to 30 mph.

TPI (TUNED PORT INJECTION)

NOTE: The idle stop screw, used to regulate the minimum idle speed, is pre-set by the OEM at the factory. The idle stop screw is covered by a plug to retain the original adjustment and to discourage readjustment. The idle speed should only be adjusted if it is absolutely necessary. Prior to adjusting the idle speed, ensure that the ignition timing is correct and the area around the throttle plates is free from dirt and debris.

1. With the proper tool, pierce the idle stop plug and remove it.

2. Leave the idle air control motor connected and ground the diagnostic lead. Turn the ignition to the on position, but do not start the engine.

3. Wait a minimum of 30 seconds, and with the ignition switch still in the on position disconnect the idle air control connector.

4. Remove the ground from the diagnostic lead and start the engine.

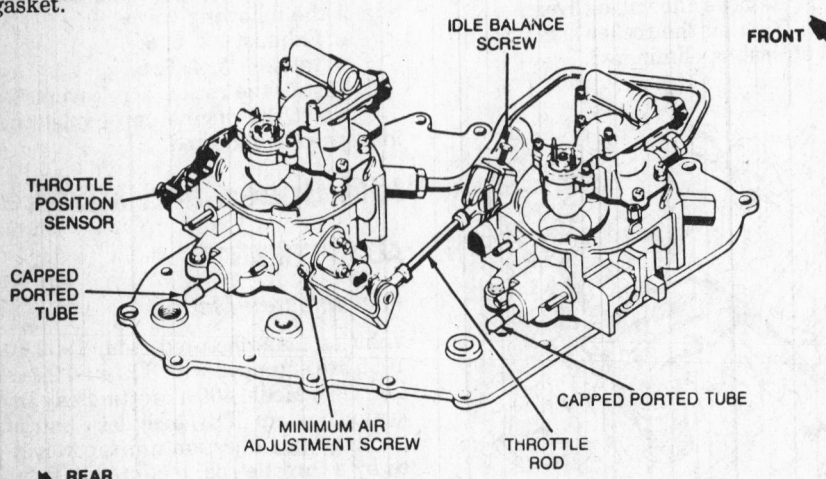

Model 400 Throttle Body Injection Unit (cross-fire injection system—twin throttle bodies

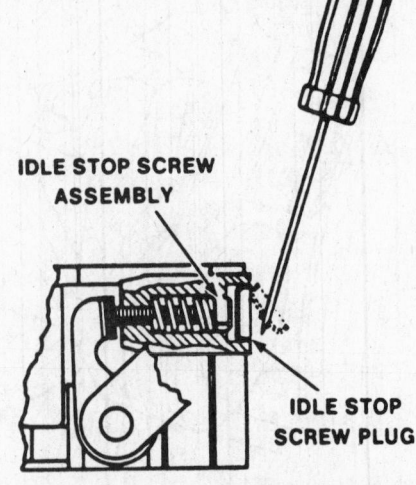

Removing the idle stop screw plug

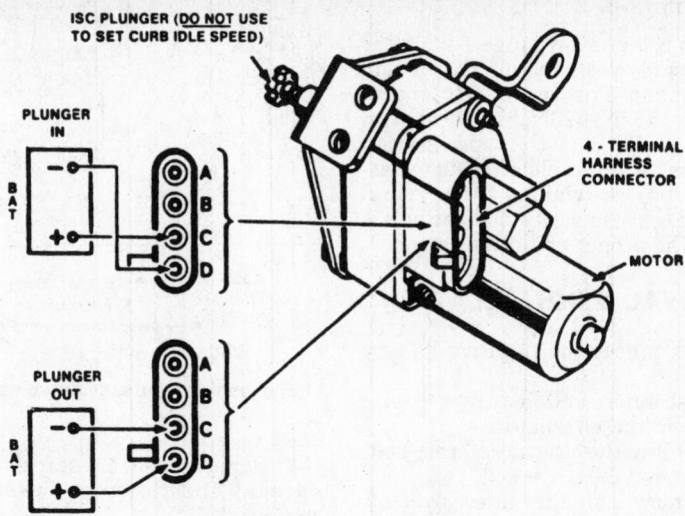

Idle speed control assembly

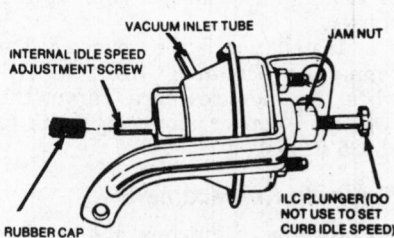

Idle load compensator

5. Allow the engine to go into the closed loop mode. Adjust the idle screw to 450 rpm in the neutral position for both manual and automatic transmissions.

6. Turn the ignition off and re-connect the idle speed control connector.

7. If necessary, adjust the throttle position sensor as follows. With the ignition switch in the "On" position, connect a "Scan" tool or 3 jumper wires to the TPS. Adjust the TPS to obtain a reading from 0.46–0.62 volts.

8. Start the engine and check the engine for proper idle operation.

ENGINE ELECTRICAL

Distributor

REMOVAL & INSTALLATION

Timing Not Disturbed

1. Disconnect the negative battery cable. Remove the air cleaner cover and distributor shield.

2. Disconnect the ignition switch battery feed wire and tachometer wire from the distributor cap (if equipped). Remove all electrical connections from the unit. Release the coil connectors from the distributor cap.

3. Remove the distributor cap retaining screws and remove the cap. Disconnect the four terminal harness from the distributor.

4. Remove the distributor hold down bolt. Note the position of the rotor and then pull the distributor assembly from the engine.

5. To insure correct ignition timing the distributor must be installed with the rotor in the same position as it was removed.

6. Installation is the reverse of the removal procedure.

Timing Disturbed

1. Disconnect the negative battery cable. Remove all the necessary components in order to gain access to the distributor assembly.

2. Remove all electrical connections from the unit. Release the coil connectors from the distributor cap.

3. Remove the distributor cap retaining screws or latches and remove the cap. Disconnect the four terminal harness from the distributor.

4. Remove the distributor hold down bolt. Note the position of the rotor and then pull the distributor assembly from the engine.

5. To insure correct ignition timing the distributor must be installed with the rotor in the same position as it was removed.

6. Installation is the reverse of the removal procedure.

7. If the engine has been cranked with the distributor out, remove the number one spark plug. Place your finger over the spark plug hole and crank the engine slowly until compression is felt.

8. Align the timing mark on the pulley to "0" on the engine timing indicator. Position the rotor between number one and number eight spark plug towers.

9. The distributor can now be correctly installed in the engine.

10. Once the distributor has been installed, check the engine timing and adjust as required.

Alternator

The vehicle is equipped with the CS type charging system. The alternator is available in two sizes; CS–130 and CS–140, denoting the outside diameter of the stator laminations. For further information on the charging system, please refer to "Charging and Starting" in the Unit Repair Section.

PRECAUTIONS

• If the battery is removed for any reason, make sure it is reconnected with the correct polarity. Reversing the battery connections may result in damage to the one-way rectifiers.

• When utilizing a booster battery as a starting aid, always connect the positive to positive terminals, and the negative terminal from the booster battery to a good engine ground on the car being started.

• Never use a fast charger as a booster to start vehicles with alternating-current (AC) circuits.

• Disconnect the battery cables when charging the battery with a fast charger.

• Never attempt to polarize an alternator.

• Avoid long soldering times when making alternator repairs. Prolonged heat will damage the alternator.

• Do not use test lamps of more than 12 volts when checking diode continuity.

• Do not short across or ground any of the alternator terminals.

• The polarity of the battery, alternator and regulator must be matched and considered before making any electrical connections within the system.

• Never separate the alternator on an open circuit. Make sure all connections within the circuit are clean and tight.

• Disconnect the battery ground terminal when performing any service on electrical components. Ensure that all the battery terminal and cable connections are clean.

• Disconnect the battery if arc welding is to be done on the vehicle.

BELT TENSION ADJUSTMENT

NOTE: On 1984–89 engines, a single serpentine belt is used to drive all accessories formerly driven with V-belts. Belt tension is maintained by a spring loaded tensioner which has the ability to maintain belt tension over a broad range of belt lengths. There is an indicator to make sure the tensioner is adjusted to within its operating range. The belt tension is adjusted with a ½ in. breaker bar inserted into the square hole in the tensioner arm and a belt tension gauge (BT-7825 or equivalent).

Except Serpentine Belt

Using belt tension gauge J–23600 or equivalent adjust the alternator belt if the tension is below 300N, as indicated on the gauge. If the belt is used the correct belt tension is 600N, as indicated on the gauge. If the belt is new the correct tension is 900N, as indicated on the gauge.

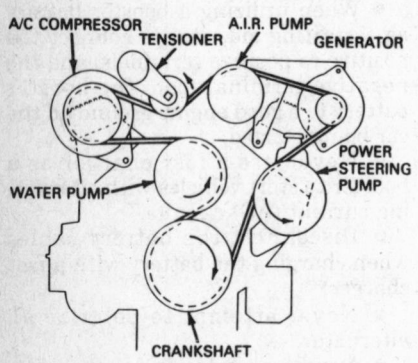

Serpentine drive belt installation

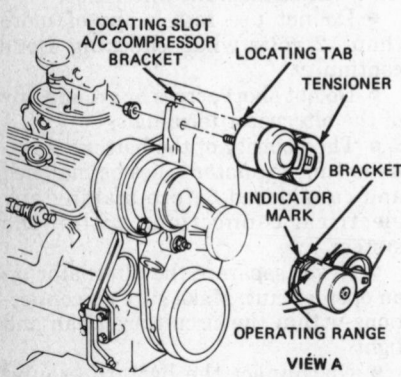

Serpentine drive belt tensioner–1984–89

Serpentine Belt

Position belt tension gauge J–23600 or BT-7825 between the alternator and the air pump. The correct belt tension should be 534N–623N, as indicated on the gauge. If not within specification adjust as required. The tensioner assembly has provisions for a visual check in order to verify that the belt is within the proper operating range.

REMOVAL & INSTALLATION

1. Disconnect the negative battery terminal.
2. Disconnect and identify the wire leads from the alternator.
3. Remove the alternator brace bolt, then remove the drive belt.
4. Remove the alternator pivot attaching bolt and remove the alternator.
5. Installation is the reverse of the removal procedure. Adjust the belt tension.

Starter

For further information on the starting system, please refer to "Charging and Starting" in the Unit Repair section.

REMOVAL & INSTALLATION

1. Disconnect the battery cables at the battery. Throughly clean all battery terminal and cable connections.
2. Raise and support the vehicle safely. Remove the flywheel cover.
3. Disconnect the wiring from the starter solenoid. Replace each connector nut as the terminals are removed as the thread sizes differ between connectors. Tag the wiring positions to avoid improper connections during installation.

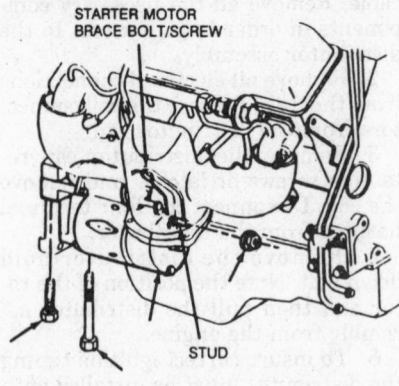

1	STARTER MOTOR
2	NUT
3	BOLT/SCREW
4	BOLT/SCREW

Removing the starter from the vehicle

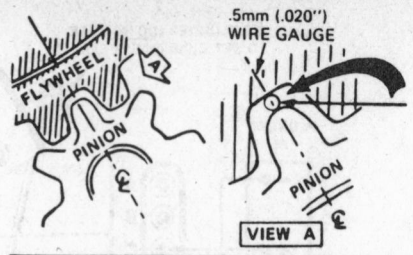

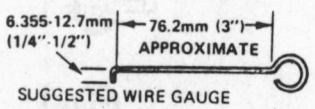

Flywheel to starter pinion clearance

4. Remove the front starter support bracket and the heat shield (if so equipped).
5. Loosen the two main starter mounting bolts, support the starter and remove the bolts. Lower the starter front end first and remove the starter.
6. Installation is the reverse of the removal procedure. Check the flywheel to pinion clearance. Torque the two main starter mounting bolts to 25–35 ft. lbs..

Solenoid Replacement

1. Remove the screw and washer from the motor connector strap terminal.
2. Remove the two solenoid retaining screws.
3. Twist the solenoid clockwise to remove the solenoid flange key from the keyway in the housing. Remove the solenoid.
4. To reinstall the unit, place the return spring on the plunger and place the solenoid body on the drive housing. Push the solenoid inward and turn counterclockwise to engage the flange key. Install and tighten the solenoid retaining screws and the screw and washer which secure the strap terminal.

ENGINE MECHANICAL

Engine

REMOVAL & INSTALLATION

NOTE: Fuel injection lines and components may be under considerable pressure even when the engine is secured. To avoid injury to personnel, be sure to relieve the

fuel pressure before disconnecting any fuel lines. Replace all worn fuel line connection O-rings as required.

1. Mark the relationship between each hood hinge, and the hood. Remove the hood.

2. Disconnect the battery cables at the battery.

3. Remove the air cleaner assembly and cover the throttle body assembly with protective tape to prevent the entry of dirt and foreign matter. Mark any disconnected hoses with their respective openings so that they may be reinstalled properly.

4. Raise and support the vehicle safely.

5. Locate and remove the engine coolant drain plugs. There is a drain plug on each side of the engine block, just above the top of the oil pan.

6. Loosen the radiator drain petcock and allow the coolant to drain from the radiator into a suitable waste container.

7. Remove the radiator hoses and the heater hoses.

8. On 1982 vehicles remove the radiator fan shroud, radiator, engine cooling fan(s) and fan clutch (if so equipped).

9. On 1984–89 vehicles, remove the serpentine belt.

10. Drain the engine oil into a suitable waste container.

11. Remove the ignition shielding and release the distributor cap hold-down screws. Move the distributor cap (with wires still intact) out of the way (away from the firewall).

12. On models so equipped, disconnect the four wire connector at the distributor.

13. On 1984–89 vehicles, remove the distributor.

14. During this step, mark the location and/or connection point of each item so that these items may be properly reinstalled/re-connected.

  a. Disconnect the wiring from the starter and distributor.

  b. Disconnect the wiring from the alternator.

  c. Disconnect the wires from both the water temperature sender and oil pressure sender.

  d. Disconnect the engine ground wires.

  e. Disconnect the wiring from the idle solenoid, if so equipped.

  f. Disconnect the wiring from the various emission control items, as applicable (e.g. oxygen sensor, barometric sensor, air control valve, etc.).

  g. Disconnect the accelerator and transmission linkage (or cables, on late models) at the throttle body injection (TBI) unit. If equipped with

cables, unbolt the cable brackets from the engine.

  h. Disconnect the flexible hoses which connect the frame mounted lines to the engine mounted lines. In either case, plug the fuel supply line to prevent fuel siphoning from the tank.

  i. On PFI equipped models, disconnect the PFI harness at the engine.

  j. Disconnect any vacuum lines which run from a body mounted item to an engine mounted item (e.g. power brake unit, cruise control, etc.).

15. Remove the drive belt(s) from both the power steering pump and the air conditioning compressor, if equipped with these items. Unbolt the pump and compressor from their respective mounting brackets and tie these units out of the way (with lines still attached—DO NOT disconnect the refrigerant lines from the A/C compressor).

16. Disconnect the cruise control chain or cable from the engine, if so equipped.

17. Disconnect the exhaust pipes from the exhaust manifold flanges.

18. Remove the starter and solenoid as an assembly.

19. Remove the flywheel splash shield or convertor underpan, as required.

20. On automatic transmission equipped vehicles, remove the torque convertor to flywheel attaching bolts. Also, remove the transmission dipstick and tube.

21. On manual transmission equipped models, disconnect the linkage from each of the two levers of the clutch cross shaft. Loosen the outer ball stud nut and slide the stud out of the bracket slot. Move the cross shaft as required to clear the inboard ball stud. Remove the cross shaft from the vehicle.

22. Unless you have a suitable plug to prevent the transmission from draining after the driveshaft is removed, drain the transmission. On automatics without drain plugs it will be necessary to carefully remove the transmission pan, drain the fluid, and reinstall the pan. Using chain or heavy wire, secure the torque convertor to the transmission so that the convertor will not fall out as the engine is removed (automatic transmission only).

23. Matchmark the driveshaft to the rear axle flange. Unbolt the universal joint straps from the flange and remove the driveshaft assembly.

24. Support the transmission using a floor jack and remove the transmission-to-engine mounting bolts (automatic transmission) or the

bellhousing-to-engine mounting bolts (manual transmission).

25. Remove the engine mount thru-bolts (one per side, positioned front-to-back).

26. Attach the engine lifting devices to the engine lifting brackets. Most engines are equipped with these brackets bolted to the intake manifold. If the engine does not have these brackets, remove the valve covers and the center head bolt from each cylinder head. Attach the lifting apparatus to the cylinder heads and secure with the cylinder head bolts.

—————— **CAUTION** ——————

Be absolutely sure that the chain which is used has a weight rating greater than the weight of the engine. If possible, use chain rated at least at 1000 lbs.. DO NOT use chains with a lesser rating; serious injury or death could result if an inferior chain is used.

27. Carefully move the engine forward, enough to disengage the engine from the transmission. Raise the engine enough to clear the front of the car and carefully move the engine over and away from the nose of the vehicle.

28. Service the existing engine as necessary, or install a replacement. Do not allow the engine to hang from the engine hoist for an extended period of time. Never work on the engine when it is attached to the hoist. Support the engine safely on the floor or on an engine stand.

29. Installation of the engine is the reverse of the removal procedure.

Cylinder Head

REMOVAL & INSTALLATION

1982

1. Disconnect the negative battery cable. Drain the cooling system. Remove the intake manifold. Remove the generator lower mounting bolt and position the unit to the side.

2. Remove the exhaust manifolds. It may be possible to remove the exhaust manifold retaining bolts and position the manifolds to the side.

3. Remove the necessary components that will interfere with removing the cylinder head. On later vehicles it will be necessary to remove the spark plugs from the cylinder head when removing the right head.

4. Remove the valve covers. Remove the rocker arms. Remove the pushrods.

5. Remove the cylinder head retaining bolts. Carefully remove the cylinder head from the engine and support on wood blocks to prevent damage.

6. Throughly clean the cylinder head and cylinder block mating surfaces to remove any foreign matter or gasket material. The cylinder head must be free of any nicks or deep scratches. Clean the cylinder bolt and block threads of dirt and grease prior to installation.

7. If the steel type gaskets were removed, coat both sides of the new steel gasket (lightly but thoroughly) with a suitable sealing compound. If composite steel asbestos type gaskets were removed, the new gaskets must be installed dry.

8. Position the gasket over the dowel pins with the bead facing up.

9. Carefully guide the cylinder head over the dowel pins and lower onto the cylinder head gasket.

10. Coat the threads of the cylinder head bolts with sealing compound No. 1052080 or equivalent and install hand tight.

11. Torque each bolt a small amount in sequence to 65 ft. lbs..

12. Install the exhaust manifolds.

13. Install the intake manifolds.

14. Adjust the valves and the alternator belt tension.

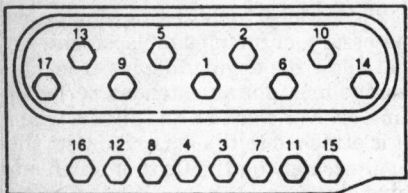

Cylinder head bolt torque sequence— 1982–89

1984–1989

RIGHT SIDE

1. Disconnect the negative battery cable and drain the cooling system. Remove the intake manifold.

2. Disconnect the rear A/C brace at the exhaust manifold.

3. Disconnect and remove the dipstick tube assembly.

4. Remove the check valve from the AIR manifold.

5. Disconnect the AIR hose at the catalitic converter AIR pipe.

6. Disconnect the temperature sending unit wire.

7. Disconnect the plug wires from the spark plugs and cylinder head/rocker arm attachment points.

8. Loosen and remove the spark plugs.

9. Raise and properly support the vehicle.

10. Disconnect the converter AIR pipe clamp at the manifold.

11. Disconnect the exhaust pipe at both manifolds.

12. Remove the front converter hanger bolts.

13. Remove the converter AIR pipe.

14. Lower the vehicle.

15. Remove the exhaust manifold bolts.

16. Remove the exhaust manifold with the EGR pipe.

17. Remove the spark plug wire retainers.

18. Remove the rocker arm cover.

19. Disconnect the serpentine belt (if equipped) at the A/C compressor.

20. Disconnect the A/C wire connectors.

21. Loosen the rear A/C mounting bolts.

22. Loosen and remove the A/C bracket nuts from the water pump studs.

23. Loosen the front A/C mounting bolt and slide the A/C unit with bracket forward.

24. Remove the push rods.

25. Loosen and remove the head bolts. Remove the right cylinder head from the cylinder head from the engine block surface.

26. Remove the cylinder head gasket and discard. Thoroughly clean all gasket mating surfaces.

NOTE: The cylinder head and engine block surfaces must be completely free of existing gasket material and free of nicks and grooves. Throughly clean the inspect the cylinder head bolt threads for damage and wear. The use of dirty or damaged bolts may produce false and inaccurate torque readings. Replace all damaged bolts as required.

27. Use new cylinder head gaskets installed with the bead facing up. Installation is the reverse of the removal procedure.

NOTE: If the steel type gaskets were removed, coat both sides of the new steel gasket (lightly but thoroughly) with a suitable sealing compound. If composite type gaskets were removed, the new gaskets must be installed dry.

28. Coat the threads of the cylinder head bolts with a suitable sealing compound (No. 1052080 or equivalent). Install the bolts finger tight.

29. Torque the bolts in the specified pattern to 60–75 ft. lbs..

LEFT SIDE

1. Remove the intake manifold.

2. Disconnect the AIR hose at the check valve.

3. Remove the alternator brace.

4. Disconnect the fan temperature sensor wire.

5. Raise and safely support the vehicle.

6. Disconnect the exhaust pipe at the manifold.

7. Lower the vehicle.

8. Remove the exhaust manifold bolts.

9. Support and remove the left hand exhaust manifold.

10. Disconnect the serpentine belt at the AIR pump.

11. Remove the rocker cover.

12. Remove the spark plugs.

13. Disconnect the P/S, alternator mounting bracket at the cylinder head.

14. Remove the push rods.

15. Loosen and remove the head bolts. Remove the right cylinder head from the cylinder head from the engine block surface.

16. Remove the cylinder head gasket and discard. Thoroughly clean all gasket mating surfaces.

NOTE: The cylinder head and engine block surfaces must be completely free of existing gasket material and free of nicks and grooves. Throughly clean then inspect the cylinder head bolt threads for damage and wear. The use of dirty or damaged bolts may produce false and inaccurate torque readings. Replace all damaged bolts as required.

17. Use new cylinder head gaskets installed with the bead facing up. Installation is the reverse of the removal procedure.

NOTE: If steel type gaskets were removed, coat both sides of the new steel gasket (thinly and evenly) with a suitable sealing compound. It is important to apply the proper amount of sealant because too much can cause the gasket to move away from the cylinder head and block surfaces. If composite type gaskets were removed, the new gaskets must be installed dry.

18. Coat the threads of the cylinder head bolts with a suitable sealing compound (No. 1052080 or equivalent). Install the bolts finger tight.

19. Torque the bolts in the specified pattern to 60–75 ft. lbs..

OVERHAUL

For all cylinder head overhaul procedures, please refer to "Engine Rebuilding" in the Unit Repair section.

Rocker Arms/Shafts

REMOVAL & INSTALLATION

1. Disconnect the negative battery cable. Remove the air cleaner.

2. If removing the left valve cover, disconnect the PCV valve and hose. Disconnect the power brake booster vacuum line. Remove the alternator.

3. If removing the right valve cover, disconnect the air hose from the exhaust check valve. As required, remove the fuel inlet and return lines from the throttle body. Loosen the required A/C compressor mounting bolts and position the compressor off to the side.

4. Remove the valve cover retaining bolts. Remove the valve covers.

5. Remove the rocker arm nuts, rocker arm balls and the rocker arms. Place all the removed components in a rack so that they may be reinstalled in their original positions.

NOTE: If new rocker arms or rocker arm balls are being installed, coat the rocker arm and rocker arm ball bearing surfaces with Molycoat ® or equivalent prior to installation.

6. Install the push rods. Ensure that the push rods seat properly in the lifter sockets.

7. Install the rocker arms, rocker arm balls and rocker arm nuts. Tighten the rocker arm nuts until no movement in the push rod can be felt. This can be determined by rotating the push rod while slowly tightening the rocker arm nut.

8. Adjust the valves.

9. Ensure that the valve cover sealing surfaces are clean and even. Bent valve cover sealing surfaces will result in oil leakage. Be sure to use new valve cover gaskets as required. Install the valve covers and the remaining components in the reverse of the removal procedure.

Intake Manifold

REMOVAL & INSTALLATION

1982–84

1. Disconnect the negative battery cable. Drain the cooling system. Remove the air cleaner.

2. Disconnect the computer command control harness and route it to a convenient location. Disconnect all electrical connections as required. Identify all electrical connections to ensure proper reinstallation.

3. Relieve the fuel system pressure. Disconnect and remove the fuel inlet and return lines. Place a shop towel over the fuel line connections to absorb excess fuel.

4. Disconnect all vacuum hoses as required. Identify each vacuum hose with its respective opening to ensure proper installation.

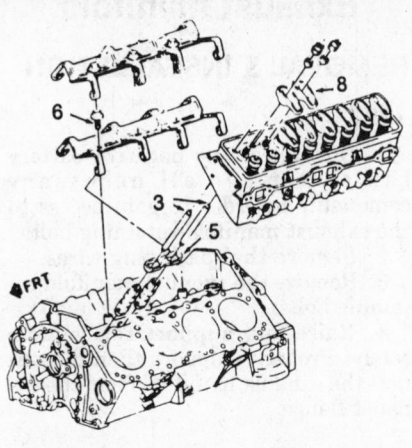

Exploded view of the rocker arms and push rods

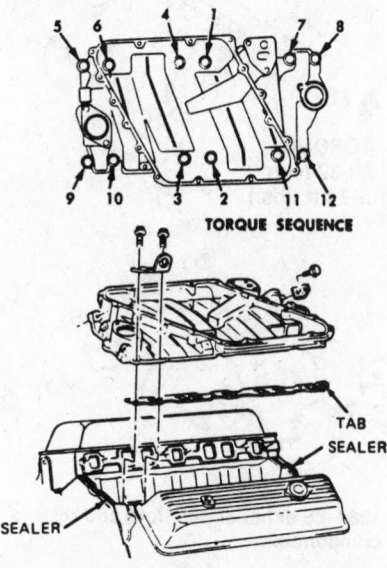

1982–84 intake manifold torque sequence

5. Disconnect the accelerator bracket cable.

6. Remove the TBI assembly (intake cover) retaining bolts, and lift the TBI assembly (with gasket) upward and away from the intake surface.

7. Drain the cooling system into a suitable fluid catch pan.

8. Disconnect the radiator hose at the thermostat opening. Remove the alternator brace.

9. Remove the distributor cap, and mark the position of the rotor, then remove the distributor.

10. Disconnect the heater hose from the rear heater intake.

11. Loosen and remove the AIR pump drive belt, pulley and valve adapter. Support the AIR pump and remove the retaining bolts. Remove the AIR pump and set it asisde.

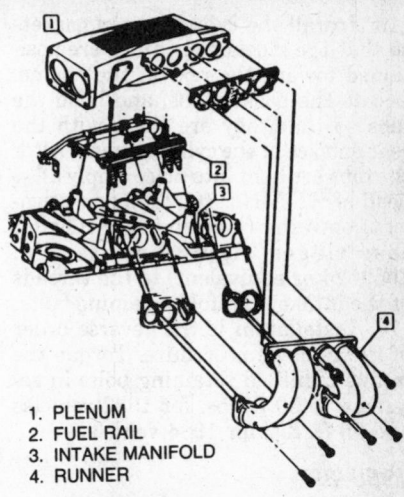

1. PLENUM
2. FUEL RAIL
3. INTAKE MANIFOLD
4. RUNNER

1985–88 PFI assembly

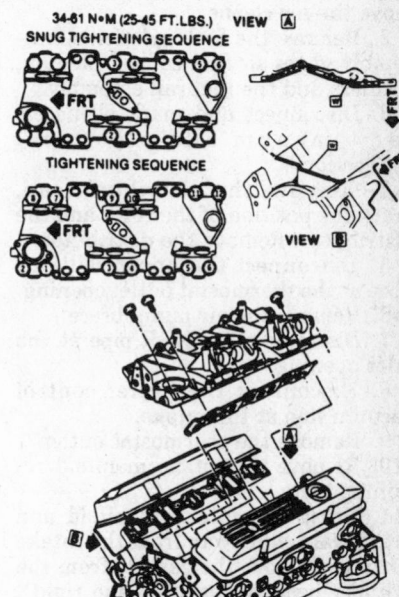

1985–88 intake manifold torque sequence

12. Disconnect the coolant temperature sensor.

13. Remove the intake manifold retaining bolts.

14. Grasp the intake manifold and lift upward and away from the intake surface. Remove the gaskets from the cylinder head surface (left and right). Discard the cylinder head gaskets.

15. Thoroughly clean the cylinder block, intake manifold and cylinder head surfaces with the proper cleaning compound to remove any traces of gasket material and RTV sealant. Any material left on these surfaces will cause installation interference and improper sealing.

16. Install the cylinder head gaskets so that the blocked openings are positioned toward the rear of the engine. Locate the gasket tabs, and bend the tabs so that they are flush with the rear surface of the cylinder head. After the tabs are bent into place, apply a $3/16$ bead of RTV (No. 1052366 or equivalent) onto the front and rear cylinder case ridges. Apply Loctite (No. 1052624 or equivalent) to the threads of the intake manifold retaining bolts.

17. Installation is the reverse order of the removal procedure. Torque the intake manifold retaining bolts in sequence to 30 ft. lbs. for 1982 vehicles and 35 ft. lbs. for 1984 vehicles.

1985–89

1. Disconnect the negative battery cable. Drain the cooling system. Remove the air cleaner.

2. Remove the fuel injection subassembly: mass air flow sensor, plenum, runners and the fuel rail assembly.

3. Disconnect and mark all necessary vacuum and electrical connections.

4. Remove the distributor cap, mark the position of the rotor and the distributor. Remove the distributor.

5. Disconnect the upper radiator hose at the thermostat outlet opening.

6. Remove the air pump brace.

7. Disconnect the EGR pipe at the inlet opening.

8. Disconnect the heater control vacuum line at the intake.

9. Remove the thermostat outlet.

10. Remove the intake manifold retaining bolts.

11. Grasp the intake manifold and lift upward and away from the intake surface. Remove the gaskets from the cylinder head surface (left and right). Discard the cylinder head gaskets.

12. Thoroughly clean the cylinder block, intake manifold and cylinder head surfaces with the proper cleaning compound to remove any traces of gasket material and RTV sealant. Any material left on these surfaces will cause installation interference and improper sealing.

13. Install the cylinder head gaskets so that the blocked openings are positioned toward the rear of the engine. Locate the gasket tabs, and bend the tabs so that they are flush with the rear surface of the cylinder head. After the tabs are bent into place, apply a $3/16$ bead of RTV (No. 1052366 or equivalent) onto the front and rear cylinder case ridges. Apply Loctite (No. 1052624 or equivalent) to the threads of the intake manifold retaining bolts.

14. Installation is the reverse order of the removal procedure. Torque the intake manifold retaining bolts in sequence to 35 ft. lbs.

Exhaust Manifold

REMOVAL & INSTALLATION

1982

1. Disconnect the negative battery cable. Remove all necessary comonents in order to gain access to the exhaust manifold retaining bolts.

2. Remove the spark plug wires.

3. Remove the exhaust manifold retaining bolts.

4. Raise and support the vehicle safely. Properly support then disconnect the exhaust manifold from the exhaust flange.

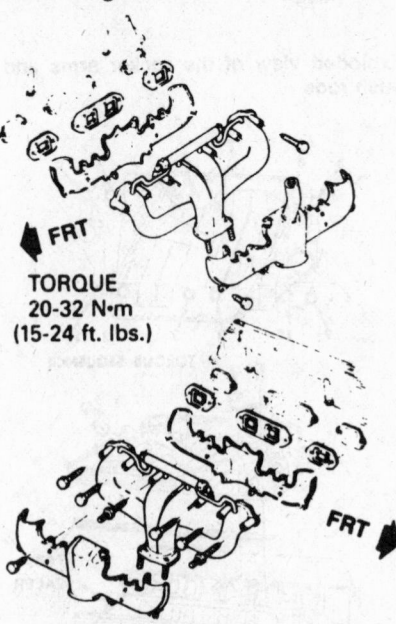

FRT

TORQUE
20-32 N•m
(15-24 ft. lbs.)

FRT

1984–85 exhaust manifold and related components

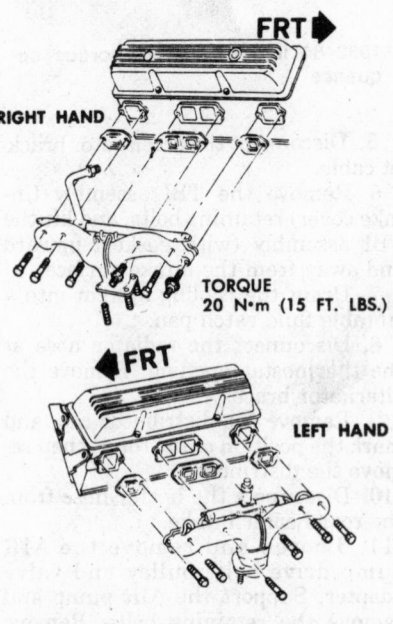

FRT

RIGHT HAND

TORQUE
20 N•m (15 FT. LBS.)

FRT

LEFT HAND

Exhaust manifold assembly–1982

5. Remove the manifold from the vehicle. Depending upon the vehicle it may be easier to remove the manifold from underneath of the vehicle.

1984–85

RIGHT SIDE

1. Disconnect the negative battery cable. Remove the air cleaner and drain the cooling system.

2. Remove the rear air condition compressor brace and allow to hang from the compressor. Disconnect the AIR hose at the exhaust check valve. Disconnect the AIR hose at the converter pipe check valve.

3. Disconnect the heater hose at the rear of the intake manifold.

4. Disconnect the spark plug wires at the valve cover. Remove the spark plugs.

5. Remove the temperature sending unit at the right cylinder head.

6. Raise and properly support the vehicle.

7. Disconnect the exhaust pipe at the exhaust manifold.

8. Disconnect the AIR pipe at the exhaust manifold.

9. Remove the two rear exhaust manifold bolts. Disconnect the dipstick tube at the exhaust manifold.

10. Lower the vehicle.

11. Remove the remaining exhaust manifold retaining bolts and support the exhaust manifold. Remove the exhaust manifold from the vehicle.

12. Replace all gaskets as required and ensure that all gasket contact surfaces are cleaned prior to reinstallation. Installation is the reverse of the removal procedure. Torque the exhaust manifold retaining bolts to 15–24 ft. lbs..

LEFT SIDE

1. Disconnect the battery negative cable.

2. Remove the air cleaner.

3. Disconnect the PCV hose from intake and rocker cover.

4. Disconnect AIR hose at the exhaust check valve.

5. Disconnect rear alternator brace at the manifold and allow it to hang from the alternator.

6. Raise and properly support the vehicle.

7. Disconnect the exhaust pipe at manifold.

8. Lower the vehicle.

9. Remove the exhaust manifold retaining bolts. Support and remove manifold.

10. Replace all gaskets as required and ensure that all gasket contact surfaces are cleaned prior to reinstallation. Installation is the reverse of the removal procedure. Torque the manifold retaining bolts to 15–24 ft. lbs..

1986–89
RIGHT SIDE

1. Disconnect the negative battery cable.
2. Remove the plenum extension.
3. Disconnect the EGR sensor wire.
4. Remove the EGR pipe bolts at the intake manifold.
5. Remove the rear A/C compressor brace, and allow it to hang from the compressor.
6. Disconnect the dipstick tube at the manifold and remove the dipstick/tube as an assembly.
7. Remove the AIR check valve at the manifold.
8. Disconnect the AIR hose at the catalytic air pipe opening.
9. Disconnect the temperature sending unit wire.
10. Disconnect the spark plug wires from the plugs, cylinder head and the valve covers.
11. Remove the spark plugs.
12. Raise and properly support the vehicle.
13. Remove the catalyic coverter AIR pipe at the manifold.
14. Disconnect the exhaust crossover pipe at the manifold.
15. Remove the bolts from the catalytic front support hanger.
16. Remove the catalytic converter AIR pipe.
17. Lower the vehicle.
18. Support the exhaust manifold and remove the retaining bolts.
19. Remove the exhaust manifold and EGR assembly from the vehicle. If the manifold is being replaced, remove the EGR pipe clamp and EGR pipe.
20. Replace all gaskets as required and ensure that all gasket contact surfaces are cleaned prior to reinstallation. Installation is the reverse of the removal procedure. Torque the manifold retaining bolts to 15–24 ft. lbs..

LEFT SIDE

1. Disconnect the negative battery cable.
2. Remove the air cleaner.
3. Disconnect the PCV hose from the intake and rocker arm cover.
4. Disconnect the AIR at the exhaust check valve.
5. Disconnect the rear alternator brace and allow to hang from the alternator.
6. Raise and properly support the vehicle.
7. Disconnect the exhaust pipe at the manifold.
8. Lower the vehicle.
9. Support the manifold and remove the retaining bolts.
10. Remove the exhaust manifold from the vehicle.

11. Replace all gaskets as required and ensure that all gasket contact surfaces are cleaned prior to reinstallation. Installation is the reverse of the removal procedure. Torque the manifold retaining bolts to 15–24 ft. lbs..

Front Cover

REMOVAL & INSTALLATION

1. Disconnect the negative battery cable. Disconnect the drive belt and remove the crankshaft pulley.
2. Install tool No. J–23523 onto the vibration dampener assembly. Remove the vibration damper from the face of the crankcase front cover.

NOTE: The use of pullers (such as the universal claw type) that pull on the outside of the hub may damage the torsional dampener. The outside ring of the dampener is bonded to the hub with rubber. The use of the wrong type puller may disturb this bond.

3. Remove the oil pan.
4. Remove the AIR management valve adapter.
5. Remove the AIR pump pulley and air pump retaining bolts. Remove the air pump.
6. Relieve the fuel system pressure, and disconnect the fuel inlet and return pipes.

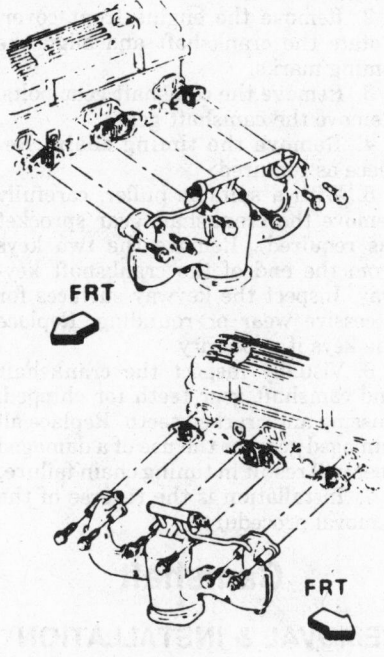

TORQUE
20-32 N·m (15-24 FT. LBS.)

Exhaust manifold and related components–1986–89

7. Disconnect the air conditioner compressor mounting bracket nuts at the water pump. Slide the mounting bracket forward and remove the compressor mounting bolt. Disconnect the electrical wires and position the unit to the side.
8. Disconnect the AIR hose at the right exhaust manifold.
9. Remove the AIR pump upper bracket, power steering brackets and the air conditioner compressor brackets.
10. Drain the radiator, and disconnect the radiator and heater hoses at the water pump. Remove the water pump.
11. Remove the front cover retaining screws. Remove the front cover and discard the gasket.
12. Thoroughly clean the gasket mating surfaces on the cylinder block and front cover. Inspect the front cover for damage and distortion. Replace the front cover if necessary. Replace the oil seal as required.
13. With a suitable cutting tool, remove any excess gasket material that may be protruding at the oil pan to engine block surface.
14. Coat the new cover gasket with a suitable sealing compound and apply the gasket onto the front cover sealing surface.
15. Position the front cover and gasket onto the cylinder block surface and hold in place. Install the cover retaining screws and make them finger tight.
16. Tighten the retaining screws evenly in an alternate pattern. While tightening the retaining screws, readjust the position of the front cover as required to ensure that the cylinder block locating dowels are evenly aligned with the holes in the cover. Do not force the cover over the locating dowels.
17. When the front cover is properly in place, torque the retaining screws to 69–139 inch lbs..
18. Prior to installing the oil pan, apply an even coating of sealant No. 1052080 or equivalent onto the front corners where the front cover and the rear main seal mate with the cranckcase. Reinstall the oil pan and pan gasket.

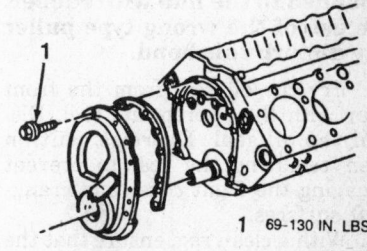

1   69-130 IN. LBS

Crankcase front cover assembly

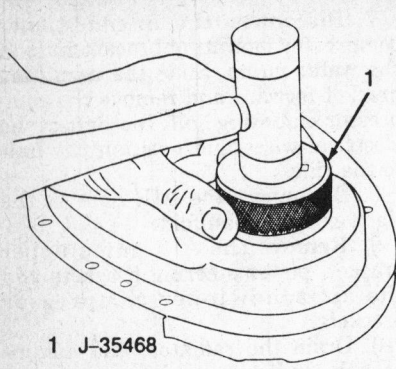

1 J—35468

Installing the crankcase front cover oil seal (front cover removed)

19. Install the remaining components in reverse of the removal procedure.

OIL SEAL REPLACEMENT

With Front Cover Removed

1. Pry the oil seal from the front cover with the appropriate tool. Discard the oil seal. Exercise caution when removing the seal to prevent damaging the front cover.

2. With a clean rag, ensure that the front cover sealing surfaces are free from dirt and grease.

3. Support the rear of the front cover and position the new seal so that the open end of the seal is toward the the inside of the front cover.

4. With tool J—35468 or equivalent, drive the new seal into the front cover. Visually inspect the seal to ensure that it is seated evenly in the front cover.

With Front Cover Installed

1. Disconnect the negative battery cable.

2. Loosen and remove the drive belt from the crankshaft pulley.

3. Remove the crankshaft pulley.

4. Install tool No. J—23523 onto the vibration dampener assembly. Remove the vibration damper from the face of the crankcase front cover.

NOTE: The use of pullers (such as the universal claw type) that pull on the outside of the hub may damage the torsional dampener. The outside ring of the dampener is bonded to the hub with rubber. The use of the wrong type puller may disturb this bond.

5. Pry the oil seal from the front cover with the appropriate tool. Discard the oil seal. Exercise caution when removing the seal to prevent damaging the front cover and crankshaft surfaces.

6. With a clean rag, ensure that the front cover sealing surfaces are free from dirt and grease.

7. With tool J—35468 or equivalent, drive the new seal into the front cover. Visually inspect the seal to ensure that it is seated evenly in the front cover.

8. With the removal tool, reinstall the vibration dampener.

9. Reinstall the crankshaft pulley and reconnect the drive belt. Adjust the drive belt tension.

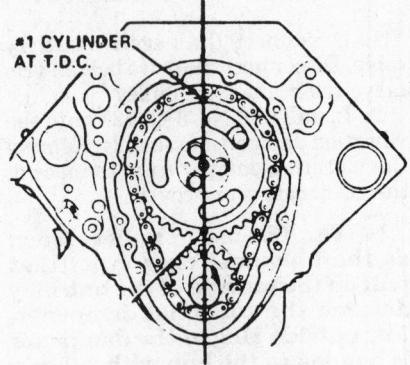

#1 CYLINDER AT T.D.C.

Timing mark alignment

Timing Chain and Sprockets

REMOVAL & INSTALLATION

1. Disconnect the negative battery cable.

2. Remove the engine front cover. Rotate the crankshaft and align the timing marks.

3. Remove the camshaft gear bolts. Remove the camshaft gear.

4. Remove the timing chain. Replace as required.

5. With a suitable puller, carefully remove the crankshaft gear sprocket (as required). Remove the two keys from the end of the crankshaft keyway. Inspect the keyway surfaces for excessive wear or rounding. Replace the keys if necessary.

6. Visually inspect the crankshaft and camshaft gear teeth for chipped, missing and cracked teeth. Replace all damaged gear, as the use of a damaged gear will result in timing chain failure.

7. Installation is the reverse of the removal procedure.

Camshaft

REMOVAL & INSTALLATION

1. Disconnect the negative battery cable.

2. Remove the intake manifold.

3. Remove the crankshaft pulley and the vibration damper.

4. Remove the power steering line in order to gain access to the vibration damper for installation.

5. Remove the air conditioning compressor brackets and position the compressor to the side. Remove the AIR pump.

6. Disconnect radiator hoses at water pump. Remove radiator hoses.

7. Remove front cover bolts. Remove front cover.

8. Rotate crankshaft and align timing marks.

9. Remove cam gear bolts remove chain and gear.

10. Remove alternator bolts and position the unit to the side.

11. Disconnect spark plug wires at spark plugs, remove rocker cover bolts. Remove rocker covers.

12. Remove all push rods. Remove lifters.

13. Disconnect air conditioning accumulator from shroud and lay aside.

14. Disconnect upper transmission cooler line at radiator. Disconnect fan wire at fan and fan shroud. Remove cooling fan. Disconnect lower transmission cooler line and remove fitting at radiator.

15. Remove upper fan shroud bolts and remove shroud. Remove radiator.

16. Disconnect air conditioning high pressure line bracket at right frame rail. Swing air conditioning condenser up and rest on top of lower shroud.

17. Remove camshaft, using care not to damage the camshaft bearings.

18. Installation is the reverse of the removal procedure.

Piston and Connecting Rod

POSITIONING

NOTE: For all piston and connecting rod overhaul procedures, please refer to "Engine Rebuilding" in the Unit Repair Section.

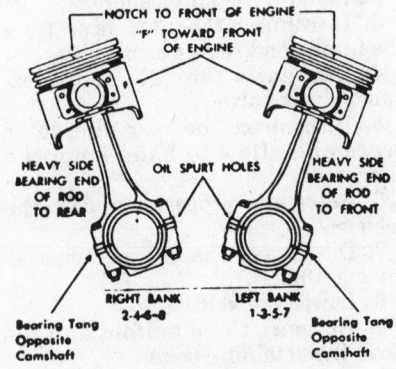

Piston identification

ENGINE LUBRICATION

Oil Pan

REMOVAL & INSTALLATION

1982–85

1. Disconnect the negative battery cable. Raise and support the vehicle safely. Drain the engine oil.

2. Remove the starter brace nut. Remove the starter from the vehicle. Remove the flywheel cover.

3. Remove the oil pan retaining bolts. Remove the oil pan from the vehicle. Thoroughly clean the cylinder block and oil pan mating surfaces.

4. Installation is the reverse of the removal procedure. Be sure to use new gaskets as required.

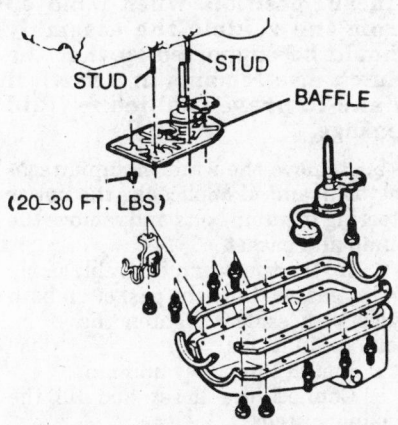

Exploded view of the oil pan assembly—1982–85

1986–89

1. Disconnect the negative battery cable. Raise the vehicle and support it safely. Drain the engine oil. Remove the oil filter.

2. If equipped disconnect the transmission oil cooler lines at the flywheel cover. Remove the starter.

3. Disconnect the catalytic converter air pipe clamps at the manifold and exhaust pipe.

4. Remove the flywheel cover. Disconnect the oil cooler line at the oil pan. Remove the ESC sensor shield.

5. Remove the front crossmember braces.

6. Remove the oil pan retaining bolts. Remove the oil pan from the engine.

7. Installation is the reverse of the removal procedure. Be sure to use a new gasket, as required.

Rear Main Bearing Oil Seal

REMOVAL & INSTALLATION

1982–85

1. Remove the oil pan. Remove the oil pump where required. Remove the rear main bearing cap.

2. Pry the lower seal out of the bearing cap with a suitable tool, being careful not to gouge the cap surface.

3. Remove the upper seal by lightly tapping on one end with a brass pin punch until the other end can be removed.

4. Clean the bearing cap, cylinder block, and crankshaft mating surfaces with a non-abrasive cleaner to remove any traces of sealant or foreign material. Inspect all these surfaces for gouges, nicks, and burrs.

5. Apply light engine oil on the seal lips and bead, but keep the seal ends clean.

NOTE: The rear oil seal installation tool may be easily fabricated from a piece of 0.004 in. shim stock.

6. Insert the tip of the installation tool between the crankshaft and the seal of the cylinder block. Place the seal between the crankshaft and the seal of the cylinder block. Place the seal between the tip of the tool and the crankshaft, so that the bead contacts the tip of the tool.

7. Be sure that the seal lip is facing the front of the engine, and work the seal around the crankshaft using the installation tool to protect the seal from the corner of the cylinder block.

NOTE: Do not remove the tool until the opposite end of the seal is flush with the cylinder block surface.

8. Remove the installation tool, being careful not to pull the seal out at the same time.

9. Using the same procedure, install the lower seal into the bearing cap. Use your finger and thumb to lever the seal into the cap.

10. Apply sealer to the cylinder block only where the cap mates to the surface. Do not apply sealer to the seal ends.

11. Install the rear cap and torque the bolts to specifications.

1986–89

1. Remove the transmission from the vehicle.

2. Using the notches provided in the rear seal retainer, pry out the seal using the proper tool.

NOTE: Care should be taken when removing the seal so as not to nick the crankshaft sealing surface.

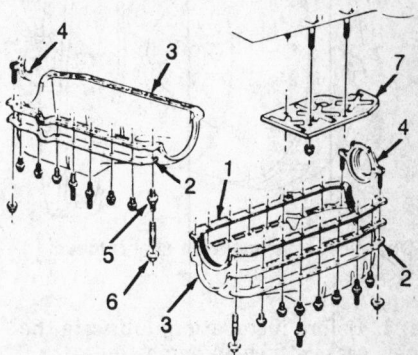

1	GASKET	5	STUD (AUTO. TRANS.)
2	REINFORCEMENT	6	NUT (MAN. TRANS.)
3	OIL PAN	7	BAFFLE
4	RETAINER		

Exploded view of the oil pan assembly—1986–89

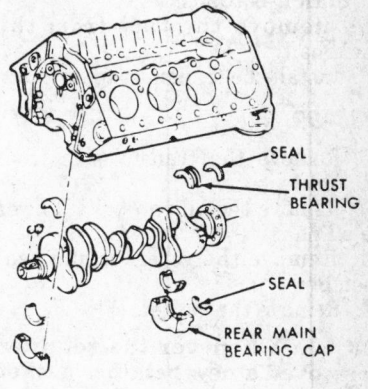

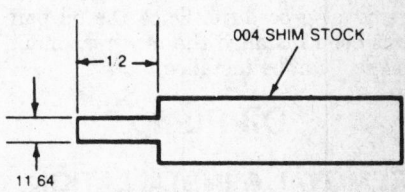

Oil seal installation tool fabrication diagram

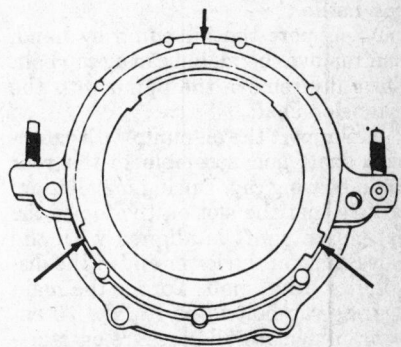

Removing the seal from the seal retainer—1986–89

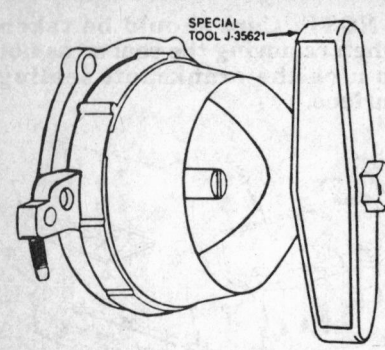

One piece rear main oil seal removal tool

3. Before installation, lubricate the new seal with clean engine oil.

4. Install the seal on tool J–3561 or equivalent. Thread the tool into the rear of the crankshaft. Tighten the screws snugly, this is to insure that the seal will be installed squarely over the crankshaft. Tighten the tool wing nut until it bottoms.

5. Remove the tool from the crankshaft.

6. Install the transmission.

1986–89

1. Remove the transmission from the vehicle.

2. Remove the oil pan bolts. Lower the oil pan.

3. Remove the retainer and seal assembly.

4. Remove the gasket.

NOTE: Whenever the retainer is removed a new retainer gasket and rear main seal must be installed.

5. Installation is the reverse of the removal procedure. Once the oil pan has been installed the new rear main oil seal can be installed.

Oil Pump

REMOVAL & INSTALLATION

1. Drain the engine oil. Remove engine oil pan. If equipped remove the oil pan baffle

2. Support the oil pump by hand, and remove the main bearing cap bolt. Carefully remove the pump with the extension shaft.

3. Support the oil pump with extension shaft and assemble to the rear main bearing cap. During installation, ensure that the slot on the top of the extension shaft is aligned with the drive tang on the lower end of the distributor drive shaft. Torque the main bearing cap bolt to 65 ft. lbs.. To ensure immediate oil pressure on start-up, the oil pump gear cavity should be packed with petroleum jelly.

ENGINE COOLING

Radiator

REMOVAL & INSTALLATION

1982

1. Disconnect the negative battery cable at the battery.

2. Drain the cooling system.

3. Remove the air cleaner snorkel.

4. Raise the vehicle and support it safely.

5. Disconnect the fan shroud from the radiator support bracket. As required, remove the fan shroud.

6. If so equipped, disconnect the automatic transmission cooler lines from the radiator.

7. Remove the radiator support brackets.

8. Disconnect the radiator upper and lower hoses and the overflow tube from the radiator.

9. Remove the radiator.

10. Installation is the reverse of the removal procedure. When installing the radiator, make sure it is seated in the mounting pads. When replacing the radiator cap make sure the arrows line up with the overflow tube.

1984–89

1. Disconnect the negative battery cable.

2. Drain the cooling system.

3. Remove the upper and lower radiator hoses.

4. Remove overflow hose at radiator.

5. Remove A/C accumulator and move aside.

6. If equipped disconnect the transmission cooler lines.

7. Remove fan wires from fan and shroud.

8. Remove fan to gain access to lower cooler line.

9. Remove upper shroud bolts. Remove upper shroud.

10. Remove the radiator from the vehicle.

11. Installation is the reverse of the removal procedure.

12. Fill the cooling system.

13. With the radiator cap removed, start the engine and allow to run at idle speed. Run the engine at idle until the upper radiator hose becomes hot (thermostat open). Inspect for coolant leaks and repair as necessary.

14. Continue running the engine while visually inspecting the coolant level. Slowly add coolant as required

until the level reaches the bottom of the filler neck.

15. Reinstall the radiator cap ensuring that the arrows on the cap are aligned with the arrows on the cap are aligned with the overflow tube.

Water Pump

REMOVAL & INSTALLATION

1982

1. Disconnect the negative battery cable. Drain the radiator and loosen the fan pulley bolts.

2. Disconnect the heater hose, lower radiator hose and, if applicable, the bypass hose at the water pump.

3. Remove the alternator upper brace. Loosen the swivel bolt and remove the fan belt.

4. Remove the fan blade and pulley. Replace a bent or damaged fan.

NOTE: Thermostatic fan clutches must be kept in an "incar" position. When removed from the vehicle the assembly should be supported so that the clutch disc remains in a vertical plane to prevent silicone fluid leakage.

5. Remove the water pump attaching bolts and, if applicable, the power steering to pump bolts and remove the pump and gasket.

6. Install the pump assembly using a new gasket. Coat the gasket on both sides with sealer. Tighten the ⅜ in. bolts to 30 ft. lbs.

7. Install the pulley and fan.

8. Connect the hoses and fill the cooling system.

9. Install the alternator upper brace and fan belt. Install the power steering pump bolt.

10. Adjust the belts, then start the engine and check for leaks.

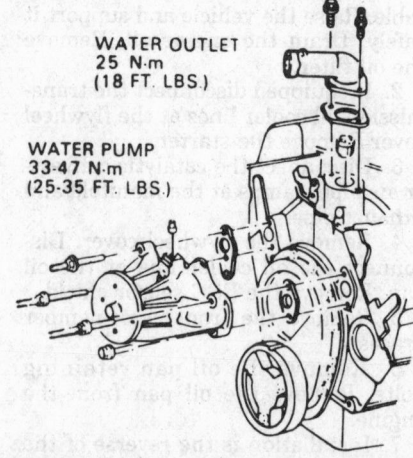

WATER OUTLET
25 N·m
(18 FT. LBS.)

WATER PUMP
33-47 N·m
(25-35 FT. LBS.)

Exploded view of the water pump assembly – 1984–89

1984–89

NOTE: If the compressor lines do not have enough slack to move the compressor out of the way without disconnecting the refrigerant lines, the air conditioning system must be evacuated, using the required tools and proper procedures, before the refrigerant lines can be disconnected. Do not disconnect any refrigerant lines unless experienced with air conditioning systems. Escaping refrigerant will freeze any surface it contacts, including skin and eyes.

1. Disconnect the negative battery cable, drain the cooling system and remove the drive belts.
2. Remove the water pump pulley and the air pump pulley along with the air management valve adapter.
3. Remove the AIR pump and disconnect the fuel inlet and return lines.
4. Remove the rear air conditioner compressor braces and the lower air condition compressor mounting bolt.
5. Remove the air condition compressor and the idler pulley bracket nuts. Disconnect the air condition compressor wires.
6. Slide the mounting bracket forward and remove the rear air condition compressor bolt along with the compressor.
7. Remove the right and left AIR hoses at the check valve and remove the AIR pipe at the intake and power steering reservoir bracket including the top alternator bolt.
8. Remove the lower AIR bracket on the water pump and the lower radiator and heater hose at the water pump.
9. Remove the water pump and gasket from the vehicle. If a new water pump is being installed, transfer the existing heater hose fitting onto the new water pump. Thoroughly clean all the water pump and cylinder block sealing surfaces to remove any sealant or foreign material.
10. Installation is the reverse order of the removal procedure, be sure to use a new gasket and RTV sealant as needed. Torque the retaining bolts to 25–35 ft lbs..

Thermostat

REMOVAL & INSTALLATION

1. Disconnect the negative battery cable and remove the air cleaner.
2. Drain the cooling system. Disconnect and remove the upper radiator hose from the outlet.
3. Remove the two retaining bolts from the thermostat housing and lift

up the housing. Withdraw the thermostat from the intake manifold.
4. Thoroughly clean all intake manifold and housing surfaces to remove any excess sealant.
5. Apply a ⅛ in. bead of RTV sealant No. 1052366 or equivalent onto the intake manifold and housing sealing surfaces.
6. Insert the new thermostat, spring end down, into the intake mainfold. While the sealant is still wet, install the housing with a new gasket. Torque the retainig bolts to 18–23 ft. lbs. (30 ft. lbs. for 1982 vehicles).
7. Fill the cooling system.
8. With the radiator cap removed, start the engine and allow to run at idle speed. Run the engine at idle until the upper radiator hose becomes hot (thermostat open). Inspect for coolant leaks and repair as necessary.
9. Continue running the engine while visually inspecting the coolant level. Slowly add coolant as required until the level reaches the bottom of the filler neck.
10. Reinstall the radiator cap ensuring that the arrows on the cap are aligned with the arrows on the cap are aligned with the overflow tube.

EMISSION CONTROLS

Please refer to "Emission Controls" in the Unit Repair section for system maintenance procedures. Due to the complex nature of modern electronic engine control systems, comprehensive diagnosis and testing procedures fall outside the confines of this repair manual. For complete information on diagnosis, testing and repair procedures concerning all modern engine and emission control systems, please refer to *Chilton's Guide To Electronic Engine Controls.*

FUEL SYSTEM

Fuel System Service Precaution

Safety is the most important factor when preforming not only fuel system maintenance, but any type of maintenance. Failure to conduct maintenance and repairs in a safe manner

may result in serious personal injury or death. Maintenance and testing of the vehicle's fuel system components can be accomplished safely and effectively by adhering to the following rules and guidelines.

• To avoid the possibility of fire and personal injury, always disconnect the negative battery cable unless the repair or test procedure requires that battery voltage be applied.

• Always relieve the fuel system pressure prior to disconnecting any fuel system component (injector, fuel rail, pressure regulator, etc...), fitting or fuel line connection. Exercise extreme caution whenever relieving fuel system pressure to avoid exposing skin, face and eyes to fuel spray. Please be advised that fuel under pressure may penetrate the skin or any part of the body that it comes in contact with.

• Always place a shop towel or cloth around the fitting or connection prior to loosening to absorb any excess fuel due to spillage. Ensure that all fuel spillage (should it occur) is quickly removed from engine surfaces. Ensure that all fuel soaked cloths or towels are deposited into a suitable waste container.

• Always have a properly charged fire extinguisher in the vincinity of the work area.

• Do not allow fuel spray or fuel vapors to come in contact with spark or open flame.

• Always use a backup wrench when loosening and tightening fuel line connection fittings. This will prevent unnecessary stress and torsion to fuel line piping. Always follow the proper torque specifications.

• Always replace worn fuel fitting O-rings with new. Do not substitute fuel hose or equivalent where fuel pipe is installed.

RELIEVING FUEL SYSTEM PRESSURE

NOTE: This procedure must be performed to relieve the fuel system pressure before any work is done to the fuel system which requires that a fuel line be disconnected.

1982–84 TBI (Throttle Body Injection) System

With the engine OFF, remove the fuse from the fuse block designated "FP" (fuel pump). Start the engine and allow it to run until it dies due to fuel starvation. Turn the ignition OFF, replace the fuel pump fuse, and service the fuel system as required.

1985–89 PFI (Port Fuel Injection) System

Disconnect the negative battery cable, then connect fuel gauge J34730-1 or equivalent to the fuel pressure tap. Wrap a shop towel around the fitting while connecting the gauge to catch any fuel spray. Install a bleed hose into a suitable container, then open the valve to bleed the fuel system pressure.

Fuel Filter

REMOVAL & INSTALLATION

1982–89

The vehicles within this period use an inline fuel filter. The filter is mounted on the passenger side frame rail, beneath the vehicle. Replacement is a simple matter of bleeding the system, disconnecting the hoses, and dismounting the filter. If the filter is supplied with screw type fitting(s), ensure that a backup wrench is used when the fuel filter fittings are disconnected. Discard all worn fuel fitting O-rings and replace with new as required. Torque the O-ring fittings to 22 ft. lbs.. Check for leaks after installing the new filter.

NOTE: A woven plastic filter is located on the lower end of the fuel pick up tube in the tank. This filter normally requires no maintenance.

Fuel Pump

The electric fuel pump is located inside the fuel tank attached to the fuel tank sending unit. The fuel pump takes its suction directly from the tank through a plastic micron filter. The pump is both cooled and lubricated by the incoming fuel. Fuel from the pump is delivered to the fuel rails, fuel injectors and then to the pressure regulator. The pump may be serviced separately, and access to the fuel pump is gained through the filler door in the body.

PRESSURE TESTING

NOTE: A special fuel pressure gauge is required to safely perform this test. On engines equipped with TBI, use gauge J-29658; on engines equipped with PFI, use gauge J-34730-1.

TBI System

1. Remove the air cleaner assembly and plug the vacuum connection(s) at the TBI unit.
2. Remove the fuel tube which connects between both TBI units.

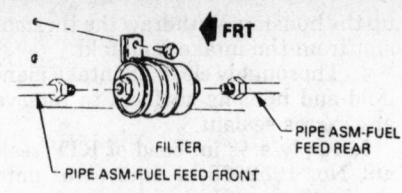

Fuel filter assembly (typical)

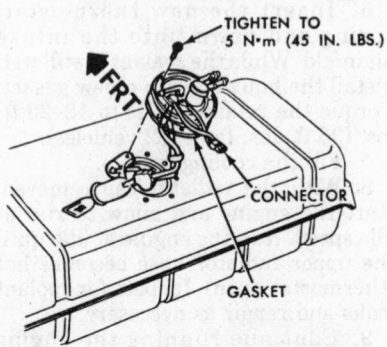

Electric fuel pump and gauge sender assembly, used with T.B.I.-equipped models

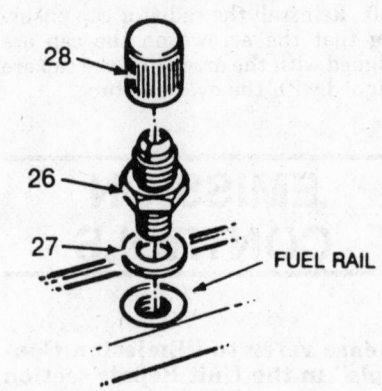

26 FUEL PRESSURE CONNECTION ASSEMBLY
27 SEAL
28 CAP

Exploded view of the fuel rail pressure tap connection

NOTE: Use two line wrenches of the appropriate sizes to disconnect each fitting, one wrench to hold the large fitting, the other to loosen the smaller fitting. A small amount of fuel will be released from the connections. Place a shop towel around the connection to collect any excess fuel that may be released.

3. Install the fuel pressure gauge between the two TBI units.
4. Turn the ignition switch On and check for fuel leakage at the gauge arrangement. If leakage is noted, turn the ignition switch OFF and correct the leak.
5. Start the engine and read the fuel pressure on the gauge. Fuel pressure should be 9–13 psi. Turn the engine OFF.

6. Remove the fuel pressure gauge, install the fuel tube assembly, and check for leaks.
7. Reinstall the air cleaner and connect the vacuum lines as originally connected.

PFI System

1. Attach fuel pressure gauge J-34730-1 to the fuel pressure tap on the fuel rail.

NOTE: A small amount of fuel may be released from the pressure tap connection. Wrap a shop towel around the connection to catch any fuel spray.

2. Turn the ignition ON and read the fuel pressure on the gauge. The fuel pump pressure should be within 40.5–47 psi and hold steady when the pump stops.

REMOVAL & INSTALLATION

1. Disconnect the battery cables at the battery.
2. Remove the fuel filler door and fuel cap.
3. Remove the fuel filler neck housing and drain hose.
4. Disconnect the fuel lines, fuel vapor line and electrical connectors from the sending unit/pump assembly, and remove the screws which retain the assembly.
5. Remove the sending unit/pump assembly and the gasket. Discard the gasket.
6. Pull the fuel pump upward and outward away from the bottom support. Take care not to damage the rubber insulator and strainer during removal. After the pump assembly is clear of the bottom support, pull the pump assembly out.
7. Separate the pump from the sending unit.
8. Inspect the fuel pump, sound insulator and strainer for signs of deterioration. Replace all components as required.
9. Push the fuel pump into its original position.
10. Install the fuel pump and fuel sending unit assemblies into the fuel tank with a new gasket.

NOTE: When installing the fuel pump/sending unit assembly, be careful not to fold or twist the strainer. If the strainer does not seat properly in the fuel tank upon installation, fuel flow will be restricted.

11. Install and tighten the attaching screws. Re-connect and tighten the fuel vapor line and fuel lines. Re-connect the electrical connectors.

12. Install the fuel tank filler neck housing and drain hose.

13. Reinstall the fuel cap and filler door.

14. Re-connect the negative battery cable.

Fuel Injection

Due to the complex nature of modern fuel injection systems, comprehensive diagnosis and testing procedures fall outside the confines of this repair manual. For complete information on fuel injection diagnosis, testing and repair procedures please refer to *Chilton's Guide to Fuel Injection and Feedback Carburetors.*

MANUAL TRANSMISSION

REMOVAL & INSTALLATION

1982

1. Disconnect the battery ground cable.

2. Remove the shifter ball and "T" handle.

3. Remove the console trim plate.

4. Raise the vehicle on a hoist.

5. Remove the right and left exhaust pipes. It may be necessary to remove the catalytic converter and its mounting bracket to gain sufficient clearance to remove the transmission.

6. Disconnect the driveshaft at the transmission, lower the driveshaft and remove the slip yoke from the transmission.

7. Remove the rear mount to bracket bolts, then jack the engine enough to raise the transmission from the mount.

8. Remove the transmission linkage mounting to frame bolts.

9. Disconnect the shift levers at the transmission.

10. Remove the bolts attaching the gearshift assembly to mounting bracket and remove the mounting bracket. Remove the shifter mechanism with the rods and levers attached.

11. Disconnect the speedometer cable.

12. Remove the transmission mount bracket.

13. Remove the transmission to clutch housing retaining bolts and the lower left extension bolt.

14. Pull the transmission rearward until it is clear of the clutch housing, then rotate it clockwise while pulling to the rear.

15. To allow room for the transmission removal slowly lower the rear of the engine until the distributor gently touches the fire wall.

NOTE: Do not allow the engine to rest against the distributor as damage may result. Place two blocks of wood directly behind the heads to keep the engine weight off the distributor.

16. Installation is the reverse of the removal procedure. Adjust the shift linkage. Torque the transmission to clutch housing bolts to 52 ft. lbs.. Torque the crossmember bolts to 25 ft. lbs.

1984–89

1. Disconnect the negative battery cable.

2. Remove the air cleaner. Disconnect the throttle valve cable at the left of the throttle body unit. Remove the distributor cap and set aside.

3. Raise the vehicle and support it safely.

NOTE: On vehicles equipped with a convertible top, remove the upper and lower underbody braces prior to removing the exhaust system components.

4. Remove the complete exhaust system as follows:

  a. Disconnect the AIR pipe at the converter.

  b. Disconnect the AIR pipe clamps at the exhaust manifold.

  c. Disconnect the oxygen sensor electrical lead.

  d. Loosen and remove the exhaust hanger bolts at the driveline support beam.

  e. Remove the bolts attaching the mufflers to the hangers.

  f. Remove the hanger bracket at the converter.

  g. Disconnect the exhaust pipes from the exhaust manifolds and remove the exhaust system.

  h. Remove the exhaust hanger at the transmission.

5. Support the transmission assembly using the proper equipment.

6. Remove the bolts attaching the driveline beam at the axle and transmission. Remove the driveline beam from the vehicle.

7. Mark the relationship of the propeller shaft to the axle companion flange. Remove the trunnion bearing straps and disengage the rear universal joint from the axle. Slide the propeller shaft slip yoke out from the overdrive unit and remove shaft from the vehicle.

8. Disconnect the transmission cooler lines at the overdrive unit. Disconnect the throttle valve at the over-

drive unit. Disconnect the shift linkage at the side cover.

9. Disconnect the electrical connectors at the side cover. Disconnect the back up light switch, 1st gear switch, overdrive unit and speedometer sensor switch.

10. Lower the transmission and support the engine.

11. Remove the bolts attaching the transmission to the bellhousing. Slide the transmission to the rear to disengage the input shaft from the clutch. Remove the transmission from the vehicle.

12. Clean and repack the clutch release bearing.

13. Install the transmission and attaching bolts.

14. Connect the oil cooler line pipes to the overdrive unit. Torque the connector fittings to 8–12 ft. lbs..

15. Install and align the driveline support beam.

16. Install the propeller shaft.

17. Connect and adjust the throttle shift linkage.

18. Connect the backup light switch, overdrive unit, speedometer sensor and 1st gear electrical connectors.

19. Refill transmission to proper level. The 4 Speed section uses SAE-80 W or SAE-80 W-90 GL-5 gear lube. The overdrive unit uses Dextron II Automatic Transmission Fluid.

20. Install the exhaust system components. Reinstall upper and lower underbody braces (if removed).

LINKAGE ADJUSTMENT

1982

1. Place the shift lever in the Neutral position.

2. Raise and support the vehicle safely.

3. Disconnect the shift rods from the transmission levers.

4. Rotate the transmission lever counterclockwise (forward detent position) then turn it back until the first detent is felt (Neutral position). This is done to verify that each transmission lever is in its Neutral position. Perform this step for each of the transmission levers individually.

5. Insert a locating gauge into the notch of the shifter housing and through the shift levers to properly align the levers. It may be necessary to move the shift lever(s) to install the locating gauge completely.

6. Loosen the locknuts of the 3–4 shift rod swivel (front of transmission side cover) and turn the swivel as necessary to allow the swivel to easily enter the hole of the 3–4 transmission lever. Apply a slight backward pressure

to the transmission lever and tighten the swivel locknuts. Attach the shift rod to the transmission lever with the retaining clip (and washer, if used).

7. Repeat Step 6 for the 1–2 and reverse shift rods.

8. Remove the locating gauge and lower the vehicle.

NOTE: After the adjustments have been made, the centerlines of the shifter levers must be aligned to prevent rubbing.

1984–89

1. Disconnect the negative battery cable.

2. Remove the left seat from the vehicle. If equipped with power seats, disconnect the electrical leads.

3. Remove the shift knob.
4. Remove the console cover.
5. Remove the glove box lock.
6. Remove the left side panel from the console.
7. Remove the shifter cover.
8. Loosen the adjusting nuts on the shifter rods.
9. With the transmission and shifter in neutral, install the alignment pin in shifter.
10. Equalize the swivels on all three shift levers. Hand tighten the forward and rear adjusting nuts at the same time with equal force. Do this for all three shifter rods and then torque the forward and rear adjusting nuts at the same time to specifications.
11. Installation is the reverse of the removal procedure. Lubricate all linkage pivot points with the proper lubricant.

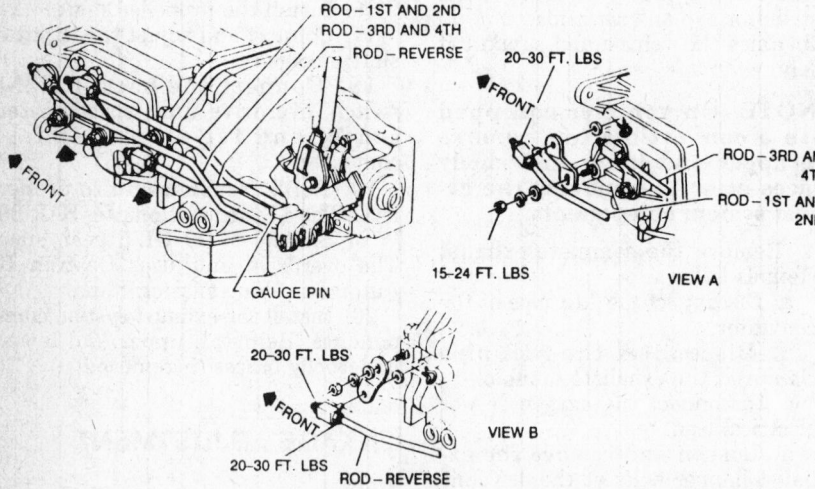

83 MM manual transmission with automatic overdrive — 1984–89

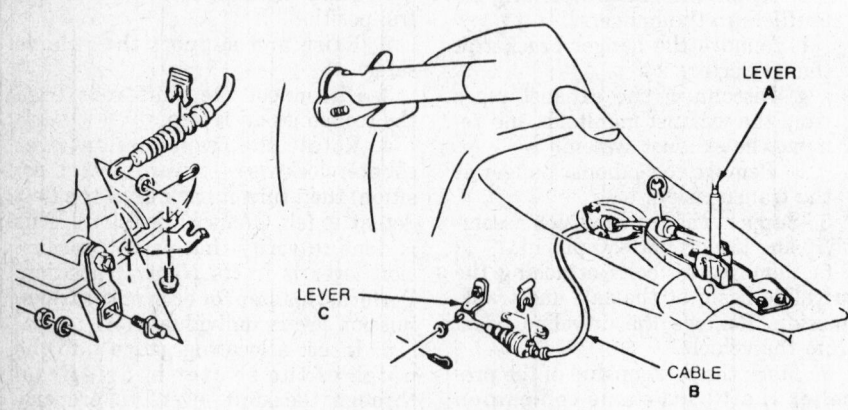

TRANSMISSION CONTROL LINKAGE ADJUSTMENT

1. Push Shift Lever (A) forward to "PARK" stop.
2. Place Trans. Lever (C) in "PARK" stop position. Obtain "PARK" stop position by rotating Trans. Lever (C) Clockwise to last detent position.
3. Attach Cable (B) to Levers (A) & (C) with attaching parts.

Automatic 700–R4 transmission — 1982

CLUTCH

REMOVAL & INSTALLATION

1. Remove the transmission from the vehicle.

2. Disconnect the clutch fork pushrod and spring. On 1984–89 vehicles, remove the slave cylinder attaching bolts.

3. Remove the flywheel housing.

4. Slide the clutch fork from the ball stud and remove the fork from the dust boot. The ball stud is threaded into the clutch housing and is easily replaced, if necessary.

5. Install a clutch pilot tool.

NOTE: Look for the assembly markings "X" on the flywheel and the clutch cover (pressure plate assembly). If there are none, scribe marks to identify the position of the clutch cover relative to the flywheel.

6. Loosen the clutch cover bolts evenly until the spring pressure is relieved, then remove the bolts and clutch assembly.

7. Before installing, clean the pressure plate and the flywheel face.

8. Position the disc and pressure plate assembly on the flywheel and install a pilot tool.

NOTE: On single disc models, the clutch disc is installed with the damper springs and slinger toward the transmission. On dual disc models, the discs are installed with the springs away from the flywheel.

9. Install the pressure plate assembly bolts. Make sure the mark on the cover is aligned with the mark on the flywheel. Tighten the bolts alternately and evenly to 35 ft. lbs..

10. Remove the pilot tool.

11. Remove the release fork and lubricate the ball socket and the fork fingers at the throwout bearing with graphite or Molycoat® grease. Reinstall the release fork.

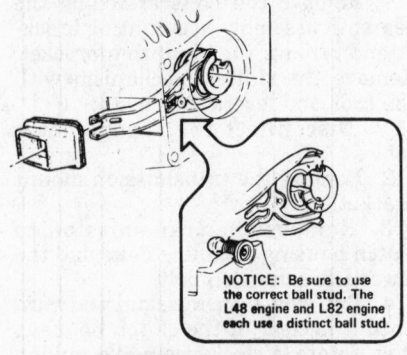

Ball stud attachment

12. Lubricate the inside recess and the fork groove of the throwout bearing with a light coat of graphite or Molycoat® grease.

13. Install the clutch release fork and dust boot in the clutch housing and the throwout bearing on the fork, then install the flywheel housing. Tighten flywheel housing bolts to 30 ft. lbs. Reinstall the slave cylinder.

14. Connect the fork pushrod and spring.

15. Adjust the shift linkage.

16. Adjust the clutch pedal free play. Bleed the hydraulic clutch system on 1984–89 vehicles.

FREE-PLAY ADJUSTMENT

1. Disconnect the return spring between the floor and the cross shaft.

2. Push the clutch lever and shaft assembly until the clutch pedal is tightly against the rubber stop under the dash.

3. Loosen the two locknuts on the shaft.

4. Push the shaft until the throwout bearing just touches the pressure plate spring.

5. Tighten the top locknut towards the swivel until the distance between it and the swivel is 0.4 in.

6. Tighten the bottom locknut against the swivel.

7. Check pedal free travel. It should be 1–1½ in.

Clutch Master Cylinder

REMOVAL & INSTALLATION

1. Disconnect the negative battery cable.

2. Remove the hush panel from underneath of the dash.

3. Disconnect the pushrod from the clutch pedal. Disconnect the hydraulic line at the master cylinder.

4. Remove the clutch master cylinder retaining bolts. Remove the clutch master cylinder from the vehicle.

5. Installation is the reverse of the removal procedure. Bleed the system, as required

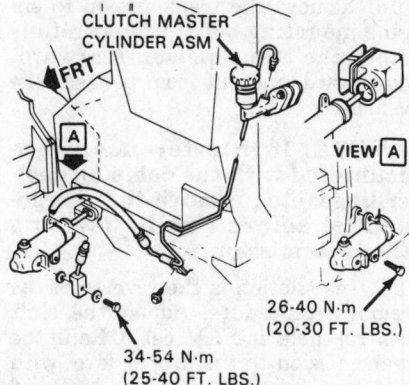

Exploded view of hydraulic clutch components

Clutch Slave Cylinder

REMOVAL & INSTALLATION

1. Disconnect the negative battery cable.

2. Raise and support the vehicle safely.

3. Disconnect the hydraulic line at the slave cylinder. Remove the slave cylinder mounting bolts from the clutch housing.

4. Remove the pushrod and the slave cylinder from the vehicle.

5. Installation is the reverse of the removal procedure. Bleed the system, as required.

BLEEDING THE HYDRAULIC CLUTCH SYSTEM

1. Fill the master cylinder reservoir with the proper grade and type brake fluid.

2. Raise the vehicle and support it safely.

3. Remove the clutch slave cylinder attaching bolts.

4. Hold the slave cylinder at about a 45 degree angle with the bleeder valve at the highest point.

5. Fully depress the clutch pedal and open the bleeder valve. Close the bleeder valve and release the clutch pedal.

6. Repeat Step 5 until all air is expelled from the system.

7. Check the fluid reservoir and replenish as required.

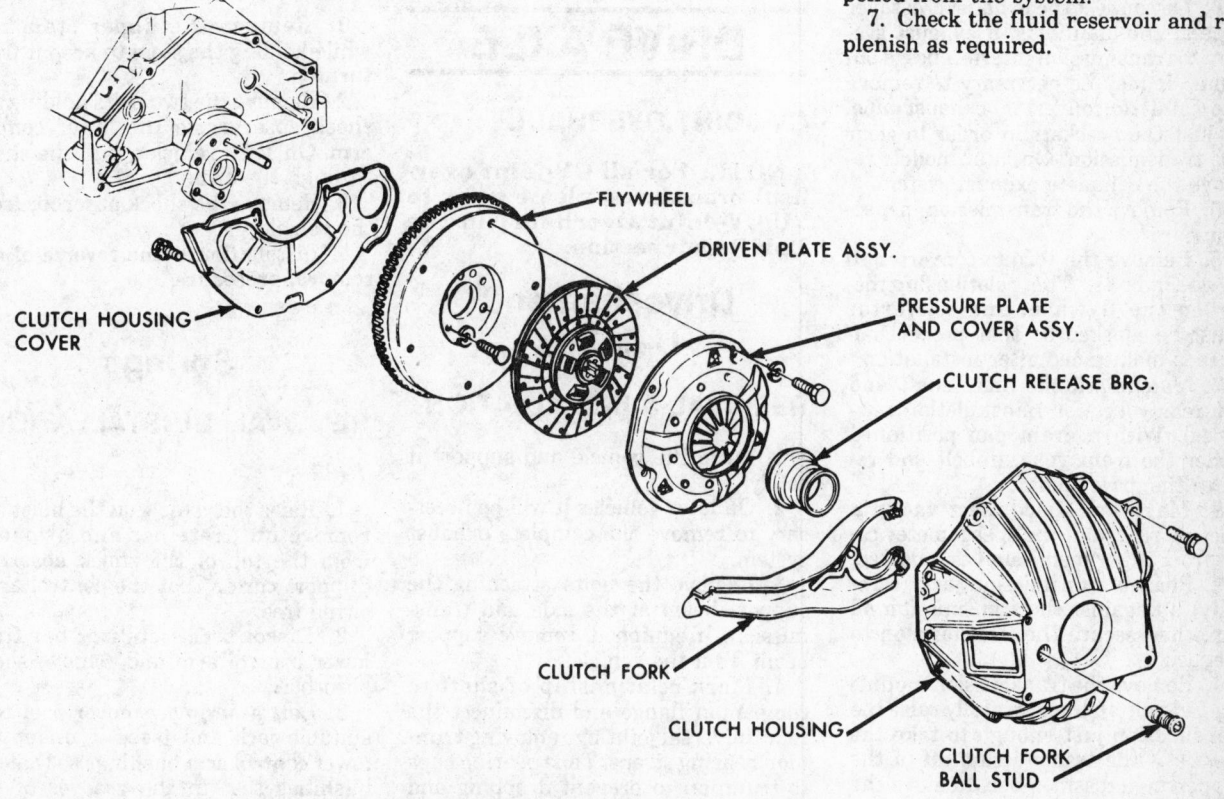

Exploded view of the clutch assembly

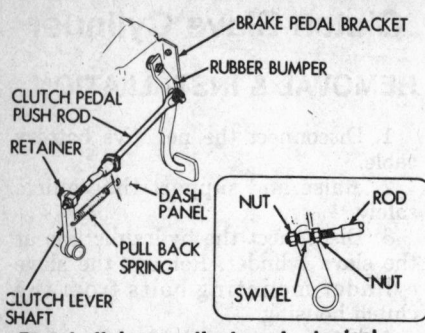

Clutch linkage adjustment—typical

Labels: BRAKE PEDAL BRACKET, RUBBER BUMPER, CLUTCH PEDAL PUSH ROD, RETAINER, DASH PANEL, PULL BACK SPRING, CLUTCH LEVER SHAFT, NUT, ROD, SWIVEL, NUT

AUTOMATIC TRANSMISSION

For further information on automatic transmissions, please refer to "Automatic Transmissions" in the Unit Repair Section.

REMOVAL & INSTALLATION

1. Disconnect the negative battery cable at the battery.
2. If so equipped, disconnect the detent/downshift cable at its upper end (accelerator pedal or carburetor).
3. Raise and support the vehicle safely.
4. Disconnect the exhaust crossover pipe at the manifolds, if exhaust system to transmission interference is obvious. It may be necessary to remove the catalytic convertor, exhaust pipe, or just the brackets in order to clear the transmission. On later models remove the complete exhaust system.
5. Remove the transmission inspection cover.
6. Remove the torque convertor to flywheel bolts. The relationship between the flywheel and convertor must be marked so that proper balance is maintained after installation.
7. Matchmark the drive shaft and the rear yoke (for reinstallation purposes). With a drain pan positioned under the front yoke, unbolt and remove the drive shaft.
8. Mark and disconnect vacuum lines, wiring, and the speedometer cable from the transmission as required.
9. Place a transmission jack (carefully) up against the transmission oil pan, then secure the transmission to the jack.
10. Remove the transmission mounting pad bolt(s), then carefully raise the transmission just enough to take the weight of the transmission off of the supporting crossmember. Remove the transmission mounting pad.

NOTE: Exercise extreme care to avoid damage to underhood components while raising or lowering the transmission.

11. Remove the transmission dipstick, then unbolt and remove the filler tube.
12. Disconnect the floor shift cable. Disconnect the oil cooler lines from the transmission.
13. Support the engine using a jack placed beneath the engine oil pan. Be sure to put a block of wood between the jack and the oil pan, to prevent damage to the pan.
14. With the proper gauge wire, fasten the torque convertor to the transmission case.
15. Remove the transmission to engine mounting bolts, then carefully move the transmission rearward, downward, and out from beneath the vehicle.

NOTE: If interference is encountered with the cable(s), cooler lines, etc., remove the component(s) before finally lowering the transmission.

16. Installation is the reverse of the removal procedure. Adjust the shift control cable and T.V. cable. Refill the transmission to the proper level with the proper type and grade fluid (Dexron II Automatic Transmission Fluid).

DRIVE AXLE

CV JOINT OVERHAUL

NOTE: For all CV-joint overhaul procedures, please refer to "U/CV-Joint Overhaul" in the Unit Repair section.

Driveshaft and U-Joints

REMOVAL & INSTALLATION

1. Raise the vehicle and support it safely.
2. On later vehicles it will be necessary to remove the complete exhaust system.
3. Remove the bolts attaching the support beam at the axle and transmission. If equipped, remove support beam from the vehicle.
4. Mark relationship of shaft to companion flange and disconnect the rear universal joint by removing trunnion bearing straps. Tape bearing cups to trunnion to prevent dropping and loss of bearing rollers.

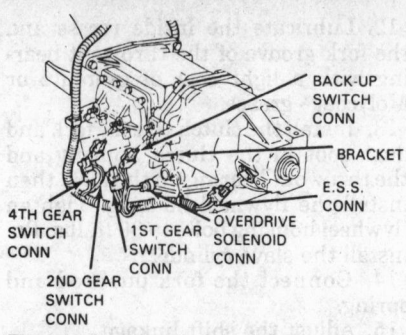

Electrical connectors on 4–speed overdrive transmission

Labels: BACK-UP SWITCH CONN, BRACKET, E.S.S. CONN, OVERDRIVE SOLENOID CONN, 1ST GEAR SWITCH CONN, 2ND GEAR SWITCH CONN, 4TH GEAR SWITCH CONN

5. Slide slip yoke from the transmission and remove shaft. Watch for oil leakage from transmission output shaft housing.
6. Installation is the reverse of the removal procedure.

FRONT SUSPENSION

Shock Absorbers

REMOVAL & INSTALLATION

1. Remove the upper stem nut while holding the stem to keep it from turning.
2. Remove the two bolts holding the shock absorber to the lower control arm. On 1982 vehicles, pull the shock through the arm.
3. Remove the shock absorber from the vehicle.
4. Installation is the reverse of the removal procedure.

Springs

REMOVAL & INSTALLATION

1982

1. Raise the vehicle on the hoist and remove nut, retainer and grommet from the top of the shock absorber. Support car so that the control arms swing free.
2. Disconnect stabilizer bar from lower control arm and remove shock absorber.
3. Bolt a spring remover tool to a suitable jack and place it under the lower control arm bushings so that the bushings seat in the grooves of the tool.

NOTE: This tool is a cradle which, when fastened to a hydraulic jack, allows the lowering of the control arm and slow decompression of the spring. A similar tool can be fabricated in the shop. Always safety chain the spring and control arm when using this method.

NOTE Spring to be installed with tape at lowest position. Bottom of spring is coiled helical, and the top is coiled flat with a gripper notch near end of wire.

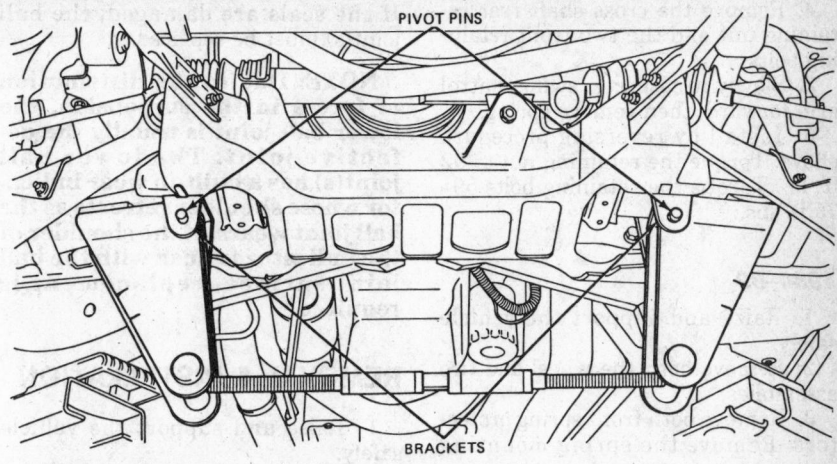

PIVOT PINS

BRACKETS

NOTE: PIVOT PINS ARE REMOVED SO THAT THE BRACKET MAY BE PLACED OVER THE TOP OF THE SPRING.

1984–89 front spring and pivot pin removal

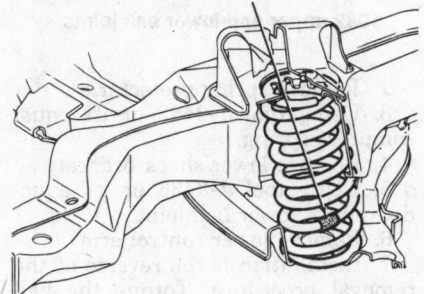

NOTE After assembly, end of spring coil must cover all or part of one inspection drain hole. The other hole must be partly exposed or completely uncovered.

1982 front spring suspension

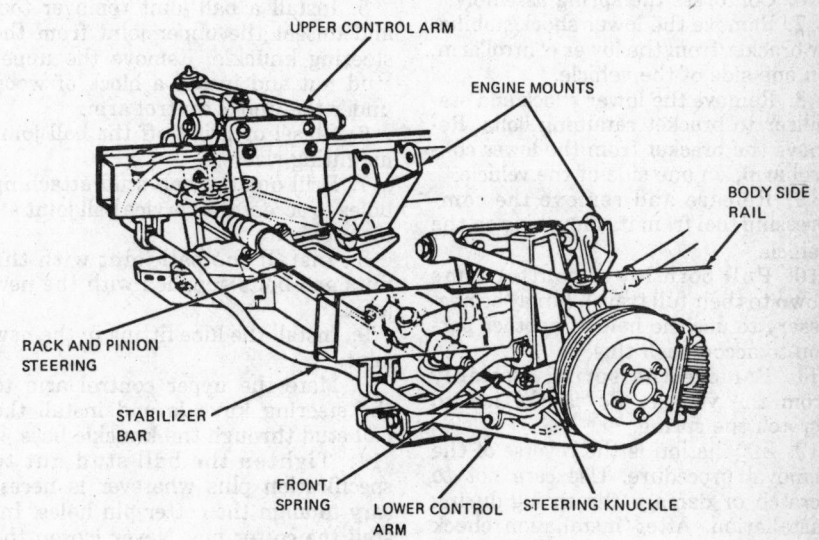

UPPER CONTROL ARM

ENGINE MOUNTS

BODY SIDE RAIL

RACK AND PINION STEERING

STABILIZER BAR

FRONT SPRING

LOWER CONTROL ARM

STEERING KNUCKLE

1984–89 front suspension components

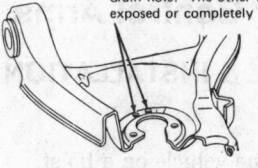

NOTE Hold stud at this point to obtain torque.

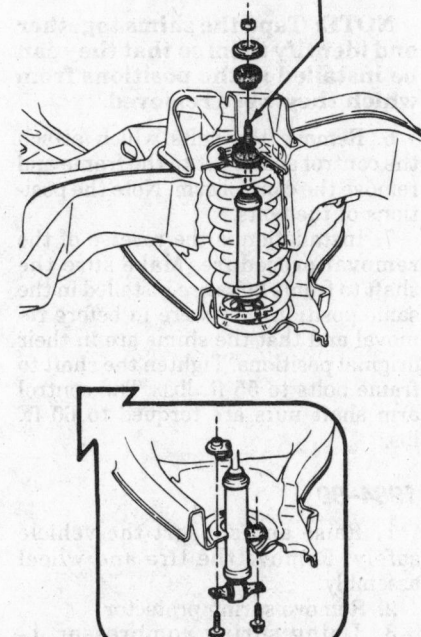

1982 front shock absorber installation

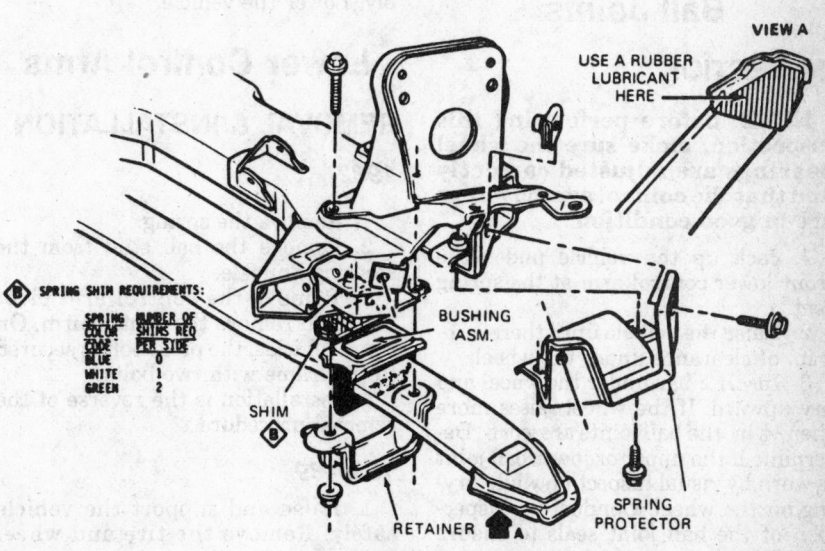

VIEW A

USE A RUBBER LUBRICANT HERE

SPRING SHIM REQUIREMENTS:

SPRING COLOR CODE	NUMBER OF SHIMS REQ PER SIDE
BLUE	0
WHITE	1
GREEN	2

BUSHING ASM.

SHIM

RETAINER

SPRING PROTECTOR

Front spring assembly

4. Remove the cross shaft rear retaining nut and the two front retaining bolts.

5. Slowly release jack, swing control arm forward, then remove spring.

6. Install by reversing procedure above. Torque the retaining nut to 92 ft. lb.. Torque the retaining bolts 59–75 ft. lbs..

1984–89

1. Raise and support the vehicle safely.

2. Remove both the wheel and tire assemblies.

3. Remove both front spring protectors. Remove the spring mounting nuts.

4. Install spring compressing tool J–3432 or equivalent.

5. Disconnect both lower ball joints using tool J–3436 or equivalent.

6. Compress the spring assembly.

7. Remove the lower shock/stabilizer bracket from the lower control arm, on one side of the vehicle.

8. Remove the lower shock and stabilizer to bracket retaining bolts. Remove the bracket from the lower control arm, on one side of the vehicle.

9. Release and remove the compressing tool from its mounting on the vehicle.

10. Pull both lower control arms down to their full travel. It may be necessary to use the help of another person to accomplish this.

11. Remove the spring assembly from the vehicle. Be careful not to scratch the spring.

12. Installation is the reverse of the removal procedure. Use care not to scratch or damage the spring during installation. After installation check wheel alignment.

Ball Joints

INSPECTION

NOTE: Before performing this inspection, make sure the wheel bearings are adjusted correctly and that the control arm bushings are in good condition.

1. Jack up the vehicle under the front lower control arm at the spring seat.

2. Raise the vehicle until there is 1–2 in. of clearance under the wheel.

3. Insert a bar under the wheel and pry upward. If the wheel raises more then ⅛ in. the ball joints are worn. Determine if the upper or lower ball joint is worn by visual inspection while prying on the wheel. Conduct an inspection of the ball joint seals to ensure that there are no cuts or tears present.

If the seals are damaged, the ball joint(s) must be replaced.

NOTE: Due to the distribution of forces in the suspension, the lower ball joint is usually the defective joint. The lower ball joint(s) has a built-in wear indicator whose shoulder retreats as the ball joint wears. If the shoulder of the indicator is flush with the ball joint surface, replacement is required.

REMOVAL & INSTALLATION

1. Raise and support the vehicle safely.

2. Remove the tire and wheel assembly.

3. Support the lower control arm with a jack.

4. Loosen the upper ball stud nut.

5. Install a ball joint remover tool and unseat the upper joint from the steering knuckle. Remove the upper stud nut and install a block of wood under the upper control arm.

6. Chisel or grind off the ball joint mounting rivets.

7. Drill out the ball stud attaching holes to accept the service ball joint attaching bolts.

8. Install the ball joint with the nuts and bolts supplied with the new joint.

9. Install the lube fitting in the new joint.

10. Mate the upper control arm to the steering knuckle and install the ball stud through the knuckle boss.

11. Tighten the ball stud nut to specification plus whatever is necessary to align the cotter pin holes. Install the cotter pin. Never loosen the nut to align the cotter pin holes.

12. Install the tire and wheel assembly. Lower the vehicle.

Lower Control Arms

REMOVAL & INSTALLATION

1982

1. Remove the spring.

2. Remove the ball stud from the steering knuckle.

3. Remove the control arm pivot bolts and remove the control arm. On some vehicles, the pivot bolt is secured to the frame with two bolts.

4. Installation is the reverse of the removal procedure.

1984–89

1. Raise and support the vehicle safely. Remove the tire and wheel assembly.

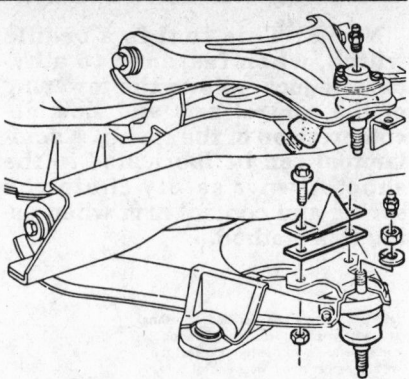

1982 upper and lower ball joints

2. Remove spring protector.

3. Using tool J–3432 or its equal compress spring.

4. Remove lower shock bracket.

5. Using tool J–3436 or its equal disconnect lower ball joint.

6. Remove lower control arm.

7. Installation is the reverse of the removal procedure. Torque the ball joint nut to specification.

Upper Control Arms

REMOVAL & INSTALLATION

1982

1. Raise the vehicle on a hoist.

2. Support the outer end of the lower control arm, with a jack.

3. Remove the wheel.

4. Separate the upper ball joint from the steering knuckle.

5. Remove the control arm shaft to frame nuts.

NOTE: Tape the shims together and identify them so that they can be installed in the positions from which they were removed.

6. Remove the bolts which attach the control arm shaft to the frame and remove the control arm. Note the positions of the bolts.

7. Installation is the reverse of the removal procedure. Make sure the shaft to frame bolts are installed in the same position they were in before removal and that the shims are in their original positions. Tighten the shaft to frame bolts to 55 ft. lbs.. The control arm shaft nuts are torqued to 60 ft. lbs..

1984–89

1. Raise and support the vehicle safely. Remove the tire and wheel assembly.

2. Remove spring protector.

3. Using spring compressor J–33432 or its equivalent, compress and loosen the spring.

4. Use tool J–33436 or its equivalent to disconnect the upper ball joint from the knuckle.

5. Remove the upper control arm.

6. Installation is the reverse of the removal procedure. Torque upper control arm bolts to specification and the ball joint nut to specification. The cotter pin at the ball joint must be installed from rear to front. Do not back off the nut for the cotter pin.

Front Wheel Bearings

ADJUSTMENT

1982

1. Raise the vehicle and support if safely.

2. Remove the dust cap from the hub. Remove the cotter pin and discard it. Remove the locknut.

3. Remove the outer wheel bearing from its mounting.

4. Remove the rotor. Remove the inner wheel bearing from its mounting.

5. Installation is the reverse of the removal procedure. To adjust, tighten the spindle nut to 12 ft. lbs. while turning the wheel. Then back off the nut ¼–½ turn.

6. Retighten the nut by hand until it is finger tight.

6. Loosen the nut no more than ⅟₆ of a turn until the nearest hole in the spindle lines up with the slot in the spindle nut, and insert a new cotter pin.

7. Feel the looseness in the hub assembly. There should be 0.001–0.005 in. endplay.

REMOVAL & INSTALLATION

1982

1. Raise and support the vehicle safely.

2. Remove the tire and wheel assembly.

3. Remove the caliper assembly and position it out of the way.

4. Remove the cotter pin, lock nut and washer.

5. Remove the outer bearing assembly.

6. Remove the rotor. Remove the inner bearing assembly.

7. Installation is the reverse of the removal procedure. Be sure to use new grease seals, as required.

1984–89

1. Raise and support the vehicle safely.

2. Remove the tire and wheel assembly.

3. Remove the caliper assembly and position it out of the way.

4. Remove the hub and bearing assembly.

5. Installation is the reverse of the removal procedure. The bearings do not require adjustment.

Front Wheel Alignment

CASTER

Caster is the tilting of the steering axis

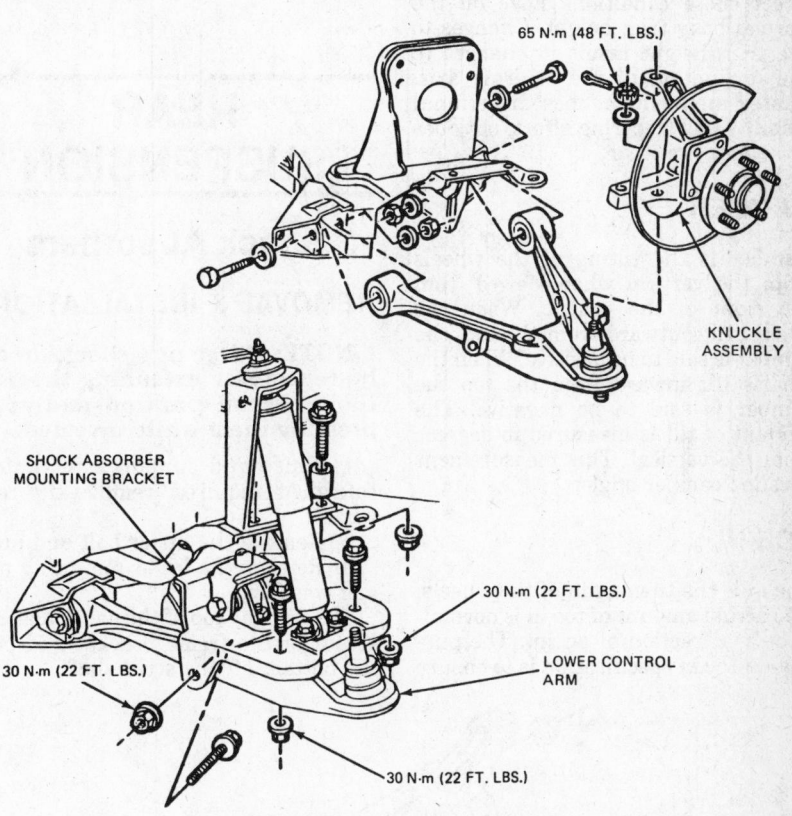

1984–89 lower control arm assembly

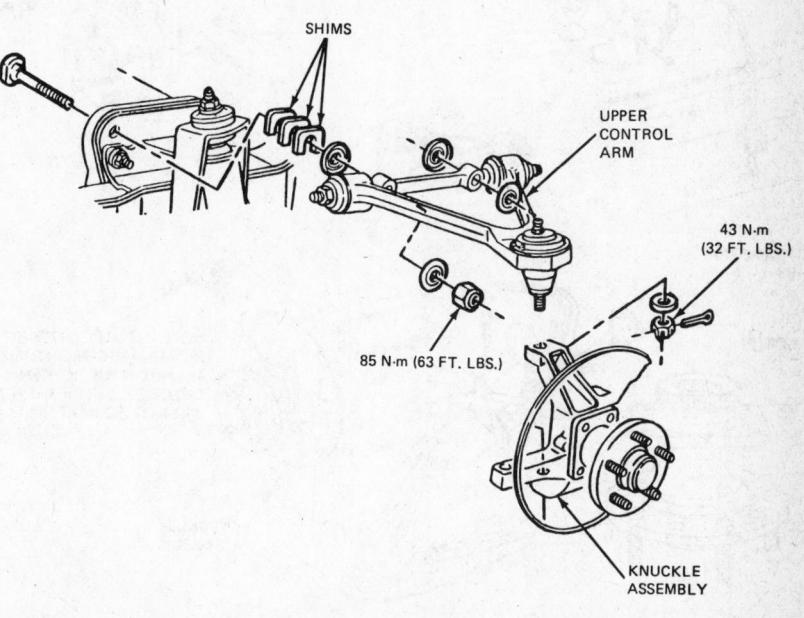

1984–88 upper control arm removal and installation

either forward or backward from the vertical, when viewed from the side of the vehicle. A backward tilt is said to be positive and a forward tilt is said to be negative. Weak springs or overloading of a vehicle effect caster due to the effect these conditions have on the normal body trim height. Changes to the trim height result in changes to the inclination of the steering axis. Caster angle influences directional stability and steeering effort, but does not effect tire wear.

CAMBER

Camber is the tilting of the wheels from the vertical when viewed from the front of the vehicle. When the wheels tilt outward from the top, the camber is said to be positive. When the wheels tilt inward from the top the camber is said to be negative. The amount of tilt is measured in degrees from the vertical. This measurement is called camber angle.

TOE IN

Toe in is the turning in of the wheels. The actual amount of toe in is normally only a fraction of an in.. The purpose of toe in specification is to ensure

parallel rolling of the wheels. Toe in also serves to offset the small deflections of the steering support system which occur when the vehicle is rolling forward.

REAR SUSPENSION

Shock Absorbers

REMOVAL & INSTALLATION

NOTE: Purge new shocks of air by repeatedly extending them in their normal position and compressing them while inverted.

1. Raise and support the vehicle safely. As required, remove the rear wheels.
2. Remove the upper bolt and nut.
3. Remove the lower mounting nut and washers.
4. Pivot the top of the shock absorber out of the frame bracket and pull the bottom off the strut shaft.

5. Slide the upper shock absorber eye into the frame bracket and install the bolt, lockwasher, and nut.
6. Install the rubber grommets on the lower shock eye and place the shock over the strut shaft. Install the washers and nut.
7. Lower the vehicle.

Springs

REMOVAL & INSTALLATION

1982

1. Raise the vehicle and support it by the frame, slightly forward of torque control pivot points. Remove the tire and wheel assemblies.
2. Place a floor jack under the spring near the link bolt, and raise the spring until it is nearly flat.
3. Tie the end of the spring to the suspension crossmember to hold this flat attitude, with a ¼ in. or ⁵/₁₆ in. chain and grab hook wrapped around the spring and crossmember. To prevent chain slipping, use a C-clamp on the spring adjacent to the chain.
4. Remove link bolt and rubber bushings.
5. Support and raise the spring end, as before, and remove chain.

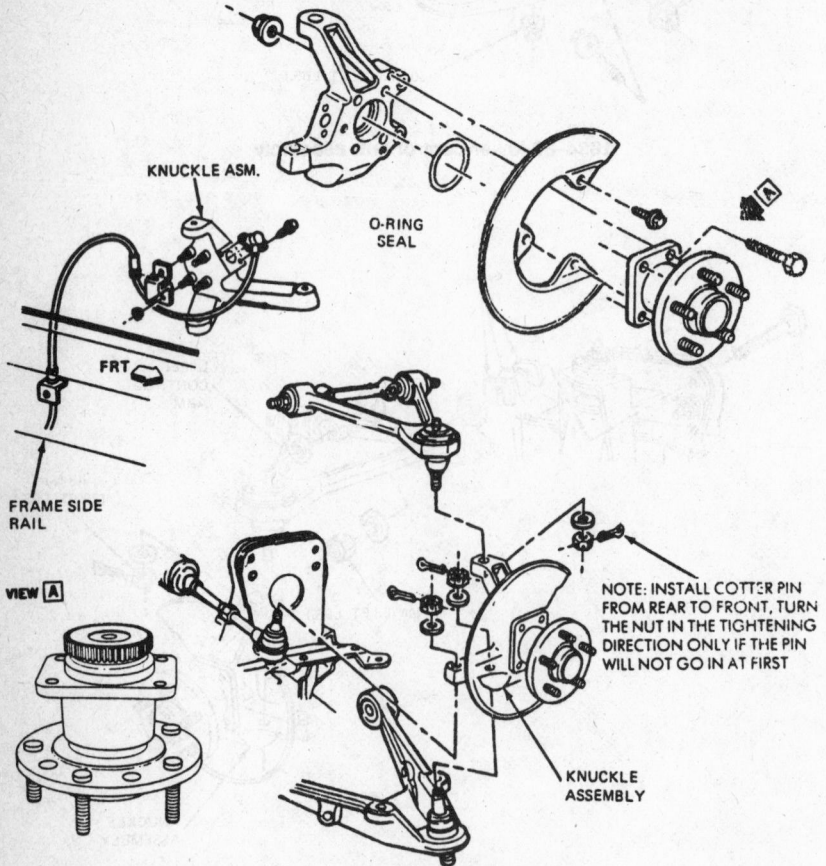

1984–89 wheel bearing assembly

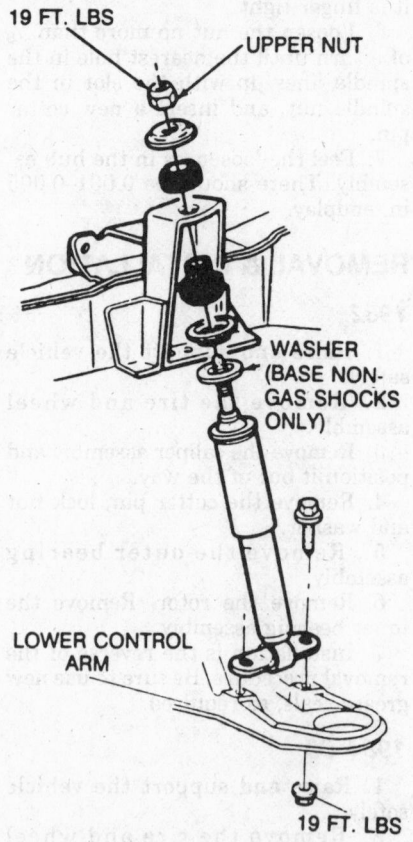

Exploded view of the rear shock absorber and mounting assemblies—1988–89

6. Carefully lower jack to completely relax spring.

7. Repeat the procedure on the other side of the vehicle.

8. Remove bolts and washers attaching the springs at the center.

9. Remove the spring by sliding it over the exhaust pipes and out one side of the vehicle.

10. Installation is the reverse of the removal procedure. Always use new link bolts and cushions. Torque the rear spring to carrier bolts to 50 ft. lbs. Install the nut on the link bolt just far enough to expose the cotter pin hole, then insert the pin.

1984–89

1. Raise and support the vehicle safely.

2. Remove both tire and wheel assemblies.

3. Remove the cotter pins, retaining nuts, rubber bushings and the link bolt that retains the spring to the knuckle.

4. Remove the spring retaining bolts, spacers and insulators. Remove the spring from the carrier beam.

5. Installation is the reverse of the removal procedure.

Rear Control Arms

REMOVAL & INSTALLATION

1984–89

1. Raise and support the vehicle safely.

2. Disconnect the spring at the knuckle.

3. Remove the control arm nut and bolt at the knuckle.

4. Remove control arm nut and bolt at the body bracket. Remove the control arm.

5. Installation is the reverse of the removal procedure.

Rear Wheel Bearings

ADJUSTMENT

1982

1. Raise and support the vehicle safely.

2. Remove the tire and wheel assembly.

3. Remove the axle driveshaft.

4. Mark the camber cam in relation to the bracket. Loosen and turn the camber bolt until the strut rod forces the torque control arm outward.

5. Mount a dial indicator on the torque control surface and rest the pointer on the flange end.

6. Grasp the rotor and move it in and out. If the bearing movement is with specifications no adjustment is

necessary. If the adjustment is not within these limits you must add or subtract shims accordingly. The rear wheel bearings should have end play of 0.001–0.008 in.

REMOVAL & INSTALLATION

1982

1. Raise and support the vehicle safely.

2. Remove the wheel and tire assembly.

3. Remove the axle drive shaft.

4. Apply the parking brake to prevent the rotors from turning.

5. Remove the cotter pin, nut and flange.

NOTE: It may be necessary to use special tool J08614–01, or its equivalent, to remove the flange.

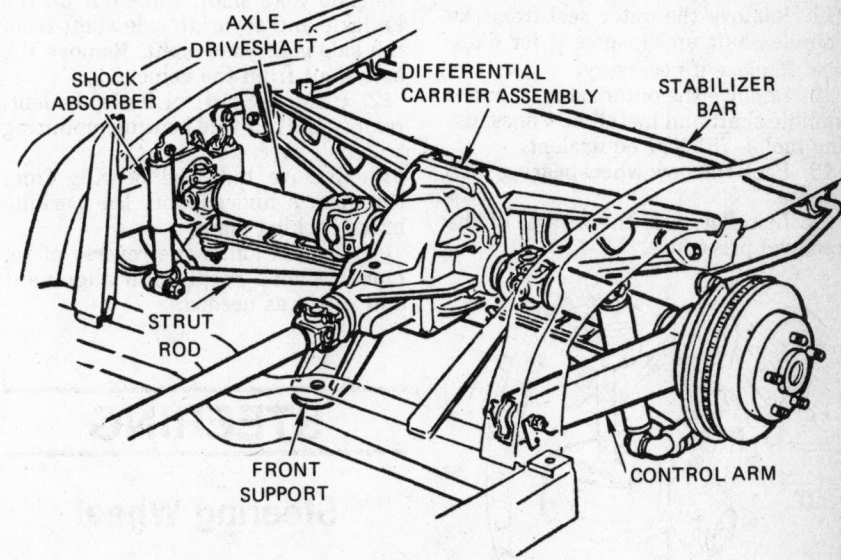

Rear suspension assembly

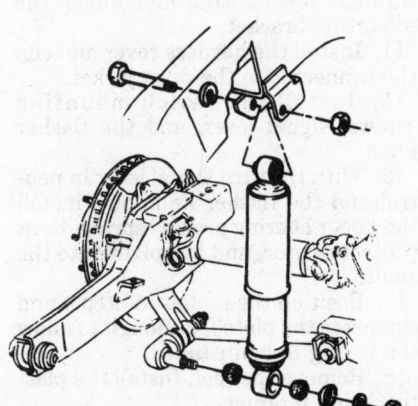

1984–89 upper control arm assembly

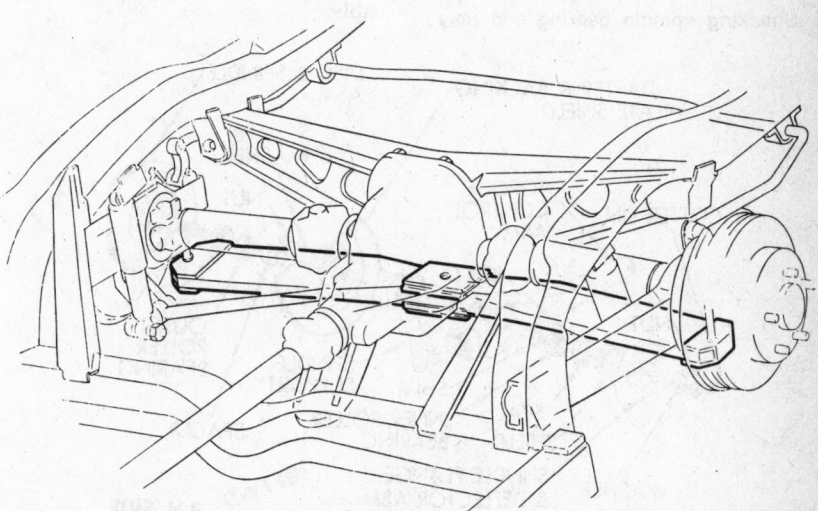

Fiberglass-reinforced plastic (F.P.R.) single leaf rear spring

6. Install tool J–21859–1, or equivalent, over the spindle threads, then remove the drive spindle from its support using tool J–22602 or equivalent. When using this tool make sure the puller plate is positioned vertically in the torque control arm before applying pressure to the puller screw.

7. When the spindle is removed, the outer bearing will remain on the spindle. The inner bearing, tubular spacer, end-play adjustment shim and both outer races will remain in the spindle support.

8. Remove the bearing, spacer and shim. Record the shim thickness for later use.

9. With the spindle assembly on the bench, position tool J24489–1, or equivalent, between the outer bearing and the seal.

10. Using puller J–8433–1, or equivalent, draw the bearing off the spindle.

11. Remove the outer seal from the spindle shaft and inspect it for damage. Replace if necessary.

12. Remove the outer races from the spindle shaft and install new ones, using tool J–7817, or equivalent.

13. Pack the new wheel bearing with grease.

14. Installation is the reverse of the removal procedure.

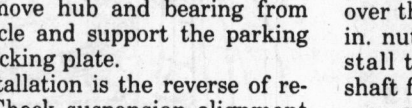

Checking spindle bearing end play

1984–89

1. Remove center cap from wheel.

2. Remove cotter pin, spindle nut and washer.

3. Raise and support the vehicle safely.

4. Remove the wheel and tire assembly.

5. Remove brake caliper and support.

6. Remove brake rotor.

7. Disconnect tie rod end from the knuckle.

8. Disconnect transverse spring from the knuckle.

9. Scribe mark on cam bolt and mounting bracket so they can be re-aligned in the same position.

10. Remove cam bolt and separate spindle support rod from the mounting bracket.

11. Remove the trunnion straps at the side yoke shaft. Push out on the knuckle and separate axle shaft from the side gear yoke shaft. Remove the axle shaft from the vehicle.

12. Using J–34161 or its equivalent, remove the hub and bearing mounting bolts.

13. Remove hub and bearing from the vehicle and support the parking brake backing plate.

14. Installation is the reverse of removal. Check suspension alignment and adjust as needed.

STEERING

Steering Wheel

REMOVAL & INSTALLATION

1. Disconnect the negative battery cable.

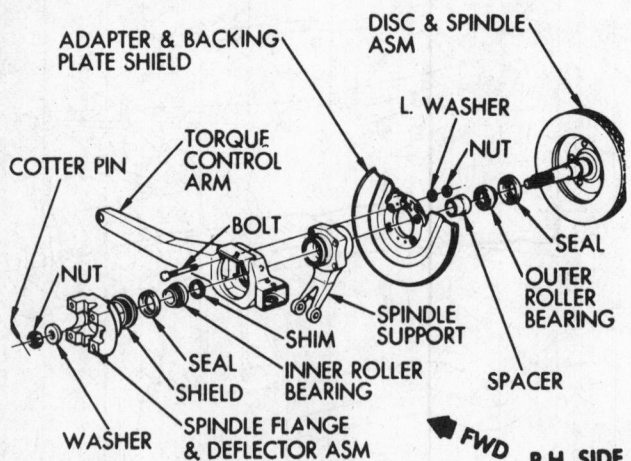

Exploded view of spindle

2. Squeeze the horn cap (top and bottom), disengage the locking fingers and remove the cap.

3. Remove the retaining screws and remove the upper horn contact assembly. disconnect the horn lead wire connector.

4. If used, remove the shim then remove the screw securing the center star screw. Remove the star screw and telescope adjusting lever assembly.

5. Remove the snapring and nut from the shaft. Remove the steering wheel assembly with a wheel puller.

6. Installation is the reverse of the removal procedure.

Turn Signal Switch

REMOVAL & INSTALLATION

1. Disconnect the negative battery cable. Remove the steering wheel.

2. Remove the steering column/dash trim cover.

3. Remove the C-ring plastic retainer, if so equipped.

4. Install the special lockplate compressing tool (J–23653 and J–23063) over the steering shaft. Position a $\frac{5}{16}$ in. nut under each tool leg and reinstall the star screw to prevent the shaft from moving.

5. Compress the lockplate by turning the shaft nut clockwise until the C-ring can be removed.

6. Remove the tool and lift out the lockplate, horn contact carrier, and the upper bearing preload spring.

7. Pull the switch connector out of the mast jacket and tape the upper part to facilitate switch removal.

8. Remove the turn signal lever. Push the flasher in and unscrew it.

9. Position the turn signal and shifter housing in Low position. Remove the switch by pulling it straight up while guiding the wiring harness out of the housing.

10. Install the replacement switch by working the harness connector down through the housing and under the mounting bracket.

11. Install the harness cover and clip the connector to the mast jacket.

12. Install the switch mounting screws, signal lever, and the flasher knob.

13. With the turn signal lever in neutral and the flasher knob out, install the upper bearing preload spring, horn contact carrier, and lockplate onto the shaft.

14. Position the tool as in Step 4 and compress the plate far enough to allow the C-ring to be installed.

15. Remove the tool. Install the plastic C-ring retainer.

16. Install the column/dash trim cover. Install the steering wheel.

Ignition Lock

REMOVAL & INSTALLATION

1. Disconnect the negative battery cable. Remove the steering wheel.
2. Remove the rubber sleeve bumper from the steering shaft.

3. Using an appropriate tool, remove the plastic retainer.
4. Using a spring compressor, compress the upper steering shaft spring and remove the C-ring. Release the steering shaft lockplate, the horn contact carrier, and the upper steering shaft preload spring.

5. Remove the four screws which hold the upper mounting bracket and then remove the bracket.
6. Slide the harness connector out of the bracket on the steering column. Tape the upper part of the harness and connector.
7. Disconnect the hazard button and position the shift bowl in park. Remove the turn signal lever from the column.
8. If the vehicle is equipped with cruise control remove the harness protector from the harness. Attach a piece of wire to the switch harness connector. Before removing the turn signal lever, loop a piece of wire and insert it into the turn signal lever opening. Use the wire to pull the cruise control harness out through the opening. Pull the rest of the harness up through and out of the column. Remove the guide wire from the connector and secure the wire to the column. Remove the turn signal lever.
9. Pull the turn signal switch up until the end connector is within the shift bowl. Remove the hazard flasher lever. Allow the switch to hang.
10. Place the ignition key in the run position.
11. Depress the center of the lock cylinder retaining tab with a suitable tool and then remove the lock cylinder.

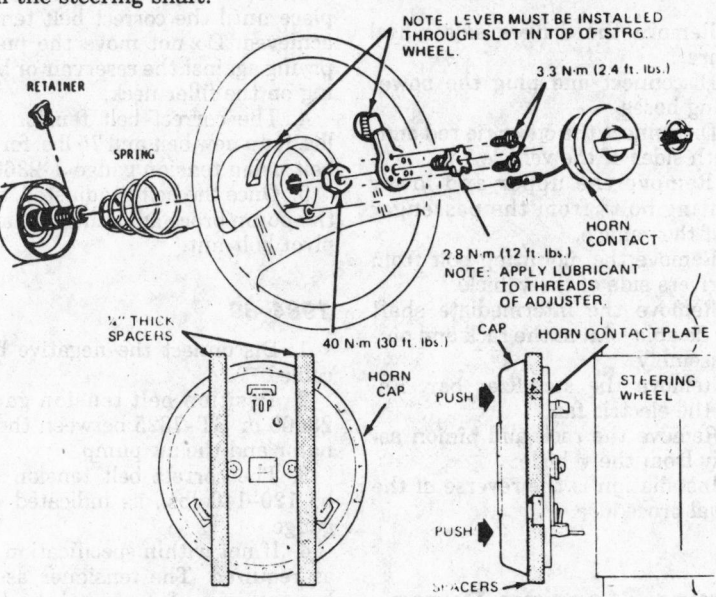

NOTE: LEVER MUST BE INSTALLED THROUGH SLOT IN TOP OF STRG. WHEEL.

3.3 N·m (2.4 ft. lbs.)

RETAINER

SPRING

HORN CONTACT

2.8 N·m (12 ft. lbs.)
NOTE: APPLY LUBRICANT TO THREADS OF ADJUSTER.

¼" THICK SPACERS

40 N·m (30 ft. lbs.)

CAP   HORN CONTACT PLATE

HORN CAP

PUSH

PUSH

SPACERS

STEERING WHEEL

Exploded view of the steering wheel assembly—1984–89

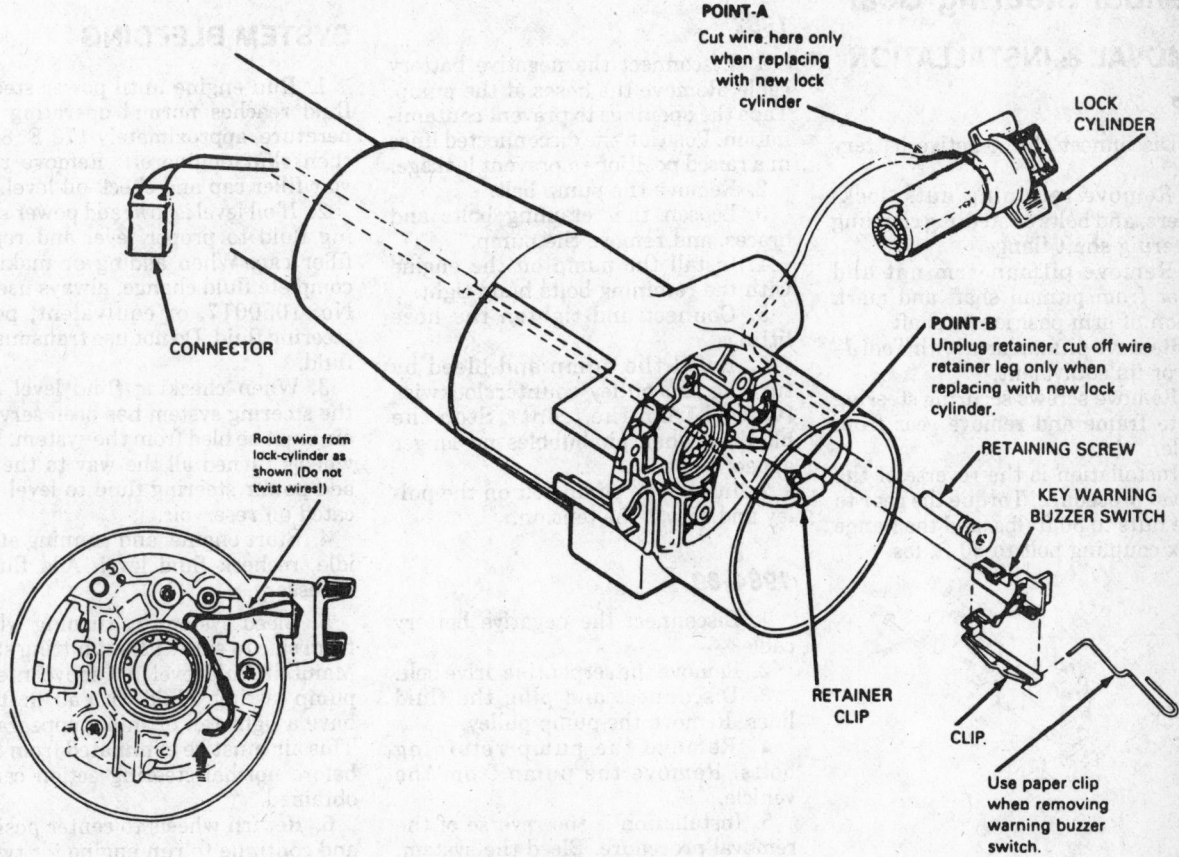

POINT-A
Cut wire here only when replacing with new lock cylinder

LOCK CYLINDER

CONNECTOR

Route wire from lock-cylinder as shown (Do not twist wires!)

POINT-B
Unplug retainer, cut off wire retainer leg only when replacing with new lock cylinder.

RETAINING SCREW

KEY WARNING BUZZER SWITCH

RETAINER CLIP

CLIP.

Use paper clip when removing warning buzzer switch.

Lock cylinder installation

12. On some vehicles it will be necessary to cut and splice an electrical wire which is a part of the lock cylinder.

13. Installation is the reverse of the removal procedure.

Ignition Switch

REMOVAL & INSTALLATION

1. Disconnect the negative battery terminal.

2. Loosen the retaining screws on the steering column.

3. Remove the column to instrument panel trim plates and attaching nuts.

4. Lower the steering column. Be sure that the steering column is supported at all times in order to prevent damage to the column. disconnect the switch wire connectors.

5. Remove the switch attaching screws and remove the switch.

6. To replace, move the key lock to the LOCK position.

7. Move the actuator rod hole in the switch to the LOCK position.

8. Install the switch with the rod in the hole.

9. Position and reassemble the steering column in reverse of the disassembly procedure.

Manual Steering Gear

REMOVAL & INSTALLATION

1982

1. Disconnect the negative battery cable.

2. Remove retaining nuts, lockwashers, and bolts at steering coupling to steering shaft flange.

3. Remove pitman arm nut and washer from pitman shaft and mark relation of arm position to shaft.

4. Remove pitman arm with Tool J–6632 or its equivalent.

5. Remove screws securing steering gear to frame and remove gear from vehicle.

6. Installation is the reverse of the removal procedure. Torque the gear to frame nuts to 30 ft. lbs. and the flange to flex coupling bolt to 30 ft. lbs.

1982 manual steering gear assembly

Power Steering Gear

REMOVAL & INSTALLATION

1984–89

1. Disconnect the negative battery cable. Raise and support the vehicle safely.

2. Remove the drivers side wheel and tire.

3. Disconnect and plug the power steering hoses.

4. Disconnect the outer tie rod ends on both sides of the vehicle.

5. Remove the upper and lower mounting bolts from the passenger side of the vehicle.

6. Remove the mounting bolt from the drivers side of the vehicle.

7. Remove the intermediate shaft lower flexible joint at the rack and pinion assembly.

8. Remove the stabilizer bar. Remove the electric fan.

9. Remove the rack and pinion assembly from the vehicle.

10. Installation is the reverse of the removal procedure.

Power Steering Pump

REMOVAL & INSTALLATION

1982

1. Disconnect the negative battery cable. Remove the hoses at the pump. Tape the openings to prevent contamination. Position the disconnected lines in a raised position to prevent leakage.

2. Remove the pump belt.

3. Loosen the retaining bolts and braces, and remove the pump.

4. Install the pump on the engine with the retaining bolts hand tight.

5. Connect and tighten the hose fittings.

6. Refill the pump and bleed by turning the pulley counterclockwise (viewed from the front). Stop the bleeding when air bubbles no longer appear.

7. Install the pump belt on the pulley and adjust the tension.

1984–89

1. Disconnect the negative battery cable.

2. Remove the serpentine drive belt.

3. Disconnect and plug the fluid lines. Remove the pump pulley.

4. Remove the pump retaining bolts. Remove the pump from the vehicle.

5. Installation is the reverse of the removal procedure. Bleed the system, as required.

BELT ADJUSTMENT

1982

1. Disconnect the negative battery cable.

2. Loosen the pivot bolt and pump brace adjusting nuts.

3. Move the pump with the belt in place until the correct belt tension is achieved. Do not move the pump by prying against the reservoir or by pulling on the filler neck.

4. The correct belt tension is 125 lbs. for a new belt and 75 lbs. for an old belt using tension gauge J–23600.

5. Once the belt is adjusted, tighten the pump brace adjusting nut and the pivot bolt nut.

1984–89

1. Disconnect the negative battery cable.

2. Position belt tension gauge J–23600 or BT–7825 between the alternator and the air pump.

3. The correct belt tension should be 120–140 lbs., as indicated on the gauge.

4. If not within specification adjust as required. The tensioner assembly has provisions for a visual check in order to verify that the belt tension is within the proper operating range.

SYSTEM BLEEDING

1. Run engine until power steering fluid reaches normal operating temperature, approximately 170°F (80°C), then shut engine off. Remove reservoir filler cap and check oil level.

2. If oil level is low, add power steering fluid to proper level and replace filler cap. When adding or making a complete fluid change, always use GM No. 1050017, or equivalent, power steering fluid. Do not use transmission fluid.

3. When checking fluid level after the steering system has been serviced, air must be bled from the system. With wheels turned all the way to the left, add power steering fluid to level indicated on reservoir.

4. Start engine, and running at fast idle, recheck fluid level. Add fluid if necessary.

5. Bleed system by turning wheels from side to side without hitting stops. Maintain fluid level just above internal pump casting. Fluid with air in it will have a light tan or milky appearance. This air must be eliminated from fluid before normal steering action can be obtained.

6. Return wheels to center position and continue to run engine for two or three minutes, then shut engine off.

7. Road test vehicle to make sure steering functions normally and is free from noise.

8. Recheck fluid level as described in Steps 1 and 2.

Tie Rod

REMOVAL & INSTALLATION

NOTE: Before attempting this procedure mark the tie rod threads with paint or chalk for easy reinstallation.

1. Remove the cotter pins and nuts from the tie rod end studs.

2. Tap on the steering arm near the tie rod end (use another hammer as backing) and pull down on the tie rod, if necessary, to free it.

3. Remove the inner stud in the same manner as the outer.

4. Loosen the clamp bolts and unscrew the ends if they are being replaced.

5. Lubricate the tie rod end threads with chassis grease if they were removed. Install each end assembly an equal distance from the sleeve.

6. Insure that the tie rod end stud threads and nut are clean. Install new seals and install the studs into the steering arms and relay rod.

7. Install the stud nuts. Tighten the nuts to 35 ft. lbs. plus as needed to align the cotter pin hole.

8. Adjust the toe-in.

NOTE: Before tightening the sleeve clamps, ensure that the clamps are positioned so that the adjusting sleeve slot is covered by the clamp.

BRAKES

For all brake system repair and service procedures not detailed below, please refer to "Brakes" in the Unit Repair section.

Master Cylinder

REMOVAL & INSTALLATION

1. Disconnect the negative battery cable. Disconnect and plug the brake lines at the master cylinder.

2. Remove the mounting nuts and lift off the cylinder.

3. Installation is the reverse of the removal procedure. Torque the nuts to 24 ft. lbs. and bleed the system.

Proportioning Valve

REMOVAL & INSTALLATION

1. Disconnect the negative battery cable. Disconnect and plug the hydraulic lines at the valve.

2. Disconnect the warning switch wiring harness from the valve switch terminal.

3. Remove the valve from its mounting.

4. Installation is the reverse of removal. Bleed the system.

Power Brake Booster

REMOVAL & INSTALLATION

1. Disconnect the negative battery cable. Remove the vacuum hose from the brake booster.

2. On 1982 vehicles remove the nuts that retain the master cylinder to

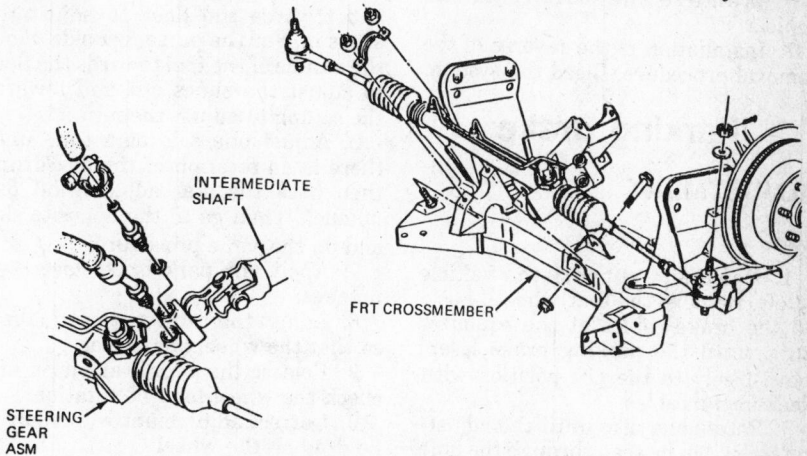

Typical rack and pinion assembly

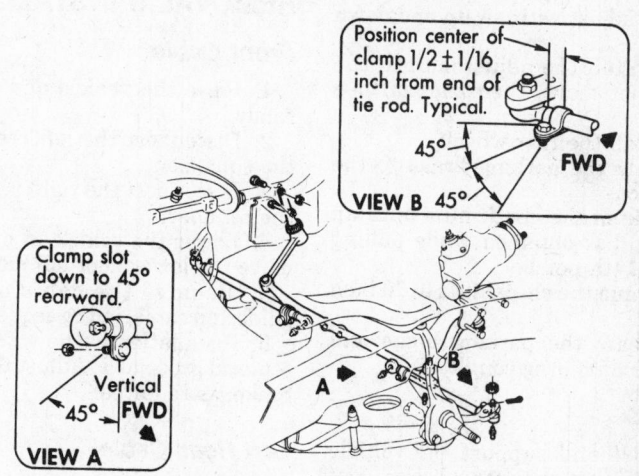

Typical steering linkage

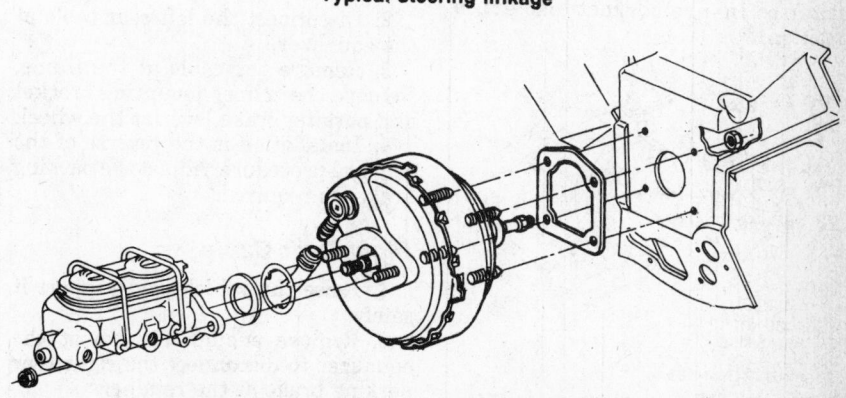

1982 power brake booster and master cylinder assembly

the brake booster and position it to the side. It is not necessary to disconnect the fluid lines.

3. On 1984–89 vehicles, disconnect and plug the hydraulic brake lines from the master cylinder. Remove the master cylinder from the brake booster.

4. Disconnect the push rod at the brake pedal.

5. Remove the nuts and lockwashers that secure the unit to the firewall.

6. Remove the unit from the vehicle.

7. Installation is the reverse of the removal procedure. Bleed the system.

Parking Brake

ADJUSTMENT

1982

1. Raise and support the vehicle safely. Remove the rear wheels. Loosen the brake cables at the equalizer nuts, until the parking brake levers move freely to the Off position with slack in the cables.

2. Rotate the disc until the adjusting screw can be seen through the hole in the disc.

3. Insert an appropriate tool in this hole and adjust with an up and down motion.

4. Tighten the adjuster until the disc cannot move, then back off 6–8 notches.

5. Install the rear wheels.

6. Apply the parking brake to the 13th notch.

7. Tighten the check nuts until an 80 lb. pull is obtained while pulling into the 14th notch.

8. Torque the check nuts to 70 inch lbs.

9. Release the parking brake and check for a no drag condition.

1984–89

1. Raise and support the vehicle safely. Remove the rear wheels, place two wheel lug nuts opposite of each other to insure correct disc/drum position.

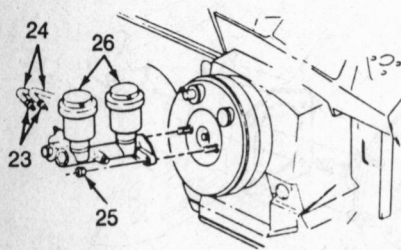

23	TUBE NUT
24	BRAKE PIPE
25	NUT
26	MASTER CYLINDER

Composite master cylinder assembly– 1988–89

2. Back the caliper piston into its bore.

3. Loosen the park brake cable so that there is no tension on the park brake shoes.

4. Rotate the disc so that the hole in the disc/drum face will align with the star adjuster.

5. To make the adjustment, insert a brake adjusting spoon through the hole in the disc face. For the driver's side, move the handle of the tool towards the roof to adjust the shoes out and towards the floor to adjust the shoes in. For the passenger side, move the handle of the tool towards the floor to adjust the shoes out and towards the ceiling to adjust them in.

6. Adjust one side at a time until there is no rotation of the disc/drum, then back the star adjuster off 5–7 notches. Then go to the opposite side and do the same procedure.

7. Apply the park brake lever two notches.

8. Adjust the cable at the equalizer so that the wheel has a drag.

9. Release the park brake lever and check the wheel for free rotation.

10. Correct adjustment will result in no drag on the wheel.

REMOVAL & INSTALLATION

Front Cable

1. Raise the vehicle and support it safely.

2. Disconnect the left rear cable at the equalizer.

3. Disconnect the right rear cable at the retainer.

4. Lower the vehicle in order to remove the lower door sill moulding.

5. Remove the cable nut, cable guide and cable, in the sequence given.

6. Installation is the reverse of the removal procedure. Adjust the parking brake, as required.

Left Rear Cable

1. Raise the vehicle and support it safely.

2. Disconnect the left rear cable at the equalizer.

3. Remove the cable at the frame. Remove the caliper mounting bracket and parking brake lever at the wheel.

4. Installation is the reverse of the removal procedure. Adjust the parking brake, as required.

Right Rear Cable

1. Raise the vehicle and support it safely.

2. Remove enough tension at the equalizer to disconnect the right rear parking brake at the retainer.

3. Remove the cable at the frame.

Remove the caliper mounting bracket and the parking brake lever at the wheel.

4. Installation is the reverse of the removal procedure. Adjust the parking brake as required.

CHASSIS ELECTRICAL

Heater Blower

REMOVAL & INSTALLATION

1982

1. Disconnect the negative battery cable at the battery.

2. Unbolt the A/C compressor and move the compressor out of the way. DO NOT disconnect the refrigerant lines from the compressor.

3. Remove the coolant recover jar, if so equipped.

4. Disconnect the wiring from the motor and the cooling tube from the motor case, if so equipped.

5. Remove the mounting screws from the blower motor and remove the motor. If the motor sticks to the case due to the sealer, pry the motor gently away from the case.

6. Installation is the reverse of the removal procedure.

1984–89

1. Disconnect the negative battery cable.

2. Remove the front wheel house rear panel and move wheel house seal aside.

3. Remove the motor cooling tube.

4. Remove the relay.

5. Remove the blower motor assembly to case attaching screws.

6. Remove the motor and impeller.

7. Installation is the reverse of the removal procedure.

Heater Core

REMOVAL & INSTALLATION

1982

1. Disconnect the negative battery cable.

2. Drain the coolant from the radiator.

3. Raise the right front of the vehicle and support it safely.

4. Disconnect the heater hoses at the heater core connections.

5. Remove the heater case retaining nut which is located on the top of the blower case.

6. Remove the glove box.

7. Remove the console side panels.

8. Remove the knobs and nuts from the radio shafts.

9. Remove the two screws which secure the console trim plate to the instrument cluster.

10. Remove the instrument cluster attaching screws.

11. Pull the cluster out slightly and disconnect the electrical connector from the rear of the cluster.

12. Remove the radio.

13. Remove the right side windshield pillar trim panel.

14. Remove the right side dash panel retaining screws and pull the panel rearward to release the upper retaining clip.

15. Remove the following ducts.

   a. Right side vent.

   b. Main vent distribution.

   c. Lower heater deflector.

   d. Heater defroster distribution duct assembly (Disconnect the vacuum line).

16. Disconnect both the temperature cable and the vacuum line at the heater housing.

17. Remove the heater core from the housing.

18. Installation is the reverse of the removal procedure.

1984–89

1. Disconnect the negative battery cable. Drain the cooling system.

2. Remove the instrument cluster bezel including the tilt wheel lever and instrument panel pad.

3. Remove the A/C distributor duct and disconnect the flex hose.

4. Remove the right side hush panel.

5. Remove the side window defroster flex hose.

6. Remove the side window defroster to heater cover screws and disconnect the extension.

7. Remove the temperature control cable and bracket assembly at heater cover including disconnecting heater door control shaft.

8. Remove the ECM (Electric Control Module) and disconnect the electrical connectors. Be sure that the ignition switch is off when disconnecting ECM.

9. Remove the tubular support brace from the door pillar to aluminum, instrument panel reinforcement brace.

10. Remove heater core cover attaching screws.

11. Remove heater pipe and heater water control bracket attaching screws.

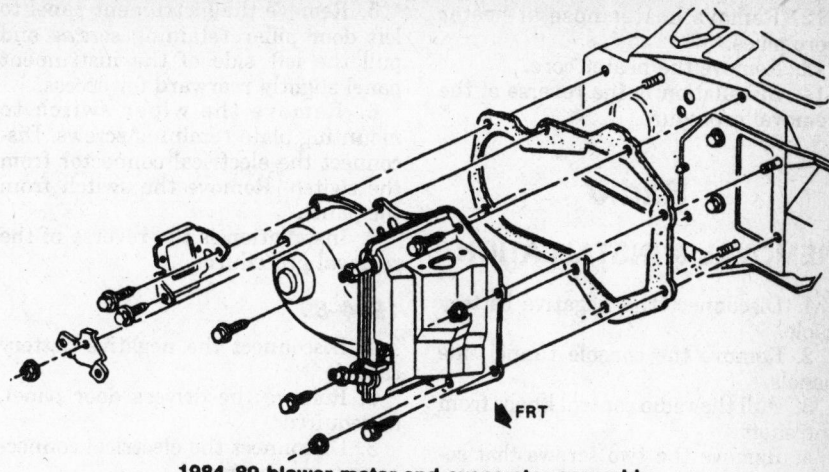

1984–89 blower motor and evaporator assembly

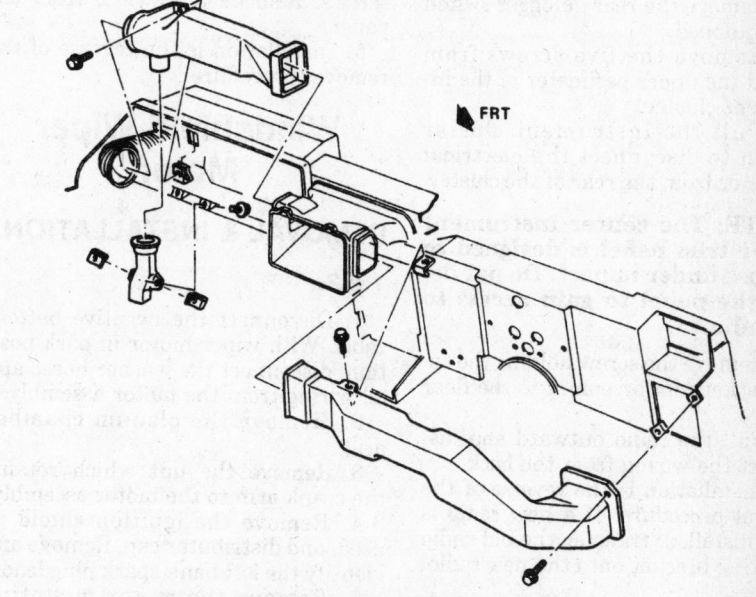

1984–89 duct assembly

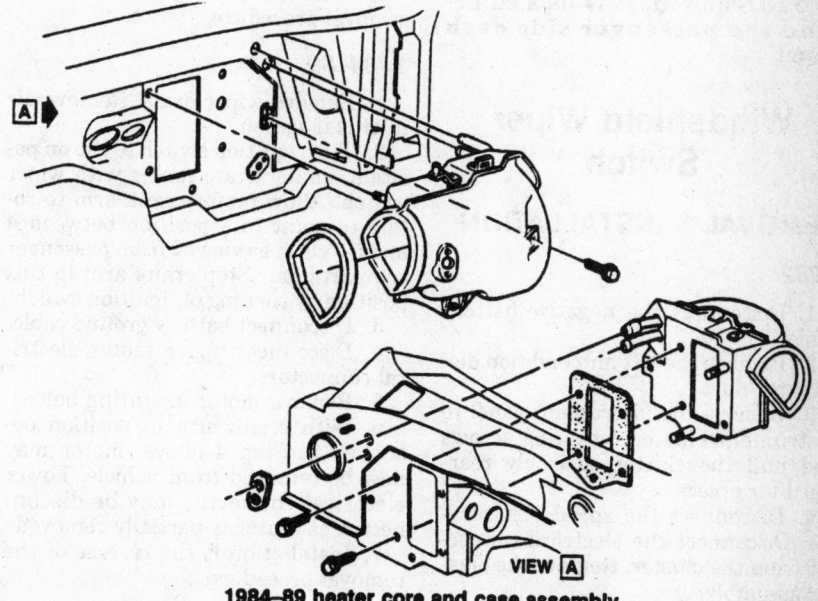

1984–89 heater core and case assembly

12. Remove heater hose at heater core pipes.

13. Remove the heater core.

14. Installation is the reverse of the removal procedure.

Radio

REMOVAL & INSTALLATION

1. Disconnect the negative battery cable.

2. Remove the console tunnel side panels.

3. Pull the radio control knobs from the shaft.

4. Remove the two screws that secure the console trim plate to the instrument cluster.

5. Remove the rear defogger switch if so equipped.

6. Remove the five screws from around the upper perimeter of the instrument cluster.

7. Pull the instrument cluster enough to disconnect the electrical connector from the rear of the cluster.

NOTE: The center instrument cluster trim panel is designed to collapse under impact. Do not deflect the panel to gain access to the radio.

8. Remove the screw holding the radio bracket reinforcement to the floor pan.

9. Pull the radio outward and disconnect the wiring from the back.

10. Installation is the reverse of the removal procedure. If a new radio is being installed, transfer the old radio mounting bracket onto the new radio.

NOTE: The radio heat sink must be removed when radio service is required. It is located behind the passenger side dash panel.

Windshield Wiper Switch

REMOVAL & INSTALLATION

1982

1. Disconnect the negative battery cable.

2. Remove the left air condition distributor duct.

3. Remove the instrument panel to instrument cluster retaining screws and pull the cluster assembly rearward for access.

4. Disconnect the speedometer cable. Disconnect the electrical connector from the cluster. Remove the cluster assembly.

5. Remove the instrument panel to left door pillar retaining screws and pull the left side of the instrument panel slightly rearward for access.

6. Remove the wiper switch to mounting plate retaining screws. Disconnect the electrical connector from the switch. Remove the switch from the panel.

7. Installation is the reverse of the removal procedure.

1984–89

1. Disconnect the negative battery cable.

2. Remove the drivers door panel, as required.

3. Disconnect the electrical connections from the switch.

4. Remove the switch retaining screws. Remove the switch from the panel.

5. Installation is the reverse of the removal procedure.

Windshield Wiper Motor

REMOVAL & INSTALLATION

1982

1. Disconnect the negative battery cable. With wiper motor in park position, disconnect the washer hoses and all wiring from the motor assembly.

2. Remove the plenum chamber grill.

3. Remove the nut which retains the crank arm to the motor assembly.

4. Remove the ignition shield, if used, and distributor cap. Remove and identify the left bank spark plug leads.

5. Remove the motor mounting screws or nuts and remove the motor.

6. Installation is the reverse of the removal procedure.

1984–89

1. Remove wiper arms. Remove air inlet leaf screen.

2. Turn ignition switch to the on position, and activate motor with wiper switch. Allow motor crank arm to rotate to point to a position between 4 and 5 o'clock as viewed from passenger compartment. Stop crank arm in this position by turning off ignition switch.

3. Disconnect battery ground cable.

4. Disconnect upper motor electrical connectors.

5. Remove motor mounting bolts.

6. With crank arm in position described in Step 4 above, motor may now be removed from vehicle. Lower electrical connector may be disconnected as motor is partially removed.

7. Installation is the reverse of the removal procedure.

Instrument Cluster

REMOVAL & INSTALLATION

1982

1. Disconnect negative battery cable.

2. Remove left air distribution duct.

3. Remove lens to bezel attaching screws and remove lens.

4. Remove cluster to instrument panel attaching screws.

5. Pull cluster assembly slightly forward to obtain clearance for removal of speedometer cable housing, headlamp switch connectors and panel illuminating lamps.

6. Installation is the reverse of removal procedure, being careful not to kink the speedometer cable casing.

1984–89

1. Disconnect battery ground cable.

2. Remove light switch knob (spring loaded), and light switch nut.

3. Remove steering column trim cover.

4. Remove the steering column attaching bolts and lower steering column for access.

5. Remove cluster bezel front and left side attaching screws.

6. Remove cluster bezel from instrument panel.

7. Remove the cluster to instrument panel attaching screws.

8. Pull cluster rearward for access to disconnect cluster electrical connectors. Metal retaining clips are located at back side of connectors.

9. Remove cluster from instrument panel. Odometer may be removed for service or replacement.

10. Installation is the reverse of the removal procedure.

Headlight Switch

REMOVAL & INSTALLATION

1. Disconnect the negative battery terminal.

2. Remove the left air distribution duct.

3. Remove the instrument cluster attaching screws and pull the cluster rearward.

4. Disconnect the speedometer cable, electrical connectors and remove the cluster.

5. Remove the instrument panel to left door pillar attaching screws and pull the left side of the instrument panel slightly forward for access.

6. Depress the shaft retainer, pull the knob and shaft assembly out and remove the switch bezel.

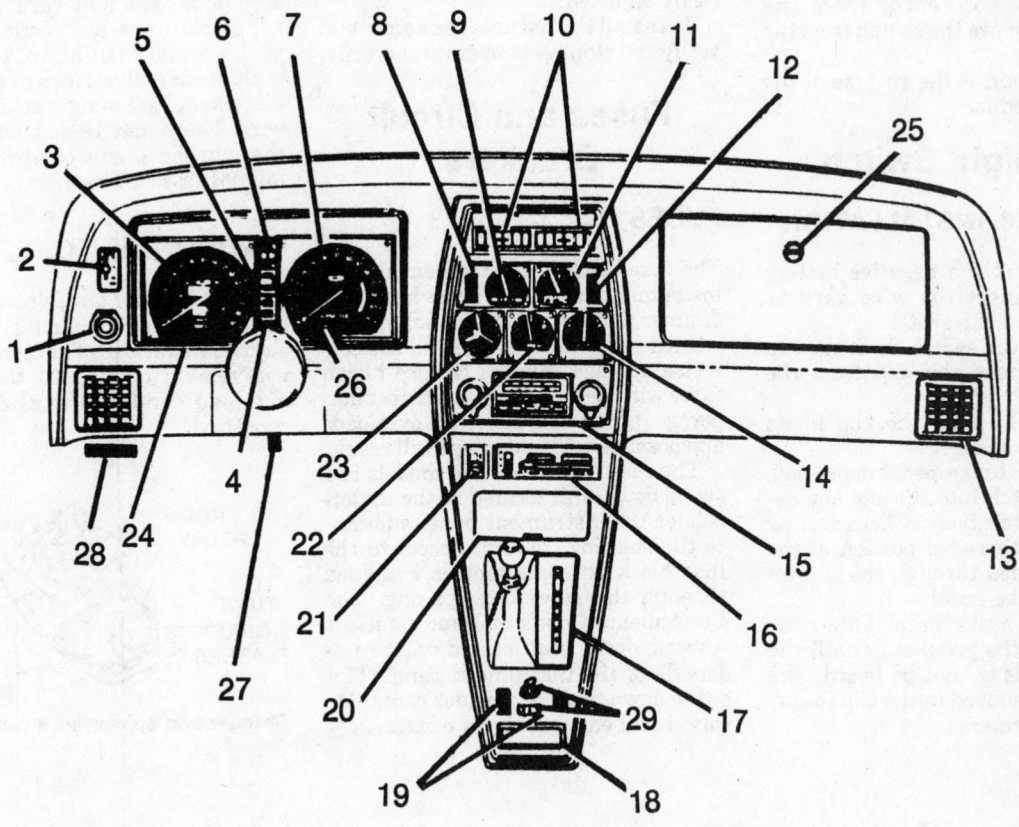

1 Light switch
2 Windshield wiper and washer switch
3 Speedometer, odometer and trip odometer
4 Brake warning indicator
5 Hi-beam indicator
6 Turn signal indicator
7 Tachometer
8 Seat belt warning indicator (upper opening), "Check Engine" (lower opening)
9 Temperature gauge
10 Air conditioning outlets
11 Fuel gauge
12 Low fuel and generator warning indicators
13 Outlets, air conditioning
14 Voltmeter

15 Radio
16 Air conditioning control
17 Transmission shift pattern or selector
18 Coin receptacle
19 Power window switches
20 Cigar lighter and ash tray
21 Rear window defog switch
22 Oil pressure gauge
23 Clock (Oil Temperature Gage W/ETR Radio)
24 Trip odometer reset pushbutton
25 Glove compartment door lock
26 Choke warning indicator light
27 Headlamp manual control knob
28 Hood release.
29 Power mirror controls

Instrument panel and related components 1982

7. Disconnect the vacuum hoses from the switch, tagging them for installation.

8. Pry the connector from the switch and remove the switch from the panel.

9. Installation is the reverse of the removal procedure.

Stoplight Switch

REMOVAL & INSTALLATION

1. Disconnect the negative battery cable. Disconnect the wire harness connector from the switch.

2. Remove the switch from the clip and then remove the clip from the bracket.

3. To install, place the clip in its bore on the bracket.

4. With the brake pedal depressed, insert the switch into the clip and depress the switch body. Clicks can be heard as the threaded portion of the switch is pushed through the clip towards the brake pedal.

5. Pull the brake pedal fully rearward against the pedal stop until the clicking sounds cannot be heard. The switch can be moved in the clip to correct the adjustment.

6. Release the brake pedal and repeat Step 5 to assure that no clicking sounds remain. The switch is now correctly adjusted.

7. Install the harness connector and verify the stoplights operate correctly.

Fuses and Circuit Breakers

FUSES

The fuse block is located beneath the instrument panel above the headlight dimmer floor switch. Fuse holders are labeled as to their service and the correct amperage. Always replace blown fuses with new ones of the correct amperage. Otherwise electrical overloads and possible wiring damage will result.

The fuse block on some models is a swing down unit located in the underside of the instrument panel adjacent to the steering column. Access to the fuse block on some models is gained through the glove box opening. The Convenience Center on some models is a swing down unit located on the underside of the instrument panel. The swing down feature provides center location and easy access to buzzers, relays and flasher units. All units are serviced by replacement components. Location of Convenience Center on specific models may vary.

Fusible links are sections of wire, with special insulation, designed to melt under electrical overload. Replacements are simply spliced into the wire. There may be as many as five of these in the engine compartment wiring harnesses. These are:

CIRCUIT BREAKER

A circuit breaker is an electrical switch which breaks the circuit during an electrical overload. The circuit breaker will remain open until the short or overload condition in the circuit is corrected.

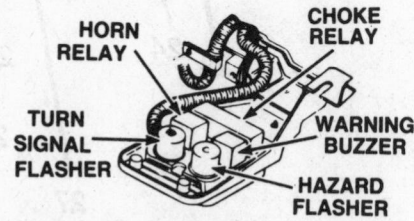

Swing–down convenience center—typical

Chevrolet

Front Wheel Drive

Nova

13

SERIAL NUMBER IDENTIFICATION

VEHICLE IDENTIFICATION CHART

It is important for servicing and ordering parts to be certain of the vehicle and engine identification. The VIN (vehicle identification number) is a 17 digit number visible through the windshield on the driver's side of the dash and contains the vehicle and engine identification codes. The tenth digit indicates model year, and the eighth digit indicates engine code. It can be interpreted as follows:

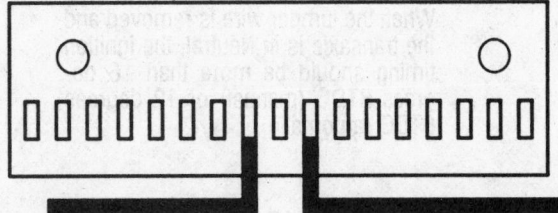

Engine Code					
Code	Cu. In.	Liters	Cyl.	Fuel Sys.	Eng. Mfg.
4	97	1.6	4	2 bbl	Toyota
5①	97	1.6	4	EFI	Toyota

① Twincam

Model Year	
Code	Year
F	1985
G	1986
H	1987
J	1988
K	1989

GENERAL ENGINE SPECIFICATIONS

Year	VIN	No. Cylinder Displacement cu. in. (liter)	Fuel System Type	Net Horsepower @ rpm	Net Torque @ rpm (ft.lbs.)	Bore × Stroke (in.)	Compression Ratio	Oil Pressure @ rpm
1985	4	4-97 (1.6)	2 bbl	70 @ 4800	85 @ 2800	3.19 × 3.03	9.0:1	34 @ 2000
1986	4	4-97 (1.6)	2 bbl	74 @ 4800	85 @ 2800	3.19 × 3.03	9.0:1	34 @ 2000
1987	4	4-97 (1.6)	2 bbl	74 @ 5200	85 @ 2800	3.19 × 3.03	9.0:1	34 @ 2000
1988-89	4	4-97 (1.6)	2 bbl	74 @ 5200	85 @ 2800	3.19 × 3.03	9.0:1	34 @ 2000
	5	4-97 (1.6)	EFI	110 @ 6600	98 @ 4800	3.19 × 3.03	9.4:1	56 @ 3000

GASOLINE ENGINE TUNE-UP SPECIFICATIONS

Year	VIN	No. Cylinder Displacement cu. in. (liter)	Spark Plugs Type	Gap (in.)	Ignition Timing (deg.) MT	AT	Compression Pressure (psi)	Fuel Pump (psi)	Idle Speed (rpm) MT	AT	Valve Clearance In.	Ex.
1985	4	4-97 (1.6)	①	.043	0	0	160	2.5-3.5	650	800	.008	.012
1986	4	4-97 (1.6)	①	.043	0	0	160	2.5-3.5	650	750	.008	.012
1987	4	4-97 (1.6)	①	.043	0	0	160	2.5-3.5	650	800	.008	.012
1988	4	4-97 (1.6)	①	.043	0	0	128-178	3.5	650	750	.008	.012
	5	4-97 (1.6)	BCPR5EP11	.043	10B④	10B④	142-179	NA	800	800	②	③
1989		SEE UNDERHOOD SPECIFICATIONS STICKER										

NA—Not available
① USA: BPR5EY11
   Calif: BPR4EY11
② Cold: 0.006-0.010 in.
   Hot: 0.008-0.012 in.
③ Cold: 0.008-0.012 in.
   Hot: 0.010-0.014 in.

④ Use jumper wire to short circuit both terminals of the check engine connector located near the wiper motor. When the jumper wire is removed and the transaxle is in Neutral, the ignition timing should be more than 16 degrees BTDC (manual) or 12 degrees BTDC (automatic)

FIRING ORDER

NOTE: To avoid confusion, always replace spark plug wires one at a time.

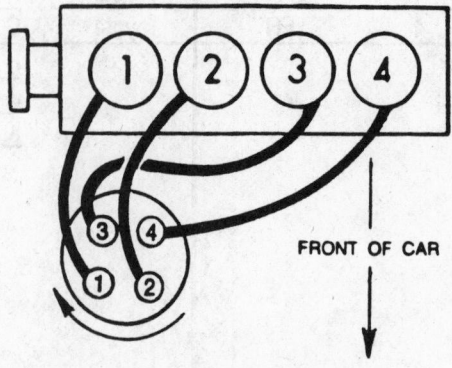

FRONT OF CAR

1.6L 4A-GE
16-valve, twincam engine
Firing order: 1–3–4–2

FIRING ORDERS

NOTE: To avoid confusion, always replace spark plug wires one at a time.

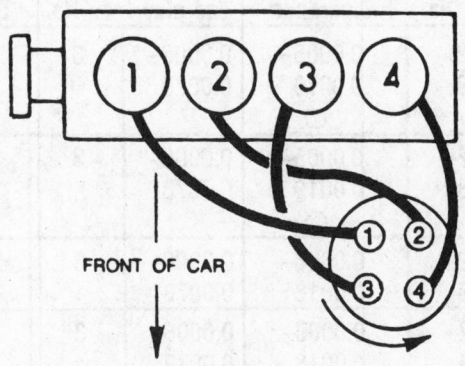

FRONT OF CAR

1.6L 4A-LC
8-valve engine
Firing order: 1–3–4–2

CAPACITIES

Year	VIN	No. Cylinder Displacement cu. in. (liter)	Engine Crankcase with Filter	Engine Crankcase without Filter	Transmission (pts.) MT	Transmission (pts.) AT	Drive Axle (pts.)	Fuel Tank (gals.)	Cooling System (qts.)
1985	4	4-97 (1.6)	3.2	3.0	5.4	11.6	–	13.3	6.2
1986	4	4-97 (1.6)	3.5	3.2	5.4	11.6	–	13.2	6.3
1987	4	4-97 (1.6)	3.5	3.2	5.4	11.6	–	13.2	6.3
1988-89	4	4-97 (1.6)	3.5	3.2	5.4	11.6	–	13.2	6.4
	5	4-97 (1.6)	3.9	3.6	5.4	17.6	–	13.2	6.3

CAMSHAFT SPECIFICATIONS
All measurements given in inches.

Year	VIN	No. Cylinder Displacement cu. in. (liter)	Journal Diameter 1	Journal Diameter 2	Journal Diameter 3	Journal Diameter 4	Journal Diameter 5	Lobe Lift In.	Lobe Lift Ex.	Bearing Clearance	Camshaft End Play
1985	4	4-97 (1.6)	1.1015–1.1022	1.1015–1.1022	1.1015–1.1022	1.1015–1.1022	–	1.5409 ①	1.5409 ①	0.0015–0.0029	0.0031–0.0071
1986	4	4-97 (1.6)	1.1015–1.1022	1.1015–1.1022	1.1015–1.1022	1.1015–1.1022	–	1.5409 ①	1.5409 ①	0.0015–0.0029	0.0031–0.0071
1987	4	4-97 (1.6)	1.1015–1.1022	1.1015–1.1022	1.1015–1.1022	1.1015–1.1022	–	1.5409 ①	1.5409 ①	0.0015–0.0029	0.0031–0.0071
1988-89	4	4-97 (1.6)	1.1015–1.1022	1.1015–1.1022	1.1015–1.1022	1.1015–1.1022	–	1.5409 ①	1.5409 ①	0.0015–0.0029	0.0031–0.0071
	5	4-97 (1.6)	1.0610–1.0616	1.0610–1.0616	1.0610–1.0616	1.0610–1.0616	1.0610–1.0616	1.3998–1.4002	1.3998–1.4002	0.0014–0.0028	0.0031–0.0075

① Minimum lobe height

CRANKSHAFT AND CONNECTING ROD SPECIFICATIONS
All measurements are given in inches.

Year	VIN	No. Cylinder Displacement cu. in. (liter)	Crankshaft Main Brg. Journal Dia.	Crankshaft Main Brg. Oil Clearance	Crankshaft Shaft End-play	Crankshaft Thrust on No.	Connecting Rod Journal Diameter	Connecting Rod Oil Clearance	Connecting Rod Side Clearance
1985	4	4-97 (1.6)	1.8892– 1.8898	0.0005– 0.0019 ①	0.0008– 0.0073	3	1.5742– 1.5748	0.0008– 0.0020	0.0059– 0.0098
1986	4	4-97 (1.6)	1.8892– 1.8898	0.0005– 0.0019 ②	0.0008– 0.0073	3	1.5742– 1.5748	0.0008– 0.0020	0.0059– 0.0089
1987	4	4-97 (1.6)	1.8892– 1.8898	0.0006– 0.0018	0.0008– 0.0073	3	1.5742– 1.5748	0.0008– 0.0020	0.0059– 0.0089
1988-89	4	4-97 (1.6)	1.8892– 1.8898	0.0006– 0.0018	0.0008– 0.0073	3	1.5742– 1.5748	0.0008– 0.0020	0.0059– 0.0089
	5	4-97 (1.6)	1.8895– 1.8898	0.0006– 0.0013	0.0008– 0.0087	3	1.6529– 1.6535	0.0008– 0.0020	0.0059– 0.0098

① Maximum clearance—.0031
② Maximum clearance—.0039

VALVE SPECIFICATIONS

Year	VIN	No. Cylinder Displacement cu. in. (liter)	Seat Angle (deg.)	Face Angle (deg.)	Spring Test Pressure (lbs.)	Spring Installed Height (in.)	Stem-to-Guide Clearance (in.) Intake	Stem-to-Guide Clearance (in.) Exhaust	Stem Diameter (in.) Intake	Stem Diameter (in.) Exhaust
1985	4	4-97 (1.6)	45	44.5	46.3	1.52	0.0010– 0.0024	0.0012– 0.0026	0.2744– 0.2750	0.2742– 0.2748
1986	4	4-97 (1.6)	45	44.5	46.3	1.52	0.0010– 0.0024	0.0012– 0.0026	0.2744– 0.2750	0.2742– 0.2748
1987	4	4-97 (1.6)	45	44.5	46.3	1.52	0.0010– 0.0024	0.0012– 0.0026	0.2744– 0.2750	0.2742– 0.2748
1988-89	4	4-97 (1.6)	45	44.5	46.3	1.52	0.0010– 0.0024	0.0012– 0.0026	0.2744– 0.2750	0.2742– 0.2748
	5	4-97 (1.6)	45	44.5	32.2	1.366	0.0010– 0.0024	0.0012– 0.0026	0.2350– 0.2356	0.2348– 0.2354

PISTON AND RING SPECIFICATIONS
All measurments are given in inches.

Year	VIN	No. Cylinder Displacement cu. in. (liter)	Piston Clearance	Ring Gap Top Compression	Ring Gap Bottom Compression	Ring Gap Oil Control	Ring Side Clearance Top Compression	Ring Side Clearance Bottom Compression	Ring Side Clearance Oil Control
1985	4	4-97 (1.6)	0.0035– 0.0043	0.0098– 0.0185	0.0059– 0.0165	0.0118– 0.0402	0.0016– 0.0031	0.0012– 0.0028	Snug
1986	4	4-97 (1.6)	0.0035– 0.0043	0.0098– 0.0185	0.0059– 0.0165	0.0118– 0.0402	0.0016– 0.0031	0.0012– 0.0028	Snug
1987	4	4-97 (1.6)	0.0035– 0.0043	0.0098– 0.0185	0.0059– 0.0165	0.0118– 0.0402	0.0016– 0.0031	0.0012– 0.0028	Snug

PISTON AND RING SPECIFICATIONS
All measurments are given in inches.

Year	VIN	No. Cylinder Displacement cu. in. (liter)	Piston Clearance	Ring Gap			Ring Side Clearance		
				Top Compression	Bottom Compression	Oil Control	Top Compression	Bottom Compression	Oil Control
1988-89	4	4-97 (1.6)	0.0035–0.0043	0.0098–0.0185	0.0059–0.0165	0.0118–0.0402	0.0016–0.0031	0.0012–0.0028	Snug
	5	4-99 (1.6)	0.0039–0.0047	0.0098–0.0138	0.0078–0.0118	0.0059–0.0031	0.0016–0.0031	0.0012–0.0028	Snug

TORQUE SPECIFICATIONS
All readings in ft. lbs.

Year	VIN	No. Cylinder Displacement cu. in. (liter)	Cylinder Head Bolts	Main Bearing Bolts	Rod Bearing Bolts	Crankshaft Pulley Bolts	Flywheel Bolts	Manifold		Spark Plugs
								Intake	Exhaust	
1985	4	4-97 (1.6)	40-47	40-47	34-39	80-94	55-61	15-21	15-21	20
1986	4	4-97 (1.6)	40-47	40-47	34-39	80-94	55-61	15-21	15-21	20
1987	4	4-97 (1.6)	43	43	29	80-94	55-61	15-21	15-21	20
1988-89	4	4-97 (1.6)	43	43	29	87	58	20	18	13
	5	4-97 (1.6)	①	44	36	101	58	20	18	13

① 1st: Torque in sequence to 22 ft. lbs.
2nd: Torque in sequence another ¼ turn
3rd: Torque in sequence another ¼ turn

BRAKE SPECIFICATIONS
All measurements in inches unless noted

Year	Model	Lug Nut Torque (ft. lbs.)	Master Cylinder Bore	Brake Disc		Standard Brake Drum Diameter	Minimum Lining Thickness	
				Minimum Thickness	Maximum Runout		Front	Rear
1985	Nova	76	NA	0.492	0.0059	7.874	0.039	0.039
1986	Nova	76	NA	0.492	0.0059	7.874	0.039	0.039
1987	Nova	76	NA	0.492	0.0059	7.874	0.039	0.039
1988-89	Nova	76	NA	0.492	0.0059	7.874	0.039	0.039

NA-Not available

WHEEL ALIGNMENT

Year	Model		Caster		Camber		Toe-in (in.)	Steering Axis Inclination (deg.)
			Range (deg.)	Preferred Setting (deg.)	Range (deg.)	Preferred Setting (deg.)		
1985	Nova	Front	¼-1¾P	1P	1¼N-¼P	½N	0 ± 0.16	11¾-13¼
		Rear	—	—	1¼N-¼P	½N	0.150 ± 0.16	—
1986	Nova	Front	⅙P-1⅔P	⅚P	¾N-¼P	¼P	0 ± 0.078	—
		Rear	—	—	1¼N-¼P	¾N	0.075-0.233	—

WHEEL ALIGNMENT

Year	Model		Caster Range (deg.)	Caster Preferred Setting (deg.)	Camber Range (deg.)	Camber Preferred Setting (deg.)	Toe-in (in.)	Steering Axis Inclination (deg.)
1987	Nova	Front	⅛-1½P	⅞	¼N-¾P	½N	0.04-0.08	—
		Rear	—	—	¼N-½P	½N	0.150-0.08	—
1988-89	Nova	Front	⅛-1⅔P	⁹⁄₁₀P	¾N-¼P	¼N	0-0.078	—
		Rear	—	—	1¼N-¼P	½N	0.070-0.228	—
	Nova	Front	1N-1½P	¼P	¾N-¼P	¼N	0-0.078	—
	Twincam	Rear	—	—	1¼N-¼P	½N	0.070-0.228	—

TUNE-UP PROCEDURES

Ignition Timing

ADJUSTMENT

Except Twincam

1. Set the parking brake and place the transaxle in Neutral. Run the engine until normal operating temperatures are reached, then, turn OFF the engine.

2. Install a timing light to the No. 1 spark plug wire according to the manufacturer's instructions.

NOTE: For inductive timing lights, the induction clip can simply be installed over the plug wire. For other lights, the pick-up wire must be connected between the spark plug boot and the spark plug. Connect a tachometer according to the manufacturer's instructions.

3. Disconnect and plug the distributor-to-intake manifold vacuum hoses.

4. Loosen the distributor flange hold-down bolt to finger tight.

5. Start the engine, then, check and/or adjust the engine rpm; it should be 750 or less.

6. Aim the timing light at the scale on the timing cover near the front pulley; the timing should be 0 degrees BTDC. If the timing is not correct, turn the distributor slightly to correct it. Once the reading is correct, tighten the hold-down bolt and recheck the timing.

7. Stop the engine, remove the timing light, then, unplug and reconnect the distributor vacuum hoses.

Twincam

1. Firmly apply the parking brake

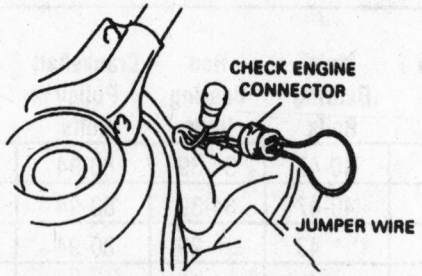

Using a jumper wire to short the check engine connector—twincam engine

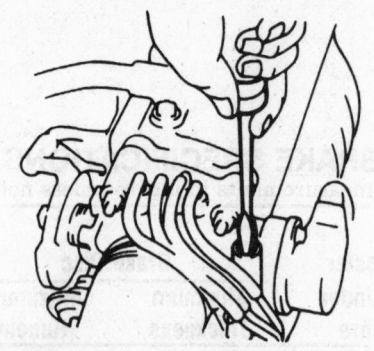

Adjusting the idle speed screw—twincam engine

and place the transaxle in Neutral.

2. Run the engine until normal operating temperatures are reached, then, stop the engine.

3. Using a jumper wire, connect it to the check engine connector located near the wiper motor.

4. Using a timing light, connect it to the No. 1 spark plug wire. Loosen the distributor hold-down bolt until it is finger tight.

5. Start the engine, then, check and/or adjust the idle speed; it should be 800 rpm.

6. Aim the timing light at the timing cover plate near the crankshaft pulley; the notch on the crankshaft pulley should align the 10 degrees BTDC timing mark on the timing plate.

7. To adjust the engine timing, turn the distributor slightly to align the marks, then, tighten the hold-down bolt and recheck the timing.

8. When the adjustment is correct, remove the jumper wire from the check engine connector and recheck the timing marks. The timing should now be more than 16 degrees BTDC (manual) or more than 12 degrees BTDC (automatic).

TACHOMETER HOOKUP

The ignition system is equipped with a service connector plug that shares a common wiring harness with the primary wiring connector leading to the distributor assembly. One lead of the tachometer is connected to that plug. Connect the tachometer leads according to the instruction manual for the instrument. Since not all types of tachometers are compatible with this ignition system, consult the instrument instruction book to make sure it will work with electronic ignition systems and will not damage the system. Never ground the TACH terminal of the distributor assembly or damage to the ignition system will result.

Valve Lash

ADJUSTMENT

Except Twincam

1. Operate the engine until normal operating temperatures are reached, then, turn the engine OFF. Remove the air cleaner and the valve cover.

NOTE: If clearances are being set because parts have been disassembled, adjust the valves COLD, then, reset them with the engine HOT.

2. Using a socket wrench on the crankshaft pulley bolt, turn the crankshaft until the No. 1 cylinder is posi-

tioned to the TDC of its compression stroke; the rocker arms of the No. 1 cylinder should be loose.

NOTE: The notch on the crankshaft pulley should align with the 0 degrees mark on the timing plate.

3. Using a 0.008 in. feeler gauge, adjust the intake valve clearance of cylinder No. 1 and 2. Using a 0.012 in. feeler gauge, adjust the exhaust valve clearance of cylinders No. 1 and 3.

4. To adjust each valve, perform the following procedures:

   a. Loosen the rocker arm adjusting nut; it may be necessary to back-off the adjusting screw.

   b. Slide the feeler gauge between the rocker arm and valve tip. The surfaces will just touch, giving a very slight pull on the gauge.

   c. Using a screwdriver (to turn the rocker arm screw) and a wrench (to hold the rocker arm lock nut), adjust the valve clearance, then, tighten the rocker arm lock nut.

   d. Recheck the clearance and re-adjust (if necessary).

5. Rotate the crankshaft one complete revolution (360 degrees), then, realign the crankshaft pulley notch with the 0 degrees mark on the timing plate.

6. Using a 0.008 in. feeler gauge, adjust the intake valve clearance of cylinder No. 3 and 4. Using a 0.012 in. feeler gauge, adjust the exhaust valve clearance of cylinders No. 2 and 4.

7. To install, use a new gasket, sealant (if necessary) and reverse the removal procedures. Install the air cleaner. Adjust the engine timing and idle speed.

Twincam

1. With the engine COLD, remove the valve covers.

2. To inspect the valve clearances, perform the following procedures:

   a. Using a socket wrench on the crankshaft pulley, rotate the crankshaft until the No. 1 cylinder is positioned to the TDC of its compression stroke; the valve lifters of the No. 1 cylinder should be loose.

NOTE: The crankshaft pulley notch will align with the 0 degrees mark on the timing plate.

   b. Using a feeler gauge, measure and record (valves not within specifications) the intake valve-to-lifter clearances of cylinders No. 1 & 2; the exhaust valve-to-lifter clearances of cylinders No. 1 & 3.

   c. Rotate the crankshaft one complete revolution (360 degrees) and realign the crankshaft pulley notch

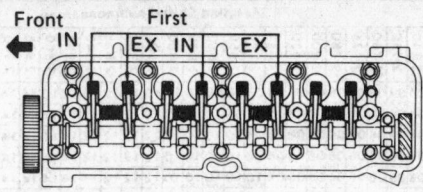

Valve adjustment sequence – step one – except twincam engine

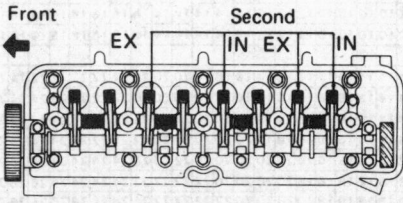

Valve adjustment sequence – step two – except twincam engine

with the 0 degrees mark on the timing plate; the valve lifters of the No. 4 cylinder should be loose.

   d. Using a feeler gauge, measure and record (valves not within specifications) the intake valve-to-lifter clearances of cylinders No. 3 & 4; the exhaust valve-to-lifter clearances of cylinders No. 2 & 4.

3. Rotate the crankshaft pulley until the cam lobe (valve being worked on) is positioned in the upward direction.

4. Using the Valve Clearance Adjustment tool set No. J-37141 or equivalent, press the valve lifter downward, then, secure it in downward position (using another tool) and remove the first tool.

5. Using a small screwdriver or a magnetic finger, remove the adjusting shim.

6. To select the correct valve shim(s), perform the following procedures:

   a. Using a micrometer, measure the thickness of the old shim.

   b. Using the valve clearance measurement (already acquired), subtract 0.008 in. (intake valve) or 0.010 in. (exhaust valve) from it; the new calculation is the difference between the old shim and the new shim.

   c. Using the difference (just calculated), add it to the old shim thickness, then, select (from the chart) a new shim with the thickness closest to the new calculation.

7. Install the new shim and remove the hold-down tool.

8. After all valves have met specifications, use new gaskets, sealant (if necessary) and reverse the removal procedures. Adjust the engine timing and idle speed.

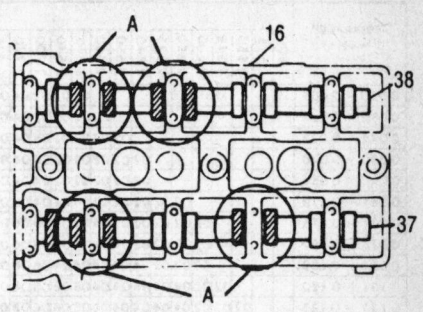

A. Adjust valves | 16. Cylinder head
(1 & 2 intake) | 37. Exhaust valve camshaft
(1 & 3 exhaust) | 38. Intake valve camshaft

Measuring the valve clearance – step one – twincam engine

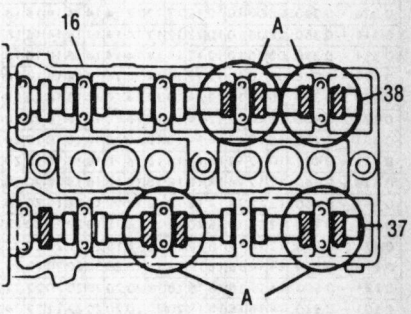

A. Adjust valves | 16. Cylinder head
(3 & 4 intake) | 37. Exhaust valve camshaft
(2 & 4 exhaust) | 38. Intake valve camshaft

Measuring the valve clearance – step two – twincam engine

Idle Speed

ADJUSTMENT

Except Twincam

1. Turn Off all of the accessories, firmly set the parking brake and position the transaxle in Neutral.

2. Check and/or adjust the ignition timing.

3. Start the engine and allow it to reach normal operating temperatures; make sure the choke is in the wide open position.

4. Inspect the fuel level sight glass on the carburetor to make sure the fuel is at the correct level.

5. At the distributor, locate the service engine connector, remove the rubber cap from it. Using a tachometer, connect the (+) positive terminal to the service connector.

NOTE: When using a tachometer, consult the manufacturer's information to be sure it is compatible with the system.

6. Adjust the idle speed screw to 650 rpm (manual transaxles), 800 rpm (1985 automatic transaxles) or 750 rpm (1986-89 automatic transaxles).

Intake valve shim size chart—twincam engine

Installed Shim Thickness (mm)

The chart lists Measured Clearance (mm) ranges in the left column against installed shim thicknesses across the top (2.500, 2.525, 2.550, 2.575, 2.600, 2.620, 2.625, 2.640, 2.650, 2.660, 2.675, 2.680, 2.700, 2.720, 2.725, 2.740, 2.750, 2.775, 2.780, 2.800, 2.820, 2.825, 2.840, 2.850, 2.860, 2.875, 2.880, 2.900, 2.920, 2.925, 2.940, 2.950, 2.960, 2.975, 2.980, 3.000, 3.020, 3.025, 3.040, 3.050, 3.075, 3.080, 3.100, 3.120, 3.125, 3.140, 3.150, 3.160, 3.175, 3.180, 3.200, 3.225, 3.250, 3.275, 3.300), with replacement shim numbers in the body.

Measured Clearance (mm) ranges (left column):

0.000 – 0.009
0.010 – 0.025
0.026 – 0.029
0.030 – 0.040
0.041 – 0.050
0.051 – 0.070
0.071 – 0.075
0.076 – 0.090
0.091 – 0.100
0.101 – 0.120
0.121 – 0.125
0.126 – 0.140
0.141 – 0.149
0.150 – 0.250
0.251 – 0.270
0.271 – 0.275
0.276 – 0.290
0.291 – 0.300
0.301 – 0.320
0.321 – 0.325
0.326 – 0.340
0.341 – 0.350
0.351 – 0.370
0.371 – 0.375
0.376 – 0.390
0.391 – 0.400
0.401 – 0.420
0.421 – 0.425
0.426 – 0.440
0.441 – 0.450
0.451 – 0.470
0.471 – 0.475
0.476 – 0.490
0.491 – 0.500
0.501 – 0.520
0.521 – 0.525
0.526 – 0.540
0.541 – 0.550
0.551 – 0.570
0.571 – 0.575
0.576 – 0.590
0.591 – 0.600
0.601 – 0.620
0.621 – 0.625
0.626 – 0.640
0.641 – 0.650
0.651 – 0.670
0.671 – 0.675
0.676 – 0.690
0.691 – 0.700
0.701 – 0.720
0.721 – 0.725
0.726 – 0.740
0.741 – 0.750
0.751 – 0.770
0.771 – 0.775
0.776 – 0.790
0.791 – 0.800
0.801 – 0.820
0.821 – 0.825
0.826 – 0.840
0.841 – 0.850
0.851 – 0.870
0.871 – 0.875
0.876 – 0.890
0.891 – 0.900
0.901 – 0.925
0.926 – 0.950
0.951 – 0.975
0.976 – 1.000
1.001 – 1.025

AVAILABLE SHIMS

Shim No.	Thickness	Shim No.	Thickness
02	2.500 (0.0984)	20	2.950 (0.1161)
04	2.550 (0.1004)	22	3.000 (0.1181)
06	2.600 (0.1024)	24	3.050 (0.1201)
08	2.650 (0.1043)	26	3.100 (0.1220)
10	2.700 (0.1063)	28	3.150 (0.1240)
12	2.750 (0.1083)	30	3.200 (0.1260)
14	2.800 (0.1102)	32	3.250 (0.1280)
16	2.850 (0.1122)	34	3.300 (0.1299)
18	2.900 (0.1142)		

Intake valve clearance (cold):
    0.15 – 0.25 mm (0.006 – 0.010 in.)

Example: A 2.800 mm shim is installed and the measured clearance is 0.450 mm. Replace the 2.800 mm shim with shim No. 24 (3.050 mm).

Installed Shim Thickness (mm)

Exhaust valve shim size chart—twincam engine. Measured Clearance (mm) listed in the left column; Installed Shim Thickness across the top (2.500 through 3.300). The body of the chart gives the replacement shim number (02–34) for each combination.

Measured Clearance (mm) rows:

Measured Clearance (mm)
0.000 – 0.009
0.010 – 0.025
0.026 – 0.040
0.041 – 0.050
0.051 – 0.070
0.071 – 0.090
0.091 – 0.100
0.101 – 0.120
0.121 – 0.140
0.141 – 0.150
0.151 – 0.170
0.171 – 0.190
0.191 – 0.199
0.200 – 0.300
0.301 – 0.320
0.321 – 0.325
0.326 – 0.340
0.341 – 0.350
0.351 – 0.370
0.371 – 0.375
0.376 – 0.390
0.391 – 0.400
0.401 – 0.420
0.421 – 0.425
0.426 – 0.440
0.441 – 0.450
0.451 – 0.470
0.471 – 0.475
0.476 – 0.490
0.491 – 0.500
0.501 – 0.520
0.521 – 0.525
0.526 – 0.540
0.541 – 0.550
0.551 – 0.570
0.571 – 0.575
0.576 – 0.590
0.591 – 0.600
0.601 – 0.620
0.621 – 0.625
0.626 – 0.640
0.641 – 0.650
0.651 – 0.670
0.671 – 0.675
0.676 – 0.690
0.691 – 0.700
0.701 – 0.720
0.721 – 0.725
0.726 – 0.740
0.741 – 0.750
0.751 – 0.770
0.771 – 0.775
0.776 – 0.790
0.791 – 0.800
0.801 – 0.820
0.821 – 0.825
0.826 – 0.840
0.841 – 0.850
0.851 – 0.870
0.871 – 0.875
0.876 – 0.890
0.891 – 0.900
0.901 – 0.925
0.926 – 0.950
0.951 – 0.975
0.976 – 1.000
1.001 – 1.025
1.026 – 1.050
1.051 – 1.075

AVAILABLE SHIMS   mm (in.)

Shim No.	Thickness	Shim No.	Thickness
02	2.500 (0.0984)	20	2.950 (0.1161)
04	2.550 (0.1004)	22	3.000 (0.1181)
06	2.600 (0.1024)	24	3.050 (0.1201)
08	2.650 (0.1043)	26	3.100 (0.1220)
10	2.700 (0.1063)	28	3.150 (0.1240)
12	2.750 (0.1083)	30	3.200 (0.1260)
14	2.800 (0.1102)	32	3.250 (0.1280)
16	2.850 (0.1122)	34	3.300 (0.1299)
18	2.900 (0.1142)		

Exhaust valve clearance (cold):
0.20 – 0.30 mm (0.008 – 0.012 in.)

Example: A 2.800 mm shim is installed and the measured clearance is 0.450 mm. Replace the 2.800 mm shim with shim No. 22 (3.000 mm).

Exhaust valve shim size chart—twincam engine

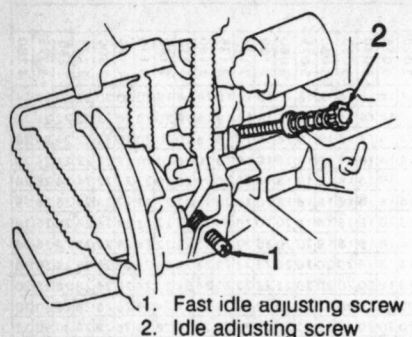

1. Fast idle adjusting screw
2. Idle adjusting screw

View of the carburetor's idle and fast idle adjusting screws—except twincam engine

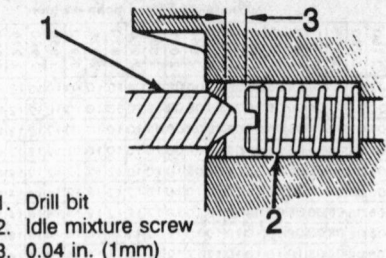

1. Drill bit
2. Idle mixture screw
3. 0.04 in. (1mm)

Drilling the mixture adjusting screw plug from the carburetor base—except twincam engine

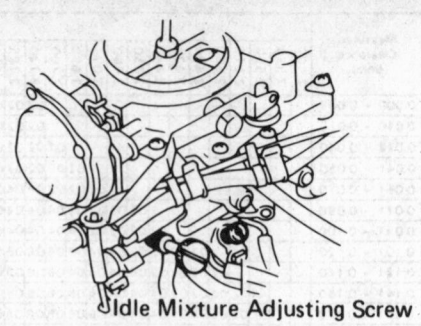

Idle Mixture Adjusting Screw

Idle mixture adjustment

Twincam

1. Refer to the "Ignition Timing, Adjustment" procedures in this section and make sure the ignition timing is correct.
2. Using a jumper wire, connect it to the check engine connector located near the wiper motor.
3. Start the engine, then, check and/or adjust the idle speed; it should be 800 rpm.
4. When the adjustment is correct, remove the jumper wire from the check engine connector and recheck the timing marks.

Idle Mixture

NOTE: The idle mixture for the twincam engine is not adjustable.

ADJUSTMENT

NOTE: Idle mixture does not require adjustment as a matter of routine maintenance. Only if the engine will not idle properly and all vacuum leaks, tune-up and mechanical problems have been eliminated as possible causes of the rough idle or stalling should the mixture adjustment be performed. Performing this procedure requires drills of 0.256 and 0.295 in. diameter. Be sure to have a source of compressed air to remove metal drillings.

1. Refer to the "Carburetor, Removal and Installation" procedures in this section and remove the carburetor.
2. To remove the mixture adjusting plug, perform the following procedures:
   a. Plug all the carburetor vacuum ports so drillings will not be able to enter them.
   b. Using a center punch, mark the center of the mixture adjusting plug. Using a 0.256 in. drill, carefully drill a hole in the center of the plug.

NOTE: Stop drilling as soon as the plug has been drilled through; there is only about 0.04 in. (1mm) clearance between the plug and the top of the mixture screw.

   c. Using a small screwdriver, reach through the drilled hole and gently turn the mixture adjusting screw inward, until it just touches bottom.

NOTE: If the screw is turned too tight, the tapered tip will become grooved, necessitating replacement.

   d. Using a 0.295 in. drill, drill to force the plug from its seat.
3. Using compressed air, remove any metal filings. Remove the mixture screw by screwing it out all the way. Inspect the tip for grooving and the top for damage to the screwdriver groove and replace the screw (if necessary).
4. Install the mixture adjusting screw, by turning it in slowly and gently until it touches bottom, then, back it out (counting the number of turns) 3¼ turns.
5. Reinstall the carburetor, then, reconnect the vacuum hoses (refer to the Vacuum Hose Information label) and air cleaner.
6. Start the engine and allow it to reach normal operating temperatures.
7. Refer to the "Idle Speed Adjustment" procedures in this section and adjust the idle speed.
8. Adjust the idle mixture screw until the highest rpm is reached, then, readjust the idle speed screw to 700 rpm. Keep adjusting both screws until the maximum speed will not rise any higher, no matter how much the idle mixture screw is adjusted.
9. Adjust the idle mixture screw until the engine speed is 650 rpm.
10. Adjust the idle speed screw to 650 rpm (manual transaxles), 800 rpm (1985 automatic transaxles) or 750 rpm (1986-89 automatic transaxles).
11. Remove the air cleaner and EGR mounting bracket. Using a hammer and drift, tap a new idle mixture adjusting plug in place with the tapered

end inward. Reinstall the air cleaner and EGR vacuum modulator bracket.

ENGINE ELECTRICAL

Distributor

REMOVAL & INSTALLATION

Except Twincam

The distributor uses vacuum and centrifugal advances for spark timing control. The voltage introduced into the pickup coil turns the ignition module On and Off. The ignition module turns the ignition coil On and Off creating high voltage for the spark plugs.

1. Disconnect the negative terminal from the battery.
2. Remove the No. 1 spark plug. Place your finger in the spark plug hole and rotate the crankshaft (clockwise) until you feel air being forced from the cylinder; this is the TDC of the No. 1 cylinder compression stroke. Align the crankshaft pulley notch with the 0 degrees mark on the timing plate.
3. Disconnect the distributor wire from the connector.
4. Disconnect the hoses and the vacuum advance unit.
5. Disconnect the distributor cap and move it aside.
6. Using a piece of chalk, make alignment marks of the distributor housing-to-engine block and the rotor-to-distributor housing.
7. Remove the distributor hold-down bolt(s) and the distributor from the engine; the rotor must be rotated slightly to remove the distributor.
8. To install, use a new O-ring on the distributor housing, lubricate the drive gear teeth with engine oil, align the protrusion at the bottom of the distributor housing with the pin on

the side of the distributor drive gear, mesh the gears and reverse the removal procedures. Check and/or adjust the ignition timing.

Twincam

The distributor uses an electronic spark advance (ESA) system. The voltage introduced into the pick-up coils is monitored by the electronic control module (ECM). The program within the ECM decides when to, using the collected data from the various sensors, turns the igniter module On and Off at precisely the right moment.

1. Disconnect the negative terminal from the battery. Disconnect the spark plug wires from the spark plugs and the ignition coil.

2. Disconnect the distributor wire from the connector.

3. To position the No. 1 cylinder on the TDC of its compression stroke, perform the following procedures:

   a. Using a socket wrench on the crankshaft pulley bolt, rotate the crankshaft pulley until the notch is aligned with the 0 degrees mark on the timing plate.

   b. Remove the oil filler cap and look for the cavity in the camshaft; if it is not visible, rotate the crankshaft pulley one complete revolution.

4. Remove the distributor-to-engine hold-down bolts and the distributor from the engine.

5. Remove the distributor from the engine and the O-ring from the distributor; discard the O-ring.

6. To install the distributor, use a new O-ring and perform the following procedures:

   a. Turn the distributor to align the drive shaft drilled mark with housing cavity.

   b. Align the center of the distributor flange with the center of the cylinder head bolt hole, then, install the distributor.

   c. Install the hold-down bolt and torque it to 14 ft. lbs.

7. To complete the installation, reverse the removal procedures. Check and/or adjust the ignition timing.

NOTE: When performing the ignition timing procedures, never allow the ignition coil terminal to touch ground for it could result in damage to the ignition coil and/or igniter.

Alternator

NOTE: For further information on the charging system, please refer to "Charging and Starting" in the Unit Repair section.

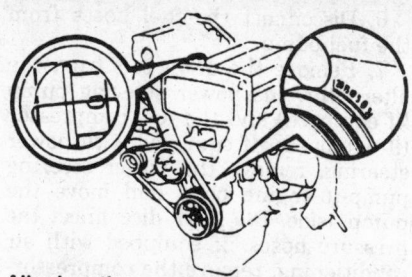

Aligning the crankshaft pulley and the camshaft cavity – twincam engine

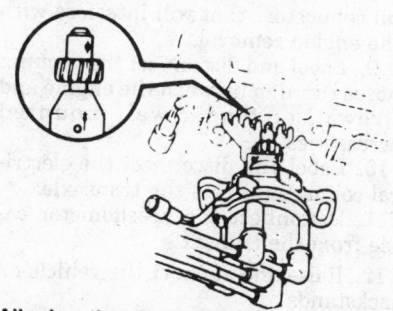

Aligning the distributor drive shaft with the housing – twincam engine

PRECAUTIONS

Several precautions must be observed with alternator equipped vehicles to avoid damage to the unit.

• If the battery is removed for any reason, make sure it is reconnected with the correct polarity. Reversing the battery connections may result in damage to the one-way rectifiers.

• When utilizing a booster battery as a starting aid, always connect the positive-to-positive terminals and the negative terminal from the booster battery to a good engine ground on the vehicle being started.

• Never use a fast charger as a booster to start vehicles with alternating-current (AC) circuits.

• Disconnect the battery cables when charging the battery with a fast charger.

• Never attempt to polarize an alternator.

• Avoid long soldering times when making alternator repairs. Prolonged head will damage the alternator.

• Do not use test lamps of more than 12V when checking diode continuity.

• Do not short across or ground any of the alternator terminals.

• The polarity of the battery, alternator and regulator must be matched and considered before making any electrical connections within the system.

• Never separate the alternator on an open circuit. Make sure all connections within the circuit are clean and tight.

• Disconnect the battery ground terminal when performing any service on electrical components.

• Disconnect the battery if arc welding is to be done on the vehicle.

BELT TENSION ADJUSTMENT

The belt tension on most components is adjusted by moving the component (alternator) within the range of the slotted bracket. Check the belt tension every 12 months or 10,000 miles. Push in on the drive belt about midway between the crankshaft pulley and the driven component. If the belt deflects more than $9/16$ in. or less than $3/8$ in., adjustment is required.

1. Loosen the adjustment nut and bolt in the slotted bracket. Slightly loosen the pivot bolt.

2. Pull (don't pry) the component outward to increase tension. Push inward to reduce tension. Tighten the adjusting nut/bolt and the pivot bolt.

3. Recheck the drive belt tension and readjust (if necessary).

REMOVAL & INSTALLATION

1. Disconnect the negative terminal from the battery.

2. Label and disconnect each alternator wiring connector.

3. Loosen the alternator adjusting lockbolt (located in the slotted bar at the bottom of the unit) and the hinge nut/bolt, located at the top of the unit. Turn the adjusting bolt to shift the alternator toward the block; remove the drive belt.

4. Remove the adjusting bolt, the hinge nut/bolt and the alternator.

5. To install, reverse the removal procedures.

NOTE: The drive belt serrations which run along its length. Make sure serrations align with indentations on the pulleys; all serrations must ride inside the pulley surface.

Voltage Regulator

ADJUSTMENT

The voltage regulator is built into the alternator and cannot be adjusted. If the voltage regulator becomes faulty, it must be replaced.

REMOVAL & INSTALLATION

1. Disconnect the negative terminal from the battery.

2. Remove the nut and terminal insulator.

3. Remove the three nuts and the end cover.

4. Remove the five screws, brush holder and IC regulator.

5. To install, reverse the removal procedures.

Starter

NOTE: For further information on the starting system, please refer to "Charging and Starting" in the Unit Repair section.

REMOVAL & INSTALLATION

1. Disconnect the negative terminal from the battery.

2. Disconnect the electrical connectors from the starter terminals.

3. Remove the transaxle cable and bracket from the transaxle.

4. Remove the starter-to-engine bolts and the starter from the vehicle.

5. To install, reverse the removal procedures. Torque the starter-to-engine bolts to 29 ft. lbs.

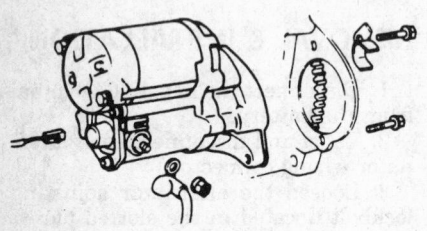

Starter removal

ENGINE MECHANICAL

Engine

REMOVAL & INSTALLATION

Except Twincam

1. Disconnect the negative terminal from the battery. Drain the cooling system into a clean container; be sure to open block drain cocks.

2. Drain the engine crankcase and transaxle fluid.

3. Using a scratch awl, scribe the hood hinge-to-hood outline, then, using an assistant remove the hood.

4. Remove the air cleaner assembly and associated ducting.

5. From the radiator, remove the upper coolant hose and the overflow hose. Disconnect the coolant hose from the coolant pipe at the rear of the cylinder head and the coolant hose from the thermostat housing.

6. Disconnect the fuel hoses from the fuel pump.

7. Remove the drive belt from the alternator, the power steering pump (if equipped) and the A/C compressor (if equipped). If equipped with power steering, remove the power steering pump-to-engine bolts and move the pump aside, DO NOT disconnect the pressure hoses. If equipped with air conditioning, remove the compressor-to-engine bolts and move it aside; DO NOT disconnect the pressure hoses.

8. Label and disconnect the electrical connectors that will interfere with the engine removal.

9. Label and disconnect the vacuum hoses running between the engine and firewall or fender well mounted accessories.

10. Label and disconnect the electrical connectors from the transaxle.

11. Disconnect the speedometer cable from the transaxle.

12. Raise and support the vehicle on jackstands.

13. Disconnect the exhaust pipe-to-exhaust manifold bolts and separate the exhaust pipe from the manifold.

14. On Federal models, disconnect the air hose from the catalytic converter.

15. If equipped with an automatic transaxle, disconnect and plug the oil cooler tubes from the radiator.

16. Remove the under covers from both sides of the vehicle.

17. Disconnect the cable and the bracket from the transaxle.

18. Disconnect the steering knuckles from the lower control arms.

19. Disconnect the halfshafts from the transaxle.

20. Remove the flywheel cover. If equipped with an automatic transaxle, mark the torque converter-to-flexplate, then, remove the torque converter-to-flexplate bolts and move the torque converter back into the transaxle.

21. Disconnect the front and rear engine mounts from the center member.

22. Lower the vehicle.

23. Remove the radiator-to-chassis bolts and the radiator (with the fans) from the vehicle.

24. Using a overhead lift, attach it to and support the engine.

25. Remove the through bolt from right-side engine mount, then, the left-side transaxle mount bolt and the mount.

26. Remove the engine/transaxle assembly from the vehicle. Remove the transaxle-to-engine bolts and separate the transaxle from the engine, then, secure the engine to a work stand.

27. To install, reverse the removal procedures. If equipped with an automatic transaxle, torque the torque converter-to-flexplate bolts to 58 ft. lbs. Torque the halfshaft-to-transaxle bolts to 27 ft. lbs., the engine-to-crossmember mount bolts to 29 ft. lbs., the exhaust pipe-to-exhaust manifold to 46 ft. lbs., the power steering pump-to-bracket bolt to 29 ft. lbs. and the power steering adjusting bolt to 32 ft. lbs. Refill the cooling system, the transaxle and the engine with clean fluid. Start the engine, allow it to reach normal operating temperatures and check for leaks.

Twincam

1. Disconnect the negative terminal from the battery.

2. Drain the cooling system into a clean container; be sure to open block drain cocks.

3. Drain the engine crankcase and transaxle fluid.

4. Using a scratch awl, scribe the hood hinge-to-hood outline, then, using an assistant remove the hood.

5. Remove the air cleaner assembly, the coolant tank reservoir and the PVC hose.

6. Disconnect the heater hoses from the water inlet housing and the fuel hose from the fuel filter.

7. If equipped with a manual transaxle, remove the clutch slave cylinder-to-transaxle bolts and the slave cylinder, then, move the cylinder aside.

8. Disconnect the vacuum hose from the charcoal canister.

9. Disconnect the speedometer cable from the transaxle and the accelerator cable from the throttle body.

10. If equipped with cruise control, perform the following procedures:

   a. Remove the cables from the throttle body.

   b. Disconnect the vacuum hose from the actuator.

   c. Remove the actuator cover bolts and the cover.

   d. Disconnect the actuator connector, then, remove the actuator.

11. Remove the ignition coil.

12. To remove the main wiring harness, perform the following procedures:

   a. Remove the right-side of the cowl panel and disconnect the No. 4 junction block connectors.

   b. Remove the ECM cover and disconnect the ECM connectors, then, pull the main wiring harness into the engine compartment.

13. Disconnect the No. 2 junction block connectors and the ground strap terminals.

14. Disconnect the windshield washer change valve connector, the battery cable from the starter, the cruise control vacuum pump and switch connectors.

15. Disconnect the vacuum hose from the power brake booster.

16. If equipped with air conditioning, perform the following procedures:

a. Remove the vane pump pulley nut.

b. Loosen the idler pulley adjusting and pulley nuts.

c. Remove the compressor-to-bracket bolts, then, move the compressor aside and secure it.

d. Disconnect the oil pressure connector.

e. Remove the compressor bracket bolts, the vane pump bolts, then, move the vane pump and bracket aside and suspend it.

17. Raise and support the front of the vehicle on jackstands.

18. Remove the splash shields.

19. If equipped with an automatic transaxle, disconnect and plug the oil cooler from the radiator.

20. Remove the exhaust pipe-to-exhaust manifold bolts and separate the pipe from the manifold. Disconnect the oxygen sensor connector.

21. Remove the flywheel housing cover.

22. Remove the front and rear engine mounts from the center member, then, the center member.

23. Disconnect the right-side control arm from the steering knuckle and halfshafts from the transaxle.

24. Lower the vehicle.

25. Using a vertical hoist, secure the engine to it and support the engine; secure the engine wiring and hoses to the lift chain.

26. Remove the right-side engine mount, then, the left-side engine mount from the transaxle bracket.

NOTE: When lifting the engine be careful not to damage the throttle position sensor or the power steering gear housing.

27. Lift the engine/transaxle assembly from the vehicle.

28. To separate the transaxle from the engine, perform the following procedures:

a. Remove the radiator fan temperature switch connector and the start injector time switch connector.

b. Disconnect the vacuum hoses from the BVSV's.

c. Remove the No. 1 and 2 hoses from the water by-pass pipes.

d. Disconnect the electrical connector from the back-up switch, the water temperature sensor and the water temperature switch.

e. If equipped with an automatic transaxle, disconnect the neutral start switch connector and the transaxle solenoid connector, then, remove the torque converter-to-flexplate bolts; be sure to push the torque converter back into the transaxle.

f. Remove the starter, the trans-

axle-to-engine bolts and the transaxle.

29. To install, reverse the removal procedures. Torque the torque converter-to-flexplate bolts to 20 ft. lbs., the starter-to-engine bolts to 29 ft. lbs., the halfshaft-to-transaxle nuts to 27 ft. lbs., the right-side control arm-to-steering knuckle nuts/bolts to 47 ft. lbs., the cross member-to-chassis bolts to 29 ft. lbs., the engine mounts-to-cross member bolts to 35 ft. lbs., the exhaust pipe-to-exhaust manifold nuts to 46 ft. lbs. Refill the cooling system, the engine crankcase and transaxle. Start the engine, allow it to reach normal operating temperatures and check for leaks.

Cylinder Head

REMOVAL & INSTALLATION

Except Twincam

1. Disconnect the negative terminal from the battery.

2. Drain the engine coolant into a clean container, opening both the radiator and cylinder block drain cocks.

3. Remove the air cleaner. Label and disconnect all vacuum hoses.

4. Raise and support the vehicle on jackstands. Drain the engine oil. Remove the exhaust pipe-to-exhaust manifold nuts and separate the exhaust pipe from the manifold. Remove the exhaust pipe bracket from the engine. Remove the hose from the catalytic converter pipe.

5. If equipped with power steering, loosen the power steering pump pivot bolt. Lower the vehicle.

6. Disconnect the accelerator and throttle cables from the carburetor and cable bracket.

7. Disconnect electrical harness from the cowl, the oxygen sensor and the distributor.

8. Disconnect the fuel hoses from the fuel pump.

9. Disconnect the upper radiator hose from the water outlet, then, remove the water outlet from the cylinder head. Remove the heater hose.

10. If equipped with power steering,

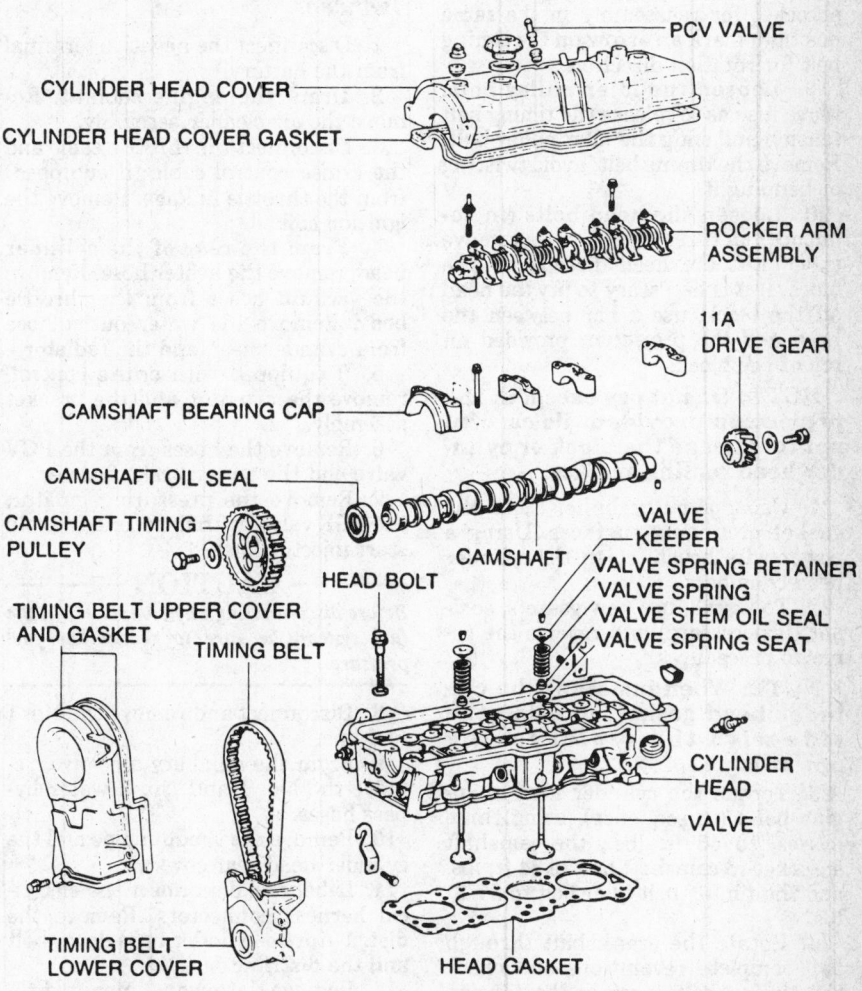

Exploded view of the cylinder head assembly—except twincam engine

remove the adjusting bracket from the engine.

11. Remove the PCV valve and the wiring harness that passes over the valve cover.

12. Label and disconnect the spark plug wires, the electrical connector and the vacuum hoses from the distributor.

13. Remove the upper timing belt cover-to-cylinder head bolts and the cover.

14. Remove the cylinder head cover-to-cylinder head bolts, the cover and the gasket.

15. Remove the alternator drive belt. Remove the water pump pulley-to-water pump bolts and the pulley.

16. Using socket wrench on the crankshaft pulley bolt, rotate the crankshaft to position the No. 1 cylinder on the TDC of its compression stroke; the crankshaft pulley notch is aligned with the 0 degrees mark on the timing plate and the No. 1 cylinder rocker arms are loose.

17. Remove the distributor-to-cylinder head hold-down bolts and the distributor.

18. Matchmark the timing belt and sprocket for reassembly in the same position; mark an arrow on the timing belt for rotation direction.

19. Loosen the idler pulley bolt. Move it so as to release the timing belt tension and snug the idler pulley bolt. Remove the timing belt; avoid twisting or bending it.

20. Loosen the head bolts (in sequence), in three stages, then, remove them. Lift the head directly off the block. If it is necessary to pry the head off the block, use a bar between the head and the projection provided on top of the block.

NOTE: Do not pry except at the projection provided. Be careful not to damage the block or cylinder head sealing surface.

21. Using a putty knife, clean the gasket mounting surfaces. Using a power wire brush, clean the cylinder head chambers.

22. To install, use new gaskets, sealant (if necessary) and reverse the removal procedures.

NOTE: When installing the cylinder head gasket, position the side with the sealer facing upwards.

23. Torque the cylinder head-to-engine bolts (in sequence), using three passes, to 43 ft. lbs., the camshaft sprocket-to-camshaft bolt to 34 ft. lbs. and the timing belt idler bolt to 27 ft. lbs.

24. Rotate the crankshaft through two complete revolutions and check the timing belt tension; the tension should be 0.024–0.28 in.

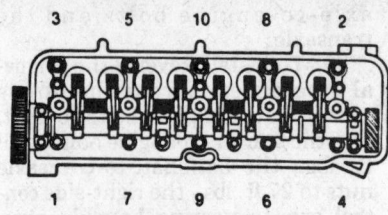

Cylinder head bolt loosening sequence – except twincam engine

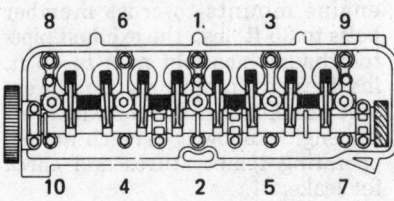

Cylinder head bolt torquing sequence – except twincam engine

25. Adjust the valves with the engine Cold. Operate the engine until normal operating temperatures are reached and check for leaks. Readjust the valves with the engine Hot. Set the ignition timing.

Twincam

1. Disconnect the negative terminal from the battery.

2. Drain the engine coolant. Remove the air cleaner assembly.

3. Disconnect the throttle cable and the cruise control cable (if equipped) from the throttle linkage. Remove the ignition coil.

4. From the rear of the cylinder head, remove the heater hose. Remove the vacuum hoses from the throttle body. Remove the water outlet hose from cylinder head and the radiator.

5. If equipped with cruise control, remove the actuator and the bracket assembly.

6. Remove the hoses from the PCV valve and the power brake booster.

7. Remove the pressure regulator, the EGR valve (with lines) and the cold start injector hose.

――――― **CAUTION** ―――――
Before disconnecting any component in the fuel system, be sure to reduce the fuel pressure.

8. Disconnect and remove the No. 1 fuel line.

9. From the auxiliary air valve, remove the No. 1 and No. 2 water by-pass hoses.

10. Remove the vacuum pipe and the cylinder head rear cover.

11. Label and disconnect the electrical harness connectors. Remove the distributor-to-cylinder hold-down bolt and the distributor.

12. Remove the exhaust manifold-to-cylinder head bolts and separate the

exhaust manifold from the cylinder head.

13. Remove the fuel delivery pipe-to-engine bolts and the delivery pipe with the injectors; DO NOT drop the fuel injectors.

14. Remove the intake manifold bracket, the intake manifold-to-cylinder head bolts (in sequence), the intake manifold and the intake air control valve.

15. If equipped with power steering, remove the drive belt. Remove the alternator drive belt and the cylinder head covers.

16. Remove the water outlet with the No. 1 by-pass pipe and drive belt adjusting bar assembly.

17. To position the No. 1 cylinder on the TDC of its compression stroke, perform the following procedures:

a. Remove the spark plugs.

b. Using a socket wrench on the crankshaft pulley, rotate the crankshaft to align the notch in the crankshaft pulley with the idler pulley bolt.

c. The valve lifters of the No. 1 cylinder should be loose; if not, rotate the crankshaft one complete revolution.

18. Remove the right-side engine mount, the right-side engine mount bracket, then, the upper and middle timing belt covers.

19. Using chalk or paint, place match-marks on the timing belt and the timing belt pulleys, then, remove the timing belt from the timing belt pulleys.

NOTE: When removing the timing belt, be sure to support it so the meshing with the timing belt pulleys does not change. DO NOT allow it to come in contact with oil or water.

20. While securing the camshafts, remove each camshaft pulley-to-camshaft bolt, washer and pulley. Remove the inner timing belt cover.

21. Remove the camshaft bearing cap-to-cylinder head bolts, the caps (keep them in order) and the camshafts (keep the in order).

22. Using the cylinder head bolt removal sequence, remove the cylinder head bolts and lift the cylinder head from the engine.

23. Using a putty knife, clean the gasket mounting surfaces. Using a power wire brush, clean the carbon from the cylinder head cavities. Inspect the cylinder head for damage and/or warpage.

NOTE: When cleaning the cylinder head, be careful, for the cylinder head is made of aluminum which is a soft material.

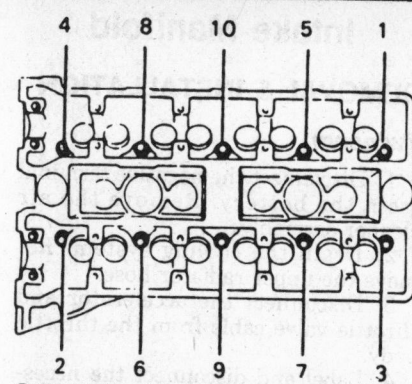

Cylinder head bolt loosening sequence — twincam engine

24. To install the cylinder head, use a new gasket (make sure it is installed in the correct direction), lubricate the bolt threads in engine oil and reverse the removal procedures.

NOTE: The intake-side bolts are 3.45 in. long and the exhaust-side bolts are 4.25 in. long.

25. To torque the cylinder head-to-engine bolts, perform the following procedures:

a. Torque the cylinder head-to-engine bolts (in sequence) to 22 ft. lbs.

b. Using paint, place a paint mark on the cylinder head bolts.

c. Torque the bolts (in sequence) ¼ turn (90 degrees).

d. Retorque the bolts (in sequence) another ¼ turn (90 degrees).

26. To install the camshafts, apply RTV sealant to the camshaft oil seal bearing cap-to-cylinder head surfaces, lightly coat the seal lip with multi-purpose grease, then, install the new oil seals and camshafts. Torque the camshaft bearing cap-to-cylinder head bolts to 9 ft. lbs.

1. EGR vlave
2. Camshaft bearing cap
3. Adjusting shim
4. Valve lifter
5. Valve keepers
6. Valve spring retainer
7. Valve spring
8. Snap ring
9. Valve guide bushing
10. Valve stem oil seal
11. Valve spring seal
12. Delivery pipe
13. O-Ring
14. Injector
15. Cylinder head rear cover
16. Cylinder head
17. Cylinder head gasket
18. Valve
19. Upper exhaust manifold insulator
20. Exhaust manifold
21. Lower exhaust manifold insulator
22. Distributor
23. No.2 timing belt cover
24. Engine mounting bracket
25. No. 3 timing belt cover
26. Exhaust camshaft timing pulley
27. Intake camshaft timing pulley
28. No. 4 timing belt cover
29. Gasket
30. Water outlet
31. Intake manifold stay
32. Intake manifold
33. Cold start injection pipe
34. Gasket
35. Air control valve
36. Gasket
37. Exhaust valve camshaft
38. Intake valve camshaft
39. Cylinder head center cover
40. Cylinder head cover

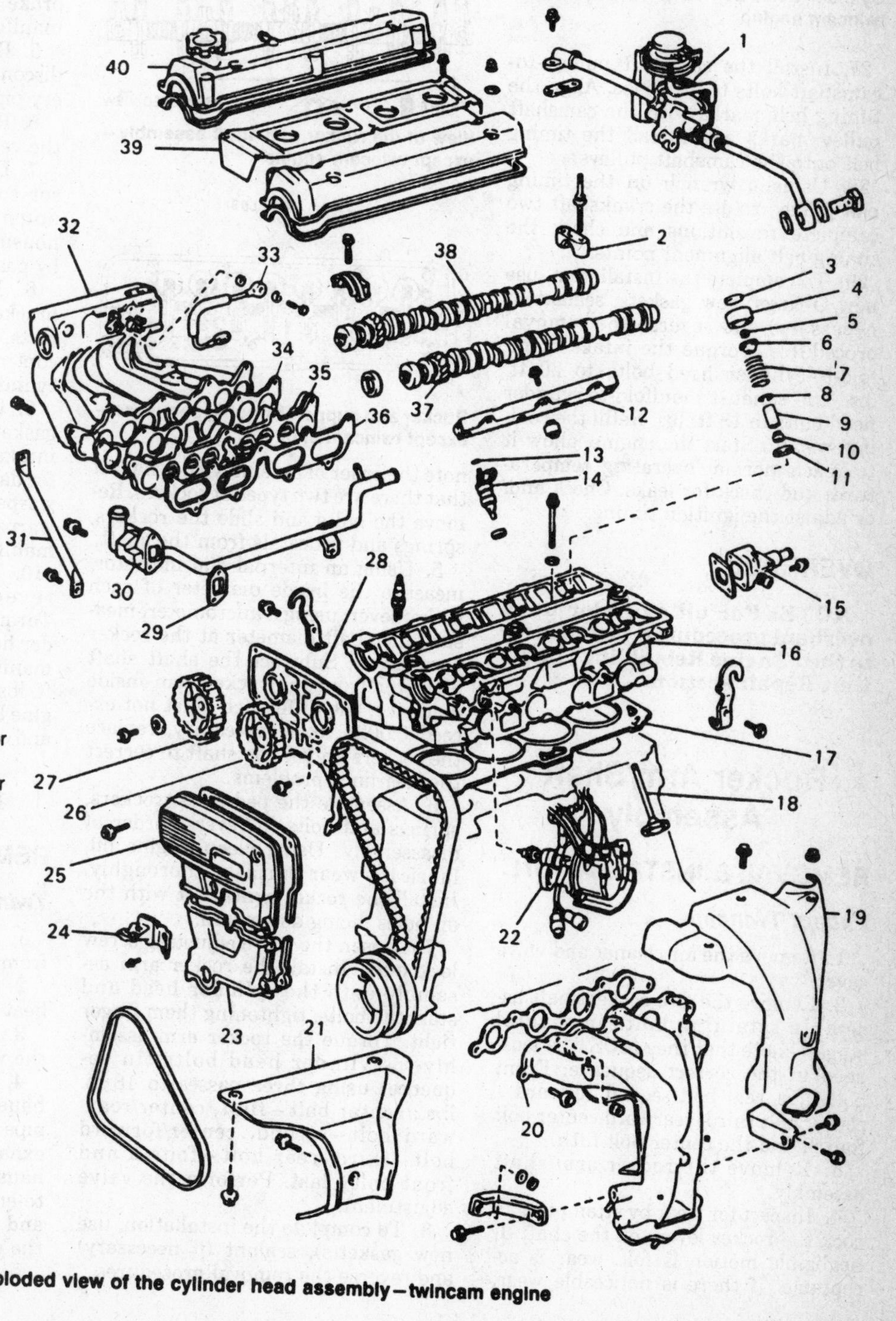

Exploded view of the cylinder head assembly — twincam engine

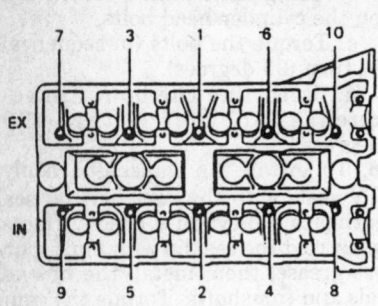

Cylinder head bolt torquing sequence—twincam engine

27. Install the camshaft pulleys-to-camshaft bolts to 34 ft. lbs. Align the timing belt marks with the camshaft pulley marks and install the timing belt onto the camshaft pulleys.

28. Using a wrench on the timing belt pulley, rotate the crankshaft two complete revolutions and check the timing belt alignment points.

29. To complete the installation, use new O-rings, new gaskets, sealant (if necessary) and reverse the removal procedures. Torque the intake manifold-to-cylinder head bolts to 20 ft. lbs., the exhaust manifold-to-cylinder head bolts to 18 ft. lbs. Refill the cooling system. Start the engine, allow it to reach normal operating temperatures and check for leaks. Check and/or adjust the ignition timing.

OVERHAUL

NOTE: For all cylinder head overhaul procedures, please refer to the "Engine Rebuilding" in the Unit Repair section.

Rocker Arm/Shaft Assembly

REMOVAL & INSTALLATION

Except Twincam

1. Remove the air cleaner and valve cover.
2. Remove the five rocker shaft assembly retaining bolts in several stages—note that they MUST be loosened in the correct sequence: Front bolt first, rear bolt second, forward-center bolt third, rearward-center bolt fourth and the center bolt fifth.
3. Remove the rocker arm/shaft assembly.
4. Inspect for wear by attempting to rock the rocker levers on the shaft. If negligible motion is felt, wear is acceptable. If there is noticeable wear,

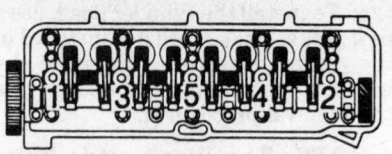

Rocker arm support loosening sequence—except twincam engine

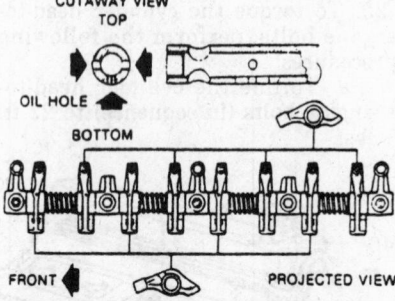

View of the rocker arm shaft assembly—except twincam engine

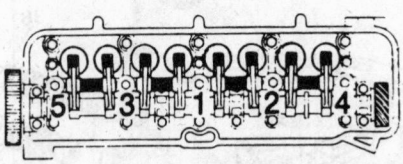

Rocker arm support torquing sequence—except twincam engine

note the order of assembly and the fact that there are two types of rockers. Remove the bolts and slide the rockers, springs and pedestals from the shaft.

5. Using an internal dial indicator, measure the inside diameter of each rocker lever; using a micrometer, measure the shaft diameter at the rocker wear areas. Subtract the shaft shaft diameter from the rocker arm inside diameter; the difference must not exceed 0.0024 in. If necessary, replace the rockers and/or the shaft to correct the clearance problems.

6. Assemble the pedestals, rockers, springs and bolts in reverse order of disassembly. Using clean engine oil, lubricate wear surfaces thoroughly. Install the rocker arm shaft with the oil holes facing downward.

7. Loosen the valve adjusting screw lock nuts. Install the rocker arm assembly onto the cylinder head and start the bolts, tightening them finger tight. Torque the rocker arm assembly-to-cylinder head bolts (in sequence) using three passes to 18 ft. lbs.: center bolt—first, center/rearward bolt—second, center/forward bolt—third, rear bolt—fourth and front bolt—last. Perform the valve adjustment.

8. To complete the installation, use new gasket(s), sealant (if necessary) and reverse the removal procedures.

Intake Manifold

REMOVAL & INSTALLATION

Twincam

1. Disconnect the negative terminal from the battery. Remove the air cleaner assembly.
2. Drain the cooling system. Remove the upper radiator hose.
3. Disconnect the accelerator and throttle valve cable from the throttle body.
4. Label and disconnect the necessary vacuum hoses. Disconnect the brake vacuum hose from the intake manifold.
5. Relieve the fuel pressure, then, disconnect and remove the fuel delivery pipe with the fuel injectors.
6. Raise and support the front of the vehicle on jackstands.
7. Disconnect the temperature sensor connector from the water outlet housing. Remove the water outlet housing-to-engine bolts with the No. 1 by-pass pipe.
8. Remove the intake manifold bracket, the intake manifold-to-engine bolts, the intake manifold (with the air control valve) and gaskets from the cylinder head.
9. Using a putty knife, clean the gasket mounting surfaces. Inspect the intake manifold and air control valve for damage and/or warpage; maximum warpage for both is 0.002 in., if the warpage is greater, replace the intake manifold or air control valve.
10. To install, use new gaskets and reverse the removal procedures. Torque the intake manifold-to-cylinder head bolts to 20 ft. lbs., the intake manifold bracket-to-engine bolts to 20 ft. lbs. and the fuel delivery pipe-to-engine bolts to 13 ft. lbs. Start the engine and check for leaks.

Exhaust Manifold

REMOVAL & INSTALLATION

Twincam

1. Disconnect the negative terminal from the battery.
2. Remove the exhaust manifold heat shield.
3. Raise and support the front of the vehicle on jackstands.
4. Remove the exhaust pipe-to-exhaust manifold nuts and separate the pipe from the manifold. Remove the exhaust manifold bracket from the exhaust manifold, the exhaust manifold-to-engine bolts, the exhaust manifold and gasket (discard the gasket) from the cylinder head.
5. Using a putty knife, clean the

gasket mounting surfaces. Inspect the exhaust manifold for damage and/or warpage; maximum warpage is 0.012 in., if the warpage is greater, replace the exhaust manifold.

6. To install, use a new gasket and reverse the removal procedures. Torque the exhaust manifold-to-cylinder head bolts to 18 ft. lbs. Start the engine and check for leaks.

Combination Manifold

REMOVAL & INSTALLATION

Except Twincam

1. Disconnect the negative terminal from the battery.
2. Remove the air cleaner assembly.

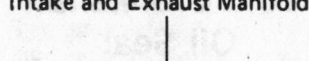

Intake and Exhaust Manifold

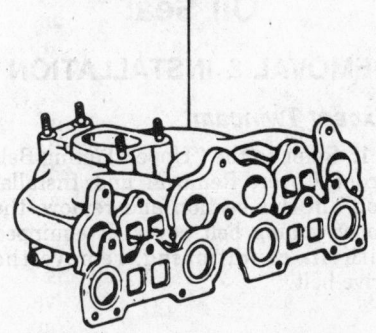

Combination manifold and gasket

Label and disconnect the vacuum hoses.

3. Disconnect the throttle valve and the accelerator cables from the carburetor. Label and disconnect the electrical connectors from the carburetor.
4. Disconnect the fuel line from the fuel pump and drain the excess fuel into a metal container.
5. Disconnect or remove any emission control hardware that may be the way. Remove the carburetor-to-combination manifold nuts and the carburetor from the combination manifold; discard the gasket.
6. Remove the Early Fuel Evaporation (EFE) gasket. Remove the vacuum line, the dashpot bracket and the carburetor heat shield.
7. Raise and support the front of the vehicle. Remove the exhaust pipe-to-combination manifold bolts, the exhaust bracket from the engine and the air hose from the catalytic converter pipe.
8. Lower the vehicle.
9. Disconnect the brake vacuum hose from the combination manifold. Remove the accelerator and throttle cable brackets.
10. Working from the center out-

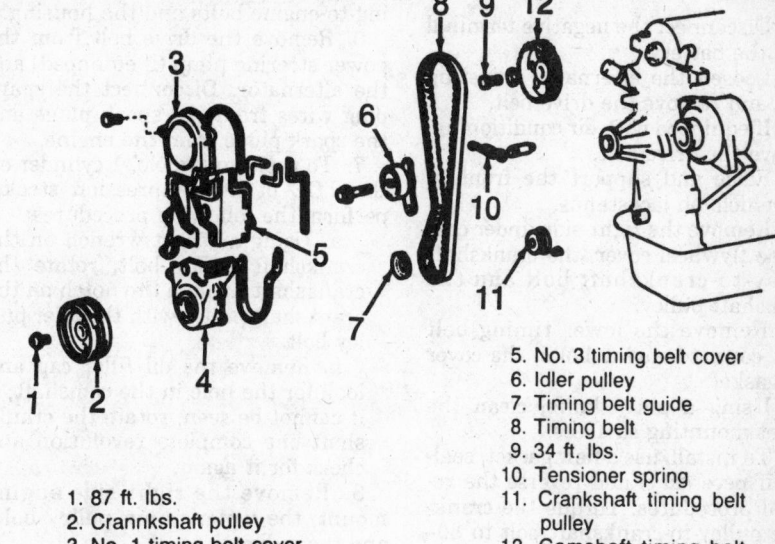

1. 87 ft. lbs.
2. Crannkshaft pulley
3. No. 1 timing belt cover
4. NO. 2 timing belt cover

5. No. 3 timing belt cover
6. Idler pulley
7. Timing belt guide
8. Timing belt
9. 34 ft. lbs.
10. Tensioner spring
11. Crankshaft timing belt pulley
12. Camshaft timing belt pulley

Exploded view of the timing belt assembly – except twincam engine

ward, remove the combination manifold-to-cylinder head nuts in several stages so tension is gradually released.

11. Remove the combination manifold from the cylinder head.
12. Using a putty knife, clean the gasket mounting surfaces. Inspect the manifold for damage and/or warpage.
13. To install, use new gaskets and reverse the removal procedures. Torque the combination manifold-to-cylinder head bolts to 18 ft. lbs. Start the engine and check for leaks.

Timing Belt Front Covers

REMOVAL & INSTALLATION

Except Twincam

This engine uses a three-piece timing belt cover assembly; any individual cover can be removed by performing one of the following procedures.

UPPER

1. Disconnect the negative terminal from the battery.
2. Loosen the water pump pulley bolts and remove the alternator/water pump drive belt. If equipped with power steering, remove the power steering pump drive belt.
3. Remove the water pump pulley bolts and pulley. Drain the cooling system.
4. Disconnect the upper radiator hose from the water pump outlet. Label and disconnect all vacuum hoses that may be in the way.
5. Remove the upper timing belt front cover-to-engine bolts.

NOTE: To remove the lower timing belt cover-to-engine bolts, it may be necessary to raise and support the vehicle, then, remove them from underneath.

6. Remove the upper timing belt front cover and gasket.
7. Using a putty knife, clean the gasket mounting surfaces.
8. To install, use a new gasket, sealant (if necessary) and reverse the removal procedures. Adjust the drive belts. Refill the cooling system. Start the engine, allow it to reach normal operating temperatures and check for leaks.

MIDDLE

1. Refer to the "Upper Timing Belt Front Cover, Removal and Installation" in this section and remove the upper timing belt front cover.
2. If equipped with air conditioning, loosen the idler pulley mounting bolt. Loosen the adjusting nut, then, remove the A/C drive belt, the idler pulley (with adjusting bolt).
3. Remove the alternator bolts and move it aside.
4. Remove the middle timing belt front cover-to-engine bolts, the cover and gasket.
5. Using a putty knife, clean the gasket mounting surfaces.
6. To install, use a new gasket, sealant (if necessary) and reverse the removal procedures. Adjust the drive bolts. Refill the cooling system. Start the engine, allow it to reach normal operating temperatures and check for leaks.

LOWER

1. Disconnect the negative terminal from the battery.

2. Loosen the alternator adjusting bolts and remove the drive belt.

3. If equipped with air conditioning, remove the drive belt.

4. Raise and support the front of the vehicle on jackstands.

5. Remove the right-side under cover, the flywheel cover, the crankshaft pulley-to-crankshaft bolt and the crankshaft pulley.

6. Remove the lower timing belt front cover-to-engine bolts, the cover and gasket.

7. Using a putty knife, clean the gasket mounting surfaces.

8. To install, use a new gasket, sealant (if necessary) and reverse the removal procedures. Torque the crankshaft pulley-to-crankshaft bolt to 80–94 ft. lbs. Adjust the drive belt(s).

Twincam

This engine uses a three-piece timing belt front cover assembly of an interlocking design. To removal any portion of the cover, disassembly must start from the top and work to the bottom.

1. Disconnect the negative terminal from the battery.

2. Raise and support the front of the vehicle, then, remove the right-side wheel assembly.

3. Remove the under carriage splash shield and drain the cooling system.

4. Disconnect the accelerator cable, the cruise control cable (if equipped), the cruise control actuator (if equipped) and the ignition coil.

5. Remove the water outlet housing-to-engine bolts and the housing.

6. Remove the drive belt from the power steering pimp (if equipped) and the alternator. Disconnect the spark plug wires from the spark plugs and the spark plugs from the engine.

7. To position the No. 1 cylinder on the TDC of its compression stroke, perform the following procedures:

a. Using a socket wrench on the crankshaft pulley bolt, rotate the crankshaft to align the notch on the crankshaft pulley with the idler pulley bolt.

b. Remove the oil filler cap and look for the hole in the camshaft; if it cannot be seen, rotate the crankshaft one complete revolution and check for it again.

8. Remove the right-side engine mount, the water pump pulley bolts and the pulley.

9. To remove the crankshaft pulley, perform the following procedures:

a. Using the Crankshaft Pulley Holding tool No. J-8614-01 or equivalent, secure and hold the pulley while removing the crankshaft pulley-to-crankshaft bolt.

b. Using the Crankshaft Pulley Puller tool No. J-1859-01 or equivalent, press the crankshaft pulley from the crankshaft.

10. Remove the timing belt front cov-

ers-to-engine bolts, the covers and the gaskets.

11. Using a putty knife, clean the gasket mounting surfaces.

12. To install, use new gaskets, sealant (if necessary) and reverse the removal procedures.

13. Using the Crankshaft Pulley Holding tool No. J-8614-01 or equivalent, secure and hold the pulley while installing the crankshaft pulley-to-crankshaft bolt.

14. To complete the installation, reverse the removal procedures. Adjust the drive belts. Refill the cooling system. Start the engine, allow it to reach normal operating temperatures and check for leaks.

Front Crankshaft Oil Seal

REMOVAL & INSTALLATION

Except Twincam

1. Refer to the "Upper Timing Belt Front Cover, Removal and Installation" in this section and remove the upper timing belt cover. If equipped with air conditioning, remove the drive belt.

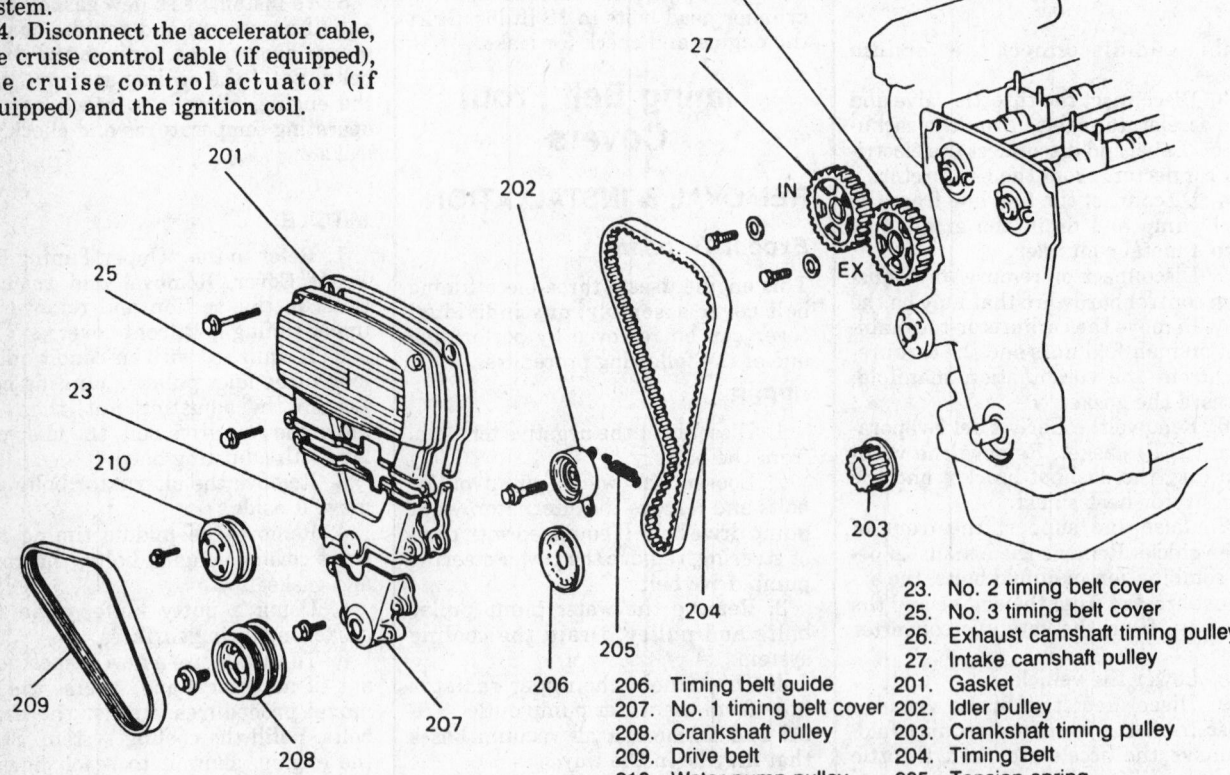

23. No. 2 timing belt cover
25. No. 3 timing belt cover
26. Exhaust camshaft timing pulley
27. Intake camshaft pulley
201. Gasket
202. Idler pulley
203. Crankshaft timing pulley
204. Timing Belt
205. Tension spring
206. Timing belt guide
207. No. 1 timing belt cover
208. Crankshaft pulley
209. Drive belt
210. Water pump pulley

Exploded view of the timing belt assembly—twincam engine

2. Remove the No. 1 cylinder spark plug. Using a socket wrench on the crankshaft pulley bolt, rotate the crankshaft clockwise until No. 1 cylinder is at TDC of its compression stroke; air is expelled from the spark plug hole as the piston approaches Top Center.

3. Raise and support the front of the vehicle on jackstands. Remove the right-side under cover and the flywheel cover.

4. Remove the crankshaft pulley-to-crankshaft bolt and the pulley.

5. Remove the lower timing belt front cover-to-engine bolts, cover and gasket. Mark the locations of the timing belt to both timing pulleys and the rotating direction of the belt.

6. Loosen the idler pulley bolt and move the idler to relieve the belt tension, then, retighten the bolt to retain the tensioner in the released position.

7. Remove the timing belt guide, the timing belt from the crankshaft timing pulley and the timing pulley from the crankshaft.

8. Using a small pry bar, pry the oil seal from oil pump; be careful not to damage the sealing surfaces.

9. To install the new oil seal, lubricate the sealing lips with multi-purpose grease, then, using the Oil Seal Driver tool No. J-35403 or equivalent, drive the new seal into the oil pump until it seats; make sure the seal is square in the bore (not cocked).

10. To complete the installation, adjust the timing belt tension and reverse the removal procedures. Rotate the crankshaft through two complete revolutions and recheck the timing. Start the engine and check for oil leaks.

Twincam

1. Refer to the "Timing Belt, Removal and Installation" procedures in this section and remove the timing belt.

2. Using a small pry bar, pry the oil seal from oil pump; be careful not to damage the sealing surfaces.

3. To install the new oil seal, lubricate the sealing lips with multi-purpose grease, then, using the Oil Seal Driver tool No. J-35403 or equivalent, drive the new seal into the oil pump until it seats; make sure the seal is square in the bore (not cocked).

4. To complete the installation, adjust the timing belt tension and reverse the removal procedures. Rotate the crankshaft through two complete revolutions and recheck the timing. Start the engine and check for oil leaks.

Timing Belt and Tensioner

ADJUSTMENT

1. Refer to the "Timing Belt Front Cover, Removal and Installation" procedures in this section and remove the cover assembly.

2. Using finger pressure on the longest span between pulleys (except twincam) or between the camshaft pulleys (twincam), measure the timing belt deflection; 4.4 lbs. @ 0.24–0.28 in. (except twincam) or 0.16 in. (twincam).

3. If adjustment is not correct, loosen the idler pulley bolt and correct the belt tension.

4. To install, the front covers, reverse the removal procedures.

REMOVAL & INSTALLATION

1. Refer to the "Timing Belt Front Cover, Removal and Installation" procedures in this section and remove the covers.

2. Remove the No. 1 spark plug. Using a socket wrench on the crankshaft pulley bolt, rotate the engine (clockwise) to position the No. 1 cylinder on the TDC of its compression stroke.

NOTE: The TDC of the No. 1 cylinder is located when air is expelled from the cylinder.

3. If reusing the timing belt, mark an arrow showing direction of rotation and matchmark the belt to both pulleys.

4. Loosen the idler pulley mounting bolt and push the idler pulley relieve the belt tension, then, retighten the mounting bolt.

5. Remove the timing belt.

NOTE: Be careful not to bend, twist or turn the belt inside out. Keep grease or water from contacting it. Inspect the belt for cracks, missing teeth or general wear, replace it (if necessary).

6. Install the timing belt by realigning the matchmarks, the belts directional arrow facing clockwise and adjust the timing belt tension. Rotate the crankshaft two complete revolutions and recheck the alignment.

7. To complete the installation, reverse the removal procedures. Torque the idler pulley mounting bolt to 27 ft. lbs. Adjust the timing belt tension. Check and/or adjust the timing.

Timing Pulleys

REMOVAL & INSTALLATION

Except Twincam

1. Refer to the "Timing Belt, Removal and Installation" procedures in this section and remove the timing belt.

2. To remove the crankshaft timing belt pulley, simply pull it and the key from the crankshaft.

3. To remove the camshaft pulley, perform the following procedures:

a. Remove the valve cover.

b. Using an open end wrench, place it on the camshaft flats to secure it.

c. Using a socket wrench on the camshaft pulley bolt, remove the camshaft pulley bolt and the camshaft pulley.

4. To install the timing belt pulleys, reverse the removal procedures. Torque the camshaft pulley-to-camshaft bolt to 34 ft. lbs.

5. After installing the crankshaft pulley bolt, rotate the crankshaft two complete revolutions and recheck the alignment. Check and/or adjust the timing belt tension. Torque the idler pulley mounting bolt to 27 ft. lbs.

6. To complete the installation, reverse the removal procedures.

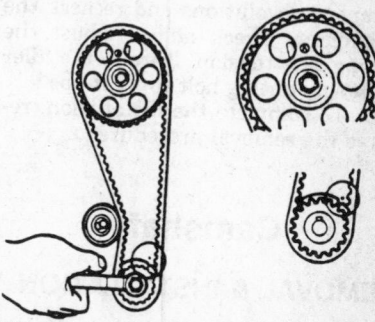

Aligning the valve timing marks—except twincam engine

Twincam

1. Refer to the "Timing Belt, Removal and Installation" procedures in this section and remove the timing belt.

2. To remove the crankshaft timing belt pulley, simply pull it and the key from the crankshaft.

3. To remove the camshaft pulleys, perform the following procedures:

a. Remove both valve covers.

b. Secure each camshaft, then, using a socket wrench on the camshaft pulley bolt, remove the camshaft pulley bolt.

c. Using the Pulley Remover tool No. J-1859-03 or equivalent, press each camshaft pulley from the camshafts.

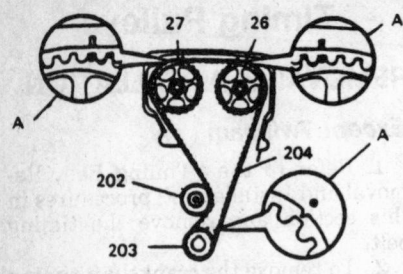

A. Valve timing marks
26. Exhaust camshaft timing pulley
27. Intake camshaft timing pulley
202. Idler pulley
203. Crankshaft timing pulley
204. Timing belt

Aligning the valve timing marks—twincam engine

4. To install the camshaft pulleys, align each with the knock pin and reverse the removal procedures. Torque the camshaft pulley-to-camshaft bolt to 34 ft. lbs.

5. To install the crankshaft timing pulley, simply align it with the keyway and slide it onto the crankshaft.

6. Align the timing belt marks with the pulley marks and install the timing belt.

7. After installing the crankshaft pulley bolt, rotate the crankshaft two complete revolutions and recheck the alignment. Check and/or adjust the timing belt tension. Torque the idler pulley mounting bolt to 27 ft. lbs.

8. To complete the installation, reverse the removal procedures.

Camshaft

REMOVAL & INSTALLATION

Except Twincam

1. Refer to the "Upper Timing Belt Front Cover, Removal and Installation" and the "Cylinder Head, Removal and Installation" procedures in this section, then, remove the upper timing belt front cover and the valve cover; DO NOT remove the timing belt.

2. Disconnect the spark plug wires, then, remove the distributor-to-engine hold-down bolt, the distributor and the distributor gear bolt.

3. Disconnect the hoses from the fuel pump, then, remove the fuel pump.

4. Using a socket wrench on the crankshaft pulley bolt, rotate the crankshaft (clockwise) to position the No. 1 cylinder on the TDC of its compression stroke; the rocker arms of the No. 1 cylinder will be loose, if not, ro-

tate the crankshaft one complete revolution.

5. Loosen the rocker arm adjusting nuts and back off the adjusting screw. Remove the rocker shaft-to-cylinder head assembly.

6. Place alignment marks on the timing belt and the timing pulleys; also, mark the direction of timing belt rotation.

7. Loosen the idler pulley bolt and push the pulley as far left as possible, then, retighten the bolt. Remove the timing belt from the camshaft timing pulleys, support it so it will remain in mesh with the crankshaft pulley; be careful not to get oil on the timing belt.

8. Use a large open-end wrench, secure the camshaft (on the flats), then, remove the camshaft pulley-to-camshaft bolt; the camshaft flats are located between the first and second cam lobes. Remove the camshaft pulley.

9. Remove the camshaft bearing cap bolts, the caps and the camshaft; keep the caps in order for reinstallation purposes.

10. Remove the distributor drive gear.

11. Inspect the camshaft for damage and/or wear; if necessary, replace the camshaft.

12. To install, insert the distributor drive gear, plate washer and bolt.

13. Using clean engine oil, coat all bearing surfaces, then, install the camshaft and No. 2, 3 and 4 bearing caps (in their proper positions and direction).

14. To install a new camshaft oil seal, apply grease the oil seal lips and sealant to the outside edge, then, slip the seal onto the camshaft; make sure it is on straight, as a crooked seal will leak.

15. Using sealant, apply it to the bottom surfaces of the No. 1 bearing cap and install it. Install all bearing cap bolts finger tight.

16. Torque the bearing cap bolts (alternately and evenly) to 8–10 ft. lbs.

17. Using a dial indicator, inspect the camshaft thrust clearance (front-to-rear movement); it should be 0.0031-0.0071 in. with a limit of 0.0098 in. Torque the distributor drive gear bolt to 22 ft. lbs.

18. To complete the installation, adjust the valves, use new gaskets, sealant (if necessary) and reverse the removal procedures. Start the engine, allow it to reach normal operating temperatures and check for leaks.

Twincam

1. Refer to the "Cylinder Head, Removal and Installation" and the "Camshaft Pulley, Removal and Installation" procedures in this section, then, remove the cylinder head covers and the camshaft pulleys.

2. Loosen and remove the camshaft bearing caps-to-cylinder head bolts in sequence. Remove the camshaft bearing caps and camshafts; be sure to keep the parts in order for reinstallation purposes.

3. Using a putty knife, clean the gasket mounting surfaces. Inspect the

Maximum clearance: 0.25 mm (0.0098 in.)
Standard clearance: 0.08-0.18 mm (0.0031-0.0071 in.)

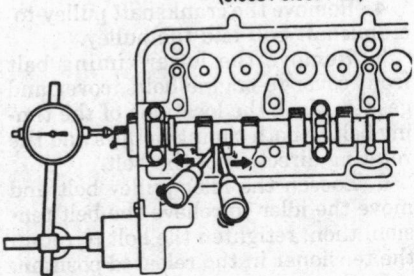

Checking the camshaft thrust clearance—except twincam engine

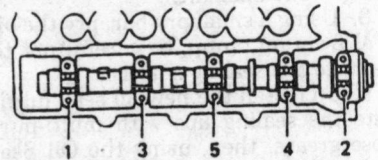

Camshaft bearing cap removal sequence—twincam engine

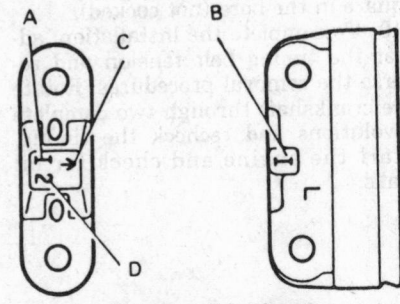

A. I = intake; E = exhaust
B. I = intake; E = exhaust
C. Front Mark
D. I.D. for bearings No. 2–5

View of the camshaft bearing caps—twincam engine

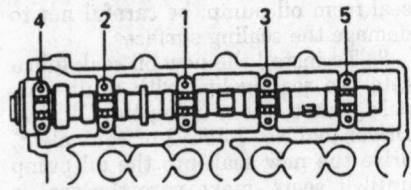

Camshaft bearing cap torque sequence—twincam engine

camshaft for wear and/or damage, if necessary, replace the camshaft.

4. Using clean engine oil, coat all bearing surfaces, then, install the camshaft and No. 2, 3 and 4 bearing

caps (in their proper positions and direction).

5. To install a new camshaft oil seal, apply grease the oil seal lips and sealant to the outside edge, then, slip the seal onto the camshaft; make sure it is on straight, as a crooked seal will leak.

6. Using sealant, apply it to the bottom surfaces of the No. 1 bearing cap and install it. Install all bearing cap bolts finger tight.

7. Torque the bearing cap bolts (alternately and evenly) to 8–10 ft. lbs.

8. Using a dial indicator, inspect the camshaft thrust clearance (front-to-rear movement; it should be 0.0031–0.0075 in. with a limit of 0.0118 in. Torque the distributor drive gear bolt to 22 ft. lbs.

9. To complete the installation, adjust the valves, use new gaskets, sealant (if necessary) and reverse the removal procedures. Start the engine, allow it to reach normal operating temperatures and check for leaks.

Piston and Connecting Rod

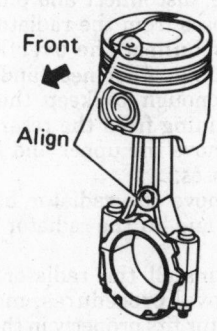

Piston alignment marks

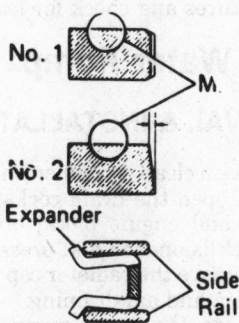

Piston ring installation. Note that the No. 2 compression ring taper faces up and that both compression rings are marked on top. Proper installation of the oil ring and side rail are also shown

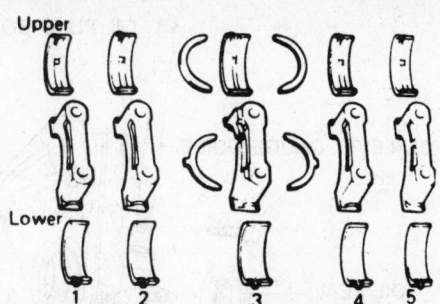

Correct positioning of crankshaft bearing shells. Note that the grooved shells must be at the top to lubricate the connecting rods

POSITIONING

Note the locations of main bearings. Upper bearings are grooved for distribution of oil to the connecting rods, while the lower mains are plain. Thrust is taken by washer shaped bearings located on both sides of the center (No. 3) bearing cap, with tabs on the lower washers which fit into notches in the lower cap. Note that both the piston crowns and connecting rods have marks which must face forward when assembling the engine. Note also the sequence of ring installation; in fact the upper outside diameter of the No. 2 compression ring is smaller than the lower O.D., while the No. 1 compression ring has an even, barrel face. Note also the positioning of the oil ring expander and side rail.

NOTE: For all piston and connecting rod overhaul procedures, please refer to "Engine Rebuilding" in the Unit Repair section.

ENGINE LUBRICATION

Oil Pan

REMOVAL & INSTALLATION

1. Disconnect the negative terminal from the battery. Raise and support the front of the vehicle on jackstands.
2. Drain the crankcase.
3. Remove the right-side undercover.
4. Remove the oil pan-to-engine bolts and the oil pan.

NOTE: When removing the oil pan, be careful not to damage the oil pan flange.

5. Using a putty knife, clean the gasket mounting surfaces.
6. To install, use a new gasket, sealant (if necessary) and reverse the removal procedures. Torque the oil pan-to-engine bolts to 4 ft. lbs. Start the engine and check for leaks.

Rear Main Oil Seal

REMOVAL & INSTALLATION

1. Refer to the "Transaxle, Removal and Installation" procedures in this section and remove the transaxle from the vehicle.
2. If equipped with a manual transaxle, perform the following procedures:

   a. Matchmark the pressure plate-to-flywheel.

   b. Remove the pressure plate-to-flywheel bolts and the clutch assembly from the vehicle.

   c. Remove the flywheel-to-crankshaft bolts and the flywheel.

3. If equipped with an automatic transaxle, perform the following procedures:

   a. Matchmark the flywheel-to-crankshaft.

   b. Remove the torque converter drive plate-to-crankshaft bolts and the torque converter drive plate.

4. Remove the rear end plate-to-engine bolts and the rear end plate.
5. If removing the rear oil seal retainer, perform the following procedures:

   a. Remove the rear oil seal retainer-to-engine bolts, rear oil seal retainer to oil pan bolts and the rear oil seal retainer.

   b. Using a small pry bar, pry the rear oil seal retainer from the mating surfaces.

   c. Using a drive punch, drive the oil seal from the rear bearing retainer.

   d. Using a putty knife, clean the gasket mounting surfaces.

6. To remove the rear oil seal, with the rear oil seal retainer installed, use a small pry bar and pry the seal from the rear oil seal retainer.

NOTE: When removing the rear oil seal, be careful not to damage the seal mounting surface.

7. Clean the oil seal mounting surface.
8. Using multi-purpose grease, lubricate the new seal lips.
9. Using an Rear Oil Seal Installation tool No. J-35388 or equivalent, tap the seal straight into the bore of the retainer.
10. If the rear oil seal retainer was removed from the vehicle, use a new gasket, sealant (if necessary) and re-

verse the removal procedures; be careful when installing the oil seal over the crankshaft.

11. To complete the installation, reverse the removal procedures. Torque the flywheel-to-crankshaft bolts to 58 ft. lbs. and the torque converter drive plate-to-crankshaft bolts to 61 ft. lbs.

Oil Pump

The oil pump is attached to the front of the engine block, behind the crankshaft pulley.

REMOVAL & INSTALLATION

1. Refer to the "Oil Pan, Removal and Installation" and the "Timing Belt Front Cover, Removal and Installation" procedures in this section, then, remove the oil pan and the timing belt cover assembly.

2. Remove the oil pickup-to-engine brace bolts and the oil pickup.

3. Attach a lifting sling to the engine lift points and securely suspend the engine.

4. Mark the timing belt alignment between the camshaft and the crankshaft pulleys; also, mark the timing belt's direction of rotation. Loosen the idler pulley bolt, relieve the timing belt tension and remove the timing belt from the crankshaft sprocket; keep it engaged with the upper pulley.

5. Remove the crankshaft timing belt pulley and the timing belt idler pulley.

6. Remove the dipstick and dipstick tube.

7. Remove the oil pump-to-engine bolts and the oil pump; it may be necessary to tap lightly on the lower rear surface of the oil pump to loosen it.

8. Using a putty knife, clean the gasket mounting surfaces.

9. To replace the oil pump seal, perform the following procedures:
   a. Using a small pry bar, pry the oil seal from the front of the oil pump; be careful not to damage the seal mounting surface.
   b. Clean the oil seal surface.
   c. Using multi-purpose grease, lubricate the lips of the new oil seal.
   d. Using the Oil Seal Driver tool No. J-35403 or equivalent, drive the new oil seal into the oil pump until it seats against the seat.

10. Inspect the oil pump for wear and/or damage; if necessary, replace or repair the oil pump.

11. Using petroleum jelly, pack the inside of the oil pump.

12. To install, use new gaskets, sealant (if necessary) and reverse the removal procedures. Engage the oil pump drive (smaller) gear with the crankshaft gear; there are both small

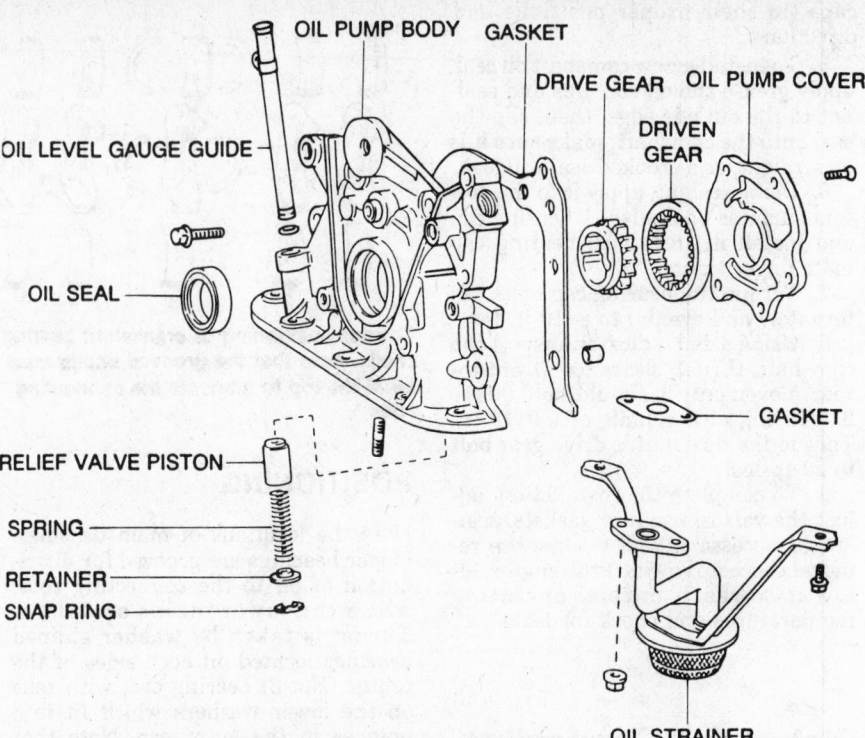

Exploded view of the oil pump assembly

and large spline teeth, make sure the teeth correspond properly. Torque the oil pick-up-to-engine bolts to 82 inch lbs. and the oil pump-to-engine bolts to 15 ft. lbs.

13. To complete the installation, reverse the removal procedures. Adjust the valve timing and the drive belt tensions. Refill the crankcase and the cooling system. Start the engine, allow it to reach normal operating temperatures and check for leaks.

ENGINE COOLING

Radiator

REMOVAL & INSTALLATION

1. Using a clean catch container, place it under the radiator, open the drain cock in the lower radiator tank and engine block, then, drain the cooling system.

2. Disconnect the electrical connector(s) from the radiator cooling fan and the A/C fan (if equipped). Remove the fan shroud, the top (4) radiator-to-chassis bolts and the bottom (2) radiator tank-to-chassis bolts (air conditioning ONLY).

3. If equipped with an a automatic transaxle, disconnect and plug the oil cooler hoses from the radiator.

4. Disconnect the overflow hose from radiator filler neck and position it high enough to keep the coolant from draining from the reservoir.

5. Remove the upper and lower radiator hoses.

6. Remove the radiator hold-down brackets and lift the radiator from the vehicle.

7. To install the radiator, reverse the removal procedures; make sure the radiator fits properly in the bottom rubber cushions. Refill both the automatic transaxle and cooling system with approved fluids. Start the engine, allow it to reach normal operating temperatures and check for leaks.

Water Pump

REMOVAL & INSTALLATION

1. Place a clean container under the radiator, open the drain cocks on the radiator and engine block; once one drain cock is opened and pressure relieved, remove the radiator cap to vent the system and aid draining.

2. Loosen the water pump pulley-to-water pump bolts. If equipped with power steering, remove the power steering pump drive belt.

3. Loosen the alternator adjusting and mounting bolts, move the alterna-

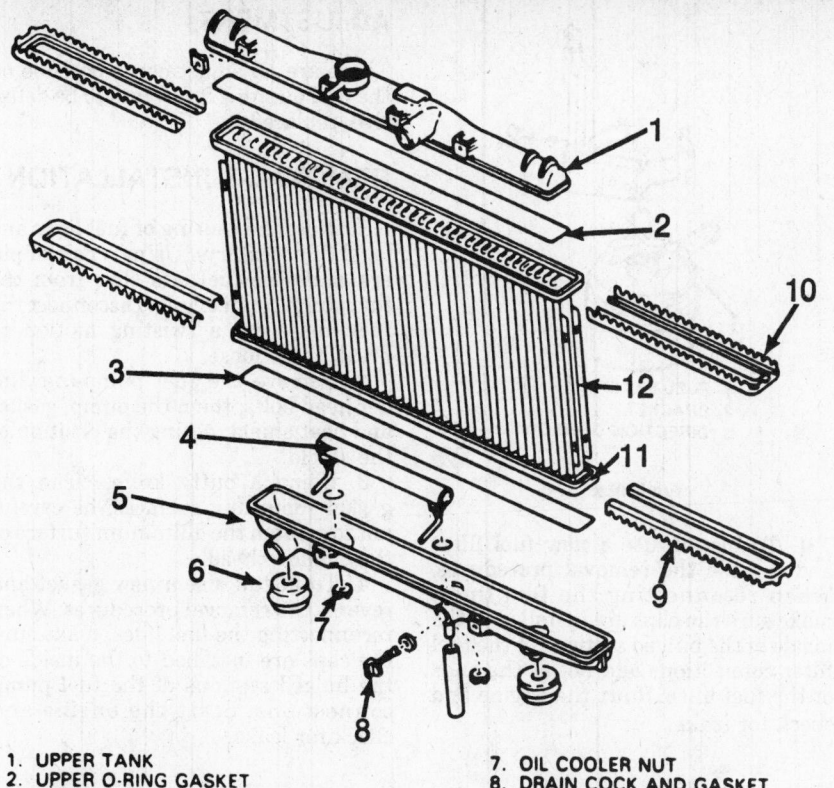

1. UPPER TANK
2. UPPER O-RING GASKET
3. LOWER O-RING GASKET
4. TRANSMISSION OIL COOLER & O-RINGS
5. LOWER TANK
6. LOWER RADIATOR SUPPORT
7. OIL COOLER NUT
8. DRAIN COCK AND GASKET
9. LOWER CLINCH RINGS
10. UPPER CLINCH RINGS
11. HEADER PLATE
12. CORE

Exploded view radiator assembly

tor to relieve the belt tension, then, remove the alternator/water pump drive belt.

4. Remove the water pump pulley-to-water pump bolts and the pulley.

5. Remove the water pump inlet-to-engine bolts (from the side of the block), the inlet pipe-to-water pump nuts and the inlet pipe (discard the O-ring).

6. Remove the dipstick tube bracket bolt and the dipstick tube; be sure to plug the hole in the block with a clean rag.

7. For the non-twincam engine, remove the upper timing belt front cover. For the twincam engine, remove the upper and middle timing belt front covers.

8. Remove the water pump-to-engine bolts and the water pump from the engine; discard the water pump-to-engine O-ring. Keep engine coolant off the timing belt!

9. Using a putty knife, clean the gasket mounting surfaces.

10. To install the water pump, use a new O-ring and reverse the removal procedures. Torque the water pump-to-engine bolts to 11 ft. lbs.

11. When installing the oil dipstick tube, use a new O-ring and coat it with engine oil.

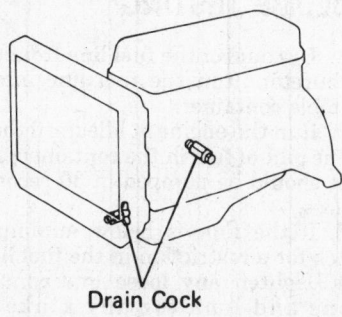

Location of drains on radiator and engine block

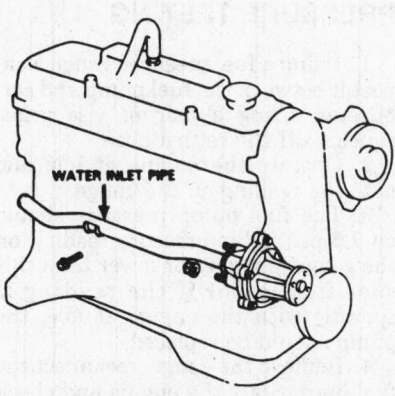

Water pump inlet pipe

12. To complete the installation, use a new O-ring and reverse the removal procedures. Refill the cooling system. Start the engine, allow it to reach normal operating temperatures and check for leaks.

Thermostat

The thermostat is installed on the water pump inlet side.

REMOVAL & INSTALLATION

1. Drain cooling system to a level below the water inlet housing.

2. Loosen water inlet hose clamps, then, disconnect the small and large hoses from the thermostat housing. Remove the water inlet-to-thermostat housing bolts and pull the water inlet housing from the thermostat housing (discard the O-ring).

3. To install a new thermostat, position the bellows side facing inward; make sure the thermostat fits squarely in the indented portion of the housing.

4. To complete the installation, use a new O-ring and reverse the removal procedures. Refill the cooling system. Start the engine, allow it to reach normal operating temperatures and check for leaks.

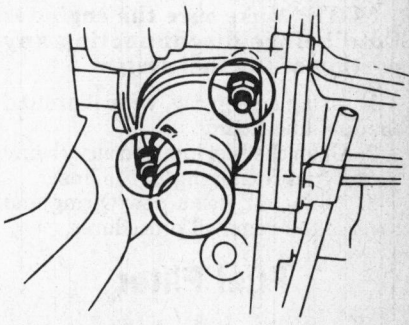

Thermostat housing fasteners

EMISSION CONTROLS

NOTE: Please refer to "Emission Control" in the Unit Repair section for system maintenance procedures. Due to the complex nature of modern electronic engine control systems, comprehensive diagnosis and testing procedures fall outside the confines of this repair manual. For complete information on diagnosis, testing

and repair procedures concerning all modern engine and emission control systems, please refer to *Chilton's Guide To Electronic Engine Controls*.

FUEL SYSTEM

Fuel System Service Precautions

- Disconnect the negative battery terminal.
- Keep a Class B dry chemical fire extinguisher available.
- Always relieve the fuel pressure before disconnecting a fuel line.
- Wrap a shop cloth around the fuel line when disconnecting a fuel line.
- Always use new O-rings.
- DO NOT replace the fuel pipes with fuel hoses.
- Always use a back-up wrench when opening or closing a fuel line.

RELIEVING FUEL SYSTEM PRESSURE

Twincam Engine

NOTE: Make sure the engine is Cold before disconnecting any portion of the fuel system.

1. Using a shop rag, wrap it around the fuel line fitting.
2. Open the fuel line and absorb any excess fuel remaining in the line.
3. To install, use a new O-ring and reverse the removal procedures.

Fuel Filter

The fuel filter is located in front of the brake master cylinder.

REMOVAL & INSTALLATION

1. Remove the fuel filler cap.

NOTE: Note the routing of the inlet/outlet lines and the direction of flow as marked on the filter; the arrow points toward the carburetor.

2. Using a pair of pliers, move the clips on the inlet/outlet hoses back and away from the filter.
3. Disconnect the fuel lines, using a twisting motion to break them loose; be sure to plug the fuel lines to prevent the spillage of fuel and the entry of dirt. Pull the filter from its retaining clip.

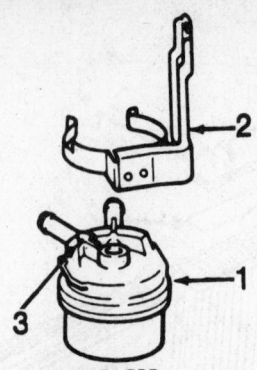

1. FUEL FILTER
2. BRACKET
3. DIRECTION OF FLOW

Fuel filter

4. To install, use a new fuel filter and reverse the removal procedures. When reconnecting the fuel lines, make sure the clips are installed to the inside of the bulged sections of the fuel filter connections and not at the ends of the fuel lines. Start the engine and check for leaks.

Mechanical Fuel Pump

The fuel pump is located on the inlet manifold side of the engine.

VOLUME TESTING

1. Disconnect the fuel line from the carburetor. Run the fuel line into a suitable container.
2. Run the engine at idle until there is one pint of fuel in the container; one pint should be pumped in 30 seconds or less.
3. If the flow is below minimum, check for a restriction in the fuel line.
4. Tighten any loose line connections and look for any kinks or restrictions.

PRESSURE TESTING

1. Using a fuel pressure gauge, connect it between the fuel pump and carburetor; using a pair of vise grips, squeeze off the return hose.
2. Operate the engine at idle and note the reading on the gauge.
3. The fuel pump pressure should be 7.6 psi; if the pressure reading on the gauge is higher or lower than this specification or if the reading is sporatic with the engine at idle, the pump should be replaced.
4. Remove the gauge, reconnect the fuel lines. Start the engine and check for fuel leaks.

ADJUSTMENT

There are no adjustments possible on the fuel pump; if it is found to be defective, replaced it.

REMOVAL & INSTALLATION

1. Note the routing of fuel lines and label (if necessary). Using a pair of pliers, slide the fuel line clips from the fuel pump connections. Disconnect the fuel lines, use a twisting motion to break them loose.
2. Remove the fuel pump-to-cylinder head bolts, then, the pump, gasket and heat shield, noting the position of the shield.
3. Using a putty knife, clean the gasket mounting surfaces; be careful not to scratch the aluminum surface of the cylinder head.
4. To install, use a new gasket and reverse the removal procedures. When reconnecting the fuel lines, make sure the clips are installed to the inside of the bulged sections of the fuel pump connections. Start the engine and check for leaks.

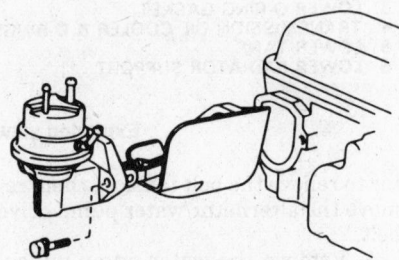

Mechanical fuel pump mounting

Electric Fuel Pump

The electric fuel pump is located in the fuel tank.

PRESSURE TESTING

1. Disconnect the negative battery terminal from the battery and the electrical connector from the cold start injector.
2. Using a shop colth, wrap it around the cold start injector pipe, loosen (slowly) the union bolt and remove the bolt; discard the gaskets.
3. Using the Pressure Gauge tools No. J-347301-1 and J-37144 or equivalent, install them onto the fuel delivery pipe.
4. Reconnect the negative battey terminal.
5. Using a jumper wire, short both terminals fo the fuel pump check con-

nector; the connector is located near the wiper motor.

6. Turn the ignition switch ON and inspect the fuel pressure; it should be 38–44 psi. If the pressure is high, replace the pressure regulator. If the pressure is low, check the fuel pump, fuel filter, pressure regulator, the hoses and connections.

7. Remove the service wire from the check connector. Start the engine.

8. Disconnect the vacuum sensing hose from the pressure regulator and pinch it off.

9. The fuel pressure at idle should still be 38–44 psi.

10. Reconnect the vacuum sensing hose to the pressure regulator and allow the engine to idle for 1½ min. Recheck the fuel pressure, it should be 30–33 psi; if no pressure, inspect the vacuum sensing hose and the pressure regulator.

11. Stop the engine and inspect the fuel pressure for 5 min.; it should remain above 21 psi. If the pressure does not remain high, inspect the fuel pump, the pressure regulator and/or the injectors.

12. After inspecting the fuel pressure, disconnect the negative battery terminal and remove the fuel pressure gauge.

13. Using new gaskets, reconnect the cold start injector hose to the delivery pipe. Check for leaks.

REMOVAL & INSTALLATION

1. Disconnect the negative terminal from the battery.

2. Drain the fuel from the fuel tank. Remove the fuel tank-to-chassis straps and lower the tank slightly. Disconnect the electrical connector and the fuel line from the fuel tube.

3. Remove the fuel pump bracket-to-fuel tank bolts and the bracket.

4. Remove the electrical connectors from the fuel pump, the fuel pump from the bracket and the fuel hose.

5. From the bottom of the fuel pump, remove the rubber cushion, the clip and pull out the filter.

6. To install, use a new bracket-to-fuel tank gasket and reverse the removal procedures. Refill the fuel tank.

Carburetor

REMOVAL & INSTALLATION

1. To remove the air cleaner, perform the following procedures.
   a. Disconnect the air intake hose.
   b. Label and disconnect the emission control hoses from the air cleaner.
   c. Remove the wingnut, mount-

ing bolts and the air cleaner from the carburetor.

2. Disconnect the accelerator cable from the carburetor. If equipped with an automatic transaxle, disconnect the transaxle throttle linkage from the carburetor.

3. Disconnect the wiring connector form the carburetor solenoid valve(s).

4. Label and disconnect the emission control hoses from the carburetor. Disconnect the fuel inlet hose, draining any fuel into a metal or ceramic container (not a styrofoam cup). Disconnect the evaporative emissions canister hose.

5. Remove the cold mixture heater wire clamp and the EGR vacuum control bracket.

6. Remove the carburetor-to-intake manifold nuts, the carburetor and gasket from the intake manifold. Using a clean shop, seal off the intake manifold opening.

7. Using a putty knife, clean the gasket mounting surfaces of the carburetor and manifold.

8. To install, use a new gasket and reverse the removal procedures. Install and adjust the throttle and transaxle linkages to the carburetor. Start the engine and check for fuel leaks.

OVERHAUL

NOTE: For all carburetor overhaul procedures, please refer to "Carburetor Service" in the Unit Repair section.

Fuel Injection

NOTE: Due to the complex nature of modern fuel injection systems, comprehensive diagnosis and testing procedures fall outside the confines of this repair manual. For complete information on fuel injection diagnosis, testing and repair procedures please refer to *Chilton's Guide To Fuel Injection and Feedback Carburetors*.

MANUAL TRANSAXLE

REMOVAL & INSTALLATION

1. Disconnect the negative terminal from the battery.

2. Remove the air cleaner and inlet duct.

3. From the transaxle, disconnect the back-up light switch connector, the speedometer cable, the thermostat housing and the ground wire.

4. Remove the clutch cable-to-transaxle (4) clips, the clutch slave cylinder-to-transaxle bolts and the slave cylinder.

5. Remove the (2) upper transaxle-to-engine bolts and the upper transaxle mount bolt.

6. Using an Engine Support tool or equivalent, attach it to and support the engine. Raise and support the front of the vehicle on jackstands.

7. Remove the left wheel assembly. From under the vehicle, remove the left, right and center splash shields. Remove the center beam-to-chassis bolts and the center beam.

8. Remove the flywheel cover-to-engine bolts and the cover.

9. From both sides of the vehicle, disconnect the lower control arms from the steering knuckles.

10. Disconnect both halfshaft from the transaxle.

11. Disconnect the battery cable and ignition switch wire from the starter. Remove the starter-to-engine bolts and the starter.

12. Using a floor jack, support the transaxle.

13. Remove the transaxle-to-engine bolts and the lower the transaxle from the vehicle.

14. Using a putty knife, clean the gasket mounting surfaces.

15. To install, make sure the input shaft splines align with the clutch disc splines and reverse the removal procedures. Torque the transaxle-to-engine bolts to 47 ft. lbs. (12mm) and to 34 ft. lbs. (10mm), the halfshaft-to-transaxle nuts to 27 ft. lbs., the crossmember-to-chassis nuts/bolts to 29 ft. lbs. and the left-side engine mount bolts to 38 ft. lbs. Check and/or refill the transaxle with fluid.

LINKAGE ADJUSTMENT

Shift Lever Free Play

Adjustment of shift lever free play is accomplished through the use of a selective shim installed in the bottom of the lower shift lever seat.

Select a shim of a thickness that allows a preload of 0.1–0.2 lbs. at the top of the lever and install it in the shift lever seat.

To install the shim, perform the following procedures:

1. Disconnect the negative terminal from the battery.

2. Remove the console and the shifter boot.

3. Remove the shifter cover, shift support and cap.

4. Remove the shifter spacer, shifter seat and the shim.

5. Install the new shim and reassemble the shifter.

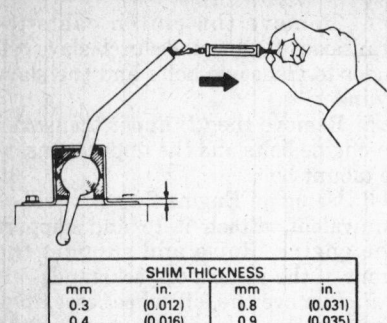

SHIM THICKNESS			
mm	in.	mm	in.
0.3	(0.012)	0.8	(0.031)
0.4	(0.016)	0.9	(0.035)
0.5	(0.020)	1.0	(0.039)
0.6	(0.024)	1.1	(0.043)
0.7	(0.028)	1.2	(0.047)

Shift lever free play

6. Check the shifter free play, using a pull scale, for the proper preload.

7. Repeat the procedure (if necessary).

RELEASE BEARING AND HUB

FLYWHEEL

CLUTCH DISC

CLUTCH COVER

RELEASE FORK

BOOT

Exploded view of the clutch assembly

CLUTCH

REMOVAL & INSTALLATION

NOTE: DO NOT allow grease or oil to contaminate any of the disc, pressure plate or flywheel friction surfaces.

1. Refer to the "Transaxle, Removal and Installation" procedures in this section and remove the transaxle from the vehicle.

2. Match-mark the pressure plate to flywheel for realignment purposes. Remove the pressure plate-to-flywheel bolts, evenly, a little at a time until the pressure is off the springs.

CAUTION

If the tension is not released in this way, the tremendous spring pressure behind the plate could be released suddenly and violently!

3. Remove the pressure plate and the clutch disc from the flywheel.

4. To install the clutch assembly, insert the Clutch Alignment tool No. J-35757 or an old transaxle pilot shaft through the clutch disc, then, insert the tool or shaft into the pilot bearing.

NOTE: The clutch disc is installed with the concave side facing the flywheel.

5. Install the pressure plate over the disc with matchmarks aligned and install the bolts. Tighten the bolts alternately and evenly until even pressure is all around. Finally, torque the pressure plate-to-flywheel bolts to 14

ft. lbs. Remove the centering tool or input shaft.

6. To complete the installation, lubricate the release bearing hub and release fork contact points with multi-purpose grease and reverse the removal procedures.

PEDAL HEIGHT/FREE-PLAY ADJUSTMENT

1. Check pedal height as measured from the insulating sheet on the floor to the front-center of the pedal; it should be 5.65–6.043 in. If the height is not correct, perform the following procedures:

   a. Remove the lower instrument finish panel and air duct.

   b. Loosen the locknut on the pedal stopper bolt (located at the top of the pedal).

   c. Turn the stopper bolt inward (to decrease) or outward (to increase) until it is within specifications.

   d. Tighten the locknut, recheck and readjust (if necessary).

2. To check and/or adjust the clutch pedal free-play, perform the following procedures:

   a. Measure the clutch pedal height.

   b. Push the pedal until you feel increased resistance as the clutch pressure plate springs begin to be compressed. Measure the pedal at this point, then, subtract the smaller figure from the larger one; this is the free-play dimension.

NOTE: The free-play dimension should be 0.51–0.91 in. (1985) or 0.20–0.59 in. (1986-89).

   c. If necessary to adjust the free-play, loosen the pushrod locknut, lo-

PUSH ROD PLAY AND FREEPLAY ADJUST POINT

PEDAL HEIGHT ADJUST POINT

PUSH ROD PLAY

PEDAL HEIGHT

View of the clutch pedal height and free-play adjustment

cated between the pedal and the clutch master cylinder. Turn the pushrod (clockwise to decrease or counter-clockwise to increase) until the dimension is within specifications.

   d. Tighten the locknut, recheck and readjust (if necessary).

Clutch Master Cylinder

REMOVAL & INSTALLATION

1. Drain or siphon the fluid from the master cylinder.

2. Remove the lower instrument finish panel and air duct.

3. Remove the pedal return spring, clevis pin and clip.

4. Disconnect the hydraulic line the clutch master cylinder.

NOTE: Do not spill brake fluid on the painted surface of the vehicle.

5. Remove the master cylinder-to-firewall nuts and withdraw the assembly.

6. To install, reverse the removal procedures. Refill the master cylinder reservoir with brake fluid. Bleed the clutch hydraulic system. Operate the clutch pedal and check the system for leaks. Check and/or adjust the clutch pedal height and free-play.

Clutch Slave Cylinder

REMOVAL & INSTALLATION

NOTE: Do not spill brake fluid on the painted surface of the vehicle.

1. Disconnect the hydraulic line from the clutch slave cylinder.

2. Remove the slave cylinder-to-engine bolts and the cylinder.

3. To install, reverse the removal procedures. Refill the clutch master cylinder reservoir with clean brake fluid. Bleed the clutch hydraulic system. Operate the clutch pedal and check for leaks.

BLEEDING THE HYDRAULIC SYSTEM

1. Fill the clutch master cylinder reservoir with brake fluid.

NOTE: DO NOT spill brake fluid on the painted surface of the vehicle for it will lift the finish.

2. Fit a vinyl bleeder tube over the bleeder screw at the front of the slave cylinder and place the other end in a clean jar half filled with brake fluid.

3. Have an assistant depress the clutch pedal several times. Loosen the bleeder screw and allow the fluid to flow into the jar.

4. Tighten the screw and have the assistant release the clutch pedal.

5. Repeat bleeding procedure until no air bubbles are present in the fluid.

6. Refill the master cylinder to the specified level, check the system for leaks, then, adjust the clutch pedal height and free-play.

AUTOMATIC TRANSAXLE

NOTE: For further information
on the automatic transaxle, please refer to "Automatic Transmissions" in the Unit Repair section.

REMOVAL & INSTALLATION

1. Disconnect the negative terminal from the battery and the ground cable from the transaxle. Label and disconnect the necessary electrical connectors. Drain the transaxle.

2. Remove the air intake duct. Disconnect the Throttle Valve cable from the carburetor (if equipped).

3. Disconnect the neutral safety switch, the speedometer cable and the shift control cable from the transaxle. Remove the shift cable bracket from the transaxle.

4. From the top of the transaxle, disconnect the thermostat housing-to-transaxle bolts.

5. Remove the single upper mount-to-bracket bolt. Remove the two upper bellhousing bolts.

6. Remove the upper (2) bell housing bolts.

7. Using a Engine Supporting tool, connect it to and support the engine. Raise and support the front of the vehicle on jackstands.

8. Remove the left wheel assembly, the left splash shield, the right splash shield and the center splash shield. Remove the crossmember-to-chassis bolts and the crossmember.

7. Remove the oil line cooler bracket. Disconnect and plug the oil cooler lines from the transaxle.

8. Remove the flywheel cover. Matchmark the torque converter-to-flywheel, then, remove the torque converter-to-flywheel bolts and separate the torque converter from the flywheel.

NOTE:The crankshaft must be rotated to gain access to the other bolts.

9. Remove both control arm-to-ball joint nuts/bolts and separate the lower control arms from the ball joints.

10. Remove both halfshaft-to-transaxle flange nuts and separate the halfshaft from the transaxle; support the halfshaft on a wire.

11. Disconnect the battery cable and ignition wire from the starter. Remove the starter-to-engine bolts and the starter.

12. Remove the lower transaxle-to-engine bolts.

13. Using a wooden block atop a floor jack, support the transaxle.

14. Remove the remaining transaxle-to-engine bolts. Separate the transaxle from the engine and lower it from the vehicle.

15. To install, align the torque con-
verter-to-flywheel alignment marks and reverse the removal procedures. Torque the transaxle-to-engine bolts to 47 ft. lbs. (12mm) and the 34 ft. lbs. (10mm), the left-side engine mount bolts to 38 ft. lbs., the torque converter-to-flywheel bolts to 13 ft. lbs. Torque the halfshaft-to-transaxle nuts/bolts to 27 ft. lbs. and the crossmember-to-chassis bolts to 29 ft. lbs. Refill the transaxle with Dexron® II transmission fluid. Start the engine, test drive it and check for leaks.

DRIVE AXLE

Halfshaft

REMOVAL & INSTALLATION

1. From the front wheel assemblies, remove the grease cup, then, loosen the wheel lug nuts and the halfshaft hub nut.

2. Raise and support the front of the vehicle on jackstands, then, remove the wheel/tire assemblies, the cotter pin, the locknut cap, hub nut and washer.

3. Loosen and remove the (6) halfshaft flange-to-transaxle flange nuts

NOTE: When removing the halfshaft-to-transaxle nuts, have an assistant depress the brake pedal to keep the shaft from turning.

4. Remove the lower control arm-to-ball joint nuts/bolts and separate the lower control arm from the steering knuckle from lower control arm.

NOTE: If the vehicle is equipped with a twincam engine, it may be necessary to remove the stabilizer bar from the lower control arm.

5. Turn the steering knuckle to separate the halfshaft from the transaxle.

6. Cover the outboard CV-joint rubber boot with a cloth to prevent damage. Using the Wheel Puller tool No. J-25287 or equivalent, press the halfshaft from the steering knuckle and remove the driveshaft.

7. To install the halfshaft, lubricate the splines with multi-puprose grease, insert the it into the steering knuckle hub, install the washer and the hub nut, then, tighten the hub nut to draw the halfshaft into the steering knuckle hub until it seats.

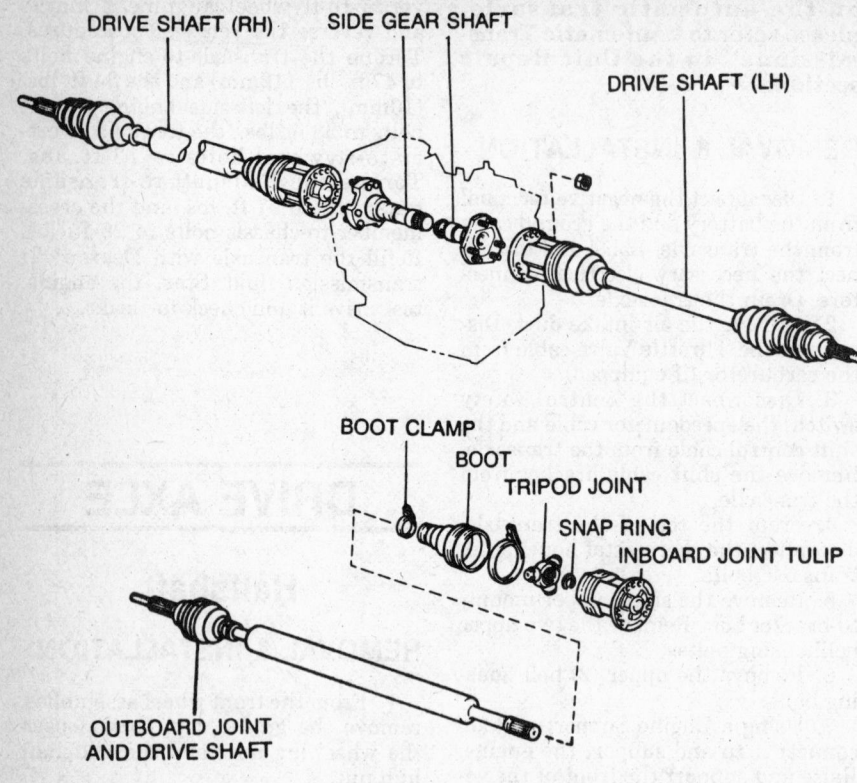

DRIVE SHAFT (RH)   SIDE GEAR SHAFT

DRIVE SHAFT (LH)

BOOT CLAMP
BOOT
TRIPOD JOINT
SNAP RING
INBOARD JOINT TULIP

OUTBOARD JOINT
AND DRIVE SHAFT

Drive axle assembly

NOTE: **When torquing the hub nut, have an assistant depress the brake pedal; it may be necessary final torque the hub nut with the vehicle resting on the ground.**

8. To complete the installation, reverse the removal procedures. Torque the lower control arm-to-ball joint nuts/bolts to 59 ft. lbs., the halfshaft-to-transaxle flange nuts to 27 ft. lbs. and the halfshaft-to-steering knuckle hub nut to 137 ft. lbs. Install a new cotter pin.

CV-JOINT OVERHAUL

NOTE: **For all CV-joint overhaul procedures, please refer to the "U/CV-Joint Overhaul" in The Unit Repair section.**

Front Wheel Drive Hub, Knuckle and Bearings

REMOVAL & INSTALLATION

1. Loosen the wheel nuts and hub nut.
2. Raise and support the front of the vehicle on jackstands. Remove the wheel/tire assembly.
3. From the strut, remove the brake hose retaining clip. Disconnect the flex hose from the brake pipe.
4. Remove the caliper bracket-to-steering knuckle bolts and support the caliper on a wire. Remove the brake disc.
5. From the tie rod ball joint, remove the cotter pin and tie rod-to-steering nut. Using the Ball Joint Removal tool No. J-24319-01 or equivalent, separate the tie rod from the steering knuckle.
6. Remove the ball joint-to-lower control arm nuts/bolts and separate the ball joint from the lower control arm.
7. Remove the halfshaft hub nut and washer. Using the Wheel Puller tool No. J-25287 or equivalent, press halfshaft from the steering knuckle; using a wire, support the halfshaft.
8. Match-mark the steering knuckle-to-strut relationship. Remove the (2) strut-to-steering knuckle nuts/bolts and remove the steering knuckle.
9. Mount the steering knuckle in a vise. Using a small pry bar, remove the dust deflector from the inside surface of the steering knuckle.
10. Using the a slide hammer puller and the Seal Extractor tool No. J-26941 or equivalent, pull the inner grease seal from the steering knuckle.
11. Using a pair of snap ring pliers, remove the inner bearing snap ring.
12. Using the Removal tools No. J-25287 and J-35378 or equivalent,

press the hub from the steering knuckle assembly. Remove the disc brake dust shield.
13. Using the Removal tools No. J-25287 and J-35378 or equivalent, press the outer bearing race from the hub.
14. Using the Seal Removal tool No. J-26941 or equivalent, remove the outer grease seal from the steering knuckle.
15. Using the Removal tools No. J-35399 and No. J-35379 or equivalent, drive the bearing assembly from the steering knuckle.
16. Clean and inspect all parts. Replace any parts that appear worn or damaged. Replace all grease seals.
17. Using the Installation tools No. J-8092 and No. J-35411 or equivalent, drive the new bearing assembly into the steering knuckle.
18. Using the Seal Installation tool No. J-35737-1 or equivalent, lubricate the seal lips with multi-purpose grease and drive the new outer grease seal into the steering knuckle.
19. Apply sealer to the dust shield and install it onto the steering knuckle.
20. Apply multi-purpose grease to the seal lip, seal and bearing. Using the Hub Installation tools No. J-8092 and No. J-35399 or equivalent, press the new wheel bearing into the steering knuckle, then, install the snap ring.
21. Lubricate the lips of the new seal with multi-purpose grease. Using the Seal Installation tool No. J-35737 or equivalent, drive the new inner grease seal into the steering knuckle.
22. Using tool No. J-35379 or equivalent (open end down), install the dust deflector ring onto the steering knuckle.
23. Install the lower ball joint-to-control arm nuts/bolts, then, torque to 59 ft. lbs.

NOTE: **If installing the ball joint-to-steering knuckle, torque the nut to 14 ft. lbs. (to seat the ball joint) and remove it. Using a new ball joint nut, torque it to 82 ft. lbs.**

24. Install the camber adjusting cam to steering knuckle, the steering steering knuckle to strut. Insert the steering knuckle-to-strut bolts (from rear to front) and align the camber adjusting marks. Torque the steering knuckle-to-strut nuts/bolts to 105 ft. lbs. (except twincam) or 166 ft. lbs. (twincam).
25. Install the tie rod-to-steering knuckle nut and torque it to 36 ft. lbs.; be sure to install a new cotter pin.
26. To complete the installation, reverse the removal procedures. Torque

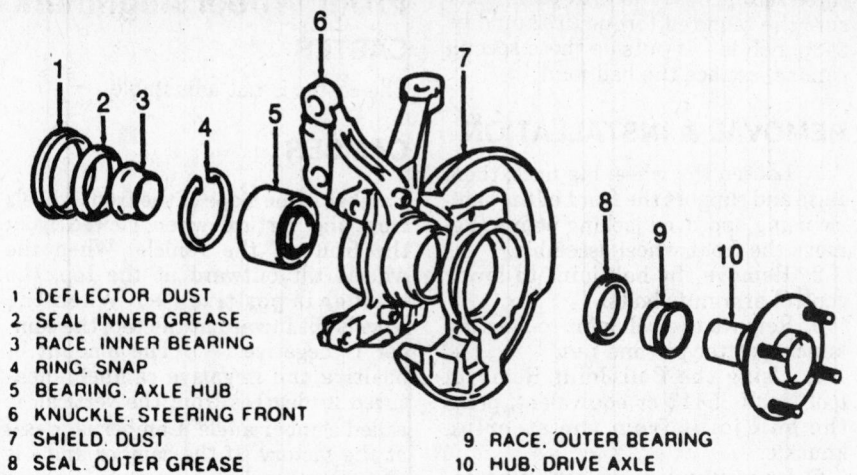

1 DEFLECTOR. DUST
2 SEAL. INNER GREASE
3 RACE. INNER BEARING
4 RING. SNAP
5 BEARING. AXLE HUB
6 KNUCKLE. STEERING FRONT
7 SHIELD. DUST
8 SEAL. OUTER GREASE
9 RACE. OUTER BEARING
10 HUB. DRIVE AXLE

Exploded view of the hub/bearing assembly

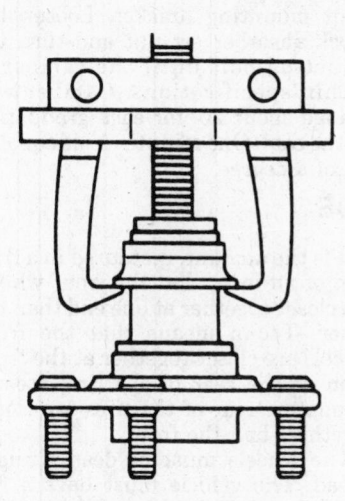

Inner race removal

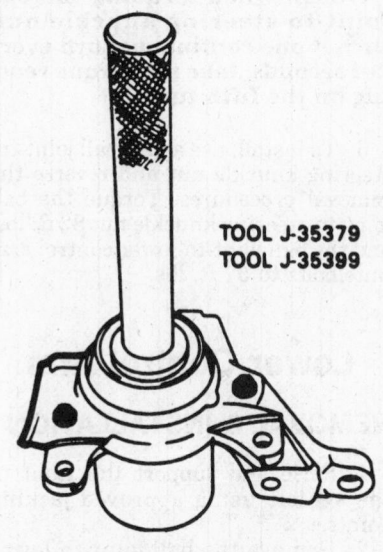

TOOL J-35379
TOOL J-35399

Bearing removal

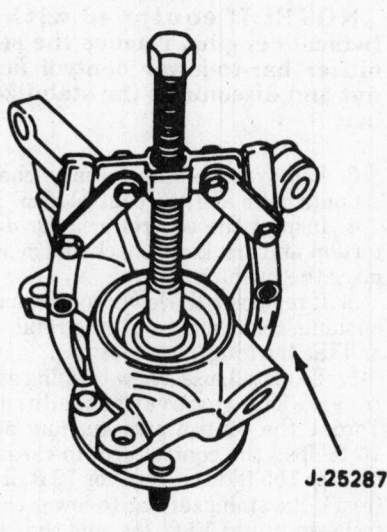

J-25287

Hub removal

the brake caliper-to-steering knuckle bolts to 65 ft. lbs.

27. Lower the vehicle so the wheels are resting on the ground. Torque the wheel nuts to 76 ft. lbs., the halfshaft hub nut 137 ft. lbs.; be sure to install a new cotter pin. Bleed the brake system.

28. Check the wheel alignment; it may be necessary to have the wheels aligned when the strut or the knuckle has been replaced with a new part.

NOTE: Never reinstall used grease seals, self locking nuts or cotter pins; always replace these parts with new ones once they have been removed.

29. If the cotter pin holes are not aligned, bend the tangs on the cap, slightly to align the holes; NEVER BACK OFF THE NUT.

FRONT SUSPENSION

MacPherson Strut

REMOVAL & INSTALLATION

1. From in the engine compartment, remove the strut-to-body nuts.
2. Loosen the wheel/tire assembly lug nuts. Raise and support the front of the vehicle so the jackstands are not under the lower control arms, then, remove the wheel/tire assemblies.
3. Detach the flexible brake line from the strut clip. Disconnect the brake hose-to-brake pipe connection

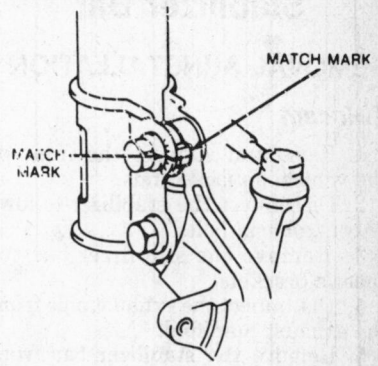

MATCH MARK
MATCH MARK

Mark the camber adjusting cam before removing the knuckle attaching nuts and bolts so camber can be restored without rechecking alignment

from the body mount. Using a catch pan, drain the excess brake fluid. Pull the brake hose back through the opening the the strut bracket; cap both open ends of the hydraulic system.

4. Remove the brake caliper-to-steering knuckle bolts. Using a wire, support the caliper out of the way; support the caliper so that the brake hose will not be under any strain (do not disconnect the hose from the caliper).

5. Mark the adjusting cam so the camber adjustment can be restored when the strut is reassembled. Remove the steering knuckle-to-strut bolts, the strut assembly and the camber adjusting cam from the steering knuckle.

6. Using a cloth, cover the drive axle boot to protect it while the strut is removed.

7. Inspect the strut for cracks, wear, distortion and/or damage; replace the strut (if necessary).

8. To install, lubricate the upper strut bearing with multi-purpose grease and reverse the removal procedures. Align the strut-to-steering

knuckle marks. Torque the steering knuckle-to-strut bolts to 105 ft. lbs. (except twincam) or 166 ft. lbs. (twincam), the strut-to-body.

9. Lower the vehicle so the strut can be aligned with body mounting holes.

10. Install and torque the strut-to-body nuts to 23 ft. lbs. (except twincam) or 29 ft. lbs. (twincam). Lower the vehicle to the ground and torque the wheel lugnuts to 76 ft. lbs. Bleed the brake system.

STRUT OVERHAUL

NOTE: For all strut overhaul procedures, please refer to the "Strut Overhaul" Unit Repair section.

Stabilizer Bar

REMOVAL & INSTALLATION

Twincam

1. Raise and support the front of the vehicle on jackstands.

2. Disconnect the stabilizer-to-lower control arm bolts.

3. Remove the stabilizer bar-to-chassis brackets.

4. Disconnect the exhaust pipe from the exhaust manifold.

5. Remove the stabilizer bar from the vehicle.

NOTE: Never reuse a self locking nut, always use a new one.

6. To install, reverse the removal procedures. Torque the exhaust pipe-to-exhaust manifold to 46 ft. lbs., the stabilizer bar-to-body bolts to 14 ft. lbs. and the stabilizer bar-to-lower control arm bolts to 13 ft. lbs.

Ball Joints

INSPECTION

1. Turn the front wheels so they are straight and chock the rear wheels. Raise the vehicle and place a wooden block of 7–8 in. under it. Then, lower the vehicle onto the block until about half its compression when the vehicle is resting on it.

2. Attempt to move the lower arm up and down. There should be no noticeable play.

3. If the ball joint is removed from the vehicle check the required rotating torque with and inch pound torque wrench. Flip the ball joint back and forth, several times. Install the nut and turn the stud with a torque wrench at a rate of about one turn in

three seconds. At the fifth turn, measure the required torque; it should be 9–30 inch lbs. If outside these specifications, replace the ball joint.

REMOVAL & INSTALLATION

1. Loosen the wheel lug nuts, then, raise and support the front of the vehicle using approved jacking points. Remove the front wheel assembly.

2. Remove the ball joint-to-lower control arm nuts/bolts.

3. Remove the ball joint-to-steering knuckle cotter pin and nut.

4. Using the Ball Joint Removal tool No. J-35413 or equivalent, press the ball joint from the steering knuckle.

5. Inspect and/or replace (if necessary) the ball joint.

NOTE: When torquing the ball joint-to-steering knuckle nut, turn it one continuous turn every 2–4 seconds; take the torque reading on the fifth turn.

6. To install, use a new ball joint-to-steering knuckle nut and reverse the removal procedures. Torque the ball joint-to-steering knuckle nut 82 ft. lbs. and the ball joint-to-lower control arm nuts/bolts to 57 ft. lbs.

Lower Control Arm

REMOVAL & INSTALLATION

1. Raise and support the front of the vehicle using approved jacking points.

2. Remove the ball joint-to-lower control arm nuts/bolts.

NOTE: If equipped with a twincam engine, remove the stabilizer bar-to-lower control arm nut and disconnect the stabilizer bar.

3. Remove the control arm-to-chassis nuts/bolts and the control arm.

4. Inspect the control arm for distortion and cracking; check and/or replace the bushing.

5. If replacing the lower control arm bushing, remove the nut, the retainer and the bushing.

6. To install, use a new bushing and reverse the removal procedures. Torque the control arm bushing nut 76 ft. lbs., the control arm-to-chassis bolts to 105 ft. lbs. (front) or 72 ft. lbs. (rear), the stabilizer bar-to-lower control arm nut to 13 ft. lbs. and the ball joint-to-lower control arm nuts/bolts to 57 ft. lbs.

Front Wheel Alignment

CASTER

The caster is not adjustable.

CAMBER

Camber is the slope of the front wheels from the vertical when viewed from the front of the vehicle. When the wheels tilt outward at the top, the camber is positive (+). When the wheels tilt inward at the top, the camber is negative (−). The amount of positive and negative camber, measured in degrees from the vertical, is called camber angle. Camber is preset at the factory. If the camber angle is out of tolerance, inspect or replace worn or damaged suspension parts.

Camber is adjustable by means of a camber adjustment bolt on the lower strut mounting bracket. Loosen the shock absorber set nut and turn the adjusting bolt until the camber is within specifications. Camber will change about 20' for each graduation on the cam. One minute (1') is equal to $\frac{1}{60}$ of a degree.

TOE

Toe is the amount, measured in a fraction of an inch, that the front wheels are closer together at one end than the other. Toe-in means that the front wheels are closer together at the front than at the rear of the tire; toe-out means the rear of the tires are closer together than the front.

The wheels must be dead straight ahead. The vehicle must have a full tank of gas, all fluids must be at their proper levels, all other suspension and steering adjustments must be correct and the tires must be properly inflated to their cold specifications.

1. Toe can be determined by measuring the distance between the centers of the tire threads, at the front of the tire and the rear. If the tread pattern makes this impossible, measure between the edges of the wheel rims but be sure to move the vehicle and measure in a few places to avoid errors caused by bent rims or wheel run-out.

2. If the measurement is not within specifications, loosen the boot clamps (small end) and slide from the boot. On the adjustable tie rods, loosen both tie rod end lock nuts.

3. Turn both tie rods equal amounts until the measurements are within specifications.

4. Reinstall the boot clamps, tighten the lock bolts and recheck the measurements. Make sure the rack boots are not twisted. Check that the steering wheel is in the proper position; if not, remove it and reposition it.

REAR SUSPENSION

MacPherson Strut

REMOVAL & INSTALLATION

1. Working inside the rear of the vehicle, remove the rear quarter window garnish molding, back window panel and the speaker grille (if necessary).

2. Raise and support the rear of the vehicle by placing jackstands under the frame, then, remove the rear wheel.

3. Disconnect the flexible brake hose from the strut. Remove the flexible hose and clip from the mounting point on the strut, then, reconnect the brake line to the flex hose to prevent an excessive amount of brake fluid from draining from the system.

NOTE: Before removing the strut from the hub carrier, be sure to mark the location of the strut to the hub carrier for reinstallation purposes.

4. Remove the strut-to-hub carrier nuts/bolts and separate the strut from the hub carrier.

5. Remove the strut-to-chassis nuts and carefully remove the strut assembly.

6. Inspect the strut for cracks, wear and/or other damage; replace it (if necessary).

7. To install, reverse the removal procedures. Torque the strut-to-chassis nuts to 17 ft. lbs., the strut-to-hub carrier nuts/bolts to 105 ft. lbs. Bleed the brake system.

OVERHAUL

NOTE: For all strut overhaul procedures, please refer to the "Strut Overhaul" in the Unit Repair section.

Rear Suspension Arms

REMOVAL & INSTALLATION

Front

1. Raise and support the rear of the vehicle by placing jackstands under the frame, then, remove the rear wheel.

2. If equipped with a twincam engine, remove the rear suspension arm-to-stabilizer bar nut, retainer and cushion.

3. Remove the front suspension arm-to-hub carrier nut/bolt.

4. Remove the front suspension arm-to-chassis nut/bolt and the suspension arm from the vehicle.

5. To install, use a new stabilizer link-to-suspension arm nut (twincam) and reverse the removal procedures. Torque the stabilizer bar-to-front suspension arm nut/bolt to 11 ft. lbs. (twincam).

6. Lower the vehicle, bounce the vehicle to stabilize the suspension, then, torque the front suspension arm bolts to 64 ft. lbs. Check and/or adjust the rear wheel alignment.

Rear

1. Raise and support the rear of the vehicle by placing jackstands under the frame, then, remove the rear wheel.

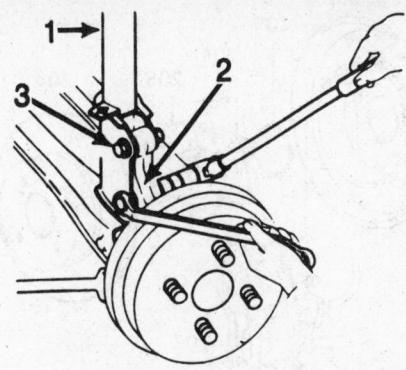

1. STRUT ASSEMBLY
2. CARRIER ASSEMBLY
3. BOLT 142 N·M (105 FT. LBS.)

Rear strut-to-carrier bolt removal

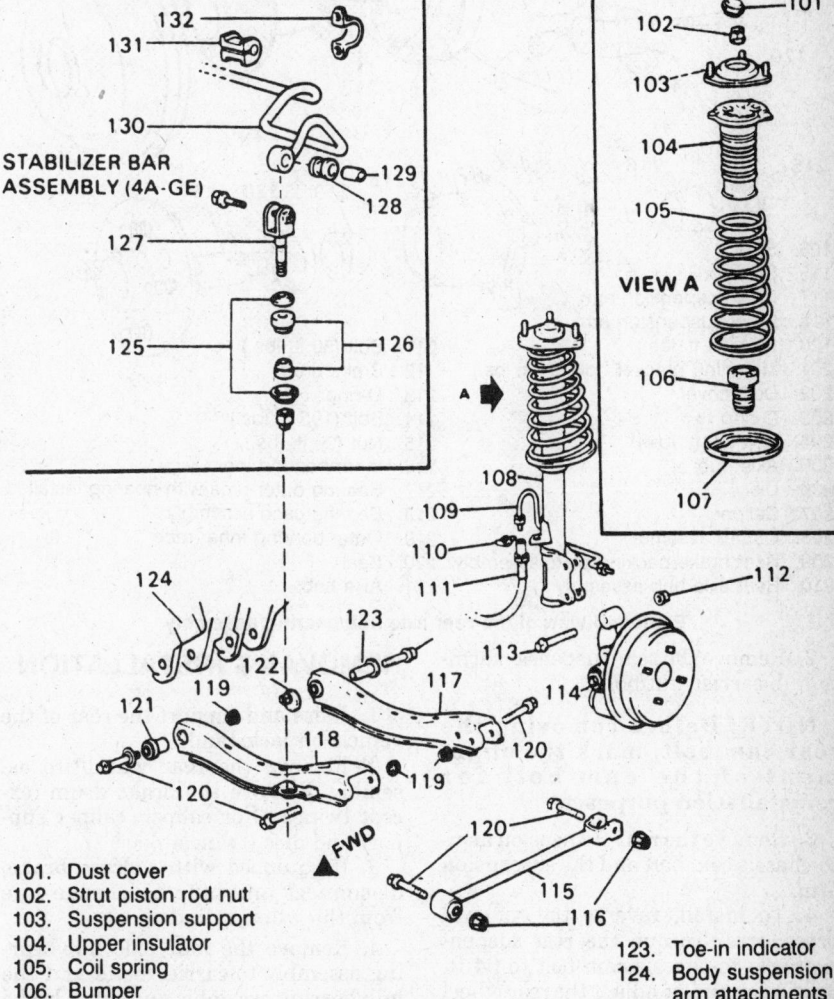

101. Dust cover	123. Toe-in indicator
102. Strut piston rod nut	124. Body suspension
103. Suspension support	arm attachments
104. Upper insulator	125. Retainer
105. Coil spring	126. Cushion
106. Bumper	127. Stabilizer link
107. Lower insulator	115. Strut rod	128. Bushing
108. Strut	116. Nut	129. Collar
109. Brake line	117. Rear suspension arm	130. Stabilizer bar
110. Retaining clip	118. Front suspension arm	131. Bushing
111. Flexible brake hose	119. Nut	132. Bracket.
112. Nut (105 ft. lbs.)	120. Bolt (64 ft. lbs.)	
113. Bolt	121. Bushing	
114. Hub carrier assembly	122. Toe-in adjusting cam nut	

Exploded view of the rear suspension

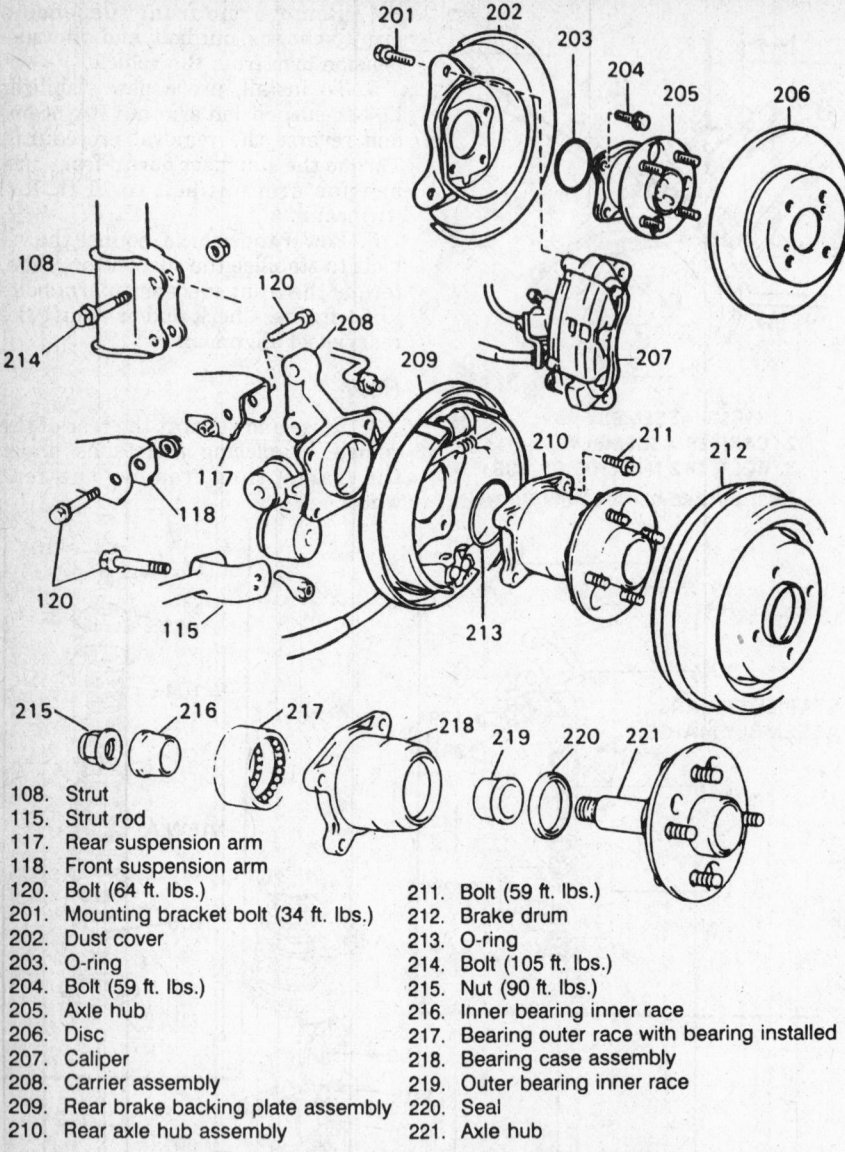

108. Strut
115. Strut rod
117. Rear suspension arm
118. Front suspension arm
120. Bolt (64 ft. lbs.)
201. Mounting bracket bolt (34 ft. lbs.)
202. Dust cover
203. O-ring
204. Bolt (59 ft. lbs.)
205. Axle hub
206. Disc
207. Caliper
208. Carrier assembly
209. Rear brake backing plate assembly
210. Rear axle hub assembly

211. Bolt (59 ft. lbs.)
212. Brake drum
213. O-ring
214. Bolt (105 ft. lbs.)
215. Nut (90 ft. lbs.)
216. Inner bearing inner race
217. Bearing outer race with bearing installed
218. Bearing case assembly
219. Outer bearing inner race
220. Seal
221. Axle hub

Exploded view of the rear axle hub/bearing assembly

2. Remove the rear suspension arm-to-hub carrier nut/bolt.

NOTE: Before removing the rear cam bolt, mark the alignment of the cam bolt for reinstallation purposes.

3. Remove the rear suspension arm-to-chassis cam bolt and the suspension arm.

4. To install, reverse the removal procedures. Torque the rear suspension arm-to-chassis cam bolt to 64 ft. lbs. Check and/or adjust the rear wheel alignment.

Rear Wheel Bearings

ADJUSTMENT

Rear wheel bearing adjustment is made by torquing the rear hub nut to 90 ft. lbs.

REMOVAL & INSTALLATION

1. Raise and support the rear of the vehicle on jackstands.

2. Remove the rear wheel/tire assembly. Remove the brake drum (except twincam) or caliper, caliper support and disc (twincam).

3. If equipped with a drum brake, disconnect and plug the brake line from the wheel cylinder.

4. Remove the four axle hub/bearing assembly-to-carrier bolts and the hub/bearing assembly and drum brake assembly (except twincam) or dust cover (twincam). Remove and discard the O-ring.

5. To disassemble the hub/bearing assembly, perform the following procedures:
   a. Using copper or aluminum, cover the vise jaws, then, insert the hub/bearing assembly into the vise.

b. Using a socket wrench, remove the hub nut from the hub/bearing assembly.

c. Using the Wheel Puller tool No. J-25287 or equivalent, press the bearing case from the axle hub, then, remove the inner race, the inner bearing and the outer bearing.

d. Using the Wheel Puller tool No. J-25287 or equivalent, press the outer bearing inner race from the axle hub.

e. Remove the seal from the axle hub.

f. Using an arbor press and the Driving tool No. J-35440 or equivalent, install outer bearing inner race onto the bearing outer race and press it from the bearing case.

NOTE: Whenever the wheel bearing assembly is disassembled, it should be replaced with a new one.

6. To install the new wheel bearing, perform the following procedures:
   a. Using multi-purpose, apply it around the bearing outer race.

b. Using an press and the Driver tool No. J-35400 or equivalent, press the new bearing outer race into the bearing case.

c. Install the new bearings and inner races into the bearing case.

d. Using multi-purpose grease, lightly coat the new seal. Using the Seal Installation tool No. J-35736 or equivalent, drive the new seal into the bearing case until it seats.

e. Using an arbor press and the Driver tool No. J-35440 or equivalent, press the bearing case onto the hub. Torque the hub nut to 90 ft. lbs.

f. Using a chisel and a hammer, stake the hub nut.

7. To install the rear hub/bearing assembly, use a new O-ring and reverse the removal procedures. Torque the hub/bearing assembly-to-axle carrier bolts to 59 ft. lbs.

NOTE: If equipped with drum brakes, reconnect the brake line to the wheel cylinder. Refill the brake master cylinder and bleed the brake system.

STEERING

Steering Wheel

REMOVAL & INSTALLATION

1. Disconnect the negative terminal from the battery.

2. Remove the screw from the bottom of the steering wheel pad and pull the pad upward and off the steering wheel.

3. Remove the steering wheel-to-steering column nut. Matchmark the steering wheel-to-steering column relationship.

4. Using the Steering Wheel Puller tool No. J-1859-03 or equivalent, screw the bolts into both sides of the steering column, turn the puller center bolt to press the steering wheel from the steering shaft.

NOTE: When working on the steering column, be careful not to strike the column in any way for it is constructed of a collapsible design and will not withstand major shock.

5. To install, align the matchmarks and reverse the removal procedures. Torque the steering wheel-to-steering column nut to 25 ft. lbs.

Combination Switch

The combination switch consists of the turn signal switch, the headlight dimmer switch, the windshield wiper switch and the hazard warning switch.

REMOVAL & INSTALLATION

1. Refer to the "Steering Wheel, Removal and Installation" procedures in this section and remove the steering wheel.

2. Remove the lower instrument finish panel, air duct and column lower cover.

3. From the base of the steering column shroud, disconnect the ignition switch and turn signal electrical connector.

4. Remove the combination switch-to-steering column screws and the combination switch with the upper column cover.

5. To install, reverse the removal procedures.

Ignition Lock and Switch

REMOVAL & INSTALLATION

1. Refer to the "Combination Switch, Removal and Installation" procedures in this section and remove the combination switch.

2. If equipped with a tilt steering column, perform the following procedures:

   a. Remove the tension springs and grommets, the tilt lever (the bolt has left-hand threads), the adjusting nut/washer.

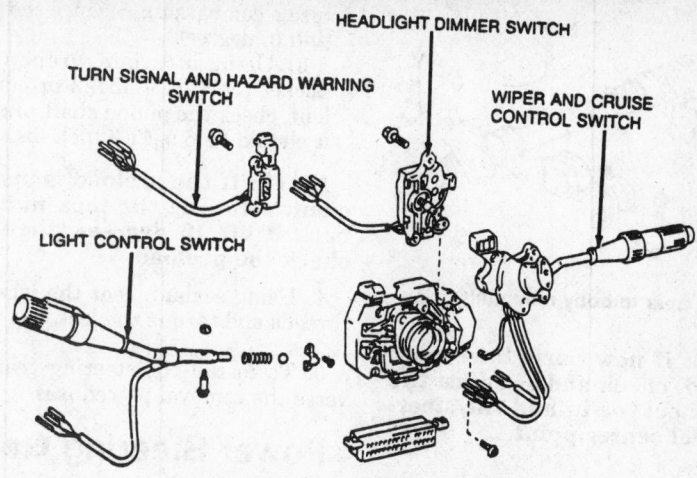

HEADLIGHT DIMMER SWITCH

TURN SIGNAL AND HAZARD WARNING SWITCH

WIPER AND CRUISE CONTROL SWITCH

LIGHT CONTROL SWITCH

Exploded view of combination switch

   b. Pull out the lock bolt, then, remove the upper and lower column supports.

3. From the lower steering column, disconnect the ignition switch electrical connector.

4. Remove the retainer-to-upper bracket screws and the retainer from the upper bracket.

5. Using snap-ring pliers, remove the snap-ring from the upper bracket.

6. Insert the key into the ignition switch and release the steering lock.

7. Using a hammer and a pin punch, drive the tapered bolt from the upper bracket.

8. Remove the upper bracket-to-steering column tube bolts and the upper bracket.

9. To install, release the steering lock and install the upper bracket-to-steering column bolts (tighten the bolts finger tight). Torque the upper bracket-to-steering column bolts to 14 ft. lbs.

10. If installing the tilt steering mechanism, perform the following procedures:

   a. Apply grease to the bushings and the O-rings, then, install the lower support-to-tube.

   b. Using multi-purpose grease, apply it to the tilt bracket-to-steering column mating surfaces, then, install the upper support and lock bolt.

NOTE: If there is any play in the adjusting support, snug-up the adjusting nut.

   c. Install the tilt lever. Move the lever to loosen the bracket-to-column bolt, adjust the column height and move the lever to lock the column position; if the lever is out of position, reposition the adjusting nut.

   d. Install the tilt lever retaining

screw (left-hand thread) and torque it. Install the tension springs and grommets.

11. To complete the installation, reverse the removal procedures.

Manual Steering Gear

REMOVAL & INSTALLATION

1. Remove the intermediate shaft cover.

2. From the steering gear pinion shaft, loosen the upper pinch bolt, then, remove the lower pinch bolt.

3. Loosen the wheel/tire assembly lug nuts.

4. Raise and support the front of the vehicle on jackstands.

5. From the tie rod ends, remove the cotter pins and nuts. Using the Ball Joint Removal tool No. J-24319-01 or equivalent, press the ball joint from the steering knuckle.

6. Remove the steering gear-to-chassis nuts/bolts and brackets, then, separate the universal joint from the steering gear and slide the steering gear through the access hole.

7. Inspect the steering gear for wear, and/or damage; replace or repair the damaged parts.

NOTE: If the ball joint seal is torn or damaged, replace the ball joint. Make sure the clamps are installed squarely over the rubber insulators so they will not be damaged when the nuts and bolts are torqued.

8. To install, reverse the removal procedures. Torque the steering gear-to-chassis nuts/bolts to 43 ft. lbs., the tie rod end-to-steering knuckle nuts to 36 ft. lbs. and the U-joint pinch clamp bolts to 26 ft. lbs.

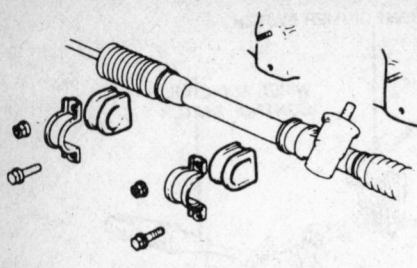

Gear to body mounting

NOTE: If new parts have been installed, check and/or adjust the front wheel toe-in and the steering wheel center point.

ADJUSTMENT

NOTE: To perform the adjustment procedure, the steering gear assembly should be removed from the vehicle.

1. Refer to the "Manual Steering Gear, Removal and Installation" procedures in this section, then, remove the steering gear and place it in a vise.
2. To adjust the pinion bearing turning torque, perform the following procedures:
   a. Using the Pinion Bearing Lock Nut Wrench tool No. J-35415 or equivalent, loosen the pinion bearing lock nut.
   b. Using a torque wrench, Pinion Spanner Wrench tool No. J-35416 or equivalent, and Socket tool No. J-35422 or equivalent, adjust the pinion bearing screw torque to 3.2 inch lbs.
   c. Loosen the adjusting screw until the turning torque is 2–2.9 inch lbs.
   d. Using sealant, coat the pinion lock nut threads, then, torque the nut to 83 ft. lbs.
   e. Recheck the turning torque, if it is incorrect, reperform this procedure.
3. To adjust the rack guide screw, perform the following procedure:
   a. At the rear of the steering gear, loosen the rack guide spring cap lock nut.
   b. Remove the rack guide adjusting plug.
   c. Install the rack guide adjusting plug and count the number of rotations, then, back-off the plug ½ the number of turns.
   d. Using a socket wrench and Socket tool No. J-35423 or equivalent, hold the rack guide adjusting plug. Using a torque wrench with a Lock Nut Wrench Adapter tool No. J-35692 or equivalent, torque the rack guide lock nut to 18 ft. lbs., then, back-off the nut 25 degrees

(use a compass to measure the position in degrees).
   e. Using a torque wrench and Socket tool No. J-35422 or equivalent, check the pinion shaft preload; it should be 6.9–11.3 inch lbs.

NOTE: If the preload is insufficient, retorque the lock nut and back it off 12 degrees, then, recheck the preload.

4. Using sealant, coat the lock nut threads and torque the lock nut to 51 ft. lbs.
5. To install the steering gear, reverse the removal procedures.

Power Steering Gear

REMOVAL & INSTALLATION

1. Remove the intermediate steering shaft protector. Loosen the upper shaft pinch bolt and remove the lower one.
2. Open the hood and place a drain pan under the steering gear assembly. Clean the area around the inlet and return lines at the steering gear valve.
3. Loosen the wheel lugnuts, then, raise and support the front of the vehicle on jackstands. Remove both front wheel/tire assemblies.
4. Remove the cotter pins and nuts from the tie rod ends. Using the Ball Joint Removal tool No. J-24319-01 or equivalent, press the tie rod ends from the steering knuckles.
5. Using a floor jack, support the transaxle. Remove the rear center engine mounting member-to-chassis mounting bolts.
6. Remove the rear engine mount-to-mount bracket nut and bolt.
7. Disconnect the pressure and return lines from the steering gear. Remove the steering gear-to-chassis nuts and bolts; raise and lower the rear of the transaxle (as necessary) to gain access to the steering gear-to-chassis nuts and bolts.
8. Remove the steering gear through the access hole.
9. To install, reverse the removal procedures. Torque the steering gear-to-chassis nuts/bolts to 43 ft. lbs., the tie rod end-to-steering knuckle nuts to 36 ft. lbs. and the U-joint pinch clamp bolts to 26 ft. lbs. Add fluid to the pump reservoir and bleed the system.

NOTE: If new parts have been installed, check and/or adjust the front wheel toe-in and the steering wheel center point.

ADJUSTMENT

NOTE: To perform the adjustment procedure, the steering gear

assembly should be removed from the vehicle.

1. Refer to the "Power Steering Gear, Removal and Installation" procedures in this section, then, remove the steering gear and place it in a vise.
2. To adjust the pinion bearing turning torque, perform the following procedures:
   a. Using the socket wrench and Socket tool No. J-35428 or equivalent, loosen the pinion bearing lock nut.
   b. Using a socket wrench and Socket tool No. J-35428 or equivalent, hold the pinion from turning. Using a torque wrench and socket, torque the lower pinion lock nut to 48 ft. lbs.
3. To adjust the rack guide cap, perform the following procedure:
   a. At the rear of the steering gear, loosen the rack guide spring cap lock nut.
   b. Using a socket wrench and Socket tool No. J-35423 or equivalent, torque the rack guide lock nut to 18 ft. lbs., then, back-off the nut 12 degrees (use a compass to measure the position in degrees).
   c. Using a torque wrench and Socket tool No. J-35428 or equivalent, check the pinion shaft preload; it should be 7–11 inch lbs.
4. Using sealant, coat the lock nut threads and torque the lock nut to 33 ft. lbs.
5. To install the steering gear, reverse the removal procedures. Bleed the power steering system.

Power Steering Pump

REMOVAL & INSTALLATION

Except Twincam

1. Place a catch pan under the power steering pump. Remove the air cleaner.
2. Remove the return hose clamp, then, disconnect the pressure and return hoses from the pump; drain the power steering fluid into the pan.
3. While pushing downward on the drive belt (to keep the belt from turning), loosen the pump pulley center nut. Remove the pump pulley and woodruff key; be sure not to loose the key.
4. Remove the pump pivot and adjusting bolts, then, move the pump to reduce the belt tension and remove the drive belt.
5. Remove the pump assembly and bracket.
6. To install, reverse the removal procedures. Torque the pressure hose-to-pump hose to 34 ft. lbs. and the power steering pump adjusting/pivot

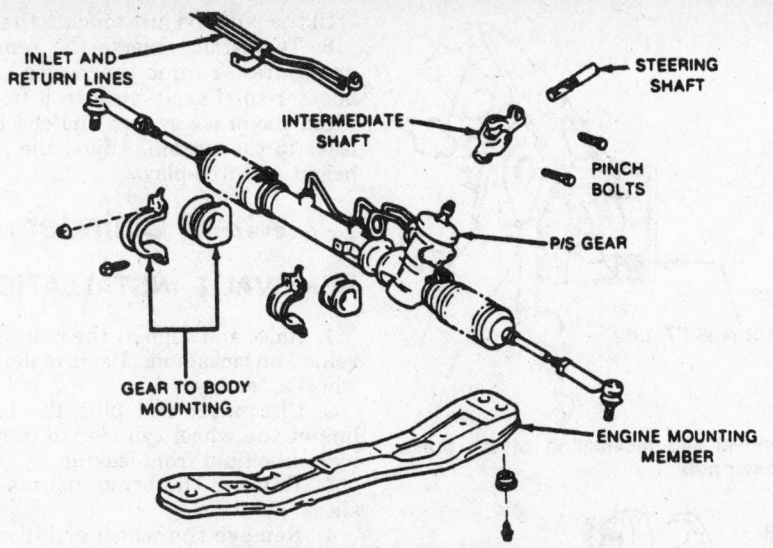

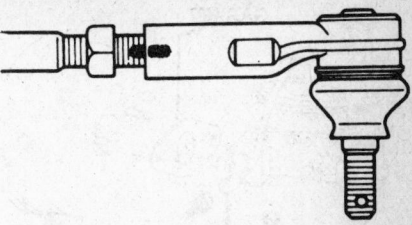

Marking tie rod end for re-installation

Power Rack and Pinion rack removal

bolts to 29 ft. lbs. Refill the power steering reservoir with Dexron® II automatic transmission fluid. Bleed the power steering system. Operate the engine, then, check and/or repair the leaks.

NOTE: If replacing the pump, switch the pulley and the mounting nut to the new pump.

Twincam

1. Remove the air cleaner.
2. Place a catch pan under the power steering pump.
3. From the power steering pump, disconnect the pressure and return hoses.
4. Remove the under engine cover.
5. Push downward of the drive belt to keep the pulley from turning, then, remove the pump pulley set nut. Remove the drive belt.
6. Remove the pump pulley and the woodruff key; be careful not to loose the key.
7. Remove the upper, lower and pivot bolts.
8. Disconnect the oil pressure switch connector.
9. Remove the power steering pulley, pump-to-bracket bolts and the pump.
10. To install, reverse the removal procedures. Torque the pressure hose-to-pump hose to 33 ft. lbs. and the power steering pump adjusting/pivot bolts to 29 ft. lbs. Refill the power steering reservoir with Dexron® II automatic transmission fluid. Bleed the power steering system. Operate the engine, then, check and/or repair the leaks.

BELT ADJUSTMENT

1. Using a Belt Tension Gauge tool

BT-33-73F or equivalent, position it on the drive belt (between the longest span of two pulleys).
2. Loosen the power steering adjusting and pivot bolts.
3. Move the pump to adjust the drive belt tension.

NOTE: The belt deflection should be 0.31–0.39 in. with moderate thumb pressure (about 20 lbs.) applied in the center of the span.

4. Torque the power steering pump pivot/adjusting bolts to 29 ft. lbs.

BLEEDING THE POWER STEERING SYSTEM

1. Raise and support the front of the vehicle on jackstands (this will minimize steering effort).
2. The engine must be turned OFF and the wheels turned all the way to the left. Fill the power steering pump reservoir with Dexron® II to the Cold mark.
3. Start the engine and allow it to run at Fast Idle for 30 seconds. Turn the engine OFF and recheck the power steering reservoir; if necessary, refill the reservoir to the Cold mark.
4. Start the engine and turn the steering wheel from lock-to-lock several times.
5. Repeat the bleeding procedure until all the air is bled from the steering system.
6. After bleeding the system, road test the vehicle to make sure the steering is functioning properly and is free of noise.

Tie Rod Ends

REMOVAL & INSTALLATION

1. Raise and support the front of

the vehicle on jacktands. Remove the wheel/tire assembly.
2. Remove the tie rod-to-steering knuckle cotter pin (discard it) and nut. Using the Ball Joint Removal tool No. J-24319-01 or equivalent, press the tie rod ends from the steering knuckles.
3. Loosen the tie rod-to-steering rack locknut. Matchmark the tie rod end-to-tie rod for installation purposes.
4. Counting the number of turns, unscrew the tie rod end from the tie rod.
5. Inspect the ball joint for wear; if necessary, replace the tie rod end.
6. To install, turn the tie rod end onto the tie rod (the same number of turns necessary to remove it), align the matchmarks and reverse the removal procedures. Torque the tie rod-to-steering rack locknut to 35 ft. lbs. and the tie rod end-to-steering knuckle nut to 36 ft. lbs. Install a new cotter pin. Check and/or adjust the front end toe.

BRAKES

NOTE: For all brake system repair and service procedures not detailed below, please refer to "Brakes" in the Unit Repair section.

Master Cylinder

REMOVAL & INSTALLATION

NOTE: Be careful not to spill brake fluid on the painted surfaces of the vehicle; it will damage the finish.

1. Using a syringe, remove the brake fluid from the master cylinder.
2. Disconnect the fluid level warning switch connector from the master cylinder.

NOTE: If planning to disassemble the master cylinder, loosen the master cylinder reservoir mounting (or set) bolts.

3. Disconnect the hydraulic lines

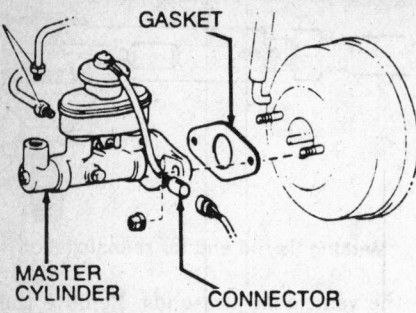

Master cylinder mounting

(GASKET, MASTER CYLINDER, CONNECTOR)

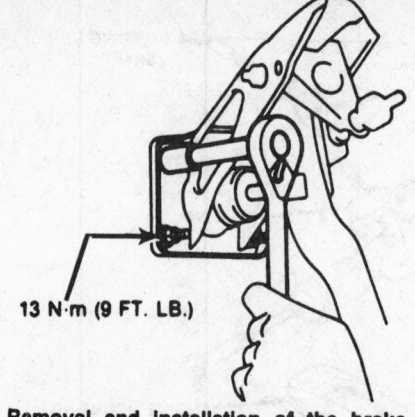

13 N·m (9 FT. LB.)

Removal and Installation of the brake booster nuts

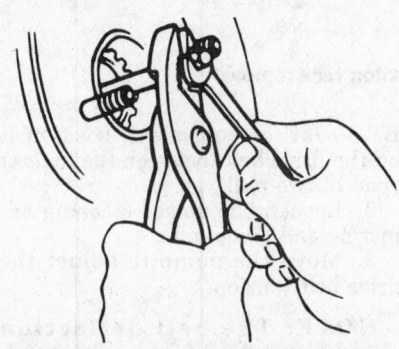

Adjusting brake booster push rod length

from the master cylinder and plug the openings.

4. Remove the master cylinder-to-power brake booster nuts and the master cylinder; discard the gasket.

5. To install the master cylinder, use a new gasket, clean out the groove on the lower installation surface, confirm that the "UP" mark on the master cylinder boot is in the correct position (at the top), adjust the pushrod and reverse the removal procedures. Torque the master cylinder-to-power brake booster nuts to 9 ft. lbs. and the brake lines to 11 ft. lbs. Connect the level warning switch connector. Refill the fluid reservoir and bleed the brake system. Check for fluid leakage and tighten or replace fittings as necessary. Adjust the pedal height and free-play.

Proportioning Valve

A proportioning valve, mounted on the bulkhead, is used on all models to reduce the hydraulic pressure to the rear brakes because of weight transfer during high speed stops. This helps to keep the rear brakes from locking up by improving front to rear brake balance.

REMOVAL & INSTALLATION

1. Disconnect and plug the brake lines from the proportioning valve unions.

2. Remove the proportioning valve-to-bulkhead bolts and the valve.

NOTE: If the proportioning valve is defective, it must be replaced as an assembly; it cannot be rebuilt.

3. To install, reverse the removal procedures. Bleed the brake system and check for leaks.

Power Brake Booster

REMOVAL & INSTALLATION

NOTE: To perform this procedure, use a booster push rod

gauge GM part No. J–34873–A or equivalent to set the booster pushrod length.

1. Refer to the "Master Cylinder, Removal and Installation" procedures in this section, then, remove the master cylinder and the 3-way union from the power brake booster.

2. Pull back the clamp and disconnect the booster vacuum line from the power brake booster.

3. Remove the instrument panel lower finish panel and the air duct.

4. Remove the brake pedal return spring.

5. Locate the clevis rod at the brake pedal (under the dash), then, pull out the clip and remove the clevis pin.

6. Remove the brake booster-to-cowl, the the booster, bracket and gasket.

7. To adjust the power brake booster pushrod, perform the following procedures:

a. Using the Push Rod Gauge tool No. J-34873-A or equivalent, set the short-side on the booster.

NOTE: The head of the pin sits near the end of the booster push rod.

b. Check the gap between the head of the tool's pin and the pushrod; it should be zero. If necessary, adjust the pushrod by turning it un-

til the pushrod just touches the pin.

8. To install, reverse the removal procedures. Torque the power brake booster-to-chassis nuts to 9 ft. lbs. Bleed the brake system and check for leaks in the system. Adjust the pedal height and free-play.

Wheel Cylinder

REMOVAL & INSTALLATION

1. Raise and support the rear of the vehicle on jackstands. Remove the rear wheel assembly.

2. Disconnect and plug the brake line at the wheel cylinder to prevent hydraulic fluid from leaking.

3. Remove the brake drums and shoes.

4. Remove the wheel cylinder-to-backing plate bolts and the wheel cylinder.

5. To install, reverse the removal procedures. Torque the wheel cylinder-to-backing plate to 7 ft. lbs. Bleed the brake system. Check the brake operation.

Parking Brake Cable

NOTE: Before performing this adjustment, make sure the rear brake shoe clearance is correct.

ADJUSTMENT

1. Release the parking brake (all the way). Using 44 lbs. of pulling pressure, slowly pull the lever upward and count the number of clicks; 4–7 clicks (except twincam) or 5–8 (twincam).

2. If the number of clicks is incorrect, adjust the parking brake cable by performing the following procedures:

a. Remove the console box.

b. At the rear of the parking brake handle, loosen the cable nut, then, turn the adjusting nut.

3. Secure the adjusting nut position when tighten the locknut. Check the adjustment and repeat Steps 2 and 3 (if necessary). Tighten the adjusting nut securely and ensure that the adjustment is correct.

REMOVAL & INSTALLATION

Front Cable

1. Raise and support the rear of the vehicle on jackstands.

2. Fully release the parking brake lever, then, remove the front parking cable-to-lever lock and adjusting nuts.

4. Disconnect the front parking brake cable from the equalizer.

5. Inspect the front cable for excessive wear and/or damage; if necessary, replace it. Lubricate the brake cable with multi-purpose grease.

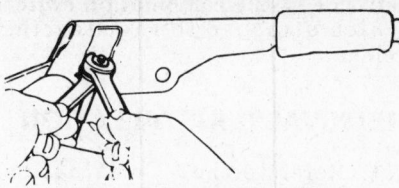

Parking brake adjustment

6. To install, reverse the removal procedures. Adjust the parking brake system.

Rear Cable(s)

1. Raise and support the rear of the vehicle on jackstands.

2. Remove the rear wheel assembly(s).

3. Fully release the parking brake lever. At the parking brake lever, back-off the front parking cable adjusting nut to provide slack on the rear cables.

4. Remove the rear brake cable(s)-to-chassis clamp bolts, then, disconnect the rear parking brake cable(s) from the equalizer.

5. If equipped with drum brakes, disassemble the rear brake assembly, then, disconnect the parking brake cable from the parking brake lever. If equipped with rear disc brakes, disconnect the brake cable from the parking brake crank.

NOTE: If the brake disc sticks, preventing removal, it will be necessary to back-off the self adjusters. This is done through the access hole in the brake disc.

6. Inspect the rear cable(s) for excessive wear and/or damage; if necessary, replace it (them). Lubricate the brake cable with multi-purpose grease.

7. To install, reverse the removal procedures. Adjust the parking brake system.

CHASSIS ELECTRICAL

Heater Blower

The heater blower motor is located inside the vehicle, behind the glove box.

REMOVAL & INSTALLATION

1. Remove the three heater assembly retainer-to-chassis screws.

2. Remove the glove box-to-chassis screws and the glove box.

3. Remove the duct-to-blower/heat-er assemblies screws and the duct; the duct is located between the blower and heater assemblies.

4. Disconnect the blower motor wiring connector and the air source selector control cable from the blower assembly case.

5. Remove the blower assembly-to-heater case nuts/bolt and blower assembly.

6. Separate the blower motor from the blower assembly.

7. To install, reverse the removal procedures and test the motor.

Heater Core

REMOVAL & INSTALLATION

— **CAUTION** —

Make sure the engine is cold before performing the following procedure, for scalding could occur.

1. Place a clean drain pan under the radiator, open the drain cock and drain the cooling system to a level below the heater core.

2. In the engine compartment, disconnect the heater hoses from the heater unit.

3. From inside the vehicle (under the dash), remove the lower heater unit case-to-heater case (6) clips and remove the lower case.

4. Using a medium prybar, separate and remove the lower portion of the case from the heater case.

5. Remove the heater core from the heater case.

6. Inspect the heater hoses for cracking and deterioration, then, the heater core for leakage and corrosion; replace the items, if necessary.

7. To install, reverse the removal procedures. Refill the cooling system. Start the engine, allow it to reach normal operating temperatures and check for leaks. Turn the heater controls to Max. Heat and check the heater operation.

Radio

REMOVAL & INSTALLATION

1. Remove the ash tray, the ash tray bracket-to-center trim panel screws and the upper center trim panel-to-dash screws.

2. Move the center panel out far enough to gain access to the cigarette

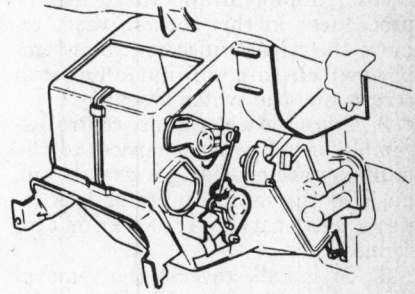

Heater core

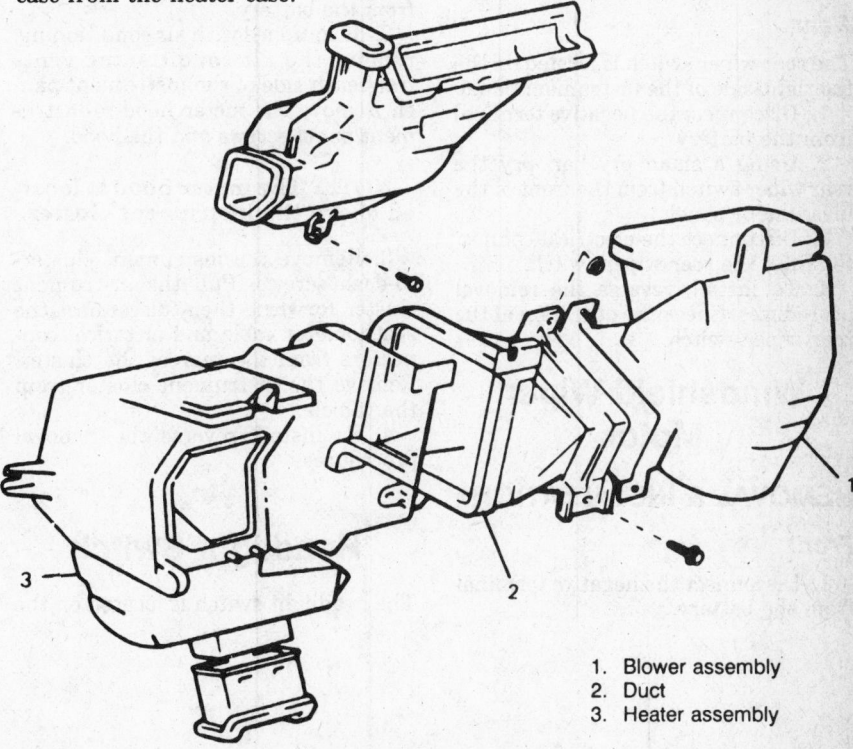

1. Blower assembly
2. Duct
3. Heater assembly

View of the heater assembly

lighter wiring and disconnect the wiring. Remove the trim panel.

3. Remove the radio-to-instrument panel screws and braces.

4. Pull the radio out (part way), then, disconnect the antenna and electrical leads from it. Remove the radio.

5. To install, reverse the removal procedures. Check the operation of the radio.

Windshield Wiper Switch

REMOVAL & INSTALLATION

Front

The front wiper switch is located on the right-side of the combination switch attached to the steering column.

1. Refer to the "Combination Switch, Removal and Installation" procedures in this section, then, remove the wiper/cruise control assembly switch-to-combination switch screws and the switch assembly.

2. Trace the wiper/cruise control assembly switch wiring harness to the multi-connector. Using a scratch awl, push in the multi-connector lock levers and pull wires from the connector.

3. To install, reverse the removal procedures. Check the operation of the windshield wiper switch and the cruise control system.

Rear

The rear wiper switch is located on the top right-side of the instrument panel.

1. Disconnect the negative terminal from the battery.

2. Using a small pry bar, pry the rear wiper switch from the front of the instrument panel.

3. Disconnect the electrical connector from the rear wiper switch.

4. To install, reverse the removal procedures. Check the operation of the rear wiper switch.

Windshield Wiper Motor

REMOVAL & INSTALLATION

Front

1. Disconnect the negative terminal from the battery.

2. From the engine compartment, disconnect the electrical connector from the windshield wiper motor.

3. Remove the wiper motor-to-chassis screws.

4. Disconnect the wiper motor from the windshield wiper crank arm; be careful not to bend the linkage.

5. To install, reverse the removal procedures. Check the operation of the front windshield wiper motor.

Rear

The rear wiper motor is located in the rear hatch.

1. Disconnect the negative terminal from the battery.

2. Remove the rear wiper arm-to-wiper motor nut and wiper arm.

3. From inside the rear hatch, remove the rear wiper cover, then, disconnect the electrical connector from the rear wiper motor.

4. Remove the wiper motor-to-hatch screws and the wiper motor from the hatch.

5. To install, reverse the removal procedures. Check the operation of the rear wiper motor.

Instrument Cluster

REMOVAL & INSTALLATION

1. Disconnect the negative terminal from the battery.

2. If equipped with air conditioning, remove the air conditioning vents from each side of the instrument panel. Remove the meter hood-to-instrument panel screws and the hood.

NOTE: The meter hood is located above the instrument cluster.

3. Remove the instrument cluster-to-dash screws. Pull the instrument cluster forward, then, disconnect the speedometer cable and electrical connectors from the rear of the cluster. Remove the instrument cluster from the vehicle.

4. To install, reverse the removal procedures.

Headlight Switch

The headlight switch is located on the left-side of the combination switch which attached to the steering column.

REMOVAL & INSTALLATION

1. Refer to the "Combination Switch, Removal and Installation" procedures in this section, then, remove the headlight/dimmer switch-to-combination switch screws and the switch assembly.

2. Trace the headlight/dimmer switch wiring harness to the multi-connector. Using a scratch awl, push in the multi-connector lock levers and pull wires from the connector.

3. To install, reverse the removal procedures. Check the operation of the headlight/dimmer switch.

Stoplight Switch

The stoplight switch is attached to a bracket at the top of the brake pedal.

REMOVAL & INSTALLATION

1. Remove the lower instrument panel cover.

2. Disconnect the electrical connector from the stoplight switch.

3. Remove the stoplight switch-to-bracket nut and the switch.

4. To install, reverse the removal procedures. Adjust the switch so the stoplights turn with slight movement of the brake pedal.

Fuses, Relays and Circuit Breakers

LOCATION

The main fuse/relay/circuit breaker box is located in the engine compartment on the left-front fender; others are located at the left and right kick panels inside the vehicle. When replacing a fuse, use a fuse puller tool.

To reset a circuit breaker, unplug them, then, using a straightened paper clip, insert it into the reset hole and press inward. If this does not restore operation, check continuity between the terminals with an ohmmeter.

Chevrolet
Rear Wheel Drive
Caprice, Impala, Malibu, Monte Carlo

SERIAL NUMBER IDENTIFICATION

VEHICLE IDENTIFICATION CHART

It is important for servicing and ordering parts to be certain of the vehicle and engine identification. The VIN (vehicle identification number) is a 17 digit number visible through the windshield on the driver's side of the dash and contains the vehicle and engine identification codes. The tenth digit indicates model year, and the eigth digit indicates engine code. It can be interpreted as follows:

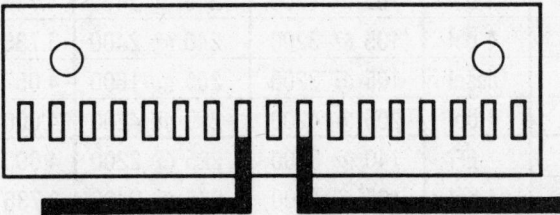

Engine Code						Model Year	
Code	Cu. In.	Liters	Cyl.	Fuel Sys.	Eng. Mfg.	Code	Year
K	229	3.8	6	Carb.	Chevy	C	1982
9	229	3.8	6	Carb.	Chevy	D	1983
A	231	3.8	6	Carb.	Buick	E	1984
V	262	4.3	6	Diesel	Olds	F	1985
Z	262	4.3	6	EFI	Chevy	G	1986
J	267	4.4	8	Carb.	Chevy	H	1987
G	305	5.0	8	Carb.	Chevy	J	1988
H	305	5.0	8	Carb.	Chevy	K	1989
Y	307	5.0	8	Carb.	Olds		
L	350	5.7	8	Carb.	Chevy		
N	350	5.7	8	Diesel	Olds		
6	350	5.7	8	Carb.	Chevy		

GENERAL ENGINE SPECIFICATIONS

Year	VIN	No. Cylinder Displacement cu. in. (liter)	Fuel System Type	Net Horsepower @ rpm	Net Torque @ rpm (ft.lbs.)	Bore × Stroke (in.)	Compression Ratio	Oil Pressure @ 2000 rpm
1982	K	6-229 (3.8)	2 bbl	110 @ 4200	170 @ 2000	3.736 × 3.480	8.2:1	37
	A	6-231 (3.8)	2 bbl	110 @ 3800	190 @ 1600	3.800 × 3.400	8.0:1	45
	V	6-262 (4.3)	Diesel	85 @ 3200	165 @ 1600	4.057 × 3.385	22.0:1	45
	J	8-267 (4.4)	2 bbl	115 @ 4000	200 @ 2400	3.500 × 3.480	8.3:1	45
	H	8-305 (5.0)	4 bbl	150 @ 3800	240 @ 2400	3.376 × 3.480	8.6:1	45
	L	8-350 (5.7)	4 bbl	—	—	4.000 × 3.480	8.2:1	45
	N	8-350 (5.7)	Diesel	105 @ 3200	205 @ 1600	4.057 × 3.385	22.5:1	40
1983	9	6-229 (3.8)	2 bbl	115 @ 4000	170 @ 2000	3.376 × 3.480	8.6:1	45
	A	6-231 (3.8)	2 bbl	110 @ 3800	190 @ 1600	3.800 × 3.400	8.0:1	45
	V	6-262 (4.3)	Diesel	85 @ 3200	165 @ 1600	4.057 × 3.385	22.0:1	45
	H	8-305 (5.0)	4 bbl	150 @ 3800	240 @ 2400	3.736 × 3.480	8.6:1	45
	N	8-350 (5.7)	Diesel	105 @ 3200	205 @ 1600	4.057 × 3.385	22.5:1	40
1984	9	6-229 (3.8)	2 bbl	115 @ 4000	170 @ 2000	3.736 × 3.480	8.6:1	45
	A	6-231 (3.8)	2 bbl	110 @ 3800	190 @ 1600	3.800 × 3.400	8.0:1	45
	V	6-262 (4.3)	Diesel	85 @ 3200	165 @ 1600	4.057 × 3.385	22.0:1	45
	H	8-305 (5.0)	4 bbl	150 @ 3800	240 @ 2400	3.736 × 3.480	8.6:1	45
	N	8-350 (5.7)	Diesel	105 @ 3200	205 @ 1600	4.057 × 3.385	22.5:1	40
1985	A	6-231 (3.8)	2 bbl	110 @ 3800	190 @ 1600	3.800 × 3.400	8.0:1	45
	Z	6-262 (4.3)	EFI	130 @ 3600	218 @ 2000	4.000 × 3.480	9.3:1	45
	H	8-305 (5.0)	4 bbl	165 @ 4200	245 @ 2400	3.736 × 3.480	9.5:1	45
	G	8-305 (5.0)	4 bbl	105 @ 3200	240 @ 2400	3.736 × 3.480	9.5:1	45
	N	8-350 (5.7)	Diesel	105 @ 3200	205 @ 1600	4.057 × 3.385	22.5:1	40
	6	8-350 (5.7)	4 bbl	205 @ 4200	290 @ 4200	4.000 × 3.480	8.2:1	45
1986	Z	6-262 (4.3)	EFI	140 @ 3800	225 @ 2200	4.000 × 3.480	9.3:1	45
	H	8-305 (5.0)	4 bbl	165 @ 4200	245 @ 2400	3.736 × 3.480	9.5:1	45
	G	8-305 (5.0)	4 bbl	105 @ 3200	240 @ 2400	3.736 × 3.480	9.5:1	45
	Y	8-307 (5.0)	4 bbl	148 @ 3800	250 @ 2400	3.800 × 3.385	8.0:1	40
	6	8-350 (5.7)	4 bbl	205 @ 4200	290 @ 4200	4.000 × 3.480	8.2:1	45
1987	Z	6-262 (4.3)	EFI	140 @ 3800	225 @ 2200	4.000 × 3.480	9.3:1	45
	H	8-305 (5.0)	4 bbl	165 @ 4200	245 @ 2400	3.736 × 3.480	9.5:1	45
	G	8-305 (5.0)	4 bbl	105 @ 3200	240 @ 2400	3.736 × 3.480	9.5:1	45
	Y	8-307 (5.0)	4 bbl	148 @ 3800	250 @ 2400	3.800 × 3.385	8.0:1	40
	6	8-350 (5.7)	4 bbl	205 @ 4200	290 @ 4200	4.000 × 3.480	8.2:1	45
1988-89	Z	6-262 (4.3)	EFI	140 @ 4200	225 @ 2000	4.000 × 3.480	9.3:1	45
	H	8-305 (5.0)	4 bbl	165 @ 4200	245 @ 2400	3.736 × 3.480	8.6:1	45
	G	8-305 (5.0)	4 bbl	105 @ 3200	240 @ 2400	3.736 × 3.480	9.5:1	45
	Y	8-307 (5.0)	4 bbl	148 @ 3800	250 @ 2400	3.800 × 3.385	8.0:1	40
	6	8-350 (5.7)	4 bbl	205 @ 4200	290 @ 4200	4.000 × 3.480	8.2:1	45

GASOLINE ENGINE TUNE-UP SPECIFICATIONS

Year	VIN	No. Cylinder Displacement cu. in. (liter)	Spark Plugs Type	Gap (in.)	Ignition Timing (deg.) MT	AT	Compression Pressure (psi)	Fuel Pump (psi)	Idle Speed (rpm) MT	AT	Valve Clearance In.	Ex.
1982	K	6-229 (3.8)	R-45TS	.045	8	12	③	4.5-6.0	—	600	Hyd.	Hyd.
	A	6-231 (3.8)	R-45TS8	.080	—	15	③	4.25–5.75	—	500	Hyd.	Hyd.
	J	8-267 (4.4)	R-45TS	.045	—	2	③	7.5-9.0	—	600	Hyd.	Hyd.
	H	8-305 (5.0)	R-45TS	.045	—	6	③	7.5-9.0	—	500	Hyd.	Hyd.
	L	8-350 (5.7)	R-45TS	.045	—	6	③	7.5-9.0	—	500	Hyd.	Hyd.
1983	9	6-229 (3.8)	R-45TS	.045	—	0	③	4.5-6.0	—	475	Hyd.	Hyd.
	A	6-231 (3.8)	R-45TS	.080	—	15	③	4.25–5.75	—	500	Hyd.	Hyd.
	H	8-305 (5.0)	R-45TS	.045	—	6	③	7.5-9.0	—	500	Hyd.	Hyd.
1984	9	6-229 (3.8)	R-45TS	.045	—	0	③	4.5-6.0	—	600	Hyd.	Hyd.
	A	6-231 (3.8)	R-45TS	.080	—	15	③	4.25–5.75	—	600	Hyd.	Hyd.
	H	8-305 (5.0)	R-45TS	.045	—	6	③	7.5-9.0	—	500	Hyd.	Hyd.
1985	A	6-231 (3.8)	R-45TS	.080	—	15	③	4.25–5.75	—	600	Hyd.	Hyd.
	Z	6-262 (4.3)	R-43TS	.035	—	0	③	—	—	400	Hyd.	Hyd.
	H	8-305 (5.0)	R-44TS	.045	—	0	③	7.5-9.0	—	500	Hyd.	Hyd.
	G	8-305 (5.0)	R-44TS	.045	—	6	③	7.5-9.0	—	500	Hyd.	Hyd.
	6	8-350 (5.7)	R-43CTS	.035	—	6	③	—	—	650	Hyd.	Hyd.
1986	Z	6-262 (4.3)	R-43TS	.035	—	0	③	—	—	400	Hyd.	Hyd.
	H	8-305 (5.0)	R-44TS	.045	—	0	③	7.5-9.0	—	500	Hyd.	Hyd.
	G	8-305 (5.0)	R-44TS	.045	—	6	③	7.5-9.0	—	500	Hyd.	Hyd.
	Y	8-307 (5.0)	FR3LS6	.060	—	20	③	6.0-7.5	—	425	Hyd.	Hyd.
	6	8-350 (5.7)	R43CTS	.035	—	6	③	—	—	650	Hyd.	Hyd.
1987	Z	6-262 (4.3)	R-45TS	.035	—	0	③	—	—	400	Hyd.	Hyd.
	H	8-305 (5.0)	R-44TS	.035	—	0	③	7.5-9.0	—	500	Hyd.	Hyd.
	G	8-305 (5.0)	R-44TS	.035	—	6	③	7.5-9.0	—	500	Hyd.	Hyd.
	Y	8-307 (5.0)	FR3CLS6	.060	—	20	③	6.0-7.5	—	450	Hyd.	Hyd.
	6	8-350 (5.7)	FR3CLS6	.060	—	6	③	—	—	500	Hyd.	Hyd.
1988	Z	6-262 (4.3)	R-45TS	.035	—	②	③	9.0-13.0	—	400	Hyd.	Hyd.
	H	8-305 (5.0)	R-45TS	.035	—	②	③	7.5-9.0	—	500①	Hyd.	Hyd.
	G	8-305 (5.0)	R-45TS	.035	—	②	③	7.5-9.0	—	600	Hyd.	Hyd.
	Y	8-307 (5.0)	FR3L56	.060	—	②	③	6.0-7.5	—	450	Hyd.	Hyd.
	6	8-350 (5.7)	FR3L56	.060	—	②	③	—	—	500	Hyd.	Hyd.
1989			SEE UNDERHOOD SPECIFICATIONS STICKER									

① Drive

② Refer to the tune-up label located in the engine compartment for the ignition timing specifications

③ When checking cylinder compression, the throttle and choke should be open, all plugs should be removed and the battery at or near full charge. The lowest reading cylinder should not be less than 70% of the highest and no cylinder reading should be less than 100 psi

DIESEL ENGINE TUNE-UP SPECIFICATIONS

Year	VIN	No. Engine Displacement cu. in. (liter)	Valve Clearance Intake (in.)	Exhaust (in.)	Intake Valve Opens (deg.)	Injection Pump Setting (deg.)	Injection Nozzle Pressure (psi) New	Used	Idle Speed (rpm)	Cranking Compression Pressure (psi)
1982	V	6-262 (4.3)	Zero Lash		16	NA	1000②	NA	NA	NA
	N	8-350 (5.7)	Zero Lash		16	NA	870	NA	600 ①	275
1983	V	6-262 (4.3)	Zero Lash		16	NA	1000②	NA	NA	NA
	N	8-350 (5.7)	Zero Lash		16	NA	1225	1025	600 ①	275
1984	V	6-262 (4.3)	Zero Lash		16	NA	1000②	NA	NA	NA
	N	8-350 (5.7)	Zero Lash		16	NA	1000	850	600 ①	300
1985	N	6-350 (5.7)	Zero Lash		16	NA	1000	850	600 ①	300

① Fast Idle 750 RPM
② Green Band or without band; 800 Red Band
NA—Not available at time of publication

FIRING ORDERS

NOTE: To avoid confusion, always replace spark plug wires one at a time.

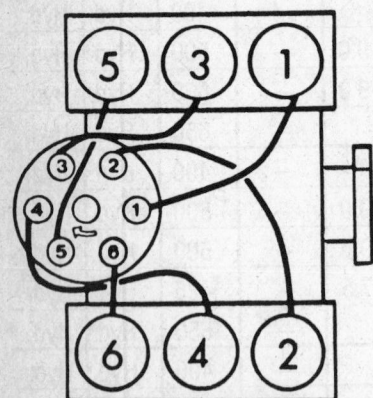

Chevrolet-built V6 engine
Engine firing order: 1-6-5-4-3-2
Distributor rotation: clockwise

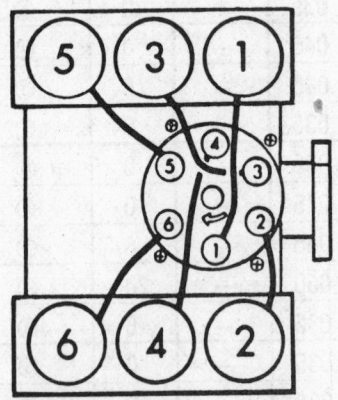

GM (Buick) 231 V6
Engine firing order: 1-6-5-4-3-2
Distributor rotation: clockwise

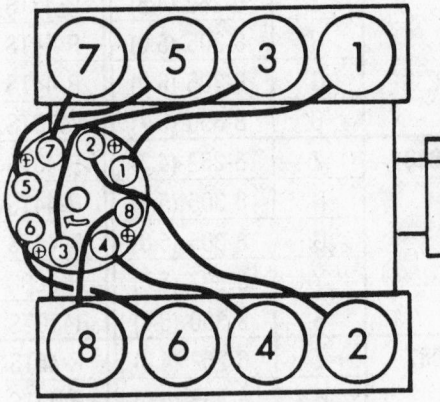

GM (Chevrolet) V8
Engine firing order: 1-8-4-3-6-5-7-2
Distributor rotation: clockwise

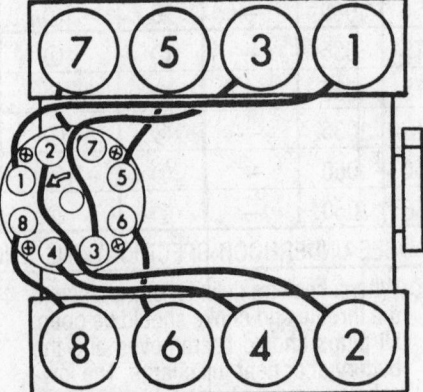

GM (Oldsmobile 307)
Firing order: 1-8-4-3-6-5-7-2
Distributor rotation: counterclockwise

CAPACITIES

Year	VIN	No. Cylinder Displacement cu. in. (liter)	Engine Crankcase with Filter	Engine Crankcase without Filter	Transmission (pts.) MT	Transmission (pts.) AT	Drive Axle (pts.)	Fuel Tank (gals.)	Cooling System (qts.)
1982	K	6-229 (3.8)	5	4	3.0	6.0	3.5	18.0	15.0
	A	6-231 (3.8)	5	4	3.0	6.0	3.5	18.0	15.0
	V	6-262 (4.3)	6	5	3.0	6.0	3.5	18.0	15.0
	J	8-267 (4.4)	5	4	3.0	6.0	3.5	18.0	15.0
	H	8-305 (5.0)	5	4	3.0	6.0	3.5	18.0	15.0
	L	8-350 (5.7)	5	4	3.0	6.0	3.5	18.0	15.0
	N	8-350 (5.7)	7	6	3.0	6.0	3.5	19.0	18.0
1983	9	6-229 (3.8)	5	4	3.0	6.0	3.5	18.0	15.0
	A	6-231 (3.8)	5	4	3.0	6.0	3.5	18.0	15.0
	V	6-262 (4.3)	6	5	3.0	6.0	3.5	18.0	15.0
	H	8-305 (5.0)	5	4	3.0	6.0	3.5	18.0	15.0
	N	8-350 (5.7)	7	6	3.0	6.0	3.5	19.0	18.0
1984	9	6-229 (3.8)	5	4	3.0	6.0	3.5	18.0	15.0
	A	6-231 (3.8)	5	4	3.0	6.0	3.5	18.0	15.0
	V	6-262 (4.3)	6	5	3.0	6.0	3.5	18.0	15.0
	H	8-305 (5.0)	5	4	3.0	6.0	3.5	18.0	15.0
	N	8-350 (5.7)	7	6	3.0	6.0	3.5	19.0	18.0
1985	A	6-231 (3.8)	5	4	3.0	6.0	3.5	18.0	15.0
	Z	6-262 (4.3)	5	4	3.0	6.0	3.5	18.0	15.0
	H	8-305 (5.0)	5	4	3.0	6.0	3.5	18.0	15.0
	G	8-305 (5.0)	5	4	3.0	6.0	3.5	18.0	15.0
	N	8-350 (5.7)	7	6	3.0	6.0	3.5	19.0	18.0
	6	8-350 (5.7)	5	4	3.0	6.0	3.5	18.0	15.0
1986	Z	6-262 (4.3)	5	4	3.0	6.0	3.5	18.0	15.0
	H	8-305 (5.0)	5	4	3.0	6.0	3.5	18.0	15.0
	G	8-305 (5.0)	5	4	3.0	6.0	3.5	18.0	15.0
	Y	8-307 (5.0)	5	4	3.0	6.0	3.5	18.0	15.0
	6	8-350 (5.7)	5	4	3.0	6.0	3.5	18.0	15.0
1987	Z	6-262 (4.3)	5	4	3.0	6.0	3.5	18.0	15.0
	H	8-305 (5.0)	5	4	3.0	6.0	3.5	18.0	15.0
	G	8-305 (5.0)	5	4	3.0	6.0	3.5	18.0	15.0
	Y	8-307 (5.0)	5	4	3.0	6.0	3.5	18.0	15.0
	6	8-350 (5.7)	5	4	3.0	6.0	3.5	18.0	15.0
1988-89	Z	6-262 (4.3)	4	4	—	6.0	3.5	18.0	12.0
	H	8-305 (5.0)	5	4	—	6.0	3.5	18.0	17.0
	G	8-305 (5.0)	5	4	—	6.0	3.5	18.0	17.0
	Y	8-307 (5.0)	5	4	—	6.0	3.5	18.0	17.0
	6	8-350 (5.7)	5	4	—	6.0	3.5	18.0	17.0

CRANKSHAFT AND CONNECTING ROD SPECIFICATIONS
All measurements are given in inches.

Year	VIN	No. Cylinder Displacement cu. in. (liter)	Crankshaft				Connecting Rod		
			Main Brg. Journal Dia.	Main Brg. Oil Clearance	Shaft End-play	Thrust on No.	Journal Diameter	Oil Clearance	Side Clearance
1982	K	6-229 (3.8)	2.4484–2.4493 ①	.0008–.0020 ②	.002–.006	4	2.0986–2.0998	.0013–.0035	.006–.014
	A	6-231 (3.8)	2.4995	.0004–.0015	.004–.008	2	2.2495–2.2487	.0005–.0026	.006–.027
	V	6-262 (4.3)	2.9993–3.0003 ③	.0005–.0021	.0035–.0135	3	2.0986–2.0998	.0013–.0035	.006–.014
	J	8-267 (4.4)	2.4484–2.4493 ①	.0008–.0020 ②	.002–.006	5	2.0986–2.0998	.0013–.0035	.006–.014
	H	8-305 (5.0)	2.4484–2.4493 ①	.0008–.0020 ②	.002–.006	5	2.0986–2.0998	.0013–.0035	.006–.014
	L	8-350 (5.7)	2.4484–2.4493 ①	.0008–.0020 ②	.002–.006	5	2.0986–2.0998	.0013–.0035	.006–.014
	N	8-350 (5.7)	2.9993–3.0003 ④	.0005–.0021	.0035–.0135	3	2.1238–2.1248	.0005–.0026	.006–.020
1983	9	6-229 (3.8)	2.4484–2.4493 ①	.0008–.0020 ②	.002–.006	4	2.0986–2.0998	.0013–.0035	.006–.014
	A	6-231 (3.8)	2.4995	.0003–.0018	.003–.011	2	2.2495–2.2487	.0005–.0026	.006–.015
	V	6-262 (4.3)	2.9993–3.0003 ③	.0005–.0021	.0035–.0135	3	2.0986–2.0998	.0013–.0035	.006–.014
	H	8-305 (5.0)	2.4484–2.4493 ①	.0008–.0020 ②	.002–.006	5	2.0986–2.0998	.0013–.0035	.006–.014
	N	8-350 (5.7)	2.9993–3.0003 ④	.0005–.0021	.0035–.0135	3	2.1238–2.1248	.0005–.0026	.006–.020
1984	9	6-229 (3.8)	2.4484–2.4493 ①	.0008–.0020 ②	.002–.006	4	2.0986–2.0998	.0013–.0035	.006–.014
	A	6-231 (3.8)	2.4995	.0003–.0018	.003–.011	2	2.2495–2.2487	.0005–.0026	.006–.015
	V	6-262 (4.3)	2.9993–3.0003 ③	.0005–.0021	.0035–.0135	3	2.0986–2.0998	.0013–.0035	.006–.014
	H	8-305 (5.0)	2.4484–2.4493 ①	.0008–.0020 ②	.002–.006	5	2.0986–2.0998	.0013–.0035	.006–.014

CRANKSHAFT AND CONNECTING ROD SPECIFICATIONS
All measurements are given in inches.

Year	VIN	No. Cylinder Displacement cu. in. (liter)	Crankshaft				Connecting Rod		
			Main Brg. Journal Dia.	Main Brg. Oil Clearance	Shaft End-play	Thrust on No.	Journal Diameter	Oil Clearance	Side Clearance
1984	N	8-350 (5.7)	2.9993–3.0003	.0005–.0021 ④	.0035–.0135	3	2.1238–2.1248	.0005–.0026	.006–.020
1985	A	6-231 (3.8)	2.4985	.0003–.0080	.003–.011	2	2.2495–2.2487	.0005–.0026	.006–.015
	Z	6-262 (4.3)	2.4484–2.4493 ①	.0008–.0020 ②	.002–.006	4	2.2487–2.2498	.0013–.0035	.006–.014
	H	8-305 (5.0)	2.4484–2.4493 ①	.0008–.0020 ②	.002–.006	5	2.0986–2.0998	.0013–.0035	.006–.014
	G	8-305 (5.0)	2.4484–2.4493 ①	.0008–.0020 ②	.002–.006	5	2.0986–2.0998	.0013–.0035	.006–.014
	N	8-350 (5.7)	2.9993–3.0003	.0005–.0021 ④	.0035–.0135	3	2.1238–2.1248	.0005–.0026	.006–.020
	6	8-350 (5.7)	2.4484–2.4493 ①	.0008–.0020 ②	.002–.006	5	2.0986–2.0998	.003–.0035	.006–.014
1986	Z	6-262 (4.3)	2.4489–2.4493 ①	.0008–.0020 ②	.002–.006	4	2.2487–2.2498	.0013–.0035	.006–.014
	H	8-305 (5.0)	2.4484–2.4493 ①	.0008–.020 ②	.002–.006	5	2.0986–2.0998	.0013–.0035	.006–.014
	G	8-305 (5.0)	2.4484–2.4493 ①	.0008–.0020 ②	.002–.006	5	2.0986–2.0998	.0013–.0035	.006–.014
	Y	8-307 (5.0)	2.4985–2.4995 ⑤	.0005–.0021 ⑥	.0035–.0135	3	2.12438–2.1248	.0004–.0033	.006–.020
	6	8-350 (5.7)	2.4484–2.4493 ①	.0008–.0020 ②	002–.006	5	2.0986–2.0998	.0013–.0035	.006–.014
1987	Z	6-262 (4.3)	2.4484–2.4493 ①	.0008–.0020 ②	.002–.006	4	2.2487–2.2498	.0013–.0035	.006–.014
	H	8-305 (5.0)	2.4484–2.4493 ①	.0008–.0020 ②	.002–.006	5	2.0986–2.0998	.0013–.0035	.006–.014
	G	8-305 (5.0)	2.4484–2.4493 ①	.0008–.0020 ②	.002–.006	5	2.0986–2.0998	.0013–.0035	.006–.014

CRANKSHAFT AND CONNECTING ROD SPECIFICATIONS
All measurements are given in inches.

Year	VIN	No. Cylinder Displacement cu. in. (liter)	Crankshaft				Connecting Rod		
			Main Brg. Journal Dia.	Main Brg. Oil Clearance	Shaft End-play	Thrust on No.	Journal Diameter	Oil Clearance	Side Clearance
1987	Y	8-305 (5.0)	2.4985–2.4995 ⑤	.0005–.0221 ⑥	.0035–.0135	3	2.1238–2.1248	.0004–.0033	.006–.020
	6	8-350 (5.7)	2.4484–2.4493 ①	.0008–.0020 ②	.002–.006	5	2.0986–2.0998	.0013–.0035	.006–.014
1988-89	Z	6-262 (4.3)	2.4484–2.4493 ①	.0008–.0020 ②	.002–.006	4	2.2487–2.2498	.0013–.0035	.006–.014
	H	8-305 (5.0)	2.4484–2.4493 ①	.0008–.0020 ②	.002–.006	5	2.0986–2.0998	.0013–.0035	.006–.014
	G	8-305 (5.0)	2.4484–2.4493 ①	.0008–.0020 ②	.002–.006	5	2.0986–2.0998	.0013–.0035	.006–.014
	Y	8-305 (5.0)	2.4988–2.4998 ⑦	.0005–.0221 ⑥	.0035–.0135	3	2.1238–2.1248	.0004–.0033	.006–.020
	6	8-350 (5.7)	2.4484–2.4493 ①	.0008–.0020 ②	.002–.006	5	2.0986–2.0998	.0013–.0035	.006–.014

① Intermediate — 2.4481-2.4490
   Rear — 2.4479-2.4488
② Intermediate — .0011-.0023
   Rear .0017-.0032
③ No. 4 — .0020–.0034
④ No. 5 — .0015–.0031
⑤ No. 2 — 2.4988–2.4998
⑥ No. 5 — .0015–.0031
⑦ Specification for No. 1 bearing shown.
   No. 2-5 — 2.4985-2.4995

CRANKSHAFT AND CONNECTING ROD SPECIFICATIONS
All measurements are given in inches.

Year	VIN	No. Cylinder Displacement cu. in. (liter)	Crankshaft				Connecting Rod		
			Main Brg. Journal Dia.	Main Brg. Oil Clearance	Shaft End-play	Thrust on No.	Journal Diameter	Oil Clearance	Side Clearance
1982	K	6-229 (3.8)	2.4484–2.4493 ①	.0008–.0020 ②	.002–.006	4	2.0986–2.0998	.0013–.0035	.006–.014
	A	6-231 (3.8)	2.4995	.0004–.0015	.004–.008	2	2.2495–2.2487	.0005–.0026	.006–.027
	V	6-262 (4.3)	2.9993–3.0003	.0005–.0021 ③	.0035–.0135	3	2.0986–2.0998	.0013–.0035	.006–.014
	J	8-267 (4.4)	2.4484–2.4493 ①	.0008–.0020 ②	.002–.006	5	2.0986–2.0998	.0013–.0035	.006–.014

CRANKSHAFT AND CONNECTING ROD SPECIFICATIONS
All measurements are given in inches.

Year	VIN	No. Cylinder Displacement cu. in. (liter)	Crankshaft				Connecting Rod		
			Main Brg. Journal Dia.	Main Brg. Oil Clearance	Shaft End-play	Thrust on No.	Journal Diameter	Oil Clearance	Side Clearance
1982	H	8-305 (5.0)	2.4484–2.4493 ①	.0008–.0020 ②	.002–.006	5	2.0986–2.0998	.0013–.0035	.006–.014
	L	8-350 (5.7)	2.4484–2.4493 ①	.0008–.0020 ②	.002–.006	5	2.0986–2.0998	.0013–.0035	.006–.014
	N	8-350 (5.7)	2.9993–3.0003	.0005–.0021 ④	.0035–.0135	3	2.1238–2.1248	.0005–.0026	.006–.020
1983	9	6-229 (3.8)	2.4484–2.4493 ①	.0008–.0020 ②	.002–.006	4	2.0986–2.0998	.0013–.0035	.006–.014
	A	6-231 (3.8)	2.4995	.0003–.0018	.003–.011	2	2.2495–2.2487	.0005–.0026	.006–.015
	V	6-262 (4.3)	2.9993–3.0003	.0005–.0021 ③	.0035–.0135	3	2.0986–2.0998	.0013–.0035	.006–.014
	H	8-305 (5.0)	2.4484–2.4493 ①	.0008–.0020 ②	.002–.006	5	2.0986–2.0998	.0013–.0035	.006–.014
	N	8-350 (5.7)	2.9993–3.0003	.0005–.0021 ④	.0035–.0135	3	2.1238–2.1248	.0005–.0026	.006–.020
1984	9	6-229 (3.8)	2.4484–2.4493 ①	.0008–.0020 ②	.002–.006	4	2.0986–2.0998	.0013–.0035	.006–.014
	A	6-231 (3.8)	2.4995	.0003–.0018	.003–.011	2	2.2495–2.2487	.0005–.0026	.006–.015
	V	6-262 (4.3)	2.9993–3.0003	.0005–.0021 ③	.0035–.0135	3	2.0986–2.0998	.0013–.0035	.006–.014
	H	8-305 (5.0)	2.4484–2.4493 ①	.0008–.0020 ②	.002–.006	5	2.0986–2.0998	.0013–.0035	.006–.014
	N	8-350 (5.7)	2.9993–3.0003	.0005–.0021 ④	.0035–.0135	3	2.1238–2.1248	.0005–.0026	.006–.020
1985	A	6-231 (3.8)	2.4985	.0003–.0080	.003–.011	2	2.2495–2.2487	.0005–.0026	.006–.015
	Z	6-262 (4.3)	2.4484–2.4493 ①	.0008–.0020 ②	.002–.006	4	2.2487–2.2498	.0013–.0035	.006–.014
	H	8-305 (5.0)	2.4484–2.4493 ①	.0008–.0020 ②	.002–.006	5	2.0986–2.0998	.0013–.0035	.006–.014

CRANKSHAFT AND CONNECTING ROD SPECIFICATIONS
All measurements are given in inches.

Year	VIN	No. Cylinder Displacement cu. in. (liter)	Crankshaft				Connecting Rod		
			Main Brg. Journal Dia.	Main Brg. Oil Clearance	Shaft End-play	Thrust on No.	Journal Diameter	Oil Clearance	Side Clearance
1985	G	8-305 (5.0)	2.4484–2.4493 ①	.0008–.0020 ②	.002–.006	5	2.0986–2.0998	.0013–.0035	.006–.014
	N	8-350 (5.7)	2.9993–3.0003 ④	.0005–.0021 ④	.0035–.0135	3	2.1238–2.1248	.0005–.0026	.006–.020
	6	8-350 (5.7)	2.4484–2.4493 ①	.0008–.0020 ②	.002–.006	5	2.0986–2.0998	.003–.0035	.006–.014
1986	Z	6-262 (4.3)	2.4489–2.4493 ①	.0008–.0020 ②	.002–.006	4	2.2487–2.2498	.0013–.0035	.006–.014
	H	8-305 (5.0)	2.4484–2.4493 ①	.0008–.020 ②	.002–.006	5	2.0986–2.0998	.0013–.0035	.006–.014
	G	8-305 (5.0)	2.4484–2.4493 ①	.0008–.0020 ②	.002–.006	5	2.0986–2.0998	.0013–.0035	.006–.014
	Y	8-307 (5.0)	2.4985–2.4995 ⑤	.0005–.0021 ⑥	.0035–.0135	3	2.12438–2.1248	.0004–.0033	.006–.020
	6	8-350 (5.7)	2.4484–2.4493 ①	.0008–.0020 ②	002–.006	5	2.0986–2.0998	.0013–.0035	.006–.014
1987	Z	6-262 (4.3)	2.4484–2.4493 ①	.0008–.0020 ②	.002–.006	4	2.2487–2.2498	.0013–.0035	.006–.014
	H	8-305 (5.0)	2.4484–2.4493 ①	.0008–.0020 ②	.002–.006	5	2.0986–2.0998	.0013–.0035	.006–.014
	G	8-305 (5.0)	2.4484–2.4493 ①	.0008–.0020 ②	.002–.006	5	2.0986–2.0998	.0013–.0035	.006–.014
	Y	8-305 (5.0)	2.4985–2.4995 ⑤	.0005–.0221 ⑥	.0035–.0135	3	2.1238–2.1248	.0004–.0033	.006–.020
	6	8-350 (5.7)	2.4484–2.4493 ①	.0008–.0020 ②	.002–.006	5	2.0986–2.0998	.0013–.0035	.006–.014
1988-89	Z	6-262 (4.3)	2.4484–2.4493 ①	.0008–.0020 ②	.002–.006	4	2.2487–2.2498	.0013–.0035	.006–.014
	H	8-305 (5.0)	2.4484–2.4493 ①	.0008–.0020 ②	.002–.006	5	2.0986–2.0998	.0013–.0035	.006–.014

CRANKSHAFT AND CONNECTING ROD SPECIFICATIONS

All measurements are given in inches.

Year	VIN	No. Cylinder Displacement cu. in. (liter)	Crankshaft				Connecting Rod		
			Main Brg. Journal Dia.	Main Brg. Oil Clearance	Shaft End-play	Thrust on No.	Journal Diameter	Oil Clearance	Side Clearance
1988-89	G	8-305 (5.0)	2.4484–2.4493 ①	.0008–.0020 ②	.002–.006	5	2.0986–2.0998	.0013–.0035	.006–.014
	Y	8-305 (5.0)	2.4988–2.4998 ⑦	.0005–.0221 ⑥	.0035–.0135	3	2.1238–2.1248	.0004–.0033	.006–.020
	6	8-350 (5.7)	2.4484–2.4493 ①	.0008–.0020 ②	.002–.006	5	2.0986–2.0998	.0013–.0035	.006–.014

① Intermediate — 2.4481-2.4490
  Rear — 2.4479-2.4488
② Intermediate — .0011-.0023
  Rear .0017-.0032
③ No. 4 — .0020–.0034
④ No. 5 — .0015–.0031
⑤ No. 2 — 2.4988–2.4998
⑥ No. 5 — .0015–.0031
⑦ Specification for No. 1 bearing shown.
  No. 2-5 — 2.4985-2.4995

VALVE SPECIFICATIONS

Year	VIN	No. Cylinder Displacement cu. in. (liter)	Seat Angle (deg.)	Face Angle (deg.)	Spring Test Pressure (lbs.)	Spring Installed Height (in.)	Stem-to-Guide Clearance (in.)		Stem Diameter (in.)	
							Intake	Exhaust	Intake	Exhaust
1982	K	6-229 (3.8)	46	45	200 @ 1.25	1.70	.0010–.0027	.0010–.0027	.3414	.3414
	A	6-231 (3.8)	45	45	168 @ 1.32	1.72	.0015–.0032	.0015–.0032	.3407	.3409
	V	6-262 (4.3)	45②	44②	210 @ 1.22	1.67	.0010–.0027	.0015–.0032	.3429	.3424
	J	8-267 (4.4)	46	45	200 @ 1.25	1.70	.0010–.0027	.0010–.0027	.3414	.3414
	H	8-305 (5.0)	46	45	200 @ 1.25	1.70	.0010–.0027	.0010–.0027	.3414	.3414
	L	8-350 (5.7)	46	45	200 @ 1.25	1.70	.0010–.0027	.0010–.0027	.3414	.3414
	N	8-350 (5.7)	45③	44④	205 @ 1.30	1.67	.0010–.0027	.0015–.0032	.3429	.3429
1983	9	6-229 (3.8)	46	45	200 @ 1.25	1.70	.0010–.0027	.0010–.0027	.3414	.3414
	A	6-231 (3.8)	45	45	168 @ 1.32	1.72	.0015–.0032	.0015–.0032	.3407	.3409
	V	6-262 (4.3)	45②	45②	210 @ 1.22	1.67	.0010–.0027	.0015–.0032	.3429	.3424
	H	8-305 (5.0)	46	45	200 @ 1.25	1.70	.0010–.0027	.0010–.0027	.3414	.3414
	N	8-350 (5.7)	45③	44④	205 @ 1.30	1.67	.0010–.0027	.0015–.0032	.3429	.3424

VALVE SPECIFICATIONS

Year	VIN	No. Cylinder Displacement cu. in. (liter)	Seat Angle (deg.)	Face Angle (deg.)	Spring Test Pressure (lbs.)	Spring Installed Height (in.)	Stem-to-Guide Clearance (in.)		Stem Diameter (in.)	
							Intake	Exhaust	Intake	Exhaust
1984	9	6-229 (3.8)	46	45	200 @ 1.25	1.70	.0010–.0027	.0010–.0027	.3414	.3414
	A	6-231 (3.8)	45	45	168 @ 1.32	1.72	.0015–.0032	.0015–.0032	.3407	.3409
	V	6-262 (4.3)	45②	44②	210 @ 1.22	1.67	.0010–.0027	.0015–.0032	.3429	.3424
	H	8-305 (5.0)	46	45	200 @ 1.25	1.70	.0010–.0027	.0010–.0027	.3414	.3414
	N	8-350 (5.7)	45③	44④	205 @ 1.30	1.67	.0010–.0027	.0015–.0032	.3429	.3424
1985	A	6-231 (3.8)	45	45	168 @ 1.32	1.72	.0015–.0032	.0015–.0032	.3407	.3409
	Z	6-262 (4.3)	46	45	200 @ 1.25	1.70	.0010–.0027	.0010–.0027	.3414	.3414
	H	8-305 (5.0)	46	45	200 @ 1.25	1.70	.0010–.0027	.0010–.0027	.3414	.3414
	G	8-305 (5.0)	46	45	200 @ 1.25	1.70	.0010–.0027	.0010–.0027	.3414	.3414
	N	8-350 (5.7)	45③	44④	205 @ 1.30	1.67	.0010–.0027	.0015–.0032	.3429	.3424
	6	8-350 (5.7)	46	45	200 @ 1.25	1.70	.0010–.0027	.0010–.0027	.3414	.3414
1986	Z	6-262 (4.3)	46	45	200 @ 1.25	1.70	.0010–.0027	.0010–.0027	.3414	.3414
	H	8-305 (5.0)	46	45	200 @ 1.25	1.70	.0010–.0027	.0010–.0027	.3414	.3414
	G	8-305 (5.0)	46	45	200 @ 1.25	1.70	.0010–.0027	.0010–.0027	.3414	.3414
	Y	8-307 (5.0)	45	44	180 @ 1.27 ①	1.70	.0010–.0027	.0015–.0032	.3425–.3432	.3420–.3427
	6	8-350 (5.7)	46	45	200 @ 1.25	1.70	.0010–.0027	.0015–.0032	.3414	.3414
1987	Z	6-262 (4.3)	46	45	200 @ 1.25	1.70	.0010–.0027	.0010–.0027	.3414	.3414
	H	8-305 (5.0)	46	45	200 @ 1.25	1.70	.0010–.0027	.0010–.0027	.3414	.3414
	G	8-305 (5.0)	46	45	200 @ 1.25	1.70	.0010–.0027	.0010–.0027	.3414	.3414
	Y	8-307 (5.0)	45	44	180-194 @ 1.27①	1.70	.0010–.0027	.0015–.0032	.3425–.3432	.3420–.3427
	6	8-350 (5.7)	46	45	200 @ 1.25	1.70	.0010–.0027	.0015–.0032	.3414	.3414

VALVE SPECIFICATIONS

Year	VIN	No. Cylinder Displacement cu. in. (liter)	Seat Angle (deg.)	Face Angle (deg.)	Spring Test Pressure (lbs.)	Spring Installed Height (in.)	Stem-to-Guide Clearance (in.) Intake	Stem-to-Guide Clearance (in.) Exhaust	Stem Diameter (in.) Intake	Stem Diameter (in.) Exhaust
1988-89	Z	6-262 (4.3)	46	45	200 @ 1.25	1.70	.0010–.0027	.0010–.0027	.3414	.3414
	H	8-305 (5.0)	46	45	200 @ 1.25	1.70	.0010–.0027	.0010–.0027	.3414	.3414
	G	8-305 (5.0)	46	45	200 @ 1.25	1.70	.0010–.0027	.0010–.0027	.3414	.3414
	Y	8-307 (5.0)	45	44	180-194 @ 1.27①	1.70	.0010–.0027	.0015–.0032	.3425–.3432	.3420–.3427
	6	8-350 (5.7)	46	45	200 @ 1.25	1.70	.0010–.0027	.0015–.0032	.3414	.3414

① Or 76-84 @ 1.67
② Exhaust – Face 30°, Seat 31°
③ Exhaust – 31°
④ Exhaust – 30°

PISTON AND RING SPECIFICATIONS
All measurments are given in inches.

Year	VIN	No. Cylinder Displacement cu. in. (liter)	Piston Clearance	Ring Gap Top Compression	Ring Gap Bottom Compression	Ring Gap Oil Control	Ring Side Clearance Top Compression	Ring Side Clearance Bottom Compression	Ring Side Clearance Oil Control
1982	K	6-229 (3.8)	.0012	.010–.020	.010–.025	.010–.035	.0012–.0032	.0012–.0032	.0020–.0070
	A	6-231 (3.8)	.0008–.0012	.010–.020	.010–.020	.015–.035	.003–.005	.003–.005	.0035 ①
	V	6-262 (4.3)	.0030–.0040	.015–.020	.015–.025	.015–.035	.005–.007	.003–.005	.0010–.0050
	J	8-267 (4.4)	.0012	.010–.020	.010–.025	.015–.055	.0012–.0032	.0012–.0032	.0020–.0070
	H	8-305 (5.0)	.0012 .0032	.010–.020	.010–.025	.015–.055	.0012–.0032	.0012–.0032	.0020–.0070
	L	8-350 (5.7)	.0012	.010–.020	.010–.025	.015–.055	.0012–.0032	.0012–.0032	.0020–.0070
	N	8-350 (5.7)	.0050–.0060	.015–.025	.015–.025	.015–.055	.005–.007	.003–.005	.0010–.0050
1983	9	6-229 (3.8)	.0012	.010–.020	.010–.020	.010–.055	.0012–.0032	.0012–.0032	.0020–.0070
	A	6-231 (3.8)	.0012	.010–.020	.010–.025	.015–.055	.0012–.0032	.0012–.0032	.0020–.0070
	V	6-262 (4.3)	.0030–.0040	.015–.025	.015–.025	.015–.035	.005–.007	.003–.005	.0010–.0050
	H	8-305 (5.0)	.0012 .0032	.010–.020	.010–.025	.015–.055	.0012–.0032	.0012–.0032	.0020–.0070
	N	8-350 (5.7)	.0050–.0060	.015–.025	.015–.025	.015–.055	.005–.007	.003–.005	.0010–.0050

PISTON AND RING SPECIFICATIONS
All measurments are given in inches.

Year	VIN	No. Cylinder Displacement cu. in. (liter)	Piston Clearance	Ring Gap			Ring Side Clearance		
				Top Compression	Bottom Compression	Oil Control	Top Compression	Bottom Compression	Oil Control
1984	9	6-229 (3.8)	.0012	.010–.020	.010–.020	.010–.055	.0012–.0032	.0012–.0032	.0020–.0070
	A	6-231 (3.8)	.0012	.010–.020	.010–.025	.015–.055	.0012–.0032	.0012–.0032	.0020–.0070
	V	6-262 (4.3)	.0030–.0040	.015–.025	.015–.025	.015–.035	.005–.007	.003–.005	.001–.005
	H	8-305 (5.0)	.0012–.0032	.010–.020	.010–.025	.015–.055	.0012–.0032	.0012–.0032	.0020–.0070
	N	8-350 (5.7)	.0050–.0060	.015–.025	.015–.025	.015–.055	.005–.007	.003–.005	.0010–.0050
1985	A	6-231 (3.8)	.0012	.010–.020	.010–.025	.015–.055	.0012–.0032	.0012–.0032	.0020–.0070
	Z	6-262 (4.3)	.0012–.0032	.010–.020	.010–.020	.015–.055	.0012–.0032	.0012–.0032	.0020–.0070
	H	8-305 (5.0)	.0012–.0032	.010–.020	.010–.025	.015–.055	.0012–.0032	.0012–.0032	.0020–.0070
	G	8-305 (5.0)	.0012–.0032	.010–.020	.010–.025	.015–.055	.0012–.0032	.0012–.0032	.0020–.0070
	N	8-350 (5.7)	.0050–.0060	.015–.025	.015–.025	.015–.055	.005–.007	.003–.005	.0010–.0050
	6	8-350 (5.7)	.0012–.0032	.010–.020	.010–.020	.015–.055	.0012–.0032	.0012–.0032	.0020–.0070
1986	Z	6-262 (4.3)	.0012–.0032	.010–.020	.010–.020	.015–.055	.0012–.0032	.0012–.0032	.0020–.0070
	H	8-305 (5.0)	.0012–.0032	.010–.020	.010–.025	.015–.055	.0012–.0032	.0012–.0032	.0020–.0070
	G	8-305 (5.0)	.0012–.0032	.010–.020	.010–.025	.015–.055	.0012–.0032	.0012–.0032	.0020–.0070
	Y	8-307 (5.0)	.0008–.0018	.009–.019	.009–.019	.015–.055	.0018–.0038	.0018–.0038	.0010–.0050
	6	8-350 (5.7)	.0012–.0032	.010–.020	.010–.020	.015–.055	.0012–.0032	.0012–.0032	.0020–.0070
1987	Z	6-262 (4.3)	.0012–.0032	.010–.020	.010–.020	.015–.055	.0012–.0032	.0012–.0032	.0020–.0070
	H	8-305 (5.0)	.0012–.0032	.010–.020	.010–.025	.015–.055	.0012–.0032	.0012–.0032	.0020–.0070
	G	8-305 (5.0)	.0012–.0032	.010–.020	.010–.025	.015–.055	.0012–.0032	.0012–.0032	.0020–.0070
	Y	8-307 (5.0)	.0008–.0018	.009–.019	.009–.019	.015–.055	.0018–.0038	.0018–.0038	.0010–.0050
	6	8-350 (5.7)	.0012–.0032	.010–.020	.010–.020	.015–.055	.0012–.0032	0012–.0032	.0020–.0070

PISTON AND RING SPECIFICATIONS
All measurments are given in inches.

Year	VIN	No. Cylinder Displacement cu. in. (liter)	Piston Clearance	Ring Gap			Ring Side Clearance		
				Top Compression	Bottom Compression	Oil Control	Top Compression	Bottom Compression	Oil Control
1988-89	Z	6-262 (4.3)	.0027 ①	.010–.020	.010–.025	.015–.055	.0012–.0032	.0012–.0032	.0020–.0070
	H	8-305 (5.0)	.0027 ①	.010–.020	.010–.025	.015–.055	.0012–.0032	.0012–.0032	.0020–.0070
	G	8-305 (5.0)	.0027 ①	.010–.020	.010–.025	.015–.055	.0012–.0032	.0012–.0032	.0020–.0070
	Y	8-307 (5.0)	.0008–.0018	.009–.019	.009–.019	.015–.055	.0018–.0032	.0018–.0032	.0010–.0050
	6	8-350 (5.7)	.0027 ①	.010–.020	.010–.025	.015–.055	.0012–.0032	0012–.0032	.0020–.0070

① Maximum

TORQUE SPECIFICATIONS
All readings in ft. lbs.

Year	VIN	No. Cylinder Displacement cu. in. (liter)	Cylinder Head Bolts	Main Bearing Bolts	Rod Bearing Bolts	Crankshaft Pulley Bolts	Flywheel Bolts	Manifold		Spark Plugs
								Intake	Exhaust	
1982	K	6-229 (3.8)	65	70	45	60	60	30	20	22
	A	6-231 (3.8)	80	100	40	175	60	45	20	20
	V	6-262 (4.3)	142②	107	42	300	48	41	29	
	J	8-267 (4.4)	65	70	45	60	60	30	20	22
	H	8-305 (5.0)	65	70	45	60	60	30	20	22
	L	8-350 (5.7)	65	70	45	60	60	30	20	22
	N	8-350 (5.7)	130①	120	42	310	60	40①	25	—
1983	9	6-229 (3.8)	65	70	45	60	60	30	20	22
	A	6-231 (3.8)	80	100	40	225	60	45	20	20
	V	6-262 (4.3)	142②	107	42	300	48	41	29	—
	H	8-305 (5.0)	65	70	45	60	60	30	20	22
	N	8-350 (5.7)	130①	120	42	310	60	40①	25	—
1984	9	6-229 (3.8)	65	70	45	60	60	30	20	22
	A	6-231 (3.8)	80	100	40	225	60	45	20	20
	V	6-262 (4.3)	142②	107	42	300	48	41	29	—
	H	8-305 (5.0)	65	70	45	60	60	30	20	22
	N	8-350 (5.7)	130①	120	42	310	60	40①	25	—
1985	A	6-231 (3.8)	80	100	40	225	60	45	20	20
	Z	6-262 (4.3)	60-75	70-85	42-47	70	70	25-45	20	22
	H	8-305 (5.0)	60-75	70-85	42-47	70	70	25-45	20	22
	G	8-305 (5.0)	60-75	70-85	42-47	70	70	25-45	20	22
	N	8-350 (5.7)	130①	120	42	310	60	40①	25	—
	6	8-350 (5.7)	60-75	70-85	42-47	70	70	25-45	20	22

TORQUE SPECIFICATIONS
All readings in ft. lbs.

Year	VIN	No. Cylinder Displacement cu. in. (liter)	Cylinder Head Bolts	Main Bearing Bolts	Rod Bearing Bolts	Crankshaft Pulley Bolts	Flywheel Bolts	Manifold Intake	Manifold Exhaust	Spark Plugs
1986	Z	6-262 (4.3)	60-75	70-85	42-47	70	70	25-45	20	22
	H	8-305 (5.0)	60-75	70-85	42-47	70	70	25-45	20	22
	G	8-305 (5.0)	60-75	70-85	42-47	70	70	25-45	20	22
	Y	8-307 (5.0)	125①	80③	42	300	60	40①	25	25
	6	8-350 (5.7)	60-75	70-85	42-47	70	70	25-45	20	22
1987	Z	6-262 (4.3)	60-75	70-85	42-47	70	70	25-45	20	22
	H	8-305 (5.0)	60-75	70-85	42-47	70	70	25-45	20	22
	G	8-305 (5.0)	60-75	70-85	42-47	70	70	25-45	20	22
	Y	8-307 (5.0)	125①	80③	42	300	60	40①	25	25
	6	8-350 (5.7)	60-75	70-85	42-47	70	70	25-45	20	22
1988-89	Z	6-262 (4.3)	60-75	70-85	42-47	—	50-70	25-45	20⑤	22
	H	8-305 (5.0)	60-75	70-85	42-47	—	50-70	25-45	14-26⑥	22
	G	8-305 (5.0)	60-75	70-85	42-47	—	50-70	25-45	14-26⑥	22.
	Y	8-307 (5.0)	130①	80③	18④	200-310	60	40①	25	25
	6	8-350 (5.7)	60-75	70-85	42-47	—	50-70	25-45	14-26⑥	22

① Dip in clean engine oil before tightening

② Nos. 5, 6, 11, 12, 13 & 14 @ 59

③ Rear Main Bearing Torque @ 120

④ 70 degrees past initial torque specification

⑤ Outer bolt specification shown. Inner bolt—25

⑥ Outer bolt specification shown. Inner bolt—20-32

BRAKE SPECIFICATIONS
All measurements in inches unless noted

Year	Model	Lug Nut Torque (ft. lbs.)	Master Cylinder Bore	Brake Disc Minimum Thickness	Brake Disc Maximum Runout	Standard Brake Drum Diameter	Minimum Lining Thickness Front	Minimum Lining Thickness Rear
1982	Malibu, Monte Carlo, Impala, Caprice	80①	NA	.965	.980	9.500	.030	.030②
1983	Malibu, Monte Carlo, Impala, Caprice	80①	NA	.965	.980	9.500	.030	.030②
1984	Monte Carlo, Impala, Caprice	80①	NA	.965	.980	9.500	.030	.030②
1985	Monte Carlo, Impala, Caprice	80①	NA	.965	.980	9.500	.030	.030②

BRAKE SPECIFICATIONS
All measurements in inches unless noted

Year	Model	Lug Nut Torque (ft. lbs.)	Master Cylinder Bore	Brake Disc		Standard Brake Drum Diameter	Minimum Lining Thickness	
				Minimum Thickness	Maximum Runout		Front	Rear
1986	Monte Carlo, Caprice	80①	NA	.965	.980	9.500	.030	.030②
1987	Monte Carlo, Caprice	80①	NA	.965	.980	9.500	.030	.030②
1988-89	Monte Carlo, Caprice	80①	1.125④	.965	.004	11.00	.030	.030②

① 88 with $7/16$ in. stud; 100 with 11 in. brake drums
② .062 bonded
③ Caprice Wagon—100
④ Specification for Caprice shown. Monte Carlo—.937

WHEEL ALIGNMENT

Year	Model	Caster		Camber		Toe-in (in.)	Steering Axis Inclination (deg.)
		Range (deg.)	Preferred Setting (deg.)	Range (deg.)	Preferred Setting (deg.)		
1982	Malibu, Monte Carlo	2-4P	3P	$3/10$N-$1 3/10$P	$1/2$P	$1/16$-$1/4$	$7 7/8$
	Impala, Caprice	2-4P	3P	0-$1 3/5$P	$1/2$P	$1/16$-$1/4$	$7 7/8$
1983	Malibu, Monte Carlo	2-4P	3P	$3/10$N-$1 3/10$P	$1/2$P	$1/16$-$1/4$	$7 7/8$
	Impala, Caprice	2-4P	3P	0-$1 3/5$P	$1/2$P	$1/16$-$1/4$	$7 7/8$
1984	Monte Carlo	2-4P	3P	$3/10$N-$1 3/10$P	$1/2$P	$1/16$-$1/4$	$7 7/8$
	Impala, Caprice	2-4P	3P	0-$1 3/5$P	$1/2$P	$1/16$-$1/4$	$7 7/8$
1985	Monte Carlo	2-4P	3P	$3/10$N-$1 3/10$P	$1/2$P	$1/16$-$1/4$	$7 7/8$
	Impala, Caprice	2-4P	3P	0-$1 3/5$P	$1/2$P	$1/16$-$1/4$	$7 7/8$
1986	Monte Carlo	2-4P	3P	$3/10$N-$1 3/10$P	$1/2$P	$1/16$-$1/4$	$7 7/8$
	Caprice	2-4P	3P	0-$1 3/5$P	$1/2$P	$1/16$-$1/4$	$7 7/8$
1987	Monte Carlo	2-4P	3P	$3/10$N-$1 3/10$P	$1/2$P	$1/16$-$1/4$	$7 7/8$
	Caprice	2-4P	3P	0-$1 3/5$P	$1/2$P	$1/16$-$1/4$	$7 7/8$
1988-89	Monte Carlo	2-4P	3P	$3/10$N-$1 3/10$P	$1/2$P	$1/16$-$1/4$	$7 7/8$
	Caprice	2-4P	3P	0-$1 3/5$P	$1/2$P	$1/16$-$1/4$	$7 7/8$

TUNE-UP PROCEDURES

Ignition Timing

ADJUSTMENT

1. Refer to the vehicle control information label which is located on the radiator support panel, for the proper timing information.

NOTE: If the vehicle is equipped with EST (Electronic Spark Timing) it will be necessary to disconnect the EST connector at the distributor to cause the engine to operate in the bypass timing mode.

2. With the ignition switch in the Off position, connect the pick-up lead of a timing light to the number one spark plug.

3. Start the engine and aim the timing light at the the timing mark. The line on the balancer (or pulley) will align with the timing mark. If the engine timing requires adjustment, loosen the distributor hold down bolt and rotate the distributor slowly in either direction, to advance or retard the engine timing.

4. Tighten the hold down bolt and re-check the engine timing.

5. Some engines incorporate a magnetic timing probe hole which is used when setting the engine timing with special electronic equipment. Consult manufacturer's instructions if using this form of timing equipment.

Valve Lash

ADJUSTMENT

Hydraulic valve lifters are used in all engines produced by General Motors Corporation. Valve adjustments are not possible on the 231 V6 (Buick produced) or the 307 V8 (Oldsmobile produced).

1. Remove the valve covers.
2. Tighten the rocker arm nuts until all lash is eliminated.
3. Adjust the valves when the lifter is on the base circle of the camshaft lobe by cranking the engine until the mark on the vibration damper lines up with the center or "0" mark on the timing tab fastened to the crankcase front cover and the engine is in the No.1 firing position.

NOTE: The No. 1 firing position may be determined by placing your fingers on the No. 1 valve as the mark on the damper comes near the "0" mark on the crankcase front cover. If the valves move as the mark comes up to the timing tab, the engine is in the No. 6 (No. 4-V6) firing position and should be turned over one more time to reach to No. 1 firing position.

4. With the engine in the No. 1 firing position, adjust the following valves:
   a. V6 engine: exhaust—1, 5, 6 intake—1, 2, 3.
   b. V8 engine: exhaust—1, 3, 4, 8 intake—1, 2, 5, 7.
5. Back out adjusting nut until lash is felt at the pushrod then turn in adjusting nut until all lash is removed. This can be determined by rotating pushrod while turning adjusting nut. When play has been removed, turn adjusting nut as follows: ½–1¼ additional turn (flat lifters); ¾–1¼ additional turn (roller lifters V8); ¾ additional turn (roller lifter V6).
6. Crank the engine one revolution until the pointer "0" mark and the vibration damper mark are again in alignment. This is the No. 6 (No.4-V6) firing position.
7. With the engine in this position, adjust the following valves:
   a. V6 engine: exhaust—2, 3, 4 intake—4, 5, 6.
   b. V8 engine: exhaust—2, 5, 6, 7 intake—3, 4, 6, 8.
8. Install the rocker arm covers with new gaskets as required.
9. Start the engine and adjust the idle speed as required.

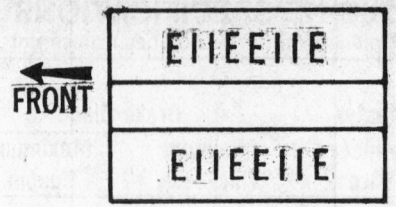

Chevrolet intake(I) and exhaust(E) valve arrangements (except the V6 engine)

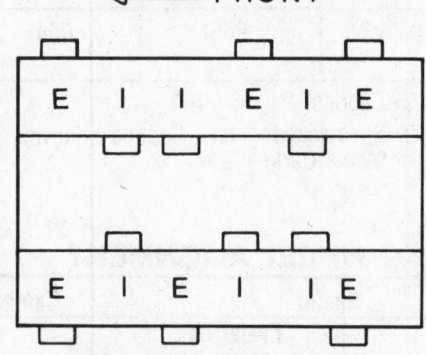

Valve arrangement of the Chevrolet-built V6 engines (E-exhaust; I-intake)

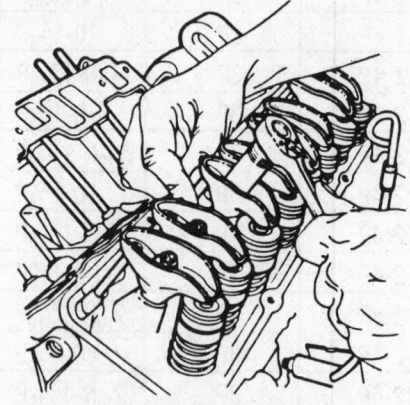

Valve adjustment procedure

Idle Speed and Mixture Gasoline Engines

ADJUSTMENT

Carbureted Models

EXCEPT 1986–89 307 V8 ENGINE

Idle mixture screws are sealed with hardened caps covering the screws during original equipment production. These plugs are not to be removed unless required for cleaning or part replacement.

Before suspecting the carburetor as the cause of poor engine performance or rough idle, check ignition system including distributor, timing, spark plugs and wires. Inspect air cleaner, evaporative emission system, EFE (Early Fuel Evaporation) system, PCV system, EGR (Exhaust Gas Recirculation) system and engine compression. Also inspect intake manifold, vacuum hoses an connections for leaks and check torque of carburetor mounting screws.

In the case of major carburetor repair, throttle body replacement or high idle carbon monoxide as indicated by state or local emission inspection, idle mixture may be adjusted. Adjusting mixture by other than the proper method may violate emissions. The following procedure must be used.

IDLE AIR BLEED VALVE ADJUSTMENT

1. Position the parking brake and block the drive wheels. Disconnect and plug the hoses as directed on the vehicle emission control label.
2. Check and adjust ignition timing. Connect a dwell meter and a tachometer.
3. Start engine, and with transmission in park or neutral, run engine at idle until fully warm and a varying dwell is noted on the dwell meter. It is essential that the engine is operated for a sufficient length of time to ensure that the engine coolant sensor, and the oxygen sensor in the exhaust, are at full operational temperature.
4. Check engine idle speed and compare to specifications on the underhood label. If necessary, adjust curb idle speed. On models with ISC (Idle Speed Control) or ILC (Idle Load Compensator), no adjustment is possible.
5. With engine idling in drive (neutral for manual transmission), observe dwell reading on the 6 cylinder scale. If varying within the 10–0 degree range, adjustment is correct. If not, proceed with Step 6.
6. Remove the idle air bleed valve cover. If the cover is staked in place, pry it off using a suitable tool and a allen wrench.
7. If the cover is riveted, cover the internal bowl vents to the bleed valve with masking tape. Cover the carburetor air intakes with masking tape in order to prevent metal chips from entering the engine.
8. Cover carburetor air intakes with masking tape to prevent metal chips from entering carburetor and engine.
9. Carefully align a No. 35 (0.110 in.) drill bit on one of the steel rivet heads holding the idle air bleed valve cover in place. Drill only enough to remove rivet head. Drill the remaining rivet head located on the other side of the tower. Use a drift and small hammer to drive the remainder of the rivets out of the idle air bleed valve tower in the air horn casting. Use care in

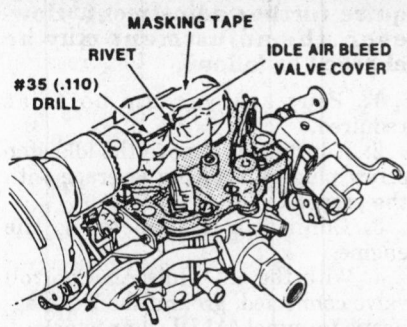

Removing the idle air bleed cover – E4ME and E4MC carburetors

drilling to prevent damage to the air horn casting.

10. Lift out cover over the idle air bleed valve and remove the rivet pieces from inside the idle air bleed valve tower.

11. Using low pressure air, carefully blow out any remaining chips from inside the tower. Discard cover after removed. A missing cover indicates that the idle air bleed valve setting has been changed from its original factory setting.

12. With cover removed, look for presence (or absence) of a letter identification on top of idle air bleed valve.

13. If an identifying letter appears on top of the valve proceed to the procedure outlined under TYPE TWO. If an identifying letter does not appear on the top of the valve proceed to the procedure outlined under TYPE ONE.

TYPE ONE

1. Presetting the idle air bleed valve to a gauge dimension if the idle air bleed valve was serviced prior to on-vehicle adjustment is accomplished as follows.

2. Install idle air bleed valve gauging tool J-33815-2, BT-8253-B, or equivalent, in throttle side ''D'' shaped vent hole in the air horn casting. The upper end of the tool should be positioned over the open cavity next to the idle air bleed valve.

3. While holding the gauging tool down lightly, so that the solenoid plunger is against the solenoid stop, adjust the idle air bleed valve so that the gauging tool will pivot over and just contact the top of the valve. The valve is now preset for on-vehicle adjustment. Remove the gauging tool.

4. Adjusting the idle air bleed valve on the vehicle to obtain correct dwell reading is accomplished as follows.

5. Start engine and allow it to reach normal operating temperature. While idling in drive (neutral for manual transmission), use a suitable tool to slowly turn valve counterclockwise or clockwise, until the dwell reading varies within the 25–35 degree range, at-

tempting to be as close to 30 degrees as possible. Perform this step carefully. The air bleed valve is very sensitive and should be turned in ⅛ turn increments only.

6. If, after performing the Step 5, the dwell reading does not vary and is not within the 25–35 degree range, it will be necessary to remove the plugs and to adjust the idle mixture needles.

7. Remove the idle mixture needle plug as follows, only if necessary. Remove the carburetor from the engine, following normal service procedures, to gain access to the plugs covering the idle mixture needles.

8. Invert carburetor and drain fuel into a suitable waste container. Place carburetor on a suitable holding fixture, with manifold side up. Use care to avoid damaging linkage, tubes, and parts protruding from air horn.

9. Make two parallel cuts in the throttle body, one on each side of the locator points beneath the idle mixture needle plug (manifold side), with a hacksaw.

10. The cuts should reach down to the steel plug, but should not extend more than ⅛ in. beyond the locator points. The distance between the saw cuts depends on the size of the punch to be used.

11. Place a flat punch near the ends of the saw marks in the throttle body. Hold the punch at a 45 degree angle and drive it into the throttle body until the casting breaks away, exposing the steel plug.

12. The hardened plug will break, rather than remaining intact. It is not necessary to remove the plug in one piece, but remove the loose pieces. Repeat this procedure with the other mixture needle.

13. Setting the idle mixture needles (if necessary) where correct dwell reading could not obtained with idle air bleed valve adjustment.

14. Using tool J-29030, BT-7610B or equivalents, turn both idle mixture needles clockwise until they are lightly seated, then turn each mixture needle counterclockwise three turns. Reinstall carburetor on engine using a new flange mounting gasket, but do not install air cleaner and gasket at this time.

15. Readjusting idle air bleed valve to finalize correct dwell reading. Start engine and run until fully warm, and adjust the air bleed valve.

16. If unable to set dwell to 25–35 degrees, and the dwell is below 25 degrees, turn both mixture needles counterclockwise an additional turn. If dwell is above 35 degrees, turn both mixture needles clockwise an additional turn. Readjust idle air bleed valve to obtain dwell limits.

17. After adjustments are complete,

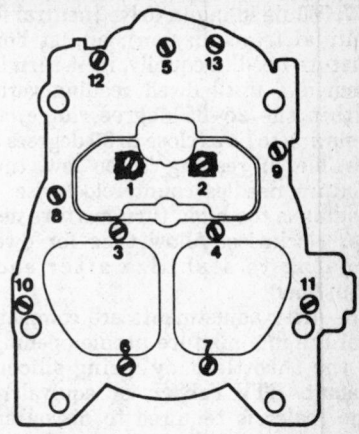

Air horn retaining screw tightening sequence – E4ME and E4MC carburetors

seal the idle mixture needle openings in the throttle body, using silicone sealant, RTV rubber, or equivalent. The sealer is required to discourage unnecessary adjustment of the setting, and to prevent fuel vapor loss in that area.

18. On vehicles without a carburetor mounted idle speed control or idle load compensator, adjust curb idle speed if necessary. Check, and only if necessary, adjust fast idle speed as described on emission control information label.

TYPE TWO

1. To set the idle air bleed valve to a gauge dimension, install air bleed valve gauging tool J-33815-2, BT-8253-B or equivalents, in throttle side ''D'' shaped vent hole in the air horn casting. The upper end of the tool should be positioned over the open cavity next to the idle air bleed valve.

2. While holding the gauging tool down lightly, so that the solenoid plunger is against the solenoid stop, adjust the idle air bleed valve so that the gauging tool will pivot over and just contact the top of the valve.

3. The valve is now set properly. No further adjustment of the valve is necessary. Remove gauging tool.

4. Adjusting the idle mixture needles on the vehicle to obtain correct dwell readings. Remove idle mixture needle plugs, following instructions in the information given under TYPE ONE.

5. Using tool J-29030-B, BT-7610-B or equivalents, turn each idle mixture needle clockwise until lightly seated, then turn each mixture needle counterclockwise three turns.

6. Reinstall carburetor on engine, using a new flange mounting gasket, but do not install air cleaner or gasket at this time. Start engine and allow it to reach normal operating temperature.

7. While idling in drive (neutral for manual transmission), adjust both mixture needles equally, in 1/8 turn increments, until dwell reading varies within the 25–35 degree range, attempting to be as close to 30 degrees as possible. If reading is too low, turn mixture needles counterclockwise. If reading is too high, turn mixture needles clockwise. Allow time for dwell reading to stabilize after each adjustment.

8. After adjustments are complete, seal the idle mixture needle openings in the throttle body, using silicone sealant, RTV rubber, or equivalent. The sealer is required to discourage unnecessary readjustment of the setting, and to prevent fuel vapor loss in that area.

9. On vehicles without a carburetor-mounted idle speed control or idle load compensator, adjust curb idle speed if necessary. Check, and if necesary, adjust fast idle speed, as described on the emission control information label.

1986–89 307 V8 ENGINE

NOTE: All carburetors have mixture needles concealed under staked in plugs. Mixture adjustments are possible only during carburetor overhaul or extreme circumstances. Vehicles equipped with the computer command control system can not use the propane enrichment or lean drop methods of idle mixture adjustment.

1. Place the transmission in the park position, set the parking brake and block the drive wheels. Connect a suitable tachometer to the engine. Remove the air cleaner assembly and plug the vacuum hose to the TVV (Thermal Vacuum Valve).

2. Disconnect and plug the vacuum hose to the EGR (Exhaust Gas Recirculation) valve and the vacuum hose to the canister purge port.

3. Disconnect and plug the vacuum hose to the (ILC) Idle Load Compensator. Back out the idle stop screw on the carburetor three turns.

4. Turn the air condition control switch to the OFF position. With the engine running and at normal operating temperature, place the transmission in the drive position. Fully extend the idle load compensator plunger (no vacuum applied).

5. Using tool J-29607, Bt-8022 or equivalents, adjust the ILC plunger to obtain a 725 ± 50 rpm. The jam nut on the plunger must be held with a suitable wrench to prevent damage to the guide tabs.

6. Measure the distance from the jam nut to the tip of the plunger. The dimension must not exceed one in.. If the dimension does exceed 1 in., check for a low idle condition. Remove the plug from the ILC vacuum hose and plug the hose back into the ILC. Adjust the idle speed to specification in the drive position.

7. If the idle speed is correct then the adjustment is over. If the idle speed does not meet specifications perform the following.

8. Stop the engine and remove the idle load compensator. It will not be necessary to remove the idle load compensator if a hex wrench is modified to clear the obstructions.

9. Remove the rubber cap from the center outlet tube. Using a 3/32 in. hex key wrench, insert it through the open center tube to engage the idle speed adjusting screw inside the tube.

10. If the idle speed was low, turn the adjusting screw counterclockwise one turn for every 75–100 rpm low. If the idle was too high, turn the adjusting screw clockwise one turn for every 75–100 rpm high. Reinstall the plug on the center of the outlet tube.

11. Reinstall the idle load compensator on the carburetor and attach the the throttle return spring and other related parts removed. Re-check the idle speed in the drive position and closed loop mode. If the idle speed is still not within specification, repeat the procedure.

12. Disconnect the power feed (fuse) to the ECM (Electronic Control Module) with the ignition off, for ten seconds. This will allow the ECM to reset the throttle position sensor value.

13. Disconnect and plug the vacuum source to the ILC. Apply a vacuum source using a hand held vacuum pump or equivalent to the ILC vacuum inlet tube to fully retract the plunger.

14. Adjust the idle stop screw on the carburetor float bowl to obtain a 450 rpm in the drive position. Place the transmission in park and stop the engine.

15. Remove the plug from the vacuum hose and install the hose on the ILC vacuum inlet tube. Remove all the plugs from the disconnected vacuum lines and reconnect the vacuum lines to their proper ports.

16. Install the air cleaner and gasket, remove the blocks from the drive wheels and road test the vehicle.

Fuel Injected Models

MINIMUM IDLE SPEED CHECK— TBI MODEL 220

NOTE: The idle stop screw, used in mechanically setting the minimum idle speed is adjusted at the factory and should not require further adjustment. However, the adjustment may be checked as follows.

1. Plug any vaccum ports as required.

2. If installed, remove the idle stop screw plug by applying leverage with the proper tool.

3. Connect a tachometer to the engine.

4. With the IAC (Idle Air Control) valve connected, ground the the diagnostic terminal (ALDL connector).

5. Turn the ignition switch to the On position, but do not start the engine. Wait at least 45 seconds to allow the the IAC valve pintle to extend and seat in the throttle body.

6. With the ignition switch in the On position and the test terminal still grounded, disconnect the IAC valve electrical connector.

7. Remove the ground from the diagnostic connector and start the engine. With the transmission in Neutral, allow the engine rpm to stabilize.

8. The tachometer should be reading 400–450 rpm. If the rpm is not within this range, rotate the idle speed adjusting screw as required until the correct reading is obtained.

9. Turn the ignition switch to the Off position and reconnect the IAC valve electrical connector.

10. Apply a small bead of RTV sealant or equivalent over the idle speed adjusting screw opening.

11. Remove the plugs from the vaccum port openings.

Idle Speed Diesel Engine

ADJUSTMENT

1. Run the engine until normal operating temperature is reached.

2. Insert the probe of the magnetic pickup tachometer into the timing indicator hole.

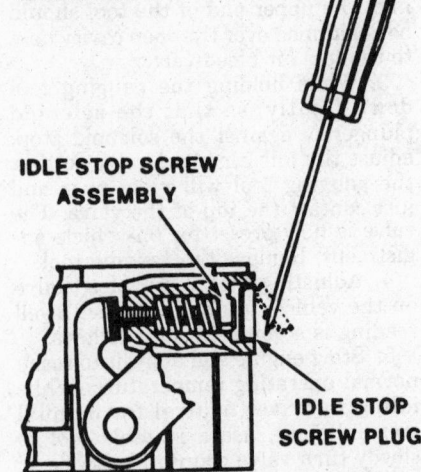

IDLE STOP SCREW ASSEMBLY

IDLE STOP SCREW PLUG

Removing the idle stop screw plug

3. Set the parking brake and block the drive wheels.

4. Position the transmission selector lever in the drive position. If equipped turn the air condition off.

5. Turn the slow idle screw on the injection pump to obtain the proper idle speed.

ENGINE ELECTRICAL

Distributor

REMOVAL & INSTALLATION

Timing Not Disturbed

1. Disconnect the negative battery cable. Remove all the necessary components in order to gain access to the distributor assembly.

2. Remove all electrical connections from the unit. Release the coil connectors from the distributor cap.

3. Remove the distributor cap retaining screws and remove the cap. Disconnect the four terminal harness from the distributor.

4. Remove the distributor hold down bolt. Note the position of the rotor and then pull the distributor assembly from the engine.

5. To insure correct ignition timing the distributor must be installed with the rotor in the same position as it was removed.

6. Installation is the reverse of the removal procedure.

Timing Disturbed

1. Disconnect the negative battery cable. Remove all the necessary components in order to gain access to the distributor assembly.

2. Remove all electrical connections from the unit. Release the coil connectors from the distributor cap.

3. Remove the distributor cap retaining screws and remove the cap. Disconnect the four terminal harness from the distributor.

4. Remove the distributor hold down bolt. Note the position of the rotor and then pull the distributor assembly from the engine.

5. To insure correct ignition timing the distributor must be installed with the rotor in the same position as it was removed.

6. Remove the No. 1 spark plug. Place your finger over the spark plug hole and crank the engine slowly until compression is felt.

7. Align the timing mark on the pulley to "0" on the engine timing indica-

tor. Position the rotor between number one and number eight spark plug towers on V8 engines and between number one and number six spark plug towers on V6 engines.

8. The distributor can now be correctly installed in the engine. Installation is the reverse of the removal procedure.

9. Once the distributor has been installed, check the engine timing and adjust as required.

Alternator

For further information on the charging system, please refer to "Charging and Starting" in the Unit Repair section.

PRECAUTIONS

Several precautions must be observed with alternator equipped vehicles to avoid damage to the unit.

• If the battery is removed for any reason, make sure it is re-connected with the correct polarity. Reversing the battery connections may result in damage to the one-way rectifiers.

• When utilizing a booster battery as a starting aid, always connect the positive to positive terminals, and the negative terminal from the booster battery to a good engine ground on the car being started.

• Never use a fast charger as a booster to start vehicles with alternating-current (AC) circuits.

• Disconnect the battery cables when charging the battery with a fast charger.

• Never attempt to polarize an alternator.

• Avoid long soldering times when making alternator repairs. Prolonged heat will damage the alternator.

• Do not use test lamps of more than 12 volts when checking diode continuity.

• Do not short across or ground any of the alternator terminals.

• The polarity of the battery, alternator and regulator must be matched and considered before making any electrical connections within the system.

• Never separate the alternator on an open circuit. Make sure all connections within the circuit are clean and tight.

• Disconnect the battery ground terminal when performing any service on electrical components.

• Disconnect the battery if arc welding is to be done on the vehicle.

BELT TENSION ADJUSTMENT

Using belt tension gauge J-23600 or

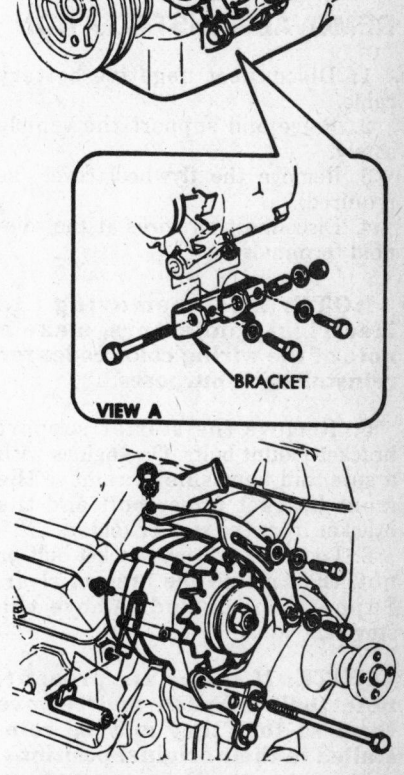

Typical alternator mounting on the Chevrolet V6 and V8 engines

equivalent adjust the alternator belt if the tension is below 300N, as indicated on the gauge. If the belt is used the correct belt tension is 600N, as indicated on the gauge. If the belt is new the correct tension is 900N, as indicated on the gauge.

REMOVAL & INSTALLATION

1. Disconnect the negative battery cable. Remove all necessary components in order to gain access to the alternator assembly.

2. Disconnect the two terminal plug and the battery lead from the back of the alternator assembly.

3. Loosen the adjusting bolts. Remove the alternator belt.

4. Support the alternator and remove the retaining bolts. Remove the alternator assembly from the vehicle.

5. Installation is the reverse of the removal procedure. Once the alternator belt is installed, check the belt tension and adjust if necessary.

Starter

For further information on the starter system, please refer to "Charging and Starting" in the Unit Repair section.

REMOVAL & INSTALLATION

1. Disconnect negative battery cable.
2. Raise and support the vehicle safely.
3. Remove the flywheel cover (as required).
4. Disconnect all wires at the solenoid terminals.

NOTE: When removing the electrical connectors, make a note of the wiring color codes for reinstallation purposes.

5. Remove the starter support bracket mount bolts. On engines with a solenoid heat shield, remove the front bracket upper bolt and the bracket from the starter motor.
6. Loosen the front bracket bolt or nut, then rotate the bracket clear. Support, lower and remove the starter.

NOTE: If shims are present, note their location and remove them so that they may be reinstalled in their original positions.

7. Installation is the reverse of the removal procedure.

Diesel Glow Plugs

REMOVAL & INSTALLATION

1. Disconnect both negative battery cables.
2. Remove all necessary components in order to gain access to the glow plugs.
3. Disconnect the glow plug electrical wire. Using the proper tool remove the glow plug from its mounting.

NOTE: A burned out glow plug tip may bulge then break off and drop into the pre-chamber when the glow plug is removed from the engine. When this occurs the cylinder head must be removed and the pre-chamber removed from the head in order to remove the broken tip.

4. Installation is the reverse of the removal procedure.

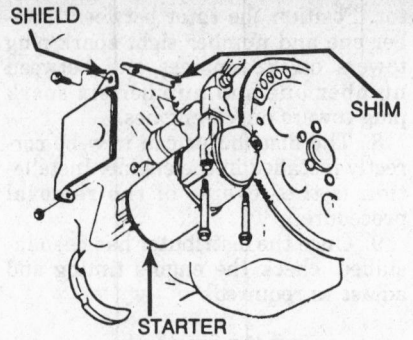

Starter motor, heat shield and mounting—5.7L V8

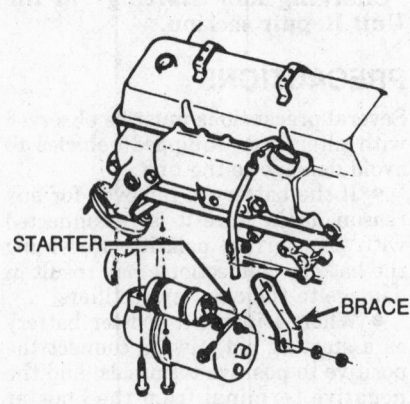

Starter motor and mounting—4.3L V6 and 5.0L V6

ENGINE MECHANICAL

NOTE: The diesel engine is produced by General Motors Oldsmobile division. For all engine service procedures, please refer to the "Oldsmobile Rear Wheel Drive" car section. The 231 V6 gas engine is produced by General Motors Buick division. For all engine service procedures refer to the "Buick Rear Wheel Drive" car section.

Engine

REMOVAL & INSTALLATION

229 V6

1. Disconnect the negative battery cable. Remove the air cleaner assembly.
2. Remove the hood from its hinges, but mark the hinges to ensure proper reassembly .

3. Drain the cooling system and remove the following: radiator hoses, heater hoses, fan shroud, radiator, drive belts and pulleys.
4. Disconnect and tag all electrical wiring, vacuum hoses and fuel lines that must be removed in order to remove the engine.
5. Disconnect the accelerator cable and if so equipped remove the air condition compressor and power steering pump from the mounting brackets and position them out of the way.
6. Remove the alternator. Raise and support the vehicle safely and drain the crankcase.
7. Disconnect the exhaust pipe at the exhaust manifold and converter bracket (if so equipped) at the transmission rear mount. Remove the starter.
8. On models equipped with automatic transmissions, remove the torque converter housing inspection cover and the converter to flex plate bolts. Remove the engine to transmission attaching bolts. On models equipped with manual transmission the transmission is removed with the engine.
9. Remove the motor mount securing bolts and the cruise control bracket (if so equipped), support the transmission and lower the vehicle.
10. Install a suitable lifting device to the engine and raise the engine high enough to allow it to be removed from the vehicle.
11. Installation is the reverse order of the removal procedure.

262 V6

1. Disconnect the negative battery cable. Remove the hood.
2. Raise and support the vehicle safely.
3. Disconnect the exhaust system at the exhaust manifold. Remove the flywheel cover.
4. Disconnect and plug the transmission lines if equipped with automatic transmission.
5. Remove the left mount mount thru bolt. Loosen the right motor mount thru-bolt.
6. Remove the flywheel to torque converter bolts. Remove the transmission bell housing bolts.
7. Disconnect the transmission CCC (Computer Command Control) electrical connections at the transmission. Disconnect the knock sensor.
8. Disconnect the fuel line hoses at the frame. Remove the lower radiator shroud.
9. Disconnect the starter wires and remove the starter (G-Models).
10. Lower the vehicle. Disconnect the ECM (Electronic Control Module) wiring harness.

11. Remove the windshield washer bottle (B-Models).

12. Disconnect the necessary electrical wires and vacuum hoses. Remove the air cleaner. Remove the accelerator and throttle valve cables.

13. Remove the upper fan shroud. Drain the radiator and remove it. Remove the radiator fan and pulley from the water pump assembly. Disconnect the heater hoses.

14. Remove the air condition compressor and position it to the side. Do not loosen any refrigerant line connections or discharge the refrigerant.

15. Remove the power steering pump and position it to the side. Remove the alternator as required.

16. Disconnect the transmission cooler lines at the radiator.

17. Disconnect the overflow tube and remove the radiator (B-Models).

18. Disconnect the A/C hose at the alternator and remove the alternator brace (B-Models).

19. Disconnect the battery cables at the frame.

20. Disconnect the intake heater hose from its bracket (B-Models).

21. Remove the fan and pulley (G-Models).

22. Remove the hood.

23. Disconnect the ground straps at the rear left cylinder head (B-Models). Disconnect both cylinder head ground straps (G-Models). Disconnect the converter AIR (Air Injection Reaction) pipe at the exhaust manifold. Disconnect the AIR hose at the converter AIR pipe.

24. Properly support the transmission assembly. Using the proper lifting equipment remove the engine from the vehicle and position in a suitable holding fixture.

25. Installation is the reverse of removal procedure.

V8 Except 5.0L (VIN Y)

1. Disconnect the negative battery cable. Remove the hood. Remove the air cleaner assembly. Drain the cooling system.

2. Remove the radiator hoses, upper fan shroud, fan assembly and heater hoses.

3. Remove the power steering pump and the air condition compressor and position them out of the way.

4. Disconnect the cooler lines at the radiator and remove the radiator from the vehicle. Disconnect the accelerator and throttle valve cables.

5. Disconnect the vacuum lines, CCC (Computer Command Control) wiring harness, AIR (Air Injection Reaction) hoses at the converter pipe. Remove the windshield washer bottle.

6. Disconnect the engine wiring harness at the bulkhead and all necessary wiring.

7. Remove the hood from its hinges and mark the hinges for easy reassembly.

8. Remove the distributor cap, disconnect the cruise control and the positive battery cable from the frame.

9. Disconnect the negative battery cable at the air condition hose bracket on the alternator bracket.

10. Raise the vehicle and support it safely, remove the crossover pipe and catalytic converter as an assembly.

11. Remove the flywheel cover and the torque converter bolts.

12. Remove the motor mount securing bolts and disconnect the fuel hose at the fuel pump.

13. Disconnect the torque converter clutch wiring at the transmission (if so equipped) and disconnect the transmission cooler lines at the clip on the engine oil pan.

14. Remove the transmission to engine bolts and support the transmission with a suitable jack.

15. Lower the vehicle and install a lifting device to the engine. Raise and remove the engine from the vehicle and position in a suitable holding fixture.

16. Installation is the reverse order of the removal procedure.

5.0L V8 (VIN Y)

1. Disconnect the negative battery cable.

2. Drain the cooling system.

3. Remove the air cleaner and the hot air pipe.

4. Mark the position of the hood hinges and remove the hood.

5. Disconnect the ground cable at the inner fender panel. Disconnect the ground cable between the right cylinder head and the engine cowl.

6. Remove the upper radiator support, fan, drive belts and radiator hoses.

7. Indentify each vacuum hose with a piece of masking tape and remove the vacuum hoses.

8. Remove the power steering pump with hoses attached.

9. Evacuate the refrigeration system and remove the A/C compressor with hoses and brackets attached. Ensure that all refrigerant hose openings are covered to prevent the entry of moisture and contamination.

10. Remove the fuel hoses from the fuel lines.

11. Disconnect all the engine wiring harness connections except the starter.

12. Disconnect the accelerator and transmission throttle valve cables.

13. Remove the AIR (Air Injection Reaction) pipe from the catalytic converter.

14. Raise the vehicle and support it safely.

15. Remove the exhaust and crossover pipes at their respective manifolds.

16. Remove the torque converter cover. Mark the relationship of the flywheel to the torque converter. Remove three of the converter to flywheel bolts.

17. Remove the engine mount bolts or nuts.

18. Remove the starter with wiring attached.

19. Remove all but the lower left hand engine to transmission bolts.

20. Lower the vehicle and connect a suitable hoist to the engine (No. BT-6606 or equivalent).

21. Place a board on top of a suitable transmission jack and raise the transmission slightly.

22. Remove the remaining converter to flywheel bolts.

23. With the hoist, remove the engine from the vehicle and position in a suitable holding fixture.

24. Installation is the reverse of the removal procedure.

Cylinder Head

REMOVAL & INSTALLATION

Except 5.0L V8 (VIN Y)

NOTE: When removing the cylinder head, ensure that the valve train components are kept together and identified so that they may be re-installed in their original locations.

1. Remove the intake manifold.

2. Remove the generator lower mounting bolt and set the generator aside.

3. Remove the exhaust manifold.

4. Remove the rocker arm covers.

5. Remove the valve assemblies.

6. Drain the coolant from the cylinder block.

7. Remove the diverter valve.

8. Remove the cylinder head bolts. Carefully lift the cylinder head away from the cylinder block and place onto two wooden blocks to prevent damage. Remove the cylinder head gasket and note the type of gasket material used. This information will be needed to properly seal the cylinder head upon installation.

9. Visually inspect the cylinder head for internal cracks in the exhaust ports, and combustion chambers. Visually inspect the water passages for external cracks. If the cylinder head is cracked in any of the above mentioned surface areas, it must be replaced.

10. With a gasket scraper, thoroughly clean the cylinder head and block surfaces to remove any traces of existing gasket material, soot or varnish.

To ensure a proper compression seal, the cylinder head and block surfaces must also be free of any nicks or cuts.

11. Thoroughly clean the cylinder head bolt threads to remove any trace of dirt or grease. Inspect the bolt threads for damage. Dirty and worn bolts may affect cylinder head bolt torque values. Replace damaged bolts as required.

NOTE: If a STEEL gasket was removed, apply a light but even coat of sealing compound to both sides of the new gasket. The use of a paint roller will accomplish this task effectively and ensure an even application. Too much or unevenly distributed sealant may raise the gasket away from the cylinder head and block. If a composition STEEL ASBESTOS gasket was removed, no sealing compound is required.

12. Place the gasket over the the dowel pins with the bead facing up.

13. Carefully guide the cylinder head over the dowel pins and gasket and lower into place.

14. Coat the threads of the cylinder head bolts with sealing compound No. 1052080 or equivalent. Install the bolts finger tight.

15. Torque each bolt a small amount in the proper sequence to 60–75 ft. lbs. No additional torque is required after the initial torque is applied.

16. Install the valve assemblies and adjust the valves.

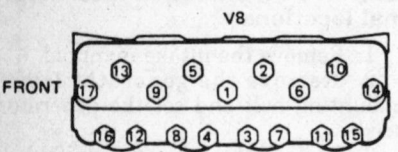

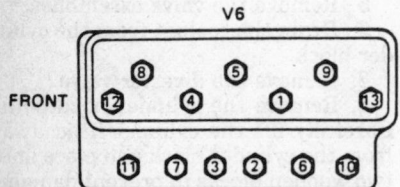

Cylinder head bolt torque sequence—V6 and V8 except 5.0L V8 (VIN Y)

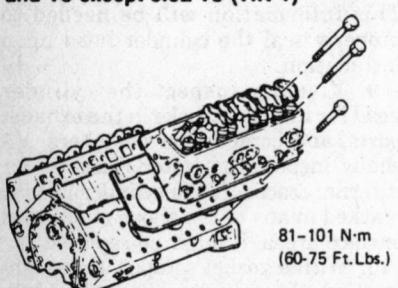

81-101 N·m
(60-75 Ft.Lbs.)

Typical cylinder head assembly—except 5.0L V8 (VIN Y)

17. Install the rocker arm covers (with new gaskets as required), exhaust manifolds, generator and intake manifold.

5.0L V8 (VIN Y)

1. Disconnect the negative battery cable.

2. Drain the radiator. Raise the vehicle approximately 2 feet to drain the remaining coolant from the engine block.

3. Remove the intake manifold.

4. Remove the valve covers, rocker arms and push rods.

5. Disconnect the ground cable from the engine cowl.

6. Remove all accessory brackets as required.

7. Remove the cylinder head bolts. If the rear cylinder head bolts or push rods on the No. 7 and 8 cylinders can not be completely removed without interference, they can be removed with the cylinder head.

8. Carefully lift the cylinder head away from the block and place onto two wooden blocks to prevent damage. Remove the cylinder head gasket and discard.

9. With a gasket scraper, thoroughly clean the cylinder head and block surfaces to remove any traces of existing gasket material, soot or varnish.

——— CAUTION ———

DO NOT use a motorized wire brush to clean the cylinder head surfaces as the wire bristles may take the cylinder head surface past bear metal.

10. Clean the threads of the cylinder bolts to remove any dirt or grease that may be present. Inspect the threads for damage and replace damaged bolts as required. Place a light film of clean engine oil onto all cylinder head bolts and allow the excess to drain.

11. Apply the new cylinder head gasket to the cylinder block surface. No sealing compound is required prior to installation. This type of gasket must be installed dry.

12. Support the cylinder block and lower onto the gasket.

13. Install the cylinder head bolts and tighten by hand. Torque the bolts in sequence to 90 ft. lbs.. Re-torque the bolts in sequence to 130 ft. lbs..

14. Install the pushrods and rocker arms. Adjust the valves then reinstall the valve covers.

15. Reinstall the accessory brackets (if removed), engine cowl ground cable, exhaust manifold and intake manifold.

16. Reconnect the negative battery cable and refill the cooling system.

OVERHAUL

For all cylinder head overhaul procedures, please refer to "Engine Rebuilding" in the unit repair section.

Rocker Arms/Shafts

REMOVAL & INSTALLATION

Except 5.0L V8 (VIN Y)

1. Disconnect the negative battery cable.

2. Remove the air cleaner.

3. Disconnect the CCC (Computer Command Control) harness from the intake manifold and the O₂ sensor.

4. Disconnect the the power brake pipe at the carburetor and booster.

5. Disconnect the AIR (Air Injection Reaction) hose from the exhaust manifold.

6. Disconnect the alternator and choke wires.

7. Disconnect the wiring harness attached to the rocker arm cover and route away from the cover.

8. Disconnect the PCV valve.

9. Disconnect the O₂ sensor electrical lead.

10. Loosen the A/C compressor upper rear bracket mounting bolts with drive belt and position the unit to the side so that the RH (right hand) rocker arm cover retaining bolts are accessible and there is sufficient clearance to remove the right hand rocker arm cover.

11. Loosen the retaining bolts and remove the left and right rocker arm covers. Remove the spark plug wires.

12. Remove the rocker arm nuts, rocker arm balls and rocker arm push rods. Identify each rocker arm assembly to ensure installation in the original positions.

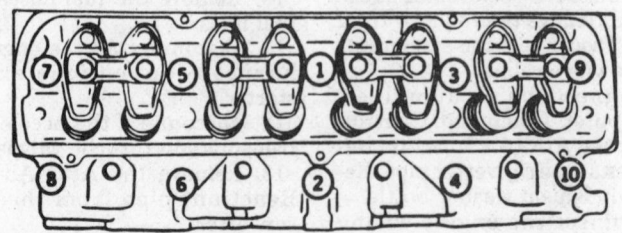

Cylinder head bolt torque sequence—5.0L V8 (VIN Y)

NOTE: If new rocker arms or rocker arm balls are being installed, coat the bearing surfaces with Molycoat® or equivalent.

13. Install the push rods. Ensure that the push rods seat properly in the lifter socket.

14. Install the rocker arms, rocker arm balls and nuts. Tighten the rocker arm nuts until all the valve lash is eliminated.

15. Adjust the valves and A/C belt tension.

16. Install the rocker arm covers and all associated components in the reverse of the removal procedure.

17. Start the engine. Check the curb idle speed and adjust if necessary.

5.0L V8 (VIN Y)

1. Disconnect the negative battery cable and remove the spark plug wires.

2. Remove the air cleaner from the crankcase inlet pipe and filter.

3. Disconnect the heater hoses and position them to the side.

4. Disconnect the PCV valve and hose.

5. Disconnect the ILC (Idle Load Compensator) anti-dieseling solenoid vacuum hoses.

6. Disconnect the following wires from their respective connectors:
   a. Generator.
   b. ILC anti-dieseling solenoid.
   c. AIR (Air Injection Reaction) and O_2 sensor.
   d. RVB (Rear Vacuum Break)/ILC (Idle Load Compensator)/EGR (Exhaust Gas Recirculation) solenoid assembly.
   e. Oil pressure, temperature and coolant sensor.

7. Remove the ILC anti-dieseling solenoid.

8. Remove the generator drive belt and rear bracket.

9. Remove the canister purge hose.

10. Loosen the right hand exhaust manifold upper shroud. Remove the EGR valve and the oil level indicator.

11. Disconnect and remove the following AIR system components:
   a. AIR hoses to the AIR switching valve and catalytic converter pipe.
   b. AIR switching valve.
   c. AIR/AC drive belt.
   d. AIR pump pulley.

12. Remove the A/C compressor rear bracket.

13. Loosen the retaining screws/nuts and remove the left and right valve covers.

14. Remove the rocker arm bolts, pivots and rocker arms. Indentify each rocker arm assembly to ensure installation in the original position.

15. Lubricate all wear points with No. 1050169 lubricant or equivalent. Install the pivots, rocker arms and

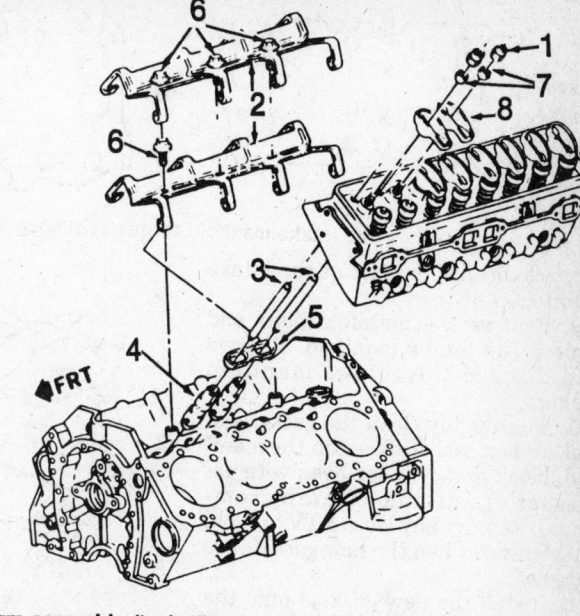

1. 55–125 inch lbs.
2. Retainer
3. Push rod
4. Lifter
5. Restrictor
6. 10–14 ft. lbs.
7. Ball
8. Rocker arm

Rocker arm assembly (typical)—except 5.0L V8 (VIN Y)

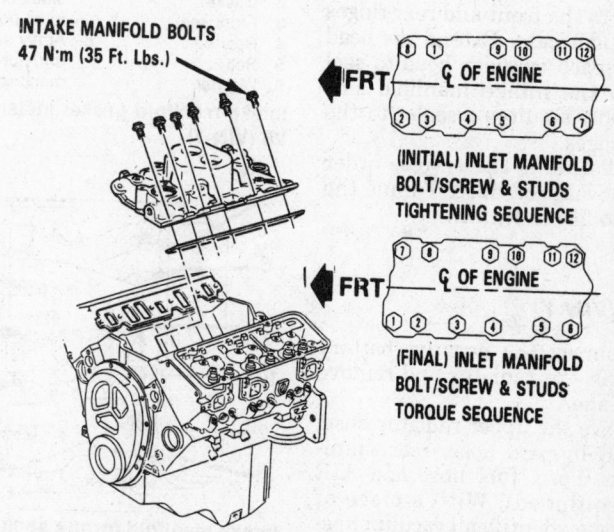

262 V6 intake manifold torque sequence

bolts. Tighten the bolts evenly to 22 ft. lbs..

16. Reinstall the valve covers and associated components in reverse of the removal procedure.

Intake Manifold

REMOVAL & INSTALLATION

Except 5.0L V8 (VIN Y) and 229 V6

1. Disconnect the negative battery cable. Drain the cooling system. Remove the air cleaner and dipstick tube at the alternator adjusting brace.

2. On the V8 models disconnect the CCC (Computer Command Control) harness and lay it to the side out of the way.

3. Remove the heater hose and radiator hose and remove the upper alternator bracket.

4. Disconnect the fuel pipes at the AIR control valve. Disconnect the fuel line and brake pipes at the carburetor. On V6 engines disconnect the fuel line clips and fuel lines at the throttle body injector.

5. Disconnect the accelerator and throttle valve cables. On V8 engines, remove the spark plug wires at the right cylinder head and exhaust manifold.

6. Remove the distributor cap, and mark the position of the rotor, then remove the distributor.

7. On the V6 models remove the coil and on the V8 models remove the carburetor.

8. Remove the A/C brace and dis-

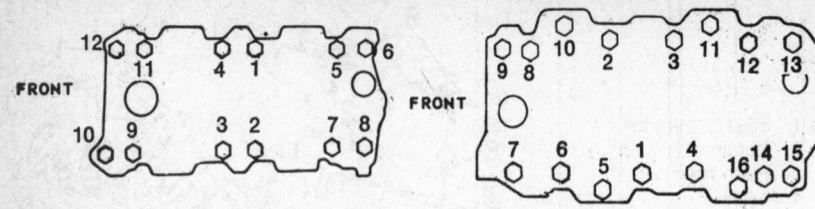

V8 intake manifold torque sequence

connect the A/C bracket at the intake manifold.

9. Remove the manifold bolts and remove the intake manifold. Remove and discard the intake manifold gaskets.

10. Thoroughly clean the gasket and seal contact seal surfaces on the manifold, block and cylinder head with degreaser or suitable cleaning compound. Remove any loose RTV to avoid interference when the new gaskets are installed.

11. Install the new gaskets onto the surface of the cylinder head. Apply a $^3/_{16}$ in. bead of RTV No. 1052366 or equivalent to the front and rear ridges of the cylinder case. Extend the bead ½ in. past each cylinder head to seal and retain the intake manifold side gasket. Apply a suitable sealer to the water passages.

10. Installation is the reverse order of the removal procedure. Torque the manifold to 25–45 ft. lbs..

5.0L V8 (VIN Y)

1. Disconnect the negative battery cable. Drain the radiator and remove the air cleaner.

2. Remove the upper radiator hose, thermostat by-pass hose, rear manifold heater hose, fuel hose and AIR hose (if equipped). With a piece of masking tape, identify all vacuum hoses that may interfere with the intake manifold removal and disconnect them.

3. Disconnect the accelerator and throttle valve cables.

4. Remove the generator rear brace. On vehicles with A/C, remove the compressor rear brace.

5. Disconnect all electrical wiring and connections routed in the vicinity of the intake manifold. Ensure that all electrical connections are marked with their respective connectors.

6. Remove the RVB (Rear Vacuum Break)/ILC (Idle Load Compensator)/EGR (Exhaust Gas Recirculation) solenoid assembly. Remove the ILC and bracket assembly.

7. Remove the EGR valve.

8. Loosen the intake manifold retaining bolts. Raise the intake manifold upward and away from the cylinder head. Remove the intake manifold

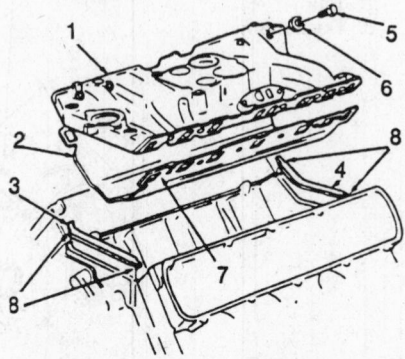

1. Intake manifold
2. Gasket
3. Front seal
4. Rear seal
5. Bolt
6. Washer
7. Apply sealant to both sides of gasket and to all port areas
8. Apply sealant to both ends of intake manifold seals

Intake manifold gasket installation—5.0L V8 (VIN Y)

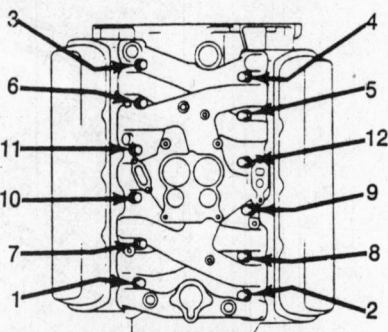

Intake manifold torque sequence—5.0L V8 (VIN Y)

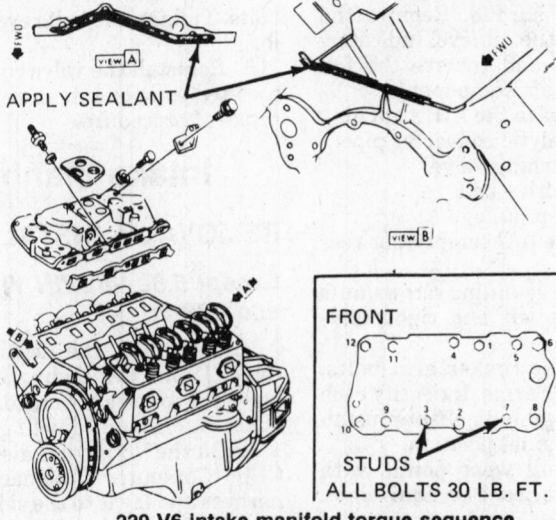

APPLY SEALANT

FRONT

STUDS
ALL BOLTS 30 LB. FT.

229 V6 intake manifold torque sequence

gasket, front seal and rear seal and discard.

9. Thoroughly clean the intake manifold and cylinder block surfaces to remove any trace of gasket material or sealant.

10. Apply an even coat of No. 1050026 sealer or equivalent to both sides of the new intake manifold gasket. Coat the new front and rear seals with No. 1052915, No. GE 1673 or equivalent RTV sealant.

11. Position and install the intake manifold gasket onto the cylinder head surface. Install the front and rear seals.

12. Support the intake manifold and lower into position.

13. Coat the intake manifold reataining bolts with clean engine oil and tighten by hand.

14. Torque the bolts in sequence to 15 ft. lbs.. Re-torque the bolts in sequence to 45 ft. lbs..

15. Install the remaining components in the reverse of the removal procedure. Adjust the throttle valve cable and drive belt tension. Refill the cooling system.

16. Operate the engine and inspect for leaks.

229 V6

1. Disconnect the negative battery cable. Drain the cooling system. Remove the air cleaner.

2. Remove the distributor.

3. Remove all the necessary components in order to gain access to the intake manifold retaining bolts.

4. Disconnect the upper radiator hose from the thermostat housing. Disconnect the fuel line at the carburetor.

5. Remove the intake manifold retaining bolts. Remove the intake manifold from the engine.

6. Installation is the reverse of the removal procedure. Be sure to use new gaskets and sealer as required.

Exhaust Manifold

REMOVAL & INSTALLATION

EXCEPT 5.0L V8 (VIN Y)

1. Disconnect the negative battery cable. On some engines it will be necessary to remove the oil dipstick tube.
2. Remove all necessary components in order to gain access to the exhaust manifold retaining bolts.
3. Raise and support the vehicle safely. Disconnect the exhaust system at the exhaust manifold flange. Lower the vehicle.
4. Remove the exhaust manifold retaining bolts. Remove the exhaust manifold from the vehicle. Depending upon the vehicle it may be easier to remove the manifold from under the vehicle.
5. Thoroughly clean the exhaust manifold and and cylinder head surfaces.
6. Installation is the reverse of the removal procedure.

5.0L V8 (VIN Y)—LEFT SIDE

1. Disconnect the negative battey cable and remove the air cleaner.
2. Raise and support the car safely.
3. Flatten the exhaust manifold locking tabs. Remove the exhaust and crossover pipes.
4. Lower the vehicle.
5. Remove the upper and lower hot air shrouds.
6. Remove the lower generator bracket.
7. Remove the exhaust manifold and gasket. Replace the gasket if required. Thoroughly clean all gasket contact surfaces.
8. Installation is the reverse of the removal procedure. Torque the retaining bolts to 25 ft. lbs.. After the bolts are torqued, bend the locking tabs around the heads of the bolts.
9. Adjust the generator drive belt tension.

5.0L V8 (VIN Y)—RIGHT SIDE

1. Disconnect the negative battery cable.
2. Disconnect the O_2 sensor lead.
3. Raise and support the vehicle safely.
4. Remove the exhaust and crossover pipes.
5. Remove the oil filter adapter and gasket.
6. Remove the right front wheel.
7. Flatten the exhaust manifold locking tabs.
8. Remove the exhaust manifold and gasket. Replace the gasket if re-

quired. Thoroughly clean all gasket contact surfaces.
9. Installation is the reverse of the removal procedure. Torque the retaining bolts to 25 ft. lbs.
10. Adjust the generator drive belt tension.

Front Cover/Oil Seal

REMOVAL & INSTALLATION

1. Disconnect the negative battery cable.
2. Remove the vibration damper assembly.

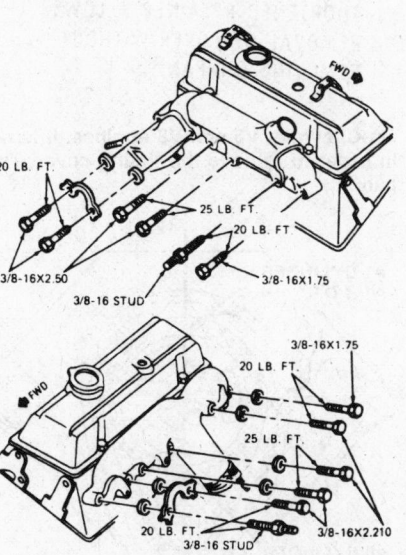

229 V6 exhaust manifold installation

3. Remove the water pump.
4. Remove the crankcase front cover retaining bolts. Remove the front cover and discard the gasket.
5. Installation is the reverse of the removal procedure.

Timing Gears

REMOVAL & INSTALLATION

Except 5.0L V8 (VIN Y)

1. Disconnect the negative battery cable.

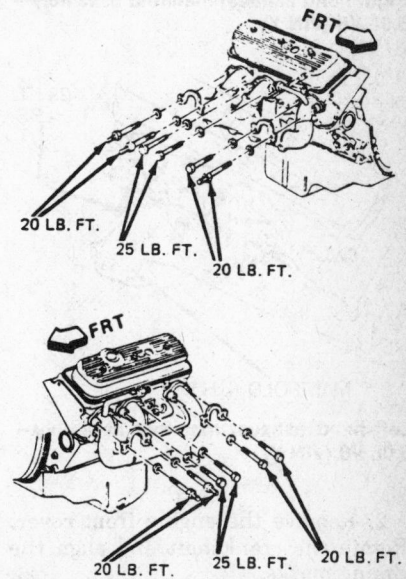

Exhaust manifold exploded view—except 5.0L V8 (VIN Y)

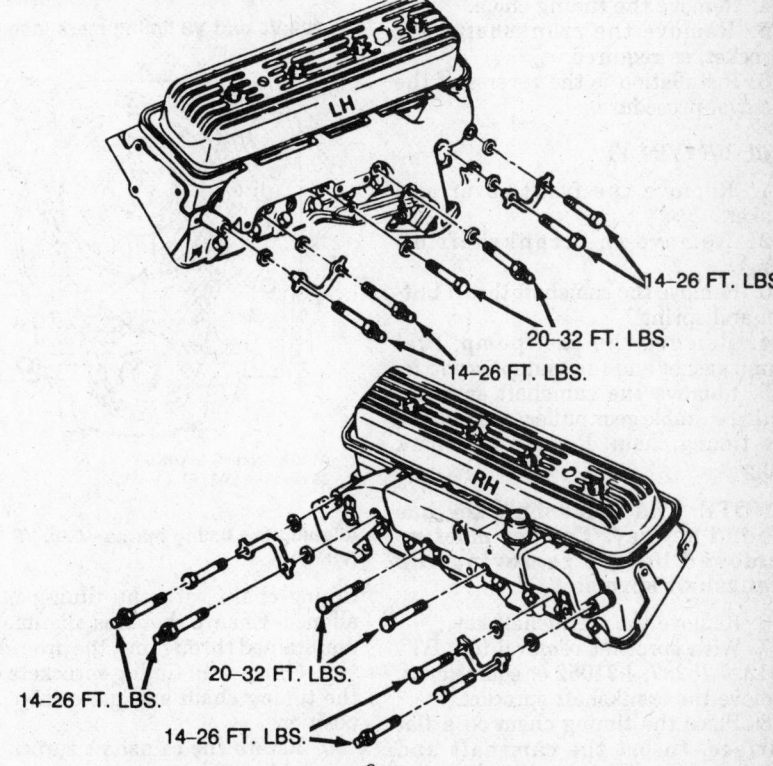

Exhaust manifold assembly exploded view—262 V8

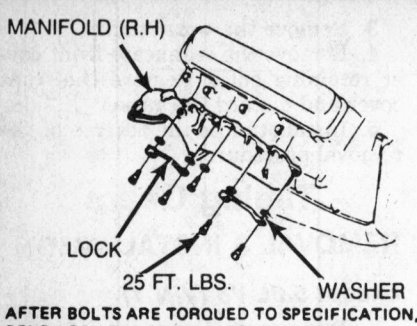

MANIFOLD (R.H)

LOCK

25 FT. LBS.   WASHER

AFTER BOLTS ARE TORQUED TO SPECIFICATION, BEND LOCK TAB AROUND BOLT HEADS

Right hand exhaust manifold assembly— 5.0L V8 (VIN Y)

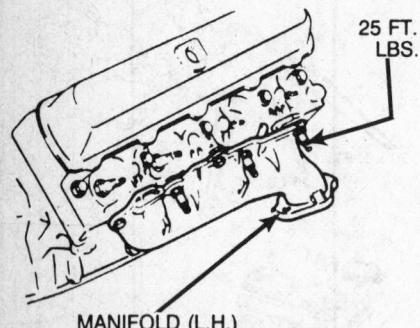

25 FT. LBS.

MANIFOLD (L.H.)

Left hand exhaust manifold assembly— 5.0L V8 (VIN Y)

2. Remove the engine front cover. Rotate the crankshaft and align the timing marks.

3. Remove the camshaft gear bolts. Remove the camshaft gear.

4. Remove the timing chain.

5. Remove the crankshaft gear sprocket, as required.

6. Installation is the reverse of the removal procedure.

5.0L V8 (VIN Y)

1. Remove the front cover and gasket.

2. Remove the crankshaft oil slinger.

3. Remove the camshaft thrust button and spring.

4. Remove the fuel pump, fuel pump gasket and fuel pump eccentric.

5. Remove the camshaft sprocket with a suitable gear puller, and remove the timing chain. Remove the spark plugs.

NOTE: The crankshaft key has a blind keyway. The key must be removed before removing the crankshaft sprocket.

6. Remove the crankshaft key.

7. With sprocket removal tool BT-6812, J 25287, J 21052 or equivalents, remove the crankshaft sprocket.

8. Place the timing chain on a flat surface. Insert the camshaft and crankshaft timing sprockets into the

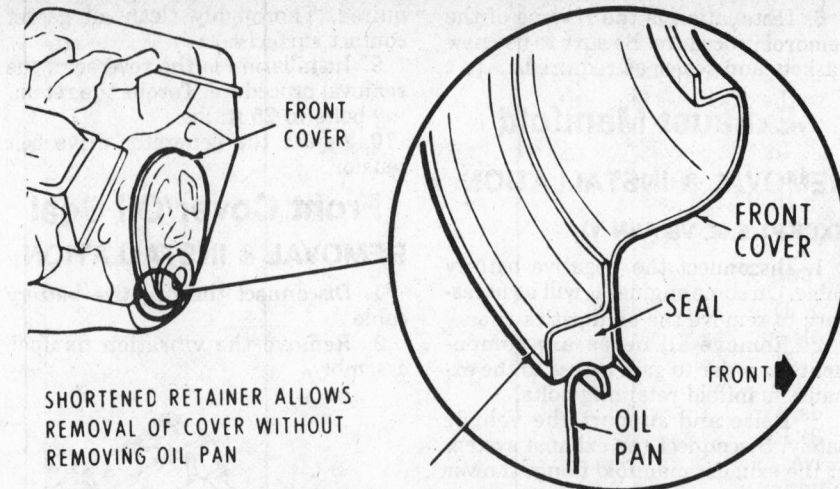

FRONT COVER

FRONT COVER

SEAL

FRONT

OIL PAN

SHORTENED RETAINER ALLOWS REMOVAL OF COVER WITHOUT REMOVING OIL PAN

On Chevrolet V6 and V8 engines, it is not necessary to lower or remove the oil pan in order to remove the timing cover. The seal retainer is short enough to clear the pan

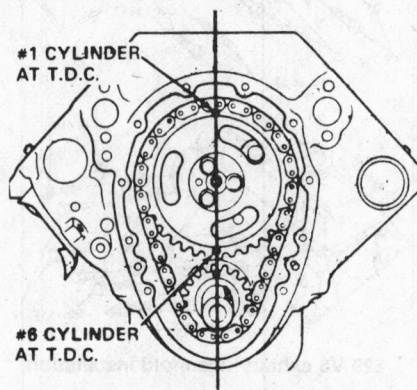

#1 CYLINDER AT T.D.C.

#6 CYLINDER AT T.D.C.

229 V6 and V8 timing mark location

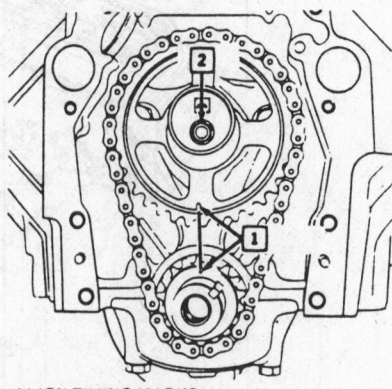

1. ALIGN TIMING MARKS
2. 88 N·m (65 LBS. FT.)

Aligning the timing marks—5.0L V8 (VIN Y)

timing chain with the timing marks aligned. Ensure that this alignment is maintained throughout the procedure.

9. Grasp both timing sprockets with the timing chain and place them into position.

10. Rotate the camshaft sprocket as required until it engages with the cam-

shaft. With the camshaft sprocket engaged, install the fuel pump eccentric (flat side toward the engine). Install the camshaft sprocket (fuel pump eccentric) bolt and make finger tight.

11. Rotate the crankshaft until the crankshaft and crankshaft timing sprocket keyways are in alignment. When the keyways are aligned, tap the crankshaft key into place with a brass hammer until the key bottoms in the keyway.

12. Check that the timing marks are still in alignment.

NOTE: When the timing marks are aligned, the No. 6 piston is at TDC. When the timing marks are on top, the No. 1 piston is in the firing position.

13. After the timing gear alignment is verified, torque the camshaft spocket (fuel pump eccentric) bolt to 65 ft. lbs..

14. Install the remaining components in the reverse of the removal procedure using new gaskets where required.

Camshaft

REMOVAL & INSTALLATION

229 V6

1. Disconnect the negative battery cable. Drain the cooling system.

2. Remove the valve covers. Remove the rocker covers and pushrods. Remove the intake manifold.

3. Remove the valve lifters.

4. As required, remove the radiator, grille and air condition condenser. Remove the water pump. Remove the front engine cover.

5. Remove the fuel pump and pushrod.

6. Install two ⁵⁄₁₆in.–18 × 4 in. bolts into the camshaft bolt holes and carefully remove the camshaft.

7. Installation is the reverse order of the removal procedure, be sure to coat the lifters and the camshaft with clean engine oil before installation.

Except 229 V6

1. Disconnect the negative battery cable. Drain the cooling system.

2. Remove the valve covers. Remove the rocker arm assemblies and pushrods. Remove the intake manifold.

3. Remove the upper fan shroud, drive belts, heater hose at the water pump and the radiator hoses. On V8 engines disconnect the transmission oil cooler lines and remove the radiator. On V8 engines, remove the fuel pump and pushrod.

4. Remove the alternator bracket and brace, remove the power steering pump and AIR pump bracket.

5. Remove the water pump and fan, align the timing marks and remove the crankshaft pulley.

6. Using pulley tool J-23523 or equivalent, remove the torsional damper and remove the front cover. Remove the timing chain and gear.

7. On V8 engine evacuate the air condition system. Remove the air condition condenser. Disconnect the grille support rods.

8. Install two ⁵⁄₁₆ in.-18 × 4 in. bolts in the camshaft bolt holes and remove the camshaft. All camshaft journals are the same diameter and caution should be used in removing the camshaft so as not to damage the camshaft bearings.

9. Installation is the reverse order of the removal procedure, be sure to coat the lifters and camshaft with clean engine oil before installation.

Piston and Connecting Rod

POSITIONING

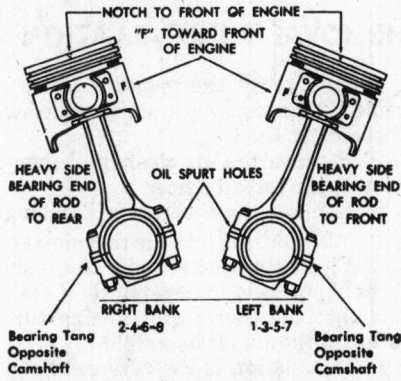

V6 and V8 piston identification

NOTE: For all piston and connecting rod overhaul procedures, please refer to "Engine Rebuilding" in the Unit Repair section.

ENGINE LUBRICATION

Oil Pan

REMOVAL & INSTALLATION

1. Disconnect the negative battery cable.

2. Raise and properly support the vehicle, then drain the engine oil. On V8 engines, remove the upper fan shroud and the retaining screws.

3. If equipped, remove the cruise control servo bracket.

4. Disconnect the AIR (Air Injection Reaction) hose at the converter pipe, and disconnect the AIR pipe at the exhaust manifold (V8 except VIN Y). Remove the exhaust crossover retaining bolts at the exhaust manifold and lower the crossover pipe.

5. Remove the starter. Remove the flywheel cover.

6. Remove the starter. Remove the flywheel cover.

7. Remove the left side mount through bolt (V8 except VIN Y). Loosen the right side mount through bolt and completely remove the left through bolt (V6). Raise the engine and reinstall the left side mount through bolt.

8. Raise the engine, and remove the oil pan retaining bolts. Remove the oil pan from the engine. Check that the forward crankshaft throw and/or counter balance weight are not extending downward so as to interfere with the oil pan removal. Rotate the crankshaft as required to position the throw on a horizontal plane.

--- **CAUTION** ---

On 5.0L V8 (VIN Y) engines, exercise caution when removing the oil pan gasket. The gaskets used with this engine have a steel core that when exposed can cause personal injury.

---

9. Thoroughly clean the cylinder case and and oil pan gasket contact surfaces. Inspect the oil pan gasket for damage and replace if necessary.

10. Apply a small amount of No. 1052751 sealant or eqivalent to the front and rear corners of the oil pan (except 5.0L V8 VIN Y). On 5.0L V8 (VIN Y) engines, apply No. 1050026 sealant or equivalent to both sides of the oil pan gasket, and coat the front and rear seal with clean engine oil.

11. Reinstall the oil pan gasket and

the front and rear seals (if installed). If installed, apply a suitable RTV sealant to the front and rear seals after they are in position on the oil pan.

12. Raise the oil pan and install the retaining bolts. Torque the bolts in an alternate diagonal pattern to 6 ft. lbs. (except 5.0L V8 VIN Y). On 5.0L V8 engines, torque the retaining bolts to 10 ft. lbs. and the nuts to 17 ft. lbs..

13. Install the remaining components in the reverse of the removal procedure. Fill the crankcase to the proper level. Start the engine and inspect for lube oil leaks.

Rear Main Bearing Oil Seal

REMOVAL & INSTALLATION

Except One Piece Seal

1. Remove the oil pan. Remove the oil pump where required. Remove the rear main bearing cap.

2. Pry the lower seal out of the bearing cap with a suitable tool, being careful not to gouge the cap surface.

3. Remove the upper seal by lightly tapping on one end with a brass pin punch until the other end can be grasped and pulled out.

4. Clean the bearing cap, cylinder block, and crankshaft mating surfaces with solvent. Inspect all these surfaces for gouges, nicks, and burrs.

5. Apply a light coat of engine oil on the seal lips and bead, but keep the seal ends clean.

6. Insert the tip of the installation tool between the crankshaft and the seal of the cylinder block. Place the seal between the crankshaft and the seal of the cylinder block. Place the seal between the tip of the tool and the crankshaft, so that the bead contacts the tip of the tool.

7. Be sure that the seal lip is facing the front of the engine, and work the seal around the crankshaft using the installation tool to protect the seal from the corner of the cylinder block.

NOTE: **Do not remove the tool until the opposite end of the seal is flush with the cylinder block surface.**

8. Remove the installation tool, being careful not to pull the seal out at the same time.

9. Using the same procedure, install the lower seal into the bearing cap. Use your finger and thumb to lever the seal into the cap.

10. Apply sealer to the cylinder block only where the cap mates to the surface. Do not apply sealer to the seal ends.

11. Install the rear cap and torque the bolts to specifications.

One Piece Seal

1. Remove the transmission from the vehicle.

2. Using the notches provided in the rear seal retainer, pry out the seal using the proper tool.

NOTE: Care should be taken when removing the seal so as not to nick the crankshaft sealing surface.

3. Before installation lubricate the inside and outside diameter of the new seal with clean engine oil.

4. Install the seal on tool J-3561 or equivalent. Thread the tool into the rear of the crankshaft. Tighten the screws snugly, this is to insure that the seal will be installed squarely over the crankshaft. Tighten the tool wing nut until it bottoms.

5. Remove the tool from the crankshaft.

6. Install the transmission.

One Piece Seal Retainer and Gasket

REMOVAL AND INSTALLATION

1. Remove the transmission from the vehicle.

2. Remove the oil pan bolts. Lower the oil pan.

3. Remove the retainer and seal assembly.

4. Remove the gasket.

NOTE: Whenever the retainer is removed a new retainer gasket and rear main seal must be installed.

5. Installation is the reverse of the removal procedure. Once the oil pan has been installed the new rear main oil seal can be installed.

Oil Pump

REMOVAL & INSTALLATION

1. Disconnect the negative battery cable. Drain the engine oil. Remove engine oil pan. If equipped remove the oil pan baffle.

2. Remove pump attaching screws or pump to rear main bearing cap bolt, and carefully remove the pump.

3. Installation is the reverse of the removal procedure. To ensure immediate oil pressure on start-up, the oil pump gear cavity should be packed with petroleum jelly.

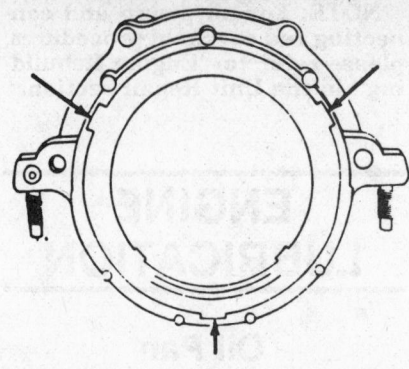

Removing the seal from the seal retainer

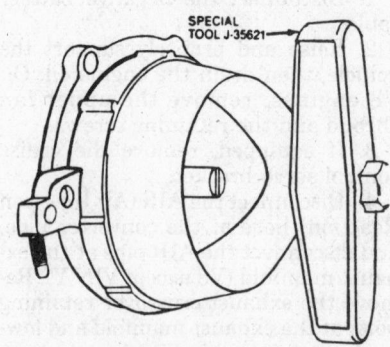

One piece rear main seal removal tool

ENGINE COOLING

Radiator

REMOVAL & INSTALLATION

Except 5.0L V8 (VIN Y)

1. Disconnect the negative battery cable. Drain the cooling system.

2. If necessary, remove the fan, the upper fan shroud or the upper support.

3. Disconnect upper and lower hoses.

4. Disconnect and plug the oil cooler lines, if equipped with automatic transmission.

5. Lift radiator from the vehicle.

6. Installation is the reverse of the removal procedure.

5.0L V8 (VIN Y)

1. Disconnect the negative battery cable. Place a fluid catch pan under the radiator and open the drain cock located at the bottom right hand corner of the radiator. Remove the radiator cap so that the coolant will flow freely.

2. Loosen the hose clamps and dis-

connect the upper and lower hoses at the radiator.

3. Loosen the hose clamp and disconnect the heater return hose at the right radiator tank.

4. Disconnect the two transmission cooling lines from the radiator. Plug or tape the connection openings to prevent loss of fluid.

5. Remove the two radiator cover to strut support rod attaching screws. Loosen one nut on each of the struts and move the support rods out of the way.

6. Remove the two screws attaching the fan shroud to the radiator cover.

7. Remove the two screws attaching the radiator cover to the support and remove the radiator cover.

8. Disconnect the reservoir hose from the filler neck.

9. Carefully grasp the radiator and lift straight up from the vehicle.

10. Installation is the reverse of the removal procedure.

Water Pump

REMOVAL & INSTALLATION

1. Disconnect the negative battery cable. Drain the cooling system. Remove the fan shroud, as required.

2. As required, loosen or remove all accessory brackets that may interfere with the water pump removal.

3. Remove the accessory drive belts. Remove the fan and pulley from the water pump hub. Disconnect all hoses from the water pump.

4. Remove the water pump retaining bolts. Remove the water pump from the engine.

5. Installation is the reverse of the removal procedure. Be sure to clean the engine to water pump mating surface before installing the pump. Use a new gasket when installing the pump assembly. If a new pump is being installed, transfer the heater hose fitting from the old pump.

Thermostat

REMOVAL & INSTALLATION

1. Disconnect the negative battery cable. Drain cooling system to below thermostat level.

2. Remove the air cleaner. Disconnect upper radiator hose.

3. Remove the thermostat housing bolts, the housing and the thermostat.

4. Clean the gasket mounting surfaces. Apply a 1/8 in. bead of RTV sealant onto the thermostat sealing surfaces on the intake manifold.

5. Installation is the reverse of the removal procedure. When installing

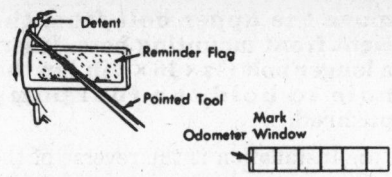

Resetting the maintenance indicator

the thermostat, place the pin side facing upwards.

EMISSION CONTROLS

Please refer to "Emission Control" in the Unit Repair section for system maintenance procedures. Due to the complex nature of modern electronic engine control systems, comprehensive diagnosis and testing procedures fall outside the confines of this repair manual. For complete information on diagnosis, testing and repair procedures concerning all modern engine and emissions control systems, please refer to *Chilton's Guide To Electronic Engine Controls.*

MAINTENANCE REMINDER SYSTEM

An emissions indicator flag may appear in the odometer window of the speedometer on some vehicles. The flag could say "Sensor", "Emissions" or "Catalyst" depending on the part or assembly that is scheduled for regular emissions maintenance replacement. The word "Sensor" indicates a need for oxygen sensor replacement and the words "Emissions" or "Catalyst" indicate the need for catalytic converter catalyst replacement.

Reset Procedure

1. Remove the instrument panel trim plate.
2. Remove the instrument cluster lens.
3. Locate the flag indicator reset notches at the drivers side of the odometer.
4. Use a pointed tool to apply light downward pressure on the notches, until the indicator is reset.
5. When the indicator is reset an alignment mark will apear in the left center of the odometer window.

GASOLINE FUEL SYSTEM

Fuel System Service Precaution

Safety is the most important factor to adhere to when preforming fuel system maintenance. Failure to conduct maintenance and repairs in a safe manner may result in serious personal injury or death. Maintenance and testing of the vehicle's fuel system components can be accomplished safely and effectively by adhering to the following rules and guidelines.

● To avoid the possibility of fire and personal injury, always disconnect the negative battery cable unless the repair or test procedure requires that battery voltage be applied.

● Always relieve the fuel system pressure prior to disconnecting any fuel system component (injector, fuel rail, pressure regulator, etc...), fitting or fuel line connection. Exercise extreme caution whenever relieving fuel system pressure to avoid exposing skin, face and eyes to fuel spray. Please be advised that fuel under pressure may penetrate the skin or any part of the body that it comes in contact with.

● Always place a shop towel or cloth around the fitting or connection prior to loosening to absorb any excess fuel due to spillage. Ensure that all fuel spillage (should it occur) is quickly contained and removed from engine surfaces. Ensure that all fuel soaked cloths or towels are deposited into a suitable waste container.

● Always have a properly charged fire extinguisher in the vincinity of the work area.

● Do not allow fuel spray or fuel vapors to come in contact with spark or open flame.

● Always use a backup wrench when loosening and tightening fuel line connection fittings. This will prevent unnecessary stress and torsion to fuel line piping. Always follow the proper torque specifications.

● Always replace worn fuel fitting O-rings with new. Do not substitute fuel hose or equivalent where fuel pipe is installed.

RELIEVING FUEL SYSTEM PRESSURE

Engines that use a mechanical fuel pump do not require fuel system pressure relief. When performing mainte-

nance on components in a mechanical fuel pump system there may be a small amount of fuel released from a component or connection. This minor leakage can be easily and safely contained with the use of a clean rag or shop towel wrapped around the fitting or connection. However, on engines where an electrical fuel pump is used, there may be considerable residual pressure remaining in the fuel lines and fuel system components even after the engine is secured. To relieve fuel pressure from these type systems, proceed as follows:

1. Disconnect the fuel pump relay connector or remove the fuel pump fuse from the fuse block.
2. Start the engine and allow to run until it stalls. At this time the majority of the fuel contained in the system should be exhausted.
3. To ensure that all the system pressure is relieved, crank the starter for an additional three seconds.
4. Reconnect the fuel pump relay connector or reinstall the fuse.

Fuel Filter

REMOVAL & INSTALLATION

Internal Filter

1. Disconnect the negative battery cable. Disconnect the fuel line connection at the fuel inlet filter nut on the carburetor.
2. Remove the fuel inlet filter nut and gasket from the carburetor.
3. Remove the filter, filter check valve and spring. Remove the gasket from the fuel inlet nut. Discard the gasket, filter check valve and filter.
4. Install the fuel filter spring and the fuel filter with check valve into the carburetor opening. Ensure that the filter assembly is installed with the check valve end facing the fuel inlet

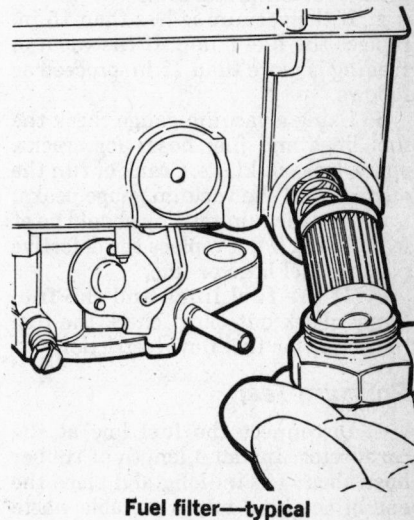

Fuel filter—typical

line. Ribs on the closed end of the filter prevent the filter from being installed incorrectly.

5. Install a new gasket onto the fuel line nut, and tighten the nut into the carburetor opening.

6. Reconnect and tighten the fuel inlet line to the fuel nut.

7. Start the engine and inspect for leaks. Correct fuel leaks immediately.

Inline Filter

1. Disconnect the fuel lines. Use a back-up wrench to hold the fuel filter connector nut stationary while disconnecting the inlet and outlet lines. Remove the O-rings from the fuel line connections. Inspect the O-rings for damage and make replacements as required.

2. Remove the fuel filter from the retainer. Discard the filter.

3. Installation is the reverse of the removal procedure. The filter has an arrow (fuel flow direction) on the side of the case to ensure proper installation. Install the filter in the retainer with the arrow facing away from the fuel tank (toward the front of the engine).

4. Start the engine and inspect for leaks. Correct fuel leaks immediately.

Mechanical Fuel Pump

TESTING

Volume Test

1. Disconnect the fuel line from the carburetor fuel feed line and position it in a suitable graduated container.

2. Start the engine and let it idle for 15 seconds. The fuel pump should supply a half pint or more of fuel, if not proceed as follows.

3. Disconnect the inlet hose at the fuel pump and install a vacuum gauge. Crank or run the engine until maximum vacuum is achieved.

4. If the vacuum is less than 15 in. replace the fuel pump. If the vacuum reading is more than 15 in. proceed as follows.

5. Using a vacuum gauge check the fuel lines and fuel hoses for cracks, splits, leaks or kinks. Crank or run the engine until the vacuum gauge peaks.

6. The vacuum reading should be at least 15 in., if not replace the defective piece of fuel hose or line.

7. If the fuel lines and the fuel pump check out okay, check the fuel tank unit for fuel flow restriction.

Pressure Test

1. Disconnect the fuel line at the carburetor. Install a length of rubber hose about ten in. long and place the end of the hose into a suitable waste

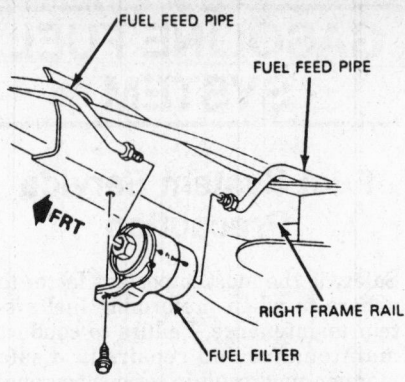

In-line fuel filter assembly (typical)

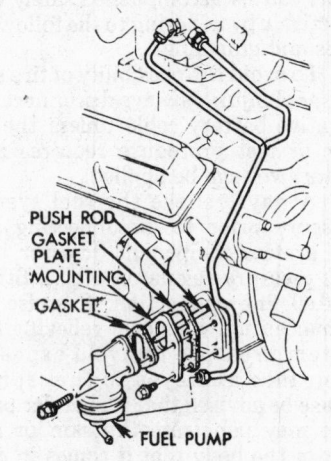

Typical small block V8 fuel pump

container. Attach a low reading pressure gauge (a 9–15 psi range is recommended).

2. Hold the gauge at least 16 in. above the fuel pump. If equipped, pinch the fuel return line.

3. Start the engine and run at slow idle, using the fuel that is left in the carburetor.

4. If the fuel pump is operating properly the pressure on the gauge should read a constant 5.5–6.5 psi.

5. If the pressure is too low, too high or significantly different at various engine speeds the pump should be replaced.

REMOVAL & INSTALLATION

1. Disconnect the negative battery cable.

2. Remove all necessary components in order to gain access to the fuel pump.

3. Remove the inlet and outlet lines from the unit.

4. Remove the fuel pump retaining bolts. Remove the pump from the vehicle.

NOTE: On some engines, if the pushrod is not to be removed, re-

move the upper bolt from the right front mounting boss. Insert a longer bolt ($\frac{3}{8} \times 16 \times 2$ in.) in this hole to hold the fuel pump pushrod.

5. Installation is the reverse of the removal procedure.

Electric Fuel Pump

PRESSURE TESTING

1. Relieve the fuel system pressure.

2. On later engines, remove the air cleaner and plug the the THERMAC vacuum port on the TBI unit.

3. Obtain two 10 in. sections of $\frac{3}{8}$ in. steel tubing. Double flare one end of each section. Install a flare nut on one end of each section.

4. Using tool J-29658-82 or equivalent, connect each of the above sections of tubing into the flare nut to flare nut adapters that are included in the tool kit.

5. Attach the pipe and adapter assemblies to the gauge from the tool kit.

6. Raise and support the vehicle safely.

7. Disconnect the fuel feed hose from the fuel pipe on the body of the vehicle.

8. Install one length of steel tubing onto the feed pipe of the body. Connect the other end of the hose onto one of the sections of the 10 in. steel pipe. Secure all hose connections with clamps.

9. Start the engine and check for leaks. Correct leaks immediately.

10. Observe the pressure reading it should be between 9–13 psi. If not within specification, correct as required.

11. Relieve the fuel system pressure and remove the test equipment.

12. Start the engine and inspect for leaks. Correct all fuel leaks immediately.

REMOVAL & INSTALLATION

The fuel pump is located inside the gas tank and is connected to the sending unit.

1. Relieve the fuel system pressure.

2. Disconnect the negative battery cable. Raise and support the vehicle safely.

3. Remove the fuel tank from the vehicle. Remove the sending unit along with the electric fuel pump.

4. Installation is the reverse order of the removal procedure, be sure to use a new gasket on the fuel sending unit. Excercise care not to fold or twist the strainer during installation of the sending unit. If the strainer is not installed properly, fuel flow will be restricted.

Carburetor

REMOVAL & INSTALLATION

1. Disconnect the negative battery cable. Remove the air cleaner.
2. Disconnect the fuel and vacuum lines. Disconnect the choke electrical connector. Disconnect the throttle linkage.
3. If equipped with an automatic transmission, disconnect the throttle valve linkage.
4. Remove the carburetor attaching nuts or bolts. Remove the assembly from the vehicle. After the carburetor is removed, cover the intake manifold with cloth or tape to prevent the entry of foreign matter.
5. If equipped, remove the electric EFE (Early Fuel Evaporation) heater and the insulator.
6. Installation is the reverse of the removal procedure. Thoroughly clean the gasket mating surfaces and install a new base gasket. Adjust idle speed as required.

OVERHAUL

For all carburetor overhaul and adjustment procedures, please refer to the "Carburetor Service" in the Unit Repair section.

Fuel Injection

Due to the complex nature of modern fuel injection systems, comprehensive diagnosis and testing procedures fall outside the confines of this repair manual. For complete information on fuel injection diagnosis, testing and repair procedures please refer to *Chilton's Guide to Fuel Injection And Feedback Carburetors.*

DIESEL FUEL SYSTEM

Fuel Filter

REPLACEMENT

1. Disconnect the negative battery cable. Relieve the fuel system pressure.
2. Disconnect the inlet and outlet lines from the fuel filter assembly. Plug the lines to prevent dirt from en-

tering the system. If equipped, disconnect the electrical connection.
3. Remove the fuel filter retaining bolts. Remove the fuel filter from the engine.
4. Installation is the reverse of the removal procedure. Start the engine and inspect for leaks. Correct fuel leaks immediately.

Diesel Injection Pump

REMOVAL & INSTALLATION

NOTE: This procedure contains throttle rod and transmission cable adjustments.

1. Disconnect the negative battery cable. Remove the air cleaner.
2. Remove the filters and pipes from the valve covers and air crossover.
3. Remove the air crossover and cap the intake manifold with screened covers or tape.
4. Disconnect the throttle rod and return spring.
5. Remove the bellcrank.
6. Remove the throttle and transmission cables from the intake manifold brackets.
7. Disconnect the fuel lines from the filter and remove the filter.
8. Disconnect the fuel inlet line at the pump.
9. Remove the rear air conditioner compressor brace and remove the fuel line.
10. Disconnect the fuel return line from the injection pump.
11. Remove the clamps and pull the fuel return lines from each injection nozzle.
12. Using two wrenches, disconnect the high pressure lines at the nozzles.
13. Remove the three injection pump retaining nuts with tool J-26987 or equivalent.
14. Remove the pump and cap all lines and nozzles to prevent the entry of grease or dirt.
15. To install, remove the protective caps from all lines and nozzles. Place the engine on TDC for the No. 1 cylinder. The mark on the harmonic balancer on the crankshaft will be aligned with the zero mark on the timing tab, and both valves for No. 1 cylinder will be closed. The index mark on the injection pump driven gear should be offset to the right when No. 1 is at TDC. Check that all of these conditions are met before continuing.
16. Line up the offset tang on the pump driveshaft with the pump driven gear and install the pump.
17. Install, but do not tighten the pump retaining nuts.
18. Connect the high pressure lines at the nozzles.

19. Using two wrenches, torque the high pressure line nuts to 25 ft. lbs.
20. Connect the fuel return lines to the nozzles and pump.
21. Align the timing mark on the injection pump with the line on the timing mark adapter and torque the mounting nuts to specification.

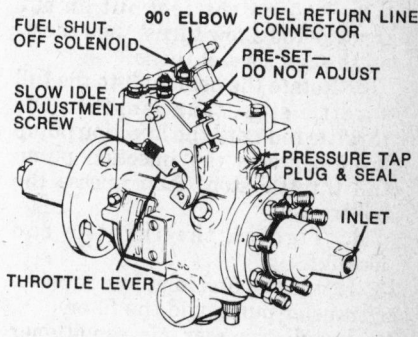

Typical diesel engine injection pump

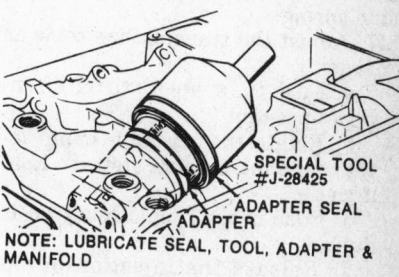

NOTE: LUBRICATE SEAL, TOOL, ADAPTER & MANIFOLD

Installing adapter seal

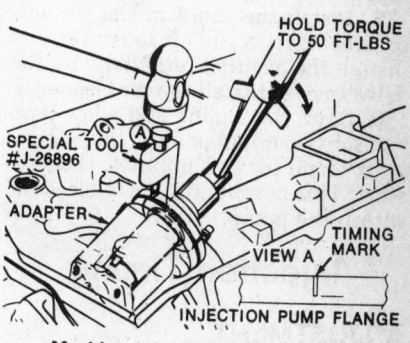

Marking injection pump adapter

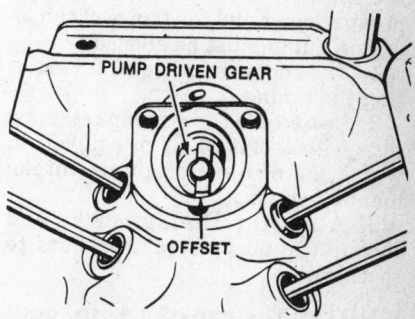

Offset on pump driven gear

NOTE: A ¾ in. open end wrench on the boss at the front of the injection pump will aid in rotating the pump to align the marks.

22. Adjust the throttle rod as follows:

   a. Remove the clip from the cruise control rod and remove the rod from the bellcrank.

   b. Loosen the locknut on the throttle rod a few turns, then shorten the rod several turns.

   c. Rotate the bellcrank to the full throttle stop, then lengthen the throttle rod until the injection pump lever contacts the injection pump full throttle stop, then release the bellcrank.

   d. Tighten the throttle rod locknut.

23. Install the fuel inlet line between the transfer pump and the filter.

24. Install the rear air conditioner compressor brace.

25. Install the bellcrank and clip.

26. Connect the throttle rod and return spring.

27. Adjust the transmission cable as follows:

   a. Push the snaplock to the disengaged position.

   b. Rotate the injection pump lever to the full throttle stop and hold it there.

   c. Push in the snaplock until it is flush.

   d. Release the injection pump lever.

28. Remove the screened covers or tape and install the air crossover.

29. Install the tubes in the air flow control valve in the air crossover and install the ventilation filters in the valve covers. Install the air cleaner.

30. Start the engine and allow it to run for two minutes. Stop the engine, let it stand for two minutes, then restart. This permits the air to bleed off within the pump.

Injection Timing

ADJUSTMENT

For the engine to be properly timed, the lines on the top of the injection pump adapter and the flange of the injection pump must be aligned.

1. The engine must be off for resetting the timing.

2. Loosen the three pump retaining nuts with tool J-26987 or equivalent, which is an injection pump intake manifold wrench.

3. Align the timing marks and torque the pump retaining nuts to specification.

NOTE: The use of a ¾ in. open end wrench on the boss at the

front of the pump will aid in rotating the pump to align the marks.

4. Adjust the throttle rod.

Injection Nozzle

REMOVAL & INSTALLATION

The injection nozzles on these engines are simply unbolted from the cylinder head, after the fuel lines are removed, in similar fashion to a spark plug. Be careful not to damage the nozzle end and make sure the copper nozzle gasket is removed from the cylinder head if it does not come off with the nozzle.

Clean the carbon off the tip of the nozzle with a soft brass wire brush and install the nozzles, with new gaskets.

NOTE: Some engines use CAV Lucas injetors and others use Diesel Equipment injectors. When installing the inlet fittings, torque the Diesel Equipment injector fitting to 45 ft. lbs. and the CAV Lucas to 25 ft. lbs.

MANUAL TRANSMISSION

REMOVAL & INSTALLATION

1. Disconnect the negative battery cable. On the 3 speed floorshift models, remove the shift knob; on the 4 speed floorshift models, remove the spring and the "T" handle.

2. Raise and support the vehicle safely.

3. Disconnect the speedometer cable at the transmission.

4. Remove the driveshaft.

5. Support the rear of the engine and remove the crossmember.

6. Detach the shift rods from the transmission levers.

NOTE: On the floorshift models, disconnect the back drive rod at the bell crank (if equipped).

7. On floorshift models, remove the shift control assembly from the transmission; pull down until the shift lever clears the rubber boot.

8. Remove the upper transmission to clutch housing bolts and replace them with headless guide pins, then remove the lower bolts.

9. Slide the transmission back along the guide pins until the input shaft clears the clutch and remove the transmission.

10. To install, reverse the removal procedures. If the input shaft won't

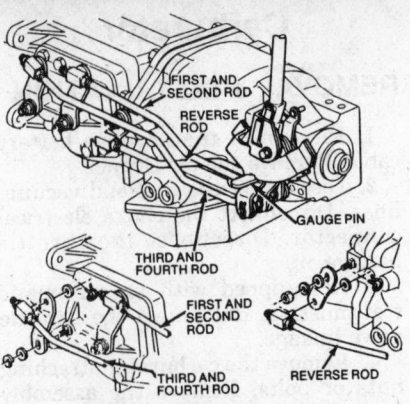

Shift linkage adjustment

engage the clutch splines, put the transmission in gear and turn the output shaft slightly.

SHIFT LINKAGE ADJUSTMENT

Floorshift

1. Turn the ignition switch off.

2. Raise and support the vehicle safely.

3. Loosen the locknuts on the shift rods; the rods should pass freely through the swivels.

4. Set the transmission levers in the Neutral position.

5. Set the floorshift lever in the Neutral position. Install a locating gauge (3.0 × ⅛ in. dia.) into the alignment slot of the control lever bracket assembly.

6. Adjust the length of the shift rods at the swivels and tighten the locknuts, then remove the locating gauge.

7. Shift the control lever into Reverse and lock the ignition switch.

NOTE: If equipped with a back drive rod, pull down slightly on the rod at the steering column, to remove any slack and tighten the locknut. The ignition switch must move freely to the LOCK position and it must not be possible to turn the key to LOCK when in any other position. If the interlock binds, leave the switch in the Lock position and readjust the back drive rod.

8. Check shifting operation and readjust if necessary.

CLUTCH

REMOVAL & INSTALLATION

1. Support the engine and remove the transmission.

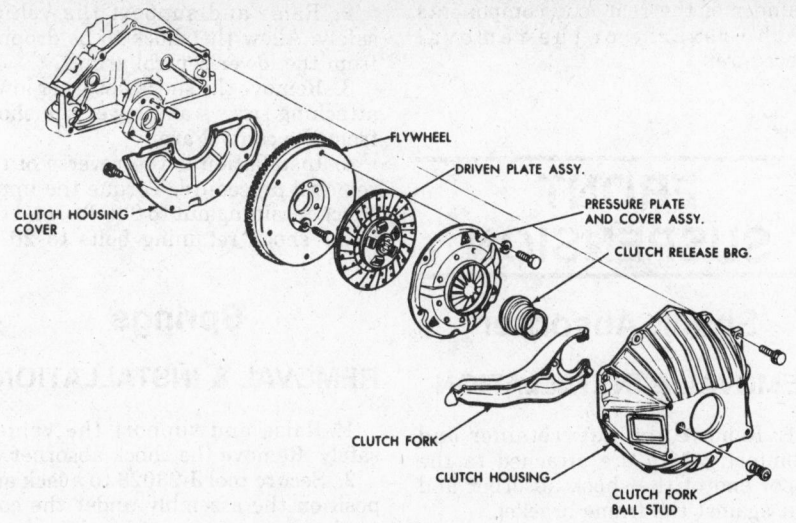

Exploded view of a typical clutch assembly

2. Disconnect the clutch fork pushrod and the spring.

3. Remove the flywheel housing.

4. Slide the clutch fork from the ball stud and remove the fork from the dust boot. The ball stud is threaded into the clutch housing and may be replaced, if necessary.

5. Install a clutch alignment tool J-5824 to support the clutch assembly during removal. Mark the relationship between the flywheel and the clutch cover for reinstallation, if they do not already have X marks.

6. Loosen the clutch to flywheel bolts evenly, one turn at a time, until the spring pressure is released, then remove bolts and the clutch assembly.

7. To install, reverse the removal procedures. Adjust the shift linkage and the clutch pedal freeplay.

FREE PLAY ADJUSTMENT

1. Disconnect the return spring at the clutch operating fork.

2. Rotate the clutch lever until the pedal is firmly against the bumper.

3. Push the outer end of the clutch operating fork to the rear until the release bearing can just be felt to contact the pressure plate fingers.

4. Detach the front end of the operating rod from the clutch pivot shaft arm and place it in the gauge hole on the arm.

5. Loosen the locknut and lengthen the rod just enough to take all the play out of the linkage, then tighten the locknut.

6. Replace the operating rod in its original location.

7. Replace the return spring and check the free play at the pedal pad, it should be about ¾–1¼ in.

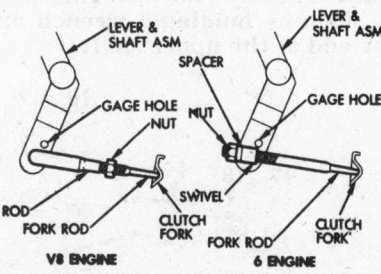

Clutch pedal free-play adjustment

AUTOMATIC TRANSMISSION

For further information on automatic transmissions, please refer to "Automatic Transmissions" in the Unit Repair section.

REMOVAL & INSTALLATION

1. Disconnect the negative battery cable.

2. Disconnect detent cable (if so equipped) from accelerator lever or carburetor.

3. Raise and support the vehicle safely. Drain the transmission fluid and remove the dipstick.

4. Remove the driveshaft. Properly support the engine assembly.

5. Remove the flywheel cover. Remove the bolts that secure the torque converter to the flex plate.

6. Remove the starter, as required. Disconnect the exhaust crossover pipe, if necessary. Disconnect the oil cooler lines at the transmission.

7. Disconnect the speedometer cable from the transmission. Disconnect all electrical and vacuum connections from the transmission assembly. Identify each connection and opening to ensure installation in the original position.

8. Properly support the transmission assembly. Remove the transmission to engine retaining bolts. Remove the transmission mount. Remove the transmission crossmember assembly.

9. Carefully remove the transmission assembly from the vehicle.

10. Installation is the reverse of the removal procedure.

DRIVE AXLE

Driveshaft and U-Joints

REMOVAL & INSTALLATION

1. Raise and support the vehicle safely.

2. Mark the relationship of the driveshaft to the pinion flange.

3. Remove the rear universal joint retainers and separate it from the pinion flange.

NOTE: If the universal joint cups are loose, tape the cups to the universal joint to keep them from falling off the joint.

4. Support the driveshaft and remove it from the transmission. When removing or installing the driveshaft, do not allow the universal joints to bend to extreme angles, this might rupture the internally injected seals.

5. Installation is the reverse of the removal procedure.

Rear Axle Shafts

REMOVAL & INSTALLATION

1. Raise and support the vehicle safely.

2. Remove the wheel and the brake drum assembly.

3. Clean the dirt from around the carrier cover.

4. Remove the carrier cover and drain the lubricant from the housing.

5. Remove the rear axle pinion shaft lock screw and the shaft.

6. Push the flanged end of the axle shaft toward the center of the vehicle and remove the C-lock from the end of the shaft.

7. Pull the axle shaft from the housing. Be careful not to damage the oil seal.

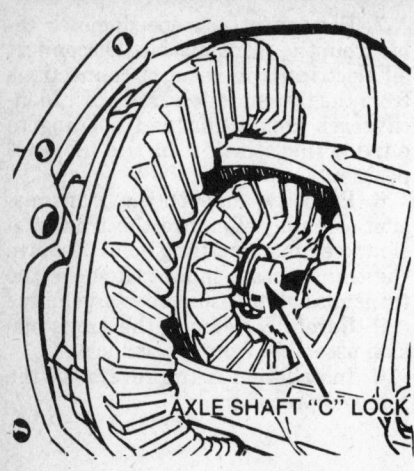

Axle shaft C-clips inside the differential

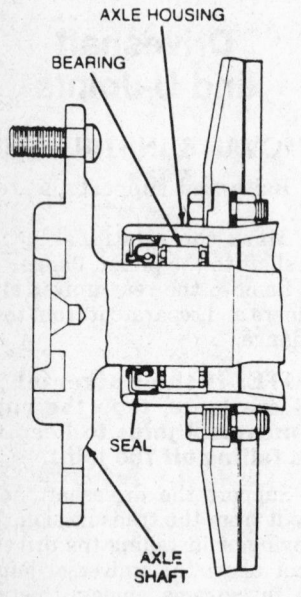

Axle shaft assembly

8. Using a pry bar, pry the oil seal from the axle housing.

9. Install bearing removal tool J-23689 or equivalent (8¾ in. axle) or J-22813 or equivalent (all other axles) to the axle bearing, connect it to a slide hammer and pull the bearing from the housing.

10. To install, lubricate a new bearing and drive it into the housing until it seats using the bearing installation tool J-23690 or equivalent.

11. Lubricate the lips of a new oil seal and drive it into the housing until it is flush with the housing, using the seal installation tool J-21128 or equivalent.

12. To complete the installation, slide the axle shaft into the housing making sure that it engages the splines of the side gear. Install the re-

mainder of the rear axle components in the reverse of the removal procedure.

FRONT SUSPENSION

Shock Absorber

REMOVAL & INSTALLATION

1. Remove the nut, retainer and grommet, which are attached to the upper end of the shock absorber and seat against the frame bracket.

NOTE: It may be necessary to hold the shock absorber upper shaft to remove the nut. This may be done by holding a wrench on the end of the upper shaft.

2. Raise and support the vehicle safely. Allow the shock to be dropped from the lower control arm.

3. Remove the shock absorber lower attaching screws and lower the shock from the control arm.

4. Installation is the reverse of the removal procedure. Torque the upper shock retaining nut to 8 ft. lbs. and the lower shock retaining bolts to 20 ft. lbs.

Springs

REMOVAL & INSTALLATION

1. Raise and support the vehicle safely. Remove the shock absorber.

2. Secure tool J-23028 to a jack and position the assembly under the control arm, supporting the inner bushing.

3. Disconnect stabilizer bar at lower control arm.

4. Raise the jack to take the tension off of the control arm pivots. Install a

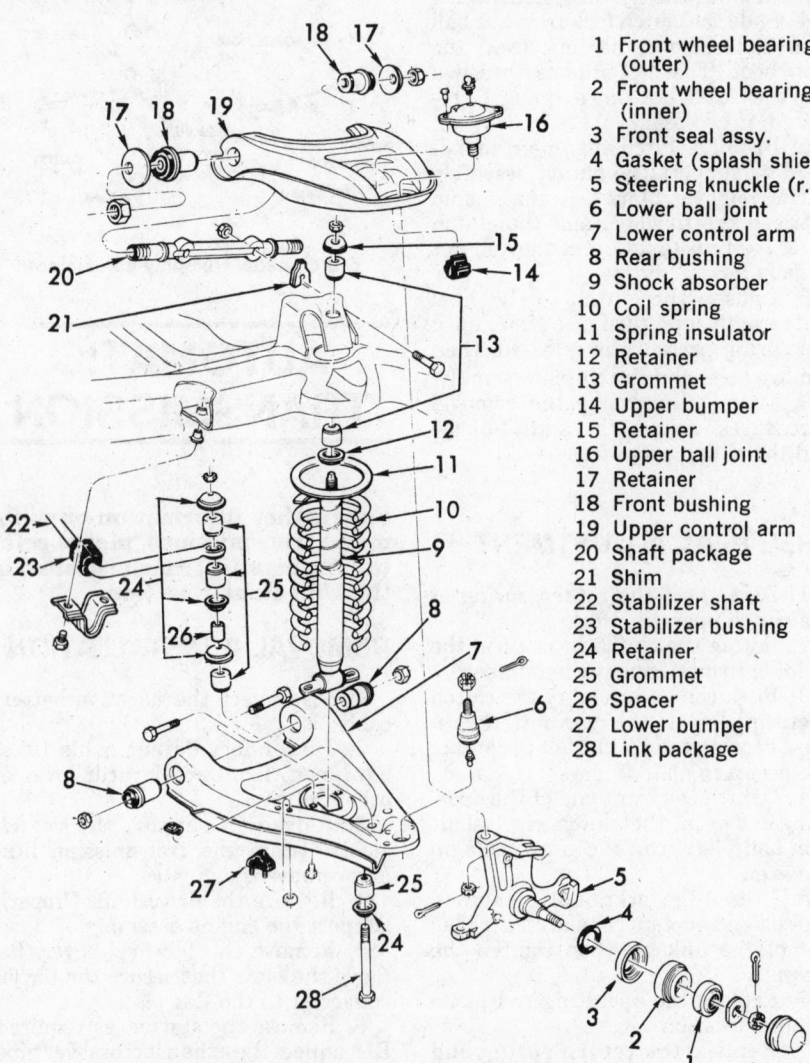

1 Front wheel bearing (outer)
2 Front wheel bearing (inner)
3 Front seal assy.
4 Gasket (splash shield)
5 Steering knuckle (r.h.)
6 Lower ball joint
7 Lower control arm
8 Rear bushing
9 Shock absorber
10 Coil spring
11 Spring insulator
12 Retainer
13 Grommet
14 Upper bumper
15 Retainer
16 Upper ball joint
17 Retainer
18 Front bushing
19 Upper control arm
20 Shaft package
21 Shim
22 Stabilizer shaft
23 Stabilizer bushing
24 Retainer
25 Grommet
26 Spacer
27 Lower bumper
28 Link package

Exploded view of the front suspension assembly

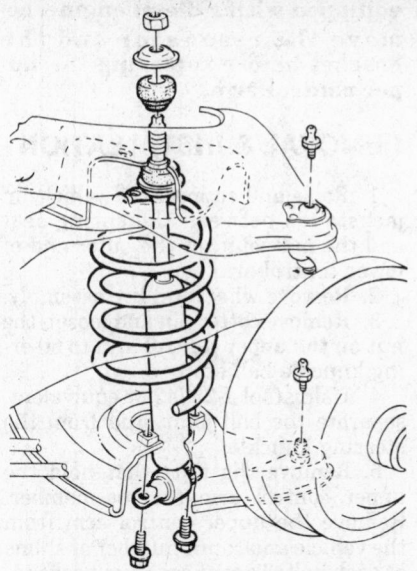

Installing the shock absorbers

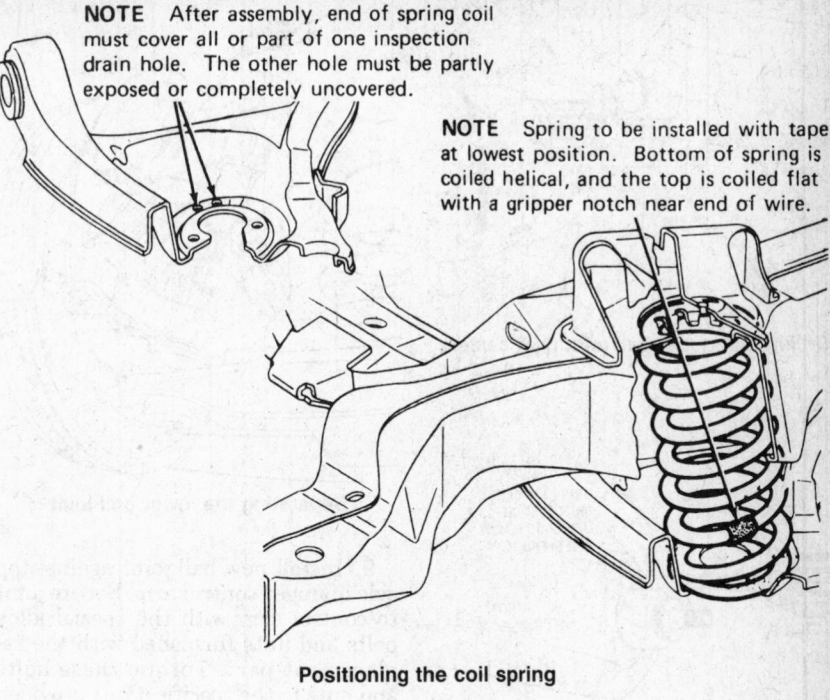

NOTE After assembly, end of spring coil must cover all or part of one inspection drain hole. The other hole must be partly exposed or completely uncovered.

NOTE Spring to be installed with tape at lowest position. Bottom of spring is coiled helical, and the top is coiled flat with a gripper notch near end of wire.

Positioning the coil spring

chain around the spring and through the control arm as a safety measure, then remove the inner control arm to crossmember pivot bolts.

5. Carefully lower the control arm, allowing the spring to relax. Allow the spring to completely expand before attempting to remove it.

NOTE: DO NOT apply force on the lower control arm and ball joint to remove the spring. Proper maneuvering of the spring will allow for easy removal. The spring must be handled carefully as not to cause damage to the corrosion protective coating. Any damage to this protective coating should be repaired prior to reinstallation.

6. Remove the chain and the spring.
7. Installation is the reverse of the removal procedure.

Ball Joints

INSPECTION

NOTE: Before performing this inspection, make sure the wheel bearings are adjusted correctly and that the control arm bushings are in good condition.

1. Raise and support the vehicle on jackstands under the front lower control arm at the spring seat. Raise the vehicle until there is 1–2 in. of clearance under the wheel. This must be done so that the weight of the car will properly load the ball joints. The car should be stable and not allowed to rock on the jackstands.

2. Insert a bar under the wheel and pry upward. If the wheel raises more

than ⅛ in., the ball joints are worn. While prying on the wheel, determine by visual inspection whether the upper or lower ball joint is worn. Visually inspect the ball joint(s) for cuts and tears. If cuts and tears are apparent, the ball joint(s) MUST be replaced.

3. Some vehicles are equipped with a lower ball joint wear indicator. Wear is indicated by the position of the ½ in. nipple into which the grease fitting is threaded. Remove all grease and dirt from the grease fitting surface. Scrape the fitting surface with your finger nail or 6 in. machinists rule. On a new joint, the nipple should project 0.050 in. beyond the ball joint cover surface. If the nipple is flush or inside the cover surface, replace the ball joint.

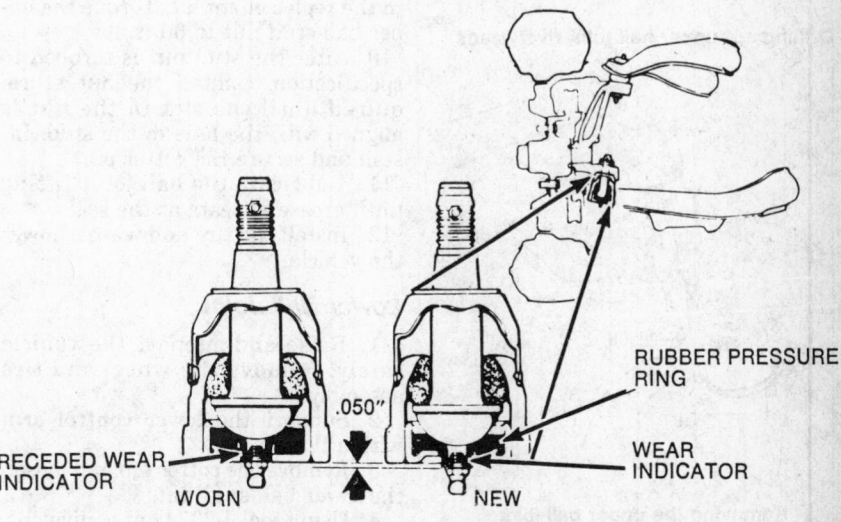

Wear indicator arrangement used on the lower ball joint

REMOVAL & INSTALLATION

Upper Ball Joint

1. Raise the front of the car and support the lower control arm with floor stands. Position the stands between the spring seats and ball joints of the lower control arm.

NOTE: The stands must remain under the control arm spring seat during removal and installation to maintain the spring and control arm in position. The weight of the car is used to relieve the spring tension on the lower control arm.

2. Remove the tire and wheel.

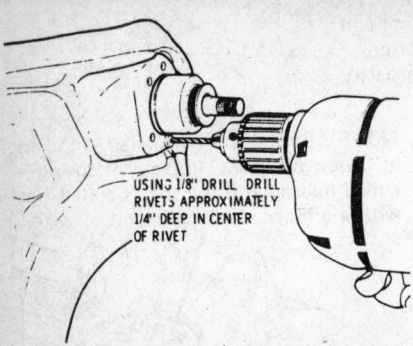

Drilling out upper ball joint rivet centers

USING 1/8" DRILL DRILL RIVETS APPROXIMATELY 1/4" DEEP IN CENTER OF RIVET

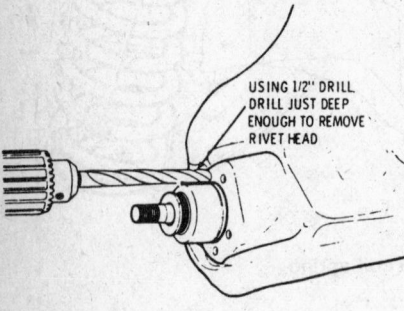

USING 1/2" DRILL DRILL JUST DEEP ENOUGH TO REMOVE RIVET HEAD

Drilling out upper ball joint rivet heads

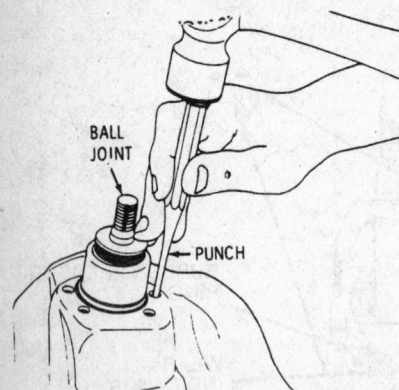

BALL JOINT

PUNCH

Removing the upper ball joint

3. Remove the cotter pin and upper ball stud nut.

4. With tool J23742 or equivalent, apply pressure on the ball joint stud nut until the stud breaks loose. Remove the tool and pull the stud free from the steering knuckle. With the stud removed, support the weight of the steering knuckle to prevent damage to the brake hose.

5. With the control arm raised, drill ¼ in. deep into the rivets using an ⅛ in. drill bit.

6. Using a ½ in. drill bit, drill off the heads of the rivets.

7. Using a center punch, punch the center of the 4 rivets.

8. Using a drift punch, drive out the remaining parts of the rivets. Remove the ball joint.

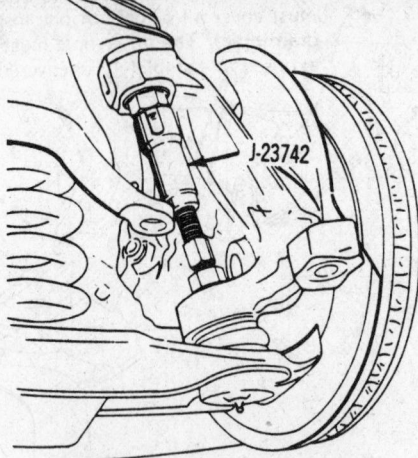

J-23742

Separating the lower ball joint

9. Install new ball joint against top side of upper control arm. Secure joint to control arm with the special alloy bolts and nuts furnished with the replacement part. Torque these bolts and nuts to the specifications provided in the replacement kit. Torque the upper ball stud nut to 60 ft. lbs.

10. After the stud nut is torqued to specification, tighten the nut as required until the slot in the nut is aligned with the hole in the stud. Install and secure the cotter pin.

11. Lubricate the ball joint fitting until grease appears at the seal.

12. Install the tire and wheel. Lower the vehicle.

Lower Ball Joint

1. Raise and support the vehicle safely. Remove the wheel and tire assembly.

2. Support the lower control arm with a floor jack.

3. Remove the cotter pin and loosen the lower ball stud nut.

4. Using tool J-23742 or equivalent, break the ball stud loose from the steering knuckle. Separate the lower control arm from the steering knuckle.

5. Using the ball joint removal tool J-9519-10 equivalent and adapter tools J-9519-16 and J-9519-22 or equivalents, press the ball stud from the lower control arm.

6. Install the new ball joint to the lower control arm. Using the installation tool J-9519-10 or equivalent and adapter tool J9519-9 or equivalent, press the ball joint into the lower control arm until it bottoms on the arm.

7. When installing the new ball joint, position the purge vent in the rubber boot facing inward.

Upper Control Arms

NOTE: If the vehicle is

equipped with a diesel engine, remove the resonator and the bracket before removing the upper control arm.

REMOVAL & INSTALLATION

1. Raise and support the vehicle on jackstands between the spring seat and the ball joint, at the outer end of lower control arm.

2. Remove wheel and tire assembly.

3. Remove cotter pin and loosen the nut on the upper control arm to steering knuckle ball stud.

4. Using tool J-23742 or equivalent, separate the ball joint stud from the steering knuckle.

5. Remove the nuts that hold the upper control arm to crossmember. Remove the upper control arm from the vehicle and count number of shims at each bolt. Tape these shim packs together and identify them with their respective bolts. These shims must be installed in their original positions.

6. Installation is the reverse of the removal procedure.

Lower Control Arms

REMOVAL & INSTALLATION

1. Loosen the wheel nuts. Raise the vehicle and support it safely.

2. Remove the wheel and tire.

3. Remove the coil spring assembly.

4. Remove the lower ball joint from the steering knuckle.

5. Remove the control arm through the splash shield opening with a putty knife or a similiar tool.

6. Installation is the reverse of the removal procedure.

Front Wheel Bearings

ADJUSTMENT

1. Raise and support the vehicle safely.

2. Remove the dust cap from the hub.

3. Remove the cotter pin and discard it.

4. Snug up the spindle nut while spinning the wheel to seat the bearings (12 ft. lbs.). Then back off the nut ¼–½ turn.

5. Retighten the nut by hand until it is finger tight.

6. Loosen the nut until the nearest hole in the spindle lines up with a slot in the spindle nut, then insert a new cotter pin. When the bearing is properly adjusted, there will be 0.001–0.005 in. end play.

7. Replace the dust cover and lower the vehicle.

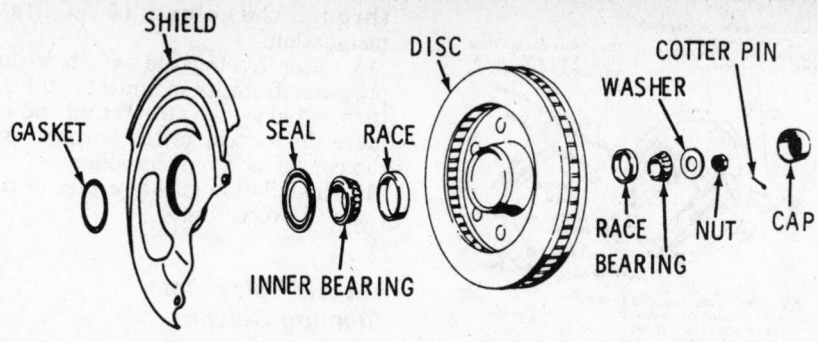

Hub and bearing assembly

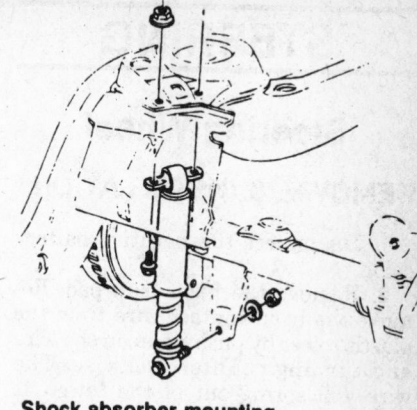

Shock absorber mounting

REMOVAL & INSTALLATION

1. Raise the vehicle and support if safely.
2. Remove the dust cap from the hub. Remove the cotter pin and discard it. Remove the locknut.
3. Remove the outer wheel bearing from its mounting.
4. Remove the rotor. Remove the inner wheel bearing from its mounting.
5. Installation is the reverse of the removal procedure. Adjust the wheel bearings.

Front Wheel Alignment

CASTER

Caster is the tilting of the steering axis either forward or backward from the vertical, when viewed from the side of the vehicle. A backward tilt is said to be positive and a forward tilt is said to be negative.

CAMBER

Camber is the tilting of the wheels from the vertical when viewed from the front of the vehicle. When the wheels tilt outward from the top, the camber is said to be positive. When the wheels tilt inward from the top the camber is said to be negative. The amount of tilt is measured in degrees from the vertical. This measurement is called camber angle.

TOE-IN

Toe-in is the turning in of the wheels. The actual amount of toe in is normally only a fraction of an in.. The purpose of toe in specification is to ensure parallel rolling of the wheels. Toe-in also serves to offset the small deflections of the steering support system which occur when the vehicle is rolling forward.

REAR SUSPENSION

Shock Absorbers

REMOVAL & INSTALLATION

1. Raise and support the vehicle safely. Position a suitable jack under the axle housing.
2. If equipped with super lift shock absorbers, disconnect the air line snap on connector at the shock absorber.
3. On some vehicles, it may be necessary to remove the wheel and tire assembly.
4. Hold the stud stationary and remove the lower end of the shock absorber from its mounting.
5. Remove the bolts, nuts and lock washers from the upper end of the shock absorber.
6. Remove the shock absorber from the vehicle.
7. Installation is the reverse of the removal procedure.

Springs

REMOVAL & INSTALLATION

1. Raise and support the vehicle safely.
2. Remove the clip that attaches the brake hose to the mounting bracket on the frame crossmember.
3. Support the rear axle using a suitable jack.
4. Disconnect the upper control arms from the axle housing.
5. If equipped with a stabilizer bar, remove the bar from the control arms.
6. Remove the brake hose support bolt. Support the brake hose to allow for additional axle drop.
7. Remove the nut and the lock washer from the shock absorber, then disconnect the shock from the axle.

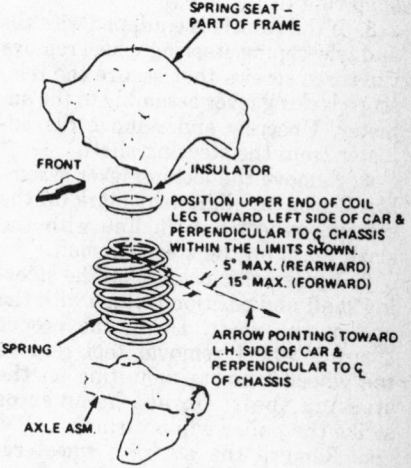

Coil spring positioning

8. Carefully lower the jack until the spring is free, then remove the spring.

NOTE: When removing the spring, mark its position so that it may be installed in the same position.

9. Installation is the reverse of the removal procedure.

Rear Control Arms

REMOVAL & INSTALLATION

NOTE: Remove and install only one lower control arm at a time. If both arms are removed at the same time, the axle could roll or slip sideways, making installation of the arms very difficult.

1. Raise and support the rear of the vehicle on jackstands under the rear axle.
2. If equipped, remove the stabilizer bar.
3. Remove the control arm attaching fasteners. Remove the control arm.
4. Installation is the reverse of the removal procedure.

STEERING

Steering Wheel

REMOVAL & INSTALLATION

1. Disconnect the negative battery cable.

2. Remove the horn trim pad. Remove the horn contact wire from the plastic tower by pushing in on the wire and turning counterclockwise. The wire will spring out of the tower. It may be necessary to turn the ignition to the on position in order to facilitate removal. Separate and remove the snap ring (if installed).

3. If the vehicle is equipped with tilt and telescoping steering wheel remove the three screws that secure the telescope locking lever assembly to the adjuster. Unscrew and remove the adjuster from the steering shaft.

4. Remove the locking lever assembly. Scribe an alignment mark on the steering wheel hub in line with the slash mark on the steering shaft.

5. Loosen the locknut on the steering shaft and position it flush with the end of the shaft. Using the proper steering wheel removal tool remove the wheel from its mounting on the steering shaft. Do not hammer or strike the puller while turning.

6. Remove the steering wheel removal tool from the steering wheel. Remove the locknut from the steering shaft. Remove the steering wheel from the vehicle.

7. Installation is the reverse of the removal procedure. When installing the steering wheel it should not be driven on the steering shaft as damage to the steering column and its components could occur.

Turn Signal Switch

REMOVAL & INSTALLATION

Standard Steering Column

1. Disconnect the negative battery cable.

2. Remove the steering wheel.

3. Insert a suitable tool into the lockplate and remove the lockplate cover assembly.

4. Install a spring compressor onto the steering shaft. Tighten the tool to compress the lockplate and the spring. Remove the snapring from the groove in the shaft.

5. Remove the lockplate and slide the turn signal cam and the upper bearing preload spring and the thrust washer off the upper steering shaft.

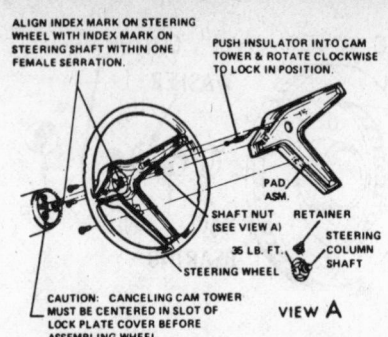

Typical steering wheel and related components

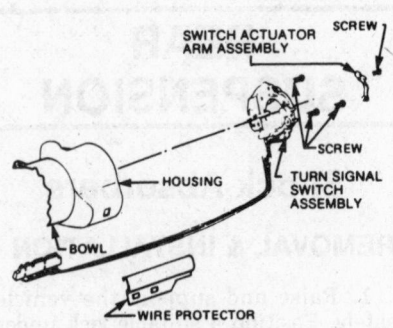

Turn signal switch assembly

6. Remove the steering column lower cover.

7. Remove the turn signal lever from the column.

8. On vehicles equipped with cruise control disconnect the cruise control wire from the harness near the bottom of the column. Remove the harness protector from the cruise control wire. Remove the turn signal lever. Do not remove the wire from the column.

9. Remove the vertical bolts at the steering column upper support. Remove the shim packs. Keep the shims in order for reinstallation.

10. Remove the screws securing the column upper mounting bracket to the column. Remove the bracket.

11. Disconnect the turn signal wiring and remove the wires from the plastic protector.

12. Remove the turn signal switch mounting screws.

13. Slide the switch connector out of the bracket on the steering column.

14. If the switch is known to be bad, cut the wires and discard the switch. Tape the connector of the new switch to the old wires, and pull the new harness down through the steering column while removing the old wires.

15. If the original switch is to be reused, wrap tape around the wire and connector and pull the harness up through the column. It may be helpful to attach a length of wire to the harness connector before pulling it up

through the column to facilitate installation.

16. After freeing the switch wiring protector from its mounting, pull the turn signal switch straight up and remove the switch, switch harness, and the connector from the column.

17. Installation is the reverse of the removal procedure.

Tilt and Telescopic Steering Column

1. Disconnect the battery and remove the steering wheel.

2. Remove the rubber sleeve bumper from the steering shaft.

3. Remove the plastic retainer and disengage the tabs on the retainer from the C-ring.

4. Compress the upper steering shaft preload spring with a spring compressor and remove the C-ring. When installing the spring compressor, pull the upper shaft up about 1 in. and turn the ignition to the lock position to hold the shaft in place.

5. Remove the spring compressor and remove the upper steering shaft lock plate, horn contact carrier and the preload spring.

6. Remove the steering column lower cover. Unscrew and remove the turn signal lever.

7. If equipped with cruise control disconnect the cruise control wire from the harness near the bottom of the steering column. Slide the protector off the cruise control wire. Remove the lever attaching screw and carefully pull the lever out enough to allow the removal of the turn signal switch.

8. Remove the nuts and shim packs from the upper column support. Keep the shims together as a unit for reinstallation.

9. Remove the bracket from the steering column by removing the two attaching screws from each side.

10. Disconnect the turn signal wiring harness and remove the wires from the plastic protector.

11. Remove the turn signal switch retaining screws and pull the switch up out of the steering column.

12. If the switch is to be replaced, cut the wires from the switch and tape the new switch connector to the old wires. Carefully pull the new harness down through the column as the old wires are removed.

13. If the old switch is to be reused, tape the connector to the wires and carefully pull the harness up out of the column.

14. Feed the wiring harness down through the steering column to replace the old switch.

15. Secure the switch in the steering column.

16. Install the upper shaft preload spring.

17. Install the lock plate and carrier assembly. Make sure that the flat on the lower end of the steering shaft is pointing up and that the small plastic tab on the carrier is up or nearest the top of the column. The flat surface of the lock plate must be installed facing down against the turn signal switch.

18. Install the spring compressor, compress the preload spring and lock plate and install the C-ring with the wide side toward the keyway.

19. Remove the spring compressor and install the plastic retainer on the C-ring.

20. Install the rubber sleeve bumper over the steering shaft and install the steering wheel.

21. Install the turn signal lever. If the vehicle is equipped with cruise control, secure the lever to the switch with the retaining screw and install the wiring harness.

22. Remove the tape from the end of the harness and connect the switch and cruise control, if so equipped, to the wire harness.

23. Cover both harnesses with the plastic protector and position it to the column. The turn signal connector slides on the tabs of the column.

24. Position the steering column upper bracket over the turn signal switch harness plastic protector.

25. Install the mounting bracket nuts and shims in their original positions.

26. Install the steering column lower cover.

Ignition Lock

REMOVAL & INSTALLATION

Standard Steering Column

1. Disconnect the negative battery cable. Remove the steering wheel.

2. Remove the lockplate cover assembly.

3. After compressing the lockplate spring, remove the snapring from the groove in the shaft.

4. Remove the lockplate and slide the turn signal cam and the upper bearing preload spring off the upper steering shaft.

5. Remove the thrust washer from the shaft.

6. Remove the hazard warning switch knob from the column along with the turn signal lever.

7. If the vehicle is equipped with cruise control attach a piece of wire to the connector on the cruise control switch harness. Gently pull the harness up and out of the column.

8. Remove the turn signal switch mounting screws.

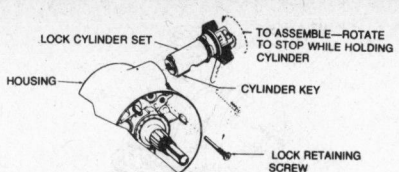

Removing ignition lock cylinder

9. Slide the switch connector out of the bracket on the steering column.

10. As required free the turn signal switch wiring protector from its mounting after disconnecting the turn signal switch electrical connectors, then pull the turn signal switch straight up and out of the steering column along with the switch harness and the connector from the steering column.

11. Turn the ignition switch to the on or run position and remove the key warning buzzer. Insert a small drift pin into the slot next to the switch mounting screw boss. Push the lock cylinder tab and remove the lock cylinder.

12. Installation is the reverse of the removal procedure.

Tilt and Telescoping Steering Wheel

1. Disconnect the negative battery cable. Remove the steering wheel.

2. Remove the rubber sleeve bumper from the steering shaft.

3. Using an appropriate tool, remove the plastic retainer.

4. Using a spring compressor, compress the upper steering shaft spring and remove the C-ring. Release the steering shaft lockplate, the horn contact carrier, and the upper steering shaft preload spring.

5. Remove the four screws which hold the upper mounting bracket and then remove the bracket.

6. Slide the harness connector out of the bracket on the steering column. Tape the upper part of the harness and connector.

7. Disconnect the hazard button and position the shift bowl in park. Remove the turn signal lever from the column.

8. If the vehicle is equipped with cruise control remove the harness protector from the harness. Attach a piece of wire to the switch harness connector. Before removing the turn signal lever, loop a piece of wire and insert it into the turn signal lever opening. Use the wire to pull the cruise control harness out through the opening. Pull the rest of the harness up through and out of the column. Remove the guide wire from the connector and secure the wire to the column. Remove the turn signal lever.

9. Pull the turn signal switch up until the end connector is within the shift bowl. Remove the hazard flasher lever. Allow the switch to hang.

10. Place the ignition key in the run position and remove the key warning buzzer.

11. Depress the center of the lock cylinder retaining tab with a suitable tool and then remove the lock cylinder.

12. Installation is the reverse of the removal procedure.

Ignition Switch

REMOVAL & INSTALLATION

1. Disconnect the negative battery terminal.

2. Loosen the toe pan screws on the steering column.

3. Remove the column to instrument panel trim plates and attaching nuts.

4. Lower the steering column. Be sure that the steering column is supported at all times in order to prevent damage to the column. Disconnect the switch wire connectors.

5. Remove the switch attaching screws and remove the switch.

6. To replace, move the key lock to the LOCK position.

7. Move the actuator rod hole in the switch to the LOCK position.

8. Install the switch with the rod in the hole.

9. Position and reinstall the steering column in the reverse of the removal procedure.

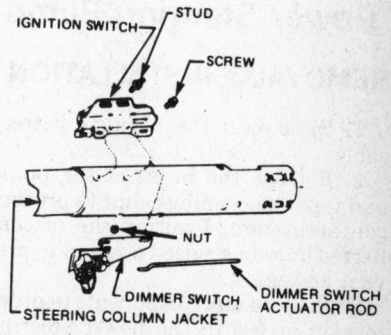

Removing ignition and dimmer switch assembly

Manual Steering Gear

REMOVAL & INSTALLATION

1. Disconnect the negative battery cable.

2. Remove coupling shield from the steering box.

3. Remove the steering coupling to steering shaft flange retaining nuts, bolts and lock washers.

4. Raise and support the vehicle

safely. Remove the pitman arm nut and washer from the pitman shaft, then mark the relationship of the arm to the shaft.

5. Using tool J-6632 or equivalent, remove the pitman arm from the steering gear.

6. Remove the steering gear to frame bolts. remove the steering gear from vehicle.

7. Installation is the reverse of the removal procedure.

Power Steering Gear

REMOVAL & INSTALLATION

1. Disconnect the negative battery cable.

2. Disconnect and plug the pressure and return hoses from the steering gear housing.

3. Remove coupling shield from the steering box. Remove the steering coupling to steering shaft flange retaining nuts, bolts and lock washers.

4. Raise and support the vehicle safely. Remove the pitman arm nut and washer from the pitman shaft, then mark the relationship of the arm to the shaft.

5. Using tool J-6632 or equivalent, remove the pitman arm from the steering gear.

6. Remove the steering gear to frame bolts. remove the steering gear from vehicle.

7. Installation is the reverse of the removal procedure.

Power Steering Pump

REMOVAL & INSTALLATION

1. Disconnect the negative battery cable.

2. Remove the hoses at the pump and tape the openings shut to prevent contamination. Position the disconnected lines in a raised position to prevent leakage.

3. Remove any components in order to gain access to the power steering pump retaining bolts. Remove the pump drive belt.

4. Loosen the retaining bolts and any braces. Remove the pump.

5. Installation is the reverse of the removal procedure.

BELT ADJUSTMENT

1. Disconnect the negative battery cable.

2. Loosen the power steering pump mounting bolts.

3. Adjust the belt tension as required by either raising or lowering the pump bracket with a suitable pry

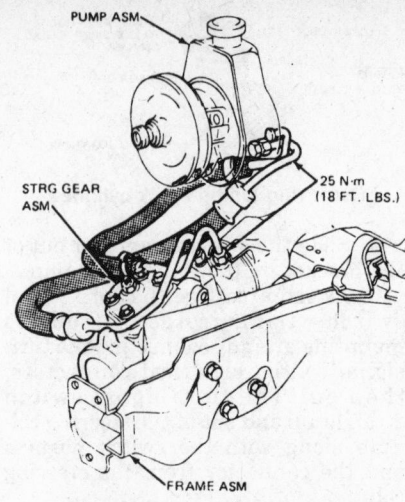

Power steering system (typical)

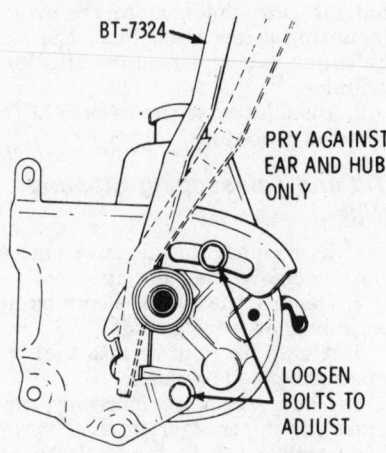

Adjusting the power steering belt

bar. Do not pry against the pump reservoir as damage to the pump may result.

4. Tighten the power steering pump retaining bolts.

5. Check the adjustment using tool J-23600-B or equivalent. A new belt should be adjusted too 170 lb. max. and a used belt should be adjusted too 90 lb. max.

SYSTEM BLEEDING

1. Raise and support the front of the vehicle safely.

2. With the wheels turned all the way to the left add power steering fluid to the "cold" mark on the dipstick.

3. Start the engine. Check the fluid level. Add fluid as necessary to bring the level to the "cold" mark on the dipstick.

4. Bleed the system by turning the steering wheel from side to side without hitting the stops.

5. Be sure to maintain the fluid level at the "hot/cold" mark on the dipstick. Fluid with air in it will have a light tan appearance. This air must be expelled from the system before normal steering action can be obtained.

6. Return the wheels to the center position. Allow the engine to run for about two minutes and then shut it off.

7. Road test the vehicle and make sure that the steering performs properly and there is no noise from the power steering pump. Correct problems as required.

8. Recheck the power steering level. Be sure that the fluid level is at the "hot" mark on the dipstick after the system has stabilized at its normal operating temperature.

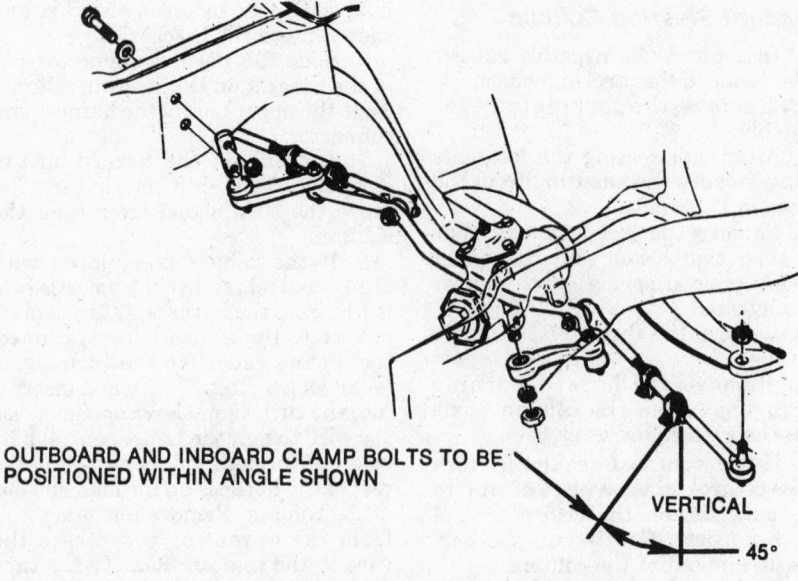

OUTBOARD AND INBOARD CLAMP BOLTS TO BE POSITIONED WITHIN ANGLE SHOWN

Typical steering linkage and related components

Tie Rod End

REMOVAL & INSTALLATION

1. Raise and support the vehicle safely.

2. Loosen the tie rod adjuster sleeve clamp nut.

3. Remove the tie rod cotter pin and nut from the ball joint stud. If the torque required to remove the nuts and bolts exceeds 7 ft. lbs., it's best to discard them and use new fasteners of equal grade quality.

4. Using tool J-6627, BT-7101 or equivalents, remove the tie rod stud from the steering knuckle. The outer tie rods have right hand threads and the inner tie rods have left hand threads.

5. Unscrew the tie rod from the adjuster sleeve. Count the number of turns the tie rod must be rotated to remove it from the adjusting sleeve; this will allow a reasonably accurate re-alignment upon reassembly.

6. To install, reverse the removal procedures. Clean all rust and dirt from the threads. Torque the tie rod to steering knuckle to 30 ft. lbs., the tie rod to intermediate rod nut to 40 ft. lbs. and the tie rod clamp nuts to 15 ft. lbs. Check and/or adjust the alignment, if necessary.

BRAKES

For all brake system repair and service procedures not detailed below, please refer to "Brakes" in the Unit Repair section.

Master Cylinder

REMOVAL & INSTALLATION

1. Disconnect the negative battery cable. Disconnect hydraulic lines at master cylinder. Cover or plug the line openings to prevent fluid loss and contamination.

2. Remove the retaining nuts and lockwashers that hold the cylinder to the brake booster.

3. Remove the master cylinder, gasket and rubber boot.

4. Installation is the reverse of the removal procedure. Fill the reservoir to the proper level with clean new brake fluid, and bleed the system.

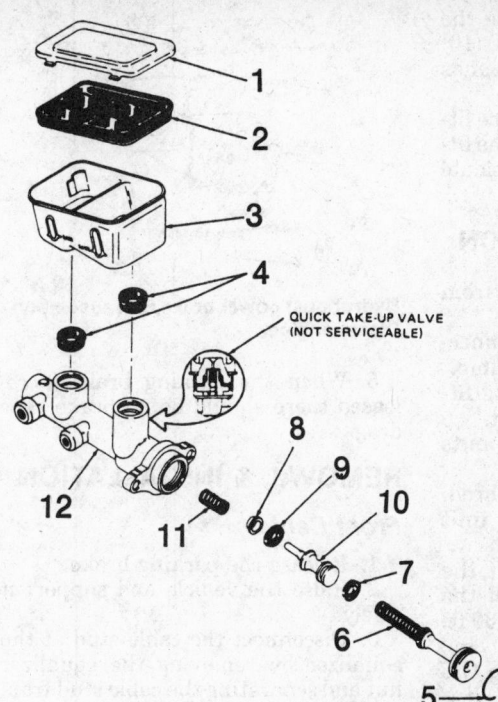

QUICK TAKE-UP VALVE
(NOT SERVICEABLE)

1. Reservoir cover
2. Reservoir diaphragm
3. Reservoir
4. Reservoir grommet
5. Lock ring
6. Primary piston assembly
7. Secondary seal
8. Spring retainer
9. Primary seal
10. Secondary piston
11. Spring
12. Cylinder body

Composite master cylinder assembly

Proportioning Valve

REMOVAL & INSTALLATION

The valve is non serviceable and is located on the frame extension on the left side of the vehicle.

1. Disconnect the electrical harness from the pressure differential switch (if installed).

2. Disconnect the brake lines at the valve. Cover or plug the line openings to prevent fluid loss and contamination.

3. Unbolt and remove the valve from the mounting bracket.

4. Installation is the reverse of the removal procedure. Fill the reservoir to the proper level with clean new brake fluid and bleed the brakes.

Power Brake Booster

REMOVAL & INSTALLATION
Gasoline Engine

1. Disconnect the negative battery cable. Remove the master cylinder retaining nuts and position the assembly out of the way.

2. Disconnect vacuum line from vacuum check valve on unit.

3. Remove steering column lower cover.

4. Remove cotter pin, washer and spring spacer that secures power unit pushrod to brake pedal arm.

5. Remove the nuts that secure the power unit to the firewall. Remove the power unit.

6. Installation is the reverse of the removal procedure.

Diesel Engine

1. Disconnect the negative battery cable. With the engine off, pump the brake pedal four or five times to empty the accumulator of pressurized fluid.

2. Disconnect the brake lines from the master cylinder and cap the lines.

3. Remove and plug the three hydraulic lines from the booster. Remove the washer and retainer that secures the booster pedal rod to the brake pedal arm.

NOTE: To avoid booster damage, do not pry the pedal rod off the pedal arm.

4. Remove the four nuts holding the booster to the firewall.

5. Loosen the booster from the firewall and move the booster pedal rod inboard until it disconnects from the brake pedal arm. Remove the spring washer from the brake pedal arm and remove the booster.

6. Installation is the reverse of the removal procedure.

Power Master Power Brake Unit

DEPRESSURING THE POWERMASTER SYSTEM

1. With the ignition switch in the

OFF position, apply and release the brake pedal a minimum of ten (10) times, using approximately 50 pounds of force on the brake pedal.

2. When loosening hoses or pipe fittings, wrap shop towels close to the fittings to prevent spraying of residual pressurized fluid.

REMOVAL & INSTALLATION

1. Disconnect the power lead from the pressure switch.
2. Disconnect the electrical connector from the electro-hydraulic pump.
3. Disconnect the brake tubing fittings from the Powermaster unit.
4. Remove the two retaining nuts for the unit to dash panel.
5. Remove the brake pedal pushrod.
6. Remove the Powermaster unit from the vehicle.
7. Install the Powermaster unit, the brake pedal pushrod and install the two retaining nuts. Torque 22 to 30 ft. lbs.
8. Install the brake pipes to the unit.
9. Install the electrical connections to the unit.

Wheel Cylinder

REMOVAL & INSTALLATION

1. Raise and support the vehicle safely. Remove the tire and wheel.
2. Remove the brake drum. Remove the brake shoes.
3. Thoroughly clean the area around the wheel cylinder assembly. Disconnect the inlet line from the wheel cylinder assembly. Plug or cover the opening to prevent the loss of fluid or contamination.
4. Remove the wheel cylinder links and retaining bolts. Remove the wheel cylinder from the vehicle.
5. Installation is the reverse of the removal procedure. Be sure to bleed the system.

Parking Brake Cable

ADJUSTMENT

1. Be sure that the rear brakes are properly adjusted before adjusting the parking brake. Check the parking brake linkage for the free movement of all the cables. Lubricate, if necessary.
2. Depress the parking brake pedal 1½ in.
3. Raise and support the vehicle safely.
4. Holding the cable stud to keep it from turning, tighten the equalizer nut until a light drag is felt on either wheel when they are spun in the forward direction.

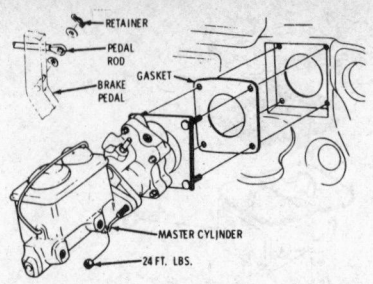

Hydroboost power brake unit assembly—Diesel engine

5. When the parking brake is released there should be no brake shoe drag.

REMOVAL & INSTALLATION

Front Cable

1. Release the parking brake.
2. Raise the vehicle and support it safely.
3. Disconnect the cable stud at the equalizer by removing the equalizer nut and separating the cable stud from the equalizer.
4. Remove the front cable from the cable connector.
5. Loosen the adjuster nut and disconnect the front cable from the connector. Compress the retainer fingers and loosen the assembly at the frame. Lower the vehicle.
6. Remove the cable at the pedal assembly.
7. Remove the cable end from the parking brake assembly clevis.
8. Pull the cable through the hole in the frame and remove it from the vehicle.
9. Installation is the reverse of the removal procedure.

Rear Cable

1. Release the parking brake.
2. Raise and support the vehicle safely.
3. Remove the rear wheel and drum on same side of the vehicle as the parking brake cable being replaced. If the right side cable is being removed, the primary shoe return spring and parking brake strut must also be removed.
4. Remove the equalizer nut and retainer. Separate the equalizer from the right rear cable stud.
5. Remove the end of the left rear cable from the cable connector and equalizer.
6. Remove the clip securing the right rear cable to control arm bracket. Remove the cable from the bracket by pulling it rearward.
7. Remove the cable from the brake backing plate. Removal can be assisted by compressing the multiple prong retainer.

8. Remove the pawl spring and the pawl lever from the actuating lever. Remove the cable end from the operating lever and remove the cable from backing plate.
9. Installation is the reverse of the removal procedure.

CHASSIS ELECTRICAL

Heater Blower

REMOVAL & INSTALLATION

1. Disconnect the negative battery cable.
2. Disconnect the electrical connections from the blower motor.
3. Remove the blower motor flange screws. Remove the blower motor assembly from the heater case.
4. Installation is the reverse of removal.

Heater Core

REMOVAL & INSTALLATION

1. Disconnect the battery negative cable. Drain the cooling system.
2. Disconnect heater hoses.
3. Remove retaining bracket and ground strap.
4. Pull off module rubber seal. Remove screws from module leaf screen and remove screen.
5. Remove right hand windshield wiper arm.
6. Remove diagnostic connector, high blower relay and thermostatic switch mounting screws.
7. Disconnect all electrical connections at the module top.
8. Remove heater core.
9. Reverse procedure for installation. Reseal with strip type caulking.

Radio

REMOVAL & INSTALLATION

1. Disconnect the negative battery cable. If installed, remove the glove box and disconnect the temperature cable at the temperature door.
2. Pull the control knobs off of the radio (as required).
3. Remove the mounting screws and the trim plate. If A/C and radio/heater control panel are installed as a unit, loosen the fasteners connecting the control panel to the dash. Withdraw the assembly from the dash.

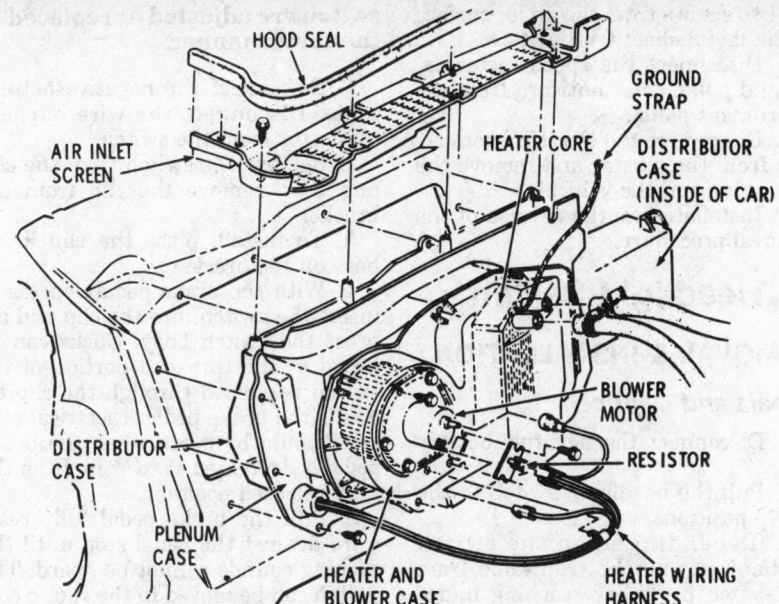

Heater module mounting—Impala and Caprice

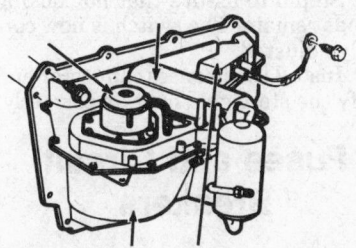

Heater module mounting—Monte Carlo and Malibu

4. Remove the receiver bracket to instrument panel screws and bottom nut.

5. Detach the electrical wiring and the antenna from the rear of the receiver. Disconnect all vacuum connections as required.

6. Remove the radio and the mounting bracket.

7. Installation is the reverse of the removal procedure. To prevent damage to the radio, always connect the speaker wiring harness before applying power to the radio.

Windshield Wiper Switch

REMOVAL & INSTALLATION

Column Mounted

1. Disconnect the negative battery cable. Remove the steering wheel. Remove the turn signal switch.

2. It may be necessary to loosen the two column mounting nuts and remove the four bracket to mast jacket screws, then separate the bracket from the mast jacket to allow the connector

clip on the ignition switch to be pulled out of the column assembly.

3. Disconnect the washer/wiper switch lower connector.

4. Remove the screws attaching the column housing to the mast jacket. Be sure to note the position of the dimmer switch actuator rod for reassembly in the same position. Remove the column housing and switch as an assembly.

NOTE: The tilt and travel columns have a removable plastic cover on the column housing. This provides access to the wiper switch without removing the entire column housing.

5. Turn the assembly upside down and use a drift to remove the pivot pin from the washer/wiper switch. Remove the switch.

6. Place the switch into position in the housing, then install the pivot pin.

7. Position the housing onto the mast jacket and attach by installing the screws. Install the dimmer switch actuator rod in the same position as noted earlier. Check switch operation.

8. Reconnect lower end of switch assembly.

9. Install remaining components in the reverse order of the removal procedure. Be sure to attach column mounting bracket in original position.

Dash Mounted

1. Disconnect the negative battery cable.

2. Remove all required trim and instrument panel bezels in order to remove the switch.

3. Disconnect the electrical connectors from the switch assembly.

4. Remove the switch retaining screws. Remove the switch.

5. Installation is the reverse of the removal procedure.

Windshield Wiper Motor

REMOVAL & INSTALLATION

1. Disconnect the negative battery cable.

2. Remove the cowl vent screen.

3. Remove the transmission drive link from the motor crank arm.

4. Disconnect the electrical connectors and the washer hoses.

5. Remove the motor retaining screws. Remove the motor from the vehicle. When removing the motor, guide the crank arm through the hole.

6. Installation is the reverse of the removal procedure. The motor must be in the "Park" position before assembling the crank arm to the transmission drive link.

Instrument Cluster

REMOVAL & INSTALLATION

Malibu (Standard Cluster)

1. Disconnect battery ground cable.

2. Remove clock set stem knob, if equipped.

3. Remove instrument bezel retaining screws.

4. Pull bezel from panel slightly and disconnect rear defogger switch, if equipped.

5. Remove bezel.

6. Remove two screws at transmission selector indicator and lower indictor assembly to disconnect cable.

7. Remove three screws at windshield wiper/light switch mounting plate and pull assembly rearward for access to lower left cluster attaching bolt and nut.

8. Remove nuts attaching cluster to instrument panel.

9. Pull cluster rearward and disconnect the speedometer cable and all wiring and cables.

10. Remove cluster from vehicle.

11. Installation is the reverse of the removal procedure.

Malibu (Optional Cluster) and Monte Carlo

1. Disconnect the negative battery cable. Remove the clock set stem knob.

2. Remove the instrument bezel retaining screws.

3. Slightly pull the bezel rearward. Disconnect the rear defogger switch. Remove the remote control mirror control knob, if equipped.

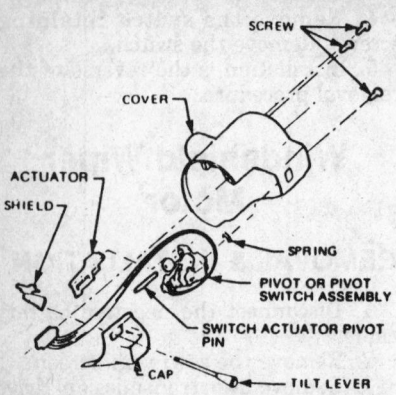

Column mounted windshield wiper switch assembly

4. Remove the dash panel bezel. Remove the speedometer assembly retaining screws. Pull the assembly from the cluster, disconnect the speedometer cable from the assembly and remove the speedometer from the vehicle.

5. Remove the fuel gauge or the tachometer retaining screws, disconnect the electrical connectors and remove the components.

6. Remove the clock or voltmeter retaining screws, disconnect the electrical connectors and remove the components.

7. Disconnect the transmission shift indicator cable from the steering column.

8. Disconnect all wiring connectors and remove the cluster case.

9. Installation is the reverse of the removal procedure.

Impala and Caprice

1. Disconnect the negative battery cable.

2. Remove the four steering column lower cover screws and the cover.

3. If equipped with automatic transmission, disconnect the shift indicator cable from the steering column.

4. Remove the steering column to instrument panel screws. Lower the steering column.

NOTE: Use extreme care when lowering the steering column in order to prevent damage to column assembly.

5. Remove the screws and the snap in fasteners from the perimeter of the instrument cluster lens.

6. Remove the screws from the lower corner of the cluster.

7. Remove the stud nuts from the lower corner of the cluster. Remove

the two screws from the upper surface of the metal sheet trim plate.

8. Disconnect the speedometer cable and pull cluster outward from the instrument panel.

9. Disconnect the electrical connectors from the cluster and remove the assembly from the vehicle.

10. Installation is the reverse of the removal procedure.

Headlight Switch

REMOVAL & INSTALLATION

Impala and Caprice

1. Disconnect the negative battery cable.

2. Pull the headlamp switch to the "ON" position.

3. Depending upon the switch mechanism, pull the trim knob from the switch by either reaching under the dash and depressing the switch shaft release button while pulling the knob and shaft from the light switch or by using a suitable tool and pushing the tang under the trim knob while pulling the knob from the shaft.

4. Remove the ferrule nut retaining the switch to the dash panel. Disconnect the electrical connector and remove the switch.

5. Installation is the reverse of the removal procedure.

Malibu and Monte Carlo

1. Disconnect the negative battery cable.

2. Remove the screws and instrument panel pad.

3. As required, remove the windshield wiper/light switch mounting screws.

4. Depending upon the switch mechanism, pull the trim knob from the switch by either reaching under the dash and depressing the switch shaft release button while pulling the knob and shaft from the light switch or by using a suitable tool and pushing the tang under the trim knob while pulling the knob from the shaft.

5. Remove ferrule nut and switch assembly from instrument panel.

6. Installation is the reverse of the removal procedure.

Stoplight Switch

REMOVAL & INSTALLATION

NOTE: The cruise control release switch and the stoplight

switch are adjusted or replaced in the same manner.

1. Disconnect the negative battery cable. Disconnect the wire harness connector from the switch.

2. Remove the switch from the clip and then remove the clip from the bracket.

3. To install, place the clip in its bore on the bracket.

4. With the brake pedal depressed, insert the switch into the clip and depress the switch body. Clicks can be heard as the threaded portion of the switch is pushed through the clip towards the brake pedal. Electrical contact should be made when the brake pedal is depressed ⅜ to ⅝ in. from the fully released position.

5. Pull the brake pedal fully rearward against the pedal stop until the clicking sounds cannot be heard. The switch can be moved in the clip to correct the adjustment.

6. Release the brake pedal and repeat Step 5 to assure that no clicking sounds remain. The switch is now correctly adjusted.

7. Install the harness connector and verify the stoplights operate correctly.

Fuses and Circuit Breakers

LOCATION

Circuit Breakers

Various circuit breakers are located under the instrument panel. In order to gain access to these components it may be necessary to first remove the under dash padding.

Fuse Panel

The fuse panel is located on the left side of the vehicle. It is under the instrument panel assembly. In order to gain access to the fuse panel it may be necessary to first remove the under dash padding.

The turn signal flasher is located behind the instrument panel bracket to the right of the steering column. In order to gain access to the turn signal flasher it may be necessary to first remove the under dash padding.

The hazard flasher is located in the fuse block. It is positioned on the lower right hand corner of the fuse block assembly. In order to gain access to the turn signal flasher it may be necessary to first remove the under dash padding.

Chevrolet
Front Wheel Drive
Spectrum

15

SERIAL NUMBER IDENTIFICATION

VEHICLE IDENTIFICATION CHART

It is important for servicing and ordering parts to be certain of the vehicle and engine identification. The VIN (vehicle identification number) is a 17 digit number visible through the windshield on the driver's side of the dash and contains the vehicle and engine identification codes. The tenth digit indicates model year, and the eigth digit indicates engine code. It can be interpreted as follows:

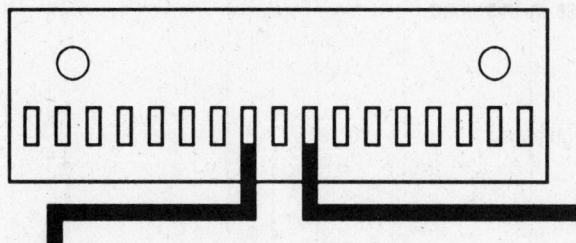

Engine Code

Code	Cu. In.	Liters	Cyl.	Fuel Sys.	Eng. Mfg.
7	90	1.5	4	2 bbl	Isuzu
9	90	1.5	4	Turbo	Isuzu

Model Year

Code	Year
F	1985
G	1986
H	1987
J	1988
K	1989

GENERAL ENGINE SPECIFICATIONS

Year	VIN	No. Cylinder Displacement cu. in. (liter)	Fuel System Type	Net Horsepower @ rpm	Net Torque @ rpm (ft.lbs.)	Bore × Stroke (in.)	Compression Ratio	Oil Pressure @ rpm
1985	7	4-90 (1.5)	2 bbl	70 @ 5400	87 @ 3400	3.031 × 3.110	9.6:1	49 @ 5200
1986	7	4-90 (1.5)	2 bbl	70 @ 5400	87 @ 3400	3.031 × 3.110	9.6:1	49 @ 5200

GENERAL ENGINE SPECIFICATIONS

Year	VIN	No. Cylinder Displacement cu. in. (liter)	Fuel System Type	Net Horsepower @ rpm	Net Torque @ rpm (ft.lbs.)	Bore × Stroke (in.)	Compression Ratio	Oil Pressure @ rpm
1987	7	4-90 (1.5)	2 bbl	70 @ 5400	87 @ 3400	3.031 × 3.110	8.2:1	49 @ 5200
	9	4-90 (1.5)	Turbo	110 @ 5400	120 @ 3400	3.031 × 3.110	8.0:1	49 @ 5200
1988-89	7	4-90 (1.5)	2 bbl	70 @ 5400	87 @ 3400	3.031 × 3.110	9.6:1	49 @ 5200
	9	4-90 (1.5)	Turbo	110 @ 5400	120 @ 3400	3.031 × 3.110	8.0:1	49 @ 5200

GASOLINE ENGINE TUNE-UP SPECIFICATIONS

Year	VIN	No. Cylinder Displacement cu. in. (liter)	Spark Plugs Type	Gap (in.)	Ignition Timing (deg.) MT	AT	Compression Pressure (psi)	Fuel Pump (psi)	Idle Speed (rpm) MT	AT	Valve Clearance In.	Ex.
1985	7	4-90 (1.5)	BPR6ES-11	.040	15①	10③	128–179	3.8-4.7	700	950	.006	.010
1986	7	4-90 (1.5)	BPR6ES-11	.040	15①	10③	128–179	3.8-4.7	700	950	.006	.010
1987	7	4-90 (1.5)	BPR6ES-11	.040	15①	10③	128–179	3.8-4.7	700	950	.006	.010
	9	4-90 (1.5)	BPR6ES-11	.040	15②	NA	128–179	28.4④	950	NA	.006	.010
1988	7	4-90 (1.5)	BPR6ES-11	.040	15①	10③	128–179	3.8-4.7	700	950	.006	.010
	9	4-90 (1.5)	BPR6ES-11	.040	15②	NA	128–179	28.4④	950	NA	.006	.010
1989		SEE UNDERHOOD SPECIFICATIONS STICKER										

NOTE: The underhood specifications sticker often reflects tune-up specification changes made in production. Sticker figures must be used if they disagree with those in this chart.

① @ 750 rpm
② @ 950 rpm
③ @ 1000 rpm
④ @ 900 rpm with pressure regulator connected

FIRING ORDERS

NOTE: To avoid confusion, always replace spark plug wires one at a time.

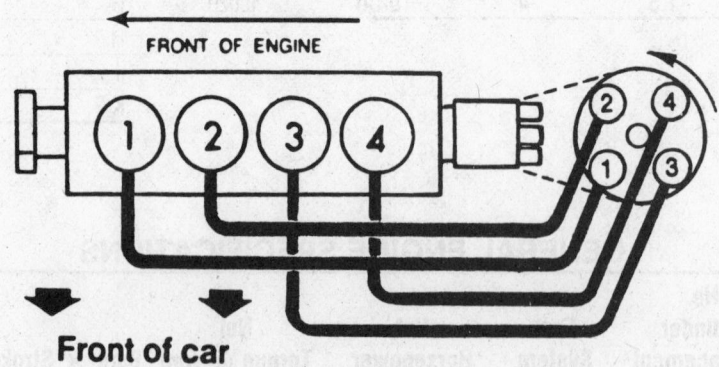

GM (Isuzu) 4-90 (1.5L)
Engine firing order: 1–3–4–2
Distributor rotation: counterclockwise

CAPACITIES

Year	VIN	No. Cylinder Displacement cu. in. (liter)	Engine Crankcase with Filter	Engine Crankcase without Filter	Transmission (pts.) MT	Transmission (pts.) AT	Drive Axle (pts.)	Fuel Tank (gals.)	Cooling System (qts.)
1985	7	4-90 (1.5)	3.4	3.0	5.4	12.2	–	11	6.8
1986	7	4-90 (1.5)	3.4	3.0	5.8	12.2	–	11	6.8
1987	7	4-90 (1.5)	3.4	3.0	5.8	12.2	–	11	6.8
	9	4-90 (1.5)	3.4	3.0	5.8	NA	–	11	7.5
1988-89	7	4-90 (1.5)	3.4	3.0	5.8	12.2	–	11	6.8
	9	4-90 (1.5)	3.4	3.0	5.8	NA	–	11	7.5

CAMSHAFT SPECIFICATIONS
All measurements given in inches.

Year	VIN	No. Cylinder Displacement cu. in. (liter)	Journal Diameter 1	2	3	4	5	Lobe Lift In.	Lobe Lift Ex.	Bearing Clearance	Camshaft End Play
1985	7	4-90 (1.5)	1.021–1.022	1.021–1.022	1.021–1.022	1.021–1.022	1.021–1.022	1.426	1.426	.0024–.0044	.0039–.0071
1986	7	4-90 (1.5)	1.021–1.022	1.021–1.022	1.021–1.022	1.021–1.022	1.021–1.022	1.426	1.426	.0024–.0044	.0039–.0071
1987	7	4-90 (1.5)	1.021–1.022	1.021–1.022	1.021–1.022	1.021–1.022	1.021–1.022	1.426	1.426	.0024–.0044	.0039–.0071
	9	4-90 (1.5)	1.021–1.022	1.021–1.022	1.021–1.022	1.021–1.022	1.021–1.022	1.426	1.426	.0024–.0044	.0039–.0071
1988-89	7	4-90 (1.5)	1.021–1.022	1.021–1.022	1.021–1.022	1.021–1.022	1.021–1.022	1.426	1.426	.0024–.0044	.0039–.0071
	9	4-90 (1.5)	1.021–1.022	1.021–1.022	1.021–1.022	1.021–1.022	1.021–1.022	1.426	1.426	.0024–.0044	.0039–.0071

CRANKSHAFT AND CONNECTING ROD SPECIFICATIONS
All measurements are given in inches.

Year	VIN	No. Cylinder Displacement cu. in. (liter)	Crankshaft Main Brg. Journal Dia.	Crankshaft Main Brg. Oil Clearance	Crankshaft Shaft End-play	Crankshaft Thrust on No.	Connecting Rod Journal Diameter	Connecting Rod Oil Clearance	Connecting Rod Side Clearance
1985	7	4-90 (1.5)	1.8865–1.8873	.0008–.0020	.0024–.0095	2	1.5720–1.5726	.0010–.0023	.0079–.0138
1986	7	4-90 (1.5)	1.8865–1.8873	.0008–.0020	.0024–.0095	2	1.5720–1.5726	.0010–.0023	.0079–.0138
1987	7	4-90 (1.5)	1.8865–1.8873	.0008–.0020	.0024–.0095	2	1.5720–1.5726	.0010–.0023	.0079–.0138
	9	4-90 (1.5)	1.8865–1.8873	.0008–.0020	.0024–.0095	2	1.5720–1.5726	.0010–.0023	.0079–.0138
1988-89	7	4-90 (1.5)	1.8865–1.8873	.0008–.0020	.0024–.0095	2	1.5720–1.5726	.0010–.0023	.0079–.0138
	9	4-90 (1.5)	1.8865–1.8873	.0008–.0020	.0024–.0095	2	1.5720–1.5726	.0010–.0023	.0079–.0138

VALVE SPECIFICATIONS

Year	VIN	No. Cylinder Displacement cu. in. (liter)	Seat Angle (deg.)	Face Angle (deg.)	Spring Test Pressure (lbs.)	Spring Installed Height (in.)	Stem-to-Guide Clearance (in.) Intake	Stem-to-Guide Clearance (in.) Exhaust	Stem Diameter (in.) Intake	Stem Diameter (in.) Exhaust
1985	7	4-90 (1.5)	45	45	47 @ 1.57	1.57	.0009–.0022	.0012–.0025	.2740–.2750	.2740–.2744
1986	7	4-90 (1.5)	45	45	47 @ 1.57	1.57	.0009–.0022	.0012–.0025	.2740–.2750	.2740–.2744
1987	7	4-90 (1.5)	45	45	47 @ 1.57	1.57	.0009–.0022	.0012–.0025	.2740–.2750	.2740–.2744
	9	4-90 (1.5)	45	45	47 @ 1.57	1.57	.0009–.0022	.0012–.0025	.2740–.2750	.2740–.2744
1988-89	7	4-90 (1.5)	45	45	47 @ 1.57	1.57	.0009–.0022	.0012–.0025	.2740–.2750	.2740–.2744
	9	4-90 (1.5)	45	45	47 @ 1.57	1.57	.0009–.0022	.0012–.0025	.2740–.2750	.2740–.2744

PISTON AND RING SPECIFICATIONS

All measurments are given in inches.

Year	VIN	No. Cylinder Displacement cu. in. (liter)	Piston Clearance	Ring Gap Top Compression	Ring Gap Bottom Compression	Ring Gap Oil Control	Ring Side Clearance Top Compression	Ring Side Clearance Bottom Compression	Ring Side Clearance Oil Control
1985	7	4-90 (1.5)	.0011–.0019	.0098–.0138	—	.0039–.0236	.0010–.0026	—	NA
1986	7	4-90 (1.5)	.0011–.0019	.0098–.0138	—	.0039–.0236	.0010–.0026	—	NA
1987	7	4-90 (1.5)	.0011–.0019	.0098–.0138	①	.0039–.0236	.0010–.0026	—	NA
	9	4-90 (1.5)	.0011–.0019	.0106–.0153	.0098–.0145	.0039–.0236	.0010–.0026	.0008–.0024	NA
1988-89	7	4-90 (1.5)	.0011–.0019	.0098–.0138	—	.0039–.0236	.0010–.0026	—	NA
	9	4-90 (1.5)	.0011–.0019	.0106–.0153	.0098–.0145	.0039–.0236	.0010–.0026	.0008–.0024	NA

① Only one compression ring used on this engine

TORQUE SPECIFICATIONS

All readings in ft. lbs.

Year	VIN	No. Cylinder Displacement cu. in. (liter)	Cylinder Head Bolts	Main Bearing Bolts	Rod Bearing Bolts	Crankshaft Pulley Bolts	Flywheel Bolts	Manifold Intake	Manifold Exhaust	Spark Plugs
1985	7	4-90 (1.5)	②	65	25	108	22 ①	17	17	18
1986	7	4-90 (1.5)	②	65	25	108	22 ①	17	17	18
1987	7	4-90 (1.5)	②	65	25	108	22 ①	17	17	18
	9	4-90 (1.5)	②	65	25	108	22 ①	17	17	18

TORQUE SPECIFICATIONS
All readings in ft. lbs.

Year	VIN	No. Cylinder Displacement cu. in. (liter)	Cylinder Head Bolts	Main Bearing Bolts	Rod Bearing Bolts	Crankshaft Pulley Bolts	Flywheel Bolts	Manifold Intake	Manifold Exhaust	Spark Plugs
1988-89	7	4-90 (1.5)	②	65	25	108	22 ①	17	17	18
	9	4-90 (1.5)	②	65	25	108	22 ①	17	17	18

① Tighten an additional 45° after torquing
② 1st step: 29 ft. lbs.; 2nd step: 58 ft. lbs.

BRAKE SPECIFICATIONS
All measurements in inches unless noted

Year	Model	Lug Nut Torque (ft. lbs.)	Master Cylinder Bore	Brake Disc Minimum Thickness	Brake Disc Maximum Runout	Standard Brake Drum Diameter	Minimum Lining Thickness Front	Minimum Lining Thickness Rear
1985	Spectrum	65	.810	.378	.0059	7.09	.039	.039
1986	Spectrum	65	.810	.378	.0059	7.09	.039	.039
1987	Spectrum	65	.810	.378	.0059	7.09	.039	.039
1988-89	Spectrum	65	.810	.378	.0059	7.09	.039	.039

WHEEL ALIGNMENT

Year	Model	Caster Range (deg.)	Caster Preferred Setting (deg.)	Camber Range (deg.)	Camber Preferred Setting (deg.)	Toe-in (in.)	Steering Axis Inclination (deg.)
1985	Spectrum	1¾P-2¾P	2¼P	⁷⁄₁₆N-1¹⁄₁₆P	¹¹⁄₃₂P	0 ± ¹⁄₁₆	①②
1986	Spectrum	1¾P-2¾P	2¼P	⁷⁄₁₆N-1¹⁄₁₆P	¹¹⁄₃₂P	0 ± ¹⁄₁₆	①②
1987	Spectrum	1¾P-2¾P	2¼P	⁷⁄₁₆N-1¹⁄₁₆P	¹¹⁄₃₂P	0 ± ¹⁄₁₆	①②
1988-89	Spectrum	1¾P-2¾P	2¼P	⁷⁄₁₆N-1¹⁄₁₆P	¹¹⁄₃₂P	0 ± ¹⁄₁₆	①②

① Inside : 37°40' full lock
② Outside: 32°30' full lock

TUNE-UP PROCEDURES

Ignition Timing

ADJUSTMENT

1. Set the parking brake and block the wheels.
2. Place the manual transmission in Neutral or the automatic transmission in Park.
3. Allow the engine to reach normal operating temperature. Make sure that the choke valve is open. Turn off all of the accessories.
4. If equipped with power steering, place the front wheels in a straight line.
5. Disconnect and plug the distributor vacuum line, the canister purge line, the EGR vacuum line and the ITC valve vacuum line at the intake manifold.
6. Connect a timing light to the No. 1 spark plug wire and a tachometer to the tachometer filter connector on the coil, tachometer filter is mounted near distributor hold down bolt.

NOTE: Check the idle speed. If the speed is not correct, refer to the "Idle Speed Adjustment" procedures in the section and set the idle speed.

7. Loosen the distributor flange bolt.
8. Using the timing light, align the notch on the crankshaft pulley with the mark on the timing cover by turning the distributor.

NOTE: Adjust the timing to 15 degrees BTDC at 750 rpm (MT) or 10 degrees BTDC at 1000 rpm (AT).

9. After the timing marks have been aligned, tighten the distributor flange bolt, then reinstall all vacuum lines.

Valve Lash

ADJUSTMENT

1. Refer to the "Rocker Arms/ Shafts, Removal & Installation" procedures in this section and remove the cylinder head cover.

2. Rotate the engine until the notched line on the crankshaft pulley aligns with the 0 degree mark on the timing gear case. The position of the No. 1 piston should be at TDC of the compression stroke.

3. Set the intake valve to 0.006 in. (Cold) for No. 1 and 2 cylinders; exhaust valves to 0.010 in. (Cold) for No. 1 and 3 cylinders.

4. Rotate the crankshaft one complete revolution. Set the intake valves to 0.006 in. (Cold) for No. 3 and 4 cylinders; exhaust valves to 0.010 in. (Cold) for No. 2 and 4 cylinders.

5. After the adjustment has been completed, replace the head cover.

Idle Speed and Mixture

ADJUSTMENT

Idle Speed

Non-turbocharged Model

1. Set the parking brake and block the wheels.

2. Place the manual transmission in Neutral or the automatic transmission in Park. Check the float level. Establish a normal operating temperature and make sure that the choke plate is open.

3. Turn off all of the accessories and wait until the cooling fan is not operating.

4. If equipped with power steering, place the wheels in the straight forward position. Remove the air filter.

5. Disconnect and plug the distributor vacuum line, canister purge line, EGR vacuum line and ITC valve vacuum line.

6. Connect a tachometer to the coil tachometer connector and a timing light to the No. 1 spark plug wire. Check the timing and idle speed.

7. If the idle speed needs adjusting, turn the idle speed adjusting screw.

8. If equipped with A/C, adjust the system to Max. Cold and place the blower on "High" position. Set the fast idle speed by turning the adjust bolt of the Fast Idle Control Diaphragm to 850 rpm (MT) or 980 rpm (AT).

9. When adjustment is completed, turn the engine off, remove the test

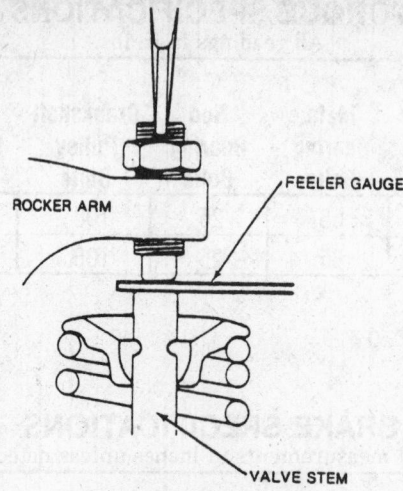

Valve lash adjustment

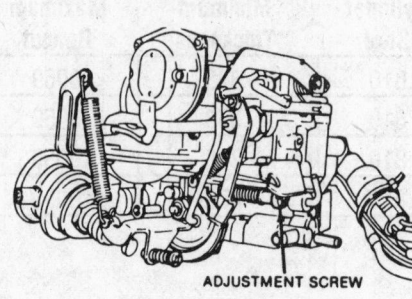

Adjusting the idle speed screw

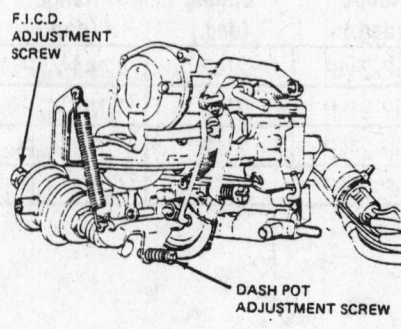

Adjustment fast idle control device

equipment, install the air filter and vacuum lines.

Turbocharged Model

1. Set the parking brake.
2. Block the front wheels.
3. Place the select lever in Neutral.
4. Make the idling speed adjustment with the engine at normal operating temperature, with A/C Off and front wheels facing straight ahead.

NOTE: All electrical equipment (lights, rear defogger, heater, etc.) should be turned off.

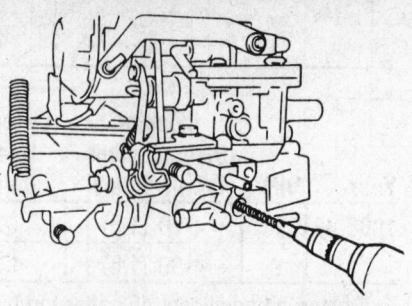

Drilling the idle mixture screw plug

5. Make sure Check Engine light is not on.
6. Ground Test terminal (ALDL connector).
7. Race over 2000 rpm to reset the position of idle air control valve.
8. Set idle adjust screw to 950 rpm.
9. Remove Test terminal, ground and clear ECM trouble code.

Idle Mixture

NOTE: The idle mixture screw is adjusted and sealed at the factory and no service adjustment is required. However, if the necessity of adjustment aries for some reason, adjusting by removing plug is possible but it must be plugged again after adjustment is completed.

1. Remove the carburetor from the engine.

2. Using a center punch, make a punch mark on the idle mixture sealing plug. Drill a hole through the plug, insert a threaded screw and pull the plug from the throttle body. The width of the plug is about 10 mm (0.39 in.).

NOTE: If the idle mixture screw is damaged from the drilling process, replace the screw.

3. Lightly seat the idle mixture screw, then back out 3 turns (MT) or 2 turns (AT). DO NOT overtighten the idle mixture screw.

4. Reinstall the carburetor and the air cleaner.

5. Adjust the idle speed.

6. Using a dwell meter, connect the positive lead to the duty monitor and the negative lead to ground. Place the meter dial on the 4 cylinder scale. Turn the idle mixture screw until the dwell meter reads 45 degrees (4 cylinder scale).

7. Turn A/C on Max. Cold and blower on High then adjust the bolt on the FICD and set the fast idle to 850 rpm (MT) or 980 (AT), if so equipped then stop the engine and remove the test equipment.

8. Drive a new idle mixture plug into the throttle body, flush with the

throttle body apply Locktite No.262 or its equivalent to the plug.

9. Recheck all adjustments and road test.

ENGINE ELECTRICAL

Distributor

REMOVAL & INSTALLATION

Undisturbed Engine

1. Disconnect the negative battery terminal from the battery.
2. Remove the distributor cap.
3. Mark and remove all electrical leads and vacuum lines connected to the distributor assembly.
4. Mark the relationship of the rotor to the distributor housing and the distributor housing to the engine.
5. Remove the hold-down bolt, clamp and distributor.
6. To install, reverse the removal procedures and check the timing.

Disturbed Engine

If the engine was cranked while the distributor was removed, you will have to place the engine on TDC of the compression stroke to obtain the proper ignition timing.

1. Remove the No. 1 spark plug.
2. Place your thumb over the spark plug hole. Crank the engine slowly until compression is felt. It will be easier if you have someone rotate the engine by hand, using a wrench on the crankshaft pulley.
3. Align the timing mark on the crankshaft pulley with the 0 degrees mark on the timing scale attached to the front of the engine. This places the engine at TDC of the compression stroke.
4. Turn the distributor shaft until the rotor points to the No. 1 spark plug tower on the cap.
5. Install the distributor into the engine. Be sure to align the distributor-to-engine block mark made earlier.
6. To complete the installation, reverse the removal procedures and check the timing.

Alternator

For further information on the charging system, please refer to "Charging and Starting" in the Unit Repair section.

PRECAUTIONS

- When installing a battery, make sure that the positive and negative cables are not reversed.
- When jump-starting the car, be sure that like terminals are connected. This also applies to using a battery charger. Reversed polarity will burn out the alternator and regulator in a matter of seconds.
- Never operate the alternator with the battery disconnected or on an otherwise uncontrolled open circuit.
- Do not short across or ground any alternator or regulator terminals.
- Do not try to polarize the alternator.
- Do not apply full battery voltage to the field (brown) connector.
- Always disconnect the battery ground cable before disconnecting the alternator lead.
- Always disconnect the battery (negative cable first) when charging it.
- Never subject the alternator to excessive heat or dampness. If you are steam-cleaning the engine, cover the alternator.
- Never use arc welding equipment on the car with the alternator connected.

BELT TENSION ADJUSTMENT

NOTE: The following procedures require the use of GM Belt Tension Gauge No. BT–33–95–ACBN (regular V-belts) or BT–33–97M (poly V-belts).

1. If the belt is cold, operate the engine (at idle speed) for 15 minutes; the belt will seat itself in the pulleys allowing the belt fibers to relax or stretch. If the belt is hot, allow it to cool, until it is warm to the touch.

NOTE: A used belt is one that has been rotated at least one complete revolution on the pulleys. This begins the belt seating process and it must never be tensioned to the new belt specifications.

2. Loosen the component-to-mounting bracket bolts.
3. Using a GM Belt Tension Gauge No. BT–33–95–ACBN (standard V-belts) or BT–33–97M (poly V-belts), place the tension gauge at the center of the belt between the longest span.
4. Applying belt tension pressure on the component, adjust the drive belt tension to the correct specifications. The belt tension should deflect about

¼ in. over a 7–10 in. span or ½ in. over a 13–16 in. span.

5. While holding the correct tension on the component, tighten the component-to-mounting bracket bolt.
6. When the belt tension is correct (70–110 inch lbs.), remove the tension gauge.

REMOVAL & INSTALLATION

1. Disconnect the negative battery terminal from the battery.

— CAUTION —

Failure to disconnect the negative cable may result in injury from the positive battery lead at the alternator and may short the alternator and regulator during the removal process.

---

2. Disconnect and label the two terminal plug and the battery leads from the rear of the alternator.
3. Loosen the mounting bolts. Push the alternator inwards and slip the drive belt off the pulley.
4. Remove the mounting bolts and remove the alternator.
5. To install, place the alternator in its brackets and install the mounting bolts. Do not tighten them yet.
6. Slip the belt back over the pulley. Pull outwards on the unit and adjust the belt tension. Tighten the mounting and adjusting bolts.
7. Install the electrical leads and the negative battery cable.

Voltage Regulator

A solid state regulator is mounted within the alternator. All regulator components are enclosed in a solid mold. The regulator is non-adjustable and requires no maintenance.

Starter

For further information on the starter system, please refer to "Charging and Starting" in the Unit Repair section

REMOVAL & INSTALLATION

1. Disconnect the negative battery terminal from the battery.
2. Disconnect the ignition switch lead wire and the battery cable from the starter motor terminal.
3. Remove the two mounting bolts from the starter and remove the starter.
4. To install, reverse the removal procedures.

ENGINE MECHANICAL

The Spectrum uses a 1.5L (90 cu. in.) overhead cam (SOHC) engine. The 4-cylinder, in-line engine utilizes one compression and one oil control ring on each piston (non-turbocharged model). The overhead camshaft, which is driven by the crankshaft through a timing belt, directly drives the rocker arms.

Engine

REMOVAL & INSTALLATION

Non-turbocharged Model

1. Remove the hood and disconnect the negative battery cable.
2. Drain the cooling system.
3. Remove the air cleaner and the throttle cable at the carburetor.
4. Disconnect the heater hoses at the intake manifold, the coolant hose at the thermostat housing and the thermostat housing at the cylinder head.
5. Remove the distributor from the cylinder head.
6. Disconnect the O_2 sensor electrical connector.
7. Support the engine using a vertical lift and remove the right motor mount.
8. Disconnect the necessary electrical connectors and vacuum hoses.
9. Disconnect the flex hose at the exhaust manifold and the lower radiator hose at the block.
10. Remove the upper A/C compressor bolt and remove the belt.
11. Disconnect the power steering bracket at the block and remove the belt.
12. Disconnect the fuel lines from the fuel pump and the electrical connectors from under the carburetor.
13. Remove the upper starter bolt and raise the vehicle.
14. Drain the oil from the crankcase and remove the oil filter.
15. Disconnect the oil temperature switch connector.
16. Disconnect the exhaust pipe bracket at the block and the exhaust pipe at the manifold.
17. Remove the A/C compressor and move to one side. Do not disconnect the A/C refrigerant lines. Remove the alternator wires.
18. Remove the flywheel cover and the converter bolts, then install the Flywheel Holding tool No. J-35271 or equivalent.

19. Disconnect the starter wires and remove the starter.
20. Remove the front right wheel and inner splash shield.
21. Lower the engine by lowering the crossmember enough to gain access to the crankshaft pulley bolts, then remove the pulley.
22. Raise the engine and crossmember. Remove the engine support.
23. Lower the vehicle and support the transmission.
24. Remove the transmission to engine bolts. Remove the engine.
25. To install, reverse the removal procedures, adjust the drive belts and refill the fluids.

Turbocharged Model

NOTE: On turbocharged model follow the above for removal & installation with exception of removal of throttle cable, fuel lines, connectors at carburetor also remove turbocharger vacuum, oil and water lines.

Cylinder Head

REMOVAL & INSTALLATION

1. Disconnect the negative battery terminal from the battery.
2. Drain the cooling system.
3. Remove the air cleaner.
4. Disconnect the flex hose and oxygen sensor at the exhaust manifold.
5. Disconnect the exhaust pipe bracket at the block and the exhaust pipe at the manifold. On turbocharged model disconnect exhaust pipe at wastegate manifold and disconnect vacumm line for turbocharger control.
6. Disconnect the spark plug wires.
7. Remove the thermostat housing, the distributor, the vacuum advance hoses and the ground cable at the cylinder head.
8. Disconnect the fuel hoses at the fuel pump on non-turbocharged model.

9. From the carburetor, if so equipped, remove the necessary hoses and the throttle cable.
10. Remove engine harness asembly from fuel injectors and fuel line from fuel injector pipe on turbocharged model.
11. Disconnect the vacuum switching valve electrical connector and the heater hoses.
12. Remove the alternator, P/S and A/C adjusting bolts, brackets and drive belts.
13. Support the engine using a vertical hoist. Remove the right hand motor mount and the bracket at the front cover.
14. Rotate the engine to align the timing marks, then remove the timing gear cover.
15. Loosen the tension pulley and remove the timing belt from the camshaft timing pulley.
16. Disconnect the carburetor fuel line at the fuel pump and remove the fuel pump.
17. Disconnect the intake manifold coolant hoses.
18. Remove the cylinder head bolts (remove the bolts from both ends at the same time, working toward the middle) and the cylinder head. Clean all of the mounting surfaces.
19. Compress the valves; then remove the keepers, springs, seals and valves.
20. To install, use new seals and gas-

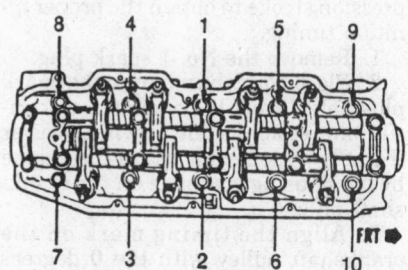

Cylinder head bolt torque sequence

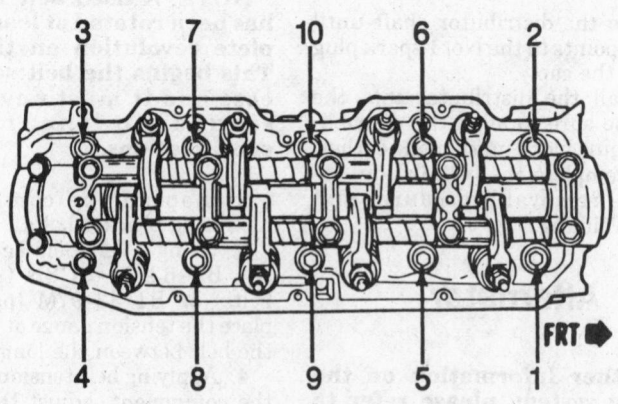

Cylinder head bolt removal sequence

1. Wing Nut
2. Air Cleaner Assembly
3. Air Duct
4. TCA Flex Hose
5. Carburetor

6. EFE Heater Assembly
7. Packing
8. Head Cover
9. Packing
10. Clip
11. Bolt; Head Cover
12. Bolt; Head Cover
13. Packing
14. Cap; Oil Filler
15. Packing

43. Camshaft
44. Oil Seal; Camshaft
45. Timing Pulley; Camshaft
46. Packing

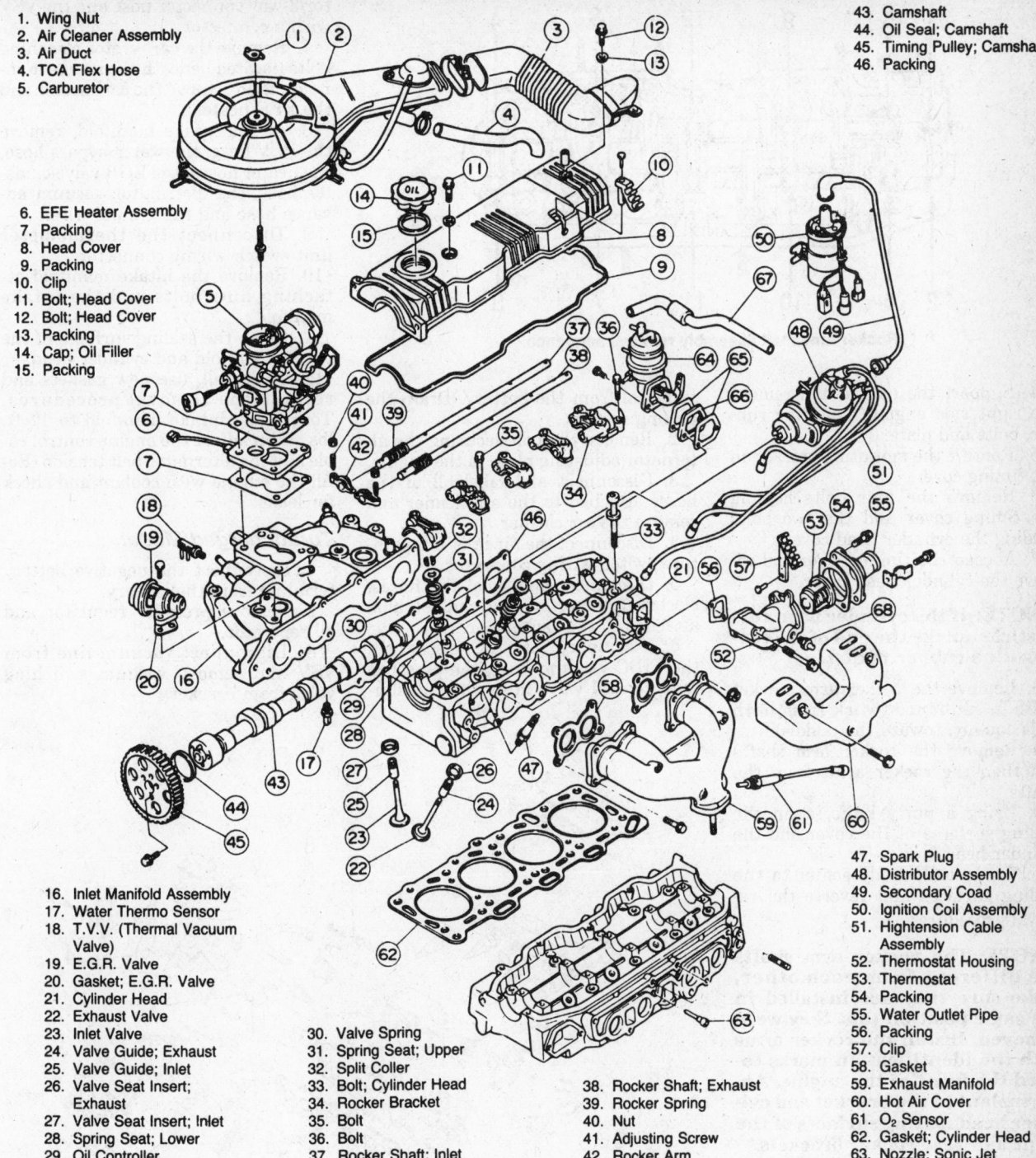

16. Inlet Manifold Assembly
17. Water Thermo Sensor
18. T.V.V. (Thermal Vacuum Valve)
19. E.G.R. Valve
20. Gasket; E.G.R. Valve
21. Cylinder Head
22. Exhaust Valve
23. Inlet Valve
24. Valve Guide; Exhaust
25. Valve Guide; Inlet
26. Valve Seat Insert; Exhaust
27. Valve Seat Insert; Inlet
28. Spring Seat; Lower
29. Oil Controller

30. Valve Spring
31. Spring Seat; Upper
32. Split Coller
33. Bolt; Cylinder Head
34. Rocker Bracket
35. Bolt
36. Bolt
37. Rocker Shaft; Inlet

38. Rocker Shaft; Exhaust
39. Rocker Spring
40. Nut
41. Adjusting Screw
42. Rocker Arm

47. Spark Plug
48. Distributor Assembly
49. Secondary Coad
50. Ignition Coil Assembly
51. Hightension Cable Assembly
52. Thermostat Housing
53. Thermostat
54. Packing
55. Water Outlet Pipe
56. Packing
57. Clip
58. Gasket
59. Exhaust Manifold
60. Hot Air Cover
61. O₂ Sensor
62. Gasket; Cylinder Head
63. Nozzle; Sonic Jet

Exploded view of the top of the engine

kets, apply oil to the bolt threads and torque the head bolts.

NOTE: When torquing the cylinder head bolts, work from the middle toward both ends at the same time. First, torque the bolts to 29 ft. lbs. and then final torque them to 58 ft. lbs.

21. After torquing, adjust the valve clearance and complete the installa-tion procedures, by reversing the re-moval procedures.

OVERHAUL

For all cylinder head overhaul procedures, please refer to the "Engine Rebuilding" in the Unit Repair section.

Rocker Arms/Shafts

REMOVAL & INSTALLATION

1. Disconnect the negative battery terminal from the battery. Remove the PCV hoses.
2. Remove the spark plug wires from the mounting clip.
3. Remove the ground wire from the right rear side of the head cover.

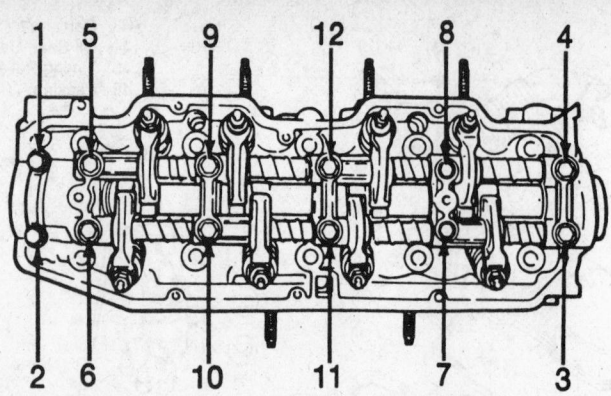

Rocker arm/shaft assembly removal sequence

4. Support the engine and remove the right side engine mounting rubber, bolts and plate.

5. Remove the mounting bracket on the timing cover.

6. Remove the four bolts holding the timing cover and the two bolts holding the cylinder head cover.

7. Loosen the timing cover and remove the cylinder head cover.

NOTE: If the cylinder head cover sticks, strike the end of the cover with a rubber mallet.

8. Remove the rocker arm bracket bolts in sequence (work from both ends equally, toward the middle).

9. Remove the rocker arm shafts and then the rocker arms from the shafts.

10. Using a putty knife, clean the sealing surfaces of the cover and the cylinder head.

11. To install, apply sealer to the sealing surfaces and reverse the removal procedures.

NOTE: The rocker arm shafts are different from each other, make sure they are installed in the same position that they were removed. Install the rocker arms with the identification marks toward the front of the engine. Apply sealant to the bracket and cylinder head mating surfaces of the front and rear rocker brackets.

12. To complete the installation, mount the rocker assemblies securely to the dowel pins on the cylinder head. Torque the rocker arm bolts to 16 ft. lbs. Start the engine and check for leaks.

Intake Manifold

REMOVAL & INSTALLATION

Non-turbocharged model

1. Disconnect the negative battery terminal from the battery. Drain the cooling system.

2. Remove the bolt securing the alternator adjusting plate to the engine.

3. Disconnect and label all of the hoses attached to the air cleaner and remove the air cleaner.

4. Disconnect the air inlet temperature switch wiring connector.

5. Disconnect and label the hoses, electrical connectors, and control cable attached to the carburetor.

6. If equipped with A/C, disconnect the FIDC vacuum hose, the pressure tank control valve hose, the distributor/3-way connector hose and the VSV wiring connector.

7. Remove the carburetor attaching bolts (located beneath the intake manifold), then remove the carburetor and the EFE heater.

8. At the intake manifold, remove the PCV hose, the water bypass hose, the heater hoses, the EGR valve/canister hose, the distributor vacuum advance hose and the ground wires.

9. Disconnect the thermometer unit switch wiring connector.

10. Remove the intake manifold attaching nuts/bolts and the intake manifold.

11. Clean the sealing surfaces of the intake manifold and cylinder head.

12. To install, use new gaskets and reverse the removal procedures. Torque the intake manifold to 17 ft. lbs.; then adjust the engine control cable and the alternator belt tension. Refill the engine with coolant and check for leaks.

Turbocharged Model

1. Disconnect the negative battery terminal from the battery.

2. Remove pressure regulator and oil seperator.

3. Disconnect vacuum line from VSV and remove vacuum switching valve from bracket.

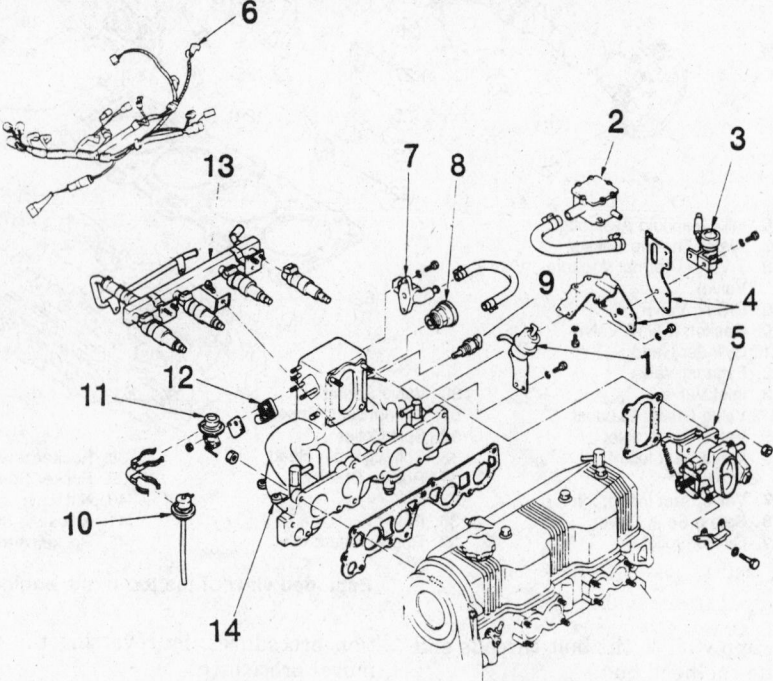

1. Pressure regulator	8.	Relief valve
2. Oil separator	9.	Map sensor
3. VSV	10.	Back pressure transducer
4. Bracket and hanger	11.	EGR valve
5. Throttle valve assembly	12.	Adaptor
6. Engine harness assembly	13.	Fuel injector with pipe
7. Idle air control valve	14.	Intake manifold

Intake manifold turbocharged model

4. Remove oil seperator/VSV bracket and hanger as an assembly.

5. Remove throttle valve assembly and engine harness assembly (mark or tag harness connections if necessary).

6. Remove Idle Air Control Valve, Relief Valve and Map sensor.

7. Disconnect vacuum line from Back Pressure transducer and unclip transducer from hold down bracket.

8. Remove EGR valve and adaptor plate.

9. Remove Fuel injectors and fuel pipe connected to rail as one unit and postion out of way then remove Intake Manifold with common chamber

10. To install, use new gaskets and reverse the removal procedures. Torque the intake manifold to 17 ft. lbs. Start and run engine check for leaks.

Exhaust Manifold

REMOVAL & INSTALLATION

NOTE: On turbocharged model refer to section on Turbocharger Removal & Installation.

1. Disconnect the negative battery terminal from the battery and the O_2 sensor wiring connector.

2. Disconnect the Thermostatic Air Cleaner (TAC) flex hose.

3. Remove the hot air cover and raise the vehicle.

4. Disconnect the exhaust pipe from the exhaust manifold and lower the vehicle.

5. Remove the nuts and bolts securing the exhaust manifold to the cylinder head. Clean the gasket mounting surfaces.

6. To install, use new gaskets and reverse the removal procedures. Torque the exhaust manifold to 17 ft. lbs. or 21 ft. lbs. turbocharged model then start the engine and check for leak

Turbocharger

REMOVAL & INSTALLATION

1. Disconnect the negative battery terminal from the battery.

2. Remove lower and upper heat protector shield covering turbocharger assembly.

3. Remove manifold heat protecter and unplug O_2 sensor.

4. Disconnect vacuum pipe from wastegate and positon out of the way.

5. Disconnect water lines.

6. Disconnect oil lines return and delivery.

7. Disconnect exhaust pipe from wastegate manifold.

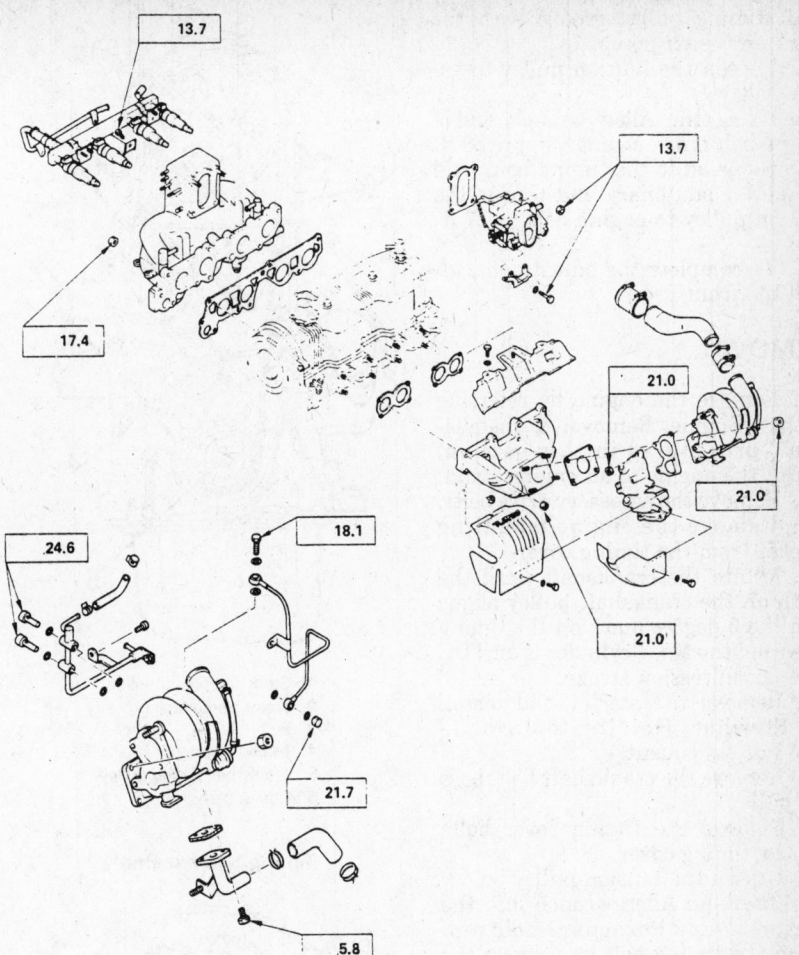

Turbocharger assembly torque specifications

NOTE: Exhaust manifold studs should be soaked with CRC or equivalent to prevent studs from breaking before removal.

8. Remove turbocharger and wastegate as an assembly.

9. To install, use new a gasket on exhaust manifold to turbocharger housing and reverse the removal procedures. Refill all fluid levels, run engine check for leaks.

TROUBLESHOOTING

NOTE: For more information on turbocharging, please refer to Turbocharging in the Unit Repair section.

Front Cover

REMOVAL & INSTALLATION

1. Disconnect negative battery cable.

2. Support the engine.

3. Remove the front mount bracket attached to the front cover.

4. Remove front cover.

5. To install, reverse the removal procedures.

Timing Belt and Tensioner

ADJUSTMENT

1. Refer to the "Front Cover, Removal & Installation" procedures in this section and remove the front cover.

2. Loosen the timing belt tension pulley bolt.

NOTE: If the belt has been removed or replaced with a new one, perform the following procedures to stretch the belt.

3. Using an Allen wrench, insert it into the hexagonal hole of the tension pulley. Hold the pulley stationary and temporarily tighten the tension pulley-to-engine bolt.

4. Rotate the crankshaft two complete revolutions and align the crank-

shaft timing pulley groove with the mark on the oil pump.

5. Loosen the tension pulley-to-engine bolt.

6. Using the Allen wrench and a timing belt tension gauge, apply 38 ft. lbs. of tension to the timing belt, hold the pulley stationary and torque the tension pulley-to-engine bolt to 37 ft. lbs.

7. To complete the adjustment, install the front cover.

REMOVAL

1. Remove the engine by referring to the "Engine, Removal & Installation" procedures in this section. Mount the engine to an engine stand.

2. Remove the accessory drive belts.

3. Remove the engine mounting bracket from the timing cover.

4. Rotate the crankshaft until the notch on the crankshaft pulley aligns with the 0 degree mark on the timing cover and the No. 4 cylinder is on TDC of the compression stroke.

5. Remove the starter and install the Flywheel Holding tool No. J–35271 or equivalent.

6. Remove the crankshaft bolt, boss and pulley.

7. Remove the timing cover bolts and the timing cover.

8. Loosen the tension pulley bolt.

9. Insert an Allen wrench into the tension pulley hexagonal hole and loosen the timing belt by turning the tension pulley clockwise.

10. Remove the timing belt.

11. Remove the head cover.

NOTE: Inspect the timing belt for signs of cracking, abnormal wear and hardening. Never expose the belt to oil, sunlight or heat. Avoid excessive bending, twisting or stretching.

INSTALLATION

1. Position the woodruff key on the crankshaft followed by the crankshaft timing gear. Align the groove on the timing gear with the mark on the oil pump.

2. Align the camshaft timing gear mark with the upper surface of the cylinder head and the dowel pin in its uppermost position.

3. Place the timing belt arrow in the direction of the engine rotation and install the timing belt. Tighten the tension pulley bolt.

4. Turn the crankshaft two complete revolutions and realign the crankshaft timing gear groove with the mark on the oil pump.

5. Loosen the tension pulley bolt and apply tension to the belt with an

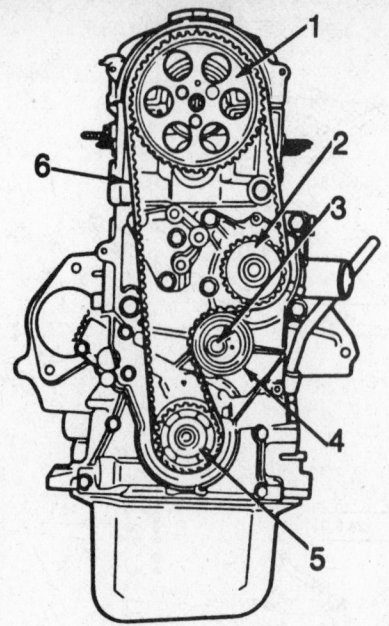

1. Camshaft timing pulley
2. Water pump timing pulley
3. Bolt
4. Tension pulley
5. Crankshaft timing pulley
6. Timing belt

Timing belt assembly

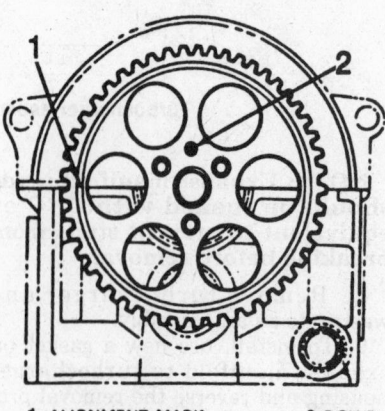

1 ALIGNMENT MARK   2 DOWEL

Alignment of the camshaft pulley

Allen wrench. Torque the pulley bolt to 37 ft. lbs. while holding the pulley stationary.

6. Adjust the valve clearances.

7. To complete the installation, reverse the removal procedures. Torque the crankshaft pulley-to-crankshaft bolt to 109 ft. lbs.

Timing Sprockets

REMOVAL & INSTALLATION

1. Disconnect the negative battery terminal from the battery.

2. Rotate the crankshaft to place the No. 4 cylinder on the TDC of compression stroke.

3. Remove the front cover-to-mount bracket bolt and the bracket from the vehicle.

4. Remove the front cover-to-engine bolts and the front cover from the engine.

NOTE: Make sure that the camshaft dowel pin is positioned at the top and the mark on the cam sprocket is aligned with the upper cylinder head surface.

5. Loosen the timing belt tension pulley-to-engine bolt, then remove the timing belt.

6. Remove the camshaft sprocket-to-camshaft bolts, the camshaft sprocket; allow the timing belt to hang.

7. If the engine has not been disturbed, reverse the removal procedures. Torque the camshaft sprocket-to-camshaft bolt to 7.2 ft. lbs. Adjust the timing belt.

8. To complete the installation, reverse the removal procedures.

OIL SEAL REPLACEMENT

The oil seal is part of the oil pump assembly; to replace the oil seal, refer to the "Oil Pump, Removal & Installation" procedures in this section.

1. With the oil pump removed from the engine, pry the oil seal from the oil pump housing with a small pry bar.

2. To install the new oil seal, drive it into the housing using the Seal Installing tool No. J–35269 or equivalent.

Camshaft

REMOVAL & INSTALLATION

1. Disconnect the negative battery terminal from the battery.

2. Align the crankshaft pulley notch with the 0 degree mark on the timing cover.

3. Remove the cylinder head cover.

4. Remove the timing cover.

5. Loosen the camshaft timing gear bolts (DO NOT rotate the engine).

6. Loosen the timing belt tensioner and remove the timing belt from the camshaft timing gear.

7. Remove the rocker arm shaft/rocker arm assembly.

8. Remove the distributor bolt and the distributor.

9. Remove the camshaft and the camshaft seal.

10. To install, drive a new camshaft seal on the camshaft using the Seal Installation tool No. J–35268 or equivalent, reverse the removal procedures, adjust the valves and the timing belt.

Piston and Connecting Rod

POSITIONING

Install the piston and rod assemblies into the same cylinder bore, facing the same direction from which they were removed. Each piston has a front directional mark stamped on the top surface.

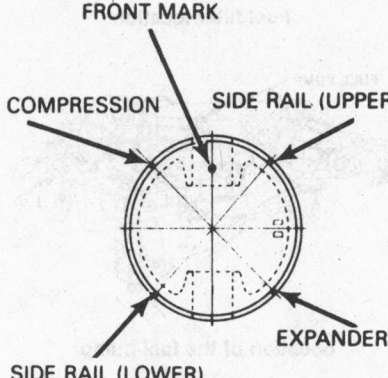

Proper piston ring installation—typical

ENGINE LUBRICATION

Oil Pan

REMOVAL & INSTALLATION

1. Disconnect the negative battery terminal from the battery.
2. Raise and support the vehicle on jackstands, then drain the crankcase.
3. Disconnect the exhaust pipe bracket from the block and the exhaust pipe at the manifold.
4. Disconnect the right hand tension rod located under the front bumper.
5. Remove the oil pan bolts and oil pan, then clean the sealing surfaces.
6. To install, use a new gasket, apply sealant to the oil pump housing and the rear retainer housing, reverse the removal procedures.

Rear Main Bearing Oil Seal

REMOVAL & INSTALLATION

1. Refer to the "Manual/Automatic

Transaxle, Removal & Installation" procedures in this section and remove the transaxle.
2. Remove the oil pan.
3. Remove the pressure plate and clutch (MT) or torque converter (AT), the flywheel bolts and the flywheel from the crankshaft.
4. Remove the rear oil seal retainer and remove the oil seal from the retainer. Clean the sealing surfaces.
5. Using a new oil seal, install the new seal in the oil seal retainer.
6. To install, use new gaskets, apply sealer to the mounting surfaces, apply oil to the seal lips, align the dowel pins of the retainer with the engine block and reverse the removal procedures.

Oil Pump

REMOVAL & INSTALLATION

1. Refer to the "Engine, Removal & Installation" procedures in this section and remove the engine.
2. Drain the crankcase.

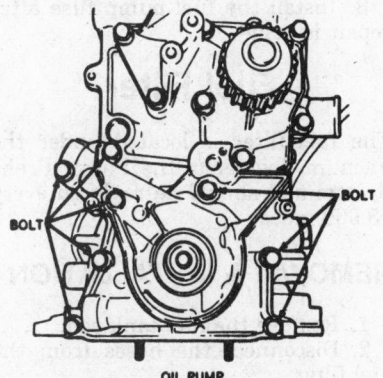

Location of the oil pump

1. Plug
2. Spring
3. Relief valve
4. Oil pump cover
5. Driven gear
6. Drive gear
7. Oil seal

3. Remove the alternator belt and the starter.
4. Install the Flywheel Holding tool No. J-35271 or equivalent, to secure the flywheel.
5. Remove the crankshaft pulley and boss.
6. Remove the timing cover bolts and the timing cover.
7. Loosen the tension pulley and remove the timing belt.
8. Remove the crankshaft timing gear and the tension pulley.
9. Remove the oil pan bolts, oil pan, oil strainer fixing bolt and the oil strainer assembly.
10. Remove the oil pump bolts and the oil pump assembly.
11. Remove the sealing material from the oil pump and engine block sealing surfaces.
12. To install, lubricate the oil pump, use new gaskets, apply sealant to the sealing surfaces and reverse the removal procedures.

ENGINE COOLING

Radiator

REMOVAL & INSTALLATION

1. Disconnect the negative battery terminal from the battery.
2. Drain the cooling system.
3. Remove the air intake duct.
4. Remove the fan motor cable from the fan motor socket.

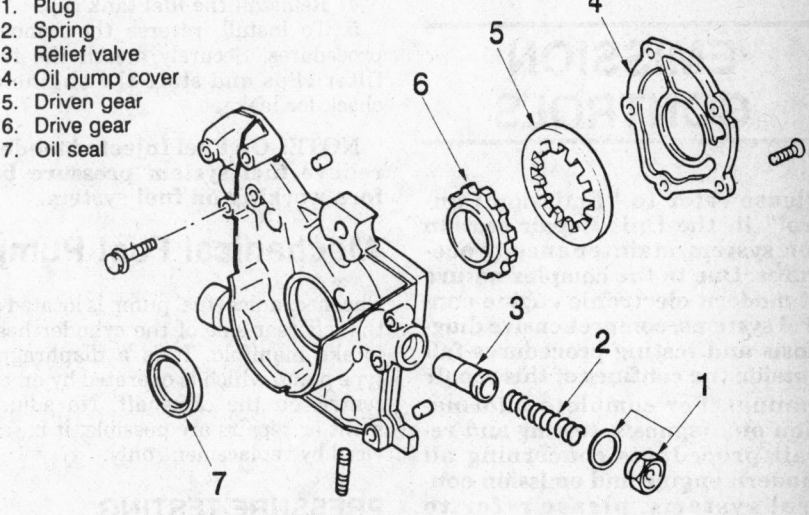

Exploded view of the oil pump

5. Disconnect the thermo switch cable.

6. Remove the fan motor assembly.

7. Remove the radiator hoses at the radiator, the coolant recovery hose at the filler neck and the oil cooler lines (AT).

8. Remove the radiator mounting bolts and the radiator.

9. To install, reverse the removal procedures.

Water Pump

REMOVAL & INSTALLATION

1. Drain the cooling system.

2. Loosen the power steering pump adjustment bolts and remove the belt.

3. Remove the timing belt.

4. Remove the tension pulley and spring.

5. Remove the water pump mounting bolts, the water pump and gasket. Clean the mounting surfaces of all gasket material.

6. To install, reverse the removal procedures. Torque the water pump to 17 ft. lbs. and the tension pulley to 30 ft. lbs.

Thermostat

REMOVAL & INSTALLATION

1. Remove the negative battery terminal. Drain the cooling system.

2. Remove the top radiator hose from the outlet pipe.

3. Remove the outlet pipe bolts, the outlet pipe, gasket and thermostat from the thermostat housing.

4. To install, reverse the removal procedures. Torque the outlet pipe-to-engine bolts to 17 ft. lbs.

EMISSION CONTROLS

Please refer to "Emission Control" in the Unit Repair section for system maintenance procedures. Due to the complex nature of modern electronic engine control systems, comprehensive diagnosis and testing procedures fall outside the confines of this repair manual. For complete information on diagnosis, testing and repair procedures concerning all modern engine and emission control systems, please refer to "Chilton's Guide to Electronic Engine Controls".

FUEL SYSTEM

Fuel System Service Precaution

Any time the fuel system is being worked on, disconnect the negative battery cable, execept for those tests where battery voltage is required and always keep a dry chemical (Class B) fire extinguisher near the work area.

RELIEVING FUEL SYSTEM PRESSURE

1. Remove the fuel pump fuse from the fuse block or disconnect the harness connector at the tank.

2. Start the engine. It should run and then stall when the fuel in the lines is exhausted. When the engine stops, crank the starter for about three seconds to make sure all pressure in the fuel lines is released.

3. Install the fuel pump fuse after repair is made.

Fuel Filter

The fuel filter is located under the Vacuum Booster of the Power Brake System and should be replaced every 15,000 miles.

REMOVAL & INSTALLATION

1. Remove the fuel tank cap.

2. Disconnect the hoses from the fuel filter.

NOTE: Cap the fuel hoses to prevent fuel spillage or dirt entry.

3. Remove the fuel filter.

4. Reinstall the fuel tank cap.

5. To install, reverse the removal procedures. Securely attach the fuel filter clips and start the engine to check for leakage.

NOTE: On Fuel Injected models relieve fuel system pressure before working on fuel system.

Mechanical Fuel Pump

The mechanical fuel pump is located at the left rear-side of the cylinder head intake manifold. It is a diaphragm-type pump which is operated by an eccentric on the camshaft. No adjustment or repairs are possible, it is serviced by replacement only.

PRESSURE TESTING

1. Disconnect the fuel line at the

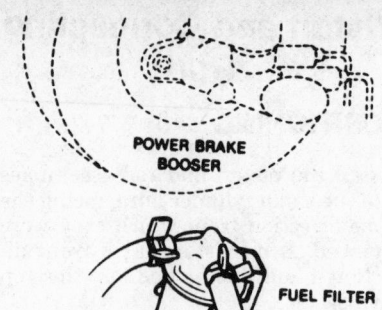

POWER BRAKE BOOSER

FUEL FILTER

Fuel filter location

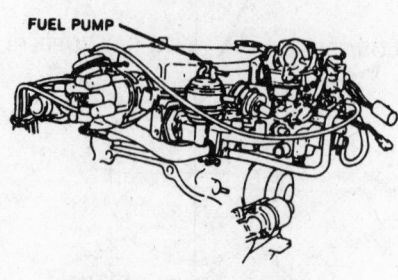

FUEL PUMP

Location of the fuel pump

carburetor. Install a rubber hose about 10 inches long. Attach a low reading pressure gauge.

2. Hold the gauge at least 16 inches above the fuel pump. If equipped, pinch the fuel return line.

3. Start the engine and run at slow idle, using the fuel that is left in the carburetor.

4. If the fuel pump is operating properly the pressure on the gauge should read a constant 3.8–4.7 psi.

5. If the pressure is too low, too high or significantly different at various engine speeds the pump should be replaced.

REMOVAL & INSTALLATION

1. Disconnect the fuel and return hoses from the fuel pump.

2. Remove the bolts, fuel pump and heat insulator assembly.

3. After removing the fuel pump, cover the mounting face of the cylinder head to prevent oil discharge.

4. To install, reverse the removal procedures. Replace the heat insulator assembly.

Electric Fuel Pump

PRESSURE TESTING

1. Relieve fuel pressure.

2. Disconnect the fuel hose between pressure regulator and fuel distributor pipe.

3. Connect a fuel pressure gauge

(J—33945) across the pressure regulator and fuel distributor pipe correctly.

4. Start engine and measure fuel pressure under these two different conditions:

    a. Vacuum hose of the pressure regulator disconnected (Intake manifold side end of hose must be plugged). The pressure should read 35.6 psi.

    b. Vacuum hose of the pressure regulator connected (At speed of 900 rpm). The pressure should read 28.4 psi.

5. After on-vechicle inspection is made remove fuel pressure gauge, reconnect fuel line and check for leaks.

REMOVAL & INSTALLATION

NOTE: Fuel is under high pressure, if the following steps are not followed the fuel could spray out and result in a fire hazard or possible injury. The fuel pump is located inside the gas tank.

1. Relieve fuel pressure then disconnect negative battery cable.

2. Drain fuel tank.

3. Remove all gas line hose connections and fuel pump ground wire.

4. Remove filler neck hose and clamp.

5. Remove breather hose and clamp.

6. Disconnect fuel tank hose to evaporator pipe.

7. Remove fuel tank mounting bolts and lower tank from car. At this point remove hose from pump to fuel fiter.

8. Remove fuel pump bracket plate and fuel pump as an assembly.

9. Remove pump bracket, rubber cushion and fuel pump filter.

10. To install, reverse the removal procedures. Be careful, to push the lower side of the fuel pump, together with the rubber cushion, into the fuel pump bracket.

Carburetor

The carburetor is a downdraft type having two stages of operation. The primary side has a small bore, double venturis, a bridge nozzle and a duty solenoid to control the fuel metering. The secondary side has a large bore and a secondary main metering system to control heavy load conditions. A high altitude emission control device is incorporated to supply clean air to the carburetor at specific altitudes, so over rich air/fuel ratio conditions will not occur.

REMOVAL & INSTALLATION

1. Disconnect the negative battery terminal from the battery.

2. Remove the air cleaner.

3. Disconnect the harness connector and hoses.

4. Remove the accelerator cable from the carburetor.

5. Remove the bolts securing the carburetor to the intake manifold. Remove the carburetor and place a cover over the intake manifold.

6. To install, reverse the removal procedures and torque carburetor fixing bolts to 7.2 ft. lbs. then start the engine and check for leaks.

OVERHAUL

For all carburetor overhaul and adjustment procedures, please refer to "Carburetor Service" in the Unit Repair section.

Fuel Injection

Due to the complex nature of modern fuel injection systems, comprehensive diagnosis and testing procedures fall outside the confines of this repair manual. For complete information on fuel injection diagnosis, testing and repair procedures please refer to *"Chilton's Guide To Fuel Injection and Feedback Carburetors"*.

MANUAL TRANSAXLE

Transaxle

REMOVAL & INSTALLATION

1. Drain the oil from the transaxle.

2. Disconnect the negative battery termninal from the battery and the transaxle.

3. Disconnect the wiring connectors, speedometer cable, clutch cable and shift cables from the transaxle.

4. Remove the air cleaner heat tube.

5. Remove the upper transaxle-to-engine bolts.

6. Raise and support the vehicle on jackstands. Remove the left-front wheel assembly and splash shield.

7. Disconnect the left tie rod at the steering knuckle and the left tension rod.

8. Disconnect the drive axles and remove the shafts by pulling them straight out from the transaxle (avoid damaging the oil seals).

9. Remove the dust cover at the clutch housing.

10. Using a floor jack, support the transaxle, then remove the transaxle-to-engine retaining bolts.

11. While sliding the transaxle away from the engine, carefully lower the jack, guiding the right axle shaft out of the transaxle.

NOTE: The right-axle shaft MUST be installed to the transaxle when the transaxle is being installed to the engine.

12. To install, reverse the removal procedures.

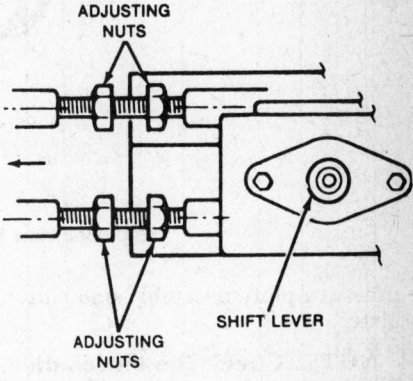

Adjusting the shift linkage of the transaxle

LINKAGE ADJUSTMENT

1. Loosen the adjusting nuts.

2. Place the transaxle and the shift lever in the Neutral position.

3. Turn the adjusting nuts until the shift lever is in the vertical position.

4. Tighten the adjusting nuts.

CLUTCH

REMOVAL & INSTALLATION

1. Refer to the "Manual Transaxle, Removal & Installation" procedures in this section and remove the transaxle.

2. Install the Pilot Shaft tool No. J—35282 or equivalent, into the pilot bearing to support the clutch assembly during the removal procedures.

NOTE: Observe the alignment marks on the clutch and the clutch cover and pressure plate assembly. If the markings are not present, be sure to add them.

3. Loosen the clutch cover and pressure plate assembly retaining bolts evenly (one at a time) until the spring pressure is released.

4. Remove the clutch cover and

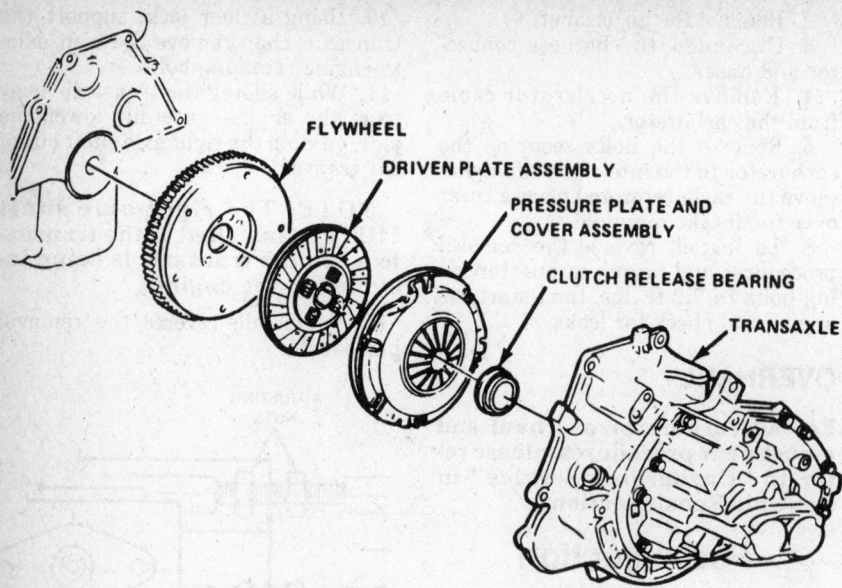

FLYWHEEL

DRIVEN PLATE ASSEMBLY

PRESSURE PLATE AND COVER ASSEMBLY

CLUTCH RELEASE BEARING

TRANSAXLE

Exploded view of the clutch assembly

pressure plate assembly and clutch plate.

NOTE: Check the clutch disc, flywheel and pressure plate for wear, damage or heat cracks. Replace all damaged parts.

5. Before installation, lightly lubricate the pilot shaft splines, pilot bearing and pilot release bearing surface with grease.

6. To install, reverse the removal procedures. Torque the clutch cover/pressure plate-to-flywheel bolts evenly to 13 ft. lbs., to avoid distortion.

FREE-PLAY ADJUSTMENT

1. Disconnect the negative battery terminal from the battery.
2. Loosen the adjusting nut and pull the cable to the rear until it turns freely.
3. Adjust the cable length by turning the adjusting nut.
4. When the clutch pedal free play travel reaches 0.39–0.79 in. release the cable.
5. When the adjustment has been completed, tighten the lock nut.

Clutch Cable

REMOVAL & INSTALLATION

1. Disconnect the negative battery terminal from the battery.
2. Loosen the clutch cable adjusting nuts. Disconnect the cable from the release arm and cable bracket.
3. At the clutch pedal, remove the cable retaining bolt.

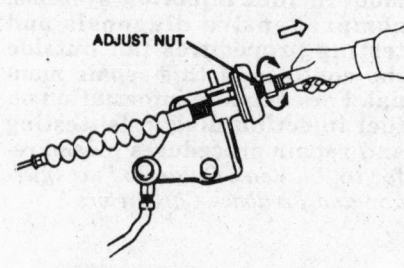

ADJUST NUT

Adjustment of the clutch cable

4. Disconnect the cable from the front of the dash.
5. Remove the clutch cable from the vehicle.
6. To install, grease the clutch cable pin and reverse the removal procedures.
7. Adjust the clutch cable.

AUTOMATIC TRANSAXLE

For further information on automatic transaxles, please refer to "Automatic Transmissions" in the Unit Repair section.

REMOVAL & INSTALLATION

1. Disconnect the negative battery terminal from the battery.
2. Remove the air duct tube from the air cleaner.
3. From the transaxle, disconnect

the shift cable, speedometer cable, vacuum diaphragm hose, engine wiring harness clamp and the ground cable.

4. At the left-fender, disconnect the inhibitor switch and the kickdown solenoid wiring connectors.
5. Disconnect the oil cooler lines from the transaxle.
6. Remove the three upper transaxle-to-engine mounting bolts. Raise and support the vehicle on jackstands.
7. Remove both front-wheels and the left-front fender splash shield.
8. Disconnect both tie rod ends at the steering knuckles.
9. Remove both front tension rod brackets and disconnect the rods from the control arms.
10. Disengage the axle shafts from the transaxle.
11. Remove the flywheel dust cover and the converter-to-flywheel attaching bolts.
12. Remove the transaxle rear mount through bolt.
13. Disconnect the starter wiring and the starter. Support the transaxle.
14. Remove the lower transaxle-to-engine mounting bolts and remove the transaxle.
15. To install, reverse the removal procedures. Torque the converter-to-flywheel at 30 ft. lbs., the transaxle-to-engine at 56 ft. lbs., adjust the shift linkage and fill the transaxle with Dexron® II automatic transmission fluid.

DRIVE AXLE

Halfshaft

REMOVAL & INSTALLATION

1. Raise and support the front of the vehicle on jackstands, allowing the wheels to hang.
2. Remove the front wheel assemblies, the hub grease caps, the hub nuts and the cotter pins.
3. Install the Drive Axle Boot Seal Protector tool No. J–28712 or equivalent, on the outer CV-joints and the Drive Axle Boot Seal Protector tool No. J–34754 or equivalent, on the inner Tri-Pot joints.

NOTE: Clean the halfshaft threads and lubricate them with a thread lubricant.

4. Have an assistant depress the brake pedal, then, remove the hub nut and washer.
5. Remove the caliper-to-steering knuckle bolts and support the caliper (on a wire) out of the way.

6. Remove the rotor. Remove the drain plug and drain the oil from the transaxle.

7. Using a Slide Hammer Puller and the Puller Attachment tool No. J–34866 or equivalent, pull the hub from the halfshaft.

8. Remove the tie rod-to-steering knuckle cotter pin and the nut. Using the Ball Joint Separator tool No. J–21687–02 or equivalent, press the tie rod ball joint from the steering knuckle.

9. Remove the lower ball joint-to-control arm nuts/bolts.

10. Swing the steering knuckle assembly outward and slide the halfshaft from the steering knuckle.

11. Place a large pry bar between the differential case and the inboard constant velocity joint. Pry the axle shaft from the differential case.

12. Remove the halfshaft assembly.

NOTE: When installing the axle shaft, press it into the differential case until it locks with with snap ring.

13. To install, use new cotter pins and reverse the removal procedures. Torque the ball joint-to-control arm nuts/bolts to 80 ft. lbs. (108 Nm), the caliper-to-steering knuckle bolts to 41 ft. lbs. (55 Nm) and the halfshaft-to-hub nut to 137 ft. lbs. (186 Nm). Check and/or adjust the front end alignment.

CV JOINT OVERHAUL

For all CV-joint overhaul procedures, please refer to "U/CV-Joint Overhaul" in the Unit Repair section.

Front Wheel Drive Hub, Knuckle and Bearings

REMOVAL & INSTALLATION

DO NOT remove the hub from the steering knuckle unless it is absolutely necessary.

1. Loosen the wheel nuts. Remove the grease cap, cotter pin, hub nut and thrust washer.

2. Remove the caliper and support it on a wire.

3. Remove the rotor.

4. Remove the tie rod nut. Using a ball joint removal tool, separate the tie rod from the steering knuckle.

5. Remove the two ball joint-to-control arm/tension rod retaining nuts and bolts.

6. Remove the two strut-to-steering knuckle retaining nuts/bolts.

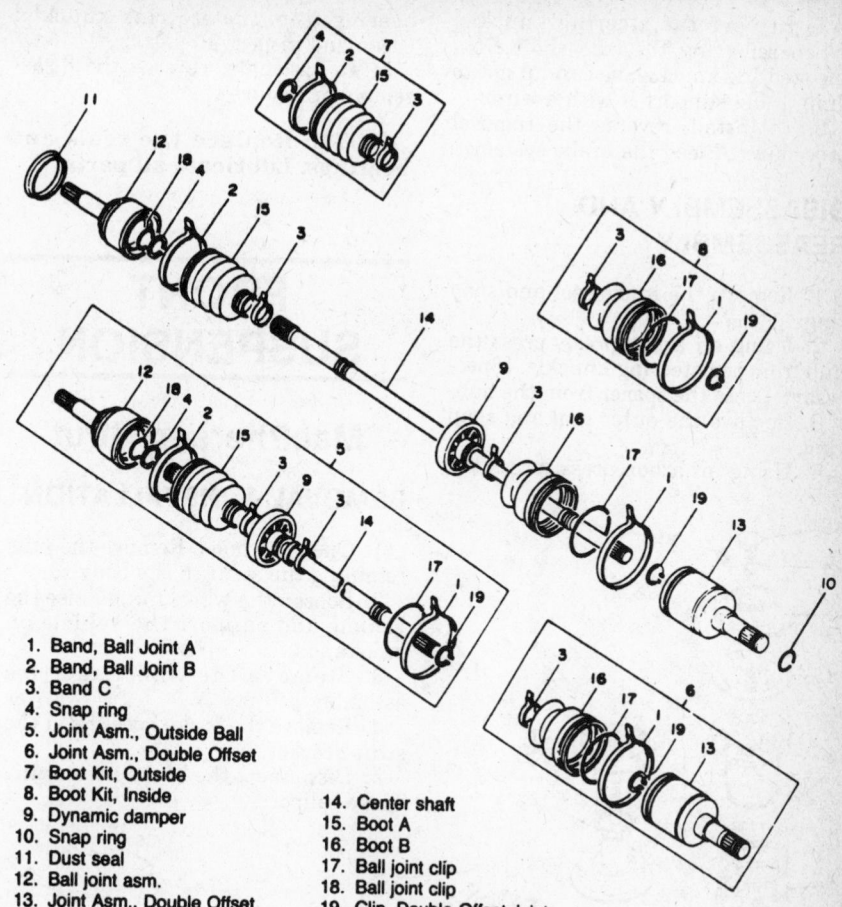

1. Band, Ball Joint A
2. Band, Ball Joint B
3. Band C
4. Snap ring
5. Joint Asm., Outside Ball
6. Joint Asm., Double Offset
7. Boot Kit, Outside
8. Boot Kit, Inside
9. Dynamic damper
10. Snap ring
11. Dust seal
12. Ball joint asm.
13. Joint Asm., Double Offset
14. Center shaft
15. Boot A
16. Boot B
17. Ball joint clip
18. Ball joint clip
19. Clip, Double Offset Joint

Exploded view of the halfshafts

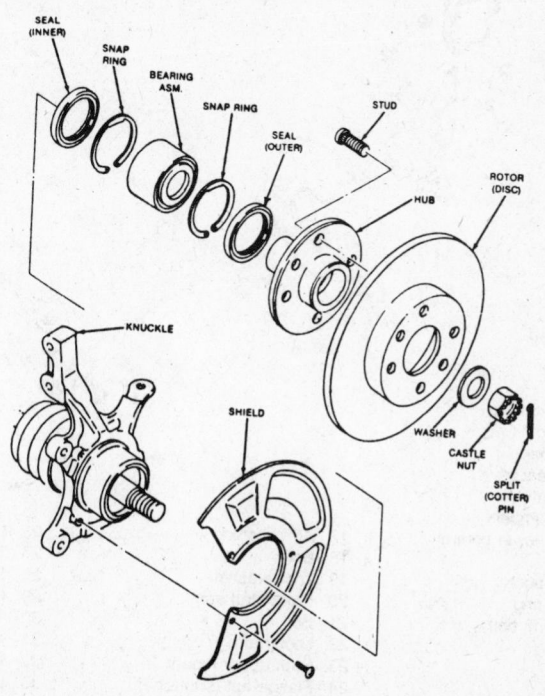

Exploded view of the front hub assembly

7. Remove the steering knuckle. When removing the axle shaft from the steering knuckle, be careful not to drop it and support it with a wire.

8. To install, reverse the removal procedures. Bleed the brake system.

DISASSEMBLY AND REASSEMBLY

1. Remove the inner seal and snap ring.

2. Using an arbor press, press the hub from the steering knuckle. If necessary, press the spacer from the hub.

3. Remove the outer seal and snap ring.

4. Using an arbor press, press the

bearing from the steering knuckle. Clean and inspect all parts.

5. To assemble, reverse the disassembly procedures.

NOTE: Replace the seals and bearings. Lubricate all parts.

FRONT SUSPENSION

MacPherson Strut

REMOVAL & INSTALLATION

1. Open the hood. Remove the nuts retaining the strut to the body.

2. Loosen the wheel nuts. Raise the vehicle and support the vehicle on jackstands.

3. Remove the wheel and tire assembly.

4. Remove the brake hose clip at the strut bracket.

5. Disconnect the brake hose at the brake caliper.

6. Tape or cap the brake hose and caliper opening.

7. Pull the brake hose through the opening in the strut bracket.

8. Remove the nuts retaining the strut to the steering knuckle.

9. Remove the strut assembly.

10. To install, reverse the removal procedures. Bleed the brake system.

OVERHAUL

For all spring and shock absorber removal & installation procedures, and all strut overhaul procedures, please refer to "Strut Overhaul" in the Unit Repair section.

Tension Bars

REMOVAL & INSTALLATION

1. Raise and support the vehicle on jackstands.

2. If equipped with a stabilizer bar, remove the nuts, bolts and insulators retaining it to the tension rod.

3. Remove the nut and washer retaining the tension rod to the body.

4. Remove the nuts and bolts retaining the tension rod to the control rod.

5. Remove the tension rod.

6. To install, reverse the removal procedures.

Ball Joints

INSPECTION

Before removing the ball joint for replacement, check it and the boot for excessive wear or damage.

REMOVAL & INSTALLATION

1. Loosen the wheel nuts.

2. Raise and support the vehicle on jackstands.

3. Remove the wheel and tire assembly.

4. Remove the two nuts retaining the ball joint to the tension rod and control arm assembly.

5. Remove the pinch bolt retaining the ball joint to the steering knuckle.

6. Remove the ball joint.

7. To install, reverse the removal procedures.

Lower Control Arm

REMOVAL & INSTALLATION

1. Raise and support the front of the vehicle on jackstands.

2. Remove the control arm to tension arm retaining nuts and bolts.

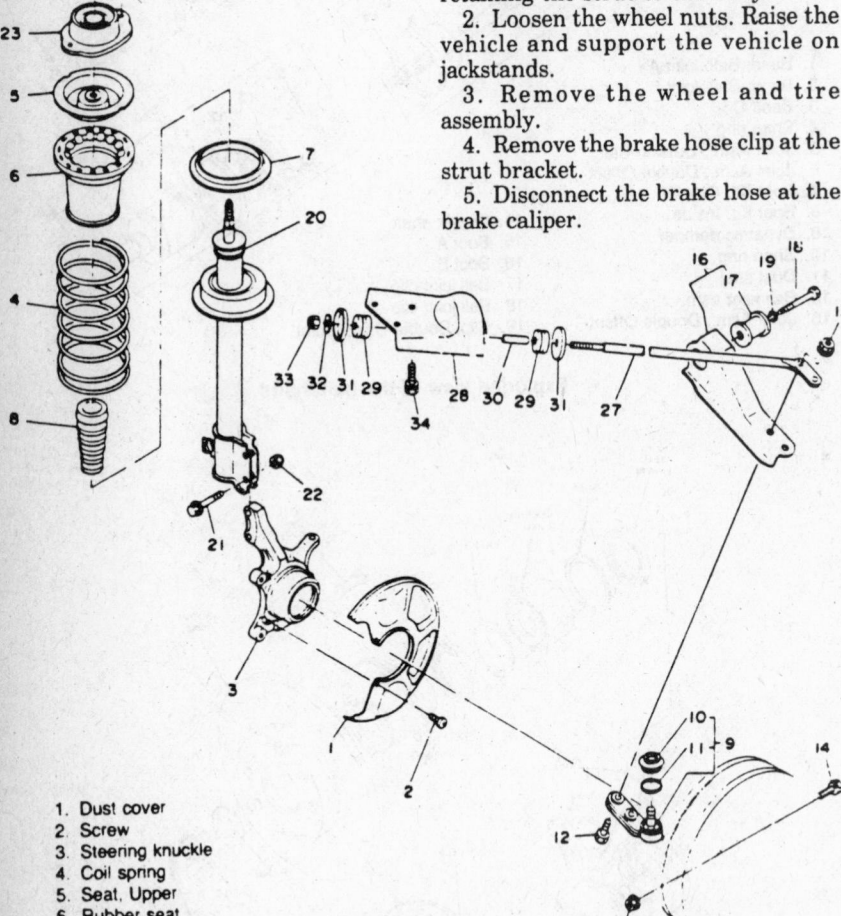

1. Dust cover
2. Screw
3. Steering knuckle
4. Coil spring
5. Seat, Upper
6. Rubber seat
7. Lower seat
8. Rubber bumper
9. Ball joint (lower control arm)
10. Ball joint boot
11. Boot clip ring
12. Control arm bolt
13. Lock nut
14. Bolt
15. Lock nut
16. Lower arm asm.
17. Arm bushing
18. Bolt
19. Lock washer
20. Front strut asm.
21. Bolt
22. Lock nut
23. Strut upper mount
24. Flange nut (strut shaft)
25. Nut
26. Cap
27. Tension rod
28. Support bracket
29. Rubber cushion
30. Tension rod spacer
31. Washer
32. Washer
33. Lock nut
34. Bolt

Exploded view of the front suspension assembly

3. Remove the nut/bolt securing the control arm to the body.

4. Remove the control arm and check for cracking or distortion.

5. To install, reverse the removal procedures.

NOTE: Raise the control arm to a distance of 15 in. from the top of the wheel well to the center of the hub. Torque the control arm-to-body bolts to 41 ft. lbs. and the control arm-to-tension rod bolts to 80 ft. lbs. This procedure aligns the bushing arm to the body.

Front Wheel Alignment

CASTER AND CAMBER ADJUSTMENT

Caster and camber cannot be adjusted. Should camber or caster be found out of specification, locate cause then repair (suspension or body related). To prevent incorrect service readings of camber or caster bumper must be moved up and down three times before inspection.

TOE ADJUSTMENT

Toe is adjusted by changing tie rod length. Loosen boot clamps and slide from the boot. Loosen right and left tie rod end lock nuts first and then turn right and left rods by the same amount to align toe to specification. After adjustment, reinstall, tighten lock nuts to specified torque and make sure that the rack boots are not twisted.

REAR SUSPENSION

Shock Absorbers

REMOVAL & INSTALLATION

1. Open the trunk and lift off the trim cover (hatch back models only). Remove the upper shock absorber nut.

2. Remove the lower bolt of the shock absorber.

3. Remove the shock absorber.

4. To install, reverse the removal procedures.

NOTE: When replacing the shock absorber, NEVER reuse the old lower bolt, ALWAYS use a new one.

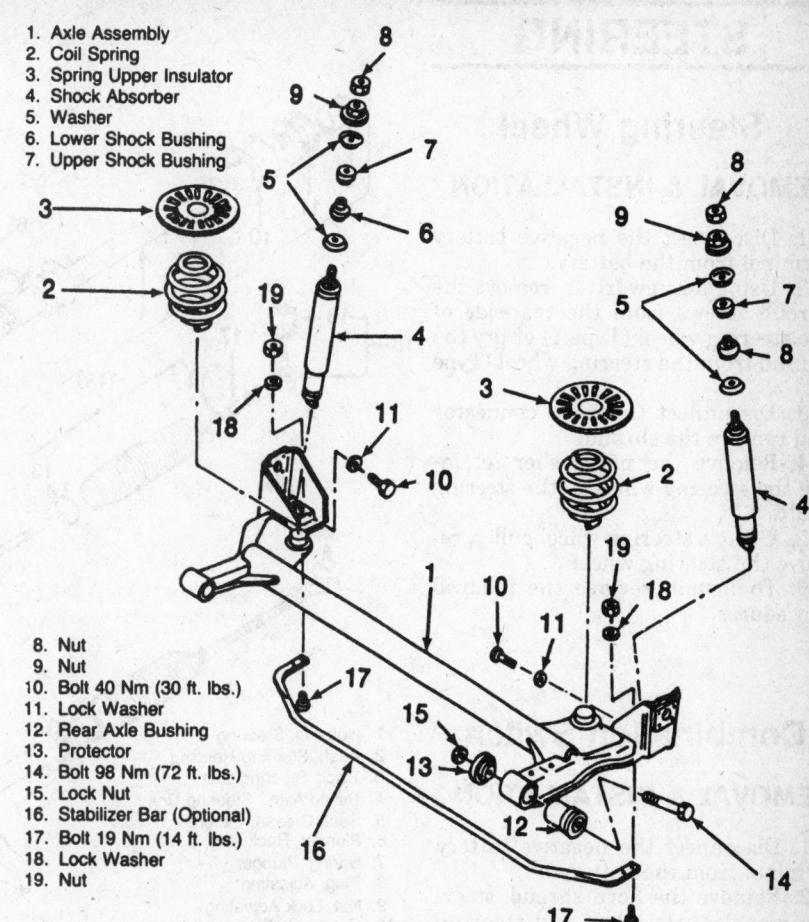

1. Axle Assembly
2. Coil Spring
3. Spring Upper Insulator
4. Shock Absorber
5. Washer
6. Lower Shock Bushing
7. Upper Shock Bushing

8. Nut
9. Nut
10. Bolt 40 Nm (30 ft. lbs.)
11. Lock Washer
12. Rear Axle Bushing
13. Protector
14. Bolt 98 Nm (72 ft. lbs.)
15. Lock Nut
16. Stabilizer Bar (Optional)
17. Bolt 19 Nm (14 ft. lbs.)
18. Lock Washer
19. Nut

Exploded view of the rear axle assembly

Coil Spring

REMOVAL & INSTALLATION

1. Raise and support the rear-end of the vehicle on jackstands.

2. Remove the rear wheels.

3. At the center of the rear axle, remove the brake line, retaining clip and flexible hose.

4. Remove the parking brake tension spring at the rear axle.

5. Disconnect the parking brake cable from the turn buckle and at the cable joint.

6. Support the axle with a jack, then remove the lower shock absorber bolt and disconnect it from the axle.

7. Lower the axle support and remove the coil spring.

8. To install, reverse the removal procedures.

NOTE: Raise the axle assembly to a distance of 15.2 in. from the top of the wheel well to the center of the axle hub, then torque the fasteners. ALWAYS replace the lower shock absorber bolt with a new one.

Rear Wheel Bearing

REMOVAL & INSTALLATION

1. Raise and support the front of the vehicle on jackstands.

2. Remove the rear wheel assemblies.

3. Remove the hub cap, cotter pin, hub nut, washer and outer bearing.

4. Remove the hub.

5. Using a slide hammer puller and attachment, pull the oil seal from the hub. Remove the inner bearing.

6. Using a brass drift and a hammer, drive both bearing races from the hub.

7. Clean, inspect and/or replace all parts.

8. To install, pack the bearings with grease, coat the oil seal lips with grease and reverse the removal procedures. Torque hub nut to 22 ft. lbs.

NOTE: If the cotter pin holes are out of alignment upon reassembly, use a wrench to tighten the nut until the hole in the shaft and a slot of the nut align.

STEERING

Steering Wheel

REMOVAL & INSTALLATION

1. Disconnect the negative battery terminal from the battery.

2. Using a screwdriver, remove the shroud screws from the rear-side of the steering wheel (Type 1) or pry the shroud from the steering wheel (Type 2).

3. Disconnect the horn connector and remove the shroud.

4. Remove the nut/washer retaining the steering wheel to the steering shaft.

5. Using a steering wheel puller, remove the steering wheel.

6. To install, reverse the removal procedures.

Combination Switch

REMOVAL & INSTALLATION

1. Disconnect the negative battery terminal from the battery.

2. Remove the horn shroud, steering wheel nut/washer and steering wheel assembly.

3. Remove the steering cowl attaching screw and steering cowl.

4. Disconnect the combination/starter switch connector.

5. Remove the turn signal/dimmer switch attaching screw and switch.

6. To install, reverse the removal procedures.

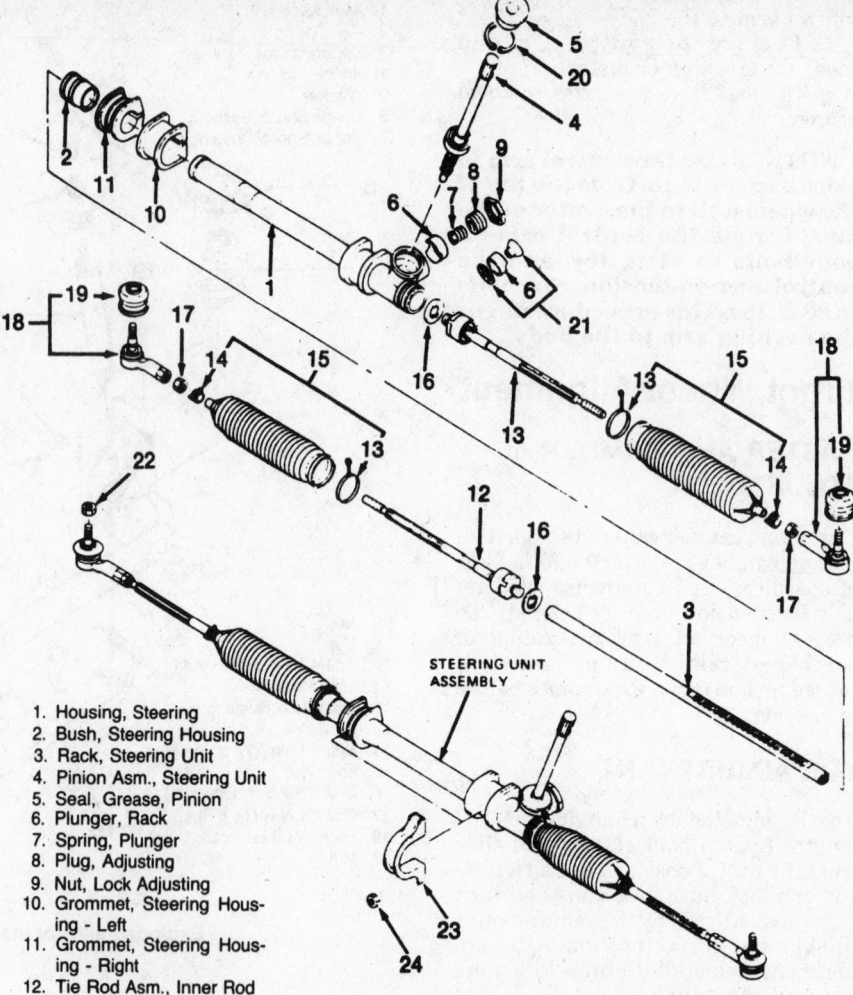

1. Housing, Steering
2. Bush, Steering Housing
3. Rack, Steering Unit
4. Pinion Asm., Steering Unit
5. Seal, Grease, Pinion
6. Plunger, Rack
7. Spring, Plunger
8. Plug, Adjusting
9. Nut, Lock Adjusting
10. Grommet, Steering Housing - Left
11. Grommet, Steering Housing - Right
12. Tie Rod Asm., Inner Rod
13. Wire, Boot Retaining
14. Clip, Boot Retaining
15. Kit, Boot
16. Washer, Locking
17. Nut, Rod End Lock
18. Tie Rod, End Asm
19. Boot, Tie Rod Sealing
20. Ring, Snap
21. Pad Asm., Pressure Rack Plunger
22. Nut, Locking Tie Rod to Knuckle
23. Bracket, Steering Unit
24. Nut, Bracket

Exploded view of the manual rack and pinion assembly

Ignition Lock/Switch

REMOVAL & INSTALLATION

1. Refer to the "Combination Switch, Removal & Installation" procedures in the this section. Remove the combination switch.

2. Insert the key into the ignition and place the key in the On position (the lock bar must be pulled all the way in).

3. Remove the snap ring and rubber cushion from the steering shaft.

4. Disconnect the switch wires at the connectors.

5. Remove the 2 screws retaining the ignition/starter switch and remove the switch.

6. To install, reverse the removal procedures.

Manual Steering Gear

REMOVAL & INSTALLATION

1. Refer to the "Tie Rod, Removal & Installation" procedures in this section. Remove both tie rod ends from the steering knuckles and the left inner tie rod from the rack.

2. Remove the intermediate shaft cover.

3. Loosen the upper pinch bolt and remove the lower pinch bolt at the pinion shaft.

4. Remove the steering gear to body retaining nuts.

5. Remove the rack and pinion assembly.

6. To install, reverse the removal procedures and check the toe-in.

Power Steering Gear

REMOVAL & INSTALLATION

1. Refer to the "Tie Rod, Removal & Installation" procedures in this section. Remove both tie rod ends from the steering knuckles and the right inner tie rod from the rack.

2. Place a drain pan under the rack assembly and clean around the pressure lines at the rack valve.

3. Cut the plastic retaining straps at the power steering lines and hose.

4. Remove the power steering pump lines, the rack valve and drain the fluid into the pan.

5. Remove the rack and pinion.

6. To install, reverse the removal procedures, add fluid, bleed the system and check the toe-in.

Power Steering Pump

REMOVAL & INSTALLATION

1. Place a drain pan below the pump.
2. Remove the pressure hose clamp, pressure hose and return hose. Drain the fluid from the pump and reservoir.
3. Remove the adjusting bolt, pivot bolt and drive belt.
4. Remove the pump assembly.
5. To install, reverse the removal procedures, tighten the pressure hose to 20 ft. lbs., adjust the drive belt, fill the reservoir and bleed the system.

BELT ADJUSTMENT

NOTE: The following procedures require the use of GM Belt Tension Gauge No. BT–33–95–ACBN (regular V-belts) or BT–33–97M (poly V-belts).

1. If the belt is cold, operate the engine (at idle speed) for 15 minutes; the belt will seat itself in the pulleys allowing the belt fibers to relax or stretch. If the belt is hot, allow it to cool, until it is warm to the touch.

NOTE: A used belt is one that has been rotated at least one complete evolution on the pulleys. This begins the belt seating process and it must never be tensioned to the new belt specifications.

2. Loosen the component-to-mounting bracket bolts.
3. Using a GM Belt Tension Gauge No. BT–33–95–ACBN (standard V-belts) or BT–33–97M (poly V-belts), place the tension gauge at the center of the belt between the longest span.
4. Applying belt tension pressure on the component, adjust the drive belt tension to the correct specifications. The belt tension should deflect about ¼ in. over a 7–10 in. span or ½ in. over a 13–16 in. span.
5. While holding the correct tension on the component, tighten the component-to-mounting bracket bolt.
6. When the belt tension is correct (70–110 inch lbs.), remove the tension gauge.

SYSTEM BLEEDING

1. Turn the wheels to the extreme left.
2. With the engine stopped, add power steering fluid to the "MIN" mark on the fluid indicator.
3. Start the engine and run it for 15 seconds at fast idle.
4. Stop the engine, recheck the fluid level and refill to the "MIN" mark.

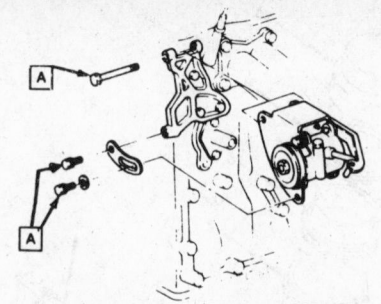

Ⓐ TORQUE: 20 N·m (15 FT. LBS.)

Power steering pump mounting and adjusting bolts

5. Start the engine and turn the wheels from side to side (3 times).
6. Stop the engine check the fluid level.

NOTE: If air bubbles are still present in the fluid, the procedures must be repeated.

Tie Rod Ends

REMOVAL & INSTALLATION

1. Raise and support the front of the vehicle on jackstands, then remove the front wheel.
2. Remove the castle nut from the ball joint. Using a ball joint removal tool, separate the tie rod from the steering knuckle.
3. Disconnect the retaining wire from the inner boot and pull back the boot.
4. Using a chisel, straighten the staked part of the locking washer between the tie rod and the rack.
5. Remove the tie rod from the rack.
6. To install, reverse the removal procedures.

BRAKES

For all brake system repair service procedures not detailed below, please refer to "Brakes" in the Unit Repair section.

Master Cylinder

REMOVAL & INSTALLATION

1. Remove some brake fluid from the master cylinder with a syringe.
2. Disconnect and cap or tape the openings of the brake tube.
3. Disconnect the brake fluid level warning switch connector.
4. Remove the 2 nuts securing the master cylinder to the power brake booster.
5. Remove the master cylinder from the power brake booster.
6. To install, reverse the removal procedures, add fluid to the reservoir and bleed the brake system.

Proportioning Valve

REMOVAL & INSTALLATION

1. Clean the area around the reservoir and brake pipe connections.
2. Remove the brake fluid from the master cylinder reservoir with a syringe.
3. Disconnect the brake pipes from the proportioning valves. Cap or tape all openings.
4. While holding the master cylinder, Use a box wrench and remove the proportioning valves from the master cylinder.

NOTE: It may be necessary to remove the master cylinder and place in a vise to sufficiently hold it while removing the proportioning valves.

5. To install, reverse the removal procedures. Fill the reservoir and bleed the system.

Power Brake Booster

REMOVAL & INSTALLATION

1. Refer to the "Master Cylinder, Removal & Installation" procedures in this section and remove the master cylinder.
2. Remove the vacuum hose from the vacuum servo.
3. Remove the clevis pin from the brake pedal.
4. Remove the 4 nuts from the brake assembly under the dash and remove the power booster from the engine compartment.
5. To install, reverse the removal procedures.

Wheel Cylinder

REMOVAL & INSTALLATION

1. Remove the brake shoe and components to gain access to the wheel cylinder.
2. Clean the area around the brake pipe and disconnect it from the wheel cylinder. Cap or tape all openings.
3. Remove the two bolts and remove the wheel cylinder.
4. To install, reverse the removal procedures. Torque the mounting nuts to 7 ft. lbs.

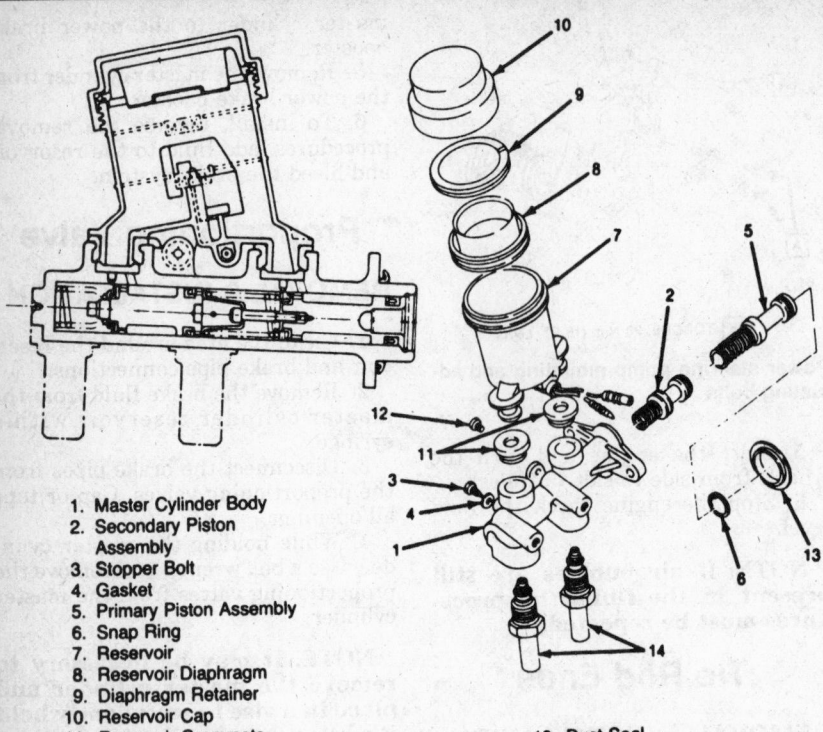

1. Master Cylinder Body
2. Secondary Piston
   Assembly
3. Stopper Bolt
4. Gasket
5. Primary Piston Assembly
6. Snap Ring
7. Reservoir
8. Reservoir Diaphragm
9. Diaphragm Retainer
10. Reservoir Cap
11. Reservoir Grommets
12. Reservoir Screw
13. Dust Seal
14. Proportioning Valves

Exploded view of the master cylinder assembly

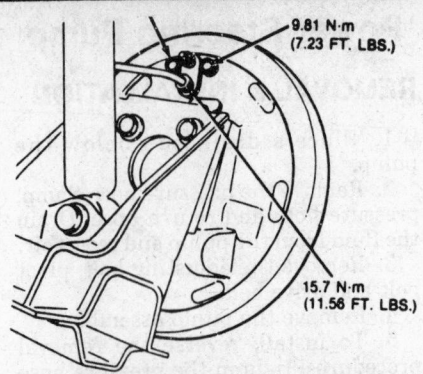

9.81 N·m
(7.23 FT. LBS.)

15.7 N·m
(11.56 FT. LBS.)

Wheel cylinder attaching bolts

Parking Brake Cable

ADJUSTMENT

The parking brake adjustment is normal when the lever moves 7–9 notches at 66 lbs. of force. If it is not within limits, adjust the rear brakes. If this adjustment does not affect the specifications, adjust the parking brake turnbuckle.

REMOVAL & INSTALLATION

1. Remove the parking brake lever assembly from inside the vehicle by performing the following procedures:
   a. Remove the console box.
   b. Disconnect the electrical wiring connector from the parking brake switch.
   c. Remove the lever-to-chassis bolts and the lever.
   d. From the parking brake lever, remove the parking brake cable and the switch.
2. Raise and support the rear of the vehicle on jackstands.
3. To remove the parking brake cable assembly, perform the following procedures:
   a. With the parking brake cable assembly in it's relaxed position, separate the front cable from the rear cable assembly.
   b. Remove the tension spring from the rear axle.
   c. Remove the rear wheel, the hub and the drum.
   d. Disconnect the parking brake cable from the rear brake lever.
   e. Remove the parking brake cable-to-chassis bolt and the cable(s) from the vehicle.
4. Inspect the parking brake lever assembly and the cable assembly for damage, wear, scoring and/or deterioration; replace the cable(s), if necessary.
5. To install, lubricate the cable(s) with grease and reverse the removal procedures. Seat the cable(s) in the

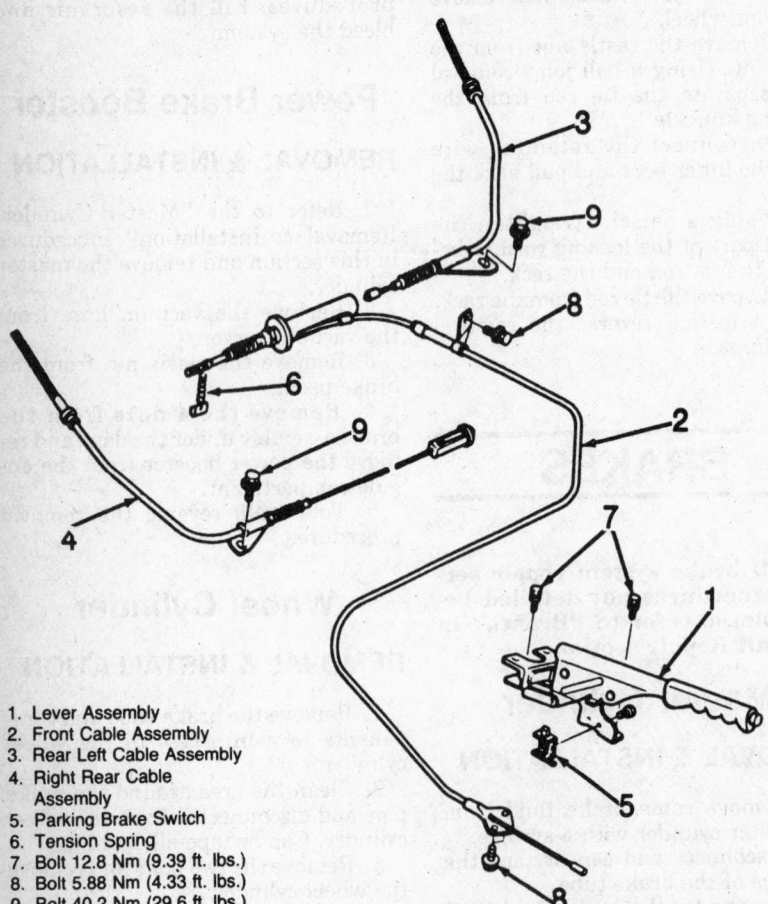

1. Lever Assembly
2. Front Cable Assembly
3. Rear Left Cable Assembly
4. Right Rear Cable
   Assembly
5. Parking Brake Switch
6. Tension Spring
7. Bolt 12.8 Nm (9.39 ft. lbs.)
8. Bolt 5.88 Nm (4.33 ft. lbs.)
9. Bolt 40.2 Nm (29.6 ft. lbs.)

Exploded view of the parking brake assembly

backing plate. Torque the backplate-to-chassis bolt to 30 ft. lbs. and the lever-to-chassis bolts to 10 ft. lbs. Adjust the parking brake.

CHASSIS ELECTRICAL

Heater Blower Motor

REMOVAL & INSTALLATION

1. Disconnect the blower motor electrical connector at the motor case.
2. If equipped with A/C, remove the rubber hose from the blower case.
3. Rotate the blower motor case counterclockwise and remove the blower motor assembly.
4. To install, reverse the removal procedures.

Heater Core

REMOVAL & INSTALLATION

1. Disconnect the heater hoses in the engine compartment.
2. At the lower part of the heater unit case, remove the 6 retaining clips.
3. Using a small pry bar, pry open the lower part of the case and remove it.
4. Remove the core assembly insulator and the core assembly.
5. To install, reverse the removal procedures.

Radio

REMOVAL & INSTALLATION

1. Remove the screws retaining the radio cover and remove the cover.
2. Remove the radio and bracket.
3. Disconnect the electrical connector, speaker connectors and the antenna cable.
4. To install, reverse the removal procedures.

Windshield Wiper Switch

REMOVAL & INSTALLATION

Front

1. Refer to the "Headlight Switch, Removal & Installation" procedures in this section and remove the instrument cluster bezel.
2. Remove the wiper switch electri-

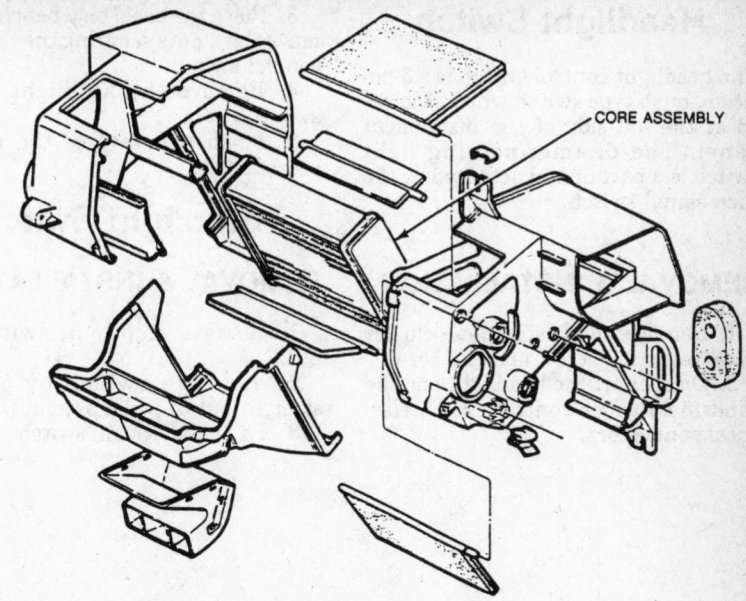

Exploded view of the heater assembly

cal connector, attaching nuts and bracket.
3. Remove the wiper switch.
4. To install, reverse the removal procedures.

Rear

1. Using a small tool, pry the switch panel from the dash.
2. Pull the switch out and disconnect the electrical connector.
3. To install, reverse the removal procedures.

Windshield Wiper Motor

REMOVAL & INSTALLATION

Front Window

1. Disconnect the negative battery terminal from the battery.
2. Remove the lock nuts retaining the wiper arms and the wiper arms.
3. Remove the cowl cover, wiper motor cover and the electrical connector.
4. Disconnect the drive arm from the wiper link.
5. Remove the mounting bolts and the wiper motor.
6. To install, reverse the removal procedures.

Rear Window

1. Disconnect the negative battery terminal from the battery.
2. Remove the trim pad and the wiper arm assemblies.
3. Remove the mounting bolts and the motor assembly.

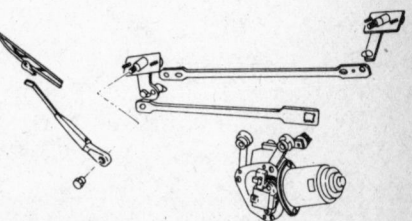

Exploded view of the front wiper assembly

4. Disconnect the electrical connector.
5. To install, reverse the removal procedures.

Instrument Cluster

REMOVAL & INSTALLATION

1. Disconnect the negative battery terminal from the battery.
2. Remove the instrument cluster bezel retaining screws and bezel.
3. Disconnect the windshield wiper and lighting switch connectors.
4. Remove the instrument cluster retaining screws and pull out the assembly.
5. Remove the trip reset knob and the assembly glass.
6. Remove the buzzer, sockets and bulbs.
7. Remove the speedometer assembly, fuel and temperature gauge.
8. Remove the tachometer, it equipped.
9. To install, reverse the removal procedures.

Headlight Switch

The headlight control switch is a 3-position, push type switch which is located at the left-side of the instrument panel. The dimmer/passing light switch is a part of and actuated by the turn signal switch.

REMOVAL & INSTALLATION

1. Remove the instrument cluster bezel retaining screw and the bezel.
2. Disconnect the headlight and the windshield wiper control switch electrical connectors.

3. Place the bezel on a bench and remove the 2 nuts securing the headlight control switch.
4. Remove the headlight control switch.
5. To install, reverse the removal procedures.

Stoplight Switch

REMOVAL & INSTALLATION

1. Remove stop light switch lock nut.
2. Remove switch by pulling straight out of pedal assembly.
3. To install push switch straight

in, push the brake pedal by turning the stop light switch, so that free play in the brake pedal is eliminated, then tighten the stop light switch lock nut.

Fuses and Circuit Breakers

LOCATION

The fuse block is located at the lower left-hand side of the instrument panel, concealed by a cover. To replace a blown fuse, pull out the fuse holder, remove the blown fuse and install one of the same amperage.

Chevrolet
Front Wheel Drive
Sprint

16

SERIAL NUMBER IDENTIFICATION

VEHICLE IDENTIFICATION CHART

It is important for servicing and ordering parts to be certain of the vehicle and engine identification. The VIN (vehicle identification number) is a 17 digit number visible through the windshield on the driver's side of the dash and contains the vehicle and engine identification codes. The tenth digit indicates model year and the eighth digit indicates engine code. It can be interpreted as follows:

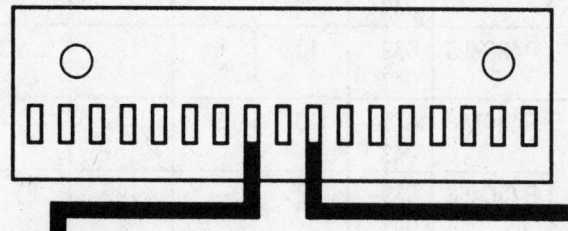

Engine Code							Model Year	
Code	Cu. In.	Liters	Cyl.	Fuel Sys.	Eng. Mfg.		Code	Year
5	61	1.0	3	2 bbl	Suzuki		F	1985
2	61	1.0	3	EFI	Suzuki		G	1986
							H	1987
							J	1988
							K	1989

GENERAL ENGINE SPECIFICATIONS

Year	VIN	No. Cylinder Displacement cu. in. (liter)	Fuel System Type	Net Horsepower @ rpm	Net Torque @ rpm (ft.lbs.)	Bore × Stroke (in.)	Compression Ratio	Oil Pressure @ rpm
1985	5	3-61 (1.0)	2 bbl	48 @ 5100	57 @ 3200	2.91 × 3.03	9.5:1	48
1986	5	3-61 (1.0)	2 bbl	48 @ 5100	57 @ 3200	2.91 × 3.03	9.5:1	48
1987	5	3-61 (1.0)	2 bbl	48 @ 5100	77 @ 3200	2.91 × 3.03	9.5:1	48
	5	3-61 (1.0)①	2 bbl	46 @ 4700	78 @ 3200	2.91 × 3.03	9.8:1	48
	2	3-61 (1.0)	EFI	70 @ 5500	107 @ 3500	2.91 × 3.03	8.3:1	48
1988–89	5	3-61 (1.0)	2 bbl	48 @ 5100	77 @ 3200	2.91 × 3.03	9.5:1	48
	5	3-61 (1.0)①	2 bbl	46 @ 4700	78 @ 3200	2.91 × 3.03	9.8:1	48
	2	3-61 (1.0)	EFI	70 @ 5500	107 @ 3500	2.91 × 3.03	8.3:1	48

① "ER" model

GASOLINE ENGINE TUNE-UP SPECIFICATIONS

Year	VIN	No. Cylinder Displacement cu. in. (liter)	Spark Plugs Type	Spark Plugs Gap (in.)	Ignition Timing (deg.) MT	Ignition Timing (deg.) AT	Compression Pressure (psi)	Fuel Pump (psi)	Idle Speed (rpm) MT	Idle Speed (rpm) AT	Valve Clearance In.	Valve Clearance Ex.
1985	5	3-61 (1.0)	R43CXLS	.039–.043	10	6	199	3.5	—	850	.006	.008
1986	5	3-61 (1.0)	R43CXLS	.039–.043	10	6	199	3.5	750	850	.006	.008
1987	5	3-61 (1.0)	R43CXLS	.039–.043	10	6	199	4.0	750 ①	850	.006	.008
	2	3-61 (1.0)	R43CXLS	.039–.043	12	—	199	25-33	750	—	.006	.008
1988	5	3-61 (1.0)	R43CXLS	.039–.043	10	6	199	4.0	750 ①	850	.006	.008
	2	3-61 (1.0)	R43CXLS	.039–.043	12	—	199	25-33	750	—	.006	.008
1989	SEE UNDERHOOD SPECIFICATIONS STICKER											

① "ER" model: 700 rpm

FIRING ORDERS

NOTE: To avoid confusion, always replace spark plug wires one at a time.

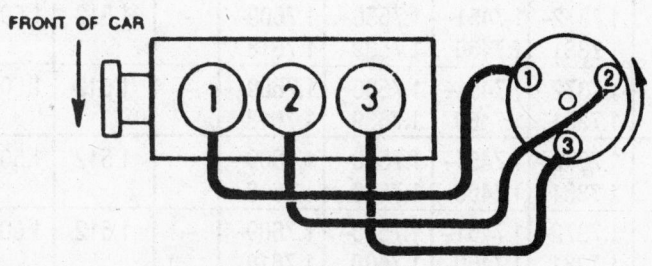

GM (SUZUKI) 63–3 (1.0L)
Engine firing order: 1–3–2
Distributor rotation: counterclockwise

CAPACITIES

Year	VIN	No. Cylinder Displacement cu. in. (liter)	Engine Crankcase with Filter	Engine Crankcase without Filter	Transmission (pts.) MT	Transmission (pts.) AT	Drive Axle (pts.)	Fuel Tank (gals.)	Cooling System (qts.)
1985	5	3-61 (1.0)	3.5	3.5	4.8	—	—	8.3	4.5
1986	5	3-61 (1.0)	3.5	3.5	4.8	9.5	—	8.3	4.5
1987	5	3-61 (1.0)	3.5	3.5	4.8	9.5	—	8.3	4.5
	2	3-61 (1.0)	3.5	3.5	4.8	—	—	8.3	4.5
1988-89	5	3-61 (1.0)	3.5	3.5	4.8	9.5	—	8.3	4.5
	2	3-61 (1.0)	3.5	3.5	4.8	—	—	8.3	4.5

CAMSHAFT SPECIFICATIONS
All measurements given in inches.

Year	VIN	No. Cylinder Displacement cu. in. (liter)	Journal Diameter 1	Journal Diameter 2	Journal Diameter 3	Journal Diameter 4	Journal Diameter 5	Lobe Lift In.	Lobe Lift Ex.	Bearing Clearance	Camshaft End Play
1985	5	3-61 (1.0)	1.7372–1.7381	1.7451–1.7460	1.7530–1.7539	1.7609–1.7618	—	1.512	1.5012	.0029	—
1986	5	3-61 (1.0)	1.7372–1.7381	1.7451–1.7460	1.7530–1.7539	1.7609–1.7618	—	1.512	1.5012	.0029	—

CAMSHAFT SPECIFICATIONS
All measurements given in inches.

Year	VIN	No. Cylinder Displacement cu. in. (liter)	Journal Diameter 1	2	3	4	5	Lobe Lift In.	Ex.	Bearing Clearance	Camshaft End Play
1987	5	3-61 (1.0)	1.7372–1.7381	1.7451–1.7460	1.7530–1.7539	1.7609–1.7618	—	1.512	1.5012	.0029	—
	2	3-61 (1.0)	1.7372–1.7381	1.7451–1.7460	1.7530–1.7539	1.7609–1.7618	—	1.512	1.5012	.0029	—
1988-89	5	3-61 (1.0)	1.7372–1.7381	1.7451–1.7460	1.7530–1.7539	1.7609–1.7618	—	1.512	1.5012	.0029	—
	2	3-61 (1.0)	1.7372–1.7381	1.7451–1.7460	1.7530–1.7539	1.7609–1.7618	—	1.512	1.5012	.0029	—

CRANKSHAFT AND CONNECTING ROD SPECIFICATIONS
All measurements are given in inches.

Year	VIN	No. Cylinder Displacement cu. in. (liter)	Crankshaft Main Brg. Journal Dia.	Main Brg. Oil Clearance	Shaft End-play	Thrust on No.	Connecting Rod Journal Diameter	Oil Clearance	Side Clearance
1985	5	3-61 (1.0)	①	.0012	.0083	3	1.6532	.0015	.0058
1986	5	3-61 (1.0)	①	.0012	.0083	3	1.6532	.0015	.0058
1987	5	3-61 (1.0)	①	.0012	.0044–.0122	3	1.6532	.0012–.0019	.0039–.0078
	2	3-61 (1.0)	①	.0012	.0044–.0122	3	1.6532	.0012–.0019	.0039–.0078
1988-89	5	3-61 (1.0)	①	.0012	.0044–.0122	3	1.6532	.0012–.0019	.0039–.0078
	2	3-61 (1.0)	①	.0012	.0044–.0122	3	1.6532	.0012–.0019	.0039–.0078

① Bearing cap stamped No. 1: 1.7710–1.7712
No. 2: 1.7714–1.7716
No. 3: 1.7712–1.7714
No. 4: 1.7710–1.7712

VALVE SPECIFICATIONS

Year	VIN	No. Cylinder Displacement cu. in. (liter)	Seat Angle (deg.)	Face Angle (deg.)	Spring Test Pressure (lbs.)	Spring Installed Height (in.)	Stem-to-Guide Clearance (in.) Intake	Exhaust	Stem Diameter (in.) Intake	Exhaust
1985	5	3-61 (1.0)	45	45	60	1.63	.0014	.0020	.2745	.2740
1986	5	3-61 (1.0)	45	45	60	1.63	.0014	.0020	.2745	.2740

VALVE SPECIFICATIONS

Year	VIN	No. Cylinder Displacement cu. in. (liter)	Seat Angle (deg.)	Face Angle (deg.)	Spring Test Pressure (lbs.)	Spring Installed Height (in.)	Stem-to-Guide Clearance (in.)		Stem Diameter (in.)	
							Intake	Exhaust	Intake	Exhaust
1987	5	3-61 (1.0)	45	45	60	1.63	.0014	.0020	.2745	.2740
	2	3-61 (1.0)	45	45	60	1.63	.0014	.0020	.2745	.2740
1988-89	5	3-61 (1.0)	45	45	60	1.63	.0014	.0020	.2745	.2740
	2	3-61 (1.0)	45	45	60	1.63	.0014	.0020	.2745	.2740

PISTON AND RING SPECIFICATIONS
All measurments are given in inches.

Year	VIN	No. Cylinder Displacement cu. in. (liter)	Piston Clearance	Ring Gap			Ring Side Clearance		
				Top Compression	Bottom Compression	Oil Control	Top Compression	Bottom Compression	Oil Control
1985	5	3-61 (1.0)	.0008–.0015	.0079–.0129	.0079–.0137	.0079–.0275	.0012–.0027	.0008–.0023	—
1986	5	3-61 (1.0)	.0008–.0015	.0079–.0129	.0079–.0137	.0079–.0275	.0012–.0027	.0008–.0023	—
1987	5	3-61 (1.0)	.0008–.0015	.0079–.0129	.0079–.0137	.0079–.0275	.0012–.0027	.0008–.0023	—
	2	3-61 (1.0)	.0008–.0015	.0079–.0119	.0079–.0119	.0079–.0237	.0012–.0030	.0008–.0023	—
	5	3-61 (1.0) ①	.0008–.0015	.0079–.0157	—	.0079–.0275	.0012–.0027	—	—
1988-89	5	3-61 (1.0)	.0008–.0015	.0079–.0129	.0079–.0137	.0079–.0275	.0012–.0027	.0008–.0023	—
	2	3-61 (1.0)	.0008–.0015	.0079–.0119	.0079–.0119	.0079–.0237	.0012–.0030	.0008–.0023	—
	5	3-61 (1.0) ①	.0008–.0015	.0079–.0157	—	.0079–.0275	.0012–.0027	—	—

① "ER" model has only one compression ring

TORQUE SPECIFICATIONS
All readings in ft. lbs.

Year	VIN	No. Cylinder Displacement cu. in. (liter)	Cylinder Head Bolts	Main Bearing Bolts	Rod Bearing Bolts	Crankshaft Pulley Bolts	Flywheel Bolts	Manifold		Spark Plugs
								Intake	Exhaust	
1985	5	3-61 (1.0)	48	38	25	50	44	17	17	20
1986	5	3-61 (1.0)	48	38	25	50	44	17	17	20
1987	5	3-61 (1.0)	48	38	25	50	44	17	17	20
	2	3-61 (1.0)	48	38	25	50	44	17	17	20
1988-89	5	3-61 (1.0)	48	38	25	50	44	17	17	20
	2	3-61 (1.0)	48	38	25	50	44	17	17	20

BRAKE SPECIFICATIONS
All measurements in inches unless noted

Year	Model	Lug Nut Torque (ft. lbs.)	Master Cylinder Bore	Brake Disc Minimum Thickness	Brake Disc Maximum Runout	Standard Brake Drum Diameter	Minimum Lining Thickness Front	Minimum Lining Thickness Rear
1985	Sprint	29-50	.825	.315	.0028	7.09	.315 ①	.110 ①
1986	Sprint	29-50	.825	.315	.0028	7.09	.315 ①	.110 ①
1987	Sprint	29-50	.825	.315	.0028	7.09	.315 ①	.110 ①
1988-89	Sprint	29-50	.825	.315	.0028	7.09	.315 ①	.110 ①

① Lining plus shoe rim

WHEEL ALIGNMENT

Year	Model	Caster Range (deg.)	Caster Preferred Setting (deg.)	Camber Range (deg.)	Camber Preferred Setting (deg.)	Toe-in (in.)	Steering Axis Inclination (deg.)
1985	Sprint	–	3³⁄₁₆	–	1	¹⁄₁₆	12³⁄₁₆
1986	Sprint	–	3³⁄₁₆	–	1	0	12³⁄₁₆
1987	Sprint	–	3³⁄₁₆	–	¼	0	12³⁄₁₆
1988-89	Sprint	–	3³⁄₁₆	–	¼	0	12³⁄₁₆

NOTE: Toe and caster settings for the rear are zero for all models

TUNE-UP PROCEDURES

Ignition Timing

ADJUSTMENT

Before checking or adjusting the ignition timing, make sure that the headlights, heater fan, engine cooling fan and any other electrical equipment is turned OFF. If any current drawing systems are operating, the idle up system will operate and cause the idle speed to be higher than normal.

1. Connect a tachometer to the negative terminal of the ignition coil. Connect a timing light to the No. 1 spark plug wire. Refer to the underhood sticker.
2. Start and run the engine until it reaches normal operating temperature.
3. Check and/or adjust the idle speed. Correct speed should be 750 rpm for models with manual transaxles and 850 rpm on models with automatic transaxles.

NOTE: To adjust the idle speed, turn the throttle adjustment screw on the carburetor.

4. With the engine at the proper idle speed, aim the timing light at the crankshaft pulley and timing marks. The "V" timing mark on the pulley should be at the 10 degrees BTDC mark on the timing plate.

NOTE: To adjust the ignition timing, loosen the distributor hold down bolt and rotate the distributor. When the "V" mark and the 10 degree mark are aligned, tighten the distributor hold down bolt and recheck the timing.

5. With the timing adjusted, stop the engine and remove the testing equipment.

Valve Lash

ADJUSTMENT

1. Remove the air cleaner and rocker arm cover.
2. Using the center crankshaft bolt, rotate the crankshaft clockwise and align the "V" mark on the crankshaft pulley with the "0" mark on the timing tab.
3. Remove the distributor cap and make sure that the rotor is facing the fuel pump. If not, rotate the crankshaft 360 degrees and check it again.

4. Check and/or adjust the valve lash for the No. 1 cylinder.

NOTE: If the engine is COLD, adjust the valve clearance to 0.006 in. (intake) and 0.008 in. (exhaust). With a WARM engine, adjust the valve clearance to 0.010 in. (intake) and 0.012 in. (exhaust). After each adjustment, tighten the lock nut on the adjusting screw to 11–13 ft. lbs. and recheck the valve lash, before proceeding with the next cylinder.

5. After adjusting the valve lash for No. 1 cylinder, rotate the crankshaft exactly 240 degrees. The "V" mark should align with the lower left oil pump mounting bolt, when facing the crankshaft pulley. Adjust the valve lash for No. 3 cylinder.
6. After adjusting the valve lash for No. 3 cylinder, rotate the crankshaft exactly 240 degrees more. The "V" mark should align with the lower right oil pump mounting bolt, when facing the crankshaft pulley. Adjust the valve lash for No. 2 cylinder.
7. After the valve lash has been adjusted on all cylinders, install the rocker cover using a new gasket. Make sure that the valve adjustment locknuts are tightened to 11–13 ft. lbs.

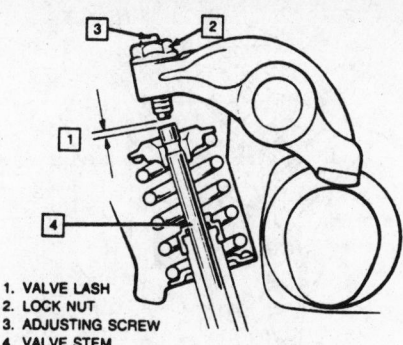

1. VALVE LASH
2. LOCK NUT
3. ADJUSTING SCREW
4. VALVE STEM

Valve lash adjusting screw location

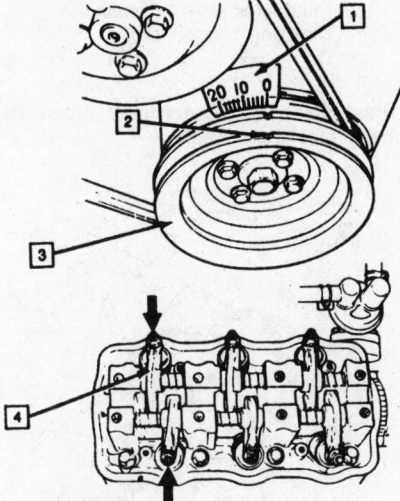

1. TIMING TAB
2. TIMING NOTCH
3. CRANKSHAFT PULLEY
4. NO. 1 CYLINDER

Timing mark alignment for adjusting valve lash for No. 1 cylinder

Idle Speed and Mixture

IDLE SPEED ADJUSTMENT

Carbureted Models

Check and/or adjust the accelerator cable free-play, ignition timing, valve lash and the emission control wiring and hoses. Make sure that the headlights, heater fan, engine cooling fan and any other electrical equipment is turned OFF. If any current drawing system is operating, the idle up system will operate and cause the idle speed to be higher than normal.

1. Connect a tachometer to the primary negative terminal of the ignition coil and refer to the underhood sticker.

2. Place the transaxle in Neutral, set the parking brake and block the wheels.

3. Start and run the engine until it reaches normal operating temperature.

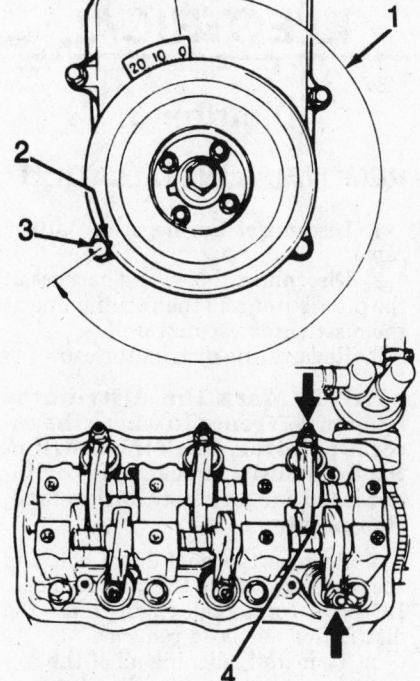

1. 240°
2. Timing notch
3. Left mounting bolt
4. No. 3 cylinder

Timing mark alignment for adjusting valve lash on No. 3 cylinder

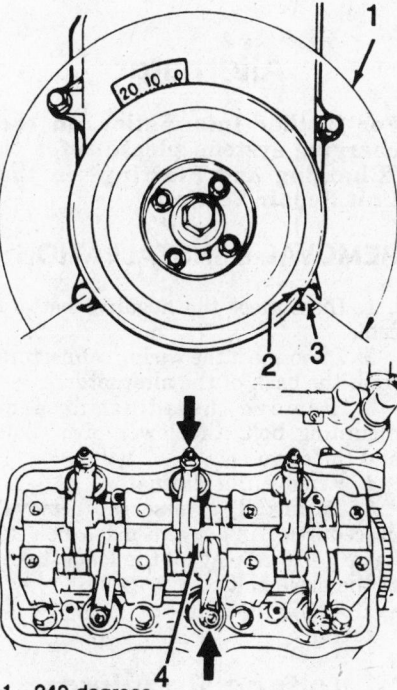

1. 240 degrees
2. Timing notch
3. Right mounting bolt
4. No. 2 cylinder

Timing mark alignment for adjusting valve lash on No. 2 cylinder

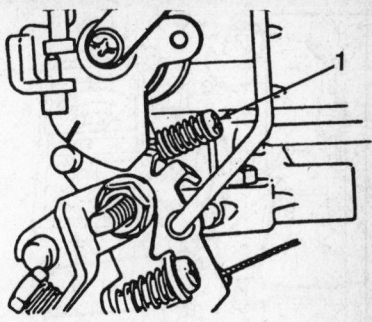

THROTTLE ADJUST SCREW

Idle speed adjustment screw—carbureted engines

4. Check and/or adjust the idle speed, it should be 700–800 rpm with manual transaxles, 800–900 rpm with automatic transaxles.

NOTE: To adjust the idle speed, turn the throttle adjustment screw on the carburetor.

5. With the engine at the proper idle speed, check and/or adjust the idle up speed.

6. Stop the engine and remove the tachometer.

Fuel Injected Models

The idle speed is controlled by the Electronic Control Module and is not adjustable.

IDLE MIXTURE ADJUSTMENT

Carbureted Models

The carburetor is adjusted at the factory and no further adjustment should be necessary. However, if the engine performance is poor, the emission test fails, or the carburetor has been replaced or overhauled, an idle mixture adjustment is necessary. Before adjusting the idle mixture, check the timing/idle speed and the valve lash. Make sure that all electrical accessories are turned OFF.

1. Refer to the "Carburetor Removal & Installation" procedures in this section and remove the carburetor from the intake manifold.

2. Using an $^{11}/_{64}$ in. bit, drill through the idle mixture screw housing, in line with the retaining pin. Use a punch to drive the pin from the housing.

3. Install the carburetor to the intake manifold by reversing the removal procedures.

4. Place the transaxle in Neutral, set the parking brake and block the wheels.

5. Start the engine and bring it to normal operating temperatures.

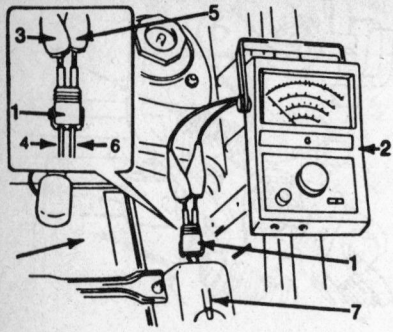

1. Duty Check Connector
2. Dwell Meter
3. Positive (+) Terminal
4. "Blue/Red" Wire
5. Negative (−) Terminal
6. "Black/Green Wire
7. Water Reservoir Tank
8. Battery

Connecting a dwell meter to the duty cycle check connector

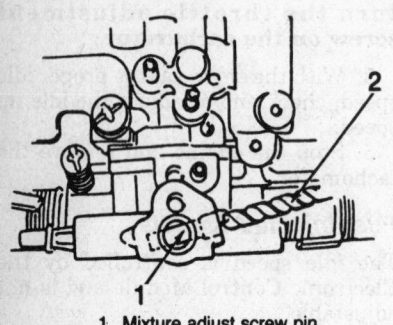

1. Mixture adjust screw pin
2. Drill

Removing the idle mixture pin

6. Disconnect the Duty Cycle Check connector, located near the water reservoir tank. Connect the positive terminal of a dwell meter to the blue/red wire and the negative terminal to the black/green wire.

7. Set the dwell meter to the 6 cylinder position, make sure that the indicator moves.

8. Check and/or adjust the idle speed.

9. Operate the engine at idle speed and adjust the idle mixture screw, allow the engine to stabilize between adjustments. Adjust the dwell to 21–27 degrees; recheck the idle speed and adjust, if necessary.

10. After completing the adjustment, stop the engine, disconnect the dwell meter and connect the Duty Cycle Check connector to the coupler.

11. Install a new idle mixture adjust screw pin in the throttle housing, drive it in place.

Fuel Injected Models

The idle mixture is controlled by the Electronic Control Module. No adjustments are possible.

ENGINE ELECTRICAL

Distributor

REMOVAL & INSTALLATION

1. Disconnect the negative battery cable.
2. Disconnect the wiring harness at the distributor and the vacuum line at the distributor vacuum unit.
3. Remove the distributor cap.

NOTE: Mark the distributor body in reference to where the rotor is pointing. Mark the distributor hold down bracket and cylinder head for a reinstallation location point.

4. Remove the hold down bolt and the distributor from the cylinder head. DO NOT rotate the engine after the distributor has been removed.

5. To install, aligning all of the reference marks and install the distributor into the off-set slot in the camshaft.

6. With the distributor installed, the hold down bolt hand tight and the cap on, run the engine and check the ignition timing.

Alternator

For further information on the charging system, please refer to "Charging and Starting" in the Unit Repair Section.

REMOVAL & INSTALLATION

1. Disconnect the negative battery cable.
2. Disconnect the wiring connectors from the back of the alternator.
3. Remove the adjusting arm mounting bolt, the lower pivot bolt and the drive belt.
4. Remove the alternator.
6. To install, reverse the removal procedures. Adjust the drive belt to have $1/4$–$3/8$ in. play on the longest run of the drive belt.

Voltage Regulator

An integral voltage regulator is part of the alternator and no adjustments are necessary or possible.

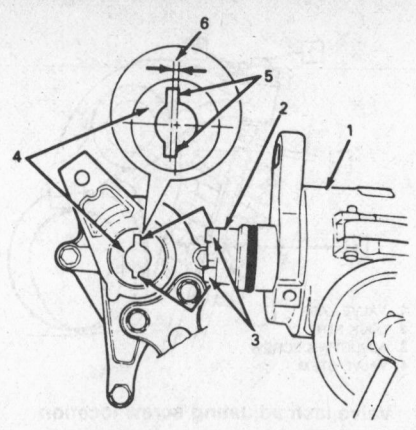

1. Distributor
2. Coupling
3. Dog
4. Camshaft
5. Slot
6. Offset

Offset slot in distributor must align with offset slot in camshaft

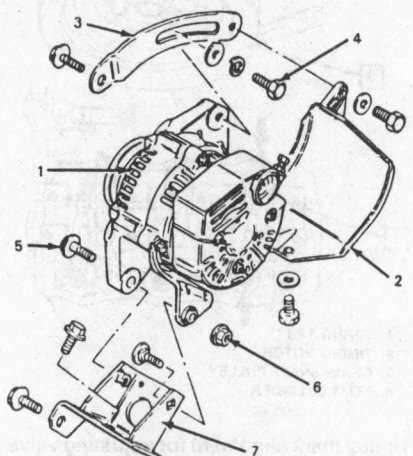

1. Alternator
2. Alternator cover
3. Alternator adjusting arm
4. Arm bolt
5. Alternator bolt
6. Alternator nut
7. Alternator bracket

Alternator mounting—all engines

Starter Motor

For further information on the starter system, please refer to "Charging and Starting" in the Unit Repair Section.

REMOVAL & INSTALLATION

1. Disconnect the negative battery cable.
2. Disconnect the ignition switch wire and the battery cable from the starter.
3. Remove the two engine-to-starter mounting bolts and remove the starter.

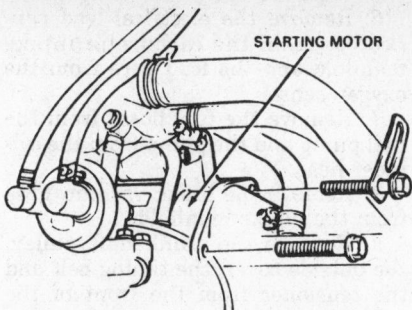

Starter motor mounting

4. To install, reverse the removal procedures.

ENGINE MECHANICAL

Engine

REMOVAL & INSTALLATION

1. Remove the battery cables.
2. Remove the hood, battery, battery tray, air cleaner and the outside air duct.
3. Drain the cooling system, engine oil and the transaxle.
4. Disconnect and tag the radiator, heater and vacuum hoses from the engine.
5. Disconnect the cooling fan wiring.
6. Remove the cooling fan, shroud and radiator as an assembly.
7. Remove the fuel hoses from the fuel pump.
8. Remove the brake booster hose from the intake manifold, accelerator cable from the carburetor and speed control cable from the transaxle.
9. Remove the clutch cable and bracket from the transaxle.
10. Disconnect and tag the necessary wiring from the engine and transaxle.
11. Remove the A/C compressor adjusting bolt and drive belt splash shield.
12. Raise and support the vehicle safely.
13. Disconnect the exhaust pipe from the exhaust manifold.
14. Remove the A/C pivot bolt, the drive belt and the mounting bracket.
15. Disconnect the gearshift control shaft and extension rod at the transaxle.
16. Disconnect the ball joints.
17. Remove the axle shafts from the transaxle.

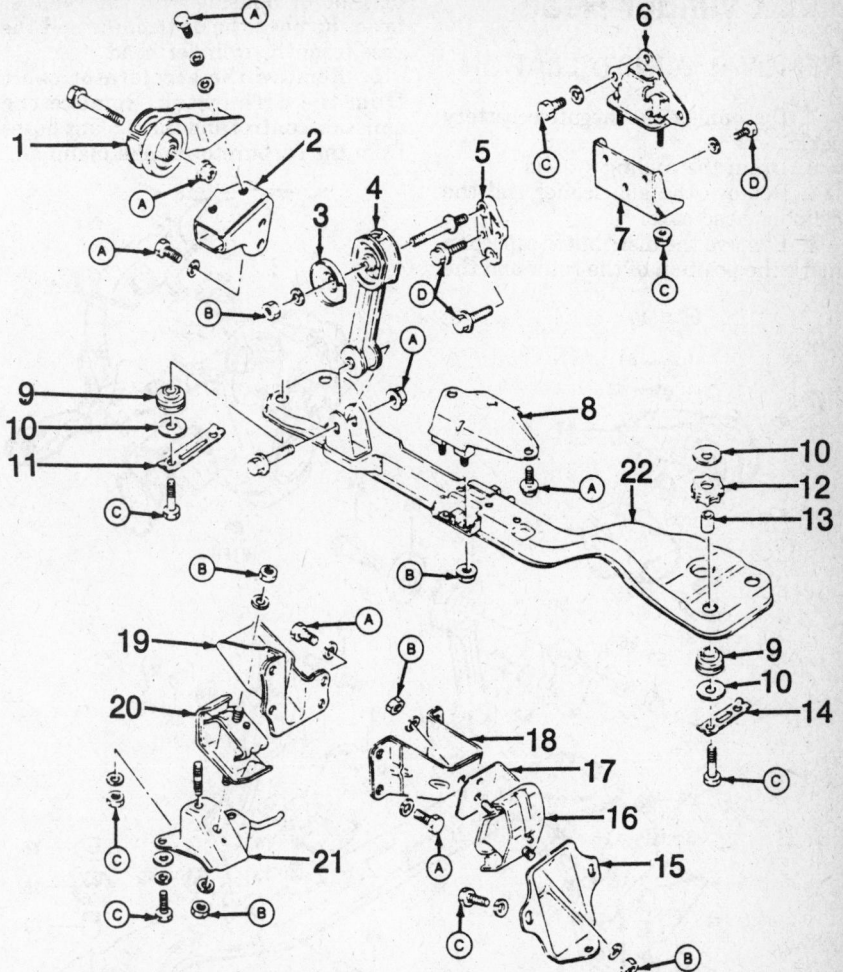

1. SIDE MOUNTING BUSHING	20. REAR MOUNTING
2. SIDE MOUNTING BRACKET	21. REAR BODY BRACKET
3. STOPPER PLATE	22. TRANSMISSION MOUNTING
4. TORQUE ROD	MEMBER
5. TORQUE ROD BRACKET	
6. TRANSMISSION L MOUNTING	
7. BRACKET	
8. TRANSMISSION MOUNTING	BOLT AND NUT TIGHTENING TORQUE:
9. LOWER CUSHION	
10. WASHER	Ⓐ: 4.0 — 6.0 Kg-m
11. REAR LOCK WASHER	40 — 60N·m
12. UPPER CUSHION	29.0 — 43.0 LB-FT
13. SPACER	Ⓑ: 4.0 — 5.0 Kg-m
14. FRONT LOCK WASHER	40 — 50 N·m
15. FRONT MOUNTING BODY BRACKET	29.0 — 36.0 LB-FT
16. FRONT MOUNTING	Ⓒ: 5.0 — 6.0 Kg-m
17. INSULATOR	50 — 60 N·m
18. FRONT MOUNTING BRACKET	36.5 — 43.0 LB-FT
19. REAR MOUNTING BRACKET	Ⓓ: 1.8 — 2.8 Kg-m
	18 — 28 N·m
	13.5 — 20.0 LB-FT

Engine mounting – automatic transaxle

18. Remove the engine torque rods and the transaxle mount nut.
19. Lower the vehicle.
20. Remove the engine side mount and the mount nuts.
21. Connect a vertical hoist to the en-

gine, then lift the engine and transaxle assembly from the vehicle.
22. To install, reverse the removal procedures. Refill the engine, the transaxle and the cooling system.

Cylinder Head

REMOVAL & INSTALLATION

1. Disconnect the negative battery cable.
2. Drain the cooling system.
3. Remove the air cleaner and the cylinder head cover.
4. Remove the distributor cap, then mark the position of the rotor and the distributor housing with the cylinder head. Remove the distributor and the case from the cylinder head.
5. Remove the accelerator cable from the carburetor. Remove the emission control and the coolant hoses from the carburetor/intake manifold.

6. Remove the electrical lead connectors from the carburetor/intake manifold and the lead wire from the oxygen sensor.
7. Remove the fuel hoses from the fuel pump and the pump from the cylinder head.
8. Remove the brake vacuum hose from the intake manifold.
9. Remove the crankshaft pulley, the outside cover, the timing belt and the tensioner from the front of the engine.
10. Remove the exhaust and the 2nd air pipes from the exhaust manifold.
11. Remove the exhaust/intake manifolds and the engine side mount from the cylinder head.
12. Loosen the rocker arm valve adjusters, turn back the adjusting screws so that the rocker arms move freely. Remove the rocker arm shaft retaining screws and pull out the shafts. Remove the rocker arms and springs from the cylinder head.

NOTE: Make a note of the differences between the rocker arm shafts. The intake shaft's stepped end is 0.55 in., which faces the camshaft pulley; the exhaust shaft's stepped end is 0.59 in., which faces the distributor.

13. Remove the mounting bolts and the cylinder head from the engine.
14. To install, use new gaskets and reverse the removal procedures. Torque the cylinder head bolts to 46–50.5 ft. lbs. and the rocker arm shaft screws to 7–9 ft. lbs. Adjust the valve clearances. Refill the cooling system. Check and/or adjust the ignition timing.

OVERHAUL

For all cylinder head overhaul procedures, please refer to "Engine Rebuilding" in the Unit Repair section.

Rocker Arms/Shafts

REMOVAL & INSTALLATION

1. Disconnect the negative battery cable.
2. Remove the air cleaner and the cylinder head cover.
3. Remove the distributor cap, then mark the position of the rotor and the distributor housing with the cylinder head. Remove the distributor and the case from the cylinder head.
4. Loosen the rocker arm valve adjusters, turn back the adjusting screws so that the rocker arms move freely.
5. Remove the rocker arm shaft retaining screws and pull out the shafts.

VIEW

FWD

Engine mounting – manual transaxle

1. Mount, Eng Frt
2. Washer, Mt Lk
3. Nut, Frt Mt
4. Insulator, Eng Frt Mt Ht
5. Bracket, Eng Frt Mt
6. Bolt, Brkt
7. Washer, Brkt Mt
8. Bracket, Frt Mt Body
9. Bolt, Brkt
10. Washer, Brkt Lk
11. Mount, Trans
12. Nut, Trans Mt
13. Bolt (M8 × 1.25 × 20)
14. Washer
15. Member, Trans Mt
16. Cushion, Mt Mbr Upr
17. Cushion, Mt Mbr Lwr
18. Washer, Mt Mbr
19. Spacer, Mbr
21. Bolt, Mbr
22. Mount, Eng Rr
23. Washer, Mt
24. Nut (M10 × 1.25 × 8)

25. Bracket, Eng Rr Mt
26. Bolt, Brkt
27. Washer, Brkt Lk
28. Bracket, Rr Mt Body
29. Bolt, Brkt
30. Washer, Brkt Lk
31. Stud, Brkt
32. Washer, Brkt Lk
33. Nut, Brkt
34. Bracket, Eng Si Mt
35. Bolt, Si Brkt
36. Washer, Brkt Lk
37. Bushing, Eng Si Mt
38. Bolt, Mt Bush
39. Nut, Mt Bush
41. Washer, Lk
42. Washer, Bush

43. Rod, Eng Frt Torq
44. Stud, Frt Rod
45. Washer, Frt Rod
46. Washer, Rod Lk
47. Nut, Frt Rod
48. Bolt, Frt Rod
49. Nut, Frt Rod
50. Bracket, Rr Torq Rod
51. Bolt, Rod Brkt
52. Washer, Brkt Lk
53. Rod, Eng Rr Torq
54. Bolt, Rr Rod
55. Plate, Rr Torq Stopper
56. Washer, Rr Rod Lk
57. Nut, Rr Rod
58. Bolt, Rr Rod
59. Nut, Rr Rod

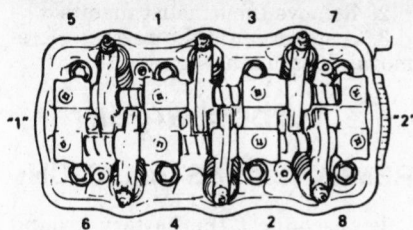

"1" Camshaft Pulley Side
"2" Distributor Side

Cylinder head mounting bolt torque sequence

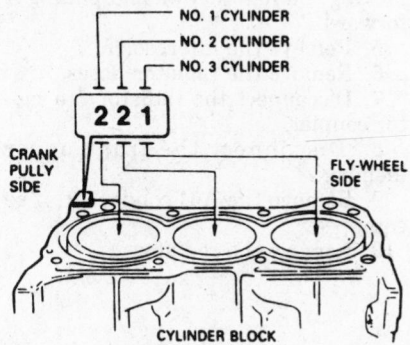

Cylinder identification

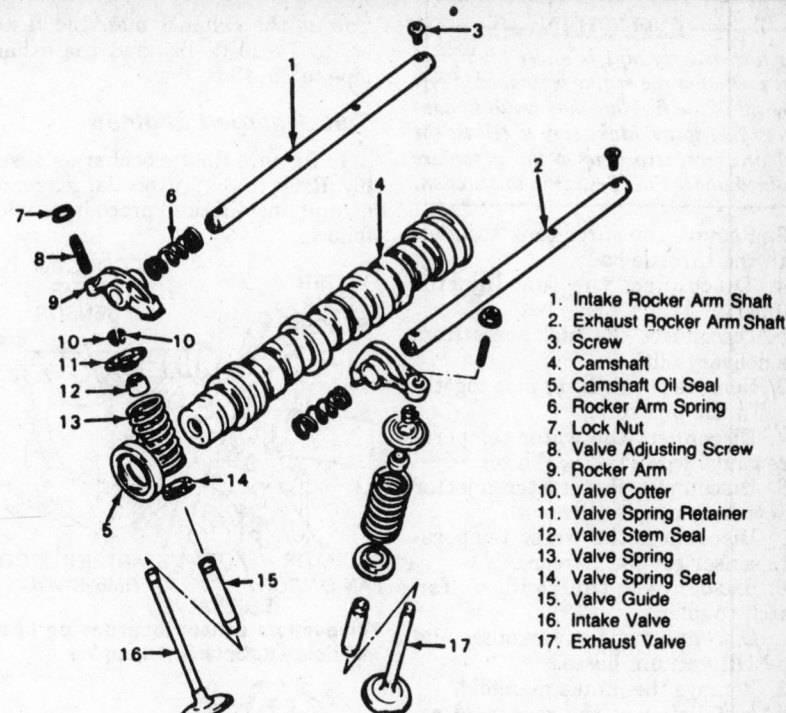

1. Intake Rocker Arm Shaft
2. Exhaust Rocker Arm Shaft
3. Screw
4. Camshaft
5. Camshaft Oil Seal
6. Rocker Arm Spring
7. Lock Nut
8. Valve Adjusting Screw
9. Rocker Arm
10. Valve Cotter
11. Valve Spring Retainer
12. Valve Stem Seal
13. Valve Spring
14. Valve Spring Seat
15. Valve Guide
16. Intake Valve
17. Exhaust Valve

Exploded view of the rocker arm assembly

Remove the rocker arms and springs from the cylinder head.

NOTE: Make a note of the differences between the rocker arm shafts. The intake shaft's stepped end is 0.55 in., which faces the camshaft pulley; the exhaust shaft's stepped end is 0.59 in., which faces the distributor.

6. To install, use new gaskets and reverse the removal procedures. Torque the rocker arm shaft screws to 7–9 ft. lbs. Adjust the valve clearances. Check and/or adjust the ignition timing.

Intake Manifold

REMOVAL & INSTALLATION

Except Turbocharged Engines

1. Disconnect the negative battery cable.
2. Drain the cooling system.
3. Disconnect the air cleaner element, the EGR modulator, the warm air, the cool air, the 2nd air and the vacuum hoses from the air cleaner case.
4. Remove the air cleaner case, the electrical lead wires and the accelerator cable from the carburetor.
5. Disconnect the emission control and the fuel hoses from the carburetor.
6. Remove the water hoses from the choke housing.

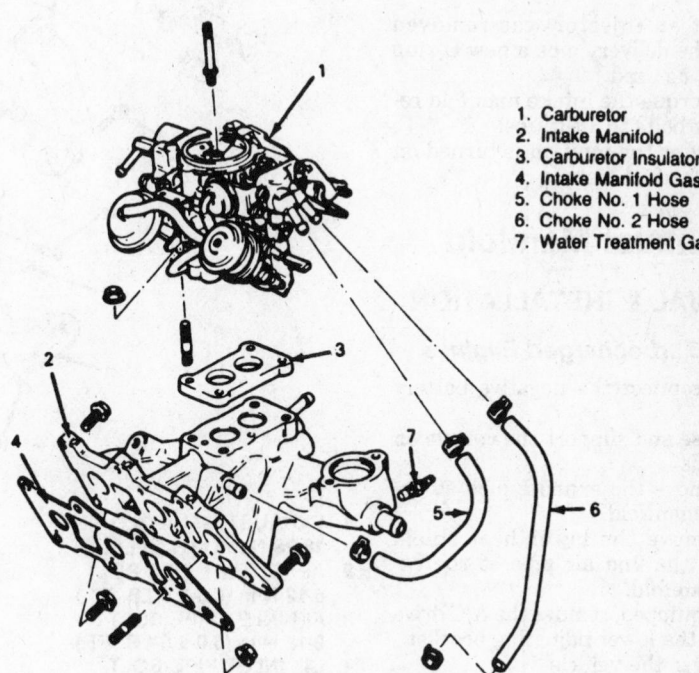

1. Carburetor
2. Intake Manifold
3. Carburetor Insulator
4. Intake Manifold Gasket
5. Choke No. 1 Hose
6. Choke No. 2 Hose
7. Water Treatment Gauge

Carburetor and intake manifold mounting

7. Remove the electrical lead wires, the emission control, the coolant and the brake vacuum hoses from the intake manifold.
8. Remove the intake manifold from the cylinder head.
9. Clean the mating gasket surfaces.
10. To install, use new gaskets and reverse the removal procedures.

Torque the intake manifold-to-cylinder head bolts to 14–20 ft. lbs. Refill the cooling system.

Turbocharged Engines

1. Disconnect the negative battery cable.
2. Drain the cooling system when the engine is cool.

CAUTION

The fuel delivery pipe is under high pressure even after the engine is stopped, direct removal of the fuel line may result in dangerous fuel spray. Make sure to release the fuel pressure according to the procedure outlined under Fuel System in this section.

3. Remove the surge tank together with the throttle body.

4. Disconnect the fuel injector couplers.

5. Disconnect the fuel hoses from the delivery pipe.

6. Remove the delivery pipe together with the injectors.

7. Disconnect the water temperature gauge wire (Yellow/White).

8. Disconnect the starter injector time switch coupler (Brown).

9. Disconnect the water temperature sensor coupler (Green).

10. Disconnect the radiator fan switch coupler.

11. Disconnect the water hoses and the EGR vacuum hoses.

12. Remove the intake manifold.

13. Installation is the reverse of removal, with the following precautions:

   a. Use a new intake manifold gasket.

   b. If an injector was removed from the delivery pipe a new O-ring should be used.

   c. Torque the intake manifold retaining bolts to 17 ft. lbs.

   d. After the ignition is turned on check for fuel leaks.

Exhaust Manifold

REMOVAL & INSTALLATION

Except Turbocharged Engines

1. Disconnect the negative battery cable.

2. Raise and support the vehicle on jackstands.

3. Remove the exhaust pipe at the exhaust manifold.

4. Remove the lower heat shield bolt and the 2nd air pipe at the exhaust manifold.

5. If equipped, remove the A/C drive belt and the lower adjusting bracket.

6. Lower the vehicle.

7. Remove the spark plug and the oxygen sensor wires.

8. Remove the hot air shroud from the exhaust manifold.

9. Remove the 2nd air valve hoses, the valve and the pipe from the exhaust manifold.

10. Remove the mounting bolts and the exhaust manifold.

11. Clean the gasket mating surfaces.

12. To install, use a new gasket and reverse the removal procedures.

Torque the exhaust manifold fasteners to 14–20 ft. lbs. and the exhaust pipe to 30–43 ft. lbs.

Turbocharged Engines

1. Remove the turbocharger assembly. Refer to the Turbocharger removal and installation procedure which follows.

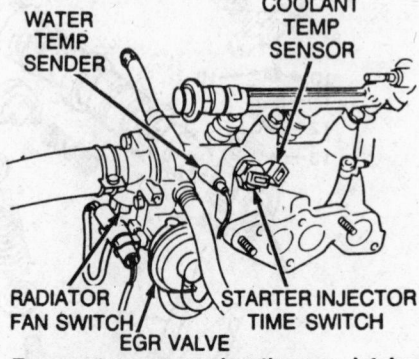

Temperature sensor locations on intake manifold—turbocharged engine

2. Remove the exhaust manifold.

3. Installation is the reverse of removal. Install a new gasket.

Turbocharger

REMOVAL & INSTALLATION

1. Disconnect the battery ground cable.

2. Drain the cooling system when the engine is cool.

3. Remove the hood.

4. Remove the front grille by removing the four screws and pulling it forward.

5. Remove the intercooler.

6. Remove the radiator hoses.

7. Disconnect the radiator fan motor coupler.

8. Disconnect the front upper member.

9. Remove the A/C condensor, if so equipped.

10. Remove the radiator.

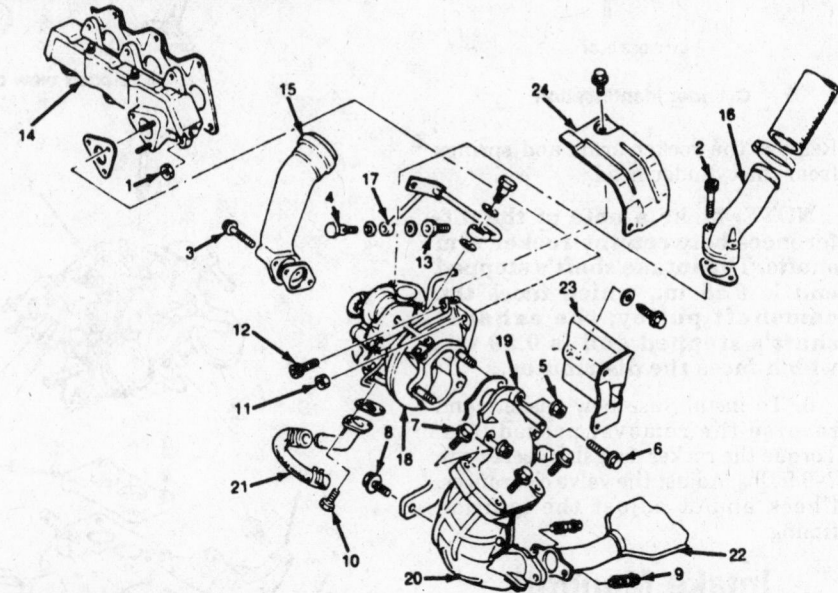

1. EXHAUST MANIFOLD NUT
   18-28 N·m (13.5-20 LB. FT.)
2. AIR OUTLET PIPE BOLT
   8-12 N·m (6.0-8.5 LB. FT.)
3. AIR INLET PIPE BOLT
   8-12 N·m (6.0-8.5 LB. FT.)
4. OIL INLET PIPE BOLT
   11-15 N·m (8.0-10.5 LB. FT.)
5. EXHAUST PIPE NUT
   18-28 N·m (13.5-20 LB. FT.)
6. EXHAUST PIPE BOLT
   25-35 N·m (18.5-25 LB. FT.)
7. LOWER EXHAUST PIPE BOLT
   40-60 N·m (29-43 LB. FT.)
8. LOWER EXHAUST PIPE
   SUPPORT BRACKET
   BOLT 25-35 N·m (18.5-25 LB. FT.)
9. EXHAUST CENTER PIPE BOLT
   30-40 N·m (22-28.5 LB. FT.)
10. OIL DRAIN PIPE BOLT
    4-7 N·m (3-5 LB. FT.)
11. TURBOCHARGER NUT
    18-28 N·m (13.5-20 LB. FT.)
12. TURBOCHARGER BOLT
    18-28 N·m (13.5-20 LB. FT.)
13. OIL INLET STAND
    10-15 N·m (7.5-10.5 LB. FT.)
14. EXHAUST MANIFOLD
15. AIR INLET PIPE
16. AIR OUTLET PIPE
17. OIL PIPE
18. TURBOCHARGER
19. UPPER EXHAUST PIPE
20. LOWER EXHAUST PIPE
21. OIL DRAIN HOSE
22. EXHAUST CENTER PIPE
23. TURBOCHARGER SIDE COVER
24. TURBOCHARGER COVER

Turbocharger and component mounting—exploded view

11. Disconnect the front bumper from the damper flange. Place a stand under the front bumper to prevent it from dropping, and remove the couplers clamps and bolts and pull the bumper towards yourself.

12. Disconnect the exhaust pipe bolts.

13. Remove the A/C compressor, if so equipped.

14. Remove the turbocharger cover.

15. Unclamp the oxygen sensor wire.

16. Remove the turbocharger side cover.

17. Lower the exhaust pipe support bracket bolt.

18. Remove the upper exhaust pipe together with the lower exhaust pipe.

19. Disconnect the air outlet pipe.

20. Disconnect the air inlet hose clamp bolt on the cylinder head.

21. Disconnect the air inlet pipe.

22. Disconnect the air inlet pipe from the cylinder block.

23. Disconnect the oil drain hose.

24. Disconnect the water pipe cylinder head clamp bolt.

25. Disconnect the water hoses.

NOTE: Never adjust or disassemble turbocharger assembly.

26. Installation is the reverse of removal. Always use new gaskets during installation. Recharge A/C system.

— **CAUTION** —
Use care when discharging and/or charging the A/C system. Please refer to "Air Conditioning" in the Unit Repair section

TROUBLESHOOTING

NOTE: For more information on Turbocharging, please refer to "Turbocharging" in the Unit Repair Section.

Timing Cover, Belt and Tensioner

REMOVAL

1. Disconnect the negative battery cable.

2. Loosen the water pump pulley bolts and the alternator adjusting bolt.

3. If equipped, remove the A/C compressor adjusting bolt.

4. Raise and support the vehicle on jackstands.

5. Remove the drive belt splash shield, the right fender plug and the drive belts.

6. Remove the crankshaft and the water pump pulleys.

7. Remove the bolts from the bottom of the belt cover.

8. Lower the vehicle.

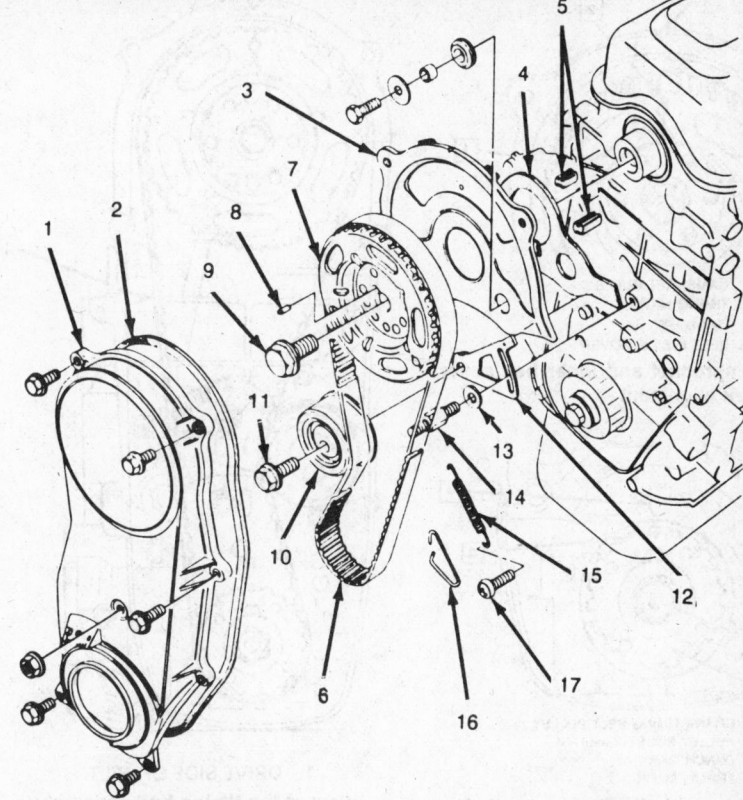

1. Outer cover	10. Tensioner
2. Outer cover seal	11. Tensioner bolt
3. Inner cover	12. Tensioner plate
4. Inner cover seal	13. Washer
5. Seal	14. Tensioner stud
6. Timing belt	15. Tensioner spring
7. Camshaft sprocket	16. Spring damper
8. Pin	17. Spring screw
9. Camshaft sprocket bolt	

Timing belt, tensioner and sprockets – exploded view

9. Remove the bolts from the top of the belt cover and the cover.

10. Remove the cylinder head cover and loosen the rocker arm adjusting bolts.

11. Remove the distributor cap.

12. Loosen the tensioner pulley and adjusting stud bolt.

13. Remove the timing belt, the tensioner, the tensioner plate and spring.

INSTALLATION

1. Install the tensioner assembly but DO NOT tighten the bolts.

2. Turn the camshaft pulley clockwise and align the mark on the pulley with the "V" mark on the inside cover.

3. Using a 17mm wrench, turn the crankshaft clockwise and align the punch mark on the crankshaft pulley with the arrow mark on the oil pump.

4. With the timing marks aligned, install the timing belt so that there is no belt slack on the right side (facing the engine) of the engine, apply belt tension with the tensioner pulley.

5. Turn the crankshaft 1 rotation clockwise to remove the belt slack. Torque the tensioner stud, first, and then the tensioner bolt to 17–21 ft. lbs.

6. To complete the installation, use new gaskets and reverse the removal procedures. Torque the crankshaft pulley to 7–9 ft. lbs. Adjust the valve clearances.

Camshaft

REMOVAL & INSTALLATION

1. Refer to "Timing Cover, Belt and Tensioner Removal & Installation"

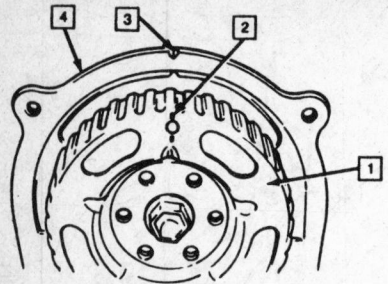

1. CAMSHAFT PULLEY
2. TIMING MARK
3. "V" MARK
4. BELT INSIDE COVER

Camshaft sprocket and inner belt cover timing mark alignment

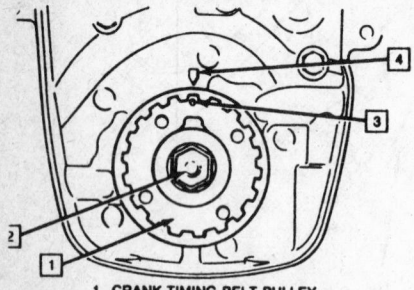

1. CRANK TIMING BELT PULLEY
2. PULLEY BOLT (17 mm)
3. PUNCH MARK
4. ARROW MARK

Crankshaft sprocket and oil pump timing mark alignment

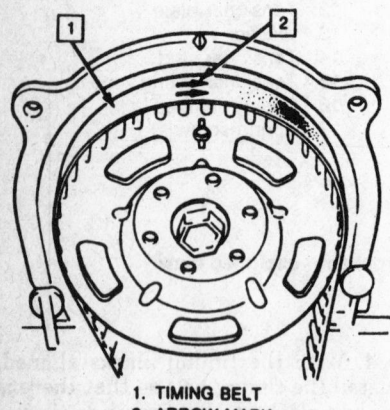

1. TIMING BELT
2. ARROW MARK

Arrow marks on timing belt show direction of rotation

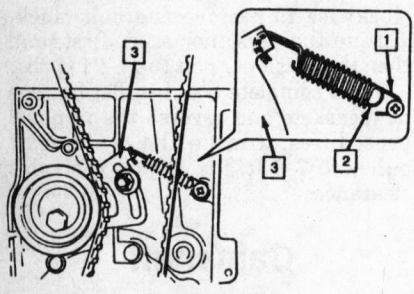

1. TENSIONER SPRING
2. SPRING DAMPER
3. TENSIONER PLATE

Installing tensioner spring and dampner

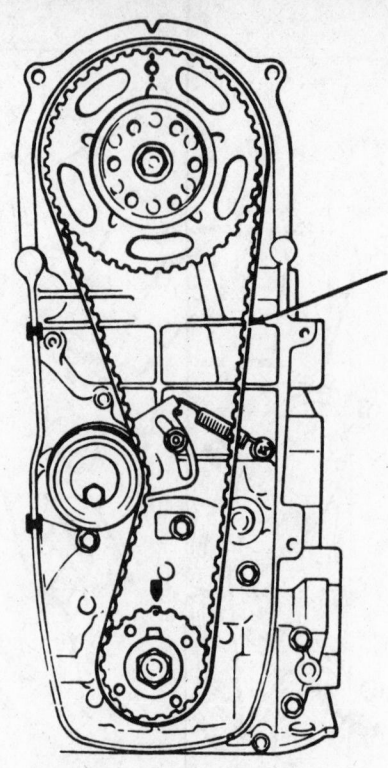

1. DRIVE SIDE OF BELT

View of the timing belt assembly

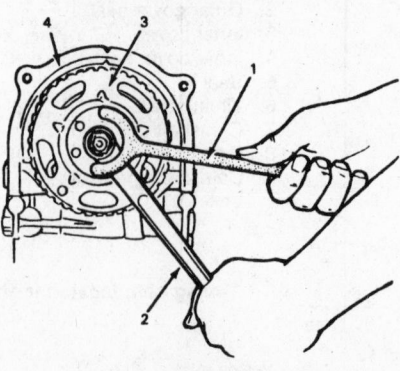

1. J–34836
2. WRENCH
3. CAMSHAFT TIMING BELT PULLEY
4. TIMING BELT INSIDE COVER

Removing the camshaft pulley bolt using a lock holder tool

procedures in this section and remove the timing belt.

2. Remove the air cleaner, rocker arm cover, distributor and distributor case. Remove the rocker arm shafts and the rocker arms.

3. Remove the fuel pump and fuel pump push rod from the cylinder head.

4. Using a spanner wrench tool J–34836 to hold the camshaft pulley, remove the camshaft pulley bolt, the pulley, the alignment pin and the inside cover.

5. Carefully slide the camshaft from the rear of the cylinder head.

6. Clean the gasket mounting surfaces. Check for wear and/or damage, replace the parts as necessary.

7. To install, use new gaskets/seals and reverse the removal procedures. Torque the camshaft pulley bolt to 41–46 ft. lbs. Adjust the valve clearances and check the timing.

Piston and Connecting Rod

POSITIONING

There are two sizes of pistons available: a No. 1 and a No. 2 (indicating the outside diameter of the piston), the numbers are stamped on top of each piston. An arrow is also stamped on top of each piston, indicating the front of the engine.

A number is stamped at the front right of the engine block, on the cylinder head gasket surface. The number indicates of the pistons sizes, in order, ranging from the front-to-rear cylinders. Install the correct diameter piston (with the arrow facing the front of the engine) and the connecting rod (with the oil hole facing the intake manifold) into the correct cylinder bore.

For all piston and connecting rod overhaul procedures, please refer to the "Engine Rebuilding" in the Unit Repair section.

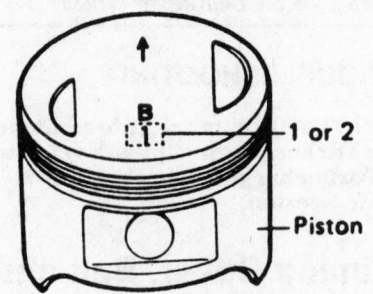

1 or 2
Piston

Piston identification

ENGINE LUBRICATION

Oil Pan

REMOVAL & INSTALLATION

1. Remove the negative battery cable.
2. Raise and support the vehicle.

3. Drain the engine oil.

4. Remove the flywheel dust cover.

5. Remove the exhaust pipe at the exhaust manifold.

6. Remove the oil pan bolts, the pan and the oil pump strainer.

7. Clean the gasket mating surfaces.

8. To install, use new gaskets and reverse the removal procedures. Torque the oil pan bolts to 9–12 ft. lbs. Refill the engine oil.

Rear Main Bearing Oil Seal

REMOVAL & INSTALLATION

1. Refer to the "Manual Transaxle Removal & Installation" procedures in this section and remove the transaxle.

2. Raise and support the vehicle. Remove the oil pan.

3. Remove the pressure plate, the clutch plate and the flywheel.

4. Remove the mounting bolts and the rear seal housing.

5. Pry the oil seal from the oil seal housing.

6. To install, use new gaskets/seals and reverse the removal procedures. Torque the oil seal housing to 7–9 ft. lbs. and the flywheel to 57–65 ft. lbs.

NOTE: After installing the oil seal housing, trim the gasket flush with the bottom of the case.

Oil Pump and Front Seal

REMOVAL & INSTALLATION

1. Refer to the "Timing Cover, Timing Belt and Tensioner Removal & Installation" procedures in this section and remove the timing belt.

2. Raise and support the vehicle. Remove the oil pan.

3. Use a suitable tool to hold the crankshaft timing belt pulley, remove the crankshaft bolt and pull the timing pulley from the shaft.

4. Remove the alternator mounting bracket and the A/C compressor bracket, if equipped.

5. Remove the alternator adjusting bolt and the upper cover bolt.

6. Remove the oil pump mounting bolts and the oil pump.

7. Pry the crankshaft oil seal from the oil pump.

8. Clean the gasket mounting surfaces. Remove the gear plate from the back of the oil pump and pack the oil pump gears with petroleum jelley.

9. To install, use new gaskets/seals

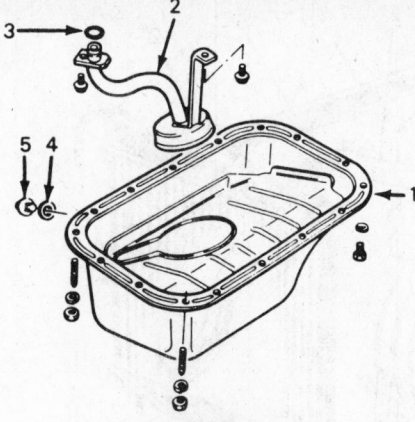

1. Oil pan
2. Oil pump strainer
3. O-ring seal
4. Drain plug gasket
5. Drain plug

Oil pan and strainer

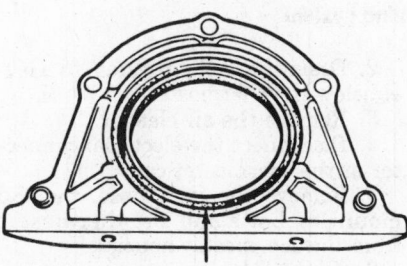

Rear main oil seal installed in seal housing

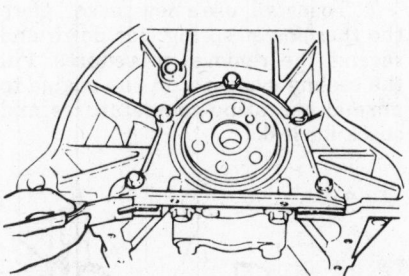

Trimming gasket on rear main oil seal housing after installation

and reverse the removal procedures. Torque the oil pump bolts to 7–9 ft. lbs. and the crankshaft timing pulley bolt to 47–54 ft. lbs. Adjust the valve clearances and check the timing.

NOTE: To install the oil pump to the engine, place the Oil Seal Guide tool J–34853 on the crankshaft and slide the oil pump onto the alignment pins. After installing the oil seal housing, trim the gasket flush with the bottom of the case.

INTERNAL GEAR TYPE– CARBURETED ENGINES ONLY

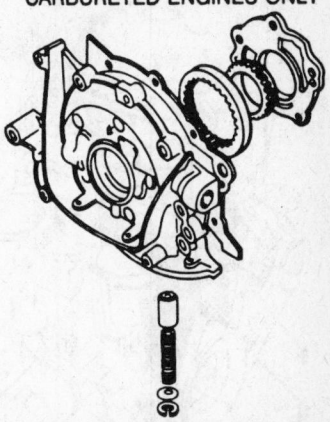

INTERNAL ROTOR TYPE– TURBOCHARGED ENGINES ONLY

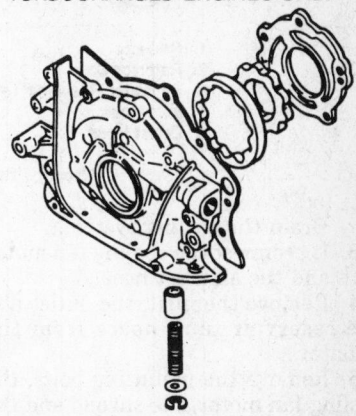

Two different oil pumps are used with turbo and non-turbo engines

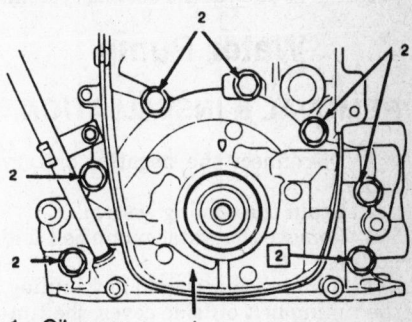

1. Oil pump
2. Oil pump mounting bolts

Tighten the oil pump mounting bolts to 7–9 ft. lbs.

ENGINE COOLING

Radiator

REMOVAL & INSTALLATION

1. Disconnect the negative battery cable.

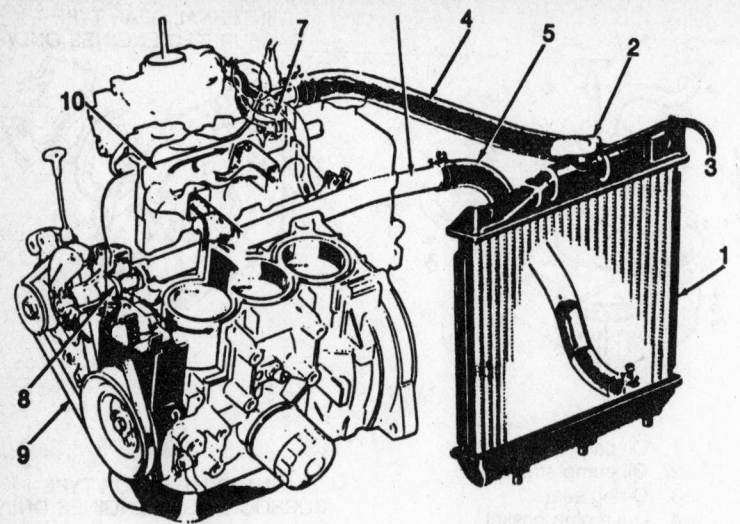

1. Radiator
2. Radiator Cap
3. To Water Reservoir Tank
4. Inlet Hose
5. Outlet Hose
6. Water Intake Pipe
7. Thermostat
8. Water Pump
9. Water Pump Belt
10. Intake Manifold

View of the cooling system

2. Drain the cooling system.

3. Disconnect the cooling fan motor wire and the air inlet hose.

4. Remove the inlet, the outlet and the reservoir tank hoses from the radiator.

5. Remove the mounting bolts, the cooling fan motor, the shroud and the radiator.

6. To install, reverse the removal procedures and fill the cooling system.

Water Pump

REMOVAL & INSTALLATION

1. Disconnect the negative battery cable.

2. Drain the cooling system.

3. Remove the water pump belt and pulley.

4. Remove the crankshaft pulley, the timing belt outside cover, the timing belt and the tensioner.

5. Remove the mounting bolts and the water pump.

6. Clean the gasket mating surfaces.

7. To install, use a new gasket/sealer and reverse the removal procedures. Torque the water pump bolts to 7.5–9 ft. lbs. Adjust the water pump belt deflection to $\frac{1}{4}$–$\frac{3}{8}$ in. between the water pump and the crankshaft pulleys.

Thermostat

REMOVAL & INSTALLATION

1. Disconnect the negative battery cable.

2. Drain the cooling system to a level below the thermostat.

3. Remove the air cleaner.

4. Disconnect the electrical connector at the thermostat cap.

5. Remove the inlet hose, the cap mounting bolts and the thermostat from the thermostat housing.

6. Clean the gasket mounting surfaces.

NOTE: Make sure that the thermostat air bleed hole is clear.

7. To install, use a new gasket, place the thermostat spring side down and reverse the removal procedures. Fill the cooling system, run the engine to normal operating temperatures and check for leaks.

COOLING SYSTEM BLEEDING

After working on the cooling system, even to replace the thermostat, it must be bled. Air trapped in the system will prevent proper filling and leave the radiator coolant level low, causing a risk of overheating.

1. To bleed the system, start with the system cool, the radiator cap off and the radiator filled to about an inch below the filler neck.

2. Start the engine and run it at slightly above normal idle speed. This will insure adequate circulation. If air bubbles appear and the coolant level drops, fill the system with an antifreeze/water mixture to bring the level back to the proper level.

3. Run the engine this way until the thermostat opens. When this happens, coolant will move abruptly across the top of the radiator and the temperature of the radiator will suddenly rise.

4. At this point, air is often expelled and the level may drop quite a bit. Keep refilling the system until the lev-

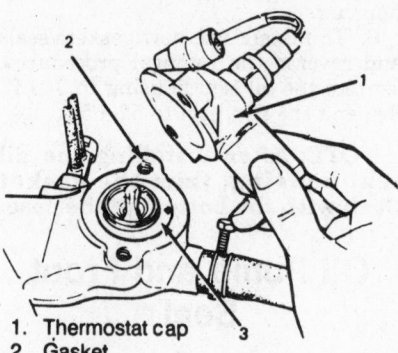

1. Thermostat cap
2. Gasket
3. Thermostat

Thermostat installation in intake manifold

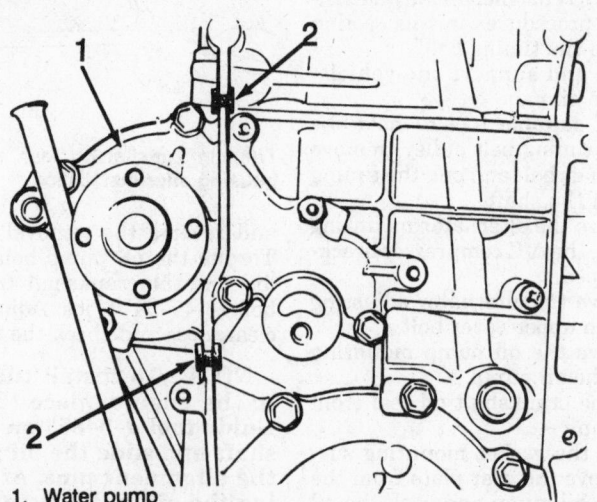

1. Water pump
2. Rubber seals

Water pump mounting. Install rubber seals after pump installation

el is near the top of the radiator and remains constant.

5. If the vehicle has an overflow tank, fill the radiator right up to the filler neck. Replace the radiator filler cap.

EMISSION CONTROLS

Please refer to "Emission Control" in the Unit Repair Section for system maintenance. Due to the complex nature of modern electronic engine control systems, comprehensive diagnosis and testing procedures fall outside the confines of this repair manual. For complete information on diagnosis, testing and repair procedures concerning all modern engine and emission control systems, please refer to *Chilton's Guide To Electronic Engine Controls.*

FUEL SYSTEM

Fuel System Service Precaution

RELIEVING FUEL SYSTEM PRESSURE

Fuel Injected Engines

The fuel delivery pipe is under high pressure even after the engine is stopped. Direct removal of the fuel line, may result in dangerous fuel spray. Make sure to release the fuel pressure according to the following procedure:

1. Release the fuel vapor pressure in the fuel tank by removing the fuel tank cap then reinstalling it.

2. With the engine running, remove the connector of the fuel pump relay and wait until the engine stops itself.

NOTE: The main relay and fuel pump relay are identical. Which one to connect to the fuel lead wire is not specified. Identify the fuel pump relay by the color of the lead wire. The fuel pump relay lead wire is Pink, Pink/White, White/Blue, White/Blue.

3. Once the engine is stopped, crank it a few times with the starter for

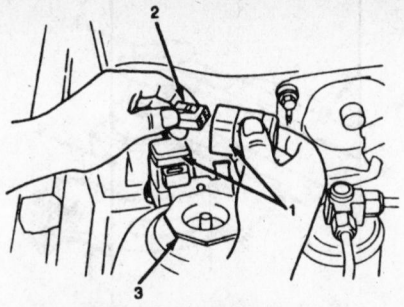

1. FUEL PUMP RELAY OR MAIN RELAY
2. FUEL PUMP RELAY LEAD WIRE (PINK, PINK/WHITE, WHITE/BLUE, WHITE/BLUE)
3. RIGHT FRONT SUSPENSION STRUT

Fuel pump relay wire identification

about three seconds each time (with the relay connector disconnected).

4. If the fuel pressure can't be released in the above manner because the engine failed to run in Step b, disconnect the negative battery cable, cover the union bolt of the high fuel pressure line with an appropriate rag and loosen the union bolt slowly to release the fuel pressure gradually.

Mechanical Fuel Pump

REMOVAL & INSTALLATION

Carbureted Engines

1. Remove and replace the fuel tank cap, this procedure releases the pressure within the fuel system.

2. Disconnect the negative battery cable.

3. Remove the air cleaner from the carburetor.

4. Remove the fuel inlet, outlet and return hoses from the fuel pump.

5. Remove the fuel pump mounting bolts, the pump and the pump rod from the cylinder head.

6. To install, lubricate the pump rod, use a new gasket and reverse the removal procedures.

Electric Fuel Pump

REMOVAL & INSTALLATION

Fuel Injected Engines

NOTE: The fuel tank must be lowered to gain access to the fuel pump which is located in the fuel tank.

1. Remove the fuel tank as follows:

a. Disconnect the negative battery cable.

b. Remove the rear seat cushion and disconnect the fuel gage and fuel pump lead wires.

c. Remove the fuel filler cap and then reinstall it to release the fuel pressure in the tank.

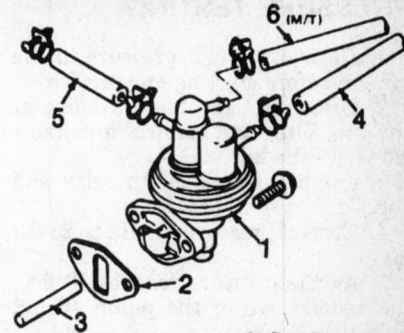

1. Fuel Pump
2. Gasket
3. Fuel Pump Rod
4. Inlet Hose
5. Outlet Hose
6. Return Hose

Fuel pump assembly, carburetted engines

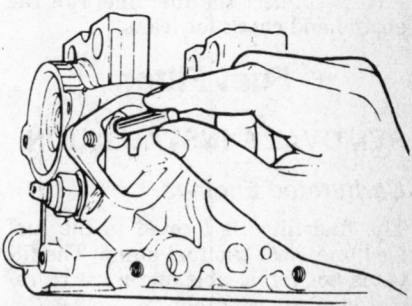

Installing fuel pump push rod in cylinder head

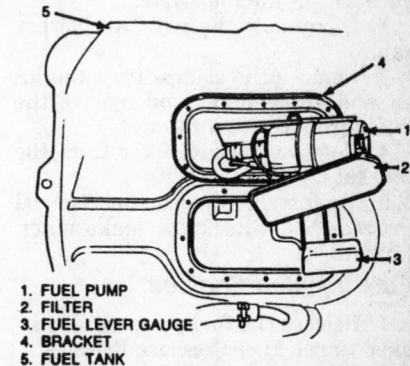

1. FUEL PUMP
2. FILTER
3. FUEL LEVER GAUGE
4. BRACKET
5. FUEL TANK

The fuel pump is located in the fuel tank on fuel injected models

d. Release the fuel line pressure as outlined under Fuel Pressure Release.

e. Since the tank does not have a drain plug, it must be drained by pumping or siphoning the fuel out through the fuel feed line (tank to fuel filter line).

f. Raise the vehicle on a hoist and disconnect all hoses and remove the tank from the vehicle.

2. Remove the fuel pump and fuel level gage bracket from the fuel tank.

3. Remove the fuel pump from the fuel tank.

4. Installation is the reverse of removal. Clean the fuel filter in the tank.

PRESSURE TESTING

1. Relieve the fuel pressure in the system before starting any service.
2. Disconnect the fuel inlet line at the fuel filter and connect a suitable gauge on the line.
3. Jump the fuel pump relay and check the system pressure.
4. Correct pressure should be 25–33 lbs.
5. As the pressure reaches 33 lbs., the relief valve in the pump should pulsate the pressure so it is always within the two limits.
6. If the pressure is not within the limits, check for restrictions in the fuel lines or replace the in-tank fuel pump.
7. Before removing the pressure gauge, relieve the fuel pressure again.
8. Reconnect the fuel line, run the engine and check for leaks.

Fuel Filter

REMOVAL & INSTALLATION

Carbureted Engines

The fuel filter is located in the fuel feed line, near the fuel pump. The filter is not serviceable and must be replaced as an assembly.

1. Remove and replace the fuel tank cap, this procedure releases the pressure within the fuel system.
2. Disconnect the negative battery cable.
3. Remove the clamps from the inlet and outlet hoses and remove the hoses from the fuel filter.
4. Remove the fuel filter from the bracket.
5. To install, reverse the removal procedures. Check for leaks when finished.

Fuel Injected Engines

1. Release the fuel pressure as outlined under Fuel Pressure Release.
2. Place an appropriate container under the fuel filter.
3. Use a 17mm and a 19mm wrench to loosen the inlet and outlet pipes and remove the fuel filter.
4. Installation is the reverse of removal with the following precautions:
- The end marked "OUT" should be placed up.
- Use new gaskets.
- Make sure the inlet and outlet pipes rest in the recesses in the plate.
- Tighten the inlet and outlet pipe bolts to 22–28 ft. lbs.
- Check for leaks when finished.

Carburetor

REMOVAL & INSTALLATION

1. Remove and replace the fuel tank

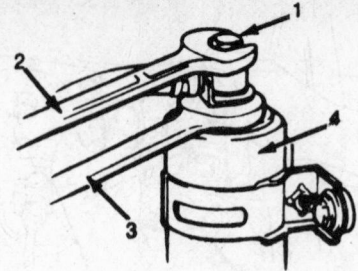

1. OUTLET PIPE BOLT
2. 17 MM (0.67 IN.) WRENCH
3. 19 MM (0.75 IN.) WRENCH
4. FUEL FILTER

Fuel filter removal, fuel injected engines

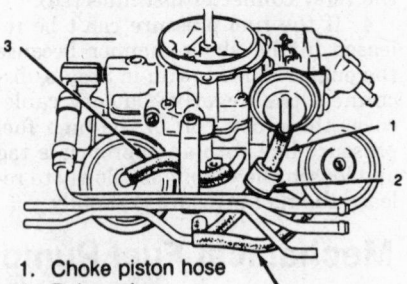

1. Choke piston hose
2. Delay valve
3. Secondary diaphragm hose
4. Idle-up actuator hose

Carburetor vacuum hose locations

cap, this procedure releases the pressure within the fuel system.
2. Disconnect the negative battery cable.
3. Disconnect the warm air, the cold air, the second air, the vacuum and the EGR modulator hoses from the air cleaner case.
4. Remove the air cleaner case from the carburetor.
5. Disconnect the accelerator cable and the electrical wiring from the carburetor.
6. Remove the emission control and the fuel hoses from the carburetor.
7. Disconnect the No. 1 and No. 2 choke hoses from the carburetor.
8. Remove the mounting bolts and the carburetor from the intake manifold.
9. To install, use new gaskets and reverse the removal procedures. Torque the carburetor mounting bolts to 18 ft. lbs.

OVERHAUL

For carburetor overhaul procedures, please refer to "Carburetor Service" in the Unit Repair Section.

Fuel Injection

Due to the complex nature of modern fuel injection systems, comprehensive diagnosis and testing procedures fall outside the confines of this repair manual. For complete information on fuel injection diagnosis, testing and repair procedures, please refer to *Chilton's Guide To Fuel Injection and Feedback Carburetors.*

MANUAL TRANSAXLE

REMOVAL & INSTALLATION

1. Disconnect the negative battery cable and the ground strap at the transaxle.
2. Remove the air cleaner and air pipe.
3. Remove the clutch cable from the clutch release lever.
4. Remove the starter and speedometer cable. Disconnect and tag the electrical wires and wiring harness from the transaxle.
5. Remove the front and rear torque rod bolts at the transaxle.
6. Raise and support the vehicle safely.
7. Drain the transaxle fluid.
8. Remove the exhaust pipe at the exhaust manifold and at the 1st exhaust hanger.
9. Remove the clutch housing lower plate.
10. Disconnect the gear shift control shaft and the extension rod at the transaxle.
11. Remove the left front wheel.
12. Using a pry bar, pry on the inboard joints of the right and left hand axle shafts. This will detach the axle shafts from the snap rings of the differential side gears.
13. On the left side, remove the stabilizer bar mounting bolts and ball joint stud bolt. Push down on the stabilizer bar and remove the ball joint stud from the steering knuckle.
14. Pull the left axle shaft out of the transaxle.
15. Remove the front torque rod.
16. Secure and support the transaxle case with a jack.
17. Remove the transaxle-to-body mounting bolts and the mounts.
18. Remove the transaxle-to-engine mounting bolts.
19. Disconnect the transaxle from the engine by sliding it to the left side and lower the jack.

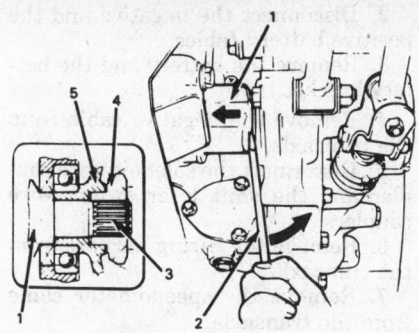

1. Inner axleshaft joint
2. Pry bar
3. Snap ring
4. Differential side gear
5. Differential carrier

Dislocating axleshafts from snap-rings in transaxle

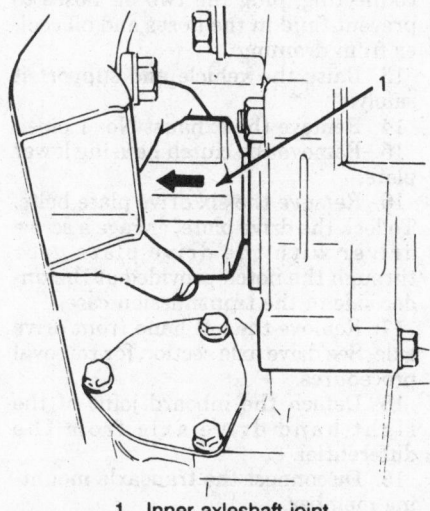

1. Inner axleshaft joint

Grasp the inner axleshaft joint and pull outwards to remove

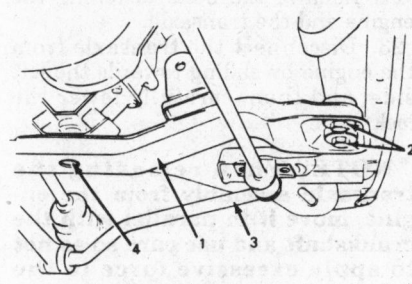

1. Mounting member
2. Mounting bolts 37–43 ft. lbs.
3. Stabilizer bar
4. Mounting nut 29–36 ft. lbs.

Transaxle mounting bolt locations

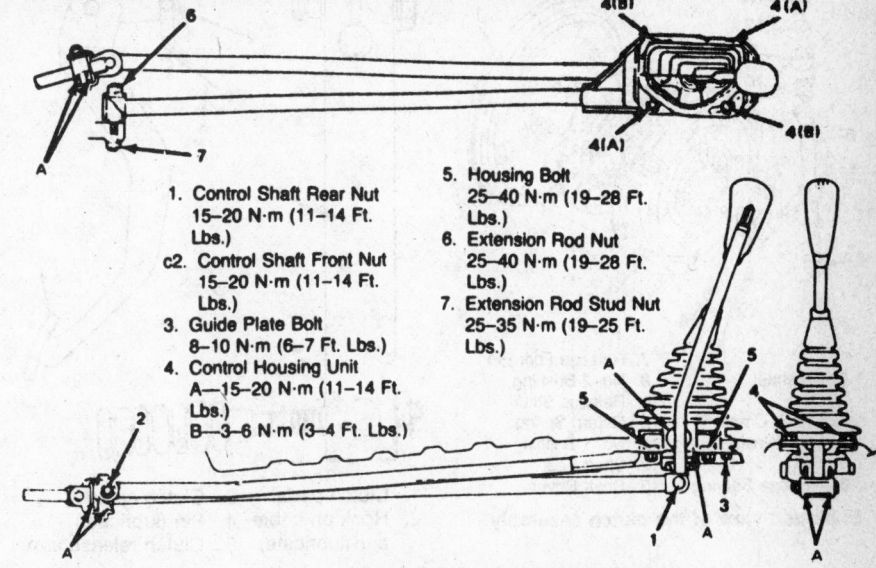

1. Control Shaft Rear Nut
   15–20 N·m (11–14 Ft. Lbs.)
c2. Control Shaft Front Nut
   15–20 N·m (11–14 Ft. Lbs.)
3. Guide Plate Bolt
   8–10 N·m (6–7 Ft. Lbs.)
4. Control Housing Unit
   A—15–20 N·m (11–14 Ft. Lbs.)
   B—3–6 N·m (3–4 Ft. Lbs.)
5. Housing Bolt
   25–40 N·m (19–28 Ft. Lbs.)
6. Extension Rod Nut
   25–40 N·m (19–28 Ft. Lbs.)
7. Extension Rod Stud Nut
   25–35 N·m (19–25 Ft. Lbs.)

View of the gear shift control assembly

NOTE: When removing the transaxle, support the right axle shaft, so it does not become damaged.

20. To install, guide the right axle shaft into the transaxle and reverse the removal procedures. Torque the transaxle-to-engine bolts to 35 ft. lbs.; the transaxle-to-mount bolts to 34 ft. lbs.; the mounting member bolts to 40 ft. lbs.; the stabilizer bar bolts to 30 ft. lbs. and the ball joint stud bolt to 44 ft. lbs. Adjust the clutch cable and refill the transaxle.

SHIFT LINKAGE ADJUSTMENT

1. At the console, loosen the gear shift control housing nuts and the guide plate bolts.
2. Adjust the guide plate, so that the shift lever is centered and at a right angle to the plate.
3. When the guide plate is positioned correctly, torque the guide plate bolts to 7 ft. lbs. and the housing nuts to 4 ft. lbs.

CLUTCH

REMOVAL & INSTALLATION

1. Refer to the "Manual Transaxle Removal & Installation" procedures in this section and remove the transaxle.
2. Install tool J–34860 into the pilot bearing to support the clutch assembly.

NOTE: Look for the "X" mark or white painted number on the clutch cover and the "X" mark on the flywheel. If there are no markings, mark the clutch cover and the flywheel for reassembly purposes.

3. Loosen the clutch cover-to-flywheel bolts, one turn at a time (evenly) until the spring pressure is released.
4. Remove the clutch cover and clutch disc.
5. Inspect the parts for wear, if necessary, replace the parts.
6. To install, reverse the removal procedures. Torque the clutch cover bolts to 14–20 ft. lbs.

FREE PLAY ADJUSTMENT

1. At the transaxle, move the clutch release arm to check the free play, it should be 0.08–0.16 in.
2. If necessary, turn the clutch cable joint nut to adjust the cable length.

PEDAL HEIGHT ADJUSTMENT

The clutch pedal height should be adjusted so that the clutch pedal is the exact same height as the brake pedal. The pedal is adjusted at the stop bolt on the upper end of the pedal pivot.

Clutch Cable

REMOVAL & INSTALLATION

1. Disconnect the negative battery cable.
2. Remove the clutch cable joint nut

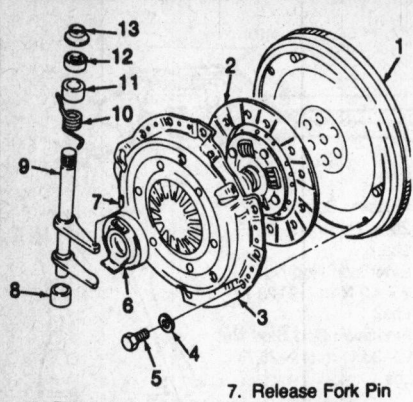

1. Flywheel
2. Disc
3. Clutch Cover
4. Lock Washer
5. Bolt
6. Release Bearing
7. Release Fork Pin
8. No. 2 Bushing
9. Release Shaft
10. Return Spring
11. No. 1 Bushing
12. Shaft Seal
13. Shaft Cover

Exploded view of the clutch assembly

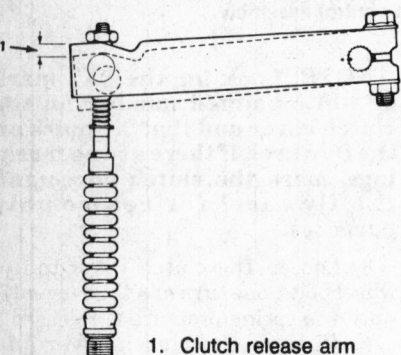

1. Clutch release arm play (0.08–0.16 in.)

Clutch release arm free-play adjustment

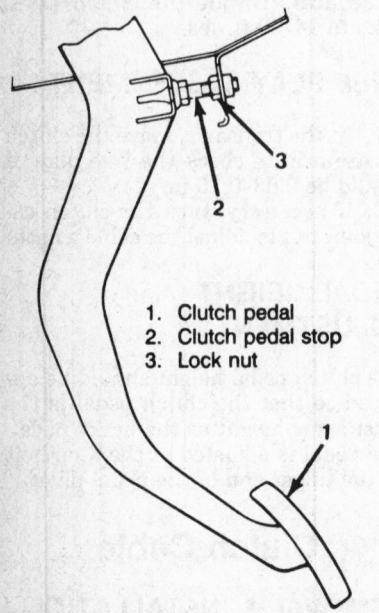

1. Clutch pedal
2. Clutch pedal stop
3. Lock nut

Clutch pedal height is adjusted at the stop-bolt. When adjusted properly, the clutch pedal should be the same height as the brake pedal.

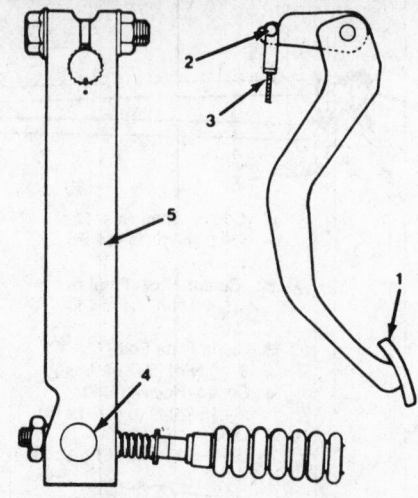

1. Clutch pedal
2. Hook on cable end (lubricate)
3. Clutch cable
4. Pin (lubricate)
5. Clutch release arm

Clutch cable mounting on release arm and at pedal. Note the matchmarks on the release arm and shaft.

and disconnect the cable from the release arm.

3. Remove the clutch cable bracket mounting nuts and remove the bracket from the cable.

4. Remove the cable retaining bolts at the clutch pedal.

5. Remove the cable from the vehicle.

6. Before installation, apply grease to the hook and pin end of the cable.

7. Connect the cable to the clutch pedal and install the retaining bolts.

8. Install the clutch cable bracket on the cable.

9. Position the bracket on the transaxle and install the mounting bolts.

10. Connect the cable to the release lever and install the joint nut on the cable.

11. Adjust the clutch cable as previously outlined and connect the negative battery cable.

AUTOMATIC TRANSAXLE

For further information on automatic transaxles, please refer to "Automatic Transmissions" in the Unit Repair Section.

REMOVAL & INSTALLATION

1. Disconnect the air suction guide from the air cleaner.

2. Disconnect the negative and the positive battery cables.

3. Remove the battery and the battery bracket tray.

4. Remove the negative cable from the transaxle.

5. Disconnect the solenoid wire coupler and the shift lever switch wire couplers.

6. Remove the wiring harness from the transaxle.

7. Remove the speedometer cable from the transaxle.

8. Disconnect the oil pressure control cable from the accelerator cable, and then the accelerator cable from the transaxle.

9. Remove the select cable from the transaxle.

10. Remove the starter motor.

11. Drain the transaxle fluid.

12. Disconnect the oil outlet and inlet hoses from the oil pipes. After disconnecting, plug the two oil hoses to prevent fluid in the hoses and oil cooler from draining.

13. Raise the vehicle and support it safely.

14. Remove the exhaust No. 1 pipe.

15. Remove the clutch housing lower plate.

16. Remove the six drive plate bolts. To lock the drive plate, engage a screw driver with the drive plate gear through the notch provided at the under side of the transmission case.

17. Remove the left hand front drive axle. See drive axle section for removal procedures.

18. Detach the inboard joint of the right hand drive axle from the differential.

19. Disconnect the transaxle mounting member.

20. Securely support the transaxle with a suitable jack for removal.

21. Remove the transaxle left mounting.

22. Remove the bolts fastening the engine and the transaxle.

23. Disconnect the transaxle from the engine by sliding towards the left side, and then, carefully lower the jack.

NOTE: When removing the transaxle assembly from the engine, move it in parallel with the crankshaft and use care so as not to apply excessive force to the drive plate and torque converter. After removing the transaxle assembly, be sure to keep it so that the oil pan is at the bottom. If the transaxle is tilted, fluid in it may flow out.

24. To install the transaxle, reverse the removal procedure noting the following important steps.

25. Before installing the transaxle

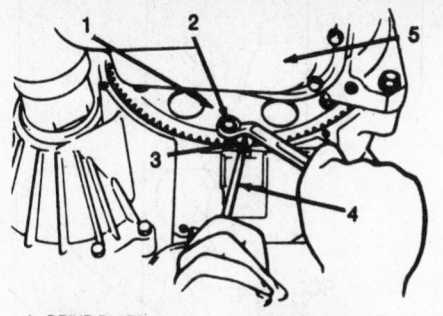

1. DRIVE PLATE
2. DRIVE PLATE BOLT
3. NOTCH
4. STANDARD SCREWDRIVER
5. ENGINE OIL PAN

Removing drive plate bolts

80-80 N·m
(57-43 LB. FT.)

1. TRANSAXLE MOUNTING MEMBER
2. TRANSAXLE OIL PAN

Transaxle mounting member and oil pan

assembly apply grease around the cup at the center of the torque converter. Then measure the distance between the torque converter flange nut and the transaxle case housing. The distance should be more than 0.85 in. (21.4mm). If the distance is less than 0.85 in. (21.4mm), the torque converter has been installed incorrectly and must be removed and reinstalled correctly.

26. When installing the transaxle, guide the right drive axle into the differential side gear as the transaxle is being raised.

27. After inserting the inboard joints of the right hand and left hand drive axles into the differential side gears, push the inboard joints into the side gears until the snap rings on the drive axles engage the side gears.

28. After connecting the oil pressure control cable to the accelerator cable, check the oil pressure control cable play and adjust if necessary.

29. Install the select cable.

30. Refill the transaxle and check the fluid level.

31. Tighten the following bolts and nuts to specifications.

a. Drive Plate Bolts—14 ft. lbs. (19 Nm).

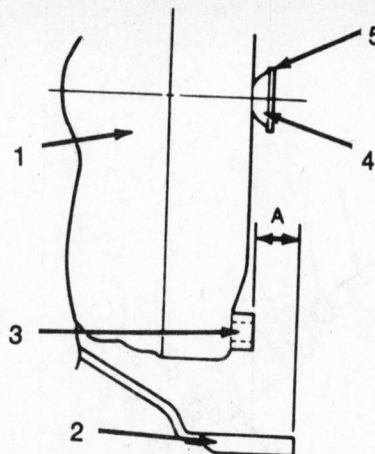

1. TORQUE CONVERTER
2. TRANSAXLE CASE HOUSING
3. FLANGE NUT
4. CUP
5. "APPLY GREASE HERE"
A: MORE THAN 21.4 mm (0.85 IN.)

Torque converter installation

b. Mounting Member Bolts—40 ft. lbs. (55 Nm).

c. Transaxle Mounting Nuts—33 ft. lbs. (45 Nm).

d. Transaxle Mounting Bolts (8mm)—40 ft. lbs. (55 Nm).

e. Transaxle Mounting Nuts—40 ft. lbs. (55 Nm).

f. Stabilizer Shaft Mounting Bolts—31 ft. lbs. (42 Nm).

g. Ball Stud Bolt—44 ft. lbs. (60 Nm).

h. Wheel Nuts—40 ft. lbs. (55 Nm).

DRIVE AXLE

Halfshaft

REMOVAL & INSTALLATION

1. Remove the grease cap, the cotter pin and the axle shaft nut from both front wheels.

2. Loosen the wheel nuts.

3. Raise and support the front of the vehicle on jackstands.

4. Remove the front wheels.

5. Drain the transaxle fluid.

6. Using a pry bar, pry on the inboard joints of the right and left hand axle shafts to detach the axle shafts from the snap rings of the differential side gears.

7. Remove the stabilizer bar mounting bolts and the ball joint stud bolt. Pull down on the stabilizer bar and remove the ball joint stud from the steering knuckle.

8. Pull the axle shafts out of the transaxle's side gear, first, and then from the steering knuckles.

NOTE: To prevent the axle shaft boots from becoming damaged, be careful not to bring them into contact with any parts. If any malfunction is found in the either of the joints, replace the joints as an assembly.

9. To install, snap the axle shaft into the transaxle, first, and then into the steering knuckle.

10. To complete the installation, reverse the removal procedures. Torque the stabilizer bar mounting bolts to 30 ft. lbs.; the ball joint stud bolt to 44 ft. lbs. and the axle shaft nut to 144 ft. lbs.

CV JOINT OVERHAUL

For all service and overhaul information, please refer to the "U-Joint/CV-Joint" Unit Repair section.

Front Hub

REMOVAL & INSTALLATION

1. Raise and support the front of the vehicle on jackstands. Remove the front wheel assembly.

2. Remove the dust cap and the cotter pin from the axle shaft.

3. Loosen the castle nut on the axle shaft.

4. Remove the brake caliper bolts and the brake caliper.

NOTE: When removing the brake caliper, DO NOT remove the brake hose, suspend it on a wire.

5. Remove the castle nut and the washer from the axle shaft.

6. Using a slide hammer tool J-2619-01 and a brake drum remover tool J-34866, pull the hub from the steering knuckle.

7. Remove the spacing ring from the rear of the hub.

8. Remove the bolts and separate the hub from the brake disc.

9. To install, place the spacing ring on the hub (install beveled side first) and reverse the removal procedures. Torque the hub-to-brake disc bolts to 29-43 ft. lbs., the brake caliper bolts to 17-26 ft. lbs. and the axle shaft nut to 108-195 ft. lbs.

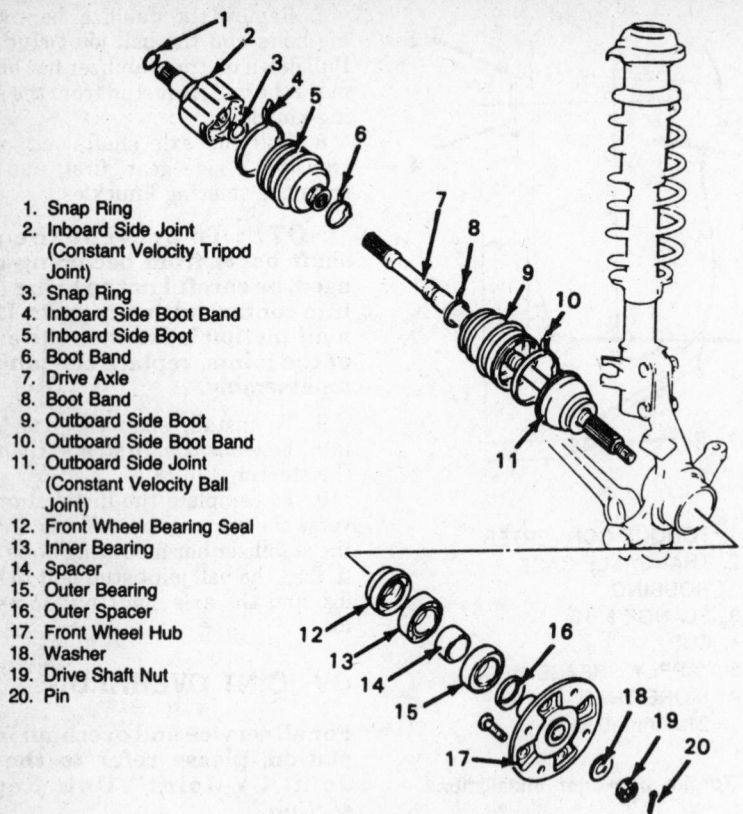

1. Snap Ring
2. Inboard Side Joint (Constant Velocity Tripod Joint)
3. Snap Ring
4. Inboard Side Boot Band
5. Inboard Side Boot
6. Boot Band
7. Drive Axle
8. Boot Band
9. Outboard Side Boot
10. Outboard Side Boot Band
11. Outboard Side Joint (Constant Velocity Ball Joint)
12. Front Wheel Bearing Seal
13. Inner Bearing
14. Spacer
15. Outer Bearing
16. Outer Spacer
17. Front Wheel Hub
18. Washer
19. Drive Shaft Nut
20. Pin

Exploded view of the axle shaft

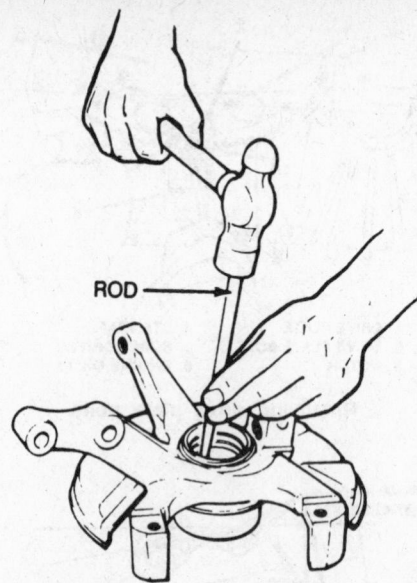

Removing outer wheel bearing from steering knuckle

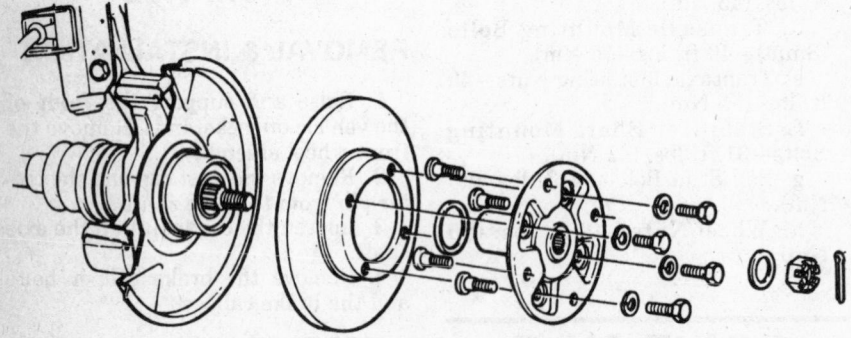

Exploded view of the front wheel hub assembly

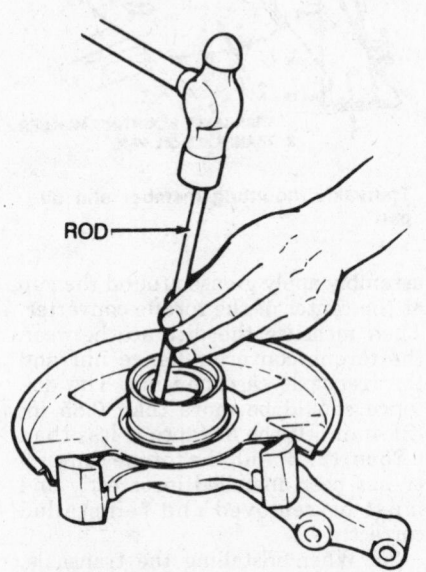

Removing inner wheel bearing from steering knuckle

NOTE: When installing the hub to the steering knuckle, tap it with a plastic hammer to align the hub, then, using the installation tool J-34856, drive the hub into the steering knuckle.

Steering Knuckle and Wheel Bearings

REMOVAL & INSTALLATION

1. Refer to the "Front Hub Removal & Installation" procedures in this section and remove the hub from the steering knuckle.

2. Remove the tie rod end cotter pin and nut.

3. Using the ball joint puller tool J-21687-02, remove the ball joint from the steering knuckle.

4. Remove the ball stud bolt from the steering knuckle.

5. Remove the strut-to-steering knuckle bolts.

6. Remove the steering knuckle and support the axle shaft on a wire.

7. Using a brass drift and a hammer, drive the wheel bearings from the steering knuckle.

8. Remove the spacer and clean the steering knuckle cavity.

9. Lubricate the new bearings and the steering knuckle cavity.

10. Using the installation tool J-34856, drive the new bearings (with the internal seals facing outward) into the steering knuckle.

11. Using the seal installation tool J-34881, drive the new seal into the steering knuckle (grease the seal lip).

12. To complete the installation, reverse the removal procedures. Torque the strut-to-steering knuckle bolts to 50–65 ft. lbs.; the ball joints-to-steering knuckle nuts to 22–40 ft. lbs. and the axle shaft castle nut to 108–195 ft. lbs.

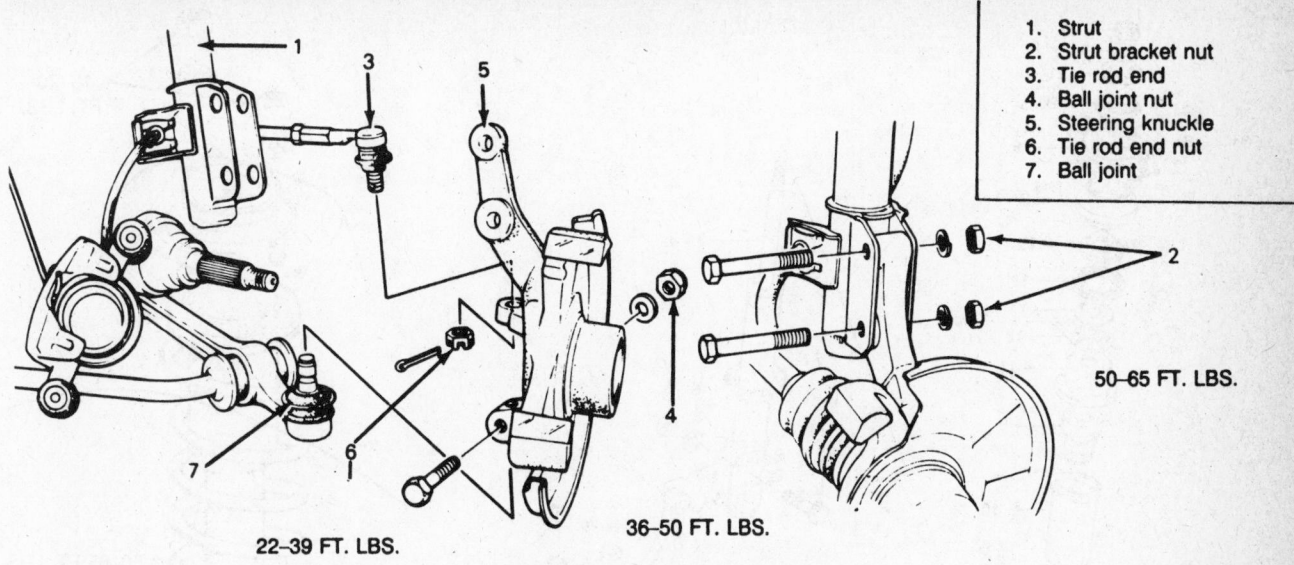

1. Strut
2. Strut bracket nut
3. Tie rod end
4. Ball joint nut
5. Steering knuckle
6. Tie rod end nut
7. Ball joint

50–65 FT. LBS.

22–39 FT. LBS.

36–50 FT. LBS.

Front steering knuckle mounting

INNER WHEEL BEARING   OUTER WHEEL BEARING

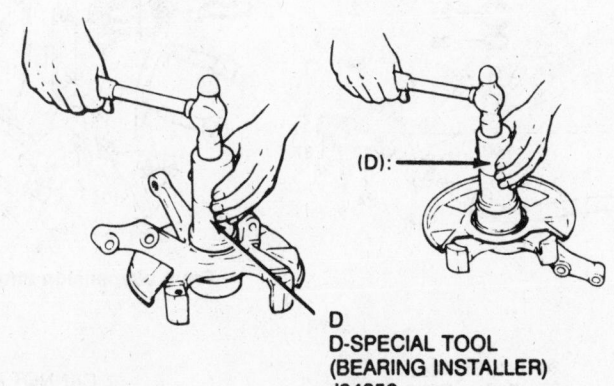

(D):

D
D-SPECIAL TOOL
(BEARING INSTALLER)
J34856

Installing inner and outer wheel bearings in steering knuckle

FRONT SUSPENSION

MacPherson Strut

REMOVAL & INSTALLATION

1. Raise and support the front of the vehicle.
2. Remove the wheel assembly.
3. Remove the brake hose securing ring and the hose from the strut.
4. Remove the upper strut support nuts from the engine compartment.
5. Remove the strut-to-steering knuckle bolts and the strut.

6. To install, reverse the removal procedures. Torque the upper mounting nuts to 13–20 ft. lbs. and the strut-to-steering knuckle bolts to 50–65 ft. lbs.

OVERHAUL

For all spring and shock absorber removal and installation procedures, and all strut overhaul procedures, please refer to the "Strut Overhaul" Unit Repair section.

Stabilizer Bar

REMOVAL & INSTALLATION

1. Raise and support the front of

the vehicle on jackstands. Remove the front wheel assemblies.
2. Remove the stabilizer bar-to-body mounting bolts.
3. Remove the cotter pin, the castle nut, the washer, the bushing and the stabilizer bar from the lower control arms.
4. To install, reverse the removal procedures. Torque the stabilizer bar-to-control arm to 29–65 ft. lbs. and the stabilizer bar-to-body bolts to 22–39 ft. lbs.

Lower Control Arm/ Ball Joint

REMOVAL & INSTALLATION

1. Raise and support the front of the vehicle safely. Remove the front wheel assembly.
2. Remove the cotter pin, the castle nut, the washer and the bushing from the stabilizer bar.
3. Remove the stabilizer bar–to-body mounting bracket bolts.
4. Remove the ball stud and the control arm bolts.
5. Remove the control arm.
6. To install, reverse the removal procedures. Torque the control arm-to-body bolt to 36–50 ft. lbs.; the ball stud-to-steering knuckle to 36–50 ft. lbs.; the stabilizer bar-to-control arm to 29–65 ft. lbs. and the stabilizer bar-to-body to 22–39 ft. lbs.

Front Wheel Alignment

CASTER AND CAMBER

Caster and camber are not adjustable.

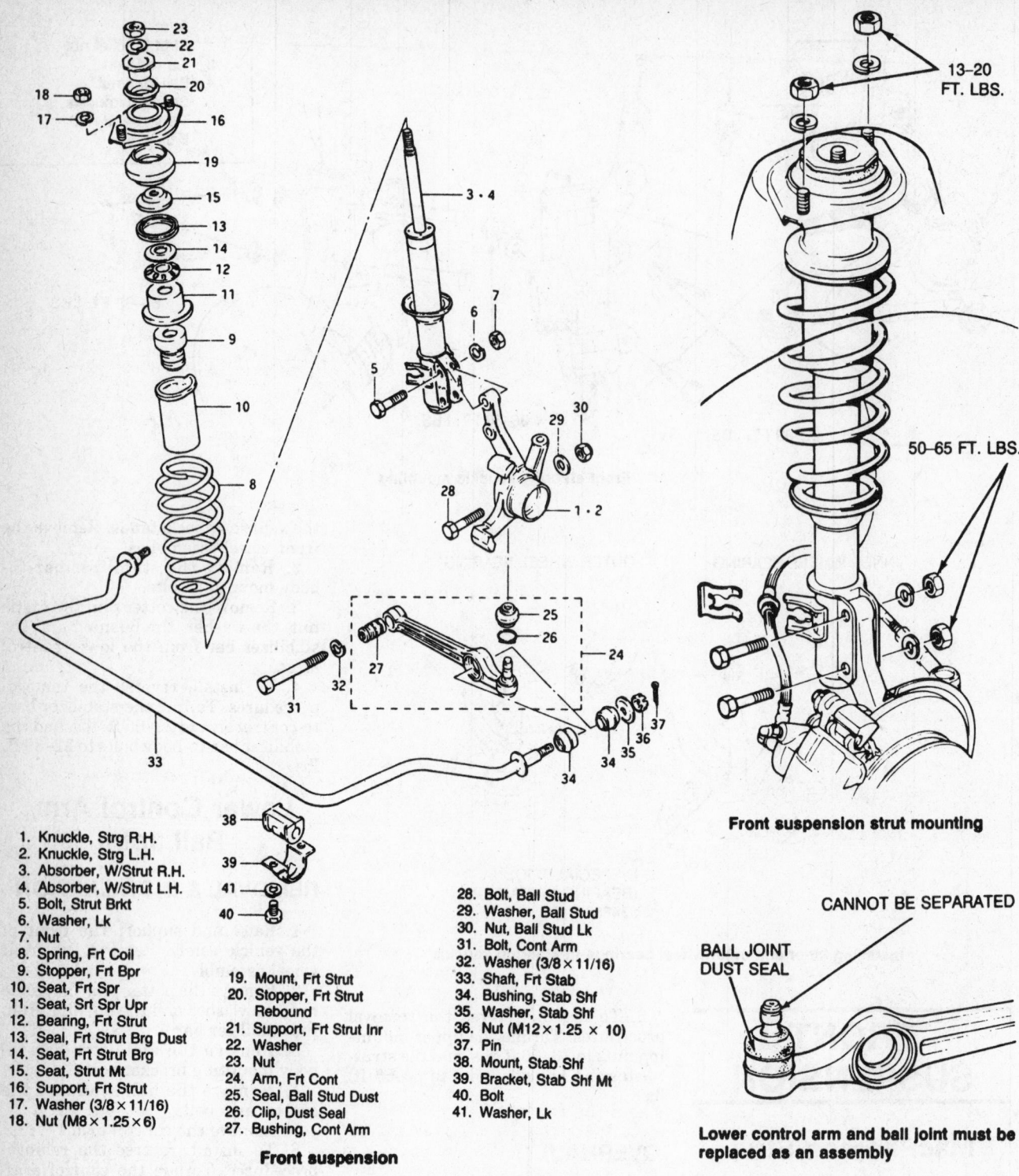

Front suspension strut mounting

13–20 FT. LBS.

50–65 FT. LBS.

1. Knuckle, Strg R.H.
2. Knuckle, Strg L.H.
3. Absorber, W/Strut R.H.
4. Absorber, W/Strut L.H.
5. Bolt, Strut Brkt
6. Washer, Lk
7. Nut
8. Spring, Frt Coil
9. Stopper, Frt Bpr
10. Seat, Frt Spr
11. Seat, Srt Spr Upr
12. Bearing, Frt Strut
13. Seat, Frt Strut Brg Dust
14. Seat, Frt Strut Brg
15. Seat, Strut Mt
16. Support, Frt Strut
17. Washer (3/8 × 11/16)
18. Nut (M8 × 1.25 × 6)

19. Mount, Frt Strut
20. Stopper, Frt Strut Rebound
21. Support, Frt Strut Inr
22. Washer
23. Nut
24. Arm, Frt Cont
25. Seal, Ball Stud Dust
26. Clip, Dust Seal
27. Bushing, Cont Arm

28. Bolt, Ball Stud
29. Washer, Ball Stud
30. Nut, Ball Stud Lk
31. Bolt, Cont Arm
32. Washer (3/8 × 11/16)
33. Shaft, Frt Stab
34. Bushing, Stab Shf
35. Washer, Stab Shf
36. Nut (M12 × 1.25 × 10)
37. Pin
38. Mount, Stab Shf
39. Bracket, Stab Shf Mt
40. Bolt
41. Washer, Lk

Front suspension

CANNOT BE SEPARATED

BALL JOINT DUST SEAL

Lower control arm and ball joint must be replaced as an assembly

If the caster and/or camber are out of specifications, check for worn, loose or broken suspension and/or steering components.

TOE ADJUSTMENT

Toe is adjusted by changing the tie rod length. Loosen the right and left tie rod end lock nuts first and then turn left and right tie rods by the same amount to align toe to specification. In this adjustment right and left tie rods should be equal in length. Toe adjustment should be (0 ± 0.157 in.).

NOTE: Before turning the tie rods, apply grease between tie rods and rack boots so that the boots won't be twisted. After adjustment, tighten lock nuts to specified torque and make sure that the rack boots are not twisted.

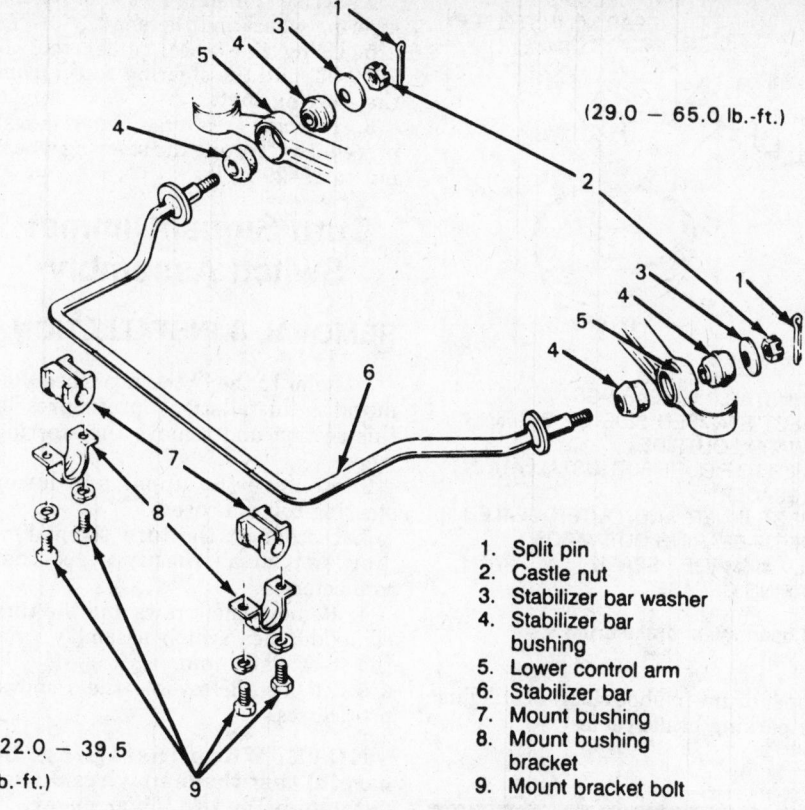

(29.0 – 65.0 lb.-ft.)

(22.0 – 39.5 lb.-ft.)

1. Split pin
2. Castle nut
3. Stabilizer bar washer
4. Stabilizer bar bushing
5. Lower control arm
6. Stabilizer bar
7. Mount bushing
8. Mount bushing bracket
9. Mount bracket bolt

Front stabilizer bar mounting

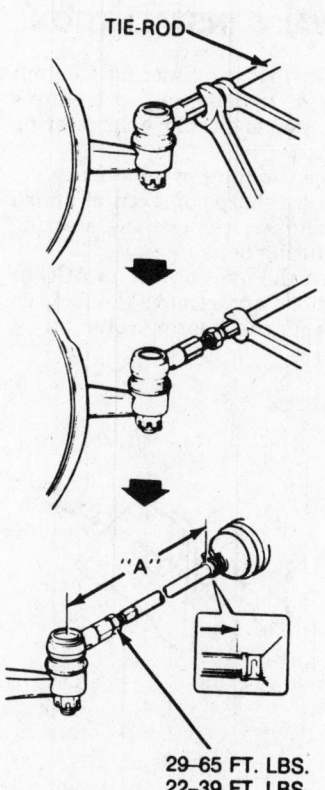

TIE-ROD

"A"

29–65 FT. LBS.
22–39 FT. LBS.

Toe adjustment

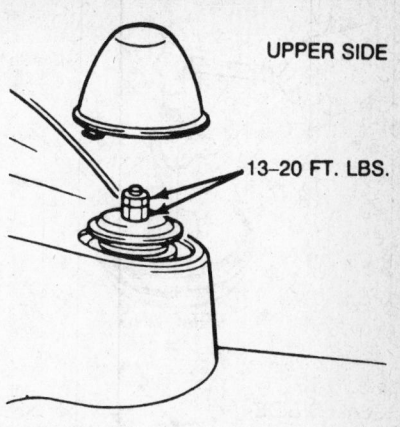

UPPER SIDE

13–20 FT. LBS.

Rear upper shock absorber mounting nut

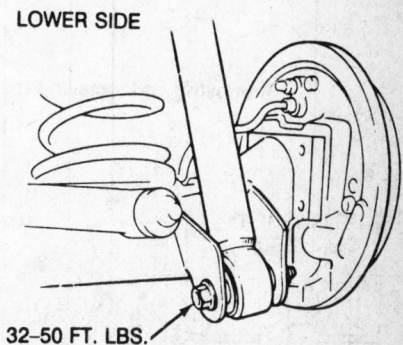

LOWER SIDE

32–50 FT. LBS.

Rear lower shock absorber mounting bolt

REAR SUSPENSION

Shock Absorber

REMOVAL & INSTALLATION

1. Raise and support the rear of the vehicle on jackstands. Remove the wheel assembly.
2. Remove the lower mounting nut, the lock washer and and the outer washer.
3. Remove the upper mounting bolt, the lock washer and nut.
4. Remove the shock absorber.
5. To install, reverse the removal procedures. Torque the upper mounting bolt to 33–50 ft. lbs. and the lower mounting nut to 8–12 ft. lbs.

Spring

REMOVAL & INSTALLATION

1. Raise and support the rear of the vehicle on jackstands. Remove the front wheel assembly.
2. Remove the U-bolt nuts.
3. Remove the shackle and leaf spring front nuts.
4. Remove the front spring bolt.
5. Remove the spring from the vehicle.

NOTE: Apply a thin coat of silicone grease to the springs bushings before installation.

6. To install, align the spring pin with the hole in the axle shaft housing and reverse the removal procedures. Torque the front spring bolt to 33–50 ft. lbs.; the rear spring shackle nuts to 22–40 ft. lbs. and the U-bolt nuts to 22–33 ft. lbs.

Rear Wheel Bearings

REMOVAL & INSTALLATION

1. Raise and support the rear of the vehicle safely.
2. Remove the wheel assembly.
3. Remove the dust cap, the cotter pin, the castle nut and the washer.
4. Loosen the adjusting nuts of the parking brake cable.
5. Remove the plug from the rear of the backing plate. Insert a screwdriver through the hole, making contact with

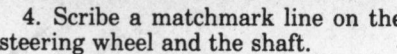

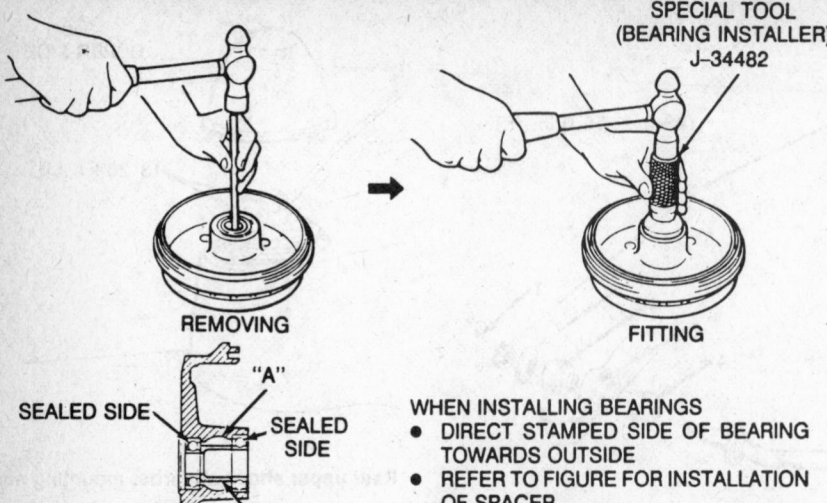

WHEN INSTALLING BEARINGS
- DIRECT STAMPED SIDE OF BEARING TOWARDS OUTSIDE
- REFER TO FIGURE FOR INSTALLATION OF SPACER
- DIRECT INNER AND OUTER SEALED SIDE OF BEARING OUTWARDS
- FILL 40% OF SPACE "A" WITH BEARING GREASE

Removing and installing rear wheel bearings in brake drum

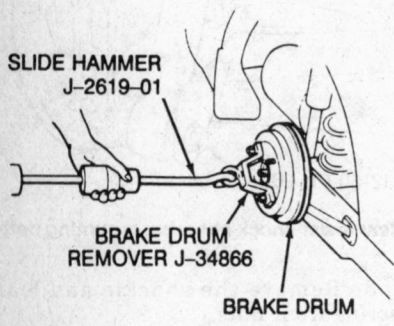

Removing rear brake drum using a slide hammer

the shoe hold down spring, then push the spring to release the parking brake shoe lever.

6. Using a slide hammer tool J–2619–01 and a brake drum remover tool J–34866, pull the brake drum from the axle shaft.

7. Using a brass drift and a hammer, drive the rear wheel bearings from the brake drum.

NOTE: When installing the wheel bearings, face the sealed sides (numbered sides) outward. Fill the wheel bearing cavity with bearing grease.

8. Drive the new bearings into the brake drum with the bearing installation tool J–34482.

9. To install, use a new seal and reverse the removal procedures. Torque the hub castle nut to 58–86 ft. lbs. Bleed the rear brake system. Operate the brakes 3–5 times to obtain the proper drum-to-shoe clearance. Adjust the parking brake cable.

STEERING

Steering Wheel

REMOVAL & INSTALLATION

1. Disconnect the negative battery cable.
2. Loosen the pad screws and remove the the pad.
3. Remove the steering wheel nut.

1. Horn pad
2. Steering shaft nut 18–28 ft. lbs.
3. Lock washer
4. Steering wheel
5. Steering shaft

4. Scribe a matchmark line on the steering wheel and the shaft.

5. Using the wheel puller tool J-1859-03, pull the steering wheel from the steering shaft.

6. To install, reverse the removal procedures. Torque the steering wheel nut to 19–29 ft. lbs.

Turn Signal/Dimmer Switch Assembly

REMOVAL & INSTALLATION

1. Refer to the "Steering Wheel Removal & Installation" procedures in this section and remove the steering wheel.

2. Remove the upper and lower steering column covers.

3. Disconnect the turn signal/dimmer switch assembly electrical connector.

4. Remove the screws and the turn signal/dimmer switch assembly from the steering column.

5. To install, reverse the removal procedures.

NOTE: When installing, be careful that the lead wires do not get caught by the lower cover.

Ignition Lock/Switch

REMOVAL & INSTALLATION

1. Refer to the "Steering Column Removal & Installation" procedures in this section and remove the steering column.

2. Place the column on a bench.

3. Using a sharp point center punch and a hammer, remove the steering lock mounting bolts.

4. Turn the ignition key to ACC or ON positions and remove the lock assembly from the steering column.

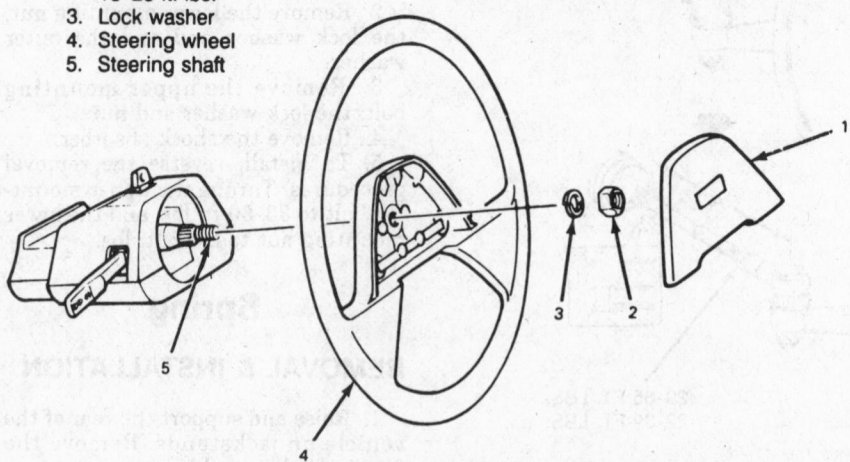

Steering wheel and horn pad mounting

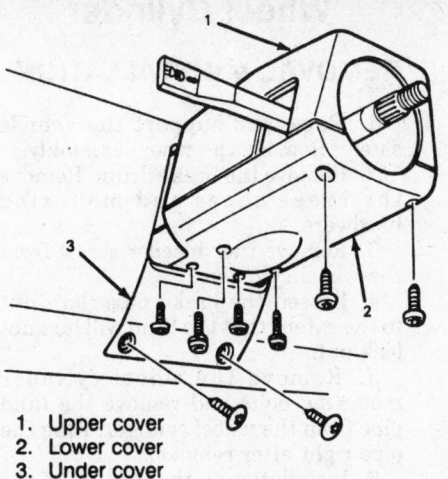

1. Upper cover
2. Lower cover
3. Under cover

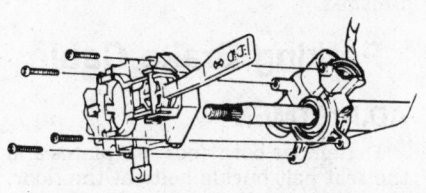

Turn signal/dimmer switch mounting

5. To install, reverse the removal procedures. After installing the lock, turn the key to LOCK position and pull out the key. Turn the steering shaft to make sure the shaft is locked. Install new mounting bolts to the lock housing, tighten until the bolt heads break off. Torque the lower bracket bolts to 8–12 ft. lbs.; the upper bracket bolts to 10 ft. lbs. and the steering shaft bolt to 15–22 ft. lbs.

Steering Gear

REMOVAL & INSTALLATION

1. Refer to the "Tie Rod Removal & Installation" procedures in this section and remove the tie rod ends from the steering knuckles.
2. Under the dash, remove the steering joint cover.
3. Remove the lower steering shaft-to-steering gear clinch bolt and separate the steering shaft from the steering gear.
4. Remove the steering gear mounting bolts, the brackets and the steering gear case from the vehicle.
5. To install, reverse the removal procedures. Torque the steering gear case bolts to 14–22 ft. lbs.; the steering gear-to-steering shaft bolt to 14–22 ft. lbs. and the tie rod end-to-steering knuckle nut to 22–40 ft. lbs.

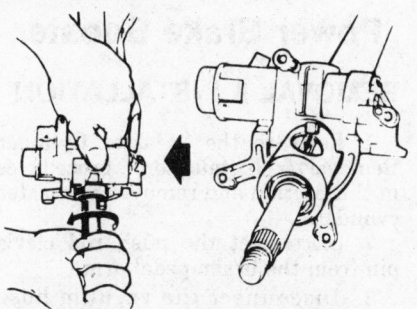

1. Lower cover
2. Key warning switch lead wire
3. Ignition key lead wire

Removing lower steering column cover

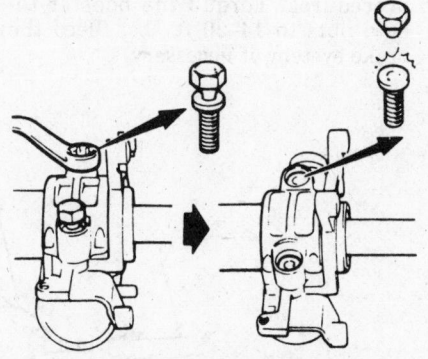

Rotate steering shaft until tab on switch aligns with the groove in the shaft

Tighten the ignition lock retaining bolts until the head of the bolt breaks off

Tie Rod Ends

REMOVAL & INSTALLATION

1. Raise and support the front of the vehicle on jackstands. Remove the front wheel assembly.
2. Remove the cotter pin and the castle nut from the tie rod end.
3. Using the ball joint remover tool J-21687-02, remove the tie rod end ball joint from the steering knuckle.
4. Loosen the lock nut on the tie rod end.

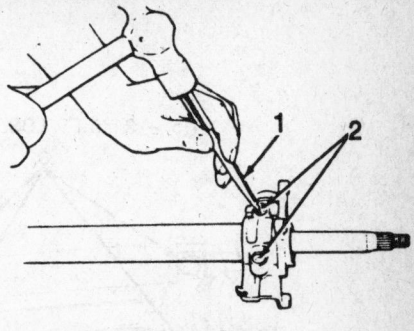

1. Center Punch (With Sharp Point)
2. Steering Lock Mounting Bolts

Removing the ignition switch/key lock assembly

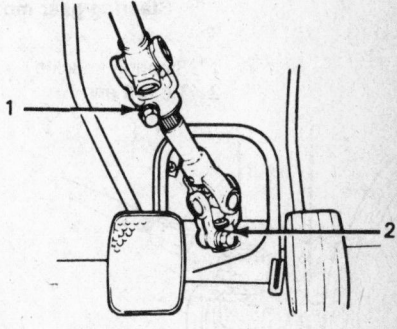

1. Steering shaft upper joint bolt
2. Steering shaft lower joint bolt

Disconnect the steering shaft from the steering gear at two locations

5. Unscrew the the tie rod end from the tie rod, count the number of revolutions necessary to remove the tie rod end, for installation purposes.
6. At the steering gear, remove the boot clamps and pull the boot back over the tie rod.
7. Using a pair of pliers, bend the lock washer back from the tie rod joint.
8. Using two wrenches, hold the steering gear and unscrew the tie rod end.
9. Remove the tie rod and slide the boot from the tie rod.
10. To install, reverse the removal procedures. Torque the tie rod-to-steering gear to 51–72 ft. lbs.; the tie rod end lock nut to 26–40 ft. lbs. and the tie rod end-to-steering knuckle to 22–40 ft. lbs. With the tie rod secured to the steering gear, bend the lock washer over the flat spot on the tie rod ball end.

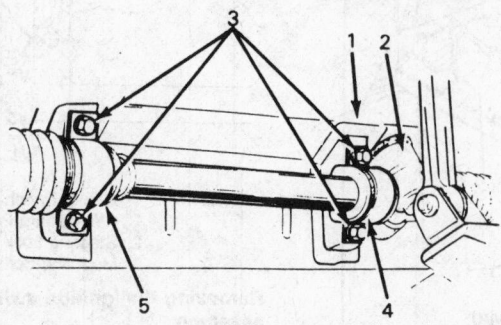

14.5 – 21.5 FT. LBS.

1. Car body
2. Steering gear case
3. Mounting bolts
4. Pinion side bracket
5. Rack side bracket

Steering gear mounting bolt locations

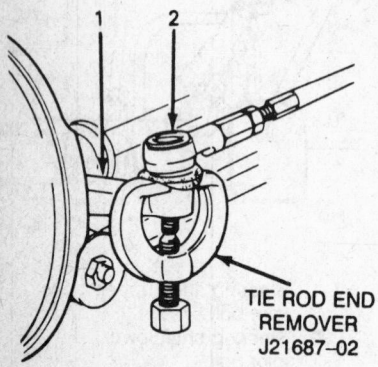

1. Steering knuckle
2. Tie rod end

TIE ROD END REMOVER J21687–02

Removing outer tie rod end from steering knuckle using a puller

BRAKES

For all brake system repair and service procedures not detailed below, please refer to "Brakes" in the Unit Repair Sction.

Master Cylinder

REMOVAL & INSTALLATION

1. Clean around the reservoir cap and take some of the fluid out with a syringe.
2. Disconnect and plug the brake tubes from the master cylinder.
3. Remove the mounting nuts and washers.
4. Remove the master cylinder.
5. To install, reverse the removal procedures. Torque the mounting bolts to 8–12 ft. lbs. Bleed the brake system.

Power Brake Booster

REMOVAL & INSTALLATION

1. Refer to the "Master Cylinder Removal & Installation" procedures in this section and remove the master cylinder.
2. Disconnect the push rod clevis pin from the brake pedal arm.
3. Disconnect the vacuum hose from the brake booster.
4. Remove the mounting nuts from under the dash and the booster.
5. To install, reverse the removal procedures. Torque the booster-to-cowl nuts to 14–20 ft. lbs. Bleed the brake system, if necessary.

Wheel Cylinder

REMOVAL & INSTALLATION

1. Raise and support the vehicle safely. Remove the wheel assembly.
2. Remove the brake drum. Remove the brake shoes and mounting hardware.
3. Remove ther bleeder screw from the wheel cylinder.
4. Loosen the brake pipe flare nut to the extent that the fluid will just not leak out.
5. Remove the wheel cylinder mounting bolts and remove the fluid pipe from the wheel cylinder. Plug the pipe right after removal.
6. Installation is the reverse of the removal procedure.
7. Fill the master cylinder with fluid and bleed the brake system when finished.

Parking Brake Cable

ADJUSTMENT

1. Remove both door seal plates and the seat belt buckle bolts at the floor.
2. Disconnect the shoulder harness bolts at the floor and the interior, bottom trim panels.
3. Raise the rear seat cushion.
4. Pull up the carpet to gain access to the parking brake lever.
5. Loosen the parking brake cable adjusting nuts.
6. Adjust the parking brake cables, so that they work evenly.
7. Adjust the cable, so that when

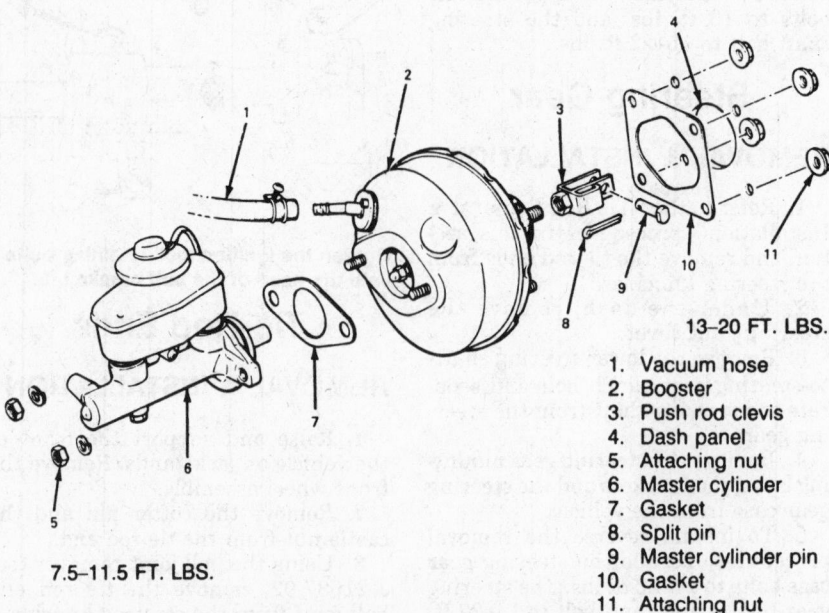

7.5–11.5 FT. LBS.

13–20 FT. LBS.

1. Vacuum hose
2. Booster
3. Push rod clevis
4. Dash panel
5. Attaching nut
6. Master cylinder
7. Gasket
8. Split pin
9. Master cylinder pin
10. Gasket
11. Attaching nut

Master cylinder and booster mounting

1. Backing plate
2. Brake fluid tube flair nut
3. Brake fluid tube
4. Wheel cylinder mounting bolts

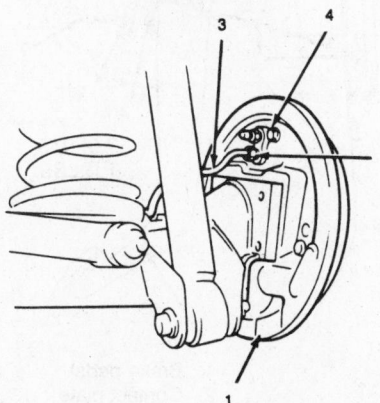

Rear wheel cylinder mounting

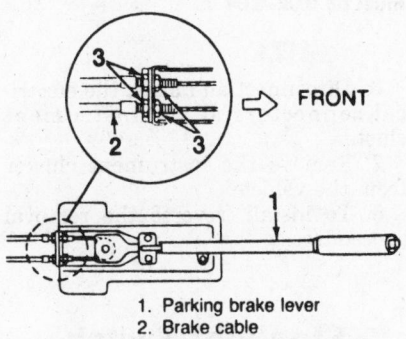

1. Parking brake lever
2. Brake cable
3. Nuts

Adjusting the parking brakes

the parking brake handle is pulled, its travel is between 5–8 notches, with 44 lbs. of force.

8. After adjustment, reverse the removal procedures.

REMOVAL & INSTALLATION

1. Raise and support the vehicle safely. Remove the wheel assembly and brake drum.

2. Disconnect the parking brake cable from the brake shoe lever and the backing plate.

3. Remove the cable(s) from the chassis mounts and remove the cable from the vehicle.

4. To install, place the white marked cable end onm the right side brakes and connect the cable to the shoe lever and backing plate.

5. Connect the cable in the chassis mounts.

6. Install the brake drum and wheel assembly.

7. Adjust the parking brake cable when finished.

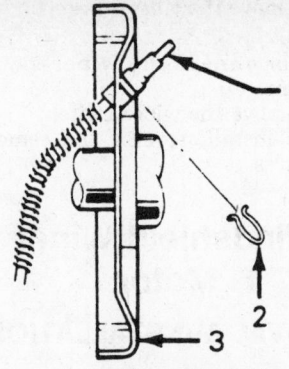

1. Parking brake cable
2. Retaining clip
3. Backing plae

Removing parking brake cable from backing plate

1. CAR HEATER ASSEMBLY
2. BLOWER MOTOR
3. SEAL
4. BLOWER FAN
5. RESISTOR
6. RESISTOR PLATE
7. CASE CLAMP
8. DEFROSTER DAMPER
9. TEMP DAMPER

10. VENT DAMPER
11. HEATER PIPE COVER
12. HEATER CORE
13. HEATER LEFT CASE
14. HEATER RIGHT CASE
15. DUCT
16. VENT LINK PLATE
17. TEMP LEVER
18. TEMP PLATE
19. LINK LEVER
20. MODE LEVER
21. LINK NO. 2 LEVER
22. DEFROSTER LINK PLATE
23. VENT LINK SHAFT
24. DEFROSTER LINK SHAFT
25. HEATER CONTROL LEVER ASSEMBLY
26. CONTROL LEVER KNOB
27. AIR CONTROL CABLE
28. HEAT CONTROL CABLE
29. FRESH AIR CONTROL CABLE
30. HEATER GROMMET
31. DEFROSTER LINK SPRING
32. DEFROSTER LINK SPRING WASHER

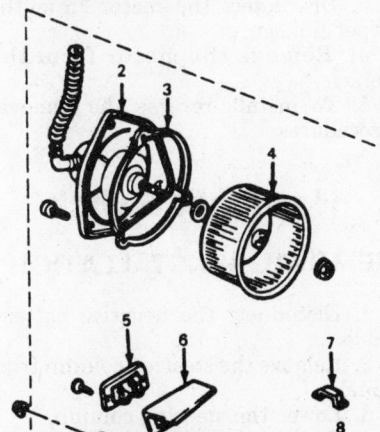

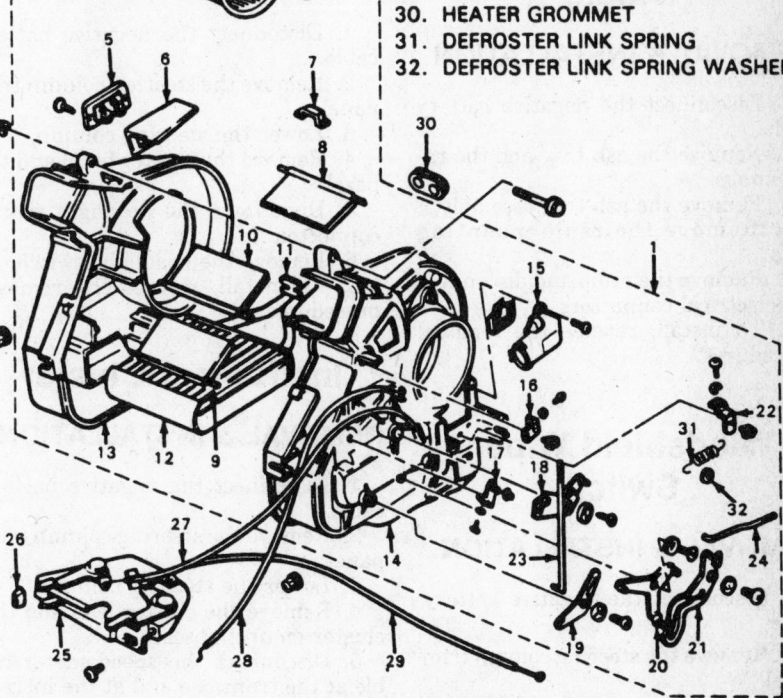

Heater unit disassembled

CHASSIS ELECTRICAL

Heater Blower Motor

REMOVAL & INSTALLATION

1. Disconnect the negative battery cable.

2. Disconnect the defroster hose on the steering column side.

3. Disconnect the blower motor electrical connector.

4. Remove the 3 mounting screws and the blower motor.

5. To install, reverse the removal procedures.

Heater Core

REMOVAL & INSTALLATION

1. Disconnect the negative battery cable. Drain the cooling system.
2. Disconnect the two water hoses from the radiator at the heater unit.
3. Remove the glove box from the upper instrument panel.
4. Remove the defroster hoses from the heater case.
5. Disconnect the electrical connectors from the blower motor and the heater resistor.
6. Disconnect the three control cables from the heater case side levers.
7. Pull out the center vent louver.
8. Disconnect both side vent ducts from the center duct vent.
9. Remove the center duct vent and the ashtray's upper plate.
10. Remove the instrument member stay and the heater assembly mounting nuts.
11. Loosen the three heater case top mounting bolts through the glove box opening.
12. Raise the dash panel and remove the heater control assembly.
13. Separate the heater case into two sections by removing the clips.
14. Pull the heater core from the heater unit.
15. To install, reverse the removal procedures. Refill the cooling system. Start the engine, bring it to normal operating temperature and check for leaks.

Radio

REMOVAL & INSTALLATION

1. Disconnect the negative battery cable.
2. Remove the ash tray and the radio knobs.
3. Remove the ash tray assembly.
4. Remove the radio mounting nuts.
5. Remove the radio and disconnect the electrical connectors.
6. To install, reverse the removal procedures.

Windshield Wiper Switch

REMOVAL & INSTALLATION

1. Disconnect the negative battery cable.
2. Remove the steering column trim panel.
3. Lower the steering column.

4. Remove the cluster bezel and the bezel.
5. Disconnect the wiper switch connector.
6. Remove the wiper switch.
7. To install, reverse the removal procedures.

Windshield Wiper Motor

REMOVAL & INSTALLATION

Front

1. Disconnect the crank arm from the wiper motor.
2. Disconnect the electrical connector from the wiper motor.
3. Remove the wiper motor from the vehicle.
4. To install, reverse the removal procedures.

Rear

1. Remove the electrical connector from the rear wiper motor.
2. Remove the rear motor mounting bracket.
3. Disconnect the motor from the wiper linkage.
4. Remove the motor from the vehicle.
5. To install, reverse the removal procedures.

Headlight Switch

REMOVAL & INSTALLATION

1. Disconnect the negative battery cable.
2. Remove the steering column trim panel.
3. Lower the steering column.
4. Remove the cluster bezel and the bezel.
5. Disconnect the headlight switch connector.
6. Remove the headlight switch.
7. To install, reverse the removal procedures.

Instrument Cluster

REMOVAL & INSTALLATION

1. Disconnect the negative battery cable.
2. Remove the steering column trim panel.
3. Lower the steering column.
4. Remove the cluster lens and the cluster mounting screws.
5. Disconnect the speedometer cable at the transaxle and at the instrument cluster.

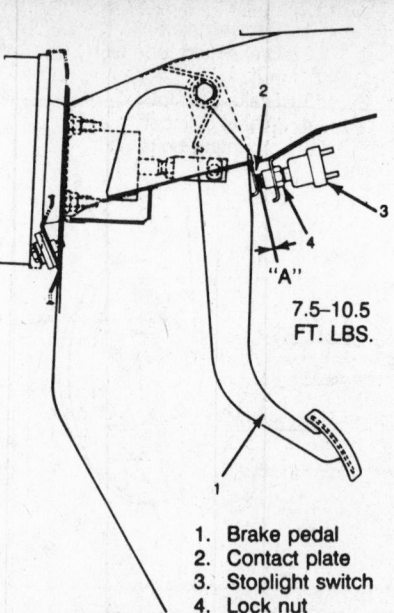

7.5–10.5 FT. LBS.

1. Brake pedal
2. Contact plate
3. Stoplight switch
4. Lock nut

Stoplight switch adjustment. Gap "A" must be 0.02–0.04 in.

6. Disconnect and mark the electrical connectors at the instrument cluster.
7. Remove the instrument cluster from the vehicle.
8. To install, reverse the removal procedures.

Stoplight Switch

REMOVAL & INSTALLATION

1. Disconnect the negative battery cable. Disconnect the stoplight switch wiring at the brake pedal.
2. Remove the switch from the plate and install the new one.
3. Adjust the switch so that there is 0.02–0.04 in. clearance between the contact plate and the end of the threads on the switch. Tighten the locknut and check the clearance again.
4. Connect the battery cable and check that the brake lights are not on with the pedal in the resting position.

Fusible Link and Fuses

LOCATION

The main fusible link is at the battery. The wiring circuits are protected by 14 fuses in the fuse block. The fuse block is located at the lower left of the instrument panel. The cover is built into the instrument panel.

Chevrolet/Pontiac
Rear Wheel Drive
Chevrolet Chevette, Pontiac 1000

SERIAL NUMBER IDENTIFICATION

VEHICLE IDENTIFICATION CHART

It is important for servicing and ordering parts to be certain of the vehicle and engine identification. The VIN (vehicle identification number) is a 17 digit number visible through the windshield on the driver's side of the dash and contains the vehicle and engine identification codes. The tenth digit indicates model year and the eigth digit indicates engine code. It can be interpreted as follows:

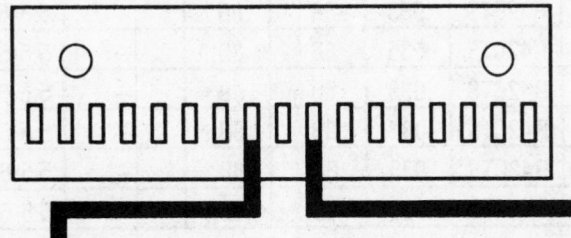

	Engine Code						Model Year	
Code	Cu. In.	Liters	Cyl.	Fuel Sys.	Eng. Mfg.		Code	Year
9	97.6	1.6	4	2 bbl	Chevy		C	1982
C	97.6	1.6	4	2 bbl	Chevy		D	1983
D	111	1.8	4	Diesel	Isuzu		E	1984
							F	1985
							G	1986
							H	1987

GENERAL ENGINE SPECIFICATIONS

Year	VIN	No. Cylinder Displacement cu. in. (liter)	Fuel System Type	Net Horsepower @ rpm	Net Torque @ rpm (ft.lbs.)	Bore × Stroke (in.)	Compression Ratio	Oil Pressure @ rpm
1982	C	4-98 (1.6)	2 bbl	65 @ 5200	80 @ 2400	3.228 × 2.980	9.0:1	55 @ 2000
	D	4-111 (1.8)	Diesel	51 @ 5000	72 @ 2000	3.310 × 3.230	22.0:1	64 @ 5000
1983	C	4-98 (1.6)	2 bbl	65 @ 5200	80 @ 2400	3.228 × 2.980	9.0:1	55 @ 2000
	D	4-111 (1.8)	Diesel	51 @ 5000	72 @ 2000	3.310 × 3.230	22.0:1	64 @ 5000
1984	C	4-98 (1.6)	2 bbl	65 @ 5200	80 @ 2400	3.228 × 2.980	9.0:1	55 @ 2000
	D	4-111 (1.8)	Diesel	51 @ 5000	72 @ 2000	3.310 × 3.230	22.0:1	64 @ 5000
1985	C	4-98 (1.6)	2 bbl	65 @ 5200	80 @ 2400	3.228 × 2.980	9.0:1	55 @ 2000
	D	4-111 (1.8)	Diesel	51 @ 5000	72 @ 2000	3.310 × 3.230	22.0:1	64 @ 5000
1986	C	4-98 (1.6)	2 bbl	65 @ 5200	80 @ 2400	3.228 × 2.980	9.0:1	55 @ 2000
	D	4-111 (1.8)	Diesel	51 @ 5000	72 @ 2000	3.310 × 3.230	22.0:1	64 @ 5000
1987	C	4-98 (1.6)	2 bbl	65 @ 5200	80 @ 2400	3.228 × 2.980	9.0:1	55 @ 2000

NOTE: Horsepower and torque are SAE net figures. They are measured at the rear of the transmission with all accessories installed and operating. Since the figures vary when a given engine is installed in different models, some are representative rather than exact.

GASOLINE ENGINE TUNE-UP SPECIFICATIONS

Year	VIN	No. Cylinder Displacement cu. in. (liter)	Spark Plugs Type	Gap (in.)	Ignition Timing (deg.) MT	AT	Compression Pressure (psi)	Fuel Pump (psi)	Idle Speed (rpm) MT	AT	Valve Clearance In.	Ex.
1982	C	4-98 (1.6)	R42CTS	.035	8B	8B	—	5.5-6.5	800	700	Hyd.	Hyd.
1983	C	4-98 (1.6)	R42CTS	.035	8B	8B	—	5.5-6.5	800	700	Hyd.	Hyd.
1984	C	4-98 (1.6)	R42CTS	.035	8B	8B	—	5.5-6.5	800	700	Hyd.	Hyd.
1985	C	4-98 (1.6)	R42CTS	.035	8B	8B	—	5.5-6.5	800	700	Hyd.	Hyd.
1986	C	4-98 (1.6)	R42CTS	.035	8B	8B	—	5.5-6.5	800	700	Hyd.	Hyd.
1987	C	4-98 (1.6)	R42CTS	.035	8B	8B	—	5.5-6.5	800	700	Hyd.	Hyd.

GASOLINE ENGINE TUNE-UP SPECIFICATIONS
See chart at end of manual for spark plug recommendations

Year	VIN	No. Cylinder Displacement cu. in. (liter)	Spark Plugs Gap (in.)	Ignition Timing (deg.) MT	AT	Compression Pressure (psi)	Fuel Pump (psi)	Idle Speed (rpm) MT	AT	Valve Clearance In.	Ex.
1982	C	4-98 (1.6)	.035	8B	8B	—	5.5-6.5	800	700	Hyd.	Hyd.
1983	C	4-98 (1.6)	.035	8B	8B	—	5.5-6.5	800	700	Hyd.	Hyd.
1984	C	4-98 (1.6)	.035	8B	8B	—	5.5-6.5	800	700	Hyd.	Hyd.
1985	C	4-98 (1.6)	.035	8B	8B	—	5.5-6.5	800	700	Hyd.	Hyd.
1986	C	4-98 (1.6)	.035	8B	8B	—	5.5-6.5	800	700	Hyd.	Hyd.
1987	C	4-98 (1.6)	.035	8B	8B	—	5.5-6.5	800	700	Hyd.	Hyd.

DIESEL ENGINE TUNE-UP SPECIFICATIONS

Year	VIN	No. Engine Displacement cu. in. (liter)	Valve Clearance Intake (in.)	Valve Clearance Exhaust (in.)	Intake Valve Opens (deg.)	Injection Pump Setting (deg.)	Injection Nozzle Pressure (psi) New	Injection Nozzle Pressure (psi) Used	Idle Speed (rpm)	Cranking Compression Pressure (psi)
1982	D	4-111 (1.8)	.010 ③	.014 ③	32	18	1848	1707	625 ①	441 ②
1983	D	4-111 (1.8)	.010 ③	.014 ③	32	11	1848	1707	625 ①	441 ②
1984	D	4-111 (1.8)	.010 ③	.014 ③	32	11	1848	1707	625 ①	441 ②
1985	D	4-111 (1.8)	.010 ③	.014 ③	32	18	1848	1707	625 ①	441 ②
1986	D	4-111 (1.8)	.010 ③	.014 ③	32	18	1848	1707	625 ①	441 ②

① 725-Automatic Transmission
② @ 200 RPM
③ Clearance with engine COLD

FIRING ORDERS

NOTE: To avoid confusion, always replace spark plug wires one at a time.

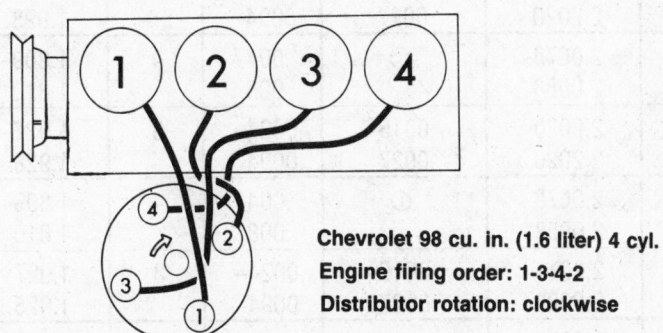

Chevrolet 98 cu. in. (1.6 liter) 4 cyl.
Engine firing order: 1-3-4-2
Distributor rotation: clockwise

CAPACITIES

Year	Model	No. Cylinder Displacement cu. in. (liter)	Engine Crankcase with Filter	Engine Crankcase without Filter	Transmission (pts.) 4-Spd	Transmission (pts.) 5-Spd	Transmission (pts.) Auto.	Drive Axle (pts.)	Fuel Tank (gal.)	Cooling System (qts.)
1982	C	4-98 (1.6)	4	3.5	3½	4	6	1¾	12½	9
	D	4-111 (1.8)	6	5	3½	3¼	6	1¾	12½	9
1983	C	4-98 (1.6)	4	3.5	3½	4	6	1¾	12½	9
	D	4-111 (1.8)	6	5	3½	3¼	6	1¾	12½	9
1984	C	4-98 (1.6)	4	3.5	3½	4	6	1¾	12½	9
	D	4-111 (1.8)	6	5	3½	3¼	6	1¾	12½	9
1985	C	4-98 (1.6)	4	3.5	3½	4	6	1¾	12½	9
	D	4-111 (1.8)	6	5	3½	3¼	6	1¾	12½	9

CAPACITIES

Year	Model	No. Cylinder Displacement cu. in. (liter)	Engine Crankcase with Filter	Engine Crankcase without Filter	Transmission (pts.) 4-Spd	Transmission (pts.) 5-Spd	Transmission (pts.) Auto.	Drive Axle (pts.)	Fuel Tank (gal.)	Cooling System (qts.)
1986	C	4-98 (1.6)	4	3.5	3½	4	6	1¾	12½	9
	D	4-111 (1.8)	6	5	3½	3¼	6	1¾	12½	9
1987	C	4-98 (1.6)	4	3.5	3½	4	6	1¾	12½	9

CRANKSHAFT AND CONNECTING ROD SPECIFICATIONS

All measurements are given in inches.

Year	VIN	No. Cylinder Displacement cu. in. (liter)	Crankshaft Main Brg. Journal Dia.	Crankshaft Main Brg. Oil Clearance	Crankshaft Shaft End-play	Crankshaft Thrust on No.	Connecting Rod Journal Diameter	Connecting Rod Oil Clearance	Connecting Rod Side Clearance
1982	C	4-98 (1.6)	2.0078–2.0088	①	.004–.008	4	1.809–1.810	.0014–.0031	.004–.012
	D	4-111 (1.8)	2.2010–2.2020	.0015–.0027	.0024–.0094	3	1.927–1.928	.0016–.0032	NA NA
1983	C	4-98 (1.6)	2.0078–2.0088	①	.004–.008	4	1.809–1.810	.0014–.0031	.004–.012
	D	4-111 (1.8)	2.2010–2.2020	.0015–.0027	.0024–.0094	3	1.927–1.928	.0016–.0032	NA NA
1984	C	4-98 (1.6)	2.0078–2.0088	①	.004–.008	4	1.809–1.810	.0014–.0031	.004–.012
	D	4-111 (1.8)	2.2020–2.2020	.0015–.0027	.0024–.0094	3	1.927–1.928	.0016–.0032	NA NA
1985	C	4-98 (1.6)	2.0078–2.0088	①	.004–.008	4	1.809–1.810	.0014–.0031	.004–.012
	D	4-111 (1.8)	2.2010–2.2020	.0015–.0027	.0024–.0094	3	1.927–1.928	.0016–.0032	NA NA
1986	C	4-98 (1.6)	2.0078–2.0088	①	.004–.008	4	1.809–1.810	.0014–.0031	.004–.012
	D	4-111 (1.8)	2.2010–2.2020	.0015–.0027	.0024–.0094	3	1.927–1.928	.0016–.0032	NA NA
1987	C	4-98 (1.6)	2.0078–2.0088	①	.004–.008	4	1.809–1.810	.0014–.0031	.004–.012

① No.5 .0009-.0026
All others .0005-.0018

VALVE SPECIFICATIONS

Year	VIN	No. Cylinder Displacement cu. in. (liter)	Seat Angle (deg.)	Face Angle (deg.)	Spring Test Pressure (lbs.)	Spring Installed Height (in.)	Stem-to-Guide Clearance (in.) Intake	Stem-to-Guide Clearance (in.) Exhaust	Stem Diameter (in.) Intake	Stem Diameter (in.) Exhaust
1982	C	4-98 (1.6)	45	46	173	1.25	.0006–.0017	.0014–.0025	.3141	.3133
	D	4-111 (1.8)	45	45	108	1.61	.0015–.0028	.0018–.0030	.3128–.3134	.3126–.3132

VALVE SPECIFICATIONS

Year	VIN	No. Cylinder Displacement cu. in. (liter)	Seat Angle (deg.)	Face Angle (deg.)	Spring Test Pressure (lbs.)	Spring Installed Height (in.)	Stem-to-Guide Clearance (in.) Intake	Exhaust	Stem Diameter (in.) Intake	Exhaust
1983	C	4-98 (1.6)	45	46	173	1.25	.0006–.0017	.0014–.0025	.3141	.3133
	D	4-111 (1.8)	45	45	108	1.61	.0015–.0028	.0018–.0030	.3128–.3134	.3126–.3132
1984	C	4-98 (1.6)	45	46	173	1.25	.0006–.0017	.0014–.0025	.3141	.3133
	D	4-111 (1.8)	45	45	108	1.61	.0015–.0028	.0018–.0030	.3128–.3134	.3126–.3132
1985	C	4-98 (1.6)	45	46	173	1.25	.0006–.0017	.0014–.0025	.3141	.3133
	D	4-111 (1.8)	45	45	108	1.61	.0015–.0028	.0018–.0030	.3128–.3134	.3126–.3132
1986	C	4-98 (1.6)	45	46	173	1.25	.0006–.0017	.0014–.0025	.3141	.3133
	D	4-111 (1.8)	45	45	108	1.61	.0015–.0028	.0018–.0030	.3128–.3134	.3126–.3132
1987	C	4-98 (1.6)	45	46	173	1.25	.0006–.0017	.0014–.0025	.3141	.3133

PISTON AND RING SPECIFICATIONS
All measurments are given in inches.

Year	VIN	No. Cylinder Displacement cu. in. (liter)	Piston Clearance	Ring Gap Top Compression	Bottom Compression	Oil Control	Ring Side Clearance Top Compression	Bottom Compression	Oil Control
1982	C	4-98 (1.6)	.0008–.0016	.009–.019	.008–.018	.015–.055	.0012–.0027	.0012–.0032	.0003–.0050
	D	4-111 (1.8)	.0006–.0014	.0078–.0157	.0078–.0157	.0078–.0157	.0035–.0049	.0014–.0020	.0012–.0028
1983	C	4-98 (1.6)	.0008–.0016	.009–.019	.008–.018	.015–.055	.0012–.0027	.0012–.0032	.0003–.0050
	D	4-111 (1.8)	.0002–.0017	.0078–.0157	.0078–.0157	.0078–.0157	.0035–.0049	.0019–.0033	.0012–.0028
1984	C	4-98 (1.6)	.0008–.0016	.009–.019	.008–.018	.015–.055	.0012–.0027	.0012–.0032	.0003–.0050
	D	4-111 (1.8)	.0002–.0017	.0078–.0157	.0078–.0157	.0078–.0157	.0035–.0049	.0019–.0033	.0012–.0028
1985	C	4-98 (1.6)	.0008–.0016	.009–.019	.008–.018	.015–.055	.0012–.0027	.0012–.0032	.0003–.0050
	D	4-111 (1.8)	.0002–.0017	.0078–.0157	.0078–.0157	.0078–.0157	.0035–.0049	.0019–.0033	.0012–.0028

PISTON AND RING SPECIFICATIONS
All measurments are given in inches.

Year	VIN	No. Cylinder Displacement cu. in. (liter)	Piston Clearance	Ring Gap			Ring Side Clearance		
				Top Compression	Bottom Compression	Oil Control	Top Compression	Bottom Compression	Oil Control
1986	C	4-98 (1.6)	.0008–.0016	.009–.019	.008–.018	.015–.055	.0012–.0027	.0012–.0032	.0003–.0050
	D	4-111 (1.8)	.0002–.0017	.0078–.0157	.0078–.0157	.0078–.0157	.0035–.0049	.0019–.0033	.0012–.0028
1987	C	4-98 (1.6)	.0008–.0016	.009–.019	.008–.018	.015–.055	.0012–.0027	.0012–.0032	.0003–.0050

TORQUE SPECIFICATIONS
All readings in ft. lbs.

Year	VIN	No. Cylinder Displacement cu. in. (liter)	Cylinder Head Bolts	Main Bearing Bolts	Rod Bearing Bolts	Crankshaft Pulley Bolts	Flywheel Bolts	Manifold		Spark Plugs
								Intake	Exhaust	
1982	C	4-98 (1.6)	75	50	40	100	50	18	25	22
	D	4-111 (1.8)	②	75	65	110	40	30	①	—
1983	C	4-98 (1.6)	75	50	40	100	50	18	25	22
	D	4-111 (1.8)	②	75	65	110	40	30	①	—
1984	C	4-98 (1.6)	75	50	40	100	50	18	25	22
	D	4-111 (1.8)	②	75	65	110	40	30	①	—
1985	C	4-98 (1.6)	75	50	40	100	50	18	25	22
	D	4-111 (1.8)	②	75	65	110	40	30	①	—
1986	C	4-98 (1.6)	75	50	40	100	50	18	25	22
	D	4-111 (1.8)	②	75	65	110	40	30	①	—
1987	C	4-98 (1.6)	75	50	40	100	50	18	25	22

① Center Bolts: 13–18
End Bolts: 19–25
② First tighten to 21-36 ft.lbs. Then retighten to 83-98 (New Bolts) or 90-105 (Used Bolts)

BRAKE SPECIFICATIONS
All measurements in inches unless noted

Year	Model	Lug Nut Torque (ft. lbs.)	Master Cylinder Bore	Brake Disc		Standard Brake Drum Diameter	Minimum Lining Thickness	
				Minimum Thickness	Maximum Runout		Front	Rear
1982	Chevette	70	.874	.374	.0005	7.874	.030	①
	1000	70	.874	.374	.0005	7.874	.030	①
1983	Chevette	70	.874	.374	.0005	7.874	.030	①
	1000	70	.874	.374	.0005	7.874	.030	①

BRAKE SPECIFICATIONS
All measurements in inches unless noted

Year	Model	Lug Nut Torque (ft. lbs.)	Master Cylinder Bore	Brake Disc Minimum Thickness	Brake Disc Maximum Runout	Standard Brake Drum Diameter	Minimum Lining Thickness Front	Minimum Lining Thickness Rear
1984	Chevette	70	.874	.374	.0005	7.874	.030	①
	1000	70	.874	.374	.0005	7.874	.030	①
1985	Chevette	80	.874	.374	.0005	7.874	.030	①
	1000	80②	.874	.374	.0005	7.874	.030	①
1986	Chevette	80	.874	.374	.0005	7.874	.030	①
	1000	80②	.874	.374	.0005	7.874	.030	①
1987	Chevette	80	.847	.374	.0005	7.874	.030	①
	1000	80②	.874	.374	.0005	7.874	.030	①

① Bonded Shoes—.062 in.
  Riveted Shoes—.030 in. over rivet head.
② Aluminum alloy wheels—100 ft. lbs.

WHEEL ALIGNMENT

Year	Model	Caster Range (deg.)	Caster Preferred Setting (deg.)	Camber Range (deg.)	Camber Preferred Setting (deg.)	Toe-in (in.)	Steering Axis Inclination (deg.)
1982	All	4P-6P	5P	¼P-½P	¼P	$\frac{1}{16}$P	NA
1983	All	4P-6P	5P	¼P-½P	¼P	$\frac{1}{16}$P	NA
1984	All	4P-6P	5P	¼P-½P	¼P	$\frac{1}{16}$P	NA
1985	All	4P-6P	5P	¼P-½P	¼P	$\frac{1}{16}$P	NA
1986	All	4P-6P	5P	¼P-½P	¼P	$\frac{1}{16}$P	NA
1987	All	4P-6P	5P	¼P-½P	¼P	$\frac{1}{16}$P	NA

TUNE-UP PROCEDURES

Ignition Timing

ADJUSTMENT

NOTE: Engines with Electronic Spark Timing (EST) can be identified by the absence of a vacuum and a mechanical spark advance on the distributor. EST allows continuous spark timing adjustments to be made by the ECM (Electronic Control Module).

1. Follow all instructions on the Vehicle Emissions Control information label located on the radiator support panel.

2. Connect the pick-up lead of the timing light to the number one spark plug. Use a jumper lead or adapter between the wire and plug, or use a timing light with an inductive type pick-up.

NOTE: Do not pierce the wire or attempt to insert a wire between the boot and the wire. Connect the timing light power leads according to the manufacturer's instructions.

3. Start and run the engine until it reaches normal operating temperature.

4. Increase the idle and disconnect the four (4) terminal EST connectors at the distributor. This will cause the engine to operate in the bypass timing mode.

NOTE: Steps 3–4 are important, because if the engine is at idle and not warm enough, when the EST terminal is disconnected, the oxygen sensor could cool off, putting the system into an open loop operation resulting in the engine shutting off.

5. With the engine running, aim the timing light at the timing mark.

6. If a change is necessary, loosen the distributor hold-down clamp bolt at the base of the distributor. While observing the mark with the timing light, slightly rotate the distributor until the correct timing is indicated. Tighten the hold-down bolt and recheck the timing.

7. Turn off the engine and reconnect all wires.

NOTE: Models with air conditioning require removal of the compressor since it is mounted directly above the distributor. Do not disconnect the refrigerant lines. Move the compressor and bracket to one side.

Valve Lash

ADJUSTMENT

Gasoline Engine

Adjustment of the hydraulic valve lash adjusters is not possible. Cleanliness should be exercised when handling the valve lash adjusters. Before installation of the valve lash adjusters, fill them with oil and check the lash adjuster oil hole in the cylinder head to make sure that it is unclogged and free of foreign matter.

Diesel Engine

NOTE: The rocker arm shaft bracket bolts and nuts should be tightened to 20 ft. lbs. before adjusting the valves.

1. Remove the cylinder head cover retaining bolts and cover.

2. Rotate the crankshaft until the No. 1 or No. 4 piston is at TDC of it's compression stroke.

3. Start with the intake valve on the No. 1 cylinder and insert a feeler gauge of the correct thickness (Intake–0.01 in., Exhaust–0.014 in.) into the gap between the valve stem cap and the rocker arm. If adjustment is required, loosen the lock nut on top of the rocker arm and turn the adjusting screw clockwise to decrease the gap and counterclockwise to increase it. When the correct clearance is reached, tighten the lock nut and then recheck the gap. Adjust the remaining three valves in this step in the same manner.

4. Rotate the crankshaft one complete revolution and adjust the remaining valves accordingly.

Idle Speed and Mixture Gasoline Engines

ADJUSTMENT

The carburetor mixture and idle speed

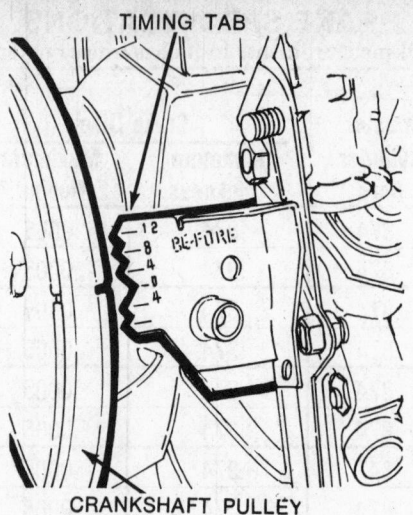

Ignition timing marks

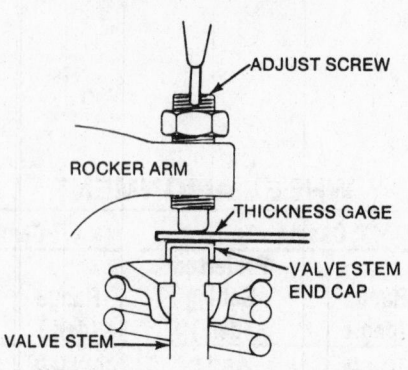

Valve adjustment—diesel engine

CYLINDER NO.	1		2		3		4	
VALVES	I	E	I	E	I	E	I	E
STEP. 1	○	○	○			○		
STEP. 2				◎	◎		◎	◎

I : INTAKE VALVE
E : EXHAUST VALVE

Valve adjustment sequence for the diesel engine

are adjusted by the Computer Command Control (CCC) System. It is not recommended to make any idle mixture adjustments, however it is possible to make two idle speed adjustments. These adjustments should be made only after all other engine systems have been checked for proper operation.

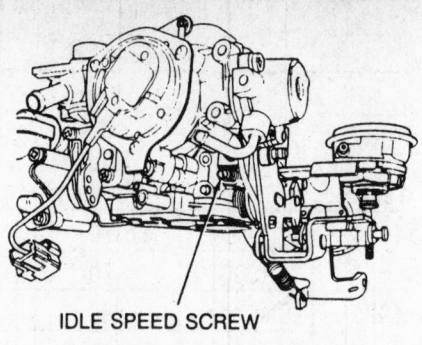

IDLE SPEED SCREW

Curb idle speed adjustment

2. Check the ignition timing. Remove air cleaner assembly.

3. Disconnect the EGR vacuum source at the carburetor and block the port. Disconnect and plug the vacuum hoses for the canister purge tank and the purge control at the canister.

4. Run engine to normal operating temperature, adjust idle speed screw to rpm specified on Vehicle Emission Control label.

5. Unplug and reconnect all vacuum lines, install air cleaner.

FAST IDLE SPEED ADJUSTMENT

1. Set the parking brake and block the drive wheels.

2. Check the ignition timing. Remove air cleaner assembly.

3. Disconnect the EGR vacuum source at the carburetor and block the port. Disconnect and plug the vacuum hoses for the canister purge tank and the purge control at the canister.

4. Place fast idle screw on highest step of fast idle cam, adjust to rpm specified on Vehicle Emission Control label.

5. Unplug and reconnect all vacuum lines, install air cleaner assembly.

HEI SYSTEM TACHOMETER HOOKUP

Connect a tachometer to the negative terminal on the coil and to a ground. Some tachometers must be connected to the negative terminal on the coil and the battery positive terminal. Check the tachometer manufacturer's instructions to make sure the tachometer is compatible with the HEI system. Never ground the TACH terminal or serious module damage could occur.

CURB IDLE SPEED ADJUSTMENT

1. Set the parking brake and block the drive wheels.

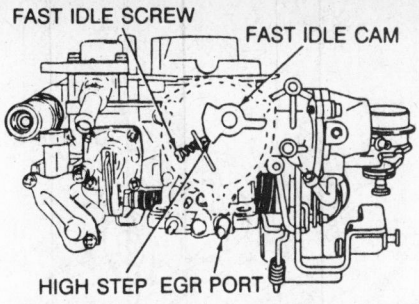

Fast idle speed adjustment

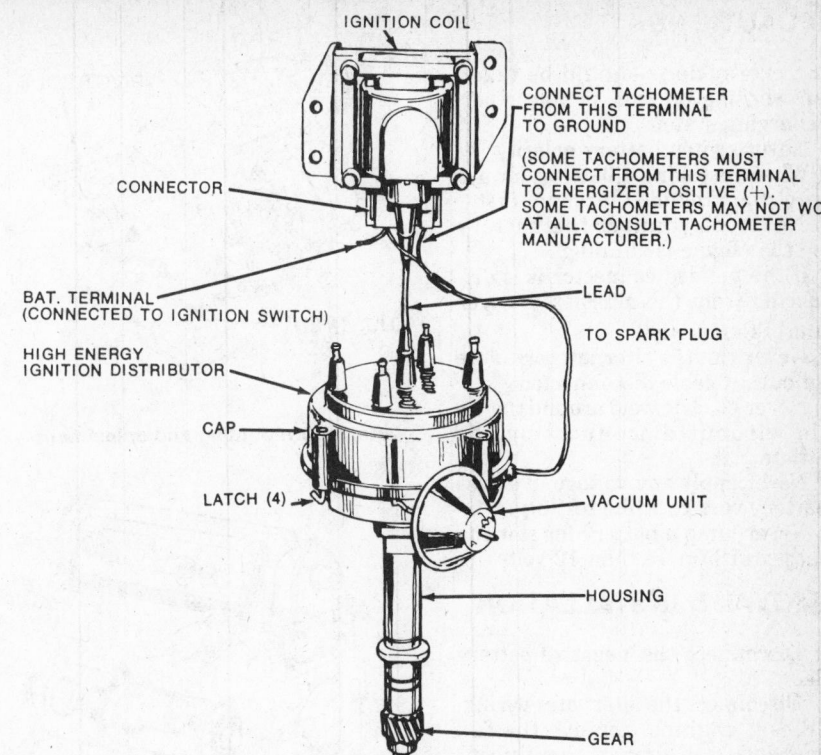

HEI tachometer hookup

IDLE MIXTURE ADJUSTMENT

The idle mixture is adjusted by the CCC system and requires no manual adjustment.

Idle Speed Diesel Engine

CURB IDLE ADJUSTMENT

1. Set the parking brake and block the wheels.
2. Place the transmission in Neutral. Connect a diesel tachometer following the manufacturer's instructions.

NOTE: A standard gasoline engine tachometer will not work on a diesel engine.

3. Start the engine and allow it to reach normal operating temperature.
4. Loosen the lock nut on the idle speed adjusting screw and turn the screw to obtain the correct idle speed.
5. Tighten the lock nut. Check the idle speed again and turn the engine off.
6. Disconnect the tachometer.

FAST IDLE SPEED ADJUSTMENT

1. Set the parking brake and block the wheels.
2. Place the transmission in Neutral.
3. Connect a diesel tachometer.
4. Start the engine and allow it to run until it reaches normal operating temperature.
5. Apply vacuum to the fast idle actuator.
6. Loosen the lock nut on the fast idle adjusting screw and adjust the knurled nut to obtain the fast idle speed specified on the emission label. After adjusting, retighten the lock nut and recheck the idle.
7. Disconnect the tachometer.

ENGINE ELECTRICAL

Distributor

REMOVAL & INSTALLATION

1. Disconnect the negative battery cable.
2. If the vehicle is equipped with air conditioning, disconnect the electrical lead at the air conditioning compressor. Remove the compressor mounting thru bolt and two adjusting bolts. Remove the compressor upper mounting bracket. Raise and safely support the vehicle on a hoist. Remove the two bolts securing the compressor lower mounting bracket and pull the bracket outward for clearance. Lower the vehicle.

—————— **CAUTION** ——————
Do not disconnect any A/C refrigerant lines.
————————————————————

3. Remove the air cleaner.
4. Remove the distributor cap.
5. Remove the ignition coil cover by prying on the flat on the front edge of the cover.
6. Remove the ignition coil mounting bracket bolts.
7. Disconnect the electrical connec-

tor with red and brown wires that goes from the ignition coil to the distributor.
8. Remove the fuel pump, gasket and push rod, noting the direction in which push rod was installed.

NOTE: The fuel pump push rod must be installed in exactly the same direction as it was removed.

9. Scribe a mark on the engine in line with the distributor rotor tip. Note the position of the distributor housing in relation to the engine.
10. Remove the distributor hold-down bolt and clamp. Remove the distributor.
11. If the engine has not been disturbed with the distributor removed, reverse the removal procedure to install, aligning the marks made during removal. If the engine has been disturbed, remove the No. 1 spark plug and place a finger over the spark plug hole. Manually turn the engine in the normal direction of rotation until compression is felt and the timing marks point to Top Dead Center. Align the marks made during removal and install the distributor.

Alternator

For further information on the charging system, please refer to "Charging and Starting" in the Unit Repair section.

PRECAUTIONS

Some precautions should be taken when working on this, or any other, AC charging system.
- Never switch battery polarity
- When installing a battery, always connect the grounded terminal first
- Never disconnect the battery while the engine is running
- If the molded connector is is disconnected from the alternator, never ground the hot wire
- Never run the alternator with the main output cable disconnected
- Never electric weld around the vehicle without disconnecting the alternator
- Never apply any voltage in excess of battery voltage while testing
- Never jump a battery for starting purposes with more than 12 volts

REMOVAL & INSTALLATION

1. Disconnect the negative battery cable.
2. Disconnect the alternator wiring. On diesel engines, remove the fan shroud and fresh air duct, then disconnect the oil and vacuum lines at the vacuum pump.
3. Remove the brace bolt and the drive belt.
4. Support the alternator, remove the mounting bolt and remove the alternator.

NOTE: On the diesel, the mounting bolts are removed from below the car.

5. Installation is the reverse of removal.

BELT TENSION ADJUSTMENT

1. Loosen the power steering pump pivot and adjustment bolts and remove the power steering belt if equipped.
2. Loosen the alternator pivot and adjustment bolt and remove the alternator belt.
3. Install the new alternator belt making sure that the belt is on the correct pulleys.
4. Adjust the alternator belt to a maximum tension of 146 lbs. for a new belt and 70 lbs. for a used belt.

— CAUTION —

Never apply pressure to the frame end of the aternator when adjusting the belt tension. Apply the pressure to the center of the alternator housing.

5. Install the power steering belt, if equipped and adjust the belt to a maxi-

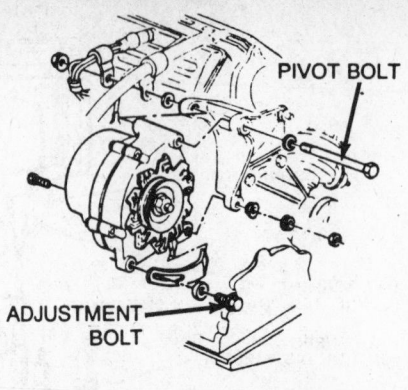

Alternator mounting and adjustment

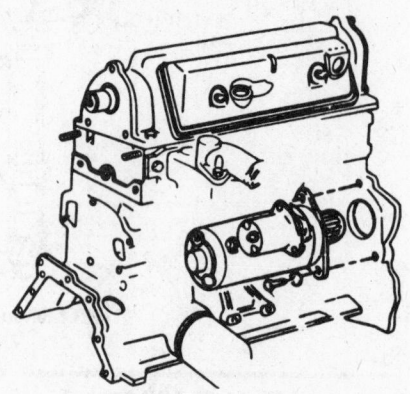

Starter motor mounting — gasoline engine

mum tension of 146 lbs. for a new belt and 70 lbs. for a used belt.
6. Start the engine and make sure that the belts are running properly.

Starter

For further information on the starting system, please refer to "Charging and Starting" in the Unit Repair section.

REMOVAL & INSTALLATION

Gasoline Engine

WITHOUT POWER BRAKES

1. Disconnect the battery negative cable.
2. Remove the air cleaner.
3. Disconnect and plug the gas line at the carburetor and move to one side.
4. Disconnect and tag the vacuum hoses at the carburetor.
5. Remove the splash shield from the distributor coil and move it to one side.
6. Using a 6 in. and 12 in. extension with a universal socket, remove the upper starter bolt.
7. Remove the lower starter bolt.
8. Disconnect and tag the starter wiring.

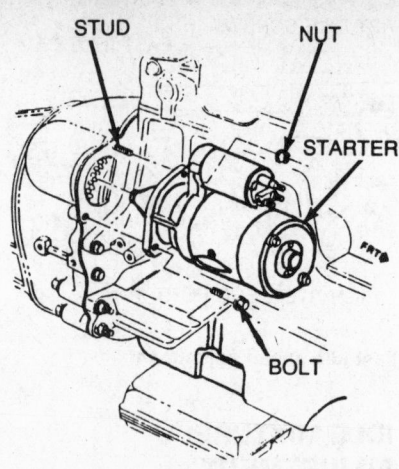

Starter motor mounting — diesel engine

NOTE: The master cylinder mounting nuts can be removed for access to remove the starter. Take care not to bend any of the brakes lines.

9. Installation is the reverse of removal.

WITH POWER BRAKES

1. Disconnect the battery ground cable.
2. Remove the air cleaner.
3. Disconnect and plug the gas line at the carburetor.
4. Remove the splash shield from the distributor coil.
5. Using a 6 in. and 12 in. extension with a universal socket, remove the upper starter bolt.
6. Remove the steering column cover screws and remove the cover.
7. Remove the steering column upper nuts and toe pan screw.
8. Raise and safely support the vehicle on a hoist and remove the steering shaft from the steering coupling.
9. Lower the vehicle and move the steering column from inside the vehicle to gain access to the starter.
10. Disconnect and tag the starter wiring.
11. Remove the starter lower bolt and remove the starter.
12. Installation is the reverse of removal.

Diesel Engine

1. Disconnect the negative battery cable.
2. Disconnect and tag the starter wiring.
3. Remove the upper mounting nut and the lower mounting bolt.
4. Remove the starter.
5. Installation is the reverse of the removal.

Diesel Glow Plugs

REMOVAL & INSTALLATION

1. Disconnect the negative battery terminal.

2. Disconnect the wire leading to the glow plug.

3. Using the proper socket, remove the glow plug from the cylinder head.

4. Installation is the reverse of the removal.

TESTING

Before removing a glow plug from the engine, check to see if there is current at the glow plug with the engine off and the ignition in the run position. If current is at the glow plug, the glow plugs can be tested by removing them from the cylinder head and checking them for continuity across the plug terminal and body. If continuity exists, the glow plug can be assumed to be good.

GASOLINE ENGINE MECHANICAL

Engine

REMOVAL & INSTALLATION

——— CAUTION ———

Do not discharge the air conditioning compressor or disconnect any of the refrigerant lines unless you have the skill and experience necessary to do so. Personal injury from the freon gas may result.

1. Remove the hood.

2. Disconnect the battery cables.

3. Remove the battery cable clips from the frame rail.

4. Drain the cooling system. Disconnect the radiator hoses from the engine and the heater hoses at the heater.

5. Tag and disconnect any wires leading from the engine.

6. Remove the radiator upper support and remove the radiator and engine fan.

7. Remove the air cleaner assembly.

8. Disconnect the following items:

   a. Fuel line at the rubber hose along the left frame rail.

   b. Automatic transmission throttle valve linkage.

   c. Accelerator cable.

9. On air conditioned cars, remove

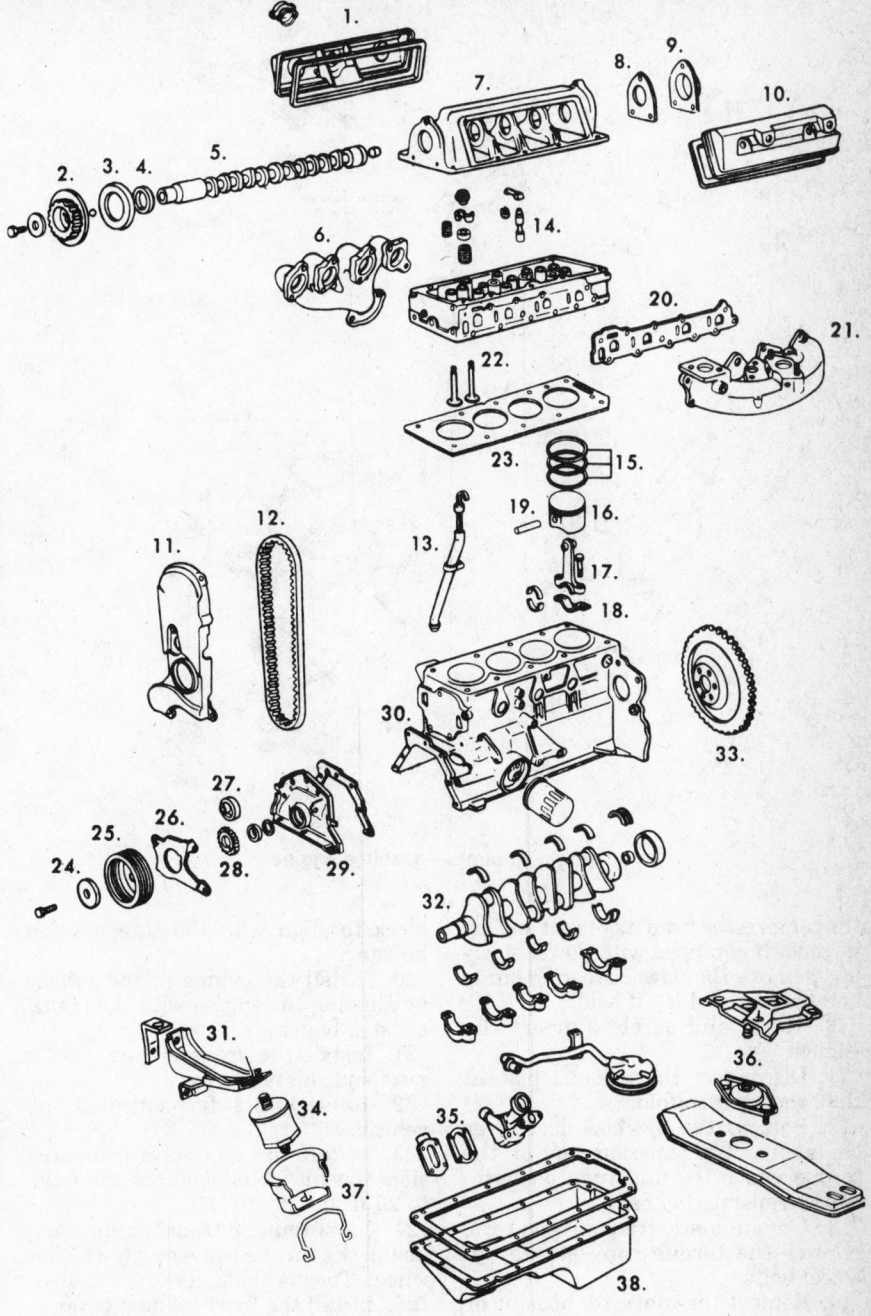

1. Camshaft Cover and Gasket	14. Rocker Arm, Adjuster, Valve Springs, Valve Spring Cap, and Keys	26. Lower Cover
2. Camshaft Sprocket	15. Piston Rings	27. Idler
3. Camshaft Sprocket Guide	16. Piston	28. Crankshaft Sprocket
4. Camshaft Oil Seal	17. Connecting Rod	29. Crankcase Front Cover
5. Camshaft	18. Connecting Rod Bearing and Cap	30. Cylinder Block
6. Exhaust Manifold	19. Piston Pin	31. Engine Mounting Bracket
7. Camshaft Housing	20. Intake Manifold Gasket	32. Crankshaft and Bearings
8. Camshaft Rear Cover Gasket	21. Intake Manifold	33. Flywheel
9. Camshaft Rear Cover	22. Valves	34. Engine Mount
10. Camshaft Housing Cover and Gasket	23. Cylinder Head Gasket	35. Oil Pump Assembly
11. Timing Belt Cover	24. Washer	36. Transmission Mounting and Support
12. Timing Belt	25. Crankshaft Pulley	37. Engine Mounting Plate and Spring
13. Oil Dipstick and Tube		38. Oil Pan and Gasket

Exploded view of the gasoline engine

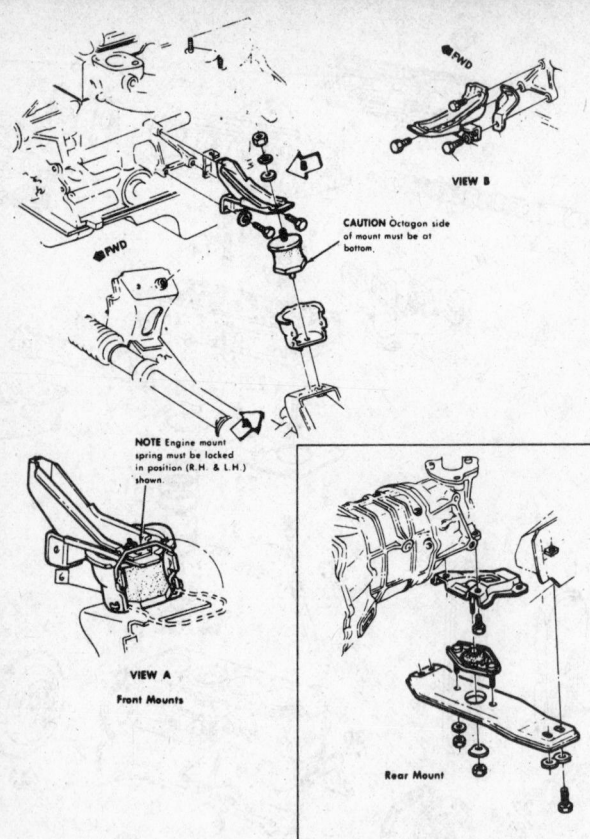

Engine mounts—gasoline engine

VIEW B

CAUTION Octagon side of mount must be at bottom.

●FWD

NOTE Engine mount spring must be locked in position (R.H. & L.H.) shown.

VIEW A
Front Mounts

Rear Mount

the compressor from its mount and lay it aside. If equipped with power steering, remove the power steering pump and bracket and lay it aside.

10. Raise and safely support the vehicle.

11. Disconnect the exhaust pipe at the exhaust manifold.

12. Remove the flywheel dust cover on manual transmission cars or the torque converter underpan on automatic transmission cars.

13. On automatic transmission cars, remove the torque converter-to-flywheel bolts.

14. Remove the converter housing or flywheel housing-to-engine retaining bolts and lower the car.

15. Position a floor jack or other suitable support under the transmission.

16. Remove the safety straps from the front engine mounts and remove the mount nuts.

17. Install the engine lifting apparatus.

18. Remove the engine by pulling it forward to clear the transmission while lifting slowly. Check to make sure that all necessary disconnections have been made and that proper clearance exists with surrounding components.

To install the engine:

19. Install guide pins in the engine block to align with the transmission housing.

20. Install the engine in the vehicle by aligning the engine with the transmission housing.

21. Install the front engine mount nuts and safety straps.

22. Raise and safely support the vehicle.

23. Install the engine-to-transmission housing bolts. Tighten the bolts to 25 ft. lbs.

24. On automatic transmission cars, install the torque converter to the flywheel. Torque the bolts to 35 ft. lbs.

25. Install the flywheel dust cover or torque converter underpan.

26. Install the exhaust pipe to the exhaust manifold and lower the car.

27. Install the air conditioning compressor or the power steering pump if equipped and adjust drive belt tension.

28. Connect the fuel lines, automatic transmission throttle valve linkage and accelerator cable.

29. Install the air cleaner.

30. Install the engine fan, radiator and radiator upper support.

31. Connect all wires previously disconnected.

32. Connect the radiator and heater hoses and fill the cooling system.

33. Install the battery cable clips along the frame rail.

34. Install the hood.

35. Connect the battery cables, start the engine and check for leaks.

Cylinder Head

REMOVAL & INSTALLATION

1. Disconnect the negative battery cable.

2. Remove all accessory drive belts.

3. Using the correct procedure in this section, remove the engine fan, timing belt cover and timing belt.

4. Remove the air cleaner and snorkel (silencer) assembly.

5. Drain the cooling system and disconnect the upper radiator hose and heater hose at the intake manifold.

6. Remove the accelerator cable support bracket.

7. Disconnect and label the spark plug wires.

8. Disconnect and label the wires from the idle solenoid, choke, temperature sender and alternator.

9. Disconnect the exhaust pipe from the exhaust manifold.

10. Remove the dipstick tube bracket-to-manifold attaching bolt.

11. Disconnect the fuel line at the carburetor.

12. Take off the coil cover. Remove the coil bracket bolts and remove the coil.

13. Remove the camshaft cover.

14. Remove the camshaft cover-to-camshaft housing attaching stubs.

15. Remove the rocker arms, rocker arm guides and valve lash adjusters. Keep the parts in order so that they can be installed in their original locations.

16. Remove the camshaft carrier bolts and remove the camshaft carrier. A sharp wedge may be necessary to separate the camshaft carrier from the cylinder head. Be very cautious not to damage the mating surfaces.

17. Remove the manifold and cylinder head assembly.

18. Install a new cylinder head gasket with the words "This Side Up" facing up over dowel pins in the block. Make sure that the gasket is absolutely clean.

19. Install the manifold and cylinder head assembly.

20. Apply a light, thin continuous bead of sealant to the jointing surfaces of the cylinder head and the camshaft carrier and install the camshaft carrier. Clean any excess sealer from the cylinder head. Apply sealing compound to the camshaft carrier/cylinder head bolts and install the bolts finger-tight. Tighten the bolts a little at a time and in the correct sequence until the final specified torque figure is reached.

21. Install the camshaft cover-to-camshaft housing attaching studs.

22. Install the valve lash adjusters and rocker arm guides. Prelube the rocker arms with engine assembly lubricant and install the rocker arms.

23. Using new gaskets, install the camshaft covers.

24. Install the coil bracket mounting bolt.

25. Connect the fuel line to the carburetor.

26. Install the dipstick tube bracket-to-manifold attaching bolt.

27. Attach the exhaust pipe to the exhaust manifold.

28. Connect the wires to the idle solenoid, choke, temperature sender and alternator.

29. Connect the spark plug wires.

30. Apply Teflon® tape or its equivalent to the threads of the accelerator cable support bracket attaching bolts and install the bracket.

31. Install the air cleaner assembly.

32. Connect the upper radiator hose and heater hose to the intake manifold.

33. Fill the cooling system.

34. Install the timing belt, timing belt cover, engine fan, drive belts and connect the negative battery cable.

OVERHAUL

For all cylinder head overhaul procedures, please refer to "Engine Rebuilding" in the Unit Repair Section.

Rocker Arms/Shafts

REMOVAL & INSTALLATION

NOTE: A special valve spring compressor is necessary for this procedure. (Tool J–25477) Also prelubricate new rocker arms with Molykote® or its equivalent.

1. Remove the camshaft cover.

2. Using the valve spring compressor, compress the valve springs and remove the rocker arms. Keep the rocker arms and guides in order so that they can be installed in their original locations.

3. To install the rocker arms, compress the valve springs and install the rocker arm guides.

4. Position the rocker arms in the guides and on the valve lash adjusters.

5. Install the camshaft cover.

Intake Manifold

REMOVAL & INSTALLATION

1. Disconnect the battery ground.

2. Drain the cooling system.

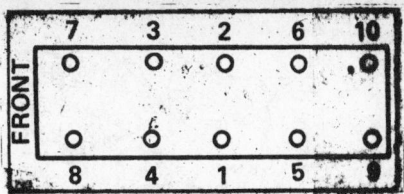

Cylinder head torque sequence—gasoline engine

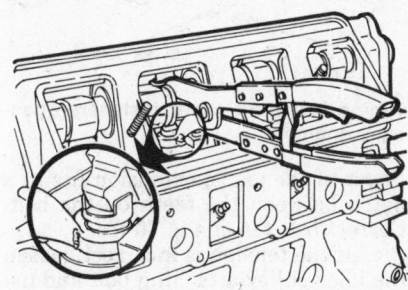

Depressing the valve spring using the special tool—gasoline engine

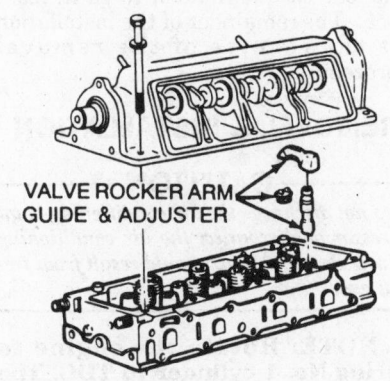

Rocker arm guide and adjuster – gasoline engine

3. Remove the air cleaner.

4. Disconnect the upper radiator and heater hoses.

5. Remove the EGR valve.

6. Disconnect all electrical wiring, vacuum hoses and the accelerator linkage from the carburetor.

7. Disconnect the fuel line from the carburetor.

8. Remove the coil.

9. Remove the manifold.

10. Installation is the reverse of removal. Torque all intake manifold bolts to 15 ft. lbs.

Exhaust Manifold

REMOVAL & INSTALLATION

1. Disconnect the negative battery cable.

2. Raise and safely support the vehicle.

3. Disconnect the exhaust pipe from the flange.

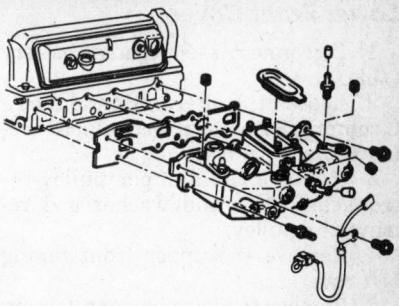

Intake manifold—gasoline engine

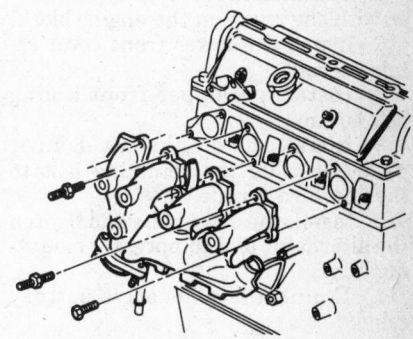

Exhaust manifold—gasoline engine

4. Lower the vehicle.

5. Remove the carburetor heat tube.

6. Remove the pulse air tubing, if so equipped.

7. Remove the exhaust manifold-to-cylinder head bolts and remove the manifold.

8. Installation is the reverse of removal. Install the two upper inner bolts first, to properly position the manifold. Tighten the bolts to the specified torque.

Timing Belt Cover

REMOVAL & INSTALLATION

Upper Front Cover

1. Disconnect the negative battery cable. Remove the radiator upper mounting panel on models without A/C or fan shroud on models with A/C.

2. Remove engine accessory drive belts.

3. Remove the engine fan.

4. Remove the cover retaining screws and nuts and remove the cover.

5. To install; align the screw slots on the upper and lower parts of the cover.

6. Install the cover retaining screws and nuts.

7. Install the engine fan.

8. Install the engine accessory drive belts.

9. Connect the negative battery cable.

Lower Front Cover

1. Disconnect the negative battery cable.
2. Loosen the alternator and the A/C compressor bolts, if so equipped. Remove the drive belts.
3. Remove the damper pulley-to-crankshaft bolt and washer and remove the pulley.
4. Remove the upper front timing belt cover.
5. Remove the lower cover retaining nut. Remove the lower cover.
6. To install the cover, align the cover with the studs on the engine block.
7. Install the lower front cover retaining nut.
8. Install the upper front timing belt cover.
9. Install the crankshaft damper pulley. Torque the retaining bolt to the specified torque.
10. Install the drive belts and tighten the alternator and compressor mounting bolts.
11. Connect the negative battery cable.

Upper Rear Cover

1. Crank the engine so that No. 1 cylinder is at TDC of the compression stroke.
2. Disconnect the negative battery cable.
3. Remove the upper and lower front cover, the timing belt and the camshaft timing sprocket.
4. Remove the three bolts retaining the camshaft sprocket cover to the camshaft carrier.
5. Inspect the condition of the cam seal. Replace the seal if necessary.
6. Position and align a new gasket over the end of the camshaft and against the camshaft carrier.
7. Install the three camshaft sprocket cover retaining screws.
8. Install the camshaft sprocket, timing belt and the upper and lower front covers.
9. Connect the negative battery cable.

Timing Belt and Sprockets

ADJUSTMENT

1. Remove the fan, fan belt, water pump pulley and upper cam belt cover.
2. Rotate the crankshaft clockwise a minimum of one revolution. Stop with No. 1 piston at TDC. DO NOT TURN THE ENGINE BACKWARD!
3. Install a belt tension gauge on the same side as the idler pulley midway between the cam sprocket and the idler pulley. Be sure that the center

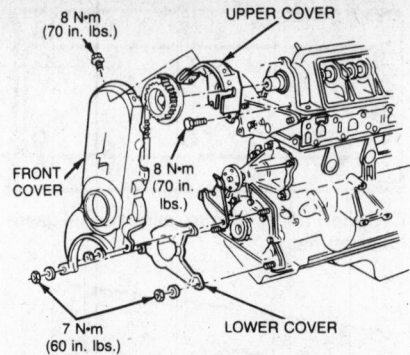

Timing belt front cover fasteners—gasoline engine

finger of the gauge extension fits in a notch between the teeth on the belt. Correct belt tension is 70 lbs..

4. If the tension is incorrect, loosen the idler pulley attaching bolt and using a ¼ in. Allen wrench, rotate the pulley counterclockwise on its attaching bolt until the correct tension is obtained. Torque the bolt to 15 ft. lbs.
5. The remainder of the installation is the reverse of the removal procedure.

REMOVAL & INSTALLATION

——— CAUTION ———

Do not discharge the air conditioning compressor or disconnect the air conditioning lines. Personal injury could result from freon gas.

NOTE: Rotate the engine to bring No. 1 cylinder to TDC. The timing mark should be at the 0 degree mark on the timing scale. With No. 1 cylinder at TDC, a ⅛ in. drill bit may be inserted through a hole in the timing belt upper rear cover into a hole in the camshaft drive sprocket. These holes are provided to facilitate and verify camshaft timing. Aligning these holes now will make installation of the new belt much easier.

1. Disconnect the negative battery cable.
2. Remove the alternator and air conditioning compressor drive belts.
3. Remove the engine fan and pulley.
4. Remove the engine upper and lower front timing belt covers.
5. Remove the timing belt idler pulley.
6. Remove the timing belt from the camshaft and crankshaft timing sprockets.
7. With the distributor cap off, mark the location of the rotor in the No. 1 spark plug firing position on the distributor housing. On air condition-

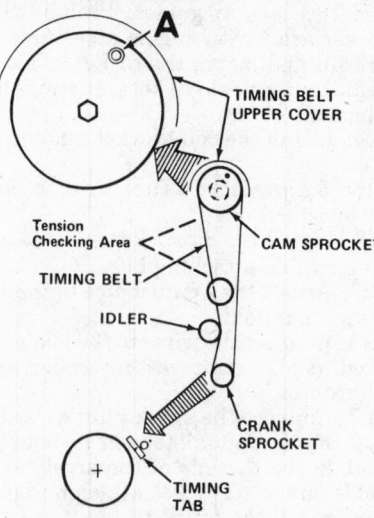

Quick Check Hole (In Sprocket) should align with hole in Timing Belt Upper Cover (A) when #1 Cyl. is at T.D.C.

Pulley timing mark should align with 0° mark on timing tab.

Timing belt installation—1.6 L Chevette. When camshaft is aligned at No. 1 cylinder TDC compression stroke, a 1/8 in. drill bit should fit through rear timing belt cover and into quick check hole in sprocket.

ed cars, remove the compressor and lower its mounting bracket.

8. Remove the camshaft timing sprocket bolt and washer and remove the camshaft sprocket.
9. Remove the crankshaft sprocket.
10. To install; place the crankshaft sprocket on the crankshaft making sure that the locating tabs face outward.
11. Install the crankshaft sprocket.
12. Align the camshaft sprocket dowel with the hole in the end of the camshaft and install the sprocket on the camshaft.
13. Apply thread locking compound to the camshaft sprocket retaining bolt and washer and torque to 65–85 ft. lbs.
14. Position the timing belt over the crankshaft sprocket.
15. Install the crankshaft pulley.
16. Align the crankshaft pulley timing mark with the "0" mark on the timing scale and the distributor rotor with the scribed mark on the distributor housing.
17. Align the hole in the camshaft sprocket with the hole in the upper rear timing belt cover. Insert a ⅛ in. drill bit to hold the sprocket in alignment.
18. Install the timing belt on the camshaft and crankshaft sprockets.
19. Using the correct procedure, adjust the timing belt tension.
20. Install the distributor cap. On air conditioned cars, install the lower

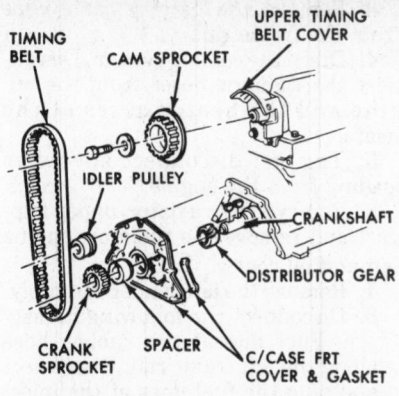

Timing belt and gears—gasoline engine

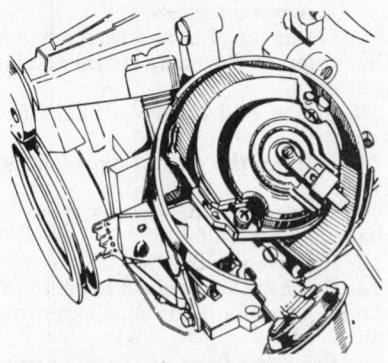

Correct distributor rotor alignment for timing belt installation

compressor bracket and the compressor.

21. Install the upper and lower front timing belt covers.
22. Install the engine fan and pulley.
23. Install the alternator and, if necessary, the air conditioning compressor drive belts.
24. Connect the negative battery cable.

OIL SEAL REPLACEMENT

1. Using the correct procedure, remove the crankcase front cover.
2. Using a suitable tool, remove the oil seal from the cover. Be careful not to distort the cover.
3. Using a proper seal driver and with the seal lip facing the rear of the cover, drive the new seal into the cover.
4. Install the cover using the correct procedure.

Camshaft

REMOVAL & INSTALLATION

NOTE: A special valve spring compressor, (J–25477), or equivalent is necessary for this procedure. If replacing the camshaft or rocker arms, prelubricate new

parts with engine assembly lubricant.

1. Disconnect the negative battery cable.
2. Remove engine accessory drive belts.
3. Remove the engine fan and pulley.
4. Remove the upper and lower front timing belt covers.
5. Loosen the idler pulley and remove the timing belt from the camshaft sprocket.
6. Remove the camshaft sprocket attaching bolt and washer and remove the camshaft sprocket.
7. Remove the camshaft cover. Using the special valve spring compressor, remove the rocker arms and guides. Keep the rocker arms and guides in order so that they can be installed in their original locations.
8. Remove the heater assembly.
9. Remove the camshaft carrier rear cover.
10. Remove the camshaft thrust plate bolts. Slide the camshaft slightly to the rear and remove the thrust plate.
11. Remove the engine mount nuts and wire retainers.
12. Using a floor jack, raise the front of the engine.
13. Remove the camshaft from the camshaft carrier. Heavy pressure will be needed to pull the camshaft and seal forward.
14. Install the camshaft into the camshaft carrier.
15. Lower the engine.
16. Install the engine mount nuts and attach the retaining wires.
17. Slide the camshaft slightly to the rear and install the thrust plate. Slide the camshaft forward and install the carrier rear cover.
18. Position and align a new gasket over the end of the camshaft, against the camshaft carrier.
19. Install the heater assembly.
20. Install the valve rocker arms and guides in their original locations using the special valve spring compressor. Install the camshaft covers.
21. Align the dowel in the camshaft sprocket with the hole in the end of the camshaft and install the sprocket.
22. Apply thread locking compound to the sprocket retaining bolt threads and install the bolt and washer. Torque the sprocket retaining bolt to 65–85 ft. lbs.
23. Turn the crankshaft clockwise to bring the No. 1 cylinder to top dead center. Make sure that the distributor rotor is in position to fire the No. 1 spark plug. Align the hole in the camshaft sprocket with the hole in the upper rear timing belt cover and install

the timing belt on the camshaft sprocket.
24. Adjust timing belt tension as previously outlined.
25. Install the upper and lower front timing belt covers.
26. Install the engine fan and pulley.
27. Install the engine accessory drive belts.
28. Connect the negative battery cable.

Piston and Connecting Rod

POSITIONING

Install piston and connecting rod assemblies into their original cylinders. Install the piston and rod assemblies with the notch on the piston crown facing to the front of the engine. The numbers on the connecting rods and bearing caps must be on the same side when installing the pistons and connecting rods.

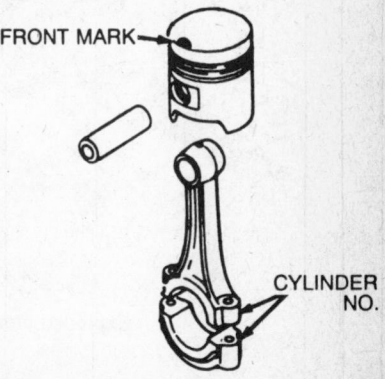

Piston and rod positioning—gasoline engine

DIESEL ENGINE MECHANICAL

Engine

REMOVAL & INSTALLATION

——— CAUTION ———

Do not discharge the air conditioning system or disconnect any refrigerant lines unless you have the skill and experience necessary to do so. Personal injury from the freon gas may result.

1. Remove the hood.
2. Disconnect the negative battery cable first then the positive cable. Remove the battery.

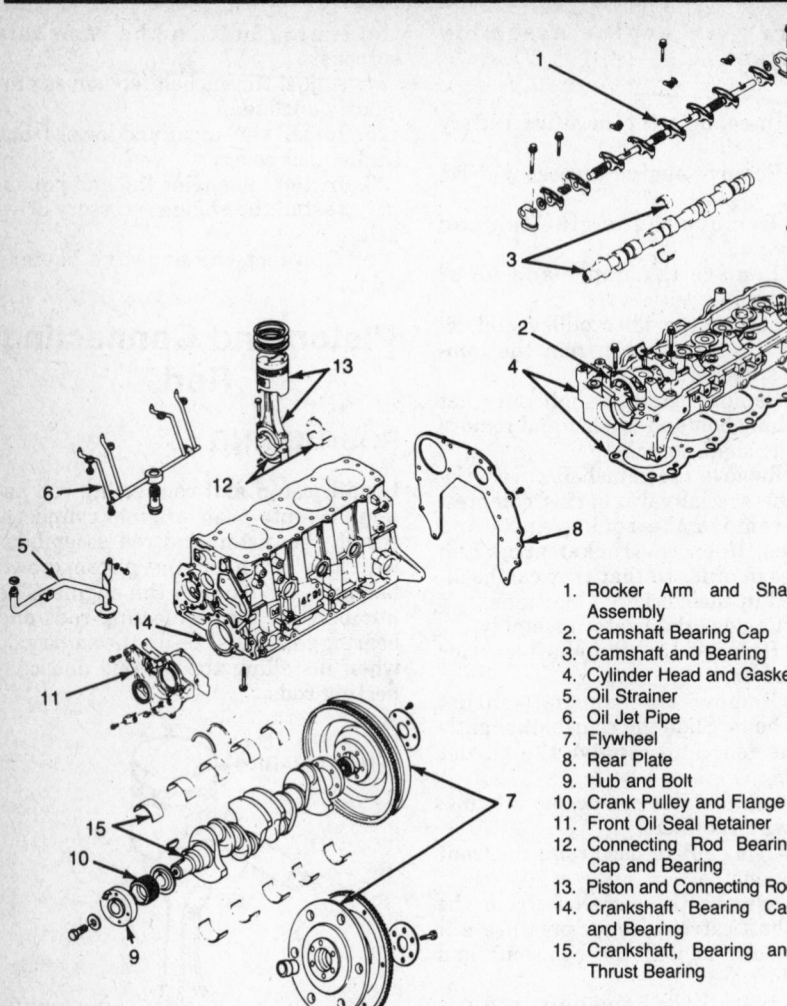

Exploded view of the diesel engine

1. Rocker Arm and Shaft Assembly
2. Camshaft Bearing Cap
3. Camshaft and Bearing
4. Cylinder Head and Gasket
5. Oil Strainer
6. Oil Jet Pipe
7. Flywheel
8. Rear Plate
9. Hub and Bolt
10. Crank Pulley and Flange
11. Front Oil Seal Retainer
12. Connecting Rod Bearing Cap and Bearing
13. Piston and Connecting Rod
14. Crankshaft Bearing Cap and Bearing
15. Crankshaft, Bearing and Thrust Bearing

3. Remove the battery cable clips from the frame rail.

4. Drain the cooling system. Disconnect the radiator hoses from the engine and the heater hoses at the heater.

5. Tag and disconnect any wires leading from the engine.

6. Remove the radiator upper support and remove the radiator, engine fan and oil cooler.

7. Remove the air cleaner assembly.

8. Disconnect the following items:

a. Fuel line at the rubber hose along the left frame rail. Disconnect and plug the fuel lines at the injection pump and position them out of the way.

b. Accelerator cable.

9. On air conditioned cars, remove the compressor from its mount and lay it aside.

10. Raise and safely support the vehicle.

11. Remove the engine strut (shock-type).

12. Disconnect the exhaust pipe at the exhaust manifold.

13. Remove the flywheel dust cover.

14. Remove the flywheel housing-to-engine retaining bolts and lower the car.

15. Position a floor jack or other suitable support under the transmission.

16. Remove the safety straps from the front engine mounts and remove the mount nuts.

17. Remove the oil filter.

18. Install an appropriate engine lifting apparatus.

19. Remove the engine by pulling forward to clear the transmission while lifting slowly. Check to make sure that all necessary disconnections have been made and that proper clearance exists with surrounding components before removing the engine from the vehicle.

To install the engine:

20. Install the engine lifting apparatus and install guide pins in the engine block.

21. Install the engine in the vehicle by aligning the engine with the flywheel housing.

22. Install the front engine mount nuts and safety straps.

23. Raise and safely support the vehicle.

24. Install the engine-to-flywheel housing bolts. Tighten to 25 ft. lbs.

25. Install the engine strut.

26. Install the exhaust pipe to the exhaust manifold and lower the car.

27. Install the air conditioning compressor and adjust the drive belt tension.

28. Connect the fuel lines and accelerator cable.

29. Install the air cleaner.

30. Install the oil cooler, engine fan,

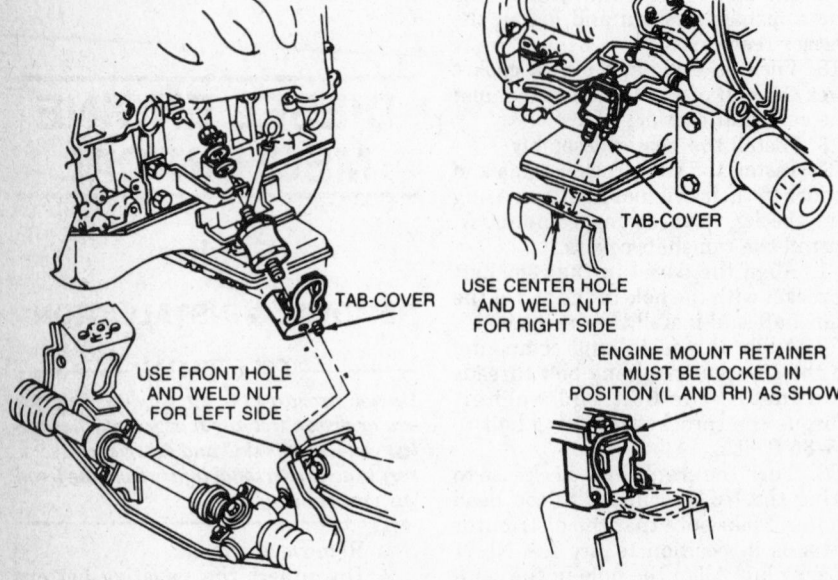

TAB-COVER

TAB-COVER

USE CENTER HOLE AND WELD NUT FOR RIGHT SIDE

USE FRONT HOLE AND WELD NUT FOR LEFT SIDE

ENGINE MOUNT RETAINER MUST BE LOCKED IN POSITION (L AND RH) AS SHOWN

Engine mounts—diesel engine

radiator and radiator upper support.

31. Connect all wires previously disconnected.

32. Connect the radiator and heater hoses and fill the cooling system.

33. Install the battery cable clips along the frame rail.

34. Install the hood.

35. Install the battery and connect the battery cables.

36. Start the engine and check for any leaks.

Cylinder Head

REMOVAL & INSTALLATION

1. Disconnect the negative battery cable.

2. Drain the cooling system.

3. Remove the cylinder head cover.

4. Disconnect the bypass hose. Remove the upper half of the front cover.

5. Loosen the tension pulley bolts and then remove the camshaft as detailed in this section.

6. Tag and disconnect the glow plug resistor wire.

7. Disconnect the injector lines at the injector pump and at the injector nozzles and then remove the injector lines. Disconnect and plug the fuel leak-off hose.

8. Disconnect the exhaust pipe at the manifold.

10. Remove the oil feed pipe from the rear of the cylinder head.

11. Disconnect the upper radiator hose and position it out of the way.

12. Remove the head bolts in the sequence shown and then remove the cylinder head with the intake and exhaust manifolds installed.

NOTE: The gasket surfaces on both the head and the block must be clean of any foreign matter and free of nicks or heavy scratches. Cylinder bolt threads in the block and on the bolt must also be clean.

13. Place a new gasket over the dowel pins with the word "TOP" facing up.

14. Apply engine oil to the threads and the seating face of the cylinder head bolts, install them and then tighten them in the proper sequence.

15. Install the camshaft and rocker arm assembly. Loosen the adjusting screws so that the entire rocker arm assembly is held in a free state.

16. Reinstall the timing belt as outlined later in this section.

17. Connect the upper radiator hose and the oil feed pipe.

18. Connect the exhaust pipe to the manifold.

19. Install the fuel leak-off hose. Connect the injector lines.

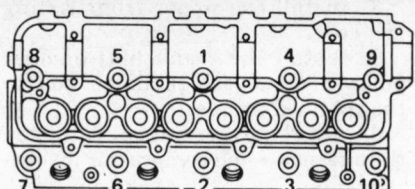

Cylinder head torque sequence—diesel engine

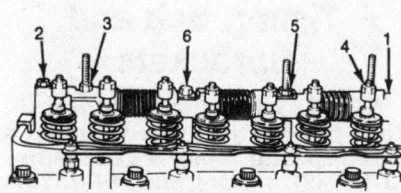

Loosening and tightening sequence for the rocker arm shaft bracket bolts and nuts—Diesel engine

20. Connect the glow plug resistor wire.

21. Adjust the valve clearance as previously detailed. Install the cylinder head cover.

22. Refill the cooling system.

OVERHAUL

For all cylinder head overhaul procedures, please refer to "Engine Rebuilding" in the Unit Repair Section.

Rocker Arms/Shaft

REMOVAL & INSTALLATION

1. Disconnect the negative battery cable.

2. Remove the cylinder head cover.

3. Remove the rocker arm shaft bracket bolts and nuts in sequence (see illustration). Remove the rocker arm shaft bracket and the rocker arm assembly.

4. Remove the rocker arms.

5. Apply a generous amount of clean engine oil to the rocker arm shaft, rocker arms and the valve stem end caps.

6. Install the rocker arm shaft assembly and then tighten the bolts to 20 ft. lbs. using the proper sequence.

7. Adjust the valves as previously detailed and reinstall the cylinder head cover.

Intake Manifold

REMOVAL & INSTALLATION

1. Disconnect the negative battery cable.

2. Disconnect the fresh air hose and the vent hose. Remove the fuel separator.

3. Tag and disconnect all electrical connectors, the accelerator linkage and the glow plug wires.

4. Disconnect the injector lines at the injection pump and at the injector nozzles. Remove the injector lines and the hold-down clamps.

5. Remove the glow plug line at the cylinder head.

6. If equipped with power steering, remove the drive belt, the idler pulley and the bracket.

7. Remove the upper half of the front cover and the bracket.

8. Remove the intake manifold.

9. Places a new gasket over the mounting studs on the cylinder head and install the manifold. Tighten the bolts to 30 ft. lbs.

10. Installation of the remaining components is in the reverse order of removal.

Exhaust Manifold

REMOVAL & INSTALLATION

1. Disconnect the battery ground.

2. Raise and safely support the vehicle.

3. Disconnect the exhaust pipe from the flange.

4. Lower the vehicle.

5. Remove the power steering belt, the flex hose and the power steering pump.

6. Remove the exhaust manifold.

7. Installation is the reverse of removal. Install the two upper inner bolts first, to properly position the manifold. Tighten the bolts to the specified torque.

Timing Belt Cover

REMOVAL & INSTALLATION

Upper Front Cover

1. Disconnect the negative battery cable. Remove the radiator upper mounting panel on models without A/C or fan shroud on models with A/C.

2. Remove the bypass hose on the engine.

3. Remove the engine fan.

4. Remove the cover retaining screws and nuts and remove the cover.

5. To install; align the screw slots on the upper and lower parts of the cover.

6. Install the cover retaining screws and nuts.

7. Install the engine fan.

8. Install the engine bypass hose.

9. Connect the negative battery cable.

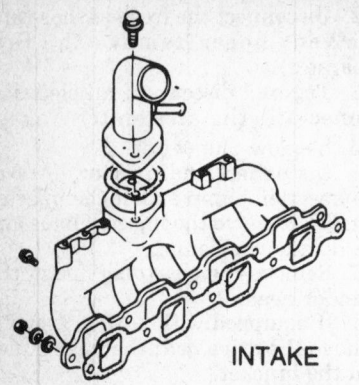

INTAKE

Intake manifold—diesel engine

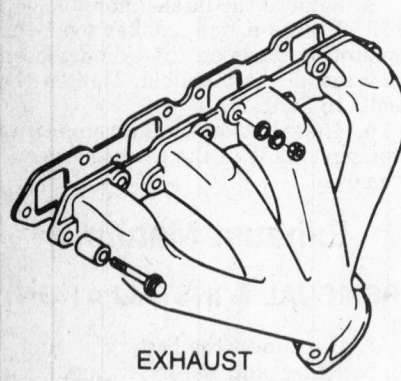

EXHAUST

Exhaust manifold—diesel engine

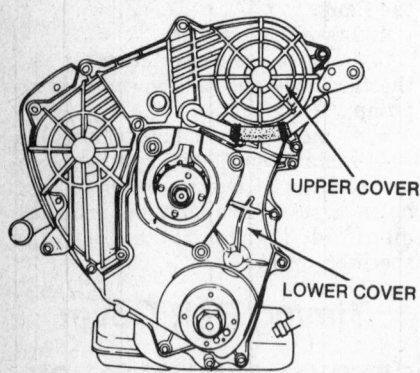

UPPER COVER

LOWER COVER

Timing belt covers—diesel engine

Lower Front Cover

1. Disconnect the negative battery cable.

2. Loosen the alternator and the A/C compressor bolts, if equipped. Remove the drive belts.

3. Remove the damper pulley-to-crankshaft bolt and washer and remove the pulley.

4. Remove the upper front timing belt cover as outlined previously.

5. Remove the lower cover retaining bolts. Remove the lower cover.

6. To install the cover, align the cover with the studs on the engine block.

7. Install the lower front cover retaining bolts.

8. Install the upper front timing belt cover.

9. Install the crankshaft damper pulley. Torque the retaining bolt to the specified torque.

10. Install the drive belts and tighten the alternator and compressor mounting bolts.

11. Connect the negative battery cable.

Timing Belt and Sprockets

NOTE: In order to complete this procedure you will need three special tools. A gear puller (J-22888), a fixing plate (J-29761) and a belt tension gauge (J-26484), or equivalent.

1. Disconnect the negative battery cable.

2. Drain the cooling system.

3. Remove the fan shroud, cooling fan and the pulley.

4. Disconnect the bypass hose and then remove the upper half of the front cover.

5. With the No. 1 piston at TDC of the compression stroke, make sure that the notch mark on the injection pump gear is aligned with the index mark on the front plate. If so, thread a lock bolt (8mm x 1.25) through the gear and into the front plate.

6. Remove the cylinder head cover and install a fixing plate J-29761 in the slot at the rear of the camshaft. This will prevent the camshaft from rotating during the procedure.

7. Remove the crankshaft damper pulley and check to make sure that the No. 1 piston is still at TDC.

8. Remove the lower half of the front cover and then remove the timing belt holder from the bottom of the front plate.

9. Remove the tension spring behind the front plate, next to the injection pump.

10. Loosen the tension pulley and slide the timing belt off the pulleys.

11. Remove the camshaft gear retaining bolt, install a gear puller and remove the gear.

12. When assembling, reinstall the camshaft gear loosely so that it can be turned smoothly by hand.

13. Slide the timing belt over the gears. The belt should be properly tensioned between the pulleys, the cogs on the belt and the gears should be properly engaged, the crankshaft should not be turned and the belt slack should be concentrated at the two tension pulleys. Push the tension pulley in with a finger and install the tension spring.

14. Partially tighten the tension pul-

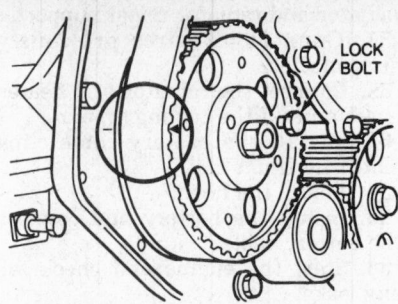

LOCK BOLT

Injection gear setting mark—diesel engine

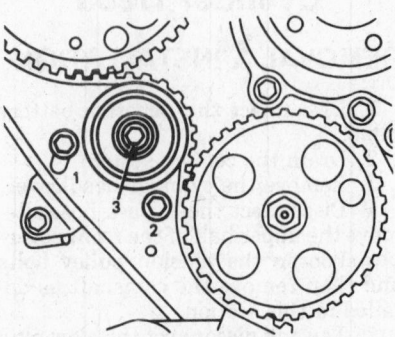

Tighten the tension pulley bolts in sequence—diesel engin

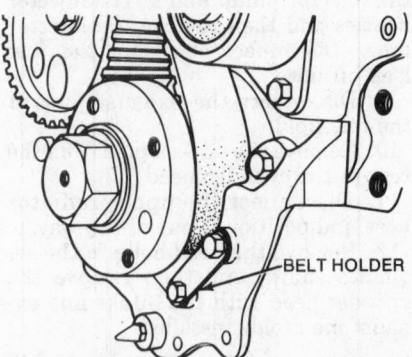

BELT HOLDER

Diesel engine: the timing belt holder must be removed before the timing belt can be taken off

ley bolts in sequence (top first, bottom second) to prevent any movement of the pulley.

15. Tighten the camshaft gear retaining bolt to 45 ft. lbs. Remove the injection pump gear lock bolt.

16. Remove the fixing plate from the end of the cam.

17. Install the crankshaft damper pulley and then check that the No. 1 piston is still at TDC. Do not try to adjust it by moving the crankshaft.

18. Check that the marks on the injection pump gear and the front plate are still aligned and that the fixing plate still fits properly into the slot on the camshaft.

19. Loosen the tensioner pulley and plate bolts, concentrate the looseness of the timing belt around the tensioner and then tighten the bolts.

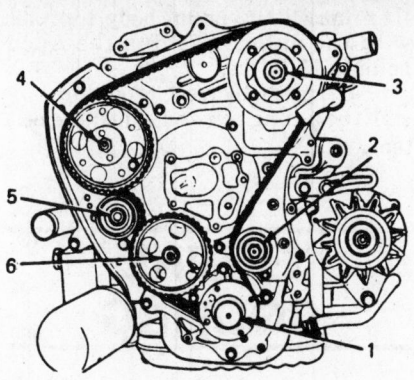

Diesel engine timing belt sequence

20. Belt tension should be 46–63 lbs., checked at a point midway between the upper two pulleys.

21. Remove the damper pulley again and install the belt holder in position away from the timing belt.

22. Installation of the remaining components is in the reverse order of removal.

OIL SEAL REPLACEMENT

1. Using the correct procedure, remove the crankcase front lower cover.

2. Using a suitable tool, remove the oil seal from the cover. Be careful not to distort the cover.

3. Using a proper seal driver and with the seal lip facing the rear of the cover, drive the new seal into the cover.

4. Install the cover using the proper procedure.

Camshaft

REMOVAL & INSTALLATION

NOTE: In order to complete this procedure you will need a gear puller J-22888 and a fixing plate J-29761, or equivalent.

1. Remove the cylinder head cover.

2. Remove the timing belt as previously detailed. Remove the plug.

3. Install the fixing plate into the slot at the rear of the camshaft.

4. Remove the camshaft gear retaining bolt and using a suitable puller, remove the cam gear.

5. Using the correct procedure, remove the rocker arms and shaft.

6. Remove the bolts attaching the front head plate and then remove the plate.

7. Remove the camshaft bearing

cap retaining bolts and remove the bearing caps with the cap side bearings.

8. Lift out the camshaft oil seal and then remove the camshaft.

9. Coat the camshaft and cylinder head journals with clean engine oil.

10. Position the camshaft in the cylinder head with a new oil seal.

11. Apply a 3 mm bead of silicone sealer to the cylinder head face of the No. 1 camshaft bearing cap.

12. Install the remaining bearing caps. Install the rocker arm shaft assembly, leaving the adjusting screws loose.

13. Install the front head plate.

14. Install the timing belt.

15. Adjust the valve clearance to specifications and then install the cylinder head cover.

Piston and Connecting Rod

POSITIONING

Install piston and connecting rod assemblies into their original cylinders. Install the piston and rod assemblies with the arrow on the piston crown facing to the front of the engine. The numbers on the connecting rods and bearing caps must be on the same side when installing pistons and connecting rods.

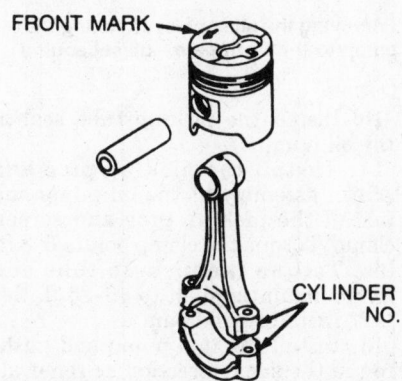

Piston and rod positioning–diesel engine

ENGINE LUBRICATION

Oil Pan
REMOVAL & INSTALLATION
Gasoline Engine

1. Disconnect the negative battery cable.

2. Drain the cooling system.

3. Remove the upper radiator support and fan shroud.

4. Disconnect the heater hoses at the heater core.

4. Remove the heater core housing.

6. Remove the engine mount retaining nuts and clips.

7. Raise and safely support the vehicle.

8. Drain the engine oil.

9. Disconnect the power steering line, if equipped.

10. Disconnect the rack and pinion unit from the crossmember and steering shaft and pull it out of the way.

11. Remove the flywheel shield.

12. Remove the heater pipe at the oil pan.

13. Remove the oil pan retaining bolts.

14. Raise the engine.

15. Remove the oil pan, oil pipe and suction screen.

16. Use a new gasket during installation.

17. The remainder of the installation is the reverse of the removal. Fill the engine with oil and check for leaks.

Diesel Engine

1. Using the correct procedure, remove the engine.

2. Support the engine in a stand.

3. Remove the bolts attaching the oil pan to the crankcase and remove the pan.

4. Clean the mating surfaces of the oil pan and the block. Install a new gasket.

5. Install the oil pan retaining bolts and tighten them to 5 ft. lbs.

6. Reinstall the engine.

Rear Main Bearing Oil Seal

REMOVAL & INSTALLATION

Gasoline Engine

1. Disconnect the battery cables. Negative cable first.

2. Using the correct procedure, remove the transmission.

3. Remove the flywheel or flexplate.

4. Remove the rack and pinion unit mounting bolts.

5. Remove the left side strut.

6. Remove the flexible coupling and pull the gear down.

7. Drain the engine oil.

8. Using the correct procedure, remove the oil pan, suction pipe and screen.

9. Remove the rear main cap.

10. Remove the seal.

11. Before replacing the seal, clean all bearing cap and case surfaces.

12. Inspect the crankshaft seal surface for any wear or nicks.

13. Install the new seal against the rear main bearing bulkhead. Apply RTV sealer or equivalent to the verticle grooves of the bearing cap. Wipe off any excess sealer.

14. Torque the bearing bolts to 10–12 ft. lbs. Tap the end of the crankshaft rearward then forward. Retorque the bearing cap bolts to 40–52 ft. lbs.

15. Reverse the removal procedure for the remainder of the installation.

Diesel Engine

1. Using the correct procedure, remove the transmission. If equipped with a manual transmission, remove the clutch.

2. Remove the flywheel.

3. Pry off the old oil seal.

4. Coat the lipped portion and the fitting face of the new oil seal with engine oil and install it into the crankshaft bearing. Make sure that the seal is properly seated.

5. Coat the threads of the new mounting bolts with Loctite® and install the flywheel. Tighten the bolts to 40 ft. lbs. in a diagonal sequence. Do not reuse the old bolts, they must be new.

6. Installation of the remaining components is in the reverse order of removal.

Oil Pump

REMOVAL & INSTALLATION

Gasoline Engine

1. Remove the ignition coil attaching bolts and lay the coil aside.

2. Raise and safely support the vehicle and remove the fuel pump, pushrod and gasket. Note the direction the push rod comes out for installation.

3. Lower the vehicle and remove the distributor. On air conditioned cars, remove the compressor mounting bolts and lay it aside. Do not disconnect any refrigerant lines.

4. Raise and safely support the vehicle. Remove the oil pan using the correct procedure.

5. Remove the oil pump pipe and screen assembly.

6. Remove the pipe and screen assembly from the oil pump.

7. Remove the pick-up tube seal from the oil pump.

8. Remove the oil pump attaching bolts and remove the oil pump.

9. Torque the oil pump bolts to 15 ft. lbs.

NOTE: Make certain that the pilot on the oil pump engages the case.

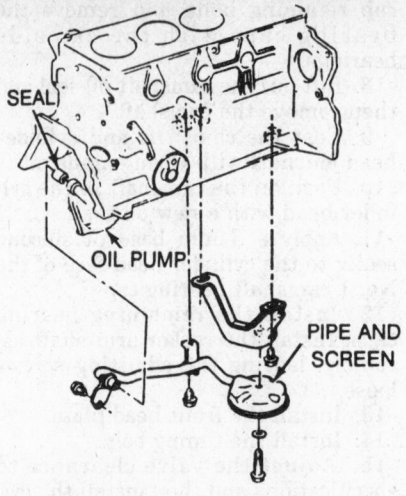

Oil pump and screen mounting

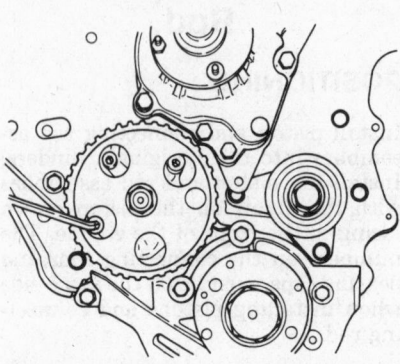

Removing the allen bolts attaching the oil pump to the front pate—diesel engine

10. Install the pick-up tube seal in the oil pump.

11. Install the pick-up pipe and screen assembly in the oil pump and install the pick-up pipe and screen clamp. Torque the clamp bolt to 6–8 ft. lbs. Torque the pick-up tube and screen mounting bolt to 19–25 ft. lbs.

12. Install the oil pan.

13. Install the fuel pump and pushrod in the same direction as removal.

14. Lower the vehicle and install the distributor and the ignition coil.

Diesel Engine

1. Using the correct procedure, remove the timing belt cover and timing belt.

2. Remove the four allen bolts attaching the oil pump to the front plate. Remove the pump with the pulley still attached.

3. Coat the pump vane with clean engine oil and then install it with the taper side toward the cylinder body.

4. Install a new O-ring, coated with engine oil, into the pump housing.

5. Position the rotor in the vane and

then install the pump body together with the pulley. Tighten the Allen bolts to 15 ft. lbs.

6. Using the correct procedure, install the timing belt and adjust the belt tension.

ENGINE COOLING

Radiator

REMOVAL & INSTALLATION

1. Disconnect the negative battery cable.

2. Drain the cooling system.

3. Remove the upper radiator support or the upper fan shroud.

4. Disconnect the coolant hoses. Disconnect and plug the automatic transmission cooler lines from the radiator.

5. Remove the radiator.

6. Installation is the reverse of the removal.

Water Pump

REMOVAL & INSTALLATION

Gasoline Engine

1. Disconnect the battery negative cable and remove the alternator and air conditioning compressor drive belts.

2. Remove the engine fan, spacer (air conditioned models) and the pulley.

3. Remove the timing belt front cover by removing the two upper bolts, center bolt and two lower nuts. Remove the timing belt lower cover retaining nut and remove the cover.

4. Drain the coolant from the engine.

5. Remove the lower radiator hose and the heater hose at the water pump.

6. Turn the crankshaft pulley so that the mark on the pulley is aligned with the "0" mark on the timing scale and that a ⅛ in. drill bit can be inserted through the timing belt upper rear cover and camshaft sprocket.

7. Remove the idler pulley and pull the timing belt off the sprocket. DO NOT disturb the crankshaft position.

8. Remove the water pump retaining bolts and remove the pump and gasket from the engine.

9. Clean off all the old gasket material from the engine.

10. With a new gasket in place on the

water pump, position the water pump in place on the engine and install the retaining bolts.

11. Install the timing belt onto the cam sprocket.

12. Apply sealer to the idler pulley attaching bolt and install the bolt and the idler pulley. Turn the idler pulley counterclockwise on its mounting bolt to remove the slack in the timing belt.

13. Use a tension gauge to adjust timing belt tension. Check belt tension midway between the tensioner and the cam sprocket on the idler pulley side. Correct belt tension is 70 lbs. Torque the idler pulley mounting bolt to 13–18 ft. lbs.

14. Remove the ⅛ in. drill bit from the upper rear timing belt cover and cam sprocket.

15. Install the lower radiator hose and the heater hose to the water pump.

16. Install the timing belt front covers.

17. Install the water pump pulley, spacer (if equipped) and engine fan.

18. Install the engine drive belt(s).

19. Refill the cooling system.

20. Connect the battery negative cable.

21. Start the engine and check for leaks. Run the engine with the heater on until the thermostat opens, then recheck the coolant level.

Diesel Engine

1. Disconnect the negative battery cable and drain the cooling system.

2. Remove the fan shroud, fan assembly and the accessory drive belt.

3. Remove the damper pulley retaining bolts and remove the pulley.

4. Remove the upper and lower halves of the front cover and then remove the bypass hose at the pump.

5. Remove the water pump retaining bolts and remove the pump assembly.

6. Installation is in the reverse order of removal.

Thermostat
REMOVAL & INSTALLATION

1. Drain the radiator and remove the radiator hose at the water outlet.

2. Remove the thermostat housing bolts and remove the housing, gasket and thermostat.

3. Remove any old gasket material. Install the thermostat. Use a new gasket on the thermostat housing and install the thermostat housing bolts.

4. Install the radiator hose at the water outlet.

5. Fill the cooling system. Run the engine with the heater on until the thermostat opens, then recheck the coolant level.

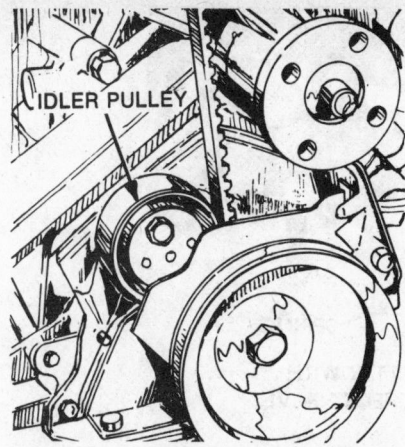

Gasoline engine timing belt idler pulley

COOLING SYSTEM BLEEDING

After working on the cooling system, even to replace the thermostat, it must be bled. Air trapped in the system will, otherwise, prevent proper filling, leaving the radiator coolant level low and causing risk of overheating.

To bleed the system, start with the system cool, the radiator cap off and the radiator filled to about an inch below the filler neck. Start the engine and run it at slightly above normal idle speed, to ensure adequate circulation. If air bubbles appear and the coolant level drops, fill the system with an antifreeze/water mixture to bring the level back to the proper level. Run the engine this way until the thermostat opens. When this happens, coolant will move abruptly across the top of the radiator and the temperature of the radiator will suddenly rise. At this point, air is often expelled and the level may drop quite a bit. Keep refilling the system until the level is near the top of the radiator and remains constant. If the vehicle has an overflow tank, fill the radiator right up to the filler neck. Replace the radiator filler cap.

EMISSION CONTROLS

Please refer to "Emission Controls" in the Unit Repair section for system maintenance procedures. Due to the complex nature of modern electronic engine control systems, comprehensive diagnosis and testing procedures fall outside the confines of this repair manual. For complete information on diagnosis, testing and re-

pair procedures, please refer to *"Chilton's Guide to Electronic Engine Controls".*

GASOLINE FUEL SYSTEM

Fuel Filter
REMOVAL & INSTALLATION

—————— CAUTION ——————
Do not perform this operation on a hot engine. Place rags under the fuel fitting to catch any spilled fuel.

1. Disconnect the small fuel line connection nut, using a flare nut wrench, while holding the large fitting nut with a standard open end wrench. A flared nut wrench is preferred over a standard open end wrench since it will not slip off and round off the corners of the tubing nut.

2. Remove the large filter retaining nut from the carburetor. There is a spring behind the filter. Remove the filter and spring.

3. Install the spring and new filter element in the same order as removal.

4. Install the new gasket on the retaining nut and tighten it into place. Do not overtighten the nut.

5. Run the engine and check for leaks.

Fuel Pump
PRESSURE TESTING

1. Disconnect the fuel line at the carburetor.

2. Attach a hose with a low pressure gauge at one end to the fuel line.

3. Start and run the engine using the gas still in the carburetor.

4. Hold the gauge about 16 in. above the fuel pump and note the reading on the gauge. The correct pressure should be 5–6 PSI constant.

5. If the pressure is too high or too low, replace the pump.

ADJUSTMENT

No adjustments are possible on the gasoline fuel pump.

REMOVAL & INSTALLATION

NOTE: Air conditioned cars require the removal of the rear compressor bracket for access to the pump.

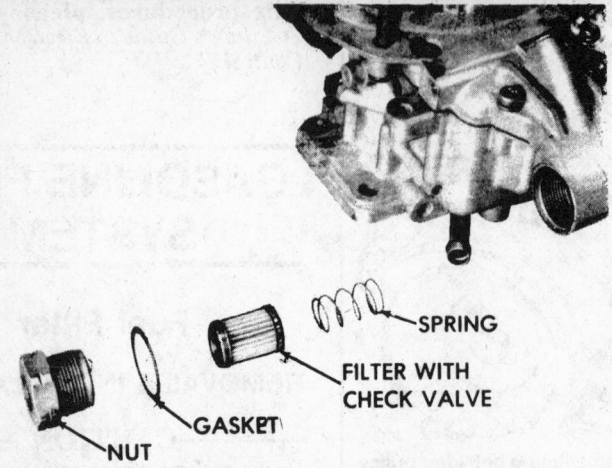

12. Connect the accelerator linkage and the electrical connectors.

13. Check and adjust the idle speed as required.

14. Install the air cleaner and gasket.

OVERHAUL

For all carburetor adjustments and specifications not above, please refer to "Carburetors" in the Unit Repair section.

Fuel filter assembly—2 bbl

DIESEL FUEL SYSTEM

Fuel Filter

REPLACEMENT

1. Disconnect the negative battery cable.

2. Disconnect the water sensor lead at the bottom of the filter, then disconnect the water filter to main body hose.

3. Remove the filter element by turning it counterclockwise using a filter strap wrench. Be careful not to spill any fuel.

4. After draining the filter, remove the water sensor from the bottom of the element.

5. Install the sensor in the new filter after apply a thin film of diesel fuel to the sensor O-ring.

6. Clean the filter mounting surface, apply a thin film of diesel fuel to the gasket on the new filter and install the filter. Continue turning the filter an additional ⅔ turn after it contacts the filter main body.

7. Connect the sensor wire. Disconnect the fuel outlet hose from the injector pump and place in a suitable container, then operate the priming pump handle several times to fill the filter with fuel. Reconnect the hose to the injector pump and start the engine to check for leaks.

DRAINING WATER FROM THE SYSTEM

1. Place a one gallon container at the end of the hose beneath the drain plug on the water separator.

2. Slowly open the drain plug 4 turns.

3. Operate the priming pump handle on the separator up and down until all of the water is drained out of the system.

4. Close the drain plug and operate

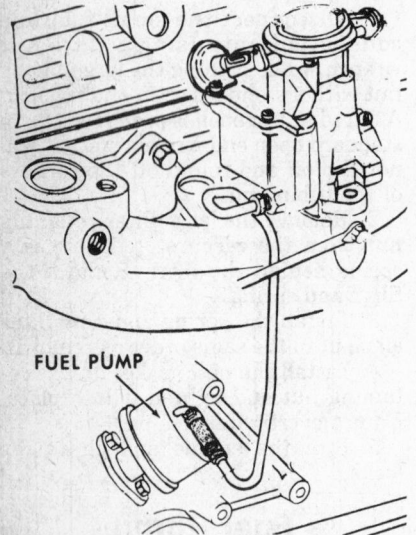

Chevette fuel pump location

1. Disconnect the negative battery cable.

2. Remove the distributor cap and the spark plug wire retaining clips.

3. Remove the coil wire and the coil assembly.

4. It may be necessary to remove the air cleaner on some models.

5. Disconnect the fuel pump hoses and remove the pump.

6. Remove the fuel pump push rod.

7. Installation is the reverse of the removal. Check for any leaks when finished.

Carburetor

REMOVAL & INSTALLATION

1. Remove air cleaner and gasket.

2. Disconnect the fuel and vacuum lines from the carburetor.

3. Disconnect the accelerator linkage and the electrical connectors.

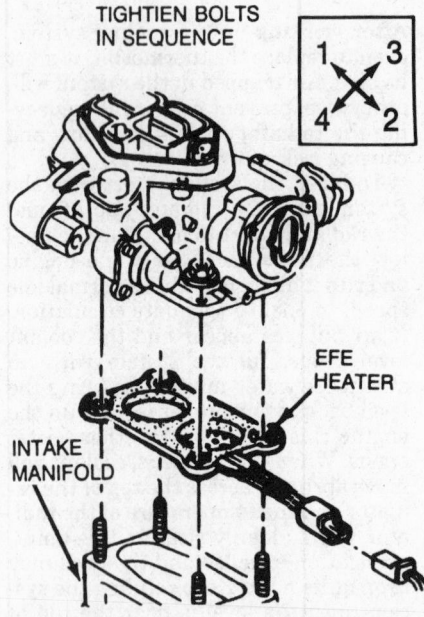

Carburetor mounting

4. Remove the carburetor attaching nuts and remove the carburetor.

5. Remove the electric Early Fuel Evaporation (EFE) heater (if so equipped) and the insulator gasket.

6. Be sure the throttle body and intake manifold sealing surfaces are clean.

7. Install a new EFE heater (if so equipped) and an insulator gasket on the manifold.

8. Install the carburetor over the manifold studs.

9. Install the vacuum lines and loosely connect the fuel line.

10. Install and tighten the attaching nuts to 12 ft. lbs.

11. Tighten the fuel inlet nut to 25 ft. lbs.

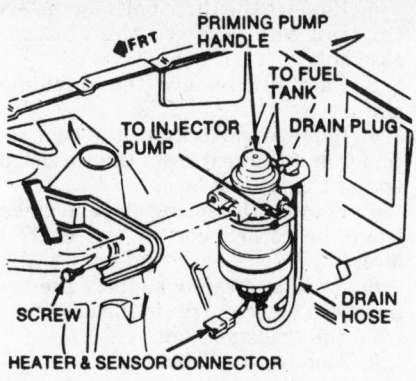

Diesel fuel filter

the priming pump again several times to fill the system with fuel.

5. Start the engine and check for leaks. Check to see that the "Water in Fuel" light is not on.

NOTE: If there is an excessive amount of water in the fuel, the filter should be replaced only after all of the water is out of the system.

Diesel Injection Pump

REMOVAL & INSTALLATION

NOTE: This procedure will require the use of two special tools: a gear puller J–22888 and a fixing plate J–29761, or equivalent. This procedure must be performed in conjunction with the following "injection timing" procedure.

1. Disconnect the negative battery cable.

2. Drain the cooling system. Remove the fan shroud, fan, radiator and coolant recovery tank.

3. Disconnect the bypass hose leading from the front cover and then remove the upper half of the front cover.

4. Loosen the timing belt tensioner pulley and plate bolts. Slide the tensioner over.

5. Remove the two retaining bolts and remove the tension spring from behind the front plate next to the injection pump.

6. Remove the injection pump gear retaining nut and remove the gear with a suitable puller.

7. Tag and disconnect all wires, hoses and cables leading from the pump. Disconnect and plug the fuel feed lines.

8. Remove the fuel filter. Disconnect the injector lines at the pump and at the injector nozzles and remove the lines.

9. Remove the four retaining bolts and remove the pump rear bracket.

10. Remove the nuts attaching the

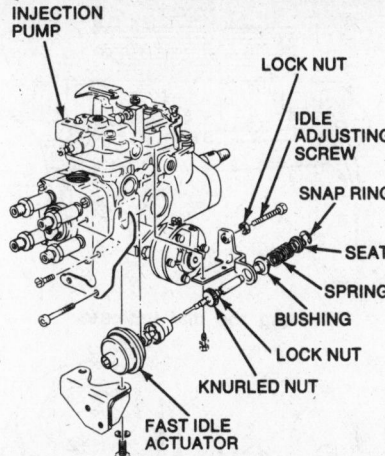

Exploded view of diesel injection pump linkage showing idle adjusting screw and fast idle adjuster (knurled nut)

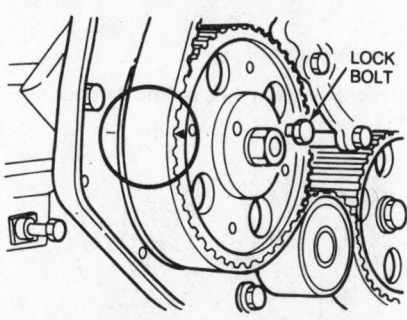

Use a lockbolt to ensure that the index marks on the injection pump gear and the front plate stay in alignment—diesel

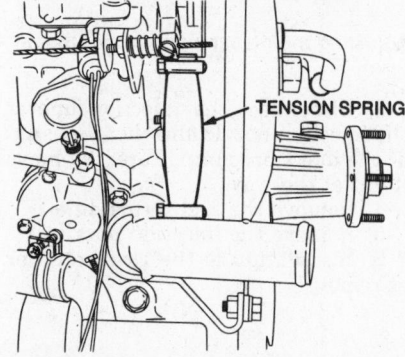

Tension spring, located behind the front plate beside the injection pump on diesel engine

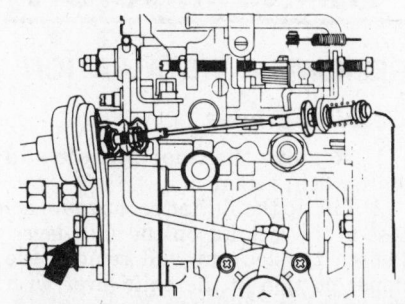

Remove the distributor head screw and washer

pump flange to the front plate. Remove the pump complete with the fast idle device and return spring.

11. To install, place the pump in position and tighten the flange bolts. Position the rear bracket and tighten the bracket-to-block bolts, then tighten the bracket-to-pump bolts. There should be no clearance between the rear bracket and the pump bracket.

12. Reconnect all wires, hoses and cables to the pump.

13. Slide the pump gear onto its shaft, making sure that it is aligned with the key groove. Turn the gear until the notch mark aligns with the index mark on the front plate. Thread a lock bolt (8mm x 1.25) through the gear and into the front plate. Tighten the retaining nut to 45 ft. lbs.

14. Remove the cylinder head cover. Position the No. 1 piston at TDC of the compression stroke and install the fixing plate into the slot in the rear of the camshaft to prevent it from rotating.

15. Remove the cam gear retaining bolt and, using a suitable puller, remove the gear. Reinstall the gear loosely so that it can be turned smoothly by hand.

16. Hold the timing belt on each side near the lower half of the front cover and move it back and forth until the cogs on the belt engage with those on the lower gears. Slide the belt first over the pump gear and then over the cam gear (the cam gear may have to be turned slightly to properly engage the cogs).

17. Make sure that any slack in the belt is concentrated around the tension pulley and NOT around or between the two upper gears. Depress the tension pulley with a finger and install the tension spring.

18. Partially tighten the tension pulley bolts; first the upper, then the lower. Tighten the cam gear retaining bolt to 45 ft. lbs.

19. Remove the pump gear lock bolt. Remove the fixing plate from the end of the camshaft.

20. Check that the No. 1 piston is still at TDC. Check that the marks on the front plate and the pump gear are still aligned. Check that the fixing plate still fits properly into the rear of the camshaft.

——— **CAUTION** ———

If Step 20 does not check out correctly, repeat the entire procedure, DO NOT attempt to compensate for any changes by moving the camshaft, pump gear or crankshaft.

21. Loosen the tension pulley and plate bolts. Make sure the belt slack is concentrated around the pulley and then tighten the bolts in the same manner as before. Belt tension should

be checked at the mid-point between the cam gear and the pump gear.

22. Installation of the remaining components is in the reverse order of removal.

23. Check the injection timing.

INJECTION TIMING ADJUSTMENT

1. Check that the No. 1 piston is at TDC of the compression stroke. Make sure that the timing belt is properly tensioned and the timing marks are aligned.

2. Remove the cylinder head cover and check that the camshaft fixing plate will still fit smoothly into the slot at the rear of the camshaft.

3. Remove the injection lines. Remove the distributor head screw and washer.

4. Position a Static Timing Gauge J–29763, or equivalent, and a dial indicator in the distributor head hole. Set the lift approximately 0.04 in. (1mm) from the end of the plunger.

5. Turn the crankshaft until the No. 1 piston is 45–60 degrees BTDC. Zero the dial indicator.

NOTE: The damper pulley is notched with eleven lines; four in one position, seven in another. The group of four are to be used for static timing.

6. Turn the crankshaft to the 18 degree position. Loosen the two nuts on the injection pump flange and move the pump until the proper reading is achieved. Swivel the pump UP to retard the timing and DOWN to advance the timing. When the adjustment is correct, tighten the pump flange nuts.

8. Remove the dial indicator. Install the distributor head screw and washer.

9. Install the cylinder head cover, injection lines and fuel filter.

10. Reconnect all wires and hoses to the pump. Installation of the remaining components is in the reverse order of removal.

Injection Nozzle

REMOVAL & INSTALLATION

NOTE: The primary function of an injection nozzle is to distribute fuel in the combustion chamber. Do not, under any circumstances, crank the engine while an injection line or injector is disconnected.

1. Disconnect the negative battery cable.

2. Remove the fresh air duct and disconnect the PCV hose.

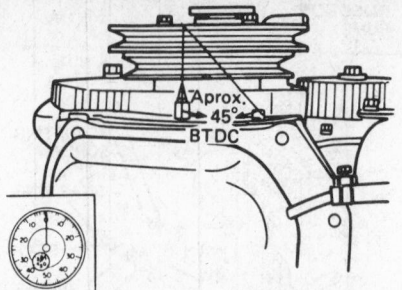

Zeroing the dial indicator

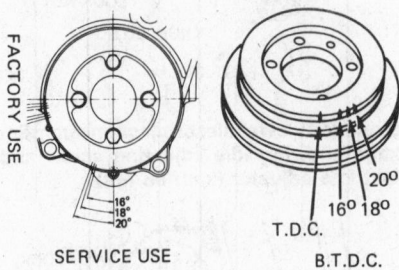

Static timing notches on the damper pulley

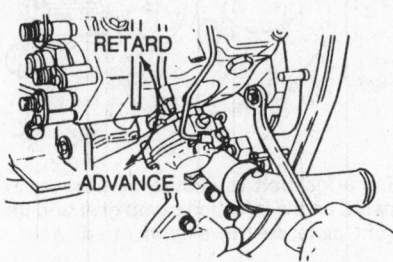

Adjusting the diesel fuel injection pump

3. Disconnect the injection line at the injection nozzle and then loosen it at the injection pump. Carefully move it out of the way.

4. Remove the fuel return line.

5. Remove the injection nozzle.

6. Installation is the reverse order of removal.

MANUAL TRANSMISSION

REMOVAL & INSTALLATION

Gasoline Engine

1. Remove the floor console and shifter boot retainer.

2. Lift up the shifter boot to gain access to the locknut on the shift lever. Loosen the locknut and remove the upper portion of the shift lever with the knob attached.

3. Remove the foam insulator.

4. Remove the three bolts on the extension and remove the control assembly.

5. Carefully remove the retaining clip.

6. Remove the locknut, the boot retainer and the seat from the threaded end of the control lever.

7. Remove the spring and the guide from the forked end of the control lever.

8. Raise and safely support the vehicle on a hoist and drain the lubricant from the transmission.

9. Remove the driveshaft.

10. Disconnect the speedometer cable and back-up light switch.

11. Disconnect the return spring and clutch cable at the clutch release fork.

12. Remove the crossmember-to-transmission mount bolts.

13. Remove the exhaust manifold nuts and converter-to-tailpipe bolts and nuts. Remove the converter-to-transmission bracket bolts and remove the converter.

14. Remove the crossmember-to-frame bolts and remove the crossmember.

15. Remove the dust cover.

16. Remove the clutch housing-to-engine retaining bolts, slide the transmission and clutch housing to the rear and remove the transmission.

17. To install, place the transmission in gear, position the transmission and clutch housing and slide forward. Turn the output shaft to align the input shaft splines with the clutch hub.

18. Install the clutch housing retaining bolts and lockwashers. Torque the bolts to 25 ft. lbs.

19. Install the dust cover.

20. Position the crossmember to the frame and loosely install the retaining bolts. Install the crossmember-to-transmission mounting bolts. Torque the center nuts to 33 ft. lbs.; the end nuts to 21 ft. lbs. Torque the crossmember-to-frame bolts to 40 ft. lbs.

21. Install the exhaust pipe to the manifold and the converter bracket on the transmission.

22. Connect the clutch cable. Adjust clutch pedal free-play.

23. Connect the speedometer cable and back-up light switch.

24. Install the driveshaft.

25. Fill the transmission to the correct level with SAE 80W or SAE 80W–90 GL-5 gear lubricant. Lower the car.

26. Install the shift lever and check operation of the transmission.

Diesel Engine

1. Disconnect the negative battery cable.

2. Remove the retaining screws and then remove the shift lever console.

3. Remove the mounting screws and remove the shift lever assembly.

4. Remove the upper starter mounting bolts.

5. Raise and safely support the front of the vehicle and drain the lubricant from the transmission.

6. Remove the driveshaft as detailed later in this section.

7. Disconnect the speedometer and the back-up light switch wires.

8. Disconnect the return spring and clutch cable at the clutch release fork.

9. Remove the starter lower bolt and support the starter.

10. Disconnect the exhaust pipe from the manifold.

11. Remove the flywheel inspection cover.

12. Remove the rear transmission support mounting bolt. Support the transmission underneath the case and then remove the rear support from the frame.

13. Lower the transmission approximately four inches.

14. Remove the transmission housing-to-engine block bolts. Pull the transmission straight back and away from the engine.

15. Installation of the remaining components is in the reverse order of removal. Please note the following:

a. Be sure to lubricate the drive gear shaft with a light coat of grease before installing the transmission.

b. After installation, fill the transmission to the level of the filler hole with 5W-30SF engine oil.

CLUTCH

REMOVAL & INSTALLATION

1. Raise and safely support the vehicle on a hoist.

2. Remove the transmission.

3. Remove the throwout bearing from the clutch fork by sliding the fork off the ball stud against spring tension. If the ball stud is to be replaced, remove the locknut and stud from the bellhousing.

4. If the balance marks on the pressure plate and the flywheel are not easily seen, mark them with paint or a centerpunch.

5. Alternately loosen the pressure plate-to-flywheel attaching bolts one turn at a time until spring tension is released.

6. Support the pressure plate and cover assembly, then remove the bolts and the clutch assembly.

—————— **CAUTION** ——————
Do not disassemble the clutch cover and pressure plate for repair. If defective, replace the assembly.

7. Check the pressure plate, clutch plate and flywheel for wear. If the flywheel is scored, worn or discolored from overheating, it should be either refaced or replaced. Replace the clutch plate as necessary.

8. Align the balance marks on the clutch disc on the pressure plate with the long end of the splined hub facing forward and the damper springs inside the pressure plate. Insert a dummy shaft through the cover and clutch disc.

9. Position the assembly against the flywheel and insert the dummy shaft into the pilot bearing in the crankshaft.

10. Align the balance marks and install the pressure plate-to-flywheel bolts finger tight.

—————— **CAUTION** ——————
Tighten all bolts evenly and gradually until tight to avoid possible clutch distortion. Torque the bolts to 18 ft. lbs. (14 ft. lbs. on diesel engine) and remove the dummy shaft.

11. Pack the groove on the inside of the throwout bearing with graphite grease. Also coat the fork groove and ball stud depression with the lubricant.

12. Install the throwout bearing and release fork assembly in the bellhousing with the fork spring hooked under the ball stud and the fork spring fingers inside the bearing groove.

13. Position the transmission and clutch housing and install the clutch housing attaching bolts and lockwashers. Torque the bolts to 25 ft. lbs.

14. Complete the transmission installation.

NOTE: Check the position of the engine in the front mounts and realign as necessary. A special gauge J–23644, or equivalent, is necessary to adjust the ball stud position if it has been removed.

15. Adjust clutch pedal free-play if necessary.

16. Lower the vehicle and check the operation of the clutch and transmission.

CLUTCH PEDAL FREE-PLAY ADJUSTMENT

Adjustment is made at the firewall end of the outer clutch cable. Pedal free-play should be ½–1 in. at the pedal.

1. Pull the adjusting ring clip from the cable at the firewall.

2. To increase free-play, move the cable into the firewall, one notch at a time and replace the clip.

3. To decrease free-play, pull the ca-

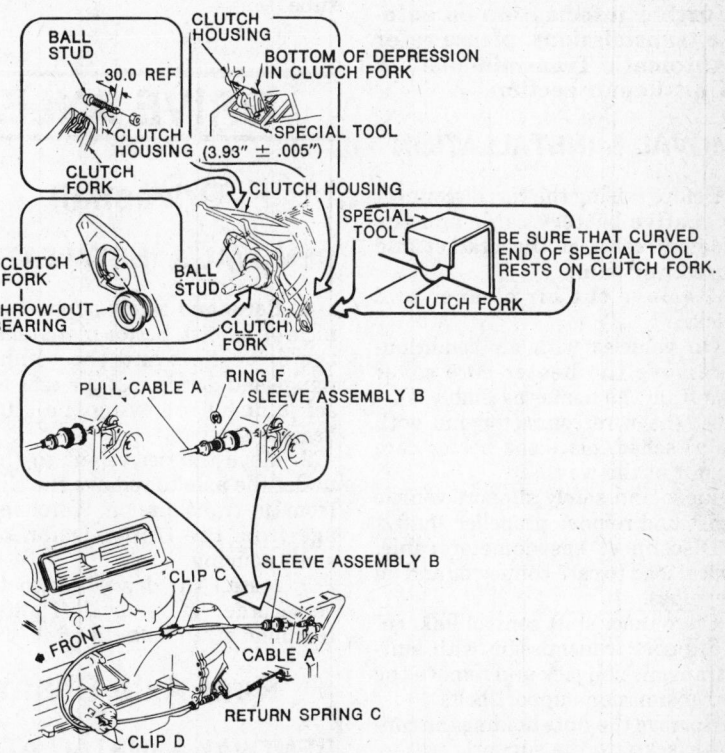

Clutch cable and ball stud adjustment details

ble out, one notch at a time and replace the clip.

4. If, after the adjustment, the pedal won't return tight against the bumper, the ball stud will have to be adjusted. Use the special gauge mentioned in the clutch replacement procedure.

Clutch Cable

REMOVAL & INSTALLATION

1. Raise and safely support the vehicle.

2. Disconnect the clutch return spring and cable from the clutch fork.

3. Dissconnect the clutch cable from the upper end of the clutch pedal.

4. Pull the clutch cable assembly through the firewall and disconnect it at the cable retainer on the fender.

5. Insert the new cable through the firewall and attach it to the clutch pedal.

6. Secure the new cable to the clutch fork.

7. Check the clutch operation and adjust the clutch as necessary.

AUTOMATIC TRANSMISSION

For further information on automatic transmissions, please refer to "Automatic Transmissions" in the Unit Repair section.

REMOVAL & INSTALLATION

1. Before raising the car, disconnect the negative battery cable and the T.V./detent cable at the bracket and carburetor or pump.

2. Remove the air cleaner and dipstick.

3. On vehicles with air conditioning, remove the heater core cover screws from the heater assembly. Disconnect the wire connector and with hoses attached, place the heater core cover out of the way.

4. Raise and safely support vehicle on hoist and remove propeller shaft.

5. Disconnect speedometer cable, electrical lead to case connector and oil cooler pipes.

6. Disconnect shift control linkage.

7. Support transmission with suitable transmission jack and remove the rear transmission support bolts.

8. Remove the nuts holding the converter bracket to the support.

9. Disconnect exhaust pipe at the rear of the catalytic converter.

10. Disconnect the exhaust pipe at manifold and remove the exhaust pipe, catalytic converter and converter bracket as an assembly.

11. Remove the torque converter dust cover.

12. Remove converter to flexplate bolts.

13. Lower transmission until jack is barely supporting it and remove transmission to engine mounting bolts.

14. Raise transmission to its normal position, then place a block of wood between the rack-and-pinion housing and the engine oil pan, then support engine with jack and slide transmission rearward from engine and lower it away from vehicle.

NOTE: The use of a converter holding tool J–5384, or equivalent, is necessary to hold the converter in when lowering the transmission. If the tool is not available, keep the rear of the transmission lower than the front so the converter will not fall out.

15. Installation is the reverse of removal. Before installing the flex plate to converter bolts, make certain that the weld nuts on the converter are flush with the flex plate and the converter rotates freely by hand in this position. Hand start the three bolts and tighten finger tight, then torque to specifications. This will insure proper converter alignment. Install new oil seal on oil filler tube before installing tube.

DRIVE AXLE

Driveshaft

REMOVAL & INSTALLATION

1. Raise and safely support the vehicle on a hoist. Scribe matchmarks on the driveshaft and the companion flange and disconnect the rear universal joint by removing the trunnion bearing straps.

2. Move the driveshaft to the rear under the axle to remove the slip yoke from the transmission. Watch for leakage from the transmission output shaft housing.

3. Install the driveshaft in the reverse order of removal. Tighten the trunnion strap bolts to 16 ft. lbs.

Rear Axle Shafts

REMOVAL & INSTALLATION

1. Raise and safely support the ve-

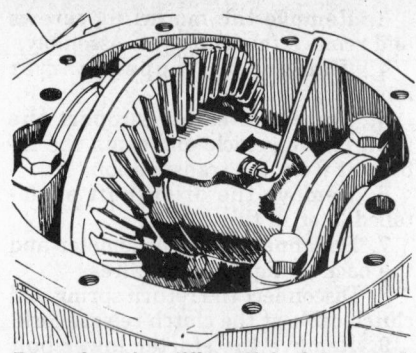

Removing the differential pinion shaft lockscrew

hicle on a hoist. Remove the wheel and tire assembly and brake drum.

2. Clean the area around the differential carrier cover.

3. Remove the differential carrier cover to drain the rear axle lubricant.

4. Use a metric Allen wrench to remove the differential pinion shaft lock-screw and remove the differential pinion shaft. It may be necessary to shorten the Allen wrench to do this.

5. Push the flanged end of the axle shaft toward the center of the vehicle and remove the C-lock from the inner end of the shaft.

6. Remove the axle shaft from the housing making sure not to damage the oil seal.

7. If replacing the seal only, remove the oil seal by using the inner end of the axle shaft. Insert the end of the shaft behind the steel case of the oil seal and carefully pry the seal out of the bore.

8. To remove bearings, insert a bearing and seal remover into the bore so that the tool head grasps behind the bearing. Slide the washer against the seal or bearing and turn the nut against the washer. Attach a slide hammer and remove the bearing.

9. Lubricate a new bearing with hypoid lubricant and install it into the housing with a bearing installer tool. Make sure that the tool contacts the end of the axle tube to ensure that the bearing is at the proper depth.

10. Lubricate the cavity between the seal lips with a high melting point wheel bearing grease. Place a new oil seal on the seal installation tool and position the seal in the axle housing bore. Tap the seal into the bore flush with the end of the housing.

11. To install the axle shaft, slide the axle shaft into place making sure that the splines on the end of the shaft do not damage the oil seal and that they engage the splines of the differential side gear. Install the C-lock on the inner end of the axle shaft and push the shaft outward so that the shaft lock seats in the counterbore of the differential side gear.

12. Position the differential pinion shaft through the case and pinions, aligning the hole in the shaft with the lockscrew hole. Install the lockscrew.

13. Clean the gasket mounting surfaces on the differential carrier and the carrier cover. Install the carrier cover using a new gasket and tighten the cover bolts in a cross-wise pattern to 22 ft. lbs.

14. Fill the rear axle with lubricant to the bottom of the filler hole.

15. Install the brake drum and the wheel and tire assembly.

16. Lower the car.

FRONT SUSPENSION

Shock Absorbers

REMOVAL & INSTALLATION

NOTE: Purge new shock absorbers of air by repeatedly extending in the normal position and compressing while inverted.

1. Hold the shock absorber upper stem and remove the nut, upper retainer and rubber grommet.

2. Raise and safely support the vehicle on a hoist.

3. Remove the bolt from the lower end of the shock absorber and remove the shock absorber.

4. With the lower retainer and rubber grommet in position, extend the shock absorber stem and install the stem through the wheelhouse opening.

5. Install and torque the lower bolt to 35–50 ft. lbs.

6. Lower the car.

7. Install the upper rubber grommet, retainer and nut to the shock absorber stem.

8. Hold the shock absorber upper stem and torque the nut to 7 ft. lbs.

Springs

REMOVAL & INSTALLATION

NOTE: The ball joint studs use a special nut which must be discarded whenever loosened and removed. On assembly, use a standard nut to draw the ball joint into position on the knuckle, then remove the standard nut and install a new special nut for final installation.

1. Raise and safely support the vehicle on a frame contact hoist.

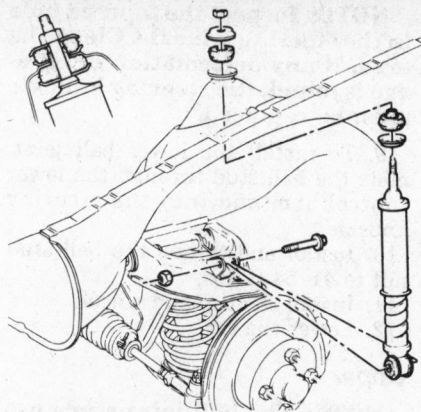

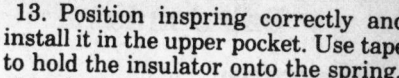

Front shock absorber mounting

2. Remove the wheel and tire.

3. Disconnect the stabilizer bar from the lower control arm and disconnect the tie rod from the steering knuckle.

4. Support the lower control arm with a jack.

5. Remove the nut from the lower ball joint, then use a ball joint removal tool to press out the lower ball joint.

6. Swing the knuckle and hub aside and attach them securely with wire.

7. Loosen the lower control arm pivot bolts.

8. As a safety precaution, install a chain through the coil spring.

9. Slowly lower the jack.

10. When the spring is extended as far as possible, use a pry bar to carefully lift the spring over the lower control arm seat. Remove the spring.

11. Remove the pivot bolts and remove the lower control arm.

12. Install the lower control arm and pivot bolts to the underbody brackets. Torque the lower control arm pivot bolts to 49 ft. lbs.

13. Position inspring correctly and install it in the upper pocket. Use tape to hold the insulator onto the spring.

14. Install the lower end of the spring onto the lower control arm. An assistant may be necessary to compress the spring far enough to slide it over the raised area of the lower control arm seat.

15. Use a jack to raise the lower control arm and compress the coil spring.

16. Install the ball joint through the lower control arm and into the steering knuckle. Install the nut on the ball stud and torque to 41–54 ft. lbs.

17. Connect the stabilizer bar to the lower control arm. Connect the tie rod to the steering knuckle. Install the wheel and tire.

18. Lower the car.

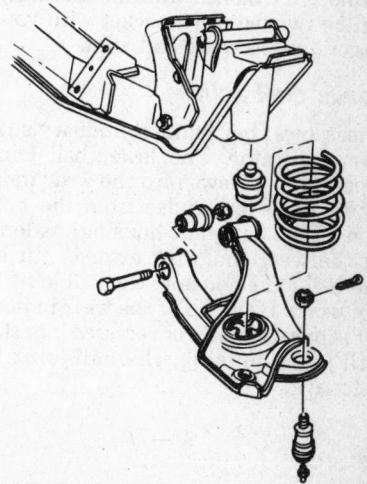

Correct position for front spring installation

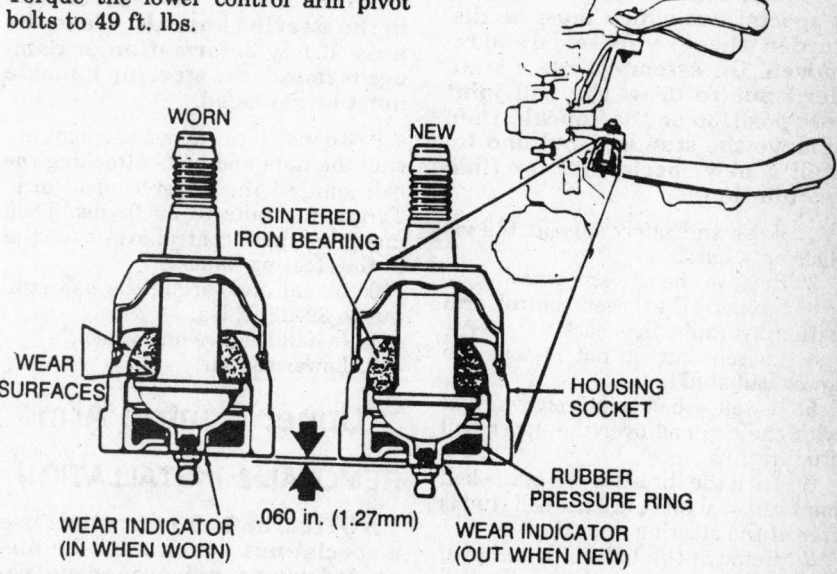

WORN | NEW
SINTERED IRON BEARING
WEAR SURFACES
HOUSING SOCKET
RUBBER PRESSURE RING
WEAR INDICATOR (IN WHEN WORN)
.060 in. (1.27mm)
WEAR INDICATOR (OUT WHEN NEW)

Lower ball joint inspection

Ball Joints

INSPECTION

Upper Ball Joint

1. Raise the vehicle and position floor stands under the left and right lower control arm as near as possible to each lower ball joint. Upper control arm bumper must not contact frame.
2. Position a dial indicator against the wheel rim.
3. Grasp the front wheel and push in on bottom of the tire while pulling out at the top. Read the guage, then reverse the push—pull procedure. Horizontal deflection on the dial indicator should not exceed 1.25 in. (3.18 mm).
4. If the indicator exceeds 1.25 in. (3.18 mm), or if ball stud (when disconnected from the knuckle assembly) can be twisted in its socket with your fingers, replace the ball joint.

Lower Ball Joint

These lower ball joints contain a visual wear indicator. The lower ball joint grease plug screws into the wear indicator which protrudes from the bottom of the ball joint housing. As long as the wear indicator extends out of the ball joint housing, the ball joint is not worn. If the tip of the wear indicator is parallel with, or recessed into the ball joint housing, the ball joint is defective.

REMOVAL & INSTALLATION

Lower

NOTE: The ball joint studs use a special nut which must be discarded whenever loosened and removed. On assembly, use a standard nut to draw the ball joint into position on the knuckle, then remove the standard nut and install a new special nut for final installation.

1. Raise and safely support the vehicle on a hoist.
2. Remove the tire and wheel.
3. Support the lower control arm with a hydraulic floor jack.
4. Loosen, but do not remove the lower ball stud nut.
5. Install a ball joint removal tool with the cup end over the upper ball stud nut.
6. Turn the threaded end of the ball joint removal tool until the ball stud is free of the steering knuckle.
7. Remove the ball joint removal tool and remove the nut from the ball stud.
8. Remove the ball joint.

NOTE: Inspect the tapered hole in the steering knuckle. Clean the area. If any deformation or damage is found, the steering knuckle must be replaced.

9. To install the lower ball joint, mate the ball stud through the lower control arm and into the steering knuckle.
10. Install and torque the ball stud nut to 41–54 ft. lbs.
11. Install the tire and wheel.
12. Lower the car.

Upper

NOTE: The ball joint studs use a special nut which must be discarded whenever loosened and removed. on assembly, use a standard nut to draw the ball joint into position on the knuckle, then remove the standard nut and install a new special nut for the final installation.

1. Raise and safely support the vehicle on a hoist.
2. Remove the tire and wheel.
3. Support the lower control arm with a floor jack.
4. Loosen, but do not remove the upper ball stud nut.
5. Install a ball joint removal tool with the cup end over the lower ball stud nut.
6. Turn the threaded end of the ball joint removal tool until the upper ball stud is free of the steering knuckle.
7. Remove the ball joint removal tool and remove the nut from the ball stud.
8. Remove the two nuts and bolts attaching the ball joint to the upper control arm and remove the ball joint.

NOTE: Inspect the tapered hole in the steering knuckle. Clean the area. If any deformation or damage is found, the steering knuckle must be replaced.

9. To install the upper ball joint, install the nuts and bolts attaching the ball joint to the upper control arm. Torque the nuts to 29 ft. lbs. Then mate the upper control arm ball stud to the steering knuckle.
10. Install and torque the ball stud nut to 29–36 ft. lbs.
11. Install the tire and wheel.
12. Lower the car.

Upper Control Arm

REMOVAL & INSTALLATION

NOTE: The ball joint studs use a special nut which must be discarded whenever loosened and removed. On assembly, use a standard nut to draw the ball joint into position on the knuckle, then remove the standard nut and install a new special nut for final installation.

1. Raise the vehicle and support it safely.
2. Remove the tire and wheel.
3. Support the lower control arm with a floor jack.
4. Remove the upper ball joint from the steering knuckle as previously described.
5. Remove the upper control arm pivot bolts and remove the upper control arm.
6. To install the upper control arm, install the upper control arm with its pivot bolts.

NOTE: The inner pivot bolt must be installed with the bolt head toward the front.

7. Install the pivot bolt nut.
8. Position the upper control arm in a horizontal plane and torque the nut to 43–50 ft. lbs.
9. Install the ball joint to the upper control arm and to the steering knuckle as previously described. Torque the ball joint-to-upper control arm attaching bolts to 29 ft. lbs. Torque the ball stud nut to 29–36 ft. lbs.
10. Install the tire and wheel.
11. Lower the car.

Lower Control Arms

REMOVAL & INSTALLATION

NOTE: The ball joint studs use a special nut which must be discarded whenever loosened and removed. On assembly, use a standard nut to draw the ball joint into position on the knuckle, then remove the standard nut and install a new special nut for final installation.

1. Raise and safely support the vehicle on a frame contact hoist.
2. Remove the wheel and tire.
3. Disconnect the stabilizer bar from the lower control arm and disconnect the tie rod from the steering knuckle.
4. Support the lower control arm with a jack.
5. Remove the nut from the lower ball joint, then use a ball joint removal tool to press out the lower ball joint.
6. Swing the knuckle and hub aside and attach them securely with wire.
7. Loosen the lower control arm pivot bolts.
8. As a safety precaution, install a chain through the coil spring.
9. Slowly lower the jack.
10. When the spring is extended as

far as possible, use a pry bar to carefully lift the spring over the lower control arm seat. Remove the spring.

11. Remove the pivot bolts and remove the lower control arm.

12. Install the lower control arm and pivot bolts to the underbody brackets. Torque the lower control arm pivot bolts to 49 ft. lbs.

13. Position inspring correctly and install it in the upper pocket. Use tape to hold the insulator onto the spring.

14. Install the lower end of the spring onto the lower control arm. An assistant may be necessary to compress the spring far enough to slide it over the raised area of the lower control arm seat.

15. Use a jack to raise the lower control arm and compress the coil spring.

16. Install the ball joint through the lower control arm and into the steering knuckle. Install the nut on the ball stud and torque to 41–54 ft. lbs.

17. Connect the stabilizer bar to the lower control arm. Connect the tie rod to the steering knuckle. Install the wheel and tire.

18. Lower the car.

Front Wheel Bearings

ADJUSTMENT

1. Raise and safely support the vehicle.

2. Remove the hub cap or wheel cover from the wheel. Remove the dust cap from the hub.

3. Remove the cotter pin from the spindle and spindle nut.

4. Spin the wheel forward by hand and tighten the spindle nut to 12 ft. lbs. This will fully seat the bearings.

5. Back off the nut to a just loose position.

6. Hand-tighten the spindle nut. Loosen the spindle nut until either hole in the spindle aligns with a slot in the nut, but not more than ½ flat.

7. Install a new cotter pin, bend the ends of the pin against the nut and cut off any extra length to avoid interference with the dust cap.

8. Proper bearing adjustment should give 0.001–0.005 in. of end-play.

9. Install the dust cap on the hub and the hub cap or wheel cover on the wheel.

10. Lower the vehicle.

REMOVAL & INSTALLATION

1. Raise and safely support the vehicle.

2. Remove the wheel and tire.

3. Remove the brake caliper leaving the brake line attached and support it so that it is not hanging on the brake line.

4. Remove the dust cap, cotter pin spindle nut and washer making sure that the rotor does not fall off.

5. Place one hand over the outer bearing and remove the rotor.

6. Using a suitable tool, drive out the inner seal and bearing race.

7. Using a suitable tool, drive out the outer bearing race.

8. Clean out the bearing seats in the rotor thoroughly.

9. Use a bearing driver and drive the inner and outer races in their proper positions.

10. Make sure that the new bearings are packed with grease properly. Place the inner bearing in the rotor and install the inner grease seal with the lip facing inward.

11. Place the outer bearing in its position and install the rotor onto the spindle. The remainder of the installation is the reverse of the removal. Adjust the bearings properly.

Front Wheel Alignment

Front wheel alignment is the relationship between the wheels, suspension parts, and the ground. This relationship is expressed in an angular term. **Example: Degrees (°).**

Several checks should be made, before an alignment is attempted, to see if any of the following conditions exist. If any of these conditions are present, they must be corrected first. Alignment specifications can be found in the front of this section.

- Loose or improperly adjusted rack and pinion.
- Excessive play in the ball joints.
- Loose tie rods or steering connections.
- Worn out or broken coil springs.
- Underinflated or out of balance tires.
- Wheel bearings out of adjustment.
- Worn out, broken, or leaking shock absorbers.

CAMBER ADJUSTMENT

The camber angle can be adjusted by 1 degree by removing the upper ball joint and rotating it one turn. Reinstall the ball joint with the flat of the upper flange on the inward side of the upper control arm. Lubricate the ball joint assembly prior to any adjustment.

CASTER ADJUSTMENT

The caster angle can be adjusted by relocating the two washers between the legs of the upper control arm. Whenever adjusting the caster, always use two washers totalling 12 mm in thickness,

with one washer at each end of the locating tube.

TOE ADJUSTMENT

The toe can be adjusted by the loosening the jam nuts on the tie rods, turning them to obtain the proper specification and retightening the nuts.

REAR SUSPENSION

NOTE: When using a hoist contacting the rear axle, be sure that the stabilizer links and the track rod are not damaged.

Shock Absorbers

REMOVAL & INSTALLATION

NOTE: Purge new shock absorbers of air by repeatedly extending them in the normal position and compressing them while inverted.

1. Raise and safely support the vehicle on a hoist.

2. Support the rear axle.

3. Remove the shock absorber upper attaching nut and lower attaching bolt and nut and remove the shock absorber.

4. Install the retainer and the rubber grommet onto the shock absorber.

5. Place the shock absorber into its installed position and install and tighten the upper retaining nut to 7 ft. lbs.

6. Install the lower shock absorber nut and bolt and torque to 21 ft. lbs.

7. Remove the rear axle supports and lower the car.

Springs

REMOVAL & INSTALLATION

1. Raise and safely support the vehicle on a hoist.

2. Support the rear axle with a floor jack.

3. Disconnect both shock absorbers from their lower brackets.

4. Disconnect the rear axle extension center support bracket from the underbody. Use caution when disconnect the extension and safely support it when disconnected.

5. Lower the rear axle and remove the springs and spring insulators.

—— **CAUTION** ——
Do not stretch the rear brake hoses when lowering the rear axle.

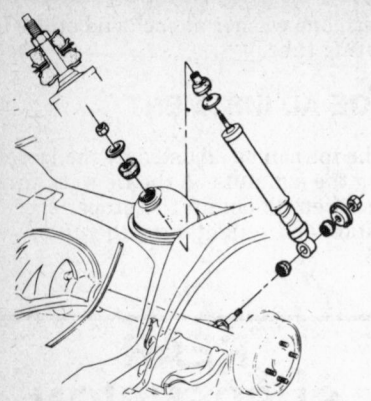

Rear shock absorber mounting

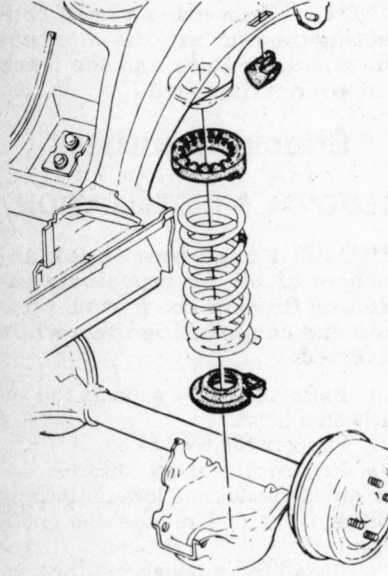

**Rear spring installation—
position both insulators as shown**

6. To install, place the insulators on top and on the bottom of the springs and position the springs between their upper and lower seats.

7. Raise the rear axle. Connect the rear axle extension center support bracket to the underbody. Torque the bolts to 37 ft. lbs.

8. Connect the shock absorbers to their lower brackets. Torque the nuts to 21 ft. lbs.

9. Remove the jack from the axle.

10. Lower the car.

Rear Control Arms

REMOVAL & INSTALLATION

NOTE: If both control arms are going to be replaced, only replace one control arm at a time. This will prevent the axle from rolling or sliding sideways.

1. Raise and safely support the vehicle.

2. Disconnect the stabalizer bar if equipped.

3. Remove the front and rear control arm mounting bolts.

4. Remove the control arm.

5. Installation is the reverse of the removal.

Rear Wheel Bearings

For Rear Wheel Bearing Removal & Installation procedures please refer to "Rear Axle Shafts."

STEERING

NOTE: This car is equipped with an steering column that is designed to collapse in the event of a collision. When working on the steering column or any related components, it is important that the column not be hammered on or banged in any way which may cause damage to the column.

Steering Wheel

REMOVAL & INSTALLATION

1. Disconnect the negative battery cable.

2. Pull up on the horn cap to remove it. Remove the horn ring-to-steering wheel attaching screws and remove the ring.

3. Remove the wheel nut retainer and the wheel nut.

— CAUTION —
Do not overexpand the retainer.

4. Using a suitable steering wheel puller, thread the puller anchor screws into the threaded holes in the steering wheel. With the center bolt of the puller butting against the steering shaft, turn the center bolt to remove the steering wheel.

5. To install, place the turn signal lever in the neutral position and install the steering wheel. Torque the steering wheel nut to 30 ft. lbs. and install the nut retainer. Use caution not to overexpand the nut retainer.

6. Connect the negative battery cable.

Combination Switch

NOTE: The turn signal switch is incorporated into the combination switch.

REMOVAL & INSTALLATION

1. Using the correct procedure, remove the steering wheel.

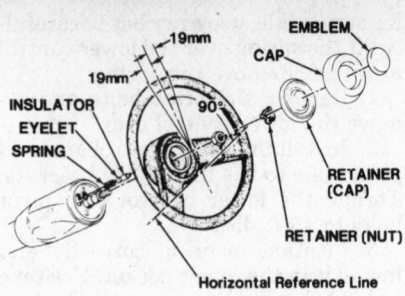

Chevette steering wheel assembly

2. Position a small prybar into one of the three cover slots. Pry up and out (at least two slots) to free the cover.

3. Press down on the lockplate, but do not relieve the full load of the spring because the ring will rotate and make removal difficult. Pry the round wire snap-ring out of the shaft groove and discard it. Lift the lockplate off the end of the shaft.

4. Slide the turn signal canceling cam, upper bearing preload spring and thrust washer off the end of the shaft.

5. Remove the multi-function lever by rotating it clockwise to its stop (off position), then pull the lever straight out to disengage it.

6. Push the hazard warning knob in and remove the knob.

7. Remove the two screws, pivot arm and spacer.

8. Wrap the upper part of the connector with tape to prevent snagging the wires during switch removal.

9. Remove the three switch mounting screws and pull the switch straight up, guiding the wiring harness through the column housing.

— CAUTION —
On installation it is extremely important that only the specified screws, bolts and nuts be used. The use of overlength screws could prevent the steering column from compresssing under impact.

10. Position the switch into the housing.

11. Install the three switch mounting screws. Replace the spacer and pivot arm. Be sure that the spacer protrudes through the hole in the arm and that the arm finger encloses the turn signal switch frame.

12. Install the hazard warning knob.

13. Make sure that the turn signal switch is in the neutral position and that the hazard warning knob is out. Slide the thrust washer, upper baring preload spring and the cancelling cam into the upper end of the shaft.

14. Place the lockplate and a new snapring onto the end of the shaft. Compress the lockplate as far as possible. Slide the new snapring into the shaft groove and remove the lockplate compressor tool.

CAUTION

On assembly, always use a new snapring.

15. Install the multi-function lever, guiding the wire harness through the column housing. Align the lever pin with the switch slot. Push on the end of the lever until it is seated securely.

16. Install the steering wheel.

Ignition Lock

REMOVAL & INSTALLATION

The ignition lock is located on the right side of the steering column and should be removed only in the Run position. Removal in any other position will damage the key buzzer switch. The ignition lock cannot be disassembled; if replacement is required, a new cylinder coded to the old key must be installed.

1. Disconnect the negative battery cable. Using the correct procedure, remove the steering wheel and turn signal switch.

2. Do not remove the buzzer switch or damage to the lock cylinder will result.

3. Place the lock cylinder in the RUN position. Remove the securing screw and remove the cylinder.

4. To install the lock cylinder, hold the cylinder sleeve and rotate knob (key in) clockwise to stop. (This retracts the actuator). Insert the cylinder into the housing bore with the key on the cylinder sleeve aligned with the keyway in the housing. Push the cylinder in until it bottoms and install the retaining screw.

5. Using the correct procedure, install the turn signal switch and the steering wheel.

Ignition Switch

REMOVAL & INSTALLATION

The ignition switch is mounted on top of the mast jacket near the front of the instrument panel. The switch is located inside the channel section of the brake pedal support and is completely inaccessible without first lowering the steering column.

1. Disconnect the negative battery cable.

2. Remove the steering wheel as previously described.

3. Move the driver's seat as far back as possible.

4. Remove the floor pan bracket screw.

5. Remove the two column bracket-

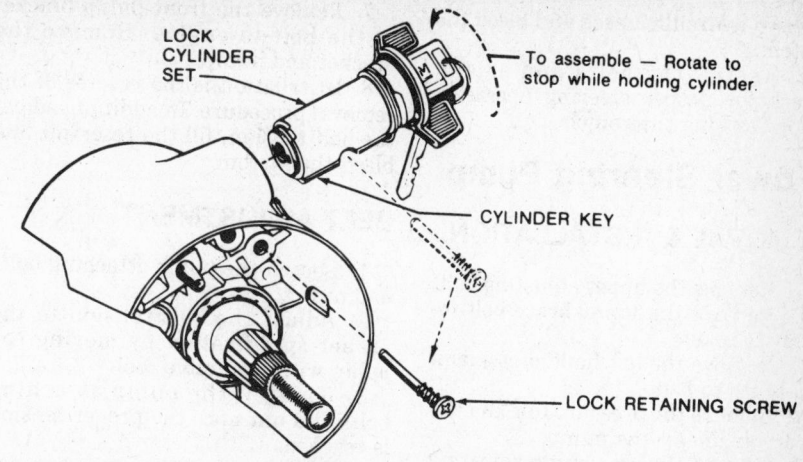

Lock cylinder installation details

to-instrument panel nuts and lower the column far enough to disconnect the ignition switch wiring harness.

CAUTION

Be sure that the steering column is properly supported before proceeding.

---

6. The switch should be in the Lock position before removal. If the lock cylinder has already been removed, the actuating rod to the switch should be pulled up until there is a definite stop, then moved down one detent to the Lock position.

7. Remove the two mounting screws and remove the ignition and dimmer switch.

8. Using the correct procedure, install the lock cylinder.

9. Turn the cylinder clockwise to stop and then counterclockwise to stop, then counterclockwise again to stop (OFF-UNLOCK) position.

10. Place the ignition switch in the OFF-UNLOCK position. Move the slider two positions to the right from ACCESSORY to the OFF-UNLOCK position.

11. Fit the actuator rod into the slider hole and install the switch on the column. Be sure to use only the correct screws. Be careful not to move the switch out of its detent.

12. Check the dimmer switch adjustment.

13. Connect the ignition switch wiring harness.

14. Loosely install the column bracket-to-instrument panel nuts.

15. Install the floor pan bracket screw and tighten it to 20 ft. lbs.

16. Tighten the column bracket-to-instrument panel nuts to 22 ft. lbs.

17. Install the steering wheel as previously outlined.

18. Connect the battery negative cable.

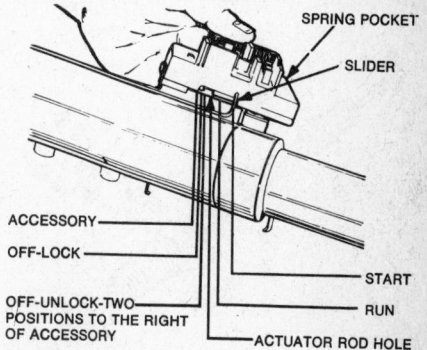

Positioning the ignition switch for installation

Steering Gear

REMOVAL & INSTALLATION

1. Raise and safely support the vehicle.

2. Remove the bolts and shield.

3. Remove the outer tie rod cotter pins and nuts on both sides.

4. Using a tie rod separating tool, disconnect the tie rods from the steering knuckles.

5. On power steering models remove the two hydraulic lines from the steering gear.

6. Remove the flexible coupling pinch bolt to the shaft.

7. Remove the four bolts at the clamps and remove the assembly from the vehicle.

8. To install, position the assembly to the vehicle with the stub shaft in position with the flexible coupling and install the clamps and four new bolts.

9. Install the flexible coupling pinch bolt to the shaft.

10. Install the tie rods into the steering knuckles and torque the nuts to 30 ft. lbs. Install a new cotter pin.

11. On power steering models install

the two hydraulic hoses and bleed the system.

12. Install the bolts and shield. Check for proper steering operation before moving the vehicle.

Power Steering Pump

REMOVAL & INSTALLATION

1. Remove the upper adjusting bolt.
2. Remove the lower brace bolt-to-pump bracket.
3. Remove the left hand crossmember brace to body.
4. Remove the pressure line and the reservoir line at the pump.
5. Remove the rear pump adjusting bracket.
6. Remove the front pivot bolt at the pump and remove the bolt.

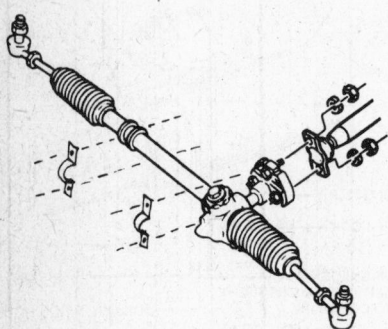

Manual rack and pinion assembly

7. Remove the front pump bracket at the bolt-to-engine. Remove the bracket and pump.
8. Installation is the reverse of the removal procedure. In addition, adjust the belt tension, fill the reservoir and bleed the system.

BELT ADJUSTMENT

1. Loosen the pump attaching bolts and nut.
2. Adjust the belt tension to the proper specification by moving the pump with a suitable tool.
3. Tighten the pump attaching bolts and nut once the proper tension is reached.
4. Run the engine to assure proper operation.

SYSTEM BLEEDING

NOTE: When checking or adjusting the fluid level after service, air must be bled from the system using the following procedure.

1. Install the pump, bracket and all hoses and lines to specifications, EXCEPT the pressure line at the pump outlet.
2. Add fluid to the reservoir until fluid begins leaving the pump at the pressure fittings.

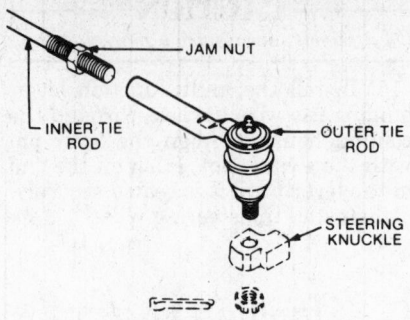

Tie rod end assembly

3. Attach the pressure line to the pump.
4. Continue filling the reservoir until the proper level is reached.
5. Road test the vehicle to make sure the steering system functions normally.
6. Recheck the fluid level and top up as necessary with power steering fluid.

Tie Rod Ends

REMOVAL & INSTALLATION

1. Loosen the jam nut located on the inner tie rod.
2. Remove the outer tie rod cotter pin and nut.
3. Using a tie rod end separating tool, remove the tie rod from the steering knuckle.
4. Remove the outer tie rod from the inner tie rod assembly. Count the number of turns it takes to remove the tie rod end.
5. Install the new outer tie rod end onto the inner tie rod assembly, turning it in the same number of turns as the old tie rod took to remove. Do not tighten the jam nut.
6. Install the outer tie rod into the steering knuckle and torque the nut to 32 ft. lbs. Install a new cotter pin.
7. Set toe-in adjustment to specification by turning the inner tie rod (an alignment rack is necessary for adjustment). Be sure not to twist the boot when making the adjustment. If an alignment rack is not available, tighten the jam nut and have the front end alignment checked as soon as possible.
8. Torque the jam nut to 50 ft. lbs.

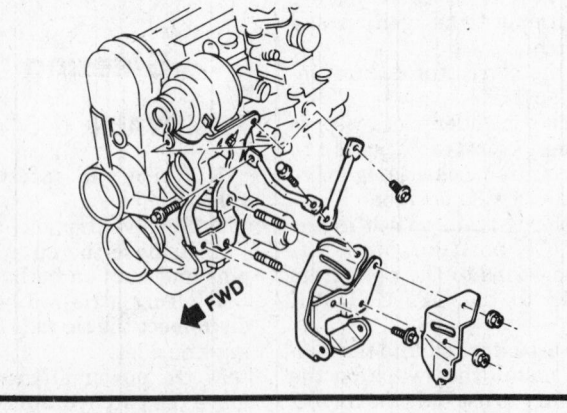

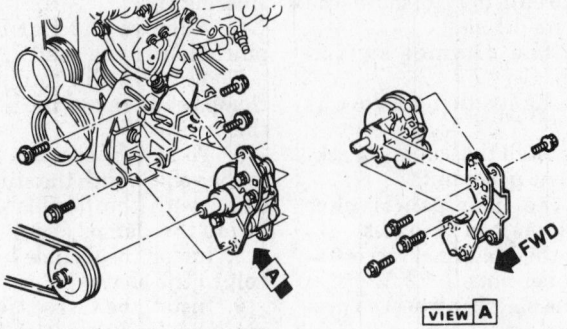

Power steering pump mounting—gasoline engine

BRAKES

For all brake system repair and service procedures not detailed below, please refer to "Brakes" in the Unit Repair section.

Master Cylinder

REMOVAL & INSTALLATION

1. Disconnect the master cylinder pushrod from the brake pedal.
2. Remove the pushrod boot.
3. Remove the air cleaner.
4. Thoroughly clean all dirt from the master cylinder and the brake lines. Disconnect the brake lines from the master cylinder and plug them to prevent the entry of dirt.
5. Remove the master cylinder securing nuts and remove the master cylinder.
6. Install the master cylinder with its spacer. Tighten the securing nuts.
7. Connect the brake lines to their ports.
8. Place the pushrod boot over the end of the pushrod. Secure the pushrod to the brake pedal with the pin and clip.
9. Fill the master cylinder and bleed the entire hydraulic system. After bleeding, fill the master cylinder to within ¼ in. from the top of the reservoir. Check for leaks.
10. Install the air cleaner.
11. Check brake operation before moving the car.

Combination Valve

REMOVAL & INSTALLATION

NOTE: If the combination valve is found defective it must be replaced.

1. Disconnect the negitive battery cable.
2. Clean all the dirt from the switch and connections.
3. Disconnect he electrical lead from the switch connection.
4. Disconnect the hydraulic lines from the connections at the switch. It may be necessary to loosen the line conncections at the master cylinder to loosen lines. Cover the open ends with a clean, lint-free rag.
5. Remove the mounting screw and remove the combination valve.
6. Installation is the reverse of removal. Bleed the brake system.

Power Brake Booster

REMOVAL & INSTALLATION

1. Remove the air cleaner.
2. Disconnect the vacuum hose from the check valve.
3. Remove the master cylinder brace.
4. Remove the master cylinder-to-power cylinder nut and pull forward

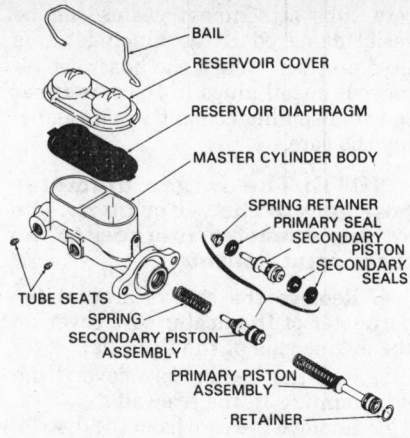

BAIL
RESERVOIR COVER
RESERVOIR DIAPHRAGM
MASTER CYLINDER BODY
SPRING RETAINER
PRIMARY SEAL
SECONDARY PISTON
SECONDARY SEALS
TUBE SEATS
SPRING
SECONDARY PISTON ASSEMBLY
PRIMARY PISTON ASSEMBLY
RETAINER

Dual master cylinder with common reservoir

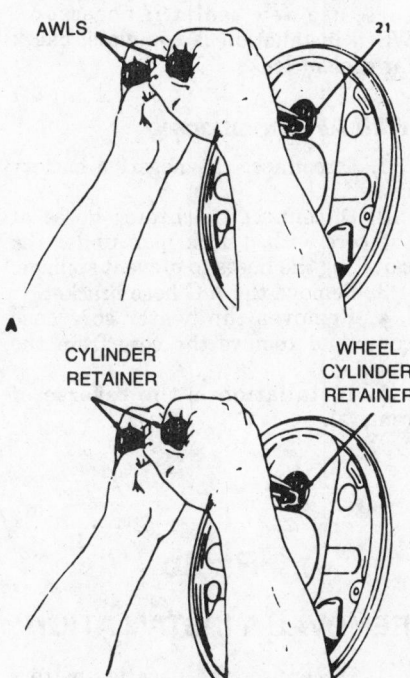

AWLS   21

CYLINDER RETAINER   WHEEL CYLINDER RETAINER

Wheel cylinder removal

on the master cylinder until it clears the power cylinder mounting studs. Move the master cylinder aside and support it, being careful of the brake lines.
5. Remove the nuts securing the power cylinder to the firewall.
6. Remove the pushrod-to-pedal retainer and slip the pushrod off the pedal pin. Remove the power cylinder.
7. Installation is the reverse of removal.

Wheel Cylinder

REMOVAL & INSTALLATION

1. Clean the area around the inlet tube line and disconnect the tube line.

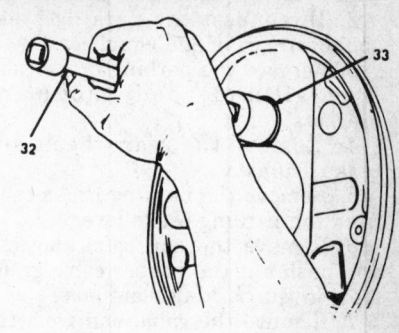

33
32

B

1 1/8 IN.
12 PT. SOCKET

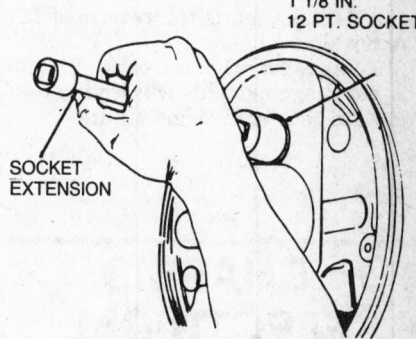

SOCKET EXTENSION

Wheel cylinder installation

2. Remove the wheel cylinder retainer by inserting two awls into the access slots between the wheel cylinder pilot and the retainer locking tabs. Bend both tabs away simutaneously and remove.
3. Place the wheel cylinder into position and hold in place using a wooden block between the cylinder and axle flange.
4. Use a 1⅛ in., 12 point socket and socket extension to aid in installing a new retainer over the wheel cylinder abutment.
5. Connect the inlet tube and torque the nut to 120–180 inch lbs.

Parking Brake Cable

ADJUSTMENT

1. Raise and safely support the vehicle on a hoist.
2. Apply the parking brake three notches from the fully released position.
3. Tighten the parking brake cable equalizer adjusting nut under the vehicle until a light drag is felt when the rear wheels are rotated forward.
4. Fully release the parking brake and rotate the rear wheels. There should be no drag.
5. Lower the car.

REMOVAL & INSTALLATION

1. Raise and safely support the vehicle.

2. Disconnect the parking brake equalizer spring and equalizer.

3. Remove the parking brake cable from all underbody mounting brackets.

4. Remove the rear wheels and brake drums.

5. Remove the parking brake cable from the parking brake lever.

6. Remove the spring locking clip and push out the rubber cable grommets in the backing plate hole.

7. Remove the cable end from the backing plate.

8. Installation is the reverse of the removal.

9. Make sure that the parking brake is not dragging. This will lead to premature rear brake shoe failure.

CHASSIS ELECTRICAL

Heater Blower

REMOVAL & INSTALLATION

1. Disconnect the negative battery cable.

2. Disconnect the electrical lead from the blower motor.

3. Scribe a mark to reference the blower motor flange-to-case position.

4. Remove the blower motor-to-case attaching screws and remove the blower motor and wheel as an assembly. Pry the flange gently if the sealer acts as an adhesive.

5. Remove the blower wheel retaining nut and separate the motor and wheel.

6. Reverse Steps 1–5 to install. Be sure to align the scribe marks made during removal.

NOTE: Assemble the blower wheel to the motor with the open end of the wheel away from the motor. If necessary, replace the sealer at the motor flange.

Heater Core

REMOVAL & INSTALLATION

Without Air Conditioning

1. Disconnect the negative battery cable.

2. Drain the radiator.

3. Disconnect the heater hoses at the heater core tube connections. Use care when removing the hoses as the core tube attachment seams can be easily damaged if too much force is used on them. When the hoses are removed, install plugs in the core tubes to avoid spilling coolant when removing the core.

NOTE: The larger diameter hose goes to the water pump: the smaller diameter hose goes to the thermostat housing.

4. Remove the screws around the perimeter of the heater core cover on the engine side of the firewall.

5. Pull the heater core cover from its mounting in the firewall.

6. Remove the core from the distributor assembly.

7. Reverse the removal procedure to install. Be sure that the core-to-case sealer is intact before replacing the core; use new sealer if necessary. When installation is complete, check for coolant leaks.

With Air Conditioning

1. Disconnect the negative battery cable.

2. Disconnect the heater hoses at the core with a drain pan under the car. Plug the hoses to prevent spillage.

3. Remove the A/C hose bracket.

4. Removes the heater core case cover and remove the core from the case.

5. Installation is the reverse of removal.

Radio

REMOVAL & INSTALLATION

1. Disconnect the negative battery cable.

2. Remove the nut from the mounting stud on the bottom of the radio.

3. Remove all control knobs and/or spacers from the right and left radio control shafts.

4. Remove the four screws from the center trim plate and pull the trim plate and the radio forward slightly.

5. Disconnect the antenna lead from the rear of the radio.

6. Disconnect the speaker and electrical connectors from the radio harness.

7. Disconnect the electrical connectors from the rear window defogger and cigarette lighter.

8. Use a deep well socket to remove the retaining nuts from both control shafts and remove the radio.

9. To install, reverse the removal procedure.

Windshield Wiper Switch

REMOVAL & INSTALLATION

1. Remove the steering wheel and the ignition and dimmer switch as outlined in the "Steering" section.

2. Remove the parts as shown in the illustration.

3. On models equipped with the standard column, assemble the rack so that the first rack tooth engages between the first and second tooth of the sector. The remainder of the installation is the reverse of removal.

Windshield Wiper Motor

REMOVAL & INSTALLATION

1. Working inside the car, reach up under the instrument panel above the steering column and loosen, but do not remove, the transmission drive link-to-motor crank arm attaching nuts.

2. Disconnect the transmission drive link from the wiper rotor crank arm.

3. Raise the hood and disconnect the wiper motor wiring.

4. Remove the three motor attaching bolts.

5. Remove the motor while guiding the crank arm through the hole.

6. To install, align the sealing gasket to the base of the motor and reverse the rest of the removal procedure.

NOTE: If the wiper motor-to-firewall sealing gasket is damaged during removal, it should be replaced with a new gasket to prevent possible water leaks.

Instrument Cluster

REMOVAL & INSTALLATION

The instrument cluster must be removed to replace light bulbs, gauges and printed circuit board.

1. Disconnect the negative battery cable.

2. Remove the clock stem knob (if equipped).

3. Remove the four screws and remove the instrument cluster bezel and lens.

4. Remove the two nuts securing the instrument cluster to the instru-

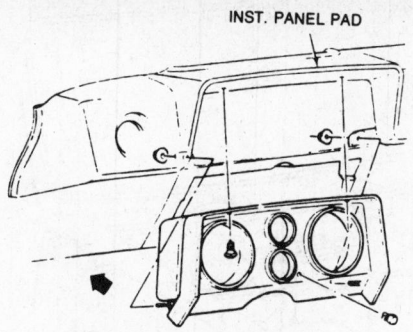

INST. PANEL PAD

Instrument cluster mounting

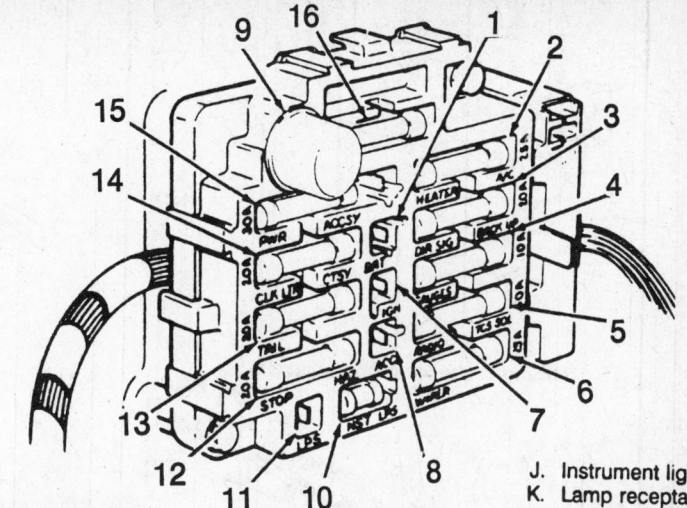

A. Battery receptacle
B. Heater/air conditioner
C. Directional signal/ backup lamp
D. Gauges
E. Radio/TCS solenoid
F. Windshield wipers
G. Ignition receptacle
H. Accessory receptacle
I. Hazard flasher
J. Instrument lights
K. Lamp receptacle
L. Stop/hazard warning lamps
M. Tail lamp
N. Clock/lighter/courtesy lamps
P. Power accessory fuse/

Fuse panel and fuse locations

ment panel and pull the cluster slightly forward.

5. Disconnect the electrical connector and speedometer cable from the cluster and remove it.

6. Attach the speedometer cable to the rear of the speedometer.

7. Installation is the reverse of removal procedures.

Headlight Switch

REMOVAL & INSTALLATION

1. Disconnect the negative battery cable.

2. Pull the headlight switch control knob to the On position.

3. Reach up under the instrument panel and depress the switch shaft retainer button while pulling on the switch control shaft knob.

4. Remove the three screws and remove the headlight switch trim plate.

5. Remove the light switch ferrule nut from the front of the instrument panel.

6. Disconnect the multi-contact connector from the bottom of the headlight switch.

7. Installation is the reverse of removal.

Stoplight Switch

REMOVAL & INSTALLATION

1. Locate the stoplight switch under the instrument panel on the brake pedal support.

2. Disconnect the wire harness at the switch.

3. Remove the switch from the mounting bracket.

4. Press the new switch into the clip until the shoulder of the switch bottoms out against the clip.

5. Adjust the switch by pulling the brake pedal back to its normal position.

6. Check the operation of the switch. Contact should be made when the brake pedal is depressed 13.5mm (0.53 in.).

Fuses and Circuit Breakers

LOCATION

The fuse panel is located under the left

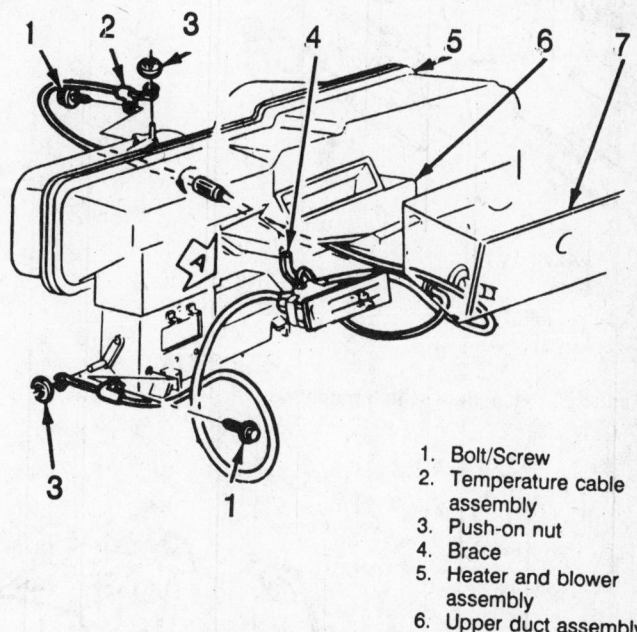

1. Bolt/Screw
2. Temperature cable assembly
3. Push-on nut
4. Brace
5. Heater and blower assembly
6. Upper duct assembly
7. Glove box

Heater and A/C case position

hand side of the instrument panel. The fuse amperage and the circuit protected is marked on the fuse panel. The headlight circuit is protected by a circuit breaker in the light switch. An electrical overload will cause the lights to go on and off, or in some case to remain off. If this condition develops, check the wiring circuits immediately. An air conditioning high blower speed fuse, 30 amp, is located in an in-line fuse holder running from the junction block to the air conditioning relay.

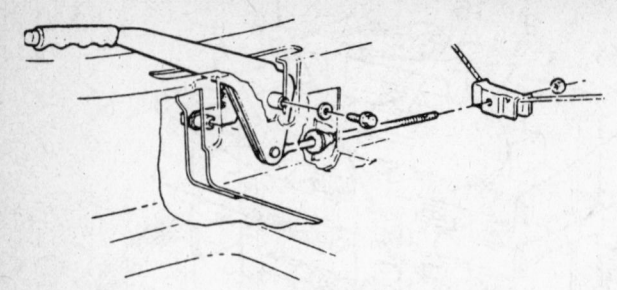

Parking brake lever and adjuster

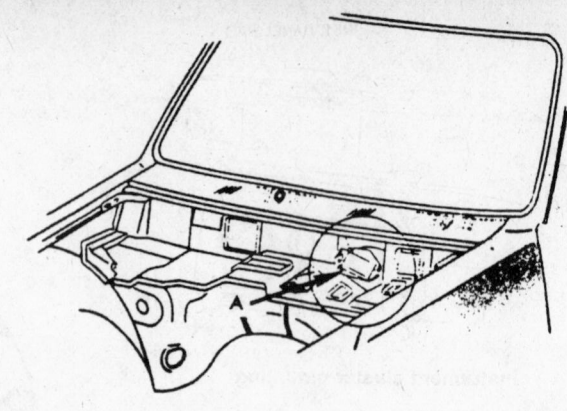

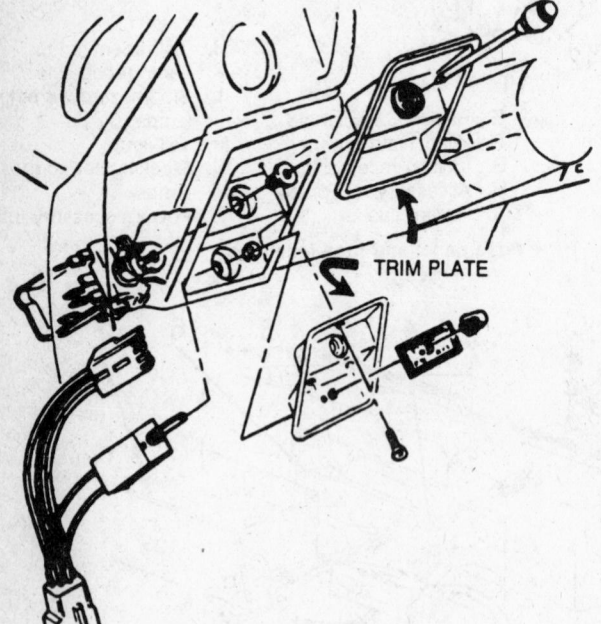

Headlight switch mounting

TRIM PLATE

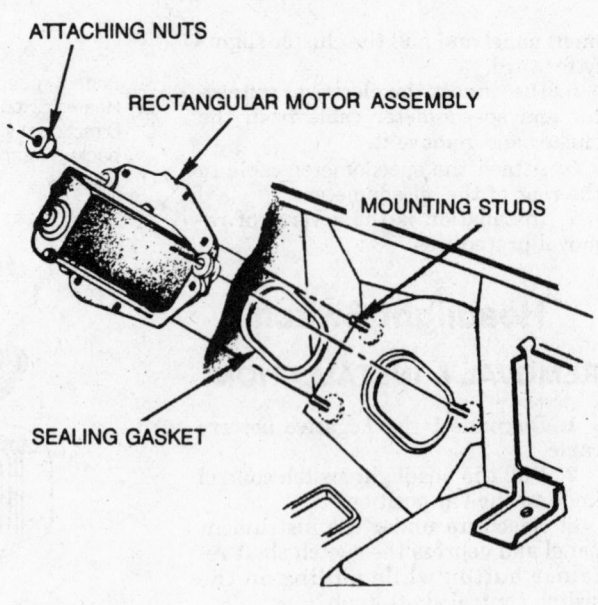

ATTACHING NUTS

RECTANGULAR MOTOR ASSEMBLY

MOUNTING STUDS

SEALING GASKET

Windshield wiper motor mounting and location

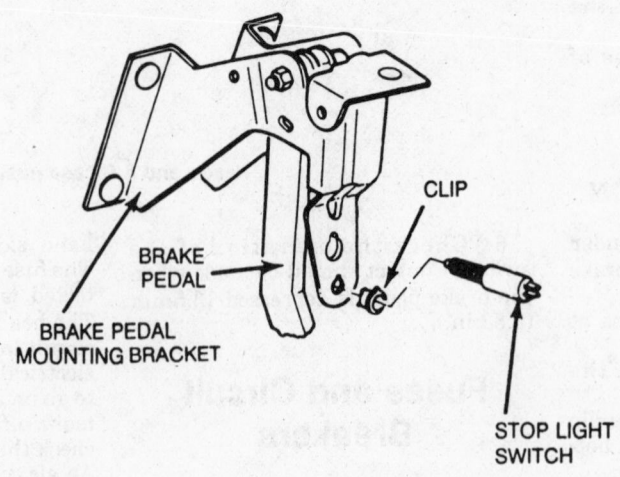

CLIP

BRAKE
PEDAL

BRAKE PEDAL
MOUNTING BRACKET

STOP LIGHT
SWITCH

Stop light switch mounting

Oldsmobile/Pontiac

Rear Wheel Drive

Oldsmobile — Cutlass Supreme, Custom Cruiser, Delta 88, Ninety Eight
Pontiac — Bonneville, Grand Am, Grand Prix, Parisienne

18

SERIAL NUMBER IDENTIFICATION

VEHICLE IDENTIFICATION CHART

It is important for servicing and ordering parts to be certain of the vehicle and engine identification. The VIN (vehicle identification number) is a 17 digit number visible through the windshield on the driver's side of the dash and contains the vehicle and engine identification codes. The tenth digit indicates model year, and the eigth digit indicates engine code. It can be interpreted as follows:

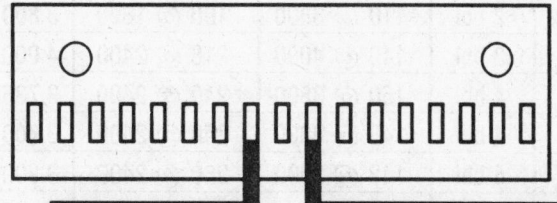

Engine Code						Model Year	
Code	Cu. In.	Liters	Cyl.	Fuel Sys.	Eng. Mfg.	Code	Year
A	231	3.8	6	2 bbl	Buick	C	1982
4	252	4.1	6	2 bbl.	Buick	D	1983
F	260	4.3	8	2bbl.	Olds	E	1984
8	260	4.3	8	2bbl.	Olds	F	1985
Z	262	4.3	6	2 bbl	Chevy	G	1986
V	263	4.3	6	Diesel	Olds	H	1987
S	265	4.3	8	2 bbl.	Pont	J	1988
W	301	4.9	8	4 bbl.	Pont	K	1989
H	305	5.0	8	4 bbl.	Chev		
Y	307	5.0	8	4bbl.	Olds		
9	307	5.0	8	4bbl.	Olds		
N	350	5.7	8	Diesel	Olds		

GENERAL ENGINE SPECIFICATIONS

Year	VIN	No. Cylinder Displacement cu. in. (liter)	Fuel System Type	Net Horsepower @ rpm	Net Torque @ rpm (ft.lbs.)	Bore × Stroke (in.)	Compression Ratio	Oil Pressure @ rpm
1982	A	6-231 (3.8)	2 bbl	110 @ 3800	190 @ 1600	3.800 × 3.400	8.0:1	37 @ 2000
	4	6-252 (4.1)	4 bbl	125 @ 4000	205 @ 2000	3.965 × 3.400	8.0:1	37 @ 2400
	8	8-260 (4.3)	2 bbl	105 @ 3600	205 @ 1800	3.500 × 3.385	7.5:1	40 @ 1500
	V	6-263 (4.3)	Diesel	85 @ 3600	165 @ 1600	4.057 × 3.385	21.6:1	40 @ 2000
	Y	8-307 (5.0)	4 bbl	148 @ 3800	250 @ 2400	3.800 × 3.385	8.0:1	30 @ 1500
	N	8-350 (5.7)	Diesel	125 @ 3600	225 @ 1600	4.057 × 3.385	22.5:1	40 @ 1500
1983	A	6-231 (3.8)	2 bbl	110 @ 3800	190 @ 1600	3.800 × 3.400	8.0:1	37 @ 2000
	4	6-252 (4.1)	4 bbl	125 @ 4000	205 @ 2000	3.965 × 3.400	8.0:1	37 @ 2400
	V	6-263 (4.3)	Diesel	85 @ 3600	165 @ 1600	4.057 × 3.385	21.6:1	40 @ 2000
	H	8-305 (5.0)	4 bbl	150 @ 3800	240 @ 2400	3.736 × 3.480	8.6:1	45 @ 2000
	Y	8-307 (5.0)	4 bbl	148 @ 3800	250 @ 2400	3.800 × 3.385	8.0:1	30 @ 1500
	N	8-350 (5.7)	Diesel	125 @ 3600	225 @ 1600	4.057 × 3.385	22.5:1	40 @ 1500
1984	A	6-231 (3.8)	2 bbl	110 @ 3800	190 @ 1600	3.800 × 3.400	8.0:1	37 @ 2000
	4	6-252 (4.1)	4 bbl	125 @ 4000	205 @ 2000	3.965 × 3.400	8.0:1	37 @ 2400
	V	6-263 (4.3)	Diesel	85 @ 3600	165 @ 1600	4.057 × 3.385	21.6:1	40 @ 2000
	H	8-305 (5.0)	4 bbl	150 @ 3800	240 @ 2400	3.736 × 3.480	8.6:1	45 @ 2000
	Y	8-307 (5.0)	4 bbl	148 @ 3800	250 @ 2400	3.800 × 3.385	8.0:1	30 @ 1500
	N	8-350 (5.7)	Diesel	125 @ 3600	225 @ 1600	4.057 × 3.385	22.5:1	40 @ 1500
1985	A	6-231 (3.8)	2 bbl	110 @ 3800	190 @ 1600	3.800 × 3.400	8.0:1	37 @ 2000
	Z	6-262 (4.3)	2 bbl	140 @ 4000	218 @ 2400	4.000 × 3.480	9.3:1	57 @ 2000
	H	8-305 (5.0)	4 bbl	150 @ 3800	240 @ 2400	3.736 × 3.480	9.5:1	45 @ 2000
	Y	8-307 (5.0)	4 bbl	148 @ 3800	250 @ 2400	3.800 × 3.385	8.0:1	30 @ 1500
	9	8-307 (5.0)	4 bbl	148 @ 3800	250 @ 2400	3.800 × 3.385	8.0:1	30 @ 1500
	N	8-350 (5.7)	Diesel	125 @ 3600	225 @ 1600	4.057 × 3.385	22.5:1	40 @ 1500
1986	A	6-231 (3.8)	2 bbl	110 @ 3800	190 @ 1600	3.800 × 3.385	8.0:1	37 @ 2000
	Z	6-262 (4.3)	2 bbl	140 @ 4000	225 @ 2200	4.000 × 3.480	9.3:1	45 @ 2000
	H	8-305 (5.0)	4 bbl	150 @ 4200①	235 @ 2000②	3.736 × 3.480	9.5:1	45 @ 2000
	Y	8-307 (5.0)	4 bbl	148 @ 3800	250 @ 2400	3.800 × 3.385	8.0:1	30 @ 1500
	9	8-307 (5.0)	4 bbl	148 @ 3800	250 @ 2400	3.800 × 3.385	8.0:1	30 @ 1500
1987	A	6-231 (3.8)	2 bbl	110 @ 3800	190 @ 1600	3.800 × 3.385	8.0:1	37 @ 2000
	H	8-305 (5.0)	4 bbl	150 @ 4200①	235 @ 2000②	3.736 × 3.480	9.5:1	45 @ 2000
	Y	8-307 (5.0)	4 bbl	148 @ 3800	250 @ 2400	3.800 × 3.385	8.0:1	30 @ 1500
	9	8-307 (5.0)	4 bbl	148 @ 3800	250 @ 2400	3.800 × 3.385	8.0:1	30 @ 1500
1988-89	Y	8-307 (5.0)	4 bbl	148 @ 3800	250 @ 2400	3.800 × 3.385	7.99:1	30 @ 1500

TBI Throttle Body Injection
① Parisienne: 165 hp
② Parisienne: 245 @ 2400

GASOLINE ENGINE TUNE-UP SPECIFICATIONS

Year	VIN	No. Cylinder Displacement cu. in. (liter)	Spark Plugs Type	Gap (in.)	Ignition Timing (deg.) MT	AT	Compression Pressure (psi)	Fuel Pump (psi)	Idle Speed (rpm) MT	AT	Valve Clearance In.	Ex.
1982	A	6-231 (3.8)	R-45TX④	.040	—	①	③	4.25-5.75	—	①	Hyd.	Hyd.
	4	6-252 (4.1)	R-45TX④	.040	—	①	③	4.25-5.75	—	①	Hyd.	Hyd.
	8	8-260 (4.3)	R-46SX	.080	—	①	③	5.5-6.5	—	①	Hyd.	Hyd.
	Y	8-307 (5.0)	R-46SX	.080	—	①	③	6-7.5	—	①	Hyd.	Hyd.
1983	A	6-231 (3.8)	R-45TX④	.040	—	①	③	4.25-5.75	—	①	Hyd.	Hyd.
	4	6-252 (4.1)	R-45TX	.040	—	①	③	4.25-5.75	—	①	Hyd.	Hyd.
	H	8-305 (5.0)	R-45TS	.045	—	①	③	5.5-7.0	—	①	Hyd.	Hyd.
	Y	8-307 (5.0)	R-46SX	.080	—	①	③	6-7.5	—	①	Hyd.	Hyd.
1984	A	6-231 (3.8)	R-45TX	.040	—	①	③	4.25-5.75	—	①	Hyd.	Hyd.
	4	6-252 (4.1)	R-45TX	.040	—	①	③	4.25-5.75	—	①	Hyd.	Hyd.
	H	8-305 (5.0)	R-45TS	.045	—	①	③	5.5-7.0	—	①	Hyd.	Hyd.
	Y	8-307 (5.0)	R-46SX	.080	—	①	③	6-7.5	—	①	Hyd.	Hyd.
1985	A	6-231 (3.8)	R-45TX⑤	.040	—	①	③	4.25-5.75	—	①	Hyd.	Hyd.
	Z	6-262 (4.3)	R-43CTS	.035	—	①	③	12.0	—	①	Hyd.	Hyd.
	H	8-305 (5.0)	R-45TS	.045	—	①	③	5.5-7.0	—	①	Hyd.	Hyd.
	Y	8-307 (5.0)	R-46SX	.080	—	①	③	6-7.5	—	①	Hyd.	Hyd.
	9	8-307 (5.0)	FR3LS	.060	—	20B	③	5.5-6.5	—	600	Hyd.	Hyd.
1986	A	6-231 (3.8)	R-45TSX	.060	—	15B	③	5.5-6.5	—	①	Hyd.	Hyd.
	Z	6-262 (4.3)	R-43TS	.035	—	①	③	12.0	—	①	Hyd.	Hyd.
	H	8-305 (5.0)	R-45TS	.045	—	①	③	5.5-7.0	—	①	Hyd.	Hyd.
	Y	8-307 (5.0)	FR3LS6⑥	.060	—	20B	③	5.5-6.5	—	600	Hyd.	Hyd.
	9	8-307 (5.0)	FR3LS	.060	—	20B	③	5.5-6.5	—	600	Hyd.	Hyd.
1987	A	6-231 (3.8)	R-45TSX	.060	—	15B	③	5.5-6.5	—	①	Hyd.	Hyd.
	H	8-305 (5.0)	R-45TS	.045	—	①	③	5.5-7.0	—	①	Hyd.	Hyd.
	Y	8-307 (5.0)	FR3LS6⑥	.060	—	20B	③	5.5-6.5	—	600	Hyd.	Hyd.
	9	8-307 (5.0)	FR3LS	.060	—	20B	③	5.5-6.5	—	600	Hyd.	Hyd.
1988	Y	8-307 (5.0)	FR3LS6⑥	.060	—	20B	③	5.5-6.5	—	600	Hyd.	Hyd.
1989		SEE UNDERHOOD SPECIFICATIONS STICKER										

NOTE: The underhood specification sticker often reflects tune-up changes made in production. Sticker figures must be used if they disagree with those in this chart. Part numbers in this chart are not recommendations by Chilton for any product by brand name.
B — Before Top Dead Center
— Not Applicable
① See underhood sticker
② Station wagon — 18B @ 1100
③ The lowest reading should not be less than 70% of the highest and no reading should be under 100 psi
④ Pontiac: R-45TS8; 0.080
⑤ Pontiac: R-45TSX; 0.060
⑥ Pontiac: R-46SX; 0.080

DIESEL ENGINE TUNE-UP SPECIFICATIONS

Year	VIN	No. Engine Displacement cu. in. (liter)	Valve Clearance		Intake Valve Opens (deg.)	Injection Pump Setting (deg.)	Injection Nozzle Pressure (psi)		Idle Speed (rpm)	Cranking Compression Pressure (psi)
			Intake (in.)	Exhaust (in.)			New	Used		
1982	V	6-260 (4.3)	Hyd.	Hyd.	NA	NA	1000	800	①	NA
	N	8-350 (5.7)	Hyd.	Hyd.	16	NA	1225	1000	①	275
1983	V	6-260 (4.3)	Hyd.	Hyd.	NA	NA	1000	800	①	NA
	N	8-350 (5.7)	Hyd.	Hyd.	16	NA	1225	1000	①	275
1984	V	6-260 (4.3)	Hyd.	Hyd.	NA	NA	1000	800	①	NA
	N	8-350 (5.7)	Hyd.	Hyd.	NA	NA	1225	1000	①	275
1985	N	8-350 (5.7)	Hyd.	Hyd.	NA	NA	1225	1000	①	275

NOTE: The underhood specifications sticker often reflects changes made in production. Sticker figures must be used if they disagree with those in this chart.

① See underhood specifications sticker

FIRING ORDER

NOTE: To avoid confusion, always replace spark plug wires one at a time.

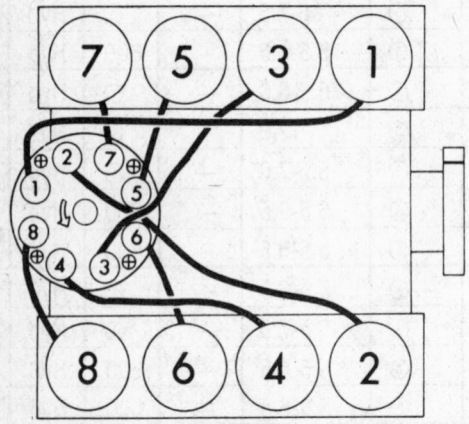

GM (Oldsmobile) 260 V8
Engine firing order: 1-8-4-3-6-5-7-2
Distributor rotation: counterclockwise

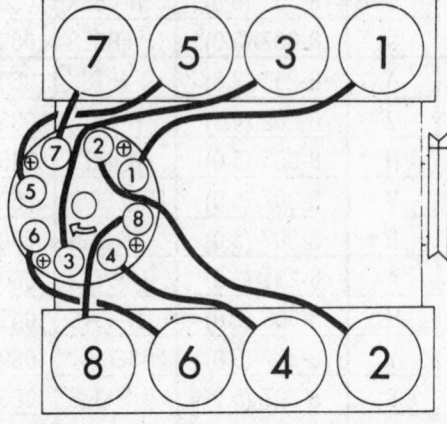

GM (Oldsmobile) 260, 307, 350 V8 GM (Pontiac) 301 V8 Engine firing order: 1–8–4–3–6–5–7–2

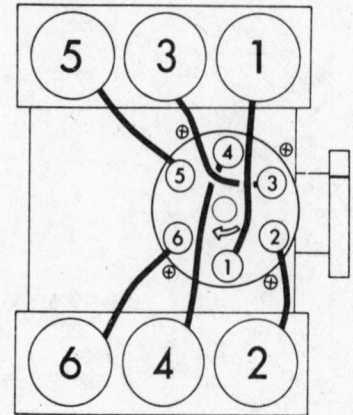

GM (Buick) 231, 252 V6 (3.2 L, 3.8 L, 4.1 L)
Engine firing order: 1–6–5–4–3–2
Distributor rotation: clockwise

V6 harmonic balancers have two timing marks: one is 1/8 in. wide, and one is 1/16 in. wide. Use the 1/16 in. mark for timing with a hand held light. The 1/8 in. mark is used only with a magnetic timing pick-up probe.

CAPACITIES

Year	VIN	No. Cylinder Displacement cu. in. (liter)	Engine Crankcase with Filter	without Fil000024T	Transmission (pts.) AT	(pts.)	Drive Axle (gals.)	Fuel Tank (qts.)	Cooling System
1982	A	6-231 (3.8)	5	4	3	7②	④	③	13.3
	4	6-252 (4.1)	5	4	3	7②	④	③	13.3
	8	8-260 (4.3)	5	4	—	7②	④	③	20.0
	Y	8-307 (5.0)	5	4	—	7②	④	③	15.5
	V	6-260 (4.3)	6①	—	—	7②	④	③	—
	N	8-350 (5.7)	7①	—	—	7②	④	20.0③	18
1983	A	6-231 (3.8)	5	4	—	7②	④	③	13.3
	4	6-252 (4.1)	5	4	—	7②	④	③	13.3
	V	6-260 (4.3)	6①	—	—	7②	④	③	12.9
	H	8-305 (5.0)	5	4	—	6②	④	17.5③	16.1
	Y	8-307 (5.0)	5	4	—	7②	④	③	15.5
	N	8-350 (5.7)	7①	—	—	7②	④	③	18
1984	A	6-231 (3.8)	5	4	—	7②	④	③	13.3
	4	6-252 (4.1)	5	4	—	7②	④	③	13.3
	V	6-260 (4.3)	6①	—	—	7②	④	③	12.9
	H	8-305 (5.0)	5	4	—	6②	④	18.1③	16.1
	Y	8-307 (5.0)	5	4	—	7②	④	③	15.5
	N	8-350 (5.7)	7①	—	—	7②	④	③	18
1985	A	6-231 (3.8)	5	4	—	7	④	③	13
	Z	8-262 (4.3)	5	4	—	7②	④	③	12.0
	H	8-305 (5.0)	5	4	—	6②	④	18.1③	16.1
	Y	8-307 (5.0)	5	4	—	7	④	③	15.5
	9	8-307 (5.0)	5	4	—	7	④	③	15.5
	N	8-350 (5.7)	7①	—	—	7	④	③	18
1986	A	6-231 (3.80)	5	4	—	7	④	③	13.5
	Z	8-262 (4.3)	5	4	—	7②	④	③	12.0
	H	8-305 (5.0)	5	4	—	6②	④	18.1③	16.1
	Y	8-307 (5.0)	5	4	—	7	④	③	15.5
	9	8-307 (5.0)	5	4	—	7	④	③	15.5
1987	A	6-231 (3.8)	5	4	—	7	④	③	13.5
	H	8-305 (5.0)	5	4	—	6②	④	22.0	16.1
	Y	8-307 (5.0)	5	4	—	7	④	③	15.6
	9	8-307 (5.0)	5	4	—	7	④	③	15.4
1988-89	Y	8-307 (5.0)	5	4	—	7	④	18.1③	15.6

① Includes mandatory filter change
② 250C – 8.0
  350C – 6.5
③ Diesel – 27.0
  Full size – 25.0
  Wagon – 22.0
④ 7.5 Ring Gear – 3.5
  8.5 Ring Gear – 4.25
  8.75 Ring Gear – 5.25

CAMSHAFT SPECIFICATIONS
All measurements given in inches.

Year	VIN	No. Cylinder Displacement cu. in. (liter)	Journal Diameter					Lobe Lift		Bearing Clearance	Camshaft End Play
			1	2	3	4	5	In.	Ex.		
1982	A	6-231 (3.8)	1.785	1.785	1.785	1.785	—	NA	NA	.0005–.0035 ①	NA
	4	6-252 (4.1)	1.785	1.785	1.785	1.785	—	NA	NA	.0005–.0035 ①	NA
	8	8-260 (4.3)	2.0361	2.0161	1.9961	1.9761	1.9561	3.96	4.00	.0039	.011–.077
	V	6-260 (4.3)	—	2.205	2.18501	2.165	—	NA	NA	.0040	.0008–.0228
	Y	8.307(5.0)	2.0361	2.0161	1.9961	1.9761	1.9561	4.00	4.00	.0039	.011–.077
	N	8-350 (5.7)	2.0361	2.0161	1.9961	1.9761	1.9561	NA	NA	.0039	.011–.077
1983	A	6-231 (3.8)	1.785	1.785	1.785	1.785	—	NA	NA	.0005–.0035 ①	NA
	4	6-252(4.1)	1.785	1.785	1.785	1.785	—	NA	NA	.0005–.0035 ①	NA
	V	6-260 (4.3)	—	2.205	2.18501	2.165	—	NA	NA	.0040	.0008–.0228
	H	8-305 (5.0)	1.8682–1.8692	1.8682–1.8692	1.8682–1.8692	1.8682–1.8692	1.8682–1.8692	.234	.257	NA	.004–.012
	Y	8-307 (5.0)	2.0361	2.0161	1.9961	1.9761	1.9561	4.00	4.00	.0039	.011–.077
	N	8-350 (5.7)	2.0361	2.0161	1.9961	1.9761	1.9561	NA	NA	.0039	.011–.077
1984	A	6-231 (3.8)	1.785	1.785	1.785	1.785	—	NA	NA	.0005–.0035 ①	NA
	4	6-252 (4.1)	1.785	1.785	1.785	1.785	—	NA	NA	.0005–.0035 ①	NA
	V	6-260 (4.3)	—	2.205	2.18501	2.165	—	NA	NA	.0040	.0008–.0228
	H	8-305 (5.0)	1.8682–1.8692	1.8682–1.8692	1.8682–1.8692	1.8682–1.8692	1.8682–1.8692	.234	.257	NA	.004–.012
	Y	8-307 (5.0)	2.0361	2.0161	1.9961	1.9761	1.9561	4.00	4.00	.0039	.011–.077
	N	8-350 (5.7)	2.0361	2.0161	1.9961	1.9761	1.9561	NA	NA	.0039	.011–.077

CAMSHAFT SPECIFICATIONS
All measurements given in inches.

Year	VIN	No. Cylinder Displacement cu. in. (liter)	Journal Diameter					Lobe Lift		Bearing Clearance	Camshaft End Play
			1	2	3	4	5	In.	Ex.		
1985	A	6-231 (3.8)	1.785	1.785	1.785	1.785	—	NA	NA	.0005–.0035 ①	NA
	Z	6-262 (4.3)	1.8682–1.8692	1.8682–1.8692	1.8682–1.8692	1.8682–1.8692	1.8682–1.8692	.234	.257	NA	.004–.012
	H	8-305 (5.0)	1.8682–1.8692	1.8682–1.8692	1.8682–1.8692	1.8682–1.8692	1.8682–1.8692	.234	.257	NA	.004–.012
	Y	8-307 (5.7)	2.0361	2.0161	1.9961	1.9761	1.9561	.247	.251	.0035	.006–.022
	9	8-307 (5.0)	2.0361	2.0161	1.9961	1.9761	1.9561	.275	.275	.0039	.006–.022
	N	8-350 (5.7)	2.0361	1.0161	1.9961	1.9761	1.9561	NA	NA	.0039	.011–.077
1986	A	6-231 (3.8)	1.785	1.785	1.785	1.785	—	NA	NA	.0005–.0035 ①	NA
	Z	6-262 (4.3)	1.8682–1.8692	1.8682–1.8692	1.8682–1.8692	1.8682–1.8692	1.8682–1.8692	.234	.257	NA	.004–.012
	H	8-305 (5.0)	1.8682–1.8692	1.8682–1.8692	1.8682–1.8692	1.8682–1.8692	1.8682–1.8692	.234	.257	NA	.004–.012
	Y	8-307 (5.0)	2.0359	2.0360	1.9959	1.9759	1.9559	.247	.251	.0038–	.006–.022
	9	8-307 (5.0)	2.0359	2.0360	1.9959	1.9759	1.9559	.272	.274	.0038–	.006–.022
1987	A	6-231 (3.8)	1.785	1.785	1.785	1.785	—	NA	NA	.0005–.0035 ①	NA
	H	8-305 (5.0)	1.8682–1.8692	1.8682–1.8692	1.8682–1.8692	1.8682–1.8692	1.8682–1.8692	.234	.257	NA	.004–.012
	Y	8-307 (5.0)	2.0359	2.0360	1.9959	1.9759	1.9559	.247	.251	.0038	.006–.022
	9	8-307 (5.0)	2.0359	2.0360	1.9959	1.9759	1.9559	.272	.274	.0038	.006–.022
1988-89	Y	8-307 (5.0)	2.0365	2.0166	1.9965	1.9765	1.9565	.251	.251	.0038	.006–.022

NA – Not available at time of publication
① No.1 – .0005-.0025

CRANKSHAFT AND CONNECTING ROD SPECIFICATIONS
All measurements are given in inches.

Year	VIN	No. Cylinder Displacement cu. in. (liter)	Crankshaft				Connecting Rod		
			Main Brg. Journal Dia.	Main Brg. Oil Clearance	Shaft End-play	Thrust on No.	Journal Diameter	Oil Clearance	Side Clearance
1982	A	6-231 (3.8)	2.4995	0.0003–0.0018	0.011–0.003	2	2.2487–2.2495	0.0005–0.0026	0.006–0.023
	4	6-252 (4.1)	2.4995	0.0003–0.0018	0.011–0.003	2	2.2487–2.2495	0.0005–0.0026	0.006–0.023
	8	8-260 (4.3)	2.4990–2.4995 ①	0.0005–0.0021 ②	0.0035–0.0135	3	2.1238–2.1248	0.0004–0.0033	0.006–0.020
	V	6-260 (4.3)	2.9993–3.0003	0.0005–0.0021 ②	0.0035–0.0135	3	2.2490–2.2510	0.0005–0.0026	0.006–0.020
	Y	8-307 (5.0)	2.4990–2.4995 ①	0.0005–0.0021 ②	0.0035–0.0135	3	2.1238–2.1238	0.0004–0.0033	0.006–0.020
	N	8-350 (5.7)	2.9993–3.0003	0.0005–0.0021 ②	0.0035 0.0135	3	2.2495–2.2500	0.0005–0.0026	0.006–0.020
1983	A	6-231 (3.8)	2.4995	0.0003–0.0018	0.011–0.003	2	2.2487–2.2495	0.0005–0.0026	0.006–0.015
	4	6-252 (4.1)	2.4995	0.0003–0.0018	0.011–0.003	2	2.2487–2.2495	0.0005–0.0026	0.006–0.015
	V	6-260 (4.3)	2.9993–3.0003	0.0005–0.0021 ①	0.0035–0.0135	3	2.2490–2.2510	0.0005–0.0026	0.006–0.020
	H	8-305 (5.0)	2.4484–2.4993 ①	0.0008–0.0020 ②	0.002–0.006	5	2.0986–2.0998	0.0013–0.0035	0.0016–0.014
	Y	8-307 (5.0)	2.4990–2.4995 ①	0.0005–0.0021 ②	0.0035–0.0135	3	2.1238–2.1248	0.0004–0.0033	0.006–0.020
	N	8-350 (5.7)	2.2993–3.0003	0.0005–0.0021 ②	0.0035–0.0135	3	2.2495–2.2500	0.0005–0.0026	0.006–0.020
1984	A	6-231 (3.8)	2.4995	0.0003–0.0018	0.011–0.003	2	2.2487–2.2495	0.0005–0.0026	0.006–0.015
	4	6-252 (4.1)	2.4995	0.0003–0.0018	0.011–0.003	2	2.2487–2.2495	0.0005–0.0026	0.006–0.015
	V	67-260 (4.3)	2.9993–3.0003	0.0005–0.0021 ②	0.0035–0.0135	3	2.2490–2.2510	0.0005–0.0026	0.006–0.020
	H	8-305 (5.0)	2.4484–2.4993 ①	0.0008–0.0020 ②	0.002–0.006	5	2.0986–2.0998	0.0013–0.0035	0.0016–0.014

CRANKSHAFT AND CONNECTING ROD SPECIFICATIONS
All measurements are given in inches.

| Year | VIN | No. Cylinder Displacement cu. in. (liter) | Crankshaft | | | | Connecting Rod | | |
			Main Brg. Journal Dia.	Main Brg. Oil Clearance	Shaft End-play	Thrust on No.	Journal Diameter	Oil Clearance	Side Clearance
1984	Y	8-307 (5.0)	2.4990–2.4995 ①	0.0005–0.0021 ②	0.0035–0.0135	3	2.1238–2.1248	0.0004–0.0033	0.006–0.020
	N	8-350 (5.7)	2.2993–3.0003	0.0005–0.0021 ②	0.0035–0.0135	3	2.2495–2.2500	0.0005–0.0026	0.006–0.020
1985	A	6-231 (3.8)	2.4995	0.0003–0.0018	0.011–0.003	2	2.2487–2.2495	0.0005–0.0026	0.006–0.015
	Z	6-262 (4.3)	2.4484–2.4993 ①	0.0008–0.0020 ②	0.002–0.006	3	2.2487–2.2498	0.0013–0.0035	0.0016–0.014
	H	8-305 (5.0)	2.4484–2.4993 ①	0.0008–0.0020 ②	0.002–0.006	5	2.0986–2.0998	0.0013–0.0035	0.0016–0.014
	Y	8-307 (5.0)	2.4990–2.4995 ①	0.0005–0.0021 ②	0.0035–0.0135	3	2.1238–2.1248	0.0004–0.0033	0.006–0.020
	9	8-307 (5.0)	2.4990–2.4995 ①	0.0005–0.0021 ②	0.0035–0.0135	3	2.1238–2.2500	0.0004–0.0026	0.006–0.015
	N	8-350 (5.7)	2.2993–3.0003	0.0005–0.0021 ②	0.0035–0.0135	3	2.2495–2.2500	0.0005–0.0026	0.006–0.020
1986	A	6-231 (3.8)	2.4995	0.0003–0.0018	0.011–0.003	2	2.2487–2.2495	0.0005–0.0026	0.006–0.015
	Z	6-262 (4.3)	2.4484–2.4993 ①	0.0008–0.0020 ②	0.002–0.006	3	2.2487–2.2498	0.0013–0.0035	0.0016–0.014
	H	8-305 (5.0)	2.4484–2.4993 ①	0.0008–0.0020 ②	0.002–0.006	5	2.0986–2.0998	0.0013–0.0035	0.0016–0.014
	Y	8-307 (5.0)	2.4990–2.4995 ①	0.0005–0.0021 ②	0.0035–0.0135	3	2.1238–2.1248	0.0004–0.0033	0.006–0.020
	9	8-307 (5.0)	2.4990–2.4995 ①	0.0005–0.0021 ②	0.0035–0.0135	3	2.1238–2.2500	0.0004–0.0026	0.006–0.015
1987	A	6-231 (3.8)	2.4995	0.0003–0.0018	0.011–0.003	2	2.2487–2.2495	0.0005–0.0026	0.006–0.015
	H	8-305 (5.0)	2.4484–2.4993 ①	0.0008–0.0020 ②	0.002–0.006	5	2.0986–2.0998	0.0013–0.0035	0.0016–0.014
	Y	8-307 (5.0)	2.4985–2.4995 ①	0.0005–0.0021 ②	0.0035–0.0135	3	2.1238–2.1248	0.0004–0.0033	0.006–0.020

CRANKSHAFT AND CONNECTING ROD SPECIFICATIONS
All measurements are given in inches.

Year	VIN	No. Cylinder Displacement cu. in. (liter)	Crankshaft				Connecting Rod		
			Main Brg. Journal Dia.	Main Brg. Oil Clearance	Shaft End-play	Thrust on No.	Journal Diameter	Oil Clearance	Side Clearance
1987	9	8-307 (5.0)	2.4990–2.4995 ①	0.0005–0.0021 ②	0.0035–0.0135	3	2.1238–2.1248	0.0004–0.0033	0.006–0.020
1988-89	Y	8-307 (5.0)	2.4985–2.4995 ①	0.0005–0.0021 ②	0.0035–0.0135	3	2.1238–2.1248	0.0004–0.0033	0.006–0.020

① Intermediate: 2.4481–2.4490
Rear: 2.4479–2.4488

② Intermediate: 0.0011–0.0034
Rear: 0.0015–0.0031

VALVE SPECIFICATIONS

Year	VIN	No. Cylinder Displacement cu. in. (liter)	Seat Angle (deg.)	Face Angle (deg.)	Spring Test Pressure (lbs.)	Spring Installed Height (in.)	Stem-to-Guide Clearance (in.)		Stem Diameter (in.)	
							Intake	Exhaust	Intake	Exhaust
1982	A	6-231 (3.8)	45	NA	98①	NA	.0015–.0035	.0015–.0032	.3412–.3401	.3412–.3405
	4	6-252 (4.1)	45	NA	98①	NA	.0015–.0035	.0015–.0032	.3412–.3401	.3412–.3405
	8	8-260 (4.3)	45-31	44-30	84①	1.96	.0010–.0027	.0015–.0032	.3425–.3432	.3420–.3427
	V	6-260 (4.3)	45-31	44-30	95①	2.09	.0010–.0027	.0015–.0032	.3425–.3432	.3420–.3427
	Y	8-307 (5.0)	45-31	44-30	84①	1.96	.0010–.0027	.0015–.0032	.3425–.3434	.3420–.3427
	N	8-350 (5.7)	45-31	44-30	95①	2.09	.0010–.0027	.0015–.0032	.3425–.3432	.3420–.3427
1983	A	6-231 (3.8)	45	NA	69①	NA	.0015–.0035	.0015–.0032	.3412–.3401	.3412–.3405
	4	6-252 (4.1)	45	NA	69①	NA	.0015–.0035	.0015–.0032	.3412–.3401	.3412–.3405
	V	6-260 (4.3)	45-31	44-30	95①	2.09	.0010–.0027	.0015–.0032	.3425–.3432	.3420–.3427
	H	8-305 (5.0)	46	45	84①	2.03	.0010–.0027	.0010–.0027	.3425	.3425
	Y	8-307 (5.0)	45-31	44-30①	84①②	1.96 ③	.0010–.0027	.0015–.0032	.3425–.3432	.3420–.3427
	N	8-350 (5.7)	45-31	44-30	95①	2.09	.0010–.0027	.0015–.0032	.3425–.3432	.3420–.3427

VALVE SPECIFICATIONS

Year	VIN	No. Cylinder Displacement cu. in. (liter)	Seat Angle (deg.)	Face Angle (deg.)	Spring Test Pressure (lbs.)	Spring Installed Height (in.)	Stem-to-Guide Clearance (in.)		Stem Diameter (in.)	
							Intake	Exhaust	Intake	Exhaust
1984	A	6-231 (3.8)	45-45	NA	64①	NA	.0015–.0035	.0015–.0032	.3412–.3401	.3412–.3405
	4	6-252 (4.1)	45-45	NA	64①	NA	.0015–.0035	.0015–.0032	.3412–.3401	.3412–.3405
	V	6-260 (4.3)	45-31	44-33	95①	2.09	.0010–.0027	.0015–.0032	.3425–.3432	.3420–.3428
	H	8-305 (5.0)	46	45	84①	2.03	.0010–.0027	.0010–.0027	.3425	.3425
	Y	8-307 (5.0)	45-31	44-30	84①	1.96	.0010–.0027	.0015–.0032	.3425–.3432	.3420–.3427
	N	8-350 (5.7)	45-31	44-30	95①	2.09	.0010–.0027	.0015–.0032	.3424–.3432	.3420–.3428
1985	A	6-231 (3.8)	45-45	NA	69①	NA	.0015–.0035	.0015–.0032	.3412–.3401	.3412–.3405
	Z	6-262 (4.3)	46	45	84①	1.70	.0010–.0027	.0010–.0027	.3425	.3425
	H	8-305 (5.0)	46	45	84①	2.03	.0010–.0027	.0010–.0027	.3425	.3425
	Y	8-307 (5.0)	45-59	46-60	84①	1.96	.0010–.0027	.0015–.0032	.3425–.3432	.3420–.3427
	9	8-307 (5.0)	45-59	46-60	95①	2.09	.0010–.0027	.0015–.0032	.3425–.3432	.3420–.3427
	N	8-350 (5.7)	45-31	44-30	95①	2.09	.0010–.0027	.0015–.0032	.3424–.3432	.3420–.3428
1986	A	6-231 (3.8)	45-45	NA	72①	NA	.0015–.0035	.0015–.0032	.3412–.3401	.3412–.3405
	Z	6-262 (4.3)	46	45	84①	1.70	.0010–.0027	.0010–.0027	.3425	.3425
	H	8-305 (5.0)	46	45	84①	2.03	.0010–.0027	.0010–.0027	.3425	.3425
	Y	8-307 (5.0)	45-59	46-60	84①	1.96	.0010–.0027	.0015–.0032	.3425–.3432	.3420–.3427
	9	8-307 (5.0)	45-59	46-60	95①	2.09	.0010–.0027	.0015–.0032	.3425–.3432	.3420–.3427
1987	A	6-231 (3.8)	45-45	NA	72①	NA	.0015–.0035	.0015–.0032	.3412–.3401	.3412–.3401
	H	8-305 (5.0)	46	45	84①	2.03	.0010–.0027	.0010–.0027	.3425	.3425
	Y	8-307 (5.0)	45	44	84①	1.96	.0010–.0027	.0015–.0032	.3425–.3432	.3420–.3427
	9	8-307 (5.0)	45	44	95①	2.09	.0010–.0027	.0015–.0032	.3425–.3432	.3420–.3427
1988-89	Y	8-307 (5.0)	45	44	84①	1.96	.0010–.0027	.0015–.0032	.3425–.3432	.3420–.3427

NA—Not available ① with valve closed ② Hurst Olds–95 ③ Hurst Olds–2.09

PISTON AND RING SPECIFICATIONS
All measurments are given in inches.

Year	VIN	No. Cylinder Displacement cu. in. (liter)	Piston Clearance	Ring Gap			Ring Side Clearance		
				Top Compression	Bottom Compression	Oil Control	Top Compression	Bottom Compression	Oil Control
1982	A	6-231 (3.8)	0.0016–0.0038	0.013–0.023	0.013–0.023	0.015–0.055	0.0030–0.0050	0.0030–0.0050	0.0015–0.0035
	4	6-252 (4.1)	0.0016–0.0038	0.013–0.023	0.013–0.023	0.015–0.055	0.0030–0.0050	0.0030–0.0050	0.0015–0.0035
	8	8-260 (4.3)	0.0008–0.0018	0.010–0.020	0.010–0.020	0.015–0.035	0.0020–0.0040	0.0020–0.0040	0.005–0.011
	V	6-260 (4.3)	0.003–0.004	0.015–0.025	0.015–0.025	—	0.005–0.007	0.0018–0.0038	0.001–0.005
	Y	8-307 (5.0)	0.0008–0.0018	0.009–0.019	0.009–0.019	—	0.0020–0.0040	0.0020–0.0040	0.000–0.0035
	N	8-350 (5.7)	0.005–0.006	0.015–0.025	0.015–0.025	—	0.005–0.007	0.0018–0.0038	0.001–0.005
1983	A	6-231 (3.8)	0.0016–0.0038	0.013–0.023	0.013–0.023	0.015–0.055	0.0030–0.0050	0.0030–0.0050	0.0015–0.0035
	4	6-252 (4.1)	0.0016–0.0038	0.013–0.023	0.013–0.023	0.015–0.055	0.0030–0.0050	0.0030–0.0050	0.0015–0.0035
	V	6-260 (4.3)	0.003–0.004	0.015–0.025	0.015–0.025	—	0.005–0.007	0.0018–0.0038	0.001–0.005
	H	8-305 (5.0)	0.0007–0.0017	0.010–0.020	0.010–0.023	0.015–0.055	0.0012–0.0032	0.0012–0.0032	0.002–0.007
	Y	8-307 (5.0)	0.0008–0.0018	0.009–0.019	0.009–0.019	—	0.0020–0.0040	0.0020–0.0040	0.000–0.0035
	N	8-350 (5.7)	0.005–0.006	0.015–0.025	0.015–0.025	—	0.005–0.007	0.0018–0.0038	0.001–0.005
1984	A	6-231 (3.8)	0.0016–0.0038	0.013–0.023	0.013–0.023	0.015–0.055	0.0030–0.0050	0.0030–0.0050	0.0015–0.0035
	4	6-252 (4.1)	0.0016–0.0038	0.013–0.023	0.013–0.023	0.015–0.055	0.0030–0.0050	0.0030–0.0050	0.0015–0.0035
	V	6-260 (4.3)	0.003–0.004	0.015–0.025	0.015–0.025	—	0.005–0.007	0.0018–0.0038	0.001–0.005
	H	8-305 (5.0)	0.0007–0.0017	0.010–0.020	0.010–0.023	0.015–0.055	0.0012–0.0032	0.0012–0.0032	0.002–0.007
	Y	8-307 (5.0)	0.0008–0.0018	0.009–0.019	0.009–0.019	—	0.0020–0.0040	0.0020–0.0040	0.000–0.0035
	N	8-350 (5.7)	0.005–0.006	0.015–0.025	0.015–0.025	—	0.005–0.007	0.0018–0.0038	0.001–0.005
1985	A	6-231 (3.8)	0.0016–0.0038	0.013–0.023	0.013–0.023	0.015–0.055	0.0030–0.0050	0.0030–0.0050	0.0015–0.0035
	Z	6-262 (4.3)	0.0007–0.0017	0.010–0.020	0.010–0.023	0.015–0.055	0.0012–0.0032	0.0012–0.0032	0.002–0.007
	H	8-305 (5.0)	0.0007–0.0017	0.010–0.020	0.010–0.023	0.015–0.055	0.0012–0.0032	0.0012–0.0032	0.002–0.007
	Y	8-307 (5.0)	0.0008–0.0018	0.009–0.019	0.009–0.019	—	0.0020–0.0040	0.0020–0.0040	0.000–0.0035

PISTON AND RING SPECIFICATIONS
All measurments are given in inches.

Year	VIN	No. Cylinder Displacement cu. in. (liter)	Piston Clearance	Ring Gap			Ring Side Clearance		
				Top Compression	Bottom Compression	Oil Control	Top Compression	Bottom Compression	Oil Control
1985	9	8-307 (5.0)	0.0008– 0.0018	0.009– 0.019	0.009– 0.019	—	0.0020– 0.0040	0.0020– 0.0040	0.000– 0.0035
	N	8-350 (5.7)	0.005– 0.006	0.015– 0.025	0.015– 0.025	—	0.005– 0.007	0.0018– 0.0038	0.001– 0.005
1986	A	6-231 (3.8)	0.0012– 0.0035	0.010– 0.020	0.010– 0.020	.0015– 0.055	0.003– 0.005	0.003– 0.005	0.005– 0.009
	Z	6-262 (4.3)	0.0007– 0.0017	0.010– 0.020	0.010– 0.023	0.015– 0.055	0.0012– 0.0032	0.0012– 0.0032	0.002– 0.007
	H	8-305 (5.0)	0.0007– 0.0017	0.010– 0.020	0.010– 0.023	0.015– 0.055	0.0012– 0.0032	0.0012– 0.0032	0.002– 0.007
	Y	8-307 (5.0)	0.00075– 0.00175	0.009– 0.019	0.009– 0.019	0.015– 0.055	0.0018– 0.0038	0.0018– 0.0038	0.001– 0.005
	9	8-307 (5.0)	0.00075– 0.00175	0.009– 0.019	0.009– 0.019	0.015– 0.055	0.0018– 0.0038	0.0018– 0.0038	0.001– 0.005
1987	A	6-231 (3.8)	0.0013– 0.0035	0.010– 0.020	0.010– 0.020	0.015– 0.055	0.003– 0.005	0.003– 0.005	0.005– 0.009
	H	8-305 (5.0)	0.0007– 0.0017	0.010– 0.020	0.010– 0.023	0.015– 0.055	0.0012– 0.0032	0.0012– 0.0032	0.002– 0.007
	Y	8-307 (5.0)	0.00075– 0.00175	0.009– 0.019	0.009– 0.019	0.015– 0.055	0.0018– 0.0038	0.0018– 0.0038	0.001– 0.005
	9	8-307 (5.0)	0.00075– 0.00175	0.009– 0.019	0.009– 0.019	0.015– 0.055	0.0018– 0.0038	0.0018– 0.0038	0.001– 0.005
1988-89	Y	8-307 (5.0)	0.00075– 0.00175	0.009– 0.019	0.009– 0.019	0.015– 0.055	0.0018– 0.0038	0.0018– 0.0038	0.001– 0.005

TORQUE SPECIFICATIONS
All readings in ft. lbs.

Year	VIN	No. Cylinder Displacement cu. in. (liter)	Cylinder Head Bolts	Main Bearing Bolts	Rod Bearing Bolts	Crankshaft Pulley Bolts	Flywheel Bolts	Manifold		Spark Plugs
								Intake	Exhaust	
1982	A	6-231 (3.8)	80	100	40	225	60	45	25	15
	4	6-252 (4.1)	80	100	40	225	60	45	25	15
	8	8-260 (4.3)	85	①	42	200-310	②	40	25	25
	V	6-260 (4.3)	142	107	42	160-350	48	41	29	③
	Y	8-307 (5.0)	130	①	42	200-310	60	40	25	25
	N	8-350 (5.7)	130	120	42	200-310	60	40	25	④
1983	A	6-231 (3.8)	80	100	40	306	60	45	25	15
	4	6-252 (4.1)	80	100	40	306	60	45	25	15
	V	6-260 (4.3)	142	107	42	160-350	57	41	29	③
	H	8-305 (5.0)	65	70	45	60	60	30	20	15

TORQUE SPECIFICATIONS
All readings in ft. lbs.

Year	VIN	No. Cylinder Displacement cu. in. (liter)	Cylinder Head Bolts	Main Bearing Bolts	Rod Bearing Bolts	Crankshaft Pulley Bolts	Flywheel Bolts	Manifold Intake	Manifold Exhaust	Spark Plugs
1983	Y	8-307 (5.0)	130	①	42	200-310	60	40	25	34
	N	8-350 (5.7)	130	120	42	200-310	60	40	25	④
1984	A	6-231 (3.8)	80	100	40	306	60	45	25	15
	4	6-252 (4.1)	80	100	40	306	60	45	25	15
	V	6-260 (4.3)	142	107	42	160-350	57	41	29	③
	H	8-305 (5.0)	65	70	45	60	60	30	20	15
	Y	8-307 (5.0)	130	①	42	200-310	60	40	25	34
	N	8-350 (5.7)	130	120	42	200-310	60	40	25	④
1985	A	6-231 (3.8)	80	100	40	306	60	45	25	15
	Z	6-262 (4.3)	65	70-85	40	70	60	30	20	—
	H	8-305 (5.0)	65	70-85	40	70	60	•30	20	—
	Y	8-307 (5.0)	130	①	42	200-310	60	40	25	34
	9	8-307 (5.0)	130	①	42	200-310	60	40	25	34
	N	8-350 (5.7)	130	120	42	200-310	60	40	25	④
1986	A	6-231 (3.8)	80	100	45	200	60	45	20	20
	Z	6-262 (4.3)	65	70-85	40	70	60	30	20	—
	H	8-305 (5.0)	65	70-85	40	70	60	30	20	—
	Y	8-307 (5.0)	125	①	43	200-310	60	40	25	25
	9	8-307 (5.0)	125	①	42	200-310	60	40	25	25
1987	A	6-231 (3.8)	80	100	40	200	60	45	37	20
	H	8-305 (5.0)	65	70-85	40	70	60	30	20	—
	Y	8-307 (5.0)	130	80 ①	48	200-310	60	40	25	25
	9	8-307 (5.0)	130	80 ①	48	200-310	60	40	25	25
1988-89	Y	8-307 (5.0)	130	80①	16⑥	200-310	60	40	25	25

① 80 on Nos. 1-4; 120 on No. 5
② AT—60 ft. lbs.
   MT—90 ft. lbs.
③ Glow Plug—21
④ Glow Plug—12

⑤ 7/16 in. bolt—70 ft. lbs.
   1/2 in. bolt—100 ft. lbs.
   Rear main bearing bolt—100 ft. lbs.

⑥ Torque in 2 steps:
   1st step—18 ft. lbs.
   2nd step—additional 70 degrees turn further

BRAKE SPECIFICATIONS
Oldsmobile
All measurements in inches unless noted

Year	Model	Lug Nut Torque (ft. lbs.)	Master Cylinder Bore	Brake Disc Minimum Thickness	Brake Disc Maximum Runout	Standard Brake Drum Diameter	Minimum Lining Thickness Front	Minimum Lining Thickness Rear
1982	Cutlass	100	15/16	.980	.004	9.500	.030	.030①
	88	100	1⅛	.980	.004	9.500	.030	.030①
	98	100	1⅛	.980	.004	11.000	.030	.030①
	Wagon	100	1⅛	.980	.004	11.000	.030	.030①

BRAKE SPECIFICATIONS
Oldsmobile
All measurements in inches unless noted

Year	Model	Lug Nut Torque (ft. lbs.)	Master Cylinder Bore	Brake Disc Minimum Thickness	Brake Disc Maximum Runout	Standard Brake Drum Diameter	Minimum Lining Thickness Front	Minimum Lining Thickness Rear
1983	Cutlass	80	15/16	.980	.004	9.500	.030	.030①
	88	100	1⅛	.980	.004	9.500	.030	.030①
	98	100	1⅛	.980	.004	11.000	.030	.030①
	Wagon	100	1⅛	.980	.004	11.000	.030	.030①
1984	Cutlass	100	15/16	.980	.004	9.500	.030	.030①
	88	100	1⅛	.980	.004	9.500	.030	.030①
	98	100	1⅛	.980	.004	11.000	.030	.030①
	Wagon	100	1⅛	.980	.004	11.000	.030	.030①
1985	Cutlass	100	15/16	.980	.004	9.500	.030	.030①
	88	100	1⅛	.980	.004	9.500	.030	.030①
	98	100	1⅛	.980	.004	11.000	.030	.030①
	Wagon	100	1⅛	.980	.004	11.000	.030	.030①
1986	Cutlass	100	15/16	.980	.004	9.500	.030.	030①
	Wagon	100	1⅛	.980	.004	11.000	.030	.030①
1987	Cutlass	100	15/16	.980	.004	9.500	.030	.030①
	Wagon	100	1⅛	.980	.004	11.000	.030	.030①
1988-89	Cutlass	100	15/16	.980	.004	9.500	.030	.030①
	Wagon	100	1⅛	.980	.004	11.000	.030	.030①

① If Bonded use .062

BRAKE SPECIFICATIONS
Pontiac
All measurements in inches unless noted

Year	Model	Lug Nut Torque (ft. lbs.)	Master Cylinder Bore	Brake Disc Minimum Thickness	Brake Disc Maximum Runout	Standard Brake Drum Diameter	Minimum Lining Thickness Front	Minimum Lining Thickness Rear
1982	All	80①	—	.980	.005	9.50⑦	1/32	⑥
1983	All	80①	—	.980	.005	9.50⑦	1/32	⑥
1984	Parisiene	80①	1⅛	.980	.004	9.50⑦	.020	—
	Parisiene②	80①	1 3/16	.980	.004	9.50⑦	.030	—
	Bonneville, Grand Prix	80①	15/16	.980	.004	9.50⑦	.030	—
	Bonneville, Grand Prix②	80①	1 1/16	.980	.004	9.50⑦	.030	—
	Bonneville, Grand Prix③	80①	1	.980	.004	9.50⑦	.030	—

BRAKE SPECIFICATIONS
Pontiac
All measurements in inches unless noted

Year	Model	Lug Nut Torque (ft. lbs.)	Master Cylinder Bore	Brake Disc Minimum Thickness	Brake Disc Maximum Runout	Standard Brake Drum Diameter	Minimum Lining Thickness Front	Minimum Lining Thickness Rear
1985	Parisienne	80①	$1\frac{1}{8}$	.980	.004	9.50⑦	.030	–
	Parisienne②	80①	$1\frac{3}{16}$	.980	.004	9.50⑦	.030	–
	Parisienne④	80①	$1\frac{1}{4}$	.980	.004	9.50⑦	.030	–
	Bonneville, Grand Prix	80①	$\frac{15}{16}$	.980	.004	9.50⑦	.030	–
	Bonneville, Grand Prix	80①	$1\frac{1}{16}$	.980	.004	9.50⑦	.030	–
1986	Parisienne	⑤	$1\frac{1}{18}$	.980	.004	9.50⑦	.030	–
	Parisienne②	⑤	$1\frac{3}{16}$	.980	.004	9.50⑦	.030	–
	Parisienne④	⑤	$1\frac{1}{4}$	.980	.004	9.50⑦	.030	–
	Bonneville, Grand Prix	100	$\frac{15}{16}$	.980	.004	9.50⑦	.030	–
	Bonneville, Grand Prix②	100	$1\frac{1}{16}$	.980	.004	9.50⑦	.030	–
1987	Safari	100	$1\frac{1}{8}$	.980	.004	9.50⑦	.030	⑥
	Grand Prix	100	$\frac{15}{16}$	.980	.004	9.50⑦	.030	⑥
1988-89	Safari	100	$1\frac{1}{8}$	.980	.004	9.50⑦	.030	⑥

① With cast aluminum wheel – 100
② With hydroboost
③ With rear discs
④ With power master
⑤ $\frac{7}{16}$ – 20-80; $\frac{1}{2}$ – 20-100
⑥ .030 over rivet head if bonded use .062
⑦ 11.00 w/11" drums

WHEEL ALIGNMENT
Oldsmobile

Year	Model	Caster Range (deg.)	Caster Preferred Setting (deg.)	Camber Range (deg.)	Camber Preferred Setting (deg.)	Toe-in (in.)	Steering Axis Inclination (deg.)
1982	Cutlass	2P-4P	3P	$\frac{5}{16}$N-$1\frac{5}{6}$	$\frac{1}{2}$P	$\frac{1}{16}$-$\frac{1}{2}$	–
	88	2P-4P	3P	0-$1\frac{5}{8}$P	$\frac{3}{4}$P	0-$\frac{1}{4}$	–
	98	2P-4P	3P	0-$1\frac{5}{8}$P	$\frac{3}{4}$P	0-$\frac{1}{4}$	–
	Wagon	2P-4P	3P	0-$1\frac{5}{8}$P	$\frac{3}{4}$P	0-$\frac{1}{4}$	–
1983	Cutlass	2P-4P	3P	$\frac{5}{16}$N-$\frac{5}{16}$	$\frac{1}{2}$P	$\frac{1}{16}$-$\frac{1}{4}$	–
	88	2P-4P	3P	0-$1\frac{5}{8}$P	$\frac{3}{4}$P	0-$\frac{1}{4}$	–
	98	2P-4P	3P	0-$1\frac{5}{8}$P	$\frac{3}{4}$P	0-$\frac{1}{4}$	–
	Wagon	2P-4P	3P	0-$1\frac{5}{8}$P	$\frac{3}{4}$P	0-$\frac{1}{4}$	–
1984	Cutlass	2P-4P	3P	$\frac{5}{16}$N-$1\frac{5}{16}$	$\frac{1}{2}$P	$\frac{1}{16}$-$\frac{1}{4}$	–
	88	2P-4P	3P	0-$1\frac{5}{8}$P	$\frac{3}{4}$P	0-$\frac{1}{4}$	–
	98	2P-4P	3P	0-$1\frac{5}{8}$P	$\frac{3}{4}$P	0-$\frac{1}{4}$	–
	Wagon	2P-4P	3P	0-$1\frac{5}{8}$P	$\frac{3}{4}$P	0-$\frac{1}{4}$	–

WHEEL ALIGNMENT
Oldsmobile

Year	Model	Caster Range (deg.)	Caster Preferred Setting (deg.)	Camber Range (deg.)	Camber Preferred Setting (deg.)	Toe-in (in.)	Steering Axis Inclination (deg.)
1985	Cutlass	2P-4P	3P	$5/16$N-$1\,5/16$	$1/2$P	$1/16$-$1/4$	—
	88	3P-4P	3P	0-$1\,5/8$P	$3/4$P	0-$1/4$	—
	98	2P-4P	3P	0-$1\,5/8$P	$3/4$P	0-$1/4$	—
	Wagon	2P-4P	3P	0-$1\,5/8$P	$3/4$P	0-$1/4$	—
1986	Cutlass	$1\,4/5$P-$2\,4/5$P	$1\,4/5$P	0-$1\,5/8$P	$3/4$P	0-$1/4$	—
	Wagon	$1\,4/5$P-$2\,4/5$P	$1\,4/5$P	0-$1\,3/5$P	$4/5$P	0-$1/4$P	—
1987	Cutlass	$1\,4/5$P-$2\,4/5$P	$1\,4/5$P	0-$1\,5/8$P	$3/4$P	0-$1/4$	—
	Wagon	$1\,4/5$P-$2\,4/5$P	$1\,4/5$P	0-$1\,3/5$P	$4/5$P	0-$1/4$P	—
1988	Cutlass	$1\,4/5$P-$2\,4/5$P	$1\,4/5$P	0-$1\,5/8$P	$3/4$P	0-$1/4$	—
	Wagon	$1\,4/5$P-$2\,4/5$P	$1\,4/5$P	0-$1\,3/5$P	$4/5$P	0-$1/4$P	—

— Not specified
N Negative
P Positive

WHEEL ALIGNMENT
Pontiac

Year	Model	Caster Range (deg.)	Caster Preferred Setting (deg.)	Camber Range (deg.)	Camber Preferred Setting (deg.)	Toe-in (in.)	Steering Axis Inclination (deg.)
1982	Grand Prix	$2\,1/2$P-$3\,1/2$P	3P	0-1P	$1/2$P	$1/16$-$3/16$	—
	Bonneville	$2\,1/2$P-$3\,1/2$P	3P	0-1P	$1/2$P	$1/16$-$3/16$	—
1983	Grand Prix	2P-3P	3P	$5/16$N-$1\,5/16$P	$1/2$P	$1/8$	8
	Bonneville	$2\,1/2$P-$3\,1/2$P	3P	$5/16$N-$1\,5/16$P	$1/2$P	$1/8$	8
1984	Grand Prix	3P-4P	$3\,1/2$P	$5/16$N-$1\,5/16$P	$1/2$P	$1/8$	8
	Bonneville	3P-4P	$3\,1/2$P	$5/16$N-$1\,5\,16$P	$1/2$P	$1/8$	8
	Parisienne	2P-4P	3P	0-$1\,5/8$P	$3/16$P	$1/8$	$9\,3/4$
1985	Grand Prix	2P-4P	3P	$5/16$N-$1\,5/16$P	$1/2$P	$1/8$	8
	Bonneville	2P-4P	3P	$5/16$N-$1\,5/16$P	$1/2$P	$1/8$	8
	Parisienne	2P-4P	3P	0-$1\,5/8$P	$1/2$P	$1/8$	$9\,3/4$
1986	Grand Prix	2P-4P	3P	$5/16$N-$1\,5/16$P	$1/2$P	$1/8$	8
	Bonneville	2P-4P	3P	$5/16$N-$1\,5/16$P	$1/2$P	$1/8$	8
	Parisienne	2P-4P	3P	0-$1\,5/8$P	$1/2$P	$1/8$	$9\,3/4$
1987	Grand Prix	$2\,13/16$P-$3\,13/16$P	$2\,13/16$P	$5/16$N-$1\,5/16$P	$1/2$P	$3/64$	8
	Safari	$2\,3/16$P-$3\,13/16$P	$2\,13/16$P	0-$1\,5/8$P	$13/16$P	$1/16$	$7\,9/16$
1988-89	Safari	$2\,3/16$P-$3\,13/16$P	$2\,13/16$P	0-$1\,5/8$P	$13/16$P	$1/16$	$7\,9/16$

N-Negative
P-Positive

TUNE-UP PROCEDURES

Ignition Timing

ADJUSTMENT

NOTE: Always consult the underhood sticker before adjusting timing. If the sticker differs from these procedures, follow the sticker.

Oldsmobile V8 Engines

1. Use an adapter between the No. 1 spark plug and No. 1 spark plug lead when connecting a timing light. Connect the timing light to the adapter; DO NOT pierce the spark plug lead. Because of the higher voltage used in the HEI system, any break in the insulation will cause electricity to jump to the nearest ground, making the No. 1 plug misfire.

2. On V8 engines ground the diagnostic terminal of the 12 terminal ALCL connector, located on the lower portion of the dashboard, by placing a jumper wire between the "A" and "B" terminals.

3. Remove the air cleaner and tape over the vacuum hose fitting.

4. Connect a timing light, loosen the distributor mounting bolt, and turn the distributor until the specified timing is obtained.

5. Tighten the mounting bolt and recheck the timing to see if it changed.

6. On V6 engines clear ECM memory by removing the ECM fuse from the fuse block. If equipped with a V8 engine unground the diagnostic terminal with the engine still running (If done before engine is shut off no trouble codes will be stored).

7. Remove the tape from the vacuum hose fitting and install and connect the hose, if so equipped.

8. Install the air cleaner and make all carburetor adjustments as required.

Pontiac V8 and Olds/Pontiac V6 Engines

1. Disconnect the 4 terminal EST connector at the distributor.

2. Remove the air cleaner and plug the vacuum hose.

3. Use an adapter between the No. 1 spark plug and No. 1 spark plug lead when connecting a timing light. Connect the timing light to the adapter; DO NOT pierce the spark plug lead. Because of the higher voltage used in the HEI system, any break in the insulation will cause electricity to jump to the nearest ground, making the No. 1 plug misfire. This can also be avoided by using an induction type timing light.

4. Set the timing by loosening the distributor mounting bolt, and turning the distributor until the specified timing is obtained. Reconnect the EST terminal.

5. Once the timing is set, the ECM must be cleared of any codes, do this by removing the ECM fuse from the fuse block and then reinstalling it.

6. Reinstall the air cleaner and vacuum hose.

NOTE: All V6 engine harmonic balancers have two timing marks, one measuring 1/8 in. wide and one measuring the normal 1/16 in. wide. The smaller mark is used for setting the timing with a hand held timing light. The 1/8 in. wide mark is required when using magnetic timing equipment. All engines have a mounting bracket on the front cover which will accept the magnetic timing pickup probe.

Valve Lash

ADJUSTMENT

Hydraulic valve lifters are used to keep all parts of the valve train in constant contact. Each lifter is an automatic adjuster maintaining zero lash under all conditions.

The engines produced for use in the Oldsmobile and Pontiac vehicle models use only hydraulic roller lifters, which are not adjustable. The rocker arm shaft assembly or the rockers, with pivot, are bolted to the cylinder head with a specific torque pressure, automatically positioning the lifter internal components for correct hydraulic operation.

Idle Speed and Mixture Gasoline Engines

ADJUSTMENT

Carbureted Models
EXCEPT 1986–89 307 V8 ENGINE

Idle mixture screws are sealed with hardened caps covering the screws during original equipment production. These plugs are not to be removed unless required for cleaning or part replacement.

Before suspecting the carburetor as the cause of poor engine performance or rough idle, check ignition system including distributor, timing, spark plugs and wires. Inspect air cleaner, evaporative emission system, EFI system, PCV system, EGR system and engine compression. Also inspect intake manifold, vacuum hoses an connections for leaks and check torque of carburetor mounting screws.

In the case of major carburetor repair, throttle body replacement or high idle CO as indicated by state or local emission inspection, idle mixture may be adjusted. Adjusting mixture by other than the proper method may violate emissions. The following procedure must be used.

IDLE AIR BLEED VALVE
ADJUSTMENT

1. Position the parking brake and block the drive wheels. Disconnect and plug the hoses as directed on the vehicle emission control label.

2. Check and adjust ignition timing. Connect a dwell meter and a tachometer.

3. Start engine, and with transmission in park or neutral, run engine at idle until fully warm and a varying dwell is noted on the dwell meter. It is essential that the engine is operated for a sufficient length of time to ensure that the engine coolant sensor, and the oxygen sensor in the exhaust, are at full operational temperature.

4. Check engine idle speed and compare to specifications on the underhood label. If necessary, adjust curb idle speed. On models with idle speed control (ISC) or idle load compensator (ILC), no adjustment is possible.

5. With engine idling in drive (neutral for manual transmission), observe dwell reading on the 6 cylinder scale. If varying within the 10–0 degree range, adjustment is correct. If not, proceed with Step 6.

6. Remove the idle air bleed valve cover. If the cover is staked in place, pry it off using a suitable tool and a allen wrench.

7. If the cover is riveted, cover the internal bowl vents to the bleed valve with masking tape. Cover the carburetor air intakes with masking tape in order to prevent metal chips from entering the engine.

8. Cover carburetor air intakes with masking tape to prevent metal chips from entering carburetor and engine.

9. Carefully align a No. 35 (0.110 in.) drill bit on one of the steel rivet heads holding the idle air bleed valve cover in place. Drill only enough to remove rivet head. Drill the remaining rivet head located on the other side of the tower. Use a drift and small hammer to drive the remainder of the rivets out of the idle air bleed valve tower in the air horn casting. Use care in drilling to prevent damage to the air horn casting.

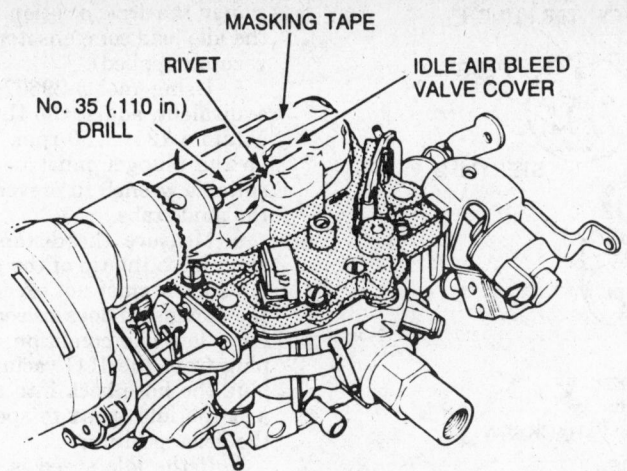

Removing air bleed valve cover

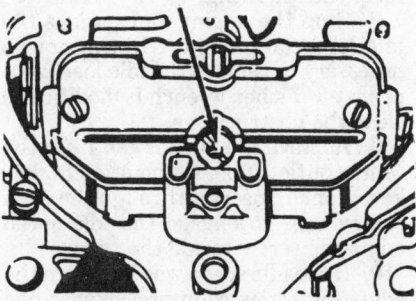

Idle air bleed valve location

10. Lift out cover over the idle air bleed valve and remove the rivet pieces from inside the idle air bleed valve tower.

11. Using shop air, carefully blow out any remaining chips from inside the tower. Discard cover after removed. A missing cover indicates that the idle air bleed valve setting has been changed from its original factory setting.

12. With cover removed, look for presence (or absence) of a letter identification on top of idle air bleed valve.

13. If an identifying letter appears on top of the valve proceed to the procedure outlined under type two. If an identifying letter does not appear on the top of the valve proceed to the procedure outlined under type one.

TYPE ONE

1. Presetting the idle air bleed valve to a gauge dimension if the idle air bleed valve was serviced prior to on-vehicle adjustment is accomplished as follows.

2. Install idle air bleed valve gauging tool J-33815-2, BT-8253-B, or equivalent, in throttle side "D" shaped vent hole in the air horn casting. The upper end of the tool should be positioned over the open cavity next to the idle air bleed valve.

3. While holding the gauging tool down lightly, so that the solenoid plunger is against the solenoid stop, adjust the idle air bleed valve so that the gauging tool will pivot over and just contact the top of the valve. The valve is now preset for on-vehicle adjustment. Remove the gauging tool.

4. Adjusting the idle air bleed valve on the vehicle to obtain correct dwell reading is accomplished as follows.

5. Start engine and allow it to reach normal operating temperature. While idling in drive (neutral for manual transmission), use a suitable tool to slowly turn valve counterclockwise or clockwise, until the dwell reading varies within the 25–35 degree range, attempting to be as close to 30 degrees as possible. Perform this step carefully. The air bleed valve is very sensitive and should be turned in 1/8 turn increments only.

6. If, after performing the step above, the dwell reading does not vary and is not within the 25–35 degree range, it will be necessary to remove the plugs and to adjust the idle mixture needles.

7. Remove the idle mixture needle plug as follows, only if necessary. Remove the carburetor from the engine, following normal service procedures, to gain access to the plugs covering the idle mixture needles.

8. Invert carburetor and drain fuel into a suitable container. Place carburetor on a suitable holding fixture, with manifold side up. Use care to avoid damaging linkage, tubes, and parts protruding from air horn.

9. Make two parallel cuts in the throttle body, one on each side of the locator points beneath the idle mixture needle plug (manifold side), with a hacksaw.

10. The cuts should reach down to the steel plug, but should not extend more than 1/8 in. beyond the locator

points. The distance between the saw cuts depends on the size of the punch to be used.

11. Place a flat punch near the ends of the saw marks in the throttle body. Hold the punch at a 45 degree angle and drive it into the throttle body until the casting breaks away, exposing the steel plug.

12. The hardened plug will break, rather than remaining intact. It is not necessary to remove the plug in one piece, but remove the loose pieces. Repeat this procedure with the other mixture needle.

13. Setting the idle mixture needles (if necessary) where correct dwell reading could not obtained with idle air bleed valve adjustment.

14. Using tool J-29030, BT-7610B, or equivalent, turn both idle mixture needles clockwise until they are lightly seated, then turn each mixture needle counterclockwise three turns. Reinstall carburetor on engine using a new flange mounting gasket, but do not install air cleaner and gasket at this time.

15. Readjusting idle air bleed valve to finalize correct dwell reading. Start engine and run until fully warm, and adjust the air bleed valve.

16. If unable to set dwell to 25–35 degrees, and the dwell is below 25 degrees, turn both mixture needles counterclockwise an additional turn. If dwell is above 35 degrees, turn both mixture needles clockwise an additional turn. Readjust idle air bleed valve to obtain dwell limits.

17. After adjustments are complete, seal the idle mixture needle openings in the throttle body, using silicone sealant, RTV rubber, or equivalent. The sealer is required to discourage unnecessary adjustment of the setting, and to prevent fuel vapor loss in that area.

18. On vehicles without a carburetor mounted idle speed control or idle load compensator, adjust curb idle speed if necessary. Check, and only if necessary, adjust fast idle speed as described on emission control information label.

TYPE TWO

1. To set the idle air bleed valve to a gauge dimension, install air bleed valve gauging tool J-33815-2, BT-8253-B, or equivalent, in throttle side "D" shaped vent hole in the air horn casting. The upper end of the tool should be positioned over the open cavity next to the idle air bleed valve.

2. While holding the gauging tool down lightly, so that the solenoid plunger is against the solenoid stop, adjust the idle air bleed valve so that the gauging tool will pivot over and just contact the top of the valve.

3. The valve is now set properly. No

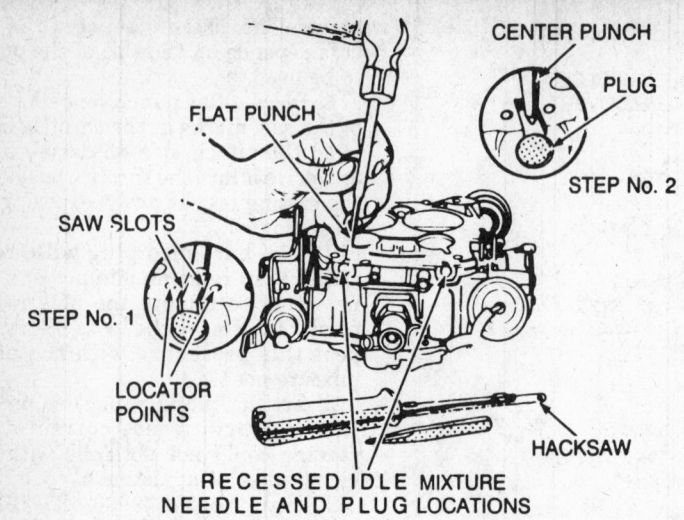

Removing idle mixture needle plugs

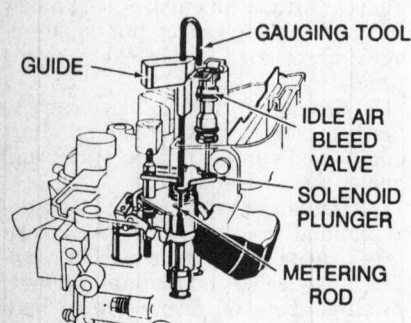

Installing idle air bleed valve gauging tool

further adjustment of the valve is necessary. Remove gauging tool.

4. Adjusting the idle mixture needles on the vehicle to obtain correct dwell readings. Remove idle mixture needle plugs, following instructions in the information given for Type 1.

5. Using tool J-29030-B, BT-7610-B, or equivalent, turn each idle mixture needle clockwise until lightly seated, then turn each mixture needle counterclockwise three turns.

6. Reinstall carburetor on engine, using a new flange mounting gasket, but do not install air cleaner or gasket at this time. Start engine and allow it to reach normal operating temperature.

7. While idling in drive (neutral for manual transmission), adjust both mixture needles equally, in 1/8 turn increments, until dwell reading varies within the 25–35 degree range, attempting to be as close to 30 degrees as possible. If reading is too low, turn mixture needles counterclockwise. If reading is too high, turn mixture needles clockwise. Allow time for dwell reading to stabilize after each adjustment.

8. After adjustments are complete, seal the idle mixture needle openings in the throttle body, using silicone sealant, RTV rubber, or equivalent. The sealer is required to discourage unnecessary readjustment of the setting, and to prevent fuel vapor loss in that area.

9. On vehicles without a carburetor-mounted idle speed control or idle load compensator, adjust curb idle speed if necessary. Check, and if necesary, adjust fast idle speed, as described on the emission control information label.

1986–89 307 V8 ENGINE

NOTE: All carburetors have mixture needles concealed under staked in plugs. Mixture adjustments are possible only during carburetor overhaul or extreme circumstances. Vehicles equipped with the computer command control system can not use the propane enrichment or lean drop methods of idle mixture adjustment.

1. Place the transmission in the park position, set the parking brake and block the drive wheels. Connect a suitable tachometer to the engine. Remove the air cleaner assembly and plug the vacuum hose to the Thermal Vacuum Valve (TVV).

2. Disconnect and plug the vacuum hose to the EGR valve and the vacuum hose to the canister purge port.

3. Disconnect and plug the vacuum hose to the idle load compensator (ILC). Back out the idle stop screw on the carburetor three turns.

4. Turn the air condition control switch to the OFF position. With the engine running and at normal operating temperature, place the transmis-

sion in the drive position. Fully extend the idle load compensator plunger (no vacuum applied).

5. Using tool J-29607, Bt-8022 or equivalent, adjust the ILC plunger to obtain a 725 ± 50 rpm. The jam nut on the plunger must be held with a suitable wrench to prevent damage to the guide tabs.

6. Measure the distance from the jam nut to the tip of the plunger. The dimension must not exceed one in.. If the dimension does exceed 1 in., check for a low idle condition. Remove the plug from the ILC vacuum hose and plug the hose back into the ILC. Adjust the idle speed to specification in the drive position.

7. If the idle speed is correct then the adjustment is over. If the idle speed does not meet specifications perform the following.

8. Stop the engine and remove the idle load compensator. It will not be necessary to remove the idle load compensator if a hex wrench is modified to clear the obstructions.

9. Remove the rubber cap from the center outlet tube. Using a $3/32$ in. hex key wrench, insert it through the open center tube to engage the idle speed adjusting screw inside the tube.

10. If the idle speed was low, turn the adjusting screw counterclockwise one turn for every 75–100 rpm low. If the idle was too high, turn the adjusting screw clockwise one turn for every 75–100 rpm high. Reinstall the plug on the center of the outlet tube.

11. Reinstall the idle load compensator on the carburetor and attach the the throttle return spring and other related parts removed. Recheck the idle speed in the drive position and closed loop mode. If the idle speed is still not within specification, repeat the procedure.

12. Disconnect the power feed (fuse) to the ECM with the ignition off, for ten seconds. This will allow the ECM to reset the throttle position sensor value.

13. Disconnect and plug the vacuum source to the ILC. Apply a vacuum source using a hand held vacuum pump or equivalent to the ILC vacuum inlet tube to fully retract the plunger.

14. Adjust the idle stop screw on the carburetor float bowl to obtain a 450 rpm in the drive position. Place the transmission in park and stop the engine.

15. Remove the plug from the vacuum hose and install the hose on the ILC vacuum inlet tube. Remove all the plugs from the disconnected vacuum lines and reconnect the vacuum lines to their proper ports.

16. Install the air cleaner and gasket, remove the blocks from the drive wheels and road test the vehicle.

Idle Speed Diesel Engine

ADJUSTMENT

1. Set the parking brake and block the drive wheels.

2. Insert the probe of a magnetic pickup tachometer into the timing indicator hole.

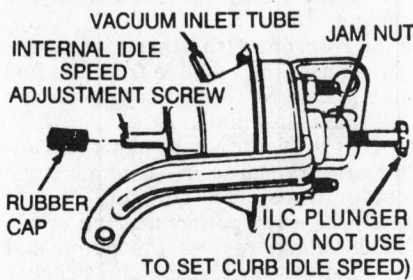

Idle load compensator assembly

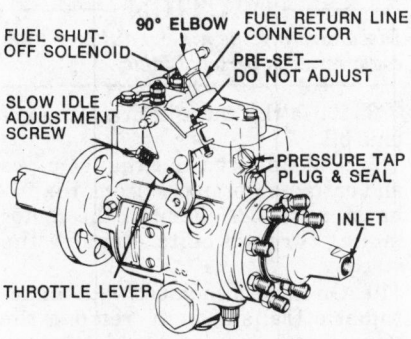

Injection pump slow idle screw

3. Run the engine until it reaches normal operating temperature.

4. Disconnect the wires to the A/C compressor and, the two wire lead to the generator, turn off all electrical accessories.

5. Put the gear selector in the drive position.

6. Turn the slow idle screw on the injection pump to obtain the idle speed specified on the emission control label.

7. Reconnect the wires to the A/C compressor and, the generator.

ENGINE ELECTRICAL

Distributor

REMOVAL & INSTALLATION

1. Remove the distributor cap, unplug the 4 terminal EST connector.

2. Mark the position of the distributor on the engine, and on the base of the distributor.

3. Remove the hold down bolt and lift the distributor from the block.

NOTE: Do not crank the engine with the distributor removed; this will change the timing.

Undisturbed Engine

If engine has not been disturbed (cranked) after removing the distributor, perform the following operations for installation:

1. Turn the rotor until it is about ⅛ turn past the locating mark previously made on the distributor housing.

2. Push the distributor down into the block. It may be necessary to turn the rotor slightly until the shaft engages in the block. The mark on the distributor housing must line up with the mark made on the engine block.

3. Tighten the hold-down bolt until it is snug, then connect the vacuum advance line.

4. Connect the primary wire to the coil or, on HEI, connect the feed wire and install the distributor cap.

5. Check the timing and adjust it as necessary. Tighten the hold down bolt.

Disturbed Engine

If engine has been disturbed (cranked) after removing distributor, perform the following operations for installation:

1. Crank the engine until No. 1 piston is at the top of its compression stroke. The compression stroke can be determined by removing the spark plug from the No. 1 cylinder and placing your thumb over the hole while an assistant slowly cranks the engine. Crank until compression is felt at the hole, then continue cranking slowly until the timing mark on the crankshaft pulley lines up with the 0 degree mark.

2. Position the distributor in the block but do not allow it to engage with its drive gear. Observe the position of the vacuum control unit on the distributor. If the distributor is located correctly, the vacuum unit will be positioned so that the vacuum hose can be easily connected to it.

3. Position the distributor rotor so that it is between terminal No. 1 and the last spark plug tower of the firing order on the distributor cap.

4. Install the distributor, making sure the distributor shaft engages the oil pump shaft, thereby allowing the distributor to fully contact the engine block.

5. Install the hold-down clamp and tighten the bolt until it is snug.

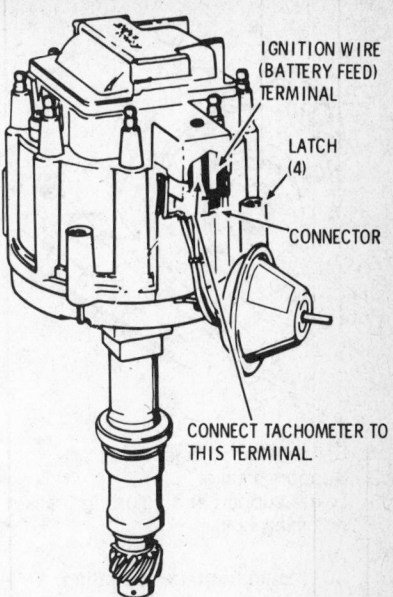

HEI system tachometer hook-up

6. Install the distributor cap.

7. Attach all wires and the vacuum advance hose.

8. Check the timing and adjust it as necessary.

Alternator

NOTE: For further information on the charging system, please refer to "Charging and Starting" in the Unit Repair section.

PRECAUTIONS

To prevent serious damage to the alternator and the rest of the charging system, the following precautions must be observed:

● When installing a battery, make sure that the positive cable is connected to the positive terminal and the negative to the negative.

● When jump-starting the vehicle with another battery, make sure that the like terminals are connected. This also applies when using a battery charger.

● Never operate the alternator with the battery disconnected or on an uncontrolled open circuit. Double-check to see that all connections are tight.

● Do not short across or ground any alternator or regulator terminals.

● Do not apply full battery voltage to the field connector.

● Always disconnect the negative battery terminal before disconnecting the alternator.

BELT TENSION ADJUSTMENT

Using belt tension gauge J-23600 or

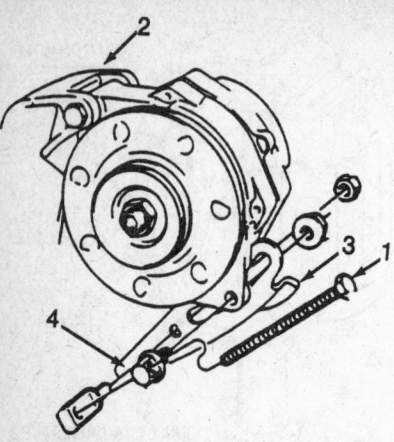

1. Belt tension adjuster
2. Support bracket
3. Lower support and adjusting bracket
4. Adjusting bolt

Typical alternator mounting

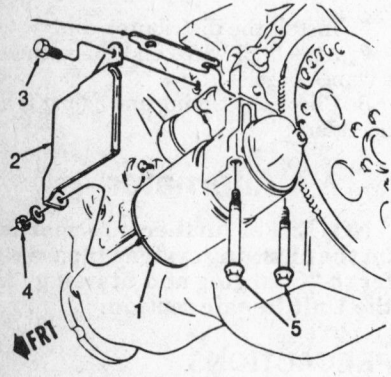

1. Starter assembly
2. Shield
3. 20 ft. lbs.
4. 35 ft. lbs.
5. 35 ft. lbs.

Typical starter mounting

equivalent adjust the alternator belt if the tension is below 300N, as indicated on the gauge. If the belt is used the correct belt tension is 600N, as indicated on the gauge. If the belt is new the correct tension is 900N, as indicated on the gauge.

REMOVAL & INSTALLATION

1. Disconnect the battery ground cable and the wiring from the alternator.
2. Remove the mounting bolt, adjusting bolt, and drive belt.
3. Lift out the alternator.
4. To install, reverse the removal procedure, connect the battery ground cable and check for proper belt tension.

Voltage Regulator

REMOVAL & INSTALLATION

This is a completely sealed unit that cannot be adjusted or disassembled. Replacement of the voltage regulator requires the disassembly of the alternator.

Starter

NOTE: For further information on the starter system, please refer to "Charging and Starting" in the Unit Repair section.

REMOVAL & INSTALLATION

1. Disconnect the battery and carefully raise the car.
2. Remove upper support attaching bolts and the brace and wire guide tube bolt, if so equipped.
3. Remove the flywheel housing cover.
4. Remove the two starter mounting bolts.
5. Lower starter, disconnect wiring, and remove starter.
6. Install by reversing the procedure. If shims were removed, they must be installed in their original location to assure proper drive pinion-to-flywheel engagement.

GASOLINE ENGINE MECHANICAL

The Chevrolet V6-262 and V8-305 and the Buick V6-231 and 252 have been used by Oldsmobile and Pontiac in various models. Service procedures for the Chevrolet built engines can be found in the "Chevrolet Rear Wheel Drive" section, and procedures for the Buick built engines can be found in the "Buick Rear Wheel Drive" section. Only engines manufactured by Oldsmobile and Pontiac will be covered in this engine section.

For engine identification, see the engine identification code chart at the beginning of this section.

Engine

REMOVAL & INSTALLATION

1. Disconnect the negative battery cable. Remove the air cleaner assembly and heat pipe.

2. Mark the position of the hood on the hood hinge supports.
3. Drain the cooling system and disconnect the radiator and heater hoses from the engine. Remove the fan blade, pulleys, and belts. Remove the radiator.
4. Disconnect the engine ground strap from the cylinder head. Remove the fan shroud.
5. Disconnect and tag all vacuum lines and electrical leads from the engine.
6. Disconnect the throttle linkage. Disconnect the fuel line from the fuel pump. Remove the clutch equalizer on manual transmission cars.
7. If the car is equipped with an automatic transmission, disconnect the cooler lines from the radiator. If equipped with power steering or air conditioning, remove the pump and bracket or compressor and bracket from the engine without disconnecting the lines.

— CAUTION —
Disconnecting the air conditioner lines could result in personal injury.

8. Raise the car and drain the engine oil.
9. Disconnect the exhaust pipes and/or crossover pipes from the exhaust manifolds. Remove the motor mount through bolts. Remove the starter.
10. On models equipped with an automatic transmission, remove the torque converter cover. Matchmark the flywheel and converter. Turn the crankshaft pulley to gain access to the three torque converter-to-flywheel attaching bolts and remove the bolts.
11. Remove the transmission or clutch housing-to-engine bolts, place a jack under the transmission, and raise the transmission slightly.
12. Attach a chain hoist to the engine and remove it from the car.
13. Reverse the procedure to install the engine.

Cylinder Head

REMOVAL & INSTALLATION

— CAUTION —
Do not disconnect the A/C lines. Severe personal injury could result.

1. Drain the cooling system.
2. Remove the intake manifold and carburetor as an assembly.
3. Remove exhaust manifolds.
4. Loosen or remove any accessory brackets which interfere.
5. Remove the valve cover(s). Loosen any accessory brackets which are in the way.

6. Remove the battery ground strap from the cylinder head.

7. Remove cylinder head bolts and cylinder head(s).

8. Install in the reverse order of removal. It is not recommended that sealer be used on the new head gasket. Dip head bolts in oil before installing and allow them to drain so oil will not fill the threads and interfere with proper torquing. Tighten all head bolts in the correct sequence to 60–70 ft. lbs., then torque, again in sequence, to 130 ft. lbs.. Re-torque the bolts after engine is warmed up. On the 1985-89 models, apply a ¼ in. bead of RTV sealer along the horizontal surface of the valve cover, running inside the bolt holes, before installation.

NOTE: The gaskets for the 260 cu. in. V8 are to be installed with the stripe facing up. The 307 cu. in. V8 gaskets do not have a stripe.

OVERHAUL

NOTE: For all cylinder head overhaul procedures, please refer to the "Engine Rebuilding" in the Unit Repair section.

Rocker Arms/Shafts

REMOVAL & INSTALLATION

1. Remove the valve covers.
2. Remove the two bolts that attach the rocker arm pivot to the cylinder head.
3. Remove the rocker arms in pairs.

NOTE: All parts for each assembly must be kept together and re-installed in the same location.

4. Install the rocker arms for each cylinder with lifters off the cam lobe and the valves closed.
5. Lubricate all pivot and rocker arm wear points with white grease.
6. Torque the retaining bolts to 25 ft. lbs. (34 Nm).
7. Install the valve covers, on the 1985-89 models, apply a ¼ in. bead of RTV sealer along the horizontal surface of the valve cover, running inside the bolt holes.

Intake Manifold

REMOVAL & INSTALLATION

1. Remove the air cleaner, drain the radiator, and disconnect the negative battery terminal.
2. Disconnect the upper radiator hose, by-pass hose, and heater hose from the manifold.

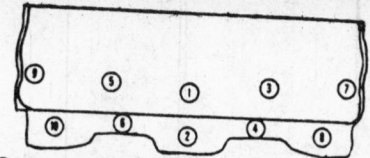

Cylinder head torque sequence—265 and 301 V8's

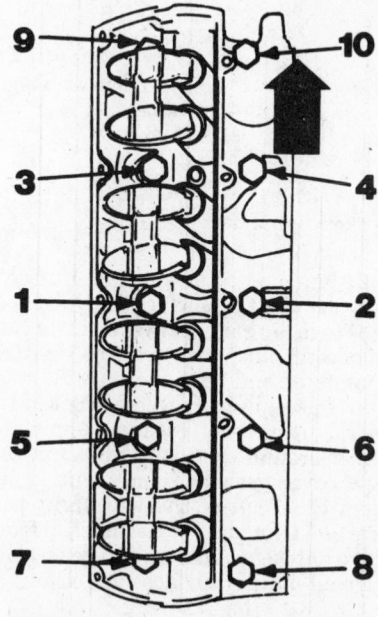

5.0L V8 head bolt torque sequence

3. Disconnect the throttle linkage, vacuum and gas lines, and the brake booster line from the carburetor.
4. Remove the accessory mounting brackets as required.

——— **CAUTION** ———
Do not disconnect the A/C lines. Personal injury could result.

5. Disconnect all necessary electrical connections.
6. Remove the intake manifold bolts and remove the manifold with the carburetor attached.
7. Install in the reverse order of removal. Coat all gasket surfaces with sealer, including both the front and rear intake seals.
7. Torque all bolts first to 15 ft. lbs. in the sequence illustrated, then tighten all bolts, again in sequence, to 40 ft. lbs..

Exhaust Manifold

REMOVAL & INSTALLATION

Right Side

OLDSMOBILE

1. Disconnect the negative battery cable.

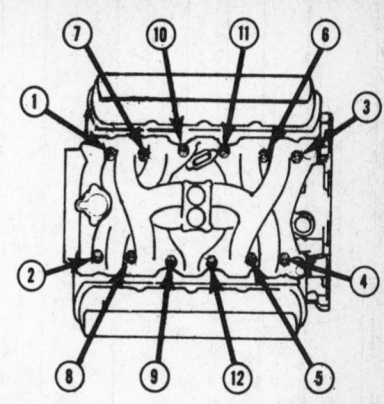

5.0L V8 intake manifold bolt tightening sequence

2. Raise the car and remove the right front wheel, the exhaust and crossover pipe(s).
3. Flatten the lock tabs on the manifold bolts and remove. If so equipped, disconnect the oxygen sensor lead.
3. Remove the lower engine mounting bolt and raise the engine slightly, if necessary for clearance.
4. Remove the manifold from below.
5. To install, use new gaskets and reverse the removal procedure. Torque the manifold bolts to specification, bend bolt lock tabs back into position.

PONTIAC

1. Disconnect the negative battery cable.
2. Raise and support the vehicle safely.
3. Remove the exhaust pipe from the exhaust manifold.
4. Lower the vehicle.
5. Disconnect the air management valve bracket, the AIR hoses and the AIR pipe at the converter, the cylinder heads and the exhaust manifold.
6. Disconnect the spark plug wires.
7. Remove the exhaust manifold bolts and the manifold.
8. To install, use a new gasket and reverse the removal procedures. Torque the exhaust manifold mounting bolts to specifications, bend bolt lock tabs back into position.

Left Side

OLDSMOBILE

1. Remove the air cleaner.
2. Remove the hot air shroud and the hot air tube.
3. Remove the lower alternator bracket, A/C drive belt and the air pump pulley.
4. Remove all air pump hoses and the AIR switching valve.
5. Raise the car and remove the crossover pipe.
6. Lower the car and, flatten the

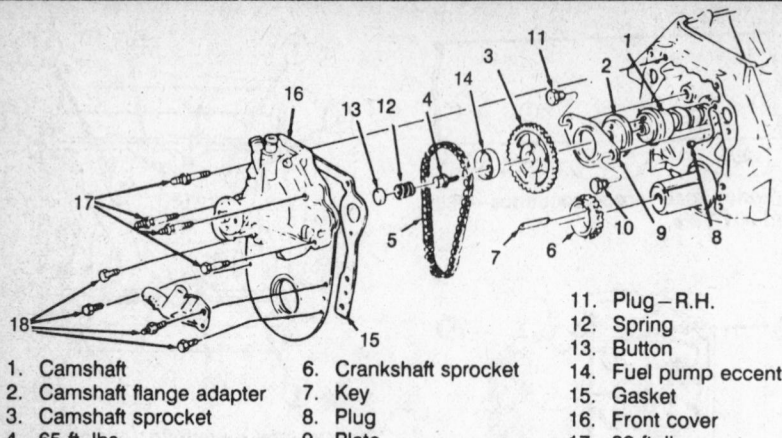

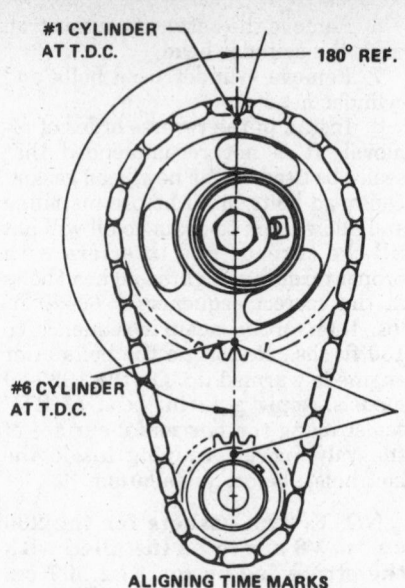

1. Camshaft
2. Camshaft flange adapter
3. Camshaft sprocket
4. 65 ft. lbs.
5. Chain
6. Crankshaft sprocket
7. Key
8. Plug
9. Plate
10. Plug—L.H.
11. Plug—R.H.
12. Spring
13. Button
14. Fuel pump eccentric
15. Gasket
16. Front cover
17. 22 ft. lbs.
18. 35 ft. lbs.

V8 front cover and timing chain assembly

#1 CYLINDER AT T.D.C.   180° REF.

#6 CYLINDER AT T.D.C.

ALIGNING TIME MARKS

V8 engine timing mark alignment

lock tabs on the manifold bolts and remove.

7. To install, use a new gasket and reverse the removal procedures. Torque the exhaust manifold mounting bolts to specifications, bend bolt lock tabs back into position.

PONTIAC

1. Disconnect the negative battery cable.

2. Raise and support the vehicle on jack stands.

3. Remove the exhaust pipe from the exhaust manifold.

4. If equipped with A/C, remove the compressor and the rear adjusting bracket, then move it aside.

5. If equipped with power steering, remove the power steering pump and lower the rear adjusting bracket, then move the pump aside.

6. Disconnect the spark plug wires from the plugs.

7. Flatten the lock tabs on the manifold bolts and remove.

8. To install, use a new gasket and reverse the removal procedures. Torque the exhaust manifold mounting bolts to specifications, bend bolt lock tabs back into position.

Front Cover

REMOVAL & INSTALLATION

1. Disconnect the negative battery cable.

2. Drain the coolant. Disconnect the radiator hose and the bypass hose. Remove the fan, belts and pulley. Remove the A/C compressor (if so equipped) and bracket.

3. Remove the vibration damper and crankshaft pulley.

4. Remove the vibration damper and crankshaft pulley.

5. Remove the front cover attaching bolts and remove the cover, timing indicator and water pump from the front of the engine.

6. Remove the dowel pins. If necessary grind a flat surface on the dowel pins to aid in removal. When installing the dowel pins, they must be inserted chamfered end first.

7. Install in the reverse order of removal using new gaskets. Apply rtv sealer around the coolant holes of the new cover gasket. Trim about 1/8 in. from each end of the new front pan seal and trim any excess material from the front edge of the oil pan gasket. Be sure all mating surfaces are clean.

OIL SEAL REPLACEMENT

5.0L V8 Engine

1. Remove the crankshaft pulley and balancer.

2. Remove the oil seal using tool BT-6406 or J-23129 and J-1859-03.

3. Coat the outside diameter of the new seal with sealer.

4. Install seal with lip facing the engine, using tool BT-6405 or J-25264-A.

5. Install crankshaft pulley and balancer. Install belts and adjust tension.

Timing Chain and Sprockets

REMOVAL & INSTALLATION

1. Remove the front cover and gasket. Remove the crankshaft oil slinger.

2. Remove the fuel pump and fuel pump eccentric.

3. Remove the camshaft sprocket and timing chain.

4. Remove the crankshaft sprocket.

5. Installation is the reverse of the removal procedure. Assemble timing chain on sprockets with timing marks in their closest together position.

Camshaft

REMOVAL & INSTALLATION

5.0L V8 Engine

1. Disconnect the negative battery cable. Drain the radiator. Remove the upper radiator baffle.

2. Disconnect the upper radiator hose.

3. Remove the radiator.

4. Disconnect the fuel line at the fuel pump.

5. Remove the air cleaner. Disconnect the throttle cable.

6. Remove the alternator belt. Remove the alternator bracket attaching bolts.

7. Remove power steering pump bracket attaching bolts and remove pump.

8. Remove air conditioning compressor mounting bracket attaching bolts and support compressor to side for access. The air conditioning lines at the compressor are flexible and should be left attached to the compressor.

—— **CAUTION** ——

Do not disconnect the A/C lines. Personal injury could result.

9. Disconnect thermostat bypass hose at water pump. Disconnect electrical and vacuum connections. Remove distributor with cap and wiring intact.

10. Remove balancer pulley. Remove balancer.

11. Remove engine front cover. Remove both valve covers.

12. Remove intake manifold and gasket, front and rear seal.

13. Remove rocker arms, push rods and valve lifters.

NOTE: All parts for each assembly must be kept together and reinstalled in the same location.

14. If equipped with air conditioning, discharge the system, remove condenser attaching bolts and remove condenser.

15. Remove bolt securing fuel pump eccentric, remove eccentric, camshaft gear, oil slinger and timing chain.

16. Remove camshaft by carefully sliding it out the front of the engine.

17. Installation is the reverse of the removal procedure. Be sure to coat the camshaft and the lifters with clean engine oil prior to installation. Be sure to use new gaskets, as required.

Piston and Connecting Rod

POSITIONING

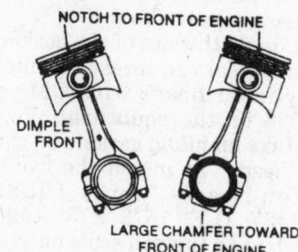

V8 engine piston and rod assembly

NOTE: For all piston and connecting rod overhaul procedures, please refer to "Engine Rebuilding" in the Unit Repair section.

DIESEL ENGINE MECHANICAL

Engine

REMOVAL & INSTALLATION

1. Drain the cooling system.
2. Remove the air cleaner.
3. Mark the hood-to-hinge position and remove the hood.
4. Disconnect the ground cables from the batteries.
5. Disconnect the ground wires at the fender panels and the ground strap at the cowl.
6. Disconnect the radiator hoses, cooler lines, heater hoses, vacuum hoses, power steering pump hoses, air conditioning compressor (hoses attached), fuel inlet hose and all attached wiring.

7. Remove the bellcrank clip.
8. Disconnect the throttle and transmission cables.
9. Remove the upper radiator support and the radiator.
10. Raise and support the car.
11. Disconnect the exhaust pipes at the manifold.
12. Remove the torque converter cover and the three bolts holding the converter to the flywheel.
13. Remove the engine mount bolts or nuts.
14. Remove the three right side transmission-to-engine bolts. Remove the starter.
15. Lower the car and attach a hoist to the engine.
16. Slightly raise the transmission with a jack.
17. Remove the three left side transmission-to-engine bolts and lift out the engine.
18. Installation is in the reverse order of removal. Converter cover bolts are torqued to 40 ft. lbs. on the 350 V8 and 35 ft. lbs. on the 263 V6.

Cylinder Head

REMOVAL & INSTALLATION

1. Remove the intake manifold.
2. Remove the rocker arm cover(s), after removing any accessory brackets which interfere with cover removal.
3. Disconnect and label the glow plug wiring.
4. If the right cylinder head is being removed, remove the ground strap from the head.
5. Remove the rocker arm bolts, the bridged pivots, the rocker arms, and the pushrods, keeping all the parts in order so that they can be returned to their original locations. It is a good practice to number or mark the parts to avoid interchanging them.
6. Remove the fuel return lines from the nozzles.
7. Remove the exhaust manifold(s), using the procedure outlined above.
8. Remove the engine block drain plug on the side of the engine from which the cylinder head is being removed. On V6s, remove the pipe-thread plugs covering the upper cylinder head bolts.
9. Remove the head bolts. Remove the cylinder head.
10. To install, first clean the mating surfaces thoroughly. Install new head gaskets on the engine block. Do not coat the gaskets with any sealer. The gaskets have a special coating that eliminates the need for sealer. The use of sealer will interfere with this coating and cause leaks. Install the cylinder head onto the block.

11. Clean the head bolts (and pipe-thread plugs-V6s) thoroughly. On the V8, dip the bolts in clean engine oil and install into the cylinder block until the heads of the bolts lightly contact the cylinder head. On V6s, coat the plug threads, bolt threads and the area under the bolt threads with sealer/lubricant part No. 1052080 or equivalent.

NOTE: The correct sealer must be used or coolant leaks and bolt torque loss will result.

12. On the V8, tighten the bolts, in the sequence illustrated, to 100 ft. lbs. When all bolts have been tightened to this figure, begin the tightening sequence again, and torque all bolts to 130 ft. lbs.

13. On V6s, tighten all head bolts in sequence to the following torques: all except bolts 5, 6, 11, 12, 13 and 14–100 ft. lbs.; bolts 5, 6, 11, 12, 13 and 14–41 ft. lbs. Finally, tighten all bolts except 5, 6, 11, 12, 13 and 14 to 142 ft. lbs., and bolts 5, 6, 11, 12, 13 and 14 to 59 ft. lbs. in the proper sequence. Install the pipe thread plugs.

14. Install the engine block drain plug(s), the exhaust manifold(s), the fuel return lines, the glow plug wiring, and the ground strap for the right cylinder head.

15. Install the valve train assembly.
16. Install the intake manifold.
17. Install the rocker cover(s). The valve covers are sealed with RTV (room temperature vulcanizing) silicone sealer instead of a gasket. Use GM No. 1052434 or its equivalent. Install the cover to the head within 10 minutes (while the sealer is still wet).

OVERHAUL

NOTE: For all cylinder head overhaul procedures, please refer to "Engine Rebuilding" in the unit repair section.

Rocker Arms/Shafts

REMOVAL & INSTALLATION

V6 Engine

NOTE: When the rocker arms are removed or loosened, the lifters must be bled down to prevent oil pressure buildup inside each lifter, which could cause it to raise up higher than normal and bring the valves within striking distance of the pistons.

1. Remove the valve cover.
2. Remove the rocker arm pivot

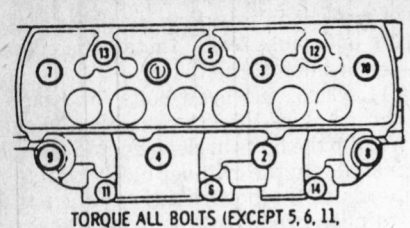

TORQUE ALL BOLTS (EXCEPT 5, 6, 11, 12, 13 & 14) TO 193 N·m (142 FT. LBS.). NUMBERS 5, 6, 11, 12 & 14 TORQUE TO 80 N·m (59 FT. LBS.).

V6 diesel engine cylinder head torque sequence

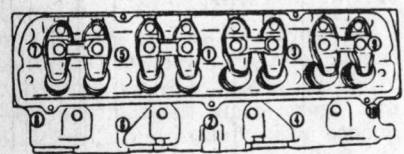

V8 Diesel cylinder head torque sequence

bolts, the bridged pivot and rocker arms.

3. Remove each rocker set as a unit.

4. Before installing any removed rocker arms, rotate the engine crankshaft so that No. 1 cylinder is 32° before top dead center. This is 2 in. counterclockwise from the 0° pointer. To verify that No. 1 cylinder TDC is coming up, if only the right valve cover was removed, remove the No. 1 cylinder glow plug, then turn the engine: compression pressure will force air out the glow plug hole. If the left valve cover was removed, rotate the crankshaft until the No. 5 cylinder intake valve pushrod ball is 0.28 in. above the No. 5 cylinder exhaust valve pushrod ball.

NOTE: Use only hand wrenches to torque the rocker arm pivot bolts to avoid engine damage.

5. If removed, install the No. 5 cylinder pivot and rocker arms, then torque the bolts alternately between the intake and exhaust valves until the intake valve begins to open, then stop.

6. Install the remaining rocker arms, except No. 3 exhaust (if this rocker was removed).

7. If removed, install the No. 3 cylinder exhaust valve pivot, but do not torque beyond the point that the valve would be fully open. This is indicated by strong resistance while still turning the pivot retaining bolts. Going beyond this point will bend the pushrod. Torque the bolts SLOWLY, allowing the lifter to bleed down.

8. Finish torquing No. 5 cylinder rocker arm pivot bolt slowly. Do not go beyond the point that the valve would be fully open, as in Step 7.

9. Do not turn the engine for at least 45 minutes.

10. Finish assembling the engine as the lifters are being bled.

V8 Engine

NOTE: When the rocker arms are removed or loosened, the lifters must be bled down to prevent oil pressure buildup inside each lifter, which could cause it to raise up higher than normal and bring the valves within striking distance of the pistons.

1. Remove the valve cover.

2. Remove the rocker arm pivot bolts, the bridged pivot and rocker arms.

3. Remove each rocker set as a unit.

4. To install, lubricate the pivot wear points and position each set of rocker arms in its proper location. Do not tighten the pivot bolts, to prevent bending the valves when the engine is turned.

5. The lifters can be bled down for six cylinders at once with the crankshaft in either of the following two positions:

a. For cylinders number 3, 5, 7, 2, 4 and 8, turn the crankshaft so the saw slot on the harmonic balancer is at 0° on the timing indicator.

b. For cylinders 1, 3, 7, 2, 4 and 6, turn the crankshaft so the saw slot on the harmonic balancer is at 4 O'clock.

6. Tighten the rocker arm pivot bolts to 28 ft. lbs. It will take 45 minutes to completely bleed down the lifters in this position. If additional lifters must be bled, rotate the engine to the other position, tighten the rocker arm pivot bolts, and again wait 45 minutes before rotating the crankshaft.

7. Assemble the remaining components in the reverse order of disassembly. The rocker covers do not use gaskets, but instead are sealed with a bead of RTV (room temperature vulcanizing) silicone sealer.

Intake Manifold

REMOVAL & INSTALLATION

1. Remove the air cleaner.

2. Drain the radiator. Loosen the upper bypass hose clamp, remove the thermostat housing bolts, and remove the housing and the thermostat from the intake manifold.

3. Remove the breather pipes from the rocker covers and the air crossover. Remove the air crossover.

4. Disconnect the throttle rod and the return spring. If equipped with cruise control, remove the servo.

5. Remove the hairpin clip at the bellcrank and disconnect the cables. Remove the throttle cable from the

bracket on the manifold; position the cable away from the engine. Disconnect and label any wiring as necessary.

6. Remove the alternator bracket if necessary. On the 350 cu. in. engine, if equipped with air conditioning, remove the compressor mounting bolts and move the compressor aside, without disconnecting any of the hoses or wiring. Remove the compressor mounting bracket from the intake manifold.

7. Disconnect the fuel line from the pump and the fuel filter. Remove the fuel filter and bracket.

8. Remove the fuel injection pump and lines. See above for procedures.

9. Disconnect and remove the vacuum pump or oil pump drive assembly from the rear of the engine.

10. Remove the intake manifold drain tube.

11. Remove the intake manifold bolts and remove the manifold. Remove the adapter seal. Remove the injection pump adapter.

12. Clean the mating surfaces of the cylinder heads and the intake manifold using a putty knife.

13. Coat both sides of the gasket surface that seal the intake manifold to the cylinder heads with GM sealer 1050026 or the equivalent. Position the intake manifold gaskets on the cylinder heads. To install the front and rear end seals, apply 1052915, 22521437, G.E. 1673 RTV sealer or equivalent to the end seals only. Then install the end seals, making sure that the ends are positioned under the cylinder heads.

14. Carefully lower the intake manifold into place on the engine.

15. Clean the intake manifold bolts thoroughly, then dip them in clean engine oil. Install the bolts and on the 350 V8 tighten to 15 ft. lbs. in the sequence shown. Next, tighten all the bolts to 30 ft. lbs., in sequence, and finally tighten to 40 ft. lbs. in sequence. On the 263 V6 engine tighten to 15 ft. lbs. in the sequence shown, then retorque to 41 ft. lbs.

16. Install the intake manifold drain tube and clamp.

17. Install injection pump adapter. If a new adapter is not being used, skip Steps 4 and 9.

18. Install the fuel injection pump.

19. Install the vacuum pump or coil pump drive assembly.

CAUTION

Do not operate the engine without vacuum pump/oil pump assembly in place as this assembly drives the engine oil pump.

---

20. Install the remaining components in the reverse sequence of their removal.

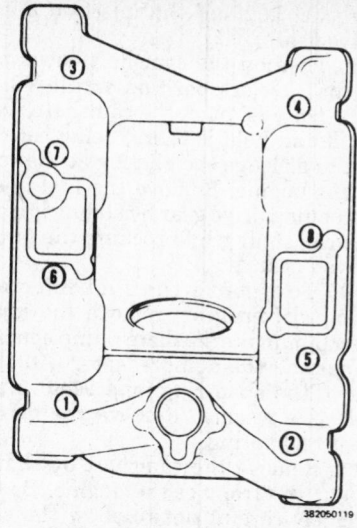

V6 intake manifold torque sequence

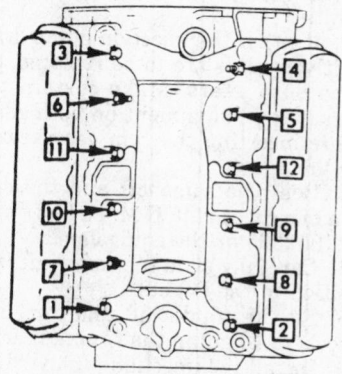

V8 Intake manifold torque sequence

Exhaust Manifold

REMOVAL & INSTALLATION

Left Side

1. Remove the air cleaner.
2. Remove the alternator lower bracket.
3. Raise and support the car.
4. Remove the crossover pipe.
5. Lower the car.
6. Remove the exhaust manifold.
7. Installation is in the reverse order of removal.

Right Side

1. Raise and support the car.
2. Remove the crossover pipe.
3. Disconnect the exhaust pipe.
4. Remove the right front wheel.
5. Remove the exhaust manifold from under the car.
6. Installation is in the reverse order of removal.

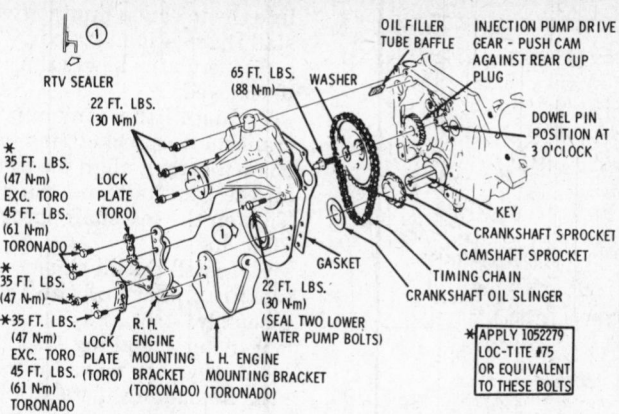

V8 diesel engine front cover and timing chain assembly

Front Cover

REMOVAL & INSTALLATION

NOTE: To perform this operation on the V8, you'll need a set of special tools designed to pull the crankshaft pulley off the crankshaft without damaging the rubber insert separating inner and outer pulley halves. Use tools equivalent to GM No. J–8614–3, J–8614–2, J–8614–1, and J–7583–3.

1. Drain the cooling system and disconnect the radiator hoses.
2. Remove all belts, fan and pulley. Remove the crankshaft pulley and balancer, utilizing the special tools described in the note above on the V8. See the illustration for proper assembly of these tools. On the V6, make sure you use a puller that will bolt to the outside of the balancer and pull it off by applying pressure to a pilot inserted into the center of the crankshaft.

— **CAUTION** —

The use of any other type of puller, such as a universal claw type which pulls on the outside of the hub, can destroy the balancer. The outside ring of the balancer is bonded in rubber to the hub. Pulling on the outside will break the bond. The timing mark is on the outside ring. If it is suspected that the bond is broken, check that the center of the keyway is 16° from the center of the timing slot. In addition, there are chiseled aligning marks between the weight and the hub.

3. Unbolt and remove the cover, timing indicator and water pump.
4. It may be necessary to grind a flat on the cover for gripping purposes.
5. Grind a chamfer on one end of each dowel pin.
6. Cut the excess material from the front end of the oil pan gasket on each side of the block.
7. Clean the block, oil pan and front cover mating surfaces with solvent.

8. Trim about ⅛ in. off each end of a new front pan seal.
9. Install a new front cover gasket on the block and a new seal in the front cover.
10. Apply sealer to the gasket around the coolant holes.
11. Apply sealer to the block at the junction of the pan and front cover. On V6, apply RTV sealer on the front cover oil pan seal retainer.
12. Place the cover on the block and press down to compress the seal. Rotate the cover left and right and guide the pan seal into the cavity using a small screwdriver. Oil bolt threads and heads, install two to hold the cover in place, then install both dowel pins (chamfered end first). Install remaining front cover bolts.
13. Apply a lubricant, compatible with rubber, on the balancer seal surface.
14. Install the balancer and bolt. Torque the bolt to 200–300 ft. lbs. on V8, 160–350 ft. lbs. on V6.
15. Install all other parts in the reverse order of removal.

OIL SEAL REPLACEMENT

1. Remove the crankshaft balancer.
2. Remove oil seal using tool BT-6406 or JT-23129 and J-1859-03.
3. Install new seal using tool BT-6405 or J-25264.

Timing Chain and Sprockets

REMOVAL & INSTALLATION

V8 Engine

1. Remove the front cover and gasket. Remove the crankshaft oil slinger.
2. Remove the fuel pump and fuel pump eccentric.
3. Remove the camshaft sprocket and timing chain.

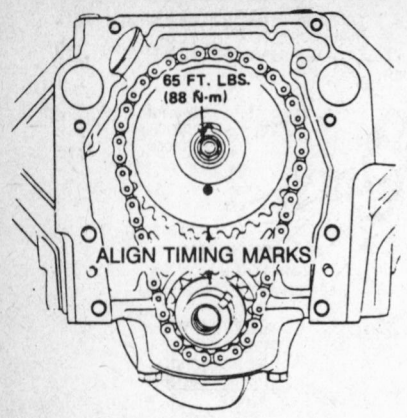

Aligning timing marks V8 diesel engine

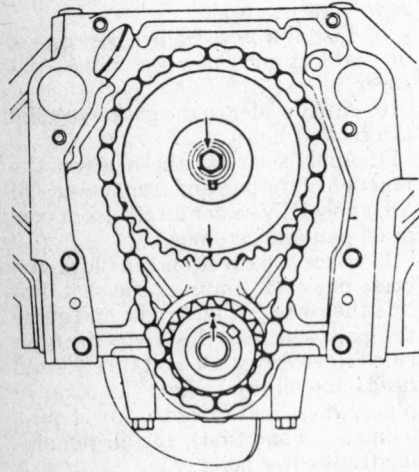

Aligning timing marks V6 diesel engine

4. Remove the crankshaft sprocket.

5. Installation is the reverse of the removal procedure. Assemble timing chain on sprockets with timing marks in their closest together position.

V6 Engine

1. Remove the front cover. Remove the valve covers.

2. Loosen all rocker arm pivot bolts evenly so that lash exists between the rocker arms and valves. It is not necessary to completely remove the rocker arms unless related service is being performed.

3. Remove the crankshaft oil slinger and the camshaft sprocket bolt and washer.

4. Remove the timing chain, camshaft and crankshaft sprockets. If the crankshaft sprocket is a tight fit on the crankshaft use an appropriate puller to remove it.

5. If the camshaft sprocket-to-cam key comes out with the camshaft sprocket, remove the front camshaft bearing retainer and install the key

into the injection pump drive gear. Install the bearing retainer.

6. Install the key in the crankshaft, if removed.

7. Install the camshaft sprocket, crankshaft sprocket and the timing chain together, align the timing marks on the camshaft and the crankshaft. Tighten the camshaft sprocket bolt to 70 ft. lbs.

8. Install the oil slinger and the remaining parts of the front cover assembly.

9. After installing the front cover, bleed down the valve lifters.

10. Remaining installation is in the reverse order of removal. Sealant is used in place of valve cover gaskets.

Camshaft

REMOVAL & INSTALLATION

NOTE: If the camshaft is to be removed the air conditioning system must be discharged by a professional and the condenser removed. Removal of the camshaft also requires removal of the injection pump drive and driven gears, removal of the intake manifold, disassembly of the valve lifters, and re-timing of the injection pump.

1. Disconnect the negative battery cables. Drain the coolant. Remove the radiator.

2. Remove the intake manifold and gasket and the front and rear intake manifold seals. Refer to the intake manifold removal and installation procedure. Remove the oil pump drive assembly on the V6.

3. Remove the balancer pulley and the balancer. Remove the engine front cover using the appropriate procedure. Rotate the engine so that the timing marks align on V6s.

4. Remove the valve covers. Remove the rocker arms, pushrods and valve lifters; see the procedure earlier in this section. Be sure to keep the parts in order so that they may be returned to their original locations.

5. On V8s, if equipped with air conditioning, the condenser must be discharged and removed from the car.

———— CAUTION ————

Compressed refrigerant expands (boils) into the atmosphere at a temperature of -26°F. It will freeze any surface it contacts, including your skin or eyes.

———————————————————

6. Remove the camshaft sprocket retaining bolt, and remove the timing chain and sprockets.

7. On V6s, remove the front camshaft bearing retainer bolt and the retainer, then remove the camshaft

sprocket key and the injection pump drive gear.

8. Position the camshaft dowel pin at the 3 o'clock position on the V8.

9. On V8s, push the camshaft rearward and hold it there, being careful not to dislodge the oil plug at the rear of the engine. Remove the fuel injection pump drive gear by sliding it from the camshaft while rocking the pump driven gear.

10. To remove the fuel injection pump driven gear, remove the injection pump intermediate pump adapter (V6s) and the pump adapter (All), remove the snap ring, and remove the selective washer. Remove the driven gear and spring.

11. Remove the camshaft by sliding it out the front of the engine. Be extremely careful not to allow the cam lobes to contact any of the bearings, or the journals to dislodge the bearings during camshaft removal. Do not force the camshaft, or bearing damage will result.

12. If either the injection pump drive or driven gears are to be replaced, replace both gears. Make certain the marks are in alignment on both gears before inserting the cam gear key on the V6.

13. Coat the camshaft and the cam bearings with GM lubricant No.1052365 or the equivalent.

14. Carefully slide the camshaft into position in the engine.

15. Fit the crankshaft and camshaft sprockets, aligning the timing marks.

16. Install the injection pump driven gear, spring, shim, and snap ring. Check the gear end play. If the end play is not within .002–.015 in. on V8s, or .002–.006 on V6s, replace the shim to obtain the specified clearance. Shims are available in 0.003 in. increments, from 0.080–0.115 in.

17. On V8s, bring the camshaft dowel pin to the 3 o'clock position. Align the zero marks on the pump drive gear and pump driven gear. Hold the camshaft in the rearward position and slide the pump drive gear onto the camshaft. On the V6, align the zero marks on the injection pump drive and driven gears, then install the camshaft sprocket key. Install the camshaft bearing retainer.

18. Install the timing chain and sprockets, making sure the timing marks are aligned.

19. Install the lifters, pushrods and rocker arms. Failure to bleed down the lifters could bend valves when the engine is turned over.

20. Install the injection pump adapter and injection pump. See the appropriate sections under "Fuel System" for procedures.

21. Install the remaining components in the reverse order of removal.

Piston and Connecting Rod

NOTE: For all piston and connecting rod overhaul procedures, please refer to "Engine Rebuilding" in the Unit Repair section.

POSITIONING

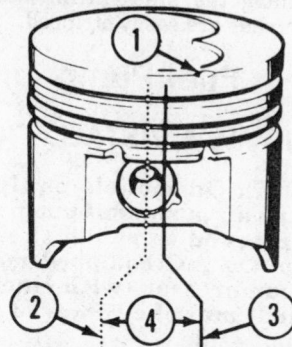

1. Notch towards front of engine
2. Piston pin center line
3. Piston center line
4. Offset

Diesel piston positioning

ENGINE LUBRICATION

Oil Pan

REMOVAL & INSTALLATION

Gasoline Engines

1. Remove the distributor cap and align the rotor to No. 1 firing position. On Cutlass, align the timing marks so No. 1 is at top dead center.
2. Disconnect the battery ground cable and remove the dipstick.
3. Remove the upper radiator support and the fan shroud attaching screws.
4. Raise the car and drain the oil.
5. Remove the flywheel cover.
6. Remove the starter motor assembly.
7. Disconnect the exhaust pipes and the crossover pipe.
8. Disconnect the engine mounts and raise the front of the engine as far as possible.
9. Remove the oil pan attaching bolts and remove the pan.
10. Coat both sides of the new gasket with sealer when installing. Installation is in the reverse order of removal. Torque the attaching bolts to 10 ft. lbs.

Diesel Engines

1. On V8s, remove the vacuum

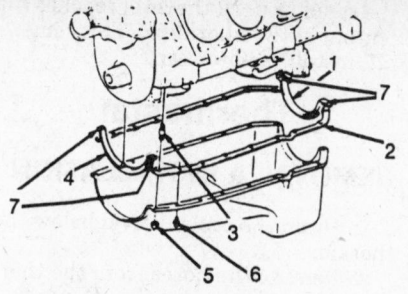

1. Rear oil pan seal
2. Side gaskets
3. Fully seat bolt
4. Front oil pan seal
5. 17 ft. lbs.
6. 10 ft. lbs.
7. Apply sealer

5.0L V8 oil pan and gaskets

pump and drive (with A/C) or the oil pump drive (without A/C). On V6s, remove the oil pump drive and vacuum pump.
2. Disconnect the batteries and remove the dipstick.
3. Remove the upper radiator support and fan shroud.
4. Raise and support the car. Drain the oil.
5. Remove the flywheel cover.
6. Disconnect the exhaust and crossover pipes.
7. Remove the oil cooler lines at the filter base.
8. Remove the starter assembly. Support the engine with a jack.
9. Remove the engine mounts from the block.
10. Raise the front of the engine and remove the oil pan.
11. Installation is in the reverse order of removal.

Rear Main Bearing Oil Seal

REMOVAL & INSTALLATION

Gasoline and Diesel Engines

The crankshaft need not be removed to replace the rear main bearing upper oil seal.

1. Drain the crankcase and remove the oil pan and rear main bearing cap.
2. Using a blunt-ended tool, drive the upper seal into its groove on each side until it is tightly packed. This is usually 1/4–3/4 in.
3. Cut pieces of new seal 1/16 in. longer than required to fill the grooves and install, packing into place.
4. Carefully trim any protruding

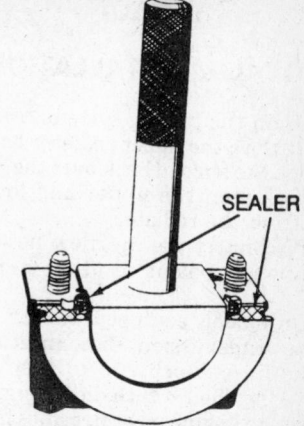

SEALER

AFTER CORRECTLY POSITIONING SEAL ROTATE TOOL SLIGHTLY AND CUT OFF EACH END OF SEAL FLUSH WITH CAP

Installing rear main oil seal into cap

seal, being sure not to scratch or damage the bearing surface.
5. Install a new seal in the bearing cap. Now, seat the seal with a tool such as BT-7923 or J-2528A. Rock the tool back and forth slightly and then cut off either end flush with the cap, holding the seal in position with the tool. Apply a thin film of chassis grease to the rope seal. Apply a sealer such as 1050026 or the equivalent to the area of the cap around the ends of the seal. Use the sealer sparingly and keep it out of the bolt threads. Install cap, tightening bolts to 120 ft. lbs. (107 ft. lbs. on V6 diesel). Install the oil pan.

Oil Pump

REMOVAL & INSTALLATION

Gasoline and Diesel Engines

1. Disconnect the negative battery cable. Drain the engine oil, remove the oil pan and baffle (if equipped).
2. Remove the pump attaching bolts and remove the pump.
3. Reinstall in reverse order. To insure immediate oil pressure on start up, the oil pump gear cavity should be packed with petroleum jelly.

ENGINE COOLING

The diesel engine cooling system is the same as that used on the gasoline engine except that the radiator tank has two oil coolers. One is connected to the transmission, the other to the oil filter base.

Radiator

REMOVAL & INSTALLATION

1. Drain the cooling system.
2. Remove the upper radiator baffle and slide the shroud back over the fan.
3. Unfasten the upper and lower hoses from the radiator.
4. Disconnect the overflow hose or the optional coolant recovery system hose.
5. On models equipped with an automatic transmission, disconnect and cap the lines which run to the fluid cooler. On vehicles with diesel engines remove the engine oil cooler lines from the radiator.
6. Unfasten the radiator's securing bolts and move the radiator upward to disengage it from its supports. Remove the radiator from the car.

NOTE: It may be necessary to rotate the fan blades in order to keep them out of the way.

7. Installation is in the reverse order of removal. Refill the cooling system.

Water Pump

REMOVAL & INSTALLATION

1. Drain the cooling system.
2. Disconnect the heater, bypass, and lower radiator hoses from the pump.
3. Loosen the drive belts. Remove the fan assembly and the four spacer bolts. On cars with A/C, remove the fan and clutch assembly.

NOTE: Keep the fan in an upright position during removal to prevent the silicone fluid from leaking out of the fan clutch.

4. Remove the alternator, A/C compressor and power steering brackets, if necessary. Do not disconnect any air conditioning hoses.
5. Unfasten the bolts which secure the water pump and remove it.
6. Installation is the reverse of the removal procedure.
7. Apply a thin coating of sealer to the pump housing gasket mounting surface.
8. Place a new gasket on the housing.
9. Install the pump assembly. Apply a thin coat of sealer to the bolts and tighten them to specifications.
10. Properly adjust all belt tensions and refill the cooling system.
11. Start engine and run, with radiator cap off, until upper hose becomes hot (thermostat open).
12. With engine idling, add coolant to

the radiator until the level reaches the bottom of the filler neck. Turn engine off, install radiator cap.

Thermostat

REMOVAL & INSTALLATION

1. Drain the coolant level below the thermostat.
2. Remove the hoses from the thermostat housing.
3. Remove the bolts, water outlet, and gasket from the thermostat housing.
4. Install the new thermostat and gasket in the engine. The thermostat may be etched with the word front; if so, front must face the radiator.
5. Connect the hoses and refill the cooling system.
6. Run engine until it reaches normal operating temperature, then check the area around the thermostat housing for leaks.

EMISSION CONTROLS

NOTE: Please refer to "Emission Control" in the Unit Repair section for system maintenance procedures. Due to the complex nature of modern electronic engine control systems, comprehensive diagnosis and testing procedures fall outside the confines of this repair manual. For complete information on diagnosis, testing and repair procedures concerning all modern engine and emission control systems, please refer to *"Chilton's Guide to Electronic Engine Controls".*

GASOLINE FUEL SYSTEM

NOTE: When working with the fuel system certain precautions should be taken; always work in a well ventilated area, keep a dry chemical (Class B) fire extinguisher near the work area. Always disconnect the negative battery cable and do not make any repairs to the fuel system until all the necessary steps for repair have been reviewed.

Fuel Filter

REPLACEMENT

All carburetors have a fuel filter in the carburetor body. To replace the filter element, remove the fuel inlet line, then remove the inlet fitting and pull out the filter element. Be careful when tightening the brass fitting because the threads are easily stripped.

Fuel Pump

REMOVAL & INSTALLATION

NOTE: On models equipped with an air pump, this pump must be removed to reach the fuel pump. On A/C equipped models the compressor (with lines attached) must be removed first and put aside.

1. Disconnect the fuel lines at the fuel pump.
2. Remove the two mounting bolts or nuts.
3. Remove the shields and oil filter on V6 engines.
4. Remove the pump and gasket. Installation is in the reverse order of removal.

—————— CAUTION ——————
Never drain or store fuel in an open container due to the possibility of fire or explosion which could result in personal injury.

TESTING

1. Connect a hose from the carburetor fuel feed line to an unbreakable container.
2. Start the engine and let it idle for 15 seconds. Pump should supply ½ pint or more in 15 seconds. If not go to Step 3, if OK go to Step 5.
3. Disconnect inlet hose at pump and connect a vacuum gage. Crank engine until maximum vacuum is reached. If less than 15 in. (50.6 kPa), replace the pump. If reading is higher than 15 in. (50.6 kPa) go to Step 4.
4. Check fuel lines and hoses for splits and leaks by disconnecting each section of line and connecting a vacuum gage. Crank the engine until gage peaks. Vacuum should be at least 15 in. (50.6 kPa). If less, replace the malfunctioning line or hose.
5. If fuel lines and pump check OK, remove the tank unit, replace the strainer and clean the fuel tank.

Carburetor

REMOVAL & INSTALLATION

1. Disconnect the negative battery cable.

2. Remove the air cleaner.

3. Disconnect the accelerator linkage.

4. Disconnect the transmission detent cable.

5. Disconnect the cruise control, if so equipped.

6. Disconnect the fuel line at the carburetor.

7. Disconnect all necessary vacuum lines. Number them for easy reinstallation.

8. Remove the attaching bolts, then the carburetor.

9. Installation is in the reverse order of removal.

10. When installing the carburetor, torque the mounting bolts to 12 ft. lbs., in an "X" pattern.

OVERHAUL

NOTE: For all carburetor overhaul and adjustment procedures, please refer to "Carburetor Service" in the Unit Repair section.

DIESEL FUEL SYSTEM

The fuel system is the heart of the diesel engine. The main components are the injection pump, injection lines and fuel injectors. The fuel injection pump is a small, high pressure rotary pump which delivers a small, metered amount of fuel to the injection nozzles at the proper time. The high pressure lines are all of equal length to avoid differences in timing. The nozzles project into the combustion chambers and inject the fuel into the chambers in a finely atomized, precisely controlled spray. A small, low pressure transfer pump is employed in the inlet line to the injection pump to keep the injection pump supplied. Engine rpm is controlled by a rotary fuel metering valve operated by the accelerator linkage. A fuel filter is located between the transfer pump and the injection pump. On all engines, the fuel pump is of the mechanical diaphragm type, mounted on the engine.

Fuel Filter

NOTE: When working with the fuel system certain precautions should be taken; always work in a well ventilated area, keep a dry chemical (Class B) fire extinguisher near the work area. Always disconnect the negative battery cable and do not make any re-

pairs to the fuel system until all the necessary steps for repair have been reviewed.

REPLACEMENT

1984-85 5.7L Diesel Engine

1. The fuel filter assembly is located on the left front side of the engine. Disconnect the fuel lines from the inlet and outlet sides of the filter.

2. Remove the drain hose and the electrical connector from the filter housing and remove the bolts on the attaching bracket.

3. Remove the filter assembly by rotating it slightly to release it. Clamp the entire assembly in a vise and carefully remove the filter cartridge. Be sure to clean the gasket surface before installing a new filter.

4. Apply a light coat of engine oil to the gasket on the new filter then install by reversing removal procedures.

1982-83 V6 (4.3L)/V8 (5.7L) Diesel Engines

1. The fuel filter is a square box located on the top—rear of the engine. Disconnect the negative battery cable.

2. Disconnect the inlet and outlet lines from the filter box. Remove the filter from its mounting bracket.

3. Install the new filter and reconnect the fuel lines, be sure not to over tighten the lines. Start the engine and check for leaks.

DRAINING WATER FROM THE SYSTEM

NOTE: Due to the chemical composition of diesel fuel, water develops in the fuel system. If the water is not periodically removed, damage may occur in the fuel system which could affect performance and the life expectancy of the components in the system.

1984-85 5.7L Diesel Engine

1. Turn ignition to the run position, but do not start the engine, this will turn on the fuel pump.

2. The water drain valve is located on the left fender well. Using a suitable container, open the valve two complete turns. Reach over to the filter assembly and push the red button in, this will allow the fuel to flow from the valve.

3. Let fuel and water drain until the

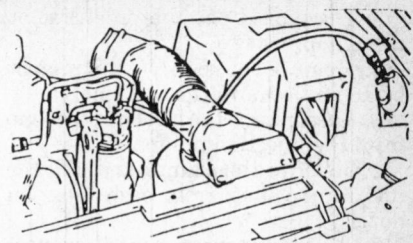

1984-85 5.7L V8 diesel fuel filter and drain valve

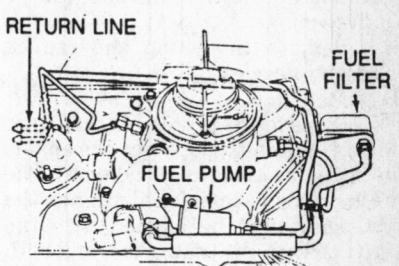

RETURN LINE

FUEL FILTER

FUEL PUMP

V6-V8 Diesel fuel filter and location

color of the fuel is uniform, this will usually take 15-20 seconds, then release button and close the drain valve.

1982-83 V6 (4.3L)/V8 (5.7L) Diesel Engines

1. Remove the negative battery cable.

2. Using a hand operated pump, drain as much fuel as possible through the fuel filler neck.

3. To complete the draining process, disconnect the main fuel line at the fuel tank or the fuel pump, and use a siphon to remove any remaining fuel.

4. Reconnect the fuel line and fill with clean fuel.

Diesel Injection Pump

REMOVAL & INSTALLATION

NOTE: This procedure contains throttle rod and transmission cable adjustments.

1. Remove the air cleaner.

2. Remove the filters and pipes from the valve covers and air crossover.

3. Remove the air crossover and cap the intake manifold with screened covers (J-26996-1 on V8's or 29657 V6), or tape.

4. Disconnect the throttle rod and return spring.

5. Remove the bellcrank.

6. Remove the throttle and transmission cables from the intake manifold brackets.

7. Disconnect the fuel lines from the filter and remove the filter.

8. Disconnect the fuel inlet line at the pump.

9. Remove the rear A/C compressor brace and remove the fuel line.

10. Disconnect the fuel return line from the injection pump.

11. Remove the clamps and pull the fuel return lines from each injection nozzle.

12. Using two wrenches, disconnect the high pressure lines at the nozzles.

13. Remove the three injection pump retaining nuts with tool J-26987 or its equivalent.

14. Remove the pump and cap all lines and nozzles.

To install:

15. Remove the protective caps from all lines and nozzles. Place the engine on TDC for the No. 1 cylinder. The mark on the harmonic balancer on the crankshaft will be aligned with the zero mark on the timing tab, and both valves for No. 1 cylinder will be closed. The index mark on the injection pump driven gear should be offset to the right when No. 1 is at TDC. Check that all of these conditions are met before continuing.

16. Line up the offset tang on the pump driveshaft with the pump driven gear and install the pump.

17. Install, but do not tighten the pump retaining nuts.

18. Connect the high pressure lines at the nozzles.

19. Using two wrenches, torque the high pressure line nuts to 25 ft. lbs.

20. Connect the fuel return lines to the nozzles and pump.

21. Align the timing mark on the injection pump with the line on the timing mark adapter and torque the mounting nuts to 35 ft. lbs. V6, 18 ft. lbs. V8.

NOTE: A ¾ in. open end wrench on the boss at the front of the injection pump will aid in rotating the pump to align the marks.

22. Adjust the throttle rod:

   a. remove the clip from the cruise control rod and remove the rod from the bellcrank.

   b. loosen the locknut on the throttle rod a few turns, then shorten the rod several turns.

   c. rotate the bellcrank to the full throttle stop, then lengthen the throttle rod until the injection pump lever contacts the injection pump full throttle stop, then release the bellcrank.

   d. tighten the throttle rod locknut.

23. Install the fuel inlet line between the transfer pump and the filter.

24. Install the rear A/C compressor brace.

25. Install the bellcrank and clip.

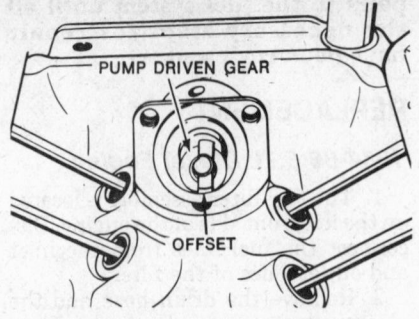

Offset on pump driven gear

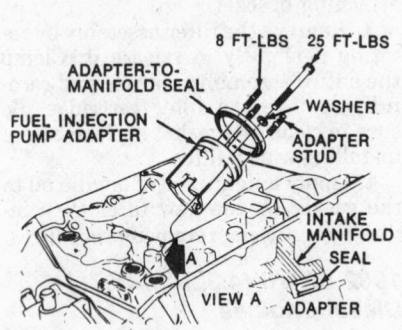

Injection pump adapter bolts

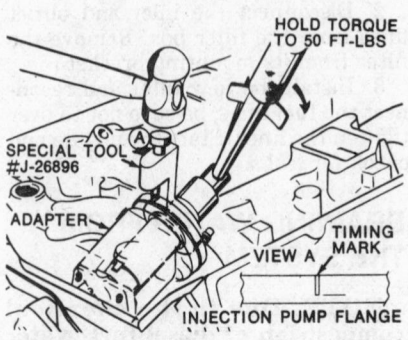

Marking Injection pump adapter

26. Connect the throttle rod and return spring.

27. Adjust the transmission cable:

   a. push the snap-lock to the disengaged position.

   b. rotate the injection pump lever to the full throttle stop and hold it there.

   c. push in the snap-lock until it is flush.

   d. release the injection pump lever.

28. Start the engine and check for fuel leaks.

29. Remove the screened covers or tape and install the air crossover.

30. Install the tubes in the air flow control valve in the air crossover and install the ventilation filters in the valve covers.

31. Install the air cleaner.

32. Start the engine and allow it to run for two minutes. Stop the engine,

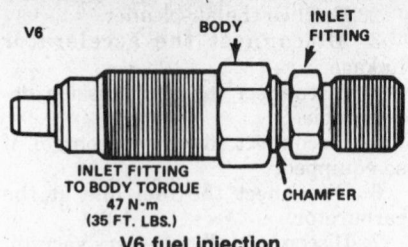

V6 fuel injection

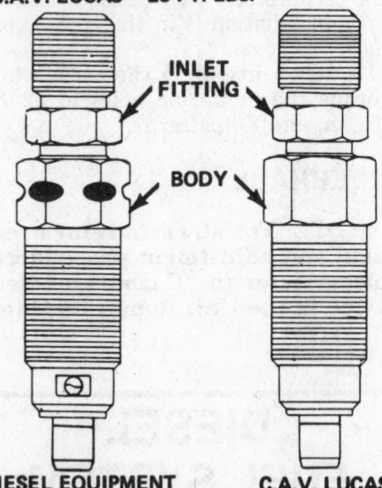

V8 diesel fuel injector identification—1980 and later

let it stand for two minutes, then restart. This permits the air to bleed off within the pump.

INJECTION TIMING

For the engine to be properly timed, the lines on the top of the injection pump adapter and the flange of the injection pump must be aligned.

1. The engine must be off for resetting the timing.

2. Loosen the three pump retaining nuts with J-26987 on V8's or J-25304 on V6's, an injection pump intake manifold wrench, or its equivalent.

3. Align the timing marks and torque the pump retaining nuts to 35 ft. lbs.

NOTE: The use of a ¾ in. open end wrench on the boss at the front of the pump will aid in rotating the pump to align the marks.

4. Adjust the throttle rod.

REMOVAL & INSTALLATION

The injection nozzles on these engines are simply unbolted from the cylinder head, after the fuel lines are removed, in similar fashion to a spark plug. Be careful not to damage the nozzle end and make sure you remove the copper nozzle gasket from the cylinder head if it does not come off with the nozzle. Clean the carbon off the tip of the nozzle with a soft brass wire brush and install the nozzles, with gaskets.

NOTE: Two types of injectors are used, CAV Lucas and Diesel Equipment. When installing the inlet fittings, torque the Diesel Equipment injector fitting to 45 ft. lbs. and the CAV Lucas to 25 ft. lbs.

MANUAL TRANSMISSION

REMOVAL & INSTALLATION

1. Disconnect throttle linkage and raise car. If applicable, disconnect T.C.S. switch.
2. Remove the driveshaft.
3. Support the rear of the engine. Remove the catalytic converter and/or brackets, if they are in the way.
4. On console equipped floorshifts, disconnect shifter assembly at transmission, allowing this unit to remain in car.
5. Disconnect parking brake cables and remove the cross member.
6. Disconnect speedometer cable and back-up light switch.
7. Remove transmission upper and lower bolts.

— CAUTION —
During removal, use aligning studs to support the transmission, otherwise distortion of the clutch driven plate will result.

8. Slide transmission rearward and remove. On models equipped with dual exhaust, it may be necessary to disconnect left exhaust pipe at the manifold.
9. Install by reversing the removal procedure.

LINKAGE ADJUSTMENT

4-Speed

1. Turn the ignition switch to the OFF position.
2. Raise and support the car.
3. Loosen the lock nuts at the swivels on the shift rods.
4. Set the transmission levers in Neutral.
5. Place the shifter in Neutral.
6. Align the control levers and place a ¼ in. gauge pin into the levers and bracket.
7. Tighten the First/Second shift

rod nut against the swivel. Torque to 10 ft. lbs.
8. Tighten the Third/Fourth shift rod nut against the swivel. Torque to 10 ft. lbs.
9. Tighten the reverse shift control rod nut to 10 ft. lbs.
10. Remove the gauge pin, check for proper operation of the levers and lower the car.

CLUTCH

REMOVAL & INSTALLATION

1. Remove the transmission.
2. Detach the clutch return spring and clutch release rod assembly.
3. Remove the throwout bearing.
4. Without removing the starter from the engine, remove the flywheel housing.

NOTE: The release yoke, boot and ball stud will remain in the housing.

5. Scribe a mark opposite the X mark on the flywheel cover. This mark is for proper flywheel balancing.
6. Loosen the pressure plate evenly, one turn at a time.

— CAUTION —
Do not lubricate the splines as the lubricant will be forced onto the damper, resulting in clutch rattle.

Clutch installation is performed in the following order:
1. Install the clutch disc/cover assembly and finger-tighten its securing bolts.

NOTE: Align the mark made during removal with the X mark on the flywheel cover.

2. Use a clutch arbor or an old input shaft to align the disc by inserting it through the disc and into the pilot bearing.
3. Tighten every other bolt until the cover assembly is within ¼ in. of the flywheel.
4. Repeat Step 3 for the three remaining bolts.
5. Tighten the first three bolts to 30 ft. lbs. and then tighten the remaining three bolts to the same torque.
6. Remove the arbor. Lubricate the inside groove of the throwout bearing and the release yoke ball stud with wheel bearing grease.
7. Install the throwout bearing.
8. Install the flywheel housing and the transmission. Adjust clutch freeplay as outlined above.

PEDAL HEIGHT/FREE-PLAY ADJUSTMENT

1. Loosen the locknut on the pushrod swivel.
2. Detach the pedal return spring.
3. Turn the clutch lever and shaft assembly until the clutch pedal seats against the rubber bumper on the dash brace.
4. Push the outer end of the clutch fork rearward, so that the throwout bearing just contacts the clutch plate.
5. Remove the retaining clip from the lower pushrod swivel and install the swivel in the upper gauge hole. Install the retaining clip.
6. Lengthen the pushrod until there is no lash.
7. Remove the retaining clip and reinstall the swivel in the lower hole on the lever and shaft assembly.
8. Tighten the locknut against the swivel. Be sure the rod length remains unchanged.
9. Install the pedal return spring and check pedal free-play.

AUTOMATIC TRANSMISSION

All Oldsmobile and Pontiac models use the Turbo Hydra-Matic automatic transmission. The transmission can be identified visually: The 200, 250 and 350 have a square or oblong pan with the right rear corner cut off. Some 200s have the word METRIC embossed in the pan. The 200 has ten pan bolts; the 350 has thirteen. The 250 has an intermediate band adjusting screw on the right side of the case. The 200, 250 and 350 have a downshift cable between the carburetor linkage and the transmission. The 200-R4 four speed automatic overdrive transmission was introduced in 1981.

NOTE: For further information on automatic transmissions, please refer to "Automatic Transmissions" in the Unit Repair section.

REMOVAL & INSTALLATION

1. Remove the air cleaner assembly.
2. Disconnect the throttle valve detent cable.
3. Remove the dipstick (and the bolt holding the dipstick tube if accessible).
4. Jack up the car and support it with jack-stands.
5. Remove the driveshaft.
6. Disconnect the speedometer cable and shift linkage.

7. Disconnect any electrical leads.

8. Remove the flywheel cover; matchmark the flywheel and converter to maintain original balance.

9. Remove the torque converter to flywheel bolts and/or nuts.

NOTE: It may be necessary to disconnect the catalytic converter support bracket.

10. Remove the transmission support bracket (rear crossmember).

11. Remove the oil cooler lines.

12. Support the transmission with a transmission jack and remove the bellhousing bolts.

13. Support the engine with a jack and remove the transmission.

NOTE: Carefully remove the transmission to prevent the torque converter from falling off the mainshaft.

14. Installation is in the reverse order of removal.

DRIVE AXLE

Driveshaft

REMOVAL & INSTALLATION

1. Matchmark the relationship of the driveshaft to the differential flange.

2. Unbolt the straps or flange. Tape the bearing caps in place to prevent losing the bearing rollers. Support the driveshaft to prevent excessive strain on the universal joint.

3. Pull the shaft back and remove it. Be careful not to damage the splines at the transmission end.

4. If the transmission splined slip yoke does not have a vent hole at the center, it should be lubricated with engine oil. If it does have a vent hole, it should be lubricated with grease. Slide the slip yoke into place.

5. Align the matchmarks and tighten the bolts. Strap bolts should be tightened to 16 ft. lbs.

Rear Axle Shafts

REMOVAL & INSTALLATION

C-lock Type

These cars use the C-lock type rear axles. The axle shafts are retained by C-shaped locks, which fit grooves at the inner end of the shaft. Bearings in the C-lock type axle consist of an outer race, bearing rollers and a roller cage, retained by snaprings.

1. Raise the vehicle and remove the wheels and brake drums.

2. Clean the area of the cover and drain the fluid from the carrier by removing the cover. Remove the differential pinion shaft.

3. Push the flanged end of the axle shaft toward the center of the vehicle and remove the C-lock from the end of the shaft.

4. Remove the axle shaft from the housing, being careful not to damage the oil seal.

5. Remove the oil seal with a pry bar inserted behind the steel case of the oil seal. Pry the seal loose from the bore.

6. Seat the legs of the bearing puller behind the bearing. Seat a washer against the bearing and hold it in place with a nut. Use a slide hammer to pull the bearing.

7. Pack the cavity between the seal lips with wheel bearing lubricant and lubricate a new wheel bearing with same.

8. Use a suitable driver and install the bearing until it bottoms. Lubricate the lips of the oil seal and tap it into place so it is flush with the axle tube.

9. Slide the axle shaft into place. Be sure that the splines on the shaft do not damage the oil seal. Make sure that the splines engage the differential side gear.

10. Install the axle shaft C-lock on the inner end of the axle shaft and push the shaft outward so that the C-lock seats in the differential side gear counterbore.

11. Position the differential pinion shaft through the case and pinions, aligning the hole in the case with the hole for the lockscrew.

12. Install the pinion shaft lockscrew.

13. Use a new gasket and install the carrier cover. Be sure that the gasket surfaces are clean before installing the gasket and cover.

14. Fill the axle with lubricant to the bottom of the filler hole.

15. Install the brake drum and wheels and lower the car. Check for leaks and road test the car.

FRONT SUSPENSION

Shock Absorber

REMOVAL & INSTALLATION

1. Remove the two bolts and lockwashers securing the shock to the lower control arm.

2. Remove the upper nut, retainer, and grommet from the shock.

3. To install, reverse the removal procedure.

NOTE: Purge new shock absorbers of air by repeatedly extending in their normal position and compressing while inverted.

Lower Control Arm and Spring

REMOVAL & INSTALLATION

1. Place the transmission in Neutral so the steering wheel is unlocked.

2. Raise the car and remove the wheel. Support the car with stands.

3. Remove the shock absorber.

4. Insert a spring removal tool into the shock hole. Rotate the tool so the plate is well seated in the lower control arm spring seat.

5. Rotate the nut on the tool to compress the spring slightly, just enough so it is free in the seat.

6. On all models remove the two lower control arm pivot bolts and disengage the arm from the frame.

7. Rotate the arm and remove the spring.

8. Loosen the lower ball joint stud nut a few turns. Using a ball joint remover, expand the tool to snap the ball joint loose from the knuckle.

9. Remove the stud nut and the control arm.

10. Installation is in the reverse order of removal. Torque the lower ball joint stud nut to 95 ft. lbs.

Torsion Bars

REMOVAL & INSTALLATION

1. Raise the vehicle and support it safely.

2. Disconnect each side of the torsion bar by removing the nut from the link bolt. Pull the bolt from the linkage and remove retainers, grommets, and spacer.

3. Remove bracket to frame or body bolts and remove torsion bar, rubber bushings, and brackets.

4. Installation is the reverse of the removal procedure. Install the torsion bar with the identification forming on the right side of the car and the slit in the rubber bushings facing the front of the car.

5. Tighten torsion bar link nut to 13 ft. lbs. (18 Nm) and the bracket bolts to 24 ft. lbs. (33 Nm).

Ball Joints

INSPECTION

Upper Ball Joint

1. Raise the vehicle and position floor stands under the left and right lower control arm as near as possible to each lower ball joint. Upper control arm bumper must not contact frame.
2. Position a dial indicator against the wheel rim.
3. Grasp the front wheel and push in on bottom of the tire while pulling out at the top. Read the guage, then reverse the push—pull procedure. Horizontal deflection on the dial indicator should not exceed 1.25 in. (3.18 mm).
4. If the indicator exceeds 1.25 in. (3.18 mm), or if ball stud (when disconnected from the knuckle assembly) can be twisted in its socket with your fingers, replace the ball joint.

Lower Ball Joint

These lower ball joints contain a visual wear indicator. The lower ball joint grease plug screws into the wear indicator which protrudes from the bottom of the ball joint housing. As long as the wear indicator extends out of the ball joint housing, the ball joint is not worn. If the tip of the wear indicator is parallel with, or recessed into the ball joint housing, the ball joint is defective.

REMOVAL & INSTALLATION

Upper Ball Joint

1. Raise the front of car and place floor stands under the lower control arm between the spring seats and the ball joints.

— CAUTION —

Leave the jack under the spring seat during removal and installation, in order to keep the spring and control arm positioned.

2. Remove the wheel.
3. Remove the cotter pin from the upper ball joint stud and loosen the upper ball joint nut.
4. Using a ball joint remover tool, break the stud loose and remove the nut and pull the stud out of the knuckle. Support the steering knuckle to prevent damage to the brake line.
5. Using a ⅛ in. diameter drill bit, drill into each of the four rivet heads to a depth of ½ in.
6. Drill off the rivet heads with a 1/2 in. diameter bit.
7. Punch out the rivets and remove the ball joint.
8. To install, place the new ball joint in the upper control arm and secure it

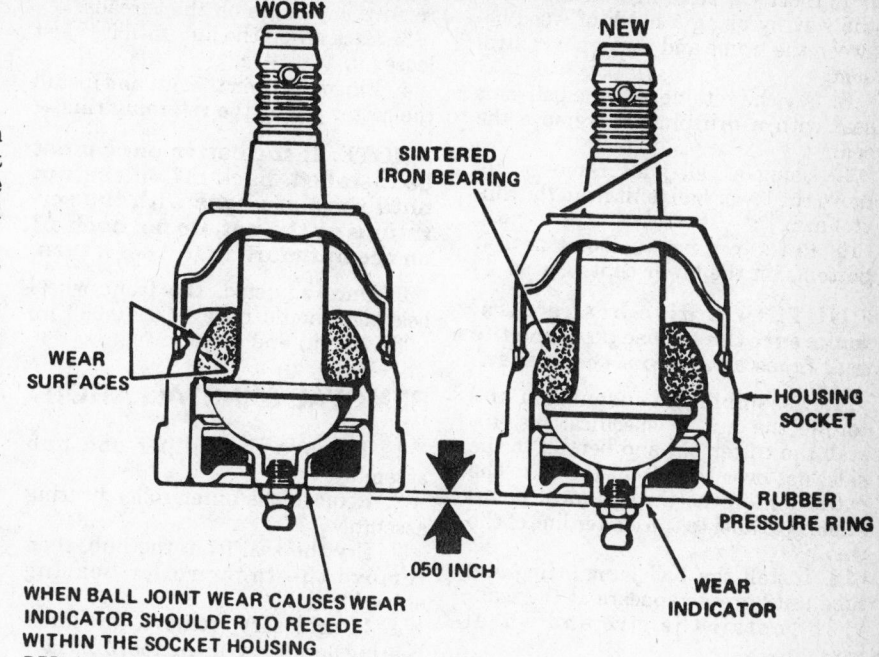

WHEN BALL JOINT WEAR CAUSES WEAR INDICATOR SHOULDER TO RECEDE WITHIN THE SOCKET HOUSING REPLACEMENT IS REQUIRED

Lower ball joint wear indicator

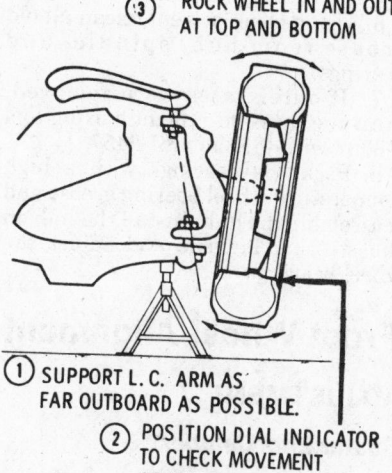

① SUPPORT L. C. ARM AS FAR OUTBOARD AS POSSIBLE.
② POSITION DIAL INDICATOR TO CHECK MOVEMENT AT THIS POINT

Checking upper ball joint

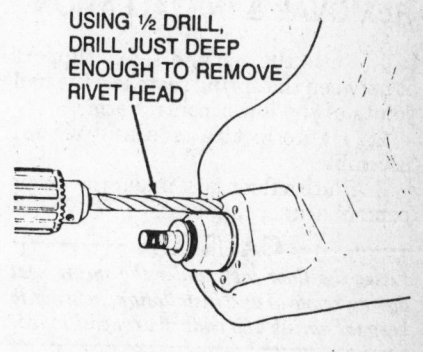

Removing upper ball joint

with four bolts and nuts in place of rivets. Torque the nuts to specifications.
9. Connect the ball joint to steering knuckle. Torque the nut to specifications.

NOTE: When replacing ball joints, use only high-quality replacement parts and bolts and nuts specified to be strong enough to endure the stress. Always advance the ball stud nut to align the cotter pin hole.

10. Install the grease fitting and lubricate until grease appears at the seal.

11. Install the wheel.

Lower Ball Joint

1. Raise the car and support the frame.
2. Remove the tire and wheel.
3. Place a floor jack under the control arm spring seat.

— CAUTION —

Leave the jack under the spring seat during removal and installation, in order to keep the spring and control arm positioned.

4. Remove the cotter pin from the ball joint stud and, using a ball joint stud removal tool, separate the ball joint from the steering knuckle.
5. When the stud comes loose, remove the stud nut.
6. Guide the lower control arm through the opening in the splash shield using a screwdriver.

7. Block the steering knuckle out of the way by using a block of wood between the frame and the upper control arm.

8. Pry the retainer off the ball joint seal with a driftpin and remove the seal.

9. Using a ball joint remover, remove the lower ball joint from the control arm.

10. Press in a new balljoint until it bottoms on the lower control arm.

NOTE: On disc brake cars, make sure the grease purge on the seal faces away from the brakes.

11. Assemble the suspension and torque the nut to specifications. Install the cotter pin and bend it to the side, not over the top of the nut. The cotter pin on the Cutlass must be installed parallel to the center line of the car.

12. Install the ball joint fitting and lube until grease appears at the seal.

13. Install the tire and wheel assembly.

Upper Control Arms

REMOVAL & INSTALLATION

1. Raise the car and safely support it between the spring seats and the ball joints of the lower control arms.

2. Remove the tire and wheel assembly.

3. Place a floor jack under the lower control arm spring seat.

——————— CAUTION ———————

Leave the floor jack under the spring seat during removal and installation, in order to keep the spring and control arm positioned.

4. Remove the ball joint from the steering knuckle. Support the hub assembly to prevent damage to the brake line.

5. Loosen pivot shaft to frame nuts and remove alignment shims. Remove the bolts to allow clearance and remove the control arm assembly from the car.

6. Installation is the reverse of the removal procedure. Install alignment shims in the same position from which they were removed and tighten all bolts to specifications. Check the wheel alignment.

Front Wheel Bearings

ADJUSTMENT

1. Raise the car so the wheel can spin freely. Remove the dust cap.

2. Tighten the adjusting nut to 12 ft. lbs. (16 Nm) while turning the wheel, this will seat the bearings and remove any burrs on the threads.

3. Back off on the nut until it is just loose.

4. Finger tighten the nut and install the cotter pin or the retaining ring.

NOTE: If the cotter pin cannot be installed, back off on the nut until the slot aligns with the serrations on the nut. Do not back off on the nut more than ¼ of a turn.

5. Once adjusted, the front wheel bearings should have 0.001–0.005 in. (.03–.13mm) end play.

REMOVAL & INSTALLATION

1. Remove the caliper and hub assembly.

2. Remove the outer roller bearing assembly.

3. Pry the seal from the hub, then remove the inner roller bearing assembly.

4. If necessary, remove the inner bearing outer race using tool J-29117.

5. To remove outer bearing outer race, insert a brass drift into hub, indexing end of drift with notches in hub and tap with a hammer.

6. Using clean solvent, clean all old grease from hub, spindle, and bearings.

7. If outer races were removed, press the races into the hub using tool J-8092 with J-8850 or J-8457.

8. Pack the bearings with a high temperature wheel bearing grease and reassemble the hub. Install the hub on the steering knuckle and adjust the wheel bearings.

Front Wheel Alignment

ADJUSTMENT

Caster and Camber

1. Loosen the upper control arm shaft to frame nuts.

2. Add or subtract shims as required per alignment correction charts.

3. Tighten the upper control arm shaft to frame nuts.

NOTE: A normal shim pack will leave at least 2 threads of the bolt exposed beyond the nut. If these requirements cannot be met in order to reach specifications, check for damaged suspension and steering components and replace parts as necessary.

Toe

1. Loosen the clamp bolts at each end of the steering tie rod adjusting sleeves.

2. With steering wheel set in the straight ahead position, turn tie rod adjusting sleeves to obtain the proper toe-in adjustment.

3. When adjustment is completed, check to see that the number of threads showing on each end of the sleeve are equal.

REAR SUSPENSION

Shock Absorber

REMOVAL & INSTALLATION

NOTE: Purge new shock absorbers of air by repeatedly extending in their normal position and compressing while inverted.

1. Raise the vehicle and support the rear axle housing.

2. Remove the lower shock mounting bolt from the shock absorber eye.

3. Unfasten the upper mounting bracket bolts and remove the shock.

4. Installation is in the reverse order of removal, except that the upper attaching bolts should remain loose while the lower (eye) is being tightened.

Springs

REMOVAL & INSTALLATION

1. Raise the rear of the car on the axle housing and place jack stands under the frame. Do not lower the jack.

2. Disconnect the brake line at the axle housing and at the differential housing.

3. Disconnect the upper control arms at the differential.

4. Remove the shock absorber lower mount and lower the jack. Be careful not to stretch the brake hose.

5. Remove the spring.

6. Installation is in the reverse order of removal.

Rear Control Arms

REMOVAL & INSTALLATION

Upper Arm

NOTE: If both control arms are to be replaced, remove and replace one control arm at a time to prevent the axle from rolling or slipping sideways as this might occur with both upper control arms removed.

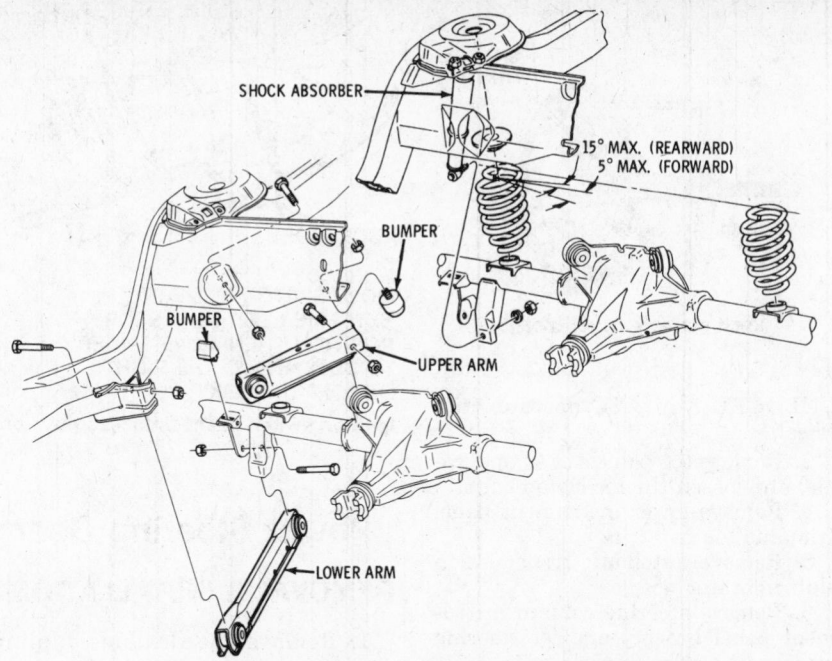

Cutlass, 88 and 98 rear suspension (except wagon)

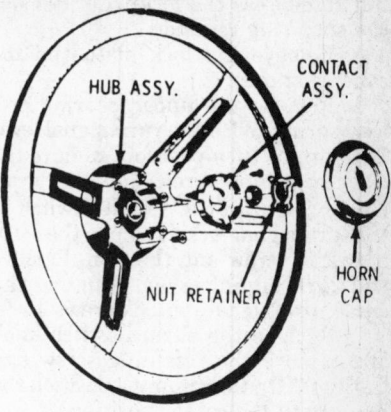

Sport steering wheel

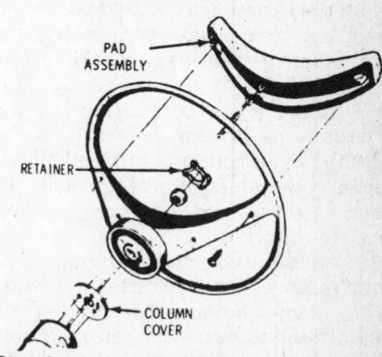

Standard steering wheel; deluxe wheel similar

1. Remove the nut from the rear arm to rear axle housing bolt and while rocking axle, remove the bolt.

2. Remove front and rear arm attaching nuts and bolts.

3. Remove the suspension arm and inspect the bushing for damage.

4. Installation is the reverse of the removal procedure. Torque nuts to specifications.

Lower Arm

1. Raise the vehicle and support it under the axle housing.

2. Remove the rear arm to axle housing bracket bolt.

3. Remove the front arm to bracket bolts and remove the lower control arm.

4. Installation is the reverse of the removal procedure. Torque nuts to specifications.

Rear Wheel Bearings

NOTE: For all rear wheel bearing removal and installation procedures, refer to Rear Axle Removal in this section.

STEERING

Steering Wheel

REMOVAL & INSTALLATION

Except Tilt and Telescope Models

1. Disconnect the battery ground cable.

2. On the stock wheel, remove the two screws attaching the horn pad assembly to the wheel. Disconnect the horn contact from the pad assembly. On the deluxe wheel, remove the pad attaching screws, lift up the pad, and disconnect the horn wire by pushing on the insulator and turning counterclockwise. On the sport steering wheel, pull up on the emblem to remove it. Remove the contact assembly attaching screws and the contact assembly.

3. On all models remove the steering wheel nut retainer.

4. Remove the retaining nut and the steering wheel, using a suitable puller.

5. Installation is in the reverse order of removal. Align the marks on the wheel hub and the steering shaft. If the spokes of the wheel are not horizontal, it is necessary to adjust the tie-rod ends. Torque the attaching bolt 30 ft. lbs. (41 Nm).

——— **CAUTION** ———

Do not hammer on the steering shaft. The energy-absorbing column will be damaged and require replacement.

Tilt and Telescope Models

1. Disconnect the battery ground.

2. Remove the three pad attaching screws, lift off the pad assembly and disconnect the horn wire.

3. Push the locking lever counterclockwise to full release.

4. Mark the plate assembly where the two attaching screws attach the plate assembly tot he locking lever and remove the two screws.

5. Unscrew and remove the plate assembly. Remove the steering wheel nut.

6. Using a puller, remove the steering wheel.

7. Install a $^5/_{16}$ in. x 18 set screw into the upper shaft at the full extended position and lock.

8. Install the steering wheel, aligning the scribe mark on the hub with the slash mark on the end of the shaft. Make sure that the attached end of the upper horn contact assembly is seated flush against the top of the horn contact assembly.

9. Install the steering wheel nut and torque to 30 ft. lbs. (41 Nm). The remainder of the installation is in the reverse order of removal. Remove the set screw after steering wheel installation.

Turn Signal Switch

REMOVAL & INSTALLATION

1. Disconnect the negative battery cable.

2. Remove the steering wheel.

3. Pry the lockplate cover off with a screwdriver.

4. Place a lock plate removal tool over the steering shaft and tighten the

nut to depress the lockplate. Remove the snap ring retainer.

5. Remove the lock plate and the cancelling cam.

6. Remove the upper bearing pre-load spring. With the turn signal lever in the right turn position, remove the lever attaching screw and the lever. On models with the dimmer switch in the turn signal lever, remove the actuator arm screw and the arm. Remove the turn signal lever. Remove the three turn signal switch screws.

7. Push in the hazard switch knob and remove the retaining screw and the knob. On tilt columns, position the housing in the center position.

8. Remove the lower trim panel from the instrument panel and disconnect the turn signal connector from the wiring harness. Remove the connector.

9. Remove the bolts attaching the surrounding bracket assembly to the jacket. On all column shift automatics remove the shift indicator needle attaching screw and remove or disconnect the needle.

10. Hold the steering column in place and remove the two attaching nuts from below. Remove the bracket assembly and the wire protector. Loosely reinstall the nuts to hold the column in place.

11. Carefully remove the turn signal switch and the wiring.

12. To install, place the switch in the right turn position and push the switch in until it is properly seated. Torque the three attaching nuts to 35 inch lbs. Return the switch to the neutral position and reverse the removal procedure.

Combination Switch

REMOVAL & INSTALLATION

1. Make sure lever is in OFF position.

2. Pull lever straight out of turn signal switch.

3. If equipped with cruise control, attach mechanic's wire to connector and pull harness through column.

4. Reverse procedure for installation. Push lever into turn signal switch.

Ignition Lock/Switch

REMOVAL & INSTALLATION

Ignition Switch

1. Disconnect negative battery cable.

2. Place ignition switch in OFF-

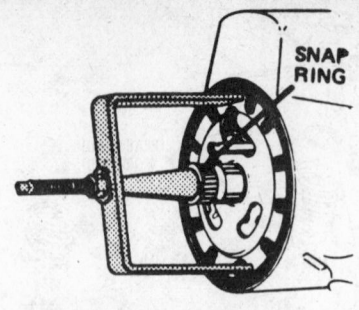

Lock plate removal tool

UNLOCKED, or ACC position (tilt wheel).

3. Remove toe pan cover (if applicable) and loosen the toe clamp bolts.

4. Remove lower instrument panel trim and toe pan trim panel.

5. Remove automatic transmission shift indicator needle.

6. Remove steering column instrument panel bracket and let steering wheel rest on the driver's seat.

7. Remove the two dimmer switch retaining screws and remove the switch.

8. Remove two ignition switch attaching screws and lift switch off actuator rod.

9. Disconnect wiring.

10. To install, check that lock cylinder is still in OFF-UNLOCKED or ACC (tilt wheel) position, and move sliding portion of switch until switch hole is positioned correctly. Hold the switch in this position with a 0.090 in. pin.

11. Connect the wiring to the switch.

12. Position switch over actuator rod, install attaching screws and remove the 0.090 in. pin.

13. Reverse Steps 1–6 to complete installation.

Lock Cylinder

1. Refer to the turn signal removal procedure, Steps 1–7.

2. Disconnect the turn signal connector from the harness. Remove the connector from the mounting bracket.

3. Carefully pull the turn signal switch from the column, allowing it to hang.

4. Position the lock assembly in the RUN position, and remove the retaining screw and the lock.

5. To install the lock cylinder, hold the lock cylinder and rotate the tabs clockwise until they stop. Insert the cylinder into the housing, aligning the keyway groove. Push the cylinder and rotate the tabs counterclockwise while lightly pushing inward on the cylinder until the drive section of the cylinder mates with drive shaft. Reverse the removal procedure.

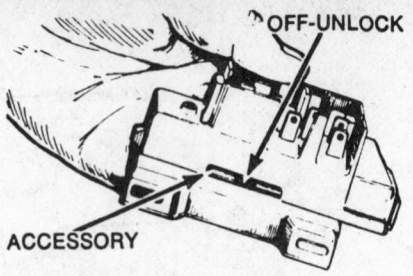

MOVE SWITCH SLIDER TO EXTREME LEFT (ACCESSORY) POSITION THEN MOVE SLIDER TO DETENTS TO THE RIGHT OF "OFF-UNLOCK"

Ignition switch in Off-Unlocked position

Power Steering Gear

REMOVAL & INSTALLATION

1. Remove the flexible coupling shield.

── **CAUTION** ──

Failure to disconnect the flexible coupling from the steering gear stub shaft can result in damage to the steering gear and/or immediate shaft. This damage can cause loss of steering control which could result in a vehicle crash and bodily injury.

2. Disconnect the hoses from the gear and cap the hose fittings.

3. Raise the vehicle and support it safely.

4. Remove the pitman shaft nut. Then disconnect the pitman arm from the pitman shaft. Special puller J29107 or its equivalent must be used.

5. Remove the three bolts attaching the gear to the frame side rail. Remove the gear.

6. Installation is in the reverse order of removal. Tighten all bolts to specification.

NOTE: If the threads are stripped, do not repair, replace the housing.

Power Steering Pump

REMOVAL & INSTALLATION

1. Disconnect negative battery cable, and remove the drive belt.

2. Use a puller to remove the pump pulley.

3. Detach and cap the hoses.

4. Remove the pump and mounting bracket.

5. Reverse the procedure for installation. Bleed the system of air by turning the wheels from side to side without hitting the stops, with the wheels off the floor and the engine running.

BELT ADJUSTMENT

NOTE: When adjusting the power steering pump belt, do not pry against the pump reservoir. Only the bracket should be pryed against when adjusting belt tension.

1. Position belt tension gage BT-33–73F or J-23600-B on pump belt.
2. Loosen the pump mounting bolts.
3. Adjust the belt by prying the pump away from the engine until the correct tension is reached.
4. Tighten pump bolts to torque specification.

SYSTEM BLEEDING

1. With the wheels turned all the way to the left, add power steering fluid to the "COLD" mark on the fluid level indicator.
2. Start the engine and run at fast idle momentarily, shut engine off and recheck fluid level. If necessary add fluid to to bring level to the "COLD" mark.
3. Start the engine and bleed the system by turning the wheels from side to side without hitting the stops.

NOTE: Fluid with air in it has a light tan or red appearance.

4. Return the wheels to the center position and keep the engine running for two or three minutes.
5. Road test the car and recheck the fluid level making sure it is at the "HOT" mark.

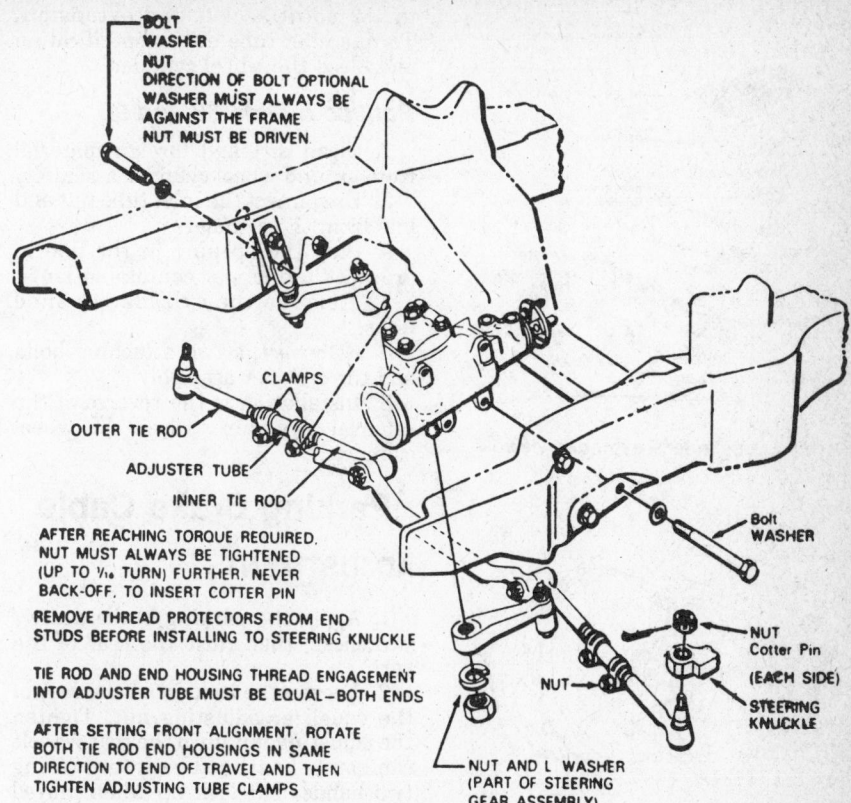

BOLT
WASHER
NUT
DIRECTION OF BOLT OPTIONAL
WASHER MUST ALWAYS BE AGAINST THE FRAME
NUT MUST BE DRIVEN

CLAMPS
OUTER TIE ROD
ADJUSTER TUBE
INNER TIE ROD

AFTER REACHING TORQUE REQUIRED. NUT MUST ALWAYS BE TIGHTENED (UP TO 1/16 TURN) FURTHER, NEVER BACK-OFF. TO INSERT COTTER PIN

REMOVE THREAD PROTECTORS FROM END STUDS BEFORE INSTALLING TO STEERING KNUCKLE

TIE ROD AND END HOUSING THREAD ENGAGEMENT INTO ADJUSTER TUBE MUST BE EQUAL—BOTH ENDS

AFTER SETTING FRONT ALIGNMENT. ROTATE BOTH TIE ROD END HOUSINGS IN SAME DIRECTION TO END OF TRAVEL AND THEN TIGHTEN ADJUSTING TUBE CLAMPS

Bolt
WASHER

NUT
Cotter Pin
(EACH SIDE)
STEERING KNUCKLE

NUT

NUT AND L WASHER (PART OF STEERING GEAR ASSEMBLY)

Steering linkage

Tie Rod Ends

REMOVAL & INSTALLATION

1. Raise and support the car.
2. Remove the cotter pins from the ball studs and remove the castellated nuts.
3. Disconnect the tie-rod end from the steering arm or knuckle with a ball joint separator.
4. Remove the inner ball stud from the intermediate rod with a puller. Mark the tie-rod end position before removal.
5. Loosen the clamp bolts and unscrew the ends from the adjuster tubes. If a force of more than 7 ft. lbs. is required to remove the ends after breakaway, the fasteners should be replaced.
6. Clean and inspect all parts. When installing, run the tie-rod end to the position marked. Torque the ball stud nuts to 30 ft. lbs. (40 Nm).

BRAKES

NOTE: For all brake system repair and service procedures not detailed below, please refer to "Brakes" in the Unit Repair section.

Master Cylinder

REMOVAL & INSTALLATION

NOTE: Be sure the area where the master cylinder is mounted is clean, before beginning removal.

1. Disconnect and cap or plug hydraulic lines. Disconnect the electrical lead, if so equipped.
2. On non-power brakes, disconnect the pushrod at the brake pedal.
3. Remove the attaching bolts and master cylinder.
4. Install in the reverse order of removal. Fill with fluid and bleed.

Proportioning Valve

REMOVAL & INSTALLATION

1. Remove the electrical wire connector from the pressure differential switch.

2. Disconnect the hydraulic lines at the combination valve.
3. Plug the lines to prevent loss of fluid and entrance of dirt.
4. Remove the combination valve.
5. Installation is the reverse of the removal procedure. Bleed the entire brake system.

Power Brake Unit

REMOVAL & INSTALLATION

1. Remove the two nuts holding the master cylinder fastened to the power unit. Carefully position the master cylinder out of the way, being careful not to kink any of the hydraulic lines. It is not necessary to disconnect the brake lines.
2. Disconnect the vacuum hose from the vacuum check valve on the front housing. Plug the hose. On cars with diesel engine, disconnect the three hydraulic lines from the power cylinder. Plug the lines immediately.
3. Loosen the four nuts that hold the power unit mounted on the firewall.
4. Disconnect the pushrod from the brake pedal. Do not force the pushrod to the side when disconnecting.
5. Remove the four mounting nuts and lift the power unit off the studs.

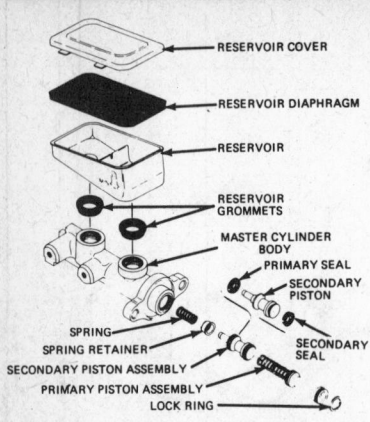

RESERVOIR COVER
RESERVOIR DIAPHRAGM
RESERVOIR
RESERVOIR GROMMETS
MASTER CYLINDER BODY
PRIMARY SEAL
SECONDARY PISTON
SECONDARY SEAL
SPRING
SPRING RETAINER
SECONDARY PISTON ASSEMBLY
PRIMARY PISTON ASSEMBLY
LOCK RING

Master cylinder – exploded view

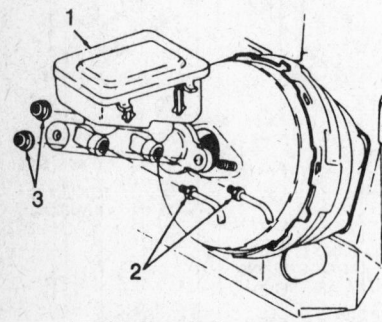

1. Master cylinder assembly
2. Brake lines
3. Mounting nut

Master cylinder to booster mounting

6. Installation is in the reverse order of removal. Torque the master cylinder-to-power brake unit mounting studs to specifications. On Diesel engine cars with power steering, refill the reservoir. See "Power Steering Pump Removal and Installation" for system bleeding.

Wheel Cylinder

REMOVAL & INSTALLATION

Cutlass

1. Clean dirt and foreign material from around wheel cylinder assembly.
2. Disconnect the inlet tube nut and line from the cylinder.
3. Plug the opening in the line to prevent fluid loss or contamination.
4. Remove the wheel cylinder retainer using tool J-29839 or two awls. Insert tool into access slots between wheel cylinder pilot and retainer locking tabs.
5. Bend both tabs away at the same time and remove the wheel cylinder.
6. To install position wheel cylinder and hold in place with wooden block between cylinder and axle flange.
7. Install new retainer using a 1⅛

in. 12 point socket and extension. Torque inlet tube nut to specification and bleed the wheel cylinder.

Pontiac & Olds 88 and 98

1. Clean dirt and foreign material from around wheel cylinder assembly.
2. Disconnect the inlet tube nut and line from the cylinder.
3. Plug the opening in the line to prevent fluid loss or contamination.
4. Remove the cylinder to shoe links.
5. Remove the two attaching bolts and the cylinder assembly.
6. Installation is the reverse of the removal procedure. Bleed the wheel cylinder.

Parking Brake Cable

ADJUSTMENT

1. Apply the parking brake exactly two clicks, then raise the rear of the car.
2. Loosen the locknut at the rear of the equalizer adjusting nut. Tighten the adjusting nut until the rear wheels can barely be turned backward (using two hands) but lock up when moved forward. Rear disc brakes will not lock up but will have a drag. Tighten the nut against the adjusting nut.
3. With the parking brake disengaged the rear wheel should turn freely in either direction with no brake drag.

REMOVAL & INSTALLATION
Front

1. Raise the vehicle and support it safely.
2. Loosen adjuster nut and disconnect the cable from the connector. Loosen the retainer at the frame.
3. Lower the vehicle.
4. Remove the lower rear bolt from the wheelhouse panel and pull the panel out to gain access to the front cable.
5. Disconnect the cable from the parking brake pedal assembly and remove the cable.
6. Installation is the reverse of the removal procedure. Adjust the parking brake.

Rear

1. Raise the vehicle and support it safely.
2. Remove the adjuster nut, compress the retainer fingers and loosen the cable from all retainers. On the left side remove the cable from the equalizer.
3. Mark the relationship of the wheel to the axle flange and remove the tire and wheel assembly.

4. Remove the brake drum, the primary shoe return spring and the parking brake strut. On the right side also remove the secondary shoe hold-down spring.
5. Compress the retainer fingers and loosen the cable from the backing plate. Disconnect the cable from the parking brake lever and remove the cable.
6. Installation is the reverse of the removal procedure. Adjust the parking brake.

CHASSIS ELECTRICAL

Heater Blower

REMOVAL & INSTALLATION

1. Disconnect the negative battery cable.
2. Disconnect all electrical connections from the blower motor.
3. Remove the retaining screws and remove the motor.
4. Installation is the reverse of the removal procedure. Use sealer as needed for a water tight seal.

Heater Core

REMOVAL & INSTALLATION

Without A/C
88 AND 98

1. Disconnect the negative battery cable, the blower motor wiring and the heater core ground strap.
2. Drain the cooling system and disconnect the heat hoses.
3. It may be necessary to move the temperature air valve by disconnecting the cable and tapping the hinge pin down to clear the upper pivot.
4. Remove the screws attaching the blower case to the heater case. Remove the heater core shroud screws and remove the shroud and core.

CUTLASS

1. Remove the glove box, the heater air distribution outlet, the upper level vent duct, and the defroster outlet attaching screw.
2. Disconnect the blower motor wiring and the cables at the blower motor.
3. Drain the cooling system.
4. Remove the right hand windshield wiper arm.
5. Remove the leaf screen.
6. Disconnect the heater hoses at the heater assembly. Remove the heat-

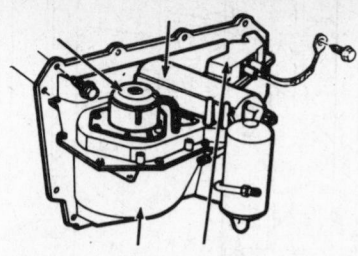

Heater module mounting—Cutlass

er assembly-to-cowl screws and remove the assembly.

7. Remove blower motor mounting screws and remove the motor from the assembly.

8. Remove the front cover screws and remove the heater core. Reverse above procedures to install.

CATALINA, LEMANS AND BONNEVILLE

1. Drain the cooling system.
2. Remove and plug the heater hoses at the heater core tubes.
3. Disconnect the electrical connectors.
4. Remove the front module cover screws and the module assembly.
5. Remove the heater core from the module.
6. To install, reverse the removal procedures. Use a strip caulk type sealer when installing the module to the cowl.

GRAND PRIX, PARISIENNE AND SAFARI

1. Disconnect and plug the heater hoses at the core tubes.
2. Remove the core cover from the module.
3. Remove the core bracket and the ground screw.
4. Lift out the heater core.
5. To install, reverse the removal procedures. Replace the damaged sealer, if necessary.

With A/C

CATALINA, CUTLASS, PARISIENNE, SAFARI

1. Drain the cooling system.
2. Disconnect the hoses at the core pipes.
3. Remove the retaining bracket and ground strap.
4. Remove the module rubber seal.
5. Remove the module screen.
6. Remove the right windshield wiper arm.
7. Remove the diagnostic connector, high blower relay and thermostatic switch mounting screws.
8. Disconnect all electrical connections at the module.
9. Remove the module top cover.

10. Lift out the core.
11. Installation is in the reverse order of removal. **Replace all insulation.**

88 AND 98

1. Disconnect the battery ground.
2. Disconnect the blower wiring.
3. Remove the thermostatic switch and diagnostic connector.
4. Remove the right end of the hood seal and the air inlet screen screws.
5. Remove the 5 case-to-firewall screws at the top, 9 upper case-to-lower case screws at the flange and two more at the plenum.
6. Lift the upper case straight up and off. Remove the pipe bracket screws from the case. Disconnect the hoses and position them to prevent spillage.
7. Disconnect and lift out the heater core.
8. Installation is in the reverse order of removal. Replace any damaged sealer.

LEMANS, GRAND PRIX AND 1982–84 BONNEVILLE

1. Position the wipers in the UP position.
2. Disconnect and unplug the heater hoses at the heater case.
3. Remove the module top cover seals.
4. Remove the module top screens.
5. Disconnect the electrical connectors from the heater case.
6. Move the lower windshield reverse molding aside.
7. Remove the cowl brackets.
8. Tape a strip of wood to the lower edge of the windshield glass, to protect the glass.
9. Remove the top cover screws.
10. Cut the sealing material along the cowl with a knife.
11. Pry the cover from the side, NOT from the top.
12. Remove the heater core and the seal.
13. To install, reverse the removal procedures. Use new sealing material.

Radio

REMOVAL & INSTALLATION

1. Disconnect the negative battery cable.
2. Remove the knobs from the radio and pull out the cigarette lighter.
3. Remove the two trim cover attaching screws and remove the cover.
4. Remove the radio bracket attaching screw from the lower tie bar.
5. Remove the four mounting plate screws and pull the radio out to obtain access to the electrical connections. Detach the wiring harness and the antenna lead.

6. Remove the mounting plate nuts and remove the radio. Installation is in the reverse order of removal.

Windshield Wiper Switch

REMOVAL & INSTALLATION

1. Disconnect the negative battery cable. Remove the steering wheel.
2. It may be necessary to loosen the two column mounting nuts and remove the four bracket-to-mast jacket screws, then separate the bracket from the mast jacket to allow the connector clip on the ignition switch to be pulled out of the column assembly.
3. Disconnect the washer/wiper switch lower connector.
4. Remove the screws attaching the column housing to the mast jacket. Be sure to note the position of the dimmer switch actuator rod for reassembly in the same position. Remove the column housing and switch as an assembly.

NOTE: The tilt and travel columns have a removable plastic cover on the column housing. This provides access to the wiper switch without removing the entire column housing.

5. Turn upside down and use a drift to remove the pivot pin from the washer/wiper switch. Remove the switch.
6. Place the switch into position in the housing and install the pivot pin.
7. Position the housing onto the mast jacket and attach by installing the screws. Install the dimmer switch actuator rod in the same position as noted earlier. Check switch operation.
8. Reconnect lower end of switch assembly.
9. Install remaining components in reverse order of removal. Be sure to attach column mounting bracket in original position.

Windshield Wiper Motor

REMOVAL & INSTALLATION

1. Remove the cowl screen or grille.
2. Loosen the linkage drive link-to-crankarm attaching nuts, and remove the link from the arm.
3. Disconnect the wiring and washer hoses.
4. Remove the three motor attaching screws, guide the crankarm through the hole in the dash, and remove the motor.
5. Reverse the above steps to install.

Instrument Cluster

REMOVAL & INSTALLATION

Cutlass

1. Disconnect the speedometer cable at the cruise control transducer, if so equipped.
2. Remove the instrument cluster pad assembly.
3. Remove the steering column trim cover.
4. Disconnect the shift indicator clip from the steering column shift bowl.
5. Remove the instrument cluster screws.
6. Pull the cluster rearward. Disconnect the speedometer cable.
7. Disconnect the speed sensor, if so equipped.
8. Remove the cluster.
9. Installation is in the reverse order of removal.

88 and 98

1. Remove the steering column trim cover.
2. Remove the screws attaching the gauge cluster to the left hand trim cover.
3. Pull the gauge cluster rearward. Disconnect gauges wiring, lamp sockets, and speedometer cable.
4. Remove the gauge cluster.
5. Installation is in the reverse order of removal.

Pontiac

1. Disconnect the negative battery cable.
2. Remove the steering column lower cover screws and cover.
3. If equipped with an automatic transmission, disconnect the shift indicator cable from the steering column.
4. Remove the two steering column-to-instrument panel screws and lower the steering column.

——— CAUTION ———

Use extreme care when lowering the steering column to prevent damage to the column assembly.

5. Remove the six screws and the three snap-in fasteners from the perimeter of the instrument cluster lens.
6. Remove the two screws from the upper surface of the grey sheet metal trim plate.
7. Remove the two stud nuts from the lower corner of the cluster.
8. Disconnect the speedometer cable and pull the cluster from the instrument panel.
9. Disconnect the electrical connec-

tors from the cluster and remove the cluster from the vehicle.
10. To install, reverse the removal procedures.

Headlight Switch

REMOVAL & INSTALLATION

Cutlass

1. Disconnect the negative battery cable.
2. Remove the instrument cluster pad.
3. Remove the two switch mounting screws.
4. Pull switch away from panel adapter to remove.
5. Installation is the reverse of the removal procedure.

88, 98 and Pontiac

1. Disconnect the negative battery cable.
2. Remove the steering column lower trim cover.
3. Remove the left hand trim cover.
4. Remove the two switch mounting plate screws and pull the switch through the opening.
5. Remove the electrical connector and remove the switch.

Stoplight Switch

REMOVAL & INSTALLATION

1. Disconnect the negative battery cable.
2. Disconnect the electrical connection from the switch.
3. Remove the switch from the tubular clip on the brake pedal mounting bracket.
4. To install and adjust, insert the switch into the clip until the switch body seats on the clip.
5. Pull the brake pedal rearwards against internal pedal stop. The switch will be moved in tubular clip providing proper adjustment.

Fuses and Circuit Breakers

LOCATION

Fuses

The fuse block is located beneath the instrument panel, drivers side of firewall. Fuse holders are labeled as to their service and the correct amperage. Always replace blown fuses with new ones of the correct amperage; otherwise, electrical overloads and possible wiring damage will result.

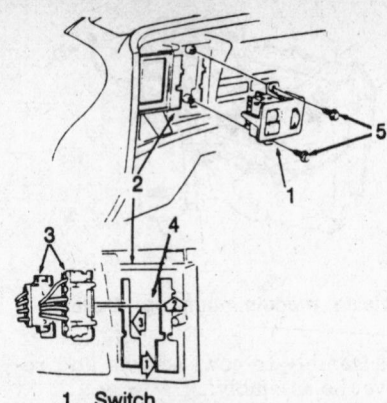

1. Switch
2. Panel adapter
3. Headlamp switch connector
4. Install connector in numbered sequence and in direction of arrows
5. Fully seat screws

Headlamp switch mounting

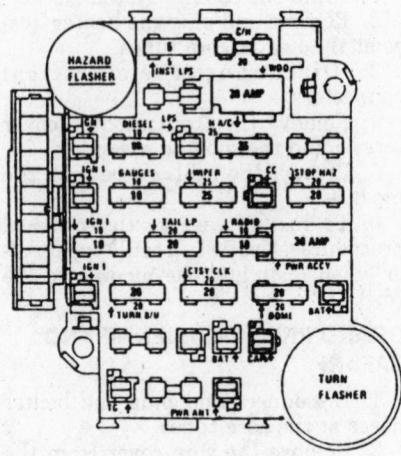

Typical fuse panel layout

Fusible Links

Fusible links are used to prevent major wire harness damage in the event of a short circuit or an overload condition in the wiring circuits which are normally not fused, due to carrying high amperage loads or because of their locations within the wiring harness. Each fusible link is of a fixed value for a specific electrical load and should a link fail, the cause of the failure must be determined and repaired prior to installing a new fusible link of the same value.

Circuit Breakers

Various circuit breakers are located under the instrument panel. In order to gain access to these components it may be necessary to first remove the under dash padding.

Pontiac
Rear Wheel Drive
Fiero

19

SERIAL NUMBER IDENTIFICATION

VEHICLE IDENTIFICATION CHART

It is important for servicing and ordering parts to be certain of the vehicle and engine identification. The VIN (vehicle identification number) is a 17 digit number visible through the windshield on the driver's side of the dash and contains the vehicle and engine identification codes. The tenth digit indicates model year, and the eighth digit indicates engine code. It can be interpreted as follows:

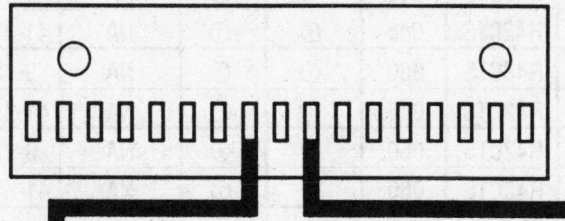

		Engine Code					Model Year	
Code	Cu. In.	Liters	Cyl.	Fuel Sys.	Eng. Mfg.		Code	Year
R	151	2.5	4	TBI	Pontiac		E	1984
9	173	2.8	6	MFI	Chevrolet		F	1985
							G	1986
							H	1987
							J	1988
							K	1989

GENERAL ENGINE SPECIFICATIONS

Year	VIN	No. Cylinder Displacement cu. in. (liter)	Fuel System Type	Net Horsepower @ rpm	Net Torque @ rpm (ft.lbs.)	Bore × Stroke (in.)	Compression Ratio	Oil Pressure @ rpm
1984	R	4-151 (2.5L)	TBI	90 @ 4000	132 @ 2800	4.000 × 3.000	9.0:1	36–41 @ 2000
1985	R	4-151 (2.5L)	TBI	90 @ 4000	132 @ 2800	4.000 × 3.000	9.0:1	36–41 @ 2000
	9	6-173 (2.8L)	MFI	130 @ 5400	160 @ 3600	3.500 × 3.000	8.5:1	30–45 @ 2000

GENERAL ENGINE SPECIFICATIONS

Year	VIN	No. Cylinder Displacement cu. in. (liter)	Fuel System Type	Net Horsepower @ rpm	Net Torque @ rpm (ft.lbs.)	Bore × Stroke (in.)	Compression Ratio	Oil Pressure @ rpm
1986	R	4-151 (2.5L)	TBI	92 @ 4400	134 @ 2800	4.000 × 3.000	9.0:1	36–41 @ 2000
	9	6-173 (2.8L)	MFI	140 @ 5200	170 @ 3600	3.500 × 3.000	8.5:1	30–45 @ 2000
1987	R	4-151 (2.5L)	TBI	92 @ 4400	134 @ 2800	4.000 × 3.000	8.3:1	36–41 @ 2000
	9	6-173 (2.8L)	MFI	140 @ 5200	170 @ 3600	3.500 × 3.000	8.5:1	30–45 @ 2000
1988	R	4-151 (2.5L)	TBI	98 @ 4500	134 @ 2800	4.000 × 3.000	8.3:1	36–41 @ 2000
	9	6-173 (2.8L)	MFI	135 @ 4500	170 @ 3600	3.500 × 3.000	8.5:1	30-45 @ 2000

TBI – Throttle Body Fuel Injection
MFI – Multiport Fuel Injection

GASOLINE ENGINE TUNE-UP SPECIFICATIONS

Year	VIN	No. Cylinder Displacement cu. in. (liter)	Spark Plugs Type	Gap (in.)	Ignition Timing (deg.) MT	AT	Compression Pressure (psi)	Fuel Pump (psi)	Idle Speed (rpm) MT	AT	Valve Clearance In.	Ex.
1984	R	4-151 (2.5)	R43CTS	.060	①	①	NA	9-13	①	①	Hyd.	Hyd.
1985	R	4-151 (2.5)	R43CTS	.060	①	①	NA	9-13	①	①	Hyd.	Hyd.
	9	6-173 (2.8)	R42CTS	.045	①	①	NA	41-47	①	①	Hyd.	Hyd.
1986	R	4-151 (2.5)	R43CTS	.060	①	①	NA	9-13	①	①	Hyd.	Hyd.
	9	6-173 (2.8)	R42CTS	.045	①	①	NA	41-47	①	①	Hyd.	Hyd.
1987	R	4-151 (2.5)	R43CTS	.060	①	①	NA	9-13	①	①	Hyd.	Hyd.
	9	6-173 (2.8)	R42CTS	.045	①	①	NA	41-47	①	①	Hyd.	Hyd.
1988	R	4-151 (2.5)	R42CTS	.060	①	①	NA	9-13	①	①	Hyd.	Hyd.
	9	6-173 (2.8)	R42CTS	.060	①	①	NA	41-47	①	①	Hyd.	Hyd.

NOTE: The underhood specifications sticker often reflects tune-up specification changes made in production. Sticker figures must be used if they disagree with those in this chart
NA – Not available
① See underhood sticker

FIRING ORDERS

NOTE: To avoid confusion, always replace spark plug wires one at a time.

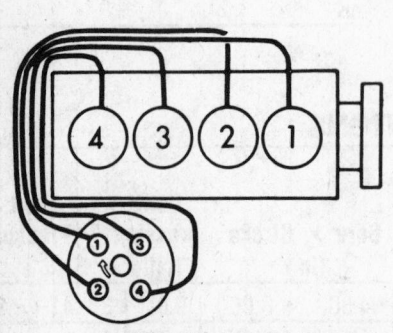

GM (Pontiac) 2.5L engine
Firing order: 1–3–4–2
Distributor rotation: clockwise

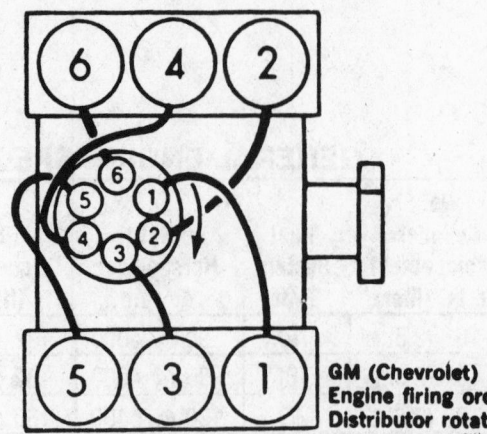

GM (Chevrolet) 173 V6 (2.8 L)
Engine firing order: 1-2-3-4-5-6
Distributor rotation: clockwise

FIRING ORDERS

NOTE: To avoid confusion, always replace spark plug wires one at a time.

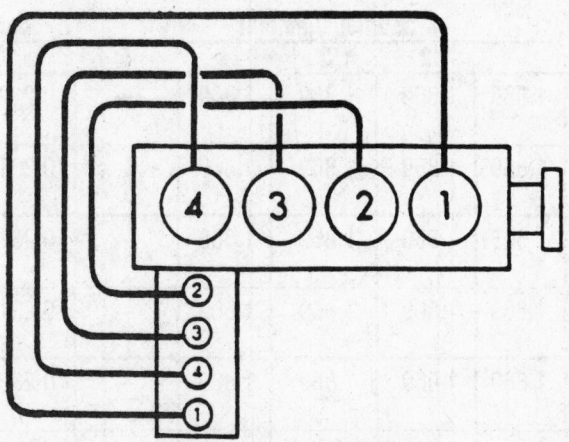

GM (Pontiac) 2.5L engine
with Direct Ignition System (DIS)
Firing order 1-3-4-2
Distributorless

CAPACITIES

Year	VIN	No. Cylinder Displacement cu. in. (liter)	Engine Crankcase with Filter	Engine Crankcase without Filter	Transmission (pts.) MT	Transmission (pts.) AT	Drive Axle (pts.)	Fuel Tank (gals.)	Cooling System (qts.)
1984	R	4-151 (2.5L)	3	3	6.0	8.0	—	10.5	13.8
1985	R	4-151 (2.5L)	3	3	6.0	8.0	—	10.3	13.8
	9	6-173 (2.8L)	4	4	5.3	8.0	—	10.3	13.8
1986	R	4-151 (2.5L)	3	3	5.9	8.0	—	10.3	13.8
	9	6-173 (2.8L)	4	4	5.3	8.0	—	10.3	13.8
1987	R	4-151 (2.5L)	3	3	4.1	8.0	—	11.9	13.8
	9	6-173 (2.8L)	4	4	5.3	8.0	—	11.9	13.8
1988	R	4-151 (2.5L)	4	4	4.1	8.0	—	11.9	13.8
	9	6-173 (2.8L)	4	4	5.3	8.0	—	11.9	13.8

CAMSHAFT SPECIFICATIONS
All measurements given in inches.

Year	VIN	No. Cylinder Displacement cu. in. (liter)	Journal Diameter 1	2	3	4	5	Lobe Lift In.	Ex.	Bearing Clearance	Camshaft End Play
1984	R	4-151 (2.5L)	1.869	1.869	1.869	1.869	—	0.232	0.232	.0007–.0027	.0015–.0050
1985	R	4-151 (2.5L)	1.869	1.869	1.869	1.869	—	0.232	0.232	.0007–.0027	.0015–.0050
	9	6-173 (2.8L)	1.869	1.869	1.869	1.869	—	0.231	0.231	.0010–.0040	—

CAMSHAFT SPECIFICATIONS
All measurements given in inches.

Year	VIN	No. Cylinder Displacement cu. in. (liter)	Journal Diameter					Lobe Lift		Bearing Clearance	Camshaft End Play
			1	2	3	4	5	In.	Ex.		
1986	R	4-151 (2.5L)	1.869	1.869	1.869	1.869	—	0.232	0.232	.0007–.0027	.0015–.0050
	9	6-173 (2.8L)	1.869	1.869	1.869	1.869	—	0.231	0.231	.0010–.0040	—
1987	R	4-151 (2.5L)	1.869	1.869	1.869	1.869	—	0.232	0.232	.0007–.0027	.0015–.0050
	9	6-173 (2.8L)	1.869	1.869	1.869	1.869	—	0.231	0.231	.0010–.0040	—
1988	R	4-151 (2.5L)	1.869	1.869	1.869	1.869	—	0.232	0.232	.0007–.0027	.0015–.0050
	9	6-173 (2.8L)	1.869	1.869	1.869	1.869	—	0.231	0.263	.0010–.0040	—

CRANKSHAFT AND CONNECTING ROD SPECIFICATIONS
All measurements are given in inches.

Year	VIN	No. Cylinder Displacement cu. in. (liter)	Crankshaft				Connecting Rod		
			Main Brg. Journal Dia.	Main Brg. Oil Clearance	Shaft End-play	Thrust on No.	Journal Diameter	Oil Clearance	Side Clearance
1984	R	4-151 (2.5L)	2.2995–2.3005	.0005–.0022	.0035–.0085	5	1.9995–2.0005	.0005–.0026	.006–.022
1985	R	4-151 (2.5L)	2.2995–2.3005	.0005–.0022	.0035–.0085	5	1.9995–2.0005	.0005–.0026	.006–.022
	9	6-173 (2.8L)	2.6473–2.6482	.0016–.0031	.0023–.0082	3	1.9984–1.9994	.0014–.0037	.006–.017
1986	R	4-151 (2.5L)	2.2995–2.3005	.0003–.0022	.0035–.0085	5	1.9995–2.0005	.0005–.0026	.006–.022
	9	6-173 (2.8L)	2.585–2.586	.0016–.0031	.002–.0067	3	1.9984–1.9994	.0014–.0037	.006–.017
1987	R	4-151 (2.5L)	2.2995–2.3005	.0005–.0022	.0035–.0085	5	1.9995–2.0005	.0005–.0026	.006–.022
	9	6-173 (2.8L)	2.6473–2.6482	.0016–.0031	.0023–.0082	3	1.9984–1.9994	.0014–.0037	.006–.017
1988	R	4-151 (2.5L)	2.2995–2.3005	.0005–.0022	.0035–.0085	5	1.9995–2.0005	.0005–.0026	.006–.022
	9	6-173 (2.8L)	2.6473–2.6482	.0016–.0031	.0023–.0082	3	1.9984–1.9994	.0014–.0037	.006–.017

VALVE SPECIFICATIONS

Year	VIN	No. Cylinder Displacement cu. in. (liter)	Seat Angle (deg.)	Face Angle (deg.)	Spring Test Pressure (lbs.)	Spring Installed Height (in.)	Stem-to-Guide Clearance (in.)		Stem Diameter (in.)	
							Intake	Exhaust	Intake	Exhaust
1984	R	4-151 (2.5L)	46	45	176	1.69	.0010–.0027	.0010–.0032	.342–.343	.342–.343
1985	R	4-151 (2.5L)	46	45	176	1.69	.0010–.0027	.0010–.0027	.342–.343	.342–.343
	9	6-173 (2.8L)	46	45	195	1.57	.0010–.0027	.0010–.0027	.3410–.3425	.3418–.3426
1986	R	4-151 (2.5L)	46	45	176	1.69	.0010–.0027	.0010–.0027	.3418–.3425	.3418–.3425
	9	6-173 (2.8L)	46	45	195	1.57	.0010–.0027	.0010–.0027	.3410–.3425	.3418–.3426
1987	R	4-151 (2.5L)	45	45	176	1.69	.0010–.0027	.0010–.0027	.3418–.3425	.3418–.3425
	9	6-173 (2.8L)	46	45	195	1.57	.0010–.0027	.0010–.0027	.3410–.3425	.3410–.3426
1988	R	4-151 (2.5L)	46	45	176	1.69	.0010–.0027	0.010–.0027	.3418–.3425	.3418–.3426
	9	6-173 (2.8L)	46	45	195	1.57	.0010–.0027	.0010–.0027	.3410–.3425	.3410–.3426

PISTON AND RING SPECIFICATIONS
All measurments are given in inches.

Year	VIN	No. Cylinder Displacement cu. in. (liter)	Piston Clearance	Ring Gap			Ring Side Clearance		
				Top Compression	Bottom Compression	Oil Control	Top Compression	Bottom Compression	Oil Control
1984	R	4-151 (2.5L)	.0025–.0033	.010–.022	.010–.027	.015–.055	.002–.003	.002–.003	Snug
1985	R	4-151 (2.5L)	.0014–.0022 ①	.010–.020	.010–.020	.020–.060	.002–.003	.001–.003	.015–.055
	9	6-173 (2.8L)	.0007–.0017	.0098–.0197	.0098–.0197	.020–.055	.0012–.0028	.0016–.0037	.008 Max
1986	R	4-151 (2.5L)	.0014–.0022	.010–.020	.010–.020	.020–.060	.002–.003	.001–.003	.015–.055
	9	6-173 (2.8L)	.0007–.0017	.0098–.0197	.0098–.0197	.020–.055	.0012–.0028	.0016–.0037	.008 Max
1987	R	4-151 (2.5L)	.0014–.0022	.010–.020	.010–.020	.020–.060	.002–.003	.001–.003	.015–.055
	9	6-173 (2.8L)	.0007–.0017	.0098–.0197	.0098–.0197	.020–.055	.0012–.0028	.0016–.0037	.008 Max
1988	R	4-151 (2.5L)	.0014–.0022	.010–.020	.010–.020	.020–.060	.002–.003	.002–.003	.015–.055
	9	6-173 (2.8L)	.0007–.0017	.0098–.0197	.0098–.0197	.020–.055	.0012–.0028	.0016–.0037	.008 Max

① Measured 1.8 in. down from piston top

TORQUE SPECIFICATIONS
All readings in ft. lbs.

Year	VIN	No. Cylinder Displacement cu. in. (liters)	Cylinder Head Bolts	Main Bearing Bolts	Rod Bearing Bolts	Crankshaft Pulley Bolts	Flywheel	Manifold Intake	Manifold Exhaust	Plugs	Spark
1984	R	4-151 (2.5L)	92	70	32	200	44	①		44	NA
1985	R	4-151 (2.5L)	92	70	32	200	44	①		44	NA
	9	6-173 (2.8L)	65-90	63-74	34-40	66-84	45-55	20-25	22-28	7-15
1986	R	4-151 (2.5L)	①	70	32	162	44	①		44	NA
	9	6-173 (2.8L)	65-90	63-74	34-40	66-84	45-55	20-25	22-28	7-15
1987	R	4-151 (2.5L)	①	70	32	162	44	①		44	NA
	9	6-173 (2.8L)	65-90	63-74	34-40	66-84	45-55	20-25	22-28	7-15
1988	R	4-151 (2.5L)	①	70	32	162	44	①		44	NA
	9	6-173 (2.8L)	65-90	63-74	34-40	66-84	45-55	22-28	44	7-15

① See text and illustration for procedure and specifications
NA — Not available

BRAKE SPECIFICATIONS
All measurements in inches unless noted

Year	Model	Lug Nut Torque (ft. lbs.)	Master Cylinder Bore	Brake Rotor Minimum Thickness	Brake Rotor Maximum Runout	Standard Brake Drum Diameter	Minimum Lining Thickness Front	Minimum Lining Thickness Rear
1984	All	①	1.00	③	0.005	②	0.062	0.062
1985	All	①	1.00	③	0.005	②	0.062	0.062
1986	All	①	1.00	③	0.004	②	0.062	0.062
1987	All	①	1.00	③	0.005	②	0.062	0.062
1988	All	①	1.00	③	0.003	②	0.062	0.062

① Steel 80; aluminum 100
② Cars equipped with four wheel disc brakes
③ Min. refinish thickness (front) 0.445
Discard thickness (front) 0.390
Min. Refinish thickness (rear) 0.0500
Discard thickness (rear) 0.450

④ Min. refinish thickness (front) 0.3858
Discard thickness (front) 0.3740
Min. Refinish thickness (rear) 0.4409
Discard thickness (rear) 0.430

⑤ Min. refinish thickness (front & rear) 0.702
Discard thickness (front& rear) 0.681

WHEEL ALIGNMENT

Year	Model	Caster Range (deg.)	Caster Preferred Setting (deg.)	Camber Range (deg.)	Camber Preferred Setting (deg.)	Toe-in (in.)	Steering Axis Inclination (deg.)
1984	All	3N-7P	5P	$\frac{5}{16}$N-1$\frac{5}{16}$P	½P	$\frac{1}{16} \pm \frac{1}{32}$	NA
1985	All	3N-7P	5P	$\frac{5}{16}$N-1$\frac{5}{16}$P	½P	$\frac{1}{16} \pm \frac{1}{32}$	NA
1986	All	3N-7P	5P	$\frac{5}{16}$N-1$\frac{5}{16}$P	½P	$\frac{1}{16} \pm \frac{1}{32}$	NA
1987	All	3N-7P	5P	$\frac{5}{16}$N-1$\frac{5}{16}$P	½P	$\frac{1}{16} \pm \frac{1}{32}$	NA
1988-89	All	3N-7P	5P	$\frac{5}{16}$N-1$\frac{5}{16}$P	½P	$\frac{1}{16} \pm \frac{1}{32}$	NA

N — Negative
P — Positive

TUNE-UP PROCEDURES

Ignition Timing

ADJUSTMENT

NOTE: Always refer to the underhood sticker for specific information, if it differs from these procedures use sticker information. 1987-88 models equipped with (DIS) Direct Ignition System, timing adjustment is not possible because the reluctor wheel is an integral part of the crankshaft and the crankshaft sensor is in a fixed position. The following procedure is for vehicles with distributors.

1. Connect a timing light to the No. 1 spark plug wire according to the timing light manufacturer's instructions. DO NOT pierce the spark plug wire to connect the timing light.
2. Follow the instructions on the underhood engine decal.
3. Ground the ALCL terminal (located in the front lower section of the console) and connect terminals A and B with a jumper wire. This puts the engine in the bypass mode, now the ignition timing can be checked. Do not disconnect the 4 wire connector at the distributor.
4. Start the engine and run it at idle speed.
5. Aim the timing light at the degree scale just over the harmonic balancer.
6. Adjust the timing by loosening the securing clamp and rotating the distributor until the desired ignition advance is achieved, then tighten the clamp.
7. Loosen the distributor retaining bolt. On the 4 cylinder engines it's nessesary to slide the clamp back slightly. Do not remove the retaining bolt.
8. Adjust the timing, then replace and tighten the clamp. To advance the timing, rotate the distributor opposite the normal direction of rotor rotation. Retard the timing by rotating the distributor in the normal direction of rotor rotation.
9. Remove jumer wire between A & B at the ALCL terminal and reconnect.

NOTE: Engines equipped with a magnetic probe hole require special timing equipment; refer to the manufactures instructions for proper usage of this equipment.

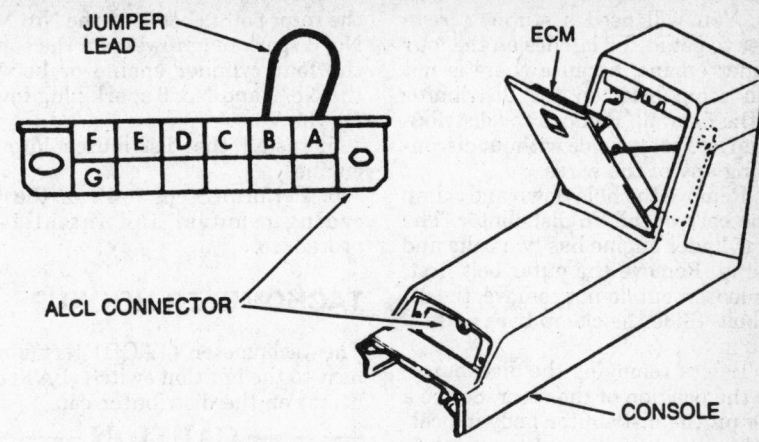

Location of the ALCL terminal

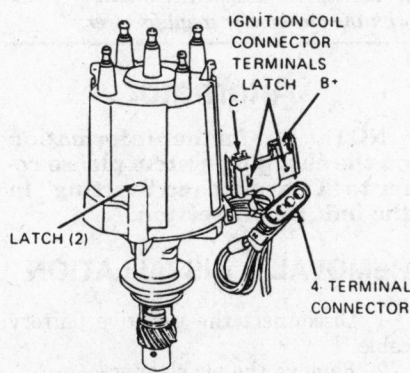

Typical distributor used with a separately mounted coil

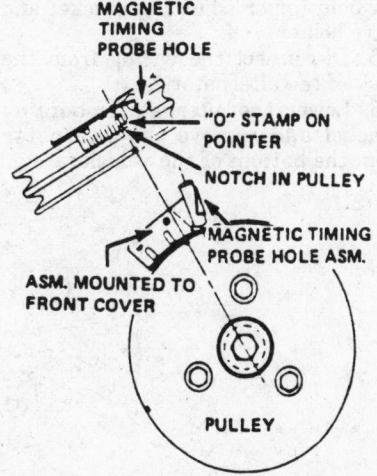

Location of the magnetic timing probe hole

Valve Lash

No routine adjustment is necessary. If it is necessary to adjust the valves on the V6 because of engine wear, follow Steps 16 a-c. in the "Rocker Arm and Pushrod Removal & Installation" procedure.

Idle Speed and Mixture

ADJUSTMENT

Idle speed is controlled by the Electronic Control Module (ECM). No adjustments are possible.

ENGINE ELECTRICAL

Test details can be found in the "Charging and Starting Systems" Unit Repair Section. The voltage regulator is a solid-state, non-adjustable unit integral with the alternator. The alternator must be disassembled to remove the regulator.

Distributor

All models are equipped with HEI distributor and ignition system. This system uses no points and is, therefore, relatively maintenance free.

——— CAUTION ———

When using an auxiliary starter switch on HEI systems, the distributor BAT. lead must be disconnected. Failure to do this may cause damage to the grounding circuit in the ignition switch.

REMOVAL & INSTALLATION

1. Disconnect the negative battery cable.
2. Tag and disconnect all wires leading from the distributor cap. Do not disconnect the plug wires.
3. Remove the external ignition coil.
4. Remove the distributor cap by turning the four latches counterclock-

wise. You will need a stubby screwdriver to get at the latches on the four cylinder engine, because there is not much room between the distributor and the firewall. Remove the distributor cap and set it a side without disconnecting any of the wires.

5. Remove the hold down and clamp at the base of the V6 distributor. The four cylinder engine has two bolts and a clamp. Remove the outer bolt first, then loosen but do not remove, the inner bolt. Slide the clamp back and remove it.

6. Before removing the distributor, note the position of the rotor. Scribe a mark on the distributor body indicating the initial position of the rotor in relationship to the the engine block.

7. Before removing the distibutor from the engine, note the position of the rotor. Scribe a mark on the distibutor body indicating the initial position of the rotor.

8. Remove the distributor from the engine. The drive gear on the distributor shaft is helical and the shaft will rotate slightly as the distributor is removed. Note and mark the position of the rotor at this second position. Do not crank the engine with the distributor removed.

9. To install the distributor, rotate the distributor shaft until the rotor aligns with the 2nd mark you made when the shaft stopped moving. Lubricate the drive gear with clean engine oil, then install the distributor into the engine.

10. Install the clamp and hold-down bolt. Tighten them until the distributor can just be moved with a little effort.

11. Connect the ignition wire and tachometer wire and install the distributor cap.

12. Set the timing and tighten the hold-down bolt.

INSTALLATION IF THE ENGINE WAS DISTURBED

If the engine was cranked while the distributor was removed, you will have to place the engine on TDC of the compression stroke to obtain proper ignition timing.

1. Remove the No. 1 spark plug.

2. Place your thumb over the spark plug hole. Crank the engine slowly until compression is felt. It will be easier if you have someone rotate the engine by hand, using a wrench on the crankshaft pulley.

3. Align the timing mark on the crankshaft pulley with the 0° mark on the timing scale attached to the front of the engine. This places the engine at TDC of the compression stroke.

4. Turn the distributor shaft until

the rotor points between the No. 1 and No. 3 spark plug towers on the cap for the four cylinder engine or between the No. 1 and No. 6 spark plug towers for the V6.

5. Install the distributor into the engine.

6. Perform Steps 9–12 of the preceding removal and installation procedure.

TACHOMETER HOOKUP

The tachometer (TACH) terminal is next to the ignition switch (BAT) connector on the distributor cap.

——— CAUTION ———
Never ground the TACH terminal; serious damage will result. If there is any doubt as to the correct tachometer hookup, check with the tachometer manufacturer.

Alternator

NOTE: For further information on the charging system please refer to "Charging and Starting" in the unit repair section.

REMOVAL & INSTALLATION

1. Disconnect the negative battery cable.

2. Remove the air cleaner.

3. Disconnect the upper strut mount.

4. Disconnect the alternator adjusting bolt, upper adjusting bracket and drive belt.

5. Disconnect the wiring from the back of the alternator.

6. Lower the alternator mounting bracket and remove the alternator from the bottom of the vehicle.

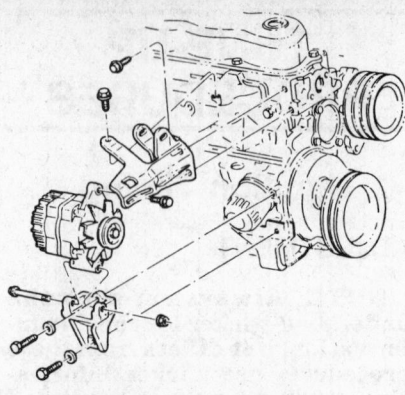

Alternator mounting

7. Installation is the reverse of removal.

Voltage Regulator

REMOVAL & INSTALLATION

An alternator with an integral voltage regulator is standard equipment. There are no adjustments possible with this unit; testing procedures will be found in the "Charging and Starting Systems" Unit Repair Section.

Starter

Starter motor troubleshooting and repairs are covered in the "Charging and Starting" Unit Repair Section.

REMOVAL & INSTALLATION

1. Disconnect the battery ground cable.

2. Raise and support the vehicle safely.

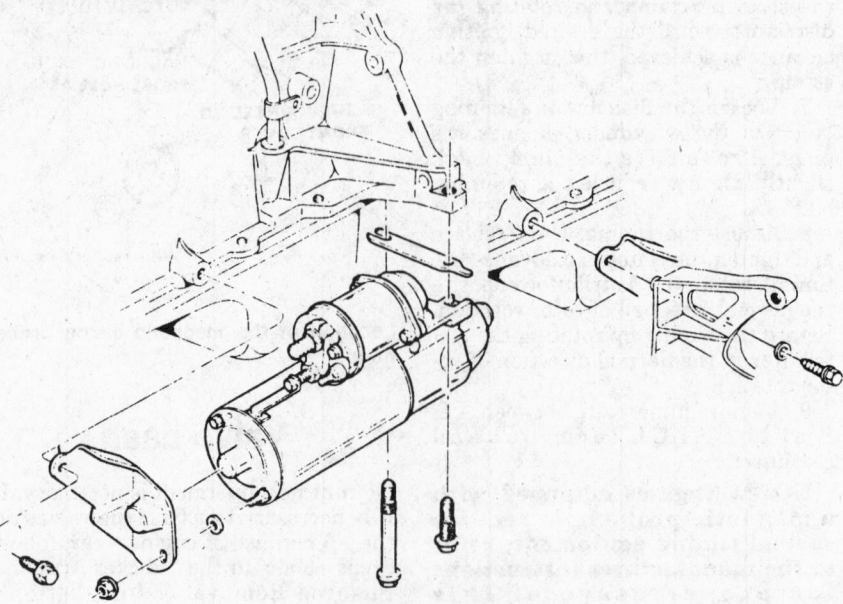

Starter motor mounting

3. Disconnect all wires at solenoid terminals. Note color coding of wires for installation.

4. Remove the starter support mount bolts.

5. Loosen the front bracket bolt or nut and rotate bracket clear. Lower and remove starter. Note the location of any shims so that they may be replaced in the same positions upon installation.

6. Reverse procedure to install.

ENGINE MECHANICAL

REMOVAL & INSTALLATION

NOTE: The engine assembly is removed from underneath the vehicle.

1. Disconnect the battery cables.
2. Drain the engine coolant.
3. Remove the rear compartment lid and also the side panels on the V6 engine.

NOTE: Do not remove the torsion rod retaining bolts.

4. Remove the air cleaner assembly.
5. Disconnect the throttle and shift cables.
6. Disconnect the heater hose at the intake manifold.
7. Disconnect vacuum hoses from all non-engine components.
8. Disconnect the fuel lines and filter.
9. Disconnect the fuel pump relay and the oxygen sensor.
10. On models equipped with automatic transaxle, disconnect the transaxle cooler lines.
11. Disconnect the slave cylinder from the manual transaxle equipped vehicles.
12. Disconnect the engine to chassis ground strap.
13. Discharge the A/C system if so equipped then disconnect the A/C lines at the compressor and seal the open ends.

— CAUTION —
Do not disconnect any refrigerant lines unless experienced with air conditioning systems. Escaping refrigerant will freeze any surface it contacts, including skin and eyes.

14. Remove the rear console.
15. Remove the ECM harness through the bulkhead.
16. Install an engine support fixture.
17. Remove the engine strut bracket and mark the bolt and bracket for reassembly.

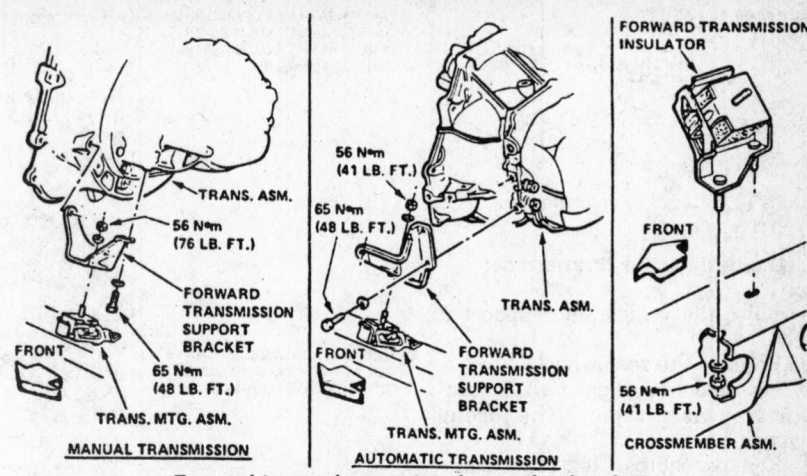

Forward transaxle mount and mounting brackets

1. Place a 4 × 4 at jacking locations
2. 4 wheel support dolly
3. Caliper supported
4. Support control arm on both sides
5. 4 × 4's
6. Wheel chocks

Engine removal and cradle support points

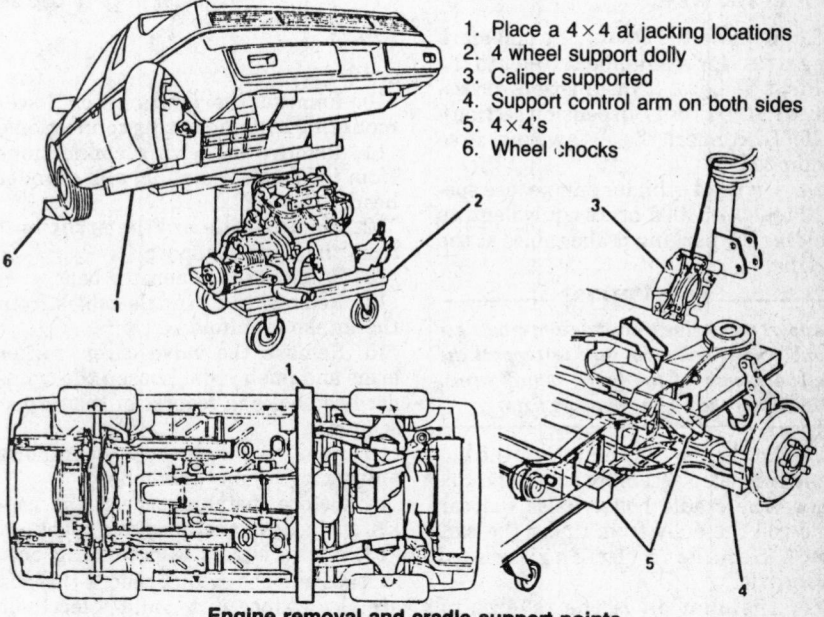

Rear transaxle mount and mounting brackets

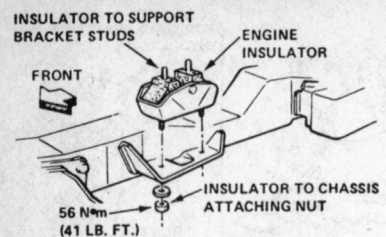

INSULATOR TO SUPPORT
BRACKET STUDS

ENGINE
INSULATOR

FRONT

56 N·m
(41 LB. FT.)

INSULATOR TO CHASSIS
ATTACHING NUT

Engine mount to crossmember

18. Raise the vehicle and support it safely.
19. Remove the rear wheels.
20. On models equipped with automatic transaxle, remove the torque converter bolts.
21. Remove the parking brake cable and calipers.

NOTE: Do not disconnect the brake hoses. Support the caliper out of the way.

22. Remove the strut bolts and mark the struts for realignment (refer to the "Strut Removal & Installation" procedure in the Front Suspension section).
23. Disconnect the A/C wiring, if so equipped.
24. On the 4 cylinder engine, use special tool J–34065 or its equivalent, to release the parking brake cables at the cradle.

─── CAUTION ───

Support the engine/transaxle and cradle assembly on a dolly. Be sure to support the outboard ends of the lower control arms. Disconnect the engine support fixture.

25. Lower the car and attach the engine/transaxle assembly to a dolly. Remove the cradle bolts. Raise the car and roll the dolly from under the car.
26. Separate the engine and transaxle.
27. Installation is the reverse of removal.

Cylinder Head

REMOVAL & INSTALLATION

4 Cylinder

1. Drain the cooling system.
2. Raise the vehicle and support safely with jack stands.
3. Remove the exhaust pipe.
4. Lower the vehicle.
5. Remove the oil level indicator tube.
6. Remove the air cleaner assembly.
7. Disconnect the EFI electrical connections and vacuum hoses. Depressurize the fuel system before disconnecting any fuel lines.
8. Remove the EGR base plate.
9. Remove the heater hose from the intake manifold.

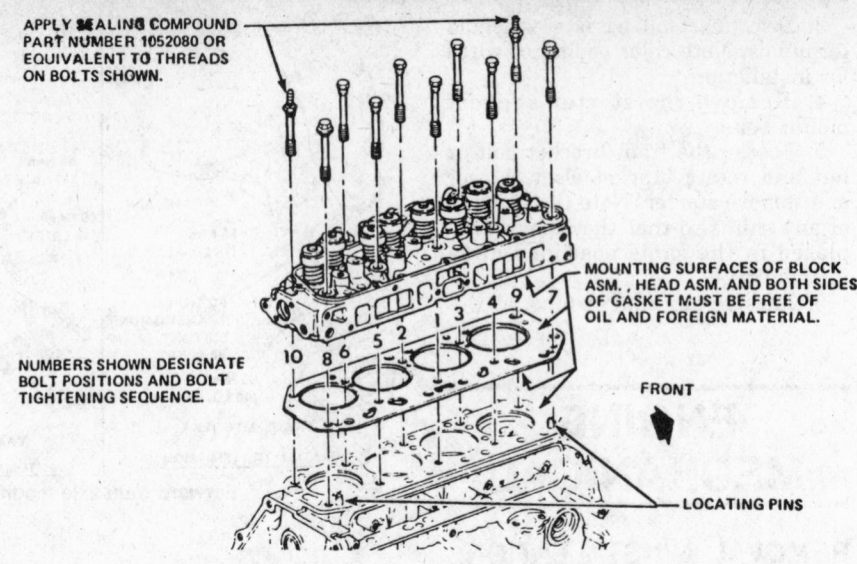

APPLY SEALING COMPOUND
PART NUMBER 1052080 OR
EQUIVALENT TO THREADS
ON BOLTS SHOWN.

NUMBERS SHOWN DESIGNATE
BOLT POSITIONS AND BOLT
TIGHTENING SEQUENCE.

MOUNTING SURFACES OF BLOCK
ASM., HEAD ASM. AND BOTH SIDES
OF GASKET MUST BE FREE OF
OIL AND FOREIGN MATERIAL.

FRONT

LOCATING PINS

Cylinder head torque sequence—four cyl. engine

10. Remove the ignition coil lower mounting bolt and wiring connections.
11. Remove all wiring connections from the intake manifold and cylinder head.
12. Remove the engine strut bolt from the upper support.
13. Remove the generator belt.
14. Remove the throttle cables from the intake manifold.
15. Remove the valve cover, rocker arms and push rods. Loosen the cylinder head bolts in reverse of the torque sequence.
16. Remove the cylinder head bolts and remove the cylinder head.
17. Before installing, clean the gasket surfaces of the head and block.
18. Make sure the retaining bolt threads and the cylinder block threads are clean since dirt could affect bolt torque.
19. Install a new gasket over the dowel pins in the cylinder.
20. Install the cylinder head into place over the dowel pins.
21. Coat the cylinder head bolt threads with sealing compound and install finger tight.
22. On 1984–85 models, tighten the cylinder head bolts gradually in the sequence shown in the illustration. Final torque is 92 ft. lbs.
23. On 1986–88 models, torque the head bolts gradually to 18 ft. lbs. in the sequence shown in the illustration. Repeat the sequence, bringing the torque to 22 ft. lbs. on all bolts except No. 9. Torque No. 9 to 29 ft. lbs. Repeat the sequence. Turn all the bolts, except No. 9, 120 degrees (two flats). Turn No. 9 1/4 turn (90 degrees).
24. The remainder of the installation is the reverse of removal.

V6 Engine

LEFT SIDE

1. Raise the vehicle and drain the coolant from the block.
2. Lower the vehicle.
3. Remove the intake manifold.
4. Disconnect the exhaust crossover pipe.
5. Disconnect the alternator bracket.
6. Remove the oil level indicator tube.
7. Loosen the rocker arms and remove the push rods. Loosen the head bolts in reverse of the torque sequence.
8. Remove the cylinder head bolts then remove the cylinder head.
9. Before installing, clean the gasket surfaces on the head, cylinder block and intake manifold.
10. Place the gasket in position over the dowel pins with the note "This Side UP" showing.
11. Place the cylinder head into position.
12. Coat the cylinder head bolt threads with a sealer and install the bolts.
13. Torque the cylinder head bolts in three steps, follow the sequence in the illustration as follows
   a. 20 ft.lbs.
   b. 45 ft.lbs.
   c. 66 ft. lbs.
13. Install the pushrods and loosely retain with the rocker arms. Make sure the lower ends of the pushrods are in the lifter seats then adjust the valve lash. Refer to the procedure under Rocker Arm, Cover and Push Rod.
14. The remainder of the installation is the reverse of removal.

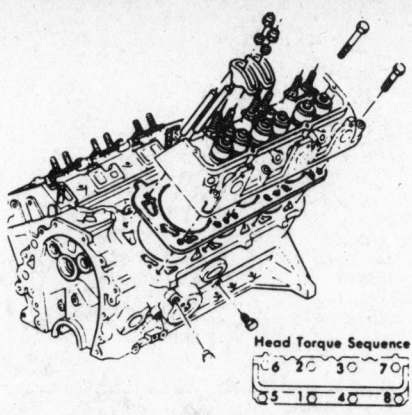

Cylinder head torque sequence—V6 engine

RIGHT SIDE

1. Raise the vehicle, support it safely, then drain the cooling system.
2. Disconnect the exhaust pipe.
3. Lower the vehicle.
4. Disconnect the cruise control servo bracket.
5. Remove the intake manifold.
6. Disconnect the exhaust crossover pipe.
7. Follow Steps 7–14 of the left side cylinder head procedure above.

OVERHAUL

NOTE: For all cylinder head overhaul procedures, please refer to "Engine Rebuilding" in the Unit Repair section.

Rocker Arms

REMOVAL & INSTALLATION

4 Cylinder

1. Remove the air cleaner.
2. Remove the PCV valve and hose.
3. Remove the valve cover bolts.
4. Disconnect the wires from the spark plugs and clips.
5. Remove the valve cover by tapping lightly with a rubber hammer.

NOTE: Prying on the cover could cause damage to the sealing surfaces.

6. Remove the rocker arm bolt and ball.
7. If replacing the push rod only, loosen the rocker arm bolt and swing the arm clear of the push rod.
8. Remove the rocker arm and push rod.
9. Installation is the reverse of removal. Torque the rocker arm bolt to 24 ft. lbs. Apply a continuous $^3/_{16}$ in. diameter bead of RTV sealant or equivalent around the cylinder head sealant surfaces inboard at the bolt holes.

V6 Engine

1. Disconnect the negative battery cable.
2. Remove the engine compartment lid and both side covers.

NOTE: Do not remove the torsion rod retaining bolts.

3. Disconnect the vacuum boost line and tube.
4. Disconnect the throttle and downshift cables and bracket.
5. Disconnect the cruise control cable, if applicable.
6. Disconnect the ground cable.
7. Remove the PCV valve from the cover.
8. Remove the oil dip stick tube.
9. Disconnect the plug wires and bracket.
10. Remove the engine lift hook.
11. Remove the rocker arm cover bolts and carefully remove the cover by bumping with your hand or a rubber mallet. If prying is necessary do not distort the sealing flange.
12. Remove the rocker arm nuts.

NOTE: Keep all components in order so that they may be installed in the same location. Keep the sealant out of the bolt holes. Keep all components in order so that they may be installed in the same location.

13. Remove the rocker arm pivot balls, arms and pushrods.
14. Before installation, coat the bearing surfaces of the rocker arms and pivot balls with Molykote® or equivalent.
15. Install the push rods, rocker arms and pivot balls. Make sure the push rods are seated in the valve lifters.
16. Adjust the rocker arm nuts until lash is eliminated.

   a. Rotate the engine until the mark on the torsional damper lines up with the "0" mark on the timing tab, with the engine in the No. 1 firing position. This may be determined by placing fingers on the No. 1 rocker arms as the mark on the damper comes near the "0" mark. If the valves are not moving, the engine is in the No. 1 firing position. With the engine in the No. 1 firing position, the following valves may be adjusted: Exhaust–1, 2, 3; Intake–1, 5, 6.

   b. Back out the adjusting nut until lash is felt at the pushrod, then turn the adjusting nut until all lash is removed. This can be determined by rotating the pushrod while turning the adjusting nut. When lash has been removed, turn the adjusting nut in 1½ additional turns to center the lifter plunger.

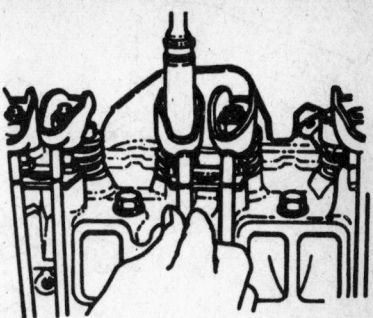

Adjusting valve lash-V6 engine

   c. Crank the engine one revolution until the timing tab "0" mark and torsional damper mark are again in alignment. This is the No. 4 firing position. With the engine in this position, the following valves may be adjusted: Exhaust–4, 5, 6; Intake–2, 3, 4.
17. Install the rocker arm covers.
   a. Clean the surfaces on the cylinder head and rocker arm cover.
   b. Place a 3mm diameter (⅛ inch) dot of RTV sealer, at the intake manifold and cylinder head split line.
   c. Install the rocker arm cover gasket, using care to line up the holes in the gasket with the bolt holes in the cylinder head.
   d. Install the rocker arm cover bolts and torque to 90 inch lbs.
18. The remainder of the installation is the reverse of removal.

Intake Manifold

REMOVAL & INSTALLATION

4 Cylinder

— CAUTION —
Relieve the pressure from the fuel system before disconnecting any fuel lines (refer to the Fuel System section).

1. Remove the air cleaner assembly.
2. Remove the PCV valve and hose.
3. Drain the cooling system.
4. Relieve the fuel system pressure and disconnect the fuel lines.
5. Disconnect the vacuum hoses.
6. Disconnect the wiring and throttle linkage from the throttle body assembly.
7. Disconnect the cruise control and linkage, if so equipped.
8. Disconnect the throttle linkage and bell crank and place to one side.
9. Disconnect the heater hose.
10. Remove the generator upper bracket.
11. Remove the ignition coil, on vehicles with the separately mounted coil.
12. Remove the retaining bolts and remove the manifolds.

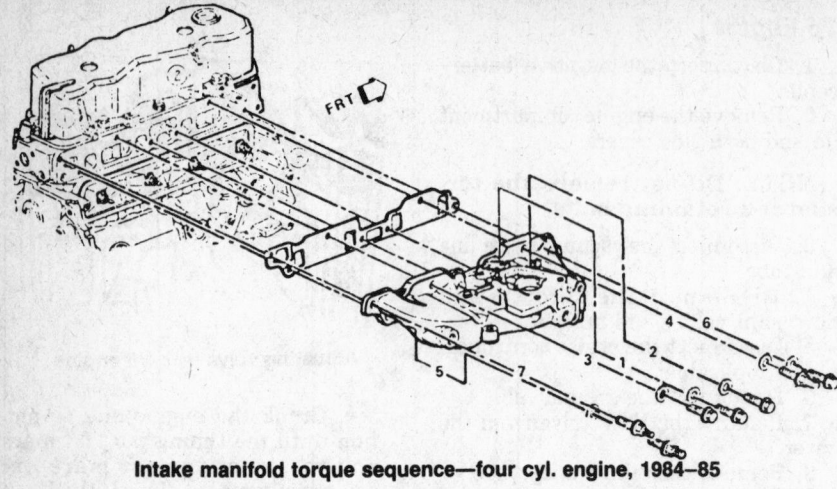

Intake manifold torque sequence—four cyl. engine, 1984–85

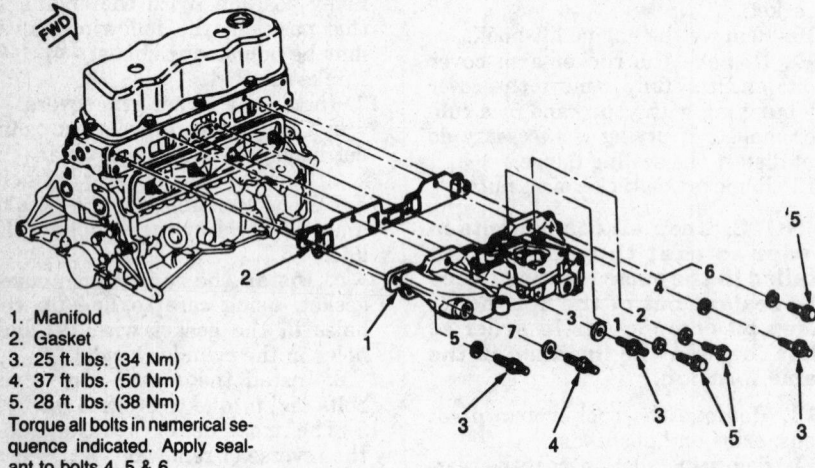

1. Manifold
2. Gasket
3. 25 ft. lbs. (34 Nm)
4. 37 ft. lbs. (50 Nm)
5. 28 ft. lbs. (38 Nm)
Torque all bolts in numerical sequence indicated. Apply sealant to bolts 4, 5 & 6

Intake manifold torque sequence—four cyl. engine, 1986 and later

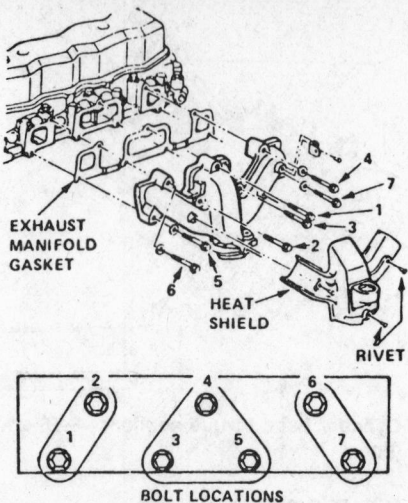

Exhaust manifold torque sequence—four cyl. engine, 1984

13. Installation is the reverse of removal. Torque all bolts in the sequence shown in the illustration.

V6 Engine

NOTE: Refer to the Fuel System section for the procedure on relieving fuel system pressure.

1. Disconnect the negative battery cable.
2. Remove both rocker arm covers.
3. Drain the engine coolant.
4. Disconnect the throttle body-to-elbow intake hose.
5. Remove the distributor and mark the position of the rotor.
6. Disconnect the shift and throttle linkage.
7. Remove the throttle body-to-upper plenum connector.
8. Disconnect the heater and radiator hoses.
9. Disconnect all wiring harness and vacuum hoses while noting their locations for reassembly.
10. Disconnect the vacuum booster pipe and bracket.

11. Disconnect the EGR pipe.
12. Remove the upper manifold plenum and gaskets.
13. Remove the intermediate intake manifold and gasket.
14. Remove the lower intake manifold and gaskets.
15. Clean all gasket surfaces on the intake manifolds and cylinder head.
16. Install the lower intake manifold and gasket and torque in sequence to 19 ft. lbs.
17. Install the intermediate intake manifold and gaskets and torque in sequence to 15 ft. lbs.
18. Install the upper manifold plenum and gaskets and torque in sequence.
19. The remainder of the installation is the reverse of removal. Check engine timing, coolant level and for leaks.

Exhaust Manifold

REMOVAL & INSTALLATION

1. Remove the air cleaner and the EFI bracket tube.

2. Raise the vehicle and support it with jack stands.
3. Remove the exhaust pipe and lower the vehicle.
4. Remove the retaining bolts and washers and remove the exhaust manifold and gasket.
5. Installation is the reverse of removal. Clean the sealing surfaces and use a new gasket. Torque the retaining bolts to the sequence shown in the illustration. Torque bolts No. 3, 4 and 5-37 ft. lbs. Torque bolts No. 1, 2, 6 and 7-16. ft. lbs.

Exhaust Manifold and Crossover

REMOVAL & INSTALLATION

V6 Engine

FRONT

1. Disconnect the negative battery cable.
2. Remove the rear compartment lid.

NOTE: Do not remove the torsion rod retaining bolts.

3. Remove the brake vacuum hose.
4. Remove the manifold heat shield.
5. Remove the front crossover bolts.
6. Raise the car and remove the front converter heat shield and the lower manifold bolts.
7. Lower the car and remove the upper manifold bolts then remove the manifold.
8. Install the manifold and torque the upper bolts to 18 ft. lbs.
9. Raise the car and torque the lower bolts to 18 ft. lbs.
10. Install the front converter heat shield.

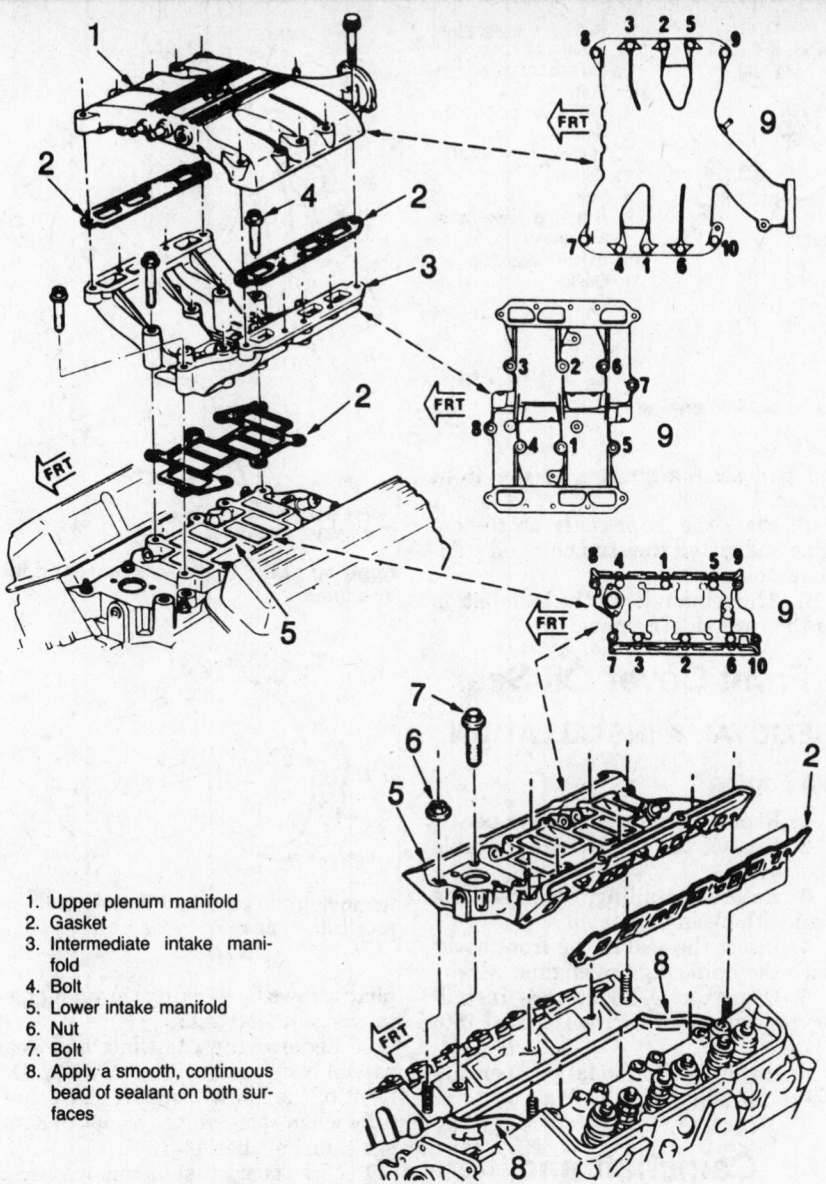

1. Upper plenum manifold
2. Gasket
3. Intermediate intake manifold
4. Bolt
5. Lower intake manifold
6. Nut
7. Bolt
8. Apply a smooth, continuous bead of sealant on both surfaces

Intake manifold installation and torque sequence—V6 engine

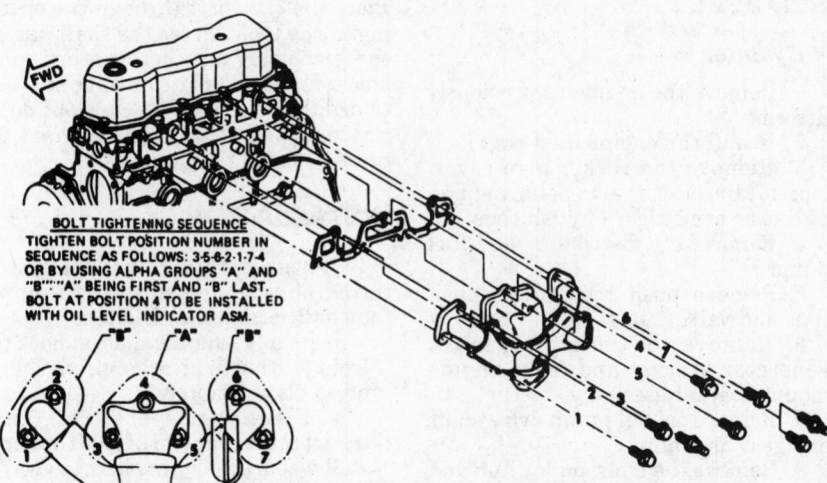

Exhaust manifold torque sequence—four cyl. engine, 1985 and later

11. Lower the car and torque the crossover bolts to 22 ft. lbs.

12. The remainder of the installation is the reverse of removal. Check for exhaust or vacuum leaks.

REAR

1. Disconnect the manifold-to-crossover bolts.

2. Remove the manifold bolts then remove the manifold.

3. Installation is the reverse of removal. Torque the manifold bolts to 18 ft. lbs. and the manifold-to-crossover bolts to 22 ft. lbs.

Timing Cover and Oil Seal

REMOVAL & INSTALLATION

4 Cylinder

1. To remove the crankshaft hub, it is necessary to remove the inner fender splash shield.

2. Remove the alternator lower bracket.

3. Remove the front engine mounts.

4. Using a floor jack, raise the engine.

5. Remove the engine mount mounting bracket-to-cylinder block bolts. Remove the bracket and mount as an assembly.

6. Remove the oil pan-to-front cover screws.

7. Remove the front cover-to-block screws.

8. Pull the cover slightly forward, just enough to allow cutting of the oil pan front seal flush with the block on both sides.

9. Remove the front cover and attached portion of the pan seal.

10. Clean the gasket surfaces throughly.

11. Cut the tabs from the new oil pan front seal.

12. Install the seal on the front cover, pressing the tips into the holes provided.

13. Coat the new gasket with sealer and position it on the front cover.

14. Apply a $\frac{1}{8}$ in. bead of silicone sealer to the joint formed at the oil pan and block.

15. Align the front cover seal with a centering tool and install the front cover. Tighten the screws.

16. Install the hub and torque the hub bolt to 160 ft. lbs.

NOTE: Coat the pulley to hub bolts with a locking sealant.

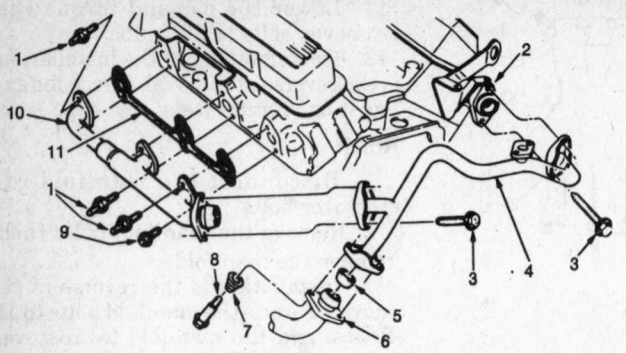

1. Bolt/stud lockwasher assembly
2. Exhaust manifold
3. Bolt
4. Crossover pipe
5. Seal
6. Muffler
7. Spring
8. Bolt
9. Bolt and lockwasher assembly
10. Exhaust manifold
11. Gasket

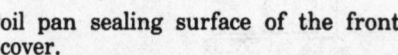

Exhaust manifold installation—V6 engine

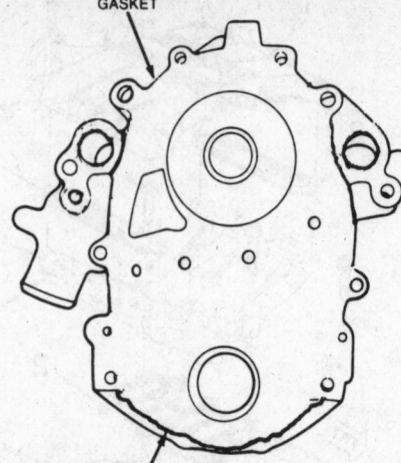

3mm BEAD OF RTV SEALANT #1052366 OR EQUIVALENT

Applying sealer to the front cover on the V6 engine

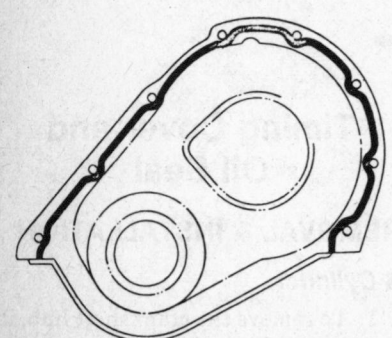

Timing cover sealer application—four cyl. engine

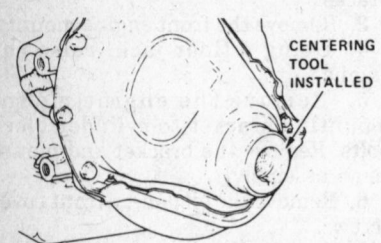

Front cover centering tool installed—four cyl. engine

Front Cover

REMOVAL & INSTALLATION

V6 Engine

1. Disconnect the negative battery cable.
2. Remove the A/C compressor and bracket, without disconnecting the refrigerant lines and position out of the way.
3. Remove the water pump.
4. Raise the vehicle and support it safely.
5. Remove the torsional damper.
6. Remove the oil pan to cover bolts.
7. Lower the vehicle and remove the front cover.
8. Before installing, clean the sealing surfaces on the front cover and cylinder block. Install a new gasket and apply a 1/8 in. bead of RTV sealer to the

oil pan sealing surface of the front cover.

9. Place the front cover on the engine and install the stud bolt and standard bolts.
10. The remainder of the installation is the reverse of removal.

Front Cover Oil Seal

REMOVAL & INSTALLATION

V6 Engine

1. Remove the torsional damper.
2. Pry out the seal using a suitable tool.
3. Before installing, lubricate the seal with clean engine oil.
4. Insert the seal in the front cover with the lip facing the engine.
5. Using tool J-23042 Seal Installer, or equivalent, drive the seal into place.
6. Install the torsional damper and check for leaks.

Camshaft and Timing Gear

REMOVAL

4 Cylinder

1. Remove the engine as previously described.
2. Install the engine on a stand.
3. Remove the rocker arm cover, loosen valve rocker arm bolts and pivot rocker arms clear of push rods.
4. Remove the distributor and fuel pump.
5. Remove push rods cover, push rods and valve lifters.
6. Remove the generator, lower generator bracket and front engine mount bracket assembly.
7. Remove the oil pump drive shaft and gear assembly.
8. Remove the front pulley hub and timing gear cover.
9. Remove the two camshaft thrust

Removing the camshaft thrust screws—four cyl. engine

plate screws by working through holes in the camshaft gear.

10. Remove the camshaft and gear assembly by pulling it out through the front of the block. Support shaft carefully when removing so as not to damage camshaft bearings.
11. If the gear must be removed from the shaft, use press plate and adaptor tool J-971 on press.
12. Place tools on table of press. Place the camshaft through the opening in the tools. Press the shaft out of the gear using a socket or other suitable tool. Thrust plate must be so positioned that woodruff key in shaft does not damage it when the shaft is pressed out of the gear.

INSTALLATION

1. To assemble camshaft gear, thrust plate and gear spacer ring to camshaft, proceed as follows:
   a. Firmly support shaft at back of front journal in an arbor press using press plate adaptors.
   b. Place gear spacer ring and thrust plate over end of shaft and install woodruff key in shaft keyway.
   c. Install the camshaft gear and press it onto the shaft until it bot-

toms against the gear spacer ring. The end clearance of the thrust plate should be replaced.

2. Throughly coat the camshaft journals with a high quality engine oil supplement.

3. Install the camshaft assembly in the engine block, being careful not to damage bearings or cam.

4. Turn crankshaft and camshaft so that the teeth will line up. Engine is now in the No. 4 cylinder firing position. Install the camshaft thrust plate to block screws and tighten 75 inch lbs.

5. Install the timing gear cover and gasket.

6. Line up the keyway in hub with the key on crankshaft and slide the hub onto the shaft. Install the center bolt and torque to 160 ft. lbs.

7. Install as previously described valve lifters, push rods, push rod cover, oil pump shaft and gear assembly and fuel pump.

8. Install the distributor as follows:

a. Turn the crankshaft 360° to firing position of number one cylinder (number one exhaust and intake valve lifters both on base circle of camshaft and timing mark on harmonic balancer indexed with top dead center mark on timing pad).

b. Install the distributor in its original position and align shaft so that rotor arm points toward number one cylinder spark plug contact.

9. Pivot the rocker arms over push rods. With lifters on base circle of camshaft, tighten rocker arm bolt to 20 ft. lbs. (27 Nm). Do not overtorque.

10. Install the front mount assembly lower generator bracket and generator.

11. Complete the engine installation as described earlier.

Timing Chain and Sprockets

REMOVAL & INSTALLATION

V6 Engine

1. Remove the crankcase front cover.

2. Place the No. 1 piston at top dead center, with the marks on the camshaft and crankshaft sprockets aligned.

3. Remove the camshaft sprocket and chain.

NOTE: It may be necessary to use a plastic mallet on the lower edge of the sprocket to dislodge it.

4. Remove the camshaft sprocket with tool J–5825.

5. Install the sprocket with tool J–5590.

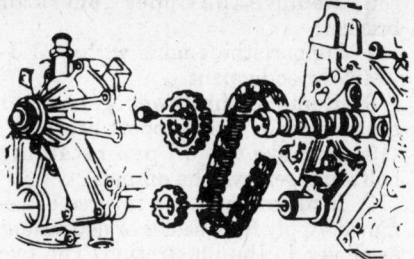

V-6 timing chain and sprockets— exploded view

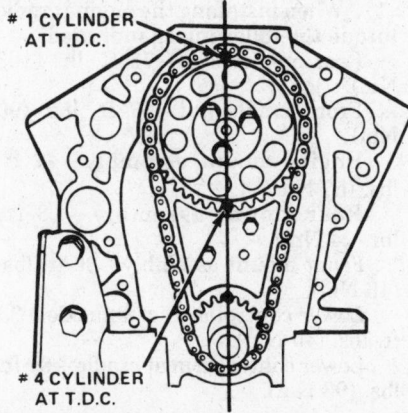

1 CYLINDER AT T.D.C.

4 CYLINDER AT T.D.C.

Align the timing marks for the camshaft and crankshaft sprockets as shown

6. Apply Molykote® or equivalent to the sprocket thrust surface.

7. Hold the sprocket with the chain hanging down and align the marks on the camshaft and crankshaft sprockets.

8. Align the dowel in the camshaft with the dowel hole in the camshaft sprocket.

9. Draw the camshaft sprocket onto the camshaft, using the mounting bolts and torque to 15–20 ft. lbs.

10. Lubricate the timing chain with engine oil.

11. Install the crankcase front cover.

Camshaft

REMOVAL & INSTALLATION

V6 Engine

1. Remove the engine (on cradle).

2. Remove the valve lifters.

3. Remove the crankcase front cover.

4. Remove the timing chain and sprocket.

5. Remove the rear cover.

6. Carefully remove the camshaft to avoid damage to the bearings.

7. Before installation, lubricate the camshaft journals with engine oil.

NOTE: If a new camshaft is to be installed, coat the lobes with

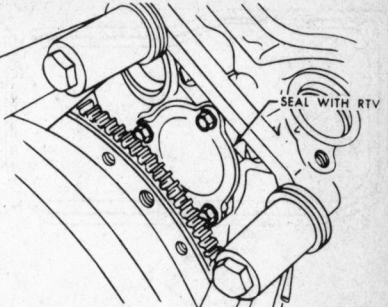

SEAL WITH RTV

The camshaft rear cover on the V6

an engine oil supplement such as GM E.O.S. or its equivalent.

8. The remainder of installation is the reverse of removal.

Piston and Connecting Rod

POSITIONING

See the accompanying illustration to properly install the piston and connecting rod assembly. Align the piston and connecting rod assembly with the piston mark (notch) toward the front of the engine. For further information on piston replacement and overhaul, please refer to the "Engine Rebuilding" Unit Repair.

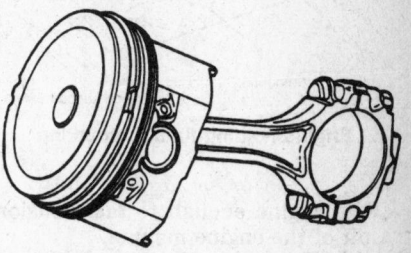

Piston and rod assembly

ENGINE LUBRICATION

Oil Pan

REMOVAL & INSTALLATION

4 Cylinder

1. Remove the engine cradle. The cradle can be removed from the car without removing the engine or transaxle.

a. Using engine support fixture tool J–28467 or equivalent, raise

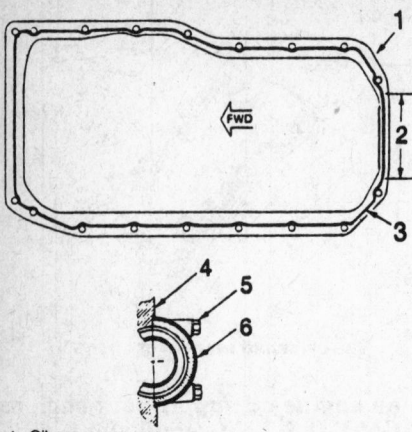

1. Oil pan
2. Apply a ³⁄₈" thick bead of RTV sealer in area indicated
3. Apply a ³⁄₁₆" wide by ⅛" thick bead of RTV sealer in area indicated
4. Engine block assy.
5. Rear bearing
6. Groove in main bearing cap must be filled flush to ⅛" above surface with RTV

Oil pan sealer application-four cylinder engine

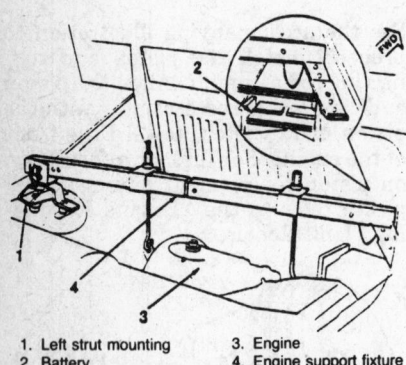

1. Left strut mounting
2. Battery
3. Engine
4. Engine support fixture

Engine holding fixture mounting

the engine enough to take tension off of the engine mounts.

b. Raise the vehicle and support safely with jack stands.

c. Remove the exhaust pipe bolts at the manifold.

d. Remove the rear wheels and tire assemblies.

e. Remove both lower control arms at the knuckle.

f. Remove both toe-link rod at the knuckle.

g. Remove the emergency brake cable at the cradle.

h. Remove the engine and transmission mounting bolts.

i. Remove the cradle bolts and remove the cradle assembly.

2. Drain the engine oil.

3. Remove the nuts from the the engine mount to the support bracket.

4. Disconnect the exhaust pipe at the manifold and the rear transaxle mount.

5. Remove the starter and flywheel cover.

6. Remove the upper generator bracket.

7. Support the engine with tool J-28467 or equivalent.

8. Remove the lower generator bracket and engine support bracket.

9. Remove the oil pan retaining bolts and remove the oil pan.

10. Installation is the reverse of removal. Apply RTV sealer or equivalent as shown in the illustration. The two bolts in the timing gear cover should be installed last after the pan bolts are tight.

11. When installing the engine cradle torque the following as indicated:

Rear cradle bolts—76 ft. lbs (103 Nm).

Front cradle nut—67 ft. lbs. (90 Nm).

Engine mount assembly—42 ft. lbs. (57 Nm).

Rear mount assembly—18 ft. lbs.(24 Nm).

Front mount assembly—36 ft. lbs. (48 Nm).

Lower control arm at knuckle—33 ft. lbs. (45 Nm).

Lower control arm at cradle—69 ft. lbs. (93 Nm).

V6 Engine

1. Disconnect the negative battery cable.

2. Raise the vehicle and support it safely.

3. Drain the crankcase.

4. Remove the flywheel shield or clutch housing cover.

5. Remove the starter.

6. Remove the oil pan.

7. Before installation, clean all mating surfaces.

8. Place a ⅛ in. bead of RTV sealant on the oil pan sealing flange.

9. Install the oil pan and torque the 1 in. bolts to 6–9 ft. lbs. and the 1.5 inch bolts to 14–22 ft. lbs.

10. The remainder of the installation is the reverse of removal.

Rear Main Bearing Oil Seal

REMOVAL & INSTALLATION

4 Cylinder

NOTE: This is a one piece seal and can be replaced without removal of the oil pan or crankshaft.

1. Remove the transaxle assembly.
2. Remove the flywheel.
3. If equipped with a manual transaxle, remove the pressure plate and disc.
4. Pry out the rear main seal.
5. Before installing, clean the block

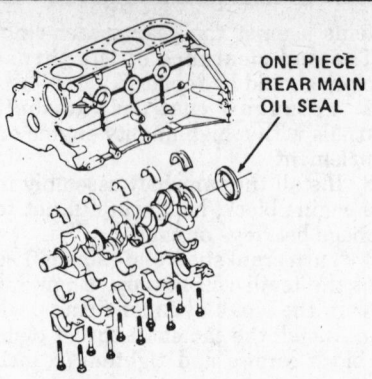

ONE PIECE REAR MAIN OIL SEAL

Crankshaft bearings and rear seal

and crankshaft-to-seal mating surfaces.

6. Lubricate the outside of the seal for ease of installation and press into the block with fingers.

7. Install the flywheel and torque the bolts to 44 ft. lbs.

8. Install the transaxle assembly.

V6 Engine (Thin Seal)

1. Remove the engine and mount it on a suitable stand.

2. Remove the oil pan and oil pump assembly.

3. Remove the front cover, then lock the chain tensioner with a pin.

4. Rotate the crankshaft until the timing marks on the cam and crank sprockets align.

5. Remove the camshaft bolt, cam sprocket and timing chain.

6. Rotate the crankshaft to the horizontal position.

7. Remove the rod bearing nuts, caps and bearings.

8. Remove the crankshaft and the old oil seal.

9. Apply a light coat of GM 1052726 or equivalent to the outside of the seal.

10. Install the new seal and tool in the rear area of the crankshaft.

11. Install the crankshaft and tool in the engine.

12. Position the seal tool so that the arrow points toward the cylinder block and remove the tool.

13. Put a light coat of oil on the crankshaft journals.

14. Seal the rear main bearing split line surface with GM 1052726 or equivalent.

15. The remainder of the installation is the reverse of removal. Torque to specifications.

Oil Pump

REMOVAL & INSTALLATION

4 Cylinder

1. Remove the oil pan as described earlier.

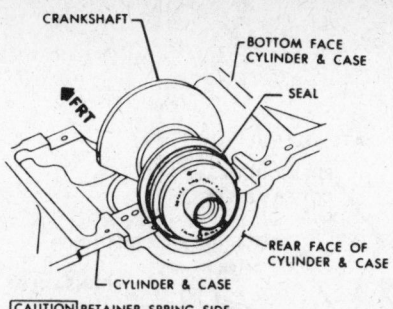

Installing the thin type oil seal—V6 engine

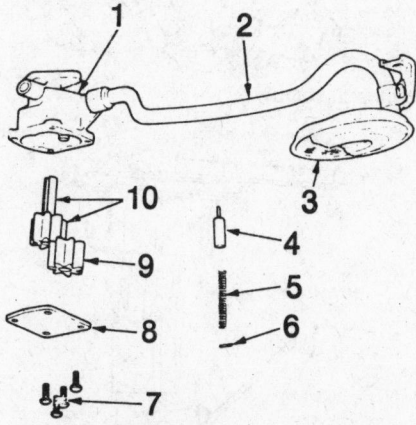

1. Pump body
2. Pickup tube
3. Pickup screen assy.
4. Pressure regulator valve
5. Pressure regulator spring
6. Spring retainer
7. Cover Screws
8. Cover
9. Idler gear
10. Drive gear and shaft

Oil pump - exploded view

2. Remove the two flange mounting bolts and the nut from the main bearing cap bolt.

3. Remove the pump and screen as an assembly.

4. Installation is the reverse of removal. Align the pump shaft with the drive shaft tang. Torque the pump retaining bolts to 20 ft. lbs.

V6 Engine

1. Remove the oil pan.

2. Remove the pump and driveshaft extension.

3. To install, engage the driveshaft extension in the cover end of the distributor drive gear.

4. Install the pump-to-rear bearing cap bolt and torque to 26–35 ft. lbs.

5. Install the oil pan and refill with oil.

ENGINE COOLING

CAUTION

Keep hands, tools and clothing away from engine cooling fan to help prevent personal injury. This fan is electric and can come on whether or not the engine is running. The fan can start automatically in response to a heat sensor with the ignition in the ON position.

Radiator

REMOVAL & INSTALLATION

1. Drain the engine coolant.

2. Disconnect the wiring harness from the fan and fan frame.

3. Remove the fan and frame assembly.

4. Disconnect the upper radiator support bracket.

5. Disconnect the coolant hoses at the radiator.

6. Disconnect the transmission/engine oil cooler lines at the radiator.

7. Remove the radiator from the car.

8. Installation is the reverse of removal. After installation run the engine and check for leaks.

Water Pump

REMOVAL & INSTALLATION

1. Disconnect battery negative cable.

2. Remove accessory drive belts. Drain the cooling system through the petcock on the bottom of the radiator.

3. Remove water pump attaching bolts and remove pump. Note that on the V6, there is a nut at the top/left position. The nut screws on to the outer end of a stud that retains the timing cover underneath.

4. If installing a new water pump, transfer pulley from old unit. With sealing surfaces cleaned, place a ⅛ in. (3mm) bead of sealant No. 1052289 or equivalent on the water pump sealing surface. While sealer is still wet, install pump and torque bolts/nut to 6 ft. lbs. on the four cylinder engine. On the V6, torque the two bottom/center bolts to 7 ft. lbs.; torque the other bolts and the nut to 22 ft. lbs.

5. Install accessory drive belts.

6. Connect battery negative cable.

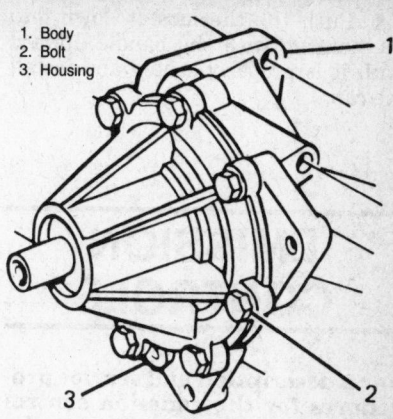

1. Body
2. Bolt
3. Housing

Water pump mounting-four cylinder engine

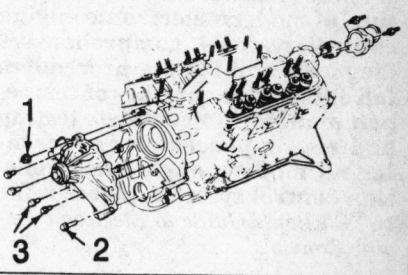

1— 30 N•m (22 FT-LBS)	2— 30 N•m (22 FT-LBS)	3— 10 N•m (7 FT-LBS)

Water pump bolt torques for the V6 engine

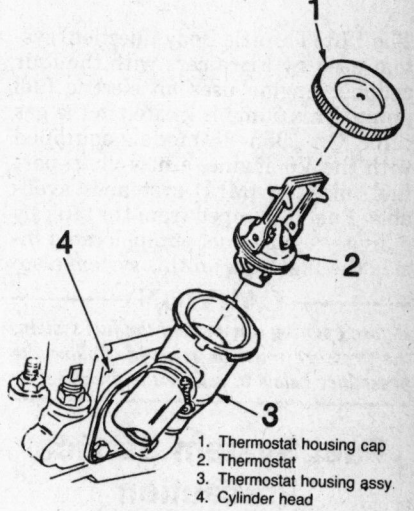

1. Thermostat housing cap
2. Thermostat
3. Thermostat housing assy.
4. Cylinder head

Thermostat and housing

Thermostat

REMOVAL & INSTALLATION

1. Remove the thermostat cap.

2. Grasp the thermostat handle and gently pull up.

3. Before installing, clean the thermostat housing and O-ring. Apply a suitable lubricant to the O-ring for easier installation.

4. Push the thermostat down into the housing with the handle upward until it is properly seated and install the cap.

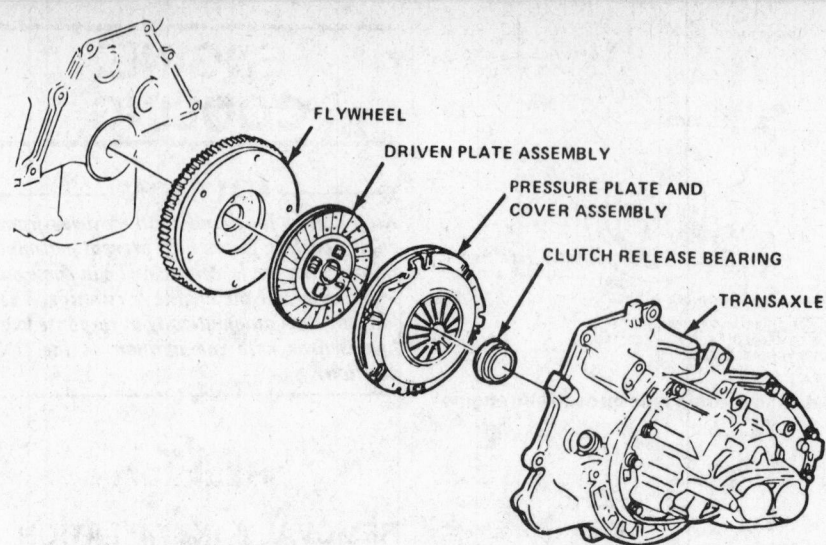

Exploded view of clutch assembly

EMISSION CONTROLS

For a description and service procedures for the emission control systems, please refer to "Emission Controls" in the Unit Repair section. Due to the complex nature of modern electronic engine control systems, comprehensive diagnosis and testing procedures fall outside the confines of this repair manual. For complete testing and repair procedures concerning all modern engine and emission control systems, please refer to "Chilton's Guide to Electronic Engine Controls".

Fuel Filter

REMOVAL & INSTALLATION

NOTE: Relieve fuel pressure (see caution above).

The filter is an inline unit ahead of the TBI or MFI unit. To remove the filter, make sure the engine is cold, unclamp and remove the fuel hose, then filter from the steel fuel line. Installation is the reverse of removal.

Electric Fuel Pump

REMOVAL & INSTALLATION

1. Relieve the fuel system pressure (refer to procedure above).
2. Drain the fuel tank.
3. Disconnect wiring from the tank.
4. Remove the ground wire retaining screw from under the body.
5. Disconnect all hoses from the tank.
6. Support the tank on a jack and remove the retaining strap nuts.
7. Lower the tank and remove it.
8. Remove the fuel gauge/pump retaining ring using a spanner wrench such as tool J—24187.
9. Remove the gauge unit and the pump.
10. Installation is the reverse of removal. Always replace the O-ring under the gauge/pump retaining ring.

Fuel Injection

NOTE: Due to the complex nature of modern fuel injection systems, comprehensive diagnosis and testing procedures fall outside the confines of this repair manual. For complete informa-

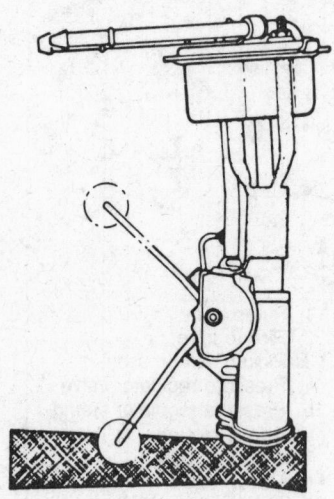

Typical electric fuel pump and sending unit

FUEL SYSTEM

The TBI (Throttle Body Injection) system used by Fiero cars with the four cylinder engine uses an electric fuel pump. This pump is located in the gas tank. On 1985–88 models equipped with the V6 engine, a new multi-port fuel injection (MFI) system is available. Fuel is pumped from the tank by a high pressure fuel pump, located inside the fuel tank on this system also.

— CAUTION —

Before opening any part of the fuel system, the pressure must be relieved. Follow the procedure below to relieve the pressure:

Fuel System Service Precaution

RELIEVING FUEL SYSTEM PRESSURE

1. Remove the fuel pump fuse from the fuse panel.
2. Start the engine and let it run until all fuel in the line is used.
3. Crank the starter an additional three seconds to relieve any residual pressure.
4. With the ignition OFF, replace the fuse.

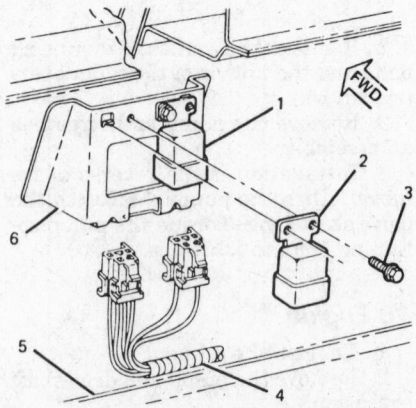

1. Fuel pump relay
2. Relay assy. (ac clutch control)
3. Bolt
4. E.F.I. harness
5. Floor pan
6. Bracket

Fuel pump relay location

tion on fuel injection diagnosis, please refer to *"Chilton's Guide To Fuel Injection And Feedback Carburetors"*.

MANUAL TRANSAXLE

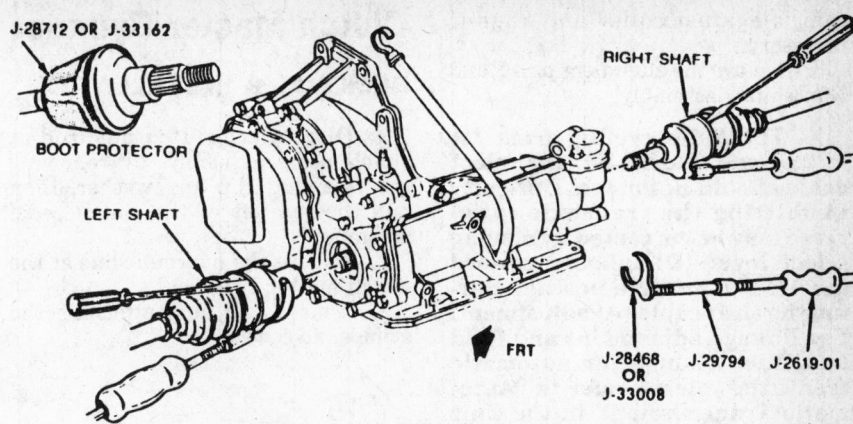

Removing the drive axle from the transaxle

REMOVAL & INSTALLATION

1. Remove the air cleaner assembly.
2. Disconnect the negative battery cable.
3. Disconnect the ground cable at the transaxle.
4. Disconnect the shift and select cable at the transaxle.
5. Remove the upper transaxle to engine bolts.
6. Install an engine support fixture tool J–28467 or equivalent.
7. Hoist the car and support it safely with jack stands.
8. Remove the rear wheels and tires.
9. Remove the axle shafts.
10. Remove the heat shield from the catalytic converter.
11. Disconnect the exhaust pipe at the exhaust manifold.
12. Remove the engine mount to cradle nuts.
13. Support the cradle with an adjustable stand.
14. Remove the rear cradle to body bolts.
15. Remove the forward cradle to body through bolts.
16. Lower the cradle and move out of the way.
17. Remove the starter and inspection cover shields and remove the starter.
18. Position a transmission stand under the transaxle.
19. Remove the lower transaxle to engine bolts and remove the transaxle.
20. Install the starter cover shield.
21. Hoist the cradle into position.

NOTE: Lower the cradle at the front and raise the car. Work cradle at rear into position on mounts then raise the front into position.

22. The remainder of the installation is the reverse of removal. Torque the retaining nuts to the following specifications:
   Starter-to-engine – 32 ft. lbs. (43 Nm).
   Front cradle-to-body nuts – 67 ft. lbs. (90 Nm).
   Rear cradle-to-body bolts – 76 ft. lbs. (103 Nm).

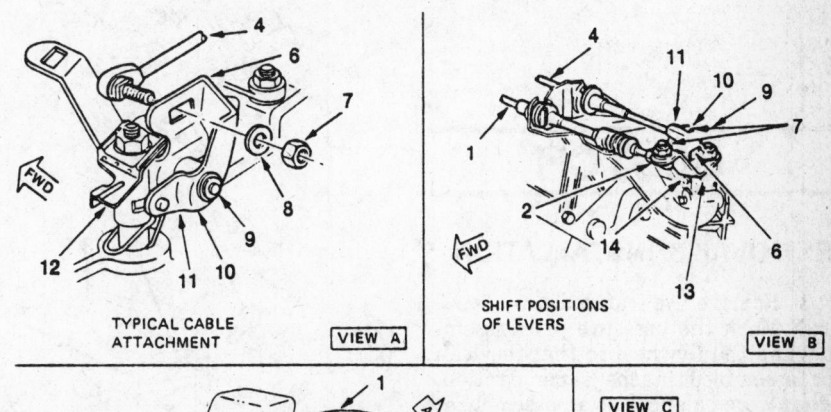

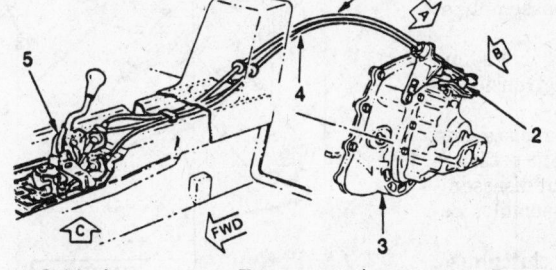

1. Cable A
2. Lever F
3. Tansaxle assy.
4. Cable B
5. Trans. control assy.
6. Lever D
7. Nut E
8. Washer P
9. R
10. 1st/2nd
11. 4th/3rd
12. Retainer clip J
13. R/3rd/1st
14. 2nd/4th
15. Alignment pin F
16. Alignment·pin G

Manual transaxle cable adjustment

Exhaust pipe-to-exhaust manifold – 25 ft. lbs. (33 Nm).
   Transaxle mounts-to-cradle nuts, rear – 8 ft. lbs. (24 Nm); front – 36 ft. lbs. (48 Nm).
   Engine mount-to-cradle nuts – 40 ft. lbs. (55 Nm).
   Upper transaxle-to-engine bolts – 55 ft. lbs. (75 Nm).
   Cooler lines – 20 ft. lbs. (27 Nm).
   Support bracket-to-transaxle (automatic) – 37 ft. lbs. (50 Nm).

CABLE ADJUSTMENT

1. Disconnect the negative (1) battery cable.
2. Place the transaxle in 1st gear.
3. Loosen the shift cable attaching nuts (E) at the transaxle levers (D) and (F).
4. Remove the console and trim plates as required for access to shifter.
5. With the shifter lever in first gear position (pulled to left and held against stop), insert alignment pins F and G as shown in view D.
6. Remove the lash from transaxle by first compressing select cable (B) and then tightening nut (E). Levers (D) and (F) should be kept from moving during this process. Similarly, shift cable (A) is first compressed and nut (E) then tightened. Again levers (D) and (F) remain stationary. Nut (E) on levers (D) and (F) tightened to 20 ft. lbs. (27 Nm).
7. Ensure that the reverse inhibit

cam is against roller and align if necessary.

8. Remove the alignment pins F and G at shifter assembly.

NOTE: While cycling from 1st to 2nd and 2nd to 1st, the select cable should not move. Difficulty in shifting the transaxle to reverse may be corrected by moving select lever (D) inboard toward the 1st-3rd-Reverse position during the shift cable (A) adjustment. For linkage adjustment and fluid and filter change for automatic transaxles, please refer to "Automatic Transmission" in the Unit Repair section.

CLUTCH

REMOVAL & INSTALLATION

1. Remove the transaxle.
2. Mark the pressure plate assembly and the flywheel so that they can be assembled in the same position. They were balanced as an assembly at the factory.
3. Loosen the attaching bolts one turn at a time until spring tension is relieved.
4. Support the pressure plate and remove the bolts. Remove the pressure plate and clutch disc. Do not disassemble the pressure plate assembly; replace it if defective.
5. Inspect the flywheel, clutch disc, pressure plate, throwout bearing and the clutch fork and pivot shaft assembly for wear. Replace the parts as required. If the flywheel shows any signs of overheating or if it is badly grooved or scored, it should be replaced.
6. Clean the pressure plate and flywheel mating surfaces throughly. Position the clutch disc and pressure plate into the installed position and support with a dummy shaft or clutch aligning tool. The clutch plate is assembled with the damper springs offset toward the transaxle. One side of the factory-supplied clutch disc is stamped "Flywheel Side".
7. Install the pressure plate-to-flywheel bolts. Tighten them gradually in a crisscross pattern.
8. Lubricate the outside groove and the inside recess of the release bearing with high temperature grease. Wipe off any excess. Install the release bearing.
9. Install the transaxle.

Clutch Master Cylinder

REMOVAL & INSTALLATION

1. Disconnect clutch pushrod at clutch pedal assembly, by removing the retaining clip and washer, then pull the rod left of the clutch pedal assemby.
2. Remove the hydraulic line at the clutch master cylinder.
3. Remove two nuts attaching the cylinder to cowl wall.

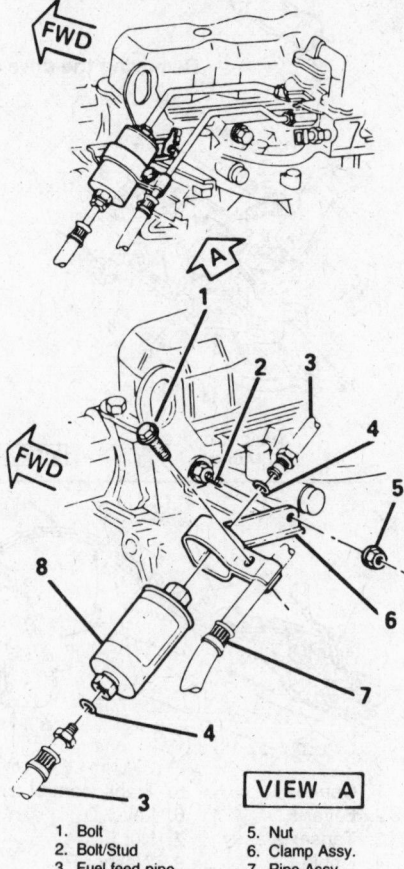

VIEW A

1. Bolt
2. Bolt/Stud
3. Fuel feed pipe
4. "O-ring
5. Nut
6. Clamp Assy.
7. Pipe Assy.
8. Filter Assy.

Fuel filter

4. Remove the clutch cylinder.
5. To install, postion clutch rod through the the cowl opening and install the cylinder to cowl nuts loosely.
6. Place the clutch master cylinder rod on the clutch pedal assembly. Install washer and clip.
7. Torque the cylinder to cowl nuts to 13 ft. lbs.
8. Reconnect the hydraulic line to the master cylinder and torque to 13 ft. lbs.
9. Fill the master cylinder with recommended fluid and bleed the system.

Clutch Slave Cylinder

REMOVAL & INSTALLATION

1. Remove the hydraulic line at the slave cylinder.
2. Remove the slave cylinder to bracket bolts and remove the cylinder.
3. To install, position slave cylinder at the bracket mounting and pilot the cylinder into the clutch release lever.
4. Install slave cylinder to bracket nuts and torque to 16 ft. lbs.
5. Install hydraulic line to slave cylinder, torque to 13 ft. lbs.
6. Fill master cylinder with recommended fluid and bleed system.

BLEEDING THE HYDRAULIC CLUTCH

1. Fill the master cylinder reservoir with Delco Supreme No. 11 Brake Fluid or an equivalent approved DOT 3 type brake fluid.
2. Have an assistant pump the clutch pedal 2-3 times and hold to the floor.
3. Open the bleeder screw at the slave cylinder one half turn and allow all air in the system to escape, close the bleeder screw as soon as brake fluid begins to flow.
4. Repeat this procedure until all air is completely out of the system.

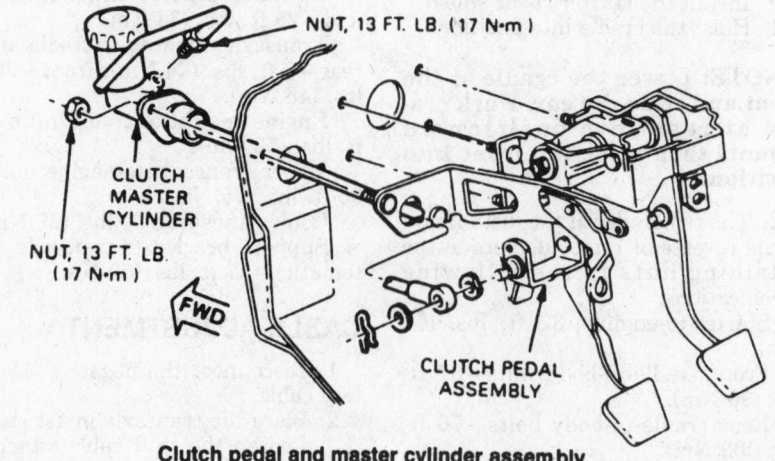

NUT, 13 FT. LB. (17 N·m)

CLUTCH MASTER CYLINDER

NUT, 13 FT. LB. (17 N·m)

CLUTCH PEDAL ASSEMBLY

Clutch pedal and master cylinder assembly

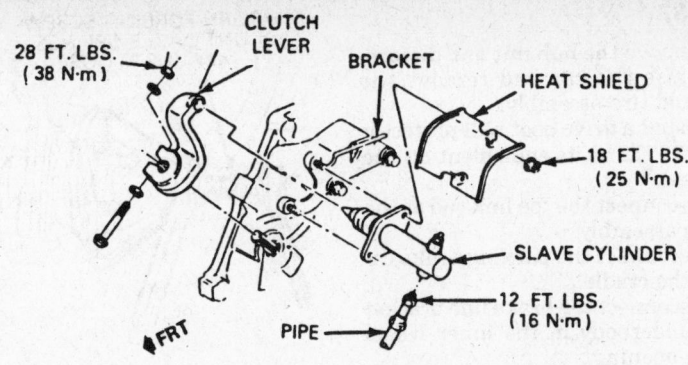

Clutch slave cylinder and clutch lever mounting

AUTOMATIC TRANSAXLE

REMOVAL & INSTALLATION

1984–87

NOTE: For further information on automatic transmissions, please refer to "Automatic Transmissions" in the Unit Repair section.

1. Remove the air cleaner assembly.
2. Disconnect the negative battery cable.
3. Disconnect the ground cable at the transaxle.
4. Disconnect the TV cable at the transaxle.
5. Disconnect the shift and select cable at the transaxle.
6. Disconnect all electrical connections at the transaxcle.

NOTE: When disconnecting the Neutral safety switch connector," extra care must be must taken," remove the connector in a straight horizontal movement away from the switch, any rocking or tipping up and down movement, will cause the electrical connector to bend inside the switch, which when reconnected may not make proper contact.

7. Remove the wiring harness at the transaxle.
8. Remove transaxle cooler line supports.
9. Remove the upper transaxle to engine bolts.
10. Install an engine support fixture tool J-28467 or equivalent.
11. Hoist the car and support it safely with jack stands.
12. Remove the rear wheels and tires.
13. Remove the axle shafts.

14. Remove the heat shield from the catalytic converter.
15. Disconnect the exhaust pipe at the exhaust manifold.
16. Remove the engine mount to cradle nuts.
17. Remove transaxle mounts to cradle nuts.
18. Support the cradle with an adjustable stand.
19. Remove the rear cradle to body bolts.
20. Remove the forward cradle to body through bolts.
21. Lower the cradle and move it out of the way.
22. Remove the starter and inspection cover shields and remove the starter.
23. Remove the flywheel to converter bolts.
24. Disconnect and plug the cooler lines.
25. Position a transmission stand under the transaxle.
26. Remove the transaxle to support mounting bolts on the right side.
27. Remove the lower bolts attaching the transaxle to the engine.
28. Remove the transaxle.

NOTE: Lower the cradle at the front and raise the car. Work cradle at rear and into position on the mounts then raise the front into position.

29. The remainder of the installation is the reverse of the removal. Torque all units to the following specifications:
 • Lower transaxle to engine bolts – 55 ft. lbs.
 • Converter to flywheel bolts – 35 ft.lbs.
 • Support bracket to transaxle – 37 ft. lbs.
 • Starter to engine bolts – 32ft. lbs.
 • Cooler lines – 20 ft. lbs.
 • Front cradle to body nut – 67ft. lbs.

 • Rear cradle to body bolts – 76ft.lbs.
 • Exhaust pipe to exhaust manifold bolts – 25 ft.lbs.
 • Engine mounts to cradle nuts – 40 ft. lbs.
 • Transaxle mounts to cradle nuts (Rear) – 18 ft. lbs. (Front) – 36ft. lbs.
 • Upper transaxle to engine bolts – 55ft. lbs.
 • Hub nut – 225ft. lbs.
 • Transaxle cooler bracket – 37 ft.lbs.

1988

1. Disconnect the negative (-) battery cable.
2. Remove the air cleaner assembly.
3. Remove the right engine vent cover.
4. Remove the left engine vent cover.
5. Remove the throttle valve cable at the transmission and carburetor.
6. Remove the shift cable at the transmission bracket.
7. Disconnect the neutral start switch electrical connection.
8. Disconnect the transmission converter clutch electrical connection.
9. Disconnect the Speedometer pick-up electrical connection.
10. Remove the wire harness at the transmission to engine retaining bolts.
11. Remove the transmission cooler line support bracket.
12. Remove the transmission to engine retaining bolts.
13. Remove the shift cable bracket to remove the neutral start switch harness.
14. Install the engine fixture tool J 28467-A or equivalent.
15. Raise the vehicle and support with jack stands.
16. Remove the rear wheels.
17. Install rear axle boot protectors.
18. Remove the fixed adjusting link/lateral control arm through bolts.
19. Diconnect the trailing arms at knuckles.

NOTE: On cars equipped with Tri-Pot joints, care must be exercised not to allow the Tri-Pot joints to become overextended. When either end or both ends of the shaft are disconnected, overextending the joint could result in separation of internal components. This could cause failure of the joint. Therefore, it is important to handle the drive axle in a manner that prevents overextending.

20. Remove rear axle shafts from transmission.
21. Support the rear axle shafts.
22. Remove the splash shields.

23. Disconnect the brake cables at the calipers.

24. Disconnect the brake control cable at the frame.

25. Disconnect the exhaust pipe at the exhaust manifold.

26. Remove the engine mounts to cradle nuts.

27. Remove the transmission mounts to cradle nuts.

28. Remove the front cradle retaining bolts.

29. Remove the rear cradle retaining bolts.

30. Remove the cradle from the vehicle.

31. Remove the starter/flexplate shield.

32. Remove the flexplate bolts.

33. Remove the cooler lines.

34. Plug the cooler lines.

35. Install the transmission support jack.

36. Remove the transmission support bracket at the right rear.

37. Remove the remaining transmission to engine retaining bolts including the ground wire.

38. Lower the transmission from the vehicle.

39. Installation is the reverse of removal. Torque all units to the following specifications:
- Lower transaxle to engine bolts—55 ft. lbs.
- Converter to flywheel bolts—35 ft.lbs.
- Support bracket to transaxle—37 ft. lbs.
- Starter to engine bolts—32ft. lbs.
- Cooler lines—20 ft. lbs.
- Front cradle to body nut—67ft. lbs.
- Rear cradle to body bolts—76ft.lbs.
- Exhaust pipe to exhaust manifold bolts—25 ft.lbs.
- Engine mounts to cradle nuts—40 ft. lbs.
- Transaxle mounts to cradle nuts (Rear)—18 ft. lbs. (Front)—36ft. lbs.
- Upper transaxle to engine bolts—55ft. lbs.
- Hub nut—225ft. lbs.
- Transaxle cooler bracket—37 ft.lbs.

DRIVE AXLE

Halfshaft

REMOVAL & INSTALLATION

—— CAUTION ——

Use care when removing the halfshaft. Tripots can be damaged if the halfshaft is overextended.

1984–87

1. Remove the hub nut and discard.

2. Raise the car and remove the wheel and tire assembly.

3. Install a drive boot seal protector tool J—28712 or its equivalent on the outer seal.

4. Disconnect the toe link rod at the knuckle assembly.

5. Disconnect the parking brake cables at the cradle.

6. Disconnect the brake line bracket at the underbody in the inner wheel housing opening.

7. Using tool J—28733 or its equivalent hub spindle remover, remove the axle shaft from the hub and bearing assembly.

8. Support the axle shaft.

9. Remove the clamp bolt from the lower control arm ball stud.

10. Separate the knuckle from the lower control arm.

11. Pull the strut, knuckle and caliper assembly away from the body and secure in this position.

12. Using tools J—33008 and J—2619–01 or their equivalents, disengage the snap rings which are retaining the halfshaft at the transaxle and remove the halfshaft.

NOTE: If the halfshaft is being replaced, replace the knuckle seal.

13. When installing the halfshaft to the transaxle, seat the axle using a small pry bar in the groove provided on the inner retainer. The remainder of the installation is the reverse of removal. Torque the hub nut to 225 ft. lbs.

1988

NOTE: Cars equipped with a silicone (gray) boot on the drive axle joints. Use boot protector J-33162 on these boots. All other boots are made of thermoplastic material (black) and DO NOT require use of the boot protector.

1. Raise the car and put the transmission in neutral.

2. Remove the wheel and tire assembly.

3. Support the front end of the vehicle with jack stands.

4. Install a drift punch through rotor and remove hub nut and washer (discard nut).

5. Remove the caliper and rotor.

6. Disconnect the trailing arm at the knuckle.

7. Remove the fixed adjusting link, lateral control arm through bolt.

8. Scribe the strut and knuckle assembly.

9. Remove the Strut mounting bolts.

10. Press the hub from the halfshaft

TURN FORCING SCREW UNTIL AXLE SPLINES ARE JUST LOOSE

Pressing half shaft the from hub

NOTE: On cars equipped with Tri-Pot joints, care must be exercised not to allow Tri-Pot joints to become overextended. When either end or both ends of the shaft are disconnected, overextending the joint could result in separation of internal compounds. This could cause failure of the joint. Therefore, it is important to handle the drive axle in a manner that prevents overextending.

11. Install special tools J—28468 or J—33008 with J—29794 and J—2619-01 or equivalent slide and remove haftshaft from the transaxle.

12. Installation is the reverse of removal. Install the hub and washer and replace with a new nut. Torque the nut to 183–208 ft. lbs.

CV-JOINT OVERHAUL

For CV-joint overhaul please refer to U-joint/CV-joint in the Unit Repair section.

FRONT SUSPENSION

Shock Absorber

REMOVAL & INSTALLATION

1. Raise the vehicle and support safely.

2. Remove the wheel and tire assembly.

3. Remove the two upper retaining bolts.

4. Remove the nut and bolt from the lower end of the shock absorber and remove the shock absorber from the vehicle.

5. To install, place the lower portion of the shock into position and hand tighten the nut and bolt.

6. Extend the shock up into the shock absorber support and torque both bolts to 20 ft. lbs.

7. Torque the lower nut and bolt to 20 ft. lbs.

8. Replace the wheel and tire assembly.

Front Spring/Lower Control Arm

REMOVAL & INSTALLATION

1. Raise the vehicle on a hoist and support the vehicle on the crossmember.

2. Remove wheel and tire assembly.

3. Disconnect the stabilizer bar from the lower control arm.

4. Disconnect the tie rod from the steering knuckle.

5. Disconnect the shock absorber at the lower control arm.

6. Support the lower control arm with a jack.

7. Remove the nut from the lower ball joint, then use tool J–26407 or its equivalent to press the ball joint out of the knuckle.

8. Move the knuckle and hub assembly out of the way.

9. Loosen the lower control arm pivot bolts.

10. Install a chain through the coil spring as a safety precaution.

——————— CAUTION ———————

The coil spring is under load and could result in personal injury if it were released too quickly. Be sure to install a chain and to slowly lower the jack.

——————————————————

11. Slowly lower the jack and remove the spring.

12. Remove the pivot bolts at the chassis and the crossmember and remove the lower control arm.

NOTE: Removal of the pivot bolt at the crossmember may require the loosening or removal of the steering assembly mounting bolts.

To install:

13. Install the lower control arm and pivot bolts at crossmember and body. Tighten slightly but do not torque.

14. Position the spring and install it into the upper pocket. Align the spring bottom to the lower control arm pocket.

15. Install the spring lower end onto lower control arm. It may be necessary to have an assistant help you compress the spring far enough to slide it over the raised area of the lower control arm seat.

16. Use a jack to raise the lower control arm and compress the coil spring.

16. Install the ball joint through the

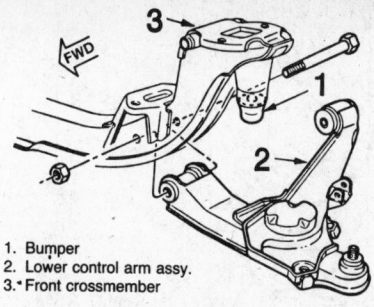

1. Bumper
2. Lower control arm assy.
3. Front crossmember

Lower control arm

lower control arm and into the steering knuckle. Install nut to ball joint stud and torque to 55 ft. lbs. Install a new cotter pin.

17. Connect the stabilizer bar and torque the bolt to 16 ft. lbs.

18. Connect the tie rod and torque to 29 ft. lbs.

19. Position the shock absorber to the lower control arm and torque the bolt to 35 ft. lbs.

20. If the bolts were removed or loosened at the steering assembly replace with new bolts and torque to 21 ft. lbs.

21. With the suspension system in its normal standing height, torque the lower control arm to body bolt at 62 ft. lbs. and the lower control arm to crossmember nut at 52 ft. lbs.

22. Check and set the front end alignment as necessary.

Upper Control Arm

REMOVAL & INSTALLATION

1984–87

1. Raise the vehicle and support safely.

2. Remove the tire and wheel assembly.

3. Remove the rivet holding the brake line clip to the upper control arm.

4. Support the lower control arm with a floor jack.

5. Remove the upper ball joint from the steering knuckle, as described earlier.

6. Remove the control arm pivot bolt and remove the control arm from vehicle.

7. Replace the ball joint if it is damaged or worn.

To install:

NOTE: Washers and shims must be reinstalled as removed unless a change in geometry is desired.

8. Install the upper control arm and pivot bolt to the vehicle. The inner pivot bolt must be installed with the bolt head toward the front.

9. Install the pivot.

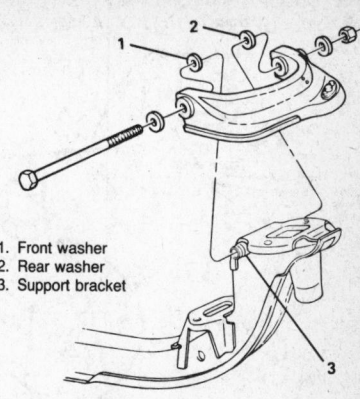

1. Front washer
2. Rear washer
3. Support bracket

Upper control arm

10. Position the control arm in a horizontal plane and torque the nut to 66 ft. lbs.

NOTE: The bolt may turn, when torqued to the minimum, if the nut is not backed up with a wrench. This does not mean the joint is loose.

11. Install the ball joint to the upper control arm and to steering knuckle, as described earlier. Install the nut, torque to 35 ft. lbs. Install a new cotter pin.

12. Install the wheel and tire assembly.

13. Lower the vehicle.

1988

1. Raise vehicle on a hoist and support the lower control arm with a jack.

——————— CAUTION ———————

This keeps the coil spring compressed. Use care to support adequately, or personal injury could result.

——————————————————

2. Remove tire and wheel assembly.

3. Remove the bolt attaching the brake line clip to the upper control arm.

4. Disconnect the tie rod end from the steering knuckle and swing the knuckle outboard.

5. Remove the ball joint stud nut from the ball joint, then use tool J–26407 or its equivalent to press the ball joint out of the knuckle.

6. Remove two bolts and paddle nut assembly attaching the upper control arm shaft to crossmember and remove the control arm from the vehicle.

To install:

7. Install upper control arm shaft bolts to crossmember with a new paddle nut assembly. Do not apply final torque until alignment is performed.

8. Visually inspect the tapered hole in the steering knuckle, remove any dirt. If any out-of-roundness, deformation or damage is noted, the knuckle MUST be replaced.

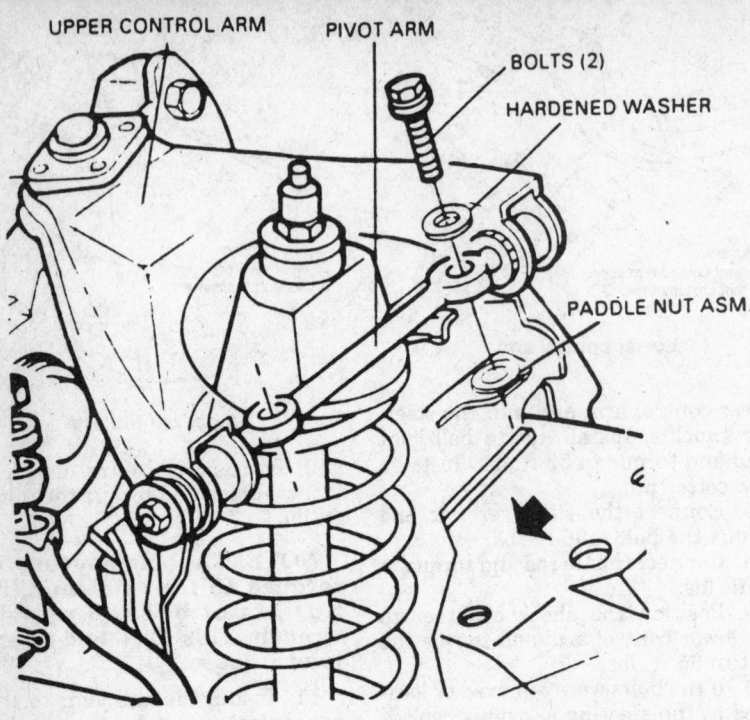

Upper control assemby—1988

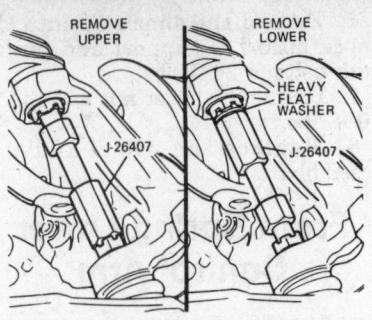

Ball joint removal

9. Position upper ball joint into steering knuckle.

10. Torque the ball joint to steering knuckle nut to 30–40–ft. lbs. ⅙ turn to align cotter pin, not to exceed 55 ft. lbs. Install a new cotter pin.

11. Install the bolt attaching the brake line clip to the upper control arm.

12. Install the wheel and tire assembly.

13. Remove the jack supporting the lower control arm and lower the vehicle to the ground.

14. Check and set alignment as necessary.

Ball Joints

INSPECTION

1. Raise the front of the car with a lift placed under the engine cradle. The front wheels should be clear of the ground.

2. Grasp the wheel at the top and bottom and shake the wheel in and out.

3. If any movement is seen of the steering knuckle relative to the control arm, the ball joints are defective and must be replaced. Note, movement elsewhere may be due to loose wheel bearings or other troubles; watch the knuckle-to-control arm connection.

4. If the ball stud is disconnected from the steering knuckle and any looseness is noted, often the ball joint

stud can be twisted in its socket with your fingers, replace the ball joints.

REMOVAL & INSTALLATION

Upper Ball Joints

1984–87

1. Raise the vehicle and support it safely.

2. Remove the tire and wheel assembly.

3. Support the lower control arm with a floor jack.

4. Remove upper ball stud nut, then reinstall nut finger tight.

5. Install tool J–26407 or equivalent with the cup end over the lower ball stud nut.

6. Turn the threaded end of tool J–26407 until upper ball stud is free of steering knuckle.

7. Remove tool J–26407 and remove the nut from the ball stud.

8. Remove the two nuts and bolts attaching the ball joint to the upper control arm. Note which way the flat section of the ball joint is pointing before removing it. The direction of this flat section of the ball joint flange should be in the same direction as the one removed, unless a change in camber is desired.

9. Remove the ball joint.

NOTE: Inspect the tapered hole in the steering knuckle. Remove any dirt and if any out-or-roundness, deformation, or damage is

noted, the knuckle must be replaced.

10. Install the bolts and nuts attaching the ball joint to the upper control arm and torque to–28 ft. lbs., then mate the upper control arm ball stud to the steering knuckle.

11. Install the ball stud nut and torque to–35 ft. lbs., then turn ⅙ of a turn to align cotter pin.

12. Install the cotter pin.

13. Install the tire and wheel assembly.

14. Lower the vehicle to the floor.

NOTE: The toe must now be checked and adjusted as necessary.

1988

1. Raise the vehicle on a hoist and support the lower control arm with a jack.

--- CAUTION ---

This keeps the coil spring compressed. Use care to support adequately or personal injury could result.

2. Remove the tire and wheel assembly.

3. Remove the bolt attaching the brake line clip to the upper control arm.

4. Disconnect the tie rod end from the steering knuckle and swing the knuckle outboard.

5. Remove the nut from the upper ball joint, then use special tool J–26407 or its equivalent to press the ball joint out of the steering knuckle.

6. Remove the upper ball joint from the control arm by drilling out the three attaching rivets.

To install:

7. Install the upper ball joint to the control arm with nuts and bolts. Torque to specifications provided in service repair package.

8. Inspect the tapered hole in the steering knuckle and remove any dirt. If any out-of-roundness, deformation or damage is noted, the knuckle MUST be replaced.

9. Position the upper ball joint to the steering knuckle and install the nut.

10. Torque the ball joint stud nut to 30–40 lb ft. ⅙ turn to align cotter pin, not to exceed 55 ft. lbs. Install a new cotter pin.

11. Install the brake line clip to the control arm.

12. Install the tire and wheel assembly.

13. Lower the vehicle to the floor.

Lower Ball Joints

1984–87

On the 1984–87 models the lower ball joint is welded to the lower control arm and cannot be serviced separately. Replacement of the entire lower control arm will be necessary if the lower ball joint requires replacement. Refer to "Front Spring/Lower Control Arm" removal.

1988

1. Raise the vehicle on a hoist and support the lower control arm with a jack.

CAUTION

This keeps the coil spring compressed. Use care to support adequately, or personal injury could result.

2. Remove the tire and wheel assembly.

3. Disconnect the tie rod end from the steering knuckle.

4. Remove the lower ball joint stud nut, then attach special tool J–26407 (or its equivalent) and press the ball joint stud from the steering knuckel. Swing the knuckle with rotor, caliper and bearing out of the way.

5. Inspect the tapered hole in the steering knuckle and remove any dirt. If any out-of-roundness, deformation, or damage is noted, the knuckle MUST be replaced.

6. Install clamp J–9591–10 and bolt J–9519–18 with removal adapters J–37161–1 and J–37161–3 or an (equivalent tool) on the lower control arm.

7. Press the ball joint out of the lower control arm.

To install:

8. Install clamp J–9519–10 and bolt J–9519–18 with installation adapters J–37161–2 and J–37161–4 on the lower control.

9. Press the ball joint into the lower control arm.

10. Position the ball stud into the steering knuckle and install the ball stud nut.

11. Torque the nut to 26 ft. lbs. + ½ turn 180 degrees. Maximum ⅙ turn to align and install a new cotter pin.

12. Reconnect the tie rod end to steering knuckle.

13. Torque the nut to 15 ft. lbs. + ½

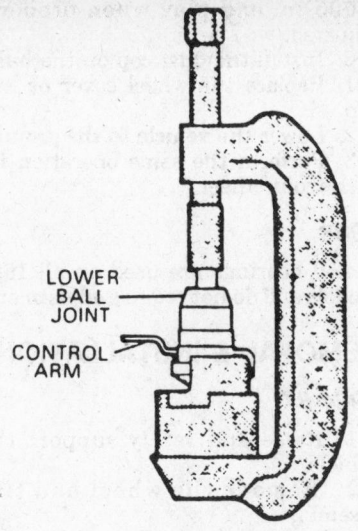

LOWER BALL JOINT

CONTROL ARM

REMOVING LOWER BALL JOINT

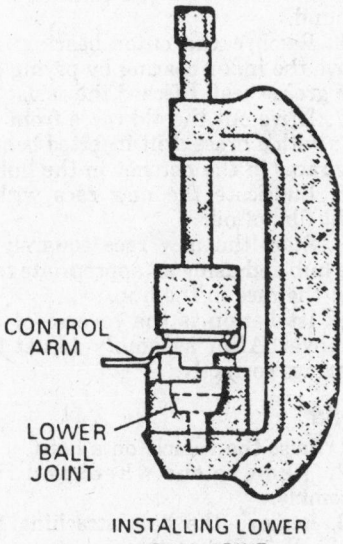

CONTROL ARM

LOWER BALL JOINT

INSTALLING LOWER BALL JOINT

Lower ball joint remove and install

turn 180 degrees. Maximum ⅙ turn to align and install the cotter pin.

14. Install the tire and wheel assembly.

15. Remove the jack supporting the lower control arm and lower the vehicle to the ground.

16. Check and align as necessary.

Steering Knuckle

REMOVAL & INSTALLATION

1984–87

1. Raise vehicle on a hoist and support the lower control arm with a jackstand.

CAUTION

This keeps the coil spring compressed. Use care to support adequately or personal injury could result.

2. Remove tire and wheel assembly.

3. Remove the disc brake caliper. Secure the caliper to the suspension using wire. Do not allow the caliper to hang by the brake hose. Insert a piece of wood between the shoes to hold the piston in the caliper bore. The block of wood should be about the same thickness as the brake disc.

4. Remove the hub and disc.

5. Remove the splash shield.

6. Remove both ball stud nuts (see Ball Joint Removal).

7. Remove the tie rod end from the steering knuckle.

8. Using tool J–26407 or its equivalent, press the upper ball stud from the steering knuckle.

9. Reverse tool J–26407 to the other ball stud and press the lower ball stud from the steering knuckle.

10. Remove the ball stud nuts and remove the steering knuckle.

11. Remove the ball stud nuts and the steering knuckle.

To install

12. Place the steering knuckle in position and insert the upper and lower ball studs into knuckle bosses.

13. Install the ball stud nuts and tighten to specifications. Torque the lower to–55 ft. lbs.; torque the upper to–35 ft. lbs. Install new cotter pins.

14. Install the splash shield to the steering knuckle. Torque to–7 ft. lbs.

15. Install tie rod end to the steering knuckle. Torque to–29 ft. lbs. and install the cotter pin.

16. Repack the wheel bearings. Then install the hub and disc, bearings and nut. Torque to specifications.

17. Install the brake caliper.

18. Install the tire wheel assembly.

19. Remove the jackstand and lower the vehicle to the ground.

1988

1. Raise the vehicle on a hoist and support the lower control arm with a jack.

CAUTION

This keeps the coil spring compressed. Use care to support adequately, or personal injury could result

2. Remove the tire and wheel assembly.

3. Remove the brake caliper and the rotor.

4. Support the caliper out of the way. Do not allow the caliper to hang by the brake hose.

5. Remove the three bolts attaching the splash shield.

6. Remove the three bolts attaching the hub and bearing assembly to the steering knuckle.

7. Disconnect the tie rod end from the steering knuckle using special tool J–6627–A or its equivalent.

8. Remove the cotter pins and loosen the stud nuts attaching the upper and lower ball joints to the steering knuckle.

9. Detach the upper ball joint using special tool J-26407 or an equivalent tool to press ball stud from the steering knuckle.

10. Detach the lower ball joint by reversing tool J-26407 to the press ball stud from the steering knuckle.

To Install

11. Place the steering knuckle in position and insert the upper an lower ball studs into into knuckle bosses.

12. Install ball stud nuts and torque to specifications.

13. Install the three bolts attaching the slash sheild to to the steering knuckle.

14. Connect the tierod to the steering knuckle.

15. Install the three bolts attaching hub and bearing asssembly. Torque to – 220 ft. lbs.

16. Install the rotor and the brake caliper.

17. Install the tire and wheel assembly.

18. Remove the jack from under the lower control arm assembly and lower the vehicle to the ground.

Front Wheel Bearing

ADJUSTMENT

1984–87

1. Raise the vehicle and support it with jack stands.

2. Remove the wheel.

3. Remove the dust cap from the hub.

4. Remove the cotter pin from spindle and spindle nut.

5. Tighten the spindle nut to – 12 ft. lbs. while turning the wheel assembly forward by hand to fully seat the bearings. This will remove any grease or burrs which could cause excessive wheel bearing play later.

6. Back off the nut to the "just loose" position.

7. Hand tighten the spindle nut. Loosen the spindle nut until either hole in the spindle lines up with a slot in the nut (not more than ½ flat).

8. Install a new cotter pin. Bend the ends of the cotter pin against nut, cut off extra length to ensure ends will not interfere with the dust cap.

9. Measure the looseness in the hub assembly. There will be from 0.001–

0.005 in. end play when properly adjusted.

10. Install the dust cap on the hub.

11. Replace the wheel cover or hub cap.

12. Lower the vehicle to the ground.

13. Perform the same operation for each front wheel.

1988

Sealed bearings are used on all 1988 models and do not require adjustment.

REMOVAL & INSTALLATION

1984-87

1. Raise and safely support the vehicle.

2. Remove the wheel and tire assembly.

3. Remove the brake caliper from the knuckle.

4. Remove the dust cup, cotter pin, spindle nut and washer.

5. Remove the hub and bearings. Do not allow the bearings to fall on the ground.

6. Remove the outer bearing. Remove the inner bearing by prying out the grease seal. Discard the seal.

7. Drive out the old races from the hub with a brass drift inserted behind the races in the notches in the hub.

8. Lubricate the new race with a light film of oil.

9. Start the new race squarely in the hub and using an appropriate tool, seat the race in the hub.

10. Istallation is the reverse of the removal. After assembly adjust the bearings correctly.

1988

1 Raise the vehicle on a hoist.

2. Remove the wheel and tire assembly.

3. Remove the bolt attaching the brake line clip to the upper control arm.

4. Remove the caliper and suspend with a wire.

5. Remove the Rotor.

6. Remove the three bolts attaching the hub and bearing assembly to the steering knuckle.

7. Remove the bearing and hub assembly.

8. Install the hub and bearing assembly. Torque the hub and bearing to steering knuckle bolt to – 220 ft. lbs.

NOTE: When ever the brake rotor has been separated from the wheel bearing, remove any rust or other foreign material from the mating surfaces of the wheel bearing flange and rotor. Failure to do so may result in lateral run-out of the rotor, causing brake pedal pulsation.

9. Install the rotor and caliper.

10. Install the bolt attaching the brake line clip to the upper control arm.

11. Install the wheel and tire assembly.

12. Lower the vehicle to the ground.

Front Wheel Alignment

CAMBER ADJUSTMENT

Camber is the tiling of the wheels from the vertical when viewed from the rear of the car. When the wheels tilt outward at the top, the camber is said to be positive (+). When the wheels tilt inward at the top, the camber is said to be negative (-). The amount of tilt is measured in degrees from the vertical and this measurement is called the camber angle.

1984–87

Camber angle can be increased approximately 1 degree by removing the upper ball joint, rotating it one-half turn, and reinstalling it with the flat of the upper flange on the inboard side of the control arm.

1988

Before adjusting camber angles, both the front and rear bumpers should be raised and released (jounced) three times each. The camber adjustment is performed by loosening the upper control arm and shaft bolts to tilt the wheel from the vertical, thus changing the Camber Angle. Toe Angle must be adjusted after caster/camber adjustments are performed.

NOTE: If the upper control arm shaft bolts are removed for any reason, the paddle nut assembly must be replaced. Final torque to upper control arm shaft bolts is – 52 ft. lbs., plus 1/4 turn 90 degrees.

CASTER ADJUSTMENT

Caster is the forward or rearward tilting of the wheel axis (at the top) from vertical. A rearward tilt (at the top) is a positive angle, and a forward tilt is a negative angle.

Weak springs or overloading of a vehicle will affect caster, because the steering axis changes when normal body "trim height" is altered.

Caster angle influences directional stability and steering effort, but does not affect tire wear.

1984–87

Caster angle can be changed with a re-alignment of washers located between the legs of the upper control arm. For adjustment, a kit containing two washers, one of 3mm thickness and one of 9mm thickness, must be used. Install to adjust caster.

1988

Before adjusting caster angles, both the front and rear bumpers should be raised and released (jounced) three times each. The Caster adjustment is performed by loosening the upper control arm and shaft bolts to tilt the wheel rearward of the vertical, thus changing the Caster Angle. Toe Angle must be adjusted after caster/camber adjustments are performed.

NOTE: Whenever adjusting caster, it is important to always use two washers totalling 12mm thickness, with one washer at each end of locating tube.

TOE-IN ADJUSTMENT

Toe adjustment is the turning in of the wheels. The actual amount of toe-in is normally only a fraction of a degree. The purpose of a toe specifications is to ensure parallel rolling of the rear wheels. (Excessive toe-in or toe-out may increase tire wear). Toe-in also serves to offset the small deflections of the wheel support system which occurs when the car is rolling forward. In other words, even when the wheels are set slightly to toe-in when the car is standing still, they tend to roll parallel on the road when the car is moving.

1984–87

1. Position the car on your alignment equipment, and follow the manufacturers instructions to obtain a toe-in reading.
2. Loosen the jam nuts on the toe link rod.
3. Rotate the toe link rods to adjust the toe to specifications.
4. Tighten the jam nuts to – 47 ft. lbs.

1988

1. Position the car on your alignment equipment and follow the manufacturer's instructions to obtain a toe-in reading.
2. Loosen the jam nut on the tie rod.
3. Rotate the tie rod to adjust the toe to specifications.
4. Tighten the jam nut to – 47 ft. lbs.

REAR SUSPENSION

MacPherson Strut

REMOVAL & INSTALLATION

1. Remove the engine compartment cover.
2. Remove the three upper strut nuts and washers.
3. Loosen the wheel lug nuts.
4. Raise the vehicle and support it on jackstands under the frame members. Support the rear control arm with a floor jack.
5. Remove the wheel and tire.
6. Remove the brake line clip.
7. Scribe the strut and knuckle.
   a. Using a sharp tool, scribe the knuckle along the lower outboard strut radius, as shown in view A.
   b. Scribe the strut flange on the inboard side, along the curve of the knuckle, as shown in view B.
   c. Make a chisel mark across the strut/knuckle interface, as shown in view C.
8. Remove the two strut mounting nuts and bolts and remove the strut assembly and spacer plate.
9. Installation is the reverse of removal. Align the scribe marks on the strut and knuckle and replace the

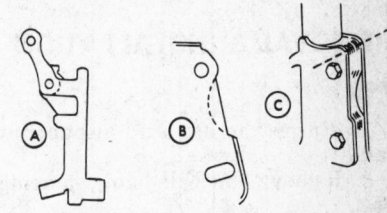

Scribing strut and knuckle

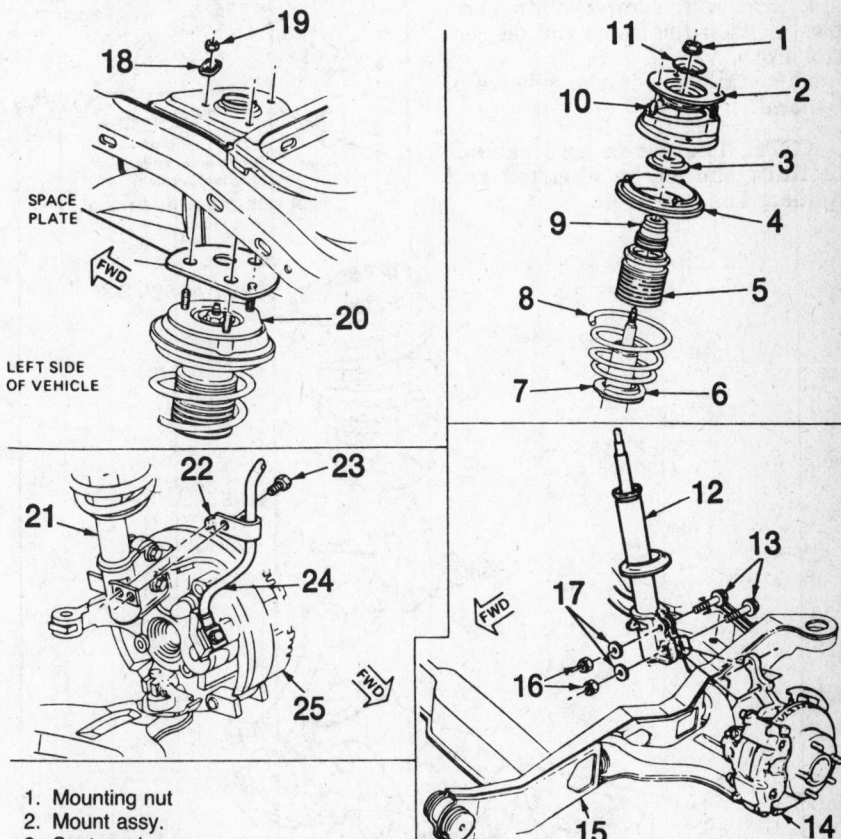

SPACE PLATE

FWD

LEFT SIDE OF VEHICLE

1. Mounting nut
2. Mount assy.
3. Seat washer
4. Upper spring insulator
5. Shield
6. Lower spring insulator
7. Lower spring seat
8. Spring
9. Bumper
10. Seat assy.
11. Upper mount washer
12. Strut assy.
13. Strut mounting bolts
14. Knuckle and hub assy.
15. Cradle assy.
16. Strut mounting nuts
17. Strut lower washers
18. Strut upper washers
19. Strut upper nuts
20. Rear strut mount assy.
21. Strut assy.
22. Brake line clip
23. Brake line clip bolt
24. Rear brake hose
25. Caliper assy.

Exploded view of strut assembly and rear suspension 1984–87

bolts in the same order in which they were removed. Tighten the strut mounting nuts to—140 ft. lbs. and the upper strut nuts to—18 ft. lbs.

OVERHAUL

For all strut overhaul procedures please refer to "Strut Overhaul" in the Unit Repair Section.

Lower Control Arm

REMOVAL & INSTALLATION

1984-87

1. Raise the car and support it safely.
2. Remove the ball joint clamping bolt.
3. Separate the knuckle from the ball joint.
4. Remove the lower control arm pivot bolts at the frame and the control arm.
5. Installation is the reverse of removal.

NOTE: The toe-in and camber settings should be checked and adjusted as required.

1988

1. Raise the car and support it safely.
2. Remove the bolts and nuts attaching the control arm to the knuckle and frame.
3. Remove the lateral control arm.
4. Installation is the reverse of removal. Torque nuts to—37 ft. lbs.

Lower Ball Joint

REMOVAL & INSTALLATION

1984-87

1. Raise the car and support it safely, then remove the wheel.

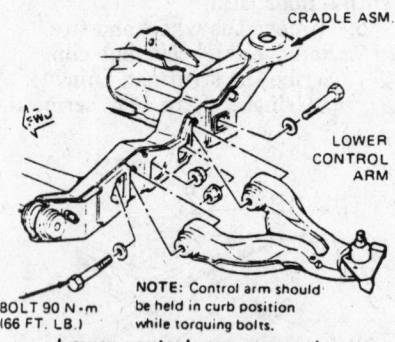

BOLT 90 N·m (66 FT. LB.)

NOTE: Control arm should be held in curb position while torquing bolts.

Lower control arm removal

2. Remove the clamp bolt from the lower control arm ball stud.
3. Disconnect the ball joint from the knuckle.

NOTE: It may be necessary to tap the ball stud with a mallet.

4. Using an $\frac{1}{8}$ in. drill, drill the rivets approximately $\frac{1}{4}$ in. deep in the center of the rivet.
5. Use a $\frac{1}{2}$ in. drill bit and drill just deep enough to remove the rivet head.
6. Remove the rivets using a hammer and a punch.
7. The ball joint is replaced using nuts and bolts. Torque to—13 ft. lbs. Check the toe-in setting and adjust as necessary.

STEERING

Steering Wheel

REMOVAL & INSTALLATION

1. Pry off the center cap, then remove the retainer clip and nut.
2. Remove the wheel using a steering wheel puller.
3. When installing align the index mark on the steering wheel with index mark on the steering shaft. Torque the retaining nut to—35 ft. lbs.

—— CAUTION ——

The cancelling cam tower must be centered in the slot of the lock plate cover before assembling the wheel.

Turn Signal Switch

REMOVAL & INSTALLATION

1. Remove the steering wheel and the trim cover.
2. Pry the cover from the steering column.
3. Position a U-shaped lockplate compressing tool on the end of the steering shaft and compress the lock plate by turning the shaft nut clockwise. Pry the wire snapring out of the shaft groove.
4. Remove the tool and lift the lockplate off the shaft.
5. Slip the cancelling cam, upper bearing preload spring and thrust washer off the shaft.
6. Remove the turn signal lever, the hazard flasher button retaining screw, the button, the spring and the knob.
7. Pull the switch connector out of the mast jacket and tape the upper part to facilitate switch removal. Attach a long piece of wire to the turn

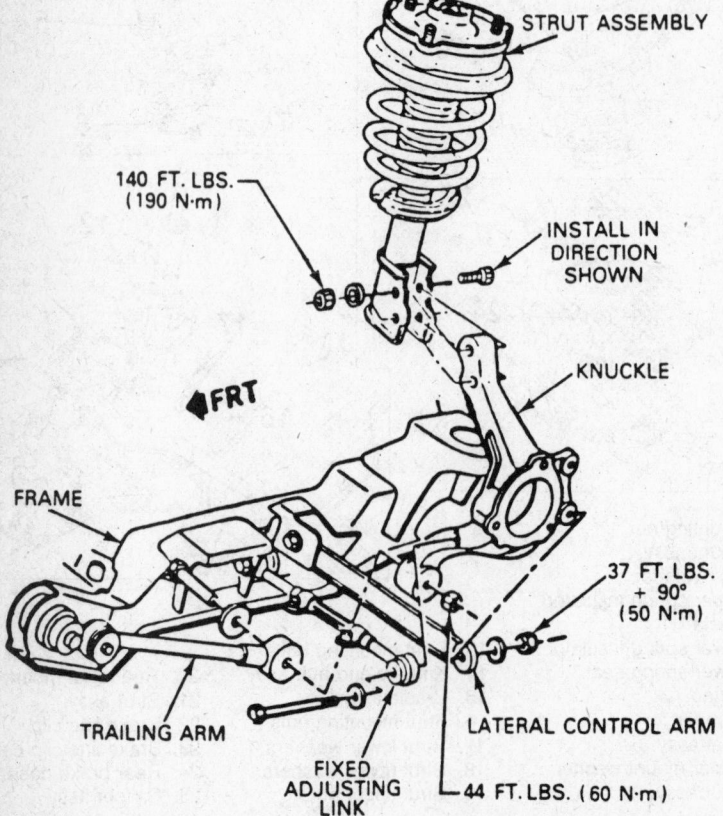

STRUT ASSEMBLY

140 FT. LBS. (190 N·m)

INSTALL IN DIRECTION SHOWN

KNUCKLE

◀FRT

FRAME

37 FT. LBS. + 90° (50 N·m)

TRAILING ARM

FIXED ADJUSTING LINK

LATERAL CONTROL ARM

44 FT. LBS. (60 N·m)

Exploded view of rear suspension—1988

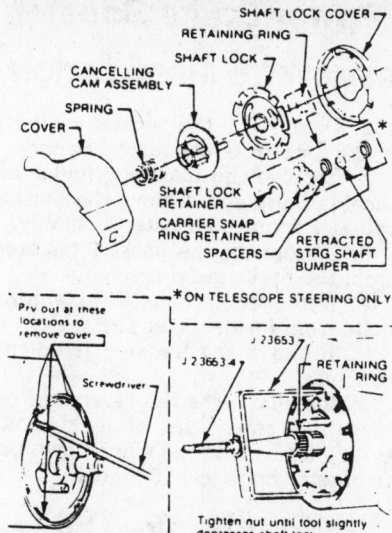

These parts must be removed to remove the turn signal switch

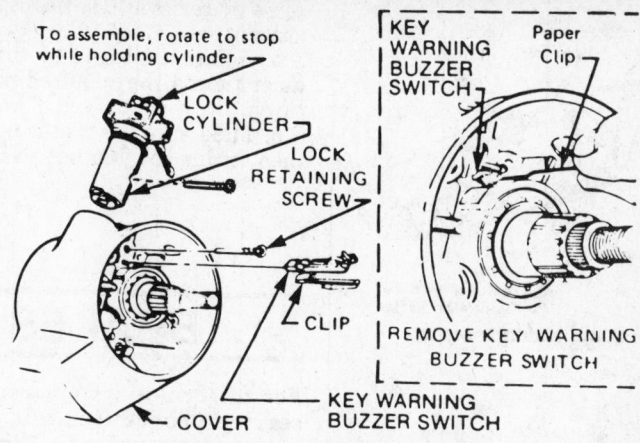

Ignition lock cylinder removal

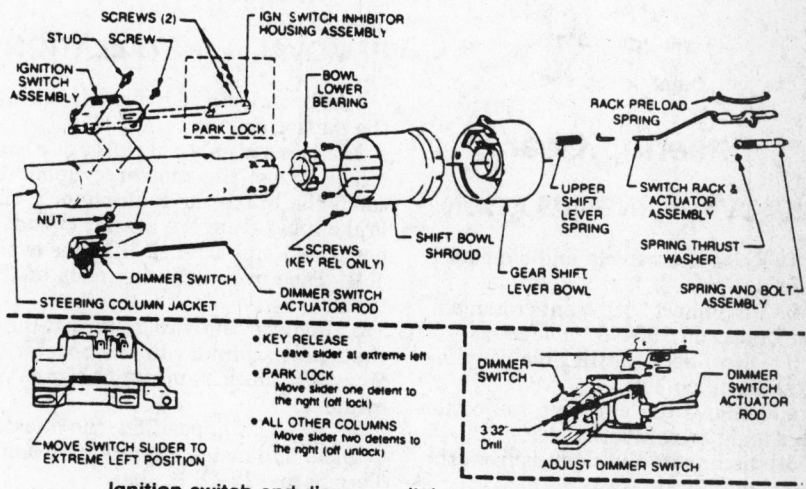

Ignition switch and dimmer switch removal and installation

signal switch connector. When installing the turn signal switch, feed this wire through the column first, then use this wire to pull the switch connector into position. On tilt wheels, place the turn signal and shifter housing in low position, then remove the harness cover.

8. Remove the three switch mounting screws. Remove the switch by pulling it straight up while guiding the wiring harness cover through the column.

9. Install the replacement switch by working the connector and cover down through the housing, then under the bracket. On tilt models, the connector is worked down through the housing and under the bracket, then the cover is installed on the harness.

10. Install the switch mounting screws and the connector on the mast jacket bracket, then the column-to-dash trim plate.

11. Install the flasher knob and the turn signal lever.

12. With the turn signal lever Neutral and the flasher knob Out, slide the thrust washer, the upper bearing preload spring and the cancelling cam onto the shaft.

13. Position the lock plate on the shaft and press it down until a new snapring can be inserted in the shaft groove. Always use a new snapring when assembling.

14. Install the cover and the steering wheel.

Ignition Lock Cylinder

REMOVAL & INSTALLATION

1. Remove the steering wheel.

2. Turn the lock to the Run position.

3. Remove the lock plate, turn signal switch or combination switch and the key warning buzzer switch. The warning buzzer switch can be fished out with a bent paper clip.

4. Remove the lock cylinder retaining screw and lock cylinder.

CAUTION

If the screw is dropped on removal, it could fall into the column, requiring complete disassembly to retrieve the screw.

---

5. Rotate the cylinder clockwise to align the cylinder key with the keyway in the housing.

6. Push the lock all the way in.

7. Install the screw. Tighten to—15 inch lbs.

8. The rest of installation is the reverse of removal. Turn the lock to the RUN position and install the key

warning buzzer switch, which is simply pushed down into place.

Ignition Switch

REMOVAL & INSTALLATION

1. Remove the (4) bolts attaching the steering column to the upper support bracket.

2. Remove the (2) bolts attaching the upper support bracket to the column support.

3. Remove (1) screw and (1) stud and nut attaching both the ignition switch and the dimmer switch to the column.

4. Remove the ignition switch from the column and disconnect the electrical connection from the switch.

5. Installation is the reverse of removal. Torque the upper support bracket to column support bolts to—25 ft. lbs. Torque the column to upper support bracket bolts to—14 ft. lbs.

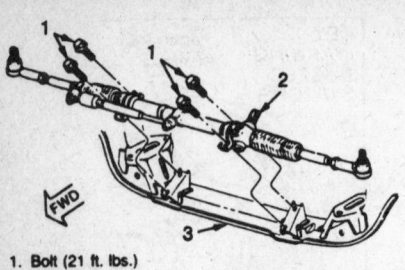

1. Bolt (21 ft. lbs.)
2. Steering assy.
3. Cross member
4. Nut (32 ft. lbs.)
5. Washer
6. Stud assy (36 ft. lbs.)
7. Steering link damper

Rack and pinion assembly

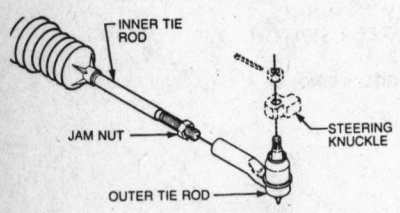

INNER TIE ROD
JAM NUT
OUTER TIE ROD
STEERING KNUCKLE

Outer tie rod end

Steering Gear

REMOVAL & INSTALLATION

1. Raise the vehicle and support it safely.
2. Disconnect both front crossmember braces on 1984–87 models.
3. Disconnect the flexible coupling to shaft pinch bolt.
4. Remove the outer tie rod cotter pins and nuts on both sides.
5. Disconnect the tie rods from the steering knuckle.
6. Remove the four bolts retaining the steering assembly to the crossmember and remove the steering assembly.
7. Installation is the reverse of removal. Tighten the flexible coupling bolt to – 46 ft. lbs., the four new steering assembly bolts to – 21 ft. lbs., the four crossmember brace bolts to – 20 ft. lbs. and the tie rod nut at each knuckle to – 29 ft. lbs., then ⅙ turn to align the cotter pin.

Tie Rod Ends

REMOVAL & INSTALLATION

1. Loosen the jam nut and remove the tie rod from the steering knuckle.

NOTE: GM recommends a special tool for this procedure; tool J-24319–01 or BT7101.

2. Count the number of threads showing on the tie rod, inboard of the jam nut. This number will be a reference for installing the new tie rod end. Remove the outer tie rod.
3. Install the outer tie-rod in the re-

verse or removal. Do not tighten the jam nut.
4. Adjust the toe-in by turning the inner tie-rod the required number of turns.
5. Make sure the boot is not twisted then torque the jam nut to 50 ft. lbs.

BRAKES

For all brake system repair and service procedures not detailed below please refer to "Brakes" in the Unit Repair section.

Master Cylinder

REMOVAL & INSTALLATION

1. Disconnect the hydraulic lines at the master cylinder.
2. Place a number of cloths or a container under the master cylinder to catch the brake fluid. Disconnect the brake tubes from the master cylinder; use a flare nut wrench if one is available. Tape over the open ends of the tubes.
3. Remove the two nuts attaching the master cylinder to the booster or firewall, then remove the master cylinder.
4. To install, position the master cylinder and install the retaining bolts. Torque to – 22–30 ft. lbs.
5. Remove the tape from the lines and reconnect to the master cylinder. Torque to – 10–15 ft. lbs. Connect the electrical lead.
6. Bleed the brakes.

Combination Valve

REMOVAL & INSTALLATION

NOTE: The combination valve is not repairable and must be replaced if found defective.

1. Disconnect and plug the hydraulic lines at the combination valve.
2. Disconnect the warning switch wiring harness from the valve switch terminal.
3. Remove the bolt attaching the valve to the bracket.
4. Remove the combination valve.
5. Installation is the reverse of removal.
5. Bleed the entire brake system.

--- CAUTION ---

Do not move the car until a firm brake pedal is obtained.

Power Brake Booster

REMOVAL & INSTALLATION

1. Disconnect the master cylinder brake lines from the master cylinder.
2. Remove the master cylinder attaching bolts and remove the master cylinder from the booster assembly.
3. Disconnect the booster pushrod from the brake pedal assembly.
4. Remove the booster attaching bolts from inside under the dash.
5. Remove the booster from the cowl.
6. Installation is the reverse of removal. Torque booster attaching bolts to – 20 ft. lbs. and the master cylinder to booster bolts to – 20 ft. lbs.

Parking Brake Cable

ADJUSTMENT

Adjustment of the parking brake cable is necessary whenever the rear brake cables have been disconnected. The need for parking brake adjustment is indicated if the hydraulic brake system operates with good reserve but parking brake hand lever travel is more than 9 ratchet clicks.

1. Place the parking brake hand lever in the released position.
2. Raise the rear wheels off floor and support safely.
3. Apply lubricant to the groove in the equalizer nut.
4. Hold the brake cable stud from turning and tighten the equalizer nut until cable slack is removed.
5. Make sure the caliper levers are against the stops on the caliper housing after tightening the equalizer nut.
6. If the levers are off the stops, loosen the cable until the levers do return to the stops.
7. Operate the parking brake lever several times to check adjustment. Properly adjusted parking brake shoes and properly adjusted brake cable will result in a parking brake handle movement of 5–8 notches when a force is applied perpendicularly at the handle grip mid-point.

NOTE: The levers must be on the caliper stops after completion of adjustment. If necessary, back off the parking brake adjuster to keep the levers on the stops.

8. Lower the rear wheels.

REMOVAL & INSTALLATION

1. Raise and safely support the vehicle.
2. Loosen the adjusting nut at the equalizer and separate the cables.

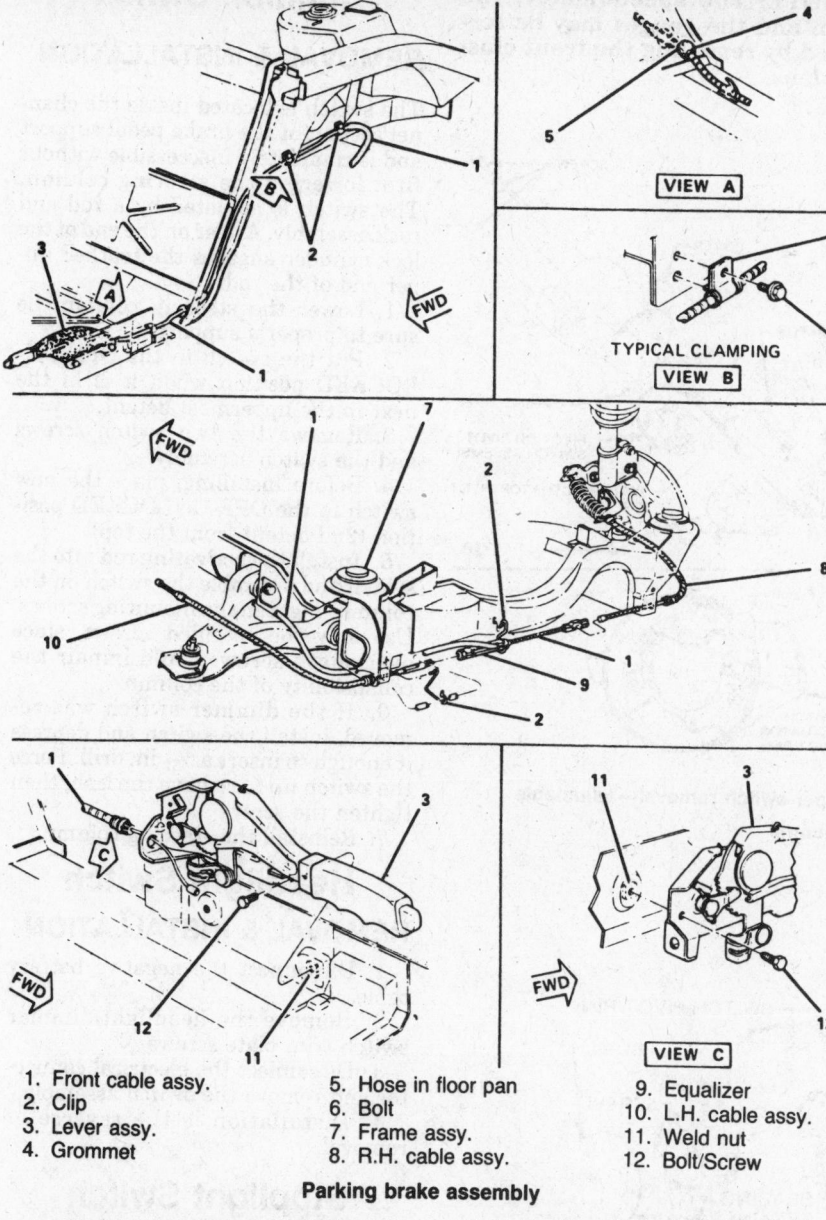

VIEW A

FWD

TYPICAL CLAMPING

VIEW B

FWD

VIEW C

FWD

1. Front cable assy.
2. Clip
3. Lever assy.
4. Grommet
5. Hose in floor pan
6. Bolt
7. Frame assy.
8. R.H. cable assy.
9. Equalizer
10. L.H. cable assy.
11. Weld nut
12. Bolt/Screw

Parking brake assembly

3. Remove the cables at the calipers.
4. Disconnect the cables at the cradle with tool J–34065 and remove the cables.
5. Install the new cables by reversing the removal procedure. Adjust the cables after installation.

CHASSIS ELECTRICAL

Heater Blower
REMOVAL & INSTALLATION

1. Disconnect the negative battery cable.

2. Remove the cooling tube.
3. Disconnect all electrical connections.
4. Remove the heater retaining screws, then the heater and the cage assembly.
5. Installation is the reverse of removal.

Heater Core
REMOVAL & INSTALLATION

With Air Conditioning

1. Under the hood, disconnect and plug the heater hoses at the heater.
2. Remove the speaker grille and the speaker.
3. Remove the heater core cover, the retainers and the heater core.

4. Installation is the reverse of removal. Refill the cooling system as required.

Without Air Conditioning

1. Disconnect the negative battery cable.
2. Disconnect the following wire connections.
   a. Heater relay.
   b. Heat blower resistor.
   c. Heater blower switch.
   d. Heater ground connection.
   e. Forward courtesy lamp socket.
3. Remove the windshield washer fluid container.
4. Disconnect the heater core inlet and outlet hoses.
5. Remove the heater core grommets.
6. Remove the heater case cover.
7. Remove the heater core retainer and the heater core.
8. Installation is the reverse of removal. Refill the cooling system as required.

Radio
REMOVAL & INSTALLATION

1. Remove the console trim plate assembly.
2. Disconnect the side retaining nuts and the rear retaining bolt.
3. Disconnect the electrical and the antenna connections.
4. Remove the radio forward of the the console.
5. Installation is the reverse of removal.

NOTE: It is important when doing any radio work to avoid pinching the speaker wires. A short circuit to ground from either wire will cause damage to the output circuit of the radio.

Windshield Wiper Motor
REMOVAL & INSTALLATION

1. Remove the wiper arms.
2. Remove the shroud top vent screen.
3. Remove the drive link from the crank arm.
4. Disconnect the electrical leads.
5. Remove the three attaching screws and the wiper motor.
6. Installation is the reverse of removal.

NOTE: Make sure the wiper motor is in the Park position before installing the wiper arms and the shroud top screen.

Windshield Wiper Switch

REMOVAL & INSTALLATION

1. Remove the steering wheel as outlined earlier in the Steering section.
2. Remove the ignition lock cylinder and the ignition switch and dimmer switch as outlined earlier in the Steering section.
3. Remove the related parts shown in the illustration and assemble in the reverse order.
4. When assembling, make sure that the first rack tooth engages between the first and second tooth of the sector.

Instrument Cluster

REMOVAL & INSTALLATION

1. Disconnect the negative battery cable.
2. Remove the rear cluster cover.
3. Remove the front trim plate.
4. Remove the steering column cover.
5. Remove the cluster attaching screws, disconnect the wiring harness and remove the cluster assembly.

NOTE: The speedometer, the tach and the gauges may be serviced by removing the front cluster lens.

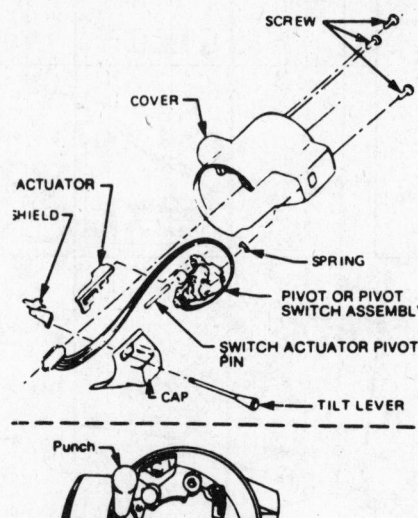

Wiper switch removal—adjustable columns

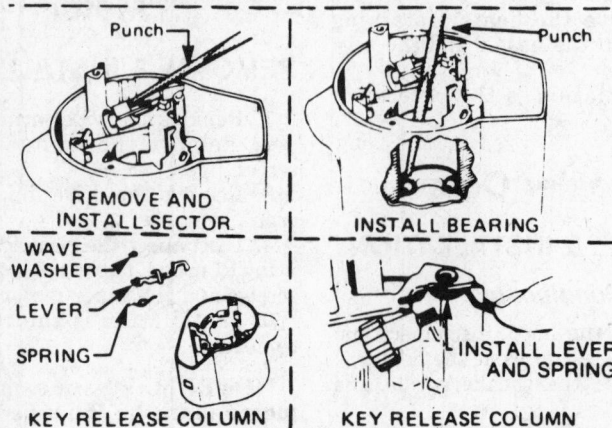

NOTE: Housing without bearing retainer and bushing has spun-in bearing. If repair is necessary, complete housing assembly replacement is necessary.

Wiper switch removal—standard columns

Ignition Switch

REMOVAL & INSTALLATION

The switch is located inside the channel section of the brake pedal support and is completely inaccessible without first lowering the steering column. The switch is actuated by a rod and rack assembly. A gear on the end of the lock cylinder engages the toothed upper end of the rod.

1. Lower the steering column; be sure to properly support it.
2. Put the switch in the OFF-UNLOCKED position when it is in the next to the uppermost detent.
3. Remove the two switch screws and the switch assembly.
4. Before installing, place the new switch in the OFF-UNLOCKED position (2nd detent from the top).
5. Install the activating rod into the switch and assemble the switch on the column. Tighten the mounting screws. Use only the specified screws, since overlength screws could impair the collapsibility of the column.
6. If the dimmer switch was removed, install the switch and depress it enough to insert a $3/32$ in. drill. Force the switch up to remove the lash, then tighten the screw.
7. Reinstall the steering column.

Headlight Switch

REMOVAL & INSTALLATION

1. Disconnect the negative battery cable.
2. Remove the headlight/dimmer switch trim plate screws.
3. Disconnect the electrical connector and remove the switch assembly.
4. Installation is the reverse of removal.

Stoplight Switch

The stoplight switch is located under the instrument panel at the brake pedal support.

REMOVAL & INSTALLATION

1. Disconnect wiring harness at the switch.
2. Remove switch from retainer.
3. Install by depressing brake pedal.
4. Install switch into retainer until switch body seats on retainer.
5. Pull brake pedal fully forward until audible clicks can no longer be heard.
6. Connect wiring harness at switch.

Fuse Block
LOCATION

The fuse block is a swing-down unit lo-

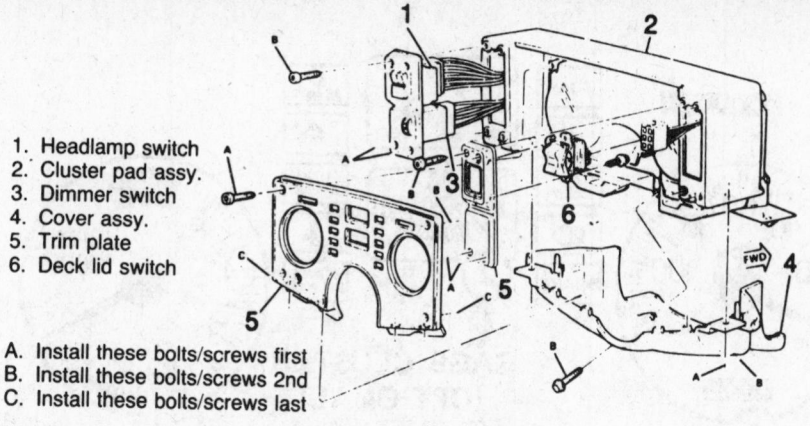

1. Headlamp switch
2. Cluster pad assy.
3. Dimmer switch
4. Cover assy.
5. Trim plate
6. Deck lid switch

A. Install these bolts/screws first
B. Install these bolts/screws 2nd
C. Install these bolts/screws last

Instrument cluster trim plates

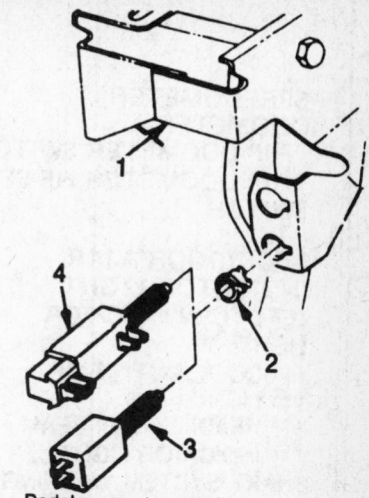

1. Pedal support assembly
2. Retainer
3. Stop light switch assembly (manual)
4. Stop light and TCC switch assembly (automatic)

Stop light and TCC switch

cated in the underside of the instrument panel left of the steering column. The fuse block uses miniaturized fuses, designed for increased circuit protection and greater reliability. Various convenience connectors, which snap-lock into the fuse block, add to the serviceability of this unit.

Convenience Center

LOCATION

The Convenience Center is a stationary unit. It is located on the right side of the heater or A/C module in the vehicle under the I.P. panel. This location provides easy access to the audio alarm, hazard warnings, the horn relay, the seatbelt key and the headlamp warning alarm. All units are serviced by plug-in replacement.

5. REMOVE AND INSTALL IGNITION AND DIMMER SWITCH

REMOVE

1. Remove parts as shown.

INSTALL

1. Install parts as shown
2. Position rod in slider hole and install ignition switch. Install lower stud and tighten to 4.0 N·m.
3. Install dimmer switch and depress switch slightly to insert 3/32" drill. Force switch up to remove lash, then tighten screw, and nut to 4.0 N·m.
4. Place shifter in neutral and install shift lever.

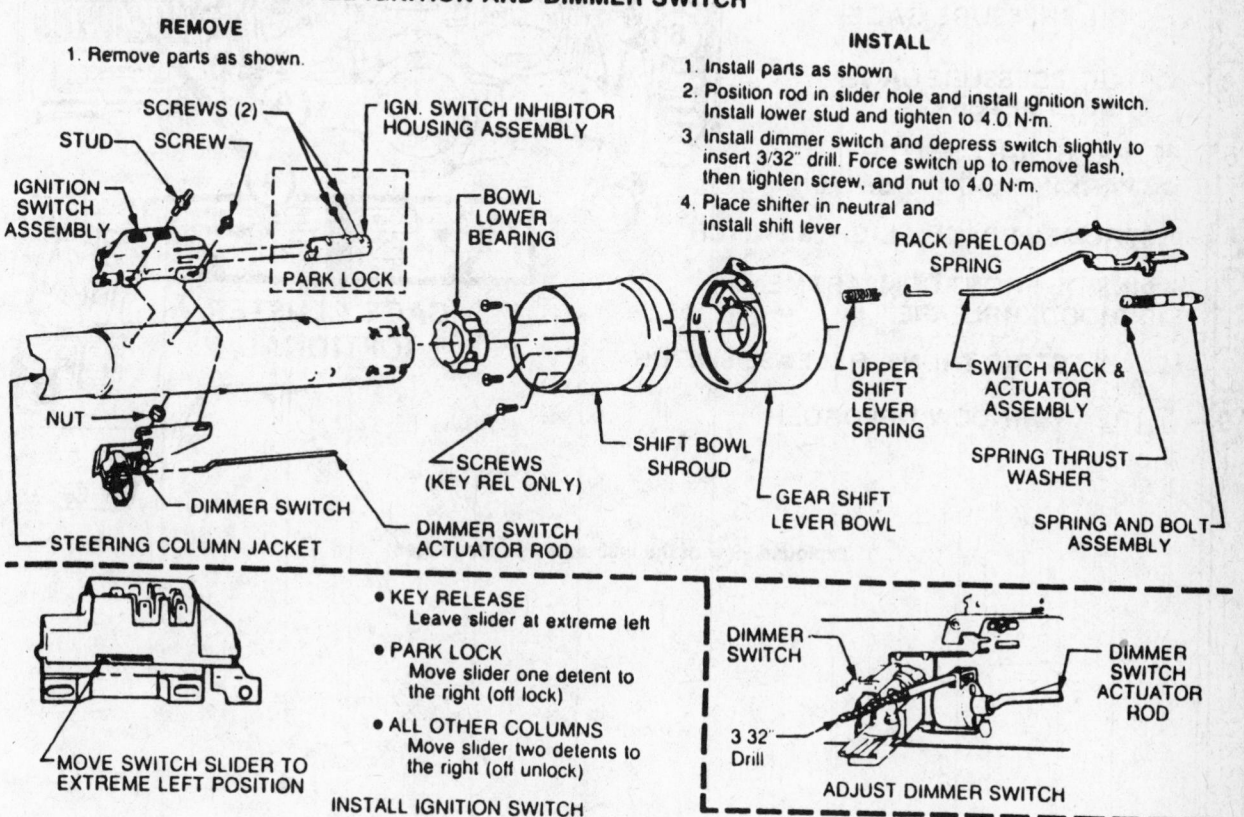

• KEY RELEASE
  Leave slider at extreme left

• PARK LOCK
  Move slider one detent to the right (off lock)

• ALL OTHER COLUMNS
  Move slider two detents to the right (off unlock)

INSTALL IGNITION SWITCH

MOVE SWITCH SLIDER TO EXTREME LEFT POSITION

ADJUST DIMMER SWITCH

Location, removal and installation of the ignition switch and dimer switch

① – SPEEDOMETER
ODOMETER
TRIP ODOMETER SWITCH
TRIP ODOMETER RE-SET
SWITCH

② – DECK/DOOR AJAR
INDICATOR LIGHT
LEFT TURN INDICATOR
LIGHT
COOLANT TEMP.
LIGHT
HEADLIGHT HI-BEAM
INDICATOR LIGHT
BRAKE SYSTEM WARNING LIGHT
COOLANT TEMPERATURE
GAGE
FUEL GAGE
SHIFT INDICATOR
LIGHT
RIGHT TURN INDICATOR LIGHT
GENERATOR LIGHT
SEAT BELT REMINDER
LIGHT
SERVICE ENGINE SOON
REMINDER LIGHT

③ – TACHOMETER
OIL PRESSURE GAGE

④ – OIL PRESSURE GAGE
VOLTMETER

⑤ – HEADLIGHT SWITCH
PARKING LIGHTS SWITCH

⑥ – INSTRUMENT PANEL LIGHTS SWITCH

⑦ – INSIDE FRONT COMPARTMENT
LID (HOOD) RELEASE

⑧ – ELECTRIC TRUNK RELEASE SWITCH

⑨ – REAR WINDOW DEFOGGER

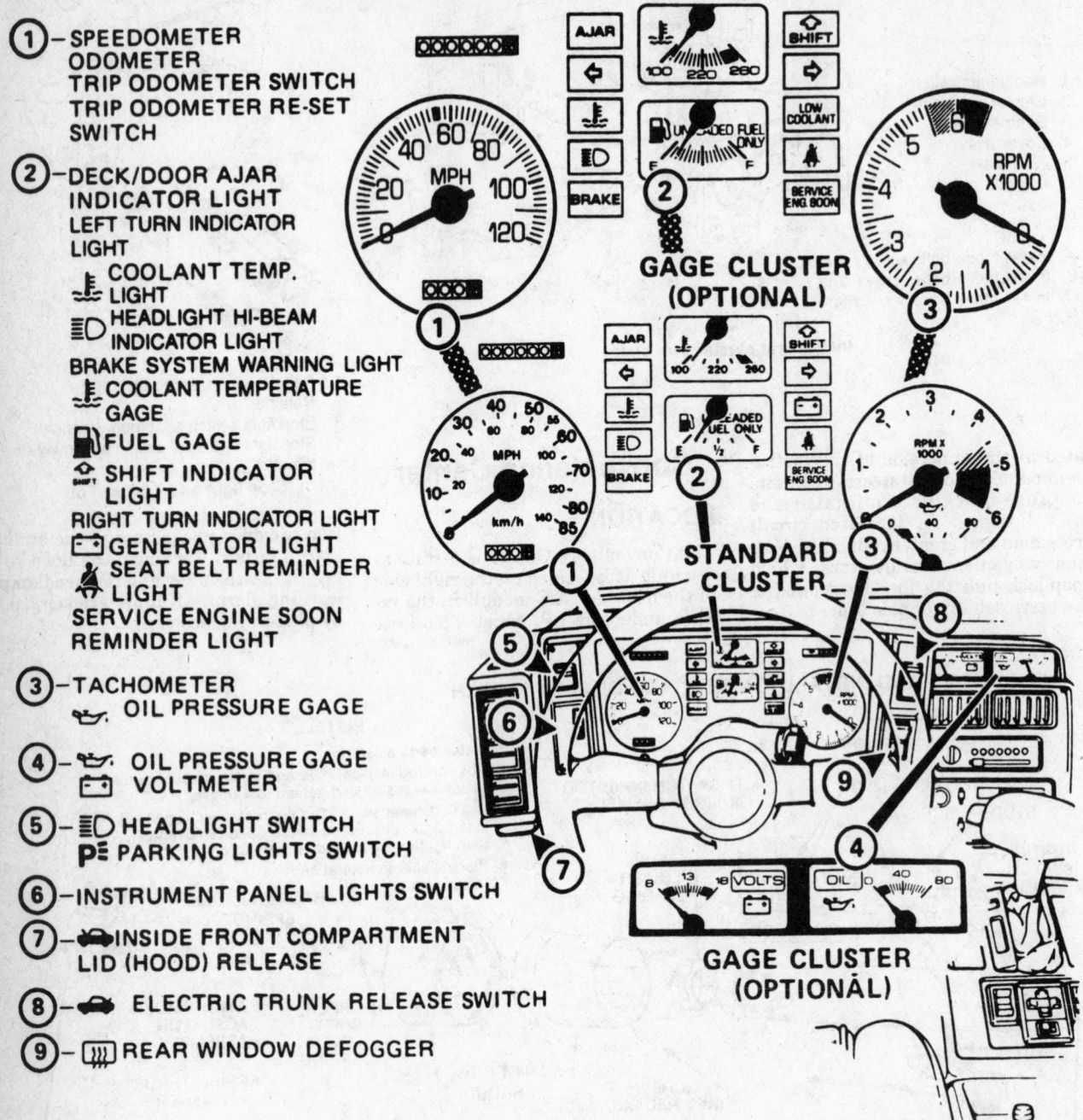

Exploded view of the instrument panel gauges

Pontiac 20
Front Wheel Drive
LeMans

SERIAL NUMBER IDENTIFICATION

VEHICLE IDENTIFICATION CHART

It is important for servicing and ordering parts to be certain of the vehicle and engine identification. The VIN (vehicle identification number) is a 17 digit number visible through the windshield on the driver's side of the dash and contains the vehicle and engine identification codes. The tenth digit indicates model year and the eighth digit indicates engine code. It can be interpreted as follows:

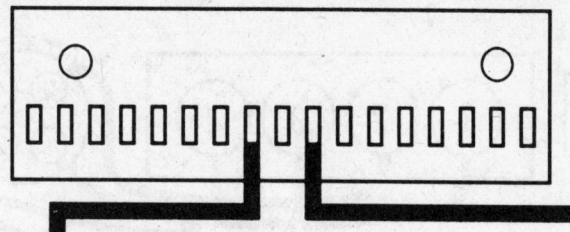

Engine Code						Model Year	
Code	Cu. In.	Liters	Cyl.	Fuel Sys.	Eng. Mfg.	Code	Year
6	98	1.6	4	TBI	Daewoo	J	1988
						K	1989

GENERAL ENGINE SPECIFICATIONS

Year	VIN	No. Cylinder Displacement cu. in. (liter)	Fuel System Type	Net Horsepower @ rpm	Net Torque @ rpm (ft.lbs.)	Bore × Stroke (in.)	Compression Ratio	Oil Pressure @ rpm
1988-89	6	4-98 (1.6)	TBI	74 @ 5200	88 @ 3400	3.11 × 3.20	8.5:1	55 @ 2000

ENGINE TUNE-UP SPECIFICATIONS

Year	VIN	No. Cylinder Displacement cu. in. (liter)	Spark Plugs Type	Spark Plugs Gap (in.)	Ignition Timing (deg.) MT	Ignition Timing (deg.) AT	Compression Pressure (psi)	Fuel Pump (psi)	Idle Speed (rpm) MT	Idle Speed (rpm) AT	Valve Clearance In.	Valve Clearance Ex.
1988	6	4-98 (1.6)	ACR44XLS6	0.06	①	①	②	9–13	①	①	NA	NA
1989		SEE UNDERHOOD SPECIFICATIONS STICKER										

① See underhood specifications sticker   ② Lowest reading not less than 70% of highest. No reading less than 100 psi

20-1

CAPACITIES

Year	Model	No. Cylinder Displacement cu. in. (liter)	Engine Crankcase with Filter	Engine Crankcase without Filter	Transmission (pts.) 4-Spd	Transmission (pts.) 5-Spd	Transmission (pts.) Auto.	Drive Axle (pts.)	Fuel Tank (gal.)	Cooling System (qts.)
1988-89	6	4-98 (1.6)	4	4	3.5	3.5	8 ①	—	13.2	8.1

① Overhaul: 12 pts.

CAMSHAFT SPECIFICATIONS
All measurements given in inches.

Year	VIN	No. Cylinder Displacement cu. in. (liter)	Journal Diameter 1	2	3	4	5	Lobe Lift In.	Ex.	Bearing Clearance	Camshaft End Play
1988-89	6	4-98 (1.6)	NA	NA	NA	NA	NA	NA	NA	0.0020–0.0044	0.016–0.064

NA Not available

FIRING ORDERS

NOTE: To avoid confusion, always replace spark plug wires one at a time.

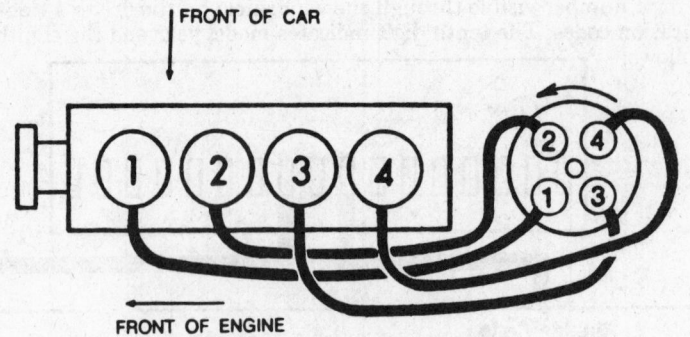

FRONT OF CAR

FRONT OF ENGINE

GM (Pontiac) 98 cu. in. (1.6L) 4-cyl
Engine firing order: 1-3-4-2
Distributor rotation: counterclockwise

CRANKSHAFT AND CONNECTING ROD SPECIFICATIONS
All measurements are given in inches.

Year	VIN	No. Cylinder Displacement cu. in. (liter)	Crankshaft Main Brg. Journal Dia.	Crankshaft Main Brg. Oil Clearance	Crankshaft Shaft End-play	Crankshaft Thrust on No.	Connecting Rod Journal Diameter	Connecting Rod Oil Clearance	Connecting Rod Side Clearance
1988-89	6	4-98 (1.6)	2.1653	0.0005–0.0018	0.0027–0.0100	3	1.6929	0.0014–0.0031	0.0027–0.0095

VALVE SPECIFICATIONS

Year	VIN	No. Cylinder Displacement cu. in. (liter)	Seat Angle (deg.)	Face Angle (deg.)	Spring Test Pressure (lbs.)	Spring Installed Height (in.)	Stem-to-Guide Clearance (in.) Intake	Stem-to-Guide Clearance (in.) Exhaust	Stem Diameter (in.) Intake	Stem Diameter (in.) Exhaust
1988-89	6	4-98 (1.6)	45	46	62	1.24	0.0006–0.0017	0.0014–0.0025	0.3141	0.3133

PISTON AND RING SPECIFICATIONS
All measurments are given in inches.

Year	VIN	No. Cylinder Displacement cu. in. (liter)	Piston Clearance	Ring Gap			Ring Side Clearance		
				Top Compression	Bottom Compression	Oil Control	Top Compression	Bottom Compression	Oil Control
1988-89	6	4-98 (1.6)	0.0008– 0.0016	0.012– 0.020	0.012– 0.020	0.016– 0.055	0.0012– 0.0027	0.0012– 0.0032	0.0000– 0.0050

TORQUE SPECIFICATIONS
All readings in ft. lbs.

Year	VIN	No. Cylinder Displacement cu. in. (liter)	Cylinder Head Bolts	Main Bearing Bolts	Rod Bearing Bolts	Crankshaft Pulley Bolts	Flywheel Bolts	Manifold		Spark Plugs
								Intake	Exhaust	
1988-89	6	4-98 (1.6)	18 ①	36 ②	18 ③	40	25 ④	16	16	18

① Cold: plus 2 turns of 60 degrees each and 1 turn of 30 degrees
  Warm: plus 30–50 degree turn after warm up (thermostat open)

② Plus a 45–60 degree turn
③ Plus a 30 degree turn
④ Plus a 30–45 degree turn

BRAKE SPECIFICATIONS
All measurements in inches unless noted

Year	Model	Lug Nut Torque (ft. lbs.)	Master Cylinder Bore	Brake Disc		Standard Brake Drum Diameter	Minimum Lining Thickness	
				Minimum Thickness	Maximum Runout		Front	Rear
1988-89	Lemans	65	0.813	0.460	0.004	7.900	0.28 ②	0.02 ①

① Above rivet head
② Shoe and lining

WHEEL ALIGNMENT

Year	Model		Caster		Camber		Toe-in (in.)	Steering Axis Inclination (deg.)
			Range (deg.)	Preferred Setting (deg.)	Range (deg.)	Preferred Setting (deg.)		
1988	Lemans	Front	¾P-2¾P	NA	1¼N-¼P	NA	0	–
		Rear	–	–	1N-0	NA	⅓	–

NA Not adjustable
P Positive
N Negative

TUNE-UP PROCEDURES

Ignition Timing

ADJUSTMENT

1. Make sure the ignition switch is turned **OFF** when connecting electrical equipment to the engine.

2. Using an induction type timing light, connect the pickup lead of the light to the No. 1 spark plug wire.

NOTE: When connecting a timing light to the No. 1 spark plug wire, be sure to use a jumper wire between the spark plug and boot; DO NOT pierce or cut the high tension wire.

3. Start the engine and aim the timing light at the timing mark.

4. The line on the harmonic balancer or crankshaft pulley should align with the mark on the timing plate. If adjustment is necessary, loosen the distributor hold down bolt and rotate the distributor until the timing mark indicates that the correct timing has been reached.

5. Tighten the distributor hold down bolt and recheck the timing, adjust as necessary.

Valve Lash

ADJUSTMENT

The valve train uses hydraulic valve compensators, located in the cylinder head, which are not adjustable and eliminate the need for valve lash adjustment.

Idle Speed and Mixture

ADJUSTMENT

Minimum Idle Speed – TBI

The throttle body is adjusted and sealed at the factory, no adjustment should be performed. All fuel control functions are controlled by the Electronic Control Module (ECM). However, if it is necessary to adjust the minimum idle speed, perform the following procedures.

1. Remove the air cleaner.

2. Using an awl, pierce the idle stop screw plug, apply leverage and remove the plug.

3. Using a tachometer, follow the manufacturer's recommendations and connect it to the engine.

4. Position the transaxle in **P** (A/T) or **N** (M/T), start the engine and allow the rpm to stabilize.

5. Using the tool BT–8528A or equivalent, position it fully into the idle air passage so that no air leak exists.

6. Using a tool No. 20 Torx Bit or equivalent, turn the idle stop screw until the engine speed is 525–575 rpm (ATX) or 575–625 rpm (MTX).

7. After correct idle speed is reached, shut off engine and remove tool. Using silicone sealant, cover the idle stop screw.

ENGINE ELECTRICAL

Distributor

REMOVAL & INSTALLATION

1. Disconnect the negative battery cable.

2. Remove the distributor cap.

3. Mark and remove all electrical leads connected to the distributor assembly.

4. Mark the relationship of the rotor to the distributor housing and the distributor housing to the engine.

5. Remove the hold down bolt, clamp and distributor.

1.	Flange gasket	
20.	Fuel meter assembly	
21.	Fuel meter body screw/washer assembly	
25.	Fuel meter-to-throttle body gasket	
35.	Injector retainer screw	
36.	Injector retainer	
40.	Fuel injector	
42.	Upper fuel injector O-ring	
43.	Lower fuel injector O-ring	
60.	Pressure regulator cover assembly	
61.	Pressure regulator screw	
65.	Spring seat	

66.	Pressure regulator spring
70.	Pressure regulator diaphragm assembly
90.	Fuel inlet nut
91.	Fuel nut seal
96.	Fuel outlet nut
200.	Throttle body assembly
205.	Idle stop screw plug
207.	Idle stop screw/washer assembly
208.	Idle stop screw spring

230.	Throttle position (TPS) sensor
232.	TPS screw/washer assembly
250.	Idle air control valve (IACV)
251.	Idle air control valve (IACV) screw
254.	Idle air control valve (IACV) gasket
270.	Manifold tubes
271.	Manifold screw
275.	Manifold tubes gasket

Exploded view of the throttle body – Model 700

1. Throttle stop screw assembly
2. Throttle stop screw plug

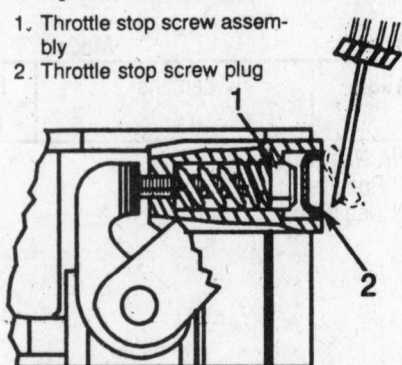

Removing the idle stop screw plug

6. To install, align the marks on the distributor housing and the engine. Install all electrical connectors and tighten distributor clamp bolt. Check and adjust the ignition timing as necessary.

If the engine was cranked with the distributor removed, it will have to be put into its compression stroke with the No. 1 cylinder at TDC. Follow the procedure listed here. This will enable the proper setting of the ignition timing.

1. Remove the No. 1 spark plug.

2. Place a finger over the spark plug hole. Crank the engine slowly until compression is felt.

3. Align the timing mark on the crankshaft pulley with the **0** degree mark on the timing scale attached to the front of the engine. This places the No. 1 cylinder at the TDC of the compression stroke.

4. Turn the distributor shaft until the rotor points to the No. 1 spark plug tower on the cap.

5. Install the distributor into the engine. Be sure to align the distributor to engine block mark made earlier.

6. Tighten the distributor hold down bolt and reconnect the electrical connections. Check the timing and adjust as necessary.

Alternator

For further information on the charging system, please refer to "Charging and Starting" in the Unit Repair section.

PRECAUTIONS

- When installing a battery, make sure that the positive and negative cables are not reversed.

- When jump starting the vehicle, be sure that like terminals are connected. This also applies to using a battery charger. Reversed polarity will burn out the alternator and regulator in a matter of seconds.

- Never operate the alternator with the battery disconnected or on an otherwise uncontrolled open circuit.

- Do not short across or ground any alternator or regulator terminals.

- Do not try to polarize the alternator.

- Do not apply full battery voltage to the field (brown) connector.

- Always disconnect the battery ground cable before disconnecting the alternator lead.

- Always disconnect the battery (negative cable first) when charging it.

- Never subject the alternator to excessive heat or dampness. If steam cleaning the engine, cover the alternator.

- Never use arc welding equipment on the car with the alternator connected.

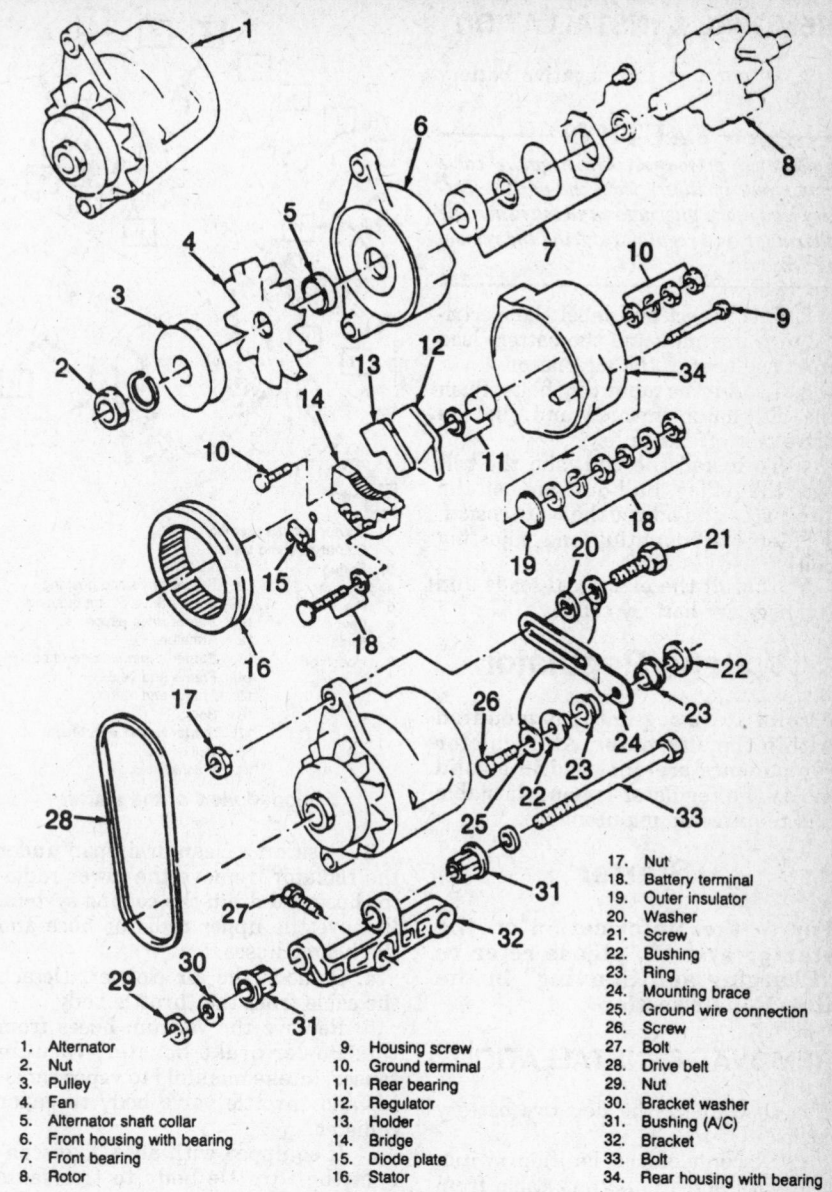

1.	Alternator	9.	Housing screw
2.	Nut	10.	Ground terminal
3.	Pulley	11.	Rear bearing
4.	Fan	12.	Regulator
5.	Alternator shaft collar	13.	Holder
6.	Front housing with bearing	14.	Bridge
7.	Front bearing	15.	Diode plate
8.	Rotor	16.	Stator

17.	Nut
18.	Battery terminal
19.	Outer insulator
20.	Washer
21.	Screw
22.	Bushing
23.	Ring
24.	Mounting brace
25.	Ground wire connection
26.	Screw
27.	Bolt
28.	Drive belt
29.	Nut
30.	Bracket washer
31.	Bushing (A/C)
32.	Bracket
33.	Bolt
34.	Rear housing with bearing

Exploded view of the alternator

BELT TENSION ADJUSTMENT

NOTE: The following procedures require the use of GM Belt Tension Gauge No. J–23600–B or equivalent.

1. If the belt is cold, operate the engine (at idle speed) until it reaches normal operating temperature; the belt will seat itself in the pulleys allowing the belt fibers to relax or stretch. If the belt is hot, allow it to cool, until it is warm to the touch.

NOTE: A used belt is one that has been rotated at least 1 complete revolution on the pulleys. This begins the belt seating process and it must never be tensioned to the new belt specifications.

2. Loosen the alternator mounting bolts.

3. Using a GM Belt Tension Gauge No. J–23600–B or equivalent, place the tension gauge at the center of the belt between the pulleys on its longest section.

4. While applying pressure on the component, adjust the drive belt tension to the correct specifications. The belt tension should deflect about ¼ in. over a 7–10 in. span or ½ in. over a 13–16 in. span.

5. While holding the correct tension on the component, tighten the component mounting bolts.

6. When the belt tension is correct (70–110 inch lbs.), remove the tension gauge.

REMOVAL & INSTALLATION

1. Disconnect the negative battery cable.

— **CAUTION** —

Failure to disconnect the negative cable may result in injury from the positive battery lead at the alternator and may short the alternator and regulator during the removal process.

2. Disconnect and label the electrical terminal plug and the battery lead from the rear of the alternator.

3. Loosen the mounting bolts. Push the alternator inwards and slip the drive belt off the pulley.

4. To install the belt, slip the belt over the pulley. Pull outwards on the alternator and adjust the belt tension. Tighten the mounting and adjusting bolts.

5. Install the electrical leads and the negative battery cable.

Voltage Regulator

A solid state regulator is mounted within the alternator. All regulator components are enclosed in a solid mold. The regulator is non-adjustable and requires no maintenance.

Starter

For further information on the starter system, please refer to "Charging and Starting" in the Unit Repair section.

REMOVAL & INSTALLATION

1. Disconnect the negative battery cable.

2. Disconnect the ignition switch lead wire and the battery cable from the starter motor terminal.

3. Remove the starter mounting bolts and the starter.

4. To install, hold the starter in place and install the mounting bolts. Reconnect the battery and ignition leads.

ENGINE MECHANICAL

Engine

REMOVAL & INSTALLATION

1. Relieve the fuel system pressure.
2. Disconnect the terminals from the battery and chassis ground wire.

---

1. Starter motor assembly
2. Starter solenoid switch
3. Spring
4. Plunger
5. Pin
6. Lever
7. Shaft
8. Housing
9. Starter drive end bushing
10. Starter drive pinion bushing
11. Starter drive pinion
12. Armature
13. Starter cummulator end bushing
14. Frame and field
15. Frame end
16. Bolt
17. Starter holder with brush
18. Bolt
19. Washer

Exploded view of the starter

---

3. Position a clean drain pan under the radiator, remove the lower radiator hose and drain the cooling system. Remove the upper radiator hose and the heater hoses.

4. Remove the air cleaner. Detach the cable from the throttle body.

5. Remove the vacuum hoses from the: Power brake booster, vacuum sensor, intake manifold to vapor canister and throttle valve body to vapor canister.

6. If equipped with an A/T, disconnect the throttle body to transaxle cable.

7. Remove the fuel lines from the throttle body.

8. Disconnect the electrical connectors from the: Distributor, oxygen sensor, oil pressure switch, intake manifold temperature sensor, injector nozzle, IAC, throttle valve. Remove the ground wires from the camshaft housing and the intake manifold, remove the the wiring harness retaining strap.

9. Disconnect the ignition coil plugs and cable, the instrument panel wiring harness multi-connector, the TCC connector (A/T) and the neutral start switch.

10. Raise and safely support the front of the vehicle.

11. Disconnect the exhaust pipe to intake manifold bolts and disconnect the rear exhaust pipe from the catalytic converter. Remove the exhaust pipe/catalytic converter assembly from the vehicle.

---

12. Remove the closure plug and the halfshaft from the transaxle.

13. Remove the clutch cover plate and the clutch housing to lower engine block bolts.

14. Lower the vehicle.

15. Using an engine sling, attach it to the engine hooks and support the engine weight.

16. Using a floor jack, support the transaxle.

17. Remove the front engine mount and the clutch housing to upper engine bolts. Separate the engine from the clutch housing and lift the engine from the vehicle.

18. To install, lower the engine into the engine compartment and align it with the clutch housing. Install the upper clutch housing bolts and the front engine mount, remove transaxle support, engine sling. Torque the engine mount bolts to 29 ft. lbs..

19. Raise the vehicle and install the lower clutch cover bolts and the clutch cover plate. Install the halfshaft and closure plug.

20. Reconnect all the wires and hoses. Refill the cooling system and the engine oil (if drained).

21. Start the engine and check operation.

Cylinder Head
REMOVAL & INSTALLATION

NOTE: Cylinder head gasket replacement is necessary if the cylinder head/camshaft carrier bolts are loosened. These bolts should only be loosened when the engine is cold. New cylinder head bolts MUST be used.

1. Relieve the fuel system pressure.
2. Disconnect the negative battery cable.

3. Position a clean drain pan under the radiator, remove the lower radiator hose and drain the cooling system. Remove the upper radiator hose and the heater hoses.

4. Remove the air cleaner. Detach the throttle cable and remove it from the intake anifold. Remove the downshift cable.

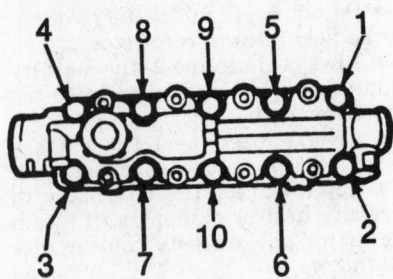

The camshaft carrier/cylinder head bolt removal sequence

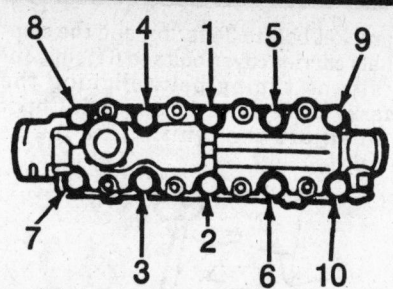

The camshaft carrier/cylinder head bolt torquing sequence

5. Disconnect the electrical wiring connectors from the throttle body, the intake manifold and the O₂ sensor. Disconnect the engine wiring harness at the thermostat housing.

6. Disconnect the exhaust pipe from the exhaust manifold. Remove the alternator bracket and lay the alternator aside.

7. Remove the accessory drive belts, the front covers and the timing belt.

8. Remove the camshaft carrier/cylinder head bolts (in sequence).

9. Remove the camshaft carrier, the rocker arms and the valve lash compensators.

10. Remove the cylinder head with the intake and exhaust manifolds attached.

11. Clean the gasket mounting surfaces.

12. To install, use a new head gasket, apply a 3mm bead of anerobic sealant to the camshaft carrier sealing surface, use new camshaft carrier/cylinder head bolts and reverse the removal procedures. Torque the camshaft carrier/cylinder head bolts to 18 ft. lbs. (in sequence), then, turn an additional 60 degrees, turn another 60 degrees (to 120 degrees) and finally to 150 degrees. Adjust the ignition timing. Refill the cooling system.

13. Start the engine and allow it to reach normal operating temperature.

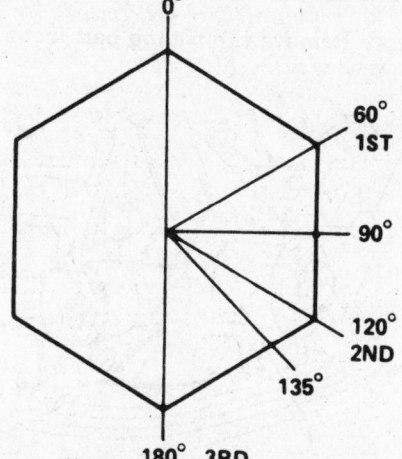

View of the camshaft carrier/cylinder head bolt torque degree chart

After operating temperature is reached, torque the camshaft carrier/cylinder head bolts an additional 30–50 degrees. Check for coolant and oil leaks.

OVERHAUL

For all cylinder head overhaul procedures, please refer to "Engine Rebuilding" in the Unit Repair section.

Rocker Arms/Valve Lash Compensators

The following procedure does not require the camshaft to be removed from the engine.

REMOVAL & INSTALLATION

1. Disconnect the negative battery cable.

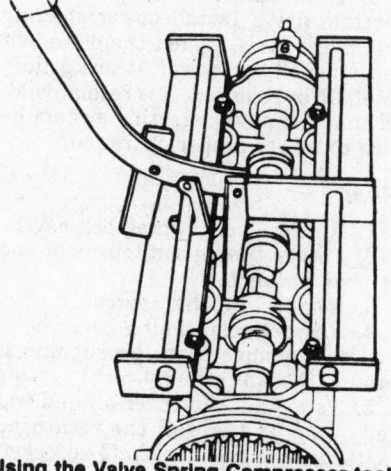

Using the Valve Spring Compressor tool No. J-33302-25 to compress the valve springs.

2. Remove the air cleaner and the breather hoses.

3. Remove the camshaft carrier cover bolts and the cover.

4. Remove the spark plugs.

NOTE: When working on a particular cylinder, be sure to rotate the crankshaft until the piston (of that cylinder) is located on the TDC of its compression stroke.

5. Using the Air Line Adapter tool No. J–22794 or equivalent, install it into the spark plug hole, of the cylinder being serviced and turn on the compressed air.

NOTE: The compressed air will hold the valves in place while the engine is being serviced.

6. Using the Valve Spring Compressor tool No. J–33302–25 or equivalent, compress the valve springs.

7. Remove the rocker arms and the valve lash compensators; it is important that all of the valve train parts are kept in the order that they were removed.

8. Inspect and/or replace the worn parts.

9. Clean the gasket mounting surfaces of the camshaft carrier and cover.

10. To install, use a new gasket and reverse the removal procedures. Install all parts in their original position. Torque the camshaft carrier cover bolts to 6 ft. lbs.

Intake Manifold
REMOVAL & INSTALLATION

1. Relieve the fuel system pressure.

2. Disconnect the negative battery cable.

3. Position a clean drain pan under the radiator, remove the lower radiator hose and drain the cooling system. Remove the cooling hoses from the intake manifold.

4. Remove the air cleaner. Detach the cable from the throttle body, the intake manifold bracket and the downshift cable.

5. Loosen the alternator and swing it aside.

6. Disconnect the electrical wiring connectors from the throttle body, the intake manifold, the engine wiring harness and the thermostat housing.

7. Remove the intake manifold mounting nuts and washers, remove the manifold from the engine.

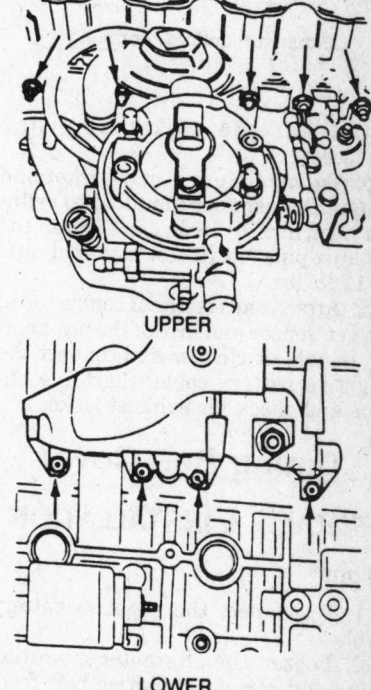

UPPER

LOWER

Intake manifold mounting

8. Clean the gasket mounting surfaces.

9. To install, use a new gasket and reverse the removal procedures. Torque the intake manifold to cylinder head nuts/washers to 16 ft. lbs. Refill the cooling system. Install the air cleaner and the negative battery cable. Start the engine and check for coolant leaks.

Exhaust Manifold

REMOVAL & INSTALLATION

1. Disconnect the negative battery cable.

2. Remove the air cleaner. Disconnect the spark plug wires from the spark plugs and the electrical connector at the oxygen sensor. Remove the manifold pre-heater.

3. Remove the exhaust pipe nuts and the exhaust manifold mounting nuts/washers. Remove the exhaust manifold from the engine.

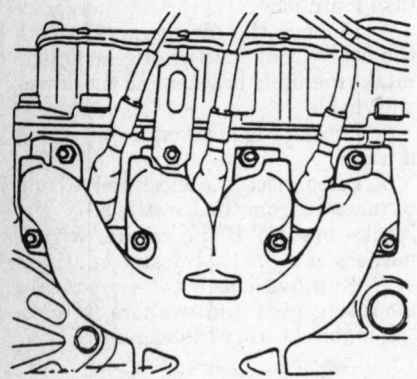

Exhaust manifold mounting

4. Clean the gasket mounting surfaces.

5. To install, use a new gasket and torque the exhaust manifold to cylinder head nuts to 16 ft. lbs. Tighten the exhaust pipe to exhaust manifold nuts to 19 ft. lbs.

6. Attach the electrical connector to oxygen sensor and install the pre-heater. Install air cleaner and connect the negative battery cable. Start the engine and check for exhaust leaks.

Timing Belt Cover

REMOVAL & INSTALLATION

Front

1. Disconnect the negative battery cable.

2. Loosen the alternator mounting bolts and remove the drive belt from the alternator pulley.

3. Loosen the A/C compressor

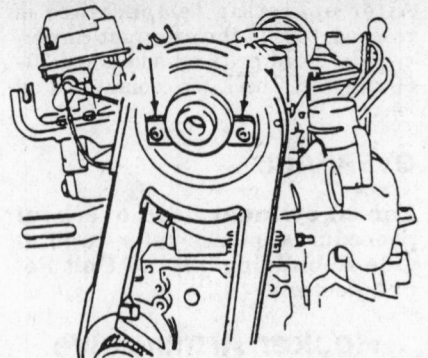

Rear timing belt cover attachment

mounting bolts and remove the drive belt from the compressor pulley.

4. Remove the power steering pump lines and mounting bolts, remove the pump.

5. Unsnap the front cover (upper half first) and remove it from the engine.

6. To install, snap cover into place (bottom first). Install power steering pump and lines. Adjust the drive belt tensions. Check power steering fluid level, fill as required. It is recommended that the power steering system be bled to insure proper operation.

Rear

1. Remove front timing belt cover.

2. Loosen timing belt tensioner and remove timing belt.

3. Remove camshaft sprocket.

4. Remove rear timing cover bolts (4), and remove cover by slipping it around the water pump.

5. To install, slip cover around water pump and install the retaining bolts. Install the camshaft sprocket, tighten to 34 ft. lbs. Slide timing belt over sprocket and adjust tension to specification. Install front cover.

Timing Belt And Sprockets

REMOVAL & INSTALLATION

Camshaft Sprocket

1. Remove the timing belt front cover.

2. Mark the relationship of the timing belt to the crankshaft and camshaft sprockets. Loosen the timing belt tensioner and remove the timing belt.

3. Remove the camshaft carrier cover to camshaft carrier bolts and remove the cover from the engine.

4. Hold the camshaft in place with an open end wrench and remove the sprocket bolt, washer and sprocket.

5. To install, reverse the removal procedures. Torque the camshaft

sprocket bolt to 34 ft. lbs. and the camshaft carrier cover bolts to 6 ft. lbs. Install the timing belt, aligning the marks made prior to removal. Check and adjust the ignition timing as needed.

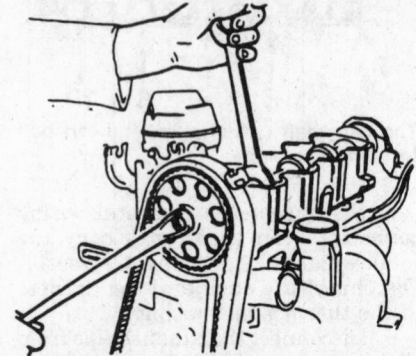

Removing the camshaft sprocket from the camshaft

Crankshaft Sprocket

1. Remove the timing belt front cover.

2. Mark the relationship of the timing belt to the crankshaft and camshaft sprockets. Loosen the timing belt tensioner and remove the timing belt.

3. Remove the crankshaft pulley bolt, pulley and thrust washer. Remove the crankshaft sprocket and the Woodruff key.

NOTE: It is recommended to replace the front oil seal when the crankshaft pulley is removed.

4. To install, reverse the removal procedures. Torque the crankshaft pulley bolt to 40 ft. lbs. Install the timing belt, aligning marks made prior to removal. Check and adjust the ignition timing. Adjust the accessory drive belt tensions.

OIL SEAL REPLACEMENT

1. Remove the timing belt front cover.

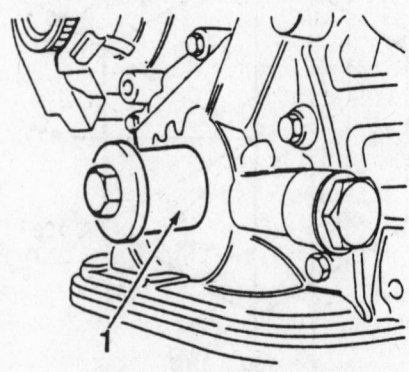

Installing the front oil seal

2. Mark the relationship of the timing belt to the crankshaft and camshaft sprockets. Loosen the timing belt tensioner and remove the timing belt.

3. Remove the crankshaft pulley retaining bolt. Remove the crankshaft sprocket and the rear thrust washer. Remove the rear timing cover mounting screws (4) and remove the cover.

4. Using a small pry bar, pry the front oil seal from the oil pump housing.

5. Using the protective sleeve of the Seal Installation tool set No. J–36534 or equivalent, install it onto the crankshaft.

6. Using a new front oil seal, lubricate the seal lips with engine oil and install it onto the protective sleeve.

7. Using the Seal Installation tool No. J–36534 or equivalent, install the new oil seal into the oil pump until it seats.

8. To complete the installation, install the rear timing cover, align the marks made prior to removing the timing belt and install the belt. Adjust the tension to specification. Install the crankshaft pulley and sprocket, tighten to 40 ft. lbs.

9. Install the front timing cover and adjust all accessory drive belts to specification. Check ignition timing.

Camshaft

REMOVAL & INSTALLATION

1. Disconnect the negative battery cable.

2. Remove the air cleaner and the breather hoses.

3. Remove the camshaft carrier cover bolts and the cover.

4. Remove the spark plugs.

NOTE: When working on a particular cylinder, be sure to rotate the crankshaft until the piston (of that cylinder) is located on the TDC of its compression stroke.

5. Using the Air Line Adapter tool No. J–22794 or equivalent, install it into the spark plug hole and turn **ON** the compressed air.

NOTE: The compressed air will hold the valves in place while the engine is being serviced.

6. Using the Valve Spring Compressor tool No. J–33302–25 or equivalent, compress the valve springs.

7. Remove the rocker arms and the valve lash compensators; be sure to keep the removed items in order for reinstallation purposes.

8. Mark the relationship of the distributor rotor to the housing and the distributor housing to the engine. Re-

move the distributor hold down clamp and the distributor from the engine.

9. Remove the thrust plate from the rear of the camshaft, remove the camshaft (rearward) from the engine.

10. Clean the gasket mounting surfaces of the carrier and the cover. Inspect and replace any worn or damaged parts.

11. To install, use new gaskets and reverse the removal procedures. Torque the rear thrust plate bolts to 70 ft. lbs., the camshaft sprocket bolt to 34 ft. lbs. and the camshaft carrier cover bolts to 6 ft. lbs. Using a feeler gauge, check the camshaft end play; it should be 0.016–0.064 in., if not, replace the rear thrust washer. Install the timing belt. Check and adjust the ignition timing as needed.

Piston and Connecting Rod

POSITIONING

For all piston and connecting rod overhaul procedures, please refer to "Engine Rebuilding" in the Unit Repair section.

ENGINE LEFT ENGINE FRONT ENGINE RIGHT

1. Oil ring spacer gap
   (Tang in hole or slot with arc)
2. Oil ring rail gaps
3. 2nd compression ring gap
4. Top compression ring gap

Location of the piston ring gaps

1. Notch towards front of engine
2. Tool No. J–8037

Installing the piston assembly into the engine block

ENGINE LUBRICATION

Oil Pan

REMOVAL & INSTALLATION

1. Disconnect the negative battery cable.

2. Raise and support the front of the vehicle.

3. Place a drain pan under the engine, remove the drain plug from the oil pan and drain the oil from the crankcase.

4. Remove the exhaust pipe from the exhaust manifold.

5. Remove the oil pan bolts and the oil pan from the engine.

6. Clean the gasket mounting surfaces.

7. To install, use a new gasket and coat the oil pan rail seams with RTV sealant. Torque the oil pan bolts to 4 ft. lbs. and the oil pan plug to 34 ft. lbs. Install the exhaust pipe, tighten the nuts to 19 ft. lbs. Refill the crankcase with new oil.

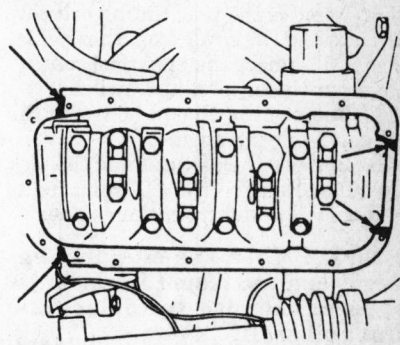

Installing sealant to the oil pan rail seams

Rear Main Bearing Oil Seal

REMOVAL & INSTALLATION

1. Remove the transaxle.

2. If equipped with a manual transaxle, remove the pressure plate/clutch disc assembly. Remove the flywheel bolts.

3. Using a small pry bar, pry the rear main oil seal from its retainer. Be sure to clean the oil seal to crankshaft and oil seal to block mating surfaces.

4. Lubricate the new oil seal lips with engine oil. Using the Seal Installation tool No. J–36792 or equivalent, drive the new rear oil seal into the block until it seats.

5. To complete the installation, re-

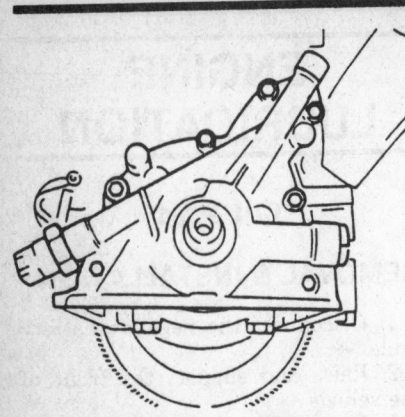

Oil pump mounting

verse the removal procedures. Torque the flywheel bolts to 25 ft. lbs. automatic transaxle, 25 ft. lbs. plus ¼ turn for manual transaxle.

Oil Pump

REMOVAL & INSTALLATION

1. Disconnect the negative battery cable.

2. Remove the accessory drive belts and remove the crankshaft pulley assembly. Remove the front timing belt cover and the timing belt.

3. Remove the rear timing belt cover bolts and the cover from the engine.

4. Disconnect the electrical connector from the oil pressure switch.

5. Remove the oil pan bolts and the oil pan from the engine.

6. Remove the oil filter and the pick up tube. Remove the oil pump bolts and the oil pump from the engine.

NOTE: When the oil pump has been removed from the engine, it is recommended to replace the front oil seal.

7. Clean the gasket mounting surfaces and the oil pump (if it is going to be re-used).

8. To install, use new oil pan and pump gaskets. Use RTV sealant or equivalent on the gasket surfaces.

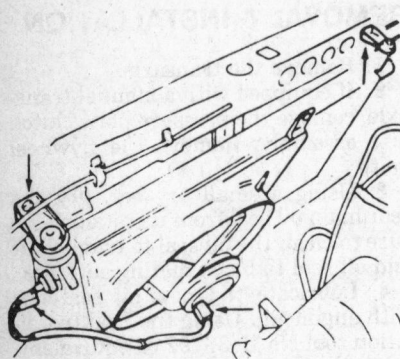

Cooling fan and radiator mounting

Torque the oil pump to engine bolts to 5 ft. lbs. and the oil pan bolts to 6 ft. lbs.

9. Install the timing belt cover, the crankshaft sprocket and the timing belt. Install and adjust the accessory drive belts. Use a new oil filter and fill the crankcase with clean engine oil. Run the engine and check for leaks, also check ignition timing.

ENGINE COOLING

Radiator

REMOVAL & INSTALLATION

1. Disconnect the negative battery cable.

2. Using a clean drain pan, place it under the radiator, remove the lower radiator hose and drain the cooling system.

3. Remove the coolant recovery bottle hose and the upper radiator hose.

4. Disconnect the electrical connectors from the fan motor, the oxygen sensor and the temperature sensor.

5. Remove the electric cooling fan assembly by removing the 2 upper mounting bolts, the fan motor and shroud assembly can then be removed as a unit. Remove the radiator support bolts and the radiator from the vehicle.

— CAUTION —
Use care when removing the radiator, even though the cooling system was drained the radiator will still contain coolant. Coolant splashed or spilled may cause personal injury.

6. Install the radiator and fan assembly by reversing the removal procedures. Fill the cooling system and bleed the air from the system. Reconnect the electrical connectors to oxygen sensor, fan motor and temperature sensor.

Water Pump

REMOVAL & INSTALLATION

1. Using a clean drain pan, place it under the radiator, remove the lower radiator hose and drain the cooling system.

2. Remove the front cover, the timing belt and the rear cover.

3. Remove the water pump mounting bolts and the water pump from the engine.

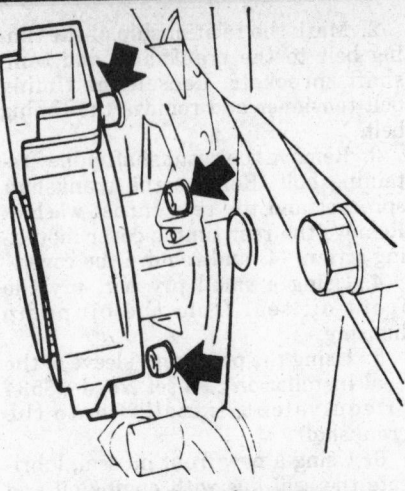

View of the water pump

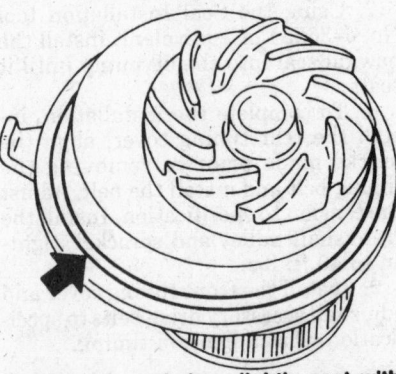

Water pump seal ring—lightly coat with grease

4. Clean the seal mounting surfaces.

5. To install, use a new water pump seal. Coat the sealing surface and the seal ring with grease (GM 1052863 or equivalent). Torque the water pump bolts to 71 inch lbs.

6. Refill the cooling system. Start the engine, allow it to reach normal operating temperatures and check for leaks, bleed cooling system. Check and adjust the ignition timing if needed.

Thermostat
REMOVAL & INSTALLATION

1. Using a clean drain pan, place it under the radiator, remove the lower radiator hose and drain the cooling system.

2. Remove the front cover, the timing belt and the rear cover (slip it over the water pump rear cover piece).

3. Remove the water inlet bolts, the water inlet housing and the thermostat.

4. Clean the gasket mounting surfaces.

5. To install, use a new seal and reverse the removal procedures. Torque the thermostat housing bolts to 78 inch lbs. Refill the cooling system and bleed the air from the system.

Exploded view of the thermostat and engine location.

COOLING SYSTEM BLEEDING

After working on the cooling system, even to replace the thermostat, it must be bled. Air trapped in the system will prevent proper filling and leave the radiator coolant level low, causing a risk of overheating.

1. To bleed the system, start with the system cool, the radiator cap off and the radiator filled to about an inch below the filler neck.

2. Start the engine and run it at slightly above normal idle speed. This will insure adequate circulation. If air bubbles appear and the coolant level drops, fill the system with an antifreeze/water mixture to bring the level back to the proper level.

3. Run the engine this way until the thermostat opens. When this happens, coolant will move abruptly across the top of the radiator and the temperature of the radiator will suddenly rise.

4. At this point, air is often expelled and the level may drop quite a bit. Keep refilling the system until the level is near the top of the radiator and remains constant.

5. If the vehicle has an overflow tank, fill the radiator right up to the filler neck. Replace the radiator filler cap.

EMISSION CONTROLS

Please refer to "Emission Control" in the Unit Repair section for system maintenance procedures. Due to the complex nature of modern electronic engine control systems, comprehensive diagnosis and testing procedures fall outside the confines of this repair manual. For complete information on diagnosis, testing and repair procedures concerning all modern engine and emission control systems, please refer to *Chilton's Guide to Electronic Engine Controls.*

FUEL SYSTEM

Fuel System Service Precaution

When working with the fuel system certain precautions should be taken; always work in a well ventilated area, keep a dry chemical (Class B) fire extinguisher near the work area. Always disconnect the negative battery cable and do not make any repairs to the fuel system until all the necessary steps for repair have been reviewed.

RELIEVING FUEL SYSTEM PRESSURE

Modern fuel injection systems operate under high pressure, this makes it necessary to first relieve the system of pressure before servicing. The pressurized fuel when released may ignite or cause personal injury. the following outlined steps may be used for most fuel systems:

● Remove the fuel punp fuse from the fuse block

● Crank the engine and let it run until the remaining fuel in the lines is consumed

● Crank engine again to make sure any fuel in the lines has been removed

● With the ignition OFF replace the fuel pump fuse

Fuel Filter

The inline fuel filter is located on the rear crossmember of the vehicle. Always use a back up wrench for removing or installing the fuel line fittings.

REMOVAL & INSTALLATION

1. Relieve fuel system pressure. Raise and safely support the rear of the vehicle.

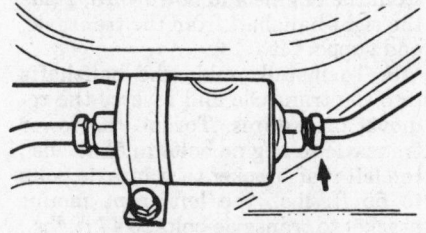

View of the inline fuel filter

2. Disconnect the fuel lines from the fuel filter.

3. Remove the fuel filter mounting bolt and the filter from the vehicle.

4. To install, use a new filter and new O-rings. Mount filter to rear crossmember and attach the fuel lines, tighten the fittings to 22 ft. lbs.

5. Start vehicle and check the line fittings for leaks.

Electric Fuel Pump

The electric fuel pump is attached to the sending unit and is located in the fuel tank.

PRESSURE TESTING

1. Relieve the fuel system pressure.
2. Remove the air cleaner.
3. Using the Fuel Pressure Gauge tool No. J–29658 or equivalent, install it on the throttle body side of the fuel filter at the rear of the vehicle, near the fuel tank.
4. Start the engine and read the fuel pressure on the gauge, it should be 9–13 psi.
5. Turn the ignition OFF, relieve the fuel system pressure and remove the fuel pressure gauge. Reconnect all fuel and vacuum lines. Install the air cleaner.

REMOVAL & INSTALLATION

1. Relieve the fuel system pressure.
2. Disconnect the negative battery cable.
3. Raise the rear seat and remove the floorpan cover.
4. Remove the fuel level sending unit bolts and the sending unit from the fuel tank.
5. To install, use a new O-ring on the sending unit. Install sending unit in tank and tighten bolts, install floorpan cover..

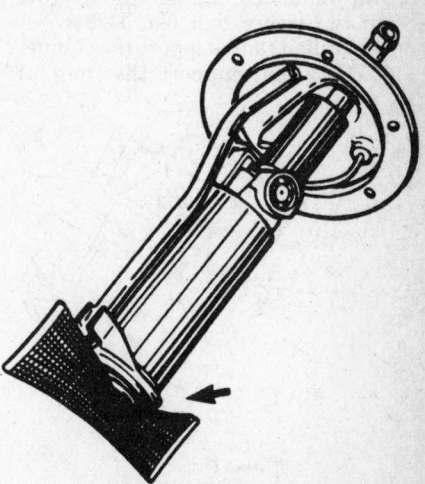

View of the electric fuel pump

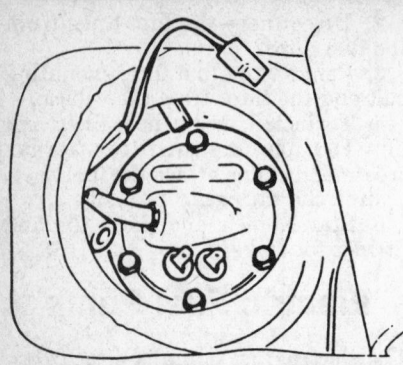

Fuel pump and sending unit mounting—
under rear seat

Fuel Injection

Due to the complex nature of modern fuel injection systems, comprehensive diagnosis and testing procedures fall outside the confines of this repair manual. For complete information on Fuel injection diagnosis, testing and repair procedures please refer to *Chilton's Guide to Fuel Injection And Feedback Carburetors.*

MANUAL TRANSAXLE

REMOVAL & INSTALLATION

1. Disconnect the negative battery cable.
2. Remove the clutch cable from the release lever.
3. From the shifter universal joint, remove the retaining clip and bolt.
4. From the transaxle, remove the speedometer cable, the speed sensor and the back up light connector.
5. Remove the upper transaxle to engine bolts (3). Install the Engine Support Fixture tool No. J-28467-A or equivalent, and support the engine.
6. Raise and support the front of

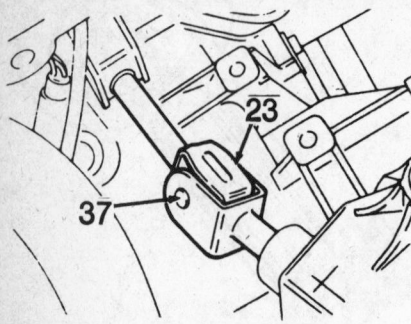

23. Clip
37. Bolt (Pin)

Removing the universal joint clip and bolt

the vehicle. Remove the left front wheel/tire assembly.

7. From the transaxle cover, remove the plug and the ground wire. Using a pair of internal snap-ring pliers, remove the snap-ring from the end of the input shaft; mark the position of the input shaft in relation to the cluster gear.
8. Using the Input Shaft Retaining Screw tool No. J-36668 or equivalent, remove the screw from the end of the input shaft.
9. Using the Input Shaft Removal and Installation tool No. J-36644 or equivalent, with the Slide Hammer tool No. J-6125 or equivalent, screw the assembly into the end of the input shaft. Using the slide hammer assembly, disengage the input shaft from the cluster gear.
10. Remove the flywheel cover bolts and the cover.
11. To remove the left lower ball joint, perform the following procedures:

   a. Remove the retainer clip from the ball joint.
   b. Remove the ball joint to steering knuckle nut.
   c. Using the Ball Joint Separator tool No. J-36226 or equivalent, separate the ball joint from the steering knuckle.

12. To remove the left tie rod end, perform the following procedures:

   a. Remove the tie rod end ball joint to steering knuckle nut.
   b. Using the Steering Linkage Puller tool No. J-24319-01 or equivalent, separate the tie rod end ball joint from the steering knuckle.

13. Using the Halfshaft Separator tool No. J-36639 or equivalent, and the tool No. J-23907 or equivalent, separate the left halfshaft from the transaxle and support it.

NOTE: When removing the halfshafts from the transaxle, be sure to swing the left strut assembly outward.

14. Using a floor jack, position it under the transaxle and support it.
15. Remove the left front mounting bracket bolts and the bracket.
16. Remove the left rear mounting bracket bolts.
17. Remove the lower transaxle to engine bolts. Move the transaxle away from the engine and downward; guide the right halfshaft from the transaxle, and support it.
18. To install, guide the halfshafts into the transaxle and reverse the removal procedures. Torque the lower transaxle to engine bolts to 55 ft. lbs., the left rear bracket to transaxle bolts to 55 ft. lbs., the left front mount bracket to transaxle bolts to 47 ft. lbs., the left front mount bracket to chassis

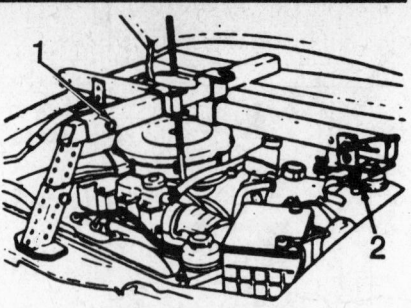

1. J-28467-A Engine support fixture
2. J-28467-20 Adapters

Supporting the engine

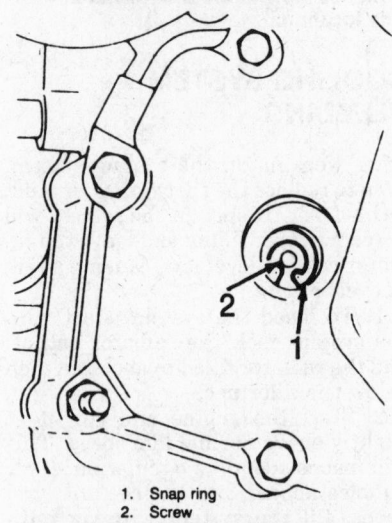

1. Snap ring
2. Screw

View of the input shaft snap ring

bolts to 55 ft. lbs., the ball joint to steering knuckle nut to 50 ft. lbs., the tie rod end to steering knuckle nut to 45 ft. lbs., the input shaft to cluster gear screw to 133 inch lbs. and the upper transaxle to engine bolts to 55 ft. lbs.

19. Check the transaxle fluid level and fill as needed.

LINKAGE ADJUSTMENT

1. Disconnect the negative battery cable.
2. Position the gear shift lever in the Neutral position.

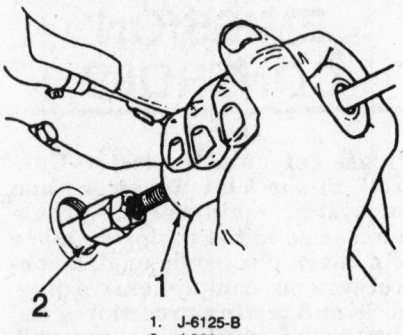

1. J-6125-B
2. J-36644

Disengaging the input shaft from the cluster gear

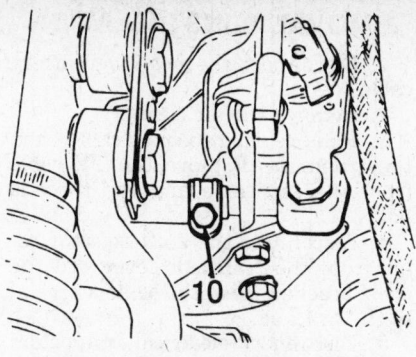

10. Rod clamp bolt

Removing the rod clamp bolt

3. Loosen the shift rod clamp bolt.

4. From the shift lever cover, remove the adjustment hole plug. Turn the shift rod left until a $\frac{3}{16}$ in. gauge pin can be inserted into the adjustment hole into the intermediate shift lever.

5. Remove the boot from the console, pull it upward to expose the shift control lever mechanism.

6. With the transaxle in Neutral, place the gear shift lever into the 1st/ 2nd gear position. With the lever against the stop and the arrow aligned with the notch, torque the rod clamp

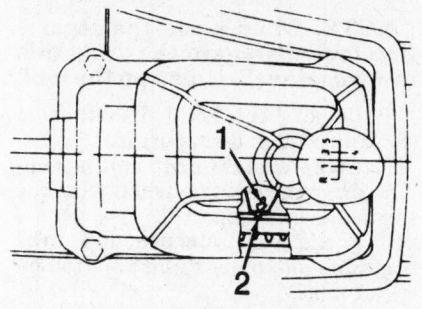

1. Alignment Arrow
2. Notch

Aligning the shift lever

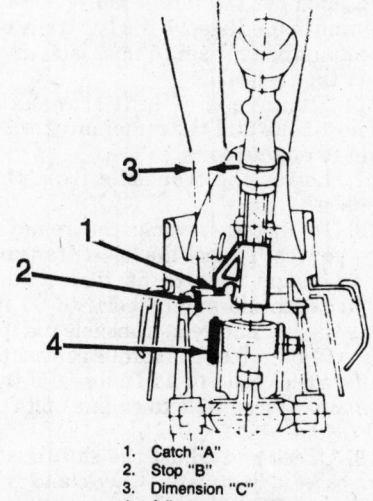

1. Catch "A"
2. Stop "B"
3. Dimension "C"
4. Adjustment nut "D"

Adjusting the shift lever measurements

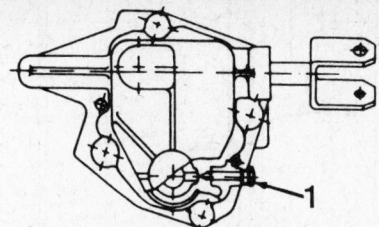

1. Adjustment hole plug

Cross-sectional view of the adjustment hole plug

bolt to 10 ft. lbs., then, turn the bolt another 90–180 degrees.

7. Using a 0.120 in. dia. gauge pin, check the clearance between the **A** catch and the **B** stop.

8. Remove the gauge pin and install the plug.

9. To further adjust the shift lever, bend back the 2 (adjusting nut) locking tabs and turn the adjusting nut **D** until the **C** dimension is 0.449–0.465 in. Bend up the locking tabs to secure the adjusting nut.

10. To complete the installation, reverse the removal procedures. The gear selector operation should be checked, to make sure that the proper gear is being selected.

CLUTCH

REMOVAL & INSTALLATION

It is not necessary to remove the transaxle from this vehicle to replace the clutch assembly.

1. Disconnect the negative battery cable. Remove the clutch cable from the release lever. Raise and safely support the front of the vehicle.

2. From the transaxle cover, remove the plug and the ground wire. Using a pair of internal snap-ring pliers, remove the snap-ring from the end of the input shaft; mark the position of the input shaft in relation to the cluster gear.

3. Using the Input Shaft Retaining Screw tool No. J–36668 or equivalent, remove the screw from the end of the input shaft.

4. Using the Input Shaft Removal and Installation tool No. J–36644 or equivalent, with the Slide Hammer tool No. J–6125 or equivalent, screw the assembly into the end of the input shaft. Using the slide hammer assembly, disengage the input shaft from the cluster gear.

5. Remove the clutch cover from the bottom of the transaxle and push back the clutch release bearing. Using the Pressure Plate Spring Clamps tool No. J–36554 or equivalent, rotate the fly-

wheel and install a clamp every 120 degrees.

NOTE: The pressure plate and clutch disc cannot be removed without installing the 3 spring clamps.

6. Remove the pressure plate to flywheel bolts, the pressure plate/clutch disc assembly; be sure to support the assembly when removing the last bolt.

7. To replace the clutch disc in the assembly, perform the following procedures:

a. Using a hydraulic press, apply pressure to the pressure plate spring fingers, then, remove the spring clamps.

b. Reduce the pressure of the press and separate the clutch disc from the pressure plate.

c. Inspect the clutch disc and the pressure plate for wear and/or damage, if necessary, replace the disc. Be sure to install the spring clamps to the pressure plate/clutch disc assembly.

d. Using grease, lightly lubricate the clutch disc spline.

e. When installing the pressure plate/clutch disc assembly, align the pressure plate **V** mark with the dot on the flywheel. Install 2 pressure plate to flywheel bolts for support and torque the bolts to 11 ft. lbs.

f. Install the input shaft by aligning the input shaft with the mark on

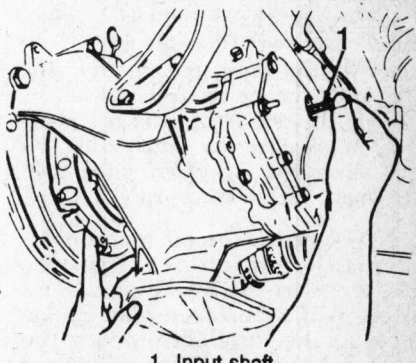

1. Input shaft

Installing the input shaft into the pressure plate/clutch disc assembly

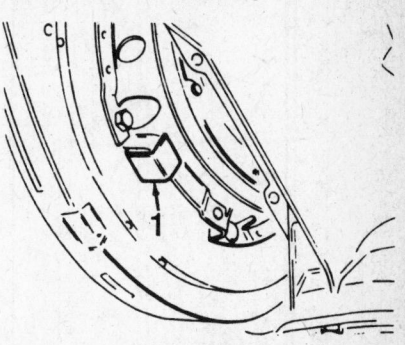

1. J–36554

View of the pressure plate spring clamps

the cluster gear. Using the Input Shaft Removal/Installation tool No. J–36644 or equivalent, and a Slide Hammer tool No. J–6125–B or equivalent, seat the input shaft with the cluster gear.

g. Install the screw into the end of the input shaft; torque it to 11 ft. lbs.

h. Install the snap ring on the end of the input shaft; the sharp edges must face the cover.

i. To complete the installation, torque the pressure plate retaining bolts to 11 ft. lbs.

NOTE: When installing a new clutch disc, make sure that the long part of the clutch disc hub faces the transaxle.

8. Using Teflon® pipe thread sealer, coat the threads of the input shaft cover plug and tighten to 36 ft. lbs..

9. Remove the spring clamps from the pressure plate/clutch disc assembly.

10. Torque the clutch cover bolts to 62 inch lbs. Install the left tire and wheel assembly, lower the vehicle. Install the clutch cable to the release lever. Check clutch engagement and operation.

PEDAL TRAVEL

1. Measure the distance from the center of the clutch pedal to the bottom edge of the steering wheel.

2. Depress the clutch pedal (fully), then, measure the distance again. Subtract the 1st measurement from the 2nd to determine the pedal travel.

3. If the pedal travel is not 5.43–5.70 in., remove the clutch cable clip and adjust the nut to bring the measurement within specifications.

NOTE: With the correct adjustment, the clutch pedal will be higher than the brake pedal and there will be no free play operation. As the clutch disc wears, the clutch pedal will move further from the brake pedal.

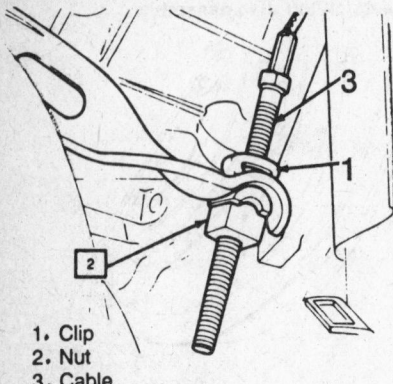

1. Clip
2. Nut
3. Cable

View of the clutch cable adjuster

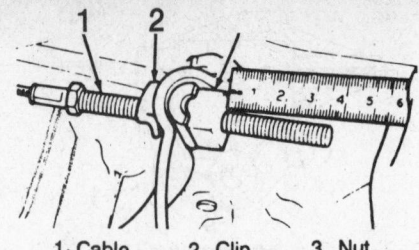

1. Cable 2. Clip 3. Nut

Measuring the end of the clutch cable

Clutch Cable

REMOVAL & INSTALLATION

1. Disconnect the negative battery cable.

2. Measure the threaded end of the clutch cable at the release lever and record the measurement for pre-adjustment procedures.

3. Remove the clutch cable clip and loosen the clutch cable adjusting nut. Disconnect the cable from the release arm and cable bracket.

4. Disconnect the clutch start safety switch.

5. At the clutch pedal, remove the cable return spring and brace. Remove the clutch pedal retaining nut, spring and shaft. Remove the pedal and pull the cable through the firewall.

6. Disconnect the spring and the cable from the pedal.

7. To install, coat the clutch pedal shaft with grease and reverse the removal procedures. Adjust the clutch cable to the measurement taken earlier. Adjust the clutch pedal travel and check the operation.

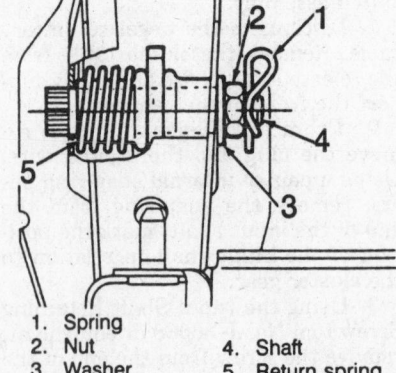

1. Spring
2. Nut
3. Washer
4. Shaft
5. Return spring

Clutch pedal and return spring mounting

AUTOMATIC TRANSAXLE

For further information on automatic transaxles, please refer to "Automatic Transaxles" in the Unit Repair section.

REMOVAL & INSTALLATION

1. Disconnect the negative battery cable.

2. Remove the air cleaner.

3. Remove the capacitor cable from the transaxle. Remove the TV cable from the transaxle and the throttle body.

4. Disconnect the shift selector cable from the transaxle lever and the cable bracket; leave the cable attached to the bracket.

5. Disconnect electrical connectors from the speed sensor, the TCC and the park/neutral/back up light switch.

6. Disconnect the speedometer drive cable.

7. Remove the top transaxle mounting bolts.

8. Using the Engine Support Fixture tool No. J–28467–A or equivalent, and the Adaptor tool No. J–228467–70 or equivalent, attach it to the engine and support its weight.

9. Raise and safely support the front of the vehicle.

10. Remove both front wheels. Using the Ball Joint Separator tool No. J–36226 or equivalent, separate the ball joints (both sides) from the steering knuckles. Remove the tie rod ends from the steering knuckles.

NOTE: When using the separation tool, disregard the "this side towards wheel" stamp on the tool.

11. Remove the left halfshaft from the transaxle and support it.

12. Using a brass drift and a hammer, drive the right halfshaft from the transaxle and support it.

13. Position a drain pan under the transaxle, disconnect and plug the oil cooler lines.

14. Remove the torque converter cover. Using a scratch awl, scribe alignment marks on the torque converter and the flywheel.

15. Remove the torque converter retaining bolts. Remove the left transaxle mount bolts. Using a floor jack, support the transaxle.

16. Remove the right transaxle mount bolts and the remaining transaxle to engine bolts.

17. Lower the transaxle from the vehicle.

18. To install, reverse the removal procedures. Torque the lower transaxle to engine bolts to 54 ft. lbs., the right transaxle mount bolts to 30 ft. lbs., the left and rear transaxle mount bolts to 16 ft. lbs., the torque converter to flywheel bolts to 44 ft. lbs. and the remaining transaxle to engine bolts to 54 ft. lbs.

19. Check and adjust the shift selector cable adjustment. Check and adjust the TV cable adjustment. Check and fill the transaxle with fluid.

DRIVE AXLE

Halfshaft

REMOVAL & INSTALLATION

1. Raise the hood. Loosen the upper strut to body nuts.

2. Remove the hub cap, then loosen the wheel lug nuts. Remove the grease cap, cotter pin and the wheel hub nut/thrust washer.

3. Raise and safely support the front of the vehicle. Remove the wheel/tire assembly.

4. From the lower ball joint, remove the retaining clip and the nut.

5. Using the Ball Joint Separator tool No. J–36226 or equivalent, separate the lower ball joint from the steering knuckle.

NOTE: When using the separation tool, disregard the "this side towards wheel" stamp on the tool.

6. Remove the tie rod ball joint nut.

7. Using the Tie Rod Separator tool No. J–24319–01 or equivalent, separate the tie rod from the steering knuckle.

8. Using the Halfshaft to Hub Separator tool No. J–3666–1 or equivalent, drive the halfshaft from the hub assembly.

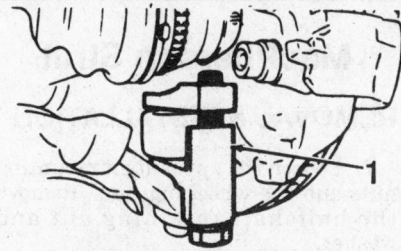

1. Ball joint separator tool No. J-36226

Separating the ball joint from the steering knuckle

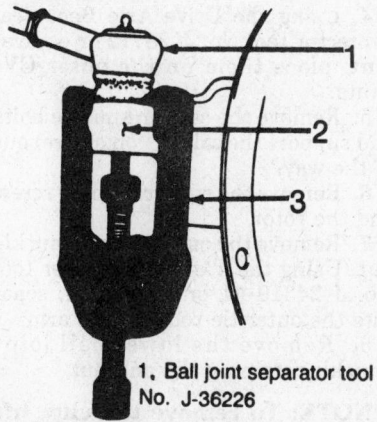

1. Ball joint separator tool No. J-36226

Separating the tie rod ball joint from the steering knuckle

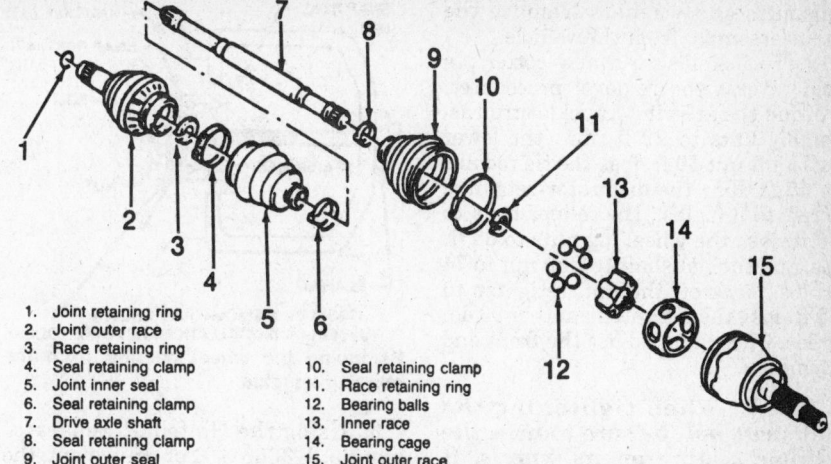

1. Joint retaining ring	
2. Joint outer race	
3. Race retaining ring	
4. Seal retaining clamp	10. Seal retaining clamp
5. Joint inner seal	11. Race retaining ring
6. Seal retaining clamp	12. Bearing balls
7. Drive axle shaft	13. Inner race
8. Seal retaining clamp	14. Bearing cage
9. Joint outer seal	15. Joint outer race

Exploded view of the halfshaft

9. Position a drain pan under the transaxle. Using the Axle Shaft to Transaxle Separator tool No. J–36639 or equivalent, and the Slide Hammer tool No. J–23907 or equivalent, separate and remove the halfshaft from the transaxle.

10. To install, use new retaining clips, cotter pins and reverse the removal procedures. Torque the lower ball joint nut to 50 ft. lbs., the tie rod nut to 45 ft. lbs.

11. Lower the vehicle to the floor. Torque the hub nut to 74 ft. lbs., the wheel lug nuts to 65 ft. lbs. and the upper strut mounting nuts to 22 ft. lbs. Check and fill the transaxle as needed.

CV JOINT OVERHAUL

For all CV-joint overhaul procedures, please refer to "U/CV-Joint Overhaul" in the Unit Repair section.

Front Wheel Drive Hub/Steering Knuckle Assembly

REMOVAL & INSTALLATION

1. Loosen the upper strut mounting nuts and the wheel lug nuts. Remove the halfshaft retaining nut and washer.

2. Raise and safely support the front of the vehicle, the front wheels must be hanging.

3. Remove the front wheel assemblies.

4. Using the Drive Axle Boot Seal Protector tool No. J–28712 or equivalent, place them on the outer CV-joints.

5. Remove the caliper knuckle bolts and support the caliper (on a wire) out of the way.

6. Remove the rotor retaining screw and the rotor.

7. Remove the outer tie rod knuckle nut. Using the Tie Rod Remover tool No. J–24319–01 or equivalent, separate the outer tie rod knuckle arm.

8. Remove the lower ball joint knuckle retaining clip and nut.

NOTE: To remove the clip, lift up on the rear of the clip, while pulling outward on the loops.

9. Using the Ball Joint Separator tool No. J–36226 or equivalent, separate the lower ball joint from the steering knuckle arm.

NOTE: When using the separator tool, disregard the "this side towards wheel" stamp on the tool.

10. Using the Front Wheel Hub Remover tool No. J–36661 or equivalent, separate the halfshaft from the steering knuckle hub. Support the halfshaft.

11. Remove the upper strut mount-

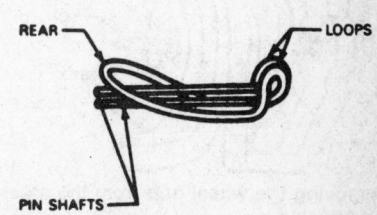

View of the retaining clip used on the lower ball joint

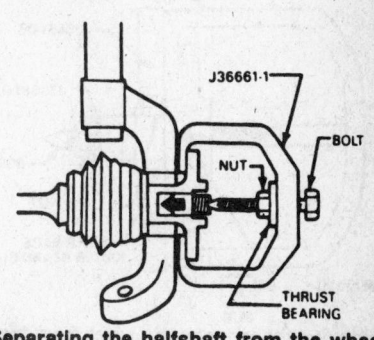

Separating the halfshaft from the wheel hub

ing nuts and washers, remove the strut assembly from the vehicle.

12. To install, use a new cotter pin and reverse the removal procedures. Torque the steering knuckle/strut assembly nuts to 22 ft. lbs., the lower ball joint nut 50 ft. lbs., the tie rod nut to 45 ft. lbs., the disc rotor retaining screw to 3 ft. lbs., the caliper bolts to 70 ft. lbs., the wheel lug nuts to 65 ft. lbs. and the halfshaft to hub nut to 74 ft. lbs., back off the nut, retighten to 15 ft. lbs., then, tighten another 90 degrees. Check and adjust the front end alignment.

NOTE: When tightening the halfshaft nut, be sure to have the vehicle resting on its wheels. If the castellated nut does not align with a shaft hole, back off the nut until it does; DO NOT tighten the nut!

Steering Knuckle, Hub and Bearing

REMOVAL & INSTALLATION

1. Remove the steering knuckle/strut assembly from the vehicle and position it on a workbench.

2. Using the Halfshaft Separator tool No. J–36661–01 or equivalent, and the Front Wheel Hub Remover tool No. J–36661–03 or equivalent, press the hub from the steering knuckle.

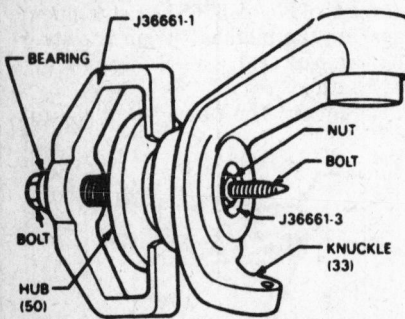

Removing the wheel hub from the steering knuckle

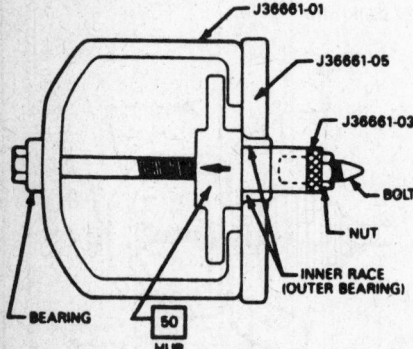

Removing the inner bearing race from the hub

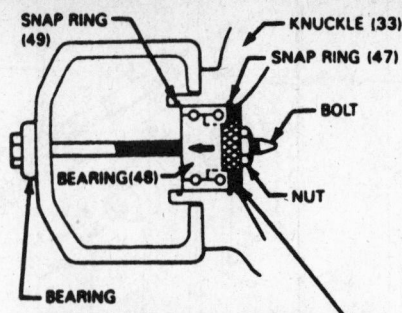

J36661-04 (REMOVAL) AS SHOWN
J36661-04 (INSTALLATION) REVERSE TOOL

Removing the wheel bearing from the steering knuckle

3. Using the Halfshaft Separator tool No. J–36661–01 or equivalent, the Front Wheel Hub Remover tool No. J–36661–03 or equivalent, and the Inner Bearing Race Remover tool No. J–36661–05 or equivalent, remove the inner bearing race from the hub.

4. From inside the steering knuckle, remove the internal snap rings.

5. Using the Halfshaft Separator tool No. J–36661–01 or equivalent, and the Bearing Remover/Installer tool No. J–36661–04 or equivalent, press the bearing from the steering knuckle.

NOTE: Whenever the wheel bearing is removed from the steering knuckle, it MUST BE discarded and replaced with a new one.

6. Using solvent, clean all of the parts and blow dry with compressed air.

7. Before assembling the parts, be sure to coat them with a layer of wheel bearing grease.

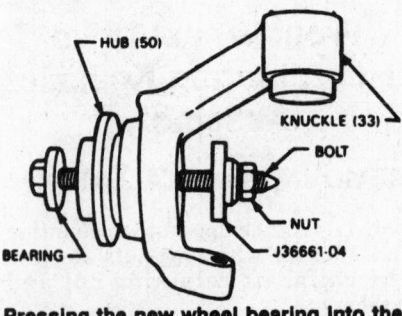

Pressing the new wheel bearing into the steering knuckle

8. Using snap ring pliers, install the outer internal snap ring into the steering knuckle.

9. Using the Halfshaft Separator tool No. J–36661–01 or equivalent, and the Bearing Remover/Installer tool No. J–36661–04 or equivalent, press the NEW wheel bearing into the steering knuckle until it butts against the snap ring.

10. Using snap ring pliers, install the inner internal snap ring into the steering knuckle.

11. Install the strut onto the body. Remove the seal protector from the halfshaft. Install the halfshaft into the steering knuckle/strut assembly, then, the washer and NEW halfshaft nut onto the halfshaft.

12. To install, use new cotter pins and reverse the removal procedures. Torque the steering knuckle/strut assembly mounting nuts to 22 ft. lbs., the lower ball joint nut to 50 ft. lbs., the tie rod nut to 45 ft. lbs., the disc rotor retaining screw to 3 ft. lbs., the caliper mounting bolts to 70 ft. lbs., the wheel lug nuts to 65 ft. lbs. and the halfshaft to hub nut to 74 ft. lbs., back off the nut, retighten to 15 ft. lbs., then, tighten another 90 degrees. Check and/or adjust the front end alignment.

NOTE: When tightening the halfshaft nut, be sure the vehicle is resting on its wheels. If the castellated nut does not align with a shaft hole, back off the nut until it does; DO NOT tighten the nut!

FRONT SUSPENSION

MacPherson Strut

REMOVAL & INSTALLATION

1. Loosen the upper strut mounting nuts and the wheel lug nuts. Remove the halfshaft retaining nut and washer.

2. Raise and safely support the front of the vehicle, the front wheels must be hanging.

3. Remove the front wheel assemblies.

4. Using the Drive Axle Boot Seal Protector tool No. J–28712 or equivalent, place them on the outer CV-joints.

5. Remove the caliper knuckle bolts and support the caliper (on a wire) out of the way.

6. Remove the rotor retaining screw and the rotor.

7. Remove the outer tie rod knuckle nut. Using the Tie Rod Remover tool No. J–24319–01 or equivalent, separate the outer tie rod knuckle arm.

8. Remove the lower ball joint knuckle retaining clip and nut.

NOTE: To remove the clip, lift up on the rear of the clip, while pulling outward on the loops.

9. Using the Ball Joint Separator tool No. J–36226 or equivalent, separate the lower ball joint from the steering knuckle arm.

NOTE: When using the separator tool, disregard the "this side towards wheel" stamp on the tool.

10. Using the Front Wheel Hub Remover tool No. J–36661 or equivalent, separate the halfshaft from the steering knuckle hub. Support the halfshaft.

11. Remove the upper strut mounting nuts and washers, remove the strut assembly from the vehicle.

12. To install, use a new cotter pin and reverse the removal procedures. Torque the steering knuckle/strut assembly nuts to 22 ft. lbs., the lower ball joint nut 50 ft. lbs., the tie rod nut to 45 ft. lbs., the disc rotor retaining screw to 3 ft. lbs., the caliper bolts to 70 ft. lbs., the wheel lug nuts to 65 ft. lbs. and the halfshaft to hub nut to 74 ft. lbs., back off the nut, retighten to 15 ft. lbs., then, tighten another 90 degrees.

OVERHAUL

For all spring and shock absorber removal and installation procedures, and all strut overhaul procedures, please refer to "Strut Overhaul" in the Unit Repair section.

Stabilizer Bar

REMOVAL & INSTALLATION

1. Loosen the left front wheel lug nuts.
2. Raise and safely support the front of the vehicle, allowing the suspension to hang free.
3. Remove the left tire and wheel assembly.
4. Remove the stabilizer shaft link assemblies from the control arms.
5. Remove the stabilizer shaft bushings and brackets from the body.
6. Remove the stabilizer shaft and bushings.

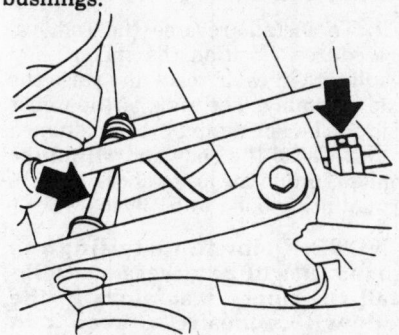

Stabilizer bar attachment

7. To install, center the stabilizer shaft and assemble all of the components. With the vehicle positioned at trim height, tighten the components. Torque the stabilizer bolts to 29 ft. lbs., the stabilizer to control arm nut to 13 ft. lbs. and wheel lug nuts to 65 ft. lbs.

Ball Joints

INSPECTION

1. Raise and safely support the front of the vehicle, allowing the front wheels to hang.
2. With the ball joint installed to the steering knuckle, perform the following procedures:
   a. Grasp the top and bottom of the wheel, move the wheel using an "in and out" shaking motion.
   b. Observe any movement between the steering knuckle and the control arm. If movement exists, replace the ball joint.
3. If the ball joint has been disconnected from the steering knuckle, perform the following procedures:
   a. Inspect the ball joint for looseness.
   b. Try to twist the ball joint in its socket.
   c. If either defect can be noticed, replace the ball joint.

REMOVAL & INSTALLATION

1. Raise and safely support the front of the vehicle, allowimg the front wheels to hang.
2. Remove the front wheel/tire assemblies.
3. If a silicone (gray) boot is used on the inboard axle joint, install a Boot Seal Protector tool No. J–28712 or equivalent. If a thermoplastic (black) boot is used, no protector is necessary.
4. Remove the retaining clip from the ball joint castle nut.
5. Remove the castle nut. Using the Ball Joint Separator tool No. J–36226 or equivalent, disconnect the ball joint from the steering knuckle arm.
6. Using a 0.47 in. bit, drill out the 3 ball joint retaining rivets.

NOTE: Be careful not to damage the halfshaft boot when drilling out the ball joint rivets.

7. Loosen the stabilizer shaft bushing assembly nut.
8. Remove the ball joint from the control arm.
9. Install the new ball joint to the control arm by bolting it in place with the nuts and bolts supplied, torque the mounting nuts to 51 ft. lbs. Tighten the stabilizer bushing clamp bolts to 13 ft. lbs. and the ball joint to steering knuckle nut to 50 ft. lbs.

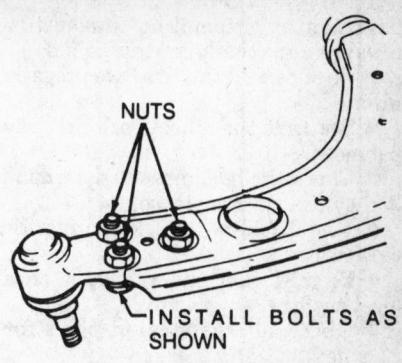

Installing new tie rod end

Lower Control Arm

REMOVAL & INSTALLATION

1. Raise and safely support the front of the vehicle, allowing the front suspension to hang freely.
2. Remove the wheel/tire assemblies.
3. Disconnect the stabilizer shaft from the control arm and support assembly.
4. Remove the ball joint to steering knuckle cotter pin and nut. Using the Ball Joint Separator tool No. J–36226 or equivalent, separate the ball joint from the steering knuckle.
5. Remove the control arm nuts/bolts and the control arm from the vehicle.

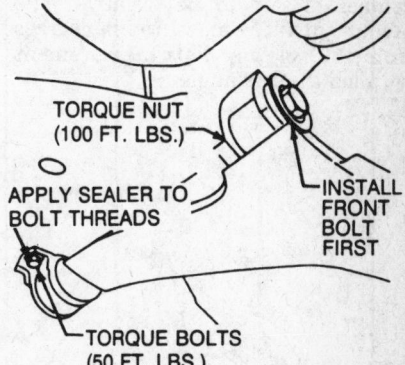

Lower control arm mounting bolt location

6. To install, use new cotter pins and reverse the removal procedures. Torque the ball joint to steering knuckle nut to 51 ft. lbs. Partially lower the vehicle until at "Curb Height", torque the front control arm bolts to 140 ft. lbs., the rear control arm bolts to 90 ft. lbs.

Front Wheel Alignment

ADJUSTMENT

Front end alignment measurements require the use of special alignment equipment. Before measuring the alignment or attempting to adjust it, always check the following points:

- Be sure that the tires are properly inflated.
- See that the wheels are properly balanced.
- Check the ball joints to determine it they are worn or loose.
- Check the wheel bearings for looseness.
- Be sure that the vehicle is on a level surface.
- Check all suspension parts for tightness.
- The fuel tank must be at least ½ filled.
- Rock the vehicle several times to make sure that the springs are stabilized.

Caster

Caster is the tilting of the steering axis either forward or backward from the vertical, when viewed from the side of the vehicle. A backward tilt is said to be positive and a forward tilt is said to be negative.

Camber

Camber is the tilting of the wheels from the vertical when viewed from the front of the vehicle. When the wheels tilt outward from the top, the camber is said to be positive. When the wheels tilt inward from the top the camber is said to be negative. The amount of tilt is measured in degrees from the vertical. This measurement is called camber angle.

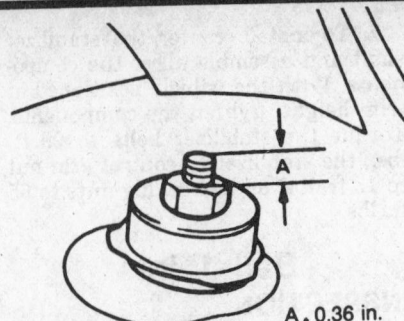

A, 0.36 in.

Tightening the rear shock absorber to the required height

Toe-In

Toe-in is the turning in of the wheels. The actual amount of toe-in is normally only a fraction of an inch. The purpose of toe-in specification is to ensure parallel rolling of the wheels. Toe-in also serves to offset the small deflections of the steering support system which occur when the vehicle is rolling forward.

REAR SUSPENSION

Shock Absorbers

REMOVAL & INSTALLATION

1. Open the rear deck lid.

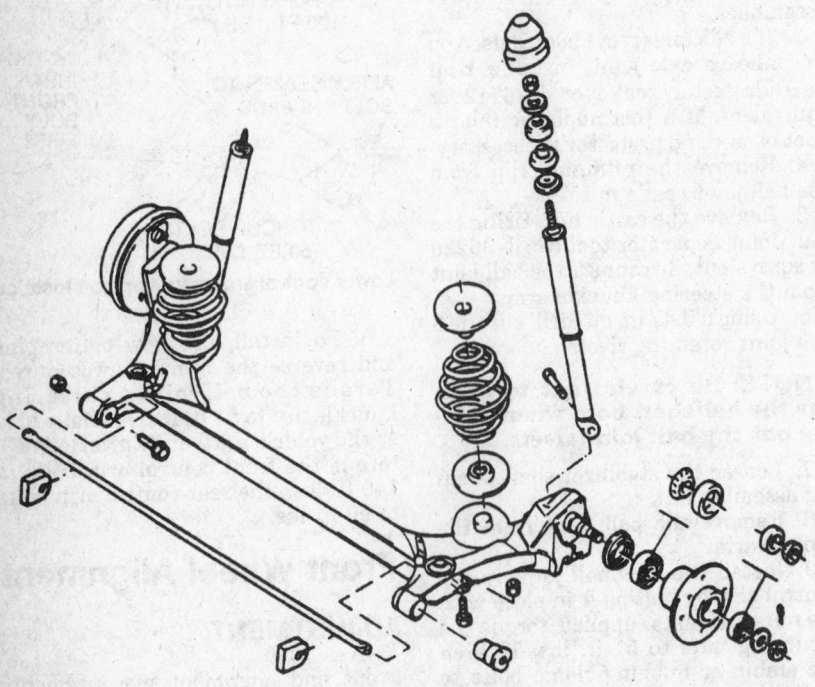

Exploded view of the rear axle assembly

2. If equipped, remove the trim cover. Remove the upper shock absorber attaching nut.

NOTE: When removing the shock absorbers, remove 1 at a time. Removing both could cause the axle to fall away, damaging the brake lines and hoses.

3. Raise and safely support the rear of the vehicle.
4. Remove the lower shock absorber mounting bolt and the shock absorber from the vehicle.
5. To install, reverse the removal procedures. Torque the lower shock absorber mounting bolt to 51 ft. lbs. and the upper shock absorber attaching nut until 0.36 in. of the shock absorber thread is showing.

OVERHAUL

For all spring and shock absorber removal and installation procedures, please refer to "Strut Overhaul" in the Unit Repair section.

Springs
REMOVAL & INSTALLATION

1. Raise and support the rear axle assembly with a floor jack.
2. Install jackstands under the frame.
3. Remove the rear wheel assemblies.
4. Remove the right and left brake line bracket attaching screws from the body and allow the brake line to hang free.
5. Remove both lower shock absorber mounting bolts.
6. With the rear axle assembly supported by a floor jack, carefully lower the rear axle and remove the springs and insulators.

NOTE: DO NOT suspend the rear axle by the brake hoses or damage to the hoses could result. Lower the axle just enough to remove the springs and support it during all service procedures.

7. To install, reverse the removal procedures. Position the springs and insulators in their seats and raise the axle assembly. The ends of the upper coil on the spring must be positioned in the seat of the body and within the limits. Torque the lower shock absorber mounting bolts to 51 ft. lbs.

NOTE: Prior to installing the spring, it will be necessary to install the upper insulators to the body with adhesive to keep it in position while raising the axle assembly and springs.

Stabilizer Bar

REMOVAL & INSTALLATION

1. Raise and safely support the rear of the vehicle.
2. Remove 1 rear wheel/tire assembly.
3. Remove the nuts/bolts at both sides of the axle assembly. Remove the insulator and stabilizer bar.
4. To install, the stabilizer bar inside the rear axle assembly. Torque the stabilizer bar retaining nuts to 59 ft. lbs. Coat the insulators with liquid detergent and insert the rear axle assembly.
5. Torque the rear wheel lug nuts to 66 ft. lbs.

Rear Wheel Bearings

ADJUSTMENT

1. Remove the grease cap from the rear wheel hub.
2. Romove the cotter pin from the spindle and the spindle nut.
3. While turning the wheel, by hand, in the forward direction, tighten the spindle nut to 12 ft. lbs.

NOTE: The tightening procedure will remove any grease or burrs which could cause excessive wheel bearing play.

4. Back off the nut to the "just loose" position.
5. Hand tighten the spindle nut and loosen it until 1 of the spindle holes aligns with a slot in the nut.
6. Install a new cotter pin and bend the ends around the nut.
7. Using a feeler gauge, measure the end play. If it is within 0.001–0.005 in., it is properly adjusted. Install the dust cap.

REMOVAL & INSTALLATION

1. Raise and safely support the rear of the vehicle.
2. Remove the wheel/tire assembly.
3. Remove the brake drum detent screw and the drum.

NOTE: To remove the brake drum, it may be necessary to loosen the parking brake cable and press the parking brake lever inwards (with a pry bar). DO NOT hammer on the brake drum, damage to the bearing may result.

4. Remove the hub/bearing assembly grease cap, cotter pin, hub nut, thrust washer and the outer bearing from the axle spindle.
5. Using a small pry bar, remove the grease seal from the inside of the hub.

Remove the inner, outer bearing from the hub.
6. If replacing the wheel bearings, perform the following procedures:
   a. Using a hammer and a drift punch, drive both outer bearing races (in opposite directions) from the wheel hub.
   b. Using a cleaning solvent (NOT gasoline), clean the bearings, races and hub. Using compressed air, blow dry the parts.
   c. Inspect the parts for damage and/or wear. If necessary, replace any defective parts.
   d. Using an arbor press, the Rear Hub Inner and Outer Bearing Race Installer tool No. J–6791 or equivalent, and the Driver Handle tool No. J–8092 or equivalent, press the outer bearing race into the wheel hub until it seats.

NOTE: Before installing the new wheel bearings, pack thoroughly with wheel bearing grease.

   e. Using an arbor press, the Rear Hub Inner and Outer Bearing Race Installer tool No. J–6791 or equivalent, and the Driver Handle tool No. J–8092 or equivalent, press the inner bearing race into the wheel hub until it seats, then, install the inner bearing.
   f. Lubricate the lips of the new grease seal. Using the Rear Hub Seal Installation tool No. J–6797 or equivalent, press the new seal into the hub.
   g. Install the wheel bearing hub onto the axle spindle, followed by the outer bearing, thrust washer and hub nut.
   h. Adjust the bearings and the parking brake.
7. To complete the installation torque the wheel lug nuts to 66 ft. lbs. and check the operation of the parking brake.

STEERING

Steering Wheel

REMOVAL & INSTALLATION

1. Disconnect the negative battery cable.
2. Remove the horn pad and wires from the steering wheel.
3. Using a scratch awl, mark the alignment of the steering wheel with the steering column.
4. Remove the steering wheel retaining nut and washer.
5. Using the Steering Wheel Puller tool No. J–36541 or equivalent, press the steering wheel from the steering column.

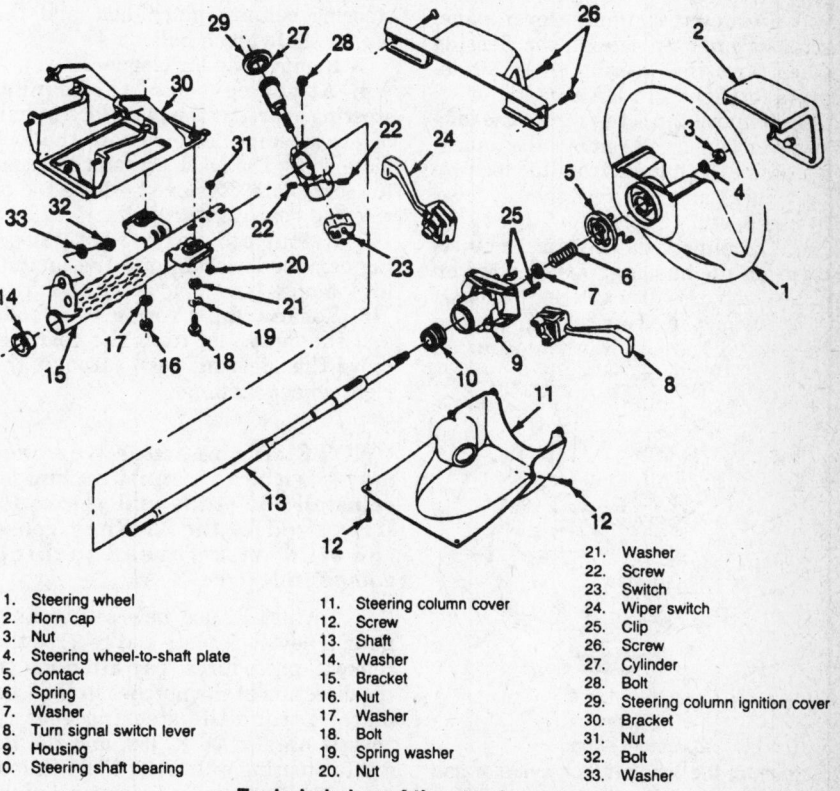

1.	Steering wheel	11.	Steering column cover
2.	Horn cap	12.	Screw
3.	Nut	13.	Shaft
4.	Steering wheel-to-shaft plate	14.	Washer
5.	Contact	15.	Bracket
6.	Spring	16.	Nut
7.	Washer	17.	Washer
8.	Turn signal switch lever	18.	Bolt
9.	Housing	19.	Spring washer
10.	Steering shaft bearing	20.	Nut
		21.	Washer
		22.	Screw
		23.	Switch
		24.	Wiper switch
		25.	Clip
		26.	Screw
		27.	Cylinder
		28.	Bolt
		29.	Steering column ignition cover
		30.	Bracket
		31.	Nut
		32.	Bolt
		33.	Washer

Exploded view of the steering column

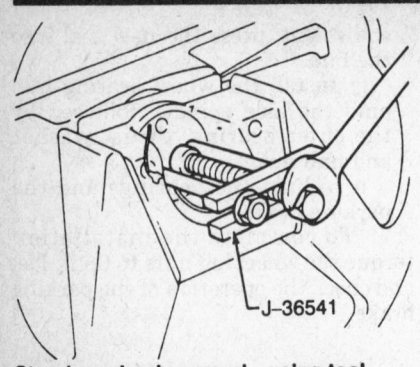

Steering wheel removal–using tool J–36541

NOTE: It may be necessary to disconnect the horn contact ring from the steering wheel. When installing the steering wheel, be sure that the turn signal return segment is positioned on the upper left side (facing the steering column).

6. To install, align the steering wheel on the column and reverse the removal procedures. Torque the steering wheel column nut to 18 ft. lbs. and bend the retaining tabs.

Turn Signal Switch

REMOVAL & INSTALLATION

1. Disconnect the negative battery cable.
2. Remove the lower instrument panel trim.
3. Remove the upper cover panel screws from both sides of the steering wheel turn the steering wheel 90 degrees for right and left access.
4. Remove the screws from the lower cover panel and remove the panel.
5. Pull the handle from the lock release lever and unscrew the tilt lever (if equipped).
6. Disconnect the electrical connector from the housing; push inward on either side of the switch and remove.
7. Install the electrical connector to the switch and clip into place. Install

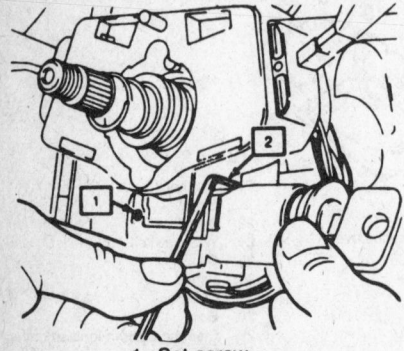

1. Set screw
2. Detent spring

Removing the ignition lock cylinder and the ignition switch

the lock release lever and the trim covers. Connect the battery cable and check switch operation.

Ignition Lock/Switch

REMOVAL & INSTALLATION

1. Disconnect the negative battery cable.
2. Remove the lower instrument cluster trim.
3. Remove the turn signal/wiper switch cover panels.
4. With the key in the ignition switch, turn the key to the II position.
5. Using a small Allen wrench, press downward on the detent spring and remove the ignition lock cylinder.
6. To remove the ignition switch, disconnect the electrical connector, then, remove the set screw and the ignition switch.
7. To install; push the ignition switch into place and attach the wiring. Place the key in the lock cylinder and install it into the ignition switch. Install the trim panels, connect the battery cable.

Manual Steering Gear

REMOVAL & INSTALLATION

1. Disconnect the negative battery cable.
2. Position the steering wheel in the straight ahead position. Remove the steering column pinch bolt and the pinion shaft pinch bolt.
3. Remove the air cleaner.
4. At the center of the manual steering gear, cut the plate lock in half before attempting to remove the lock plate bolts; DO NOT attempt to reuse the lock plate. Remove both tie rod to steering gear (center) bolts.
5. If equipped, remove both steering damper brackets and the mounting clamps.
6. Remove the steering gear bolts and the dash seal from the gear, remove the steering gear through the right wheel opening.

NOTE: If the studs were removed with the mounting clamps, reinstall the studs and retorque. If removed for the 2nd time, reuse the stud with thread locking compound.

7. To install, use new self locking nuts, a new lock plate and reverse the removal procedures; pay attention to the direction of the notches in the lock plate. Torque the steering gear to chassis nuts to 28 ft. lbs. and the tie rod to steering gear bolts to 65 ft. lbs. Adjust the manual steering gear play.

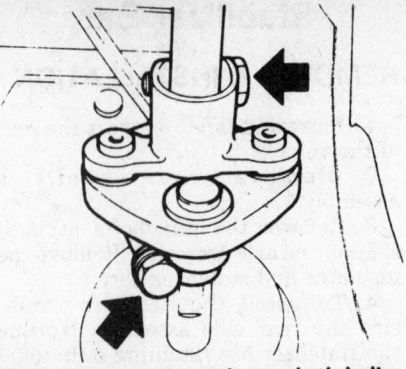

View of the steering column pinch bolts

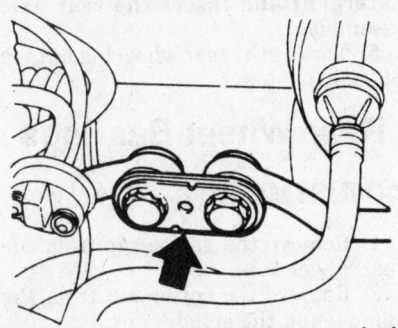

View of the manual steering gear lock plate

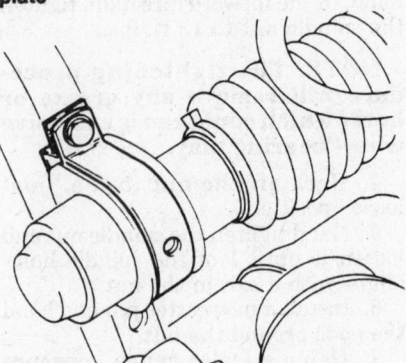

Steering rack mounting clamp

NOTE: When installing the coupling onto the steering pinion, push it downward, then, torque the pinion pinch bolt to 29 ft. lbs. When installing the steering spindle, pull it upwards until it stops on the spindle ball bearing, then, torque the upper pinch bolt to 34 ft. lbs.

ADJUSTMENT

1. Raise and safely support the front of the vehicle.
2. Center the steering wheel.
3. Loosen the adjuster plug lock nut. Turn the adjuster plug clockwise until it bottoms, then, back it out 50–70 degrees.
4. Inspect the steering pinion torque, it should be 8–20 inch lbs.
5. After adjusting the pinion

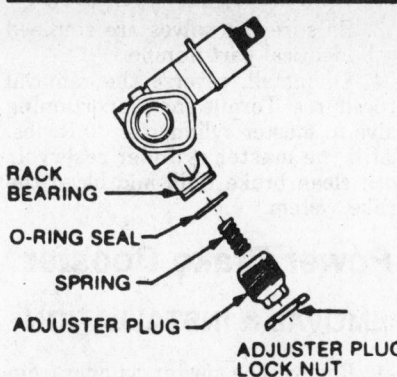

RACK
BEARING

O-RING SEAL

SPRING

ADJUSTER PLUG

ADJUSTER PLUG
LOCK NUT

Exploded view of the manual steering gear adjustment assembly

torque, hold the adjuster stationary and torque the adjuster plug lock nut to 50 ft. lbs.

Power Steering Gear

REMOVAL & INSTALLATION

1. Disconnect the negative battery cable.
2. Position the steering wheel in the straight ahead position. Remove the steering column pinch bolt and the pinion shaft pinch bolt.
3. Remove the air cleaner.
4. At the center of the power steering gear, cut the lock plate in half before attempting to remove the lock plate bolts; DO NOT attempt to reuse the lock plate. Remove both tie rod to steering gear (center) bolts.
5. Remove the high pressure hoses from the power steering gear and plug.
6. Remove the steering gear mounting bolts/clamps and the dash seal from the gear, remove the steering gear through the right wheel opening.

NOTE: If the studs were removed with the mounting clamps, reinstall the studs and retorque. If removed for the 2nd time, reuse the stud with thread locking compound.

7. To install, use new self locking nuts, a new lock plate and reverse the removal procedures; pay attention to the direction of the notches in the lock plate. Torque the steering gear to chassis nuts to 28 ft. lbs. and the tie rod bolts to 65 ft. lbs. Adjust the power steering gear play.

NOTE: When installing the coupling onto the steering pinion, push it downward, then, torque the pinion pinch bolt to 37 ft. lbs. When installing the steering spindle, pull it upwards until it stops on the spindle ball bearing, then, torque the upper pinch bolt to 34 ft. lbs.

8. Refill the power steering system reservoir and bleed the system.

ADJUSTMENT

1. Raise and safely support the front of the vehicle.
2. Center the steering wheel.
3. Loosen the adjuster plug lock nut. Turn the adjuster plug clockwise until it bottoms, then, back it out 50–70 degrees.
4. Inspect the steering pinion torque, it should be 16 inch lbs.
5. After adjusting the pinion torque, hold the adjuster stationary and torque the adjuster plug lock nut to 50 ft. lbs.

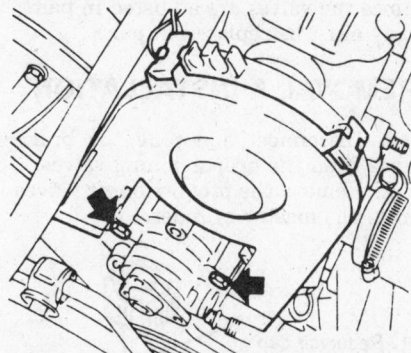

Power steering pump location and mounting

Power Steering Pump

REMOVAL & INSTALLATION

1. Loosen the alternator and remove the accessory drive belt.
2. Remove the power steering pump pulley bolts and the pulley.
3. Disconnect the fluid lines from the power steering pump and plug.
4. Remove the front timing belt cover from the engine.
5. Remove the power steering pump mounting bolts and the pump from the engine.
6. To install, clean the mounting surfaces and install the steering pump. Install the pump drive pulley and belt, adjust the drive belt tension. Refill the power steering reservoir with new power steering fluid. Start the engine and check for leaks. Bleed the power steering system.

BELT ADJUSTMENT

The drive belt should be inspected and/or replaced every 30,000 miles or 24 months.
1. Using the Belt Tension Gauge tool No. J–26486–B or equivalent, position it on the center of the longest belt span.
2. If the belt tension is not correct,

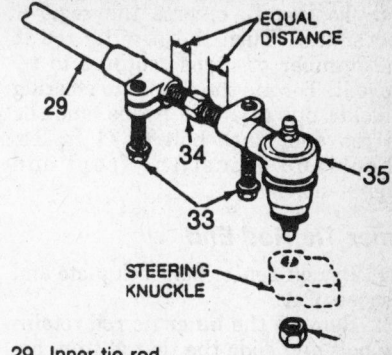

EQUAL
DISTANCE

29

34

35

33

STEERING
KNUCKLE

29. Inner tie rod
33. Pinch bolt   35. Outer tie rod
34. Tie rod adjuster   39. Hex lock nut

Outer tie rod mounting

loosen the alternator adjuster bolt, then, move the alternator until the correct tension is attained.
3. Tighten the alternator bolts.

SYSTEM BLEEDING

If the power steering system has been serviced, an accurate fluid level reading cannot be obtained until the air is bled from the system.
1. With the wheels turned all the way to the left, add power steering fluid to the **COLD** mark on the fluid level indicator.
2. Start the engine and run at fast idle momentarily, shut engine off and recheck fluid level. If necessary add fluid to to bring level to the **COLD** mark.
3. Start the engine and bleed the system by turning the wheels from side to side without hitting the stops.

NOTE: Fluid with air in it has a light tan or red appearance.

4. Return the wheels to the center position and keep the engine running for two or three minutes.
5. Road test the car and recheck the fluid level making sure it is at the **HOT** mark.

Tie Rod Ends
REMOVAL & INSTALLATION
Outer Tie Rod End

1. Raise and safely support the front of the vehicle.
2. Remove the tie rod ball joint to steering knuckle nut.
3. Loosen the tie rod end pinch bolt.
4. Using the Steering Linkage Puller tool No. J–24319–01 or equivalent, separate the tie rod from the steering knuckle.
5. Remove the tie rod end from the tie rod adjuster. When unscrewing the tie rod, record the number of revolutions to remove it, this will aid in installation.

6. To install, reverse the removal procedures. Turn the new tie rod in the number of turns required to remove it. Torque the tie rod to steering knuckle nut to 43–50 ft. lbs. and the tie rod end pinch bolt to 41 ft. lbs. Check and adjust the front end alignment.

Inner Tie Rod End

1. Pry off center bolt lock plate and dispose of it.
2. Remove the inner tie rod retaining bolt and slide the tie rod from behind the bolt support. Loosen the pinch bolt at the outer tie rod and remove the inner tie rod.

Removing inner tie rod assemblies

NOTE: If both tie rods are to be removed the rack and pinion must be kept in position. This can be accomplished by install a retaining bolt in the tie rod bolt hole of the rack after removing the first tie rod.

3. Install the inner tie rod to the outer tie rod and tighten the pinch bolt to 41 ft. lbs. Slip the inside end of the tie rod behind the bolt support and install the lock plate and bolt. Tighten the mounting bolt to 65 ft. lbs.

BRAKES

For all brake system repair service procedures not detailed below, please refer to "Brakes" in the Unit Repair section.

Master Cylinder

REMOVAL & INSTALLATION

1. Disconnect the electrical connector from the reservoir cap.
2. Disconnect and plug the brake lines from the master cylinder.
3. Remove the master cylinder to cowl or master cylinder to power brake booster nuts.
4. Remove the master cylinder from the vehicle.
5. To install, use new self locking nuts and reverse the removal procedures. Torque the master cylinder to cowl (or power brake booster) nuts to

Master cylinder to booster attachment

13 ft. lbs. Refill the master cylinder reservoir with clean brake fluid and bleed the brake system.

Proportioning Valve

Since the valves are adjusted in pairs, they must be replaced in pairs.

REMOVAL & INSTALLATION

1. Disconnect and plug the brake lines from the proportioning valves.
2. Remove the proportioning valves from the master cylinder.

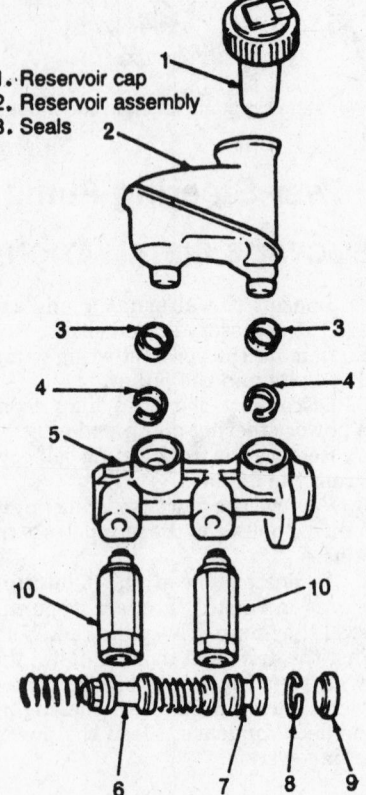

1. Reservoir cap
2. Reservoir assembly
3. Seals
4. Retaining clamps
5. Cylinder body
6. Secondary piston assembly
7. Primary piston
8. Retainer
9. Seal ring
10. Proportioning valves

Exploded view of the master cylinder

3. Be sure the valves are stamped with identical part numbers.
4. To install, reverse the removal procedures. Torque the proportioning valve to master cylinder to 30 ft. lbs. Refill the master cylinder reservoir with clean brake fluid and bleed the brake system.

Power Brake Booster

REMOVAL & INSTALLATION

1. Remove the master cylinder from the booster, do not disconnect the brake lines.
2. Remove the vacuum hose from the intake manifold.
3. Remove the windshield washer reservoir.
4. From under the dash, remove the brake light switch and the brake spring.
5. Remove the push rod retainer and the pin.
6. If not equipped with power steering, remove the brake pedal bracket to dash nuts. If equipped with power

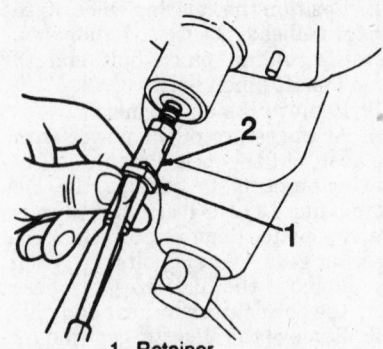

1. Retainer
2. Adjustment sleeve

Removing the retaining ring from the push rod

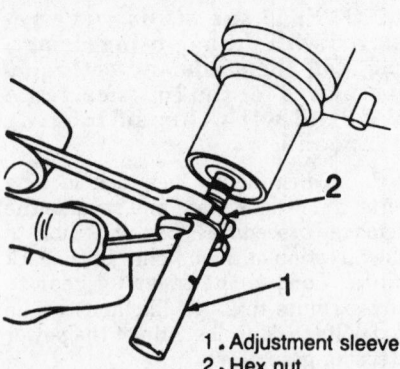

1. Adjustment sleeve
2. Hex nut

Removing the hex nut from the adjustment sleeve

steering, remove the lower mounting screw from behind the fluid lines using a flat head socket wrench.
7. To remove the power brake booster and bracket, tilt the brake servo slightly and remove it upwards.

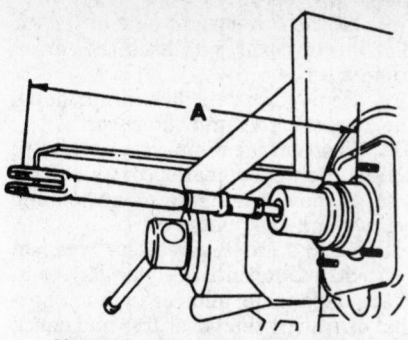

Measuring the push rod length

8. From the power brake booster, remove the 2 part support bracket and the rubber boot.

9. Remove the push rod retainer and push rod, then, unscrew and remove the adjuster sleeve from the piston rod.

10. Unscrew the hex nut.

11. To install, reverse the removal procedures. Adjust the adjuster sleeve so the distance **A** is 10.96 in. Torque the 2 booster bracket nuts to 16 ft. lbs., the power booster/bracket to dash bolts to 16 ft. lbs., the master cylinder mounting nuts to 13 ft. lbs. Start the engine and check the brake operation.

Wheel Cylinder

REMOVAL & INSTALLATION

1. Raise and safely support the rear of the vehicle.

2. Using a piece of chalk, mark the relative position of the wheels to the wheel hub. Remove the wheel/tire assemblies.

3. Remove the brake drum to wheel hub detent screw and the brake drum.

4. Remove the upper return spring and push the brake shoes slightly outward.

NOTE: Note the position of the adjuster assembly and the adjuster actuator to the spring.

5. Clean all dirt and foreign material from the around the wheel cylinder inlet line, the pilot and the bolt.

6. Remove and plug the brake line from the wheel cylinder.

7. Remove the wheel cylinder mounting bolt and the wheel cylinder.

8. To install, reverse the removal procedures. Torque the wheel cylinder mounting bolt to 7 ft. lbs. Adjust the rear wheel brakes and the parking brake. Bleed the brake system.

BLEEDING THE BRAKE SYSTEM

1. To bleed the brakes, first carefully clean all dirt from around the master cylinder filler cap.

2. If a bleeder tank is used, follow the manufacturer's instructions.

3. Remove the filler cap and fill the master cylinder to the lower edge of the filler neck.

4. Clean off the bleeder connections at all of the wheel cylinders or disc brake calipers. Attach the bleeder hose and fixture to the right rear wheel cylinder bleeder screw and place the end of the tube in a glass jar, submerged in brake fluid.

5. Open the bleeder valve $1/2$–$3/4$ of a turn. Have an assistant depress the brake pedal and allow it to return slowly. Continue this pumping action to force any air out of the system.

6. When bubbles cease to appear at the end of the bleeder hose, close the bleeder valve and remove the hose. Check the level of the brake fluid in the master cylinder and add fluid, if necessary.

7. After the bleeding operation at each caliper or wheel cylinder has been completed, fill the master cylinder reservoir and replace the filler plug.

Parking Brake Cable

ADJUSTMENT

1. Raise and safely support the rear of the vehicle.

2. Release the parking brake.

3. Inspect the parking brake cable for free movement.

4. At the equalizer, adjust the self locking nut until the wheels are difficult to turn.

5. Back off the self locking nut until the rear wheels are just free to turn.

REMOVAL & INSTALLATION

1. Release the parking brake lever.

2. Raise and safely support the rear of the vehicle. Remove the rear wheel/tire assemblies.

3. Remove the brake drum mounting screw and the brake drum.

NOTE: If the brake drum is hard to remove, press the parking brake shoe lever backwards through the access hole in the backing plate.

4. At the transaxle tunnel, remove the parking brake cable from the guides.

5. Remove the plastic guides from the fuel tank bracket.

6. Remove the parking brake cable from the rear axle assembly guides.

7. Using a pointed tool, remove the retaining ring from the plastic sleeve in the backing plate.

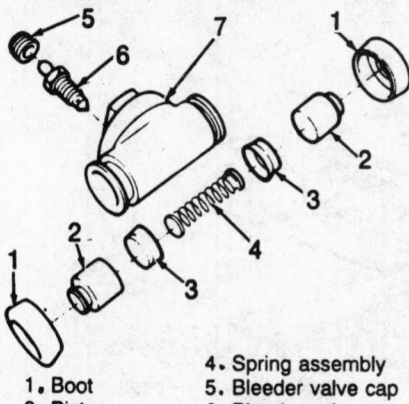

1. Boot
2. Piston
3. Seal
4. Spring assembly
5. Bleeder valve cap
6. Bleeder valve
7. Wheel cylinder

Exploded view of the rear wheel cylinder

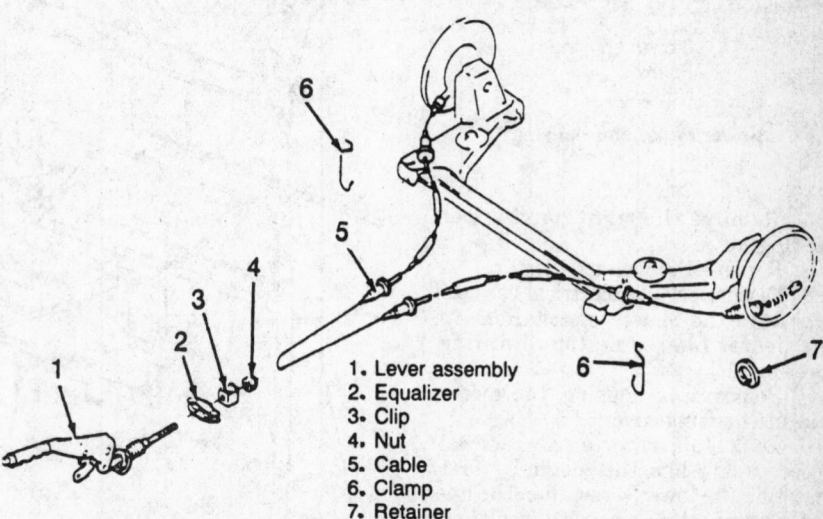

1. Lever assembly
2. Equalizer
3. Clip
4. Nut
5. Cable
6. Clamp
7. Retainer

Exploded view of the parking brake cable system

8. Remove the parking brake cable from the parking brake shoe lever and the brake anchor plate.

9. To install, use a new plastic insert in the backing plate, a new plastic insert in the fuel tank bracket and reverse the removal procedures. Adjust the parking brake cable.

CHASSIS ELECTRICAL

Heater Blower

The heater blower motor is located in the engine compartment attached to the cowl.

REMOVAL & INSTALLATION

1. Disconnect the negative battery cable.
2. Remove the wiper arms.
3. Remove the wind deflector screws and the deflector halves.
4. Remove the right hand windshield washer nozzle from the water deflector.
5. Remove the dash panel seal and clip.

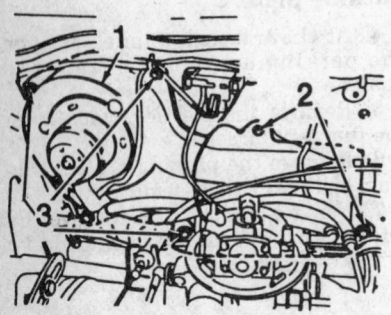

1. Blower housing
2. Screw
3. Nut

Blower motor and housing

6. Remove the right hand wiper bearing nut.
7. Remove the water deflector.
8. Disconnect the electrical connectors from the blower motor. Remove the heater blower motor retaining screws.
9. Remove the housing, the motor and the housing cover.
10. To install, reverse the removal procedures. Align the motor by first inserting the lower screw then the upper. Reconnect all electrical leads and check operation.

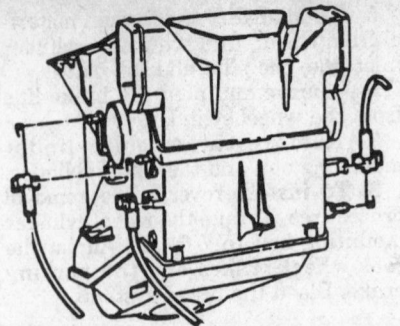

Heater core housing and plenum chamber

Heater Core

The heater core is located under the center of the dash.

REMOVAL & INSTALLATION

1. Disconnect the negative battery cable.
2. Place a clean drain pan under the radiator, remove the lower coolant hose and drain the cooling system.
3. Using spring clips, close off, label and disconnect the heater hoses from the heater core.
4. Using a pointed plastic tool, remove the package panel from in front of the console.
5. Position the heater control levers to the lowest position on the control unit.
6. Remove the temperature control cable from the air distributor and the actuating lever.
7. From under the glove box, remove the kick panel.
8. Remove the temperature valve linkage from the right side of the air distributor.

9. At the lower right side of the air distributor cover, pull back the carpet to access the screw.
10. Remove the air distributor housing cover screws and the cover.
11. Position the temperature valve to access the upper heater core screws.
12. Remove the heater core housing screws and the heater core.
13. To install, reverse the removal procedures. Refill the cooling system. Start the engine, allow it to reach normal operating temperatures and check for leaks.

Radio

REMOVAL & INSTALLATION

1. Disconnect the negative battery cable.
2. From both sides of the console, remove the radio mounting bracket screws.
3. Pull the radio from the dash.
4. Disconnect the electrical connectors and the antenna lead from the radio.
5. To install, plug in electrical connectors and antenna lead. Slide the radio into the dash panel and attach the mounting bracket.

Windshield Wiper Switch

REMOVAL & INSTALLATION

1. Disconnect the negative battery cable.
2. Remove the lower instrument panel trim.
3. Remove the upper steering column panel screws from both sides;

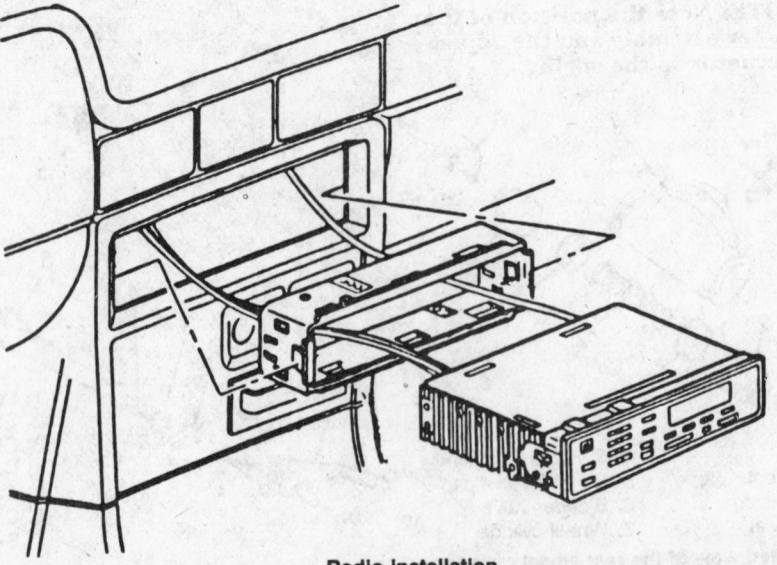

Radio installation

turn the steering wheel 90 degrees for right and left access.

4. Remove the screws from the lower cover panel and remove the panel.

5. Pull the handle from the lock release lever and unscrew the tilt lever (if equipped).

6. Disconnect the electrical connector from the switch housing; push inward on either side of the switch to release it from the retaining clips.

7. To install, push the switch into the retaining clips and connect the electrical lead. Install the lock release lever and tilt lever (if equipped). Install the column cover panels and check switch operation.

Windshield Wiper Motor

REMOVAL & INSTALLATION

1. Disconnect the negative battery cable.

2. Remove the right wiper arm and the right side cowl vent grille.

3. Disconnect the electrical connectors at the wiper motor.

4. Remove the nut securing the crankarm to the motor and the wiper motor mounting nuts. Remove the wiper motor.

5. To install, bolt wiper motor into place and attach the crankarm, electrical connectors. Install the cowl vent grille and attach the wiper arm. Check the operation of the wipers.

Instrument Cluster

REMOVAL & INSTALLATION

1. Disconnect the negative battery cable.

2. Remove the instrument cluster trim plate retaining screws and the trim plate.

3. Pull the instrument cluster forward, disconnect the speedometer cable and the electrical connectors from the rear of the instrument cluster.

4. To install, connect the speedometer and the electrical connectors to the instrument cluster. Install the cluster in the dash and install the retaining screws. Check for the proper operation of the speedometer and the gauges.

Headlight Switch

REMOVAL & INSTALLATION

1. Disconnect the negative battery cable.

2. Using an offset tool, depress the headlight switch retaining clips and pull the switch from the dash.

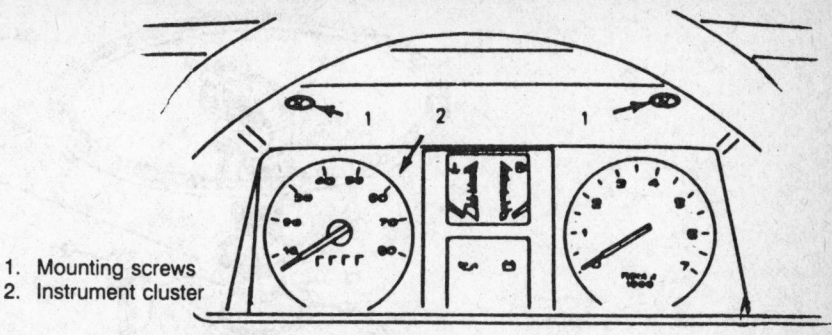

1. Mounting screws
2. Instrument cluster

Instrument cluster retaining screw locations

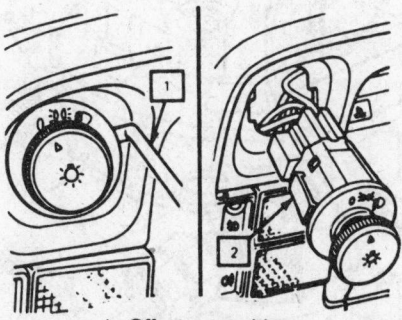

1. Offset screwdriver
2. Retainer

Replacing the headlight switch in the instrument panel

3. Disconnect the electrical connector from the rear of the switch.

4. To install, connect the electrical lead and push switch into position in the dash.

Stoplight Switch

REMOVAL & INSTALLATION

1. Disconnect the negative battery cable.

2. Disconnect the electrical connector from the brake light switch (located above the brake pedal).

3. Remove the switch from the tubular clip on the brake pedal mounting bracket.

4. To install and adjust, insert the switch into the clip until the switch body seats on the clip.

5. Pull the brake pedal rearward against the internal pedal stop. The switch will be moved in the tubular clip providing the proper adjustment.

Fuses and Circuit Breakers

LOCATION

The fuse block is located at the left side of the instrument panel and is reached by pulling the release handle and swinging the panel downward. Always return the fuse block to its full upward, latched position before driving the vehicle.

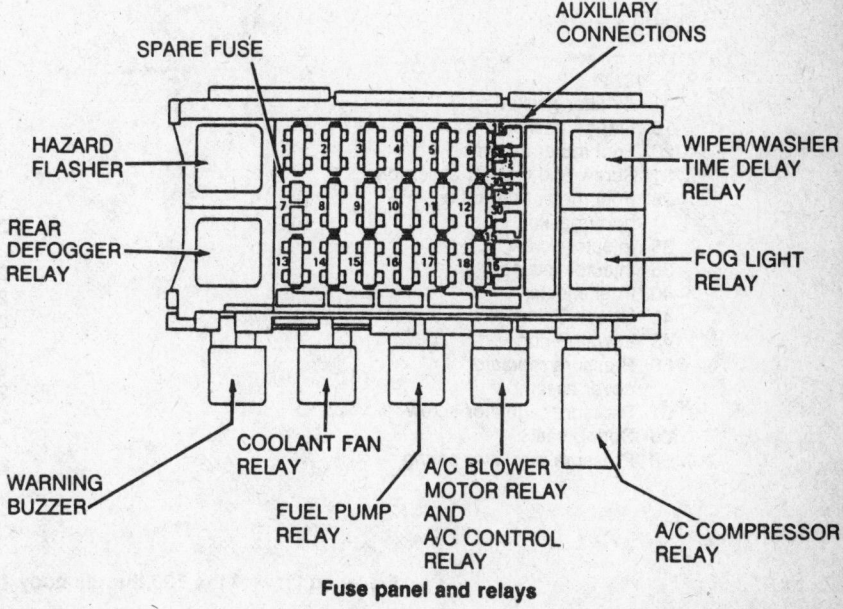

Fuse panel and relays

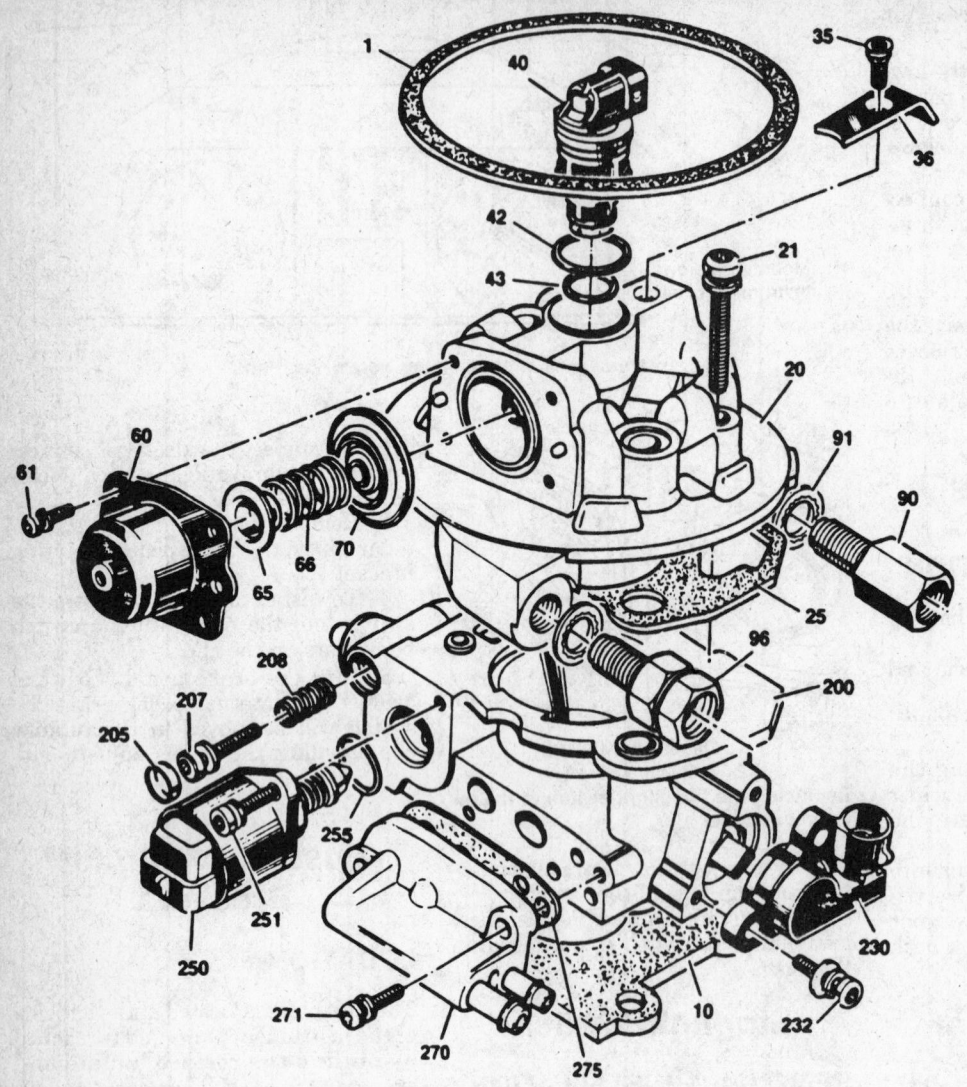

1 Air filter gasket
10 Flange gasket
20 Fuel meter assembly
21 Screw and washer assembly
25 Fuel meter-to-throttle
body gasket
35 Injector screw
36 Injector retainer
40 Fuel injector
42 Upper O-ring
43 Lower O-ring
60 Pressure regulator
cover assembly
61 Pressure regulator screw
65 Spring seat
66 Pressure regulator spring

70 Pressure regulator
diaphragm assembly
90 Fuel inlet nut
91 Fuel nut seal
96 Fuel outlet nut
200 Throttle body assembly
205 Idle stop screw spring
207 Screw and washer assembly
208 Idle stop screw spring
230 Throttle position sensor
232 Screw and washer
250 Idle air control valve
251 Screw
254 Gasket
270 Manifold tubes
271 Manifold Screw
275 Manifold tube gaskets

Exploded view of the 700 throttle body

GM "A" & "X" Body
Front Wheel Drive
"A" Body—Buick Century, Chevrolet Celebrity,
Oldsmobile Cutlass Ciera, Pontiac 6000
"X" Body—Buick Skylark, Chevrolet Citation,
Oldsmobile Omega, Pontiac Phoenix

SERIAL NUMBER IDENTIFICATION

VEHICLE IDENTIFICATION CHART

It is important for servicing and ordering parts to be certain of the vehicle and engine identification. The VIN (vehicle identification number) is a 17 digit number visible through the windshield on the driver's side of the dash and contains the vehicle and engine identification codes. The tenth digit indicates model year and the eigth digit indicates engine code. It can be interpreted as follows:

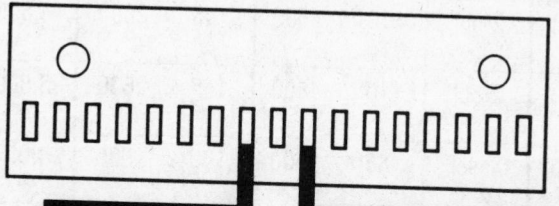

Engine Code						Model Year	
Code	Cu. In.	Liters	Cyl.	Fuel Sys.	Eng. Mfg.	Code	Year
5	151	2.5	4	2 bbl	Pontiac	C	1982
R	151	2.5	4	TBI	Pontiac	D	1983
X	173	2.8	6	2 bbl	Chevrolet	E	1984
Z	173	2.8	6	2 bbl	Chevrolet	F	1985
W	173	2.8	6	MFI	Chevrolet	G	1986
E	181	3.0	6	2 bbl	Buick	H	1987
L	181	3.0	6	MFI	Buick	J	1988
3	231	3.8	6	SFI	Buick	K	1989
B	231	3.8	6	SFI	Buick		
T	263	4.3	6	Diesel	Oldsmobile		

GENERAL ENGINE SPECIFICATIONS

Year	VIN	No. Cylinder Displacement cu. in. (liter)	Fuel System Type	Net Horsepower @ rpm	Net Torque @ rpm (ft.lbs.)	Bore × Stroke (in.)	Compression Ratio	Oil Pressure @ rpm
1982	R	4-151 (2.5)	TBI	90 @ 4000	134 @ 2400	4.000 × 3.000	8.2:1	37.5@2000
	X	6-173 (2.8)	2 bbl	112 @ 5100	148 @ 2400	3.500 × 3.000	8.42:1	30-45 @ 2000
	Z	6-173 (2.8)①	2 bbl	135 @ 5400	142 @ 2400	3.500 × 3.000	8.9:1	30-45 @ 2000
1983	R	4-151 (2.5)	TBI	92 @ 4000	134 @ 2800	4.000 × 3.000	8.2:1	37.5@2000
	X	6-173 (2.8)	2 bbl	112 @ 4800	145 @ 2100	3.500 × 3.000	8.5:1	50-65 @ 1200
	Z	6-173 (2.8)①	2 bbl	135 @ 5400	145 @ 2400	3.500 × 3.000	8.9:1	50-65 @ 1200
	E	6-181 (3.0)	2 bbl	110 @ 4800	145 @ 2600	3.800 × 2.660	8.45:1	35-42 @ 2000
	L	6-181 (3.0)	2 bbl	110 @ 4800	145 @ 2600	3.800 × 2.660	8.45:1	35-42 @ 2000
	T	6-263 (4.3)	Diesel	85 @ 3600	165 @ 1600	4.057 × 3.385	21.6:1	40-45 @ 2000
1984	R	4-151 (2.5)	TBI	92 @ 4000	134 @ 2800	4.000 × 3.000	8.2:1	37.5@2000
	X	6-173 (2.8)	2 bbl	112 @ 4800	145 @ 2100	3.500 × 3.000	8.5:1	50-65 @ 1200
	Z	6-173 (2.8)①	2 bbl	135 @ 5400	145 @ 2400	3.500 × 3.000	8.9:1	50-65 @ 1200
	E	6-181 (3.0)	2 bbl	110 @ 4800	145 @ 2600	3.800 × 2.660	8.45:1	35-42 @ 2000
	L	6-181 (3.0)	2 bbl	110 @ 4800	145 @ 2600	3.800 × 2.660	8.45:1	35-42 @ 2000
	T	6-263 (4.3)	Diesel	85 @ 3600	165 @ 1600	4.057 × 3.385	21.6:1	40-45 @ 2000
1985	R	4-151 (2.5)	TBI	92 @ 4000	134 @ 2800	4.000 × 3.000	8.2:1	37.5@2000
	X	6-173 (2.8)	2 bbl	112 @ 4800	145 @ 2100	3.500 × 3.000	8.5:1	50-65 @ 1200
	W	6-173 (2.8)	MFI	130 @ 4800	155 @ 3600	3.503 × 2.992	8.5:1	50-65 @ 1200
	E	6-181 (3.0)	2 bbl	110 @ 4800	145 @ 2600	3.800 × 2.660	8.45:1	35-42 @ 2000
	3	6-231 (3.8)	MFI	125 @ 4800	195 @ 2000	3.800 × 3.400	8.0:1	35-42 @ 2000
	T	6-263 (4.3)	Diesel	85 @ 3600	165 @ 1600	4.057 × 3.385	21.6:1	40-45 @ 2000
1986	R	4-151 (2.5)	TBI	92 @ 4000	134 @ 2800	4.000 × 3.000	8.3:1	37.5@2000
	X	6-173 (2.8)	2 bbl	112 @ 4800	145 @ 2100	3.500 × 3.000	8.5:1	50-65 @ 1200
	W	6-173 (2.8)	MFI	130 @ 4800	155 @ 3600	3.503 × 2.992	8.9:1	50-65 @ 1200
	3	6-231 (3.8)	SFI	150 @ 4400	200 @ 2000	3.800 × 3.400	8.0:1	37@2400
	B	6-231 (3.8)	SFI	150 @ 4400	200 @ 2000	3.800 × 3.400	8.0:1	37@2400

GENERAL ENGINE SPECIFICATIONS

Year	VIN	No. Cylinder Displacement cu. in. (liter)	Fuel System Type	Net Horsepower @ rpm	Net Torque @ rpm (ft.lbs.)	Bore × Stroke (in.)	Compression Ratio	Oil Pressure @ rpm
1987	R	4-151 (2.5)	TBI	92 @ 4000	134 @ 2800	4.000 × 3.000	8.3:1	37.5@2000
	W	6-173 (2.8)	MFI	130 @ 4800	155 @ 3600	3.503 × 2.992	8.9:1	50-65 @ 1200
	3	6-231 (3.8)	SFI	150 @ 4400	200 @ 2000	3.800 × 3.400	8.0:1	37@2400
1988-89	R	4-151 (2.5)	TBI	92 @ 4000	134 @ 2800	4.000 × 3.000	8.3:1	37.5@2000
	W	6-173 (2.8)	MFI	130 @ 4800	155 @ 3600	3.503 × 2.992	8.9:1	50-65 @ 1200
	3	6-231 (3.8)	SFI	150 @ 4400	200 @ 2000	3.800 × 3.400	8.0:1	37@2400

TBI Throttle Body Injection
MFI Multi-port Fuel Injection
SFI Sequential Multi-port Fuel Injection
① H.O. — High output

GASOLINE ENGINE TUNE-UP SPECIFICATIONS

Year	VIN	No. Cylinder Displacement cu. in. (liter)	Spark Plugs Type	Gap (in.)	Ignition Timing (deg.) MT	Ignition Timing (deg.) AT	Compression Pressure (psi)	Fuel Pump (psi)	Idle Speed (rpm) MT	Idle Speed (rpm) AT	Valve Clearance In.	Valve Clearance Ex.
1982	R	4-151 (2.5)	R-44TSX	.060	8B	8B	NA	6.0-8.0	950	750	Hyd.	Hyd.
	X	6-173 (2.8)	R-43CTS	.045	10B	10B	NA	6.0-8.0	800	600	Hyd.	Hyd.
	Z	6-173 (2.8)①	R-42CTS	.045	6B	10B	NA	6.0-8.0	850②	750	Hyd.	Hyd.
1983	R	4-151 (2.5)	R-44TSX	.060	8B	8B	NA	6.0-8.0	950	750	Hyd.	Hyd.
	X	6-173 (2.8)	R-43CTS	.045	10B	10B	NA	6.0-7.5	800	600	Hyd.	Hyd.
	Z	6-173 (2.8)①	R-42CTS	.045	6B	10B	NA	6.0-7.5	850②	750	Hyd.	Hyd.
	L	6-181 (3.0)	R-44TS8	.080	—	15B	NA	6.0-8.0	—	④	Hyd.	Hyd.
	E	6-181 (3.0)	R-44TS8	.080	—	15B	NA	6.0-8.0	—	④	Hyd.	Hyd.
1984	R	4-151 (2.5)	R-44TSX	.060	8B	8B	NA	6.0-8.0	950	750	Hyd.	Hyd.
	X	6-173 (2.8)	R-43CTS	.045	10B	10B	NA	6.0-7.5	800	600	Hyd.	Hyd.
	Z	6-173 (2.8)①	R-42CTS	.045	6B	10B	NA	6.0-7.5	850②	750	Hyd.	Hyd.
	L	6-181 (3.0)	R-44TS8	.080	—	15B	NA	4.0-8.0	—	④	Hyd.	Hyd.
	E	6-181 (3.0)	R-44TS8	.080	—	15B	NA	6.0-8.0	—	④	Hyd.	Hyd.
1985	R	4-151 (2.5)	R-43TSX	.060	③	③	NA	6.0-7.0	③	③	Hyd.	Hyd.
	X	6-173 (2.8)	R-43CTS	.045	③	③	NA	6.0-7.0	③	③	Hyd.	Hyd.
	W	6-173 (2.8)	R-42CTS	.045	③	③	NA	9.0-13.0	③	③	Hyd.	Hyd.
	E	6-181 (3.0)	R-44TS	.060	①	①	NA	4.0-6.5	③	③	Hyd.	Hyd.
	3	6-231 (3.8)	R-44TS8	.080	③	③	NA	34.0-40.0	③	③	Hyd.	Hyd.
1986	R	4-151 (2.5)	R-43TSX	.060	③	③	NA	6.0-7.0	③	③	Hyd.	Hyd.
	X	6-173 (2.8)	R-43CTS	.045	③	③	NA	6.0-7.0	③	③	Hyd.	Hyd.
	W	6-173 (2.8)	R-42CTS	.045	③	③	NA	40.0-46.0	③	③	Hyd.	Hyd.
	3	6-231 (3.8)	R-44TS8	.080	③	③	NA	34.0-40.0	③	③	Hyd.	Hyd.
	B	6-231 (3.8)	R-44LTS	.045	①	①	NA	34.0-40.0	③	③	Hyd.	Hyd.

GASOLINE ENGINE TUNE-UP SPECIFICATIONS

Year	VIN	No. Cylinder Displacement cu. in. (liter)	Spark Plugs Type	Spark Plugs Gap (in.)	Ignition Timing (deg.) MT	Ignition Timing (deg.) AT	Compression Pressure (psi)	Fuel Pump (psi)	Idle Speed (rpm) MT	Idle Speed (rpm) AT	Valve Clearance In.	Valve Clearance Ex.
1987	R	4-151 (2.5)	R-43TSX	.060	③	③	NA	6.0-7.0	③	③	Hyd.	Hyd.
	W	6-173 (2.8)	R-42CTS	.045	③	③	NA	40.0-46.0	③	③	Hyd.	Hyd.
	3	6-231 (3.8)	R-44TS8	.080	③	③	NA	34.0-40.0	③	③	Hyd.	Hyd.
1988	R	4-151 (2.5)	R-43TS6	.060	③	③	NA	6.0-7.0	③	③	Hyd.	Hyd.
	W	6-173 (2.8)	R-43LTSE	.045	③	③	NA	40.0-46.0	③	③	Hyd.	Hyd.
	3	6-231 (3.8)	R-44LTS	.080	③	③	NA	34.0-40.0	③	③	Hyd.	Hyd.
1989		SEE UNDERHOOD SPECIFICATIONS STICKER										

① High Output
② California: 750
③ Refer to underhood specifications sticker
④ See text

DIESEL ENGINE TUNE-UP SPECIFICATIONS

Year	VIN	No. Engine Displacement cu. in. (liter)	Valve Clearance Intake (in.)	Valve Clearance Exhaust (in.)	Intake Valve Opens (deg.)	Injection Pump Setting (deg.)	Injection Nozzle Pressure (psi) New	Injection Nozzle Pressure (psi) Used	Idle Speed (rpm)	Cranking Compression Pressure (psi)
1983	T	6-263 (4.3)	Hyd.	Hyd.	16	①	1000	850	650	300
1984	T	6-263 (4.3)	Hyd.	Hyd.	16	①	1000	850	650	300
1985	T	6-263 (4.3)	Hyd.	Hyd.	16	①	1000	850	650	300

① Refer to the underhood sticker

FIRING ORDERS

NOTE: To avoid confusion, always replace sparkplug wires one at a time.

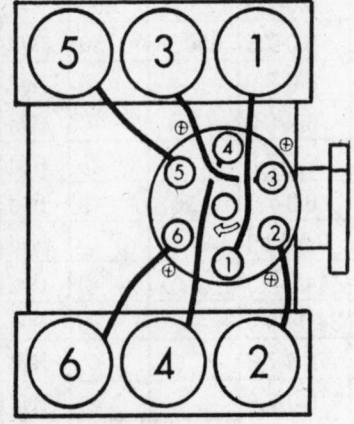

GM (Buick) 181 V6 (3.0L)
GM (Buick) 231 V6 (3.8 L)
Engine firing order: 1-6-5-4-3-2
Distributor rotation: clockwise

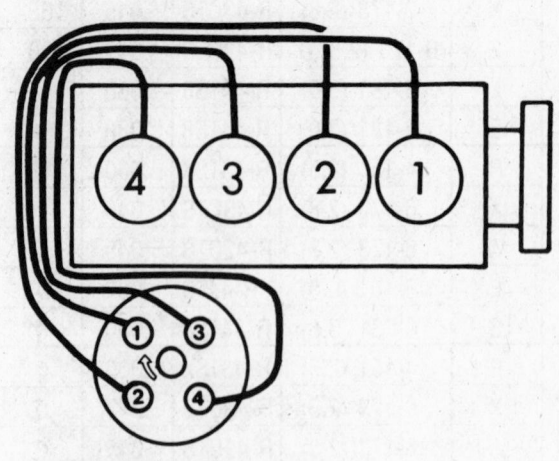

GM (Pontiac) 151-4
Engine firing order: 1-3-4-2
Distributor rotation: clockwise

FIRING ORDERS

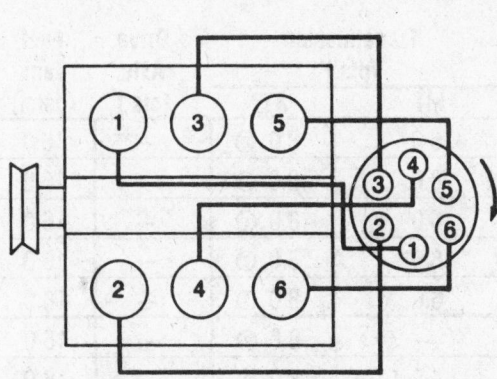

GM (Chevrolet) 173 V6 (2.8L)
Engine firing order: 1–2–3–4–5–6
Distributor rotation: clockwise

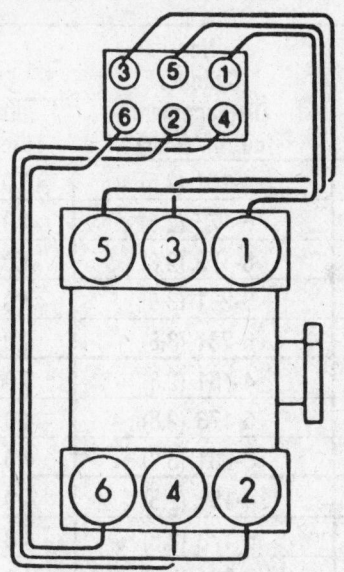

GM (Buick) 181 V6 (3.0 L)
Engine firing order: 1–6–5–4–3–2
Distributor rotation: clockwise

CAPACITIES
A Body

Year	VIN	No. Cylinder Displacement cu. in. (liter)	Engine Crankcase		Transmission (pts.)		Drive Axle (pts.)	Fuel Tank (gals.)	Cooling System (qts.)
			with Filter	without Filter	MT	AT			
1982	R	4-151 (2.5)	3.0	2.8	6.0	10.0	—	16.0	9.5
	X	6-173 (2.8)	4.0	3.0	6.0	10.0	—	16.0	11.5
1983	R	4-151 (2.5)	3.0	2.8	6.0	10.0	—	16.0	9.5
	X	6-173 (2.8)	4.0	3.0	6.0	10.0	—	16.0	11.5
	E	6-181 (3.0)	4.0	3.0	—	10.0 ①	—	16.0	14.25
	L	6-181 (3.0)	4.0	3.0	—	10.0 ①	—	16.0	11.5
	T	6-263 (4.3)	6.0	5.5	—	10.0 ①	—	16.0	13.5
1984	R	4-151 (2.5)	3.0	2.8	6.0	10.0	—	16.0	9.5
	X	6-173 (2.8)	4.0	3.0	6.0	10.0	—	16.0	11.5
	E	6-181 (3.0)	4.0	3.0	—	10.0 ①	—	16.0	14.25
	L	6-181 (3.0)	4.0	3.0	—	10.0 ①	—	16.0	11.5
	T	6-263 (4.3)	6.0	5.5	—	10.0 ①	—	16.0	13.5
1985	R	4-151 (2.5)	3.0	2.8	6.0	10.0	—	16.0	9.5
	X	6-173 (2.8)	4.0	3.0	6.0	10.0	—	16.0	11.5
	W	6-173 (2.8)	4.0	3.0	6.0	10.0	—	16.0	11.5
	E	6-181 (3.0)	4.0	3.0	—	10.0 ①	—	16.0	14.25
	3	6-231 (3.8)	4.0	4.0	—	13.0	—	16.0	12.5
	T	6-263 (4.3)	6.0	5.5	—	10.0 ①	—	16.0	13.5

CAPACITIES
A Body

Year	VIN	No. Cylinder Displacement cu. in. (liter)	Engine Crankcase with Filter	without Filter	Transmission (pts.) MT	AT	Drive Axle (pts.)	Fuel Tank (gals.)	Cooling System (qts.)
1986	R	4-151 (2.5)	3.0	3.0	6.0	8.0 ②	—	16.0	9.6
	X	6-173 (2.8)	4.0	4.0	6.0	8.0 ②	—	16.0	12.5
	W	6-173 (2.8)	4.0	4.0	6.0	8.0 ①	—	16.0	12.5
	3	6-231 (3.8)	4.0	4.0	6.0	8.0 ②	—	16.0	12.0
	B	6-231 (3.8)	4.0	4.0	6.0	8.0 ②	—	16.0	12.0
1987	R	4-151 (2.5)	3.0	3.0	—	8.0 ②	—	16.0	9.5
	W	6-173 (2.8)	4.0	4.0	4.5	8.0 ②	—	16.0	12.5
	3	6-231 (3.8)	4.0	4.0	4.5	8.0 ②	—	16.0	12.0
1988-89	R	4-151 (2.5)	4.0	4.0	4.5	8.0 ②	—	15.7	12.0
	W	6-173 (2.8)	4.0	4.0	4.5	8.0 ②	—	15.7	13.5
	3	6-231 (3.8)	4.0	4.0	4.5	8.0 ②	—	15.7	12.7

① 8.0 pts. with 440 T4 transaxle   ② 12.0 pts. with 125C transaxle

CAPACITIES
X Body

Year	VIN	No. Cylinder Displacement cu. in. (liter)	Engine Crankcase with Filter	without Filter	Transmission (pts.) MT	AT	Drive Axle (pts.)	Fuel Tank (gals.)	Cooling System (qts.)
1982	R	4-151 (2.5)	3.0	3.0	5.9	10.5	—	14	8.5
	X	6-173 (2.8)	4.0	3.0	5.9	10.5	—	14	10.5
1983	R	4-151 (2.5)	3.0	3.0	5.9	10.5	—	14	8.5
	X	6-173 (2.8)	4.0	3.0	5.9	10.5	—	14	10.5
	Z	6-173 (2.8)	4.0	3.0	5.9	10.5	—	14	10.5
1984	R	4-151 (2.5)	3.0	3.0	5.9	10.5	—	15	8.5
	X	6-173 (2.8)	4.0	3.0	5.9	10.5	—	15	10.5
	Z	6-173 (2.8)	4.0	3.0	5.9	10.5	—	15	10.5
1985	R	4-151 (2.5)	3.0	3.0	5.9	10.5	—	15	8.5
	X	6-173 (2.8)	4.0	3.0	5.9	10.5	—	15	10.5
	W	6-173 (2.8)	4.0	3.0	5.9	10.5	—	15	10.5
	Z	6-173 (2.8)	4.0	3.0	5.9	10.5	—	15	10.5

CAMSHAFT SPECIFICATIONS
All measurements given in inches.

Year	VIN	No. Cylinder Displacement cu. in. (liter)	Journal Diameter 1	2	3	4	5	Lobe Lift In.	Ex.	Bearing Clearance	Camshaft End Play
1982	R	4-151 (2.5)	1.869	1.869	1.869	—	—	0.398	0.398	0.0007–0.0027	0.0015–0.0050

CAMSHAFT SPECIFICATIONS
All measurements given in inches.

Year	VIN	No. Cylinder Displacement cu. in. (liter)	Journal Diameter 1	2	3	4	5	Lobe Lift In.	Ex.	Bearing Clearance	Camshaft End Play
1982	X	6-173 (2.8)	1.869	1.869	1.869	1.869	—	0.231	0.263	0.0010–0.0040	—
	Z	6-173 (2.8)	1.869	1.869	1.869	1.869	—	0.231	0.263	0.0010–0.0040	—
1983	R	4-151 (2.5)	1.869	1.869	1.869	—	—	0.398	0.398	0.0007–0.0027	0.0015–0.0050
	X	6-173 (2.8)	1.869	1.869	1.869	1.869	—	0.231	0.263	0.0010–0.0040	—
	Z	6-173 (2.8)	1.869	1.869	1.869	1.869	—	0.231	0.263	0.0010–0.0040	—
	E	6-181 (3.0)	1.786	1.786	1.786	1.786	1.786	0.406	0.406	①	—
	L	6-181 (3.0)	1.786	1.786	1.786	1.786	1.786	0.406	0.406	①	—
	T	6-263 (4.3)	②	2.205	2.185	2.165	—	NA	NA	0.0020–0.0059	0.0008–0.0228
1984	R	4-151 (2.5)	1.869	1.869	1.869	—	—	0.398	0.398	0.0007–0.0027	0.0015–0.0050
	X	6-173 (2.8)	1.869	1.869	1.869	1.869	—	0.231	0.263	0.0010–0.0040	—
	Z	6-173 (2.8)	1.869	1.869	1.869	1.869	—	0.231	0.263	0.0010–0.0040	—
	E	6-181 (3.0)	1.786	1.786	1.786	1.786	1.786	0.406	0.406	①	—
	L	6-181 (3.0)	1.786	1.786	1.786	1.786	1.786	0.406	0.406	①	—
	T	6-263 (4.3)	②	2.205	2.185	2.165	—	NA	NA	0.0020–0.0059	0.0008–0.0228
1985	R	4-151 (2.5)	1.869	1.869	1.869	—	—	0.232	0.232	0.0007–0.0027	0.0015–0.0050
	X	6-173 (2.8)	1.869	1.869	1.869	1.869	—	0.231	0.263	0.0010–0.0040	—
	W	6-173 (2.8)	1.869	1.869	1.869	1.869	—	0.231	0.263	0.0010–0.0040	—
	E	6-181 (3.0)	1.786	1.786	1.786	1.786	1.786	0.406	0.406	①	—
	3	6-231 (3.8)	1.786	1.786	1.786	1.786	1.786	0.406	0.406	①	—
	T	6-263 (4.3)	②	2.205	2.185	2.165	—	NA	NA	0.0020–0.0059	0.0008–0.0228
1986	R	4-151 (2.5)	1.869	1.869	1.869	—	—	0.232	0.232	0.0007–0.0027	0.0015–0.0050
	X	6-173 (2.8)	1.869	1.869	1.869	1.869	—	0.263	0.273	0.0010–0.0040	—
	W	6-173 (2.8)	1.869	1.869	1.869	1.869	—	0.263	0.273	0.0010–0.0040	—
	3	6-231 (3.8)	1.786	1.786	1.786	1.786	1.786	0.397	0.397	①	—
	B	6-231 (3.8)	1.786	1.786	1.786	1.786	1.786	0.397	0.397	①	—

CAMSHAFT SPECIFICATIONS
All measurements given in inches.

Year	VIN	No. Cylinder Displacement cu. in. (liter)	Journal Diameter 1	2	3	4	5	Lobe Lift In.	Ex.	Bearing Clearance	Camshaft End Play
1987	R	4-151 (2.5)	1.869	1.869	1.869	—	—	0.232	0.232	0.0007–0.0027	0.0015–0.0050
	W	6-173 (2.8)	1.869	1.869	1.869	1.869	—	0.263	0.273	0.0010–0.0040	—
	3	6-231 (3.8)	1.786	1.786	1.786	1.786	1.786	0.397	0.397	①	—
1988-89	R	4-151 (2.5)	1.869	1.869	1.869	—	—	0.232	0.232	0.0007–0.0027	0.0015–0.0050
	W	6-173 (2.8)	1.8678–1.8815	1.8678–1.8815	1.8678–1.8815	1.8678–1.8815	—	0.262	0.273	0.0010–0.0040	—
	3	6-231 (3.8)	1.785–1.786	1.785–1.786	1.785–1.786	1.785–1.786	1.785–1.786	0.245	0.245	0.0005–0.0035	—

NA—Not available
① No.1: 0.0005–0.0025
  No.2-5: 0.0005–0.0035

② No. 1 bearing is not boreable, but must be replaced separately

CRANKSHAFT AND CONNECTING ROD SPECIFICATIONS
All measurements are given in inches.

Year	VIN	No. Cylinder Displacement cu. in. (liter)	Crankshaft Main Brg. Journal Dia.	Main Brg. Oil Clearance	Shaft End-play	Thrust on No.	Connecting Rod Journal Diameter	Oil Clearance	Side Clearance
1982	R	4-151 (2.5)	2.2995–2.3005	0.0005–0.0022	0.0035–0.0085	5	1.9995–2.0005	0.0005–0.0026	0.006–0.022
	X	6-173 (2.8)	2.4397–2.4946	0.0017–0.0030	0.0020–0.0067	3	1.9984–1.9994	0.0014–0.0036	0.006–0.017
	Z	6-173 (2.8)	2.4397–2.4946	0.0017–0.0030	0.0020–0.0067	3	1.9984–1.9994	0.0014–0.0036	0.006–0.017
1983	R	4-151 (2.5)	2.2995–2.3005	0.0005–0.0022	0.0035–0.0085	5	1.9995–2.0005	0.0005–0.0026	0.006–0.022
	X	6-173 (2.8)	2.4397–2.4946	0.0017–0.0030	0.0020–0.0067	3	1.9984–1.9994	0.0014–0.0036	0.006–0.017
	Z	6-173 (2.8)	2.4397–2.4946	0.0017–0.0030	0.0020–0.0067	3	1.9984–1.9994	0.0014–0.0036	0.006–0.017
	E	6-181 (3.0)	2.4990–2.5000	0.0003–0.0018	0.0030–0.0090	2	2.2487–2.2495	0.0005–0.0026	0.006–0.022
	L	6-181 (3.0)	2.4990–2.5000	0.0003–0.0018	0.0030–0.0090	2	2.2487–2.2495	0.0005–0.0026	0.006–0.022
	T	6-263 (4.3)	2.9993–3.0003	①	0.0035–0.0135	4	2.2490–2.2510	0.0003–0.0025	0.008–0.021
1984	R	4-151 (2.5)	2.2995–2.3005	0.0005–0.0022	0.0035–0.0085	5	1.9995–2.0005	0.0005–0.0026	0.006–0.022
	X	6-173 (2.8)	2.4397–2.4946	0.0017–0.0030	0.0020–0.0067	3	1.9984–1.9994	0.0014–0.0036	0.006–0.017

CRANKSHAFT AND CONNECTING ROD SPECIFICATIONS
All measurements are given in inches.

Year	VIN	No. Cylinder Displacement cu. in. (liter)	Crankshaft Main Brg. Journal Dia.	Crankshaft Main Brg. Oil Clearance	Crankshaft Shaft End-play	Thrust on No.	Connecting Rod Journal Diameter	Connecting Rod Oil Clearance	Connecting Rod Side Clearance
1984	Z	6-173 (2.8)	2.4397–2.4946	0.0017–0.0030	0.0020–0.0067	3	1.9984–1.9994	0.0014–0.0036	0.006–0.017
	E	6-181 (3.0)	2.4990–2.5000	0.0003–0.0018	0.0030–0.0090	2	2.2487–2.2495	0.0005–0.0026	0.006 0.022
	L	6-181 (3.0)	2.4990–2.5000	0.0003–0.0018	0.0030–0.0090	2	2.2487–2.2495	0.0005–0.0026	0.006 0.022
	T	6-263 (4.3)	2.9993–3.0003	①	0.0035–0.0135	4	2.2490–2.2510	0.0003–0.0025	0.008–0.021
1985	R	4-151 (2.5)	2.2995–2.3005	0.0005–0.0022	0.0035–0.0085	5	1.9995–2.0005	0.0005–0.0026	0.006–0.022
	X	6-173 (2.8)	2.4397–2.4946	0.0017–0.0030	0.0020–0.0067	3	1.9984–1.9994	0.0014–0.0036	0.006–0.017
	W	6-173 (2.8)	2.4397–2.4946	0.0017–0.0030	0.0020–0.0067	3	1.9984–1.9994	0.0014–0.0036	0.006–0.017
	E	6-181 (3.0)	2.4990–2.5000	0.0003–0.0018	0.0030–0.0090	2	2.2487–2.2495	0.0005–0.0026	0.006 0.022
	T	6-263 (4.3)	2.9993–3.0003	①	0.0035–0.0135	4	2.2490–2.2510	0.0003–0.0025	0.008–0.021
1986	R	4-151 (2.5)	2.2995–2.3005	0.0005–0.0022	0.0035–0.0085	5	1.9995–2.0005	0.0005–0.0026	0.006–0.022
	X	6-173 (2.8)	2.4397–2.4946	0.0017–0.0030	0.0020–0.0067	3	1.9984–1.9994	0.0014–0.0036	0.006–0.017
	W	6-173 (2.8)	2.4397–2.4946	0.0017–0.0030	0.0020–0.0067	3	1.9984–1.9994	0.0014–0.0036	0.006–0.017
	3	6-231 (3.8)	2.4995	0.0003–0.0018	0.003–0.011	2	2.2487–2.2495	0.0005–0.0026	0.006–0.023
	B	6-231 (3.8)	2.4995	0.0003–0.0018	0.003–0.011	2	2.2487–2.2487	0.0005–0.0026	0.006–0.023
1987	R	4-151 (2.5)	2.2995–2.3005	0.0005–0.0022	0.0035–0.0085	5	1.9995–2.0005	0.0005–0.0026	0.006–0.022
	W	6-173 (2.8)	2.6473–2.6483	0.0016–0.0033	0.002–0.008	3	1.9983–1.9993	0.0013–0.0026	0.006–0.017
	3	6-231 (3.8)	2.4995	0.0003–0.0018	0.003–0.011	2	2.2487–2.2495	0.0005–0.0026	0.004–0.015
1988-89	R	4-151 (2.5)	2.3000	0.0005–0.0022	0.0035–0.0085	5	1.9995–2.0005	0.0005–0.0026	0.006–0.022
	W	6-173 (2.8)	2.6473–2.6483	0.0016–0.0033	0.002–0.008	3	1.9983–1.9993	0.0013–0.0026	0.006–0.017
	3	6-231 (3.8)	2.4988–2.4998	0.0003–0.0018	0.003–0.011	2	2.2487–2.2495	0.0005–0.0026	0.006–0.023

① No. 1, 2, 3: 0.0005–0.0021
No. 4: 0.0020–0.034

VALVE SPECIFICATIONS

Year	VIN	No. Cylinder Displacement cu. in. (liter)	Seat Angle (deg.)	Face Angle (deg.)	Spring Test Pressure (lbs.)	Spring Installed Height (in.)	Stem-to-Guide Clearance (in.)		Stem Diameter (in.)	
							Intake	Exhaust	Intake	Exhaust
1982	R	4-151 (2.5)	46	45	176 @ 1.254	1.660	0.0010–0.0027	0.0010–0.0027	0.3418–0.3425	0.3418–0.3425
	X	6-173 (2.8)	46	45	155 @ 1.160	1.610	0.0010–0.0027	0.0010–0.0027	0.3410–0.3416	0.3410–0.3416
	Z	6-173 (2.8)	46	45	155 @ 1.160	1.610	0.0010–0.0027	0.0010–0.0027	0.3410–0.3416	0.3410–0.3416
1983	R	4-151 (2.5)	46	45	176 @ 1.254	1.660	0.0010–0.0027	0.0010–0.0027	0.3418–0.3425	0.3418–0.3425
	X	6-173 (2.8)	46	45	155 @ 1.160	1.610	0.0010–0.0027	0.0010–0.0027	0.3410–0.3416	0.3410–0.3416
	Z	6-173 (2.8)	46	45	155 @ 1.160	1.610	0.0010–0.0027	0.0010–0.0027	0.3410–0.3416	0.3410–0.3416
	E	6-181 (3.0)	45	45	220 @ 1.340	1.727	0.0015–0.0035	0.0015–0.0035	0.3401–0.3412	0.3402–0.3415
	T	6-263 (4.3)	①	②	210 @ 1.220	1.670	0.0010–0.0027	0.0015–0.0032	0.3425–0.3432	0.3420–0.3427
1984	R	4-151 (2.5)	46	45	176 @ 1.254	1.660	0.0010–0.0027	0.0010–0.0027	0.3418–0.3425	0.3418–0.3425
	X	6-173 (2.8)	46	45	155 @ 1.160	1.610	0.0010–0.0027	0.0010–0.0027	0.3410–0.3416	0.3410–0.3416
	Z	6-173 (2.8)	46	45	155 @ 1.160	1.610	0.0010–0.0027	0.0010–0.0027	0.3410–0.3416	0.3410–0.3416
	E	6-181 (3.0)	45	45	220 @ 1.340	1.727	0.0015–0.0035	0.0015–0.0035	0.3401–0.3412	0.3402–0.3415
	T	6-263 (4.3)	①	②	210 @ 1.220	1.670	0.0010–0.0027	0.0015–0.0032	0.3425–0.3432	0.3420–0.3427
1985	R	4-151 (2.5)	46	45	176 @ 1.254	1.660	0.0010–0.0027	0.0010–0.0027	0.3418–0.3425	0.3418–0.3425
	X	6-173 (2.8)	46	45	155 @ 1.160	1.610	0.0010–0.0027	0.0010–0.0027	0.3410–0.3416	0.3410–0.3416
	W	6-173 (2.8)	46	45	155 @ 1.160	1.610	0.0010–0.0027	0.0010–0.0027	0.3410–0.3416	0.3410–0.3416
	E	6-181 (3.0)	45	45	220 @ 1.340	1.727	0.0015–0.0035	0.0015–0.0035	0.3401–0.3412	0.3402–0.3415
	T	6-263 (4.3)	①	②	210 @ 1.220	1.670	0.0010–0.0027	0.0015–0.0032	0.3425–0.3432	0.3420–0.3427
1986	R	4-151 (2.5)	46	45	176 @ 1.260	1.690	0.0010–0.0027	0.0010–0.0027	0.3420–0.3430	0.3420–0.3430
	3	6-231 (3.8)	45	45	220 @ 1.340	1.727	0.0015–0.0032	0.3405–0.0032	0.3405–0.3412	0.3405–0.3412
	B	6-231 (3.8)	45	45	220 @ 1.340	1.727	0.0015–0.0032	0.0015–0.0032	0.3405–0.3412	0.3405–0.3412

VALVE SPECIFICATIONS

Year	VIN	No. Cylinder Displacement cu. in. (liter)	Seat Angle (deg.)	Face Angle (deg.)	Spring Test Pressure (lbs.)	Spring Installed Height (in.)	Stem-to-Guide Clearance (in.)		Stem Diameter (in.)	
							Intake	Exhaust	Intake	Exhaust
1987	R	4-151 (2.5)	46	45	176 @ 1.254	1.690	0.0010–0.0027	0.0010–0.0032	0.3410–0.3140	0.3410–0.313
	W	6-173 (2.8)	46	45	215 @ 1.291	1.727	0.0015–0.0027	0.0015–0.0027	0.3412–0.3416	0.3412–0.3416
	3	6-231 (3.8)	45	45	195 @ 1.340	1.727	0.0015–0.0032	0.0015–0.0032	0.3405–0.3412	0.3405–0.3412
1988-89	R	4-151 (2.5)	46	46	176 @ 1.254	1.440	–	–	0.3130–0.3140	0.3120–0.3130
	W	6-173 (2.8)	46	45	215 @ 1.291	1.727	0.0010–0.0027	0.0010–0.0027	0.3412–0.3416	0.3412–0.3416
	3	6-231 (3.8)	45	45	195 @ 1.340	1.727	0.0015–0.0035	0.0015–0.0032	0.3405–0.3412	0.3405–0.3412

① Intake: 45 degrees
Exhaust: 32 degrees
② Intake: 44 degrees
Exhaust: 30 degrees

PISTON AND RING SPECIFICATIONS
All measurments are given in inches.

Year	VIN	No. Cylinder Displacement cu. in. (liter)	Piston Clearance	Ring Gap			Ring Side Clearance		
				Top Compression	Bottom Compression	Oil Control	Top Compression	Bottom Compression	Oil Control
1982	R	4-151 (2.5)	0.0025–0.0033	0.010–0.022	0.010–0.027	0.0015–0.055	0.0015–0.0030	0.0015–0.0030	0.015–0.055
	X	6-173 (2.8)	0.0017–0.0027	0.010–0.020	0.010–0.020	0.020–0.055	0.0012–0.0028	0.0016–0.0037	0.008
	Z	6-173 (2.8)	0.0017–0.0027	0.010–0.020	0.010–0.020	0.020–0.055	0.0012–0.0028	0.0016–0.0037	0.008
1983	R	4-151 (2.5)	0.0025–0.0033	0.010–0.022	0.010–0.027	0.0015–0.055	0.0015–0.0030	0.0015–0.0030	0.015–0.055
	X	6-173 (2.8)	0.0017–0.0027	0.010–0.020	0.010–0.020	0.020–0.055	0.0012–0.0028	0.0016–0.0037	0.008
	Z	6-173 (2.8)	0.0017–0.0027	0.010–0.020	0.010–0.020	0.020–0.055	0.0012-0.0028	0.0016–0.0037	0.008
	E	6-181 (3.0)	0.0008–0.0020	0.013–0.023	0.013–0.023	0.015–0.035	0.0030–0.0050	0.0030–0.0050	0.0035
	L	6-181 (3.0)	0.0008–0.0020	0.013–0.023	0.013–0.023	0.015–0.035	0.0030–0.0050	0.0030–0.0050	0.0035
	T	6-263 (4.3)	0.0030–0.0040	0.015–0.025	0.015–0.025	0.015–0.055	0.0050–0.0070	0.0030–0.0070	0.001–0.005
1984	R	4-151 (2.5)	0.0025–0.0033	0.010–0.022	0.010–0.027	0.0015–0.055	0.0015–0.0550	0.0015–0.0550	0.015–0.055
	X	6-173 (2.8)	0.0017–0.0027	0.010–0.020	0.010–0.020	0.020–0.055	0.0012–0.0028	0.0016–0.0037	0.008

PISTON AND RING SPECIFICATIONS

All measurments are given in inches.

Year	VIN	No. Cylinder Displacement cu. in. (liter)	Piston Clearance	Ring Gap			Ring Side Clearance		
				Top Compression	Bottom Compression	Oil Control	Top Compression	Bottom Compression	Oil Control
1984	Z	6-173 (2.8)	0.0017–0.0027	0.010–0.020	0.010–0.020	0.020–0.055	0.0012–0.0028	0.0016–0.0037	0.008
	E	6-181 (3.0)	0.0008–0.0020	0.013–0.023	0.013–0.023	0.015–0.035	0.0030–0.0050	0.0030–0.0050	0.0035
	L	6-181 (3.0)	0.0008–0.0020	0.013–0.023	0.013–0.023	0.015–0.035	0.0030–0.0050	0.0030–0.0050	0.0035
	T	6-263 (4.3)	0.0030–0.0040	0.015–0.025	0.015–0.025	0.015–0.055	0.0050–0.0070	0.0030–0.0070	0.001–0.005
1985	R	4-151 (2.5)	0.0014–0.0022 ①	0.010–0.020	0.010–0.020	0.020–0.060	0.002–0.003	0.001–0.0550	0.015–0.0550
	X	6-173 (2.8)	0.0017–0.0027	0.010–0.020	0.010–0.020	0.020–0.055	0.0012–0.0028	0.0016–0.0037	0.008
	W	6-173 (2.8)	0.0017–0.0027	0.010–0.020	0.010–0.020	0.020–0.055	0.0012–0.0028	0.0016–0.0037	0.008
	E	6-181 (3.0)	0.0008–0.0020	0.013–0.023	0.013–0.023	0.015–0.035	0.0030–0.0050	0.0030–0.0050	0.0035
	3	6-231 (3.8)	0.0008–0.0020	0.010–0.020	0.010–0.020	0.015–0.055	0.003–0.005	0.003–0.005	0.0035
	T	6-263 (4.3)	0.0035–0.0045	0.019–0.027	0.013–0.021	0.015–0.055	0.005–0.007	0.003–0.007	0.001–0.005
1986	R	4-151 (2.5)	0.0014–0.0022 ①	0.010–0.020	0.010–0.020	0.020–0.060	0.002–0.003	0.001–0.003	0.015–0.055
	X	6-173 (2.8)	0.0017–0.0027	0.010–0.020	0.010–0.020	0.020–0.055	0.0012–0.0028	0.0016–0.0037	0.008
	W	6-173 (2.8)	0.0017–0.0027	0.010–0.020	0.010–0.020	0.020–0.055	0.0012–0.0028	0.0016–0.0037	0.008
	3	6-231 (3.8)	0.001–0.002	0.013–0.023	0.013–0.023	0.015–0.035	0.003–0.005	0.003–0.005	0.0035
	B	6-231 (3.8)	0.001–0.002	0.013–0.023	0.013–0.023	0.015–0.035	0.003–0.005	0.003–0.005	0.0035
1987	R	4-151 (2.5)	0.0014–0.0022 ①	0.010–0.020	0.010–0.020	0.020–0.060	0.002–0.003	0.001–0.003	0.015–0.055
	W	6-173 (2.8)	0.0020–0.0028	0.010–0.020	0.010–0.020	0.020–0.055	0.001–0.003	0.001–0.003	0.005–0.008
	3	6-231 (3.8)	0.001–0.002	0.013–0.023	0.013–0.023	0.015–0.035	0.003–0.005	0.003–0.005	0.0035
1988-89	R	4-151 (2.5)	0.0014–0.0022 ①	0.010–0.020	0.010–0.020	0.020–0.060	0.002–0.003	0.001–0.003	0.015–0.055

PISTON AND RING SPECIFICATIONS
All measurments are given in inches.

Year	VIN	No. Cylinder Displacement cu. in. (liter)	Piston Clearance	Ring Gap			Ring Side Clearance		
				Top Compression	Bottom Compression	Oil Control	Top Compression	Bottom Compression	Oil Control
1988-89	W	6-173 (2.8)	0.0020– 0.0028	0.010– 0.020	0.010– 0.020	①0.020– 0.055	0.001– 0.003	0.001– 0.003	0.005– 0.008
	3	6-231 (3.8)	0.001– 0.002	0.013– 0.023	0.013– 0.023	0.015– 0.035	0.003– 0.005	0.003– 0.005	0.0035

① Measured ⅛ in. down from piston top

TORQUE SPECIFICATIONS
All readings in ft. lbs.

Year	VIN	No. Cylinder Displacement cu. in. (liter)	Cylinder Head Bolts	Main Bearing Bolts	Rod Bearing Bolts	Crankshaft Pulley Bolts	Flywheel Bolts	Manifold		Spark Plugs
								Intake	Exhaust	
1982	R	4-151 (2.5)	85	70	32	200	44	29	44	NA
	X	6-173 (2.8)	70	68	37	75	50	23	25	7-15
	Z	6-173 (2.8)	70	68	37	75	50	23	25	7-15
1983	R	4-151 (2.5)	85	70	32	200	44	29	44	NA
	X	6-173 (2.8)	70	68	37	75	50	23	25	7-15
	Z	6-173 (2.8)	70	68	37	75	50	23	25	7-15
	E	6-181 (3.0)	80	100	40-45	225	60	32	25-37	13
	L	6-181 (3.0)	80	100	40-45	225	60	32	25-37	13
	T	6-263 (4.3)	①	107	42	②	76	41	29	—
1984	R	4-151 (2.5)	92	70	32	200	44	29	44	NA
	X	6-173 (2.8)	70	68	37	75	50	23	25	7-15
	Z	6-173 (2.8)	70	68	37	75	50	23	25	7-15
	E	6-181 (3.0)	80	100	40-45	225	60	32	25-37	13
	L	6-181 (3.0)	80	100	40-45	225	60	32	25-37	13
	T	6-263 (4.3)	①	107	42	②	76	41	29	—
1985	R	4-151 (2.5)	92	70	32	200	44	29	③	15
	X	6-173 (2.8)	70	68	37	75	50	23	25	15
	W	6-173 (2.8)	70	68	37	75	50	23	25	15
	E	6-181 (3.0)	80	100	40-45	200	60	47	25-37	13
	3	6-231 (3.8)	80	100	45	200	60	47	25	13
	T	6-263 (4.3)	①	107	42	②	76	41	29	—
1986	R	4-151 (2.5)	92	70	32	200	44	25	③	15
	X	6-173 (2.8)	65-90	68	37	75	50	23	25	7-15
	W	6-173 (2.8)	65-90	68	37	75	50	23	25	7-15
	3	6-231 (3.8)	③	100	45	200	60	32	37	20
	B	6-231 (3.8)	③	100	45	200	60	32	37	20
1987	R	4-151 (2.5)	③	70	32	162	④	25	③	15
	W	6-173 (2.8)	③	68	37	75	⑤	25	15-23	10-25
	3	6-231 (3.8)	③	100	45	219	60	32	37	20

TORQUE SPECIFICATIONS
All readings in ft. lbs.

Year	VIN	No. Cylinder Displacement cu. in. (liter)	Cylinder Head Bolts	Main Bearing Bolts	Rod Bearing Bolts	Crankshaft Pulley Bolts	Flywheel Bolts	Manifold Intake	Manifold Exhaust	Spark Plugs
1988-89	R	4-151 (2.5)	③	70	32	162	④	25	③	15
	W	6-173 (2.8)	③	68	37	75	⑤	25	15-23	10-25
	3	6-231 (3.8)	③	100	45	219	60	32	37	20

NA Not available

① All exc. No. 5, 6, 11, 12, 13, 14: 142 ft. lbs.
  No. 5, 6, 11, 12, 13, 14: 59 ft. lbs.
② Range 160-350 ft. lbs.
③ Refer to sequence and torque procedure in text
④ Manual Trans.: 69 ft. lbs.
  Automatic Trans.:55 ft. lbs.
⑤ Manual Trans.: 52 ft. lbs.
  Automatic Trans.:46 ft. lbs.

BRAKE SPECIFICATIONS
All measurements in inches unless noted

Year	Model	Lug Nut Torque (ft. lbs.)	Master Cylinder Bore	Brake Disc Minimum Thickness	Brake Disc Maximum Runout	Standard Brake Drum Diameter	Minimum Lining Thickness Front	Minimum Lining Thickness Rear
1982	A Body	100	0.874	0.830	0.002	8.858	0.030	①
	X Body	100	0.874	0.830	0.002	7.880	0.030	①
1983	A Body	100	0.874	0.830	0.002	8.858	0.030	①
	X Body	100	0.874	0.830	0.002	7.880	0.030	①
1984	A Body	100	0.874	0.830	0.004	8.858	0.030	①
	X Body	100	0.874	0.830	0.004	8.858	0.030	①
1985	A Body	100	0.874	0.830	0.004	8.858	0.030	①
	X Body	100	0.874	0.830	0.004	8.858	0.030	①
1986	All	100	0.875	0.830	0.004	8.858	0.030	①
1987	All	100	0.875	0.830	0.004	8.858	0.030	①
1988-89	All	100	0.875	0.830	0.004	8.858	0.030	①

① 0.030 in. over rivet head; if bonded, 0.062 in. over shoe

WHEEL ALIGNMENT

Year	Model	Caster Range (deg.)	Caster Preferred Setting (deg.)	Camber Range (deg.)	Camber Preferred Setting (deg.)	Toe-in (in.)	Steering Axis Inclination (deg.)
1982	All	1P–3P	2P	½N–½P	0	$^3/_{32}$N–$^3/_{32}$P	NA
1983	All	1P–3P	2P	½N–½P	0	$^3/_{32}$N–$^3/_{32}$P	NA
1984	All	1P–3P	2P	½N–½P	0	$^3/_{32}$N–$^3/_{32}$P	NA
1985	All	1P–3P	2P	½N–½P	0	$^3/_{32}$N–$^3/_{32}$P	NA
1986	All	1P–3P	2P	½N–½P	0	$^3/_{32}$N–$^3/_{32}$P	NA
1987	All	1P–3P	2P	½N–½P	0	$^3/_{32}$N–$^3/_{32}$P	NA
1988-89	All	1P–3P	2P	½N–½P	0	$^3/_{32}$N–$^3/_{32}$P	NA

NA Not available
① The caster angle is preset and is not adjustable

N Negative
P Positive

TUNE-UP PROCEDURES

All models are equipped with the HEI distributor and ignition system. When using an auxiliary starter switch on HEI systems, the distributor BATT lead must be disconnected. Failure to do this may cause damage to the grounding circuit in the ignition switch.

HEI SYSTEM TACHOMETER HOOKUP

On all models models with the V6 engine, there is a terminal on the distributor cap marked TACH. On all models with the L4 engine, there is a terminal on the ignition coil where the brown wire is connected. Connect one tachometer lead to this terminal and the other lead to a suitable ground. On some tachometers, the leads must be connected to the TACH terminal and then to the positive battery terminal.

Never ground the TACH terminal; serious module and ignition coil damage will result. If there is any doubt as to the correct tachometer hookup, check with the tachometer manufacturer.

Ignition Timing

ADJUSTMENT

1982–86 Carbureted Models

NOTE: Always consult the underhood sticker on your car before adjusting timing. If the sticker differs from these procedures, follow the sticker.

Timing adjustment is not possible on 1987–89 models with the C³I system, the reluctor wheel is an integral part of the crankshaft and the crankshaft sensor is in a fixed position.

1. Connect a timing light to the No. 1 spark plug wire according to the light manufacturer's instructions. DO NOT PIERCE THE SPARK PLUG WIRE TO CONNECT THE TIMING LIGHT.
2. Disconnect the distributor spark advance hose (if equipped) and plug the vacuum opening.
3. On models with Electronic Spark Timing (EST) distributor, disconnect the 4 terminal plug at the distributor.
4. Start the engine and run it at idle speed.
5. Aim the timing light at the de-

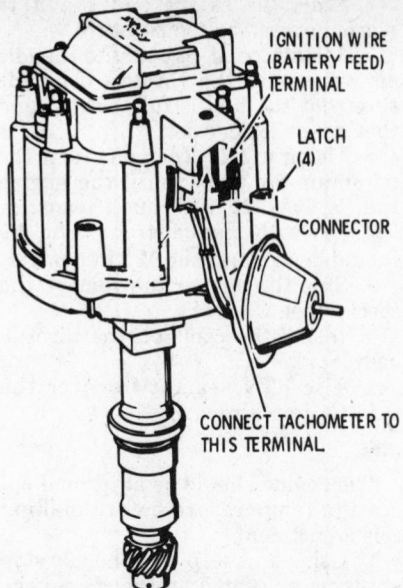

HEI coil-in-cap distributor tachometer hookup

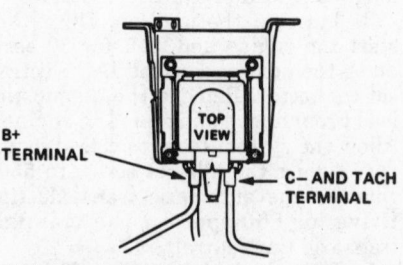

HEI external coil tachometer connection is opposite the BATT (B+) terminal

gree scale just over the harmonic balancer.
6. Adjust the timing by loosening the securing clamp and rotating the distributor until the desired ignition advance is achieved, then tighten the clamp.
7. On the 4 cylinder, loosen the distributor clamp outer bolt, then slide the clamp back slightly. Do not remove the retaining bolt.
8. Adjust the timing, then replace and tighten the clamp. To advance the timing, rotate the distributor opposite the normal direction of rotor rotation. Retard the timing by rotating the distributor in the normal direction of rotor rotation.

NOTE: Before completion of the ignition timing adjustment The ECM should be cleared of trouble codes.

Fuel Injected Models

1. Connect a timing light to the No. 1 spark plug wire according to the light manufacturer's instructions. DO NOT PIERCE THE SPARK PLUG WIRE

TO CONNECT THE TIMING LIGHT.
2. On models with fuel injection, the 4 terminal connector must not be disconnected or the engine will not run. The EST distributor uses no mechanical or vacuum advance and is easily identified by the absence of a vacuum advance and the presence of a 4 terminal connector.
3. To time the fuel injected engines, the Diagnostic Terminal in the ALDL (or ALCL) must be grounded (terminals A and B shorted).
4. Start the engine and run it at idle speed.
5. Aim the timing light at the degree scale just over the harmonic balancer.
6. Adjust the timing by loosening the securing clamp and rotating the distributor until the desired ignition advance is achieved, then tighten the clamp.
7. On the 4 cylinder, loosen the distributor clamp outer bolt, then slide the clamp back slightly. Do not remove the retaining bolt.
8. Adjust the timing, then replace and tighten the clamp. To advance the timing, rotate the distributor opposite the normal direction of rotor rotation. Retard the timing by rotating the distributor in the normal direction of rotor rotation.

NOTE: Before completion of the ignition timing adjustment The ECM should be cleared of trouble codes.

Valve Lash

ADJUSTMENT

4–151, 6–181, 6–231 and 6–263 Engines

Hydraulic valve lifters are used on these engines, no routine adjustment is necessary.

6–173 Engine

Anytime the V6 valve train is disturbed, the valve lash must be adjusted. Crank the engine until the timing mark aligns with the "0" mark on the timing scale, and both valves in the No. 1 cylinder are closed. If the valves are moving as the timing marks align, the engine is in the No. 4 firing position. Turn the crankshaft one more revolution. With the engine in the No. 1 firing position, adjust the following valves:

- Exhaust – 1,2,3
- Intake – 1,5,6

Rotate the crankshaft one full revolution, until it is in the No. 4 firing position. Adjust the following valves:

- Exhaust—4,5,6
- Intake—2,3,4

Adjustment is made by backing off the rocker arm adjusting nut until there is play in the pushrod. Tighten the nut to remove the pushrod clearance (this can be determined by rotating the pushrod with your fingers while tightening the adjusting nut). When the pushrod cannot be freely turned, tighten the nut 1½ additional turns to place the hydraulic lifter in the center of its travel. No further adjustment is required.

Idle Speed and Mixture Gasoline Engines

ADJUSTMENT

Carbureted Models

Mixture adjustments are a function of the Computer Command Control (CCC) system. The idle speed on models equipped with an Idle Speed Control (ISC) motor is also automatically adjusted by the Computer Command Control System, making manual adjustment unnecessary. The underhood specifications sticker will indicate ISC motor use.

On non-A/C models not equipped with ISC, the idle speed is adjusted at the idle speed screw on the carburetor. Before adjusting, check the underhood sticker for any preparations required. On A/C equipped models which do not have an ISC motor, an idle speed solenoid similar to the ones on earlier models is used. This solenoid is adjusted at the solenoid screw, using the same procedures as on earlier models. Consult the underhood specifications sticker for special instructions.

Fuel Injected Models

TBI

This procedure should be performed only when the throttle body parts have been replaced.

NOTE: The following procedure requires the use of a special tool.

1. Remove the air cleaner and gasket.
2. Plug the vacuum port on the TBI marked THERMAC.
3. If the car is equipped with a tamper resistant plug cover the throttle stop screw, the TBI unit must be removed as instructed above, to remove the plug.
4. Remove the throttle valve cable from the throttle control bracket to allow access to the throttle stop screw.
5. Connect a tachometer to the engine.

6. Start the engine and run it to normal operating temperature.
7. Install tool J–33047 into the idle air passage of the throttle body. Be sure that the tool is fully seated and that no air leaks exist.
8. Using a #20 Torx bit, turn the minimum air screw until the engine rpm is 675–725 with auto. trans. or 725–825 with manual trans. The AT should be in Park; the MT in neutral.
9. Stop the engine and remove the special tool.
10. Install the cable on the throttle body.
11. Use RTV sealant to cover the throttle stop screw.

MFI

The engine should be at normal operating temperature before making this adjustment

1. Using an awl, pierce the idle stop screw plug (located on the side of the throttle body) and remove it by prying it from the housing.
2. Using a jumper wire, ground the diagnostic lead of the IAC motor.
3. Turn on the ignition, DO NOT start the engine and wait for 30 seconds, then disconnect the IAC electrical connector. Remove the diagnostic lead ground lead and start the engine. Allow the system to go to closed loop.
4. Adjust the idle set screw to 550 rpm for the automatic transaxle (in Drive) or 650 rpm for the manual transaxle (in Neutral).
5. Turn the ignition Off and reconnect the IAC motor lead.
6. Using a voltmeter, adjust the TPS to 0.55 ± 0.1 volt and secure the TPS.
7. Recheck the setting, then start the engine and check for proper idle operation.
8. Seal the idle stop screw with silicone sealer.

Idle Speed Diesel Engine

ADJUSTMENT

1. Apply the parking brake, place the transmission selector lever in Park and block the drive wheels.
2. Start engine and allow it to run until warm, usually 10–15 minutes.
3. Shut off the engine, remove the air cleaner assembly.
4. Clean the front cover rpm counter (probe holder) and the crankshaft balancer rim.
5. Install the magnetic pick-up probe of tool J–26925 fully into the rpm counter. Connect the battery leads; red to positive (+) and black to negative (–).

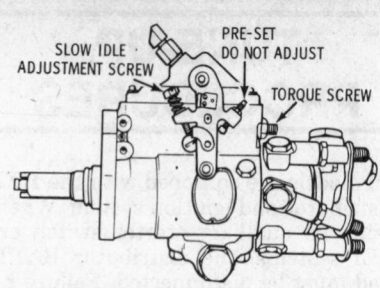

Idle speed adjustment points, CAV pump shown

6. Disconnect the 2-lead connector at the generator.
7. Turn off all electrical accessories.
8. Allow no one to touch either the steering wheel or service brake pedal.
9. Start the engine and place the transmission selector lever in Drive.
10. Check the slow idle speed reading against the one given on the underhood emission control sticker. Reset if required.
11. Unplug the connector from the fast idle cold advance (engine temp.) switch and install a jumper between the connector terminals. Do not allow the jumper to touch ground.
12. Check the fast idle solenoid speed against the one given on the underhood sticker and reset if required.
13. Remove the jumper and reconnect the connector to the temperature switch.
14. Recheck and reset the slow idle speed if necessary.
15. Shut off the engine.
16. Reconnect the lead at the generator.
17. Disconnect and remove the tachometer.
18. If equipped with cruise control adjust the servo throttle cable to minimum slack then install the clip on the servo stud.

ENGINE ELECTRICAL

Distributor

REMOVAL & INSTALLATION

Engine Not Disturbed

——— CAUTION ———

On Chevrolet V6 models the distributor body is involved in the engine lubricating system. The lubricating circuit to the right bank valve train can be interrupted by misalignment of the distributor body.

NOTE: On 4 cylinder engines, it may be necessary to remove the 2 rear cradle attaching bolts and lower the cradle enough to allow access to the distributor. If so, also disconnect the brake line support from the floor pan.

1. Disconnect the negative battery cable.

2. Tag and disconnect all wires leading from the distributor cap.

3. Remove the ignition coil on the 1982–89 L4 engine.

4. Remove the distributor cap by turning the 4 latches counterclockwise. You will need a stubby screwdriver to get at the latches on the 4 cylinder engine because there isn't much room between the distributor and the firewall. Remove the distributor cap and set it aside without disconnecting any of the wires.

5. Remove the vacuum hose from the vacuum advance unit.

6. Remove the hold-down clamp and bolt at the base of the V6 distributor. The 4 cylinder engine has 2 bolts, and a clamp. Remove the outer bolt first, then loosen, but do not remove, the inner bolt. Slide the clamp back and remove it.

7. Before removing the distributor, note the position of the rotor. Scribe a mark on the distributor body indicating the initial position of the rotor.

8. Remove the distributor from the engine. The drive gear on the distributor shaft is helical, and the shaft will rotate slightly as the distributor is removed. Note and mark the position of the rotor at this second position. Do not crank the engine with the distributor removed.

9. To install the distributor, rotate the distributor shaft until the rotor aligns with the second mark you made (when the shaft stopped moving). Lubricate the drive gear with clean engine oil, then install the distributor into the engine. As the distributor is installed, the rotor should move to the mark you made first, indicating rotor position before the distributor was removed. This will ensure proper timing. If the marks do not align properly, remove the distributor and try again.

10. Install the clamp and hold-down bolt. Tighten them until the distributor can just be moved with a little effort.

11. Connect the ignition wire and tachometer wire, and install the distributor cap. Plug the vacuum advance hose (if so equipped). Set the ignition timing. Connect the vacuum hose.

Installation If The Engine Was Disturbed

If the engine was cranked while the distributor was removed, you will have

to place the engine on TDC of the compression stroke to obtain proper ignition timing.

1. Remove the No. 1 spark plug.

2. Place your thumb over the spark plug hole. Crank the engine slowly until compression is felt. It will be easier if you have someone rotate the engine by hand, using a wrench on the crankshaft pulley.

3. Align the timing mark on the crankshaft pulley with the 0° mark on the timing scale attached to the front of the engine. This places the engine at TDC of the compression stroke.

4. Turn the distributor shaft until the rotor points between the No. 1 and No. 3 spark plug towers on the cap for the 4 cylinder engine, or between the No. 1 and No. 6 spark plug towers for the V6.

5. Install the distributor into the engine.

6. Perform Steps 9–11 of the preceding Removal & Installation procedure.

Alternator

For further information on the charging system, please refer to "Charging and Starting" in the Unit Repair section.

PRECAUTIONS

Several precautions must be observed with alternator equipped vehicles to avoid damage to the unit.

● If the battery is removed for any reason, make sure it is reconnected with the correct polarity. Reversing the battery connections may result in damage to the one-way rectifiers.

● When utilizing a booster battery as a starting aid, always connect the positive to positive terminals, and the negative terminal from the booster battery to a good engine ground on the car being started.

● Never use a fast charger as a booster to start vehicles with alternating-current (AC) circuits.

● Disconnect the battery cables when charging the battery with a fast charger.

● Never attempt to polarize an alternator.

● Avoid long soldering times when making alternator repairs. Prolonged head will damage the alternator.

● Do not use test lamps of more than 12 volts when checking diode continuity.

● Do not short across or ground any of the alternator terminals.

● The polarity of the battery, alternator and regulator must be matched and considered before making any electrical connections within the system.

● Never separate the alternator on an open circuit. Make sure all connections within the circuit are clean and tight.

● Disconnect the battery ground terminal when performing any service on electrical components.

● Disconnect the battery if arc welding is to be done on the vehicle.

REMOVAL, INSTALLATION AND BELT TENSION ADJUSTMENT

1. Disconnect battery ground cable to prevent diode damage.

2. Disconnect and label the alternator wiring.

3. Remove the brace bolt. If power steering equipped, loosen pump brace and mount nuts. Detach drive belt(s).

4. On 4 cylinder engines, remove the upper bracket.

5. Support the alternator and remove mount bolt(s). Remove unit from vehicle.

6. Reverse procedure to install. Adjust drive belt to have $1/4$–$1/2$ in. play on longest run of belt.

Voltage Regulator

An alternator with an integral voltage regulator is standard equipment. There are no adjustments possible with this unit; testing procedures will be found in the Charging and Starting Systems Unit Repair Section.

Starter

For further information on the charging system, please refer to "Charging and Starting" in the Unit Repair section.

REMOVAL & INSTALLATION

All Except Diesel

1. Disconnect battery ground cable.

2. Raise and support vehicle.

3. Disconnect all wires at solenoid terminals. Note color coding of wires for reinstallation.

4. Remove starter support bracket mount bolts (4 cylinder engines use 2 nuts; V6 engines use one nut). On engines with solenoid heat shield, remove front bracket upper bolt and detach bracket from starter motor.

5. Loosen the front bracket bolt or nut and rotate bracket clear. Lower and remove starter. Note the location of any shims so that they may be replaced in the same positions upon installation.

6. Reverse procedure to install.

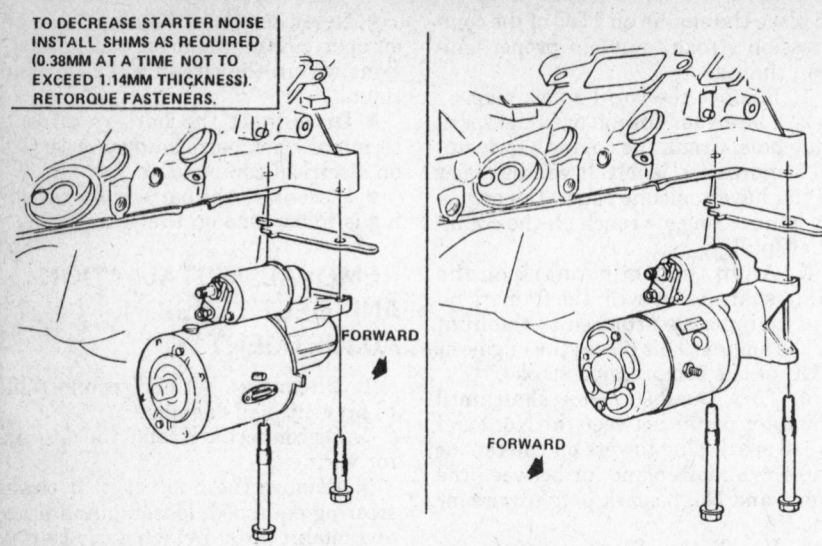

TO DECREASE STARTER NOISE INSTALL SHIMS AS REQUIRED (0.38MM AT A TIME NOT TO EXCEED 1.14MM THICKNESS). RETORQUE FASTENERS.

FORWARD

FORWARD

Diesel starter mounting

21 N·m (15 FT. LBS.)

GLOW PLUG

APPLY LUBE TO THREADS ONLY

Diesel glow plug Installation

Diesel

1. Disconnect the negative cable at the battery(s).
2. Raise and support the car on jackstands.
3. Remove the lower starter shield nut and bend the shield out of the way.
4. Disconnect the wires from the starter. It's a good idea to tag the wires.
5. Remove the front starter bolt. Loosen the rear starter bolt and remove the starter with the rear bolt remaining in the starter housing.
6. Installation is the reverse of removal.

Diesel Glow Plugs

NOTE: A burned out Fast Glow glow plug may bulge then break off and drop into the pre-chamber when the glow plug is removed. When this occurs the cylinder head must be removed and the pre-chamber removed from the head to remove the broken tip. When installing a glow plug, apply lubricant 1052771 or equavalent to the threads only when the engine is equipped with aluminum cylinder heads.

—— CAUTION ——

It is important that the pre-chamber be fully installed flush to the surface of the cylinder head. If this is not done, cylinder head gasket or piston damage can occur.

REMOVAL & INSTALLATION

1. Remove the engine support strut.
2. Rotate the intermediate steering shaft so that the steering gear stub shaft clamp bolt is in the up position and remove the clamp bolt. Then disconnect the intermediate shaft from the stub shaft.

—— CAUTION ——

Failure to disconnect the intermediate shaft from the rack and pinion stub shaft can result in damage to the steering gear and/or intermediate shaft. This damage can cause loss of steering control which could result in a vehicle crash with possible bodily injury.

---

3. Place a floor jack under the front crossmember of the cradle and raise the jack until the jack just starts to raise the car.
4. Remove the front 2 body mount bolts with the lower cushions and retainers. Then remove the cushions from the bolts.
The removal of any one body mount requires the loosening of the adjacent body mounts to permit the cradle to seperate from the body. Take care to prevent breaking the plastic fan shroud, or damaging frame attachments such as steering hoses and brake pipes, during replacement of body mounts.
When installing a body mount, take care to ensure that the body is seated

properly in the frame mounting hole; otherwise, direct metal to metal contact will result between the frame and the body. The tube spacer should be in all bolt-in-body mounts. The insulator and metal washer should be positioned to prevent contact with the frame rail. Do not overtighten the body mount; a collasped tube spacer or stripped bolt may result.

Proper clamping by the mount depends on clean dry surfaces. If the body mount bolt doesn't screw in smoothly, it may be necessary to run a tap through the cage nut in the body to remove foreign material. Take care to ensure that the tap does not punch through the underbody.

Whenever the body is going to be moved in relation to the cradle, the intermediate shaft should be disconnected from the rack and pinion steering gear stub shaft.

—— CAUTION ——

Failure to disconnect the intermediate shaft from the rack and pinion steering gear stub shaft can result in damage to the steering gear and/or intermediate shaft. This damage can cause loss of steering control which could result in a vehicle crash with possible bodily injury.

---

5. Thread the body mount bolts with retainers a minimum of three turns into the cage nuts so that the bolts retain cradle movement.
6. Release the floor jack slowly until the crossmember contacts the body mount bolt retainers. As the jack is being lowered, watch and correct any interference with hoses, lines, pipes and cables.

—— CAUTION ——

Do not place your hands between the crossmember and body mount to remove objects or correct interference while the jack is lowering.

NOTE: Do not lower the cradle without it being restrained as possible damage can occur to the body and underhood items.

7. Reverse the procedure for installation. Torque the intermediate steering shaft clamp bolt to 46 ft. lbs. and the body mount bolts to 77 ft. lbs.

TESTING

For complete diagnosis, testing and repair procedures of the diesel glow plug system, please refer to "Diesel Maintenance" in the Unit Repair section.

GASOLINE ENGINE MECHANICAL

Engine

REMOVAL & INSTALLATION

4-151

WITH MANUAL TRANSAXLE

NOTE: Before attempting this procedure, relieve the pressure in the fuel system as described under "Relieving Fuel Pressure" in the Fuel Section.

1. Disconnect battery cables at battery.
2. Raise the car and support it safely.
3. Remove front mount-to-cradle nuts.
4. Remove forward exhaust pipe.
5. Remove starter assembly (wires attached and swing to side).
6. Remove flywheel inspection cover.
7. Lower the car.
8. Remove air cleaner.
9. Remove all bellhousing bolts.
10. Remove forward torque reaction rod from engine and core support.
11. If equipped with A/C, remove A/C belt and compressor and swing to side.
12. Remove emission hoses at canister.
13. Remove power steering hose (if so equipped).
14. Remove vacuum hoses and electrical connectors at solenoid.
15. Remove heater blower motor.
16. Disconnect throttle cable.
17. Drain cooling system.
18. Disconnect heater hose.
19. Disconnect engine harness at bulkhead connector.
20. With engine lifting tool, hoist engine (remove heater hose at intake manifold and disconnect fuel line).
21. Installation is the reverse of removal.

4-151

WITH AUTOMATIC TRANSAXLE

1. Disconnect battery cables at battery.
2. Drain cooling system.
3. Remove air cleaner and preheat tube.
4. Disconnect engine harness connector.
5. Disconnect all external vacuum hose connections.
6. Remove throttle and transaxle

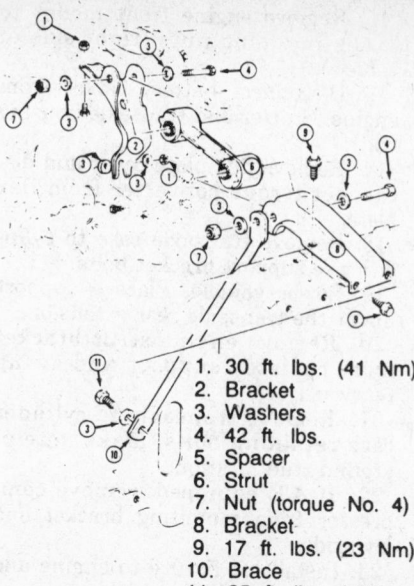

1. 30 ft. lbs. (41 Nm)
2. Bracket
3. Washers
4. 42 ft. lbs.
5. Spacer
6. Strut
7. Nut (torque No. 4)
8. Bracket
9. 17 ft. lbs. (23 Nm)
10. Brace
11. 35 ft. lbs. (48Nm)

Engine mounting strut and bracket

linkage at EFI assembly and intake manifold.
7. Remove upper radiator hose.
8. If equipped with air conditioning, remove A/C compressor from mounting brackets and set aside. Do not disconnect hoses.
9. Remove front engine strut assembly.
10. Disconnect heater hose at intake manifold.
11. Remove transaxle to engine bolts leaving the upper 2 bolts in place.
12. Remove front mount-to-cradle nuts.
13. Remove forward exhaust pipe.
14. Remove flywheel inspection cover and remove starter motor.
15. Remove torque converter to flywheel bolts.
16. Remove power steering pump and bracket and move to one side.
17. Remove heater hose and lower radiator hose.
18. Remove 2 rear transaxle support bracket bolts.
19. Remove fuel supply line at fuel filter.
20. Using a floor jack and a block of wood placed under the transaxle, raise engine and transaxle until engine front mount studs clear cradle.
21. Connect engine lift equipment and put tension on engine.
22. Remove 2 remaining transaxle bolts.
23. Slide engine forward and left from car. Install engine on stand.
24. Installation is the reverse of removal. Do not completely lower the engine with a jack supporting the transaxle.

6-173

WITH MANUAL TRANSAXLE

1. Disconnect cables from battery.
2. Remove air cleaner.
3. Drain cooling system.
4. Disconnect vacuum hosing to all nonengine mounted components.
5. Disconnect accelerator linkage from carburetor.
6. Disconnect engine harness connector.
7. Disconnect radiator hoses from radiator.
8. Disconnect heater hoses from engine.
9. If equipped, remove power steering pump and bracket assembly from engine.
10. Disconnect clutch cable from transaxle.
11. Disconnect shift linkage from transaxle shift levers. Remove cables from transaxle bosses.
12. Disconnect speedometer cable from transaxle.
13. Install engine support fixture. Raise engine until weight is relieved from mount assemblies.
14. Remove exhaust crossover.
15. Remove all but the transaxle to engine retaining bolts.
16. Remove side and crossmember assembly.
17. Disconnect exhaust pipe.
18. Remove all powertrain mount to cradle attachments.
19. Using tool J–28468 or J–33008, pull both axle drive shafts from transaxle assembly.
20. Lower vehicle.
21. Lower left side of engine/transaxle assembly by loosening tool J–22825.
22. Place jack under transaxle.
23. Remove the final transaxle to engine attaching bolt and separate transaxle from engine and lower.
24. Lower vehicle.
25. Install engine lifting fixture.
26. If A/C equipped, remove compressor from mounting bracket and swing aside.
27. Disconnect forward strut bracket from radiator support. Swing aside.
28. Lift engine out of vehicle.
29. Installation is the reverse of removal.

6-173

WITH AUTOMATIC TRANSAXLE

1. Disconnect battery cables from battery.
2. Remove air cleaner.
3. Drain cooling system.
4. Disconnect vacuum hosing to all non-engine mounted components.
5. Disconnect detent cable from carburetor lever.
6. Disconnect accelerator linkage.

7. Disconnect engine harness connector.

8. Disconnect ground strap from engine at engine forward strut.

9. Disconnect radiator hoses from radiator.

10. Disconnect heater hoses from engine.

11. Remove power steering pump and bracket assembly from engine, if equipped.

12. Raise the vehicle and support it safely.

13. Disconnect exhaust pipe.

14. Disconnect fuel lines at rubber hose connections at right side of engine.

15. Remove engine front mount to cradle retaining nuts (right side of vehicle).

16. Disconnect battery cables from engine (Starter and transaxle housing bolt).

17. Remove flex plate cover and disconnect torque convertor from flex plate.

18. Remove transaxle case to cylinder case support bracket bolts.

19. Lining bolts. Make note of ground stud location.

23. If A/C equipped, remove compressor from mounting bracket and lay aside.

24. Install lift fixture to engine and remove engine from vehicle.

25. Installation is the reower vehicle. Place a support under the transaxle rear extension.

20. Remove engine strut bracket from radiator support and swing rearward.

21. Remove exhaust crossover pipe.

22. Remove transaxle to cylinder case retaverse of removal.

6–181 and 231 Engines

1. Disconnect battery cables from battery.

2. Remove air cleaner.

3. Drain cooling system.

4. Disconnect vacuumhosing to all nonengine mounted components.

5. Disconnect detent cable from carburetor lever.

6. Disconnect accelerator linkage.

7. Disconnect engine harness connector.

8. Disconnect ground strap from engine at engine forward strut.

9. Disconnect radiator hoses from radiator.

10. Disconnect heater hoses from engine.

11. Remove power steering pump and bracket assembly from engine.

12. Raise the vehicle and support it safely.

13. Disconnect exhaust pipe at manifold.

14. Disconnect fuel lines at rubber hose connections.

15. Remove engine front mount to cradle retaining nuts (right side of vehicle).

16. Disconnect battery cables from engine (Starter and transaxle housing bolt).

17. Remove flex plate cover and disconnect torque converter from flex plate.

18. Remove transaxle case to cylinder case support bracket bolts.

19. Lower vehicle. Place a support under the transaxle rear extension.

20. Remove engine strut bracket from radiator support and swing rearward.

21. Remove transaxle to cylinder case retaining bolts. Make note of ground stud location.

22. If A/C equipped, remove compressor from mounting bracket and lay aside.

23. Install lift fixture to engine and remove engine from vehicle.

24. Installation is the reverse of removal.

Cylinder Head

REMOVAL & INSTALLATION

4–151 Engine

—————— CAUTION ——————

On fuel injected engines, relieve the pressure in the fuel system before disconnecting any fuel line connections. Refer to the procedure under Gasoline Fuel System. The engine should be overnight cold.

1. Drain the cooling system into a clean container.

2. Remove the air cleaner.

3. Remove the intake and exhaust manifolds as previously outlined.

1. Apply sealing compound No. 102080 or equivalent to bolts shown

2. Mounting surfaces of block assy., head assy. and both sides of gasket must be free of oil.

3. Locating pins

4. Remove the alternator bracket bolts.

5. Remove the A/C compressor bracket bolts and position the compressor to one side. Do not disconnect any of the refrigerant lines.

6. Disconnect all vacuum and electrical connections from the cylinder head.

7. Disconnect the upper radiator hose.

8. Disconnect the spark plug wires and remove the plugs.

9. Remove the rocker arm cover, rocker arms, and pushrods.

10. Unbolt and remove the cylinder head.

11. Clean the gasket surfaces thoroughly.

12. Install a new gasket over the dowels and position the cylinder head.

13. Coat the head bolt threads with sealer and install finger tight.

14. On models through 1986, tighten the bolts in sequence, in three equal steps to the specified torque.

15. On 1987–89 models torque the cylinder head bolts as follows:

• Torque the cylinder head bolts gradually to 25 ft.lbs in the sequence shown in the illustration.

• Torque all bolts except No. 9 in sequence again to 22 ft. lbs. Torque No. 9 to 29 ft. lbs.

• Repeat sequence. Turn all bolts, except No. 9, 120 degrees (2 flats). Turn No. 9 ¼ turn (90 degrees).

16. Install all parts in the revere of removal.

6–173 Engine

LEFT SIDE

1. Raise the vehicle and support it safely.

2. Drain the coolant from the block and lower the car.

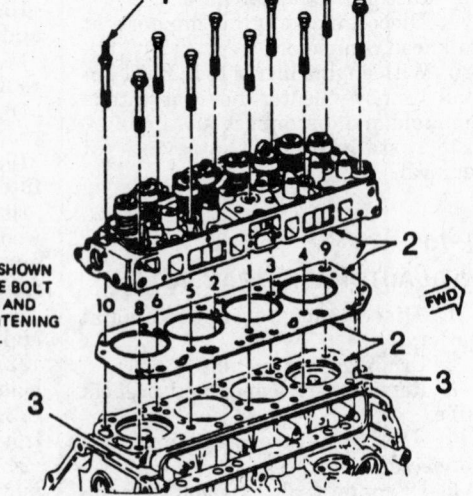

NUMBERS SHOWN DESIGNATE BOLT POSITIONS AND BOLT TIGHTENING SEQUENCE.

4–151 Cylinder head torque sequence, thru 1988

3. Remove the intake manifold.

4. Remove the crossover.

5. Remove the alternator and AIR pump brackets.

6. Remove the dipstick tube.

7. Loosen the rocker arm bolts and remove the pushrods. Keep the pushrods in the same order as removed.

8. Remove the cylinder head bolts in stages and in the reverse order of the tightening sequence.

9. Remove the cylinder head. Do not pry on the head to loosen it.

10. Installation is the reverse of removal. The words "This Side Up" on the new cylinder head gasket should face upwards. On models through 1986, coat the cylinder head bolts with sealer and tighten them to specifications in the sequence shown. On 1987–89 models coat the threads with sealer and using a 12 in. clicker torque wrench torque in sequence to 33 ft. lbs. Rotate the wrench an additional 90 degrees (¼ turn). Make sure the lower ends of the pushrods seat in the lifter seats and adjust the valves.

RIGHT SIDE

1. Raise the vehicle and drain the coolant from the block.

2. Disconnect the exhaust pipe and lower the vehicle.

3. If equipped, removes the cruise control servo bracket.

4. Remove the air management valve and hose.

5. Remove the intake manifold.

6. Remove the exhaust crossover.

7. Loosen the rocker arm nuts and remove the pushrods. Keep the pushrods in the order in which they were removed.

8. Remove the cylinder head bolts in stages and in the reverse order of the tightening sequence.

9. Remove the cylinder head. Do not pry on the cylinder head to loosen it.

10. Installation is the reverse of removal. The words "This Side Up" on the new cylinder head gasket should face upwards. On models through 1986, coat the cylinder head bolts with sealer and tighten them to specifications in the sequence shown. On 1987–89 models coat the threads with sealer and using a 12 in. clicker torque wrench torque in sequence to 33 ft. lbs. Rotate the wrench an additional 90 degrees (¼ turn). Make sure the lower ends of the pushrods seat in the lifter seats and adjust the valves.

6–181 and 6–231 Engine

1. Disconnect negative battery cable.

2. Remove intake manifold.

3. Loosen and remove belt(s).

4. When removing LEFT cylinder head:

    a. Remove oil dipstick.

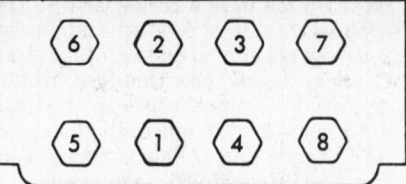

6-173 head bolt torque sequence

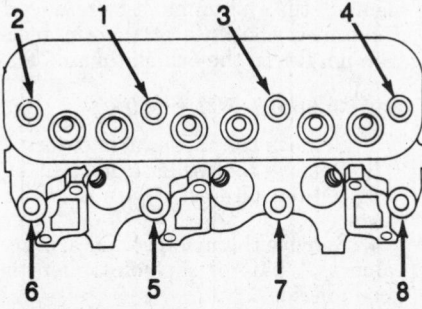

6–181, 231 cylinder head bolt torque sequence, 1982

    b. Remove air and vacuum pumps with mounting bracket if present, and move out of the way with hoses attached.

5. When removing RIGHT cylinder head:

    a. Remove alternator.

    b. Disconnect power steering gear pump and brackets attached to cylinder head.

6. Disconnect wires from spark plugs, and remove the spark plug wire clips from the rocker arm cover studs.

7. Remove exhaust manifold bolts from head being removed.

8. With air hose and cloths, clean dirt off cylinder head and adjacent area to avoid getting dirt into engine. It is extremely important to avoid getting dirt into the hydraulic valve lifters.

9. Remove rocker arm cover and rocker arm and shaft assembly from cylinder head. Lift out pushrods. If lifters are to be serviced, remove them at this time and place them in a container with numbered holes or a similar device, to keep them identified as to engine position. If they are not to be removed, protect lifters and camshaft from dirt by covering area with a clean cloth.

10. Loosen all cylinder head bolts, then remove bolts and lift off the cylinder head.

11. With cylinder head on bench, remove all spark plugs for cleaning and to avoid damaging them during work on the head.

12. Installation is the reverse of removal. Clean all gasket surfaces thoroughly. Always use a new head gasket. The head gasket is installed with the bead downward. Coat the head bolt

threads with thread sealer. On models through 1985, torque the head bolts in three equal stages in the sequence shown and to the specification listed in the Torque Specification Chart. Recheck head bolt torque after the engine has been warmed to operating temperature. On 1986–89 models torque the cylinder head bolts as follows:

- Torque the bolts to 25 ft. lbs. in the sequence shown.
- Then turn each bolt ¼ turn (90 degrees) in sequence.
- Turn each bolt an additional ¼ turn (90 degrees) in sequence.

NOTE: If you should reach 60 ft. lbs. at any time in either of the last 2 steps, you should NOT complete the balance of the 90 degree turn.

OVERHAUL

For all cylinder head overhaul procedures, please refer to "Engine Rebuilding" in the Unit Repair Section.

Rocker Arms/Shafts

REMOVAL & INSTALLATION

4–151 Engine

1. Remove the valve cover.

2. On fuel injected engines, relieve pressure in the fuel system before disconnecting any fuel lines.

3. If only the pushrod is being removed, loosen the rocker arm bolt and swing the rocker arm aside.

4. Remove the rocker arm nut and ball.

5. Lift the rocker arm off the stud, keeping rocker arms in order for installation.

6–173 Engine

NOTE: Some engines are assembled using RTV (Room Temperature Vulcanizing) silicone sealant in place of rocker arm cover gasket. If the engine was assembled using RTV, never use a gasket when reassembling. Conversely, if the engine was assembled using a rocker arm cover gasket, never replace it with RTV. When using RTV, a ⅛ in. bead is sufficient. Always run the bead on the inside of the bolt holes.

Rocker arms are removed by removing the adjusting nut. Be sure to adjust valve lash after replacing rocker arms. When replacing an exhaust rocker,

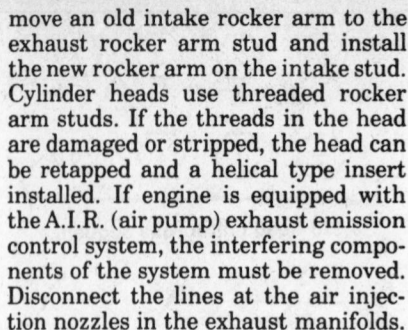

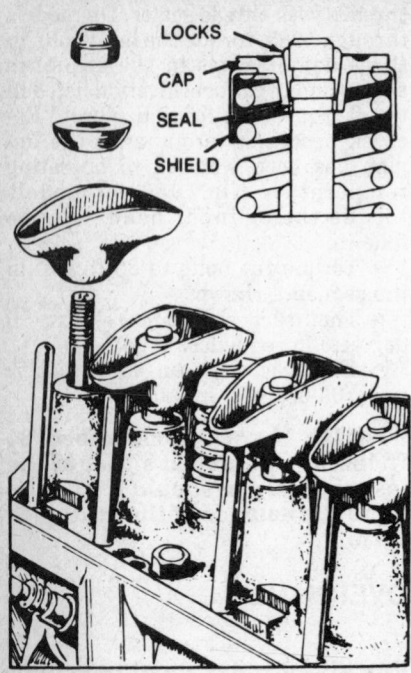

4-151 and 6-173 rocker arm, pivot and nut

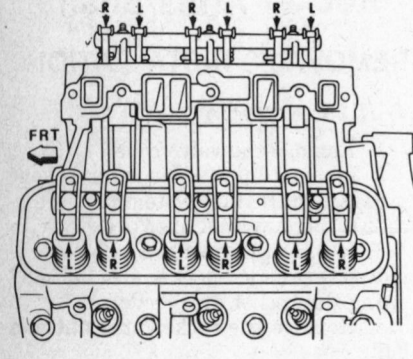

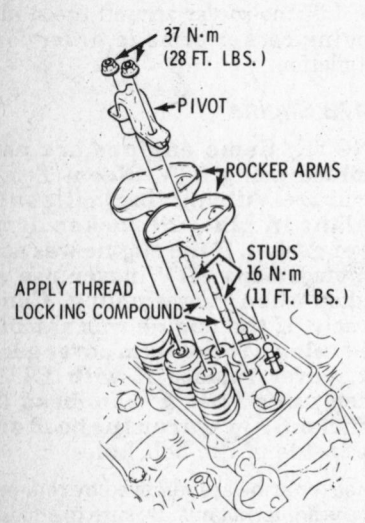

Position of rocker arms on shaft—6-181

move an old intake rocker arm to the exhaust rocker arm stud and install the new rocker arm on the intake stud. Cylinder heads use threaded rocker arm studs. If the threads in the head are damaged or stripped, the head can be retapped and a helical type insert installed. If engine is equipped with the A.I.R. (air pump) exhaust emission control system, the interfering components of the system must be removed. Disconnect the lines at the air injection nozzles in the exhaust manifolds.

6-181 and 6-231 Engines

1. Remove the rocker arm cover(s).
2. Remove the rocker arm shaft(s).
3. Place the shaft on a clean surface.
4. Remove the nylon rocker arm retainers. A pair of slip joint pliers is good for this.
5. Slide the rocker arms off the shaft and inspect them for wear or damage. Keep them in order.
6. Installation is the reverse of removal. If new rocker arms are being installed, note that they are stamped R (right) or L (left). Each rocker arm must be centered over its oil hole. New nylon retainers must be used.

Intake Manifold

REMOVAL & INSTALLATION

4-151 Engine

— CAUTION —

Bleed pressure from the fuel system, if equipped with fuel injection, before attempting this procedure.

1. Remove the air cleaner and the PCV valve.
2. Drain the cooling system into a clean container.
3. Disconnect the fuel and vacuum lines and the electrical connections at the carburetor and manifold.
4. Disconnect the throttle linkage at the EFI unit and disconnect the transaxle downshift linkage and cruise control linkage.
5. Remove the carburetor and the spacer.
6. Remove the bell crank and the throttle linkage. Position to the side for clearance.
7. Remove the heater hose at the intake manifold.
8. Remove the pulse air check valve bracket from the manifold.
9. Remove the manifold attaching bolts and remove the manifold.
10. Install the intake manifold with a new gasket and tighten the retaining bolts in sequence and to the torque value in the appropriate illustration.

6-173 Engine

WITH CARBURETOR

1. Remove the rocker covers.
2. Drain the cooling system.
3. If equipped, remove the A.I.R. pump and bracket.
4. Remove the distributor cap. Mark the position of the ignition rotor in relation to the distributor body, and remove the distributor. Do not crank the engine with the distributor removed.
5. Remove the heater and radiator hoses from the intake manifold.
6. Remove the power brake vacuum hose.
7. Disconnect and label the vacuum hoses. Remove the EFE pipe from the rear of the manifold.
8. Remove the carburetor linkage. Disconnect and plug the fuel line.
9. Remove the manifold retaining bolts and nuts.
10. Remove the intake manifold. Remove and discard the gaskets, and scrape off the old silicone seal from the front and rear ridges.

To install:

1. The gaskets are marked for right and left side installation; do not interchange them. Clean the sealing surface of the engine block and apply a $\frac{3}{16}$ in. bead of silicone sealer to each ridge.
2. Install the new gaskets onto the heads. The gaskets will have to be cut slightly to fit past the center pushrods. Do not cut any more material than necessary. Hold the gaskets in place by extending the ridge bead of sealer ¼ in. onto the gasket ends.
3. Install the intake manifold. The area between the ridges and the manifold should be completely sealed.
4. Install the retaining bolts and nuts, and tighten in sequence to 23 ft. lbs. Do not overtighten; the manifold is made from aluminum, and can be warped or cracked with excessive force.
5. The rest of installation is the reverse of removal. Adjust the ignition timing after installation, and check the coolant level after the engine has warmed up.

6-173 Engine

With MFI

— CAUTION —

Release the fuel pressure from the fuel system. Refer to the procedure under Gasoline Fuel System.

1. Disconnect the battery ground cable.
2. Disconnect the accelerator and T.V. cable bracket at the plenum.
3. Disconnect the throttle body at the plenum.

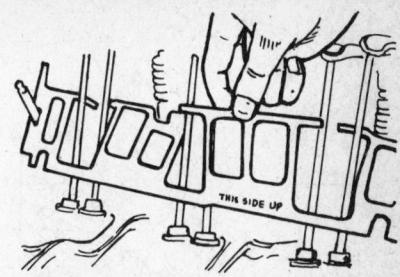

1 34 N.M. (25 LB. FT.)

2 50 N.M. (37 LB. FT.)

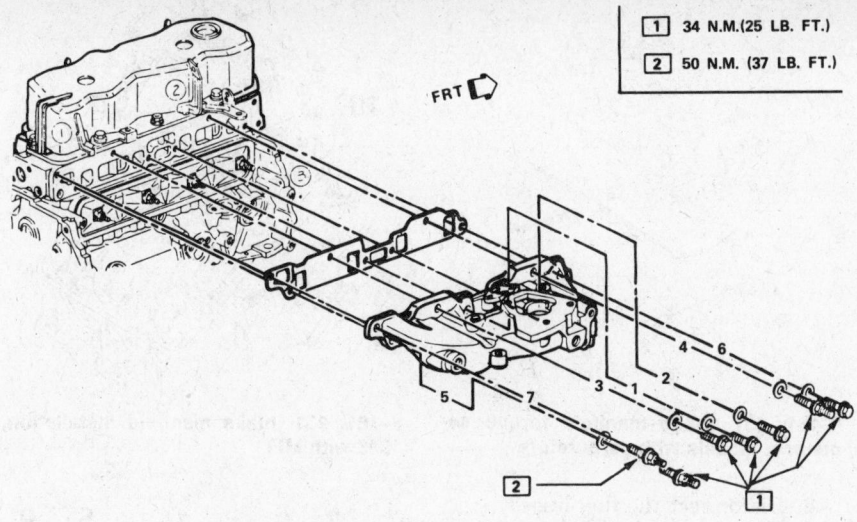

4–151 intake manifold torque sequence, 1982–1985

Cut the 6-173 intake manifold gasket as necessary

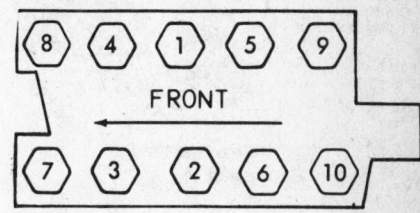

6–173 intake manifold torque sequence, 1982–86

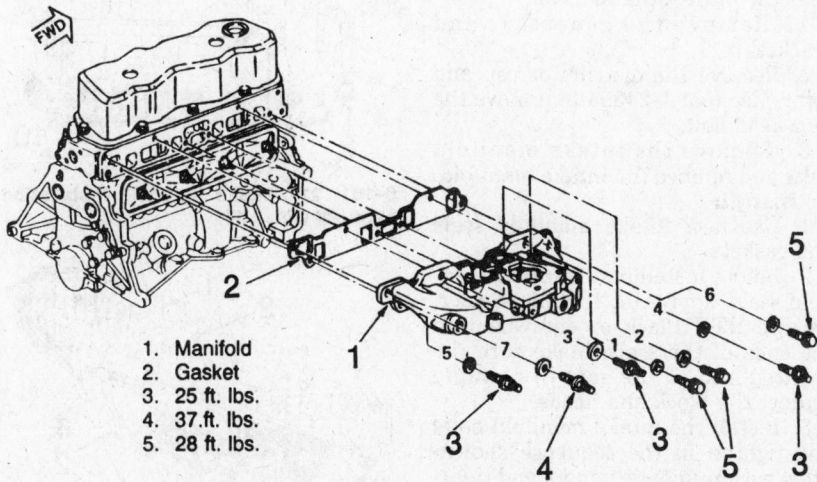

1. Manifold
2. Gasket
3. 25 ft. lbs.
4. 37 ft. lbs.
5. 28 ft. lbs.

4–151 intake manifold torque sequence, 1986

4. Disconnect the EGR valve at the plenum.

5. Remove the plenum.

6. Disconnect the fuel inlet and return pipes at the fuel rail.

7. Remove the serpintine belt.

8. Disconnect the power steering pump and lay it aside.

9. Disconnect the generator and lay it aside.

10. Loosen the generator bracket.

11. Disconnect the idle air vacuum hose at the throttle body.

12. Disconnect the wires at the injectors.

13. Disconnect the fuel rail.

14. Remove the breather tube.

15. Remove both rocker covers.

16. Drain the cooling system.

17. Disconnect the radiator hose at the thermostat housing.

18. Disconnect the wires at the coolant sensor and the oil sending switch.

19. Remove the coolant sensor.

20. Disconnect the bypass hose at the fill neck and head.

21. Loosen the rocker arms and remove the push rods.

22. Remove the intake manifold bolts and remove the intake manifold.

To install:

1. Place a 5mm diameter diameter ($^3/_{16}$ in.) bead GM 1052917 RTV sealant or equvalent on each ridge.

2. Position a new intake manifold gasket.

3. Install the push rods and tighten the rocker arm nuts to 14–20 ft. lbs.

4. Install the intake manifold and torque the bolts to specifications.

5. The remainder of the installation is the reverse of removal.

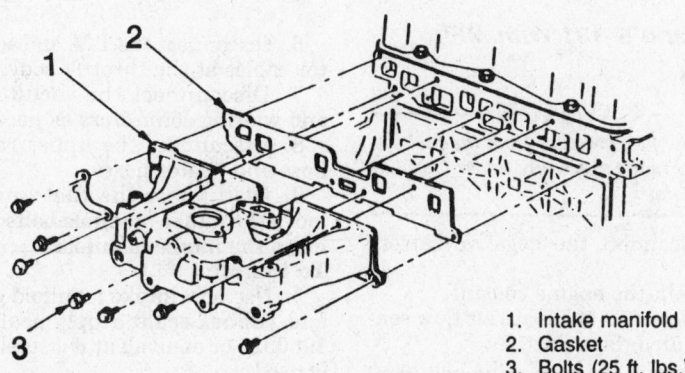

1. Intake manifold
2. Gasket
3. Bolts (25 ft. lbs.)

4–151 intake manifold torque sequence, 1987–89

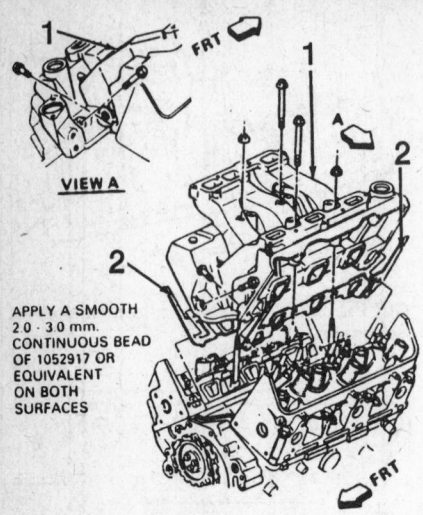

APPLY A SMOOTH
2.0 - 3.0 mm.
CONTINUOUS BEAD
OF 1052917 OR
EQUIVALENT
ON BOTH
SURFACES

1. Intake manifold
2. Gasket

6-173 Intake manifold installation, 1987-89

6-181 and 6-231 Engines

WITH CARBURETOR

1. Disconnect the battery ground.
2. Drain the cooling system.
3. Remove the air cleaner.
4. Disconnect all hoses and wiring from the manifold.
5. Disconnect the accelerator linkage and cruise control chain.
6. Disconnect the fuel line at carburetor.
7. Remove the distributor cap and rotor and remove the Torx® head bolt from the left side of the manifold.
8. Unbolt and remove the manifold.
9. Installation is the reverse of removal. When installing the front and rear seals, make sure that the ends of the seals fit snugly against the block and head. Install Nos. 1 & 2 bolts first and tighten them until snug, then install the other bolts in order.

6-231 Engine With MFI

1985

——— CAUTION ———
Release the fuel pressure from the fuel system. Refer to the procedure under Gasoline Fuel System.

1. Disconnect the negative battery cable.
2. Drain the engine coolant.
3. Disconnect the mass air flow sensor and air intake duct.
4. Disconnect the T.V. and accelerator cables at the throttle body.
5. Disconnect the crankcase ventilation pipe.
6. Disconnnect the vacuum lines at the throttle body.
7. Disconnect the upper radiator hose and heater hoses.

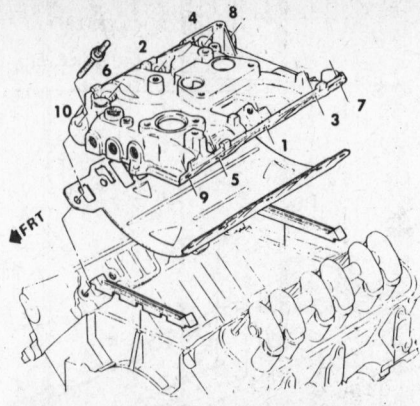

6-181, 231 intake manifold torque sequence, models with carburetors

8. Disconnect the fuel lines.
9. Disconnect the wiring harness connectors at the T.P.S. switch, IAC connector at the throttle body, water temperature switch, coolant temperature switch and fan control.
10. Disconnect the fuel rail.
11. Remove the generator and bracket.
12. Remove the distributor cap and rotor. Use tool J-24394 to remove the torx head bolt.
13. Remove the intake manifold bolts and remove the intake manifold.
To install:
1. Use new intake manifold seals and gaskets.
2. Before installing the intake manifold seals, apply GM 1052366 Sealer, Fel-Pro RTV Black or equivalent to the ends of the seals. Make sure the pointed end of the seal fits snugly against the block and heads.
3. Install the intake manifold bolts and tighten in the sequence shown. Start with numbers 1 and 2 and tighten gradually until both are snug. Tighten all bolts to the specification listed in the Torque Specifications Chart.
4. The remainder of the installation is the reverse of removal.

6-231 and 6-181 With MFI

1986-89

——— CAUTION ———
Release the fuel pressure from the fuel system. Refer to the procedure under Gasoline Fuel System.

1. Disconnect the negative battery cable.
2. Drain the engine coolant.
3. Disconnect the mass air flow sensor and air intake duct.
4. Remove the serpintine belt, generator and bracket.
5. Remove the C³I ignition module and wiring.

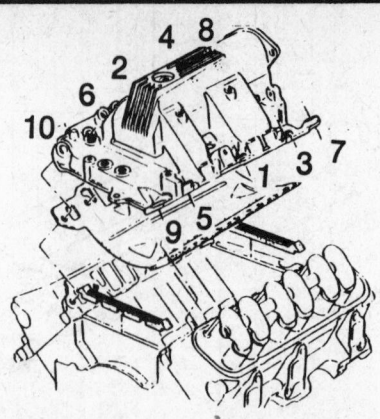

6-181, 231 intake manifold installation, 1985 with MFI

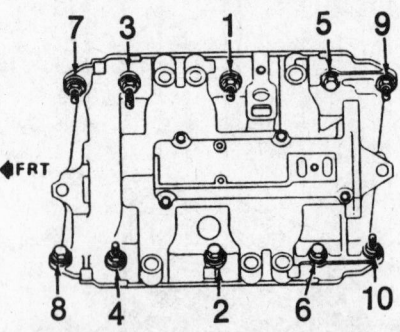

6-181, 231 intake manifold installation, 1986-89 with MFI

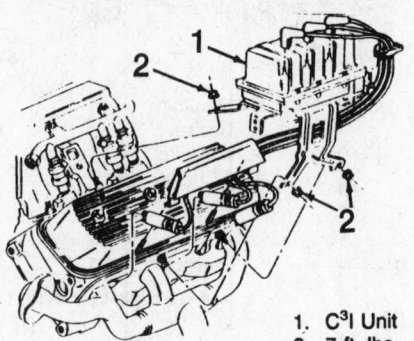

1. C³I Unit
2. 7 ft. lbs.

6-181, 231 C³ ignition module unit mounting, 1986-89

6. Disconnect the T.V. and accelerator cables at the throttle body.
7. Disconnnect the vacuum lines and wioring connectors as necessary.
8. Disconnect the upper radiator hose and heater hoses.
9. Disconnect the fuel lines. Remove the intake manifold bolts and remove the intake manifold.
To install:
1. Use new intake manifold gaskets and rubber seals. Apply sealer GM 1050026 or equivalent if a steel gasket is used.
2. Apply sealer/lubricant GM 1052080 or equivalent to all pipe threads.

3. Tighten the intake manifold bolts in the sequence shown and to the specifications listed in the Torque Specifications Chart.

Exhaust Manifold

REMOVAL & INSTALLATION

4–151 Engine

1. Remove the air cleaner and the EFI preheat tube.

2. Remove the manifold strut bolts from the radiator support panel and the cylinder head.

3. Remove the A/C compressor bracket to one side. Do not disconnect any of the refrigerant lines.

4. If necessary, remove the dipstick tube attaching bolt, and the engine mount bracket from the cylinder head.

5. Raise the car and disconnect the exhaust pipe from the manifold.

6. Remove the manifold attaching bolts and remove the manifold.

7. Installation is the reverse of removal. Refer to the illustrations for the torque specification and sequence for 1985–88 models.

6–173 Engine

LEFT SIDE

1. Remove the air cleaner. Remove the carburetor heat stove pipe.

2. Remove the air supply plumbing from the exhaust manifold.

3. Raise and support the car. Unbolt and remove the exhaust pipe at the manifold.

4. Unbolt and remove the manifold.

To install:

1. Clean the mating surfaces of the cylinder head and manifold. Install the manifold onto the head, and install the retaining bolts finger tight.

2. Tighten the manifold bolts in a circular pattern, working from the center to the ends, to the value in the Torque Specifications Chart in 2 stages.

3. Connect the exhaust pipe to the manifold.

4. The remainder of installation is the reverse of removal.

RIGHT SIDE

1. Raise and support the car.

2. Tighten the exhaust pipe-to-manifold flange bolts until they break off. Remove the pipe from the manifold. Later models are equipped with flange bolts.

3. Lower the car. Remove the spark plug wires from the plugs. Number them first if they are not already labeled.

4. Remove the air supply pipes from the manifold. Remove the PULSAIR bracket bolt from the rocker cover, on

models so equipped, then remove the pipe assembly.

5. Remove the manifold retaining bolts and remove the manifold.

To install:

1. Clean the mating surfaces of the cylinder head and manifold. Position the manifold against the head and install the retaining bolts finger tight.

2. Tighten the bolts in a circular pattern, to the value in the Torque Specifications Chart working from the center to the ends, in 2 stages.

3. Install the air supply system.

4. Install the spark plug wires.

5. Raise and support the car. Connect the exhaust pipe to the manifold and install new flange bolts.

6–181 and 6–231 Engines

1. Disconnect the battery ground cable.

2. Remove the pinch bolt at the steering gear intermediate shaft and separate the intermediate shaft from the stub shaft.

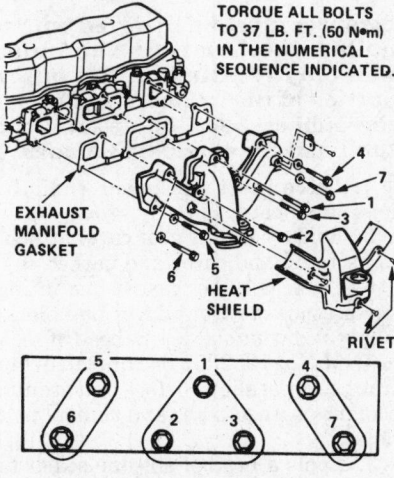

TORQUE ALL BOLTS TO 37 LB. FT. (50 N•m) IN THE NUMERICAL SEQUENCE INDICATED.

EXHAUST MANIFOLD GASKET

HEAT SHIELD

RIVET

BOLT LOCATIONS

4–151 exhaust manifold torque sequence, 1982–1984

3. Raise and support the car on jackstands.

4. Unbolt the exhaust pipe from the manifold.

5. Lower the car.

6. Remove the upper engine support strut.

7. Place a floor jack under the front crossmember and take up the weight of the car.

8. Remove the 2 front body mount bolts along with their cushions and retainers.

9. Remove the cushions from the bolts and thread the bolts and their retainers a minimum of three turns into the cradle cage nuts so that the bolts serve to hold the cradle and prevent movement.

10. Lower the floor jack so that the crossmember contacts the body mount bolt retainers. Check for any hose or wire interference problems.

11. Remove the alternator, disconnect the power steering pump and remove its bracket.

12. Disconnect the manifold from the crossover pipe.

13. Unbolt and remove the manifold.

14. Installation is the reverse of removal.

LEFT SIDE

1. Disconnect the battery ground.

2. Unbolt and remove the crossover pipe.

3. Remove the upper engine support strut.

4. Unbolt and remove the manifold.

5. Installation is the reverse of removal.

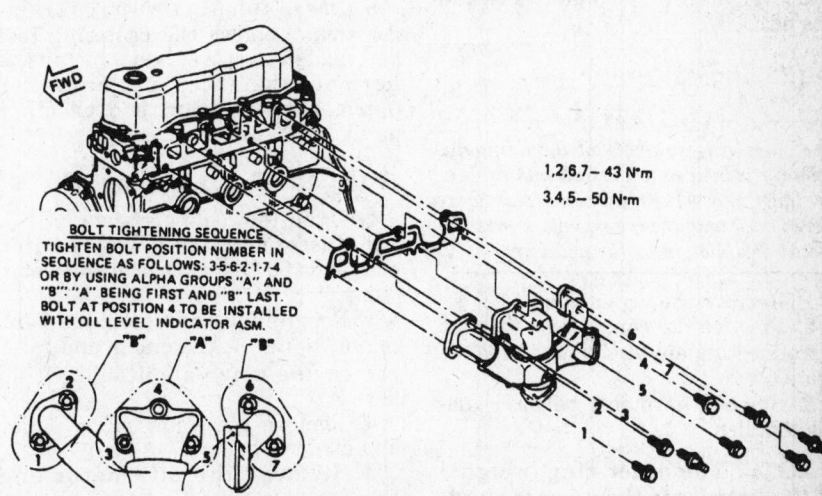

FWD

BOLT TIGHTENING SEQUENCE
TIGHTEN BOLT POSITION NUMBER IN SEQUENCE AS FOLLOWS: 3-5-6-2-1-7-4 OR BY USING ALPHA GROUPS "A" AND "B"; "A" BEING FIRST AND "B" LAST. BOLT AT POSITION 4 TO BE INSTALLED WITH OIL LEVEL INDICATOR ASM.

1,2,6,7 – 43 N•m
3,4,5 – 50 N•m

4–151 exhaust manifold torque sequence, 1985–89

Front Cover

REMOVAL & INSTALLATION

4-151 Engine

─────── CAUTION ───────

On fuel injected engines, relieve the pressure in the fuel system before disconnecting the fuel line connections. Please refer to the procedure under the Fuel System section.

1. Remove the crankshaft hub. It is necessary to remove the inner fender splash shield.
2. Remove the alternator lower bracket.
3. Remove the front engine mounts.
4. Using a floor jack, raise the engine.
5. Remove the engine mount mounting bracket-to-cylinder block bolts. Remove the bracket and mount as an assembly.
6. Remove the oil pan-to-front cover screws.
7. Remove the front cover-to-block screws.
8. Pull the cover slightly forward, just enough to allow cutting of the oil pan front seal flush with the block on both sides.
9. Remove the front cover and attached portion of the pan seal.
10. Clean the gasket surfaces thoroughly.
11. Cut the tabs from the new oil pan front seal.
12. Install the seal on the front cover, pressing the tips into the holes provided.
13. Coat the new gasket with sealer and position it on the front cover.
14. Apply a ⅛ in. bead of silicone sealer to the joint formed at the oil pan and block.
15. Align the front cover seal with a centering tool and install the front cover. Tighten the screws and install the hub.

6-173 Engine

─────── CAUTION ───────

The outer ring (weight) of the harmonic balancer is bonded to the hub with rubber. Breakage may occur if the balancer is hammered back onto the crankshaft. A press or special installation tool is necessary.

1. Remove the water pump.
2. Remove the compressor without disconnecting any A/C lines and lay it aside.
3. Remove harmonic balancer, using a puller.

NOTE: The outer ring (weight) of the harmonic balancer is bonded to the hub with rubber. The

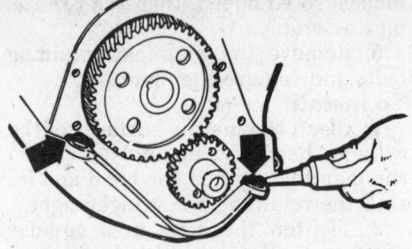

Apply sealant where shown on the 4-151

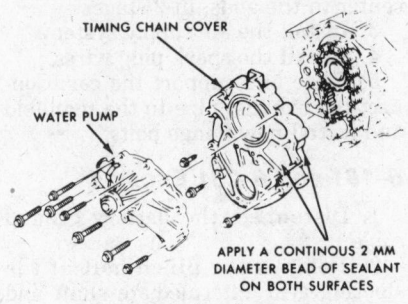

TIMING CHAIN COVER

WATER PUMP

APPLY A CONTINOUS 2 MM DIAMETER BEAD OF SEALANT ON BOTH SURFACES

6-173 timing cover removal

balancer must be removed with a puller which acts on the inner hub only. Pulling on the outer portion of the balancer will break the rubber bond or destroy the tuning of the torsional damper.

4. Disconnect the lower radiator hose and heater hose.
5. Remove timing gear cover attaching screws, and cover and gasket.
6. Clean all the gasket mounting surfaces on the front cover and block. Apply a continuous ³⁄₂₂ in. bead of sealer (GM No. 1052357 or equivalent) to front cover sealing surface and around coolant passage ports and central bolt holes.
7. Apply a bead of silicone sealer to the oil pan-to-cylinder block joint.
8. Install a centering tool in the crankshaft snout hole in the front cover and install the cover.
9. Install the front cover bolts finger tight, remove the centering tool and tighten the cover bolts. Install the harmonic balancer, pulley, water pump, belts, radiator, and all other parts.

6-181 and 6-231 Engines

1. Drain the cooling system.
2. Disconnect the lower radiator hose and the heater hose at the water pump.
3. Remove the 2 nuts from the front engine mount at the cradle and raise the engine using a suitable lifting device.
4. Remove the water pump pulley and all drive belts.
5. Remove the alternator and brackets.
6. Remove the distributor.

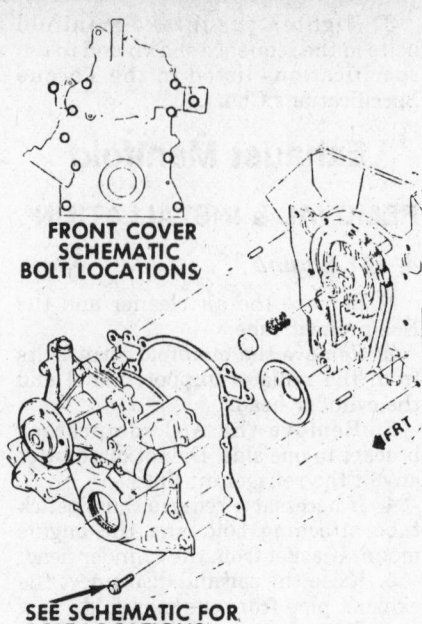

FRONT COVER SCHEMATIC BOLT LOCATIONS

FRT

SEE SCHEMATIC FOR BOLT LOCATIONS

Timing cover removal—6-181 and 6-231

NOTE: If the timing chain and sprockets are not going to be disturbed, note the position of the distributor rotor for reinstallation in the same position.

7. Remove the balancer bolt and washer, and using a puller, remove the balancer.
8. Remove the cover-to-block bolts. Remove the 2 oil pan-to-cover bolts.
9. Remove the cover and gasket.
10. Installation is the reverse of removal. Always use a new gasket coated with sealer. Remove the oil pump cover and pack the area around the gears with petroleum jelly so that no air space is left within the pump. Apply sealer to the cover bolt threads.

OIL SEAL REPLACEMENT

1. After removing the timing cover, pry oil seal out of front of cover.
2. Install new lip seal with lip (open side of seal) inside and drive or press seal carefully into place.

NOTE: The timing cover oil seal can be replaced without removing the cover. Remove the fan belts, crankshaft pulley and harmonic balancer. Pry the oil seal out the cover working carefully to prevent damage to the seal mating surface. Lubricate the new seal and drive it into place with the open side toward the engine. Use a seal installer to avoid damaging or cocking the seal.

Timing Gear and/or Chain

REMOVAL & INSTALLATION

4–151 Engine

CAUTION

On fuel injected engines, relieve the pressure in the fuel system before disconnecting the fuel line connections. Please refer to the procedure under the Fuel System section.

1. Remove the crankshaft hub. It is necessary to remove the inner fender splash shield.
2. Remove the alternator lower bracket.
3. Remove the front engine mounts.
4. Using a floor jack, raise the engine.
5. Remove the engine mount mounting bracket-to-cylinder block bolts. Remove the bracket and mount as an assembly.
6. Remove the oil pan-to-front cover screws.
7. Remove the front cover-to-block screws.
8. Pull the cover slightly forward, just enough to allow cutting of the oil pan front seal flush with the block on both sides.
9. Remove the front cover and attached portion of the pan seal.
10. Remove the rocker cover, rocker arms, and pushrods.
11. Remove the distributor, spark plugs, and fuel pump.
12. Remove the pushrod cover and gasket. Remove the lifters.
13. Remove the oil pump driveshaft and gear assembly.
14. Remove the crankshaft hub and timing gear cover.
15. Remove the 2 camshaft thrust plate screws by working through the holes in the gear.
16. Remove the camshaft and gear assembly by pulling it through the front of the block. Take care not to damage the bearings.
17. Installation is the reverse of removal.
18. Align the front cover seal with a centering tool and install the front cover. Tighten the screws and install the hub.

6–173 Engine

1. Remove the crankcase front cover. This will allow access to the timing chain.
2. Crank the engine until the marks punched on both sprockets are closest to one another and in line between the shaft centers.

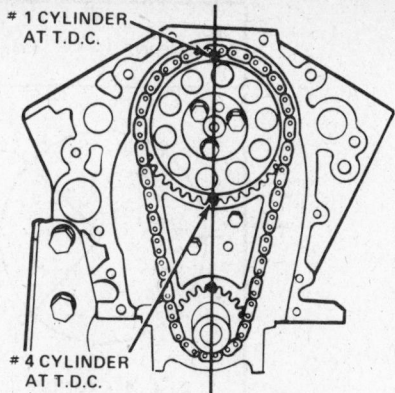

6-173 timing gear alignment

6-173 timing chain and sprockets

3. Take out the three bolts that hold the camshaft sprocket to the camshaft. This sprocket is a light press fit on the camshaft and will come off readily. It is located by a dowel. The chain comes off with the camshaft sprocket. A gear puller will be required to remove the crankshaft sprocket.
4. Without disturbing the position of the engine, mount the new crank sprocket on the shaft, then mount the chain over the camshaft sprocket.
5. Arrange the camshaft sprocket in such a way that the timing marks will line up between the shaft centers and the camshaft locating dowel will enter the dowel hole in the cam sprocket.
6. Place the cam sprocket, with its chain mounted over it, in position on the front of the camshaft and pull up with the three bolts that hold it to the camshaft.
7. After the sprockets are in place, turn the engine 2 full revolutions to make certain that the timing marks are in correct alignment between the shaft centers.

6–181 and 6–231 Engines

1. Remove the timing chain cover as outlined earlier.
2. Turn the crankshaft so that the timing marks are aligned.
3. Remove the crankshaft oil slinger.

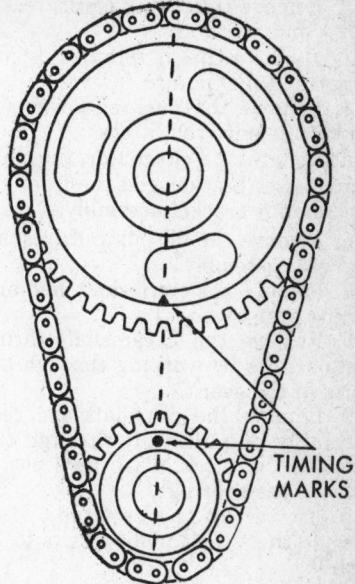

Timing gear alignment—6–181 and 6–231

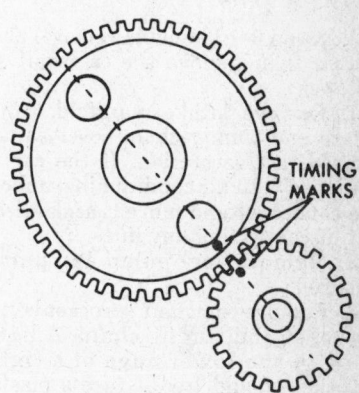

4-151 timing gear alignment

4. Remove the camshaft sprocket bolts.
5. Use 2 prybars to alternately pry the camshaft and crankshaft sprocket free along with the chain.
6. Installation is the reverse of removal. If the engine was turned, make sure that the No. 1 cylinder is at TDC.

Camshaft

REMOVAL & INSTALLATION

4–151 Engine

CAUTION

Relieve the pressure in the EFI system on fuel injected engines before disconnecting the fuel line connections.

1. Remove the engine as previously outlined.

2. Remove the rocker cover, rocker arms, and pushrods.

3. Remove the distributor, spark plugs, and fuel pump.

4. Remove the pushrod cover and gasket. Remove the lifters.

5. Remove the alternator, the alternator lower bracket and the front engine mount bracket assembly.

6. Remove the oil pump driveshaft and gear assembly.

7. Remove the crankshaft hub and timing gear cover.

8. Remove the 2 camshaft thrust plate screws by working through the holes in the gear.

9. Remove the camshaft and gear assembly by pulling it through the front of the block. Take care not to damage the bearings.

10. Install in the reverse order. Torque the thrust plate screws to 75 inch lbs.

6-173 Engine

Follow the 6-173 engine removal procedure then remove the camshaft as follows:

1. Remove intake manifold, valve lifters and timing chain cover as described in this section. If the car is equipped with air conditioning, unbolt the condenser and move it aside without disconnecting any lines.

2. Remove fuel pump and pump pushrod.

3. Remove camshaft sprocket bolts, sprocket and timing chain. A light blow to the lower edge of a tight sprocket should free it (use a plastic mallet).

4. Install 2 bolts in cam bolt holes and pull cam from block.

5. To install, reverse removal procedure aligning the sprocket timing marks.

6-181 and 6-231 Engines

1. Remove the engine as described earlier.

2. Remove the intake manifold.

3. Remove the rocker arm covers.

4. Remove the rocker arm assemblies, pushrods and lifters.

5. Remove the timing chain cover.

NOTE: Align the timing marks of the camshaft and crankshaft sprockets to avoid burring the camshaft journals by the crankshaft.

6. Remove the timing chain and camshaft sprocket as described earlier.

7. Installation is the reverse of removal.

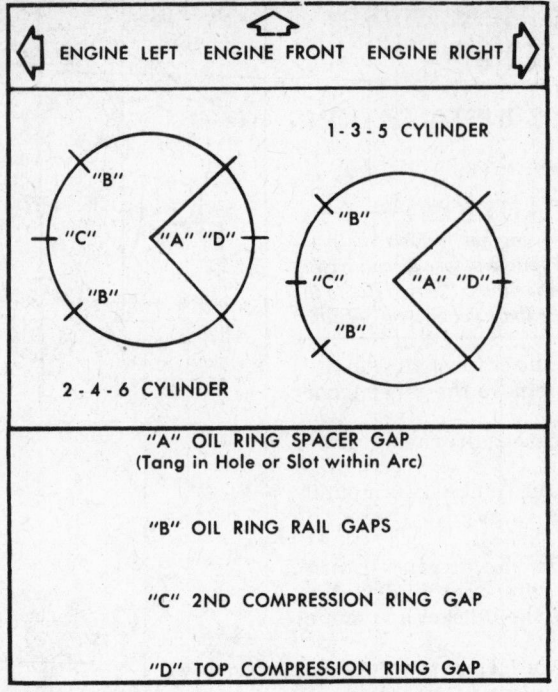

Arrange the piston rings on all V6 engines as shown

1-3-5 CYLINDER

2-4-6 CYLINDER

"A" OIL RING SPACER GAP
(Tang in Hole or Slot within Arc)

"B" OIL RING RAIL GAPS

"C" 2ND COMPRESSION RING GAP

"D" TOP COMPRESSION RING GAP

Piston and Connecting Rod

FRONT OF ENGINE

NOTCH

On all engines, the piston assemblies are installed with the notch facing forward

POSITIONING

For all piston and connecting rod overhaul procedures, please refer to "Engine Rebuilding" in the Unit Repair Section.

DIESEL ENGINE MECHANICAL

Engine
REMOVAL & INSTALLATION
6-263

1. Drain the cooling system. Remove the serpentine drive belt (and vacuum pump drive belt, if A/C equipped).

2. Remove air cleaner and install cover J-26996.

3. Disconnect battery negative cable(s) at batteries and ground wires at inner fender panel. Disconnect engine ground strap, rear (right) head to cowl.

4. Raise the car and support it safely.

5. Remove the flywheel cover.

6. Remove the flywheel to torque converter bolts.

7. Disconnect the exhaust pipe from the rear exhaust manifold.

8. Remove the engine to transaxle brace.

9. Remove the engine mount to cradle retaining nuts and washers.

10. Disconnect the leads to the starter motor, No. 2 cylinder glow plug and battery ground cable to engine bolt.

11. Disconnect the lower oil cooler hose and cap the openings.

12. Remove the accessible power steering pump bracket fasteners.

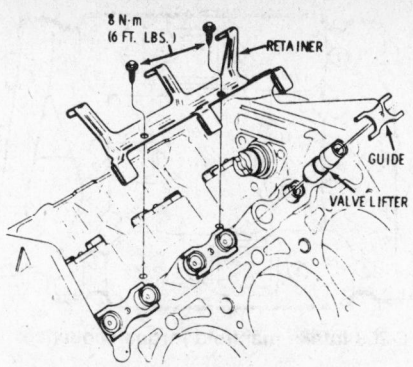

Diesel valve lifters, guides and retainers

13. Lower the car.

14. Remove the remaining power steering pump bracket/brace fasteners and lower the power steering pump with hoses out of the way.

15. Remove heater water return pipe.

16. Disconnect all remaining glow plug leads at the glow plugs.

17. Disconnect all other leads at the engine, disconnect the engine harness at the cowl connector and body mounted relays and position the engine harness aside.

18. If A/C equipped, disconnect the compressor with brackets and lines attached and position aside.

19. Disconnect the fuel and vacuum hoses, cap all fuel line openings.

20. Disconnect the throttle and T.V. cables at the injection pump and cable bracket. Position cables aside.

21. Disconnect the upper oil cooler hose and cap the openings.

22. Remove the exhaust crossover pipe heat shield.

23. Disconnect and move aside the transaxle filler tube.

24. Remove the exhaust crossover pipe.

25. Remove the engine mounting strut and strut brackets.

26. Install a suitable engine lifting device. Make certain that when installing chains to the cylinder heads that washers are used under the chains and bolt heads and that the bolts are torqued to 20 ft. lbs.

——— CAUTION ———

Failure to properly secure the engine lift to the aluminum cylinder heads can result in personal injury.

27. Position a support under the transaxle rear extension. It may be necessary to raise the support as the engine is being removed.

28. Remove the engine to transaxle bolts and remove the engine.

29. Installation is the reverse of removal. Note the following:

a. Before installing the flex plate-to-converter bolts, make sure that

the weld nuts on the converter are flush with the flex plate, and the converter rotates freely by hand.

b. Use only new O-rings at all connections.

c. Adjust the throttle valve cable.

Cylinder Head

REMOVAL & INSTALLATION

6–263 Engine

NOTE: This procedure requires the complete disassembly of the valve lifters.

1. Remove intake manifold.

2. Remove valve cover. Loosen or remove any accessory brackets or pipe clamps which interfere.

3. Disconnect glow plug wiring (and block heater lead if so equipped on rear bank).

4. Remove the ground strap from right (rear) cylinder head.

5. Remove rocker arm nuts, pivots, rocker arms and pushrods. Scribe pivots and keep rocker arms separated so they can be installed in their original locations.

6. Disconnect the exhaust crossover pipe from the exhaust manifold on the side being worked on and loosen it on the other.

7. Remove engine block drain plug, from side of the block where head is being removed.

8. Remove the pipe plugs covering the upper cylinder head bolts.

9. Remove all the cylinder head bolts and remove the cylinder head.

10. If necessary to remove the prechamber, remove the glow plug and injection nozzle, then tap out with a small blunt 1/8 in. drift. DO NOT use a tapered drift.

11. Installation is the reverse of removal. Do not use sealer on the head gasket. If a pre-chamber was replaced, measure the chamber height and grind the new one to within 0.001 in. of the old chamber's height, using No. 80 grit wet sandpaper to polish it. Coat the head bolts with sealer.

OVERHAUL

For all cylinder head overhaul procedures, please refer to "Engine Rebuilding" in the Unit Repair Section.

Rocker Arm/Shafts

REMOVAL & INSTALLATION

NOTE: This procedure requires that the valve lifters be bled.

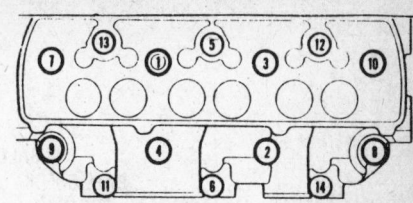

6-263 head bolt torque sequence

6–263 Engine

1. Remove the valve cover(s).

2. Remove the rocker arm nuts, pivot and rocker arms.

3. If rocker arms are being replaced, they must be replaced in cylinder sets. Never replace just one rocker arm per cylinder. If a stud was replaced, coat the threads with locking compound and torque it to 11 ft. lbs.

4. Installation is the reverse of removal. Perform the "Valve lifter bleed-down" procedure. This is absolutely necessary; if lifters are not bled, engine damage will be unavoidable. Torque the rocker arm nuts to 28 ft. lbs.; the cover to 5 ft. lbs.

To bleed the lifters proceed as follows:

1. Before installing any removed rocker arms, rotate the engine crankshaft to a position of No. 1 cylinder being 32 degrees BTDC. This is about 2 in. (50mm) counterclockwise from the 0 degrees pointer. If only the right valve cover was removed, remove No. 1 cylinder glow plug to determine if the position of the piston is the correct one. The compression pressure will indicate the right position. If the left valve cover was removed, rotate the crankshaft until the No. 5 cylinder intake valve pushrod ball is 0.28 in. (7.0mm) above the No. 5 cylinder exhaust valve pushrod ball.

NOTE: Use only hand wrenches to torque the rocker arm pivot nuts to avoid engine damage.

2. If removed, install the No. 5 cylinder pivot and rocker arms. Torque the nuts alternately between the intake and exhaust valves until the intake valve begins to open, then stop.

3. Install remaining rocker arms except No. 3 exhaust valve (if this rocker arm was removed).

4. If removed, install but do not torque No. 3 valve pivots beyond the point that the valve would be fully open. This is indicated by strong resistance while still turning the pivot retaining bolts. Going beyond this would bend the pushrod. Torque the nuts SLOWLY allowing the lifter to bleed down.

5. Finish torquing No. 5 cylinder rocker arm pivot nut SLOWLY. Do not go beyond the point that the valve

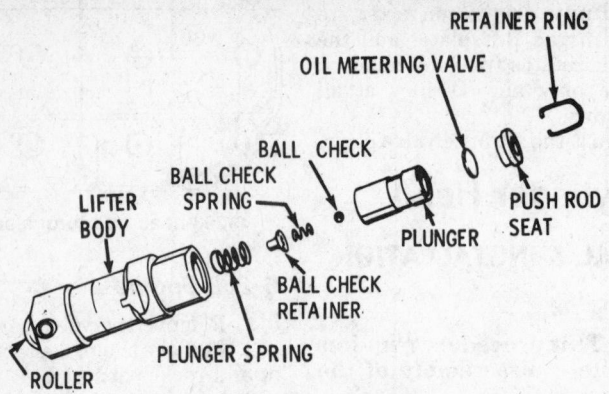

Valve lifter disassembled

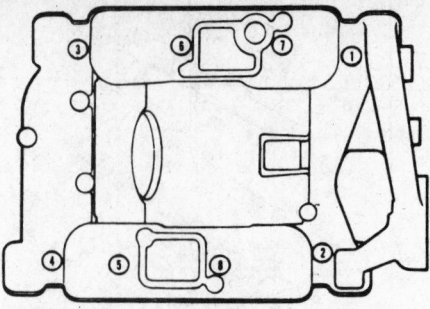

6-263 intake manifold torque sequence

would be fully open. This is indicated by strong resistance while still turning the pivot retaining bolts. Going beyond this would bend the pushrod.

6. DO NOT turn the engine crankshaft for at least 45 minutes.

7. Finish reassembling the engine as the lifters are being bled.

NOTE: Do not rotate the engine until the valve lifters have been bled down, or damage to the engine will occur.

Intake Manifold

REMOVAL & INSTALLATION

6-263 Engine

NOTE: This procedure requires the removal, disassembly draining and reassembly of the valve lifters.

1. Remove the air cleaner assembly.
2. Drain the radiator, then disconnect the upper radiator hose from the water outlet.
3. Disconnect the heater inlet hose from the outlet on the intake manifold and disconnect the heater outlet pipe from the intake manifold attachments and move it aside.
4. Remove air crossover and the fuel injection pump.
5. Disconnect wiring as necessary at the generator, A/C compressor and switches, if so equipped.
6. Remove the cruise control servo if so equipped.
7. Remove the A/C compressor bracket and brace bolts and position the compressor (if so equipped) with lines attached out of the way.
8. Remove the generator assembly.
9. Disconnect the engine mounting strut.
10. Remove the fuel lines, filter and brackets. Cap all openings.
11. Disconnect the electrical leads to the glow plug controller and sending units.

12. Disconnect the exhaust crossover pipe head shield.
13. Remove the left (forward) injection lines and cap all openings. Use a backup wrench on the nozzles.
14. Disconnect the throttle and T.V. cables from the bracket.
15. Remove the drain tube.
16. Remove the intermediate pump adapter.
17. Remove pump adapter and seal.
18. Remove the intake manifold.
19. Clean the machined surfaces of cylinder head and intake manifold with a putty knife. Use care not to gouge or scratch the machined surfaces. Clean all bolts and bolt holes.
20. Coat both sides of gasket sealing surface that seal the intake manifold to the head with 1050026 sealer or equivalent and position intake manifold gasket. Install end seals, making sure that ends are positioned under the cylinder heads. The seals and mating surfaces must be dry. Any liquid, including sealer will act as a lubricant and cause the seal to move during assembly. Use RTV sealer only on each end of the seal.
21. Position intake manifold on engine. Lubricate the entire intake manifold bolt (all) with lubricant 1052080 or equivalent.
22. Torque the bolts in sequence shown to 20 ft. lb. Then retorque to 41 ft. lbs.
23. Install the drain tube.
24. Install the pump adapter.
25. Apply chassis lube to seal area of intake manifold and pump adapter.
26. Apply chassis lube to inside and outside diameter of seal and seal area of tool J–28425.
27. Install seal on tool and install the seal.
28. Install intermediate pump adapter.
29. Reverse the order of removal and install all other removed parts except the air crossover.
30. Fill the cooling system.
31. Install manifold covers, J–29657.

32. Start engine and check for leaks.
33. Check and reset the injection pump timing, if necessary.
34. Remove screen covers from manifold.
35. Install air crossover.
36. Install the air cleaner.
37. Road test car and inspect for leaks.

Exhaust Manifold

REMOVAL & INSTALLATION

6-263 Engine

LEFT SIDE

1. Remove the crossover pipe from the manifolds.
2. Raise and support the car on jackstands.
3. Unbolt and remove the manifold.
4. Installation is the reverse of removal. Lubricate the entire length of each manifold bolt with lubricant 1052080 or its equivalent.

RIGHT SIDE

1. Remove the engine support strut.
2. Place a floor jack under the front crossmember and take up the weight of the car.
3. Remove the 2 front body mount bolts. Remove the cushions from the bolts.
4. Thread the body mount bolts with their retainers into the cage nuts so that the bolts restrict movement of the engine cradle.
5. Lower the jack until the crossmember contacts the body mount bolt retainers. Check for any hose or wire interference.
6. Remove the crossover pipe.
7. Raise and support the car on jackstands.
8. Disconnect the exhaust pipe from the manifold.
9. Lower the car.
10. Unbolt and remove the manifold.
11. Installation is the reverse of removal. Lubricate the entire length of each manifold bolt with lubricant 1052080 or its equivalent.

Front Cover

REMOVAL & INSTALLATION

6–263 Engine

1. Drain the cooling system.
2. Disconnect the lower radiator hose and the heater hose at the water pump. Disconnect the heater outlet pipe at the manifold.
3. Disconnect the power steering pump, vacuum pump, belt tensioner, air conditioning compressor and alternator brackets.

——— **CAUTION** ———

Do not disconnect any refrigerant lines.

4. Remove the crankshaft balancer using a puller.
5. Unbolt and remove the front cover and gasket.
6. Installation is the reverse of removal. Grind a chamfer on the end of each dowel pin to aid in cover installation. Trim ⅛ inch from the ends of the new front pan seal. Apply RTV sealer to the oil pan seal retainer. After the cover gasket is in place, apply sealer to the junction of the pan, gasket and block. When installing the cover, rotate it right and left while guiding the pan seal into place with a small screwdriver.

OIL SEAL REPLACEMENT

1. After removing the timing cover, pry oil seal out of front of cover.
2. Install new lip seal with lip (open side of seal) inside and drive or press seal carefully into place.

NOTE: The timing cover oil seal can be replaced without removing the cover. Remove the fan belts, crankshaft pulley and harmonic balancer. Pry the oil seal out the cover working carefully to prevent damage to the seal mating surface. Lubricate the new seal and drive it into place with the open side toward the engine. Use a seal installer to avoid damaging or cocking the seal.

Timing Gear and/or Chain

REMOVAL & INSTALLATION

6–263 Engine

NOTE: The following procedure requires the bleed-down of the valve lifters. Read that procedure before proceeding.

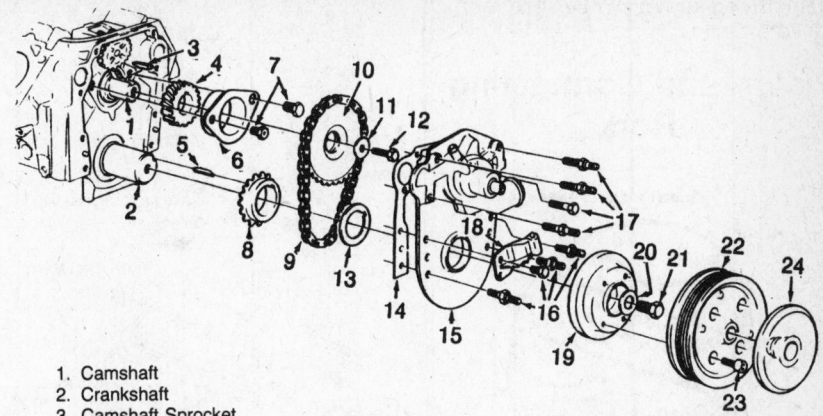

1. Camshaft
2. Crankshaft
3. Camshaft Sprocket Key
4. Injection Pump Drive Gear
5. Crankshaft Sprocket Key
6. Front Camshaft Bearing Retainer
7. 65 N·m (48 Ft. Lbs.)
8. Crankshaft Sprocket
9. Timing Chain
10. Camshaft Sprocket
11. Washer
12. 87 N·m (64 Ft. Lbs.)
13. Slinger
14. Gasket
15. Front Cover
16. 55 N·m (41 Ft. Lbs.)
17. 28 N·m (21 Ft. Lbs.)
18. Probe Holder (RPM Counter)
19. Crankshaft Balancer
20. Washer
21. 217–475 N·m (160 - 350 Ft. Lbs.)
22. Pulley Assembly
23. 40 N·m (30 Ft. Lbs.)
24. Cover

6-263 timing cover and chain removal

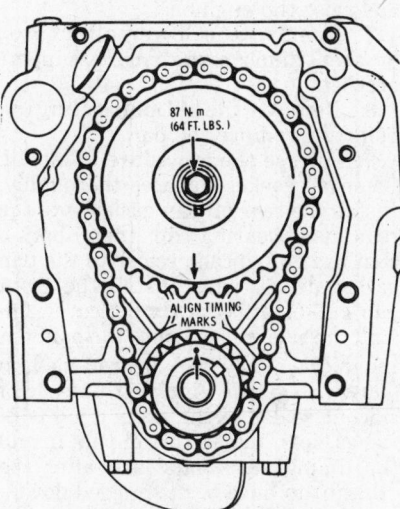

6-263 timing gear alignment

1. Remove the front cover.
2. Loosen all the rocker arms.
3. Remove the crankshaft oil slinger.
4. Remove the camshaft sprocket bolt.
5. Using 2 prybars, work the camshaft and crankshaft sprockets alternately off their shafts along with the chain. It may be necessary to remove the crankshaft sprocket with a puller.
6. Installation is the reverse of removal. If the engine was turned, make sure that the No. 1 piston is at TDC. Bleed the lifters following the procedure under "Diesel Engine Valve Lifter Bleed-Down."

Camshaft

REMOVAL & INSTALLATION

6–263 Engine

NOTE: This procedure requires the removal, disassembly, cleaning, reassembly and bleed-down of all the valve lifters. Read that procedure, described earlier, before proceeding.

1. Remove the engine as described earlier.
2. Remove the intake manifold.
3. Remove the oil pump drive assembly.
4. Remove the timing chain cover.
5. Align the timing marks.
6. Remove the rocker arms, pushrods and lifters, keeping them in order for reassembly.
7. Remove the timing chain and camshaft sprocket as described earlier.
8. Remove the camshaft bearing retainer.
9. Remove the cam sprocket key.
10. Remove the injection pump drive gear.
11. Remove the injection pump driven gear, intermediate pump adapter and pump adapter. Remove the snap ring and selective washer. Remove the driven gear and spring.
12. Carefully slide the camshaft out of the block.
13. If the camshaft bearings are being replaced, you'll have to remove the oil pan.
14. Installation is the reverse of removal. Perform the complete valve

lifter bleed-down procedure mentioned earlier.

Piston and Connecting Rod

On all engines, the piston assemblies are installed with the notch facing forward

POSITIONING

For all piston and connecting rod overhaul procedures, please refer to "Engine Rebuilding" in the Unit Repair Section. See the accompanying illustration to properly install piston and connecting rod assemblies.

ENGINE LUBRICATION

Oil Pan

REMOVAL & INSTALLATION

4-151 Engine

1. Raise and support the vehicle safely. Drain the oil.
2. Remove the engine cradle-to-front engine mounts.
3. Disconnect the exhaust pipe at both the exhaust manifold and at the rear transaxle mount.
4. Disconnect and remove the starter. Remove the flywheel housing or torque converter cover.

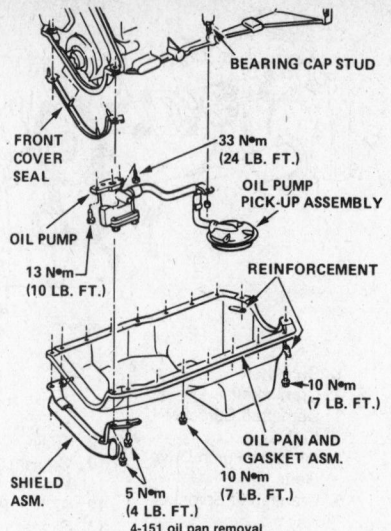

4-151 oil pan removal

5. Remove the alternator upper bracket.
6. Install an engine lifting chain and raise the engine.
7. Remove the lower alternator bracket. Remove the engine support bracket.
8. Remove the oil pan retaining bolts and remove the pan.
9. Reverse the procedure to install. Clean all gasket surfaces thoroughly. Install the rear oil pan gasket into the rear main bearing cap, then apply a thin bead of silicone sealer to the pan gasket depressions. Install the front pan gasket into the timing cover. Install the side gaskets onto the pan, not the block. They can be retained in place with grease. Apply a thin bead of silicone sealer to the mating joints of the gaskets. Install the oil pan; install the timing gear bolts last, after the other bolts have been snugged down.

6-173 Engine

1. Disconnect the battery ground.
2. Raise and support the car on jackstands.
3. Drain the oil.
4. Remove the bellhousing cover.
5. Remove the starter.
6. Support the engine.
7. Unbolt the engine from its mounts.
8. Remove the oil pan bolts.
9. Raise the engine with a jack, just enough to remove the oil pan.
10. Installation is the reverse of removal. The pan is installed using RTV gasket material in place of a gasket. Make sure that the sealing surfaces are free of old RTV material. Use a ⅛ in. bead of RTV material on the pan sealing flange. Torque the pan bolts to 8–10 ft. lbs.

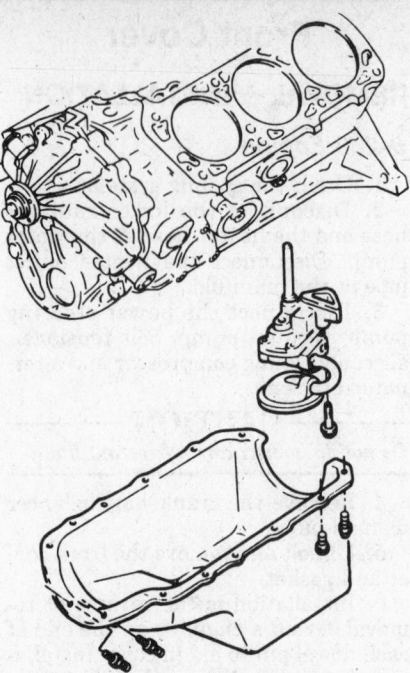

6-173 oil pan removal

6-181 and 6-231 Engines

1. Disconnect the battery ground cable.
2. Raise and support the car on jackstands.
3. Drain the oil.
4. Remove the bellhousing cover.
5. Unbolt and remove the oil pan.
6. Installation is the reverse of removal. RTV gasket material is used in place of a gasket. Make sure that the sealing surfaces are free of all old RTV material. Use a ⅛ in. bead of RTV material on the oil pan sealing flange. Torque the pan bolts to 10–14 ft. lbs.

6-263 Engine

— CAUTION —

The following procedure will be personally hazardous unless the procedures are followed exactly.

1. Install the engine support fixture assembly shown in the accompanying illustration. Be certain to arrange washers on the fixture so that the bolt securing the chain to the cylinder head can be torqued to 20 ft. lbs. THIS IS ABSOLUTELY NECESSARY.
2. Raise the front and rear of the car and support it on jackstands with the rear slightly lower than the front. The front jackstands should be located at the front lift points.
3. Drain the oil.
4. Remove the left side steering gear cradle bolt and loosen the right side cradle bolts.
5. Remove the front stabilizer bar.

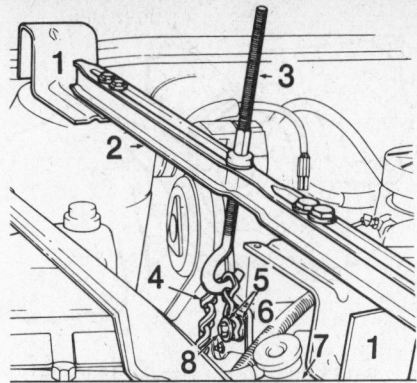

1. J-22825-45 Supports
2. BT-6603 or J-22825-1 Bar
3. J-22825-48 Hook
4. Chain
5. Washers
6. Right Cylinder Head
7. Radiator Support
8. 27 N·m (20 Ft. Lbs.)

6-263 engine support fixture

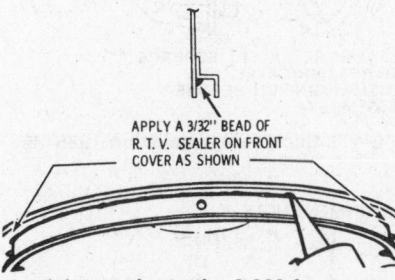

APPLY A 3/32" BEAD OF R.T.V. SEALER ON FRONT COVER AS SHOWN

Applying sealer to the 6-263 front cover

6. Using a ½ in. drill bit, drill through the spot weld located between the rear holes at the left front stabilizer bar mounting.

7. Remove the nuts securing the engine and transaxle to its cradle.

8. Disconnect the left lower ball joint from the knuckle.

9. Place a wood block on a floor jack and raise the transaxle under the pan until the mount studs clear the cradle.

10. Remove the bolts securing the front crossmember to the right side of the cradle.

11. Remove the bolts from the left side front body mounts.

12. Remove the left side and front crossmember assemblies. It will be necessary to lower the rear crossmember below the left side of the body through the careful use of a large prybar.

13. Remove the bellhousing cover.

14. Remove the starter.

15. Remove the engine front mount bracket.

16. Unbolt and remove the oil pan.

17. Installation is the reverse of removal. Apply sealer to both sides of the oil pan gasket and make sure that the tabs on the gaskets are installed in the seal notches. Apply RTV sealer to the front cover oil pan seal retainer, and to each seal where it contacts the block. Wipe the seal area of the pan with clean engine oil before installing the pan. Torque the pan bolts to 10 ft. lbs.

Rear Main Bearing Oil Seal

REMOVAL & INSTALLATION

4-151 Engine

1. Remove the transaxle and flywheel.

2. Being careful not to scratch the crankshaft, pry out the old seal with an suitable pry tool.

3. Coat the new seal with clean engine oil, and install it by hand (or use tool J-34924 Seal Installer) onto the crankshaft. The seal backing must be flush with the block opening.

4. Install all other parts in reverse of removal.

6-173 Engine

1982-84

1. Remove the oil pan and pump.

2. Remove the rear main bearing cap.

3. Gently pack the upper seal into the groove approximately ¼ in. on each side.

4. Measure the amount the seal was driven in on one side and add $\frac{1}{16}$ in. Cut this length from the old lower cap seal. Be sure to get a sharp cut. Repeat for the other side.

5. Place the piece of cut seal into the groove and pack the seal into the block. Do this for each side.

NOTE: GM makes a guide tool (J-29114-1) which bolts to the block via an oil pan bolt hole, and a packing tool (J-29114-2) which are machined to provide a built-in stop for the installation of the short cut pieces. Using the packing tool, work the short pieces of seal onto the guide tool, then pack them into the block with the packing tool.

6. Install a new lower seal in the rear main cap.

7. Install a piece of Plastigage® or the equivalent on the bearing journal. Install the rear cap and tighten to 70 ft. lbs. Remove the cap and check the gauge for bearing clearance. If out of specification, the ends of the seal may be frayed or not flush, preventing the cap from proper sealing. Correct as required.

8. Clean the journal, and apply a thin film of sealer to the mating sur-

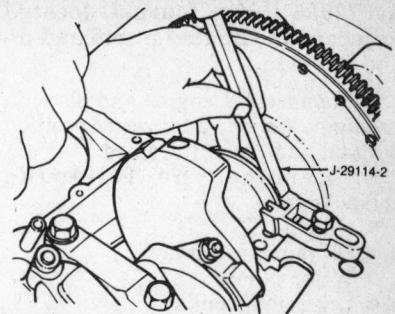

6-173 upper rear main seal installation, 1982-1984

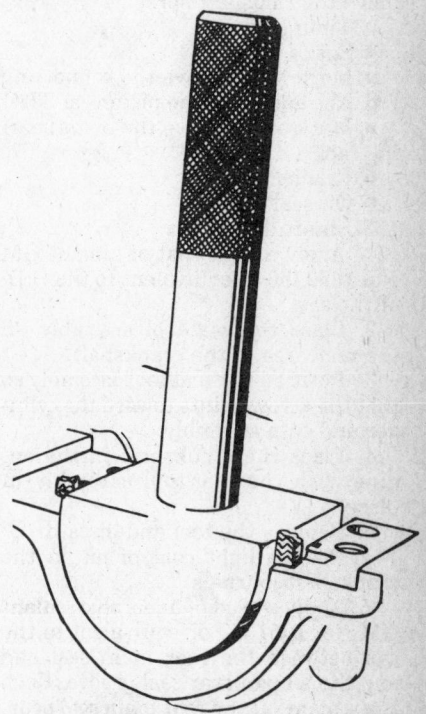

AFTER CORRECTLY POSITIONING SEAL, ROTATE TOOL SLIGHTLY AND CUT OFF EACH END OF SEAL FLUSH WITH BLOCK

Installing the lower seal half

faces of the cap and block. Do not allow any sealer to get onto the journal or bearing. Install the bearing cap and tighten to 70 ft. lbs. Install the pan and pump.

1985 WITH THIN SEAL

NOTE: 1985 models could have either a thin or thick designed rear main seal. The thin seal is used on models with a No. 4 journal size of 63.3 mm, also with the cylinder and case casting No. 14054832 (small journal) located adjacent to the fuel pump pad on the LH side. The thick seal is used on models with a No. 4 journal size of 67.2 mm, also with the cylinder and case casting No.

14072065 (large journal) located adjacent to the fuel pump pad on the LH side.

1. Remove the engine and place on an engine stand in an inverted position with oil and coolant drained.
2. Remove the following components:
- Oil pan
- Oil pump assembly
- Water pump
- Crankshaft pulley
- Harmonic balancer
- Front cover
- Align the timing marks and remove the camshaft sprocket
- Timing chain
- Spark plugs
- Mark and remove the connecting rod caps and place the pistons at TDC
- Mark and remove the main bearing caps
  - Crankshaft
  - Oil seal

To install:

1. Apply a light coat of sealant GM No. 1052756 or equivalent to the O.D. of the seal.
2. Place the seal/tool assembly on the rear area of the crankshaft.
3. Position the seal/tool assembly so that the arrow points toward the cylinder and case assembly.
4. Place the crankshaft in the engine with the seal/tool assembly in place.
5. Remove the tool and discard.
6. Place a light coat of oil on the crankshaft journals.
7. Apply a bead of anaerobic sealant GM No. 1051357 or equivalent to the cap between the rear main seal end and the oil pan rear seal groove. Keep the sealant off the rear main seal bearing and out of the drain slots.
8. Install the following parts:
- Rear main cap
- Main bearing caps
- Rod bearing caps
- Camshaft sprocket
- Align the timing marks and install the timing chain
  - Spark plugs
  - Front cover
  - Harmonic balancer
  - Crankshaft pulley
  - Water pump
  - Oil pump assembly
  - Oil pan

1985–89 WITH THICK SEAL

1. Remove the transaxle.
2. Remove the flexplate.
3. Insert an appropriate pry tool through the dust lip at the angle shown, and pry out the old seal by moving the handle of the tool towards the end of the crankshaft. Repeat as required around the seal until it is removed.

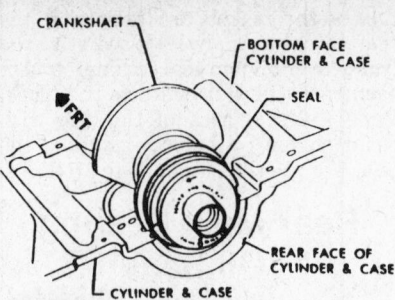

6–173 thin seal installation, 1985

NOTE: Be careful not to damage the crankshaft surface with the pry tool.

4. Check the I.D. of the bore for knicks or burrs on the surface which contacts the seal.
5. Install a new seal using Tool J–34686. Apply a light coat of oil to the I.D. of the new seal and install it over the mandril, slide the seal on the mandril until the dust lip (back of seal) bottoms squarely against the collar of the tool.
6. Align the dowel pin of the tool with the dowel pin hole in the crankshaft and attach the tool to the crankshaft by hand or torque screw to 2–5 ft. lbs.
7. Turn the "T" handle of the tool so that the collar pushes the seal into the bore, turn the handle until the collar is tight against the case. This will insure that the seal is seated properly.
8. Loosen the "T" handle of the tool until it comes to a stop. This will insure that the collar will be in the proper position for installing a new seal. Remove the attaching screws.
9. Check the seal to make sure it is seated squarely in the bore.
10. Install the flywheel and transmission.

6–181, 6–231 and 6–263 Engines

Braided fabric seals are pressed into grooves formed in crankcase and rear bearing cap to rear of the oil collecting groove, to seal against leakage of oil around the crankshaft.

A new braided fabric seal can be installed in crankcase only when crankshaft is removed, but it can be repaired while crankshaft is installed, as outlined under "Rear Main Bearing Upper Oil Seal Repair". The seal can be replaced in cap whenever the cap is removed. Remove old seal and apply GM 1052756 sealer, Fel Pro-Set and Seal or equivalent to the seal groove. Within in one minute and place new seal in groove with both ends projecting

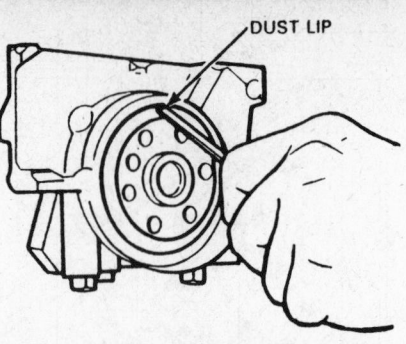

6–173 thick seal removal, 1985–89

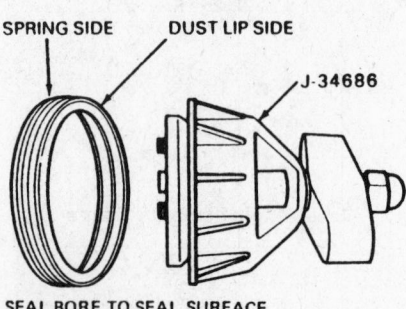

SEAL BORE TO SEAL SURFACE TO BE LUBRICATED WITH ENGINE OIL BEFORE ASSEMBLY

6–173 thick seal installation 1985–89

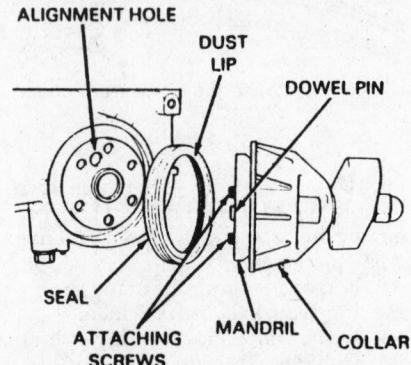

6–173 thick seal installation 1985–89

above parting surface of cap. Force seal into groove rubbing down with hammer handle or smooth stick until seal projects above the groove not more than $\frac{1}{16}$ in. Cut ends off flush with surface of cap, using sharp knife or razor blade. Apply a thin film of grease to the rope seal.

NOTE: Use sealer sparingly. Keep sealer out of bolt threads.

The engine must be operated at slow speed when first started after a new braided seal is installed. Neoprene composition seals are placed in grooves in the sides of bearing cap to seal against leakage at the joints between cap and crankcase. The neoprene composition swells in the presence of oil and heat. The seals are undersize when newly installed and may even leak for a short time until the seals have had time to swell and seal the opening.

The neoprene seals are slightly longer than the grooves in the bearing cap. The seals must not be cut to length. Before installation of seals, soak for 5 minutes in light oil or kerosene. After installation of bearing cap in crankcase, install seal in bearing cap.

To help eliminate oil leakage at the joint where the cap meets the crankcase, apply silicone sealer, or equivalent, to the rear main bearing cap split line. When applying sealer, use only a thin coat as an over abundance will not allow the cap to seat properly. After seal is installed, force seals up into the cap with a blunt instrument to be sure of a seal at the upper parting line between the cap and case.

Oil Pump

REMOVAL & INSTALLATION

4-151 and 6-173 Engines

1. Remove the oil pan as described earlier.
2. Unbolt and remove the oil pump and pickup.
3. Installation is the reverse of removal. Torque the 4-151 pump to 22 ft. lbs. and the 6-173 pump bolts to 26-35 ft. lbs.

6-181 and 6-231 Engines

1. Remove the oil filter.
2. Unbolt the oil pump cover from the timing chain cover.
3. Slide out the oil pump gears. Clean all parts thoroughly in solvent and check for wear. Remove the oil pressure relief valve cap, spring and valve.
4. Installation is the reverse of removal. Torque the pressure relief valve cap to 35 ft. lbs. Install the pump gears and check their clearances:
   a. End clearance: 0.002-0.006 in.
   b. Side clearance: 0.002-0.005 in.

Place a straightedge across the face of the pump cover and check that it is flat to within 0.001 in. Pack the oil pump cavity with petroleum jelly so that there is no air space. Install the cover and torque the bolts to 10 ft. lbs.

6-263 Engine

1. Remove the oil pan.
2. Unbolt and remove the oil pump and drive extension.
3. Installation is the reverse of removal. Torque the pump bolts to 18 ft. lbs.

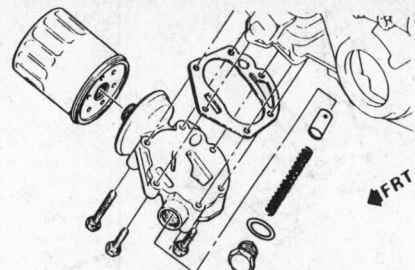

Oil pump—6-181 and 6-231

ENGINE COOLING

Radiator

REMOVAL & INSTALLATION

1. Disconnect the negative battery cable.
2. Drain the cooling system.
3. Remove the forward strut bracket for the engine at the radiator. Loosen the bolt to prevent shearing the rubber bushing, then swing the strut rearward.
4. Disconnect the headlamp wiring harness from the fan frame. Unplug the fan electrical connector.
5. Remove the attaching bolts for the fan.
6. Scribe the hood latch location on the radiator support, then remove the latch.
7. Disconnect the coolant hoses from the radiator. Remove the coolant recover tank hose from the radiator neck. Disconnect and plug the automatic transmission fluid cooler lines from the radiator, if so equipped.
8. Remove the radiator attaching bolts and remove the radiator. If the car has air conditioning, it first may be necessary to raise the left side of the radiator so that the radiator neck will clear the compressor.

To install:

1. Install the radiator in the car, tightening the mounting bolts to 7 inch lbs. Connect the transmission cooler lines and hoses. Install the coolant recovery hose.
2. Install the hood latch. Tighten to 6 ft. lbs.
3. Install the fan, making sure the bottom leg of the frame fits into the rubber grommet at the lower support. Install the fan wires and the headlamp wiring harness. Swing the strut and brace forward, tightening to 11 ft. lbs. Connect the engine ground strap to

the strut brace. Install the negative battery cable, fill the cooling system, and check for leaks.

Water Pump

REMOVAL & INSTALLATION

4-151 Engine

1. Disconnect battery negative cable.
2. Remove accessory drive belts.
3. Remove water pump attaching bolts and remove pump.
4. If installing a new water pump, transfer pulley from old unit. With sealing surfaces cleaned, place a ⅛ in. (3mm) bead of sealant No. 1052289 or equivalent on the water pump sealing surface. While sealer is still wet, install pump and torque bolts to 6 ft. lbs.
5. Install accessory drive belts.
6. Connect battery negative cable.

6-173 Engine

1. Disconnect battery negative cable.
2. Drain cooling system and remove heater hose.
3. Remove water pump attaching bolts and nut and remove pump.
4. With the sealant surfaces cleaned, place a ³⁄₃₂ in. (2mm) bead of sealant No. 1052357 or equivalent on the water pump sealing surface.
5. Clean old sealant from pump.
6. Coat bolt threads with pipe sealant No. 1052080 or equivalent.
7. Install pump and torque bolts to 10 ft. lbs.
8. Connect battery negative battery cable.

NOTE: When replacing the water pump on a car equipped with the 6 engine, the timing cover must be clamped to the cylinder block prior to removing the water pump bolts. Certain bolts holding the water pump pass through the front cover, and when removed, may allow the front cover to pull away from the cylinder block, breaking the seal. This may or may not be readily apparent and if left undetected, could allow coolant to enter the crankcase. To prevent this possible separation during water pump removal, Special Tool No. J29176 will have to be installed.

1982–83 6-181 Engine

1. Disconnect the negative battery cable.
2. Remove accessory drive belts.
3. Remove water pump attaching bolts.
4. Remove the engine support strut.

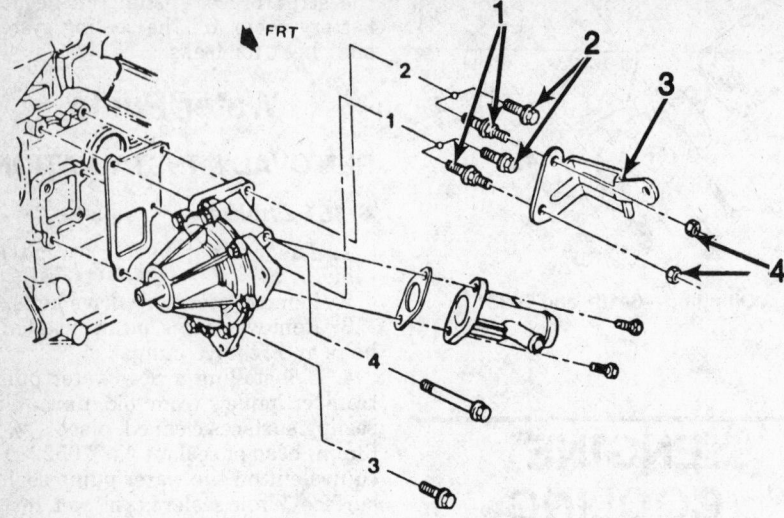

4-151 water pump installation

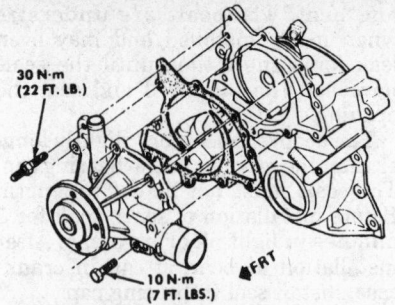

Water pump installation—6-181 and 6-231

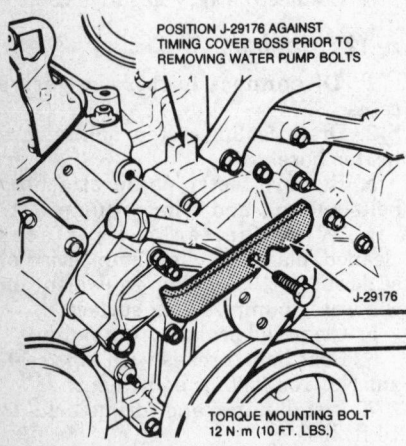

Install the special tool on the 6-173 to insure that the front cover does not separate from the crankcase when the pump is removed

5. Place a floor jack under the front crossmember of the cradle and raise the jack until the jack just starts to raise the car.

6. Remove the front 2 body mount bolts with the lower cushions and retainers.

7. Thread the body mount bolts with retainers a minimum of three turns into the cage so that the bolts restrain cradle movement.

8. Release the floor jack slowly until the crossmember contacts the body mount bolt retainers. As the jack is being lowered watch and correct any interference with hoses, lines, pipes and cables.

NOTE: Do not lower the cradle without its being restrained as possible damage can occur to the body and underhood items.

9. Remove water pump from engine.

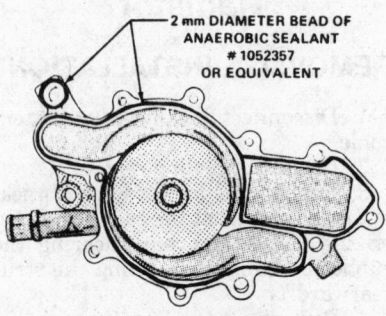

Applying sealer to the 6-173 water pump

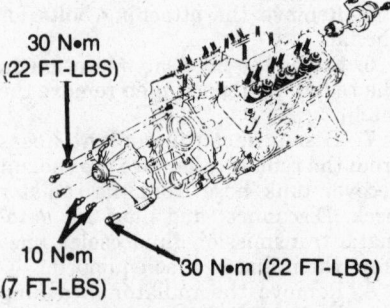

6-173 water pump installation

10. Reverse removal procedure.
11. Install pump and torque to 25 ft. lbs.
12. Connect negative battery cable.
13. Fill with coolant and check for leaks.

1984–89 6–181, 231 Engines

1. Disconnect the negative cable at the battery.
2. Drain the cooling system.
3. Remove the accessory drive belts.
4. Disconnect the radiator and heater hoses at the water pump.
5. Remove the water pump pulley bolts (long bolt removed through ac-

cess hole provided in the body side rail), then remove the pulley.
6. Remove the water pump attaching bolts, then remove the water pump.
7. Clean all gasket mating surfaces.
8. Using a new gasket, install the water pump on the engine. Torque the bolts to specifications.
9. Install the water pump pulley, then torque the bolts to specifications.
10. The remainder of the installation is the reverse of removal.

6–263 Engine

1. Drain radiator.
2. Disconnect lower radiator hose at water pump.
3. Disconnect the heater return hose at the water pump, remove the bolt retaining the heater water return pipe to the intake manifold and position the pipe out of the way.
4. If equipped with A/C, remove the vacuum pump drive belt.
5. Remove the serpentine drive belt.
6. Remove the generator. A/C compressor or vacuum pump brackets.
7. Remove the water pump attaching bolts and remove the water pump assembly.
8. Remove the water pump pulley.
9. Clean gasket material from engine block.
10. Apply a thin coat of 1050026 sealer or equivalent to the water pump housing to retain the gasket, then position new gasket on the housing. Also apply sealer to water pump mounting bolts. Torque bolts to 12–15 ft. lbs.

Thermostat

REMOVAL & INSTALLATION

1. Disconnect the negative battery cable.
2. Drain the cooling system.
3. Some models with cruise control have a vacuum modulator attached to the thermostat housing with a bracket. If equipped, remove the bracket from the housing.
4. On the 4 cylinder engine, unbolt

the water outlet from the thermostat housing, remove the outlet and lift the thermostat out of the housing. On all other models, unbolt the water outlet from the intake manifold, remove the outlet and lift the thermostat out of the manifold.

5. Clean both of the mating surfaces and run a ⅛ in. bead of RTV sealer in the groove of the water outlet.

6. Install the thermostat with the spring toward the engine and bolt the water outlet into place while the sealer is still wet. Torque the bolts to 21 ft. lbs. The remainder of the installation is in the reverse of the removal procedures. Check for leaks after the car is started and correct as required.

EMISSION CONTROLS

For all routine maintenance and service information on emission control systems, please refer to "Emission Controls" in the Unit Repair section. Due to the complex nature of modern electronic engine and emission control systems, comprehensive diagnosis and testing procedures fall outside the confines of this repair manual. For complete information on diagnosis, testing and repair procedures concerning all modern engine and emission control systems, please refer to *Chilton's Guide To Electronic Engine Controls*.

GASOLINE FUEL SYSTEM

Fuel System Service Precaution

RELIEVING FUEL SYSTEM PRESSURE

Throttle Body Injection (TBI)

1. On a COLD engine, remove the fuse marked "Fuel Pump" from the fuse block in the passenger compartment.

2. Crank the engine, engine will start and run until the fuel supply remaining in the fuel lines is exhausted.

When the engine stops, engage the starter again for 3.0 seconds to assure dissapation of any remaining pressure.

3. With the ignition OFF, replace the "Fuel pump" fuse.

─── **CAUTION** ───

Unless this procedure is followed before servicing fuel lines or connections, fuel spray could occur.

Port Fuel Injection (MFI)

1. On a COLD engine, connect fuel gauge J34730–1 or equavalent to fuel valve. Wrap a shop towel around the fitting while connecting gauge to avoid spillage.

2. Install bleed hose into an approved container and open valve to relieve system pressure.

Fuel Filter

REMOVAL & INSTALLATION

Carbureted Engines

1. An in-carburetor filter is used. With the engine cold, disconnect the fuel inlet line at the carburetor. Hold the large nut with a wrench while turning the smaller nut.

2. Remove the large nut from the carburetor inlet.

3. Remove the filter and spring from the carburetor.

4. New filters usually come with a new inlet nut gasket. If not, obtain one. Never reuse the old gasket. Install the new filter, gasket and nut. Do not overtighten the nut.

5. Install the fuel line. Use 2 wrenches to avoid distorting the fuel pipe.

Fuel Injected Models

─── **CAUTION** ───

Before servicing any part of the fuel system, it is necessary to releave the fuel system pressure. This will reduce the risk of fire or personal injury. The system contains an orafice, in the pressure regulator, which allows the fuel pressure to bleed off after the engine has been shut off. Make sure the engine is COLD and follow the Fuel System Pressure Relief procedure above.

The filter is an inline unit ahead of the TBI unit or in the fuel feed line under the vehicle to the left of the fuel tank on later models. To remove the filter, make sure the engine is COLD, unclamp and remove the fuel hose, then unscrew the filter from the steel fuel line. Installation is the reverse of removal.

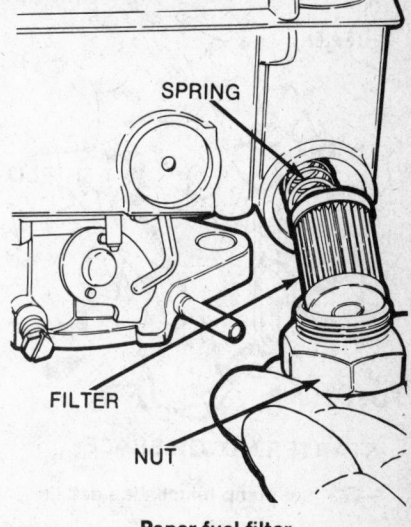

Paper fuel filter

Mechanical Fuel Pump

PRESSURE TESTING

1. Disconnect the fuel line at the carburetor and connect a fuel pump pressure gauge. Fill the carburetor float bowl with gasoline.

2. Start the engine and check the pressure with the engine at idle. If the pump has a vapor return hose, squeeze it off so that an accurate reading can be obtained. Pressure should measure 6.0–7.5 psi.

3. If the pressure is incorrect, replace the pump. If it is ok, go on to the volume test.

VOLUME TESTING

1. Disconnect the pressure gauge. Run the fuel line into a graduated container.

2. Run the engine at idle until one pint of gasoline has been pumped. One pint should be delivered in 30 seconds or less. There is normally enough fuel in the carburetor float bowl to perform this test, but refill it if necessary.

3. If the delivery rate is below the minimum, check the lines for restrictions or leaks, then replace the pump.

REMOVAL & INSTALLATION

1. Disconnect the negative battery cable. Raise the front of the vehicle and support it on jackstands.

2. Disconnect the fuel inlet and outlet lines at the pump and plug pump inlet line.

3. If necessary, on the V6, remove the shields and the oil filter.

4. Remove 2 pump mounting bolts and lockwashers; remove pump and gasket.

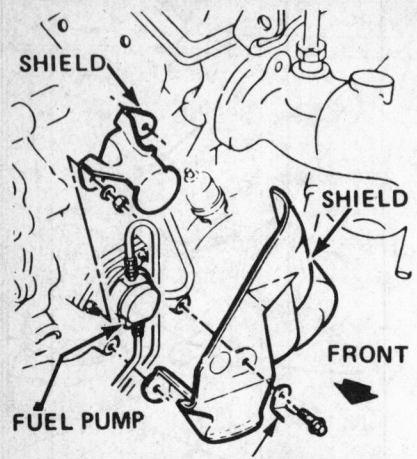

SHIELD

SHIELD

FRONT

FUEL PUMP

STARTER MOTOR BRACE

6–173 fuel pump installation details

5. Install pump with new gasket coated with sealer. Coat mounting bolt threads with sealer and tighten bolts.

NOTE: On Chevrolet V6 engines, mechanical fingers or heavy grease can be used to hold pump pushrod in place during installation. Coat pipe plug threads or adapter gasket with sealer if pushrod was removed.

6. Install the shields and oil filter on the V6, if removed.

7. Connect inlet and outlet lines, start engine and check for leaks.

Electric Fuel Pump

PRESSURE TESTING

1. On TBI or MFI equipped engines, disconnect the fuel line from the EFI, or on carburetor equipped engines, disconnect the fuel line from the fuel filter, then connect the fuel line to a pressure gauge.

NOTE: If the system is equipped with a fuel return hose, squeeze it off so that an accurate reading can be obtained.

2. If equipped with a carburetor, be sure to fill the float bowl with fuel.

3. On the TBI or MFI equipped engines, connect a jumper wire from the positive battery terminal to the **G** terminal of the ALCL unit or on the carbureted engines, start the engine, then check the fuel pressure.

4. The fuel pressure on the carburetor model is 5½–6½ psi, on the TBI unit, it is 9–13 psi and on the MFI system, it is 34–46 psi.

NOTE: If the pressures do not indicate correctly, check the fuel line for restrictions or the pump for malfunctions.

VOLUME TESTING

This test should be completed after the pressure test has been performed.

1. Disconnect the pressure gauge from the fuel line and connect a flexible tube from the fuel line to an unbreakable container.

NOTE: If the engine is equipped with a fuel return line, squeeze off the line to obtain an accurate reading.

2. If equipped with a carburetor, start the engine; if equipped with a TBI or an MFI unit, connect a jumper wire from the positive battery cable to the **G** terminal of the ALCL unit.

3. In 15 seconds, the fuel pump should supply ½ pint of fuel.

NOTE: If the fuel volume is below minimum, check the fuel line for restrictions.

4. After testing, reconnect the fuel line to the carburetor or the EFI unit.

REMOVAL & INSTALLATION

—— CAUTION ——
Before opening any part of the fuel system, the pressure must be relieved. Follow the procedure below to relieve the pressure:

1. Remove the fuel pump fuse from the fuse panel.

2. Start the engine and let it run until all fuel in the line is used.

3. Crank the starter an additional three seconds to relieve any residual pressure.

4. With the ignition OFF, replace the fuse.

5. Drain the fuel tank.

6. Disconnect wiring from the tank.

7. Remove the ground wire retaining screw from under the body.

8. Disconnect all hoses from the tank.

9. Support the tank on a jack and remove the retaining strap nuts.

10. Lower the tank and remove it.

11. Remove the fuel gauge/pump retaining ring using a spanner wrench such as tool J–24187.

12. Remove the gauge unit and the pump.

13. Installation is the revere of removal. Always replace the O-ring under the gauge/pump retaining ring.

Carburetor

REMOVAL & INSTALLATION

1. Disconnect the battery.

2. Remove the air cleaner.

3. Disconnect the accelerator linkage.

4. Disconnect the transmission detent cable.

5. If equipped, disconnect the cruise control cable.

6. Disconnect all electrical connectors at the carburetor, or which might interfere with carburetor removal. Tag the wires for installation.

7. Disconnect and tag all vacuum lines at the carburetor.

8. Disconnect the fuel line at the carburetor inlet.

9. Installation is the reverse of removal. Torque the long bolts to 7 ft. lbs.; the short bolts to 11 ft. lbs.

OVERHAUL

For all carburetor overhaul and adjustment procedures, please refer to "Carburetor Service" in the Unit Repair section.

Fuel Injection

Due the complex nature of modern fuel injection systems, comprehensive diagnosis and testing procedures fall outside the confines of this repair manual. For complete information on fuel injection diagnosis, testing and repair procedures please refer to *Chilton's Guide To Fuel Injection and Feedback Carburetors.*

DIESEL FUEL SYSTEM

Fuel Filter

REMOVAL & INSTALLATION

Models with NB9

NB9 is an assembly which performs several functions:
- Filtration
- Water seperation
- Water detection
- Water drainage and fuel heating (fuel heating is optional)

To remove the fuel filter:

1. Disconnect the fuel lines from the inlet and outlet ports.

2. Disconnect the drain hose, drain fuel filter lamp, harness connector and fuel heater harness connector (if equipped).

3. Remove the filter assembly clamp to bracket bolts and remove the clamp.

4. Rotate the filter assembly to dis-

engage it from the bracket and remove the filter assembly.

5. Carefully clamp the filter assembly into a vise. Then, using a cloth, clamp it at the line openings and at the flat at the opposite side of the cover.

6. Remove the filter and clean the filter cover gasket surface.

7. Coat the new filter's gasket with engine oil or diesel fuel.

8. Install the filter on the cover and tighten the filter ⅔ turn beyond intial gasket contact.

9. Loosely assemble the filter assembly in the bracket. Engage the bracket lock tab into the bracket. Using new "0" rings, loosely assemble the fuel lines to the filter assembly.

10. Install the clamps and tighten the bolts to specification.

11. Install the drain hose and torque the clamp.

12. Torque the fuel lines to specification.

13. Connect the harness connectors to the drain fuel filter lamp module and fuel heater.

14. Carefully expand the clamps that retain the fuel hoses to the in-line filter (sight glass).

15. Disconnect the hoses and remove the in-line filter.

16. Install a new in-line filter on the hoses with the arrow pointing to the engine. Carefully expand the clamps and position them in the origional location.

17. Loosen the air bleed screw.

18. Turn the ignition switch to the RUN position. This will energize the fuel pump.

19. Close the air bleed screw when fuel is present at the air bleed ports. Clean any spilled fuel.

20. Start the engine and inspect for leaks.

Models Without NB9

1. Remove the air cleaner and install J–26996–1 air crossover cover.

2. Place a rag under the fuel filter to catch any fuel that will drop out.

3. Disconnect the fuel lines from the filter.

4. Remove the wing nut and remove the filter assembly.

5. Place a new filter into position.

6. Loosely assemble the fuel lines to the filter. The filter can only be installed one way because the fittings are different sizes.

7. Install and tighten the wing nut.

8. Torque the lines to the proper specification.

NOTE: It is suggested that after changing the fuel filter on a diesel, that the Housing Pressure Cold Advance be activated manually, if the engine temperature is above 125°F (52°C). Activating the H.P.C.A. solenoid will reduce cranking time.

To activate the H.P.C.A. solenoid:

a. Disconnect the 2 lead connector at the engine temperature switch.

b. Bridge the connector with a jumper and start the engine.

c. After the engine is running, remove the jumper and reconnect the connector to the engine temperature switch.

9. Start the engine and check for leaks in the fuel lines and fittings.

DRAINING WATER FROM THE SYSTEM

NOTE: Due to the chemical composition of diesel fuel, water develops in the fuel system. If the water is not periodically removed, damage may occur in the fuel system which could affect performance and the life expectancy of the components in the system.

1. Turn ignition to the run position, but do not start the engine, this will turn on the fuel pump.

2. Using a suitable container, open the water drain valve (located near the left fender well) 2 complete turns. Reach over to the filter assembly and push the red button in, this will allow the fuel to flow from the valve.

—————— CAUTION ——————
Never drain or store fuel in an open container due to the possibility of fire or explosion which could result in personal injury.

3. Let fuel and water drain until the color of the fuel is uniform, this will usually take 15–20 seconds, then release button and close the drain valve.

BLEEDING FUEL SYSTEM

Refer to the last three steps of the fuel filter removal and installation procedure.

Diesel Injection Pump

REMOVAL

1. Remove the air cleaner assembly.

2. Remove the crankcase ventilation filter and pipes from the valve cover and air crossover.

3. Remove the air crossover and install intake manifold screened covers J–29657. Remove the fuel lines, filter and fuel pump as an assembly.

4. Disconnect the throttle cable and T.V. cable from the pump throttle lever. Disconnect the throttle return spring.

5. Remove the throttle and T.V./Detent cables from the intake manifold brackets. Position the cables away from the engine.

6. Disconnect the fuel return line from the injection pump.

7. Disconnect the injection line clamps that are closest to the pump.

8. Disconnect the injection lines from the pump and cap all openings. Carefully reposition the lines to gain enough clearance for pump removal.

9. Remove the 2 bolts retaining the injection pump.

10. Remove the pump and discard the pump to adapter O-ring.

INSTALLATION

1. Position engine No. 1 cylinder to firing position by aligning the mark on the balancer with zero mark on the indicator located on the front of the engine (the index is offset to the right when No. 1 cylinder is at TDC).

2. Line up offset tang on pump driveshaft with the pump driven gear. Install a new pump to adapter O-ring, then install the pump fully, seating the pump by hand.

3. If a new or intermediate adapter is installed, set the injection pump at the center of the slots in the pump mounting flange. If the original intermediate adapter is being retained, align the pump timing mark with the mark on the intermediate adapter. Install the 2 bolts and washers retaining the pump and torque to 35 ft. lbs.

4. Remove the caps from the openings and connect the injection lines to the pump. Install the disconnected injection line clamps.

5. Connect the fuel return line.

6. Install the throttle and T.V. cables into the intake manifold bracket.

7. Connect the throttle cable and T.V. cable to the pump throttle lever. Connect the throttle return spring. Adjust the T.V. cable.

8. Install all remaining fuel lines and fuel filter.

9. Start the engine and check for leaks.

10. Check and if necessary reset the pump timing.

11. Adjust the vacuum regulator valve.

12. Adjust the idle speeds.

13. Remove the screened covers from intake manifold, then install the air crossover.

14. Install tubes and hoses in the air crossover and ventilation filters in the valve cover.

15. Install the air cleaner being certain to reconnect the EGR valve hose.

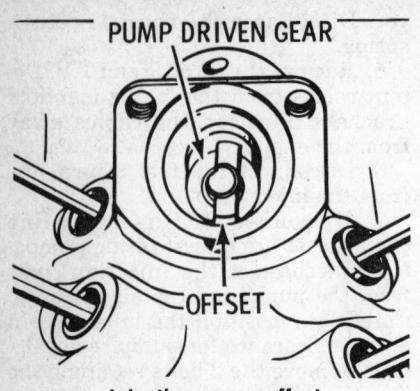

PUMP DRIVEN GEAR

OFFSET

Injection pump offset

Injection Timing

CHECKING AND/OR ADJUSTING TIMING USING J–33075 TIMING METER

The timing meter picks up the engine speed and crankshaft position from the crankshaft balancer. It uses a luminosity signal through a glow plug probe to determine combustion timing. Certain engine malfunctions may cause incorrect timing readings. Engine malfunctions should be corrected before timing adjustment is made. The marks on the pump and adapter flange will normally be aligned within 0.050 in. (1.27mm).

NOTE: Alignment of timing marks may be used in emergency situations (i.e. timing meter not available). However for optimum engine operation, the timing should be adjusted with the timing meter as soon as possible.

1. Place the transmission selector lever in Park, apply the parking brake and block the drive wheels.
2. Start the engine and let it run at idle until fully warmed up. Then shut off the engine.

NOTE: Failure to have the engine fully warmed up will result in incorrect timing reading and adjustments.

3. Remove the air cleaner assembly and install cover J–26996–1. The EGR valve hose must be disconnected.
4. Clean any dirt from the engine probe holder (rpm counter) and crankshaft balancer rim.
5. Clean the lens on both ends of the glow plug probe and clean the lens in the photo-electric pick-up. Use a dulled tooth pick to scrape the carbon from the combustion chamber side of the glow plug probe. Look through the probe to be sure it's clean. Retarded readings will result if the probe is not clean.

6. Install the rpm probe into the crankshaft rpm counter (probe holder).
7. Remove the glow plug from No. 1 cylinder. Install the glow plug from No. 1 cylinder. Install the glow plug probe in the glow opening. Torque the probe to 9 ft. lbs.
8. Set the timing meter offset selector to A (20).
9. Connect the battery leads; red to positive, black to negative.
10. Start the engine and adjust the engine rpm to the speed specified on the underhood emission control sticker.
11. Observe the timing reading, then at 2 minute intervals, again observe the reading. When the readings stabilize over the 2 minute interval, compare that reading to the one specified on the underhood sticker. The timing reading when set to specification will be ATDC (after top dead center).
12. Disconnect the timing meter.
13. Lubricate only the threads of the removed glow plug with lubricant 9985462 or equivalent.

NOTE: Failure to apply the correct lubricant can cause engine damage.

14. Install the removed glow plug. Torque the glow plug to 15 ft. lbs.
15. Install the air cleaner being certain to reconnect the EGR valve hose.

ADJUSTMENT

1. Shut off the engine.
2. Note the relative position of the marks on the pump flange and pump intermediate adapter.
3. Loosen the bolts holding the pump to the adapter to a point where the pump can be rotated. Use a 1 in. open end wrench. Tool J–25304 has the proper offset on the handle to clear the fuel return line.
4. Rotate the pump to the left to advance the timing and to the right to retard the timing. The width of the mark on the intermediate adapter is about ⅔ degree. Move the pump the amount that is needed and tighten the pump retaining bolts to 35 ft. lbs.
5. Start the engine and recheck the timing reading as outlined previously. Reset and recheck the timing if needed.
6. Reset the idle speed. Please note the following:
   a. Sooty or dirty probes will result in retarded readings.
   b. The luminosity probe will soot up very fast when used in a cold engine.
   c. Wild needle fluctuations on the timing meter indicate a cylinder not firing properly. Correction of this

condition must be made prior to adjusting the timing.

Electric Fuel Transfer Pump

The pump is located at the front of the engine next to the fuel heater.

REMOVAL & INSTALLATION

1. Place the ignition in the OFF position.
2. Remove the air cleaner.
3. Disconnect the pump electrical supply wire.
4. Using a ¼ in. wrench on the inlet fitting, unscrew the fuel pipe inlet tube.
5. Using the same method, unscrew the outlet pipe.
6. Unbolt the pump mounting bracket and the pump.
7. Installation is the reverse of removal. Using the 2 wrench method, torque the fuel lines to 19 ft. lbs. The pump bracket is torqued to 18 ft. lbs. In some cases, it may be necessary to adjust the pump location slightly to get a good alignment on the fuel lines. When the pump is installed, disconnect the fuel line at the filter, and run the pump with the key ON to bleed the lines.

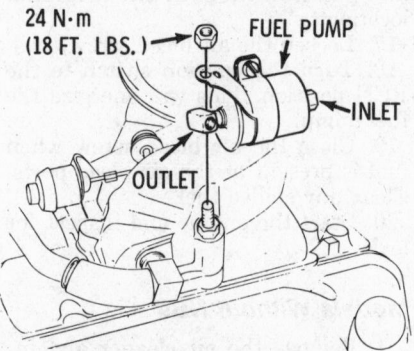

24 N·m (18 FT. LBS.)   FUEL PUMP   INLET   OUTLET

Diesel fuel transfer pump

Injection Nozzle

REMOVAL & INSTALLATION

NOTE: Whenever lines are disconnected, use a backup wrench to avoid line distortion.

1. Remove the injection lines as described earlier. When working on the right side, leave the engine in the position described under line removal, for injection removal.
2. Remove the nozzle by applying the wrench to the larger hex on the nozzle.
3. Remove the copper gasket from

the head if it did not remain on the nozzle.

4. Installation is the revere of removal. Use lubricant 9985462 or its equivalent on the nozzle threads. Always use a new copper gasket on each nozzle. Torque the nozzle and the lines to 25 ft. lbs. each.

MANUAL TRANSAXLE

All 1982–86 models were equipped with 4 speed transaxles. In 1987–89 Muncie 5 speed transaxles were used. The 4 speed transaxles use cable actuated clutches while the 5 speed clutches are hydraulically controlled utilizing a clutch master and slave cylinder.

REMOVAL & INSTALLATION

4 Speed Transaxle

1. Disconnect the negative battery cable from the transaxle case.
2. Remove the 2 transaxle strut bracket bolts on the left side of the engine compartment, if equipped.
3. On some models equipped with a V6 engine, disconnect the fuel lines and fuel line clamps at the clutch cable bracket.
4. Remove the top 4 engine-to-transaxle bolts, and the one at the rear near the firewall. The one at the rear is installed from the engine side.
5. Loosen the engine-to-transaxle bolt near the starter, but do not remove.
6. Disconnect the speedometer cable at the transaxle, or at the speed control transducer on cars so equipped.
7. Remove the retaining clip and washer from the shift linkage at the transaxle. Remove the clips holding the cables to the mounting bosses on the case.
8. Support the engine with a lifting chain.
9. Unlock the steering column and raise and support the car. Drain the transaxle. Remove the 2 nuts attaching the stabilizer bar to the left lower control arm. Remove the 4 bolts which attach the left retaining plate to the engine cradle. The retaining plate covers and holds the stabilizer bar.
10. Loosen the 4 bolts holding the right stabilizer bracket.
11. Disconnect and remove the exhaust pipe and crossover if necessary.

12. Pull the stabilizer bar down on the left side.
13. Remove the 4 nuts and disconnect the front and rear transaxle mounts from the engine cradle. Remove the 2 rear center crossmember bolts.
14. Remove the three right side front cradle attaching bolts. They are accessible under the splash shield.
15. Remove the top bolt from the lower front transaxle shock absorber if equipped.
16. Remove the left front wheel. Remove the front cradle-to-body bolts on the left side, and the rear cradle-to-body bolts.
17. Pull the left side drive shaft from the transaxle using G.M. special tool J–28468 or the equivalent. The right side axle shaft will simply disconnect from the case. When the transaxle is removed, the right shaft can be swung out of the way. A boot protector should be used when disconnecting the driveshafts.
18. Swing the cradle to the left side. Secure out of the way, outboard of the fender well.
19. Remove the flywheel and starter shield bolts, and remove the shields.
20. Remove the 2 transaxle extension bolts from the engine-to-transaxle bracket, if equipped.
21. Place a jack under the transaxle case. Remove the last engine-to-transaxle bolt. Pull the transaxle to the left, away from the engine, then down and out from under the car.
22. Installation is the reverse of removal. Position the right axle shaft into its bore as the transaxle is being installed. When the transaxle is bolted to the engine, swing the cradle into position and install the cradle-to-body bolts immediately. Be sure to guide the left axle shaft into place as the cradle is moved back into position.

5 Speed Transaxle

1. Disconnect the negative battery cable.
2. Remove the air cleaner and air intake duct assembly.
3. Remove the sound insulator from inside the car.
4. Remove the clutch master cylinder push rod from the clutch pedal.
5. Remove the clutch slave cylinder from the transaxle.
6. Disconnect the exhaust crossover pipe.
7. Disconnect the shift cables at the transaxle.
8. Install the engine support fixture J–28467.

9. Remove the top engine to transaxle bolts.
10. Raise the car and suitably support it.
11. Install the drive axle boot seal protectors with special Tool J–34754.
12. Remove the L.H. front wheel and tire.
13. Remove the L.H. side frame and disconnect the rear transaxle mount from the bracket.
14. Drain the transaxle.
15. Disengage the R.H. and L.H. drive axles from the transaxle.
16. Remove the clutch housing cover bolts.
17. Disconnect the speedometer cable.
18. Attach a jack to the transaxle case.
19. Remove the remaining transaxle to engine bolts.
20. Slide the transaxle away from the engine. Carefully lower the jack while guiding the R.H. drive axle out of the transaxle.
21. When installing the transaxle, position the right drive axle shaft into its bore as the transaxle is being installed. The R.H. shaft CANNOT be readily installed after the transaxle is connected to the engine.
22. After the transaxle is fastened to the engine and the L.H. drive axle is installed at the transaxle, position the L.H. side frame and install the frame to body bolts.
23. Connect the transaxle to the front and rear mounts.
24. The remainder of the installation is the reverse of removal.

LINKAGE ADJUSTMENT

4 Speed Models

1. Remove the shifter boot and retainer inside the car. Shift into first gear.
2. Install 2 No. 22 drill bits, or 2 $\frac{5}{32}$ in. rods, into the 2 alignment holes in the shifter assembly to hold it in first gear.
3. Place the transaxle into first gear by pushing the rail selector shaft down just to the point of feeling the resistance of the inhibitor spring. Then rotate the shift lever all the way counterclockwise.
4. Install the stud, with the cable attached, into the slotted area of the select lever, while gently pulling on the lever to remove all lash.
5. Remove the 2 drill bits or pins from the shifter.
6. Check the shifter for proper operation. It may be necessary to fine tune the adjustment after road testing.

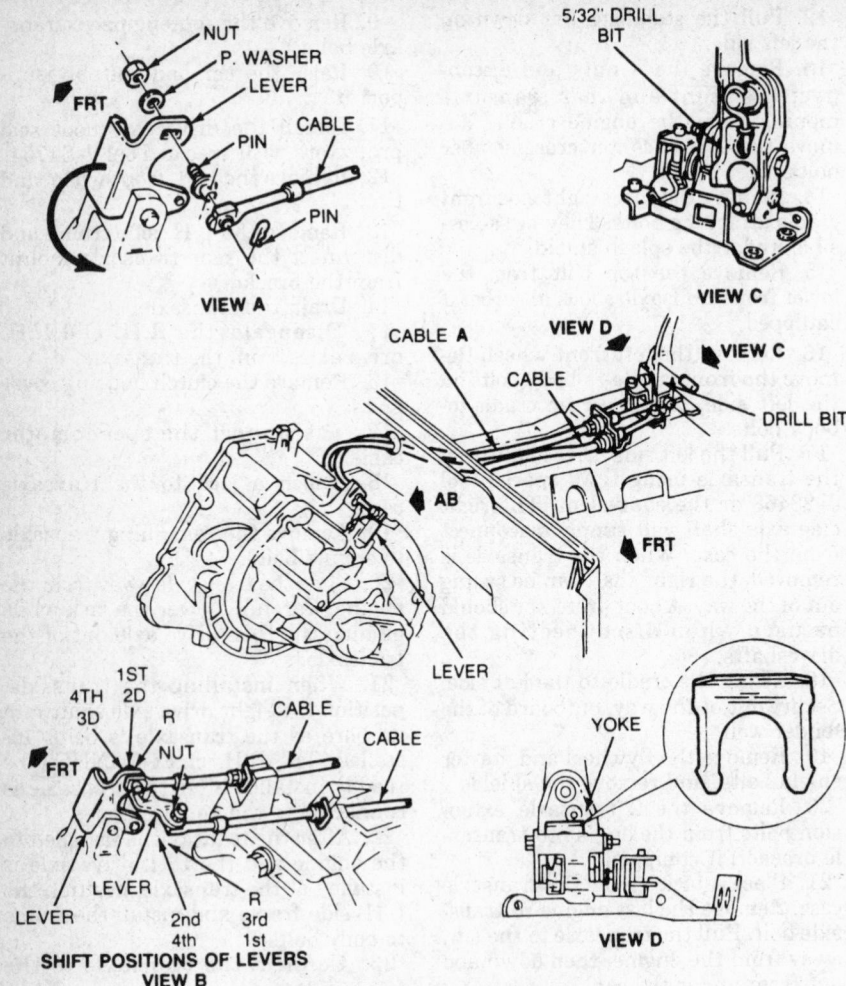

VIEW A

VIEW C

Four speed transaxle shift linkage

SHIFT POSITIONS OF LEVERS
VIEW B

VIEW D

CLUTCH

On 1982–86 models the only service adjustment necessary on the clutch is to maintain the correct pedal free play. Clutch pedal free play, or throwout bearing lash, decreases with driven disc wear. On 1987–89 models a hydraulic clutch system provides automatic clutch adjustment.

REMOVAL & INSTALLATION

1. On 1987–89 models disconnect the negative battery cable, remove the hush panel from inside the vehicle then disconnect the clutch master cylinder push rod from the clutch pedal.
2. Remove the transaxle.
3. Mark the pressure plate assembly and the flywheel so that they can be assembled in the same position. They were balanced as an assembly at the factory.
4. Loosen the attaching bolts one

turn at a time until spring tension is relieved.
5. Support the pressure plate and remove the bolts. Remove the pressure plate and clutch disc. Do not disassemble the pressure plate assembly; replace it if defective.
6. Inspect the flywheel, clutch disc, pressure plate, throwout bearing and the clutch fork and pivot shaft assembly for wear. Replace the parts as required. If the flywheel shows any signs of overheating, or if it is badly grooved or scored, it should be replaced.
7. Clean the pressure plate and flywheel mating surfaces thoroughly. Position the clutch disc and pressure plate into the installed position, and support with a dummy shaft or clutch aligning tool. The clutch plate is assembled with the damper springs offset toward the transaxle. One side of the factory-supplied clutch disc is stamped "Flywheel side".
8. Install the pressure plate-to-flywheel bolts. Tighten them gradually in a crisscross pattern.
9. Lubricate the outside groove and

the inside recess of the release bearing with high temperature grease. Wipe off any excess. Install the release bearing.
10. Install the transaxle.
11. On 1987–89 models connect the clutch master cylinder push rod to the clutch pedal and install the retaining clip.
12. On 1987–89 models, if equipped with cruise control, check the switch adjustment at the clutch pedal bracket.

NOTE: When adjusting the cruise control switch, do not exert an upward force on the clutch pedal pad of more than 20 lbs. or damage to the master cylinder push rod retaining ring may result.

13. On 1987–89 models, install the hush panel and reconnect the negative battery cable.

CLUTCH LINKAGE AND PEDAL HEIGHT/FREE—PLAY ADJUSTMENT

1982–86 Models

All cars use a self-adjusting clutch mechanism which may be checked as follows. As the clutch friction material wears, the cable must be lengthened. This is accomplished by simply pulling the clutch pedal up to its rubber bumper. This action forces the pawl against its stop and rotates it out of mesh with the quadrant teeth, allowing the cable to play out until the quadrant spring load is balanced against the load applied by the release bearing. This adjustment procedure is required every 5000 miles or less.

1. With engine running and brake on, hold the clutch pedal approximately ½ in. from floor mat and move shift lever between first and reverse several times. If this can be done smoothly without clashing into reverse, the clutch is fully releasing. If shift is not smooth, clutch is not fully releasing and linkage should be inspected and corrected as necessary.
2. Check clutch pedal bushings for sticking or excessive wear.
3. Have an assistant sit in the driver's seat and fully apply the clutch pedal to the floor. Observe the clutch fork level travel at the transaxle. The end of the clutch fork lever should have a total travel of approximately 1.5–1.7 in.
4. If fork lever is not correct, check the adjusting mechanism by depressing the clutch pedal and looking for pawl to firmly engage with the teeth in the quadrant.

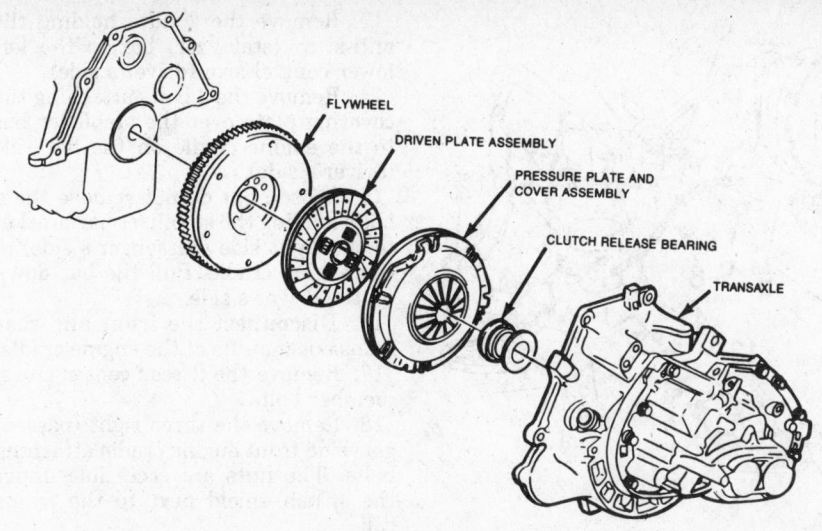

FLYWHEEL

DRIVEN PLATE ASSEMBLY

PRESSURE PLATE AND COVER ASSEMBLY

CLUTCH RELEASE BEARING

TRANSAXLE

Clutch components

Clutch Cable

REMOVAL

1. Support the clutch pedal upward against the bumper stop to release the pawl from the quadrant. Disconnect the end of the cable from the clutch release lever at the transaxle. Be careful to prevent the cable from snapping rapidly toward the rear of the car. The quadrant in the adjusting mechanism can be damaged by allowing the cable to snap back.

2. Disconnect the clutch cable from the quadrant. Lift the locking pawl away from the quadrant, then slide the cable out on the right side of the quadrant.

3. From the engine side of the cowl disconnect the 2 upper nuts holding the cable retainer to the upper studs. Disconnect the cable from the bracket mounted to the transaxle, and remove the cable.

4. Inspect the clutch cable for frayed wires, kinks, worn ends and excessive friction. If any of these conditions exist, replace the cable.

INSTALLATION

1. With the gasket in position on the 2 upper studs, position a new cable with the retaining flange against the bracket.

2. Attach the end of the cable to the quadrant, being sure to route the cable underneath the pawl.

3. Attach the 2 upper nuts to the retainer mounting studs, and torque to specifications.

4. Attach the cable to the bracket mounted to the transaxle.

5. Support the clutch pedal upward against the bumper stop to release the

pawl from the quadrant. Attach the outter end of the cable to the clutch release lever. Be sure not to yank on the cable, since overloading the cable could damage the quadrant.

6. Check clutch operation and adjust by lifting the clutch pedal up to allow the mechanism to adjust the cable length. Depress the pedal slowly several times to set the pawl into mesh with the quadrant teeth.

Clutch Master and Slave Cylinder

NOTE: The clutch hydraulic system is serviced as a complete unit, it has been bled of air and filled with fluid.

REMOVAL & INSTALLATION

1987–89

1. Disconnect the negative battery cable.

2. Remove the hush panel from inside the vehicle.

3. Remove the clutch master cylinder retaining nuts at the front of the dash.

4. Remove the slave cylinder retaining nuts at the transaxle.

5. Remove the hydraulic system as a unit from the vehicle.

6. Install the slave cylinder to the transmission support bracket aligning the push rod into the pocket on the clutch fork outer lever. Tighten the retaining nuts evenly to prevent damage to the slave cylinder. Torque the nuts to 40 ft. lbs.

NOTE: Do not remove the plastic push rod retainer from the slave cylinder. The straps will

break on the first clutch pedal application.

7. Position the clutch master cylinder to the front of the dash. Torque the nuts evenly to 20 ft. lbs.

8. Remove the pedal restrictor from the push rod. Lube the push rod bushing on the clutch pedal. Connect the push rod to the clutch pedal and install the retaining clip.

9. If equipped with cruise control, check the switch adjustment at the clutch pedal bracket.

NOTE: When adjusting the cruise control switch, do not exert an upward force on the clutch pedal pad of more than 20 lbs. or damage to the master cylinder push rod retaining ring may result.

10. Install the hush panel.

11. Press the clutch pedal down several times. This will break the plastic retaining straps on the slave cylinder push rod. Do not remove the plastic button on the end of the push rod.

12. Connect the negative battery cable.

BLEEDING THE HYDRAULIC CLUTCH SYSTEM

Bleeding air from the system is necessary any time part of the system has been disconnected, or the fluid level in the reservoir has been allowed to fall so low that air has been drawn into the master cylinder.

—————— CAUTION ——————

Never under any circumstance use fluid that has been bled from the system as it could be contaminated with air or moisture.

1. Clean the cap then remove the cap and diaphragm and fill the reservoir to the top with certified DOT 3 brake fluid.

2. Fully loosen the bleed screw which is in the slave cylinder body next to the inlet connection. Fluid will now begin to move from the master cylinder down the tube to the slave. It is important that for efficent gravity fill, the reservoir must be filled at all times.

3. At this point bubbles will be noticeable at the bleed screw outlet showing air is being expelled. When the slave is full, a steady stream of fluid will come from the slave outlet. At this point, tighten the bleed screw.

4. Install the diaphragm and cap to the reservoir. The fluid in the reservoir should be level with the step.

5. The hydraulic system should now be fully bled and should release the clutch. Check the vehicle by starting, then push the clutch pedal to the floor

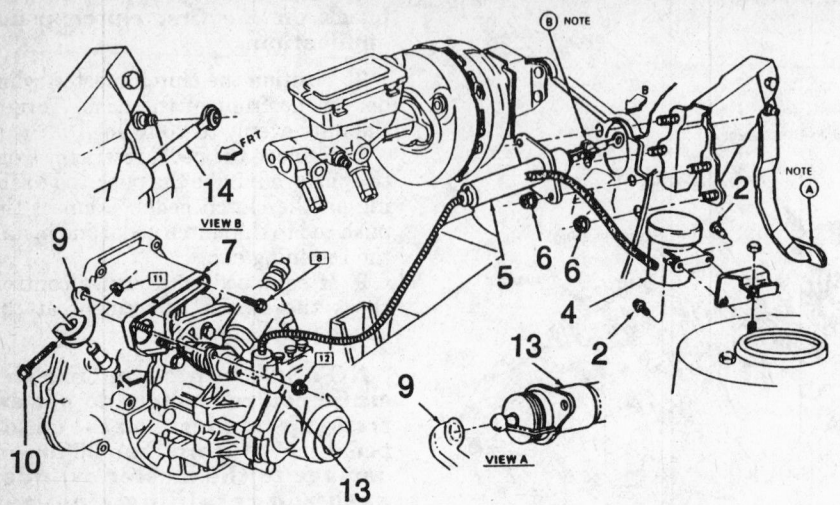

1. Clutch pedal assembly
2. Bolt
3. Bracket
4. Reservoir
5. Master cylinder
6. 20 ft. lbs.
7. Slave cylinder bracket
8. Bolt 40 ft. lbs.
9. Lever
10. Bolt 37 ft. lbs.
11. Nut
12. Nut 40 ft. lbs.
13. Slave cylinder
14. Master cylinder push rod

Clutch hydraulic system

and selecting reverse gear. There should be no grinding of gears, if there is, the hydraulic system still contains air. If so, bleed the system again.

AUTOMATIC TRANSAXLE

For further information on automatic transmissions, please refer to "Automatic Transmissions" in the Unit Repair section.

CAUTION

Any inaccuracies in shift linkage adjustments may result in premature failure of the transmission due to operation without the controls in full detent. Such operation results in reduced fluid pressure and in turn, partial engagement of the affected clutches. Partial engagement of the clutches, with sufficient pressure to permit apparently normal vehicle operation will result in failure of the clutches and/or other internal parts after only a few miles of operation.

REMOVAL & INSTALLATION

125 and 125C Transaxle

1. Disconnect the negative battery cable from the transaxle. Tape the wire to the upper radiator hose to keep it out of the way.
2. Remove the air cleaner and dis-connect the detent cable. Slide the detent cable in the opposite direction of the cable to remove it from the carburetor.
3. Unbolt the detent cable attaching bracket at the transaxles.
4. Pull up on the detent cable cover at the transaxle until the cable is exposed. Disconnect the cable from the rod.
5. Remove the 2 transaxle strut bracket bolts at the transaxle, if equipped.
6. Remove all the engine-to-transaxle bolts except the one near the starter. The one nearest the firewall is installed from the engine side; you will need a short handled box wrench or ratchet to reach it.
7. Loosen, but do not remove the engine-to-transaxle bolt near the starter.
8. Disconnect the speedometer cable at the upper and lower coupling. On cars with cruise control, remove the speedometer cable at the transducer.
9. Remove the retaining clip and washer from the shift linkage at the transaxle. Remove the 2 shift linkage at the transaxle. Remove the 2 shift linkage bracket bolts.
10. Disconnect and plug the 2 fluid cooler lines at the transaxle. These are inch-size fittings ($\frac{1}{2}$ and $\frac{11}{16}$); use a back-up wrench to avoid twisting the lines.
11. Install an engine holding chain or hoist. Raise the engine enough to take its weight off the mounts.
12. Unlock the steering column and raise the car.

13. Remove the 2 nuts holding the anti-sway (stabilizer) bar to the left lower control arm (driver's side).
14. Remove the 4 bolts attaching the covering plate over the stabilizer bar to the engine cradle on the left side (driver's side).
15. Loosen but do not remove the 4 bolts holding the stabilizer bar bracket to the right side (passenger's side) of the engine cradle. Pull the bar down on the driver's side.
16. Disconnect the front and rear transaxle mounts at the engine cradle.
17. Remove the 2 rear center cross-member bolts.
18. Remove the three right (passenger) side front engine cradle attaching bolts. The nuts are accessible under the splash shield next to the frame rail.
19. Remove the top bolt from the lower front transaxle shock absorber, if equipped (V6 engine only).
20. Remove the left (driver) side front and rear cradle-to-body bolts.
21. Remove the left front wheel. Attach an axle shaft removing tool (GM No. J–28468 or equivalent) to a slide hammer. Place the tool behind the axle shaft cones and pull the cones out away from the transaxle. Remove the right shaft in the same manner. Set the shafts out of the way. Plug the openings in the transaxle to prevent fluid leakage and the entry of dirt.
22. Swing the partial engine cradle to the left (driver) side and wire it out of the way outboard of the fender well.
23. Remove the 4 torque converter and starter shield bolts. Remove the 2 transaxle extension bolts from the engine-to-transaxle bracket.
24. Attach a transaxle jack to the case.
25. Use a felt pen to matchmark the torque converter and flywheel. Remove the three torque converter-to-flywheel bolts.
26. Remove the transaxle-to-engine bolt near the starter. Remove the transaxle by sliding it to the left, away from the engine.
27. Installation is the reverse of removal. As the transaxle is installed, slide the right axle shaft into the case. Install the cradle-to-body bolts before the stabilizer bar is installed. To aid in stabilizer bar installation, a pry hole has been provided in the engine cradle.

440 T4 Transaxle

1. Disconnect the negative battery cable.
2. Remove the air cleaner and disconnect the T.V. cable at the throttle body.
3. Disconnect the shift linkage at the transaxle.
4. Install the engine support fixture. Tool J–28467 is recommended.

5. Disconnect all electrical connectors.

6. Remove the three bolts from the transaxle to the engine.

7. Disconnect the vacuum line at the modulator.

8. Raise the car and suitably support it.

9. Remove the left front wheel and tire assembly.

10. Remove the L.H. ball joint from the steering knuckle.

11. Disconnect the brake line bracket at the strut.

NOTE: A drive axle seal protector Tool J–34754 should be modified and installaed on any drive axle prior to service procedures on or near the drive axle. Failure to do so could result in seal damage or joint failure.

12. Remove the drive axles from the transaxle.

13. Disconnect the pinch bolt at the intermediate steering shaft. Failure to do so could cause damage to the steering gear.

14. Remove the frame to stabilizer bolts.

15. Remove the stabilizer bolts at the control arm.

16. Remove the left front frame assembly.

17. Disconnect the speedometer cable or wire connector from the transaxle.

18. Remove the extension housing to engine block support bracket.

19. Disconnect the cooler pipes.

20. Remove the converter cover, and converter to flywheel bolts.

21. Remove all of the remaining transaxle to engine bolts except one.

22. Position a jack under the transaxle.

23. Remove the remaining transaxle to engine bolt and remove the transaxle.

24. Installation is the reverse of removal. Torque the transaxle to engine bolts to 55 ft. lbs. Flush the oil cooler lines with Tool J–35944 or equivalent and adjust the T.V. cable and shift linkage as necessary.

DRIVE AXLE

Halfshaft
REMOVAL & INSTALLATION

―――― CAUTION ――――
Use care when removing the drive axle. Tripots can be damaged if the drive axle is overextended.

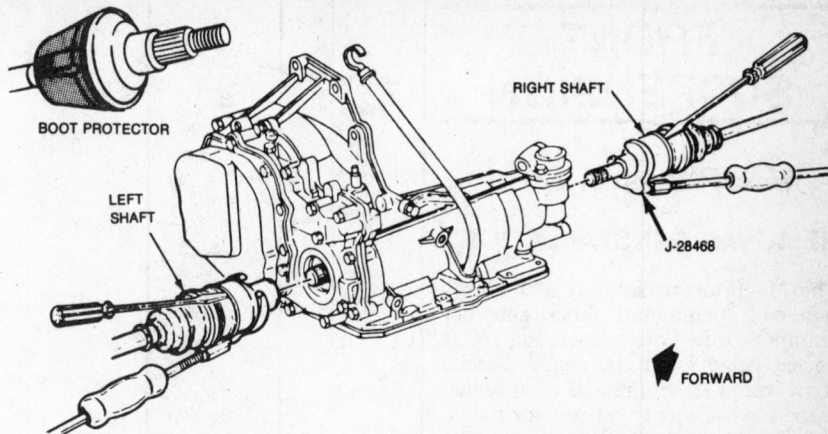

Halfshaft removal using special tools attached to slidehammers

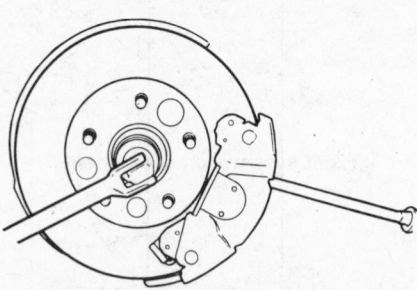

Insert a drift into the caliper when tightening the hub nut

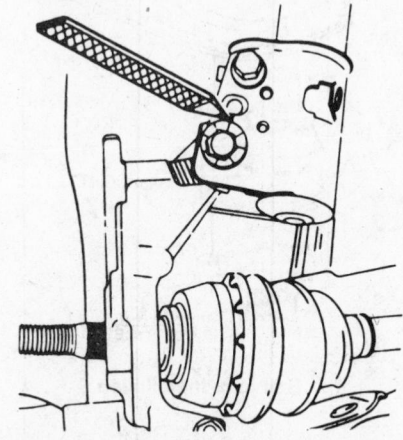

Mark the camber eccentric before removal

1. Remove the hub nut.

2. Raise the front of the car. Remove the wheel and tire.

3. Install an axle shaft boot seal protector, GM special tool No. J–28712 or equivalent, onto the seal.

4. Disconnect the brake hose clip from the MacPherson strut, but do not disconnect the hose from the caliper. Remove the brake caliper from the spindle, and hang the caliper out of the way by a length of wire. Do not allow the caliper to hang by the brake hose.

5. Mark the camber alignment cam bolt for reassembly. Remove the cam

bolt and the upper attaching bolt from the strut and spindle.

6. Pull the steering knuckle assembly from the strut bracket.

7. Using GM special tool J–28733 or the equivalent spindle remover, remove the axle shaft from the hub and bearing assembly.

8. If a new drive axle is to be installed, a new knuckle seal should be installed first.

9. Loosely install the drive axle into the transaxle and steering knuckle.

10. Loosely attach the steering knuckle to the suspension strut.

11. The drive axle is an interference fit in the steering knuckle. Press the axle into place, then install the hub nut. When the shaft begins to turn with the hub, insert a drift through the caliper into one of the cooling slots in the rotor to keep it from turning. Insert a long bolt in the hub flange to prevent the shaft from turning. Tighten the hub nut to 70 ft. lbs. to completely seat the shaft.

12. Install the brake caliper. Tighten the bolts to 30 ft. lbs.

13. Load the hub assembly by lowering it onto a jackstand. Align the camber cam bolt marks made during removal, install the bolt and tighten to 140 ft. lbs. Tighten the upper nut to the same value.

14. Install the axle shaft all the way into the transaxle using a screwdriver inserted into the groove provided on the inner retainer. Tap the screwdriver until the shaft seats in the transaxle. Remove the boot seal protector.

15. Connect the brake hose clip to the strut. Install the tire and wheel, lower the car, and tighten the hub nut to 225 ft. lbs. (1982); 185 ft. lbs. (1983–89).

CV-JOINT OVERHAUL

For all CV-joint overhaul procedures, please refer to " U/CV-joint Overhaul" in the Unit Repair section.

FRONT SUSPENSION

MacPherson Strut

REMOVAL & INSTALLATION

The MacPherson strut is a combination coil spring and shock absorber (damper) unit. The strut is removed as an assembly from the car. A special strut compressor must be used to disassemble the strut and coil spring.

1. Loosen the wheel nuts, raise the car, and remove the wheel and tire.
2. Remove the brake hose clip-to-strut bolt (if equipped). Do not disconnect the hose from the caliper. Install a drive axle cover to protect the axle boot.
3. Mark the camber cam eccentric adjuster for assembly.
4. Remove the 2 lower strut-to-steering knuckle bolts and the three upper strut-to-body nuts. Remove the strut.

OVERHAUL

For all spring and shock absorber Removal & Installation procedures, and all strut overhaul procedures, please refer to "Strut Overhaul" in the Unit Repair section.

Ball Joints

INSPECTION

1. Raise the front of the car with a lift placed under the engine cradle. The front wheels should be clear of the ground.
2. Grasp the wheel at the top and bottom and shake the wheel in and out.
3. If any movement is seen of the steering knuckle relative to the control arm, the ball joints are defective and must be replaced. Note that movement elsewhere may be due to loose wheel bearings or other troubles; watch the knuckle-to-control arm connection.
4. If the ball stud is disconnected from the steering knuckle and any looseness is noted, often the ball joint stud can be twisted in its socket with your fingers, replace the ball joints.

REMOVAL & INSTALLATION

NOTE: These cars use only a lower ball joint.

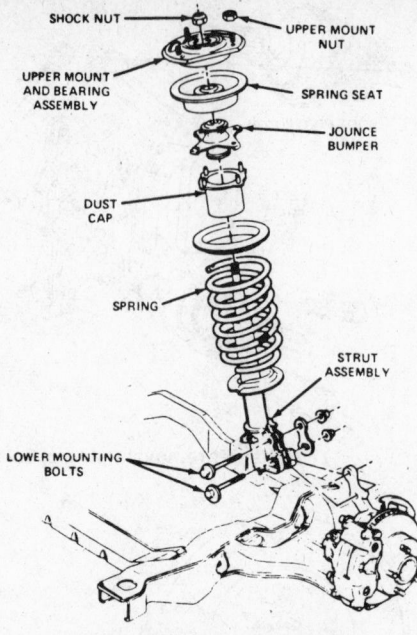

Front suspension components

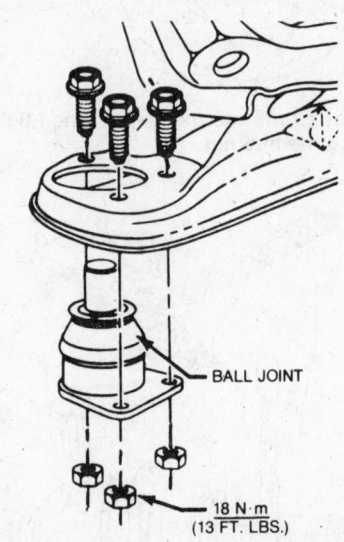

Ball joint installation

1. Loosen the wheel nuts, raise the car, and remove the wheel.
2. Use a ⅛ in. drill bit to drill a hole approximately ¼ in. deep in the center of each of the three ball joint rivets.
3. Use a ½ in. drill bit to drill off the rivet heads. Drill only enough to remove the rivet head.
4. Use a hammer and punch to remove the rivets. Drive them out from the bottom.
5. Loosen the ball joint pinch bolt in the steering knuckle.
6. Remove the ball joint.
7. Install the new ball joint in the control arm. Tighten the bolts supplied with the replacement joint to 13 ft. lbs.
8. Install the ball stud into the steering knuckle pinch bolt fitting. It should go in easily; if not, check the stud alignment. Install the pinch bolt from the rear to the front. Tighten to 45 ft. lbs.
9. Install the wheel and lower the car.

Lower Control Arm

REMOVAL & INSTALLATION

1. Loosen the wheel nuts, raise the car, and remove the wheel.
2. Remove the stabilizer bar from the control arm.
3. Remove the ball joint from the steering knuckle.
4. Remove the control arm pivot bolts and the control arm.
5. To install, insert the control arm into its fittings. Install the pivot bolts from the rear to the front. Tighten the bolts to 50 ft. lbs.
6. Insert the ball stud into the pinch bolt fitting. It should go in easily; if not, check the ball joint stud alignment.
7. Install the pinch bolt from the rear to the front. Tighten to 40 ft. lbs.
8. Install the stabilizer bar attachment. Tighten to 35 ft. lbs.
9. Install the wheel and lower the car.

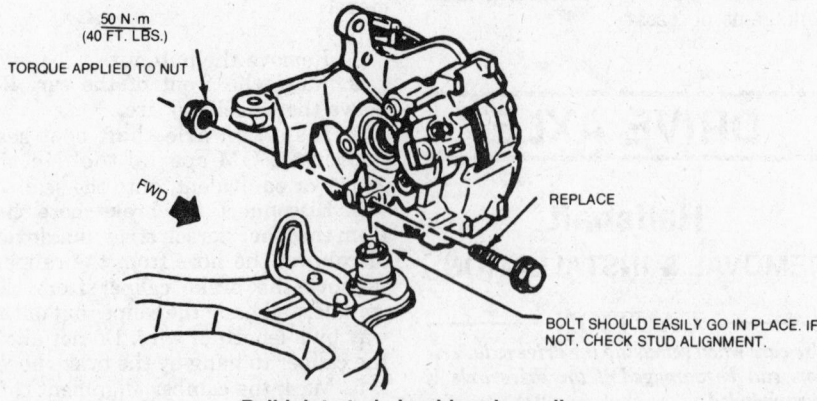

Ball joint stud should go in easily

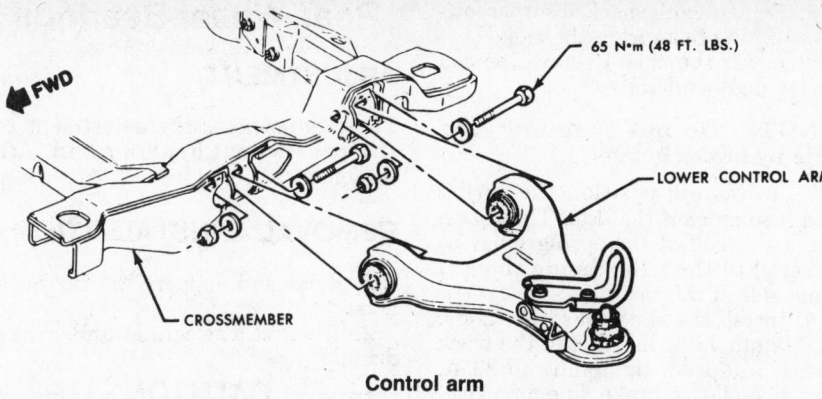

65 N•m (48 FT. LBS.)

LOWER CONTROL ARM

FWD

CROSSMEMBER

Control arm

Front Wheel Bearings

ADJUSTMENT

The front wheel bearings are sealed, non-adjustable units which require no periodic attention. They are bolted to the steering knuckle by means of an integral flange.

NOTE: You will need a special tool to pull the bearing free of the halfshaft tool J–28733 or the equivalent. You should also use a halfshaft boot protector tool J–28712 (Double-Offset joint) or J–33162 (Tri-Pot joint) to protect the parts from damage.

REMOVAL & INSTALLATION

1. Remove the wheel cover, loosen the hub nut, and raise and support the car. Remove the front wheel.
2. Install the boot cover, tool J–28712 (Double-Offset joint) or J–33162 (Tri-Pot joint).
3. Remove and discard the hub nut. Be sure to use a new one on assembly, not the old one.
4. Remove the brake caliper and rotor:
   a. Remove the allen head caliper mounting bolts;
   b. Remove the caliper from the knuckle and suspend from a length of wire. Do not allow the caliper to hang from the brake hose. Pull the rotor from the knuckle.
5. Remove the three hub and bearing attaching bolts and remove the hub. If the old bearing is to be reused, match mark the bolts and holes for installation. The brake rotor splash shield will have to come off, too.
6. Attach a puller, tool J–28733 or the equivalent, and remove the bearing. If corrosion is present, make sure the bearing is loose in the knuckle before using the puller.
7. Clean the mating surfaces of all dirt and corrosion. Check the knuckle bore and knuckle seal for damage. If a

new bearing is to be installed, remove the old knuckle seal and install a new one. Grease the lips of the new seal before installation; install with a seal driver made for the purpose, tool J–28671 (1982–84) or J–34657 (1985–88).
8. Push the bearing onto the halfshaft. Install a new washer and hub nut.
9. Tighten the new hub nut on the halfshaft until the bearing is seated. If the rotor and hub start to rotate as the hub nut is tightened, insert a drift through the caliper and into the rotor cooling fins to prevent rotation. Do not apply full torque to the hub nut at this time—just seat the bearing.
10. Install the brake shield and the bearing retaining bolts. Tighten the bolts evenly to 63 ft.lb. (85 Nm).
11. Install the caliper and rotor. Be sure that the caliper hose isn't twisted. Install the caliper bolts and tighten to 28 ft.lb. (38 Nm) for 1982–84 or 38 ft.lb. (51 Nm) for 1985–88.
12. Install the wheel. Lower the car. Tighten the hub nut to 214 ft.lb. (290 Nm) for '82 or 192 ft.lb. (260 Nm) for 1983–88.

Front Wheel Alignment

ADJUSTMENT

Caster

Caster is not adjustable.

Camber

Camber is adjusted by loosening the cam and through bolts on the Mac-Pherson strut-to-knuckle bolts and rotating the cam bolt to move the upper knuckle and wheel in or out. Tighten the bolts to 140 ft. lbs. after adjustment and check that the cam is seated between the inner and outer guide surfaces.

NOTE: It may be necessary to apply only partial torque because of inaccessability to the bolts. Torque just enough to hold the

correct camber position, then remove the wheel and tire and apply final torque.

Toe

Toe is adjusted with the steering linkage tie rods. Loosen the jamnuts at the steering knuckle end of the tie rods, and remove the boot clamps. Rotate the tie rods to align the toe. Tighten the jamnuts to 40 ft. lbs., and replace the boot clamps.

REAR SUSPENSION

Shock Absorber

REMOVAL & INSTALLATION

1. Open the deck or trunk lid, remove the trim cover, and remove the upper shock nut. Remove and replace one shock at a time when replacing both shocks.
2. Jack the car to a convenient working height. Support the rear axle assembly.
3. Remove the lower attaching bolt and remove the shock absorber. On cars equipped with air shocks, disconnect the air line.

NOTE: Purge new shocks of air by repeatedly compressing them while inverted and extending them in their normal installed position.

4. Install the shock absorber in a reverse of the removal procedure. Torque the lower nuts to 43 ft. lbs.; the upper nut to 13 ft. lbs.

Spring

REMOVAL & INSTALLATION

1. Raise and support the car on a hoist. Do not use twin-post hoist. The swing arc of the axle may cause it to slip from the hoist when the bolts are removed. If a suitable hoist is not available, raise and support the car on jackstands, and use a jack under the axle.
2. Support the axle with a jack that can be raised and lowered.
3. Remove the brake hose attaching brackets (right and left), allowing the hoses to hang freely. Do not disconnect the hoses.
4. Remove the track bar attaching bolts from the rear axle.

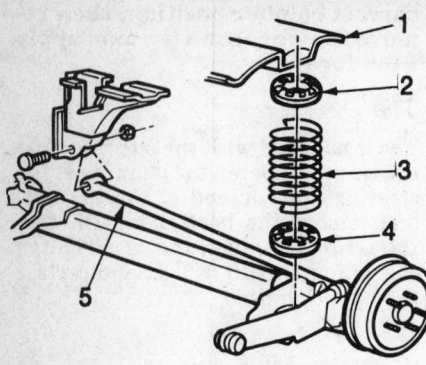

1. Underbody
2. Insulator Upper
3. Spring
4. Lower Insulator on a Series Only
5. Track Bar

A-Body Rear suspension

5. Remove both shock absorber lower attaching bolts from the axle.

6. Lower the axle. Remove the coil spring and insulator.

NOTE: Do not suspend rear axle by brake hoses.

7. To install, position the spring and insulator on the axle. The leg on the upper coil of the spring must be parallel to the axle, facing the left hand side of the car.

8. Install the shock absorber bolts. Tighten to 43 ft. lbs. Install the track bar, if equipped, tightening to 33 ft. lbs. Install the brake line brackets. Tighten to 8 ft. lbs.

Shock absorber installation

Rear Wheel Bearings

ADJUSTMENT

There is no necessary adjustment to the rear wheel bearing and hub assembly.

REMOVAL & INSTALLATION

1. Raise and support the car on a hoist.

2. Remove the wheel and brake drum.

--- **CAUTION** ---

Do not hammer on the brake drum as damage to the bearing could result.

3. Remove the hub and bearing assembly to rear axle attaching bolts and remove the rear axle.

NOTE: The bolts which attach the hub and bearing assembly also support the brake assembly. When removing these bolts, support the brake assembly with a wire or other means. Do not let the brake line support the brake assembly.

4. Install the hub and bearing assembly to the rear axle and torque the hub and bearing bolts to 45 ft. lbs.

5. Install the brake drum, tire and wheel assembly and lower the car.

STEERING

Steering Wheel

REMOVAL & INSTALLATION

--- **CAUTION** ---

Disconnect the battery ground cable before removing the steering wheel. When installing a steering wheel, always make sure that the turn signal lever is in the neutral position.

1. Remove the trim retaining screws from behind the wheel. On wheels with a center cap, pull off the cap.

2. Lift the trim off and pull the horn wires from the turn signal cancelling cam.

3. Remove the retainer and the steering wheel nut.

4. Mark the wheel-to-shaft relationship, and then remove the wheel with a puller.

5. Install the wheel on the shaft aligning the previously made marks. Tighten the nut to 30 ft. lbs.

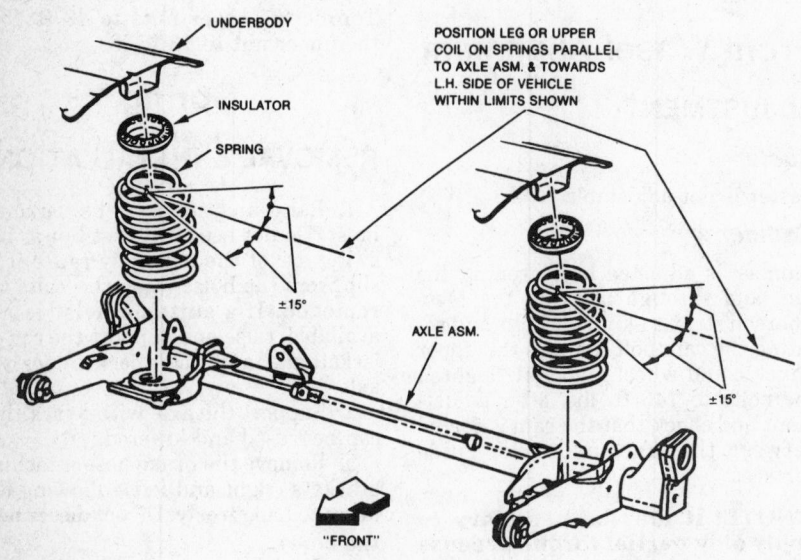

Spring installation

6. Insert the horn wires into the cancelling cam.

7. Install the center trim and reconnect the battery cable.

Turn Signal Switch

REMOVAL & INSTALLATION

1. Remove the steering wheel as previously outlined. Remove the trim cover.

2. Loosen the cover screws. Pry the cover off with a screwdriver, and lift the cover off the shaft.

3. Position the U-shaped lockplate compressing tool on the end of the steering shaft and compress the lockplate by turning the shaft nut clockwise. Pry the wire snapring out of the shaft groove.

4. Remove the tool and lift the lockplate off the shaft.

5. Slip the cancelling cam, upper bearing preload spring, and thrust washer off the shaft.

6. Remove the turn signal lever. Push the flasher knob in and unscrew it. Remove the button retaining screw and remove the button, spring and knob.

7. Pull the switch connector out the mast jacket and tape the upper part to facilitate switch removal. Attach a long piece of wire to the turn signal switch connector. When installing the turn signal switch, feed this wire through the column first, and then use this wire to pull the switch connector into position. On tilt wheels, place the turn signal and shifter housing in low position and remove the harness cover.

8. Remove the three switch mounting screws. Remove the switch by pulling it straight up while guiding the wiring harness cover through the column.

9. Install the replacement switch by working the connector and cover down through the housing and under the bracket. On tilt models, the connector is worked down through the housing, under the bracket, and then the cover is installed on the harness.

10. Install the switch mounting screws and the connector on the mast jacket bracket. Install the column-to-dash trim plate.

11. Install the flasher knob and the turn signal lever.

12. With the turn signal lever in neutral and the flasher knob out, slide the thrust washer, upper bearing preload spring, and cancelling cam onto the shaft.

13. Position the lockplate on the shaft and press it down until a new snapring can be inserted in the shaft

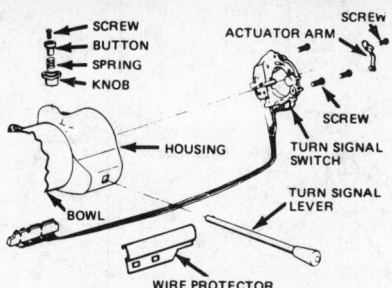

Turn signal switch

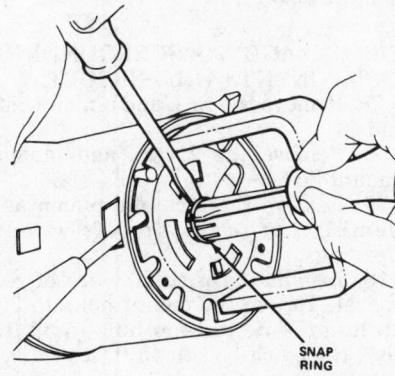

Depress the lockplate and remove the snapring

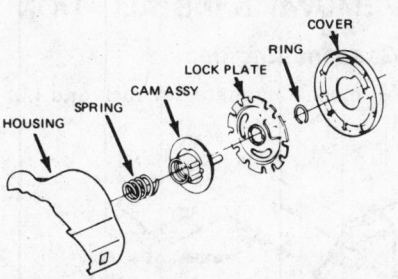

Remove these parts for access to the turn signal switch

groove. Always use a new snapring when assembling.

14. Install the cover and the steering wheel.

Ignition Switch

REPLACEMENT

The switch is located inside the channel section of the brake pedal support and is completely inaccessible without first lowering the steering column. The switch is actuated by a rod and rack assembly. A gear on the end of the lock cylinder engages the toothed upper end of the rod.

1. Lower the steering column; be sure to properly support it.

2. Put the ignition switch in the OFF–UNLOCKED position. With the cylinder removed, the rod is in LOCK

when it is in the next to the uppermost detent. OFF–UNLOCKED is 2 detents from the top.

3. Remove the 2 switch screws and remove the switch assembly.

4. Before installing, place the new switch in OFF–UNLOCKED position and make sure the lock cylinder and actuating rod are in OFF–UNLOCKED (third detent from the top) position.

5. Install the activating rod into the switch and assemble the switch on the column. Tighten the mounting screws. Use only the specified screws since overlength screws could impair the collapsibility of the column.

6. Reinstall the steering column.

Ignition Lock Cylinder

REPLACEMENT

1. Place the lock in the RUN position.

2. Remove the lockplate, turn signal switch and buzzer switch.

3. Remove the screw and lock cylinder.

— CAUTION —
If the screw is dropped on removal, it could fall into the column, requiring complete disassembly to retrieve the screw.

4. Rotate the cylinder clockwise to align cylinder key with the keyway in the housing.

5. Push the lock all the way in.

6. Install the screw. Tighten the screw to 14 inch lbs. for adjustable columns and 25 inch lbs. for standard columns.

Power Steering Gear

REMOVAL & INSTALLATION

1. Raise and support the front end of the car with jackstands under the frame members. Allow the front suspension to hang freely. Disconnect the power steering hoses from the gear, where equipped.

2. Move the intermediate shaft seal upward and remove the intermediate shaft-to-stub shaft pinch bolt.

3. Remove both front wheels.

4. Remove the cotter pins and nut from both tie rod ends. Disconnect the tie rod ends from the steering knuckles.

5. Remove the air management system pipe bracket bolt from the crossmember.

6. Support the engine cradle with a floor jack. Remove the 2 rear cradle mount bolts and, using a jack, lower the rear of the engine cradle about 4–5 inches. DON'T LOWER IT TOO FAR

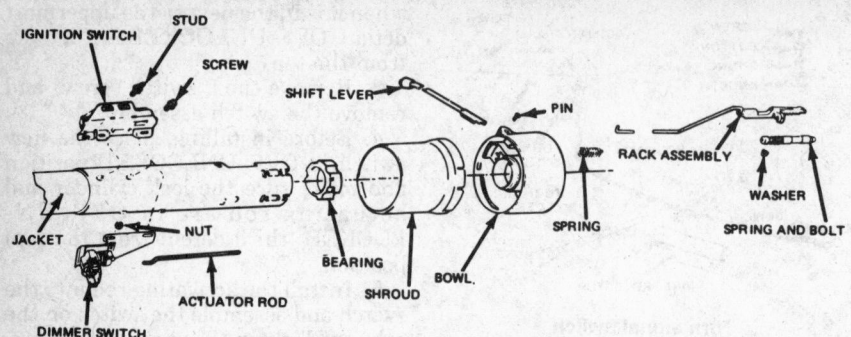

Exploded view, steering column

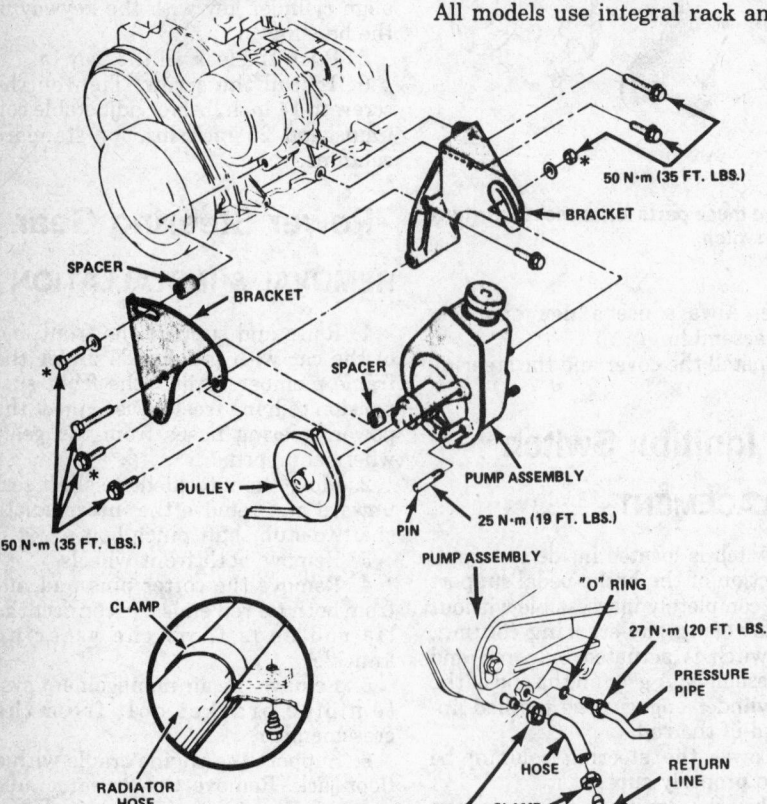

Ignition lock cylinder

OR DAMAGE TO SURROUNDING COMPONENTS WILL RESULT.

7. Remove the rack and pinion heat shield.

8. Remove the 2 rack and pinion mount bolts.

9. Remove the rack and pinion assembly through the left wheel opening.

10. Installation is the reverse of removal. Torque the mount bolts to 70 ft. lbs.; the tie rod end nuts to 30 ft. lbs.; the pinch bolt to 45 ft. lbs.

Power Steering Pump

REMOVAL & INSTALLATION

Gasoline Engines

All models use integral rack and pin-ion power steering. A pump delivers hydraulic pressure through 2 hoses to the steering gear itself.

1. Remove the hoses at the pump and tape the openings shut to prevent contamination. Position the disconnected lines in a raised position to prevent leakage.

2. Remove the pump belt.

3. On the 4 cylinder, remove the radiator hose clamp bolt. On the 6–173, disconnect the negative battery cable and the electrical connector at the blower motor, drain the cooling system, and remove the heater hose at the water pump. On the 6–183, remove the alternator.

4. Loosen the retaining bolts and any braces, and remove the pump.

5. Install the pump on the engine with the retaining bolts hand tight.

6. Connect and tighten the hose fittings.

7. Refill the pump with fluid and bleed by turning the pulley counterclockwise (viewed from the front). Stop the bleeding when air bubbles no longer appear.

8. Install the pump belt on the pulley and adjust the tension.

9. Replace all other parts in reverse order of removal.

Diesel Engine

1. Remove the drive belt.

2. Siphon the fluid from the power steering reservoir.

3. Disconnect the hoses from the pump.

4. Remove the three bolts from the front of the pump through the access holes in the pulley.

5. Remove the 2 nuts holding the lower brace to the engine. Remove the brace.

6. Remove the pump.

7. Installation is the reverse of removal. Torque the brace nuts to 40 ft. lbs; the pump bolt to 40 ft. lbs.

BELT ADJUSTMENT

NOTE: When adjusting the power steering pump belt, do not pry against the pump reservoir. Only the bracket should be pried against when adjusting belt tension.

1. Position the belt tension gauge on pump belt.

2. Loosen the pump mounting bolts.

3. Adjust the belt by prying the pump away from the engine until the correct tension is reached.

4. Tighten pump bolts to torque specification.

Power steering pump removal, 4-151

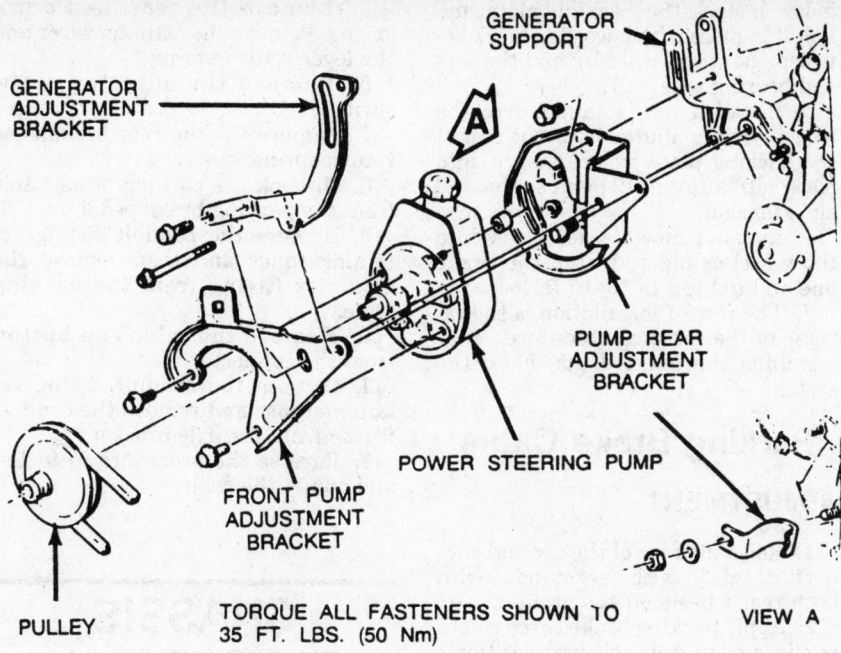

Power steering pump removal—6-181

TORQUE ALL FASTENERS SHOWN TO 35 FT. LBS. (50 Nm)

VIEW A

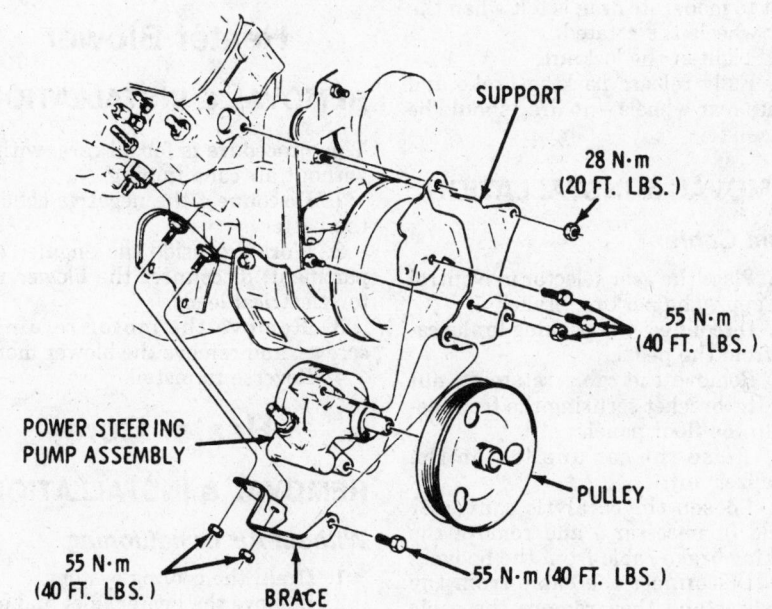

Power steering pump removal, 6-263

BLEEDING THE POWER STEERING SYSTEM

1. Fill the fluid reservoir.
2. Let the fluid stand undisturbed for 2 minutes, then crank the engine for about 2 seconds. Refill reservoir if necessary.
3. Repeat Steps 1 and 2 above until the fluid level remains constant after cranking the engine.
4. Raise the front of the car until the wheels are off the ground, then start the engine. Increase the engine speed to about 1500 rpm.
5. Turn the wheels lightly against the stops to the left and right, checking the fluid level and refilling if necessary.

Tie Rod End

REMOVAL & INSTALLATION

1. Loosen the jam nut on the steering rack (inner tie rod).

2. Remove the tie rod end nut. Separate the tie rod end from the steering knuckle using a puller.
3. Unscrew the tie rod end, counting the number of turns.
4. To install, screw the tie rod end onto the steering rack (inner tie rod) the same number of turns as counted for removal. This will give approximately correct toe.
5. Install the tie rod end into the knuckle. Install the nut and tighten to 40 ft. lbs.
6. If the toe must be adjusted, use pliers to expand the boot clamp. Turn the inner tierod to adjust. Replace the clamp.
7. Tighten the jamnut to 50 ft. lbs.

BRAKES

For all brake system repair procedures no detailed below, please refer to "Brakes" in the Unit Repair section.

Master Cylinder

REMOVAL & INSTALLATION

1. Disconnect hydraulic lines at master cylinder.
2. Remove the retaining nuts and lockwashers that hold cylinder to firewall or the brake booster. Disconnect pushrod at brake pedal (non-power brakes only).
3. Remove the master cylinder, gasket and rubber boot.
4. On non-power brakes, position master cylinder on firewall, making sure pushrod goes through the rubber boot into the piston. Reconnect pushrod clevis to brake pedal. With power brakes, install the cylinder on the booster. Torque the attaching nuts to 25 ft. lbs.
5. Install nuts and lockwashers.
6. Install hydraulic lines then check brake pedal free play.
7. Bleed brakes, as described in Unit Repair section.

NOTE: Cars having disc brakes do not have a check valve in the front outlet port of the master cylinder. If one is installed, front discs will quickly wear out due to residual pressure holding pads against rotor.

Power Brake Booster

REMOVAL & INSTALLATION

1. Disconnect vacuum hose from vacuum check valve.

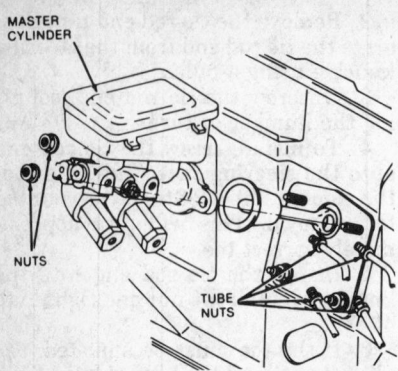

Typical master cylinder installation

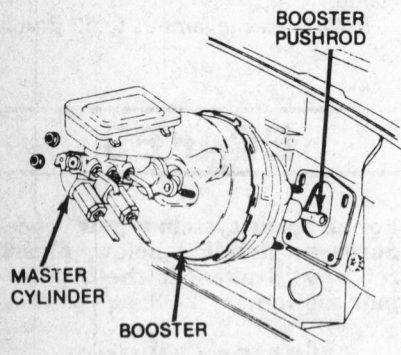

Power booster removal

2. Unbolt the master cylinder and carefully move it aside without disconnecting the hydraulic lines.

3. Disconnect pushrod at brake pedal assembly.

4. Remove nuts and lockwashers that secure booster to firewall and remove booster from engine compartment.

5. Install by reversing removal procedure. Torque the mounting nuts to 25 ft. lbs. Make sure to check operation of stop lights. Allow engine vacuum to build before applying brakes.

Wheel Cylinder

REMOVAL & INSTALLATION

1. Loosen the wheel lug nuts, raise and support the vehicle properly, and remove the wheel. Remove the drum and brake shoes. Leave the hub and wheel bearing assembly in place.

2. Remove any dirt from around the brake line fitting. Disconnect the brake line.

3. Remove the wheel cylinder retainer by using 2 awls or punches with a tip diameter of ⅛ in. or less. Insert the awls or punches into the access slots between the wheel cylinder pilot and retainer locking tabs. Bend both tabs away simultaneously. Remove the wheel cylinder from the backing plate.

4. To install, position the wheel cyl-

inder against the backing plate and holt it in place with a wooden block between the wheel cylinder and the hub and bearing assembly.

5. Install a new retainer over the wheel cylinder abutment on the rear of the backing plate by pressing it into place with a 1⅛ in. 12 point socket and an extension.

6. Install a new bleeder screw into the wheel cylinder. Install the brake line and tighten to 10–15 ft. lbs.

7. The rest of installation is the reverse of the removal procedure. After installing the brake drum, bleed the system.

Parking Brake Cable

ADJUSTMENT

1. Raise the rear of the car and support it safely with jackstands, with both rear wheels off the ground.

2. Apply parking brake three ratchet clicks from fully released position.

3. Loosen the equalizer locknut, then tighten the adjusting nut until a light to moderate drag is felt when the rear wheels are rotated.

4. Tighten the locknut.

5. Fully release parking brake and rotate rear wheels—no drag should be felt.

REMOVAL & INSTALLATION

Front Cable

1. Place the gear selector in Neutral and apply the parking brake.

2. Disconnect the parking brake cable from the pedal.

3. Remove the cable retaining nut and the bracket securing the front cable to the floor panel.

4. Raise the car and loosen the equalizer nut.

5. Loosen the catalytic converter shield (if necessary) and remove the parking brake cable from the body.

6. Disconnect the cable from the equalizer and then remove the cable from the guide and the underbody clips.

7. Reverse the procedure and adjust the cable.

Rear Cables

1. Raise and support the rear of the car.

2. Back off the equalizer nut until the cable tension is eliminated.

3. Remove the tires, wheels and brake drums.

4. Insert a screwdriver between the brake shoe and the top part of the brake adjuster bracket. Push the bracket to the front and then release the top brake adjuster rod.

5. Remove the rear hold down spring. Remove the actuator lever and the lever return spring.

6. Remove the adjuster screw spring.

7. Remove the top rear brake shoe return spring.

8. Unhook the parking brake cable from the parking brake pedal.

9. Depress the conduit fitting retaining tangs and then remove the conduitx fitting from the backing plate.

10. Remove the cable end button from the connector.

11. Depress the conduit fitting retaining tangs and remove the conduit fitting from the axle bracket.

12. Reverse the procedure to install and adjust the cable.

CHASSIS ELECTRICAL

Heater Blower

REMOVAL & INSTALLATION

This procedure is for all cars, with or without air conditioning.

1. Disconnect the negative cable at the battery.

2. Working inside the engine compartment, disconnect the blower motor electrical leads.

3. Remove the motor retaining screws, and remove the blower motor.

4. Reverse to install.

Heater Core

REMOVAL & INSTALLATION

Without Air Conditioning

1. Drain the cooling system.

2. Remove the heater inlet and outlet hoses at the firewall, inside the engine compartment.

3. Remove the radio noise suppression strap.

4. Remove the heater core cover retaining screws. Remove the cover.

5. Remove the core. Reverse to install.

With Air Conditioning

A–BODY CARS

1. Drain the cooling system.

2. On the diesel, raise and support the car on jackstands.

3. Disconnect the hoses at the core.

4. On the diesel, remove the instrument panel lower sound absorber.

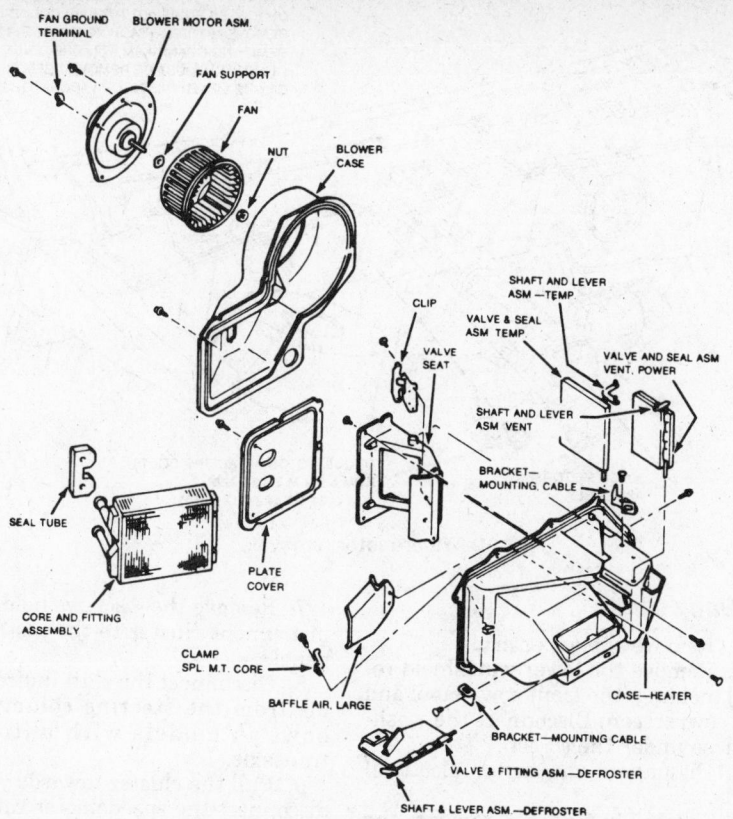

Heater assembly, without air conditioning

5. Remove the heater duct and lower side covers.

6. Remove the lower heater outlet.

7. Remove the 2 housing cover-to-air valve housing clips.

8. Remove the housing cover.

9. Remove the core restraining straps.

10. Remove the core tubing retainers and lift out the core.

11. Installation is the reverse of removal.

X–BODY CARS

1. Drain the cooling system.

2. Remove the heater hoses from the core tubes at the firewall.

3. Remove the heater duct and heater case side cover from under the instrument panel.

4. Remove the core retaining clamps. Remove the inlet and outlet tube support clamps.

5. Remove the core. Reverse to install.

Radio

REMOVAL & INSTALLATION

Celebrity

1. Disconnect the battery ground.

2. Remove the steering column trim panel including hush panel.

3. Remove the ashtray and ashtray assembly fuse block, seperate ashtray assembly from fuse block. Move both for access.

4. Disconnect the cigarette lighter and rear defogger switch connectors.

5. Remove the cigarette lighter.

6. Remove the glove box.

7. Remove the instrument panel center trim panel attaching nuts.

8. Pull the trim panel away from the instrument panel (enough to remove the radio).

9. Remove the radio.

10. Installation is the reverse of removal.

Century

1. Disconnect the battery ground.

2. Remove the instrument panel trim plate.

3. Remove the right side instrument panel rocker switch trim panel by removing the 3 screws and gently rocking it out.

4. Remove the 4 radio mounting screws.

5. Unplug the antenna and all other wires.

6. Remove the radio.

7. Installation is the reverse of removal.

Ciera

1. Disconnect the battery ground.

2. Remove the left instrument panel trim pad.

3. Remove the instrument panel cover.

4. Unbolt the radio from the upper and lower mounting brackets.

5. Pull the radio out to disconnect the wires, then remove it.

6. Installation is the reverse of removal.

6000

1. Disconnect the battery ground.

2. Remove the lower center instrument panel trim plate.

3. Unbolt and remove the radio.

4. Installation is the reverse of removal.

Citation

1. Disconnect the negative battery cable.

2. Remove the radio knobs, the shaft nuts, and the clock knob, if equipped.

3. Remove the instrument cluster trim bezel attaching screws and pull the bezel rearward.

4. Remove the headlamp shaft and knob. Reach behind the instrument panel bezel with a long screwdriver and push the headlamp shaft release button to release the knob.

5. Disconnect the wiring and remove the bezel.

6. Remove the 2 screws attaching the radio bracket to the instrument panel.

7. Pull the radio rearward while at the same time twisting it slightly to the left, and disconnect the electrical connectors and antenna lead. Remove the lamp socket.

8. Remove the radio.

9. Installation is the reverse of removal.

Omega

1. Remove the instrument panel molding.

2. Remove the ash tray receiver.

3. Remove the 4 screws attaching the ash tray assembly and remove the ash tray light bulb and socket assembly.

4. Pull the radio and ash tray retainer assembly out far enough to disconnect the radio wiring and remove the radio.

5. Installation is the reverse of removal.

Skylark

1. Disconnect the negative battery cable.

2. Remove the center instrument panel trim plate.

3. Remove the radio attaching screws and pull the radio out to gain

access to the wiring. You may have to remove the ashtray retainer assembly to gain access to the radio wiring.

4. Disconnect the wiring. Remove the knobs and separate the face plate from the radio.

5. Installation is the reverse of removal.

Phoenix

1. Disconnect the negative battery cable.

2. Remove the center instrument panel trim plate.

3. Remove the radio attaching screws and pull the radio out to gain access to the wiring.

Windshield Wiper Switch

REMOVAL & INSTALLATION

1. Disconnect the negative battery cable.

2. Remove the steering wheel, the cover and the lock plate assembly.

3. Remove the turn signal actuator arm, the lever and the hazard flasher button.

4. Remove the turn signal switch screws, the lower steering column trim panel and the steering column bracket bolts.

5. Disconnect the the turn signal switch and the wiper switch connectors.

6. Pull the turn signal switch rearward 6–8 inches, then remove the key buzzer switch and cylinder lock.

7. Remove and pull the steering column housing rearward, then remove the housing cover screw.

8. Remove the wiper switch pivot and the switch.

9. To install, reverse the removal procedure.

Windshield Wiper Motor

REMOVAL & INSTALLATION

A–Body Cars

1. Raise the hood.

2. Remove the grille.

3. Loosen the wiper linkage to drive arm attaching nuts.

4. Remove the transmission link from the drive arm.

5. Disconnect the wiring and hoses from the motor.

6. Unbolt and remove the motor.

7. Installation is the reverse of removal.

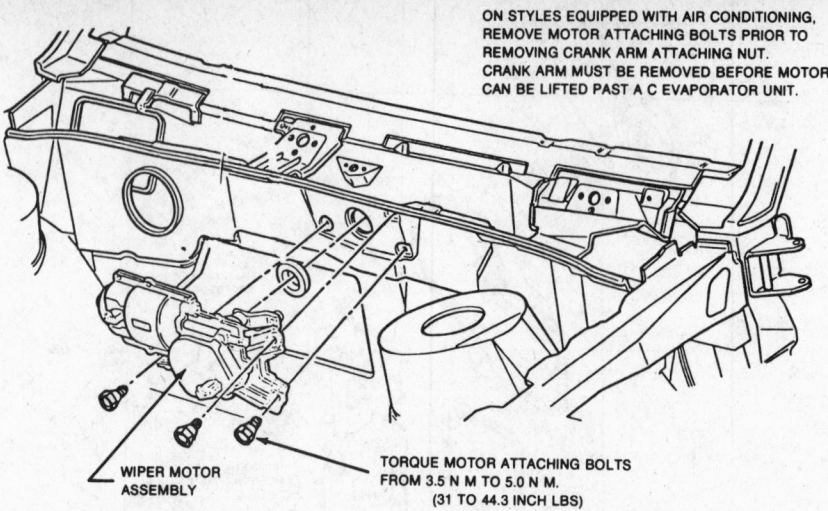

ON STYLES EQUIPPED WITH AIR CONDITIONING, REMOVE MOTOR ATTACHING BOLTS PRIOR TO REMOVING CRANK ARM ATTACHING NUT. CRANK ARM MUST BE REMOVED BEFORE MOTOR CAN BE LIFTED PAST A C EVAPORATOR UNIT.

WIPER MOTOR ASSEMBLY

TORQUE MOTOR ATTACHING BOLTS FROM 3.5 N M TO 5.0 N M. (31 TO 44.3 INCH LBS)

Wiper motor removal

X–Body Cars

1. Remove the wiper arms.

2. Remove the lower windshield reveal molding, the front cowl panel and the cowl screen. Disconnect the washer hose under the screen.

3. Disconnect the motor electrical leads.

4. Loosen, but do not remove, the transmission drive link attaching nuts to the motor crank arm.

5. Disconnect the drive link from the motor crank arm.

6. Remove the three motor attaching bolts. On models with air conditioning, remove the bolts and while supporting the motor, remove the motor crank arm nut using lock-ring type pliers and a closed end wrench. The motor attaching bolts must be removed first to avoid damage to the nylon gear inside the motor. On all models, rotate the motor up and out to remove.

7. Reverse the procedure to install.

Instrument Cluster

REMOVAL & INSTALLATION

Citation

1. Disconnect the negative battery cable.

2. Remove the radio knobs (pull off), the shaft nuts, and the clock knob.

3. Remove the instrument cluster bezel (trim plate) attaching screws; there are three at the top and 1 each in the 2 lower corners. Pull the bezel slightly rearward.

4. Remove the headlamp shaft and knob.

5. Disconnect the accessory switch wiring.

6. Remove the bezel.

7. Remove the 4 screws holding the instrument cluster to the instrument panel.

8. Disconnect the shift indicator cable from the steering column shift bowl on models with automatic transaxle.

9. Pull the cluster towards you and disconnect the speedometer cable and instrument electrical connections.

10. Remove the instrument cluster. Installation is the reverse of removal.

Omega

1. Remove the steering column trim cover.

2. Lower the steering column.

3. Remove the 4 screws holding the instrument panel trim cover to the panel.

4. Pull the trim cover rearward and disconnect the switch wiring, and the remote control mirror cable if your car has one. Remove the trim panel.

5. Remove the 4 screws holding the instrument cluster to the panel.

6. Disconnect the shift indicator cable from the steering column shift bowl, if your Omega has an automatic transaxle.

7. Pull the cluster towards you and disconnect the speedometer cable and electrical wiring.

8. Remove the instrument cluster. Installation is the reverse.

Phoenix

1. Disconnect the negative battery cable.

2. Remove the speedometer cluster trim plate. There is 1 screw in each corner.

3. Remove the screws attaching the steering column trim cover to the instrument panel and remove the trim cover.

4. Remove the 4 cluster attaching screws.

5. With automatic transaxle, disconnect the shift indicator cable, marking the cable location on the steering column shift bowl prior to disconnecting.

6. Disconnect the speedometer cable and pull the cluster toward you. Disconnect the electrical wiring from the back of the cluster and remove the cluster. Installation is the reverse of removal.

Skylark

1. Disconnect the negative battery cable.

2. Remove the radio and accessory switch knobs.

3. Remove the instrument panel trim plate.

4. With automatic transaxle, disconnect the shift indicator cable from the steering column shift bowl.

5. Remove the 4 cluster attaching screws.

6. Disconnect the speedometer cable and electrical wiring from the back of the cluster. Remove the cluster. Installation is the reverse of removal.

Century

1. Disconnect the battery ground.

2. Disconnect the speedometer cable and pull it through the firewall.

3. Remove the left side hush panel by removing the 3, 7mm screws and one 11mm nut.

4. Remove the right side hush panel by removing the 5, 7mm screws and the 2, 11mm nuts.

5. Remove the shift indicator cable clip.

6. Remove the steering column trim plate.

7. Put the gear selector in LOW, remove the nine retaining screws and gently pull out the instrument panel trim plate.

8. Disconnect the parking brake cable at the lever by pushing it forward and sliding it out of its slot.

9. Unbolt and lower the steering column (3 bolts and 1 nut).

10. Remove the gauge cluster by removing the 4 screws and pulling the cluster out far enough to disconnect any wires, then pull the cluster out.

11. Installation is the reverse of removal.

Celebrity

1. Disconnect battery ground cable.

2. Remove instrument panel hush panel.

3. Remove vent control housing (heater only vehicles).

4. On non A/C cars remove steering column trim cover screws and lower

cover with vent cables attached. On A/C equipped vehicles, remove trim cover attaching screws (6) and remove cover.

5. Remove instrument cluster trim pad as outlined in this section.

6. Remove ash try, retainer and fuse block, disconnect wires as necessary.

7. Remove headlamp switch knob and instrument panel trim plate and disconnect electrical connectors of any accessory switches in trim plate.

8. Remove cluster assembly and disconnect speedometer cable. PRNDL and cluster electrical connectors.

9. Installation is the reverse of removal.

Ciera

1. Remove left instrument panel trim pad.

2. Remove instrument panel cluster trim cover.

3. Disconnect speedometer cable at transmission or cruise control transducer if equipped.

4. Remove steering column trim cover.

5. Disconnect shift indicator clip from steering column shift bowl.

6. Remove 4 screws attaching cluster assembly to instrument panel.

7. Pull assembly out far enough to reach behind cluster and disconnect speedometer cable.

8. Remove cluster assembly.

9. Installation is the reverse of removal.

6000

1. Remove the center and left-hand lower instrument panel trim plates.

2. Remove 6–8 screws holding instrument cluster to instrument panel carrier.

3. Remove instrument cluster lens to gain access to speedometer head and instrument/gauges.

4. Installation is the reverse of removal.

Headlight Switch

REPLACEMENT

Citation

1. Disconnect the negative battery cable.

2. Pull the headlamp switch knob out to the last detent.

3. Remove the spring clip retainer on the knob shaft and remove the shaft.

4. Disconnect all accessory switch connectors.

5. Remove the headlamp switch ferrule nut and push switch forward out of the mounting hole.

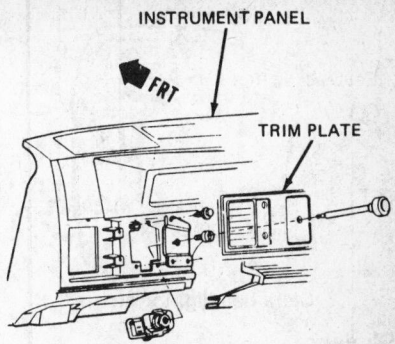

INSTRUMENT PANEL

TRIM PLATE

FRT

Celebrity headlight switch

6. Lift the switch up and out through the opening above the switch mounting and disconnect the switch electrical connector.

7. Remove the switch from the instrument panel.

8. Installation is the reverse of removal.

Celebrity

1. Disconnect the battery ground.

2. Remove the headlamp switch knob.

3. Remove the instrument panel trim pad.

4. Unbolt the switch mounting plate from the instrument panel carrier.

5. Disconnect the wiring from the switch.

6. Remove the switch.

7. Installation is the reverse of removal.

Ciera and Omega

1. Remove the left side instrument panel trim pad.

2. Remove the three screws that attach the switch to the instrument panel.

3. Pull the switch rearward and remove it.

4. Installation is the reverse of removal.

6000 and Phoenix

1. Disconnect the battery ground.

2. Remove the steering column trim cover and headlight rod and knob by reaching behind the instrument panel and depressing the lock tab with a screwdriver.

3. Remove the left instrument panel trim plate.

4. Unbolt and remove the switch and bracket assembly from the instrument panel.

5. Loosen the bezel and remove the switch from the bracket.

6. Installation is the reverse of removal.

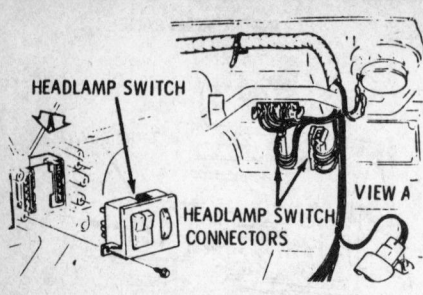

Ciera headlight switch

Skylark

1. Disconnect the negative battery cable.

2. Remove the light switch knob by depressing the retaining clip behind the knob and removing the knob from the shaft.

3. Turn the sleeve counterclockwise and spin the knob off the shaft.

4. Remove the instrument panel trim plate.

5. Remove the mounting screws and unplug the switch.

6. Installation is the reverse of removal.

Century

1. Disconnect the battery ground.

2. Remove the instrument panel trim plate.

3. Remove the left side instrument panel switch trim panel by removing the three screws and gently rocking the panel out.

4. Remove the three screws and pull the switch straight out.

5. Installation is the reverse of removal.

Stoplight Switch

REMOVAL & INSTALLATION

1. Disconnect the negative battery terminal.

2. Disconnect the wiring connector at the switch.

3. Remove the switch.

4. Installation is the reverse of the removal procedure and adjust.

Fuses, Fusible Links and Circuit Breakers

LOCATION

On some models, the fuse block is a swingdown unit located in the underside of the instrument panel, adjacent to the steering column. On other models, access to the fuse block is gained through the glove box. All models use miniaturized plug type fuses which are color-coded and stamped with the amperage rating.

Fusible links are provided in all circuits and fed directly from the battery. Fusible links are lengths of copper wire, about 4 in. long and 4 gauge sizes smaller than the wire that they protect. Burned out fusible links should be replaced with the same gauge wire for continued circuit protection.

The head lights are protected by a circuit breaker in the headlamp switch. If the circuit breaker trips, the headlights will either flash on and off, or stay off all toeghter. The circuit breaker resets automatically after the overload is removed.

The windshield wipers are also protected by a circuit breaker. If the motor overheats, the circuit breaker will trip, remaining off until the motor cools and the overload is removed.

The circuit breakers for the power door locks and power windows are located in the fuse box.

GM "C" Body
Front Wheel Drive
Buick—Electra, Park Avenue
Cadillac—DeVille, Fleetwood
Oldsmobile—Ninety Eight Regency Brougham, Touring Sedan

SERIAL NUMBER IDENTIFICATION

Vehicle Identification Number

The vehicle identification number is stamped on a plate which is attached to the left side of the instrument pan-el; the plate is visible through the windshield.

The VIN is also stamped on a plate in the engine compartment which is usually located on the firewall and a third VIN plate is attached to the driver's door jam.

The serial number is a 17 digit for-mat. The first three digits are the World Manufacturer Identification number. The next five digits are the Vehicle Description Section. The re-maining nine numbers are the produc-tion numbers.

VEHICLE IDENTIFICATION CHART

It is important for servicing and ordering parts to be certain of the vehicle and engine identification. The VIN (vehicle iden-tification number) is a 17 digit number visible through the windshield on the driver's side of the dash and contains the vehicle and engine identification codes. The tenth digit indicates model year and the eigth digit indicates engine code. It can be interpreted as follows:

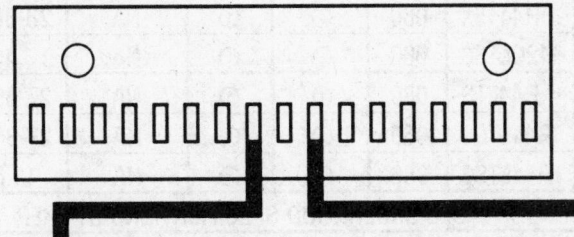

Engine Code							Model Year	
Code	Cu. In.	Liters	Cyl.	Fuel Sys.	Eng. Mfg.		Code	Year
3	231	3.8	6	SFI	Buick		F	1985
B	231	3.8	6	SFI	Buick		G	1986
C	231	3.8	6	SFI	Buick		H	1987
T	263	4.3	6	Diesel	Oldsmobile		J	1988
8	250	4.1	8	DFI	Cadillac		K	1988
5	273	4.5	8	DFI	Cadillac			

GENERAL ENGINE SPECIFICATIONS

Year	VIN	No. Cylinder Displacement cu. in. (liter)	Fuel System Type	Net Horsepower @ rpm	Net Torque @ rpm (ft.lbs.)	Bore × Stroke (in.)	Compression Ratio	Oil Pressure @ rpm
1985	3	6-231 (3.8)	SFI	195 @ 2000	195 @ 2000	3.800 × 3.400	8.0:1	35-40 @ 2000
	T	6-263 (4.3)	Diesel	165 @ 1600	165 @ 1600	4.057 × 3.385	21.6:1	30-45 @ 2000
	8	8-250 (4.1)	DFI	190 @ 2000	190 @ 2000	3.465 × 3.307	8.5:1	30 @ 2000
1986	3	6-231 (3.8)	SFI	150 @ 4400	200 @ 2000	3.800 × 3.400	8.5:1	37 @ 2000
	B	6-231 (3.8)	SFI	140 @ 4400	200 @ 2000	3.800 × 3.400	8.5:1	37 @ 2000
	8	8-250 (4.1)	DFI	130 @ 4200	200 @ 2000	3.465 × 3.307	8.5:1	30 @ 2000
1987	3	6-231 (3.8)	SFI	150 @ 4400	200 @ 2000	3.800 × 3.400	8.5:1	37 @ 2000
	8	8-250 (4.1)	DFI	130 @ 4200	200 @ 2000	3.465 × 3.307	9.0:1	30 @ 2000
1988-89	3	6-231 (3.8)	SFI	150 @ 4400	200 @ 2000	3.800 × 3.400	8.5:1	37 @ 2000
	C	6-231 (3.8)	SFI	.165 @ 5200	210 @ 2000	3.800 × 3.400	8.5:1	37 @ 2400
	5	8-273 (4.5)	DFI	155 @ 4000	240 @ 2800	3.622 × 3.307	9.0:1	37 @ 1500

SFI Sequential Fuel Injection
DFI Digital Fuel Injection

GASOLINE ENGINE TUNE-UP SPECIFICATIONS

Year	VIN	No. Cylinder Displacement cu. in. (liter)	Spark Plugs Type	Gap (in.)	Ignition Timing (deg.) MT	AT	Compression Pressure (psi)	Fuel Pump (psi)	Idle Speed (rpm) MT	AT	Valve Clearance In.	Ex.
1985	3	6-231 (3.8)	R44TS8	.080	①	①	NA	28-36	①	①	Hyd.	Hyd.
	8	6-250 (4.1)	R42CLTS6	.060	①	①	NA	40	①	①	Hyd.	Hyd.
1986	3	6-231 (3.8)	R44TSX	.080	①	①	NA	28-36	①	①	Hyd.	Hyd.
	B	6-231 (3.8)	R44TSX	.080	①	①	NA	28-36	①	①	Hyd.	Hyd.
	8	6-250 (4.1)	R42CLTS6	.060	①	①	NA	40	①	①	Hyd.	Hyd.
1987	3	6-231 (3.8)	R44TSX	.080	①	①	NA	28-36	①	①	Hyd.	Hyd.
	8	6-250 (4.1)	R42CLTS6	.060	①	①	NA	40	①	①	Hyd.	Hyd.
1988	3	6-231 (3.8)	R44LTS	.080	①	①	NA	27-36	①	①	Hyd.	Hyd.
	C	6-231 (3.8)	R44LTS6	.060	①	①	NA	27-36	①	①	Hyd.	Hyd.
	5	8-273 (4.5)	R44LTS6	.060	①	①	NA	11.6	①	①	Hyd.	Hyd.
1989				SEE UNDERHOOD SPECIFICATIONS STICKER								

NOTE: The underhood specifications sticker often reflects tune-up specification changes made in production. Sticker figures must be used if they disagree with those in this chart. Part numbers in this chart are not recommendations by Chilton for any product by brand name

NA Not available

Hyd. Hydraulic: There is no adjustment possible on hydraulic lifters

① Only vehicles equipped with computerized emissions systems (which have no distributor vacuum advance unit), the idle speed and ignition timing are controlled by the emissions computer.

DIESEL ENGINE TUNE-UP SPECIFICATIONS

Year	VIN	No. Engine Displacement cu. in. (liter)	Valve Clearance Intake (in.)	Exhaust (in.)	Intake Valve Opens (deg.)	Injection Pump Setting (deg.)	Injection Nozzle Pressure (psi) New	Used	Idle Speed (rpm)	Cranking Compression Pressure (psi)
1985	T	6-263 (4.3)	Hyd.	Hyd.	16 BTDC	NA	800	650	①	NA

① See the Underhood Specifications Sticker
NA Not available

CAPACITIES

Year	VIN	No. Cylinder Displacement cu. in. (liter)	Engine Crankcase with Filter	without Filter	Transmission (pts.) MT	AT	Drive Axle (pts.)	Fuel Tank (gals.)	Cooling System (qts.)
1985	3	6-231 (3.8)	5.0	4.0	—	13	—	18	13.2
	T	6-263 (4.3)	6.0	5.5	—	13	—	18	13.3
	8	6-250 (4.1)	5.0	4.0	—	13	—	18	13.2 ①
1986	3	6-231 (3.8)	5.0	4.0	—	13	—	18	13.2
	B	6-231 (3.8)	5.0	4.0	—	13	—	18	13.2
	8	6-250 (4.1)	5.0	4.0	—	13	—	18	13.2 ①
1987	3	6-231 (3.8)	5.0	4.0	—	13	—	18	13.2
	8	6-250 (4.1)	5.0	4.0	—	13	—	18	13.2 ①
1988-89	3	6-231 (3.8)	5.0	4.0	—	22	—	18	13.0
	C	6-231 (3.8)	5.0	4.0	—	22	—	18	13.0
	5	6-273 (4.5)	6.0	5.0	—	22	—	18	13.2 ①

Specifications do not include torque converter.
NA Not available

① Use a coolant solution specifically designed for use in aluminum engines. Be sure that the coolant used meets GM spec. No. 1825M or is labeled for use in aluminum engines

FIRING ORDERS

NOTE: To avoid confusion, always replace spark plug wires one at a time.

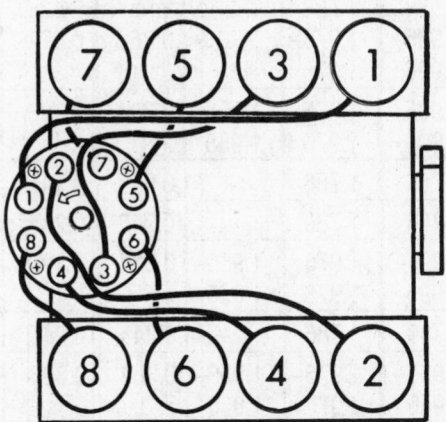

Cadillac 250 cu. in. (4.1L) and 273 cu. in. (4.5L) V8 engines
Firing order: 1–8–4–3–6–5–7–2
Distributor rotation: counterclockwise

FIRING ORDERS

NOTE: To avoid confusion, always replace spark plug wires one at a time.

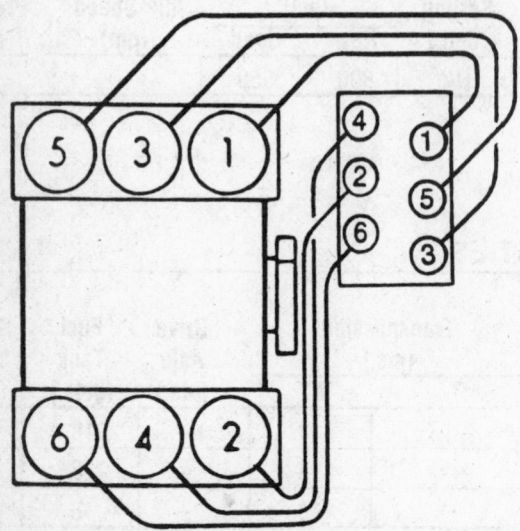

Buick 231 cu. in. (3.8L VIN C) V6 engine
Firing order: 1–6–5–4–3–2
C³I ignition system

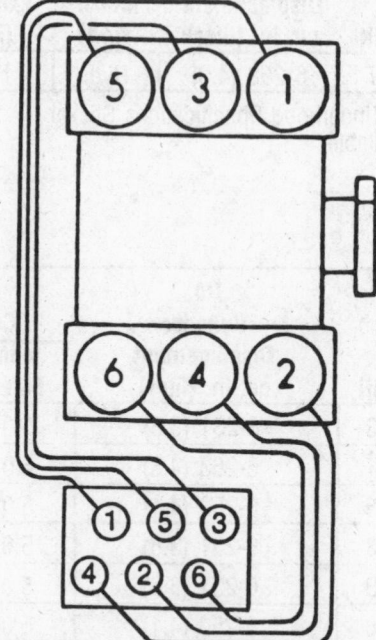

Buick 231 cu. in. (3.8L VIN 3) V6 engine
Firing order: 1–6–5–4–3–2
C³I ignition system

CAMSHAFT SPECIFICATIONS
All measurements given in inches.

Year	VIN	No. Cylinder Displacement cu. in. (liter)	Journal Diameter					Lobe Lift		Bearing Clearance	Camshaft End Play
			1	2	3	4	5	In.	Ex.		
1985	3	6-231 (3.8)	1.785	1.786	1.786	1.786	—	0.245	0.245	①	NA
	T	6-263 (4.3)	②	2.015–2.016	1.995–1.996	1.975–1.976	—	0.252	0.271	0.0020–0.0059	0.0008–0.0228
	8	8-250 (4.1)	2.035–2.036	2.015–2.016	1.995–1.996	1.975–1.976	1.955–1.956	0.384	0.396	0.0018–0.0037	NA
1986	3	6-231 (3.8)	1.785	1.786	1.786	1.786	—	0.245	0.245	①	NA
	B	6-231 (3.8)	1.785	1.786	1.786	1.786	—	0.245	0.245	①	NA
	8	8-250 (4.1)	2.035–2.036	2.015–2.016	1.995–1.996	1.975–1.976	1.955–1.956	0.384	0.396	0.0018–0.0037	NA
1987	3	6-231 (3.8)	1.785	1.786	1.786	1.786	—	0.245	0.245	①	NA
	8	8-250 (4.1)	2.035–2.036	2.015–2.016	1.995–1.996	1.975–1.976	1.955–1.956	0.384	0.396	0.0018–0.0037	NA

CAMSHAFT SPECIFICATIONS
All measurements given in inches.

Year	VIN	No. Cylinder Displacement cu. in. (liter)	Journal Diameter					Lobe Lift		Bearing Clearance	Camshaft End Play
			1	2	3	4	5	In.	Ex.		
1988-89	3	6-231 (3.8)	1.785	1.786	1.786	1.786	—	0.245	0.245	①	NA
	C	6-231 (3.8)	1.785	1.786	1.786	1.786	—	0.272	0.272	①	NA
	5	8-273 (4.5)	2.035–2.036	2.015–2.016	1.995–1.996	1.975–1.976	1.955–1.956	0.384	0.396	0.0018–0.0037	NA

NA Not available
① No. 1:0.0005–0.0025
No. 2–5: 0.0005–0.0035
② No. 1 bearing is not borable, but must be replaced separately.

CRANKSHAFT AND CONNECTING ROD SPECIFICATIONS
All measurements are given in inches.

Year	VIN	No. Cylinder Displacement cu. in. (liter)	Crankshaft				Connecting Rod		
			Main Brg. Journal Dia.	Main Brg. Oil Clearance	Shaft End-play	Thrust on No.	Journal Diameter	Oil Clearance	Side Clearance
1985	3	6-231 (3.8)	2.4990–2.5000	0.0003–0.0018	0.0030–0.0110	2	2.2487–2.2499	0.0003–0.0028	0.003–0.015
	T	6-263 (4.3)	2.9993–3.0003	①	0.0035–0.0135	4	2.2490–2.2500	0.0005–0.0025	0.008–0.018
	8	8-250 (4.1)	2.6400	0.0004–0.0027	0.0010–0.0070	3	1.9291	0.0005–0.0028	0.008–0.020
1986	3	6-231 (3.8)	2.4990–2.5000	0.0003–0.0018	0.0030–0.0110	2	2.2487–2.2499	0.0003–0.0028	0.003–0.015
	B	6-231 (3.8)	2.4990–2.5000	0.0003–0.0018	0.0030–0.0110	2	2.2487–2.2499	0.0003–0.0028	0.003–0.015
	8	8-250 (4.1)	2.6400	0.0004–0.0027	0.0010–0.0070	3	1.9291	0.0005–0.0028	0.008–0.020
1987	3	6-231 (3.8)	2.4995	0.0003–0.0018	0.0030–0.0110	2	2.2487–2.2499	0.0003–0.0028	0.003–0.015
	8	8-250 (4.1)	2.6354–2.6364	0.0004–0.0027	0.0010–0.0070	3	1.9291	0.0005–0.0028	0.008–0.020
1988-89	3	6-231 (3.8)	2.4988–2.4998	0.0003–0.0018	0.0030–0.0110	2	2.2487–2.2495	0.0003–0.0028	0.003–0.015
	C	6-231 (3.8)	2.4988–2.4998	0.0003–0.0018	0.0030–0.0110	2	2.2487–2.2495	0.0003–0.0028	0.0003–0.015
	5	8-273 (4.5)	2.6354–2.6364	0.0004–0.0027	0.0010–0.0070	3	1.9291	0.0005–0.0028	0.008–0.020

① No. 1, 2 & 3: 0.0005–0.0020 in.
No. 4: 0.0020–0.0034 in.

VALVE SPECIFICATIONS

Year	VIN	No. Cylinder Displacement cu. in. (liter)	Seat Angle (deg.)	Face Angle (deg.)	Spring Test Pressure (lbs.)	Spring Installed Height (in.)	Stem-to-Guide Clearance (in.) Intake	Stem-to-Guide Clearance (in.) Exhaust	Stem Diameter (in.) Intake	Stem Diameter (in.) Exhaust
1985	3	6-231 (3.8)	46	45	90	1.727	0.0015–0.0035	0.0015–0.0032	0.3401–0.3412	0.3405–0.3412
	T	6-263 (4.3)	①	②	210	1.670	0.0010–0.0027	0.0015–0.0032	0.3425–0.3432	0.3420–0.3427
	8	8-250 (4.1)	45	44	182	1.730	0.001–0.003	0.001–0.003	0.3413–0.3420	0.3411–0.3418
1986	3	6-231 (3.8)	46	45	90	1.727	0.0015–0.0035	0.0015–0.0032	0.3401–0.3412	0.3405–0.3412
	B	6-231 (3.8)	45	45	105	1.727	0.0015–0.0035	0.0015–0.0032	0.3401–0.3412	0.3405–0.3412
	8	8-250 (4.1)	45	44	185	1.730	0.001–0.003	0.001–0.003	0.3413–0.3420	0.3411–0.3418
1987	3	6-231 (3.8)	46	45·	90	1.727	0.0015–0.0035	0.0015–0.0032	0.3401–0.3412	0.3405–0.3412
	8	8-250 (4.1)	45	44	185	1.730	0.001–0.003	0.001–0.003	0.3413–0.3420	0.3411–0.3418
1988-89	3	6-231 (3.8)	46	45	90	1.727	0.0015–0.0035	0.0015–0.0032	0.3401–0.3412	0.3405–0.3412
	C	6-231 (3.8)	45	45	105	1.730	0.0015–0.0035	0.0015–0.0032	0.3401–0.3412	0.3405–0.3412
	5	6-273 (4.5)	45	44	185	1.730	0.0010–0.0030	0.0010–0.0030	0.3413–0.3420	0.3411–0.3418

① Intake: 45
  Exhaust: 31
② Intake: 44
  Exhaust: 30

PISTON AND RING SPECIFICATIONS
All measurments are given in inches.

Year	VIN	No. Cylinder Displacement cu. in. (liter)	Piston Clearance	Ring Gap Top Compression	Ring Gap Bottom Compression	Ring Gap Oil Control	Ring Side Clearance Top Compression	Ring Side Clearance Bottom Compression	Ring Side Clearance Oil Control
1985	3	6-231 (3.8)	0.0008–0.0020	0.010–0.020	0.010–0.020	0.015–0.055	0.0030–0.0050	0.0030–0.0050	0.0035 Max.
	T	6-263 (4.3)	0.0035–0.0045	0.019–0.027	0.013–0.021	0.010–0.022	0.005–0.007	0.003–0.005	0.001–0.005
	8	8-250 (4.1)	0.0010–0.0018	0.023–0.025	0.023–0.025	0.010–0.050	0.0016–0.0037	0.0016–0.0037	None (side sealing)
1986	3	6-231 (3.8)	0.0008–0.0020	0.010–0.020	0.010–0.020	0.015–0.055	0.0030–0.0050	0.0030–0.0050	0.0035 Max.
	B	6-231 (3.8)	0.0008–0.0020	0.010–0.020	0.010–0.020	0.015–0.055	0.0030–0.0050	0.0030–0.0050	0.0035 Max.

PISTON AND RING SPECIFICATIONS
All measurments are given in inches.

Year	VIN	No. Cylinder Displacement cu. in. (liter)	Piston Clearance	Ring Gap			Ring Side Clearance		
				Top Compression	Bottom Compression	Oil Control	Top Compression	Bottom Compression	Oil Control
1986	8	8-250 (4.1)	0.0010–0.0018	0.023–0.025	0.023–0.025	0.010–0.050	0.0016–0.0037	0.0016–0.0037	None (side sealing)
1987	3	6-231 (3.8)	0.0008–0.0020	0.010–0.020	0.010–0.020	0.015–0.055	0.0030–0.0050	0.0030–0.0050	0.0035 Max.
	8	8-250 (4.1)	0.0010–0.0018	0.023–0.025	0.023–0.025	0.010–0.050	0.0016–0.0037	0.0016–0.0037	None (side sealing)
1988-89	3	6-231 (3.8)	①	0.010–0.020	0.010–0.022	0.015–0.055	0.0010–0.0030	0.0010–0.0030	0.0005–0.0065
	C	6-231 (3.8)	0.0004–0.0022	0.010–0.025	0.010–0.025	0.015–0.0055	0.0013–0.0031	0.0013–0.0031	0.0011–0.0081
	5	6-273 (3.8)	0.0010–0.0018	0.023–0.025	0.023–0.025	0.010–0.050	0.0016–0.0037	0.0016–0.0037	None (side sealing)

① Skirt top: 0.0007–0.0027
Skirt bottom: 0.0010–0.0045

TORQUE SPECIFICATIONS
All readings in ft. lbs.

Year	VIN	No. Cylinder Displacement cu. in. (liter)	Cylinder Head Bolts	Main Bearing Bolts	Rod Bearing Bolts	Crankshaft Pulley Bolts	Flywheel Bolts	Manifold		Spark Plugs
								Intake	Exhaust	
1985	3	6-231 (3.8)	80	100	40	200	60	47	37	20
	T	6-263 (4.3)	①	89	42	②	76	41	31	–
	8	8-250 (4.1)	90③	85	22	18	63	④	18	11
1986	3	6-231 (3.8)	60⑤	100	40	200	60	32	37	20
	B	6-231 (3.8)	60⑤	100	40	200	60	32	25	20
	8	8-250 (4.1)	90③	85	22	18	63	41	18	11
1987	3	6-231 (3.8)	60⑤	100	40	200	60	32	37	20
	8	8-250 (4.1)	90③	85	22	18	63	41	18	11
1988-89	3	6-231 (3.8)	60⑤	100	40	219	60	80⑥	37	20
	C	6-231 (3.8)	60⑤	100	40	219	60	80⑥	37	20
	5	8-273 (4.5)	90③	85	22	18	63	41	18	11

① All exc. bolt No.5, 6, 11, 12, 13, 14: 142 ft.lbs.
Bolt No.5, 6, 11, 12, 13, 14: 59 ft.lbs.
② Crankshaft balancer to crankshaft bolt: 203–350 ft.lbs.
Crankshaft pulley to balancer bolts: 30 ft.lbs.
③ See text for proper tightening sequence

④ Bolts No.1, 2, 3, 4: 15 ft.lbs.
Bolts No.5–16: 22 ft.lbs.
All bolts: 22 ft.lbs.
Repeat 3rd Step
⑤ Torque (in sequence) to 25 ft. lbs.
Torque additional ¼ turn (90 degrees) until 60 ft. lbs. is reached
⑥ Inch lbs.

BRAKE SPECIFICATIONS
All measurements in inches unless noted

Year	Model	Lug Nut Torque (ft. lbs.)	Master Cylinder Bore	Brake Disc Minimum Thickness	Brake Disc Maximum Runout	Standard Brake Drum Diameter	Minimum Lining Thickness Front	Minimum Lining Thickness Rear
1985	Buick	100	0.973	0.972	0.004	8.880	0.79	0.60
	Oldsmobile	100	0.944	0.972	0.004	8.920	0.79	0.60
	Cadillac	100	0.940	0.972	0.004	8.900	0.79	0.60
1986	Buick	100	0.973	0.972	0.004	8.880	0.79	0.60
	Oldsmobile	100	0.944	0.972	0.004	8.920	0.79	0.60
	Cadillac	100	0.940	0.972	0.004	8.900	0.79	0.60
1987	Buick	100	0.973	0.972	0.004	8.880	0.79	0.60
	Oldsmobile	100	0.944	0.972	0.004	8.920	0.79	0.60
	Cadillac	100	0.940	0.972	0.004	8.900	0.79	0.60
1988-89	Buick	100	0.944	0.972	0.004	8.860	0.79	0.60
	Oldsmobile	100	0.944	0.972	0.004	8.920	0.79	0.60
	Cadillac	100	0.944	0.972	0.004	8.900	0.79	0.60

WHEEL ALIGNMENT

Year	Model	Caster Range (deg.)	Caster Preferred Setting (deg.)	Camber Range (deg.)	Camber Preferred Setting (deg.)	Toe-in (in.)	Steering Axis Inclination (deg.)
1985	Buick	2P-3P	2½P	L—1-0 R—0-1	½P	$7/32$P①	—
	Oldsmobile	2P-3P	2½P	L—1-0 R—0-1	½N ½	$3/32$P①	—
	Cadillac	1½P-3½P	2½P	$5/16$N—1¼P	½	$3/32$P①	—
1986	Buick	2P-3P	2½P	L—1-0 R—0-1	½P	$7/32$P①	—
	Oldsmobile	2P-3P	2½P	L—1-0 R—0-1	½N ½	$3/32$P①	—
	Cadillac	1½P-3½P	2½P	$5/16$N—1¼P	½P	$3/32$P①	—
1987	Buick	2P-3P	2½P	L—1-0 R—0-1	½P	$7/32$P①	—
	Oldsmobile	2P-3P	2½P	L—1-0 R—0-1	½N ½	$3/32$P①	—
	Cadillac	1½P-3½P	2½P	$5/16$N—1¼P	½P	$3/32$P①	—
1988-89	Buick	2P-3P	2½P	⅓N-⅔P	⅕P	0	—
	Oldsmobile	2½P-3½P	3P	⅓N-⅔P	⅕P	0	—
	Cadillac	2½P-3½P	3P	1N-0	½N	0	—

① In or out pref: 0
L Left
R Right
N Negative
P Positive

TUNE UP PROCEDURES

Ignition Timing

The 4.1L and 4.5L engines are equipped with High Energy Ignition (HEI) system, utilizing Electronic Spark Timing (EST). The EST distributor uses no mechanical or vacuum advance and is easily identified by the absence of a vacuum advance and the presence of a four terminal connector.

The 3.8L engines use a Computer Controlled Coil Ignition (C³I) system. The system does not use a distributor; instead, it uses a coil pack, an ignition module, a crankshaft sensor and a camshaft sensor; no adjustment is necessary.

ADJUSTMENT

NOTE: The 4.1L and 4.5L V8 engines incorporate a magnetic timing probe hole for use with special electronic timing equipment. Consult the manufacturer's instructions before using this system. The following procedure is for use with the HEI-EST distributor. For instructions on initial timing of C³I systems, see the underhood emission sticker and follow the procedure given.

1. Connect a timing light to the No. 1 spark plug wire according to the light manufacturer's instructions; DO NOT PIERCE the spark plug wire to connect the timing light.
2. Follow the instructions on the emission control label located in the engine compartment.
3. If equipped with an Electronic Spark Timing (EST) distributor, disconnect the 4-wire terminal plug from the distributor. Ground the diagnostic connector (ALCL) located under the left side of the dash.
4. Start the engine and allow it to run at idle speed.
5. Aim the timing light at the degree scale just over the harmonic balancer.
6. Adjust the timing by loosening the hold-down clamp and rotate the distributor until the desired ignition advance is achieved. When the correct timing marks are aligned, tighten the clamp.

NOTE: On the 4.1L and 4.5L V8 engines, use the Distributor Wrench tool No. J-29791 is used to loosen the hold down nut.

7. Adjust the timing, replace and

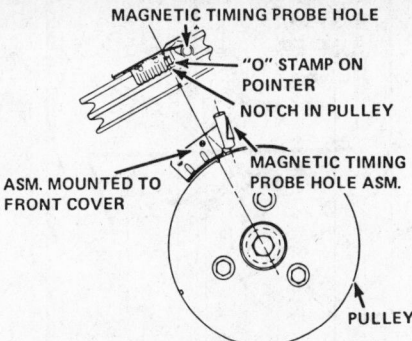

The 4·1L V8 incorporates a special magnetic timing probe hole

tighten the hold-down clamp. To advance the timing, rotate the distributor opposite the normal direction of rotor rotation. Retard the timing by rotating the distributor in the normal direction of rotor rotation.

NOTE: On DFI systems (Digital Fuel Injection), the malfunction trouble codes must be cleared after removal or adjustment of the distributor. This is accomplished by removing battery voltage to terminal R for 10 seconds.

Valve Lash

ADJUSTMENT

All engines use hydraulic lifters. Valve systems with hydraulic lifters operate with zero clearance in the valve train. The rocker arms are non-adjustable. The lifter itself will compensate if there is slack in the system but if there is excessive play, the entire system should be checked.

If the valve guides are found to be worn past allowable limits, they will have to be rebored and valves with oversize stem installed.

Idle Speed and Mixture Gasoline Engines

ADJUSTMENT

Idle Speed

**DIGITAL FUEL INJECTION
CADILLAC**

NOTE: The engine idle speed is controlled by the electronic control module. Idle adjustment is only necessary when the idle speed control motor or the throttle body has been replaced. Before adjusting the idle speed, record, diagnosis, repair and clear all trouble codes in the ECM memory.

1. Remove the air cleaner assembly. Connect a suitable tachometer and timing light. Start the engine and allow it to reach normal operating temperatures.
2. Turn all the accessories OFF. Check and adjust the ignition timing.
3. Place the steering wheel in the center position and the transmission selector in the PARK position.
4. To retract the idle speed control motor (ISC) plunger, unlock the ISC motor connector but do not disconnect the motor. Open the throttle and hold it at approximately 1,500 rpm.
5. Close the throttle switch by depressing the ISC plunger. When the plunger is fully retracted, continue to hold the throttle open and the throttle switch closed, while disconnecting the ISC motor.
6. Return the throttle to idle; be sure not to power the ISC motor in the fully retracted position for more than four seconds or damage to the electronic control module may occur.
7. The ISC plunger should now be retracted. If the plunger still contacts the throttle lever, turn the plunger in so it is not touching. With the ISC plunger fully retracted and not touching the throttle lever, the idle speed should be 450 rpm.
8. Check the throttle position sensor adjustment. With the ISC motor fully retracted and the throttle against the stop screw. Turn the ISC plunger adjustment screw to obtain a 0.160 in. gap between the throttle lever and the plunger.
9. Shut the engine OFF, disconnect all the test equipment and reconnect all harness connectors. Turn the ignition OFF for a least 10 seconds. Start the engine and check the ISC motor for proper operation.

NOTE: This procedure may have recorded intermittent trouble codes in the DFI computer. After all the connections have been made and the system is restored to normal operations, these codes must be cleared.

10. To remove the codes from the ECM, on all models except Cadillac, perform the following procedures:
    a. Turn the ignition switch to the OFF position; this will prevent damage to the ECM when disconnecting or reconnecting the power cable.
    b. Remove the ECM fuse from the fuse panel.
    c. Remove the ECM pigtail.
    d. Disconnect the negative terminal from the battery for 30 seconds.

NOTE: Disconnecting the battery cable should only be done as a last resort as it will also clear

the digital radio, digital clock, trip odometer, etc.

11. To clear the ECM codes, perform the following porcedures:

   a. Turn the key to the **ON** position.

   b. Then simultaneously press the **OFF** and **HI** buttons in the climate control panel until E.O.O appears in the readout.

12. To clear the Body Computer Module **BCM**, depress the **OFF** and **LO** buttons simultaneously until F.O.O appears.

PORT FUEL INJECTION EXCEPT CADILLAC

NOTE: This adjustment should be performed only when the throttle body parts have been replaced. Engine must be at normal operating temperatures before making an adjustment.

1. With a scratch awl or equivalent, piece the idle stop screw plug and apply leverage to remove it.

2. Ground the ALDL diagnostic test lead and turn ignition switch **ON** position, without starting engine for at least 30 seconds.

3. After 30 seconds, disconnect the Idle Air Control (IAC) electrical connector.

4. Remove ground wire from diagnostic lead. Firmly set the parking brake and block the front drive wheels.

5. Start the engine and place the transaxle in **DRIVE**. Using the minimum idle stop set screw and adjust the idle speed to 450–550 rpm.

6. Turn ignition switch **OFF** and reconnect connector at IAC motor.

7. Adjust Throttle Position Sensor **TPS** to 0.36–0.44V.

8. Recheck setting, start engine and inspect for proper idle operation.

Fuel Mixture

On all models, the fuel mixture is computer-controlled and not adjustable. No periodic adjustment or maintenance is required.

Idle Speed Diesel Engines

ADJUSTMENT

Tools necessary to perform this procedure are: Air Crossover tool No. J–26996–1 or equivalent, and Tachometer tool No. J–26925 or equivalent.

1. Apply the parking brake, place the transaxle selector lever in Park and block the front wheels.

2. Adjust the throttle linkage (if necessary).

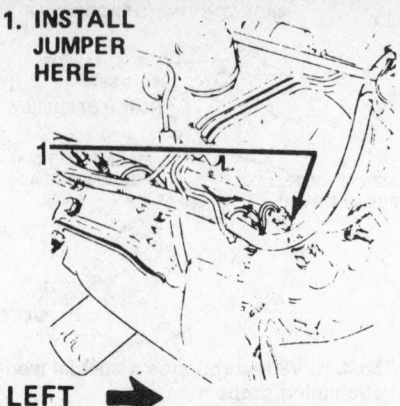

1. INSTALL JUMPER HERE

LEFT ➡

Install a jumper wire to the HPCA and fast idle temperature switch (internal EGR) — diesel engine

Unplugging the engine coolant temperature sensor — diesel engine

3. Start the engine and allow it to reach normal operating temperature.

4. Turn the engine **OFF** and remove the air cleaner cover. Remove the MAP sensor retainer and move the sensor aside (with the leads and hose attached).

5. Using the Air Crossover Cover tool No. J–26996–1 or equivalent, remove the air cleaner assembly and install the cover.

6. Clean the front cover RPM counter (probe holder) and the crankshaft balancer rim.

7. Using the Magnetic Pick-up Timing Probe tool No. J–26925 or equivalent, install it fully into the RPM counter. Connect the battery leads; red-to-positive and black-to-negative.

8. If equipped with air conditioning, disconnect the clutch lead from the compressor.

9. If equipped with cruise control, remove the cruise control servo throttle rod retainer. Remove the servo cable retainer and disconnect the servo throttle cable from the servo blade.

10. Turn **OFF** all electrical accessories.

11. Do not touch the steering wheel or the service brake pedal.

12. Start the engine and place the transaxle selector lever in Drive.

13. Check the slow idle speed reading against the one given on the Vehicle Emissions Information Label; reset it (if necessary).

14. Turn **OFF** the engine.

15. If equipped with an internal EGR, unplug the connector from the HPCA and the fast idle temperature switch, install a jumper wire between the connector terminals. Do not allow the jumper to touch ground.

NOTE: If the vehicle DOES NOT have an internal EGR, unplug the connector from the engine coolant temperature sensor.

16. Make sure the parking brake has not been released and the front wheels are still blocked. Start the engine and shift the transaxle into Drive.

17. Check the fast idle solenoid speed against the one given on the Vehicle Emissions Information Label; reset it (if necessary). Open the throttle valve (slightly) and allow the plunger to extend.

18. If equipped with an internal EGR, remove the jumper wire and reconnect the harness connector to the HPCA temperature switch. If not equipped with an internal EGR, reconnect the harness connector to the engine coolant temperature sensor.

19. Recheck and reset the slow idle speed, if necessary.

20. Turn **OFF** the engine.

21. If equipped with air conditioning, reconnect the clutch lead to the compressor.

22. Disconnect and remove the tachometer.

23. If equipped with cruise control, pull the cruise control cable toward the servo blade. If the hole in the servo blade aligns with the cable pin, install the pin (in the hole) and the retainer. If the hole does not align with the pin, install the pin in the next hole away from the servo assembly.

24. Remove the air crossover cover. Install the air cleaner assembly and reconnect the EGR valve hose.

25. Install the MAP sensor and the air cleaner cover.

ENGINE ELECTRICAL

Distributor

HEI SYSTEM TACHOMETER HOOKUP

On the HEI distributor cap, there is a

terminal marked TACH (usually next to the BAT terminal). Connect one tachometer lead to this terminal and the other lead to a suitable ground. On some tachometers, the leads must be connected to the TACH terminal and the positive battery terminal.

NOTE: Never ground the TACH terminal; serious module and ignition coil damage will result. If there is any doubt as to the correct tachometer hookup, check with the tachometer manufacturer.

REMOVAL & INSTALLATION

HEI Distributor

1. Disconnect the negative terminal from the battery.
2. Label and disconnect all wires leading from the distributor cap.
3. Remove the distributor cap by turning the four latches counterclockwise. Lift off the distributor cap and carefully move it aside.

NOTE: The location of the distributor cap doghouse must be in the same position on reinstallation in order to provide sufficient clearance for adjustment.

4. Disconnect the four terminal ECM connector harness from the distributor, if not already done.
5. Remove the distributor hold-down nut and clamp.

NOTE: On the 4.1L and 4.5L engines, use Distributor Hold-down Clamp Bolt tool No. J–29791 or equivalent, to loosen the hold-down nut and clamp.

6. Using a piece of chalk or paint, mark the rotor-to-distributor body and the distributor body-to-engine positions. Pull the distributor upward until the rotor just stops turning (counterclockwise); note the position of the rotor once again. Remove the distributor.

NOTE: DO NOT crank the engine with the distributor removed.

7. On certain models, a thrust washer is used between the distributor drive gear and the crankcase. This washer may stick to the bottom of the distributor when it is removed. Always make sure that this washer is at the bottom of the distributor bore before installation. On DFI systems (Digital Fuel Injection), the malfunction trouble codes must be cleared after removal or adjustment of the distributor. This is accomplished by removing battery voltage to terminal **R** for 10 seconds.

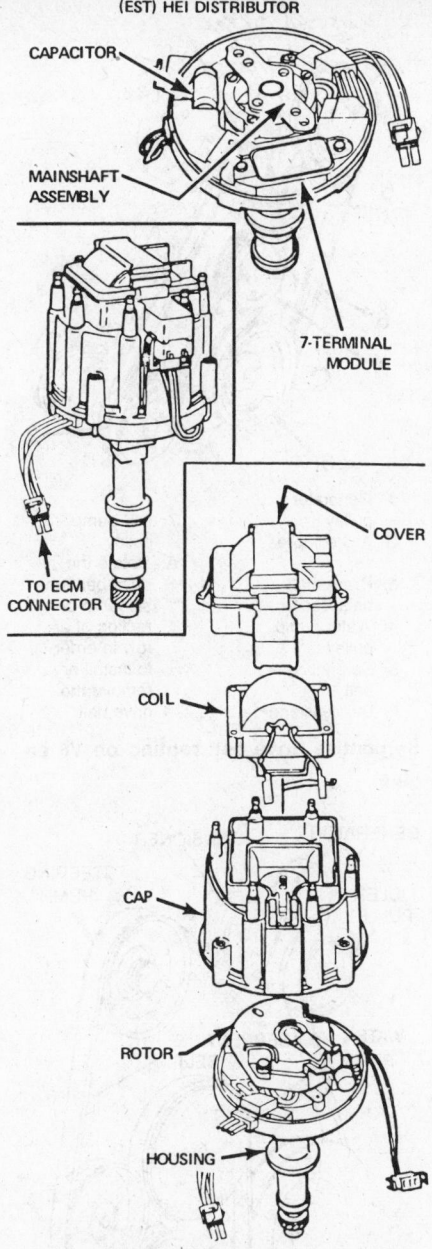

Exploded view of the HEI distributor

8. To install the distributor, rotate the distributor shaft until the rotor aligns with the second mark (when the shaft stopped moving). Lubricate the drive gear with clean engine oil and install the distributor into the engine. As the distributor is installed, the rotor should rotate to the first alignment mark; this will ensure proper timing. If the marks do not align properly, remove the distributor and reset; be sure to install the thrust washer (if equipped).
9. Install the clamp and hold-down nut. Tighten the nut until the distributor can just be moved with a little effort.
10. Connect all wires and hoses. In-

stall the distributor cap. Check and/or adjust the ignition timing.

INSTALLATION
ENGINE DISTURBED

If the engine has been disturbed (cranked) after the distributor was removed, perform the following installation procedure:

1. Remove the No. 1 spark plug.
2. Rotate the crankshaft until No. 1 piston is at the TDC of its compression stroke.

NOTE: The compression stroke can be determined by placing your thumb over the hole while an assistant slowly cranks the engine. Crank until compression is felt at the hole and continue cranking slowly until the timing mark on the crankshaft pulley aligns with the 0 degrees timing mark located on the timing chain cover.

3. Position the distributor in the block but do not, at this time, allow it to engage with the drive gear.
4. Rotate the distributor shaft until the rotor points between No. 1 and No. 8 spark plug towers (V8) or No. 1 and No. 6 (V6) and lower the distributor to engage the camshaft.

NOTE: It may be necessary to turn the rotor a small amount in either direction in order to achieve this engagement. The rotor will rotate slightly as the distributor gear engages. If installed correctly, the rotor should point toward the No. 1 spark plug terminal in the distributor cap.

5. Press down firmly on the distributor housing. This will ensure that the distributor shaft engages the oil pump shaft, thereby allowing the distributor to fully contact the engine block.
6. Install the hold-down clamp and tighten the nut until it is snug (not tight).
7. Install the distributor cap, making sure that the rotor points to No. 1 terminal in the cap.
8. Attach all wires and hoses.
9. Start the engine. Check and/or adjust the ignition timing. Torque the distributor hold-down nut to 20 ft. lbs.

Alternator

NOTE: For further information on the charging system, please refer to "Charging And Starting" in the Unit Repair Section.

PRECAUTIONS

Several precautions must be observed

with alternator equipped vehicles to avoid damage to the unit.

• If the battery is removed for any reason, make sure it is reconnected with the correct polarity. Reversing the battery connections may result in damage to the one-way rectifiers.

• When utilizing a booster battery as a starting aid, always connect the positive to positive terminals, and the negative terminal from the booster battery to a good engine ground on the vehicle being started.

• Never use a fast charger as a booster to start vehicles with alternating-current (AC) circuits.

• Disconnect the battery cables when charging the battery with a fast charger.

• Never attempt to polarize an alternator.

• Avoid long soldering times when making alternator repairs. Prolonged head will damage the alternator.

• Do not use test lamps of more than 12V when checking diode continuity.

• Do not short across or ground any of the alternator terminals.

• The polarity of the battery, alternator and regulator must be matched and considered before making any electrical connections within the system.

• Never separate the alternator on an open circuit. Make sure all connections within the circuit are clean and tight.

• Disconnect the battery ground terminal when performing any service on electrical components.

• Disconnect the battery if arc welding is to be done on the vehicle.

BELT TENSION ADJUSTMENT

The engines utilize a serpentine drive; the belt tension pulley is spring loaded to maintain constant pressure on the drive belt. Using a Belt Tension Gauge tool No. J–23600 or equivalent, inspect the serpentine drive belt on the longest span between the pulleys. The drive belt tension should be 100–140 lbs. (diesel), 110 lbs. (4.1L and 4.5L) or never below 67 lbs. (3.8L). If the belt tensioner is adjusted beyond it movable limit, replace the serpentine drive belt.

REMOVAL & INSTALLATION

1. Disconnect the negative terminal from the battery.
2. Label and disconnect the electrical connectors from the back of the alternator.
3. Remove the brace at the back of the alternator (if equipped).

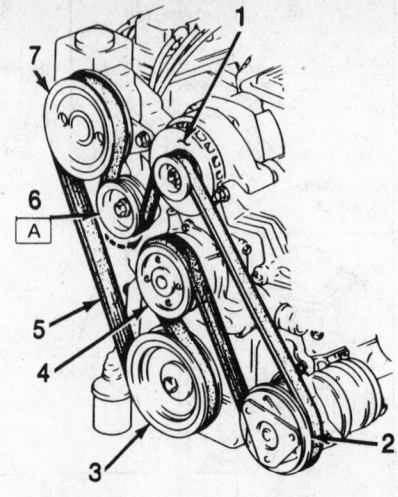

1. Generator pulley
2. A/C compressor
3. Crankshaft balancer
4. Water pump pulley
5. Serpentine belt
6. Belt tensioner
7. P/S pump pulley
A. Rotate the drive belt tensioner in direction of arrow in order to install or remove the drive belt

Serpentine drive belt routing on V6 engine

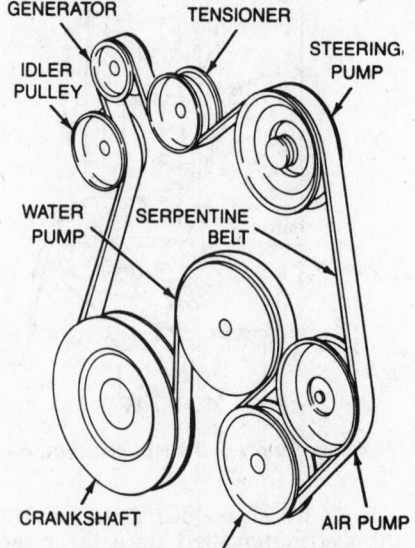

Serpentine drive belt routing on V8 engine.

4. Loosen the adjusting bolts, move the alternator inward and remove the drive belt. If a serpentine drive belt is used, loosen the belt tensioner and rotate it counterclockwise to remove the drive belt.
5. While supporting the alternator, remove the mounting bolts and the alternator.
6. To install, reverse the removal procedures. If not equipped with a ser-

pentine drive belt, adjust the drive belt to have ¼–½ in. play midway along the longest free span of the belt. If a serpentine drive belt is used, tighten the tensioner pulley.

Voltage Regulator

An alternator with an integral voltage regulator is standard equipment. There are no adjustments possible with this unit. Testing procedures can be found in the Unit Repair section.

Starter

NOTE: For further information on the starter system, please refer to "Charging and Starting" in the Unit Repair section.

REMOVAL & INSTALLATION

All Except Diesel

1. Disconnect the negative terminal from the battery.
2. Raise and support the vehicle on jackstands.
3. If equipped, remove the splash shields and/or braces which may be in the way.
4. Label and disconnect the electrical connectors from the starter.

NOTE: On some models it may be necessary to remove the crossover pipe to complete this procedure.

5. Remove the starter-to-engine bolts and the starter.

NOTE: Note the location of any shims so that they may be replaced in the same positions upon installation.

6. To install, reverse the removal procedures; be sure to install the shims. Check the starter operation.

Diesel

1. Disconnect the negative terminal from the battery.
2. Raise and support the vehicle on jackstands.
3. Remove the lower starter shield nut and carefully bend the shield out of the way.
4. Label and disconnect the electrical connectors from the starter.
5. Remove the front starter bolt. Loosen the rear starter mounting bolt and remove the starter with the rear bolt still in housing.
6. To install, reverse the removal procedures. Check the starter operation.

Diesel Glow Plugs

REMOVAL & INSTALLATION

1. Disconnect both negative terminals from the batteries.
2. Remove all necessary components in order to gain access to the glow plugs.
3. Disconnect the electrical connector from the glow plug(s). Using a deep socket remove the glow plug.
4. Inspect and test the glow plug.

NOTE: A burned out glow plug tip may bulge, break off and drop into the prechamber when the glow plug is removed from the engine. When this occurs the cylinder head must be removed and the prechamber removed from the head in order to remove the broken tip.

5. To install, reverse the removal procedures.

TESTING

1. Disconnect the electrical connector from the glow plug.
2. Using a test light, connect it between the glow plug terminal and the positive battery terminal.
3. If the test light turns **ON**, the glow plug is working.
4. Test all other glow plugs; replace any glow plug which does not work.

GASOLINE ENGINE MECHANICAL

Engine

REMOVAL & INSTALLATION

3.8L Engines

1. Disconnect the negative terminal from the battery. Using a scribing tool, matchmark the hood hinges and remove the hood.
2. If equipped with fuel injection, label and disconnect the air flow sensor wiring. Depressurize the fuel system.
3. Remove the air intake duct. If equipped with fuel injection, remove the throttle cable and bracket from the throttle body. Place a clean drain pan under the radiator, open the drain cock and drain the cooling system.

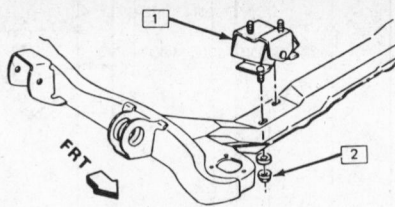

1. ENGINE MOUNT
2. NUT 41 N·m (30 FT. LBS.)

Exploded view of the right-side engine mount—3.8L engine

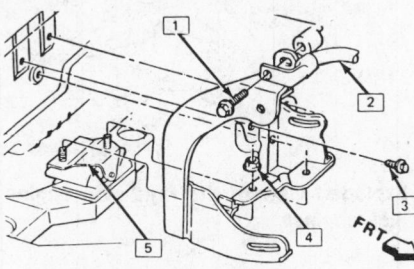

1. BOLT 50 N·m (37 FT. LBS.)
2. NEGATIVE BATTERY CABLE
3. BOLT 95 N·m (70 FT. LBS.)
4. NUT 35 N·m (25 FT. LBS.)
5. ENGINE MOUNT

Exploded view of the left-side engine mount—3.8L engine

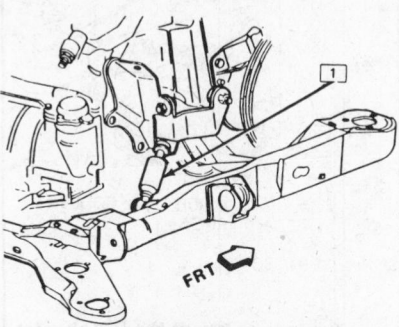

1. DRIVELINE VIBRATION ABSORBER

Typical driveline vibration absorber

4. Raise and support the front of the vehicle on jackstands.
5. Remove the exhaust pipe-to-exhaust manifold bolts and separate the exhaust pipe.
6. Remove the engine mount bolts.
7. If equipped with a driveline vibration absorber, remove the bolts and disconnect the absorber.
8. Label and disconnect the electrical connectors from the starter. Remove the starter-to-engine bolts and the starter.
9. If equipped with air conditioning, disconnect the compressor and position it out of the way; DO NOT disconnect the refrigerant lines.
10. Place a catch pan under the pow-

er steering gear, disconnect the hydraulic lines, drain the fluid and wire the hoses out of the way.
11. Remove the lower transaxle-to-engine bolts.

NOTE: One bolt is situated between the transaxle case and the engine block; it is installed in the opposite direction of the other bolts.

12. Remove the flywheel cover. Matchmark the flexplate-to-torque converter relationship to insure proper alignment upon installation. Remove the flexplate-to-torque converter bolts.
13. Remove the engine support bracket-to-transaxle bolts and the bracket. Lower the vehicle.
14. Using a vertical engine hoist, attach it to the engine and support the weight.
15. Remove the radiator and heater hoses from the engine; position them out of the way.
16. Remove hoses from the vacuum modulator and canister purge lines.
17. Disconnect the engine electrical wiring harness(es) and tie it (them) out of way.
18. Remove the upper transaxle-to-engine bolts.
19. To install, reverse the removal procedures. Refill the cooling system. Start the engine, allow it to reach normal operating temperatures and check for leaks.

4.1L and 4.5L V8

1. Disconnect the negative terminal from the battery. Place a clean drain pan under the radiator, open the drain cock and drain the cooling system.
2. Remove the air cleaner. Using a scribing tool, matchmark the hood to the support brackets and remove the hood.
3. If equipped with air conditioning, perform the following procedures:
   a. Remove the hose strap from the right-strut tower.
   b. Remove the accumulator from its bracket and position it out of the way.
   c. Remove the canister hoses from the accumulator bracket.
   d. Remove the accumulator bracket from the wheel house.
4. Remove the cooling fans, the accessory drive belt, the radiator and heater hoses.
5. Label and disconnect the electrical connectors from the following items:
   a. Oil pressure switch
   b. Coolant temperature sensor
   c. Distributor
   d. EGR solenoid
   e. Engine temperature switch

6. Label and disconnect the cables from the following items:
   a. Accelerator
   b. Cruise control linkage
   c. Transmission TV cable

7. If equipped with cruise control, remove the diaphragm (with the bracket) and move it aside.

8. Remove the vacuum supply hose and the exhaust crossover pipe.

9. Disconnect the oil cooler lines from the oil filter adapter, the oil line cooler bracket from the transaxle and position them aside.

10. Remove the air cleaner mounting bracket.

11. Using a catch pan or a shop rag, carefully bleed the fuel pressure from the Schraeder valve. Disconnect the fuel lines from the throttle body. Remove the fuel line bracket from the transaxle and secure the fuel lines out of the way.

— CAUTION —

When bleeding the fuel system, be sure to have a container or rags on hand to catch excess fuel. Take precautions to avoid the risk of fire.

12. Remove the small vacuum line from the brake booster.

13. Label and disconnect the AIR solenoid electrical and hose connections. Remove the AIR valves with the bracket.

14. Label and disconnect the electrical connectors from the following:
   a. Idle Speed Control (ISC) motor
   b. Throttle Position Switch (TPS)
   c. Fuel injectors
   d. Manifold Air Temperature (MAT) sensor
   e. Oxygen sensor
   f. Electric Fuel Evaporator (EFE) grid
   g. Alternator bracket

15. Remove the power steering pump hose strap from the stud-headed bolt in front of the right cylinder head and the stud-headed bolt.

16. Remove the AIR pipe clip located near the No. 2 spark plug.

17. Remove the power steering pump and belt tensioner (with bracket); wire them out of the way.

18. Raise and support the front of the vehicle on jackstands.

19. Label and disconnect the electrical connectors from the starter and the ground wire from the cylinder block.

20. Remove the two flywheel covers. Remove the starter-to-engine bolts and the starter. Matchmark the flywheel-to-torque converter location. Remove the three flywheel-to-torque converter bolts and slide the converter back into the bell housing.

21. If equipped with air conditioning, perform the following procedures:

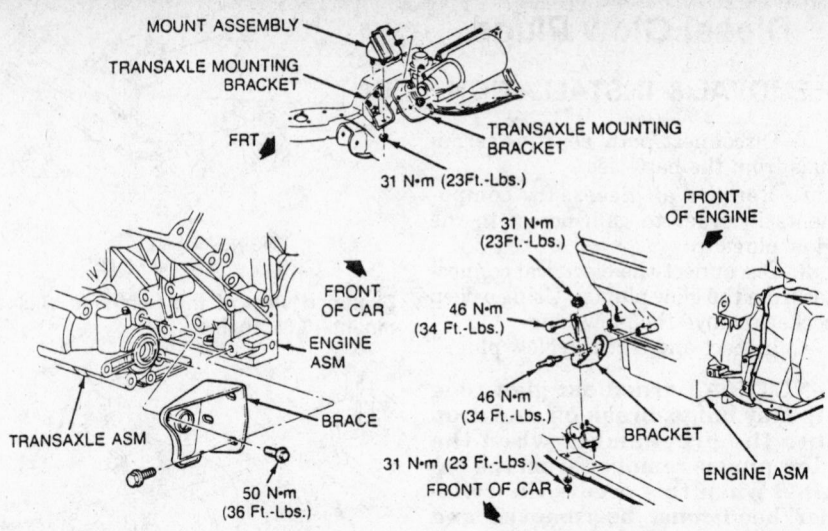

Exploded view of the right-side engine brace and transaxle mount—4.1L and 4.5L engines

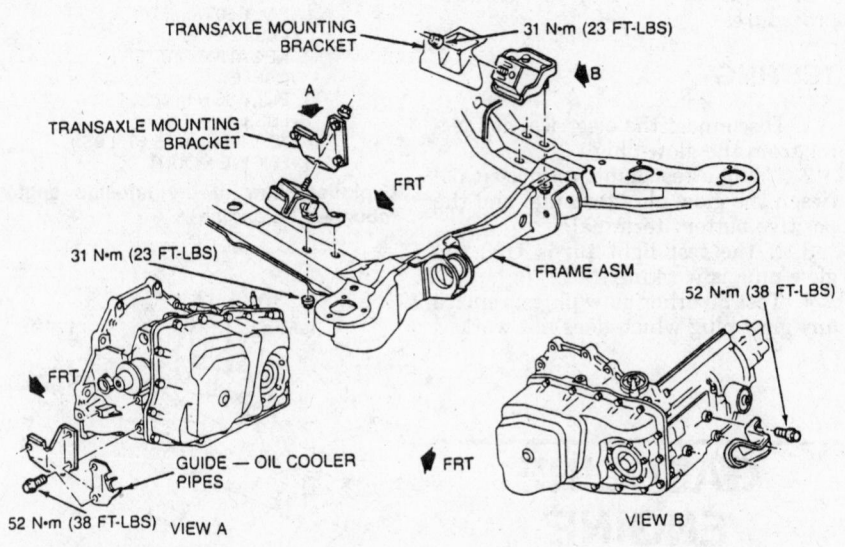

Exploded view of the left-side transaxle mount—4.1L and 4.5L engines

   a. Remove the compressor lower dust shield.
   b. Remove the right front wheel/tire assembly and outer wheelhouse plastic shield.
   c. Remove the compressor-to-bracket bolts and lower the compressor from the engine; DO NOT disconnect the refrigerant lines.

22. Remove the lower radiator hose.

23. From the lower right front of the engine and cradle, remove the driveline vibration dampener (with brackets) and the engine-to-transaxle bracket bolts. Pull the alternator wire (with plastic cover), down and out of the way.

24. Remove the exhaust pipe-to-manifold bolts (with springs) and the AIR pipe-to-converter bracket from the exhaust manifold stud.

   NOTE: Be careful not to lose the springs when detaching the exhaust pipe.

25. Remove the lower right side bell housing-to-engine bolt. Lower the vehicle.

26. Using a vertical engine hoist, attach it to the engine and support it.

27. Remove the upper bell housing-to-engine bolts and left front engine mount bracket-to-engine bolts. Remove the engine from the vehicle.

28. To install, reverse the removal procedures. Refill the cooling system. Start the engine, allow it to reach normal operating temperatures and check for leaks.

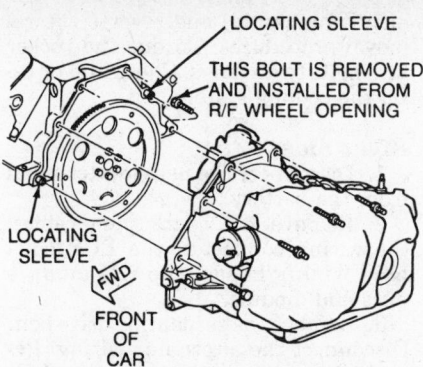

Exploded view of the transaxle-to-engine assembly—4.1L and 4.5L engines

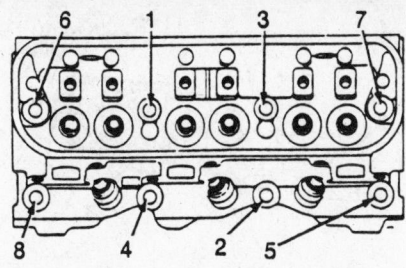

View of the cylinder head bolt torquing sequence—3.8L engine

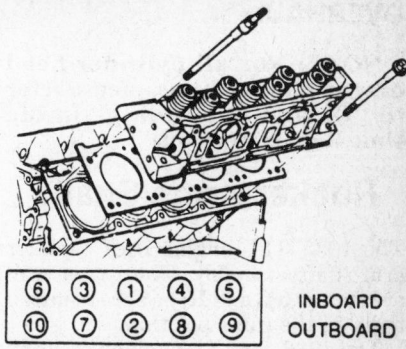

View of the cylinder head bolt torquing sequence—4.1L and 4.5L engines

Cylinder Head

REMOVAL & INSTALLATION

3.8L Engine

LEFT SIDE

1. Refer to "Intake Manifold, Removal and Installation" in this section and remove the intake manifold.

2. Remove the exhaust manifold-to-cylinder head bolts and the exhaust manifold.

3. Remove the valve cover-to-cylinder head screws and the valve cover.

4. Label and remove the spark plug wires. If equipped, remove the C³I unit-to-cylinder head bolts and the unit.

5. Remove the serpentine drive belt, the alternator-to-bracket bolts, the alternator, the alternator bracket-to-engine bolts and the bracket.

6. If equipped with air conditioning, remove the compressor-to-bracket bolts and move it aside; DO NOT disconnect the refrigerant lines.

7. Remove the rocker arm assemblies, the guide plate and the pushrods; keep them in order for reinstallation purposes.

8. Remove the cylinder head bolts and the cylinder head.

9. Using a putty knife, clean and inspect the gasket mounting surfaces.

10. To install, use new gaskets, apply P/N sealant No. 1052080 or equivalent, on the cylinder head bolt threads and reverse the removal procedures. Torque the cylinder head-to-engine bolts (in sequence, using 3 torquing steps) to 25 ft. lbs., an additional ¼ turn (90 degrees) and additional ¼ turn (90 degrees).

NOTE: Should 60 ft. lbs. be reached at any time, STOP; DO NOT complete the balance of the torquing sequence.

11. To complete the installation, reverse the removal procedures. Torque the rocker arm bolts to 43 ft. lbs. Refill the cooling system. Start the engine, allow it to reach normal operating temperatures and check for leaks.

RIGHT SIDE

1. Refer to "Intake Manifold, Removal and Installation" in this section and remove the intake manifold.

2. Remove the exhaust manifold-to-cylinder head bolts and the exhaust manifold.

3. Remove the valve cover-to-cylinder head screws and the valve cover.

4. Label and remove the spark plug wires.

5. Remove the serpentine drive belt, the power steering pump-to-bracket bolts, the belt tensioner assembly and the fuel line heat shield.

6. Remove the rocker arm assemblies, the guide plate and the pushrods; keep them in order for reinstallation purposes.

7. Remove the cylinder head bolts and the cylinder head.

8. Using a putty knife, clean and inspect the gasket mounting surfaces.

9. To install, use new gaskets, apply P/N sealant No. 1052080 or equivalent, on the cylinder head bolt threads and reverse the removal procedures. Torque the cylinder head-to-engine bolts (in sequence, using 3 torquing steps) to 25 ft. lbs., an additional ¼ turn (90 degrees) and additional ¼ turn (90 degrees).

NOTE: Should 60 ft. lbs. be reached at any time, STOP; DO NOT complete the balance of the torquing sequence.

10. To complete the installation, reverse the removal procedures. Torque the rocker arm bolts to 43 ft. lbs. Refill the cooling system. Start the engine, allow it to reach normal operating temperatures and check for leaks.

4.1L and 4.5L Engines

LEFT SIDE

1. Refer to the "Intake Manifold, Removal and Installation" in this section, remove the intake manifold.

2. Remove both cooling fans.

3. Disconnect the exhaust manifold crossover pipe, the exhaust pipe-to-exhaust manifold bolts, the exhaust manifold-to-cylinder head bolts and the exhaust manifold.

4. Remove the cylinder head-to-engine bolts and the cylinder head.

5. Using a putty knife, clean the gasket mounting surfaces.

6. To install, use new gaskets, sealant (if necessary), apply GM lubricant No. 1052356 or equivalent, to the cylinder head bolt threads and reverse the removal procedures. Torque the cylinder head bolts (in sequence) using three steps: 1st to 38 ft. lbs., 2nd to 68 ft. lbs. and 3rd to 90 ft. lbs. (bolts No. 1, 3 & 4).

7. To complete the installation, reverse the removal procedures. Refill the cooling system, start the engine, allow it to reach normal operating temperatures and check for leaks.

RIGHT SIDE

1. Refer to the "Intake Manifold, Removal and Installation" in this section, remove the intake manifold.

2. Disconnect the exhaust manifold crossover pipe, the exhaust pipe-to-exhaust manifold bolts, the exhaust manifold-to-cylinder head bolts and the exhaust manifold.

3. Remove the cylinder head-to-engine bolts and the cylinder head.

4. Using a putty knife, clean the gasket mounting surfaces.

5. To install, use new gaskets, sealant (if necessary), apply GM lubricant No. 1052356 or equivalent, to the cylinder head bolt threads and reverse the removal procedures. Torque the cylinder head bolts (in sequence) using three steps: 1st to 38 ft. lbs., 2nd to 68 ft. lbs. and 3rd to 90 ft. lbs. (bolts No. 1, 3 & 4).

6. To complete the installation, reverse the removal procedures. Refill the cooling system, start the engine, allow it to reach normal operating temperatures and check for leaks.

OVERHAUL

NOTE: For all cylinder head overhaul procedures, please refer to "Engine Rebuilding" in the Unit Repair Section.

Rocker Arms/Shafts

The 1985 3.8L engine uses a rocker arm shaft assembly. The rocker arm are stamped **L** and **R**; be sure to install them in the same position.

The 1986–89 3.8L engine uses individual rocker arm and pedestal assemblies.

REMOVAL & INSTALLATION

3.8L Engine

1985

1. Disconnect the negative terminal from the battery.
2. Remove the rocker arm cover.
3. Remove the rocker arm shaft assembly-to-cylinder head bolts and the assembly. Remove the bolts from the shaft and disassemble the rocker arms from the shaft.
4. Using a small pry bar, pry the nylon arm retainers.
5. To install, lubricate the rocker arms with engine oil and position them on the shaft. Center each arm on the ¼ in. hole in the shaft. Install new nylon rocker arm retainers in the holes using a ½ in. drift. Locate the push rods in the rocker arms and insert the shaft-to-cylinder head bolts.
6. To install, use new gaskets, sealant (if necessary) and reverse the removal procedures. Torque (a little at a time) the rocker arm shaft assembly-to-cylinder head bolt to 30 ft. lbs.

1986–89

Left Side

1. Disconnect the negative terminal from the battery.
2. If equipped, remove the upper engine support strut and bracket.
3. Remove the PCV valve and pipe.
4. Remove the spark plug wiring harness cover and disconnect the spark plug wires from the spark plugs.
5. Remove the rocker arm cover nuts, washers, seals, the cover and gasket (discard the gasket).
6. Remove the rocker arm pedestal-to-cylinder head bolts, the pedestals, the rocker arms and the pedestal retainers.

NOTE: Be sure to keep the parts in order for reassembly purposes.

7. Using a putty knife, clean the gasket mounting surfaces.
8. To install, use a new gasket, seal-

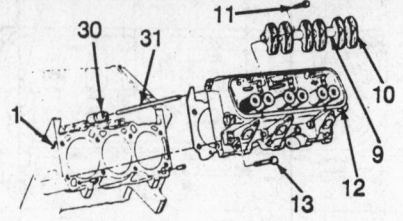

1. Cylinder block
9. Rocker arm shaft
10. Rocker arm
11. Bolt (30 ft. lbs.)
12. Cylinder head
13. Bolt (80 ft. lbs.)
30. Lifter
31. Pushrod

Exploded view of the rocker arm assembly—3.8L (1985) engine

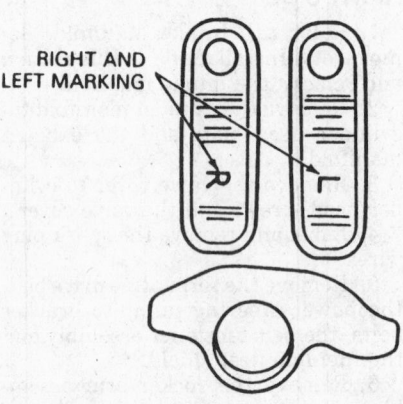

RIGHT AND LEFT MARKING

View of the rocker arm/shaft assembly—3.8L (1985) engine

ant (if necessary) and reverse the removal procedures. Torque the rocker arm bolts to 45 ft. lbs. Check and/or refill the cooling system.

Right Side

1. Disconnect the negative terminal from the battery.
2. Remove the spark plug cables, the wiring connector, the EGR solenoid wiring/hoses, the C³I module nuts and module.
3. Remove the serpentine drive belt. Disconnect the alternator wiring. Remove the alternator mounting bolt and rotate the alternator toward the front of the vehicle.
4. Remove the power steering pump from the belt tensioner and the belt tensioner.
5. Remove the engine lifting bracket and the rear alternator brace.
6. Place a clean drain pan under the radiator, open the drain cock and drain the cooling system to a level below the heater hose level.
7. Remove the heater hoses from the throttle body.
8. Remove the rocker arm cover nuts, washers, seals, the cover and gasket (discard the gasket).
9. Remove the rocker arm pedestal-to-cylinder head bolts, the pedestals, the rocker arms and the pedestal retainers.

NOTE: Be sure to keep the parts in order for reassembly purposes.

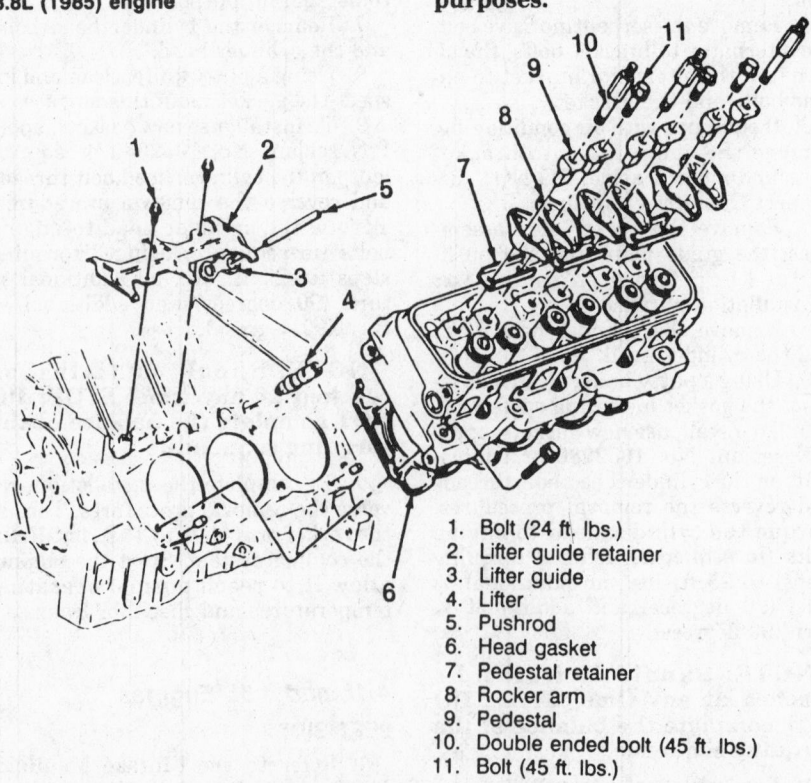

1. Bolt (24 ft. lbs.)
2. Lifter guide retainer
3. Lifter guide
4. Lifter
5. Pushrod
6. Head gasket
7. Pedestal retainer
8. Rocker arm
9. Pedestal
10. Double ended bolt (45 ft. lbs.)
11. Bolt (45 ft. lbs.)

Exploded view of the rocker arm assembly—3.8L (1986–89) engine

10. Using a putty knife, clean the gasket mounting surfaces.

11. To install, use a new gasket, sealant (if necessary) and reverse the removal procedures. Torque the rocker arm bolts to 45 ft. lbs. Check and/or refill the cooling system, start the engine, allow it to reach normal operating temperatures and check for leaks.

4.1L and 4.5L V8 Engines

LEFT SIDE

1. Disconnect the negative terminal from the battery. Remove the air cleaner, the PCV valve, the throttle return spring and the serpentine drive belt.

2. Loosen the lower power steering pump bracket nuts.

3. Remove the power steering pump, the belt tensioner, the bracket-to-engine bolts and the bracket. Move the power steering pump assembly toward the front of the vehicle; DO NOT disconnect the pressure hoses.

4. Remove the left side spark plug wires and conduit.

5. Remove the rocker arm cover-to-cylinder screws, the cover and the gasket/seals (discard them).

6. Remove the rocker arm pivot-to-rocker arm support bolts, the pivots and the rocker arms.

7. If necessary, remove the rocker arm support-to-cylinder head nuts/bolts and the support.

8. Using a putty knife, clean the gasket mounting surfaces. Inspect the parts for wear and/or damage and replace the parts (if necessary).

9. To install, lubricate the parts with clean engine oil, use a new gasket (coat both sides with RTV sealant), install RTV sealant between the intake manifold-to-cylinder head mating surfaces and reverse the removal procedures. Torque the rocker arm support-to-cylinder head nuts to 37 ft. lbs., the rocker arm support-to-cylinder head bolts to 7 ft. lbs., the rocker arm pivots-to-rocker arm support bolts to 22 ft. lbs. and the rocker arm cover-to-cylinder head screws to 8 ft. lbs. Check and/or refill the crankcase. Start the engine and check for leaks.

RIGHT SIDE

1. Disconnect the negative terminal from the battery. Remove the air cleaner and the AIR management valve with bracket (move the assembly aside).

2. From the throttle body, remove the Manifold Absolute Pressure (MAP) hose.

3. Remove the right side spark plug wires and conduit.

4. Remove the fuel vapor canister pipe bracket from the valve cover stud.

5. Drain the cooling system to a lev-

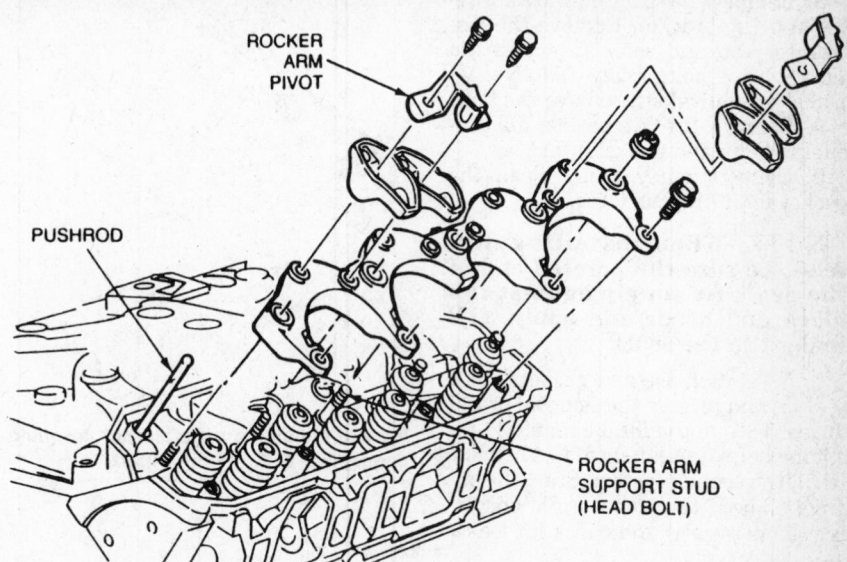

Exploded view of the rocker arm assembly—4.1L and 4.5L engines

APPLY CONTINUOUS BEAD OF RTV SEALER TO TWO SIDES OF TRIANGULAR SEALS SO AS TO CONTACT CYLINDER HEAD AND INTAKE MANIFOLD.

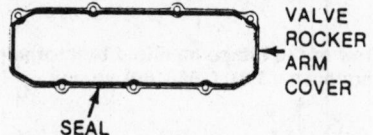

View of the RTV sealant installation—4.1L and 4.5L engines

el below the thermostat housing. Remove the heater hose from the thermostat housing and move it aside.

6. Remove the brake booster vacuum hose from the intake manifold.

7. Remove the rocker arm cover-to-cylinder screws, the cover and the gasket/seals (discard them).

8. Remove the rocker arm pivot-to-rocker arm support bolts, the pivots and the rocker arms.

9. If necessary, remove the rocker arm support-to-cylinder head nuts/bolts and the support.

10. Using a putty knife, clean the gasket mounting surfaces. Inspect the parts for wear and/or damage and replace the parts (if necessary).

11. To install, lubricate the parts with clean engine oil, use a new gasket (coat both sides with RTV sealant), install RTV sealant between the intake manifold-to-cylinder head mating surfaces and reverse the removal procedures. Torque the rocker arm support-to-cylinder head nuts to 37 ft. lbs., the

rocker arm support-to-cylinder head bolts to 7 ft. lbs., the rocker arm pivots-to-rocker arm support bolts to 22 ft. lbs. and the rocker arm cover-to-cylinder head screws to 8 ft. lbs. Check and/or refill the crankcase. Start the engine and check for leaks.

Intake Manifold

REMOVAL & INSTALLATION
3.8L V6 Engines

1985

1. Refer to "Relieving Fuel Pressure" in this section and reduce the fuel pressure.

2. Disconnect the negative terminal from the battery. Place a clean drain pan under the radiator, open the drain cock and drain the cooling system.

3. Remove the mass air flow sensor. From the throttle body, remove the air intake duct, the T.V. cable, the accelerator cable and the cruise control cable (if equipped).

4. From the throttle body, disconnect the vacuum lines. Remove the PCV valve

5. Remove the upper radiator hose and the heater hose from the intake manifold. Remove the serpentine drive belt

6. Remove the fuel lines and the booster vacuum pipe from the intake manifold.

7. From the rear of the engine, remove the electrical connectors from the TPS switch and the IAC connector (throttle body). From the front of the engine, disconnect the electrical connectors from the coolant temperature switch, the water temperature switch and the fan control.

8. Remove the fuel rail, the alternator and the bracket. Remove the distributor cap and rotor to access the Torx® head bolt; using tool No. J–24394 or equivalent, remove the bolt.

9. Remove the intake manifold-to-engine bolts and the manifold.

10. Using a putty knife, clean the gasket mounting surfaces.

NOTE: When installing new seals, be sure the pointed end of the seals fit snugly against the block and heads and apply RTV sealant to the seals.

11. To install, use new gaskets, RTV sealant and reverse the removal procedures. Torque the intake manifold-to-engine bolts (in sequence) to 47 ft. lbs. Refill the cooling system. Start the engine, allow it to reach normal operating temperatures and check for leaks.

1986–89

1. Refer to "Relieving Fuel Pressure" in this section and reduce the fuel pressure.

2. Disconnect the negative terminal from the battery. Place a clean drain pan under the radiator, open the drain cock and drain the cooling system.

3. Remove the serpentine drive belt, the alternator and the bracket.

4. Remove the power steering pump, the braces and move it aside; DO NOT disconnect the pressure lines.

5. Remove the coolant bypass hose, the heater pipe and the upper radiator hose from the intake manifold.

6. Remove the vacuum hoses and disconnect the electrical connectors from the intake manifold.

7. Remove the EGR pipe, the EGR valve and the adapter from the throttle body.

8. Remove the throttle body coolant pipe, the throttle body and the throttle body adapter.

9. Disconnect the rear spark plug wires. Remove the intake manifold-to-engine bolts and the manifold.

10. Using a putty knife, clean the gasket mounting surfaces.

11. To install, use new gaskets, sealant No. 12345336 or equivalent (on the ends of the manifold seals) and reverse the removal procedures. Torque the intake manifold (in sequence) to 47 ft. lbs. (1985), 37 ft. lbs. (1986–87) or 80 inch lbs. (1988–89). Refill the cooling system. Start the engine, allow it to reach normal operating temperatures and check for leaks.

4.1L and 4.5L V8 Engine

NOTE: Some vehicles equipped with the 4.1L and 4.5L engines have been experiencing oil leakage at the intake manifold to block seal, due to a split intake

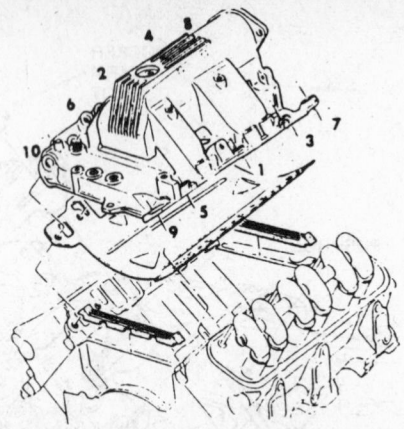

View of the intake manifold bolt torquing sequence—3.8L (1985) engine

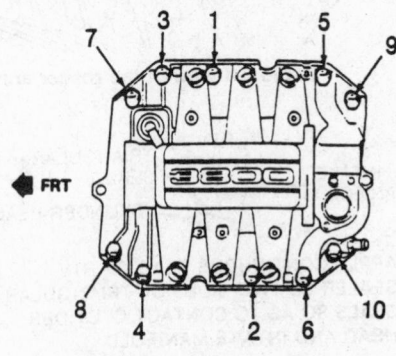

View of the intake manifold bolt torquing sequence—3.8L (1986–89) engine

manifold seal. When repairing this leak, replace the old seal with a new silicone seal (Part No. 3634619) The new seal is easily identified by its gray color.

1. Disconnect the negative terminal from the battery. Drain the cooling system to a level below the intake manifold. Disconnect the upper radiator hose from the thermostat housing.

2. Remove the air cleaner and the serpentine drive belt. Label and disconnect the spark plug wires from the spark plugs.

3. Remove the upper power steering pump bracket-to-engine bolts and loosen the lower nuts.

4. Disconnect the following electrical connections and position the wiring harness out of the way: distributor, oil pressure switch, EGR solenoid, coolant sensor, mass airflow temperature sensor, throttle position sensor, four way connector at the distributor, electric fuel evaporator grid, idle speed control motor and fuel injectors.

5. From the throttle lever, disconnect the accelerator, cruise control (if equipped) and transaxle TV cables.

6. Using a shop rag at the fuel line

schraeder valve (test port), bleed off the fuel pressure. Disconnect the fuel inlet and return lines from the throttle body. From the transaxle, remove the fuel line brackets and move the lines aside; disconnect the modulator vacuum line.

7. Disconnect the heater hose from the nipple at the rear of the intake manifold.

8. From the intake manifold, remove the cruise control bracket (if equipped). Remove the vacuum line from the left rear engine lift bracket and the throttle body.

9. Disconnect the electrical connectors from the alternator and AIR management solenoid. Remove the alternator, the idler pulley, the AIR management valve/bracket and EGR solenoid/bracket. Disconnect the hose from the MAP hose.

10. From the right cylinder head, remove the power steering pipe and the AIR pipe. Remove the oil filter.

11. Remove the distributor. Remove both rocker arm covers. Remove the rocker arm support with the rocker arms intact by first alternately and evenly removing the four bolts followed by the five nuts. Keep the pushrods in sequence so they may be reassembled in their original positions.

12. If equipped with air conditioning, partially remove the compressor; DO NOT discharge the system. Remove the vacuum harness connections from the TVS at the rear of the intake manifold.

13. Remove the intake manifold bolts and remove the two bolts securing the lower thermostat housing to the front cover. Remove the engine lift brackets or bend them out of the way.

14. Remove the intake manifold and lower thermostat housing as an assembly by lifting it straight up off of the dowels.

15. Using a putty knife, clean the gasket mounting surfaces.

16. To install, use new gaskets, apply RTV sealant No. 1052366 to the four corners where the end seals meet and reverse the removal procedures.

17. To torque the intake manifold-to-engine bolts, perform the following procedures:

   a. Torque the No. 1–4 bolts (in sequence) to 15 ft. lbs.

   b. Torque the No. 5–16 bolts (in sequence) to 22 ft. lbs.

   c. Retorque all bolts (in sequence) to 22 ft. lbs.

   d. Recheck all bolts (in sequence) to 22 ft. lbs.

18. To complete the installation, use new gaskets and reverse the removal procedures. Refill the cooling system. Start the engine allow it to reach normal operating temperatures and check for leaks.

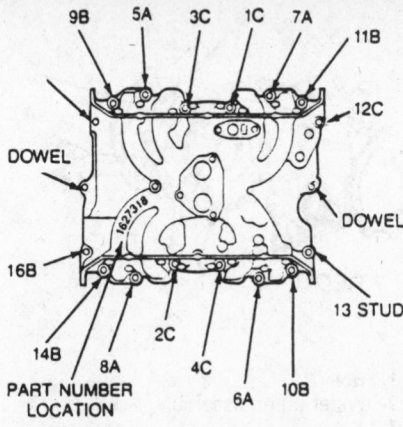

View of the intake manifold bolt size location and torquing sequence — 4.1L and 4.5L engines

Exhaust Manifold

REMOVAL & INSTALLATION

3.8L V6

LEFT SIDE

1. Disconnect the negative terminal from the battery.
2. If necessary, remove the mass air flow sensor, air intake duct and crankcase ventilation pipe.
3. Remove the exhaust crossover pipe-to-exhaust manifold bolts.
4. Label and disconnect the spark plug wires.
5. Remove the exhaust manifold-to-cylinder head bolts and the manifold.
6. If necessary, remove the oil dipstick tube to provide access to the manifold bolts.
7. Using a putty knife, clean the gasket mounting surfaces.
8. To install, use a new gasket and reverse the removal procedures. Torque the exhaust manifold-to-cylinder head bolts to 37 ft. lbs. and the exhaust crossover pipe-to-manifold bolts to 22 ft. lbs. Start the engine and check for exhaust leaks.

RIGHT SIDE

1. Disconnect the negative terminal from the battery.
2. If necessary, disconnect the mass air flow sensor, air intake duct, the crankcase ventilation pipe and the IAC connector from the throttle body.
3. Label and disconnect the wires from the spark plugs. Disconnect the oxygen sensor lead.
4. If equipped, disconnect the heater inlet pipe from the manifold studs.
5. Remove the exhaust crossover pipe-to-exhaust manifold bolts and the pipe.
6. Remove the serpentine drive belt. On the 1985–87 models, remove the

front alternator-to-engine support bracket. On the 1985 models, remove the power steering pump and bracket.

7. Raise and support the front of the vehicle on jackstands. Remove the exhaust pipe-to-manifold bolts, the exhaust manifold-to-cylinder head bolts and the manifold.
8. Remove the EGR pipe from the exhaust manifold.
9. Using a putty knife, clean the gasket mounting surfaces.
10. To install, use a new gasket and reverse the removal procedures. Torque the exhaust manifold-to-cylinder head bolts to 37 ft. lbs. and the exhaust crossover pipe-to-manifold bolts to 22 ft. lbs. Start the engine and check for exhaust leaks.

4.1L and 4.5L V8

RIGHT SIDE

1. Disconnect the negative battery cable. Remove the air cleaner.
2. Remove the exhaust crossover pipe. Disconnect the oxygen and coolant temperature sensors.
3. Remove the catalytic converter-to-AIR pipe clip bolt.
4. Remove the two front manifold-to-cylinder head bolts. Raise and support the front of the vehicle.
5. Disconnect the converter air pipe bracket from the stud and remove the converter-to-manifold exhaust pipe.
6. Remove the remaining exhaust manifold-to-cylinder head bolts, the AIR pipe and the manifold.
7. Using a putty knife, clean the gasket mounting surfaces.
8. To install, use new gaskets and reverse the removal procedures. Torque the intake manifold-to-engine bolts to 18 ft. lbs. Start the engine and check for exhaust leaks.

LEFT SIDE

1. Disconnect the negative terminal from the battery.
2. Remove both cooling fans and the exhaust crossover pipe.
3. Remove the serpentine drive belt and the AIR pump pivot bolt.
4. Remove the belt tensioner and the power steering pump brace.
5. Remove the exhaust manifold-to-cylinder head bolts, the AIR pipe and the manifold.
6. Using a putty knife, clean the gasket mounting surfaces.
7. To install, use new gaskets and reverse the removal procedures. Torque the exhaust manifold-to-engine bolts to 18 ft. lbs. Start the engine and check for exhaust leaks.

Front Cover and Oil Seal

REMOVAL & INSTALLATION

3.8L V6 Engines

COVER REMOVED

1. Disconnect the negative terminal from the battery.
2. PLace a clean drain pan under the radiator, open the drain cock and drain the engine coolant. Remove the lower radiator hose and the coolant bypass hose from the front cover. Remove the heater pipes.
3. Remove the front engine cradle mount bolts. Using a vertical lifting device, secure it to the engine and raise it slightly.
4. Remove the serpentine drive belt and the water pump pulley.
5. Label and disconnect the alternator wiring. Remove the alternator and the alternator bracket.

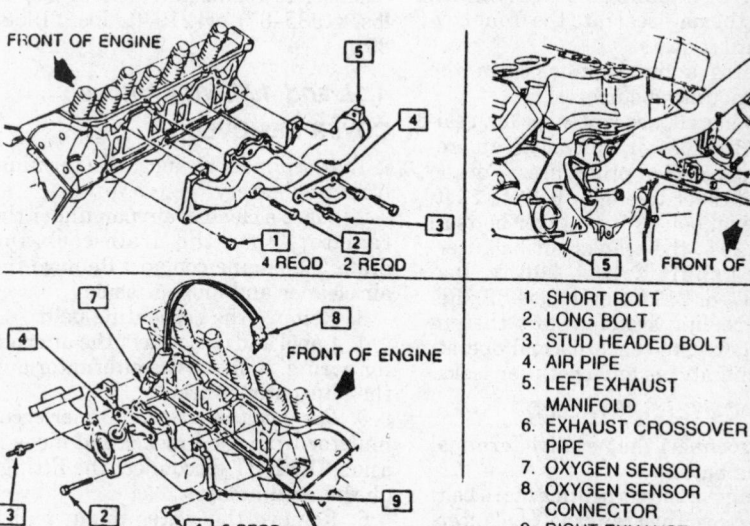

1. SHORT BOLT
2. LONG BOLT
3. STUD HEADED BOLT
4. AIR PIPE
5. LEFT EXHAUST MANIFOLD
6. EXHAUST CROSSOVER PIPE
7. OXYGEN SENSOR
8. OXYGEN SENSOR CONNECTOR
9. RIGHT EXHAUST MANIFOLD

Exploded view of the exhaust manifolds — 4.1L and 4.5L engines

6. On the 1985 models, mark the position of the distributor rotor and remove the distributor.

7. On the 1988–89 models, remove the inner splash shield.

8. Remove the crankshaft balancer bolt/washer and the balancer.

9. Disconnect the electrical connectors from the crankshaft sensor, the camshaft sensor and the oil pressure switch.

10. Remove the oil pan-to-front cover bolts, the front cover-to-engine bolts and the front cover. Using a small pry bar, remove the oil seal and discard it.

11. To replace the front oil seal, perform the following procedures:

a. Using a small pry bar, pry the

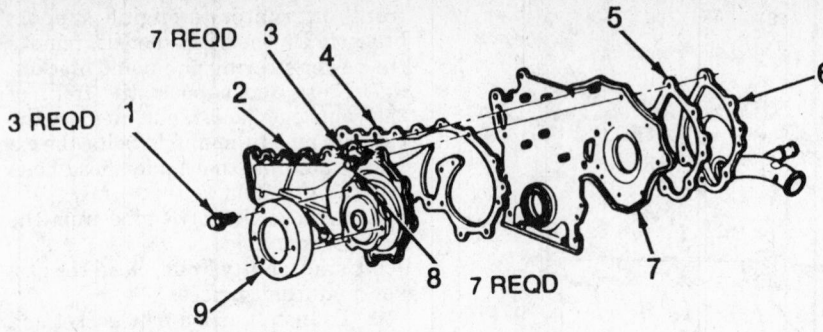

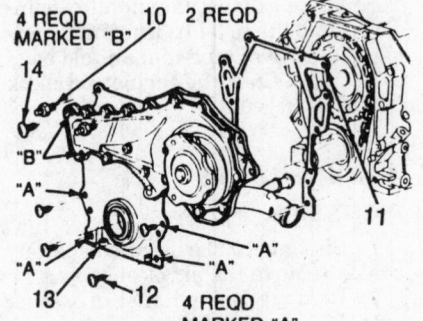

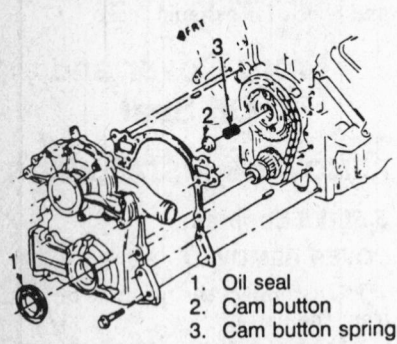

1. Oil seal
2. Cam button
3. Cam button spring

Exploded view of the front cover assembly—3.8L engines

1. Bolt
2. Water pump assembly
3. Nut
4. Water pump gasket
5. Inlet gasket
6. Inlet
7. Front cover
8. Bolt
9. Water pump pulley
10. Stud headed bolt
11. Front cover gasket
12. Torx® screw
13. Front cover/water pump/inlet assembly
14. Torx® screw

Exploded view of the front cover assembly—4.1L and 4.5L engines

oil seal from the front cover; be careful not to damage the sealing surfaces.

b. Clean the oil seal mounting surface.

c. Using GM lubricant No. 1050169 or equivalent, coat the outside of the seal and the crankshaft balancer.

d. Using the Oil Seal Installation tool No. J–35354 or equivalent, drive the new seal into the front cover until it seats.

12. Using a putty knife, clean the gasket mounting surfaces.

13. To install, use a new gasket, sealant No. 1052080 or equivalent, and reverse the removal procedures. Torque the front cover-to-engine bolts to 22 ft. lbs., the oil pan-to-front cover bolts to 88 inch lbs., the crankshaft balancer-to-crankshaft bolt to 200 ft. lbs. (1985–87) or 219 ft. lbs. (1988–89). Refill the cooling system. Start the engine, allow it to reach normal operating temperatures and check for leaks.

FRONT COVER INSTALLED

1. Disconnect the negative terminal from the battery.

2. Remove the serpentine drive belt.

3. Remove the crankshaft balancer-to-crankshaft bolts.

4. Using a small pry bar, pry the oil seal from the front cover; be careful not to damage the sealing surfaces.

5. Clean the oil seal mounting surface.

6. Using GM lubricant No. 1050169 or equivalent, coat the outside of the seal and the crankshaft balancer.

7. Using the Oil Seal Installation tool No. J–35354 or equivalent, drive the new seal into the front cover until it seats.

8. To install, reverse the removal procedures. Torque the crankshaft balancer-to-crankshaft bolt to 200 ft. lbs. (1985–87) or 219 ft. lbs. (1988–89).

4.1L and 4.5L V8 Engines
COVER REMOVED

1. Disconnect the negative terminal from the battery.

2. Place a clean drain pan under the radiator, open the drain cock and drain the engine coolant. Remove the air cleaner and move it aside.

3. Remove the serpentine belt.

4. Label and disconnect the alternator wiring. Remove the alternator and the alternator bracket.

5. Remove the air conditioner accumulator from the bracket and move it aside; DO NOT disconnect the fittings on the accumulator.

6. Remove the water pump pulley bolts and the pulley. If necessary, remove the idler pulley.

7. Raise and support the front of the vehicle on jackstands.

8. Remove the crankshaft pulley-to-crankshaft pulley bolt. Using the Puller tool No. J–24420–B or equivalent, attach it to the crankshaft pulley; using the center bolt, press the crankshaft pulley from the crankshaft. Remove the woodruff key from the crankshaft.

9. Remove the front cover-to-engine bolts, the oil pan-to-front cover bolts and the front cover.

10. Using a putty knife, clean the gasket mounting surfaces.

11. Using a small pry bar, pry the oil seal from the front cover (discard it).

12. Clean the oil seal mounting surface. Lubricate the new seal with engine oil.

13. Using a hammer and the Oil Seal Installation tool No. J–29662 or equivalent, drive the new oil seal in to the front cover until it seats.

14. To complete the installation, use a new gasket, RTV sealant (on the oil pan lip) and reverse the removal procedures. Torque the front cover-to-engine bolts to 15 ft. lbs., the crankshaft pulley-to-crankshaft bolt to 18 ft. lbs.

FRONT COVER INSTALLED

1. Refer to the "Crankshaft Pulley, Removal and Installation" in this section and remove the crankshaft pulley.

2. Using the Oil Seal Removal tools No. J–23129, J–21052–4, J–1859–03

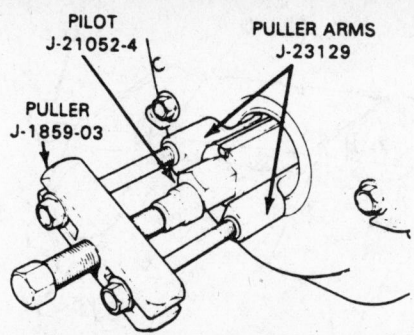

Removing the front oil seal from the front cover—4.1L and 4.5L engines

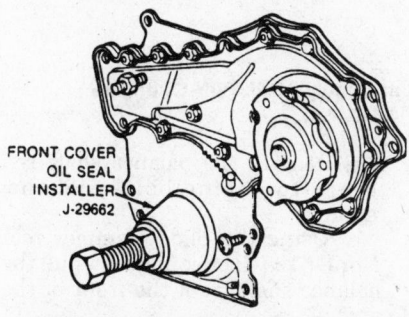

Installing the front oil seal to the front cover—4.1L and 4.5L engines

or equivalent, press the oil seal from the front cover.

3. Clean the oil seal mounting surface.

4. Lubricate the new seal with engine oil.

5. Using a hammer and the Oil Seal Installation tool No. J–29662 or equivalent, drive the new oil seal in to the front cover until it seats.

6. To complete the installation, reverse the removal procedures. Torque the crankshaft pulley-to-crankshaft bolt to 18 ft. lbs.

Timing Chain and Sprocket

REMOVAL & INSTALLATION

3.8L V6 Engines

1. Refer to the "Front Cover, Removal and Installation" procedures in this section and remove the front cover.

2. Remove the button and spring from the center of the camshaft.

3. Rotate the crankshaft to align the marks of the timing sprockets; they must be close together.

4. Remove the camshaft sprocket bolts, the sprocket and the timing chain.

5. Remove the crankshaft sprocket and the woodruff key (be sure not to lose the key).

6. Using a putty knife, clean the

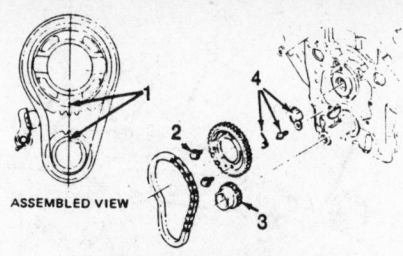

1. Timing marks (aligned)
2. 19 ft. lbs.
3. Crankshaft sprocket
4. Damper assembly

Exploded view of the timing chain and sprockets—3.8L (VIN 3) engine

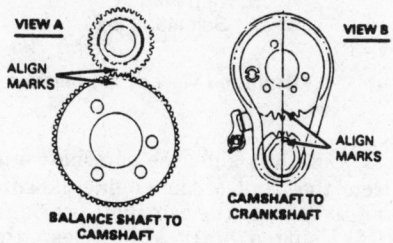

View of the timing chain/sprockets and balancer shaft alignment—3.8L (VIN C) engine

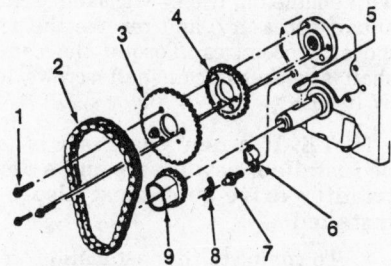

1. 27 ft. lbs.
2. Timing chain
3. Camshaft sprocket
4. Camshaft gear
5. Key
6. Damper
7. Special bolt (14 ft. lbs.)
8. Spring
9. Crankshaft sprocket

Exploded view of the timing chain, sprockets and balancer shaft sprocket—3.8L (VIN C) engine

gasket mounting surfaces. Inspect the parts for wear and/or damage; if necessary, replace the parts.

7. To install the timing chain and sprockets, perform the following procedures:

a. Assemble the timing chain on the camshaft sprocket and crankshaft sprockets.

b. Align the O marks on the sprockets; they must face each other.

c. Slide the assembly onto the camshaft and crankshaft. Install the camshaft sprocket-to-camshaft bolts. Torque the camshaft sprocket-to-camshaft sprocket bolts to 20 ft. lbs. (1985–86) or 28 ft. lbs. (1987–89).

NOTE: On the 1988–89 (VIN C) engine, align the camshaft sprocket mark with the balancer shaft sprocket mark.

8. Using petroleum jelly, pack the oil pump.

9. To complete the installation, use new gaskets, sealant (if necessary) and reverse the removal procedures. Refill the cooling system. Start the engine, allow it to reach normal operating temperatures and check for leaks.

4.1L and 4.5L V8 Engine

1. Refer to the "Front Cover, Removal and Installation" procedures in this section and remove the front cover.

2. Remove the oil slinger from the crankshaft. Rotate the engine to align the sprocket timing marks; the No. cylinder will be on the TDC of its compression stroke.

3. From the camshaft, remove the camshaft thrust button (discard it) and the camshaft sprocket-to-camshaft screw. Slide the camshaft sprocket, the crankshaft sprocket and timing chain from the engine as an assembly.

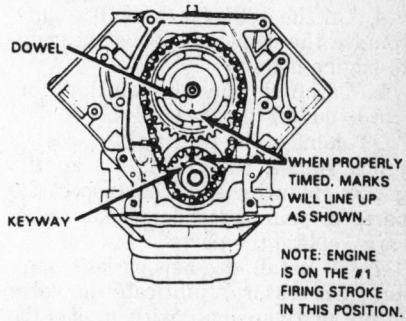

View of the timing chain sprocket alignment—4.1L and 4.5L engines

4. Using a putty knife, clean the gasket mounting surfaces. Inspect the parts for wear and/or damage; if necessary, replace the parts.

5. To install the timing chain and sprockets, perform the following procedures:

a. Assemble the timing chain on the camshaft sprocket and crankshaft sprockets.

b. Align the timing marks on the sprockets; they must face each other.

c. Align the dowel pin in the camshaft with the index hole in the sprocket.

d. Slide the assembly onto the camshaft and crankshaft. Install the camshaft sprocket-to-camshaft bolts. Torque the camshaft sprocket-to-camshaft sprocket bolts to 37 ft. lbs.

6. To complete the installation, use new gaskets, sealant (if necessary) and

reverse the removal procedures. Refill the cooling system. Start the engine, allow it to reach normal operating temperatures and check for leaks.

Camshaft

REMOVAL & INSTALLATION

3.8L V6 Engines

1. Refer to the "Intake Manifold, Removal and Installation" and the "Timing Chain and Sprocket, Removal and Installation" procedures in this section and remove the intake manifold, the timing chain and camshaft sprockets.

2. Remove the rocker arm covers, the rocker arm shaft or rocker arm assemblies, the push rods and the hydraulic lifters.

NOTE: When removing the valve components, be sure to keep them in order for reinstallation purposes.

3. On the 1988–89 (VIN C) engine, remove the camshaft gear from the camshaft.

4. On the 1985–89 (VIN 3) engine, remove the camshaft thrust bearing-to-engine bolts.

5. Carefully, slide the camshaft forward, out of the bearing bores; DO NOT damage the bearing surfaces.

6. Using a putty knife, clean the gasket mounting surfaces. Inspect the parts for wear and/or damage; if necessary, replace the parts.

7. To install, use new gaskets, sealant (if necessary), lubricate the valve lifters and camshaft with multi-lube No. 1052365 or equivalent and reverse the removal procedures. Refill the cooling system. Start the engine, allow it to reach normal operating temperatures and check for leaks.

NOTE: On the 1988–89 (VIN C) engine, align the camshaft gear with the balancer shaft gear timing marks.

4.1L and 4.5L V8

To perform this procedure, the engine must be removed from the vehicle and attached to an engine stand.

1. Refer to the "Intake Manifold, Removal and Installation" and the "Timing Chain, Removal and Installation" procedures in this section and remove the intake manifold and the timing chain.

2. Remove the valve lifters.

NOTE: When removing the valve components, be sure to keep the parts in order for reinstallation purposes.

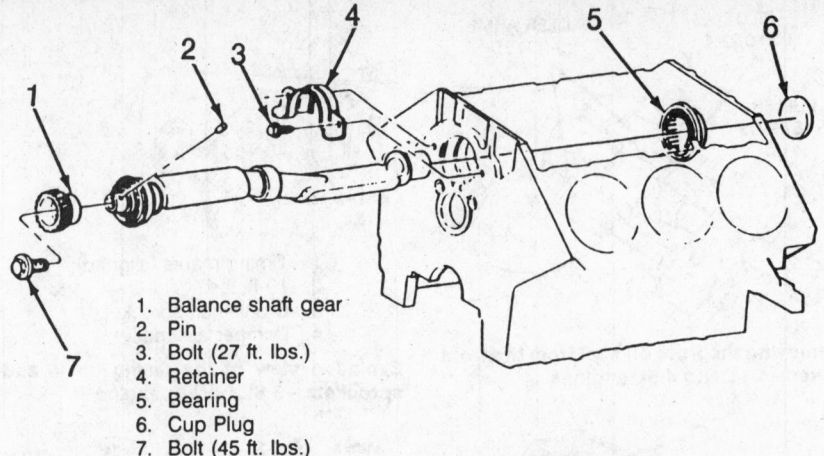

1. Balance shaft gear
2. Pin
3. Bolt (27 ft. lbs.)
4. Retainer
5. Bearing
6. Cup Plug
7. Bolt (45 ft. lbs.)

Exploded view of the balance shaft assembly – 3.8L (VIN C) engine

3. Carefully slide the camshaft out from the front of the engine; be sure not to damage the camshaft bearings.

4. Using a putty knife, clean the gasket mounting surfaces. Inspect the parts for wear and/or damage; if necessary, replace the parts.

5. To install, lubricate the camshaft with engine oil, use new gaskets, sealant (if necessary) and reverse the removal procedures. Torque the camshaft sprocket-to-camshaft screws to 37 ft. lbs.

NOTE: If a new camshaft is to be installed, new lifters and a distributor drive gear must also be installed.

6. To complete the installation, reverse the removal procedures. Refill the cooling system. Start the engine, allow it to reach normal operating temperatures and check for leaks.

Balance Shaft

REMOVAL & INSTALLATION

3.8L Engine – VIN C

1. Refer to the "Engine, Removal and Installation" procedures in this section, remove the engine and secure it to a workstand.

2. Remove the flywheel-to-crankshaft bolts and the flywheel.

3. Remove the timing chain cover-to-engine bolts and the cover.

4. Remove the camshaft sprocket-to-camshaft gear bolts, the sprocket, the timing chain and the gear.

5. To remove the balance shaft, perform the following procedures:

a. Remove the balance shaft gear-to-shaft bolt and the gear.

b. Remove the balance shaft retainer-to-engine bolts and the retainer.

c. Using the Slide Hammer tool No. J–6125–B or equivalent, pull the balance shaft from the front of the engine.

6. If replacing the rear balance shaft bearing, perform the following procedures:

a. Drive the rear plug from the engine.

b. Using the Camshaft Remover/Installer tool No. J–33049 or equivalent, press the rear bearing from the rear of the engine.

c. Dip the new bearing in clean engine oil.

d. Using the Balance Shaft Rear Bearing Installer tool No. J–36995 or equivalent, press the new rear bearing into the rear of the engine.

e. Install the rear cup plug.

7. Using the Balance Shaft Installer tool No. J–36996 or equivalent, screw it into the balance shaft and install the shaft into the engine; remove the installer tool.

8. Using a putty knife, clean the gasket mounting surfaces. Inspect the parts for wear and/or damage; replace the parts, if necessary.

9. Install the balance shaft retainer. Torque the balance shaft retainer-to-engine bolts to 27 ft. lbs.

10. Align the balance shaft gear with the camshaft gear timing marks. Install the balance shaft gear onto the balance shaft. Torque the balance gear-to-balance shaft bolt to 45 ft. lbs.

11. To complete the installation, use new gaskets, sealant (if necessary) and reverse the removal procedures. Torque the flywheel-to-crankshaft bolts to 60 ft. lbs. Refill the cooling system. Start the engine, allow it reach normal operating temperatures and check for leaks.

Piston and Connecting Rod

POSITIONING

On the V6 engines, starting at the front, the cylinders in the right bank are numbered 2-4-6 and in the left bank are numbered 1-3-5.

All compression rings are marked with a dimple, a letter **T**, a letter **O** or the word **TOP** to identify the side of the ring which must face toward the top of the piston.

When the piston and connecting rod assembly is properly installed, the oil spurt hole in the connecting rod will face the camshaft. The notch on the piston will face the front of the engine. The chamfered corners of the bearing caps should face toward the front of the left bank and toward the rear of the right bank. The boss on the connecting rod should face toward the front of the engine for the right bank and to the rear of the engine on the left bank.

NOTE: For all piston and connecting rod overhaul procedures, please refer to "Engine Rebuilding" in the Unit Repair section.

View of the piston alignment mark

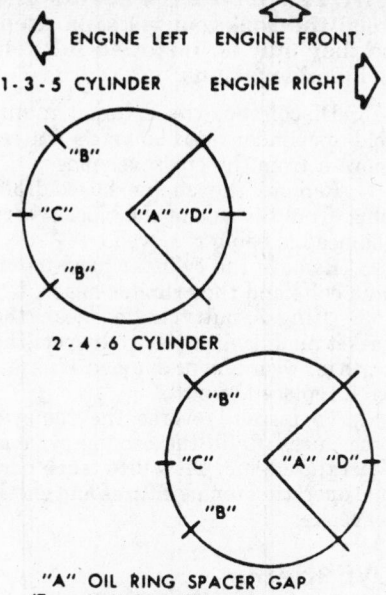

"A" OIL RING SPACER GAP
(Tang in Hole or Slot within Arc)

"B" OIL RING RAIL GAPS

"C" 2ND COMPRESSION RING GAP

"D" TOP COMPRESSION RING GAP

View of the piston rings alignment points

DIESEL ENGINE MECHANICAL

Engine

REMOVAL & INSTALLATION

4.3L V6

1. Disconnect the negative terminal from the battery. Using a scribing tool, matchmark the hood to the support brackets and remove the hood. Drain the cooling system.

2. Remove the serpentine drive belt and the vacuum pump drive belt.

3. Remove the air cleaner. Using the Air Crossover Cover tool No. J-26996-1 or equivalent, install it over the intake manifold opening.

4. Label and disconnect the ground wires from the inner fender panel and the engine.

5. Raise and support the front of the vehicle on jackstands.

6. Remove the engine-to-transaxle brace.

7. Remove the flywheel cover. Matchmark the flywheel-to-torque converter location and remove the flywheel-to-torque converter bolts.

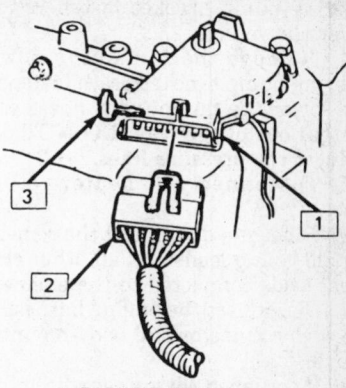

1. PARK/NEUTRAL & BACKUP LAMP SWITCH
2. SWITCH CONN.
3. "T" LATCH

T-latch connector

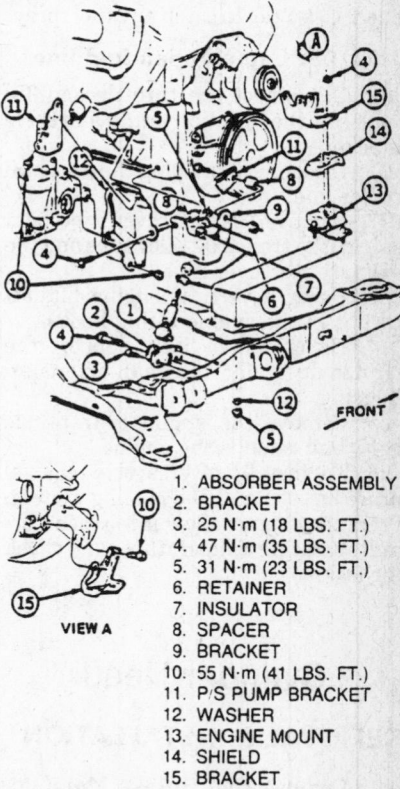

1. ABSORBER ASSEMBLY
2. BRACKET
3. 25 N·m (18 LBS. FT.)
4. 47 N·m (35 LBS. FT.)
5. 31 N·m (23 LBS. FT.)
6. RETAINER
7. INSULATOR
8. SPACER
9. BRACKET
10. 55 N·m (41 LBS. FT.)
11. P/S PUMP BRACKET
12. WASHER
13. ENGINE MOUNT
14. SHIELD
15. BRACKET

Engine mounting—4.3L V6 (diesel)

8. Disconnect the exhaust pipe from the rear exhaust manifold.

9. Remove the engine mount-to-cradle retaining nuts and washers.

10. Remove the engine absorbers assembly from the frame bracket.

11. Label and disconnect the following:
   a. Starter motor wires
   b. Glow plug wire from the No. 2 cylinder
   c. Battery ground cable

12. Disconnect and plug the lower oil cooler hose.

13. Remove the accessible power

steering pump bracket fasteners and lower the vehicle.

14. Remove the remaining power steering pump bracket/brace fasteners and lower the pump (with hoses connected) out of the way; DO NOT disconnect the pressure lines.

15. Disconnect the heater return pipe.

16. Label and disconnect the remaining glow plug leads and all other electrical leads connected to the engine.

17. Disconnect the engine harness at the cowl connector and body-mounted relays.

18. If equipped with air conditioning, remove the A/C compressor (with the lines/brackets attached) and move it aside.

19. Disconnect all fuel and vacuum lines. Exercise caution as some fuel may spray from the fittings when loosened. Use a rag to catch any fuel spray.

NOTE: Cap all open fuel lines.

20. Disconnect the throttle and TV cables at the injection pump and cable brackets.

21. Disconnect and plug the upper oil cooler line.

22. Remove the crossover pipe heat shield, the transaxle filler tube and the exhaust crossover pipe.

23. Using a vertical engine lift, attach it to the engine lifting hooks.

24. Using a floor jack, support the transaxle under the rear extension housing.

25. Remove the engine-to-transaxle bolts and remove the engine.

26. To install, reverse the removal procedures. Refill the cooling system. Start the engine, allow it to reach normal operating temperatures and check for leaks.

Cylinder Head

REMOVAL & INSTALLATION

1. Remove the "Intake Manifold, Removal and Installation" procedures in this section and remove the intake manifold.

NOTE: If removing the left cylinder head, remove the oil level indicator tube.

2. Remove the fuel lines and injection nozzles.

3. Disconnect the glow plug wiring and block the heater lead on the rear bank (if equipped).

4. Disconnect the ground strap from the rear of the right cylinder head.

5. Remove the rocker arms and push rods.

NOTE: Scribe the pivots and keep the rocker arms separated, so they may be installed in their original locations.

6. Disconnect the exhaust manifold-to-cylinder head bolts; do not remove it from the crossover pipe.

7. Remove the engine block drain plug, from the side of the block where the head is being removed.

8. Remove the cylinder head-to-engine bolts and the cylinder head.

9. Using a putty knife, clean the gasket mounting surfaces. Inspect the parts for wear and/or damage; if necessary, replace the parts.

10. To install, reverse the removal procedures. Refill the cooling system. Start the engine, allow it to reach normal operating temperatures and check for leaks.

OVERHAUL

NOTE: For all cylinder head overhaul procedures, please refer to "Engine Rebuilding" in the Unit Repair Section.

Rocker Arms/Shafts

REMOVAL & INSTALLATION

NOTE: When the diesel engine rocker arms are removed or loosened, the lifters must be bled down to prevent oil pressure buildup inside each lifter, which could cause it to raise higher than normal and bring the valves within striking distance of the pistons.

1. Remove the valve cover.

2. Remove the rocker arm pivot bolts, the bridged pivot and rocker arms; remove each rocker set as a unit.

3. Before installing any removed rocker arms, rotate the engine crankshaft to position the No. 1 cylinder at 32 degrees BTDC. This is 2 in. counterclockwise from the 0 degrees pointer. To verify that No. 1 cylinder is approaching TDC, with right valve cover removed, remove the No. 1 cylinder glow plug, turn the engine: compression pressure will force air out the glow plug hole. With the left valve cover removed, rotate the crankshaft until the No. 5 cylinder intake valve pushrod ball is 0.28 in. above the No. 5 cylinder exhaust valve pushrod ball.

NOTE: Use only hand wrenches to torque the rocker arm pivot bolts to avoid engine damage.

4. If removed, install the No. 5 cylinder pivot and rocker arms. Torque the bolts alternately between the intake and exhaust valves until the intake valve begins to open.

5. Install the remaining rocker arms, except the No. 3 exhaust (if removed).

6. If removed, install the No. 3 cylinder exhaust valve pivot, but do not torque beyond the point that the valve would be fully open. This is indicated by strong resistance while still turning the pivot retaining bolts. Going beyond this point will bend the pushrod. Torque the bolts SLOWLY, allowing the lifter to bleed down.

7. Finish torquing No. 5 cylinder rocker arm pivot bolt slowly. Do not go beyond the point that the valve would be fully open.

8. Allow the engine to stand for at least 45 minutes.

9. To complete the installation, use new gaskets, sealant (if necessary) and reverse the removal procedures.

Intake Manifold

REMOVAL & INSTALLATION

1. Disconnect the negative terminal from the battery. Remove the air cleaner.

2. Drain the cooling system. Loosen the upper bypass hose clamp. Remove the thermostat housing bolts, the housing and the thermostat from the intake manifold.

3. Remove the breather pipes from the rocker covers and the air crossover. Remove the air crossover.

4. Disconnect the throttle rod and the return spring. If equipped with cruise control, remove the servo.

5. From the bottom of the bellcrank, remove the hairpin clip and disconnect the cables. From the intake manifold, remove the throttle cable from the bracket and position the cable aside. Disconnect and label any electrical connectors which may be in the way.

6. Remove the alternator bracket (if necessary). If equipped with air conditioning, remove the compressor, with the mounting bracket and move it aside.

7. Disconnect the fuel line from the pump and the fuel filter. Remove the fuel filter and bracket.

8. Remove the fuel injection pump and lines.

9. From the rear of the engine, disconnect and remove the vacuum pump or oil pump drive assembly.

10. Remove the intake manifold drain tube, intake manifold-to-cylinder head bolts and the manifold. Remove the adapter seal and the injection pump adapter.

11. Using a putty knife, clean the gasket mounting surfaces. Inspect the parts for wear and/or damage; replace the parts (if necessary).

12. To install, use new gaskets, sealant (if necessary) and reverse the removal procedures. Coat both sides of the gasket surface that seal the intake manifold to the cylinder heads with GM sealer 1050026 or the equivalent. Position the intake manifold gaskets on the cylinder heads. To install the front and rear end seals, apply 1052915, 22521437, G.E. 1673 RTV sealer or equivalent, to the end seals only. Install the end seals, making sure the ends are positioned under the cylinder heads.

13. To complete the installation, reverse the removal procedures. Torque the intake manifold-to-cylinder head bolts (in sequence): 1st to 15 ft. lbs. and 2nd to 41 ft. lbs. Adjust the fuel injection pump timing

NOTE: Do not operate the engine without vacuum pump/oil pump assembly in place for this assembly drives the engine oil pump.

14. Install the remaining components in the reverse sequence of their removal. Perform the throttle rod and transaxle cable adjustments. Refill the cooling system. Start the engine, allow it to reach normal operating temperatures and check for leaks.

Exhaust Manifold

REMOVAL & INSTALLATION

LEFT SIDE

1. Disconnect the negative terminal from the battery.
2. Remove the exhaust crossover pipe.
3. Raise and support the front of the vehicle on jackstands.
4. Remove the right engine splash shield.
5. Remove the vacuum pump-to-exhaust manifold brace.
6. Remove the manifold-to-cylinder head bolts and the manifold.
7. Using a putty knife, clean the gasket mounting surfaces. Inspect the parts for wear and/or damage; replace the parts, if necessary.
8. To install, reverse the removal procedures. Torque the exhaust manifold-to-cylinder head bolts to 28 ft. lbs. Start the engine and check for exhaust leaks.

RIGHT SIDE

1. Disconnect the negative terminal from the battery.
2. Remove the exhaust crossover pipe.
3. Raise and support the front of the vehicle on jackstands.
4. Disconnect the exhaust pipe from the manifold.

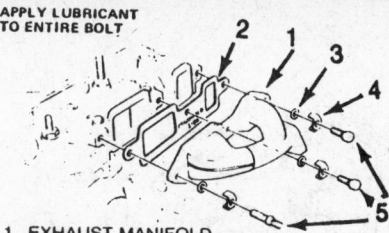

APPLY LUBRICANT TO ENTIRE BOLT

1. EXHAUST MANIFOLD
2. GASKET
3. WASHER (3)
4. LOCK (3)
5. BOLT-38 N·m (28 LB. FT.)

Left (front) exhaust manifold removal—4.3L V6 (diesel).

5. Remove the manifold-to-cylinder head bolts and the manifold.
6. Using a putty knife, clean the gasket mounting surfaces. Inspect the parts for wear and/or damage; replace the parts, if necessary.
7. To install, reverse the removal procedures. Torque the exhaust manifold-to-cylinder head bolts to 28 ft. lbs. Start the engine and check for exhaust leaks.

Front Cover and Oil Seal

REMOVAL & INSTALLATION

1. Drain the cooling system and disconnect the radiator hoses.
2. Remove the drive belts, the fan and pulley. Remove the crankshaft pulley bolt, the pulley and balancer. Use a puller that will bolt to the outside of the balancer and pull it off by applying pressure to a pilot inserted into the center of the crankshaft.

NOTE: The use of any other type of puller, such as a universal claw type which pulls on the outside of the hub, can destroy the balancer. The outside ring of the balancer is bonded in rubber to the hub. Pulling on the outside will break the bond. The timing mark is located on the outside of the ring. If it is suspected that the bond is broken, check that the center of the keyway is 16 degrees from the center of the timing slot. In addition, there are chiseled alignment marks between the weight and the hub.

3. Remove the front cover-to-engine bolts, the timing indicator and water pump; it may be necessary to grind a flat on the cover for gripping purposes.
4. Grind a chamfer on one end of each dowel pin.
5. From each side of the engine block, cut the excess material from the front end of the oil pan gasket.

6. Using a putty knife, clean the gasket mounting surfaces.
7. Trim about ⅛ in. off each end of a new front pan seal.
8. To install, use new gaskets, sealant and reverse the removal procedures. Using a small pry bar, rotate the cover left-to-right and guide the pan seal into the cavity. Oil the bolt threads, install two to hold the cover in place, install both dowel pins (chamfered end first). Apply a lubricant, compatible with rubber, on the balancer seal surface. Torque balancer bolt to 203–350 ft. lbs.
9. To complete the installation, reverse the removal procedures. Refill the cooling system. Start the engine, allow it to reach normal operating temperatures and check for leaks.

Timing Chain and Sprocket

REMOVAL & INSTALLATION

NOTE: Whenever the timing chain and gears are replaced on the diesel engine, it will be necessary to retime the engine.

1. Refer to the "Front Cover, Removal and Installation" procedures in this section and remove the front cover.
2. Remove the valve covers.
3. Loosen all rocker arm pivot bolts evenly so lash exists between the rocker arms and valves. It is not necessary to completely remove the rocker arms unless related service is being performed.
4. Remove the crankshaft oil slinger, the camshaft sprocket bolt and washer.
5. Remove the timing chain, camshaft and crankshaft sprockets. If the crankshaft sprocket is a tight fit on the crankshaft, use a threaded wheel puller to press it from the crankshaft.
6. If the camshaft sprocket-to-cam key comes out with the camshaft sprocket, remove the front camshaft bearing retainer and install the key into the injection pump drive gear. Install the bearing retainer.
7. Using a putty knife, clean the gasket mounting surfaces. Inspect the parts for wear and or damage; replace the parts, if necessary.
8. To install, use new gaskets, sealant and reverse the removal procedures. Install the sprockets onto the timing chain, align the sprocket alignment marks and install the sprockets onto the engine. Torque the camshaft sprocket-to-camshaft bolt to 70 ft. lbs.
9. After installing the front cover, bleed down the valve lifters.
10. To complete the installation, use

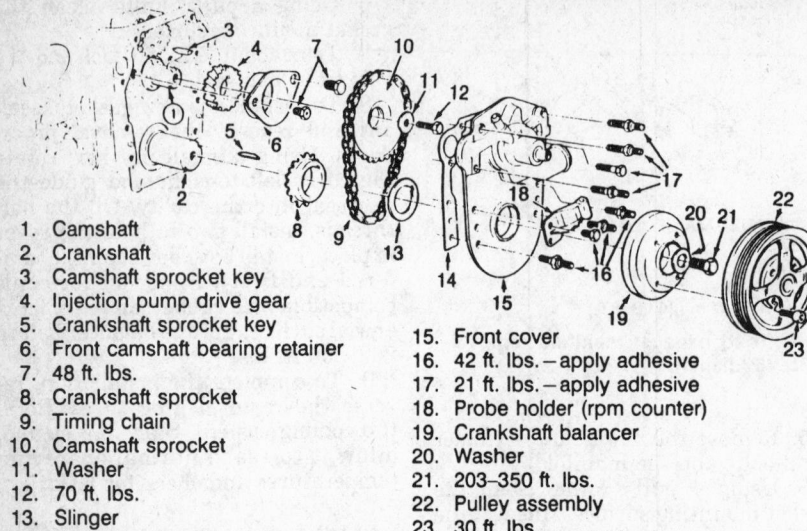

1. Camshaft
2. Crankshaft
3. Camshaft sprocket key
4. Injection pump drive gear
5. Crankshaft sprocket key
6. Front camshaft bearing retainer
7. 48 ft. lbs.
8. Crankshaft sprocket
9. Timing chain
10. Camshaft sprocket
11. Washer
12. 70 ft. lbs.
13. Slinger
14. Gasket
15. Front cover
16. 42 ft. lbs. – apply adhesive
17. 21 ft. lbs. – apply adhesive
18. Probe holder (rpm counter)
19. Crankshaft balancer
20. Washer
21. 203–350 ft. lbs.
22. Pulley assembly
23. 30 ft. lbs.

Exploded view of the front cover assembly – 4.3L diesel engine

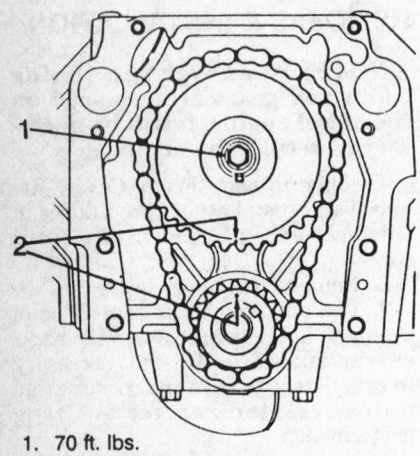

1. 70 ft. lbs.
2. Align timing marks

View of the timing chain sprocket alignment – 4.3L diesel engine

new gaskets, sealant (if necessary) and reverse the removal procedures. Refill the cooling system. Check and/or adjust the ignition timing. Start the engine, allow it to reach normal operating temperatures and check for leaks.

Camshaft
REMOVAL & INSTALLATION

NOTE: If the camshaft is to be removed the air conditioning system must be discharged by a professional and the condenser removed. Removal of the camshaft also requires removal of the injection pump drive and driven gears, removal of the intake manifold, disassembly of the valve lifters, and re-timing of the injection pump.

1. Disconnect the negative terminal from the battery. Drain the coolant and remove the radiator.

2. Refer to the "Intake Manifold, Removal and Installation" procedures in this section and remove the intake manifold. Remove the oil pump drive assembly.

3. Remove the crankshaft balancer pulley and the balancer. Remove the front cover-to-engine bolts and the front cover. Rotate the crankshaft until the engine timing sprocket marks align (facing each other).

4. Remove the valve covers, the rocker arms, pushrods and valve lifters; be sure to keep the parts in order so they may be returned to their original locations.

5. Remove the camshaft sprocket-to-camshaft bolts, the timing chain and sprockets.

6. Remove the front camshaft bearing retainer bolt, the retainer, the camshaft sprocket key and the injection pump drive gear.

7. To remove the fuel injection pump driven gear, remove the injection pump intermediate pump adapter, the pump adapter, the snap ring, the selective washer, the driven gear and spring.

8. Remove the camshaft by sliding it out the front of the engine. Be extremely careful not to allow the cam lobes to contact any of the bearings or the journals to dislodge the bearings during camshaft removal; DO NOT force the camshaft or bearing damage may result.

9. If either the injection pump drive or driven gears are to be replaced, replace both gears. Make certain the alignment marks are aligned on both gears before inserting the cam gear key.

10. Coat the camshaft and the cam bearings with GM lubricant No. 1052365 or equivalent.

11. Carefully slide the camshaft into position in the engine.

12. Fit the crankshaft and camshaft sprockets, aligning the timing marks. Remove the sprockets without disturbing the timing.

13. Install the injection pump driven gear, spring, shim and snap ring. Check the gear end play; if it is not within 0.002–0.006, replace the shim to obtain the specified clearance. Shims are available in 0.003 in. increments, from 0.080–0.115 in.

14. Align the **0** marks on the injection pump drive and driven gears. Install the camshaft sprocket key and the camshaft bearing retainer.

15. Install the timing chain and sprockets, making sure the timing marks are aligned.

16. Install the lifters, pushrods and rocker arms; allow the lifter at least 45 min. to bleed down. Failure to bleed down the lifters could bend valves when the crankshaft is turned over.

17. Install the injection pump adapter and injection pump. See the appropriate sections under "Fuel System" for procedures.

18. To complete the installation, reverse the removal procedures. Refill the cooling system. Start the engine, allow it to reach normal operating temperatures and check for leaks.

Piston and Connecting Rod

POSITIONING

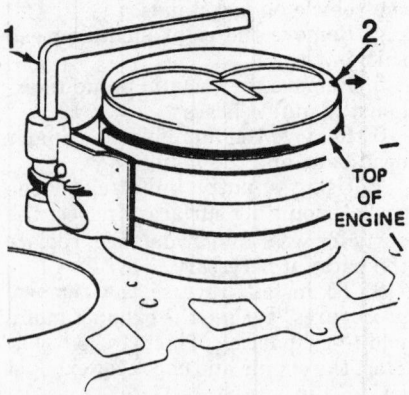

1. TOOL J-8037
2. NOTCH FACES FRONT OF ENGINE

Using a ring compressor to install the piston assembly

NOTE: For all piston and connecting rod overhaul procedures, please refer to "Engine Rebuilding" in the Unit Repair section.

ENGINE LUBRICATION

Oil Pan

REMOVAL & INSTALLATION

3.8L Engines

1. Disconnect the negative terminal from the battery.

2. Raise and support the front of the vehicle on jackstands. Drain the crankcase.

3. Remove the flywheel cover.

4. On the 1987–89 models, remove the oil filter and the starter motor.

5. Remove the oil pan-to-engine bolts and the oil pan.

6. Using a putty knife, clean the gasket mounting surfaces.

7. To install, use new gaskets, sealant and reverse the removal procedures. Torque the oil pan-to-engine bolts to 88 inch lbs. Refill the crankcase. Start the engine and check for leaks.

4.1L and 4.5L Engines

1. Disconnect the negative terminal from the battery. Raise and support the front of the vehicle on jackstands.

2. Drain the crankcase and remove the oil filter. Remove the flywheel inspection cover and the support struts.

3. Disconnect the exhaust "Y" pipe at the exhaust manifolds and remove the bolt at the catalytic converter bracket. Lower the exhaust pipe.

4. Remove the oil pan-to-engine bolts and the oil pan.

NOTE: If the pan is difficult to remove, lightly tap the edges with a plastic hammer.

5. Using a putty knife, clean the gasket mounting surfaces.

6. To install, use a new gasket, sealant and reverse the removal procedures. Torque the oil pan-to-engine bolts to 11 ft. lbs. Refill the crankcase. Start the engine and check for leaks.

4.3L V6 Diesel

1. Remove the oil pump drive and vacuum pump.

2. Disconnect the negative terminals from the batteries. Remove the dipstick.

3. Remove the upper radiator support and fan shroud.

4. Raise and support the front of the vehicle on jackstands. Drain the crankcase.

5. Remove the flywheel cover.

6. Disconnect the exhaust and crossover pipes.

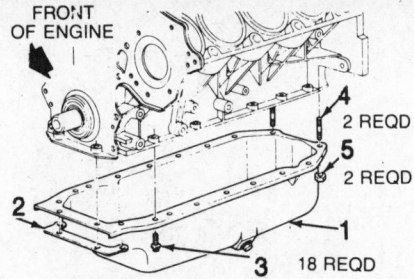

FRONT OF ENGINE

2 REQD
2 REQD
18 REQD

1. OIL PAN
2. REINFORCEMENT
3. BOLT
4. STUD
5. NUT

Exploded view of the oil pan—4.1L and 4.5L engines

7. Disconnect and plug the oil cooler lines at the filter base.

8. Remove the starter assembly. Using a floor jack, support the engine.

9. Remove the engine mounts from the block.

10. Raise the front of the engine. Remove the oil pan-to-engine bolts and the oil pan.

11. Using a putty knife, clean the gasket mounting surfaces.

12. To install, use a new gasket, sealant and reverse the removal procedures. Refill the crankcase. Start the engine and check for leaks.

Rear Main Bearing Oil Seal

REMOVAL & INSTALLATION

3.8L and 4.3L (Diesel) Engines

Braided fabric rope seals are used. The upper seal half cannot be replaced without removing the crankshaft, unless the Time Saver in this section is used.

LOWER HALF-SEAL

1. Refer to the "Oil Pan, Removal and Installation" procedures in this section and remove the oil pan.

2. Remove the rear main bearing cap-to-engine bolts and the cap.

3. Remove the old seal from the bearing cap.

4. To replace the oil seal, perform the following procedures:

   a. Using sealant No. GM 1052621, Loctite® 414 or equivalent, apply it to the main bearing cap seal groove and wait for 1 minute.

   b. Using a new rope seal and a wooden dowel or hammer handle, roll the new seal into the cap so both ends projecting above the parting surface of the cap; force the seal into the groove by rubbing it down, until the seal projects above the groove not more than $\frac{1}{16}$ in.

   c. Using a sharp razor blade, cut the ends off flush with the surface of the cap.

   d. Using chassis grease, apply a thin coat to the seals surface.

5. To install the neoprene sealing strips (side seals), perform the following procedures:

   a. Using light oil or kerosene, soak the strips for 5 minutes.

NOTE: The neoprene composition seals will swell up once exposed to the oil and heat. It is normal for the seals to leak for a short time, until they become properly seated. The seals must not be cut to fit.

   b. Place the sealing strips in the grooves on the sides of the bearing cap.

6. Using sealer No. GM 1052621 or equivalent, apply it to the main bearing cap mating surface; DO NOT apply sealer to the bolt holes.

7. To install, reverse the removal procedures. Torque the main bearing cap-to-engine bolts to 100 ft. lbs. (3.8L) or 107 ft. lbs. (4.3L diesel). Refill the crankcase. The engine must be operated at low rpm when first started, after a new seal is installed.

UPPER HALF-SEAL

Engine removal is not necessary if the following Time Saver procedure is followed.

1. Refer to the "Oil Pan, Removal and Installation" procedures in this section and remove the oil pan.

2. Remove the rear main bearing cap-to-engine bolts and the cap.

3. Using the Seal Packing tool No. J–21526–1 or equivalent, insert it against each side of the upper seal and drive the seal until it is tight.

4. Measure the amount the seal was driven into the engine and add about $\frac{1}{16}$ in. Using a razor blade, cut that amount off the old lower seal.

5. Using the Seal Packing tool No. J–21526–1 or equivalent, work the short packing pieces into the cylinder block; a small amount of oil on the seal will help the installation.

6. Repeat this process on the other side.

7. Install the lower bearing cap.

8. To complete the installation, reverse the removal procedures. Torque the main bearing cap-to-engine bolts to 100 ft. lbs. (3.8L) or 107 ft. lbs. (4.3L diesel). Refill the crankcase. The engine must be operated at low rpm when first started, after a new seal is installed.

4.1L and 4.5L Engines

1. Refer to the "Transaxle, Remov-

al and Installation" procedures in this section and remove the transaxle.

2. Remove the flywheel-to-crankshaft bolts and the flywheel.

3. Using a shop rag, clean around the seal area.

4. Using the Rear Main Oil Seal Removal tool No. J–26868 or equivalent, pry the oil seal from the rear of the engine.

5. Lubricate the new seal lips with wheel bearing grease and position it on crankshaft with the spring side facing the inside of the engine.

6. Using the Rear Main Oil Seal Installing tool No. J–34604 or equivalent, press the seal into the engine block until it is flush.

7. To complete the installation, reverse the removal procedures. Start the engine and check for leaks.

Oil Pump

REMOVAL & INSTALLATION

3.8L Engines

The oil pump, located at the bottom of the front cover, is an integral part of the front cover; the crankshaft passes through it.

1. Refer to the "Front Cover, Removal and Installation" procedures in this section and remove the front cover.

2. Using a putty knife, clean the gasket mounting surfaces.

3. To inspect the pump gears, perform the following procedures:

   a. Remove the oil pump cover-to-front cover screws and the cover.

   b. Remove the inner and outer pump gears.

   c. Using solvent, clean the gears.

   d. Inspect the gears for wear and/or damage; if necessary, replace the parts.

   e. Using petroleum jelly, pack the pump and reinstall the parts. Torque the oil pump cover-to-front cover screws to 88 inch lbs.

NOTE: Unless the pump is primed this way, it won't produce any oil pressure when the engine is started.

4. To complete the installation, use new gaskets, sealant (if necessary) and reverse the removal procedures. Check and/or refill the crankcase. Replace the oil filter. Start the engine and check for leaks.

4.1L and 4.5L V8 Engine

1. Refer to the "Oil Pan, Removal and Installation" procedures in this section and remove the oil pan.

2. Remove the oil pump-to-engine screws/nut and the oil pump from the engine.

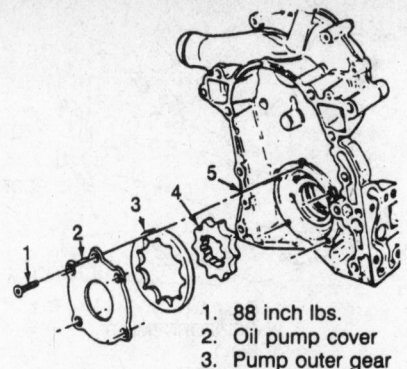

1. 88 inch lbs.
2. Oil pump cover
3. Pump outer gear
4. Pump inner gear
5. Front cover

Exploded view of the oil pump assembly – 3.8L engines

3. To disassemble, remove the oil pump cover-to-housing screws, slide the drive shaft, drive gear and driven gear from the pump housing.

4. Remove the oil pressure regulator valve and spring from the bore in the housing assembly.

5. Inspect the oil pressure regulator valve for nicks and burrs.

6. Measure the free length of the regulator valve spring. It should be 2.57–2.69 in.

7. Inspect the drive gear and driven gear for nicks and burrs.

8. Assemble the pump drive gear over the drive shaft so the retaining ring is inside the gear. Position the drive gear over the pump housing shaft closest to the pressure regulator bore.

9. Slide the driven gear over the remaining shaft in the pump housing, meshing the driven gear with the drive gear.

10. Install the oil pressure regulator spring and valve in the bore of the pump housing assembly.

11. Install the pump cover-to-pump housing screws to 5 ft. lbs., the oil pump-to-engine screws to 15 ft. lbs. and nut to 22 ft. lbs.

12. To complete the installation, use new gaskets and reverse the removal procedures. Refill the crankcase. Start the engine and check for leaks.

4.3L V6 Diesel

1. Refer to the "Oil Pan, Removal and Installation" procedures in this section and remove the oil pan.

2. Remove the oil pump-to-rear main bearing cap bolts and the oil pump.

3. Using a putty knife, clean the gasket mounting surfaces.

4. To install, use new gaskets, sealant (if necessary) and reverse the removal procedures. Torque the oil pump-to-rear main bearing cap bolts to 18 ft. lbs. Refill the crankcase. Start the engine and check for leaks.

ENGINE COOLING

The diesel engine cooling system is the same as that used on the gasoline engine except that the radiator tank has two oil coolers. One is connected to the transmission, the other to the oil filter base.

Radiator

REMOVAL & INSTALLATION

1. Disconnect the negative terminal(s) from the battery(s). Drain the cooling system.

2. Remove the upper fan-to-radiator bolts.

3. Remove the air cleaner duct and/or the silencer. Remove the upper radiator panel.

4. Remove the upper/lower hoses from the radiator and the coolant recovery tank hose from the radiator neck.

5. Disconnect the electrical connector from the fan.

6. Disconnect and cap the oil cooler lines from the radiator side tank. If equipped with an oil cooler, disconnect and plug the lines from it.

7. Remove the radiator-to-chassis bolts and the radiator from the vehicle.

8. To install, reverse the removal procedures. Torque the radiator-to-chassis bolts to 20 ft. lbs. Refill the cooling system. Start the engine, allow it to reach normal operating temperatures and check for leaks.

Water Pump

REMOVAL & INSTALLATION

3.8L and 4.3L (Diesel) Engines

1. Disconnect the negative terminal(s) from the battery(s).

2. Drain the cooling system.

3. Remove the serpentine drive belt.

4. Remove the coolant hoses from the water pump.

5. Remove the water pump pulley bolts and the pulley; the long bolt can be removed through the access hole in the body side rail.

6. Remove the water pump-to-engine bolts and the pump.

7. Using a putty knife, clean the gasket mounting surfaces. Inspect the parts for damage and/or wear; replace the parts, if necessary.

8. To install, use a new gasket, sealant (if necessary) and reverse the removal procedures. Torque the water

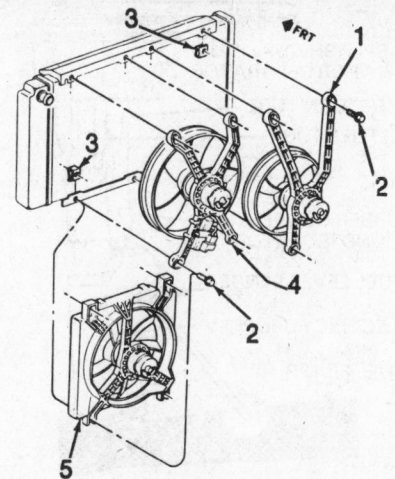

1. FAN ASM.
2. 9.5 N·m (84 LBS. IN.)
3. NUT
4. FAN ASM.—DIESEL
5. FAN ASM.—GAS

Certain models utilize two cooling fans

pump-to-engine bolts to 29 ft. lbs. (long) and 97 inch lbs. (short). Refill and bleed the cooling system.

4.1L and 4.5L V8

1. Disconnect the negative terminal from the battery.

2. Drain the cooling system.

3. If equipped with air conditioning, remove the accumulator from its bracket, the bracket and move the accumulator aside.

4. Remove the right cross-car brace.

5. Remove the accessory drive belt.

6. Remove the water pump pulley-to-water pump bolts and the pulley.

7. Remove the water pump-to-engine bolts and the water pump.

8. Using a putty knife, clean the gasket mounting surfaces.

9. To install, use new gasket, sealant (if necessary) and reverse the removal procedures. Torque the water pump-to-engine Torx® screws to 30 ft. lbs. (A), nut to 5 ft. lbs. (B), screws to 30 ft. lbs. (C) and 5 ft. lbs. (D). Refill the cooling system. Start the engine, allow it to reach normal operating temperatures and check for leaks.

Thermostat

REMOVAL & INSTALLATION

3.8L Engine

1. Disconnect the negative battery cable. Drain the cooling system until the coolant level is below the thermostat housing.

2. Remove the upper radiator hose at the thermostat housing. Remove the thermostat housing retaining bolts.

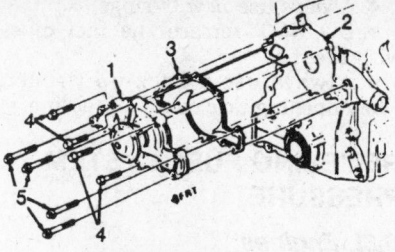

1. Water pump
2. Engine front cover assembly
3. Gasket
4. 97 inch lbs.
5. 29 ft. lbs.

Exploded view of the water pump—3.8L engines

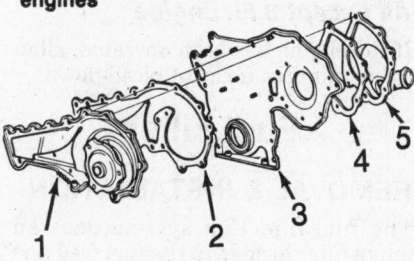

1. WATER PUMP ASSEMBLY
2. WATER PUMP GASKET
3. FRONT COVER
4. WATER PUMP INLET GASKET
5. WATER PUMP INLET

Exploded view of the water pump—4.1L and 4.5L engines

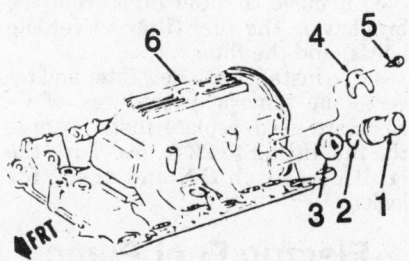

1. Water outlet
2. O-ring
3. Thermostat
4. Clamp
5. 20 ft. lbs.
6. Intake manifold

Exploded view of the thermostat housing assembly—3.8L engine

3. Remove the thermostat from the engine.

4. Using a putty knife, clean the gasket mounting surfaces.

5. To install, use a new gasket, sealant and reverse the removal procedures.

4.1L and 4.5L Engines

There are both an upper and a lower thermostat housing. DO NOT remove the lower housing to replace the thermostat.

1. Drain the cooling system to a level below the thermostat housing.

REFER TO FIGURE 1

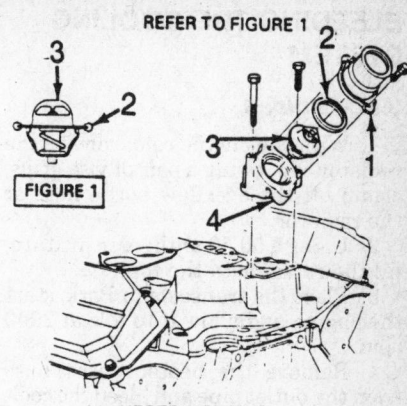

FIGURE 1

1. UPPER HOUSING
2. GASKET
3. THERMOSTAT ASSEMBLY
4. LOWER HOUSING

Exploded view of the thermostat assembly—4.1L and 4.5L engines

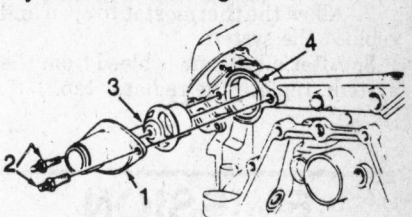

1. Water outlet
2. Studs—dip in thread sealer
3. Thermostat
4. Apply RTV sealant

Exploded view of the thermostat housing assembly—4.3L diesel engine

2. Remove the upper thermostat housing-to-lower thermostat housing bolts and separate the housings.

3. Remove the O-ring gasket and the thermostat.

4. Using a putty knife, clean the gasket mounting surfaces.

5. To install, use a new O-ring and reverse the removal procedures. Refill the cooling system. Start the engine, allow it to reach normal operating temperatures and check for leaks.

4.3L Diesel Engine

The thermostat is located at the rear of the intake manifold.

1. Drain the cooling system to a level below the thermostat housing.

2. Remove the thermostat housing-to-intake manifold bolts and the housing.

3. Remove the thermostat.

4. Using a putty knife, clean the gasket mounting surfaces.

5. To install, coat the gasket mounting surface with RTV sealant and reverse the removal procedures. Torque the thermostat housing-to-intake manifold stud bolts to 18 ft. lbs. Refill the cooling system. Start the engine, allow it to reach normal operating temperatures and check for leaks.

BLEEDING THE COOLING SYSTEM

3.8L Engines

1. With the engine cold, remove the radiator cap. Using a pair of vise-grips, clamp off the overflow bottle hose at the radiator.
2. Using a 50/50 antifreeze mixture, fill the radiator to the top.
3. Place the transaxle in Park, start the engine and allow it to idle at 2000 rpm.
4. Remove the heater outlet hose from the outlet pipe and bleed the cooling system (approx. 5 sec.).
5. Reconnect the hose and refill the radiator to the neck.
6. Throttle the engine to 3000 rpm (at least 10 times) and rebleed the system.
7. Allow the thermostat to open and rebleed the system.
8. After all the air is bleed from the system, replace the radiator cap.

EMISSION CONTROLS

Please refer to "Emission Control" in the Unit Repair section for system maintenance procedures. Due to the complex nature of modern electronic engine control systems, comprehensive diagnosis and testing procedures fall outside the confines of this repair manual. For complete information on diagnosis, testing and repair procedures concerning all modern engine and emission control systems, please refer to Chilton's Guide To Electronic Engine Controls.

GASOLINE FUEL SYSTEM

Fuel System Service Precaution

- Disconnect the negative battery terminal.
- Keep a Class B dry chemical fire extinguisher available.
- Always relieve the fuel pressure before disconnecting a fuel line.
- Wrap a shop cloth around the fuel line when disconnecting a fuel line.

- Always use new O-rings.
- DO NOT replace the fuel pipes with fuel hoses.
- Always use a back-up wrench when opening or closing a fuel line.

RELIEVING FUEL SYSTEM PRESSURE

3.8L Engines

1. From the fuse panel, remove the fuel pump fuse.
2. Start the engine and allow it run until it uses all the fuel.
3. Replace the fuse.

All Except 3.8L Engine

If the engine has been operated, allow a few minutes for it to bleed-down.

Fuel Filter

REMOVAL & INSTALLATION

The fuel injection system uses an inline filter located in the fuel feed line under the hood, attached to the frame rail or on the rear crossmember of the vehicle.

1. Refer to "Relieving the Fuel Pressure" in this section and relieve the fuel pressure.
2. Using a backup wrench (on the fittings), disconnect the fuel lines from the fuel filter.
3. Remove the fuel filter from the bracket or the fuel filter-to-vehicle bolt(s) and the filter.
4. To install, use a new filter and reverse the removal procedures. If O-rings are used, replace them. Torque the fuel fitting to 22 ft. lbs. Turn the ignition switch **ON** and check for leaks.

Electric Fuel Pump

PRESSURE TESTING

1. Refer to "Relieving the Fuel Pressure" in this section and relieve the fuel pressure.
2. Disconnect the inlet fuel line from the throttle body.
3. Using a fuel pressure gauge, connect it to fuel line.
4. Turn the ignition switch **ON**; the fuel pressure should be 27–36 psi (3.8L), 40 psi (4.1L) or 11.6 psi (4.3L).
5. Remove the fuel pressure gauge and reconnect the fuel line.

REMOVAL & INSTALLATION

The electric fuel pump is located in the fuel tank.
1. Refer to "Fuel Tank, Removal and Installation" in this section and remove the fuel tank.

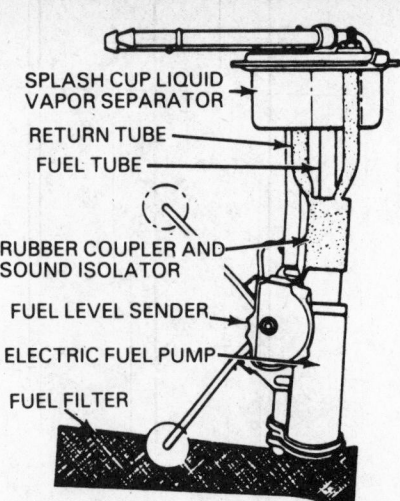

SPLASH CUP LIQUID VAPOR SEPARATOR
RETURN TUBE
FUEL TUBE
RUBBER COUPLER AND SOUND ISOLATOR
FUEL LEVEL SENDER
ELECTRIC FUEL PUMP
FUEL FILTER

Electric fuel pump assembly used with V8 engine

2. Using a brass drift and a hammer, drive (turn) the cam lock ring-to-fuel tank counterclockwise and lift the assembly from the fuel tank.
3. Pull the fuel pump up into the attaching hose while pulling outward away from the bottom support. Take care to prevent damage to the rubber sound insulator and strainer during removal. Once the pump assembly is clear of the bottom support, pull it out of the rubber connector.
4. To install, use a new O-ring and reverse the removal procedures. When installing the fuel tank, make sure all rubber sound isolators or anti-squeak spacers are replaced in their original locations. Refill the fuel tank.

Fuel Injection

Due to the complex nature of modern fuel injection systems, comprehensive diagnosis and testing procedures fall outside the confines of this repair manual. For complete information on Fuel injection diagnosis, testing and repair procedures please refer to Chilton's Guide to Fuel Injection And Feedback Carburetors.

DIESEL FUEL SYSTEM

Fuel Filter

REPLACEMENT

The fuel filter is a square assembly lo-

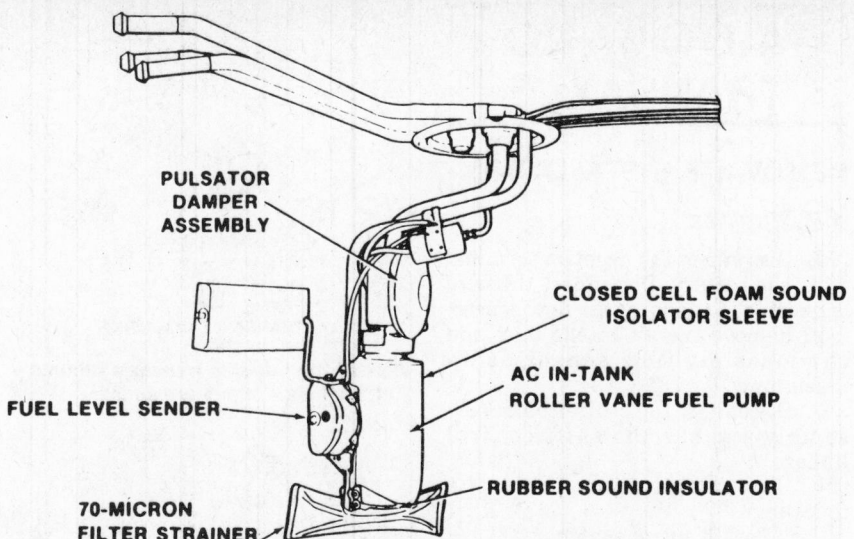

PULSATOR
DAMPER
ASSEMBLY

CLOSED CELL FOAM SOUND
ISOLATOR SLEEVE

AC IN-TANK
ROLLER VANE FUEL PUMP

FUEL LEVEL SENDER

RUBBER SOUND INSULATOR

70-MICRON
FILTER STRAINER

Electric fuel pump assembly used with V6 engine

cated at the back of the engine above the intake manifold. Disconnect the fuel lines and remove the filter. Install the lines to the new filter. Start the engine and check for leaks.

Electric Fuel Pump

NOTE: The electric fuel pump is located on top of the engine, next to the fuel heater; it's purpose is to push fuel to the fuel injection pump.

1. Disconnect negative terminal from the battery. Remove the air cleaner and disconnect all electrical leads from the pump.
2. Using a shop rag, place it under the pump inlet and outlet fittings.
3. Using two wrenches (one for backup), carefully unscrew the inlet and the outlet fittings; cap all fittings to keep dirt out.
4. Remove the fuel pump mounting bracket nut and the fuel pump.
5. To install, reverse the removal procedures. Torque the pump-to-bracket nut to 18 ft. lbs. and inlet/outlet line fittings to 18 ft. lbs.

NOTE: In some cases the pump's position may have to be adjusted slightly to align pump fittings with the fuel lines.

6. After installing the fuel pump, position a catch basin under the fuel filter and disconnect the fuel line from the fuel filter. Turn the ignition switch **ON** to prime and bleed the fuel lines.

NOTE: If after torquing the fuel line, the pump runs with a click-like sound or the fuel bubbles, check for leaks in the fuel lines. When the pump quiets

down, tighten the fuel line at the filter.

Diesel Fuel Injection Pump

The fuel injection pump is located at the top front center of the engine.

REMOVAL & INSTALLATION

NOTE: This procedure contains throttle rod and transmission cable adjustments.

1. Remove the air cleaner.
2. Remove the filters and pipes from the valve covers and air crossover.
3. Remove the air crossover. Using the Air Crossover Screen tool No. J–229657 or equivalent.
4. Disconnect the throttle rod and return spring.
5. Remove the bellcrank.
6. Remove the throttle and transmission cables from the intake manifold brackets.
7. Disconnect the fuel lines from the filter and remove the filter.
8. Disconnect the fuel inlet line from the pump.
9. If equipped with air conditioning, remove the rear compressor brace and the fuel line.
10. Disconnect the fuel return line from the injection pump.
11. Remove the clamps and pull the fuel return lines from each injection nozzle.
12. Using two wrenches, disconnect the high pressure lines from the nozzles.
13. Using tool No. J–26987 or equiv-

alent, remove the three injection pump retaining nuts.
14. Remove the pump and cap all lines and nozzles.
15. To install the pump, perform the following procedures:
    a. Remove the protective caps from all lines and nozzles.
    b. Rotate the crankshaft to position the No. 1 cylinder on TDC of its compression stroke.

NOTE: The mark on the harmonic balancer on the crankshaft will be aligned with the "0" mark on the timing tab and both valves for No. 1 cylinder will be closed. The index mark on the injection pump driven gear should be offset to the right. Make sure all of these conditions are met before continuing.

    c. Align the offset tang on the pump driveshaft with the pump driven gear and install the pump.
    d. Install, but do not tighten the pump retaining nuts.
    e. Connect the high pressure lines at the nozzles.
    f. Using two wrenches, torque the high pressure line nuts to 25 ft. lbs.
    g. Connect the fuel return lines to the nozzles and pump.
    h. Align the timing mark on the injection pump with the line on the timing mark adapter and torque the mounting nuts to 35 ft. lbs.

NOTE: A ¾ in. open end wrench on the boss at the front of the injection pump will aid in rotating the pump to align the marks.

16. To adjust the throttle rod, perform the following procedures:
    a. Remove the clip from the cruise control rod and the rod from the bellcrank.
    b. Loosen the locknut on the throttle rod a few turns, shorten the rod several turns.
    c. Rotate the bellcrank to the full throttle stop, lengthen the throttle rod until the injection pump lever contacts the injection pump full throttle stop, release the bellcrank.
    d. Tighten the throttle rod locknut.
17. Install the fuel inlet line between the transfer pump and the fuel filter.
18. If equipped, install the rear compressor brace.
19. Install the bellcrank and clip.
20. Connect the throttle rod and return spring.
21. Adjust the transmission cable, perform the following procedures:
    a. Push the snap-lock to the disengaged position.
    b. Rotate the injection pump lever to the full throttle stop and hold it.

c. Push in the snap-lock until it is flush.

d. Release the injection pump lever.

22. Start the engine and check for fuel leaks.

23. Remove the screened cover and install the air crossover.

24. Install the tubes in the air flow control valve in the air crossover and install the ventilation filters in the valve covers.

25. To complete the installation, reverse the removal procedures. Start the engine and allow it to run for two minutes. Stop the engine, allow it stand for two minutes and restart it; this permits the air to bleed off within the pump.

INJECTION TIMING

For the engine to be properly timed, the lines on the top of the injection pump adapter and the flange of the injection pump must be aligned.

1. The ignition switch must be turned **OFF** for resetting the timing.

2. Using the Injection Pump Intake Manifold Wrench tool No. J-25304 or equivalent, loosen the three pump retaining nuts.

3. Align the timing marks and torque the pump retaining nuts to 35 ft. lbs.

NOTE: The use of a ¾ in. open end wrench on the boss at the front of the pump will aid in rotating the pump to align the marks.

4. Refer to the "Fuel Injection Pump, Removal and Installation" in this section to adjust the throttle rod.

Injection Nozzle

REMOVAL & INSTALLATION

The injection nozzles on these engines are simply unbolted from the cylinder head, after the fuel lines are removed, in similar fashion to a spark plug. Be careful not to damage the nozzle end and make sure to remove the copper nozzle gasket from the cylinder head if it does not come off with the nozzle.

Using a soft brass wire brush, clean the carbon from the tip of the nozzle and install the nozzles, with new gaskets.

NOTE: Two types of injectors are used, CAV Lucas and Diesel Equipment. When installing the inlet fittings, torque the Diesel Equipment injector fitting to 45 ft. lbs. and the CAV Lucas to 25 ft. lbs.

AUTOMATIC TRANSAXLE

REMOVAL & INSTALLATION

3.8L Engines

1. Disconnect the negative terminal from the battery. Disconnect the wire connector at the mass air flow sensor.

2. Remove the air intake duct and the mass air flow sensor as an assembly.

3. Disconnect the cruise control assembly and the the shift control linkage.

4. Label and disconnect the following:

a. Park/Neutral switch

b. Torque converter clutch

c. Vehicle speed sensor

d. Vacuum modulator hose at the modulator

NOTE: Care must be exercised on reassembly of the Park/Neutral switch to ensure a proper fit of both the connector and the T-latch. Failure to do so may result in intermittent loss of switch functions.

5. Remove the three top transaxle-to-engine block bolts and install an engine support fixture.

6. Remove both front wheels and turn the steering wheel to the full left position.

7. Remove the right front ball joint nut and separate the control arm from the steering knuckle.

8. Remove the right drive axle.

NOTE: Be careful not to allow the drive axle splines to contact any portion of the lip seal.

9. Using a medium pry bar, remove the left drive axle; be careful not to damage the pan. Install drive axle boot seal protectors.

10. Remove three bolts at the transaxle and three nuts at the cradle member. Remove the left front transaxle mount.

11. Remove the right front mount-to-cradle nuts. Remove the left rear transaxle mount-to-transaxle bolts.

12. Remove the right rear transaxle mount. Remove the engine support bracket-to-transaxle case bolts.

13. Remove the flywheel cover, matchmark the flywheel-to-torque converter and remove the flywheel-to-converter bolts.

NOTE: Be sure to matchmark the flywheel-to-converter relationship for proper alignment upon reassembly.

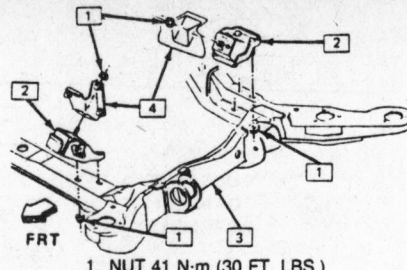

1. NUT 41 N·m (30 FT. LBS.)
2. MOUNT ASM.
3. FRAME ASM.
4. TRANSAXLE MOUNTING BRACKET

View of the left-side transaxle mounts— 3.8L engines—others are similar

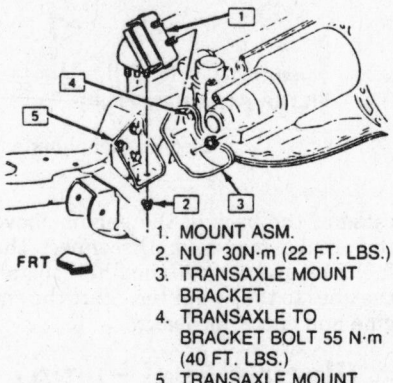

1. MOUNT ASM.
2. NUT 30N·m (22 FT. LBS.)
3. TRANSAXLE MOUNT BRACKET
4. TRANSAXLE TO BRACKET BOLT 55 N·m (40 FT. LBS.)
5. TRANSAXLE MOUNT BRACKET

View of the right-side transaxle mounts— 3.8L engines—others are similar

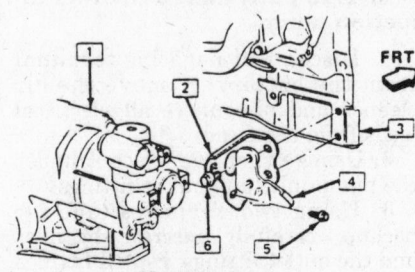

1. TRANSAXLE
2. BRACE—TRANSAXLE
3. ENGINE ASM.
4. BRACKET—DRIVELINE ABSORBER
5. BOLT 45N·m (33 FT. LBS.)
6. BOLT 95N·m (70 FT. LBS.)

View of the transaxle brace and brackets—3.8L engines—others are similar

14. Remove the rear-cradle member-to-front cradle dog leg.

15. Remove the front left cradle-to-body bolt and the front cradle dog leg-to-right cradle member bolts.

16. Install a transaxle support fixture into position.

17. Remove the cradle assembly by swinging it aside and supporting it with jackstand.

18. Disconnect and plug the oil cooler lines at the transaxle.

NOTE: One bolt is located between the transaxle and the engine block; it is installed in the opposite direction.

19. Remove the remaining lower transaxle-to-engine bolts and lower the transaxle from the vehicle.

20. To install, reverse the removal procedures. Check the fluid level and all adjustments.

4.1L and 4.5L Engines

1. Disconnect the negative terminal from the battery. Remove the air cleaner and the TV cable.

2. Disconnect the shift linkage from the transaxle. Using an Engine Support Fixture tool, connect it to and support the engine.

3. Label and disconnect the electrical connectors from the following items:

  a. Converter clutch
  b. Vehicle speed sensor
  c. Neutral start/back-up light switch
  d. Vacuum line at the modulator

4. Remove the upper bell housing-to-engine bolts and studs.

5. Raise and support the front of the vehicle on jackstands. Remove both front wheels.

6. From the left side of the vehicle, disconnect the lower ball joint from steering knuckle. Remove both drive axles from the transaxle.

7. Remove the stabilizer bar-to-left control arm bolt.

8. Remove the left front cradle assembly.

9. Remove the extension housing-to-engine support bracket.

10. Disconnect and plug the oil cooler lines at the transaxle case.

11. Remove the right and left transaxle mount attachments.

12. Remove the flywheel splash shield. Matchmark the torque converter-to-flyheel and remove the converter-to-flywheel bolts.

13. Remove the lower bellhousing bolts except the lower rear on (No. 6).

14. Using a floor jack, position it under the transaxle and remove the last bell housing bolt.

NOTE: To reach the last bell housing bolt, use a 3 in. socket wrench extension through the right wheel arch opening.

15. Remove the transaxle assembly.

16. To install, reverse the removal procedures. Check the fluid level and all adjustments.

4.3L V6 Diesel

1. Disconnect the negative terminal from the battery. Disconnect the TV

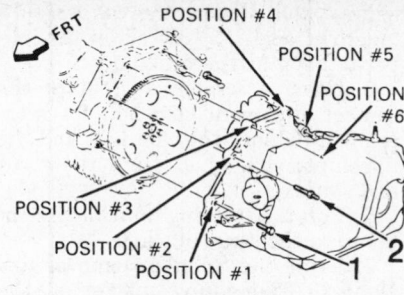

1. BOLT (75 N·m/55 FT. LBS.)
2. STUD (75 N·m/55 FT. LBS.)

View of the transaxle-to-engine assembly, remove No. 6 bolt last — 4.1L and 4.5L engines

cable from the injection pump and transaxle.

2. Remove the crossover pipe shield and disconnect the shift control linkage.

3. Label and disconnect electrical connectors from the following items:

  a. Park/Neutral switch
  b. Torque converter clutch
  c. Vehicle speed sensor
  d. Vacuum hose at the modulator

4. Remove the three upper engine-to-transaxle bolts.

5. Loosen, but do not remove, the engine-to-transaxle bolt at the starter.

6. Using an Engine Support Fixture tool, attach it to the engine and support it.

7. Raise and support the vehicle. Remove both front wheels and turn the steering wheel to the full left position.

8. From the right side of the vehicle, disconnect the ball joint from the steering knuckle. Remove the right drive axle from the transaxle.

9. Remove both front/rear transaxle-to-cradle mounts.

10. Remove the transaxle brace and bracket.

11. Disconnect the speedometer cable.

12. Remove the right rear transaxle mount and disconnect the left stabilizer link.

13. Remove the flywheel cover, matchmark the torque converter-to-flyweel and remove the flywheel-to-torque converter bolts.

14. Remove the rear cradle member-to-front cradle dog leg bolts. Remove one stabilizer brace and loosen the other.

15. Remove the front cradle-to-body bolt and the right front motor mount.

16. Remove the wiring harness cover on the cradle and position it aside.

17. Using a Transaxle Support Fixture tool, attach it to the transaxle and support it.

18. Disconnect and plug the oil cooler lines at the transaxle.

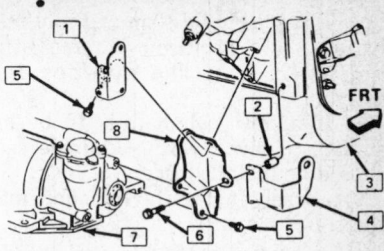

1. POWER STEERING PUMP BRACKET
2. SPACER
3. ENGINE
4. SHOCK ABSORBER BRACKET
5. BOLT 55N·m (40 FT. LBS.)
6. BOLT 45N·m (33 FT. LBS.)
7. TRANSAXLE
8. BRACE

Transaxle brace and brackets—4.3L V6 (diesel)

19. Remove the exhaust connector pipe and the rear exhaust manifold.

20. Remove the remaining engine-to-transaxle bolts.

NOTE: One engine-to-transaxle bolt is installed in the opposite direction.

21. Lower the transaxle and remove it.

22. To install, reverse the removal procedures. Check the fluid level and all adjustments.

DRIVE AXLE

Halfshaft

REMOVAL & INSTALLATION

NOTE: Use care when removing the drive axle. Tri-pots can be damaged if the drive axle is overextended.

1. Remove the hub nut.

2. Raise and support the front of the vehicle on jackstands. Remove the wheel and tire assembly.

3. Using the Axle Shaft Boot Seal Protector tool No. J–28712 or equivalent, install it onto the seal.

4. Disconnect the brake hose clip from the MacPherson strut, DO NOT disconnect the hose from the caliper. Remove the brake caliper from the spindle and hang the caliper out of the way, using a length of wire; DO NOT allow the caliper to hang by the brake hose.

5. Mark the camber alignment cam bolt for reassembly. Remove the cam bolt and the upper strut-to-steering knuckle bolt.

6. Pull the steering knuckle assembly from the strut bracket.

7. Using Spindle Removal tool tool No. J–28733 or equivalent, remove the halfshaft from the hub/bearing assembly.

8. If a new halfshaft is to be installed, a new steering knuckle seal should be installed first.

9. Loosely install the halfshaft into the transaxle and steering knuckle.

10. Loosely attach the steering knuckle-to-strut bolts.

11. The halfshaft is an interference fit in the steering knuckle. Press the axle into place and install the hub nut. When the shaft begins to turn with the hub, insert a drift through the caliper into one of the cooling slots in the rotor to keep it from turning. Insert a long bolt in the hub flange to prevent the shaft from turning. Torque the hub nut to 70 ft. lbs., the brake caliper-to-steering knuckle bolts to 30 ft. lbs.

12. Load the hub assembly by lowering it onto a jackstand. Align the camber cam bolt marks made during removal, install the bolt and tighten to 140 ft. lbs. Tighten the upper nut to the same value.

13. Install the halfshaft all the way into the transaxle, using a small prybar inserted into the groove provided on the inner retainer. Tap the prybar until the shaft seats in the transaxle. Remove the boot seal protector.

14. Connect the brake hose clip to the strut. Install the tire and wheel, lower the vehicle. Torque the hub nut to 185 ft. lbs.

CV JOINT OVERHAUL

NOTE: For all CV-joint overhaul procedures, please refer to "U/CV-Joint Overhaul" in the Unit Repair section.

Front Wheel Drive Hub, Knuckle and Bearings

REMOVAL & INSTALLATION

NOTE: Use caution during halfshaft removal, damage to the tri-pots may occur if the halfshaft is overextended.

1. Remove the hub nut.

2. Raise and support the front of the vehicle on jackstands. Remove the wheel and tire assembly.

3. Install a Halfshaft Boot Seal Protector tool No. J–28712 or equivalent, onto the boot.

4. Disconnect the brake hose clip from the MacPherson strut; DO NOT disconnect the hose from the caliper. Remove the brake caliper from the

spindle and support the caliper on a length of wire; DO NOT allow the caliper to hang by the brake hose.

5. Using a scratch awl, mark the camber alignment cam bolt for reassembly. Remove the cam bolt and the upper attaching bolt from the strut and spindle.

6. Pull the steering knuckle assembly from the strut bracket.

7. Using the Spindle Removal tool No. J–28733 or equivalent, remove the halfshaft from the hub/bearing assembly.

8. Press the bearing from the hub assembly and install a new bearing.

9. Loosely install the halfshaft into the transaxle and steering knuckle.

10. Loosely attach the steering knuckle-to-strut bolts.

11. Press the halfshaft into place and install the hub nut. When the shaft begins to turn with the hub, insert a drift through the caliper into one of the cooling slots in the rotor to keep it from turning. Insert a long bolt in the hub flange to prevent the shaft from turning. Torque the hub nut to 70 ft. lbs. to completely seat the shaft.

12. Torque the caliper-to-steering knuckle bolts to 30 ft. lbs.

13. Load the hub assembly by lowering it onto a jackstand. Align the camber cam bolt marks made during removal, install the bolt and torque to 140 ft. lbs. Tighten the upper nut to the same value.

14. Install the halfshaft all the way into the transaxle using a small prybar inserted into the groove provided on the inner retainer. Tap the prybar until the shaft seats in the transaxle. Remove the boot seal protector.

15. Connect the brake hose clip to the strut. Install the tire/wheel assembly, lower the vehicle and torque the hub nut 185 ft. lbs.

FRONT SUSPENSION

MacPherson Strut

REMOVAL & INSTALLATION

1. Remove the three strut-to-chassis nuts.

2. Raise and support the front of the vehicle on jackstands (under the engine cradle).

3. Lower the vehicle slightly so the weight rests on the jackstands.

4. Remove the wheel/tire assemblies.

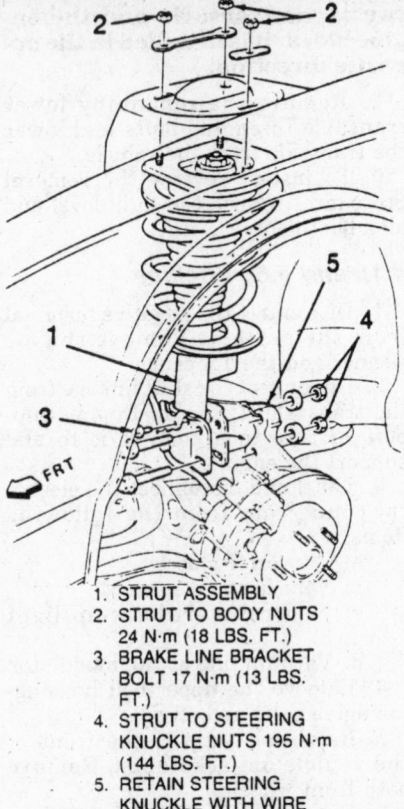

1. STRUT ASSEMBLY
2. STRUT TO BODY NUTS 24 N·m (18 LBS. FT.)
3. BRAKE LINE BRACKET BOLT 17 N·m (13 LBS. FT.)
4. STRUT TO STEERING KNUCKLE NUTS 195 N·m (144 LBS. FT.)
5. RETAIN STEERING KNUCKLE WITH WIRE ONCE STRUT ASSEMBLY IS REMOVED

Front MacPherson strut assemlby

NOTE: Always install halfshaft boot seal protectors. Care must be taken to prevent overextension of the inner Tri-Pot joints.

5. Remove the brake line bracket bolt from the strut assembly. Do not disconnect the brake line from the caliper.

6. Remove the strut-to-steering knuckle bolts and carefully remove the strut assembly.

7. To install, reverse the removal procedures. Check and/or adjust the wheel alignment. Torque the strut-to-body nuts to 18 ft. lbs. and the strut-to-steering knuckle bolts to 144 ft. lbs.

OVERHAUL

NOTE: For all spring and shock absorber removal and installation procedures, and all strut overhaul procedures, please refer to "Strut Overhaul" in the Unit Repair section.

Ball Joints

INSPECTION

1. Raise and support the front of the vehicle with a jackstands placed

under the engine cradle; the front wheel should be off the ground.

2. Grasp the wheel at the top and bottom and shake the wheel in and out.

3. If any movement is seen of the steering knuckle relative to the control arm, the ball joints are defective and must be replaced. Note that movement elsewhere may be due to loose wheel bearings or other troubles; watch the knuckle-to-control arm connection.

4. If the ball stud is disconnected from the steering knuckle and any looseness is noted and the ball joint stud can be twisted in its socket with finger pressure, replace the ball joints.

REMOVAL & INSTALLATION

1. Raise and support the front of the vehicle and with jackstands positioned underneath the engine cradle; lower the vehicle slightly so the weight rests primarily on the jack stands.

2. Remove the wheel and tire assemblies.

3. Install halfshaft covers to protect the halfshaft boot seals.

4. Remove the cotter pin and nut from the ball joint. Using a Ball Joint Separator tool, separate the ball joint from the steering knuckle.

5. Using an ⅛ in. drill bit, drill a hole approximately ¼ in. deep in the center of each of the three ball joint rivets.

6. Using a ½ in. drill bit, drill off the rivet heads; drill only enough to remove the rivet head.

7. Use a hammer and punch to remove the rivets; drive them out from the bottom.

8. Loosen the stabilizer bar bushing assembly nut.

9. Pull the control arm downward to remove the ball joint from the steering knuckle and control arm.

10. Install the new ball joint in the steering knuckle and align the holes with those in the control arm. Install the three ball joint-to-lower control arm bolts facing down. Torque the ball joint-to-lower control arm nuts to 50 ft. lbs. and the ball joint-to-steering knuckle nut to 81 ft. lbs.

NOTE: Tightening the nut for cotter pin alignment is allowed but do not loosen it once the torque value has been reached.

11. To complete the installation, use a new cotter pin and reverse the removal procedures.

Lower Control Arm

REMOVAL & INSTALLATION

1. Refer to the "Ball Joint, Removal

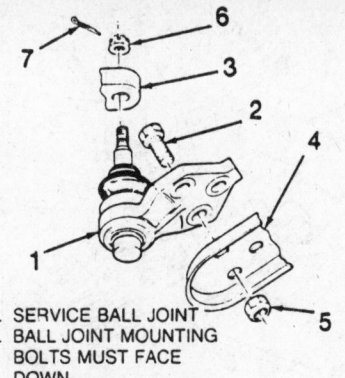

1. SERVICE BALL JOINT
2. BALL JOINT MOUNTING BOLTS MUST FACE DOWN
3. STEERING KNUCKLE
4. CONTROL ARM
5. BALL JOINT MOUNTING NUTS 68 N·m (50 LBS. FT.)
6. BALL JOINT TO STEERING KNUCKLE NUT 110 N·m (81 LBS. FT.) BEFORE COTTER PIN INSTALLATION
7. COTTER PIN

Ball joint installation

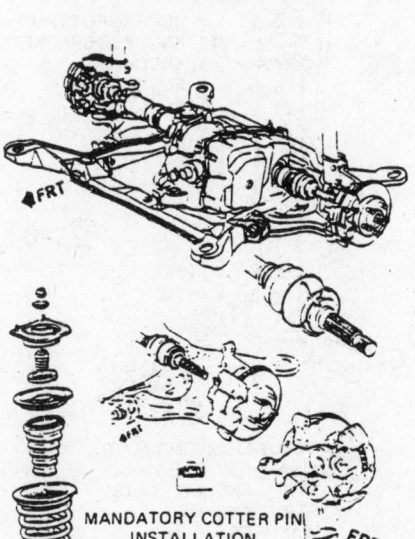

MANDATORY COTTER PIN INSTALLATION

Front suspension assembly

and Installation" procedures in this section and separate the ball joint from the lower control arm.

2. Remove the control arm-to-chassis bolts and the control arm from the vehicle.

3. To install, position the control arm and install the mounting bolts; DO NOT torque them.

4. Install the stabilizer bar bushing assembly. Reconnect the ball joint to the steering knuckle.

5. Hoist the vehicle (slightly) so the weight of the vehicle is supported by the control arms.

NOTE: The weight of the vehicle MUST be supported by the

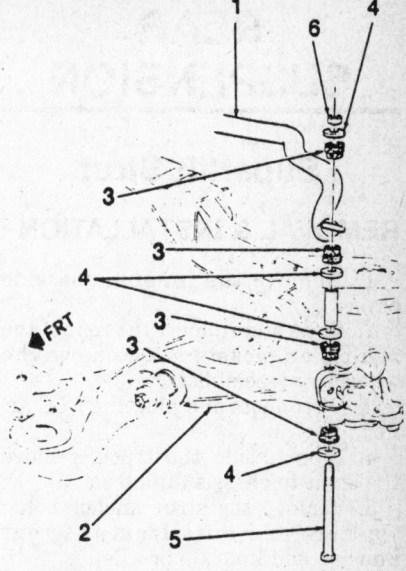

1. Stabilizer Bar
2. Control Arm
3. Insulator (4)
4. Retainer (4)
5. Bolt
6. Nut 17 N·m (13 LBS. FT.)

Stabilizer bar bushing assembly

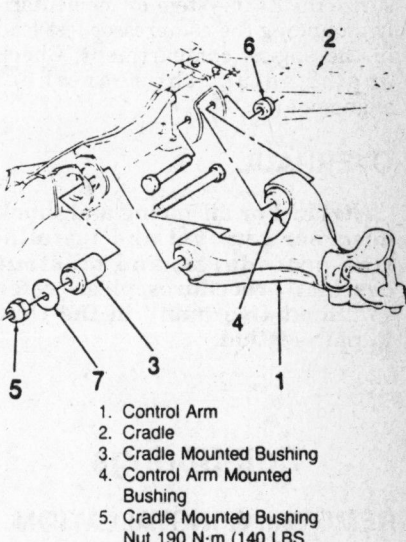

1. Control Arm
2. Cradle
3. Cradle Mounted Bushing
4. Control Arm Mounted Bushing
5. Cradle Mounted Bushing Nut 190 N·m (140 LBS. FT.)
6. Control Arm Mounted Bushing Nut 123 N·m (90 LBS. FT.)
7. Washer

Lower control arm assembly

control arms when tightening the mounting nuts.

6. To complete the installation, reverse the removal procedures. Torque the stabilizer bar bushing nut to 13 ft. lbs., the rear control arm-to-chassis nut to 90 ft. lbs., the front control arm-to-chassis nut to 140 ft. lbs. and the ball joint-to-steering knuckle nut to 81 ft. lbs. (110 Nm).

REAR SUSPENSION

Superlift Strut

REMOVAL & INSTALLATION

1. Remove the inner trunk side cover.

2. Raise and support the rear of the vehicle on jackstands. Remove the wheel/tire assemblies.

3. Disconnect and plug the ELC air line.

4. From inside the truck, remove the strut-to-chassis nuts from.

5. Remove the strut anchor bolts, washers and nuts from the rear knuckle and knuckle bracket.

6. Remove the strut.

7. To install, reverse the removal procedures. Torque the strut-to-chassis nuts to 19 ft. lbs. and the strut anchor nuts to 144 ft. lbs., Lightly pressurize the ELC system by momentarily grounding the compressor test lead in the engine compartment. Check and/or adjust the rear wheel alignment.

OVERHAUL

NOTE: For all spring and shock absorber removal and installation procedures, and all strut overhaul procedures, please refer to "Strut Overhaul" in the Unit Repair section.

Coil Springs

REMOVAL & INSTALLATION

1. Raise and support the rear of the vehicle on jackstands placed under the frame; support it so that the control arms hang free. Remove the rear wheels.

2. Remove the rear stabilizer bar from the knuckle bracket.

3. Disconnect the ELC height sensor link (right control arm) and/or the parking brake cable retaining clip (left control arm).

4. Using the tool No. J-23028-01 or equivalent, position it cradle the control arm bushings.

NOTE: Special tool No. J-23028-01 or equivalent, should be secured to a suitable jack.

5. Raise the jack to remove the tension from the control arm pivot bolts.

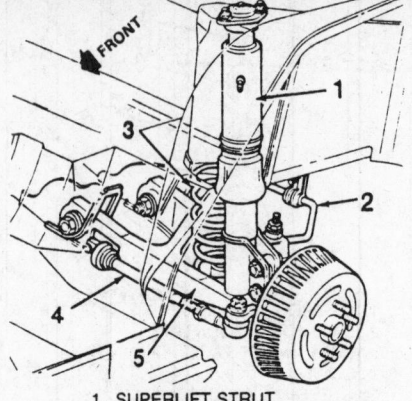

1. SUPERLIFT STRUT
2. STABILIZER BAR
3. COIL SPRING
4. SUSPENSION ADJUSTMENT LINK
5. LOWER CONTROL ARM

Rear suspension

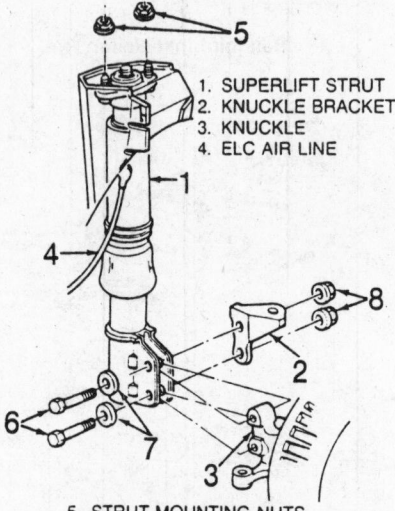

1. SUPERLIFT STRUT
2. KNUCKLE BRACKET
3. KNUCKLE
4. ELC AIR LINE

5. STRUT MOUNTING NUTS (25 N·m/19 FT. LBS.)
6. STRUT ANCHOR BOLTS
7. STRUT ANCHOR WASHERS
8. STRUT ANCHOR NUTS (195 N·m/144 FT. LBS.)

Rear strut installation

CAUTION

Secure a chain around the spring and through the control arm as a safety precaution.

6. Remove the rear control arm-to-chassis pivot bolt and nut.

7. Slowly maneuver the jack to relieve any tension in the front control arm pivot bolt and remove the nut/bolt.

8. Lower the jack to allow the control arm to pivot downward.

9. When all pressure is removed from the coil spring, remove the safety chain, spring and insulators.

NOTE: The spring insulators

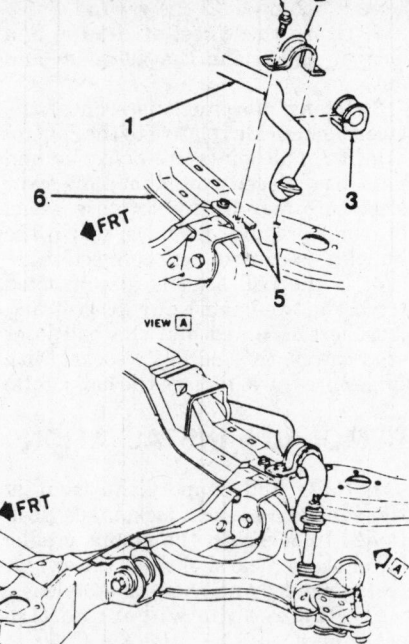

VIEW A

1. Stabilizer Bar
2. Stabilizer Bar Mounting Bracket
3. Stabilizer Bar Mounting Bushing
4. 50 N·m (37 LBS. FT.)
5. Frame Welded Nuts
6. Cradle

Stabilizer bar installation

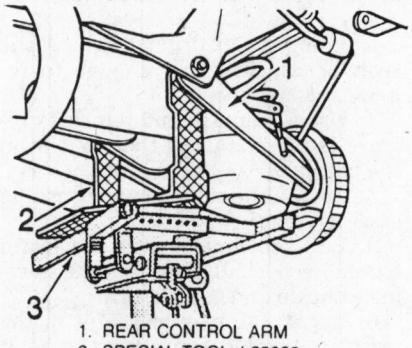

1. REAR CONTROL ARM
2. SPECIAL TOOL J-23028-01
3. TRANSMISSION JACK

Use the special tool and a transmission jack to cradle the control arm

should be inspected for cuts or tears. They should be replaced if the vehicle has over 50,000 miles.

10. To install, snap the upper insulator onto the spring. Position the lower insulator and the spring in the control arm. Install the coil springs so the upper ends are positioned in the slot.

11. To complete the installation, reverse the removal procedures. Control arm mounting nuts should not be tightened until the vehicle is unsupported and resting on its wheels at normal trim height.

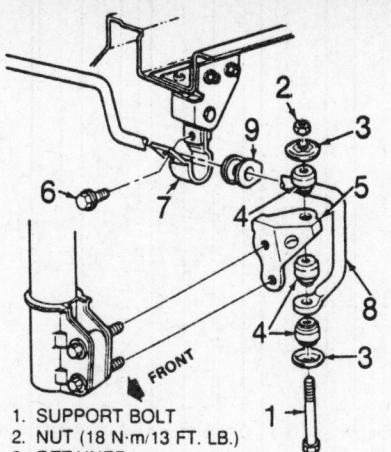

1. SUPPORT BOLT
2. NUT (18 N·m/13 FT. LB.)
3. RETAINER
4. INSULATORS
5. KNUCKLE BRACKET
6. BUSHING CLIP BOLT (50 N·m/37 FT. LB.)
7. SUPPORT ASSEMBLY
8. STABILIZER BAR
9. BUSHING

Rear stabilizer bar bushing assembly

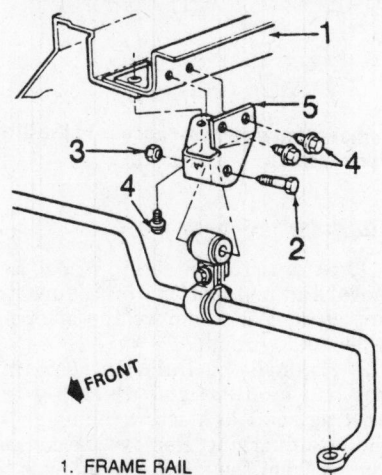

1. FRAME RAIL
2. BUSHING ASSEMBLY BOLT
3. NUT (50 N·m/37 FT. LB.)
4. MOUNTING BRACKET BOLTS (18N·m/13 FT. LB.)
5. MOUNTING BRACKET

Rear stabilizer bar mounting bracket

Ball Joint

REMOVAL & INSTALLATION

1. Raise and support the rear of the vehicle on jackstands positioned under the frame. Remove the wheels.

2. Disconnect the ELC height sensor link (right control arm) and/or the parking brake cable retaining link (left control arm).

3. Remove the cotter pin and castellated nut from the outer suspension adjustment link.

4. Separate the outer suspension link from the knuckle.

5. Using a floor jack, support the control arm; the lower control arm

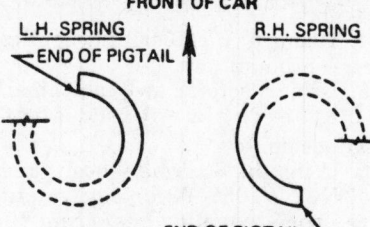

TOP VIEW OF UPPER END OF SPRING

FRONT OF CAR

L.H. SPRING   R.H. SPRING
END OF PIGTAIL

END OF PIGTAIL

Rear coil spring positioning

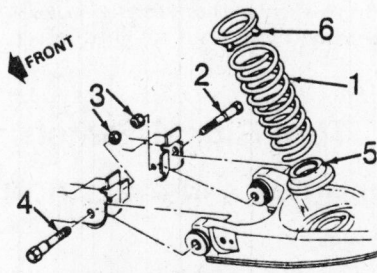

1. COIL SPRING
2. CONTROL ARM PIVOT BOLT-REAR (170 N·m/125 FT. LB.)
3. CONTROL ARM PIVOT NUTS (115 N·m/85 FT. LB.)
4. CONTROL ARM PIVOT BOLT-FRONT (170 N·m/125 FT. LB.)
5. LOWER COIL SPRING INSULATOR
6. UPPER COIL SPRING INSULATOR

Rear coil spring installation

MUST be supported to prevent the coil spring from forcing the control arm downward.

6. Remove the ball stud cotter pin.

7. Remove the castellated nut and reinstall it with the flat side facing upward; DO NOT tighten the nut.

8. Usng the Ball Joint Separator tool, separate the knuckle from the ball stud by backing off the inverted nut against the tool.

9. Separate the ball joint from the control arm.

10. To install, use a new castellated nut, cotter pin and reverse the removal procedures. Torque the a NEW castellated nut: 1st to 7.5 ft. lbs. and 2nd an additional ⅔ turn.

NOTE: Align the slot in the nut to the cotter pin hole by tightening only; DO NOT loosen the nut to align the holes.

Rear Control Arms

REMOVAL & INSTALLATION

1. Refer to the "Coil Spring, Re-

REMOVE CASTELLATED NUT AND REINSTALL WITH FLAT SIDE FACING UPWARD.
PLACE J-34505 INTO POSITION AS SHOWN. LOOSEN NUT AND BACK OFF UNTIL. . .

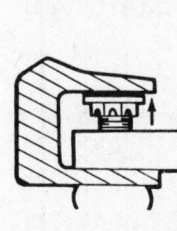
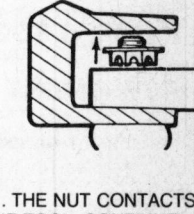

... THE NUT CONTACTS THE TOOL. CONTINUE BACKING OFF THE NUT UNTIL THE NUT FORCES THE BALL STUD OUT OF THE KNUCKLE.

Separating the ball joint from the steering knuckle

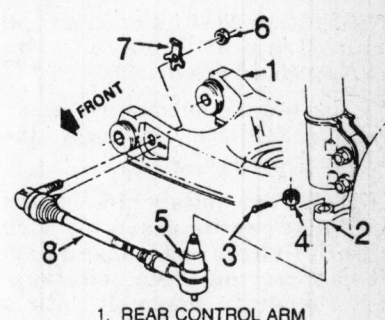

1. REAR CONTROL ARM
2. KNUCKLE
3. COTTER PIN
4. CASTELLATED NUT (50 N·m/37 FT. LB.)
5. OUTER SUSPENSION ADJUSTMENT LINK
6. LINK RETAINING NUT (85 N·m/63 FT. LB.)
7. LINK RETAINER
8. SUSPENSION ADJUSTMENT LINK ASSEMBLY

Rear suspension adjustment link

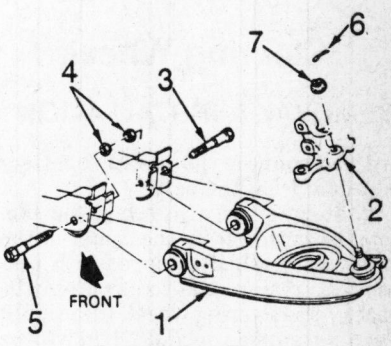

1. REAR CONTROL ARM
2. KNUCKLE
3. CONTROL ARM PIVOT BOLT—REAR
4. CONTROL ARM PIVOT NUTS (115 N·m/85 FT-LB)
5. CONTROL ARM PIVOT BOLT—FRONT
6. COTTER PIN
7. CASTELLATED NUT

Rear control arm

moval and Installation" and the "Ball Joint, Removal and Installation" procedures in this section and remove the the rear control arm from the vehicle.

2. To install, reverse the removal procedures.

Rear Wheel Bearings

ADJUSTMENT

There is no necessary adjustment to the rear wheel bearing and hub assembly.

REMOVAL & INSTALLATION

1. Raise and support the rear of the vehicle on jackstands.

2. Remove the wheel/tire assembly and the brake drum.

NOTE: DO NOT hammer on the brake drum as damage to the bearing could result.

3. Remove the hub/bearing assembly-to-knuckle bolts and remove the hub/bearing assembly.

NOTE: The bolts which attach the hub/bearing assembly also support the brake assembly. When removing these bolts, support the brake assembly with a wire or other means; DO NOT allow the brake line support the brake assembly.

4. To install, reverse the removal procedures. Torque the hub/bearing assembly-to-rear knuckle Torx® bolts to 52 ft. lbs.

STEERING

Steering Wheel

REMOVAL & INSTALLATION

1. Disconnect the negative battery terminal from the battery.

2. If equipped with a horn button, pry the button from the center of the steering wheel. If equipped with center pad, remove the screws from the rear of the steering wheel. If equipped with an air bag module, remove the screws from the rear of the steering wheel.

--- CAUTION ---
When removing the air bag module, place it on a flat surface with the air bag facing upwards. If this is not done, the air module could inflate prematurely causing bodily harm.

3. Disconnect the horn electrical connector from the steering wheel assembly.

4. Remove the steering wheel-to-steering column nut.

5. Using a scratch awl, matchmark the steering wheel-to-shaft relationship.

6. Using the Steering Wheel Puller tool No. J-1859-03 or equivalent, press the steering wheel from the steering column.

7. To install, align the matchmarks and the reverse the removal procedures. Torque the steering wheel-to-steering column nut to 30 ft. lbs.

Turn Signal Switch

REMOVAL & INSTALLATION

1985–87

1. Refer to the "Steering Wheel, Removal and Installation" procedures in this section and remove the steering wheel. Remove the trim cover.

2. Loosen the cover screws. Pry the cover off with a screwdriver and lift the cover off the shaft.

3. Using the Lock Plate Compression tool No. J-23653-A or equivalent, position it on the end of the steering shaft and compress the lock plate by turning the shaft nut clockwise. Pry the wire snapring out of the shaft groove.

4. Remove the tool and lift the lock plate from the shaft.

5. Slip the cancelling cam, upper bearing preload spring and thrust washer off the shaft.

6. Remove the turn signal lever. Push the flasher knob in and unscrew it. Remove the button retaining screw and the button, spring and knob.

7. Pull the switch connector out the mast jacket and tape the upper part to facilitate switch removal. If equipped with tilt steering, place the steering housing in low position and remove the harness cover.

8. Remove the turn signal switch assembly-to-steering housing screws and pull the switch straight up while guiding the wiring harness cover through the column.

9. To install the turn signal switch, attach a long piece of wire to the turn signal switch connector, feed the wire through the steering column and pull the switch connector into position. On tilt steering models, the connector is worked down through the housing, under the bracket and the cover is installed on the harness.

10. To complete the installation, reverse the removal procedures. Check the operation of the components.

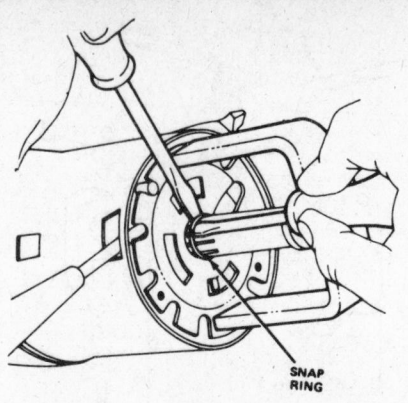

Depress the lockplate and remove the snapring

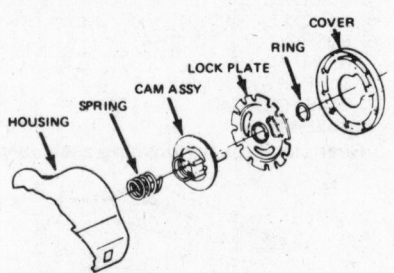

Remove these parts for access to the turn signal switch

1988–89

1. Refer to the "Steering Wheel, Removal and Installation" procedures in this section and remove the steering wheel and shroud.

2. Remove the inflation restraint (air bag module) coil assembly-to-steering shaft lock screw (home boss) and retaining ring. Remove the coil assembly from the shaft and allow it to hang freely.

3. Using the Lock Plate Compression tool No. J-23653-A or equivalent, position it on the end of the steering shaft and compress the lock plate by turning the shaft nut clockwise. Pry the wire snapring out of the shaft groove.

4. Remove the tool and lift the lock plate from the shaft.

5. Remove the cancelling cam, upper bearing preload spring, bearing seat and inner race from the shaft.

6. Position the turn signal switch in the Right Turn position. Remove the turn signal lever screw and the lever.

7. To remove the turn signal switch, perform the following procedures:

   a. Remove the switch-to-steering column screws, pull the switch out and allow it to hang freely.

   b. From under the dash, remove the retainer spring and wiring protector.

   c. Remove the hazard knob.

d. Disconnect the electrical connector from the lower steering column and gently pull the wiring connector through the gear shift lever bowl, the column housing and the lock housing cover.

8. To install, reverse the removal procedures. Torque the turn signal switch-to-steering column screws to 30 inch lbs. and the turn signal lever screw to 20 inch lbs.

9. To install the inflation restraint coil, perform the following procedures:

a. Install the home boss-to-steering column lock screw, allowing the hub to rotate.

b. While holding the coil assembly (in one hand) with the steering wheel connector facing upwards, rotate the coil hub counterclockwise until it stops; the coil ribbon is now wound snug.

c. Rotate the coil hub 2½ turns clockwise until the center lock hole is even with the notch in the coil housing.

d. While holding the hub in position, install the lock screw into the center lock hole.

e. Install the coil assembly using the horn tower on the inner ring cancelling cam and outer ring projections for alignment purposes.

10. To complete the installation, reverse the removal procedures.

Ignition Switch

REMOVAL & INSTALLATION

The switch is located inside the channel section of the brake pedal support and is completely inaccessible without first lowering the steering column. The switch is actuated by a rod and rack assembly. A gear on the end of the lock cylinder engages the toothed upper end of the rod.

1. Lower the steering column; be sure to properly support it.

2. Position the switch in the **OFF-UNLOCKED** position. With the cylinder removed, the rod is in **LOCK** when it is in the next to the uppermost detent; **OFF-UNLOCKED** is two detents from the top.

3. Remove the two switch screws and the switch assembly.

4. To install, position the new switch in **OFF-UNLOCKED** position; make sure the lock cylinder and actuating rod are in **OFF-UN-LOCKED** (third detent from the top) position.

5. Install the activating rod into the switch and assemble the switch on the column. Tighten the mounting screws.

NOTE: Use only the specified screws since overlength screws

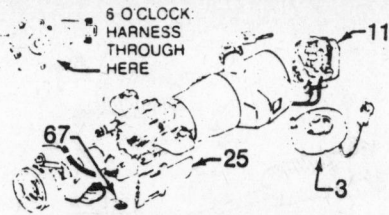

3. Inflation restraint coil assembly
11. Turn signal switch assembly
25. Wiring protector
67. Retaining spring

View of the inflation restraint equipped steering column

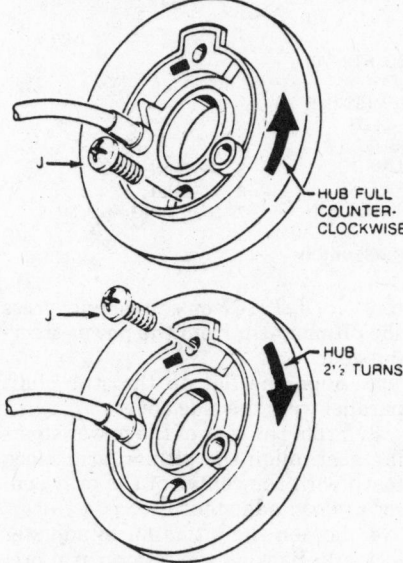

J. Lock retaining screw

Centering the inflation restraint coil assembly

could impair the collapsibility of the column.

6. To complete the installation, reverse the removal procedures.

Ignition Lock Cylinder

REMOVAL & INSTALLATION

1985–87

1. Refer to the "Turn Signal Switch, Removal and Installation" procedures in this section and remove the turn signal switch assembly.

2. Position the ignition switch in the RUN position.

3. Remove the buzzer switch, the lock cylinder-to-steering column screw and the lock cylinder.

NOTE: If the screw is dropped on removal, it could fall into the column, requiring complete disassembly to retrieve the screw.

4. To install the lock cylinder, rotate the cylinder clockwise to align cylinder key with the keyway in the housing.

5. Push the lock all the way in.

6. Install the lock cylinder-to-steering column screw. Torque the lock cylinder-to-steering column screw to 14 inch lbs. (tilt columns) and 25 inch lbs. (standard).

1988–89

1. Refer to the "Turn Signal Switch, Removal and Installation" procedures in this section and remove the turn signal switch assembly.

2. Remove the key from the lock cylinder. Remove the buzzer switch and clip.

3. Reinsert the key into the lock cylinder and turn it to the Lock position.

4. Remove the cylinder lock-to-steering column screw and the lock set.

5. To install the cylinder lock and torque the lock-to-steering column screw to 22 inch lbs.

6. Position the key in the Run position and reverse the removal procedures. Torque the turn signal switch-to-steering column screws to 30 inch lbs. and the turn signal lever screw to 20 inch lbs.

Power Steering Gear

REMOVAL & INSTALLATION

1. Raise and support the front of the vehicle with jackstands positioned under the frame members. Allow the front suspension to hang freely. Disconnect the pressure lines from the steering gear and drain the excess fluid into a container; be sure to plug the openings.

2. Move the intermediate shaft cover upward and remove the intermediate shaft-to-stub shaft pinch bolt.

3. Remove both front wheel assemblies.

4. Remove the cotter pins and nut from both tie rod ends. Disconnect the tie rod ends from the steering knuckles.

5. Remove the line retainer.

6. Remove the outlet and pressure hose.

7. Remove the rack/pinion assembly-to-chassis bolts.

8. Loosen the front engine cradle mounting bolts and the lower the rear of the cradle about 3 in. (76mm) onto jackstands.

———— **CAUTION** ————
DO NOT lower the rear of the engine cradle too far.
————————————————

9. Remove the rack and pinion assembly.

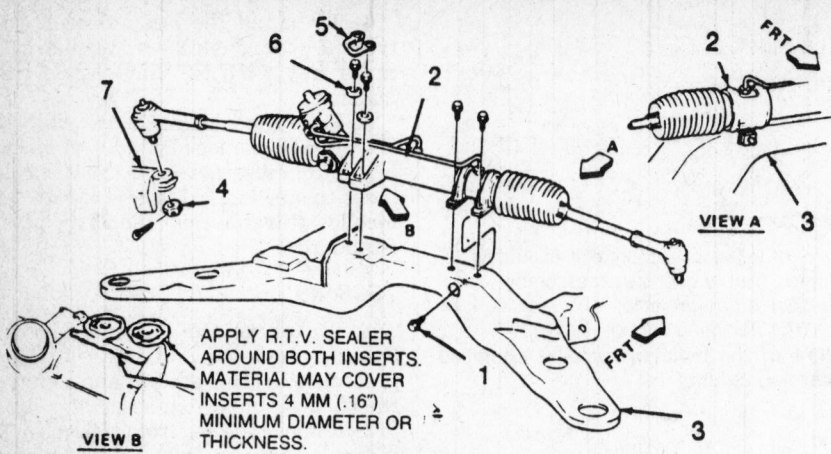

APPLY R.T.V. SEALER
AROUND BOTH INSERTS.
MATERIAL MAY COVER
INSERTS 4 MM (.16")
MINIMUM DIAMETER OR
THICKNESS.

VIEW B

1. BOLT 68 N·m (50 LBS. FT.) AFTER SECOND REUSE OF BOLT, LOCTITE THREAD LOCKING KIT, #1052624 MUST BE USED
2. STEERING GEAR
3. FRAME
4. 50 N·m (35 LBS. FT.), 70 N·m (52 LBS. FT.) MAXIMUM PERMISSIBLE TORQUE TO ALIGN COTTER PIN SLOT. (1/6 TURN MAXIMUM) DO NOT BACK OFF FOR COTTER PIN INSERTION
5. RETAINER
6. WASHER
7. STEERING KNUCKLE

Rack and pinion assembly

10. To install, reverse the removal procedures. Tighten the rack mounting bolts to 50 ft. lbs. (68 Nm). Tighten the tie rod end nut to 35–52 ft. lbs. (50–70 Nm). Refill the power steering pump reservoir. Bleed the power steering system and check for leaks. Check and/or adjust the front wheel alignment.

ADJUSTMENT

NOTE: For the following adjustments, the power steering gear should be removed from the vehicle and positioned it in a vise.

Thrust Bearing Preload

1. Using a punch and a hammer, loosen the power steering gear stub shaft lock nut and remove the lock nut.
2. Using the Spanner Wrench tool No. J–7624 or equivalent, tighten the stub shaft adjuster plug until the thrust bearing is firmly bottomed; 20 ft. lbs.
3. Place alignment marks on the adjuster plug and the housing.
4. Using a ruler, measure back (counterclockwise) ½ in. and place a second mark.
5. Using the Spanner Wrench tool No. J–7624 or equivalent, turn the adjuster plug counterclockwise until it aligns with the second mark.
6. While holding the adjuster plug stationary, to maintain the alignment, tighten the adjuster plug lock nut.

Over-Center Adjustment
Pitman Shaft

1. Using the Pitman Arm Puller

tool No. J–29107 or equivalent, press the pitman arm from the power steering gear.
2. Align the flat on the stub shaft parallel with the side cover.
3. From the rear of the power steering gear, align the pitman arm block tooth with the center of the over-center preload adjuster.
4. Loosen the pitman arm adjuster lock nut. Back off the pitman arm preload adjuster until it stops and rotate it inward 1 full turn.
5. Using an inch lb. torque wrench and socket on the stub, record the torque reading (pressure required to move the shaft).
6. Using the torque reading, add 6–10 inch lbs. to it; tighten the preload adjuster to acquire the new calculated reading.
7. After the new torque reading is achieved, maintain the preload adjuster from turning and torque the preload adjuster lock nut to 20 ft. lbs.
8. Install the power steering gear into the vehicle. Torque the pitman arm-to-power steering gear nut to 185 ft. lbs. Refill the power steering pump reservoir. Bleed the power steering system.

Power Steering Pump

REMOVAL & INSTALLATION

3.8L V6 Engines

1. Disconnect the negative terminal from the battery.
2. Remove the serpentine drive belt, the alternator bolts and the alternator.

3. Raise and support the front of the vehicle and on jackstands.
4. Disconnect and plug the pressure and return lines from the pump.
5. Remove the rear pump adjustment bracket-to-pump nut.
6. Remove the alternator adjustment bracket and support brace.
7. Remove the rear pump adjustment bracket and the pump assembly.
8. Remove the front pump adjustment bracket and the pulley.
9. To install, reverse the removal procedures. Refill the power steering pump reservoir. Bleed the power steering system.

4.1L and 4.5L V8 Engines

1. Disconnect the negative terminal from the battery.
2. Remove the serpentine drive belt, the power steering pump pulley.
3. Disconnect and plug the high pressure and feed lines from the pump.
4. Remove the power steering pump-to-bracket bolts and the pump.
5. To install, reverse the removal procedures. Torque the power steering pump-to-bracket bolts to 30 ft. lbs. Refill the power steering pump reservoir. Bleed the power steering system.

4.3L V6 Diesel

1. Disconnect the negative terminal from the battery. Raise and support the front of the vehicle on jackstands.
2. Remove the engine splash shield, the crankshaft pulley and the engine shock absorber.
3. Disconnect the reservoir hose from the power steering pump and drain the reservoir.
4. Remove the high pressure hose support. Disconnect and plug the high pressure hose.
5. Remove the power steering pump bracket-to-engine bolts and the pump assembly along with its brackets.
6. To install, reverse the removal procedures. Refill the power steering pump reservoir. Bleed the power steering system and check for leaks.

BELT ADJUSTMENT

Deflection Method

1. Loosen the power steering pump adjusting bolt.
2. Move the pump until the drive belt deflection is 3/8–1/2 in. on the longest span between the pulleys.
3. Retorque the power steering pump bolts.

Gauge Method

1. Using the Belt Tension Gauge tool No. J–23600-B, BT-33-73F or equivalent, attach it to the drive belt

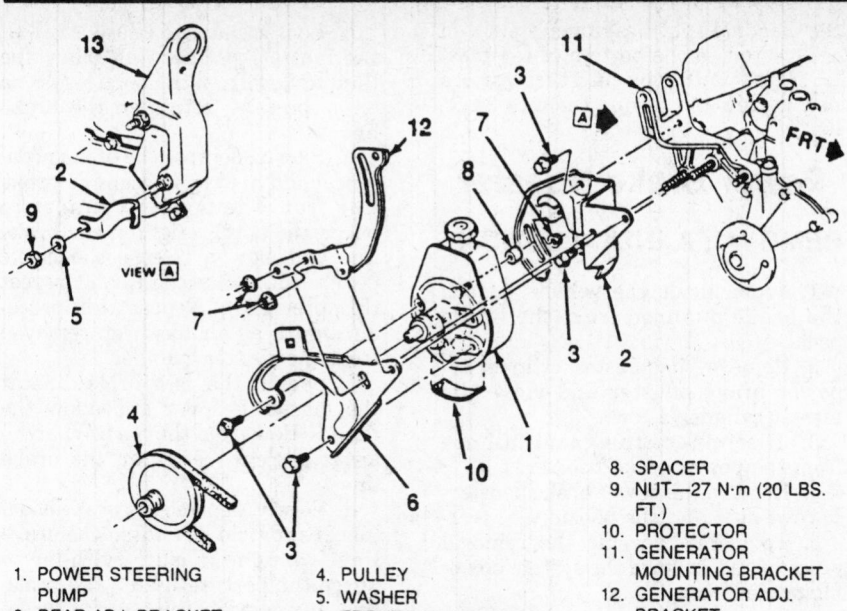

1. POWER STEERING PUMP
2. REAR ADJ. BRACKET
3. BOLT—50 N·m (37 LBS. FT.)
4. PULLEY
5. WASHER
6. FRONT ADJ. BRACKET
7. NUT—50 N·m (37 LBS. FT.)
8. SPACER
9. NUT—27 N·m (20 LBS. FT.)
10. PROTECTOR
11. GENERATOR MOUNTING BRACKET
12. GENERATOR ADJ. BRACKET
13. ENGINE LIFT BRACKET & SHIELD

Exploded view of the power steering pump assembly—3.8L engine

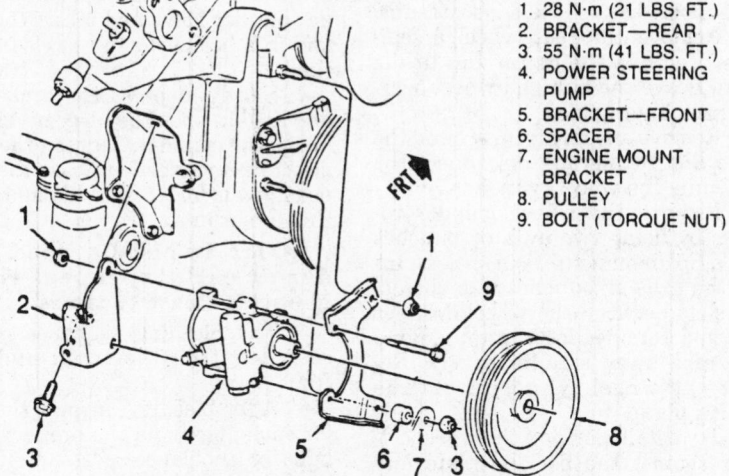

1. 28 N·m (21 LBS. FT.)
2. BRACKET—REAR
3. 55 N·m (41 LBS. FT.)
4. POWER STEERING PUMP
5. BRACKET—FRONT
6. SPACER
7. ENGINE MOUNT BRACKET
8. PULLEY
9. BOLT (TORQUE NUT)

Power steering pump mounting—4.3L V6 (diesel)

on the longest span between the pulleys.

2. The belt tension should be 170 lbs. (new) or 90 lbs. (used).

3. If necessary, loosen the power steering pump bolts and adjust the belt to the correct tension.

SYSTEM BLEEDING

1. Fill the fluid reservoir.

2. Let the fluid stand undisturbed for 2 minutes, crank the engine for about two seconds. Refill the reservoir, if necessary.

3. Repeat Steps 1 and 2 above until the fluid level remains constant after cranking the engine.

4. Raise and support the front of the vehicle (until the wheels are off the ground). Start the engine and increase the engine speed to about 1500 rpm.

5. Turn the wheels lightly against the stops to the left and right, checking the fluid level and refilling (if necessary).

Tie Rod Ends

REMOVAL & INSTALLATION

1. Loosen the jam nut on the steering rack (inner tie rod).

2. Remove the cotter pin and nut from the outer tie rod end. Using the Ball Joint Puller tool No. J–6627, BT–7101 or equivalent, press the tie rod end from the steering knuckle.

3. Unscrew the tie rod end, counting the number of turns.

4. To install, screw the tie rod end onto the steering rack (inner tie rod) the same number of turns as counted for removal. This will give approximately correct toe.

5. To complete the installation, use a new cotter pin and reverse the removal procedures. Torque the tie rod end-to-steering knuckle nut to 30 ft. lbs. and the tie rod end-to-adjuster tube clamp nut to 14 ft. lbs. Check and/or adjust the toe.

BRAKES

NOTE: For all brake system repair service procedures not detailed below, please refer to "Brakes" in the Unit Repair section.

Master Cylinder

REMOVAL & INSTALLATION

Diagonal Split System

1. Disconnect the electrical connector from the level sensor unit.

2. Disconnect and plug hydraulic lines from the master cylinder. Using a catch pan drain the fluid from the master cylinder.

3. If not equipped with a power brake booster, perform the following procedures:

   a. Remove the push rod from the brake pedal.

   b. Remove the master cylinder-to-cowl nuts and the master cylinder.

4. If equipped with a power brake booster, remove the master cylinder-to-power brake booster nuts and the master cylinder.

5. To install, reverse the removal procedures. Refill the master cylinder with clean brake fluid. Bleed the brake system.

Anti-Lock System

— CAUTION —

The hydraulic accumulator is under pressure and MUST BE depressurized before attempting to dismantle the system.

1. Disconnect the negative terminal from the battery.

2. Firmly apply the parking brake.

3. Using at least 50 lbs. pressure on the brake pedal, depress the pedal at least 20 times; a noticable change in pedal pressure will be noticed when the accumulator is discharged.

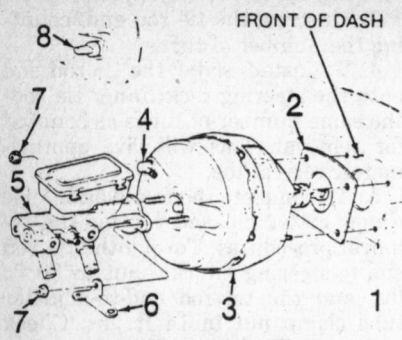

FRONT OF DASH

1. NUT (20 N·m/14 FT. LB.)
2. SEAL
3. POWER BOOSTER
4. CHECK VALVE
5. MASTER CYLINDER
6. VACUUM SWITCH
   BRACKET (DIESEL)
7. NUT (30 N·m/22 FT. LB.)
8. VACUUM SWITCH (GAS)

Typical master cylinder and power booster mounting

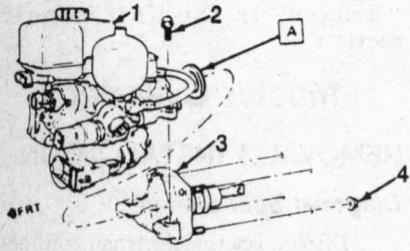

1. Hydraulic unit
2. Bolt—37 ft. lbs.
3. Pushrod assembly
4. Nut—177 inch lbs.
5. Seal ring

View of the anti-lock hydraulic brake unit

4. Disconnect the electrical connectors from the hydraulic brake unit.

5. Remove the pump-to-hydraulic unit bolt and move the unit aside to gain access to the hydraulic lines.

6. Using a back-up wrench, disconnect the hydraulic lines from the hydraulic unit.

7. From under the dash, disconnect the pushrod from the brake pedal.

8. Move the dust boot forward, past the pushrod hex and unscrew the two pushrod halves.

9. Remove the hydraulic unit-to-pushrod bracket bolts and separate the hydraulic unit from the pushrod bracket; half of the pushrod will remain locked in the hydraulic unit.

10. Disassemble the master cylinder from the hydraulic unit.

11. To install, assemble the master cylinder to the hydraulic unit and reverse the removal procedures. Torque the hydraulic unit-to-pushrod bracket bolts to 37 ft. lbs. Bleed the brake system.

Proportioning Valve

Two proportioning valves are used on the diagonal split braking system and are located on the bottom of the master cylinder. If replacing them, use a new O-ring and torque them to 24 ft. lbs.

Power Brake Booster

REMOVAL & INSTALLATION

1. From inside the vehicle, detach the brake pushrod from the brake pedal.

2. Remove the master cylinder-to-power brake booster and move the master cylinder aside.

3. Disconnect the vacuum hose from the power brake booster.

4. Remove the power brake booster-to-cowl nuts and the booster.

5. To install, reverse the removal procedures. Perform the system bleeding procedure.

Wheel Cylinder

REMOVAL & INSTALLATION

1. Loosen the wheel lug nuts. Raise and support the vehicle on jackstands.

2. Remove the rear wheel assemblies. Remove the drum and brake shoes. Leave the hub and wheel bearing assembly in place.

3. Remove any dirt from around the brake line fitting and disconnect the brake line the wheel cylinder.

4. Remove the wheel cylinder retainer by using two awls or punches with a tip diameter of ⅛ in. or less. Insert the awls or punches into the access slots between the wheel cylinder pilot and retainer locking tabs. Bend both tabs away simultaneously. Remove the wheel cylinder from the backing plate.

5. To install, position the wheel cylinder against the backing plate and hold it in place with a wooden block between the wheel cylinder and the hub and bearing assembly.

6. Install a new retainer over the wheel cylinder abutment on the rear of the backing plate by pressing it into place with a 1⅛ in. 12 point socket and an extension.

7. Install a new bleeder screw into the wheel cylinder. Install the brake line and tighten to 10–15 ft. lbs.

8. To complete the installation, reverse the removal procedures. Bleed the brake system.

SYSTEM BLEEDING
Diagonal Split System

1. Check and/or refill the master cylinder reservoir.

2. If the master cylinder has air in it, perform the following procedures:

a. Loosen the front brake line at the master cylinder and allow the fluid to flow from the port. When no air is present, retighten the brake line.

b. Slowly, depress the brake pedal (once) and hold it. Loosen the brake line from the master cylinder to purge the port, retighten the brake line and slowly, release the brake pedal. Wait 15 seconds and repeat this procedure. Repeat this procedure until all air has been removed from the master cylinder.

c. Loosen the rear brake line at the master cylinder and allow the fluid to flow from the port. When no air is present, retighten the brake line.

d. Slowly, depress the brake pedal (once) and hold it. Loosen the brake line from the master cylinder to purge the port, retighten the brake line and slowly, release the brake pedal. Wait 15 seconds and repeat this procedure. Repeat this procedure until all air has been removed from the master cylinder.

3. Using a transparent vinyl tube, connect it to the right rear wheel cylinder bleeder valve and insert the other end in a beaker ½ full of clean brake fluid.

4. Slowly, depress the brake pedal and hold it, open the bleeder valve and purge the cylinder. Tighten the bleeder screw and slowly release the brake pedal; wait for 15 seconds and repeat this procedure.

NOTE: To bleed a wheel cylinder or caliper, repeat the sequence at least 10 times.

5. The bleeding sequence is right rear, left front, left rear and right front.

6. After bleeding, inspect the pedal for sponginess and the brake warning light for unbalanced pressure; if either of the conditions exist, repeat the bleeding procedure.

Anti-Lock System
FRONT BRAKES

1. Check and/or refill the master cylinder reservoir.

2. Using a transparent vinyl tube, connect it to the right rear wheel cylinder bleeder valve and insert the other end in a beaker ½ full of clean brake fluid.

3. Slowly, depress the brake pedal and hold it, open the bleeder valve and purge the cylinder. Tighten the bleeder screw and slowly release the brake pedal; wait for 15 seconds and repeat this procedure.

NOTE: To bleed a wheel cylinder or caliper, repeat the sequence at least 10 times.

4. The bleeding sequence is either front caliper.

5. After bleeding, inspect the pedal for sponginess and the brake warning light for unbalanced pressure; if either of the conditions exist, repeat the bleeding procedure.

REAR BRAKES

1. Check and/or refill the master cylinder reservoir.

2. Turn the ignition switch **ON** and allow the system to charge.

NOTE: The pump will turn off when the system is charged.

3. Using a transparent vinyl tube, connect it to a rear wheel bleeder valve and insert the other end in a beaker ½ full of clean brake fluid.

4. Open the bleeder valve and slightly depress the brake pedal for at least 10 seconds or until air is removed from the brake system.

5. Repeat the bleeding procedure for the other rear wheel.

6. After bleeding, inspect the pedal for sponginess and the brake warning light for unbalanced pressure; if either of the conditions exist, repeat the bleeding procedure.

Parking Brake Cable

ADJUSTMENT

1. Depress the parking brake pedal 3 ratchet clicks.

2. Raise and support the rear of the vehicle on jackstands.

3. Using multi-purpose grease, lubricate the equalizer nut groove.

4. Tighten the adjusting nut until the right rear wheel can just be turned rearward with both hands but is locked when forward rotation is attempted.

5. With the mechanisms totally disengaged, both rear wheels should turn freely in either direction with no brake drag.

NOTE: Do not adjust the parking brake cable to tight for brake drag may result.

6. Lower the vehicle.

REMOVAL & INSTALLATION

Front Cable

1. Raise and support the vehicle on jackstands.

2. Loosen the equalizer assembly. Separate the cable from the equalizer assembly.

3. From under the body, remove the cable casing-to-chassis nut.

4. From the control assembly, separate the cable casing and cable.

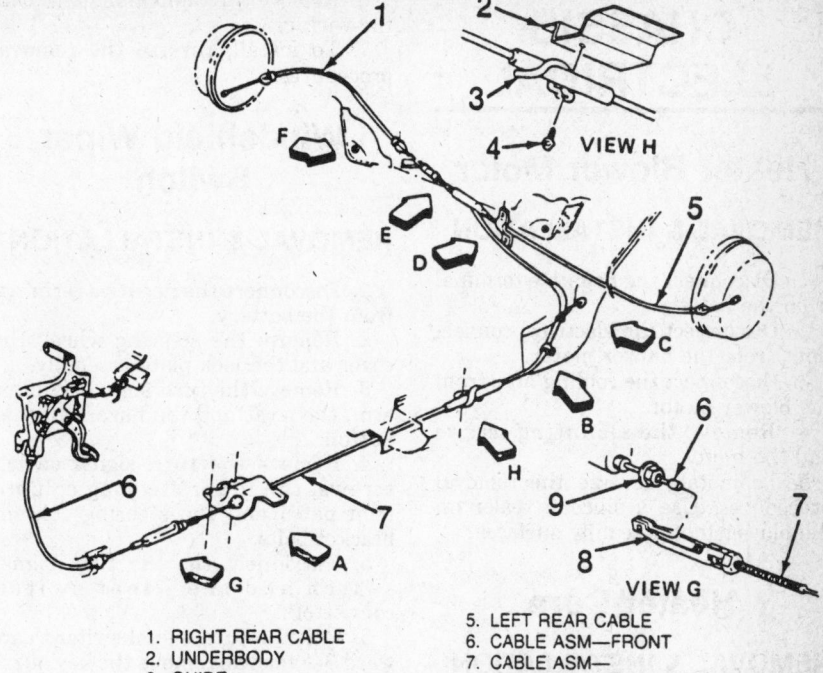

1. RIGHT REAR CABLE
2. UNDERBODY
3. GUIDE
4. BOLT/SCREW 38 N·m (28 FT. LB.)
5. LEFT REAR CABLE
6. CABLE ASM—FRONT
7. CABLE ASM—INTERMEDIATE.
8. EQUALIZER ASM
9. NUT

Parking brake cable routing

5. Using multi-purpose grease, lubricate the cable.

6. To install, reverse the removal procedures. Torque the cable casing-to-chassis nut to 22 ft. lbs. Adjust the parking brake assembly.

Intermediate Cable

1. Raise and support the vehicle on jackstands.

2. Loosen the equalizer assembly and disconnect the intermediate cable from it.

3. Remove the intermediate cable housing from the front bracket, the clip and the underbody guide.

4. Disconnect the cable from the rear equalizer assembly.

5. Using multi-purpose grease, lubricate the cable.

6. To install, reverse the removal procedures. Adjust the parking brake assembly.

Rear Cables

1. Raise and support the vehicle on jackstands.

2. Loosen the equalizer assembly and disconnect the intermediate cable from it.

3. Remove the wheel/tire assembly and the brake drum.

4. Using a small pry bar, insert it between the brake shoe and the top of the brake adjuster bracket. Push the

bracket forward and release the top adjuster bracket rod.

5. Remove the rear hold-down spring, the actuator lever and the lever return spring, the adjuster screw spring and the top rear brake shoe spring.

6. Disconnect the parking brake cable from the parking brake lever.

7. Depress the conduit fitting retaining tangs and the conduit fitting from the backing plate.

8. To replace the left rear cable, perform the following procedures:

a. Back off the equalizer nut and disconnect the left cable from the equalizer.

b. Depress the conduit fitting retaining tangs and the conduit fitting from the axle bracket.

c. Remove the conduit fitting-to-bracket screws and the conduit fitting.

d. To install, reverse the removal procedures.

9. To replace the left rear cable, perform the following procedures:

a. Disconnect the cable end button on the connector.

b. Depress the conduit fitting retaining tangs and the conduit fitting from the axle bracket.

c. To install, reverse the removal procedures.

10. To complete the installation, reverse the removal procedures. Torque the conduit fitting-to-underbody bracket screws to 84 ft. lbs.

CHASSIS ELECTRICAL

Heater Blower Motor

REMOVAL & INSTALLATION

1. Disconnect the negative terminal from the battery.
2. Disconnect the electrical connections from the blower motor.
3. Disconnect the cooling hose from the blower motor.
4. Remove the mounting screws and the motor.
5. To install, reverse the removal procedures. Use a silicone sealer on the blower motor sealing surfaces.

Heater Core

REMOVAL & INSTALLATION

——— CAUTION ———
Make sure the engine is cool before attempting this procedure.

1. Drain the cooling system to a level below the heater core.
2. Disconnect and plug the heater hoses from the heater core.
3. Remove the instrument panel.
4. Remove the four defroster nozzle screws from the cowl, the case screw and the nozzle.
5. Disconnect the vacuum hoses.
6. Disconnect the electrical connector from the programmer.
7. From under the hood, remove the heater case-to-cowl screws.
8. From under the instrument panel, remove the heater case-to-cowl screw.
9. Remove the heater case.
10. Remove the four case-to-core screws and the core.
11. To install, reverse the removal procedures. Refill and bleed the cooling system.

Radio

REMOVAL & INSTALLATION

1. Disconnect the negative terminal from the battery.
2. Remove the screws from the top of the instrument panel center insert.
3. Remove the radio knobs and the insert.
4. Remove the rear window defogger switch to gain access to the left side mounting screw (if equipped).
5. Remove the mounting screws.

6. Remove the radio and disconnect the wiring.
7. To install, reverse the removal procedures.

Windshield Wiper Switch

REMOVAL & INSTALLATION

1. Disconnect the negative terminal from the battery.
2. Remove the steering wheel, the cover and the lock plate assembly.
3. Remove the turn signal actuator arm, the lever and the hazard flasher button.
4. Remove the turn signal switch screws, the lower steering column trim panel and the steering column bracket bolts.
5. Disconnect the the turn signal switch and the wiper switch connectors.
6. Pull the turn signal switch rearward 6–8 inches, remove the key buzzer switch and cylinder lock.
7. Remove and pull the steering column housing rearward. Remove the housing cover screw.
8. Remove the wiper switch pivot and the switch.
9. To install, reverse the removal procedure.

Windshield Wiper Motor

REMOVAL & INSTALLATION

1. Remove the cowl screen or grille.
2. Loosen the linkage drive link-to-crankarm attaching nuts and the link from the arm.
3. Disconnect the wiring and washer hoses.
4. Remove the three motor-to-chassis screws, guide the crankarm through the hole in the dash and remove the motor.
5. To install, reverse the removal procedures.

Instrument Cluster

REMOVAL & INSTALLATION

Standard

1. Disconnect the negative terminal from the battery.
2. Remove the left sound insulator. Lower the steering column (if necessary) in order to gain working clearance.
3. If equipped with Quartz Clusters, removal of the steering column

trim cover may be required in order to remove the shift indicator clip.
4. Remove the instrument panel trim in order to gain access to the instrument panel retaining bolts. Remove the instrument panel retaining bolts.
5. Pull the instrument panel forward. Label and disconnect all the electrical connectors.
6. Remove the instrument panel assembly from the vehicle.
7. To install, reverse the removal procedures. Be sure the shift indicator is properly aligned.

Digital

1. Disconnect the negative terminal from the battery. Remove the defroster grille.
2. Remove the instrument panel top cover-to-instrument panel screws.
3. If equipped with a twilight sentinel, pop up the photocell retainer and turn the photocell counterclockwise in the retainer and pull it down-and-out.
4. Slide the instrument panel top cover out far enough to disconnect the aspirator hose, electrical connector to the in-car sensor and the electrical connector to the electro-luminescent inverter.
5. Remove the instrument panel top cover from the instrument panel. If equipped with Quartz Electronic Speedometer clusters, remove the steering column trim cover, so the shift indicator can be removed.
6. Remove the instrument cluster-to-instrument panel carrier screws. Pull the cluster housing assembly straight out; this will separate the electrical connectors from the cluster.

NOTE: It may be helpful to tilt the wheel all the way down and pull the gear select lever to low, when removing the cluster.

7. To install, reverse the removal procedures.

Headlight Switch

REMOVAL & INSTALLATION

1. Disconnect negative terminal from the battery. Remove the steering column lower cover or the instrument panel trim plate covering the headlamp switch, if equipped with a rocker-type headlamp switch.
2. Disconnect the electrical harness retainer below headlight switch assembly. On Buick models, the switch connector is integral with the instrument panel; simply pull the switch outward to disconnect it.
3. On knob-type switches, depress spring loaded release button on top of

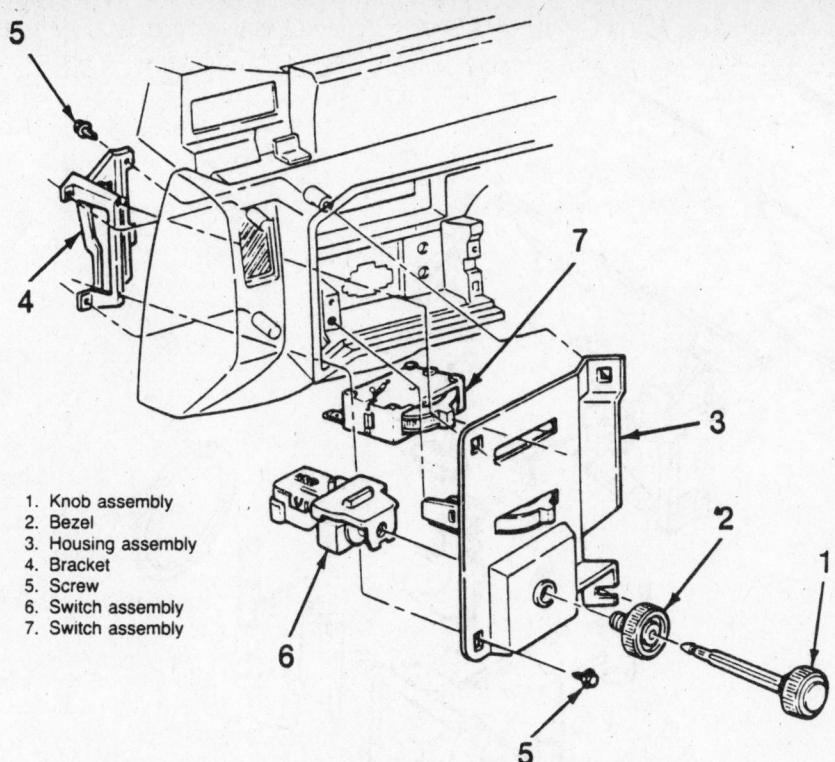

1. Knob assembly
2. Bezel
3. Housing assembly
4. Bracket
5. Screw
6. Switch assembly
7. Switch assembly

Cadillac knob type headlamp switch mounting

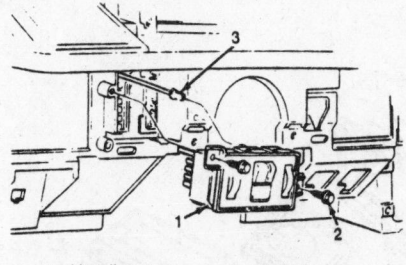

1. Headlamp switch
2. Fully driven, seated and not stripped
3. Plug fiber optic into rear of switch

Oldsmobile rocker type headlamp switch mounting—Buick similar

headlight switch and remove switch, knob and rod assembly (switch **ON**).

4. Remove screw with ground wire at bottom of switch housing and any other mounting screws.

5. Pull assembly down and rearward, disconnect wiring harness connectors, bulb(s) and remove assembly.

6. To install, reverse the removal procedures.

Stoplight Switch

REMOVAL & INSTALLATION

1. Disconnect the negative terminal from the battery.

2. Loosen the tubular clip from the stoplight switch assembly.

3. Disconnect the electrical connector from the rear of the switch assembly.

4. Remove the stoplight switch from the vehicle.

5. To install, reverse the removal procedures.

ADJUSTMENT

1. Install the switch into the tubular clip until the switch assembly seats itself on the tubular clip.

2. Pull the brake pedal rearward against the pedal stop.

3. The switch will be moved in the tubular clip which will adjust itself properly.

NOTE: Certain 1986–88 models may light up the brake warning light for no apparent reason. After careful inspection of the braking system and no problem is found, the problem may be found in the parking brake mechanism. A small rubber stop may have been lost from the braking mechanism. This allows the brake switch to be compressed, shorting it and causing the brake warning light to operate. If this problem is found, replace the rubber stop with part number 25527682 and install a new switch assembly in the mechanism.

Fuses and Circuit Breakers

LOCATION

The fuse block is located under the instrument panel above the headlight dimmer floor switch. Fuse holders are labeled as to their service and the correct amperage. Always replace blown fuses with new ones of the correct amperage. Otherwise electrical overloads and possible wiring damage will result.

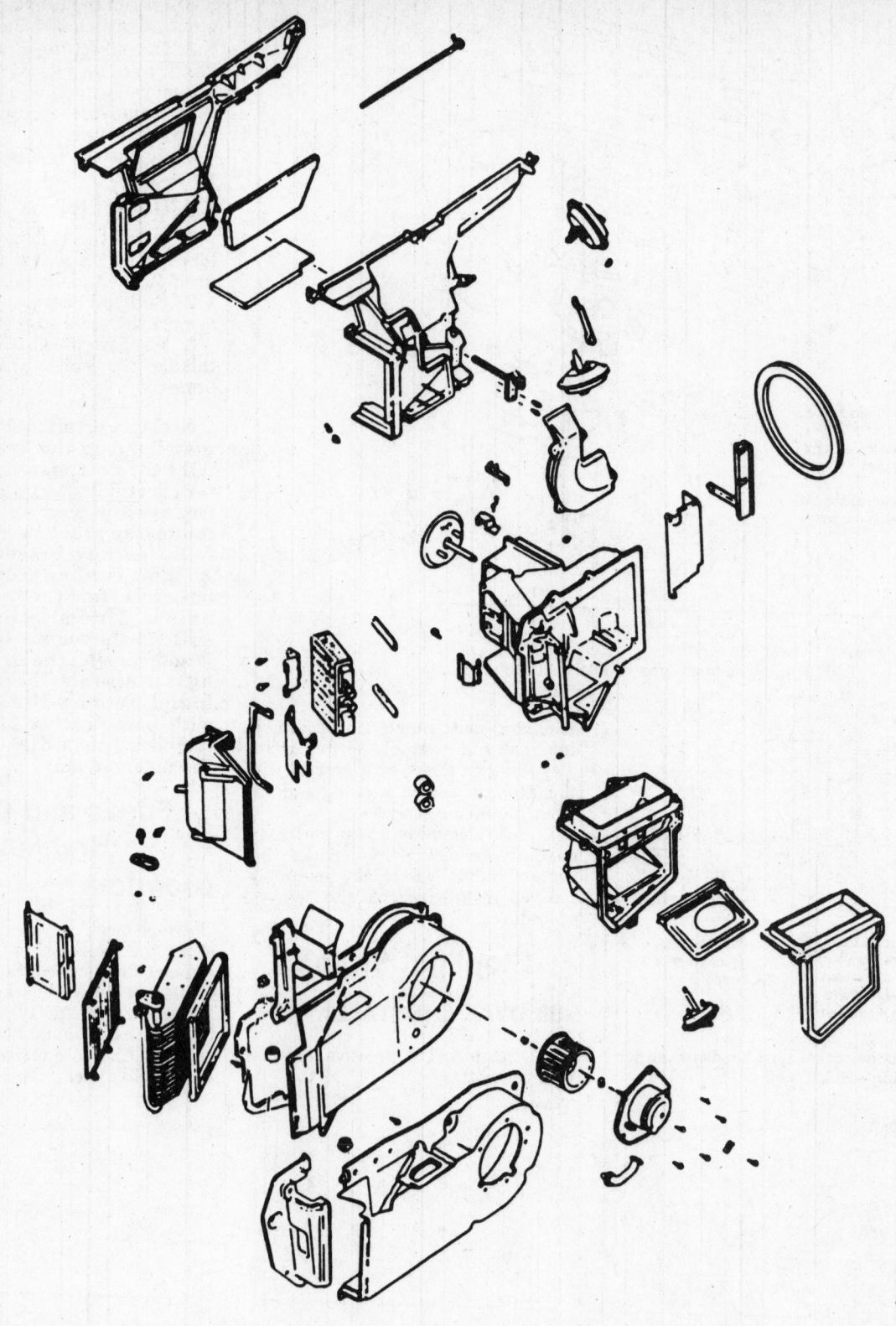

Heater assembly

GM "E, K, V, Z" Body

Front Wheel Drive

"E" Body—Buick Riviera, Cadillac Eldorado, Oldsmobile Tornado, Oldsmobile Trofeo
"K" Body—Cadillac Seville
"V" Body—Cadillac Allante
"Z" Body—Buick Reatta

SERIAL NUMBER IDENTIFICATION

VEHICLE IDENTIFICATION CHART

It is important for servicing and ordering parts to be certain of the vehicle and engine identification. The VIN (vehicle identification number) is a 17 digit number visible through the windshield on the driver's side of the dash and contains the vehicle and engine identification codes. The tenth digit indicates model year and the eighth digit indicates engine code. It can be interpreted as follows:

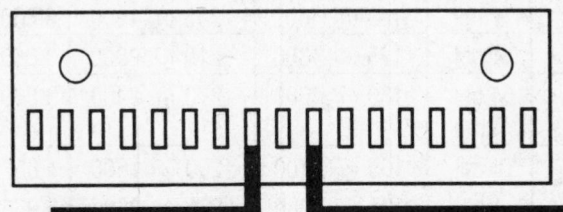

Engine Code						Model Year	
Code	Cu. In.	Liters	Cyl.	Fuel Sys.	Eng. Mfg.	Code	Year
3 ('82)	231	3.8	6	4 bbl①	Buick	C	1982
9 ('83-'85)	231	3.8	6	SFI①	Buick	D	1983
3 ('86-'87)	231	3.8	6	SFI	Buick	E	1984
8 ('82-'87)	250	4.1	8	DFI	Cadillac	F	1985
7 ('87-'89)	250	4.1	8	MFI	Cadillac	G	1986
4 ('82-'85)	252	4.1	6	4 bbl	Buick	H	1987
Y ('82-'85)	307	5.0	8	4 bbl	Oldsmobile	J	1988
N ('82-'86)	350	5.7	8	Diesel	Oldsmobile	K	1989
5 ('88-'89)	273	4.5	8	DFI	Cadillac		
C ('88-'89)	231	3.8	6	SFI	Buick		

DFI Digital Fuel Injection
SFI Sequential Fuel Injection
MFI Multi-Port Fuel Injection
① Turbo

GENERAL ENGINE SPECIFICATIONS

Year	VIN	No. Cylinder Displacement cu. in. (liter)	Fuel System Type	Net Horsepower @ rpm	Net Torque @ rpm (ft.lbs.)	Bore × Stroke (in.)	Compression Ratio	Oil Pressure @ rpm
TORONADO								
1982	4	6-252 (4.1)	4 bbl	125 @ 4000	205 @ 2000	3.965 × 3.400	8.0:1	37 @ 2400
	Y	8-307 (5.0)	4 bbl	148 @ 3800	250 @ 3800	3.800 × 3.385	8.0:1	40 @ 1500
	N	8-350 (5.7)	Diesel	125 @ 3600	225 @ 1600	4.057 × 3.385	22.5:1	38 @ 1500
1983	4	6-252 (4.1)	4 bbl	125 @ 4000	205 @ 2000	3.965 × 3.400	8.0:1	37 @ 2400
	Y	8-307 (5.0)	4 bbl	140 @ 3600	240 @ 1600	3.800 × 3.385	8.0:1	40 @ 1500
	N	8-350 (5.7)	Diesel	105 @ 3200	200 @ 1600	4.057 × 3.385	22.5:1	38 @ 1500
1984	4	6-252 (4.1)	4 bbl	125 @ 4000	205 @ 2000	3.965 × 3.400	8.0:1	37 @ 2400
	Y	8-307 (5.0)	4 bbl	140 @ 3600	240 @ 1600	3.800 × 3.385	8.0:1	40 @ 1500
	N	8-350 (5.7)	Diesel	105 @ 3200	200 @ 1600	4.057 × 3.385	22.5:1	38 @ 1500
1985	Y	8-307 (5.0)	4 bbl	140 @ 3600	240 @ 1600	3.800 × 3.385	8.0:1	40 @ 1500
	N	8-350 (5.7)	Diesel	105 @ 3200	200 @ 1600	4.057 × 3.385	22.5:1	38 @ 1500
1986	3	6-231 (3.8)	SFI	140 @ 4400	200 @ 2000	3.800 × 3.400	8.5:1	37 @ 2400
1987	3	6-231 (3.8)	SFI	140 @ 4400	200 @ 2000	3.800 × 3.400	8.5:1	37 @ 2400
1988-89	3	6-231 (3.8)	SFI	165 @ 5200	210 @ 2000	3.800 × 3.400	8.5:1	37 @ 2400
RIVIERA								
1982	Y	8-307 (5.0)	4 bbl	140 @ 3600	245 @ 1600	3.800 × 3.385	8.0:1	37 @ 1500
	4	6-252 (4.1)	4 bbl	125 @ 3800	210 @ 2000	3.965 × 3.400	8.0:1	35 @ 2000
	3	6-231 (3.8)	4 bbl Turbo	180 @ 4000	270 @ 2400	3.800 × 3.400	8.0:1	37 @ 2600
	N	8-350 (5.7)	Diesel	105 @ 3200	200 @ 1600	4.057 × 3.385	22.5:1	38 @ 1500
1983	4	6-252 (4.1)	4 bbl	125 @ 4000	205 @ 2000	3.965 × 3.400	8.0:1	35 @ 2000
	Y	8-307 (5.0)	4 bbl	140 @ 3600	240 @ 1600	3.800 × 3.385	8.0:1	37 @ 1500
	N	8-350 (5.7)	Diesel	105 @ 3200	200 @ 1600	4.057 × 3.385	22.5:1	38 @ 1500
	9	6-231 (3.8)	SFI Turbo	190 @ 4000	300 @ 2400	3.800 × 3.400	8.0:1	37 @ 2600
1984	4	6-252 (4.1)	4 bbl	125 @ 4000	205 @ 2000	3.965 × 3.400	8.0:1	35 @ 2000
	Y	8-307 (5.0)	4 bbl	140 @ 3600	240 @ 1600	3.800 × 3.385	8.0:1	37 @ 1500
	N	8-350 (5.7)	Diesel	105 @ 3200	200 @ 1600	4.057 × 3.385	22.5:1	38 @ 1500
	9	6-231 (3.8)	SFI Turbo	190 @ 4000	300 @ 2400	3.800 × 3.400	8.0:1	37 @ 2600
1985	4	6-252 (4.1)	4 bbl	125 @ 4000	205 @ 2000	3.965 × 3.400	8.0:1	35 @ 2000
	Y	8-307 (5.0)	4 bbl	140 @ 3600	240 @ 3600	3.800 × 3.385	8.0:1	37 @ 1500
	9	6-231 (3.8)	SFI Turbo	190 @ 4000	300 @ 2400	3.800 × 3.400	8.0:1	37 @ 2600
1986	3	6-231 (3.8)	SFI	140 @ 4400	200 @ 2000	3.800 × 3.400	8.5:1	37 @ 2400
1987	3	6-231 (3.8)	SFI	140 @ 4400	200 @ 2000	3.800 × 3.400	8.5:1	37 @ 2400
1988-89	3	6-231 (3.8)	SFI	165 @ 5200	210 @ 2000	3.800 × 3.400	8.5:1	37 @ 2400

GENERAL ENGINE SPECIFICATIONS

Year	VIN	No. Cylinder Displacement cu. in. (liter)	Fuel System Type	Net Horsepower @ rpm	Net Torque @ rpm (ft.lbs.)	Bore × Stroke (in.)	Compression Ratio	Oil Pressure @ rpm
SEVILLE/ELDORADO								
1982	8	8-250 (4.1)	DFI	135 @ 4200	190 @ 2000	3.465 × 3.307	8.5:1	40 @ 1500
	N	8-350 (5.7)	Diesel	105 @ 3200	205 @ 1600	4.057 × 3.385	22.5:1	40 @ 2000
	4	6-252 (4.1)	4 bbl	125 @ 3800	210 @ 2000	3.965 × 3.400	8.0:1	35 @ 2000
1983	8	8-250 (4.1)	DFI	135 @ 4200	180 @ 2000	3.465 × 3.307	8.5:1	40 @ 1500
	N	8-350 (5.7)	Diesel	105 @ 3200	205 @ 1600	4.057 × 3.385	22.5:1	35 @ 2000
1984	8	8-250 (4.10)	DFI	135 @ 4200	190 @ 2000	3.465 × 3.307	8.5:1	40 @ 1500
	N	8-350 (5.7)	Diesel	105 @ 3200	205 @ 1600	4.057 × 3.385	22.5:1	35 @ 2000
1985	8	8-250 (4.1)	DFI	135 @ 4200	200 @ 2000	3.465 × 3.307	8.5:1	35 @ 2000
	N	8-350 (5.7)	Diesel	105 @ 3200	205 @ 1600	4.057 × 3.385	22.5:1	35 @ 2000
1986	8	8-250 (4.1)	DFI	130 @ 4200	200 @ 2200	3.465 × 3.307	9.0:1	40 @ 1500
1987	8	8-250 (4.1)	DFI	130 @ 4200	200 @ 2200	3.465 × 3.310	9.0:1	37 @ 1500
1988-89	5	8-273 (4.5)	DFI	155 @ 4200	240 @ 2800	3.620 × 3.310	9.0:1	37 @ 1500
REATTA								
1988-89	C	8-231 (3.8)	SFI	165 @ 5200	210 @ 2000	3.800 × 4.060	8.5:1	37 @ 2400
ALLANTE								
1987	7	8-250 (4.1)	MFI	170 @ 4300	235 @ 3200	3.460 × 3.310	8.5:1	37 @ 1500
1988-89	7	8-250 (4.1)	MFI	170 @ 4300	235 @ 3200	3.460 × 3.310	8.5:1	37 @ 1500

NOTE: Horsepower and torque are SAE net figures. They are measured at the rear of the transmission with all accessories installed and operating. Since the figures vary when a given engine is installed in different models, some are representative, rather than exact.

PFI Port Fuel Injection
SFI Sequential Fuel Injection
DFI Digital Fuel Injection
MFI Multi-Port Fuel Injection
NA Not available

GASOLINE ENGINE TUNE-UP SPECIFICATIONS

Year	VIN	No. Cylinder Displacement cu. in. (liter)	Spark Plugs Type	Spark Plugs Gap (in.)	Ignition Timing (deg.) MT	Ignition Timing (deg.) AT	Compression Pressure (psi)	Fuel Pump (psi)	Idle Speed (rpm) MT	Idle Speed (rpm) AT	Valve Clearance In.	Valve Clearance Ex.
TORONADO												
1982	4	6-252 (4.1)	R–45TS8	0.080	—	15B	100	6–7.5	—	550④	①	①
	Y	8-307 (5.0)	R–46SX	0.080	—	15B②	100	6–7.5	—	550③	①	①
1983	4	6-252 (4.1)	R–45TS8	0.080	—	15B	100	6–7.5	—	470④	①	①
	Y	8-307 (5.0)	R–46SX	0.080	—	20B②	100	6–7.5	—	550③	①	①
1984	4	6-252 (4.1)	R–45TS8	0.080	—	15B	100	6–7.5	—	450④	①	①
	Y	8-307 (5.0)	R–46SX	0.080	—	20B②	100	6–7.5	—	550③	①	①
1985	Y	8-307 (5.0)	FR3LS6	0.060	—	20B②	100	6–7.5	—	550③	①	①
1986	3	6-231 (3.8)	R44LTS	0.045	—	⑤	100	38	—	500	①	①
1987	3	6-231 (3.8)	R44LTS	0.045	—	⑤	100	38	—	500	①	①
1988	C	6-231 (3.8)	R44LTS6	0.060	—	⑤	—	27–36	—	⑤	Hyd.	Hyd.
1989		SEE UNDERHOOD SPECIFICATIONS STICKER										

GASOLINE ENGINE TUNE-UP SPECIFICATIONS

Year	VIN	No. Cylinder Displacement cu. in. (liter)	Spark Plugs Type	Gap (in.)	Ignition Timing (deg.) MT	AT	Compression Pressure (psi)	Fuel Pump (psi)	Idle Speed (rpm) MT	AT	Valve Clearance In.	Ex.
RIVIERA												
1982	Y	8-307 (5.0)	R–46SX	0.080	—	15B②	100	6–7.5	—	550③	①	①
	4	6-252 (4.1)	R–45TS8	0.080	—	15B	100	6–7.5	—	550④	①	①
	3	6-231 (3.8)	R–45TS	0.040	—	15B	100	6–7.5	—	450④	①	①
1983	4	6-252 (4.1)	R–45TS8	0.080	—	15B	100	6–7.5	—	470④	①	①
	Y	8-307 (5.0)	R–46SX	0.080	—	20B②	100	6–7.5	—	550③	①	①
	9	6-231 (3.8)	R–45TS	0.045	—	⑥	100	28–50	—	475⑦	①	①
1984	4	6-252 (4.1)	R–45TSB	0.080	—	15B	100	6–7.5	—	450④	①	①
	Y	8-307 (5.0)	R–46SX	0.080	—	20B②	100	6–7.5	—	550④	①	①
	9	6-231 (3.8)	R–45TSX	0.045	—	⑥	100	28–50	—	475⑦	①	①
1985	4	6-252 (4.1)	R–45TS8	0.080	—	15B	100	6–7.5	—	450④	①	①
	Y	8-307 (5.0)	FR3LS6	0.060	—	20B②	100	6–7.5	—	550③	①	①
	9	6-231 (3.8)	R–45TSX	0.060	—	⑤	100	28–50	—	475⑦	①	①
1986	3	6-231 (3.8)	R44LTS	0.045	—	⑤	100	38	—	500	①	①
1987	3	6-231 (3.8)	R44LTS	0.045	—	⑤	100	38	—	500	①	①
1988	C	6-231 (3.8)	R44LTS6	0.060	—	⑤	—	27–36	—	⑤	Hyd.	Hyd.
1989		SEE UNDERHOOD SPECIFICATIONS STICKER										
ELDORADO AND SEVILLE												
1982	8	8-250 (4.1)	R–43NTS	0.060	—	10B⑧	120	9–12	—	⑤	①	①
	4	6-252 (4.1)	R–45TS8	0.080	—	15B	100	6–7.5	—	550④	①	①
1983	8	8-250 (4.1)	R–43NTS6	0.080	—	10B⑧	120	9–12	—	⑤	①	①
1984	8	8-250 (4.1)	R–42CLTS6	0.060	—	10B⑧	120	9–12	—	⑤	①	①
1985	8	8-250 (4.1)	R–42CLTS6	0.060	—	10B⑧	140	9–12	—	⑤	①	①
1986	8	8-250 (4.1)	R–44LTS6	0.060	—	10B⑧	140	9–12	—	⑤	①	①
1988	5	8-273 (4.5)	R–44LTS6	0.060	—	⑤	140–165	46.5	—	⑤	Hyd.	Hyd.
1989		SEE UNDERHOOD SPECIFICATIONS STICKER										
REATTA												
1988	C	6-231 (3.8)	R44LTS6	0.060	—	⑤	—	27–36	—	⑤	Hyd.	Hyd.
1989		SEE UNDERHOOD SPECIFICATIONS STICKER										
ALLANTE												
1988	7	8-250 (4.1)	R44LTS6	0.060	—	⑤	140–165	65–95	—	⑤	Hyd.	Hyd.
1989		SEE UNDERHOOD SPECIFICATIONS STICKER										

Note: Check the underhood emission control sticker for correct timing procedure. Some engines require grounding 2 connector or disconnecting a distributor plug to set base timing. Use the sticker specifications if different from above.
B Before Top Dead Center

① Zero Lash
② 1100 rpm in Park
③ 650 with solenoid energized
④ 900 with solenoid energized
⑤ Controlled by ECM
⑥ 0 degrees @ 1200
⑦ 850 with solenoid energized
⑧ 800 in Park

DIESEL ENGINE TUNE-UP SPECIFICATIONS

Year	VIN	No. Engine Displacement cu. in. (liter)	Valve Clearance Intake (in.)	Exhaust (in.)	Intake Valve Opens (deg.)	Injection Pump Setting (deg.)	Injection Nozzle Pressure (psi) New	Used	Idle Speed (rpm)	Cranking Compression Pressure (psi)
1982	N	8-350 (5.7)	③	③	16	99.5	1125–1325	NA	600①	275②
1983	N	8-350 (5.7)	③	③	16	99.5	1125–1325	NA	600①	275②
1984	N	8-350 (5.7)	③	③	16	99.5	1125–1325	NA	600①	275②
1985	N	8-350 (5.7)	③	③	16	99.5	1112–1325	NA	600①	275②

NA Not available
① Hot; Cold: 750 rpm
② Minimum pressure
③ Zero Lash

FIRING ORDERS

NOTE: To avoid confusion, always replace spark plug wires one at a time.

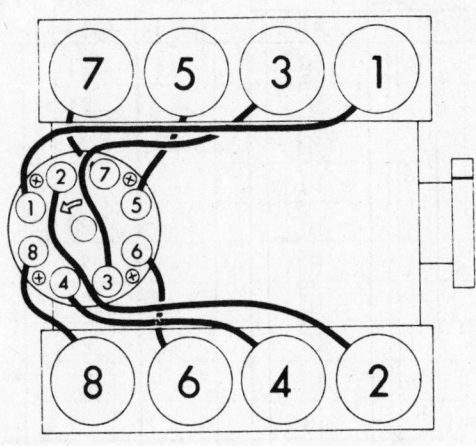

GM 250 (4.1L), 273 (4.5L) & 307 (5.0L) V8s
Engine firing order: 1-8-4-3-6-5-7-2
Distributor rotation: Counterclockwise

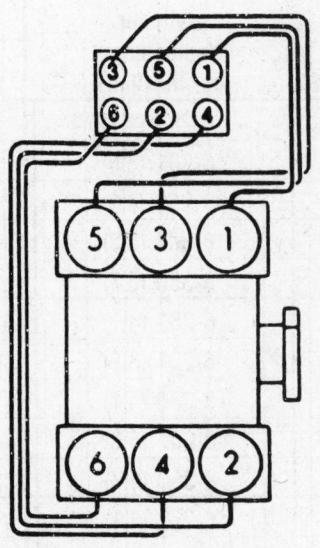

GM Buick 231 (3.8L) V6 Code 3
Firing order with the C³I
Coilless Ignition System

FIRING ORDERS

NOTE: To avoid confusion, always replace spark plug wires one at a time.

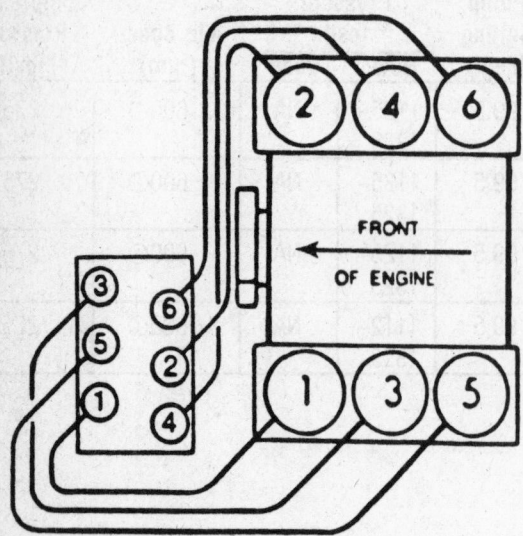

GM Buick 231 (3.8L) Code C
Firing order with the C³I
Coiless Ignition System

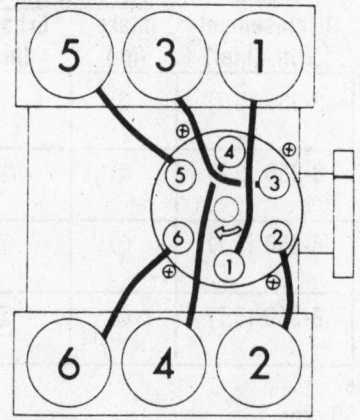

GM (Buick) 231 and 252 V6 (3.8 and 4.1L)
Engine firing order: 1-6-5-4-3-2
Distributor rotation: clockwise
V6 Harmonic balancers have two timing
marks: one is ⅛ in. wide, and one is 1/16
in. wide. Use the 1/16 in. mark for timing
with a hand held light. The ⅛ in. mark is
used only with a magnetic timing pick-up
probe.

CAPACITIES

Year	VIN	No. Cylinder Displacement cu. in. (liter)	Engine Crankcase with Filter	Engine Crankcase without Filter	Transmission (pts.) MT	Transmission (pts.) AT	Drive Axle (pts.)	Fuel Tank (gals.)	Cooling System (qts.)
1982	4	6-252 (4.1)	5	4	—	10	—	21	13
	3	6-231 (3.8)	4.5	4	—	10	—	21	13
	8	8-250 (4.1)	5	4	—	10	—	21	11
	Y	8-307 (5.0)	5	4	—	10	—	21	16
	N	8-350 (5.7)	7	6	—	10	—	23	18
1983	4	6-252 (4.1)	5	4	—	10	—	21	13
	9	6-231 (3.8)	4.5	4	—	10	—	21	15
	8	8-250 (4.1)	5	4	—	10	—	21	11
	Y	8-307 (5.0)	5	4	—	10	—	21	16
	N	8-350 (5.7)	7	6	—	10	—	23	18
1984	4	6-252 (4.1)	5	4.5	—	10	—	21	13
	9	6-231 (3.8)	5	4.5	—	10	—	21	13
	8	8-250 (4.1)	5	4	—	10	—	21	13
	Y	8-307 (5.0)	5	4	—	10	—	21	16
	N	8-350 (5.7)	7	6	—	10	—	23	18
1985	4	6-252 (4.1)	5	4.5	—	10	—	21	13
	9	6-231 (3.8)	5	4.5	—	10	—	21	13
	8	8-250 (4.1)	5	4	—	10	—	21	13

CAPACITIES

Year	VIN	No. Cylinder Displacement cu. in. (liter)	Engine Crankcase with Filter	Engine Crankcase without Filter	Transmission (pts.) MT	Transmission (pts.) AT	Drive Axle (pts.)	Fuel Tank (gals.)	Cooling System (qts.)
1985	Y	8-307 (5.0)	5	4	—	10	—	21	16
	N	8-350 (5.7)	7	6	—	10	—	23	18
1986	3	6-231 (3.8)	4.5	4	—	13	—	18	12
	8	250 (4.1)	5.5	5	—	13	—	18	13
1987	3	6-231 (3.8)	5.0	4.0	—	13	—	18	13
	7	8-250 (4.1)	6.0	5.0	—	13	—	22	12.1
	8	8-250 (4.1)	6.0	5.0	—	13	—	18	12.6
1988-89	C	6-231 (3.8)	5.0	4.0	—	13	—	18	13
	7	8-250 (4.1)	6.0	5.0	—	13	—	22	12.1
	5	8-273 (4.5)	6.0	5.0	—	13	—	18.8	12.1

CAMSHAFT SPECIFICATIONS
All measurements given in inches.

Year	VIN	No. Cylinder Displacement cu. in. (liter)	Journal Diameter 1	2	3	4	5	Lobe Lift In.	Lobe Lift Ex.	Bearing Clearance	Camshaft End Play
1982	4	6-252 (4.1)	1.785–1.786	1.785–1.786	1.785–1.786	1.785–1.786	—	NA	NA	0.0005–0.0035 ①	NA
	3	6-231 (3.8)	1.785–1.786	1.785–1.786	1.785–1.786	1.785–1.786	—	NA	NA	0.0005–0.0035 ①	NA
	8	8-250 (4.1)	NA	NA	NA	NA	NA	0.384	0.396	0.0020–0.0040	NA
	Y	8-307 (5.0)	2.0357–2.0365	2.0157–2.0165	1.9957–1.9965	1.9757–1.9765	1.9557–1.9565	0.400	0.400	0.0020–0.0058	0.011–0.077
	N	8-350 (5.7)	2.0357–2.0365	2.0157–2.0165	1.9957–1.9965	1.9757–1.9765	1.9557–1.9565	NA	NA	0.0020–0.0058	0.011–0.077
1983	4	6-252 (4.1)	1.785–1.786	1.785–1.786	1.785–1.786	1.785–1.786	—	NA	NA	0.0005–0.0035 ①	NA
	9	6-231 (3.8)	1.868–1.869	1.868–1.869	1.868–1.869	1.868–1.869	—	0.357	0.390	NA	NA
	8	8-250 (4.1)	NA	NA	NA	NA	NA	0.384	0.396	0.0020–0.0040	NA
	Y	8-307 (5.0)	2.0357–2.0365	2.0157–2.0165	1.9957–1.9965	1.9757–1.9765	1.9557–1.9565	0.400	0.440	0.0020–0.0058	0.011–0.077
	N	8-350 (5.7)	2.0357–2.0365	2.0157–2.0165	1.9957–1.9965	1.9757–1.9765	1.9557–1.9557	NA	NA	0.0020–0.0058	0.011–0.077
1984	4	6-252 (4.1)	1.785–1.786	1.785–1.786	1.785–1.786	1.785–1.786	—	NA	NA	0.0005–0.0035 ①	NA

CAMSHAFT SPECIFICATIONS
All measurements given in inches.

Year	VIN	No. Cylinder Displacement cu. in. (liter)	Journal Diameter					Lobe Lift		Bearing Clearance	Camshaft End Play
			1	2	3	4	5	In.	Ex.		
1984	9	6-231 (3.8)	1.785–1.786	1.785–1.786	1.785–1.786	1.785–1.786	—	NA	NA	0.0005–0.0035 ①	NA
	8	8-250 (4.1)	NA	NA	NA	NA	NA	0.384	0.396	0.0020–0.0040	NA
	Y	8-307 (5.0)	2.0357–2.0365	2.0157–2.0165	1.9957–1.9965	1.9757–1.9765	1.9957–1.9565	NA	NA	0.0020–0.0058	0.011–0.077
	N	8-350 (5.7)	2.0357–2.0365	2.0157–2.0165	1.9957–1.9965	1.9757–1.9765	1.9557–1.9565	NA	NA	0.0020–0.0058	0.011–0.077
1985	4	6-252 (4.1)	1.785–1.786	1.785–1.786	1.785–1.786	1.785–1.786	—	NA	NA	0.0005–0.0035 ①	NA
	9	6-231 (3.8)	1.785–1.786	1.785–1.786	1.785–1.786	1.785–1.786	—	NA	NA	0.0005–0.0035 ①	NA
	8	8-250 (4.1)	NA	NA	NA	NA	NA	0.384	0.396	0.0020–0.0040	NA
	Y	8-307 (5.0)	2.0357–2.0365	2.0157–2.0165	1.9957–1.9965	1.9757–1.9765	1.9557–1.9565	NA	NA	0.0020–0.0058	0.011–
	N	8-350 (5.7)	2.0357–2.0365	2.0157–2.0165	1.9957–1.9965	1.9757–1.9765	1.9557–1.9565	NA	NA	0.0020–0.0058	0.011–0.077
1986	3	6-231 (3.8)	1.785–1.786	1.785–1.786	1.785–1.786	1.785–1.786	—	0.397	0.397	0.0005–0.0035 ①	NA
	8	8-250 (4.1)	NA	NA	NA	NA	NA	0.384	0.396	0.0020–0.0040	NA
1987	3	6-231 (3.8)	1.785	1.786	1.786	1.786	—	0.245	0.245	0.0005–0.0035 ①	NA
	8	8-250 (4.1)	NA	NA	NA	NA	NA	0.384	0.396	0.0018–0.0037	NA
	7	8-250 (4.1)	NA	NA	NA	NA	NA	0.384	0.396	0.0018–0.0037	NA
1988-89	C	6-231 (3.8)	1.785	1.786	1.786	1.786	—	0.272	0.272	0.0005–0.0035	NA
	7	8-250 (4.1)	NA	NA	NA	NA	NA	0.384	0.396	0.0018–0.0037	NA
	5	8-273 (4.5)	NA	NA	NA	NA	NA	0.384	0.396	0.0018–0.0037	NA

NA Not available

① Journal No.1: 0.0005-0.0025 in.

CRANKSHAFT AND CONNECTING ROD SPECIFICATIONS
All measurements are given in inches.

Year	VIN	No. Cylinder Displacement cu. in. (liter)	Crankshaft				Connecting Rod		
			Main Brg. Journal Dia.	Main Brg. Oil Clearance	Shaft End-play	Thrust on No.	Journal Diameter	Oil Clearance	Side Clearance
1982	4	6-252 (4.1)	2.4995	0.0003–0.0018	0.003–0.009	2	2.2491	0.0005–0.0026	0.006–0.023
	3	6-231 (3.8)	2.4995	0.0003–0.0017	0.004–0.008	2	2.2491	0.0005–0.0026	0.006–0.027
	8	8-250 (4.1)	2.6400	0.0004–0.0030	0.001–0.007	3	1.929	0.0005–0.0028	0.008–0.020
	Y	8-307 (5.0)	2.4995–2.4990 ①	0.0005–0.0021 ②	0.0035–0.0135	3	2.1243	0.0004–0.0033	0.006–0.020
	N	8-350 (5.7)	2.9998	0.0005–0.0021 ②	0.0035–0.0135	3	2.1243	0.0004–0.0033	0.006–0.020
1983	4	6-252 (4.1)	2.4995	0.0003–0.0018	0.003–0.011	2	2.2491	0.0005–0.0026	0.006–0.027
	9	6-231 (3.8)	2.4995	0.0003–0.0018	0.003–0.011	2	2.2491	0.0005–0.0026	0.006–0.023
	8	8-250 (4.1)	2.6400	0.0004–0.0027	0.001–0.007	3	1.929	0.0005–0.0028	0.008–0.020
	Y	8-307 (5.0)	2.4995–2.4990 ①	0.0005–0.0021 ②	0.0035–0.0135	3	2.1238–2.1248	0.0004–0.0033	0.006–0.020
	N	8-350 (5.7)	2.9993–3.0003	0.0005–0.0021 ③	0.0035–0.0135	3	2.1238–2.1248	0.0005–0.0026	0.006–0.020
1984	4	6-252 (4.1)	2.4995	0.0003–0.0018	0.003–0.011	2	2.2491	0.0005–0.0026	0.006–0.027
	9	6-231 (3.8)	2.4995	0.0003–0.0018	0.003–0.011	2	2.2491	0.0005–0.0026	0.006–0.023
	8	8-250 (4.1)	2.6400	0.0004–0.0027	0.001–0.007	3	1.929	0.0005–0.0028	0.008–0.020
	Y	8-307 (5.0)	2.4995–2.4990 ①	0.0005–0.0021 ②	0.0035–0.0135	3	2.1238–2.1248	0.0004–0.0033	0.006–0.020
	N	8-350 (5.7)	2.9993–3.0003	0.0005–0.0021 ③	0.0035–0.0135	3	2.1238–2.1248	0.0005–0.0026	0.006–0.020
1985	4	6-252 (4.1)	2.4995	0.0003–0.0018	0.003–0.011	2	2.2491	0.0005–0.0026	0.006–0.023
	9	6-231 (3.8)	2.4995	0.0003–0.0018	0.003–0.011	2	2.2491	0.0005–0.0026	0.006–0.027
	8	8-250 (4.1)	2.6400	0.0004–0.0027	0.001–0.007	3	1.929	0.0005–0.0028	0.008–0.020

CRANKSHAFT AND CONNECTING ROD SPECIFICATIONS
All measurements are given in inches.

Year	VIN	No. Cylinder Displacement cu. in. (liter)	Crankshaft				Connecting Rod		
			Main Brg. Journal Dia.	Main Brg. Oil Clearance	Shaft End-play	Thrust on No.	Journal Diameter	Oil Clearance	Side Clearance
1985	Y	8-307 (5.0)	2.4995–2.4990 ①	0.0005–0.0021 ②	0.0035–0.0135	3	2.1238–2.1248	0.0004–0.0033	0.006–0.020
	N	8-350 (5.7)	2.9993–3.0003	0.0005–0.0021 ③	0.0035–0.0135	3	2.1238–2.1248	0.0005–0.0026	0.006–0.020
1986	3	6-231 (3.8)	2.4995	0.0003–0.0018	0.003–0.011	2	2.2487–2.2495	0.0009–0.0026	0.003–0.015
	8	8-250 (4.1)	2.6374–2.6384	0.0016–0.0039 ④	0.0010–0.0070	3	1.929	0.0005–0.0028	0.008–0.020
1987	3	6-231 (3.8)	2.4995	0.0003–0.0018	0.003–0.011	2	2.2487–2.2495	0.0003–0.0028	0.003–0.015
	7	8-250 (4.1)	2.6374–2.6384	0.0016–0.0039 ④	0.0010–0.0070	3	1.929	0.0005–0.0028	0.008–0.020
	8	8-250 (4.1)	2.6374–2.6384	0.0016–0.0039 ④	0.0010–0.0070	3	1.929	0.0005–0.0028	0.008–0.020
1988-89	C	6-231 (3.8)	2.4998–2.4998	0.0003–0.0018	0.003–0.011	2	2.2487–2.2495	0.0003–0.0028	0.003–0.015
	7	8-250 (4.1)	2.6374–2.6384	0.0016–0.0039 ④	0.0010–0.0070	3	1.929	0.0005–0.0028	0.008–0.020
	5	8-273 (4.5)	2.6374–2.6384	0.0016–0.0039 ④	0.0010–0.0070	3	1.929	0.0005–0.0028	0.008–0.020

① No. 1 — 2.4998–2.4993
② No. 2 — 0.0015–0.0031
③ No. 3 — 0.0020–0.0034
④ No. 4 — 0.0008–0.0031

VALVE SPECIFICATIONS

Year	VIN	No. Cylinder Displacement cu. in. (liter)	Seat Angle (deg.)	Face Angle (deg.)	Spring Test Pressure (lbs.)	Spring Installed Height (in.)	Stem-to-Guide Clearance (in.)		Stem Diameter (in.)	
							Intake	Exhaust	Intake	Exhaust
1982	4	6-252 (4.1)	45	45	220 @ 1.34	1²⁵⁄₃₂	0.0015–0.0035	0.0015–0.0032	0.3407	0.3409
	3	6-231 (3.8)	45	45	164 @ 1.34 ③	1²⁵⁄₃₂	0.0015–0.0035	0.0015–0.0032	0.3406	0.3408
	8	8-250 (4.1)	45	44	182 @ 1.28	1²⁵⁄₃₂	0.0010–0.0027	0.0012–0.0029	0.3420	0.3408
	Y	8-307 (5.0)	45①	44②	187 @ 1.27	1²³⁄₃₂	0.0010–0.0027	0.0015–0.0032	0.3429	0.3424
	N	8-350 (5.7)	45①	44②	210 @ 1.30	1²³⁄₃₂	0.0010–0.0027	0.0015–0.0032	0.3429	0.3424

VALVE SPECIFICATIONS

Year	VIN	No. Cylinder Displacement cu. in. (liter)	Seat Angle (deg.)	Face Angle (deg.)	Spring Test Pressure (lbs.)	Spring Installed Height (in.)	Stem-to-Guide Clearance (in.) Intake	Stem-to-Guide Clearance (in.) Exhaust	Stem Diameter (in.) Intake	Stem Diameter (in.) Exhaust
1983	4	6-252 (4.1)	45	45	182 @ 1.34	$1^{25}/_{32}$	0.0015–0.0035	0.0015–0.0032	0.3401–0.3412	0.3405–0.3412
	9	6-231 (3.8)	45	45	182 @ 1.34	$1^{25}/_{32}$	0.0015–0.0035	0.0015–0.0032	0.3401–0.3412	0.3405–0.3412
	8	8-250 (4.1)	45	44	182 @ 1.28	$1^{23}/_{32}$	0.0010–0.0030	0.0010–0.0030	0.3413–0.3420	0.3411–0.3418
	Y	8-307 (5.0)	45	44	187 @ 1.27	$1^{23}/_{32}$	0.0010–0.0027	0.0015–0.0032	0.3425–0.3432	0.3420–0.3427
	N	8-350 (5.7)	45①	44②	210 @ 1.22	$1^{23}/_{32}$	0.0010–0.0027	0.0015–0.0032	0.3425–0.3432	0.3420–0.3427
1984	4	6-252 (4.1)	45	45	182 @ 1.34	$1^{25}/_{32}$	0.0015–0.0035	0.0015–0.0032	0.3401–0.3412	0.3405–0.3412
	9	6-231 (3.8)	45	45	220 @ 1.34	$1^{25}/_{32}$	0.0015–0.0035	0.0015–0.0032	0.3401–0.3412	0.3405–0.3412
	8	8-250 (4.1)	45	44	182 @ 1.28	$1^{23}/_{32}$	0.0010–0.0030	0.0010–0.0030	0.3413–0.3420	0.3411–0.3418
	Y	8-307 (5.0)	45	44	187 @ 1.27	$1^{23}/_{32}$	0.0010–0.0027	0.0015–0.0032	0.3425–0.3432	0.3420–0.3427
	N	8-350 (5.7)	45①	44②	210 @ 1.22	$1^{23}/_{32}$	0.0010–0.0027	0.0015–0.0032	0.3425–0.3432	0.3420–0.3427
1985	4	6-252 (4.1)	45	45	182 @ 1.34	$1^{25}/_{32}$	0.0015–0.0035	0.0015–0.0032	0.3401–0.3412	0.3405–0.3412
	9	6-231 (3.8)	45	45	220 @ 1.34	$1^{25}/_{32}$	0.0015–0.0035	0.0015–0.0032	0.3401–0.3412	0.3405–0.3412
	8	8-250 (4.1)	45	44	182 @ 1.28	$1^{23}/_{32}$	0.0010–0.0030	0.0010–0.0030	0.3413–0.3420	0.3411–0.3418
	Y	8-307 (5.0)	45	44	187 @ 1.27	$1^{23}/_{32}$	0.0010–0.0027	0.0015–0.0032	0.3425–0.3432	0.3420–0.3427
	N	8-350 (5.7)	45①	44②	210 @ 1.22	$1^{23}/_{32}$	0.0010–0.0027	0.0015–0.0032	0.3425–0.3432	0.3420–0.3427
1986	3	6-231 (3.8)	45	45	185 @ 1.34	$1^{25}/_{32}$	0.0015–0.0035	0.0015–0.0032	0.3401–0.3412	0.3405–0.3412
	8	8-250 (4.1)	45	44	182 @ 1.28	$1^{25}/_{32}$	0.0010–0.0030	0.0010–0.0030	0.3420–0.3413	0.3411–0.3418
1987	3	6-231 (3.8)	46	45	90 @ 1.727	$1^{23}/_{32}$	0.0015–0.0035	0.0015–0.0032	0.3401–0.3412	0.3405–0.3412
	7	8-250 (4.1)	45	44	99 @ 1.730	$1^{23}/_{32}$	0.0010–0.0030	0.0010–0.0030	0.3413–0.3420	0.3411–0.3418
	8	8-250 (4.1)	45	44	99 @ 1.730	$1^{23}/_{32}$	0.0010–0.0030	0.0010–0.0030	0.3413–0.3420	0.3411–0.3418
1988-89	C	6-231 (3.8)	45	45	105 @ 1.730	$1^{23}/_{32}$	0.0015–0.0035	0.0015–0.0032	0.3401–0.3412	0.3405–0.3412
	7	8-250 (4.1)	45	44	99 @ 1.730	$1^{23}/_{32}$	0.0010–0.0030	0.0010–0.0030	0.3413–0.3420	0.3411–0.3418

VALVE SPECIFICATIONS

Year	VIN	No. Cylinder Displacement cu. in. (liter)	Seat Angle (deg.)	Face Angle (deg.)	Spring Test Pressure (lbs.)	Spring Installed Height (in.)	Stem-to-Guide Clearance (in.)		Stem Diameter (in.)	
							Intake	Exhaust	Intake	Exhaust
1988-89	5	8-250 (4.1)	45	44	99 @ 1.730	1²³⁄₃₂	0.0010– 0.0030	0.0010– 0.0030	0.3413– 0.3420	0.3411– 0.3418

① Exhaust valve seat 31°   ③ Exhaust valve: 182 @ 1.34
② Exhaust valve face 30°

PISTON AND RING SPECIFICATIONS
All measurments are given in inches.

Year	VIN	No. Cylinder Displacement cu. in. (liter)	Piston Clearance	Ring Gap			Ring Side Clearance		
				Top Compression	Bottom Compression	Oil Control	Top Compression	Bottom Compression	Oil Control
1982	4	6-252 (4.1)	0.0008– 0.0020	0.013– 0.023	0.013– 0.023	0.015– 0.035	0.0030– 0.0050	0.0030– 0.0050	0.0035 Max
	3	6-231 (3.8)	0.0008– 0.0020	0.013– 0.023	0.013– 0.023	0.015– 0.035	0.0030– 0.0050	0.0030– 0.0050	0.0035 Max
	8	8-250 (4.1)	0.0010– 0.0018	0.009– 0.020	0.009– 0.020	0.010– 0.050	0.0016– 0.0037	0.0016– 0.0037	None ②
	Y	8-307 (5.0)	0.0007– 0.0017	0.009– 0.019	0.009– 0.019	0.015– 0.055	0.0020– 0.0040	0.0020– 0.0040	0.0015– 0.0055
	N	8-350 (5.7)	0.0005– 0.0006	0.015– 0.025	0.015– 0.025	0.015– 0.055	0.0040– 0.0060	0.0018– 0.0038	0.0010– 0.0050
1983	4	6-252 (4.1)	0.0008– 0.0020	0.010– 0.020	0.010– 0.020	0.015– 0.055	0.0030– 0.0050	0.0030– 0.0050	0.0035 Max
	9	6-231 (3.8)	0.0022– 0.0034 ③	0.010– 0.020	0.010– 0.020	0.015– 0.055	0.0030– 0.0050	0.0030– 0.0050	0.0035 Max
	8	8-250 (4.1)	0.0010– 0.0018	0.009– 0.020	0.009– 0.020	0.010– 0.050	0.0016– 0.0037	0.0016– 0.0037	None ①
	Y	8-307 (5.0)	0.0007– 0.0017	0.009– 0.019	0.009– 0.019	0.015– 0.055	0.0020– 0.0040	0.0020– 0.0040	0.0015– 0.0055
	N	8-350 (5.7)	0.0005– 0.0006	0.019– 0.027	0.013– 0.021	0.015– 0.055	0.0050– 0.0070	0.0030– 0.0050	0.0010– 0.0050
1984	4	6-252 (4.1)	0.0008– 0.0020	0.010– 0.020	0.010– 0.020	0.015– 0.055	0.0030– 0.0050	0.0030– 0.0050	0.0035 Max
	9	6-231 (3.8)	0.0022– 0.0034 ③	0.010– 0.020	0.010– 0.020	0.015– 0.055	0.0030– 0.0050	0.0030– 0.0050	0.0035 Max
	8	8-250 (4.1)	0.0010– 0.0018	0.009– 0.020	0.009– 0.020	0.015– 0.050	0.0016– 0.0037	0.0016– 0.0037	None ②
	Y	8-307 (5.0)	0.0007– 0.0017	0.009– 0.019	0.009– 0.019	0.015– 0.055	0.0020– 0.0040	0.0020– 0.0040	0.0015– 0.0055
	N	8-350 (5.7)	0.0005– 0.0006	0.019– 0.027	0.013– 0.021	0.015– 0.055	0.0050– 0.0070	0.0030– 0.0050	0.0010– 0.0050
1985	4	6-252 (4.1)	0.0008– 0.0020	0.010– 0.020	0.010– 0.020	0.015– 0.055	0.0030– 0.0050	0.0030– 0.0050	0.0035 Max

PISTON AND RING SPECIFICATIONS
All measurments are given in inches.

Year	VIN	No. Cylinder Displacement cu. in. (liter)	Piston Clearance	Ring Gap			Ring Side Clearance		
				Top Compression	Bottom Compression	Oil Control	Top Compression	Bottom Compression	Oil Control
1985	9	6-231 (3.8)	0.0022–0.0034 ③	0.010–0.020	0.010–0.020	0.015–0.055	0.0030–0.0050	0.0030–0.0050	0.0035 Max
	8	8-250 (4.1)	0.0010–0.0018	0.009–0.020	0.009–0.020	0.015–0.050	0.0016–0.0037	0.0016–0.0037	None ②
	Y	8-307 (5.0)	0.0007–0.0017	0.009–0.019	0.009–0.019	0.015–0.055	0.0020–0.0040	0.0020–0.0040	0.0015–0.0055
	N	8-350 (5.7)	0.0005–0.0006	0.019–0.027	0.013–0.021	0.015–0.055	0.0050–0.0070	0.0030–0.0050	0.0010–0.0050
1986	3	6-231 (3.8)	0.0013–0.0035 ④	0.013–0.023	0.013–0.023	0.015–0.035	0.0030–0.0050–	0.0030–0.0050–	0.0035
	8	8-250 (4.1)	0.0010–0.0018 ①	0.015–0.025	0.015–0.025	0.010–0.050	0.0020–0.0040	0.0020–0.0040	None ②
1987	3	6-231 (3.8)	0.0004–0.0022	0.010–0.020	0.010–0.022	0.015–0.055	0.0010–0.0030	0.0010–0.0030	0.0005 0.0065
	7	8-250 (4.1)	0.0010–0.0018	0.015–0.024	0.015–0.024	0.010–0.050	0.0016–0.0037	0.0016–0.0037	None ②
	8	8-250 (4.1)	0.0010–0.0018	0.015–0.024	0.015–0.024	0.010–0.050	0.0016–0.0037	0.0016–0.0037	None ②
1988-89	C	6-231 (3.8)	⑤	0.010–0.025	0.010–0.025	0.015–0.055	0.0013–0.0031	0.0013–0.0031	0.0011–0.0081
	7	8-250 (4.1)	0.0010–0.0018	0.015–0.024	0.015–0.024	0.010–0.050	0.0016–0.0037	0.0016–0.0037	None ②
	5	8-250 (4.5)	0.0010–0.0018	0.015–0.024	0.015–0.024	0.010–0.050	0.0016–0.0037	0.0016–0.0037	None ②

① Measured at top of skirt
② Side sealing
③ Measured at piston pin center line
④ Measured at bottom of piston skirt
⑤ Skirt top–0.0007–0.0027
   Skirt bottom–0.0010–0.0045

TORQUE SPECIFICATIONS
All readings in ft. lbs.

Year	VIN	No. Cylinder Displacement cu. in. (liter)	Cylinder Head Bolts	Main Bearing Bolts	Rod Bearing Bolts	Crankshaft Pulley Bolts	Flywheel Bolts	Manifold		Spark Plugs
								Intake	Exhaust	
1982	4	6-252 (4.1)	80	100	40	225	60	45	25	15
	3	6-231 (3.8)	80	100	40	225	60	45	25	20
	8	8-250 (4.1)	②④	85①	22	225	75	20②	18	11
	Y	8-307 (5.0)	130②	80①	42	200-310	60	40②	25③	25
	N	8-350 (5.7)	130②	120	42	200-310	60	40②	25	26

TORQUE SPECIFICATIONS
All readings in ft. lbs.

Year	VIN	No. Cylinder Displacement cu. in. (liter)	Cylinder Head Bolts	Main Bearing Bolts	Rod Bearing Bolts	Crankshaft Pulley Bolts	Flywheel Bolts	Manifold Intake	Manifold Exhaust	Spark Plugs
1983	4	6-252 (4.1)	80	100	40	225	60	45	25	15
	9	6-231 (3.8)	80	100	40	225	60	45	25	20
	8	8-250 (4.1)	④	85	20	20	35	20	20	11
	Y	8-307 (5.0)	130②	80①	42	200-310	60	40②	25	25
	N	8-350 (5.7)	130②	120	42	200-310	60	40②	25	12
1984	4	6-252 (4.1)	80	100	40	225	60	45	25	15
	9	6-231 (3.8)	80	100	40	225	60	45	25	20
	8	8-250 (4.1)	④	85	20	20	35	20	20	11
	Y	8-307 (5.0)	125②	80①	42	200-310	60	40②	25	25
	N	8-350 (5.7)	130②	120	42	200-310	60	40②	25	12
1985	4	6-252 (4.1)	80	100	40	225	60	45	25	16
	9	6-231 (3.8)	80	100	40	225	60	45	25	20
	8	8-250 (4.1)	④	85	20	20	35	20	20	11
	Y	8-307 (5.0)	125②	80①	42	200-310	60	40②	25	25
	N	8-350 (5.7)	130②	120	42	200-310	60	40②	25	12
1986	3	6-231 (3.8)	⑤	100	40	200	60	32	37	20
	8	8-250 (4.1)	⑤	85	22	18	37	22	18	11
1987	3	6-231 (3.8)	60⑤	100	40	219	60	32	37	20
	7	8-250 (4.1)	90⑤	85	22	18	37	22⑤	18	11
	8	8-250 (4.1)	90⑤	85	22	18	37	22⑤	18	11
1988-89	C	6-231 (3.8)	60⑤	100	40	219	60	88⑥	37	20
	7	8-250 (4.1)	90⑤	85	22	18	37	22⑤	18	11
	5	8-273 (4.5)	90⑤	85	22	18	70	22⑤	18	11

① 120 ft. lbs. on No. 5
② Oil bolt before torquing
③ 12 ft. lbs. for short bolt
④ Torque in sequence to 45 ft. lbs.; then torque to 90 ft. lbs. in sequence
⑤ See text
⑥ Inch lbs.

BRAKE SPECIFICATIONS
All measurements in inches unless noted

Year	Model	Lug Nut Torque (ft. lbs.)	Master Cylinder Bore	Brake Disc Minimum Thickness	Brake Disc Maximum Runout	Standard Brake Drum Diameter	Minimum Lining Thickness Front	Minimum Lining Thickness Rear
1982	Toronado	100	1.000	0.960	0.005	9.590	0.030	0.030
	Eldorado	100	1.000	0.960	0.004	NA	0.030	0.030
	Seville	100	1.000	0.960	0.004	NA	0.030	0.030
	Riviera	100	0.945	0.960	0.003	9.590	0.030	0.030
1983	Toronado	100	1.000	0.956	0.004	NA	0.030	0.030
	Eldorado	100	1.000	0.980	0.004	NA	0.030	0.030

BRAKE SPECIFICATIONS
All measurements in inches unless noted

| Year | Model | Lug Nut Torque (ft. lbs.) | Master Cylinder Bore | Brake Disc | | Standard Brake Drum Diameter | Minimum Lining Thickness | |
				Minimum Thickness	Maximum Runout		Front	Rear
1983	Seville	100	1.000	0.980	0.004	NA	0.030	0.030
	Riviera	100	1.125	0.956	0.004	9.560	0.030	0.030
1984	Toronado	100	1.000	0.980	0.004	NA	0.030	0.030
	Eldorado	100	1.000	0.980	0.004	NA	0.030	0.030
	Seville	100	1.000	0.980	0.004	NA	0.030	0.030
	Riviera	100	1.125	0.980	0.004	9.560	0.030	0.030
1985	Toronado	100	②	0.980	0.004	NA	0.030	0.030
	Eldorado	100	②	0.980	0.004	NA	0.030	0.030
	Seville	100	②	0.980	0.004	NA	0.030	0.030
	Riviera	100	②	0.980	0.004	9.560①	0.030	0.030
1986	Toronado	100	②	0.980	0.004	NA	0.030	0.030
	Eldorado	100	②	0.980	0.004	NA	0.030	0.030
	Seville	100	②	0.980	0.004	NA	0.030	0.030
	Riviera	100	②	0.980	0.004	NA	0.030	0.030
1987	Toronado	100	③	0.971④	0.004⑤	NA	0.030	0.030
	Eldorado	100	③	0.971④	0.004⑤	NA	0.030	0.030
	Seville	100	③	0.971④	0.004⑤	NA	0.030	0.030
	Riviera	100	③	0.971④	0.004⑤	NA	0.030	0.030
1988-89	Toronado	100	③	0.971④	0.004⑤	NA	0.030	0.030
	Eldorado	100	③	0.971④	0.004⑤	NA	0.030	0.030
	Seville	100	③	0.971④	0.004⑤	NA	0.030	0.030
	Riviera	100	③	0.971④	0.004⑤	NA	0.030	0.030
	Reatta	100	③	0.971④	0.004⑤	NA	0.030	0.030
	Alante	100	③	0.971④	0.004⑤	NA	0.030	0.030

NA Not applicable
① 11.060 in., if equipped with 11 in. brake drums
② 1.000 in. with vacuum boost
0.937 in. with quick take up
1.062 in. with hydro boost
③ Standard— 1.126 in.
Quick Take-up—1.574 in.
Anti-Lock—1.000 in.
④ Rear—0.444 in.
⑤ Rear—0.003 in.

WHEEL ALIGNMENT

| Year | Model | | Caster | | Camber | | Toe-in (in.) | Steering Axis Inclination (deg.) |
			Range (deg.)	Preferred Setting (deg.)	Range (deg.)	Preferred Setting (deg.)		
1982	Toronado	Front	2P-3P	$2\frac{1}{2}$P	$\frac{1}{2}$N-$\frac{1}{2}$P	0	$\frac{1}{16}$P-$\frac{1}{16}$N	—
	Eldorado	Front	$1\frac{1}{2}$P-$3\frac{1}{2}$P	$2\frac{1}{2}$P	$\frac{3}{16}$N-$\frac{3}{16}$P	0	$\frac{1}{8}$P-$\frac{1}{8}$N	—
	Seville	Front	$1\frac{1}{2}$P-$3\frac{1}{2}$P	$2\frac{1}{2}$P	$\frac{3}{16}$N-$\frac{3}{16}$P	0	$\frac{1}{8}$P-$\frac{1}{8}$N	—
	Riviera	Front	$1\frac{1}{2}$P-$3\frac{1}{2}$P	$2\frac{1}{2}$P	$\frac{13}{16}$N-$\frac{13}{16}$P	0	$\frac{1}{8}$P-$\frac{1}{8}$N	—
1983	Toronado	Front	$1\frac{1}{2}$P-$3\frac{1}{2}$P	$2\frac{1}{2}$P	$\frac{1}{2}$N-$\frac{1}{2}$P	0	$\frac{1}{8}$P-$\frac{1}{8}$N	—
	Eldorado	Front	2P-3P	$2\frac{1}{2}$P	$\frac{1}{2}$N-$\frac{1}{2}$P	0	$\frac{1}{8}$P-$\frac{1}{8}$N	—

WHEEL ALIGNMENT

Year	Model		Caster Range (deg.)	Caster Preferred Setting (deg.)	Camber Range (deg.)	Camber Preferred Setting (deg.)	Toe-in (in.)	Steering Axis Inclination (deg.)
1983	Seville	Front	2P-3P	$2\frac{1}{2}$P	$\frac{1}{2}$N-$\frac{1}{2}$P	0	$\frac{1}{8}$P-$\frac{1}{8}$N	—
	Riviera	Front	2P-3P	$2\frac{1}{2}$	$\frac{1}{2}$N-$\frac{1}{2}$P	0	$\frac{1}{8}$P-$\frac{1}{8}$N	—
1984	Toronado	Front	$1\frac{1}{2}$P-$3\frac{1}{2}$P	$2\frac{1}{2}$P	$\frac{1}{2}$N-$\frac{1}{2}$P	0	$\frac{1}{8}$P-$\frac{1}{8}$N	—
		Rear	—	—	—	—	0-$\frac{5}{16}$①	—
	Eldorado	Front	2P-3P	$2\frac{1}{2}$P	$\frac{1}{2}$N-$\frac{1}{2}$P	0	$\frac{1}{8}$P-$\frac{1}{8}$N	—
		Rear	—	—	—	—	0-$\frac{2}{5}$①	—
	Seville	Front	2P-3P	$2\frac{1}{2}$P	$\frac{1}{2}$N-$\frac{1}{2}$P	0	$\frac{1}{8}$P-$\frac{1}{8}$N	—
		Rear	—	—	—	—	0-$\frac{2}{5}$①	—
	Riviera	Front	2P-3P	$2\frac{1}{2}$P	$\frac{1}{2}$N-$\frac{1}{2}$P	0	$\frac{1}{8}$P-$\frac{1}{8}$N	—
		Rear	—	—	—	—	0-$\frac{2}{5}$①	—
1985	Toronado	Front	$1\frac{1}{2}$P-$3\frac{1}{2}$P	$2\frac{1}{2}$P	$\frac{1}{2}$N-$\frac{1}{2}$P	0	$\frac{1}{8}$P-$\frac{1}{8}$N	—
		Rear	—	—	—	—	0-$\frac{5}{16}$①	—
	Eldorado	Front	2P-$2\frac{1}{2}$P	$2\frac{1}{2}$P	$\frac{1}{2}$N-$\frac{1}{2}$P	0	$\frac{1}{16}$P-$\frac{1}{16}$N	—
		Rear	—	—	—	—	0-$\frac{2}{5}$①	—
	Seville	Front	2P-$2\frac{1}{2}$P	$2\frac{1}{2}$P	$\frac{1}{2}$N-$\frac{1}{2}$P	0	$\frac{1}{16}$P-$\frac{1}{16}$N	—
		Rear	—	—	—	—	0-$\frac{2}{5}$①	—
	Riviera	Front	2P-3P	$2\frac{1}{2}$P	$\frac{1}{2}$N-$\frac{1}{2}$P	0	$\frac{1}{8}$P-$\frac{1}{8}$N	—
		Rear	—	—	—	—	0-$\frac{2}{5}$①	—
1986	Toronado	Front	$1\frac{1}{2}$P-$3\frac{1}{2}$P	$2\frac{1}{2}$P	$\frac{1}{2}$N-$\frac{1}{2}$P	0	$\frac{1}{10}$P-$\frac{1}{10}$N	—
		Rear	—	—	—	—	0-$\frac{2}{5}$①	—
	Eldorado	Front	$1\frac{1}{2}$P-$3\frac{1}{2}$P	$2\frac{1}{2}$P	$\frac{1}{2}$N-$\frac{1}{2}$P	0	$\frac{1}{5}$P-$\frac{3}{5}$N	—
		Rear	—	—	—	—	0-$\frac{2}{5}$①	—
	Seville	Front	$1\frac{1}{2}$P-$3\frac{1}{2}$P	$2\frac{1}{2}$P	$\frac{1}{2}$N-$\frac{1}{2}$P	0	$\frac{1}{5}$P-$\frac{3}{5}$N	—
		Rear	—	—	—	—	0-$\frac{2}{5}$①	—
	Riviera	Front	$1\frac{1}{2}$P-$3\frac{1}{2}$N	$2\frac{1}{2}$P	$\frac{1}{2}$N-$\frac{1}{2}$P	0	$\frac{1}{10}$P-$\frac{1}{10}$N	—
		Rear	—	—	—	—	0-$\frac{2}{5}$①	—
1987	Toronado	Front	1½P-3½N	$2\frac{1}{2}$P	$\frac{4}{5}$N-$\frac{4}{5}$P	0	$\frac{1}{10}$P-$\frac{1}{10}$N	—
		Rear	—	—	1N-$\frac{2}{5}$P	$\frac{7}{10}$N	0-$\frac{1}{5}$N①	—
	Riviera	Front	$1\frac{3}{10}$P-$3\frac{3}{10}$N	$2\frac{3}{10}$P	$\frac{4}{5}$N-$\frac{4}{5}$P	0	$\frac{1}{10}$P-$\frac{1}{10}$N	—
		Rear	—	—	1N-$\frac{2}{5}$P	$\frac{7}{10}$N	0-$\frac{1}{5}$N①	—
	Eldorado	Front	2P-3P	$2\frac{1}{2}$P	$\frac{1}{2}$N-$\frac{1}{2}$P	0	$\frac{1}{10}$P-$\frac{1}{10}$N	—
		Rear	—	—	—	—	0-$\frac{1}{5}$P①	—
	Seville	Front	2P-3P	$2\frac{1}{2}$P	$\frac{1}{2}$N-$\frac{1}{2}$P	0	$\frac{1}{10}$P-$\frac{1}{10}$N	—
		Rear	—	—	—	—	0-$\frac{1}{5}$P①	—
	Allante	Front	2P-3P	$2\frac{1}{2}$P	$\frac{1}{2}$N-$\frac{1}{2}$P	0	$\frac{1}{10}$P-$\frac{1}{10}$N	—
		Rear	—	—	—	—	0-$\frac{1}{5}$P①	—
1988	Toronado	Front	$1\frac{3}{10}$P-$3\frac{3}{10}$N	$2\frac{3}{10}$P	$\frac{4}{5}$N-$\frac{4}{5}$P	0	$\frac{1}{10}$P-$\frac{1}{10}$N	—
		Rear	—	—	—	—	0-$\frac{1}{5}$P①	—
	Riviera	Front	$1\frac{3}{10}$P-$3\frac{3}{10}$N	$2\frac{3}{10}$P	$\frac{4}{5}$N-$\frac{4}{5}$P	0	$\frac{1}{10}$P-$\frac{1}{10}$N	—
		Rear	—	—	—	—	0-$\frac{1}{5}$P①	—

WHEEL ALIGNMENT

Year	Model		Caster Range (deg.)	Caster Preferred Setting (deg.)	Camber Range (deg.)	Camber Preferred Setting (deg.)	Toe-in (in.)	Steering Axis Inclination (deg.)
1988	Eldorado	Front	$1\frac{3}{10}$P-$3\frac{3}{10}$N	$2\frac{3}{10}$P	$\frac{4}{5}$N-$\frac{4}{5}$P	0	$\frac{1}{10}$P-$\frac{1}{10}$N	—
		Rear	—	—	—	—	0-$\frac{1}{5}$P①	—
	Seville	Front	$1\frac{3}{10}$P-$3\frac{3}{10}$N	$2\frac{3}{10}$P	$\frac{4}{5}$N-$\frac{4}{5}$P	0	$\frac{1}{10}$P-$\frac{1}{10}$N	—
		Rear	—	—	—	—	0-$\frac{1}{5}$P①	—
	Allante	Front	$2\frac{3}{10}$P-$3\frac{3}{10}$N	$2\frac{4}{5}$P	$\frac{4}{5}$N-$\frac{4}{5}$P	0	0-$\frac{1}{5}$N	—
		Rear	—	—	—	—	0-$\frac{1}{5}$P①	—
	Reatta	Front	$1\frac{4}{5}$P-$3\frac{4}{5}$P	$2\frac{4}{5}$P	$\frac{1}{2}$N-$\frac{1}{2}$P	0	$\frac{1}{5}$N-$\frac{1}{5}$P	—
		Rear	—	—	—	—	0-$\frac{1}{5}$P①	—

P Positive
N Negative
① Degrees

TUNE-UP PROCEDURES

Ignition Timing

ADJUSTMENT

Gasoline Engines

NOTE: Always consult the underhood sticker before adjusting timing. If the underhood sticker differs from the following procedures, follow the sticker.

V6 – 3.8L (231 CU. IN.)

The 3.8L (Code 3 and C) engines are equipped with a C³I ignition system which do not incorporate a distributor. For instructions on initial timing, see the underhood emission sticker and follow the procedures.

V6 – 4.1L (252 CU. IN.)

1. Connect a timing light to the No. 1 spark plug wire according to the light manufacturer's instructions. DO NOT pierce the spark plug wire to connect the timing light.
2. Set the parking brake and position the transaxle in the **PARK** position.
3. Turn the **ON** and allow it to reach normal operating temperatures. Be sure the air cleaner is installed and the air conditioning turned **OFF**.
4. Inspect the instrument panel to be sure the **CHECK ENGINE** light is turned **OFF**.
5. Disconnect the 4-wire terminal connector from the distributor. See the Underhood sticker for identification. The **CHECK ENGINE** light will turn **ON**.
6. If necessary, loosen the distributor hold-down bolt and turn the distributor until the specified timing is obtained.

NOTE: All V6 engines harmonic balancers have 2 timing marks, 1 measuring ⅛ in. wide and 1 measuring the normal $\frac{1}{16}$ in. wide. The smaller mark is used for setting the timing with a hand held timing light. The ⅛ in. wide mark is required when using magnetic timing equipment. All engines have a mounting bracket on the front cover which will accept a magnetic timing pick-up probe.

7. Tighten the mounting bolt and recheck timing to see if it changed during tightening.
8. Reconnect the electrical connector to the distributor.
9. Stop the engine, then, temporarily disconnect the negative battery terminal to cancel any stored trouble codes.

V8 – 4.1L (250 CU. IN.) AND V8 – 4.5L (273 CU. IN.)

NOTE: The engine incorporates a magnetic timing probe hole for use with special electronic timing equipment. Consult manufacturer's instructions before using this system. The following procedure is for use with the HEI – EST distributor.

1. Connect a timing light to the No. 1 spark plug wire according to the light manufacturer's instructions. DO NOT pierce the spark plug wire to connect the timing light.
2. Set the parking brake and position the transaxle in the **PARK** position.
3. Follow the instructions on the emission control label located in the engine compartment.

NOTE: DO NOT attempt to time the engine if it is operating on 7 cylinders for damage to the catalytic converter may occur.

4. On the 4.5L (273 cu. in.) engine, connect a jumper wire between pins **A** (ground) and **B** of the Assembly Line Data Link (ALDL) connector (located

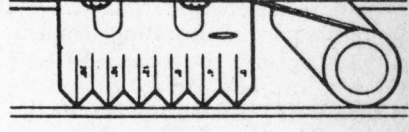

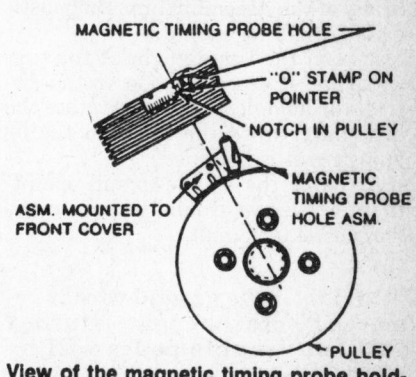

View of the magnetic timing probe holder – 4.1L (250 cu. in.) and 4.5L (273 cu. in.) V8 engines

near the parking brake pedal under the dash).

NOTE: By jumping the Assembly Line Data Link (ALDL) connector, the ECM will command the BCM to display a SET TIMING message on the Climate Control Driver Information Panel (CCDIC). The engine will now operate at base timing. The timing can now be checked with a standard timing light at 10 degrees BTDC at 900 rpm or less.

5. Start the engine and run it at idle speed until normal operating temperatures are reached.

6. Aim the timing light at the degree scale just over the harmonic balancer; the line on the pulley should align with the mark on the timing plate.

7. If necessary to adjust the timing, use the Distributor Wrench tool No. J–29791 or equivalent, to loosen the hold-down clamp, then, rotate the distributor until the desired ignition advance is achieved. When the correct timing is set, torque the hold-down clamp nut/bolt to 20 ft. lbs.

NOTE: To advance the timing, rotate the distributor opposite the normal direction of rotor rotation. Retard the timing by rotating the distributor in the normal direction of rotor rotation.

V8–5.0L (307 CU. IN.)

1. Connect a timing light to the No. 1 spark plug wire according to the light manufacturer's instructions. DO NOT pierce the spark plug wire to connect the timing light.

2. Set the parking brake and position the transaxle in the **PARK** position.

3. Turn the engine **ON** and allow it to reach normal operating temperatures. Make sure the choke is **FULLY OPEN** and the air conditioning turned **OFF**. Ground the No. 12 terminal of the Assembly Line Diagnostic Link (ALDL).

4. Aim the timing light at the timing plate. If necessary, loosen the distributor hold-down nut and rotate the distributor until the specified timing adjustment is obtained.

5. While the engine is still operating, remove the ground wire from the diagnostic terminal.

NOTE: If the ground wire is removed before the engine is turned OFF, no trouble codes will be stored.

6. Remove the timing light.

Diesel Engines

V8–5.7L (350 CU. IN.)

The engine is properly timed when the injection pump timing mark is aligned between the edges of the pump adapter. If the engine is not aligned, perform the following procedures:

1. Loosen the injection pump-to-bracket nuts.

2. Turn the injection pump to align the timing marks with the adapter. Torque the injection pump-to-bracket nuts to 18 ft. lbs.

NOTE: Using a ¾ in. wrench on the boss at the front of the injection pump will aid in the rotation of the pump.

3. If necessary, check and/or tighten the fuel lines. Adjust the throttle linkage. Start the engine and check the operation.

Valve Lash

ADJUSTMENT

All engines use hydraulic lifters. Valve systems with hydraulic lifters operatewith zero clearance in the valve train. The rocker arms are non-adjustable. The lifter itself will compensate if there is slack in the system but if there is excessive play, the entire system should be checked.

If the valve guides are found to be worn past allowable limits, they will have to be rebored and valves with oversize stem installed.

Idle Speed and Mixture Gasoline Engines

ADJUSTMENT

Carbureted Models

1982–85 M4MC/M4ME WITH IDLE SPEED SOLENOID

1. Run the engine to normal operating temperatures are reached.

2. Make sure that the choke is **FULLY OPENED**, turn the air conditioning **OFF**, set the parking brake and block the wheels.

3. Connect a tachometer to the engine according to the manufacturer's instructions.

4. Disconnect the purge hose from the vapor canister.

5. Disconnect and plug the EGR vacuum hose at the valve. If equipped, disconnect and plug the vacuum advance hose.

6. Place the transaxle in **PARK**.

7. Check and adjust the timing. Reconnect the vacuum advance hose. Place the transaxle in **DRIVE**.

8. If not equipped with air conditioning, turn the idle speed screw to attain specified rpm.

9. If equipped with air conditioning, perform the following procedures:

a. Turn the idle speed screw to set the specified curb idle.

b. Turn the air conditioning **ON** and disconnect the compressor clutch wire.

c. Open the throttle momentarily to extend the solenoid plunger.

d. Adjust the solenoid screw to obtain the solenoid idle speed shown on the underhood sticker.

e. Reconnect the compressor clutch and turn the air conditioning **OFF**.

10. Reconnect all hoses and remove the tachometer.

1982–85 M4MC/M4ME WITHOUT IDLE SPEED SOLENOID

Most 1982–85 models are equipped with an Idle Speed Control (ISC) mounted on the float bowl. Idle speeds are computer controlled and the ICS should not be adjusted.

On some V8 models an Idle Load Compensator (ILC) is mounted on the float bowl to control the curb idle speed. The ILC is adjusted at the factory and capped to prevent readjustment.

On vehicles that do not include either an ISC or ILC but are equipped with air conditioning, an idle speed solenoid is used to maintain idle speed. For adjustment of these refer to the previous 1982–85 adjustment procedures.

NOTE: The underhood sticker specifies which idle system the vehicle is equipped with.

Fuel Injected Models

NOTE: Idle speed adjustment is not required unless throttle body parts have been replaced, the Throttle Position Sensor (TPS) and/or the Idle Speed Control (ISC) have been adjusted.
Before performing the minimum idle speed adjustment, visually inspect the vacuum hoses for leaks, splits or cuts, the throttle body and intake manifold for vacuum leaks. Vacuum leaks can cause the engine(s) to run at a high rpm.

NOTE: If instructions on the underhood sticker differ from these, follow the underhood sticker.

MULTI–PORT FUEL INJECTION (MFI)

1. Using a scratch awl, pierce and pry the idle speed screw plug from the

throttle body; it can be discarded and not replaced.

2. Connect a tachometer to the engine. Set the parking brake, place the transaxle in the **PARK**, position the steering wheel in the **STRAIGHT AHEAD** position and turn **OFF** the air conditioning and all accessories.

3. Operate the engine until normal operating temperatures are reached.

4. Check and/or adjust the timing.

5. On the Climate Control Driver Information Panel (CCDIC), press the "COOLER" button and wait for at least 20 seconds; this will cause the ISC motor plunger to retract. Once the motor has retracted, inspect the throttle lever to make sure it is resting on the minimum idle speed screw.

6. If the minimum idle speed it too high, use a T–20 Torx® Driver to adjust the minimum idle speed screw. The minimum idle speed should be 450–550 rpm (0–500 miles) or 450–600 rpm (above 500 miles).

7. After adjustment, disconnect the test equipment and turn the ignition switch **OFF** for 10 seconds.

8. Turn the engine **ON**, check the ISC operation and inspect the ECM and/or BCM readout for stored codes or telltale lights. Perform the diagnostics.

9. Disconnect the negative battery cable for 10 seconds; this will reset the TPS learned value in the ECM.

DIGITAL FUEL INJECTION (DFI)

1. Connect a tachometer to the engine. Set the parking brake, place the transaxle in the **PARK**, position the steering wheel in the **STRAIGHT AHEAD** position. Turn **OFF** the air conditioning and all accessories. Ground the green test connector located near the alternator.

2. Operate the engine until normal operating temperatures are reached.

3. Check and/or adjust the timing.

4. Remove the air cleaner and plug the THERMAC vacuum tap.

5. To retract plunger of the ISC motor, perform the following procedures.

  a. Disconnect the ISC connector and connect the jumper harness to the ISC.

  b. Connect the jumper wire leading to the ISC terminal **C** to 12V at the battery or junction block.

  c. Apply finger pressure to the ISC plunger (close the throttle switch). Touch the jumper wire connected to the ISC terminal **D** to ground until the ISC plunger retracts fully and stops; DO NOT allow the ground wire to be connected for longer than necessary for damage to the ISC motor can result.

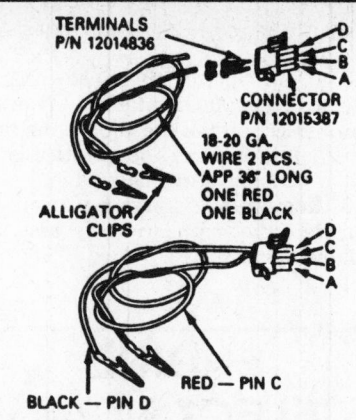

TERMINALS P/N 12014836

CONNECTOR P/N 12015387

18-20 GA. WIRE 2 PCS. APP 36" LONG ONE RED ONE BLACK

ALLIGATOR CLIPS

RED — PIN C

BLACK — PIN D

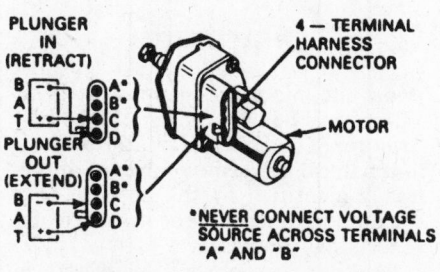

PLUNGER IN (RETRACT)

PLUNGER OUT (EXTEND)

4 — TERMINAL HARNESS CONNECTOR

MOTOR

*NEVER CONNECT VOLTAGE SOURCE ACROSS TERMINALS "A" AND "B"

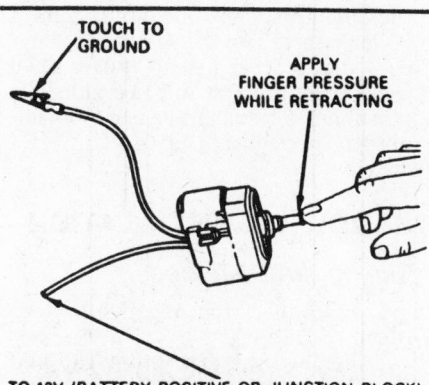

TOUCH TO GROUND

APPLY FINGER PRESSURE WHILE RETRACTING

TO 12V (BATTERY POSITIVE OR JUNCTION BLOCK)

Using a jumper harness to retract/extend the Idle Speed Control (ISC) unit

NOTE: Never connect a voltage source to the ISC motor terminals A and B as damage to the internal throttle switch contacts will result.

  d. Once the motor has retracted, inspect the throttle lever to make sure it is resting on the minimum idle speed screw.

6. If the minimum idle speed it too high, adjust the minimum idle speed screw. The minimum idle speed should be 375–500 rpm (0–500 miles) or 475–550 rpm (above 500 miles).

7. After adjustment, disconnect the test equipment and turn the ignition switch **OFF** for 10 seconds.

8. Turn the engine **ON**, check the ISC operation and inspect the ECM and/or BCM readout for stored codes or telltale lights. Perform the diagnostics.

9. Disconnect the negative battery

cable for 10 seconds; this will reset the TPS learned value in the ECM.

SEQUENTIAL FUEL INJECTION (SFI)

1. Set the parking brake, place the transaxle in the **PARK**, position the steering wheel in the **STRAIGHT AHEAD** position. Turn **OFF** the air conditioning and all accessories.

2. With the ignition switch turned **OFF**, enter ECM outputs mode "EO07" and wait for 30 seconds.

3. Turn the ignition switch **ON** and disconnect the electrical connector from the Idle Air Control (IAC) motor.

4. Operate the engine until normal operating temperatures are reached and enter the ECM diagnostic data "ED11" to read rpm.

5. If necessary, adjust the idle spot screw to 450–550 rpm.

6. Turn the engine **OFF** and reconnect the electrical connector to the IAC motor.

7. To the ECM, enter data "ED01". Loosen the Throttle Position Sensor (TPS) screw(s), adjust the TPS to 350–450MV and retorque the screws.

8. Start the engine and inspect the idle speed.

IDLE AIR CONTROL VALVE

The Idle Air Control valve controls engine idle speed by bypassing air around the throttle valve. It responds to a number of electronic signals, actually compensating for changes in engine load. It is not adjustable.

IDLE MIXTURE ADJUSTMENT

On these models the air/fuel mixture is controlled by the electronic control module of the Computer Command Control (CCC) system. No adjustment should be attempted.

Idle Speed Diesel Engine

ADJUSTMENT

Hot Slow Idle

1. Block the drive wheels and set the parking brake.

2. Place the transaxle gear selector in the **PARK** position.

3. Start the engine and allow it to reach normal operating temperatures.

4. Stop the engine. Remove the air cleaner assembly, the MAP sensor and retainer from the side of the air cleaner; move the MAP sensor/bracket (with hose attached) aside.

5. Using the Crossover Cover tool No. J–26996–1 or equivalent, install it onto the throttle body.

6. Clean the front cover probe holder (rpm counter) and the crankshaft

balancer rim. Using the magnetic pickup, of Tachometer tool No. J–26925 or equivalent, insert it into the front cover probe holder.

7. Connect the tachometer leads to the battery; red to positive and black to negative.

8. If equipped with air conditioning, disconnect the compressor clutch wire from the compressor.

9. If equipped with a parking brake release vacuum line, disconnect it.

NOTE: If equipped with a parking brake release vacuum line, DO NOT touch the steering wheel or brake pedal during adjustment, for the load may alter the engine speed.

10. Turn all of the electrical accessories **OFF**. Start the engine and place the transaxle in the **DRIVE** position.

11. On the fuel injection pump, turn the idle speed screw to 600 rpm.

Cold Fast Idle

1. Block the drive wheels and set the parking brake.

2. Place the transaxle gear selector in the **PARK** position.

3. If equipped with an internal EGR, perform the following procedures:

   a. Disconnect the coolant temperature sensor connector.

   b. Disconnect the Housing Pressure Cold Advance (HPCA) connector and the fast idle temperature switch; DO NOT allow the jumper wire to touch ground.

4. Start the engine and place the transaxle in **DRIVE**. Check and/or ad-

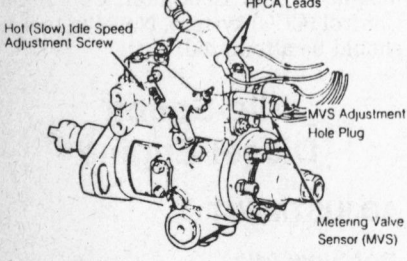

Hot (Slow) Idle Speed Adjustment Screw

HPCA Leads

MVS Adjustment Hole Plug

Metering Valve Sensor (MVS)

View of the diesel fuel injection pump

just the fast idle speed.

5. Open the throttle slightly and allow the plunger to extend.

NOTE: If the idle and fast idle speeds are different (on the underhood decal), always use the decal information.

6. If equipped with an internal EGR, remove the HPCA jumper wire. On all other models, reconnect the temperature sensor connector.

7. Check and/or adjust the slow idle speed. Turn the engine **OFF**. Reconnect the air conditioning compressor

clutch wire and remove the tachometer.

8. If equipped with cruise control, adjust the servo throttle rod for minimum slack; install the clip on the first free hole closest to the throttle lever but within the servo ball.

9. Remove the crossover cover. To complete the installation, reverse the removal procedures.

ENGINE ELECTRICAL

Distributor

Most models are equipped with an Electronic Spark Timing (EST) distributor. The EST distributor uses no mechanical or vacuum advance and is easily identified by the absence of a vacuum advance and the presence of a 4 terminal connector.

Another type of ignition system is the Computer Controlled Coil Ignition (C^3I) system. The C^3I system does not use a distributor; instead, it uses a coil pack, an ignition module, a crankshaft sensor and a camshaft sensor. The following procedure is for the HEI distributor.

REMOVAL & INSTALLATION

Timing Not Disturbed

1. Disconnect the negative battery cable.

2. Remove the distributor cap and electrical harness connector from the distributor.

3. Using a piece of chalk, matchmark the rotor to the distributor body and the distributor body to the block.

4. Remove the hold-down clamp and lift the distributor from the engine until the rotor stops turning. Mark the position of the rotor again and remove the distributor.

5. Insert the distributor into the engine, making sure the tip of the rotor is aligned with the alignment marks on the distributor housing and the engine.

6. Make sure the oil pump intermediate drive shaft is properly seated in the oil pump.

7. Install the distributor lock but DO NOT tighten.

8. Reconnect the electrical harness connector(s) to the distributor, then, install distributor cap.

9. Start the engine and allow it to reach normal operating temperatures. Check and/or adjust the timing.

Timing Disturbed

1. Disconnect the negative battery cable.

2. Remove the distributor cap and the electrical harness connector from the distributor.

3. Using a piece of chalk, matchmark the rotor to the distributor body and the distributor body to the block.

4. Remove the hold-down clamp and lift the distributor from the engine until the rotor stops turning. Mark the position of the rotor again and remove the distributor.

5. Remove the No. 1 spark plug and place a finger over the hole. Using a wrench on the crankshaft pulley bolt, slowly turn the engine until compression is felt.

6. Align the timing marks so the No. 1 cylinder is on TDC of the compression stroke.

7. Position the distributor in the engine with the rotor at No. 1 firing position. Make sure the oil pump intermediate drive shaft is properly seated in the oil pump.

8. Install the distributor retainer and lock bolt, tighten the lock bolt.

9. Reconnect the electrical harness connector(s) to the distributor and install distributor cap.

10. Start the engine and allow it to reach normal operating temperatures. Check and/or adjust the timing.

Alternator

For further information on the charging system, please refer to "Charging and Starting" in the Unit Repair section.

PRECAUTIONS

To prevent damage to the on-board computer, alternator and regulator, the following precautionary measures must be taken when working with the electrical system.

• Never reverse the battery connections. Always check the battery polarity visually. This is to be done before any connections are made to be sure that all of the connections correspond to the battery ground polarity.

• Booster batteries for starting must be connected properly. Make sure that the positive cable of the booster battery is connected to the positive terminal of the battery that is getting the boost. This applies to both negative and ground cables.

• Make sure the ignition switch is **OFF** when connecting or disconnecting any electrical component, especially on vehicles equipped with an on-board computer control system.

- Disconnect the battery cables before using a fast charger; the charger has a tendency to force current through the diodes in the opposite direction for which they were designed. This burns out the diodes.
- Never use a fast charger as a booster for starting the vehicle.
- Never disconnect the voltage regulator while the engine is running.
- Do not ground the alternator output terminal.
- Do not operate the alternator on an open circuit with the field energized.
- Do not attempt to polarize an alternator.

BELT TENSION ADJUSTMENT

NOTE: The V6 engine is equipped with a serpentine, self adjusting drive belt; no adjustment is necessary.

REMOVAL & INSTALLATION

1. Disconnect the negative battery cable.
2. Label and disconnect the electrical connectors from the back of the alternator.
3. Release the tension from the drive belt and remove the belt from the alternator pulley. Do not remove the belt from any other pulleys.
4. Remove the alternator-to-bracket bolts and the alternator from the vehicle.
5. To install, reverse the removal procedures.

NOTE: If equipped with air conditioning, it may be necessary to remove the compressor retaining bracket.

Integral Voltage Regulator

An alternator with an integral voltage regulator is standard equipment. There are no adjustments possible with this unit; testing procedures will be found in the "Charging and Starting Systems" Unit Repair Section.

Starter

For further information on the starter system, please refer to "Charging and Starting" in the Unit Repair section.

REMOVAL & INSTALLATION

NOTE: On some models it may be necessary to move the fuel lines out of the way. Remove the fuel lines from the retaining clamp and loosen the regulator.

CAUTION

If equipped with fuel injection, relieve the pressure from the fuel system before disconnecting the fuel lines.

1. Disconnect the negative battery cable.
2. Raise and support the front of the vehicle on jackstands.
3. If equipped with a starter splash shield, remove it.
4. Disconnect and label the wires from the solenoid.
5. Remove the starter-to-engine bolts and the starter.
6. To install, reverse the removal procedures.

NOTE: If starter shims were removed, they must be installed in their original location to assure proper drive pinion-to-flywheel engagement.

Diesel Glow Plugs

REMOVAL & INSTALLATION

1. Disconnect the electrical connector from the glow plug.
2. Using a deep socket, remove the glow plug from the engine.
3. Inspect and test the glow plug.
4. To install, reverse the removal procedures. Torque the glow plug-to-engine to 15 ft. lbs.

TESTING

1. Disconnect the electrical connector from the glow plug.
2. Using a test light, connect it between the glow plug terminal and the positive battery terminal.
3. If the test light turns **ON**, the glow plug is working.
4. Test all other glow plugs; replace any glow plug which does not work.

ENGINE MECHANICAL

Engine

REMOVAL & INSTALLATION

Toronado 1982–85

1. Position a drain pan under the radiator, open the drain cock and drain the cooling system.
2. Using a scratch awl, mark the outline of the hood hinges on the hood and remove hood.
3. If equipped with a fan shroud, remove the strap and the venturi ring seal clips; move the seal toward the radiator. Remove the air cleaner.
4. Disconnect the negative battery cable.
5. Disconnect the radiator hoses, the oil cooler lines, the heater hoses, the vacuum hoses, the engine-to-body ground strap, the fuel hose(s), the electrical wiring connectors and throttle cable. Remove the air conditioning compressor and the power steering pump without disconnecting lines and move them aside.
6. Remove the throttle control switch bracket, the radiator support and the radiator.
7. Raise and support the front of the vehicle on jackstands.
8. Disconnect the exhaust pipes from the exhaust manifold. Loosen but DO NOT remove the upper left flywheel cover attaching bolt.
9. Disconnect starter electrical connectors and remove starter.
10. Remove the torque converter cover and the converter-to-flywheel bolts. Using a scratch awl, scribe alignment marks on the converter and the flywheel for reassembly. Remove the splash shield.
11. Support the final drive assembly.
12. Remove the right side output shaft support bracket bolts and the 1 left side final drive-to-engine bolt. Using a scratch awl, scribe alignment marks around the washers for reassembly purposes.
13. Remove the engine mount-to-crossmember nuts and the front engine mount nuts. Remove the lower right engine-to-transaxle bolt.
14. Support the final drive assembly with a chain stretched under and across the final drive assembly and attached to holes in the frame members.
15. Lower the vehicle.
16. Using a vertical lifting device, attach it to and support engine.
17. Remove the remaining transaxle-to-engine bolts.
18. Lift the engine from the vehicle.

CAUTION

If the vehicle is to be moved, install a torque converter holding tool. If it is necessary to reposition the air conditioner compressor, DO NOT disconnect the refrigerant lines.

19. To install, reverse removal procedures. Refill the cooling system. Start the engine, allow it to reach normal operating temperatures and check for leaks.

Eldorado and Seville 1982–85

1. Using a scratch awl, mark the outline of the hood hinges on the hood and remove hood.

2. Position a drain pan under the radiator, open the drain cock and drain the cooling system.

3. Disconnect the battery terminals from the battery and remove the battery.

4. Remove the air cleaner assembly.

5. Loosely install a special valve compressor tool on the EFI line pressure fitting. Place a towel around the fitting to catch any spray. Slowly tighten the tool to relieve fuel pressure.

6. Raise and support the front of the vehicle on jackstands. Remove the exhaust pipe flange-to-exhaust manifold bolts. Separate the left side pipe from the Y-pipe and remove the exhaust pipe from the vehicle.

7. Disconnect the shift linkage from the transaxle.

8. Disconnect the flexible fuel line from the main fuel pipe; use a new clamp on installation.

9. Remove the drive axle-to-output shaft screws from both sides.

10. Remove the engine and transaxle mount nuts.

11. Remove the lower fan shroud screws and the lower radiator hose.

12. Lower the vehicle. Disconnect the upper radiator hose and the transaxle cooler lines.

13. Remove the radiator upper cover and the radiator.

14. Remove the water pump-to-fan clutch nuts and the fan shroud.

15. Disconnect and plug the power steering hoses at the steering gear.

16. Disconnect the flexible fuel line from the pressure regulator fuel return pipe; use a new clamp on installation.

17. If equipped with cruise control, disconnect the vacuum lines from the power unit. Pull the hoses out of the tie-down straps and position them out of the way.

18. Disconnect the following items:

    a. The carbon canister hoses.

    b. The throttle cable from the throttle body or carburetor.

    c. The heater hoses from the water valve and the water pump.

    d. The brake vacuum line at the brake pipe.

    e. The speedometer cable from the transaxle.

    f. The engine electrical harness-to-center bulkhead connector.

    g. The distributor wiring.

    h. The heater wire from the water valve.

    i. Wiring at the windshield wiper motor and the washer bottle.

    j. The engine ground strap from the cowl.

    k. The wiring from the air conditioning compressor.

19. Remove the coolant reservoir tank.

20. Loosen the AIR pump and remove the belt from the air conditioning compressor.

21. Remove the compressor-to-bracket screws and position the compressor out of the way; DO NOT disconnect any of the lines.

22. Install a vertical lifting device to the engine and remove the engine, transaxle and final drives as a unit.

23. To install, reverse the removal procedures. Torque the engine mounts to 65 ft. lbs., transaxle mounts to 48 ft. lbs. and the output shaft-to-drive axle bolts to 60 ft. lbs. Refill the cooling system. Start the engine, allow it to reach normal operating temperatures and check for leaks.

Riviera 1982–85

1. Using a scratch awl, mark the outline of the hood hinges on the hood and remove hood.

2. Position a drain pan under the radiator, open the drain cock and drain the cooling system.

3. Disconnect the battery terminals from the battery and remove the battery.

4. Remove the air cleaner assembly.

5. Raise and support the front of the vehicle on jackstands. Remove the exhaust pipe flange-to-exhaust manifold bolts. Separate the left side pipe from the Y-pipe and remove the exhaust pipe from the vehicle.

6. Remove the lower fan shroud screws and the lower radiator hose.

7. Lower the vehicle. Disconnect the upper radiator hose and the transaxle cooler lines.

8. Disconnect the flexible fuel line from the main fuel pipe; use a new clamp on installation.

9. Remove the drive axle-to-output shaft screws from both sides.

10. Remove the engine and transaxle mount nuts.

11. Remove the radiator upper cover and the radiator.

12. If equipped with a turbocharger, disconnect the turbo outlet exhaust pipe from the turbocharger.

13. Remove the starter electrical connectors, the starter-to-engine bolts and the starter.

14. Matchmark the torque converter-to-flywheel, remove the torque convertor cover and the converter-to-flywheel bolts.

15. Remove the transaxle-to-engine bolts.

16. Remove the right output shaft support bolts and the front engine mounts.

17. Install chain to support the final drive.

18. Remove the final drive-to-engine bracket.

19. Using a vertical lifting device, install to the engine and remove it from the vehicle.

20. To install, reverse the removal procedures. Refill the cooling system. Start the engine, allow it to reach normal operating temperatures and check for leaks.

Toronado and Riviera — V6 3.8L 1986–87

1. Disconnect the negative battery cable. Using a scratch awl, matchmark the hood hinges and remove the hood.

2. Position a drain pan under the radiator, open the drain cock and drain the cooling system.

3. Remove the air inlet and radiator hoses.

4. Disconnect the following electrical connectors:

    a. Fuel rail and other injection system connectors

    b. Engine ground wires

    c. Oil pressure sending unit.

    d. EGR solenoid

    e. Coolant temperature sending units

    f. Throttle body electrical connections

    g. Crankshaft and camshaft sensors

    h. Alternator

5. Remove the serpentine drive belt. Remove the power steering pump and move it aside; DO NOT disconnect the pressure hoses (if possible).

6. Remove the alternator. Disconnect and remove the heater hoses.

7. Remove the throttle cable bracket and the cruise control cables from the throttle lever.

8. Disconnect both fuel lines.

9. Remove the cooling fan and radiator.

10. Disconnect the exhaust Y-pipe, remove the exhaust manifold on the forward side of the engine. Label and disconnect the vacuum lines between the engine and components mounted on the firewall.

11. Remove the engine-to-transaxle bolts, the vibration damper and bracket from the engine.

12. Remove the ground strap and wiring harness bolts. Remove the engine-to-transaxle bracket. Raise the vehicle and support it securely.

13. Remove the air conditioning compressor-to-bracket bolts, move it aside and support it without disturbing the refrigerant hoses. Remove the exhaust pipe.

14. Remove the engine-to-mount nuts. Matchmark the torque convert-

er-to-flywheel and remove the torque converter-to-flywheel bolts.

15. Remove the left front wheel and the remaining engine-to-transaxle bolts. Make sure to remove the 1 bolt that faces in the opposite direction.

16. Remove the engine-to-transaxle bracket and lower the vehicle. Using an engine vertical lifting device, connect it to the engine and lift the engine from the vehicle.

17. To install, reverse the removal procedures. Align the torque converter-to-flywheel matchmarks. Torque the damper pulley-to-crankshaft bolt to 200 ft. lbs., the exhaust manifold-to-cylinder head bolts to 37 ft. lbs., the transaxle-to-engine bolts to 55 ft. lbs. and the engine mount-to-engine nuts 70 ft. lbs. Refill the cooling system. Start the engine, allow it to reach normal operating temperatures and check for leaks.

NOTE: When installing the torque converter-to-flywheel, make sure the weld nuts on the converter are flush with the flywheel.

Eldorado and Seville 1986–89

1. Disconnect the negative battery cable. Position a drain pan under the radiator, open the drain cock and drain the cooling system.

2. Remove the air cleaner. Using a scratch awl, matchmark the hood hinge-to-hood and remove the hood.

3. Remove the cooling fan and the accessory drive belt.

4. Remove the upper radiator hose and disconnect the heater hose from the thermostat housing.

5. Disconnect the following electrical connectors, positioning the wires out of the way:
   a. Oil pressure sending unit
   b. Coolant temperature sensor
   c. Distributor
   d. EGR solenoid
   e. Engine temperature switch
   f. Idle Speed Control
   g. Throttle position sensor
   h. Injector electrical connections
   i. MAT sensor
   j. Oxygen sensor
   k. Throttle body base warmer
   l. Alternator
   m. Ground wires at the alternator mounting bracket.

6. Disconnect the accelerator, the cruise control and the transaxle throttle valve cables from the throttle lever.

7. Disconnect the cruise control diaphragm/bracket and move them out of the way.

8. Disconnect the transaxle oil cooler lines from the radiator. Remove the radiator.

9. Disconnect and remove the oil cooler lines from the oil filter adapter.

10. Remove the oil cooler lines-to-transaxle bracket.

11. Remove the air cleaner bracket and the oil filter housing adapter.

12. Disconnect the air injection tubes from the diverter valve.

13. Remove the right front and right rear body braces.

14. Remove the right front heater hose and the coolant reservoir.

15. Remove the Air Injection Reactor (AIR) filter box and bracket. Remove the idler pulley for the accessory drive belt.

16. Remove the power steering line brace from the right cylinder head. Remove the pump and belt tensioner as an assembly and position them forward of the engine.

——— CAUTION ———

Make sure to follow carefully the instructions in the next 2 steps. Air conditioning refrigerant has a boiling point of −26°F and must not be handled except by a qualified person. Follow fuel pressure release procedures carefully to avoid injury.

17. Discharge the air conditioning system (by someone trained and experienced in refrigeration repair) and remove the air conditioning lines from the accumulator and condenser.

18. Position a metal container and a rag so as to catch the fuel and carefully depress the center pin at the Schrader valve on the fuel line until all fuel pressure is exhausted. Disconnect supply and return fuel lines from the throttle body. Remove the fuel line bracket from the transaxle and move the fuel lines aside.

19. Remove the EGR lines and brackets. Remove the vacuum modulator line and the fuel filter; reposition them aside.

20. Raise and support the front of the vehicle on jackstands.

21. Remove the starter heat shield. Label and disconnect the electrical connectors from the starter. Disconnect any ground wires still connected at the block.

22. Disconnect and remove the exhaust crossover pipe. Remove the starter-to-engine bolts and the starter.

23. Remove the torque converter covers. Matchmark the torque converter-to-flywheel and remove the flywheel-to-torque converter bolts.

24. Remove the air conditioning compressor lower dust shield, the right front tire and the outer wheelhouse plastic shield.

25. Remove the right rear transaxle-to-engine mount bolt and the lower engine mounting damper nut.

26. Remove the front engine mount nuts and the right rear transaxle mount nuts.

27. Remove the alternator. Remove the O_2 sensor wires. Remove the heater bypass bracket from the right side of the vehicle.

28. Remove the right side engine brace and lower the vehicle to the ground.

29. Remove the engine-to-transaxle bolts; the bolts are accessible from the top.

30. Run a chain from a lifting crane down to the 2 lift points on top of the engine and ensure it is secure. Lift the engine out of the vehicle.

31. To install, first situate a floorjack under the transaxle and raise it slightly so it will align with the engine. Lower the engine into the engine compartment, being careful not to damage accessories that are still in position. Change the engine and transaxle angles as necessary to get good alignment and then engage the dowels that are on the engine block with the corresponding holes in the transaxle.

32. Install the 5 transaxle-to-engine bolts that are accessible from above into the bell housing. Lower the engine, directing it squarely onto its mounts. Remove the lifting equipment.

33. To complete the installation, reverse the removal procedures. Make sure to replenish all fluids with the required type and quantity. Recharge the air conditioning system charged. Operate the engine until normal operating temperatures are reached and check for leaks.

Toronado, Riviera and Reatta 1988–89

1. Using a scratch awl, matchmark the hood hinge-to-hood and remove the hood.

2. Relieve the fuel pressure and disconnect the fuel lines from the fuel rail.

3. Disconnect the negative battery cable. Remove the air intake duct.

4. Remove the upper engine strut. From the throttle body, remove the throttle cable bracket and the cables.

5. Raise and support the front of the vehicle on jackstands.

6. Position a drain pan under the radiator, open the drain cock and drain the cooling system.

7. Remove the exhaust pipe from the rear exhaust manifold.

8. Using a vertical lifting device, secure it to the engine and support its weight. Remove the engine mounting bolts.

9. Disconnect the electrical connectors from the starter. Remove the starter-to-engine bolts and the starter.

10. Remove the serpentine drive belt. Remove the air conditioning compressor-to-bracket bolts and move the

compressor aside; DO NOT disconnect the pressure hoses.

11. Disconnect and plug the power steering hoses at the steering gear.

12. Remove the lower transaxle-to-engine bolts.

NOTE: One of the lower transaxle bolts is located between the transaxle case and the engine block; it is installed in the opposite direction.

13. Remove the flywheel cover. Matchmark the torque converter-to-flywheel for alignment purposes. Remove the torque converter-to-flywheel bolts and slide the torque converter rearward.

14. Remove the engine support bracket-to-transaxle bolts and the bracket.

15. Lower the vehicle.

16. Disconnect the vacuum hoses from the vacuum modulator and the emission control canister. Disconnect and move aside any electrical harness connectors which may be in the way.

17. Remove the radiator and heater hoses from the engine.

18. Remove the remaining transaxle-to-engine bolts. Lift the engine assembly from the vehicle and attach it to a work stand.

19. To install, reverse the removal procedures. Align the torque converter-to-flywheel matchmarks. Torque the torque converter-to-flywheel bolts to 46 ft. lbs. Refill the cooling system and the power steering reservoir. Start the engine, allow it to reach normal operating temperatures and check for leaks.

Allante 1987–89

1. Disconnect the negative battery cable. Position a drain pan under the radiator, open the drain cock and drain the cooling system.

2. Remove the air cleaner. Using a scratch awl, matchmark the hood hinge-to-hood and remove the hood.

3. Remove the cooling fans and the accessory drive belt.

4. Remove the upper intake manifold. Remove the upper radiator hose and disconnect the heater hose from the thermostat housing.

5. Disconnect the following electrical connectors, positioning the wires out of the way:
   a. Oil pressure sending unit
   b. Coolant temperature sensor
   c. Distributor
   d. EGR solenoid
   e. Engine temperature switch
   f. Idle Speed Control
   g. Throttle position sensor
   h. Injector electrical connections
   i. MAT sensor
   j. Oxygen sensor

k. Throttle body base warmer
   l. Alternator
   m. Ground wires at the alternator mounting bracket.

6. Disconnect the accelerator, the cruise control and the transaxle throttle valve cables from the throttle lever.

7. Disconnect the cruise control diaphragm/bracket and move them aside.

8. Disconnect the transaxle oil cooler lines from the radiator. Remove the radiator.

9. Disconnect and remove the oil cooler lines from the oil filter adapter.

10. Remove the oil cooler lines-to-transaxle bracket.

11. Remove the air cleaner bracket and the oil filter adapter.

12. Disconnect the air injection tubes from the diverter valve.

13. Remove the cross car brace.

14. Remove the right front heater hose and the coolant reservoir.

15. Remove the Air Injection Reactor (AIR) filter and bracket.

16. Remove the power steering line brace from the right cylinder head. Remove the pump and belt tensioner as an assembly and position them forward of the engine.

CAUTION

Make sure to follow carefully the instructions in the next 2 steps. Air conditioning refrigerant has a boiling point of −26°F and must not be handled except by a qualified person. Follow fuel pressure release procedures carefully to avoid injury.

---

17. Discharge the air conditioning system (by someone trained and experienced in refrigeration repair) and remove the air conditioning lines from the accumulator and condenser.

18. Position a metal container and a rag so as to catch the fuel and carefully depress the center pin at the Schrader valve on the fuel line until all fuel pressure is exhausted. Disconnect supply and return fuel lines from the fuel rail. Remove the fuel line bracket from the transaxle and move the fuel lines aside.

19. Raise and support the front of the vehicle on jackstands.

20. Label and disconnect the electrical connectors from the starter. Disconnect any ground wires still connected at the block.

21. Disconnect the O_2 level sensor wire and the remove the O_2 sensors.

22. Disconnect and remove the exhaust Y-pipe. Remove the starter-to-engine bolts and the starter.

23. Remove the torque converter covers. Matchmark the torque converter-to-flywheel and remove the flywheel-to-torque converter bolts.

24. Remove the air conditioning compressor lower dust shield, the

right front tire and the outer wheelhouse plastic shield.

25. Remove the right rear transaxle-to-engine mount bolt, the front engine mount nuts and the right rear transaxle mount bolts.

26. Remove the alternator. Remove the O_2 sensor wires. Remove the heater bypass bracket from the right side of the vehicle.

27. Remove the right side engine brace and lower the vehicle to the ground.

28. Remove the engine-to-transaxle bolts; the bolts are accessible from the top.

29. Run a chain from a lifting crane down to the 2 lift points on top of the engine and ensure it is secure. Lift the engine out of the vehicle.

30. To install, first situate a floorjack under the transaxle and raise it slightly so it will align with the engine. Lower the engine into the engine compartment, being careful not to damage accessories that are still in position. Change the engine and transaxle angles as necessary to get good alignment; engage the dowels that are on the engine block with the corresponding holes in the transaxle.

31. Install the 5 transaxle-to-engine bolts that are accessible from above into the bell housing. Lower the engine, directing it squarely onto its mounts. Remove the lifting equipment.

32. To complete the installation, reverse the removal procedures. Make sure to replenish all fluids with the required type and quantity. Recharge the air conditioning system charged. Operate the engine until normal operating temperatures are reached and check for leaks.

Cylinder Head

REMOVAL & INSTALLATION

Gasoline

3.8L and 4.1L V6 1982–85

1. Disconnect the negative battery cable.

2. Remove the intake manifold-to-engine bolts and the manifold.

3. Loosen and remove the drive belt(s).

4. When removing the left cylinder head, remove the oil dipstick, the air pump (if equipped) with the mounting bracket and move it aside with the hoses attached.

5. When removing the right cylinder head, remove the alternator, disconnect the power steering gear pump and the brackets.

6. Label and disconnect the spark plug wires; remove the spark plug wire

clips from the rocker arm cover studs.

7. Remove the exhaust manifold-to-cylinder head bolts.

8. Using an air hose and/or cloths, clean the dirt from the cylinder head and adjacent area to avoid getting dirt into the engine.

9. Remove the rocker arm cover and the rocker arm/shaft assembly from the cylinder head. Lift out the push rods.

10. Loosen the cylinder head-to-engine bolts, then, remove the bolts and the cylinder head.

11. Using a putty knife, clean the gasket mounting surfaces.

12. To install, reverse the removal procedures. Refill the cooling system. Operate the engine until normal operating temperatures are reached and check for leaks.

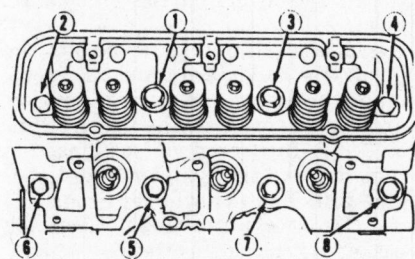

Cylinder head torquing sequence — V6 1981–85

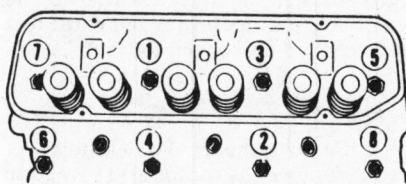

◄ FRONT OF VEHICLE

Cylinder head torquing sequence — 3.8L (1986–87) engine

3.8L V6 1986–87

1. Disconnect the negative battery cable. Remove the air cleaner.

2. Place a drain pan under the radiator, open the drain cock and drain the cooling system.

3. If equipped with air conditioning, remove the compressor from the mounting bracket and position it out of the way; DO NOT disconnect any lines. Disconnect the AIR hose at the check valve.

4. If equipped with a turbocharger assembly, depressurize the fuel system before removing any fuel lines or components.

5. Remove the intake manifold-to-engine bolts and the manifold.

6. If removing the right cylinder head, loosen the alternator belt, disconnect the electrical connectors and remove the alternator.

7. If removing the left cylinder head, remove the dipstick, power steering pump and air pump (if equipped).

8. Disconnect and label the spark plug wires.

9. Disconnect the exhaust manifold-to-cylinder head bolts and the manifold.

10. Remove the rocker arm cover and the rocker shaft assembly, then, lift out the pushrods. Be extremely careful to avoid getting dirt in the valve lifters. Keep the pushrods in order; they must be returned to their original positions.

11. Remove the cylinder head bolts, the cylinder head and gasket.

12. Using a putty knife, clean the gasket mounting surfaces.

13. To install, reverse the removal procedures. Torque the cylinder head-to-engine bolts in the following matter:

a. Use a heavy duty thread sealer on the head bolts.

b. Torque the head bolts to 25 ft. lbs. in the sequence shown in the illustration.

NOTE: Should 60 ft. lbs. be reached at any time in the next 2 steps, stop; DO NOT complete the balance of the 90 degree turn.

c. Tighten each bolt ¼ turn (90 degrees) in sequence.

d. Tighten each bolt an additional ¼ turn (90 degrees) in sequence.

14. To complete the installation, reverse the removal procedures. Refill the cooling system. Operate the engine until normal operating temperatures are reached and check for leaks.

3.8L V6 1988–89

Left Side

1. Remove the intake manifold.

2. Remove the exhaust manifold-to-cylinder head bolts and the exhaust manifold.

3. Remove the valve cover-to-cylinder head screws and the valve cover.

4. Label and remove the spark plug wires. Remove the C³I unit-to-cylinder head bolts and the unit.

5. Remove the serpentine drive belt, the alternator-to-bracket bolts, the alternator, the alternator bracket-to-engine bolts and the bracket.

6. If equipped with air conditioning, remove the compressor-to-bracket bolts and move it aside; DO NOT disconnect the refrigerant lines.

7. Remove the rocker arm assemblies, the guide plate and the pushrods; keep them in order for reinstallation purposes.

8. Remove the cylinder head bolts and the cylinder head.

9. Using a putty knife, clean and inspect the gasket mounting surfaces.

10. To install, use new gaskets, apply

P/N sealant No. 1052080 or equivalent, on the cylinder head bolt threads and reverse the removal procedures. Torque the cylinder head-to-engine bolts (in sequence, using 3 torquing steps) to 25 ft. lbs., an additional ¼ turn (90 degrees) and additional ¼ turn (90 degrees).

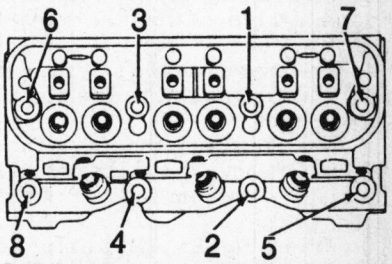

Cylinder head torquing sequence — 3.8L (1988–89) engine

NOTE: Should 60 ft. lbs. be reached at any time, STOP; DO NOT complete the balance of the torquing sequence.

11. To complete the installation, reverse the removal procedures. Torque the rocker arm bolts to 43 ft. lbs. Refill the cooling system. Start the engine, allow it to reach normal operating temperatures and check for leaks.

Right Side

1. Remove the intake manifold.

2. Remove the exhaust manifold-to-cylinder head bolts and the exhaust manifold.

3. Remove the valve cover-to-cylinder head screws and the valve cover.

4. Label and remove the spark plug wires.

5. Remove the serpentine drive belt, the power steering pump-to-bracket bolts, the belt tensioner assembly and the fuel line heat shield.

6. Remove the rocker arm assemblies, the guide plate and the pushrods; keep them in order for reinstallation purposes.

7. Remove the cylinder head bolts and the cylinder head.

8. Using a putty knife, clean and inspect the gasket mounting surfaces.

9. To install, use new gaskets, apply P/N sealant No. 1052080 or equivalent, on the cylinder head bolt threads and reverse the removal procedures. Torque the cylinder head-to-engine bolts (in sequence, using 3 torquing steps) to 25 ft. lbs., an additional ¼ turn (90 degrees) and additional ¼ turn (90 degrees).

NOTE: Should 60 ft. lbs. be reached at any time, STOP; DO NOT complete the balance of the torquing sequence.

10. To complete the installation, reverse the removal procedures. Torque the rocker arm bolts to 43 ft. lbs. Refill the cooling system. Start the engine,

allow it to reach normal operating temperatures and check for leaks.

4.1L V8 1982–87

1. Disconnect the negative battery cable. Drain the engine coolant.
2. Remove the intake and exhaust manifolds.
3. Disconnect all electrical and ground connections from the cylinder head.
4. When removing the left cylinder head, partially remove the power steering pump.
5. When removing the right cylinder head, remove the alternator and the heater hose from the rear of the head.
6. Remove the air pump, if equipped.
7. Remove bolts holding the rocker arm cover to the heads and remove the cover.
8. Remove nuts holding the rocker arm support to cylinder head, then remove the support and rocker arm assemblies. Store these assemblies so that they may be reinstalled in their correct locations.
9. Remove the pushrods and store them with their respective rocker arm assemblies.
10. Remove the cylinder head bolts.
11. Lift the cylinder head off of the block.

NOTE: Install cylinder liner holders to prevent loss of the bottom seal.

12. Remove all gasket material from the cylinder head and block mating surfaces.

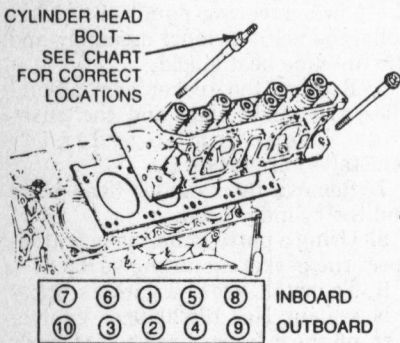

Cylinder head torquing sequence—4.1L (1982–87) engine

13. To install, reverse the removal procedures.
14. When torquing the head bolts, use the 3 step method. Torque the bolts to ⅓ of the total torque listed in the sequence shown. Once this is done, repeat the same procedure, this time torquing all the bolts to ⅔ of the total listed torque. Finally torque the bolts to the recommended torque of 90 ft. lbs. Refill the cooling system. Operate the engine until normal operating

temperatures are reached and check for leaks.

4.1L AND 4.5L 1988–89 ENGINES
Left Side

1. Disconnect the negative battery cable.
2. Drain the cooling system.
3. Remove the rocker arm covers.
4. Remove the intake manifold-to-engine bolts and intake manifold.
5. Remove the exhaust manifold crossover pipe, the exhaust pipe-to-exhaust manifold bolts, the exhaust manifold-to-cylinder head bolts and the exhaust manifold.
6. Remove the engine lifting bracket and the dipstick tube.
7. Remove the AIR bracket-to-engine bolts and move the bracket aside.
8. Remove the cylinder head-to-engine bolts and the cylinder head.
9. Using a putty knife, clean the gasket mounting surfaces.
10. To install, use new gaskets, sealant (if necessary), apply GM lubricant No. 1052356 or equivalent, to the cylinder head bolt threads and reverse the removal procedures. Torque the cylinder head bolts (in sequence) using three steps: 1st to 38 ft. lbs., 2nd to 68 ft. lbs. and 3rd to 90 ft. lbs. (bolts No. 1, 3 & 4).

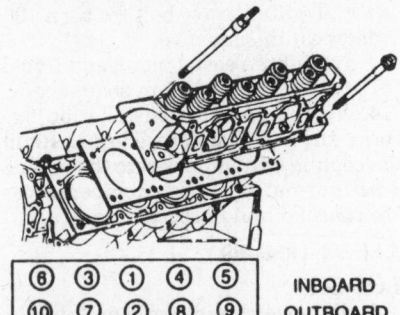

Cylinder head torquing sequence—4.1L and 4.5L (1988–89) engines

11. To complete the installation, reverse the removal procedures. Refill the cooling system. Start the engine, allow it to reach normal operating temperatures and check for leaks.

Right Side

1. Remove negative battery cable.
2. Drain the cooling system.
3. Remove the rocker arm covers.
4. Remove the intake manifold-to-engine bolts and intake manifold.
5. Disconnect the exhaust manifold crossover pipe, the exhaust pipe-to-exhaust manifold bolts, the exhaust manifold-to-cylinder head bolts and the exhaust manifold.
6. Remove the engine lifting bracket.
7. Remove the AIR bracket-to-engine bolts and move the bracket aside.
8. Remove the cylinder head-to-engine bolts and the cylinder head.

9. Using a putty knife, clean the gasket mounting surfaces.
10. To install, use new gaskets, sealant (if necessary), apply GM lubricant No. 1052356 or equivalent, to the cylinder head bolt threads and reverse the removal procedures. Torque the cylinder head bolts (in sequence) using three steps: 1st to 38 ft. lbs., 2nd to 68 ft. lbs. and 3rd to 90 ft. lbs. (bolts No. 1, 3 & 4).
11. To complete the installation, reverse the removal procedures. Refill the cooling system. Start the engine, allow it to reach normal operating temperatures and check for leaks.

5.0L V8 1982–85

1. Remove the intake manifold.
2. Remove the exhaust manifold-to-cylinder head bolts and the manifold.
3. Remove the valve cover. Remove the ground strap from the left cylinder head.
4. Remove the rocker arm bolts, the pivots, the rocker arms and push rods. Mark the pivots and store the rocker arms separated so they can be installed in their original locations.
5. Remove the cylinder head-to-engine bolts and the cylinder head.
6. Using a putty knife, clean the gasket mounting surfaces.
7. To install, use new gaskets and reverse the removal procedures. Refill the cooling system. Check and/or adjust the timing. Operate the engine until normal operating temperatures are reached and check for leaks.

Diesel—5.7L 1982–85

1. Remove the intake manifold.
2. Remove the rocker arm cover and any accessory brackets which may interfere with the cylinder head removal.
3. From the right side head, disconnect the glow plug wiring and the ground strap.
4. Remove the rocker arm bolts, the pivots, the rocker arms and push rods; be sure to keep the parts in order for reinstallation purposes.
5. Remove the exhaust manifold-to-cylinder head, leave the cross-over pipe attached to the exhaust manifold.
6. From the cylinder head (side of the engine being removed) remove the block drain plugs.
7. Remove the cylinder head-to-en-

Cylinder head torquing sequence—5.7L Diesel and 5.0L

gine bolts and cylinder head from the engine.

8. Using a putty knife, clean the gasket mounting surfaces.

9. To install, use new gaskets and reverse the removal procedures. The prechamber shield of the cylinder head gasket MUST face the cylinder head. Torque the cylinder head-to-engine bolts (in sequence): 1st, to 100 ft. lbs. and 2nd, to 130 ft. lbs. Refill the cooling system. Check and/or adjust the timing. Start the engine, allow it to reach normal operating temperatures and check for leaks.

OVERHAUL

For all cylinder head overhaul procedures, please refer to the "Engine Rebuilding" in the Unit Repair section.

Rocker Arms/Shafts

REMOVAL & INSTALLATION

3.8L

The 1982–85 3.8L engine uses a rocker arm shaft assembly. The rocker arm are stamped "L" and "R"; be sure to install them in the same position.

The 1986–89 3.8L engine uses individual rocker arm and pedestal assemblies.

1982–85

1. Disconnect the negative battery cable.

2. Remove the rocker arm cover.

3. Remove the rocker arm shaft assembly-to-cylinder head bolts and the assembly. Remove the bolts from the shaft and disassemble the rocker arms from the shaft.

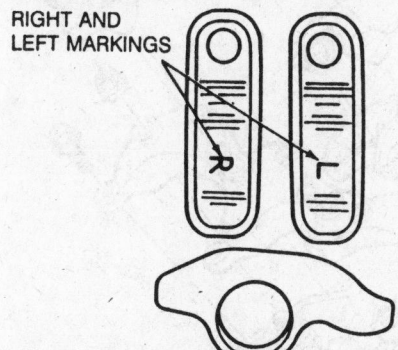

Service rocker arm identification marks — 3.8L (1982–85) engines

4. Using a small pry bar, pry the nylon arm retainers.

5. To install, lubricate the rocker arms with engine oil and position them on the shaft. Center each arm on the ¼ in. hole in the shaft. Install new nylon rocker arm retainers in the holes using a ½ in. drift. Locate the

push rods in the rocker arms and insert the shaft-to-cylinder head bolts.

6. To install, use new gaskets, sealant (if necessary) and reverse the removal procedures. Torque (a little at a time) the rocker arm shaft assembly-to-cylinder head bolt to 30 ft. lbs.

1986–87

1. Remove the rocker arm cover nuts, washers, seals, the cover and gasket (discard the gasket).

2. Remove the rocker arm pedestal-

to-cylinder head bolts, the pedestals, the rocker arms and the pedestal retainers.

NOTE: Be sure to keep the parts in order for reassembly purposes.

3. Using a putty knife, clean the gasket mounting surfaces.

4. To install, use a new gasket, sealant (if necessary) and reverse the removal procedures. Torque the rocker arm bolts to 45 ft. lbs. Check and/or re-

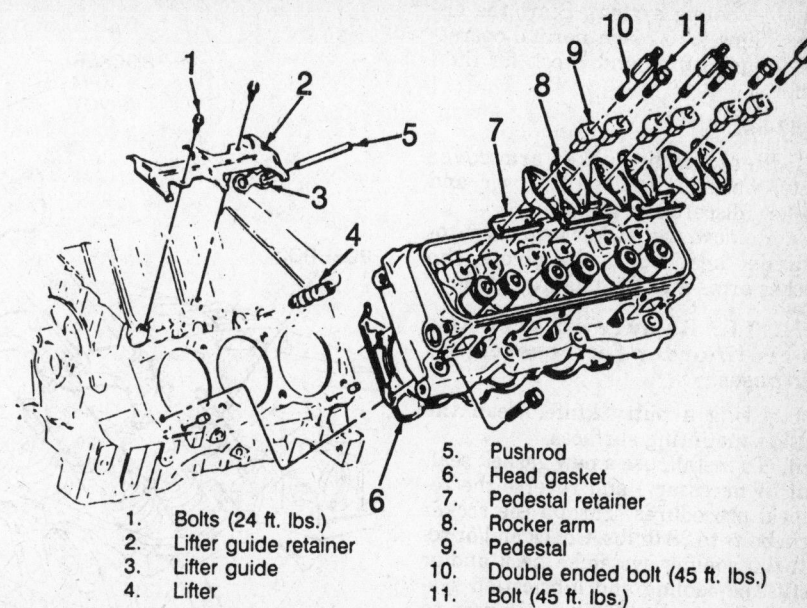

1.	Bolts (24 ft. lbs.)	5.	Pushrod
2.	Lifter guide retainer	6.	Head gasket
3.	Lifter guide	7.	Pedestal retainer
4.	Lifter	8.	Rocker arm
		9.	Pedestal
		10.	Double ended bolt (45 ft. lbs.)
		11.	Bolt (45 ft. lbs.)

Exploded view of the rocker arm assembly — 3.8L (1986–87) V6 engines

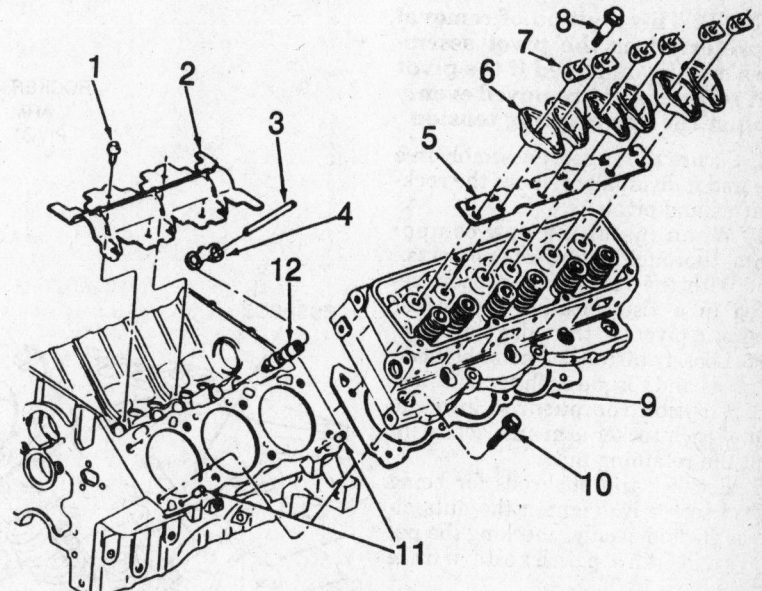

1.	Bolt (27 ft. lbs.)	5.	Pushrod guide	9.	Head gasket
2.	Lifter guide retainer	6.	Rocker arm	10.	Head bolt
3.	Pushrod	7.	Rocker arm pivot	11.	Dowel pin
4.	Lifter guide	8.	Bolt (28 ft. lbs.)	12.	Valve lifter

Exploded view of the rocker arm assembly — 3.8L (1988–89) V6 engines

fill the cooling system. Start the engine, allow it to reach normal operating temperatures and check for fluid leaks.

1988-89

1. Remove the rocker arm cover nuts, washers, seals, the cover and gasket (discard the gasket).
2. Remove the rocker arm pivot-to-cylinder head bolts, the pivots, the rocker arms and the pushrod guide.

NOTE: Be sure to keep the parts in order for reassembly purposes.

3. Using a putty knife, clean the gasket mounting surfaces.
4. To install, use a new gasket, sealant (if necessary) and reverse the removal procedures. Torque the rocker arm bolts to 28 ft. lbs. Check and/or refill the cooling system. Check and/or refill the cooling and lubrication systems. Start the engine, allow it to reach normal operating temperatures and check for leaks.

4.1L V8 1982–84

1. Disconnect the negative battery cable. Remove the necessary components in order to gain access to the rocker arm cover retaining bolts. Remove the rocker arm covers.
2. Remove the rocker arm support-to-cylinder head nuts, a little at a time until pressure is relieved from the assembly. Remove the rocker arm support with the rocker arms and pivots attached as an assembly.

NOTE: This method of removal is preferred as the pivot assemblies may be damaged if the pivot bolt torque is not removed evenly against the valve spring tension.

3. Secure the support assembly in a vise and individually remove the rocker arms and pivots.
4. When installing new components, thoroughly lubricate all parts.
5. With the valve train support secured in a vise, position the rocker arms and pivots to the valve train support. Loosely install the pivot bolts on all studs and torque each to 22 ft. lbs.
6. Position the pushrod into the seat of each rocker arm and loosely install the retaining nuts.
7. Recheck the pushrods for being seated correctly. Tighten the nuts alternately and evenly, checking the position of the pushrods while tightening.
8. When the nuts have been seated and the pushrods are correct, tighten the nuts to 37 ft. lbs. torque.
9. To complete the installation, reverse the removal procedures. Start the engine and check for leaks.

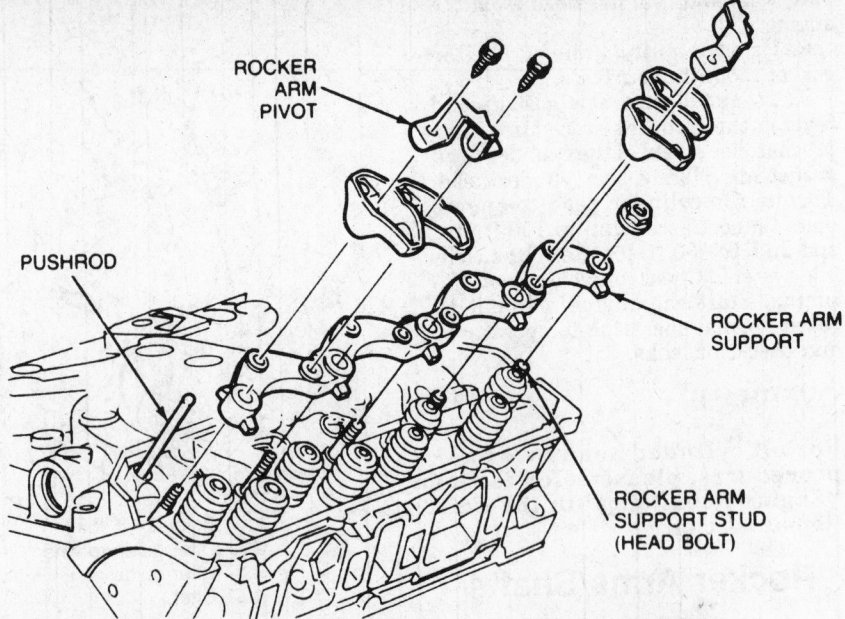

Exploded view of the rocker arm assembly—4.1L (1982–84) V8 engine

4.1L 1985–89 and 4.5L 1988–89

1. Remove the rocker arm cover.
2. Remove the 4 rocker arm support-to-cylinder head bosses bolts.
3. Remove the 5 rocker arm support-to-cylinder head stud nuts.

NOTE: This method of removal is preferred as the pivot assemblies may be damaged if the pivot bolt torque is not removed evenly against the valve spring tension.

4. Place the rocker arm support in a vise and remove the rocker arm pivot-to-rocker arm support bolts.
5. To install, lubricate all parts with Axle Lube No. 1052271 or equivalent, and reverse the removal procedures. Torque the rocker arm pivot-to-rocker arm support bolts to 22 ft. lbs.

NOTE: The pivot bolts are self-tapping.

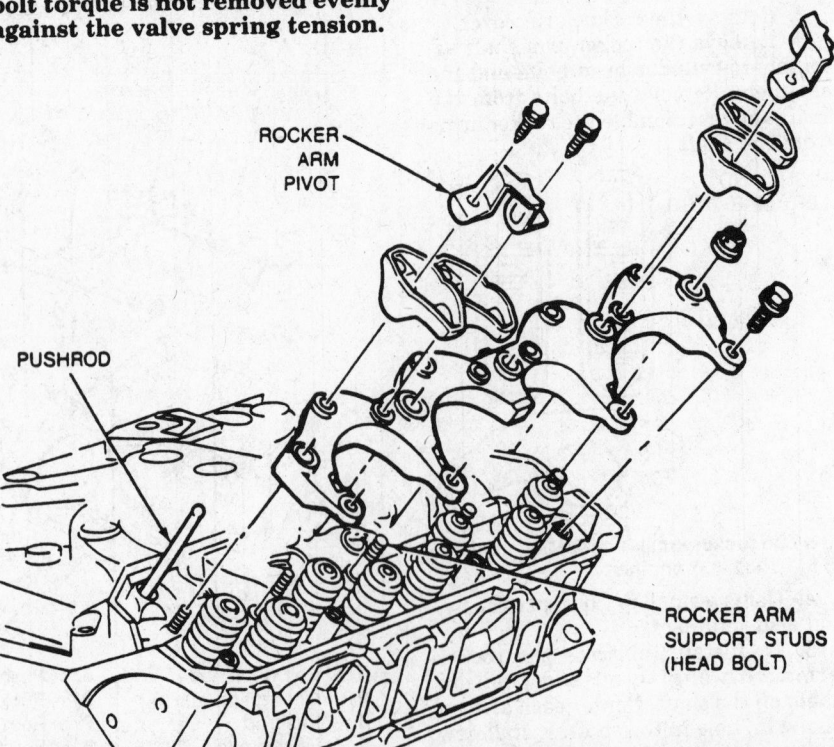

Exploded view of the rocker arm assembly—4.1L (1985–89) V8 and 4.5L (1988–89) engines

6. Position the pushrod into the seat of each rocker arm and loosely install the retaining nuts.

7. Recheck the pushrods for being seated correctly. Tighten the nuts alternately and evenly, checking the position of the pushrods while tightening.

8. When the nuts have been seated and the pushrods are correct. Torque the rocker arm support-to-cylinder head nuts to 37 ft. lbs. and the rocker arm support-to-cylinder head bolts to 7 ft. lbs.

9. To complete the installation, reverse the removal procedures. Start the engine and check for leaks.

4.1L V6, 5.0L and 5.7L (Diesel)

1. Remove the rocker arm cover.

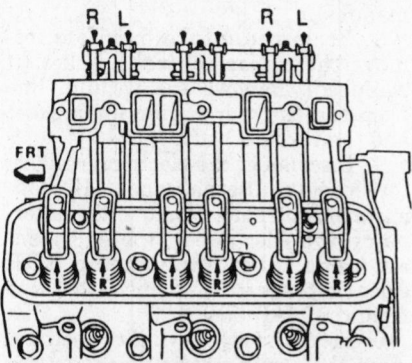

Removing the nylon rocker arm retainers – 3.8L (1982-85) and 4.1L V6 engines – 5.0L and 5.7L (diesel) engines are similar

2. Remove the rocker arm shaft assembly bolts and the assembly.

3. Remove the nylon arm retainers by prying them out.

4. Remove the rocker arms.

5. Install the rocker arms on the shaft and lubricate them with oil.

6. Center each arm on the ¼ in. hole in the shaft. Install new nylon rocker arm retainers in the holes using a ½ in. drift.

7. Locate the pushrods in the rocker arms and insert the shaft-to-cylinder head bolts. Tighten the bolts a little at a time until they are tightened to 30 ft. lbs.

8. To install the rocker cover, use a new gasket(s) and reverse the removal procedures.

Intake Manifold

REMOVAL & INSTALLATION

Carburetor

V8 ENGINE

1. Disconnect the negative battery cable. Remove the air cleaner, the heat tube and PCV valve.

2. Disconnect the throttle and cruise control linkages.

3. Remove the HEI electrical connection from the distributor.

4. Remove the distributor cap and the ignition wires; mark the wires for easy reinstallation.

5. Disconnect the temperature sending unit and the electrical connection from the air conditioning compressor.

6. Disconnect the 2 wires from the downshift switch. Disconnect the throttle return spring and downshift switch bracket. Disconnect the electric choke (if equipped).

7. Remove the plug from the anti-dieseling solenoid and any other necessary electrical connections.

8. Disconnect the power brake booster vacuum and vacuum modulator lines. Remove the cruise control mechanism (if equipped). Disconnect the air conditioning vacuum hose from the rear of the manifold.

9. Disconnect the fuel line from the carburetor.

10. Disconnect the vacuum advance line (if equipped) and the canister purge hoses; move them aside.

11. Remove the air conditioning compressor and move it aside; DO NOT disconnect the refrigerant lines.

12. Disconnect the coolant bypass hose from the manifold (if equipped).

13. Remove the carburetor, the manifold bolts and the manifold.

14. Using a putty knife, clean the gasket mounting surfaces.

15. To install, use new gaskets and reverse the removal procedures.

V6 ENGINES

1. Disconnect the negative battery cable and drain the radiator.

2. Remove the air cleaner. Remove the mass air flow sensor on fuel injected engines.

3. Disconnect the upper radiator hose and heater hose at the manifold. Remove the serpentine drive belt, if equipped.

4. Disconnect the accelerator linkage and linkage bracket at the manifold. Remove the cruise control chain, if equipped.

5. Remove the fuel line from the carburetor and the booster vacuum pipe from the manifold. Remove turbocharger, if equipped.

6. Disconnect and tag the transmission vacuum modulator line, idle stop solenoid wire (if equipped), distributor wires and temperature sending unit wire.

7. Disconnect and tag the vacuum hoses at the distributor and carburetor.

8. Disconnect the coolant bypass hose at the manifold.

9. Remove the distributor cap and wires to gain access to the Torx® head bolt. Remove the bolt.

10. Remove the throttle linkage springs.

11. Remove the air conditioning compressor top mounting bracket.

12. Remove the intake manifold from the engine.

13. When installing, always use new gaskets. Use sealer on the ends of the rubber gasket seals. Carefully guide the manifold onto the engine block dowel pin. Observe "Turbocharger Precautions" given with the Turbocharger information. Tighten the bolts in the proper order.

Fuel Injected Engines

3.8L V6 Engines

1983-85

1. Relieving the fuel pressure.

2. Disconnect the negative battery cable. Place a clean drain pan under the radiator, open the drain cock and drain the cooling system.

3. Remove the mass air flow sensor. From the throttle body, remove the air intake duct, the T.V. cable, the accelerator cable and the cruise control cable (if equipped).

4. From the throttle body, disconnect the vacuum lines. Remove the PCV valve.

5. Remove the upper radiator hose and the heater hose from the intake manifold. Remove the drive belt.

6. Remove the fuel lines and the booster vacuum pipe from the intake manifold.

7. From the rear of the engine, remove the electrical connectors from the TPS switch and the IAC connector (throttle body). From the front of the engine, disconnect the electrical connectors from the coolant temperature switch, the water temperature switch and the fan control.

8. Remove the alternator and the bracket. Remove the distributor cap and rotor to access the Torx® head bolt; using tool No. J-24394 or equivalent, remove the bolt.

9. Remove the intake manifold-to-engine bolts and the manifold.

10. Using a putty knife, clean the gasket mounting surfaces.

NOTE: When installing new seals, be sure the pointed end of the seals fit snugly against the block and heads and apply RTV sealant to the seals.

11. To install, use new gaskets, RTV sealant and reverse the removal procedures. Torque the intake manifold-to-engine bolts (in sequence) to 47 ft. lbs. Refill the cooling system. Start the engine, allow it to reach normal operating temperatures and check for leaks.

1986-87

1. Relieve the fuel pressure.
2. Disconnect the negative battery battery cable. Drain the cooling system. Remove the air intake duct and mass airflow sensor.
3. Remove the serpentine drive belt, alternator and alternator bracket.
4. Remove the ignition module and associated wiring. Disconnect wiring and vacuum lines that will interfere with removal of the manifold.
5. Disconnect and remove the throttle, cruise control and transaxle valve cables from the throttle body.
6. Remove the upper radiator hose. Disconnect the heater hoses at the throttle body.
7. Disconnect the electrical connections for the injectors.
8. Remove the fuel rail bolts and the fuel rail. Replace all O-rings on injectors that are to be reused.
9. Label and remove the spark plug wires.
10. Remove the intake manifold bolts, the manifold and gasket.
11. Using a putty knife, clean all mating surfaces.
12. To install, use new gaskets, sealant (GM Part No. 1050026, for a steel gasket) and reverse the removal procedures. Pipe thread fittings must be sealed with a sealer and lubricant such as GM Part No. 1052080. Torque the intake manifold-to-engine bolts to 37 ft. lbs. (in sequence).

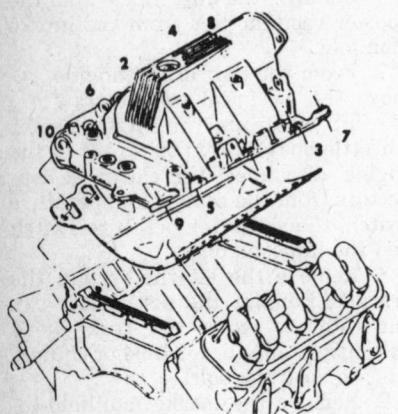

Intake manifold bolt torquing sequence— 3.8L V6 (1986-87) engine.

13. To complete the installation, reverse the removal procedures. Replenish all fluids. Start the engine, operate it until normal temperatures are reached and check for leaks.

1988-89

1. Relieve the fuel pressure.
2. Disconnect the negative battery cable. Place a clean drain pan under the radiator, open the drain cock and drain the cooling system.
3. Remove the serpentine drive belt, the alternator and the bracket.

4. Remove the power steering pump, the braces and move it aside; DO NOT disconnect the pressure lines.
5. Remove the coolant bypass hose, the heater pipe and the upper radiator hose from the intake manifold.
6. Remove the vacuum hoses and disconnect the electrical connectors from the intake manifold.
7. Remove the EGR pipe, the EGR valve and the adapter from the throttle body.
8. Remove the throttle body coolant pipe, the throttle body and the throttle body adapter.
9. Disconnect the rear spark plug wires. Remove the intake manifold-to-engine bolts and the manifold.
10. Using a putty knife, clean the gasket mounting surfaces.

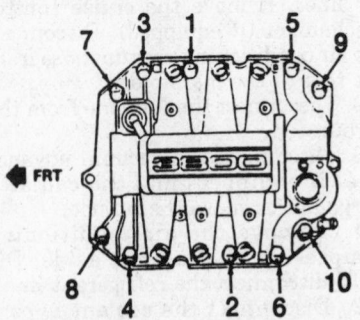

◄ FRT

Intake manifold bolt torquing sequence— 3.8L V6 (1988-89)

11. To install, use new gaskets, sealant No. 12345336 or equivalent (on the ends of the manifold seals) and reverse the removal procedures. Torque the intake manifold (in sequence) to 88 inch lbs. Refill the cooling system. Start the engine, allow it to reach normal operating temperatures and check for leaks.

4.1L V8 1982-89 AND
4.5L V8 1988-89

NOTE: Some vehicles equipped with the 4.1L and 4.5L engines have been experiencing oil leakage at the intake manifold to block seal, due to a split intake manifold seal. When repairing this leak, replace the old seal with a new silicone seal (Part No. 3634619) The new seal is easily identified by its gray color.

1. Disconnect the negative battery cable. Drain the cooling system to a level below the intake manifold. Disconnect the upper radiator hose from the thermostat housing.
2. Remove the air cleaner and the drive belt. Label and disconnect the spark plug wires from the spark plugs.
3. Remove the upper power steering pump bracket-to-engine bolts and loosen the lower nuts.

4. Disconnect the following electrical connections and position the wiring harness out of the way: distributor, oil pressure switch, EGR solenoid, coolant sensor, mass airflow temperature sensor, throttle position sensor, 4-way connector at the distributor, electric fuel evaporator grid, idle speed control motor and fuel injectors.
5. From the throttle lever, disconnect the accelerator, cruise control (if equipped) and transaxle TV cables.
6. Using a shop rag at the fuel line Schraeder valve (test port), bleed off the fuel pressure. Disconnect the fuel inlet and return lines from the throttle body. From the transaxle, remove the fuel line brackets and move the lines aside; disconnect the modulator vacuum line.
7. Disconnect the heater hose from the nipple at the rear of the intake manifold.
8. From the intake manifold, remove the cruise control bracket (if equipped). Remove the vacuum line from the left rear engine lift bracket and the throttle body.
9. Disconnect the electrical connectors from the alternator and AIR management solenoid. Remove the alternator, the idler pulley, the AIR management valve/bracket and EGR solenoid/bracket. Disconnect the hose from the MAP hose.
10. From the right cylinder head, remove the power steering pipe and the AIR pipe. Remove the oil filter.
11. Remove the distributor. Remove both rocker arm covers. Remove the rocker arm support with the rocker arms intact by first alternately and evenly removing the 4 bolts followed by the 5 nuts. Keep the pushrods in sequence so they may be reassembled in their original positions.
12. If equipped with air conditioning, partially remove the compressor; DO NOT discharge the system. Remove the vacuum harness connections from the TVS at the rear of the intake manifold.
13. Remove the intake manifold bolts and remove the 2 bolts securing the lower thermostat housing to the front cover. Remove the engine lift brackets or bend them out of the way.
14. Remove the intake manifold and lower the thermostat housing as an assembly by lifting it straight up off of the dowels.
15. Using a putty knife, clean the gasket mounting surfaces.

NOTE: The right intake manifold gasket for 1985 vehicles, contains a restrictor which controls the flow of the exhaust gas into the intake manifold. The gaskets that do not have this restrictor are identified by a tab which pro-

trudes from between the cylinder head and the intake manifold. On the left side of the engine the tab will protrude from the rear of the engine. If a gasket without a restrictor is used on the right side of the engine the tab will protrude from the front of the engine. The manifold gasket with the restrictor has "Right Bank" printed on it to aid identification when the gasket is out of the vehicle.

16. To install, use new gaskets, apply RTV sealant No. 1052366 to the 4 corners where the end seals meet and reverse the removal procedures.

17. To torque the intake manifold-to-engine bolts, perform the following procedures:

a. Torque the No. 1–4 bolts (in sequence) to 15 ft. lbs.

b. Torque the No. 5–16 bolts (in sequence) to 22 ft. lbs.

c. Retorque all bolts (in sequence) to 22 ft. lbs.

d. Recheck all bolts (in sequence) to 22 ft. lbs.

18. To complete the installation, use new gaskets and reverse the removal procedures. Refill the cooling system.

Diesel Engine

1. Remove the air cleaner.

2. Drain the radiator. Loosen the upper bypass hose clamp, remove the thermostat housing bolts, and remove the housing and the thermostat from the intake manifold.

3. Remove the breather pipes from the rocker covers and the air crossover. Remove the air crossover.

4. Disconnect the throttle rod and the return spring. If equipped with cruise control, remove the servo.

5. Remove the hairpin clip at the bellcrank and disconnect the cables. Remove the throttle cable from the bracket on the manifold; position the cable away from the engine. Disconnect and label any wiring as necessary.

6. Remove the alternator bracket, if necessary. If equipped with air conditioning, remove the compressor mounting bolts and move the compressor aside, without disconnecting any of the hoses or wiring. Remove the compressor mounting bracket from the intake manifold.

7. Disconnect the fuel line from the pump and the fuel filter. Remove the fuel filter and bracket.

8. Remove the fuel injection pump and lines.

9. Disconnect and remove the vacuum pump or oil pump drive assembly from the rear of the engine.

10. Remove the intake manifold drain tube.

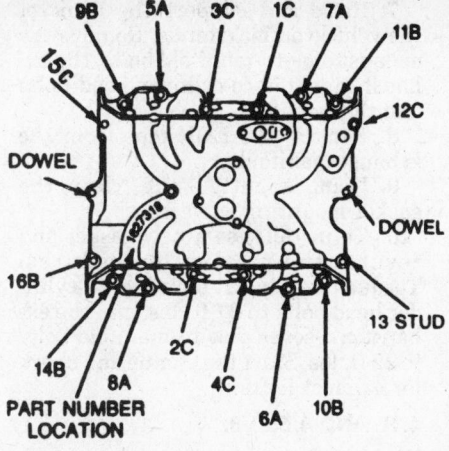

DOWEL

DOWEL

16B

PART NUMBER LOCATION

14B   8A   4C   6A   10B

2C

13 STUD

◁ FRONT OF ENGINE

BOLT TIGHTENING SEQUENCE

1. TIGHTEN BOLTS 1, 2, 3, & 4 IN SEQUENCE TO 20.0 N·m (15 FT-LBS).

2. TIGHTEN BOLTS 5 THRU 16 IN SEQUENCE TO 30.0 N·m (22 FT-LBS).

3. RETIGHTEN ALL BOLTS IN SEQUENCE TO 30.0 N·m (22 FT-LBS).

4. REPEAT STEP 3.

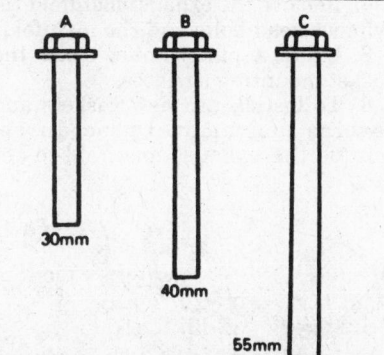

A   B   C

30mm

40mm

55mm

Intake manifold bolt torquing sequence – 4.1L (1982–89) and 4.5L (1988–89) V8 engines – 4.1L MFI (Allante 1987–89) is similar

11. Remove the intake manifold bolts and remove the manifold. Remove the adapter seal. Remove the injection pump adapter.

12. Clean the mating surfaces of the cylinder heads and the intake manifold using a putty knife.

13. Coat both sides of the gasket surface that seal the intake manifold to the cylinder heads with GM sealer 1050026 or the equivalent. Position the intake manifold gaskets on the cylinder heads. To install the front and rear end seals, apply 1052915, 22521437, G.E. 1673 RTV sealer or equivalent, to the end seals only. Then install the end seals, making sure that the ends are positioned under the cylinder heads.

14. Carefully lower the intake manifold into place on the engine.

15. Clean the intake manifold bolts

thoroughly and dip them in clean engine oil. Install the bolts and torque to 15 ft. lbs. in the sequence. Next, tighten all the bolts to 30 ft. lbs., in sequence, and finally tighten to 40 ft. lbs. in sequence.

16. Install the intake manifold drain tube and clamp.

17. Install injection pump adapter. If a new adapter is not being used, skip Steps 4 and 9.

18. Install the fuel injection pump.

19. Install the vacuum pump or coil pump drive assembly.

— CAUTION —

Do not operate the engine without vacuum pump/oil pump assembly in place as this assembly drives the engine oil pump.

20. Install the remaining components and reverse the removal procedures. Start the engine, allow it to reach normal operating temperatures and check for leaks.

Exhaust Manifold

REMOVAL & INSTALLATION

Carbureted

V8 ENGINES

Left Side

1. Remove the air cleaner and the heat shroud.

2. Remove the lower alternator bracket. Raise and support the front of the vehicle on jackstands.

3. Disconnect the exhaust pipe from the exhaust manifold.

4. Lower the vehicle. Remove the exhaust manifold-to-engine bolts and the exhaust manifold.

5. Using a putty knife, clean the gasket mounting surfaces.

6. To install, use a new gasket and reverse the removal procedures. Start the engine and check for leaks.

Right Side

1. Raise and support the front of the vehicle on jackstands.

2. Disconnect the exhaust pipe from the exhaust manifold. Remove the right front wheel.

3. Remove the exhaust manifold-to-engine bolts, lower the manifold down and out from under the vehicle.

4. Using a putty knife, clean the gasket mounting surfaces.

5. To install, use a new gasket and reverse the removal procedures. Start the engine and check for leaks.

V6 ENGINES

Left Side

1. Raise and support the front of the vehicle on jackstands.

2. Disconnect the exhaust crossover pipe.

3. Remove the left front engine

mount through bolt and loosen the through bolt on the right mount.

4. Raise the engine slightly. Remove the exhaust manifold-to-engine bolts and the manifold.

5. Using a putty knife, clean the gasket mounting surfaces.

6. To install, reverse the removal procedures. Start the engine and check for leaks.

Right Side

1. Raise and support the front of the vehicle on jackstands.

2. Disconnect the exhaust pipe from both manifolds and lower it.

3. Remove the exhaust manifold-to-engine bolts and the manifold from under the vehicle.

4. Using a putty knife, clean the gasket mounting surfaces.

5. To install, reverse the removal procedures. Start the engine and check for leaks.

Fuel Injected

3.8L V6

Left Side

1. Disconnect the negative terminal from the battery.

2. If necessary, remove the mass air flow sensor, air intake duct and crankcase ventilation pipe.

3. Remove the exhaust crossover pipe-to-exhaust manifold bolts.

4. Label and disconnect the spark plug wires.

5. Remove the exhaust manifold-to-cylinder head bolts and the manifold.

6. If necessary, remove the oil dipstick tube to provide access to the manifold bolts.

7. Using a putty knife, clean the gasket mounting surfaces.

8. To install, use a new gasket and reverse the removal procedures. Torque the exhaust manifold-to-cylinder head bolts to 37 ft. lbs. and the exhaust crossover pipe-to-manifold bolts to 22 ft. lbs. Start the engine and check for exhaust leaks.

Right Side

1. Disconnect the negative terminal from the battery.

2. If necessary, disconnect the mass air flow sensor, air intake duct and the IAC connector from the throttle body.

3. Label and disconnect the wires from the spark plugs. Disconnect the oxygen sensor lead.

4. If equipped, disconnect the heater inlet pipe from the manifold studs.

5. Remove the exhaust crossover pipe-to-exhaust manifold bolts and the pipe.

6. Remove the serpentine drive belt. On the 1985–87 models, remove the front alternator-to-engine support bracket. On the 1985 models, remove the power steering pump and bracket.

7. Raise and support the front of the vehicle on jackstands. Remove the exhaust pipe-to-manifold bolts, the exhaust manifold-to-cylinder head bolts and the manifold.

8. Remove the EGR pipe from the exhaust manifold.

9. Using a putty knife, clean the gasket mounting surfaces.

10. To install, use a new gasket and reverse the removal procedures. Torque the exhaust manifold-to-cylinder head bolts to 37 ft. lbs. and the exhaust crossover pipe-to-manifold bolts to 22 ft. lbs. Start the engine and check for exhaust leaks.

4.1L AND 4.5L V8

Right Side

1. Disconnect the negative battery cable. Remove the air cleaner.

2. Remove the EGR pipe from the mainfold.

3. Raise and support the front of the vehicle.

4. Disconnect the Y-pipe from the manifold.

5. From the front of the manifold, remove the engine mount brace.

6. Disconnect the O_2 sensor wire.

7. Remove the exhaust manifold-to-cylinder head bolts and the manifold.

8. Using a putty knife, clean the gasket mounting surfaces.

9. To install, use new gaskets and reverse the removal procedures. Torque the exhaust manifold-to-en-

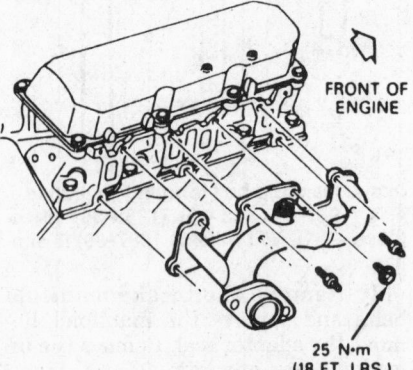

25 N·m
(18 FT. LBS.)

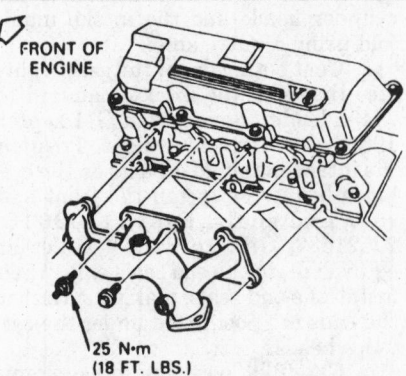

FRONT OF ENGINE

25 N·m
(18 FT. LBS.)

Exploded view of the exhaust manifolds—4.1L and 4.5L engines

gine bolts to 18 ft. lbs. Start the engine and check for exhaust leaks.

Left Side

1. Disconnect the negative battery cable, the O_2 sensor wire and the spark pulg wires.

2. Remove both cooling fans.

3. Remove the serpentine drive belt and the A.I.R. pipe from the air pump.

4. Remove the belt tensioner and the power steering pump brace.

5. Raise and support the front of the vehicle on jackstands.

6. Remove the exhaust Y-pipe and the air conditioning-to-manifold brace.

7. Remove the exhaust manifold-to-cylinder head bolts, the AIR pipe and the manifold.

8. Using a putty knife, clean the gasket mounting surfaces.

9. To install, use new gaskets and reverse the removal procedures. Torque the exhaust manifold-to-engine bolts to 18 ft. lbs. Start the engine and check for exhaust leaks.

Diesel

LEFT SIDE

1. Remove the air cleaner.

2. Remove the alternator lower bracket.

3. Raise and support the car.

4. Remove the crossover pipe.

5. Lower the car.

6. Remove the exhaust manifold.

7. Installation is in the reverse order of removal.

RIGHT SIDE

1. Raise and support the car.

2. Remove the crossover pipe.

3. Disconnect the exhaust pipe.

4. Remove the right front wheel.

5. Remove the exhaust manifold from under the car.

6. Installation is in the reverse order of removal.

Turbocharger

REMOVAL & INSTALLATION

1. Disconnect the turbocharger exhaust inlet pipe and the exhaust outlet pipe at the turbocharger.

2. Disconnect the oil feed pipe from the center housing.

3. Remove the air intake elbow-to-carburetor nut and the elbow (still attached to the flex tube) from the carburetor.

4. Disconnect the accelerator, cruise and detent linkages from the carburetor. Disconnect the linkage bracket from the plenum.

5. Remove the 2 bolts attaching the plenum to the side bracket.

6. Disconnect the carburetor fuel line and necessary vacuum hoses.

7. Drain the cooling system.

8. Disconnect the coolant hoses from the front and rear of the plenum.

9. Disconnect the power brake vacuum line from the plenum.

10. Remove the turbo housing-to-intake manifold bracket bolts.

11. Remove the EGR valve manifold-to-plenum bolts. Loosen the EGR valve manifold-to-intake manifold bolts.

12. Loosen the AIR by-pass-to-pipe hose clamp to the check valve. Remove the hose from the pipe.

13. Remove the compressor housing-to-intake manifold bolts.

14. Remove the turbocharger and actuator, still attached to the carburetor/plenum assembly, from the engine. Label and disconnect any vacuum hoses (as necessary).

15. Remove the turbo/actuator unit-to-plenum/carburetor assembly bolts.

16. Remove the oil drain from the turbo center housing.

17. To install, reverse the removal procedures. Refill the cooling system.

NOTE: Before installing the turbo unit, make certain that all parts and connections are clean. Serious damage to the turbo unit and engine will result if dirt and/or foreign matter enters into the engine.

TROUBLESHOOTING

For more information on turbocharging, please refer to "Turbocharging" in the Unit Repair section.

Front Cover and Oil Seal

REMOVAL & INSTALLATION

3.8L V6 Engines
COVER REMOVED

1. Disconnect the negative battery cable.

2. PLace a clean drain pan under the radiator, open the drain cock and drain the engine coolant. Remove the lower radiator hose and the coolant by-pass hose from the front cover. Remove the heater pipes.

3. Remove the front engine cradle mount bolts. Using a vertical lifting device, secure it to the engine and raise it slightly.

4. Remove the serpentine drive belt and the water pump pulley.

5. Label and disconnect the alternator wiring. Remove the alternator and the alternator bracket.

6. On the 1982-85 models, mark the position of the distributor rotor and remove the distributor.

7. On the 1988-89 models, remove the inner splash shield.

8. Remove the crankshaft balancer bolt/washer and the balancer.

9. Disconnect the electrical connectors from the crankshaft sensor, the camshaft sensor and the oil pressure switch.

10. Remove the oil pan-to-front cover bolts, the front cover-to-engine bolts and the front cover. Using a small pry bar, remove the oil seal and discard it.

11. To replace the front oil seal, perform the following procedures:

   a. Using a small pry bar, pry the oil seal from the front cover; be careful not to damage the sealing surfaces.

   b. Clean the oil seal mounting surface.

   c. Using GM lubricant No. 1050169 or equivalent, coat the outside of the seal and the crankshaft balancer.

   d. Using the Oil Seal Installation tool No. J-35354 or equivalent, drive the new seal into the front cover until it seats.

12. Using a putty knife, clean the gasket mounting surfaces.

13. To install, use a new gasket, sealant No. 1052080 or equivalent, and reverse the removal procedures. Torque the front cover-to-engine bolts to 22 ft. lbs., the oil pan-to-front cover bolts to 88 inch lbs., the crankshaft balancer-to-crankshaft bolt to 200 ft. lbs. (1982-87) or 219 ft. lbs. (1988-89). Refill the cooling system. Start the engine, allow it to reach normal operating temperatures and check for leaks.

FRONT COVER INSTALLED

1. Disconnect the negative battery cable.

2. Remove the drive belt.

3. Remove the crankshaft balancer-to-crankshaft bolts.

4. Using a small pry bar, pry the oil seal from the front cover; be careful not to damage the sealing surfaces.

5. Clean the oil seal mounting surface.

6. Using GM lubricant No. 1050169 or equivalent, coat the outside of the seal and the crankshaft balancer.

7. Using the Oil Seal Installation tool No. J-35354 or equivalent, drive the new seal into the front cover until it seats.

8. To install, reverse the removal procedures. Torque the crankshaft balancer-to-crankshaft bolt to 200 ft. lbs. (1982-87) or 219 ft. lbs. (1988-89).

4.1L and 4.5L V8 Engines
COVER REMOVED

1. Disconnect the negative battery cable.

2. Place a clean drain pan under the radiator, open the drain cock and drain the engine coolant. Remove the air cleaner and move it aside.

3. Remove the serpentine belt.

4. Label and disconnect the alternator wiring. Remove the alternator and the alternator bracket.

5. Remove the air conditioner accumulator from the bracket and move it aside; DO NOT disconnect the fittings on the accumulator.

6. Remove the water pump pulley bolts and the pulley. If necessary, remove the idler pulley.

7. Raise and support the front of the vehicle on jackstands.

8. Remove the crankshaft pulley-to-crankshaft pulley bolt. Using the Puller tool No. J-24420-B or equivalent, attach it to the crankshaft pulley; using the center bolt, press the crankshaft pulley from the crankshaft. Remove the woodruff key from the crankshaft.

9. Remove the front cover-to-engine bolts, the oil pan-to-front cover bolts and the front cover.

10. Using a putty knife, clean the gasket mounting surfaces.

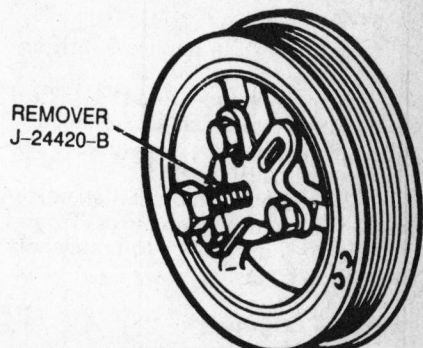

REMOVER
J-24420-B

Using the Wheel Puller tool to remove the damper pulley—4.1L and 4.5L engines

11. Using a small pry bar, pry the oil seal from the front cover (discard it).

12. Clean the oil seal mounting surface. Lubricate the new seal with engine oil.

13. Using a hammer and the Oil Seal Installation tool No. J-29662 or equivalent, drive the new oil seal in to the front cover until it seats.

14. To complete the installation, use a new gasket, RTV sealant (on the oil pan lip) and reverse the removal procedures. Torque the front cover-to-engine bolts to 15 ft. lbs., the crankshaft pulley-to-crankshaft bolt to 18 ft. lbs.

COVER INSTALLED

1. Remove the crankshaft pulley.

2. Using the Oil Seal Removal tools No. J-23129, J-21052-4, J-1859-03 or equivalent, press the oil seal from the front cover.

3. Clean the oil seal mounting surface.

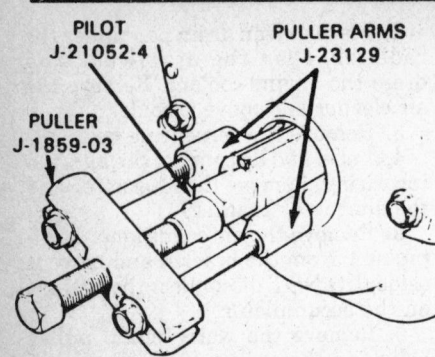

Removing the front oil seal—4.1L and 4.5L engines

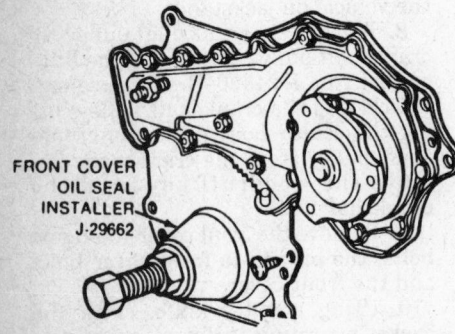

Installing the front oil seal—4.1L and 4.5L engines

4. Lubricate the new seal with engine oil.

5. Using a hammer and the Oil Seal Installation tool No. J-29662 or equivalent, drive the new oil seal in to the front cover until it seats.

6. To complete the installation, reverse the removal procedures. Torque the crankshaft pulley-to-crankshaft bolt to 18 ft. lbs.

5.0L V8 Engine

COVER REMOVED

1. Drain the cooling system. Disconnect the upper/lower radiator, heater and bypass hoses.

2. Remove the radiator, drive belt(s), fan/fan pulley, crankshaft pulley and the harmonic balancer.

3. Remove the timing cover-to-engine bolts and the cover. If necessary, remove the timing pointer and water pump.

4. Remove both front cover dowel pins. Grind a chamfer on 1 end of each dowel pin.

5. Using a putty knife, clean the gasket mounting surfaces.

6. To install, use new gaskets, sealant and reverse the removal procedures. Use sealer around the coolant

CHAMFER

Chamfer the alignment pin

holes and at the junction of the block pan and front cover.

7. To complete the installation, reverse the removal procedures. Refill the cooling system. Start the engine, allow it to reach normal operating temperatures and check for leaks.

COVER INSTALLED

1. Disconnect the negative battery cable. Remove the air pump belt, power steering pump belt and vacuum belt.

2. Remove the crankshaft pulley-to-crankshaft screws. Remove the damper-to-hub, the pulley and damper. Remove the plug from the end of the crankshaft.

3. Install the Puller Pilot tool No. J-21052-4 or equivalent, in the bore in end of the crankshaft.

4. Install the Holding Base tool No. J-21052-02 or equivalent, on the front hub, aligning the 2 base holes with the 2 tapped holes in the hub and install the 2 screws with washers finger tight.

5. Thread the Puller tool No. J-21052-2 or equivalent, into the base until the screw contact point. Using a suitable wrench remove the hub from the crankshaft by tightening the screw.

NOTE: If available, the use of compressed air pressure to hold a piston within its compression stroke may be necessary to remove the hub without turning the crankshaft. Remove a spark plug and install Adapter tool No. J-

22794 or equivalent, into the spark plug port (finger tight) and apply air pressure to the hold piston within its compression stroke. The adapter should not be tightened with a wrench.

6. Remove the pilot from the end of the crankshaft and the puller from the hub.

7. Using the tools No. J-1859-03 and No. J-23129 or equivalent, remove the oil seal.

8. To install, coat the new oil seal lips with engine oil and position the seal on the end of the crankshaft with the spring side toward the engine.

9. Using the Seal Installer tool No. J-29662 or equivalent, and a hammer, drive the seal into the front cover until the tool bottoms out against the front cover.

NOTE: The tool No. J-29662 is designed is such a way that the front cover seal can also be pressed on, by using the Balancer Hub Installer tool No. J-29774 or equivalent.

10. Lubricate the bore of the hub and seal with extreme pressure lubricant to prevent seizure to the crankshaft and provide lubrication of the oil seal lip. Position the hub on the crankshaft, aligning the key slot in the hub with the crankshaft key.

11. Install the Thread Installer Screw tool No. J-29774 or equivalent, into the end of the crankshaft. Position the thrust bearing with the inner race forward, washer next and Installer Nut last. Using a suitable wrench

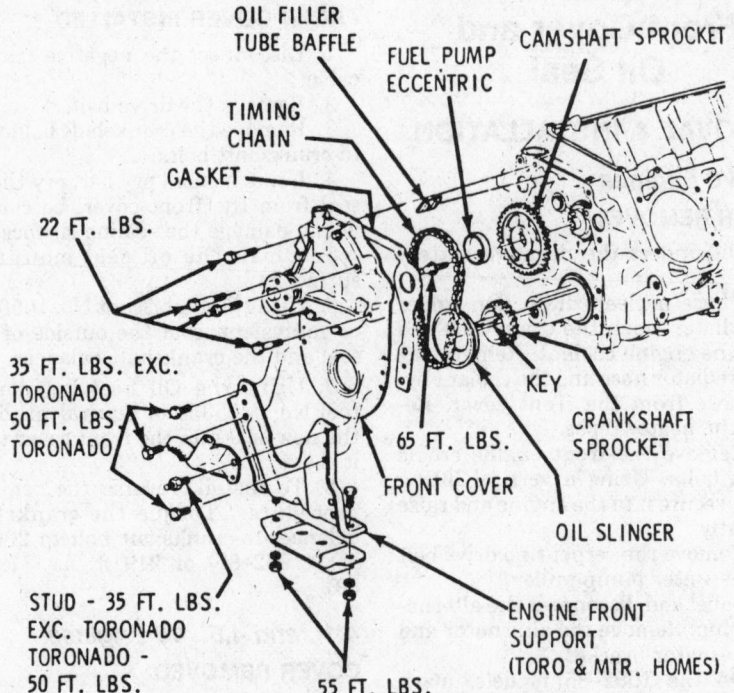

Exploded view of the front cover—V8 engine

install the hub on the crankshaft by tightening the installer nut.

12. To complete the installation, reverse the removal procedures. Torque the crankshaft pulley-to-damper screws to 20 ft. lbs.

Diesel Engines

NOTE: To perform this operation on the V8, secure a set of special tools designed to pull the crankshaft pulley off the crankshaft without damaging the rubber insert separating inner and outer pulley halves. Use tools equivalent to GM No. J-8614-3, J-8614-2, J-8614-1, and J-7583-3.

1. Drain the cooling system and disconnect the radiator hoses.

2. Remove all belts, fan and pulley. Remove the crankshaft pulley and balancer, utilizing the special tools described in the note above on the V8. See the illustration for proper assembly of these tools.

CAUTION

The use of any other type of puller, such as a universal claw type which pulls on the outside of the hub, can destroy the balancer. The outside ring of the balancer is bonded in rubber to the hub. Pulling on the outside will break the bond. The timing mark is on the outside ring. If it is suspected that the bond is broken, check that the center of the keyway is 16° from the center of the timing slot. In addition, there are chiseled aligning marks between the weight and the hub.

---

3. Unbolt and remove the cover, timing indicator and water pump.

4. It may be necessary to grind a flat on the cover for gripping purposes.

5. Grind a chamfer on one end of each dowel pin.

6. Cut the excess material from the front end of the oil pan gasket on each side of the block.

7. Clean the block, oil pan and front cover mating surfaces with solvent.

8. Trim about ⅛ in. off each end of a new front pan seal.

9. Install a new front cover gasket on the block and a new seal in the front cover.

10. Apply sealer to the gasket around the coolant holes.

11. Apply sealer to the block at the junction of the pan and front cover. On V6, apply RTV sealer on the front cover oil pan seal retainer.

12. Place the cover on the block and press down to compress the seal. Rotate the cover left and right and guide the pan seal into the cavity using a small screwdriver. Oil bolt threads and heads, install 2 to hold the cover in place, then install both dowel pins (chamfered end first). Install remaining front cover bolts.

13. Apply a lubricant, compatible

with rubber, on the balancer seal surface.

14. Install the balancer and bolt. Torque the bolt to 200–300 ft. lbs.

15. Install all other parts in the reverse order of removal.

Timing Chain and Sprockets

REMOVAL & INSTALLATION

3.8L V6 Engines

1. Remove the front cover.

2. Remove the button and spring from the center of the camshaft.

3. Rotate the crankshaft to align the marks of the timing sprockets; they must be close together.

4. Remove the camshaft sprocket bolts, the sprocket and the timing chain.

5. Remove the crankshaft sprocket and the Woodruff key (be sure not to lose the key).

6. Using a putty knife, clean the gasket mounting surfaces. Inspect the parts for wear and/or damage; if necessary, replace the parts.

7. To install the timing chain and

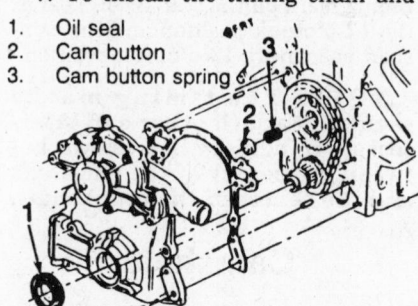

1. Oil seal
2. Cam button
3. Cam button spring

Exploded view of the front cover assembly—3.8L engines

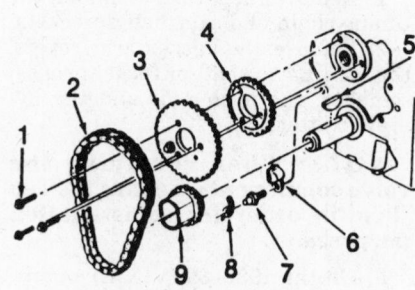

1. 27 ft. lbs.
2. Timing chain
3. Camshaft sprocket
4. Camshaft gear
5. Key
6. Damper
7. Bolt—14 ft. lbs.
8. Spring
9. Crankshaft sprocket

Exploded view of the timing chain assembly—3.8L (Code C) 1988–89 engine—other 3.8L engines are similar

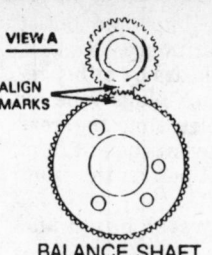
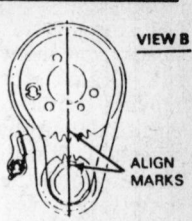

View of the timing sprocket alignment—3.8L engines—the balance shaft gear alignment is used on the 3.8L (Code C) 1988–89 engines ONLY

sprockets, perform the following procedures:

a. Assemble the timing chain on the camshaft sprocket and crankshaft sprockets.

b. Align the **0** marks on the sprockets; they must face each other.

c. Slide the assembly onto the camshaft and crankshaft. Install the camshaft sprocket-to-camshaft bolts. Torque the camshaft sprocket-to-camshaft sprocket bolts to 20 ft. lbs. (1982–86) or 28 ft. lbs. (1987–89).

NOTE: On the 1988–89 (VIN C) engine, align the camshaft sprocket mark with the balancer shaft sprocket mark.

8. Using petroleum jelly, pack the oil pump.

9. To complete the installation, use new gaskets, sealant (if necessary) and reverse the removal procedures. Refill the cooling system. Start the engine, allow it to reach normal operating temperatures and check for leaks.

4.1L and 4.5L V8 Engine

1. Disconnect the negative battery cable. Drain the radiator.

2. Remove the screws on each side of the radiator securing the support rod. Move the support rods out of the way.

3. Remove the wiring harness from the upper fan shroud clamps.

4. Remove the power steering pump reservoir from the upper radiator shroud.

5. Remove the upper fan shroud from the lower fan shroud by removing the staples.

6. Remove the clutch fan assembly.

7. Remove the alternator, air pump, vacuum pump and air condition compressor drive belts.

8. Partially remove the air condition compressor from the engine mounting brackets without discharging the system.

9. Remove the alternator and support bracket from the engine.

10. Loosen the clamp and disconnect the coolant reservoir hose from the water pump.

11. Disconnect the inlet and outlet hoses from the water pump.

12. Drain the crankcase by either removing the crankcase plugs (one on each side) or by elevating the rear wheels. This will prevent coolant from draining into the oil pan as the front cover is removed.

13. Remove the water pump and crankcase pulleys.

14. Remove the air conditioning bracket from the water pump.

15. Remove the timing mark tab from the front cover.

16. Remove the crankcase pulley to hub bolts and separate the pulley from the hub.

17. Remove the plug from the end of the crankshaft. Install a puller and remove the hub.

18. Remove the remaining front cover-to-engine screws and the cover with the water pump and lower thermostat housing as an assembly.

19. Remove the oil slinger from the crankshaft. Rotate the crankshaft and align the timing marks to **TDC**.

20. Remove the camshaft sprocket-to-camshaft screw, the camshaft and crankshaft sprockets with the chain attached.

21. To install, reverse the removal procedures. After installing the timing chain over the camshaft sprocket rotate the crankshaft until the crankshaft sprocket timing mark is positioned **STRAIGHT UP**.

22. Install the cam sprocket and timing chain over the crankshaft so that the timing marks are aligned.

23. Hold the camshaft sprocket in position against the end of the camshaft and press the sprocket on the camshaft by hand. Make sure the camshaft index pin is align with the sprocket index hole.

24. If necessary, keep the engine from rotating while torquing the camshaft sprocket screw to 37 ft. lbs.

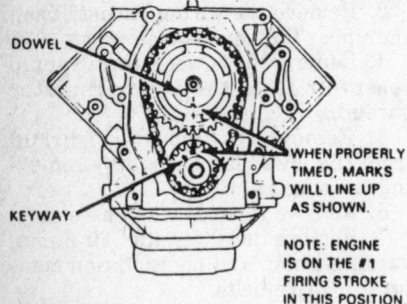

Aligning the timing marks—4.1L and 4.5L V8 engines

NOTE: Engine timing has been set so that the No. 1 cylinder is in the TDC firing position. If the distributor was removed make sure the rotor is positioned on the No. 1 cylinder firing position.

25. Install the oil slinger on the crankshaft with the smaller end of the slinger against the crankshaft sprocket. Install the engine front cover.

26. To complete the installation, reverse the removal procedures.

5.0L V8 Engine

1. Disconnect the negative battery cable.

2. Remove the engine front cover. Rotate the crankshaft and align the timing marks.

3. Remove the camshaft gear bolts. Remove the camshaft gear.

NOTE: Be sure the locating dowel is in place on the camshaft for the camshaft gear.

4. Remove the timing chain.

5. Remove the crankshaft gear sprocket, as required.

6. Installation is the reverse of the removal procedure. Position the No. 1 or 6 cylinder pistons in the TDC Position. Assemble the gears and chain in the following manner.

7. Assemble timing chain on sprockets and slide the sprocket and chain assembly on the shafts with the timing mark on the crankshaft gear at the **12 o'clock** position and the camshaft gear in its **12 o'clock** position.

NOTE: The timing marks should face each other and intersect an imaginary line drawn between the center of the camshaft and the center of the crankshaft.

Camshaft

REMOVAL & INSTALLATION

3.8L V6 Engines

1. Remove the intake manifold, the timing chain and camshaft sprockets.

2. Remove the rocker arm covers, the rocker arm shaft or rocker arm assemblies, the push rods and the hydraulic lifters.

NOTE: When removing the valve components, be sure to keep them in order for reinstallation purposes.

3. On the 1988–89 (VIN C) engine, remove the camshaft gear from the camshaft.

4. On all except the 1988–89 engines, remove the camshaft thrust bearing-to-engine bolts.

5. Carefully, slide the camshaft forward, out of the bearing bores; DO NOT damage the bearing surfaces.

6. Using a putty knife, clean the gasket mounting surfaces. Inspect the parts for wear and/or damage; if necessary, replace the parts.

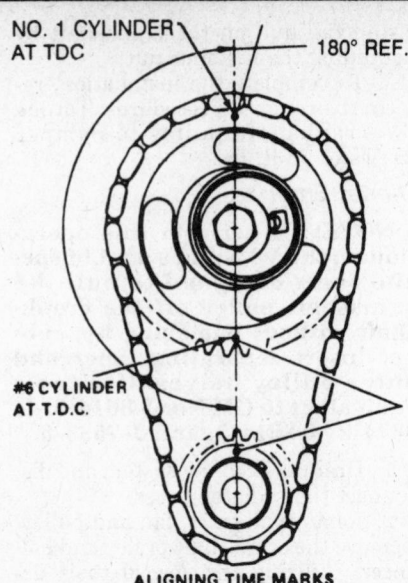

ALIGNING TIME MARKS

Aligning the timing marks—5.0L V8 engine

7. To install, use new gaskets, sealant (if necessary), lubricate the valve lifters and camshaft with multi-lube No. 1052365 or equivalent and reverse the removal procedures. Refill the cooling system. Start the engine, allow it to reach normal operating temperatures and check for leaks.

NOTE: On the 1988–89 (VIN C) engine, align the camshaft gear with the balancer shaft gear timing marks.

4.1L and 4.5L V8

To perform this procedure, the engine must be removed from the vehicle and attached to an engine stand.

1. Remove the intake manifold and the timing chain.

2. Remove the valve lifters.

NOTE: When removing the valve components, be sure to keep the parts in order for reinstallation purposes.

3. Carefully slide the camshaft out from the front of the engine; be sure not to damage the camshaft bearings.

4. Using a putty knife, clean the gasket mounting surfaces. Inspect the parts for wear and/or damage; if necessary, replace the parts.

5. To install, lubricate the camshaft with engine oil, use new gaskets, sealant (if necessary) and reverse the removal procedures. Torque the camshaft sprocket-to-camshaft screws to 37 ft. lbs.

NOTE: If a new camshaft is to be installed, new lifters and a distributor drive gear must also be installed.

6. To complete the installation, re-

verse the removal procedures. Refill the cooling system. Start the engine, allow it to reach normal operating temperatures and check for leaks.

5.0L V8 Engine

1. Disconnect the negative battery cable.

2. Drain the cooling system. Remove the upper radiator baffle. Disconnect the upper radiator hose. Remove the radiator.

3. Disconnect the fuel line from the fuel pump.

4. Remove the air cleaner. Disconnect the throttle cable.

5. Remove the alternator drive belt and the alternator bracket-to-engine bolts.

6. Remove the power steering pump bracket-to-engine bolts and pump.

7. If equipped, remove the air conditioning compressor bracket-to-engine bolts and move aside; the air conditioning lines (at the compressor) are flexible and should be left attached to the compressor.

8. Disconnect thermostat bypass hose from the water pump. Disconnect the electrical and vacuum connections. Remove distributor with cap and wiring intact.

9. Remove the balancer pulley and the balancer.

10. Remove the engine front cover and both valve covers.

11. Remove the intake manifold and gasket, front and rear seal.

12. Remove the rocker arms, push rods and valve lifters.

13. Record the position of the parts so they may be installed in their original position.

14. Remove the fuel pump eccentric pump, the eccentric, the camshaft gear, the oil slinger and timing chain.

15. Carefully slide the camshaft out the front of the engine.

16. Using a putty knife, clean the gasket mounting surfaces.

17. To install, use new gaskets and reverse the removal procedures. Be sure to coat the camshaft and the lifters with clean engine oil prior to installation.

Balance Shaft

REMOVAL & INSTALLATION

3.8L Engine 1988–89

1. Remove the engine and secure it to a workstand.

2. Remove the flywheel-to-crankshaft bolts and the flywheel.

3. Remove the timing chain cover-to-engine bolts and the cover.

4. Remove the camshaft sprocket-to-camshaft gear bolts, the sprocket, the timing chain and the gear.

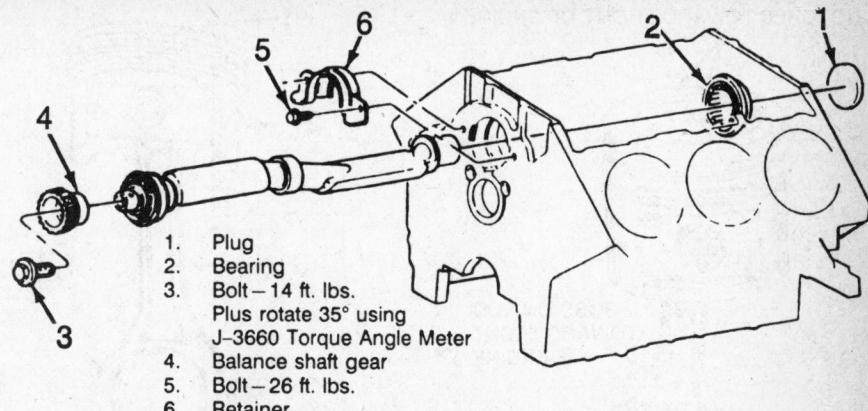

1. Plug
2. Bearing
3. Bolt – 14 ft. lbs.
   Plus rotate 35° using
   J–3660 Torque Angle Meter
4. Balance shaft gear
5. Bolt – 26 ft. lbs.
6. Retainer

Exploded view of the camshaft – 3.8L (Code C) 1988–89 engine

5. To remove the balance shaft, perform the following procedures:

   a. Remove the balance shaft gear-to-shaft bolt and the gear.

   b. Remove the balance shaft retainer-to-engine bolts and the retainer.

   c. Using the Slide Hammer tool No. J–6125–B or equivalent, pull the balance shaft from the front of the engine.

6. If replacing the rear balance shaft bearing, perform the following procedures:

   a. Drive the rear plug from the engine.

   b. Using the Camshaft Remover/Installer tool No. J–33049 or equivalent, press the rear bearing from the rear of the engine.

   c. Dip the new bearing in clean engine oil.

   d. Using the Balance Shaft Rear Bearing Installer tool No. J–36995 or equivalent, press the new rear bearing into the rear of the engine.

   e. Install the rear cup plug.

7. Using the Balance Shaft Installer tool No. J–36996 or equivalent, screw it into the balance shaft and install the shaft into the engine; remove the installer tool.

8. Using a putty knife, clean the gasket mounting surfaces. Inspect the parts for wear and/or damage; replace the parts, if necessary.

9. Install the balance shaft retainer. Torque the balance shaft retainer-to-engine bolts to 27 ft. lbs.

10. Align the balance shaft gear with the camshaft gear timing marks. Install the balance shaft gear onto the balance shaft. Torque the balance gear-to-balance shaft bolt to 45 ft. lbs.

11. To complete the installation, use new gaskets, sealant (if necessary) and reverse the removal procedures. Torque the flywheel-to-crankshaft bolts to 60 ft. lbs. Refill the cooling system. Start the engine, allow it reach normal operating temperatures and check for leaks.

Piston and Connecting Rod

POSITIONING

On the V6 engines, starting at the front, the cylinders in the right bank are numbered 2-4-6 and in the left bank are numbered 1-3-5.

All compression rings are marked with a dimple, a letter **T**, a letter **O** or the word **TOP** to identify the side of the ring which must face toward the top of the piston.

When the piston and connecting rod assembly is properly installed, the oil spurt hole in the connecting rod will face the camshaft. The notch on the piston will face the front of the engine. The chamfered corners of the bearing caps should face toward the front of the left bank and toward the rear of the right bank. The boss on the connecting rod should face toward the front of the engine for the right bank and to the rear of the engine on the left bank.

For all piston and connecting rod overhaul procedures, please refer to "Engine Rebuilding" in the Unit Repair section.

ENGINE LUBRICATION

Oil Pan

REMOVAL & INSTALLATION

V8 Engines

TORONADO 1982–85

1. Disconnect the negative battery cable.

2. Remove the 3 final drive-to-transaxle bolts.

3. Raise and support the front of the vehicle on jackstands.

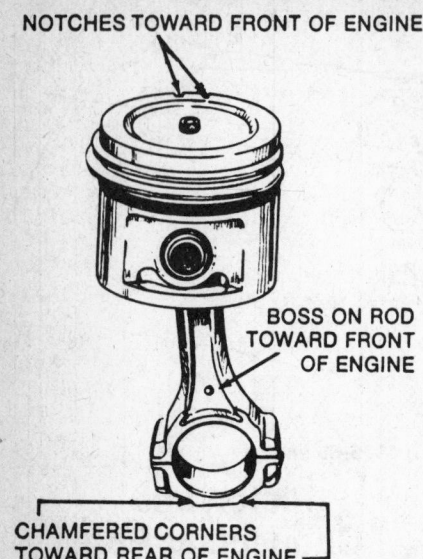

NOTCHES TOWARD FRONT OF ENGINE

BOSS ON ROD
TOWARD FRONT
OF ENGINE

CHAMFERED CORNERS
TOWARD REAR OF ENGINE

RIGHT NO. 2-4-6
View of the right-bank piston and rod positioning—3.8L and 4.1L V6 engines

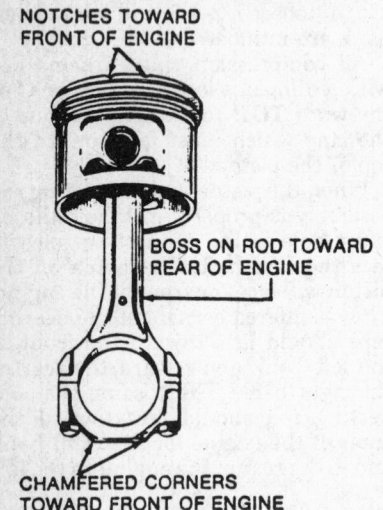

NOTCHES TOWARD
FRONT OF ENGINE

BOSS ON ROD TOWARD
REAR OF ENGINE

CHAMFERED CORNERS
TOWARD FRONT OF ENGINE

LEFT NO. 1-3-5
View of the left-bank piston and rod positioning—3.8L and 4.1L V6 engines

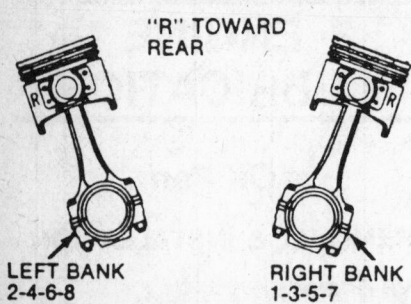

"R" TOWARD
REAR

LEFT BANK
2-4-6-8

RIGHT BANK
1-3-5-7

View of the piston/connecting rod assembly—5.0L engines

4. Disconnect the 2 lower frame braces, if necessary for working clearance.

5. Disconnect the idler and the pitman arms from the relay rod.

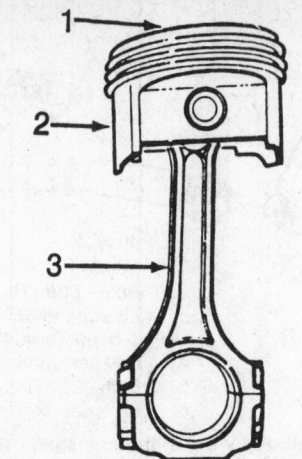

1. Notch (installed toward front of engine)
2. Piston
3. Connecting rod

View of the piston assembly using 1 notch on the piston and the oil hole on the side of the connecting rod

6. Disconnect the right and left side drive axles from their respective output shafts.

7. Disconnect the battery terminal bracket from the output shaft support and the support (itself) from the engine block.

8. Remove the remaining final drive-to-transaxle bolts, position a transaxle jack under the final drive and remove the final drive.

9. Disconnect the starter electrical connectors. Remove the starter and the splash shield.

10. Remove the 2 front motor mount nuts and loosen the front motor mount bolts from the side of the engine block. Raise the engine 1–1½ in. to gain working clearance. Drain the crankcase. Remove the oil pan bolts and the oil pan.

11. Using a putty knife, clean the gasket mounting surfaces.

12. To install, use new gaskets, sealant (on both sides of the gasket) and reverse the removal procedures. Torque the oil pan-to-engine bolts to 10 ft. lbs.

ELDORADO AND SEVILLE

1982–85

1. Disconnect the negative battery cable.

2. Raise and support the vehicle on jackstands.

3. Remove the frame brace front attaching bolts (both sides) and pivot the braces outward.

4. Remove the 6 drive axle-to-output shaft bolts (both sides). Separate the flanges of the output shafts and drive axles to gain clearance for removal with the shafts attached.

5. Remove the battery terminal-to-output shaft retaining screws and the 2 support-to-engine block screws.

6. Remove the final drive-to-transaxle screw that holds the front of the shield. Remove the shield.

7. Remove the remaining final drive-to-transaxle bolts.

8. Remove the final drive support bracket-to-engine block screw.

9. Using a puller, separate the steering linkage intermediate shaft from the pitman arm and the idler arm. Push the linkage toward the front of the vehicle.

10. With the aid of a helper, slide the final drive assembly forward, off the transaxle splined shaft and remove the unit with the output shaft attached. DO NOT use the shafts as handles, as damage to the seals will occur.

11. Remove the battery terminal and the wiring harness connectors from the starter solenoid **BAT** terminal.

12. Remove the electrical connector from the solenoid **S** terminal.

13. Remove the harness from the clip on the solenoid and position it out of the way.

14. Remove the starter-to-engine bolts and the starter.

15. Drain the crankcase.

16. Remove the oil pan-to-engine screws and the oil pan.

NOTE: On vehicles equipped with diesel engines it is necessary to loosen the motor mounts and raise the engine slightly to remove the oil pan.

17. Using a putty knife, clean the gasket mounting surfaces.

18. To install, use new gaskets, sealant and reverse the removal procedures. Torque the oil pan screws to 10 ft. lbs., the final drive-to-transaxle bolts to 30 ft. lbs., the front support bracket-to-block to 50 ft. lbs., the output shaft-to-drive axle screws to 60 ft. lbs. and the steering linkage intermediate shaft-to-pitman arm clamp to 60 ft. lbs.

1986–87

1. Disconnect the negative battery cable. Raise and support the front of the vehicle on jackstands. Drain the crankcase.

2. Remove the torque converter

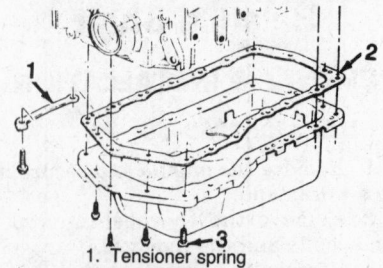

1. Tensioner spring
2. Gasket (formed rubber)
3. Torque to 88 in. lbs.

Replacing the oil pan on the 1986–87 231 V6. Note the location of the tensioner spring (1)

cover from the lower side of the transaxle.

3. Remove the oil pan-to-engine bolts and the pan; DO NOT lose the tensioner spring located at a corner.

4. Using a putty knife, clean the gasket mounting surfaces.

5. To install, use new gaskets, sealant and reverse the removal procedures. Torque the oil pan-to-engine bolts to 88 inch lbs. Make sure to install the tensioner spring as shown in the illustration. Refill the crankcase. Start the engine and check for leaks.

1988–89

1. Disconnect the negative battery cable.

2. Raise and support the front of the vehicle on jackstands.

3. Drain the crankcase.

4. Remove the 2 torque converter covers.

5. Disconnect the exhaust crossunder pipe and move it aside.

6. Remove the oil pan-to-engine bolts and the oil pan.

7. Using a putty knife, clean the gasket mounting surfaces.

8. To install, use a new gasket, RTV sealant at the rear main bearing cap and the front cover-to-block joints and reverse the removal procedures. Torque the oil pan-to-engine bolts to 12 ft. lbs. Refill the crankcase. Start the engine and check for leaks.

RIVIERA 1982–85

1. Disconnect negative battery cable.

2. Remove top 3 final drive-to-transaxle bolts.

3. Raise and support the front of the vehicle on jackstands.

4. Disconnect 2 frame braces, the idler arm and the pitman arm from relay rod.

5. Disconnect drive axles from output shafts.

6. Disconnect battery terminal bracket from output shaft support.

7. Disconnect output shaft support from engine block.

8. Remove 3 final drive-to-transaxle bolts.

9. Using a transaxle jack, remove the final drive unit.

10. Remove splash shield and disconnect starter wires.

11. Remove the starter-to-engine bolts and the starter.

12. Drain the crankcase. Remove oil pan bolts and the pan.

13. Using a putty knife, clean the gasket mounting surfaces.

14. To install, use new gaskets, sealant and reverse the removal procedures. Torque oil pan-to-engine bolts to 10 ft. lbs.

ALLANTE 1987–89

1. Disconnect the negative battery

cable.

2. Raise and support the front of the vehicle on jackstands.

3. Drain the crankcase and disconnect the oil level sensor.

4. Remove the troque converter cover.

5. Remove the exhaust Y-pipe.

6. Remove the oil pan-to-engine bolts/nuts and the oil pan.

7. Using a putty knife, clean the gasket mounting surfaces.

8. To install, use a new gasket, RTV sealant at the rear main bearing cap and the front cover-to-block joints and reverse the removal procedures. Torque the oil pan-to-engine bolts to 12 ft. lbs. Refill the crankcase. Start the engine and check for leaks.

V6 Engines

TORONADO 1982–85

1. Disconnect the negative battery cable. Raise and support the front of the vehicle on jackstands.

2. Drain the crankcase. Remove the flywheel cover and the crossover pipe.

3. Disconnect the engine mounts from the frame brackets. Raise the engine by the vibration damper for clearance.

4. Remove the oil pan-to-engine bolts and the pan.

5. Using a putty knife, clean the gasket mounting surfaces.

6. To install, use new gaskets, sealant and reverse the removal procedures. Torque the oil pan-to-engine bolts to 14 ft. lbs.

ELDORADO AND SEVILLE 1982

1. Disconnect the negative battery cable. Raise and support the front of the vehicle on jackstands.

2. Drain the crankcase.

3. Remove the final drive assembly as described later in this section.

4. Remove the exhaust crossover pipe. Remove the oil pan-to-engine bolts and the oil pan.

5. Using a putty knife, clean the gasket mounting surfaces.

6. To install, use new gaskets, sealant and reverse the removal procedures. Torque the pan bolts to 14 ft. lbs. Refill the crankcase.

RIVIERA AND TORONADO 1986–87

1. Disconnect the negative battery cable. Raise and support the vehicle on jackstands. Drain the crankcase.

2. Remove the flywheel or torque converter cover and the crossover pipe.

3. While supporting the engine from above, unbolt the engine mounts from the frame brackets.

4. Raise the engine until there will be clearance to remove the oil pan

from underneath. Remove the oil pan-to-engine bolts and the pan.

5. Using a putty knife, clean the gasket mounting surfaces.

6. To install, use a new gasket, sealant and reverse the removal procedures. Torque the oil pan-to-engine bolts to 6–9 ft. lbs. Refill the crankcase. Operate the engine and check for leaks.

RIVIERA, TORONADO AND REATTA 1988–89

1. Disconnect the negative battery cable.

2. Raise and support the front of the vehicle on jackstands.

3. Drain the crankcase.

4. Remove the torque converter cover and the oil filter.

5. Disconnect the electrical connectors from the starter. Remove the starter-to-engine bolts and the starter.

6. Remove the oil pan-to-engine bolts and the oil pan.

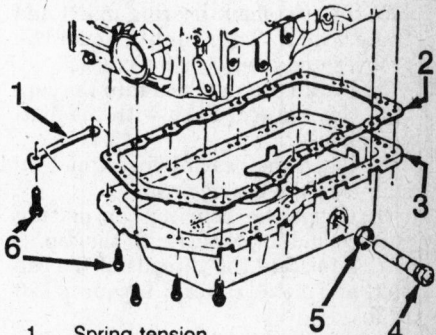

1. Spring tension
2. Oil pan gasket
3. Oil pan
4. Oil level indicator switch – 40 ft. lbs.
5. Seal
6. Bolt – 124 inch lbs.

Exploded view of the oil pan assembly – 3.8L (code C) 1988–89 engine

7. Using a putty knife, clean the gasket mounting surfaces.

8. To install, use new gasket(s) and reverse the removal procedures. Torque the oil pan-to-engine bolts to 124 inch lbs. Refill the crankcase. Start the engine, allow it to reach normal operating temperatures and check for leaks.

Rear Main Bearing Oil Seal

REMOVAL & INSTALLATION

Toronado 1982–85

1. Remove the oil pan.

2. Remove the rear main bearing cap. Using a blunt-ended tool, drive the upper seal into its groove on each side until it is tightly packed; usually ¼–¾ in.

3. Cut pieces of the old bearing cap

seal $\frac{1}{16}$ in. longer than the distance each side of the upper seal was compressed.

4. Install these pieces into each side of the upper seal seat, packing them into place. Carefully trim any protruding seal, being sure not to scratch or damage the bearing surface.

5. Install a new seal in the bearing cap and install the cap.

6. To complete the installation, reverse the removal procedures. Refill the crankcase. Start the engine and check for leaks.

Eldorado and Seville

ALL ENGINES EXCEPT 4.1L AND 4.5L V8

In order to replace the upper main bearing seal, the crankshaft must be removed from the engine. Only the lower rear main oil seal is covered here.

1. Remove the oil pan.
2. Remove the rear main bearing cap, the rear main bearing insert and the old seal. Thoroughly clean the grooves and inspect it for cracks.
3. Install the new seal into the cap.
4. Cut the seal flush with the mating surface.
5. Clean the bearing insert and install it in the bearing cap.
6. Clean the bearing cap mating surface and apply sealer to the cap.
7. Lubricate the threads of the cap bolts and install the cap. Torque to 120 ft. lbs.
8. Install the oil pan. To complete the installation, reverse the removal procedures.

4.1L AND 4.5L V8 ENGINE

NOTE: To perform this procedure, use a Seal Removal tool No. J–26868 or equivalent, and a Seal Installer tool No. J–34604 or equivalent.

1. Remove the transaxle.
2. Unbolt and remove the flexplate from the rear end of the crankshaft.
3. Using a Seal Removal tool No. J–26868 or equivalent, remove the old seal. Thoroughly clean the seal bore of any leftover seal material with a clean rag.
4. Lubricate the lip of a new seal with wheel bearing grease. Position it over the crankshaft and into the seal bore with the spring facing inside the engine.
5. Using a Seal Installer tool No. J–34604 or equivalent, press the seal into place. The seal must be square (this is the purpose of the installer) and flush with the block to 1mm indented.
6. To complete the installation, reverse the removal procedures. Torque the flexplate-to-crankshaft bolts to 37

ft. lbs. Refill the crankshaft. Operate the engine and check for leaks.

Allante 1987–89

1. Remove the transaxle.
2. Remove the flywheel-to-crankshaft bolts and the flywheel.
3. Using a shop rag, clean around the seal area.
4. Using the Rear Main Oil Seal Removal tool No. J–26868 or equivalent, pry the oil seal from the rear of the engine.
5. Lubricate the new seal lips with wheel bearing grease and position it on crankshaft with the spring side facing the inside of the engine.
6. Using the Rear Main Oil Seal Installing tool No. J–34604 or equivalent, press the seal into the engine block until it is flush.
7. To complete the installation, reverse the removal procedures. Start the engine and check for leaks.

Reatta 1988–89 and Toronado 1986–89

Braided fabric rope seals are used. The upper seal half cannot be replaced without removing the crankshaft.

LOWER HALF-SEAL

1. Remove the oil pan.
2. Remove the rear main bearing cap-to-engine bolts and the cap.
3. Remove the old seal from the bearing cap.
4. To replace the oil seal, perform the following procedures:

   a. Using sealant No. GM 1052621, Loctite® 414 or equivalent, apply it to the main bearing cap seal groove and wait for 1 minute.

   b. Using a new rope seal and a wooden dowel or hammer handle, roll the new seal into the cap so both ends projecting above the parting surface of the cap; force the seal into the groove by rubbing it down, until the seal projects above the groove not more than $\frac{1}{16}$ in.

   c. Using a sharp razor blade, cut the ends off flush with the surface of the cap.

   d. Using chassis grease, apply a thin coat to the seals surface.

5. To install the neoprene sealing strips (side seals), perform the following procedures:

   a. Using light oil or kerosene, soak the strips for 5 minutes.

NOTE: The neoprene composition seals will swell up once exposed to the oil and heat. It is normal for the seals to leak for a short time, until they become properly seated. The seals must not be cut to fit.

   b. Place the sealing strips in the

grooves on the sides of the bearing cap.

6. Using sealer No. GM 1052621 or equivalent, apply it to the main bearing cap mating surface; DO NOT apply sealer to the bolt holes.

7. To install, reverse the removal procedures. Torque the main bearing cap-to-engine bolts to 100 ft. lbs. Refill the crankcase. The engine must be operated at low rpm when first started, after a new seal is installed.

UPPER HALF-SEAL

Engine removal is not necessary if the following Time Saver procedure is followed.

1. Remove the oil pan.
2. Remove the rear main bearing cap-to-engine bolts and the cap.
3. Using the Seal Packing tool No. J–21526–1 or equivalent, insert it against each side of the upper seal and drive the seal until it is tight.
4. Measure the amount the seal was driven into the engine and add about $\frac{1}{16}$ in. Using a razor blade, cut that amount off the old lower seal.
5. Using the Seal Packing tool No. J–21526–1 or equivalent, work the short packing pieces into the cylinder block; a small amount of oil on the seal will help the installation.
6. Repeat this process on the other side.
7. Install the lower bearing cap.
8. To complete the installation, reverse the removal procedures. Torque the main bearing cap-to-engine bolts to 100 ft. lbs. Refill the crankcase. The engine must be operated at low rpm when first started, after a new seal is installed.

Oil Pump

REMOVAL & INSTALLATION

3.8L and 4.1 V6 Engines

The oil pump, located in the bottom of the front cover, is an integral part of the front cover; the crankshaft passes through it.

1. Remove the front cover.
2. Using a putty knife, clean the gasket mounting surfaces.
3. To inspect the pump gears, perform the following procedures:

   a. Remove the oil pump cover-to-front cover screws and the cover.

   b. Remove the inner and outer pump gears.

   c. Using solvent, clean the gears.

   d. Inspect the gears for wear and/or damage; if necessary, replace the parts.

   e. Using petroleum jelly, pack the pump and reinstall the parts. Torque the oil pump cover-to-front cover screws to 88 inch lbs.

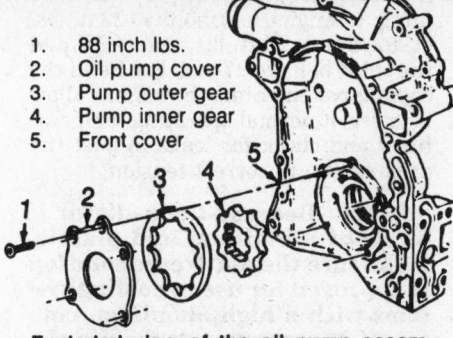

1. 88 inch lbs.
2. Oil pump cover
3. Pump outer gear
4. Pump inner gear
5. Front cover

Exploded view of the oil pump assembly — 3.8L engine — 4.1L V6 similar

NOTE: Unless the pump is primed this way, it won't produce any oil pressure when the engine is started.

4. To complete the installation, use new gaskets, sealant (if necessary) and reverse the removal procedures. Check and/or refill the crankcase. Replace the oil filter. Start the engine and check for leaks.

4.1L and 4.5L V8 Engines

1. Remove the oil pan.
2. Remove the oil pump-to-engine screws/nut and the oil pump from the engine.
3. To disassemble, remove the oil pump cover-to-housing screws, slide the drive shaft, drive gear and driven gear from the pump housing.
4. Remove the oil pressure regulator valve and spring from the bore in the housing assembly.
5. Inspect the oil pressure regulator valve for nicks and burrs.
6. Measure the free length of the regulator valve spring. It should be 2.57–2.69 in.
7. Inspect the drive gear and driven gear for nicks and burrs.
8. Assemble the pump drive gear over the drive shaft so the retaining ring is inside the gear. Position the drive gear over the pump housing shaft closest to the pressure regulator bore.
9. Slide the driven gear over the remaining shaft in the pump housing, meshing the driven gear with the drive gear.
10. Install the oil pressure regulator spring and valve in the bore of the pump housing assembly.
11. Install the pump cover-to-pump housing screws to 5 ft. lbs., the oil pump-to-engine screws to 15 ft. lbs. and nut to 22 ft. lbs.
12. To complete the installation, use new gaskets and reverse the removal procedures. Refill the crankcase. Start the engine and check for leaks.

5.0L V8 Engine

1. Disconnect the negative battery

cable. Drain the engine oil. Remove the engine oil pan.
2. Remove pump attaching screws and carefully lower the pump and extension.
3. Install the extension with the washer end in the oil pump drive shaft, making certain that the extension is fully engaged. Continue installation in reverse order of removal procedure.

NOTE: To insure immediate oil pressure on start-up, the oil pump gear cavity should be packed with petroleum jelly. If the pump is not packed, severe engine damage may result.

5.7L Diesel

1. Remove the oil pan.
2. Remove the oil pump-to-rear main bearing cap, the remove the pump and the drive shaft extension.
3. Using a putty knife, clean the gasket mounting surfaces.
4. To install, new gaskets, sealant and reverse the removal procedures. Be sure the shaft is properly mated with the distributor drive gear. Torque the bolts to 35 ft. lbs.

Oil Pump Cover and Gears

REMOVAL & INSTALLATION

3.8L and 4.1L V6 Engines

1. Disconnect the negative battery cable.
2. Raise and support the front of the vehicle on jackstands. Remove the oil filter.
3. Remove the oil pump cover-to-timing chain cover bolts, the oil pump cover assembly, drive gear and the driven gear.
4. Remove the oil pump pressure relief valve cap, spring and relief valve.
5. Clean all the parts in solvent and blow them dry with compressed air.

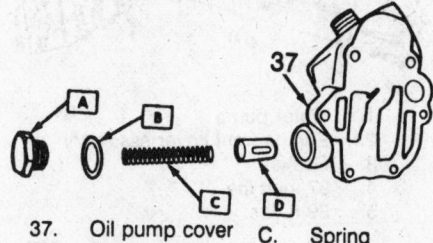

37. Oil pump cover
A. Plug
B. Washer
C. Spring
D. Relief valve

Exploded view of the oil pump cover — 3.8L and 4.1L V6 engines

6. To install, reverse the removal procedures. Make sure you lubricate all the relief valve parts with clean engine oil. After reassembling the gears

into the pump housing, thoroughly pack all the voids between gears and the housing with petroleum jelly to ensure that the pump will prime itself.

NOTE: Failure to pack the oil pump with petroleum jelly before reassembling the pump and starting the engine will cause engine damage.

7. To complete the installation, use new gaskets and reverse the removal procedures. Torque the cap for the pressure regulator valve to 35 ft. lbs. Torque the bolts for the pump cover alternately and in several stages to 12 ft. lbs. Refill the oil pan. Operate the engine and check for leaks.

ENGINE COOLING

Radiator

REMOVAL & INSTALLATION

1982–85

1. Drain the cooling system. Disconnect the upper/lower hoses and the transaxle coolant lines.
2. Disconnect the coolant recovery hose.
3. Remove the fan shroud-to-radiator screws. Lift the shroud out of the clips and hang the shroud over the fan.
4. Remove the radiator upper mounting panel and the radiator.
5. To install, reverse the removal procedures. Refill the cooling system. Start the engine and check for leaks.

1986–87

1. Disconnect the negative battery cable and drain the engine coolant.
2. Remove the forward strut brace from the radiator and swing the strut rearward.

NOTE: To prevent shearing the rubber bushings, loosen the bolt before swinging the strut.

3. Disconnect the fan electrical connector and the forward lamp harness.
4. Remove the electric fan bolts and the fan/frame assembly.
5. Using a scratch awl, scribe the hood latch location and remove the hood latch.
6. Disconnect the radiator hoses and coolant recovery hose from the radiator. Disconnect the transaxle-to-radiator oil cooling lines.
7. Remove the radiator-to-radiator

support bolts/clamps and the radiator from the vehicle.

8. To install, reverse the removal procedures. Torque the radiator support attaching clamp bolts to 7 inch lbs., the transaxle oil cooler lines-to-radiator to 15 ft. lbs. and the fan assembly-to-support bolts to 85 inch lbs. Refill the cooling system with a 50/50 antifreeze mix.

NOTE: Because the 4.1L and 4.5L V8 engines use an aluminum block, make sure the antifreeze solution is approved for use in cooling systems with a high aluminum content. GM recommends the use of a supplement/sealant No. 3634621, or equivalent, specifically designed for use in aluminum engines to protect the engine from damage.

1988–89

ALLANTE, ELDORADO AND SEVILLE

1. Disconnect the negative battery cable.
2. Drain the cooling system. Remove the cooling fans.
3. From the radiator filler neck, remove the coolant reservoir hose.
4. Remove the upper radiator hose, the engine oil cooler lines, the transaxle cooler lines and the lower radiator hose from the radiator.
5. Remove the radiator from the vehicle.
6. To install, reverse the removal procedures. Refill the cooling system. Check and/or refill the crankcase and transaxle fluids. Operate the engine until normal operating temperatures are reached and check for leaks.

NOTE: Because the 4.1L and 4.5L V8 engines use an aluminum block and the radiator is made of aluminum, make sure the antifreeze solution is approved for use in cooling systems with a high aluminum content. GM recommends the use of a supplement/sealant No. 3634621, or equivalent, specifically designed for use in aluminum engines to protect the engine from damage.

REATTA AND TORONADO

1. Disconnect the negative battery cable.
2. Drain the cooling system. Remove the cooling fans.
3. Remove the upper air cleaner duct and/or silencer.
4. Remove the upper radiator-top-chassis panel screws and the panel.
5. Remove the upper hose, the lower hose and the coolant recovery hose from the radiator. From the radiator

side tank, remove the transaxle cooler lines.

6. Disconnect the fan electrical connector.
7. Remove the radiator from the vehicle.
8. To install, reverse the removal procedures. Refill the cooling system. Check and/or refill the transaxle fluid. Operate the engine until normal operating temperatures are reached and check for leaks.

NOTE: Because the radiator is made of aluminum and plastic, make sure the antifreeze solution is approved for use in cooling systems with a high aluminum content. GM recommends the use of a supplement/sealant No. 3634621, or equivalent, specifically designed for use in aluminum engines to protect the engine from damage.

Water Pump

REMOVAL & INSTALLATION

All Engines Except 4.1L and 4.5L V8

1. Disconnect the negative battery cable.
2. Position a drain pan under the radiator, open the drain cock and drain the cooling system.
3. Disconnect the hoses from the water pump.
4. Remove the drive belt(s).
5. Remove the water pump pulley bolts and the pulley.

NOTE: The long bolt is removed through the access hole provided in the body side rail.

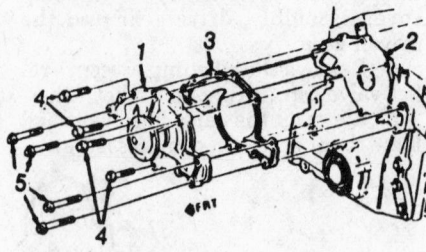

1. Water pump
2. Engine front cover assembly
3. Gasket
4. 97 inch lbs.
5. 29 ft. lbs.

Exploded view of the water pump – 3.8L engine

6. Remove the water pump-to-engine bolts and the pump.
7. Using a putty knife, clean the gasket mounting surfaces.
8. To install, use a new gasket, sealant (if necessary) and reverse the re-

moval procedures. Torque the water pump-to-engine long bolts to 22 ft. lbs. (1982–87) or 29 ft. lbs. (1988–89) and the short bolts to 97 inch lbs. Refill the cooling system. Start the engine, allow it to reach normal operating temperatures and check for leaks. Adjust the drive belt(s) to correct tension.

NOTE: Because the radiator is made of aluminum and plastic, make sure the antifreeze solution is approved for use in cooling systems with a high aluminum content. GM recommends the use of a supplement/sealant No. 3634621, or equivalent, specifically designed for use in aluminum engines to protect the engine from damage.

4.1L and 4.5L V8 Engines

1. Disconnect the negative battery cable.
2. Position a drain pan under the radiator, open the drain cock and drain the cooling system.
3. Remove the air filter assembly. Disconnect and remove the coolant recovery tank.
4. Disconnect and remove the cross car brace.
5. While applying tension to the drive belt, to hold the water pump pulley from moving, remove the water pulley bolts.
6. Remove the drive belt and the water pump pulley.
7. Remove the water pump-to-engine bolts and the pump.
8. Using a putty knife, clean the gasket mounting surfaces.
9. To install, use a new gasket, sealant (if necessary) and reverse the removal procedures. Torque the pulley-to-water pump bolts to 25 ft. lbs., the water pump-to-engine Torx® bolts and stud nuts to 30 ft. lbs. and the remaining fasteners to 5 ft. lbs.

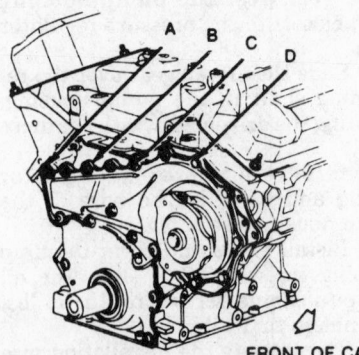

FRONT OF CAR

Locations for fasteners on the 250 V8 water pump. A fasteners are Torx screws; B fasteners are nuts; C fasteners are studs; and D fasteners are hex screws. Torque A and C to 30 ft. lbs. and B and D to 5 ft. lbs.

NOTE: Because the engines use an aluminum block and the radiator is made of aluminum, make sure the antifreeze solution is approved for use in cooling systems with a high aluminum content. GM recommends the use of a supplement/sealant No. 3634621, or equivalent, specifically designed for use in aluminum engines to protect the engine from damage.

Thermostat

REMOVAL & INSTALLATION

The thermostat is located in the rear of the intake manifold.

NOTE: If only silicone sealer was used from the factory, use only sealer during assembly.

1. Drain the cooling system below the level of the thermostat.
2. Remove the bolt fastening the housing mounting clamp.
3. Pull the thermostat housing from the manifold. Remove the sealing ring and thermostat.
4. Using a putty knife, clean the gasket mounting surfaces of the intake manifold and the thermostat housing.

NOTE: On some Cadillac 4.1L and 4.5L engines, there are both an upper and a lower thermostat housing; do not remove the lower housing to replace the thermostat. Make sure to replace the ring seal after the thermostat is in place.

5. To install, use a new gasket or O-ring and reverse the removal procedures. Torque the thermostat housing-to-intake manifold bolts to 18 ft. lbs. Operate the engine until normal operating temperatures are reached and check for leaks.

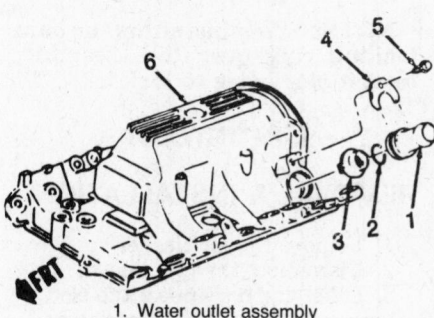

1. Water outlet assembly
2. O-ring seal
3. Thermostat assembly
4. Clamp
5. Torque to 20 ft. lbs.
6. Intake manifold

Replacing the thermostat on the 231 V6 with injection

NOTE: Be sure not to install the thermostat upside down. The spring and wax pellet must always be positioned downward or on the cylinder block side.

EMISSION CONTROLS

Please refer to "Emission Control" in the Unit Repair section for system maintenance procedures. Due to the complex nature of modern electronic engine control systems, comprehensive diagnosis and testing procedures fall outside the confines of this repair manual. For complete information on diagnosis, testing and repair procedures concerning all modern engine and emission control systems, please refer to *Chilton's Guide to Electronic Engine Controls.*

GASOLINE FUEL SYSTEM

Fuel System Service Precaution

- Disconnect the negative battery terminal.
- Keep a Class B dry chemical fire extinguisher available.
- Always relieve the fuel pressure before disconnecting a fuel line.
- Wrap a shop cloth around the fuel line when disconnecting a fuel line.
- Always use new O-rings.
- DO NOT replace the fuel pipes with fuel hoses.
- Always use a back-up wrench when opening or closing a fuel line.

RELIEVING FUEL SYSTEM PRESSURE

All Except 3.8L Engines

If the engine has been operated, allow a few minutes for it to bleed-down.

3.8L Engines

1. From the fuse panel, remove the "fuel pump" fuse.
2. Start the engine and allow it run until it stalls.

3. Crank the starter for at least 3 full seconds to ensure that there is no fuel pressure in the system.
4. Turn the ignition switch OFF and replace the fuse.

Fuel Filter

REMOVAL & INSTALLATION

Carbureted Engines

1. Disconnect the fuel line connection from the carburetor inlet.
2. Remove the inlet fuel filter nut from the carburetor with a box wrench.
3. Remove the filter element and spring.
4. If it's a bronze element, blow through the cone end; the element should allow air to pass through freely.
5. Install the spring and a new element into the carburetor. Bronze elements are installed with the small section of the cone facing outward.
6. Install a new gasket on the fitting nut and install the nut.
7. Install the fuel line and tighten it securely. Start the engine and check for leaks.

Fuel Injected Engines

On most vehicles, except Allante, the fuel filter is located on the left side, behind the front tire, where the fuel hoses connect to the body fuel pipes.

On the Allante, the fuel filter is located in front of the left rear wheel

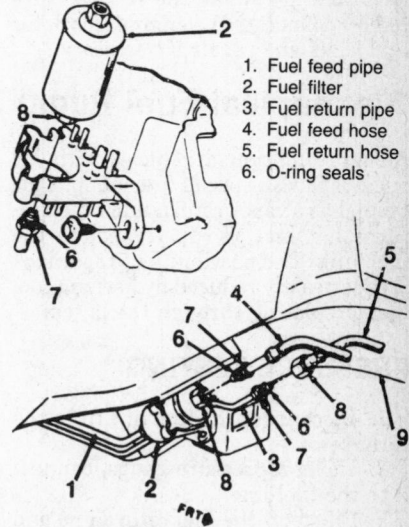

1. Fuel feed pipe
2. Fuel filter
3. Fuel return pipe
4. Fuel feed hose
5. Fuel return hose
6. O-ring seals

7. Torque these fittings to 26 ft. lbs.
8. Flats for use of a backup wrench
9. Left hand frame rail in the engine compartment

View of the fuel filter—fuel injected engines (1985 and later), except Allante

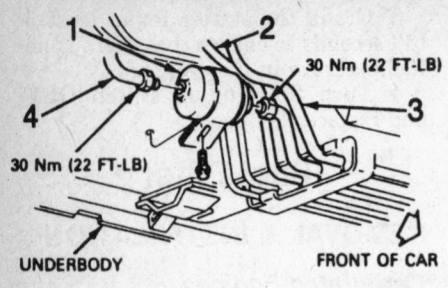

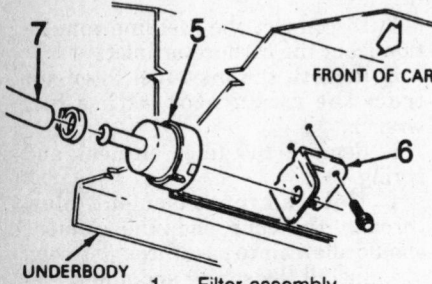

1. Filter assembly
2. Vapor pipe
3. Return pipe
4. Fuel feed pipe
5. Vent valve
6. Vent valve bracket
7. Vent hose

View of the fuel filter — Allante (1988 and later)

near the frame.

1. Relieve the fuel pressure. Raise and support the front of the vehicle on jackstands.
2. Using a backup wrench, disconnect both fuel lines from the filter.
3. Remove the fuel line-to-filter clamps and the filter from the bracket.
4. To install, use a new filter, new O-rings and reverse the removal procedures. Operate the engine, check for fuel leaks and repair if necessary.

Mechanical Fuel Pump

All air conditioned vehicles with V8 engines have a special fuel pump. This pump has a vapor return line which returns hot fuel and fuel vapor to the fuel tank. The possibility of vapor lock is thus greatly reduced by keeping cool fuel circulating through the pump.

PRESSURE TESTING

1. Disconnect the fuel line from the carburetor.
2. Using a pressure gauge, connect it to the fuel line.
3. Pinch off the fuel return line and hold the gauge about 16 in. above the fuel pump.
4. Start the engine and allow it idle (using the gas in the carburetor).
5. Observe the pressure gauge, it should be 4–7 psi (V6) or 6–9 psi. (V8).
6. If the pressure is too high, too low or varies within the engine speed, replace the pump.

REMOVAL & INSTALLATION

1. Disconnect the fuel inlet, the outlet and vapor (if equipped) hoses from the pump.
2. Remove the fuel pump-to-engine bolts and the fuel pump from the engine.
3. Using a putty knife, clean the gasket mounting surfaces.
4. To install, use a new gasket, a new pump (if necessary) and bolts. Torque the bolts alternately and evenly. Reconnect the hoses, start the engine and check for fuel leaks.

Electric Fuel Pump

PRESSURE TESTING

1. Disconnect the fuel line from the injector "T" inlet.
2. Using a pressure gauge, install it to the line and reconnect it to the injector.

NOTE: Some models are equipped with a "T" fitting which allows a pressure test without disconnecting the fuel lines.

3. Pinch off the fuel return line (if equipped). Hold the pressure gauge about 16 inches above the fuel pump.
4. Start the engine and observe the pressure; it should be 27–36 psi (sequential fuel injection), 9–13 psi (digital fuel injection) or 46 psi (multi-port fuel injection).
5. If the pressure is too high, too low or varies within the engine speed, replace the pump.

REMOVAL & INSTALLATION

— CAUTION —

Because of the large amount of fuel under pressure in the injection system, it is dangerous to disassemble system parts unless fuel system pressure is first relieved. There is considerable risk of fire unless the proper procedures are followed.

1. Relieve the fuel pressure.
2. Disconnect the negative battery cable.
3. Raise and support the rear of the vehicle on jackstands.

NOTE: Make sure the rear end is supported securely so that in the next step, weight distribution changes will not cause it to become unbalanced.

4. Drain the fuel tank and remove it from the vehicle.
5. Using a hammer and the brass bar, drive the cam locking ring counterclockwise to release it and lift the sending unit from the tank.

6. Pull the fuel pump up into the attaching pipe while pulling it outward, away from the support on the bottom of the tank. Make sure not to damage the rubber insulator and the strainer. When the pump is entirely clear of the bottom support, pull it out of the rubber connector to remove it.

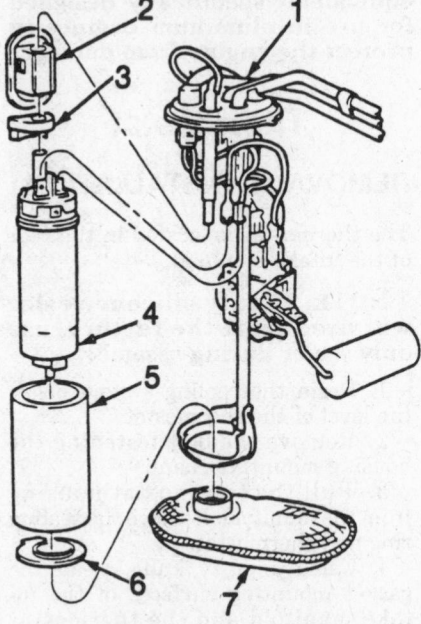

1. Fuel tank meter assembly
2. Pulsator
3. Bumper
4. Fuel pump
5. Sound isolator sleeve
6. Sound insulator
7. Filter strainer

Exploded view of the electric fuel pump/sending unit assembly

7. Inspect the attaching hose and the rubber sound insulator from the bottom of the pump for signs of deterioration and replace parts (if necessary).
8. To install, use a new O-ring, push the fuel pump into the attaching hose and reverse the removal procedures. Start the engine and check for leaks.

NOTE: When installing the cam locking ring over the assembly, turn it clockwise to lock it.

Carburetor

REMOVAL & INSTALLATION

1. Remove the air cleaner.
2. Disconnect the fuel line(s).
3. Label and disconnect the electrical connectors from the carburetor.
4. Label and disconnect the vacuum lines from the carburetor.
5. Remove the carburetor-to-intake manifold bolts and the carburetor.
6. Using a putty knife, clean the gasket mounting surfaces.

7. To install, use a new gasket and reverse the removal procedures.

OVERHAUL

For all carburetor overhaul and adjustment procedures, please refer to "Carburetor Service" in the Unit Repair section.

Fuel Injection

Due to the complex nature of modern fuel injection systems, comprehensive diagnosis and testing procedures fall outside the confines of this repair manual. For complete information on Fuel injection diagnosis, testing and repair procedures please refer to *Chilton's Guide to Fuel Injection And Feedback Carburetors.*

DIESEL FUEL SYSTEM

For diesel engine fuel injection adjustments, timing, removal and installation procedures, see the Oldsmobile/Pontiac Rear Wheel Drive section. For additional information on the fuel system, please refer to "Carburetors" or "Diesel Maintenance" in the Unit Repair section.

Fuel Filter

REPLACEMENT

1. Disconnect the negative battery cable.
2. Disconnect the electrical connector from the water sensor.
3. Disconnect the fuel hoses from the fuel filter.
4. Remove the fuel filter-to-bracket screws and the filter assembly from the barcket.
5. To install, reverse the removal procedures. Drain the water and air from the fuel filter.

DRAINING WATER FROM THE SYSTEM

1. Disconnect the electrical connector from the fuel filter.
2. Disconnect the fuel outlet hose and place it in a suitable container.
3. Operate the the priming handle several times to expell any air from the system.

NOTE: If an excessive amount of water is present in the fuel filter, it may be necessary to drain the fuel tank.

4. To complete the installation, reverse the removal procedures. Start the engine and check for leaks.

Diesel Injection Pump

REMOVAL & INSTALLATION

1. Remove the air cleaner, the crankcase ventilation filter and the pipes from the valve covers.
2. Disconnect the throttle rod and spring.

NOTE: If equipped with air conditioning, disconnect the rear compressor brace.

3. Remove the Crankcase Depression Regulator Valve (CDRV) and fuel filter.
4. Disconnect the fuel return line from the injection pump.
5. Disconnect and plug the fuel injection lines from the pump.
6. Remove the injection pump-to-engine nuts/bolts and the injection pump; discard the O-ring.

NOTE: If the pump is to be sent to an authorized dealer for repair, remove the MVS.

7. To install, use a new O-rings, apply Loctite® 242 to the MVS threads and torque the screws to 30 inch lbs.

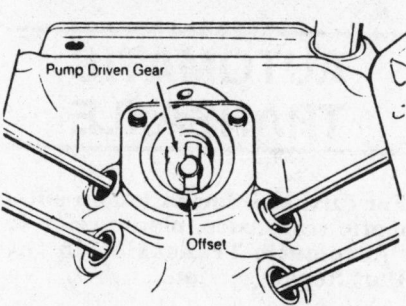

Positioning the pump driven gear to align with the fuel injection pump—diesel

8. Position the No. 1 cylinder on the TDC of its compression stroke. Align the pumps drive shaft with the pump driven gear and reverse the removal procedures. Torque the injection pump-to-engine nuts to 18 ft. lbs. Perform the injection timing adjustment. Start the engine and check for leaks.

INJECTION TIMING

Checking

1. The engine must be at normal operating temperatures.
2. Position the transaxle selector lever in the **PARK** position.
3. Remove the air cleaner. Using the Cover Screen tool No. J–26996–1

or equivalent, install it on the throttle body.

4. Remove the MAP sensor and disconnect the EGR valve hose.
5. Clean the probe holder (rpm counter) and the crankshaft balancer rim. On both sides of the glow plug probe and the photo-electric pick-up, clean the lens.
6. Using a dull toothpick, scrape the carbon from the combustion chamber side of the glow plug probe.

NOTE: If the carbon is cleaned from the glow plug probe, retarded reading will result.

7. Install the rpm probe into the crankshaft probe holder. Remove the glow plug from the No. 3 cylinder and install the glow plug probe. Torque the probe to 8 ft. lbs.
8. Adjust the timing meter offset selector to **B** (99.5). Disconnect the 2-lead electrical connector from the alternator.

NOTE: If the alternator lead is difficult to remove, remove the gauge fuse (with the engine NOT running).

9. Start the engine and check the injection timing; it should be 4 degrees ATDC @ 1250 rpm. If the timing is not correct, adjust the injection pump timing.

Adjusting

PUMP TIMING

1. With the engine turned **OFF**, note the position of the marks on the pump flange and the pump adapter.
2. Loosen the pump-to-retainer nuts/bolts.

NOTE: Rotate the pump left to advance the timing and/or right to retard the timing. The width of a mark on the intermediate adaptor is ⅔ degrees.

3. Adjust the timing and tighten the bolts to 35 ft. lbs.
4. Start the engine and recheck the timing. Adjust the throttle linkage assembly. Reset the fast and curb idle.

THROTTLE ROD LINKAGE

1. Disconnect the T.V. (detent) cable and the cruise control servo rod (if equipped) from the throttle body.
2. Loosen the injection pump rod lock nut and shorten the rod several turns.
3. Rotate the bellcrank assembly to **FULL** throttle and hold. Lengthen the pump rod until the injection pump lever contacts the full throttle stop.
4. Release the bellcrank assembly and tighten the pump rod lock nut.
5. Depress and hold the metal lock tab on the upper cable end of the T.V.

cable. Move the slider through the fitting, away from the bellcrank assembly, until the slider stops against the metal fitting. Release the metal tab.

6. If equipped, install the cruise control rod, then, rotate the bellcrank lever to the full throttle stop and release it.

7. Adjust the vacuum regulator and the idle speed.

VACUUM REGULATOR

1. Remove the air cleaner. Using the Cover Screen tool No. J-26996–1 or equivalent, install it on the throttle body.

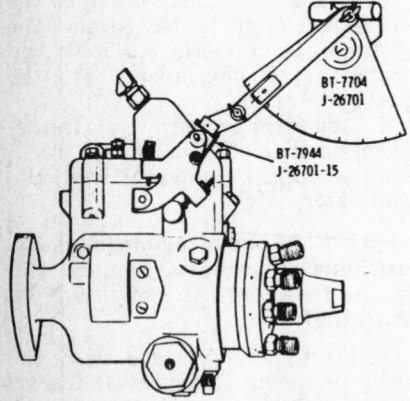

Adjusting the vacuum regulator—diesel engine

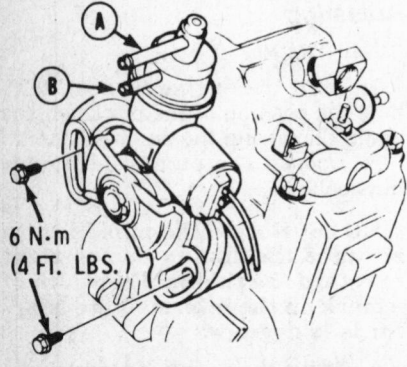

View of the injection pumps vacuum regulator—diesel

2. Disconnect the throttle rod from the injection pump.

3. Loosen the vacuum regulator valve-to-injection pump bolts.

4. Using the Angle Gauge Adapter tool No. J-26701–15, BT-7944 or equivalent, install it onto the injection pump throttle lever.

5. Using the Angle Gauge tool No. J-26701, BT-7704 or equivalent, connect it onto the adapter tool. Rotate the throttle lever to the WIDE OPEN THROTTLE position. Set the angle gauge to the 0 degrees position and level the center bubble.

6. Set the angle gauge to 58 degrees, rotate the throttle lever so the bubble is centered.

7. Install a vacuum pump to port "A" and a gauge to port "B". Apply 22 inch (hg) vacuum to port "A", then, rotate the vacuum valve clockwise to obtain 10.6 inch (hg) vacuum.

8. While holding the valve in this position, torque the valve-to-injection pump bolts to 48 inch lbs.

9. After adjustment is complete, disconnect the equipment and reverse the removal procedures.

Injection Nozzle

REMOVAL & INSTALLATION

1. Using a back-up wrench on the upper injector hex, disconnect the fuel line from the injector.

NOTE: Be sure to cap the fuel injector and plug the fuel line.

2. Remove the fuel injector from the engine.

3. If the copper gasket did not stay on the injector, remove it from the cylinder head.

4. To install, reverse the removal procedures. Torque the fuel injector-to-cylinder head to 35 ft. lbs.

5. Start the engine and check for leaks.

AUTOMATIC TRANSAXLE

For further information on automatic transaxles, please refer to "Automatic Transaxle" in the Unit Repair section.

REMOVAL & INSTALLATION

All Models 1982–85

1. Open the hood and disconnect the negative battery cable (2 terminals on diesels).

NOTE: If equipped with a turbocharger, refer to the "Turbocharger, Removal and Installation" procedures in this section and remove the turbocharger.

2. Disconnect the speedometer cable from the transaxle. Remove the transaxle oil dipstick tube.

3. Remove the air cleaner.

4. Disconnect the throttle valve (T.V./detent) cable from the transaxle, at it's upper end. Disconnect the linkage by removing 1 nut from shaft on left side of transaxle, if equipped.

5. Using an engine holding fixture between the cowl and radiator support, safely support the engine.

6. Remove the top and 2 upper left final drive-to-transaxle bolts.

7. Remove the remaining accessible engine-to-transaxle bolts.

8. Raise and support the front of the vehicle on jackstands.

9. Remove the starter-to-transaxle bolts and starter from the transaxle.

10. Disconnect the transaxle converter clutch connector.

11. Disconnect and plug the transaxle oil cooler lines.

12. Remove the flywheel inspection cover (loosen the top left bolt). Matchmark the flywheel-to-converter relationship for later assembly.

13. On the V8's, disconnect the exhaust Y-pipe connection to the left exhaust pipe. On all models, disconnect the right exhaust pipe at the manifold. On gasoline vehicles, disconnect the catalytic converter hanger bolts (2). On all models, lower the exhaust system about 5 in. and support it.

14. Remove the crossmember-to-frame bolts.

15. Using a floor jack and a wooden block (to protect the transaxle case), position it under the transaxle case, then raise the transaxle slightly.

16. Remove the remaining final drive-to-transaxle bolts.

17. Remove the torque converter-to-flywheel bolts.

18. Disconnect the shift linkage from the transaxle.

19. Remove the final drive support bracket bolt.

20. Remove the right transaxle mount (through bolt and 3 bracket bolts).

21. Remove the left transaxle mount through bolt. Remove the lower bracket-to-transaxle bolt. Raise the transaxle assembly about 2 in. for access to the remaining upper bracket-to-transaxle bolts. Remove the remaining transaxle-to-engine bolts.

22. Carefully lower the transaxle unit while disengaging the final drive.

23. Install a C-clamp or torque converter holding clamp in front of the torque converter (attached to the bell housing) to hold the converter in place. Remove the transaxle from the vehicle.

24. To install, use a new gasket and reverse the removal procedures.

NOTE: Use care when engaging the final drive-to-transaxle splines and make sure the final drive-to-transaxle mounting faces are in alignment with each other.

25. After the splines are engaged, loosely install the 2 final drive-to-transaxle lower bolts.

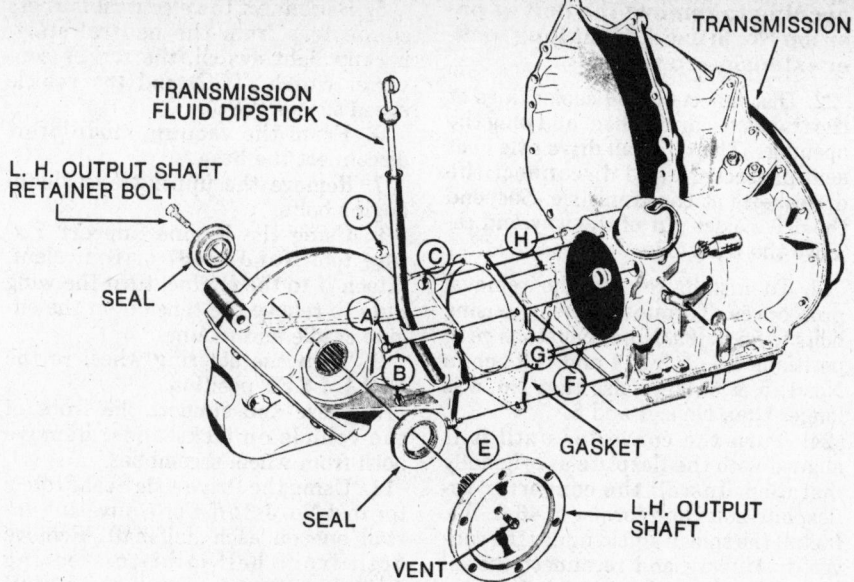

Typical transmission attachment points

TRANSMISSION FLUID DIPSTICK

L. H. OUTPUT SHAFT RETAINER BOLT

SEAL

TRANSMISSION

GASKET

L.H. OUTPUT SHAFT

SEAL

VENT

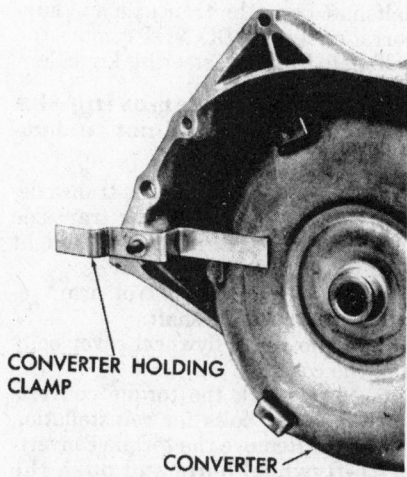

CONVERTER HOLDING CLAMP

CONVERTER

Converter holding clamp. A C-clamp will also work

NOTE: Time can be saved here by installing 2 engine-to-transaxle bolts from above first to aid alignment.

26. After the final drive and transaxle are aligned, install the attaching bolts. Before torquing the flywheel-to-converter bolts, make sure the weld nuts on the converter are flush with the flywheel and that the converter rotates freely by hand. Then hand start all 3 bolts and tighten finger tight. This will insure proper converter alignment. Torque the transaxle-to-engine bolts to 35 ft. lbs., the final drive-to-transaxle bolts to 30 ft. lbs. and the final drive support bracket to final drive bolts to 35 ft. lbs.

Riviera and Toronado 1986–87

NOTE: To perform this procedure, secure an Engine Support

tool No. J–28467 or equivalent, and a Drive Axle Remover tool No. J–33008 or equivalent.

1. Disconnect the negative battery cable. Install the engine support fixture.
2. Disconnect the: vacuum line from the modulator; electrical connections involved with the transaxle; transaxle valve cable at the throttle body and at the transaxle; the cruise control servo.
3. Disconnect the shift selector bracket and cable from the transaxle. Disconnect the neutral start switch.
4. Remove the top 3 transaxle mounting bolts.
5. Remove the bolts that fasten the wiring harness to the transaxle. Remove the driveline dampener bracket.
6. Raise and support the front of the vehicle on jackstands.
7. Disconnect and drain the transaxle oil cooler lines at the transaxle.
8. Remove the torque converter cover. Scribe the relationship between the flexplate and the converter so the same relationship may be established on reinstallation for balance. Remove the converter-to-flexplate bolts, turning the crankshaft (as necessary).
9. Remove the left side transaxle mounting bolts. Remove the engine mounting nuts.
10. Disconnect the sway bar links. Disconnect the left side ball joint from the knuckle.
11. Disconnect the left side driveshaft from the transaxle using a special tool No. J–33008 or equivalent.
12. Disconnect the left side of the frame by removing the bolts.
13. Position a floor jack under the transaxle and support it securely.

14. Remove the 2 remaining engine-to-transaxle bolts.

NOTE: One of the bolts is located between the transaxle case and the block, it is installed in the direction opposite to the others.

15. Remove the engine-to-transaxle bracket.
16. Remove the right drive axle from the transaxle and hang it securely.
17. Remove the transaxle.
18. To install the transaxle, first slide it into position and then install the 2 lower engine-to-transaxle bolts, torquing to 55 ft. lbs.
19. Install the engine-to-transaxle bracket. Install the left side frame assembly bolts.
20. Install the engine mounting nuts. Install the left side transaxle mounting bolts.
21. To complete the installation, reverse the removal procedures. Torque the transaxle mounting bolts to 55 ft. lbs., the converter-to-flexplate bolts to 46 ft. lbs. Make sure that the scribe marks are aligned.

Eldorado and Seville 1986–89 Allante 1987–89

1. Disconnect the negative battery cable. Remove the air cleaner assembly. Disconnect the transaxle throttle valve cable.
2. Remove the cruise control servo and bracket assembly. Disconnect the electrical connectors going to the distributor, oil pressure sending unit and transaxle.
3. Remove the bracket for the engine oil cooler lines.
4. Remove the shift linkage bracket from the transaxle and the manual shift lever from the manual shift

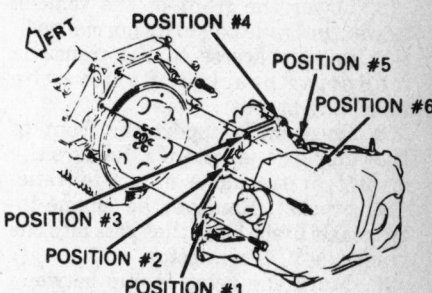

POSITION #4
POSITION #5
POSITION #6
POSITION #3
POSITION #2
POSITION #1

Removing the transaxle-to-engine mounting bolts on the 1986 and later Eldorado and Seville

shaft; leave the cable attached to the lever and bracket.

5. Remove the fuel line bracket and disconnect the neutral safety switch connector.
6. Remove the vacuum modulator.
7. Remove the throttle valve cable support bracket and engine oil cooler line bracket. Remove the bell housing

bolts which are in positions 2, 3, 4 and 5 (see illustration).

8. Remove the air injection reactor crossover pipe fitting and reposition the pipe. Remove the radiator hose bracket and transaxle mount-to-bracket nuts.

9. Install an engine support fixture, noting the positions of the hooks.

10. Raise and support the front of the vehicle on jackstands.

11. Remove both front wheels, the right and left stabilizer link bolts. Remove the ball joint cotter pins and nuts, and press the ball joints from the steering knuckles.

12. Remove the air conditioner splash shield and the mount cover for the forwardmost cradle insulator.

13. Remove the hose connections from the ends of the air injection reactor pipes. Remove the vacuum hoses and the wire loom from the clips at the front of the cradle.

14. Remove the engine mount and dampener-to-cradle attachments. Remove the transaxle mount-to-cradle attachments. Remove the wire loom clip from the transaxle mount bracket and lower the vehicle.

15. Using the 2 left side support hooks on the engine support fixture to raise the transaxle 2 in. from its normal position. Raise and support the front of the vehicle on jackstands.

16. Remove the right front and left rear transaxle-to-cradle bolts and the left stabilizer mount bolts. Remove the foremost cradle mount insulator bolt and the left cradle member, separate the right front corner first.

17. Remove the air injection reactor management valve/bracket assembly from the transaxle mount bracket and reposition the bracket to the transaxle stud bolts.

18. Lower the front of the vehicle. Lower the transaxle to its normal position to gain access to the transaxle mounting bracket. Remove the mounting bracket.

19. Raise and support the front of the vehicle on jackstands. Remove the right rear transaxle mount-to-transaxle bracket. Remove the engine-to-transaxle brace bolts that pass into the transaxle VSS connector.

20. Mark the relationship between torque converter and flexplate for reassembly in the same position. Remove the flywheel covers, then, remove the torque converter bolts, rotating the crankshaft with a socket wrench as necessary to gain access. Position a jack under the transaxle to support it.

21. Remove the bell housing bolts in positions No. 1 and No. 6.

NOTE: Access may be gained through the right wheelhouse

opening to remove the bolt at position No. 6; use a 3 foot long socket extension to reach it.

22. Disconnect the oil cooler lines at the transaxle, drain them and plug the openings. Then, install drive axle boot seal protectors and disconnect the driveshafts at the transaxle. Suspend the drive axles out of the way and remove the transaxle.

23. To install, reverse the removal procedures. Torque the bell housing bolts to 55 ft. lbs. Note that studs go in positions No. 2, 3 & 4 and bolts go in No. 1, 5 & 6. Note also that No. 6 is longer than No's. 1 and 5.

24. Turn the converter until it is aligned with the flexplate as originally installed. Install the converter-to-flexplate bolts and torque to 46 ft. lbs. Install the splash shield under the converter. Unplug and reconnect the oil cooler lines to the transaxle case. Torque the fittings to 15 ft. lbs.

25. To complete the installation, reverse the removal procedures, observing the following torque figures:

    a. Forward most insulator mount bolt — 74 ft. lbs.

    b. Cradle-to-cradle mounting bolts — 74 ft. lbs.

    c. Upper transaxle mount bracket stud bolts — 74 ft. lbs.

    d. Side transaxle mount bracket stud bolts — 50 ft. lbs.

    e. Left or rear transaxle mount nuts — 35 ft. lbs.

    f. Engine mount-to-cradle attachments — 35 ft. lbs.

    g. Right rear mount bracket-to-transaxle bolts — 50 ft. lbs.

    h. Right rear mount bracket nuts — 35 ft. lbs.

    i. Stabilizer mount bolts — 38 ft. lbs.

    j. Ball joint nuts — 81 ft. lbs.

    k. Shift cable bracket-to-transaxle bolts — 18 ft. lbs.

    l. Lug nuts — 100 ft. lbs.

26. Adjust the transaxle valve cable and the shift linkage. Refill the transaxle to the proper level. Operate the engine until hot and adjust the level until it is correct.

Reatta, Riviera and Toronado 1988–89

1. Disconnect the negative battery cable. Remove the air intake duct.

2. Disconnect the throttle valve (T.V.) cable from the transaxle and the throttle body. Disconnect the cruise control servo and cable.

3. Remove the exhaust pipe crossover.

4. Disconnect the shift control linkage lever from from the manual shaft and the mounting bracket from the transaxle.

5. Disconnect the electrical harness connectors from the neutral start/backup light switch, the torque converter clutch (TCC) and the vehicle speed sensor (VSS).

6. From the vacuum modulator, disconnect the hose.

7. Remove the upper transaxle-to-engine bolts.

8. Using the Engine Support Fixture tool No. J-28467 or equivalent, attach it to the engine, turn the wing nuts to relieve the tension on the engine cradle and mounts.

9. Turn the steering wheel to the **FULL LEFT** position.

10. Raise and support the front of the vehicle on jackstands. Remove both from wheel assemblies.

11. Using the Drive Axle Seal Protector tool No. J-34754 or equivalent, install one on each halfshaft. Remove both front ball joint-to-steering knuckle nuts and separate the control arms from the steering knuckles.

12. Using a medium pry bar, pry the halfshaft from the transaxle and support it on a wire; DO NOT remove the halfshaft from the steering knuckle.

NOTE: When removing the halfshaft, be careful not to damage the seal lips.

13. Remove the right rear transaxle-to-frame nuts, the left rear transaxle mount-to-transaxle bolts and the right rear transaxle mount.

14. From the left control arm, remove the stabilizer shaft.

15. Remove the flywheel cover bolts and the cover.

16. Matchmark the torque converter-to-flywheel bolts for reinstallation purposes. Remove the torque converter-to-flywheel bolts and push the torque converter back into the transaxle.

17. Remove the partial frame-to-main frame bolts, the partial frame-to-body bolts and the partial frame.

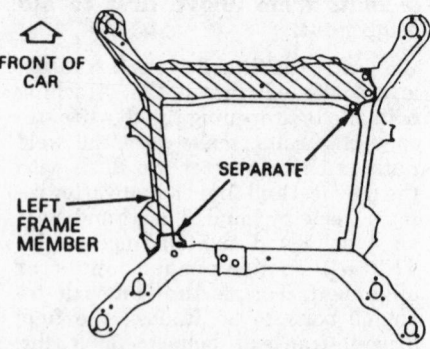

View of the frame separation points

18. Disconnect and plug the oil cooler tubes from the transaxle.

19. Remove the lower transaxle-to-engine bolts.

NOTE: One bolt is located between the engine and the transaxle case and is positioned in the opposite direction.

20. Lower the transaxle from the vehicle; be careful not to damage the hoses, lines and wiring.

21. To install, reverse the removal procedures. Align the torque converter-to-flywheel matchmarks and torque the bolts to 46 ft. lbs. Check and/or adjust the T.V. and shift control cables. Check and/or refill the transaxle fluid. Road test the vehicle and check for leaks.

NOTE: When installing the halfshafts, be careful not to damage the oil seals.

FINAL DRIVE

REMOVAL & INSTALLATION

All Models 1982–85

1. Disconnect the negative battery cable. Raise and support the front of the vehicle on jackstands.

NOTE: If using a twin post hoist, place the jackstands under the front frame horns and the lower the hoist front post.

2. Remove the right side frame brace bolts and pivot the braces outward in order to gain access.

3. If service is being performed on the final drive, perform the following procedures:

   a. Place a drain pan under the final drive cover, loosen the final drive cover screws and allow the fluid to drain.

   b. Remove the cover and gasket material.

4. Remove the output shaft-to-drive axle screws from both sides of the vehicle. Separate the shaft and axle flanges to obtain clearance.

NOTE: The final drive assembly will be removed with the output shafts installed.

5. Remove the battery cable retaining screws from the right output shaft support and the support-to-engine screws.

6. If equipped with a diesel, remove the rear final drive shield-to-transaxle screw, loosen the front final drive shield-to-support bracket screw and remove the shield.

7. Remove the remaining final drive-to-transaxle screws.

8. Using the Puller tool No. J–24319 or equivalent, separate the

steering linkage intermediate rod from the pitman arm. Push the linkage toward the front of the vehicle above the frame crossmember.

9. Remove the final drive support bracket-to-engine block screws.

10. Using a transaxle jack, slide the final drive assembly forward, off the transaxle shaft and remove the unit. DO NOT hold the unit by the output shafts as the seals or splines could easily be damaged.

11. Using a putty knife, clean the gasket mounting surfaces.

12. To install, use a new gasket, a thin coat of anaerobic sealant No. 1052756 or equivalent (on both sides of the gasket).

NOTE: To aid in the installation, tie the right side output shaft support arm to the shaft flange hole, closest to the 12 o'clock position. The support must be in this upward position before installation.

13. Align the final drive assembly with the output shafts attached to the transaxle.

NOTE: If equipped with a diesel engine, install 5 final drive-to-transaxle screws, omitting 1 at the 12 o'clock position until the shield is installed. If not equipped with a diesel engine, install all of the final drive-to-transaxle screws. Torque final drive-to-transaxle screws (in rotation) to 30 ft. lbs.

14. Loosen the front support bracket-to-housing pad screws and install the bracket to the engine block while holding the bracket flush on the housing pad. Torque to 70 ft. lbs.

15. Install the final drive shield (diesel engine). Torque the final drive-to-transaxle screw to 30 ft. lbs. and the shield-to-housing screws to 33 ft. lbs.

NOTE: DO NOT allow the shaft and support assemblies to hang from the final drive unit for damage may occur to the seals.

16. Align the right side output shaft support with the attaching holes in the engine block. By moving the flange end of the shaft up and down and installing the screws and washers loosely, locate the centered position. Torque the screws to 50 ft. lbs.

17. Install the battery cable retainer-to-support screws.

18. Align the right drive axle to the output shaft and install the attaching screws. Torque the screws to 60 ft. lbs. Repeat this procedure for the left side.

19. Position a new cover gasket or apply silicone sealer on the final drive cover. Install the final drive cover and torque the screws to 89 inch lbs. Using

3.2 pints of transaxle fluid, refill the unit. Torque the filler plug to 36 ft. lbs.

20. Install the steering linkage-to-pitman arm and torque the bolt to 60 ft. lbs. If the cotter pin hole does not align properly, tighten the nut slightly. DO NOT loosen to align. Install a new cotter pin.

21. Install the frame braces and torque the nuts to 50 ft. lbs.

22. To complete the installation, reverse the removal procedures. Check and/or refill the transaxle. Start the vehicle. When the final drive has reached operating temperature, check it for leaks.

DRIVE AXLE

Drive axles consist of a halfshaft with an inner and outer constant velocity joint. The right halfshaft has a torsional damper mounted in the center. The inner constant velocity (CV) joint has complete flexibility, plus inward and outward movement. The outer constant velocity (CV) joint has complete flexibility but doesn't allow for inward and outward movement.

Halfshaft

REMOVAL & INSTALLATION

All Models 1982–85

RIGHT SIDE

1. Raise and support the vehicle with jackstands placed under the lower control arms. Remove the wheel.

2. Remove drive axle cotter pin, retainer, nut and washer from the wheel hub.

3. If equipped with a V8, remove oil filter.

4. Remove the inner constant velocity joint-to-final drive bolts.

5. Push the inner constant velocity joint outward (enough) to disengage the right hand final drive output shaft and remove it rearward.

6. Remove the right hand output shaft bracket support-to-engine/final drive bolts.

7. Remove right hand output shaft and drive axle assembly.

NOTE: Care must be exercised so that CV joints DO NOT turn to full extremes and that seals are not damaged against the shock absorber or stabilizer bar.

8. Carefully place the right hand drive axle assembly into the lower con-

trol arm and insert the outer race splines into the steering knuckle.

9. Using special seal lubricant, lubricate the final drive output shaft seal.

10. Install the right hand output shaft into the final drive and attach the support-to-engine/brace bolts. Torque the bolts to 50 ft. lbs.

11. Move right hand drive axle assembly toward front of vehicle and align with right hand output shaft. Install the bolts and torque to 60 ft. lbs.

12. To complete the installation, reverse the removal procedures. Torque the drive axle-to-hub nut to 175 ft. lbs., then, install the retainer and cotter pin. If equipped with a V8, check and/or adjust the oil level.

LEFT SIDE

1. Raise and support the front of the vehicle with jackstands under the lower control arms.

2. Remove wheel assembly and the brake disc.

3. Remove drive axle cotter pin, nut and washer.

4. Remove tie rod end cotter pin and nut.

5. Using a puller, separate the tie rod end from the steering knuckle.

6. Remove the drive axle assembly and left output shaft bolts. Insert a spacer between the axle shaft and lower control arm.

7. Remove the upper control arm ball joint cotter pin and nut.

8. Using a hammer and brass drift, drive the upper ball joint stud free of the steering knuckle.

9. Remove the steering knuckle/support assembly and support the knuckle with wire or string.

10. Carefully remove the drive axle assembly.

NOTE: Care must be exercised so that CV joints DO NOT turn to full extremes and that seals are not damaged against shock absorber or stabilizer bar.

11. Carefully guide the left hand drive axle assembly onto lower control arm and into position on the spacer.

12. Center the left hand drive axle assembly in steering knuckle opening and insert the upper ball joint stud.

13. Place brake hose clip over the upper ball joint stud and install nut; DO NOT torque.

14. Insert the tie rod end stud into the steering knuckle and attach the nut, then, torque to 35 ft. lbs. Install cotter pin and crimp.

15. Align the inner CV joint with the output shaft and install bolts, then, torque to 60 ft. lbs.

16. Torque the lower ball joint stud nuts to 65 ft. lbs. and the upper nuts to 55 ft. lbs. (1982). Install cotter pins and crimp.

NOTE: Upper ball joint cotter pin must be crimped toward the upper control arm to prevent interference with outer CV joint seal.

17. Install the drive axle washer/nut and torque to 175 ft. lbs. Install cotter pin and crimp.

18. To complete the installation, reverse the removal procedures. Check and/or adjust the Front End Alignment.

1986–87

RIVIERA AND TORONADO

NOTE: Secure a Drive Axle Spindle Remover Set tool No. J–33008, J–28733 or equivalent. Also, if the vehicle uses silicone boot seals, drive axle boot seal protectors must be installed before the driveshaft is disconnected. If the vehicle uses thermoplastic seals, these are not required. They are needed with the silicone seals because, without them, the joint may turn to too sharp an angle, causing the seal to be damaged in a way that is not readily detectible. These are identified by GM tool No. J–28712 or equivalent (for the outer seal), and tool No. J–33162 or equivalent (for the inner seal).

1. Remove the hub nut and washer for each axle. Raise and support the front of the vehicle on jackstands. Remove the wheel(s) involved.

NOTE: If the vehicle has silicone seals, install the protectors described in the note above.

2. Remove the brake caliper, the caliper support and the rotor.

3. Remove the steering knuckle-to-strut bolts and pull the knuckle out of the strut bracket.

4. Using the special tool, pull the driveshafts from the transaxle.

NOTE: Support the shafts at the center so there will be no downward force on the outer joints.

5. Using the Spindle Removal tool No. J–28733 or equivalent, remove the axles from the hub/bearing assembly and the vehicle. DO NOT remove the boot seal protectors unless complete disassembly is necessary.

6. To install, 1st, loosely position the drive axle into the steering knuckle and transaxle.

7. Place the the steering knuckle into position in the strut bracket and install the bolts. Torque to 144 ft. lbs.

8. To complete the installion, reverse the removal procedures.

If the vehicle uses a prevailing torque hub nut, use a new 1, torque it to specifications, make sure the threads are undamaged, free of oil and grease. Otherwise, the drive axle may not be retained safely.

9. Install a new prevailing torque hub nut and washer and torque them to 74 ft. lbs. Remove the object used to hold the rotor stationary.

10. Seat the drive axle into the trans-

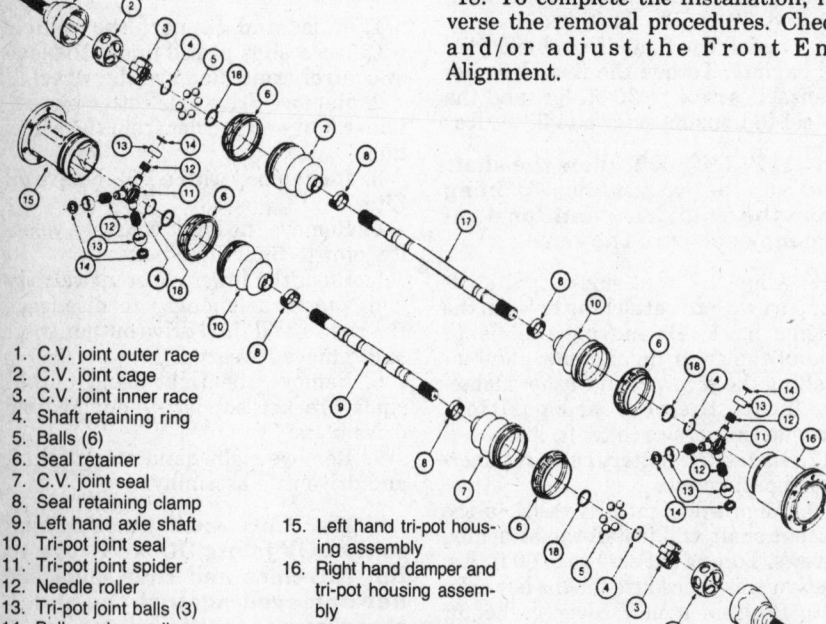

1. C.V. joint outer race
2. C.V. joint cage
3. C.V. joint inner race
4. Shaft retaining ring
5. Balls (6)
6. Seal retainer
7. C.V. joint seal
8. Seal retaining clamp
9. Left hand axle shaft
10. Tri-pot joint seal
11. Tri-pot joint spider
12. Needle roller
13. Tri-pot joint balls (3)
14. Ball and needle retainer (3)
15. Left hand tri-pot housing assembly
16. Right hand damper and tri-pot housing assembly
17. Right hand axle shaft
18. Spacer ring

Exploded view of the drive axle—tri-pot design, first type

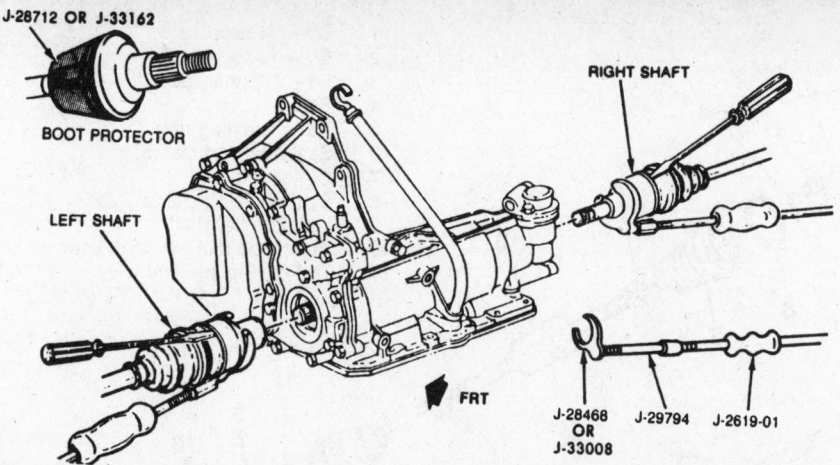

BOOT PROTECTOR

J-28712 OR J-33162

LEFT SHAFT

RIGHT SHAFT

FRT

J-28468 OR J-33008   J-29794   J-2619-01

Use a screwdriver and the special tool shown to pull the drive axles out of the transaxle. Make sure to support the axles at the center to avoid putting downward force on the outer joint

axle with a screwdriver resting against the groove provided on the inner retainer, as shown. Tap the screwdriver lightly to seat the snapring and lock the driveshaft into the transaxle. Verify that the snapring has been seated by grasping the housing (NOT the shaft itself) and pulling it outboard. If the shaft is locked, it will not pull free.

11. Torque the lugnuts to 100 ft. lbs.

ELDORADO AND SEVILLE

NOTE: To perform this procedure, use a special puller tool No. J–28733 or equivalent, and new prevailing torque nut for each axle.

1. Remove the hub nut and washer. Raise and support the front of the vehicle on jackstands.
2. Remove the wheel/tire assembly.
3. Remove the brake caliper and rotor.
4. Disconnect the stabilizer bar from the control arm, the tie rod end from the steering knuckle and the lower ball joint stud from the steering knuckle. Use a pry bar and a wood block (to protect the case), pry the drive axle from the transaxle case.
5. Using the Puller tool No. J–28733 or equivalent, force the drive axle from the hub and remove the axle from the vehicle. Inspect the boot seals for damage and replace (if necessary).
6. Position the drive axle ends into the steering knuckle and transaxle without fully seating them.
7. Reconnect the lower ball joint-to-steering knuckle and torque the nut as described later under "Front Suspension." Reconnect the stabilizer bar-to-lower control arm and the tie rod end-to-steering knuckle, again referring to "Front Suspension."
8. Using new bolts, reinstall the brake caliper.
9. Install a washer and new prevail-

ing torque nut; torque the nut to 74 ft. lbs. Insert a prybar into a slot in the brake caliper to prevent the axle from turning when torquing the nut.
10. Position a prybar into the CV-joint housing groove, tap it with a hammer until the axle is seated in the drive axle. Grab the drive axle housing (not the driveshaft) and pull it outward to make sure the axle is properly seated.
11. To complete the installation, reverse the removal procedures. Torque the hub nut to 183 ft. lbs.

1988–89

ALL MODELS

1. Remove the hub nut and washer.
2. Raise and support the front of the vehicle on jackstands. Remove the front wheel assembly(s).
3. Remove the brake caliper and rotor.
4. Remove the stabilizer link from the control arm(s).
5. Remove the tie rod end-to-steering knuckle cotter pin and nut. Using a ball joint removal tool, separate the tie rod end from the steering knuckle.
6. Remove the lower ball joint-to-steering knuckle cotter pin and nut. Using a ball joint removal tool, separate the lower ball joint from the steering knuckle.
7. Using a pry bar and a wooden block, pry the halfshaft from the steering knuckle and suspend it on a wire.

NOTE: When removing the halfshaft, be careful not to allow the shaft to drop causing damage to the CV-joints. DO NOT allow the halfshaft to overextend for the Tri-Pot (S-plan) joint can disengage from the bearing blocks.

8. Using the Halfshaft Removal tool No. J–28733 or equivalent, press the halfshaft from the steering knuckle hub and remove it from the vehicle.

NOTE: If equipped with an anti-lock brake system, be careful not to damage the toothed sensor ring (on halfshaft) and the wheel speed sensor (on steering knuckle).

9. Inspect the CV-joint seals for tears, damage and/or leakage.
10. To install, grease the splines and reverse the removal procedures. Torque the hub nut to 74 ft. lbs.

NOTE: To keep the halfshaft from turning, place a small drift pin in one of the rotor's slots.

11. Using a small pry bar, place it in the halfshaft CV-joint groove and tap the halfshaft into the transaxle until the snapring seats. Lower the vehicle. Torque the hub nut to 183 ft. lbs.

CV JOINT OVERHAUL

For all CV-joint overhaul procedures, please refer to "U/CV-Joint Overhaul" in the Unit Repair section.

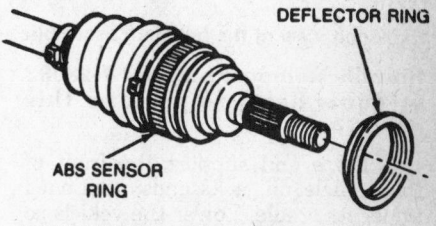

DEFLECTOR RING

ABS SENSOR RING

ANTI-LOCK BRAKE EQUIPPED

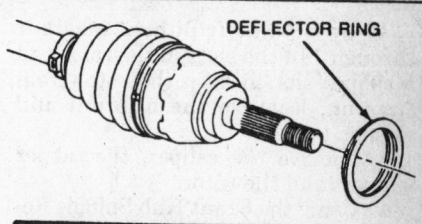

DEFLECTOR RING

STANDARD BRAKE EQUIPPED

View of the two types of outer CV-joint assemblies and deflector rings—1988–89

Front Wheel Drive Hub and Bearings

NOTE: All models have front and rear sealed wheel bearings. The bearings are preadjusted and require no lubrication maintenance or adjustment. There are darkened areas on the bearing assembly. These darkened areas are from a heat treatment process and do not indicate a need for bearing replacement.

REMOVAL & INSTALLATION

NOTE: Secure a Front Hub

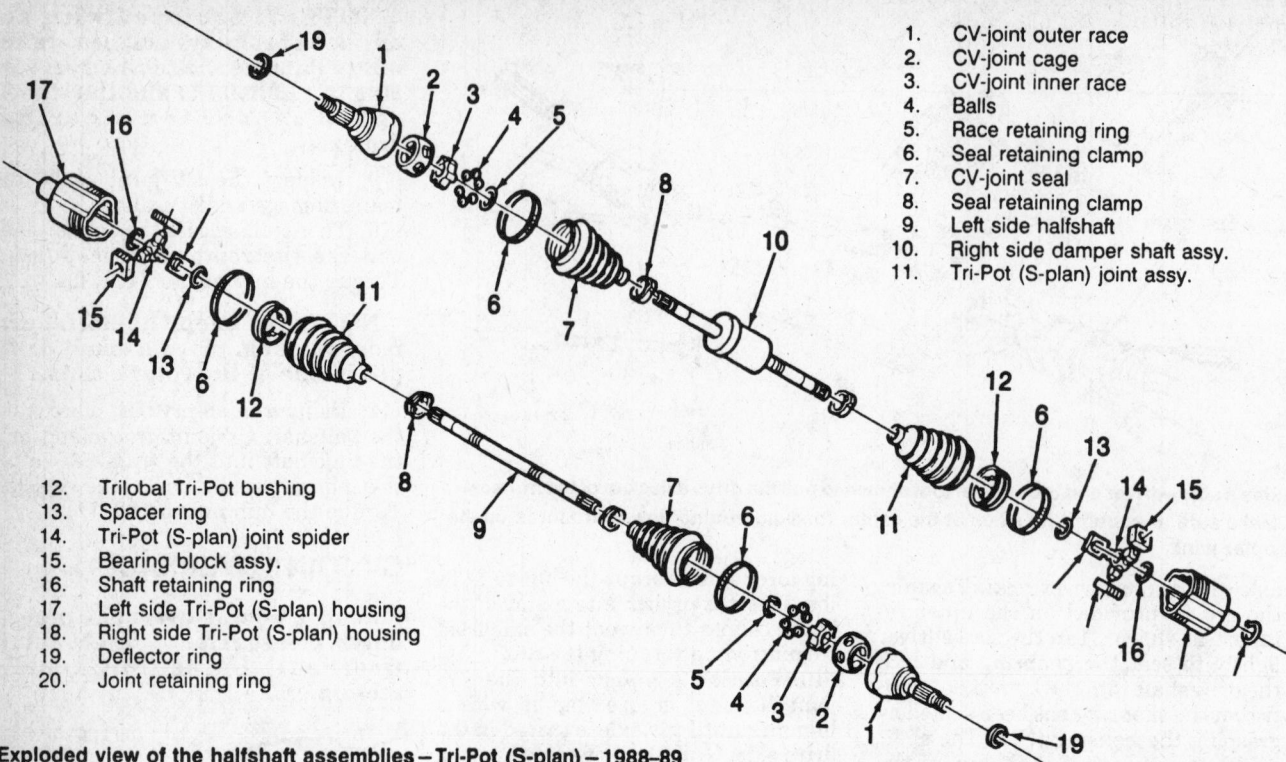

1. CV-joint outer race
2. CV-joint cage
3. CV-joint inner race
4. Balls
5. Race retaining ring
6. Seal retaining clamp
7. CV-joint seal
8. Seal retaining clamp
9. Left side halfshaft
10. Right side damper shaft assy.
11. Tri-Pot (S-plan) joint assy.

12. Trilobal Tri-Pot bushing
13. Spacer ring
14. Tri-Pot (S-plan) joint spider
15. Bearing block assy.
16. Shaft retaining ring
17. Left side Tri-Pot (S-plan) housing
18. Right side Tri-Pot (S-plan) housing
19. Deflector ring
20. Joint retaining ring

Exploded view of the halfshaft assemblies — Tri-Pot (S-plan) — 1988–89

Spindle Remover tool No. J–28733 or equivalent, to perform this operation.

1. Raise and support the front of the vehicle on jackstands positioned under its cradle. Lower the vehicle so the jackstands support it and the control arms are free. Remove the front wheel.

2. Using a drift punch, insert it through 1 of the slots in the rotor and a caliper slot to keep the rotor from turning. Remove the hub nut and washer.

3. Remove the caliper, the caliper support and the rotor.

4. Using the Front Hub Spindle Remover tool No. J–28733 or equivalent, press the halfshaft from the hub.

5. Remove the hub/bearing assembly bolts and the hub/bearing assembly. Remove the seal by driving it toward the center of the vehicle and cut it off the halfshaft.

6. To install, lubricate the lip of a new seal with wheel bearing grease and install it with a Hub Seal Installer tool No. J–34657–A or equivalent.

7. The complete the installation, use new caliper-to-steering knuckle bolts and reverse the removal procedures. Torque the hub/bearing assembly-to-steering knuckle bolts to 70 ft. lbs. Install the wheel and lower the vehicle. Torque the hub nut to 180 ft. lbs. and the wheel lug nuts to 100 ft. lbs. If equipped with a wheel speed sensor, torque the mounting bracket-to-steering knuckle bolts to 9 ft. lbs.

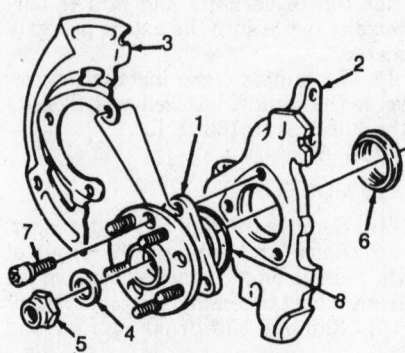

1. Hub and bearing assembly
2. Steering knuckle
3. Shield
4. Washer
5. Hub nut — 180 ft. lbs.
6. Seal
7. Hub and bearing retaining bolt — 70 ft. lbs.
8. O-ring

Exploded view of the hub/bearing assembly

FRONT SUSPENSION

MacPherson Strut

REMOVAL & INSTALLATION

1. Open the hood and remove the nuts attaching the top of the strut to the body.

2. Raise and support the front of the vehicle with jackstands placed under the cradle (not the control arms).

CAUTION

Support all vehicles at the rear so as components are removed, the weight will not shift, causing the vehicle to fall off the supports.

---

3. Remove the tire and wheel assemblies.

4. Using a sharp tool, scribe the knuckle along the lower/outboard radius of the strut. Scribe the strut flange on the inboard side, right along the curve of the knuckle. Finally, make a scribe mark across the strut/knuckle interface. These scribe marks will be used on reassembly to properly match the components.

5. Remove the brake line mounting bracket from the strut.

NOTE: When working near the drive axles, make sure you don't permit the inner Tri-Pot joints to become overextended, as this could cause undetectible damage. Also, DO NOT scratch the spring coating, as this could result in premature failure of the spring.

6. Remove the strut-to-knuckle nuts/bolts and carefully support the knuckle from the body with wire.

7. Remove the strut.

8. To install the strut, aligning all scribe marks to ensure it is in the proper position. Install the strut-to-

knuckle nuts/bolts and tighten just slightly.

9. Install the brake line bracket back onto the strut.

10. Install the nuts attaching the top of the strut to the body. Torque the strut-to-body nuts to 18 ft. lbs. Torque the strut-to-knuckle bolts/nuts to 145 ft. lbs. (all models—1982–87 and Allante—1987–89) or 136 ft. lbs. (all models—1988–89 except Allante).

11. Install the tire/wheel assemblies and torque the lug nuts to 100 ft. lbs. Lower the vehicle.

OVERHAUL

For all spring and shock absorber removal and installation procedures, and all strut overhaul procedures, please refer to "Strut Overhaul" in the Unit Repair section.

Steering Knuckle

REMOVAL & INSTALLATION

1. Remove the hub/bearing assembly.

2. Using a sharp scribing tool, scribe the strut outline on the steering knuckle.

3. Remove the tie rod end-to-steering knuckle cotter pin and nut. Using the Tie Rod Remover tool No. J–6627–A or equivalent, separate the tie rod end from the steering knuckle.

4. Remove the ball joint-to-steering knuckle cotter pin. Using the Ball Joint Nut Wrench tool No. J–35551 or equivalent, remove the nut from the ball joint. Using the Ball Joint Separator tool No. J–35315 or equivalent, separate the ball joint from the steering knuckle.

5. If equipped with anti-lock brakes, remove the wheel speed sensor and bracket from the steering knuckle.

6. Remove the strut-to-steering knuckle bolts and the steering knuckle.

7. To install, align the matchmarks and reverse the removal procedures. Torque the steering knuckle-to-strut bolts to 136 ft. lbs. and the ball joint nut to 37 ft. lbs. Check and/or adjust the front end alignment.

NOTE: When tightening the ball joint nut, torque it to 84 inch lbs., retorque it 120 degrees (37 ft. lbs.). To install the cotter pin, it may be necessary to torque the nut an additional 60 degrees.

Torsion Bars

REMOVAL & INSTALLATION

All Models 1982–85

1. Raise and support the vehicle with jackstands under the cradle.

2. Install a Torsion Bar Remover tool No. J–22517–02, BT–6601 or equivalent, remove the torsion bar adjusting bolt and nut.

NOTE: Record the number of turns necessary to remove and relax the torsion bar. Do the same on the other torsion bar.

3. Remove the bolts and retainer from the torsion bar crossmember. Move the crossmember back until the bars are free and the adjusting arms can be removed. It may be necessary to slide the torsion bars forward.

4. To install, reverse the removal procedures.

Ball Joints

INSPECTION

1. Raise and support the front of the vehicle on jackstands under both lower control arms, as near as possible to each lower ball joint.

NOTE: The vehicle must be stable and should not rock on jackstands. The upper control arm bumper must not contact the frame. The wheel bearing must be correctly adjusted.

2. Position the dial indicator to register vertical movement at the base of the tire rim for upper ball joint and at center of hub for lower ball joint.

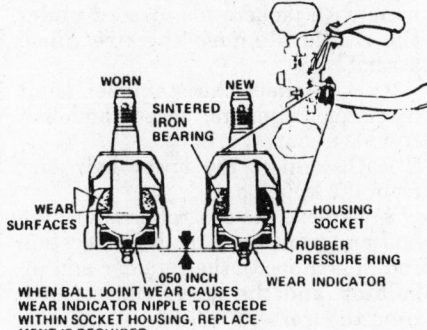

Lower ball joint wear indicator, typical

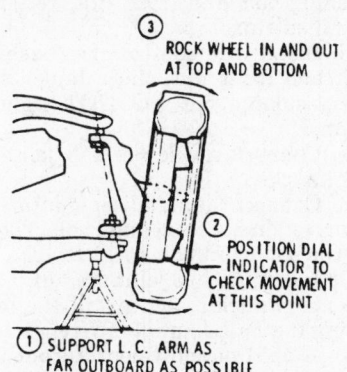

Upper ball joint check

3. Grasp the tire at the 12 o'clock and 6 o'clock positions and rock it in and out for upper ball joint. Pry with a pry bar between the lower control arm and the outer race of the CV-joint for lower ball joint. The vertical reading must not exceed 0.125 in. in either case.

REMOVAL & INSTALLATION

All Models 1982–85

NOTE: Although not absolutely necessary, removal of the individual control arm will facilitate ball joint removal.

1. Remove the steering knuckle.

2. Drill the top rivet head off.

3. Drill the rivets just deep enough to remove the rivet head.

4. Using a hammer and punch, drive the rivets out of the control arm.

5. To install, reverse the removal procedures. Torque the ball joint-to-control arm nuts/bolts to 8 ft. lbs., the upper ball joint-to-steering knuckle nut to 90 ft. lbs. and the lower ball joint-to-steering knuckle nut to 65 ft. lbs. Stake the upper nut.

All Models 1986–89

NOTE: To perform this job, use a Ball Joint Separator tool No. J–35315 or equivalent, and a Ball Joint Nut Wrench tool No. J–35551 or equivalent.

1. Raise and support the front of the vehicle with jackstands located under the cradle in a secure manner, so the control arms will hang free.

2. Remove the wheel/tire assembles.

3. Remove the stabilizer bar insulators, retainers, spacer and bolt.

4. Using a ¼ in. drill bit for the 1st pass and a ½ inch bit for the 2nd, drill out the 3 rivets retaining the joint. Remove the cotter pin, the nut and the ball joint.

5. Using the Ball Joint Separator tool No. J–35315 or equivalent, press the ball joint from the steering knuckle.

6. To install, reverse the removal procedure, replacing the ball joint mounting rivets with bolts and torque them to 50 ft. lbs.

7. Insert the ball joint stud into the steering knuckle and install the nut. Using the Ball Joint Nut Wrench tool No. J–35551 or equivalent, torque the nut to 84 inch lbs.; turn it an additional 120 degrees (180 degrees—1986–87 Cadillac and 1987–89 Allante) while watching the required torque. It must reach at least 37 ft. lbs. torque (48 ft. lbs.—1986–87 Cadillac and 1987–89 Allante) in that 120 degrees. The nut may be turned an additional 60 de-

grees to install the cotter pin. Install the cotter pin.

8. To complete the installation, reverse the removal procedures.

Upper Control Arms

REMOVAL & INSTALLATION

All Models 1982–85

NOTE: The upper control arm is serviced as an assembly, less bushings.

1. Raise and support the front of the vehicle with jackstands located under the lower control arm. Remove the wheel/tire assembly.

2. Remove the upper shock attaching bolt; this is not necessary but it does allow more working room.

3. Remove the cotter pin and nut from the upper ball joint.

4. Disconnect the brake hose clamp from ball joint stud.

5. Using a hammer and drift, separate the upper ball joint stud from steering knuckle.

6. Guide the upper control arm over the shock absorber and install the bushing ends into frame horns.

7. Install the cam assemblies, the ball joint stud into the steering knuckle and the brake hose clip onto ball joint stud.

8. To complete the installation, reverse the removal procedures. Torque the ball joint-to-steering knuckle nut to 55 ft. lbs. (Riviera and Toronado) or 61 ft. lbs. (Eldorado and Seville) and insert the cotter pin and crimp.

NOTE: Cotter pin must be crimped toward upper shock attaching bolt and nut. Torque to 95 ft. lbs.

9. Torque the upper shock-to-body bolts to 95 ft. lbs.

10. Install the wheel assembly and lower the vehicle. Check and/or adjust the front end alignment.

Lower Control Arms

REMOVAL & INSTALLATION

All Models 1982–85

1. Raise and support the vehicle with jackstands under lift points. Remove wheel/tire assembly.

2. Place the torsion bar remover and installer tool over the crossmember so that center screw is seated in dimple of torsion adjusting arm.

3. Remove the torsion bar adjusting bolt and nut, counting the number of turns necessary.

NOTE: This number of turns will be used when installing, to obtain initial ride height.

4. Turn the center screw of tool until torsion bar is completely relaxed.

5. Disconnect the shock absorber and stabilizer link from the lower control arm.

6. Remove the drive axle nut. Remove the bolt and nut from the front of the frame brace. Loosen the rear bolt and move the brace out.

7. Remove the cotter pin and nut from the lower ball joint stud.

8. Using a puller, remove the ball joint stud from the steering knuckle.

9. Push the drive axle in and pull steering knuckle outward to gain clearance, then, remove the lower control arm from the steering knuckle and torsion bar.

10. To install, reverse the removal procedures. Check and adjust ride height if necessary.

All Models 1986–89

NOTE: Throughout this procedure, take care not to overextend the tri-pot joints. Overextension could result in separation of internal components, resulting in eventual failure of the joint. The damage done would not be readily detectible. Secure a 90 degree angle Torque Wrench tool No. J–35551 or equivalent.

1. Raise and support front of the vehicle with jackstands located under the cradle. Remove the tire/wheel assembly.

2. Disconnect the stabilizer shaft insulator, retainers, spacer and bolt from the control arm.

3. Disconnect the lower ball joint from the knuckle.

4. Remove the control arm bushing bolt and front nut, the brake reaction rod (if equipped), the retainer and insulator, and the lower control arm from the frame.

5. To install, assemble the lower control arm onto the frame with the bushing bolt and front nut, retainer and insulator.

6. Install the control arm bushing bolt and front nut, the retainer and the insulator but DO NOT tighten them.

7. Connect the lower ball joint to the knuckle.

8. Connect the stabilizer shaft insulator, retainers, spacer and bolt. Tighten the shaft nut/bolt to 13 ft. lbs.

9. Insert the ball joint stud into the steering knuckle and install the nut. Using the Ball Joint Nut Wrench tool No. J–35551 or equivalent, torque the nut to 84 inch lbs.; turn it an additional 120 degrees (180 degrees 1986–87–

Cadillac – 1986–87 and Allante – 1987–89) while watching the required torque. It must reach at least 37 ft. lbs. torque (48 ft. lbs. Cadillac – 1986–87 and Allante – 1987–89) in that 120 degrees. Install the cotter pin.

10. Install the tire/wheel assembly and lower the vehicle to the ground, leaving it unsupported by any jacking equipment. Torque the wheel nuts to 100 ft. lbs., the control arm bushing bolt to 100 ft. lbs. or a nut, to 91 ft. lbs. and the retaining nut to 52 ft. lbs.

Front Wheel Bearing

For the front wheel bearing replacement procedures, refer to Drive Axle in this section and remove the front wheel bearing.

Front Wheel Alignment

ADJUSTMENT

Front end alignment measurements require the use of special alignment equipment. Before measuring the alignment or attempting to adjust it, always check the following points:

1. Be sure that the tires are properly inflated.

2. See that the wheels are properly balanced.

3. Check the ball joints to determine it they are worn or loose.

4. Check the front wheel bearing adjustment.

5. Be sure that the vehicle is on a level surface.

6. Check all suspension parts for tightness.

Caster

Caster is the tilt of the front steering axis either forward or backward away from the front of the vehicle. When the strut is tilted rearward, the center is (+) positive. The amount of tilt is measured in degrees from vertical.

1. Bounce the vehicle several times to settle the suspension.

2. Inspect and/or correct the tire pressure and worn steering/suspensions comnponents.

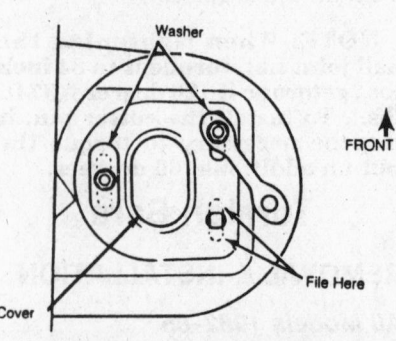

Adjusting the caster angle

3. With the vehicle resting on its wheels, remove the top strut-to-body nuts and the 2 special washers.

4. Lift the front of the body to separate the top strut mount from the inner wheelhouse.

NOTE: If necessary, drill two $^{11}/_{32}$ in. holes at each side of the slot to reduce the filing time.

5. Using a rat-tail file, file the material from the oval strut mounting hole.

6. To install, reverse the removal procedures. Using primer, apply a coat to the exposed area.

7. To adjust the caster, move the top of the strut forward or backward. Torque the strut-to-bdoy nuts to 18 ft. lbs.

Camber

Camber is the slope of the front wheels from vertical when viewed from the front of the vehicle. When the wheels tilt outward (at the top), the camber is (+) positive; when the wheels tilt inward (at the top), the camber is (−) negative. The amount of tilt is measured in degrees from vertical and is called the camber angle.

1. Loosen both strut-to-steering knuckle bolts.

2. Using the adjusting bolt next to the top mounting bolt, adjust the camber to specifications.

3. After adjustment, torque the strut-to-steering knuckle bolts to 136 ft. lbs. (except Allante) or 144 ft. lbs. (Allante) and the camber adjusting bolt to 7 ft. lbs.

Toe-in

Toe is the amount measured in the fraction of an inch, that the front wheels are closer together at 1 end than the other. Toe-in means that the front wheels are closer together at the front of the tire than at the rear; the toe is (+) positive. Toe-out means that the rear of the tires are closer together than the front; the toe is (−) negative.

REAR SUSPENSION

Shock Absorbers

REMOVAL & INSTALLATION

All Models 1982–84

1. Raise and support the rear of the vehicle on jackstands; position the jack under the control arm to take the load off of the shock.

2. Remove the wheel/tire assembly.

3. Remove the lower shock retaining bolt. Using a plastic hammer, gently tap the shock out of it's retainer.

4. Remove the upper shock-to-body bolt and the shock from the vehicle.

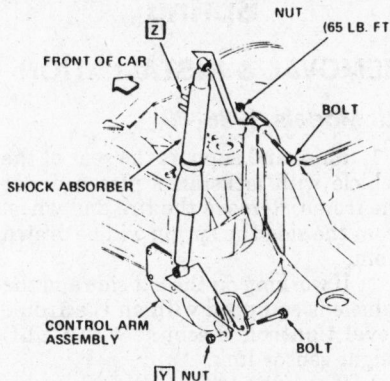

Y **LOWER ATTACHING MUST BE TORQUED WITH WEIGHT ON SUSPENSION AND IN CURB POSITION**

Z **EXTEND SHOCK ABSORBERS PRIOR TO INSTALLATION. INSTALL SHOCK ABSORBERS WITH PORTS TOWARD FRONT OF CAR.**

Typical rear shock absorber mounting

5. To install, reverse the removal procedures. Torque the retaining bolts to 65 ft. lbs. Follow any special instructions in the shock absorber packages.

MacPherson Strut

REMOVAL & INSTALLATION

All Models 1985–89

1. Raise and support the rear of the vehicle on jackstands; position the jackstand under the outboard end of the control arm to slightly compress the spring.

2. Remove the wheel/tire assembly. Install 2 lug nuts to retain the rotor.

NOTE: If equipped with Electronic Load Control (ELC), disconnect the air lines before removing shocks. Purge the new shocks of air before installing (on all models) by repeatedly extending and compressing them. On ALC equipped models, the shocks should be fully extended before installing air lines.

3. If equipped, remove the stabilizer bar-to-strut bolt. Remove and support the caliper on a wire.

NOTE: Before removing the left strut, disconnect the ELC height sensor link.

4. Remove the knuckle pinch bolt from the outboard end of the control arm; DO NOT remove it.

5. Remove the upper strut-to-body nut, retainer and the upper insulator. Slowly remove the jackstand to relieve the spring pressure. Compress the strut (by hand).

6. Using a plastic hammer, gently tap the shock out of it's retainer. Remove the lower insulator and the strut from the vehicle.

7. To install, seat the strut in the knuckle with the tang on the strut bottom (in the knuckle slot) and reverse the removal procedures. Torque the knuckle pinch bolt to 40 ft. lbs., the upper strut-to-suspension support nut to 65 ft. lbs., the knuckle-to-control arm nut/bolt to 59 ft. lbs. and the stabilizer shaft bolt to 43 ft. lbs. (if equipped). Follow any special instructions in the air strut package.

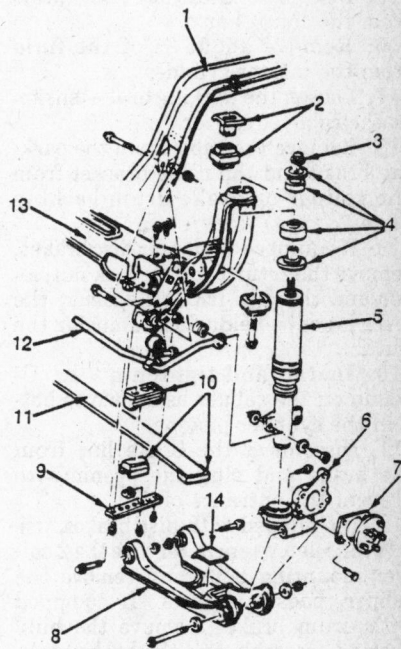

1. Underbody assembly
2. Suspension support insulators
3. Upper strut mounting nut
4. Strut mount insulators
5. Strut
6. Knuckle
7. Hub/bearing assembly
8. Control arm
9. Spring retainer
10. Spring insulators
11. Single leaf spring
12. Stabilizer shaft
13. Suspension support
14. Trim height adjustment spacer

Exploded view of the rear suspension system—1985 and later

OVERHAUL

For all spring and shock absorber removal and installation procedures, and all strut overhaul procedures, please refer to "Strut Overhaul" in the Unit Repair section.

Springs and Rear Control Arms

REMOVAL & INSTALLATION

All Models 1982–85

1. Raise and support the rear of the vehicle on jackstands. Remove the wheel assemblies.
2. Remove the front stabilizer bar-to-control arm bolt.
3. Remove the inner bolt and loosen the outer bolt from both sides of the stabilized link.
4. Position the bottom parts of the link aside and remove the stabilizer bar.
5. Disconnect the brake line bracket from the control arm.
6. Remove about ⅔ of the fluid from the master cylinder.
7. Loosen the parking brake tension at the cable equalizer.
8. Remove the cable from the parking brake and the cable bracket from the caliper or brake drum backing plate.
9. If equipped with rear disc brakes, remove the return spring, lock nut, lever and the anti-friction washer; the lever must be held while removing the nut.
10. Install and tighten a 7 in. C-clamp on the caliper as shown to bottom the cylinder pistons.
11. Disconnect the brake line from the brake and plug the openings to prevent the entrance of dirt.
12. If equipped with disc brakes, use a ⅜ in. Allen wrench, remove the 2 caliper mounting bolts and remove the caliper, pads and rotor. If equipped with drum brakes, remove the hub/bearing assembly and the brake backing plate, along with the brake shoes.
13. If working on the left side, snap the Electronic Level Control link off the control arm.
14. Support the bottom of the control arm with a floor jack.
15. Remove the ELC line from the shock and the shock absorber.
16. Lower the control arm to relieve tension on the spring. Remove the spring and the insulators.
17. Remove the 2 control arm mounting bolts and the control arm.
18. To install, reverse the removal procedures. Torque the control arm-to-frame bolts to 98 ft. lbs., the shock absorbers to 65 ft. lbs., the brake caliper mounting bolts to 30 ft. lbs., the brake lines to 15 ft. lbs. and the wheel lug nuts to 100 ft. lbs.

Transverse Rear Spring

REMOVAL & INSTALLATION

All Models 1986–89

1. Raise and support the rear of the vehicle with jackstands placed under the frame. Remove the tire and wheel from the side the spring will be drawn from.
2. If working on the left side and the vehicle is equipped with an Electronic Level Control, disconnect the ELC height sensor link.
3. If equipped with a stabilizer bar, disconnect the mounting bolt from the strut.
4. Reinstall 2 wheel nuts opposite each other to hold the rotor onto the hub/bearing assembly.
5. Remove and suspend the brake caliper on a wire.
6. Loosen but DO NOT remove the knuckle pivot bolt on the outboard end of the control arm.
7. Remove the strut rod cap, mounting nut, retainer and upper insulator. Compress the strut by hand and remove the lower insulator.
8. If equipped with anti-lock brakes, disconnect the wheel speed sensor.
9. Remove the inner control arm nuts. Support the knuckle and control arm with a floorjack and remove the inner control arm bolts. Remove control arm, knuckle, strut, hub/bearing and rotor as an assembly.
10. Using a jackstand, capable of suspending the entire weight of the vehicle, suspend the outer end of the spring securely.

———— CAUTION ————

Make sure the jackstand is squarely positioned under the spring so that the stand will not shift or personal injury could result.

11. Gradually and cautiously lower the vehicle until its weight compresses the spring so there is no weight on the spring retainer. Remove the retainer mounting bolts, the retainer and the lower insulator from that side of the vehicle. Raise the vehicle slowly until the jackstand is free of downward pressure from the spring and remove it.
12. Draw the spring out of the rear suspension. Remove the upper spring insulators as necessary.
13. Install any insulators that required replacement. Upper/outboard insulators must be installed so that the molded arrow points toward the vehicle centerline. Torque the center and outboard insulator nuts to 21 ft. lbs.
14. Position the spring into the crossmember. Make sure the outboard and center insulator locating bands are centered on the insulators.
15. Using a jackstand, capable of suspending the entire weight of the vehicle, suspend the outer end of the spring securely.

———— CAUTION ————

Make sure the jackstand is squarely positioned under the spring so that the stand will not shift or personal injury could result.

16. Carefully and gradually lower the vehicle until its weight will permit easy installation of the spring retainer.
17. Install the lower insulator and spring retainer and torque the bolts to 21 ft. lbs. Raise the vehicle carefully and when the spring is clear, remove the jackstand.
18. Position the assembled control arm, knuckle, strut, hub/bearing and rotor assembly into the crossmember assembly. Install the inner control arm bolts and nuts JUST HAND TIGHT.
19. If equipped with an anti-lock brakes, reconnect the wheel speed sensor.
20. Install the lower strut insulator and position the strut rod into the suspension support assembly.
21. Install the upper strut insulator, retainer and nut. Torque the upper strut nut to 65 ft. lbs., the knuckle pivot bolt to 59 ft. lbs. and the inner control arm bolts to 66 ft. lbs.
22. Install the strut rod cap. Install the stabilizer mounting bolt (if equipped) and torque this bolt to 43 ft. lbs.
23. Remove the 2 wheel nuts retaining the brake rotor. Install the remaining parts in reverse of the removal procedure. Check and/or adjust the rear end alignment.

Rear Wheel Bearings

No adjustment procedures are available for the hub/bearing assembly.

REMOVAL & INSTALLATION

1. Raise and support the rear of the vehicle on jackstands.
2. Remove the wheel and tire assembly.
3. Remove the caliper and suspend it with a wire; DO NOT disconnect the brake line.
4. If equipped with rotor retainers, remove and discard them. Remove the rotor.
5. Remove the hub/bearing assem-

bly-to-knuckle bolts and the assembly from the vehicle.

NOTE: The hub/bearing assembly is to replaced as an assembly; no overhaul procedure is available.

6. To install, reverse the removal procedures. Torque the hub/bearing assembly bolts to 52 ft. lbs. and the new caliper/caliper bracket bolts to 83 ft. lbs.

STEERING

Steering Wheel

REMOVAL & INSTALLATION

Allante, Eldorado and Seville

1. Disconnect the negative battery cable.
2. For the Allante, pry the horn trim pad from the steering wheel. For the Eldorado/Seville, remove the steering wheel-to-horn pad screws (located behind the steering wheel) and the horn trim pad. Remove the horn contact wire, ground connector and cruise control wiring connector.
3. Remove the 3 screws that secure the telescope locking lever assembly to the adjuster. Unscrew and remove the telescoping adjuster from the steering shaft.
4. Remove the telescoping lever assembly. Scribe an alignment mark on the steering wheel hub in line with the slash mark on the steering shaft.
5. Remove the steering wheel-to-steering shaft locknut. Using the Steering Wheel Puller tool No. J-23072 or equivalent, press the steering wheel from the steering shaft.

NOTE: When removing the steering wheel, be sure to remove the cruise control wire from it.

6. To install, feed the cruise control wire through the steering wheel, align the matchmark and reverse the removal procedures. Torque the steering wheel-to-steering shaft to 35 ft. lbs.

NOTE: For ease of installation, fully extent the steering shaft and install the Lock Plate Compressor Screw tool No. J-23653-10 or equivalent, hand tight; this will keep the shaft extended when installing the steering wheel. Feed the cruise control wire through the wheel.

7. Remove the tool No. J-23653-10 and place the telescoping lever in the **5 O'CLOCK** position.
8. Thread the telescope adjuster as-

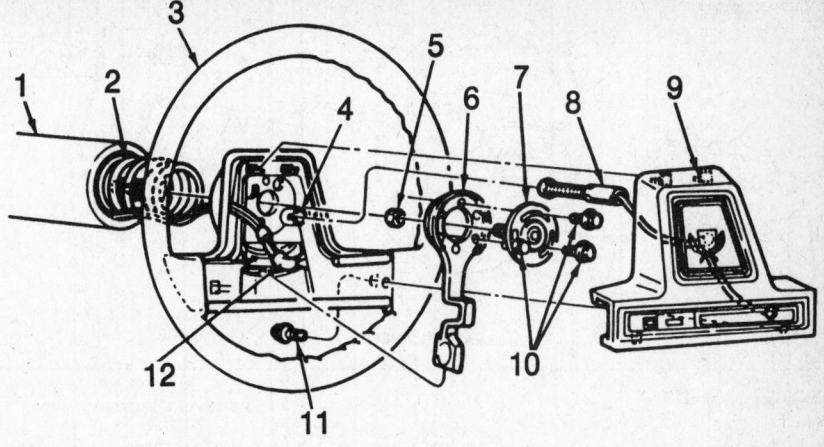

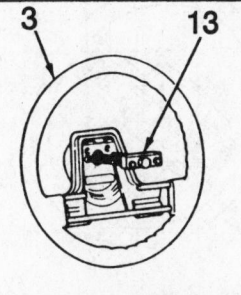 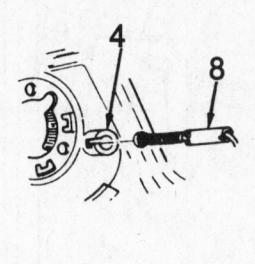 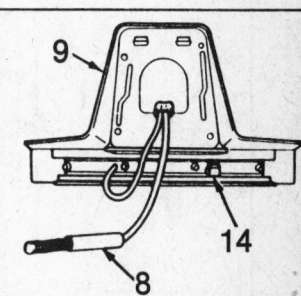

1.	Steering column	8.	Horn lead
2.	Telescoping spring	9.	Horn pad
3.	Steering wheel	10.	Telescope adjuster screws—13 inch lbs.
4.	Cam tower	11.	Horn pad mounting screws—13 inch lbs.
5.	Nut—35 ft. lbs.	12.	Cruise control connector (column)
6.	Telescope lever	13.	Steering Wheel Puller tool No. J-23072
7.	Telescope adjuster	14.	Cruise control connector

Exploded view of the steering wheel assembly—Eldorado and Seville—Allante is similar

sembly finger tight onto the shaft. Install the 3 screws into the telescoping adjuster lever.

9. Move the adjuster lever all the way to the right. The steering wheel should move freely in and out. Move the adjuster lever to the left. The steering wheel should be **LOCKED** in place with the telescope lever approximately ¼ in. from the left side of the shroud opening. The lever must not contact the shroud in the **FULLY LOCKED** position. Loosen and adjust the lever as required.

Reatta, Riviera and Toronado

1. Disconnect the negative battery cable.
2. Depending on the type of horn pad used, pry the horn trim pad or remove the steering wheel-to-horn pad screws (located behind the steering wheel) and lift the pad from the steering wheel.
3. Remove the steering wheel-to-shaft retainer (if equipped) and nut.
4. Scribe an alignment mark on the steering wheel hub in line with the slash mark on the steering shaft.
5. Using the Steering Wheel Puller tool No. J-1859-03, BT-61-9 or equiv-

alent, press the steering wheel from the steering shaft.

6. To install, reverse the removal procedures. Torque the steering wheel-to-steering shaft nut to 35 ft. lbs.

Combination Switch

The combination switch is a multi-function switch which consists of the turn signal, headlight beam, cruise control, windshield washer and wiper switches.

REMOVAL & INSTALLATION

1. Remove the steering wheel.
2. Remove the bumper and the carrier snap ring retainer from the steering shaft.
3. Using the Lock Plate Compressor Screw tool No. J-23653-10 or equivalent, install it in the upper steering shaft, torque it to 40 inch lbs., to keep the shaft from telescoping.
4. Using the Lock Plate Compressor tool No. J-23653-A or equivalent, install it on the upper steering shaft, tighten it to depress the shaft lock. Remove the shaft lock retainer, the com-

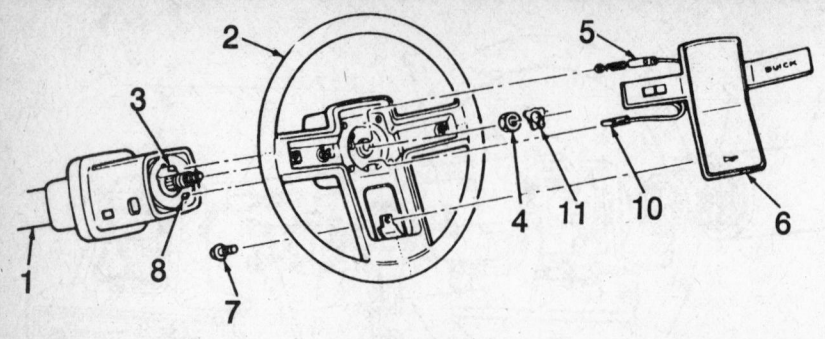

LEATHER WHEEL

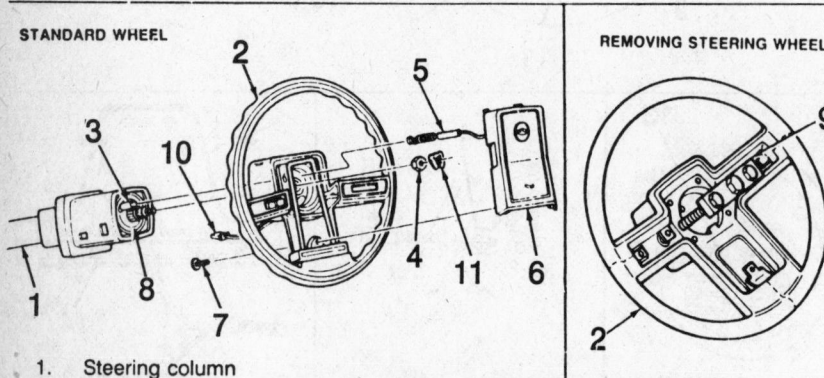

STANDARD WHEEL

REMOVING STEERING WHEEL

1.   Steering column
2.   Steering wheel
3.   Cam tower
4.   Nut – 35 ft. lbs.
5.   Horn lead
6.   Horn pad

7.   Horn pad mounting screws – 13 inch lbs.
8.   Cruise control connector (column)
9.   Steering Wheel Puller tool No. J-23072
10. Cruise control connector
11. Retainer

Exploded view of the steering wheel assembly – Reatta, Riviera and Toronado

pressor tool and the steering shaft lock.

5.   Remove the turn signal cancelling cam assembly. Place the turn signal switch in the **NEUTRAL** position and remove the upper bearing spring.

6.   Position the turn signal switch so the mounting screws can be removed through the holes in the switch and remove the turn signal lever.

7.   Remove the turn signal switch-to-steering column screws and lift the turn signal switch. Remove the wire protector and disconnect the turn signal switch connector.

8.   Using the Terminal Remover tool No. J–35689–A or equivalent, disconnect the buzzer switch wires from the turn signal switch connector. Using needle-nose pliers, remove the buzzer switch assembly.

9.   Place the lock cylinder in the **ACCESSORY** position, remove the lock retaining screw and the lock cylinder set.

10. Lifting the turn signal switch assembly, gently pull the wires through the steering column shroud.

11. To install, reverse the removal procedures. Torque the lock retaining screw to 22 inch lbs., the turn signal switch screws to 59 inch lbs. and the turn signal lever screw to 53 inch lbs.

Check the operation of the switches and the steering column.

Ignition Lock/Switch

REMOVAL & INSTALLATION

1.   Remove the steering wheel.
2.   Remove the bumper and the carrier snap ring retainer from the steering shaft.
3.   Using the Lock Plate Compressor Screw tool No. J–23653–10 or equivalent, install it in the upper steering shaft, torque it to 40 inch lbs., to keep the shaft from telescoping.
4.   Using the Lock Plate Compressor tool No. J–23653–A or equivalent, install it on the upper steering shaft, tighten it to depress the shaft lock. Remove the shaft lock retainer, the compressor tool and the steering shaft lock.
5.   Remove the turn signal cancelling cam assembly. Place the turn signal switch in the **NEUTRAL** position and remove the upper bearing spring.
6.   Position the turn signal switch so the mounting screws can be removed through the holes in the switch and remove the turn signal lever.
7.   Remove the turn signal switch-

to-steering column screws and lift the turn signal switch. Remove the wire protector and disconnect the turn signal switch connector.

8.   Using the Terminal Remover tool No. J–35689–A or equivalent, disconnect the buzzer switch wires from the turn signal switch connector. Using needle-nose pliers, remove the buzzer switch assembly.

9.   Place the lock cylinder in the **ACCESSORY** position, remove the lock retaining screw and the lock cylinder set.

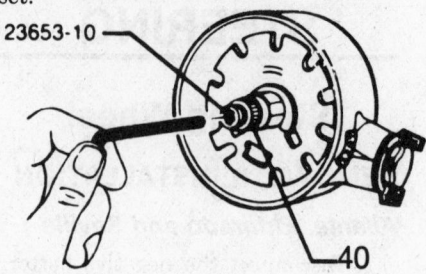

40.   Upper steering shaft

Installing the lock plate compressor screw

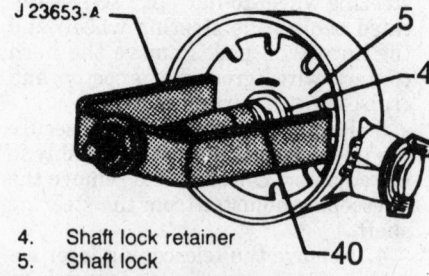

4.   Shaft lock retainer
5.   Shaft lock
40. Upper steering shaft

Compressing the shaft lock

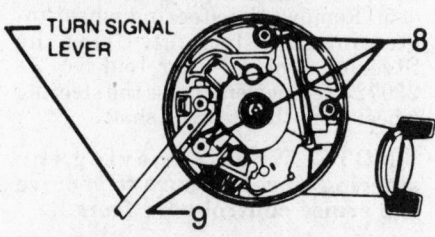

8.   Screw
9.   Turn signal switch assembly

Positioning the turn signal lever to remove the turn signal switch screws

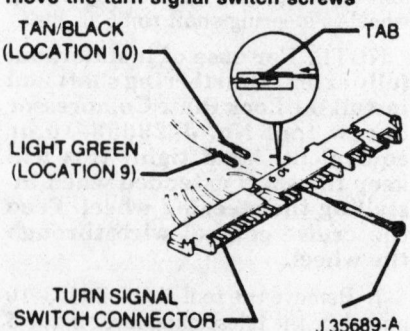

TAN/BLACK (LOCATION 10)
TAB
LIGHT GREEN (LOCATION 9)
TURN SIGNAL SWITCH CONNECTOR
J 35689-A

Releasing the buzzer wires from the turn signal switch connector

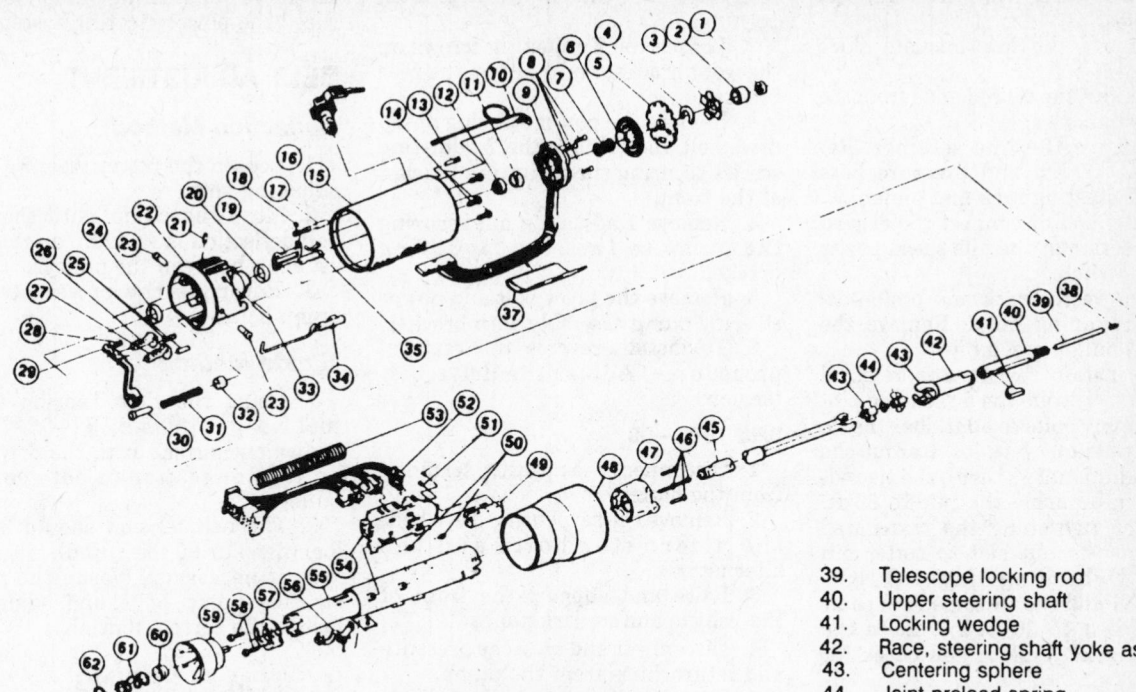

39. Telescope locking rod
40. Upper steering shaft
41. Locking wedge
42. Race, steering shaft yoke assembly
43. Centering sphere
44. Joint preload spring
45. Lower steering shaft assembly
46. Screw
47. Steering column housing support assembly
48. Steering column housing shroud
49. Ignition switch inhibitor housing assembly
50. Screw
51. Screw
52. Wiring assembly
53. Convoluted conduit
54. Ignition switch assembly
55. Steering column jacket assembly
56. Clip
57. Adapter and bearing assembly
58. Screw
59. Bearing retainer
60. Lower bearing seat
61. Lower bearing spring
62. Lower spring retainer

1. Jam nut
2. Retracted steering shaft bumper
3. Carrier snap ring retainer
4. Shaft lock retainer
5. Shaft lock
6. Turn signal cancel cam assembly
7. Upper bearing spring
8. Screws
9. Turn signal switch assembly
10. Buzzer switch assembly
11. Upper bearing inner race seat
12. Inner race
13. Lock retaining screw
14. Screw
15. Lock housing cover assembly
16. Lock cylinder set
17. Bolt/spring assembly

18. Spring thrust washer
19. Switch actuator rack
20. Bearing assembly
21. Releaser lever pin
22. Steering column housing
23. Pivot pin
24. Bearing assembly
25. Shoe spring
26. Steering wheel lock shoe
27. Steering wheel lock shoe
28. Release lever spring
29. Shoe release lever
30. Spring guide
31. Wheel tilt spring
32. Spring retainer
33. Dowel pin
34. Ignition switch actuator assembly
35. Rack preload spring
37. Wiring protector
38. Lock retaining screw

Exploded view of the steering column

10. To install, reverse the removal procedures. Torque the lock retaining screw to 22 inch lbs., the turn signal switch screws to 59 inch lbs. and the turn signal lever screw to 53 inch lbs. Check the operation of the switches and the steering column.

Steering Gear

ADJUSTMENT

1. Raise and support the front of the vehicle on jackstands.
2. Turn the steering linkage until the inner tie rod end stud is under the upper control arm bolt.
3. Place a socket on the end of the upper control bolt. Measure from the socket to the center of the inner tie rod end stud on both sides.

4. If the difference between the right and left dimension is more than $1/16$ in. (2mm), adjust the linkage at the idler arm.

REMOVAL & INSTALLATION

1. Position a fluid catch pan under the steering gear, disconnect the pressure and return lines from the steering gear assembly. Plug the opening to prevent entrance of dirt.
2. If equipped, disconnect the stone shield from the return pipe.
3. Remove the pinch bolt from the flex coupling and disconnect the coupling from the gear.
4. Raise and support the front of the vehicle on jackstands.
5. Remove the pitman arm nut and washer. Remove the pitman arm from

the sector shaft with a pitman arm puller tool.
6. Remove the 3 retaining bolts and washer holding the steering gear to the side rail. Lower the gear assembly from the vehicle.
7. To install, reverse the removal procedures. Tighten the pitman arm nut to 185 ft. lbs., the 3 mounting bolts to 70 ft. lbs. and the flex coupling pinch bolt to 30 ft. lbs.

Steering Rack and Pinion

REMOVAL & INSTALLATION

1. Disconnect the negative battery cable.
2. Raise and support the front of the vehicle on jackstands.

3. Remove both front tire and wheel assemblies.

4. Remove the intermediate shaft lower pinch bolt.

5. Remove the tie rod ends from the steering knuckles.

6. Remove the line retainer. Remove the return and pressure hose from the steering rack and pinion.

7. Label and disconnect the electrical connection at the idle speed power steering switch.

8. Remove the rack and pinion assembly retaining bolts. Remove the rack and pinion assembly.

9. To install, reverse the removal procedures Torque the 5 rack and pinion attaching bolts to 50 ft. lbs., the tie rod end nuts to 7.5 ft. lbs. (torque the nut an additional ⅓ turn). the tie rod-to-steering knuckle the nut to 33 ft. lbs. (after tightening the castellated nut, align the nut slot to cotter pin hole by tightening only. DO NOT LOOSEN) and the intermediate shaft coupling bolt to 30 ft. lbs. Bleed the power steering system and check for leaks.

ADJUSTMENT

1. Loosen the adjuster plug lock nut.

2. Turn the adjuster plug clockwise until it bottoms and back it off 50–70 degrees.

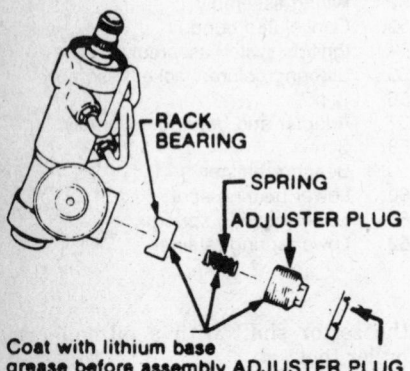

Coat with lithium base grease before assembly ADJUSTER PLUG LOCK NUT

Exploded view of the power steering rack adjustment assembly

3. Check the pinion torque; it should be 16 inch lbs.

4. While holding the adjuster plug, torque the lock nut to 50 ft. lbs.

Power Steering Pump

REMOVAL & INSTALLATION

NOTE: On some models, it may be necessary to remove the alternator with its adjusting bracket.

V6 Engine

ALL EXCEPT 3.8L 1986–89

1. Disconnect the pressure and re-

turn lines from the pump and plug all openings.

2. Loosen the 2 adjusting screws on the front bracket and 1 nut on the rear bracket.

3. Remove the power steering pump drive belt and remove the 2 adjusting screws securing the mounting bracket at the front.

4. Remove 1 adjusting nut securing the pump to the rear mounting bracket.

5. Remove the pivot bolt and power steering pump assembly with bracket.

6. To install, reverse the removal procedures. Adjust the drive belt tension.

3.8L 1986–89

1. Disconnect the negative terminal from the battery.

2. Remove the serpentine drive belt, the alternator bolts and the alternator.

3. Raise and support the front of the vehicle and on jackstands.

4. Disconnect and plug the pressure and return lines from the pump.

5. Remove the rear pump adjustment bracket-to-pump nut.

6. Remove the alternator adjustment bracket and support brace.

7. Remove the rear pump adjustment bracket and the pump assembly.

8. Remove the front pump adjustment bracket and the pulley.

9. To install, reverse the removal procedures. Refill the power steering pump reservoir. Bleed the power steering system.

V8 Engine

ALL EXCEPT 4.1L AND 4.5L

1. Loosen the air conditioning mounting bracket and vacuum pump bracket. Remove the belts from the pulley.

2. Disconnect the pressure and return lines and plug all openings.

3. Remove 2 bolts securing the pump to the engine block, through the access holes in the drive pulley. Remove the pump assembly from the vehicle.

4. To install, reverse the removal procedures. Adjust the drive belt.

4.1L AND 4.5L

1. Disconnect the negative terminal from the battery.

2. Remove the serpentine drive belt, the power steering pump pulley.

3. Disconnect and plug the high pressure and feed lines from the pump.

4. Remove the power steering pump-to-bracket bolts and the pump.

5. To install, reverse the removal procedures. Torque the power steering pump-to-bracket bolts to 30 ft. lbs. Re-

fill the power steering pump reservoir. Bleed the power steering system.

BELT ADJUSTMENT

Deflection Method

1. Loosen the power steering pump adjusting bolt.

2. Move the pump until the drive belt deflection is ⅜–½ in. on the longest span between the pulleys.

3. Retorque the power steering pump bolts.

Gauge Method

1. Using the Belt Tension Gauge tool No. J–23600–B, BT–33–73F or equivalent, attach it to the drive belt on the longest span between the pulleys.

2. The belt tension should be 170 lbs. (new) or 90 lbs. (used).

3. If necessary, loosen the power steering pump bolts and adjust the belt to the correct tension.

SYSTEM BLEEDING

1. Fill the fluid reservoir.

2. Let the fluid stand undisturbed for 2 minutes, crank the engine for about two seconds. Refill the reservoir, if necessary.

3. Repeat Steps 1 and 2 above until the fluid level remains constant after cranking the engine.

4. Raise and support the front of the vehicle (until the wheels are off the ground). Start the engine and increase the engine speed to about 1500 rpm.

5. Turn the wheels lightly against the stops to the left and right, checking the fluid level and refilling (if necessary).

Tie Rod Ends

REMOVAL & INSTALLATION

1. Loosen the jam nut on the steering rack (inner tie rod).

2. Remove the cotter pin and nut from the outer tie rod end. Using the Ball Joint Puller tool No. J–24319–01, BT–7101 or equivalent, press the tie rod end from the steering knuckle.

3. Unscrew the tie rod end, counting the number of turns.

4. To install, screw the tie rod end onto the steering rack (inner tie rod) the same number of turns as counted for removal. This will give approximately correct toe.

5. To complete the installation, use a new cotter pin and reverse the removal procedures. Torque the tie rod end nuts to 7.5 ft. lbs. (torque the nut an additional ⅓ turn). the tie rod-to-steering knuckle the nut to 33 ft. lbs.

(after tightening the castellated nut, align the nut slot to cotter pin hole by tightening only. DO NOT LOOSEN). Check and/or adjust the toe.

BRAKES

For all brake system repair service procedures not detailed below, please refer to "Brakes" in the Unit Repair section.

Master Cylinder

REMOVAL & INSTALLATION

Diagonal Split System

1. If equipped with a fluid level sensor switch, disconnect the electrical connector.
2. Disconnect and plug hydraulic lines. Drain the master cylinder.
3. Remove the master cylinder-to-power brake booster nuts and the master cylinder.
4. To install, reverse the removal procedures. Torque the mounting nuts to 26 ft. lbs. Refill the master cylinder and bleed the system.

Anti-Lock System

TEVES—EXCEPT ALLANTE

—————— CAUTION ——————

The hydraulic accumulator is under pressure and MUST BE depressurized before attempting to dismantle the system.

1. Disconnect the negative battery cable.
2. Firmly apply the parking brake.
3. Using at least 50 lbs. pressure on the brake pedal, depress the pedal at least 20 times; a noticable change in pedal pressure will be noticed when the accumulator is discharged.
4. Disconnect the electrical connectors from the hydraulic brake unit.
5. Remove the pump-to-hydraulic unit bolt and move the unit aside to gain access to the hydraulic lines.
6. Using a back-up wrench, disconnect the hydraulic lines from the hydraulic unit.
7. From under the dash, disconnect the pushrod from the brake pedal.
8. Move the dust boot forward, past the pushrod hex and unscrew the 2 pushrod halves.
9. Remove the hydraulic unit-to-pushrod bracket bolts and separate the hydraulic unit from the pushrod bracket; half of the pushrod will remain locked in the hydraulic unit.
10. Disassemble the master cylinder from the hydraulic unit.

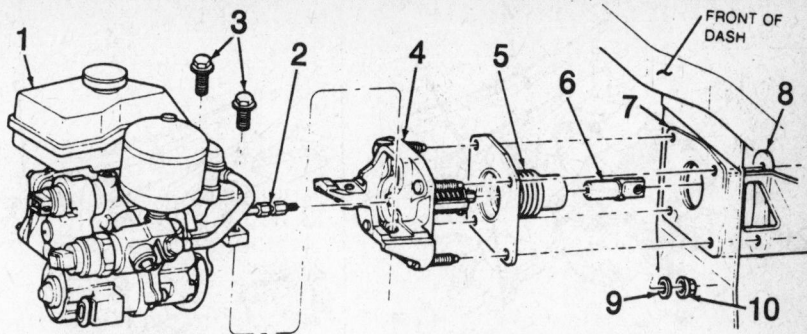

1. Hydraulic unit
2. Front pushrod half
3. Bolts—37 ft. lbs.
4. Pushrod bracket assembly
5. Rubber boot
6. Rear pushrod half
7. Gasket
8. Reinforcement washer
9. Washer—used on lower right stud only
10. Nuts—15 ft. lbs.

Exploded view of the anti-lock brake system hydraulic unit—Teves—all except Allante

11. To install, assemble the master cylinder to the hydraulic unit and reverse the removal procedures. Torque the hydraulic unit-to-pushrod bracket bolts to 37 ft. lbs. Bleed the brake system.

BOSCH III—ALLANTE

—————— CAUTION ——————

The hydraulic accumulator is under pressure and MUST BE depressurized before attempting to dismantle the system.

1. Disconnect the negative terminal from the battery.
2. Firmly apply the parking brake.
3. Using at least 50 lbs. pressure on the brake pedal, depress the pedal at least 25 times; a noticable change in pedal pressure will be noticed when the accumulator is discharged.
4. If working on an Allante, remove the air intake duct from the air cleaner and the throttle body.
5. Remove the cross-car brace.
6. Disconnect the electrical connectors from the hydraulic brake unit and the pump motor. Using a siphon, remove as much fluid from the reservoir as possible.
7. Remove the pressure hose fitting (banjo bolt) from the hydraulic unit; be careful not to drop the fitting washers. Disconnect the return hose from the reservoir fitting.
8. Using a back-up wrench, disconnect the hydraulic lines from the hydraulic unit.
9. From under the dash, remove the driver's side sound insulator panel. From the pedal hub pin, remove the pushrod retainer and the foam washer.
10. From the engine compartment, remove the hydraulic unit-to-mounting adapter nuts.
11. Move the hydraulic unit to disengage the pushrod-to-pedal hub pin.

12. Remove the hydraulic unit from the vehicle.
13. To install, reverse the removal procedures. Torque the hydraulic unit-to-mounting bracket nuts to 20 ft. lbs. Refill the reservoir to the **FULL** mark. Turn the ignition **ON** and allow the pump to charge the hydraulic accumulator. Bleed the brake system.

Proportioning Valve

REMOVAL & INSTALLATION

Diagonal Split System

NOTE: Individual proportioning valves are installed to the master cylinder outlets.

1. Disconnect and plug the fluid lines from the proportioning valves.
2. Remove the proportioning valves and O-rings from the master cylinder.
3. To install, use new O-rings and reverse the removal procedures. Torque the proportioning valve-to-master cylinder to 18–30 ft. lbs. Refill the master cylinder reservoir with clean brake fluid. Bleed the brake system.

Anti-Lock System

TEVES—EXCEPT ALLANTE

The Teves system uses a single proportioner valve located near the left rear wheel. The valve is not to be disassembled.

1. Turn the ignition switch **OFF** and keep it off throughout this procedure.
2. Using at least 50 lbs. pressure on the brake pedal, depress the pedal at least 25 times; a noticable change in pedal pressure will be noticed when the accumulator is discharged.
3. Disconnect the fluid lines from the proportioner valve and the valve from the vehicle.

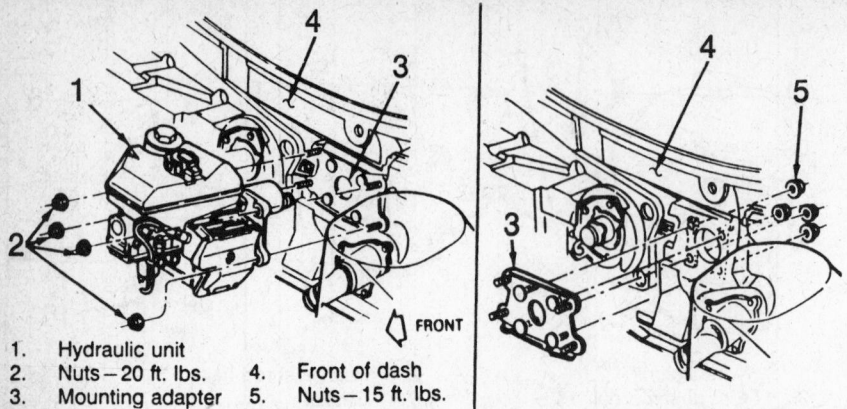

1. Hydraulic unit
2. Nuts – 20 ft. lbs.
3. Mounting adapter
4. Front of dash
5. Nuts – 15 ft. lbs.

FRONT

View of the anti-lock brake system hydraulic unit and mounting bracket – Bosch III – Allante

4. To install, reverse the removal procedures. Bleed the rear brake system.

BOSCH III – ALLANTE

The Bosch III system uses individual proportioning valves installed to the master cylinder. The valve are not to be disassembled.

1. Turn the ignition switch **OFF** and keep it **OFF** throughout this procedure.
2. Using at least 50 lbs. pressure on the brake pedal, depress the pedal at least 25 times; a noticable change in pedal pressure will be noticed when the accumulator is discharged.
3. Disconnect and plug the fluid line(s) from the proportioning valve(s).
4. Remove the proportioning valve(s) from the hydraulic unit.
5. To install, reverse the removal procedures. Torque the proportioning valve(s)-to-hydraulic unit to 11 ft. lbs. Bleed the brake circuit(s).

Power Brake Booster

This procedure is used only with the diagonal split system.

REMOVAL & INSTALLATION

1. Remove the master cylinder-to-power booster nuts and move the master cylinder aside.
2. From inside the vehicle, detach the brake pushrod from the brake pedal.
3. Detach the vacuum hose at the vacuum cylinder.
4. Remove the nuts from the mounting studs which hold the unit to the dash panel. Remove the unit and clean it prior to installation.
5. To install, reverse the removal procedures. Torque the power booster-to-cowl nuts to 28 ft. lbs. and the master cylinder-to-power booster nuts to 28 ft. lbs. Bleed the brake system.

Parking Brake Cable

ADJUSTMENT

1. Lube the cables at the underbody rub points and at the equalizer hooks. Set and release the parking brake several times and check for free movement of all cables.

NOTE: With the ignition switch turned ON, the parking brake warning light should be OFF.

2. Set the parking brake pedal in the fully released position, raise and support the rear of the vehicle.
3. Hold the brake cable stud and tighten the equalizer nut until all cable slack is removed. Make sure the caliper levers are against the stops on the caliper housing; if not, loosen the cable until they are.
4. Operate the parking brake pedal several times to check the adjustment, it should travel approximately 4–5½ in. (1982–85 models). On 1986–88 models, note that the pedal should become firm after 3½ strokes.
5. Lower the vehicle and check that the caliper levers are still on their stops. If not, back off the parking brake adjuster until they are.

REMOVAL & INSTALLATION

Front

1. Raise and support the rear of the vehicle on jackstands.
2. If not equipped with an intermediate cable, remove the adjuster nut from the equalizer. If equipped with an intermediate cable, disconnect the front cable from the intermediate cable.
3. From the left fender, remove the lower rear wheelhouse panel bolt and screw. Pull the panel outward to gain access to the front cable.
4. Disconnect the cable from the parking brake assembly and remove it from the vehicle.

5. To install, reverse the removal procedures. Perform the adjustment procedures.

Intermediate

NOTE: Some vehicles do not use an intermediate cable.

1. Raise and support the vehicle on jackstands.
2. Disconnect the front cable from the intermediate at the adjuster.
3. Remove the adjuster from the intermidiate cable.
4. Disconnect the right rear, left rear and the intermediate cables from the equalizer. Remove the intermediate cable from the vehicle.
5. To install, reverse the removal procedures. Adjust the parking brake.

Rear

1. Release the parking brake.
2. Raise and support the rear of the vehicle on jackstands. Loosen the cable adjuster.
3. If not equipped with an intermediate cable, loosen the equalizer nut, remove the equalizer and the cable from the equalizer. If equipped with an intermediate cable, disconnect the intermediate, left rear and right rear cables from the equalizer.
4. From the left side and both caliper support plate, remove the parking brake cable-to-lower control arm retaining clips.
5. Remove the cable ends from the parking brake actuator.
6. Remove the control arm hooks, the conduit from the exhaust hanger clip (if equipped) and the cable.
7. To install, reverse the removal procedures. Adjust the parking brake.

CHASSIS ELECTRICAL

Heater Blower

REMOVAL & INSTALLATION

Reatta and Riviera

1982–85

1. Disconnect the blower motor wires.
2. On air conditioning equipped vehicles, disconnect the cooling tube from the case.
3. Remove the motor attaching screws and lift the motor from the case.
4. To install, reverse the removal procedures. Replace any damaged sealer.

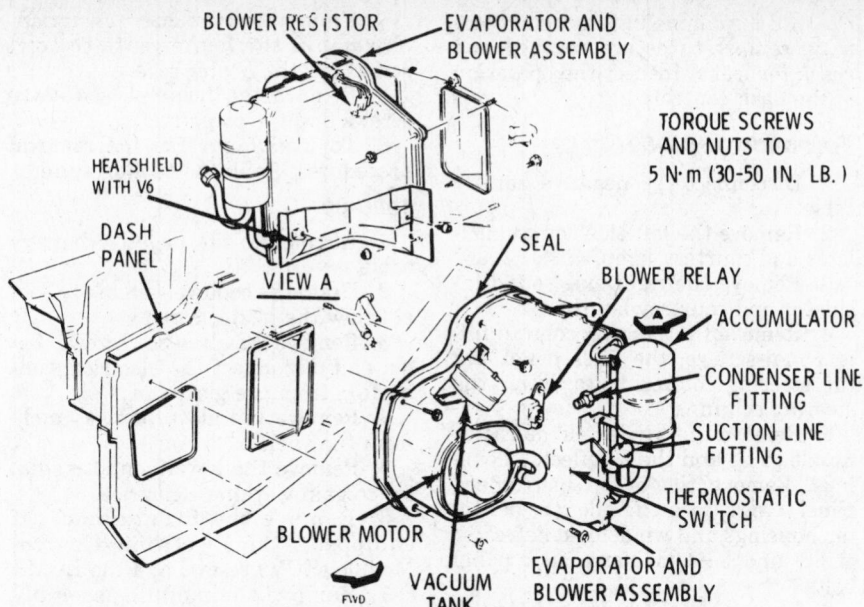

Blower assembly

Labels in figure:
BLOWER RESISTOR
EVAPORATOR AND BLOWER ASSEMBLY
TORQUE SCREWS AND NUTS TO 5 N·m (30-50 IN. LB.)
HEATSHIELD WITH V6
DASH PANEL
VIEW A
SEAL
BLOWER RELAY
A ACCUMULATOR
CONDENSER LINE FITTING
SUCTION LINE FITTING
THERMOSTATIC SWITCH
BLOWER MOTOR
VACUUM TANK
FWD
EVAPORATOR AND BLOWER ASSEMBLY

1986–89

1. Disconnect the negative battery cable.

2. Remove the 2 front of cowl shields.

3. Disconnect the electrical harness from the blower motor. Remove the harness from the retaining clips and move it aside.

4. Remove the cooling tube from the blower motor.

5. Remve the blower motor screws and the motor from the vehicle.

6. To install, reverse the removal procedures.

Eldorado and Seville

1982–85

1. Disconnect the negative battery cable.

2. Disconnect the electrical wiring connectors from the blower motor.

3. Disconnect the cooling hose from the blower motor.

4. Remove the mounting screws and the blower motor.

5. To install, reverse the removal procedures. Use a silicone sealer on the blower motor sealing surfaces.

1986–87

1. Disconnect the negative battery cable.

2. Remove the air cleaner assembly and the cross tower brace.

3. Disconnect the electrical harness support bracket.

4. Label and disconnect the electrical wiring connectors. Remove the cooling hose and mounting screws.

5. Tilt the blower motor in the case and remove the fan from the blower motor.

NOTE: Be careful not to bend the fan upon removal as a fan imbalance will result after reassembly.

6. Remove the blower motor and fan assembly from the vehicle.

7. To install, reverse the removal procedures.

1988–89

1. Disconnect the negative battery cable.

2. Remove the cowl relay center bracket nuts and move the bracket aside.

3. Remove the air cleaner assembly and the cross tower brace.

4. Disconnect the electrical harness support bracket.

5. Label and disconnect the electrical wiring connectors. Remove the cooling hose and mounting screws.

6. Tilt the blower motor in the case and remove the fan from the blower motor.

NOTE: Be careful not to bend the fan upon removal as a fan imbalance will result after reassembly.

7. Remove the blower motor and fan assembly from the vehicle.

8. To install, reverse the removal procedures.

Toronado 1986–89

1. Disconnect the negative battery cable.

2. Remove the front of the cowl shield.

3. Remove the bulkhead retaining screw and the bulkhead electrical connector.

4. Remove the Electronic Spark Control (ESC) module electrical connector.

5. Remove the ESC module and bracket assembly.

6. Remove the power steering pump bracket support.

7. Remove the coil bracket nuts. Label and disconnect the electrical connector from the coil.

8. Remove the plug wire guides. Remove the coil/bracket assembly and move it aside. Remove the wiring harness conduit.

9. Remove the blower motor cooling tube.

10. Tag and disconnect the electrical connectors from the blower motor. Remove the blower motor mounting screws.

11. Remove the blower motor mounting screws and the blower motor.

12. To install, reverse of the removal procedures.

Allante 1987–89

1. Disconnect the negative battery cable.

2. Remove the cross tower brace.

3. Partially remove the upper intake manifold by performing the following procedures.

   a. Remove the 2 EGR pipe bolts.

   b. Remove the transaxle dipstick bolt.

   c. Remove the rear bracket bolt.

   d. Remove the 4 lower intake manifold nuts.

   e. Position the upper intake manifold aside.

4. Remove the electrical harness bracket and disconnect the electrical connector.

5. Remove the cooling hose, the mounting screws and the blower motor.

6. To install, reverse the removal procedures.

Heater Core

REMOVAL & INSTALLATION

Toronado and Riviera 1982–87

NOTE: This procedure involves removing the dashboard.

1. Disconnect the negative battery cable.

2. Drain the cooling system. Remove the heater hoses from the heater core.

3. Remove the instrument panel sound absorbers which cover the underside of the dash area.

4. Loosen and lower the steering column and remove the left hand trim cover.

5. To remove the instrument clus-

ter, perform the following procedures:

a. Remove the headlight switch.

b. Remove the windshield wiper switch, the radio and heater/air conditioning control assembly.

c. Remove all cluster electrical connections and disconnect the speedometer cable.

d. Remove the mounting screws and remove the cluster.

6. Remove the front speakers, the manifold-to-heater case screws, the upper/lower instrument panel screws, then, disconnect the brake release cable.

7. Disconnect the instrument panel wiring harness from the dash wiring assembly and the right hand remote control mirror cable from the instrument panel.

8. Disconnect the speedometer cable from its clip and the heater control cable from the heater case.

9. Disconnect all vacuum lines and wiring necessary to remove the instrument panel. If vehicle is equipped with pulse wipers, remove the wiper switch, unlock the connector from the cluster carrier and separate the pulse jumper harness from the connector.

10. Remove the instrument panel and harness assembly.

11. Remove the defroster ducts, disconnect vacuum hoses and temperature cable; remove the blower resistor and the heater assembly nuts.

12. Remove the heater assembly-to-dash screw and clip from inside the vehicle.

13. Remove the heater assembly and the heater core.

14. To install, reverse the removal procedures. Refill the cooling system.

Reatta and Riviera 1988–89

1. Disconnect the negative battery cable.

2. Drain the cooling system.

3. Disconnect the hoses from the heater core.

4. Remove the right side sound insulator and courtesy lamp.

5. Remove the glove box.

6. Disconnect the air conditioning programmer the electrical and vacuum connectors. Remove the air conditioning programmer screws and the programmer.

7. Disconnect the ECM electrical connectors. Remove the ECM and bracket.

8. Disconnect the BCM electrical connectors. Remove the BCM and bracket.

9. Remove the heater core cover screws, the cover, the retaining clip, the heater core screws and the heater core.

10. To install, reverse the removal procedures. Refill the cooling system.

Operate the engine until normal operating temperatures are reached and check for leaks. Inspect the operation of the dash controls.

Toronado 1988–89

1. Disconnect the negative battery cable.

2. Remove the left side sound insulator and courtesy lamp.

3. Remove the right side sound insulator and courtesy lamp.

4. Remove the steering column filler panel screws, the filler panel and the steering column bolts; lower the steering column.

5. Remove the windshield defroster nozzle grille and the 2 deflector housings. Remove the 5 top instrument panel screws (located under the deflector housings and windshield defroster grille) and bottom instrument panel bolts.

6. Disconnect the bulkhead electrical connector and move the instrument rearward. Remove the aspirator duct.

7. Disconnect the electrical connectors from the fuel filler door release, the rear compartment lid release and the antenna. Remove the fuse panel and the instrument panel from the vehicle.

8. Drain the cooling system to a level below the heater core. Disconnect the hoses from the heater core.

9. Disconnect the air conditioning programmer the electrical and vacuum connectors. Remove the air conditioning programmer screws and the programmer.

10. Disconnect the power module electrical connectors. Remove the power module screws and the module.

11. Remove the heater core cover screws, the cover, the retaining clip, the heater core screws and the heater core.

12. To install, reverse the removal procedures. Refill the cooling system. Operate the engine until normal operating temperatures are reached and check for leaks. Inspect the operation of the dash controls.

Eldorado and Seville

1982–85

1. Drain the cooling system.

2. Remove the heater hoses from the core and plug the hoses and the nipples to prevent spillage.

3. Remove the instrument panel.

4. Remove the defroster nozzle-to-cowl screws, the case-to-nozzle screw and the nozzle.

5. Disconnect the vacuum hoses and the electrical connector from the programmer.

6. From the engine compartment, remove the heater case-to-cowl screws.

7. From under the instrument panel, remove the heater case-to-cowl screw and the heater case.

8. Remove the heater case-to-core screws and the core.

9. To install, reverse the removal procedures. Refill the cooling system.

1986–89

1. Disconnect the negative battery cable.

2. Drain the cooling system to a level below the heater core.

3. Remove the glove box screws. Label and disconnect the electrical connectors from the glove box.

4. Remove the glove box assembly from the vehicle.

5. Remove the lower sound insulator to gain working clearance.

6. Remove the Programmer (if equipped), the Electronic Control Module (ECM) screws and the ECM.

7. Remove the module assembly heater core cover. Disconnect the hoses from the heater core.

8. Remove the heater core screws and the heater core.

9. To install, reverse the removal procedures. Refill the cooling system.

Allante 1987–89

1. Disconnect the negative battery cable.

2. Drain the cooling system to a level below the heater core.

3. Remove the glove box screws. Label and disconnect the electrical connectors from the glove box.

4. Remove the glove box assembly from the vehicle.

5. Remove the lower sound insulator to gain working clearance.

6. Remove the radio.

7. Remove the Programmer (if equipped), the Electronic Control Module (ECM) screws and the ECM.

8. Remove the module assembly heater core cover. Disconnect the hoses from the heater core.

9. Remove the heater core screws and the heater core.

10. To install, reverse the removal procedures. Refill the cooling system.

Radio

REMOVAL & INSTALLATION

Toronado

1. Disconnect the negative battery cable.

2. Remove the instrument panel trim plate. Remove the radio/air conditioning/heater control bracket screws, pull the bracket rearward and disconnect the electrical connectors and antenna lead.

3. Remove the radio-to-bracket nuts and the radio.

4. To install, reverse the removal procedures. Inspect the radio operation.

Eldorado and Seville

1982–85

1. Disconnect the negative battery cable.
2. Remove the screws from the top of the instrument panel center insert.
3. Remove the radio knobs and the insert.
4. Remove the rear window defogger switch to gain access to the left side mounting screw (if equipped).
5. Remove the mounting screws.
6. Remove the radio and disconnect the wiring.
7. To install, reverse the removal procedures.

1986–89

1. Disconnect the negative battery cable. Remove the radio trim plate.
2. Remove the instrument panel trim plate-to-instrument panel screws and remove it.
3. Remove the mounting nuts under the radio. Disconnect the electrical connectors and antenna lead. Remove the radio.
4. To install, reverse the removal procedures. Check the radio operation.

Reatta and Riviera

1982–85

1. Disconnect the negative battery cable.
2. Remove the center trim plate by grasping it firmly and pulling out. Be careful not to lose the spring retaining clips.
3. Remove the ashtray and bracket.
4. Pull off the radio knobs and trim washers.
5. Remove the lower left air duct.
6. Remove the 2 retaining nuts from the control shafts.
7. Disconnect the power lead, speaker wire and antenna lead.
8. Remove the rear radio mounting nut.

1986–87

1. Remove the left side trim cover from the instrument panel.
2. Remove the right hand switch trim plate.
3. Remove the radio-to-dash screws in place. Disconnect the 3 electrical connectors, antenna lead and the clock connector. Remove the radio.
4. To install, reverse the removal procedures.

1988–89

The radio is mounted in the rear of the console.
1. Remove the console assembly-to-chassis screws, lift the console and dis-

connect the electrical connector.
2. From the radio, disconnect the antenna lead and the electrical connectors.
3. Remove the radio-to-chassis screws and the radio from the vehicle.
4. To install, reverse the removal procedures.

Allante 1987–89

1. Remove the glove box assembly.
2. Remove the radio-to-chassis screws, nut and washer.
3. Pull the radio outward and disconnect the antenna lead and the 3 electrical connectors.
4. Remove the radio from the vehicle.
5. To install, reverse the removal procedures. Check the radio operation.

Windshield Wiper Switch

REMOVAL & INSTALLATION

Eldorado and Seville 1982–85, Riviera 1982–87 and Toronado 1982–89

1. Disconnect the negative battery cable. Remove the steering wheel.
2. It may be necessary to loosen the 2 column mounting nuts and remove the 4 bracket—to—mast jacket screws. Separate the bracket from the mast jacket to allow the connector clip on the ignition switch to be pulled out of the column assembly.
3. Disconnect the washer/wiper switch lower connector.
4. Remove the screws attaching the column housing to the mast jacket. Be sure to note the position of the dimmer switch actuator rod for reassembly in the same position. Remove the column housing and switch as an assembly.

NOTE: The tilt and travel columns have a removable plastic cover on the column housing. This provides access to the wiper switch without removing the entire column housing.

5. Turn upside down and use a drift to remove the pivot pin from the washer/wiper switch. Remove the switch.
6. Place the switch into position in the housing and install the pivot pin.
7. Position the housing onto the mast jacket and attach by installing the screws. Install the dimmer switch actuator rod in the same position as noted earlier. Check switch operation.
8. Reconnect lower end of switch assembly.
9. Install remaining components in reverse order of removal. Be sure to at-

tach column mounting bracket in original position.

Eldorado and Seville 1986–89 Reatta and Riviera 1988–89

The windshield wiper switch is attached to switch pod, located on the instrument panel to the right side of the steering wheel.
1. Disconnect the negative battery cable.
2. Remove the switch trim panel from the instrument panel.
3. Remove the switch-to-instrument panel screws.
4. Pull the switch outward and disconnect the electrical connectors from the rear of the switch.
5. To install, reverse the removal procedures.

Allante 1987–89

The windshield wiper switch is attached to switch pod, located on the instrument panel to the right side of the steering wheel.
1. Disconnect the negative battery cable.
2. Remove the bottom instrument panel trim plate.
3. Remove the switch pod-to-instrument panel screws, pull the pod outward and disconnect the electrical connectors. Remove the switch pod from the vehicle.
4. To install, reverse the removal procedures. Check the switch pod operation.

Windshield Wiper Motor

REMOVAL & INSTALLATION

1. Remove both wiper arms.
2. Remove the cowl cover.
3. Remove the wiper arm drive link from the crank arm.
4. Disconnect the electrical connectors.
5. Remove the wiper motor-to-chassis bolts and the motor; guide the crank arm through the hole.
6. To install, reverse the removal procedures. Check the wiper motor operation.

Instrument Cluster

REMOVAL & INSTALLATION

Reatta and Riviera

1982–85

1. Disconnect the negative battery cable.
2. Slide the steering column collar

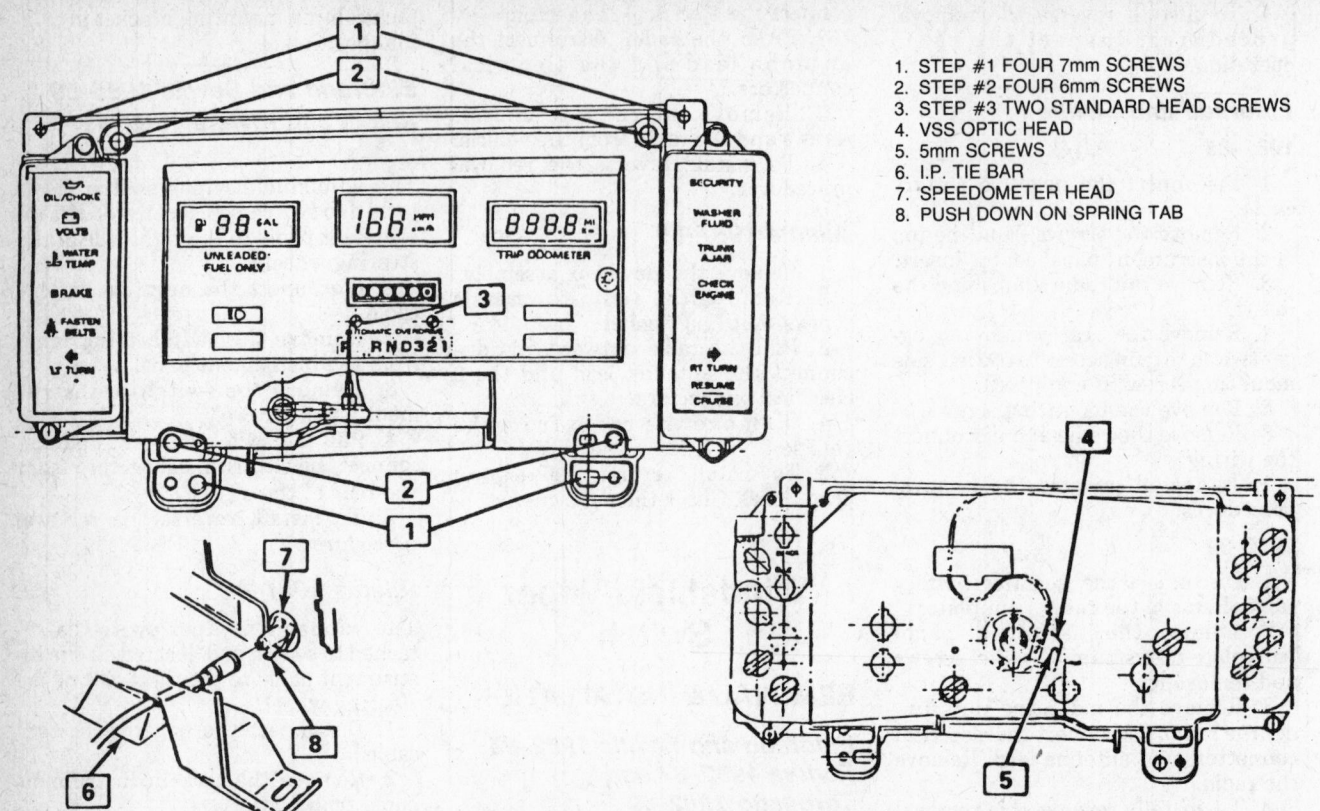

1. STEP #1 FOUR 7mm SCREWS
2. STEP #2 FOUR 6mm SCREWS
3. STEP #3 TWO STANDARD HEAD SCREWS
4. VSS OPTIC HEAD
5. 5mm SCREWS
6. I.P. TIE BAR
7. SPEEDOMETER HEAD
8. PUSH DOWN ON SPRING TAB

Typical Riviera digital instrument cluster

upward on the steering column.

3. Remove the headlight knob, escutcheon assembly and all remaining knobs.

4. Depending on the vehicle model, pry either the right or left (or both) trim plates from the instrument panel.

NOTE: Remove the center trim plate by first removing the right and left trim plates. Then remove the radio knobs and screws securing the center trim plate.

5. Disconnect the seelite and remove.

6. Remove all cluster retaining screws. Pull the cluster out slightly and disconnect the speedometer cable. Remove the instrument cluster assembly.

7. To install, attach the cluster assembly and speedometer cable and reverse the removal procedures. Secure the center trim plate. Hold the left and right trim plates in position, press into place and reposition the rubber filler ring and headlight knob assembly.

1986–89 DIGITAL CLUSTER

1. Disconnect the negative battery cable.

2. Remove the center, left and right trim covers.

3. Remove the instrument cluster-to-dash screws, then, pull the cluster straight out of the housing.

4. To install, reverse of removal procedures.

Seville and Eldorado

1982–85

1. Disconnect the negative battery cable.

2. Remove the left sound insulator.

3. Remove the instrument panel insert and applique trim from the instrument panel.

4. Place the shift lever in the **PARK** position and remove the shift indicator clip from the steering column.

5. Remove the steering column-to-upper mounting bracket nuts and lower the steering column.

6. Remove the upper steering column mounting bracket-to-cowl screws and lower the bracket.

7. Remove the cluster retaining screws, disconnect the speedometer cable, printed circuit connector and remove the cluster.

8. To install, reverse the removal procedures. Be sure the shift indicator is properly aligned.

1986–89

1. Remove the 7 screws located along the top and remove the instrument panel trim plate.

2. Remove the 4 mounting screws and the filter lens.

3. Remove the warning light lens screws and the lens. Remove the trip odometer reset button.

4. Remove the instrument panel cluster screws. Pull the cluster off the electrical connections and remove it. Using a pair of pliers, hold the retaining tabs at either end of the cluster board and remove the board.

5. To install the cluster, align it with the electrical connectors, push it into the instrument panel and reverse the removal procedures.

Toronado

1982–85

NOTE: To remove the left side sound absorber from under the dash take out 2 screws and 1 nut. Pull the absorber down the slide from the steering column.

1. Disconnect the ALCL computer connector, if equipped.

2. Remove 4 screws from bottom side of trim cover.

3. Remove the steering column trim cover.

4. Remove the headlamp switch knob and the radio knobs.

5. Carefully pull left hand trim cover rearward to remove; the trim cover is retained by clips.

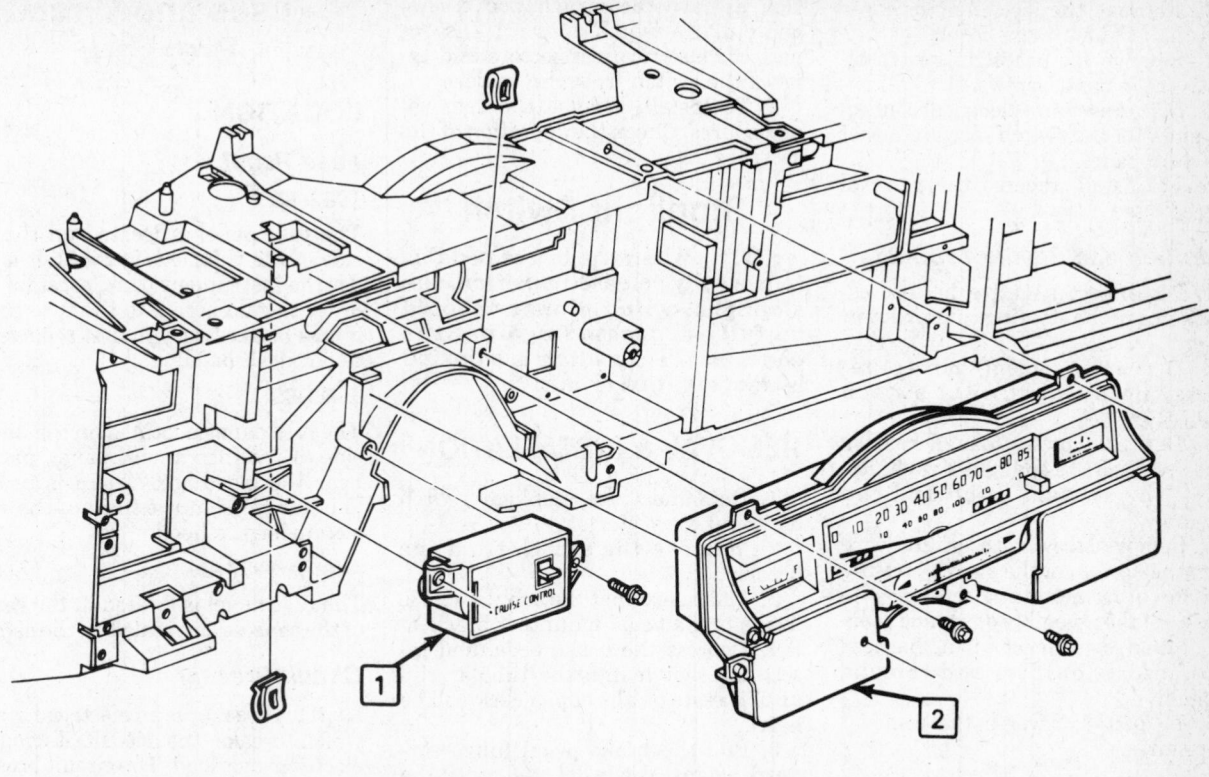

☐1 CRUISE CONTROL DASH SWITCH ☐2 INSTRUMENT CLUSTER

Typical instrument cluster (Eldorado and Seville)

NOTE: It may be necessary to disconnect the shift indicator clip and lower the steering column slightly to obtain clearance needed for trim cover removal.

6. Remove trip odometer knob by turning counterclockwise.

7. Remove the cluster lens screws, the face plate-to-cluster carrier, the lens and the face plate.

8. Remove 2 screws, attaching gauge assembly to cluster housing.

9. Pull the gauge assembly rearward to remove.

10. Disconnect the shift indicator cable end from shift indicator pointer.

11. Remove the speedometer-to-cluster housing screws.

12. If the printed circuit is to be removed, remove both gauge assemblies by removing the upper gauge assemblies-to-cluster housing screws and pull the assemblies rearward.

13. Remove the lower cluster housing-to-cluster carrier screws.

14. Disconnect speedometer cable at transaxle or at transducer on vehicles equipped with cruise control.

15. Pull cluster housing rearward (far enough) to reach behind it, then, disconnect the speedometer cable by depressing speedometer cable clip.

16. If equipped, remove the speed sensor pickup-to-speedometer head screw and remove the pickup.

17. Remove the cluster housing and speedometer assembly.

18. Remove the cluster housing-to-speedometer screws and the speedometer.

19. To install, reverse the removal procedures.

1986–89

1. Disconnect the negative battery cable.

2. Remove the steering column trim cover. Lower the steering column.

3. Remove the instrument panel trim plate.

4. Remove the cluster-to-instrument panel screws.

5. Pull the cluster rearward and remove it.

6. To install, reverse the removal procedures.

Headlight Switch

REMOVAL & INSTALLATION

Toronado 1982–85

1. To remove the left hand trim cover, perform the following procedures:

a. Remove the headlight switch knob and the radio knobs.

b. Remove the steering column trim cover and the 4 screws beneath the cover.

c. Remove the left hand sound absorber and carefully pull the trim cover rearward.

2. Remove the switch-to-dash screws.

3. Pull the switch rearward to remove.

4. To install, reverse the removal procedures.

Riviera

1982

1. Disconnect the negative battery cable.

2. Pull the switch knob to the last notch and depress the spring loaded latch button on top of the switch, while pulling the knob and rod out of the switch.

3. Remove the escutcheon, the trim plate and the retaining nut/screws. Remove the switch from the cluster.

4. Disconnect the multiple connector.

5. To install, reverse the removal procedures.

1983–85

1. Disconnect the negative battery cable.

2. Remove the switch trim cover and the left hand trim cover.

3. Remove the headlight switch-to-instrument panel screws.

4. Disconnect any electrical connector and pull the switch forward out of the dash panel.

5. To install, reverse the removal procedures.

Eldorado and Seville 1982–85

1. Disconnect negative battery cable. Remove the steering column lower cover.

2. Disconnect wiring harness retainer below headlight switch assembly.

3. Depress spring loaded release button on top of headlight switch. Remove the switch, knob and rod assembly.

4. Remove screw with ground wire from the bottom of the switch housing and any other mounting screws.

5. Pull the assembly down and rearward, then, disconnect wiring harness connectors, bulb(s) and remove assembly.

6. To install, reverse the removal procedures.

All Models 1986–89

The headlight switch is located on a switch pod, located on the left side of the instrument panel.

1. Remove the instrument panel trim plate.

2. Remove the switch pod screws and pull the switch outward. Disconnect the electrical connectors and remove the switch from the vehicle.

3. To install, reverse the removal procedures. Check the operation of the switches.

Stoplight Switch

NOTE: When the brake pedal is in the fully released position, the stoplight switch plunger should be fully depressed against the pedal arm. The switch is adjusted by moving it in or out.

REMOVAL & INSTALLATION

1. Disconnect the stoplight switch electrical connector(s).

2. Remove the switch from the bracket.

3. Make sure that the tubular clip is in the brake pedal mounting bracket.

4. Depress the brake pedal and insert the switch into the tubular clip until it seats on the clip; a click will be heard.

5. Pull the brake pedal fully rearward, against the pedal stop, until the clicking sounds can no longer be heard; the switch is adjusting itself in the bracket.

6. Release the brake pedal and pull the pedal rearward again to assure that the adjustment is complete.

Fuses and Circuit Breakers

LOCATION

Fuse Panel

1982–85

The fuse panel is located on the left side of the vehicle (1982–85); it is under the instrument panel assembly. In order to gain access to the fuse panel, it may be necessary to first remove the under dash padding.

1986–89

The fuse panel is located on the underside of the instrument panel, usually near the glove box. There is usually another panel at the front of the vehicle, under the hood.

Allante 1987–89

The fuse panel is located in the center of the console, concealed by the ashtry.

Circuit Breaker

A circuit breaker is an electrical switch which breaks the circuit during an electrical overload. The circuit breaker will remain open until the short or overload condition in the circuit is corrected.

GM "F" Body
Rear Wheel Drive
Chevrolet Camaro, Pontiac Firebird

24

VEHICLE IDENTIFICATION CHART

It is important for servicing and ordering parts to be certain of the vehicle and engine identification. The VIN (vehicle identification number) is a 17 digit number visible through the windshield on the driver's side of the dash and contains the vehicle and engine identification codes. The tenth digit indicates model year and the eighth digit indicates engine code. It can be interpreted as follows:

Engine Code					
Code	Cu. In.	Liters	Cyl.	Fuel Sys.	Eng. Mfg.
F	151	2.5	4	Carb.	Pontiac
2	151	2.5	4	TBI	Pontiac
1	173	2.8	6	Carb.	Chevy
L	173	2.8	6	Carb.	Chevy
S	173	2.8	6	MFI	Chevy
A	231	3.8	6	Carb.	Buick
K	229	3.8	6	Carb.	Chevy
S	265	4.3	8	Carb.	Pontiac
J	267	4.4	8	Carb.	Chevy
T	301	4.9	8	Turbo	Pontiac
W	301	4.9	8	Turbo	Pontiac
H	305	5.0	8	Carb.	Chevy
S	305	5.0	8	EFI	Chevy
G	305	5.0	8	Carb.	Chevy
F	305	5.0	8	TPI	Chevy
E	305	5.0	8	EFI	Chevy
L	350	5.7	8	Carb.	Chevy
7	350	5.7	8	TBI	Chevy
8	350	5.7	8	TPI	Chevy

Model Year	
Code	Year
C	1982
D	1983
E	1984
F	1985
G	1986
H	1987
J	1988
K	1989

24-1

GENERAL ENGINE SPECIFICATIONS

Year	VIN	No. Cylinder Displacement cu. in. (liter)	Fuel System Type	Net Horsepower @ rpm	Net Torque @ rpm (ft.lbs.)	Bore × Stroke (in.)	Compression Ratio	Oil Pressure @ 2000 rpm
1982	2	4-151 (2.5)	TBI	90 @ 4000	134 @ 2400	4.000 × 3.000	8.2:1	40
	1	6-173 (2.8)	Carb.	102 @ 4800	145 @ 2400	3.500 × 3.000	8.5:1	40
	H	8-305 (5.0)	Carb.	145 @ 4000	240 @ 2400	3.736 × 3.480	8.6:1	40
	7	8-305 (5.7)	TBI	165 @ 4200	240 @ 2400	3.736 × 3.480	9.5:1	40
1983	F	4-151 (2.5)	Carb.	92 @ 4200	130 @ 2800	4.000 × 3.000	8.2:1	40
	2	4-151 (2.5)	TBI	90 @ 4000	134 @ 2400	4.000 × 3.000	8.2:1	40
	1	6-173 (2.8)	Carb.	102 @ 4800	145 @ 2400	3.500 × 3.000	8.5:1	40
	L	6-173 (2.8)	Carb.	125 @ 5400	145 @ 2400	3.500 × 3.000	8.9:1	55
	S	8-305 (5.0)	EFI	175 @ 4200	250 @ 2800	3.736 × 3.480	9.5:1	55
	H	8-305 (5.0)	Carb.	145 @ 4000	240 @ 2400	3.736 × 3.480	8.6:1	40
1984	F	4-151 (2.5)	Carb.	92 @ 4200	130 @ 2800	4.000 × 3.000	8.2:1	40
	2	4-151 (2.5)	TBI	90 @ 4000	134 @ 2400	4.000 × 3.000	8.2:1	40
	1	6-173 (2.8)	Carb.	102 @ 4800	145 @ 2400	3.500 × 3.000	8.5:1	40
	G	8-305 (5.0)	Carb.	165 @ 4400	250 @ 2000	3.736 × 3.480	9.5:1	55
	H	8-305 (5.0)	Carb.	150 @ 4000	240 @ 2400	3.736 × 3.480	8.6:1	55
1985	2	2-151 (2.5)	EFI	92 @ 4000	134 @ 2800	4.000 × 3.000	9.0:1	40
	S	6-173 (2.8)	MFI	135 @ 5100	165 @ 3600	3.500 × 3.000	8.9:1	55
	G	8-305 (5.0)	Carb.	165 @ 4400	250 @ 2000	3.740 × 3.480	9.5:1	55
	H	3-305 (5.0)	Carb.	150 @ 4000	240 @ 2400	3.736 @ 3.480	8.6:1	55
	F	8-305 (5.0)	TPI	190 @ 4800	240 @ 3200	3.740 × 3.480	9.5:1	55
1986	2	2-151 (2.5)	EFI	92 @ 4000	134 @ 2800	4.000 × 3.000	9.0:1	40
	S	6-173 (2.8)	MFI	135 @ 5100	165 @ 3600	3.500 × 3.000	8.9:1	55
	G	8-305 (5.0)	Carb.	165 @ 4400	250 @ 2000	3.740 × 3.480	9.5:1	55
	H	3-305 (5.0)	Carb.	150 @ 4000	240 @ 2400	3.736 . × 3.480	8.6:1	55
	F	8-305 (5.0)	TPI	190 @ 4800	240 @ 3200	3.740 × 3.480	9.5:1	55
	8	8-350 (5.7)	TPI	230 @ 4000	300 @ 3200	3.736 × 3.480	9.5:1	55
1987	S	6-173 (2.8)	MFI	135 @ 5100	165 @ 3600	3.500 × 3.000	8.9:1	55
	H	3-305 (5.0)	Carb.	150 @ 4000	240 @ 2400	3.736 × 3.480	8.6:1	55
	F	8-305 (5.0)	TPI	190 @ 4800	240 @ 3200	3.740 × 3.480	9.3:1	55
	8	8-350 (5.7)	TPI	230 @ 4000	300 @ 3200	4.000 × 3.480	9.5:1	55
1988-89	S	6-173 (2.8)	MFI	135 @ 5100	165 @ 3600	3.736 × 3.480	9.3:1	55
	F	8-305 (5.0)	TPI	190 @ 4800	240 @ 3200	3.736 × 3.480	9.3:1	55
	E	8-305 (5.0)	EFI	150 @ 4000	240 @ 3200	3.736 × 3.480	9.3:1	55
	8	8-350 (5.7)	TPI	230 @ 4000	300 @ 3200	4.000 × 3.480	9.5:1	55

GASOLINE ENGINE TUNE-UP SPECIFICATIONS

Year	VIN	No. Cylinder Displacement cu. in. (liter)	Spark Plugs Type	Gap (in.)	Ignition Timing (deg.) MT	AT	Compression Pressure (psi)	000030 Fuel Pump (psi)	Speed (rpm) MT	AT	Valve Clearance In.	Ex.
1982	2	4-151 (2.5)	R-44TSX	.060	8	8	NA	9.0-13.0	775	500	Hyd.	Hyd.
	1	6-173 (2.8)	R-43TS	.045	10	10	NA	5.5-6.5	850	700	Hyd.	Hyd.
	H	8-305 (5.0)	R-45TS	.045	6	6	NA	5.5-6.5	750	575	Hyd.	Hyd.
	7	8-350 (5.7)	R-45TS	.045	—	6	NA	9.0-13.0	—	500	Hyd.	Hyd.
1983	F	4-151 (2.5)	R-44TS	.060	8	8	NA	5.5-6.5	775	500	Hyd.	Hyd.
	2	4-151 (2.5)	R-44TSX	.060	8	8	NA	9.0-13.0	775	500	Hyd.	Hyd.
	1	6-173 (2.8)	R-43CTS	.045	10	10	NA	5.5-6.5	850	700	Hyd.	Hyd.
	L	6-173 (2.8)	R-42CTS	.045	10	10	NA	6.0-7.5	850	750	Hyd.	Hyd.
	S	8-305 (5.0)	R-45TS	.045	—	6	NA	9.0-13.0	—	475	Hyd.	Hyd.
	H	8-305 (5.0)	R-45TS	.045	6	6	NA	5.5-6.5	750	575	Hyd.	Hyd.
1984	F	4-151 (2.5)	R-44TS	.060	8	8	NA	5.5-6.5	775	500	Hyd.	Hyd.
	2	4-151 (2.5)	R-44TSX	.060	8	8	NA	9.0-13.0	775	500	Hyd.	Hyd.
	1	6-173 (2.8)	R-43CTS	.045	10	10	NA	5.5-6.5	850	700	Hyd.	Hyd.
	G	8-305 (5.0)	R-45TS	.045	6	6	NA	5.5-6.5	750	550	Hyd.	Hyd.
	H	8-305 (5.0)	R-45TS	.045	6	6	NA	5.5-6.5	750	575	Hyd.	Hyd.
1985	2	4-151 (2.5)	R-43TSX	.060	8	8	NA	9.0-13.0	775	500	Hyd.	Hyd.
	S	6-173 (2.8)	R-42CTS	.045	10	10	NA	6.0-7.5	600	500	Hyd.	Hyd.
	G	8-305 (5.0)	R-43CTS	.045	6	6	NA	9.0-13.0	750	550	Hyd.	Hyd.
	H	8-305 (5.0)	R-43CTS	.045	6	6	NA	9.0-13.0	750	550	Hyd.	Hyd.
	F	8-305 (5.0)	R-43CTS	.045	—	6	NA	9.0-13.0	—	500	Hyd.	Hyd.
1986	2	4-151 (2.5)	R-43TSX	.060	8	8	NA	9.0-13.0	775	500	Hyd.	Hyd.
	S	6-173 (2.8)	R-42CTS	.045	10	10	NA	6.0-7.5	600	500	Hyd.	Hyd.
	G	8-305 (5.0)	R-43CTS	.045	6	6	NA	9.0-13.0	750	550	Hyd.	Hyd.
	H	8-305 (5.0)	R-43CTS	.045	6	6	NA	9.0-13.0	750	550	Hyd.	Hyd.
	F	8-305 (5.0)	R-43CTS	.045	—	6	NA	9.0-13.0	—	500	Hyd.	Hyd.
	8	8-350 (5.7)	R-43CTS	.045	6	6	NA	9.0-13.0	450	400	Hyd.	Hyd.
1987	S	6-173 (2.8)	R-43LTSE	.045	10	10	NA	9.0-13.0	600	500	Hyd.	Hyd.
	H	8-305 (5.0)	R-44TS	.035	6	6	NA	9.0-13.0	500	500	Hyd.	Hyd.
	F	8-305 (5.0)	R-44TS	.035	6	6	NA	9.0-13.0	500	500	Hyd.	Hyd.
	8	8-350 (5.7)	R-44TS	.035	6	6	NA	9.0-13.0	450	400	Hyd.	Hyd.
1988	S	6-173 (2.8)	R-42CTS	.045	10	10	NA	9.0-13.0	450	400	Hyd.	Hyd.
	F	8-305 (5.0)	R-43TS	.035	6	6	NA	9.0-13.0	500	500	Hyd.	Hyd.
	E	8-305 (5.0)	R-45TS	.035	6	6	NA	9.0-13.0	450	400	Hyd.	Hyd.
	8	8-350 (5.7)	R-43TS	.035	6	6	NA	9.0-13.0	450	400	Hyd.	Hyd.
1989		SEE UNDERHOOD SPECIFICATIONS STICKER										

FIRING ORDERS

NOTE: To avoid confusion, always replace spark plug wires one at a time.

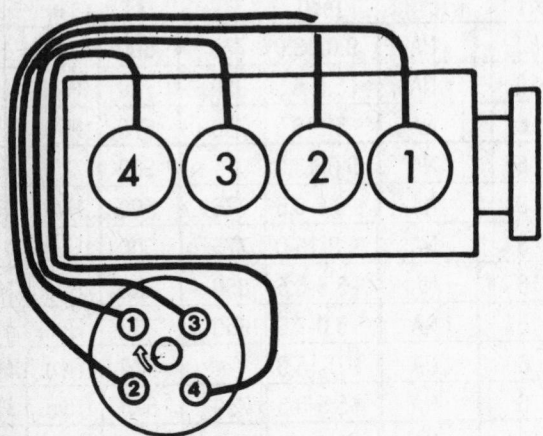

Pontiac-built 151-4 cylinder engine
Engine firing order: 1-3-4-2
Distributor rotation: clockwise

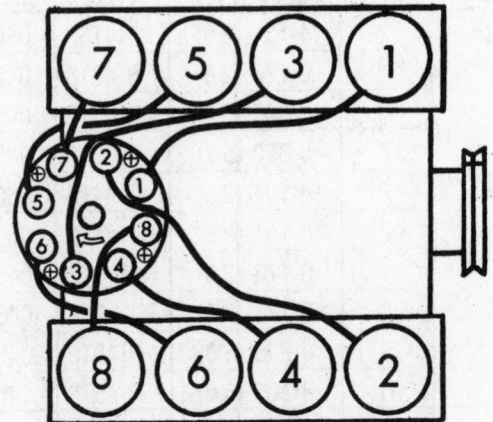

Chevrolet-built V8 engines
Engine firing order: 1-8-4-3-6-5-7-2
Distributor rotation: clockwise

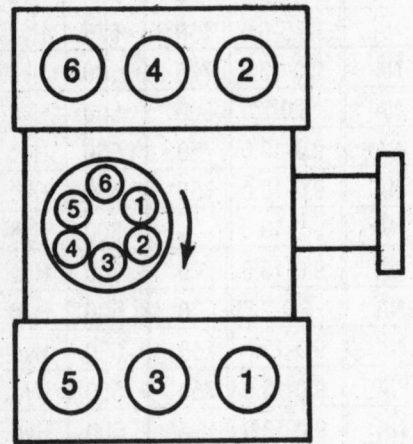

Chevrolet-built 173-V6 engine
Engine firing order: 1-2-3-4-5-6
Distributor rotation: clockwise

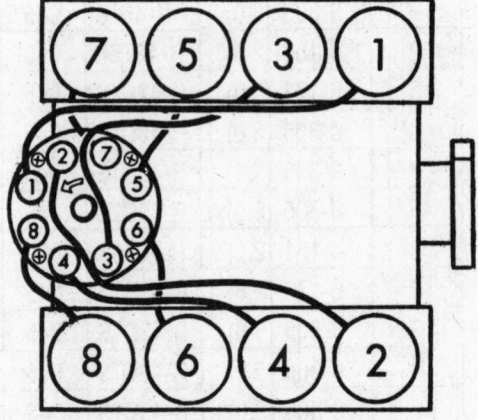

Pontiac-built V8 engines
Engine firing order: 1-8-4-3-6-5-7-2
Distributor rotation: counterclockwise

CAPACITIES

Year	VIN	No. Cylinder Displacement cu. in. (liter)	Engine Crankcase with Filter	Engine Crankcase without Filter	Transmission (pts.) MT	Transmission (pts.) AT	Drive Axle (pts.)	Fuel Tank (gals.)	Cooling System (qts.)
1982	2	4-151 (2.5)	3.5	3	4.3 ②	8.5 ①	3.5	16	13
	1	6-173 (2.8)	4	4	4.3 ②	8.5 ①	3.5	16	13
	H	8-305 (5.0)	5	4	4.3 ②	8.5 ①	3.5	16	17
	7	8-350 (5.7)	5	4	4.3 ②	8.5 ①	3.5	16	16
1983	F	4-151 (2.5)	3.5	3	4.3 ②	8.5 ①	3.5	16	13
	2	4-151 (2.5)	3.5	3	4.3 ②	8.5 ①	3.5	16	13
	1	6-173 (2.8)	4	4	4.3 ②	8.5 ①	3.5	16	13

CAPACITIES

Year	VIN	No. Cylinder Displacement cu. in. (liter)	Engine Crankcase with Filter	Engine Crankcase without Filter	Transmission (pts.) MT	Transmission (pts.) AT	Drive Axle (pts.)	Fuel Tank (gals.)	Cooling System (qts.)
1983	L	6-173 (2.8)	5	4	4.3 ②	8.5 ①	3.5	16	13
	S	8-305 (5.0)	5	4	4.3 ②	8.5 ①	3.5	16	16
	H	8-305 (5.0)	5	4	4.3 ②	8.5 ①	3.5	16	17
1984	F	4-151 (2.5)	3.5	3	3.5 ③	8.5 ①	3.5	16	9
	2	4-151 (2.5)	3.5	3	3.5 ③	8.5 ①	3.5	16	9
	1	6-173 (2.8)	4	4	3.5 ③	8.5 ①	3.5	16	13
	G	8-305 (5.0)	5	4	3.5 ③	8.5 ①	3.5	16	17
	H	8-305 (5.0)	5	4	3.5 ③	8.5 ①	3.5	16	9
1985	2	4-151 (2.5)	3.5	3	3.5 ③	8.5 ①	3.5	16	9
	S	6-173 (2.8)	4	4	3.5 ③	8.5 ①	3.5	16	15
	G	8-305 (5.0)	5	4	3.5 ③	8.5 ①	3.5	16	17
	H	8-305 (5.0)	5	4	3.5 ③	8.5 ①	3.5	16	17
	F	8-305 (5.00	5	4	3.5 ③	8.5 ①	3.5	16	17
1986	2	4-151 (2.5)	3.5	3	3.5 ③	8.5 ①	3.5	16	9
	S	6-173 (2.8)	4	4	3.5 ③	8.5 ①	3.5	16	15
	G	8-305 (5.0)	5	4	3.5 ③	8.5 ①	3.5	16	17
	H	8-305 (5.0)	5	4	3.5 ③	8.5 ①	3.5	16	17
	F	8-305 (5.00	5	4	3.5 ③	8.5 ①	3.5	16	17
	8	8-350 (5.7)	5	4	3.5 ③	8.5 ①	3.5	16	17
1987	S	6-173 (2.8)	4	4	3.5 ③	8.5 ①	3.5	16	13
	H	8-305 (5.0)	5	4	3.5 ③	8.5 ①	3.5	16	17
	F	8-305 (5.00	5	4	3.5 ③	8.5 ①	3.5	16	17
	8	8-350 (5.7)	5	4	3.5 ③	8.5 ①	3.5	16	17
1988-89	S	6-173 (2.8)	4	4	3.5 ③	8.5 ①	3.5	16	13
	F	8-305 (5.0)	5	4	3.5 ③	8.5 ①	3.5	16	17
	E	8-305 (5.0)	5	4	3.5 ③	8.5 ①	3.5	16	15.5
	8	8-305 (5.7)	5	4	3.5 ③	8.5 ①	3.5	16	17

① 10.0 if equipped with overdrive   ② 5.3 if equipped with overdrive   ③ 6.6 if equipped with overdrive

CAMSHAFT SPECIFICATIONS
All measurements given in inches.

Year	VIN	No. Cylinder Displacement cu. in. (liter)	Journal Diameter 1	2	3	4	5	Lobe Lift In.	Lobe Lift Ex.	Bearing Clearance	Camshaft End Play
1982	2	4-151 (2.5)	1.8690	1.8690	1.8690	1.8690	1.8690	.2350	.2660	NA	.004–.012
	1	6-173 (2.8)	1.8976–1.8996	1.8976–1.8996	1.8976–1.8996	1.8976–1.8996	1.8976–1.8996	.2380	.2600	NA	.004–.012
	H	8-305 (5.0)	1.8682–1.8692	1.8682–1.8692	1.8682–1.8692	1.8682–1.8692	1.8682–1.8692	.2600	.2730	NA	.004–.012

CAMSHAFT SPECIFICATIONS
All measurements given in inches.

Year	VIN	No. Cylinder Displacement cu. in. (liter)	Journal Diameter 1	2	3	4	5	Lobe Lift In.	Ex.	Bearing Clearance	Camshaft End Play
1982	7	8-350 (5.7)	1.8682–1.8692	1.8682–1.8692	1.8682–1.8692	1.8682–1.8692	1.8682–1.8692	.2600	.2730	NA	.004–.012
1983	F	4-151 (2.5)	1.8690	1.8690	1.8690	1.8690	1.8690	.3980	.3980	NA	.0015–.0050
	2	4-151 (2.5)	1.8690	1.8690	1.8960	1.8960	1.8960	.3980	.3980	NA	.0015–.0050
	1	6-173 (2.8)	1.8976–1.8996	1.8976–1.8996	1.8976–1.8996	1.8976–1.8996	1.8976–1.8996	.2350	.2660	NA	NA
	L	6-173 (2.8)	1.8976–1.8996	1.8976–1.8996	1.8976–1.8996	1.8976–1.8996	1.8976–1.8996	.2350	.2660	NA	NA
	S	8-305 (5.0)	1.8682–1.8692	1.8682–1.8692	1.8682–1.8692	1.8682–1.8692	1.8682–1.8692	.2340 ①②	.2570 ①②	NA	.004–.012
	H	8-305 (5.0)	1.8682–1.8692	1.8682–1.8692	1.8682–1.8692	1.8682–1.8692	1.8682–1.8692	.2340 ①②	.2570 ①②	NA	.004–.012
1984	F	4-151 (2.5)	1.8690	1.8690	1.8690	1.8690	1.8690	.3980	.3980	NA	.0015–.0050
	2	4-151 (2.5)	1.8690	1.8690	1.8960	1.8960	1.8960	.3980	.3980	NA	.0015–.0050
	1	6-173 (2.8)	1.8976–1.8996	1.8976–1.8996	1.8976–1.8996	1.8976–1.8996	1.8976–1.8996	.2350	.2660	NA	NA
	G	8-305 (5.0)	1.8682–1.8692	1.8682–1.8692	1.8682–1.8692	1.8682–1.8692	1.8682–1.8692	.2340 ①②	.2570 ①②	NA	.004–.012
	H	8-305 (5.0)	1.8682–1.8692	1.8682–1.8692	1.8682–1.8692	1.8682–1.8692	1.8682–1.8692	.2340 ①②	.2570 ①②	NA	.004–.012
1985	2	4-151 (2.5)	1.8690	1.8690	1.8960	1.8960	1.8960	.3980	.3980	NA	.0015–.0050
	S	6-173 (2.8)	1.8976–1.8996	1.8976–1.8996	1.8976–1.8996	1.8976–1.8996	1.8976–1.8996	.2350	.2660	NA	NA
	G	8-305 (5.0)	1.8682–1.8692	1.8682–1.8692	1.8682–1.8692	1.8682–1.8692	1.8682–1.8692	.2340 ①②	.2570 ①②	NA	.004–.012
	H	8-305 (5.0)	1.8682–1.8692	1.8682–1.8692	1.8682–1.8692	1.8682–1.8692	1.8682–1.8692	.2340 ①②	.2570 ①②	NA	.004–.012
	F	8-305 (5.0)	1.8682–1.8692	1.8682–1.8692	1.8682–1.8692	1.8682–1.8692	1.8682–1.8692	.2340 ①②	.2570 ①②	NA	.004–.012
1986	2	4-151 (2.5)	1.8690	1.8690	1.8960	1.8960	1.8960	.3980	.3980	NA	.0015–.0050
	S	6-173 (2.8)	1.8976–1.8996	1.8976–1.8996	1.8976–1.8996	1.8976–1.8996	1.8976–1.8996	.2350	.2660	NA	NA
	G	8-305 (5.0)	1.8682–1.8692	1.8682–1.8692	1.8682–1.8692	1.8682–1.8692	1.8682–1.8692	.2340 ①②	.2570 ①②	NA	.004–.012
	H	8-305 (5.0)	1.8682–1.8692	1.8682–1.8692	1.8682–1.8692	1.8682–1.8692	1.8682–1.8692	.2340 ①②	.2570 ①②	NA	.004–.012
	F	8-305 (5.0)	1.8682–1.8692	1.8682–1.8692	1.8682–1.8692	1.8682–1.8692	1.8682–1.8692	.2340 ①②	.2570 ①②	NA	.004–.012

CAMSHAFT SPECIFICATIONS
All measurements given in inches.

Year	VIN	No. Cylinder Displacement cu. in. (liter)	Journal Diameter					Lobe Lift		Bearing Clearance	Camshaft End Play
			1	2	3	4	5	In.	Ex.		
1986	8	8-350 (5.7)	1.8682–1.8692	1.8682–1.8692	1.8682–1.8692	1.8682–1.8962	1.8682–1.8962	.2730	.2828	NA	.004–.012
1987	S	6-173 (2.8)	1.8976–1.8996	1.8976–1.8996	1.8976–1.8996	1.8976–1.8996	1.8976–1.8996	.2350	.2660	NA	NA
	H	8-305 (5.0)	1.8682–1.8692	1.8682–1.8692	1.8682–1.8692	1.8682–1.8692	1.8682–1.8692	.2340 ①②	.2570 ①②	NA	.004–.012
	F	8-305 (5.0)	1.8682–1.8692	1.8682–1.8692	1.8682–1.8692	1.8682–1.8692	1.8682–1.8692	.2340 ①②	.2570 ①②	NA	.004–.012
	8	8-350 (5.7)	1.8682–1.8692	1.8682–1.8692	1.8682–1.8692	1.8682–1.8962	1.8682–1.8962	.2730	.2828	NA	.004–.012
1988-89	S	6-173 (2.8)	1.8976–1.8996	1.8976–1.8996	1.8976–1.8996	1.8976–1.8996	1.8976–1.8996	.2350	.2660	NA	NA
	F	8-305 (5.0)	1.8682–1.8692	1.8682–1.8692	1.8682–1.8692	1.8682–1.8692	1.8682–1.8692	.2690	.2760	NA	.004–.012
	E	8-305 (5.0)	1.8682–1.8692	1.8682–1.8692	1.8682–1.8692	1.8682–1.8692	1.8682–1.8692	.2340	.2570	NA	.004–.012
	8	8-350 (5.7)	1.8682–1.8692	1.8682–1.8692	1.8682–1.8692	1.8682–1.8692	1.8682–1.8692	.2730	.2820	NA	.004–.012

① TBI — .2570-Intake; .2690-Exhaust
② 4 bbl HO — .2690-Intake; .2760-Exhaust

CRANKSHAFT AND CONNECTING ROD SPECIFICATIONS
All measurements are given in inches.

Year	VIN	No. Cylinder Displacement cu. in. (liter)	Crankshaft				Connecting Rod		
			Main Brg. Journal Dia.	Main Brg. Oil Clearance	Shaft End-play	Thrust on No.	Journal Diameter	Oil Clearance	Side Clearance
1982	2	4-151 (2.5)	2.300	.0005–.0022	.0035–.0085	5	2.000	.0014 .0035	.0060 .0220
	1	6-173 (2.8)	2.4930–2.4940	.0017–.0029	.0019–.0066	3	1.998–1.998	.0018–.0039	.0060–.0170
	H	8-305 (5.0)	①	②	.0020–.0060	5	2.098–2.099	.0018–.0039	.0080–.0140
	7	8-305 (5.7)	①	②	.0020–.0060	5	2.098–2.099	.0018–.0039	.0080–.0140
1983	F	4-151 (2.5)	2.300	.0005–.0022	.0035–.0085	5	2.000	.0005–.0026	.0060–.0020
	2	4-151 (2.5)	2.300	.0005–.0022	.0035–.0085	5	2.000	.0005–.0026	.0060–.0020
	1	6-173 (2.8)	2.4930–2.4940	.0017–.0029	.0019–.0066	3	1.998–1.998	.0018–.0039	.0060–.0170
	L	6-173 (2.8)	2.4930–2.4940	.0017–.0029	.0019–.0066	3	1.998–1.998	.0018–.0039	.0060–.0170

CRANKSHAFT AND CONNECTING ROD SPECIFICATIONS
All measurements are given in inches.

Year	VIN	No. Cylinder Displacement cu. in. (liter)	Crankshaft				Connecting Rod		
			Main Brg. Journal Dia.	Main Brg. Oil Clearance	Shaft End-play	Thrust on No.	Journal Diameter	Oil Clearance	Side Clearance
1983	S	8-305 (5.0)	①	②	.0020–.0060	5	2.098–2.099	.0018–.0039	.0080–.0140
	H	8-305 (5.0)	①	②	.0020–.0060	5	2.098–2.099	.0018–.0039	.0080–.0140
1984	F	4-151 (2.5)	2.300	.0005–.0022	.0035–.0085	5	2.000	.0005–.0026	.0060–.0020
	2	4-151 (2.5)	2.300	.0005–.0022	.0035–.0085	5	2.000	.0005–.0026	.0060–.0020
	1	6-173 (2.8)	2.4930–2.4940	.0017–.0029	.0019–.0066	3	1.998–1.998	.0018–.0039	.0060–.0170
	G	8-305 (5.0)	①	②	.0020–.0060	5	2.098–2.099	.0018–.0039	.0080–.0140
	H	8-305 (5.0)	①	②	.0020–.0060	5	2.098–2.099	.0018–.0039	.0080–.0140
1985	2	4-151 (2.5)	2.300	.0005–.0022	.0035–.0085	5	2.000	.0005–.0026	.0060–.0020
	S	6-173 (2.8)	2.493–2.494	.0017–.0029	.0019–.0066	3	1.998–1.999	.0014–.0035	.0060–.0170
	G	8-305 (5.0)	①	②	.0020–.0060	5	2.098–2.099	.0018–.0039	.0080–.0140
	H	8-305 (5.0)	①	②	.0020–.0060	5	2.098–2.099	.0018–.0039	.0080–.0140
	F	8-305 (5.0)	①	②	.0020–.0060	5	2.098–2.099	.0018–.0039	.0080–.0140
1986	2	4-151 (2.5)	2.300	.0005–.0022	.0035–.0085	5	2.000	.0005–.0026	.0060–.0020
	S	6-173 (2.8)	2.493–2.494	.0017–.0029	.0019–.0066	3	1.998–1.999	.0014–.0035	.0060–.0170
	G	8-305 (5.0)	①	②	.0020–.0060	5	2.098–2.099	.0018–.0039	.0080–.0140
	H	8-305 (5.0)	①	②	.0020–.0060	5	2.098–2.099	.0018–.0039	.0080–.0140
	F	8-305 (5.0)	①	②	.0020–.0060	5	2.098–2.099	.0018–.0039	.0080–.0140
	8	8-305 (5.0)	①	②	.0020–.0060	5	2.098–2.099	.0018–.0039	.0080–.0140
1987	S	6-173 (2.8)	2.493–2.494	.0017–.0029	.0019–.0066	3	1.998–1.999	.0014–.0035	.0060–.0170
	H	8-305 (5.0)	①	②	.0020–.0060	5	2.098–2.099	.0018–.0039	.0080–.0140
	F	8-305 (5.0)	①	②	.0020–.0060	5	2.098–2.099	.0018–.0039	.0080–.0140
	8	8-305 (5.0)	①	②	.0020–.0060	5	2.098–2.099	.0013–.0035	.0060–.0140

CRANKSHAFT AND CONNECTING ROD SPECIFICATIONS
All measurements are given in inches.

Year	VIN	No. Cylinder Displacement cu. in. (liter)	Crankshaft				Connecting Rod		
			Main Brg. Journal Dia.	Main Brg. Oil Clearance	Shaft End-play	thrust on No.	Journal Diameter	Oil Clearance	Side Clearance
1988-89	S	6-173 (2.8)	2.493–2.494	.0017–.0029	.0019–.0066	3	1.998–1.999	.0014–.0035	.0060–.0170
	F	8-305 (5.0)	①	②	.0020–.0060	5	2.098–2.099	.0018–.0039	.0080–.0140
	E	8-305 (5.0)	①	②	.0020–.0060	5	2.098–2.099	.0018–.0039	.0080–.0140
	8	8-305 (5.0)	①	②	.0020–.0060	5	2.098–2.099	.0013–.0035	.0060–.0140

① No. 1 – 2.4484–2.4493
   Nos. 2, 3, 4 – 2.4481–2.4490
   No. 5 – 2.4479–2.4488

② No. 1 – .000–.0020
   Nos. 2, 3, 4 – .0011–.0023
   No. 5 – .0-017–.0032

VALVE SPECIFICATIONS

Year	VIN	No. Cylinder Displacement cu. in. (liter)	Seat Angle (deg.)	Face Angle (deg.)	Spring Test Pressure (lbs.)	Spring Installed Height (in.)	Stem-to-Guide Clearance (in.)		Stem Diameter (in.)	
							Intake	Exhaust	Intake	Exhaust
1982	2	4-151 (2.5)	46	45	122-180 @ 1.25	1.69	.0010–.0027	.0010–.0027	.3418–.3425	.3418–.3425
	1	6-173 (2.8)	46	45	194 @ 1.18	1.57	.0010–.0027	.0010–.0027	.3410–.3420	.3410–.3420
	H	8-305 (5.0)	46	45	198-206 @ 1.25	1²³⁄₃₂	.0010–.0027	.0010–.0027	.3410–.3420	.3410–.3420
	7	8-350 (5.7)	46	45	194-206 @ 1.25	1²³⁄₃₂	.0010–.0027	.0010–.0027	.3410–.3420	.3410–.3420
1983	F	4-151 (2.5)	46	45	122-180 @ 1.25	1.69	.0010–.0027	.0010–.0027	.3418–.3425	.3418–.3425
	2	4-151 (2.5)	46	45	122-180 @ 1.25	1.69	.0010–.0027	.0010–.0027	.3418–.3425	.3418–.3425
	1	6-173 (2.8)	46	45	194 @ 1.18	1.57	.0010–.0027	.0010–.0027	.3410–.3420	.3410–.3240
	L	6-173 (2.8)	46	45	194 @ 1.18	1.57	.0010–.0027	.0010–.0027	.3410–.3420	.3410–.3240
	S	8-305 (5.0)	46	45	194-206 @ 1.25	1²³⁄₃₂	.0010–.0027	.0010–.0027	.3410–.3420	.3410–.3420
	H	8-305 (5.0)	46	45	194-206 @ 1.25	1²³⁄₃₂	.0010–.0027	.0010–.0027	.3410–.3420	.3410–.3420
1984	F	4-151 (2.5)	46	45	122-180 @ 1.25	1.69	.0010–.0027	.0010–.0027	.3418–.3425	.3418–.3425
	2	4-151 (2.5)	46	45	122-180 @ 1.25	1.69	.0010–.0027	.0010–.0027	.3418–.3425	.3418–.3425
	1	6-173 (2.8)	46	45	194 @ 1.18	1.57	.0010–.0027	.0010–.0027	.3410–.3420	.3410–.3240

VALVE SPECIFICATIONS

Year	VIN	No. Cylinder Displacement cu. in. (liter)	Seat Angle (deg.)	Face Angle (deg.)	Spring Test Pressure (lbs.)	Spring Installed Height (in.)	Stem-to-Guide Clearance (in.) Intake	Exhaust	Stem Diameter (in.) Intake	Exhaust
1984	G	8-305 (5.0)	46	45	194-206 @ 1.25	$1\frac{23}{32}$	.0010–.0027	.0010–.0027	.3410–.3420	.3410–.3420
	H	8-305 (5.0)	46	45	194-206 @ 1.25	$1\frac{23}{32}$	.0010–.0027	.0010–.0027	.3410–.3420	.3410–.3420
1985	2	4-151 (2.5)	46	45	122-180 @ 1.25	1.69	.0010–.0027	.0010–.0027	.3418–.3425	.3418–.3425
	S	6-173 (2.8)	46	45	194 @ 1.18	1.57	.0010–.0027	.3410–.0027	.0010–.3420	.3410–.3420
	G	8-305 (5.0)	46	45	194-206 @ 1.25	$1\frac{23}{32}$	.0010–.0027	.0010–.0027	.3410–.3420	.3410–.3420
	H	8-305 (5.0)	46	45	194-206 @ 1.25	$1\frac{23}{32}$	.0010–.0027	.0010–.0027	.3410–.3420	.3410–.3420
	F	8-305 (5.0)	46	45	194-206 @ 1.25	$1\frac{23}{32}$	.0010–.0027	.0010–.0027	.3410–.3420	.3410–.3420
1986	2	4-151 (2.5)	46	45	122-180 @ 1.25	1.69	.0010–.0027	.0010–.0027	.3418–.3425	.3418–.3425
	S	6-173 (2.8)	46	45	194 @ 1.18	1.57	.0010–.0027	.3410–.0027	.0010–.3420	.3410–.3420
	G	8-305 (5.0)	46	45	194-206 @ 1.25	$1\frac{23}{32}$	.0010–.0027	.0010–.0027	.3410–.3420	.3410–.3420
	H	8-305 (5.0)	46	45	194-206 @ 1.25	$1\frac{23}{32}$	.0010–.0027	.0010–.0027	.3410–.3420	.3410–.3420
	F	8-305 (5.0)	46	45	194-206 @ 1.25	$1\frac{23}{32}$	.0010–.0027	.0010–.0027	.3410–.3420	.3410–.3420
	8	8-350 (5.7)	46	45	194-206 @ 1.25	$1\frac{23}{32}$	.0010–.0027	.0010–.0027	.3410–.3420	.3410–.3420
1987	S	6-173 (2.8)	46	45	194 @ 1.18	1.57	.0010–.0027	.3410–.0027	.0010–.3420	.3410–.3420
	H	8-305 (5.0)	46	45	194-206 @ 1.25	$1\frac{23}{32}$	.0010–.0027	.0010–.0027	.3410–.3420	.3410–.3420
	F	8-305 (5.0)	46	45	194-206 @ 1.25	$1\frac{23}{32}$	.0010–.0027	.0010–.0027	.3410–.3420	.3410–.3420
	8	8-350 (5.7)	46	45	194-206 @ 1.25	$1\frac{23}{32}$	.0010–.0027	.0010–.0027	.3410–.3420	.3410–.3420
1988-89	S	6-173 (2.8)	46	45	194 @ 1.18	1.57	.0010–.0027	.3410–.0027	.0010–.3420	.3410–.3420
	E	8-305 (5.0)	46	45	194-206 @ 1.25	①	.0010–.0027	.0010–.0027	.3410–.3420	.3410–.3420
	F	8-305 (5.0)	46	45	194-206 @ 1.25	①	.0010–.0027	.0010–.0027	.3410–.3420	.3410–.3420
	8	8-350 (5.7)	46	45	194-206 @ 1.25	①	.0010–.0027	.0010–.0027	.3410–.3420	.3410–.3420

① Intake — $1\frac{23}{32}$
Exhaust — $1\frac{19}{32}$

PISTON AND RING SPECIFICATIONS

All measurments are given in inches.

Year	VIN	No. Cylinder Displacement cu. in. (liter)	Piston Clearance	Ring Gap			Ring Side Clearance		
				Top Compression	Bottom Compression	Oil Control	Top Compression	Bottom Compression	Oil Control
1982	2	4-151 (2.5)	NA	.0100–.0200	.0100–.0270	.0150–.0550	.0015–.0030	.0015–.0030	.0010–.0050
	1	6-173 (2.8)	NA	.0098–.0196	.0098–.0196	.0020–.0550	.0011–.0027	.0015–.0037	.0078 Max.
	H	8-305 (5.0)	NA	.0100–.0200	.0100–.0250	.0150–.0550	.0012–.0032	.0012–.0032	.0020–.0070
	7	8-350 (5.7)	NA	.0100–.0200	.0100–.0250	.0150–.0550	.0012–.0032	.0012–.0032	.0020–.0070
1983	F	4-151 (2.5)	NA	.0100–.0200	.0100–.0270	.0150–.0550	.0015–.0030	.0015–.0030	.0010–.0050
	2	4-151 (2.5)	NA	.0100–.0200	.0100–.0270	.0150–.0550	.0015–.0030	.0015–.0030	.0010–.0050
	1	6-173 (2.8)	NA	.0098–.0196	.0098–.0196	.0020–.0550	.0011–.0027	.0015–.0037	.0078 Max.
	L	6-173 (2.8)	NA	.0098–.0196	.0098–.0196	.0020–.0550	.0011–.0027	.0015–.0037	.0078 Max.
	S	8-305 (5.0)	NA	.0100–.0200	.0100–.0250	.0150–.0550	.0012–.0032	.0012–.0032	.0020–.0070
	H	8-305 (5.0)	NA	.0100–.0200	.0100–.0250	.0150–.0550	.0012–.0032	.0012–.0032	.0020–.0070
1984	F	4-151 (2.5)	NA	.0100–.0200	.0100–.0270	.0150–.0550	.0015–.0030	.0015–.0030	.0010–.0050
	2	4-151 (2.5)	NA	.0100–.0200	.0100–.0270	.0150–.0550	.0015–.0030	.0015–.0030	.0010–.0050
	1	6-173 (2.8)	NA	.0098–.0196	.0098–.0196	.0020–.0550	.0011–.0027	.0015–.0037	.0078 Max.
	G	8-305 (5.0)	NA	.0100–.0200	.0100–.0250	.0150–.0550	.0012–.0032	.0012–.0032	.0020–.0070
	H	8-305 (5.0)	NA	.0100–.0200	.0100–.0250	.0150–.0550	.0012–.0032	.0012–.0032	.0020–.0070
1985	2	4-151 (2.5)	NA	.0100–.0200	.0100–.0270	.0150–.0550	.0015–.0030	.0015–.0030	.0010–.0050
	S	6-173 (2.8)	NA	.0098–.0196	.0098–.0196	.0020–.0550	.0011–.0027	.0015–.0037	.0078 Max.
	G	8-305 (5.0)	NA	.0100–.0200	.0100–.0250	.0150–.0550	.0012–.0032	.0012–.0032	.0020–.0076
	H	8-305 (5.0)	NA	.0100–.0200	.0100–.0250	.0150–.0550	.0012–.0032	.0012–.0032	.0020–.0076
	F	8-305 (5.0)	NA	.0100–.0200	.0100–.0250	.0150–.0550	.0012–.0032	.0012–.0032	.0020–.0076
1986	2	4-151 (2.5)	NA	.0100–.0200	.0100–.0270	.0150–.0550	.0015–.0030	.0015–.0030	.0010–.0050
	S	6-173 (2.8)	NA	.0098–.0196	.0098–.0196	.0020–.0550	.0011–.0027	.0015–.0037	.0078 Max.

PISTON AND RING SPECIFICATIONS
All measurments are given in inches.

Year	VIN	No. Cylinder Displacement cu. in. (liter)	Piston Clearance	Ring Gap			Ring Side Clearance		
				Top Compression	Bottom Compression	Oil Control	Top Compression	Bottom Compression	Oil Control
1986	G	8-305 (5.0)	NA	.0100–.0200	.0100–.0250	.0150–.0550	.0012–.0032	.0012–.0032	.0020–.0076
	H	8-305 (5.0)	NA	.0100–.0200	.0100–.0250	.0150–.0550	.0012–.0032	.0012–.0032	.0020–.0076
	F	8-305 (5.0)	NA	.0100–.0200	.0100–.0250	.0150–.0550	.0012–.0032	.0012–.0032	.0020–.0076
	8	8-305 (5.0)	NA	.0100–.0200	.0100–.0250	.0150–.0550	.0012–.0032	.0012–.0032	.0020–.0076
1987	S	6-173 (2.8)	NA	.0098–.0196	.0098–.0196	.0020–.0550	.0011–.0027	.0015–.0037	.0078 Max.
	H	8-305 (5.0)	NA	.0100–.0200	.0100–.0250	.0150–.0550	.0012–.0032	.0012–.0032	.0020–.0070
	F	8-305 (5.0)	NA	.0100–.0200	.0100–.0250	.0150–.0550	.0012–.0032	.0012–.0032	.0020–.0070
	8	8-305 (5.0)	NA	.0100–.0200	.0100–.0250	.0150–.0550	.0012–.0032	.0012–.0032	.0020–.0070
1988-89	S	6-173 (2.8)	NA	.0098–.0196	.0098–.0196	.0020–.0550	.0011–.0027	.0015–.0037	.0078 Max.
	F	8-305 (5.0)	NA	.0100–.0200	.0100–.0250	.0150–.0550	.0012–.0032	.0012–.0032	.0020–.0070
	E	8-305 (5.0)	NA	.0100–.0200	.0100–.0250	.0150–.0550	.0012–.0032	.0012–.0032	.0020–.0070
	8	8-350 (5.7)	NA	.0100–.0200	.0100–.0250	.0150–.0550	.0012–.0032	.0012–.0032	.0020–.0070

TORQUE SPECIFICATIONS
All readings in ft. lbs.

Year	VIN	No. Cylinder Displacement cu. in. (liter)	Cylinder Head Bolts	Main Bearing Bolts	Rod Bearing Bolts	Crankshaft Pulley Bolts	Flywheel Bolts	Manifold		Spark Plugs
								Intake	Exhaust	
1982	2	4-151 (2.5)	85	70	32	160	44	15	44	15-20
	1	6-173 (2.8)	70	70	37	75	50	23	25	15-20
	H	8-305 (5.0)	65	70	45	60	60	30	20	15-20
	7	8-350 (5.7)	65	70	45	60	60	30	20	15-20
1983	F	4-151 (2.5)	85	70	32	160	44	30	44	15-20
	2	4-151 (2.5)	85	70	32	160	44	15	44	15-20
	1	6-173 (2.8)	70	70	37	75	50	23	25	15-20
	L	6-173 (2.8)	70	70	37	75	50	23	25	15-20
	S	8-305 (5.0)	65	70	45	60	60	30	20	15-20
	H	8-305 (5.0)	65	70	45	60	60	30	20	15-20

TORQUE SPECIFICATIONS
All readings in ft. lbs.

Year	VIN	No. Cylinder Displacement cu. in. (liter)	Cylinder Head Bolts	Main Bearing Bolts	Rod Bearing Bolts	Crankshaft Pulley Bolts	Flywheel Bolts	Manifold Intake	Manifold Exhaust	Spark Plugs
1984	F	4-151 (2.5)	85	70	32	160	44	30	44	15-20
	2	4-151 (2.5)	85	70	32	160	44	15	44	15-20
	1	6-173 (2.8)	70	70	37	75	50	23	25	15-20
	G	8-305 (5.0)	65	70	45	60	60	30	20	15-20
	H	8-305 (5.0)	65	70	45	60	60	30	20	15-20
1985	2	4-151 (2.5)	92	70	32	200	44	15	44	15-20
	S	6-173 (2.8)	③	83	34-45	75	50	13-25	19-31	7-15
	G	8-305 (5.0)	60-75	60-75	42-47	60	65	25-45	②	15-20
	H	8-305 (5.0)	60-75	60-75	42-47	60	65	25-45	②	15-20
	F	8-305 (5.0)	60-75	60-75	42-47	60	65	25-45	②	15-20
1986	2	4-151 (2.5)	92	70	32	200	44	15	44	15-20
	S	6-173 (2.8)	③	83	34-45	75	50	13-25	19-31	7-15
	G	8-305 (5.0)	65-90	①	42-47	60	75	25-45	②	15-20
	H	8-305 (5.0)	65-90	①	42-47	60	75	25-45	②	15-20
	F	8-305 (5.0)	65-90	①	42-47	60	75	25-45	②	15-20
	8	8-350 (5.7)	65-90	①	42-47	60	75	25-45	②	15-20
1987	S	6-173 (2.8)	③	63-83	34-45	75	50	13-25	25	7-15
	H	8-305 (5.0)	60-70	63-85	42-47	60	75	25-45	②	15-20
	F	8-305 (5.0)	60-75	63-85	42-47	60	75	25-45	②	15-20
	8	8-350 (5.7)	60-75	63-85	42-47	60	75	25-45	②	15-20
1988-89	S	6-173 (2.8)	④	63-83	34-45	75	50	13-25	19-31	7-15
	F	8-305 (5.0)	60-75	63-85	42-47	60	75	25-45	②	15-20
	E	8-305 (5.0)	60-75	63-85	42-47	60	75	25-45	②	15-20
	8	8-350 (5.7)	60-75	63-85	42-47	60	75	25-45	②	15-20

① Inner—70-85
   Outer—60-75
② Outer bolts—14-26
   Inner bolts—20-32
③ Torque in 2 steps:
   1st step—Tighten to 40 ft. lbs.
   2nd step—Rotate wrench an additional 90 degrees

BRAKE SPECIFICATIONS
All measurements in inches unless noted

Year	Model	Lug Nut Torque (ft. lbs.)	Master Cylinder Bore	Brake Disc Minimum Thickness	Brake Disc Maximum Runout	Standard Brake Drum Diameter	Minimum Lining Thickness Front	Minimum Lining Thickness Rear
1982	Camaro, Firebird	80 ②	NA	.965	.004	9.500	.030	.030①③
1983	Camaro, Firebird	80 ②	NA	.965	.004	9.500	.030	.030①③
1984	Camaro, Firebird	80 ②	NA	.965	.004	9.500	.030	.030①③

BRAKE SPECIFICATIONS
All measurements in inches unless noted

Year	Model	Lug Nut Torque (ft. lbs.)	Master Cylinder Bore	Brake Disc		Standard Brake Drum Diameter	Minimum Lining Thickness	
				Minimum Thickness	Maximum Runout		Front	Rear
1985	Camaro, Firebird	80 ②	NA	.965	.004	9.500	.030	.030①③
1986	Camaro, Firebird	80	NA	.965	.005	9.500	.030	.030①③
1987	Camaro, Firebird	80	NA	.965	.005	9.500	.030	.030①③
1988-89	Camaro, Firebird	80	NA	.965	.005	9.500	.030	.030①③

① .062 bonded
② Aluminum wheels 105
③ Rear disc .030

WHEEL ALIGNMENT

Year	Model	Caster		Camber		Toe-in (in.)	Steering Axis Inclination (deg.)
		Range (deg.)	Preferred Setting (deg.)	Range (deg.)	Preferred Setting (deg.)		
1982	Camaro	2½P–3½P	3P	½P–1½P	1P	$7/32$P	NA
	Z28	2½P–3½P	3P	½P–1½P	1P	$5/32$P	NA
	Firebird	2½P–3½P	3	½P–1½P	1P	$1/16$P	NA
1983	Camaro	2P–4P	3P	$3/16$P–$1^{13}/16$P	1P	$7/32$P	NA
	Z28	2P–4P	3P	$3/16$P–$1^{13}/16$P	1P	$5/32$P	NA
	Firebird	2P–4P	3P	$3/16$P–$1^{13}/16$P	1P	$1/16$P	NA
1984	Camaro	2P–4P	3P	$3/16$P–$1^{13}/16$P	1P	$7/32$P	NA
	Z28	2P–4P	3P	$3/16$P–$1^{13}/16$P	1P	$5/32$P	NA
	Firebird	2P–4P	3P	$3/16$P–$1^{13}/16$P	1P	$1/16$P	NA
1985	Camaro	2½P–3½P	3P	½P–1½P	1P	$5/32$P	NA
	Z28	3P–3½P	4P	½P–1½P	1P	$1/16$P	NA
	Firebird	$2^5/16$P–$3^5/16$P	$2^{13}/16$P	½P–1½P	1P	$1/16$P	NA
1986	Camaro	2½P–3½P	3P	½P–1½P	1P	$5/32$P	NA
	Z28	3P–3½P	4P	½P–1½P	1P	$5/32$P	NA
	Firebird	3–3½	4	½–1½	1	$1/16$	NA
1987	Camaro, Firebird	4½P–5½P	5P	½P–1½P	1P	$3/64$P	NA
1988–89	Camaro, Firebird	4½P–5½P	5P	½N–1½P	0	$3/64$P	NA

NA Not available
P Positive
N Negative

TUNE-UP PROCEDURES

Ignition Timing
ADJUSTMENT

NOTE: On vehicles equipped with the LU5 V8 engine with TBI and on all 1986–88 vehicles it will be necessary to put the EST in the bypass mode by disconnecting the single wire timing connector. This wire is tan with a black tracer and breaks out of the wiring harness conduit near the rear of the right hand valve cover. Do not disconnect the four prong EST connector from the distributor assembly.

1. Refer to the vehicle control information label which is located on the radiator support panel, for the proper timing information.

2. If equipped, disconnect and plug the vacuum advance hose from the distributor. As required, disconnect the EST connector at the distributor assembly.

3. If the engine timing requires adjustment, loosen the distributor hold down bolt and rotate the distributor slowly in either direction, to advance or retard the engine timing.

4. Tighten the hold down bolt and recheck the engine timing.

5. Some engines incorporate a magnetic timing probe hole which is used when setting the engine timing with special electronic equipment. Consult manufacturer's instructions if using this form of timing equipment.

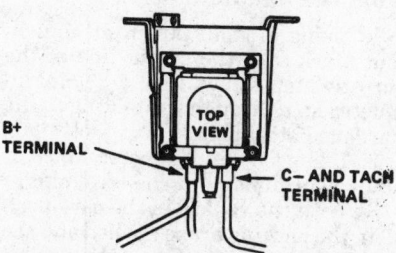

HEI external coil tachometer connection is opposite the BATT (B⁺) terminal

Valve Lash

ADJUSTMENT

Hydraulic valve lifters are used in all engines produced by General Motors Corporation. The following procedure is for Chevrolet produced engines only.

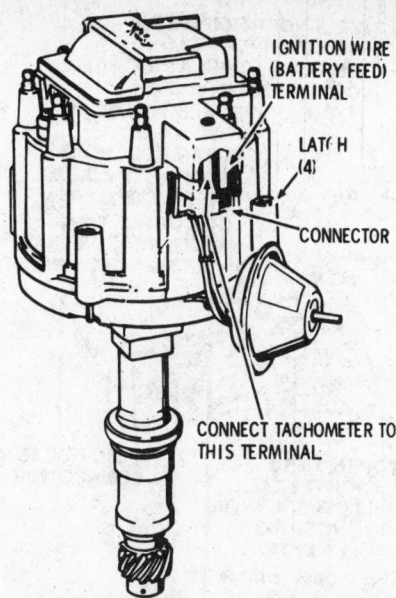

Typical coil in cap tachometer hookup

1. Disconnect the negative battery cable. Remove the valve covers.

2. Tighten the rocker arm nuts until all lash is eliminated.

3. Adjust the valves when the lifter is on the base circle of the camshaft lobe by cranking the engine until the mark on the vibration damper lines up with the center or 0 mark on the timing tab fastened to the crankcase front cover and the engine is in the No.1 firing position.

NOTE: This may be determined by placing your fingers on the No. 1 valve as the mark on the damper comes near the "0" mark on the crankcase front cover. If the valves move as the mark comes up to the timing tab, the engine is in the No. 6 (No. 4–V6) firing position and should be turned over one more time to reach to No. 1 firing position.

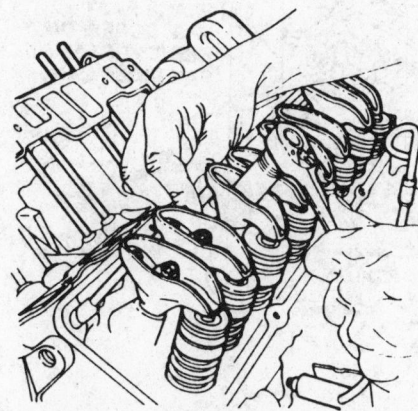

Typical valve adjustment procedure

4. With the engine in the No. 1 firing position, adjust the following valves:

V6 engine:
- exhaust — 1, 5, 6
- intake — 1, 2, 3

V8 engine:
- exhaust — 1, 3, 4, 8
- intake — 1, 2, 5, 7

5. Back out the adjusting nut until lash is felt at the push rod then turn in adjusting nut until all lash is removed. This can be determined by rotating push rod while turning adjusting nut. When play has been removed, turn adjusting nut in one full additional turn.

6. Crank the engine one revolution until the pointer 0 mark and the vibration damper mark are again in alignment. This is the No. 6 (No.4–V6) firing position.

7. With the engine in this position, adjust the following valves:

V6 engine:
- exhaust — 2, 3, 4
- intake — 4, 5, 6

V8 engine:
- exhaust — 2, 5, 6, 7
- intake — 3, 4, 6, 8

8. Install the rocker arm covers.

9. Start the engine and adjust the idle speed as required.

Idle Speed and Mixture

ADJUSTMENT

Carbureted Models

1982–84 VEHICLES WITH E2SE CARBURETOR

1. Refer to the emission label in the engine compartment and follow the instructions to prepare the vehicle for adjustment.

2. Place the A/T in **DRIVE** or the M/T in **NEUTRAL** and increase the enginr speed slightly to allow the solenoid plunger to fully extend.

3. Turn the solenoid screw to adjust the curb idle rpm, then disconnect the solenoid lead.

4. Turn the idle speed screw to set the basic idle speed. Reconnect the solenoid electrical lead after adjustment.

1982–88 VEHICLES WITH E4ME CARBURETOR

1. Run the engine until it reaches normal operating temperature. Make sure that the choke is open and the air conditioning is **OFF**.

2. Connect a tachometer and a timing light.

3. Set the parking brake and block the wheels.

4. Tag, disconnect and plug all carbon canister and EGR vacuum hoses.

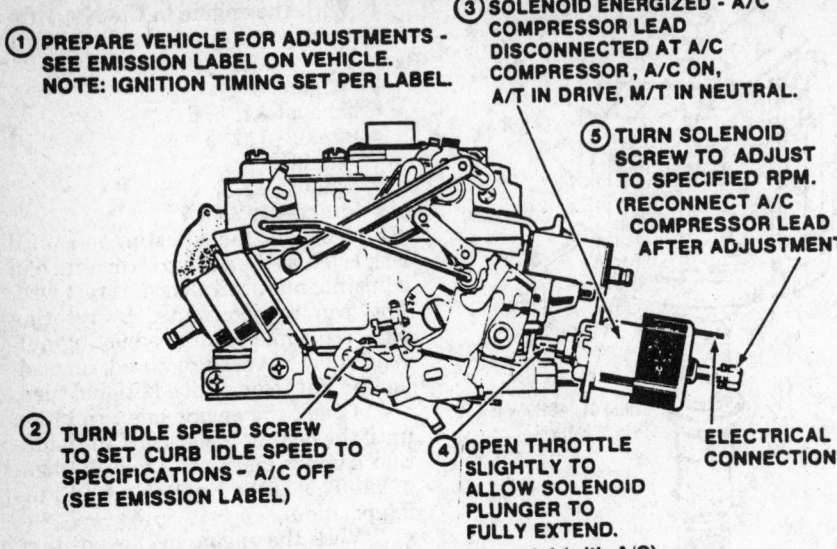

① PREPARE VEHICLE FOR ADJUSTMENTS - SEE EMISSION LABEL ON VEHICLE. NOTE: IGNITION TIMING SET PER LABEL.

③ SOLENOID ENERGIZED - A/C COMPRESSOR LEAD DISCONNECTED AT A/C COMPRESSOR, A/C ON, A/T IN DRIVE, M/T IN NEUTRAL.

⑤ TURN SOLENOID SCREW TO ADJUST TO SPECIFIED RPM. (RECONNECT A/C COMPRESSOR LEAD AFTER ADJUSTMENT).

② TURN IDLE SPEED SCREW TO SET CURB IDLE SPEED TO SPECIFICATIONS - A/C OFF (SEE EMISSION LABEL)

④ OPEN THROTTLE SLIGHTLY TO ALLOW SOLENOID PLUNGER TO FULLY EXTEND.

ELECTRICAL CONNECTION

Idle speed adjustment—E2SE model (with A/C)

① PREPARE VEHICLE FOR ADJUSTMENTS - SEE EMISSION LABEL ON VEHICLE. NOTE: IGNITION TIMING SET PER LABEL

④ TURN SOLENOID SCREW TO ADJUST CURB IDLE SPEED TO SPECIFIED RPM (SOLENOID ENERGIZED)

② SOLENOID ENERGIZED - A/T IN DRIVE, M/T IN NEUTRAL

⑥ TURN IDLE SPEED SCREW TO SET BASIC IDLE SPEED TO SPECIFICATIONS. RECONNECT SOLENOID ELECTRICAL LEAD AFTER ADJUSTMENT

③ OPEN THROTTLE SLIGHTLY TO ALLOW SOLENOID PLUNGER TO FULLY EXTEND

⑤ DISCONNECT ELECTRICAL LEAD TO DE-ENERGIZE SOLENOID

Idle speed adjustment—E2SE model (without A/C)

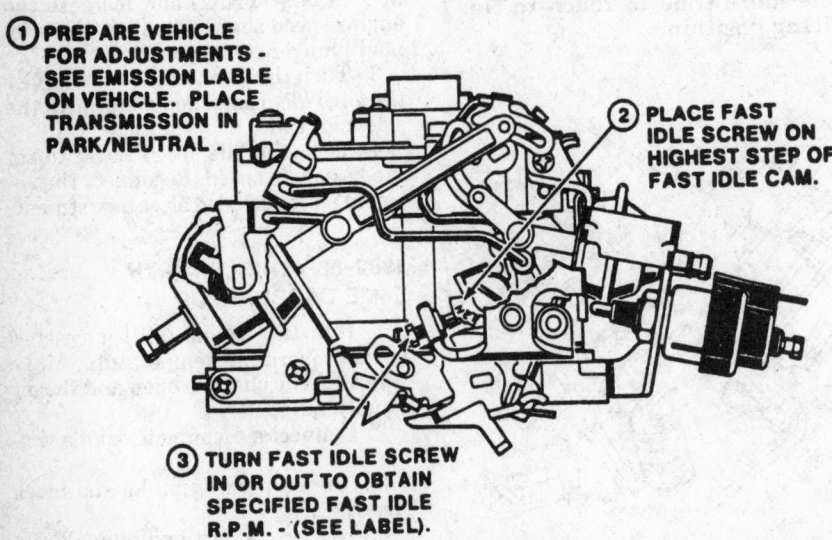

① PREPARE VEHICLE FOR ADJUSTMENTS - SEE EMISSION LABLE ON VEHICLE. PLACE TRANSMISSION IN PARK/NEUTRAL.

② PLACE FAST IDLE SCREW ON HIGHEST STEP OF FAST IDLE CAM.

③ TURN FAST IDLE SCREW IN OR OUT TO OBTAIN SPECIFIED FAST IDLE R.P.M. - (SEE LABEL).

Fast Idle speed adjustment

5. Disconnect the air conditioner compressor clutch connector.

6. Start the engine and place the transmission in **DRIVE** for automatic, **NEUTRAL** for standard.

7. Set the ignition timing.

8. On vehicles equipped with air conditioning, adjust the idle stop screw to the specified rpm, turn the air condition switch to the on position. Disconnect the electrical connector at the air condition compressor. Open the throttle momentarily to ensure that the solenoid plunger is fully extended. Adjust the idle speed solenoid to the speed given on the underhood sticker. Turn the air condition switch to the off posdition.

9. On vehicles without air conditioning, turn the idle speed screw until you obtain the specified rpm.

10. Position the transmission selector in **PARK**.

11. Disconnect and plug the vacuum hose running from the EGR valve.

12. Adjust the fast idle screw on the second step of the fast idle cam until you obtain the specified rpm.

13. Stop the engine and reconnect the EGR vacuum hose, the vapor canister hose and the air conditioner compressor clutch connector.

Fuel Injected Models

2.5L ENGINE

NOTE: The throttle stop screw that is used to adjust the idle speed of the vehicle, is adjusted to specifications at the factory. The throttle stop screw is then covered with a steel plug to prevent the unnecessary readjustment in the field. If it is necessary to gain access to the throttle stop screw without removing the TBI unit from the manifold.

1. Using a small punch or equivalent mark over the center line of the throttle stop screw. Drill a $5/32$ in. diameter hole through the casting to the hardened steel plug.

2. Using a $1/16$ in. diameter punch or equivalent punch out the steel plug.

3. With the vehicle in the park position, the parking brake applied and the drive wheels blocked, remove the air cleaner and plug the thermac vacuum port.

4. Remove the transmission T.V. cable from the throttle control bracket in order to gain access to the minimum air adjustment screw (automatic transmission only).

5. Connect a tachometer to the engine and disconnect the idle air control motor connector.

6. Start the engine and let the engine reach normal operating temperature and the rpm to stabilize.

7. Install the special tool No. J–33047 or equivalent to the idle air passage of the throttle body.

8. Using a No. 20 torx head bit or equivalent, turn the throttle stop screw until the rpm reachers specifications (500 ± 25 rpm on the automatic models and 775 ± 25 on the manual transmission models.

9. Reinstall the transmission T.V. cable into the throttle control bracket (automatic transmission only).

10. Shut down the engine and remove the special tool or equivalent from the throttle body.

11. Reconnect the idle air control motor connector and seal the drilled hole through the throttle body housing with solicone sealant or equivalent.

12. Check the throttle position sensor voltage. Reinstall the air cleaner and thermac vacuum lines.

TBI (THROTTLE BODY INJECTION)

1. Remove the air cleaner and the gasket.

2. Disconnect and plug the thermac vacuum port at the rear TBI unit.

3. If necessary, remove the plug covering the minimum air adjusting screw.

4. Block the wheels and set the parking brake. Connect a tachometer to the engine, start the engine and allow the engine speed to stabilize.

5. Place the automatic transmission in **DRIVE**.

6. Using 2 tools J-33047, plug the idle air passages of each throttle body. Make sure that the tools are seated and no air leaks exist.

NOTE: When the plugs are installed, the rpm should drop below the curb idle speed. If the speed does not drop, check for an air leak.

7. At the rear TBI unit, remove the cap from the ported tube and connect a water manometer J-23951 or equivalent.

8. Adjust the minimum air adjustment screw to obtain 6 in. of water on the manometer. Remove the manometer and install the cap on the ported tube.

9. At the front TBI unit, remove the cap from the ported tube and connect the water manometer J-23951. The reading should be 6 in. of water on the manometer.

10. If the manometer reading is not correct, locate the idle balance screw on the throttle linkage. If the screw is welded, break the weld and install a new screw with thread sealing compound. Adjust the screw to obtain 6 in. of water on the manometer.

11. Remove the manometer and install the cap on the ported tube.

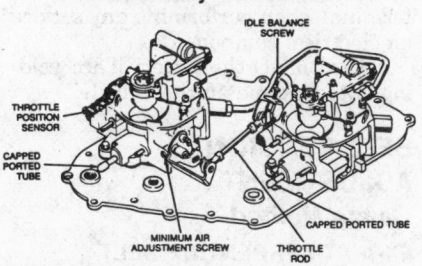

Throttle body—model 300

Cross fire injection system—model 400

12. At the rear TBI unit, adjust the minimum air adjustment screw to obtain 475 rpm.

13. Stop the engine and remove the idle air passage plugs.

14. Place the transmission in **NEUTRAL** and start the engine.

NOTE: The engine will run at a high rpm but will decrease when the IAC motors close the air passages. When the rpm drops, stop the engine.

15. Check the Throttle Position Sensor (TPS) voltage and adjust, if necessary.

NOTE: To reset the IAC motors, drive the vehicle at 30 mph or if equipped with cruise control, disconnect the speedometer cable at the transducer, turn the key ON and rotate the cable to 30 mph.

TPI (TUNED PORT INJECTION)

NOTE: The idle speed should only be adjusted if it is absolutely necessary.

1. Using an awl or equivalent, pierce the idle stop plug and remove it.

2. Leave the idle air control motor connected and ground the diagnostic lead. Turn the ignition to the on position, but do not start the engine.

3. Wait 30 seconds, and with the ignition switch still in the on position disconnect the idle air control connector.

4. Remove the ground from the diagnostic lead and start the engine.

5. Allow the engine to go into the closed loop mode and adjust the idle screw to specification.

6. Turn the ignition off and reconnect the idle speed control connector.

7. Adjust the throttle position sensor, start the engine and check the engine for proper idle operation.

ENGINE ELECTRICAL

Distributor

REMOVAL & INSTALLATION

1. Disconnect the negative battery cable. Remove all the necessary components in order to gain access to the distributor assembly.

2. Remove all electrical connections from the unit. Release the coil connectors from the distributor cap.

3. Remove the distributor cap retaining screws and remove the cap. Disconnect the four terminal harness from the distributor.

4. Remove the distributor hold down bolt. Mark the distributor location on the block and note the position of the rotor, then pull the distributor assembly from the engine.

5. To insure correct ignition timing the distributor must be installed with the rotor in the same position as it was removed.

6. Reinstall all electrical connections and components removed.

7. If the engine has been cranked with the distributor out, remove the number one spark plug. Place your finger over the spark plug hole and crank the engine slowly until compression is felt.

8. Align the timing mark on the pulley to **0** degree mark on the engine timing indicator. Position the rotor between the No. 1 and No. 8 spark plug towers on V8 engines and between the No. 1 and No. 6 spark plug towers on V6 engines.

9. The distributor can now be correctly installed in the engine.

10. Once the distributor has been installed, check the engine timing and adjust as required.

Alternator

For further information on the charging system, please refer to "Charging and Starting" in the Unit Repair section.

PRECAUTIONS

Several precautions must be observed

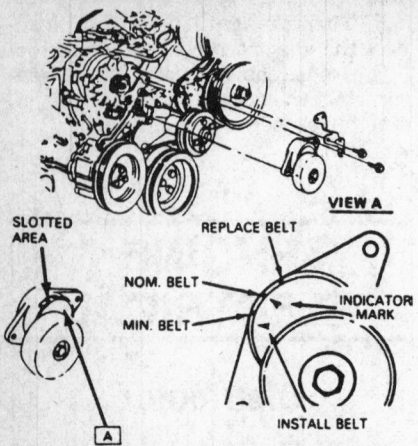

VIEW A

SLOTTED AREA

REPLACE BELT

NOM. BELT

MIN. BELT

INDICATOR MARK

INSTALL BELT

THE INDICATOR MARK ON THE MOVEABLE PORTION OF THE TENSIONER MUST BE WITHIN THE LIMITS OF THE SLOTTED AREA ON THE STATIONARY PORTION OF THE TENSIONER. ANY READING OUTSIDE THESE LIMITS INDICATES EITHER A DEFECTIVE BELT OR TENSIONER.

Serpentine drive belt tensioner and related components

with alternator equipped vehicles to avoid damage to the unit.

• If the battery is removed for any reason, make sure it is reconnected with the correct polarity. Reversing the battery connections may result in damage to the one-way rectifiers.

• When utilizing a booster battery as a starting aid, always connect the positive to positive terminals, and the negative terminal from the booster battery to a good engine ground on the car being started.

• Never use a fast charger as a booster to start vehicles with alternating-current (AC) circuits.

• Disconnect the battery cables when charging the battery with a fast charger.

• Never attempt to polarize an alternator.

• Avoid long soldering times when making alternator repairs. Prolonged heat will damage the alternator.

• Do not use test lamps of more than 12 volts when checking diode continuity.

• Do not short across or ground any of the alternator terminals.

• The polarity of the battery, alternator and regulator must be matched and considered before making any electrical connections within the system.

• Never separate the alternator on an open circuit. Make sure all connections within the circuit are clean and tight.

• Disconnect the battery ground terminal when performing any service on electrical components.

• Disconnect the battery if arc welding is to be done on the vehicle.

BELT TENSION ADJUSTMENT
Gauge Method
EXCEPT SERPENTINE BELT

Using belt tension gauge J-23600 or equivalent adjust the alternator belt if the tension is below 300N, as indicated on the gauge. If the belt is used the correct belt tension is 350N, as indicated on the gauge. If the belt is new the correct tension is 575N, as indicated on the gauge.

SERPENTINE BELT

The correct belt tension is indicated on the indicator mark of the belt tensioner. If the indicator mark is not within specification replace the belt or the tensioner.

REMOVAL & INSTALLATION

1. Disconnect the negative battery cable.
2. Tag and disconnect the alternator wiring.

3. Remove the alternator brace bolt. As required, loosen the power steering pump brace and mount nuts. Remove the drive belts.
4. Support the alternator and remove the mount bolts. Remove the unit from the vehicle.
5. Installation is the reverse of the previous steps. Tighten belt enough to allow approximately ½ in. of play on the longest run between pulleys.

Starter

For further information on the charging system, please refer to "Charging and Starting" in the Unit Repair section.

REMOVAL & INSTALLATION

1. Disconnect the battery cable.
2. As required, raise the vehicle and support it safely.
3. Disconnect all wiring from the starter.
4. As required, remove the frame support. This support runs from the corner of the frame to the front crossmember.
5. Remove the starter motor retaining bolts. If equipped, remove the solenoid heat shield.
6. Remove the starter from the vehicle.
7. Installation is the reverse of the removal procedure.
8. If shims were used, they must be replaced in their original locations.

ENGINE MECHANICAL

Engine

REMOVAL & INSTALLATION
2.8L, 5.0L and 5.7L Engines

1. Disconnect the negative battery cable.
2. Mark the position of the hood on the hood hinges and remove the hood from the vehicle.
3. Drain the cooling system. Remove the lower raditor hose and the upper fan shroud. Remove the fan assembly.
4. Remove the upper radiator hose and the coolant recovery hose. Remove the radiator.
5. Remove the transmission cooler lines. Remove the heater hoses.
6. Disconnect the carburetor linkage. If the vehicle is equipped with

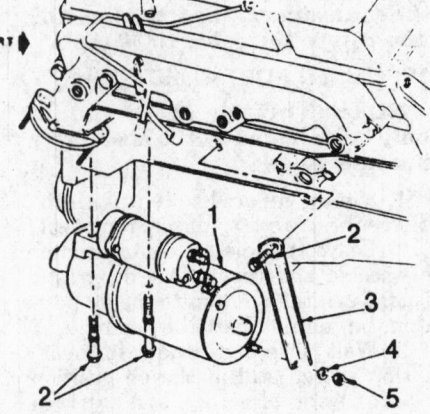

1. Starter motor
2. Bolt
3. Bracket
4. Washer
5. Nut

Starter mounting V6–V8 engines

cruise control, disconnect the detent cable.

7. If equipped with fuel injection, properly relieve the fuel line pressure. Disconnect and plug the fuel lines.

8. Remove the vacuum brake booster line.

9. As required, remove the distributor cap and lay aside with the wiring to gain working clearance.

10. Disconnect all necessary wires and hoses.

11. Remove the power steering pump and lay aside.

12. Raise the vehicle and support safely.

13. Remove the exhaust pipes from the manifold. Remove the dust cover from the vehicle. Remove the converter assembly.

14. Disconnect the starter wires and remove the starter assembly.

15. Remove the bellhousing bolts. Remove the motor mount through bolts.

16. On carbureted engines, disconnect the fuel lines at the fuel pump.

17. Lower the vehicle and support the transmission using a suitable fixture.

18. Remove the air injection reaction system, if equipped.

19. Attach a suitable engine lifting device and remove the engine from the vehicle.

20. Install engine in the reverse order of removal, making sure to align the engine with transmission bell housing. Install the top 2 bolts before removing or lowering transmission support, raise vehicle and install the remaining bolts.

2.5L

1. Disconnect the negative battery cable.

2. Mark the location of the hood on the hood hinges and remove the hood.

3. Drain the cooling system.

4. Remove the A/C compressor and any necessary brackets to gain working clearance.

—————— CAUTION ——————

Do not disconnect the A/C pressure lines. The release of the refrigerant in the system can cause personal injury.

5. Remove the radiator hoses from the engine. Remove the fan assembly. Remove the radiator shroud and radiator.

6. If equipped, remove the power steering pump.

7. Tag and disconnect the electrical connector at the bulkhead connector.

8. If equipped with fuel injection, properly relieve the fuel line pressure. Disconnect and plug the fuel lines.

9. Remove the brake hoses from the

filter and the ground strap from the rear of the cylinder head.

10. Working from inside the vehicle, remove the right hand hush panel and the ECM harness at the main ECM connector. Remove the right hand splash shield from the right fender and feed the ECM harness out from inside the vehicle.

11. Disconnect the heater hoses from the heater core. Remove the canister hose and the throttle cable from the electronic fuel injection if equipped.

12. Raise the vehicle and support safely. Disconnect the electrical connections from the transmission.

13. Remove the flywheel dustcover. If the vehicle is an automatic, remove the torque converter to flywheel holding bolts.

14. Remove the bolts holding the bellhousing to the engine. Remove the bellhousing to engine exhaust pipe support.

15. Remove the exhaust pipe at the manifold. Remove the catalytic converter assembly.

16. Remove the starter assembly.

17. Remove the clutch fork return spring if vehicle is equipped with a manual transmission.

18. Remove the motor mount bolts.

19. Lower the vehicle and install a suitable engine lifting device.

20. Position a floor jack under the transmission to support the transmission.

21. Lift the engine from the vehicle and place in a suitable engine holding fixture.

22. Install engine in the reverse order of removal, making sure to align the engine with transmission bell housing. Install the top 2 bolts before removing or lowering transmission support, raise vehicle and install remaining bolts.

Cylinder Head

REMOVAL & INSTALLATION

2.8L, 5.0L and 5.7L Engines

1. Disconnect the negative battery cable.

2. Drain the engine coolant from the radiator. Disconnect the radiator hoses from the intake manifold.

3. Remove the intake manifold. Remove the exhaust manifold.

4. Remove the alternator lower mounting bolt and lay aside to gain working clearance.

5. If the vehicle is equipped with power steering, remove the pump and bracket to gain access.

6. Remove the rocker arm covers and the rocker assemblies. Remove the push rods.

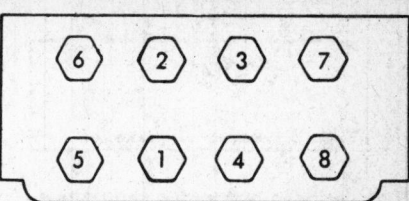

Cylinder head bolt torque sequence—2.8L engine

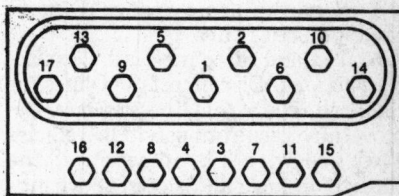

Cylinder head bolt torque sequence—V8 Chevy produced engine

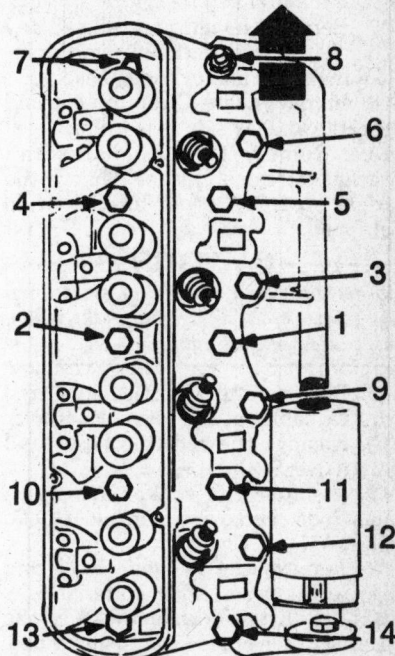

Cylinder head bolt torque sequence—V8 Pontiac produced engine

7. Remove all vacuum hoses from the cylinder head assembly. Tag and disconnect the spark plug wires.

8. Remove the cylinder head bolts. Remove the cylinder head and discard the old gasket.

9. Installation is the reverse of the removal procedure. Carefully guide the cylinder head over the dowel pins and onto the cylinder block. Tighten the cylinder head bolts in sequence to the torque specified.

2.5L

1. Disconnect the negative battery cable.

2. Drain the cooling system.

3. Raise and support the vehicle safely. Disconnect the exhaust pipe. Lower the vehicle.

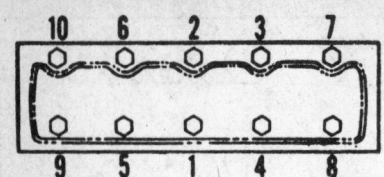

Cylinder head bolt torque sequence—
2.5L engine

4. Remove the air cleaner. Remove the oil dipstick tube.

5. Tag and disconnect all electrical connections. Disconnect fuel lines, as required relieve fuel line pressure. Remove any vacuum hoses. On vehicles equipped with TBI, disconnect the throttle linkage and electrical wiring.

6. Remove the EGR baseplate if equipped and the heater hose from the intake manifold.

7. Remove the ignition coil and any other wiring connections from the intake manifold and cylinder head.

8. Remove the A/C compressor and brackets and lay side to working clearance. Remove the alternator and bracket for same reason. Remove the power steering upper bracket if so equipped.

CAUTION

Do not disconnect the A/C pressure lines. The release of the refrigerant in the system can cause personal injury.

9. Remove the throttle valve and throttle cables at the intake manifold.

10. Remove the radiator hoses and valve cover.

11. Remove the rocker arms and push rods. Remove the cylinder head bolts.

12. Remove the cylinder head and discard the used gasket material.

13. Install the cylinder head in the reverse order of removal, using a new gasket. Prior to installing the cylinder head, apply a suitable thread sealer to the stud bolts at both ends of the head. Torque the cylinder head bolts in sequence until a final torque of 92 ft. lbs. has been reached.

OVERHAUL

For all cylinder head overhaul procedures, please refer to the "Engine Rebuilding" in the Unit Repair section.

Rocker Arms/Shafts

REMOVAL & INSTALLATION

2.5L Engine

1. Disconnect negative battery terminal. Remove air cleaner, PCV valve and hose. Remove EGR valve and spark plug wires.

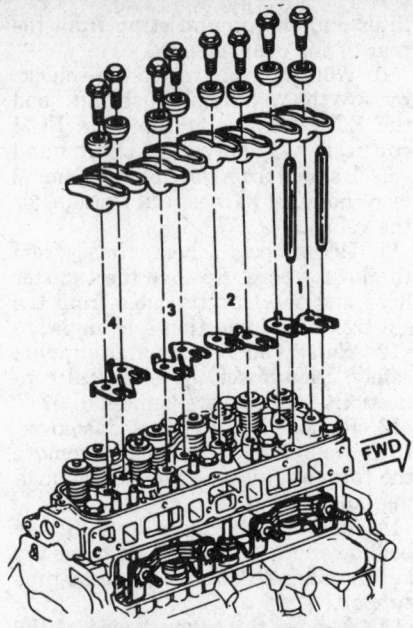

View of rocker arm and pushrod assembly—2.5L engine

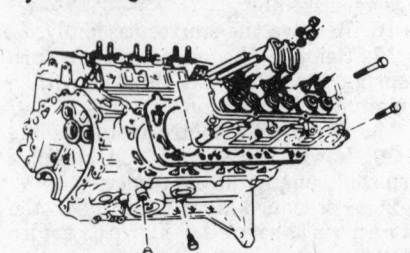

View of rocker arm and pushrod assembly—Chevy V6 shown Chevy V8 similar

2. Remove rocker arm cover retaining bolts and remove cover.

3. Remove rocker arm bolts, rocker arms and pivot balls. It is important to keep all valve train parts in the order that they were removed and to install them in the same location.

4. Install the rocker arms, bolts and pivot balls. Torque the bolts to 24 ft. lbs. Install the rocker arm cover using a new gasket and tighten bolts to 4 ft. lbs.

5. Reinstall all hoses and wiring that was disconnected. Connect battery and run engine to check for leaks.

NOTE: For valve adjustment procedure refer to "Valve Lash Adjustment" in this section.

2.8L, 5.0L and 5.7L Engines

1. Disconnect the negative battery terminal. Remove air cleaner, if equipped.

2. On models equipped with TBI fuel injection remove the plenum and runners.

3. Remove A/C bracket, coil and coil bracket. On V8 engines remove the air management hoses and valve, EGR solenoid.

4. Remove rocker arm cover bolts and remove.

5. Remove rocker arm bolts, rocker arms and pivot balls. It is important to keep all valve train parts in the order that they were removed and to install them in the same location.

6. Install rocker arms, bolts and pivot balls. Tighten the bolts until no lash is felt. Install the rocker arm covers using new gaskets and tighten to 6 ft. lbs.

7. Reinstall all hoses and wiring that was disconnected. Connect battery and run engine to check for leaks.

Intake Manifold

REMOVAL & INSTALLATION

2.5L Engine

1. Disconnect the negative battery cable.

2. Remove the air cleaner, PCV valve and hose.

3. Drain the cooling system. Tag and disconnect the vacuum hoses.

4. Disconnect the fuel lines from the carburetor. Relieve fuel pump pressure, as required.

5. If the vehicle is equipped with

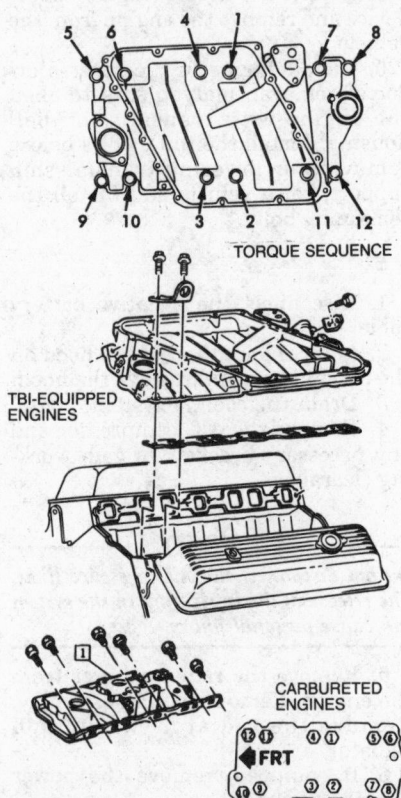

Intake manifold bolt tightening sequence of all Chevrolet-built V8 engines. Note that the lower sequence is used for all carbureted engines, whereas the upper sequence is used for all TBI-equipped engines

EFI, remove the throttle linkage and wiring.

6. Disconnect the transmission downshift linkage.

7. Disconnect the cruise control linkage if needed.

8. Remove the heater hoses to gain working clearance.

9. Disconnect the alternator bracket and lay aside.

10. Disconnect the ignition coil assembly.

11. Remove the intake manifold retaining bolts and remove the intake manifold.

12. Install the intake manifold by reversing the removal procedure, making sure to tighten all bolts in sequence and to the specified torque. Install all hoses and wires that were removed, reconnect the battery and fill the cooling system. Run the engine to normal operating temperature and check for fluid leaks.

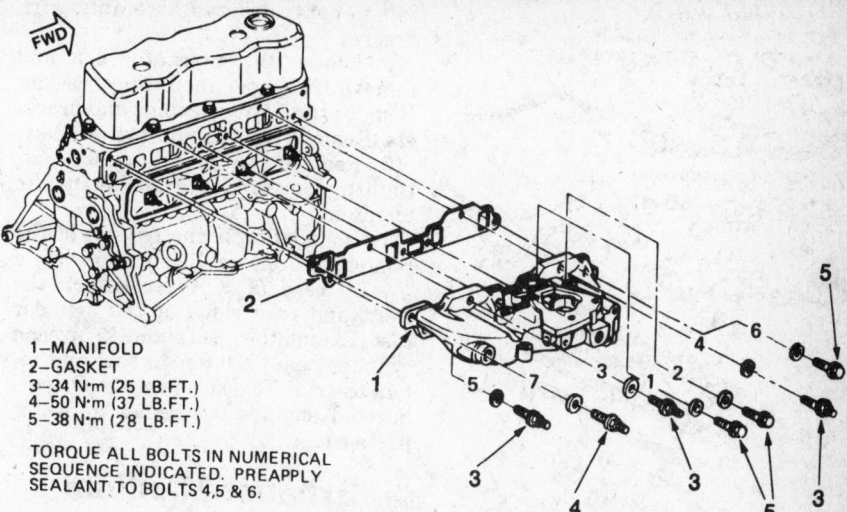

1—MANIFOLD
2—GASKET
3—34 N·m (25 LB.FT.)
4—50 N·m (37 LB.FT.)
5—38 N·m (28 LB.FT.)

TORQUE ALL BOLTS IN NUMERICAL SEQUENCE INDICATED. PREAPPLY SEALANT TO BOLTS 4,5 & 6.

Intake manifold tightening sequence—1986-87 2.5L

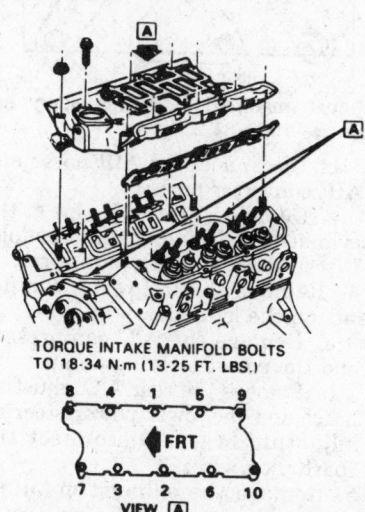

TORQUE INTAKE MANIFOLD BOLTS TO 18-34 N·m (13-25 FT. LBS.)

VIEW [A]

View of the PFI intake manifold

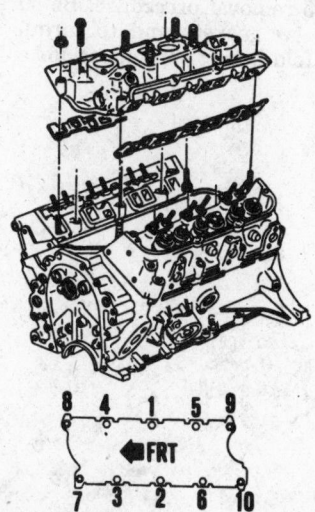

Intake manifold bolt tightening sequence—2.8L engine

2.8L Engine

1. Disconnect the negative battery cable. Remove the air cleaner assembly. Drain the coolant system.

2. As required, remove the carburetor assembly.

3. On vehicles equipped with fuel injection remove the following subassemblies: plenum, fuel rail and runner.

4. Remove the spark plug wires from the spark plugs and disconnect the wires at the coil.

5. Remove the distributor cap along with the spark plug wires, mark the position of the distributor, remove the distributor hold down bolt and lift the distributor out of the vehicle.

6. If equipped, remove the air management hose and bracket.

7. Disconnect the emission canister hoses. Remove the pipe bracket on the front left valve cover and remove the left valve cover.

8. Remove the right valve cover and the upper radiator hose. Disconnect the coolant switches.

9. Remove the manifold bolts along with the intake manifold. Discard the old gaskets and any loose RTV sealant from the front and rear ridges of the cylinder case.

10. Installation is the reverse order of the removal procedure. Be sure to apply a $\frac{3}{16}$ in. bead of RTV sealant on the front and rear ridge of the cylinder case.

11. Install the new gaskets on the cylinder heads, note the position of the gaskets (new gaskets will be marked **LEFT/RIGHT**). Hold the gaskets in place by extending the RTV bead up onto the gasket ends. New GM intake gaskets will have to be cut to install behind the pushrods. Cut these gaskets as required and only where necessary.

5.0L and 5.7L Engines

1. Disconnect the negative battery cable.

2. Remove the air cleaner assembly.

3. Drain the radiator. Disconnect the upper radiator hose and the heater hoses at the manifold.

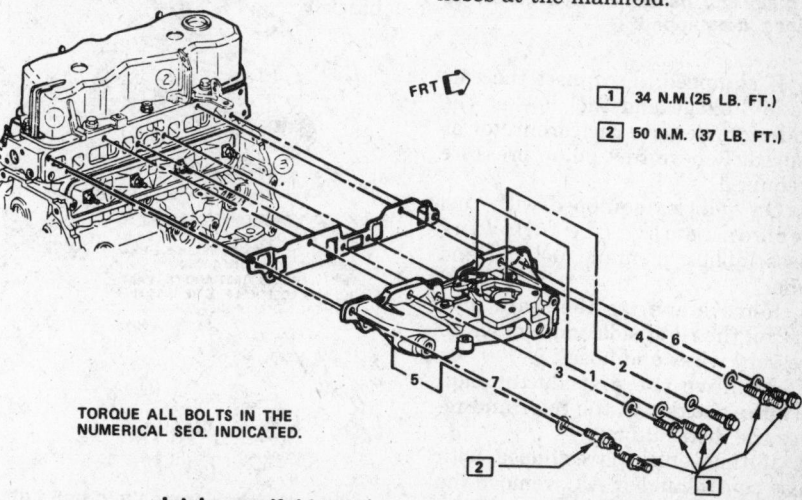

| 1 | 34 N.M. (25 LB. FT.) |
| 2 | 50 N.M. (37 LB. FT.) |

TORQUE ALL BOLTS IN THE NUMERICAL SEQ. INDICATED.

Intake manifold tightening sequence—1982-86 2.5L

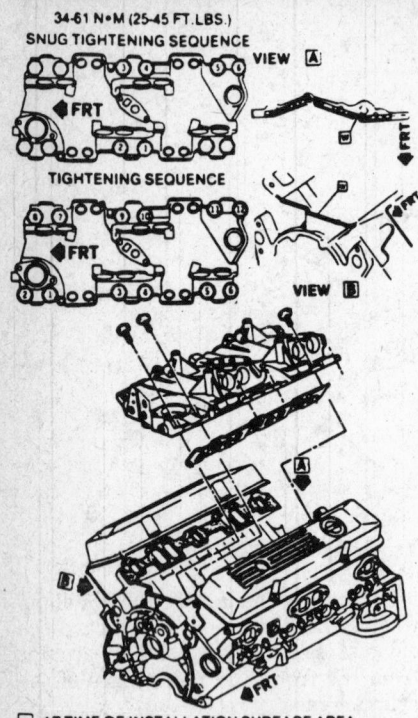

34-61 N•M (25-45 FT.LBS.)
SNUG TIGHTENING SEQUENCE
VIEW Ⓐ
FRT
TIGHTENING SEQUENCE
FRT
VIEW Ⓑ

Ⓦ AT TIME OF INSTALLATION SURFACE AREA MUST BE FREE OF OIL AND SEALING COMPOUND MUST BE WET TO TOUCH WHEN BOLT/SCREWS ARE TORQUED. APPLY SEALING COMPOUND .12 THICK.

View of the MFI intake manifold

27-46 N•m (20-34 FT. LBS.)

27-46 N•m (20-34 FT. LBS.)

27-46 N•m (20-34 FT. LBS.)

TBI plate and gasket installation on V8 engines, if equipped

4. If equipped, disconnect the carburetor linkage and fuel line at the carburetor. Remove the carburetor as required. Relieve fuel pump pressure as required.

5. On vehicles equipped with fuel injection remove the following subassemblies: plenum, fuel rail and runner.

6. Remove and tag the spark plug wires on the right side and remove all necessary wires and hoses.

7. Remove the distributor cap. Mark the position of the rotor and remove the distributor.

8. If the vehicle is equipped with cruise control and/or A/C, remove the compressor with brackets and the

cruise control servo assembly with bracket.

9. Loosen the alternator belt and remove the upper mounting bracket. Remove the EGR solenoids and brackets. Remove the vacuum brake line.

10. Remove the intake manifold attaching bolts. Remove the intake manifold.

11. Installation is the reverse of the removal procedure. Be sure to apply a $^3/_{16}$ in. bead of RTV sealant on the front and rear ridge of the cylinder case. Extend the bead about ½ up each cylinder head in order to seal and retain the manifold side gaskets. On carbureted engines use sealer at water passages.

Exhaust Manifold

REMOVAL & INSTALLATION

2.5L Engine

1. Disconnect the negative battery cable.

2. Remove the air cleaner and EFI preheat tube if equipped. Remove the oxygen sensor if equipped.

3. Remove the exhaust pipe from the exhaust manifold.

4. Remove the oil dipstick tube to gain working clearance.

5. Remove the exhaust manifold bolts. Remove the exhaust manifold.

6. Installation is the reverse of the removal procedure. Inspect for exhaust leaks.

2.8L Engine

1. Disconnect the negative battery cable and raise and support the vehicle safely.

2. Disconnect the exhaust pipe from the exhaust manifold.

3. Remove the following components on the right side.

a. Lower the vehicle and disconnect the air management valve bracket.

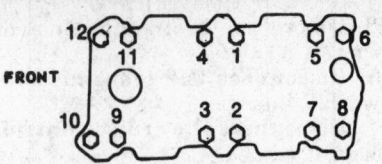

FRONT

Intake manifold bolt tightening sequence — V8 Chevy produced engines with carburetor

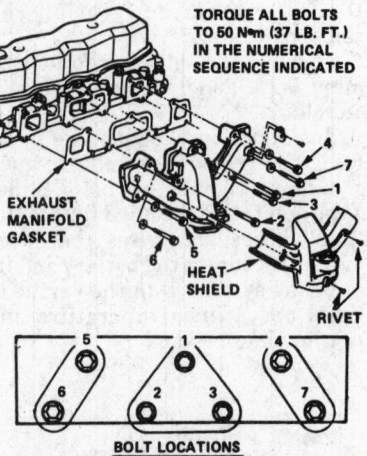

TORQUE ALL BOLTS TO 50 N•m (37 LB. FT.) IN THE NUMERICAL SEQUENCE INDICATED

EXHAUST MANIFOLD GASKET

HEAT SHIELD

RIVET

BOLT LOCATIONS

Exhaust manifold bolt tightening sequence — 1982-84 2.5L

b. Disconnect the AIR hoses and AIR converter pipe.

c. Disconnect the AIR pipe at the cylinder heads and at the manifold. Disconnect the spark plug wires.

4. Remove the following components on the left side:

a. Remove the A/C compressor and the power steering pump.

b. Remove the rear A/C adjusting brace and the lower power steering adjusting brace. Disconnect the spark plug wires.

5. Remove the exhaust manifold bolts and remove the exhaust manifold.

6. Installation is the reverse order of the removal procedure. Be sure to use new gaskets and to torque the manifold bolts to specifications.

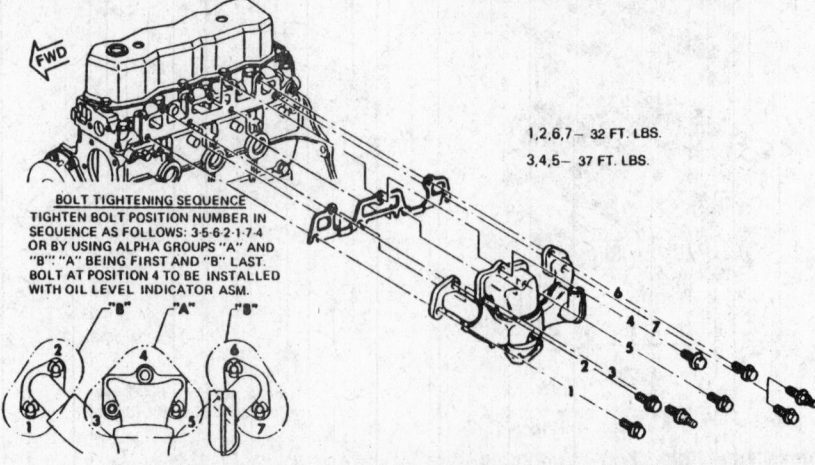

FWD

BOLT TIGHTENING SEQUENCE
TIGHTEN BOLT POSITION NUMBER IN SEQUENCE AS FOLLOWS: 3-5-6-2-1-7-4 OR BY USING ALPHA GROUPS "A" AND "B". "A" BEING FIRST AND "B" LAST. BOLT AT POSITION 4 TO BE INSTALLED WITH OIL LEVEL INDICATOR ASM.

"B" "A" "B"

1,2,6,7 — 32 FT. LBS.
3,4,5 — 37 FT. LBS.

Exhaust manifold bolt tightening sequence — 1985-87 2.5L

5.0L and 5.7L Engines

1. Disconnect the negative battery cable and raise and support the vehicle safely.

2. Disconnect the exhaust pipe from the exhaust manifold and lower the vehicle.

3. On the right side, remove the air cleaner, spark plugs and disconnect the vacuum hoses at the early fuel evaporator canister.

4. On the left side, remove the power steering pump and loosen the A/C bracket at the front of the head, remove the rear A/C bracket and the A/C compressor. Remove the lower power steering adjusting bracket.

5. Remove the vacuum hose at the air injection reactor (AIR) valve.

6. On the right side, remove the alternator belt and lower alternator bracket, also remove the AIR valve. Disconnect the converter AIR pipe at the back of the manifold.

7. Remove the exhaust manifold bolts, and on the left side remove the wire loom holder at the valve cover, remove the exhaust manifold.

8. Installation in the reverse order of removal, and torque the manifold bolts to specifications. Run engine and check for exhaust leaks.

Front Cover/Oil Seal
REMOVAL & INSTALLATION

2.5L Engine

1. Disconnect the negative battery terminal.

2. Raise and support vehicle, drain the cooling system.

3. Remove the lower radiator hose and lower fan shroud. Lower vehicle.

4. Remove the upper radiator hose and the upper fan shroud. Remove all belts and the fan assembly.

5. Remove the crankshaft pulley and hub. Remove the front cover retaining bolts and remove the cover. Remove the front cover seal and discard.

6. Clean all mating surfaces. Install new seal to front cover using tool J-34995, or equivalent.

7. Apply a bead of RTV sealer to the block mating surfaces of the front cover. Using tool J-34995 as an centering tool, insert it into the front cover seal and install cover to block.

8. Install all front cover attaching bolts and tighten to 90 inch lbs., remove centering tool. Install crankshaft hub and pulley. Reinstall all hoses and belts, fan assembly and shroud. Fill cooling system and run engine to check for leaks.

2.8L Engine

1. Disconnect the negative battery cable.

2. Remove the drive belts and pulley. If equipped with A/C, remove the compressor from the mounting bracket and lay it aside. Remove the compressor mounting bracket. Remove the AIR pump and bracket if so equipped.

3. Drain the cooling system. Disconnect the lower radiator hose at the front cover and the heater at the water pump. Remove the water pump. Raise the vehicle and support safely.

4. Remove the crankshaft pulley. Remove the torsional damper retaining bolt.

5. Install tool J-23523 or equivalent on the torsional damper. Remove the torsional damper. Remove the oil pan to front cover bolts.

6. Lower the vehicle. Remove the remaining front cover to block attaching bolts. Remove the front cover. Discard the gasket material.

7. Remove the front oil seal from the front cover using a suitable tool.

8. Installation is the reverse of the removal procedure. Be sure to apply a continuous bead of a suitable sealant to the front cover mating surface. Then apply a continuous bead of sealer to the oil pan surface of the front cover. Also be sure to install the components within 5 minutes of sealant application. Install the new oil seal so that the open end of the seal is facing the inside of the cover.

5.0L, 5.7L Engines

1. Disconnect the negative battery cable. Drain the cooling system.

2. Remove the drive belts and accessory belts. Remove the fan assembly and fan pulley. Using Torsional Damper Puller J-23523 or equivalent remove the torsional damper.

3. On engines equipped with TBI, remove the air injection pump pulley and air management valve adapter, then remove the air injection pump. Disconnect the fuel inlet and outlet lines at the TBI unit.

4. On vehicles equipped with A/C, remove the rear A/C compressor braces and lower the A/C mount bolts. Remove the compressor bracket and nuts at the water pump. Slide the mounting bracket forward and remove the compressor mount bolt. Disconnect the wires at the compressor and lay the unit aside. Disconnect the air injection hose at the right exhaust manifold.

5. Remove the compressor mount bracket. Remove the upper air injection pump bracket with the power steering reservoir. Remove the lower air injection pump bracket.

6. Disconnect the heater and radiator hoses to the water pump. Remove the water pump. Remove the front cover reatining bolts, cover and old gasket.

Camshaft thrust plate screw removal — 2.5L engine

7. To install clean the gasket surfaces. Apply a suitable sealer to the new gasket. Apply a suitable RTV sealant to the joint formed where the oil pan meets the cylinder block, be sure to trim the excess material the sticks out from the junction. Place the gasket on the cover and install the cover to oil pan seal. The rest of the installation procedure is the reverse order of the removal procedure.

Timing Chain and Sprockets

REMOVAL & INSTALLATION

2.5L Engine

1. Disconnect the negative battery cable.

2. Remove the camshaft.

3. With the camshaft removed, use a press plate and Adapter J-971 or equivalent on the press to remove the timing gear from the camshaft. Be sure to place the camshaft through the opening in the tools on the table of the press and press the camshaft out of the timing gear. Position the thrust plate so that the Woodruff key in the camshaft does no damage during removal.

4. If the crankshaft gear needs to be replaced, use a suitable gear puller to remove it from the crankshaft.

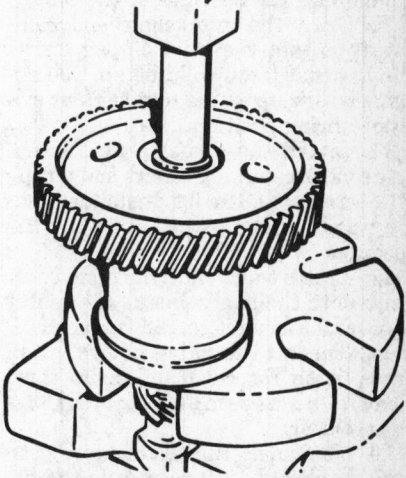

Timing gear removal — 2.5L engine

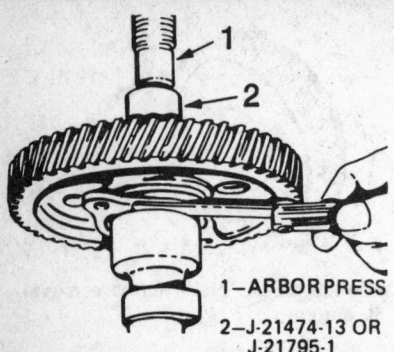

1—ARBOR PRESS

2—J-21474-13 OR J-21795-1

Checking thrust plate end clearance— 2.5L engine

Timing gear alignment—2.5L

5. To install support the camshaft at the back of the front journal in a arbor press using the press plate adaptors. Install the spacer ring and thrust plate over the end of the camshaft.

6. Install the woodruff key in the shaft keyway. Install the timing gear on the camshaft until it bottoms against the gear ring spacer ring. Measure the end clearance of the thrust plate. The clearance should be 0.0015–0.0050 in.

7. If the clearance is less than specified, replace the spacer ring. If the clearance is more than specified, replace the thrust plate.

8. Coat the camshaft journals with a high quality engine oil supplement.

9. Install the camshaft assembly into the engine block, being careful not to damage the bearings or the cam.

10. Turn the crankshaft and camshaft so that the valve timing marks on the gear teeth will line up. The engine is now up on the number four cylinder firing position.

11. Install the thrust plate, the engine block retaining screws and torque the screws to 88 in. lbs. Install the timing gear cover as outlined in this section.

12. Line up and slide the crankshaft hub onto the shaft. Install the center bolt and torque it to 162 ft. lbs.

13. Install the valve lifters, push rods, push rod cover, oil pump shaft and gear assembly. Install the distributor.

14. To install the distributor, turn the crankshaft 360 degrees to the firing position of the number one cylin-der (number one exhaust and intake valve lifters both are on the base circle of the camshaft and timing mark on the harmonic balancer indexed with the top dead center mark on the timing pad) Install the distributor in the original position and align the shaft with the rotor arm towards the number one plug contact.

15. Position the push rods and install the rocker arms and rocker arm bolts. Torque the rocker arm bolts to 20 ft. lbs.

16. Install the water pump pulley and fan assembly. Install the A/C condenser and recharge the A/C system. Install the radiator and shroud assembly. Refill engine coolant and engine oil to specifications.

2.8L, 5.0L and 5.7L Engines

1. Disconnect the negative battery cable. Remove the timing chain cover. Remove the crankshaft oil slinger if so equipped.

2. Crank the engine until the No. 1 piston is at TDC and the timing marks on the camshaft and crankshaft sprockets are aligned.

3. Remove the camshaft sprocket bolts and remove the camshaft sprocket and chain.

4. Install the timing chain on the camshaft sprocket and lubricate the thrust surface.

5. Hold the sprocket vertically with the chain hanging down and align the marks on the camshaft and crankshaft sprockets.

6. Align the dowel in the camshaft with the dowel hole in the camshaft sprocket, and install the sprocket on the camshaft.

7. Slowly and evenly draw the camshaft sprocket onto the camshaft using the mounting bolts and torque the bolts to specifications. Do not drive the sprocket onto the camshaft, this could cause the rear freeze plug to be dislodged and cause fluid leaks.

8. Lubricate the timing chain and install the timing chain cover.

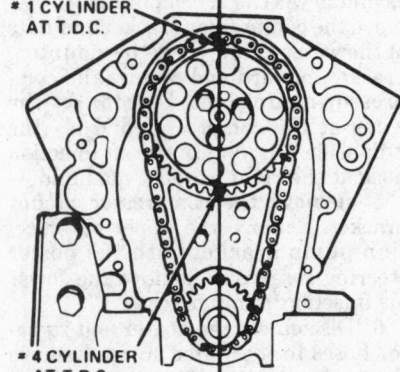

\# 1 CYLINDER AT T.D.C.

\# 4 CYLINDER AT T.D.C.

Timing chain alignment—Chevy produced V6 engine

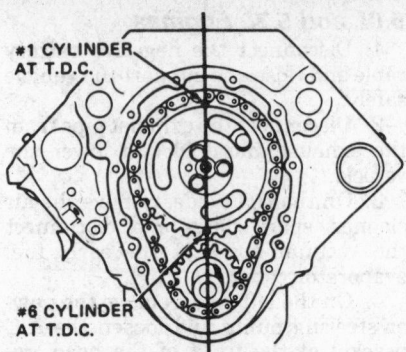

#1 CYLINDER AT T.D.C.

#6 CYLINDER AT T.D.C.

Timing chain alignment—Chevy produced V8 engine

Camshaft

REMOVAL & INSTALLATION

2.5L Engine

1. Disconnect the negative battery cable.

2. Drain the engine oil and coolant from the engine. Remove the radiator. If equipped with A/C, remove the A/C condenser.

3. Remove the water pump pulley and the fan assembly.

4. Remove the valve cover and discard the gasket. Loosen the valve rocker bolts and turn the rocker arms to clear the push rods.

5. Remove the oil pump drive shaft and gear assembly. On some vehicles it may be necessary to remove the spark plugs.

6. Mark the location of the distributor and remove it.

7. Remove the push rod cover, push rods, guides and valve lifters.

8. Remove the crankshaft pulley and hub assembly. Remove the timing gear cover.

9. Remove the two camshaft thrust plate screws, by working through the holes in the camshaft gear. Remove the camshaft assembly by pulling it out through the front of the engine block.

10. To install, coat the camshaft journals with a high quality engine oil supplement.

11. Install the camshaft assembly into the engine block, being careful not to damage the bearings or the cam.

12. Turn the crankshaft and camshaft so that the valve timing marks on the gear teeth will line up. The engine is now up on the No. 4 cylinder firing position.

13. Install the thrust plate to the engine block retaining screws and torque the screws to 24 in. lbs. Install the timing gear cover.

14. Line up and slide the crankshaft hub onto the shaft. Install the center bolt and torque it to 162 ft. lbs.

15. Install the valve lifters, push

rods, push rod cover, oil pump shaft and gear assembly. Install the distributor.

16. Turn the crankshaft 360 degrees to the firing position of the No.1 cylinder (No. 1 exhaust and intake valve lifters both are on the base circle of the camshaft and timing mark on the harmonic balancer indexed with the TDC mark on the timing pad).Install the distributor in the original position and align the shaft with the rotor arm towards the No. 1 plug contact.

17. Position the push rods and install the rocker arms and rocker arm bolts. Torque the rocker arm bolts to 20 ft. lbs.

18. Install the water pump pulley and fan assembly. Install the A/C condenser and recharge the A/C system. Install the radiator and shroud assembly. Refill engine coolant and engine oil to specifications.

19. Start the vehicle and check for leaks.

2.8L, 5.0L and 5.7L Engines

1. Disconnect the negative battery cable. Drain the cooling system. As required, remove the distributor assembly.

2. Remove the intake manifold. Remove the rocker covers, rocker arm assemblies, push rods, and lifters.

3. Remove all necessary wires and hoses. Disconnect the upper and lower transmission cooler lines.

4. Remove the radiator shroud assembly and radiator. Remove the front grille if necessary. If necessary properly discharge the air condition system and remove the air condition condenser. Remove the cooling fan.

5. Remove the power steering pump if so equipped. Remove the drive belts, crankshaft pulley and torsional damper.

6. Remove the A/C compressor mount bolts, brackets, accumulator and compressor and position it out of the way. Remove the air injection pump with brackets and set it aside.

7. Remove the water pump assembly, remove the front engine cover. Remove the fuel pump push rod, if equipped. Rotate the crankshaft and align the timing marks.

8. Remove the camshaft bolts, gear and chain. Install two $5/16$ in. × 4 in. bolts in the camshaft bolt holes and carefully remove the camshaft.

9. Installation is the reverse order of the removal procedure. Lubricate the camshaft journals with a suitable engine oil supplement, before installing the camshaft. Once the camshaft has been installed, install the chain on the camshaft sprocket. Hold the sprocket vertically with the chain hanging down and align the marks on the camshaft and crankshaft sprockets.

10. Align the dowel in the camshaft sprocket with the dowel hole in the camshaft sprocket then install the sprocket on the camshaft. Draw the camshaft sprocket onto the camshaft using the mounting bolts.

Piston and Connecting Rod

POSITIONING

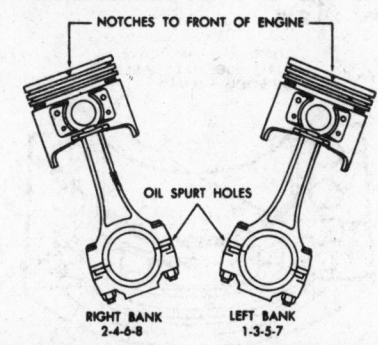

Piston identification—Chevy produced engines

ENGINE LUBRICATION

Oil Pan

REMOVAL & INSTALLATION

2.5L Engine

1. Disconnect the negative battery cable.

2. Raise the vehicle and support it safely.

3. Drain the engine oil.

4. Disconnect the exhaust pipe at the manifold.

5. Loosen the exhaust pipe at the manifold.

6. Remove the starter assembly, if necessary.

7. Remove the flywheel dust cover, if necessary.

8. Remove the front engine mount through bolts.

9. Carefully raise the engine enough to provide sufficient clearance to lower the oil pan.

10. Remove the oil pan retaining bolts and remove the oil pan.

11. Clean all old RTV from the mating surfaces.

12. Install the rear gasket into the rear main bearing cap and apply a small amount of RTV where the gasket engages into the engine block.

13. Install the front gasket.

14. Install the side gaskets and apply a continuous bead of RTV sealer around the perimeter of the oil pan. Apply a small amount of RTV where the side gaskets meet the front gasket.

15. Install the oil pan tightening all bolts to 7 ft. lbs..

NOTE: Install the oil pan to timing cover bolts last, as these holes will not align until the other pan bolts are snug.

16. Lower the engine and install motor mount bolts, starter and exhaust pipes.

17. Add engine oil to the specified level. Connect negative battery cable.

2.8L, 5.0L and 5.7L Engines

1. Disconnect the negative battery cable. Remove the air cleaner assembly. Remove the distributor cap and lay it aside.

2. Remove the upper half of the fan shroud assembly. On some vehicles it may be necessary to position the air condition compressor to one side.

3. Raise the vehicle and support it safely. Drain the engine oil.

4. Remove the air injection pipe at the catalytic convertor. Remove the catalaytic converter hanger bolts.

5. Remove the torque converter dust shield.On some vehicles equipped with manual transmissions, it may be necesary to remove the oil filter in order to remove the dust shield.

6. Remove the exhaust pipe at the manifolds.

7. Remove the starter bolts, loosen the starter brace, then lay the starter aside. On V8 engines remove the front starter brace.

8. Remove the front engine mount through bolts.

9. Raise the engine enough to provide sufficient clearance for oil pan removal.

10. Remove the oil pan bolts. If the front crankshaft throw prohibits removal of the pan, turn the crankshaft to position the throw horizontally.

11. Remove the oil pan from the vehicle.

12. Remove all old RTV from the oil pan and engine block.

13. Install new gasket and apply a small amount of RTV sealer to the corners of the oil pan.

14. Install oil pan tightening all bolts to 7 ft. lbs..

15. Lower engine and install motor mount through bolts. Install starter, exhaust pipes, dust sheild and oil filter. Fill the engine, to specification with oil. Connect the negative battery cable.

Rear Main Bearing Oil Seal

REMOVAL & INSTALLATION

2 Piece Seal

1. Remove the oil pan. Remove the oil pump where required. Remove the rear main bearing cap.

2. Pry the lower seal out of the bearing cap with a suitable tool, being careful not to gouge the cap surface.

3. Remove the upper seal by lightly tapping on one end with a brass pin punch until the other end can be grasped and pulled out with pliers.

4. Clean the bearing cap, cylinder block, and crankshaft mating surfaces with solvent. Inspect all these surfaces for gouges, nicks, and burrs.

5. Apply light engine oil on the seal lips and bead, but keep the seal ends clean.

6. Insert the tip of the installation tool between the crankshaft and the seal of the cylinder block. Place the seal between the crankshaft and the cylinder block. Place the seal between the tip of the tool and the crankshaft, so that the bead contacts the tip of the tool.

7. Be sure that the seal lip is facing the front of the engine, and work the seal around the crankshaft using the installation tool to protect the seal from the corner of the cylinder block.

NOTE: Do not remove the tool until the opposite end of the seal is flush with the cylinder block surface.

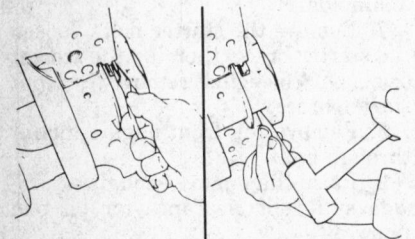

Removing the oil seal from the upper half—V8 engine

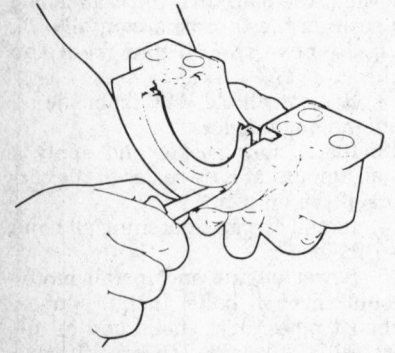

Removing the oil seal from the lower half—V8 engine

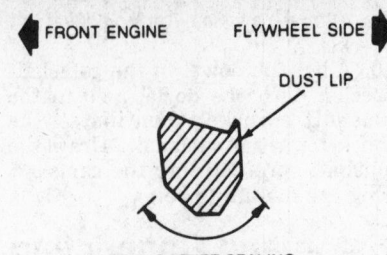

FRONT ENGINE   FLYWHEEL SIDE

DUST LIP

APPLY GASKET SEALING COMPOUND TO THIS AREA

END VIEW OF SEAL

New style rear main seal installation—1985–89 2.8L

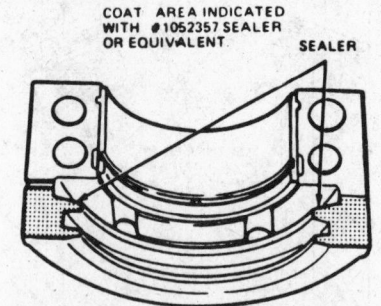

COAT AREA INDICATED WITH #1052357 SEALER OR EQUIVALENT.

SEALER

Rear main bearing cap sealer location—1985–89 2.8L

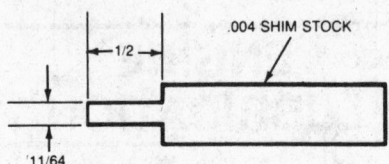

.004 SHIM STOCK

1/2

11/64

Oil seal installation tool

8. Remove the installation tool, being careful not to pull the seal out at the same time.

9. Using the same procedure, install the lower seal into the bearing cap. Use your finger and thumb to lever the seal into the cap.

10. Apply sealer to the cylinder block only where the cap mates to the surface. Do not apply sealer to the seal ends.

11. Install the rear main bearing cap and torque the bolts to specifications. Install the oil pan.

1 Piece Seal

1. Remove the transmission from the vehicle.

2. Using the notches provided in the rear seal retainer, pry out the seal using the proper tool.

NOTE: Care should be taken when removing the seal so as not to nick the crankshaft sealing surface.

3. Before installation lubricate the new seal with clean engine oil.

4. Install the seal on tool J-3561 or equivalent. Thread the tool into the

rear of the crankshaft. Tighten the screws snugly, this is to insure that the seal will be installed squarely over the crankshaft. Tighten the tool wing nut until it bottoms.

5. Remove the tool from the crankshaft.

6. Install the transmission.

1 Piece Seal Retainer and Gasket

1. Remove the transmission from the vehicle.

2. Remove the oil pan bolts and lower the oil pan.

3. Remove the retainer and seal assembly.

4. Remove the gasket. Whenever the retainer is removed a new retainer gasket and rear main seal must be installed.

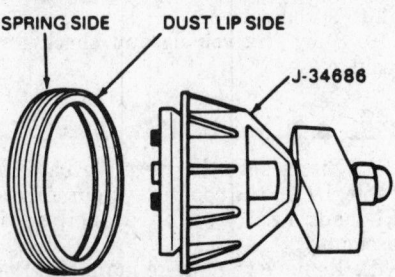

SPRING SIDE   DUST LIP SIDE

J-34686

SEAL BORE TO SEAL SURFACE TO BE LUBRICATED WITH ENGINE OIL BEFORE ASSEMBLY

One piece seal installation tool positioning

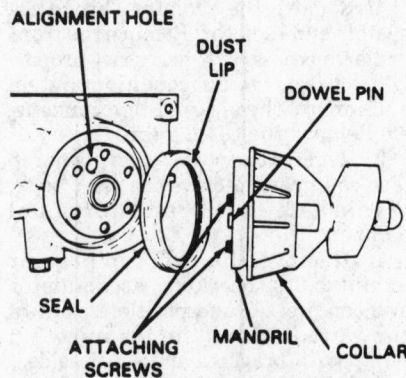

ALIGNMENT HOLE

DUST LIP

DOWEL PIN

SEAL

ATTACHING SCREWS

MANDRIL

COLLAR

One piece seal installation procedure

5. Installation is the reverse of the removal procedure. Once the oil pan has been installed the new rear main oil seal can be installed.

Oil Pump

REMOVAL & INSTALLATION

All Engines

1. Raise the vehicle and support safely.

2. Drain the oil pan.

3. Remove the oil pan as outlined in

this section. Discard the old gasket material.

4. Remove the oil pump bolts and the bolt or nuts from the main bearing cap. Remove the oil pump.

5. Installation is the reverse of the removal procedure. Use a new gasket or equivalent prior to installing. All parts should be coated with clean engine oil before installation.

ENGINE COOLING

Radiator

REMOVAL & INSTALLATION

1. Disconnect the negative battery cable.

2. Drain the cooling system.

3. Remove the engine cooling fan. If equipped with a fan clutch, the clutch be set aside in an upright position to prevent seal leakage.

4. Disconnect the radiator hoses from the radiator.

5. If equipped with an automatic transmission, disconnect and plug the transmission cooler lines at the radiator.

6. If equipped, remove the fan shield assembly.

7. Remove the radiator and shroud assembly, then lift the radiator straight up and out of the vehicle.

8. Install radiator and shroud assembly by reversing removal procedures.

9. Reconnect all hoses, install fan and fill cooling system.

Water Pump

REMOVAL & INSTALLATION

1. Disconnect the negative battery cable. Drain the cooling system.

2. If equipped, remove the fan shroud and the upper radiator support.

3. Remove the drive belts.

4. Remove the fan and the pulley from the water pump.

NOTE: Viscous drive fans should not be stored horizontally. The silicone fluid can leak out of the fan assembly if it is not kept upright.

5. As required, remove the upper and lower brackets, the air brace, the bracket and the lower power steering pump bracket.

6. Disconnect the heater and lower radiator hoses, from the water pump. On vehicles equipped with a bypass hose, remove it.

7. Remove the water pump retaining bolts. Remove the water pump.

NOTE: On the 2.5L engine, remove the pump by pulling it straight out of the block.

8. Installation is the reverse of the removal procedure. Use new gaskets or RTV sealant as required. Fill cooling system and run engine to normal operating temperature. Check pump area for leaks.

Thermostat

REMOVAL & INSTALLATION

1. Disconnect the negative battery cable. Drain the cooling system.

2. As required, remove the air cleaner assembly.

3. As required, remove the upper radiator hose.

4. Remove the thermostat housing bolts, the thermostat housing and the thermostat.

5 Install new thermostat in engine block, use new housing gasket and install housing. Tighten housing bolts to 20–25 ft. lbs. Fill cooling system and run engine to check for leaks.

COOLING SYSTEM BLEEDING

After working on the cooling system, even to replace the thermostat, it must be bled. Air trapped in the system will prevent proper filling and leave the radiator coolant level low, causing a risk of overheating.

1. To bleed the system, start with the system cool, the radiator cap off and the radiator filled to about an inch below the filler neck.

2. Start the engine and run it at slightly above normal idle speed. This will insure adequate circulation. If air bubbles appear and the coolant level drops, fill the system with an antifreeze/water mixture to bring the level back to the proper level.

3. Run the engine this way until the thermostat opens. When this happens, coolant will move abruptly across the top of the radiator and the temperature of the radiator will suddenly rise.

4. At this point, air is often expelled and the level may drop quite a bit. Keep refilling the system until the level is near the top of the radiator and remains constant.

5. If the vehicle has an overflow tank, fill the radiator right up to the filler neck. Replace the radiator filler cap.

EMISSION CONTROLS

For all information on emission control systems please refer to "Emission Controls" in the Unit Repair section. Due to the complex nature of modern electronic engine control systems, comprehensive diagnosis and testing procedures fall outside the confines of this repair manual. For complete information on diagnosis, testing and repair procedures concerning all modern engine and emission control systems, please refer to *"Chilton's Guide To Electronic Engine Controls".*

FUEL SYSTEM

NOTE: When working with the fuel system certain precautions should be taken; always work in a well ventilated area, keep a dry chemical (Class B) fire extinguisher near the work area. Always disconnect the negative battery cable and do not make any repairs to the fuel system until all the necessary steps for repair have been reviewed.

FUEL SYSTEM PRESSURE RELIEF

Modern fuel injection systems operate under high pressure, this makes it necessary to first relieve the system of pressure before servicing. The pressurized fuel when released may ignite or cause personal injury. The following outlined steps may be used for most fuel systems:

• Remove the fuel pump fuse from the fuse block

• Crank the engine and let it run until the remaining fuel in the lines is consumed

• Crank engine again to make sure any fuel in the lines has been removed

• With the ignition **OFF** replace the fuel pump fuse

Fuel Filter

REMOVAL & INSTALLATION

Carbureted Vehicles

1. Disconnect the fuel line connection at the fuel inlet filter nut on the carburetor.

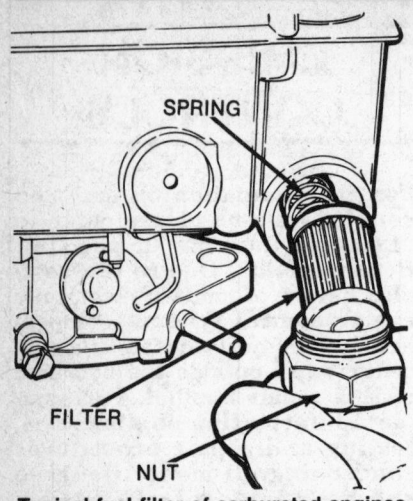

Typical fuel filter of carbureted engines

2. Remove the fuel inlet filter nut from the carburetor.

3. Remove the filter and the spring.

4. Installation is the reverse of the removal procedure. Start the engine and check for leaks.

Fuel Injected Vehicles

1. Relieve the fuel line pressure. Disconnect the negative battery cable.

2. Disconnect the fuel lines. Remove the fuel filter from the retainer or mounting bolt.

3. Installation is the reverse of the removal procedure. Start the engine and check for leaks.

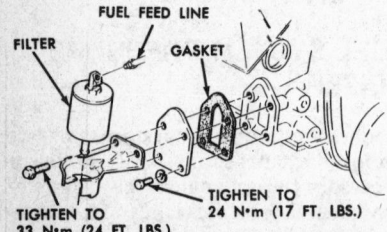

Fuel filter mounting on a TBI-equipped V8 engine. Note that the mounting location is the same as that for the fuel pump on carbureted engines

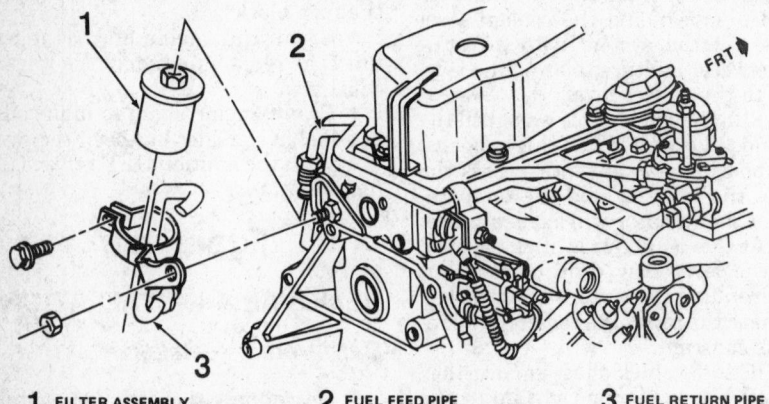

| 1 FILTER ASSEMBLY | 2 FUEL FEED PIPE | 3 FUEL RETURN PIPE |

Fuel filter location—2.5L engine with TBI

Mechanical Fuel Pump

TESTING

Volume Test

1. Disconnect the fuel line from the carburetor fuel feed line and position it in a suitable container.

2. Start the engine and let it idle for 15 seconds. The fuel pump should supply a half pint or more of fuel, if not proceed as follows.

3. Disconnect the inlet hose at the fuel pump and install a vacuum gauge. Crank or run the engine until maximum vacuum is achieved.

4. If the vacuum is less than 15 in. replace the fuel pump. If the vacuum reading is more than 15 in. proceed as follows.

5. Using a vacuum gauge check the fuel lines and fuel hoses for cracks, splits, leaks or kinks. Crank or run the engine until the vacuum gauge peaks.

6. The vacuum reading should be at least 15 in., if not replace the defective piece of fuel hose or line.

7. If the fuel lines and the fuel pump check out okay, check the fuel tank unit for fuel flow restriction.

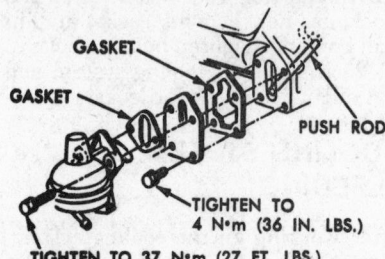

Typical mechanical fuel pump installation on a V8 engine

Pressure Test

1. Disconnect the fuel line at the carburetor. Install a rubber hose about 10 in. long. Attach a low reading pressure gauge.

2. Hold the gauge at least 16 in.

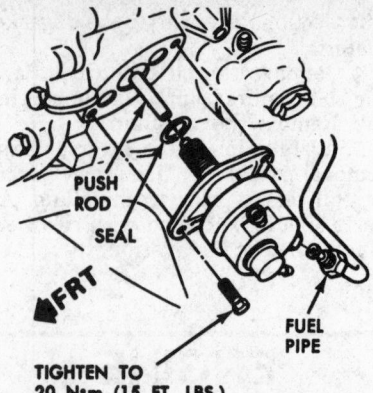

Fuel pump location—2.8L engine

above the fuel pump. If equipped, pinch the fuel return line.

3. Start the engine and run at slow idle, using the fuel that is left in the carburetor.

4. If the fuel pump is operating properly the pressure on the gasuge should read a constant 5.5-6.5 psi.

5. If the pressure is too low, too high or significantly different at various engine speeds the pump should be replaced.

REMOVAL & INSTALLATION

1. Disconnect the negative battery cable. Remove all the necessary components in order to gain access to the fuel pump assembly.

2. Disconnect and plug the fuel intake and outlet lines at the fuel pump.

3. On Chevrolet produced V6 and V8 engines remove the upper bolt from the right front mounting boss. Insert a longer bolt (3/8–16 × 2 in.) in this hole to hold the fuel pump pushrod.

4. Remove the 2 pump mounting bolts and lockwashers. Remove the fuel pump from the vcehicle.

5. If the rocker arm pushrod is to be removed from Chevrolet produced V6 or V8 engines, remove the 2 adapter bolts and lockwashers and remove the adapter and its gasket.

6. Installation is the reverse of the removal procedure.

Electric Fuel Pump

PRESSURE TESTING

1. Obtain 2 sections of 3/8 in. steel tubing 10 in. long.. Double flare one end of each section. Install a flare nut on 1 end of each section.

2. Using tool J-29658-82, connect each of the above sections of tubing into the flare nut to flare nut adapters that are included in the tool kit.

3. Attach the pipe and adapter assemblies to the gauge from the tool kit.

4. Raise and support the vehicle safely.

5. Disconnect the fuel feed hose from the fuel pipe on the body of the vehicle.

6. Install one length of steel tubing onto the feed pipe of the body. Connect the other end of the hose onto one of the sections of the 10 in. steel pipe. Secure all hose connections with clamps.

7. Start the engine and check for leaks. Correct leaks immediately.

8. Observe the pressure reading it should be between 9–13 psi. If not within specification, correct as required.

9. Depressurize the fuel system and remove the test equipment.

REMOVAL & INSTALLATION

The electric pump used with fuel injected models is an integral part of the fuel tank sending unit. The pump may be serviced separately after the pump/sending unit assembly is removed from the tank.

1. Disconnect the negative battery cable.

2. Drain the fuel from the fuel tank.

3. Disconnect the exhaust pipe at the catalytic convertor and the rear hanger. Allow the exhaust system to hang over the rear axle assembly.

4. Remove the tailpipe and muffler heat shields.

5. Remove the fuel filler neck shield from behind the left rear tire.

6. Remove the rear suspension track bar and the track bar brace.

7. Disconnect the fuel pump/sending unit electrical connector, at the body harness connector. Do not pry up on the cover connector, as the pump/sending unit wiring harness is an integral part of the sending unit.

8. Disconnect the fuel pipes.

9. Remove the fuel pipe retaining bracket on the left side and the brakeline clip from the retaining bracket.

10. Position a jack under the rear axle assembly in order to support the rear axle.

11. Disconnect the lower ends of the shock absorbers, lower the axle assembly enough to release the tension on the coil springs. Remove the coil springs.

12. Lower the rear axle assembly as far as possible without causing damage to the brake lines and cables.

13. Remove the fuel tank strap bolts.

14. Remove the tank by rotating the front of the tank downward and sliding it to the right side.

15. Remove the fuel pump/sending unit from the tank, by loosening the cam nut. When removing the cam nut, use brass tools to tap the nut loose. Do not use standard metal tools, as sparks could be generated.

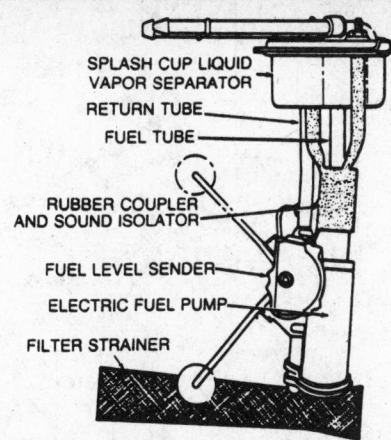

Electric fuel pump and fuel gauge meter assembly of a TBI-equipped engine

16. Remove the O-ring from beneath the unit. Replace the O-ring if defective.

17. Separate the fuel pump from the sending unit and install the new pump in the same manner.

18. Install the pump/sending unit assembly into the fuel tank and install the fuel tank. Reinstall the rear sususpension componenets, exhaust system and fuel lines. After installation is complete, check all fuel line connections for leaks.

Carburetor

REMOVAL & INSTALLATION

1. Disconnect the negative battery cable. Remove the air cleaner.

2. Disconnect the fuel and vacuum lines. Disconnect the choke electrical connector and the throttle linkage.

3. If equipped with an automatic transmission, disconnect the throttle valve linkage.

4. If equipped, disconnect the EGR line and the idle stop solenoid.

5. Remove the carburetor retaining bolts. Remove the carburetor assembly from the vehicle.

6. Install the carburetor in the reverse order of removal.

OVERHAUL

For all carburetor overhaul and adjustments procedures, please refer to the "Carburetor Service" in the Unit Repair section.

Fuel Injection

Due to the complex nayure of modern fuel injection systems, comprehensive diagnosis and testing procedures fall outside the confines of this repair manual. For complete information on fuel injection diagnosis, testing and repair procedures please refer to *Chilton's Guide to Fuel Injection And Feedback Carburetors.*

MANUAL TRANSMISSION

REMOVAL & INSTALLATION

4 Speed

1. Disconnect the negative battery cable.

2. Raise the vehicle and support it safely.

3. Drain the lubricant from the transmission.

4. Remove the torque arm from the vehicle.

5. Mark the driveshaft and the rear axle pinion flange to indicate their relationship. Remove the driveshaft from the vehicle.

6. Disconnect the speedometer cable and the electrical connectors from the transmission.

7. Remove the exhaust pipe brace.

8. Remove the transmission shifter support attaching bolts from the transmission.

9. Disconnect the shift linkage at the shifter.

10. Raise the transmission slightly with a jack, then remove the crossmember attaching bolts.

11. Remove the transmission mount attaching bolts and remove the mount and crossmember from the vehicle.

12. Remove the transmission attaching bolts and carefully move the transmission rearward and downward out of the vehicle.

13. Installation is the reverse of the removal procedure.

14. Refill the transmission with the proper amount and quality of transmission lubricant. Install the driveshaft with the matchmarks aligned, install all linkages in their proper location.

5 Speed

1. Disconnect the negative battery cable.

2. Remove the shift lever boot attaching screws and slide the boot up the shift lever.

3. Remove the shift lever from the transmission.

4. Raise the vehicle and support it safely.

5. Drain the lubricant from the transmission.

6. Remove the torque arm from the vehicle.

7. Mark the driveshaft and the rear axle pinion flange to indicate their relationship. Remove the driveshaft from the vehicle.

8. Disconnect the speedometer cable and the electrical connectors from the transmission.

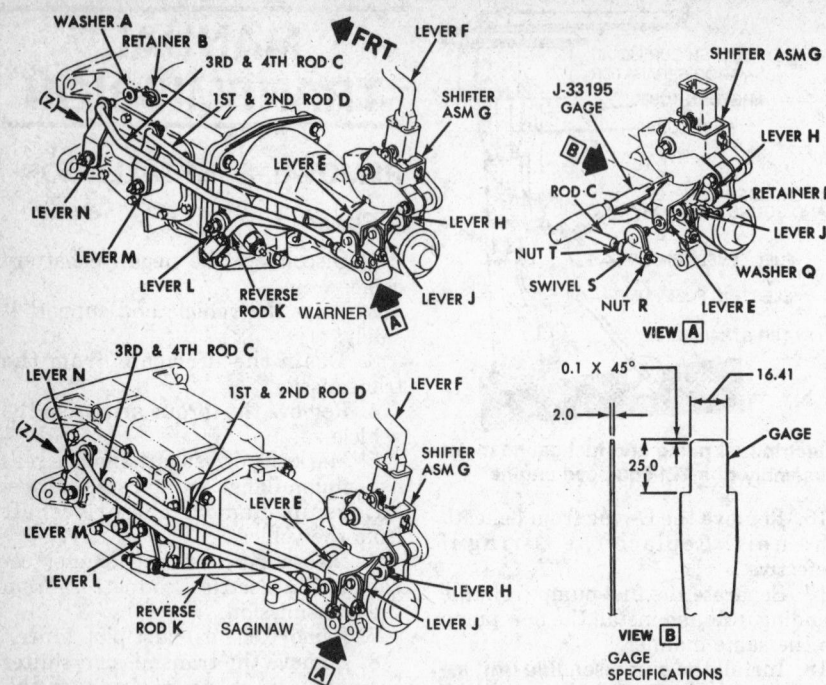

Transmission shift linkage adjustment on 1982–84 models. Note that all component references in the illustration match those in the text and that the dimensions are expressed in millimeters.

9. Disconnect the clutch cable at the transmission.

10. Remove the catalytic converter hanger.

11. Remove the exhaust pipe brace.

12. Remove the transmission shifter support attaching bolts from the transmission.

13. Disconnect the shift linkage at the shifter.

14. Raise the transmission slightly with a jack, then remove the cross-member attaching bolts.

15. Remove the transmission mount attaching bolts and remove the mount and crossmember from the vehicle.

16. Remove the transmission attaching bolts and carefully move the transmission rearward and downward out of the vehicle.

17. Installation is the reverse of the removal procedure.

LINKAGE ADJUSTMENT

4 Speed

1982–84

1. Disconnect the negative battery cable.

2. Place the shift control lever in **Neutral**.

3. Raise and support the vehicle safely.

4. Remove the swivel retainers from the levers.

5. Remove the swivels from the the shifter assembly and loosen the swivel locknuts.

6. Make sure that all levers in the center detents.

7. Align the holes of levers and with the notch in the shifter assembly. Insert an alignment gauge (J-33195) to hold the levers in this position.

8. Insert the rear swivel into the rear ever and install the washer. Secure with retainer.

9. Apply rearward pressure to the lever. Tighten the locknuts against swivel, torque to 25 ft. lbs.

10. Repeat Steps 8 and 9 for the other rods and levers.

11. Remove the alignment gauge, lower the vehicle and check the operation of the shifting mechanism.

5 Speed

The 5 speed transmission gearshift lever is floor mounted and is located on top of the extension housing. The shift mechanism does not require adjustment.

CLUTCH

REMOVAL & INSTALLATION

1. Support engine and remove the transmission.

2. Disconnect the clutch fork push rod and spring.

3. Remove the flywheel housing.

4. Slide the clutch fork from the ball stud and remove the fork from the dust boot. The ball stud is threaded into the clutch housing and may be replaced, if necessary. As required, remove the clutch fork from the slave cylinder.

5. Install an alignment tool to support the clutch assembly during removal. Mark the flywheel and clutch cover for reinstallation, if they do not already have **X** marks.

6. Loosen the clutch to flywheel attaching bolts evenly, one turn at a time, until spring pressure is released. Remove the bolts and clutch assembly.

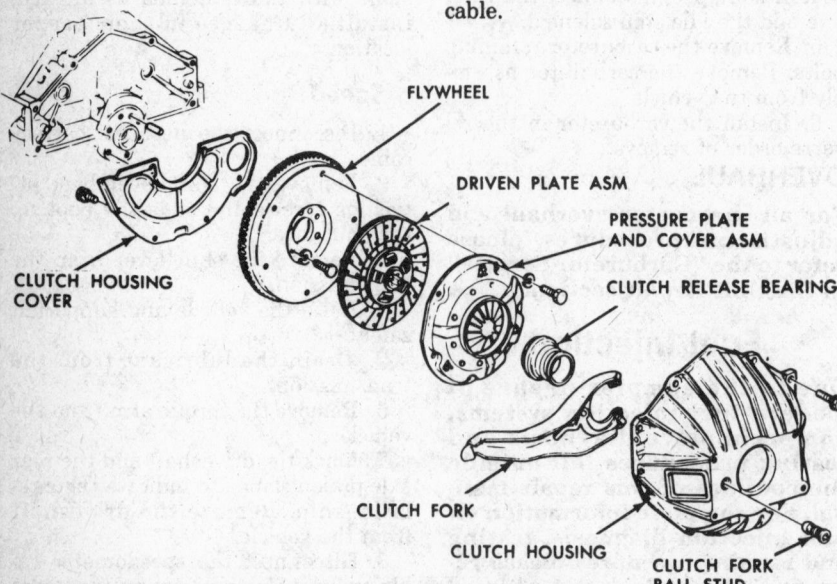

Exploded view of the clutch assembly

7. Installation is the reverse of removal. Be sure to install the driven disc with the damper springs facing the transmission.

FREE-PLAY ADJUSTMENT

1. Disconnect the return spring at the clutch fork.
2. Hold the pedal against the rubber bumper on the dash brace.
3. Push the clutch fork so that the throwout bearing lightly contacts the pressure plate fingers.
4. Loosen the locknut and adjust the length of the rod so that the swivel or rod can slip freely into the gauge hole of the lever. Increase the length of the rod until the freeplay is removed.
5. Remove the rod or swivel from the gauge hole and insert it in the other (original) hole on the lever. Install the retainer and tighten the locknut.
6. Install the return spring and check freeplay measurement from the floor mat to top of the pedal pad. It should measure 7/8–1 1/8 in.

Clutch Hydraulic System

REMOVAL & INSTALLATION

1. Disconnect the negative battery cable. Remove the steering column trim cover and hush panel.
2. Remove the master cylinder push rod from the clutch pedal.
3. Remove the clutch master cylinder to cowl nuts.
4. Remove the brake booster to cowl nuts. Remove the clutch fluid reservoir from the bracket.
5. Pull the brake master cylinder forward for access to the clutch master cylinder. Remove the clutch master cylinder from the cowl.
6. Raise and support the vehicle safely. Remove the slave cylinder heat shield.
7. Disconnect the slave cylinder from the clutch fork. Remove the slave cylinder retaining bolts and remove the slave cylinder from the bell housing.
8. Lower the vehicle and remove the complete clutch hydraulic system from the engine compartment.
9. Install in the reverse order of removal making sure to properly connect the clutch pedal linkage. Bleed the system.

BLEEDING THE HYDRAULIC CLUTCH SYSTEM

1. Clean all dirt and grease from the cap to make sure that no foreign substances enter the system.

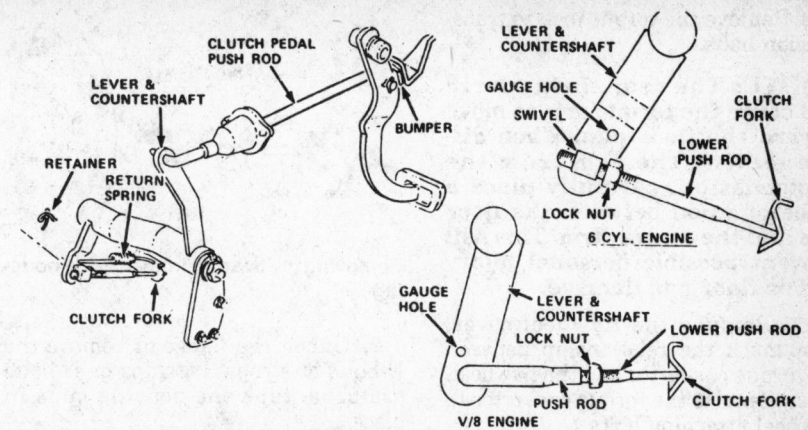

Typical clutch linkage and adjustment points

2. Remove the cap and diaphragm and fill the reservoir to the top with the approved DOT 3 brake fluid. Fully loosen the bleed screw which is in the slave cylinder body next to the inlet connection.
3. At this point bubbles of air will appear at the bleed screw outlet. When the slave cylinder is full and a steady stream of fluid comes out of the slave cylinder bleeder, tighten the bleed screw.
4. Assemble the diaphragm and cap to the reservoir, fluid in the reservoir should be level with the step. Exert a light load of about 20 lbs. to the slave cylinder piston by pushing the release lever towards the cylinder and loosen the bleed screw. Maintain a constant light load, fluid and any air that is left will be expelled through the bleed port. Tighten the bleed screw when a steady flow of fluid and no air is being expelled.
5. Fill the reservoir fluid level back to normal capacity and if necessary repeat Step 4.

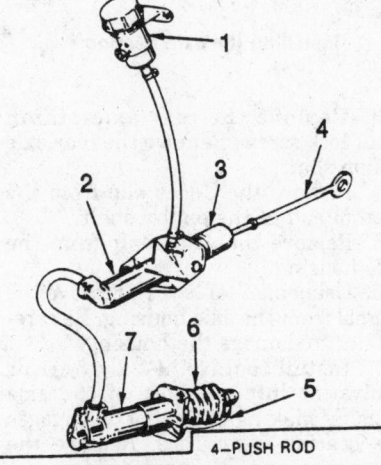

1—FLUID RESERVOIR
2—CLUTCH MASTER CYLINDER
3—BOOT
4—PUSH ROD
5—SHIPPING STRAP
6—BOOT
7—CLUTCH SLAVE CYLINDER

Hydraulic clutch assembly

6. Exert a light load to the release lever, but do not open the bleeder screw as the piston in the slave cylinder will move slowly down the bore. Repeat this operation 2–3 times, the fluid movement will force any air left in the system into the reservoir. The hydraulic system should now be fully bled.
7. Check the the operation of the clutch hydraulic system and repeat this procedure if necesary. Check the push rod travel at the slave cylinder to insure the minimum travel 0.57 in.

AUTOMATIC TRANSMISSION

For further information on automatic transmissions, please refer to "Automatic Transmissions" in the Unit Repair section.

REMOVAL & INSTALLATION

1. Disconnect the negative battery cable.
2. Remove the air cleaner assembly.
3. Disconnect the throttle valve (TV) control cable at the carburetor.
4. Remove the transmission oil dipstick. Unbolt and remove the dipstick tube.
5. Raise the vehicle and support it safely.
6. Mark the relationship between the driveshaft and the rear pinion flange so that the driveshaft may be reinstalled in its original position.
7. Remove the driveshaft from the vehicle.
8. Disconnect the catalytic convertor support bracket at the transmission.
9. Disconnect the speedometer cable, electrical connectors and the shift control cable from the transmission.

10. Remove the torque arm to transmission bolts.

NOTE: The rear spring force will cause the torque arm to move toward the floor pan. When disconnecting the arm from the transmission, carefully place a piece of wood between the floor pan and the torque arm. This will prevent possible personal injury and/or floor pan damage.

11. Remove the flywheel cover, then mark the relationship between the torque convertor and the flywheel.

12. Remove the torque convertor to flywheel attaching bolts.

13. Support the transmission with a jack, then remove the transmission mount bolt.

14. Unbolt and remove the transmission crossmember.

15. Lower the transmission slightly. Disconnect the T.V. cable and oil cooler lines from the transmission.

16. Support the engine. Remove the transmission to engine mounting bolts.

17. Remove the transmission from the vehicle. Keep the rear of the transmission lower than the front to avoid the possibility of the torque convertor disengaging from the transmission.

18. Installation is the reverse of the removal procedure. Check all cooling lines for leakage. Torque the converter to flywheel bolts to 35 ft. lbs..

DRIVE AXLE

Driveshaft and U-Joints

REMOVAL & INSTALLATION

1. Raise and support the vehicle safely. Matchmark the pinion flange and driveshaft for assembly.

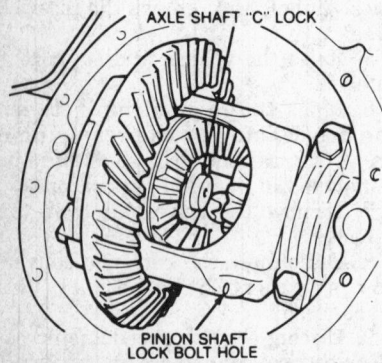

AXLE SHAFT "C" LOCK

PINION SHAFT LOCK BOLT HOLE

Removing the "C" lock from the axle shaft

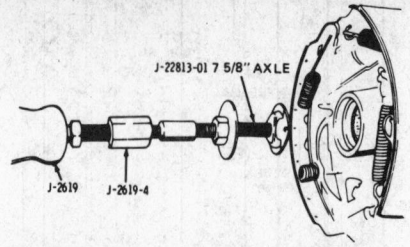

J-22813-01 7 5/8" AXLE

J-2619 J-2619-4

Removing the bearing from the axle housing

2. Unbolt the flange or remove the U-bolts or straps. If straps or U-bolts are used, tape the bearing cups in place.

3. Drop the driveshaft down at the rear, then pull it backwards out from the transmission extension housing. The transmission housing should be plugged to prevent leakage.

4. Installation is the reverse of the removal procedure.

Rear Axle Shafts

REMOVAL & INSTALLATION

Except Borg Warner Rear Assembly

1. Raise the vehicle and support it safely. Remove the rear wheels and drums.

2. Remove the carrier cover and drain the lubricant.

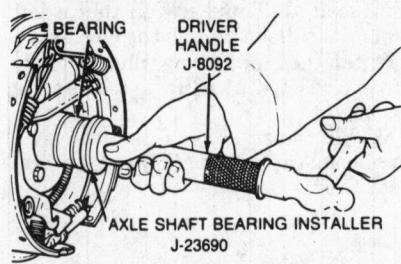

BEARING   DRIVER HANDLE J-8092

AXLE SHAFT BEARING INSTALLER J-23690

Installing the axle bearing

3. Remove the rear axle pinion shaft lock screw. Remove the rear axle pinion shaft.

4. Remove the C-lock clip from the bottom end of the pinion shaft.

5. Remove the axle shaft from the axle housing.

6. Using a suitable tool, remove the oil seal from the axle housing. Be careful not to damage the housing.

7. Install tool No. J-22813-01 or equivalent into the bore of the axle housing making sure that it engages the bearing outer race. Remove the bearing using slide hammer.

8. Installation is the reverse of the removal procedure. Lubricate the new bearing with gear lube before installing.

Borg Warner Rear Assembly

1. Raise the vehicle and support it safely.

2. Remove the rear wheels and drums. Remove the brake components as required.

3. Remove the 4 nuts holding the brake anchor plate and outer bearing retainer.

4. Remove the axle shaft and wheel bearing assembly using axle shaft removal tool J-21597 and slide hammer J-2619 or equivalent.

5. To remove the inner bearing retainer and the bearing from the axle shaft, split the retainer with a chisel and remove it from the shaft. Using tool J-22912-01 press the bearing off the shaft.

6. Install the axle assembly in the reverse order of removal. LIghtly lubricate the oil seal to install it in the axle housing.

FRONT SUSPENSION

Shock Absorber

REMOVAL & INSTALLATION

1. Remove the upper shock retaining nut from its mounting.

2. Raise and support the vehicle safely.

3. Remove the bolts holding the shock absorber to lower control arm and pull the shock through the arm.

4. Installation is the reverse of the removal procedure.

McPherson Strut

REMOVAL & INSTALLATION

1. Position the ignition key in the unlocked position so that the front wheels can be moved.

2. At the front wheelhouse reinforcement, remove the strut to upper mount cover and nut. Do not attempt to move the vehicle with the upper strut fastener disconnected.

3. Raise and support the vehicle safely. Position a suitable jack under the lower control arms.

4. Remove the wheel and tire assembly.

5. Remove the brake hose from the strut bracket.

6. Remove the bolts attaching the strut to steering knuckle.

7. Lift the strut up from the steering knuckle to compress the rod, then pull down and remove the strut.

8. Installation is the reverse of the removal procedure.

OVERHAUL

For all spring and shock absorber removal and installation procedures, and all strut overhaul procedures, please refer to "Strut Overhaul" in the Unit Repair section.

Coil Spring

REMOVAL & INSTALLATION

1. Disconnect the negative battery cable. Raise and support the vehicle safely.

2. Remove the front wheel and tire assembly.

3. Disconnect the stabilizer link from the lower control arm. If the steering gear hinders removal procedures, detach the unit and move it aside.

4. Disconnect the tie rod from the steering knuckle using a ball joint removal tool J-24292A.

5. Using an internal fit coil spring compressor, compress the coil spring so that it is loose in its seat.

6. To remove the coil spring, disconnect the lower control arm from the crossmember at the pivot bolts. If additional clearance is necessary, disconnect the lower control arm from the steering knuckle at the ball joint.

7. To install, compress the coil spring until spring height is the same as when removed, then position the spring on the control arm. Make sure the lower end of the coil spring is properly positioned in the lower control arm and that the upper end fits correctly in its pad.

8. To complete the installation, reverse the removal procedures. Torque the lower control arm to steering knuckle to 78 ft. lbs., the pivot bolt nuts to 63 ft. lbs., the tie rod to steering knuckle to 35 ft. lbs. and the stabilizer to control arm to 13 ft. lbs.

Ball Joints

INSPECTION

1. Raise and support the front of the vehicle, until there is 1–2 in. of clearance under the wheels.

2. Before performing this inspection, make sure the wheel bearings are adjusted and that the control arm bushings are in good condition.

3. Insert a bar under the wheel and pry upward. If the wheel raises more than ⅛ in., the ball joints are worn. Determine if the upper or lower ball

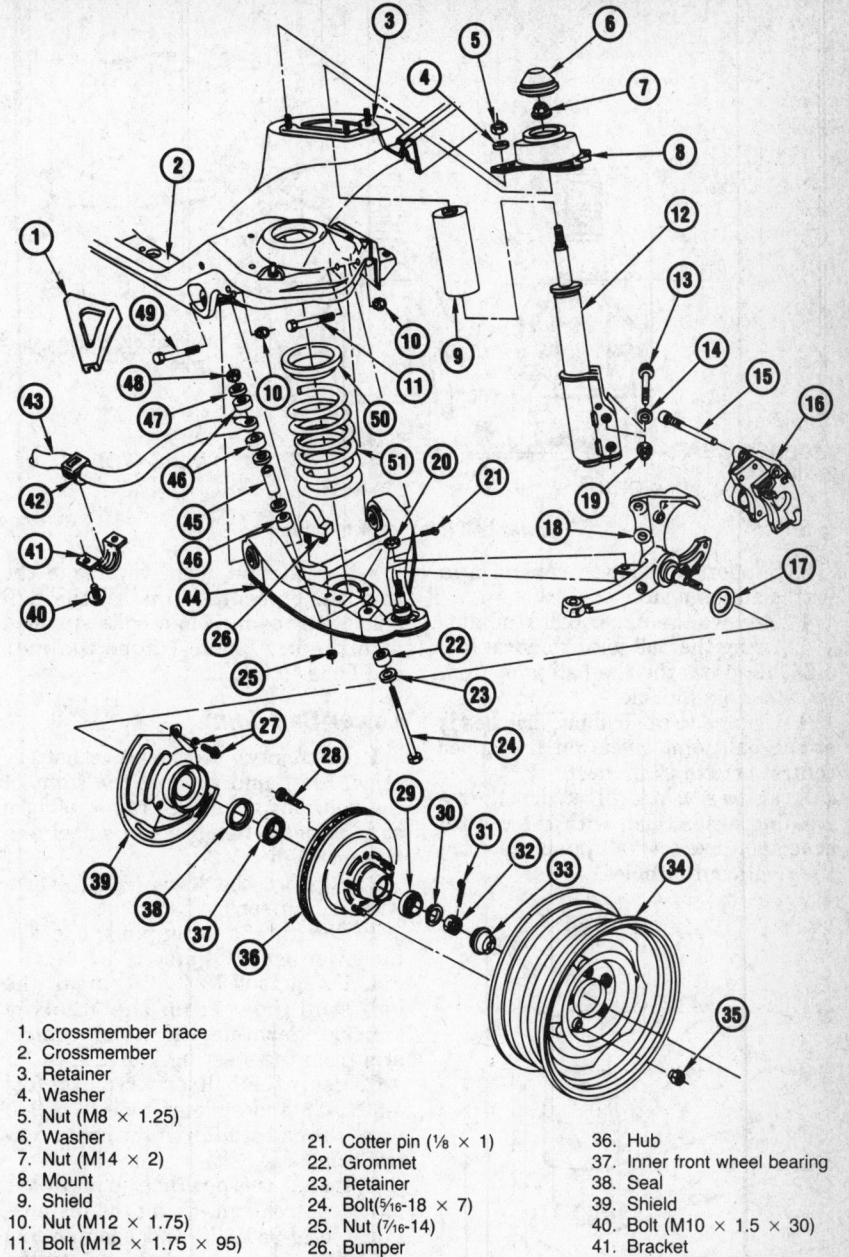

1. Crossmember brace
2. Crossmember
3. Retainer
4. Washer
5. Nut (M8 × 1.25)
6. Washer
7. Nut (M14 × 2)
8. Mount
9. Shield
10. Nut (M12 × 1.75)
11. Bolt (M12 × 1.75 × 95)
12. Absorber w/strut
13. Bolt
14. Washer
15. Bolt
16. Caliper
17. Gasket
18. Knuckle
19. Nut (M16 × 2)
20. Nut (9⁄16-18)

21. Cotter pin (⅛ × 1)
22. Grommet
23. Retainer
24. Bolt(9⁄16-18 × 7)
25. Nut (7⁄16-14)
26. Bumper
27. Bolt
28. Bolt
29. Outer front wheel bearing
30. Washer
31. Cotter pin (M3.2 × 25)
32. Nut
33. Cap
34. Wheel
35. Nut

36. Hub
37. Inner front wheel bearing
38. Seal
39. Shield
40. Bolt (M10 × 1.5 × 30)
41. Bracket
42. Insulator
43. Front stabilizer shaft
44. Lower control arm
45. Spacer
46. Grommet
47. Retainer
48. Nut
49. Bolt (M12 × 1.75 × 115)
50. Insulator

Front suspension and related components — 1982–89

joint is worn by visual inspection while prying on the wheel.

4. The upper ball joint can be further inspected after partial suspension disassembly. If the stud has any detectable side to side movement or if it can be twisted easily by hand, it should be replaced.

REMOVAL & INSTALLATION

Upper Ball Joint

1. Raise and support the vehicle safely.

2. Remove the tire and wheel assembly.

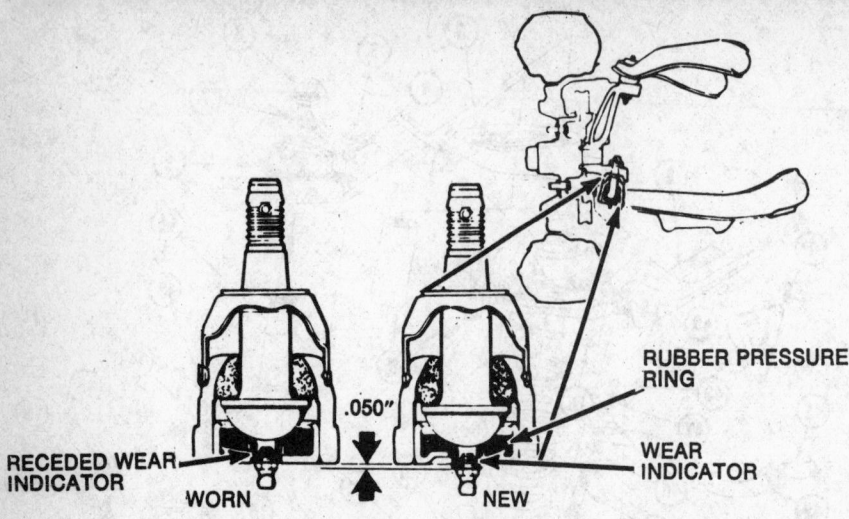

Lower ball joint wear indicator

3. Support the lower control arm with a suitable jack.

4. Remove the upper ball stud nut.

5. Using the ball joint removal tool J-23742, press the the ball joint from the steering knuckle.

6. Using a ⅛ in. drill bit, drill heads of the ball joint rivets on the upper control arm to ¼ in. deep.

7. Using a ½ in. drill bit, drill the remaining heads flush with the control arm, then use a small punch to drive the rivets out of holes.

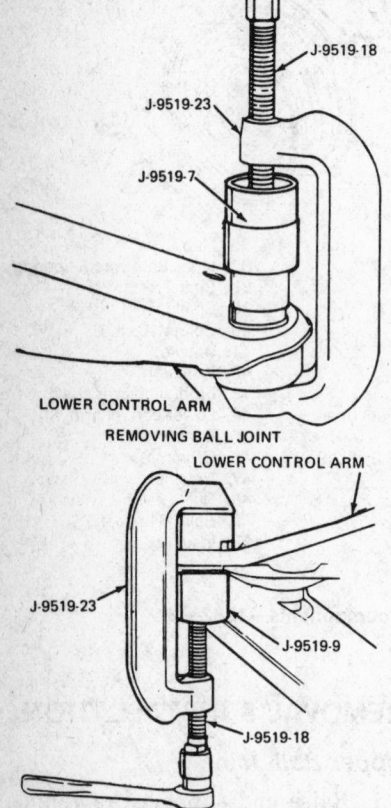

Removing and installing the lower ball joint

8. Installation is the reverse of the removal procedure. Install the ball joint with the nuts and bolts supplied with the new joint. Torque the nuts and bolts to 8 ft. lbs.

Lower Ball Joint

1. Disconnect the negative battery cable. Raise and support the front of the vehicle under the frame using a suitable jack. Remove the wheel and tire assembly.

2. Support the lower control arm with the proper jack.

3. Remove the cotter pin and loosen the lower ball stud nut.

4. Using tool J-24292A, break the ball stud loose from the steering knuckle. Separate the lower control arm from the steering knuckle.

5. Using the ball joint removal tool J-9519-23 and adapter tool J-9519-7, press the ball stud from the lower control arm.

6. Install the new ball joint to the lower control arm. Using the installation tool J-9519-23 and adapter tool J9519-9, press the ball joint into the lower control arm until it bottoms on the arm.

NOTE: When installing the new ball joint, position the purge vent in the rubber boot facing inward.

7. To complete the installation, connect the ball joint to control arm assembly to the steering knuckle and torque the ball joint nut to 77 ft. lbs., then reverse the removal procedures.

Upper Control Arm

REMOVAL & INSTALLATION

1. Separate the upper ball joint from the steering knuckle.

2. Remove the upper control arm shaft pivot nuts. Tape the shims together and identify them so that they can be installed in the position from which they were removed.

3. Support the hub assembly to prevent damage to the brake line.

4. Remove the upper control arm from the vehicle.

5. Installation is the reverse the removal procedures. Make sure the shaft to frame bolts are installed in the same position they were in before removal and that the shims are in their original positions. Torque the control arm pivot bolt nuts to 85 ft. lbs.

Lower Control Arm

REMOVAL & INSTALLATION

1. Remove the coil spring assembly.

2. Remove the ball stud from the steering knuckle.

3. Remove the pivot bolts and the lower control arm.

4. Installation is the reverse of the removal procedure. Torque the control arm pivot bolts to 63 ft. lbs. (1982–89).

Front Wheel Bearing

ADJUSTMENT

1. Raise and support the vehicle safely.

2. Remove the hub dust cover, the cotter pin and loosen the hub nut.

3. Spin the wheel and tighten the nut to seat the bearings. Do not exert over 12 ft. lbs. of force on the nut.

4. Back the nut off until it is just loose. Line up the cotter pin hole in the spindle with the hole in the nut.

5. Insert a new cotter pin and bend the ends of the pin. The end-play should be between 0.001–0.005 in. If the play exceeds this tolerance, the wheel bearings should be replaced.

REMOVAL & INSTALLATION

1. Raise and support the vehicle safely. Remove the wheel assembly. Remove the caliper.

2. Pry off the dust cap. Tap out and discard the cotter pin. Remove the locknut.

3. Being careful not to drop the outer bearing, pull off the brake disc and wheel hub.

4. Remove the grease inside the wheel hub.

5. Using a brass drift, carefully drive the outer bearing race out of the hub.

6. Remove the inner grease seal and bearing.

7. Check the bearings for wear or damage and replace them if necessary.

8. Coat the inner surface of the hub with grease.

9. Grease the outer surface of the bearing race and drift it into place in the hub.

10. Pack the inner and outer wheel bearings with grease. If the brake disc has been removed and/or replaced, tighten the retaining bolts to specification.

11. Install the inner bearing in the hub. Being careful not to distort it, install the oil seal with its lip facing the bearing. Drive the seal on until its outer edge is even with the edge of the hub.

12. Install the hub/disc assembly on the spindle, being careful not to damage the oil seal.

13. Install the outer bearing, washer and spindle nut. Adjust the bearing.

Front Wheel Alignment
ADJUSTMENT

Caster

Caster is the tilting of the steering axis either forward or backward from the vertical, when viewed from the side of the vehicle. A backward tilt is said to be positive and a forward tilt is said to be negative.

Camber

Camber is the tilting of the wheels from the vertical when viewed from the front of the vehicle. When the wheels tilt outward from the top, the camber is said to be positive. When the wheels tilt inward from the top the camber is said to be negative. The amount of tilt is measured in degrees from the vertical. This measurement is called camber angle.

Toe-In

Toe-in is the turning in of the wheels. The actual amount of toe-in is normally only a fraction of an inch. The purpose of toe-in specification is to ensure parallel rolling of the wheels. Toe-in also serves to offset the small deflections of the steering support system which occur when the vehicle is rolling forward.

REAR SUSPENSION

Shock Absorber

REMOVAL & INSTALLATION

1. Raise and support the vehicle safely.

2. Pull back the carpet in the rear hatch area and disconnect the upper shock attaching nut.

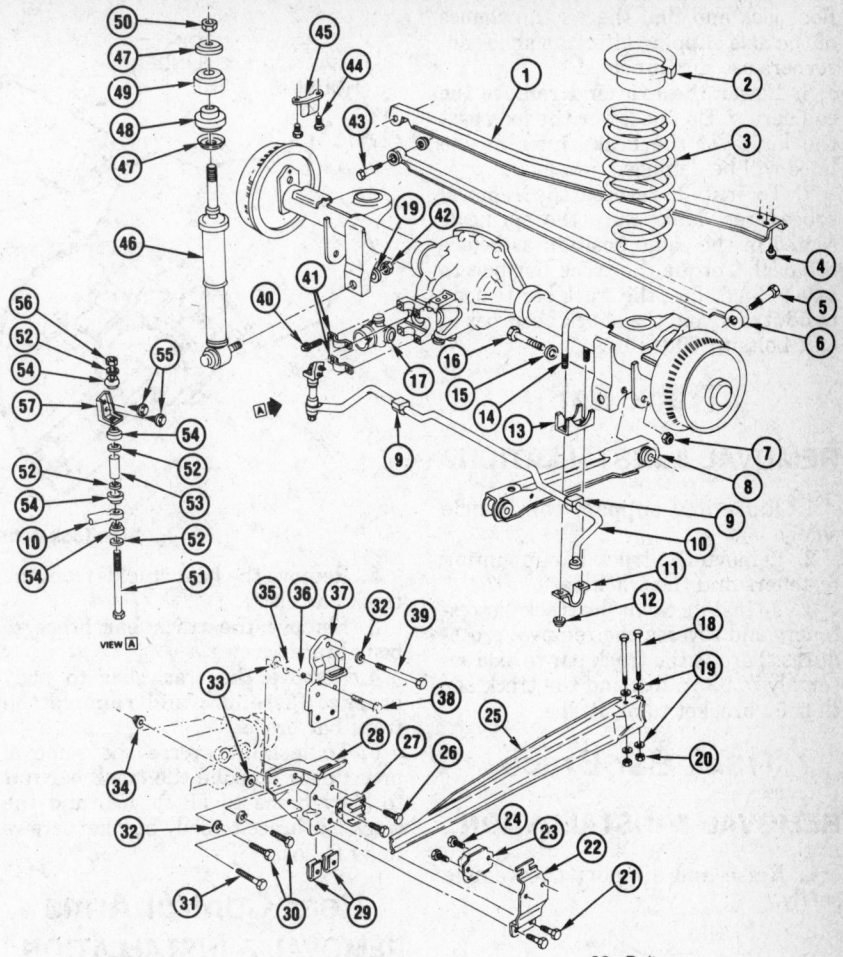

VIEW A

1. Tie rod bracket brace
2. Upper spring insulator
3. Coil spring
4. Screw (M10 × 1.5 × 32)
5. Bolt
6. Tie rod
7. Nut (M12 × 1.75)
8. Lower control arm
9. Insulator
10. Rear stabilizer shaft
11. Clamp
12. Nut (M8 × 1.25)
13. Bracket
14. Bolt
15. Washer
16. Bolt (M12 × 1.75 × 95)
17. Driveshaft w/universal joint
18. Bolt (M14 × 2 × 185)
19. Washer
20. Nut (M14 × 2)
21. Bolt (M8 × 1.25 × 25)
22. Bracket
23. Insulator
24. Bolt (M5 × 0.8 × 10)
25. Torque arm
26. Bolt (M5 × 0.8 × 10)
27. Torque arm insulator
28. Torque arm bracket
29. Nut; "U" (M8 × 1.25)
30. Bolt (M10 × 1.5 × 20)
31. Bolt (M10 × 1.5 × 70)
32. Washer (M10 × 18.3)
33. Spacer
34. Bolt (M4 × 0.7 × 20)
35. Push-nut
36. Spacer
37. Bracket
38. Bolt
39. Bolt (M10 × 1.5 × 110)
40. Bolt
41. Strap
42. Nut (M 14.0 × 2)
43. Bolt w/screw
44. Bolt (M8 × 1.25 × 16)
45. Bumper
46. Rear shock absorber
47. Retainer
48. Grommet
49. Grommet
50. Nut (M10 × 1.5)
51. Bolt (M8 × 1.25 × 180)
52. Washer
53. Spacer
54. Grommet
55. Screw (M10 × 1.5 × 32)
56. Nut (M8 × 1.25)(*2)
57. Bracket

Rear suspension and related components—1982–89

3. Remove the lower shock to axle mounting bolt. Remove the shock absorber from the vehicle.

4. Installation is the reverse of the removal procedure. Torque the upper shock attaching nut to 13 ft. lbs., the lower attaching bolts to 70 ft. lbs..

Springs
REMOVAL & INSTALLATION

1. Raise and support the vehicle so that the rear axle can be independently raised and lowered.

2. Support the rear axle with a suitable jack.

3. If equipped with brake hose attachment brackets, disconnect the brackets allowing the hoses to hang free. Do not disconnect the hoses. Perform this step only if the hoses will be unduly stretched when the axle is lowered.

4. Disconnect the track bar from the axle.

5. Remove the lower shock absorber bolts and lower the axle. Make sure the axle is supported securely on the

floor jack and that there is no chance of the axle slipping after the shock absorbers are disconnected.

6. Lower the axle and remove the coil spring. Do not lower the axle past the limits of the brake lines or the lines will be damaged.

7. To install, reverse the removal procedures. Make sure the spring is seated in the same position as before removal. Torque the track bar bolt to axle to 93 ft. lbs., the track bar to body to 58 ft. lbs. and the shock absorber to axle bolts to 70 ft. lbs.

Track Bar

REMOVAL & INSTALLATION

1. Raise and support the vehicle safely.

2. Remove the track bar mounting fasteners and the track bar.

3. To install, clean the track bar fasteners and reverse the removal procedures. Torque the track bar to axle assembly to 93 ft. lbs. and the track bar to body bracket to 58 ft. lbs.

Track Bar Brace

REMOVAL & INSTALLATION

1. Raise and support the vehicle safely.

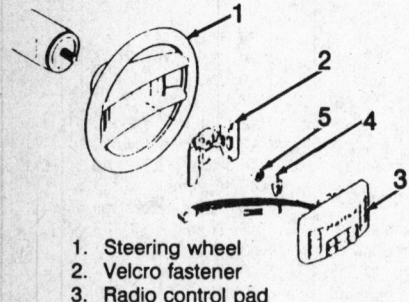

1. Steering wheel
2. Velcro fastener
3. Radio control pad
4. Retainer
5. Hex nut

Removing in-steering wheel radio controls

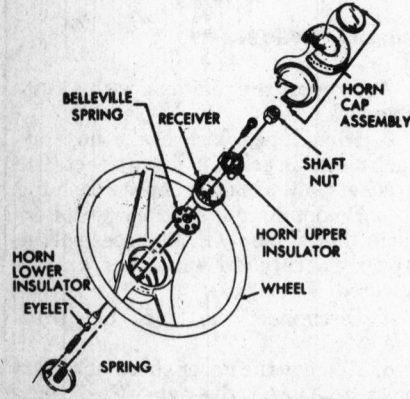

Cushioned rim steering wheel assembly

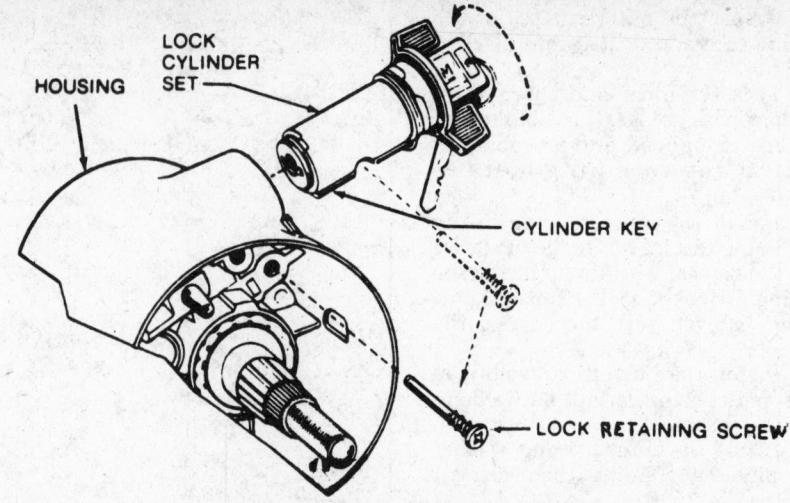

Ignition lock cylinder replacement

2. Remove the heat shields from the track bar brace.

3. Remove the track bar brace to body brace screws.

4. Remove the track bar to body bracket fasteners and remove the track bar brace.

5. To install, reverse the removal procedures. Torque the track bar nut to body brace to 58 ft. lbs. and the track bar brace to body bracket screws to 34 ft. lbs.

Rear Control Arms

REMOVAL & INSTALLATION

NOTE: Remove and install one lower control arm at a time. If both arms are removed at the same time, the axle could roll or slip sideways, making installation of the arms very difficult.

1. Raise and support the vehicle safely.

2. Remove the control arm attaching fasteners. Remove the control arm.

3. To install, reverse the removal procedures. Torque the control arm bolts to 68 ft. lbs.

STEERING

Steering Wheel

REMOVAL & INSTALLATION

1. Disconnect the negative battery cable.

2. Remove the horn trim pad. Remove the horn contact wire from the plastic tower by pushing in on the wire and turning counterclockwise. The wire will spring out of the tower. It may be necessary to turn the ignition

to the on position in order to facilitate removal.

3. If the vehicle is equipped with tilt and telescoping steering wheel remove the three screws that secure the telescope locking lever assembly to the adjuster. Unscrew and remove the adjuster from the steering shaft.

4. Remove the locking lever assembly. Scribe an alignment mark on the steering wheel hub in line with the slash mark on the steering shaft.

5. Loosen the locknut on the steering shaft and position it flush with the end of the shaft. Using the proper steering wheel removal tool remove the wheel from its mounting on the steering shaft.

6. Remove the steering wheel removal tool from the steering wheel. Remove the locknut from the steering shaft. Remove the steering wheel from the vehicle.

7. Installation is the reverse of the removal procedure. When installing the steering wheel it should not be driven on the steering shaft as damage to the steering column and its components could occur.

Turn Signal Switch

REMOVAL & INSTALLATION

1. Disconnect the negative battery cable.

2. Remove the steering wheel.

3. Insert a suitable tool into the lockplate and remove the lockplate cover assembly.

4. Install a spring compressor onto the steering shaft. Tighten the tool to compress the lockplate and the spring. Remove the snapring from the groove in the shaft.

5. Remove the lockplate and slide the turn signal cam and the upper bearing preload spring and the thrust washer off the upper steering shaft.

Depressing the lock cylinder spring latch

6. Remove the steering column lower cover.

7. Remove the turn signal lever from the column.

8. On vehicles equipped with cruise control disconnect the cruise control wire from the harness near the bottom of the column. Remove the harness protector from the cruise control wire. Remove the turn signal lever. Do not remove the wire from the column.

9. Remove the vertical bolts at the steering column upper support. Remove the shim packs. Keep the shims in order for reinstallation.

10. Remove the screws securing the column upper mounting bracket to the column. Remove the bracket.

11. Disconnect the turn signal wiring and remove the wires from the plastic protector.

12. Remove the turn signal switch mounting screws.

13. Slide the switch connector out of the bracket on the steering column.

14. If the switch is known to be bad, cut the wires and discard the switch. Tape the connector of the new switch to the old wires, and pull the new harness down through the steering column while removing the old wires.

15. If the original switch is to be reused, wrap tape around the wire and connector and pull the harness up through the column. It may be helpful to attach a length of wire to the harness connector before pulling it up through the column to facilitate installation.

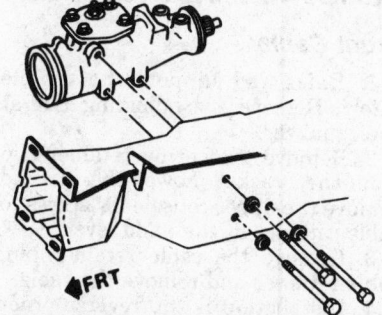

◄FRT

Power steering gear mounting—typical of all models

16. After freeing the switch wiring protector from its mounting, pull the turn signal switch straight up and remove the switch, switch harness, and the connector from the column.

17. Installation is the reverse of the removal procedure. Check operation of the turn signal switch and of the cancelling mechanism.

Steering Gear

REMOVAL & INSTALLATION

1. Disconnect the negative battery cable. Remove coupling shield, if equipped.

2. Remove the retaining nuts, lock washers and bolts at the steering coupling to steering shaft flange.

3. If equipped with power steering. Disconnect and plug the pressure and return lines from the steering gear box. Plug the hoses and gearbox openings.

4. Remove the pitman arm nut and washer. Matchmark the arm to the shaft.

5. With a puller, remove the pitman arm from the shaft.

6. Remove the bolts retaining the steering gear box to the side frame rail and remove the gear box from the vehicle.

7. Installation is the reverse of the removal procedure.

8. Fill and bleed the hydraulic system.

Power Steering Pump
REMOVAL & INSTALLATION

1. Disconnect the negative battery cable. Remove the hoses at the pump and tape the openings shut to prevent contamination. Position the disconnected lines in a raised position to prevent leakage.

2. Remove the pump drive belt.

3. Loosen the retaining bolts and braces. Remove the pump from the engine.

4. Installation is the reverse of removal. Tighten pump retaining bolts to 25–37 ft. lbs. After installing pump power steering system must be bled.

SYSTEM BLEEDING

1. Fill the reservoir with power steering fluid.

NOTE: The use of automatic transmission fluid in the power steering system is NOT recommended. Use power steering fluid only.

2. Allow the reservoir and fluid to be undisturbed for a few minutes.

3. Start the engine, allow it to run for approximately 3–5 minutes to warm up the fluid, then turn it off.

4. Check the reservoir fluid level and add fluid, if necessary.

5. Repeat the above steps until the fluid level stabilizes.

6. Raise and support the vehicle safely.

7. Start the engine and increase the engine speed to about 1500 rpm.

8. Turn the front wheels right to left (and back) several times, lightly contacting the wheel stops at the ends of travel.

9. Check the reservoir fluid level. Add fluid as required.

10. Repeat Step 8 until the fluid level in the reservoir stabilizes.

11. Lower the vehicle and repeat Steps 8 and 9.

Tie Rod Ends

REMOVAL & INSTALLATION

1. Raise and support the vehicle safely.

2. Remove the cotter pins and the castle nuts from the ball studs.

3. Using the ball joint removal tool J-24319-01 or J-6627, remove the ball joint. If necessary, pull downward on the tie rod to disconnect it from the steering arm.

4. Using the same removal tool, remove the inner ball stud from the relay rod. When removing the tie rod ends from the tie rod, be sure to mark their positions or count the number of turns necessary to remove them.

5. To remove the tie rod end or ends from the tie rod, loosen the clamp bolt and unscrew the ends.

NOTE: Lubricate tie rod threads with chassis grease and install new tie rod. Make sure both ends are an equal distance from the tie rod and tighten clamp bolts. Make sure ball studs, tapered surfaces and the threaded surfaces are clean and smooth and free of grease. Install new seals on ball studs, then position them in the steering knuckle and the relay rod.

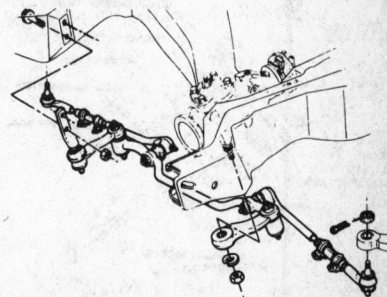

Steering linkage—typical of all models

6. Make sure clamp slots and sleeve slots are aligned before tightening clamps. Make sure tightening bolts will be in a horizontal position to 50 degrees upward (in the forward direction) when the tie rod is in its normal position.

7. To install, reverse the removal procedures. Torque the ball joint nuts to 35 ft. lbs. and the tie rod clamps to 14 ft. lbs. Install the new cotter pins. Lubricate new tie rod ends. Check the wheel alignment.

BRAKES

For all brake system repair and service procedures not detailed below, please refer to "Brakes" in the Unit Repair section.

Master Cylinder

REMOVAL & INSTALLATION

1. Disconnect the negative battery cable. Disconnect hydraulic lines at master cylinder.
2. Remove the retaining nuts and lockwashers that hold the cylinder to the brake booster.
3. Remove the master cylinder, gasket and rubber boot.
4. Installation is the reverse of the removal procedure. Bleed the system as required.

Proportioning Valve

REMOVAL & INSTALLATION

1. Disconnect the negative battery cable.

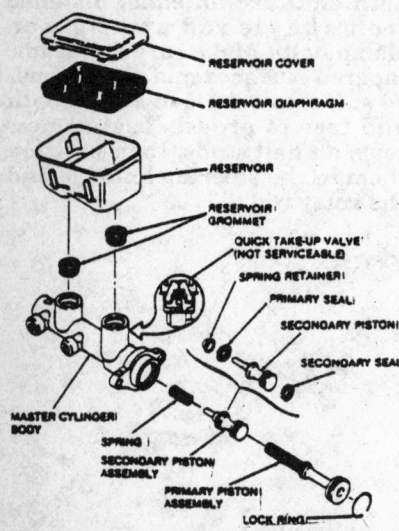

Exploded view of the master cylinder

2. Disconnect the electrical connector at the pressure differential switch.
3. Disconnect and plug the hydraulic lines at the valve.
4. Remove the valve from the vehicle. It may be necessary to raise the vehicle in order to gain access to the assembly.
5. Installation is the reverse of removal. Bleed the system. Do not move the vehicle until a firm brake pedal is obtained.

Power Brake Booster

REMOVAL & INSTALLATION

1. Disconnect the negative battery cable. Remove the master cylinder retaining nuts and position the assembly out of the way.
2. Disconnect vacuum line from vacuum check valve on unit.
3. Remove steering column lower cover, as required.
4. Remove cotter pin, washer and spring spacer that secures power unit pushrod to brake pedal arm.
5. Remove the nuts that secure the power unit to the firewall. Remove the power brake unit.
6. Installation is the reverse of the removal procedure. Tighten booster mounting nuts to 20 ft. lbs. and master cylinder to booster nuts to 25–37 ft. lbs..

Wheel Cylinder

REMOVAL & INSTALLATION

1. Raise and support the vehicle safely. Remove the tire and wheel assembly. Remove the brake shoes.
2. Insert awls or pins, 1/8 in. diameter or less, into the access slots between the wheel cylinder pilot and retainer locking tabs.
3. Bend both tabs away simultanously until they spring over the abutment shoulder releasing the wheel cylinder. Discard the old retaining clip.
4. For ease of installation hold the wheel cylinder against the backing plate by inserting a block betwen the wheel cylinder and the axle shaft flange.
5. Position the wheel cylinder retainer clip so the tabs will be away from and in a horizontal position with the backing plate when installing.
6. Press the new retaining clip over the wheel cylinder abutment and into position using a 1 1/8 in. 12 point socket. Make sure the retainer tabs are properly snapped under the abutment shoulder.

7. Install the brake shoes, drum and wheel. Bleed the hydraulic system.

Parking Brake Cable

ADJUSTMENT

Except Rear Disc Brakes

1. Depress the parking brake pedal exactly two ratchet clicks.
2. Raise the rear of the vehicle and support it safely.
3. Tighten the brake cable adjusting nut until the left rear wheel can be turned rearward with both hands, but locks when forward rotation is attempted.
4. Release the parking brake pedal; both rear wheels must turn freely in either direction without brake drag. Be sure that the parking brake cables are not adjusted too tightly causing the brakes to drag.
5. Lower the vehicle.

Rear Disc Brakes

1. Check for free movement of the parking brake cables and lubricate the underbody rub points of the cables. Also lubricate the equalizer hooks.
2. Release the parking brake pedal completely.
3. Raise the rear of the vehicle and support it safely.
4. Hold the brake cable stud from turning, then tighten the adjusting nut until all cable slack is taken up.

NOTE: Check that the parking brake levers on the rear calipers are against the stops on the caliper housing. If the levers are not contacting the stops, loosen the cable adjusting nut until the levers just contact the stops.

5. Operate the parking brake cable several times. Parking brake pedal travel should be 14 clicks with approximately 150 ± 20 lbs. of forced applied to the pedal.
6. Readjust if necessary.
7. Make sure that the levers contact the caliper stops after adjustment.
8. Lower the vehicle.

REMOVAL & INSTALLATION

Front Cable

1. Raise and support the vehicle safely. Remove the adjusting nut at the equalizer.
2. Remove the spring retainer clip from the bracket. Lower the car and remove the upper console for access to cable retainer at the hand lever.
3. Remove the cable retainer pin, cable retainer and remove the cable.
4. Installation is the reverse order of the removal procedure. Adjust the parking brake cable.

Rear Cable

DRUM BRAKES

1. Raise and support the vehicle safely. Remove the adjusting nut at the equalizer.

2. Disengage the rear cable at the connector. Mark the relationship of the wheel to the axle flange and remove the wheel assembly and brake drum.

3. Bend the retainer fingers. Disengage the cable at the brake shoe operating lever.

4. Install the new cable by reversing the removal procedure. Adjust the parking brake cable.

REAR DISC BRAKES

1. Raise and support the vehicle safely. Remove the adjusting nut at the equalizer.

2. Disengage the rear cable at the connector. Push forward on the caliper parking brake apply lever. This will allow the cable to be removed from the tang in the lever. Release the lever.

3. Installation is the reverse order of the removal procedure. Adjust the parking brake. Apply the parking brake 3 or more times with heavy pressure and repeat the adjustment.

CHASSIS ELECTRICAL

Heater Blower

REMOVAL & INSTALLATION

1. Disconnect the negative battery cable.

2. Tag and disconnect the wiring from the blower motor and the resistor.

3. Remove the blower motor cooling tube.

4. Remove the blower motor retaining screws.

5. Remove the blower motor and fan assembly from the case.

6. Installation is the reverse of the removal procedure.

Heater Core

REMOVAL & INSTALLATION

1982–86

1. Disconnect the negative battery cable.

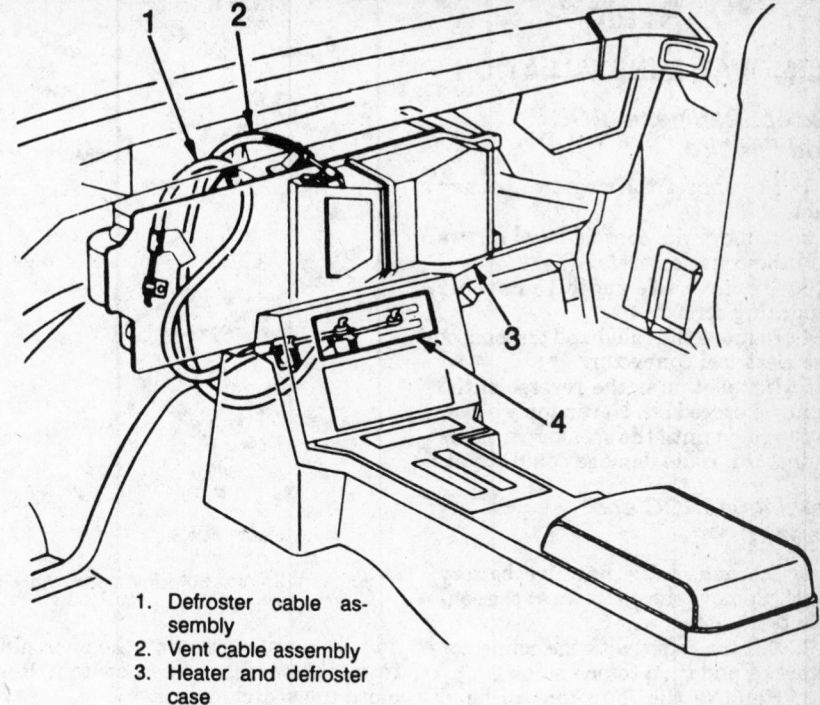

1. Defroster cable assembly
2. Vent cable assembly
3. Heater and defroster case
4. Contol assembly

Heater and A/C box location

2. Drain the cooling system.

3. Disconnect the coolant hoses from the heater core.

4. Remove the right side lower hush panel.

5. Remove the right side lower instrument panel trim panel.

6. On fuel injected V8 engines, remove the electronic spark control (ESC) module from under the right side of the instrument panel.

7. Remove the right side lower instrument panel carrier to cowl screw.

8. Remove the four heater case cover screws.

NOTE: The upper left heater case cover screw may be reached with a long socket extension placed through the instrument panel openings which were exposed by the removal of the lower instrument panel trim panel. Carefully lift the lower right corner of the instrument panel to align the socket extension.

9. Remove the heater case cover.

10. Remove the heater core support plate and the baffle screws.

11. Remove the heater core, support plate, and baffle from the heater case.

12. Installation is the reverse of the removal procedure. When installing case cover be sure case sealer is in place.

1987–89

1. Disconnect the nagative battery cable. Drain the cooling system. Disconnect the heater hoses.

2. Remove the right and left lower hush panel. Remove the upper dash pad.

3. Remove both front speaker retaining nuts. Remove the side window defrost duct retaining nuts, front carrier braces and carrier shelf. Remove both side window defrost ducts.

4. Remove the two screws securing the right speaker and bracket. Disconnect the electronic control module and position it to the side.

5. Remove the radio trim plate. Remove the upper console trim. Remove the console glove box assembly. Remove the emergency brake handle grip.

6. Remove the screws that secure the console body and position the assembly out of the way.

7. Remove the trim plate from under the steering column. Remove the steering column retaining nuts and lower the column.

8. Remove the nuts and screws that retain the instrument panel carrier.

9. Move the instrument panel carrier back to gain access to the heater core and the heater core upper bolt.

10. Remove the screws that secure the heater core housing cover. Remove the screws that secure the heater core and shroud. Remove the heater core from the shroud assembly.

11. Installation is the reverse of the removal procedure.

Radio

REMOVAL & INSTALLATION

Except Berlinetta/IROC and Firebird

1. Disconnect the negative battery cable.
2. Remove the console bezel screws and the console bezel.
3. Remove the radio to console mounting screws.
4. Remove the radio and disconnect the electrical connector.
5. Installation is the reverse of the removal procedure. Never apply power to the radio until the speaker wiring is connected, radio damage could result.

Berlinetta/IROC and Firebird

1. Disconnect the negative battery cable. Remove the 4 screws at the console trim plate.
2. Lift the radio, with the connector attached and turn to one side.
3. Remove the four control head mounting bracket screws. Remove the control head by pulling back on the pawl spring and pulling up on the control head.
4. Disconnect the electrical connectors from the control head.
5. Remove the four screws at the radio bracket and the slotted screw at the radio.
6. Disconnect the electrical connector and remove the radio.
7. Installation is the reverse of the removal procedure. Never apply power to the radio until the speaker wiring is connected, radio damage could result.

Windshield Wiper Switch

REMOVAL & INSTALLATION

Column Mounted

1. Disconnect the negative battery cable. Remove the steering wheel. Remove the turn signal switch.
2. It may be necessary to loosen the two column mounting nuts and remove the four bracket to mast jacket screws, then separate the bracket from the mast jacket to allow the connector clip on the ignition switch to be pulled out of the column assembly.
3. Disconnect the washer/wiper switch lower connector.
4. Remove the screws attaching the column housing to the mast jacket. Be sure to note the position of the dimmer switch actuator rod for reassembly in the same position. Remove the column housing and switch as an assembly.
5. Turn the assembly upside down

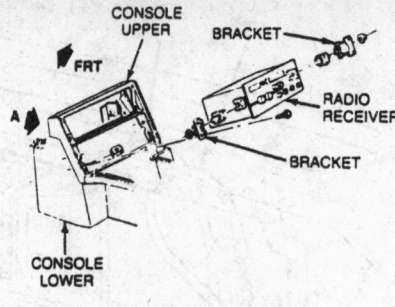

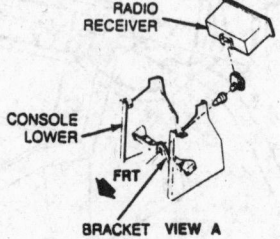

Typical radio and holddown assembly

and use a drift to remove the pivot pin from the washer/wiper switch. Remove the switch.
6. Place the switch into position in the housing, then install the pivot pin.
7. Position the housing onto the mast jacket and attach by installing the screws. Install the dimmer switch actuator rod in the same position as noted earlier. Check switch operation.
8. Reconnect lower end of switch assembly.
9. Install remaining components in reverse order of removal. Be sure to attach column mounting bracket in original position.

Dash Mounted

1. Disconnect the negative battery cable.
2. Remove the trim panel. Remove the switch retaining screws.
3. Pull the switch forward and disconnect the electrical connection. Remove the switch from the vehicle.
4. Installation is the reverse of the removal procedure.

Windshield Wiper Motor

REMOVAL & INSTALLATION

1. Disconnect the negative battery cable.
2. Remove the wiper arms. Remove the cowl screen.
3. Loosen the transmission drive link to crank arm retaining bolts. Remove the drive link from the motor crank arm.
4. Disconnect the electrical wiring and the washer hoses from the motor assembly.

5. Remove the motor retaining screws. Remove the windshield wiper motor while guiding the crank arm through the hole.
6. Installation is the reverse of the removal procedure. The motor must be in the park position before assembling the crank arm to the drive link.

Instrument Cluster

REMOVAL & INSTALLATION

Camaro without Electronic Cluster

1. Disconnect the negative battery cable. As required, lower the steering column.
2. Remove the instrument cluster bezel.
3. Remove the cluster retaining screws. Pull the cluster assembly forward and disconnect the speedometer cable and all electrical connections.
4. As required, remove the trip odometer, reset knob and the cluster lens.
5. Remove the speedometer assembly from the vehicle.
6. Installation is the reverse of the removal procedure.

Firebird without Electronic Cluster

1. Disconnect the negative battery cable. As required, lower the steering column.
2. Remove the instrument cluster bezel.
3. Remove the cluster retaining screws. Pull the cluster assembly forward and disconnect the speedometer cable and all electrical connections.
4. As required, remove the trip odometer, reset knob and the cluster lens.
5. Remove the speedometer assembly from the vehicle.
6. Installation is the reverse of the removal procedure.

Camaro/Firebird with Electronic Cluster

1. Disconnect the negative battery cable.
2. Remove the screws holding the steering column trim cover to the instrument panel. Remove the trim cover.
3. Remove the screws at the bottom of the right hand pod. Pull the pod rearward and disconnect the electrical connector. Slide the pod from the track as a unit.
4. Remove the screws at the bottom of the left hand pod. Pull the pod rearward and disconnect the electrical con-

nector. Slide the pod from the track as a unit.

5. Disconnect the electrical connector from under the instrument panel.

6. Remove the cluster bezel screws and remove the bezel. Remove the cluster lens screws and remove the cluster lens.

7. Remove the steering column bolts and lower the column to gain working clearance.

8. Pull the cluster forward and disconnect the electrical connection.

9. Installation is the reverse of the removal procedure.

Ignition Switch
REMOVAL & INSTALLATION

1. Disconnect the negative battery terminal.

2. Loosen the toe pan screws on the steering column.

3. Remove the column to instrument panel trim plates and attaching nuts.

4. Lower the steering column. Be sure that the steering column is supported at all times in order to prevent damage to the column. disconnect the switch wire connectors.

5. Remove the switch attaching screws and remove the switch.

6. To replace, move the key lock to the **LOCK** position.

7. Move the actuator rod hole in the switch to the **LOCK** position.

8. Install the switch with the rod in the hole.

9. Position and reassemble the steering column in reverse of the disassembly procedure.

Headlamp Switch
REMOVAL & INSTALLATION

1982–87 Camaro Except Berlinetta/IROC

1. Disconnect the negative battery cable. Remove the left and right lower trim plates.

2. Remove the instrument panel trim plate and the two switch assembly retaining screws.

3. Depress the side tangs and remove the switch from the instrument panel.

4. Installation is the reverse order of the removal procedure.

1983–86 Berlinetta and 1987–89 IROC

NOTE: The headlight switch on the Berlinetta and IROC, is located in the left pod assembly. In order to replace the switch assembly, the pod assembly must be removed as a unit.

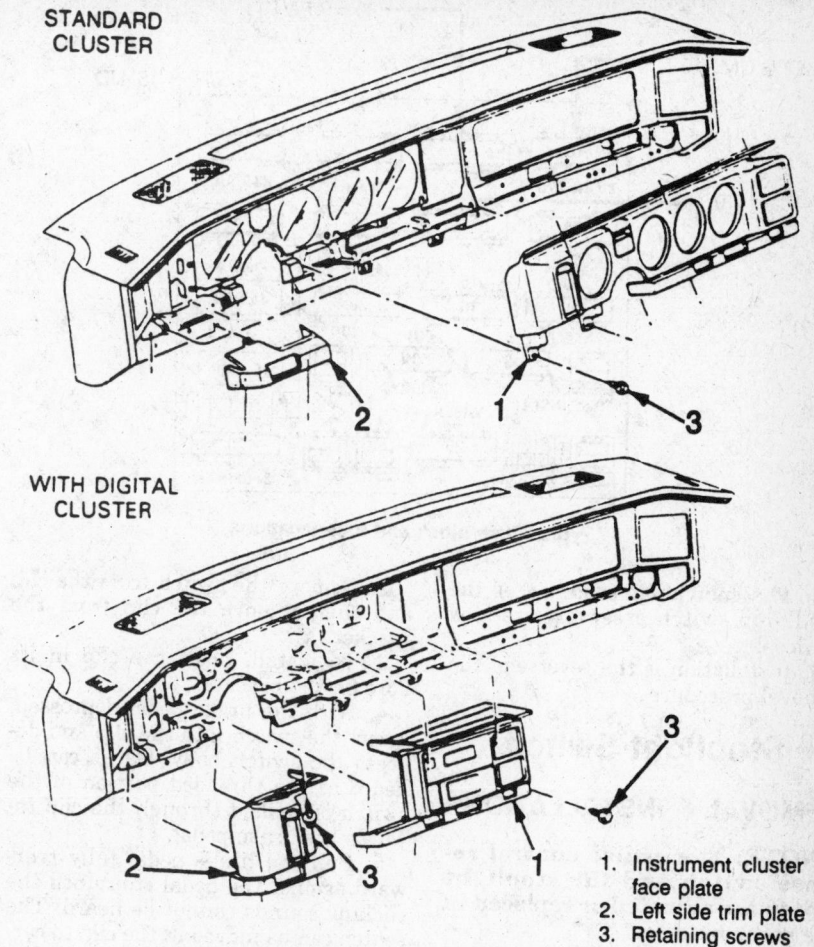

1. Instrument cluster face plate
2. Left side trim plate
3. Retaining screws

Standard and Electronic instrument cluster mounting

1. Disconnect the negative battery cable.

2. Remove the instrument panel trim plate screws. Remove the instrument panel trim plate.

3. Remove the lower steering column trim cover.

4. Remove the left control head attaching screw at the bottom front. Release the holding tab.

5. Disconnect the electrical connector located below the instrument panel.

6. Remove the pod assembly. Slide the control off the track to remove.

7. Installation is the reverse of the removal procedure.

Firebird

1. Disconnect the negative battery cable. Remove the right and left lower trim plates. Remove the instrument panel lower cover, as required.

2. Remove the instrument panel cluster trim plate.

3. Remove the two switch mounting screws.

4. Depress the side tangs of the switch and pull the switch out of the instrument panel.

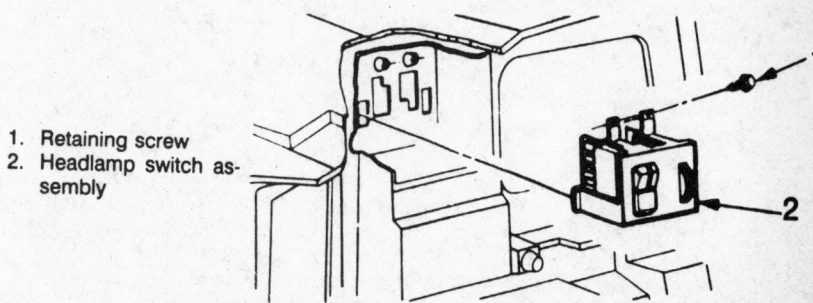

1. Retaining screw
2. Headlamp switch assembly

Headlamp switch mounting—Berlinetta/IROC and Firebird

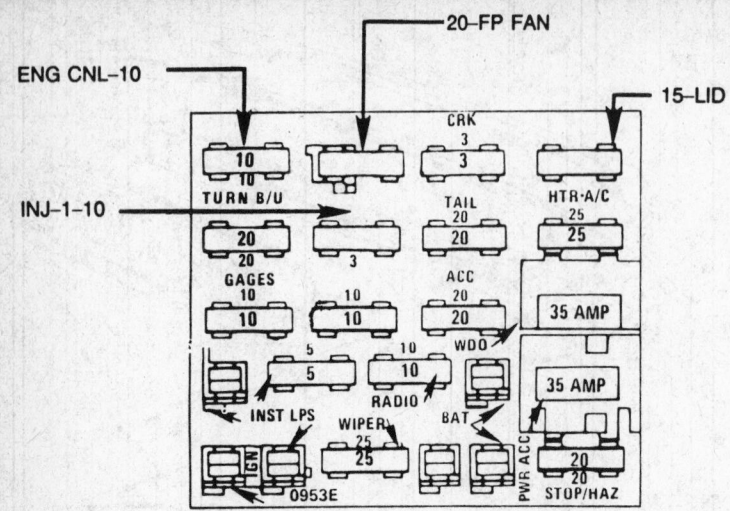

Typical fuse block and fuse locations

5. The individual switches of the headlamp switch assembly are now serviceable.

6. Installation is the reverse of the removal procedure.

Stoplight Switch

REMOVAL & INSTALLATION

NOTE: The cruise control release switch and the stoplight switch are adjusted or replaced in the same manner.

1. Disconnect the negative battery cable. Disconnect the wire harness connector from the switch.

2. Remove the switch from the clip and then remove the clip from the bracket.

3. To install, place the clip in its bore on the bracket.

4. With the brake pedal depressed, insert the switch into the clip and depress the switch body. Clicks can be heard as the threaded portion of the switch is pushed through the clip towards the brake pedal.

5. Pull the brake pedal fully rearward against the pedal stop until the clicking sounds cannot be heard. The switch can be moved in the clip to correct the adjustment.

6. Release the brake pedal and repeat Step 5 to assure that no clicking sounds remain. The switch is now correctly adjusted.

7. Install the harness connector and verify the stoplights operate correctly.

Fuses and Circuit Breakers

LOCATION

Fuseable Links

Fusible links are used to prevent major wire harness damage in the event of a short circuit or an overload condition in the wiring circuits which are normally not fused, due to carrying high amperage loads or because of their locations within the wiring harness. Each fusible link is of a fixed value for a specific electrical load and should a link fail, the cause of the failure must be determined and repaired prior to installing a new fusible link of the same value.

Circuit Breakers

Various circuit breakers are located under the instrument panel. In order to gain access to these components it may be necessary to first remove the under dash padding.

Fuse Panel

The fuse panel is located on the left side of the vehicle. It is under the instrument panel assembly. In order to gain access to the fuse panel it may be necessary to first remove the under dash padding.

GM "H" Body
Front Wheel Drive
Buick LeSabre, Oldsmobile Delta 88, Pontiac Bonneville

SERIAL NUMBER IDENTIFICATION

VEHICLE IDENTIFICATION CHART

It is important for servicing and ordering parts to be certain of the vehicle and engine identification. The VIN (vehicle identification number) is a 17 digit number visible through the windshield on the driver's side of the dash and contains the vehicle and engine identification codes. The tenth digit indicates model year and the eighth digit indicates engine code. It can be interpreted as follows:

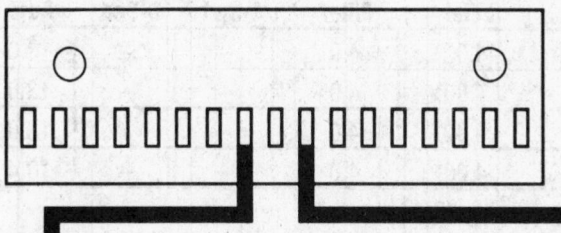

Engine Code						Model Year	
Code	Cu. In.	Liters	Cyl.	Fuel Sys.	Eng. Mfg.	Code	Year
L	181	3.0	6	MFI	Buick	G	1986
B	231	3.8	6	SFI	Buick	H	1987
3	231	3.8	6	SFI	Buick	J	1988
C (3800)	231	3.8	6	SFI	Flint Powertrain	K	1989

GENERAL ENGINE SPECIFICATIONS

Year	VIN	No. Cylinder Displacement cu. in. (liter)	Fuel System Type	Net Horsepower @ rpm	Net Torque @ rpm (ft.lbs.)	Bore × Stroke (in.)	Compression Ratio	Oil Pressure @ rpm
1986	L	6-181 (3.0)	MFI	125 @ 4900	150 @ 2400	3.80 × 2.66	9.0:1	37 @ 2400
	B	6-231 (3.8)	SFI	150 @ 4400	200 @ 2000	3.80 × 3.40	8.5:1	37 @ 2400
	3	6-231 (3.8)	SFI	150 @ 4400	200 @ 2000	3.80 × 3.40	8.5:1	37 @ 2400
1987	B	6-231 (3.8)	SFI	150 @ 4400	200 @ 2000	3.80 × 3.40	8.5:1	37 @ 2400
	3	6-231 (3.8)	SFI	150 @ 4400	200 @ 2000	3.80 × 3.40	8.5:1	37 @ 2400
1988-89	3	6-231 (3.8)	SFI	150 @ 4400	200 @ 2000	3.80 × 3.40	8.5:1	37 @ 2400
	C	6-231 (3.8)	SFI	165 @ 5200	210 @ 2000	3.80 × 3.40	8.5:1	37 @ 2400

GASOLINE ENGINE TUNE-UP SPECIFICATIONS

Year	VIN	No. Cylinder Displacement cu. in. (liter)	Spark Plugs Type	Spark Plugs Gap (in.)	Ignition Timing (deg.) MT	Ignition Timing (deg.) AT	Compression Pressure (psi)	Fuel Pump (psi)	Idle Speed (rpm) MT	Idle Speed (rpm) AT	Valve Clearance In.	Valve Clearance Ex.
1986	L	6-181 (3.0)	R44LTS	.045	—	①	NA	34-44	—	①	Hyd.	Hyd.
	B	6-231 (3.8)	R44LTS	.045	—	①	NA	26-36	—	①	Hyd.	Hyd.
	3	6-231 (3.8)	R44LTS	.045	—	①	NA	26-36	—	①	Hyd.	Hyd.
1987	B	6-231 (3.8)	R44LTS	.080	—	①	NA	26-36	—	①	Hyd.	Hyd.
	3	6-231 (3.8)	R44LTS	.080	—	①	NA	26-36	—	①	Hyd.	Hyd.
1988	3	6-231 (3.8)	R44LTS	.080	—	①	NA	26-36	—	①	Hyd.	Hyd.
	C	6-231 (3.8)	R44LTS	.080	—	①	NA	26-36	—	①	Hyd.	Hyd.
1989		SEE UNDERHOOD SPECIFICATIONS STICKER										

① Timing adjustment is not required on engines with Computer Controlled Coil Ignition (C³I)

CAPACITIES

Year	Model	No. Cylinder Displacement cu. in. (liter)	Engine Crankcase with Filter	Engine Crankcase without Filter	Transmission (pts.) 4-Spd	Transmission (pts.) 5-Spd	Transmission (pts.) Auto.	Drive Axle (pts.)	Fuel Tank (gal.)	Cooling System (qts.)
1986	All	6-181 (3.0)	4.0①	4.0	—	—	13.0	—	18.0	12.2
	All	6-231 (3.8)	4.0①	4.0	—	—	13.0	—	18.0	12.6
1987	All	6-231 (3.8)	4.0①	4.0	—	—	13.0	—	18.0	13.3
1988-89	All	6-231 (3.8)	4.0①	4.0	—	—	10.4	—	18.0	11.7②

① Additional oil may be necessary to bring the level to full
② Engine VIN Code 3 — 13.0 qts.

FIRING ORDERS

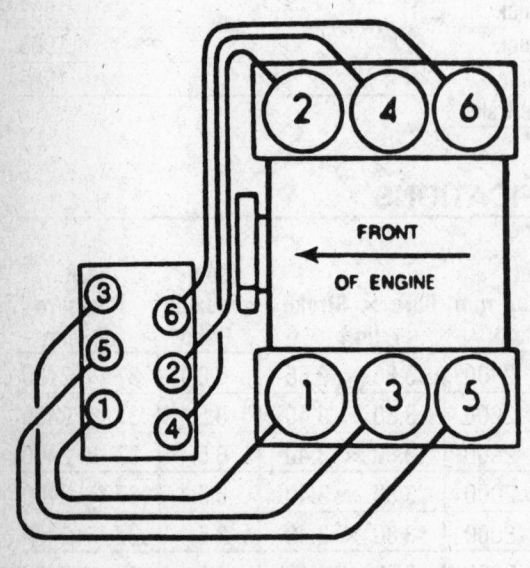

231 cu. in. (3.8L) C (3800) engine
Firing order: 1-6-5-4-3-2

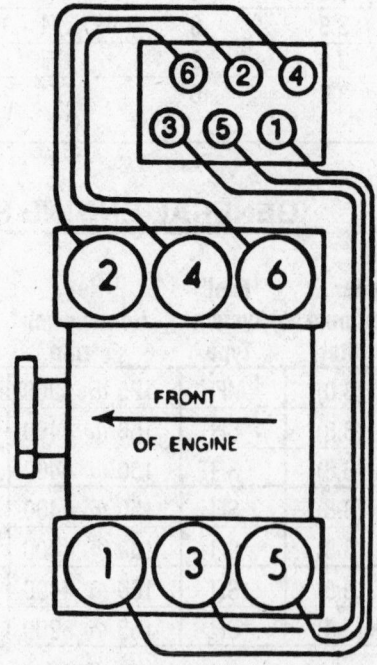

181 cu. in. (3.0L) L engine
231 cu. in. (3.8L) 3 engine
231 cu. in. (3.8L) B engine
Firing order: 1-6-5-4-3-2

CAMSHAFT SPECIFICATIONS
All measurements given in inches.

| Year | VIN | No. Cylinder Displacement cu. in. (liter) | Journal Diameter | | | | | Lobe Lift | | Bearing Clearance | Camshaft End Play |
			1	2	3	4	5	In.	Ex.		
1986	L	6-181 (3.0)	1.7800–1.7865	1.7800–1.7865	1.7800–1.7865	1.7800–1.7865	—	0.358	0.384	①	NA
	B	6-231 (3.8)	1.7800–1.7865	1.7800–1.7865	1.7800–1.7865	1.7800–1.7865	—	0.392	0.392	①	NA
	3	6-231 (3.8)	1.7800–1.7865	1.7800–1.7865	1.7800–1.7865	1.7800–1.7865	—	0.368	0.384	①	NA
1987	B	6-231 (3.8)	1.7800–1.7865	1.7800–1.7865	1.7800–1.7865	1.7800–1.7865	—	0.392	0.392	①	NA
	3	6-231 (3.8)	1.7800–1.7865	1.7800–1.7865	1.7800–1.7865	1.7800–1.7865	—	0.368	0.384	①	NA
1988-89	3	6-231 (3.8)	1.7800–1.7865	1.7800–1.7865	1.7800–1.7865	1.7800–1.7865	—	0.245	0.245	①	NA
	C	6-231 (3.8)	1.7850–1.7860	1.7850–1.7860	1.7850–1.7860	1.7850–1.7860	—	0.272	0.272	①	NA

NA Not available
① No. 1: 0.0005–0.00025
No. 2-5: 0.0005–0.0035

CRANKSHAFT AND CONNECTING ROD SPECIFICATIONS
All measurements are given in inches.

| Year | VIN | No. Cylinder Displacement cu. in. (liter) | Crankshaft | | | | Connecting Rod | | |
			Main Brg. Journal Dia.	Main Brg. Oil Clearance	Shaft End-play	Thrust on No.	Journal Diameter	Oil Clearance	Side Clearance
1986	L	6-181 (3.0)	2.4995	.0003–.0018	.003–.011	2	2.2487–2.2495	.0005–.0026	.006–.023
	B	6-231 (3.8)	2.4995	.0003–.0018	.003–.011	2	2.2487–2.2495	.0005–.0026	.006–.023
	3	6-231 (3.8)	2.4995	.0003–.0018	.003–.011	2	2.2487–2.2495	.0005–.0026	.006–.023
1987	B	6-231 (3.8)	2.4995	.0003–.0018	.003–.011	2	2.2487–2.2495	.0005–.0026	.006–.023
	3	6-231 (3.8)	2.4995	.0003–.0018	.003–.011	2	2.2487–2.2495	.0005–.0026	.006–.023
1988-89	3	6-231 (3.8)	2.4988–2.4998	.0003–.0018	.003–.011	2	2.2487–2.2499	.0003–.0028	.003–.015
	C	6-231 (3.8)	2.4988–2.4998	.0003–.0018	.003–.011	2	2.2487–2.2499	.0003–.0028	.003–.015

VALVE SPECIFICATIONS

Year	VIN	No. Cylinder Displacement cu. in. (liter)	Seat Angle (deg.)	Face Angle (deg.)	Spring Test Pressure (lbs.)	Spring Installed Height (in.)	Stem-to-Guide Clearance (in.) Intake	Exhaust	Stem Diameter (in.) Intake	Exhaust
1986	L	6-181 (3.0)	45	45	220 @ 1.340	1.727	.0015–.0035	.0015–.0032	.3401–.3412	.3405–.3412
	B	6-231 (3.8)	45	45	185 @ 1.340	1.727	.0015–.0035	.0015–.0032	.3401–.3412	.3405–.3412
	3	6-231 (3.8)	45	45	185 @ 1.340	1.727	.0015–.0035	.0015–.0032	.3401–.3412	.3405–.3412
1987	B	6-231 (3.8)	45	45	185 @ 1.340	1.727	.0015–.0035	.0015–.0032	.3401–.3412	.3405–.3412
	3	6-231 (3.8)	45	45	185 @ 1.340	1.727	.0015–.0035	.0015–.0032	.3401–.3412	.3405–.3412
1988-89	3	6-231 (3.8)	46	45	185 @ 1.340	1.690–1.750	.0015–.0035	.0015–.0032	.3401–.3412	.3405–.3412
	C	6-231 (3.8)	45	45	225 @ 1.255	1.690–1.750	.0015–.0035	.0015–.0032	NA	NA

NA Not available

PISTON AND RING SPECIFICATIONS
All measurments are given in inches.

Year	VIN	No. Cylinder Displacement cu. in. (liter)	Piston Clearance	Ring Gap Top Compression	Bottom Compression	Oil Control	Ring Side Clearance Top Compression	Bottom Compression	Oil Control
1986	L	6-181 (3.0)	①	.010–.020	.010–.022	.015–.055	.0030–.0050	.0030–.0050	.0035 Max
	B	6-231 (3.8)	①	.010–.020	.010–.022	.015–.055	.0030–.0050	.0030–.0050	.0035 Max
	3	6-231 (3.8)	①	.010–.020	.010–.022	.015–.055	.0030–.0050	.0030–.0050	.0035 Max
1987	B	6-231 (3.8)	①	.010–.020	.010–.022	.015–.055	.0030–.0050	.0030–.0050	.0035 Max
	3	6-231 (3.8)	①	.010–.020	.010–.022	.015–.055	.0030–.0050	.0030–.0050	.0035 Max
1988-89	3	6-181 (3.0)	②	.010–.020	.010–.022	.015–.055	.0010–.0030	.0010–.0030	.0005–.0065
	C	6-181 (3.0)	.0004–.0022	.010–.025	.010–.025	.015–.055	.0010–.0030	.0010–.0030	.0011–.0081

① Top Land—.046–.056 in.
  Skirt Top—.0008–.0020 in.
  Skirt Bottom—.0013–.0035 in.
② Skirt top—.0007–.0027
  Skirt bottom—.001–.0045

TORQUE SPECIFICATIONS
All readings in ft. lbs.

Year	VIN	No. Cylinder Displacement cu. in. (liter)	Cylinder Head Bolts	Main Bearing Bolts	Rod Bearing Bolts	Crankshaft Pulley Bolts	Flywheel Bolts	Manifold		Spark Plugs
								Intake	Exhaust	
1986	L	6-181 (3.0)	①	100	40	200	60	32	37	20
	B	6-231 (3.8)	①	100	45	200	60	32	37	20
	3	6-231 (3.8)	①	100	45	200	60	32	37	20
1987	L	6-181 (3.0)	①	100	40	229	60	32	37	20
	B	6-231 (3.8)	①	100	45	219	60	32	37	20
	3	6-231 (3.8)	①	100	45	219	60	32	37	20
1988-89	3	6-231 (3.8)	①	100	40	219	60	32	37	20
	C	6-231 (3.8)	①	100	40	219	60	②	37	20

① 3 step procedure: should you reach 60 ft. lbs. at any time in Step 2 or Step 3, stop tightening. Do not complete the balance of the 90 degree turn of this bolt
Step 1: 25 ft. lbs.
Step 2: 90 degrees
Step 3: 90 degrees
② 80 inch lbs.

BRAKE SPECIFICATIONS
All measurements in inches unless noted

Year	Model	Lug Nut Torque (ft. lbs.)	Master Cylinder Bore	Brake Disc		Standard Brake Drum Diameter	Minimum Lining Thickness	
				Minimum Thickness	Maximum Runout		Front	Rear
1986	LeSabre, Delta 88	100①	.937②	.972	.004	8.86	3/32	3/32
1987	LeSabre, Delta 88, Bonneville	100①	.937②	.972	.004	8.86	3/32	3/32
1988-89	LeSabre, Delta 88, Bonneville	100①	.937②	.972	.004	8.86	3/32	3/32

① 7/16 in. stud — 80 ft. lbs.
② Anti-lock brakes; standard brakes — .945

WHEEL ALIGNMENT

Year	Model		Caster Range (deg.)	Caster Preferred Setting (deg.)	Camber Range (deg.)	Camber Preferred Setting (deg.)	Toe-in (in.)	Steering Axis Inclination (deg.)
1986	LeSabre	Front	2-3	2½P	①	①	0	—
		Rear	—	—	$3/16$P–$13/16$N	$5/16$N	$1/8$P	—
	Delta 88	Front	2-3	2½P	①	①	0	$12^{13}/_{16}$P
		Rear	—	—	$3/16$P–$13/16$P	$5/16$N	$3/32$P	—
1987	LeSabre	Front	2-3	2½P	$5/16$N–$11/16$P	$3/16$P	0	—
		Rear	—	—	$3/16$P–$13/16$N	$5/16$N	$3/64$P	—
	Delta 88	Front	2-3	2½P	$5/16$N–$11/16$P	$3/16$P	0	$12^{13}/_{16}$P
		Rear	—	—	$3/16$P–$13/16$N	$5/16$N	$1/16$P	—
	Bonneville	Front	2-3	2½P	$5/16$N–$11/16$P	$3/16$P	0	—
		Rear	—	—	$3/16$P–$13/16$N	$5/16$N	$3/64$P	—
1988-89	LeSabre	Front	2-3	2½P	$5/16$N–$11/16$P	$3/16$P	0	—
		Rear	—	—	$3/16$P–$13/16$N	$5/16$N	$3/64$P	—
	Delta 88	Front	2-3	2½P	$5/16$N–$11/16$P	$3/16$P	0	$12^{13}/_{16}$P
		Rear	—	—	$3/16$P–$13/16$N	$5/16$N	$1/16$P	—
	Bonneville	Front	2-3	2½P	$5/16$N–$11/16$P	$3/16$P	0	—
		Rear	—	—	$3/16$P–$13/16$N	$5/16$N	$3/64$P	—

① Left wheel
    Min. — 1N
    Pref. — ½N
    Max. — 0
  Right wheel
    Min. — 0
    Pref. — ½P
    Max. — 1P

TUNE-UP PROCEDURES

Ignition Timing

ADJUSTMENT

The C³I ignition system does not require timing adjustments, therefore the engine timing procedures are not available.

Valve Lash

ADJUSTMENT

All engines use hydraulic valve lifters which run at zero clearance. The rocker arms are non adjustable. The lifters will compensate if there is any lash in the system. If there is excessive noise or lash in the valve train the entire system should be checked.

Idle Speed and Mixture

ADJUSTMENT

NOTE: The idle speed and mixture are all controlled by the ECM. This adjustment should be performed only when the throttle body or throttle body parts have been replaced.

1. With a scratch awl or equivalent, piece the idle stop screw plug and apply leverage to remove it.

2. Ground the ALDL diagnostic test lead and turn ignition switch ON position, without starting engine for at least 30 seconds.

3. After 30 seconds, disconnect the Idle Air Control (IAC) electrical connector.

4. Remove ground wire from diagnostic lead. Firmly set the parking brake and block the front drive wheels.

5. Start the engine and place the transaxle in DRIVE. Using the minimum idle stop set screw and adjust the idle speed to 450–550 rpm.

6. Turn ignition switch OFF and reconnect connector at IAC motor.

7. Check and clear any trouble codes. Start engine and inspect for proper idle operation.

ENGINE ELECTRICAL

Computer Controlled Coil Ignition (C³I) System

All models are equipped with Computer Controlled Coil Ignition (C³I), which eliminates the distributor. The 3.0L with C³I is slightly different than the 3.8L engine. It is not a sequentially injected engine, therefore a discrete camshaft signal is not necessary. The ECM provides multiport injection from processing the crankshaft signal only.

The C³I system consists of the coil pack, ignition module, various hall effect sensors, interrupter rings and electronic control module (ECM). There are three types of C³I systems used. Type 1 coils have three plug wires on each side of the coil assembly; Type 2 coils have all six wires connected on one side of the coil. All components are serviced as complete assemblies, although individual coils are available for Type 2 coil packs. The third system, know as type 3 or fast start is similar in appearance to type 1. In fact the coil packs are interchangeable; however, the module is electronically different and the harness connector plugs are not compatible. There are differences in the harness, the crankshaft sensor and the harmonic balancer. When troubleshooting or replacing components, it is important to determine which C³I system is installed on the engine. Since the ECM controls the ignition timing, no timing adjustments are necessary or possible.

Crankshaft Sensor

REMOVAL & INSTALLATION

1. Disconnect the negative battery cable.
2. Remove the serpentine drive belt.
3. Raise the car and support it safely.
4. Remove the right front tire.
5. Remove the inner fender splash shield.
6. Remove the crankshaft balancer bolt and balancer if necessary.
7. Remove the mounting bolts and remove the crankshaft sensor from the front cover. Disconnect the electrical connector and remove the sensor from the vehicle.

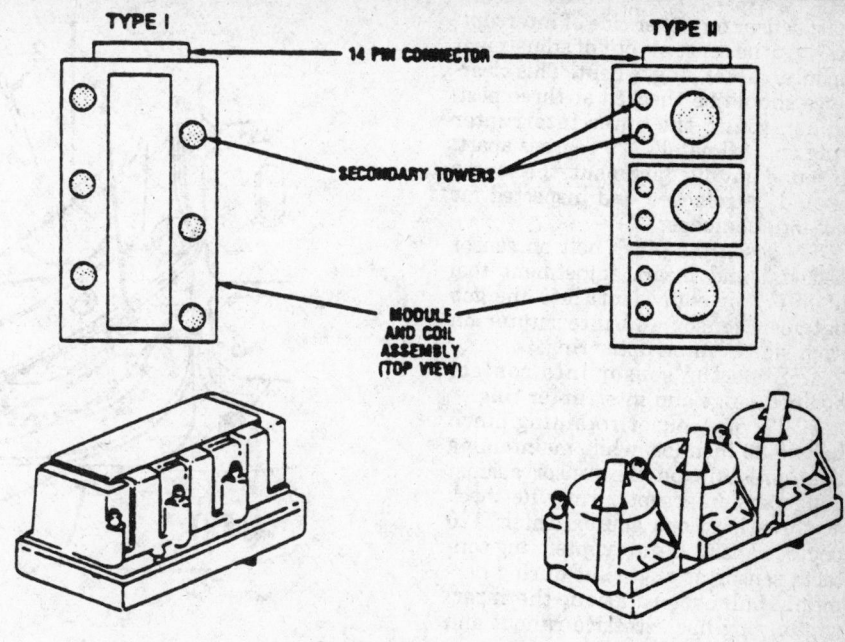

C³I system identification

1. Crankshaft sensor
2. Mounting bolt
3. Camshaft sensor
4. Mounting bolts

Crankshaft and camshaft sensor location

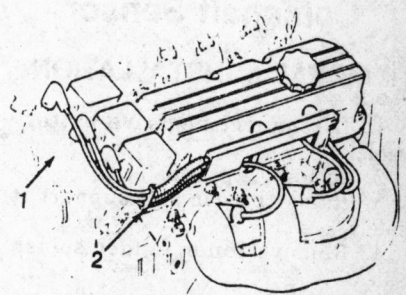

1. C³I unit
2. Spark plug harness

C³I ignition system – 3800 engine

8. Installation is the reverse of removal. Sensor must be adjusted before engine is cranked. Make sure the electrical T-latch connector is assembled properly or an intermittent loss of operation may occur. Tighten the crankshaft sensor mounting bolts to 22 ft. lbs. and the crankshaft balancer bolt to 200 ft. lbs.

ADJUSTMENT

1. Rotate harmonic balancer, using a 28mm socket and pull handle, until the interrupter ring(s) full the sensor slot(s) and edge of interrupter window is aligned with edge of the deflector on the pedestal.
2. Insert adjustment tool (J–36179 or equivalent) into the gap between sensor and interrupter on each side of interrupter ring. If gauge will not slide

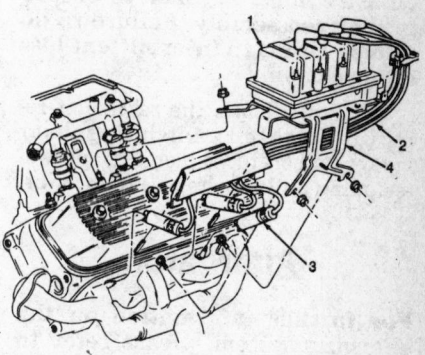

1. C3I coil and module assembly
2. Rear spark plug wire harness
3. Spark plug heat shield
4. Coil and module bracket

C³I ignition system

past sensor on either side of interrupter ring, the sensor is out of adjustment or interrupter ring is bent. This clearance should be checked at three positions around the outer interrupter ring approximately 120 degrees apart. If found out of adjustment, the sensor should be removed and inspected for potential damage.

3. Loosen the pinch bolt on sensor pedestal and insert adjustment tool (J–38179 or equivalent) into the gap between sensor and interrupter on each side of interrupter ring.

4. Slide the sensor into contact against gauge and interrupter ring.

5. Torque sensor retaining pinch bolt to 30 inch lbs. while maintaining light pressure on the sensor against gauge and interrupter ring. Re-check at three locations approximately 120 degrees apart. If interrupter ring contacts sensor at any point during harmonic balancer rotation, the interrupter ring has excessive runout and must be replaced.

Camshaft Sensor

REMOVAL & INSTALLATION

1. Disconnect negative battery cable.
2. Remove serpentine belt.
3. Raise the car and support it safely.
4. Remove inner fender splash shield.
5. Remove water pump pulley retaining bolts and water pump pulley.
6. Remove camshaft sensor bolt and sensor.
7. Remove sensor electrical connection.

When servicing requires that the T-latch type wiring is disconnected, care must be taken to ensure proper reassembly. Failure to do so may result in intermittent loss of operation.

8. Installation is the reverse of removal. Tighten camshaft sensor mounting bolt to 75 inch lbs. and water pump pulley bolts to 115 inch lbs.

Alternator

For further information on the charging system, please refer to "Charging and Starting" in the Unit Repair section.

PRECAUTIONS

Several precautions must be observed with alternator equipped vehicles to avoid damage to the unit.

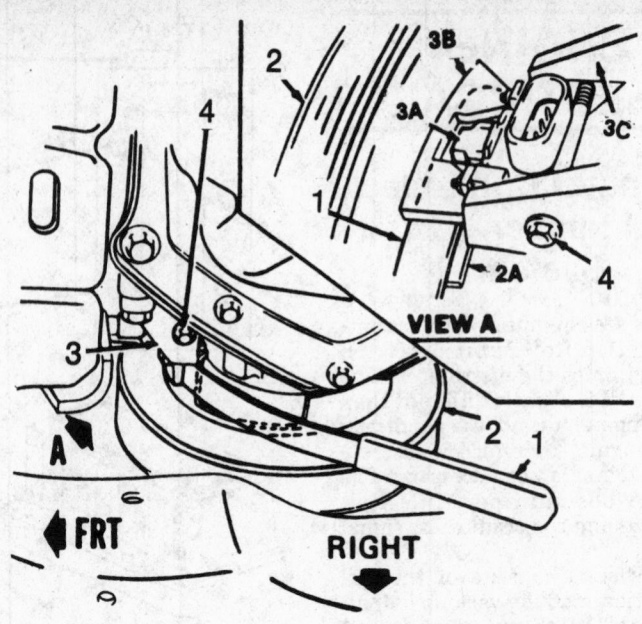

1. TOOL J 38179
2. CRANKSHAFT HARMONIC BALANCER ASSY.
   A. INTERRUPTER RING
3. CRANKSHAFT POSITION SENSOR ASSY.
   A. SENSOR
   B. DEFLECTOR
   C. PEDESTAL
4. PINCH BOLT

Crankshaft sensor adjustment

● If the battery is removed for any reason, make sure it is reconnected with the correct polarity. Reversing the battery connections may result in damage to the one-way rectifiers.

● When utilizing a booster battery as a starting aid, always connect the positive to positive terminals, and the negative terminal from the booster battery to a good engine ground on the car being started.

● Never use a fast charger as a booster to start vehicles with alternating-current (AC) circuits.

● Disconnect the battery cables when charging the battery with a fast charger.

● Never attempt to polarize an alternator.

● Avoid long soldering times when making alternator repairs. Prolonged heat will damage the alternator.

● Do not use test lamps of more than 12 volts when checking diode continuity.

● Do not short across or ground any of the alternator terminals.

● The polarity of the battery, alternator and regulator must be matched and considered before making any electrical connections within the system.

● Never separate the alternator on an open circuit. Make sure all connections within the circuit are clean and tight.

● Disconnect the battery ground terminal when performing any service on electrical components.

● Disconnect the battery if arc welding is to be done on the vehicle.

REMOVAL & INSTALLATION

1. Disconnect the negative battery cable.
2. Tag and disconnect the battery charge wire, 3-prong connector and the ground wire at the back of the alternator.
3. Remove the brace at the back of the alternator (if equipped).
4. Loosen the serpentine belt tensioner and rotate it counterclockwise to remove the drive belt.
5. Support the alternator, remove the mounting bolts and then remove the alternator.
6. Installation is in the reverse order of removal. Tighten the serpentine belt tensioner pulley.

BELT TENSION ADJUSTMENT

A single (serpentine) belt is used to drive all engine mounted accessories. Drive belt tension is maintained by a spring loaded tensioner. A belt squeak when the engine is started or stopped is normal and has no effect on belt durability. The drive belt tensioner can control belt tension over a broad range belt lengths; however, there are limits to the tensioner's ability to compensate.

1. Inspect tensioner markings to see if the belt is within operating lengths. Replace belt if the belt is excessively worn or is outside of the tensioner's operating range.

2. Run engine with no accessories on until the engine is warmed up. Shut the engine Off and read belt tension with tool J–23600–B belt tension gage or equivalent placed halfway between the alternator and the A/C compressor. For non-A/C applications read tension between the power steering pump and crankshaft pulley. Remove tool.

3. Start the engine (with accessories off) and allow the system to stabilize for 15 seconds. Turn the engine off. Using an 18mm box end wrench, apply clockwise force (tighten) to the tensioner pulley bolt. Release the force and immediately take a tension reading without disturbing belt tensioner position.

4. Using the same wrench, apply a counterclockwise force to the tensioner pulley bolt and raise the pulley to the "install" position. Slowly lower the pulley to the "at rest" position and take a tension reading without disturbing the belt tensioner position.

5. Average the three readings. If the average of the three readings is lower than 67 lbs. and the belt is within the tensioner's operating range, replace the belt tensioner.

Voltage Regulator

An alternator with an integral voltage regulator is standard equipment. There are no adjustments possible with this unit. Testing procedures can be found in the Unit Repair section.

Starter

For all information concerning the starter which is not detailed below, please refer to "Charging and Starting" in the Unit Repair section.

REMOVAL & INSTALLATION

1. Disconnect the negative battery cable.

2. Raise and support the vehicle safely. Remove the starter splash shield and any braces which may be in the way.

3. Remove the two starter mounting bolts and lower the starter slightly to gain access to the wires.

4. Tag and disconnect all wires at the solenoid. Note the color coding of the wires for reinstallation.

5. Installation is in the reverse order of removal. Install any shims, if present.

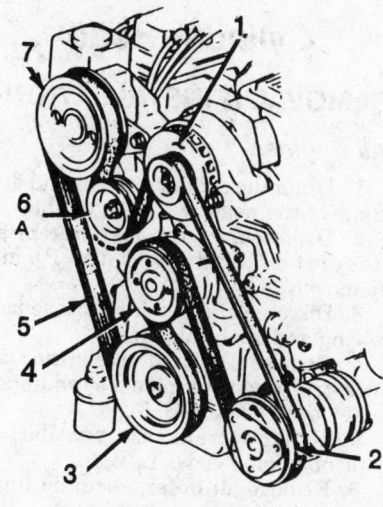

1. Alternator pulley
2. A/C compressor
3. Crankshaft balancer
4. Water pump pulley
5. Serpentine belt
6. Belt tensioner
7. Power steering pump
A. Rotate drive belt tensioner in direction of arrow to remove or install belt

Serpentine drive belt routing

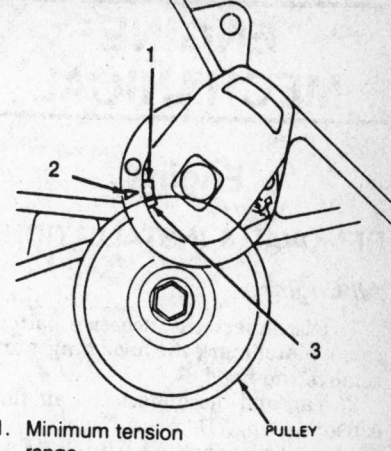

1. Minimum tension range
2. Pointer
3. Maximum tension range

Belt tensioner range

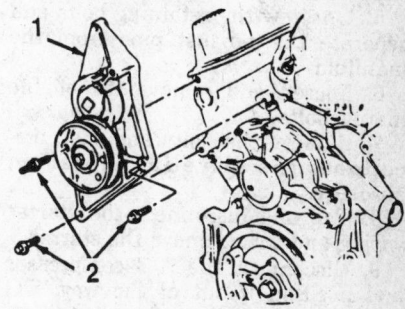

1. Drive belt tensioner
2. Torque 37 ft. lbs.

Serpentine belt tensioner

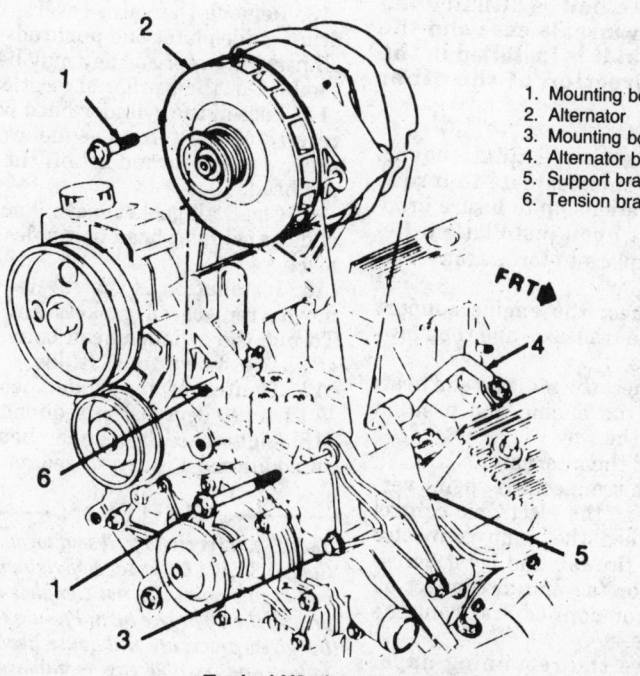

1. Mounting bolt
2. Alternator
3. Mounting bolt
4. Alternator brace
5. Support bracket
6. Tension bracket

Typical V6 alternator mounting

ENGINE MECHANICAL

Engine

REMOVAL & INSTALLATION

All Engines

1. Disconnect the negative battery cable. Matchmark the hood hinges and remove the hood.
2. Tag and disconnect the air flow sensor wiring. Depressurize the fuel system as described under "Fuel Pump Removal."
3. Disconnect the air intake duct. Drain the engine coolant.
4. Raise the front of the vehicle and support it on jackstands.
5. Unscrew the retaining bolts and separate the exhaust pipe from the manifold.
6. Loosen and remove the engine mount bolts.
7. Remove the bolts and then disconnect the driveline vibration absorber.
8. Tag and disconnect the starter wiring and then remove the starter.
9. Disconnect the A/C compressor and position it out of the way. DO NOT disconnect the refrigerant lines.
10. Disconnect the hydraulic lines at the power steering pump and wire them out of the way.
11. Loosen and remove the lower transaxle-to-engine bolts.

NOTE: One bolt is situated between the transaxle case and the engine block. It is installed in the opposite direction of the other bolts.

12. Remove the flexplate cover. Matchmark the flexplate-to-torque converter relationship to insure proper alignment upon installation. Remove the flexplate-to-torque converter bolts.
13. Disconnect the engine support bracket at the transaxle and then lower the vehicle.
14. Disconnect the radiator and heater hoses at the engine and position them out of the way.
15. Remove the alternator.
16. Either disconnect the engine wiring harness at the electronic control unit, then feed the main connector through the firewall and lay it across the engine, or tag and disconnect all engine sensor connectors from the wiring harness.
17. Remove the remaining upper transaxle-to-engine bolts.

18. Install a lifting fixture to the engine and remove the engine from the vehicle. Lift the engine slowly and make sure no wiring or hoses are snagged as the engine is removed.
19. Installation is the reverse of the removal procedure.

Cylinder Head

REMOVAL & INSTALLATION

All Engines

1. Drain the cooling system and disconnect the negative battery cable.
2. Depressurize the fuel system as described under "Fuel Pump Removal."
3. Disconnect Mass Air Flow sensor wiring and air intake duct.
4. Remove T.V. and accelerator cables, cruise control cable if so equipped on engine codes L, B, 3.
5. Remove crankcase ventilation pipe on engine codes L, B, 3.
6. Remove all hoses, vacumm lines and wiring to gain access.
7. Remove fuel rail.
8. Remove the intake manifold.
9. Remove from front (left) cylinder head the C³I unit, spark plug wires, alternator bracket and one A/C compressor bracket bolt on engine code C (3800).
10. Remove from rear (right) cylinder head the power steering pump, belt tensioner assembly and fuel line heat shield on engine code C (3800).
11. Disconnect the exhaust crossover pipe.
12. Remove the exhaust manifolds.
13. Remove the valve covers, rocker arms, guide plates and pushrods. Keep all parts in order so they may be reassembled in their original locations.
14. Loosen the cylinder head bolts in reverse of the torque sequence, then remove the bolts and lift off the cylinder head.
15. Clean all gasket mating surfaces and the cylinder head bolt holes in the block.
16. Installation is the reverse of removal, replace all gaskets and seals. Torque the cylinder head bolts in the sequence shown to 25 ft. lbs.
17. Tighten each cylinder head bolt ¼ turn (90 degrees) in sequence.
18. Tighten each cylinder head bolt an additional ¼ turn in sequence.

CAUTION

Should you reach 60 ft. lbs. of torque at any time in Steps 17 and 18, stop tightening the bolt at this point. Do not complete the balance of the 90 degree turn. Failure to follow the given procedure will cause head gasket failure and possible engine damage.

---

19. Torque the rocker arm pedestal bolts to 37 ft. lbs. on engine code C (3800) and all others to 43 ft. lbs. the valve cover bolts to 53 in. lbs. on engine code C (3800) and all others to 88 in. lbs. and lifter guide retainer bolts to 27 ft. lbs on engine code C all others to 25 ft. lbs.
20. Check oil and coolant level, road test and check for leaks.

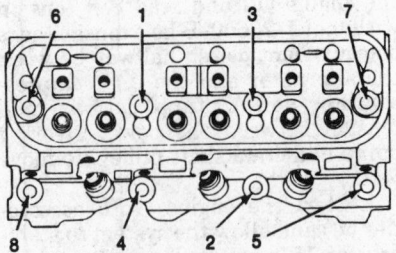

Cylinder head bolt torque sequence

OVERHAUL

For all cylinder head overhaul procedures, please refer to "Engine Rebuilding" in the unit repair section.

Rocker Arm Assembly

REMOVAL & INSTALLATION

1. Remove the valve cover.
2. Remove the rocker arm pedestal retaining bolts.
3. Remove the pedestal and rocker arm assembly. Place the assemblies in order on a clean workbench so they can be reassembled in their original locations.

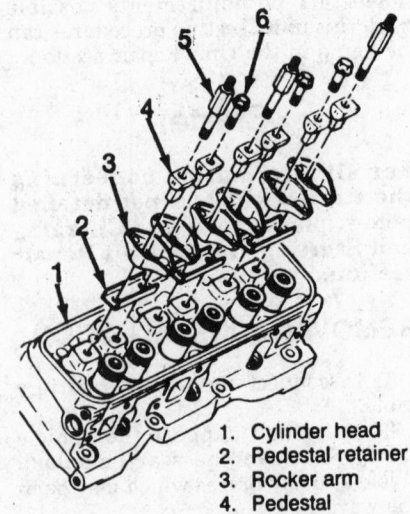

1. Cylinder head
2. Pedestal retainer
3. Rocker arm
4. Pedestal
5. 43 ft. lbs.
6. 43 ft. lbs.

Exploded view of rocker arm assembly

4. Installation is the reverse of removal. Torque the rocker arm pedestal bolts to 37 ft. lbs. on engine code C (3800) and all others to 43 ft. lbs., the valve cover bolts to 53 in. lbs. on engine code C (3800) and all others to 88 in. lbs. and lifter guide retainer bolts to 27 ft. lbs on engine code C and all others to 25 ft. lbs.

Intake Manifold

REMOVAL & INSTALLATION

1. Disconnect the negative battery cable.
2. Remove the Mass Air Flow sensor wiring and air intake duct.
3. Remove the serpentine drive belt, alternator and bracket.
4. Remove the C³I ignition module and wiring on engine codes L, 3, B and rear spark plug wiring on engine code C (3800).
5. Tag and disconnect all vacuum hoses and wiring connectors as necessary.
6. Disconnect the throttle, cruise control if so equipped and throttle valve cables from the throttle body.
7. Disconnect EGR pipe on engine code C (3800).
8. Drain the cooling system.

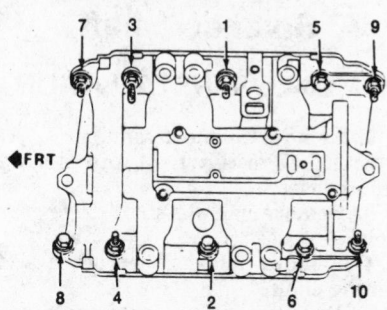

Intake manifold bolt torque sequence

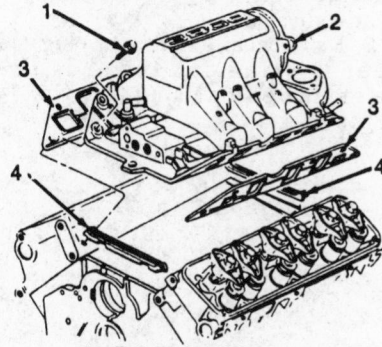

1. Bolt 80 inch lbs.
2. Intake manifold
3. Intake manifold gasket
4. Intake manifold seal

Intake manifold and gaskets—3800 engine

9. Disconnect the heater hoses from the throttle body.
10. Disconnect the upper radiator hose from the intake manifold.
11. Depressurize the fuel system and remove the fuel lines, fuel rail and injectors as an assembly.
12. Remove the intake manifold bolts in reverse of the torque sequence and lift off the intake manifold.
13. Installation is the reverse of removal. Clean all gasket mating surfaces and apply sealer if a steel gasket is used. Torque the intake manifold bolts in the sequence shown to 32 ft. lbs on engine codes L, 3, B and on code C (3800) torque manifold bolts to 80 in. lbs.

NOTE: On engine code C (3800) a special intake gasket is used for improved sealability between the intake manifold and cylinder head. It requires a very low torque to seal.

Exhaust Manifold

REMOVAL & INSTALLATION

Left Side

1. Disconnect the negative battery cable.
2. Disconnect the Mass Air Flow sensor wiring, air intake duct and crankcase ventilation pipe.
3. Remove the two bolts attaching the exhaust crossover pipe to the manifold.
4. Tag and disconnect the spark plug wires.
5. Remove the mounting bolts and remove the manifold.

NOTE: The oil dipstick tube may have to be removed to provide access to the manifold bolts.

6. Installation is in the reverse order of removal. Apply sealer as illustrated.

Right Side

1. Disconnect the negative battery cable.
2. Disconnect the Mass Air Flow sensor wiring, air intake duct and crankcase ventilation pipe.
3. Disconnect the IAC connector at the throttle body on engine codes L, 3, B and any other electrical connections on engine code C (3800).
4. Tag and disconnect the spark plug wires and the oxygen sensor lead.
5. Disconnect the heater inlet pipe from the manifold studs on engine codes L, 3, B and on engine code C (3800) remove EGR pipe and transaxle oil level indicator tube.

6. Remove the exhaust crossover pipe.
7. Remove the front alternator support bracket on engine codes L, 3, B.
8. Remove the exhaust manifold mounting bolts. Raise and support the front of the vehicle.
9. Disconnect the exhaust pipe from the manifold.
10. Remove the front exhaust pipe. Remove the manifold.
11. Installation is in the reverse order of removal. Apply sealer as illustrated.

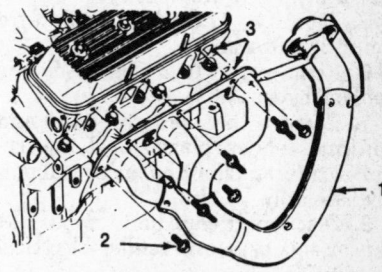

1. Exhaust manifold
2. 37 ft. lbs.
3. Apply sealant between manifold and cylinder head

Left exhaust manifold mounting

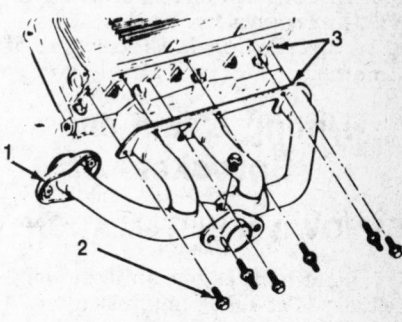

1. Exhaust manifold
2. 37 ft. lbs.
3. Apply sealant between manifold and cylinder head

Right exhaust manifold mounting

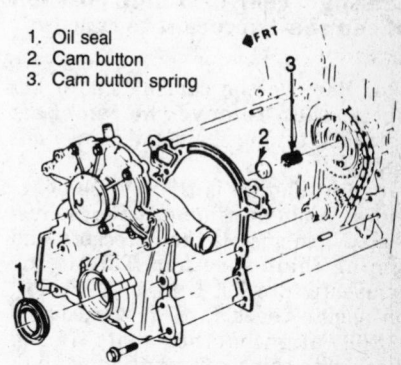

1. Oil seal
2. Cam button
3. Cam button spring

Timing chain cover

Front Cover and Seal

REMOVAL & INSTALLATION

1. Disconnect the negative battery cable and drain the cooling system.
2. Disconnect the upper and lower radiator hoses disconnect the heater return hose.
3. Remove the two nuts from the front engine mount at the cradle and raise the engine slightly with a suitable lifting device.
4. Remove the serpentine drive belt and the water pump pulley.
5. Remove the alternator and mounting bracket.
6. Remove the front clamp on the coolant bypass hose.
7. Remove the right front tire and the inner fender splash shield, then remove the crankshaft balancer and pulley assembly.
8. Disconnect camshaft, crankshaft sensor, oil pressure sender electrical connection.
9. Remove the timing chain cover mounting bolts at the block and oil pan.
10. Remove the timing chain cover. Clean all gasket mating surfaces and pry out the old oil seal with a suitable tool. Install a new oil seal using tool J–35354 or equivalent.
11. Installation is the reverse of removal.

Timing Chain and Sprockets

REMOVAL & INSTALLATION

1. Rotate the engine until the No. 1 cylinder is at TDC/compression.
2. Remove the front cover as described above.
3. Remove the camshaft thurst button, button spring and timing chain dampener.

NOTE: On engine code C (3800) remove camshaft sprocket from camshaft gear also note position of camshaft sprocket to camshaft gear.

4. Remove the camshaft sprocket bolts, then remove the camshaft sprocket, timing chain and crankshaft sprocket.
5. Installation is the reverse of removal. Align the timing marks as illustrated and install the sprockets and timing chain together. Torque the camshaft sprocket bolts to 19 ft. lbs. on engine codes L, 3, B. On code C (3800) align balance shaft timing mark with camshaft gear timing mark if either of two was disturbed after camshaft sprocket was removed.

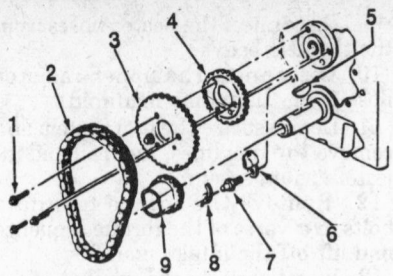

1. 27 ft. lbs.
2. Timing chain
3. Camshaft sprocket
4. Camshaft gear
5. Key
6. Damper
7. Bolt (special) 14 ft. lbs.
8. Spring
9. Crankshaft sprocket

Timing chain and sprockets – 3800 engine

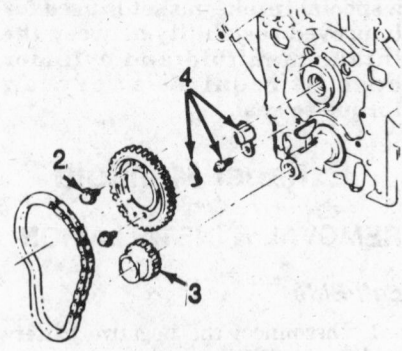

1. Timing mark alignment
2. 19 ft. lbs.
3. Crankshaft sprocket
4. Dampener assembly

Timing chain and sprockets

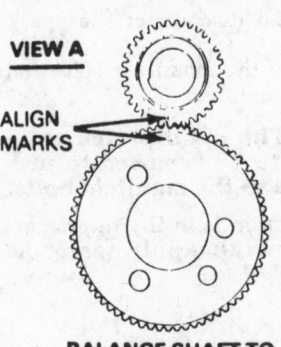

VIEW A

ALIGN MARKS

BALANCE SHAFT TO CAMSHAFT

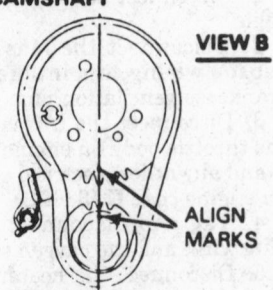

VIEW B

ALIGN MARKS

CAMSHAFT TO CRANKSHAFT

Timing balance shaft and camshaft marks

Torque sprocket to camshaft gear bolts to 27 ft. lbs.

Camshaft

REMOVAL & INSTALLATION

1. Remove engine assembly.
2. Remove intake manifold.
3. Remove the valve covers, rocker arms, guide plates, pushrods and valve lifters. Keep all parts in order so they may be reassembled in their original locations.
4. Remove crankshaft balancer assembly.
5. Remove camshaft thurst button.
6. Remove the timing chain cover, chain, sprockets and camshaft gear on engine code C (3800)

NOTE: When removing or installing camshaft, avoid marring the camshaft bearing surfaces.

7. Remove camshaft from engine.
8. Installation is the reverse of removal. Align all timing marks on camshaft, crankshaft and balance shaft on engine code C (3800). Coat camshaft with P/N 1052365 or equivalent before installation and dip the valve lifters in P/N 1052365 or equivalent before installation.

Balance Shaft

REMOVAL & INSTALLATION

1. Remove engine assembly.
2. Remove flywheel and timing chain cover.
3. Remove balance shaft drive gear bolt.
4. Remove camshaft sprocket and timing chain.
5. Remove balance shaft retainer bolts, retainer and gear.
6. Remove balance shaft from engine assembly using tool No. J–6125–B or equivalent.
7. Drive balance shaft rear plug and rear bearing out towards the bellhousing side using tool No. J–33049 or equivalent.

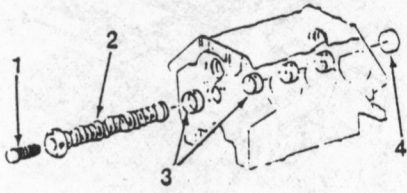

1. Button and spring assembly
2. Camshaft
3. Bearings
4. Cup plug

Camshaft assembly

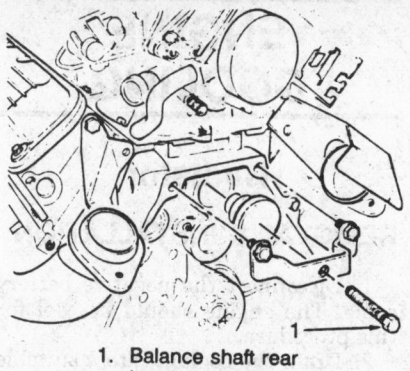

1. Balance shaft rear bearing installer (J–36995)

Balance shaft rear bearing installation— 3800 engine

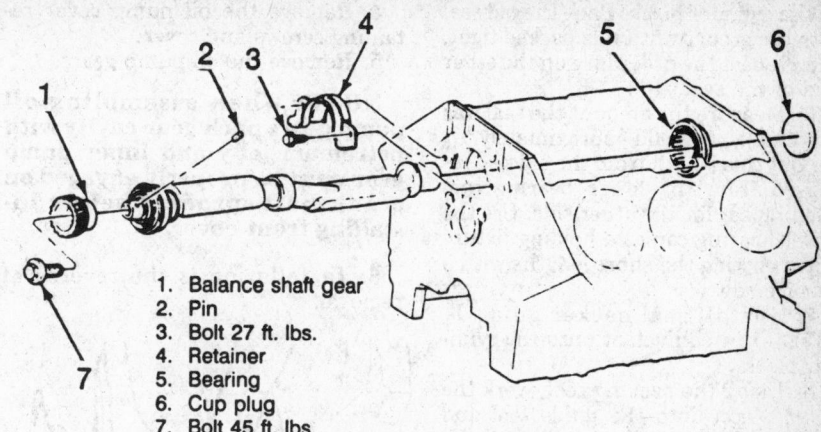

1. Balance shaft gear
2. Pin
3. Bolt 27 ft. lbs.
4. Retainer
5. Bearing
6. Cup plug
7. Bolt 45 ft. lbs.

Balance shaft assembly—3800 engine

NOTE: Check balance shaft rear journal and bearing for scoring and always replace the front balance shaft bearing whenever the balance shaft is removed.

8. To install dip rear balance shaft bearing in clean engine oil and install bearing in engine block using J–36995 or equivalent.

9. Install balance shaft rear plug in engine block.

10. Install balance shaft in block using tool J–36996 or equivalent and balance shaft front bearing retainer and bolts, tighten bolts to 27 ft. lbs.

11. Install balance shaft drive gear and tighten bolt to 45 ft. lbs.

12. Turn the crankshaft so that No. 1 is at TDC, turn the camshaft, with the sprocket temporarily installed so timing mark is straight down.

13. With the camshaft sprocket removed, turn the balance shaft so that the timing mark on the gear points straight down.

14. Install camshaft gear align the marks on the balance shaft gear and the camshaft gear.

15. Install timing chain and camshaft sprocket, tighten balance shaft drive gear bolt to 45 ft. lbs.

16. Install timing chain cover and flywheel, torque flywheel bolts to 60 ft. lbs.

17. Install engine assembly, check fluid levels and for any leaks, roadtest vehicle.

Piston and Connecting Rod

POSITIONING

NOTE: For all piston and connection rod overhaul procedures, please refer to "Engine Rebuilding" in the Unit Repair section.

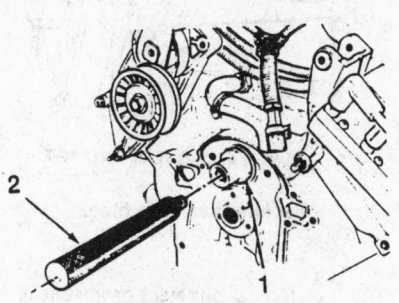

1. Balance shaft installer (J–36996)
2. Driver handle (J–21465–13)

Balance shaft installation—3800 engine

ENGINE LUBRICATION

Oil Pan

REMOVAL & INSTALLATION

1. Disconnect the negative battery cable.
2. Raise the car and support it safely.
3. Drain the engine oil into a suitable container and discard.
4. Remove the transaxle converter cover.
5. Remove starter motor and oil filter.
6. Remove the oil pan mounting bolts and lower the oil pan. Clean all gasket mating surfaces.

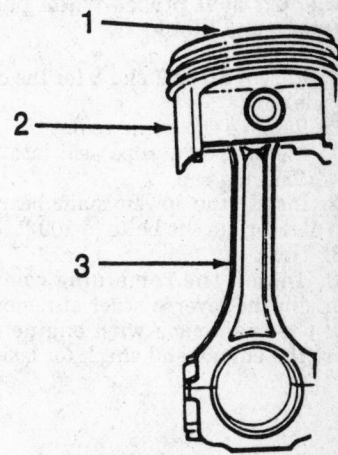

1. Notch (install toward front of engine)
2. Piston
3. Connecting rod

Piston and connecting rod assembly

7. Installation is the reverse of removal. Use a new oil pan gasket and tighten the retaining bolts to 88 in. lbs. Do not overtighten or leakage may occur.

Rear Main Bearing Oil Seal

REMOVAL & INSTALLATION

1. Raise the vehicle and support it safely.
2. Drain the engine oil and remove the oil pan.
3. Remove the rear main bearing cap.
4. Remove the old seal from the bearing cap.
5. Insert packing tool J–21526–2 or equivalent against one end of the seal

in the cylinder block. Pack the old seal into the groove until it is packed tight, then repeat the procedure on the other end of the seal.

6. Measure the amount the seal was driven up, then add approximately $\frac{1}{16}$ in. Cut this length from the old seal removed from the lower bearing cap, then repeat for the other side. Use the lower bearing cap as a holding fixture when cutting the short lengths with a razor blade.

7. Install seal packer guide J–21526–1 or equivalent onto the cylinder block.

8. Using the packing tool, work the short pieces into the guide tool and pack into the cylinder block until the tool hits the built-in stop.

NOTE: It may help to use oil on the short seal pieces when packing into the block.

9. Repeat Steps 7 and 8 for the other side.

10. Remove the guide tool.

11. Install a new rope seal into the lower bearing cap.

12. Install the lower main bearing cap and torque the bolts to 100 ft. lbs. (135 Nm).

13. Install the remaining components in the reverse order of removal. Fill the crankcase with engine oil, start the engine and check for leaks.

Oil Pump

REMOVAL & INSTALLATION

1. Disconnect the negative battery cable.

2. Remove the front cover from the engine as outlined under "Front Cover and Oil Seal."

3. Remove the oil filter adapter, pressure regulator valve and valve spring.

4. Remove the oil pump cover retaining screws and cover.

5. Remove the oil pump gears.

NOTE: When assembling oil pump gears pack gear cavity with petroleum jelly and inner pump gear must be properly engaged on crankshaft sprocket before installing front cover.

6. Installation is the reverse of removal.

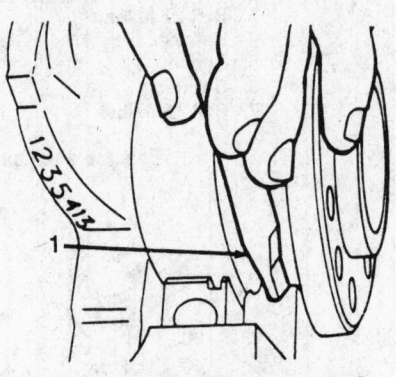

1. PACKING TOOL J-21526-2

Packing seal into block

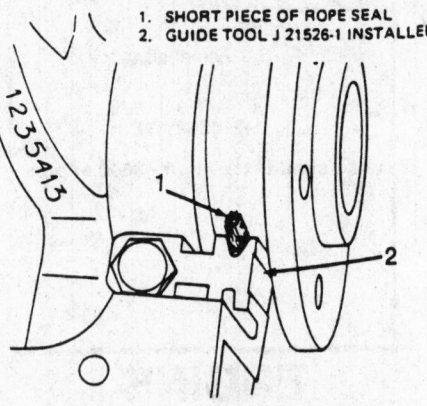

1. SHORT PIECE OF ROPE SEAL
2. GUIDE TOOL J 21526-1 INSTALLED

Guide tool installed on block

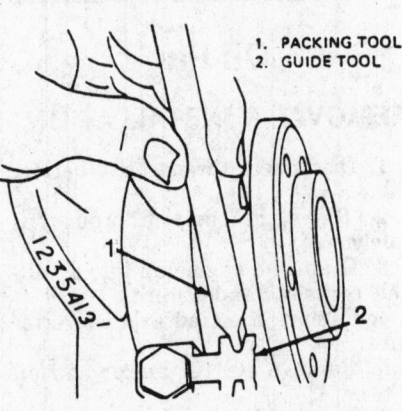

1. PACKING TOOL
2. GUIDE TOOL

Packing short pieces of rope seal into guide tool

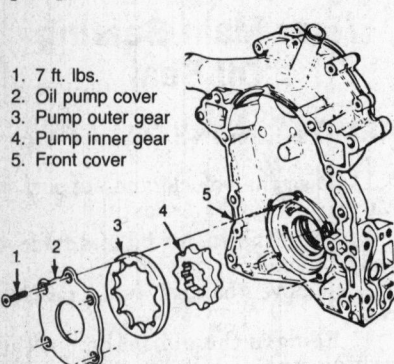

1. 7 ft. lbs.
2. Oil pump cover
3. Pump outer gear
4. Pump inner gear
5. Front cover

Oil pump and housing

ENGINE COOLING

Radiator

REMOVAL & INSTALLATION

1. Disconnect the negative battery cable. The engine should be cool for this procedure.

2. Drain the coolant into a suitable container. Unless contaminated, the coolant may be reused.

3. Disconnect the forward strut brace at the radiator and swing it out of the way. Detach the electrical connector, remove the mounting bolts and then remove the cooling fan from the radiator assembly.

4. Loosen the clamp-screws and remove the coolant reservoir and upper radiator hoses. It may be necessary to remove the hood latch; if so, scribe alignment marks around the latch assembly before removing it from the radiator support.

5. Disconnect the transaxle and auxiliary oil cooler lines at the radiator. Wire the lines out of the way.

6. Disconnect the lower radiator hose at the radiator.

7. Remove the mounting bolts and lift out the radiator.

8. Installation is in the reverse order of removal.

Water Pump

REMOVAL & INSTALLATION

1. Disconnect the negative battery cable.

2. Drain the cooling system.

3. Remove the serpentine drive belt.

4. Disconnect the coolant hoses at the water pump.

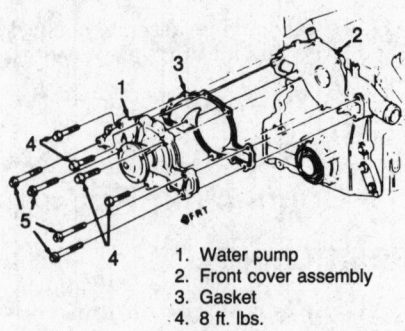

1. Water pump
2. Front cover assembly
3. Gasket
4. 8 ft. lbs.
5. 29 ft. lbs.

Typical water pump mounting

5. Remove the water pump pulley bolts. The long bolt is removed through the access hole provided in the body side rail. Remove the pulley.

6. Remove the water pump attaching bolts and remove the water pump from the engine.

7. Installation is the reverse of removal. Clean all gasket mating surfaces and use a new gasket. Torque the short water pump mounting bolts to 8 ft. lbs. and the long mounting bolts to 29 ft. lbs.

Thermostat

REMOVAL & INSTALLATION

To replace the thermostat, drain the cooling system below the level of the thermostat and remove the bolt(s) holding the water neck in place. Remove the water neck and the thermostat will lift out. Clean the mating surfaces of both the intake manifold and the water neck. Use a new gasket when installing a new thermostat. If only silicone sealer was used from the factory, use only silicone sealer during assembly. Some late model engines only use an O-ring to seal the thermostat water neck.

CAUTION

Be sure the thermostat is not reversed in its installed position. The spring should be installed toward the engine.

COOLING SYSTEM BLEEDING

After working on the cooling system, even to replace the thermostat, it must be bled. Air trapped in the system will, otherwise, prevent proper filling, leaving the radiator coolant level low and causing risk of overheating.

To bleed the system, start with the system cool, the radiator cap off, and the radiator filled to about an inch below the filler neck. Start the engine and run it at slightly above normal idle speed, to ensure adequate circulation. If air bubbles appear and the coolant level drops, fill the system with antifreeze/water mix to bring the level back to the proper level. Run the engine this way until the thermostat opens. When this happens, coolant will move abruptly across the top of the radiator and the temperature of the radiator will suddenly rise. At this point, air is often expelled, and the level may drop quite a bit. Keep refilling the system until the level is near the top of the radiator and remains constant. If the car has an overflow tank, fill the radiator right up to the filler neck. Replace the radiator filler cap.

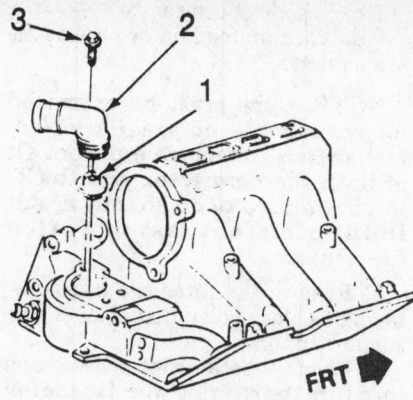

1. Thermostat
2. Water outlet
3. Bolt/Screw

Thermostat and housing asembly—3800 engine

EMISSION CONTROLS

For a description of and service for each system, please refer to "Emission Controls" in the Unit Repair section.

Due to the complex nature of modern electronic engine control systems, comprehensive diagnosis and testing procedures fall outside the confines of this repair manual. For complete information on diagnosis, testing and repair procedures concerning all modern engine and emission control systems, please refer to *Chilton's Guide To Electronic Engine Controls.*

FUEL SYSTEM

Fuel System Service Precaution

Any time the fuel system is being worked on, disconnect the negative battery cable, except for those tests where battery voltage is required and always keep a dry chemical (Class B) fire extinguisher near the work area.

RELIEVING FUEL SYSTEM PRESSURE

1. Remove the fuel pump fuse from the fuse block or disconnect the harness connector at the tank.

2. Start the engine. It should run and then stall when the fuel in the lines is exhausted. When the engine stops, crank the starter for about three seconds to make sure all pressure in the fuel lines is released.

3. Install the fuel pump fuse after repair is made.

Fuel Filter

REMOVAL & INSTALLATION

CAUTION

Fuel system is under pressure. See the procedure under "Relieving Fuel System Pressure" to relieve fuel pressure before attempting to remove any fuel lines.

The fuel injection system uses an inline filter located in the fuel feed line under the hood, attached to the frame rail, or on the rear crossmember of the vehicle. Always use the proper wrench on the fittings any time a fuel filter is removed or installed, and never replace a metal fuel line with a rubber insert. The high pressure fuel system used with all fuel injection systems requires metal fuel lines to contain the pressure. Replace the O-ring at the connection and torque the fuel fitting to 22 ft. lbs. (30 Nm).

Electric Fuel Pump

PRESSURE TESTING

1. Relieve the fuel system pressure. Use pressure gauge J-34730-1 or equivalent, mounting the gauge to the test fitting on the fuel rail, wrap a shop towel around the pressure fitting to absorb any small amount of fuel that may leak during installation.

2. Turn ignition OFF for ten seconds and turn off the A/C.

3. Turn ignition ON. Fuel pump should run for about two seconds and shut off.

4. Note the fuel pressure when the pump stops this is initial pump pressure.

5. Pressure should be 40–47 psi for 3.8L engine code C, 37–43 psi for the 3.8L engine codes 3, B and 37–43 psi for the 3.0L engine and hold steady.

ADJUSTMENT

No adjustments are possible on these systems. If fuel pressure is inadequate additional diagnosis is necessary.

REMOVAL & INSTALLATION

CAUTION

Fuel system pressure must be relieved before attempting any service procedures.

---

1. Relieve the fuel system pressure.
2. Disconnect the negative battery cable.
3. Raise the car and support it safely.
4. Drain and remove the fuel tank.
5. Remove the fuel lever sending unit and pump assembly by turning the cam lock ring counterclockwise and lifting the assembly from the fuel tank. There is a special tool made for turning the lock ring, but careful tapping with a brass drift will work.
6. Pull the fuel pump up into the attaching hose while pulling outward away from the bottom support. Take care to prevent damage to the rubber sound insulator and strainer during removal. Once the pump assembly is clear of the bottom support, pull it out of the rubber connector.
7. Installation is the reverse of removal. Use a new O-ring when installing the assembly into the fuel tank. When installing the fuel tank, make sure all rubber sound isolators or anti-squeak spacers are replaced in their original locations.

Fuel Injection

Due to the complex nature of modern fuel injection systems, comprehensive diagnosis and testing procedures fall outside the confines of this repair manual. For complete information on fuel injection diagnosis and testing procedures, please refer to *Chilton's Guide To Fuel Injection And Feedback Carburetors.*

AUTOMATIC TRANSAXLE

For further information on automatic transaxles, please refer to "Automatic Transmissions" in the Unit Repair section.

REMOVAL & INSTALLATION

1. Disconnect the negative battery cable. Disconnect the wire connector at the mass air flow sensor.
2. Remove the air intake duct and the mass air flow sensor as an assembly.
3. Disconnect the cruise control assembly. Disconnect the shift control linkage.
4. Tag and disconnect the following:
   a. Park/Neutral switch
   b. Torque converter clutch

c. Vehicle speed sensor
   d. Vacuum modulator hose at the modulator.

NOTE: Care must be exercised on reassembly of the Park/Neutral switch to ensure a proper fit of both the connector and the T-latch. Failure to do so may result in intermittent loss of switch functions.

5. Remove the three top transaxle-to-engine block bolts. Install an engine support fixture.
6. Remove both front wheels and then turn the steering wheel to the full left position.
7. Remove the right front ball joint nut and separate the control arm from the steering knuckle.
8. Remove the right drive axle as detailed later in this section.

NOTE: Be careful not to allow the drive axle splines to contact any portion of the lip seal.

9. Remove the left drive axle using a suitable pry bar. Be careful not to damage the pan. Install drive axle boot seal protectors.
10. Remove three bolts at the transaxle and three nuts at the cradle member. Remove the left front transaxle mount.
11. Remove the right front mount-to-cradle nuts. Remove the left rear transaxle mount-to-transaxle bolts.
12. Remove the right rear transaxle mount as in Step 10. Remove the engine support bracket-to-transaxle case bolts.
13. Remove the flywheel cover. Remove the flywheel-to-converter bolts.

NOTE: Be sure to matchmark the flywheel-to-converter relationship for proper alignment upon reassembly.

14. Remove the bolts attaching the rear cradle member to the front cradle dog leg.
15. Remove the front left cradle-to-body bolt. Remove the front cradle dog leg-to-right cradle member bolts.
16. Install a transaxle support fixture into position.
17. Remove the cradle assembly by swinging it aside and supporting it with a suitable stand.
18. Disconnect and cap the oil cooler lines at the transaxle.

NOTE: One bolt is located between the transaxle and the engine block and is installed in the opposite direction.

19. Remove the remaining lower transaxle-to-engine bolts. And then lower the transaxle assembly away from the car.
20. Installation is in the reverse order or removal. Check the fluid level and all adjustments.

DRIVE AXLE

Halfshafts

REMOVAL & INSTALLATION

1. Raise car and remove wheel and tire.
2. Insert drift into rotor and caliper to prevent rotor from turning.
3. Remove hub nut and washer using tool No. J–34826 or equivalent.
4. Remove caliper and/or caliper bracket from steering knuckle. Suspend caliper assembly with wire. Never allow caliper to hang with the brake hose.

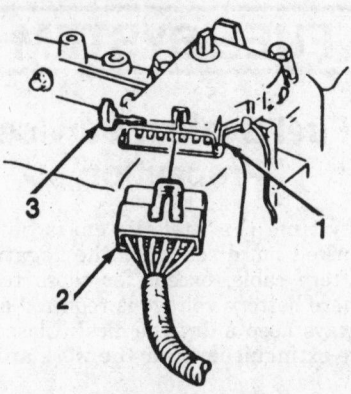

1. Park/Neutral and backup lamp switch
2. Switch connector
3. T-latch connector

T-latch connector assembly

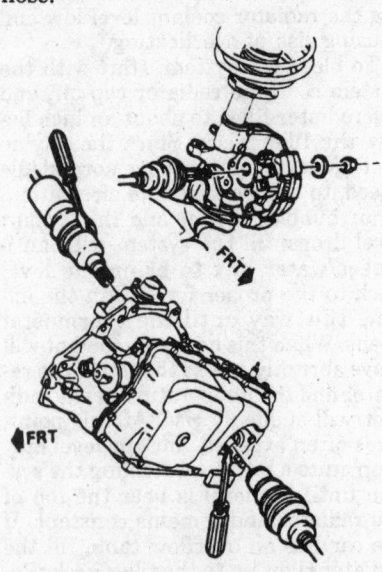

Halfshaft removal

5. Remove the rotor from the hub.

6. Disconnect the stabilizer link.

7. Disconnect the ball joint from the steering knuckle.

8. Disconnect drive axle from transaxle.

9. Remove drive axle from hub using tool No. J–28733 or equivalent.

10. Installation is reverse of removal. Torque hub nut 191 ft. lbs. (260 Nm.)

CV JOINT OVERHAUL

For all CV-Joint overhaul procedures, please refer to "U-Joints and CV-Joints" in the Unit Repair section.

Front Wheel Drive Hub, Knuckle, and Bearings

NOTE: The hub and bearing are replaced only as an assembly.

REMOVAL & INSTALLATION

1. Raise and support vehicle.

2. Lower vehicle slightly so that the weight of the vehicle rests on the jack stands and not on the control arms.

3. Remove the wheel and tire assembly.

4. Insert drift punch through caliper into the rotor to hold the rotor from turning.

5. Remove the axle shaft nut and washer.

6. Remove drift punch.

7. Remove caliper bolts and support caliper properly.

8. Remove the rotor.

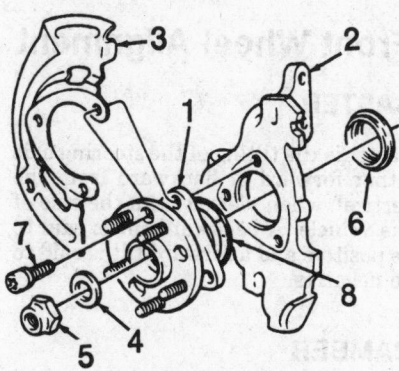

1. Hub and bearing assembly
2. Steering knuckle
3. Shield
4. Washer
5. Hub nut
6. Seal
7. Hub and bearing retaining bolt
8. "O" ring

Hub & bearing-Exploded view

9. Attach tool No. J–28733, or equivalent, and separate hub and drive axle.

10. Remove three hub and bearing bolts, shield, hub and bearing assembly and O-ring.

11. Using a punch, tap the seal towards the engine. When the seal is removed from the steering knuckle, cut it off the drive axle using side cutters.

NOTE: The factory seal is installed from the engine side of the steering knuckle. The service replacement is installed from the wheel side of the steering knuckle.

12. Install new hub and bearing seal in steering knuckle using a proper seal installation tool.

13. Lubricate hub and bearing seal with grease.

14. Install a new O-ring around hub and bearing assembly.

15. Install hub and bearing assembly into steering knuckle.

16. The remainder of the installation is the reverse of the removal. Torque the hub and bearing retaining bolts to 70 ft. lbs. (95 Nm.). Torque the caliper bolts to 38 ft. lbs. (51 Nm.). Torque the axle shaft nut to 180 ft. lbs. (245 Nm.).

FRONT SUSPENSION

MacPherson Strut

REMOVAL & INSTALLATION

For spring and shock absorber removal and installation, and any other strut overhaul procedures, please refer to "Strut Overhaul" in the Unit Repair section.

1. Remove the three nuts attaching the top of the strut assembly to the body.

2. Raise the car and support it with jack stands under the engine cradle.

3. Lower the car slightly so that the weight rests on the jack stands.

4. Remove the wheels and tires.

NOTE: Always install drive axle boot seal protectors. Care must be taken to prevent overextension of the inner Tri-Pot joints.

5. Remove the brake line bracket bolt from the strut assembly. Do not disconnect the brake line from the caliper.

6. Remove the strut-to-steering knuckle bolts and then carefully remove the strut assembly.

7. Installation is in the reverse order of removal. Please note the following:

 a. Check wheel alignment

 b. Tighten the strut-to-body bolts to 18 ft. lbs. (24 Nm)

 c. Tighten the strut-to-steering knuckle bolts to 144 ft. lbs. (195 Nm).

Ball Joints

INSPECTION

1. Raise the front of the car with a lift placed under the engine cradle. The front wheel should be clear of the ground.

2. Grasp the wheel at the top and bottom and shake the wheel in and out.

3. If any movement is seen of the steering knuckle relative to the control arm, the ball joints are defective and must be replaced. Note that movement elsewhere may be due to loose wheel bearings or other troubles; watch the knuckle-to-control arm connection.

4. If the ball stud is disconnected from the steering knuckle and any looseness is noted, often the ball joint stud can be twisted in its socket with your fingers, replace the ball joints.

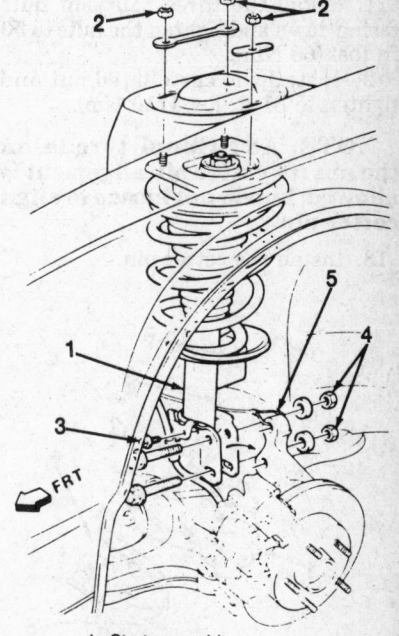

1. Strut assembly
2. 18 ft. lbs.
3. 13 ft. lbs.
4. 144 ft. lbs.
5. Retain knuckle with wire once strut assembly is removed

Strut assembly mounting

REMOVAL & INSTALLATION

1. Raise the front of the car and support it with jackstands underneath the engine cradle. Lower the car slightly so that the weight rests primarily on the jack stands.

2. Remove the wheel and tire assemblies.

3. Install drive axle covers to protect the drive axle boot seals.

4. Pull the cotter pin from the ball joint and remove castellated nut from stud. Use ball joint/knuckle separator or equivalent detach ball joint stud from knuckle.

5. Use a ⅛ in. drill bit to drill a hole approximately ¼ in. deep in the center of each of the three ball joint rivets.

6. Use a ½ in. drill bit to drill off the rivet heads. Drill only enough to remove the rivet head.

NOTE: If ball joints were replaced there will be bolts not rivets.

7. Use a hammer and punch to remove the rivets. Drive them out from the bottom.

8. Loosen the stabilizer bar bushing assembly nut.

9. Pull down on the control arm and remove the ball joint from the steering knuckle and control arm.

10. Install the new ball joint in the steering knuckle and line up the holes with those in the control arm.

11. Install the three ball joint nuts facing down and tighten the nuts to 50 ft. lbs. (68 Nm).

12. Install the castellated nut and tighten to 81 ft. lbs. (110 Nm).

NOTE: Additional torque on the nut for cotter pin alignment is allowed, but do not loosen to align cotter pin.

13. Install the cotter pin.

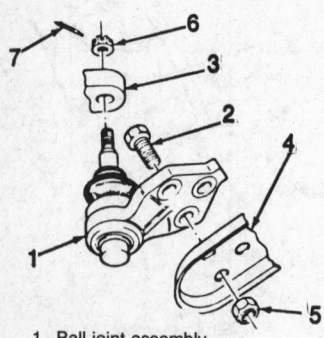

1. Ball joint assembly
2. Mounting bolt
3. Steering knuckle
4. Control arm
5. 50 ft. lbs.
6. 81 ft. lbs.
7. Cotter pin

Ball joint replacement

14. Installation of the remaining components is in the reverse order of removal.

Lower Control Arm

REMOVAL & INSTALLATION

1. Perform Steps 1–3 of the "Ball Joint Removal and Installation" procedure.

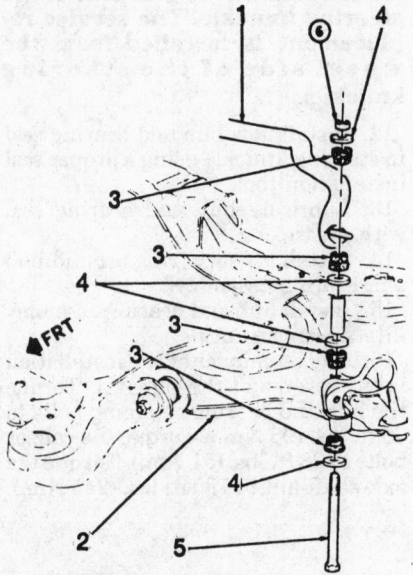

1. Stabilizer Bar
2. Control Arm
3. Insulator (4)
4. Retainer (4)
5. Bolt
6. Nut 17 N·m (13 LBS. FT.)

Stabilizer bar bushing assembly

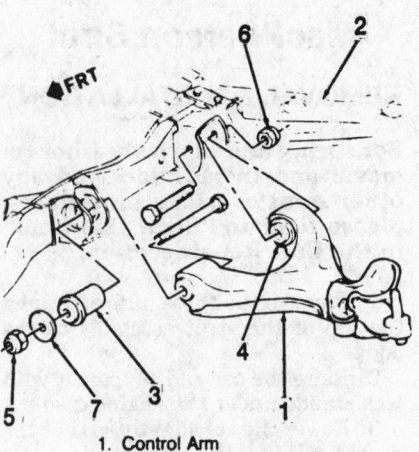

1. Control Arm
2. Cradle
3. Cradle Mounted Bushing
4. Control Arm Mounted Bushing
5. Cradle Mounted Bushing Nut 190 N·m (140 LBS. FT.)
6. Control Arm Mounted Bushing Nut 123 N·m (90 LBS. FT.)
7. Washer

Lower control arm assembly

2. Remove the stabilizer bar bushing-to-control arm bolt.

3. Pull the cotter pin from the ball joint and remove castellated nut from stud. Use ball joint/knuckle separator or equivalent detach ball joint stud from knuckle.

4. Remove the remaining control arm bolts and remove the control arm from the vehicle.

5. Position the control arm and install the mounting bolts, but DO NOT tighten.

6. Install the stabilizer bar bushing assembly. Reconnect the ball joint to the steering knuckle.

7. Hoist the vehicle slightly so the weight of the vehicle is supported by the control arms.

NOTE: The weight of the vehicle MUST be supported by the control arms when tightening the mounting nuts.

8. Tighten the:
   a. Stabilizer bar bushing nut to 13 ft. lbs. (17 Nm)
   b. Rear control arm mounting nut to 90 ft. lbs. (123 Nm)
   c. Front control arm mounting nut to 140 ft. lbs. (190 Nm)
   d. Ball joint nut to 81 ft. lbs. (110 Nm).

9. Installation of the remaining components is in the reverse order of removal.

Front Wheel Bearings

For front wheel bearing replacement refer to Drive Axle in this section.

Front Wheel Alignment

CASTER

Caster is the tilting of the steering axis either forward or backward from the vertical, when viewed from the side of the vehicle. A backward tilt is said to be positive and a forward tilt is said to be negative.

CAMBER

Camber is the tilting of the wheels from the vertical when viewed from the front of the vehicle. When the wheels tilt outward from the top, the camber is said to be positive. When the wheels tilt inward from the top the camber is said to be negative. The amount of tilt is measured in degrees from the vertical. This measurement is called camber angle.

TOE IN

Toe in is the turning in of the wheels. The actual amount of toe in is normally only a fraction of an inch. The purpose of toe in specification is to ensure parallel rolling of the wheels. Toe in also serves to offset the small deflections of the steering support system which occur when the vehicle is rolling forward.

REAR SUSPENSION

Superlift Strut

REMOVAL & INSTALLATION

1. Remove the inner trunk side cover.
2. Raise and support the rear of the vehicle. Remove the wheels and tires.
3. Disconnect and plug the ELC air line.
4. Remove the strut tower mounting nuts from inside the trunk.
5. Remove the strut anchor bolts, washers and nuts from the rear knuckle and knuckle bracket.
6. Remove the strut.
7. Installation is in the reverse order of removal. Please note the following:
   a. Tighten the strut tower mounting nuts to 19 ft. lbs. (25 Nm)

b. Tighten the strut anchor nuts to 144 ft. lbs. (195 Nm)
   c. Lightly pressurize the ELC system by momentarily grounding the compressor test lead in the engine compartment.
   d. Check rear wheel alignment.

Coil Springs

REMOVAL & INSTALLATION

1. Raise the rear of the vehicle and support it so that the control arms hang free. Remove the rear wheels.
2. Separate the rear stabilizer bar from the knuckle bracket and remove it.
3. Disconnect the ELC height sensor link (right control arm) and/or the parking brake cable retaining clip (left control arm).
4. Position the special tool J–23028–01 or its equivalent, so as to cradle the control arm bushings.

NOTE: Special tool J–23028–01 should be secured to a suitable jack.

5. Raise the jack to remove the tension from the control arm pivot bolts.

─────── **CAUTION** ───────
Secure a chain around the spring and through the control arm as a safety precaution.

6. Remove the rear control arm pivot bolt and nut.
7. Slowly maneuver the jack so as to relieve any tension in the front control arm pivot bolt and then remove the bolt and nut.
8. Lower the jack to allow the control arm to pivot downward.

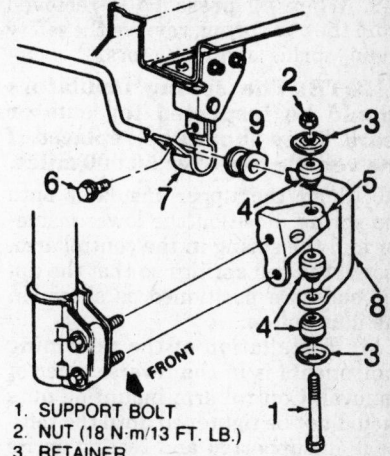

1. SUPPORT BOLT
2. NUT (18 N·m/13 FT. LB.)
3. RETAINER
4. INSULATORS
5. KNUCKLE BRACKET
6. BUSHING CLIP BOLT (50 N·m/37 FT. LB.)
7. SUPPORT ASSEMBLY
8. STABILIZER BAR
9. BUSHING

Rear stabilizer bar bushing assembly

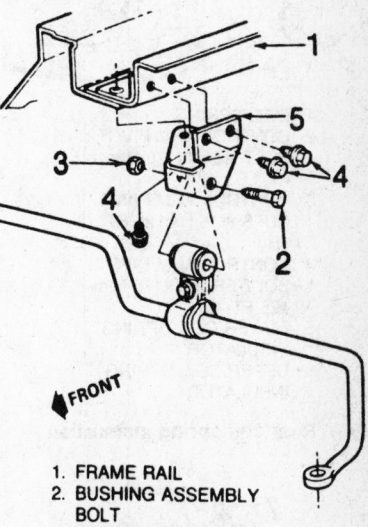

1. FRAME RAIL
2. BUSHING ASSEMBLY BOLT
3. NUT (50 N·m/37 FT. LB.)
4. MOUNTING BRACKET BOLTS (18N·m/13 FT. LB.)
5. MOUNTING BRACKET

Rear stabilizer bar mounting bracket

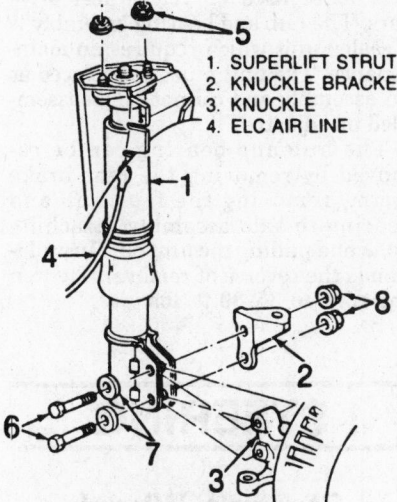

1. SUPERLIFT STRUT
2. KNUCKLE BRACKET
3. KNUCKLE
4. ELC AIR LINE

5. STRUT MOUNTING NUTS (25 N·m/19 FT. LBS.)
6. STRUT ANCHOR BOLTS
7. STRUT ANCHOR WASHERS
8. STRUT ANCHOR NUTS (195 N·m/144 FT. LBS.)

Rear strut installation

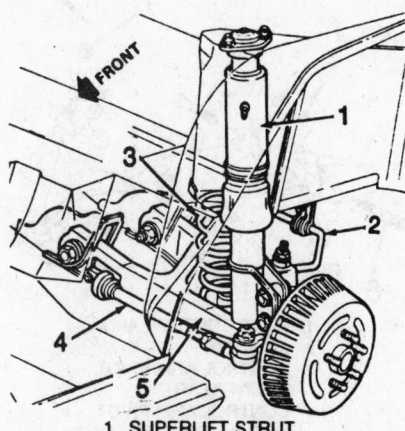

1. SUPERLIFT STRUT
2. STABILIZER BAR
3. COIL SPRING
4. SUSPENSION ADJUSTMENT LINK
5. LOWER CONTROL ARM

Rear suspension

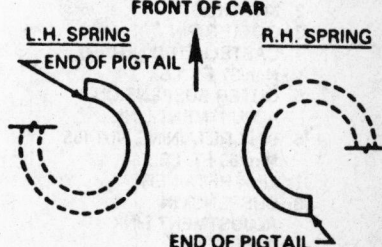

TOP VIEW OF UPPER END OF SPRING

FRONT OF CAR

L.H. SPRING   R.H. SPRING
←END OF PIGTAIL

END OF PIGTAIL

Rear coil spring positioning

9. When all pressure is removed from the coil spring, remove the safety chain, spring and insulators.

NOTE: The spring insulators should be inspected for cuts or tears. They should be replaced if the vehicle has over 50,000 miles.

10. Snap the upper insulator onto the spring. Position the lower insulator and the spring in the control arm. Install the coil springs so that the upper ends are positioned as shown in the illustration.

11. Installation of the remaining components is in the reverse order of removal. Control arm mounting nuts should not be tightened until the vehicle is unsupported and resting on its wheels at normal trim height.

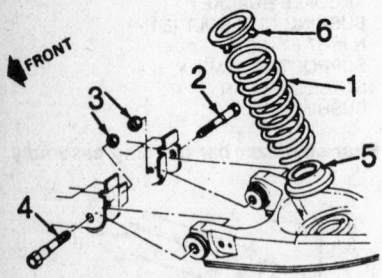

1. COIL SPRING
2. CONTROL ARM PIVOT BOLT-REAR (170 N·m/125 FT. LB.)
3. CONTROL ARM PIVOT NUTS (115 N·m/85 FT. LB.)
4. CONTROL ARM PIVOT BOLT-FRONT (170 N·m/125 FT. LB.)
5. LOWER COIL SPRING INSULATOR
6. UPPER COIL SPRING INSULATOR

Rear coil spring installation

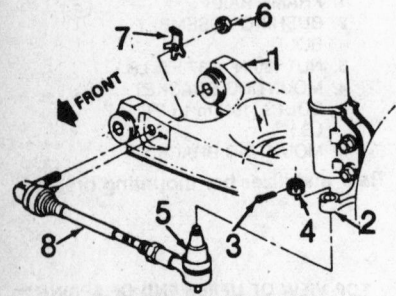

1. REAR CONTROL ARM
2. KNUCKLE
3. COTTER PIN
4. CASTELLATED NUT (50 N·m/37 FT. LB.)
5. OUTER SUSPENSION ADJUSTMENT LINK
6. LINK RETAINING NUT (85 N·m/63 FT. LB.)
7. LINK RETAINER
8. SUSPENSION ADJUSTMENT LINK ASSEMBLY

Rear suspension adjustment link

Rear Ball Joint

REMOVAL & INSTALLATION

1. Raise and support the rear of the vehicle and remove the wheels.
2. Disconnect the ELC height sensor link (right control arm) and/or the parking brake cable retaining link (left control arm).
3. Remove the cotter pin and castellated nut from the outer suspension adjustment link.
4. Separate the outer suspension link from the knuckle.
5. Support the control arm with a suitable jack. The lower control arm MUST be supported to prevent the coil spring from forcing the control arm downward.
6. Remove the ball stud cotter pin.
7. Remove the castellated nut.
8. Install a ball joint separator tool and separate the knuckle from the ball stud.
9. Press the ball joint from the control arm.
10. Installation is in the reverse order of removal. Please note following:
    a. Tighten a NEW castellated nut to 7.5 ft. lbs. (10 Nm). Tighten the nut an additional ⅔ of a turn.
    b. Align the slot in the nut to the cotter pin hole by tightening only. Do not loosen the nut to align the holes.

Control Arm

REMOVAL & INSTALLATION

1. Perform Steps 1–2 of the "Rear Ball Joint Removal & Installation" procedures.

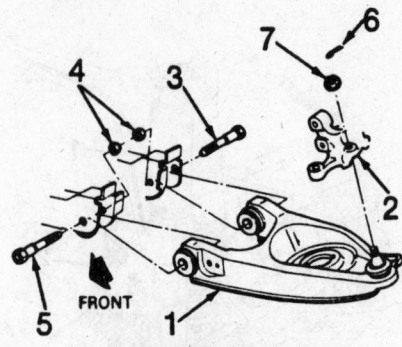

1. REAR CONTROL ARM
2. KNUCKLE
3. CONTROL ARM PIVOT BOLT—REAR
4. CONTROL ARM PIVOT NUTS (115 N·m/85 FT-LB)
5. CONTROL ARM PIVOT BOLT—FRONT
6. COTTER PIN
7. CASTELLATED NUT

Rear control arm

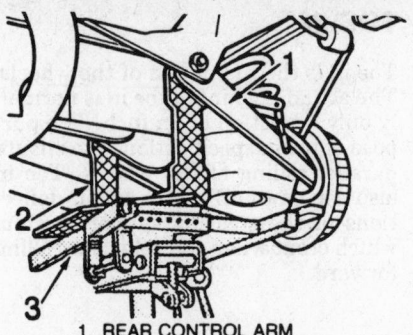

1. REAR CONTROL ARM
2. SPECIAL TOOL J-23028-01
3. TRANSMISSION JACK

Use the special tool and a transmission jack to cradle the control arm

2. Remove the suspension adjustment link retaining nut and retainer.
3. Separate the link assembly from the control arm.
4. Remove the coil spring as detailed previously.
5. Perform Steps 6–9 of the "Ball Joint Removal & Installation" procedure.
6. Remove the control arm.
7. Installation is in the reverse order of removal.

Rear Wheel Hub and Bearing

REMOVAL & INSTALLATION

A single unit hub and bearing assembly is bolted to both ends of the rear axle assembly. These take the place of rear axles used on rear wheel drive cars. The hub and bearing assembly is a sealed unit which requires no maintenance. The unit must be replaced as an assembly and cannot be disassembled or adjusted.

The hub and bearing can be removed by removing the rear brake drum, removing the four hub and bearing-to-axle assembly attaching bolts and pulling the unit out. Installation is the reverse of removal. Tighten the bolts to 35–39 ft. lbs.

STEERING

Steering Wheel

REMOVAL & INSTALLATION

————— CAUTION —————

The Delta 88 Oldsmobile Royale and Royal Brougham are equipped with a Inflatable Restraint System (IRS) as an option. The

IRS equipped vehicle can be identified by Inflatable Restraint marked on steering wheel hub, instrument cluster light and code 3 for seventh digit of Vehicle Identification Number. Improper maintenance, including incorrect removal and installation of related components, can lead to personal injury caused by unintentional activation of the Airbag. Related components on these models should be serviced only by authorized service technicians.

1. Disconnect battery ground cable and place turn signal lever in neutral position.
2. Remove the trim retaining screws from behind the wheel. On wheels with a center cap, pull off the cap.
3. Lift the trim off and pull the horn wires from the turn signal cancelling cam.
4. Remove the retainer and the steering wheel nut.
5. Mark the wheel-to-shaft relationship, and then remove the wheel with a puller.
6. Install the wheel on the shaft aligning the previously made marks. Tighten the nut.
7. Insert the horn wires into the cancelling cam.
8. Install the center trim and reconnect the battery cable.

NOTE: Some vehicles equipped with tilt steering columns may experience a squeaking noise when turning the steering wheel in a tilted position. This can be caused by insufficient grease in the tilting mechanism.

Turn Signal Switch

REMOVAL & INSTALLATION

1. Remove the steering wheel as previously outlined.
2. Loosen the cover screws. Pry the cover off with a screwdriver, and lift the cover off the shaft.
3. Position the U-shaped lockplate compressing tool on the end of the steering shaft and compress the lock plate by turning the shaft nut clockwise. Pry the wire snapring out of the shaft groove.
4. Remove the tool and lift the lock plate off the shaft.
5. Slip the cancelling cam, upper bearing preload spring, and thrust washer off the shaft.
6. Remove the turn signal lever. Push the flasher knob in and unscrew it. Remove the button retaining screw and remove the button, spring and knob.

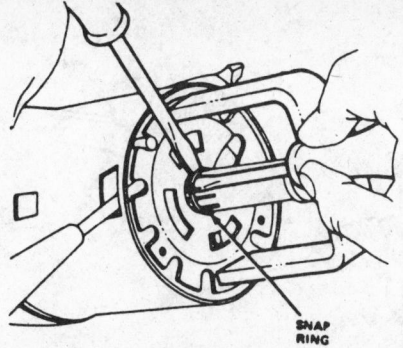

Depress the lockplate and remove the snapring

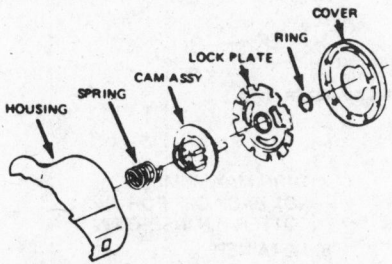

Remove these parts for access to the turn signal switch

7. Pull the switch connector out the mast jacket and tape the upper part to facilitate switch removal. Attach a long piece of wire to the turn signal switch connector. When installing the turn signal switch, feed this wire through the column first, and then use this wire to pull the switch connector into position. On tilt wheels, place the turn signal and shifter housing in low position and remove the harness cover.
8. Remove the three switch mounting screws. Remove the switch pulling it straight up while guiding the wiring harness cover through the column.
9. Install the replacement switch by working the connector and cover down through the housing and under the bracket. On tilt models, the connector is worked down through the housing, under the bracket, and then the cover is installed on the harness.
10. Install the switch mounting screws and the connector on the mast jacket bracket. Install the column-to-dash trim plate.
11. Install the flasher knob and the turn signal lever.
12. With the turn signal lever in neutral and the flasher knob out, slide the thrust washer, upper bearing preload spring, and cancelling cam onto the shaft.
13. Position the lock plate on the shaft and press it down until a new snapring can be inserted in the shaft groove. Always use a new snapring when assembling.
14. Install the cover and the steering wheel.

Ignition Switch

REMOVAL & INSTALLATION

The switch is located inside the channel section of the brake pedal support and is completely inaccessible without first lowering the steering column. The switch is actuated by a rod and rack assembly. A gear on the end of the lock cylinder engages the toothed upper end of the rod.

1. Lower the steering column; be sure to properly support it.
2. Put the switch in the OFF-UNLOCKED position. With the cylinder removed, the rod is in LOCK when it is in the next to the uppermost detent. OFF-UNLOCKED is two detents from the top.
3. Remove the two switch screws and remove the switch assembly.
4. Before installing, place the new switch in OFF-UNLOCKED position and make sure the lock cylinder and actuating rod are in OFF-UNLOCKED (third detent from the top) position.
5. Install the activating rod into the switch and assemble the switch on the column. Tighten the mounting screws. Use only the specified screws since overlength screws could impair the collapsibility of the column.
6. Reinstall the steering column.

Ignition Lock Cylinder

REMOVAL & INSTALLATION

1. Place the lock in the RUN position.
2. Remove the lock plate, turn signal switch and buzzer switch.
3. Remove the screw and lock cylinder.

—— **CAUTION** ——
If the screw is dropped on removal, it could fall into the column, requiring complete disassembly to retrieve the screw.

4. Rotate the cylinder clockwise to align cylinder key with the keyway in the housing.
5. Push the lock all the way in.
6. Install the screw. Tighten the screw to 14 inch lbs. for adjustable columns and 25 inch lbs. for standard columns.

Power Steering Gear

REMOVAL & INSTALLATION

1. Raise and support the front end of the car with jackstands under the frame members. Allow the front suspension to hang freely. Disconnect the

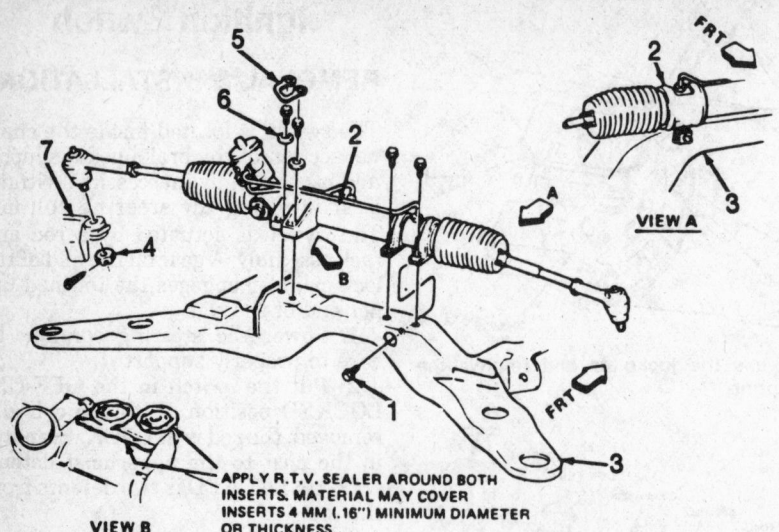

APPLY R.T.V. SEALER AROUND BOTH
INSERTS. MATERIAL MAY COVER
INSERTS 4 MM (.16") MINIMUM DIAMETER
OR THICKNESS.

VIEW B

1. BOLT 68 N·m (50 LBS. FT.) AFTER SECOND REUSE OF BOLT, LOCTITE THREAD LOCKING KIT, #1052624 MUST BE USED
2. STEERING GEAR
3. FRAME
4. 50 N·m (35 LBS. FT.), 70 N·m (52 LBS. FT.) MAXIMUM PERMISSIBLE TORQUE TO ALIGN COTTER PIN SLOT. (⅛

TURN MAXIMUM) DO NOT BACK OFF FOR COTTER PIN INSERTION
5. RETAINER
6. WASHER
7. STEERING KNUCKLE

APPLY R.T.V. SEALER AROUND BOTH INSERTS. MATERIAL MAY COVER INSERTS 4 MM (.16") MINIMUM DIAMETER OR THICKNESS.

Rack and pinion assembly

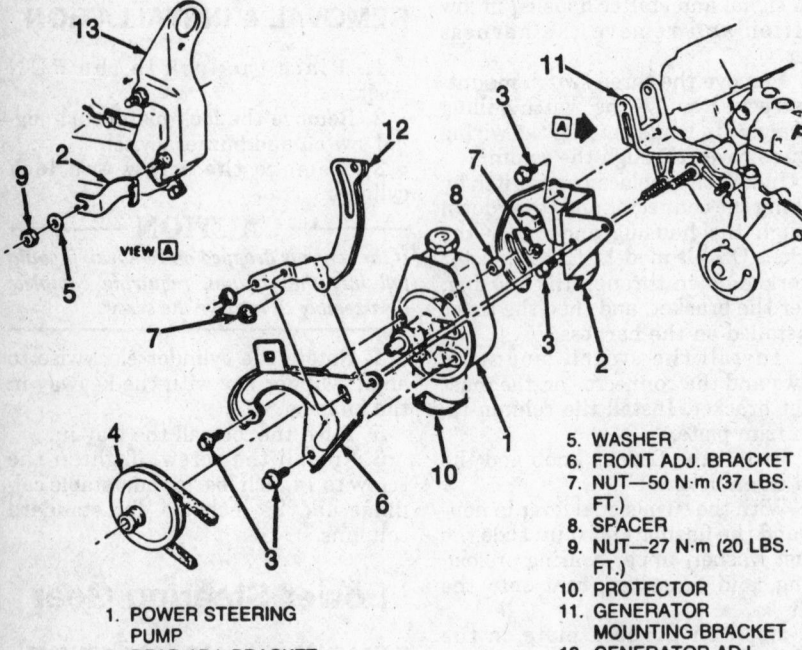

1. POWER STEERING PUMP
2. REAR ADJ. BRACKET
3. BOLT—50 N·m (37 LBS. FT.)
4. PULLEY

5. WASHER
6. FRONT ADJ. BRACKET
7. NUT—50 N·m (37 LBS. FT.)
8. SPACER
9. NUT—27 N·m (20 LBS. FT.)
10. PROTECTOR
11. GENERATOR MOUNTING BRACKET
12. GENERATOR ADJ. BRACKET
13. ENGINE LIFT BRACKET & SHIELD

Power steering pump mounting

power steering hoses from the gear, where equipped.

2. Move the intermediate shaft seal upward and remove the intermediate shaft-to-stub shaft pinch bolt.

3. Remove both front wheels.

4. Remove the cotter pins and nut from both tie-rod ends. Disconnect the tie-rod ends from the steering knuckles.

5. Remove the line retainer.

6. Remove the outlet and pressure hose.

7. Remove the five rack and pinion assembly mounting bolts.

8. Loosen the front engine cradle mounting bolts. Install jack stands and the lower the rear of the cradle about 3 in. (76mm).

— CAUTION —

Do not lower the rear of the engine cradle too far.

9. Remove the rack and pinion assembly.

10. Installation is in the reverse order of removal. Tighten the rack mounting bolts to 50 ft. lbs. (68 Nm). Tighten the tie rod end nut to 35–52 ft. lbs. (50–70 Nm). Bleed the power steering system and check for leaks.

Power Steering Pump

REMOVAL & INSTALLATION

1. Disconnect the negative battery cable.

2. Remove the air cleaner assembly on the 3.0L.

3. Remove the drive belt and then the alternator itself.

4. Raise the front of the vehicle and support it on jack stands.

5. Disconnect and plug the pressure and return lines at the pump.

6. Remove the rear pump adjustment bracket-to-pump nut. Remove the power steering belt and lower the vehicle.

7. Remove the alternator adjustment bracket and support brace.

8. Remove the rear pump adjustment bracket and then remove the pump assembly.

9. Remove the front pump adjustment bracket and then remove the pulley.

10. Installation is in the reverse order of removal. Adjust the drive belts and bleed the power steering system.

BLEEDING THE POWER STEERING SYSTEM

1. Fill the fluid reservoir.

2. Let the fluid stand undisturbed for two minutes, then crank the engine for about two seconds. Refill reservoir if necessary.

3. Repeat Steps 1 and 2 above until the fluid level remains constant after cranking the engine.

4. Raise the front of the car until the wheels are off the ground, then start the engine. Increase the engine speed to about 1500 rpm.

5. Turn the wheels lightly against the stops to the left and right, checking the fluid level and refilling if necessary.

Tie Rod Ends

REMOVAL & INSTALLATION

1. Loosen the jam nut on the steering rack (inner tie rod).

2. Remove the tie rod end nut. Separate the tie rod end from the steering knuckle using a puller.

3. Unscrew the tie rod end, counting the number of turns.

4. To install, screw the tie rod end onto the steering rack (inner tie rod) the same number of turns as counted for removal. This will give approximately correct toe.

5. Install the tie rod end into the knuckle. Install the nut and tighten to 40 ft. lbs.

6. If the toe must be adjusted, use pliers to expand the boot clamp. Turn the inner tie rod to adjust. Replace the clamp.

7. Tighten the jam nut to 50 ft. lbs.

BRAKES

For all brake system removal, installation and adjustment procedures, please refer to "Brakes" in the Unit Repair section.

Master Cylinder

REMOVAL & INSTALLATION

1. Disconnect electrical connector from fluid level sensor switch.

2. Disconnect and plug hydraulic lines, and drain the cylinder.

3. Remove the attaching nuts and remove the master cylinder from the power booster unit.

4. Reverse to install. Bleed master cylinder assembly before installing, bleed complete brake system if necessary.

Power Brake Booster

REMOVAL & INSTALLATION

1. From inside the car, detach the brake pushrod from the brake pedal.

2. Disconnect the hydraulic lines from the front of the master cylinder.

3. Remove the nuts from the mounting studs which hold the brake booster to the firewall. Remove the brake booster from car, then remove master cylinder from the booster assembly.

4. Installation is the reverse of removal. Bleed the brake system.

Parking Brake Cable

ADJUSTMENT

1. Depress the parking brake pedal 1½ in. (35mm).

2. Raise the vehicle and support it with jack stands.

3. Tighten the adjusting nut until the left rear wheel can just be turned to the rear with both hands, but is locked when forward rotation is attempted.

4. Lower the vehicle.

Do not adjust the parking brake cable so tight as to cause brake drag when parking brake is disengaged.

REMOVAL & INSTALLATION

Front Cable

1. Raise and suppport the vehicle on jackstands.

2. Loosen the equalizer assembly. Separate the cable from the equalizer assembly.

3. From under the body, remove the cable casing-to-chassis nut.

4. From the control assembly, separate the cable casing and cable.

5. To install, reverse the removal procedures. Torque the cable casing-to-chassis nut to 22 ft. lbs. Adjust the parking brake assembly.

Intermediate Cable

1. Raise and support the vehicle on jackstands.

2. Loosen the equalizer assembly and disconnect the intermediate cable from it.

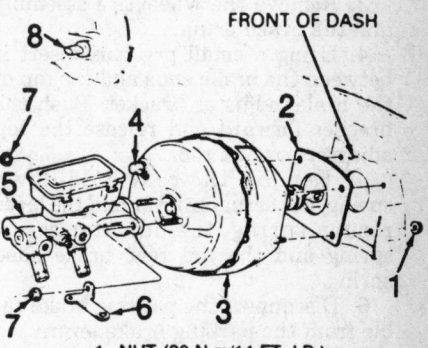

FRONT OF DASH

1. NUT (20 N·m/14 FT. LB.)
2. SEAL
3. POWER BOOSTER
4. CHECK VALVE
5. MASTER CYLINDER
6. VACUUM SWITCH BRACKET (DIESEL)
7. NUT (30 N·m/22 FT. LB.)
8. VACUUM SWITCH (GAS)

Typical master cylinder and power booster mounting

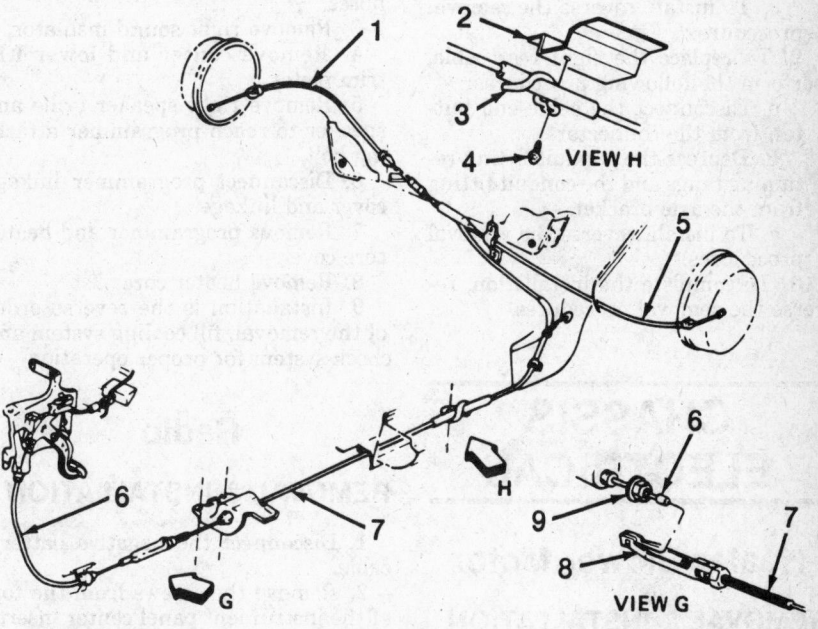

1. Right rear cable	4. 28 ft. lbs.	7. Intermediate cable
2. Underbody	5. Left rear cable	8. Equalizer assembly
3. Guide	6. Front cable assembly	9. Nut

Parking brake cable assembly

3. Remove the intermediate cable housing from the front bracket, the clip and the underbody guide.

4. Disconnect the cable from the rear equalizer assembly.

5. To install, reverse the removal procedures. Adjust the parking brake assembly.

Rear Cables

1. Raise and support the vehicle on jackstands.

2. Loosen the equalizer assembly and disconnect the intermediate cable from it.

3. Remove the wheel/tire assembly and the brake drum.

4. Using a small pry bar, insert it between the brake shoe and the top of the brake adjuster bracket. Push the bracket forward and release the top adjuster bracket rod.

5. Remove the rear hold-down spring, the actuator lever and the lever return spring, the adjuster screw spring and the top rear brake shoe spring.

6. Disconnect the parking brake cable from the parking brake lever.

7. Depress the conduit fitting retaining tangs and the conduit fitting from the backing plate.

8. To replace the left rear cable, perform the following procedures:

   a. Back off the equalizer nut and disconnect the left cable from the equalizer.

   b. Depress the conduit fitting retaining tangs and the conduit fitting from the axle bracket.

   c. To install, reverse the removal procedures.

9. To replace the right rear cable, perform the following procedures:

   a. Disconnect the cable end button from the connector.

   b. Depress the conduit fitting retaining tangs and the conduit fitting from the axle bracket.

   c. To install, reverse the removal procedures.

10. To complete the installation, reverse the removal procedures.

CHASSIS ELECTRICAL

Heater Blower Motor

REMOVAL & INSTALLATION

1. Disconnect the negative battery cable.

2. Disconnect the electrical connections at the blower motor.

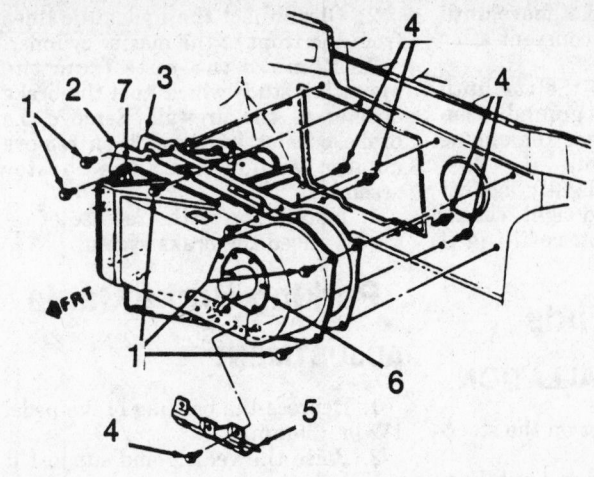

1. 27 inch lbs.
2. Module
3. Gasket
4. 30 inch lbs.
5. Shield
6. Blower motor
7. Evaporator

Blower module

3. Disconnect the cooling hose from the blower motor.

4. Remove the mounting screws and remove the motor.

5. Reverse to install. Use a silicone sealer on the blower motor sealing surfaces.

Heater Core

REMOVAL & INSTALLATION

1. Disconnect negative battery and drain cooling system.

2. Remove splash cover to gain access to heater hoses and remove heater hoses.

3. Remove right sound insulator.

4. Remove center and lower I.P. trim plates.

5. Remove right speaker grille and speaker to reach programmer attaching bolt.

6. Disconnect programmer linkage cover and linkage.

7. Remove programmer and heater core cover.

8. Remove heater core.

9. Installation is the reverse order of the removal, fill cooling system and check system for proper operation.

Radio

REMOVAL & INSTALLATION

1. Disconnect the negative battery cable.

2. Remove the screws from the top of the instrument panel center insert.

3. Remove the radio knobs and remove the insert.

4. Remove the rear window defogger switch to gain access to the left side mounting screw if so equipped.

5. Remove the mounting screws.

6. Remove the radio and disconnect the wiring. Reverse to install.

Windshield Wiper Switch

REMOVAL & INSTALLATION

1. Disconnect the negative battery cable.

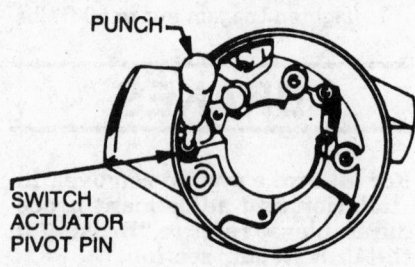

PUNCH

SWITCH ACTUATOR PIVOT PIN

Removing pivot and switch assembly

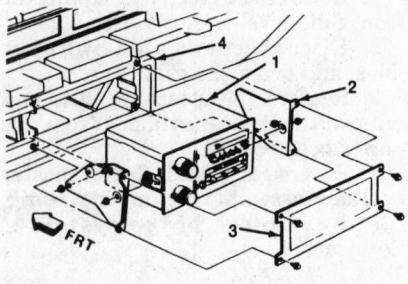

1. Radio
2. Bracket
3. Cover (if no radio)
4. Instrument panel

Typical radio mounting

2. Remove the steering wheel and directional switch.

3. It may be necessary to loosen the steering column nuts and remove the bracket to mast retaining screws, then separate the bracket from the mast jacket to allow the connector clip on the ignition switch to be pulled out of the steering column assembly.

4. Disconnect the wiper/washer switch lower connector.

5. Remove the screws attaching the column housing to the mast jacket. Be sure to note the position of the dimmer switch actuator rod for reassembly. Remove the column housing and switch as an assembly.

NOTE: The tilt and travel columns have a removable plastic cover on the column housing. This provides access to the wiper switch without removing the entire column housing.

6. Remove the pivot pin from the wiper/washer switch using a brass drift. Remove the switch.

7. To install, position the switch in the housing, then install the pivot pin.

8. Position the housing onto the mast jacket and install the retaining screws.

9. Install the dimmer switch accuator rod. Check for proper switch operation.

10. Reconnect the lower end of the switch assembly. Remainder of the installation is the reverse order of the removal.

Windshield Wiper Motor

REMOVAL & INSTALLATION

1. Remove the cowl screen or grille.
2. Loosen the linkage drive link-to-crankarm attaching nuts, and remove the link from the arm.
3. Disconnect the wiring and washer hoses.
4. Remove the three motor attaching screws, guide the crankarm through the hole in the dash, and remove the motor.
5. Reverse the above steps to install.

Instrument Cluster

REMOVAL & INSTALLATION

NOTE: When handling an electronic part that has an (ESD) Electrostatic Discharge sensitive label avoid any possible electrostatic charge build up on your body or on the part.

1. Disconnect the negative battery cable.
2. Remove the left sound insulator.
3. Remove the instrument panel insert and applique trim from the instrument panel.
4. Place the shift lever in the Park position and remove the shift indicator clip from the steering column.
5. Remove the nuts securing the steering column to the upper mounting bracket and lower the steering column.
6. Remove the screw securing the upper steering column mounting bracket to the cowl and lower the bracket.
7. Remove the cluster retaining screws, disconnect the speedometer cable, printed circuit connector and remove the cluster.
8. The installation is the reverse of the removal procedure. Be sure the shift indicator is properly aligned.

Headlight Switch

REMOVAL & INSTALLATION

1. Disconnect negative battery cable. Remove the steering column lower cover or the instrument panel trim plate covering the headlamp switch, if a rocker-type headlamp switch is used.

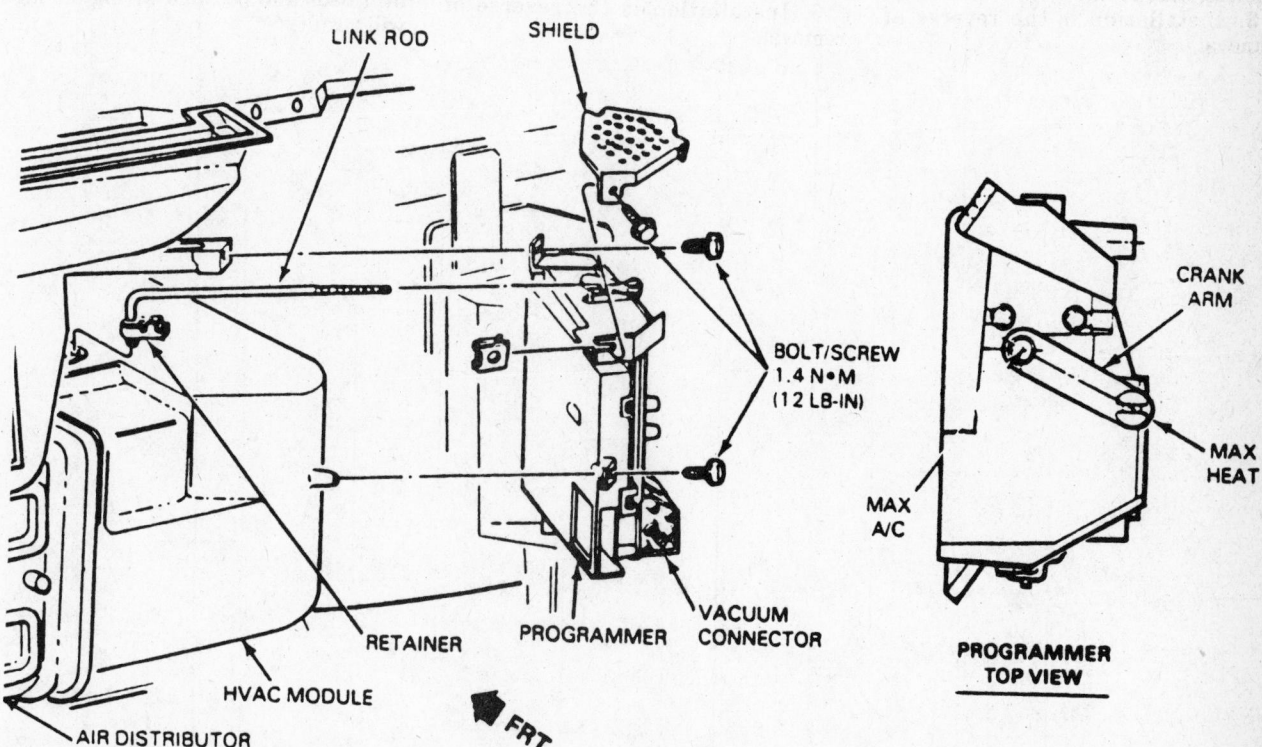

LINK ROD   SHIELD

BOLT/SCREW 1.4 N•M (12 LB-IN)

RETAINER   PROGRAMMER   VACUUM CONNECTOR

HVAC MODULE

AIR DISTRIBUTOR ASSEMBLY

FRT

CRANK ARM

MAX HEAT

MAX A/C

PROGRAMMER TOP VIEW

Programmer assembly

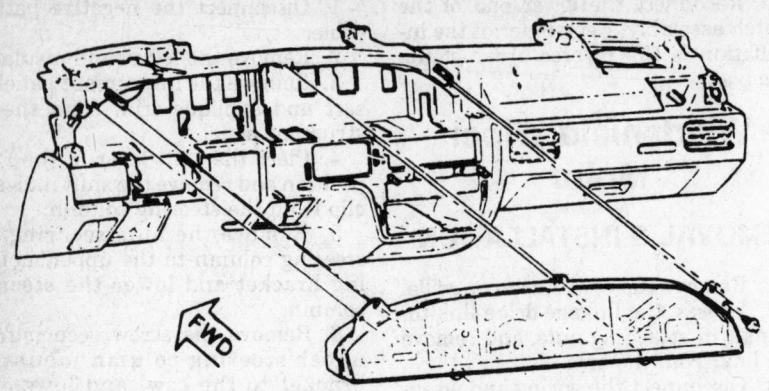

Instrument cluster assembly

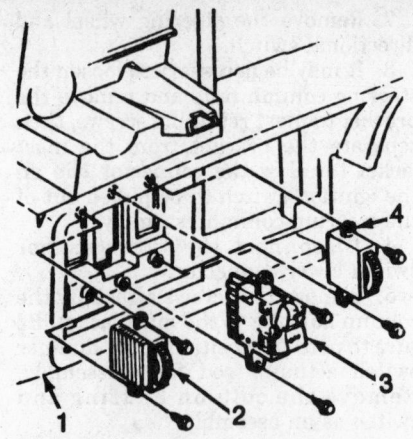

1. Instrument panel
2. Interior light dimmer
3. Headlamp switch
4. Twilight sentinal switch

Light switch assemblies—rocker type

2. Disconnect wiring harness retainer below headlight switch assembly. On some models the switch connector is integral with the instrument panel; simply pull the switch outward to disconnect it.

3. On knob-type switches, depress spring loaded release button on top of headlight switch and remove switch, knob and rod assembly (switch ON).

4. Remove screw with ground wire at bottom of switch housing and any other mounting screws.

5. Pull assembly down and rearward, disconnect wiring harness connectors, bulb(s) and remove assembly.

6. Installation is the reverse of removal.

Stoplight Switch

REMOVAL & INSTALLATION

1. Disconnect the negative battery cable.

2. Remove the necessary trim panels in order to gain access to the stoplight switch mounting bracket.

3. Loosen the tubular clip from the switch assembly.

4. Disconnect the electrical connector from the rear of the switch.

5. Remove the switch assembly from the vehicle.

6. Installation is the reverse of removal.

Fuses

LOCATION

The fuse block is located behind a cover on the instrument panel to the left of the steering column. Fuse holders are labeled as to their service and the correct amperage. Always replace blown fuses with new ones of the correct amperage. Otherwise electrical overloads and possible wiring damage will result.

GM "J" Body

Front Wheel Drive

Buick Skyhawk, Cadillac Cimarron, Chevrolet Cavalier,
Oldsmobile Firenza, Pontiac Sunbird

26

SERIAL NUMBER IDENTIFICATION

VEHICLE IDENTIFICATION CHART

It is important for servicing and ordering parts to be certain of the vehicle and engine identification. The VIN (vehicle identification number) is a 17 digit number visible through the windshield on the driver's side of the dash and contains the vehicle and engine identification codes. The tenth digit indicates model year, and the eighth digit indicates engine code. It can be interpreted as follows:

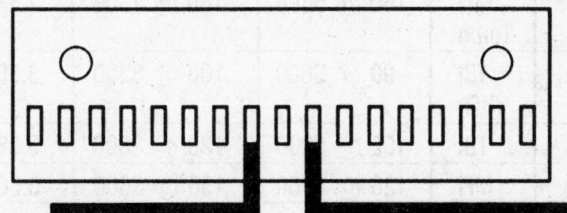

Engine Code						Model Year	
Code	Cu. In.	Liters	Cyl.	Fuel Sys.	Eng. Mfg.	Code	Year
G	110 (OHV)	1.8	4	2 bbl	Chevrolet	C	1982
0	110 (OHC)	1.8	4	TBI	Pontiac	D	1983
J	110 (OHC)	1.8	4	MFI Turbo	Pontiac	E	1984
B	122 (OHV)	2.0	4	2 bbl	Chevrolet	F	1985
P	122 (OHV)	2.0	4	TBI	Chevrolet	G	1986
M	122 (OHC)	2.0	4	MFI Turbo	①	H	1987
1	122 (OHV)	2.0	4	TBI HO	Chevrolet	J	1988
K	122 (OHC)	2.0	4	TBI	①	K	1989
W	173	2.8	V6	MFI	Chevrolet		

HO High Output
OHV Overhead Valve engine
OHC Overhead Cam engine
TBI Throttle Body Injection
MFI Multi-Port Fuel Injection
① Chevrolet-Pontiac-GM of Canada

GENERAL ENGINE SPECIFICATIONS

Year	VIN	No. Cylinder Displacement cu. in. (liter)	Fuel System Type	Net Horsepower @ rpm	Net Torque @ rpm (ft.lbs.)	Bore × Stroke (in.)	Compression Ratio	Oil Pressure @ rpm
1982	G	4-110 (1.8)	2 bbl	88 @ 5100	100 @ 2800	3.50 × 2.91	9.0:1	45 @ 2400
	B	4-122 (2.0)	2 bbl	90 @ 5100	111 @ 2800	3.50 × 3.15	9.0:1	45 @ 2400
1983	0	4-110 (1.8)	TBI	84 @ 5200	102 @ 2800	3.34 × 3.13	8.8:1	45 @ 2400
	J	4-110 (1.8)	MFI Turbo	150 @ 5600	150 @ 2800	3.34 × 3.13	8.0:1	65 @ 2500
	P	4-122 (2.0)	TBI	86 @ 4900	100 @ 3000	3.50 × 3.15	9.3:1	68 @ 1200
	B	4-122 (2.0)	TBI	86 @ 4900	110 @ 3000	3.50 × 3.15	9.3:1	45 @ 2400
1984	0	4-110 (1.8)	TBI	84 @ 5200	102 @ 2800	3.34 × 3.13	8.8:1	45 @ 2400
	P	4-122 (2.0)	TBI	86 @ 4900	100 @ 3000	3.50 × 3.15	9.3:1	68 @ 1200
	B	4-122 (2.0)	TBI	86 @ 4900	110 @ 3000	3.50 × 3.15	9.3:1	45 @ 2400
1985	0	4-110 (1.8)	TBI	84 @ 5200	102 @ 2800	3.34 × 3.13	8.8:1	45 @ 2400
	J	4-110 (1.8)	MFI Turbo	150 @ 5600	150 @ 2800	3.34 × 3.13	8.0:1	65 @ 2500
	P	4-122 (2.0)	TBI	86 @ 4900	100 @ 3000	3.50 × 3.15	9.3:1	68 @ 1200
	W	6-173 (2.8)	MFI	120 @ 4800	155 @ 3600	3.50 × 2.99	8.9:1	50 @ 2400
1986	0	4-110 (1.8)	TBI	84 @ 5200	102 @ 2800	3.34 × 3.13	8.8:1	45 @ 2400
	J	4-110 (1.8)	MFI Turbo	150 @ 5600	150 @ 2800	3.34 × 3.13	8.0:1	65 @ 2500
	P	4-122 (2.0)	TBI	86 @ 4900	100 @ 3000	3.50 × 3.15	9.3:1	68 @ 1200
	W	6-173 (2.8)	MFI	120 @ 4800	155 @ 3600	3.50 × 2.99	8.9:1	50 @ 2400
1987	M	4-122 (2.0)	MFI Turbo	160 @ 5600	160 @ 2800	3.38 × 3.38	8.0:1	65 @ 2500
	1	4-122 (2.0)	TBI (HO)	90 @ 5600	108 @ 3200	3.50 × 3.15	9.0:1	63–77 @ 1200
	K	4-122 (2.0)	TBI	102 @ 5200	130 @ 2800	3.38 × 3.38	8.8:1	45 @ 2000
	W	6-173 (2.8)	MFI	120 @ 4800	155 @ 3600	3.50 × 2.99	8.9:1	50 @ 2400
1988-89	M	4-122 (2.0)	MFI Turbo	160 @ 5600	160 @ 2800	3.38 × 3.38	8.0:1	65 @ 2500
	1	4-122 (2.0)	TBI (HO)	90 @ 5600	108 @ 3200	3.50 × 3.15	9.0:1	63–77 @ 1200
	K	4-122 (2.0)	TBI	102 @ 5200	130 @ 2800	3.38 × 3.38	8.8:1	45 @ 2000
	W	6-173 (2.8)	MFI	120 @ 4800	155 @ 3600	3.50 × 2.99	8.9:1	50 @ 2400

GASOLINE ENGINE TUNE-UP SPECIFICATIONS

Year	VIN	No. Cylinder Displacement cu. in. (liter)	Spark Plugs Type	Gap (in.)	Ignition Timing (deg.) MT	AT	Compression Pressure (psi)	Fuel Pump (psi)	Idle Speed (rpm) MT	AT	Valve Clearance In.	Ex.
1982	G	4-110 (1.8)	R-42TS	0.045 ①	12B	12B	NA	4.5–6.0	②	②	Hyd.	Hyd.
	B	4-122 (2.0)	②	②	②	②	NA	4.5–6.0	②	②	Hyd.	Hyd.

GASOLINE ENGINE TUNE-UP SPECIFICATIONS

Year	VIN	No. Cylinder Displacement cu. in. (liter)	Spark Plugs Type	Gap (in.)	Ignition Timing (deg.) MT	AT	Compression Pressure (psi)	Fuel Pump (psi)	Idle Speed (rpm) MT	AT	Valve Clearance In.	Ex.
1983	0	4-110 (1.8)	R-42XLS6	0.060	8B	8B	NA	9–13	②	②	Hyd.	Hyd.
	J	4-110 (1.8)	R-42CXLS	0.035	②	②	NA	26–32	②	②	Hyd.	Hyd.
	P	4-122 (2.0)	R-42CTS	0.035	②	②	NA	12	②	②	Hyd.	Hyd.
	B	4-122 (2.0)	R-42CTS	0.035	—	12B	NA	12	②	②	Hyd.	Hyd.
1984	0	4-110 (1.8)	R-44XLS	0.060	8B	8B	NA	9–13	②	②	Hyd.	Hyd.
	P	4-122 (2.0)	R-42CTS	0.035	②	②	NA	12	②	②	Hyd.	Hyd.
	B	4-122 (2.0)	R-42CTS	0.035	—	12B	NA	12	②	②	Hyd.	Hyd.
1985	0	4-110 (1.8)	R-44XLS	0.060	8B	8B	NA	9–13	②	②	Hyd.	Hyd.
	J	4-110 (1.8)	R-42CXLS	0.035	②	②	NA	26–32	②	②	Hyd.	Hyd.
	P	4-122 (2.0)	R-42CTS	0.035	②	②	NA	12	②	②	Hyd.	Hyd.
	W	6-173 (2.8)	R-42CTS	0.045	②	②	NA	30–37	②	②	Hyd.	Hyd.
1986	0	4-110 (1.8)	R-44XLS6	0.060	8B	8B	NA	9–13	②	②	Hyd.	Hyd.
	J	4-110 (1.8)	R-42CXLS	0.035	②	②	NA	26–32	②	②	Hyd.	Hyd.
	P	4-122 (2.0)	R-42CTS	0.035	②	②	NA	12	②	②	Hyd.	Hyd.
	B	4-122 (2.0)	R-42CTS	0.035	—	12B	NA	4.5–6	②	②	Hyd.	Hyd.
	W	6-173 (2.8)	R-42CTS	0.045	②	②	NA	30–37	②	②	Hyd.	Hyd.
1987	M	4-122 (2.0)	RN9YC4	0.060	②	②	NA	25–30	②	②	Hyd.	Hyd.
	1	4-122 (2.0)	RC12LYC	0.035	②	②	NA	10–12	②	②	Hyd.	Hyd.
	K	4-122 (2.0)	RN12YC6	0.060	②	②	NA	10	②	②	Hyd.	Hyd.
	W	6-173 (2.8)	R-42CTS	0.045	②	②	NA	30–37	②	②	Hyd.	Hyd.
1988	M	4-122 (2.0)	RN9YC4	0.060	②	②	NA	25–30	②	②	Hyd.	Hyd.
	1	4-122 (2.0)	RC12LYC	0.035	②	②	NA	10–12	②	②	Hyd.	Hyd.
	K	4-122 (2.0)	RN12YC6	0.060	②	②	NA	10	②	②	Hyd.	Hyd.
	W	6-173 (2.8)	RS13LYC	0.045	②	②	NA	30–37	②	②	Hyd.	Hyd.
1989	All					SEE UNDERHOOD SPECIFICATIONS STICKER						

NOTE: The underhood specifications sticker often reflects tune-up specifications changes made in production. Sticker figures must be used if they disagree with those in this chart.

Part numbers in this chart are not recommendations by Chilton for any product by brand name

B Before top dead center

NA Not available at time of publication

① Certain models may use 0.035 in. gap. See underhood specifications sticker to be sure

② See underhood specifications sticker

FIRING ORDERS

NOTE: To avoid confusion, always replace spark plug wires one at a time.

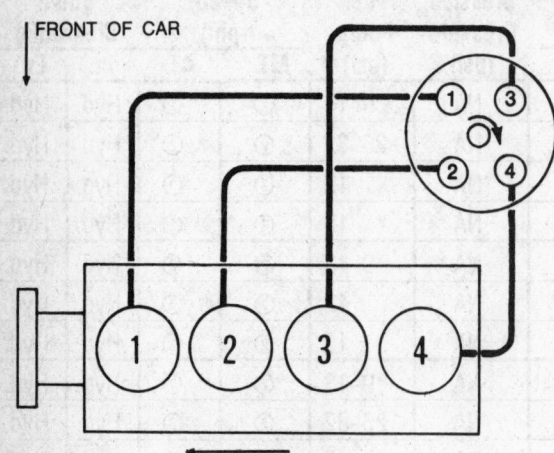

GM (Chevrolet) 110 and 122 overhead valve (OHV)
Engine firing order: 1-3-4-2
Distributor rotation: clockwise

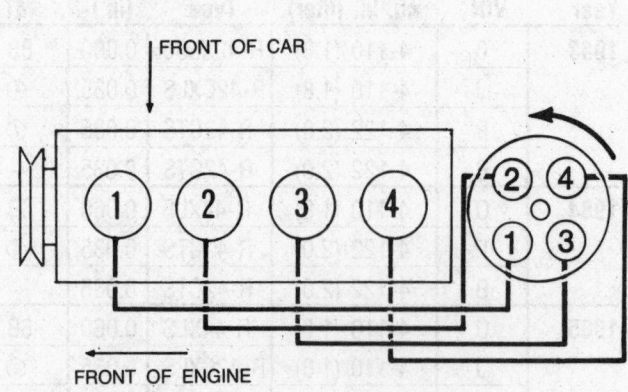

GM (Pontiac) 110 overhead camshaft (OHC)
Engine firing order: 1-3-4-2
Distributor rotation: counterclockwise

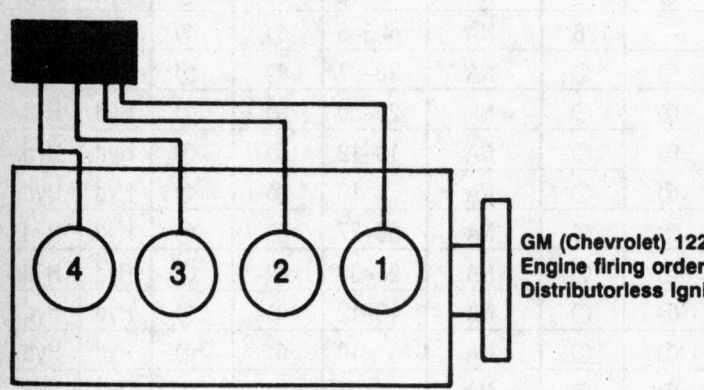

GM (Chevrolet) 122 L4 (2.0)
Engine firing order: 1–3–4–2
Distributorless Ignition

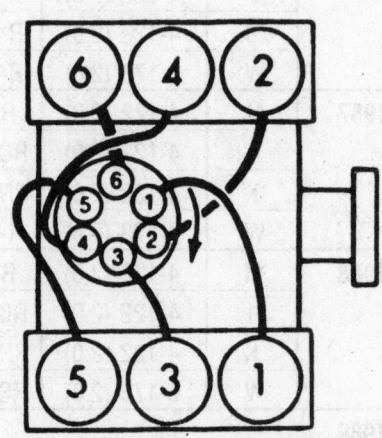

GM (Chevrolet) 173 V6 (2.8L)
Engine firing order: 1–2–3–4–5–6
Distributor rotation: Clockwise

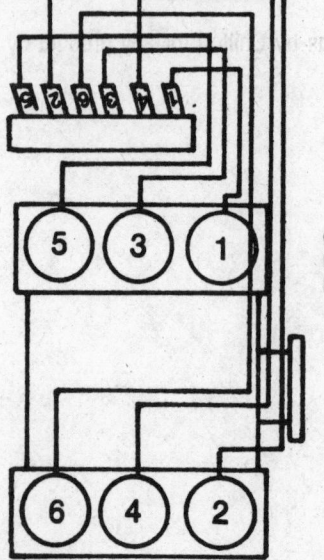

GM (Chevrolet) 173 V6 (2.8L)
Engine firing order: 1–2–3–4–5–6
Distributorless Ignition

CAPACITIES

Year	Model	No. Cylinder Displacement cu. in. (liter)	Engine Crankcase with Filter	Engine Crankcase without Filter	Transmission (pts.) 4-Spd	Transmission (pts.) 5-Spd	Transmission (pts.) Auto.	Drive Axle (pts.)	Fuel Tank (gal.)	Cooling System (qts.)
1982	All	4-110 (1.8)	4.0④	4.0	5.9	—	10.5	—	14	8.0
	All	4-122 (2.0)	4.0④	4.0	5.9	—	10.5	—	14	8.3
1983	All	4-110 (1.8)	①	①	—	5.0	10.5	—	14	7.9
	All	4-122 (2.0)	4.0④	4.0	5.9	—	10.5	—	14	8.3
1984	All	4-110 (1.8)	①	①	—	5.0	10.5	—	14	7.9
	All	4-122 (2.0)	4.0④	4.0	5.9	—	10.5	—	14	8.3
1985	All	4-110 (1.8)	①	①	—	5.0	10.5	—	14	7.9
	All	4-122 (2.0)	4.0④	4.0	5.9	—	10.5	—	14	8.3
	All	6-173 (2.8)	4.0④	4.0	6.0	—	8.0	—	14③	12.4
1986	All	4-110 (1.8)	①	①	—	5.0	10.5	—	14	7.9
	All	4-122 (2.0)	4.0④	4.0	5.9	—	10.5	—	14	8.3
	All	6-173 (2.8)	4.0④	4.0	6.0	—	8.0	—	14	12.4
1987	All	4-122 (2.0)	4.0④	4.0	5.9	5.36	11.0	—	13.6	8.8
	All	6-173 (2.8)	4.0④	4.0	5.36	—	11.0	—	14③	11.4
1988-89	All	4-122 (2.0)	4.0④	4.0	5.9	5.36	11.0	—	13.5	8.8
	All	6-173 (2.8)	4.0④	4.0	5.36	—	11.0	—	13.5③	11.4

① Add 3 quarts, check oil level at dip-stick and add as necessary
② Cimarron 8.0 pints
③ Cimarron 16.0 gallons
④ When changing oil filter, additional oil may be needed

CAMSHAFT SPECIFICATIONS
All measurements given in inches.

Year	VIN	No. Cylinder Displacement cu. in. (liter)	Journal Diameter 1	Journal Diameter 2	Journal Diameter 3	Journal Diameter 4	Journal Diameter 5	Lobe Lift In.	Lobe Lift Ex.	Bearing Clearance	Camshaft End Play
1982	G	4-110 (1.8)	1.8677–1.8696	1.8677–1.8696	1.8677–1.8696	1.8677–1.8696	1.8677–1.8696	0.2625	0.2625	0.0010–0.0039	NA
	B	4-122 (2.0)	1.8677–1.8696	1.8677–1.8696	1.8677–1.8696	1.8677–1.8696	1.8677–1.8696	0.2600	0.2600	0.0010–0.0039	NA
1983	O	4-110 (1.8)	1.6714–1.6720	1.6812–1.6816	1.6911–1.6917	1.7009–1.7015	1.7108–1.7114	0.2409	0.2409	NA	0.016–0.064
	J	4-110 (1.8)	1.6714–1.6720	1.6812–1.6816	1.6911–1.6917	1.7009–1.7015	1.7108–1.7114	0.2409	0.2409	NA	0.016–0.064
	P	4-122 (2.0)	1.8677–1.8696	1.8677–1.8696	1.8677–1.8696	1.8677–1.8696	1.8677–1.8696	0.2600	0.2600	0.0010–0.0039	NA
	B	4-122 (2.0)	1.8677–1.8696	1.8677–1.8696	1.8677–1.8696	1.8677–1.8696	1.8677–1.8696	0.2600	0.2600	0.0010–0.0039	NA
1984	O	4-110 (1.8)	1.6714–1.6720	1.6812–1.6816	1.6911–1.6917	1.7009–1.7015	1.7108–1.7114	0.2409	0.2409	NA	0.016–0.064
	P	4-122 (2.0)	1.8677–1.8696	1.8677–1.8696	1.8677–1.8696	1.8677–1.8696	1.8677–1.8696	0.2600	0.2600	0.0010–0.0039	NA
	B	4-122 (2.0)	1.8677–1.8696	1.8677–1.8696	1.8677–1.8696	1.8677–1.8696	1.8677–1.8696	0.2600	0.2600	0.0010–0.0039	NA

CAMSHAFT SPECIFICATIONS
All measurements given in inches.

Year	VIN	No. Cylinder Displacement cu. in. (liter)	Journal Diameter 1	2	3	4	5	Lobe Lift In.	Ex.	Bearing Clearance	Camshaft End Play
1985	O	4-110 (1.8)	1.6714–1.6720	1.6812–1.6816	1.6911–1.6917	1.7009–1.7015	1.7108–1.7114	0.2409	0.2409	NA	0.016–0.064
	J	4-110 (1.8)	1.6174–1.6720	1.6812–1.6816	1.6911–1.6917	1.7009–1.7015	1.7108–1.7114	0.2409	0.2409	NA	0.016–0.064
	P	4-122 (2.0)	1.8677–1.8696	1.8677–1.8696	1.8677–1.8696	1.8677–1.8696	1.8677–1.8696	0.2600	0.2600	0.0010–0.0039	NA
	W	6-173 (2.8)	1.8678–1.8815	1.8678–1.8815	1.8678–1.8815	1.8678–1.8815	1.8678–1.8815	0.2626	0.2732	NA	NA
1986	O	4-110 (1.8)	1.6714–1.6720	1.6812–1.6816	1.6911–1.6917	1.7009–1.7015	1.7108–1.7114	0.2409	0.2409	NA	0.016–0.064
	J	4-110 (1.8)	1.6174–1.6720	1.6812–1.6816	1.6911–1.6917	1.7009–1.7015	1.7108–1.7114	0.2409	0.2409	NA	0.016–0.064
	P	4-122 (2.0)	1.8677–1.8696	1.8677–1.8696	1.8677–1.8696	1.8677–1.8696	1.8677–1.8696	0.2600	0.2600	0.0010–0.0039	NA
	W	6-173 (2.8)	1.8678–1.8815	1.8678–1.8815	1.8678–1.8815	1.8678–1.8815	1.8678–1.8815	0.2626	0.2732	NA	NA
1987	M	4-122 (2.0)	1.6714–1.6720	1.6812–1.6816	1.6911–1.6917	1.7009–1.7015	1.7108–1.7114	0.2409	0.2409	0.0008	0.016–0.064
	1	4-122 (2.0)	1.8670–1.8690	1.8670–1.8690	1.8670–1.8690	1.8670–1.8690	1.8670–1.8690	0.2600	0.2600	0.0010–0.0040	NA
	K	4-122 (2.0)	1.6714–1.6720	1.6812–1.6816	1.6911–1.6917	1.7009–1.7015	1.7108–1.7114	0.2409	0.2409	0.0008	0.016 0.064
	W	6-173 (2.8)	1.8678–1.8815	1.8678–1.8815	1.8678–1.8815	1.8678–1.8815	1.8678–1.8815	0.2626	0.2732	NA	NA
1988-89	M	4-122 (2.0)	1.6714–1.6720	1.6812–1.6816	1.6911–1.6917	1.7009–1.7015	1.7108–1.7114	0.2409	0.2409	0.0008	0.016–0.064
	1	4-122 (2.0)	1.8670–1.8690	1.8670–1.8690	1.8670–1.8690	1.8670–1.8690	1.8670–1.8690	0.2600	0.2600	0.0010–0.0040	NA
	K	4-122 (2.0)	1.6714–1.6720	1.6812–1.6816	1.6911–1.6917	1.7009–1.7015	1.7108–1.7114	0.2409	0.2409	0.0008	0.016–0.064
	W	6-173 (2.8)	1.8678–1.8815	1.8678–1.8815	1.8678–1.8815	1.8678–1.8815	1.8678–1.8815	0.2626	0.2732	NA	NA

NA Not available

CRANKSHAFT AND CONNECTING ROD SPECIFICATIONS
All measurements are given in inches.

Year	VIN	No. Cylinder Displacement cu. in. (liter)	Crankshaft Main Brg. Journal Dia.	Main Brg. Oil Clearance	Shaft End-play	Thrust on No.	Connecting Rod Journal Diameter	Oil Clearance	Side Clearance
1982	G	4-110 (1.8)	2.4944–2.4954 ②	0.0006–0.0018 ③	0.0019–0.0071	4	1.9983–1.9993	0.0009–0.0031	0.0039–0.0240

CRANKSHAFT AND CONNECTING ROD SPECIFICATIONS
All measurements are given in inches.

Year	VIN	No. Cylinder Displacement cu. in. (liter)	Crankshaft Main Brg. Journal Dia.	Crankshaft Main Brg. Oil Clearance	Crankshaft Shaft End-play	Thrust on No.	Connecting Rod Journal Diameter	Connecting Rod Oil Clearance	Connecting Rod Side Clearance
1982	B	4-122 (2.0)	2.4944– 2.4954 ②	0.0006– 0.0018 ③	0.0019– 0.0071	4	1.9983– 1.9993	0.0009– 0.0031	0.0039– 0.0240
1983	O	4-110 (1.8)	①	0.0006– 0.0016	0.0027– 0.0118	3	1.9278– 1.9286	0.0007– 0.0024	0.0027– 0.0095
	J	4-110 (1.8)	①	0.0006– 0.0016	0.0027– 0.0118	3	1.9278– 1.9286	0.0007– 0.0024	0.0027– 0.0095
	P	4-122 (2.0)	2.4944– 2.4954 ②	0.0006– 0.0018 ③	0.0019– 0.0071	4	1.9983– 1.9993	0.0009– 0.0031	0.0039– 0.0240
	B	4-122 (2.0)	2.4944– 2.4954 ②	0.0006– 0.0018 ③	0.0019– 0.0071	4	1.9983– 1.9993	0.0009– 0.0031	0.0039– 0.0240
1984	O	4-110 (1.8)	①	0.0006– 0.0016	0.0027– 0.0118	3	1.9278– 1.9286	0.0007– 0.0024	0.0027– 0.0095
	P	4-122 (2.0)	2.4944– 2.4954 ②	0.0006– 0.0018 ③	0.0019– 0.0071	4	1.9983– 1.9993	0.0009– 0.0031	0.0039– 0.0240
	B	4-122 (2.0)	2.4944– 2.4954 ②	0.0006– 0.00018 ③	0.0019– 0.0071	4	1.9983– 1.9993	0.0009– 0.0031	0.0039– 0.0240
1985	O	4-110 (1.8)	①	0.0006– 0.0016	0.0027– 0.0118	3	1.9278– 1.9286	0.0007– 0.0024	0.0027– 0.0095
	J	4-110 (1.8)	①	0.0006– 0.0016	0.0027– 0.0118	3	1.9278– 1.9286	0.0007– 0.0024	0.0027– 0.0095
	P	4-122 (2.0)	2.4944– 2.4954 ②	0.0006– 0.0018 ③	0.0019– 0.0071	4	1.9983– 1.9993	0.0009– 0.0031	0.0039– 0.0240
	W	6-173 (2.8)	2.6473– 2.6482	0.0016– 0.0033	0.0024– 0.0083	3	1.9983– 1.9994	0.0014– 0.0037	0.0063– 0.0173
1986	O	4-110 (1.8)	①	0.0006– 0.0016	0.0027– 0.0118	3	1.9278– 1.9286	0.0007– 0.0024	0.0027– 0.0095
	J	4-110 (1.8)	①	0.0006– 0.0016	0.0027– 0.0118	3	1.9278– 1.9286	0.0007– 0.0024	0.0027– 0.0095
	P	4-122 (2.0)	2.4944– 2.4955 ②	0.0006– 0.0018 ③	0.0019– 0.0071	4	1.9983– 1.9993	0.0009– 0.0031	0.0039– 0.0240
	W	6-173 (2.8)	2.6473– 2.6482	0.0016– 0.0033	0.0024– 0.0083	3	1.9983– 1.9994	0.0014– 0.0037	0.0063– 0.0173
1987	M	4-122 (2.0)	①	0.0006– 0.0016	0.0030– 0.0120	3	1.9278– 1.9286	0.0007– 0.0024	0.0027– 0.0095
	1	4-122 (2.0)	2.4945– 2.4954	0.0006– 0.0019	0.0020– 0.0080	4	1.9983– 1.9994	0.0010– 0.0031	0.0040– 0.0150

CRANKSHAFT AND CONNECTING ROD SPECIFICATIONS

All measurements are given in inches.

Year	VIN	No. Cylinder Displacement cu. in. (liter)	Crankshaft Main Brg. Journal Dia.	Crankshaft Main Brg. Oil Clearance	Crankshaft Shaft End-play	Crankshaft Thrust on No.	Connecting Rod Journal Diameter	Connecting Rod Oil Clearance	Connecting Rod Side Clearance
1987	K	4-122 (2.0)	①	0.0006–0.0016	0.0030–0.0120	3	1.9278–1.9286	0.0007–0.0024	0.0027–0.0095
	W	6-173 (2.8)	2.6473–2.6482	0.0016–0.0033	0.0024–0.0083	3	1.9983–1.9994	0.0014–0.0037	0.0063–0.0173
1988-89	M	4-122 (2.0)	①	0.0006–0.0016	0.0030–0.0120	3	1.9278–1.9286	0.0007–0.0024	0.0027–0.0095
	1	4-122 (2.0)	2.4945–2.4954	0.0006–0.0019	0.0020–0.0080	4	1.9983–1.9994	0.0010–0.0031	0.0040–0.0150
	K	4-122 (2.0)	①	0.0006–0.0016	0.0030–0.0120	3	1.9278–1.9286	0.0007–0.0024	0.0027–0.0095
	W	6-173 (2.8)	2.6473–2.6482	0.0016–0.0033	0.0024–0.0083	3	1.9983–1.9994	0.0014–0.0037	0.0063–0.0173

① Bearings are identified by color:
Brown 2.2830–2.2832;
Green 2.2827–2.2830

② No.5: 2.4936–2.4946
③ No.5: 0.0014–0.0027

VALVE SPECIFICATIONS

Year	VIN	No. Cylinder Displacement cu. in. (liter)	Seat Angle (deg.)	Face Angle (deg.)	Spring Test Pressure (lbs.)	Spring Installed Height (in.)	Stem-to-Guide Clearance (in.) Intake	Stem-to-Guide Clearance (in.) Exhaust	Stem Diameter (in.) Intake	Stem Diameter (in.) Exhaust
1982	G	4-110 (1.8)	46	45	183 @ 1.33	1.60	0.0011–0.0026	0.0014–0.0031	0.3139–0.3144	0.3129–0.3136
	B	4-122 (2.0)	46	45	183 @ 1.33	1.60	0.0011–0.0026	0.0014–0.0031	0.3139–0.3144	0.3129–0.3136
1983	O	4-110 (1.8)	46	46	NA	NA	0.0006–0.0016	0.0012–0.0024	NA	NA
	J	4-110 (1.8)	46	46	NA	NA	0.0006–0.0016	0.0012–0.0024	NA	NA
	P	4-122 (2.0)	46	45	183 @ 1.33	1.60	0.0011–0.0026	0.0014–0.0031	0.3139–0.3144	0.3129–0.3136
	B	4-122 (2.0)	46	45	183 @ 1.33	1.60	0.0011–0.0026	0.0014–0.0031	0.3139–0.3144	0.3129–0.3136
1984	O	4-110 (1.8)	46	46	NA	NA	0.0006–0.0016	0.0012–0.0024	NA	NA
	P	4-122 (2.0)	46	45	183 @ 1.33	1.60	0.0011–0.0026	0.0014–0.0031	0.3139–0.3144	0.3129–0.3136
	B	4-122 (2.0)	46	45	183 @ 1.33	1.60	0.0011–0.0026	0.0014–0.0031	0.3139–0.3144	0.3129–0.3136
1985	O	4-110 (1.8)	46	46	NA	NA	0.0006–0.0016	0.0012–0.0024	NA	NA
	J	4-110 (1.8)	46	46	NA	NA	0.0006–0.0016	0.0012–0.0024	NA	NA
	P	4-122 (2.0)	46	45	183 @ 1.33	1.60	0.0011–0.0026	0.0014–0.0031	0.3139–0.3144	0.3129–0.3136

VALVE SPECIFICATIONS

Year	VIN	No. Cylinder Displacement cu. in. (liter)	Seat Angle (deg.)	Face Angle (deg.)	Spring Test Pressure (lbs.)	Spring Installed Height (in.)	Stem-to-Guide Clearance (in.)		Stem Diameter (in.)	
							Intake	Exhaust	Intake	Exhaust
1985	W	6-173 (2.8)	46	45	195 @ 1.18	1.57	0.0010–0.0027	0.0010–0.0027	NA	NA
1986	O	4-110 (1.8)	46	46	NA	NA	0.0006–0.0016	0.0012–0.0024	NA	NA
	J	4-110 (1.8)	46	46	NA	NA	0.0006–0.0016	0.0012–0.0024	NA	NA
	P	4-122 (2.0)	46	45	183 @ 1.33	1.60	0.0011–0.0026	0.0014–0.0031	0.3139–0.3144	0.3129–0.3136
	W	6-173 (2.8)	46	45	195 @ 1.18	1.57	0.0010–0.0027	0.0010–0.0027	NA	NA
1987	M	4-122 (2.0)	45	46	NA	NA	0.0006–0.0020	0.0010–0.0024	NA	NA
	1	4-122 (2.0)	46	45	183 @ 1.33	1.60	0.0011–0.0026	0.0014–0.0030	0.049–0.056	0.063–0.075
	K	4-122 (2.0)	45	46	NA	NA	0.0006–0.0020	0.0010–0.0024	NA	NA
	W	6-173 (2.8)	46	45	195 @ 1.18	1.57	0.0010–0.0027	0.0010–0.0027	0.061–0.073	0.067–0.079
1988-89	M	4-122 (2.0)	45	46	NA	NA	0.0006–0.0020	0.0010–0.0024	NA	NA
	1	4-122 (2.0)	46	45	183 @ 1.33	1.60	0.0011–0.0026	0.0014–0.0030	0.049–0.056	0.063–0.075
	K	4-122 (2.0)	45	46	NA	NA	0.0006–0.0020	0.0010–0.0024	NA	NA
	W	6-173 (2.8)	46	45	195 @ 1.18	1.57	0.0010–0.0027	0.0010–0.0027	0.061–0.073	0.067–0.079

NA Not available

PISTON AND RING SPECIFICATIONS
All measurments are given in inches.

Year	VIN	No. Cylinder Displacement cu. in. (liter)	Piston Clearance	Ring Gap			Ring Side Clearance		
				Top Compression	Bottom Compression	Oil Control	Top Compression	Bottom Compression	Oil Control
1982	G	4-110 (1.8)	0.0008–0.0018	0.0098–0.0197	0.0098–0.0197	Snug	0.0012–0.0027	0.0012–0.0027	0.0078
	B	4-122 (2.0)	0.0008–0.0018	0.0098–0.0197	0.0098–0.0197	Snug	0.0012–0.0027	0.0012–0.0027	0.0078
1983	O	4-110 (1.8)	0.0008	0.0010–0.0020	0.0010–0.0020	0.0010–0.0020	0.0020–0.0030	0.0010–0.0024	Sung
	J	4-110 (1.8)	①	0.0010–0.0020	0.0010–0.0020	0.0010–0.0020	0.0020–0.0030	0.0010–0.0024	Sung
	P	4-122 (2.0)	0.0008–0.0018	0.0098–0.0197	0.0098–0.0197	Snug	0.0012–0.0027	0.0012–0.0027	0.0078
	B	4-122 (2.0)	0.0008–0.0018	0.0098–0.0197	0.0098–0.0197	Snug	0.0012–0.0027	0.0012–0.0027	0.0078

PISTON AND RING SPECIFICATIONS
All measurments are given in inches.

Year	VIN	No. Cylinder Displacement cu. in. (liter)	Piston Clearance	Ring Gap			Ring Side Clearance		
				Top Compression	Bottom Compression	Oil Control	Top Compression	Bottom Compression	Oil Control
1984	O	4-110 (1.8)	0.0008	0.0010–0.0020	0.0010–0.0020	0.0010–0.0020	0.0020–0.0030	0.0010–0.0024	Sung
	P	4-122 (2.0)	0.0007–0.0017	0.0098–0.0197	0.0098–0.0197	Snug	0.0012–0.0027	0.0012–0.0027	0.0078
	B	4-122 (2.0)	0.0007–0.0017	0.0098–0.0197	0.0098–0.0197	Snug	0.0012–0.0027	0.0012–0.0027	0.0078
1985	O	4-110 (1.8)	0.0008	0.0010–0.0020	0.0010–0.0020	0.0010–0.0020	0.0020–0.0030	0.0010–0.0024	Sung
	J	4-110 (1.8)	①	0.0010–0.0020	0.0010–0.0020	0.0010–0.0020	0.0020–0.0030	0.0010–0.0024	Sung
	P	4-122 (2.0)	0.0007–0.0017	0.0098–0.0197	0.0098–0.0197	Snug	0.0012–0.0027	0.0012–0.0027	0.0078
	W	6-173 (2.8)	0.0007–0.0017	0.0098–0.0197	0.0098–0.0197	0.020–0.055	0.0012–0.0027	0.0016–0.0037	0.0078 Max
1986	O	4-110 (1.8)	0.0008	0.0010–0.0020	0.0010–0.0020	0.0010–0.0020	0.0020–0.0030	0.0010–0.0024	Sung
	J	4-110 (1.8)	①	0.0010–0.0020	0.0010–0.0020	0.0010–0.0020	0.0020–0.0030	0.0010–0.0024	Sung
	P	4-122 (2.0)	0.0008–0.0018	0.0098–0.0197	0.0098–0.0197	Snug	0.0012–0.0027	0.0012–0.0027	0.0078
	W	6-173 (2.8)	0.0007–0.0017	0.0098–0.0197	0.0098–0.0197	0.020–0.055	0.0012–0.0027	0.0016–0.0037	0.0078 Max
1987	M	4-122 (2.0)	0.0012–0.0020	0.012–0.020	0.012–0.020	0.016–0.055	0.0020–0.0030	0.0010–0.0024	–
	1	4-122 (2.0)	0.0098–0.0220	0.0100–0.0200	0.0100–0.0200	0.010–0.050	0.0010–0.0030	0.0010–0.0030	0.0006–0.0090
	K	4-122 (2.0)	0.0004–0.0012	0.012–0.020	0.012–0.020	0.016–0.055	0.0020–0.0030	0.0010–0.0024	–
	W	6-173 (2.8)	0.0007–0.0017	0.0098–0.0197	0.0098–0.0197	0.020–0.055	0.0012–0.0027	0.0016–0.0037	0.0078 Max
1988-89	M	4-122 (2.0)	0.0012–0.0020	0.012–0.020	0.012–0.020	0.016–0.055	0.0020–0.0030	0.0010–0.0024	–
	1	4-122 (2.0)	0.0098–0.0220	0.0100–0.0200	0.0100–0.0200	0.010–0.050	0.0010–0.0030	0.0010–0.0030	0.0006–0.0090
	K	4-122 (2.0)	0.0004–0.0012	0.012–0.020	0.012–0.020	0.016–0.055	0.0020–0.0030	0.0010–0.0024	–
	W	6-173 (2.8)	0.0022–0.0035	0.010–0.020	0.010–0.020	0.010–0.050	0.002–0.0035	0.002–0.0035	0.008 Max

① 0.0004–0.0012

TORQUE SPECIFICATIONS
All readings in ft. lbs.

Year	VIN	No. Cylinder Displacement cu. in. (liter)	Cylinder Head Bolts	Main Bearing Bolts	Rod Bearing Bolts	Crankshaft Pulley Bolts	Flywheel Bolts	Manifold Intake	Manifold Exhaust	Spark Plugs
1982	G	4-110 (1.8)	65-75	63-74	34-40	66-84⑩	45-55	20-25	22-28	15
	B	4-122 (2.0)	65-75	63-77	34-40	66-84⑩	45-63②	18-25	20-30	15
1983	O	4-110 (1.8)	①	57	39	115⑪	45	25	16	15
	J	4-110 (1.8)	①	57	39	115⑪	45	25	16	15
	P	4-122 (2.0)	65-75	63-77	34-40	68-84⑩	45-63②	18-25	20-30	15
	B	4-122 (2.0)	65-75	63-77	34-40	66-84⑩	45-63②	18-25	20-30	15
1984	O	4-110 (1.8)	①	57	39	115⑪	45	25	16	15
	P	4-122 (2.0)	65-75	63-77	34-40	66-84⑩	45-63②	18-25	20-30	15
	B	4-122 (2.0)	65-75	63-77	34-40	66-84⑩	45-63②	18-25	20-30	15
1985	O	4-110 (1.8)	①	57	39	115⑪	45	25	16	15
	J	4-110 (1.8)	①	57	39	115⑪	45	25	16	15
	P	4-122 (2.0)	65-75	63-77	34-40	66-84⑩	45-63②	18-25	20-30	15
	W	6-173 (2.8)	70	68	37	75	45	23	16	15
1986	O	4-110 (1.8)	①	57	39	115⑪	45	25	16	15
	J	4-110 (1.8)	①	57	39	115⑪	45	25	16	15
	P	4-122 (2.0)	65-75	63-77	34-40	66-84⑩	45-63②	18-25	20-30	15
	W	6-173 (2.8)	70	68	37	75	45	23	16	15
1987	M	4-122 (2.0)	③	44④	26⑤	20⑥	48⑦	16	16	15
	1	4-122 (2.0)	⑧	63-77	34-43	68-89	63②	15-22	6-13	15
	K	4-122 (2.0)	③	44④	26⑤	20⑥	48⑦	16	16	15
	W	6-173 (2.8)	33⑨	63-83	34-45	66-84	45	18	14-22	15
1988-89	M	4-122 (2.0)	③	44④	26⑤	20⑥	48⑦	16	16	15
	1	4-122 (2.0)	⑧	63-77	34-43	68-89	63②	15-22	6-13	15
	K	4-122 (2.0)	③	44④	26⑤	20⑥	48⑦	16	16	15
	W	6-173 (2.8)	33⑨	63-83	34-45	66-84	45	18	14-22	15

CAUTION: Verify the correct original equipment engine is in the vehicle by referring to the VIN engine code before torquing any bolts.

① Torque bolts to 18 ft.lb., then turn each bolt 60 degrees, in sequence, 3 times for a 180 degree rotation, then run the engine to normal operating temperature and turn each bolt, in sequence, an additonal 30–50 degrees
② Auto. Trans.—45-59
③ Step 1—18 ft. lbs.

Step2—Tighten additional 180 degrees in 3 steps of 60 degrees each
Step3—Warm engine—tighten bolts additional 30–50 degree turn
④ Plus additional 45–50 degree turn
⑤ Plus additional 45 degree turn
⑥ Crankshaft pulley to sprocket bolts

⑦ Plus additional 30 degree turn
⑧ Long bolts—73–83 ft. lbs.
  Short bolts—62–70 ft. lbs.
⑨ Coat thread with sealer an additional 90 degree turn
⑩ Crankshaft pulley center
⑪ Crankshaft sprocket retaining bolts

BRAKE SPECIFICATIONS
All measurements in inches unless noted

Year	Model	Lug Nut Torque (ft. lbs.)	Master Cylinder Bore	Brake Disc Minimum Thickness	Brake Disc Maximum Runout	Maximum Brake Drum Diameter	Minimum Lining Thickness Front	Minimum Lining Thickness Rear
1982	Cavalier	100	.94	0.815	0.002	7.929	⅛	⅛
	2000	100	.94	0.815	0.002	7.929	⅛	⅛
	Firenza	100	.94	0.815	0.002	7.929	⅛	⅛

BRAKE SPECIFICATIONS
All measurements in inches unless noted

| Year | Model | Lug Nut Torque (ft. lbs.) | Master Cylinder Bore | Brake Disc | | Maximum Brake Drum Diameter | Minimum Lining Thickness | |
				Minimum Thickness	Maximum Runout		Front	Rear
1982	Skyhawk	100	.94	0.815	0.002	7.929	1/8	1/8
	Cimarron	100	.94	0.815	0.002	7.929	1/8	1/8
1983	Cavalier	100	.94	0.815	0.002	7.929	1/8	1/8
	2000	100	.94	0.815	0.002	7.929	1/8	1/8
	Firenza	100	.94	0.815	0.002	7.929	1/8	1/8
	Skyhawk	100	.94	0.815	0.002	7.929	1/8	1/8
	Cimarron	100	.94	0.815	0.002	7.929	1/8	1/8
1984	Cavalier	100	.94	0.815	0.004	7.929	1/8	1/8
	2000 Sunbird	100	.94	0.815	0.004	7.929	1/8	1/8
	Firenza	100	.94	0.815	0.004	7.929	1/8	1/8
	Skyhawk	100	.94	0.815	0.004	7.929	1/8	1/8
	Cimarron	100	.94	0.815	0.004	7.929	1/8	1/8
1985	Cavalier	100	.94	0.815	0.004	7.929	1/8	1/8
	2000 Sunbird	100	.94	0.815	0.004	7.929	1/8	1/8
	Firenza	100	.94	0.815	0.004	7.929	1/8	1/8
	Skyhawk	100	.94	0.815	0.004	7.929	1/8	1/8
	Cimarron	100	.94	0.815	0.004	7.929	1/8	1/8
1986	Cavalier	100	.94	0.815	0.004	7.929	1/8	1/8
	Sunbird	100	.94	0.815	0.004	7.929	1/8	1/8
	Firenza	100	.94	0.815	0.004	7.929	1/8	1/8
	Skyhawk	100	.94	0.815	0.004	7.929	1/8	1/8
	Cimarron	100	.94	0.815	0.004	7.929	1/8	1/8
1987	Cavalier	100	.94	0.815	0.004	7.929	1/8	1/8
	Sunbird	100	.94	0.815	0.004	7.929	1/8	1/8
	Firenza	100	.94	0.815	0.004	7.929	1/8	1/8
	Skyhawk	100	.94	0.815	0.004	7.929	1/8	1/8
	Cimarron	100	.94	0.815	0.004	7.929	1/8	1/8
1988-89	Cavalier	100	.94	0.815	0.004	7.929	1/8	1/8
	Sunbird	100	.94	0.815	0.004	7.929	1/8	1/8
	Firenza	100	.94	0.815	0.004	7.929	1/8	1/8
	Skyhawk	100	.94	0.815	0.004	7.929	1/8	1/8
	Cimarron	100	.94	0.815	0.004	7.929	1/8	1/8

WHEEL ALIGNMENT

Year	Model	Caster Range (deg.)	Caster Preferred Setting (deg.)	Camber Range (deg.)	Camber Preferred Setting (deg.)	Toe-in (in.)	Steering Axis Inclination (deg.)
1982	Cavalier	NA	NA	$\frac{1}{16}$P-1$\frac{1}{16}$P	$\frac{9}{16}$P	$\frac{1}{4}$-0①	13$\frac{1}{2}$
	2000	NA	NA	$\frac{1}{16}$P-1$\frac{1}{16}$P	$\frac{9}{16}$P	$\frac{1}{4}$-0①	13$\frac{1}{2}$
	Firenza	NA	NA	$\frac{1}{16}$P-1$\frac{1}{16}$P	$\frac{9}{16}$P	$\frac{1}{4}$-0①	13$\frac{1}{2}$
	Skyhawk	NA	NA	$\frac{1}{16}$P-1$\frac{1}{16}$P	$\frac{9}{16}$P	$\frac{1}{4}$-0①	13$\frac{1}{2}$
	Cimarron	NA	NA	$\frac{1}{16}$P-1$\frac{1}{16}$P	$\frac{9}{16}$P	$\frac{1}{4}$-0①	13$\frac{1}{2}$
1983	Cavalier	NA	NA	$\frac{7}{32}$P-1$\frac{17}{32}$P	$\frac{23}{32}$P	$\frac{5}{16}$-$\frac{1}{16}$①	13$\frac{1}{2}$
	2000	NA	NA	$\frac{7}{32}$P-1$\frac{17}{32}$P	$\frac{23}{32}$P	$\frac{5}{16}$-$\frac{1}{16}$①	13$\frac{1}{2}$
	Firenza	NA	NA	$\frac{7}{32}$P-1$\frac{17}{32}$P	$\frac{23}{32}$P	$\frac{5}{16}$-$\frac{1}{16}$①	13$\frac{1}{2}$
	Skyhawk	NA	NA	$\frac{7}{32}$P-1$\frac{17}{32}$P	$\frac{23}{32}$P	$\frac{5}{16}$-$\frac{1}{16}$①	13$\frac{1}{2}$
	Cimarron	NA	NA	$\frac{7}{32}$P-1$\frac{17}{32}$P	$\frac{23}{32}$P	$\frac{5}{16}$-$\frac{1}{16}$①	13$\frac{1}{2}$
1984	Cavalier	NA	NA	$\frac{3}{16}$P-1$\frac{3}{16}$P	$\frac{13}{16}$P	$\frac{1}{4}$-0①	13$\frac{1}{2}$
	2000 Sunbird	NA	NA	$\frac{3}{16}$P-1$\frac{3}{16}$P	$\frac{13}{16}$P	$\frac{1}{4}$-0①	13$\frac{1}{2}$
	Firenza	NA	NA	$\frac{3}{16}$P-1$\frac{3}{16}$P	$\frac{13}{16}$P	$\frac{1}{4}$-0①	13$\frac{1}{2}$
	Skyhawk	NA	NA	$\frac{3}{16}$P-1$\frac{3}{16}$P	$\frac{13}{16}$P	$\frac{1}{4}$-0①	13$\frac{1}{2}$
	Cimarron	NA	NA	$\frac{3}{16}$P-1$\frac{3}{16}$P	$\frac{13}{16}$P	$\frac{1}{4}$-0①	13$\frac{1}{2}$
1985	Cavalier	NA	NA	$\frac{3}{16}$P-1$\frac{3}{16}$P	$\frac{13}{16}$P	$\frac{1}{4}$-0①	13$\frac{1}{2}$
	2000 Sunbird	NA	NA	$\frac{3}{16}$P-1$\frac{3}{16}$P	$\frac{13}{16}$P	$\frac{1}{4}$-0①	13$\frac{1}{2}$
	Firenza	NA	NA	$\frac{3}{16}$P-1$\frac{3}{16}$P	$\frac{13}{16}$P	$\frac{1}{4}$-0①	13$\frac{1}{2}$
	Skyhawk	NA	NA	$\frac{3}{16}$P-1$\frac{3}{16}$P	$\frac{13}{16}$P	$\frac{1}{4}$-0①	13$\frac{1}{2}$
	Cimarron	NA	NA	$\frac{3}{16}$P-1$\frac{3}{16}$P	$\frac{13}{16}$P	$\frac{1}{4}$-0①	13$\frac{1}{2}$
1986	Cavalier	NA	NA	$\frac{3}{16}$P-1$\frac{3}{16}$P	$\frac{13}{16}$P	$\frac{1}{4}$-0①	13$\frac{1}{2}$
	2000 Sunbird	NA	NA	$\frac{3}{16}$P-1$\frac{3}{16}$P	$\frac{13}{16}$P	$\frac{1}{4}$-0①	13$\frac{1}{2}$
	Firenza	NA	NA	$\frac{3}{16}$P-1$\frac{3}{16}$P	$\frac{13}{16}$P	$\frac{1}{4}$-0①	13$\frac{1}{2}$
	Skyhawk	NA	NA	$\frac{3}{16}$P-1$\frac{3}{16}$P	$\frac{13}{16}$P	$\frac{1}{4}$-0①	13$\frac{1}{2}$
	Cimarron	NA	NA	$\frac{3}{16}$P-1$\frac{3}{16}$P	$\frac{13}{16}$P	$\frac{1}{4}$-0①	13$\frac{1}{2}$
1987	Cavalier	NA	NA	$\frac{3}{16}$P-1$\frac{3}{16}$P	$\frac{13}{16}$P	0③	13$\frac{1}{2}$
	2000 Sunbird	NA	NA	$\frac{3}{16}$P-1$\frac{3}{16}$P	$\frac{13}{16}$P	0③	13$\frac{1}{2}$
	Firenza	NA	NA	$\frac{3}{16}$P-1$\frac{3}{16}$P	$\frac{13}{16}$P	0③	13$\frac{1}{2}$
	Skyhawk	NA	NA	$\frac{3}{16}$P-1$\frac{3}{16}$P	$\frac{13}{16}$P	0③	13$\frac{1}{2}$
	Cimarron	NA	NA	$\frac{3}{16}$P-1$\frac{3}{16}$P	$\frac{13}{16}$P	0③	13$\frac{1}{2}$
1988-89	Cavalier	NA	NA	$\frac{3}{16}$P-1$\frac{3}{16}$P②	$\frac{13}{16}$P②	0	13$\frac{1}{2}$
	2000 Sunbird	NA	NA	$\frac{3}{16}$P-1$\frac{3}{16}$P	$\frac{13}{16}$P	0	13$\frac{1}{2}$
	Firenza	NA	NA	$\frac{3}{16}$P-1$\frac{3}{16}$P	$\frac{13}{16}$P	0	13$\frac{1}{2}$
	Skyhawk	NA	NA	$\frac{3}{16}$P-1$\frac{3}{16}$P	$\frac{13}{16}$P	0	13$\frac{1}{2}$
	Cimarron	NA	NA	$\frac{3}{16}$P-1$\frac{3}{16}$P	$\frac{13}{16}$P	0	13$\frac{1}{2}$

NA Not adjustable
① Preferred setting—$\frac{1}{8}$ degree out
② Z-24: 1N–1P. Preferred setting is 0 camber
③ If vehicle is equipped with P215-60R14 tires setting is $\frac{1}{8}$ degree out

TUNE-UP PROCEDURES

Ignition Timing

ADJUSTMENT

Distributorless Ignitions Systems

The ignition timing on engines with distributorless ignitions, is controlled by the Electronic Control Module (ECM). No adjustments are possible.

HEI Ignitions Systems

2.0L (EXC. ENG. CODE B) AND 2.8L ENGINES

1. Refer to the underhood emission control label and follow all of the timing instructions if they differ from below.
2. Warm engine to normal operating temperature.
3. Place transmission in **NEUTRAL** or **PARK**. Apply parking brake and block wheels.
4. A/C, cooling fan and choke must be off. Do not remove air cleaner, except as noted.
5. Connect inductive timing light to coil lead. Peel back the protective covering on the coil lead to make good connection.

NOTE: On engine code P, 1 and W disconnect the single wire HEI bypass connector (tan/black wire) usually near the distributor on 4 cylinder engines and near the left shock tower on 6 cylinder engines, to cause the engine to operate in the bypass timing mode instead of grounding test terminal.

6. Ground the ALCL connector under the dash by installing a jumper wire between the **A** and **B** terminals. The **Check Engine** light should begin flashing.
7. Using the timing light, check the position of the timing mark.
8. Optimum timing of all cylinders is achieved when the apparent notch width is centered with the timing mark.

NOTE: A notch for the No.1 cylinder is scribed across all 3 edges of the double groove pulley. Another notch is scribed 180 degrees away only across the center edge of the pulley. Since the coil high tension lead is triggering the timing light, timing for all cylinders is shown, causing a slight "jiggling" of the timing notch and an apparent increase in the width of the timing notch.

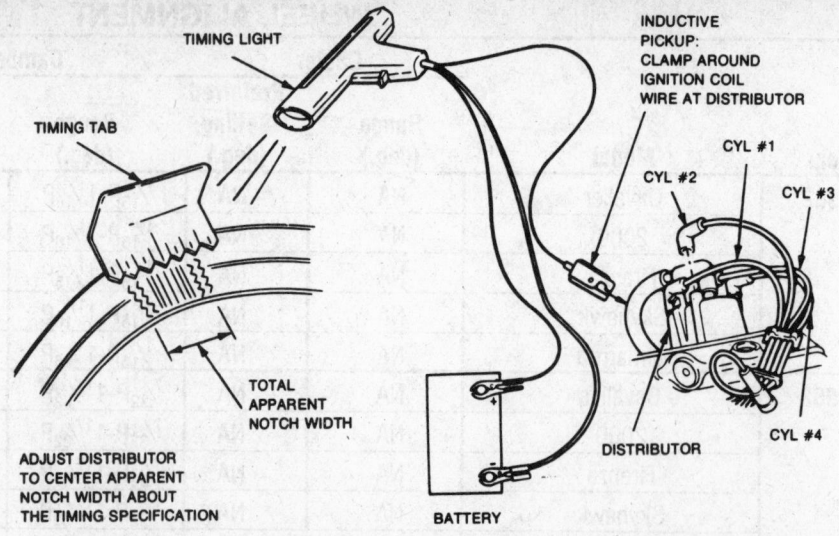

Ignition timing is accomplished by using the averaging method; see the text

9. To correct the timing, loosen the distributor hold down clamp, adjust the distributor and retighten the hold down bolt.
10. Once the timing is properly set, remove the jumper wire from the ALCL connector.
11. If necessary to clear the ECM memory, disconnect the ECM harness from the positive battery pigtail for 10 seconds with the key in the **OFF** position.

1.8L (ENGINE CODE 0, J)

1. Refer to the underhood emission control label and follow all of the timing instructions if they differ from below.
2. Warm engine to normal operating temperature.
3. Place transmission in **NEUTRAL** or **PARK**. Apply parking brake and block wheels.
4. A/C, cooling fan and choke must be off. Do not remove air cleaner, except as noted.
5. Ground the ALCL connector under the dash by installing a jumper wire between the **A** and **B** terminals. The **Check Engine** light should begin flashing.
6. Connect inductive timing light to No.1 spark plug wire lead and record timing.
7. Connect inductive timing light to No.4 spark plug wire lead and record timing.
8. Add the 2 timing numbers and divide by 2 to obtain "average timing"

NOTE: For example: No. 1 timing = 4 degrees and No. 4 timing = 8 degrees; 4 + 8 = 12 ÷ 2 = 6 degrees average timing. If a change is necessary, subtract the average timing from the timing specification to determine the

amount of timing change to No. 1 cylinder. For example: if the timing specification is 8 degrees and the average timing is 6 degrees, advance the No. 1 cylinder 2 degrees to set the timing.

9. To correct the timing, loosen the distributor hold down clamp, adjust the distributor and retighten the hold down bolt.
10. Once the timing is properly set, remove the jumper wire from the ALCL connector.
11. If necessary to clear the ECM memory, disconnect the ECM harness from the positive battery pigtail for 10 seconds with the key in the **OFF** position.

1.8L (CODE G) AND 2.0L (CODE B)

1. Refer to the underhood emission control label and follow all of the timing instructions if they differ from below.
2. Disconnect the 4 wire EST connector at distributor.
3. Place transmission in **NEUTRAL** or **PARK**. Apply parking brake and block wheels.
4. A/C, cooling fan and choke must be off. Do not remove air cleaner, except as noted.
5. Make sure the timing marks are clean and readable. Start the engine and let it run until it reaches normal operating temperature.
6. Stop the engine and connect a timing light to **No.1** cylinder. Connect a suitable tachometer.
7. Loosen the distributor clamp.
8. Start the engine. Rotate the distributor until the correct marks line up. Tighten the distributor clamp and recheck the timing.
9. Adjust the engine idle rpm if necessary.

Valve Lash

ADJUSTMENT

NOTE: No routine valve lash adjustments are required. Adjustments should only be performed if the valve system has been overhauled, or if noise is present.

1.8L and 2.0L OHV Engines

1982–86

1. Rotate the engine until the mark on the crankshaft pulley lines up with the **0** mark on the timing tab. Remove the rocker cover.

2. Determine that the engine is in the No. 1 firing position. While rotating the engine, check the No. 1 rocker arm as the mark on the crankshaft pulley comes near the **0** mark. If the valves are not moving, the engine is in the No. 1 firing position. If the valves are moving, rotate the engine 1 complete revolution.

3. The following valves may be adjusted with the engine in the No. 1 firing position:
- **Exhaust 1 and 3**
- **Intake 1 and 2**

4. To adjust the valves, loosen the adjusting nut until lash is felt at the push rod. Turn the adjusting nut clockwise until all lash is removed. With all lash removed, turn the nut in another 1½ turns.

5. Rotate the engine 1 complete revolution. Line up the crankshaft pulley with the **0** mark. This is the No. 4 firing position. Adjustment the following valves:
- **Exhaust 2 and 4**
- **Intake 3 and 4**

6. When all valves have been adjusted, install the rocker arm cover with a new gasket. Start the engine and check the ignition timing and idle speed.

1.8L And 2.0L OHC Engines

1983–89

The valve lash on 1.8L and 2.0L OHC engines, is automatically adjusted by the hydraulic rocker arms and valve lash compensators. No adjustments are possible.

2.8L V6 Engine

1985–89

1. Rotate the engine until the mark on the harmonic balancer lines up with the **0** mark on the timing tab. Remove the rocker covers.

2. To determine that the engine is in the No. 1 firing position, while rotating the engine, place a finger on the No. 1 rocker arms as the timing mark nears the **0** mark. If the valves are not

moving, the engine is in the No. 1 firing position. If the valves are moving, the engine is in the No. 4 firing position and should be rotated 1 complete revolution.

3. With the engine in the No. 1 firing position, the following valves may be adjusted:
- **Intake 1, 5, 6**
- **Exhaust 1, 2, 3**

4. To adjust the valves, back the adjusting nut out until lash is felt at the pushrod. Turn the adjusting in just until all lash is removed.

5. When all lash has been removed, turn the adjusting nut in 1½ additional turns.

6. Rotate the engine 1 complete revolution until the timing tab **0** mark and balancer mark are aligned. The engine is now in the No. 4 firing position. With the engine is in this position, adjust following valves:
- **Intake 2, 3, 4**
- **Exhaust 4, 5, 6**

7. When all valves have been adjusted, install the rocker covers using new gaskets. Start the engine and check idle speed and ignition timing.

2.0L and 2.8L Engines

1987–89

The valve systems on 1987–89 2.0L and 2.8L engines with aluminum cylinder heads, use hydraulic lifters and are not adjustable. If noise is present in the valve system of these engines, check the rocker arm nut torque. The correct torque should be 11–18 ft. lbs. for 2.0L engines, and 14–20 ft. lbs. for 2.8L V6 engines. No other adjustments are necessary. If noise is still present, check the condition of the camshaft, lifters, rocker arms, push rods and valves.

Idle Speed and Mixture

ADJUSTMENT

1.8L (Code G) and 2.0L (Code B) Engines

IDLE SPEED CONTROL (ISC)

The idle speed control motor (ISC), is controlled by the electronic control module (ECM). The ECM has the desired idle speed programmed in it's memory. The ECM compares the actual idle speed to the desired idle speed and automatically adjusts the throttle to maintain an idle rpm independent of the engine loads.

An integral part of the ISC is the throttle contact switch. The position of the switch determines whether or not the ISC should control idle speed. When the throttle lever is resting against the ISC plunger, the switch contacts are closed, at which time the

ECM moves the ISC to the programmed idle speed. When the throttle lever is not contacting the ISC plunger, the switch contacts are open; the ECM stops sending idle speed commands and the driver controls engine speed.

NOTE: Before starting engine, place transmission selector lever in PARK or NEUTRAL, set the parking brake and block drive wheels.

When a new ISC assembly is installed, a base (minimum authority) and high (minimum authority) rpm speed check must be performed and adjustment made as required. These adjustment limit the low and high rpm speeds to the ECM. When making a low and high speed adjustment, the low speed adjustment is always made first. DO NOT use the ISC plunger to adjust curb idle speed as the idle speed is controlled by the ECM.

NOTE: Do not disconnect or connect ISC connector with ignition ON. Damage to the ECM may occur.

1. Connect tachometer (distributor side of tach filter, if used).

2. Connect dwell meter to mixture control (M/C) solenoid dwell lead. Remember to set dwell meter on the 6 cylinder scale.

3. Turn A/C off.

4. Start engine and run until stabilized by entering "closed loop" (dwell meter needle starts to vary).

5. Turn ignition **OFF**.

6. Unplug connector from ISC motor.

7. Fully retract ISC plunger by applying 12 volts DC (battery voltage) to terminal **C** of the ISC motor connection and ground lead to terminal **D** of the ISC motor connection. It may be necessary to install jumper leads from the ISC motor in order to make proper connections.

NOTE: Do not apply battery voltage to motor longer than necessary to retract ISC plunger. Prolonged contact will damage motor. Also, never connect voltage source across terminals "A" and "B" as damage to the internal throttle contact switch will result.

8. Start engine and wait until dwell meter needle starts to vary, indicating "closed loop" operation.

9. With parking brake applied and drive wheels blocked, place transaxle in **DRIVE** or **NEUTRAL** on manual transaxle models.

10. With ISC plunger fully retracted, adjust carburetor base (slow) idle stop

IDLE SPEED CONTROL (ISC) ADJUSTMENT

CARBURETOR PART NUMBER	BASE (SLOW) IDLE STOP SCREW (1)		ISC ADJUSTMENT RPM (2)	
	AUTO	MAN	AUTO	MAN
17081600	700		2300	
17081601		750		1700
17081607		700		1200
17081700	680		1600	
17081701	680		1900	

(1) ISC plunger fully retracted   (2) ISC plunger fully extended

screw to the specified rpm (see chart). ISC plunger should not be left in full retracted position.

11. Place transaxle in **PARK** or **NEUTRAL** and fully extend ISC plunger by applying 12 volts DC to terminal **D** of the ISC motor connection and ground lead to terminal **C** of the ISC motor connection.

NOTE: Never connect voltage source across terminal "A" and "B" as damage to the internal throttle contact switch will result.

12. With ISC plunger fully extended, using Tool J–29831 or equivalent, turn ISC plunger to obtain ISC adjustment rpm. Verify ISC adjustment rpm with voltage applied to motor, it will ratchet in and out.

Auto transaxle only; place transmission in **DRIVE** and readjust ISC plunger to ISC adjustment rpm.

13. Place transaxle in **PARK** or **NEUTRAL** and turn ignition **OFF**. Disconnect 12 volt DC power source, jumper leads, ground lead, tachometer, and dwell meter.

14. Reconnect 4 terminal harness connector to ISC motor.

15. "Tricking" the ISC motor as described will cause the "Check Engine" light to come on and an ISC motor trouble code to be set. By restoring the system to normal operation, the light will go out, but the trouble code will continue to be stored as an intermittent problem. In this case, it will be necessary to clear the diagnostic trouble code.

16. After a fault has been corrected, it will will be necessary to remove battery voltage for 10 seconds to clear any stored codes. Voltage can be removed by removing ECM fuse.

FAST IDLE

1. Prepare the vehicle for adjust-

ment as specified on the underhood emission label. Place the transmission in **PARK** or **NEUTRAL**.

2. Place the fast idle screw on the highest step of the fast idle cam.

3. Turn the fast idle screw in or out to obtain the specified fast idle speed.

1983–89 1.8L, 2.0L and 2.8L Fuel Injected Engines

The idle speed on fuel injected engines is controlled by the Electronic Control Module (ECM). No adjustments are possible.

IDLE MIXTURE

1.8L (Code G) and 2.0L (Code B) Engines

1.8L and 2.0L Engines use the E2SE carburetor with the Computer Command Control system (CCC). The carburetor is equipped with a mixture control solenoid.

NOTE: Before checking or resetting the carburetor as the cause of poor engine performance or rough idle, check ignition system including distributor, timing, spark plugs and wires. Check air cleaner, evaporative emission system, EFE system, PCV system, EGR valve and engine compression. Also inspect intake manifold vacuum hose gaskets and connections for leaks and check torques of carburetor mounting bolts/nuts.

1. Remove the carburetor.

2. Remove the idle mixture screw plugs. Lightly seat the screws.

3. Back out the screws 5 turns each for the 4 cylinder engine.

4. Remove the idle air bleed screw plug from the air horn. Lightly seat the air bleed screw. Back it out 3 turns for the 4 cylinder engine.

5. Remove the vent stack and screen assembly in order to gain access to the lean mixture screw. Lightly seat the lean mixture screw. Back it out 2 1/2 turns.

6. Reinstall the carburetor on the engine, but DO NOT install the air cleaner and gasket.

7. Disconnect the bowl vent line at the carburetor.

8. Disconnect and plug the vacuum hose at the tee in the bowl vent line (if so equipped).

9. Disconnect the canister purge and EGR hose at the carburetor. Plug the carburetor fitting.

10. Connect a dwell meter to the mixture control solenoid test lead (green connector) and set the dwell meter to the 6 cylinder position.

11. Connect a tachometer to the distributor TACH lead (brown connector).

12. Block the drive wheels, place the transaxle in **PARK** (auto. trans.) or **NEUTRAL** (man. trans.), and apply the parking brake.

13. Start the engine and let it idle until the cooling fan starts to cycle, indicating that the engine is warm and operating in the closed loop mode.

14. Run the engine at 3000 rpm and adjust the lean mixture screw in small increments (allowing the dwell to stabilize after each adjustment) until the average dwell is 35 degrees. If unable to adjust to this specification, check the carburetor main metering circuit for leaks, restrictions, etc.

NOTE: While idling, it is normal for the dwell to increase and decrease fairly constantly over a relatively narrow range, such as 5 degrees. The dwell reading may also vary 10–15 degrees momentarily due to temporary mixture changes.

15. Allow the engine to return to idle and adjust the idle speed to 700 rpm, with the cooling fan in the off cycle.

16. Adjust the idle mixture screw (in the same manner as in Step 14) until a dwell (average) of 25 degrees is obtained. The adjustment is very sensitive-the final check must be made with the adjusting tool removed. If unable to set the dwell to specification, check the carburetor idle system for leaks, restrictions, etc.

17. Raise the engine speed to 3000 rpm, and make sure that the dwell stabilizes and averages 35 degrees at this rpm. Repeat Steps 14–17 if required.

18. Remove the tachometer and dwell meter, reattach the hoses as they were originally, and reinstall the items removed.

19. Set the idle speed to the figure given on the underhood emissions label.

1983–89 1.8L, 2.0L and 2.8L Fuel Injected Engines

The idle mixture on fuel injected engines is controlled by the Electronic Control Module (ECM). No adjustments are possible.

ENGINE ELECTRICAL

Distributor

REMOVAL & INSTALLATION

OHV Engines

1. Disconnect the negative battery cable.
2. Tag and disconnect all wires leading from the distributor cap.
3. Remove the air cleaner housing.
4. Remove the distributor cap.
5. Disconnect the AIR pipe-to-exhaust manifold hose at the air management valve.
6. Unscrew the rear engine lift bracket bolt and nut, lift it off the stud and position the entire assembly out of the way to facilitate better access to the distributor.
7. Mark the position of the distributor, relative to the engine block and scribe a mark on the distributor body indicating the initial position of the rotor.
8. Remove the hold-down nut and clamp from the base of the distributor. Remove the distributor from the engine. The drive gear on the distributor shaft is helical and the shaft will rotate slightly as the distributor is removed. Note and mark the position of the rotor at this second position. Do not

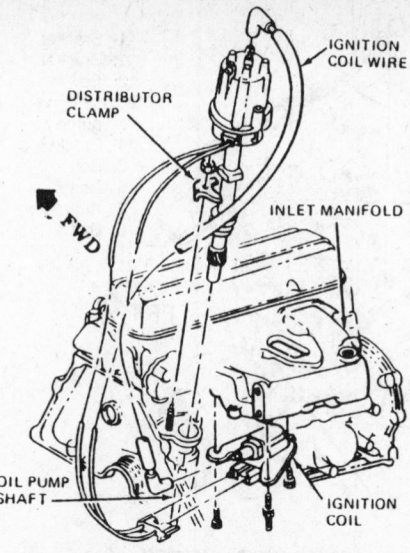

Distributor mounting OHV engines

crank the engine while the distributor is removed.

9. To install the distributor, rotate the shaft until the rotor aligns with the second mark made (when the shaft stopped moving). Lubricate the drive gear with clean engine oil and install the distributor into the engine. As the distributor is installed, the rotor should move to the first mark made. This will ensure proper timing. If the marks do not align properly, remove the distributor and try again.
10. Install the clamp and hold-down nut.
11. Installation of the remaining components is in the reverse order of removal. Run the engine and check the ignition timing.

OHC Engines

1. Disconnect the negative battery cable.
2. Tag the spark plug wires and remove the wires and ignition coil.
3. Disconnect the wiring from the distributor.
4. Remove the 2 distributor hold-down nuts.
5. Remove the distributor.
6. Installation is the reverse of removal. Torque the hold-down nuts to 13 ft. lbs. Check and adjust the ignition timing.

REMOVAL & INSTALLATION

ENGINE DISTURBED

1. Remove the No. 1 cylinder spark plug.
2. Place a finger over the spark plug hole while rotating the engine slowly by hand, until compression is felt.
3. Align the timing mark on the crankshaft pulley with the 0° mark on

the timing scale attached to the front of the engine. This places the engine at TDC of the compression stroke for No. 1 cylinder.

4. Rotate the distributor shaft until the rotor points to the No. 1 spark plug tower on the distributor cap.
5. Install the distributor in the engine. Be sure to align the distributor-to-engine block matchmarks.
6. Install the hold down clamp and bolt. Start and run the engine.
7. Check and/or adjust the ignition timing.

Alternator

NOTE: For further information on the charging system, please refer to "Charging and Starting" in the Unit Repair section.

PRECAUTIONS

- When installing a battery, make sure that the positive and negative cables are not reversed.
- When jump-starting the vehicle, be sure that like terminals are connected. This also applies to using a battery charger. Reversed polarity will burn out the alternator and regulator in a matter of seconds.
- Never operate the alternator with the battery disconnected or on an otherwise uncontrolled open circuit.
- Do not short across or ground any alternator or regulator terminals.
- Do not try to polarize the alternator.
- Do not apply full battery voltage to the field (brown) connector.
- Always disconnect the battery ground cable before disconnecting the alternator lead.
- Always disconnect the battery (negative cable first) when charging it.
- Never subject the alternator to excessive heat or dampness. If steam-cleaning the engine, cover the alternator.
- Never use arc-welding equipment on the vehicle with the alternator connected.

BELT TENSION ADJUSTMENT

Gauge Method

V-BELTS

Using belt tension gauge J–23600 or equivalent, adjust the alternator belt if the tension is below 300N, as indicated on the gauge. If the belt is used the correct belt tension is 350N, as indicated on the gauge. If the belt is new, the correct tension is 600N, as indicated on the gauge.

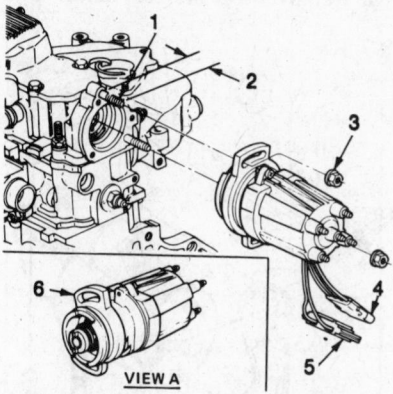

1. Stud
2. 20 ± 1.0
3. Nut
4. EST connector
5. Coil Connector
6. Distributor

Distributor mounting on OHC engines

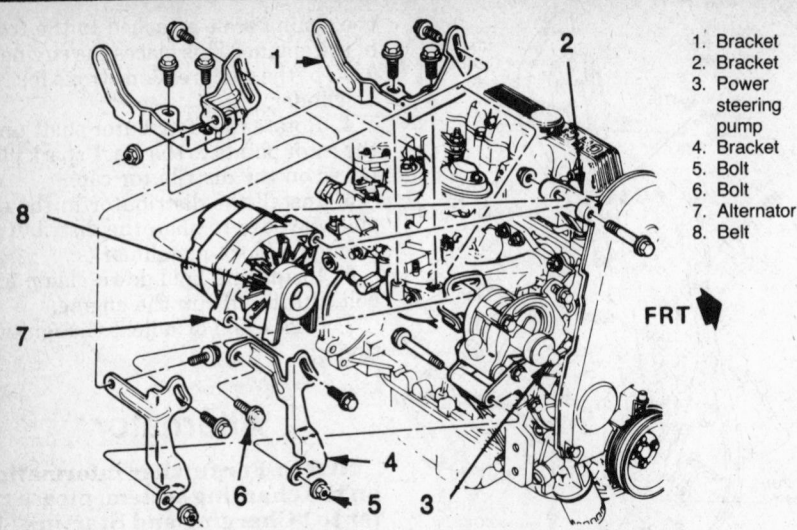

1. Bracket
2. Bracket
3. Power steering pump
4. Bracket
5. Bolt
6. Bolt
7. Alternator
8. Belt

FRT

Alternator installation, OHC engines with power steering

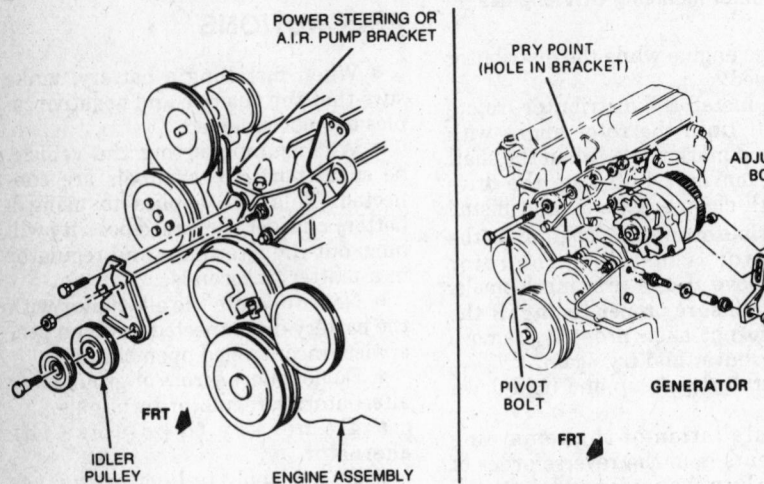

POWER STEERING OR A.I.R. PUMP BRACKET

IDLER PULLEY

FRT

ENGINE ASSEMBLY

PRY POINT (HOLE IN BRACKET)

ADJUSTING BOLTS

PIVOT BOLT

GENERATOR

FRT

Alternator installation, OHV engines

SERPENTINE BELTS

The correct belt tension is indicated on the indicator mark of the belt tensioner. If the indicator mark is not within specification, replace the belt or the tensioner.

REMOVAL & INSTALLATION

V-Belt

1. Disconnect the negative battery cable.

— CAUTION —

Failure to disconnect the negative cable may result in injury from the positive battery lead at the alternator, and may short the alternator and regulator during the removal process.

2. Disconnect and tag the 2 terminal plug and the battery lead from the rear of the alternator.

3. Loosen the mounting bolts. Push the alternator inwards and slip the drive belt off the pulley.

4. Remove the mounting bolts and remove the alternator.

5. To install, position the alternator in its brackets and install the mounting bolts. Do not tighten the bolts.

6. Slip the drive belt over the pulley. Pull outwards on the alternator and adjust the belt tension. Tighten the mounting and adjusting bolts.

7. Connect the electrical leads.

8. Connect the negative battery cable.

Serpentine Belts

Serpentine belts are tensioned by loosening and rotating the belt tensioner. The correct belt tension is indicated on the indicator mark of the belt tensioner. If the indicator mark is not within specification, replace the belt or the tensioner.

1. Disconnect the negative battery cable.

2. Disconnect and tag the alternator wiring at the rear of the alternator.

3. Loosen the belt tensioner pivot

bolt and rotate the tensioner to remove the belt.

4. Support the alternator and remove the mounting bolts.

5. Remove the alternator from the engine.

6. To install, place the alternator in the mounts and install the bolts.

7. Install the serpentine belt and tighten the belt tensioner.

8. Connect the alternator wiring and negative battery cable.

Voltage Regulator

All models are equipped with a solid state regulator inside the alternator. All regulator components are sealed and non-adjustable. Removal and installation requires alternator disassembly.

Starter

For further information on the starting system, please refer to "Charging and Starting" in the Unit Repair section.

REMOVAL & INSTALLATION

NOTE: The procedures below may vary slightly for different models and years.

OHV Engines

1. Disconnect the negative battery cable. Raise and support the vehicle safely.

2. Disconnect and tag the solenoid wires and battery cable at the starter.

3. Remove the rear starter motor support bracket. Remove the A/C compressor support rod, if equipped.

4. Support the starter motor and remove the 2 starter-to-engine bolts.

5. Remove the starter motor and

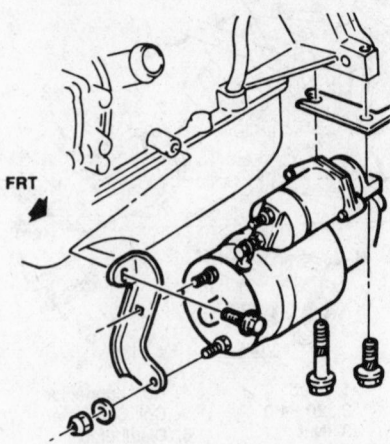

FRT

Starter mounting, OHV engines

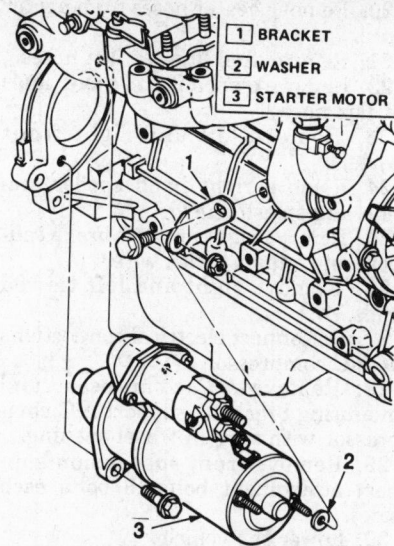

[1] BRACKET
[2] WASHER
[3] STARTER MOTOR

Starter mounting, OHC engines

note the location and number of any shims.

6. Install the starter motor, placing any shims removed in the original location.

7. Tighten the mounting bolts to 25–35 ft. lbs.

8. Install the support bracket and A/C compressor rod, if removed.

9. Connect the starter wiring.

10. Connect the negative battery cable and check the starter operation.

OHC Engines

1. Disconnect the negative battery cable.

2. Remove the air cleaner assembly.

3. Remove the lower starter motor mounting bolt.

4. Remove the rear starter motor brace.

5. Disconnect and tag the wiring at the starter.

6. Remove the upper starter motor mounting bolt.

7. Raise and support the vehicle safely.

8. Disconnect the speedometer cable on automatic transaxle models only.

9. Push the shifter cable up and guide the starter, armature end first, down between the stabilizer bar the engine on automatic transaxle models only.

10. Install the starter motor from under the vehicle, armature end first.

11. Connect the speedometer cable and lower the vehicle.

12. Install the upper and lower mounting bolts. Connect the wiring.

13. Install the rear starter motor brace. Install the air cleaner assembly.

14. Connect the negative battery cable and check the starter motor operation.

ENGINE MECHANICAL

Engine

REMOVAL & INSTALLATION

1982–84 2.0L Engines (Codes B and P)

NOTE: This procedure requires the use of a special powertrain alignment bolt No. M6X1X65. The engine is removed from the top of vehicle.

1. Disconnect the battery cables at the battery and relieve fuel pressure.

2. Remove the air cleaner. Drain the cooling system.

3. Remove the power steering pump, if equipped. Position it out of the way. Leave the lines connected. Remove the windshield washer bottle.

4. If equipped with A/C, remove the relay bracket at the bulkhead connector. Remove the bulkhead connector and separate the wiring harness connections.

5. If equipped with cruise control, remove the servo bracket and position it out of the way.

6. Tag and disconnect all vacuum hoses and wires.

7. Remove the master cylinder from the power brake booster.

8. Disconnect the heater and radiator hoses. Position them out of the way.

9. Remove the fan assembly. Remove the horn.

10. Disconnect the carburetor linkage if so equipped. Raise and support the front of the vehicle safely.

11. Disconnect the fuel line at the intake manifold.

12. Remove the air conditioning brace, if equipped.

13. Remove the exhaust manifold shield. Remove the starter motor.

14. Disconnect the exhaust pipe at the manifold. Remove the front wheel assemblies.

15. Disconnect the stabilizer bar from the lower control arms. Disconnect the ball joints from the steering knuckle.

16. Remove the axleshafts from the transaxle. Remove the transaxle strut.

17. If equipped with A/C, remove the inner fender shield. Remove the drive belt. Tag and disconnect the wires and remove the A/C compressor, without disconnecting any refrigerant lines.

18. Remove the rear engine mount nuts and plate.

19. If equipped with an automatic

transaxle, remove the oil filter.

20. Disconnect the speedometer cable and lower the vehicle.

21. If equipped with an automatic transaxle, remove the oil cooler at the transaxle.

22. Remove the front engine mount nuts.

23. Disconnect the clutch cable on the manual transaxle. Disconnect the detent cable on the automatic transaxle.

NOTE: It may be necessary to remove the engine hood. Using an awl, scribe marks around the hood hinges to help aid correct hood alignment upon installation.

24. Install an engine lifting device. Remove the transaxle mount and bracket. Lift the engine out of the vehicle.

25. Install the engine mount alignment bolt No. M6X1X65 to ensure proper power train alignment.

26. To install, lower the engine into the vehicle, leaving the lifting device attached.

27. Install the transaxle bracket. Install the mount to the side frame and secure with new bolts.

28. With the engine weight not on the mounts, tighten the transaxle bolts. Tighten the right front mount nuts.

29. Lower the engine weight onto the mounts. Remove the lifting device. Raise and support the vehicle safely.

30. Installation of the remaining components is in the reverse order of removal. Check the powertrain alignment bolt; if excessive force is required to remove the bolt, loosen the transaxle bolts and realign the powertrain.

1985–89 2.0L Engines (Codes P And 1)

NOTE: Special tool J–24420 crankshaft pulley hub remover is required. The engine is removed from the top of vehicle.

1. Disconnect battery and relieve fuel pressure.

2. Drain cooling system.

3. Remove air cleaner.

4. Disconnect accelerator and T. V. cables.

5. Disconnect ECM harness at engine.

6. Disconnect necessary vacuum hoses.

7. Disconnect all cooling hoses at engine.

8. Remove exhaust heat shield.

9. If equipped with A/C, remove adjustment bolt at motor mount.

10. Disconnect engine wiring harness at bulkhead.

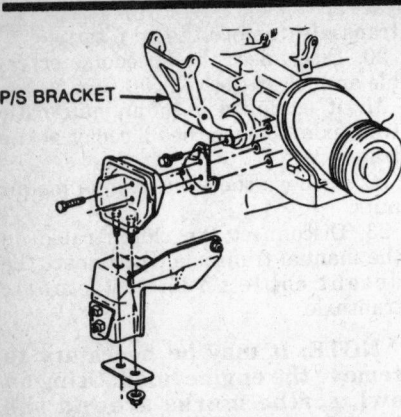

Rear engine mounts on OHV engines

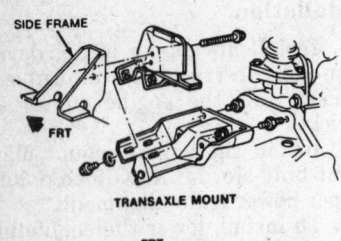

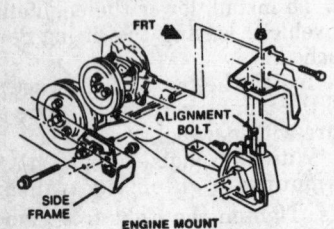

Front engine mounts on OHV engines

11. Remove windshield washer bottle.

12. Remove alternator and power steering belt.

13. Disconnect fuel hoses.

14. Raise vehicle. If equipped with A/C, remove A/C brace.

15. Remove inner fender splash shield.

16. If equipped with A/C, remove A/C compressor.

17. Remove flywheel splash shield.

18. Disconnect and tag starter wires.

19. Disconnect front starter brace.

20. Remove starter.

21. Remove torque converter bolts.

22. Remove crankshaft pulley and hub using tool J–24420 or equivalent.

23. Remove oil filter.

24. Disconnect engine to transmission bracket.

25. Disconnect right rear mount.

26. Disconnect exhaust at manifold and at center hanger.

27. Disconnect T.V. and shift cable.

28. Remove lower 2 bellhousing bolts.

29. Lower vehicle.

30. Remove right front motor mount nuts.

31. Remove alternator and adjusting brace.

32. Disconnect master cylinder and push aside.

NOTE: It may be necessary to remove the engine hood. Using an awl, scribe marks around the hood hinges to help aid correct hood alignment upon installation.

33. Install lifting device.

34. Remove right front motor mount bracket.

35. Remove upper bellhousing bolts.

36. Remove power steering pump while lifting engine.

37. Remove engine.

38. To install reverse removal procedures making sure to adjust all drive belts. On manual transaxle adjust clutch cable. Check fluid all levels and road test vehicle.

1982–86 1.8L Engines
1987–89 2.0L Engines (Codes K and M)

NOTE: This procedure requires the use of a special powertrain alignment bolt No. M6X1X65. The engine is removed from the bottom of the vehicle.

1. Disconnect the negative battery cable and relieve fuel pressure.

2. Drain the cooling system.

3. Remove the air cleaner assembly.

4. Disconnect the engine electrical harness at bulkhead.

5. Disconnect the electrical connector at brake cylinder.

6. Remove the throttle cable from bracket and EFI assembly.

7. Remove and tag the vacuum hoses from EFI assembly.

8. Remove the power steering high pressure hose at cut-off switch.

9. Remove and tag the vacuum hoses at map sensor and canister.

10. Disconnect the air conditioning relay cluster switches.

11. Remove the power steering return hose at pump.

12. Disconnect the ECM wire connections, feed harness through bulkhead and lay harness over engine.

13. Remove the upper and lower radiator hoses from engine.

14. Remove the electrical connections from temperature switch at thermostat housing.

15. Raise and support the vehicle safely.

16. Disconnect the transmission shift cable at transmission.

17. Remove speedometer cable at transmission and bracket.

18. Disconnect exhaust pipe at exhaust manifold.

19. Remove exhaust pipe from converter.

20. Remove heater hoses from heater core.

21. Remove fuel lines at flex hoses.

22. Remove transmission cooler lines at flex hoses.

23. Remove left and right front wheels.

24. Remove right hand spoiler section and splash shield.

25. Remove right and left brake calipers and support with wire.

26. Remove right and left tie rod ends.

27. Disconnect electrical connections at A/C compressor.

28. Remove A/C compressor and mounting brackets, support A/C compressor with wire in wheel opening.

29. Remove front suspension support attachment bolts (6 bolts each side).

30. Lower the vehicle.

31. Support front of vehicle by placing 2 short stands under core support.

32. Position front post hoist to the rear of cowl.

33. Position a 4 x 4 x 6 timber on front post hoist.

34. Raise vehicle enough to remove stands.

35. Position a 4-wheel dolly under engine and transaxle assembly.

36. Position three 4 x 4 x 12 blocks under engine and transaxle assembly only, letting support rails hang free.

37. Lower vehicle onto 4-wheel dolly slightly.

38. Remove rear transaxle mount attachment bolts.

39. Remove left front engine mount attachment bolts.

40. Remove 2 engine support to body attachment bolts behind right hand inner axle U-joint.

41. Remove 1 attaching bolt and nut from right hand chassis side rail to engine mount bracket.

42. Remove 6 strut attachment nuts.

43. Raise vehicle letting engine, transaxle and suspension resting on 4-wheel dolly.

Reverse removal procedure for engine installation with the following exceptions:

1. Position the engine and transaxle assembly in chassis.

2. Install transaxle and left front mounts to side rail bolts loosely.

3. Install M6X1X65 alignment bolt in left front mount to prevent powertrain misalignment.

4. Torque transaxle mount bolts to 42 ft. lbs. and left front mount bolts to 18 ft. lbs.

5. Install right rear mount to body bolts and torque to 38 ft. lbs.

6. Install right rear mount to chassis side rail bolt and nut torque to 38 ft. lbs.

7. Place a lifting device under the control arms. Raise them into position

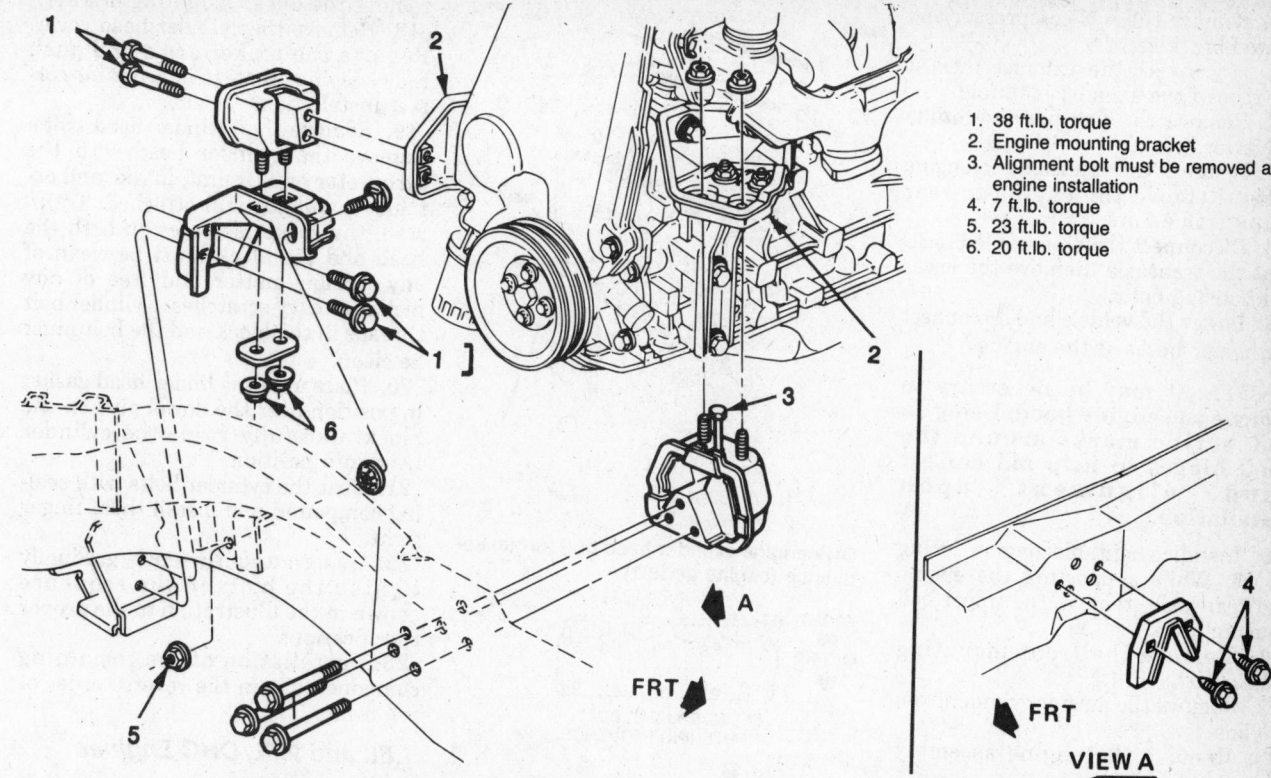

1. 38 ft.lb. torque
2. Engine mounting bracket
3. Alignment bolt must be removed after engine installation
4. 7 ft.lb. torque
5. 23 ft.lb. torque
6. 20 ft.lb. torque

FRT

VIEW A

Front engine mounts on OHC engines. The right mount is for cars without air conditioning

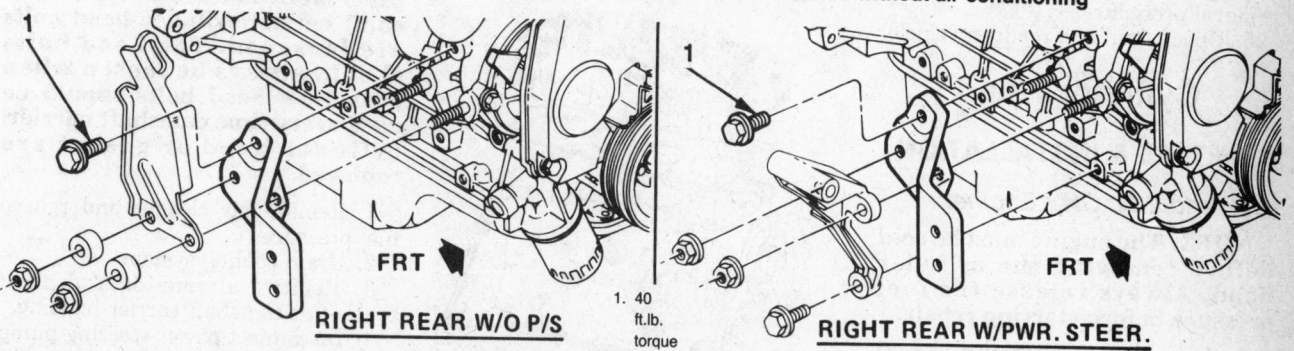

RIGHT REAR W/O P/S

1. 40 ft.lb. torque

RIGHT REAR W/PWR. STEER.

Rear engine mounts on OHC engines

1. 23 ft.lb. torque
2. 38 ft.lb. torque

FRT

RIGHT HAND FRONT W/A.C.

Front right engine mount on OHC engines with air conditioning

and install retaining nuts.

8. Raise and support the vehicle safely.

9. Using suitable lifting equipment, raise the control arms and attach tie rod ends.

10. Check all fluids and roadtest.

1985–89 2.8L V6 Engine

NOTE: Always release the fuel pressure before starting repair. The engine is removed from the top of the vehicle.

1. Disconnect the negative battery cable. Drain the cooling system and remove the air cleaner assembly.

2. Remove the air flow sensor. Remove the exhaust crossover heat shield and remove the crossover pipe.

3. Remove the serpentine belt tensioner and belt.

4. Remove the power steering pump mounting bracket. Disconnect the heater pipe at the power steering pump mounting bracket.

5. Disconnect the radiator hoses from the engine.

6. Disconnect the accelerator and throttle valve cable at the throttle valve.

7. Remove the alternator. Tag and disconnect the wiring harness at the engine.

8. Relieve the fuel pressure and disconnect the fuel hose. Disconnect the coolant bypass and the overflow hoses at the engine.

9. Tag and remove the vacuum hoses to the engine.

10. Raise the vehicle and support it safely.

11. Remove the inner fender splash shield. Remove the harmonic balancer.

12. Remove the flywheel cover. Remove the starter bolts. Tag and disconnect the electrical connections to the starter. Remove the starter.

13. Disconnect the wires at the oil sending unit.

14. Remove the A/C compressor and related brackets.

15. Disconnect the exhaust pipe at the rear of the exhaust manifold.

16. Remove the flex plate-to-torque converter bolts.

17. Remove the transaxle-to-engine bolts. Remove the engine-to-rear mount frame nuts.

18. Disconnect the shift cable bracket at the transaxle. Remove the lower bell housing bolts.

19. Lower the vehicle and disconnect the heater hoses at the engine.

NOTE: It may be necessary to remove the engine hood. Using an awl, scribe marks around the hood hinges to help aid correct hood alignment upon installation.

20. Install a suitable engine lifting device. While supporting the engine and transaxle, remove the upper bell housing bolts.

21. Remove the front mounting bolts.

22. Remove the master cylinder from the booster.

23. Remove the engine assembly from the vehicle.

24. Installation is the reverse of the removal procedure.

25. Check fluid and roadtest vehicle.

Cylinder Head

REMOVAL & INSTALLATION

1.8L and 2.0L OHV Engines

NOTE: The engine must be cold before removing the cylinder head. Always release the fuel pressure before starting repair.

1. Disconnect the negative battery cable.

2. Drain the cooling system into a clean container; the coolant can be reused if it is still good.

3. Remove the air cleaner. Raise and support the front of the vehicle.

4. Remove the exhaust shield. Disconnect the exhaust pipe.

5. Remove the heater hose from the intake manifold. Lower the vehicle.

6. Unscrew the mounting bolts and remove the engine lift bracket (includes air management).

7. Remove the distributor. Disconnect the vacuum manifold at the alternator bracket.

8. Tag and disconnect the remaining vacuum lines at the intake manifold and thermostat.

9. Remove the air management pipe at the exhaust check valve.

10. Disconnect the accelerator linkage at the carburetor or TBI unit and remove the linkage bracket.

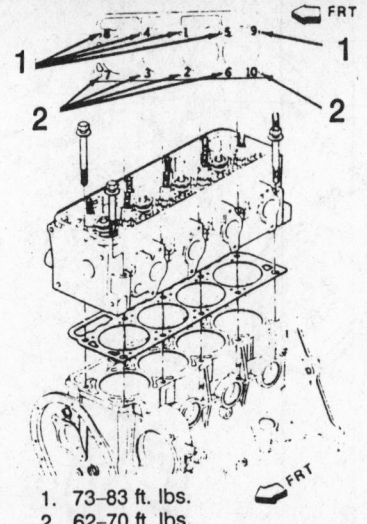

1. 73–83 ft. lbs.
2. 62–70 ft. lbs.

OHV engine cylinder head bolt torque sequence (engine code 1)

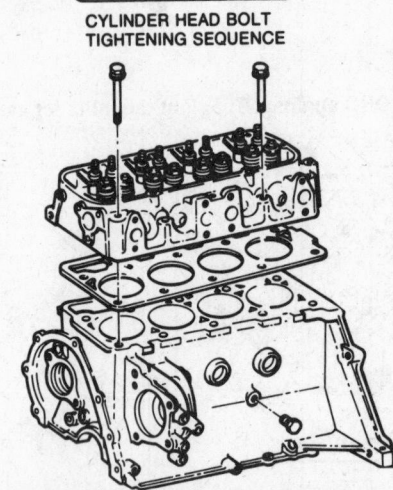

OHV engine cylinder head bolt torque sequence (engine codes B, P, G)

11. Tag and disconnect all necessary wires. Remove the upper radiator hose at the thermostat.

12. Remove the bolt attaching the dipstick tube and hot water bracket.

13. Remove the idler pulley. Remove the A.I.R. and power steering pump drive belts.

14. Remove the A.I.R. bracket-to-intake manifold bolt. If equipped with power steering, remove the air pump pulley, the A.I.R. thru-bolt and the power steering adjusting bracket.

15. Loosen the A.I.R. mounting bracket lower bolt so that the bracket will rotate.

16. Disconnect and plug the fuel line at the carburetor if so equipped.

17. Remove the alternator. Remove the alternator brace from the head and

remove the upper mounting bracket.

18. Remove the cylinder head cover. Remove the rocker arms and push rods keeping all parts in order for correct installation.

19. Remove the cylinder head bolts. Remove the cylinder head with the carburetor or TBI unit, intake and exhaust manifolds still attached. To install, the gasket surfaces on both the head and the block must be clean of any foreign matter and free of any nicks or heavy scratches. Cylinder bolt threads in the block and the bolt must be clean.

20. Place a new cylinder head gasket in position over the dowel pins on the block. Carefully guide the cylinder head into position.

21. Coat the cylinder bolts with sealing compound and install them finger tight.

22. Using a torque wrench, gradually tighten the bolts in the sequence shown in the illustration to the proper specifications.

23. Installation of the remaining components is in the reverse order of removal.

1.8L and 2.0L OHC Engines

NOTE: Cylinder head gasket replacement is necessary if camshaft carrier/cylinder head bolts are loosened. The head bolts should always be loosen when cold. New head bolts should be used every time camshaft carrier/cylinder head or gasket are replaced.

1. Remove air cleaner and relieve fuel pressure.

2. Drain cooling system.

3. Remove alternator and pivot bracket at camshaft carrier housing.

4. Disconnect power steering pump and bracket and lay to one side.

5. Disconnect ignition coil electrical connections and remove coil.

6. Disconnect spark plug wires and distributor cap and remove.

7. Remove throttle cable from bracket at intake manifold.

8. Disconnect throttle cable, downshift cable and T.V. cable from EFI assembly.

9. Disconnect the ECM connectors from the EFI assembly.

10. Remove vacuum brake hose at filter.

11. Disconnect inlet and return fuel lines at flex joints.

12. Remove water pump bypass hose at intake manifold and water pump.

13. Disconnect ECM harness connectors at intake manifold.

14. Disconnect heater hose from intake manifold.

15. Disconnect exhaust pipe at exhaust manifold.

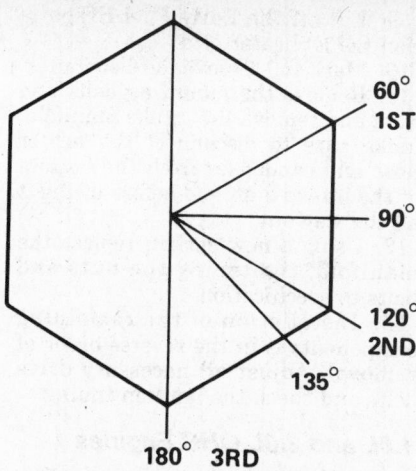

OHC engine cylinder head bolt torque degree sequence

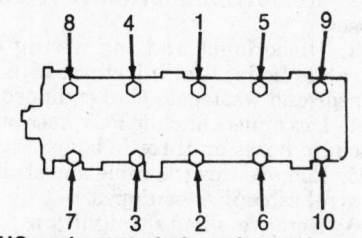

OHC engine camshaft carrier and head bolt tightening sequence

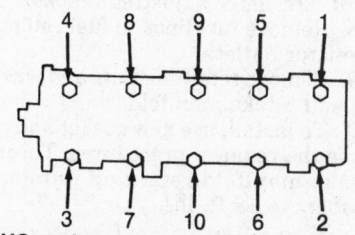

OHC engine camshaft carrier and head bolt loosening sequence

NOTE: On engine code M, remove exhaust manifold to turbo connection and O₂ sensor connection.

16. Disconnect breather hose at camshaft carrier.

17. Remove upper radiator hose.

18. Disconnect engine electrical harness and wires from thermostat housing.

19. Remove timing cover.

20. Remove timing probe holder.

21. Loosen water pump retaining bolts and remove timing belt.

22. Loosen camshaft carrier and cylinder head attaching bolts a little at a time in sequence shown.

23. Remove camshaft carrier assembly.

24. Remove cylinder head, intake manifold and exhaust manifold as an assembly.

25. To install use new gasket and reverse the removal procedures. Apply continuous 3mm bead of anerobic sealer to sealing surface of cam carrier. Torque head bolts in the sequence shown. Make sure to follow the correct torque procedures as stated in the specifications chart.

NOTE: If cylinder head is made of aluminum contamination such as debris, dirt leaves etc. in the spark plug recess area can cause spark plug hole thread damage.

2.8L V6 Engine

LEFT SIDE

1. Drain the cooling system. Remove the rocker cover.

2. Remove the intake manifold. Disconnect the exhaust crossover at the right exhaust manifold.

3. Disconnect the oil level indicator tube bracket.

4. Loosen the rocker arms nuts enough to remove the push rods.

5. Starting with the outer bolts, remove the cylinder head bolts. Remove the cylinder head with the exhaust manifold.

6. Clean and inspect the surfaces of the cylinder head, block and intake manifold. Clean the threads in the block and the threads on the bolts.

7. Align the new gasket over the dowels on the block with the note "This Side Up" facing the cylinder head.

8. Install the cylinder head and exhaust manifold crossover assembly on the engine.

9. Coat the cylinder head bolts with a proper sealer and install the bolts hand tight.

10. Following the correct sequence, torque the bolts to the correct specifications.

11. Install the push rods in the same order that they were removed in. Adjust the valve lash.

NOTE: The valve system on 1987–89 2.8L engine is not adjustable. The correct rocker arm torque is 14–20 ft. lbs.

12. Install the intake manifold using a new gasket and following the correct sequence, torque the bolts to the correct specification.

13. The remainder of the installation is the reverse of the removal.

RIGHT SIDE

1. Disconnect the negative battery cable. Drain the cooling system.

2. Raise and safely support the vehicle. Disconnect the exhaust manifold from the exhaust pipe.

3. Lower the vehicle. Disconnect the exhaust manifold from the cylinder head and remove the manifold.

4. Remove the rocker cover. Remove the intake manifold.

5. Loosen the rocker arms enough so that the push rods can be removed. Note the position of the push rods for assembly.

6. Starting with the outer bolts, remove the cylinder head bolts and remove the cylinder head.

7. Inspect and clean the surfaces of the cylinder head, engine block and intake manifold.

8. Clean the threads in the engine block and the threads on the cylinder head bolts.

9. Align the new gasket on the dowels on the engine block with the note "This Side Up" facing the cylinder head.

10. Install the cylinder head on the engine. Coat the head bolts with a proper sealer. Install and tighten the bolts hand tight.

11. Using the correct sequence, torque the bolts to the correct specifications.

12. Install the push rods in the same order as they were removed. Adjust the valve lash.

NOTE: The valve system on 1987–89 2.8L engine is not adjustable. The correct rocker arm torque is 14–20 ft. lbs.

13. Install the intake manifold using a new gasket. Following the correct sequence, torque the bolts to the proper specification.

14. The remainder of the installation is the reverse of the removal.

OVERHAUL

For all cylinder head overhaul procedures, please refer to "Engine Rebuilding" in the Unit Repair section.

Rocker Arms and Push Rods

REMOVAL & INSTALLATION

OHV Engines

1. Remove the air cleaner. Remove the rocker cover.

2. Remove the rocker arm nut and ball. Lift the rocker arm off the stud and the push rods from the engine. Always keep the valve system parts in order. Install in the same location.

3. To install, coat the rocker arm balls with Molykote®, or equivalent.

4. Install the push rods in the order removed, making sure that they seat properly in the lifter.

5. Install the rocker arms, balls and nuts in the order removed and adjust the valve lash.

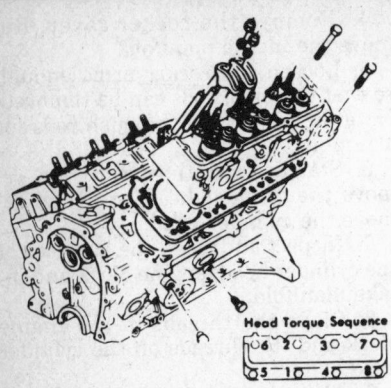

2.8L V6 cylinder head installation

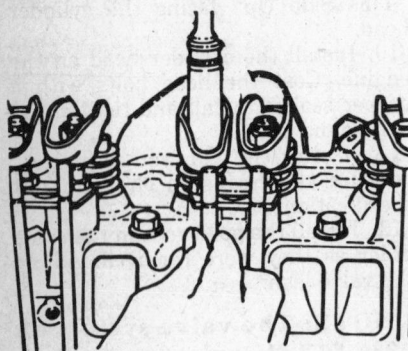

On OHV engines, tighten the rocker arm nut until the pushrod can't be rotated between your fingers

NOTE: 1987-89 the torque should be 11-18 ft. lbs. for 2.0L engine and 14-20 ft. lbs. for 2.8L V6 engine. No other adjustments are necessary.

6. Installation of the remaining components is in the reverse order of removal.

OHC Engines

1. Remove camshaft carrier cover.
2. Hold valves in place with compressed air, using air adapter J-22794 or equivalent in spark plug hole.
3. Compress valve springs with special tool J-33302-25.
4. Remove rocker arms. Keep rocker arms in order for re-assembly.
5. To install reverse the removal procedures using new gasket.

Intake Manifold

REMOVAL & INSTALLATION

1.8L and 2.0L OHV Engines

1. Disconnect the negative battery cable and relieve fuel pressure.
2. Remove the air cleaner. Drain the cooling system.
3. Tag and disconnect all necessary vacuum lines and wires. Remove the idler pulley.

NOTE: AT TIME OF INSTALLATION, FLANGES MUST BE FREE OF OIL. A ⅛ BEAD OF SEALANT MUST BE APPLIED TO FLANGES AND SEALANT MUST BE WET TO TOUCH WHEN BOLTS ARE TORQUED.

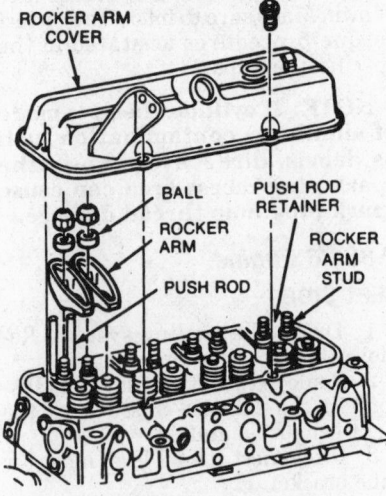

OHV engine rocker arm assembly

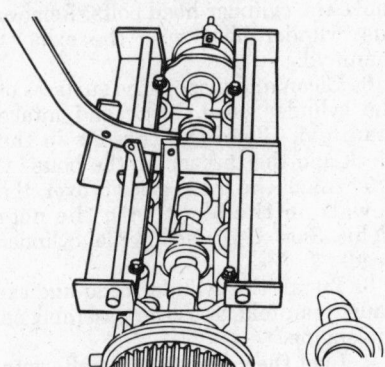

Compressing the valve spring using the valve train compressing tool J-33302, on OHC engines

4. Remove the A.I.R. drive belt. If equipped with power steering, remove the drive belt and remove the pump with the lines attached. Position the pump out of the way.
5. Remove the A.I.R. bracket-to-intake manifold bolt. Remove the air pump pulley.
6. If equipped with power steering, remove the A.I.R. thru-bolt and the power steering pump adjusting bracket.
7. Loosen the lower bolt on the air pump mounting bracket so that the bracket will rotate.
8. Disconnect the fuel line at the carburetor. Disconnect the carburetor linkage and remove the carburetor if so equipped.

NOTE: If fuel injected remove fuel inlet line, TBI linkage and assembly.

9. Lift off the Early Fuel Evaporation (EFE) heater grid.
10. Mark and remove the distributor.
11. Remove the mounting bolts and nuts and remove the intake manifold. Make sure to disconnect the heater hose and condenser from the bottom of the intake manifold before lifting it all the way out.
12. Using a new gasket, replace the manifold, tightening the nuts and bolts to specification.
13. Installation of the remaining components is in the reverse order of removal. Adjust all necessary drive belts and check the ignition timing.

1.8L and 2.0L OHC Engines

1. Release the fuel pressure. Disconnect the negative battery terminal from the battery.
2. Remove induction tube and hoses.
3. Disconnect and tag wiring to throttle body, fuel injectors, M.A.P sensor and wastegate if so equipped.
4. Disconnect and tag PCV hose and vacuum hoses on throttle body.
5. Remove throttle cable and cruise control cable if so equipped.
6. Remove wiring to ignition coil and remove manifold support bracket.
7. Remove rear bolt from alternator bracket, P/S adjusting bracket and front alternator adjusting bracket.
8. Remove fuel lines to fuel rail and regulator outlet.
9. Remove retaining nuts and washers and intake manifold.
10. To install, use new gasket and reverse the removal procedures. Torque intake manifold retaining nuts and washers to 18 ft. lbs.

NOTE: The rear adjusting bracket must be the last part secured to prevent distorting the accessory drive system this will prevent the belt from coming off.

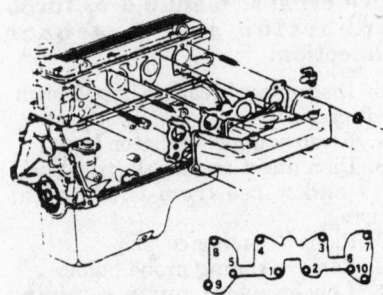

Intake manifold installation and torque sequence (engine code 1)

2.8L V6 Engine

1. Disconnect the negative battery cable and relieve fuel pressure.
2. Disconnect the accelerator cable bracket at the plenum.

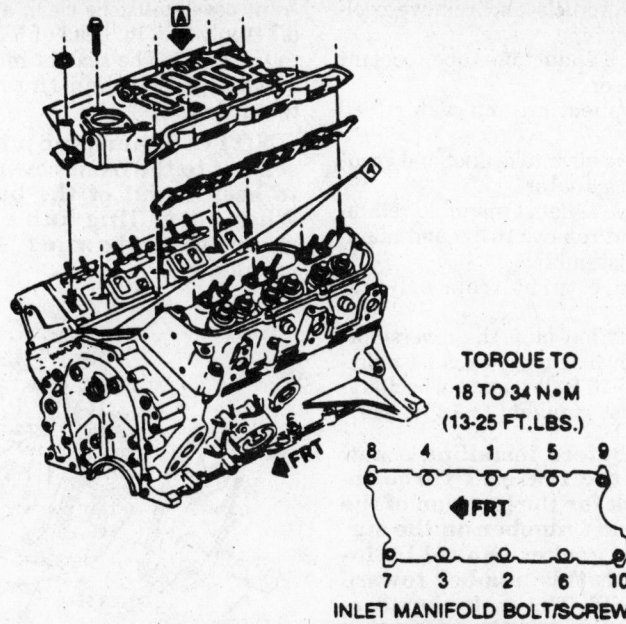

**TORQUE TO
18 TO 34 N•M
(13-25 FT.LBS.)**

```
8   4   1   5   9
        ◀FRT
7   3   2   6   10
```

**INLET MANIFOLD BOLT/SCREW
& NUT TIGHTENING SEQUENCE**

(A) **NOTE** APPLY A SMOOTH CONTINUOUS BEAD
APPROX. 2.0-3.0 WIDE AND 3.0-5.0 THICK
ON BOTH SURFACES. BEAD CONFIGURATION
MUST INSURE COMPLETE SEALING OF WATER
AND OIL. SURFACE MUST BE FREE OF OIL
AND DIRT TO INSURE ADEQUATE SEAL.

2.8L V6 intake manifold installation

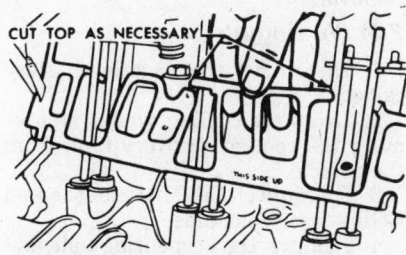

Installing intake manifold gasket on 2.8L V6 engine

3. Disconnect the throttle body and the EGR pipe from the EGR valve. Remove the plenum assembly.

4. Disconnect the fuel line along the fuel rail.

5. Disconnect the serpentine drive belt. Remove the power steering pump mounting bracket.

6. Remove the heater pipe at the power steering pump bracket.

7. Tag and disconnect the wiring at the alternator and remove the alternator.

8. Disconnect the wires from the cold start injector assembly. Remove the injector assembly from the intake manifold.

9. Disconnect the idle air vacuum hose at the throttle body. Disconnect the wires at the injectors.

10. Remove the fuel rail, breather tube and the fuel runners from the engine.

11. Tag and disconnect the coil wires.

12. Remove the rocker arm covers. Drain the cooling system, the disconnect the radiator hose at the thermostat housing. Disconnec the heater hose from the thermostat housing and the thermostat wiring.

13. Mark and remove the distributor.

14. Remove the thermostat assembly housing.

15. Remove the intake manifold bolts and remove the intake manifold from the engine.

16. Installation is the reverse of removal. Upon installation, note that the gaskets are marked for right and left sides. Torque the intake manifold bolts to specifications in the sequence shown.

Exhaust Manifold

REMOVAL & INSTALLATION

1.8L and 2.0L OHV Engines

1. Disconnect the negative battery cable.

2. Remove the air cleaner. Remove the exhaust manifold shield. Raise and support the front of the vehicle.

3. Disconnect the exhaust pipe at the manifold and lower the vehicle.

4. Disconnect the air management-to-check valve hose and remove the bracket. Disconnect the oxygen sensor lead wire.

5. Remove the alternator belt. Remove the alternator adjusting bolts, loosen the pivot bolt and pivot the alternator upward.

6. Remove the alternator brace and the A.I.R. pipes bracket bolt.

7. Unscrew the mounting bolts and remove the exhaust manifold. The manifold should be removed with the A.I.R. plumbing as an assembly. If the manifold is to be replaced, transfer the plumbing to the new one.

8. Clean the mating surfaces on the manifold and the head, position the manifold and tighten the bolts to the proper specifications.

9. Installation of the remaining components is in the reverse order of removal.

1.8L and 2.0L OHC Engines

1. Disconnect the negative battery cable.

2. Remove turbo induction tube if so equipped.

3. Remove and tag spark plug wires.

4. Remove turbo assembly from exhaust manifold if so equipped.

5. Remove exhaust manifold retaining nuts and manifold.

6. Installation is in the reverse order of removal. Torque exhaust manifold bolts to 16 ft. lbs. and turbocharger-to-exhaust manifold to 18 ft. lbs. if so equipped.

NOTE: Before installing a new gasket on the 1.8L MFI Turbo engine (code J), check for the location of the stamped part number on the surface. This gasket should be installed with this number toward the manifold. The gasket appears to be the same in either direction but it is not. Installing the gasket backwards will result in a leak.

2.8L V6 Engine

LEFT SIDE

1. Disconnect the negative battery cable and drain coolant.

2. Remove the air cleaner assembly and inlet hose.

3. Remove the air flow sensor. Remove the engine heat shield.

4. Disconnect the crossover pipe at the manifold.

5. Remove the exhaust manifold bolts.

6. Remove the exhaust manifold.

7. Installation is the reverse of removal.

RIGHT SIDE

1. Disconnect the negative battery cable.

2. Remove the air cleaner assembly.

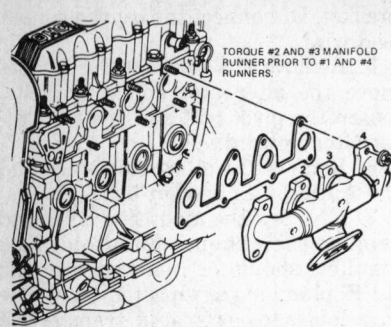

Exhaust manifold torque sequence—1.8 turbocharged engine

3. Remove the air flow sensor. Remove the engine heat shield.

4. Disconnect the crossover pipe at the manifold.

5. Disconnect the accelerator and throttle valve cable at the throttle lever and the plenum. Move aside to gain working clearance.

6. Disconnect the power steering line at the power steering pump.

7. Remove the EGR valve assembly.

8. Raise the vehicle and support it safely.

9. Disconnect the exhaust pipe at the exhaust manifold.

10. Lower the vehicle.

11. Remove the manifold bolts and remove the exhaust manifold.

12. Installation is the reverse of removal.

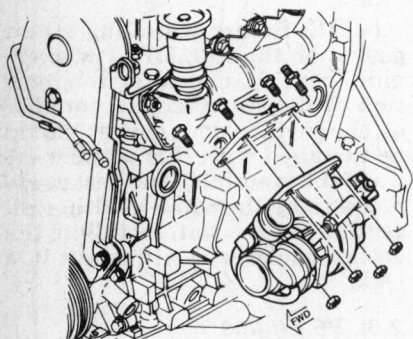

Turbocharger mounting

Turbocharger

REMOVAL & INSTALLATION

1.8L and 2.0L OHC Engines

1. Disconnect the negative battery cable.

2. Raise car and suitably support.

3. Lower fan retaining screws.

4. Disconnect exhaust pipe.

5. Remove A/C rear support bracket.

6. Remove turbo support bracket to engine.

7. Disconnect oil drain and water return pipe at turbo.

8. Lower vehicle and remove coolant recovery pipe.

9. Remove induction tube, coolant fan, O_2 sensor.

10. Disconnect oil and water feed pipe.

11. Remove air intake duct and vacuum hose at actuator.

12. Remove exhaust manifold retaining nuts and remove turbo and manifold as an assembly.

13. Remove turbo from exhaust manifold.

14. Installation is in the reverse order of removal. Torque exhaust manifold bolts to 16 ft. lbs. and turbocharger-to-exhaust manifold to 18 ft. lbs.

NOTE: Before installing a new gasket on the 1.8L MFI Turbo engine, check for the location of the stamped part number on the surface. This gasket should be installed with this number toward the manifold. The gasket appears to be the same in either direction but it is not. Installing the gasket backwards will result in a leak.

TROUBLESHOOTING

NOTE: For more information on turbocharging, please refer to "Turbocharging" in the Unit Repair section.

Front Cover

REMOVAL & INSTALLATION

1.8L and 2.0L OHV Engines

NOTE: The following procedure requires the use of a front cover centering tool J–35468 and crankshaft puller J–24420.

1. Disconnect battery cables. Remove the engine drive belts.

2. Although not absolutely necessary, removal of the right front inner fender splash shield will facilitate access to the front cover.

3. Remove the center bolt from the crankshaft pulley and retaining bolts and remove pulley. Using a puller J–24420 or equivalent remove hub from the crankshaft.

4. Remove the alternator lower bracket.

5. Remove the oil pan-to-front cover bolts.

NOTE: It may be necessary to remove oil pan to remove front cover.

6. Remove the front cover-to-block bolts and remove the front cover. If the front cover is difficult to remove, use a plastic mallet.

7. The surfaces of the block and front cover must be clean and free of oil. Apply a $\frac{1}{8}$ in. bead of RTV sealant to the cover. The sealant must be wet to the touch when the bolts are torqued down.

NOTE: When applying RTV sealant to the front cover, be sure to keep it out of the bolt holes. When installing hub or pulley note position of key on crankshaft.

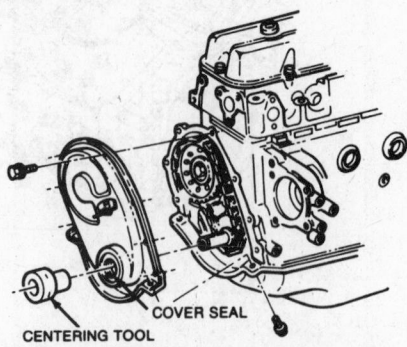

Front cover installation on OHV engines; a centering tool will aid in positioning

8. Position the front cover on the block using a centering tool J–35468 and tighten the screws.

9. Installation of the remaining components is in the reverse order of removal.

2.8L V6 Engine

1. Disconnect the negative battery cable.

2. Drain the cooling system and remove the coolant recovery tank from the vehicle.

3. Disconnect the MAP sensor and EGR sensor solenoids.

4. Remove the serpentine belt and adjusting pulley.

5. Tag and disconnect the heater hose at the power steering bracket.

6. Tag and disconnect the alternator wiring and remove the alternator.

7. Raise the vehicle and support it safely.

8. Remove the inner fender splash shield.

9. Remove the harmonic balancer with tool J–24420 or equivalent puller.

10. Remove the pan to block bolts. Remove the lower cover bolts.

11. Lower the vehicle and disconnect the radiator hoses at the water pump.

12. Remove the heater hose from the thermostat housing.

13. Disconnect the overflow hoses and the canister purge hose.

14. Remove the front cover.

15. Installation is the reverse of removal. Upon installation, apply a 3mm coninuous bead of RTV sealant to the oil pan surface and make sure all mating surfaces are clean of old gasket material.

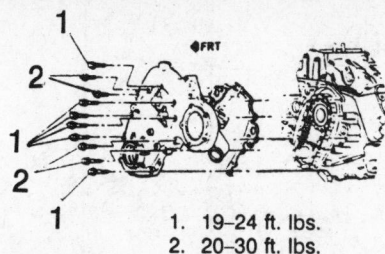

1. 19–24 ft. lbs.
2. 20–30 ft. lbs.

Front cover assembly 2.8L engine

1.8L OHC Engine

1. Disconnect negative battery cable.
2. Remove alternator pivot bolts and power steering belt.
3. Disconnect canister purge hose.
4. Remove upper timing belt cover retaining bolts.
5. Raise vehicle and support safely.
6. Remove right front wheel assembly and remove splash shield.
7. Remove lower timing belt cover retaining bolts.
8. Remove timing belt cover.
9. To install reverse removal procedures.

2.0L OHC Engine

1. Disconnect negative battery cable.
2. Remove tensioner and bolt.
3. Remove serpentine belt.
4. Unsnap upper and lower cover.
5. To install reverse the removal procedures.

OIL SEAL REPLACEMENT

OHV Engines

The oil seal can be replaced with the front cover either on or off the engine. If the cover is on the engine, remove the crankshaft pulley and hub first. Pry out the seal using a suitable tool, being careful not to distort the seal mating surfaces. Install the new seal so that the open, or helical side, is towards the engine. Press it into place with a seal driver. Install the hub and pulley, if removed.

OHC Engines

1. Remove the crankshaft sprocket.
2. Remove the crankshaft key and rear thrust washer.
3. Using a suitable prybar, pry out the front oil seal.
4. Place the protective sleeve of special tool set J33083 (Seal Installer), onto the crankshaft.
5. Lubricate the lip of the new seal. Using special tool J33083, install the seal.
6. Remove the protective.
7. Install the rear thrust washer and key on the crankshaft.
8. Install the crankshaft sprocket.

Timing Chain and Sprockets

REMOVAL & INSTALLATION

1.8L and 2.0L OHV Engines

1. Remove the front cover.
2. Place the No. 1 piston at **TDC** of the compression stroke so that the marks on the camshaft and crankshaft sprockets are in alignment.
3. Loosen the timing chain tensioner nut as far as possible without actually removing it.
4. Remove the camshaft sprocket bolts and remove the sprocket and chain together. If the sprocket does not slide from the camshaft easily, a light blow with a soft tool at the lower edge of the sprocket will dislodge it.
5. Use a gear puller J–2288–8–20 and remove the crankshaft sprocket.
6. Press the new crankshaft sprocket back onto the crankshaft.
7. Install the timing chain over the camshaft sprocket and around the crankshaft sprocket. Make sure that the marks on the 2 sprockets are in alignment. Lubricate the thrust surface with Molykote®, or equivalent.
8. Align the dowel in the camshaft with the dowel hole in the sprocket and install the sprocket onto the camshaft. Use the mounting bolts to draw the sprocket onto the camshaft and tighten them to 27–33 ft. lbs.

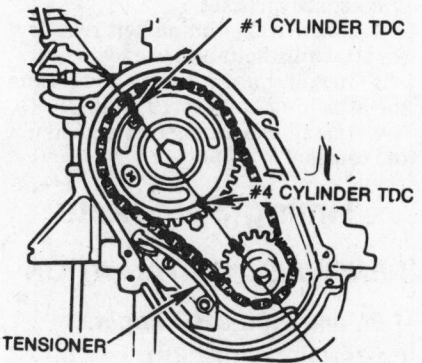

Timing mark alignment on OHV engines

9. Lubricate the timing chain with clean engine oil. Tighten the chain tensioner.
10. Installation of the remaining components is in the reverse order of the removal procedure.

2.8L V6 Engine

1. Disconnect the negative battery cable.
2. Remove the front cover.
3. Position the No. 1 piston at **TDC** with the marks on the crankshaft and camshaft sprockets aligned.

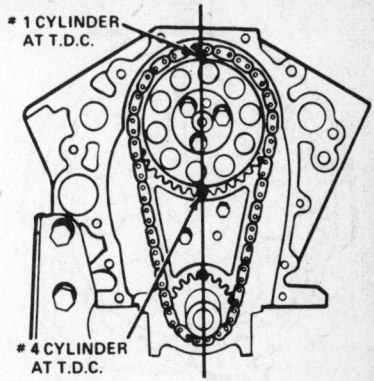

Timing mark alignment on 2.8L V6 engine

4. Remove the camshaft sprocket bolts.
5. Remove the camshaft sprocket and chain from the front of the engine.

NOTE: If the sprocket does not move freely from the camshaft, a light blow using a plastic tool on the lower edge of the sprocket should dislodge it.

6. Installation is the reverse of removal. Draw the camshaft sprocket onto the camshaft using the mounting bolts. Lubricate the timing chain with engine oil prior to installation.

Timing Belt and Tensioner

REMOVAL/INSTALLATION & ADJUSTMENT

1.8L and 2.0L OHC Engines

NOTE: The following procedure requires the use of special tools.

1. Disconnect negative battery cable.
2. Remove timing belt cover.
3. Remove crankshaft pulley.
4. Drain radiator and remove coolant reservoir.
5. Loosen water pump bolts and remove timing belt.
6. Install new timing belt and crankshaft pulley.

NOTE: Check if the mark on the camshaft sprocket lines up with mark on the rear timing belt cover. The timing mark on the crankshaft pulley should line up at 10 degrees BTDC on the indicator scale. DO NOT turn camshaft. Use only crankshaft nut to turn. Turning the nut on the camshaft directly can damage the camshaft bearings.

7. Adjust timing belt to specifica-

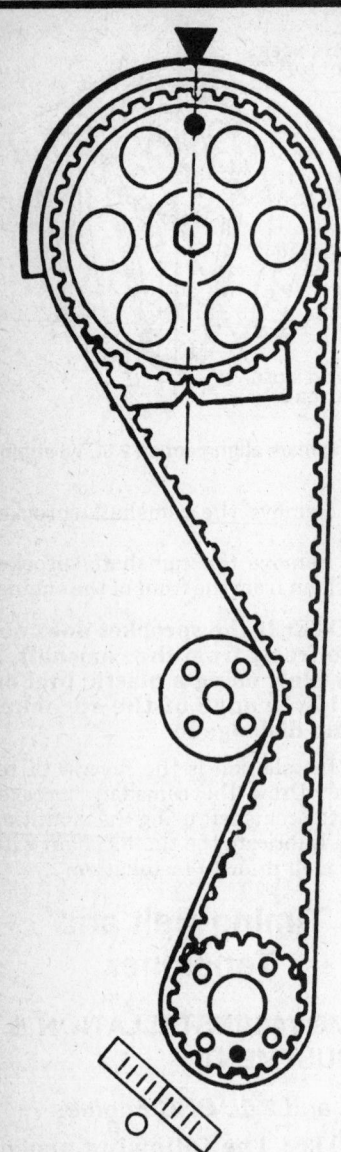

OHC timing belt installation—typical

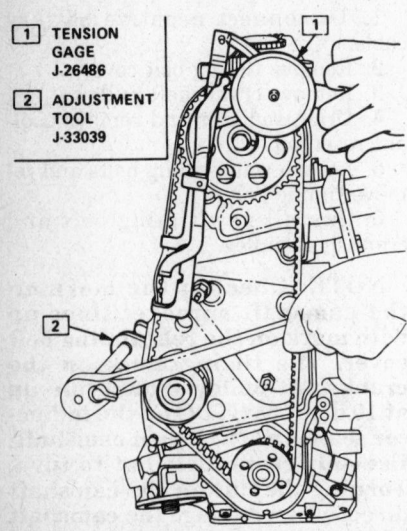

| 1 | TENSION GAGE J-26486 |
| 2 | ADJUSTMENT TOOL J-33039 |

Timing belt tension adjustment on OHC engines

tions using tool J – 26486 – A or equivalent. Tool J-33039 or equivalent is used to adjust water pump which removes slack from timing belt. The correct adjusting tension for timing belt is a band marked on the tool. Never adjust belt tension with gauge installed this will result in an incorrect reading.

8. Crank engine (without starting) 10 revolutions. As new belt takes position tension loss will occur. Recheck tension with gauge.

NOTE: The timing mark on the camshaft gear and rear timing belt cover must be aligned during the final tension recheck or reset.

9. Tighten water pump bolts to 19 ft. lbs.
10. Reverse the remaining removal procedures.

NOTE: Whenever a timing belt is replaced on a 1.8L OHC (code 0, J) engine it must be adjusted when the engine is at normal operating temperature (thermostat open).

Timing Belt Rear Cover

REMOVAL & INSTALLATION

1.8L and 2.0L OHC Engines

1. Remove the timing belt from the crankshaft sprocket.
2. Remove the timing belt rear covers attaching bolts and the rear covers.
3. Install the rear covers and torque the attaching bolts to 19 ft. lbs.
4. Install the timing belt and adjust the tension.

Timing Sprockets

REMOVAL & INSTALLATION

1.8L and 2.0L OHC Engines
CAMSHAFT SPROCKET

1. Remove the timing belt front cover.
2. Align the mark on camshaft sprocket with mark on camshaft carrier.
3. Remove timing probe holder if so equipped.
4. Loosen the water pump retaining bolts and remove the timing belt from the camshaft sprocket.
5. Remove the camshaft carrier cover.
6. Hold the camshaft with an open-end wrench. For this purpose a hexagonal is provided in the camshaft. Remove the camshaft sprocket retaining bolt and washer and sprocket.

Camshaft sprocket removal on OHC engines

7. Install the camshaft sprocket and align marks on camshaft sprocket and camshaft carrier.
8. Hold the camshaft with a open-end wrench. Install the sprocket washer and retaining bolt. Torque to 34 ft. lbs.
9. Install the camshaft carrier cover.
10. Install the timing belt on sprockets and adjust.
11. Install timing probe holder. Torque nuts to 19 ft. lbs.
12. Install timing belt front cover.

CRANKSHAFT SPROCKET

1. Remove the timing belt from the crankshaft sprocket.
2. Remove the crankshaft sprocket to crankshaft attaching bolt and the thrust washer.
3. Remove the sprocket.
4. Position the sprocket over the key on end of crankshaft.
5. Install the thrust washer and the attaching bolt. Torque to 115 ft. lbs.
6. Install the timing belt and adjust.

Camshaft

REMOVAL & INSTALLATION

1.8L and 2.0L OHV Engines

1. Remove the engine.
2. Remove the intake manifold.
3. Remove the cylinder head cover, pivot the rocker arms to the sides, and remove the pushrods, keeping them in order. Remove the valve lifters, keeping them in order. There are special tools which make lifter removal easier.
4. Remove the front cover.
5. Remove the distributor.
6. Remove the fuel pump and its pushrod.
7. Remove the timing chain and sprocket.
8. Carefully pull the camshaft from the block, being sure that the camshaft lobes do not contact the bearings.

9. To install, lubricate the camshaft journals with clean engine oil. Lubricate the lobes with Molykote® or the equivalent. Install the camshaft into the engine, being extremely careful not to contact the bearings with the cam lobes.

10. Install the timing chain and sprocket. Install the fuel pump and pushrod. Install the timing cover. Install the distributor.

11. Install the valve lifters. If a new camshaft has been installed, new lifters should be used to ensure durability of the cam lobes.

12. Install the pushrods and rocker arms and the intake manifold. Adjust the valve lash after installing the engine. Install the cylinder head cover.

1.8L and 2.0L OHC Engines

NOTE: The following procedure requires the use of a special tool.

1. Remove camshaft carrier cover.

2. Hold valves in place with compressed air, using an air adapter J-22794 or equivalent in the spark plug hole. Compress the valve springs with a special tool J-33302–25 and remove rocker arms. Keep rocker arms in order for re-assembly.

3. Remove timing belt front cover.

4. Remove timing belt.

5. Remove camshaft sprocket.

6. Mark and remove distributor.

7. Remove camshaft thrust plate from rear of camshaft carrier.

8. Slide camshaft rearward and remove it from the carrier.

9. Install a new camshaft carrier front oil seal using Tool J–33085 or equivalent.

10. Place camshaft in the carrier.

NOTE: Take care not to damage the carrier front oil seal when installing the camshaft.

11. Install camshaft thrust plate retaining bolts. Torque bolts to 70 inch lbs.

12. Check camshaft end play, which should be within 0.016–0.064 in.

13. Install the distributor.

14. Install the camshaft sprocket.

15. Install the timing belt.

16. Install the timing belt front cover.

17. Using an air adapter J-22794 or equivalent in spark plug hole to hold valve closed and valve train compressing fixture J-33302, compress valve springs and replace rocker arms.

18. Install camshaft carrier cover.

2.8L V6 Engine

1. Disconnect the negative battery cable. Remove the engine assembly from the vehicle.

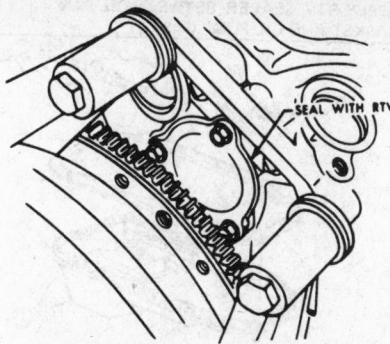

Camshaft rear cover on 2.8L V6

2. Remove the intake manifold as described earlier.

3. Remove the rocker arm covers. Remove the rocker arm nuts, balls, rocker arms and pushrods.

NOTE: Always keep valve train parts in order for correct installation.

4. Remove the upper front cover bolts. Remove the lower cover bolts and the front cover.

5. Remove the camshaft sprocket bolts, camshaft sprocket and timing chain.

6. Remove the camshaft by carefully sliding it out the front of the engine. Measure the camshaft bearing journals using a micrometer and replace the camshaft if the journals exceed 0.0009 in. (0.025mm) out of round.

7. Installation is the reverse of removal. When installing a new camshaft, lubricate the camshaft lobes with GM E.O.S. or equivalent.

Camshaft Carrier

REMOVAL & INSTALLATION

1.8L and 2.0L OHC Engines

NOTE: Whenever the camshaft carrier bolts are loosened, it is necessary to remove the cylinder head and replace the cylinder head gasket.

1. Disconnect the crankcase ventilation hose from the camshaft carrier.

2. Remove the distributor.

3. Remove the camshaft sprocket.

4. Loosen the camshaft carrier and cylinder head attaching bolts a little at a time in sequence.

NOTE: Camshaft carrier and cylinder head bolts should be loosened in sequence and only when the engine is cold.

5. Remove the camshaft carrier.

6. Remove the camshaft thrust plate from the rear of the camshaft carrier.

7. Slide the camshaft rearward and remove it from the carrier.

8. Remove the carrier front oil seal.

9. Install a new carrier front oil seal using Tool J-33085.

10. Place the camshaft in the carrier.

NOTE: Take care not to damage the carrier front oil seal when installing the camshaft.

11. Install the camshaft thrust plate and the retaining bolts. Torque the bolts to 70 inch lbs.

12. Check the camshaft end-play which should be within 0.016–0.064 in. (0.04–0.16mm).

13. Clean the sealing surfaces on cylinder head and carrier. Apply a continuous 3mm bead of RTV sealer.

14. Install the camshaft carrier on the cylinder head.

15. Install the camshaft carrier and cylinder head attaching bolts.

16. Torque the bolts a little at a time in the proper sequence, to 18 ft. lbs. Turn each bolt 60 degrees clockwise in the proper sequence for 3 times until a 180 degrees rotation is obtained, or equivalent to ½ turn.

NOTE: After remainder of installation is completed, start engine and let it run until thermo-

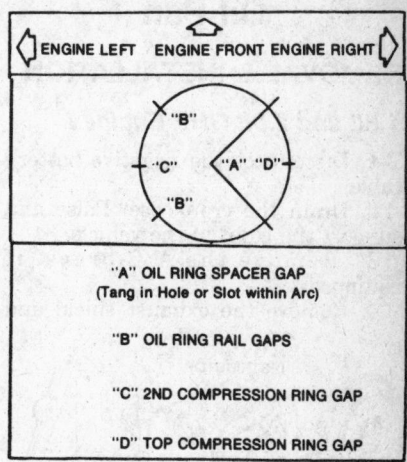

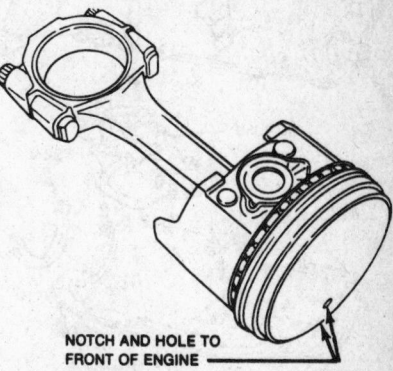

NOTCH AND HOLE TO FRONT OF ENGINE

Install the piston and rod with the notch and/or hole facing front (engine's front end)

stat opens. Torque all bolts an additional 30–50 degrees in the proper sequence.

17. Install the camshaft sprocket.
18. Install the distributor.
19. Connect the positive crankcase ventilation hose to the camshaft carrier.

Piston and Connecting Rod

POSITIONING

Pistons are installed with the notch in the top of the piston facing the front end of the engine.

For all piston and connecting rod overhaul procedures, please refer to "Engine Rebuilding" in the Unit Repair section.

ENGINE LUBRICATION

Oil Pan

REMOVAL & INSTALLATION

1.8L and 2.0L OHV Engines

1. Disconnect the negative battery cable.
2. Drain the crankcase. Raise and support the front of the vehicle.
3. Remove the A/C brace, if equipped.
4. Remove the exhaust shield and

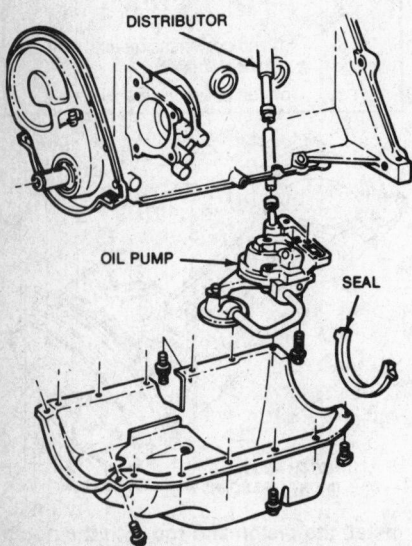

OHV engine oil pan and pump mounting

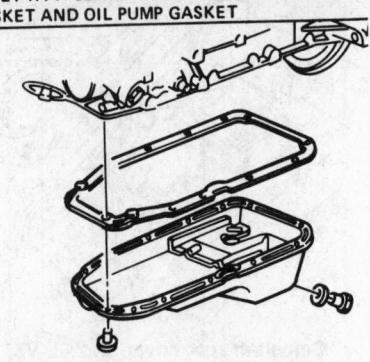

APPLY RTV SEALER BETWEEN OIL PAN GASKET AND OIL PUMP GASKET

OHC engine oil pan mounting

disconnect the exhaust pipe at the manifold.
5. Remove the starter motor and position it out of the way.
6. Remove the flywheel cover. Remove the oil pan.

NOTE: Prior to oil pan installation, check that the sealing surfaces on the pan, cylinder block and front cover are clean and free of oil. If installing the old oil pan, be sure that all old RTV has been removed.

7. Apply a ⅛ in. bead of RTV sealant to the oil pan sealing surface. Use a new oil pan rear seal and install the pan in place. Tighten the bolts to 9–13 ft. lbs.
8. Installation of the remaining components is in the reverse order of removal.

1.8L and 2.0L OHC Engines

1. Disconnect the negative battery terminal from the battery.
2. Raise and support the vehicle.
3. Remove right front wheel assembly.
4. Remove front splash shield.
5. Drain crankcase.
6. Remove exhaust pipe from manifold on turbocharged models remove exhaust pipe from wastegate.
7. Remove flywheel cover and oil pan scraper.
8. To install reverse removal procedures. Use gasket and sealant. Torque oil pan bolts to 4 ft. lbs.

2.8L V6 Engine

1. Disconnect the negative battery cable.
2. Raise the vehicle and support it safely.
3. Drain the engine oil.
4. Remove the flywheel dust cover.
5. Tag and disconnect the electrical connections at the starter motor.
6. Remove the starter retainer bolts and remove the starter.

7. Remove the oil pan bolts and remove the oil pan.
8. Installation is the reverse of the removal procedure. Clean the gasket surfaces and install a new gasket.
9. Fill the engine with oil, start the engine and check for leaks.

Rear Main Bearing Oil Seal

REMOVAL & INSTALLATION

1.8L and 2.0L OHV Engines
1982–84

1. Remove the oil pan and pump.
2. Remove the rear main bearing cap.
3. Gently pack the upper seal into the groove approximately ¼ in. on each side.
4. Measure the amount the seal was driven in on one side and add ¹⁄₁₆ in. Cut this length from the old lower cap seal. Be sure to get a sharp cut. Repeat for the other side.
5. Place the piece of cut seal into the groove and pack the seal into the block. Do this for each side.
6. Install a piece of Plastigage or the equivalent on the bearing journal. Install the rear cap and tighten to 70 ft. lbs. Remove the cap and check the gauge for bearing clearance. If out of specification, the ends of the seal may be frayed or not flush, preventing the cap from proper seating. Correct as required.
7. Clean the journal, and apply a thin film of sealer to the mating surfaces of the cap and tighten to 70 ft. lbs. Install the pan and pump.

1985–89

1. Disconnect the negative battery cable.
2. Support the engine and remove the transaxle assembly.
3. Remove the flywheel and verify that the leak is originating from the rear main seal.
4. Remove the seal from the dust lip.
5. Clean the cylinder block and crankshaft sealing surface.
6. Inspect the crankshaft for damage. Coat the seal and engine mating surface with engine oil.
7. Install the new seal using seal installation tool J–34686 or equivalent. For remainder of installation, reverse the removal procedure.

NOTE: Some 1982 1.8L OHV engines, may experience a rear main seal oil leak. To correct this condition a new crankshaft part No. 14086053 and a 1 piece rear main seal kit part No. 14081761 has

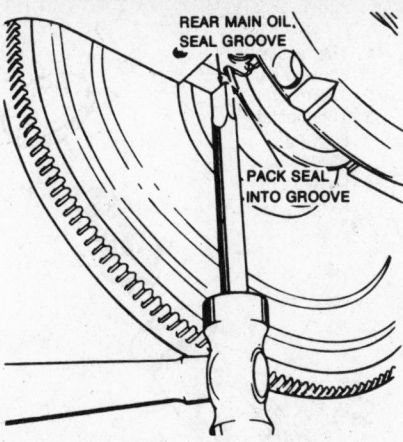

On OHV engines, pack the upper seal into its groove, ¼ inch on each side

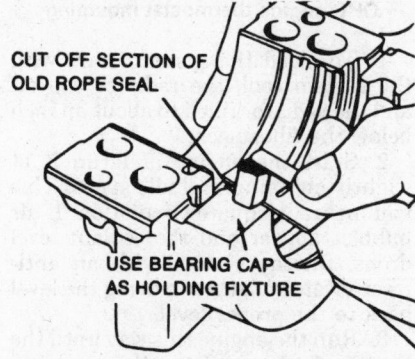

On OHV engines, use the bearing cap to hold the lower seal while you cut it

COATED AREA INDICATED WITH #1052357 SEALER OR EQUIVALENT.

Applying sealer to the rear cap on OHV engines

been released for service. The 1 piece seal kit contains an installation tool, rear main seal and instruction sheet.

1.8L and 2.0L OHC Engines

NOTE: The rear main bearing oil seal is a 1 piece unit and can be replaced without the removal of the oil pan or crankshaft.

1. Remove the transaxle.
2. If equipped with a manual transaxle remove the pressure plate and clutch disc.

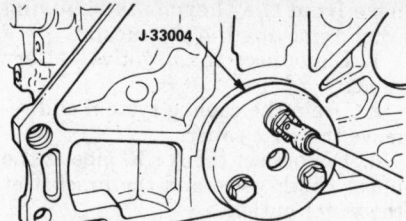

Rear main seal installation on OHC engines

3. Remove the flywheel-to-crankshaft bolts and the flywheel.
4. Using a medium pry bar, pry out the old seal; Be careful not to scratch the crankshaft surface.
5. Clean the block and crankshaft-to-seal mating surfaces.
6. Using the Seal Installation tool No. J–34924 or equivalent, install the new rear seal into the block. Lubricate the outside of the seal to aid installation and press the seal in evenly with the tool.
7. To install, reverse the removal procedures. Use new bolts and torque flywheel to specifications. If equipped with flexplate torque to specification and using same bolts.

2.8L V6 Engine

1. Disconnect the negative battery cable.
2. Support the engine and remove the transaxle assembly.
3. Remove the flywheel and verify that the leak is originating from the rear main seal.
4. Remove the seal from the dust lip.

NOTE: Care must be exercised during removal so as not to damage the crankshaft outside diameter area.

5. Clean the cylinder block and crankshaft sealing surface.
6. Inspect the crankshaft for nicks, burrs, scratches, etc.
7. Coat the seal and the engine mating surface with engine oil.
8. Install the new seal using seal installation tool J–34686 or equivalent.
9. To complete installation reverse remaining removal procedure.

Oil Pump

REMOVAL & INSTALLATION

1.8L and 2.0L OHV Engines

1. Remove the engine oil pan.
2. Remove the pump attaching bolts and carefully lower the pump.
3. Install in reverse order. To ensure immediate oil pressure on start-

up, the oil pump gear cavity should be packed with petroleum jelly. Installation torque is 26–35 ft. lbs.

1.8L and 2.0L OHC Engines

1. Remove the crankshaft sprocket.
2. Remove the timing belt rear cover.
3. Disconnect the connector at oil pressure switch.
4. Remove the oil pan.
5. Remove the oil filter.
6. Unbolt and remove the oil pick-up tube.
7. Unbolt and remove the oil pump.
8. Installation is the reverse of removal. Use new gaskets in all instances. Torque the oil pump bolts to 5 ft. lbs. Torque the oil pan bolts to 4 ft. lbs., and the oil pick-up tube bolts to 5 ft. lbs.

2.8L V6 Engine

1. Disconnect the negative battery cable.
2. Drain the engine oil and remove the oil pan.
3. Remove the rear main bearing cap.
4. Remove the oil pump and extension shaft.
5. Installation is the reverse of the removal procedure.

ENGINE COOLING

Radiator

REMOVAL & INSTALLATION

All Models

1. Disconnect the negative battery cable.
2. Drain the cooling system.
3. Disconnect the electrical lead at the fan motor.
4. Remove the fan frame-to-radiator support attaching bolts and remove the fan assembly.
5. Disconnect the upper and lower radiator hoses and the coolant recovery hose from the radiator.
6. Disconnect the transmission oil cooler lines on automatic transaxle models, from the radiator and wire them out of the way.
7. Remove the radiator-to-radiator support attaching bolts and clamps. Remove the radiator.
8. Place the radiator in the vehicle so that the bottom is located in the lower mounting pads. Tighten the attaching bolts and clamps.

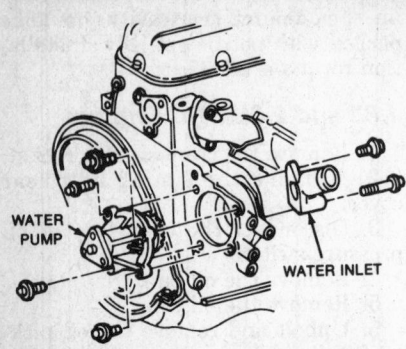

OHV engine water pump installation

9. Connect the transmission oil cooler lines and tighten the bolts to 20 ft. lbs.

10. Installation of the remaining components is in the reverse order of the removal procedure. Fill and bleed the cooling system when finished.

Water Pump

REMOVAL & INSTALLATION

All OHV Engines

1. Disconnect the negative battery cable.
2. Drain the cooling system.
3. Remove all drive belts.
4. Remove the alternator.
5. Unscrew the water pump pulley mounting bolts and remove the pulley.
6. Remove the mounting bolts and remove the water pump.
7. Place a 1/8 in. bead of RTV sealant on the water pump sealing surface. While the sealer is still wet, install the pump and tighten the bolts to 15–22 ft. lbs on 4 cylinder engine and 6–9 ft. lbs. on 6 cylinder engine.
8. Installation of the remaining components is in the reverse order of removal.

All OHC Engines

1. Disconnect negative battery cable.
2. Drain cooling system.
3. Remove timing belt.
4. Remove water pump retaining bolts, water pump and seal ring.
5. To install reverse removal procedures. Torque water pump bolts to 18 ft. lbs.

Thermostat

REMOVAL & INSTALLATION

All OHV Engines

The thermostat is located inside a housing either on the cylinder head (4 cylinder), or in the thermostat housing on the intake manifold (V6 engine). It is not necessary to remove the radiator

hose from the thermostat housing when removing the thermostat.

1. Disconnect the negative battery cable.
2. Drain the cooling system and remove the air cleaner.
3. Disconnect the A.I.R. pipe at the upper check valve and the bracket at the water outlet.
4. Disconnect the electrical lead.
5. Remove the 2 retaining bolts from the thermostat housing and lift up the housing with the hose attached. Lift out the thermostat.
6. Insert the new thermostat, spring end down. Apply a thin bead of silicone sealer to the housing mating surface and install the housing while the sealer is still wet. Tighten the housing retaining bolts 15–22 ft. lbs. on 6 cylinder engine and 6–9 ft. lbs on 4 cylinder engine.
7. Installation of the remaining components is in the reverse order of removal.

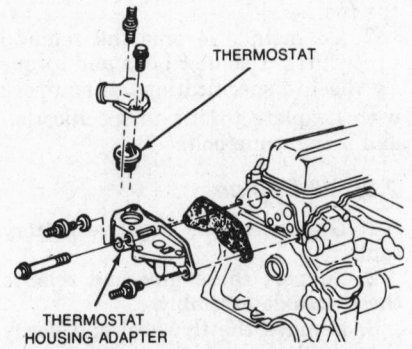

OHV engine thermostat mounting

All OHC Engines

— CAUTION —
The engine must be COLD for this procedure.

1. Remove the thermostat housing cap.
2. Grasp the handle of the thermostat assembly and gently pull upward.
3. Clean the thermostat housing and O-ring.
4. Apply a suitable lubricant to the O-ring, then install the thermostat into the housing, pushing down to ensure that the thermostat is firmly seated.
5. Replace the thermostat housing cap.

COOLING SYSTEM BLEEDING

After working on the cooling system, even to replace the thermostat, it must be bled. Air trapped in the system will prevent proper filling and leave the radiator coolant level low, causing a risk of overheating.

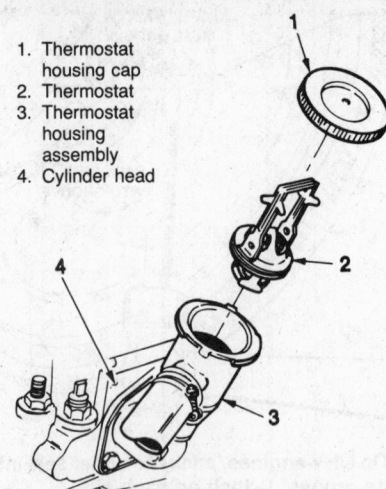

1. Thermostat housing cap
2. Thermostat
3. Thermostat housing assembly
4. Cylinder head

OHC engine thermostat mounting

1. To bleed the system, start with the system cool, the radiator cap off and the radiator filled to about an inch below the filler neck.
2. Start the engine and run it at slightly above normal idle speed. This will insure adequate circulation. If air bubbles appear and the coolant level drops, fill the system with an antifreeze/water mixture to bring the level back to the proper level.
3. Run the engine this way until the thermostat opens. When this happens, coolant will move abruptly across the top of the radiator and the temperature of the radiator will suddenly rise.
4. At this point, air is often expelled and the level may drop quite a bit. Keep refilling the system until the level is near the top of the radiator and remains constant.
5. If the vehicle has a coolant recovery tank, fill the radiator up to the filler neck then install the radiator cap and fill recovery tank to correct level.

EMISSION CONTROLS

Please refer to "Emission Control" in the Unit Repair section for system maintenance procedures. Due to the complex nature of modern electronic engine control systems, comprehensive diagnosis and testing procedures fall outside the confines of this repair manual. For complete information on diagnosis, testing and repair procedures concerning all modern engine and emission control systems, please refer to *"Chilton's Guide To Electronic Engine Controls".*

FUEL SYSTEM

Fuel System Service Precaution

RELIEVING FUEL SYSTEM PRESSURE

Fuel Injected Engines

The fuel delivery pipe is under high pressure even after the engine is stopped. Direct removal of the fuel line, may result in dangerous fuel spray. Make sure to release the fuel pressure according to the following procedure:

1. Release the fuel vapor pressure in the fuel tank by removing the fuel tank cap and reinstalling it.

2. With the engine running, remove the connector of the fuel pump relay and wait until the engine stops.

3. Once the engine is stopped, crank it a few times with the starter for about 3 seconds with the relay disconnected.

4. If the fuel pressure can't be released in the above manner because the engine failed to run, disconnect the negative battery cable, cover the union bolt of the fuel line with an absorbant rag and loosen the union bolt slowly to release the fuel pressure gradually.

Fuel Filter

REMOVAL & INSTALLATION

Carbureted Engines

The fuel filter located within the carburetor body. When the filter is replaced, make sure the new one is of the same type.

1. Place absorbent rags underneath the fuel line where it joins the carburetor.

2. Disconnect the fuel line connection at the fuel inlet nut using a backup wrench on filter housing and a line wrench or equivalent on the line fitting.

NOTE: If filter is installed wrong engine will starve for fuel.

3. Unscrew the fuel inlet nut from the carburetor. As the nut is removed, the filter will be pushed partway out by spring pressure.

4. Remove the filter and spring.

5. Install the new spring and filter. The hole in the filter faces the nut.

6. Install a new gasket on the inlet nut and install the nut into the carburetor. Tighten securely.

7. Install the fuel line, using a back-

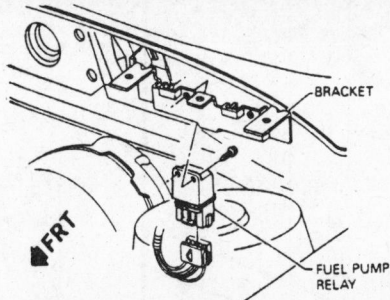

The fuel pump relay used on fuel injected engines—typical location

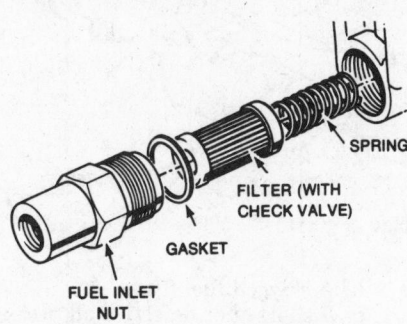

Carburetor-mounted fuel filter

up wrench on filter housing and a line wrench or equivalent on the line fitting.

8. Run the engine and check for leaks.

Fuel Injected Engines

All models have a filter located in-line before throttle body.

1. Relieve the fuel system pressure and disconnect battery cable.

2. Disconnect the fuel line connections at the fuel filter using a backup wrench on filter housing and a line wrench or equivalent on the line fitting.

3. Remove the filter housing bracket retaining bolt and remove filter.

4. To install reverse removal procedures.

Mechanical Fuel Pump

A mechanical fuel pump is used on carbureted engines. It is of the diaphragm-type and because of the design is serviced by replacement only. No adjustments or repairs are possible. The pump is operated by an eccentric on the camshaft. An electric, in-tank fuel pump is used with fuel injected engines. No adjustments are possible.

PRESSURE TESTING

To determine if the pump is in good condition, tests for both volume and pressure should be performed. The

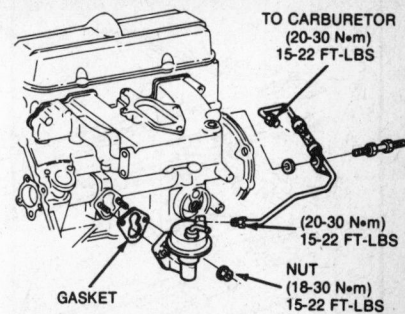

Fuel pump mounting on carbureted engines

tests are made with the pump installed, and the engine at normal operating temperature and idle speed. Never replace a fuel pump without first performing these simple tests. Be sure that the fuel filter has been changed at the specified interval. If in doubt, install a new filter first.

1. Disconnect the fuel line at the carburetor and connect a fuel pump pressure gauge. Fill the carburetor float bowl with gasoline.

2. Start the engine and check the pressure with the engine at idle. If the pump has a vapor return hose, squeeze it off so that an accurate reading can be obtained. Pressure should not be below 4.5 psi.

3. If the pressure is incorrect, replace the pump. If it is ok, go on to the volume test.

VOLUME TESTING

1. Disconnect the pressure gauge. Run the fuel line into a graduated container.

2. Run the engine at idle until 1 pint of gasoline has been pumped. 1 pint should be delivered in 30 seconds or less. There is normally enough fuel in the carburetor float bowl to perform this test, but refill it if necessary.

3. If the delivery rate is below the minimum, check the lines for restrictions or leaks and replace the pump.

REMOVAL & INSTALLATION

The fuel pump is located at the center rear of the engine.

1. Disconnect the negative battery cable. Raise and support the vehicle safely.

2. Disconnect the inlet line from the pump. Disconnect the vapor return hose, if equipped.

3. Loosen the fuel line at the carburetor and fuel pump. Disconnect the outlet line from the pump.

4. Remove the 2 mounting bolts and remove the fuel pump from the engine.

5. To install, place a new gasket on the fuel pump and install the pump to

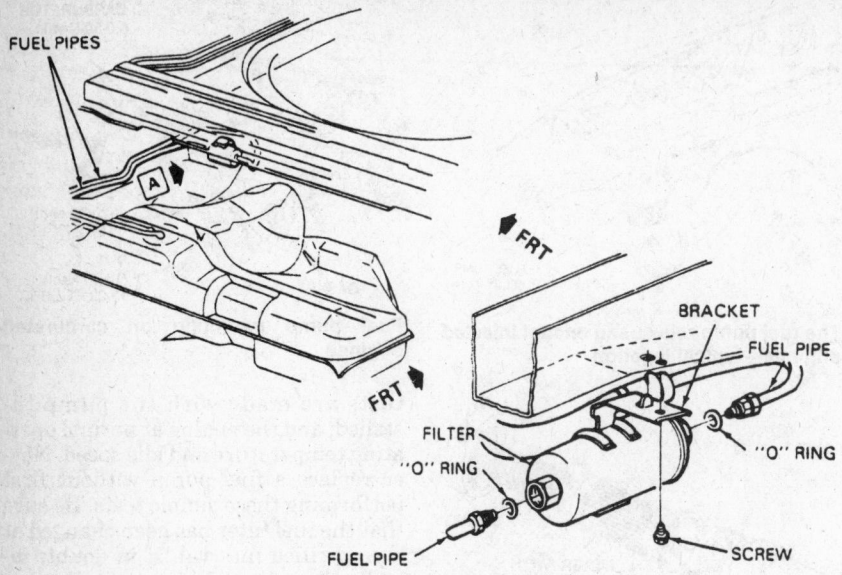

FUEL PIPES

FRT

FRT

BRACKET

FUEL PIPE

"O" RING

"O" RING

FILTER

FUEL PIPE

SCREW

Fuel filter—fuel injected engines

the engine. Tighten the mounting bolts alternately and evenly.

6. Install the pump outlet line. This is easier if the line is disconnected from the carburetor. Tighten the fitting while backing up the pump nut with another wrench. Install the line at the carburetor.

7. Install the inlet line and vapor hose if so equipped. Lower the vehicle and connect the negative battery cable. Start the engine and check for leaks.

Electric Fuel Pump

TBI PRESSURE TESTING

──── **CAUTION** ────

Before performing any tests, do the following to prevent personal injury: Remove the fuel pump fuse from the fuse panel in the passenger compartment. Start the engine and run it until all fuel in the system is used. Crank the engine for an additional 3 seconds to relieve any residual pressure. Turn the ignition to OFF and replace the fuse.

1. Remove the air cleaner and plug the thermal vacuum port on the throttle body unit.

2. Remove the steel fuel line from between the throttle body unit and the fuel filter.

3. Install a fuel pressure gauge with at least a 15 psi capacity between the throttle body and the filter.

4. Start the engine and observe the pressure reading. Pressure should be 9–13 psi. If the pressure is not within these limits, one or more of the following could be at fault:

a. A short in the system

b. A clogged fuel filter

c. A shorted or defective oil pressure switch

d. Defective fuel pump relay

e. Defective fuel pump

Check each of these components in turn to diagnose the problem before replacing the pump.

5. Follow the cautions at the start of this procedure to depressurize the system. Remove the pressure gauge and install the fuel line. Torque the nuts to 19–25 ft. lbs.

6. Start the engine and check for leaks.

7. Unplug the thermal vacuum port on the throttle body.

MFI PRESSURE TESTING

1. Wrap a shop towel around fuel pressure connector on the fuel rail to absorb any leakage that may occur when installing gauge.

2. Install a fuel pressure gauge J–34730–1 or equivalent to pressure connector.

3. With ignition **ON** pump pressure should be 40.5–47 psi on 2.8L engine (code W), 35–38 psi on 2.0L engine (code M), 30–40 psi on 2.0L engine (code J).

4. When engine is idling pressure should drop 3–10 psi on 2.8L engine (code W), pressure should be 25–30 psi on 2.0L engine (code M) and the pressure should drop 3–6 psi on the 2.0L engine (code J).

NOTE: The application of vacuum to the pressure regulator should result in a fuel pressure drop.

5. Remove fuel pressure gauge J–34730–1 or equivalent from pressure connector.

REMOVAL & INSTALLATION

The electric fuel pump is located in the fuel tank.

1. Depressurize the fuel system.

2. Disconnect the battery ground.

3. Raise and support the vehicle safely.

4. Remove the fuel filler cap.

5. Drain the fuel tank. Due to a restrictor in the fuel filler neck, a siphon cannot be used to drain the tank. Disconnect the fuel feed hose from the chassis feed pipe at the rear of the vehicle. Connect a length of hose to the feed line and into a container. Apply voltage to the pump at the pump test lead, terminal **G** on the ALCL (Assembly Line Communication Link) and

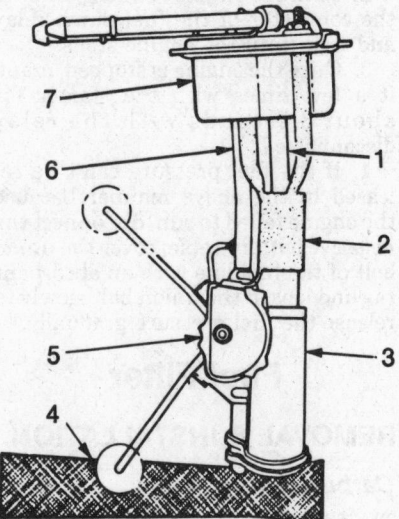

1. Fuel line
2. Rubber coupler and sound insulator
3. Electric fuel pump
4. Filter/strainer
5. Fuel level sender
6. Return tube
7. Splash cup liquid/vapor separator

Fuel injected engine fuel pump

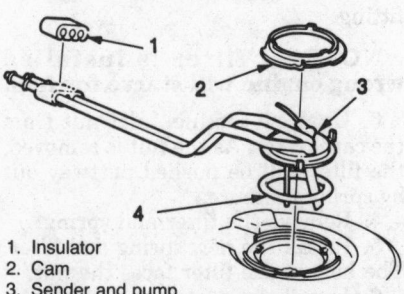

1. Insulator
2. Cam
3. Sender and pump
4. Gasket

Fuel meter removal from the fuel tank on cars with fuel injection

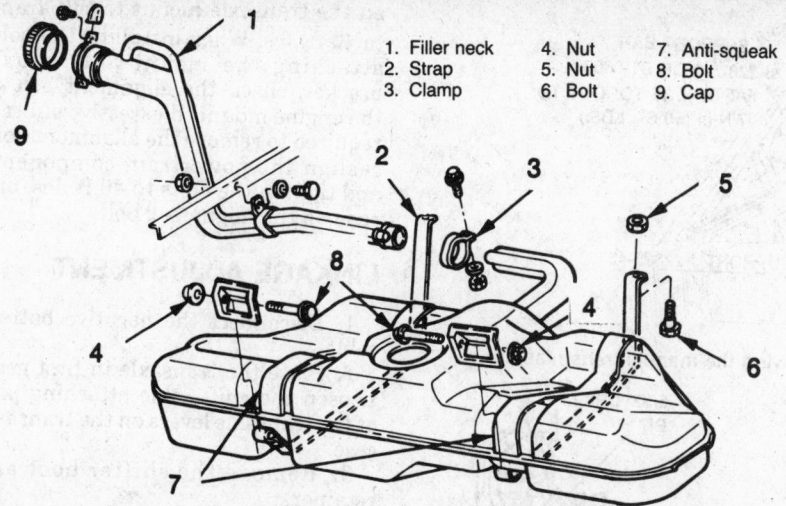

1. Filler neck
2. Strap
3. Clamp
4. Nut
5. Nut
6. Bolt
7. Anti-squeak
8. Bolt
9. Cap

Fuel tank mounting on cars with fuel injection. The tank must be removed to remove the electric fuel pump

run the pump until the tank is empty. Do not run the pump after the tank is empty, as this will damage the pump.

6. Disconnect the wiring from the tank.

7. Disconnect the filler neck hose and the vent hose.

8. Remove the fuel tank strap rear support bolts and lower the tank on a jack, just enough to disconnect the fuel feed line, return and vapor lines from the fuel meter.

9. Remove the tank.

10. Remove the fuel meter/pump assembly by turning the cam lockring counterclockwise. Lift the assembly from the tank and remove the pump from the meter.

11. Pull the pump up onto the attaching hose while pulling outward from the bottom support. Take care not to damage the rubber insulator and strainer. After the pump is clear of the bottom support pull it out of the rubber connector.

12. Installation is the reverse of removal. Use a new O-ring on the tank cam lockring.

Carburetor

REMOVAL & INSTALLATION

1. Remove the air cleaner and gasket.

2. Disconnect the fuel pipe and all vacuum lines.

3. Tag and disconnect all electrical connections.

4. Disconnect the downshift cable.

5. If equipped with cruise control, disconnect the linkage.

6. Remove the carburetor mounting bolts and remove the carburetor.

7. Inspect the EFE heater for dam-

age. Be sure that the throttle body and EFE mating surfaces are clean.

8. Install the carburetor and tighten the nuts alternately.

9. Installation of the remaining components is in the reverse order of removal.

OVERHAUL

For all carburetor overhaul and adjustment procedures, please refer to "Carburetor Service" in the Unit Repair section.

Fuel Injection

Due to the complex nature of modern fuel injection systems, comprehensive diagnosis and testing procedures fall outside the confines of this repair manual. For all fuel injection system diagnosis and testing procedures, please refer to *"Chilton's Guide To Fuel Injection And Feedback Carburetors"*.

MANUAL TRANSAXLE

REMOVAL & INSTALLATION

All Models

1. Disconnect the negative battery cable.

2. Install an engine holding bar so that one end is supported on the cowl tray over the wiper motor and the other end rests on the radiator support.

Use padding and be careful not to damage the paint or body work with the bar. Attach a lifting hook to the engine lift ring and to the bar and raise the engine enough to take the pressure off the motor mounts.

NOTE: If a lifting bar and hook is not available, a chain hoist can be used, however, during the procedure the vehicle must be raised, at which time the chain hoist must be adjusted to keep tension on the engine/transaxle assembly.

3. Remove the heater hose clamp at the transaxle mount bracket. Disconnect the electrical connector and remove the horn assembly.

4. Remove the transaxle mount attaching bolts. Discard the bolts attaching the mount to the side frame; new bolts must be used at installation.

NOTE: Starting in 1985, J-body vehicles use a hydraulic clutch system. Disconnect the clutch master cylinder push rod from the clutch pedal and disconnect the clutch slave cylinder from the transaxle support bracket and move it aside.

5. Disconnect the clutch cable from the clutch release lever. Remove the transaxle mount bracket attaching bolts and nuts.

6. Disconnect the shift cables and retaining clips at the transaxle. Disconnect the ground cables at the transaxle mounting stud.

7. Remove the 4 upper transaxle-to-engine mounting bolts.

8. Raise the vehicle and support it on stands. Remove the left front wheel.

9. Remove the left front inner splash shield. Remove the transaxle strut and bracket.

10. Remove the clutch housing cover bolts.

11. Disconnect the speedometer cable at the transaxle.

12. Disconnect the stabilizer bar at the left suspension support and control arm.

13. Disconnect the ball joint from the steering knuckle.

14. Remove the left suspension support attaching bolts and remove the support and control arm as an assembly.

15. Install boot protectors and disengage the drive axles at the transaxle. Remove the left side shaft from the transaxle.

16. Position a jack under the transaxle case, remove the lower 2 transaxle-to-engine mounting bolts and remove the transaxle by sliding it towards the driver's side, away from the engine. Carefully lower the jack, guiding the right shaft out the transaxle.

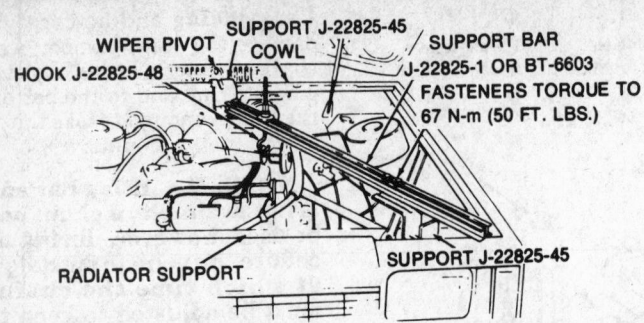

Install an engine holding bar when removing the manual transmission

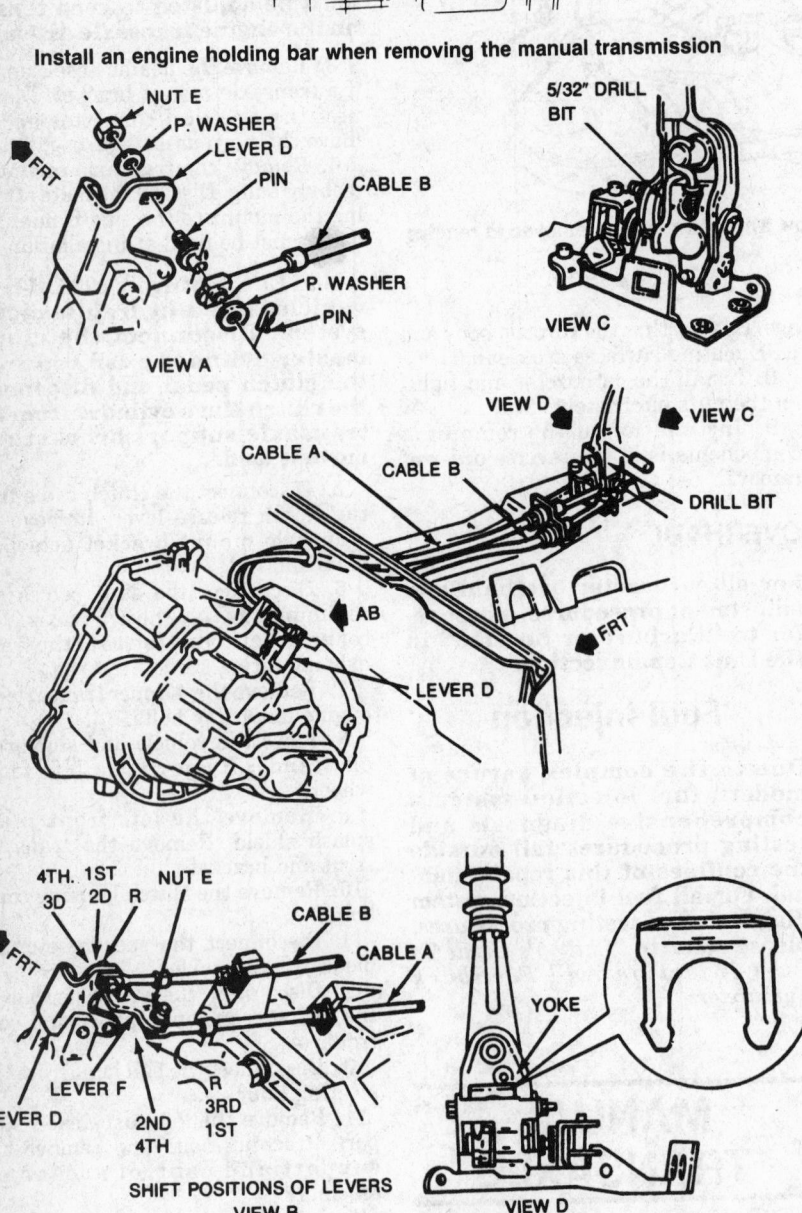

Shift linkage adjustment

17. When installing the transaxle, guide the right drive axle into its bore as the transaxle is being raised. The right drive axle CANNOT be readily installed after the transaxle is connected to the engine. Installation of the remaining components is in the reverse order of removal with the following notes. Tighten the transaxle-to-engine mounting bolts to 55 ft. lbs. Tighten the suspension support-to-body attaching bolts to 75 ft. lbs. and the clutch housing cover bolts to 10 ft. lbs. Using new bolts, install and tight-

en the transaxle mount-to-side frame to 40 ft. lbs. When installing the bolts attaching the mount-to-transaxle bracket, check the alignment bolt at the engine mount. If excessive effort is required to remove the alignment bolt, realign the powertrain components and tighten the bolts to 40 ft. lbs. and remove the alignment bolt.

LINKAGE ADJUSTMENT

1. Disconnect the negative battery cable.
2. Place the transaxle in first gear. Loosen the shift cable attaching pins at the transaxle levers on the transaxle case.
3. Remove the shifter boot and retainer.
4. Install a No. 22 ($^5/_{32}$ in.) drill bit into the alignment hole at the side of the shifter assembly. Install a yoke clip between the shifter tower and carrier.
5. Remove the lash from the transaxle by rotating the upright select lever (lever D) while tightening the cable attaching pin nut.
6. Remove the drill bit and yoke at the shifter assembly, install the shifter boot and retainer and connect the negative battery cable.
7. Road test the vehicle to check for good gate feel during shifting. Fine tune the adjustment as necessary.

CLUTCH

REMOVAL & INSTALLATION

All Models

1. Remove the transaxle.
2. Mark the pressure plate assembly and the flywheel so that they can be assembled in the same position. They were balanced as an assembly at the factory.
3. Loosen the attaching bolts 1 turn at a time until spring tension is relieved.
4. Support the pressure plate and remove the bolts. Remove the pressure plate and clutch disc. Do not disassemble the pressure plate assembly; replace it if defective.
5. Inspect the flywheel, clutch disc, pressure plate, throwout bearing and the clutch fork and pivot shaft assembly for wear. Replace the parts as required. If the flywheel shows any signs of overheating, or if it is badly grooved or scored, it should be refaced or replaced.
6. Clean the pressure plate and flywheel mating surfaces thoroughly. Position the clutch disc and pressure

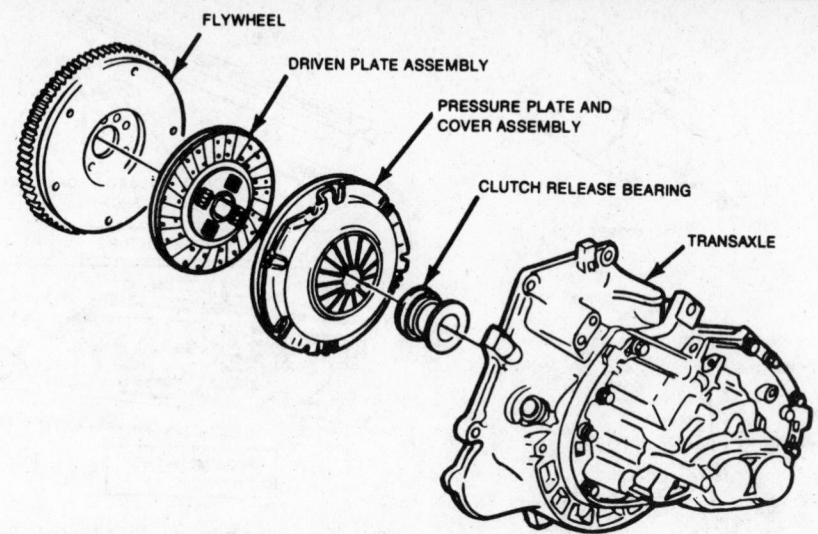

FLYWHEEL

DRIVEN PLATE ASSEMBLY

PRESSURE PLATE AND COVER ASSEMBLY

CLUTCH RELEASE BEARING

TRANSAXLE

Clutch components

plate into the installed position, and support with a dummy shaft or clutch aligning tool. The clutch plate is assembled with the damper springs offset toward the transaxle. 1 side of the factory-supplied clutch disc is stamped "Flywheel Side."

7. Install the pressure plate-to-flywheel bolts. Tighten them gradually in a criss-cross pattern.

8. Lubricate the outside groove and the inside recess of the release bearing with high temperature grease. Wipe off any excess. Install the release bearing.

9. Install the transaxle.

FREE-PLAY ADJUSTMENT

A self-adjusting clutch mechanism is located on the clutch pedal, eliminating the need for periodic free play adjustments. The self-adjusting mechanism should be inspected periodically as follows:

1. Depress the clutch pedal and look for the pawl on the self-adjusting mechanism to firmly engage the teeth on the ratchet.

2. Release the clutch. The pawl should be lifted off of the teeth by the metal stop on the bracket.

NOTE: Starting in 1985, J-body vehicles use a hydraulic system which provides automatic clutch adjustment, no adjustment of the clutch linkage or pedal height is required.

Neutral Start Switch

A neutral start switch is located on the clutch pedal assembly; the switch prevents the engine from starting unless the clutch is depressed. If the switch is faulty, it can be unbolted and replaced without removing the pedal assembly from the vehicle. No adjustments for the switch are provided.

Clutch Cable

REMOVAL & INSTALLATION

1. Press the clutch pedal up against the bumper stop so as to release the pawl from the detent. Disconnect the clutch cable from the release lever at the transaxle assembly. Be careful that the cable does not snap back toward the rear of the vehicle as this could damage the detent in the adjusting mechanism.

2. Remove the hush panel from inside the vehicle.

3. Disconnect the clutch cable from the detent end tangs. Lift the locking pawl away from the detent and pull the cable forward between the detent and the pawl.

4. Remove the windshield washer bottle.

5. From the engine side of the cowl, pull the clutch cable out to disengage it from the clutch pedal mounting bracket. The insulators, dampener and washers may separate from the cable in the process.

6. Disconnect the cable from the transaxle mounting bracket and remove it.

7. Install the cable into both insulators, damper and washer. Lubricate the rear insulator with tire mounting lube or the like to ease installation into the pedal mounting bracket.

8. From inside the vehicle, attach the end of the cable to the detent. Be sure to route the cable underneath the pawl and into the detent cable groove.

9. Press the clutch pedal up against the bumper stop to release the pawl from the detent. Install the other end of the cable at the release lever and the transaxle mount bracket.

10. Install the hush panel and the windshield washer bottle.

11. Check the clutch operation.

Clutch Master/Slave Cylinder

REMOVAL & INSTALLATION

NOTE: The clutch hydraulic system is serviced as a complete unit. Individual components of the system are not available separately.

1. Disconnect the negative battery terminal from the battery.

2. Remove the hush panel from the under the dash.

NOTE: On 6 cylinder engine remove air cleaner, mass air flow sensor and air intake duct as an assembly. Disconnect electrical lead at the washer bottle and remove washer bottle from vehicle.

3. Disconnect the master cylinder push rod from the clutch pedal.

4. Remove the master cylinder-to-cowl brace nuts and remove master cylinder.

5. Remove the slave cylinder retaining nuts at the transaxle and remove slave cylinder. Remove the hydraulic system as a unit from the vehicle.

6. To install reverse removal procedures. Bleed hydraulic system.

NOTE: Do not remove the plastic push rod retainer from the slave cylinder. The strap will break on the first clutch pedal application.

BLEEDING THE HYDRAULIC SYSTEM

1. Clean dirt and grease from the cap to ensure no foreign substances enter the system.

2. Fill reservoir to the top with approved brake fluid only.

NOTE: Brake fluid must be certified to DOT 3 specification.

3. Fully loosen bleed screw which is in the slave cylinder body.

4. Fluid will now begin to move from the master cylinder down the tube to the slave cylinder. The reservoir must be kept full at all times.

5. When slave cylinder is full, a steady stream of fluid will come from

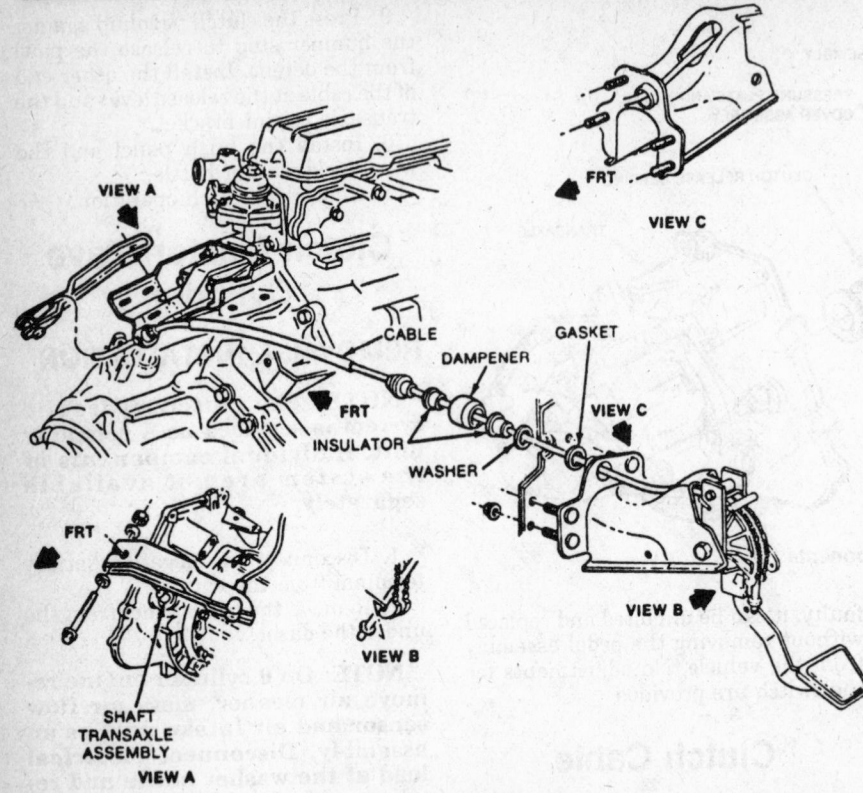

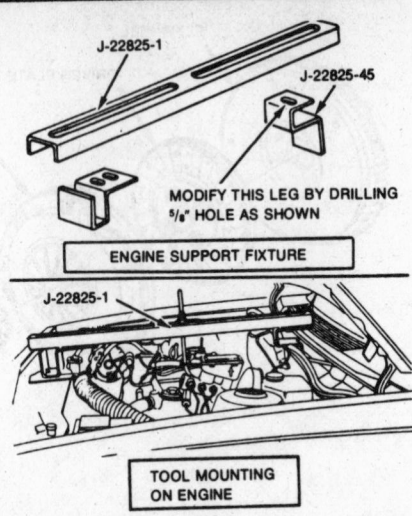

MODIFY THIS LEG BY DRILLING 5/8" HOLE AS SHOWN

ENGINE SUPPORT FIXTURE

J-22825-1

TOOL MOUNTING ON ENGINE

Clutch cable and brackets

Supporting the engine with a holding bar when removing the automatic transmission

the slave outlet. At this point, tighten bleed screw.

6. Start engine, push clutch pedal to the floor and select reverse gear. There should be no grating of gears, if there is the system still contains air.

AUTOMATIC TRANSAXLE

For further information on automatic transaxles, please refer to "Automatic Transmissions" in the Unit Repair section.

REMOVAL & INSTALLATION

All Models

1. Disconnect the negative battery cable where it attaches to the transaxle.

2. Insert a ¼ x 2 in. bolt into the hole in the right front motor mount to prevent any mislocation during the transaxle removal.

3. Remove the air cleaner. Disconnect the T.V. cable at the carburetor if so equipped.

4. Unscrew the bolt securing the T.V. cable to the transaxle. Pull up on the cable cover at the transaxle until

the cable can be seen. Disconnect the cable from the transaxle rod.

5. Remove the wiring harness retaining bolt at the top of the transaxle.

6. Remove the hose from the air management valve and pull the wiring harness up and out of the way.

7. Install an engine support bar as shown in the illustration. Raise the engine just enough to take the pressure off the motor mounts.

—— CAUTION ——

The engine support bar must be located in the center of the cowl and the bolts must be tightened before attempting to support the engine.

8. Remove the transaxle mount and bracket assembly. It may be necessary to raise the engine slightly to aid in removal.

9. Disconnect the shift control linkage from the transaxle.

10. Remove the top transaxle-to-engine mounting bolts. Loosen, but do not remove, the transaxle-to-engine bolt nearest to the starter.

11. Unlock the steering column. Raise and support the front of the vehicle. Remove the front wheels.

12. Pull out the cotter pin and loosen the castellated ball joint nut until the ball joint separates from the control arm. Repeat on the other side of the vehicle.

13. Disconnect the stabilizer bar from the left lower control arm.

14. Remove the 6 bolts that secure the left front suspension support assembly.

15. Connect an axle shaft removal tool (J-28468) to a slide hammer (J-23907).

16. Position the tool behind the axle shaft cones and pull the cones out and away from the transaxle. Remove the axle shafts and plug the transaxle bores to reduce fluid leakage.

17. Remove the nut that secures the transaxle control cable bracket to the transaxle. Remove the engine-to-transaxle stud.

18. Disconnect the speedometer cable at the transaxle.

19. Disconnect the transaxle strut (stabilizer) at the transaxle.

20. Remove the 4 retaining screws and remove the torque converter shield.

21. Remove the 3 bolts securing the torque converter to the flex plate.

22. Disconnect and plug the oil cooler lines at the transaxle. Remove the starter.

23. Remove the screws that hold the brake and fuel line brackets to the left side of the underbody. This will allow the lines to be moved slightly for clearance during transaxle removal.

24. Remove the bolt that was loosened in Step 10.

25. Remove the transaxle to the left. Installation is in the reverse order of removal.

NOTE: Guide the right hand drive axle shaft into its bore as the transaxle is being raised. The right hand drive axle shaft cannot not be readily installed after the transaxle is bolted to the engine.

DRIVE AXLE

Halfshaft

REMOVAL & INSTALLATION

1. Raise and support the front of the vehicle with jackstands positioned under the frame.

NOTE: When servicing suspension components in the area of the outer drive axle seal or when removing a drive axle, always install J–34754 seal protector or equivalent.

2. Lower the vehicle slightly so that the weight rests on the frame and not on the lower control arms.

3. Remove the wheel/tire assemblies.

4. Install a drift punch through the brake rotor cooling holes to lock the rotor in place. Clean the halfshaft threads of dirt, then using a suitable socket and breaker bar, lubricate and remove the hub nut and washer.

5. Remove the caliper mounting bolts and support the caliper on a wire. DO NOT let the caliper hang by the brake hose.

6. Remove the brake rotor.

7. Remove the lower ball joint-to-control arm nut and separate the ball joint from the control arm.

8. Remove the stabilizer-to-lower control arm nuts/bolts and separate the stabilizer from the lower control arm.

9. Using the tool No. J–28733 or equivalent, install it to the axle hub and press the halfshaft in and away from the hub. The halfshaft should only be pressed in until the press fit between the halfshaft and hub is loose.

NOTE: Be careful not to press the halfshaft in too far as damage to the joint may occur.

10. Separate the halfshaft from the hub by pulling the hub assembly out away from the halfshaft.

NOTE: If equipped with Tri-Pot joints, care must be taken not to allow the joints to become overextended. When either end or both ends of the shaft are disconnected, overextending the joint could result in separation of internal components. This could cause failure of the joint, so it's important to handle the halfshaft in a manner that prevents overextension.

11. Using a slide hammer or equivalent remove the halfshaft from the differential assembly.

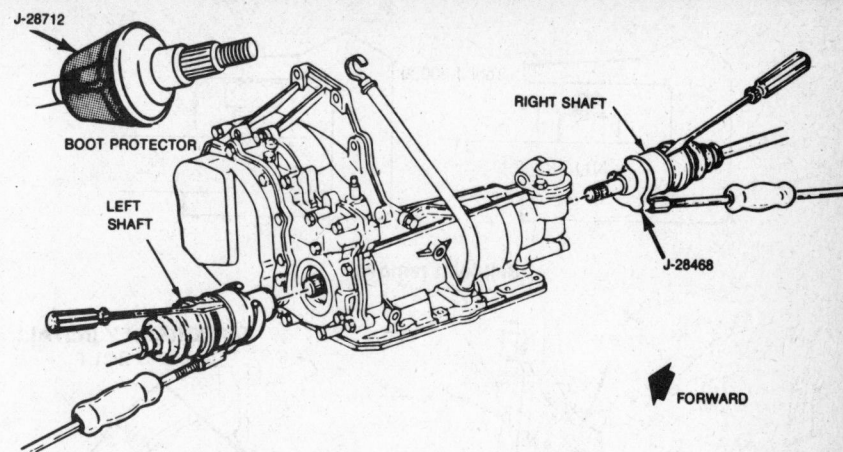

Halfshaft removal; the special tools are attached to slide hammers in this diagram

12. To install, use a new hub nut, cotter pins and reverse the removal procedures. Start the splines of the halfshaft into the transaxle and push until the axle snaps into place. Torque the caliper-to-steering knuckle bolts to 28 ft. lbs., the ball joint-to-steering knuckle nut to 42 ft. lbs. and the halfshaft (new) nut to 191 ft. lbs.

CV-JOINT OVERHAUL

For all CV-Joint overhaul procedures, please refer to "U/CV-Joint Overhaul" in the Unit Repair section.

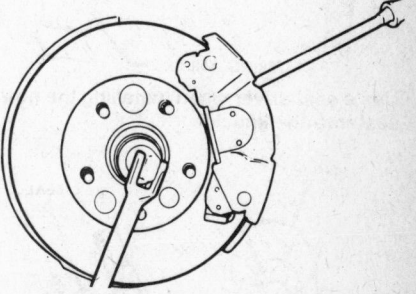

Insert a holding tool, such as a drift or punch into the caliper when tightening the hub nut

Front Hub, Knuckle and Bearings

REMOVAL & INSTALLATION

1. Remove the wheel cover, loosen the hub nut, and raise and support the car safely. Remove the front wheel.

2. Install the boot cover protector on 4 cylinder engine with automatic transaxle.

3. Remove the hub nut.

4. Remove the brake caliper and rotor.

NOTE: Do not allow the brake caliper to hang from the brake hose.

5. Remove the 3 hub and bearing attaching bolts.

6. Remove splash shield.

7. Install special tool J–28733 or equivalent and press the hub and bearing assembly off the halfshaft.

8. Disconnect the stabilizer link bolt at the lower control arm.

9. Separate the ball joint from sterring knuckle.

10. Remove halfshaft from knuckle and support out of the way.

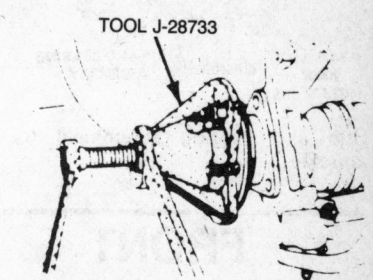

Removal of the hub and bearing assembly

11. Remove inner knuckle seal using brass drift pin or equivalent.

NOTE: To remove steering knuckle at this point remove both strut to knuckle mounting bolts. Before removing the steering knuckle from the strut, be sure to scribe alignment marks between them, so that the installation can be easily performed.

12. To install, use new O-rings, new bearing seals, new cotter pins, new hub nut and reverse the removal procedures. Torque the steering knuckle-to-strut bolts to 129 ft. lbs. Torque ball joint nut to 42 ft. lbs. Torque new hub and bearing nut to 74 ft. lbs. Lower vehicle and apply final torque to hub and bearing nut, 191 ft. lbs.

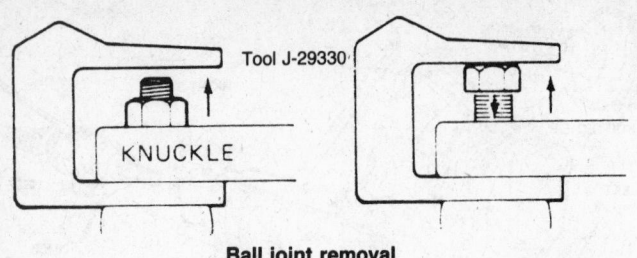

Ball joint removal

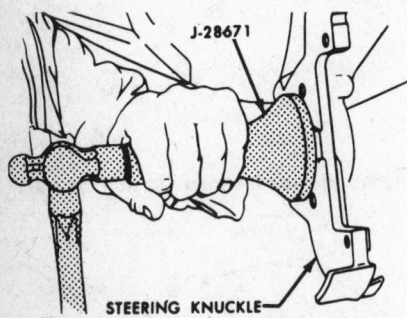

Use a seal driver when installing the new seal into the knuckle

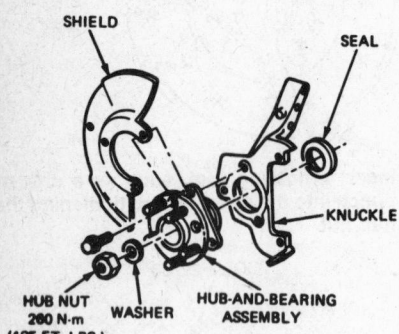

Hub and bearing attachment to the knuckle

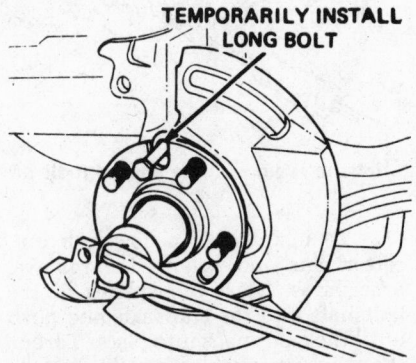

Insert a bolt into the rotor when tightening the hub nut

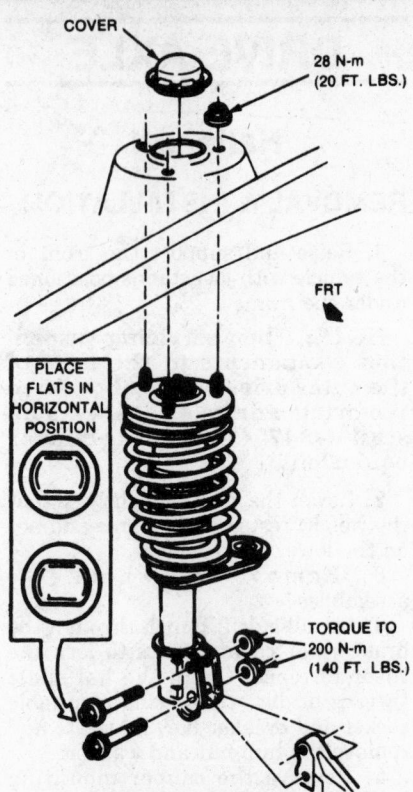

Strut assembly mounting

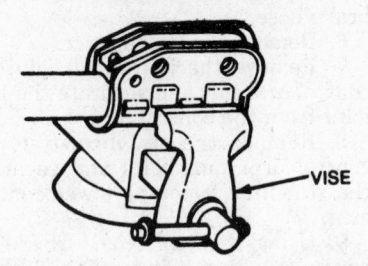

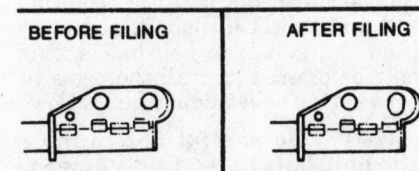

Modifying the strut mounting holes

FRONT SUSPENSION

MacPherson Struts

REMOVAL & INSTALLATION

NOTE: Before removing front suspension components, their positions should be marked so they may be assembled correctly.

1. Remove the strut-to-body nuts.
2. Raise and support the front of the vehicle on jackstands; position the jackstands under the frame.
3. Lower the vehicle slightly so that the weight rests on the jackstands and not on the control arms.
4. Remove the front wheel assemblies and tie rod from strut assembly using tool J-24319 or equivalent.

5. Some vehicles may use a silicone (gray) boot on the inboard axle joint. Use the Boot Protector tool No. J-33162 or equivalent, on these boots. All other boots are made from a thermoplastic material (black) and do not require the use of a boot seal protector.
6. Disconnect the brake line bracket from the strut assembly.
7. Remove the strut-to-steering knuckle bolts.

NOTE: Support steering knuckle to prevent tension from being applied to brake hose.

8. Remove the strut assembly from the vehicle. Care should be taken to avoid chipping or cracking the spring coating when handling the front suspension coil spring assembly.
9. To install, reverse the removal procedures. Align the strut-to-steering knuckle bolts and tighten (lightly). Torque the strut-to-body nuts to 20 ft. lbs. and the strut-to-steering knuckle bolts to 140 ft. lbs. Check and/or adjust the front end alignment.

NOTE: On 1982–86 Firenza models, struts can be serviced by replacing cartridges only. On 1987–89 Firenza models, the entire strut assembly must be replaced.

OVERHAUL

For all spring and shock absorber removal and installation procedures, and all strut overhaul procedures, please refer to "Strut Overhaul" in the Unit Repair section.

STRUT MODIFICATION

This modification is made only if a camber adjustment is required.

1. Place the strut in a vise. This step is not absolutely necessary; filing can be accomplished by disconnecting the strut from the steering knuckle.
2. File the holes in the outer flanges so as to enlarge the bottom holes until they match the slots already in the inner flanges.
3. Adjust the camber.

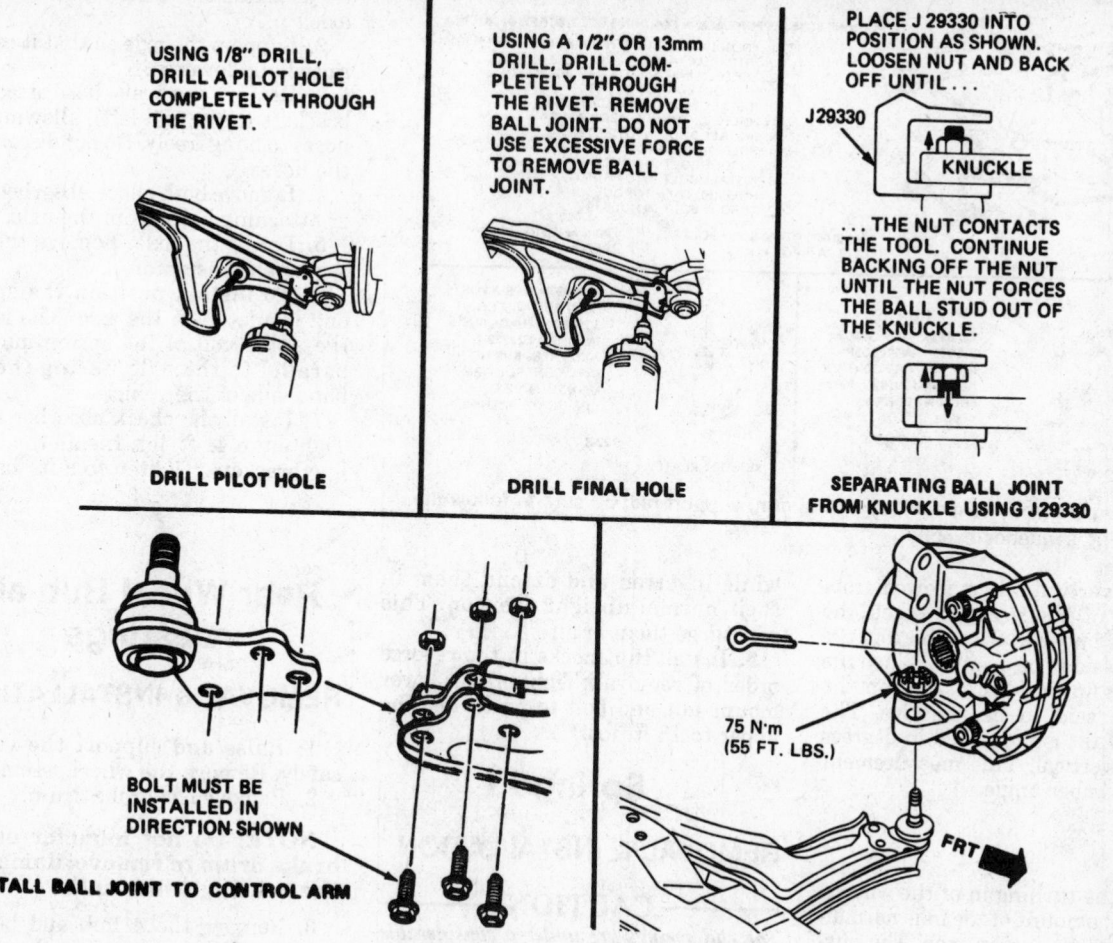

USING 1/8" DRILL, DRILL A PILOT HOLE COMPLETELY THROUGH THE RIVET.

DRILL PILOT HOLE

USING A 1/2" OR 13mm DRILL, DRILL COMPLETELY THROUGH THE RIVET. REMOVE BALL JOINT. DO NOT USE EXCESSIVE FORCE TO REMOVE BALL JOINT.

DRILL FINAL HOLE

PLACE J 29330 INTO POSITION AS SHOWN. LOOSEN NUT AND BACK OFF UNTIL . . .

J29330
KNUCKLE

. . . THE NUT CONTACTS THE TOOL. CONTINUE BACKING OFF THE NUT UNTIL THE NUT FORCES THE BALL STUD OUT OF THE KNUCKLE.

SEPARATING BALL JOINT FROM KNUCKLE USING J29330

BOLT MUST BE INSTALLED IN DIRECTION SHOWN

INSTALL BALL JOINT TO CONTROL ARM

75 N·m (55 FT. LBS.)

FRT

Ball joint removal and installation

Ball Joints

INSPECTION

1. Raise and support the front of the vehicle allowing the suspension hang free.
2. Grasp the wheel at the top and the bottom and shake it in an "in-and-out" motion. Check for any horizontal movement of the steering knuckle relative to the lower control arm. Replace the ball joint if such movement is noted.
3. If the ball stud is disconnected from the steering knuckle and any looseness is detected, or if the ball stud can be twisted in its socket using finger pressure, replace the ball joint.

REMOVAL & INSTALLATION

NOTE: This procedure requires the use of a special tool. The Mac-Pherson strut design does not use an upper ball joint.

1. Raise and support the vehicle safely. Remove the wheel assembly.
2. Use a ⅛ in. drill bit to drill a hole through the center of each of the 3 ball joint rivets.
3. Use a ½ in. drill bit to drill completely through the rivet.
4. Use a hammer and punch to remove the rivets. Drive them out from the bottom.
5. Use the special tool J29330 or a ball joint removal tool to separate the ball joint from the steering knuckle.
6. Disconnect the stabilizer bar from the lower control arm. Remove the ball joint.
7. Install the new ball joint into the control arm with the 3 bolts supplied as shown. Installation of the remaining components is in the reverse order of removal. Use a new cotter pin when installing the castellated nut on the ball joint. Check the toe setting and adjust as necessary.

Lower Control Arm

REMOVAL & INSTALLATION

1. Raise and support the front of the vehicle safely. Remove the wheel assembly.

2. Disconnect the stabilizer bar from the control arm and/or support.
3. Separate the ball joint from the steering knuckle.
4. Remove the 2 control arm-to-support bolts and remove the control arm.
5. If control arm support bar removal is necessary, unscrew the 6 mounting bolts and remove the support.
6. Installation is in the reverse order of removal. Tighten the control arm support rail bolts in sequence. Check the toe and adjust as necessary.

Front Wheel Alignment

CASTER

Caster is the tilting of the steering axis either forward or backward from the vertical, when viewed from the side of the vehicle. A backward tilt is said to be positive and a forward tilt is said to be negative.

CAMBER

Camber is the tilting of the wheels

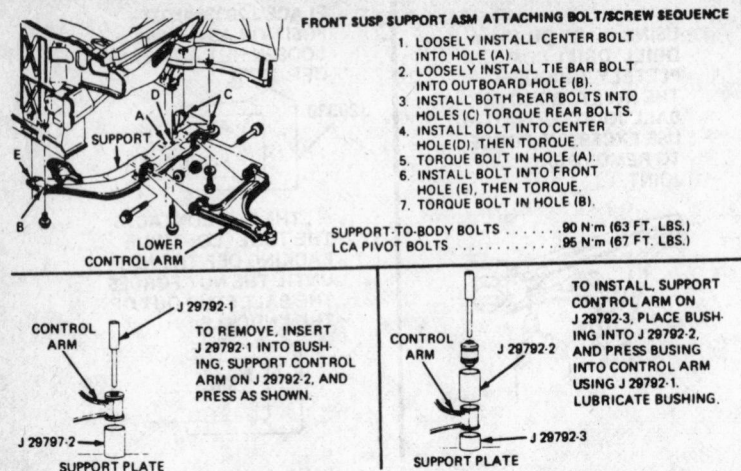

FRONT SUSP SUPPORT ASM ATTACHING BOLT/SCREW SEQUENCE

1. LOOSELY INSTALL CENTER BOLT INTO HOLE (A).
2. LOOSELY INSTALL TIE BAR BOLT INTO OUTBOARD HOLE (B).
3. INSTALL BOTH REAR BOLTS INTO HOLES (C) TORQUE REAR BOLTS.
4. INSTALL BOLT INTO CENTER HOLE(D), THEN TORQUE.
5. TORQUE BOLT IN HOLE (A).
6. INSTALL BOLT INTO FRONT HOLE (E), THEN TORQUE.
7. TORQUE BOLT IN HOLE (B).

SUPPORT-TO-BODY BOLTS . . . . .90 N·m (63 FT. LBS.)
LCA PIVOT BOLTS . . . . .95 N·m (67 FT. LBS.)

J 29792-1
TO REMOVE, INSERT J 29792-1 INTO BUSHING, SUPPORT CONTROL ARM ON J 29792-2, AND PRESS AS SHOWN.

TO INSTALL, SUPPORT CONTROL ARM ON J 29792-3, PLACE BUSHING INTO J 29792-2, AND PRESS BUSING INTO CONTROL ARM USING J 29792-1. LUBRICATE BUSHING.

Installing the front suspension (control arm) support rail; be sure to follow the tightening sequence exactly

from the vertical when viewed from the front of the vehicle. When the wheels tilt outward from the top, the camber is said to be positive. When the wheels tilt inward from the top the camber is said to be negative. The amount of tilt is measured in degrees from the vertical. This measurement is called camber angle.

TOE IN

Toe in is the turning in of the wheels. The actual amount of toe in is normally only a fraction of an inch. The purpose of toe in specification is to ensure parallel rolling of the wheels. Toe in also serves to offset the small deflections of the steering support system which occur when the vehicle is rolling forward.

REAR SUSPENSION

Shock Absorbers

REMOVAL & INSTALLATION

1. Open the hatch or trunk lid, remove the trim cover if present, and remove the upper shock absorber nut.
2. Raise and support the vehice to a convenient working height. It is not necessary to remove the weight of the vehicle from the shock absorbers, however, the vehicle can be left on the ground if preferred.
3. Remove the lower attaching bolt and remove the shock.
4. If new shock absorbers are being installed, repeatedly compress them

while inverted and extend them in their normal upright position. This will purge them of air.
5. Install the shocks in the reverse order of removal. Tighten the lower mount nut and bolt to 55 ft. lbs. the upper to 13 ft. lbs.

Springs

REMOVAL & INSTALLATION

—— CAUTION ——
The coil springs are under a considerable amount of tension. Be very careful when removing or installing them; they can exert enough force to cause very serious injuries.

1. Raise and support the vehicle safely. Do not use a twin-post hoist. The swing arc of the axle may cause it to slip from the hoist when the bolts are removed. If a suitable hoist is not available, raise and support the vehicle

on jackstands. Use a jack under the axle.
2. Support the axle so that it can be raised and lowered.
3. Remove the brake hose attaching brackets (right and left), allowing the hoses to hang freely. Do not disconnect the hoses.
4. Remove both shock absorber lower attaching bolts from the axle.
5. Lower the axle. Remove the coil spring and insulator.
6. To install, position the spring and insulator on the axle. The leg on the upper coil of the spring must be parallel to the axle, facing the left hand side of the vehicle.
7. Install the shock absorber bolts. Tighten to 41 ft. lbs. Install the brake line brackets. Tighten to 8 ft. lbs.

Rear Wheel Hub and Bearings

REMOVAL & INSTALLATION

1. Raise and support the vehicle safely. Remove the wheel assembly.
2. Remove the brake drum.

NOTE: Do not hammer on the brake drum to remove; damage to the bearing will result.

3. Remove the 4 hub and bearing retaining bolts and remove the assembly from the axle. The top rear attaching bolt will not clear the brake shoe when removing the hub and bearing assembly. Partially remove the hub and bearing assembly prior to removing this bolt.
4. Installation is in the reverse. Hub and bearing bolt torque is 39 ft. lbs.

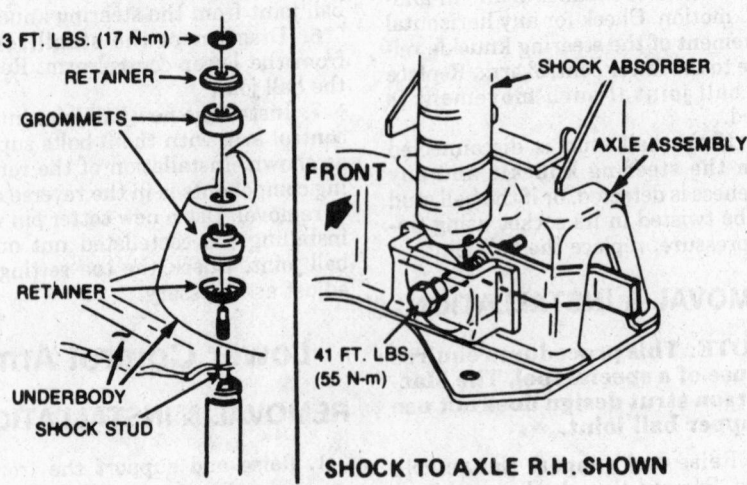

13 FT. LBS. (17 N-m)
RETAINER
GROMMETS
RETAINER
UNDERBODY
SHOCK STUD

SHOCK ABSORBER
AXLE ASSEMBLY
FRONT
41 FT. LBS. (55 N-m)

SHOCK TO AXLE R.H. SHOWN

Shock absorber mounting

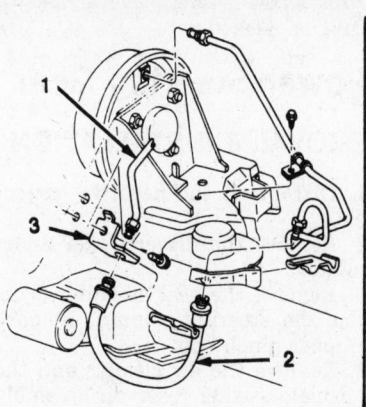

1. Center Brake Pipe
2. Brake Hose
3. Brake Pipe Bracket
4. Underbody

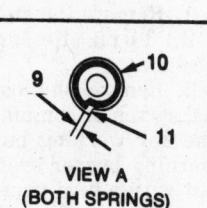

VIEW A
(BOTH SPRINGS)

5. Spring Insulator
6. Spring
7. Compression Bumper

8. Axle Assembly
9. .549 Inch (15mm) Max.
10. Spring

11. Spring Stop Part of Spring Seat

Rear spring mounting

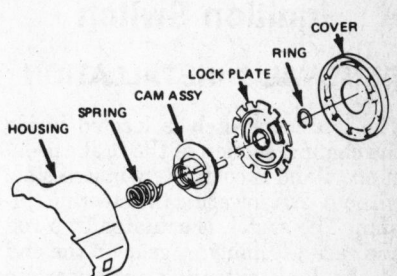

Depress the lockplate and remove the snap ring

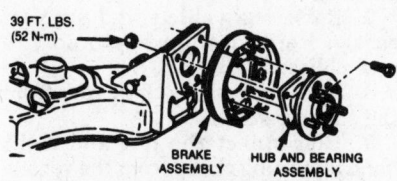

39 FT. LBS. (52 N-m)

BRAKE ASSEMBLY

HUB AND BEARING ASSEMBLY

Rear hub and bearing

Remove these parts to get at the turn signal switch

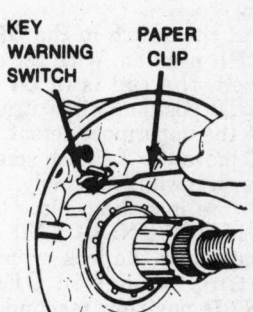

KEY WARNING SWITCH

PAPER CLIP

Remove the key warning buzzer switch with a paper clip

STEERING

Steering Wheel

REMOVAL & INSTALLATION

Standard Steering Wheel

1. Disconnect the negative cable.
2. Pull the pad from the wheel. The horn lead is attached to the pad at one end; the other end of the pad has a wire with a spade connector. The horn lead is disconnected by pushing and turning; the spade connector is simply unplugged.
3. Remove the retainer under the pad, if equipped.
4. Remove the steering shaft nut.
5. There should be alignment marks already present on the wheel and shaft. If not, matchmark the parts.
6. Remove the wheel with a puller.
7. Install the wheel on the shaft, aligning the matchmarks. Install the shaft nut and tighten to 30 ft. lbs.
8. Install the retainer.
9. Plug in the spade connector, and push and turn the horn lead to connect. Install the pad. Connect the negative battery cable.

Sport Steering Wheel

1. Disconnect the negative cable.

2. Pry the center cap from the wheel.
3. Remove the retainer, if equipped.
4. Remove the shaft nut.
5. If the wheel and shaft do not have factory-installed alignment marks, matchmark the parts before removal of the wheel.
6. Install a puller and remove the wheel. A horn spring, eyelet and insulator are underneath; don't lose the parts.
7. Install the spring, eyelet and insulator into the tower in the column.
8. Align the matchmarks and install the wheel onto the shaft. Install the retaining nut and tighten to 30 ft. lbs.
9. Install the retainer. Install the center cap. Connect the negative battery cable.

Combination Switch

REMOVAL & INSTALLATION

1. Remove the steering wheel. Remove the trim cover.
2. Remove the cover from the steering column.
3. Position a U-shaped lockplate compressing tool on the end of the steering shaft and compress the lock plate by turning the shaft nut clockwise. Pry the wire snap-ring out of the shaft groove.
4. Remove the tool and lift the lockplate off the shaft.
5. Slip the cancelling cam, upper bearing preload spring, and thrust washer off the shaft.
6. Remove the turn signal lever. Remove the hazard flasher button retaining screw and remove the button, spring and knob.
7. Pull the switch connector out of the mast jacket and tape the upper

part to facilitate switch removal. Attach a long piece of wire to the turn signal switch connector. When installing the turn signal switch, feed this wire through the column first. Use this wire to pull the switch connector into position. On tilt wheels, place the turn signal and shifter housing in low position and remove the harness cover.

8. Remove the 3 switch mounting screws. Remove the switch by pulling it straight up while guiding the wiring harness cover through the column.
9. Install the replacement switch by working the connector and cover down through the housing and under the bracket. On tilt models, the connector is worked down through the housing and under the bracket. The cover is installed on the harness.
10. Install the switch mounting screws and the connector on the mast

jacket bracket. Install the column-to-dash trim plate.

11. Install the flasher knob and the turn signal lever.

12. With the turn signal lever in neutral and the flasher knob out, slide the thrust washer, upper bearing preload spring, and cancelling cam onto the shaft.

13. Position the lock plate on the shaft and press it down until a new snap-ring can be inserted in the shaft groove. Always use a new snap-ring when assembling.

14. Install the cover and the steering wheel.

Ignition Switch

REMOVAL & INSTALLATION

The ignition switch is located inside the channel section of the brake pedal support and is completely inaccessible without first lowering the steering column. The switch is actuated by a rod and rack assembly. A gear on the end of the lock cylinder engages the toothed upper end of the rod.

1. Disconnect the negative battery cable. Lower and support the steering column.

2. Put the switch in the **OFF-UN-LOCKED** position. With the cylinder removed, the rod is in **OFF-UN-LOCKED** position when it is in the next to the uppermost detent.

3. Remove the 2 switch screws and remove the switch assembly.

4. Before installing, place the new switch in **OFF-UNLOCKED** position and make sure the lock cylinder and actuating rod are in **OFF-UN-LOCKED** position (second detent from the top).

5. Install the activating rod into the switch and assemble the switch on the column. Tighten the mounting screws. Use only the specified screws, since

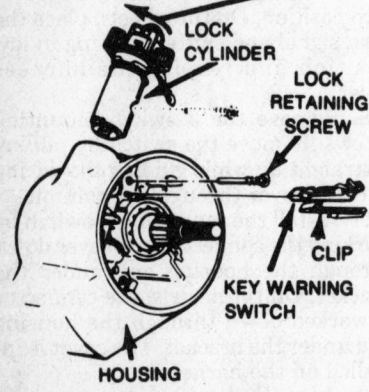

TO ASSEMBLE, ROTATE TO STOP WHILE HOLDING CYLINDER

LOCK CYLINDER

LOCK RETAINING SCREW

CLIP

KEY WARNING SWITCH

HOUSING

Lock cylinder installation

overlength screws could impair the collapsibility of the column.

6. Reinstall the steering column.

Ignition Lock Cylinder

REMOVAL & INSTALLATION

1. Remove the steering wheel.

2. Turn the lock to the **RUN** position.

3. Remove the lock plate, turn signal switch or combination switch, and the key warning buzzer switch. The warning buzzer switch can be fished out with a bent paper clip.

4. Remove the lock cylinder retaining screw and lock cylinder.

— **CAUTION** —

If the screw is dropped on removal, it could fall into the column, requiring complete disassembly to retrieve the screw.

---

5. Rotate the cylinder clockwise to align the cylinder key with the keyway in the housing.

6. Push the lock all the way in.

7. Install the screw. Tighten to 15 inch lbs.

8. The rest of installation is in the reverse of removal. Turn the lock to **RUN** position to install the key warning buzzer switch, which is simply pushed down into place.

Manual Steering Gear

REMOVAL & INSTALLATION

1. Disconnect the negative battery cable.

2. Remove the driver's side sound insulator.

3. Remove the seal assembly from under the steering column. Remove the upper pinch bolt.

4. Remove the air cleaner and the windshield washer reservoir assembly.

5. Raise the vehicle and support safely. Remove the wheel and tire assemblies.

6. Disconnect both tie rods from the support struts.

7. Disconnect the left and right hand mounting clamp from the vehicle chassis.

8. Remove the lower pinch bolt from the flexible coupling. Separate the flexible coupling from the rack assembly.

9. Remove the dash seal from the rack assembly.

10. Remove the splash shield from the driver's side inner fender if equipped.

11. Slide the rack and pinion assembly through the driver's side fender opening.

12. Installation is in the reverse or-

der of removal. Check and adjust toe setting as needed.

Power Steering Gear

REMOVAL & INSTALLATION

1. Disconnect the negative battery cable.

2. Remove the driver's side sound insulator.

3. Remove the seal assembly from under the steering column. Remove the upper pinch bolt.

4. Remove the air cleaner and the windshield washer reservoir assembly if necessary to gain working clearance.

5. Disconnect the pressure line from the rack assembly and the switch block. Remove the pressure line to gain access to the return line fitting.

6. Disconnect the return line from the rack assembly.

7. Raise the vehicle and support safely. Remove the wheel and tire assemblies.

8. Disconnect the both tie rods from the support struts.

9. Disconnect the left and right hand mounting clamp from the vehicle chassis.

10. Remove the lower pinch bolt from the flexible coupling. Separate the flexible coupling from the rack assembly.

11. Remove the dash seal from the rack assembly.

12. Remove the splash shield from the driver's side inner fender.

13. Slide the rack and pinion assembly through the driver's side fender opening.

14. Installation is in the reverse order of removal. Check and adjust toe setting as needed.

NOTE: 1982–84 J-Body vehicles equipped with power steering may exhibit a temporary reduction of power steering when vehicle is cold. After a short period of engine operation, full assist is restored. This indicates a internal power steering rack problem. Contact General Motors about Special Policy covering this item.

Power Steering Pump

REMOVAL & INSTALLATION

1. Disconnect the negative battery cable.

2. Disconnect the vent hose at the carburetor.

3. Loosen the adjusting bolt and pivot bolt on the pump. Remove the pump drive belt.

4. Remove the 3 pump-to-bracket bolts and remove the adjusting bolt.

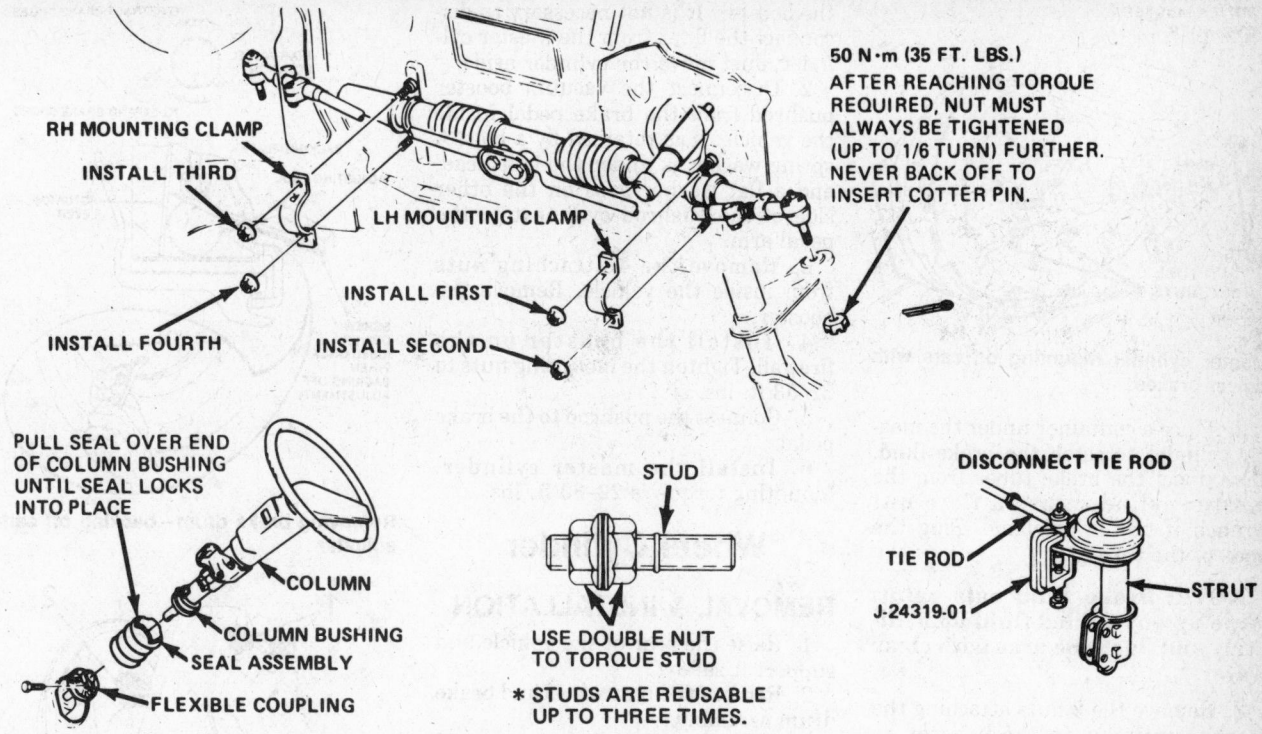

RH MOUNTING CLAMP

INSTALL THIRD

LH MOUNTING CLAMP

INSTALL FIRST

INSTALL FOURTH

INSTALL SECOND

50 N·m (35 FT. LBS.)
AFTER REACHING TORQUE
REQUIRED, NUT MUST
ALWAYS BE TIGHTENED
(UP TO 1/6 TURN) FURTHER.
NEVER BACK OFF TO
INSERT COTTER PIN.

PULL SEAL OVER END
OF COLUMN BUSHING
UNTIL SEAL LOCKS
INTO PLACE

COLUMN

COLUMN BUSHING

SEAL ASSEMBLY

FLEXIBLE COUPLING

STUD

USE DOUBLE NUT
TO TORQUE STUD

* STUDS ARE REUSABLE
UP TO THREE TIMES.

Manual rack and pinion unit mounting

DISCONNECT TIE ROD

TIE ROD

J-24319-01

STRUT

5. Remove the high pressure fitting from the pump.

6. Disconnect the reservoir-to-pump hose from the pump.

7. Remove the pump.

8. Installation is in the reverse order of removal. Adjust the belt tension and bleed the system.

BELT ADJUSTMENT

1. Loosen the adjustment nut and bolt in the slotted bracket. Slightly loosen the pivot bolt.

2. Pull (don't pry) the component outward to increase tension. Push inward to reduce tension. Tighten the adjusting nut and bolt and the pivot bolt.

3. Recheck the drive belt tension which is 135 lbs. on a new belt, 75 lbs. on a used belt and readjust if necessary.

NOTE: On a serpentine belt the correct tension is indicated on the indicator mark of the belt tensioner. If the indicator mark is not within specification, replace the belt or the tensioner.

SYSTEM BLEEDING

1. Raise the front of the vehicle and support safely.

2. With the wheels turned all the way to the left, add power steering fluid to the **COLD** mark on the fluid level indicator.

3. Start the engine and check the fluid level at fast idle. Add fluid, if necessary to bring the level up to the **COLD** mark.

4. Bleed air from the system by turning the wheels from side-to-side without hitting the stops. Keep the fluid level just above the internal pump casting or at the **COLD** mark.

5. Return the wheels to the center position and continue running the engine for 2–3 minutes.

6. Road test the vehicle to check steering function and recheck the fluid level with the system at its normal operating temperature. Fluid should be at the **HOT** mark.

Tie Rod Ends

REMOVAL & INSTALLATION

1. Loosen both pinch bolts at the outer tie rod.

2. Remove the tie rod end from the strut assembly using a suitable removal tool.

3. Unscrew the outer tie rod end from the tie rod adjuster, counting the number of turns required before they are disconnected.

4. Install the new tie rod end, screwing it on the same number of turns as counted in Step 3. When the tie rod end is installed, the tie rod adjuster must be centered between the tie rod and the tie rod end, with an equal number of threads exposed on

both sides of the adjuster nut. Tighten the pinch bolts to 20 ft. lbs.

5. Install the tie rod end to the strut assembly and tighten to 50 ft. lbs. If the cotter pin cannot be installed, tighten the nut up to $\frac{1}{16}$ in. further. Never back off the nut to align the holes for the cotter pin.

6. Check front end alignment.

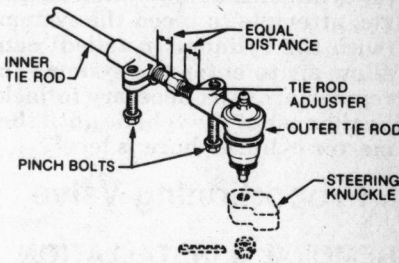

INNER TIE ROD

EQUAL DISTANCE

TIE ROD ADJUSTER

OUTER TIE ROD

PINCH BOLTS

STEERING KNUCKLE

Tie rod end removal and installation

BRAKES

For all brake system repair and service procedures not detailed below, please refer to "Brakes" in the Unit Repair section.

Master Cylinder

REMOVAL & INSTALLATION

1. Disconnect the electrical connector from the master cylinder.

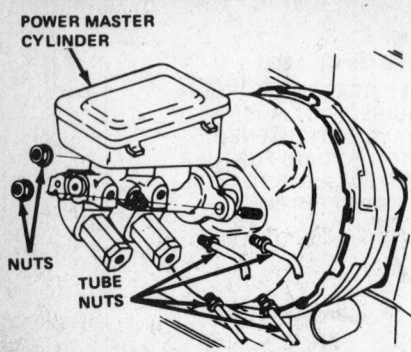

POWER MASTER CYLINDER

NUTS

TUBE NUTS

Master cylinder mounting on cars with power brakes

2. Place a container under the master cylinder to catch the brake fluid. Disconnect the brake tubes from the master cylinder; use a flare nut wrench if one is available. Plug the ends of the tubes.

NOTE: Brake fluid eats paint. Wipe up any spilled fluid immediately and flush the area with clear water.

3. Remove the 2 nuts attaching the master cylinder to the booster or firewall.
4. Remove the master cylinder.
5. To install, attach the master cylinder to the booster with the nuts. Torque to 22–30 ft. lbs.
6. Remove the tape from the lines and connect to the master cylinder. Torque to 10–15 ft. lbs. Connect the electrical lead.
7. Bleed the brakes.

NOTE: When installing a master cylinder that mounts on an angle, attempts to bleed the system (with the cylinder installed) can allow air to enter the system. To remove air, it is necesary to jack up the rear of the vehicle until the master cylinder bore is level.

Proportioning Valve

REMOVAL & INSTALLATION

There is a front and a rear proportioning valve located at the lower left side of the master cylinder. To remove the proportioning valves, disconnect the brake lines from the valves. Disconnect the valves from the master cylinder and remove the O-rings. Replace the old O-rings and proportioning valves with new ones and reinstall into the master cylinder. Torque the proportioning valves to 18–30 ft. lbs.

Power Brake Booster

REMOVAL & INSTALLATION

1. Remove the master cylinder from

the booster. It is not necessary to disconnect the lines from the master cylinder. Just move the cylinder aside.
2. Disconnect the vacuum booster pushrod from the brake pedal inside the vehicle. It is retained by a bolt. A spring washer is under the bolt head, and a flat washer goes on the other side of the pushrod eye, next to the pedal arm.
3. Remove the 4 attaching nuts from inside the vehicle. Remove the booster.
4. Install the booster on the firewall. Tighten the mounting nuts to 22–33 ft. lbs.
5. Connect the pushrod to the brake pedal.
6. Install the master cylinder. Mounting torque is 22–33 ft. lbs.

Wheel Cylinder

REMOVAL & INSTALLATION

1. Raise the rear of the vehicle and support it safely.
2. Remove the rear wheel and brake drum assembly.
3. Disconnect the inlet tube nut and line from the wheel cylinder.
4. Remove the wheel cylinder retainer using 2 awls or pins $1/8$ in. diameter or less.
   a. Insert the awls or pins into the access slots between the wheel cylinder pilot and the retainer locking tabs.
   b. Bend both tabs away simultaneously.
5. Remove the wheel cylinder.
To install:
6. Position the wheel cylinder and hold it in place using a wooden block placed between the the wheel cylinder and the axle flange.
7. Install a new wheel cylinder retainer over the wheel cylinder abutment using a 1⅛ inch 12 point socket and extension.
8. Reconnect the inlet tube nut and torque to 12 ft. lbs.
9. Reinstall the brake drum and bleed the brake system.
10. Install the wheels, lower the vehicle and check for leaks.

Parking Brake Cable

ADJUSTMENT

1. Raise and support the vehicle with both rear wheels off the ground.
2. Pull the parking brake lever exactly 2 ratchet clicks.

NOTE: To prevent damage to the threaded adjusting rod, thoroughly clean and lubricate the threads before turning the adjusting nut.

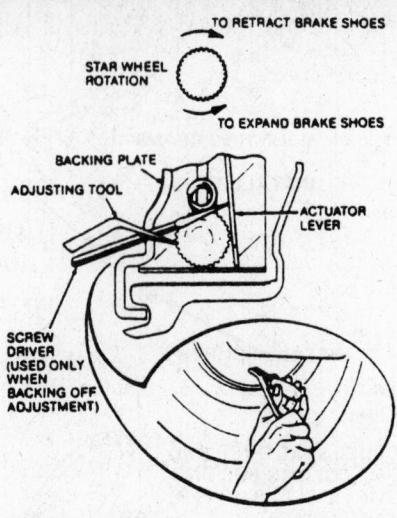

TO RETRACT BRAKE SHOES

STAR WHEEL ROTATION

TO EXPAND BRAKE SHOES

BACKING PLATE

ADJUSTING TOOL

ACTUATOR LEVER

SCREW DRIVER (USED ONLY WHEN BACKING OFF ADJUSTMENT)

Removing brake drum—backing off self-adjuster

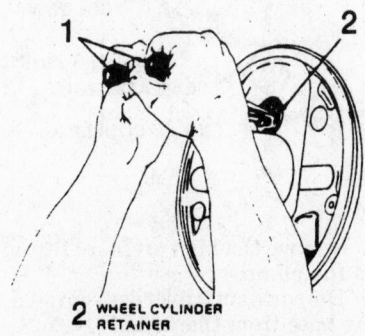

1
2
2 WHEEL CYLINDER RETAINER

1. Awls
2. Wheel cylinder retainer

Removing wheel cylinder retainer

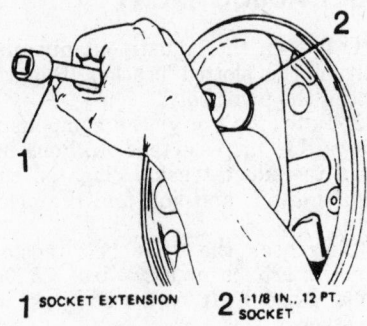

2
1
1 SOCKET EXTENSION
2 1-1/8 IN. 12 PT. SOCKET

1. Socket extension
2. 1⅛ in., 12 pt socket

Installing wheel cylinder retainer

3. Loosen the equalizer locknut and tighten the adjusting nut until the left rear wheel can just be turned backward using 2 hands, but is locked in forward rotation.
4. Tighten the locknut.
5. Release the parking brake. Rotate the rear wheels—there should be no drag.
6. Lower the vehicle.

REMOVAL & INSTALLATION

Front Cable

1. Place the gear selector in **NEU-TRAL** and apply the parking brake.
2. Remove the center console.
3. Disconnect the parking brake cable from the lever.
4. Remove the cable retaining nut and the bracket securing the front cable to the floor panel.
5. Raise the vehicle and loosen the equalizer nut.
6. Loosen the catalytic converter shield and remove the parking brake cable from the body.
7. Disconnect the cable from the equalizer and remove the cable from the guide and the underbody clips.
8. Reverse the procedure and adjust the cable.

Rear Cables

1. Raise and support the rear of the vehicle.
2. Back off the equalizer nut until the cable tension is eliminated.
3. Remove the wheel assembly and brake drums.
4. Insert a small prybar or equivalent between the brake shoe and the top part of the brake adjuster bracket. Push the bracket to the front and release the top brake adjuster rod.
5. Remove the rear hold down spring. Remove the actuator lever and the lever return spring.
6. Remove the adjuster screw spring.
7. Remove the top rear brake shoe return spring.
8. Unhook the parking brake cable from the parking brake lever.
9. Depress the conduit fitting retaining tangs and remove the conduit fitting from the backing plate.
10. Remove the cable end button from the connector.
11. Depress the conduit fitting retaining tangs and remove the conduit fitting from the axle bracket.
12. Reverse the procedure to install and adjust the cable.

CHASSIS ELECTRICAL

Heater Blower

REMOVAL & INSTALLATION

1. Disconnect the negative battery cable.
2. Disconnect the electrical connec-

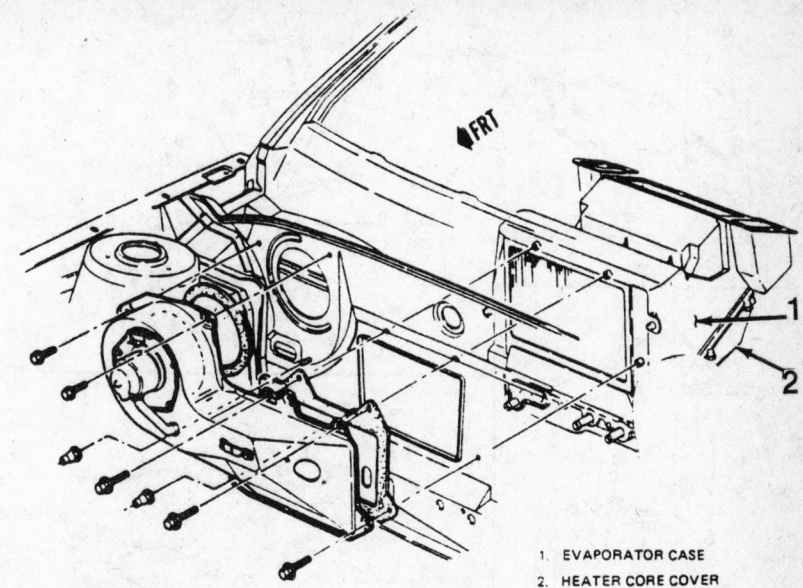

1. EVAPORATOR CASE
2. HEATER CORE COVER

Heater assembly

tions at the blower motor and blower resistor.
3. Remove the plastic water shield from the right side of the cowl.
4. Remove the blower motor retaining screws and remove the blower motor and cage.
5. Hold the blower motor cage and remove retaining nut from the blower motor shaft.
6. Remove the blower motor and cage.
7. Install the cage on the new motor.
8. Check that the retaining nut is on tight, the motor rotates and the fan cage is not interferring with the motor.
9. Install the motor in the heater assembly, connect the wiring and check the motor operation in all speeds.

Heater Core

REMOVAL & INSTALLATION

Without Air Conditioning

1. Disconnect the negative battery cable and drain the cooling system.
2. Remove the heater hoses at the heater core.
3. Remove the heater outlet deflector.
4. Remove the heater core cover retaining screws. Remove the heater core cover.
5. Remove the heater core retaining straps and remove the heater core.
6. Install the new heater core and retaining straps.
7. Install the heater oulet deflector and heater core cover.

8. Connect the heater hoses to the core.
9. Fill and bleed the cooling system when finished. Check for leaks and the heater operation.

With Air Conditioning

1. Disconnect the negative battery cable and drain the cooling system.
2. Raise and support the front of the vehicle.
3. Disconnect the drain tube from the heater case.
4. Remove the heater hoses from the heater core.
5. Lower the vehicle. Remove the right and left hush panels, steering column trim cover, heater outlet duct and glove box.
6. Remove the heater core cover. Pull the cover straight to the rear so it does not damage the drain tube.
7. Remove the heater core clamps and remove the heater core.
8. Install the heater core and clamps.
9. Install the heater core cover using care not to damage the drain tube.
10. Install the glove box, heater outlet duct, steering column trim cover and hush panels.
11. Raise and support the vehicle safely.
12. Connect the heater hoses to the heater core and the drain tube to the case.
13. Lower the vehicle, fill the cooling system and connect the negative battery cable.
14. Check the heater operation and bleed the cooling system. Check for leaks.

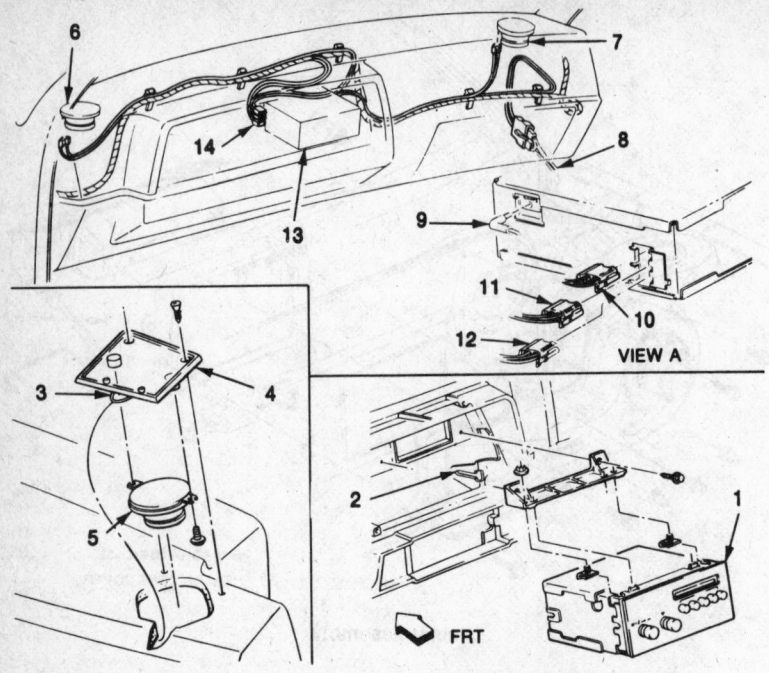

1. Radio
2. Screw on side of radio fits here
3. Retainer
4. Grille
5. Speaker
6. Front speaker
7. Front speaker
8. Rear speaker wire
9. Antenna
10. Rear speakers
11. Front speakers
12. Instrument panel harness
13. Receiver
14. Instrument panel harness

Radio removal and installation

NOTE: If evaporator drain hose becomes pluged a water leak at passenger side floor carpet will develope. To repair working from under the hood cut of the bottom of the drain hose.

Radio

REMOVAL & INSTALLATION

NOTE: Do not operate the radio with the speaker leads disconnected. Operating the radio without an electrical load will damage the output transistors.

1. Disconnect the negative battery cable.
2. Remove the center instrument panel trim plate.
3. Check the right side of the radio to determine whether a nut or a stud is used for side retention.
4. If a nut is used, remove the hush panel and loosen the nut from below on models without air conditioning. On models with air conditioning, remove the hush panel, A/C duct and A/C control head for access to the nut. Do not remove the nut; loosen it just enough to pull the radio out. If a rubber stud is used, go to Step 5.
5. Remove the 2 radio bracket-to-instrument panel attaching screws.

Pull the radio forward far enough to disconnect and tag the wiring and antenna. Remove the radio.
6. Installation is the reverse of the removal procedure.

Windshield Wiper Switch

REMOVAL & INSTALLATION

1. Disconnect the negative battery cable. Remove the steering wheel and turn signal switch.

NOTE: It may be necessary to loosen the 2 column mounting nuts and remove the 4 bracket-to-mast jacket to allow the connector clip on the ignition switch to be pulled out of the column assembly.

2. Disconnect the wiper switch lower connector.
3. Remove the screws attaching the column housing to the mast jacket. Note the position of the dimmer switch actuator rod for reassembly. Remove the column housing and switch as an assembly.

NOTE: Tilt and travel columns have a removable plastic cover on the column housing. This pro- vides access to the wiper switch without removing the entire column housing.

4. Turn the switch upside down and use a drift to remove the pivot pin from the switch. Remove the switch.
5. Place the switch into the housing and install the pivot pin.
6. Position and attach the housing onto the mast jacket by installing the screws.
7. Install the dimmer switch actuator rod in the same position as noted earlier. Check the switch operation.
8. Reconnect lower switch wiring.
9. Install the remaining components in reverse order of removal. Be sure to attach column mounting bracket in the original position.

Windshield Wiper Motor

REMOVAL & INSTALLATION

1. Loosen, but do not remove, the drive link-to-crank arm attaching nuts. Detach the drive link from the motor crank arm.
2. Tag and disconnect all electrical leads from the wiper motor.
3. Remove the motor mounting bolts, rotate the motor up and outward and remove the motor.
4. To install, guide the crank arm through the opening in the body and tighten the mounting bolts to 4–6 ft. lbs.
5. Install the drive link to the crank arm with the motor in the park position.
6. Check that all tools, rags, etc. are removed from the linkage area and check the motor operation.

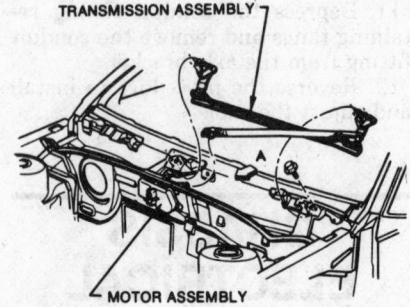

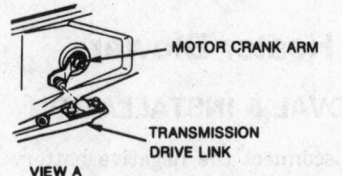

Wiper motor and linkage

Instrument Cluster

REMOVAL & INSTALLATION

1. Disconnect the negative battery cable.

2. Remove the right and left hush panels. Remove the steering column trim cover. Disconnect the vent panels from the bottom of the panel, if equipped.

3. Remove the glove box. Disconnect the temperature and mode control cables on models without air conditioning. On models with air conditioning, remove the lower A/C outlet duct.

4. Remove the 3 steering column retaining bolts (2 at the instrument panel pad and one at the cowl). Lower and support the steering column.

5. Remove the lower right hand trim plate. Disconnect and tag the cigar lighter and accessory switches.

6. Pull the heater or A/C control head out far enough to disconnect and tag any wiring or vacuum harnesses. Remove the control head.

7. Disconnect the front end and engine wiring harnesses from the bulkhead connector in the engine compartment. Remove the bulkhead connector from the cowl, (2) screws.

8. Loosen the set screw and remove the hood release cable handle. Remove the retaining nut and pull the hood release cable loose.

9. Remove the 4 upper instrument panel retaining screws, in the defroster duct openings.

10. Remove the 2 lower corner instrument panel retaining nuts. Remove the screw for the instrument panel brace from the left side of the glove box opening.

11. Pull the instrument panel out far enough to disconnect and tag the ignition, dimmer switch and turn signal switch wiring. Tag and disconnect all other wiring and vacuum lines.

12. Remove the instrument panel with the wiring harness intact.

13. Installation is the reverse of the removal procedure.

Headlight Switch

REMOVAL & INSTALLATION

1. Disconnect the negative battery cable.

2. Pull the knob out fully. Remove the knob from the rod by depressing the retaining clip with a small tool from the underside of the knob.

3. Remove the switch trimplate from the dashboard.

4. Remove the retaining nut from the switch.

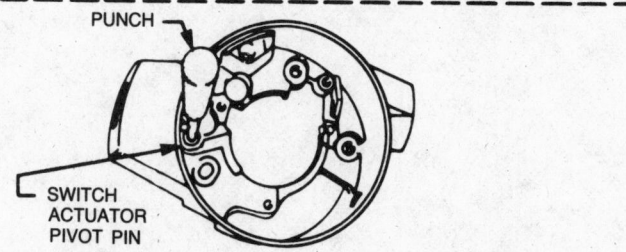

Removal and installation of the wiper switch

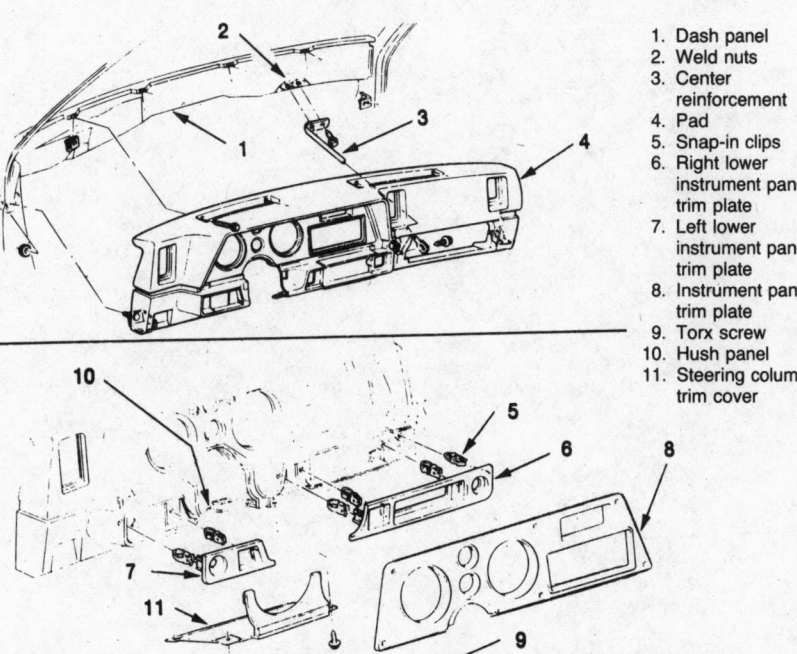

1. Dash panel
2. Weld nuts
3. Center reinforcement
4. Pad
5. Snap-in clips
6. Right lower instrument panel trim plate
7. Left lower instrument panel trim plate
8. Instrument panel trim plate
9. Torx screw
10. Hush panel
11. Steering column trim cover

Instrument panel and trim plate mounting

5. Rotate the switch 180 degrees, tilt it forward and pull it out.

6. Disconnect and tag the wiring from the switch.

7. Installation is the reverse of the removal procedure.

Stoplight Switch

REMOVAL & INSTALLATION

1. Disconnect the negative battery cable.

2. Disconnect the wiring connector at the switch.

3. Remove the switch.

4. Install the switch and adjust it so the brake lights are not on unless the brake pedal is depressed.

Fuses and Circuit Breakers

LOCATION

The fuse box is located under the left side of the instrument panel. The amperage of each fuse and the circuit it protects is stamped on the fuse box.

NOTE: All major electrical systems are protected by fuses. In the event of an overload, the fuse melts, protecting the component. If a fuse melts, the cause should be investigated and repaired before replacing the fuse.

The headlights, windshield wipers, power door locks and power windows are protected by circuit breakers. The circuit breaker for the headlights is located in the headlight switch. The breaker for the wipers is located in the wiper switch. The breakers for the power door locks and power windows are located in the fuse box.

Breakers reset themselves automatically when the problem is relieved. A convenience center is located on the underside of the instrument panel, providing a central location for various relays, the hazard flasher and buzzer. All units are plug-in modules. The turn signal flasher is locted directly under the steering column. In order to gain access, it may be necessary to remove the under dash cover panel.

GM "N" Body
Front Wheel Drive
Buick Somerset Regal, Buick Skylark,
Oldsmobile Calais, Pontiac Grand Am

27

SERIAL NUMBER IDENTIFICATION

VEHICLE IDENTIFICATION CHART

It is important for servicing and ordering parts to be certain of the vehicle and engine identification. The VIN (vehicle identification number) is a 17 digit number visible through the windshield on the driver's side of the dash and contains the vehicle and engine identification codes. The tenth digit indicates model year, and the eighth digit indicates engine code. It can be interpreted as follows:

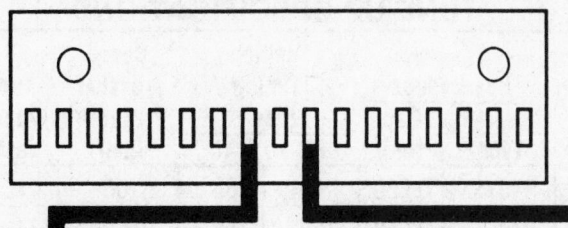

Engine Code						Model Year	
Code	Cu. In.	Liters	Cyl.	Fuel Sys.	Eng. Mfg.	Code	Year
U	151	2.5	4	TBI	Pontiac	F	1985
M	122	2.0	4	MFI①	Pontiac	G	1986
D	138	2.3	4	MFI②	Olds	H	1987
L	181	3.0	6	MFI	Buick	J	1988
						K	1989

TBI Throttle Body Injection
MFI Multi-port Fuel Injection
① Turbo
② Quad-4 engine

GENERAL ENGINE SPECIFICATIONS

Year	VIN	No. Cylinder Displacement cu. in. (liter)	Fuel System Type	Net Horsepower @ rpm	Net Torque @ rpm (ft.lbs.)	Bore × Stroke (in.)	Compression Ratio	Oil Pressure @ rpm
1985	U	4–151 (2.5)	TBI	92 @ 4400	134 @ 2800	4.00 × 3.00	9.0:1	37 @ 2000
	L	6–181 (3.0)	MFI	125 @ 4900	150 @ 2400	3.80 × 2.70	9.0:1	37 @ 2400
1986	U	4–151 (2.5)	TBI	92 @ 4400	134 @ 2800	4.00 × 3.00	9.0:1	37 @ 2000
	L	6–181 (3.0)	MFI	125 @ 4900	150 @ 2400	3.80 × 2.70	9.0:1	37 @ 2400
1987	M	4-122 (2.0)	MFI①	167 @ 4500	175 @ 4000	3.50 × 3.15	9.0:1	—
	D	4–138 (2.3)	MFI	150 @ 4500	150 @ 2400	3.62 × 3.35	9.5:1	25 @ 2000
	U	4–151 (2.5)	TBI	92 @ 4400	132 @ 2800	4.00 × 3.00	9.0:1	37 @ 2000
	L	6–181 (3.0)	MFI	125 @ 4900	150 @ 2400	3.80 × 2.70	9.0:1	37 @ 2400
1988-89	M	4-122 (2.0)	MFI①	167 @ 4500	175 @ 4000	3.50 × 3.15	9.0:1	—
	D	4–138 (2.3)	MFI	150 @ 4500	150 @ 2400	3.62 × 3.35	9.5:1	25 @ 2000
	U	4–151 (2.5)	TBI	92 @ 4400	132 @ 2800	4.00 × 3.00	9.0:1	37 @ 2000
	L	6–181 (3.0)	MFI	125 @ 4900	150 @ 2400	3.80 × 2.70	9.0:1	37 @ 2400

TBI Throttle Body Injection
MFI Multi-port Fuel Injection
① Turbo

TUNE-UP SPECIFICATIONS

Year	VIN	No. Cylinder Displacement cu. in. (liter)	Spark Plugs Type	Gap (in.)	Ignition Timing (deg.) MT	AT	Compression Pressure (psi)	Fuel Pump (psi)	Idle Speed (rpm) MT	AT	Valve Clearance In.	Ex.
1985	U	4–151 (2.5)	R43TSX	0.060	8B	8B	100	12	①	①	Zero	Zero
	L	6–181 (3.0)	R44LTS	0.040	15B	15B	100	34–44	①	①	Zero	Zero
1986	U	4–151 (2.5)	R43TS6	0.060	8B	8B	100	12	①	①	Zero	Zero
	L	6–181 (3.0)	R44LTS	0.040	15B	15B	100	34–44	①	①	Zero	Zero
1987	M	4–122 (2.0)②	R42XLS	0.035	8B	8B	100	—	①	①	Zero	Zero
	D	4–138 (2.3)	FR3LS	0.035	—	—	—	34–44	—	—	Zero	Zero
	U	4–151 (2.5)	R43TS6	0.060	8B	8B	100	12	①	①	Zero	Zero
	L	6–181 (3.0)	R44LTS	0.040	15B	15B	100	34–44	①	①	Zero	Zero
1988	M	4–122 (2.0)②	R42XLS	0.035	8B	8B	100	—	①	①	Zero	Zero
	D	4–138 (2.3)	FR3LS	0.035	—	—	—	34–44	—	—	Zero	Zero
	U	4–151 (2.5)	R43TS6	0.060	8B	8B	100	9–13	①	①	Zero	Zero
	L	6–181 (3.0)	R44LTS	0.045	③	③	100	34–44	①	①	Zero	Zero
1989					SEE UNDERHOOD SPECIFICATIONS STICKER							

NOTE: The Underhood Specifications sticker often reflects tune-up specification changes made in production. Sticker figures must be used if they disagree with those in this chart.
B Before Top Dead Center
① See Underhood Specifications sticker
② Turbocharged model
③ No timing adjustment required with C³I ignition

FIRING ORDERS

NOTE: To avoid confusion, always replace spark plug wires one at a time.

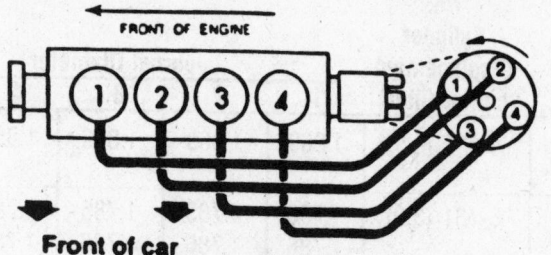

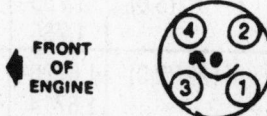

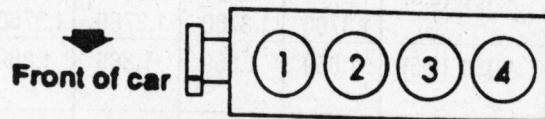

GM (Pontiac) 122–2.0L
Engine firing order: 1–3–4–2
Distributor rotation: counterclockwise

GM (Pontiac) 151–2.5L
Engine firing order: 1–3–4–2
Distributor rotation: clockwise

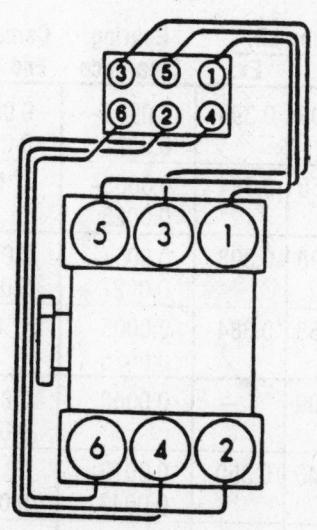

Buick V6 with C3I ignition system, Engine firing order: 1–6–5–4–3–2

CAPACITIES

Year	VIN	No. Cylinder Displacement cu. in. (liter)	Engine Crankcase		Transaxle (pts.)		Drive Axle (pts.)	Fuel Tank (gals.)	Cooling System (qts.)
			with Filter	without Filter	MT	AT			
1985	U	4–151 (2.5)	3.5	3.0	5.4	11.7	—	13.6	7.9①
	L	6–181 (3.0)	4.5	4.0	—	18.0	—	13.6	5.5①
1986	U	4–151 (2.5)	3.5	3.0	5.4	11.7	—	13.6	7.9①
	L	6–181 (3.0)	4.5	4.0	—	18.0	—	13.6	5.5①
1987	M	4–122 (2.0)	4.0	3.8	6.0	11.0	—	13.6	8.3
	D	4–138 (2.3)	②	4.0	6.0③	8.0④	—	13.6	7.6
	U	4–151 (2.5)	3.5	3.0	5.4	11.7	—	13.6	7.8①
	L	6–181 (3.0)	4.5	4.0	—	18.0	—	13.6	9.7①
1988-89	M	4–122 (2.0)	②	4.0	6.0③	8.0④	—	13.6	7.8①
	D	4–138 (2.3)	②	4.0	6.0③	8.0④	—	13.6	7.6
	U	4–151 (2.5)	②	4.0	6.0③	8.0④	—	13.6	7.8
	L	6–181 (3.0)	②	4.0	6.0③	8.0④	—	13.6	10.4

① With A/C
② When changing oil filter, additional oil may be needed
③ Manual 5 speed MK7 or MT2 — 5.4 pts.
③ Manual 5 speed MG1 or MG2 — 4.4 pts.
④ Drain and refill after complete overhaul — 12 pts.

CAMSHAFT SPECIFICATIONS
All measurements given in inches.

Year	VIN	No. Cylinder Displacement cu. in. (liter)	Journal Diameter 1	2	3	4	5	Lobe Lift In.	Ex.	Bearing Clearance	Camshaft End Play
1985	U	4-151 (2.5)	1.869	1.869	1.869	1.869	1.869	0.398	0.398	0.0007–0.0027	0.0015–0.0050
	L	6-181 (3.0)	1.785–1.786	1.785–1.786	1.785–1.786	1.785–1.786	–	0.358	0.384	0.0005–0.0025	NA
1986	U	4-151 (2.5)	1.869	1.869	1.869	1.869	1.869	0.398	0.398	0.0007–0.0027	0.0015–0.0050
	L	6-181 (3.0)	1.785–1.786	1.785–1.786	1.785–1.786	1.785–1.786	–	0.358	0.384	0.0005–0.0025	NA
1987	M	4-122 (2.0)	1.6720–1.6714	1.6816–1.6812	1.6917–1.6911	1.7015–1.7009	1.7114–1.7108	0.2409	–	0.0008	0.0016–0.0064
	D	4-138 (2.3)	1.3751–1.3760	1.3751–1.3760	1.3751–1.3760	1.3751–1.3760	1.3751–1.3760	0.340	0.350	0.0019–0.0043	0.006–0.0014
	U	4-151 (2.5)	1.869	1.869	1.869	1.869	1.869	0.398	0.398	0.0007–0.0027	0.0015–0.0050
	L	6-181 (3.0)	1.785–1.786	1.785–1.786	1.785–1.786	1.785–1.786	–	0.358	0.384	0.0005–0.0025	NA
1987-88	M	4-122 (2.0)	1.6720–1.6714	1.6816–1.6812	1.6917–1.6911	1.7015–1.7009	1.7114–1.7108	0.2409	–	0.0008	0.0016–0.0064
	D	4-138 (2.3)	1.3751–1.3760	1.3751–1.3760	1.3751–1.3760	1.3751–1.3760	1.3751–1.3760	0.340	0.350	0.0019–0.0043	0.006–0.0014
	U	4-151 (2.5)	1.869	1.869	1.869	1.869	1.869	0.398	0.398	0.0007–0.0027	0.0015–0.0050
	L	6-181 (3.0)	1.785–1.786	1.785–1.786	1.785–1.786	1.785–1.786	–	0.358	0.384	0.0005–0.0025	NA

NA Not available

CRANKSHAFT AND CONNECTING ROD SPECIFICATIONS
All measurements are given in inches.

Year	VIN	No. Cylinder Displacement cu. in. (liter)	Crankshaft Main Brg. Journal Dia.	Main Brg. Oil Clearance	Shaft End-play	Thrust on No.	Connecting Rod Journal Diameter	Oil Clearance	Side Clearance
1985	U	4–151 (2.5)	2.3000	0.0005–0.0022	0.0035–0.0085	5	2.000	0.0005–0.0022	0.006–0.022
	L	6–181 (3.0)	2.4995	0.0003–0.0018	0.0030–0.0150	2	2.487	0.0005–0.0026	0.003–0.015
1986	U	4–151 (2.5)	2.3000	0.0005–0.0022	0.0035–0.0085	5	2.000	0.0005–0.0022	0.006–0.022
	L	6–181 (3.0)	2.4995	0.0003–0.0018	0.0030–0.0150	2	2.487	0.0005–0.0026	0.003–0.015

CRANKSHAFT AND CONNECTING ROD SPECIFICATIONS
All measurements are given in inches.

Year		Engine Displacement cu. in. (cc)	Crankshaft				Connecting Rod		
			Main Brg. Journal Dia.	Main Brg. Oil Clearance	Shaft End-play	Thrust on No.	Journal Diameter	Oil Clearance	Side Clearance
1987	M	4–122 (2.0)	2.2830–2.2833 ①	0.0006–0.0016	0.003–0.012	3	1.9278–1.9286	0.0007–0.0024	0.0027–0.0095
	D	4–138 (2.3)	2.0470–2.0474	0.0005–0.0020	0.0034–0.0095	3	1.8887–1.8897	0.0005–0.0025	0.0059–0.0177
	U	4–151 (2.5)	2.3000	0.0005–0.0022	0.0035–0.0085	5	2.000	0.0005–0.0022	0.006–0.022
	L	6–181 (3.0)	2.4995	0.0003–0.0018	0.0030–0.0085	2	2.487	0.0005–0.0026	0.003–0.015
1988-89	M	4–122 (2.0)	2.2830–2.2833	0.0006–0.0016	0.003–0.012	3	1.9278–1.9286	0.0007–0.0024	0.0027–0.0095
	D	4–138 (2.3)	2.0470–2.0474	0.0005–0.0020	0.0034–0.0095	3	1.8887–1.8897	0.0005–0.0025	0.0059–0.0177
	U	4–151 (2.5)	2.3000	0.0005–0.0022	0.0035–0.0085	5	2.000	0.0005–0.0022	0.006–0.022
	L	6–181 (3.0)	2.4988–2.4998	0.0003–0.0018	0.0030–0.0011	2	2.487	0.0003–	0.003–0.015

① Brown; Green — 2.2827–2.2830

VALVE SPECIFICATIONS

Year	VIN	No. Cylinder Displacement cu. in. (liter)	Seat Angle (deg.)	Face Angle (deg.)	Spring Test Pressure (lbs.)	Spring Installed Height (in.)	Stem-to-Guide Clearance (in.)		Stem Diameter (in.)	
							Intake	Exhaust	Intake	Exhaust
1985	U	4–151 (2.5)	46	45	82	1.66	0.0010–0.0027	0.0010–0.0027	0.3420–0.3430	0.3420–0.3430
	L	6–181 (3.0)	45	45	220	1.34	0.0015–0.0035	0.0015–0.0032	0.3401–0.3412	0.3405–0.3412
1986	U	4–151 (2.5)	46	45	82	1.66	0.0010–0.0027	0.0010–0.0027	0.3130–0.3140	0.3120–0.3130
	L	6–181 (3.0)	45	45	220	1.34	0.0015–0.0035	0.0015–0.0032	0.3401–0.3412	0.3405–0.3412
1987	M	4–122 (2.0)	45	46	—	—	0.0006–0.0020	0.0001–0.0024	—	—
	D	4–138 (2.3)	45	②	③	1.423–1.443	0.0009–0.0027	0.0015–0.0032	0.2751–0.2744	0.2754–0.2739
	U	4–151 (2.5)	46	45	75	1.44	—	—	0.3130–0.3140	0.3120–0.3130
	L	6–181 (3.0)	45	45	90	1.73	0.0015–0.0035	0.0015–0.0032	0.3401–0.3412	0.3405–0.3412

VALVE SPECIFICATIONS

Year	VIN	No. Cylinder Displacement cu. in. (liter)	Seat Angle (deg.)	Face Angle (deg.)	Spring Test Pressure (lbs.)	Spring Installed Height (in.)	Stem-to-Guide Clearance (in.)		Stem Diameter (in.)	
							Intake	Exhaust	Intake	Exhaust
1988-89	M	4–122 (2.0)	45	46	—	—	0.0006–0.0020	0.0001–0.0024	—	—
	D	4–138 (2.3)	45	②	③	1.423–1.443	0.0009–0.0027	0.0015–0.0032	0.2751–0.2744	0.2754–0.2739
	U	4–151 (2.5)	46	45	①	1.44	—	—	0.3130–0.3140	0.3120–0.3130
	L	6–181 (3.0)	46	45	90	1.73	0.0015–0.0035	0.0015–0.0032	0.3401–0.3412	0.3405–0.3412

① 71–78 ft. lbs. @ 1.440 in.
② 44 degrees intake face angle
   44.5 degrees exhaust face angle
③ 64–70 ft. lbs. @ 1.4370 in.

PISTON AND RING SPECIFICATIONS
All measurments are given in inches.

Year	VIN	No. Cylinder Displacement cu. in. (liter)	Piston Clearance	Ring Gap			Ring Side Clearance		
				Top Compression	Bottom Compression	Oil Control	Top Compression	Bottom Compression	Oil Control
1985	U	4–151 (2.5)	0.0014–0.0022 ①	0.010–0.020	0.010–0.020	0.020–0.060	0.002–0.003	0.001–0.003	0.015–0.055
	L	6–181 (3.0)	0.0008–0.0020 ②	0.013–0.028	0.013–0.023	0.015–0.035	0.003–0.005	0.003–0.005	0.0035
1986	U	4–151 (2.5)	0.0014–0.0022 ①	0.010–0.020	0.010–0.020	0.020–0.060	0.002–0.003	0.001–0.003	0.015–0.055
	L	6–181 (3.0)	0.0008–0.0020 ②	0.013–0.028	0.013–0.023	0.015–0.035	0.003–0.005	0.003–0.005	0.0035
1987	M	4–122 (2.0)	0.0012–0.0020	0.012–0.020	0.012–0.020	0.016–0.055	0.002–0.003	0.001–0.0024	—
	D	4–138 (2.3)	0.0007–0.0020	0.016–0.025	0.016–0.025	0.016–0.055	0.002–0.0035	0.0016–0.0031	—
	U	4–151 (2.5)	0.0014–0.0022 ①	0.010–0.020	0.010–0.020	0.020–0.060	0.002–0.003	0.001–0.003	0.015–0.055
	L	6–181 (3.0)	0.0008–0.0020 ②	0.013–0.028	0.013–0.023	0.015–0.035	0.003–0.005	0.003–0.005	0.0035

PISTON AND RING SPECIFICATIONS
All measurments are given in inches.

Year	VIN	No. Cylinder Displacement cu. in. (liter)	Piston Clearance	Ring Gap			Ring Side Clearance		
				Top Compression	Bottom Compression	Oil Control	Top Compression	Bottom Compression	Oil Control
1988-89	M	4–122 (2.0)	0.0012–0.0020	0.012–0.020	0.012–0.020	0.016–0.055	0.002–0.003	0.001–0.0024	–
	D	4–138 (2.3)	0.0007–0.0020	0.016–0.025	0.016–0.025	0.016–0.055	0.002–0.0035	0.0016–0.0031	–
	U	4–151 (2.5)	0.0014–0.0022 ①	0.010–0.020	0.010–0.020	0.020–0.060	0.002–0.003	0.001–0.003	0.015–0.055
	L	6–181 (3.0)	0.001–0.0045 ②	0.010–0.020	0.010–0.022	0.015–0.055	0.001–0.003	0.001–0.003	0.0005–0.0065

① Measured 1.8 in. from piston top
② Measured at top of piston skirt

TORQUE SPECIFICATIONS
All readings in ft. lbs.

Year	VIN	No. Cylinder Displacement cu. in. (liter)	Cylinder Head Bolts	Main Bearing Bolts	Rod Bearing Bolts	Crankshaft Pulley Bolts	Flywheel Bolts	Manifold		Spark Plugs
								Intake	Exhaust	
1985	U	4–151 (2.5)	⑬	70	32	200	44	37①	32⑥	20
	L	6–181 (3.0)	⑫	100	41	200	60	32	37	15
1986	U	4–151 (2.5)	⑭	70	32	162	44	37①	32⑥	15
	L	6–181 (3.0)	⑫	100	45	200	60	32	37	20
1987	M	4–122 (2.0)	②	44③	26④	20	48⑦	16	16	15
	D	4–138 (2.3)	⑧	15⑨	15⑩	74⑨	46	18⑪	27	15–18
	U	4–151 (2.5)	⑭	70	32	162	44	37①	32⑥	15
	L	6–181 (3.0)	⑫	100	45	219	60	32	37	20
1988-89	M	4–122 (2.0)	②	44③	26④	20	48⑦	16	16	15
	D	4–138 (2.3)	⑧	15⑨	15⑩	74⑨	46	40⑪	27	15–18
	U	4–151 (2.5)	⑮	70	32	162	55④	32	32⑥	15–18
	L	6–181 (3.0)	⑫	100	45	219	60	32	37	20

① See exploded view of intake manifold
② Step 1: 18 ft. lbs.
　Step 2: Tighten additional 180 degrees in 3 steps of 60 degrees each
　Step 3: Warm engine—tighten bolts additional 30-50 degree turn
③ Plus additional 45-50 degree turn
④ Plus additional 45 degrees turn
⑤ Manual trans.—69 ft. lbs.
⑥ Bolts 3–5—to 37 ft. lbs.
⑦ Plus 30 degree turn
⑧ Short bolts—26 ft. lbs. plus 80 degree turn
　Long bolts—26 ft. lbs. plus 90 degree turn
⑨ Plus 90 degree turn
⑩ Plus 75 degree turn

TORQUE SPECIFICATIONS
All readings in ft. lbs.

Year	VIN	No. Cylinder Displacement cu. in. (liter)	Cylinder Head Bolts	Main Bearing Bolts	Rod Bearing Bolts	Crankshaft Pulley Bolts	Flywheel Bolts	Manifold Intake	Manifold Exhaust	Spark Plugs

⑪ Brace-to-manifold stud nut—18 ft. lbs.
Brace-to-block stud nut—40 ft. lbs.
Brace-to-manifold—40 ft. lbs.

⑫ Should you reach 60 ft. lbs. at any time, do not complete Steps 2 and 3
Step 1—Tighten bolts 25 ft. lbs. in sequence
Step 2—Tighten each bolt ¼ turn in sequence
Step 3—Tighten each bolt an additional ¼ turn in sequence

⑬ Torque head bolts in sequence and in 3 steps. Final torque is 92 ft. lbs.

⑭ Torque head bolts in sequence to 18 ft. lbs. Repeat sequence bringing torque to 22 ft. lbs. on all bolts except No. 9, torque to 29 ft. lbs. Repeat sequence. Turn all bolts 120 degrees (2 flats). Torque No. 9 ¼ turn

⑮ Torque all head bolts in sequence to 18 ft. lbs. Repeat sequence bringing torque to 26 ft. lbs. on all bolts except No. 9, torque to 18 ft. lbs. Repeat sequence turning all bolts 90 degrees

BRAKE SPECIFICATIONS
All measurements in inches unless noted

Year	Model	Lug Nut Torque (ft. lbs.)	Master Cylinder Bore	Brake Disc Minimum Thickness	Brake Disc Maximum Runout	Standard Brake Drum Diameter	Minimum Lining Thickness Front	Minimum Lining Thickness Rear
1985	All	80②	0.875	0.830	0.004	7.879	0.030①	0.030①
1986	All	80②	0.875	0.830	0.004	7.879	0.030①	0.030①
1987	All	80②	0.875	0.830	0.004	7.879	0.030①	0.030①
1988-89	All	80②	0.937	0.830	0.004	7.879	0.030①	0.030①

① Measured above the rivet heads
② Aluminum wheels—100 ft. lbs.

WHEEL ALIGNMENT

Year	Model	Caster Range (deg.)	Caster Preferred Setting (deg.)	Camber Range (deg.)	Camber Preferred Setting (deg.)	Toe-in (in.)	Steering Axis Inclination (deg.)
1985	Somerset	1P–3P	2P	½N–½P	0	0	NA
	Calais	$^{11}/_{16}$P–2$^{11}/_{16}$P	1$^{11}/_{16}$P	$^{7}/_{32}$N–1$^{13}/_{32}$P	$^{13}/_{16}$P	$^{1}/_{16}$N	13½
	Grand Am	$^{11}/_{16}$P–2$^{11}/_{16}$P	1$^{11}/_{16}$P	$^{7}/_{32}$N–1$^{13}/_{32}$P	$^{13}/_{16}$P	$^{1}/_{16}$N	13½
1986	Somerset	$^{23}/_{34}$P–2$^{23}/_{32}$P	1$^{23}/_{32}$P	¼P–1$^{7}/_{16}$P	$^{27}/_{32}$P	0	13½
	Calais	$^{11}/_{16}$P–2$^{11}/_{16}$P	1$^{11}/_{16}$P	$^{7}/_{32}$N–1$^{13}/_{32}$P	$^{13}/_{16}$P	$^{1}/_{16}$N	13½
	Grand Am	$^{11}/_{16}$P–2$^{11}/_{16}$P	1$^{11}/_{16}$P	$^{7}/_{32}$N–1$^{13}/_{32}$P	$^{13}/_{16}$P	$^{1}/_{16}$N	13½
1987	Skylark	$^{23}/_{34}$P–2$^{23}/_{32}$P	1$^{23}/_{32}$P	¼P–1$^{7}/_{16}$P	$^{27}/_{32}$P	0	13½
	Somerset	$^{23}/_{34}$P–2$^{23}/_{32}$P	1$^{23}/_{32}$P	¼P–1$^{7}/_{16}$P	$^{27}/_{32}$P	0	13½
	Calais	$^{11}/_{16}$P–2$^{11}/_{16}$P	1$^{11}/_{16}$P	$^{7}/_{32}$N–1$^{13}/_{32}$P	$^{13}/_{16}$P	$^{1}/_{16}$N	13½
	Grand Am	$^{11}/_{16}$P–2$^{11}/_{16}$P	1$^{11}/_{16}$P	$^{7}/_{32}$N–1$^{13}/_{32}$P	$^{13}/_{16}$P	$^{1}/_{16}$N	13½
1988-89	Skylark	$^{13}/_{16}$N–4$^{3}/_{16}$P	1$^{11}/_{16}$P	$^{3}/_{16}$N–1$^{13}/_{16}$P	$^{13}/_{16}$	0	13½
	Calais	$^{13}/_{16}$N–4$^{3}/_{16}$P	1$^{11}/_{16}$P	$^{3}/_{16}$N–1$^{13}/_{16}$P	$^{13}/_{16}$	0	13½
	Grand Am	$^{13}/_{16}$N–4$^{3}/_{16}$P	1$^{11}/_{16}$P	$^{3}/_{16}$N–1$^{13}/_{16}$P	$^{13}/_{16}$	0	13½

TUNE-UP PROCEDURES

Ignition Timing

ADJUSTMENT

Timing specifications for each engine are listed in the Tune-Up Specifications Chart and on the underhood emission control label. The ignition timing marks are located on the engine front cover; a notch on the harmonic balancer indicates top dead center (TDC).

2.5L TBI Engine

NOTE: Begining in 1987, the 2.5L engine uses a Direct Ignition System (DIS) and timing is controlled by ECM and is not adjustable. Earlier years use the "Averaging Method" to set the ignition timing. This involves the use of BOTH the No. 1 and No. 4 spark plug wires to trigger the timing light.

1. Refer to the underhood emission control label and follow all of the timing instructions if they differ from below.
2. The engine should be at normal operating temperature, air cleaner installed, air conditioner off, electric cooling fan off and parking brake set firmly.
3. Place the automatic transaxle in PARK or the manual transaxle in NEUTRAL.

NOTE: The engines are equipped with a magnetic probe timing light receptacle, located at 9.5 degrees ATDC. DO NOT use a normal timing light with this receptacle.

4. Using an inductive timing light, connect it to the No. 1 plug wire and make sure the "Check Engine" light is not on.
5. Ground the ALCL connector under the dash by installing a jumper wire between the A and B terminals. The Check Engine light should begin flashing.
6. Using the timing light, check and record the position of the timing mark.
7. Repeat Step 4, but connect the timing light inductive pick-up to the No. 4 spark plug wire. Take the total of the two recorded timing marks and divide by two to arrive at an average timing position.

NOTE: For example: No. 1 timing = 4 degrees and No. 4 timing = 8 degrees; 4 + 8 = 12 ÷ 2 = 6 degrees average timing. If a change is necessary, subtract the average timing from the timing specification to determine the amount of timing change to No. 1 cylinder. For example: if the timing specification is 8 degrees and the average timing is 6 degrees, advance the No. 1 cylinder 2 degrees to set the timing.

8. To correct the timing, loosen the distributor hold down clamp, adjust the distributor and retighten the hold down bolt.
9. Once the timing is properly set, remove the jumper wire from the ALCL connector.
10. If necessary to clear the ECM memory, disconnect the ECM harness from the positive battery pigtail for 10 seconds with the key in the OFF position.

2.0L MFI Engine

1. Refer to the underhood emission control label and follow all of the timing instructions if they differ from below.
2. Warm engine to normal operating temperature.
3. Place transmission in NEUTRAL or PARK. Apply parking brake and block wheels.
4. A/C, cooling fan and choke must be off. Do not remove air cleaner, except as noted.

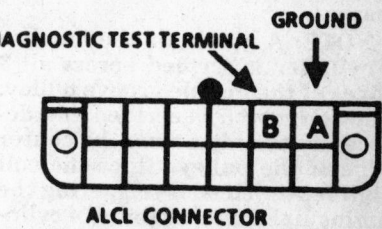

Install a jumper wire to terminals A and B of the ALCL connector to set ignition timing

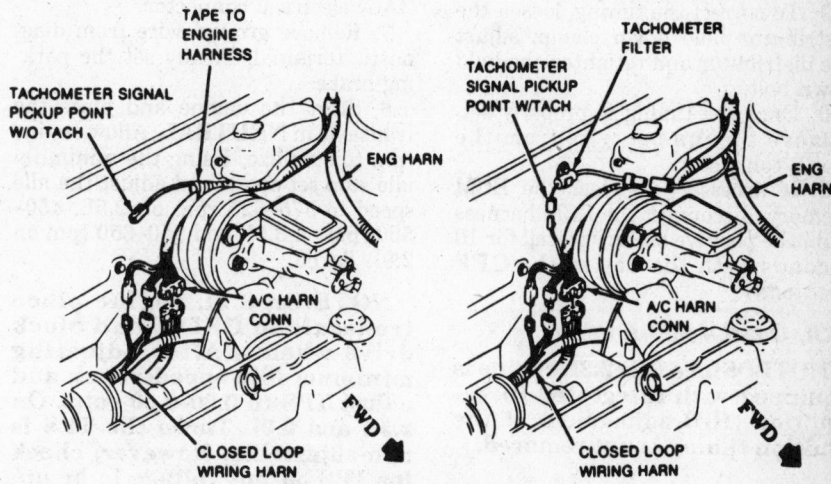

Tachometer hookup on the HEI distributor

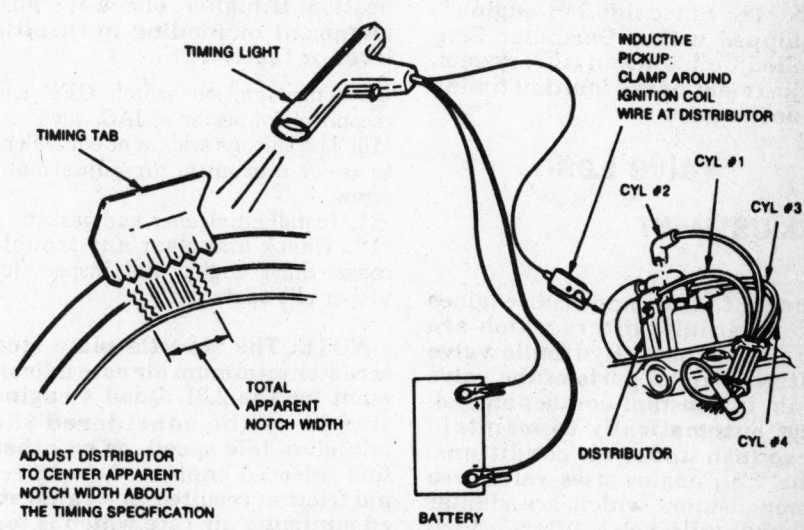

Ignition timing is accomplished using the averaging method

5. Connect inductive timing light to coil lead. Peel back the protective covering on the coil lead to make good connection.

6. Ground the ALCL connector under the dash by installing a jumper wire between the **A** and **B** terminals. The **Check Engine** light should begin flashing.

7. Using the timing light, check the position of the timing mark.

8. Optimum timing of all cylinders is achieved when the apparent notch width is centered with the timing mark.

NOTE: A notch for the number 1 cylinder is scribed across all 3 edges of the double groove pulley. Another notch is scribed 180 degrees away only across the center edge of the pulley. Since the coil high tension lead is triggering the timing light, timing for all 4 cylinders is shown, causing a slight "jiggling" of the timing notch and an apparent increase in the width of the timing notch.

9. To correct the timing, loosen the distributor hold down clamp, adjust the distributor and retighten the hold down bolt.

10. Once the timing is properly set, remove the jumper wire from the ALCL connector.

11. If necessary to clear the ECM memory, disconnect the ECM harness from the positive battery pigtail for 10 seconds with the key in the **OFF** position.

2.3L Quad 4 MFI Engine

NOTE: Since this 2.3L engine is equipped with Integrated Direct Ignition (IDI) adjustment of the ignition timing is not required.

3.0L MFI Engine

NOTE: Since this 3.0L engine is equipped with a Computer Controlled Coil Ignition (C³I) system, adjustment of the ignition timing is not required.

Valve Lash

ADJUSTMENT

The 2.3L, 2.5L and 3.0L engines use hydraulic lifters which are non-adjustable. Hydraulic valve lifters keep all parts of the valve train in constant contact and adjust automatically to maintain zero lash under all conditions. The 2.0L engine uses valve lash compensators which are similar to hydraulic valve lifters which require no adjustment.

Idle Speed and Mixture

MINIMUM IDLE SPEED ADJUSTMENT

NOTE: The idle speed and mixture are electronically controlled by the electronic control module (ECM). All adjustments are preset at the factory. The only time the idle speed should be adjusted is when the throttle body assembly has been replaced.

1. Remove air cleaner and gasket.
2. With a scratch awl or equivalent, piece the idle stop screw plug and apply leverage to remove it.
3. Connect tachometer to engine.
4. Ground the ALDL diagnostic terminal with IAC valve connected.
5. Turn ignition switch to **ON** position, without starting engine for at least 45 seconds. This allows IAC valve pintle to extend and seat in throttle body.
6. Disconnect the Idle Air Control (IAC) electrical connector.
7. Remove ground wire from diagnostic terminal. Firmly set the parking brake.
8. Start the engine and place the transaxle in **NEUTRAL**. Allow engine rpm to stabilize. Using the minimum idle stop set screw and adjust the idle speed to 575–625 rpm on 2.5L, 450–550 rpm on 3.0L and 550–650 rpm on 2.0L Turbo.

NOTE:On 3.0L engine place transaxle in DRIVE and block drive wheels. After adjusting minimum idle speed check and adjust TPS to 0.50–0.60 volts. On 2.5L and 2.0L Turbo the TPS is non-adjustable. However, check for TPS output voltage to be under 1.25 volts at closed throttle postion. If higher, check for misalignment or binding in throttle lever or faulty TPS.

9. Turn ignition switch **OFF** and reconnect connector at IAC valve.
10. Use silicone sealant or equivalent to cover minimum air adjustment screw.
11. Install air cleaner and gasket.
12. Check and clear any trouble codes. Start engine and inspect for proper idle operation.

NOTE: The throttle plate stop screw or minimum air rate adjustment for the 2.3L Quad 4 engine should not be considered the minimum idle speed, as on other fuel injected engines. Low internal friction resulted in a calibrated minimum air rate which is too low to allow most engines to idle.

The adjustment is preset at the factory and no further adjustment should be necessary.

ENGINE ELECTRICAL

Distributor

NOTE: There are 4 types of ignition systems used on N-Body vehicles. The HEI system, Direct Ignition System (DIS), Integrated Direct Ignition (IDI) and the Computer Controlled Coil Ignition (C³I) system. The C³I, IDI and DIS systems do not use a distributor; instead, they use a coil pack, an ignition module, a combination sensor (3.0L) and a magnetic or single sensor and a reluctor (2.3L and 2.5L). The following procedure is for the HEI distributor.

REMOVAL & INSTALLATION

Undisturbed Engine

1. Disconnect the negative battery terminal from the battery.
2. Disconnect the ignition switch battery feed wire and the tachometer lead (if equipped) from the distributor cap.
3. Release the coil connectors from the cap. Remove the distributor cap and position it out of the way. DO NOT remove the ignition wires from the cap.

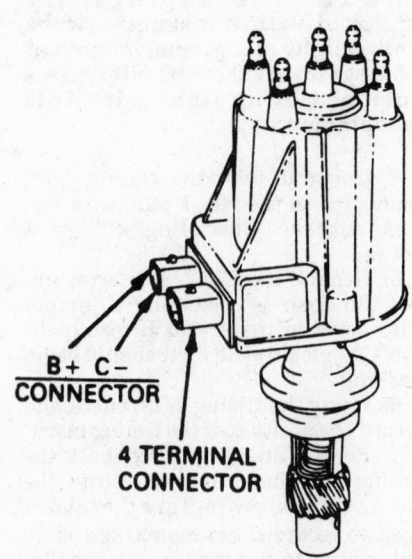

B+ C−
CONNECTOR

4 TERMINAL CONNECTOR

Typical 4 cyl HEI/EST distributor

4. Disconnect the 4-wire ECM harness from the distributor.

5. Remove the distributor clamp screw and hold down clamp.

6. Using a piece of chalk, mark the rotor position on the distributor housing and the distributor position with the block. Carefully pull the distributor up until the rotor just stops turning and again mark the rotor position for installation.

NOTE: The drive gear on the shaft is helical and the shaft will rotate slightly as the distributor is removed. DO NOT crank the engine while the distributor is removed.

7. To install the distributor, perform the following procedures:

a. Rotate the shaft until the rotor aligns with the second mark.

b. Using clean engine oil, lubricate the drive gear and install the distributor into the engine.

c. When installing the distributor, turn the rotor to the first mark made during removal; this ensures proper timing.

NOTE: If the marks do not align properly, remove the distributor and try again.

8. To complete the installation, install the clamp, the hold down nut and reverse the removal procedures. Start the engine and check the ignition timing.

Disturbed Engine

If the engine was accidently cranked while the distributor was removed, use the following procedure for installation. The engine must be set on TDC of the compression stroke to obtain the proper spark timing.

1. Remove the No. 1 spark plug.

2. Place finger over the No. 1 spark plug hole and crank the engine slowly until compression is felt.

3. Align the timing mark on the damper pulley with the **0** degree mark on the engine timing plate.

4. To install the distributor, perform the following procedures:

a. Rotate the shaft until the rotor aligns with the second mark.

b. Using clean engine oil, lubricate the drive gear and install the distributor into the engine.

c. When installing the distributor, turn the rotor to the first mark made during removal; this ensures proper timing.

NOTE: If the marks do not align properly, remove the distributor and try again.

5. To complete the installation, install the clamp, the hold down nut and reverse the removal procedures. Start the engine. Check and/or adjust the ignition timing.

Computer Controlled Coil Ignition (C³I)

REMOVAL & INSTALLATION

Ignition Coil

TYPE 1

NOTE: There are 3 types of C³I systems used. Type 1 coils have 3 plug wires on each side of the coil assembly; Type 2 coils have all 6 wires connected on one side of the coil. All components are serviced as complete assemblies, although individual coils are available for Type 2 coil packs. The third system, know as Type 3 or fast start is similar in appearance to Type 1. When troubleshooting or replacing components, it is important to determine which C³I system is installed on the engine. On 1985–88 N-Body vehicles Type 1, C³I system is used.

Direct Ignition system

1. Disconnect the negative battery terminal from the battery.

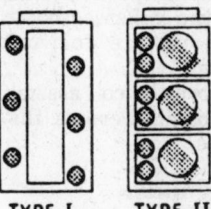

Module/coil assembly

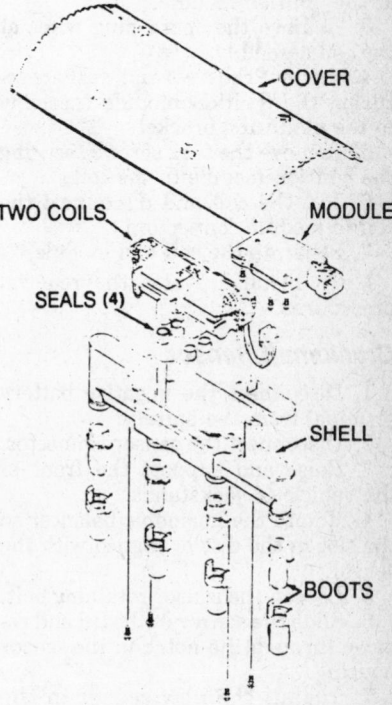

Integrated Direct Ignition

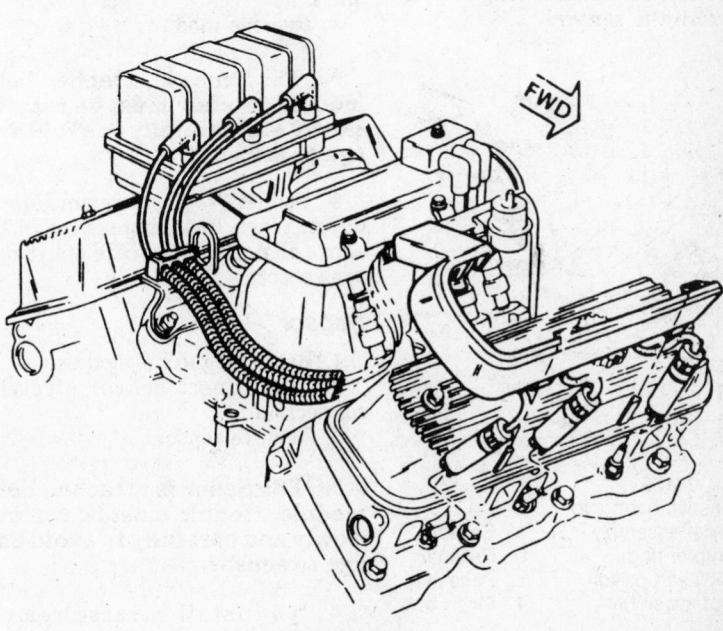

C³I system

2. Remove the spark plug wires.

3. Remove the torx screws holding the coil to the ignition module.

4. Tilt the coil assembly to the rear and remove the coil to module connectors.

5. Remove the coil assembly.

6. To install, reverse the removal procedures.

Ignition Module

1. Disconnect the negative battery terminal from the battery.

2. Disconnect the 14-pin connector at the ignition module.

3. Remove the spark plug wires at the coil assembly.

4. Remove the nuts and washers securing the ignition module assembly to the mounting bracket.

5. Remove the torx screws securing the ignition module to the coil.

6. Tilt the coil and disconnect the coil to module connectors.

7. Separate the coil and module.

8. To install, reverse the removal procedures.

Crankshaft Sensor

1. Disconnect the negative battery terminal from the battery.

2. Disconnect the sensor connector.

3. Raise and support the front of the vehicle on jackstands.

4. Rotate the harmonic balancer so the slot in the disc is aligned with the sensor.

5. Loosen the sensor retaining bolt.

6. Slide the sensor outboard and remove through the notch in the sensor housing.

7. Install the new sensor in the housing and rotate the harmonic balancer so the interrupter ring is positioned with the sensor.

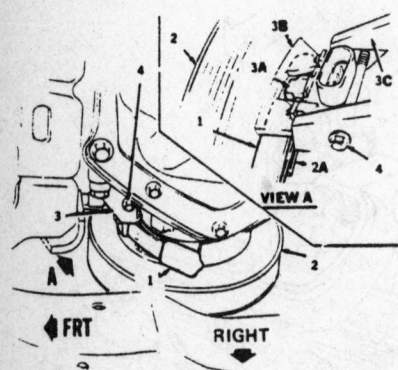

1. Tool J–36179
2. Crankshaft harmonic
   balancer assembly
   a. Interrupter ring
3. Crankshaft position
   sensor assembly

a. Sensor
b. Deflector
c. Pedestal
4. Pinch bolt

Crankshaft sensor adjustment

8. Adjust the sensor so there is equal distance on each side of the interrupter ring. There should be approximately 0.030 in. (0.76mm) clearance between the and interrupter ring and the sensor. Check in 4 places.

9. Tighten the pinch bolt to 30 inch lbs.

NOTE: When servicing requires that the T-latch type wiring is disconnected, care must be taken to ensure proper reassembly. Failure to do so may result in intermittent loss of operation. Interrupter rings should never touch the crankshaft sensor. Never crank engine till sensor is adjusted properly.

10. Reconnect negative battery cable.

Direct Ignition System (DIS)

REMOVAL & INSTALLATION

Ignition Coil

1. Remove negative battery cable.
2. Remove and tag spark plug wires.
3. Remove coil attaching nuts.
4. Remove coil (do not bend module prongs).
5. To install reverse removal procedures.

Ignition Module

1. Remove negative battery cable.
2. Disconnect module connectors.
3. Remove and tag spark plug wires at coil.
4. Remove module attaching bolts and nuts.
5. Remove module.

NOTE: Senor is attached below module. Module must be removed slowly and carefully to avoid damage to sensor.

6. To install reverse removal procedures. When installing sensor in hole above oil pan rail use care not to damage sensor.

Sensor

1. Remove ignition module.
2. Disconnect sensor electrical connection.
3. Remove sensor

NOTE: Senor is attached below module. Module must be removed slowly and carefully to avoid damage to sensor.

4. To install reverse removal procedures.

Alternator

For further information on the charging system, please refer to "Charging and Starting" in the Unit Repair section.

PRECAUTIONS

To prevent damage to the on-board computer, alternator and regulator, the following precautionary measures must be taken when working with the electrical system.

• Never reverse the battery connections. Always check the battery polarity visually. This is to be done before any connections are made to be sure that all of the connections correspond to the battery ground polarity.

• Booster batteries for starting must be connected properly. Make sure that the positive cable of the booster battery is connected to the positive terminal of the battery that is getting the boost. This applies to both negative and ground cables.

• Make sure the ignition switch is **OFF** when connecting or disconnecting any electrical component, especially on trucks equipped with an on-board computer control system.

• Disconnect the battery cables before using a fast charger; the charger has a tendency to force current through the diodes in the opposite direction for which they were designed. This burns out the diodes.

• Never use a fast charger as a booster for starting the vehicle.

• Never disconnect the voltage regulator while the engine is running.

• Do not ground the alternator output terminal.

• Do not operated the alternator on an open circuit with the field energized.

• Do not attempt to polarize an alternator.

BELT TENSION ADJUSTMENT

2.0L, 2.3L and 3.0L Engines

A single (serpentine) belt is used to drive all engine mounted accessories. Drive belt tension is maintained by a spring loaded tensioner. The drive belt tensioner can control belt tension over a broad range belt lengths; however, there are limits to the tensioner's ability to compensate.

1. Inspect tensioner markings to see if the belt is within operating lengths. Replace belt if the belt is excessively worn or is outside of the tensioner's operating range.

NOTE: On early production models, some serpentine belts wre slightly short. This will position the tensioner justed outside of its marked range. There is no need to replace any parts since normal function is not affected.

2. Run engine with no accessories on until the engine is warmed up. Shut the engine off and read belt tension with tool J–23600–B belt tension gage or equivalent placed halfway between the alternator and the A/C compressor. For non-A/C applications read tension between the power steering pump and crankshaft pulley. Remove tool.

3. Using an 18mm box end wrench, apply clockwise force (tighten) to the tensioner pulley bolt. Release the force and immediately take a tension reading without disturbing belt tensioner position.

4. Using the same wrench, apply a counterclockwise force to the tensioner pulley bolt and raise the pulley to the "install" position. Slowly lower the pulley to the "at rest" position and take a tension reading without disturbing the belt tensioner position.

5. Average the 3 readings. If the average of the 3 readings is lower than 50 lbs. on 2.0L and 2.3L and 79 lbs. on the 3.0L the belt is within the tensioner's operating range, replace the belt tensioner.

2.5L Engine

1. Loosen the alternator mounting bolts.

2. Using a standard Belt Tension

Gauge, install it onto the center (longest span) of the drive belt.

3. Using a medium pry bar, apply pressure to the center of the alternator, not against either end frame. When the drive belt tension is 90–100 lbs. (used belt) or 165–175 lbs. (new belt), tighten the alternator mounting bolts.

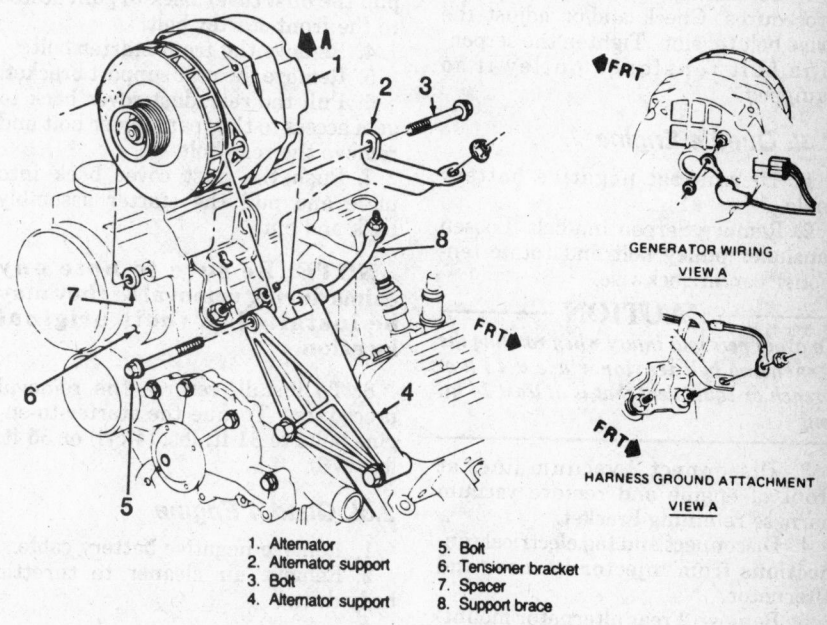

1. Alternator
2. Alternator support
3. Bolt
4. Alternator support
5. Bolt
6. Tensioner bracket
7. Spacer
8. Support brace

V6 alternator mounting and wiring attachments

REMOVAL & INSTALLATION

All Engines Except 2.3L Quad 4

1. Disconnect the negative battery terminal from the battery.

2. Remove the two-terminal plug and the battery lead from the back of the alternator assembly.

GENERATOR WIRING
VIEW A

HARNESS GROUND ATTACHMENT
VIEW A

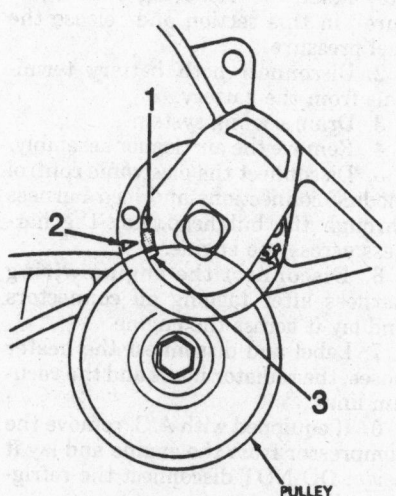

1. Minimum tension range
2. Pointer
3. Maximum tension range

Tensioner operating range

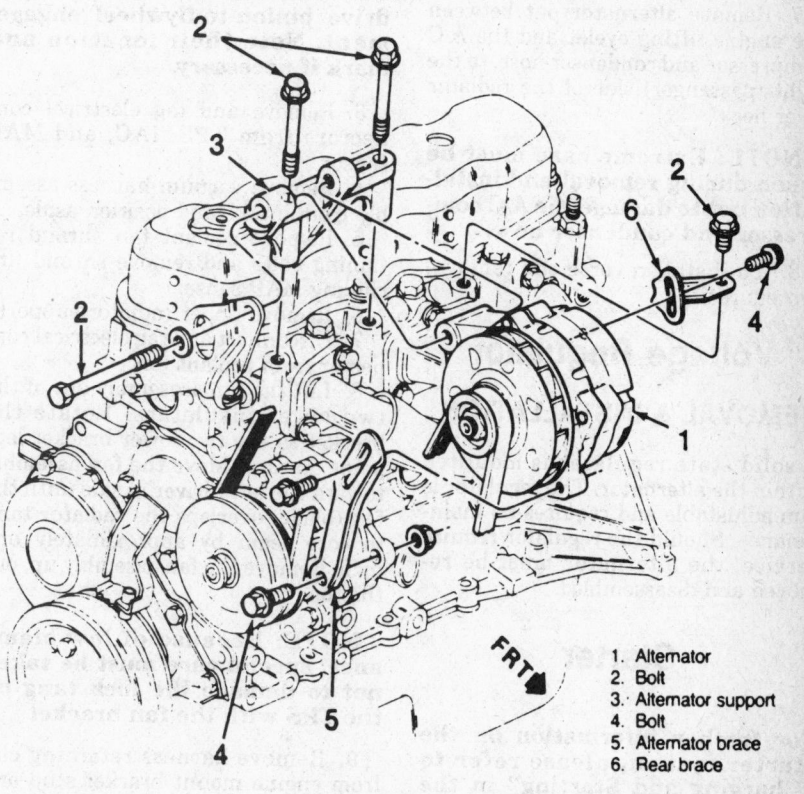

1. Alternator
2. Bolt
3. Alternator support
4. Bolt
5. Alternator brace
6. Rear brace

4 cyl alternator mounting

3. Loosen the adjusting bolts and remove the alternator belt. On engines with a serpentine belt loosen the serpentine belt tensioner and rotate it counterclockwise to remove the drive belt.

4. Remove the alternator retaining bolts and lift the alternator assembly from the vehicle.

5. To install, reverse the removal procedures. Check and/or adjust the drive belt tension. Tighten the serpentine belt tensioner pulley if so equipped.

2.3L Quad 4 Engine

1. Disconnect negative battery cable.

2. Remove Serpentine belt. Loosen tensioner pulley bolt and rotate tensioner conterclockwise.

── CAUTION ──

To avoid personal injury when rotating the serpentine belt tensioner use a 13 mm wrench or equivalent that is at least 24 in. long.

3. Disconnect 2 vacuum lines at front of engine and remove vacuum harness retaining bracket.

4. Disconnect and tag electrical connections from injector harness and alternator.

5. Remove 2 rear alternator mounting bolts.

6. Remove front alternator bolt and engine harness clip.

7. Remove alternator out between the engine lifting eyelet and the A/C compressor and condenser hose, to the right (passenger) side of the radiator filler neck.

NOTE: Extreme care must be taken during removal and installation not to damage the A/C compressor and condenser hose.

8. To install reverse the removal procedures.

Voltage Regulator

REMOVAL & INSTALLATION

A solid state regulator is mounted within the alternator. The regulator is non-adjustable and requires no maintenance. Should the regulator require service, the alternator must be removed and disassembled.

Starter

For further information on the starter system, please refer to "Charging and Starting" in the Unit Repair section.

REMOVAL & INSTALLATION

All Engines except 2.3L Quad 4

1. Disconnect the negative battery terminal from the battery.

2. Raise and support the front of the vehicle on jackstands. Disconnect the electrical wiring from the starter.

3. Remove the dust cover bolts and pull the dust cover back to gain access to the front starter bolt.

4. Remove the front starter bolt.

5. Remove the rear support bracket.

6. Pull the rear dust cover back to gain access to the rear starter bolt and remove the rear bolt.

7. Push the dust cover back into place and pull the starter assembly back and out.

NOTE: Be sure to note any shims during removal so they may be installed in their original location.

8. To install, reverse the removal procedures. Torque the starter-to-engine bolts to 31 ft. lbs. (4-cyl) or 35 ft. lbs. (V6).

2.3L Quad 4 Engine

1. Remove negative battery cable.

2. Remove air cleaner to throttle body duct.

NOTE: If shims are used they must be reinstalled in their original location to assure proper drive pinion-to-flywheel engagement. Note their location and mark if necessary.

3. Remove and tag electrical connectors from TPS, IAC, and MAP sensor.

4. Remove vacuum harness assembly from intake and position aside.

5. Remove coolant fan shroud retaining bolts and remove shroud (including MAP sensor).

6. Remove upper radiator support.

7. Disconnect and tag electrical connector from coolant fan.

8. Lift the fan asesembly out of the two lower insulators. Rotate the bracket so the two lower bracket legs point upward. Move the fan assembly toward the left (driver's) side until the fan (blade) overlaps the radiator tank to core seam by approximately one inch. Remove the fan assembly up, out the top

NOTE: Because of low clearance, special care must be taken not to damage the lock tang on the TPS with the fan bracket

9. Remove harness retaining clip from engine mount bracket stud and starter mounting bolts.

10. Tilt rear of starter towards the radiator, pull the starter out and rotate solenoid towards the radiator to gain access to the electrical connections.

NOTE: Take care not to damage the crank sensor mounted directly to the rear of the starter.

11. Disconnect and tag electrical connections at solenoid.

12. Move starter to the left (driver) side of the vehicle and remove out the top.

13. To install reverse removal procedures. If shims are present they must be installed in their original location. Torque starting mounting bolts to 74 ft. lbs.

ENGINE MECHANICAL

Engine

REMOVAL & INSTALLATION

2.5L, 2.0L and 2.3L Quad 4 Engines

NOTE: The following procedure is for removing the engine and transaxle as a unit. The engines are removed from the bottom of the car. The procedures below may differ slighty on the 2.3L Quad 4.

1. Refer to "Relieving Fuel Pressure" in this section and release the fuel pressure.

2. Disconnect both battery terminals from the battery.

3. Drain cooling system.

4. Remove the air cleaner assembly.

5. Disconnect the electronic control module connections and feed harness through the bulkhead. Lay the harness across the engine.

6. Disconnect the engine wiring harness after tagging all connectors and lay it across the engine.

7. Label and disconnect the heater hoses, the radiator hoses and the vacuum lines.

8. If equipped with A/C, remove the compressor from the engine and lay it aside; DO NOT disconnect the refrigerant lines.

9. If equipped with power steering, remove the power steering pump from its mount and lay it aside. Remove the power steering pump bracket from the engine.

10. Remove the front transaxle strut.

11. If equipped with a M/T disconnect the clutch and transaxle linkage. Remove the throttle cable from the TBI unit.

12. If equipped with an A/T disconnect the transaxle cooler lines, shifter linkage, downshift cable and throttle cable from the TBI unit.

13. Disconnect the redundant ground and multi-relay bracket.

14. Raise and support the front of the vehicle on jackstands.

15. Remove the front wheels. Remove the calipers and wire them up out of the way. DO NOT allow the calipers to hang by the brake hoses.

16. Remove the brake rotors.

17. Remove the knuckle-to-strut bolts (2/side).

18. Disconnect the exhaust pipe-to-manifold bolts and move it aside.

19. Remove the 4 body-to-cradle bolts at the lower control arms. Loosen the remaining 8 body-to-cradle bolts at their ends. Remove 1 bolt at each cradle side, leaving 1 bolt per corner.

20. Place stands under the front of the body, then move the hoist back to the body pan. Using a 6 x 4 x 4 in. timber, positioned between the hoist and the vehicle, raise the hoist and remove the stands.

21. Position a sturdy dolly under the engine/transaxle assembly, then, use 4 x 4 in. blocks to maintain the position on the dolly.

22. Lower the vehicle slightly, allowing the engine/transaxle assembly to rest on the dolly.

23. Remove the engine mount bolts and the right-front bracket. Remove the remaining cradle-to-body bolts.

24. Raise car leaving engine, transaxle and suspension on dolly.

25. To install, reverse the removal procedures. Refill the cooling system. Start the engine and check for leaks.

3.0L V6 Engine

NOTE: The engine is removed from the top of the car.

1. Refer to "Relieving Fuel Pressure" in this section and release the fuel pressure.

2. Disconnect the battery terminal from the battery.

3. Using an awl, scribe marks around the hood hinges and remove the hood.

4. Raise and support the front of the vehicle on jackstands. Position a clean drain pan under the radiator, open the drain cock and drain the cooling system.

5. Remove the starter and torque converter cover.

6. Remove the torque converter-to-flywheel bolts. Matchmark the torque

converter to the flywheel for reassembly.

7. If equipped with A/C, remove the compressor from the engine and position it aside; DO NOT disconnect any refrigerant lines.

8. Disconnect the heater hoses and the lower radiator hose from the engine.

9. Remove the front motor mount bolts and the right-inner fender splash shield.

10. Remove the transaxle-to-engine mount bolt located between the transaxle and the cylinder block.

11. Remove the two right-rear motor mount bolts.

12. Disconnect the exhaust pipe from the exhaust manifold flange.

13. Lower the vehicle.

14. Remove the serpentine drive belt. Label and disconnect the alternator wiring and the alternator.

15. If equipped with power steering, remove the power steering pump and the fluid lines.

16. Disconnect the mass air flow sensor and the air intake duct. Disconnect the top radiator hose.

17. Disconnect the electric fan wiring and remove the fan assembly. Remove the radiator.

18. Install an vertical lifting device to the engine and support the engine, remove the left-upper transaxle mount.

19. If necessary, disconnect and remove the master cylinder.

20. Disconnect and remove the fuel lines from the fuel rail.

21. Disconnect the throttle, the TV and the cruise control cables.

22. Remove the remaining engine-to-transaxle bolts. Lift the engine from the vehicle using the lifting device.

23. To install, reverse the removal procedures. Refill the cooling system. Start the engine and check for fluid leaks.

Cylinder Head

REMOVAL & INSTALLATION

2.5L Engine

1. Refer to "Relieving Fuel Pressure" in this section and release the fuel pressure.

2. Disconnect the negative battery terminal from the battery.

3. Position a drain pan under the radiator, open the drain cock and drain the cooling system. Remove the dipstick tube.

4. Remove the air cleaner assembly.

5. Disconnect the exhaust pipe-to-manifold bolts and separate the exhaust pipe from the manifold.

6. Label and disconnect the electrical wiring and throttle linkage from the TBI assembly.

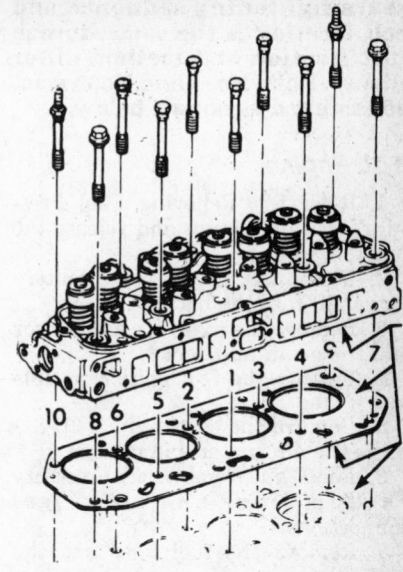

2.5L cylinder head bolt torque sequence

7. Remove the heater hose from the intake manifold.

8. Remove the ignition coil. Label and disconnect the electrical wiring connectors from the intake manifold and the cylinder head. Remove the alternator.

9. If equipped with A/C, remove the compressor and lay it aside; DO NOT disconnect the refrigerant lines.

10. If equipped with power steering, remove the upper bracket from the power steering pump.

11. Remove the radiator hoses from the engine.

12. Remove the rocker arm covers, rocker arms and pushrods.

13. Remove the cylinder head-to-engine bolts, then lift the cylinder head from the engine.

14. Using a gasket scraper, clean the gasket mating surfaces.

15. To install, use new gaskets and reverse the removal procedures. Refill the cooling system. Start the engine and check for leaks.

NOTE: On 1985 models, torque head bolts gradually or in 3 stages in sequence shown below. Final torque is 92 ft. lbs. On 1986–87 models, torque head bolts in sequence in stages to 18. ft. lbs. Repeat sequence, bringing torque to 22 ft. lbs. on all bolts except No. 9 torque to 29 ft. lbs. Repeat sequence turn all bolts 120 degrees (2 flats). Torque No. 9 additional ¼ turn. On 1988 models torque all head bolts in sequence gradually to 18 ft. lbs. Repeat sequence, bringing torque to 26 ft. lbs. on all bolts except No. 9 torque to 18 ft. lbs. Repeat sequence, turning all bolts 90 degrees. On all model years tightening sequence and bolt location is the same, torque specification and method differ slighty. Bolts No. 1 and No. 9 must be installed as shown below.

3.0L Engine

1. Refer to "Relieving Fuel Pressure" in this section and release the fuel pressure.

2. Disconnect the negative battery terminal from the battery.

3. Remove the mass air flow sensor and the air intake duct.

4. Remove the C³I ignition module and wiring.

5. Remove the serpentine belt. Remove the alternator and bracket.

6. Label and remove all necessary vacuum lines and electrical connections.

7. Remove the fuel lines and the fuel rail. Remove the spark plug wires.

8. Position a drain pan under the radiator, open the drain cock and drain the cooling system. Remove the heater and radiator hoses from the throttle body and intake manifold. Remove the radiator and cooling fan.

9. Remove the intake manifold-to-engine bolts and the manifold from the engine.

10. Remove the valve covers. Remove the rocker arms, the pedestals and pushrods.

NOTE: When removing the valve parts, be sure to keep the parts in order, so they may be assembled in their original locations.

11. Remove the left exhaust manifold-to-engine bolts and the manifold from the engine.

12. If equipped with power steering, remove the power steering pump. Remove the dipstick and dipstick tube.

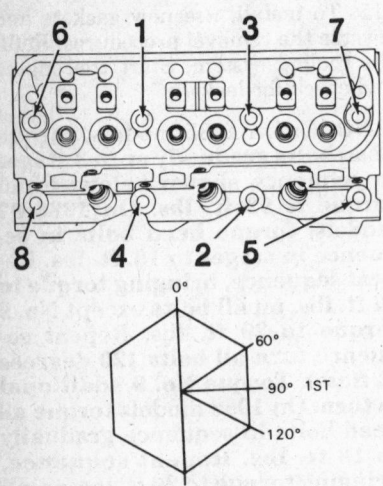

3.0L cylinder head bolt torque sequence and angle—tightening procedure

13. Remove the left cylinder head-to-engine bolts (in reverse of the torque sequence) and lift the left cylinder head from the engine.

14. Raise and support the front of the vehicle on jackstands. Remove the right exhaust manifold-to-engine bolts.

15. Remove the right cylinder head-to-engine bolts (in reverse of the torque sequence) and lift the right cylinder head from the engine.

16. Using a gasket scraper, clean the gasket mounting surfaces.

17. To install, use new gaskets, sealant (if necessary) and reverse the removal procedures. Torque the cylinder head bolts in 3 steps. Step 1 tighten all bolts in sequence to 25 ft. lbs. Step 2 tighten each bolt in sequence ¼ turn. Step 3 tighten each bolt in sequence additional ¼ turn. Note should you reach 60 ft. lbs. at any time do not complete Step 2 and Step 3. Torque the intake manifold mounting bolts to specifications in the sequence illustrated under "Intake Manifold, Removal & Installation."

2.0L Engine

NOTE: Cylinder head gasket replacement is necessary if camshaft carrier/cylinder head bolts are loosened. The head bolts should always be loosen when cold. New head bolts should be used every time camshaft carrier/cylinder head or gasket are replaced.

1. Refer to "Relieving Fuel Pressure" in this section and release the fuel pressure. Remove induction tube.

2. Drain coolant and remove negative battery cable.

3. Remove alternator and bracket.

4. Remove ignition coil.

5. Remove distributor and wiring, but first mark distributor housing to block, then mark rotor position to housing. Tag spark plug wires and all electrical connections.

6. Disconnect all cables from throttle body.

7. Disconnect and tag all electrical connections TBI and intake manifold.

8. Remove hoses from vacuum brake, fuel inlet and return lines. Remove heater hoses.

9. Remove intake manifold and water pump.

10. Remove breather from camshaft carrier.

11. Remove upper radiator support.

12. Remove exhaust manifold to turbo connection and O₂ sensor connection.

13. Disconnect and tag wiring at engine harness and thermostat housing.

14. Remove timing belt.

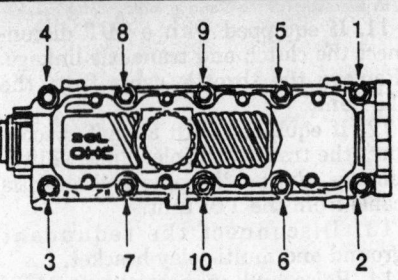

Camshaft carrier and cylinder head bolt loosening sequence 2.0L

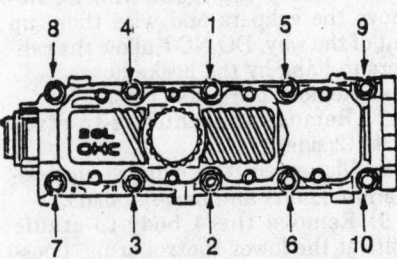

Camshaft carrier and cylinder head bolt torque sequence 2.0L

15. Loosen cam carrier/cylinder head gradually in sequence. Engine must be cold.

16. Remove cam carrier, rocker arms and valve lash compensators.

17. Remove cylinder head and exhaust manifold as an assembly.

18. To install use new gasket and reverse the removal procedures. Apply continuous 3mm bead of anerobic sealer to sealing surface of cam carrier. Always replace cam carrier/cylinder head retaining bolts. Torque head bolts in sequence to proper specification as stated in the "Torque Specification Chart".

2.3L Quad 4 Engine

1. Remove negative battery cable and drain cooling system.

2. Disconnect heater inlet and throttle body heater hoses from water outlet. Disconnect upper radiator hose from water outlet.

3. Remove exhaust manifold.

4. Remove intake and exhaust camshaft housings.

5. Remove oil cap and dipstick. Pull oil fill tube upward to unseat from block.

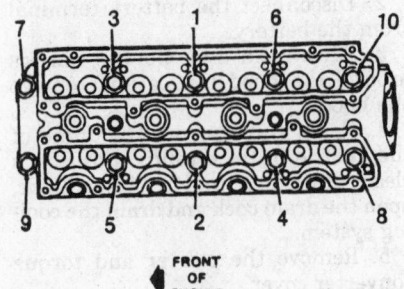

Cylinder head bolt torque sequence 2.3L Quad 4

6. Disconnect and tag injector harness electrical connector.

7. Disconnect throttle body to air cleaner duct. Remove throttle cable and bracket an position aside.

8. Remove throttle body from intake manifold with electrical harness, hoses, cable attached and position aside.

9. Disconnect and tag MAP sensor vacuum hose from intake manifold.

10. Remove intake manifold bracket to block bolt.

11. Disconnect and tag 2 coolant sensor connections.

12. Remove cylinder head to block bolts.

NOTE: When removing cylinder head to block bolts follow reverse of tighten sequence.

13. Remove cylinder head and gasket.

NOTE: Clean all gasket surfaces with plastic or wood scraper. Do not use any sealing material.

14. Installation is the reverse of the removal. Torque cylinder head to block short bolts to 26 ft. lbs. plus 80 degree turn. Torque cylinder head to block long bolts to 26 ft. lbs. plus 90 degree turn.

OVERHAUL

For all cylinder head overhaul procedures, please refer to the "Engine Rebuilding" in the Unit Repair section.

Rocker Arms/Shafts

REMOVAL & INSTALLATION

2.3L Quad 4 Engine

The valve train consists of 2 chain driven overhead camshafts with direct acting lifters.

2.5L Engine

1. Disconnect the negative battery terminal from the battery.

NOTE: Do not pry on cover or damage to sealing surfaces may result.

2. Label and disconnect all electrical wiring connectors and the vacuum hoses which inhibit the valve cover removal.

3. Remove the valve cover-to-cylinder head bolts and lift off the valve cover.

4. Remove the rocker arm bolts and balls, then lift off the rocker arms.

NOTE: If only the pushrods are being replaced, simply loosen the rocker arm bolt and swing them aside. Keep all removed components in order so they may be assembled in their original locations.

5. Using a gasket scraper, clean the gasket mounting surfaces. Inspect and/or replace any damaged parts.

6. Install the push rods, making sure they seat properly in the lifters.

7. Install the rocker arms, balls and nuts. Torque all retaining nuts to 24 ft. lbs.

8. To complete the installation, use new gaskets or sealant and reverse the removal procedures.

3.0L Engine

1. Disconnect the negative battery terminal from the battery.

2. Remove the valve covers.

NOTE: It will be necessary to remove the C³I ignition coil module to gain access to the rear valve cover bolts. It may also be necessary to remove the alternator, alternator brace, engine lift bracket and power steering belt tensioner.

3. Label and disconnect any necessary vacuum hoses.

4. Remove the rocker arm pedestal-to-cylinder head bolts, then the rocker arm, the pedestal assembly and the pushrods.

NOTE: Check the position of the double ended bolts and note for reassembly.

5. Place all removed components on a clean surface in order so they may be installed in their original locations.

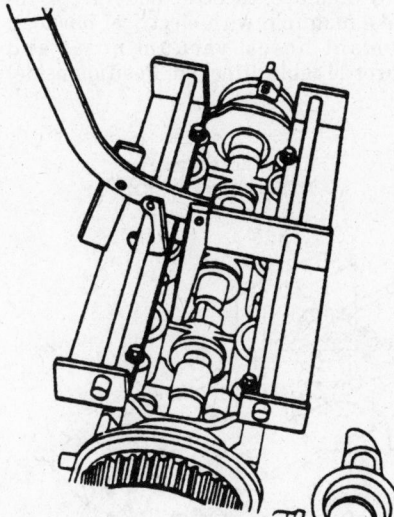

Compressing valve spring with tool J–33302–25 2.0L

6. To install, use new gaskets and reverse the removal procedures. Torque all rocker arm pedestal bolts to 45 ft. lbs. (60 Nm).

7. To complete the installation, reverse the removal procedures. Make sure the drive belt is tensioned properly.

2.0L Engine

1. Remove camshaft carrier cover.

2. Hold valves in place with compressed air, using air adapter J–22794 or equivalent in spark plug hole.

3. Compress valve springs with special tool J–33302–25.

4. Remove rocker arms. Keep rocker arms in order for re-assembly.

5. To install reverse the removal procedures using new gasket.

Intake Manifold

REMOVAL & INSTALLATION

2.5L Engine

1. Refer to "Relieving Fuel Pressure" in this section and release the fuel pressure.

2. Disconnect the negative battery terminal from the battery.

3. Remove the air cleaner, then the PCV valve and hose.

4. Position a drain pan under the radiator, open the drain cock and drain the cooling system.

5. Label and remove the vacuum lines. Disconnect the fuel lines from the TBI unit.

6. Label and disconnect the electrical wiring and throttle linkage from the TBI.

7. If equipped, disconnect the transaxle downshift linkage and the cruise control linkage.

8. Disconnect the throttle linkage and bell crank; position the assembly to the side for clearance.

9. Disconnect the heater hose(s). If equipped with power steering, disconnect and remove the upper power steering pump bracket.

10. Remove the ignition coil.

11. Remove the intake manifold-to-cylinder head bolts and the intake manifold.

12. Using a gasket scraper, clean the gasket mounting surfaces.

13. To install, use new gaskets, sealant (if necessary) and reverse the removal procedures. Torque the intake manifold-to-engine bolts in sequence to specifications.

3.0L Engine

1. Refer to "Relieving Fuel Pressure" in this section and release the fuel pressure.

2. Disconnect the negative battery terminal from the battery.

3. Disconnect the mass air flow sensor and remove the air intake duct.

4. Remove the serpentine drive belt, alternator and bracket.

5. Remove the C³I ignition module and bracket.

6. Label and remove all the necessary vacuum and electrical wiring connectors.

7. Remove the throttle, cruise control and TV cables from the throttle body assembly.

8. Position a drain pan under the radiator, open the drain cock and drain the cooling system. Disconnect the heater hoses from the throttle body.

9. Remove the upper radiator hose from the intake manifold.

10. Remove the fuel lines, the fuel rail and the fuel injectors. Remove the spark plug wires.

11. Remove the intake manifold-to-engine bolts and the intake manifold.

12. Using a gasket scraper, clean the gasket mounting surfaces.

13. To install, use new gaskets, sealant (if necessary) and reverse the removal procedures. Torque intake manifold-to-cylinder head bolts in sequence to 32 ft. lbs.

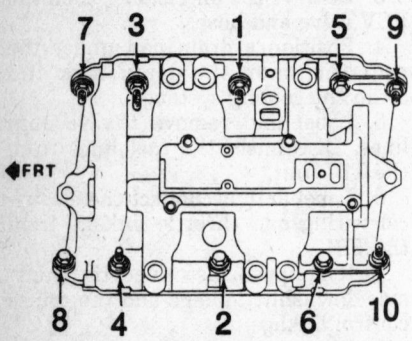

3.0L intake manifold bolt torque sequence

2.0L Engine

1. Refer to "Relieving Fuel Pressure" in this section and release the fuel pressure. Disconnect the negative battery terminal from the battery.

2. Remove induction tube and hoses.

3. Disconnect and tag wiring to throttle body, fuel injectors, M.A.P sensor and wastegate.

4. Disconnect and tag PCV hose and vacuum hoses on throttle body.

5. Remove throttle cable and cruise control cable if so equipped.

6. Remove wiring to ignition coil and remove manifold support bracket.

7. Remove rear bolt from alternator bracket, P/S adjusting bracket and front alternator adjusting bracket.

8. Remove fuel lines to fuel rail and regulator outlet.

9. Remove retaining nuts and washers and intake manifold.

10. To install, use new gasket and reverse the removal procedures. Torque intake manifold retaining nuts and washers to 18 ft. lbs.

NOTE: The rear adjusting bracket must be the last part secured to prevent distorting the accessory drive system this will prevent the belt from coming off.

2.3L Quad 4 Engine

1. Remove negative battery cable.

2. Remove coolant fan shroud (including vacuum hose and electrical connector from MAP sensor).

3. Disconnect throttle body to air cleaner duct.

4. Remove throttle cable bracket.

5. Remove power brake vacuum hose (including retaining bracket to power steering bracket) and position aside.

6. Remove throttle body from intake manifold with electrical harness, coolant hoses, vacuum hoses and throttle cable attached. Position aside.

7. Remove oil/air separator 2 bolts and 4 hoses. Leave the hoses attached to the separator, disconnect from the oil fill, chain housing, and the intake manifold. Remove as an assembly.

8. Remove oil fill cap and oil level indicator stick.

9. Pull oil tube fill upward to unseat from block and remove.

10. Disconnect Injector harness connector.

11. Remove fill tube out top, rotating as necessary to gain clearance for oil/air separator nipple between intake tubes and fuel rail electrical harness.

12. Remove intake manifold support bracket 2 bolts and 1 nut. Remove intake manifold retaining nuts and bolts.

13. Remove intake manifold.

To install:

NOTE: Intake manifold mounting hole closest to chain housing is slotted for additional clearance.

14. Install intake manifold and gasket. Tightening intake manifold bolts/nuts in sequence and to correct specification. Tighten intake manifold brace and retainers hand tight. Then tighten to specifications in the following sequence:

    a. Nut to stud bolt.

    b. Bolt to intake manifold.

    c. Bolt to cylinder block.

15. Lubricate a new oil fill tube ring seal with engine oil and install tube down between No. 1 and 2 intake tubes. Rotate as necessary to gain clearance for oil/air separator nipple on fill tube.

16. Locate the oil fill tube in its cylinder block opening. Align the fill tube so it is approximately in its installed position. Place the palm of your hand over the oil fill opening and press straight down to seat fill tube and O-ring into cylinder block.

17. Install oil/air separator assembly (it may be necessary to lubricate the hoses for ease of assembly).

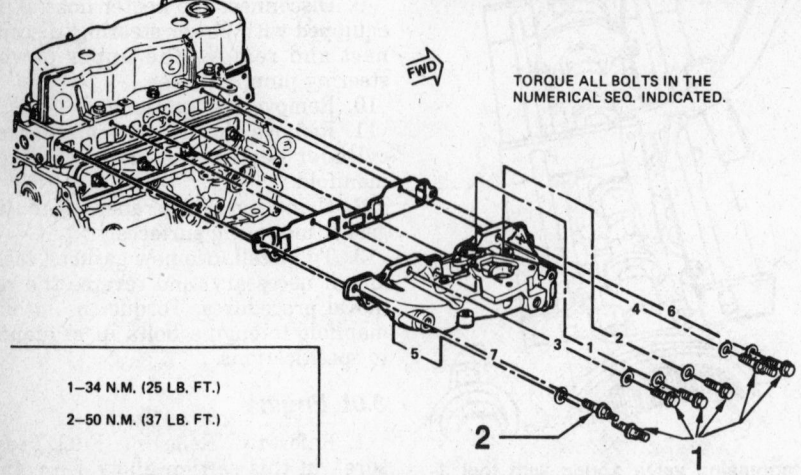

FWD

TORQUE ALL BOLTS IN THE NUMERICAL SEQ. INDICATED.

1—34 N.M. (25 LB. FT.)

2—50 N.M. (37 LB. FT.)

2.5L intake manifold bolt torque sequence

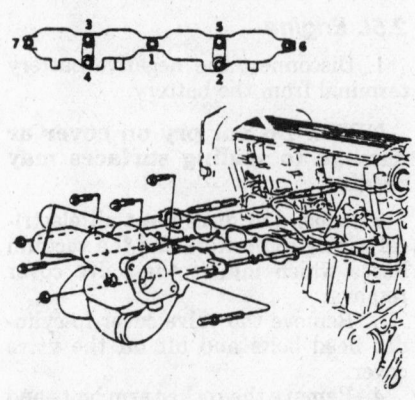

Intake manifold installation 2.3L Quad 4

18. Install throttle body to intake manifold using a new gasket.

19. Reverse the remaining removal procedures. Torque intake manifold brace-to-block 40 ft. lbs., brace-to-manifold 40 ft. lbs., brace-to-manifold stud 18 ft. lbs. and intake manifold to cylinder head bolts in sequence to 18 ft. lbs.

Exhaust Manifold

REMOVAL & INSTALLATION

2.5L Engine

1. Disconnect the negative battery terminal from the battery.

2. Remove the air cleaner.

3. Remove the alternator top engine mount and position the unit to one side.

4. Disconnect the O_2 sensor connector.

5. Raise and support the front of the vehicle on jackstands.

6. Disconnect the exhaust pipe-to-exhaust manifold bolts and lower the exhaust pipe.

7. Lower the vehicle.

8. Remove the exhaust manifold-to-cylinder head retaining bolts and lift the exhaust manifold from the engine.

9. Using a gasket scraper, clean the gasket mounting surfaces.

10. To install, use new gaskets and reverse the removal procedures. Torque the exhaust manifold-to-cylinder head (in sequence) to 32 ft. lbs.(bolts 1, 2, 6, 7) and 37 ft. lbs (bolts 3, 4, 5).

3.0L Engine

LEFT SIDE (FRONT)

1. Disconnect the negative battery cable.

2. Disconnect air cleaner mounting bolts.

3. Remove the two bolts attaching the exhaust crossover pipe to the manifold.

4. Tag and disconnect the spark plug wires.

5. Remove engine cooling fan.

6. Remove the mounting bolts and remove the manifold.

NOTE: The oil dipstick tube may have to be removed to provide access to the manifold bolts.

7. Installation is in the reverse order of removal. Apply sealer between manifold and cylinder head.

RIGHT SIDE (REAR)

1. Disconnect the negative battery cable.

2. Remove the 2 bolts attaching exhaust pipe to manifold.

3. Disconnect O_2 sensor wire.

4. Disconnect and tag spark plug wires.

5. Remove 2 nuts retaining crossover pipe to manifold.

6. Remove serpentine belt.

7. Remove power steering pump.

8. Remove heater hose from tube, heat shield and C^3I bracket nuts.

9. Remove 6 bolts attaching manifold to cylinder head

10. Installation is in the reverse order of removal. Apply sealer between manifold and cylinder head.

2.0L Engine

1. Disconnect the negative battery cable.

2. Remove turbo induction tube.

3. Remove and tag spark plug wires.

4. Remove turbo assembly from exhaust manifold.

5. Remove exhaust manifold retaining nuts and manifold.

6. Installation is in the reverse order of removal. Torque exhaust manifold bolts to 16 ft. lbs. and turbocharger to exhaust manifold to 18 ft. lbs.

2.3L Quad 4 Engine

1. Disconnect the negative battery cable and O_2 sensor connector.

2. Remove upper and lower exhaust manifold heat shields.

3. Remove exhaust manifold brace to manifold bolt.

4. Break loose the manifold- to-exhaust pipe spring loaded bolts using a 13mm box wrench.

5. Raise and support car.

6. Remove the manifold to exhaust pipe bolts out of the exhaust pipe flange by using a $^7/_{32}$ in. (5.5mm) socket and **rotate clockwise** (as if tightening a bolt with right hand threads or removing a bolt with left hand threads). It is necessary to relieve the spring pressure from one bolt prior to removing the second bolt. If the spring

pressure is not relieved it will cause the exhaust pipe to twist and bind up the bolt as it is removed. Relieve the spring pressure by:

a. Thread one bolt out 4 turns.

b. Move to the other bolt and turn it all the way out of the exhaust pipe flange.

c. Return to the first bolt and rotate it the rest of the way out of the exhaust pipe flange.

7. Pull down and back on the exhaust pipe to disengage it from the exhaust manifold bolts.

8. Lower car.

9. Remove exhaust manifold to cylinder head retaining nuts and remove exhaust manifold.

10. Installation is in the reverse order of removal. In sequence torque exhaust manifold bolts to head 27 ft. lbs., manifold to exhaust pipe 22 ft. lbs. and manifold to brace 19 ft. lbs.

NOTE: Turn bolts in evenly to avoid cocking the exhaust pipe and binding the bolts. Turn bolts in until fully seated.

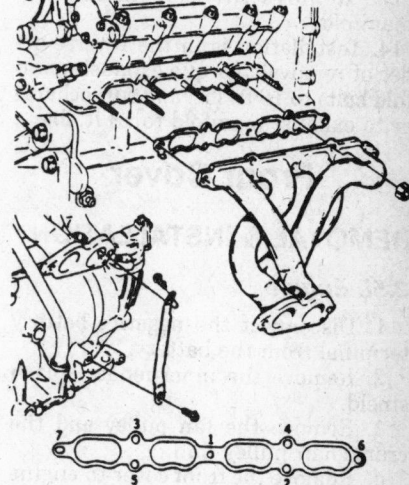

Exhaust manifold installation 2.3L Quad 4

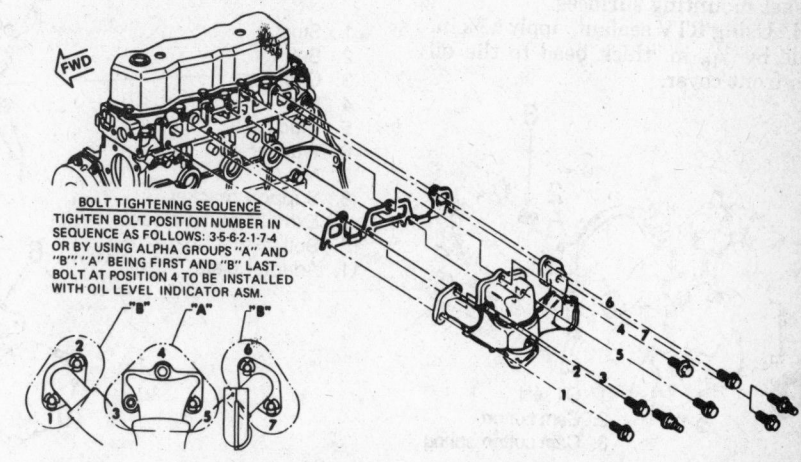

BOLT TIGHTENING SEQUENCE
TIGHTEN BOLT POSITION NUMBER IN SEQUENCE AS FOLLOWS: 3-5-6-2-1-7-4 OR BY USING ALPHA GROUPS "A" AND "B" "A" BEING FIRST AND "B" LAST. BOLT AT POSITION 4 TO BE INSTALLED WITH OIL LEVEL INDICATOR ASM.

2.5 L exhaust manifold bolt torque sequence

Turbocharger

REMOVAL & INSTALLATION

2.0L Engine

1. Disconnect the negative battery cable.
2. Raise car and suitably support.
3. Lower fan retaining screws.
4. Disconnect exhaust pipe.
5. Remove A/C rear support bracket.
6. Remove turbo support bracket to engine.
7. Disconnect oil drain and water return pipe at turbo.
8. Lower vehicle and remove coolant recovery pipe.
9. Remove induction tube, coolant fan, O_2 sensor.
10. Disconnect oil and water feed pipe.
11. Remove air intake duct and vacuum hose at actuator.
12. Remove exhaust manifold retaining nuts and remove turbo and manifold as an assembly.
13. Remove turbo from exhaust manifold.
14. Installation is in the reverse order of removal. Torque exhaust manifold bolts to 16 ft. lbs. and turbocharger to exhaust manifold to 18 ft. lbs.

Front Cover

REMOVAL & INSTALLATION

2.5L Engine

1. Disconnect the negative battery terminal from the battery.
2. Remove the inner-fender splash shield.
3. Remove the fan pulley and the crankshaft pulley hub.
4. Remove the front cover-to-engine bolts and the front cover.
5. Using a gasket scraper, clean the gasket mounting surfaces.
6. Using RTV sealant, apply a 3/8 in. wide by 3/16 in. thick bead to the oil pan/front cover.

7. Using RTV sealant, apply a 1/4 in. wide by 1/8 in. thick bead to the front cover at the engine block mating surfaces.
8. Using the Installation tool No. J–34995 or equivalent, install a new front oil seal.

NOTE: Tool No. J–34995 is also used as a centering tool which fits over the crankshaft seal and is used to correctly position the front cover during installation.

9. Partially tighten the two timing case cover opposing screws, then tighten the remaining cover screws and remove the centering tool from the front cover. Torque timing case to block screws 90 inch lbs.
10. To complete the installation, reverse the removal procedures.

2.0L Engine

1. Disconnect negative battery cable.
2. Remove tensioner and bolt.
3. Remove serpentine belt.
4. Unsnap upper and lower cover.
5. To install reverse the removal procedures.

3.0L Engine

1. Disconnect the negative battery terminal from the battery.
2. Position a drain pan under the radiator, open the drain cock and drain the cooling system.
3. Loosen, but DO NOT remove, the water pump pulley bolts. Remove the serpentine drive belt and the pulley.

4. Remove the water pump-to-engine bolts and the water pump.
5. Raise and support the front of the vehicle on jackstands. Remove the right wheel assembly and the right-inner fender splash shield.
6. Remove the crankshaft harmonic balancer.
7. Place an oil drain pan under the crankcase, remove the drain plug and drain the crankcase. Remove the oil filter.
8. Remove the radiator and heater hoses.
9. Remove the crankshaft sensor and the engine oil pan.
10. Remove the front cover-to-engine bolts, the the front cover and the gasket.
11. Using a gasket scraper, clean the gasket mounting surfaces. Replace the front oil seal.
12. To install, use new gaskets, sealant (if necessary) and reverse the removal procedures. Coat all front cover bolts with thread sealer prior to installation. Refill the cooling system and the crankcase. Torque water pump bolts to 97 inch lbs., front cover bolts to 22 ft. lbs. and oil pan bolts to 88 inch lbs.

2.3L Quad 4 Engine

1. Disconnect the negative battery terminal from the battery. Remove coolant recovery reservoir.
2. Remove the serpentine drive belt.

--- CAUTION ---

To avoid personal injury when rotating the serpentine belt tensioner, use a 13mm wrench that is at least 24 in. long.

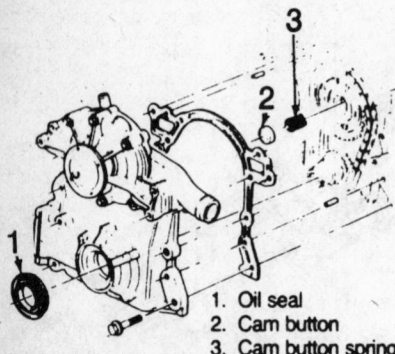

1. Oil seal
2. Cam button
3. Cam button spring

V6 front cover and seal

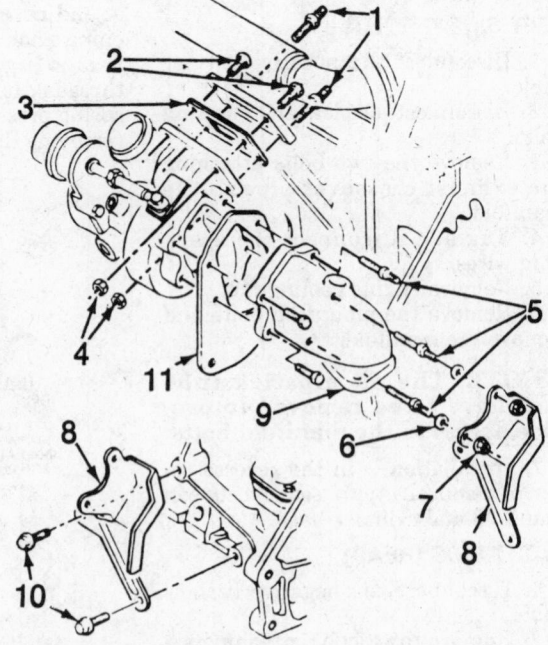

1. Stud
2. Bolt
3. Gasket
4. Nut
5. Stud
6. Washer
7. Nut
8. Support bracket
9. Exhaust outlet elbow
10. Bolt
11. Adapter plate

Turbocharger mounting

3. Remove upper cover fasteners.

4. Raise car and suitably support.

5. Remove right front wheel assembly.

6. Remove right lower splash shield.

7. Remove crankshaft balancer assembly.

8. Remove lower cover fasteners and lower car.

9. Remove front cover

10. Installation is in the reverse order of removal. Torque retaining bolt and washer for balancer assembly to 74 ft. lbs.

NOTE: The automatic transaxle crankshaft balancer must NOT be installed on a manual transaxle engine.

OIL SEAL REPLACEMENT

1. Refer to the "Front Cover, Removal & Installation" procedures in this section and remove the front cover.

2. Using a small pry bar, pry out the old oil seal.

NOTE: Use care to avoid damage to seal bore or seal contact surfaces.

3. Be sure to clean the oil seal mounting surface.

4. Using the Installation tool No. J–34995 (2.5L), J–36010 (2.3L Quad 4) and J–35354 (3.0L) or equivalent, drive the oil seal into the front cover.

5. Lubricate balancer and seal lip with clean engine oil.

6. To complete the installation, use new gaskets, sealant (if necessary) and reverse the removal procedures.

Timing Gears

REMOVAL & INSTALLATION

2.5L Engine

NOTE: If the camshaft gear is to be replaced, the engine must be removed from the vehicle. The crankshaft gear may be replaced with the engine in the vehicle.

1. Disconnect the negative battery terminal from the battery.

2. Raise and support the front of the vehicle on jackstands.

3. Remove the inner-fender splash shield.

4. Remove the accessory drive belt(s). Remove the crankshaft pulley-to-crankshaft pulley bolt and slide the pulley from the crankshaft.

5. If replacing the camshaft gear, perform the following procedures:

a. Refer to the "Engine, Removal & Installation" procedures in this

section and remove the engine from the vehicle; secure it to a workstand.

b. Refer to the "Camshaft, Removal & Installation" procedures in this section and remove the camshaft from the engine.

c. Using an arbor press, press the camshaft gear from the camshaft.

d. To install the camshaft gear onto the camshaft, press the gear onto the shaft until a thrust clearance of 0.0015–0.0050 in. exists.

6. If removing the crankshaft gear, perform the following procedures:

a. Remove the front cover-to-engine bolts.

b. Remove the retaining bolt and slide the crankshaft gear forward off of the crankshaft.

View of the timing gears – 2.5L (4-cyl) engine

7. Using a gasket scraper, clean the gasket mounting surfaces. Inspect the parts for damage and/or wear; if necessary, replace the damaged parts.

8. To install, align the timing marks, use new gaskets and sealant (on the timing cover), then reverse the removal procedures. Torque the crankshaft pulley-to-crankshaft bolt to 200 ft. lbs. (1985) or 162 ft. lbs. (1986–89) and the camshaft thrust plate-to-engine bolts to 90 inch lbs. and the front cover-to-engine bolts to 90 inch lbs.

Timing Chain and Sprockets

REMOVAL & INSTALLATION

3.0L Engine

1. Disconnect the negative battery terminal from the battery.

2. Position a drain pan under the radiator, open the drain cock and drain the cooling system. Disconnect the cooling hose from the water pump.

3. Raise and support the front of the vehicle on jackstands.

4. Remove the inner-fender splash shield.

5. Remove the serpentine drive belt.

6. Remove the crankshaft pulley-to-crankshaft bolt and slide the pulley from the crankshaft.

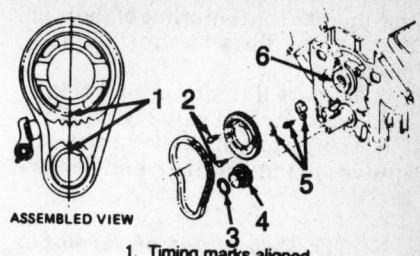

ASSEMBLED VIEW

1. Timing marks aligned
2. 22 ft. lbs. (30 Nm)
3. Seal
4. Crankshaft gear
5. Dampner assembly
6. Camshaft

V6 timing chain and sprocket

7. Remove the front cover-to-engine bolts and the cover.

8. Rotate the crankshaft to align the timing marks on the sprockets.

9. Remove the camshaft sprocket-to-camshaft bolts, then remove the camshaft sprocket and chain.

10. Remove the crankshaft sprocket by sliding it forward.

11. Using a gasket scraper, clean the gasket mounting surfaces. Inspect the timing chain and the sprockets for damage and/or wear; if necessary, replace the damaged components.

12. To install, use a new gasket, sealant and reverse the removal procedures. Make sure the timing marks are aligned on the sprockets. Torque the camshaft sprocket-to-camshaft bolts to 19 ft. lbs., the front cover-to-engine bolts to 22 ft. lbs., the crankshaft pulley bolt to 200–225 ft. lbs., the oil pan-to-front cover bolts to 88 inch lbs. and the water pump pulley bolts to 97 inch lbs. Refill the cooling system. Start the engine, allow the engine to reach normal operating temperatures and check for leaks.

Timing Chain and Sprockets

REMOVAL & INSTALLATION

2.3L Quad 4 Engine

NOTE: Prior to removing the timing chain review the entire procedure.

1. Disconnect the negative battery terminal from the battery.

2. Remove front engine cover and crankshaft oil slinger.

3. Rotate crankshaft clockwise (as viewed from front of engine/normal rotation) until the camshaft sprockets' timing dowel pin holes line up with the holes in the timing chain housing. The mark on the crankshaft sprocket should line up with the mark on the cylinder block. The crankshaft sprocket keyway should point upwards and

line up with the centerline of the cylinder bores. This is the "Timed" position.

4. Remove 3 timing chain guides.
5. Raise car and suitably support.
6. Gently pry off timing chain tensioner spring retainer and remove spring.

NOTE: Two styles of tensioner are used. One with a spring post (early production), and one without a spring post (late production). Both styles are identical in operation and are interchangeable.

7. Remove timing chain tensioner shoe retainer.
8. Make sure all the slack in the timing chain is above the tensioner assembly; then remove the chain tensioner shoe. The timing chain must be disengaged from the wear grooves in the tensioner shoe in order to remove the shoe. Slide a screwdriver blade under the timing chain while pulling shoe outward.
9. If difficulty is encountered removing chain tensioner shoe, proceed as follows:
   a. Lower the vehicle.
   b. Hold intake camshaft sprocket with tool J–36013 and remove the sprocket bolt and washer.
   c. Remove the washer from the bolt and rethread the bolt back into the camshaft by hand (the bolt provides a surface to push against).
   d. Remove intake cam sprocket using a three-jaw puller in the three relief holes in the sprocket. Do not attempt tp pry sprocket off camshaft or damage to the sprocket or chain housing could occur.
10. Remove tensioner assembly retaining bolts and tensioner.

――――――― **CAUTION** ―――――――
Tensioner piston is spring loaded and could come out causing personal injury.

11. Remove chain housing to block stud (timing chain tensioner shoe pivot).
12. Remove timing chain

To install:

NOTE: Failure to follow this procedure could result in severe engine damage.

13. Tighten intake camshaft sprocket retaining bolt and washer, to specification while holding sprocket with tool J–36013 if removed.
14. Install special tool J–36008 through holes in camshaft sprockets into holes in timing chain housing (this positions the camshafts for correct timing).

15. If the camshafts are out of position and must be rotated more than ⅛ turn in order to install the alignment dowel pins:
   a. The crankshaft **MUST** be rotated 90 degrees clockwise off of TDC in order to give the valves adequate clearance to open.
   b. Once the camshafts are in position and the dowels installed, rotate the crankshaft counter clockwise back to top dead center. Do not rotate the crankshaft clockwise to TDC, valve or piston damage could occur.
16. Install timing chain over exhaust camshaft sprocket around idler sprocket and around crankshaft sprocket.
17. Remove the aligment dowel pin from the intake camshaft. Using tool J–36013 rotate the intake camshaft sprocket counterclockwise enough to slide the timing chain over the intake cam sprocket. Release the camshaft sprocket wrench. The length of chain between the 2 camshaft sprockets will tighten. If properly timed the intake cam alignment dowel pin should slide in easily. If the dowel pin does not fully index the camshafts are not timed correctly, the procedure must be repeated.
18. Leave the alignment dowel pins installed.
19. With slack removed from chain between intake cam sprocket and crankshaft sprocket the timing marks on the crankshaft and the cylinder block should be aligned. If marks are not aligned move the chain one tooth forward or rearward, remove slack and recheck marks.
20. Tighten chain housing to block stud (timing chain tensioner shoe pivot). Stud is installed under the timing chain. Tighten to 19 ft. lbs.

NOTE: Two styles of tensioner are used. One with a spring post (early production), and one without a spring post (late production). Both styles are identical in operation and are interchangeable.

21. Reload timing chain tensioner assembly to its **0** position as follows:
   a. Assemble restraint cylinder, spring and nylon plug into plunger. Index slot in restraint cylinder with peg in plunger. While rotating the restraint cylinder clockwise, push the restraint cylinder into the plunger until it bottoms. Keep rotating the restraint cylinder clockwise but allow the spring to push it out of the plunger. The pin in the plunger

will lock the restraint in the loaded position.
   b. Install tool J–36589 onto plunger assembly.
   c. Install plunger assembly into tensioner body with the long end toward the crankshaft when installed.
22. Install tensioner assembly to chain housing. Recheck plunger assembly installation, it is correctly installed when the long end is toward the crankshaft.
23. Install and tighten timing chain tensioner bolts and tighten to 10 ft. lbs.
24. Install tensioner shoe and tensioner shoe retainer.
25. Remove special tool J–36589 and squeeze plunger assembly into tensioner body to unload the plunger assembly.
26. Lower car enough to reach and remove the alignment dowel pins. Rotate crankshaft clockwise (normal rotation) 2 full rotations. Align crankshaft timing mark with mark on cylinder block and reinstall alignment dowel pins. Alignment dowel pins will slide in easily if engine is timed correctly.

NOTE: If the engine is not correctly timed, severe engine damage could occur.

27. Install 3 timing chain guides and crankshaft oil slinger.
28. Install engine front cover.
29. Start engine and check for oil leaks.

Timing Belt and Tensioner

REMOVAL & INSTALLATION

2.0L Engine

1. Disconnect negative battery cable.
2. Remove timing belt cover.
3. Remove crankshaft pulley.
4. Drain radiator and remove coolant reservoir.
5. Loosen water pump bolts and remove timing belt.
6. Install new timing belt and crankshaft pulley.

NOTE: Check if the mark on the camshaft sprocket lines up with mark on the rear timing belt cover. The timing mark on the crankshaft pulley should line up at 10 degrees BTDC on the indicator scale. DO NOT turn camshaft. Use only crankshaft nut to turn. Turning the nut on the camshaft directly can damage the camshaft bearings.

7. Adjust timing belt to specifications using tool J—26486—A. The correct adjusting tension for timing belt is a band marked on the tool. Never adjust belt tension with gage installed this will result in an incorrect reading.

8. Crank engine (without starting) 10 revolutions. As new belt takes position tension loss will occur. Recheck tension with gage.

NOTE: The timing mark on the camshaft gear and rear timing belt cover must be aligned during the final tension recheck or reset.

9. Tighten water pump bolts to 18 ft. lbs.

10. Reverse the remaining removal procedures.

Camshaft
REMOVAL & INSTALLATION
2.5L Engine

NOTE: Relieve the fuel system pressure before disconnecting any fuel lines.

1. Refer to the "Engine, Removal & Installation" procedures in this section and remove the engine from the vehicle. Secure the engine to a workstand.

2. Remove the rocker cover, rocker arms and pushrods.

3. Remove the distributor, the spark plug wires and the spark plugs.

4. Remove the pushrod cover and gasket, then remove the lifters.

5. Remove the alternator, alternator lower bracket and the front engine mount bracket assembly.

6. Remove the oil pump driveshaft and gear assembly.

7. Remove the crankshaft pulley and front cover.

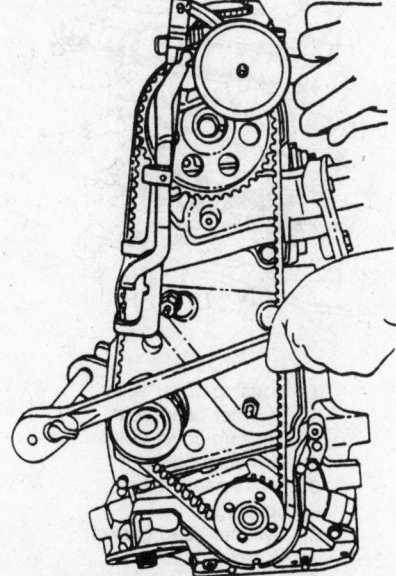

Timing belt adjustment 2.0L

8. Remove the two camshaft thrust plate screws by working through the holes in the gear.

9. Remove the camshaft and gear assembly by pulling it through the front of the block. Take care not to damage the bearings while removing the camshaft.

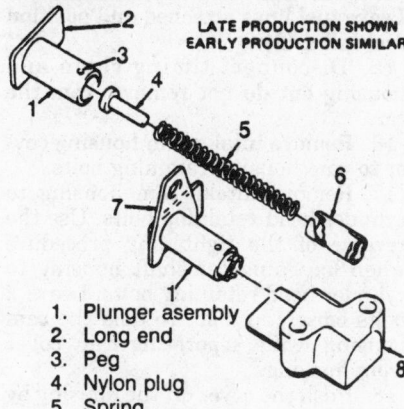

LATE PRODUCTION SHOWN
EARLY PRODUCTION SIMILAR

1. Plunger asembly
2. Long end
3. Peg
4. Nylon plug
5. Spring
6. Restraint cylinder
7. J—36589 anti-release devise
8. Tensioner body

Timing chain tensioner 2.3L Quad 4

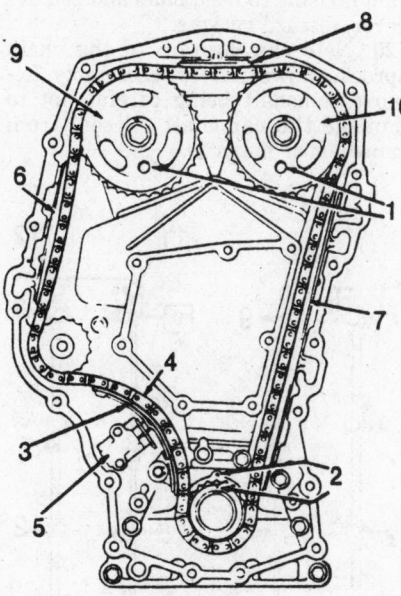

1. Camshaft timing marks
2. Crankshaft timing mark
3. Tensioner shoe assembly
4. Timing chain
5. Tensioner
6. R/H guide
7. L/H guide
8. Upper guide
9. Exhaust camshaft sprocket
10. Intake camshaft sprocket

Timing chain installation 2.3L Quad 4

10. Using a gasket scraper, clean the gasket mounting surfaces. Inspect the parts for wear, scoring and/or damage; if necessary, replace the damaged parts.

NOTE: Coat the camshaft with a liberal amount of clean engine oil before installing

11. To install, use new gaskets, sealant (if necessary) and reverse the removal procedures. Torque the crankshaft pulley-to-crankshaft bolt to 200 ft. lbs. (1985) or 162 ft. lbs. (1986–89) and the camshaft thrust plate-to-engine bolts to 90 inch lbs. and the front cover-to-engine bolts to 90 inch lbs.

3.0L Engine

NOTE: Relieve the fuel system pressure before disconnecting any fuel lines.

1. Refer to the "Engine, Removal & Installation" procedures in this section and remove the engine from the vehicle.

2. Remove the serpentine drive belt from the front of the engine.

3. Remove the intake manifold-to-engine bolts and the manifold.

4. Remove the valve covers, rocker arm assemblies, push rods and lifters. Keep all parts in order for reassembly.

5. Remove the crankshaft balancer from the crankshaft.

6. Remove the front cover-to-engine bolts and the front cover.

7. Rotate the crankshaft to align the timing marks on the timing sprockets. Remove the camshaft sprocket-to-camshaft bolts, then the camshaft sprocket and the timing chain.

8. Remove the camshaft retainer bolts and slide the camshaft forward out of the engine block. Take care not to damage the bearings while removing the camshaft.

9. Using a gasket scraper, clean the gasket mounting surfaces. Inspect the parts for wear, scoring and/or damage; if necessary, replace the damaged parts.

NOTE: Coat the camshaft with a liberal amount of clean engine oil prior to installation.

10. To install, use new gaskets, sealant (if necessary) and reverse the removal procedures. Torque the camshaft sprocket-to-camshaft bolts to 19 ft. lbs., the front cover-to-engine bolts to 22 ft. lbs., the crankshaft pulley bolt to 200–225 ft. lbs., the oil pan-to-front cover bolts to 88 inch lbs. and the water pump pulley bolts to 97 inch lbs. Refill the cooling system. Start the engine, allow the engine to reach normal operating temperatures and check for leaks.

2.0L Engine

1. Remove camshaft carrier cover.
2. Hold valves in place with compressed air, using air adapter J–22794 or equivalent in spark plug hole.
3. Compress valve springs with special tool J–33302–25.
4. Remove rocker arms. Keep rocker arms in order for re-assembly.
5. Remove camshaft sprocket.
6. Using a piece of chalk, mark the rotor position on the distributor housing and the distributor position with the block. Carefully pull the distributor up until the rotor just stops turning and again mark the rotor position for installation. Remove the distributor.
7. Remove camshaft thrust plate from rear of carrier.
8. Remove camshaft by sliding it to the rear.
9. To install, use new gaskets, sealant (if necessary) and reverse the removal procedures. Torque the rear thrust plate to 70 inch lbs. and camshaft sprocket retaining bolts to 34 ft. lbs.

2.3L Quad 4 Engine

INTAKE CAMSHAFT

NOTE: Any time the camshaft housing to cylinder head bolts are loosened or removed the camshaft housing-to-cylinder head gasket must be replaced.

1. Remove negative battery cable.
2. Remove ignition coil and module assembly electrical connections mark or tag if necessary.
3. Remove 4 ignition coil and module assembly to camshaft housing bolts and remove assembly by pulling straight up. Use special tool J–36011 to remove connector assembly(s) if stuck to the spark plugs.
4. Remove the idle speed power steering pressure switch connector.
5. Loosen 3 power steering pump pivot bolts and remove drive belt.
6. Disconnect the 2 rear power steering pump bracket to transaxle bolts.
7. Remove the front power steering pump bracket to cylinder block bolt.
8. Disconnect the power steering pump assembly and position aside.
9. Using special tools J–36014 and J–29785–A or equivalent remove power steering pump drive pulley from intake camshaft.
10. Remove oil/air separator bolts and hoses. Leave the hoses attached to the separator, disconnect from the oil fill, chain housing, and intake manifold. Remove as an assembly.
11. Remove vacuum line from fuel pressure regulator and fuel injector harness connector.

12. Disconnect fuel line retaining clamp from bracket on top of intake cam housing.
13. Remove fuel rail to camshaft housing retaining bolts.
14. Remove fuel rail from cylinder head. Cover injector openings in cylinder head and cover injector nozzles. Leave fuel lines attached and position fuel rail aside.
15. Disconnect timing chain and housing but do not remove from the car.
16. Remove intake cam housing cover to cam housing retaining bolts.
17. Remove intake cam housing to cylinder head retaining bolts. Use the reverse of the tightening procedure when loosening camshaft housing to cylinder head retaining bolts. Leave 2 bolts loosely in place to hold the cam housing while separating cam cover from housing.
18. Push the cover off the housing by threading 4 of the housing to head retaining bolts into the tapped holes in the cam housing cover. Tighten the bolts in evenly so the cover does not bind on the dowel pins.
19. Remove the 2 loosely installed cam housing to head bolts and remove cover, discard gaskets.
20. Note the position of the chain sprocket dowel pin for reassembly. Remove camshaft being careful not to damage the camshaft oil seal from camshaft or journals.

21. Remove intake camshaft oil seal from camshaft and discard seal. This seal must be replaced any time the housing and cover are separated.

To install:

NOTE: If the camshaft is being replaced, the lifters must also be replaced. Lube camshaft lobes, journals and lifters with part No. 1052365 camshaft and lifter prelube. The camshaft lobes and journals must be adequately lubricated or serious engine damage wil occur upon start up.

22. Install camshaft in same position as when removed. The timing chain sprocket dowel pin should be straight up and line up with the centerline of the lifter bores.
23. Install new camshaft housing-to-camshaft housing cover seals into cover (no sealer needed).

NOTE: Cam housing to cover seals are all different.

24. Apply Part No. 1052080, 3M® 08166, Fel-Pro® TST, Loctite® 592 or equivalent to camshaft housing and cover retaining bolt threads.
25. Install bolts and torque to 11 ft. lbs., Then rotate the bolts additional 75 degrees in sequence.

NOTE: The 2 rear bolts that hold fuel pipe to camshaft housing are torque to 11 ft. lbs. then rotate the bolts additional 25 degrees.

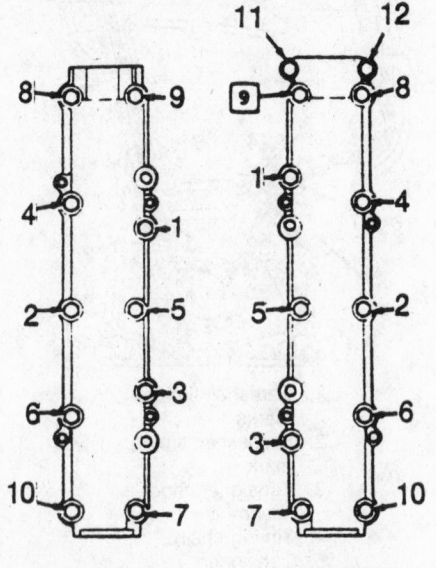

EXHAUST   INTAKE

FRONT
OF
ENGINE

Camshaft housing bolt torque sequence 2.3L Quad 4

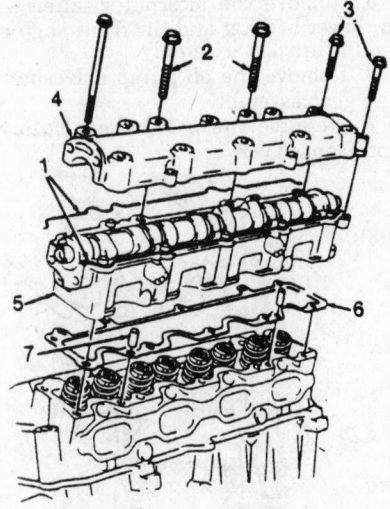

1. Housing cover seals
2. Cylinder head bolts
3. Housing cover bolts
4. Camshaft cover
5. Intake camshaft housing
6. Cylinder head gasket
7. Dowel pins

Camshaft housing assembly 2.3L Quad 4

26. Install timing chain housing and timing chain.

27. Uncover fuel injectors and install new fuel injector ring seals lubed with engine oil.

28. Reverse the remaining removal procedures.

NOTE: Clean any loose lubricant that is present on the ignition coil and module assembly to camshaft housing bolts. Apply LOCTITE® 592 or equivalent onto the ignition coil and module assembly to camshaft housing bolts. Hand start the ignition coil and module assembly to housing bolts then torque to 13 ft.lbs.

2.3L Quad 4 Engine

EXHAUST CAMSHAFT

NOTE: Any time the camshaft housing to cylinder head bolts are loosened or removed the camshaft housing-to-cylinder head gasket must be replaced.

1. Remove negative battery cable.

2. Remove electrical connection from ignition coil and module assembly.

3. Remove 4 ignition coil and module assembly to camshaft housing bolts and remove assembly by pulling straight up. Use special tool J—36011 to remove connector assembly(ies) if stuck to the spark plugs.

4. Remove electrical connection from oil pressure switch.

5. Remove transaxle fluid level indicator tube assembly from exhaust camshaft cover and position aside.

6. Remove exhaust camshaft cover and gasket.

7. Disconnect timing chain and housing but do not remove from the car.

8. Remove exhaust camshaft housing-to-cylinder head bolts. Use the reverse of the tightening procedure when loosening camshaft housing while separating camshaft cover from housing.

9. Push the cover off the housing by threading 4 of the housing-to-head retaining bolts into the tapped holes in the camshaft cover. Tighten the bolts in evenly so the cover does not bind on the dowel pins.

10. Remove the 2 loosely installed cam housing-to-cylinder head bolts and remove cover, discard gaskets.

11. Loosely reinstall 1 camshaft housing to cylinder head bolt to retain the housing during camshaft and lifter removal.

12. Note the position of the chain sprocket dowel pin for reassembly. Remove camshaft being careful not to damage the camshaft or journals

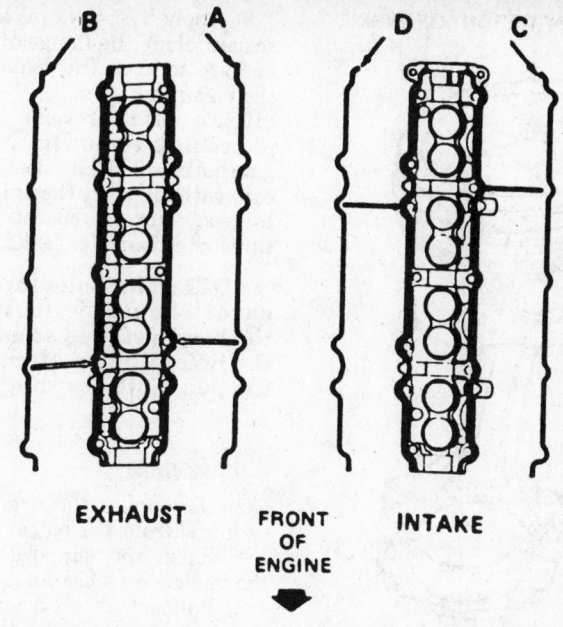

EXHAUST · FRONT OF ENGINE · INTAKE

A. Seal—inner (exhaust—red)
B. Seal—outer (exhaust—red)
C. Seal—outer (intake—blue)
D. Seal—inner (intake—blue)

Camshaft cover seals 2.3L Quad 4

To install:

NOTE. If the camshaft is being replaced, the lifters must also be replaced. Lube camshaft lobe, journals and lifters with Part No. 1052365 camshaft and lifter prelube. The camshaft lobes and journals must be adequately lubricated or serious engine damage will occur upon start up.

13. Install camshaft in same position as when removed. The timing chain sprocket dowel pin should be straight up and line up with the centerline of the lifter bores.

14. Install new camshaft housing to camshaft housing cover seals into cover (no sealer needed).

NOTE. Cam housing to cover seals are all different.

15. Apply Part No. 1052080, 3M® 08166, FEL-PRO® TST, Loctite® 592 or equivalent to camshaft housing and cover retaining bolt threads.

16. Install camshaft housing cover to camshaft housing.

17. Install bolts and torque in sequence to 11 ft. lbs. Then rotate the bolts 75 degrees in sequence.

18. Install timing chain housing and timing chain.

19. Install exhaust camshaft housing cover and new gasket and torque to 10 ft. lbs.

20. Reverse the remaining removal procedures.

NOTE: Clean any loose lubricant that is present on the ignition coil and module assembly-to-camshaft housing bolts. Applly LOCTITE® 592 or equivalent onto the ignition coil and module assembly-to-camshaft housing bolts. Hand start the ignition coil and module assembly to housing bolts then torque to 13 ft. lbs.

Piston and Connecting Rod

POSITIONING

See the illustrations for proper piston and connecting rod installation.

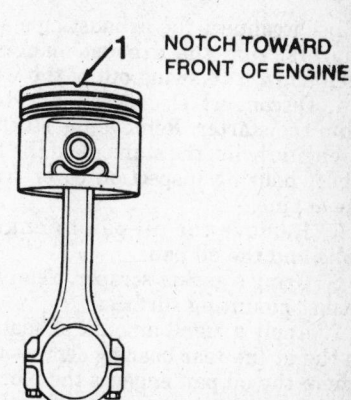

1 — NOTCH TOWARD FRONT OF ENGINE

3.0L piston identification

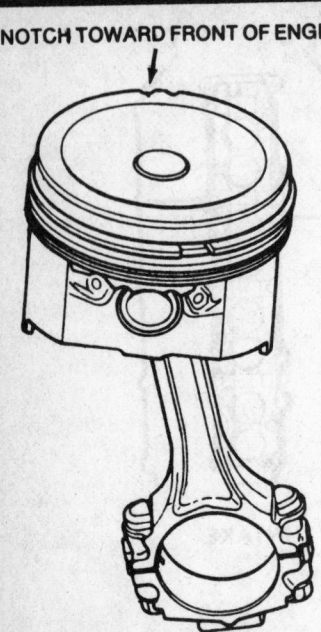

NOTCH TOWARD FRONT OF ENGINE

2.5L piston identification

ENGINE LUBRICATION

Oil Pan

REMOVAL & INSTALLATION

2.5L Engine

1. Disconnect the negative battery terminal from the battery.

2. Raise and support the front of the vehicle on jackstands. Position a drain pan under the crankcase, remove the drain plug and drain the engine oil.

NOTE: On manual transaxle it is necessary to remove engine from car.

3. Disconnect the exhaust pipe and hangers from the exhaust manifold, then allow it to swing out of the way.

4. Disconnect electrical connectors from the starter. Remove the starter-to-engine bolts, the starter and the flywheel housing inspection cover from the engine.

5. Remove the oil pan-to-engine bolts and the oil pan.

6. Using a gasket scraper, clean the gasket mounting surfaces.

7. Apply a small amount of sealant in the at the rear bearing depressions where the oil pan engages the block.

8. Apply a small amount of sealant in the at the front bearing depressions where the oil pan engages the block.

9. Apply a 1/8 x 1/4 in. long bead of sealant along the flange of the oil pan; be sure to keep the sealant inside of the bolt holes.

10. To install, reverse the removal procedures. Torque the oil pan-to-engine bolts to 20 ft. lbs. Refill the crankcase with oil, start the engine, allow it to reach normal operating temperatures and check for leaks.

NOTE: The bolts into the front cover should be installed last; they are installed at an angle and the holes line up after the rest of the pan bolts are snugged up.

3.0L Engine

1. Disconnect the negative battery terminal from the battery.

2. Raise and support the front of the vehicle on jackstands.

3. Position an oil drain pan under the engine, remove the drain plug and drain the engine oil. Remove the oil filter.

4. Remove the flywheel cover.

5. Remove the oil pan-to-engine bolts and the oil pan tensioner spring (located behind the oil filter adapter).

6. Remove the oil pan from the engine.

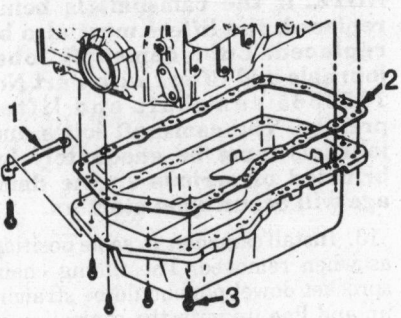

1. Tension spring
2. Rubber gasket
3. Bolt

V6 oil pan installation

7. Using a gasket scraper, clean the gasket mounting surfaces.

8. To install, use sealant (if necessary) and reverse the removal procedures. Torque the oil pan-to-engine bolts to 88 inch lbs. Refill the crankcase, operate the engine to normal operating temperatures and check for leaks.

2.0L Engine

1. Disconnect the negative battery terminal from the battery.

2. Raise and support the vehicle.

3. Remove right front wheel assembly.

4. Remove front splash shield.

5. Drain crankcase.

6. Remove exhaust pipe from wastegate.

7. Remove flywheel cover and oil pan scraper.

8. To install reverse removal procedures. Use gasket and sealant. Torque oil pan bolts to 4 ft. lbs.

2.3L Quad 4 Engine

1. Disconnect the negative battery terminal from the battery.

2. Remove flywheel inspection cover.

3. Remove splash shield to suspension support bolt.

4. Remove radiator outlet pipe to oil pan bolt.

5. Remove transaxle to oil pan nut then stud using a 7mm socket or equivalent.

6. Gently pry spacer out from between oil pan and transaxle.

7. Remove oil pan bolts.

NOTE: The crankshaft may have to be rotated to gain clearance. Use only enough RTV sealer to restore the silicone strip to its original dimension.

8. To install reverse the removal procedures. Torque vertical retaining

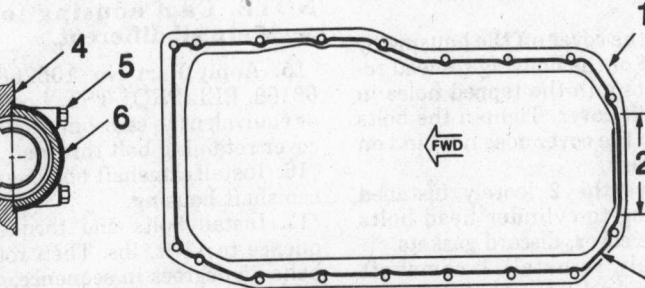

1—OIL PAN

2—APPLY A 3/8" WIDE BY 3/16" THICK BEAD OF RTV SEALER IN AREA INDICATED

3—APPLY A 3/16" WIDE BY 1/8" THICK BEAD OF RTV SEALER IN AREA INDICATED

4—ENGINE BLOCK ASSEMBLY

5—REAR BEARING

6—GROOVE IN MAIN BEARING CAP MUST BE FILLED FLUSH TO 1/8" ABOVE SURFACE WITH RTV

2.5L oil pan installation

bolts **A** and **C** (looking straight up at installed oil pan) to 106 inch lbs. Torque horizontal retaining bolts **B** to 17 ft. lbs.

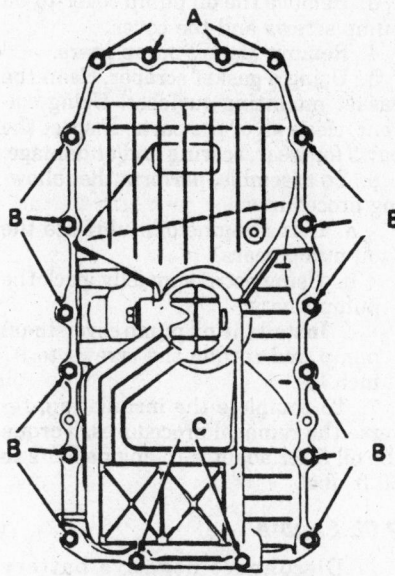

A. Chain housing bolts
B. Block bolts
C. Carrier seal bolts

Oil pan installation 2.3L Quad 4

Rear Main Bearing Oil Seal

REMOVAL & INSTALLATION

2.5L and 2.0L Engines

NOTE: The rear main bearing oil seal is a one piece unit and can be replaced without the removal of the oil pan or crankshaft.

1. Remove the transaxle.
2. If equipped with a manual transaxle remove the pressure plate and clutch disc.
3. Remove the flywheel-to-crankshaft bolts and the flywheel.
4. Using a medium pry bar, pry out the old seal; Be careful not to scratch the crankshaft surface.
5. Clean the block and crankshaft-to-seal mating surfaces.
6. Using the Seal Installation tool No. J–34924 or equivalent, install the new rear seal into the block. Lubricate the outside of the seal to aid installation and press the seal in evenly with the tool.
7. To install, reverse the removal procedures. Torque the flywheel-to-crankshaft bolts to 44 ft. lbs. (1985), 55 ft. lbs. (1986–89–AT) or 69 ft. lbs. (1986–89–MT). On 2.0L engine use new bolts and torque flywheel (MT) to 48 ft. lbs. plus 30 degrees turn and on flexplate (AT) torque to 48 ft. lbs. use same bolts.

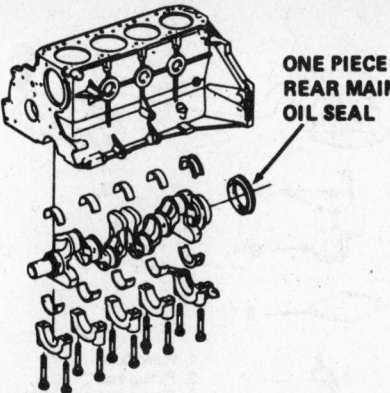

Exploded view of 4 cyl crankshaft and bearings

3.0L Engine

The rear main oil seal is a 2-piece, rope type and is located inside the rear main bearing.

1. Raise and support the front of the vehicle on jackstands.
2. Position a oil drain pan under the engine, remove the drain plug and drain the oil. Remove the oil pan-to-engine bolts and the oil pan.
3. Remove the rear main bearing cap-to-engine bolts and the bearing cap from the engine.
4. Remove the old seal from the bearing cap.
5. Using a Seal Packing tool No. J–21526–2 or equivalent, insert it against one end of the seal in the cylinder block. Pack the old seal into the groove until it is packed tight, then repeat the procedure on the other end of the seal.
6. Measure the amount the seal was driven up, then add approximately $1/16$ in. Cut this length from the old seal removed from the lower bearing cap, then repeat for the other side.

NOTE: When cutting the seal into short lengths, use a razor blade and the lower bearing cap as a holding fixture.

7. Using the Seal Packer Guide tool No. J–21526–1 or equivalent, install it onto the cylinder block.
8. Using the packing tool, work the short pieces into the guide tool and pack into the cylinder block until the tool hits the built-in stop.

NOTE: It may help to use oil on the short seal pieces when packing into the block.

9. Repeat Steps 7–8 for the other side.
10. Remove the guide tool.
11. Install a new rope seal into the lower bearing cap.

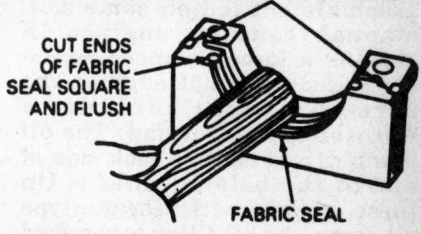

Installing rear main bearing cap oil seal on V6

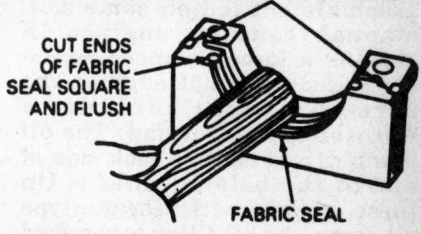

Applying sealer to bearing cap on V6

12. Install the lower main bearing cap and torque the bolts to 100 ft. lbs. (135 Nm).
13. To complete the installation, reverse the removal procedures. Torque the oil pan-to-engine bolts to 88 in. lbs. Refill the crankcase. Start the engine, allow it to reach normal operating temperatures and check for leaks.

2.3L Quad 4 Engine

1. Remove the transaxle.
2. If equipped with a manual transaxle remove the pressure plate and clutch disc.
3. Remove the flywheel-to-crankshaft bolts and the flywheel.
4. Remove 2 oil pan to seal housing bolts and 6 block to seal housing bolts.

NOTE: Drive seal evenly out the transaxle side of the seal housing using small chisel in the relief grooves.

5. To install reverse the removal procedures. Torque flywheel to crankshaft to 22 ft. lbs. plus 45 degree turn. Torque flywheel to converter 46 ft. lbs.

Oil Pump

REMOVAL & INSTALLATION

2.5L Engine

1. Disconnect the negative battery terminal from the battery.

NOTE: In 1987 a force balancer assembly is used on some 2.5L manual transaxle engines. In 1988–89 a force balancer assembly is used on all 2.5L engines. The force balancer includes a Gerotor-type oil pump. The oil pump drives off the back side of one of the balance shafts. On these engines with Gerotor-type oil pump the oil filter is serviced through an opening in the oil pan. The engine still must be removed on manual transaxle to lower oil pan to replace pump. The procedure below is for gear-type oil pump which is driven off the camshaft.

2. Raise and support the front of the vehicle on jackstands.

3. Remove the oil pan-to-engine bolts and the oil pan.

4. Remove the oil pump-to-engine bolts.

5. Remove the oil pump, pipe and screen as an assembly.

6. To install, reverse the removal procedures. Torque the oil pump-to-engine bolts to 22 ft. lbs., the oil pan-to-engine bolts to 20 ft. lbs. Refill the crankcase with new oil. Start the engine, allow it to reach normal operating temperatures and check for leaks.

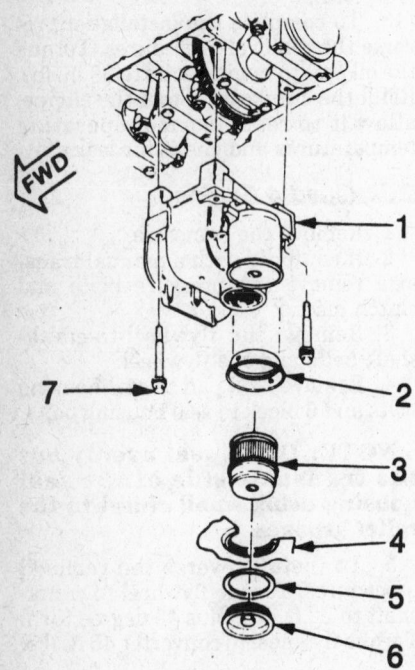

1. Balancer assembly
2. Restrictor
3. Filter
4. Oil pan
5. Gasket
6. Plug
7. Bolt

Force balancer assembly 2.5L

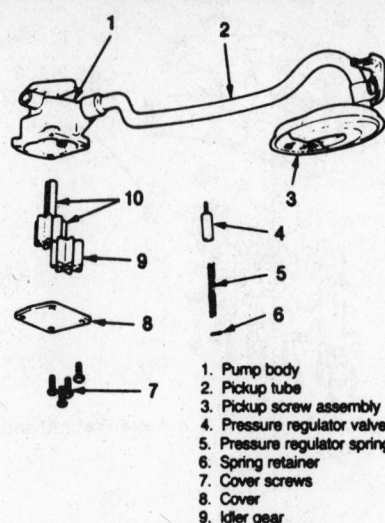

1. Pump body
2. Pickup tube
3. Pickup screw assembly
4. Pressure regulator valve
5. Pressure regulator spring
6. Spring retainer
7. Cover screws
8. Cover
9. Idler gear
10. Drive gear and shaft

2.5L oil pump assembly

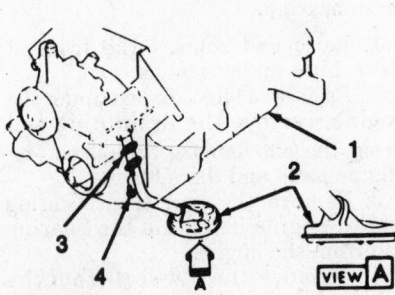

1. Engine block
2. Oil pump pipe and screen
3. Gasket
4. Bolt

V6 oil pipe and screen assembly

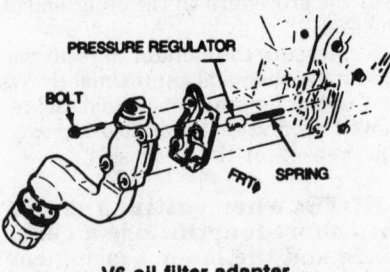

V6 oil filter adapter

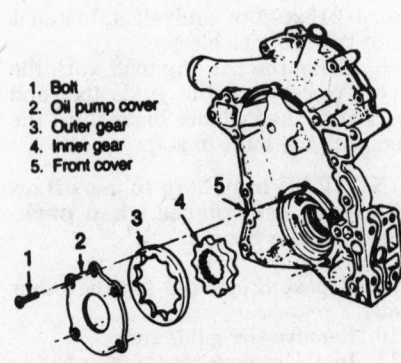

1. Bolt
2. Oil pump cover
3. Outer gear
4. Inner gear
5. Front cover

V6 oil pump assembly

3.0L Engine

1. Remove the front cover
2. Remove the oil filter adapter, the pressure regulator valve and the valve spring.
3. Remove the oil pump cover-to-oil pump screws and the cover.
4. Remove the oil pump gears.
5. Using a gasket scraper, clean the gasket mounting surfaces. Using solvent, clean all of the parts. Inspect the parts for wear, scoring and/or damage.
6. To assemble, perform the following procedures:
   a. Using engine oil, lubricate the oil pump gears.
   b. Using petroleum jelly, pack the pump cavity.
   c. Install the oil pump cover-to-oil pump and torque the screws to 97 inch lbs.
7. To complete the installation, reverse the removal procedures. Torque the oil filter adapter-to-engine bolts to 30 ft. lbs.

2.0L Engine

1. Disconnect negative battery cable.
2. Remove crankshaft sprocket.
3. Remove rear timing belt cover.
4. Disconnect and tag oil pressure electrical connection.
5. Remove oil pan and oil filter.
6. Remove oil pump and pick-up tube.
7. Remove front oil seal from housing.
8. To install reverse removal porocedures. Torque oil pump to 5 ft. lbs. and use a new O-ring for pick-up tube.

2.3L Quad 4 Engine

1. Disconnect the negative battery terminal from the battery.
2. Remove oil pan.
3. Remove oil pump assembly retainers 2 bolts and 1 nut.
4. Remove oil pump assembly and shims if so equipped.

NOTE: Oil pump drive gear backlash must be checked when any of the following components are replaced: oil pump assembly, oil pump drive gear, crankshaft and cylinder block.

5. To install reverse removal procedures. Torque oil pump to block bolts 33 ft.lbs.

OIL PUMP DRIVE GEAR BACKLASH ADJUSTMENT

1. With oil pump assembly off engine remove 3 retaining bolts and separate the driven gear cover and screen assembly from the oil pump.

2. Install the oil pump on the block using the original shim(s). Tighten the bolts to 33 ft. lbs.

3. Install the dial indicator assembly J–26900–13 and J–8001 or equivalent to measure backlash between oil pump to drive gear.

4. Record oil pump drive to driven gear backlash correct backlash clearance is 0.010–0.014. When taking measurement crankshaft cannot move.

5. Remove shims to decrease clearance and add shims to increase clearance.

6. When proper clearance is reached rotate crankshaft ½ turn and recheck clearance.

7. Remove oil pump from block reinstall driven gear cover and screen assembly to pump and tighten to 106 in. lbs.

8. Reinstall pump assembly on block. Torque oil pump to block bolts 33 ft.lbs.

ENGINE COOLING

Radiator

REMOVAL & INSTALLATION

1. Disconnect the negative battery terminal from the battery.

2. Position a drain pan under the radiator, open the drain cock and drain the fluid from the cooling system.

3. Disconnect the forward strut brace from the radiator and swing it rearward.

NOTE: To prevent shearing of the rubber bushing, loosen the bolt before swinging the strut brace.

4. Remove the forward lamp harness from the fan frame and disconnect the fan connector.

5. Remove the fan bolts, then remove the fan and frame assembly.

6. Using an awl, scribe a reference mark on the hood latch assembly, then remove the hood latch from the radiator support.

7. Disconnect the coolant hoses from the radiator and remove the coolant recovery hose from the radiator neck.

8. If equipped with an automatic transaxle, disconnect and plug the transaxle oil cooler lines from the radiator.

9. Remove the radiator-to-radiator support attaching bolts and clamps, then lift the radiator from the engine compartment. It may be necessary to raise the right-hand (driver) side of the radiator first to allow the neck to clear the A/C compressor.

10. To install, reverse the removal procedures. Torque the radiator-to-chassis bolts to 7.5 ft. lbs. (10 Nm), the oil cooling lines-to-radiator to 20 ft. lbs. (27 Nm), the hood latch bolts to 18 ft. lbs. (25 Nm), the fan bolts to 88 inch lbs. and the brace-to-radiator support bolts to 37 ft. lbs. Refill the cooling system and the automatic transaxle. Start the engine, allow it to reach normal operating temperatures and check for leaks.

NOTE: On 1988–89 3.0L and 2.3L Quad 4 the radiator utilizes an aluminum core with plastic side tanks.

Water Pump

REMOVAL & INSTALLATION

2.5L and 3.0L Engines

NOTE: Special pulley removal and installation tools are required to remove and install the water pump pulley on the 2.5L engine.

1. Disconnect the negative battery terminal from the battery.

2. Position a drain pan under the radiator, open the drain cock and drain the cooling system.

3. Remove the drive belt(s).

4. Remove the fan, pulley and radiator shroud, as required to gain working clearance and access to the water pump bolts.

5. Remove the radiator and heater hose(s) from the water pump.

6. Remove the water pump-to-engine bolts.

NOTE: On the V6 engine, the long bolt is removed through the access hole that is provided in the body side rail.

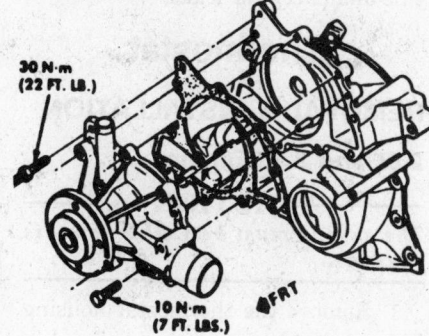

30 N·m
(22 FT. LB.)

10 N·m
(7 FT. LBS.)

FRT

Water pump mounting on V6

7. Remove the water pump from the vehicle.

NOTE: On 2.5L engines, remove the water pump pulley and transfer it to the replacement assembly; using the removal tool No. J–29785–A, J–25034 or equivalent, and the installation tool No. J–25033–B or equivalent.

8. Using a gasket scraper, clean the gasket mounting surfaces.

9. To install, use sealant and reverse the removal procedures. Clean all gasket mating surfaces and place a ⅛ in. bead of RTV sealant on all sealing surfaces. Water pump mounting bolts must also be coated with RTV sealer to avoid coolant leaks. Torque the water pump mounting bolts to 25 ft. lbs. 2.5L or 97 inch lbs. on 3.0L Refill the cooling system. Start the engine, allow it to reach normal operating temperatures and check for leaks.

2.0L Engine

1. Disconnect negative battery cable.

2. Drain cooling system.

3. Remove timing belt.

4. Remove water pump retaining bolts, water pump and seal ring.

5. To install reverse removal procedures. Torque water pump bolts to 18 ft. lbs.

2.3L Quad 4 Engine

1. Disconnect the negative battery cable and O₂ sensor connector.

2. Drain coolant. Remove heater hose from thermostat housing for more complete coolant drain.

3. Remove upper and lower exhaust manifold heat shields.

4. Remove exhaust manifold brace to manifold bolt.

5. Break loose the manifold to exhaust pipe spring loaded bolts using a 13 mm box wrench.

6. Raise and support car.

7. Remove the manifold to exhaust pipe bolts out of the exhaust pipe flange by using a ⁷⁄₃₂ in. (5.5mm) socket and **rotate clockwise** (as if tightening a bolt with right hand threads or removing a bolt with left hand threads). It is necessary to relieve the spring pressure from one bolt prior to removing the second bolt. If the spring pressure is not relieved it will cause the exhaust pipe to twist and bind up the bolt as it is removed. Relieve the spring pressure by:

a. Thread one bolt out 4 turns.

b. Move to the other bolt and turn it all the way out of the exhaust pipe flange.

c. Return to the first bolt and rotate it the rest of the way out of the exhaust pipe flange.

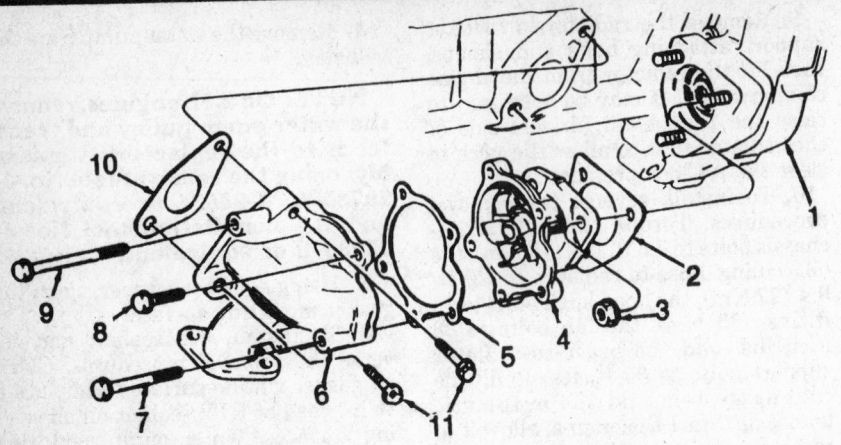

1. Timing chain housing
2. Water pump to timing chain housing gasket
3. Nut
4. water pump
5. Water pump body cover gasket
6. Water pump cover
7. Bolt
8. Bolt
9. Bolt
10. Water pump gasket cover to block gasket
11. water pump cover bolts

Water pump Installation 2.3L Quad 4

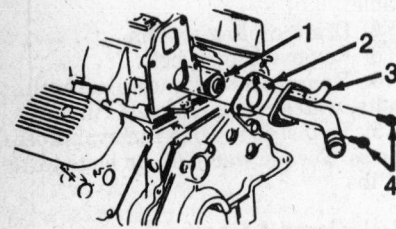

1. Thermostat   3. Thermostat housing
2. Gasket   4. Bolt

V6 thermostat housing

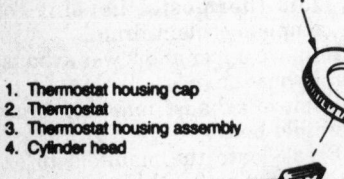

1. Thermostat housing cap
2. Thermostat
3. Thermostat housing assembly
4. Cylinder head

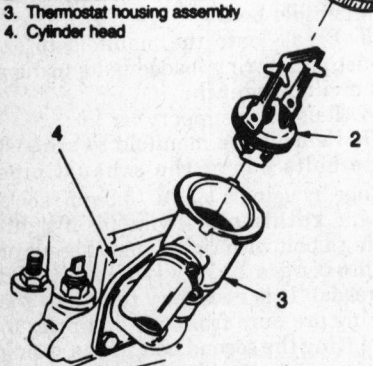

4 cyl thermostat housing

8. Pull down and back on the exhaust pipe to disengage it from the exhaust manifold bolts.

9. Remove radiator outlet pipe from oil pan and transaxle. Leave the lower radiator hose attached and pull down on the outlet pipe to remove it from the water pump.

10. Lower vehicle.
11. Remove exhaust manifold, seals and gaskets.
12. Remove water pump cover to block bolts and water pump assembly to timing chain housing nuts.

NOTE: On early production models it may be necessary to loosen and reposition the rear engine mount, mount to engine block bracket to gain clearance.

13. Remove water pump and cover assembly.
14. To install reverse the removal procedure. Start all bolts hand tight. Torque bolts/nuts to specifications in order
   a. Pump assembly to chain housing nuts — 19 ft. lbs.
   b. Pump cover to pump assembly — 106 inch lbs.
   c. Cover to block — 19 inch lbs.
   d. Radiator outlet pipe assembly to cover — 125 inch lbs.
15. Refill cooling system, start engine and check for leaks.

Thermostat

REMOVAL & INSTALLATION

2.0L and 2.5L Engines

—— CAUTION ——
The engine must be COLD for this procedure.

1. Remove the thermostat housing cap.
2. Grasp the handle of the thermostat assembly and gently pull upward.

3. Clean the thermostat housing and O-ring.
4. Apply a suitable lubricant to the O-ring, then install the thermostat into the housing, pushing down to ensure that the thermostat is firmly seated.
5. Replace the thermostat housing cap.

3.0L Engine

1. Disconnect the negative battery terminal from the battery.
2. Drain the engine coolant below the level of the thermostat housing.
3. Remove the water outlet-to-thermostat housing bolts.
4. Remove the thermostat housing and lift out the thermostat.
5. Using a gasket scraper, clean the gasket mounting surfaces.
6. To install, reverse the removal procedures. Using RTV sealant, coat the thermostat housing with a 1/8 in. bead. Make sure the thermostat is installed correctly (wax pellet toward the engine). Torque the thermostat housing-to-engine bolts to 21 ft. lbs. (28 Nm).

NOTE: On the 2.3L Quad 4 the procedure is similar to 3.0L. The 2 heater hoses and upper radiator hose must be position aside.

EMISSION CONTROLS

Please refer to "Emission Control" in the Unit Repair section for system maintenance procedures. Due to the complex nature of modern electronic engine control systems, comprehensive diagnosis and testing procedures fall outside the confines of this repair manual. For complete information on diagnosis, testing and repair procedures concerning all modern engine and emission control systems, please refer to "Chilton's Guide to Electronic Engine Controls".

FUEL SYSTEM

Fuel System Service Precaution

Any time the fuel system is being worked on, disconnect the negative battery cable, except for those tests where battery voltage is required and always keep a dry chemical (Class B) fire extinguisher near the work area.

RELIEVING FUEL SYSTEM PRESSURE

2.5L and 2.3L Quad 4 Engines

1. Remove the fuel pump fuse from the fuse block or disconnect the harness connector at the tank.
2. Start the engine. It should run and then stall when the fuel in the lines is exhausted. When the engine stops, crank the starter for about three seconds to make sure all pressure in the fuel lines is released.
3. Install the fuel pump fuse after repair is made.

2.0L and 3.0L Engines

1. Using a Fuel Pressure Gauge tool No. J–34730–1 or equivalent, connect it to the fuel pressure valve.

NOTE: Wrap a clean shop towel around the fitting while making connections to catch any fuel spray.

2. Install a bleed hose onto the gauge assembly and place the end in a suitable container.
3. Open the pressure gauge valve and bleed the fuel pressure from the system.
4. Close the pressure gauge bleed screw.

Fuel Filter

REMOVAL & INSTALLATION

An inline fuel filter is used on all fuel injected models. It is located on a frame crossmember near the rear of the vehicle.
1. Raise and support the rear of the vehicle on jackstands.
2. Refer to "Relieving Fuel Pressure" procedures in this section and relieve the fuel pressure.
3. Using a back-up wrench, remove the fuel line fittings from the fuel filter.
4. Remove the fuel filter-to-crossmember screws and the filter from the vehicle.
5. To install, use a new fuel filter, O-rings and reverse the removal procedures.

Electric Fuel Pump

PRESSURE TESTING

TBI System

1. Refer to "Relieving Fuel Pres-

sure" procedures in this section and relieve the fuel pressure.
2. Remove the air cleaner and plug the THERMAC vacuum port on the throttle body.
3. Using the Pressure Gauge tool No. J–29658 or equivalent, install it on the throttle body side of the fuel filter at the rear of the vehicle near the fuel tank.
4. Start the engine and read the fuel pressure on the gauge, it should be 9–13 psi.
5. Turn the ignition **OFF**, relieve the fuel system pressure and remove the fuel pressure gauge. Reconnect all fuel and vacuum lines. Install the air cleaner.

MFI System

1. Refer to "Relieving Fuel Pressure" procedures in this section and relieve the fuel pressure.
2. Using the Pressure Gauge tool No. J–34730–1 or equivalent, to the fuel pressure test point (Shrader fitting) on the fuel rail.
3. Using a clean shop cloth, wrap it around the fitting to catch any fuel leakage when connecting the gauge.
4. Turn the ignition **ON** and read the fuel pressure (on the gauge), it should be 37–43 psi.
5. Start the engine and again note the fuel pressure on the gauge.
6. With the engine idling, the fuel pressure should be 33–40 psi. This idle pressure will vary somewhat depending on barometric pressure but in any case it should be lower.
7. Relieve the fuel pressure and disconnect the gauge.

REMOVAL & INSTALLATION

1. Refer to "Relieving Fuel Pressure" procedures in this section and relieve the fuel pressure.
2. Disconnect the negative battery terminal from the battery.
3. Raise and support the vehicle on jackstands. Drain the fuel tank.

—— CAUTION ——
DO NOT drain or store fuel in an open container. Serious explosion and fire hazard exists. Empty the contents of the fuel tank into an approved gasoline storage container and take precautions to avoid the risk of fire.

4. Remove the fuel tank by supporting it and disconnecting the two retaining straps. Lower the tank enough to disconnect the sending unit wires, hoses and ground strap (if equipped).
5. Lower the fuel tank from the vehicle and remove the sending unit.

NOTE: The sending unit is retained by a cam lock ring. The fuel

pump is attached to the tank sending unit.

6. To install, use new O-rings, anti-squeak pieces on top of the tank and reverse the removal procedures. Tighten the retaining straps.

Fuel Injection

Due to the complex nature of modern fuel injection systems, comprehensive diagnosis and testing procedures fall outside the confines of this repair manual. For complete information on fuel injection diagnosis, testing and repair procedures please refer to *"Chilton's Guide to Fuel Injection and Feedback Carburetors".*

MANUAL TRANSAXLE

REMOVAL & INSTALLATION

1. Disconnect the negative battery terminal from the battery.
2. Using the Engine Support Fixture tool No. J–28467 or equivalent, attach it to the engine lift ring and raise the engine enough to take the pressure off the engine mounts.

NOTE: If a lifting bar is not available a chain hoist can be used. However, during the removal procedure the vehicle must be raised and the chain hoist adjusted to keep tension on the engine/transaxle assembly.

3. Remove the hush panel from inside the vehicle.
4. Disconnect the clutch master cylinder push rod from the clutch pedal.
5. Disconnect the clutch slave cylinder from the transaxle support bracket and move it aside.
6. Remove the transaxle mount-to-transaxle bolts. Discard the bolts attaching the mount to the side frame. New bolts must be used upon installation.
7. Remove the transaxle mount bracket attaching bolts and nuts.
8. Disconnect the shift cables and retaining clips from the transaxle. Disconnect the ground cables from the transaxle mounting stud.
9. Remove the air management valve-to-chassis bolts to gain clearance to remove the upper-right transaxle-to-engine bolt.
10. Raise and support the front of the vehicle on jackstands. Remove the left-front wheel/tire assembly.

11. Remove the left-front inner splash shield. Remove the transaxle strut and bracket.

12. Remove the clutch housing cover bolts.

13. Disconnect the speedometer cable or sensor from the transaxle.

14. Disconnect the stabilizer bar from the left-suspension support and control arm.

15. Disconnect the ball joint-to-steering knuckle nut and separate the ball joint from the steering knuckle.

16. Remove the left-suspension support attaching bolts, the support and control arm as an assembly.

17. Using boot protectors, install them and disengage the halfshafts from the transaxle. Remove the left-side shaft from the transaxle.

18. Using a transmission jack, position it under and secure it to the transaxle case. Remove the transaxle-to-engine mounting bolts.

19. Remove the transaxle by sliding it toward the driver's side, away from the engine. Carefully lower the jack, guiding the right-shaft out of the transaxle. Place the transaxle on a work bench.

20. To install the transaxle, guide the right halfshaft into its bore as the transaxle is being raised.

NOTE: The right halfshaft cannot be readily installed after the transaxle is connected to the engine.

21. To complete the installation, reverse the removal procedures. Torque the transaxle-to-engine bolts to 55 ft. lbs., the suspension support-to-chassis bolts to 75 ft. lbs. and the clutch housing cover bolts to 10 ft. lbs. Using new bolts, install and torque the transaxle mount-to-side frame to 35 ft. lbs. Adjust the shift linkage cables.

NOTE: When installing the mount-to-transaxle bracket bolts, check the alignment bolt at the engine mount.

LINKAGE ADJUSTMENT

1. Disconnect the negative battery terminal from the battery.

2. Shift the transaxle into 3rd gear.

3. On top of the transaxle, remove the lock pin (H) and reinstall the tapered end down; this will lock the transaxle in 3rd gear.

4. Loosen the shift cable nuts (E) at the transaxle levers (G & F).

5. Remove the trim plate from the console and slide the shifter boot up the shifter handle, then remove the console.

6. Using a ⁵⁄₃₂ in. or No. 22 drill bit, install it into the alignment hole at the side of the shifter assembly.

7. Using a ³⁄₁₆ in. drill bit, install it into the select lever hole and the slot in the shifter plate.

8. Tighten the (E) nuts at the (G & F) levers, then remove the drill bits from the alignment holes. Remove the lockpin (H) and reinstall it with the tapered end up.

9. To complete the installation, reverse the removal procedures. Road test the vehicle.

NOTE: When shifting, there should be a good NEUTRAL gate feel.

CLUTCH

— CAUTION —

The clutch plate contains asbestos, which has been determined to be a cancer causing agent. Never clean the clutch surfaces with compressed air! Avoid inhaling any dust from any clutch surface! When cleaning clutch surfaces, use a commercially available brake cleaning fluid.

REMOVAL & INSTALLATION

1. Remove the transaxle.

2. Mark the pressure plate assembly and the flywheel so that they may be assembled in their original position. They are balanced as an assembly at the factory.

3. Loosen the attaching bolts one turn at a time until all spring tension is released.

4. Support the pressure plate and remove the bolts, then remove the pressure plate, clutch disc, throwout bearing and the clutch fork and pivot shaft assembly. Replace any parts found to be defective.

5. Inspect the flywheel, pressure plate, clutch disc, throwout bearing and the clutch fork and pivot shaft for signs of wear and replace the parts as necessary.

6. Using a stiff bristle brush (NOT WIRE), clean the pressure plate and flywheel mating surfaces. Position the clutch disc and pressure plate into the installed position and support with a

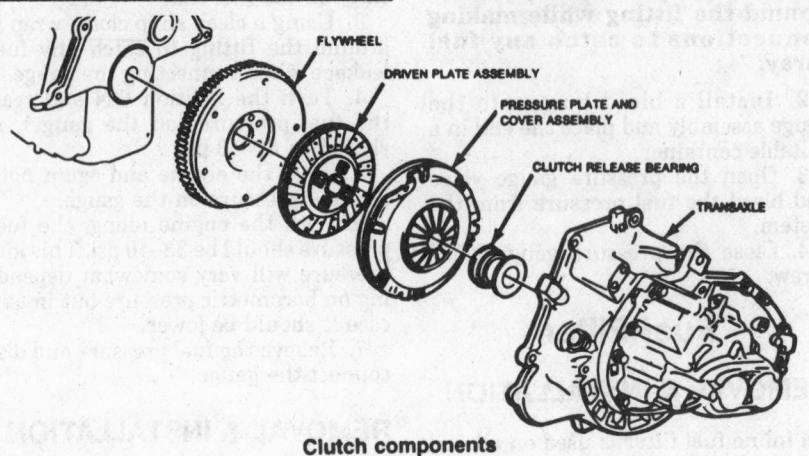

Clutch components

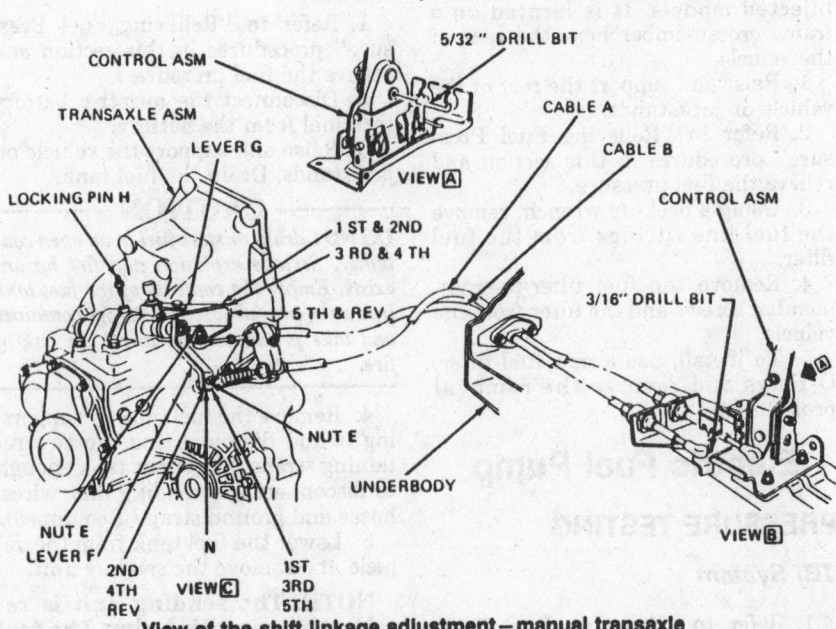

View of the shift linkage adjustment—manual transaxle

Clutch Alignment tool No. J–29074 or equivalent. The clutch plate is assembled with the damper springs offset toward the transaxle.

7. Install the pressure plate-to-flywheel bolts and tighten gradually in a criss-cross pattern to 15 ft. lbs. (20 Nm).

8. Lubricate the outside grooves and the inside recess of the release bearing with high temperature grease. Wipe off the excess and install the bearing.

9. To complete the installation, reverse the removal procedures.

PEDAL HEIGHT/FREE-PLAY ADJUSTMENT

Since the hydraulic system provides automatic clutch adjustment, no adjustment of the clutch linkage or pedal height is required.

Clutch Master Cylinder

The clutch master cylinder is located in the engine compartment, on the left side of the firewall, above the steering column.

REMOVAL & INSTALLATION

1. Disconnect the negative battery terminal from the battery.

2. Remove the hush panel from the under the dash.

3. Disconnect the push rod from the clutch pedal.

4. Disconnect the hydraulic line from the clutch master cylinder.

5. Remove the master cylinder-to-cowl brace nuts. Remove the master cylinder and overhaul (if necessary).

6. Using a gasket scraper, clean the master cylinder and cowl mounting surfaces.

7. To install reverse the removal procedures. Torque the master cylinder-to-cowl nuts to 15–25 ft. lbs. Refill the master cylinder with new hydraulic fluid conforming to Dot 3 specifications. Bleed and check the hydraulic clutch system for leaks.

Clutch Slave Cylinder

The slave cylinder is located on the top left-side of the transaxle and controls the clutch release fork operation.

REMOVAL & INSTALLATION

1. Disconnect the negative battery terminal from the battery.

2. Raise and support the front of the vehicle on jackstands.

3. Disconnect the hydraulic line from clutch master cylinder. Remove the hydraulic line-to-chassis screw and the clip from the chassis.

NOTE: Be sure to plug the line opening to keep dirt and moisture out of the system.

4. Remove the slave cylinder-to-transaxle nuts.

5. Remove the push rod and the slave cylinder from the vehicle, then overhaul it (if necessary).

6. To install, reverse the removal procedures. Lubricate the leading end of the slave cylinder with Girling® Rubber Lube or equivalent. Torque the slave cylinder-to-transaxle nuts to 18–26 ft. lbs. Refill the master cylinder with new brake fluid conforming to Dot 3 specifications. Bleed the hydraulic clutch system.

BLEEDING THE HYDRAULIC CLUTCH

Bleeding air from the hydraulic clutch system is necessary whenever any part of the system has been disconnected or the fluid level (in the reservoir) has been allowed to fall so low, that air has been drawn into the master cylinder.

1. Fill master cylinder reservoir with new brake fluid conforming to Dot 3 specifications.

NOTE: Never, under any circumstances, use fluid which has been bled from a system to fill the reservoir as it may be aerated.

2. Raise and support the front of the vehicle on jackstands.

3. Remove the slave cylinder-to-transaxle nuts.

4. Hold the slave cylinder at approximately 45 degrees with the bleeder at highest point. Fully depress clutch pedal and open the bleeder screw.

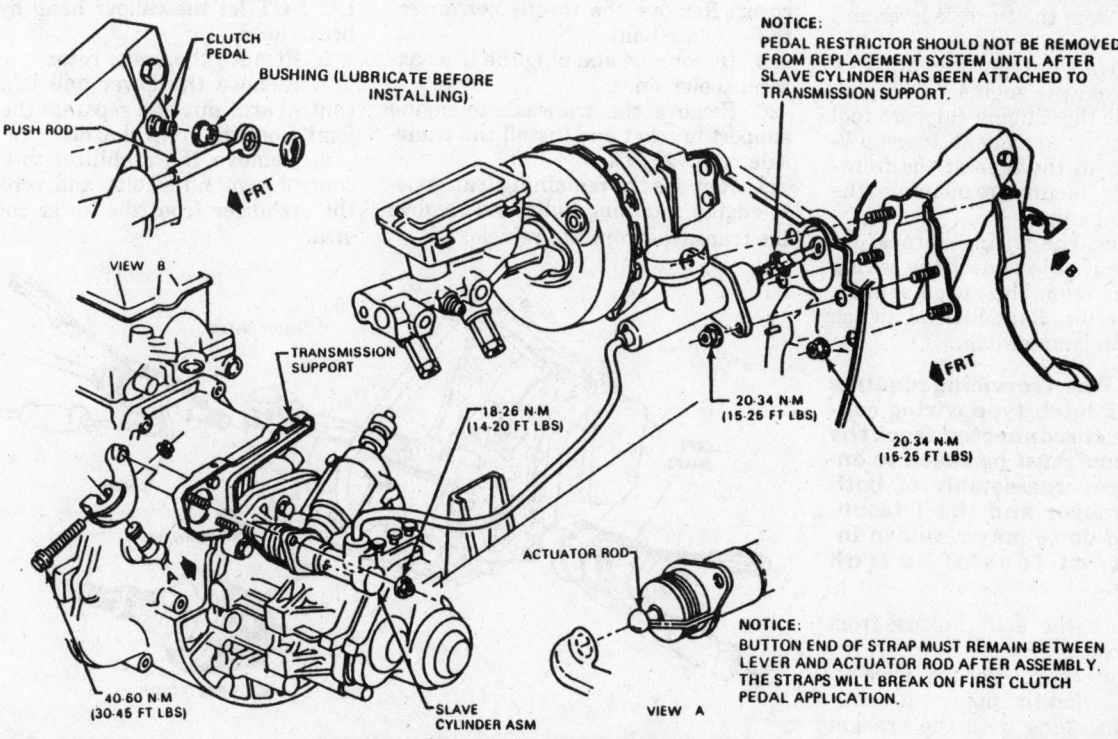

CLUTCH PEDAL

BUSHING (LUBRICATE BEFORE INSTALLING)

PUSH ROD

FRT

VIEW B

TRANSMISSION SUPPORT

18-26 N·M (14-20 FT LBS)

20-34 N·M (15-25 FT LBS)

20-34 N·M (15-25 FT LBS)

FRT

NOTICE:
PEDAL RESTRICTOR SHOULD NOT BE REMOVED FROM REPLACEMENT SYSTEM UNTIL AFTER SLAVE CYLINDER HAS BEEN ATTACHED TO TRANSMISSION SUPPORT.

ACTUATOR ROD

40-60 N·M (30-45 FT LBS)

SLAVE CYLINDER ASM

VIEW A

NOTICE:
BUTTON END OF STRAP MUST REMAIN BETWEEN LEVER AND ACTUATOR ROD AFTER ASSEMBLY. THE STRAPS WILL BREAK ON FIRST CLUTCH PEDAL APPLICATION.

Exploded view of the hydraulic clutch assembly

5. Close the bleeder screw and release clutch pedal.

6. Repeat the procedure until all of the air is evacuated from the system. Check and refill master cylinder reservoir as required to prevent air from being drawn through the master cylinder.

NOTE: Never release a depressed clutch pedal with the bleeder screw open or air will be drawn into the system.

AUTOMATIC TRANSAXLE

For further information on automatic transaxles, please refer to "Automatic Transaxles" in the Unit Repair section.

REMOVAL & INSTALLATION

NOTE: When removing the transaxle from the 2.3L Quad 4 the procedure may slighty differ.

1. Disconnect the negative battery terminal from the battery.

2. Remove the air cleaner assembly. If equipped with a 3.0L engine, remove the mass air flow sensor and air intake duct.

3. Disconnect the throttle valve (TV) cable from the throttle lever and the transaxle.

4. Remove the transaxle dipstick and tube from the engine.

5. Install the Engine Support tool No. J–28467 or equivalent. Insert a ¼ x 2 in. bolt in the hole at the front-right motor mount to maintain the driveline alignment.

6. Remove the wiring harness-to-transaxle nut. Disconnect the wiring connectors from the speed sensor, TCC connector, Park/Neutral switch and back-up lamp switch.

NOTE: When servicing requires that the T-latch type wiring connector be disconnected from the switch, care must be taken to ensure proper reassembly of both the connector and the T-latch. Failure to do so may result in intermittent loss of switch functions.

7. Remove the shift linkage from the transaxle.

8. Remove the top two transaxle-to-engine bolts and the upper-left transaxle mount along with the bracket assembly.

9. Remove the rubber hose from the transaxle vent pipe. Remove the remaining upper engine-to-transaxle bolts.

10. Raise and support the vehicle safely, then remove both front wheel/tire assemblies.

11. Position an oil drain pan under the transaxle, remove the drain plug and drain the transaxle fluid.

12. Remove the shift linkage and bracket from the transaxle.

13. Using a Drive Axle Boot Seal Protector tool No. J–33162 or equivalent, install it on the inner seals.

NOTE: Some vehicles may use a silicone (gray) boot on the inboard axle joint. Use the tool No. J–33162 or equivalent, on these boots. All other boots are made from a thermo-plastic material (black) and do not require use of a boot seal protector.

14. Remove both ball joints-to-control arms nuts and separate the ball joints from the control arms.

15. Remove both halfshafts and support them with a cord or wire.

16. Remove the transaxle mounting strut.

17. Remove the left stabilizer bar link pin bolt, left frame bushing clamp nuts and left frame support assembly.

NOTE: Before disconnecting, be sure to match mark the flex plate and torque converter for installation purposes.

18. Remove the transaxle converter cover. Remove the torque converter-to-flex plate bolts.

19. Disconnect and plug the transaxle oil cooler lines.

20. Remove the transaxle-to-engine support bracket and install the transaxle removal jack.

21. Remove the remaining transaxle-to-engine retaining bolts and remove the transaxle from the vehicle.

22. To install, reverse the removal procedures. Refill the transaxle with the proper grade and type automatic transaxle fluid.

DRIVE AXLE

Halfshaft

REMOVAL & INSTALLATION

NOTE: Some vehicles use a silicone (gray) boot on the right hand inboard joint. Use the Boot Protector tool No. J–33162 or equivalent, on these boots during removal. All other boots are made of thermoplastic material (black) and do not require the use of a boot protector.

1. Raise and support the front of the vehicle with jackstands positioned under the frame.

2. Lower the vehicle slightly so that the weight rests on the frame and not on the lower control arms.

3. Remove the wheel/tire assemblies.

4. Install a drift punch through the brake rotor cooling holes to lock the rotor in place. Clean the halfshaft threads of dirt, then, using a suitable socket and breaker bar, lubricate and remove the hub nut and washer.

5. Remove the caliper mounting bolts and support the caliper on a wire. DO NOT let the caliper hang by the brake hose.

6. Remove the brake rotor.

7. Remove the lower ball joint-to-control arm nut and separate the ball joint from the control arm.

8. Remove the stabilizer-to-lower control arm nuts/bolts and separate the stabilizer from the lower control arm.

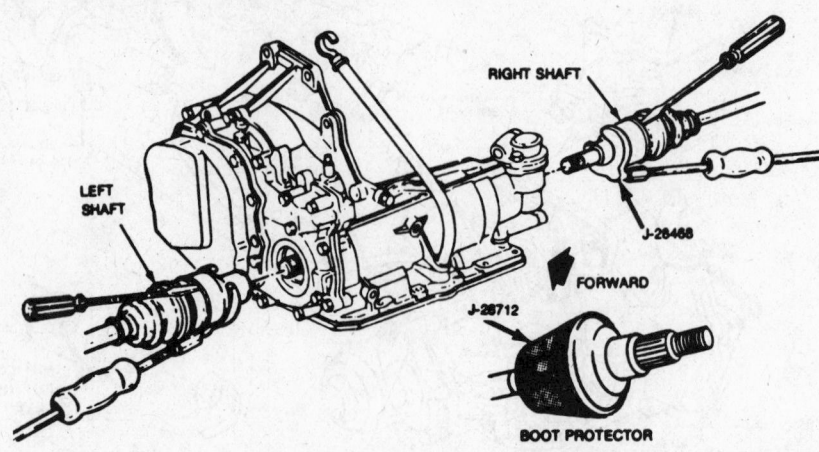

Halfshaft removal; the special tools are attached to a slide hammer in this diagram

9. Using the tool No. J–28733 or equivalent, install it to the axle hub and press the halfshaft in and away from the hub. The halfshaft should only be pressed in until the press fit between the halfshaft and hub is loose.

NOTE: Be careful not to press the halfshaft in too far as damage to the joint may occur.

10. Separate and remove the lower ball joint from the steering knuckle.
11. Separate the halfshaft from the hub by pulling the hub assembly out away from the halfshaft.

NOTE: If equipped with Tri-Pot joints, care must be taken not to allow the joints to become overextended. When either end or both ends of the shaft are disconnected, overextending the joint could result in separation of internal components. This could cause failure of the joint, so it's important to handle the halfshaft in a manner that prevents overextension.

12. Using a slide hammer and a boot protector (if necessary), remove the halfshaft from the differential assembly.
13. To install, use a new hub nut, cotter pins and reverse the removal procedures. Start the splines of the halfshaft into the transaxle and push until the axle snaps into place. Torque the caliper-to-steering knuckle bolts to 28 ft. lbs., the ball joint-to-steering knuckle nut to 44 ft. lbs. and the halfshaft (new) nut to 185 ft. lbs.

CV-JOINT OVERHAUL

For all CV-joint overhaul procedures, please refer to "U/CV-Joint Overhaul" in the Unit Repair section.

Front Wheel Drive Hub, Steering Knuckle and Bearings

REMOVAL & INSTALLATION

1. Raise and support the front of the vehicle on jackstands, allowing the wheels to hang.
2. Remove the front wheel assemblies.
3. Using the Drive Axle Boot Seal Protector tool No. J–28712 or equivalent, on the outer CV-joints and the Drive Axle Boot Seal Protector tool No. J–34754 or equivalent, on the inner Tri-Pot joints.

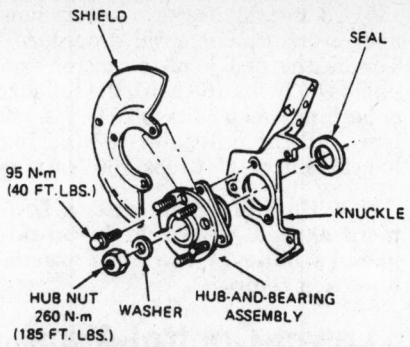
Exploded view of the front wheel hub and bearing assembly

SHIELD · SEAL · 95 N·m (40 FT.LBS.) · KNUCKLE · HUB NUT 260 N·m (185 FT. LBS.) · WASHER · HUB-AND-BEARING ASSEMBLY

4. Insert a long punch through the caliper and into a rotor vent to keep it from turning.
5. Clean the halfshaft threads and lubricate them with a thread lubricant.
6. Remove the hub nut and washer.
7. Remove the caliper-to-steering knuckle bolts and support the caliper (on a wire) out of the way.
8. Remove the rotor.
9. Using the Puller tool No. J–28733 or equivalent, loosen the splined fit between the hub and shaft.
10. Remove the 3 hub bolts, the shield, the hub, the bearing assembly and the O-ring. Remove the bearing seal from the knuckle.

NOTE: The hub and bearing are serviced as an assembly only.

11. To remove the steering knuckle, perform the following procedures:
   a. At the ball joint-to-steering knuckle and the tie-rod-to-steering knuckle intersections, remove the cotter pins and nuts.
   b. Using the Ball Joint Removal tool No. J–29330 or equivalent, separate the ball joint and the tie-rod end from the steering knuckle.

NOTE: Before removing the steering knuckle from the strut, be sure to scribe alignment marks between them, so that the installation can be easily performed.

   c. While supporting the steering knuckle, remove the steering knuckle-to-strut bolts and the steering knuckle from the vehicle.
12. To install, use new O-rings, new bearing seals, new cotter pins and reverse the removal procedures. Lubricate the new bearing seal and the bearing with wheel bearing grease. Torque the steering knuckle-to-strut bolts to 140 ft. lbs., the ball joint-to-steering knuckle nut 55 ft. lbs., the tie rod-to-steering knuckle nut to 35 ft. lbs., the wheel hub-to-steering knuckle bolts to 40 ft. lbs. (55 Nm), the caliper-to-steering knuckle bolts to 28 ft. lbs. (38

Nm) and the halfshaft-to-hub nut to 185 ft. lbs. (260 Nm). Check and/or adjust the front end alignment.

FRONT SUSPENSION

MacPherson Strut

REMOVAL & INSTALLATION

NOTE: Before removing front suspension components, their positions should be marked so they may assembled correctly. Scribe the knuckle along the lower outboard strut radius, the strut flange on the inboard side along the curve of the knuckle and make a chisel mark across the strut/knuckle interface. When reassembling, carefully match the marks to the components.

1. Remove the strut-to-body nuts.
2. Raise and support the front of the vehicle on jackstands; position the jackstands under the frame.
3. Lower the vehicle slightly so that the weight rests on the jackstands and not on the control arms.
4. Remove the front wheel/tire assemblies.

— **CAUTION** —
Whenever working near the halfshafts, take care to prevent the inner Tri-Pot joints from being overextended. Overextension of the joint could result in separation of internal components which could go undetected and result in failure of the joint.

5. Some vehicles may use a silicone (gray) boot on the inboard axle joint. Use the Boot Protector tool No. J–33162 or equivalent, on these boots. All other boots are made from a thermoplastic material (black) and do not require the use of a boot seal protector.
6. Disconnect the brake line bracket from the strut assembly.
7. Remove the strut-to-steering knuckle bolts.
8. Remove the strut assembly from the vehicle. Care should be taken to avoid chipping or cracking the spring coating when handling the front suspension coil spring assembly.
9. To install, reverse the removal procedures. Align the strut-to-steering knuckle bolts and tighten (lightly). Torque the strut-to-body nuts to 20 ft. lbs. and the strut-to-steering knuckle bolts to 140 ft. lbs. Check and/or adjust the front end alignment.

OVERHAUL

For all spring and shock absorber removal and installation procedures, and all strut overhaul procedures, please refer to "Strut Overhaul" in the Unit Repair section.

Ball Joints

INSPECTION

1. Raise and support the front of the vehicle on jackstands.
2. With the ball joint installed to the steering knuckle, perform the following procedures:
   a. Grasp the top and bottom of the wheel, then move the wheel using a "in and out" shaking motion.
   b. Observe any movement between the steering knuckle and the control arm. If movement exists, replace the ball joint.
3. If the ball joint has been disconnected from the steering knuckle, perform the following procedures:
   a. Inspect the ball joint for looseness.
   b. Try to twist the ball joint in its socket.
   c. If either defect can be noticed, replace the ball joint.
4. To complete the installation, reverse the removal procedures.

REMOVAL & INSTALLATION

1. Raise and support the front of the vehicle on jackstands positioned under the frame.
2. Lower the vehicle slightly so that the weight rests on the jackstands and not the control arm.
3. Remove the front wheel/tire assemblies.
4. If a silicone (gray) boot is used on the inboard axle joint, install a Boot Seal Protector tool No. J-33162 or equivalent. If a thermoplastic (black) boot is used, no protector is necessary.
5. Remove and discard the cotter pin from the ball joint castle nut.
6. Remove the castle nut. Using the Ball Joint Separator tool No. J-34505 or equivalent, disconnect the ball joint from the steering knuckle.
7. Using a drill, drill out the three ball joint-to-steering knuckle rivets.

NOTE: Be careful not to damage the halfshaft boot when drilling out the ball joint rivets.

8. Loosen the stabilizer shaft bushing assembly nut.
9. Remove the ball joint from the control arm.

10. To install, use new cotter pins and reverse the removal procedures. Torque the ball joint-to-control arm nuts to 50 ft. lbs. (68 Nm), the stabilizer bushing clamp bolts to 15 ft. lbs. (20 Nm) and the ball joint-to-steering knuckle nut to 45 ft. lbs. (60 Nm).

NOTE: The front-end alignment should be checked and adjusted whenever the strut assemblies are removed.

Lower Control Arms

REMOVAL & INSTALLATION

1. Raise and support the front of the vehicle on jackstands. Place the jackstands under the frame so that the suspension hangs freely.
2. Remove the wheel/tire assemblies.

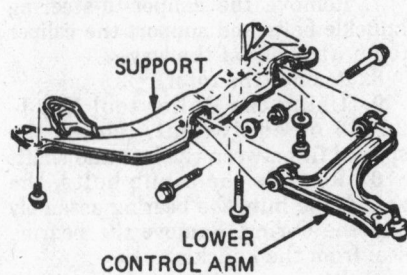

Exploded view of the control arm

3. Disconnect the stabilizer shaft from the control arm and/or support assembly.
4. Remove the ball joint-to-steering knuckle cotter pin and nut. Using the Ball Joint Separator tool No. J-29330 or equivalent, separate the ball joint from the steering knuckle.
5. Remove the control arm-to-support arm nuts/bolts and the control arm from the vehicle.
6. To install, use new cotter pins and reverse the removal procedures. Torque the ball joint-to steering knuckle nut to 45 ft. lbs. (60 Nm). Lower the vehicle to the floor. With the weight of the vehicle on the control arm, torque the control arm-to-support arm bolts to 60 ft. lbs. (85 Nm).

CASTER

Caster is the tilt of the front steering axis either forward or backward away from the front of the vehicle. When the strut is tilted rearward, the center is (+) positive. The amount of tilt is measured in degrees from vertical.

CAMBER

Camber is the slope of the front wheels from vertical when viewed from the front of the vehicle. When the wheels tilt outward (at the top), the camber is (+) positive; when the wheels tilt inward (at the top), the camber is (−)

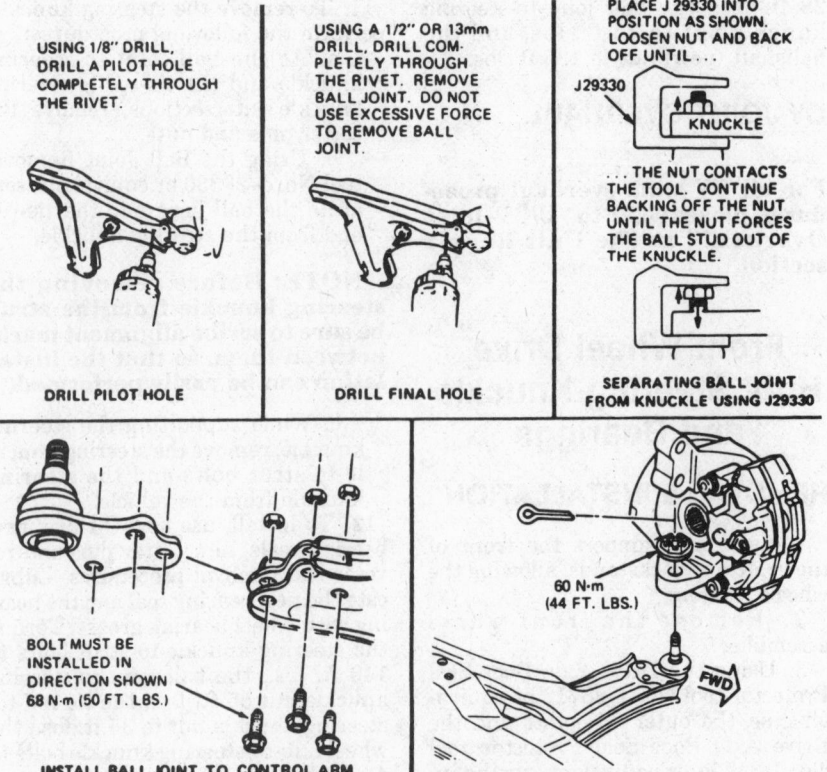

USING 1/8" DRILL, DRILL A PILOT HOLE COMPLETELY THROUGH THE RIVET.

USING A 1/2" OR 13mm DRILL, DRILL COMPLETELY THROUGH THE RIVET. REMOVE BALL JOINT. DO NOT USE EXCESSIVE FORCE TO REMOVE BALL JOINT.

PLACE J 29330 INTO POSITION AS SHOWN. LOOSEN NUT AND BACK OFF UNTIL...

J29330

KNUCKLE

... THE NUT CONTACTS THE TOOL. CONTINUE BACKING OFF THE NUT UNTIL THE NUT FORCES THE BALL STUD OUT OF THE KNUCKLE.

DRILL PILOT HOLE

DRILL FINAL HOLE

SEPARATING BALL JOINT FROM KNUCKLE USING J29330

BOLT MUST BE INSTALLED IN DIRECTION SHOWN 68 N·m (50 FT. LBS.)

INSTALL BALL JOINT TO CONTROL ARM

60 N·m (44 FT. LBS.)

FWD

Removing ball joint assembly

negative. The amount of tilt is measured in degrees from vertical and is called the camber angle.

TOE

Toe is the amount measured in the fraction of an inch, that the front wheels are closer together at one end than the other. Toe-in means that the front wheels are closer together at the front of the tire than at the rear; the toe is (+) positive. Toe-out means that the rear of the tires are closer together than the front; the toe is (−) negative.

Before performing the toe adjustment, be certain the following items are correct: The wheels must be straight ahead, the fuel tank must be Full, all fluids must be at their proper level, all suspension/steering adjustments must be correct and the tires must be at their correct Cold specifications.

REAR SUSPENSION

Shock Absorbers

REMOVAL & INSTALLATION

1. Open the trunk and remove the trim cover (if equipped) over the shock absorber-to-body nuts.
2. Remove the upper shock absorber attaching nut.

NOTE: DO NOT remove both shock absorbers at the same time as suspending the rear axle at full length could result in damage to brake lines and hoses.

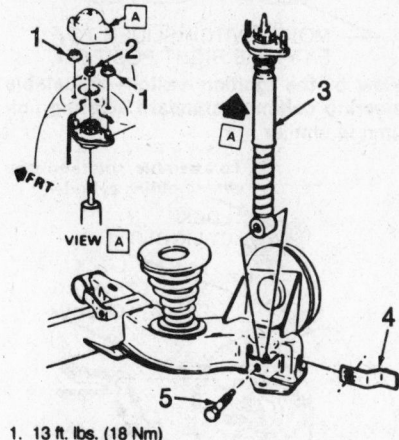

1. 13 ft. lbs. (18 Nm)
2. 28 ft. lbs. (38 Nm)
3. Shock absorber
4. 35 ft. lbs. (48 Nm)
5. Tab nut
A. Arrow should point to left side

Rear shock absorber mounting

3. Raise and support the rear of the vehicle on jackstands.
4. Remove the lower shock absorber-to-axle assembly nut/bolt and shock absorber.
5. To install, reverse the removal procedures. Torque the lower shock absorber-to-axle assembly nut/bolt to 35 ft. lbs., the upper shock absorber-to-mount nut to 28 ft. lbs. and the upper shock absorber mount-to-body nuts to 27 ft. lbs.

Springs

REMOVAL & INSTALLATION

1. Raise and support the rear axle assembly with a floor jack.
2. Install jackstands under the frame.
3. Remove the rear wheel assemblies.
4. Remove the right and left-brake line bracket attaching screws from the body and allow the brake line to hang free.
5. Remove both lower shock absorber-to-rear axle assembly nuts/bolts.
6. With the rear axle assembly supported by a floor jack, carefully lower the rear axle and remove the springs and/or insulators.

NOTE: DO NOT suspend the rear axle by the brake hoses or damage to the hoses could result. Lower the axle just enough to remove the springs and support it during all service procedures.

7. To install, reverse the removal procedures. Position the springs and insulators in their seats and raise the axle assembly. The ends of the upper coil on the spring must be positioned in the seat of the body and within the limits. Torque the lower shock absorber-to-axle assembly nut/bolt to 35 ft. lbs.

NOTE: Prior to installing the spring it will be necessary to install the upper insulators to the body with adhesive to keep it in position while raising the axle assembly and springs.

Stabilizer Bar

REMOVAL & INSTALLATION

1. Raise and support the rear of the vehicle on jackstands.
2. Remove the nuts/bolts at both the axle and control arm attachments. Remove the bracket, insulator and stabilizer bar.
3. Install the U-bolts, upper clamp, spacer and insulator in the trailing axle. Position the stabilizer bar in the

insulators and loosely install the lower clamp and nuts.
4. Torque the stabilizer bar-to-control arms nuts to 15 ft. lbs. (20 Nm).

Rear Wheel Bearings

ADJUSTMENT

The rear wheel bearing assembly is non-adjustable, it is serviced by replacement only.

REMOVAL & INSTALLATION

1. Raise and support the rear of the vehicle on jackstands.
2. Remove the wheel/tire assembly.
3. Remove the brake drum.

NOTE: DO NOT hammer on the brake drum during removal or damage to the assembly could result.

4. Remove the four hub/bearing assembly-to-rear axle assembly nuts/bolts and the hub/bearing assembly from the axle.

NOTE: The top rear attaching bolt will not clear the brake shoe when removing the hub and bearing assembly. Partially remove the hub prior to removing this bolt.

5. To install, reverse the removal procedures. Torque the hub/bearing assembly-to-rear axle assembly nuts/bolts to 39 ft. lbs.

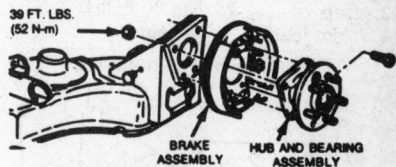

Rear hub and bearing assembly

STEERING

Steering Wheel

REMOVAL & INSTALLATION

1. Disconnect the negative battery terminal from the battery.

NOTE: When installing a steering wheel, make sure the turn signal lever is in the Neutral position.

2. Remove the trim retaining screws from behind the wheel. If

equipped with a center cap, pull off the cap.

3. Lift off the trim and pull the horn wires from the turn signal canceling cam.

4. Remove the retainer and the steering wheel nut.

5. Mark the wheel-to-shaft relationship. Using a Steering Wheel Puller tool No. J–1859, BT–61–9 or equivalent, remove the steering wheel.

6. To install, place the wheel on the shaft and align the previously made marks. Torque the steering wheel-to-steering column nut to 30 ft. lbs.

7. Insert the horn wires into the canceling cam, then install the center trim and reconnect the battery terminal.

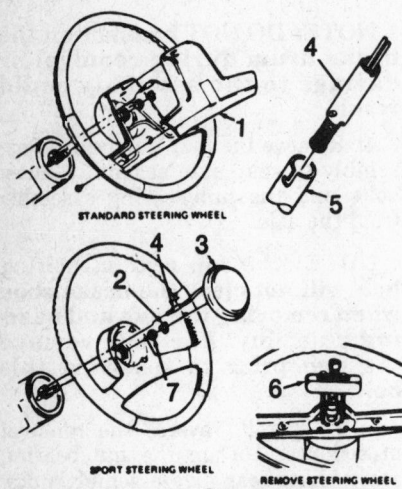

1. Pad
2. Retainer
3. Cap
4. Horn lead
5. Cam tower
6. J-1859-03 or BT-61-9
7. Nut 30 ft. lbs. (41 Nm)

Steering wheel mounting

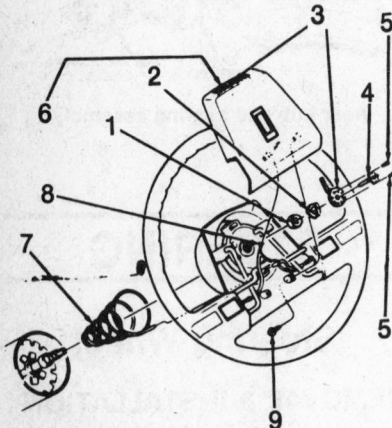

1. Steering wheel nut 41 N·m (30 ft. lbs.)
2. Steering wheel nut retainer
3. Telescoping adjuster lever
4. Steering shaft lock knob bolt
5. Steering shaft lock knob bolt positioning screw (2)
6. Steering wheel pad
7. Horn contact spring
8. Horn lead
9. Fully driven, seated and not stripped

Tilt wheel mounting

Combination Switch

REMOVAL & INSTALLATION

1. Refer to the "Steering Wheel, Removal & Installation" procedures in this section and remove the steering wheel.

2. Loosen the cover screws, pry the cover off with a screwdriver, then lift the cover off the shaft.

3. Position the U-shaped lockplate compressor on the end of the steering shaft and compress the lock plate by turning the shaft nut clockwise. Pry the wire snapring out of the shaft groove.

4. Remove the tool and lift the lockplate off the shaft.

5. Slip the canceling cam, upper bearing preload spring and thrust washer off the shaft.

6. Remove the turn signal lever. Push the flasher knob in and unscrew it. Remove the button retaining screw, the button, spring and knob.

7. Pull the switch connector out the mast jacket and tape the upper part to aid the switch removal. Attach a long piece of wire to the turn signal switch connector. When installing the turn signal switch, feed this wire through the column first, then use the wire to pull the switch connector into position. If equipped with a tilt steering column, position the turn signal and shifter housing in **LOW** position, then remove the harness cover.

8. Remove the 3 switch mounting screws and the switch by pulling it straight up while guiding the wiring harness connector through the column.

9. Install the replacement switch by working the connector and cover down through the housing, under the bracket. On tilt models, the connector is worked down through the housing and under the bracket, then the cover is installed on the harness.

10. Install the switch mounting screws and the connector on the mast jacket bracket. Install the column-to-dash trim plate.

11. Install the flasher knob and the turn signal lever.

12. With the turn signal lever in Neutral and the flasher knob pulled Out, slide the thrust washer, upper bearing preload spring and canceling cam onto the shaft.

13. Position the lock plate on the shaft and press it down until a new snapring can be inserted in the shaft groove. Always use a new snapring when assembling.

14. To complete the installation, reverse the removal procedures.

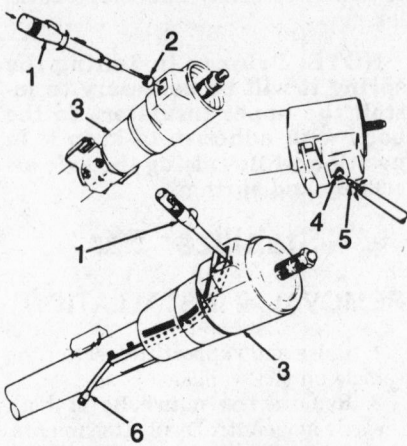

1. Turn signal lever
2. Insulator
3. Housing
4. Switch notch
5. Tang
6. Cruise control wiring

Multi-function switch removal

Ignition Switch

REMOVAL & INSTALLATION

The ignition switch is located on the upper-side of the lower steering column area and is completely inaccessible without first lowering the steering column. The switch is actuated by a rod and rack assembly. A gear on the end of the lock cylinder engages the toothed upper end of the rod.

1. Lower the steering column; be sure to properly support it.

2. Disconnect the wiring from the ignition switch.

3. Remove the ignition switch-to-steering column screws and the ignition switch assembly from the steering column.

MOVE SWITCH SLIDER TO EXTREME RIGHT POSITION

View of the ignition switch—adjustable steering column—standard steering column is similar

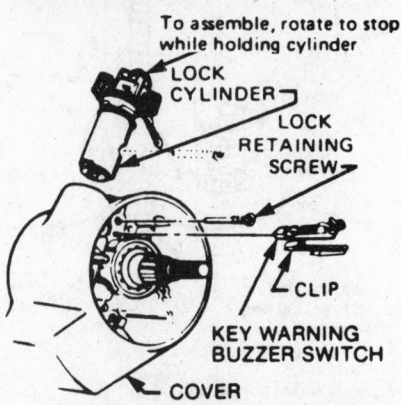

To assemble, rotate to stop while holding cylinder

LOCK CYLINDER

LOCK RETAINING SCREW

CLIP

KEY WARNING BUZZER SWITCH

COVER

View of the ignition lock cylinder

4. Before installing, place the slider on the new switch in one of the following positions, depending on the steering column and accessories:

    a. Standard column with key release—extreme left detent.

    b. Standard column with Park Lock—one detent from extreme left.

    c. All other standard columns—two detents from extreme left.

    d. Adjustable column with key release—extreme right detent.

    e. Adjustable column with Park Lock—one detent from extreme right.

    f. All other adjustable columns—two detents from extreme right.

5. Install the activating rod into the switch and assembly the switch to the column. Tighten the mounting screws. DO NOT use oversize screws as they could impair the collapsibility of the column.

6. To complete the installation, reverse the removal procedures.

Ignition Lock Cylinder

REMOVAL & INSTALLATION

1. Place the lock cylinder in the **RUN** position.

2. Remove the lock plate, the turn signal switch and the buzzer switch.

3. Remove the the screw and the lock cylinder.

NOTE: If the screw is dropped on removal, it could fall into the column, requiring complete disassembly to retrieve the screw.

4. Rotate the cylinder clockwise to align the cylinder key with the keyway in the housing.

5. Push the lock all the way in.

6. Install the screw and tighten to 14 inch lbs. (adjustable columns) or 25 inch lbs. (standard columns).

Power Steering Gear

REMOVAL & INSTALLATION

1. Remove the left-side sound insulator.

2. Disconnect the upper-pinch bolt on the coupling assembly.

3. Disconnect the clamp nuts.

4. Raise and support the front of the vehicle on jackstands.

5. Remove the clamp nut.

6. Remove both front wheel/tire assemblies.

7. Remove the tie rod end-to-steering knuckle cotter pin and castle nut. Using the Puller tool No. J-24319-01 or equivalent, disconnect the tie rod ends from the steering knuckles.

8. Lower the vehicle.

9. Disconnect the fluid line retainer.

10. Disconnect and plug the pressure tubes from the power steering gear.

11. Move the steering gear forward and remove the lower pinch bolt on the coupling assembly.

12. Disconnect the coupling from the steering gear.

13. Remove the rack and pinion assembly with the dash seal through the left-wheel opening.

NOTE: If the studs were removed with the mounting clamps, reinstall the studs into the cowl and torque to specifications. If the stud has been reused for the 2nd time, use thread Loctite® to secure the threads.

14. To install, use new cotter pins and reverse the removal procedures. Torque the power steering gear-to-chassis clamp nuts to 28 ft. lbs., the tie rod end-to-steering knuckle nut to 35-50 ft. lbs. and the steering coupling-to-power steering unit pinch bolt to 29 ft. lbs. Refill the power steering pump reservoir and bleed the system.

ADJUSTMENT

1. Raise and support the front of the vehicle on jackstands.

2. Make sure that the steering wheel is centered.

3. Loosen the adjuster plug lock nut.

4. Turn the adjuster plug (counterclockwise) until it is loose in the housing.

5. With the rack centered, turn the adjuster plug (clockwise) until it bottoms, then back it off 50-70 degrees.

6. While holding the adjuster plug stationary, torque the adjuster plug locknut to 50 ft. lbs.

Power Steering Pump

REMOVAL & INSTALLATION

2.5L Engine

1. Remove the drive belt.

2. Disconnect and plug the pressure tubes from the power steering pump.

3. Remove the front adjustment bracket-to-rear adjustment bracket bolt.

4. Remove the front adjustment bracket-to-engine bolt and spacer.

5. Remove the pump with the front adjustment bracket.

6. If installing a new pump, transfer the pulley and front adjustment bracket to the new pump.

7. To install, reverse the removal procedures. Torque the pump-to-bracket bolts to 20 ft. lbs. and the front

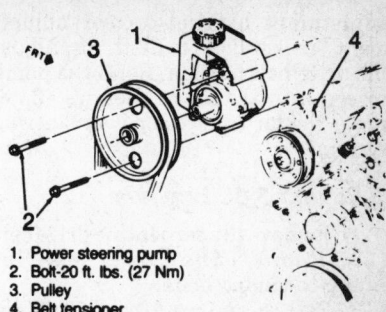

1. Power steering pump
2. Bolt-20 ft. lbs. (27 Nm)
3. Pulley
4. Belt tensioner

V6 power steering pump mounting

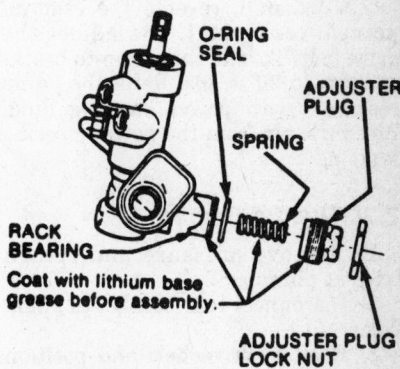

Exploded view of the power steering gear rack bearing

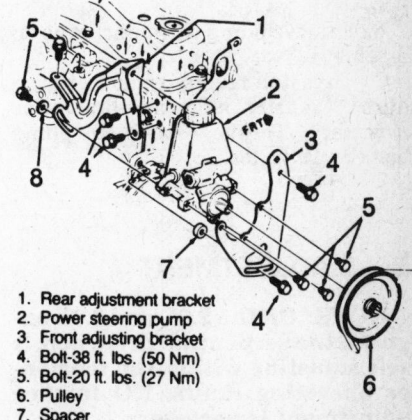

1. Rear adjustment bracket
2. Power steering pump
3. Front adjusting bracket
4. Bolt-38 ft. lbs. (50 Nm)
5. Bolt-20 ft. lbs. (27 Nm)
6. Pulley
7. Spacer
8. Washer

4cyl power steering pump mounting

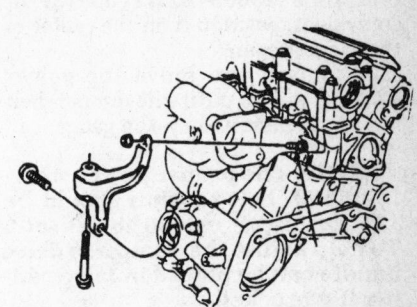

Intake manifold brace 2.3L Quad 4

adjustment bracket-to-rear adjustment bracket bolts to 38 ft. lbs. Adjust the drive belt tension. Refill the pump reservoir with power steering fluid. Bleed the air from the power steering system.

2.0L and 3.0L Engines

1. Remove the serpentine drive belt.
2. Remove the power steering pump-to-engine bolts.
3. Pull the pump forward and disconnect the pressure tubes.
4. Remove the pump and transfer the pulley as necessary.
5. To install, reverse the removal procedures. Install and adjust the drive belt. Torque the pump-to-bracket bolts to 20 ft. lbs. Refill the pump reservoir with power steering fluid. Bleed the air from the power steering system.

2.3L Quad 4 Engine

1. Remove pressure and return lines at pump.
2. Disconnect rear bracket to pump bolts.
3. Remove drive belt and position aside.
4. Remove rear bracket to transaxle bolts.
5. Remove front bracket to engine bolt.
6. Remove pump with bracket as an assembly.
7. To install reverse removal procedures. Transfer pulley and bracket as necessary. Torque bracket to pump bolts to 19 ft. lbs.

BELT ADJUSTMENT

NOTE: On the 2.0L and 3.0L engines, the serpentine drive belt is self adjusting within the tensioner operating limits; NO further adjustment is necessary.

2.5L and 2.3L Quad 4 Engines

1. Using the Belt Tension Gauge tool No. J–23600–B, BT–33–73F or equivalent, position it on the center of the longest span.
2. Loosen and move the power steering pump until the proper belt tension is indicated on the gauge.

NOTE: The proper power steering pump belt tension should be 175 lbs. (new) or 100 lbs. (used). To help adjust the pump a ½ drive handle can be placed in tab or adjusting bracket.

3. Torque the pump-to-bracket bolts to 38 ft. lbs.

SYSTEM BLEEDING

If the power steering hydraulic system has been serviced, an accurate fluid level reading cannot be obtained unless air is bled from the system.

1. With the wheels turned all the way to the left, add power steering fluid to the **COLD** mark on the fluid level indicator.
2. Start the engine and check the fluid level at fast idle. Add fluid, if necessary to bring the level up to the **COLD** mark.
3. Bleed air from the system by turning the wheels from side-to-side without hitting the stops. Keep the fluid level just above the internal pump casting or at the **COLD** mark. Fluid with air in it has a light tan or red appearance.
4. Return the wheels to the center position and continue running the engine for 2–3 minutes.
5. Road test the vehicle to check steering function and recheck the fluid level with the system at its normal operating temperature. Fluid should be at the **HOT** mark.

Tie Rod Ends

REMOVAL & INSTALLATION

1. Raise and support the front of the vehicle on jackstands.
2. Remove the front wheel/tire assemblies.
3. From the tie rod end-to-strut connection, remove the cotter pin (discard it) and the castle nut.
4. Using the Puller tool No. J–24319–01, BT–7101 or equivalent, press the tie rod end from the strut (or steering knuckle).

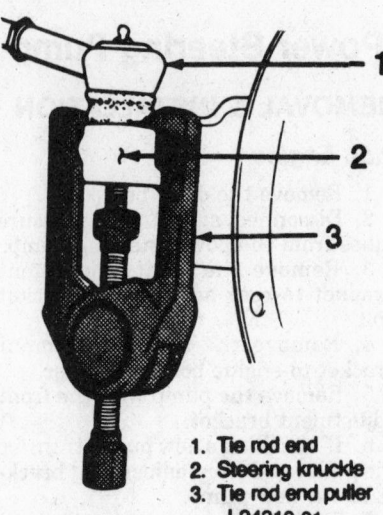

1. Tie rod end
2. Steering knuckle
3. Tie rod end puller
J-24319-01

Seperating tie rod end from knuckle

5. Loosen the tie rod end pinch bolt, then remove the tie rod end from the power steering gear.

NOTE: When installing the tie rod end, be sure to allow equal distance between the inner tie rod and the tie rod end.

6. To install, use new tie rod ends (if necessary), use new cotter pin(s) and reverse the removal procedures. Torque the tie rod end pinch bolts to 41 ft. lbs. and the tie rod end-to-strut (or steering knuckle) nut to 35–50 ft. lbs.

BRAKES

For all brake system repair service procedures not detailed below, please refer to "Brakes" in the Unit Repair section.

Master Cylinder

REMOVAL & INSTALLATION

1. If not equipped with power brakes, disconnect the brake push rod from the brake pedal.
2. Disconnect the electrical connector from the warning switch.
3. Disconnect and plug the hydraulic lines to prevent the entry of dirt into the system.
4. Drain and discard the brake fluid from the master cylinder.

NOTE: Exercise caution when handling the brake fluid as it will damage painted surfaces.

5. Remove the master cylinder-to-cowl (or power booster) nuts, then lift the master cylinder from the vehicle.

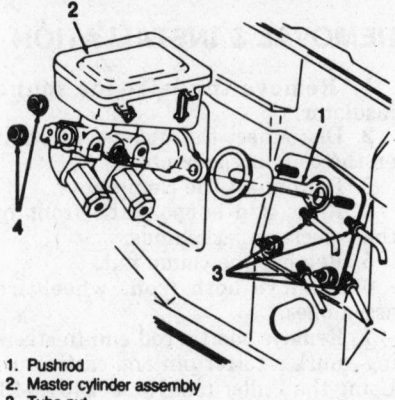

1. Pushrod
2. Master cylinder assembly
3. Tube nut
4. Nut

Master cylinder mounting

6. To install, reverse the removal procedures. Torque the master cylinder-to-cowl (or power booster) nuts to 22–30 ft. lbs. Refill the master cylinder reservoir with clean brake fluid. Bleed the brake system.

Proportioning Valve

NOTE: Individual proportioning valves are installed to the master cylinder outlets.

REMOVAL & INSTALLATION

1. Disconnect and plug the fluid lines from the proportioning valves.
2. Remove the proportioning valves and O-rings from the master cylinder.
3. To install, use new O-rings and reverse the removal procedures. Torque the proportioning valve-to-master cylinder to 18–30 ft. lbs. Refill the master cylinder reservoir with clean brake fluid. Bleed the brake system.

Power Brake Booster

REMOVAL & INSTALLATION

1. Working inside the vehicle, detach the brake pushrod from the brake pedal.
2. Disconnect the hydraulic lines from the master cylinder and the vacuum line from the power booster.
3. Remove the power booster-to-cowl nuts and the booster/master cylinder assembly. Continue disassembly to separate the booster and master cylinder on the bench.
4. To install, reverse the removal procedures. Torque the master cylinder-to-power booster nuts and the power booster-to-cowl nuts to 28 ft. lbs. Bleed the brake system.

Wheel Cylinder

REMOVAL & INSTALLATION

1. Raise and support the rear of the vehicle on jackstands.
2. Remove the wheel/tire assemblies. Remove the brake drum(s).
3. Remove the brake shoes and springs.
4. Clean the area around the brake line, then disconnect and plug the brake line at the wheel cylinder.
5. Using two awls, ⅛ in. diameter, insert them into the access slots between the wheel cylinder pilot and the retainer locking tabs. Bend both tabs away simultaneously.
6. Remove the wheel cylinder.
7. Using a wooden block between the cylinder and the axle flange, posi-

tion the wheel cylinder and hold it in place.
8. Using a 1⅛ in.–12 point socket and extension, install a new retainer on the wheel cylinder.
9. To complete the installation, torque the brake tube to 150 inch lbs. and reverse the removal procedures. Bleed the brake system.

Parking Brake Cable

ADJUSTMENT

1. Depress the parking brake pedal exactly five ratchet clicks.
2. Raise and support the rear of the vehicle on jackstands.
3. Check that the equalizer nut groove is liberally lubricated with chassis lube. Tighten the adjusting nut until the right-rear wheel can just be turned to the rear with both hands but is locked when forward rotation is attempted.
4. With the mechanism totally disengaged, both rear wheels should turn freely in either direction with no brake drag. DO NOT adjust the parking brake so tightly as to cause brake drag.

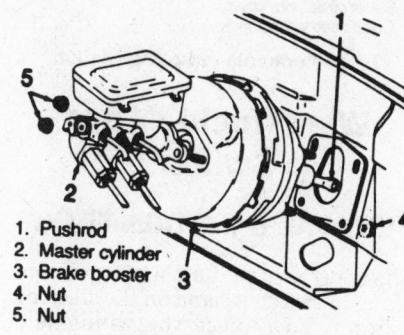

1. Pushrod
2. Master cylinder
3. Brake booster
4. Nut
5. Nut

Brake booster location

REMOVAL & INSTALLATION
Front Cable

1. Raise and support the vehicle on jackstands.
2. Remove the adjusting nut from the equalizer.
3. Remove the spring retainer clip from the bracket.
4. From inside the vehicle, remove the upper console cover rear screws.
5. Lift the rear of the lower console for access to the cable retainer at the hand lever.
6. Remove the cable retainer pin, cable retainer, then the cable.
7. To install, reverse the removal procedures. Adjust the parking brake.

Rear Cable

1. Raise and support the vehicle on jackstands.
2. Loosen the adjusting nut from the equalizer.
3. Disengage the rear cable from the connector.
4. Remove the wheel assembly and brake drum.
5. Bend the retainer fingers.
6. Disengage the cable from the brake shoe operating lever.
7. To install, reverse the removal procedures. Adjust the parking brake.

CHASSIS ELECTRICAL

Heater Blower

REMOVAL & INSTALLATION

1. Disconnect negative battery terminal from the battery.
2. If equipped with a V6 engine, remove the serpentine drive belt and the two power steering pump-to-bracket bolts, then move the pump aside.
3. Remove the blower motor screws.

1. Right rear cable
2. 6 ft. rear cable
3. Front cable
4. Nut-20 ft. lbs. (28 Nm)
5. Bolt-13 ft. lbs. (18 Nm)

Parking brake cable routing

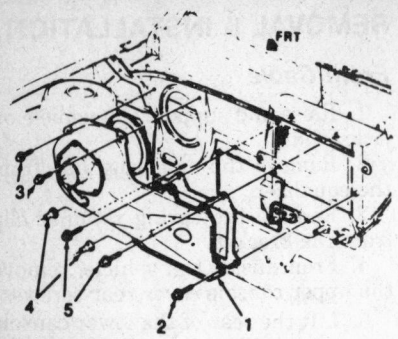

1. Blower assembly
2. Install first
3. Install second
4. 23 inch lbs.
5. 30 inch lbs.

Removing blower motor assembly

4. Disconnect wiring connector.
5. Slide blower motor assembly forward enough to remove nut retaining fan.
6. Slide fan out of housing.
7. Remove the blower motor.
8. If necessary, remove the fan from the blower motor.
9. To install, reverse the removal procedures.

Heater Core

REMOVAL & INSTALLATION

1. Disconnect negative battery terminal from the battery.
2. Place a clean drain pan under the radiator, open the drain cock and drain cooling system.
3. Remove the console extensions and the console ducts.
4. Remove the hush panel, the plenum and the housing.
5. Raise and support the front of the vehicle on jackstands.
6. Loosen the hoses.
7. Lower the vehicle.
8. Remove the heater core.
9. To install, reverse the removal procedures. Refill the cooling system.

Radio

REMOVAL & INSTALLATION

1. Disconnect the negative battery terminal from the battery.
2. Remove radio panel trim plate by pulling rearward.
3. Remove two 7mm screws from radio mounting bracket.
4. Pull radio rearward and unplug digital clock connector, the radio connector and the antenna lead.
5. To install, reverse the removal procedures.

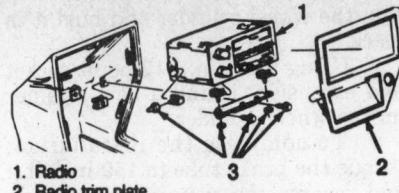

1. Radio
2. Radio trim plate
3. Fully driven, seated and not stripped

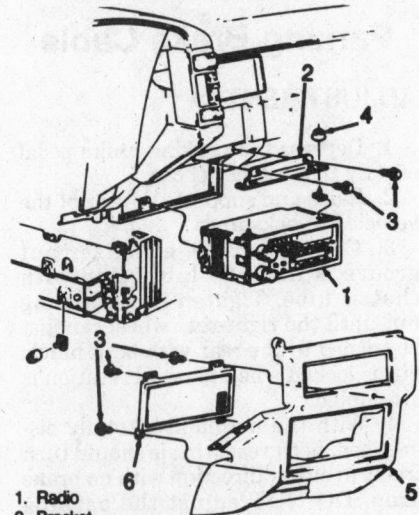

1. Radio
2. Bracket
3. Fully driven, seated and not stripped
4. Tighten to 23 inch lbs.
5. Lower center trim cover
6. Cover used without radio

Typical console radio installation

Windshield Wiper Switch

REMOVAL & INSTALLATION

The wiper switch if a part of the combination switch located on the steering column. To replace the windshield wiper switch, refer to the "Combination Switch, Removal & Installation" procedures in this section and remove the combination switch.

Windshield Wiper Motor

REMOVAL & INSTALLATION

1. Disconnect the negative battery terminal from the battery.
2. Remove the wiper arm assemblies.
3. Loosen but DO NOT remove the retaining nuts that secure the transaxle drive link to the motor crank arm.
4. Remove the air inlet screw panel, then the transaxle drive link from the motor crank arm.
5. Remove the wiper motor retaining bolts, then the wiper motor and linkage by guiding it through the access hole in the upper shroud panel.

6. To install, reverse the removal procedures.

Instrument Cluster

REMOVAL & INSTALLATION

Calais

1. Disconnect the negative battery terminal from the battery.
2. Remove the steering column collar and the steering column opening filler screws.
3. Remove the cluster trim plate screws and the trim plate.
4. Remove the steering column support bolts, then lower the steering column.
5. Remove the cluster-to-instrument panel pad screws and the cluster by pulling it rearward.
6. To install, reverse the removal procedures.

Grand Am, Somerset and Skylark

1. Disconnect the negative battery terminal from the battery.
2. Remove the cluster lower trim plate.
3. Lower the steering column.
4. Remove the upper cluster trim plate.
5. Remove the cluster retaining screws and the cluster, by pulling it rearward.
6. To install, reverse the removal procedures.

Headlight Switch

REMOVAL & INSTALLATION

Calais

1. Disconnect the negative battery terminal from the battery.
2. Remove the lower steering column collar.
3. Remove the instrument panel cluster trim plate.
4. Remove the headlight switch mounting screws, then pull the switch assembly rearward and unplug both electrical connections.
5. Remove the headlight switch from the vehicle.
6. To install, reverse the removal procedures.

Grand Am

1. Disconnect the negative battery terminal from the battery.
2. Remove the headlight switch trim plate.
3. Remove the head light switch screws, then pull the switch rearward and unplug the electrical connectors.

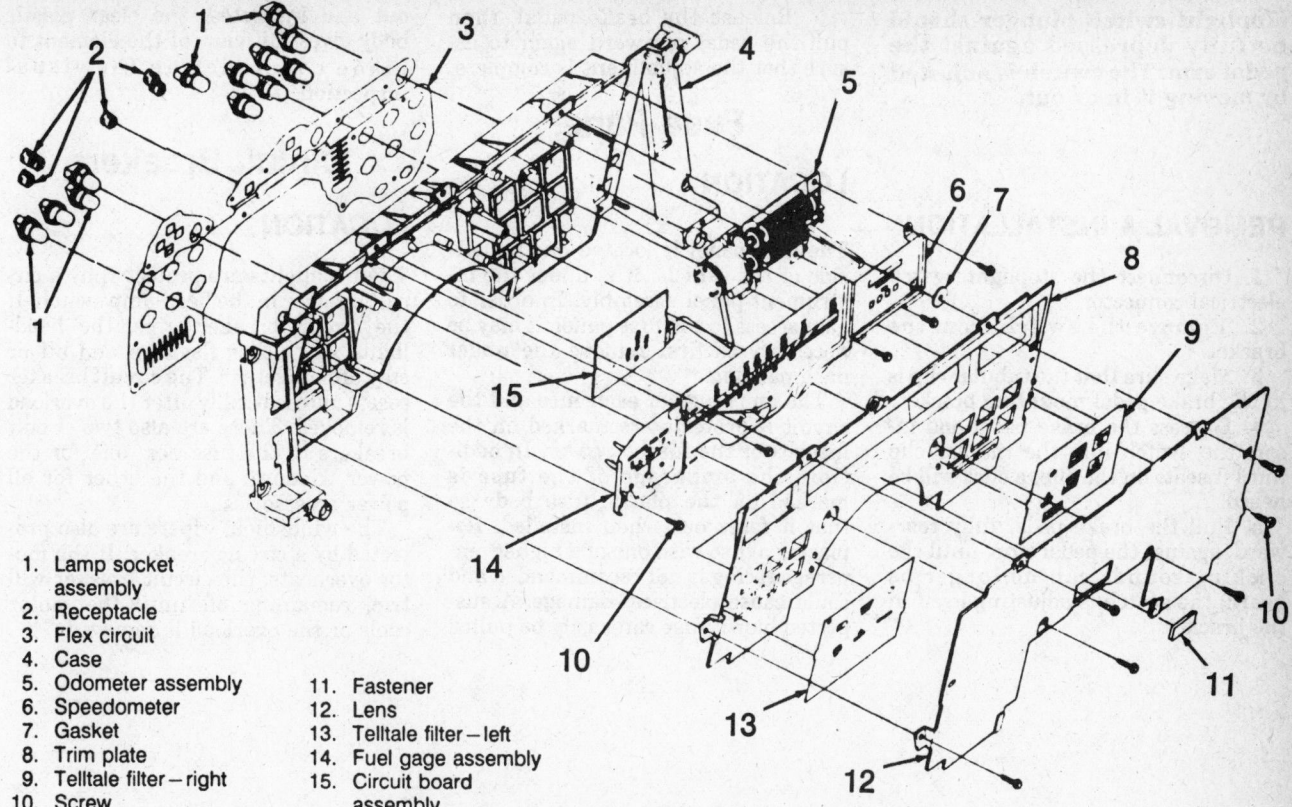

1. Lamp socket
   assembly
2. Receptacle
3. Flex circuit
4. Case
5. Odometer assembly
6. Speedometer
7. Gasket
8. Trim plate
9. Telltale filter — right
10. Screw
11. Fastener
12. Lens
13. Telltale filter — left
14. Fuel gage assembly
15. Circuit board
    assembly

Disassembled view of base cluster (Analog)

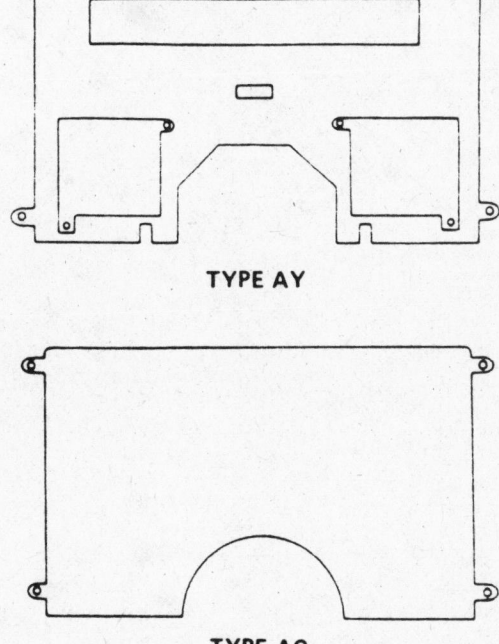

TYPE AY

TYPE AC

Outline of 2 types of electronic instrument clusters

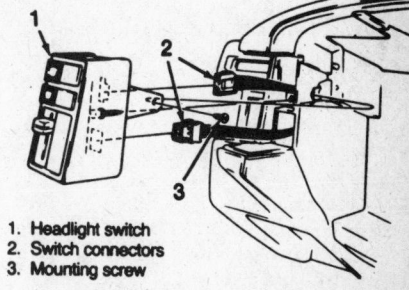

1. Headlight switch
2. Switch connectors
3. Mounting screw

Typical head lamp switch installation

4. Remove the headlight switch from the vehicle.
5. To install, reverse the removal procedures.

Somerset and Skylark

1. Disconnect the negative battery terminal from the battery.
2. Remove the instrument panel trim cover and the headlight switch trim panel.
3. Remove the switch retaining screws and the switch from the vehicle.
4. To install, reverse the removal procedures.

Stoplight Switch

NOTE: When the brake pedal is in the fully released position, the

stoplight switch plunger should be fully depressed against the pedal arm. The switch is adjusted by moving it in or out.

REMOVAL & INSTALLATION

1. Disconnect the stoplight switch electrical connector(s).

2. Remove the switch from the bracket.

3. Make sure that the tubular clip is in the brake pedal mounting bracket.

4. Depress the brake pedal and insert the switch into the tubular clip until it seats on the clip; a click will be heard.

5. Pull the brake pedal fully rearward, against the pedal stop, until the clicking sounds can no longer be heard; the switch is adjusting itself in the bracket.

6. Release the brake pedal, then pull the pedal rearward again to assure that the adjustment is complete.

Fuse Panel

LOCATION

The fuse panel is located on the left-side of the vehicle. It is under the instrument panel assembly. In order to gain access to the fuse panel, it may be necessary to first remove the under dash padding.

The amperage of each fuse and the circuit it protects are marked on the fusebox or the fusebox cover. In addition, the amperage of the fuse is marked on the plastic fuse body so that it faces out when installed. Replacing a fuse with one of a higher amperage rating is not recommended and could cause electrical damage. A suspected blown fuse can easily be pulled out and inspected; the clear plastic body gives full view of the element to blade construction for visual inspection.

Circuit Breakers

LOCATION

The headlights are protected by a circuit breaker in the headlamp switch. If the circuit breaker trips, the headlights will either flash on and off or stay off altogether. The circuit breaker resets automatically after the overload is removed. There are also two circuit breakers in the fuse box, one for the power windows and the other for all power accessories.

The windshield wipers are also protected by a circuit breaker. If the motor overheats, the circuit breaker will trip, remaining off until the motor cools or the overload is removed.

GM "W" Body
Front Wheel Drive
Buick Regal, Oldsmobile Cutlass Supreme, Pontiac Grand Prix

28

SERIAL NUMBER IDENTIFICATION

VEHICLE IDENTIFICATION CHART

It is important for servicing and ordering parts to be certain of the vehicle and engine identification. The VIN (vehicle identification number) is a 17 digit number visible through the windshield on the driver's side of the dash and contains the vehicle and engine identification codes. The tenth digit indicates model year and the eighth digit indicates engine code. It can be interpreted as follows:

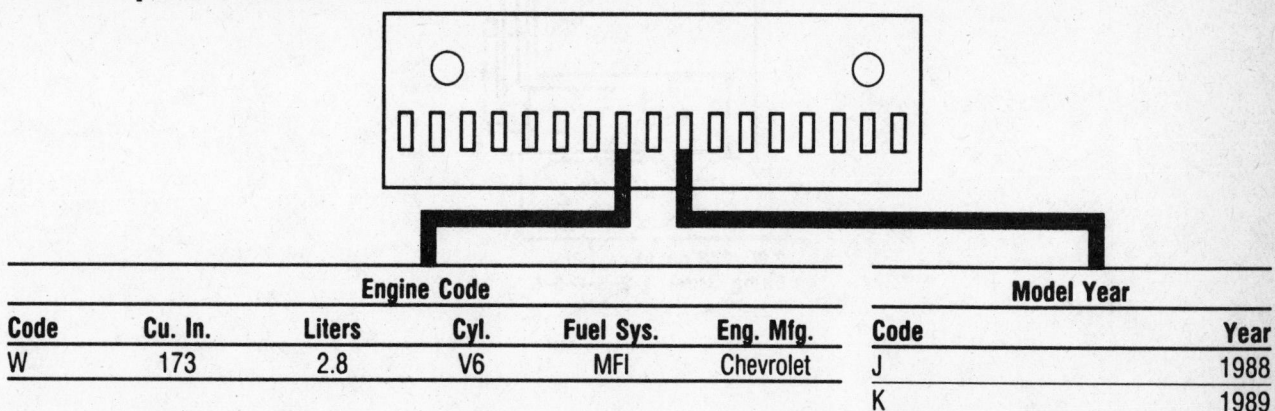

Engine Code						Model Year	
Code	Cu. In.	Liters	Cyl.	Fuel Sys.	Eng. Mfg.	Code	Year
W	173	2.8	V6	MFI	Chevrolet	J	1988
						K	1989

GENERAL ENGINE SPECIFICATIONS

Year	VIN	No. Cylinder Displacement cu. in. (liter)	Fuel System Type	Net Horsepower @ rpm	Net Torque @ rpm (ft.lbs.)	Bore × Stroke (in.)	Compression Ratio	Oil Pressure @ rpm
1988-89	W	6-173 (2.8)	MFI	125 @ 4500	160 @ 3600	3.500 × 2.990	8.9:1	50–65@2000

GASOLINE ENGINE TUNE-UP SPECIFICATIONS

Year	VIN	No. Cylinder Displacement cu. in. (liter)	Spark Plugs Type	Gap (in.)	Ignition Timing (deg.) MT	AT	Com- pression Pressure (psi)	Fuel Pump (psi)	idle Speed (rpm) MT	AT	Valve Clearance In.	Ex.
1988	W	6-173 (2.8)	R43CTLSE	.045	①	①	②	10–12	①	①	Hyd.	Hyd.
1989		SEE UNDERHOOD SPECIFICATION STICKER										

① Ignition timing and idle speed are controlled by the Electronic Control Module. No adjustment is necessary

② Look for uniformity between cylinders rather than pressure. Lowest reading not less than 70% of the highest. No reading less than 100 psi

FIRING ORDERS

NOTE: To avoid confusion, always replace spark plug wires one at a time.

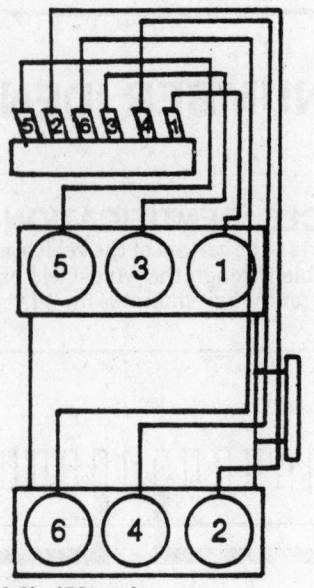

2.8L, 173 cu. in.
Firing Order: 1–2–3–4–5–6

CAPACITIES

Year	Model	No. Cylinder Displacement cu. in. (liter)	Engine Crankcase with Filter	without Filter	Transmission (pts.) 4-Spd	5-Spd	Auto.	Drive Axle (pts.)	Fuel Tank (gal.)	Cooling System (qts.)
1988-89	Cutlass Supreme	6-173 (2.8)	4.0	3.8	—	5	16①	—	16	12.6
	Grand Prix	6-173 (2.8)	4.0	3.8	—	5	16①	—	16	12.6
	Regal	6-173 (2.8)	4.0	3.8	—	—	16①	—	16	12.6

① Drain and refill only. Complete overhaul—11 qts.

CAMSHAFT SPECIFICATIONS
All measurements given in inches.

Year	VIN	No. Cylinder Displacement cu. in. (liter)	Journal Diameter					Lobe Lift		Bearing Clearance	Camshaft End Play
			1	2	3	4	5	In.	Ex.		
1988-89	W	6-173 (2.8)	1.867–1.881	1.867–1.881	1.867–1.881	1.867–1.881	1.867–1.881	0.262	0.273	.001–.004	NA

CRANKSHAFT AND CONNECTING ROD SPECIFICATIONS
All measurements are given in inches.

Year	VIN	No. Cylinder Displacement cu. in. (liter)	Crankshaft				Connecting Rod		
			Main Brg. Journal Dia.	Main Brg. Oil Clearance	Shaft End-play	Thrust on No.	Journal Diameter	Oil Clearance	Side Clearance
1988-89	W	6-173 (2.8)	2.6473–2.6483	0.0016–0.0032	0.0024–0.0083	3	1.9983–1.9993	0.0013–0.0026	0.0060–0.0170

VALVE SPECIFICATIONS

Year	VIN	No. Cylinder Displacement cu. in. (liter)	Seat Angle (deg.)	Face Angle (deg.)	Spring Test Pressure (lbs.)	Spring Installed Height (in.)	Stem-to-Guide Clearance (in.)		Stem Diameter (in.)	
							Intake	Exhaust	Intake	Exhaust
1989-89	W	6-173 (2.8)	46	45	90 @ 1.70①	1.70	0.0010–0.0027	0.0010–0.0027	NA	NA

① Valve closed

PISTON AND RING SPECIFICATIONS
All measurments are given in inches.

Year	VIN	No. Cylinder Displacement cu. in. (liter)	Piston Clearance	Ring Gap			Ring Side Clearance		
				Top Compression	Bottom Compression	Oil Control	Top Compression	Bottom Compression	Oil Control
1988-89	W	6-173 (2.8)	0.002–0.003	0.016–0.020	0.010–0.020	0.020–0.055	0.001–0.003	0.001–0.003	0.008

TORQUE SPECIFICATIONS
All readings in ft. lbs.

Year	VIN	No. Cylinder Displacement cu. in. (liter)	Cylinder Head Bolts	Main Bearing Bolts	Rod Bearing Bolts	Crankshaft Pulley Bolts	Flywheel Bolts	Manifold		Spark Plugs
								Intake	Exhaust	
1988-89	W	6-173 (2.8)	①	72	40	77	46	23	19	18

① Torque in 2 steps:
1st step—33 ft. lbs.
2nd step—Turn an additional 90 degrees (¼) turn

BRAKE SPECIFICATIONS
All measurements in inches unless noted

| Year | Model | Lug Nut Torque (ft. lbs.) | Master Cylinder Bore | Brake Disc | | Standard Brake Drum Diameter | Minimum Lining Thickness | |
				Minimum Thickness	Maximum Runout		Front	Rear
1988-89	Cutlass Supreme	100	0.945	0.972	0.003	—	$^3/_{32}$	$^3/_{32}$
	Grand Prix	100	0.945	0.972	0.003	—	$^3/_{32}$	$^3/_{32}$
	Regal	100	0.945	0.972	0.003	—	$^3/_{32}$	$^3/_{32}$

WHEEL ALIGNMENT

| Year | Model | Caster | | Camber | | Toe-in (in.) | Steering Axis Inclination (deg.) |
		Range (deg.)	Preferred Setting (deg.)	Range (deg.)	Preferred Setting (deg.)		
1988-89	Cutlass Supreme	1½N-2½P	½P	$^3/_{16}$P–1$^3/_{16}$P	$^{11}/_{16}$P	$^3/_{16}$N–$^3/_{16}$P	NA
	Grand Prix	1½N-2½P	½P	$^3/_{16}$P–1$^3/_{16}$P	$^{11}/_{16}$P	$^3/_{16}$N–$^3/_{16}$P	NA
	Regal	1½N-2½P	½P	$^3/_{16}$P–1$^3/_{16}$P	$^{11}/_{16}$P	$^3/_{16}$N–$^3/_{16}$P	NA

NA Not adjustable

TUNE-UP PROCEDURES

Ignition Timing

ADJUSTMENT

Ignition timing is controlled by the Electronic Control Module (ECM). No adjustment is necessary.

Valve Lash

ADJUSTMENT

This engine uses hydraulic valve lifters, which are not adjustable. If valve system noise is present, check the torque on the rocker arm nuts. It should be 14-20 ft. lbs. If the noise is still present check the condition of the the valve train components.

Idle speed and Mixture

MINIMUM IDLE SPEED ADJUSTMENT

NOTE: The idle speed and mixture are electronically controlled

by the electronic control module (ECM). All adjustments are preset at the factory. The only time the idle speed should be adjusted is when the throttle body assembly has been replaced.

1. Remove air cleaner and gasket.
2. With a scratch awl or equivalent, piece the idle stop screw plug and apply leverage to remove it.
3. Connect tachometer to engine.
4. Ground the ALDL diagnostic terminal with IAC valve connected.
5. Turn ignition switch to **ON** position, without starting engine for at least 45 seconds. This allows IAC valve pintle to extend and seat in throttle body.
6. Disconnect the Idle Air Control (IAC) electrical connector.
7. Remove ground wire from diagnostic terminal. Firmly set the parking brake.
8. Start the engine and place the transaxle in **NEUTRAL**. Allow engine rpm to stabilize. Using the minimum idle stop set screw and adjust the idle speed to 450–550 rpm.
9. Turn ignition switch **OFF** and reconnect connector at IAC valve.
10. Use silicone sealant or equivalent to cover minimum air adjustment screw.
11. Install air cleaner and gasket.
12. Check and clear any trouble

codes. Start engine and inspect for proper idle operation.

ENGINE ELECTRICAL

Distributor

All engines use a distributor-less ignition. Distributor-less ignition systems use a "Waste-Spark" method of spark distribution. Each cylinder is paired with its opposing cylinder in the firing order. This makes one cylinder that is on the compression stroke fire with the opposing cylinder that is on the exhaust stroke. The cylinder that is on the exhaust stroke uses very little spark allowing most of the spark to go to the cylinder on the compression stroke. This process reverses when the cylinder roles reverse. There are 3 coils for the Direct Ignition System (DIS).

Components of the DIS system are a coil pack, ignition module, crankshaft reluctor ring, magnetic sensor and the ECM. The coil pack consists of 3 interchangeable ignition coils. Three coils are needed because each coil only fires 2 cylinders. The ignition module is located under the coil pack and is connected to the ECM by a 6 pin connector. The ignition module controls the primary circuit to the coils and it also controls the ignition timing below 400 rpm.

The magnetic pickup sensor inserts through the engine block, just above the pan rail. Notches in the crankshaft reluctor ring trigger the magnetic pickup sensor to provide timing information to the ECM.

Alternator

For further information on the charging system, refer to "Charging and Starting" in the Unit Repair section.

PRECAUTIONS

- When installing a battery, make sure that the positive and negative cables are not reversed.
- When jump-starting the vehicle, be sure that like terminals are connected. This also applies to using a battery charger. Reversed polarity will burn out the alternator and regulator in a matter of seconds.
- Never operate the alternator with the battery disconnected or on an otherwise uncontrolled open circuit.
- Do not short across or ground any alternator or regulator terminals.
- Do not try to polarize the alternator.
- Do not apply full battery voltage to the field (brown) connector.
- Always disconnect the battery ground cable before disconnecting the alternator lead.
- Always disconnect the battery (negative cable first) when charging it.
- Never subject the alternator to excessive heat or dampness. If you are steam-cleaning the engine, cover the alternator.
- Never use arc welding equipment on the car with the alternator connected.

BELT TENSION ADJUSTMENT

A single serpentine belt is used to drive all engine mounted components. Drive belt tension is maintained by a spring loaded tensioner.

NOTE: The drive belt tensioner can control the belt tension over a wide range of belt lengths; however, there are limits to the tensioners ability to compensate for various belt lengths. Installing the wrong size belt and using the tensioner outside of its operating

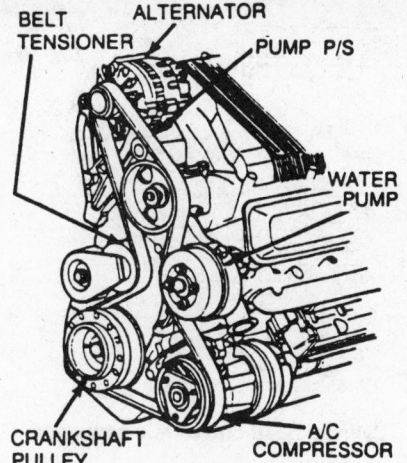

Accessory drive belt routing

range can result in poor tension control and damage to the tensioner, drive belt and driven components.

To remove the accessory drive belt, use a ¾ in. open end wrench and relive the tension from the belt. This will allow the belt to be removed.

REMOVAL & INSTALLATION

1. Disconnect the negative battery cable.
2. Disconnect the electrical connector at the rear of the alternator.
3. Remove the accessory drive belt.
4. Remove the mounting bolts and remove the alternator from the vehicle.
5. Install the alternator, tighten the upper mounting bolt to 18 ft. lbs. and the lower bolt to 37 ft. lbs.
6. Attach the electrical connector. Install the accessory drive belt.
7. Connect the negative battery cable.

Voltage Regulator

REMOVAL & INSTALLATION

A solid state regulator is mounted within the alternator. The regulator is non-adjustable and requires no maintenance. Should the regulator require service, the alternator must be removed and disassembled.

Starter

For further information on the starter system, refer to "Charging and Starting" in the Unit Repair section.

REMOVAL & INSTALLATION

1. Disconnect the negative battery cable.
2. Raise and safely support the vehicle.
3. Tag and disconnect the wires from the starter.
4. Remove the starter motor cover and the 2 bolts retaining the starter.
5. Remove the starter and any shims.
6. Install the starter, install shims in their original location.
7. Attach the starter cover and the wiring.
8. Lower the vehicle. Connect the negative battery cable.

ENGINE MECHANICAL

Engine

REMOVAL & INSTALLATION

1. Disconnect the battery cables. Matchmark the hood and the hood hinges, remove the hood.
2. Disconnect and remove the air inlet tube from the throttle body and the air cleaner.
3. Disconnect the throttle cable, T.V. linkage, cruise control cable and all other electrical wiring from the engine.
4. Relieve the fuel system pressure and remove the fuel lines from the fuel rails.
5. Relieve the serpentine belt tension and remove the belt.
6. Drain the cooling system and remove the radiator and heater hoses.
7. Remove the A/C compressor mounting bolts and remove the compressor, DO NOT disconnect the refrigerant lines. Lay the compressor to the side.
8. Remove the power steering pump mounting bolts and lay the pump aside.
9. Disconnect the brake booster vacuum line.
10. Raise and safely support the vehicle. Remove the flywheel cover and remove the starter.
11. Remove the torque converter bolts. Remove the transaxle bracket.
12. Remove the front engine retaining nuts. Remove the exhaust pipe at the crossover.
13. Lower the vehicle. Remove the engine torque struts.
14. Remove the coolant recovery bot-

tle. Remove the left crossover pipe-to-manifold clamp.

15. Pull the engine forward and support it. Disconnect the bulkhead connector.

16. Remove the right crossover pipe-to-manifold clamp. Remove the engine support and allow the engine to return to its normal position.

17. Support the transaxle and remove the transaxle-to-engine bolts.

18. Attach a suitable lifting device and remove the engine assembly.

To install:

19. Install the engine, align it with the transaxle housing and insert the transaxle-to-engine bolts. Tighten the bolts to 55 ft. lbs.

20. Remove the lifting device. Install the left and right crossover pipe clamps.

21. Attach the bulkhead connector. Install the coolant recovery bottle and the engine torque struts.

22. Raise and safely support the vehicle. Attach the crossover pipe.

23. Install the front engine mount nuts and tighten to 63 ft. lbs.

24. Attach the transaxle bracket and install the torque converter bolts. Install the flywheel cover.

25. Install the starter. Install the A/C compressor and lower the vehicle.

26. Attach the heater and radiator hoses. Install the power steering pump.

27. Install the accessory drive belt. Connect the fuel lines to the fuel rail. Connect any electrical wiring that was disconnected.

28. Connect the throttle cable, T.V. linkage and the cruise control cable.

29. Attach the air inlet tube. Align the matchmarks on the hood and hinges and install the hood.

30. Connect the negative battery cable. Fill the cooling system.

Cylinder Head

REMOVAL & INSTALLATION

Left Side

1. Drain the cooling system. Remove the rocker cover.

2. Remove the intake manifold-to-cylinder head bolts and the intake manifold. Disconnect the exhaust crossover from the right exhaust manifold.

3. Disconnect the oil level indicator tube bracket.

4. Loosen the rocker arms nuts, turn the rocker arms and remove the push rods.

NOTE: Be sure to keep the parts in order for installation purposes.

5. Remove the cylinder head-to-en-

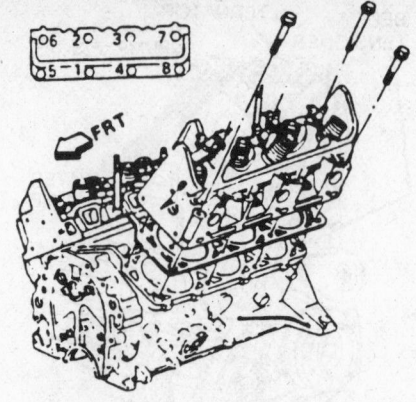

Cylinder head bolt torque sequence

gine bolts; start with the outer bolts and work toward the center. Remove the cylinder head with the exhaust manifold as an assembly.

6. Clean the gasket mounting surfaces. Inspect the surfaces of the cylinder head, block and intake manifold for damage and/or warpage. Clean the threaded holes in the block and the cylinder head bolt threads.

To install:

7. Use new gaskets, align the new cylinder head gasket over the dowels on the block with the note "This Side Up" facing the cylinder head.

8. Install the cylinder head and exhaust manifold crossover assembly on the engine.

9. Using GM Sealant No. 1052080 or equivalent, coat the cylinder head bolts and install the bolts hand tight.

10. Using the correct sequence, torque the bolts to 33 ft. lbs. After all bolts are torqued to 33 ft. lbs., rotate the torque wrench another 90 degrees or ¼ turn. This will apply the correct torque to the bolts.

11. Install the push rods in the same order that they were removed. Torque the rocker arm nuts to 14–20 ft. lbs.

12. Install the intake manifold using a new gasket and following the correct sequence, torque the bolts to the correct specification.

13. Install the oil level indicator tube and install the rocker cover. Install the air inlet tube.

14. Refill the cooling system. Operate the engine until it reaches normal operating temperatures and check for leaks.

Right Side

1. Disconnect the negative battery terminal from the battery. Drain the cooling system.

2. Raise and safely support the front of the vehicle. Remove the exhaust manifold-to-exhaust pipe bolts and separate the pipe from the manifold.

3. Lower the vehicle. Remove the

exhaust manifold-to-cylinder head bolts and the manifold.

4. Remove the rocker arm cover. Remove the intake manifold-to-cylinder head bolts and the intake manifold.

5. Loosen the rocker arms nuts, turn the rocker arms and remove the push rods.

NOTE: Be sure to keep the components in order for reassembly purposes.

6. Remove the cylinder head-to-engine bolts (starting with the outer bolts and working toward the center) and the cylinder head.

7. Clean the gasket mounting surfaces. Inspect the parts for damage and/or warpage.

8. Clean the engine block's threaded holes and the cylinder head bolt threads.

9. To install, use new gaskets and reverse the removal procedures. Using GM Sealant No. 1052080 or equivalent, coat the cylinder head bolts and install the bolts hand tight.

NOTE: Place the cylinder head gasket on the engine block dowels with the note "This Side Up" facing the cylinder head.

10. Using the torquing sequence, torque the bolts to 33 ft. lbs. After all bolts are torqued to 33 ft. lbs., rotate the torque wrench another 90 degrees or ¼ turn. This will apply the correct torque to the bolts.

11. Install the push rods in the same order as they were removed. Torque the rocker arm nuts to 14–20 ft. lbs.

12. Follow the torquing sequence, use a new gasket and install the intake manifold.

13. Install the oil level indicator tube and install the rocker cover. Install the air inlet tube.

14. Refill the cooling system. Start the engine, allow it to reach normal operating temperatures and check for leaks.

OVERHAUL

For all cylinder head overhaul procedures, refer to "Engine Rebuilding" in the Unit Repair section.

Rocker Arms/Shafts

REMOVAL & INSTALLATION

Left Side

1. Disconnect the negative battery cable. Disconnect the bracket tube from the rocker cover.

2. Remove the spark plug wire cov-

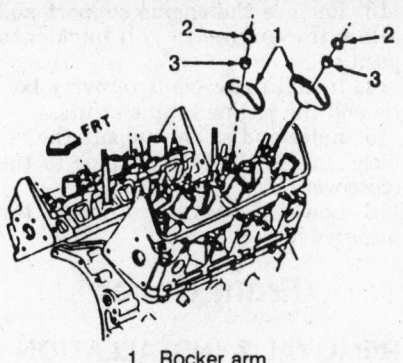

1. Rocker arm
2. 14–20 ft. lbs.
3. Ball

Rocker arm installation

er. Drain the cooling system and remove the heater hose from the filler neck.

3. Remove the rocker arm cover-to-cylinder head bolts and the rocker cover.

NOTE: If the rocker arm cover will not lift off the cylinder head easily, strike the end with the palm of the hand or a rubber mallet.

4. Remove the rocker arm nuts and remove the rocker arms, keep the components in order for installation purposes.

5. Clean the gasket mounting surfaces.

6. To install, use new rocker cover gaskets apply a bead of sealant, GM No. 1052917 or equivalent, to the rocker cover and install it.

7. Install the spark plug wire cover and attach the heater hose to the filler neck. Fill the cooling system.

8. Torque the rocker arm nuts to 14–20 ft. lbs. Start the engine and check for leaks.

Right Side

1. Disconnect the negative battery cable. Disconnect the brake booster vacuum line from the bracket.

2. Disconnect the cable bracket from the plenum.

3. Disconnect the vacuum line bracket from the cable bracket.

4. Disconnect the lines from the alternator brace stud.

5. Remove the rear alternator brace and the serpentine drive belt.

6. Remove the alternator and support it out of the way.

7. Remove the PCV valve.

8. Loosen the alternator bracket.

9. Disconnect the spark plug wires from the spark plugs. Remove the rocker cover-to-cylinder head bolts and the rocker cover.

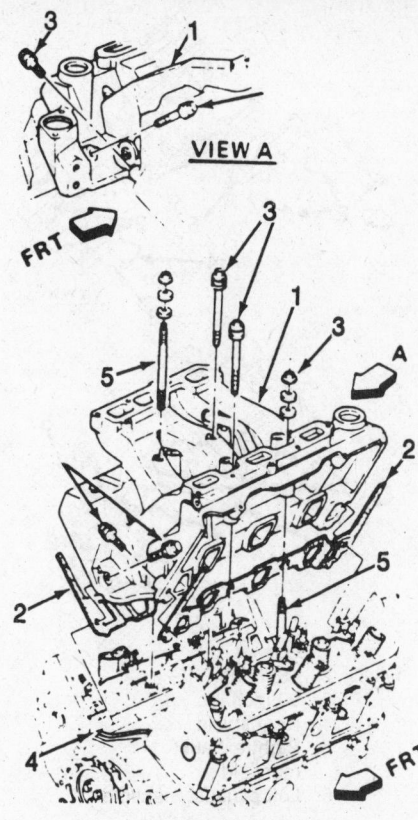

VIEW A

1. Intake manifold
2. Gasket
3. 23 ft. lbs.
4. Apply sealer
5. 24 ft. lbs.

Intake manifold installation

NOTE: If the rocker arm cover will not lift off the cylinder head easily, strike the end with the palm of the hand or a rubber mallet.

10. Remove the rocker arm nuts and the rocker arms; be sure to keep the components in order for installation purposes.

11. Clean the gasket mounting surfaces.

12. To install, use new rocker cover gaskets apply a bead of sealant, GM No. 1052917 or equivalent, to the rocker cover and install it.

13. Install the spark plug wire cover and attach the heater hose to the filler neck. Fill the cooling system.

14. Torque the rocker arm nuts to 14–20 ft. lbs. Start the engine and check for leaks.

Intake Manifold

REMOVAL & INSTALLATION

1. Disconnect the negative terminal from the battery. Drain the cooling system.

2. Disconnect the T.V. and accelerator cables from the plenum.

3. Remove the throttle body-to-plenum bolts and the throttle body. Remove the EGR valve.

4. Remove the plenum-to-intake manifold bolts and the plenum. Disconnect and plug the fuel lines and return pipes at the fuel rail.

5. Remove the serpentine drive belt. Remove the power steering pump-to-bracket bolts and support the pump out of the way; DO NOT disconnect the pressure hoses.

6. Remove the alternator-to-bracket bolts and support the alternator out of the way.

7. Loosen the alternator bracket. From the throttle body, disconnect the idle air vacuum hose.

8. Label and disconnect the electrical connectors from the fuel injectors. Remove the fuel rail.

9. Remove the breather tube. Disconnect the runners.

10. Remove both rocker arm cover-to-cylinder head bolts and the covers. Remove the radiator hose from the thermostat housing.

11. Label and disconnect the electrical connectors from the coolant temperature sensor and oil pressure sending unit. Remove the coolant sensor.

12. Remove the bypass hose from the filler neck and cylinder head.

13. Remove the intake manifold-to-cylinder head bolts and the manifold.

14. Loosen the rocker arm nuts, turn them 90 degrees and remove the push rods; be sure to keep the components in order for installation purposes.

15. Clean all of the gasket mounting surfaces.

To install:

16. Place a bead of RTV sealer or equivalent on each ridge where the intake manifold and blosk meet. Install the intake manifold gasket in place on the block.

17. Install the pushrods and reposition the rocker arms, tighten the rocker arm nuts to 18 ft. lbs.

18. Mount the intake manifold on the engine and tighten the bolts to 23 ft. lbs.

19. Connect the heater inlet pipe to the manifold. Install and connect the coolant sensor.

20. Attach the radiator hoses. Connect the wire at the oil sending switch.

21. Install the rocker covers, tighten the retaining bolts to 90 inch lbs.

22. Install the runners, breather tube, fuel rail and connect the wires at the fuel injectors.

23. Install the alternator bracket and the alternator. Install the power steering pump.

24. Connect the fuel lines to the fuel rail. Install the EGR valve.

25. Install the plenum and mount the throttle body to the plenum.

26. Connect the accelerator cable and the T.V. cable.

27. Fill the cooling system. Connect the negative battery cable.

28. Run the engine until it reaches normal operating temperature and check for coolant and oil leaks.

Exhaust Manifold

REMOVAL & INSTALLATION

Left Side

1. Disconnect the negative battery cable.

2. Remove the coolant recovery bottle.

3. Relieve the accessory drive belt tension and remove the belt.

4. Remove the A/C compressor mounting bolts and support the compressor aside.

5. Remove the right side engine torque strut. Remove the bolts retaining the A/C compressor and torque strut mounting bracket, remove the bracket.

6. Remove the heat shield and crossover pipe at the manifold.

7. Remove the exhaust manifold mounting bolts and remove the manifold.

To install:

8. Clean the gasket mounting surfaces.

9. Install the exhaust manifold to the engine, loosely install the mounting bolts.

10. Install the exhaust crossover pipe. Tighten the exhaust manifold bolts to 18 ft. lbs.

11. Attach the heat shield. Install the A/C and torque strut mounting bracket.

12. Install the torque strut. Mount the A/C compressor and install the accessory drive belt.

13. Install the coolant recovery bottle and connect the negative battery cable.

Right Side

1. Disconnect the negative battery cable.

2. Raise and safely support the vehicle.

3. Remove the exhaust pipe at the crossover. Lower the vehicle.

4. Remove the coolant recovery bottle and remove the engine torque struts.

5. Pull the engine forward and support it.

6. Remove the air cleaner, breather, mass air flow sensor and heat shield.

7. Remove the crossover at the manifold. Disconnect the accelerator and T.V. cables.

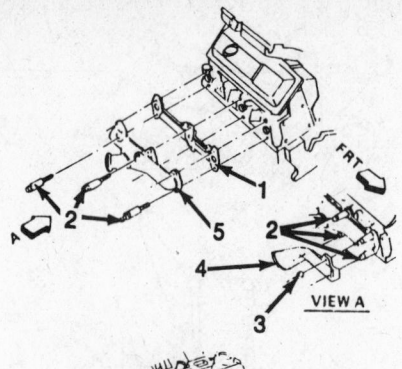

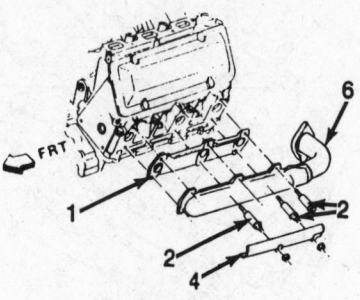

1. Gasket
2. 18 ft. lbs.
3. 90 inch lbs.
4. Heat shield
5. Right exhaust manifold
6. Left exhaust manifold

Exhaust manifold installation

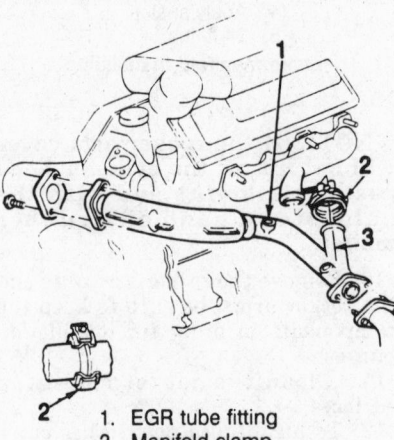

1. EGR tube fitting
2. Manifold clamp
3. Welded seam — orient the clamp to the seam

Exhaust crossover mounting

8. Remove the manifold mounting bolts and remove the manifold. Clean the manifold mounting surfaces.

To install:

9. Install the exhaust manifold, loosely install the mounting bolts.

10. Attach the crossover at the manifold. Tighten the manifold mounting bolts to 18 ft. lbs.

11. Connect the accelerator and T.V. cables.

12. Attach the air cleaner, breather and mass air flow sensor.

13. Remove the engine support and allow the engine to roll back into position.

14. Install the coolant recovery bottle and the engine torque struts.

15. Raise and safely support the vehicle. Install the exhaust pipe to the crossover.

16. Lower the vehicle. Connect the negative battery cable.

Front Cover

REMOVAL & INSTALLATION

1. Disconnect the negative terminal from the battery. Drain the cooling system.

2. Remove the serpentine belt and the belt tensioner.

3. Remove the alternator-to-bracket bolts and remove the alternator, with the wires attached, support it out of the way.

4. Remove the power steering pump-to-bracket bolts and support it out of the way; DO NOT disconnect the pressure hoses.

5. Raise and safely support the vehicle.

6. Remove the right side inner fender splash shield. Remove the flywheel dust cover.

7. Using the crankshaft pulley puller tool No. J–24420 or equivalent, remove the crankshaft damper.

8. Label and disconnect the starter wires, remove the starter.

9. Remove the oil pan. Remove the lower front cover bolts.

10. Lower the vehicle. Disconnect the radiator hose from the water pump.

11. Disconnect the heater coolant hose from the cooling system filler pipe.

12. Remove the bypass and overflow hoses.

13. Remove the water pump pulley. Disconnect the canister purge hose.

14. Remove the spark plug wire shield from the water pump.

15. Remove the upper front cover-to-engine bolts and remove the front cover.

16. Clean front cover mounting surfaces.

To install:

17. Apply a thin bead of silicone sealant on the front cover mating surface and using a new gasket, install the front cover on the engine with the top bolts to hold it in place.

18. Raise and safely support the vehicle.

19. Install the oil pan. Install the lower front cover bolts, tighten all of the front cover bolts to 26–35 ft. lbs.

20. Install the serpentine belt and idler pulley. Install the damper on the

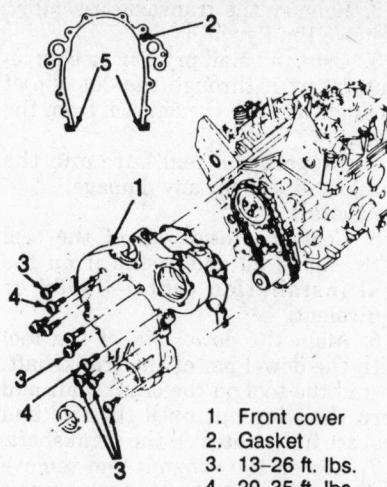

1. Front cover
2. Gasket
3. 13–26 ft. lbs.
4. 20–35 ft. lbs.
5. Apply sealer

Front cover assembly removal

engine using tool J–29113 or equivalent. Install the starter.

21. Install the inner fender splash shield. Lower the vehicle.

22. Attach the radiator hose too the water pump and attach the heater hoses.

23. Install the power steering pump and the alternator.

24. Attach the spark plug wire shield. Fill the cooling system.

25. Connect the negative battery cable. Run the engine to normal operating temperature and check for coolant and oil leaks.

OIL SEAL REPLACEMENT

1. Disconnect the negative terminal from the battery. Remove the serpentine belt.

2. Raise and safely support the vehicle. Remove the right side inner fender splash shield.

3. Remove the damper retaining bolt.

4. Using the crankshaft pulley puller tool No. J–24420 or equivalent, press the damper pulley from the crankshaft.

5. Using a small pry bar, pry out the seal in the front cover.

NOTE: Use care not to damage the seal seat or the crankshaft while removing or installing the seal. Inspect the crankshaft seal surface for signs of wear.

To install:

6. Coat the new seal with oil. Using a seal installer tool No. J–35468 or equivalent, drive the new seal in the cover with the lip facing towards the engine.

7. Crankshaft pulley installer tool No. J–29113 or equivalent, press the

crankshaft pulley onto the crankshaft. Torque the damper bolt to 67–85 ft. lbs.

8. Install the inner fender splash shield. Lower the vehicle.

9. Install the serpentine belt. Connect the negative battery cable. Run the engine to normal operating temperature and check for leaks.

Timing Chain and Sprockets

REMOVAL & INSTALLATION

1. Disconnect the negative battery cable.

2. Remove the front cover assembly.

3. Place the No. 1 piston at TDC with the marks on the crankshaft and the camshaft aligned (No. 4 firing position).

4. Remove the camshaft sprocket and the timing chain.

NOTE: If the camshaft sprocket does not come off easily, a light blow on the lower edge of the sprocket with a rubber mallet should loosen the sprocket.

5. Remove the crankshaft sprocket.
To install:

6. Install the crankshaft sprocket. Apply a coat of Molykote® or equivalent, to the sprocket thrust surface.

7. Hold the camshaft sprocket with the chain hanging down and align the marks on the camshaft and crankshaft sprockets.

8. Align the dowel in the camshaft with the dowl hole in the camshaft sprocket. Install the camshaft sprocket and chain, use the camshaft sprocket bolts to draw the sprocket on to the camshaft. Tighten the sprocket bolts to 18 ft. lbs.

9. Lubricate the timing chain with engine oil. Install the front cover assembly.

10. Connect the negative battery cable.

Camshaft

REMOVAL & INSTALLATION

NOTE: The engine assembly must be removed in order to remove the camshaft.

1. Remove the engine assembly from the vehicle.

2. Remove the rocker covers and remove the valve lifters.

3. Remove the front cover assembly, timing chain and sprockets.

4. Remove the camshaft by sliding it from the block.

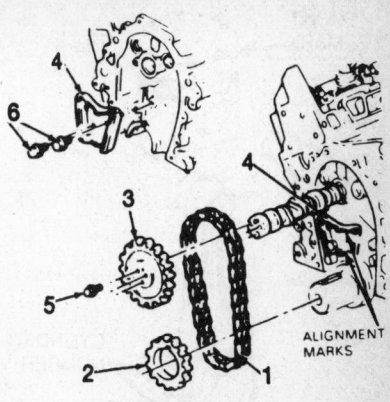

1. Timing chain
2. Crank sprocket
3. Camshaft sprocket
4. Damper
5. 15–20 ft. lbs.
6. 13–18 ft. lbs.

Timing chain and sprockets

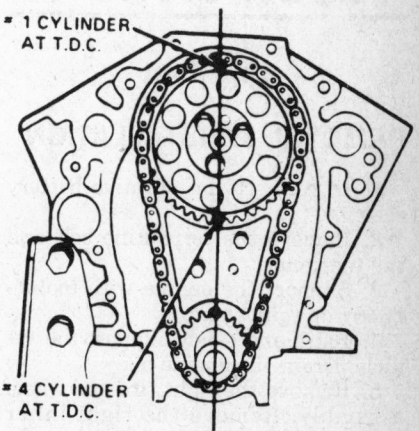

Timing mark alignment

To install:

5. Coat the camshaft journals with engine oil. Coat the camshaft lobes with GM Engine Oil Supplement 1052367 or equivalent.

6. Slide the camshaft into the block.

7. Install the timing chain and sprockets, making sure to align the timing marks.

8. Install the front cover assembly. Install the valve lifters.

9. Install the engine assembly into the vehicle. Run the engine to normal operating temperature and check for leaks. Check the timing.

Piston and Connecting Rod Positioning

For all piston and connecting rod overhaul procedures, refer to "Engine Rebuilding" in the Unit Repair section.

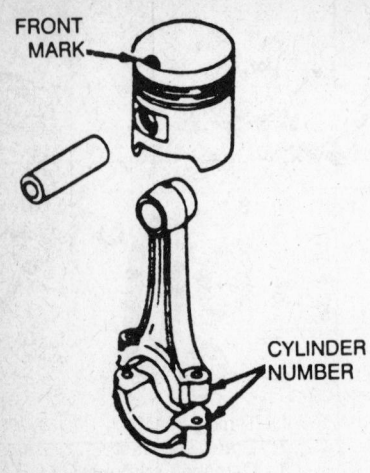

Piston and connecting rod positioning

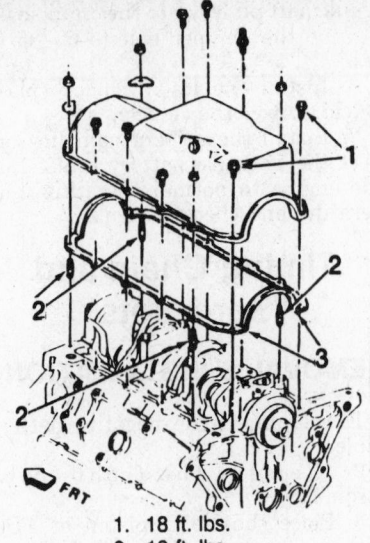

1. 18 ft. lbs.
2. 13 ft. lbs.
3. Apply sealer

Oil pan and gasket installation

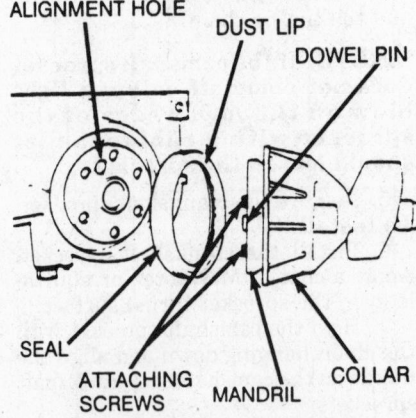

Installing the rear main seal

ENGINE LUBRICATION

Oil Pan

REMOVAL & INSTALLATION

1. Disconnect the negative battery cable.
2. Remove the serpentine belt and the tensioner.
3. Support the engine with tool J–28467 or equivalent.
4. Raise and safely support the vehicle. Drain the engine oil.
5. Remove the right tire and wheel assembly. Remove the right inner fender splash shield.
6. Remove the steering gear pinch bolt. Remove the transaxle mount retaining bolts.
7. Remove the engine-to-cradle mounting nuts. Remove the front engine collar bracket from the block.
8. Remove the starter shield and the flywheel cover. Remove the starter.
9. Loosen, but DO NOT remove the rear engine cradle bolts.
10. Remove the front cradle bolts. Remove the oil pan retaining bolts and nuts. Remove the oil pan.

To install:

11. Clean the gasket mating surfaces.
12. Install a new gasket on the oil pan. Apply silicon sealer to the portion of the pan that contacts the rear of the block.
13. Install the oil pan, nuts and retaining bolts. Tighten to 13–18 ft. lbs.
14. Install the front cradle bolts and tighten the rear cradle bolts. Install

the starter and splash shield. Install the flywheel shield.
15. Attach the collar bracket to the block, install the engine-to-cradle nuts. Install the transaxle mount nuts.
16. Install the steering pinch bolt. Install the right inner fender splash shield and tire assembly. Lower the vehicle.
17. Remove the engine support tool. Install the serpentine belt and tensioner.
18. Fill the crankcase to the correct level. Connect the negative battery cable. Run the engine to normal operating temperature and check for leaks.

Rear Main Bearing Oil Seal

REMOVAL & INSTALLATION

1. Support the engine with tool J–28467 or equivalent. Raise and safely support the vehicle.

2. Remove the transaxle assembly. Remove the flywheel.
3. Using a small pry bar or equivalent, insert it through the dust lip at an angle and pry the old seal from the block.
4. Inspect the seal bore and the crankshaft end for any damage.

To install:

5. Coat the inside lip of the seal with engine oil and install it on the seal installation tool J–34686 or equivalent.
6. Align the dowel pin of the tool with the dowel pin of the crankshaft. Install the tool on the crankshaft and turn the wing nut until the tool and seal are fully seated on the crankshaft.
7. Loosen the wingnut and remove the tool. Check the seal to make sure it is properly seated.
8. Install the flywheel and the transaxle.
9. Remove the engine support tool. Run the engine and check for leaks.

Oil Pump

REMOVAL & INSTALLATION

1. Raise and safely support the vehicle.
2. Drain the engine oil.
3. Remove the oil pan.
4. Remove the oil pump retaining bolts, remove the oil pump and pump driveshaft.
5. Install the oil pump and pump driveshaft. Tighten the oil pump mounting bolts to 30 ft. lbs.
6. Install the oil pan. Lower the vehicle.
7. Fill the crankcase to the correct level with oil. Run the vehicle and check for leaks.

ENGINE COOLING

Radiator

REMOVAL & INSTALLATION

1. Disconnect the negative battery cable.
2. Drain the cooling system.
3. Remove the front engine torque strut support braces and swing the torque strut rearward.
4. Remove the coolant recovery bottle. Remove the bolts retaining the electric cooling fan and frame assembly and remove.
5. Remove the transaxle cooler lines

from the radiator and remove the radiator hoses.

6. Remove the bolts retaining the radiator and remove the radiator from the vehicle.

To install:

7. Install the radiator in the vehicle bottom first and align it in the rubber mounts.

8. Install the radiator support bolts. Attach the transaxle cooler lines and the radiator hoses.

9. Install the cooling fan assembly. Install the coolant recovery bottle.

10. Attach the engine torque strut braces and swing the torque strut into position.

11. Fill the cooling system to the correct level. Connect the negative battery cable.

Water Pump

REMOVAL & INSTALLATION

1. Disconnect the negative battery cable.
2. Drain the cooling system.
3. Remove the accessory drive belt.
4. Remove the radiator.
5. Remove the water pump pulley.
6. Remove the water pump mounting bolts and remove the water pump.
7. Clean the gasket mating surfaces.

To install:

8. Install the water pump to the engine and tighten the mounting bolts to 89 inch lbs.
9. Attach the water pump pulley. Install the accessory drive belt.
10. Fill the cooling system and connect the negative battery cable.

Thermostat

REMOVAL & INSTALLATION

1. Drain the cooling system to a level below the thermostat.
2. Remove the thermostat housing-to-engine bolts and the housing.
3. Using a putty knife, clean the gasket mounting surfaces.
4. To install, use new gaskets and reverse the removal procedures. Torque the thermostat housing-to-engine bolts to 15–22 ft. lbs. Refill and bleed the cooling system. Start the engine, allow it to reach normal operating temperatures and check for leaks.

COOLING SYSTEM BLEEDING

After working on the cooling system, even to replace the thermostat, it must be bled. Air trapped in the system will prevent proper filling and leave the ra-

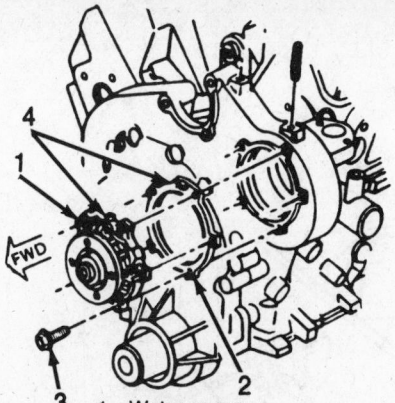

1. Water pump
2. Gasket
3. Mounting bolts
4. Pump locator — must be vertical

Water pump mounting

diator coolant level low, causing a risk of overheating.

1. To bleed the system, start with the system cool, the radiator cap off and the radiator filled to about an inch below the filler neck.

2. Start the engine and run it at slightly above normal idle speed. This will insure adequate circulation. If air bubbles appear and the coolant level drops, fill the system with an antifreeze/water mixture to bring the level back to the proper level.

3. Run the engine this way until the thermostat opens. When this happens, coolant will move abruptly across the top of the radiator and the temperature of the radiator will suddenly rise.

4. At this point, air is often expelled and the level may drop quite a bit. Keep refilling the system until the level is near the top of the radiator and remains constant.

5. If the vehicle has an overflow tank, fill the radiator right up to the filler neck. Replace the radiator filler cap.

EMISSION CONTROLS

Please refer to "Emission Control" in the Unit Repair section for system maintenance procedures. Due to the complex nature of modern electronic engine control systems, comprehensive diagnosis and testing procedures fall outside the confines of this repair manual. For complete information on diagnosis, testing and repair procedures concerning all modern engine and emission control systems, please refer to

Chilton's Guide to Electronic Engine Controls.

FUEL SYSTEM

Fuel System Service Precautions

When working with the fuel system certain precautions should be taken; always work in a well ventilated area, keep a dry chemical (Class B) fire extinguisher near the work area. Always disconnect the negative battery cable and do not make any repairs to the fuel system until all the necessary steps for repair have been reviewed.

RELIEVING FUEL SYSTEM PRESSURE

1. Connect fuel pressure gauge J–34730-1, or equivalent to the fuel pressure connection.
2. Wrap a shop cloth around the fitting while connecting the gauge to catch any leaking fuel.
3. Install the bleed hose into an approved container and open the valve.
4. When the repair to the fuel system is complete check all of the fittings for leaks.

Fuel Filter

REMOVAL & INSTALLATION

The fuel filter is located at the rear of the vehicle attached to the crossmember.

1. Relieve the fuel system pressure.
2. Raise and safely support the vehicle.
3. Disconnect the fuel lines from the fuel filter. Remove the filter from the vehicle.
4. Using new O-rings install the fuel lines into the filter. Tighten the fuel line fittings to 22 ft. lbs.
5. Secure the filter to the crossmember. Lower the vehicle.
6. Run the vehicle and check for leaks.

Electric Fuel Pump

PRESSURE TESTING

1. Relieve the fuel system pressure.
2. Place a shop cloth under the fuel pressure connector on the fuel rail. Using the Fuel Pressure Gauge tool No. J–34730-1 or equivalent, connect it to the fuel rail pressure connector.

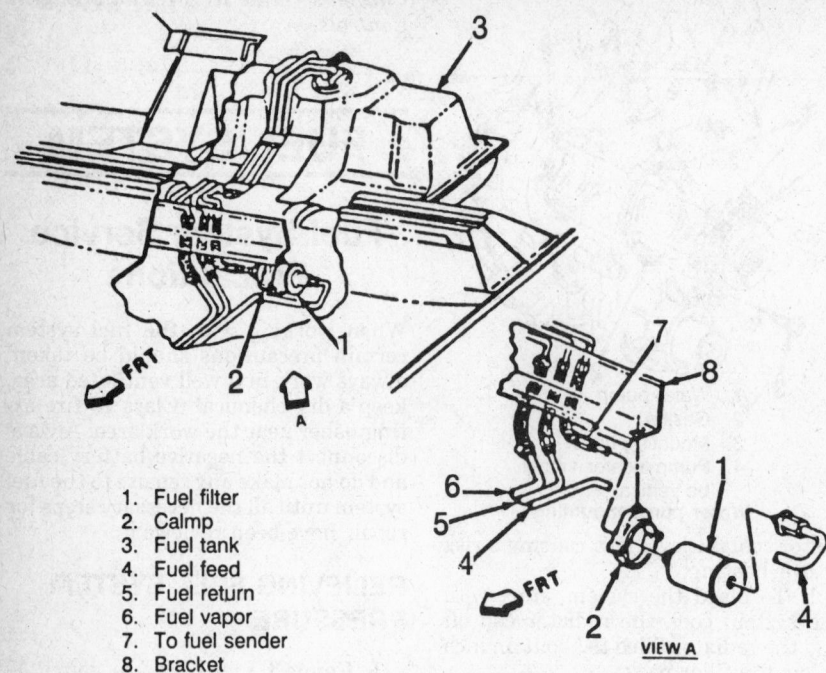

1. Fuel filter
2. Calmp
3. Fuel tank
4. Fuel feed
5. Fuel return
6. Fuel vapor
7. To fuel sender
8. Bracket

VIEW A

Location and mounting of the In line fuel filter

modern fuel injection systems, comprehensive diagnosis and testing procedures fall outside the confines of this repair manual. For complete information on fuel injection diagnosis, testing and repair procedures refer to *Chilton's Guide To Fuel Injection And Feedback Carburetors.*

MANUAL TRANSAXLE

REMOVAL & INSTALLATION

Cutlass Supreme and Grand Prix

NOTE: Before performing any maintenance that requires the removal of the slave cylinder, transaxle or clutch housing, the clutch master cylinder push rod must first be disconnected from the clutch pedal. Failure to disconnect the push rod will result in permanent damage to the slave cylinder if the clutch pedal is depressed with the slave cylinder disconnected.

1. Disconnect the negative battery cable.
2. Install the engine support tool J–28467 or equivalent.
3. Remove the air cleaner housing and intake tube. Disconnect the clutch actuator from the transaxle.
4. Disconnect the electrical connection at the speed sensor assembly. Disconnect the clutch and shift cables from the transaxle.
5. Remove the exhaust crossover pipe at the left manifold and remove the EGR tube from the crossover.
6. Loosen the crossover-to-right exhaust manifold clamp and move the crossover pipe to gain access to the transaxle bolts.
7. Remove the 2 upper transaxle mounting bolts and remove the 2 upper mounting studs. Leave 1 bottom bolt and stud attached.
8. Disconnect the electrical connection at the backup lamp switch. Raise and safely support the vehicle.
9. Drain the transaxle fluid. Remove the clutch housing cover. Remove the wheels.
10. Remove the inner fender splash shields from both side of the vehicle. Disconnect the power steering lines from the frame.
11. Remove the rack and pinion heat shield and remove the rack and pinion from the frame.
12. Disconnect the right and left ball

3. Turn the ignition switch **ON**; the fuel pressure should be 40–46 psi.
4. Start the engine and allow it to idle; the fuel pressure will be lower.

NOTE: The manifold pressure (being lower) operates the fuel pressure regulator.

5. Stop the engine, relieve the fuel pressure and remove the fuel pressure gauge.
6. If the fuel pressure is not to specification, check the system components.

ADJUSTMENT

The fuel system pressure is not adjustable. If the pressure is not within specifications, problems could be caused by a faulty fuel pump, clogged fuel filter, a leaking coupling or hose, a faulty regulator or an injector sticking open.

REMOVAL & INSTALLATION

The fuel pump is an integral part of the fuel level sensor assembly, located in the fuel tank.

1. Disconnect the negative battery cable.
2. Drain all fuel from the fuel tank.
3. Raise and safely support the vehicle. Support the fuel tank and remove the retaining straps.
4. Lower the fuel tank slightly and

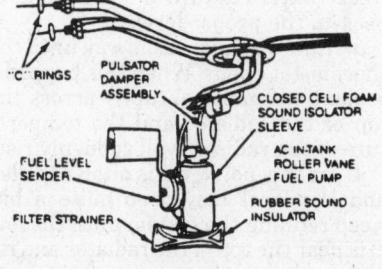

"C" RINGS
PULSATOR DAMPER ASSEMBLY
CLOSED CELL FOAM SOUND ISOLATOR SLEEVE
FUEL LEVEL SENDER
AC IN-TANK ROLLER VANE FUEL PUMP
FILTER STRAINER
RUBBER SOUND INSULATOR

Fuel pump and sending unit assemblies

disconnect the fuel lines, hoses and the sending unit electrical connectors.

5. Remove the tank from the vehicle.
6. Remove the sending unit retaining cam using tool J–24187 or equivalent, and remove the sending unit assembly from the tank.

To install:

7. Use a new O-ring and install the sending unit assembly into the tank.
8. Raise the tank into position and install the retaining straps. Tighten the tank retaining strap bolts to 26 ft. lbs.
9. Attach all fuel lines, hoses and electrical connectors to the tank.
10. Lower the vehicle and refill the tank. Connect the negative battery cable.

Fuel Injection

Due to the complex nature of

joints. Remove the upper transaxle mount retaining bolts. Remove the lower engine mount retaining nuts.

13. Remove the sub-frame retaining bolts and remove the sub-frame from the vehicle. Remove the starter and support it aside.

14. Remove the right and left drive axles from the transaxle. Support the transaxle and remove the remaining bolt and stud. Remove the transaxle from the vehicle.

To install:

15. Align the transaxle with the engine and install. Install the lower transaxle-to-engine mounting bolt and stud, tightening to 55 ft. lbs.

16. Install the starter assembly. Install the left and right drive axles.

17. Install the sub-frame and retaining bolts. Install the lower engine mount retaining nuts.

18. Install the upper transaxle retaining bolts, tightening to 55 ft. lbs. Install the right and left ball joints to the steering knuckles.

19. Install the rack and pinion, heat shield and lines to the frame. Install the right and left inner fender splash shields.

20. Install the clutch housing cover, tighten the screws to 115 inch lbs. Lower the vehicle.

21. Attach the crossover pipe to the manifolds and attach the EGR pipe to the crossover.

22. Attach the shift and clutch cables to the transaxle. Connect all of the electrical connectors. Install the air cleaner housing and tube. Remove the engine support tool.

23. Fill the transaxle with fluid. Connect the negative battery cable.

LINKAGE ADJUSTMENT

No adjustments are possible on the manual transaxle shifting cables or linkage. If the transaxle is not engaging completely, check for stretched cables, broken shifter components or a faulty transaxle.

CLUTCH

A hydraulic clutch release mechanism is used. This mechanism uses a clutch master cylinder with a remote reservoir and a slave cylinder connected to the master cylinder. Whenever the system is disconnected for repair or replacement, the clutch system must be bleed to insure proper operation.

REMOVAL & INSTALLATION

1. Disconnect the negative terminal from the battery.

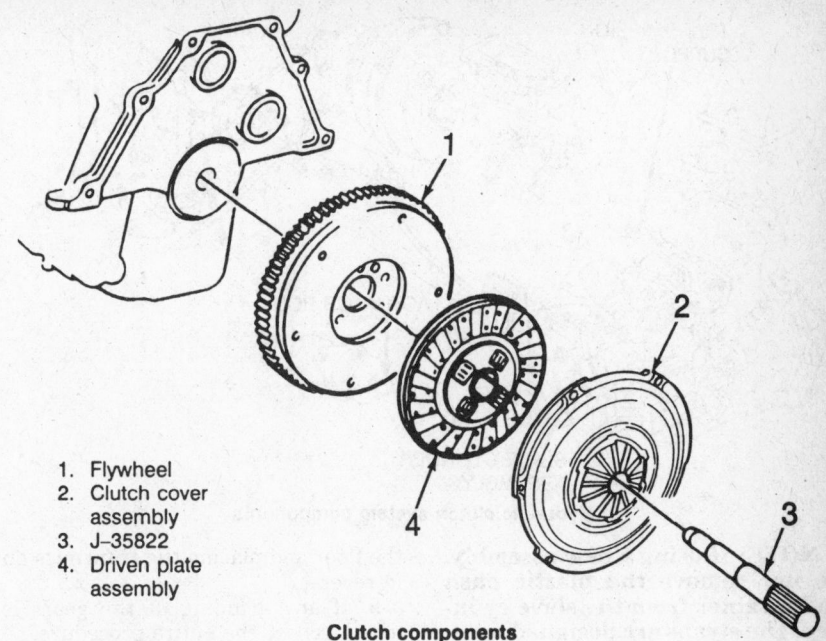

1. Flywheel
2. Clutch cover assembly
3. J–35822
4. Driven plate assembly

Clutch components

2. From inside the vehicle, remove the hush panel.

3. Disconnect the clutch master cylinder push rod from the clutch pedal.

4. Remove the transaxle.

5. With the transaxle removed, matchmark the pressure plate and flywheel assembly to insure proper balance during reassembly.

6. Loosen the pressure plate-to-flywheel bolts (a turn at a time) until the spring pressure is removed.

7. Support the pressure plate and remove the bolts.

8. Remove the pressure plate and disc assembly; be sure to note the flywheel side of the clutch disc.

To install:

9. Clean and inspect the clutch assembly, flywheel, release bearing, clutch fork and pivot shaft for signs of wear. Replace any necessary parts.

10. Position the clutch disc and pressure plate in the appropriate position, support the assembly with alignment tool No. J–29074, J–35822 or equivalent.

NOTE: Make sure the clutch disc is facing the same direction it was removed. If the same pressure plate is being reused, align the marks made during removal and install, install the pressure plate retaining bolts and tighten them gradually and evenly.

11. Remove the alignment tool and torque the pressure plate-to-flywheel bolts to 15 ft. lbs. Lightly lubricate the clutch fork ends. Fill the recess ends of the release bearing with grease. Lubricate the input shaft with a light coat of grease.

12. Install the transaxle assembly.

Install the clutch master cylinder pushrod and install the interior hush panel.

NOTE: The clutch lever must not be moved towards the flywheel until the transaxle is bolted to the engine. Damage to the transaxle, release bearing and clutch fork could occur if this is not followed.

13. Connect the negative battery cable. Bleed the clutch system and check the clutch operation.

Clutch Master Cylinder and Slave Cylinder

REMOVAL & INSTALLATION

NOTE: The clutch master and slave cylinders are serviced as an assembly.

1. Disconnect the negative battery cable. Remove the air cleaner and air inlet duct.

2. Remove the left side lower trim panel in the vehicle.

3. Disconnect the clutch master cylinder push rod from the clutch pedal.

4. Remove the clutch master cylinder mounting nuts. Remove the remote fluid reservoir mounting screws.

5. Remove the slave cylinder retaining nuts at the transaxle. Remove the clutch master and slave cylinders from the vehicle.

To install:

6. Attach the slave cylinder to the transaxle support bracket by aligning the the push rod into the pocket on the clutch fork outer lever.

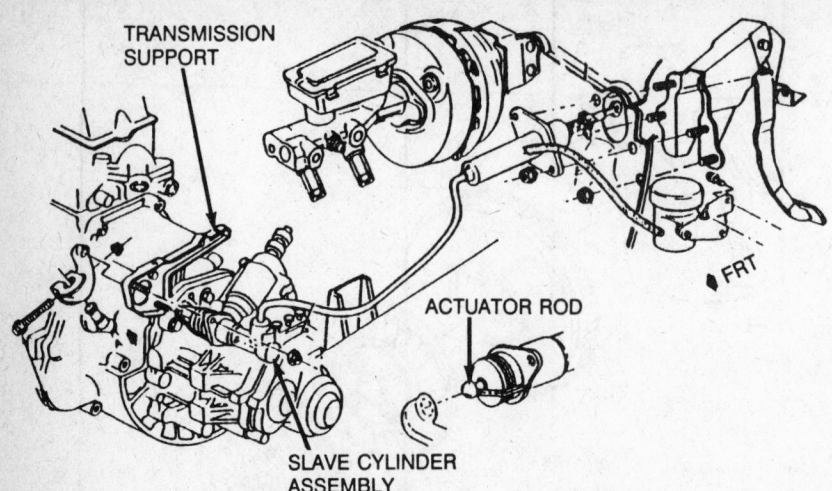

TRANSMISSION
SUPPORT

FRT

ACTUATOR ROD

SLAVE CYLINDER
ASSEMBLY

Hydraulic clutch system components

NOTE: If using a new assembly, do not remove the plastic push rod retainer from the slave cylinder. The straps are designed to retain the push rod and break during the first application of the clutch pedal.

7. Install the slave cylinder retaining nuts, tightening to 14 ft. lbs.

8. Install the clutch master cylinder and retaining nuts, tightening to 15 ft. lbs.

9. Install the fluid reservoir. Install the push rod on the clutch pedal.

10. Install the interior trim panel.

11. Press the clutch pedal down several times to break the retaining straps on the slave cylinder.

12. Fill and bleed the system.

BLEEDING THE HYDRAULIC CLUTCH SYSTEM

1. Remove any dirt or grease around the reservoir cap so that dirt cannot enter the system.

2. Fill the reservoir with an approved DOT 3 brake fluid.

3. Loosen, but do not remove, the bleeder screw on the slave cylinder.

4. Fluid will now flow from the master cylinder to the slave cylinder.

NOTE: It is important that the reservoir remain filled throughout the procedure.

5. Air bubbles should now appear at the bleeder screw.

6. Continue this procedure until a steady stream of fluid without any air bubbles is present.

7. Tighten the bleeder screw. Check the fluid level in the reservoir and fill to the proper mark.

8. The system is now fully bled. Check the clutch operation by starting the engine, pushing the clutch pedal to

the floor and placing the transmission in reverse.

9. If any grinding of the gears is noted, repeat the entire procedure.

NOTE: Never under any circumstances reuse fluid that has been in the system. The fluid may be contaminated with dirt and moisture.

AUTOMATIC TRANSAXLE

For further information on automatic transaxles, refer to "Automatic Transmissions" in the Unit Repair section.

1. Disconnect the negative terminal from the battery. Remove the air cleaner, bracket, mass air flow (MAF) sensor and air tube as an assembly.

2. Disconnect the exhaust crossover from the right-side manifold and remove the left-side exhaust manifold, then, raise and support the manifold/crossover assembly.

3. Disconnect the T.V. cable from the throttle lever and the transaxle.

4. Remove the vent hose and the shift cable from the transaxle.

5. Remove the fluid level indicator and the filler tube.

6. Using the Engine Support Fixture tool No. J–28467 or equivalent, and the Adapter tool No. J–35953 or equivalent, install them on the engine.

7. Remove the wiring harness-to-transaxle nut.

8. Label and disconnect the wires for the speed sensor, TCC connector and the neutral safety/back up light switch.

9. Remove the upper transaxle-to-engine bolts.

10. Remove the transaxle-to-mount through bolt, the transaxle mount bracket and the mount.

11. Raise and safely support the vehicle.

12. Remove the front wheel assemblies.

13. Disconnect the shift cable bracket from the transaxle.

14. Remove the left-side splash shield.

15. Using a modified Drive Axle Seal Protector tool No. J–34754 or equivalent, install one on each drive axle to protect the seal from damage and the joint from possible failure.

16. Using care not to damage the halfshaft boots, disconnect the halfshafts from the transaxle.

17. Remove the torsional and lateral strut from the transaxle. Remove the left-side stabilizer link pin bolt.

18. Remove the left frame support bolts and move it out of the way.

19. Disconnect the speedometer wire from the transaxle.

20. Remove the transaxle converter cover and matchmark the converter to the flywheel for assembly.

21. Disconnect and plug the transaxle cooler pipes.

22. Remove the transaxle-to-engine support.

23. Using a transmission jack, position and secure it to the transaxle and remove the remaining transaxle-to-engine bolts.

24. Make sure that the torque converter does not fall out and remove the transaxle from the vehicle.

NOTE: The transaxle cooler and lines should be flushed any time the transaxle is removed for overhaul, or to replace the pump, case or converter.

To install:

25. Put a small amount of grease on the pilot hub of the converter and make sure that the converter is properly engaged with the pump.

26. Raise the transaxle to the engine while guiding the right-side halfshaft into the transaxle.

27. Install the lower transaxle mounting bolts, tighten to 55 ft. lbs. and remove the jack.

28. Align the converter with the marks made previously on the flywheel and install the bolts hand tight.

29. Torque the converter bolts to 46 ft. lbs.; retorque the first bolt after the others.

30. Install the starter assembly. Install the left side halfshaft.

31. Install the converter cover, oil cooler lines and cover. Install the subframe assembly. Install the lower en-

gine mount retaining bolts and the transaxle mount nuts.

32. Install the right and left ball joints. Install the power steering rack, heat shield and cooler lines to the frame.

33. Install the right and left inner fender splash shields. Install the tire assemblies.

34. Lower the vehicle. Connect all electrical leads. Install the upper transaxle mount bolts, tighten to 55 ft. lbs.

35. Attach the crossover pipe to the exhaust manifold. Connect the EGR tube to the crossover.

36. Connect the T.V. cable and the shift cable. Install the air cleaner and inlet tube.

37. Remove the engine support tool. Connect the negative battery cable.

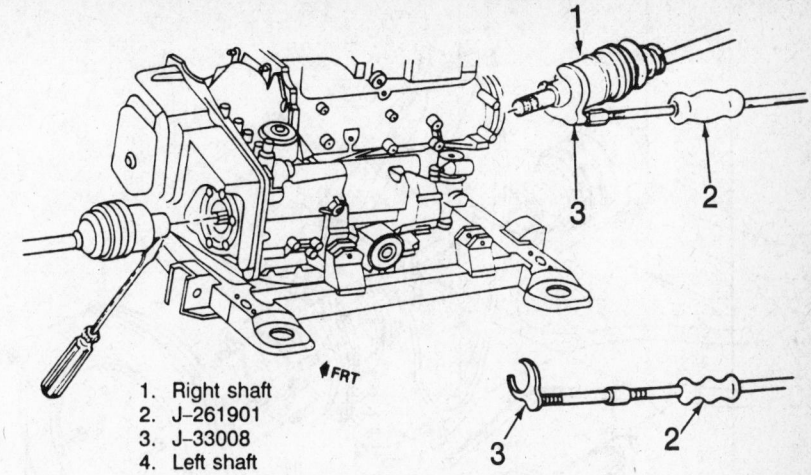

1. Right shaft
2. J-261901
3. J-33008
4. Left shaft

Halfshaft removal and installation

DRIVE AXLE

Halfshaft

REMOVAL & INSTALLATION

On models equipped with an automatic transaxle, the left half shaft uses a female spline which installs over a stub shaft protruding from the transaxle. The right half shaft uses a male and interlocks with the transaxle gears using barrel type snap-rings. On models equipped with a manual transaxle, the left half shaft uses a male spline locking into the gear assembly. The right half shaft uses a female spline that installs into the intermediate axle shaft.

1. With the weight of the vehicle on the tires, loosen the hub nut.

2. Raise and safely support the vehicle.

3. Remove the hub nut.

4. Install boot protectors on the boots.

5. Remove the brake caliper with the line attached and safely support it out of the way; DO NOT allow the caliper to hang from the line.

6. Remove the brake rotor and caliper mounting bracket.

7. Remove the strut-to-steering knuckle bolts. Pull the steering knuckle out of the strut bracket.

8. Using the Halfshaft Removal tool J-33008 or equivalent and the Extention tool No. J-29794 or equivalent, remove the halfshafts from the transaxle and support them safely.

9. Using a Spindle Remover tool No. J-28733 or equivalent, remove the halfshaft from the hub and bearing.

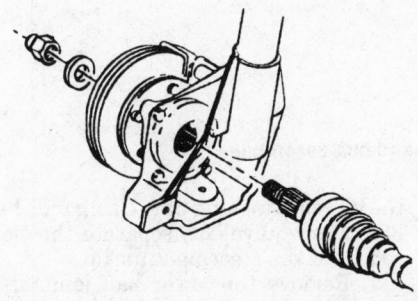

Removing the halfshaft from the hub/ knuckle assembly

To install:

10. Loosely place the halfshaft on the transaxle and in the hub and bearing.

11. Properly position the steering knuckle to the strut bracket and install the bolt. Torque the bolts to 133 ft. lbs.

12. Install the brake rotor, caliper bracket and caliper. Place a holding device in the rotor to prevent it from turning.

13. Install the hub nut and washer. Torque the nut to 71 ft. lbs.

14. Seat the halfshafts into the transaxle using a small pry bar on the groove on the inner retainer.

15. Verify that the shafts are seated by grasping the CV-joint and pulling outwards. DO NOT grasp the shaft. If the snap ring is seated, the halfshaft will remain in place.

16. Remove the boot protectors and lower the vehicle.

17. When the vehicle is lowered with the weight on the wheels, final torque the hub nut to 191 ft. lbs.

CV-JOINT OVERHAUL

For all CV-joint overhaul proce- dures, refer to "U/CV-Joint Overhaul" in the Unit Repair section.

Front Wheel Hub, Knuckle and Bearings

REMOVAL & INSTALLATION

The hub and bearing are replaced as an assembly only.

1. With the vehicle weight on the tires, loosen the hub nut.

2. Raise and support the vehicle. Remove the wheel and tire assembly.

3. Install a boot cover over the outer CV-joint boot.

4. Remove the hub nut. Remove the brake caliper and support it out of the way; DO NOT allow the caliper to hang on the brake line.

5. Remove the 3 hub and bearing mounting bolts.

6. Remove the brake rotor splash shield.

7. Install the hub puller tool No. J-28733 or equivalent, and press the hub and bearing from the halfshaft.

8. Disconnect the stabilizer link from the lower control arm.

9. Using the ball joint puller tool No. J-29330 or equivalent, separate the ball joint from the steering knuckle.

10. Remove the halfshaft from the knuckle and support it out of the way.

11. Using a brass drift, remove the inner knuckle seal.

12. Clean and inspect the steering knuckle bore and the bearing mating surfaces.

13. Install a new O-ring between the bearing and knuckle assembly.

14. Install the hub and bearing assembly and torque the nuts to 90 ft. lbs.

15. Using a seal driver tool No. J-

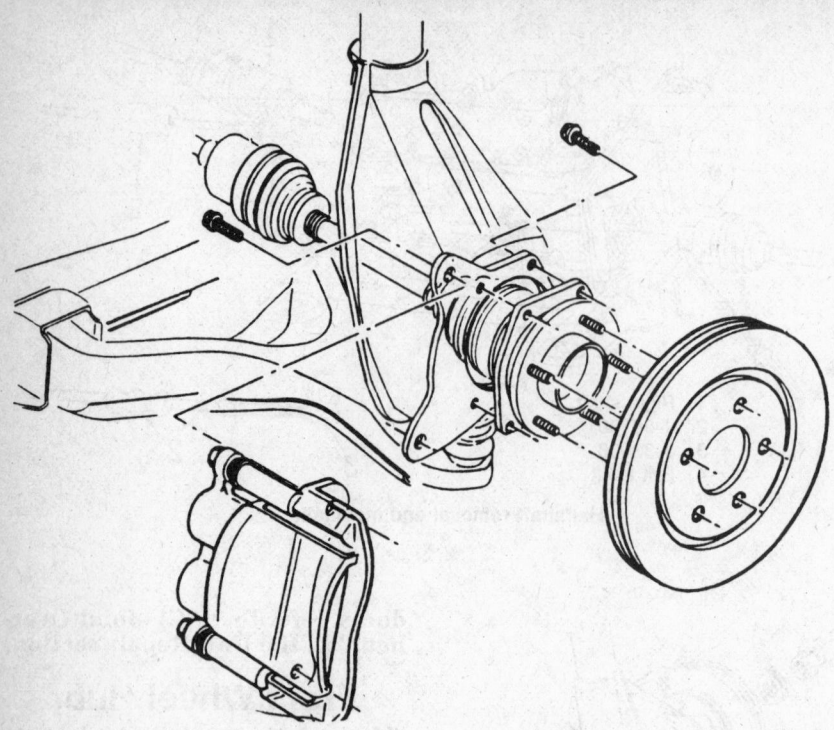

Removing the front rotor and hub assemblies

34658 or equivalent, install it into the steering knuckle; be sure to lubricate the new seal and the bearing with a high temperature wheel bearing grease.

16. Reconnect the lower ball joint.

17. Install the hub, bearing nut and washer on the halfshaft, torque the nut to 71 ft. lbs.

18. Install the brake rotor and caliper. Install the wheel and tire.

19. Lower the vehicle and torque the hub nut to 191 ft. lbs.

FRONT SUSPENSION

MacPherson Strut

REMOVAL & INSTALLATION

1. Disconnect the negative battery cable.

2. Loosen the cover plate bolts.

3. Loosen the wheel nuts. Raise and safely support the vehicle.

4. Remove the wheel assembly. Remove the brake caliper and bracket assembly, hang the caliper aside. DO NOT hang the caliper by the brake lines.

5. Remove the brake rotor. Remove the hub and bearing attaching bolts.

6. Remove the halfshaft. Remove

the tie rod attaching nut. Using tool J–35917 or equivalent, separate the tie rod from the steering knuckle.

7. Remove the lower ball joint attaching nut and separate the lower ball from the lower control arm.

8. Remove the cover plate bolts and remove the strut from the vehicle.

To install:

9. Install the strut mount cover plate, tighten the nuts after lowering the vehicle. Install the lower ball joint and install the tie rod.

10. Install the halfshaft and install the hub and bearing-to-knuckle attaching bolts, tighten to 59 ft. lbs.

11. Install the brake rotor and caliper assembly.

12. Install the wheel assembly, tighten the wheel nuts after lowering the vehicle.

13. Lower the vehicle, tighten the strut cover bolts to 17 ft. lbs. and tighten the wheel nuts.

14. Connect the negative battery cable.

OVERHAUL

For all spring and shock absorber removal and installation, and all strut overhaul procedures, please refer to "Strut Overhaul" in the Unit Repair section.

Ball Joint

INSPECTION

1. Raise and safely support the ve-

hicle, allowing the front suspension to hang freely.

2. Grasp and shake the wheel at the top and bottom to feel if there is any in and out movement.

3. Replace the ball joint if any movement is detected.

4. When the ball joint is disconnected from the knuckle, check for any looseness or if the ball joint can be twisted freely in the socket by hand.

REMOVAL & INSTALLATION

1. Raise and safely support the vehicle.

2. Remove the wheel assembly.

3. Remove the ball joint heat shield retaining nuts and remove the heat shield.

4. Remove the ball joint cotter pin and nut.

5. Loosen, but do not remove, the stabilizer bar bushing bolts.

6. Using tool J–35917 or equivalent, remove the ball joint from the lower control arm.

7. Using an ⅛ in. drill bit, make a pilot hole in each of the rivets retaining the ball joint to the lower control arm. Using a ½ in. drill bit, drill the rivets out and remove the ball joint.

To install:

8. Install the ball joint to the lower control arm, install the retaining nut hand tight.

9. Install the ball joint to the steering knuckle. Install the 4 ball joint retaining nuts and bolts, supplied with the replacement joint.

10. Tighten the stabilizer bushing bar bushing bolts to 35 ft. lbs. Tighten the ball joint retaining nut to 7 ft. lbs. and an additional 120 degrees. Install a new cotter pin.

NOTE: DO NOT at any time loosen the ball joint nut to align it when installing the cotter pin.

11. Install the ball joint heat shield and tighten the retaining bolts to 5 ft. lbs.

Lower Control Arms

REMOVAL & INSTALLATION

1. Loosen the wheel nuts. Raise and safely support the vehicle.

2. Remove the wheel assembly.

3. Remove the stabilizer shaft-to-lower control arm bolts. Remove the ball joint retaining nut and cotter pin.

4. Using tool J–35917 or equivalent, Separate the ball joint from the control arm.

5. Remove the lower control arm-to-frame attaching nuts and bolts. Remove the lower control arm from the vehicle.

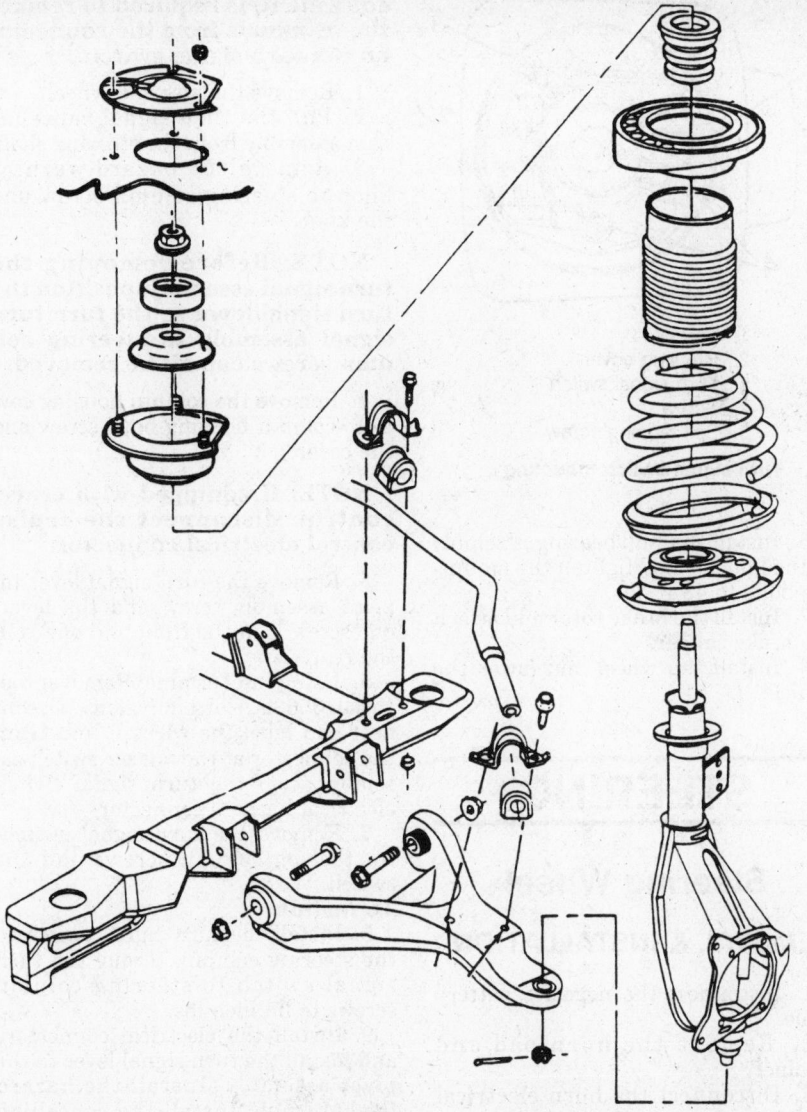

Front suspension components

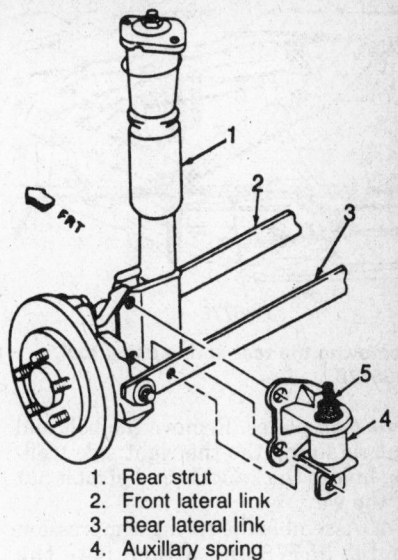

1. Rear strut
2. Front lateral link
3. Rear lateral link
4. Auxillary spring assembly
5. J–37098

Rear strut assembly

6. Install the lower control arm to the frame and pivot it to the ball joint.

7. Tighten the lower control arm bolts to 52 ft. lbs. and the ball joint nut to 7 ft. lbs plus an additional 120 degrees. Install a new cotter pin.

8. Install the stabilizer shaft to the lower control arm, tighten the bolts to 35 ft. lbs.

9. Install the wheel assembly and lower the vehicle. Tighten the wheel nuts to 100 ft. lbs.

Front Wheel Alignment

ADJUSTMENT

Caster and camber are preset at the factory and are not adjustable. Toe can be adjusted by loosening the clamps on the outer tie rods and rotating the tie rods to obtain the proper specification. Torque the tie rod clamp to 33 ft. lbs.

REAR SUSPENSION

MacPherson Strut

REMOVAL & INSTALLTION

1. Raise and safely support the vehicle.

2. Remove the wheel assembly.

3. Using tool J–37098 or equivalent, compress the auxiliary spring assembly.

4. Remove the brake caliper and support it aside. Remove the brake rotor.

5. Matchmark the strut mounting bracket and the knuckle assembly. Remove the upper strut mounting bolts and let the assembly drop down.

6. Remove the strut-to-knuckle bolts/nuts and remove the strut assembly from the vehicle.

To install:

7. Attach the strut assembly to the knuckle, aligning the matchmarks made prior to removal. Tighten the strut-to-knuckle bolts to 133 ft. lbs.

8. Install the upper strut mounting bolts, tighten to 34 ft. lbs.

9. Install the brake rotor and attach the brake caliper. Remove the compression tool from the auxiliary spring assembly.

10. Install the wheel assembly and lower the vehicle.

OVERHAUL

For all spring and shock absorber removal and installation procedures and all strut overhaul procedures, refer to "Strut Overhaul" in the Unit Repair section.

Spring

REMOVAL & INSTALLATION

NOTE: The rear spring used is a single transverse mounted fiberglass spring. The removal of this spring requires the use of a special tool, J–35778 rear spring compression tool. It is not recommended that rear spring removal be attempted unless this tool is used.

1. Raise and safely support the vehicle.

2. Remove the bolts retaining the jackpad and remove the jackpad.

3. Remove the right and left spring

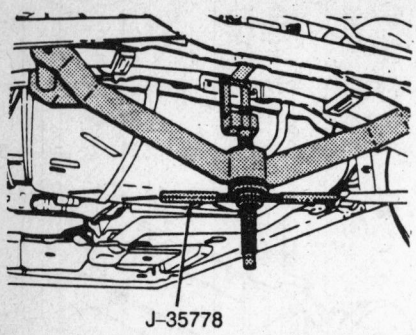

J–35778

Removing the rear spring using tool J–35778

retention plates. Remove the bolt and nut retaining the the right side trailing link to the knuckle and pivot it out of the way.

4. Assemble the spring compression tool J–35778 and attach it to the spring.

5. Fully compress the spring. Slide the spring to the left side, relax the spring until removal clearance is reached. Remove the spring from the vehicle.

To install:

6. Install the spring into the position, with the compression tool attached, by sliding it to the left.

7. With the spring in position, loosen the compression tool slightly.

8. Attach the right side trailing link to the knuckle, tighten the mounting bolt to 192 ft. lbs.

9. Install the right and left retention plates. Tighten the retention plate bolts to 15 ft. lbs.

NOTE: The retention plates are designed with tabs on one end. The tabs must be aligned with the support assembly to prevent damage to the fuel tank.

10. Remove the spring compression tool.

11. Install the jack pad, tighten the retaining bolts to 18 ft. lbs.

12. Lower the vehicle.

Rear Wheel Bearings

REMOVAL & INSTALLATION

The rear wheel bearing and hub are non-serviceable. The bearing and hub are replaced as an assembly.

1. Raise and safely support the vehicle.

2. Remove the wheel assembly.

3. Remove the brake caliper and support it aside.

4. Remove the brake rotor.

5. Remove the hub/bearing assembly mounting bolts and remove the assembly from the knuckle.

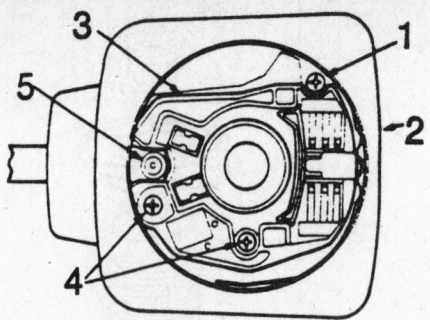

1. Screw
2. Housing cover
3. Turn signal switch
4. Screw
5. Self tapping screw

Turn signal switch mounting

6. Install the hub/bearing assembly to the knuckle and tighten the mounting bolts to 48 ft. lbs.

7. Install the brake rotor and attach the brake caliper.

8. Install the wheel and lower the vehicle.

STEERING

Steering Wheel

REMOVAL & INSTALLATION

1. Disconnect the negative battery cable.

2. Remove the horn pad and retainer.

3. Disconnect the horn electrical lead from the canceling cam tower.

4. Turn the ignition switch to the **ON** position.

5. Scribe an alignment mark on the steering wheel hub in line with the slash mark on the steering shaft.

6. Loosen the steering shaft nut and install steering wheel puller J–185903 or equivalent. Remove the steering wheel.

7. Align the matchmarks on the wheel hub and shaft and install the steering wheel. Tighten the steering shaft nut to 30 ft. lbs.

8. Connect the horn electrical lead and install the horn pad.

9. Connect the negative battery cable.

Turn Signal Switch/ Combination Switch

REMOVAL & INSTALLATION

NOTE: Tool No. J–35689-A or

equivalent, is required to remove the terminals from the connector on the turn signal switch.

1. Remove the steering wheel.

2. Pull the turn signal canceling cam assembly from the steering shaft.

3. Remove the hazard warning knob-to-steering column screw and the knob.

NOTE: Before removing the turn signal assembly, position the turn signal lever so the turn turn signal assembly to steering column screws can all be removed.

4. Remove the column housing cover-to-column housing bowl screw and the cover.

NOTE: If equipped with cruise control, disconnect the cruise control electrical connector.

5. Remove the turn signal lever-to-pivot assembly screw and the lever; one screw is in the front and one is in the rear.

6. Using the Terminal Remover tool No. J–35689-A or equivalent, disconnect and label the wires **F** and **G** on the connector at the buzzer switch assembly from the turn signal switch electrical harness connector.

7. Remove the turn signal switch-to-steering column screws and the switch.

To install:

8. Install the turn signal switch to the steering column, torque the turn signal switch-to-steering column screws to 35 inch lbs.

9. Install the electrical connectors and install the turn signal lever to the pivot assembly. Install the hazard flasher knob. Install the cancelling cam.

10. Install the steering wheel. Connect the negative battery cable.

Ignition Lock/Switch

REMOVAL & INSTALLATION

1. Disconnect the negative terminal from the battery. Remove the left-side lower trim panel.

2. Remove the steering column-to-support screws and lower the steering column.

3. Disconnect the dimmer switch and turn signal switch connectors.

4. Remove the wiring harness-to-firewall nuts.

5. Remove the steering column-to-steering gear bolt and the steering column from the vehicle.

6. Remove the combination switch.

7. Place the lock cylinder in the **RUN** position.

8. Remove the steering shaft assem-

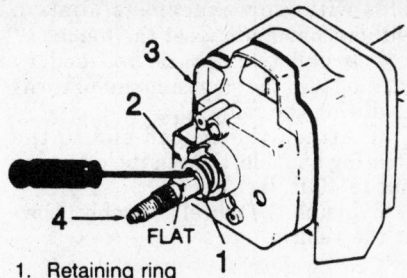

1. Retaining ring
2. Thrust washer
3. Turn signal switch housing
4. Steering shaft assembly

Removing the turn signal switch housing

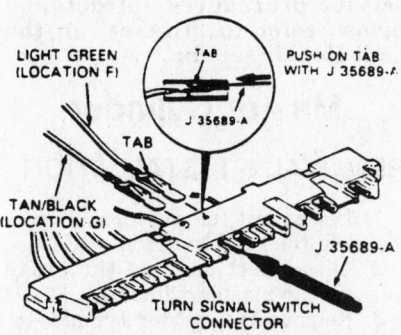

Removing the turn signal switch connector

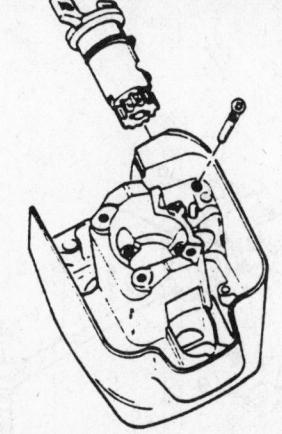

Removing the ignition lock cylinder

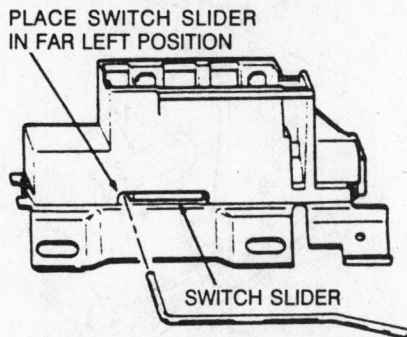

Ignition switch installation position

bly and turn signal switch housing as an assembly.

9. Using the Terminal Remover tool No. J–35689-A or equivalent, disconnect and label the wires **F** and **G** on the connector at the buzzer switch assembly from the turn signal switch electrical harness connector.

10. With the lock cylinder in the **RUN** position, remove the buzzer switch.

11. Place the lock cylinder in the **ACCESSORY** position, remove the lock cylinder retaining screw and the lock cylinder.

12. Remove the dimmer switch nut/bolt, the dimmer switch and actuator rod.

13. Remove the dimmer switch mounting stud (the mounting nut was mounted to it).

14. Remove the ignition switch-to-steering column screws and the ignition switch.

15. Remove the lock bolt screws and the lock bolt.

16. Remove the switch actuator rack and ignition switch.

17. Remove the steering shaft lock and spring.

To install:

18. To install the lock bolt, lubricate it with lithium grease and install the lock bolt, spring and retaining plate.

19. Lubricate the teeth on the switch

actuator rack, install the rack and the ignition switch through the opening in the steering bolt until it rests on the retaining plate.

20. Install the steering column lock cylinder set by holding the barrel of the lock cylinder, inserting the key and turning the key to the **ACCESSORY** position.

21. Install the lock set in the steering column while holding the rack against the lock plate.

22. Install the lock retaining screw. Insert the key in the lock cylinder and turn the lock cylinder to the **START** position and the rack will extend.

23. Center the slotted holes on the ignition switch mounting plate and install the ignition switch mounting screw and nut.

24. Install the dimmer switch and actuator rod into the center slot on the switch mounting plate.

25. Install the buzzer switch and turn the lock cylinder to the **RUN** position. Push the switch in until it is bottomed out with the plastic tab that covers the lock retaining screw.

26. Install the steering shaft and turn signal housing as an assembly.

27. Install the turn signal switch. Install the steering wheel to the column, torque the steering shaft nut to 30 ft. lbs.

28. Install the steering column in the

vehicle. Connect all electrical leads. Install the lower trim panels.

30. Connect the negative battery cable.

Power Steering Gear

REMOVAL & INSTALLATION

1. Disconnect the negative battery cable. Remove the air cleaner.

2. Raise and safely support the vehicle.

3. Remove both front wheel assemblies.

4. Remove the intermediate shaft lower pinch bolt at the steering gear. Remove the intermediate shaft from the stub shaft.

5. Disconnect the electrical lead at the power steering idle switch.

6. Separate the tie rod ends from the knuckle assembly. Remove the rear sub-frame mounting bolts and lower the rear of the sub-frame approximately 4 in.

7. Remove the steering rack heat shield. Disconnect the pressure lines at the steering gear.

8. Remove the rack and pinion mounting bolts, remove the rack and pinion through the left wheel opening.

To install:

9. Install the rack and pinion through the left wheel opening. Tighten the mounting bolts to 59 ft. lbs. Connect the pressure lines, tighten the fittings to 20 ft. lbs.

10. Install the rack heat shield, tighten the retaining bolts to 53 inch lbs. Attach the tie rod ends to the steering knuckle.

11. Connect the electrical lead to the power steering idle switch. Attach the intermediate shaft to the stub shaft, tighten the pinch bolt to 35 ft. lbs.

12. Install both wheel assemblies. Lower the vehicle.

13. Install the air cleaner. Connect the negative battery cable. Fill and bleed the power steering system.

Power Steering Pump

REMOVAL & INSTALLATION

1. Disconnect the negative terminal from the battery.

2. Remove the pressure and return hoses from the pump and drain the system into a suitable container.

3. Cap the fittings at the pump.

4. Remove the serpentine belt.

5. Locate the pump attaching bolts through the pulley and remove the bolts.

6. Remove the pump assembly.

7. Install the pump and torque the mounting bolts to 18 ft. lbs.

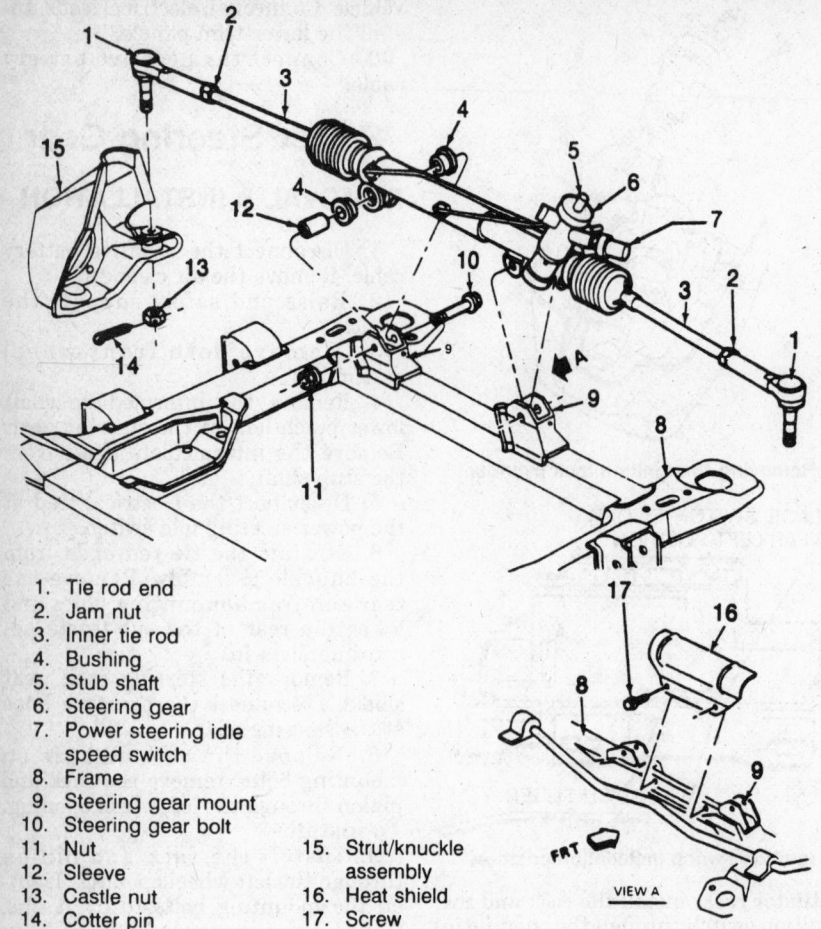

1. Tie rod end
2. Jam nut
3. Inner tie rod
4. Bushing
5. Stub shaft
6. Steering gear
7. Power steering idle
   speed switch
8. Frame
9. Steering gear mount
10. Steering gear bolt
11. Nut
12. Sleeve
13. Castle nut
14. Cotter pin
15. Strut/knuckle
    assembly
16. Heat shield
17. Screw

Steering gear components and mounting

8. Reconnect the hoses to the pump and install the serpentine belt.

9. Refill the power steering pump reservoir and bleed the system. Connect the negative battery cable.

BELT ADJUSTMENT

The serpentine accessory drive belt used on this engine, is adjusted automatically by an spring loaded tensioner. No adjustment is necessary.

SYSTEM BLEEDING

────────── **CAUTION** ──────────
Automatic transmission fluid is NOT compatible with the seals and hoses of the power steering system. Under no circumstances should automatic transmission be used in place of power steering fluid in this system.

1. With the engine turned **OFF**, turn the wheels all the way to the left.

2. Fill the reservoir with power steering fluid until the level is at the cold mark on the reservoir.

3. Start and run the engine at fast idle for 15 seconds. Turn the engine **OFF**.

4. Recheck the fluid level and fill it to the cold mark.

5. Start the engine and bleed the system by turning the wheels in both directions slowly to the stops.

6. Stop the engine and check the fluid. Fluid that still has air in it will be a light tan color.

7. Repeat this procedure until all of the air is removed from the system.

Tie Rod Ends

REMOVAL & INSTALLATION

1. Raise and safely support the vehicle. Remove the wheel assembly.

2. Remove the tie rod-to-steering knuckle retaining nut. Using tool J–35917 or equivalent, remove the tie rod from the steering knuckle.

3. Remove the outer tie rod from the adjuster by counting the exact number of turns required to remove it.

This will allow proper installation without having to reset the toe in.

4. Install the new tie rod end by turning it in the same amount of turns as during the removal.

5. Attach the tie rod end to the steering knuckle, tighten the retaining nut to 40 ft. lbs.

6. Install the wheel assembly. Lower the vehicle.

BRAKES

For all brake system repair and service procedures not detailed below, refer to "Brakes" in the Unit Repair section.

Master Cylinder

REMOVAL & INSTALLATION

1. Disconnect the electrical connector from the fluid level sensor.

2. Disconnect and cap the brake lines on the master cylinder.

3. Remove the master cylinder-to-power booster nuts and the master cylinder with the reservoir attached.

4. Install the master cylinder-to-booster and torque the master cylinder-to-power booster nuts to 20 ft. lbs.

5. Connect the brake lines-to-master cylinder and tighten the fittings to 13 ft. lbs.

6. Connect the fluid level electrical sensor wires. Refill the reservoir with an approved DOT 3 brake fluid and bleed the brake system.

Proportioning Valve

REMOVAL & INSTALLATION

NOTE: It may be necessary to remove the reservoir in order to remove the proportioning valve. If the reservoir is removed, bleed the brake system when finished.

1. Remove the proportioning valve cap on the master cylinder.

2. Remove and discard the O-rings.

3. Remove the springs, the proportioning valve pistons and the seals from the valves.

4. Inspect the valves for corrosion or abnormal wear; to replace, if necessary.

5. Clean all parts in denatured alcohol and dry them with air before reassembling.

6. To install, use new O-rings (coated with silicone grease) and install the new seals on the pistons with the lip facing the cap. Torque the caps to 20 ft. lbs.

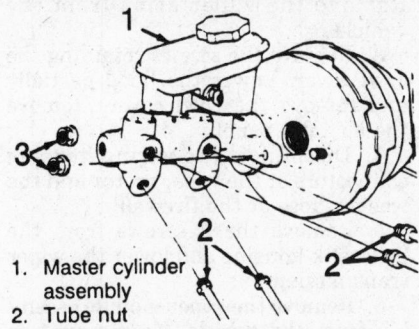

1. Master cylinder
   assembly
2. Tube nut
3. Nut

Removing the master cylinder assembly

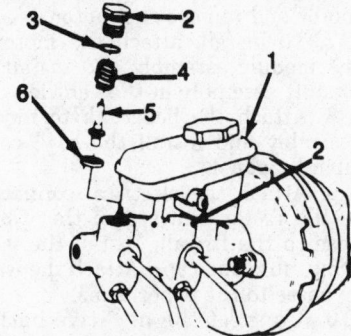

1. Master cylinder
2. Proportioner valve
   cap assembly
3. O-ring
4. Spring
5. Proportioner valve piston
6. Proportioner valve seal

Proportioning valve removal and installation

7. Refill the reservoir and bleed the brake system.

Power Brake Booster
REMOVAL & INSTALLATION

1. Remove the left side under-dash panel.
2. Remove the booster grommet bolt and remove the grommet.
3. Remove the pushrod from the brake pedal. Remove the master cylinder from the booster.
4. Using tool J–2280501 or equivalent, unlock the booster from the mounting flange by turning it counterclockwise. Remove the booster from the vehicle.
5. Install the booster to the mounting flange. Install the pushrod to the brake pedal.
6. Install the master cylinder to the booster. Install the booster grommet and bolt.
7. Install the trim panel.

Parking Brake Cable
ADJUSTMENT

1. Depress the service brake pedal 3 times.

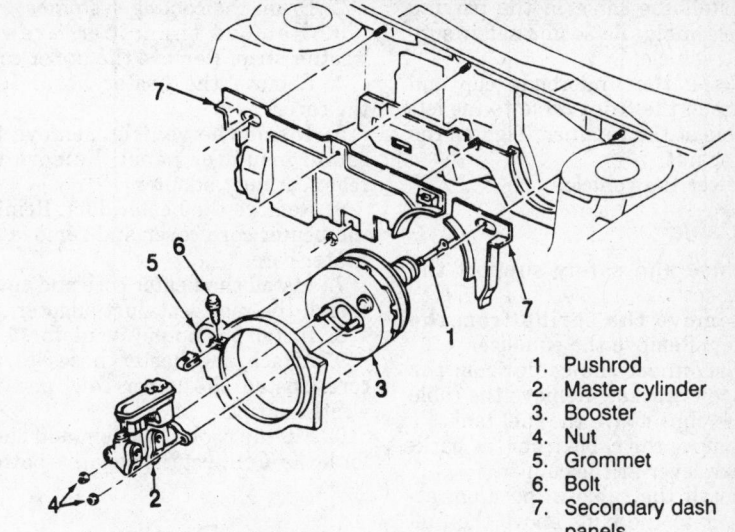

1. Pushrod
2. Master cylinder
3. Booster
4. Nut
5. Grommet
6. Bolt
7. Secondary dash
   panels

Removing the power brake booster

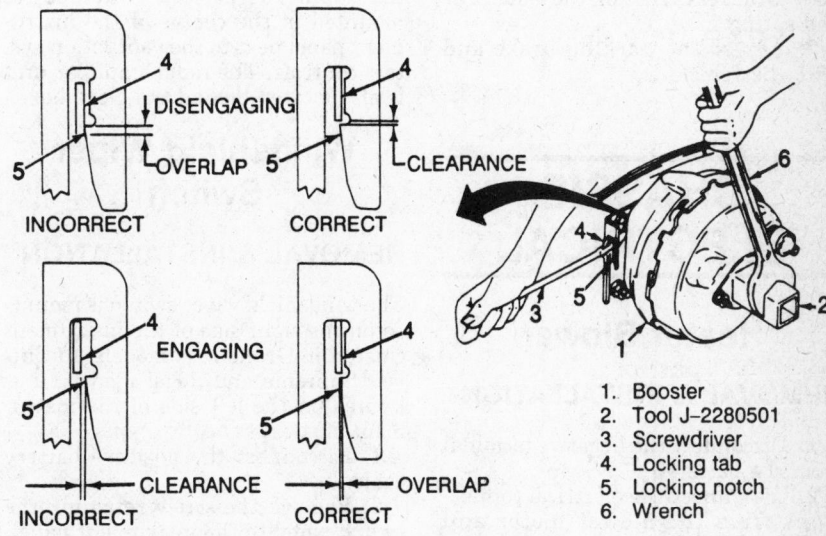

1. Booster
2. Tool J–2280501
3. Screwdriver
4. Locking tab
5. Locking notch
6. Wrench

Unlocking the brake booster from the mounting flange

2. Fully apply and release the parking brake 3 times.
3. Raise and safely support the vehicle. Remove the rear wheel assemblies. Install 2 lug nuts on each rear hub to retain the rotors.
4. The parking brake levers on both calipers should be against the lever stops on the caliper housings. If the levers are not against the stops, check for binding in the rear cables and loosen the cables at the adjuster until both of the levers are against their stops.
5. Tighten the parking brake cable at the adjusters until the levers just start to move off the stop.
6. Operate the parking brake several times to check the adjustment. A firm pedal should be reached with 2 strokes of the pedal. The rear wheels

should not move forward when the brake is applied.
7. Install the wheels and tires. Lower the vehicle.

REMOVAL & INSTALLATION

Front Cable

1. Raise and safely support the vehicle.
2. Loosen, but do not remove the equalizer nut.
3. Disconnect the front cable from the left rear cable at the retainer.
4. Remove the nut from the underbody bracket and remove the clip.
5. Lower the vehicle and remove the cable from the parking brake control assembly.

6. Install the cable in the parking brake assembly. Raise and safely support the vehicle.

7. Install the underbody clip and nut. Attach the front cable to the left rear cable at the retainer. Tighten the equalizer nut.

8. Lower the vehicle.

Rear Cable

1. Raise and safely support the vehicle.

2. Remove the spring from the equalizer. Remove the equalizer.

3. Disconnect the cable from the underbody bracket. Remove the cable from the clips above the fuel tank.

4. Remove the cable from the parking brake lever at the caliper.

5. Install the cable in position, attaching it to the clips above the fuel tank.

6. Attach the cable to the lever at the caliper.

7. Attach the cable to the underbody brackets. Install the equalizer and spring.

8. Adjust the parking brake and lower he vehicle.

CHASSIS ELECTRICAL

Heater Blower

REMOVAL & INSTALLATION

1. Disconnect the negative terminal from the battery.

2. Disconnect the electrical connections from the blower motor and resistor.

3. Remove the plastic water shield from the right-side of the cowl.

4. Remove the blower motor-to-chassis screws and the blower motor.

5. Remove the cage retaining nut and the cage.

6. Install the cage on the new blower motor with the opening facing away from the motor.

7. Install the blower motor and screws. Connect the electrical leads to the motor and resistor.

8. Install the water shield to the cowl. Connect the negative battery cable.

Heater Core

REMOVAL & INSTALLATION

1. Disconnect the negative battery cable.

2. Drain the cooling system.

3. Remove the upper firewall weatherstrip. Remove the upper cowl.

4. Remove the heater hoses from the core.

5. Inside the vehicle, remove the sound insulator panel. Remove the rear seat duct adapter.

6. Remove the heater duct. Remove the heater core cover and remove the heater core.

7. Install the heater core and cover. Install the rear seat duct adapter.

8. Install the sound insulator.

9. Attach the heater hoses to the core. Install the upper cowl and the weatherstrip.

10. Fill the cooling system and check for leaks. Connect the negative battery cable.

Radio

The radio receiver used is remotely mounted behind the glove box. All of the radio operational controls are mounted in the center of the instrument panel next to the ventilation system controls. The radio amplifier unit is also located behind the glove box.

Windshield Wiper Switch

REMOVAL & INSTALLATION

The windshield wiper switch is mounted on the right side of the instrument cluster, in Grand Prix models. In Cutlass Supreme and Regal models, it is located on the left side of the instrument cluster.

1. Disconnect the negative battery cable.

2. Remove the screw retaining the switch panel to the instrument panel.

3. Remove the switch from the instrument panel by pulling the bottom out and releasing the top retaining clips.

4. Disconnect the electrical connector from the switch and remove it from the vehicle.

5. To install the switch, connect the electrical leads and push the switch into position.

6. Install the retaining screw. Connect the negative battery cable.

Windshield Wiper Motor

REMOVAL & INSTALLATION

1. Disconnect the negative battery cable.

2. Remove the washer hose, cap and retaining nut from each wiper arm.

Remove the wiper arms from the vehicle.

3. Remove the screws retaining the cowl cover. Lower the hood partially and remove the cowl cover. Remove the air inlet panel.

4. Disconnect the wiring harness connectors at the wiper motor and the washer hose at the firewall.

5. Remove the 3 screws from the bellcrank housing and lower the wiper transmission.

6. Remove the wiper module assembly from the vehicle. To remove the wiper motor from the module assembly, remove the 3 screw retaining the motor and remove the motor.

7. To install, attach the motor to the module assembly and install the module assembly in the vehicle.

8. Attach the bellcrank to module assembly and install the cowl cover, air inlet panel.

9. Attach the electrical connectors to the motor and attach the washer hose to the firewall. Install the wiper arms, nuts and caps. Attach the washer hoses to the wiper arms.

10. Connect the negative battery cable.

Instrument Cluster

REMOVAL & INSTALLATION

Cutlass Supreme and Regal

1. Disconnect the negative battery cable.

2. Remove the 5 screws retaining the cluster trim plate. Pull the bottom of the trim plate out and remove it from the vehicle.

3. Open the glove box and remove the lower storage compartment. Remove the 2 screws in the glove box opening.

4. Remove the defroster grille and remove the 2 screws inside the opening. Remove the 2 screws at the side of the instrument cluster.

5. Lift up on the upper panel pad and remove the pad. Remove the screws retaining the instrument cluster and remove the cluster from the instrument panel. Disconnect the electrical connectors.

To install:

6. Install the cluster to the instrument panel. Connect the electrical leads.

7. Install the upper panel pad. Install the defroster grille and the glove box compartment.

8. Install the cluster trim panel. Connect the negative battery cable.

Grand Prix

1. Disconnect the negative battery cable.

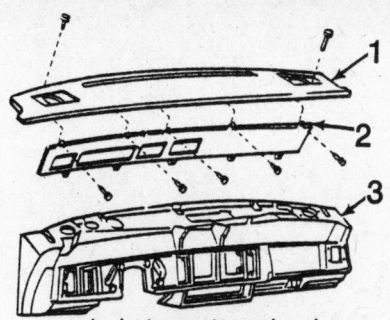

1. Instrument panel pad
2. Instrument panel cluster bezel
3. Instrument panel carrier

Instrument panel pad and cluster trim removal – Regal

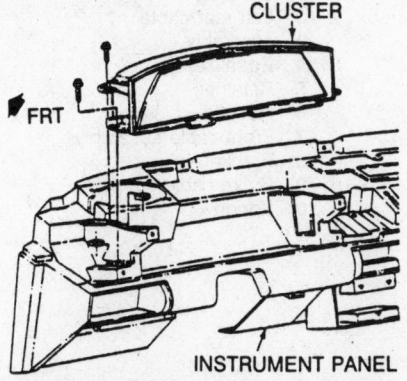

Instrument cluster removal – Grand Prix

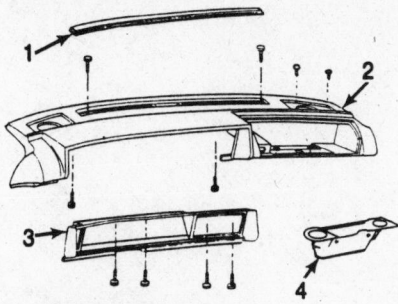

1. Defroster grille
2. Instrument panel pad
3. Instrument cluster trim plate
4. Lower glove compartment

Instrument panel pad and cluster trim removal – Cutlass Supreme

2. Remove the wiper and headlight switch assemblies.

3. Remove the 2 screws in each of the switch openings and remove the 2 screws from the top of the cluster trim plate. Remove the cluster trim plate.

4. Remove the glove box and remove the screw above the glove box opening.

5. Lift the front of the instrument panel pad and pull it back to release it from the instrument panel. Remove it from the vehicle.

6. Remove the 4 screws retaining the instrument cluster and pull the cluster forward. Disconnect the elec-

trical connectors and remove the cluster from the vehicle.

To install:

7. Install the cluster to the instrument panel. Connect the electrical leads.

8. Install the upper panel pad. Install the glove box.

9. Install the cluster trim panel.

10. Connect the negative battery cable.

Headlight Switch

REMOVAL & INSTALLATION

Cutlass Supreme and Regal

1. Disconnect the negative battery cable.

2. Remove the instrument cluster trim plate.

3. Remove the 4 screws retaining the switch and remove the switch from the instrument panel.

4. Disconnect the electrical connector from the switch and remove the switch.

5. To install the switch, connect the electrical connector and install the switch in the instrument panel.

6. Install the cluster trim plate.

7. Connect the negative battery cable.

Grand Prix

1. Disconnect the negative battery cable.

2. Remove the screw retaining the headlight switch to the instrument panel.

3. Pull the top of the switch out to release the lower retaining clips and remove it from the instrument panel.

4. Disconnect the electrical connector and remove the switch from the vehicle.

5. To install the switch, connect the electrical connector and install the switch in the instrument panel.

6. Connect the negative battery cable.

Stoplight Switch

REMOVAL & INSTALLATION

1. Disconnect the negative terminal from the battery.

2. Remove the lower-left trim panel. Locate the stoplight switch on the brake pedal support.

3. Disconnect the plug on the switch and remove the switch by twisting it out of the tubular retaining clip. If the vehicle is equipped with cruise control unplug the vacuum line from the cruise control cut-off switch.

4. Install the new switch using a

new retaining clip and connect the wire.

5. Adjust the switch by pulling back on the brake pedal noting the "clicks" as the switch is pushed through the retaining clip.

6. Repeat the procedure until no "clicks" can be heard.

7. Connect the negative battery cable and check the switch operation.

Fuses and Circuit Breakers

LOCATION

The fuse box is located behind the right side of the instrument panel. To reach the fuse block, open the glove compartment and pull out the storage container. The fuse block is at the back of the container opening. Spare fuses and a removal tool are stored in the glove compartment lid under a plastic cover.

Various circuit breakers are used through out the electrical system. The breakers are designed to "trip" when an overload is placed on the system. The breaker automatically resets when the overload is removed. The majority of the breakers are located within the fuse block.

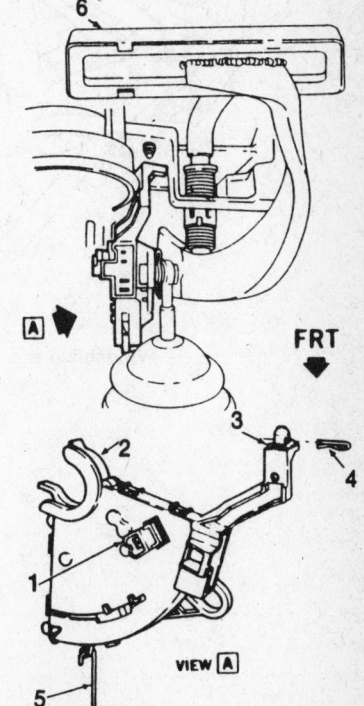

1. Cruise control connector
2. Switch assembly
3. Wave washer
4. Retainer clip
5. Wire hook
6. Brake pedal

Stoplight switch mounting and removal

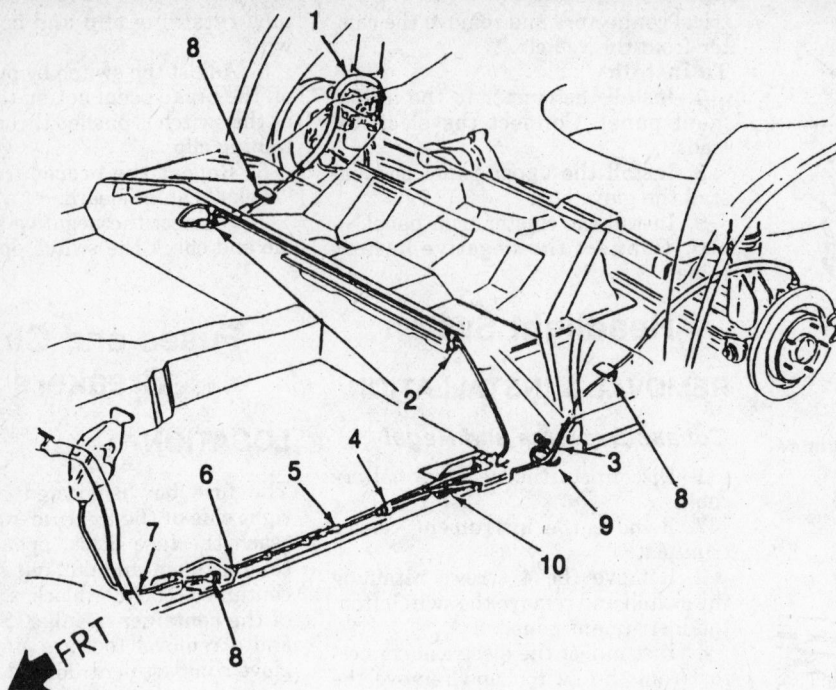

1. Right rear cable
   assembly
2. Bolt/screw
3. Left rear cable
   assembly
4. Equalizer
5. Retainer
6. Nut
7. Front cable assembly
8. Bracket
9. Brake cable support
10. Spring

Parking brake cable routing

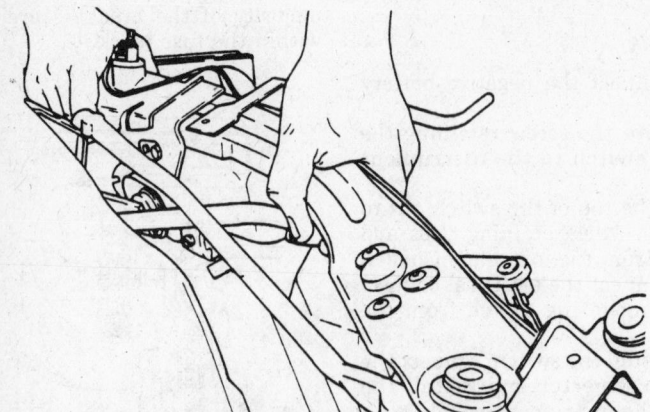

Windshield wiper module removal

Unit Repair Sections

29 General Maintenance

Introduction

Routine maintenance is probably the most important part of automobile care and the easiest to neglect. A regular program aimed at monitoring essential systems ensures that all components are in good and safe working order, and can prevent small problems from developing into major headaches. Routine maintenance also pays off big dividends in keeping major repair costs at a minimum and extending the life of the car.

The vehicle owner's manual includes a maintenance schedule indicating service intervals in numbers of months or thousands of miles. This schedule should always be followed. We have provided in this section a guide to service intervals based on an averaging of manufacturer's recommendations. In most cases the suggested interval offered here will be close to that given by the manufacturer of your car, but the manufacturer's schedule should always take precedence.

We have divided the maintenance work to be done into three categories: Under Hood, Under Car, and Exterior. The checks in each section require only a few minutes of attention every few weeks and the services to be performed can be easily accomplished in a morning. The most important part of any maintenance program is regularity. The few minutes or occasional morning spent on these seemingly trivial tasks will forestall or eliminate major problems later.

Under Hood Maintenance

AUTOMATIC TRANSMISSION, AUTOMATIC TRANSAXLE

The fluid level in the automatic transmission or transaxle should be checked every three months or 6000 miles. All automatic transmissions have a dipstick for fluid level checks.

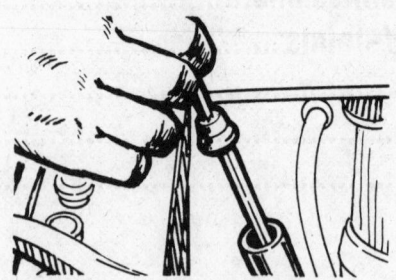

Check the automatic transmission fluid level with the dipstick provided

1. Drive the car until it is at normal operating temperature. The level should not be checked immediately after the car has been driven for a long time at high speed, or in city traffic in hot weather; in those cases, the transmission should be given a half hour to cool down.
2. Stop the car, apply the parking brake, then shift slowly through all gear positions, ending in Park. Leave the engine running.

3. Remove the dipstick, wipe it clean, then reinsert it, pushing it fully home.
4. Pull the dipstick again and, holding it horizontally, read the fluid level.
5. Cautiously feel the end of the dipstick to determine the temperature. Most dipsticks are marked with both cool and hot levels. If the fluid is not up to the correct level, more will have to be added.

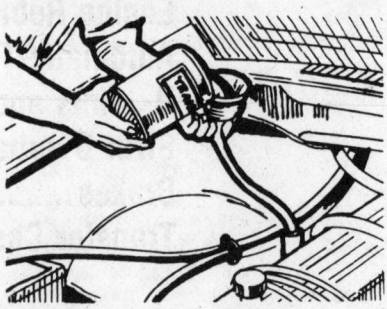

Fill the automatic transmission through the dipstick tube

NOTE: On General Motors Citation, Omega, Phoenix, Skylark, Cavalier, Cimarron, J2000, Celebrity, Cierra and 6000 models, the "Cold" level marks (dimples) are above the "Hot" level area.

6. Fluid is added through the dipstick tube. You will probably need the aid of a spout or a long-necked funnel. Be sure that whatever you pour through is perfectly clean and dry. Fluid recommendations can be found in the owner's manual or the Auto-

matic Transmission Unit Repair Section in this book. Add fluid slowly and in small amounts, checking the level frequently between additions. Do not overfill, which will cause foaming, fluid loss, slippage, and possible transmission damage.

BATTERY

Fluid Level (Except "Maintenance Free" Batteries)

Check the battery electrolyte level at least once a month, or more often in hot weather or during periods of extended car operation. The level can be checked through the case on translucent polypropylene batteries; the cell caps must be removed on other models. The electrolyte level in each cell should be kept filled to the split ring inside, or the line marked on the outside of the case.

If the level is low add only distilled water or colorless, odorless drinking water through the opening until the level is correct. Each cell is completely separate from the others, so each must be checked and filled individually.

If water is added in freezing weather, the car should be driven several miles to allow the water to mix with the electrolyte. Otherwise, the battery could freeze.

Specific Gravity (Except "Maintenance Free" Batteries)

At least once a year, check the specific gravity of the battery. It should be between 1.20 and 1.26 at room temperature. See the "Charging and Starting Systems" Section in this book for details.

Cables ana Clamps

Once a year, the battery terminals and the cable clamps should be cleaned. Loosen the clamps and remove the cables, negative cable first. On batteries with posts on top, the use of a puller specially made for the purpose is recommended. These are inexpensive, and available in auto parts stores. Side terminal battery cables are secured with a bolt.

Clean the cable clamps and the battery terminal with a wire brush, until all corrosion, grease, etc. is removed and the metal is shiny. It is especially important to clean the inside of the clamp thoroughly, since a small deposit of foreign material or oxidation there will prevent a sound electrical connection and inhibit either starting or charging. Special tools are available for cleaning these parts, one type for conventional batteries and another type for side terminal batteries.

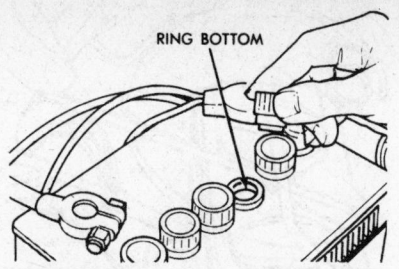

Fill the battery cell to the bottom of the split ring

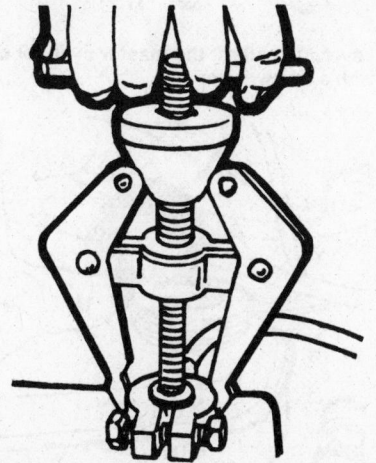

Use a puller to remove the clamp on post-type batteries

Clean the clamp with a wire brush

Before installing the cables, loosen the battery hold-down clamp or strap, remove the battery and check the battery tray. Clear it of any debris, and check it for soundness. Rust should be wire brushed away, and the metal given a coat of anti-rust paint. Replace the battery and tighten the hold-down clamp or strap securely, but be careful not to overtighten, which will crack the battery case.

After the clamps and terminals are clean, reinstall the cables, negative cable last; do not hammer on the clamps to install. Tighten the clamps securely, but do not distort them. Give

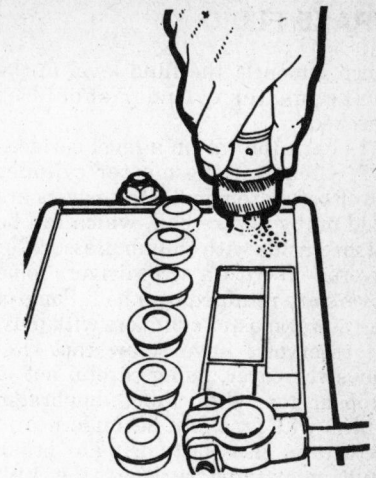

The posts are easily cleaned with a wire brush, or the battery post tool shown

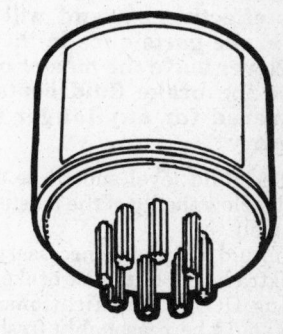

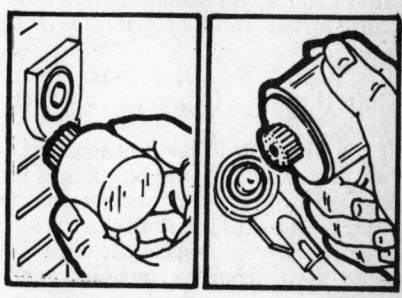

A special tool is required to clean the terminals and clamps on side terminal batteries

the clamps and terminals a thin external coat of grease after installation, to retard corrosion.

Check the cables at the same time that the terminals are cleaned. If the cable insulation is cracked or broken, or if the ends are frayed, the cable should be replaced with a new cable of the same length and gauge.

CAUTION

Keep flame or sparks away from the battery; it gives off explosive hydrogen gas. Battery electrolyte contains sulphuric acid. If you should splash any on your skin or in your eyes, flush the affected area with plenty of clear water; if it lands in your eyes, get medical help immediately.

BRAKE FLUID

Once a month, the fluid level in the brake master cylinder should be checked.

1. Park the car on a level surface.

2. Clean off the master cylinder cover before removal. Most covers are held on by a wire bail, which can be pushed aside with thumb pressure, or levered off with a screwdriver. Some covers are retained by a bolt. Some of the newer master cylinders with plastic reservoirs have screw caps. Remove the cover, being careful not to drop or tear the rubber diaphragm which will probably be underneath. Be careful also not to drip any brake fluid on painted surfaces; the stuff eats paint.

NOTE: Brake fluid absorbs moisture from the air, which reduces effectiveness and will corrode brake parts once in the system. Never leave the master cylinder or the brake fluid container uncovered for any longer than necessary.

3. The fluid level should be about $\frac{1}{4}$ inch below the lip of the master cylinder well.

4. If fluid addition is necessary, use only extra heavy duty disc brake fluid meeting DOT 3 specifications. The fluid should be reasonably fresh, because brake fluid deteriorates with age.

5. Replace the cover, making sure that the diaphragm is correctly seated.

If the brake fluid level is constantly low, the system should be checked for leaks. However, it is normal for the fluid level to fall gradually as the disc brake pads wear; expect the fluid level to drop about $\frac{1}{8}$ inch for every 10,000 miles of wear.

BELT TENSION ADJUSTMENT

Every six months or 12,000 miles, check the water pump, alternator, power steering pump, air pump, and air conditioning compressor drive belts for proper tension. Also look for signs of wear, fraying, separation, glazing and so on, and replace the belts as required.

Belt tension should be checked with a gauge made for the purpose. If a gauge is not available, tension can be checked with moderate thumb pressure applied to the belt at its longest span midway between pulleys. If the belt has a free span less than twelve inches, it should deflect approximately $\frac{1}{8}$–$\frac{1}{4}$ inch. If the span is longer

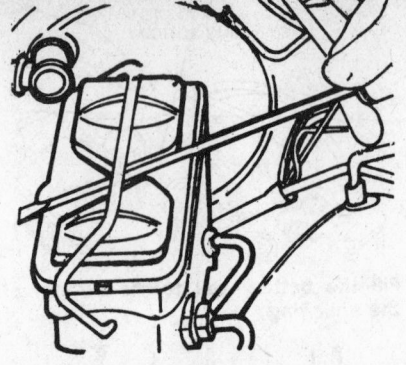

Lever the bail off the master cylinder cap with a screwdriver

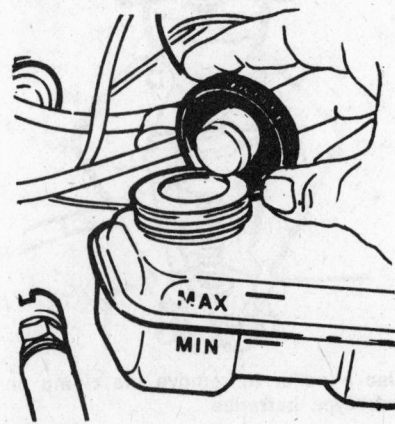

Screw caps are used on some master cylinders

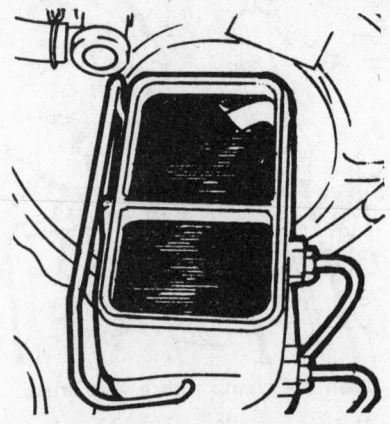

Proper brake fluid level

than twelve inches, deflection can range between $\frac{1}{8}$–$\frac{3}{8}$ inches.

NOTE: On cars except American Motors models which use a one-piece "serpentine" belt to drive all accessories, belt tension is automatically adjusted. On cars which have two "serpentine" belts, or one "serpentine" belt as well as conventional V-belts, and on all American Motors models with the "serpentine" belt, belt

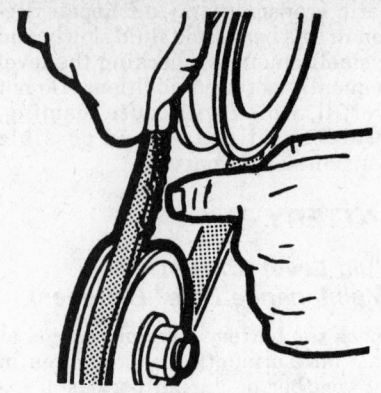

Check the belts for wear

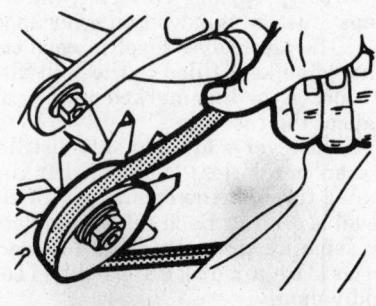

Check the belt tension at the middle of the longest span between pulleys

tensions usually must be checked and adjusted. Belt tension is higher on "serpentine" belts and cannot be tested with thumb pressure. Some Ford models (Thunderbird/XR-7 with AOD transmission) require special tools for adjustment. American Motors "serpentine" belts are adjusted at the alternator.

To adjust or replace belts:

1. Loosen the driven accessory's pivot and mounting bolts. Some air conditioning compressor belts are tensioned by an idler pulley; in this case, loosen the idler pulley and use a $\frac{1}{2}$ in. drive ratchet in the square hole provided to lever the idler pulley up or down.

2. Move the accessory toward or away from the engine until the tension is correct. You can use a wooden hammer handle or broomstick as a lever, but do not use anything metallic.

3. Tighten the bolts and recheck the tension. If new belts have been installed, run the engine for a few minutes, then recheck and readjust as necessary.

NOTE: If the driven component has two drive belts, the belts should be replaced in pairs to maintain proper tension.

It is better to have belts too loose

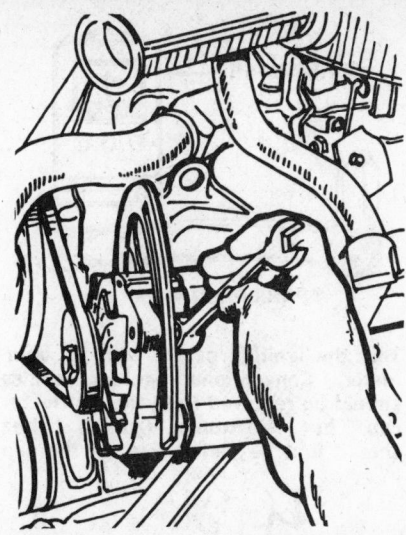

To either adjust or remove a belt, loosen the driven component's adjusting bolt

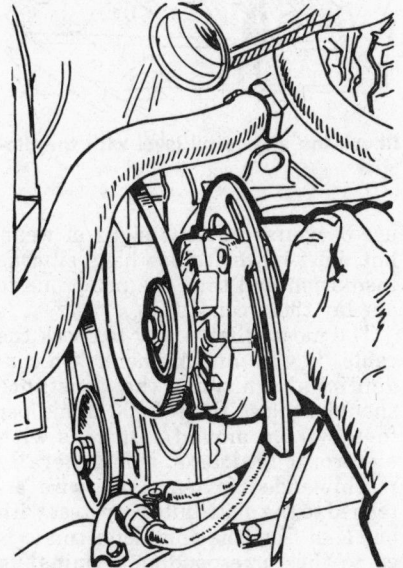

Push the component toward the engine to remove the belt

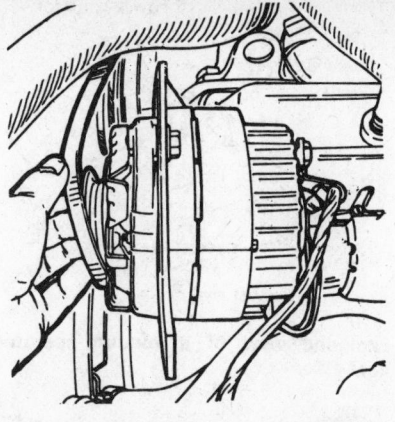

Slip the replacement belt over the pulley

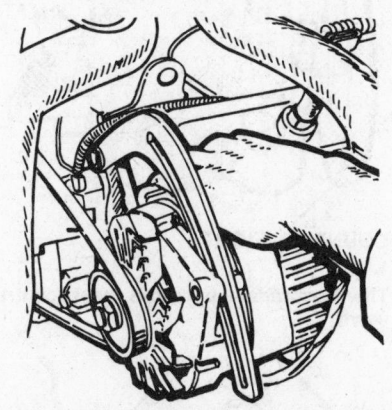

Pull outwards on the component to tension the belt, then tighten the bolts; recheck the belt tension after tightening

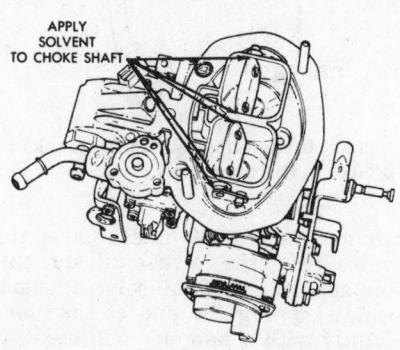

APPLY SOLVENT TO CHOKE SHAFT

Use a spray solvent on the choke shaft, but do not apply any lubricants

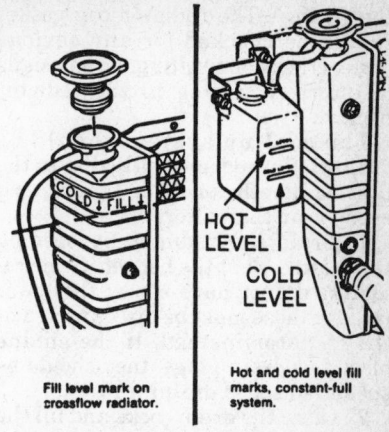

Fill level mark on crossflow radiator.

Hot and cold level fill marks, constant-full system.

Proper coolant level is about one inch below the radiator neck, or between the lines on the recovery tank

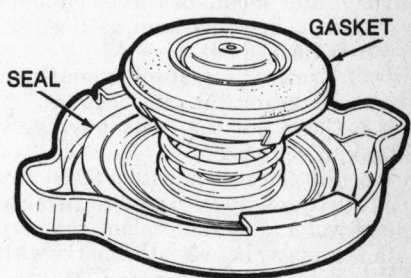

GASKET

SEAL

Check the radiator cap gasket and sealing surface

CAUTION

To avoid injury when working with a hot engine, cover the radiator cap with a thick cloth. Wear a heavy glove to protect your hand. Turn the radiator cap slowly to the first stop, and allow all the pressure to vent (indicated when the hissing noise stops). When the pressure has been released, remove the cap the rest of the way.

---

than too tight, because overtight belts will lead to bearing failure, particularly in the water pump and alternator. However, loose belts place an extremely high impact load on the driven component due to the whipping action of the belt.

CARBURETOR AND CHOKE LINKAGE

Every 12 months or 6000 miles, examine the carburetor linkage and choke plate for free movement. The choke plate action can generally be freed, if necessary, with the application of a solvent made for the purpose to the ends of the choke shaft. This solvent will also clean grease and dirt from the throttle linkage.

COOLING SYSTEM

Once a month, the engine coolant level should be checked. On cars without a coolant recovery system, this should only be done when the engine is cold.

Remove the radiator cap, the coolant level should be about one inch below the radiator filler neck.

On cars with a coolant recovery tank, coolant should be visible within the tank; as long as the coolant is between the markings on the tank, the level is correct.

If coolant is needed, a 50/50 mix of ethylene glycol-based antifreeze and water should always be used, both winter and summer. This is imperative on cars with air conditioning; without the antifreeze, the heater core could freeze when the air conditioning is used. Add coolant to the radiator if the car does not have a coolant recovery system. Add coolant to the recovery tank on cars so equipped.

The radiator hoses and clamps and the radiator cap should be checked at the same time as the coolant level. Hoses which are brittle, cracked, or swollen should be replaced. Clamps should be checked for tightness (screwdriver tight only; do not allow the clamp to cut into the hose or crush the fitting). The radiator cap gasket should be checked for any obvious tears, cracks or swelling, or any signs of incorrect seating in the radiator neck.

The cooling system should be drained, flushed and refilled after the first 24 months or 24,000 miles, and every year thereafter.

1. Drain the radiator by opening the drain cock at the bottom. Some radiators do not have these; the lower radiator hose must be disconnected at the radiator instead. If the engine block has drain plugs, they should be opened to speed draining.

2. Close the drain cocks and fill the system with clear water. A cooling system flushing additive can be used, if desired.

3. Run the engine until it is hot. The heater should be turned on to its maximum heat position so that the core is flushed out.

4. Drain the system, then flush with water until it runs clear.

5. Clean out the coolant recovery tank, if equipped.

6. Fill the system with a 50/50 mix of ethylene glycol-based antifreeze and water. Fill the coolant recovery tank midway between the marks with this mixture also (except G.M. cars, which should be filled to the "Full Cold" mark).

7. Run the engine until it is hot, then let it cool and top up the radiator or coolant recovery tank as necessary with the anti-freeze/water mixture.

HEAT RISER

The heat riser is a thermostatically or vacuum operated valve in the exhaust manifold. (Not all cars have one.) It closes when the engine is warming up, to direct hot exhaust gases to the intake manifold, in order to preheat the incoming fuel/air mixture. If it sticks open, the result will be frequent stalling during warmup, especially in cold and damp weather. If it sticks shut, the result will be a rough idle after the engine is warm.

NOTE: Some 1981 and later GM engines are equipped with an electrically heated ceramic grid mounted below the carburetor which takes the place of a heat riser.

The heat riser should move freely. It can be checked easily when the engine is cold by giving the counterweight on the valve shaft a twirl, or pulling the vacuum rod to open and shut the valve. If the valve is sticking or binding, a quick shot of solvent made for the purpose will free it up. This solvent should be applied every

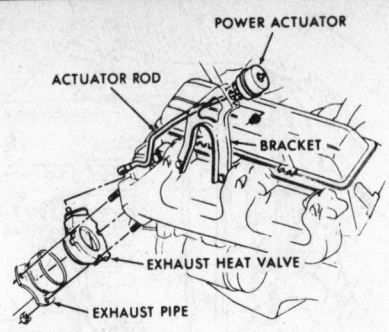

Exploded view of a vacuum-operated heat riser

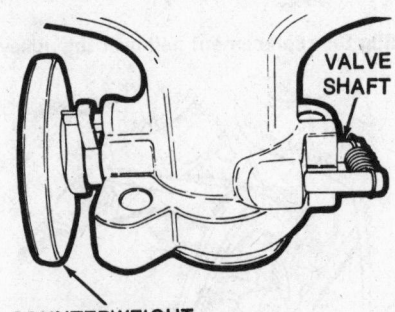

Thermostatically-operated heat control valve

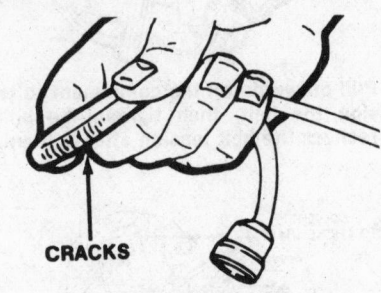

Inspect the ignition cables for cracks or breaks in the insulation

six months or 6000 miles to keep the valve free. If the valve is still stuck after application of the solvent, sometimes rapping the end of the shaft lightly with a hammer will break it loose. Otherwise, the components will have to be removed for further repairs.

IGNITION WIRES

The ignition system receives regular attention in the form of a tune-up, and thus is not covered here. But one of the most commonly overlooked components is the ignition cable, or spark plug wire.

Although they rarely show any visible signs of deterioration, the ignition cables should be checked at every tune-up, and replaced every 50,000 miles. Cracking and embrittlement

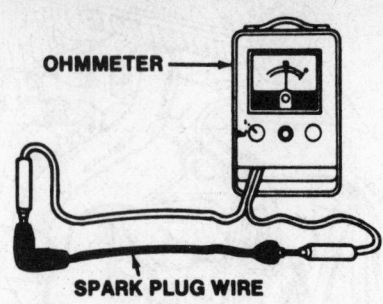

Test the ignition cables with an ohmmeter. Conventional ignition cables should be removed from the distributor cap, but electronic ignition wires should first be tested through the cap

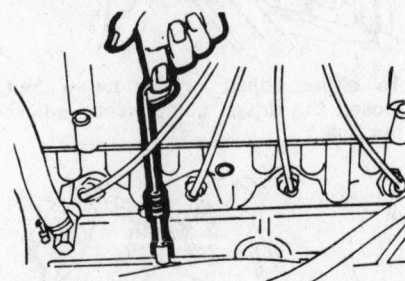

Check the engine oil level with the dipstick

are of course obvious signs of wear, but most newer cables have silicone insulation and thus are not prone to display these conditions.

The most reliable way to check the cables is with an ohmmeter. On conventional ignitions, the resistance should be less than 7,000 ohms per foot (wire removed). On cars with electronic ignitions, it is generally recommended to leave the wire attached to the distributor cap, test with one lead from the ohmmeter connected to the corresponding terminal in the distributor cap, the other lead touched to the disconnected end of the cable at the spark plug. Then, if resistance seems close to the limit, remove the wire from the cap and retest. In general, the spark plug wires on electronic ignitions should be replaced if the total resistance is over 36,000 ohms. (50,000 ohms on Ford and Chrysler products).

Always replace the cables with new ones of the same type. Replace the wires one at a time, working from the longest to the shortest.

OIL LEVEL

The engine oil should be checked on a regular basis, ideally at each fuel stop, or once a week. It is best to check when the engine is at operating temperature, but checking the level immediately after shutting off the engine will give a false reading, because all of the oil will not yet have drained back into the crankcase. The car should be parked on a level surface to obtain an accurate reading.

1. Remove the oil dipstick. Wipe it clean, then replace it, seating it firmly.

2. Remove the dipstick again and hold it horizontally to prevent the oil from running. The level should be between the "Add" and "Full" marks on the dipstick. The dipstick may be marked "Add" and "Safe", or may have lines scribed on it; in any case, the oil level should be above the lower marking.

3. If the oil is below the lower mark, enough oil should be added to the engine to raise the level to the upper mark. The markings are usually spaced so that one-half to one quart of oil will raise the level from the "Add" mark to the "Full" mark. Oil is added through the capped opening in the valve cover. Only oils labeled SE or SF should be used; select a viscosity that will be compatible with the temperatures expected until the next drain interval.

NOTE: The diesel engines used in GM cars require the use of SF/CC or SF/CD type oils only. Do not use oil which is rated for SE or SF use only, or which is rated for CD use. Do not use the oil if the rating CD appears anywhere on the can, either alone or in combination with ratings other than SF, such as SE/CD. The use of CD type oil will void the manufacturer's warranty, and may cause expensive engine damage and leakage.

4. Replace the dipstick, then check the level again after any additions of oil. Be careful not to overfill, which will lead to leakage and seal damage.

POWER STEERING

The power steering fluid level is checked with a dipstick inserted into the pump reservoir. The dipstick may be attached to the reservoir cap, or inserted into a tube on the pump body. The level should be checked at every oil change. On all cars except Ford products, the level can be checked with the fluid either warm or cold; on Fords, the engine must be at operating temperature.

1. On Ford products, with the engine hot and idling, turn the steering wheel back and forth to the full right and full left stops several times, then center the wheels and shut off the engine.

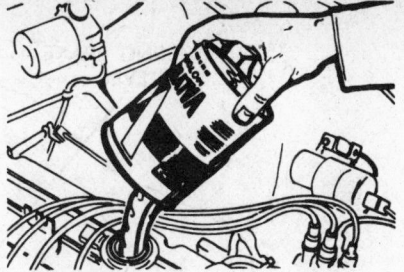

Add oil through the valve cover

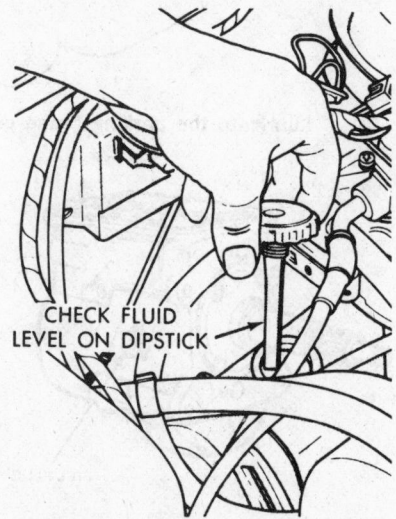

CHECK FLUID LEVEL ON DIPSTICK

The power steering level is checked with the dipstick installed in the reservoir

2. On all cars, with the engine off, pull or unscrew the dipstick and check the level. If the engine is warm, the level should be between the "Hot" and "Cold" marks on the dipstick; on Fords, the level should be between the "Cold Full" and "Hot Full" marks. If the engine is cold, the fluid should be between the "Add" and "Cold" marks; this does not apply to Ford products.

3. If the level is low, add power steering fluid until correct. Be careful not to overfill, which will cause fluid loss and seal damage.

WINDSHIELD WASHER FLUID

Check the fluid level in the windshield washer tank at every oil level check. The fluid can be mixed in a 50% solution with water, if desired, as long as temperatures remain above freezing. Below freezing, the fluid should be used full strength. Never add engine coolant antifreeze to the washer fluid, because it will damage the car's paint.

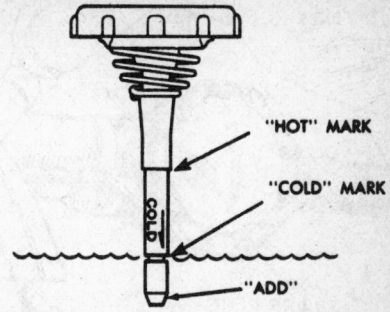

"HOT" MARK

"COLD" MARK

"ADD"

Power steering dipstick markings, typical of all types except Ford

Under Car

AXLE

The fluid level in the drive axle should be checked every 12 months or 12,000 miles. On the front wheel drive Omni, Horizon, Aries, Reliant LeBaron and Dodge 400 with automatic transmission, the drive axle lubricant is separate from the automatic fluid and must be checked separately. The level can be checked through the fill plug in the drive axle housing.

On the American Motors Eagle, SX/4 and Kammback, both drive axles should be checked. Both assemblies have fill plugs for this purpose.

1. With the car parked on a level surface, remove the filler plug. The plug can be found either in the rear cover of the differential, or on the front of the pinion housing.

2. If lubricant dribbles out when the plug is removed, the level is correct. Otherwise, stick in your finger (watch out for sharp threads); the fluid should be even with or just a little below the filler hole.

3. If lubricant is needed, use SAE 80W-90 GL-5 gear oil (SAE 80W GL-5 in very cold climates) to fill standard axles. Limited slip axles require a special lubricant, available in auto parts stores. The Omni, Horizon, Aries, Reliant Dodge 400 and LeBaron drive axles should be filled with DEXRON II ATF fluid.

4. When the level is correct, install the plug and tighten until snug. Do not overtighten.

Drive axles should be drained and refilled according to the manufacturer's maintenance schedule, usually found in the owner's manual. If the unit is used in severe driving conditions (trailer towing, etc.) the lubricant should be changed more often. Some later model drive axles do not require regular draining and refilling. Refer to the owner's manual for information on this subject. The axle may be drained by removing the drain

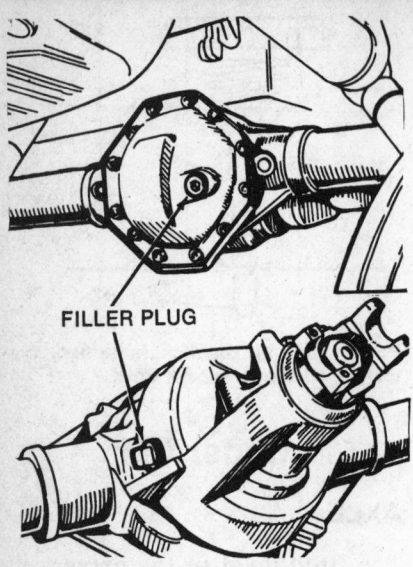

FILLER PLUG

Rear axle filler plug locations

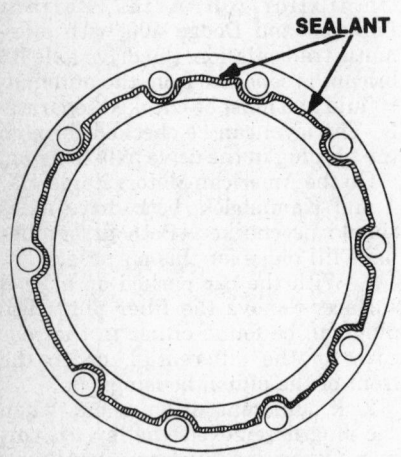

SEALANT

Apply a bead of silicone sealer to the rear cover if no gasket is used

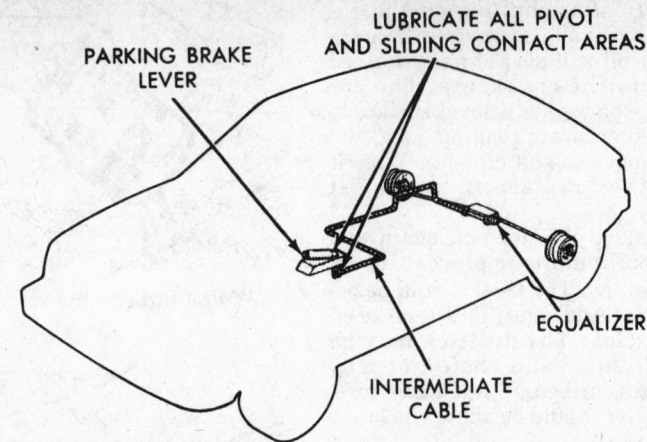

PARKING BRAKE LEVER

LUBRICATE ALL PIVOT AND SLIDING CONTACT AREAS

EQUALIZER

INTERMEDIATE CABLE

Lubricate the parking brake cable with white waterproof grease

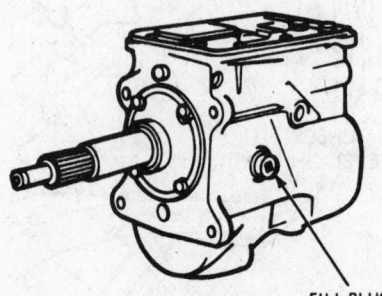

FILL PLUG

MANUAL TRANSMISSION
FILL TO BOTTOM OF FILLER HOLE WITH VEHICLE ON LEVEL GROUND.

Typical manual transmission filler plug location

plug at the bottom of the axle housing, if present. Otherwise the rear cover (if equipped) must be removed or a suction gun used through the filler hole. Always use silicone sealer or a gasket when re-installing the rear cover. Run sealer around the insides of the bolt holes. Tighten the bolts a few turns at a time in a crisscross pattern.

EXHAUST SYSTEM

The exhaust system should be checked twice a year for general soundness. Inspect the pipes for holes, broken welds, leaking seams, or loose connections. Leaks at connections can sometimes be successfully repaired with the use of a commercial exhaust pipe sealer, but holes or breaks warrant replacement of the part. The exhaust pipe hangers and straps should be examined for any breaks or cracks;

replace these as necessary. Some slight cracking of rubber hangers is normal, but deep cracks or cuts are cause for replacement.

CAUTION
Check the exhaust system only when it is cold. The temperature on an exhaust system using a catalytic converter can reach 1000°F after only a short period of engine operation.

MANUAL TRANSMISSION OR MANUAL TRANSAXLE

The fluid level in the manual transmission (or transaxle on front wheel drive cars) should be checked twice a year, or every 6000 miles.
1. Park the car on a level surface. The transmission should be cool to the touch.
2. Remove the filler plug from the side of the transmission or transaxle. If lubricant trickles out as the plug is removed, the fluid level is correct. If not, stick in your finger (watch out for

sharp threads); the lubricant should be right up to the edge of the filler hole.
3. If lubricant is needed, use SAE 80W-90 GL-5 gear lubricant (SAE 80W GL-5 in extremely cold climates) in manual transmission.
Front wheel drive transaxles use different lubricants. The Omni and Horizon with the A412 transaxle (starter on the radiator side of the engine) require GL-4 hypoid gear lubricant; the same SAE viscosities apply (80W-90 or 80W; 75W in temperatures below -30°F). GL-5 classification lubricants are specifically not recommended. Omnis and Horizons with the A460 transaxle (starter on the firewall side of the engine), and all Aries, Reliant LeBaron and Dodge 400 models use DEXRON II automatic transmission fluid.
The front wheel drive Citation, Omega, Phoenix, Skylark Cavalier, J2000, Cimarron, Celebrity, Cierra and 6000 require DEXRON II automatic transmission fluid. The use of a manual transmission lubricant is specifically not recommended.
The Ford Escort, EXP, and Mercury Lynx and LN-7 use Ford Type F automatic transmission fluid. The use of a manual transmission lubricant is specifically not recommended.
4. When the level is correct, install the filler plug and tighten until snug.

PARKING BRAKE LINKAGE
The parking brake cable assembly should be inspected twice a year for fraying, kinks, and binding. A smooth white waterproof lubricant should be applied at the same time to all pivot points and areas in sliding contact.

SUSPENSION LUBRICATION
Depending on the year of manufac-

ture, there may be as many as twelve grease fittings on the suspension parts, or as few as two. Typical locations for grease nipples are on the ball joints, control arm pivot points, steering linkage, and the tie-rod ends.

Lubricate these fittings with a small hand operated grease gun filled with EP chassis lubricant. Pump grease into the fitting slowly, until it begins to ooze out around the joint, or until the grease begins to expand the rubber boot around the fitting. Be extremely careful not to rupture any seals or boots, as this will lead to lubricant loss and contamination of the parts involved.

Occasionally, the grease nipples may become clogged with dirt or hardened grease. If so, unscrew them with a wrench of the proper size and clean them out with solvent. When reinstalled, they may be covered with plastic caps made for the purpose, or a piece of aluminum foil.

The chassis and suspension parts should be lubricated once a year, or every 7500 miles, whichever comes first.

TRANSFER CASE

If you have a four-wheel drive AMC car, you should check the transfer case lubricant level every 5000 miles.

1. Park the car on a level surface.
2. Check the build date tag on the rear of the transfer case.
3. If the transfer case was built after March 1980, the fill plug will be at location "A" in the illustration. Remove the fill plug. The lubricant should be right up to the edge of the filler hole. Check and correct as necessary.
4. If the transfer case was built before March, 1980, the filler plug may be in any one of the four locations shown in the illustration. Check to see which one you have, then remove the filler plug. Use a length of wire to measure the distance from the bottom edge of the fill hole to the lubricant. The correct distance depends on the location of the hole:
   • "A" 0.56 inch
   • "B" 1.13 inch
   • "C" 1.20 inch
   • "D" 0.56 inch
5. The correct fluid to use is 10W-30 SE or SF motor oil. Capacity is 4.0 pints, regardless of when the transfer case was built. Some early owner's manuals may have listed the capacity as 3.0 pints, but this is incorrect; revised publications call for a capacity of 4.0 pints.

The transfer case should be drained and refilled every 15,000 miles. The drain plug is located at the lower edge

of the rear face of the case. Installation torque for the plugs is 18 ft. lbs. The case is made from aluminum, so this figure should not be exceeded.

Exterior

DRAIN HOLES AND UNDERBODY

Most cars have drain holes spaced along the lower edge of the rocker panels and doors. These holes should be cleared of any debris or rust twice a year. A small screwdriver can be used to open plugged drain holes.

Every spring, the underbody should be flushed with clear water to remove deposits of mud, road salt, and debris. It is advisable to loosen any packed-in sediment before flushing to assure a more thorough cleaning.

HINGES AND LOCKS

Once a year, the door, hood, and trunk hinges, and all locks should be lubricated to ensure smooth operation. The hinge points should be lightly oiled. Lock cylinders may be easily lubricated with a shot of silicone spray directed into the keyhole. Silicone lubricant also works well on the door latch mechanisms, and keeps the door, trunk, and window weather seals pliable when applied in a light film.

TIRES

Tires should be checked weekly for proper air pressure. A chart, located either in the glove compartment or on the driver's or passenger's door, gives the recommended inflation pressures. Maximum fuel economy and tire life will result if the pressure is maintained at the highest figure given on the chart.

Pressures should be checked before driving since pressure can increase as much as six pounds per square inch (psi) due to heat buildup. It is a good idea to have your own accurate pressure gauge, because not all gauges on service station air pumps can be trusted. When checking pressures, do not neglect the spare tire. Note that some spare tires require pressures considerably higher than those used in the other tires.

While you are about the task of checking air pressure, inspect the tire treads for cuts, bruises and other damage. Check the air valves to be sure that they are tight. Replace any missing valve caps.

Check the tires for uneven wear that might indicate the need for front end alignment or tire rotation. Tires

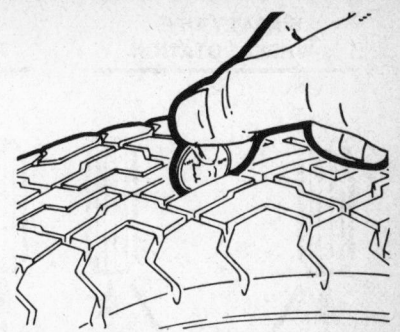

Tire tread depth can be checked with a penny. If the top of Lincoln's head is visible, the tires are due for replacement

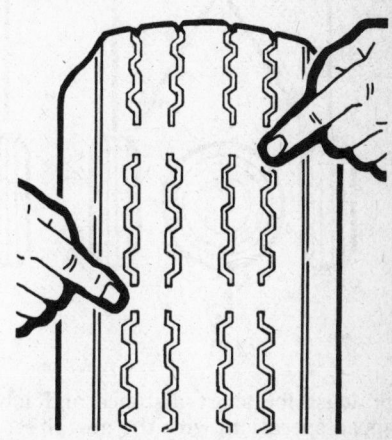

Tread wear indicators will appear as a band across the tire when the tread has worn out.

should be replaced when a tread wear indicator appears as a solid band across the tread.

When buying new tires, give some thought to the following points, especially if you are considering a switch to larger tires or a different profile series:

1. All four tires must be of the same construction type. This rule cannot be violated. Radial, bias, and bias-belted tires must not be mixed.
2. The wheels should be the correct width for the tire. Tire dealers have charts of tire and rim compatibility. A mismatch will cause sloppy handling and rapid tire wear. The tread width should match the rim width (inside bead to inside bead) within an inch. For radial tires, the rim width should be 80% or less of the tire (not tread) width.
3. The height (mounted diameter) of the new tires can change speedometer accuracy, engine speed at a given road speed, fuel mileage, acceleration, and ground clearance. Tire manufacturers furnish full measurement specifications.
4. The spare tire should be usable,

BIAS PLY TIRE 4-WHEEL ROTATION	BIAS PLY TIRE 5-WHEEL ROTATION	RADIAL PLY TIRES 4-WHEEL ROTATION	RADIAL PLY TIRES 5-WHEEL ROTATION

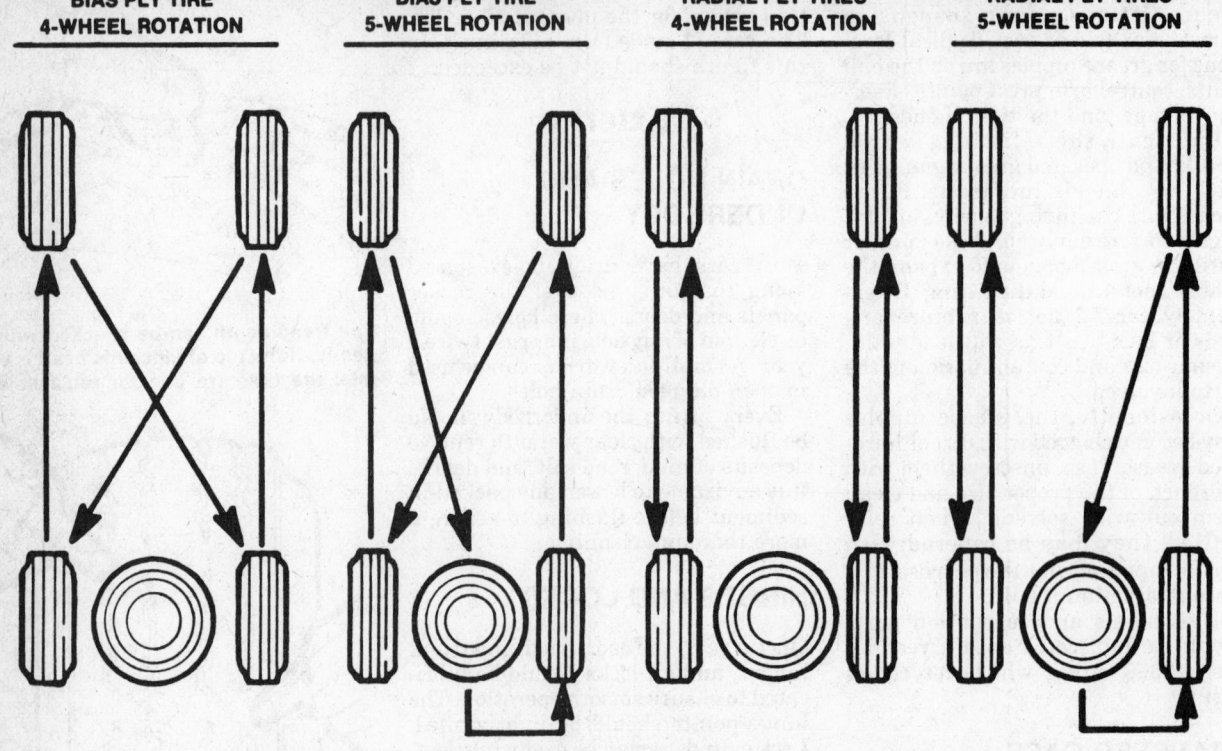

Tire rotation diagrams

at least for short distance and low speed operation, with the new tires.

5. There shouldn't be any body interference when loaded, on bumps, or in turns.

Tire Rotation

Tire rotation is recommended every 6000 miles or so, to obtain maximum tire wear. The pattern you use depends on whether or not your car has a usable spare. Radial tires should not be cross-switched (from one side of the car to the other); they last longer if their direction of rotation is not changed. Snow tires sometimes have directional arrows molded into the side of the carcass; the arrow shows the direction of rotation. They will wear very rapidly if the rotation is reversed. Studded tires will lose their studs if their rotational direction is reversed.

NOTE: Mark the wheel position or direction of rotation on radial tires or studded snow tires before removing them.

Storage

Store the tires at the proper inflation pressure if they are mounted on wheels. Keep them in a cool dry place, laid on their sides. If the tires are stored in the garage or basement, do not let them stand on a concrete floor; set them on strips of wood.

WINDSHIELD WIPERS AND WASHERS

For maximum effectiveness and longest element life, the windshield and wiper blades should be kept clean. Dirt, tree sap, road tar and so on will cause streaking, smearing and blade deterioration if left on the glass. It is advisable to wash the windshield carefully with a commercial glass cleaner at least once a month. Wipe off the rubber blades with the wet rag afterwards.

For access to the blades on wiper systems which park below the hood line, turn the ignition key to "On" and run the wipers to the center of the windshield. Shut the wipers off with the ignition key, not the wiper switch. Do not attempt to move the wipers by hand; damage to the motor and drive mechanism will result.

If the blades are found to be cracked, broken or torn, they should be replaced immediately. Replacement intervals will vary with usage, although ozone deterioration usually limits blade life to about one year. If the wiper pattern is smeared or streaked, or if the blade chatters across the glass, the elements should be replaced. It is easiest and most sensible to replace the elements in pairs.

There are basically three different types of refills, which differ in their method of replacement. One type has two release buttons, approximately one-third of the way up from the ends of the blade frame. Pushing the buttons down releases a lock and allows the rubber filler to be removed from the frame. The new filler slides back into the frame and locks in place.

The second type of refill has two metal tabs which are unlocked by squeezing them together. The rubber filler can then be withdrawn from the frame jaws. A new refill is installed by inserting the refill into the front frame jaws and sliding it rearward to engage the remaining frame jaws. There are usually four jaws; be certain when installing that the refill is engaged in all of them. At the end of its travel, the tabs will lock into place on the front jaws of the wiper blade frame.

The third type is a refill made from polycarbonate. The refill has a simple locking device at one end which flexes downward out of the groove into which the jaws of the holder fit, allowing easy release. By sliding the new refill through all the jaws and pushing through the slight resistance when it reaches the end of its travel, the refill will lock into position.

Regardless of the type of refill used, make sure that all of the frame jaws are engaged as the refill is pushed into place and locked. The metal blade holder and frame will scratch the glass if allowed to touch it.

TRICO

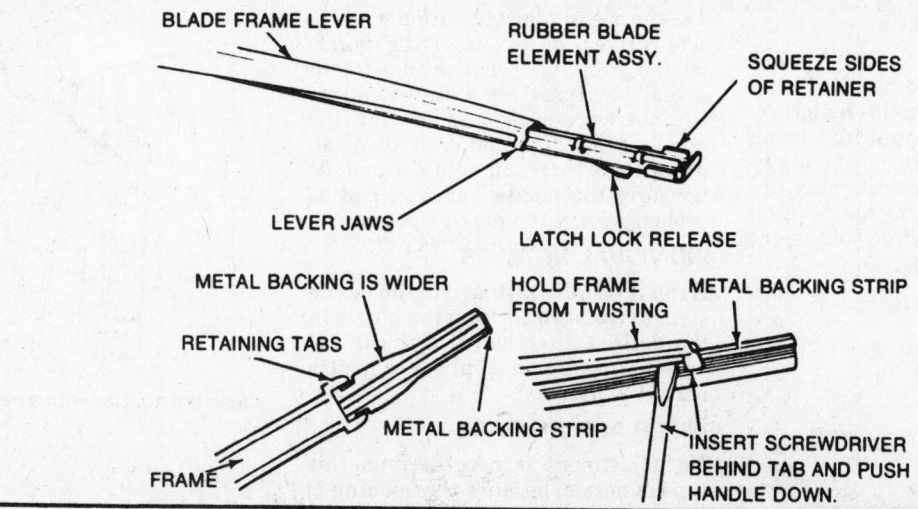

ANCO

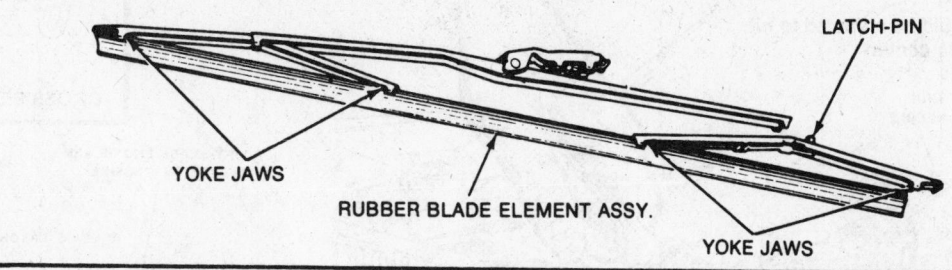

POLYCARBONATE

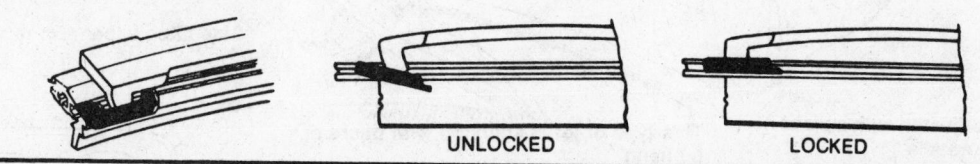

TRIDON

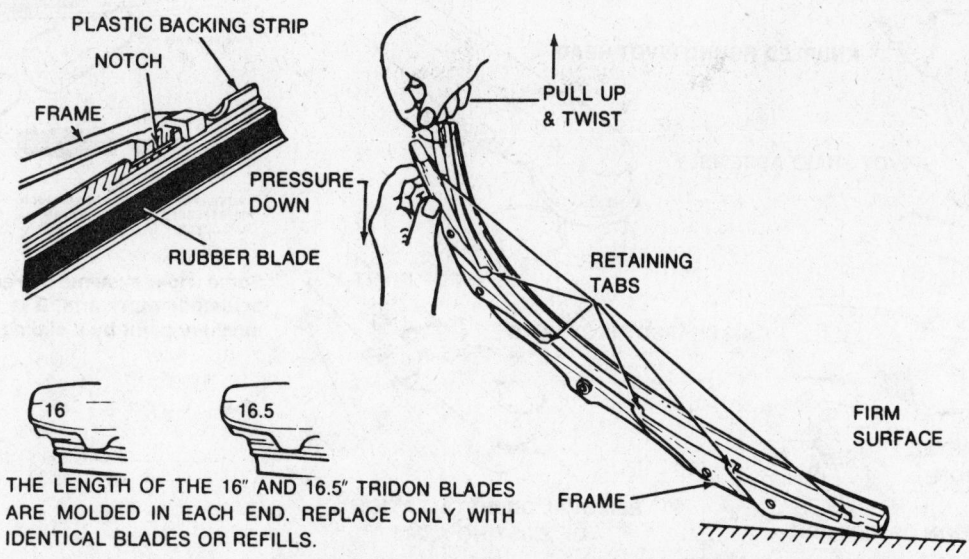

THE LENGTH OF THE 16" AND 16.5" TRIDON BLADES ARE MOLDED IN EACH END. REPLACE ONLY WITH IDENTICAL BLADES OR REFILLS.

Windshield wiper blade replacement methods

Washer Nozzle Adjustment

CENTERED SINGLE POST—NON-ADJUSTABLE NOZZLES

This type is usually located on the rear center of the hood panel, directly in front of the windshield. By loosening the body retaining nut from under the hood, the nozzle body can be turned to provide the best spray discharge to cover the windshield. Tighten the retaining nut while holding the nozzle body in position.

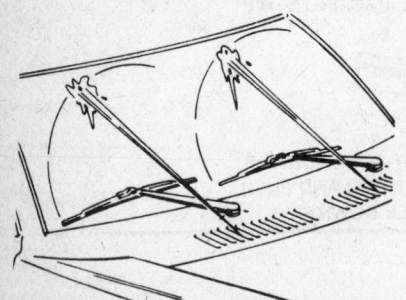

Washer nozzles should be adjusted to hit the windshield above center

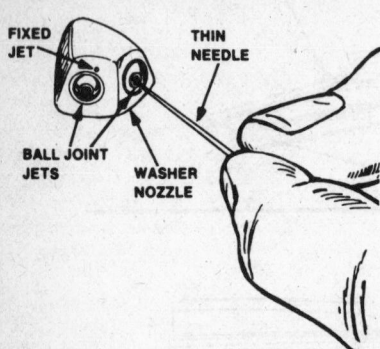

Some jets can be adjusted with a piece of fine wire or a thin needle

CENTERED SINGLE POST—ADJUSTABLE NOZZLES

This nozzle is adjusted with a wrench, screwdriver, or pliers. If the nozzle has no gripping area, the adjustment is made by inserting a stiff wire into the nozzle opening and moving the nozzle in the direction desired. When using the wire as an adjuster tool, do not force the nozzle; the wire can be broken within the nozzle opening.

INDIVIDUAL NOZZLES

A tab is usually fastened to the nozzle stem to assist in turning the nozzle in the desired direction. If a tab is not present, use a pair of pliers to gently move the nozzle.

WIPER ARM NOZZLES

No adjustment is necessary on this type of nozzle, because the opening is centered on the wiper arm and moves along with the arm.

This type of jet is adjusted with pliers or by hand

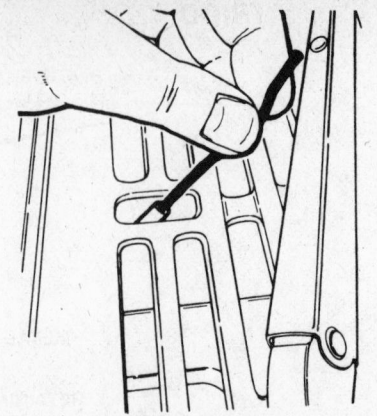

Clean the nozzles with a piece of fine wire

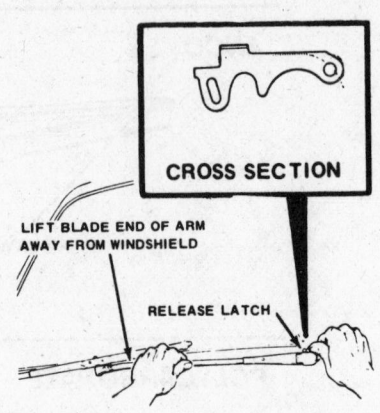

Side latch wiper arm replacement

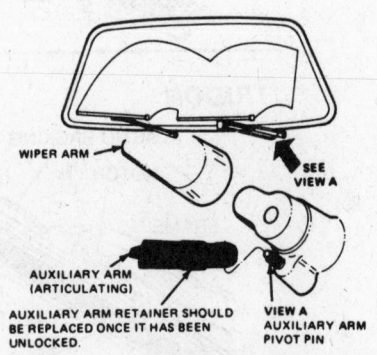

Some wiper systems use an auxiliary (articulated) wiper arm. It is secured to an auxiliary pivot by a sliding lock.

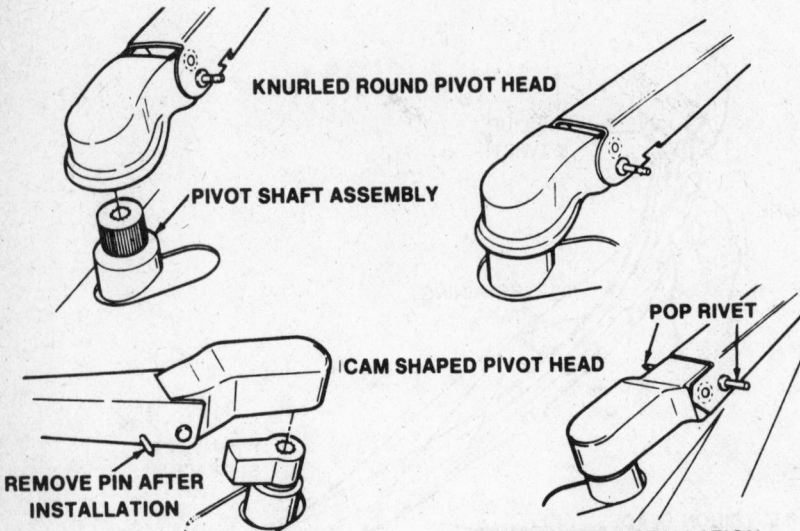

Pin and hole type wiper arm replacement

Diesel Maintenance 30

NOTE: Standard maintenance procedures are given here while component removal, installation and adjustment procedures are given in the appropriate car section.

How The Diesel Engine Works

Four-stroke diesels require four piston strokes for the complete cycle of actions, exactly like a gasoline engine. The difference lies in how the fuel mixture is ignited. A diesel engine does not rely on a conventional spark ignition to ignite the fuel mixture for the power stroke. Instead, a diesel relies on the heat produced by compressing air in the combustion chamber to ignite the fuel and produce a power stroke. This is known as a compression-ignition engine. No fuel enters the cylinder on the intake stroke, only air. At the end of the compression stroke, fuel is sprayed into the precombustion chamber (prechamber). The mixture ignites and spreads out into the main combustion chamber, forcing the piston downward (power stroke). The fuel/air mixture ignites because of the very high combustion chamber temperatures generated by the extraordinarily high compression ratios used in diesel engines. Typically, the compression ratios used in automotive diesels run anywhere from 16:1 to 23:1. A typical spark-ignition engine has a ratio of about 8:1. This is why a spark-ignition engine which contin-

ues to run after you have shut off the engine is said to be "dieseling". It is running on combustion chamber heat alone.

Designing an engine to ignite on its own combustion chamber heat poses certain problems. For instance, although a diesel engine has no need for a coil, spark plugs, or a distributor, it does need what are known as "glow plugs". These superficially resemble spark plugs, but are only used to warm the combustion chambers when the engine is cold. Without these plugs, cold starting would be impossible, due to the enormously high compression ratios and the characteristics of the diesel fuel itself.

All diesel engines use fuel injection, because unlike spark-ignited engines, the fuel cannot be drawn through the

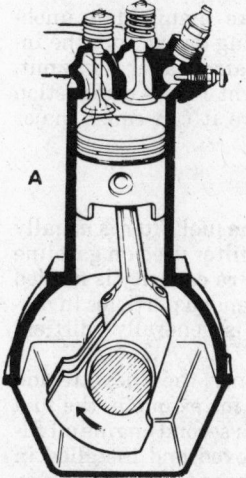 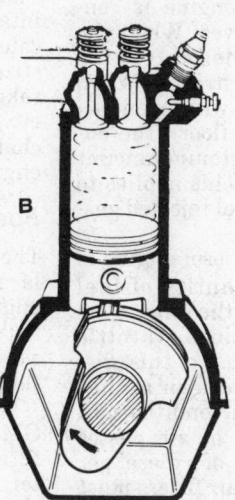 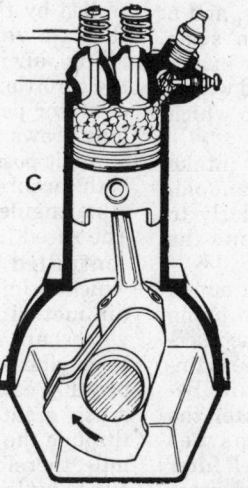 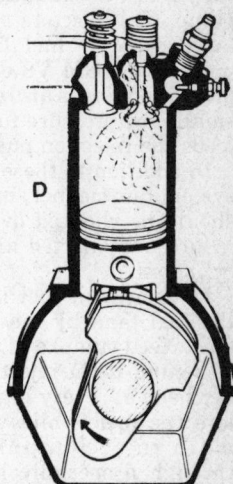

Cycles of a four-stroke cycle diesel engine. (A) Intake stroke: The downward movement of the piston draws air into the cylinder through the open intake valve. (B) Compression: The intake valve closes and the piston moves upward, compressing the air in the cylinder. (C) Ignition: While the piston is at approximately top dead center, fuel is injected into the cylinder. The superheated air (from compression) ignites the fuel, causing an explosion which forces the piston downward. (D) Exhaust: The piston begins moving upward, forcing the exhaust gas out of the cylinder, through the open exhaust valve.

intake tract and into the cylinders. The introduction of fuel into a diesel engine must be precisely timed so that each cylinder "fires" at the proper moment. Also, the fuel injection pressure (at the cylinder) must be great enough to overcome the high compression pressures, and properly atomize the fuel without the aid of a moving air mass (as in a carbureted gas engine). It is not uncommon for diesel engine fuel injection pressures to be set at 1500–1700 psi.

Diesel engines share many of their basic mechanical components with gasoline engines, though the cylinder block, head(s), crankshaft, connecting rods, pistons, etc. are manufactured to be much stronger for use in diesel engines. The additional strength of the components is necessary due to the very high cylinder pressure generated within the diesel engine.

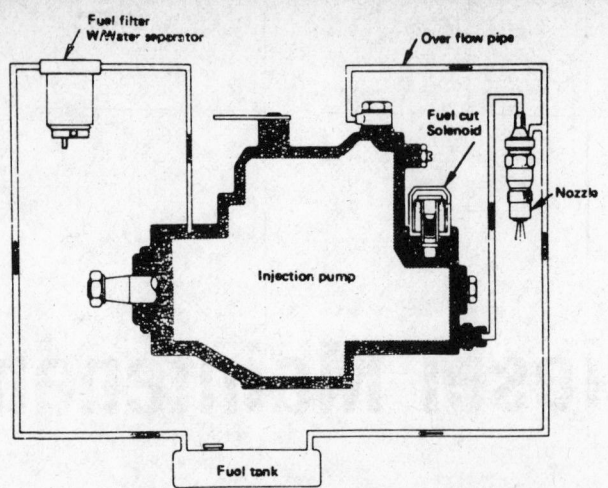

Chevette diesel fuel system schematic

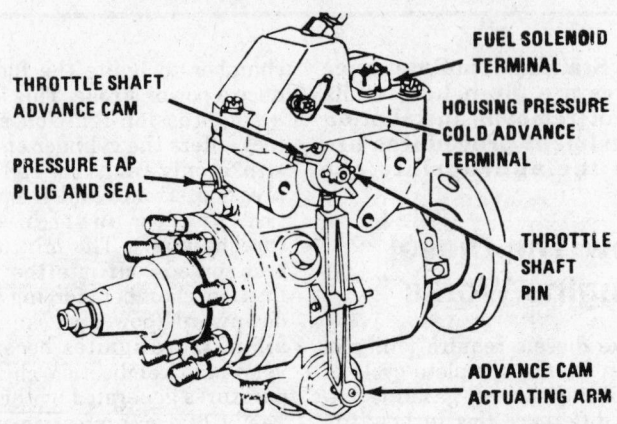

1981 and later GM V8 diesel fuel injection pump with Housing Pressure Cold Advance (HPCA) system

Maintenance Procedures

Maintenance procedures for the diesel engine generally fall into three categories:
1. Fuel system
2. Starting system
3. Engine mechanical systems
Of these, the fuel system is usually the most likely source of engine troubles, and should be high on the list for regular maintenance attention.

FUEL SYSTEM

The typical diesel engine fuel system consists of fuel tank, fuel feed and return lines, mechanical fuel injection pump, fuel injectors and lines, and a large capacity fuel filter. On some models, the GM V8 diesel for example, the engine is also equipped with a small, low pressure fuel pump which feeds the injection pump.

In addition to these, the air intake system (air cleaner, intake manifold) should be checked over regularly to insure unrestricted air flow into the cylinders.

In operation, fuel is drawn out of the fuel tank by the injection pump (or its feed pump) and fed by the injection pump to the injectors in the cylinder head at a very high pressure. Before the fuel is allowed to enter the main injection pump, it passes through a specially built fuel filter which traps solid particles (and water on some models) in the fuel. Fuel that is not used is pumped back to the fuel tank through the fuel return lines. This recirculated fuel helps cool the injection pump.

Air Cleaner

On a gasoline engine, the volume of air taken in by the engine is controlled by throttle valves. When the throttle valves are closed (engine idling), air intake is restricted. When the throttle valves are wide open (accelerator pedal to the floor), the engine draws in the maximum amount of air it possibly can. This applies to both carbureted and fuel injected gasoline engines.

The speed (rpm) of a diesel engine is controlled by the quantity of fuel which is injected into the engine; no air metering restrictions (throttle valves) are used. Because of this, diesel engines ingest as much air as they possibly can under all conditions. A much greater volume of air passes through the air cleaner of a diesel per mile, therefore, diesel air filters must either be larger or the filter replacement intervals more frequent than those of a similarly sized gasoline engine.

One word of caution; never remove the air cleaner on a diesel with the engine running, and never run the engine with the air cleaner removed. The volume of air drawn through the intake manifold is very great and, because the intake manifold is unobstructed, anything drawn into the intake manifold (air cleaner wing nut, etc.) goes straight to the combustion chambers, where it can cause major engine damage.

Fuel Filter

The diesel engine fuel filter is usually larger than the filter used on gasoline engines. The extra capacity is needed to trap the suspended particles in diesel fuel, which is generally "dirtier" than gasoline.

On some engines, the Chevette and GM V6 diesels, for example, the fuel filter looks like a second engine oil filter, and is removed and installed in the same manner as the canister-type oil filter. On GM V8 engines, the fuel filter is located at the rear of the engine and is unbolted from its bracket after its fuel lines are disconnected. See the Chevette car section for diesel fuel filter removal and installation. The fuel filter must be changed according to the manufacturer's suggested interval. See the owner's manual for information.

After installing the fuel filter on GM V8s, start the engine and check for leaks. Run the engine for about two minutes, then stop the engine for the same amount of time to allow any air trapped in the injection system to bleed off. Many diesels also have a small, in-tank filter which is usually maintenance-free.

Water In Fuel

Diesel fuel is a hydrophilic fluid; it naturally attracts water. Since diesel fuel and water do not mix, the water remains floating beneath the fuel at the bottom of the tank. This water must be removed every now and then, or it will be drawn into the fuel circuit and pass through the injection system, causing corrosion and possible component failure (injection pumps can cost up to $1,000). Water in the fuel system will also cause the engine to run poorly, if at all.

Most diesel fuel tanks are equipped with a separator which can isolate from 1 to 3 gallons of water from the fuel. Many GM diesels are also equipped with "Water in Fuel" lights in the dashboard which warn of the presence of H_2O in the fuel tank. These warning systems can be installed by the dealer on GM models not so equipped.

On some diesels, such as the Chevette, there is a water catcher in the bottom of the fuel filter which can easily be bled off. In addition, there are several bolt-on water filters on the market which attach to the fuel line under the hood and separate water from the fuel. Depending on which kind you buy, draining water from the system is simply a matter of opening the petcock at the bottom of the filter and letting the water drain out, or, if money is no object, a separator is available on which water is drained from the filter simply by activating a switch on the dashboard.

Bleeding Water From The Chevette Diesel Fuel Filter

1. Place a 4 pint see-through container at the end of the vinyl hose beneath the drain plug on the filter.
2. Open the drain plug approximately 4 turns.
3. Operate the priming pump handle at the top of the filter by pumping it about 10 times or until all the water is drained out. The water will collect at the bottom of the see-through container and the diesel fuel will float on

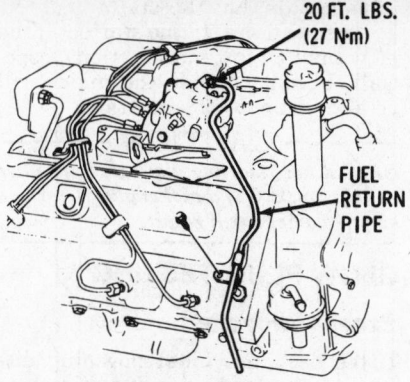

Fuel return pipe

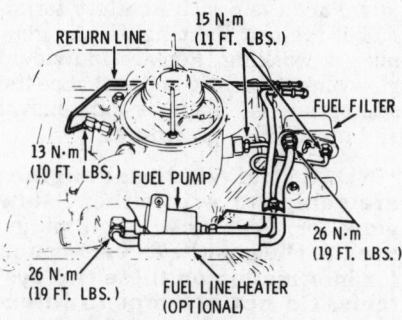

Top view of the GM V6 diesel engine. Note the location of the fuel filter.

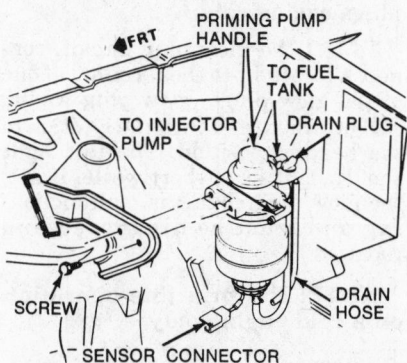

Chevette diesel fuel filter assembly, showing drain plug and hose and fuel priming pump

top of it. When the pump is pushing through nothing but diesel fuel system bleeding is complete.

4. Close the drain plug and again operate the pump handle up and down several times to prime the fuel system.
5. Start the engine and check for leaks. Make sure the "Water in Fuel" light in the instrument panel goes off. If it doesn't the water in the fuel tank will have to be drained. See procedure below.

Removing Water From The Fuel Tank

Treat diesel fuel with the same re-

spect you would gasoline, and after the procedure, properly dispose of the fuel.

1. Remove the fuel tank cap.
2. Connect a pump or siphon hose to the $\frac{1}{4}$ in. fuel return hose (smaller of the two fuel hoses) above the rear axle, or under the hood near the fuel pump (on the passenger's side of the engine, near the front).
3. Siphon until all water is removed from the tank. Do not use your mouth to create siphon vacuum, EVER! The best method is to siphon the water into a large capacity see-through container. The water will collect at the bottom of the container. There are several different types of siphon pumps available in auto parts and hardware stores that makes fuel tank draining both easy and safe.
4. When all water has been removed from the tank, be sure to reinstall the fuel return hose and fuel cap.

NOTE: If the entire fuel system (not just the tank) is contaminated by water, the vehicle must be stopped immediately and the fuel system must be purged. This includes draining and removing the fuel tank, blowing low pressure compressed air backwards through the fuel feed and return lines, and bleeding the water out of all injection components. This job should be referred to a qualified technician.

COLD WEATHER FUEL SYSTEM MAINTENANCE

——— CAUTION ———
NEVER use "starting aids" such as ether to help start a GM diesel engine — serious engine damage will result.

As will be explained later under "Fuel Recommendations", diesel fuel tends to become "cloudy", or thicker, as the temperature drops. The thicker the diesel fuel becomes, the slower it flows through the fuel system, until finally it stops flowing altogether somewhere near the bottom of the thermometer. One way to fight sluggish fuel flow is to use winterized blends of diesel fuel or straight No. 1 diesel fuel.

Another way is to install an aftermarket fuel system pre-heater. These are generally canisters which connect into the fuel line and use coolant from the engine cooling system to heat the fuel before it reaches the injection pump. The one drawback with this system is the engine must be started before the pre-heater begins to work. Also available are electric fuel warmers. These pre-heat the fuel going into the filter and can be used in conjunction with the coolant-type fuel heater.

For 1981 and later Diesels, GM offers an optional electric diesel fuel heater (V6 and V8 only) and an engine block heater (all GM diesels). The fuel heater is thermostatically controlled to heat the fuel before it enters the fuel filter when fuel temperature is 20°F or lower. The fuel heater works only when the ignition key is in the RUN position. On these models, the fuel tank filter has a bypass valve which allows fuel to flow to the heater when the tank filter is covered with fuel wax. The engine block heater is equipped with an electrical cord wrapped up on the right side of the engine compartment. The cord plugs into regular 110 volt household current. The block heater can be used, according to the type of oil in the crankcase, up to eight hours or overnight to warm up the block. Consult the manufacturer's Diesel Engine Supplement for more information.

1981 and later GM V6 and V8 diesel engine fuel injection pumps are equipped with a Housing Pressure Cold Advance (HPCA) system which advances the injection timing about 3° during cold operation to promote easier cold starts, better idle and less noise when cold. The system should be maintenance free.

Starting System

The diesel starting system includes one (sometimes two) heavy duty battery, the starter, and the glow plug circuit. In addition to the heavy duty battery(ies), the majority of diesel engines also have starters and battery cables designed specifically as heavy duty items for diesel usage only. Because of the high compression of any diesel, the torque required to turn the engine is much greater than a gasoline engine. The starter must be powerful enough to handle the increased load; the battery cables must be thick enough to withstand the heat generated by the starter load.

For battery maintenance, see the regular "Maintenance" section. Jump starting procedures for a dual battery car are given below. Starter maintenance is included in the appropriate car section, or the "Charging and Starting Systems" section.

The glow plug circuit is used on the diesel to initially start the engine. When the ignition switch is turned to the ON position, a light will come on in the instrument panel signalling that the glow plugs are preheating the combustion chambers. After a certain interval (depending on how cold the engine is), the light will go off.

This signals that the starter may be engaged and the engine started. If the glow plug circuit malfunctions, especially in cold weather, the engine will be almost impossible to start.

— CAUTION —

NEVER use "starting aids" such as ether to help start a GM diesel engine — serious engine damage will result.

GLOW PLUG TESTING

Except Chevette

To test each individual glow plug, disconnect the busbar and/or wire connector from the glow plug and connect a test light between the glow plug terminal and the positive battery terminal. If the test light lights, the glow plug is working. Replace individual glow plugs which do not work. See the appropriate car sections for removal and installation procedures.

NOTE: GM V8 diesel engines are equipped with either "slow glow" or "fast glow" glow plugs. See the Oldsmobile 88 car section for information on these two systems. Do not attempt to interchange any parts of these two glow plug systems. The GM V6 diesel uses the "fast glow" style glow plugs exclusively.

To test the glow plug circuit, connect a test light to the terminal of one of the glow plugs (glow plug wiring still attached) and turn the ignition to the heating position. The test light should light for a short while. If not, the glow plug circuit is malfunctioning and must be diagnosed and repaired.

NOTE: Perform this operation on a cold engine only.

Chevette

To test the glow plugs of the Chevette, check for continuity across the plug terminals and the body with an ohmmeter. If there is continuity between these points, the glow plugs is okay; if not, replace the glow plug.

Jump-Starting a Dual Battery Diesel

Many GM diesels are equipped with two 12 volt batteries. The batteries are connected in parallel circuit (positive terminal to positive terminal, negative terminal to negative terminal). Hooking the batteries up in parallel circuit increases battery cranking power without increasing total battery voltage output (12 volts). On the other hand, hooking two 12 volt batteries up in a series circuit (positive terminal to negative terminal)

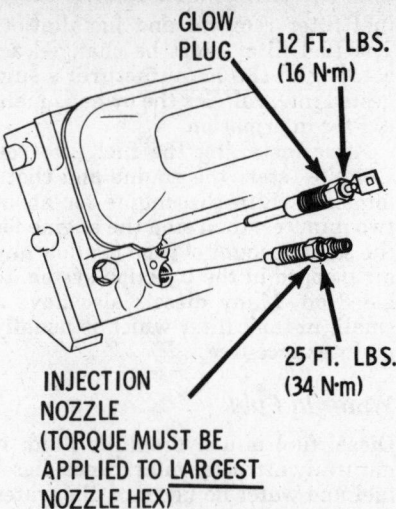

GM V8 diesel engine glow plug and injection nozzle—1980 and later models shown. Nozzles of 1978–79 models are retained by a collar clamp and bolt.

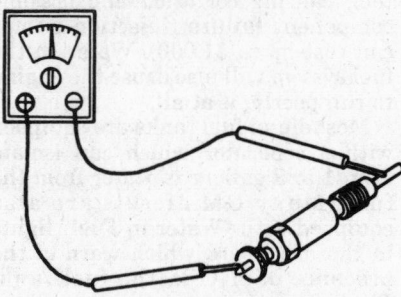

Testing the Chevette diesel glow plug with an ohmmeter

increases total battery output to 24 volts (12 volts + 12 volts).

— CAUTION —

NEVER hook the batteries up in a series circuit; SEVERE electrical system damage will result.

In the event that a dual battery diesel must be jump started, use the following procedure.

1. Open the hood and locate the batteries. On GM diesels, the manufacturer usually suggests using the battery on the driver's side of the car to make the connection.

2. Position the donor car so that the jumper cables will reach from its battery (must be 12 volt, negative ground) to the appropriate battery in the diesel. Do not allow the cars to touch.

3. Shut off all electrical equipment on both vehicles. Turn off the engine of the donor car, set the parking brakes on both vehicles and block the wheels. Also, make sure both vehicles are in Neutral (manual transmission models) or Park (automatic transmission models).

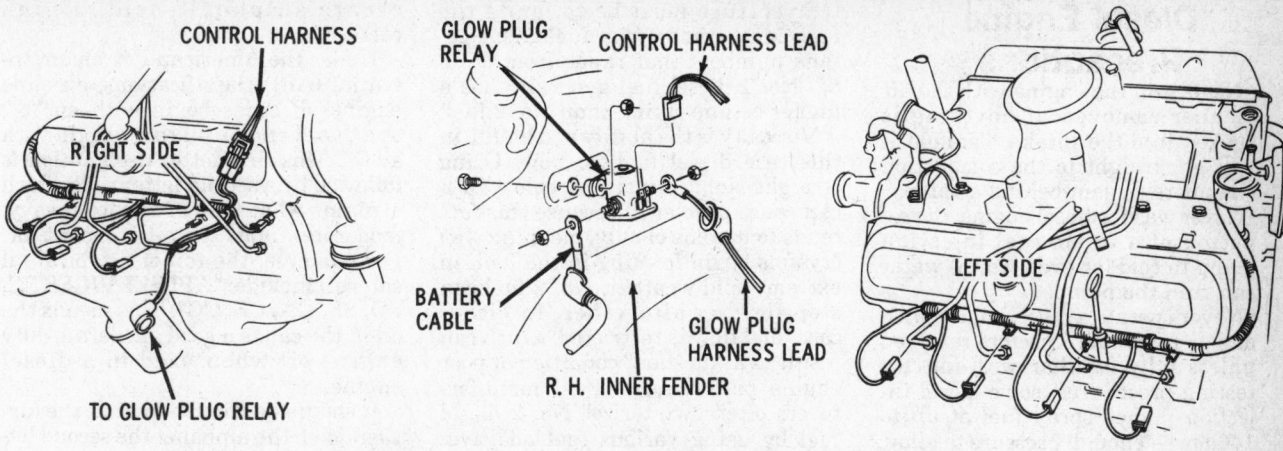

Typical GM V8 diesel glow plug harness arrangement—V6 similar.

4. Using the jumper cables, connect the positive (+) terminal of the donor car battery to the positive terminal of one (not both) of the diesel batteries.

5. Using the second jumper cable, connect the negative (-) terminal of the donor battery to a solid, stationary, metallic point on the diesel (alternator bracket, engine block, etc.). Be very careful to keep the jumper cables away from moving parts (cooling fan, alternator belt, etc.) on both vehicles.

6. Start the engine of the donor car and run it at moderate speed.

7. Start the engine of the diesel.

8. When the diesel starts, disconnect the battery cables in the reverse order of attachment.

Engine Mechanical Systems

Although diesel engines are very low in carbon monoxide (CO) and hydrocarbon (HC) emissions, "particulate" emission output is very high. This is evident from the black smoke emitted by diesels, which is most noticeable during hard acceleration or high engine loads. The particulates are made up of mostly soot (carbon) and sulphur particles. The majority of these particulates are released into the atmosphere. However, some of the particulate matter, because it is produced within the engines cylinders, is left inside the engine and gradually contaminates the engine oil. This contamination makes the oil corrosive, due to the sulphur, and abrasive, due to the carbon. Serious engine damage will result if these contaminants continue to accumulate in the oil. Engine oil and filters of diesel engines must be changed more frequently than those of gasoline engines, due to the increased rate at which the contami-

nants form in the diesel. Consult the "Maintenance" section for oil and filter change procedures. The manufacturer's recommended oil change interval will be given in the owner's manual. An explanation of diesel engine oils is given at the end of this section.

As explained earlier, very high cylinder compression is the key to the operation of the diesel engine. The normal compression of most gasoline engines will rarely exceed 180 psi; whereas with diesel engines, compression pressures of 350–400 psi are commonplace.

CAUTION

DO NOT attempt to check the compression of a diesel engine with a standard compression gauge—personal injury could result. A special, high pressure compression gauge is needed to safely check the compression of any diesel.

COMPRESSION TEST

GM V6 and V8 Diesel Engines

1. Remove the air cleaner and install air crossover cover (Tool No. J-26996-1).

2. Disconnect the wire from the fuel shutoff solenoid terminal of the injection pump.

3. Disconnect the wires from the glow plugs and remove all glow plugs.

4. Screw compression gauge J-26999 into the glow plug hole in the cylinder being checked.

5. Crank the engine, allowing six "puffs" for each cylinder. The lowest reading cylinder should not be less than 70% of the highest, and no cylinder should be less than 275 pounds.

Chevette Diesel

1. Start the engine and bring it to normal operating temperature.

2. Disconnect or remove the following:
   a. Sensing resistor
   b. Glow plug connector
   c. Glow plugs (4)
   d. Fuel cut-off solenoid connector
   e. Disconnect the in-line fusible link wire of Q.S.S. (Quick Start and Silent idling) system at the connector.

3. Install an adapter (special tool J-29762) into the glow plug hole, then hook a compression gauge (must read to 600 psi) to the adapter.

4. Engage the starter motor to take the reading. Standard compression is 441 psi at 200 rpm or more. Limit is 370 psi at 200 rpm or less.

CONNECTING A TACHOMETER TO A DIESEL ENGINE

As mentioned earlier, the diesel engine does not require an electrical ignition system. Because of this, problems arise when attempts are made to connect a tachometer to the engine for the purpose of idle adjustments, etc. The average gasoline engine tachometer senses the ignition spark pulses and converts them into a readable engine rpm signal. This type of tachometer is useless on the diesel engine, as you may have guessed, because of the diesel's compression ignition system.

There are several magnetic and photoelectric tachometers available from various tool manufacturers (Kent-Moore Corp., Snap-on Tools, etc.) which were designed specifically for use with the diesel engine. These units can run into a little more money than the average do-it-yourselfer may be willing to spend, in which case any adjustments requiring the monitoring of engine rpm should be performed by a competent service technician.

Diesel Engine Precautions

• Never run the engine with the air cleaner removed; if anything is sucked into the intake manifold it will go straight to the combustion chambers, or jam behind a valve.
• Never wash a diesel engine; the reaction of a warm fuel injection pump to cold (or even warm) water can ruin the pump.
• Never operate a diesel engine with one or more fuel injectors removed unless fully familiar with injector testing procedures; some diesel injection pumps spray fuel at up to 1400 psi—enough pressure to allow the fuel to penetrate your skin.
• Do not skip engine oil and filter changes.
• Strictly follow the manufacturer's oil and fuel recommendations as given in the owner's manual.
• Do not use home heating oil as fuel for any diesel unless it's a dire emergency.
• Do not use "starting aids" such as ether in the automotive diesel engine, as these can cause severe internal engine damage.
• Do not run a diesel engine with the "Water in Fuel" warning light on in the dashboard.
• If removing water from the fuel tank, use the same caution as when working around gasoline engine fuel components.
• Do not allow diesel fuel to come in contact with rubber hoses or components on the engine, as it can damage them.

Fuel and Oil Recommendations

FUEL

Fuel makers produce two grades of diesel fuel, No. 1 and No. 2, for use in automotive diesel engines. Generally speaking, No. 2 fuel is recommended over No. 1 for driving in temperatures above 20°F. In fact, in many areas, No. 2 diesel is the only fuel available. By comparison, No. 2 diesel fuel is less volatile than No. 1 fuel, and gives better fuel economy. No. 2 fuel is also a better injection pump lubricant. Two important characteristics of diesel fuel are its cetane number and its viscosity.

The cetane number of a diesel fuel refers to the case with which a diesel fuel ignites. High cetane numbers mean that the fuel will ignite with relative ease or that it ignites well at low temperatures. Naturally, the lower the cetane number, the higher the temperature must be to ignite the fuel. Most commercial fuels have cetane numbers that range from 35 to 65. No. 1 diesel fuel generally has a higher cetane rating than No. 2 fuel.

Viscosity is the ability of a liquid, in this case diesel fuel, to flow. Using straight No. 2 diesel fuel below 20°F can cause problems, because this fuel tends to become cloudy, meaning wax crystals begin forming in the fuel. In extreme cold weather, No. 2 fuel can stop flowing altogether. In either case, fuel flow is restricted, which can result in a "no start" condition or poor engine performance. Fuel manufacturers often "winterize" No. 2 diesel fuel by using various fuel additives and blends (No. 1 diesel fuel, kerosene, etc.) to lower its winter-time viscosity. Generally speaking, though, No. 1 diesel fuel is more satisfactory in extremely cold weather.

NOTE: No. 1 and No. 2 diesel fuels will mix and burn with no ill effects, although the engine manufacturer will undoubtedly recommend one or the other. Consult the owner's manual for information.

Depending on local climate, most fuel manufacturers make winterized No. 2 fuel available seasonally. Many automobile manufacturers (Oldsmobile, for example) publish pamphlets giving the locations of diesel fuel stations nationwide. Contact the local dealer for information.

Do not substitute home heating oil for automotive diesel fuel. While in some cases, home heating oil refinement levels equal those of diesel fuel, many times they are far below diesel engine requirements. The result of using "dirty" home heating oil will be a clogged fuel system, in which case the entire system may have to be dismantled and cleaned.

One more word on diesel fuels. Don't thin diesel fuel with gasoline in cold weather. The lighter gasoline, which is more explosive, will cause rough running at the very least, and may cause extensive engine damage if enough is used. In addition, the combination of diesel fuel and gasoline produces an extremely explosive mixture that is even more volatile than gasoline, making the simple act of adding gasoline to a diesel fuel tank very dangerous.

OIL

Diesel engines require different engine oil from those used in gasoline engines. Besides doing the things gasoline engine oil does, diesel oil must also deal with increased engine heat and the diesel blow-by-gases, which create sulphuric acid, a high corrosive.

Under the American Petroleum Institute (API) classifications, gasoline engine oil codes begin with an "S", and diesel engine oil codes begin with a "C". This first letter designation is followed by a second letter code which explains what type of service (heavy, moderate, light) the oil is meant for. For example, the top of a typical oil can will include: "API SERVICES SC, SD, SE, CA, CB, CC". This means the oil in the can is a good, moderate duty engine oil when used in a diesel engine.

It should be noted here that the further down the alphabet the second letter of the API classification is, the greater the oil's protective qualities are (CD is the severest duty diesel engine oil, CA is the lightest duty oil, etc.). The same is true for gasoline engine oil classifications (SF is the severest duty gasoline engine oil, SA is the lightest duty oil, etc.).

Many diesel manufacturers recommend an oil with both gasoline and diesel engine API classifications. Consult the owner's manual for specifications.

The top of the oil can will also contain an SAE (Society of Automotive Engineers) designation, which gives the oil's viscosity. A typical designation will be: SAE 10W–30, which means that the oil is a "winter" viscosity oil, meaning it will flow and give protection at low temperatures.

On the diesel engine, oil viscosity is critical, because the diesel is much harder to start (due to its higher compression) than a gasoline engine. Obviously, if you fill the crankcase with a very heavy oil during winter (SAE 20W–50, for example), the starter is going to require a lot of current from the battery to turn the engine. And, since batteries don't function well in cold weather in the first place, you may find yourself stranded some morning. Consult the owner's manual for recommended oil specifications for the climate you live in.

Aftermarket Fuel System Accessories

Due to reasons described previously, most diesel engine problems can be attributed to either fuel contamination or cold weather fuel performance characteristics. Diesel-engined vehicle manufacturers have designed and installed various systems to combat these problems, but ultimately, their best efforts are limited by cost.

Inconvenience is a major concern to diesel owners. Excepting the Chevette, for example, if water accumulates (in substantial quantities) in the diesel fuel system, the fuel and water must be siphoned from the fuel tank and purged from the remainder of the fuel system. It goes without saying that this operation is a messy, time-consuming process. Even if the vehicle is equipped with a water/fuel separator having a drain valve, the owner must manually open the valve from either under the hood or beneath the vehicle. Although the fuel filter installed by the manufacturer offers adequate performance when maintained properly, the addition of another, separate diesel fuel filter is a wise improvement.

If you live in an extremely cold climate, you've probably experienced cold starting problems due to fuel "waxing", plugged filters "gelled" fuel, etc. If your vehicle is not factory-equipped with the optional fuel line or cylinder block heaters, these heaters can be purchased from the aftermarket (retail auto parts manufacturers). The installation of either of these items can improve cold-starting dramatically.

WATER/FUEL SEPARATORS

Centrifugal Action

Sometimes referred to as a "cyclonic" water/fuel separator, this device uses baffles which spin the fuel as it comes through the separator intake. Since water is heavier than diesel fuel, the water will spin away from the fuel, sink to the bottom of the separator, and collect in the sediment bowl.

This type of separator is most efficient in dealing with large water droplets. If the water is an emulsion with the fuel, that is, if the water is equally dispersed through the fuel in very small droplets, some of the water will remain with the fuel to travel through the fuel system.

Coalescing Action

In this type of separator, the fuel must pass through a coalescent filtering media before proceeding through the fuel system. The idea behind the coalescent media is to trap even the smallest droplets of water on the media. As the small droplets combine into larger, heavier droplets, gravity acts on the droplets to pull them downward, off of the media and into the sediment bowl.

FUEL FILTER/SEPARATOR COMBINATION UNITS

Most separators of either the centrifugal or coalescent types are available with disposeable fuel filtering elements which are built into the separator unit. If your car already has a large, disposeable filter, it would probably be more cost-effective to stay with a separator only, and to change the factory-equipped filter at the recommended intervals. Should your vehicle have a fairly small filter, and/or an inconveniently located water drain (or none at all), choose the filter/separator combination. The filter/separator offers both increased fuel filtering ability and efficient water separation.

CONVENIENCE ADD-ONS

Available with many separators and filter/separators are items such as dash-mounted water-in-fuel indicator lamps, audible water-in-fuel alarms, and dash-controlled water ejection systems. A properly chosen system would warn you of water in the fuel, and allow you to eject the water by simply flipping a dash-mounted switch.

Installing a Separator

Clear installation instructions and the necessary installation parts will be provided with the separator kit. Follow those instructions exactly. A general list of suggestions follows:

1. Fuel additives should not be used unless approved by the separator manufacturer.

2. Do not install a separator less than 4 in. away from any exhaust system component.

3. If plastic fittings are supplied with the kit, do not replace them with metal fittings. Also, use extreme caution when tightening the fittings, especially those made of plastic.

4. Use a fuel-proof sealer on all fitting threads, only if the threads are not factory-coated with sealer.

5. Use only fuel-proof hoses for the installation.

6. Do not eliminate the original equipment fuel filter, even if a filter/separator is installed.

7. For new car warranty purposes, a filter/separator should be located BEFORE the original equipment filter. The fuel must pass through the original filter last, before entering the fuel injection pump.

8. If any type of fuel line heater is installed, it is best to position the heater between the fuel tank and the separator intake.

9. To ease the job of the separator,

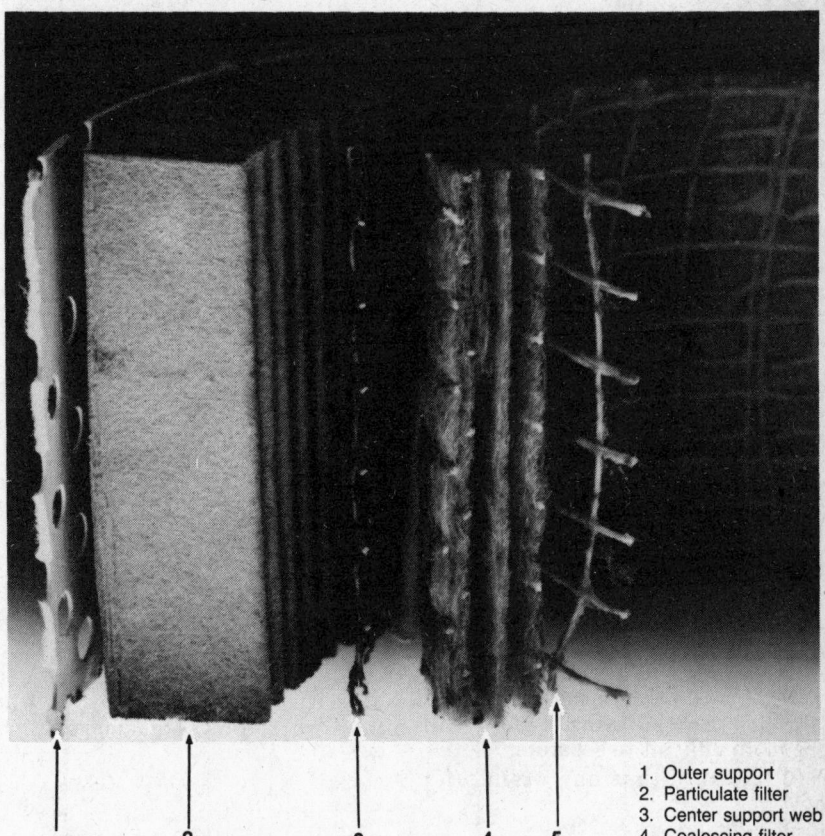

1. Outer support
2. Particulate filter
3. Center support web
4. Coalescing filter
5. Inner support web

Cross section of a coalescing filter/fuel filter combination (© CR Industries)

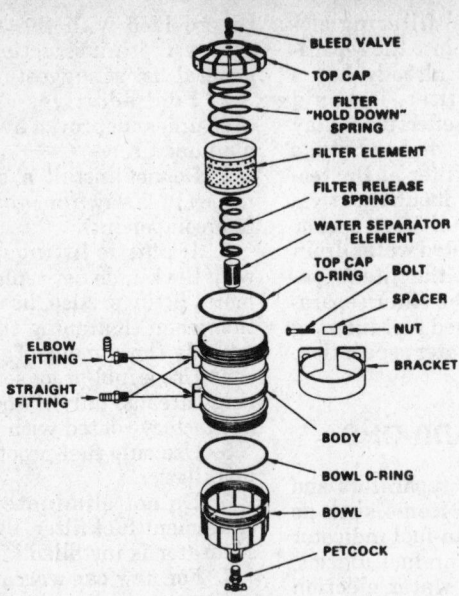

Exploded view of a fuel filter/water separator combination unit (© CR Industries)

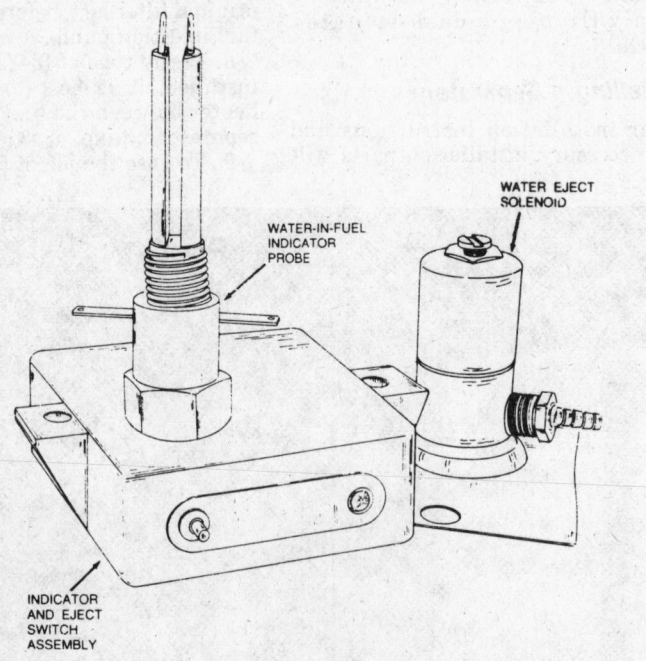

Typical convenience accessories for a water-in-fuel detection system (© CR Industries)

the separator should be installed between the fuel transfer pump and the tank (unless the separator manufacturer specifies otherwise). Fuel and water which have been churned through the fuel transfer pump will be more difficult to separate.

10. Be sure that any wiring (for warning lamps, water ejection, etc.) is routed and connected properly. If the wiring must pass through a drilled hole, be sure to use a rubber grommet between the drilled component(s) and the wire to prevent damage to the wire.

FUEL LINE HEATERS

Two popular types of fuel line heaters are available for diesel passenger cars. Both types raise the temperature of the fuel to prevent "waxing" and "gelling" of the fuel in the lines during cold weather operation. One type uses engine coolant as a heating source. In order for this type to heat the fuel, the engine must first be started and allowed to run until the coolant temperature increases. Though this type of heater will usually increase fuel mileage, it offers no aid in starting ability.

The other type of heater uses a 12V DC electric heating element. This type is recommended, due to its ability to warm the fuel BEFORE the engine is started. This type of heater will also usually increase the overall fuel mileage.

Installation

Follow the manufacturer's instructions exactly. Also, see suggestions 5, 8, and 9 under Separator Installation.

CYLINDER BLOCK HEATERS

A cylinder block heater electrically (usually 110V house current) heats the engine coolant, which in turn warms the cylinder block, heads, and engine oil. In this case, the warmth is not used to alter the characteristics of the fuel. Block heaters offer two main advantages when starting a diesel in cold weather.

1. The reduced viscosity (thinning) of the engine oil from the warmth allows the engine to be "turned over" easier (and faster) by the starter. Less strain is imposed on the starting system.

2. Because the diesel relies on the heat of compression to ignite the fuel, the increase in the base combustion chamber temperature results in a higher temperature during compression. This allows the fuel to ignite easier than if just the glow plugs were used.

Installation

Most cylinder block heaters replace one of the existing freeze (or expansion) plugs of the cylinder block. Follow the manufacturers installation instructions exactly. Also, refer to the manufacturers recommendations for usage.

Tools and Equipment 31

In addition to the normal assortment of screwdrivers and pliers, automotive service work requires an investment in wrenches, sockets and the handles needed to drive them, and various measuring tools such as torque wrenches and feeler gauges.

The best approach to gathering the required equipment is to proceed slowly, buying high-quality tools as they are needed. An initial investment should be made in a set of quality wrenches, ranging in size from $\frac{1}{4}$ inch to one inch, if your car has standard bolts, or from 5mm to 19mm if your car has metric fasteners. High quality forged wrenches are available in three styles; open end, box end, and combination open/box end. The combination tools are generally the most desirable as a starter set; the wrenches shown in the illustration are of the combination type.

NOTE: Many later model American cars use both metric and standard nuts and bolts.

The other set of tools inevitably required is a ratchet handle and socket set. This set should have the same size range as your wrench set. The ratchet, extension, and flex drives fro the sockets are available in many sizes; it is advisable to choose a $\frac{3}{8}$ inch drive set initially. One break in the inch/metric sizing war is that metric-sized sockets sold in the U.S. have inch-sized drive ($\frac{1}{4}$, $\frac{3}{8}$, $\frac{1}{2}$, etc.). Sockets are available in six and twelve point versions; six point types are generally cheaper and are a good choice for a first set.

The choice of a drive handle for the sockets should be made with some care. If this is your first set, take the plunge and invest in a flexhead ratchet; it will get into many places otherwise accessible only through a long chain of universal joints, extensions and adapters. An alternative is a flex handle; such a tool is shown in the illustration, below the ratchet handle. In addition to the range of sockets mentioned, a rubber-lined spark plug socket should be purchased. Spark plugs have either a $\frac{13}{16}$ or a $\frac{5}{8}$ inch hex; get the correct socket for the plugs in your car.

The most important thing to consider when purchasing hand tools is quality. Don't be misled by the low cost of "bargain" tools. Forged wrenches, tempered screwdriver blades, and fine tooth ratchets are a much better investment than their less expensive counterparts. The skinned knuckles and frustration inflicted by poor quality tools make any job an unhappy core. Another consideration is that quality tools sold by reputable firms come with an on-the-spot replacement guarantee; if the tool breaks, you get a new one, no questions asked.

The tools needed for basic maintenance jobs, in addition to those just mentioned, include:

1. Jackstands, for support;
2. Oil filter wrench;
3. Oil filler spout or funnel;
4. Grease gun;
5. Battery hydrometer;
6. Battery post and clamp cleaner;
7. Container for draining oil;
8. Many rags for the inevitable spills.

In addition to these items there are several others which are not absolutely necessary, but handy to have around. These include a transmission funnel and filler tube, a drop (trouble) light on a long cord, an adjustable wrench (crescent wrench), and slip joint pliers.

A more extensive list of tools, suitable for tune-up work, can be drawn up easily. While the tools involved are slightly more sophisticated, they need not be outrageously expensive. For example, there are several inexpensive tach/dwell meters on the market that are every bit as good for the average mechanic as a $100.00 professional model. The key to these purchases is to make them with an eye towards adaptability and wide range. Using the tach/dwell meter example again, if the model you buy runs up to at least 1,500 rpm on the tachometer scale, the dwell meter works on 4, 6, or 8 cylinder engines, and the tachometer unit is adaptable to both conventional and electronic ignitions, it will serve for a long time on a variety of automobiles. A basic list of tune-up tools could include:

1. A tach/dwell meter;
2. Spark plug gauge and gapping tool;
3. Feeler blades;
4. Timing light.

In this list, the choice of a timing light should be made carefully. A light which works on the DC current supplied by the car battery is the best choice; it should have a xenon tube for brightness. If your car has electronic ignition, the light should have an inductive pick-up (the timing light illustrated has one of these), and since nearly all cars will have electronic ignition in the future, this feature is a reasonable one to look for.

In addition to these basic tools, there are several other tools and gauges you may find useful. These include:

1. A compression gauge. The screw-in type is slower to use, but eliminates the possibility of a faulty reading due to escaping pressure.
2. A manifold vacuum gauge.
3. A test light.
4. An induction meter. This is used

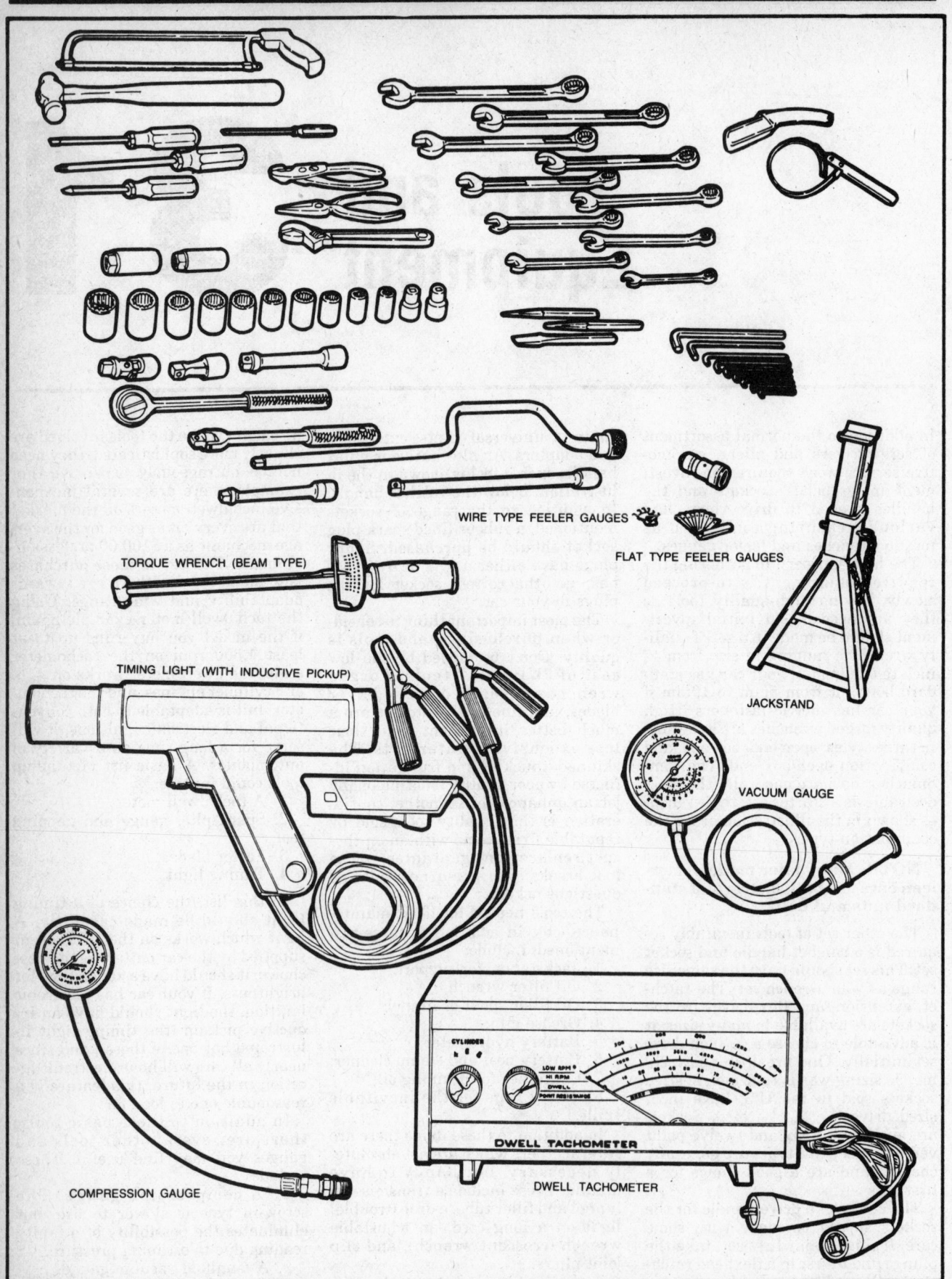

WIRE TYPE FEELER GAUGES

FLAT TYPE FEELER GAUGES

TORQUE WRENCH (BEAM TYPE)

JACKSTAND

TIMING LIGHT (WITH INDUCTIVE PICKUP)

VACUUM GAUGE

COMPRESSION GAUGE

DWELL TACHOMETER

A basic tool collection will handle almost any automotive repair work

to determine whether or not there is current flowing in a wire, and thus is extremely helpful in electrical troubleshooting.

Finally, you will probably find a torque wrench necessary for all but in the most basic of work. The beam type models are perfectly adequate, although the newer click (break-away) type are more precise. Whichever type you choose, plan on having it recalibrated every once in a while.

Special Tools

Several procedures in this manual refer to special tools needed to make repairs or adjustments. These tools can be purchased from the following companies:

AMC, GM
Special Tool Division
Kent-Moore Corp.
29784 Little Mack
Roseville, MI 48066

Ford
Owatonna Tool Co.
Owatonna, MN 55060

Chrysler
Miller Special Tools
A Division of Utica Tool Co.
32615 Park Lane
Garden City, MI 48135

SPECIAL TEST EQUIPMENT

A variety of diagnostic tools are available to help troubleshoot and repair computerized engine and emission control systems. The most sophisticated of these devices are the console-type engine analyzers that usually occupy a garage service bay, but there are several types of aftermarket electronic testers available that will allow quick circuit tests of the engine control system by plugging directly into a special test connector located in the engine compartment or under the dashboard. Several tool and equipment manufacturers offer simple, hand-held testers that measure various circuit voltage levels on command to check all system components for proper operation. Although these testers usually cost about $300–500, consider that the average computer-controlled carburetor can cost twice as much and the money saved by not replacing perfectly good sensors in an attempt to correct a problem could justify the purchase price of a special diagnostic tester.

These testers can allow quick and easy test measurements while the en-

Aftermarket hand-held testers can make diagnosing computer-controlled systems easier

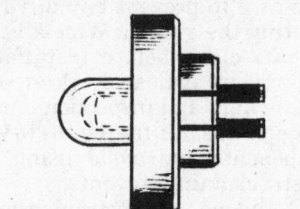

Throttle body fuel injector tester

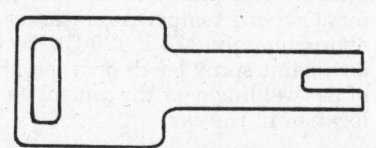

Special key for activating GM on-board diagnosis system. Insert the prongs into the diagnostic test terminals located under the dash

gine is operating or while the car is being driven. In addition, the on-board computer memory can be read to access any stored trouble codes; in effect allowing the computer to tell you where it hurts and aid trouble diagnosis by pinpointing exactly which circuit or component is malfunctioning. In the same manner, repairs can be tested to make sure the problem has been corrected. The biggest advantage these special testers have is their relatively easy hookups that minimize or eliminate the chances of making the wrong connections and getting false voltage readings or damaging the on-board computer.

NOTE: It should be remembered that these testers check voltage levels in circuits; they don't detect mechanical problems or failed components if the circuit voltage falls within the preprogrammed limits stored in the tester PROM unit. Also, most of the

hand-held testes are designed to work only on one or two systems made by a specific manufacturer.

A variety of aftermarket testers are available to help diagnose different computerized engine control systems. Owatonna Tool Company (OTC), for example, markets a device called the OTC Monitor 2000 which plugs directly into the assembly line diagnostic link (ALDL). When the correct manufacturer cartridge is plugged into the unit, the OTC tester makes diagnosis a simple matter of pressing the correct buttons. An adapter is supplied with the tester to allow connection to all types of ALDL links, regardless of the number of pin terminals used.

Servicing Your Car Safely

It is virtually impossible to anticipate all of the hazards involved with automotive maintenance and service, but care and common sense will prevent most accidents. The rules of safety for mechanics range from "don't smoke around gasoline," to "use the proper tool for the job." The trick to avoiding injuries is to develop safe work habits and take every possible precaution.

Any computer-based electronic engine control system is extremely sensitive to electrical voltages and cannot tolerate careless or haphazard testing or service procedures. An inexperienced individual can literally do major damage looking for a minor problem by using the wrong kind of test equipment or connecting test leads or connectors with the ignition switch ON. When selecting test equipment, make sure the manufacturers instructions state that the tester is compatible with whatever type of electronic control system is being serviced. Read all instructions carefully and double check all test points before installing probes or making any connections.

Aftermarket electronic testers are available from a variety of sources, as well as from the manufacturer, but care should be taken that the test equipment being used is designed to diagnose a particular system accurately without damaging the control unit (ECU) or components being tested.

DO'S

• DO keep a fire extinguisher and first aid kit within easy reach.
• DO wear safety glasses or goggles when cutting, drilling, grinding or prying, even if you have 20-20 vi-

sion. If you wear glasses for the sake of vision, they should be made of hardened glass that can serve also as safety glasses, or wear safety goggles over your regular glasses.

• DO shield your eyes whenever you work around the battery. Batteries contain sulphuric acid. In case of contact with the eyes or skin, flush the area with water or a mixture of water and baking soda and get medical attention immediately.

• DO remove the battery cables before charging the battery. Never use a high-output charger on an installed battery or attempt to use any type of "hot shot" (24 volt) starting aid.

• DO use safety stands for any undercar service. Jacks are for raising vehicles; safety stands are for making sure the vehicle stays raised until you want it to come down. Whenever the car is raised, block the wheels remaining on the ground and set the parking brake.

• DO use adequate ventilation when working with any chemicals or hazardous materials. Follow the manufacturer's directions for usage. Brake fluid, anti-freeze, solvents, paints, etc. are all deadly poisons if taken internally. Seal the containers tightly after use and store them safely, out of the reach of children.

• DO use caution when working on clutches or brakes. The asbestos used in the friction material will cause lung cancer if inhaled. Wipe the component with a damp rag to remove dust, and dispose of the rag after use.

• DO disconnect the negative battery cable when working on the electrical system. The secondary ignition system can contain up to 40,000 volts.

• DO properly maintain your tools. Loose hammerheads, mushroomed punches and chisels, frayed or poorly grounded electrical cords, excessively worn screwdrivers, spread open-end wrenches, cracked sockets, slipping ratchets, or faulty droplight sockets can cause accidents.

• DO use the proper size and type of tool for the job being done.

• DO when possible, pull on a wrench handle rather than push on it, and adjust your stance to prevent a fall.

• DO be sure that adjustable wrenches are tightly closed on the nut or bolt and pulled so that the face is on the side of the fixed jaw.

• DO select a wrench or socket that fits the nut or bolt. The wrench or socket should sit straight, not cocked.

• DO strike squarely with a hammer; avoid glancing blows.

• DO set the parking brake and block the drive wheels if the work requires the engine running.

• DO depressurize the fuel system before attempting to disconnect any fuel lines. Although only fuel injection vehicles use a pressurized fuel system, it's a good idea to exercise caution whenever disconnecting any fuel line or hose during service procedures. Take precautions to avoid a fire hazard.

• DO use clean rags and tools when working on an open fuel system and take care to prevent any dirt from entering the system. Wipe all components clean before installation and prepare a clean work area for disassembly and inspection of components. Use lint-free cloths to wipe components and avoid using any caustic cleaning solvents.

• DO remove the electronic control unit (on-board computer) if the vehicle is to be placed in an environment where temperatures exceed approximately 176°F (80°C), such as a paint spray booth or when arc or gas welding near the control unit location in the car.

DON'TS

• DON'T run an engine in a garage or anywhere else without proper ventilation—EVER! Carbon monoxide is poisonous; it takes a long time to leave the human body and you can build up a deadly supply of it in your system by simply breathing in a little every day. You may not realize you are slowly poisoning yourself. Always use power vents, windows, fans or open the garage doors.

• DON'T work around moving parts while wearing a necktie or other loose clothing. Short sleeves are much safer than long, loose sleeves; hard-toed shoes with neoprene soles protect your toes and give a better grip on slippery surfaces. Jewelry such as watches, rings, fancy belt buckles, beads or body adornment of any kind is not safe working around a car. Long hair should be hidden under a hat or cap.

• DON'T use pockets for toolboxes. A fall or bump can drive a screwdriver deep into your body. Even a wiping cloth hanging from the back pocket can wrap around a spinning shaft or fan.

• DON'T smoke when working around gasoline, cleaning solvent or other flammable material.

• DON'T use gasoline to wash your hands; there are excellent soaps available. Gasoline may contain lead, and lead can enter the body through a cut, accumulating in the body until you are very ill. Gasoline also removes all the natural oils from the skin so that bone dry hands will suck up oil and grease.

• DON'T service the air conditioning system unless you are equipped with the necessary tools and training. The refrigerant, R-12, is extremely cold when compressed, and when released into the air will instantly freeze any surface it contacts, including your eyes. Although the refrigerant is normally non-toxic, R-12 becomes a deadly poisonous gas in the presence of an open flame. One good whiff of the vapors from burning refrigerant can be fatal.

• DON'T install or remove battery cables with the key ON or the engine running. Jumper cables should be connected with the key OFF to avoid power surges that can damage electronic control units. Engines equipped with computer controlled systems should avoid both giving and getting jump starts due to the possibility of serious damage to components from arcing in the engine compartment when connections are made with the ignition ON.

• DON'T remove or attach wiring harness connectors with the ignition switch ON, especially to the electronic control unit.

• DON'T drop any components during service procedures and never apply 12 volts directly to any component (like a fuel injector) unless instructed specifically to do so. Some component electrical windings are designed to safely handle only 4 or 5 volts and can be destroyed in seconds if 12 volts are applied directly to the connector.

Air Conditioning Service 32

AIR CONDITIONING SYSTEMS

Automotive air conditioning systems are basic in design and operation, but many different components are used by the vehicle manufacturers to operate and control the systems to their specifications.

Basic System

The basic air conditioning system utilizes the compressor, condenser, evaporator, receiver-drier, expansion valve and a thermostatic or ambient type switch to control evaporator freeze-up. The controls are manually operated and the unit is basic in design. This system is usually installed as an add-on or after-market unit. A sight glass may be used in the system.

GENERAL SERVICING PROCEDURES

The most important aspect of air conditioning service is the maintenance of a pure and adequate charge of refrigerant in the system. A refrigeration system cannot function properly if a significant percentage of the charge is lost. Leaks are common be-

cause the severe vibration encountered in an automobile can easily cause a sufficient cracking or loosening of the air conditioning fittings; as a result, the extreme operating pressures of the system force refrigerant out.

The problem can be understood by considering what happens to the system as it is operated with a continuous leak. Because the expansion valve regulates the flow of refrigerant to the evaporator, the level of refrigerant there is fairly constant. The receiver-drier stores any excess of refrigerant, and so a loss will first appear there as a reduction in the level of liquid. As this level nears the bottom of the vessel, some refrigerant vapor bubbles will begin to appear in the stream of liquid supplied to the expansion valve. This vapor decreases the capacity of the expansion valve very little as the valve opens to compensate for

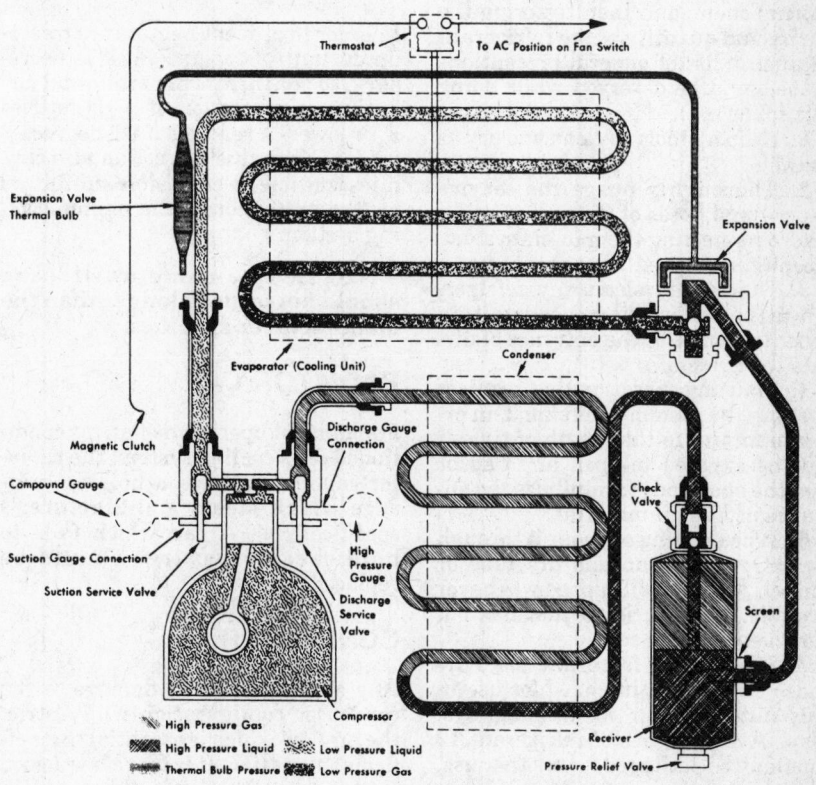

Basic air conditioning system

32–1

its presence. As the quantity of liquid in the condenser decreases, the operating pressure will drop there and throughout the high side of the system. As the R-12 continues to be expelled, the pressure available to force the liquid through the expansion valve will continue to decrease, and, eventually, the valve's orifice will prove to be too much of a restriction for adequate flow even with the needle fully withdrawn.

At this point, low side pressure will start to drop, and severe reduction in cooling capacity, marked by freeze-up of the evaporator coil, will result. Eventually, the operating pressure of the evaporator will be lower than the pressure of the atmosphere surrounding it, and air will be drawn into the system wherever there are leaks in the low side.

Because all atmospheric air contains at least some moisture, water will enter the system and mix with the R-12 and the oil. Trace amounts of moisture will cause sludging of the oil, and corrosion of the system. Saturation and clogging of the filter-drier, and freezing of the expansion valve orifice will eventually result. As air fills the system to a greater and greater extent, it will interfere more and more with the normal flows of refrigerant and heat.

From this description, it should be obvious that much of the repairman's time will be spent detecting leaks, repairing them, and then restoring the purity and quantity of the refrigerant charge. A list of general precautions that should be observed while doing this follows:

1. Keep all tools as clean and dry as possible.

2. Thoroughly purge the service gauges and hoses of air and moisture before connecting them to the system. Keep them capped when not in use.

3. Thoroughly clean any refrigerant fitting before disconnecting it, in order to minimize the entrance of dirt into the system.

4. Plan any operation that requires opening the system beforehand, in order to minimize the length of time it will be exposed to open air. Cap or seal the open ends to minimize the entrance of foreign material.

5. When adding oil, pour it through an extremely clean and dry tube or funnel. Keep the oil capped whenever possible. Do not use oil that has not been kept tightly sealed.

6. Use only refrigerant 12. Purchase refrigerant intended for use in only automatic air conditioning systems. Avoid the use of refrigerant 12 that may be packaged for another use, such as cleaning, or powering a horn, as it is impure.

7. Completely evacuate any system that has been opened to replace a component, or that has leaked sufficiently to draw in moisture and air. This requires evacuating air and moisture with a good vacuum pump for at least one hour.

If a system has been open for a considerable length of time it may be advisable to evacuate the system for up to 12 hours (overnight).

8. Use a wrench on both halves of a fitting that is to be disconnected, so as to avoid placing torque on any of the refrigerant lines.

9. When overhauling a compressor, pour some of the oil into a clean glass and inspect it. If there is evidence of dirt or metal particles, or both, flush all refrigerant components with clean refrigerant before evacuating and recharging the system. In addition, if metal particles are present, the compressor should be replaced.

10. Schrader valves may leak only when under full operating pressure. Therefore, if leakage is suspected but cannot be located, operate the system with a full charge of refrigerant and look for leaks from all Schrader valves. Replace any faulty valves.

Additional Preventive Maintenance Checks

ANTIFREEZE

In order to prevent heater core freeze-up during A/C operation, it is necessary to maintain permanent type antifreeze protection of +15 degrees F, or lower. A reading of -15 degrees F is ideal since this protection also supplies sufficient corrosion inhibitors for the protection of the engine cooling system.

NOTE: The same antifreeze should not be used longer than the manufacturer specifies.

RADIATOR CAP

For efficient operation of an air conditioned car's cooling system, the radiator cap should have a holding pressure which meets manufacturer's specifications. A cap which fails to hold these pressures should be replaced.

CONDENSER

Any obstruction of or damage to the condenser configuration will restrict the air flow which is essential to its efficient operation. It is therefore a good rule to keep this unit clean and in proper physical shape.

NOTE: Bug screens are regarded as obstructions.

CONDENSATION DRAIN TUBE

This single molded drain tube expels the condensation, which accumulates on the bottom of the evaporator housing, into the engine compartment. If this tube is obstructed, the air conditioning performance can be restricted and condensation buildup can spill over onto the vehicle's floor.

Safety Precautions

Because of the importance of the necessary safety precautions that must be exercised when working with air conditioning systems and R-12 refrigerant, a recap of the safety precautions are outlined.

1. Avoid contact with a charged refrigeration system, even when working on another part of the air conditioning system or vehicle. If a heavy tool comes into contact with a section of copper tubing or a heat exchanger, it can easily cause the relatively soft material to rupture.

2. When it is necessary to apply force to a fitting which contains refrigerant, as when checking that all system couplings are securely tightened, use a wrench on both parts of the fitting involved, if possible. This will avoid putting torque on refrigerant tubing. (It is advisable, when possible, to use tube or line wrenches when tightening these flare nut fittings.)

3. Do not attempt to discharge the system by merely loosening a fitting, or removing the service valve caps and cracking these valves. Precise control is possible only when using the service gauges. Place a rag under the open end of the center charging hose while discharging the system to catch any drops of liquid that might escape. Wear protective gloves when connecting or disconnecting service gauge hoses.

4. Discharge the system only in a well ventilated area, as high concentrations of the gas can exclude oxygen and act as an anaesthetic. When leak testing or soldering, this is particularly important, as toxic gas is formed when R-12 contacts any flame.

5. Never start a system without first verifying that both service valves are back-seated, if equipped, and that all fittings throughout the system are snugly connected.

6. Avoid applying heat to any refrigerant line or storage vessel. Charging may be aided by using wa-

ter heated to less than 125° to warm the refrigerant container. Never allow a refrigerant storage container to sit out in the sun, or near any other source of heat, such as a radiator.

7. Always wear goggles when working on a system to protect the eyes. If refrigerant contacts the eyes, it is advisable in all cases to see a physician as soon as possible.

8. Frostbite from liquid refrigerant should be treated by first gradually warming the area with cool water, and then gently applying petroleum jelly. A physician should be consulted.

9. Always keep refrigerant drum fittings capped when not in use. Avoid sudden shock to the drum, which might occur from dropping it, or from banging a heavy tool against it. Never carry a drum in the passenger compartment of a car.

10. Always completely discharge the system before painting the vehicle (if the paint is to be baked on), or before welding anywhere near refrigerant lines.

AIR CONDITIONING TOOLS AND GAUGES

Test Gauges

Most of the service work performed in air conditioning requires the use of a set of two gauges, one for the high (head) pressure side of the system, the other for the low (suction) side.

The low side gauge records both pressure and vacuum. Vacuum readings are calibrated from 0 to 30 inches and the pressure graduations read from 0 to no less than 60 psi.

The high side gauge measures pressure from 0 to at least 600 psi. Both gauges are threaded into a manifold that contains two hand shut-off valves. Proper manipulation of these valves and the use of the attached test hoses allow the user to perform the following services:

1. Test high and low side pressures.
2. Remove air, moisture, and contaminated refrigerant.
3. Purge the system (of refrigerant).
4. Charge the system (with refrigerant).

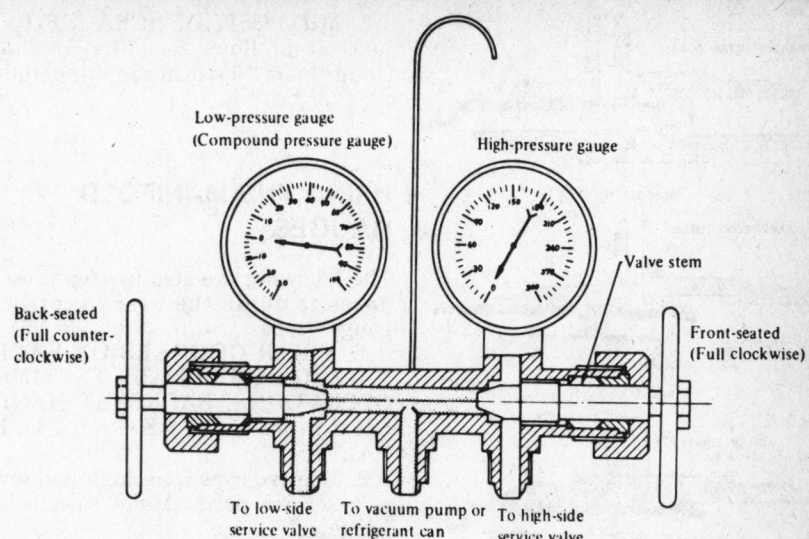

Typical manifold gauge set

NOTE: Chrysler Corp. requires the use of a third gauge on those units that have an evaporator pressure regulator (EPR) valve mounted on the suction side of the compressor.

The manifold valves are designed so they have no direct effect on gauge readings, but serve only to provide for, or cut off, flow of refrigerant through the manifold. During all testing and hook-up operations, the valves are kept in a closed position to avoid disturbing the refrigeration system. The valves are opened only to purge the system of refrigerant or to charge it.

When purging the system, the center hose is uncapped at the lower end, and both valves are cracked open slightly. This allows refrigerant pressure to force the entire contents of the system out through the center hose. During charging, the valve on the high side of the manifold is closed, and the valve on the low side is cracked open. Under these conditions, the low pressure in the evaporator will draw refrigerant from the relatively warm refrigerant storage container into the system.

Service Valves

For the user to diagnose an air conditioning system he or she must gain "entrance" to the system in order to observe the pressures. There are two types of terminals for this purpose, the hand shut off type and the familiar Schrader valve.

The Schrader valve is similar to a tire valve stem and the process of connecting the test hoses is the same as threading a hand pump outlet hose to a bicycle tire. As the test hose is threaded to the service port the valve

core is depressed, allowing the refrigerant to enter the test hose outlet. Removal of the test hose automatically closes the system.

Extreme caution must be observed when removing test hoses from the Schrader valves as some refrigerant will normally escape, usually under high pressure. (Observe safety precautions.)

Some systems have hand shut-off valves (the stem can be rotated with a special ratcheting box wrench) that can be positioned in the following three ways:

1. FRONT SEATED—Rotated to full clockwise position.

   a. Refrigerant will not flow to

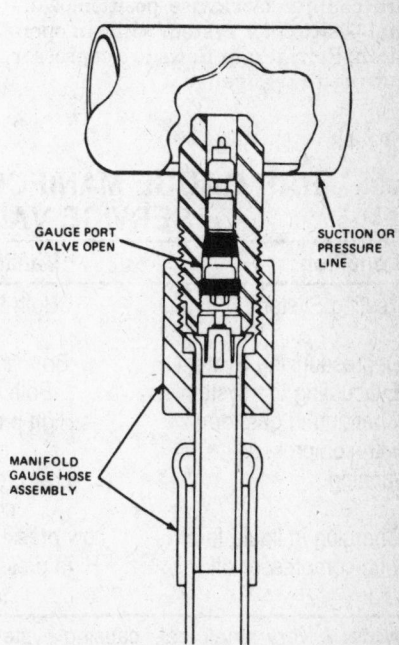

Manifold gauge hose connected to a Schraeder type service port

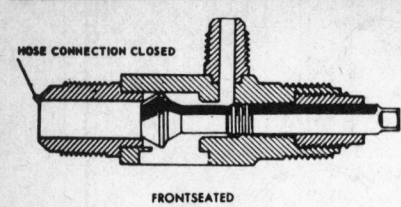

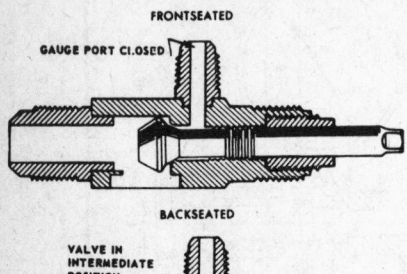

Manual service valve positions

compressor, but will reach test gauge port. COMPRESSOR WILL BE DAMAGED IF SYSTEM IS TURNED ON IN THIS POSITION.

b. The compressor is now isolated and ready for service. However, care must be exercised when removing service valves from the compressor as a residue of refrigerant may still be present within the compressor. Therefore, remove service valves slowly observing all safety precautions.

2. BACK SEATED – Rotated to full counter clockwise position. Normal position for system while in operation. Refrigerant flows to compressor but not to test gauge.

3. MID-POSITION (CRACKED) – Refrigerant flows to entire system. Gauge port (with hose connected) open for testing.

USING THE MANIFOLD GAUGES

The following are step-by-step procedures to guide the user to correct gauge usage.

1. WEAR GOGGLES OR FACE SHIELD DURING ALL TESTING OPERATIONS. BACKSEAT HAND SHUT-OFF TYPE SERVICE VALVES.

2. Remove caps from high and low side service ports. Make sure both gauge valves are closed.

3. Connect low side test hose to service valve that leads to the evaporator (located between the evaporator outlet and the compressor).

4. Attach high side test hose to service valve that leads to the condenser.

5. Mid-position hand shutoff type service valves.

6. Start engine and allow for warm-up. All testing and charging of the system should be done after engine and system have reached normal operation temperatures (except when using certain charging stations).

7. Adjust air conditioner controls to maximum cold.

8. Observe gauge readings.

When the gauges are not being used it is a good idea to:

a. Keep both hand valves in the closed position.

b. Attach both ends of the high and low service hoses to the manifold, if extra outlets are present on the manifold, or plug them if not.

Also, keep the center charging hose attached to an empty refrigerant can. This extra precaution will reduce the possibility of moisture entering the gauges. If air and moisture have gotten into the gauges, purge the hoses by supplying refrigerant under pressure to the center hose with both gauge valves open and all openings unplugged.

DISCHARGING, EVACUATING AND CHARGING

Discharging the System

—— CAUTION ——
Perform operation in a well-ventilated area.

When it is necessary to remove (purge) the refrigerant pressurized in the system, follow this procedure:

1. Operate air conditioner for at least 10 minutes.

2. Attach gauges, shut off engine and air conditioner.

3. Place a container or rag at the outlet of the center charging hose on the gauge. The refrigerant will be discharged there and this precaution will avoid its uncontrolled exposure.

4. Open low side hand valve on gauge slightly.

5. Open high side hand valve slightly.

NOTE: Too rapid a purging process will be identified by the appearance of an oily foam. If this occurs, close the hand valves a little more until this condition stops.

6. Close both hand valves on the gauge set when the pressures read 0 and all the refrigerant has left the system.

Evacuating the System

Before charging any system it is necessary to purge the refrigerant and draw out the trapped moisture with a suitable vacuum pump. Failure to do so will result in ineffective charging and possible damage to the system.

Use this hook-up for the proper evacuation procedure:

1. Connect both service gauge hoses to the high and low service outlets.

BAR GAUGE MANIFOLD AND COMPRESSOR SERVICE VALVE SETTINGS

Condition	Manifold Valves	Compressor Valves
Testing System	Both fully closed	Both cracked off backseat
Depressurizing System	Both cracked open	Both at mid position
Evacuating the system	Both wide open	Both at mid position
Charging in gas form with compressor running	High pressure valve closed	High pressure valve cracked off backseat
	Low pressure valve cracked	Low pressure valve at mid position
Charging in liquid form with compressor off	Low pressure valve closed	Both valves mid positioned
	High pressure valve wide open	

Note: A very small leak, causing system discharge about every two weeks, can be caused by a leaky Schrader type service valve. Check these valves with extra care when testing for a small leak.

2. Open high and low side hand valves on gauge manifold.

3. Open both service valves a slight amount (from back seated position), allow refrigerant to discharge from system.

4. Install center charging hose of gauge set to vacuum pump.

5. Operate vacuum pump for at least one hour. (If the system has been subjected to open conditions for a prolonged period of time it may be necessary to "pump the system down" overnight. Refer to "System Sweep" procedure.)

NOTE: If low pressure gauge does not show at least 28" hg. within 5 minutes, check the system for a leak or loose gauge connectors.

6. Close hand valves on gauge manifold.

7. Shut off pump.

8. Observe low pressure gauge to determine if vacuum is holding. A vacuum drop may indicate a leak.

System Sweep

An efficient vacuum pump can remove all the air contained in a contaminated air conditioning system very quickly, because of its vapor state. Moisture, however, is far more difficult to remove because the vacuum must force the liquid to evaporate before it will be able to remove it from the system. If a system has become severely contaminated, as, for example, it might become after all the charge was lost in conjunction with vehicle

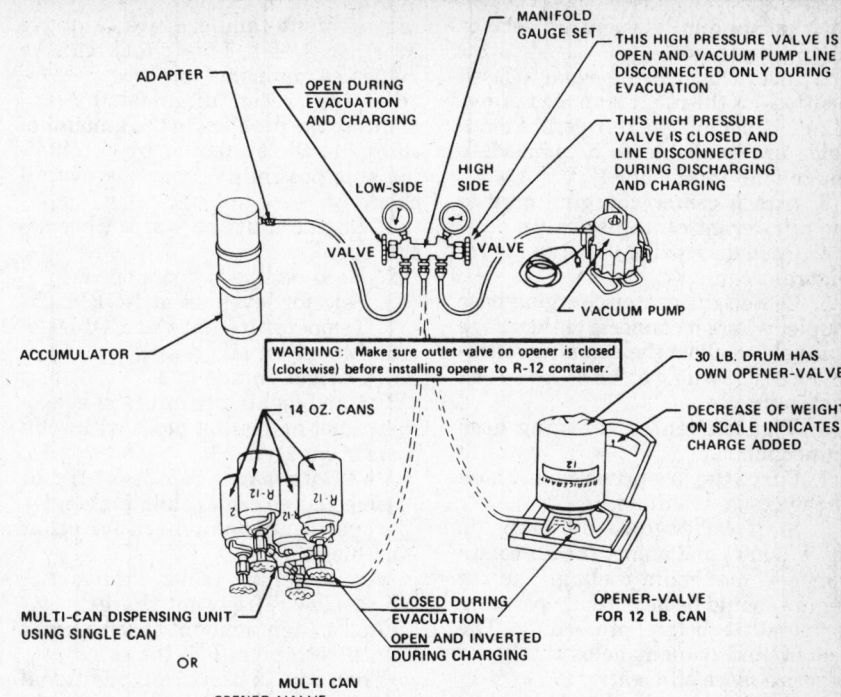

WARNING: Make sure outlet valve on opener is closed (clockwise) before installing opener to R-12 container.

Typical gauge connections for discharge, evacuation and charging the system

accident damage, moisture removal is extremely time consuming. A vacuum pump could remove all of the moisture only if it were operated for 12 hours or more.

Under these conditions, sweeping the system with refrigerant will speed the process of moisture removal considerably. To sweep, follow the following procedure:

1. Connect vacuum pump to

gauges, operate it until vacuum ceases to increase, then continue operation for ten more minutes.

2. Charge system with 50% of its rated refrigerant capacity.

3. Operate system at fast idle for ten minutes.

4. Discharge the system.

5. Repeat twice the process of charging to 50% capacity, running the system for ten minutes, and discharging it, for a total of three sweeps.

6. Replace drier.

7. Pump system down as in Step 1.

8. Charge system.

Charging the System

——— CAUTION ———

Never attempt to charge the system by opening the high pressure gauge control while the compressor is operating. The compressor accumulating pressure can burst the refrigerant container, causing sever personal injuries.

BASIC SYSTEM

In this procedure the refrigerant enters the suction side of the system as a vapor while the compressor is running. Before proceeding, the system should be in a partial vacuum after adequate evacuation. Both hand valves on the gauge manifold should be closed.

1. Attach both test hoses to their respective service valve ports. Mid-

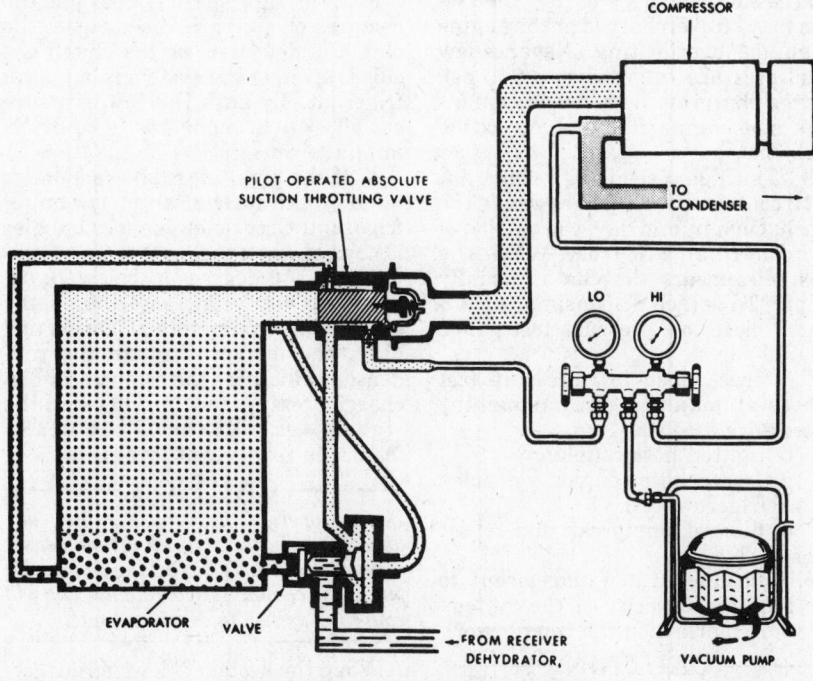

Schematic for evacuating the system

position manually operated service valves, if present.

2. Install dispensing valve (closed position) on the refrigerant container. (Single and multiple refrigerant manifolds are available to accommodate one to four 15 oz. cans.)

3. Attach center charging hose to the refrigerant container valve.

4. Open dispensing valve on the refrigerant can.

5. Loosen the center charging hose coupler where it connects to the gauge manifold to allow the escaping refrigerant to purge the hose of contaminants.

6. Tighten center charging hose connection.

7. Purge the low pressure test hose at the gauge manifold.

8. Start car engine, roll down the car windows and adjust the air conditioner to maximum cooling. The car engine should be at normal operating temperature before proceeding. The heated environment helps the liquid vaporize more efficiently.

9. Crack open the low side hand valve on the manifold. Manipulate the valve so that the refrigerant that enters the system does not cause the low side pressure to exceed 40 psi. Too sudden a surge may permit the entrance of unwanted liquid to the compressor. Since liquids cannot be compressed, the compressor will suffer damage if compelled to attempt it. If the suction side of the system remains in a vacuum the system is blocked. Locate and correct the condition before proceeding any further.

NOTE: Placing the refrigerant can in a container of warm water (no hotter than 125°F) will speed the charging process. Slight agitation of the can is helpful too, but be careful not to turn the can upside down.

Some manufacturers allow for a partial charging of the A/C system in the form of a liquid (can inverted and compressor off) by opening the high side gauge valve only, and putting the high side compressor service valve in the middle position (if so equipped). The remainder of the refrigerant is then added in the form of a gas in the normal manner, through the suction side only.

SYSTEMS WITHOUT SIGHT GLASS, EXCEPT CCOT SYSTEM

The following procedure can be used to quickly determine whether or not an air conditioning system has the proper charge of refrigerant (providing ambient temperature is above 70°F, or 21°C). This check can be made in a manner of minutes, thus facilitating system diagnosis by pinpointing the problem to the amount of charge in the system or by eliminating this possibility from the overall checkout.

1. Engine must be warm (thermostat open).

2. Hood and body doors open.

3. Selector lever set at NORM.

4. Temperature lever at COLD.

5. Blower on HI.

6. Normal engine idle.

7. Hand-feel temperature of evaporator inlet and outlet pipes with compressor engaged.

a. Both same temperature or some degree cooler than ambient—proper condition: check for other problems.

b. Inlet pipe cooler than outlet pipe—low refrigerant charge.
• Add a slight amount of refrigerant until both pipes feel the same.
• Then add 15 oz. (1 can) additional refrigerant.

c. Inlet pipe has frost accumulation—outlet pipe warmer: proceed as in Step b above.

If during the charging process the head pressure exceeds 200 psi, place an electric fan in front of the car and direct the turbulent air to the condenser. If no fan is available, repeatedly pour cool water over the top of the condenser. These cooling actions may be necessary on an extremely warm day to help dissipate the heat emitted by the engine during idle.

If this fails and pressure on the discharge side continues to rise, the system may be overcharged or the engine might be overheating. Never allow head pressure to go beyond 240 psi. during charging. If this condition occurs, stop engine, find and correct the problem.

8. Continue dispensing refrigerant until container is no longer cool to the touch. On a humid day, the outside of the container will frost. When the frost disappears the can is usually empty. To detach dispensing can:

a. close low pressure test gauge hand valve.

b. crack open low pressure test hose at manifold until remaining pressure escapes.

c. tighten hose coupler.

d. loosen hose coupler connected to refrigerant can.

e. discard empty can and repeat Steps 2–8.

9. Continue to add refrigerant to the required capacity of the system. (Usually marked on the compressor).

———— CAUTION ————
DO NOT OVERCHARGE. This condition is usually indicated by an abnormally high side pressure reading and a noisy compressor resulting in ineffective cooling and damage to the system.

SYSTEMS WITH A SIGHT GLASS

The air conditioning systems that use a sight glass as a means to check the refrigerant level, should be carefully checked to avoid under or over charging. The gauge set should be attached to the system for verification of pressures.

To check the system with the sight glass, clean the glass and start the vehicle engine. Operate the air conditioning controls on maximum for approximately five minutes to stabilize the system. The room temperature should be above 70 degrees. Check the sight glass for one of the following conditions:

1. If the sight glass is clear, the compressor clutch is engaged, the compressor discharge line is warm and the compressor inlet line is cool, the system has a full charge of refrigerant.

2. If the sight glass is clear, the compressor clutch is engaged and there is no significant temperature difference between the compressor inlet and discharge lines, the system is empty or nearly empty. By having the gauge set attached to the system a measurement can be taken. If the gauge reads less than 25 psi, the low pressure cutoff protection switch has failed.

3. If the sight glass is clear and the compressor clutch is disengaged, the clutch is defective, or the clutch circuit is open, or the system is out of refrigerant. By-pass the low pressure cut-off switch momentarily to determine the cause.

4. If the sight glass shows foam or bubbles, the system can be low on refrigerant. Occasional foam or bubbles is normal when the room temperature is above 110 degrees or below 70 degrees. To verify, increase the engine speed to approximately 1500 rpm and block the airflow through the condenser to increase the compressor discharge pressure to 225–250 psi. If the sight glass still shows bubbles or foam, the refrigerant level is low.

———— CAUTION ————
Do not operate the vehicle engine any longer than necessary with the condenser airflow blocked. This blocking action also blocks the cooling system radiator and will cause the system to overheat rapidly.

When the system is low on refrigerant, a leak is present or the system was not properly charged. Use a leak detector and locate the problem area and repair. If no leakage is found, charge the system to its capacity. (Refer to the refrigerant capacity chart at the end of this section).

— CAUTION —

It is not advisable to add refrigerant to a system utilizing the suction throttling valve and a sight glass, because the amount of refrigerant required to remove the foam or bubbles will result in an overcharge and potentially damaged system components.

CCOT SYSTEM

When charging the CCOT system, attach only the low pressure line to the low pressure gauge port, located on the accumulator. Do not attach the high pressure line to any service port or allow it to remain attached to the vacuum pump after evacuation. Be sure both the high and the low pressure control valves are closed on the gauge set. To complete the charging of the system, follow the outline supplied.

1. Start the engine and allow to run at idle, with the cooling system at normal operating temperature.
2. Attach the center gauge hose to a single or multi-can dispenser.
3. With the multi-can dispenser inverted, allow one pound or the contents of one or two 14 oz. cans to enter the system through the low pressure side by opening the gauge low pressure control valve.
4. Close the low pressure gauge control valve and turn the A/C system on to engage the compressor. Place the blower motor in its high mode.
5. Open the low pressure gauge control valve and draw the remaining charge into the system. Refer to the capacity chart at the end of this section for the individual vehicle or system capacity.
6. Close the low pressure gauge control valve and the refrigerant source valve, on the multi-can dispenser. Remove the low pressure hose from the accumulator quickly to avoid

Check item \ Amount of refrigerant	Almost no refrigerant	Insufficient	Suitable	Too much refrigerant
Temperature of high pressure and low pressure lines.	Almost no difference between high pressure and low pressure side temperature.	High pressure side is warm and low pressure side is fairly cold.	High pressure side is hot and low pressure side is cold.	High pressure side is abnormally hot.
State in sight glass.	Bubbles flow continuously. Bubbles will disappear and something like mist will flow when refrigerant is nearly gone.	The bubbles are seen at intervals of 1 - 2 seconds.	Almost transparent. Bubbles may appear when engine speed is raised and lowered. No clear difference exists betwen these two conditions.	No bubbles can be seen.
Pressure of system.	High pressure side is abnormally low.	Both pressure on high and low pressure sides are slightly low.	Both pressures on high and low pressure sides are normal.	Both pressures on high and low pressure sides are abnormally high.
Repair.	Stop compressor immediately and conduct an overall check.	Check for gas leakage, repair as required, replenish and charge system.		Discharge refrigerant from service valve of low pressure side.

Using a sight glass to determine the relative refrigerant charge

loss of refrigerant through the Schrader valve.

7. Install the protective cap on the gauge port and check the system for leakage.

8. Test the system for proper operation.

Leak Testing the System

There are several methods of detecting leaks in an air conditioning system; among them, the two most popular are (1) halide leak-detection or the "open flame method," and (2) electronic leak-detection.

The halide leak detection is a torch like device which produces a yellow-green color when refrigerant is introduced into the flame at the burner. A purple or violet color indicates the presence of large amounts of refrigerant at the burner.

An electronic leak detector is a small portable electronic device with an extended probe. With the unit activated the probe is passed along those components of the system which contain refrigerant. If a leak is detected, the unit will sound an alarm signal or activate a display signal depending on the manufacturer's design. It is advisable to follow the manufacturer's instructions as the design and function of the detection may vary significantly.

— CAUTION —

Caution should be taken to operate either type of detector in well ventilated areas, so as to reduce the chance of personal injury, which may result from coming in contact with poisonous gases produced when R-12 is exposed to flame or electric spark.

REFRIGERANT CAPACITIES CHART

Auto Manufacturer	1980		1981		1982–87	
	Models	Recharge Capacities (lbs.)①	Models	Recharge Capacities (lbs.)①	Models	Recharge Capacities (lbs.)①
AMERICAN MOTORS CORP.	Concord	2	Concord	2	All	2.00
	Pacer	2⅛	Spirit	2		
	Spirit	2	Eagle	2		
	Eagle	2				

REFRIGERANT CAPACITIES CHART

Auto Manufacturer	1980		1981		1982–87	
	Models	Recharge Capacities (lbs.) ①	Models	Recharge Capacities (lbs.) ①	Models	Recharge Capacities (lbs.) ①
BUICK MOTOR DIVISION	Skyhawk	2½	Skyhawk	2½	Electra, LeSabre	3.50
	Skylark	2¾	Skylark	2¾	Regal, Century, Skylark	2.75
	Electra, LeSabre	3¾	Electra, LeSabre	3¾	Riviera, Somerset Regal	3.25
	Century, Regal, Riviera	3½	Century, Regal, Riviera	3½	Skyhawk	2.50
CADILLAC MOTOR CAR DIVISION	Seville, Eldorado	3½	Seville, Eldorado	3½	Cimarron	1.87
	All others	3¾	All others	3¾	Seville	2.75
					All others	3.50
CHEVROLET MOTOR DIVISION	Monza, Nova	3½	Monza, Nova	3½	Corvette, Camaro	3.00
	Chevette	2¼	Chevette	2¼	Caprice, Impala	3.50
	Camaro	3¼	Camaro	3¼	Monte Carlo	3.25
	Corvette	3	Corvette	3	Malibu, Celebrity, Citation, Cavalier	2.75
	Citation	2¾	Citation	2¾	Chevette	2.25
	Malibu, Impala, Caprice	3¾	Malibu, Impala, Caprice	3¾		
CHRYSLER CORPORATION	All, except below	2⅝	All, except below	2⅝	Diplomat, Gran Fury, New Yorker, Mirada, Cordoba, Imperial	2.62
	Omni, Horizon	2⅛	Omni, Horizon, Aries, Reliant	2⅛	Aries, Reliant, LeBaron, E-Class, 400, 600	2.37 ③
					Omni, Horizon, 024, TC3, Charger, Turismo	2.12
FORD DIVISION	Pinto	2¼	Escort, EXP	2½	Thunderbird, Fairmont, Granada, Mustang, Escort, EXP	2.56
	All others ②	3½	All others ②	3½	LTD, Crown Victoria	3.25
LINCOLN-MERCURY DIVISION	Bobcat	2¼	Lynx, LN7	2½	Lincoln Continental, XR-7, Zephyr, Cougar, Capri, Lynx, LN7	2.56
	All others ②	3½	All others ②	3½	Lincoln, Mark VI	3.00
					Marquis, Grand Marquis	3.25
OLDSMOBILE DIVISION	Cutlass, 88, 98	3¾	Cutlass, 88, 98	3¾	88, 98	3.50
	Toronado	3½	Toronado	3½	Cutlass, Cutlass Ciera, Omega	2.75
	Starfire	2½	Starfire	2½	Toronado	3.25
	Omega	2¾	Omega	2¾	Firenza	2.50
PONTIAC MOTOR DIVISION	Catalina, Bonneville	3½	Catalina, Bonneville Lemans, Gran Am	3½	Firebird	3.00
	Firebird	3¼	Firebird	3¼	Bonneville, Parisienne, Grand Am	3.30
	Sunbird	2½	Sunbird	2½	Grand Prix	3.30
	Phoenix	2¾	Phoenix	2¾	6000, Phoenix	2.75
					J-2000, Fiero, Sunbird	2.50
					T-1000	2.25

① All refrigerant charges listed are approximate and represent a minimal reserve with moderate head pressures. Check label on or near compressor for correct charge.

② Ford, Mercury and Lincoln vehicles using Frigidaire 6 cylinder compressor—4¼ lbs.

③ 1985 and later Aries, Reliant, LeBaron, E class, 400 & 600 recharge capacities are 2.12 lbs.

Charging and Starting 33

SOLENOID AND NEUTRAL SAFETY SWITCH

IDENTIFICATION

Solenoids Without Relays

This type of starter solenoid is always mounted on the starter. It makes electrical contact for the starter, it pulls the starter and the drive clutch into mesh with the flywheel. The Chrysler reduction gear starter has this solenoid embodied in the starter housing, however an internal relay is integral to the brush plate. The ignition by-pass terminal is usually marked **R** or **IGN**, if it is used.

Solenoids With Separate Relays

The solenoid is always mounted on the starter. In addition to making contact for the starter, it also pulls the starter drive clutch gear into mesh with the flywheel. A single control terminal is used on the solenoid. The relay is usually found mounted to the inner fender panel or on the firewall.

Solenoids With Built-In Relays

These units are mounted on the starter and are connected, through linkage, to the starter clutch. The relay portion is built into the solenoid assembly.

Neutral Safety Switches

The purpose of the neutral safety switch is to prevent the starter from cranking the engine except when the transmission is in the **NEUTRAL** or the **PARK** positions. On some vehicles, the neutral safety switch is located on the transmission; it serves to ground the solenoid or magnetic switch, whichever is used. On other vehicles, the neutral safety switch is located either at the bottom of the steering column (where it contacts the shift mechanism), on the steering column, underneath the dash or on the shift linkage (console).

Some manual transmission models have a clutch linkage safety switch to prevent starter operation unless the clutch pedal is depressed. On most cars, the neutral safety switch and the back-up light switch are combined into a single switch mechanism.

TROUBLESHOOTING NEUTRAL SAFETY SWITCHES – QUICK TEST

If the starter fails to function and the neutral safety switch is to be checked, a jumper can be placed across its terminals. If the starter then functions, the safety switch is defective. In the case of the neutral safety switches having 1 wire, the wire must be grounded for testing purposes. If the starter works with the wire grounded, the switch is defective.

NEUTRAL SAFETY SWITCH BACK-UP LIGHT SWITCH

When the neutral safety switch is built in combination with the back-up light switch, the easiest way to tell which terminals are for the back-up lights is to place a jumper on and across each pair of wires. The pair of wires which light the back-up lamps should be ignored when testing the neutral safety switch. Once the back-up light wires have been located, jump the other pair of wires to test the neutral safety switch. If the starter functions only when the jumper is placed across these 2 wires, the neutral safety switch is defective or requires adjustment.

STARTER MOTORS

Chrysler Reduction Gear Starter Motor

DISASSEMBLY & ASSEMBLY

1. Support the assembly in a vise equipped with soft jaws; do not clamp. Care must be used not to distort or damage the die cast aluminum housing.

2. Remove the housing bolts and remove the end housing.

3. Carefully pull the armature up and out of the gear housing, remove the starter frame and the field assembly. Remove the steel and the fiber thrust washers.

NOTE: On V8 engines the starting motors have the wire of the shunt field coil soldered to the brush terminal. The 6 cylinder engines have the 4 coils in series and do not have a wire soldered to the brush terminal. One pair of brushes is connected to this terminal, while the other pair is at-

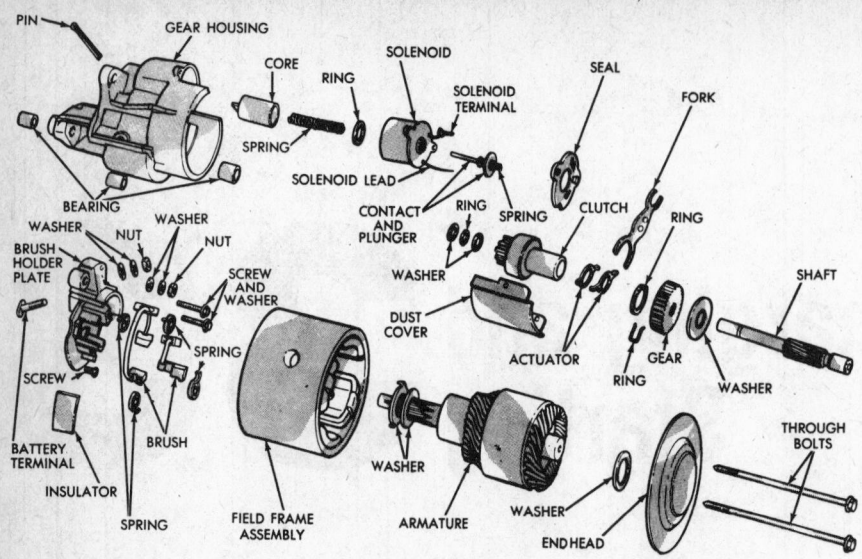

Rear wheel drive reduction gear motor—Chrysler Corp.

tached to the series field coils by means of a terminal screw. Carefully pull the frame and the field assembly up enough to expose the terminal screw and the solder connection of the shunt field at the brush terminal. Place 2 wooden blocks between the starter frame and gear housing to facilitate removal of the terminal screw and unsoldering of the shunt field wire at the brush terminal.

4. Support the brush terminal with a finger behind the terminal and remove the screw.

5. On the V8 engine starters, unsolder the shunt field coil lead from the brush terminal and the housing.

6. The brush holder plate with the terminal, the contact and the brushes is serviced as an assembly.

7. Clean the old sealant from around the plate and the housing, remove the brush holder attaching screw.

8. On the shunt type, unsolder the solenoid winding from the brush terminal, remove the $^{11}/_{32}$ in. nut, the washer and the insulator from solenoid terminal.

9. Remove the brush holder plate with the brushes as an assembly.

10. Remove gear housing ground screw and remove the solenoid assembly from the well. Remove the nut, the washer and the seal from starter (battery) terminal, remove the terminal from the plate.

11. Remove the solenoid contact and plunger from the solenoid. Remove the coil sleeve. Remove the solenoid return spring, coil retaining washer, retainer and the dust cover from the gear housing.

12. Release the snap-ring which locates the driven gear pinion shaft and remove the front retaining ring. Push the pinion shaft rearward, remove the snap-ring, thrust washers, clutch and the pinion. Remove the 2 shift fork nylon actuators.

13. Remove the driven gear and the friction washer. Pull the shifting fork forward and remove the moving core.

14. Remove the fork retainer pin and the shifting fork assembly. The gear housing with bushings is serviced as an assembly.

15. Any brushes that are worn more than ½ the length of new brushes or are oil soaked, should be replaced.

16. When resoldering the shunt field and the solenoid lead, make a strong low resistance connection using a high temperature solder and a resin flux. Do not use acid or acid core solder. Do not break the shunt field wire units when removing and installing the brushes.

17. Do not immerse the starter clutch unit in a cleaning solvent. The outside of the clutch and the pinion must be cleaned with a cloth so as not to wash the lubricant from the inside of the clutch.

18. Rotate the pinion, the pinion gear should rotate smoothly and in 1 direction only. If the starter clutch unit does not function properly or if the pinion is worn, chipped or burred, replace the starter clutch unit.

19. Inspect the commutator and the brush contact surface when the starter is assembled, for flat spots, out of roundness or excessive wear.

20. Reface the commutator (if necessary), by removing only a sufficient amount of metal to provide a smooth, even surface.

21. Using light pressure, clean the

grooves of the face of the commutator with a pointed tool. Do not remove any metal or widen the grooves.

22. Assembly is the reverse of the disassembly procedure. After lubricating the plates with a small amount of SAE 10 engine oil, they should have about $^{1}/_{16}$ in. side movement to insure proper pinion gear engagement.

Bosch, 1982–86 Nippondenso and Mitsubishi Starter

DISASSEMBLY & ASSEMBLY

1. Position the assembly in the proper holding fixture. Disconnect the field coil wire from the solenoid terminal.

2. Remove the solenoid mounting screws (and the solenoid Bosch automatic transmission) and work the solenoid (plunger Bosch automatic transmission) off the shift fork.

3. On Nippondenso units remove the bearing cover, armature shaft lock, washer, spring and seal.

4. On Bosch units remove the 2 screws holding down the end shield bearing cap and remove the cap and washers.

5. Remove the through bolts and the commutator end frame cover. Remove the 2 brushes and the brush plate. Slide the field frame off over the armature.

6. Take out the shift lever pivot bolt. Take off the rubber gasket and metal plate.

7. For the Bosch (automatic transmission) and all Nippondenso units remove the armature assembly and shift lever from the drive end housing. For the Bosch (manual transmission) press the stop collar off the snap-ring, remove the snap-ring, remove the clutch assembly and remove the drive end housing from the armature.

8. For all except the Bosch (manual transmission), press the stop collar off the snap-ring and remove the snap-ring, stop collar and clutch.

9. Brushes that are worn more than one half the length of new brushes, or are oil soaked should be replaced. New brushes are $^{11}/_{16}$ in. long.

10. Do not immerse the starter clutch unit in cleaning solvent. Solvent will wash the lubricant from the clutch.

11. Place the drive unit on the armature shaft and while holding the armature rotate the pinion. The drive pinion should rotate smoothly in 1 direction only. The pinion may not rotate easily but as long as it rotates smoothly it is in good condition. If the clutch unit does not function properly or if

the pinion is worn, chipped or burred replace the unit.

12. Assembly is the reverse of the disassembly procedure. Lubricate the armature shaft and splines with SAE 10 or 30 W oil.

13. On all except the Bosch (manual transmission) install the clutch, stop collar, lock ring and shaft fork on the armature. On the Bosch (manual transmission) install the drive end housing on the armature. Install the clutch, stop collar and snap-ring on the armature.

14. On all except the Bosch (manual transmission) install the armature assembly and shift fork in the drive end housing. On Bosch units install the shim and armature shaft lock. Check the end play it should be 0.002–0.021 in.

1987–89 Nippondenso Starter

DISASSEMBLY & ASSEMBLY

1. Position the assembly in a suitable holding fixture. Remove the rubber boot from the field coil terminal. Remove the nut from the field coil terminal stud. Remove the field coil terminal from the stud.

2. Remove the through bolts. Remove the splash shield. Remove the end shield screws from the brush plate. Remove the starter end shield.

3. Slide the brushes from their holders. Pry the retaining springs back for access and remove the brush plate.

4. Slide the armature out of the starter housing. Remove the starter housing from the gear housing. Remove the solenoid terminal cover.

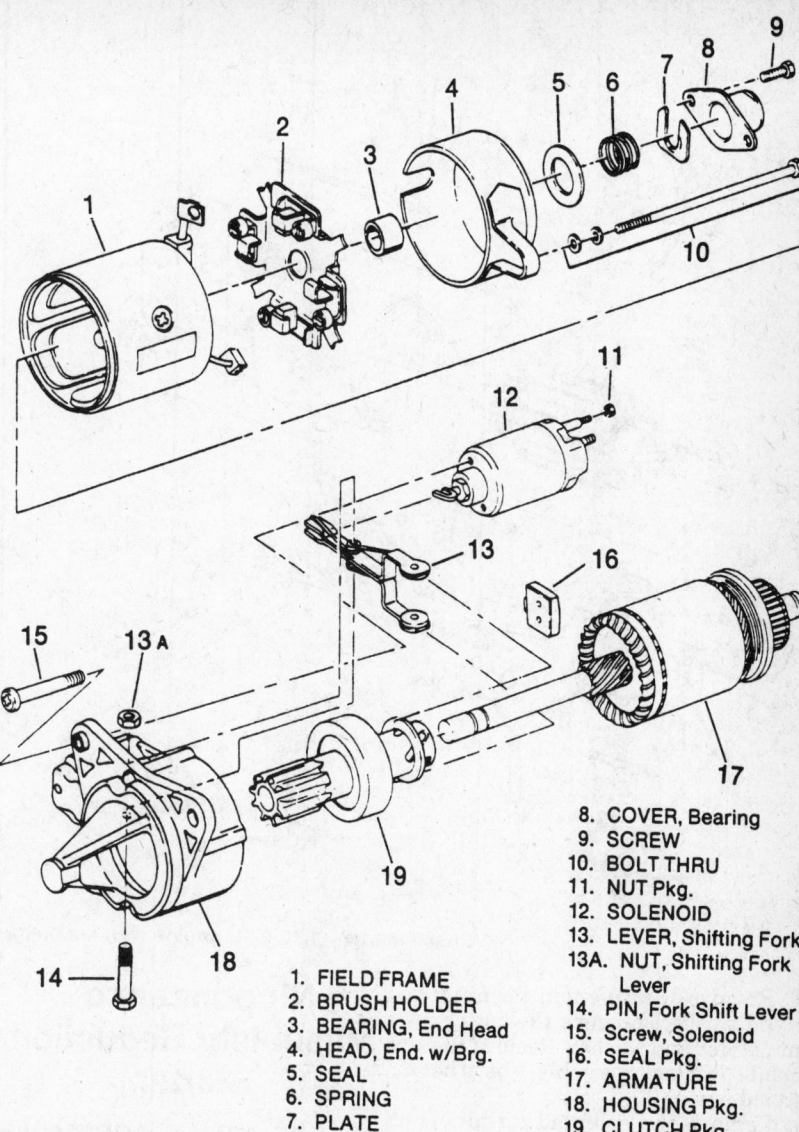

1. FIELD FRAME
2. BRUSH HOLDER
3. BEARING, End Head
4. HEAD, End. w/Brg.
5. SEAL
6. SPRING
7. PLATE
8. COVER, Bearing
9. SCREW
10. BOLT THRU
11. NUT Pkg.
12. SOLENOID
13. LEVER, Shifting Fork
13A. NUT, Shifting Fork Lever
14. PIN, Fork Shift Lever
15. Screw, Solenoid
16. SEAL Pkg.
17. ARMATURE
18. HOUSING Pkg.
19. CLUTCH Pkg.

Nippondenso starter – 1.7L engine with manual transmission

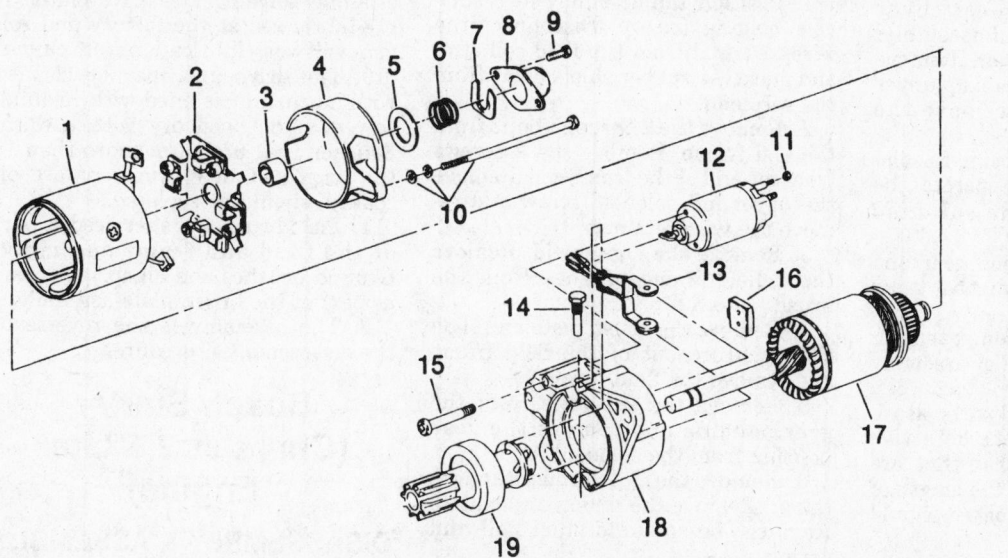

1. FIELD FRAME
2. BRUSH HOLDER
3. BEARING, End Head
4. HEAD, End w/Brg.
5. SEAL
6. SPRING
7. PLATE
8. COVER, Bearing
9. SCREW
10. BOLT THRU
11. NUT Pkg.
12. SOLENOID
13. LEVER, Shift Fork
14. PIN, Fork Shift Lever
15. SCREW, Solenoid
16. SEAL Pkg.
17. ARMATURE Pkg.
18. HOUSING Pkg.
19. CLUTCH Pkg.

Nippondenso starter – typical except 1.7 with manual transmission

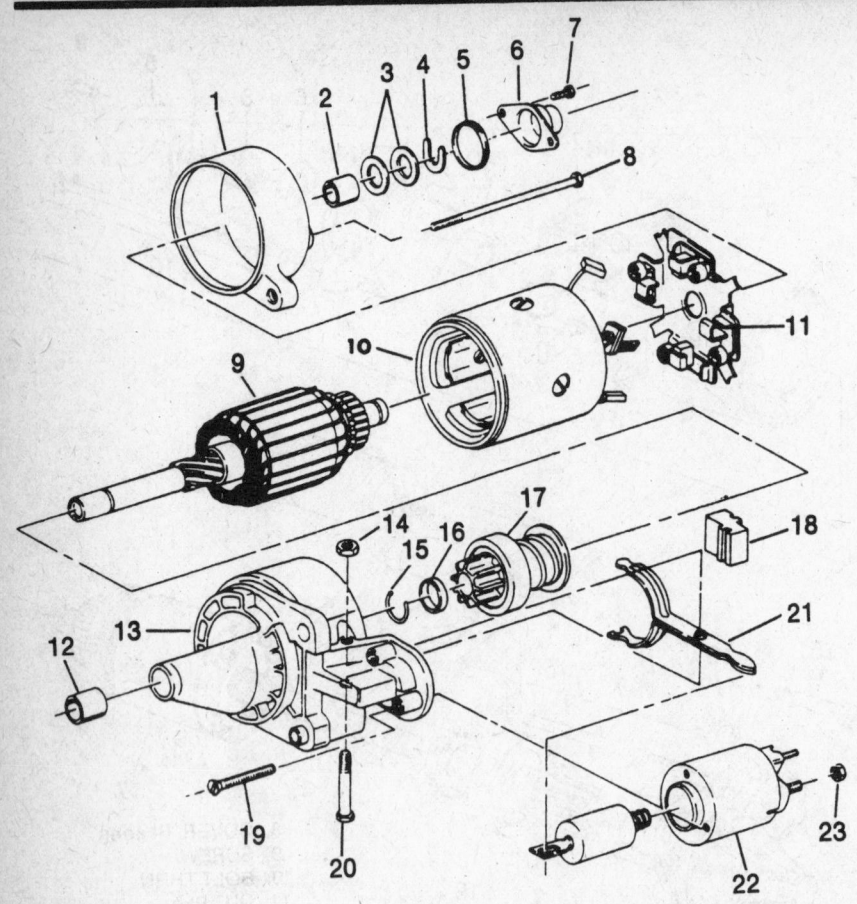

1. HEAD, End
2. BEARING, End Head
3. SHIM PKG.
4. WASHER, Retaining
5. SEAL
6. COVER, Bearing
7. SCREW, Bearing Cover
8. BOLT THRU
9. ARMATURE
10. FIELD FRAME
11. BRUSH HOLDER
12. BEARING, Housing
13. HOUSING
14. NUT, Fork shift Lever
15. SNAP RING
16. SEAL
17. CLUTCH
18. SEAL
19. SCREW, Solenoid
20. PIN, Shift Fork Lever
21. LEVER, Shift Fork
22. SOLENOID
23. NUT, Connecting Terminal

Bosch starter – 1.7L 2.2L engine with automatic transmission

5. Remove the solenoid terminal nut and washer. Remove the battery terminal nut and washer. Remove the solenoid terminal assembly from the terminal posts.

6. Remove the solenoid terminal from the insulator. Remove the battery terminal from the insulator.

7. Remove the solenoid cover screws from the solenoid assembly. Remove the solenoid cover. Remove the seal. Remove the solenoid plunger from the housing and remove the plunger spring.

8. Remove the gear housing-to-solenoid retaining screws. Separate the gear housing from the solenoid housing.

9. Remove the reduction gear and clutch assembly from the gear housing.

10. Remove the reduction gear, pinion gear, retainer and roller assembly from the gear housing.

11. Inspect and clean all parts, as required. Repair or replace defective parts as required. Brushes that are worn more than one half the length of new brushes, or are oil soaked should be replaced.

12. Assembly is the reverse of the disassembly procedure.

Nippondenso/ Mitsubishi Reduction Starter

DISASSEMBLY & ASSEMBLY

1. Position the assembly in a suitable holding fixture. Disconnect the wire terminal from the field coil stud and remove the rubber shield away from the wire end.

2. Remove the 2 through bolts from the end frame. Remove the 2 screws from the end of the frame cap. Remove the upper left solenoid screw and remove the wire retainer.

3. Remove the end shield. Remove the 2 field frame brushes from the brush plate.

4. Remove the brush plate and slide the armature out of the field frame and remove the field frame.

5. Remove the 2 screws from the gear housing and remove the gear housing from the solenoid.

6. Remove the clutch rollers and retainer. Remove the pinion and clutch. Remove the solenoid steel ball and spring.

7. Remove the solenoid cover

screws, remove the solenoid cover and remove the solenoid plunger.

8. Do not immerse parts in cleaning solvent. Immersing the field frame, coil assembly and armature will damage insulation. Wipe these parts with a cloth only.

9. Do not immerse drive unit in cleaning solvent. The drive clutch is pre-lubricated at the factory and solvent will wash lubrication from clutch.

10. The drive unit may be cleaned with a brush moistened with cleaning solvent and wiped dry with a cloth. Brushes that are worn more than ½ the length of new brush, or are oil soaked, should be replaced.

11. Field brushes are serviced as part of the field and frame assembly. Ground brushes and all springs come as part of the brush plate assembly.

12. The assembly is the reverse of the disassembly procedure.

Bosch Starter (Chrysler 2.5 Liter Engine)

DISASSEMBLY & ASSEMBLY

1. Position the assembly in a suit-

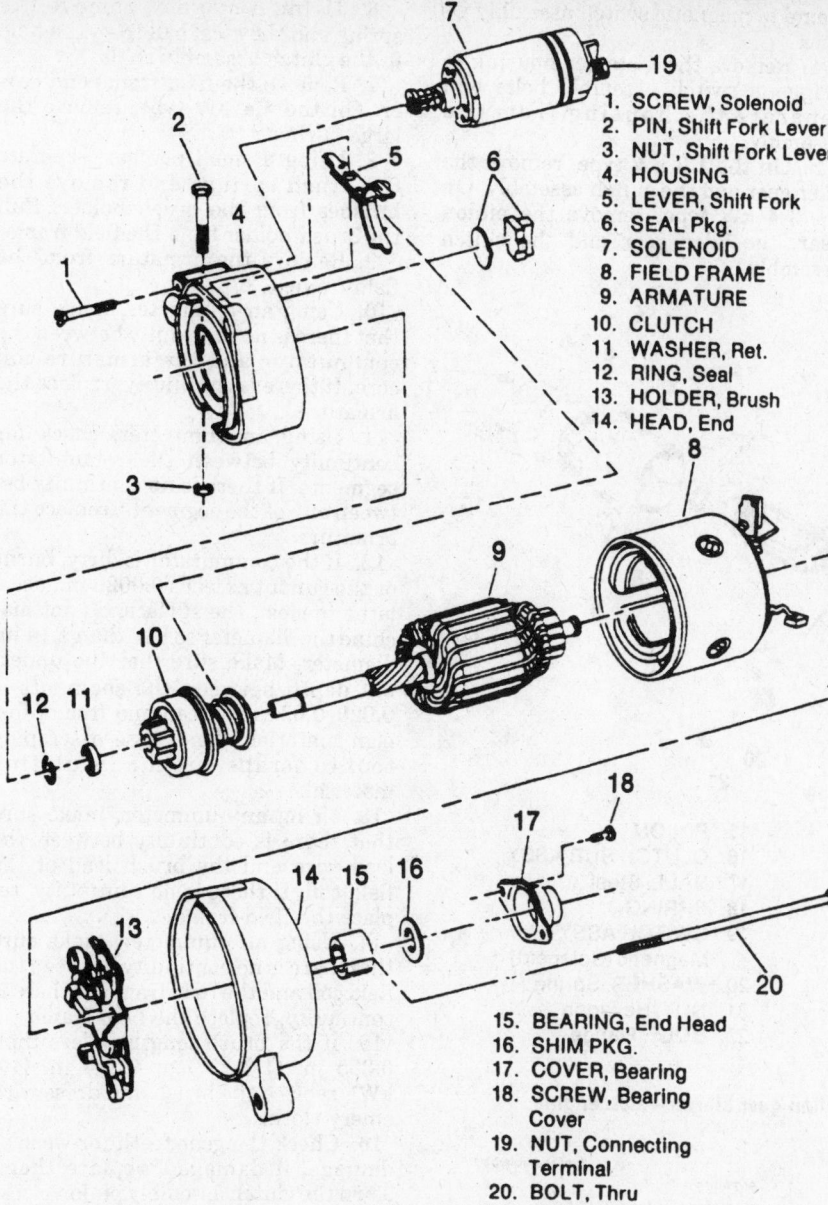

1. SCREW, Solenoid
2. PIN, Shift Fork Lever
3. NUT, Shift Fork Lever
4. HOUSING
5. LEVER, Shift Fork
6. SEAL Pkg.
7. SOLENOID
8. FIELD FRAME
9. ARMATURE
10. CLUTCH
11. WASHER, Ret.
12. RING, Seal
13. HOLDER, Brush
14. HEAD, End

15. BEARING, End Head
16. SHIM PKG.
17. COVER, Bearing
18. SCREW, Bearing Cover
19. NUT, Connecting Terminal
20. BOLT, Thru

Bosh starter – 1.7L engine with manual transmission

able holding fixture. Remove the field terminal nut. Remove the field terminal. Remove the field washer.

2. Remove the solenoid mounting screws. Work the solenoid off of the shift fork and remove the solenoid from the starter.

3. Remove the 2 starter end shield bushing cap screws. Remove the starter end shield bushing cap. Remove the end shield bushing and C-washer.

4. Remove the starter end shield bushing washer. Remove the starter end shield bushing seal.

5. Remove the two starter through bolts. Remove the starter end shield. Remove the brush plate.

6. Slide the field frame off of the starter and over the armature. Remove the armature assembly from the drive end housing.

7. Remove the rubber seal from the drive end housing. Remove the starter drive gear train.

8. Remove the dust plate. Press the stop collar off the snap-ring using the proper tool. Loosen the snap-ring using a snap-ring pliers.

9. Remove the output shaft snap-ring. Remove the clutch stop ring collar. Remove the clutch assembly from the starter.

10. Remove the clutch shift lever bushing. Remove the clutch shift lever. Position a suitable tool and remove the C-clip retainer.

11. Remove the retaining washer. Remove the sun and the planetary gears from the annulus gear,

12. Assembly is the reverse of the disassembly procedure. Replace all defective components as required.

Nippondenso Gear Reduction Starter
DISASSEMBLY & ASSEMBLY
Nova

1. Position the assembly in a suit-

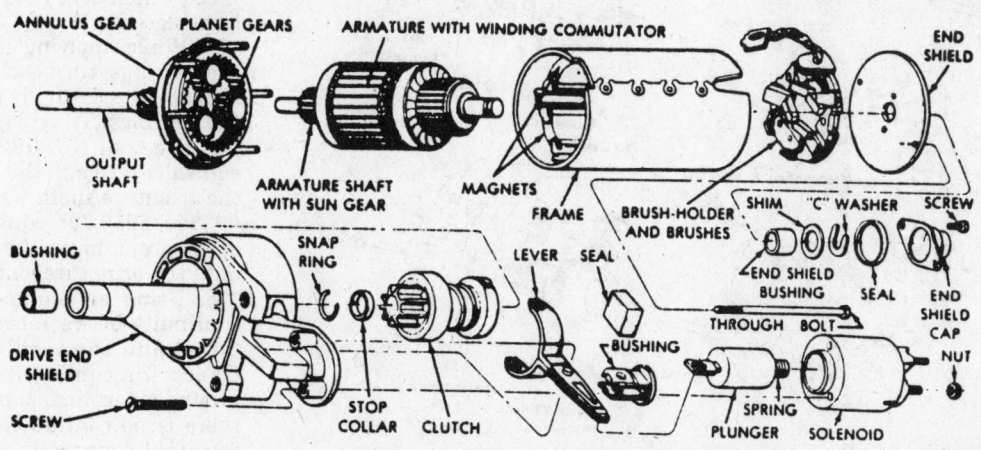

Bosch starter – 2.5L engine

able holding fixture. Remove the nut and disconnect the motor wire from the magnetic switch terminal.

2. Remove the 2 through bolts and pull the field frame (with the armature) from the magnetic switch assembly.

3. On the 1.0 kW type, remove the felt seal from the armature shaft; on the 1.4 kW type, remove the field

frame to magnetic switch assembly O-ring.

4. Remove the 2 starter housing to magnetic switch assembly bolts and separate the housing from the assembly.

5. On the 1.0 kW type, remove the idler gear and the clutch assembly. On the 1.4 kW type, remove the pinion gear, the idler gear and the clutch assembly.

6. Using a magnet, remove the spring and the steel ball from the hole in the clutch assembly shaft.

7. Remove the field frame end cover. On the 1.4 kW type, remove the large O-ring.

8. Using a small pry bar, separate the brush springs and remove the brushes from the brush holder. Pull the brush holder from the field frame.

9. Remove the armature from the field frame.

10. Using an ohmmeter, make sure that there is no continuity between the commutator and the armature coil core. If there is continuity, replace the armature.

11. Using an ohmmeter, check for continuity between the commutator segments. If there is no continuity between any of the segments, replace the armature.

12. If the commutator is dirty, burnt or the runout exceeds 0.0020 in., use a lathe to clean the surface; do not machine the diameter to less than 1.14 in. diameter. Make sure that the undercut depth between the segments is 0.020–0.031 in., clean and free of foreign material. If not, use a scraping tool to scrape out the insulating material.

13. Using an ohmmeter, make sure that there is continuity between the lead wire and the brush lead of the field coil. If there is no continuity, replace the field frame.

14. Using an ohmmeter, make sure that there is no continuity between the field coil and the field frame. If there is continuity, replace the field frame.

15. If the brush length is less than 0.335 in. (1.0 kW) or 0.394 in. (1.4 kW), replace the brush and dress with emery cloth.

16. Check the gear teeth for wear or damage, if damaged, replace them. Turn the clutch assembly pinion clockwise and make sure that it rotates freely, try to turn the pinion counterclockwise and make sure that it locks. If the pinion does not respond correctly, replace it.

17. While applying inward force on the bearings, turn each by hand; if resistance or sticking is noticed, replace the bearings. To replace the bearings, use the tool No. 09286–46011 (or equivalent) to pull the bearing(s) from the armature shaft. Using the tool No. 09285–76010 (or equivalent) and an arbor press, press the new bearing(s) onto the armature shaft.

18. Using an ohmmeter, check for continuity between the grounded terminal and the insulated terminal. Check for continuity between the grounded terminal and the housing. If there is no continuity in either case, replace the magnetic switch assembly.

19. Assembly is the reverse of the

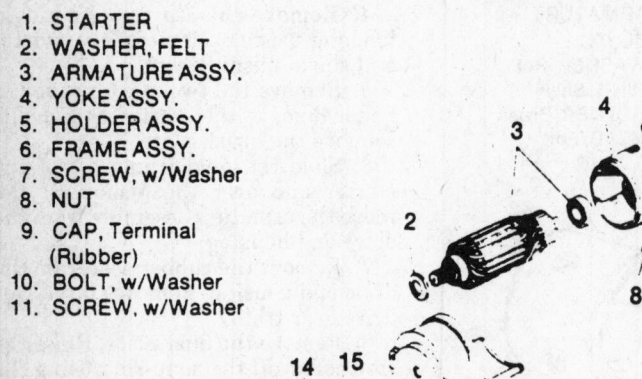

1. STARTER
2. WASHER, FELT
3. ARMATURE ASSY.
4. YOKE ASSY.
5. HOLDER ASSY.
6. FRAME ASSY.
7. SCREW, w/Washer
8. NUT
9. CAP, Terminal (Rubber)
10. BOLT, w/Washer
11. SCREW, w/Washer

12. HOUSING SUB ASSY.
13. RETAINER
14. ROLLER, Clutch

15. PINION
16. CLUTCH SUB ASSY.
17. BALL, Steel
18. SPRING
19. SWITCH ASSY., Magnetic (Solenoid)
20. WASHER, Spring
21. NUT, Hexagon
22. BOLT, Flange

Nippondenso and Mitsubishi reduction gear starter – 2.6L engine

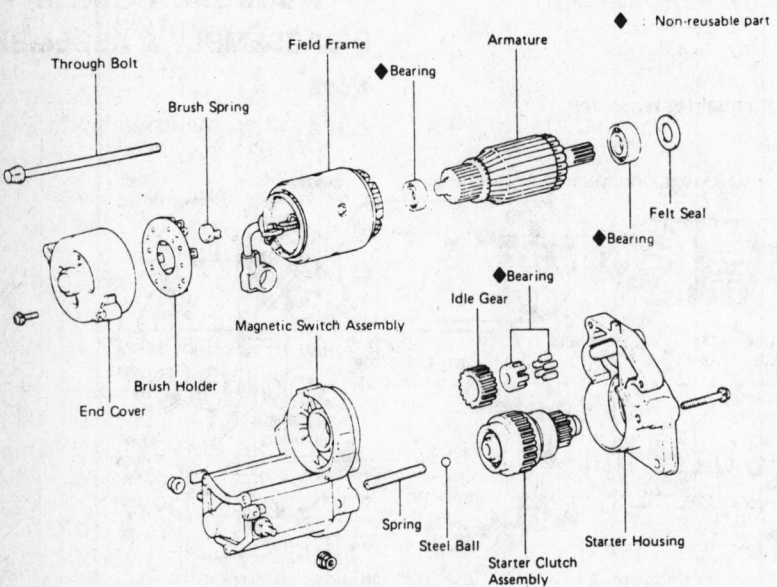

◆ : Non-reusable part

Through Bolt
Field Frame
Armature
Brush Spring
◆ Bearing
◆ Bearing
Felt Seal
◆ Bearing
◆ Bearing
Idle Gear
Magnetic Switch Assembly
Brush Holder
End Cover
Spring
Steel Ball
Starter Clutch Assembly
Starter Housing

Exploded view of the 1.0 kW type starter – G.M. reduction type

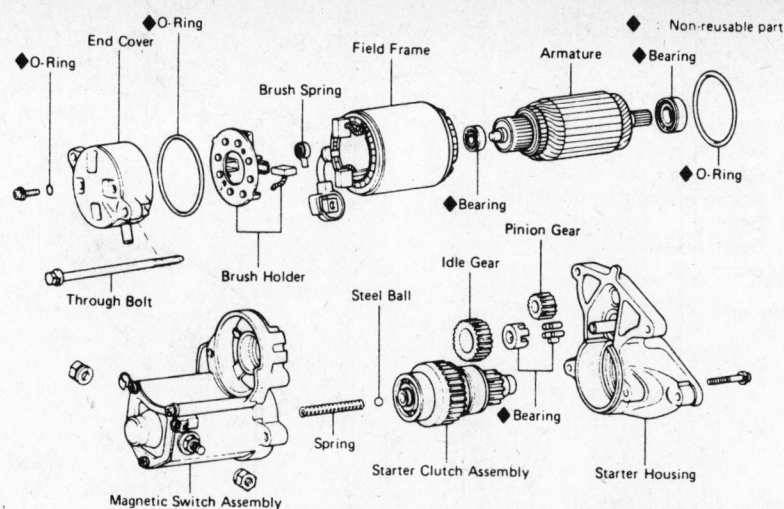

Exploded view of the 1.4 kW type starter—G.M. reduction type

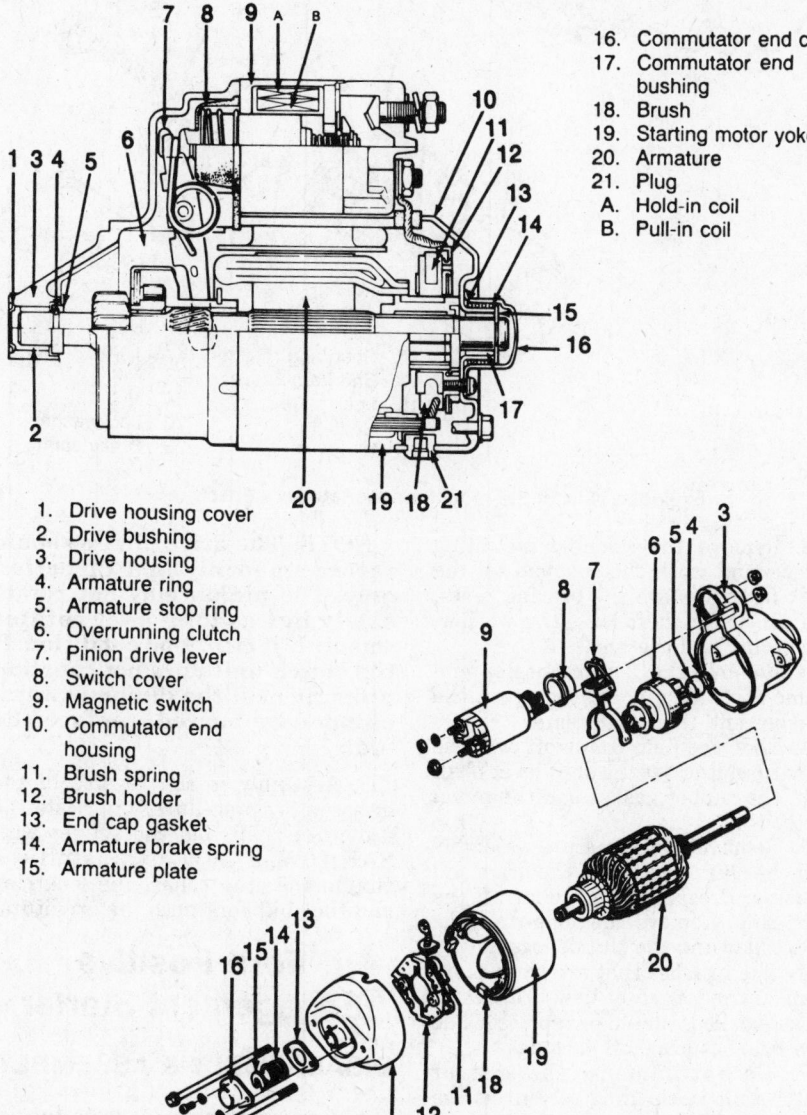

16. Commutator end cap
17. Commutator end bushing
18. Brush
19. Starting motor yoke
20. Armature
21. Plug
A. Hold-in coil
B. Pull-in coil

1. Drive housing cover
2. Drive bushing
3. Drive housing
4. Armature ring
5. Armature stop ring
6. Overrunning clutch
7. Pinion drive lever
8. Switch cover
9. Magnetic switch
10. Commutator end housing
11. Brush spring
12. Brush holder
13. End cap gasket
14. Armature brake spring
15. Armature plate

Exploded view of the reduction gear starter—Sprint

disassembly procedure. Before installing the gears and the bearings, lubricate them with high temperature grease.

Sprint with Automatic Transmission

1. Position the starter in a suitable holding fixture. Remove the nut and disconnect the motor wire from the magnetic switch terminal.

2. Remove the 2 through bolts and pull the field frame (with the armature) from the magnetic switch assembly.

3. Remove the 2 starter housing to magnetic switch assembly bolts and separate the housing from the assembly. Remove the pinion gear, the pinion retainer, bearings and the clutch assembly.

4. Using a magnet, remove the spring and the steel ball from the hole in the clutch assembly shaft. Remove the field frame end cover.

5. Using a small pry bar, separate the brush springs. Remove the brushes from the brush holder and pull the brush holder from the field frame.

6. Remove the armature from the field frame. Using an ohmmeter, make sure that there is no continuity between the commutator and the armature coil core. If there is continuity, replace the armature.

7. Using an ohmmeter, check for continuity between the commutator segments. If there is no continuity between any of the segments, replace the armature.

8. If the commutator is dirty, burnt or the runout exceeds 0.002 in., use a lathe to clean the surface; do not machine the diameter to less than 1.14 in. diameter. Make sure that the undercut depth between the segments is 0.018–0.030 in., clean and free of foreign material. If not, use a scraping tool to scrape out the insulating material.

9. Using an ohmmeter, make sure that there is continuity between the lead wire and the brush lead of the field coil. If there is no continuity, replace the field frame.

10. Using an ohmmeter, make sure that there is no continuity between the field coil and the field frame. If there is continuity, replace the field frame.

11. If the brush length is less than 0.394 in., replace the brush and dress with emery cloth.

12. Check the gear teeth for wear or damage, if damaged, replace them. Turn the clutch assembly pinion clockwise and make sure that it rotates freely, try to turn the pinion counterclockwise and make sure that it locks. If the pinion does not respond correctly, replace it.

13. While applying inward force on the bearings, turn each by hand; if resistance or sticking is noticed, replace the bearings. To replace the bearings, use the tool No. 09286-46011 (or equivalent) to pull the bearing(s) from the armature shaft. Using the tool No. 09285-76010 (or equivalent) and an arbor press, press the new bearing(s) onto the armature shaft.

14. Using an ohmmeter, check for continuity between the grounded terminal and the insulated terminal. Check for continuity between the grounded terminal and the housing. If there is no continuity in either case, replace the magnetic switch assembly.

15. Assembly is the reverse of the disassembly procedure. Before installing the gears and the bearings, lubricate them with a high temperature grease.

Hitachi Gear Reduction Starter

DISASSEMBLY & ASSEMBLY

1. Position the assembly in a suitable holding fixture. Disconnect the wire lead at the solenoid. Remove the solenoid to starter bolts and the solenoid from the shift lever.

2. Remove the torsion spring from the solenoid. Remove the starter through bolts and the rear cover.

3. Remove the 4 brushes from the brush holder. Remove the frame, the armature and the brush holder as a unit, from the gear case.

4. Carefully remove the brushes and the commutator, do not allow them to contact the adjacent parts.

5. Remove the brush holder and pull the armature assembly from the frame. Remove the bearing retainer and the pinion from the gear case. Remove the retaining clip and disassemble the pinion assembly. Inspect the component parts, replace any that are damaged or worn.

6. To assemble, apply lubricant to the pinion assembly and reverse the removal procedures. After the armature has been installed, raise the end of the brush springs and install the brushes. Install the brush holder by aligning it with the frame.

Nippondenso Starter

DISASSEMBLY & ASSEMBLY

Spectrum and Sprint with Manual Transmission

1. Position the starter in a suitable holding fixture. Disconnect the field coil wire from the solenoid terminal.

1. Starter yoke assembly
2. Brush
3. Armature
4. Overrunning clutch
5. Gear case assembly
6. Bearing
7. Gear case cover
8. Frame assembly
9. Bearing
10. Brush holder
11. Brush
12. Brush spring
13. Shift lever
14. Magnetic switch
15. Snap ring

16. Snap ring retainer
17. End frame cover
18. Lock plate
19. Seal
20. Screw
21. Nut
22. Through bolt
23. Nut
24. Nut
25. Lockwasher
26. Brake spring

Exploded view of the reduction gear starter — Spectrum

2. Remove the solenoid mounting screws and work the solenoid off the shift fork. Remove the bearing cover, the armature shaft lock, the washer, the spring and the seal.

3. Remove the 2 commutator end frame cover thru-bolts, the cover, the brushes and the brush plate.

4. Slide the field frame off over the armature. Remove the shift lever pivot bolt, the rubber gasket and the metal plate.

5. Remove the armature assembly and the shift lever from the drive end housing. Press the stop collar off the snap-ring. Remove the snap-ring, the stop collar and the clutch assembly.

6. The brushes that are worn more than ½ the length of new brushes or are oil-soaked, should be replaced. The new brushes are 0.63 in. long.

7. Do not immerse the starter clutch unit in cleaning solvent as the solvent will wash the lubricant from the clutch. Place the drive unit on the armature shaft and while holding the armature, rotate the pinion.

NOTE: The drive pinion should rotate smoothly in 1 direction only. The pinion may not rotate easily but as long as it rotates smoothly it is in good condition. If the clutch unit does not function properly or if the pinion is worn, chipped or burred, replace the unit.

8. Assembly is the reverse of the disassembly procedure. Lubricate the armature shaft and the splines with SAE 10W or 30W oil. Install the clutch, the stop collar, the lock ring and the shift fork onto the armature.

Ford Positive Engagement Starter

DISASSEMBLY & ASSEMBLY

1. Remove the starter from the vehicle. Position the unit in a suitable holding fixture.

2. Remove the cover screw. Remove

the cover, through bolts, starter drive end housing and the starter drive plunger lever return spring.

3. Remove the pivot pin retaining the starter gear plunger lever. Remove the lever and the armature. Remove the stop ring retainer and the thrust washer from the armature shaft.

4. Remove the stop ring from the groove in the armature shaft and discard it. Remove the starter drive gear assembly. Remove the brush end plate and insulator assembly.

5. Remove the brushes from the plastic brush holder. Lift out the brush holder. Note the location of the holder in relation to the end terminal.

6. Remove the 2 ground brush retaining screws. Remove the sleeve and the retainer by bending up the edge of the sleeve which is inserted in the rectangular hole of the frame.

7. Remove the 3 pole retaining screws, using tool 10044–A or equivalent. An arbor press may have to be used in conjunction with the special tool.

8. Cut the positive brush leads from the coil fields as close to the field connection as possible.

9. Check the commutator for runout. If the commutator is rough, has flat spots, or is more than 0.005 in. out of round, reface the commutator. Clean the grooves in the commutator face.

10. Inspect the armature shaft and the 2 bearings for scoring and excessive wear. Replace if necessary. Inspect the starter drive. If the gear teeth are pitted, broken, or excessively worn, replace the starter drive.

11. Assemble the starter in the reverse order of the disassembly procedure.

Delco 5MT, 10MT and 27MT Starters

DISASSEMBLY & ASSEMBLY

1. Remove the starter from the vehicle. Position the unit in a suitable holding fixture.

2. Remove the screw from the field coil connector and the solenoid mounting screws. Rotate the solenoid 90 degrees and remove it along with the plunger return spring.

3. Remove the starter through bolts. Remove the commutator end frame and washer.

4. Remove the field frame assembly from the drive gear housing.

5. If equipped, remove the center bearing screws. Remove the drive gear housing from the armature shaft.

6. To remove the overrunning clutch from the armature shaft, first

remove the washer or collar from the armature shaft.

7. Slide a ⅝ in. deep socket over the shaft and against the retainer. Use the socket as a driving tool and tap the socket to move the retainer of the snap-ring.

8. Remove the snap-ring from the groove in the shaft. If the snap-ring is distorted, replace it.

9. Remove the retainer and the clutch assembly from the armature shaft.

10. If required, the shaft lever and

the plunger can be disassembled by removing the roll pin.

11. To replace the starter brushes, remove the brush holder pivot pin which positions the insulated and the ground brushes. Remove the brush spring.

12. On 5MT starters, to replace the brushes remove the screw from the brush holder and separate the brushes from the holder.

13. Inspect armature commutator, shaft and bushings, overrunning clutch pinion, brushes and springs for

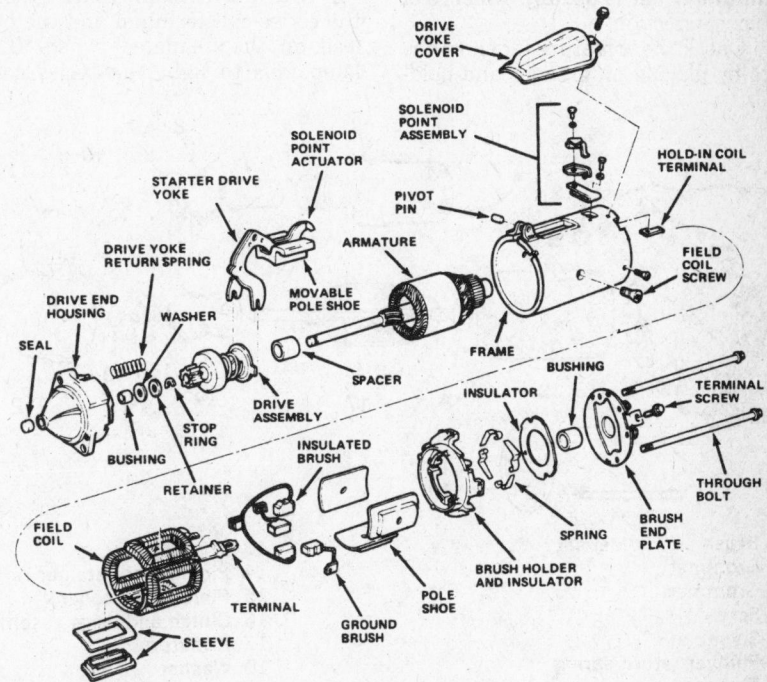

Exploded view of the Ford positive engagement starter motor—AMC similar

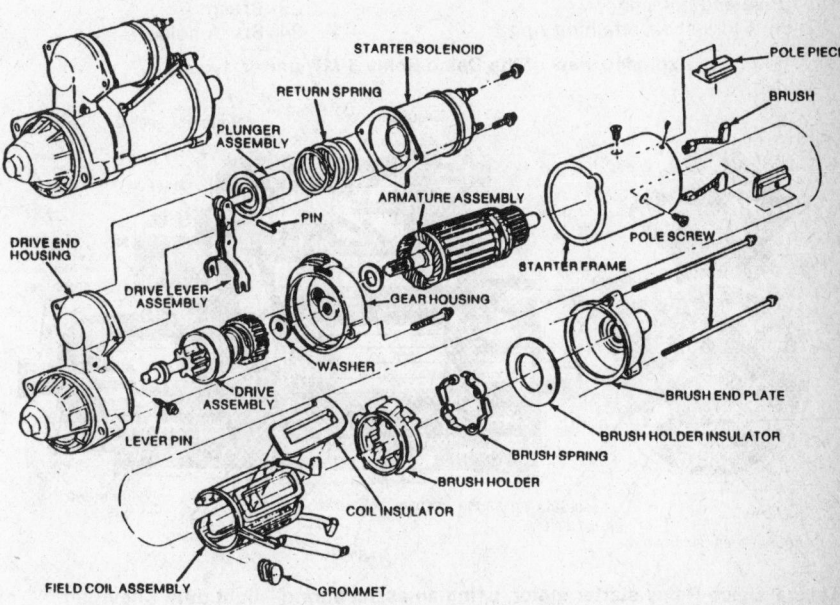

Ford 2.2L diesel engine starter

discoloration, damage or wear. Replace as required.

14. Check fit of armature shaft in bushing in drive housing. Shaft should fit snugly in the bushing. If the bushing is worn, it should be replaced.

15. Inspect armature commutator. If commutator is rough, it should be turned down. Do not undercut or turn to less than 1.65 in. O.D. Do not turn out of round commutators. Inspect the points where the armature conductors join the commutator bars to make sure they have a good connection. A burned commutator bar is usually evidence of a poor connection.

16. Check the armature for short circuits by placing on growler and hold-ing back saw blade over armature core while armature is rotated. If saw blade vibrates, armature is shorted. Recheck after cleaning between the commutator bars. If the saw blade still vibrates, replace the armature.

17. Using a test lamp place 1 lead on the shunt coil terminal and connect the other lead to a ground brush. This test should be made from both ground brushes to insure continuity through both brushes and leads. If the lamp fails to light, the field coil is open and will require replacement.

18. Using a test lamp place 1 lead on the series coil terminal and the other lead on the insulated brush. If the lamp fails to light the series coil is open and will require repair or replacement. This test should be made from each insulated brush to check brush and lead continuity.

19. On starters with shunt coil separate series and shunt coil strap terminals during this test. Do not let strap terminals touch case or other ground. Using a test lamp place 1 lead on the grounded brush holder and the other lead on either insulated brush. If the lamp lights a grounded series coil is indicated and must be repaired or replaced.

NOTE: If the solenoid has not been removed from the starter the connector strap terminals must be removed before making the following tests. Complete the tests as fast as possible in order to prevent overheating the solenoid.

20. To check the starter winding connect an ammeter in series with 12 volt battery and the switch terminal on the solenoid. Connect a voltmeter to the switch terminal and to ground. Connect a carbon pile across battery. Adjust the voltage to 10 volts and note the ammeter reading. It should be 14.5 to 16.5 amperes.

21. To check both windings, connect as for previous test. Ground the solenoid motor terminal. Adjust the voltage to 10 volts and note the ammeter reading. It should be 41–47 amperes.

22. Current draw readings that are over specifications indicate shorted turns on a ground in the windings of the solenoid and the solenoid should be replaced. Current draw readings that are under specifications indicate excessive resistance. No reading indicates an open circuit. Check the connections and replace solenoid if necessary. Current readings will decrease as the windings heat up.

23. Assembly of the starter is the

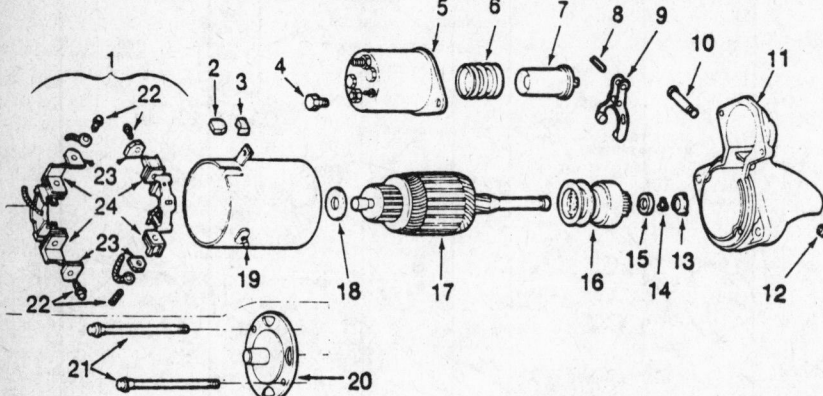

1 Brush and holder set
2 Grommet
3 Grommet
4 Screw
5 Solenoid
6 Plunger return spring
7 Plunger
8 Plunger pin
9 Shift fork
10 Shift fork shaft
11 Drive end housing
12 Shift fork shaft retaining ring
13 Thrust collar
14 Pinion stop retainer ring
15 Pinion stop collar
16 Clutch and drive assembly
17 Armature
18 Washer
19 Frame and field assembly
20 Commutator end frame
21 Through bolts
22 Screw
23 Brush
24 Brush holder

Exploded view of the Delco-Remy 5 MT starter, typical

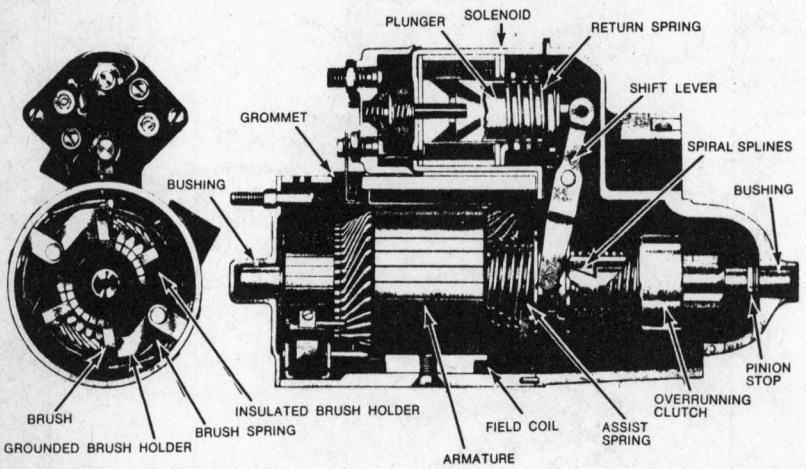

Typical Delco-Remy starter motor, using an assist spring—light duty Chevrolet illustrated

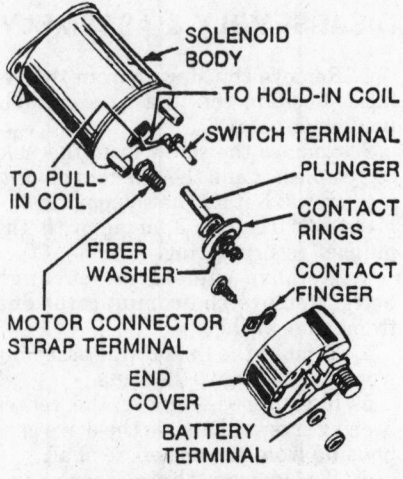

Delco-Remy starter solenoid

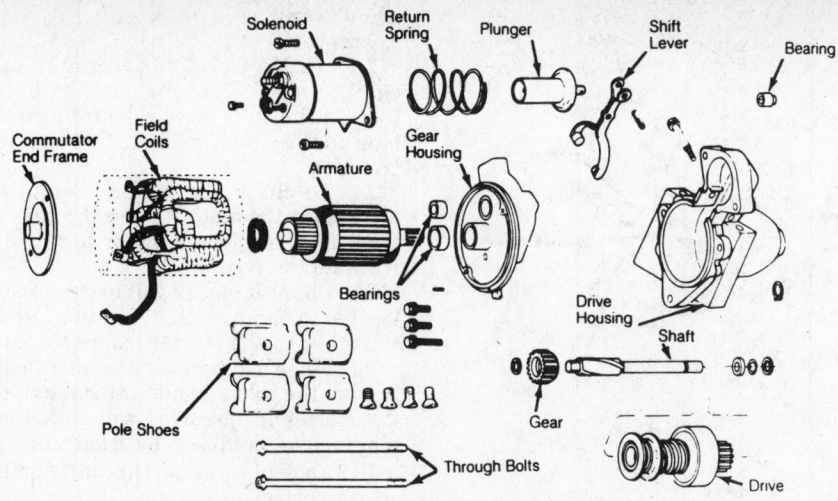

Exploded view of the GM 15MT/GR starter

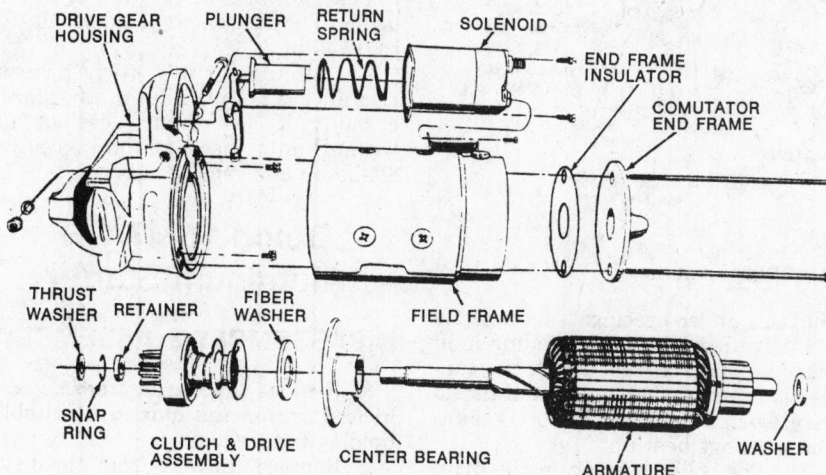

Exploded view of the GM 27 MT starter

reverse of the disassembly procedure. Be sure to replace or repair all defective components as required.

24. When the starter has been disassembled or the solenoid replaced it is necessary to check the pinion clearance.

25. Pinion clearance must be checked in order to prevent the buttons on the shift lever yoke from rubbing on the clutch collar during engine cranking.

26. To check the pinion clearance, disconnect the motor field coil connector from the solenoid motor terminal. Insulate the terminal.

27. Connect one 12 volt battery lead to the solenoid switch terminal and the other to the starter frame.

28. Flash a jumper lead momentarily from the solenoid motor terminal to the starter frame. This will shift the pinion into cranking position and it will remain so until the battery is disconnected.

29 Push the pinion back as far as possible to take up any movement and check the clearance with a feeler gauge. The clearance should be 0.0100 to 0.140 in.

30. Means for adjusting pinion clearance is not provided on the starter motor. If the clearance does not fall within limits check for improper installation and replace all worn parts.

Delco 15MT/GR Starter

DISASSEMBLY & ASSEMBLY

1. Remove the starter from the vehicle. Position the unit in a suitable holding fixture.

2. Remove the field coil screw. Remove the field frame through bolts. Separate the field frame assembly from the drive gear assembly. Separate the armature and the commutator end frame from the field frame.

3. Remove the solenoid mounting screws. Remove the solenoid from the drive housing.

4. Remove the retaining ring, shift lever shaft and housing through bolts to separate the drive assembly, drive housing and gear assembly.

5. To remove the overrunning clutch from the armature shaft, first remove the washer or collar from the armature shaft.

6. Slide a ⅝ in. deep socket over the shaft and against the retainer. Use the socket as a driving tool and tap the socket to move the retainer off of the snap-ring.

7. Remove the snap-ring from the groove in the shaft. If the snap-ring is distorted, replace it.

8. Remove the retainer and the clutch assembly from the armature shaft. To replace the starter brushes, remove the brush holder pivot pin which positions the insulated and the ground brushes. Remove the brush spring.

9. Inspect armature commutator, shaft and bushings, overrunning clutch pinion, brushes and springs for discoloration, damage or wear. Replace as required. Check fit of armature shaft in bushing in drive housing. Shaft should fit snugly in the bushing. If the bushing is worn, it should be replaced.

10. Inspect armature commutator. If commutator is rough, it should be turned down. Do not undercut or turn to less than 1.650 in. O.D. Do not turn out of round commutators. Inspect the points where the armature conductors join the commutator bars to make sure they have a good connection. A burned commutator bar is usually evidence of a poor connection.

11. Check the armature for short circuits by placing on growler and holding hack saw blade over armature core while armature is rotated. If saw blade vibrates, armature is shorted. Recheck after cleaning between the commutator bars. If saw blade still vibrates, replace the armature.

12. Using a test lamp place 1 lead on the shunt coil terminal and connect the other lead to a ground brush. This test should be made from both ground brushes to insure continuity through both brushes and leads. If the lamp fails to light the field coil is open and will require replacement.

13. Using a test lamp place 1 lead on the series coil terminal and the other lead on the insulated brush. If the lamp fails to light the series coil is open and will require repair or replacement. This test should be made from each insulated brush to check brush and lead continuity.

14. On starters with shunt coil sepa-

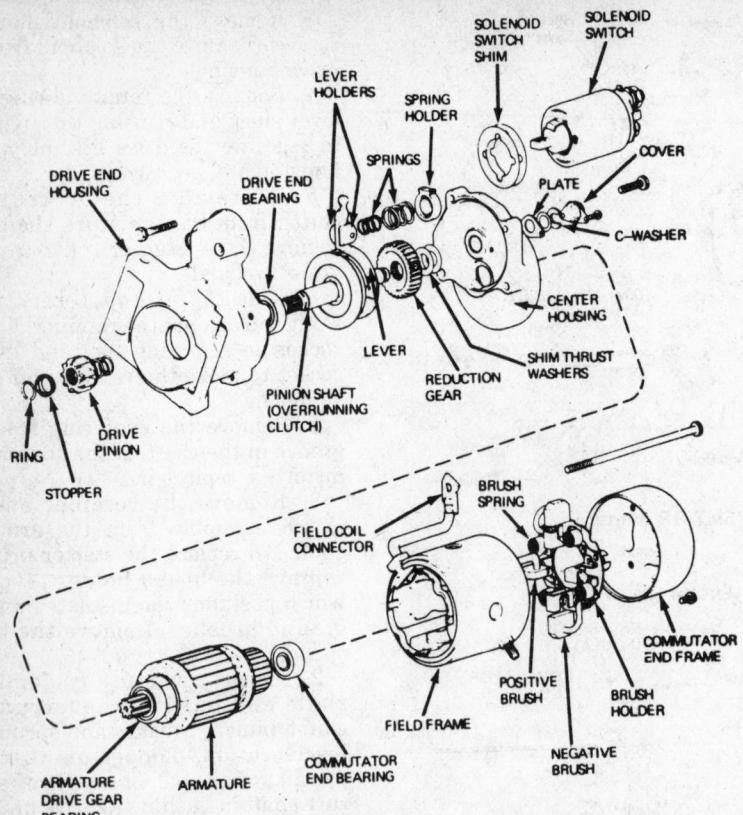

Exploded view of the GM ALU/GR diesel starter

rate series and shunt coil strap terminals during this test. Do not let strap terminals touch case or other ground. Using a test lamp place 1 lead on the grounded brush holder and the other lead on either insulated brush. If the lamp lights a grounded series coil is indicated and must be repaired or replaced.

NOTE: If the solenoid has not been removed from the starter the connector strap terminals must be removed before making the following tests. Complete the tests as fast as possible in order to prevent overheating the solenoid.

15. To check the starter winding connect an ammeter in series with a 12-volt battery and the switch terminal and to ground. Connect carbon pile across battery. Adjust the voltage to 10 volts and note the ammeter reading. It should be 14.5–16.5 amperes.

16. To check both windings, connect as for previous test. Ground the solenoid motor terminal. Adjust the voltage to 10 volts and note the ammeter reading. It should be 41–47 amperes.

17. Current draw readings that are over specifications indicate shorted turns or a ground in the windings of the solenoid and the solenoid should be replaced. Current draw readings

that are under specifications indicate excessive resistance. No reading indicates an open circuit. Check the connections and replace solenoid if necessary. Current readings will decrease as the windings heat up.

18. The roller bearing in the drive housing and the roller bearings in the gear housing must be replaced if they are dry. Do not lubricate or re-use the bearings.

19. To replace the gear housing bearing use a tube or solid cylinder that just fits inside the housing to push bearing out toward armature side. In the opposite direction use a tube or cylinder to press the bearing in flush with the housing.

20. To replace the gear housing drive shaft bearing push bearing out and use a tube or collar that just fits inside the housing. Press against the open end of the bearing. To press new bearing in, press against closed end, using a thin wall tube or collar that fits in space between bearing and housing. Do not press against the flat end of the bearing; this will bend the thin metal of the bearing. As required, replace the drive housing bearing.

21. Assembly of the starter is the reverse of the disassembly procedure. Be sure to replace or repair all defective components as required.

22. When the starter has been disassembled or the solenoid replaced it is

necessary to check the pinion clearance.

23. Pinion clearance must be checked in order to prevent the buttons on the shift lever yoke from rubbing on the clutch collar during engine cranking.

24. To check the pinion clearance disconnect the motor field coil connector from the solenoid motor terminal. Insulate the terminal.

25. Connect one 12 volt battery lead to the solenoid switch terminal and the other to the starter frame.

26. Flash a jumper lead momentarily from the solenoid motor terminal to the starter frame. This will shift the pinion into cranking position and it will remain so until the battery is disconnected.

27. Push the pinion back as far as possible to take up any movement and check the clearance with a feeler gauge. The clearance should be 0.0010 to 0.140 in.

28. Means for adjusting pinion clearance is not provided on the starter motor. If the clearance does not fall within limits check for improper installation and replace worn parts.

Delco 15MT/GR Aluminum Starter

DISASSEMBLY & ASSEMBLY

1. Remove the starter from the vehicle. Position the unit in a suitable holding fixture.

2. Remove the nut from the field connector and the 2 solenoid switch mounting screws. Remove the solenoid.

3. Some starters may have shims between the solenoid and the drive end housing. These shims are used to set the drive pinion position.

4. Remove the starter through bolts and the 2 brush holder retaining bolts. Remove the commutator end frame from the armature and bearing assembly. Remove the field frame assembly and the armature from the center housing.

5. Pry back each brush spring so that each brush can be backed away from the armature about ¼ in. Release the spring to hold the brushes in the backed out position. Remove the armature from the field frame and brush holder.

6. Remove the shaft cover on the center housing by removing the 2 retaining screws. Remove the C-shaped washer and plate. Remove the 2 center housing bolts. Remove the center housing shim and thrust washers.

7. Remove the reduction gear. Remove the spring holder. Remove the 2

lever springs. To remove the drive pinion. slide a ⅝ in. socket over the shaft against the stopper. Tap the tool to move the stopper off of the ring. Remove the stopper and the drive pinion.

8. Remove the pinion shaft and the lever assembly. Note the direction of the lever and the lever holders.

9. Clean all parts in the proper cleaning solution. Inspect all parts for wear and damage. Replace or repair defective components as required. Inspect all bearings for wear, roughness or dryness. Replace damaged bearings with new ones.

10. Inspect the armature commutator. If the commutator is rough, it should be turned down. Do not turn the commutator down less than 1.48 in. outside diameter.

11. With the brush holder assembly still attached to the field frame, test the field coils for open circuits. Using a test lamp, put 1 test lead on the field coil connector and the other test lead on the positive brush.

12. The test light should light. If the test light fails to light the field coil is open. The field coil must be replaced. Repeat this test on the other positive brush.

13. To test the field coil for ground use a test light and put 1 lead on the field coil connector and the other test lead on the field frame.

14. The test light should not light. If the test lamp lights the field coils are grounded to the field frame assembly. The field frame must be replaced.

15. To replace the brushes remove the brush holder and the negative brush assembly from the field frame by removing the positive brushes from the brush holder.

16. Cut the old brush leads off of their mountings as close to brush connection point as possible. Solder the new brushes as required. Careful installation of the positive side is necessary to prevent grounding of the brush connection point having no insulation.

17. Reinstall the positive and negative brushes in the brush holder assembly. Position it in the backed out position in the starter housing.

18. In order to replace the drive end bearing it will be necessary to press the bearing out of the drive end housing using a press.

19. Replace the armature commutator end bearing and the armature drive end bearing as required using the proper bearing removal tool.

20. Assemble the starter in the reverse order of the disassembly procedure. Be sure to check all parts for wear and damage. Repair or replace defective components as required.

21. If either the drive end housing, pinion shaft, reduction gear, shim washers, or center housing were re-

placed it will be necessary to check the end play for the pinion shaft. Install the plate and C-shaped washer onto the end of the pinion shaft.

22. With the drive end housing mounted in a suitable holding fixture, measure end play. Insert a feeler gauge between C-washer and cover plate. Move the pinion shaft in the axial direction with a suitable tool to see whether a proper end play of 0.004 to 0.020 in. is obtained.

23. If the end play does not fall within limits, remove the plate, C-shaped washer and center bracket. Add or remove the shim thrust washers to adjust the end play and recheck. Shim thrust washers are available in 2 thicknesses 0.010 in. and 0.020 in.

24. When the starter has been disassembled or the solenoid switch has been replaced, it is necessary to check the pinion position. Pinion position must be correct to prevent the top of the lever from rubbing on the clutch collar during cranking.

25. Connect 1 12 volt battery lead to the terminal **S** on the switch and momentarily connect the other to the starter frame. This will shift the pinion into cranking position and it will remain so until the battery is disconnected. Do not leave it engaged more than 30 seconds at a time.

26. Set up dial indicator with the pinion engaged. Push the pinion shaft back by hand and measure the amount of pinion shaft movement. The amount corresponds to the pinion clearance of current starters and should be 0.020 to 0.080 in.

27. If the amount does not fall within the limit, adjust it by adding or removing the shims which are located between the switch and the front bracket. Adding shims decreases the amount of the movement. Solenoid switch shims are available in 2 thicknesses 0.020 in. and 0.010 in.

ALTERNATORS

Chrysler Alternators

Alternator disassembly, repair and assembly procedures are basically the same for all Chrysler alternators. Certain variations in design, or production modifications, could require slightly different procedures that should be obvious upon inspection of the unit being serviced.

DISASSEMBLY & ASSEMBLY

To prevent damage to the brush as-

semblies (114 and 117 amp), they should be removed before proceeding with the disassembly of the alternator. The brushes are mounted in a plastic holder that positions the brushes vertically against the slip-rings.

1. Remove the retaining screw, flat washer, nylon washer and field terminal and carefully lift the plastic holder containing the spring and brush assembly from the end housing.

2. The ground brush (60 amp) is positioned horizontally against the slip-ring and is retained in the holder that is integral with the end housing. Remove the retaining screw and lift the clip, spring and brush assembly from the end housing. The stator is laminated, use care not to damage it or the end housing.

3. Remove the through bolts and pry between the stator and drive end housing with a suitable tool. Carefully separate the drive end housing, pulley and rotor assembly from the stator and rectifier housing assembly.

4. The pulley is an interference fit on the rotor shaft. Remove with a puller and special adapters.

5. Remove the 3 nuts and washers, while supporting the end frame, tap the rotor shaft with a plastic hammer and separate the rotor and end housing.

6. The drive end ball bearing is an interference fit with the rotor shaft. Remove the bearing with puller and adapters.

NOTE: Further dismantling of the rotor is not advisable, as the remainder of the rotor assembly is not serviced separately.

7. Remove the DC output terminal nuts and washers and remove the terminal screw. Remove the inside capacitor (on units so equipped).

8. Remove the insulator.

NOTE: Positive rectifiers are pressed into the heat sink and negative rectifiers in the end housing. When removing the rectifiers it is necessary to support the end housing and the heat sink in order to prevent damage to the castings. Don't subject the diode rectifiers to unnecessary jolting. Heavy vibration or shock may ruin them. Cut rectifier wires at the point of crimp. Support rectifier housing. The factory tool is cut away and slotted to fit over the wires and around the bosses in the housing. Be sure that the bore of the tool completely surrounds the rectifier, press the rectifier out of the housing. The roller bearing in the rectifier end frame is a press fit. To protect the end housing, it is necessary to

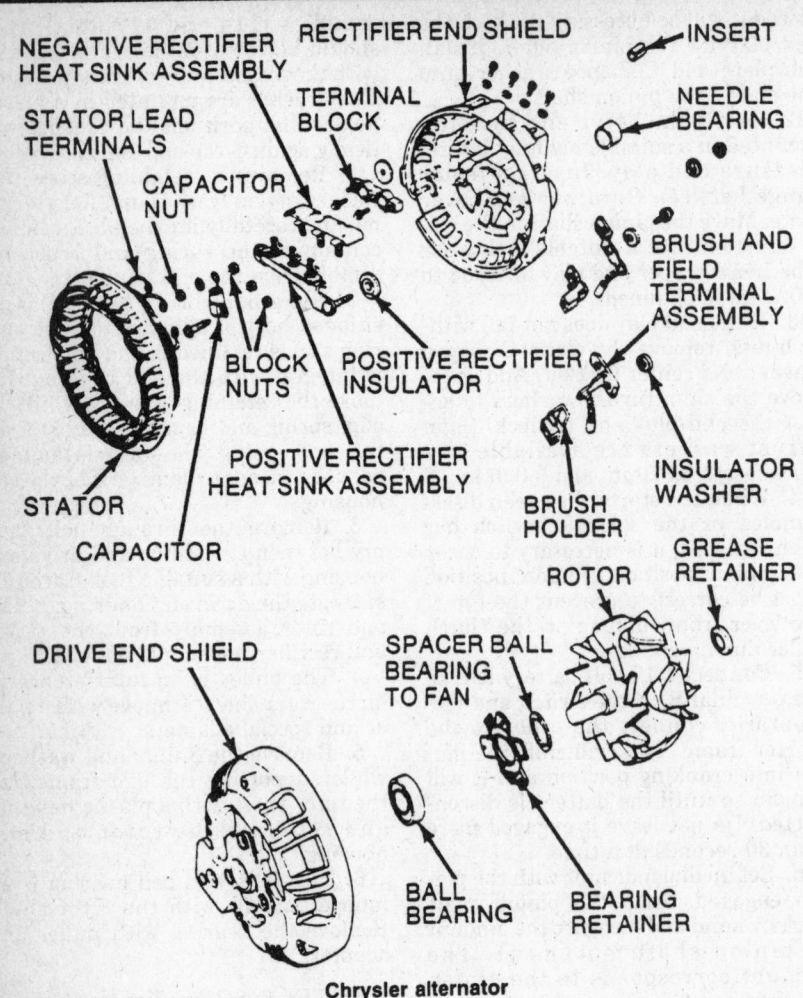

NEGATIVE RECTIFIER HEAT SINK ASSEMBLY

STATOR LEAD TERMINALS

CAPACITOR NUT

RECTIFIER END SHIELD

TERMINAL BLOCK

INSERT

NEEDLE BEARING

BRUSH AND FIELD TERMINAL ASSEMBLY

BLOCK NUTS

POSITIVE RECTIFIER INSULATOR

POSITIVE RECTIFIER HEAT SINK ASSEMBLY

STATOR

CAPACITOR

BRUSH HOLDER

ROTOR

INSULATOR WASHER

GREASE RETAINER

DRIVE END SHIELD

SPACER BALL BEARING TO FAN

BALL BEARING

BEARING RETAINER

Chrysler alternator

support the housing with a tool when pressing out the bearing.

9. To assemble, support the heat sink or rectifier end housing on a circular plate.

10. Check the rectifier identification to be sure the correct rectifier is being used. The part numbers are stamped on the case of the rectifier. They are also marked red for positive and black for negative.

11. Start the new rectifier into the casting and press it in squarely. Do not start rectifier with a hammer or it will be ruined.

12. Crimp the new rectifier wire to the wires disconnected at removal or solder using a heat sink with rosin core solder.

13. Support the end housing on tool so that the notch in the support tool will clear the raised section of the heat sink, press the bearing into position with tool SP–3381, or equivalent. New bearings are pre-lubricated, additional lubrication is not required.

14. Insert the drive end bearing in the drive end housing and install the bearing plate, washers and nuts to hold the bearing in place.

15. Position the bearing and drive end housing on the rotor shaft and, while supporting the base of the rotor shaft, press the bearing and housing in position on the rotor shaft with an arbor press and arbor tool. Be careful that there is no cocking of the bearing at installation; or damage will result. Press the bearing on the rotor shaft until the bearing contacts the shoulder on the rotor shaft.

16. Install pulley on rotor shaft. Shaft of rotor must be supported so that all pressing force is on the pulley hub and rotor shaft. Do not exceed 6800 lbs. pressure. Pulley hub should just contact bearing inner race.

17. Some alternators will be found to have the capacitor mounted internally. Be sure the heat sink insulator is in place.

18. Install the output terminal screw with the capacitor attached through the heat sink and end housing.

19. Install insulating washers, lockwashers and locknuts.

20. Make sure the heat sink and insulator are in place and tighten the locknut.

21. Position the stator on the rectifi-

er end housing. Be sure that all of the rectifier connectors and phase leads are free of interference with the rotor fan blades and that the capacitor (internally mounted) lead has clearance.

22. Position the rotor assembly in the rectifier end housing. Align the through bolt holes in the stator with both end housings.

23. Enter stator shaft in the rectifier end housing bearing, compress stator and both end housings manually and install through bolts, washers and nuts.

24. Install the insulated brush and terminal attaching screw.

25. Install the ground screw and attaching screw.

26. Rotate pulley slowly to be sure the rotor fan blades do not hit the rectifier and stator connectors.

Chrysler 40/90 And 50/120 Amp Alternator with External Regulator

DISASSEMBLY & ASSEMBLY

1. Remove the dust cover mounting nut. Remove the dust cover.

2. Remove the 2 brush holder assembly mounting screws. Remove the brush holder assembly.

3. Remove the 3 stator to rectifier mounting screws. Remove the 2 stator to rectifier assembly mounting screws. Remove the rectifier insulator. Remove the capacitor mounting screw. Remove the rectifier assembly.

4. Remove the 4 through bolts. Carefully pry between the stator and the drive end shield. Using a suitable tool, separate the end shields. The stator is laminated, do not burr the stator or the end shield.

5. Position the drive end of the alternator over the bosses of the holding fixture. Do not position the plastic rotor termination plate over the fixture boss or damage to the assembly will result.

6. Bolt the drive end of the assembly to shield fixture. Loosen the pulley mounting nut. Remove the pulley mounting nut. Remove the pulley washer.

7. Remove the poly-vee pulley. Remove the fan. Remove the front bearing spacer. Press the rotor assembly out of the drive end shield.

8. Remove the inner bearing spacer. Position the alternator bearing puller tool under the rear rotor bearing. Tighten the right puller bolt ½ turn. Tighten the left puller bolt ½ turn. Continue tightening the tool ½ turn on each bolt until the rear rotor bear-

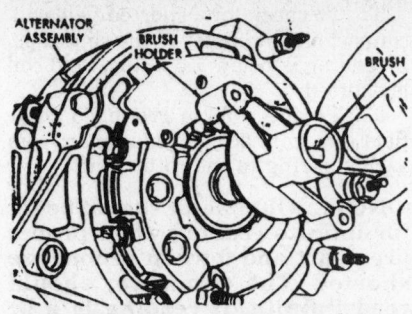

Removing the brush assembly – Chrysler 40/90 alternator

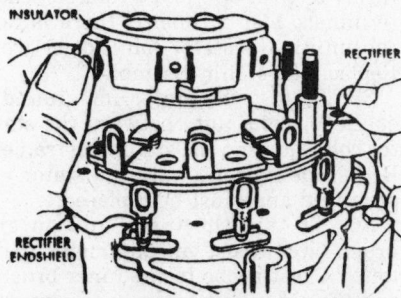

Removing and installing the rectifier assembly – Chrysler 40/90 alternator

ing is free. Remove the rear rotor bearing assembly from the rotor.

9. Position the rotor assembly in the holding fixture. Position the rear rotor bearing onto the rotor shaft.

10. Drive the rear rotor bearing onto the rotor until it bottoms. The rear rotor position is critical and must be installed using special tools C–4885 and C–4894.

11. Remove the 4 front bearing retaining screws. Press the front bearing out of the drive end shield.

12. Carefully remove the stator from the rectifier end shield.

13. Assembly is the reverse of the disassembly procedure.

14. Be sure to repair or replace defective components as required.

Mitsubshi Alternator with Internal Regulator

DISASSEMBLY & ASSEMBLY

1. Place the alternator in a vise or similar holding fixture, mark the body components and remove the 3 through body bolts.

2. Pry between the stator and the drive end shield and carefully separate the drive end plate, the pulley and the rotor assembly from the stator and rectifier end shield assembly.

3. Carefully clamp the rotor and remove the pulley nut from the end of the shaft. Remove the pulley, the pulley fan, the pulley fan spacer and the

alternator drive end shield from the rotor shaft.

4. The front bearing can be removed from the front drive housing by the removal of the dust seals, front and rear, the 3 bearing retainer screws, the retainer, exposing the bearing so that it can be tapped from the drive housing.

5. To remove the stator assembly. The 6 stator leads must be unsoldered from the rectifiers, as per the manufacturer's recommendation.

6. Remove the rectifiers from the stator end shield housing.

7. Remove the brush holder and regulator retaining screw.

8. Remove the battery terminal retaining nut and remove the capacitor from the terminal.

9. Remove the regulator and rectifier assembly. Unsolder 1 rectifier to regulator assembly and remove the other rectifier assembly by sliding the battery stud out of the regulator.

10. Inspect the rotor bearing surface for scores and make the necessary off vehicle test on the electrical components.

11. The assembly of the alternator is the reverse of the removal procedure. Certain steps must be performed as the alternator is assembled.

12. Install the seals in the front and in the rear of the front bearing with the angled lip away from the bearing.

13. Push the brushes into the brush holder and insert a wire to hold them in the raised position. Install the rotor and remove the holding wire.

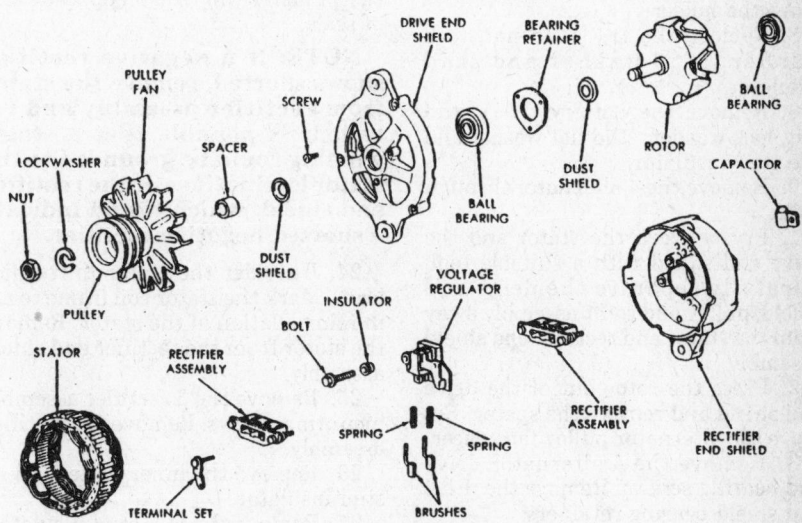

Mitsubishi alternator

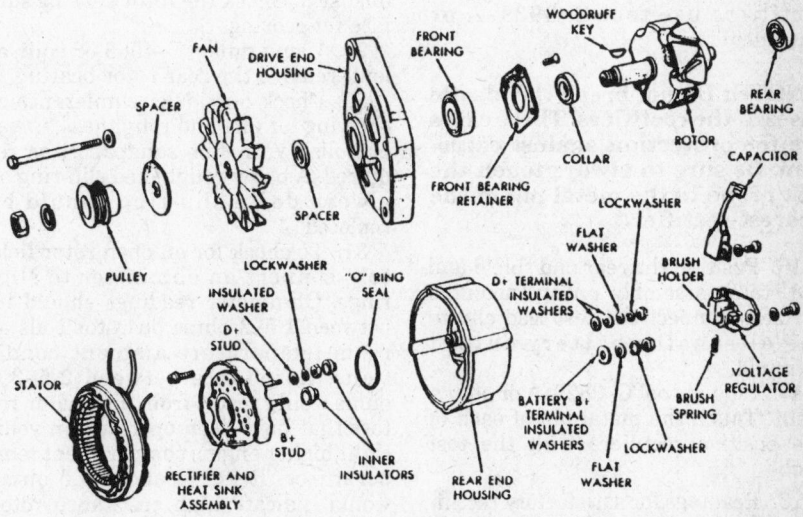

Bosch alternator with internal regulator

Bosch Alternator with Internal Regulator

DISASSEMBLY & ASSEMBLY

1. Remove the alternator from the vehicle.
2. Position the unit in a suitable holding fixture.
3. Remove the pulley nut, lock washer and pulley.
4. Remove the fan spacer and the pulley fan from the alternator shaft.
5. Remove the Woodruff key from the rotor shaft.
6. From the rear of the alternator disconnect the capacitor terminal and remove the capacitor mounting screw. Remove the capacitor from the alternator.
7. Remove the voltage regulator and brush holder mounting screw. Remove the holder.
8. Remove the D+ stud nut, lock washer, stud washer and stud insulators.
9. Remove the battery (B+) stud nut, lock washer, stud flat washer and the stud insulator.
10. Remove the 4 alternator through bolts.
11. Pry between the stator and the drive end shield with a suitable tool. Carefully separate the drive end shield, pulley and rotor assembly away from the stator and rectifier end shield assembly.
12. Press the rotor out of the drive end shield and remove the spacer. Remove the alternator pulley fan spacer.
13. Remove the 4 alternator drive end bearing screws. Remove the drive end shield bearing retainer.
14. Press out the drive end shield bearing. Remove the front drive bearing from the front drive end shield.
15. To test the positive and negative rectifiers use tool C–3929–A or equivalent.

NOTE: Do not break the plastic cases of the rectifiers. These cases are for protection against corrosion. Be sure to always touch the test probe to the metal pin of the nearest rectifier.

16. Position the rear end shield and the stator assembly on an insulated surface. Connect the test lead clip to the alternator battery output terminal.
17. Plug in tool C–3829–A or equivalent. Touch the metal pin of each of the positive rectifiers with the test probe.
18. Readings for satisfactory rectifiers will be 1¾ amperes or more. Readings should be approximately the same and the meter needle must move in same direction for all 3 rectifiers.
19. When some rectifiers are good and one is shorted, the reading taken at good rectifiers will be low and reading taken at shorted rectifiers will be 0. Disconnect stator lead to rectifiers reading 0 and retest. Reading of good rectifiers will now be within satisfactory range.
20. When 1 rectifier is open it will read approximately 1 ampere and good rectifiers will read within satisfactory range.
21. To test the negative rectifiers connect the test clip of tool C–3829–A to the rectifier end housing.
22. Touch the metal pin of each of the negative rectifiers with the test probe.
23. Test specifications are the same and test results will be approximately the same as for positive case rectifiers, except meter will read on opposite side of scale.

NOTE: If a negative rectifier shows shorted, remove the stator from rectifier assembly and retest. It is possible that a stator winding could be grounded to the stator laminations or the rectifier end shield, which would indicate a shorted negative rectifier.

24. Unsolder the stator to rectifier leads. Mark the stator coil frame to aid in reinstallation of the stator. Remove the stator from the rectifier end shield assembly.
25. Remove the 3 rectifier assembly mounting screws. Remove the rectifier assembly.
26. Remove the inner battery (B+) stud insulator.
27. Remove the D+ stud insulator, stud nut, stud flatwasher and stud insulating washer.
28. Remove the rear bearing oil and dust seal. Check the rotor bearing surface for scoring.
29. Using puller C–4068 or equivalent, remove the rear rotor bearing.
30. Check outside circumference of slip-ring for dirt and roughness. Clean or polish with fine sandpaper, as required. A badly roughened slip-ring or a worn down slip-ring should be replaced.
31. To check for an open rotor field coil, connect an ohmmeter to slip-rings. Ohmmeter readings should be between 1.5–2 ohms on rotor coils at room temperature ambient conditions. Resistance between 2.5–3.0 ohms would result from alternator rotors that have been operated on vehicle at higher engine compartment temperatures. Reading above 3.5 ohms would indicate high resistance rotor coils and further testing or replacement may be required.
32. To check for a shorted field coil, connect an ohmmeter to the slip-rings. If reading is below 1.5 ohms, field coil is shorted.
33. To check for a grounded rotor field coil; connect an ohmmeter from each slip-ring to the rotor shaft.

NOTE: Ohmmeter should be set for infinite reading when probes are apart and 0 when probes are shorted. The ohmmeter should read infinite. If reading is 0 or higher, rotor is grounded.

34. Check for continuity between leads of stator coil. Press test probe firmly to each of 3 phase (stator) lead terminals 1 at a time. If there is no continuity, the stator coil is defective. Replace the stator assembly.
35. To test the stator for ground, check for continuity between the stator coil leads and the stator coil frame. If there is no continuity the stator is grounded and must be replaced.
36. To test the inner and outer brush circuit, use an ohmmeter and touch 1 test probe to the inner brush and the other test probe to the brush terminal. If continuity does not exist replace the brush assembly. Repeat the same procedure for the outer brush.
37. To assemble the alternator reverse the disassembly procedure.
38. Be sure to check all parts for wear. Replace defective components as required.
39. Push the brushes into the brush holder and insert a wire to hold them in the raised position. Install the rotor and remove the holding wire.

Bosch Alternator with External Regulator

DISASSEMBLY & ASSEMBLY

1. Remove the alternator from the vehicle. Mount the unit in a suitable holding fixture.
2. Hold the alternator pulley and remove the pulley retaining nut.
3. Remove the pulley lockwasher, pulley fan spacer and pulley from the alternator assembly.
4. Remove the Woodruff key from the rotor shaft.
5. From the rear of the alternator remove the brush holder retaining screws. Remove the brush holder.
6. To test the inner and outer brush circuits, use an ohmmeter and touch 1 test probe to the inner brush and the other test probe to the brush terminal. If continuity does not exist replace the brush assembly. Repeat the same test for the outer brush circuit.
7. Disconnect the capacitor electri-

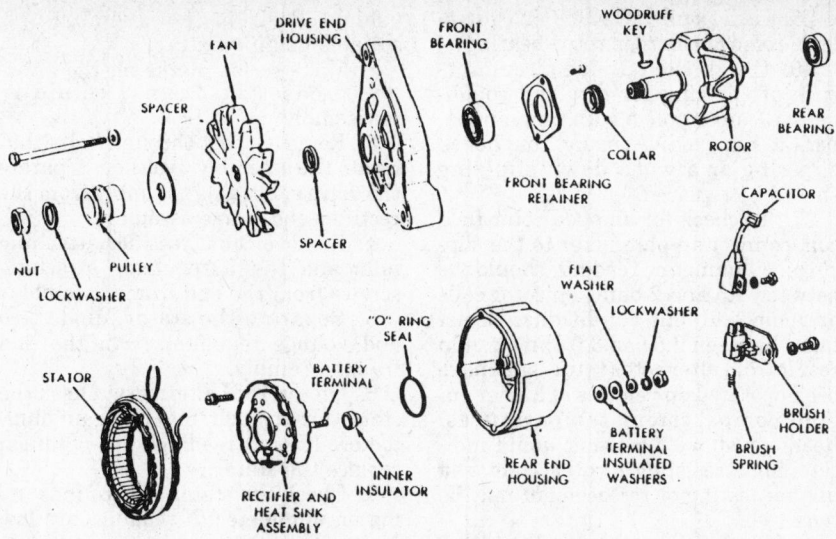

Bosch alternator with external regulator

cal connection and remove the capacitor retaining screw. Remove the capacitor from its mounting on the alternator.

8. Remove the ground stud nut and stud washer.

9. Remove the 4 alternator through bolts that retain the unit together.

10. Using the proper tool, separate the stator and the drive end shield.

11. To test the positive and negative rectifiers use tool C–3929–A or equivalent.

NOTE: Do not break the plastic cases of the rectifiers. These cases are for protection against corrosion. Be sure to always touch the test probe to the metal pin of the nearest rectifier.

12. Position the rear end shield and the stator assembly on an insulated surface. Connect the test lead clip to the alternator battery output terminal.

13. Plug in tool C–3829–A or equivalent. Touch the metal pin of each of the positive rectifiers with the test probe.

14. Reading for satisfactory rectifiers will be 1¾ amperes or more. Reading should be approximately the same and meter needle must move in the same direction for all 3 rectifiers.

15. When some rectifiers are good and 1 is shorted the reading taken at good rectifiers will be low and reading at shorted rectifiers will be 0. Disconnect stator lead to rectifiers reading 0 and retest. Reading of good rectifiers will now be within satisfactory range.

16. When 1 rectifier is open it will read approximately 1 ampere and good rectifiers will read within satisfactory range.

17. To test the negative rectifiers

connect the test clip of tool C–3829–A to the rectifier end housing.

18. Touch the metal pin of each of the negative rectifiers with the test probe.

19. Test specifications are the same and test results will be approximately same as for positive case rectifiers except that the meter will read on opposite side of scale.

NOTE: If a negative rectifier shows shorted, remove stator from rectifier assembly and retest. It is possible that a stator winding could be grounded to stator laminations or rectifier end shield which would indicate a shorted negative rectifier.

20. Remove the battery (B+) stud nut, stud lockwasher, stud flatwasher and stud insulator.

21. Remove the rectifier assembly retaining screws. Remove the stator assembly along with the rectifier unit. Unsolder the stator to rectifier leads.

22. Check for continuity between stator coil leads. Press test probe firmly to each of the 3 phase (stator) lead terminals 1 at a time. If there is no continuity, stator coil is defective. Replace stator assembly.

23. To test the stator for ground. Check for continuity between stator coil leads and the stator coil frame. If there is continuity, the stator is grounded. Replace the stator assembly.

24. Remove the rear bearing oil and dust seals. Check the rotor bearing surface for wear and scoring. Replace as required.

25. Remove the inner battery (B+) stud insulator.

26. Press the rotor out of the drive end shield and remove the spacer.

27. Check outside circumference of slip-ring for dirt and roughness. Clean or polish with fine sandpaper, if required. A badly roughened slip-ring or a worn down slip-ring should be replaced.

28. Check for continuity between field coil and slip-rings. If there is no continuity, field coil is defective. Replace rotor assembly.

29. Check for continuity between slip-rings and shaft (or core). If there is continuity, it means that coil or slip-ring is grounded. Replace the rotor assembly.

30. Using a puller remove the rotor bearing.

31. Remove the front bearing from the drive end shield by removing the front bearing retaining screws.

32. Press out the drive end shield bearing. Remove the front drive bearing from the front drive end shield.

33. To assemble the alternator reverse the disassembly procedure.

34. Be sure to check all parts for wear. Replace defective components as required.

35. Push the brushes into the brush holder and insert a wire to hold them in the raised position. Install the rotor and remove the holding wire.

Bosch 40/90 And 40/100 Amp Alternator

DISASSEMBLY & ASSEMBLY

1. Remove the alternator from the vehicle. Position the unit in a suitable holding fixture.

2. Remove the pulley nut and lockwasher. Remove the alternator pulley.

3. Remove the pulley to fan spacer and pulley fan.

4. Remove the Woodruff key from the rotor shaft.

5. From the rear of the alternator disconnect the electrical terminal from the capacitor. Remove the capacitor retaining screw and the capacitor.

6. Remove the brush holder retaining screw and remove the brush holder from its mounting on the rear of the alternator.

7. Remove the alternator through bolts. Using a suitable tool pry between the stator and the drive end shield and carefully separate the assembly.

8. Press the rotor out of the drive end shield and remove the spacer. Remove the pulley fan spacer.

9. Remove the front alternator drive end bearing screws.

10. Remove the drive end shield bearing retainer and press out the drive end shield bearing.

11. Remove the front drive bearing from the front of the drive end shield.

12. To test the positive and negative rectifiers use tool C–3929–A or equivalent.

NOTE: Do not break the plastic cases of the rectifiers. These cases are for protection against corrosion. Be sure to always touch the test probe to the metal pin of the nearest rectifier.

13. Position the rear end shield and the stator assembly on an insulated surface. Connect the test lead clip to the alternator battery output terminal.

14. Plug in tool C–3829–A or equivalent. Touch the metal pin of each of the positive rectifiers with the test probe.

15. Reading for satisfactory rectifiers will be 1¾ amperes or more. Reading should be approximately the same and meter needle must move in same direction for all 3 rectifiers.

16. When some rectifiers are good and 1 is shorted the reading taken at good rectifiers will be low and the reading at shorted rectifiers will be 0. Disconnect stator lead to the rectifiers reading 0 and retest. Reading of good rectifiers will now be within satisfactory range.

17. When a rectifier is open it will read approximately 1 ampere and the good rectifiers will read within the satisfactory range.

18. Touch the metal pin of each of the negative rectifiers with the test probe.

19. Test specifications are the same and the test results will be approximately the same as for positive case rectifiers except that the meter will read on opposite side of scale.

NOTE: If a negative rectifier shows shorted remove stator from the rectifier assembly and retest. It is possible that a stator winding could be grounded to stator laminations or rectifiers end shield which would indicate a shorted negative rectifier.

20. Unsolder the stator to rectifier leads. Mark the stator coil frame, to aid in reinstallation of the stator. Remove the stator from the rectifier end shield assembly.

21. Remove the 3 rectifier assembly mounting screws. Remove the rectifier assembly.

22. Remove the inner battery (B+) stud insulator.

23. Remove the D+ stud insulator, stud nut, stud flatwasher and stud insulating washer.

24. Remove the rear bearing oil and dust seals. Check the rotor bearing surface for scoring.

25. Using puller C–4068 or equivalent, remove the rear rotor bearing.

26. Check the outside circumference of slip-ring for dirt and roughness. Clean or polish with fine sandpaper, if required. A badly roughened slip-ring or a worn down slip-ring should be replaced.

27. To check for an open rotor field coil, connect an ohmmeter to the slip-rings. Ohmmeter reading should be between 1.5 and 2 ohms on rotor coils at room ambient conditions. Resistance between 2.5 and 3.0 ohms would result from alternator rotors that have been operated on vehicles at higher engine compartment temperatures. Readings above 3.5 ohms would indicate high resistance rotor coils and further testing or replacement may be required.

28. To check for a shorted field coil connect an ohmmeter to the slip-rings. If reading is below 1.5 ohms, the field coil is shorted.

29. To check for a grounded rotor field coil connect an ohmmeter from each slip-ring to the rotor shaft.

NOTE: Ohmmeter should be set for infinite reading when probes are apart and 0 when probes are shorted. The ohmmeter should read infinite. If reading is 0 or higher, rotor is grounded.

30. Check for continuity between leads of stator coil. Press test probe firmly to each of 3 phase (stator) lead terminals 1 at a time. If there is no continuity, stator coil is defective. Replace stator assembly.

31. To test the stator for ground check for continuity between the stator coil leads and the stator coil frame. If there is no continuity the stator is grounded and must be replaced.

32. To test the inner and outer brush circuit, use an ohmmeter and touch 1 test probe to the inner brush and the other test probe to the brush terminal. If continuity does not exist replace the brush assembly. Repeat the same procedure for the outer brush.

33. To assemble the alternator reverse the disassembly procedure.

34. Be sure to check all parts for wear. Replace defective components as required.

35. Push the brushes into the brush holder and insert a wire to hold them in the raised position. Install the rotor and remove the holding wire.

Delcotron SI Alternators

DISASSEMBLY & ASSEMBLY

1. Remove the alternator from the vehicle. Position the assembly in a suitable holding fixture.

2. Make scribe marks on the alternator case end frames to aid in reassembly.

3. Remove the 4 through bolts that retain the assembly together. Separate the drive end frame assembly from the rectifier end frame assembly.

4. Remove the 3 rectifier attaching nuts and the 3 regulator attaching screws from the end frame assembly.

5. Separate the stator, diode trio and voltage regulator from the end frame assembly.

6. On the 10SI alternator, check the stator for open circuits using an ohmmeter. If high readings are obtained replace the stator.

7. Check the stator for grounds using an ohmmeter. If readings are low replace the stator.

8. Using an ohmmeter check the rotor for grounds. The ohmmeter reading should be very high if not replace the rotor.

9. Using an ohmmeter, check the rotor for opens. If the ohmmeter reading is not 2.4–3.5 ohms replace the rotor.

10. To check the diode trio connect the ohmmeter to the diode trio and reverse the lead connections. The ohmmeter should read high and low if not replace the diode trio. Repeat the same test between the single connector and each of the other connectors.

11. Check rectifier bridge with ohmmeter connected from grounded heat sink to flat metal on terminal. Reverse the leads. If both readings are the same replace rectifier bridge.

12. Repeat test between the grounded heat sink and the other 2 flat metal clips.

13. Repeat test between the insulated heat sink and 3 flat metal clips.

14. Clean or replace the alternator brushes as required. Position the brushes in the brush holder and retain them in place using the brush retainer wire or equivalent.

15. To remove the rotor and drive end bearing, remove the shaft nut, washer and pulley, fan and collar. Push the rotor from the housing.

16. Remove the retainer plate from inside the drive end frame. Push the bearing out. Clean or replace parts as required.

17. Press against the outer bearing race to push the bearing in. On early production alternators it will be necessary to fill the bearing cavity with lubricant. Late production alternators use a sealed bearing and lubricant is not required for assembly.

18. Press rotor into the end frame. Assemble the collar, fan, pulley, washer and nut. Torque the shaft nut to 40–60 ft. lbs.

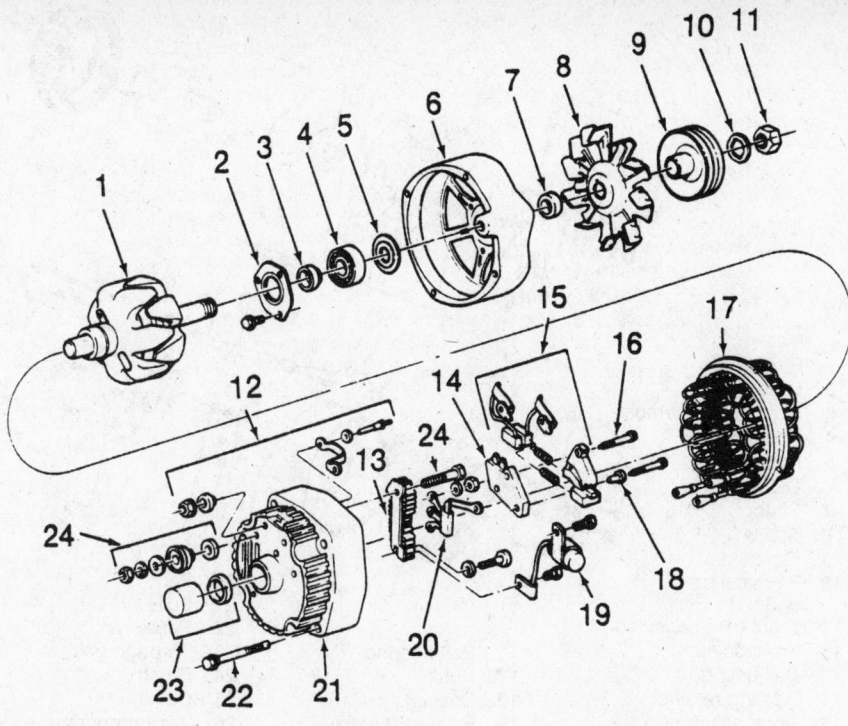

1 Rotor
2 Front bearing retainer
3 Inner collar
4 Bearing
5 Washer
6 Front housing
7 Outer collar
8 Fan
9 Pulley
10 Lockwasher
11 Pulley nut
12 Terminal assembly
13 Rectifier bridge
14 Regulator
15 Brush assembly
16 Screw
17 Stator
18 Insulating washer
19 Capacitor
20 Diode trio
21 Rear housing
22 Through bolt
23 Bearing and seal assembly
24 Terminal assembly

Delcotron 10-SI alternator—exploded view

19. Push slip-ring end bearing out from the outside toward inside of end frame.

20. On 10SI and 15SI, place flat plate over new bearing and press from outside toward inside until bearing is flush with the end frame.

21. On 15SI alternators use the thin wall tube in the space between the grease cup and the housing to push the bearing in flush with the housing.

22. Assemble the brush holder, regulator, resistor, diode trio, rectifier bridge and stator to slip-ring end frame.

23. Assemble end frames together with through bolts. Remove the brush retainer wire.

Delcotron CS Alternators

DISASSEMBLY & ASSEMBLY

Type CS 144

1. Remove the alternator from the vehicle. Scribe marks on the end frames to facilitate assembly.

2. Remove the through bolts and separate the end frames.

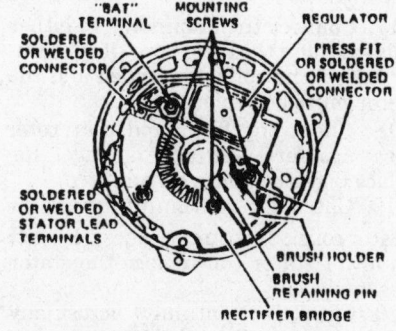

GM Delcotron alternator component location

3. Check the rotor for grounds using an ohmmeter. The reading should be infinite, if not, replace the rotor.

4. Check the rotor for shorts and open circuits. Replace the rotor as required.

5. Remove the 3 attaching nuts and remove the stator from the end frame.

6. Check the stator for grounds using an ohmmeter. If the reading is low replace the stator.

7. Unsolder the connections, remove the retaining screws and connector from the end frame. Separate the

regulator and the brush holder from the end frame.

8. Check the rectifier bridge using an ohmmeter. Replace as required. Check the heat sink, using an ohmmeter. Replace as required. Clean the brushes. Replace them as required.

9. To remove the rotor and drive end bearing, hold the rotor using a hex wrench in the shaft end while removing the nut. Push the rotor from the housing. Remove the plate and push the bearing out.

10. Assembly is the reverse of the disassembly procedure. Repair or replace defective components as required.

Type CS 130

1. Remove the alternator from the vehicle. Scribe marks on the end frames to facilitate assembly. Remove the through bolts and separate the end frames.

2. Remove the cover rivets or pins. Remove the cover on the slip-ring end frame.

3. Unsolder the stator leads at the 3 terminals on the rectifier bridge. Avoid excessive heat, as damage to the assembly will occur. Remove the stator.

4. Drive out the 3 baffle pins. Remove the baffle from inside of the slip-ring end frame.

5. Check the rotor for grounds using an ohmmeter. The reading should be infinite, if not, replace the rotor. Check the rotor for shorts and open circuits, the ohmmeter should read 1.7–2.3 ohms. Replace the rotor as required.

6. Check the stator for grounds using an ohmmeter. If the reading is low replace the stator.

7. Remove the brush holder screw. Disconnect the terminal and remove the brush holder assembly. Check and replace the brushes, as required.

8. Unsolder and pry open the terminal between the regulator and the rectifier bridge. Remove the terminal and the retaining screws. Remove the regulator and the rectifier bridge from the end frame.

9. To check the rectifier bridge, connect the proper (analog reading) ohmmeter, using the low scale, to 1 terminal and the heat sink, record the reading. Reverse the test leads and record the reading. If both readings are the same replace the rectifier bridge. Check the other diodes in the same manner.

10. To remove the rotor and drive end bearing, hold the rotor using a hex wrench in the shaft end while removing the nut. Push the rotor from the housing. Remove the plate and push the bearing out.

11. Assembly is the reverse of the disassembly procedure. Repair or replace defective components as required.

Delcotron Alternator with Rear Vacuum Pump

DISASSEMBLY & ASSEMBLY

1. Remove the alternator from the vehicle. Position the unit in a suitable holding fixture.

2. Remove the vacuum pump retaining bolts. Remove the vacuum pump from the rear of the alternator while holding the center plate.

3. Remove the brush cover retaining bolts and brushes. Wrap the pump drive shaft spline with tape in order to protect the rear seal from damage.

4. Inspect the vacuum pump for wear and damage, replace defective components as required. Measure the length of the vanes, replace if not within specification (0.511–0.531 in.) Measure the inside diameter of the housing and replace if not within specification (2.440–2.441 in.).

5. Examine the check valve for damage. Apply light pressure to the valve and make sure that the valve operates properly. Replace as required.

6. Check the inner face of the rear cover on the vacuum pump for oil leakage. Check the inner face of the oil seal for wear and damage. Replace the oil seal in the rear end housing of the vacuum pump as required.

7. Remove the alternator through bolts which hold the unit together. Matchmark the assembly to aid in reassembly. Separate the front end housing from the stator and rear end housing.

8. Remove the pulley nut, fan and front end housing from the rotor.

9. Remove the front bearing retainer screws. Remove the front bearing retainer and the bearing from the front end housing.

10. Remove the bolt and nuts retaining the stator, diodes and brush holder to the rear end housing. Note the position of the insulating washers for reassembly.

11. Separate the rear end housing from the stator and diode assembly.

12. Remove the diodes from the stator by melting the solder from the terminals. Be sure to protect the diodes while melting the solder.

13. Remove the solder from the voltage regulator holder plate terminal. Remove the voltage regulator.

14. Check the slip-ring surfaces of the rotor for wear and damage, repair or replace as required.

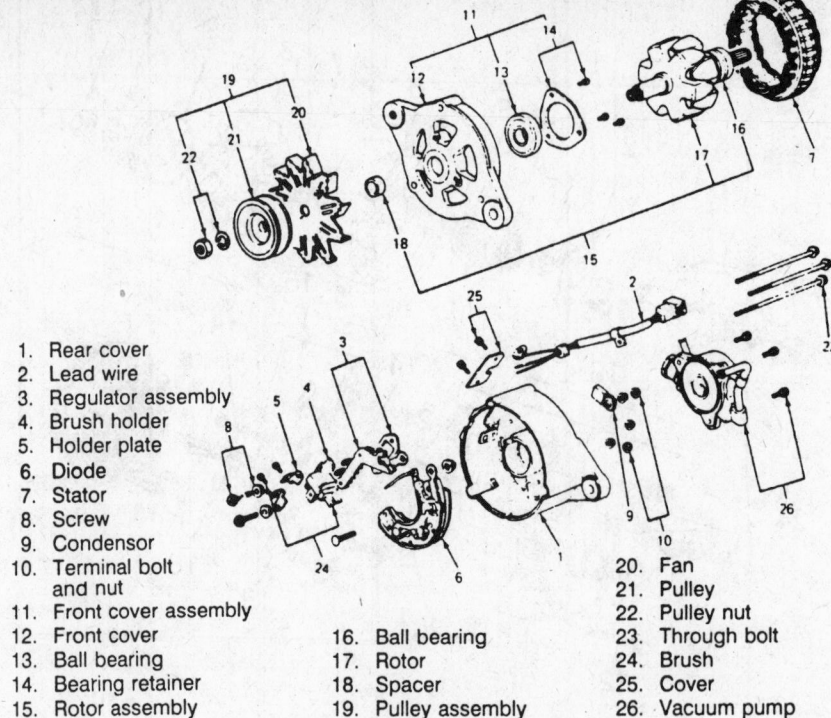

1. Rear cover
2. Lead wire
3. Regulator assembly
4. Brush holder
5. Holder plate
6. Diode
7. Stator
8. Screw
9. Condensor
10. Terminal bolt and nut
11. Front cover assembly
12. Front cover
13. Ball bearing
14. Bearing retainer
15. Rotor assembly
16. Ball bearing
17. Rotor
18. Spacer
19. Pulley assembly
20. Fan
21. Pulley
22. Pulley nut
23. Through bolt
24. Brush
25. Cover
26. Vacuum pump

Delcotron alternator with vacuum pump

15. Measure the outside diameter of the rotor slip-rings. If ring diameter is not 1.18–1.24 in., replace the rotor.

16. Connect the ohmmeter test leads to each slip-ring. Resistance should be 4.2 ohms at 68°F. If continuity does not exist the coil is open and the rotor must be replaced.

17. Connect the ohmmeter to either slip-ring and the rotor core. If continuity exists the coil is grounded and the rotor must be replaced.

18. Check the front and rear rotor bearings for wear and damage. Replace defective parts as required.

19. Check for continuity across the stator coils. If continuity does not exist in any 1 stator coil replace the stator assembly.

20. Check for continuity across any of the stator coils and the stator core. If continuity exists, 1 of the stator coils is grounded and the stator must be replaced.

21. Coil resistance should be 0.05 ohms at 68°F and should be measured from the coil lead to terminal N.

22. Inspect the alternator brush assembly for wear and damage. Replace defective components as required.

23. Check for continuity of positive diodes between each stator coil terminal and the battery terminal of rectifier assembly. Reverse the ohmmeter leads and recheck for continuity.

24. If continuity exists in both polarity directions or does not exist in both directions diode is defective and must

be replaced.

25. Check for continuity of negative diodes between each stator lead and E terminal or rectifier assembly. Reverse ohmmeter leads and recheck for continuity. Continuity should exist in 1 direction only.

26. Assemble a test circuit using the following components: One 10 ohm 3 watt resistor (R_1) one 0–300 ohm 3 watt variable resistor (R_2), two 12 volt batteries (BAT_1 and BAT_2) and one 0–30 volt DC voltmeter.

27. Adjust variable resistor (R_2) until voltage at V_4 reads the same as voltage at V_3 (this should be all the way to 1 end of travel or 0 ohms).

28. Connect the test circuit to the integrated circuit regulator terminals. Measure voltage at V_1 and V_2. Voltage should measure 10–13 volts at V_1 and 0–2 volts at V_2.

29. Disconnect terminal S from circuit and measure voltage at V_3. Voltage at V_3 should be 20–26 volts. Reconnect terminal S.

30. Measure voltage at V_4 while increasing resistance at R_2 from 0 ohms. V_4 voltmeter reading should increase from 2 volts to 10–13 volts. Stop increasing R_2 when voltage reaches 10–13 volts.

31. If increase at V_4 is interrupted at any point up to 10–13 volts, while increasing resistance at R_2, regulator is defective.

32. Measure voltage at V_4 with R_2 at same setting as previous step that produced 10–13 volt reading at V_2. If V_4

not within 14–14.6 volts, regulator is defective.

33. Disconnect wire at terminal S. Connect it to terminal B. Repeat Step 30. If V_2 does not vary or V_4 is not within 14.5–16.6 volts, regulator is defective.

34. To assemble the alternator reverse the disassembly procedure. Be sure to check all parts for wear and damage. Replace defective components as required.

35. Insert the brushes into the brush holder and insert a wire to retain them in place. Install the rotor and remove the retaining wire.

Delcotron Alternator Sprint, Spectrum and Nova

DISASSEMBLY & ASSEMBLY

1. Remove the alternator from the vehicle. Position the assembly in a suitable holding fixture.

2. Remove the nut and the terminal insulator. Remove the nuts and the end cover.

3. Remove the screws, brush holder and IC regulator. Remove the screws securing the rectifier holder and rubber insulators.

4. Using tool J–35452 and a breaker bar loosen and remove the alternator pulley.

5. Using an ohmmeter inspect the rotor assembly for an open circuit. Check for continuity between the slip-rings. If continuity does not exist, replace the rotor.

6. Using an ohmmeter inspect the rotor assembly for ground. Check for continuity between the slip-ring and the rotor. If continuity exists, replace the rotor.

7. Check that the slip-rings are not rough or scored. If the slip-rings are rough or scored replace the rotor.

8. Using a measuring caliper, measure the slip-ring diameter. If not within specification, replace the rotor assembly.

9. Using an ohmmeter inspect the stator assembly for open circuits. Check all leads for continuity. If continuity does not exist, replace the drive end.

10. Using an ohmmeter inspect the stator assembly to insure that it is not grounded. Check that there is no continuity between the coil leads and the drive end frame. If continuity exists, replace the drive end frame.

11. Replace the brush assembly if less than 0.177 in. Check the front bearing and if necessary, replace it.

12. Assembly of the alternator is the reverse of the disassembly procedure.

Ford Alternator with External Regulator

DISASSEMBLY & ASSEMBLY

All Except 65, 70 and 90 Amp Alternators

1. Mark both end housings with a scribe mark for assembly.

2. Remove the 3 housing through bolts.

3. Separate the front housing and rotor from the stator and rear housing.

4. Remove the nuts from the rectifier to rear housing mounting studs and remove rear housing.

5. Remove the brush holder mounting screws and the holder, brushes, springs, insulator and terminal.

6. If replacement is necessary press the bearing from the rear end housing while supporting the housing on the inner boss.

7. If rectifiers are to be replaced carefully unsolder the leads from the terminals. Use only a 100 watt soldering iron. Leave the soldering iron in contact with the diode terminals only long enough to remove the wires. Use a heat sink in order to protect the diodes.

8. There are various types of rectifier assembly circuit boards installed in production. One type has the circuit board spaced away from the diode plates and the diodes are exposed. Another type consists of a single circuit board with integral diodes; and still another has integral diodes with an additional booster diode plate containing 2 diodes.

9. This last type is used only on the 8 diode (61 amp) alternator. To disassemble use the following procedures. Exposed diodes, remove the screws from the rectifier by rotating bolt heads ¼ turn clockwise to unlock and remove. Integral diodes, press out the stator terminal screw, making sure not to twist it while doing this. Do not remove the grounded screw. Booster diodes, press out the stator terminal screw about ¼ in., remove the nut from the end of the screw and lift screw from circuit board. Be sure not to twist it as it comes out.

10. Remove the drive pulley and fan. On alternator pulleys with threaded holes in the outer end of the pulley use a standard puller for removal.

11. Remove the 3 screws that hold the front bearing retainer and remove the front housing. If the bearing is to be replaced press it from the housing.

Assembly:

12. Press the front bearing into the front housing boss by putting pressure

on outer race only. Install bearing retainer.

13. If the stop ring on the driveshaft was damaged install a new stop ring. Push the new ring onto the shaft and into the groove.

14. Position the front bearing spacer on the driveshaft against the stop ring.

15. Place the front housing over the shaft with the bearing positioned in the front housing cavity.

16. Install fan spacer, fan, pulley, lockwasher and retaining nut and tighten the nut 60–100 ft. lbs. holding the drive shaft with an Allen key.

17. If rear bearing was removed, press a new one into rear housing.

18. Assemble brushes, springs, terminal and insulator in the brush holder, retract the brushes and insert a short length of ⅛ in. rod or stiff wire through the hole in the holder to hold the brushes in the retracted position.

19. Position the brush holder assembly in the rear housing and install mounting screws. Position the brush leads to prevent shorting.

20. Wrap the 3 stator winding leads around the circuit board terminals and solder them using only rosin core solder and a solder iron. Position the stator neutral lead eyelet on the stator terminal screw and install the screw in the rectifier assembly.

21. Alternators with exposed diodes, insert the special screws through the wire lug, dished washers and circuit board. Turn ¼ turn counterclockwise to lock in place. Alternators with Integral diodes, insert the screws straight through the holes.

NOTE: The dished washers are to be used on the molded circuit boards only. Using these washers on a fiber board will result in a serious short circuit, as only a flat insulating washer between the stator terminal and the board is used on fiber circuit boards.

22. Alternators with booster diodes, position the stator wire terminal on the stator terminal screw, position the screw on rectifier. Position the square insulator over the screw and into the square hole in the rectifier, rotate terminal screw until it locks, press it in fingertight. Position the stator wire and press the terminal screw into the rectifier and insulator with a vise.

23. Place the radio noise suppression condenser on the rectifier terminals. With molded circuit board and install the STA and BAT terminal insulators. With fiber circuit board place the square stator terminal insulator in the square hole in the rectifier assembly. Position the BAT terminal insulator.

24. Position the stator and rectifier

assembly in the rear housing, making sure that all terminal insulators are seated properly in the recesses. Position the STA, BAT and FLD insulators on terminal bolts and install the nuts.

25. Clean the rear bearing surface of the rotor shaft with a rag and then position rear housing and stator assembly over rotor. Align matchmarks made during disassembly and install the through bolts. Remove brush retracting wire and place a dab of silicone sealer over the hole.

65, 70, 90 and 100 Amp Alternators

NOTE: When disassembling the side terminal alternator the brush holder would be removed after the rectifier is removed. During the assembly the brush holder would be installed in the reverse order.

1. Remove the brush holder and cover assembly from the rear housing.
2. Mark both end housings and the stator.
3. Remove the 3 housing through bolts.
4. Separate the front housing and rotor from the stator and rear housing.
5. Remove the drive pulley nut, lockwasher, flat washer, pulley, fan, fan spacer and rotor from the front housing.
6. Remove the 3 screws that hold the front bring retainer and remove the retainer. If the bearing is damaged or has lost its lubricant, support the housing close to the bearing boss and press out the bearing.
7. Remove all the nut and washer assemblies and insulators from the rear housing and remove the rear housing from the stator and rectifier assembly.
8. If necessary press the rear bearing from the housing while supporting the housing on the inner boss.
9. Unsolder the 3 stator leads from the rectifier assembly and separate the stator from the assembly. Use a 200 watt soldering iron. Perform a diode test and an open and grounded stator coil test.

To install:
10. If the front bearing is being replaced press the new bearing into the bearing boss by putting pressure on the outer race only. Install the bearing retainer and tighten the retainer screws until the tips of the retainer touch the housing.
11. Position the rectifier assembly to the stator, wrap the 3 stator leads around the diode plate terminals and solder them using a 200 watt soldering iron.
12. If the rear housing bearing was

removed press in a new bearing from the inside of the housing by putting pressure on the other race only.

13. Install at the BAT/GRD insulator and position the stator and rectifier assembly in the rear housing.
14. Install the STA (purple) and BAT (red) terminal insulators on the terminal bolts and install the nut and washer assemblies. Make certain that the shoulders on all insulators, both inside and outside of the housing, are seated properly before tightening the nuts.
15. Position the front housing over the rotor and install the fan spacer, fan, pulley, flat and lockwashers. Install the nut on the rotor shaft.
16. Wipe the rear bearing surface of the rotor shaft with a clean rag.
17. Position the rotor with the front housing into the stator and rear housing assembly and align the matchmarks made during disassembly. Seat the machined portion of the stator core into the step in both housings and install the through bolts.
18. If the field brushes have worn to less than ⅜ in., replace both brushes. Hold the brushes in position by inserting a stiff wire into the brush holder.
19. Position the brush holder assembly into the rear housing and install the 3 mounting screws. Remove the brush retracting wire and put a dab of silicone cement over the hole.

BRUSH REPLACEMENT

65, 70, 90 and 100 Amp Alternators

1. Remove the brush holder and cover assembly from the rear housing.
2. Remove the terminal bolts from the brush holder and cover assembly. Remove the brush assemblies.
3. Position the new brush terminals on the terminal bolts and assemble the terminals, bolts, brush holder washers and nuts. The insulating washer mounts under the FLD terminal nut. The entire brush and cover assembly is also available for service.
4. Depress the brush springs in the brush holder cavities and insert the brushes on top of the springs. Hold the brushes in position by inserting a stiff wire in the brush holder.
5. Install the brush holder and cover assembly into the rear housing. Remove the brush retracting wire and put a dab of silicone cement over the hole.

Ford Alternator with Internal Regulator

DISASSEMBLY & ASSEMBLY

1. Remove the alternator from the

vehicle. Position the unit in a suitable holding fixture.

2. Remove the voltage regulator and the brush holder from the rear of the alternator assembly.
3. Remove the 2 screws retaining the brush holder to the voltage regulator. Separate the 2 components.
4. Matchmark the alternator end housings and stator frame to aid in assembly.
5. Remove the alternator through bolts. Separate the front housing and the rotor assembly from the stator and the rear housing.
6. Unsolder the 3 stator leads from the rectifier assembly. Be careful that the rectifiers are not in contact with the solder iron as overheating them will cause damage.
7. Remove the rectifier assembly from the rear of the alternator housing. Press the rear alternator housing bearing from the rear housing.
8. From the front housing of the alternator remove the drive pulley nut from the rotor shaft.
9. Remove the lockwasher, drive pulley, fan and fan spacer from the rotor shaft.
10. Remove the rotor from the front housing. Remove the front bearing spacer from the rotor shaft. Do not remove the rotor stop ring unless it must be replaced.
11. Remove the front housing bearing retainer and bearing.
12. Assembly of the alternator is the reverse of the disassembly procedure. Be sure to clean and check all parts for wear and defects. Repair or replace defective components as required.

Ford Side Terminal Alternator

DISASSEMBLY & ASSEMBLY

1. Mark both end housings and stator with a scribe mark for assembly.
2. Remove 4 housings through bolts and separate front housing and rotor from rear housing and stator. Slots are provided in front housing to aid in disassembly. Do not separate rear housing from stator at this time.
3. Remove drive pulley nut. Remove the lockwasher, pulley, fan and fan spacer from rotor shaft.
4. Pull rotor and shaft from front housing and remove spacer from rotor shaft.
5. Remove 3 screws retaining bearing to front housing. If bearing is damaged or has lost lubricant, remove bearing from housing. To remove bearing, support housing close to bearing boss and press bearing from housing.

6. Unsolder and disengage 3 stator leads from the rectifier. Work quickly to prevent overheating the rectifier.

7. Lift stator from rear housing.

8. Unsolder and disengage the brush holder lead from rectifier. Work quickly to prevent overheating rectifier.

9. Remove screw attaching capacitor lead to the rectifier.

10. Remove the 4 screws attaching rectifier to rear housing.

11. Remove the 2 terminal nuts and insulator from outside housing. Remove rectifier from the housing.

12. Remove 2 screws attaching the brush holder to housing. Remove brushes and holder.

13. Remove any sealing compound from rear housing and brush holder.

14. Remove 1 screw attaching capacitor to rear housing and remove capacitor.

15. If bearing replacement is necessary, support rear housing close to the bearing boss and press the bearing out of housing.

16. Wipe rotor, stator and bearings with a clean cloth. Do not clean these parts with solvent.

17. Rotate front bearing on drive end of rotor shaft. Check for any scraping noise, looseness or roughness. Look for excessive lubricant leakage. If any of these conditions exist, replace bearing.

18. Inspect rotor shaft rear bearing surface for roughness or severe chatter marks. Replace rotor assembly if shaft is not smooth.

19. Place rear bearing on slip-ring end of rotor shaft and rotate bearing. Make the same check for noise, looseness, or roughness as was made for the front bearing. Inspect rollers and cage for damage. Replace bearing if these conditions exist, or if lubricant is lost or contaminated.

20. Check pulley and fan for excessive looseness on rotor shaft. Replace any pulley that is loose or bent out of shape.

21. Check both the front and rear housings for cracks, particularly in the webbed areas and at the mounting ear. Replace damaged or cracked housing.

22. Check all wire leads on both stator and rotor assemblies for loose or broken soldered connections and for burned insulation. Resolder poor connections. Replace parts that show signs of burned insulation.

23. Check slip-rings for nicks and surface roughness. Nicks and scratches may be removed by turning down slip-rings. Do not go beyond minimum diameter of 1.22 in. If rings are badly damaged, replace rotor assembly.

24. Replace brushes if they are worn shorter than ¼ in.

25. If front housing bearing is being replaced, press new bearing in housing. Apply pressure on bearing outer race only. Install the bearing retaining screws and tighten to 25–40 inch lbs.

26. Place inner spacer on rotor shaft and insert rotor shaft into front housing and bearing.

27. Install fan spacer, fan, pulley, lockwasher and nut on rotor shaft. Use the proper tool to tighten pulley nut.

28. If rear bearing is being replaced, press a new bearing in from inside housing until rear bearing face is flush with boss outer surface.

29. Position brush terminal on brush holder. Install springs and brushes in brush holder and insert a piece of stiff wire to hold brushes in place.

30. Brushes and springs are serviced as part of brush holder assembly. Position brush holder in rear housing and install attaching screws. Brush retaining wire must stick out enough to be grabbed and pulled from housing assembly.

31. Waterproof glue sealer may have to be pushed out of pin hole in housing. Push brush holder toward brush holder attaching screws. Reseal crack between brush holder and brush cavity in rear housing with Caulking Cord or equivalent body sealer. Do not use silicone base sealer for this application.

32. Position capacitor to rear housing and install attaching screw. Place 2 rectifier insulators on bosses inside housing.

33. Place insulator on BAT (large) terminal of rectifier and position rectifier in rear housing. Place outside insulator on BAT terminal and install the nuts on BAT and GRD terminals fingertight. Install, but do not tighten, 4 rectifier attaching screws.

34. Tighten the BAT terminal nuts to 35–50 inch lbs. and GRD terminal nuts to 25–35 inch lbs. on outside of rear housing. Tighten the 4 rectifier attaching screws to 40–50 inch lbs.

35. Position capacitor lead to rectifier and install attaching screw.

36. Press brush holder lead on rectifier pin and solder securely. Work quickly to prevent overheating of rectifier.

37. Position stator in rear housing and align scribe marks. Press 3 stator leads on rectifier pins and solder securely using rosin core electrical solder. Work quickly to prevent overheating rectifier.

38. Position rotor and front housing into stator and rear housing. Align scribe marks and install 4 through bolts. Tighten 2 opposing bolts and

then the 2 remaining bolts.

39. Spin fan and pulley to be sure nothing is binding within alternator.

40. Remove brush retracting wire and place a daub of waterproof cement over hole to seal it. Do not use silicone sealer on the hole.

Paris-Rhone 75/90 Amp Alternator

DISASSEMBLY & ASSEMBLY

1. Remove the alternator from the vehicle.

2. Position the unit in a suitable holding fixture.

3. Remove the pulley nut, lock washer and pulley.

4. Remove the fan spacer and the pulley fan from the alternator shaft.

5. Remove the Woodruff key from the rotor shaft.

6. From the rear of the alternator disconnect the capacitor terminal and remove the capacitor mounting screw. Remove the capacitor from the alternator.

7. Remove the voltage regulator and brush holder mounting screw. Remove the holder.

8. Remove the D+ stud nut, lock washer, stud washer and stud insulators.

9. Remove the battery (B+) stud nut, lock washer, stud flat washer and the stud insulator.

10. Remove the 4 alternator through bolts.

11. Pry between the stator and the drive end shield with a suitable tool. Carefully separate the drive end shield, pulley and rotor assembly away from the stator and rectifier end shield assembly.

12. Press the rotor out of the drive end shield and remove the spacer. Remove the alternator pulley fan spacer.

13. Remove the 4 alternator drive end bearing screws. Remove the drive end shield bearing retainer.

14. Press out the drive end shield bearing. Remove the front drive bearing from the front drive end shield.

15. To test the positive and negative rectifiers use tool J–21008–A or equivalent.

NOTE: Do not break the plastic cases of the rectifiers. These cases are for protection against corrosion. Be sure to always touch the test probe to the metal pin of the nearest rectifier.

16. Position the rear end shield and the stator assembly on an insulated surface. Connect the test lead clip to the alternator battery output terminal.

17. Plug in tool J–21008–A or equivalent. Touch the metal pin of each of the positive rectifiers with the test probe.

18. Readings for satisfactory rectifiers will be 1¾ amperes or more. Readings should be approximately the same and the meter needle must move in same direction for all 3 rectifiers.

19. When some rectifiers are good and one is shorted, the reading taken at good rectifiers will be low and reading taken at shorted rectifiers will be 0. Disconnect stator lead to rectifiers reading 0 and retest. Reading of good rectifiers will now be within satisfactory range.

20. When 1 rectifier is open it will read approximately 1 ampere and good rectifiers will read within satisfactory range.

21. To test the negative rectifiers connect the test clip of tool J–21008–A to the rectifier end housing.

22. Touch the metal pin of each of the negative rectifiers with the test probe.

23. Test specifications are the same and test results will be approximately the same as for positive case rectifiers, except meter will read on opposite side of scale.

NOTE: If a negative rectifier shows shorted, remove the stator from rectifier assembly and retest. It is possible that a stator winding could be grounded to the stator laminations or the rectifier end shield, which would indicate a shorted negative rectifier.

24. Unsolder the stator to rectifier leads. Mark the stator coil frame to aid in reinstallation of the stator. Remove the stator from the rectifier end shield assembly.

25. Remove the 3 rectifier assembly mounting screws. Remove the rectifier assembly.

26. Remove the inner battery (B+) stud insulator.

27. Remove the D+ stud insulator, stud nut, stud flatwasher and stud insulating washer.

28. Remove the rear bearing oil and dust seal. Check the rotor bearing surface for scoring.

29. Remove the rear rotor bearing.

30. Check outside circumference of slip-ring for dirt and roughness. Clean or polish with fine sandpaper, as required. A badly roughened slip-ring or a worn down slip-ring should be replaced.

31. To check for an open rotor field coil, connect an ohmmeter to slip-rings. Ohmmeter readings should be between 1.5–2 ohms on rotor coils at room temperature ambient conditions. Resistance between 2.5–3.0 ohms would result from alternator rotors that have been operated on vehicle at higher engine compartment temperatures. Reading above 3.5 ohms would indicate high resistance rotor coils and further testing or replacement may be required.

32. To check for a shorted field coil, connect an ohmmeter to the slip-rings. If reading is below 1.5 ohms, field coil is shorted.

33. To check for a grounded rotor field coil; connect an ohmmeter from each slip-ring to the rotor shaft.

NOTE: Ohmmeter should be set for infinite reading when probes are apart and 0 when probes are shorted. The ohmmeter should read infinite. If reading is 0 or higher, rotor is grounded.

34. Check for continuity between leads of stator coil. Press test probe firmly to each of 3 phase (stator) lead terminals 1 at a time. If there is no continuity, the stator coil is defective. Replace the stator assembly.

35. To test the stator for ground, check for continuity between the stator coil leads and the stator coil frame. If there is no continuity the stator is grounded and must be replaced.

36. To test the inner and outer brush circuit, use an ohmmeter and touch 1 test probe to the inner brush and the other test probe to the brush terminal. If continuity does not exist replace the brush assembly. Repeat the same procedure for the outer brush.

37. To assemble the alternator reverse the disassembly procedure.

38. Be sure to check all parts for wear. Replace defective components as required.

39. Push the brushes into the brush holder and insert a wire to hold them in the raised position. Install the rotor and remove the holding wire.

Carburetor Service 34

FUNCTIONS

Gasoline is the source of fuel for power in the automobile engine and the carburetor is the mechanism which automatically mixes liquid fuel with air in the correct proportions to provide the desired power output from the engine. The carburetor performs this function by metering, atomizing and mixing fuel with air flowing through the engine. A carburetor also regulates the volume of air/fuel mixture which enters the engine. It is the carburetor's regulation of the mixture flow which gives the operator control of the engine speed.

Metering

The automotive internal combustion engine operates efficiently within a relatively small range of air/fuel ratios. It is the function of the carburetor to meter the fuel in exact proportions to the air flowing into the engine, so that the optimum ratio of air/fuel is maintained under all operating conditions. Regulations governing exhaust gas emissions have made the proper metering of fuel by the carburetor an increasingly important factor. Too rich a mixture will result in poor economy and increased emissions, while too lean a mixture will result in loss of power and generally poor performance. Carburetors are matched to engines so that metering can be accomplished by using carefully calibrated metering jets which allow fuel to enter the engine at a rate proportional to the engine's ability to draw air.

Atomization

The liquid fuel must be broken up into small particles so that it will more readily mix with air and vaporize. The more contact the fuel has with the air, the better the vaporization. Atomization can be accomplished in 2 ways; air may be drawn into a stream of fuel which will cause a turbulence and break the solid stream of fuel into smaller particles; or a nozzle can be positioned at the point of highest air velocity in the carburetor and the fuel will be torn into a fine spray as it enters the air stream.

Distribution

The carburetor is the primary device involved in the distribution of fuel to the engine. The more efficiently fuel and air are combined in the carburetor, the smoother the flow of vaporized mixture through the intake manifold to each combustion chamber. Hence, the importance of the carburetor in fuel distribution.

PRINCIPLES

Vacuum

All carburetors operate on the basic principle of pressure difference. Any pressure less than atmospheric pressure is considered vacuum or a low pressure area. In the engine, as the piston moves down on the intake stroke with the intake valve open, a partial vacuum is created in the intake manifold. The farther the piston travels downward, the greater the vacuum created in the manifold. As vacuum increases in the manifold, a difference in pressure occurs between the carburetor and cylinder. The carburetor is positioned in such a way that the high pressure above it and the vacuum or low pressure above it and the vacuum or low pressure beneath it, causes air to be drawn through it. Fuel and air always move from high to low pressure areas.

Venturi Principle

To obtain greater pressure drop at the tip of the fuel nozzle so that fuel will flow, the principle of increasing the air velocity to create a low pressure area is used. The device used to increase the velocity of the air flowing through the carburetor is called a venturi. A venturi is a specially designed restriction placed in the air flow. In order for the air to pass through the restriction, it must accelerate causing a pressure drop or vacuum as it passes.

CARBURETOR CIRCUITS

Float Circuit

The float circuit includes the float, float bowl and a needle valve and seat. This circuit controls the amount of gas allowed to flow into the carburetor. As the fuel level rises, it causes the float to rise which pushes the needle valve into its seat. As soon as the valve and seat make contact, the flow of gas is cut off from the fuel inlet. When the level of fuel drops, the float sinks and releases the needle valve from its seat which allows the gas to flow in. In actual operation, the fuel is maintained at practically a constant level. The float tend to hold the needle valve partly closed so that the incoming fuel just balances the fuel being withdrawn.

Idle and Low Speed Circuit

When the throttle is closed or only

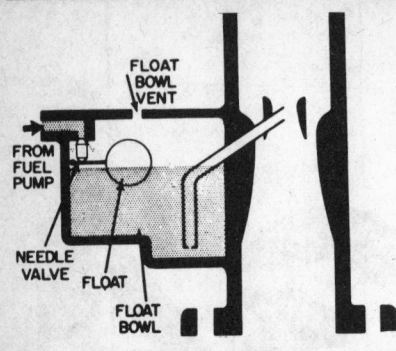

Float circuit

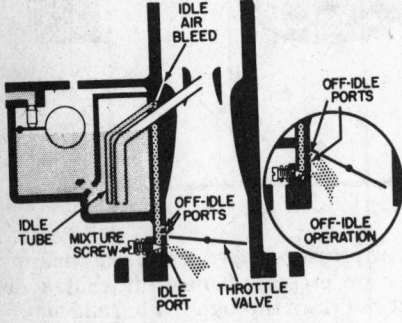

Idle and low speed circuit

High Speed Full Power Circuit

For high-speed, full-power, wide open throttle operation, the air/fuel mixture must be enriched; this is done either mechanically or by intake manifold vacuum.

Full Power Circuit (Mechanical)

This circuit includes a metering rod jet and a metering rod. The rod has 2 steps of different diameters and is attached to the throttle linkage. When the throttle is wide open, the metering rod is lifted bringing the smaller diameter of the rod into the jet. When the throttle is partly closed, the larger diameter of the metering rod is in the jet. This restricts fuel flow to the main nozzle but adequate amounts of fuel do flow for part-throttle operation.

Full Power Circuit (Vacuum)

This circuit is operated by intake manifold vacuum. It includes a vacuum diaphragm or piston linked to a valve. When the throttle is opened so that intake manifold vacuum is reduced, the spring raises the diaphragm or piston. This allows more fuel to flow in, either by lifting a metering rod or by opening a power valve.

Accelerator Pump Circuit

For acceleration, the carburetor must deliver additional fuel. A sudden inrush of air is caused by rapid acceleration or applying full throttle. When the throttle is opened, the pump lever pushes the plunger down and this forces fuel to flow through the accelerator pump circuit and out the pump jet. This fuel enters the air passage through the carburetor to supply additional fuel demands.

Choke

When starting an engine, it is necessary to increase the amount of fuel delivered to the intake manifold. This increase is controlled by the choke. The choke consists of a valve in the top of the air horn controlled mechanically by an automatic device. When the choke valve is closed, only a small amount of air can get past it.
When the engine is cranked, a fairly high vacuum develops in the air horn. This vacuum causes the main nozzle to discharge a heavy stream of fuel. The quantity delivered is sufficient to produce the correct air/fuel mixture needed for starting the engine. The choke is released either manually or by heat from the engine.

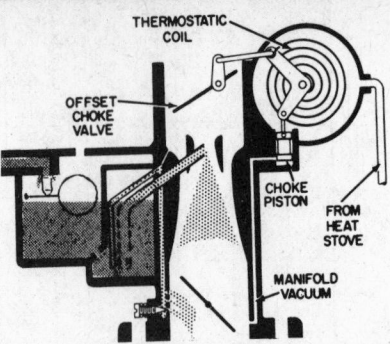

Choke system

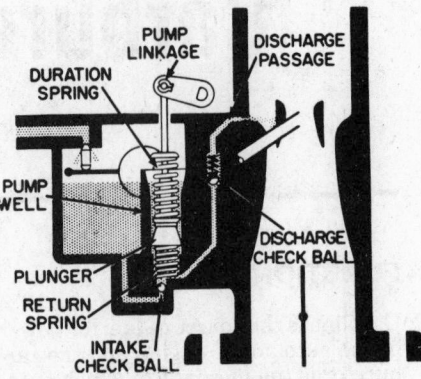

Accelerator pump circuit

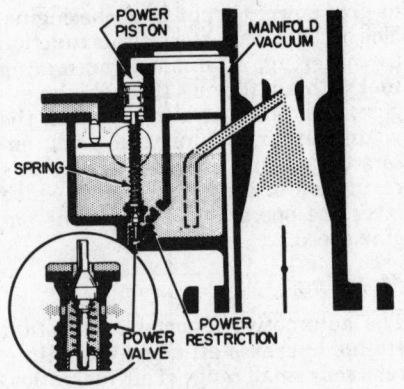

Power circuit

slightly opened, the air speed is low and practically no vacuum develops in the venturi. This means that the fuel nozzle will not feed. Thus, the carburetor must have another circuit to supply fuel during operation with a closed or slightly opened throttle. This circuit is called the idle and low speed circuit. It consists of passages in which air and fuel can flow beneath the throttle plate. With the throttle plate closed, there is high vacuum from the intake manifold. Atmospheric pressure pushes the air/fuel mixture through the passages of the idle and low speed circuit and past the tapered point of the idle adjustment screw, which regulates engine idle mixture volume.

High Speed Partial Load Circuit

When the throttle plate is opened sufficiently, there is little difference in vacuum between the upper and lower part of the air horn. Thus, little air/fuel mixture will discharge from the low speed and idle circuit. However, under this condition enough air is moving through the air horn to produce vacuum in the venturi to cause the main nozzle or high speed nozzle to discharge fuel. The circuit from the float bowl to the main nozzle is called the high speed partial load circuit. A nearly constant air/fuel ratio is maintained by this circuit from part to full-throttle.

CARTER CARBURETORS

Model BBD

The BBD carburetor is a 2 barrel unit. It is equipped with a dashpot on some applications.

VACUUM STEP-UP PISTON ADJUSTMENT

1. Remove the dust cover.
2. Be sure not to disturb the adjust-

TROUBLE SHOOTING

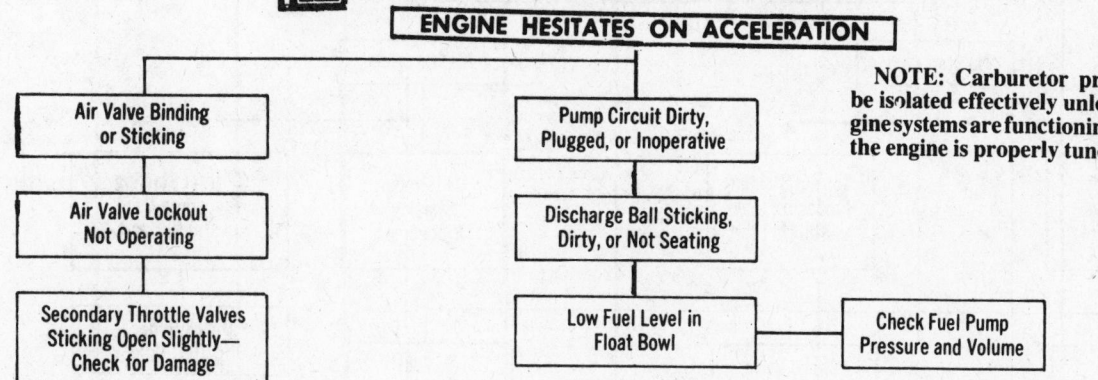

ENGINE HESITATES ON ACCELERATION

- Air Valve Binding or Sticking
- Air Valve Lockout Not Operating
- Secondary Throttle Valves Sticking Open Slightly— Check for Damage

- Pump Circuit Dirty, Plugged, or Inoperative
- Discharge Ball Sticking, Dirty, or Not Seating
- Low Fuel Level in Float Bowl → Check Fuel Pump Pressure and Volume

NOTE: Carburetor problems cannot be isolated effectively unless all other engine systems are functioning correctly and the engine is properly tuned.

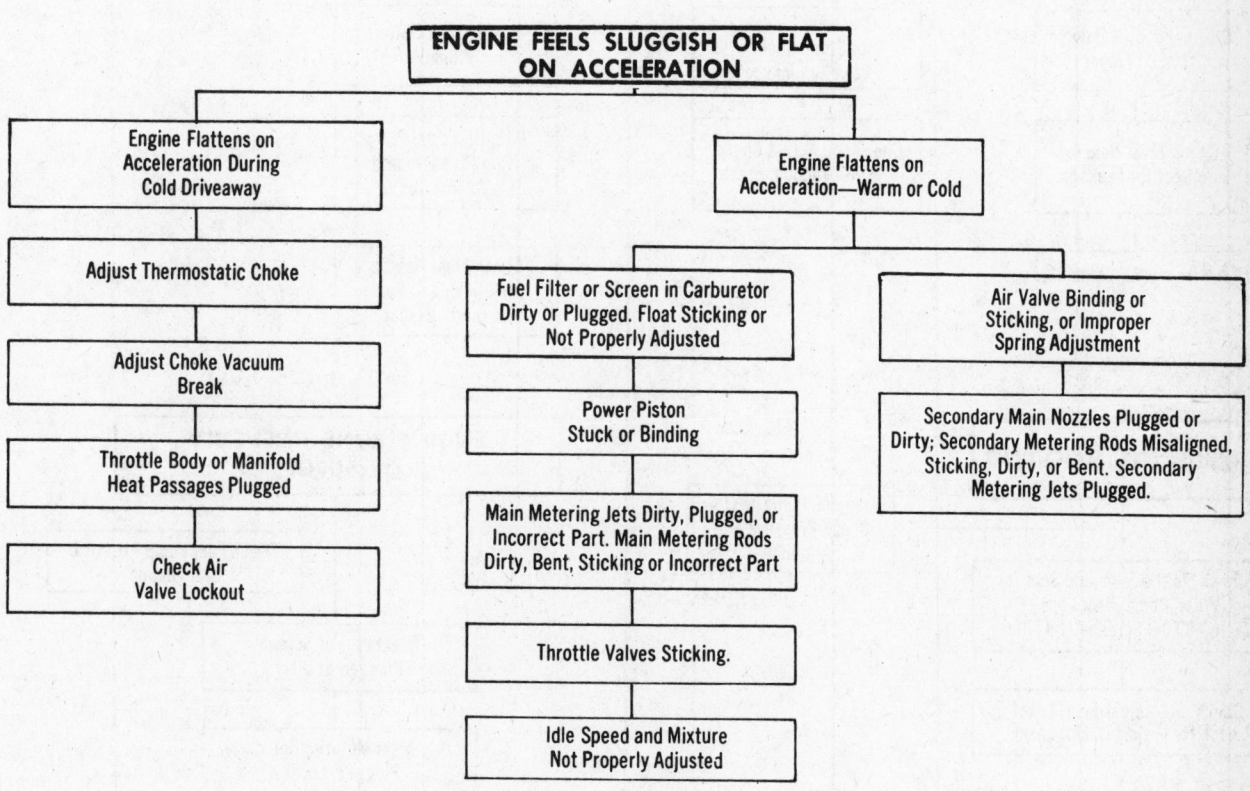

ENGINE FEELS SLUGGISH OR FLAT ON ACCELERATION

- Engine Flattens on Acceleration During Cold Driveaway
  - Adjust Thermostatic Choke
  - Adjust Choke Vacuum Break
  - Throttle Body or Manifold Heat Passages Plugged
  - Check Air Valve Lockout

- Engine Flattens on Acceleration—Warm or Cold
  - Fuel Filter or Screen in Carburetor Dirty or Plugged. Float Sticking or Not Properly Adjusted
  - Power Piston Stuck or Binding
  - Main Metering Jets Dirty, Plugged, or Incorrect Part. Main Metering Rods Dirty, Bent, Sticking or Incorrect Part
  - Throttle Valves Sticking.
  - Idle Speed and Mixture Not Properly Adjusted

  - Air Valve Binding or Sticking, or Improper Spring Adjustment
  - Secondary Main Nozzles Plugged or Dirty; Secondary Metering Rods Misaligned, Sticking, Dirty, or Bent. Secondary Metering Jets Plugged.

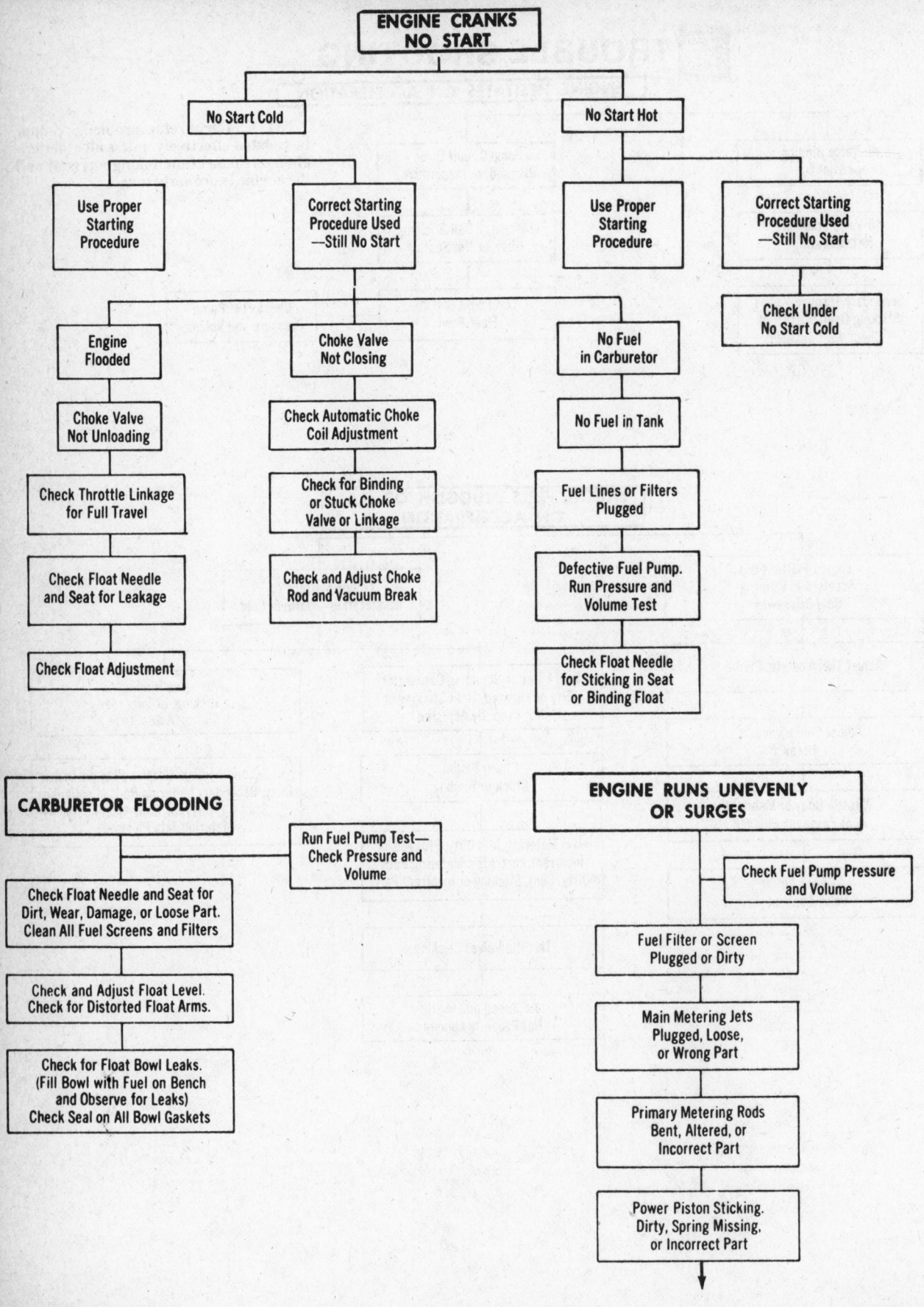

ENGINE CRANKS NO START

No Start Cold
- Use Proper Starting Procedure
- Correct Starting Procedure Used —Still No Start
  - Engine Flooded
    - Choke Valve Not Unloading
    - Check Throttle Linkage for Full Travel
    - Check Float Needle and Seat for Leakage
    - Check Float Adjustment
  - Choke Valve Not Closing
    - Check Automatic Choke Coil Adjustment
    - Check for Binding or Stuck Choke Valve or Linkage
    - Check and Adjust Choke Rod and Vacuum Break

No Start Hot
- Use Proper Starting Procedure
- Correct Starting Procedure Used —Still No Start
  - Check Under No Start Cold
  - No Fuel in Carburetor
    - No Fuel in Tank
    - Fuel Lines or Filters Plugged
    - Defective Fuel Pump. Run Pressure and Volume Test
    - Check Float Needle for Sticking in Seat or Binding Float

CARBURETOR FLOODING
- Run Fuel Pump Test— Check Pressure and Volume
- Check Float Needle and Seat for Dirt, Wear, Damage, or Loose Part. Clean All Fuel Screens and Filters
- Check and Adjust Float Level. Check for Distorted Float Arms.
- Check for Float Bowl Leaks. (Fill Bowl with Fuel on Bench and Observe for Leaks) Check Seal on All Bowl Gaskets

ENGINE RUNS UNEVENLY OR SURGES
- Check Fuel Pump Pressure and Volume
- Fuel Filter or Screen Plugged or Dirty
- Main Metering Jets Plugged, Loose, or Wrong Part
- Primary Metering Rods Bent, Altered, or Incorrect Part
- Power Piston Sticking. Dirty, Spring Missing, or Incorrect Part

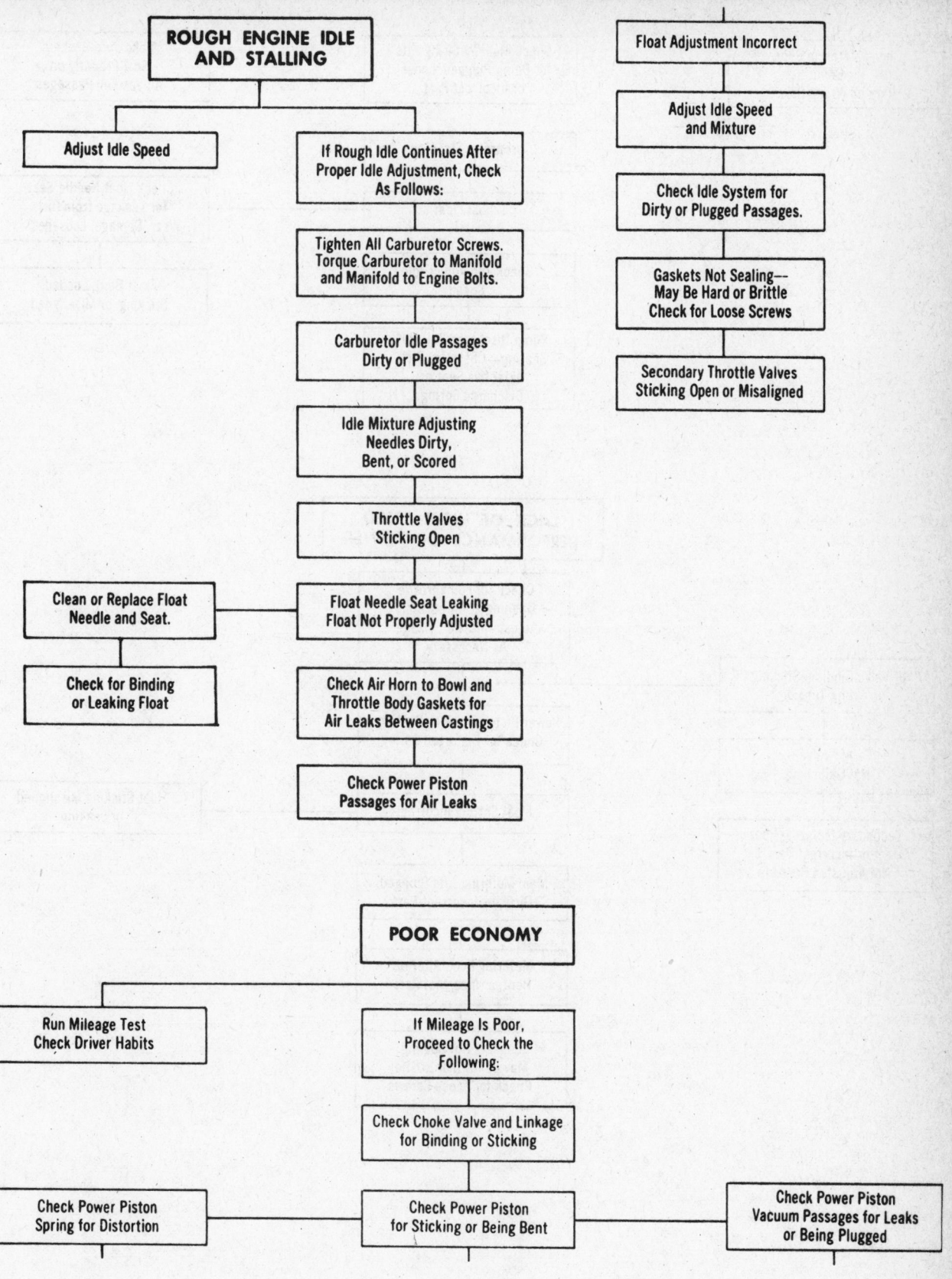

ROUGH ENGINE IDLE AND STALLING

Adjust Idle Speed

If Rough Idle Continues After Proper Idle Adjustment, Check As Follows:

Tighten All Carburetor Screws. Torque Carburetor to Manifold and Manifold to Engine Bolts.

Carburetor Idle Passages Dirty or Plugged

Idle Mixture Adjusting Needles Dirty, Bent, or Scored

Throttle Valves Sticking Open

Clean or Replace Float Needle and Seat.

Float Needle Seat Leaking Float Not Properly Adjusted

Check for Binding or Leaking Float

Check Air Horn to Bowl and Throttle Body Gaskets for Air Leaks Between Castings

Check Power Piston Passages for Air Leaks

Float Adjustment Incorrect

Adjust Idle Speed and Mixture

Check Idle System for Dirty or Plugged Passages.

Gaskets Not Sealing— May Be Hard or Brittle Check for Loose Screws

Secondary Throttle Valves Sticking Open or Misaligned

POOR ECONOMY

Run Mileage Test Check Driver Habits

If Mileage Is Poor, Proceed to Check the Following:

Check Choke Valve and Linkage for Binding or Sticking

Check Power Piston Spring for Distortion

Check Power Piston for Sticking or Being Bent

Check Power Piston Vacuum Passages for Leaks or Being Plugged

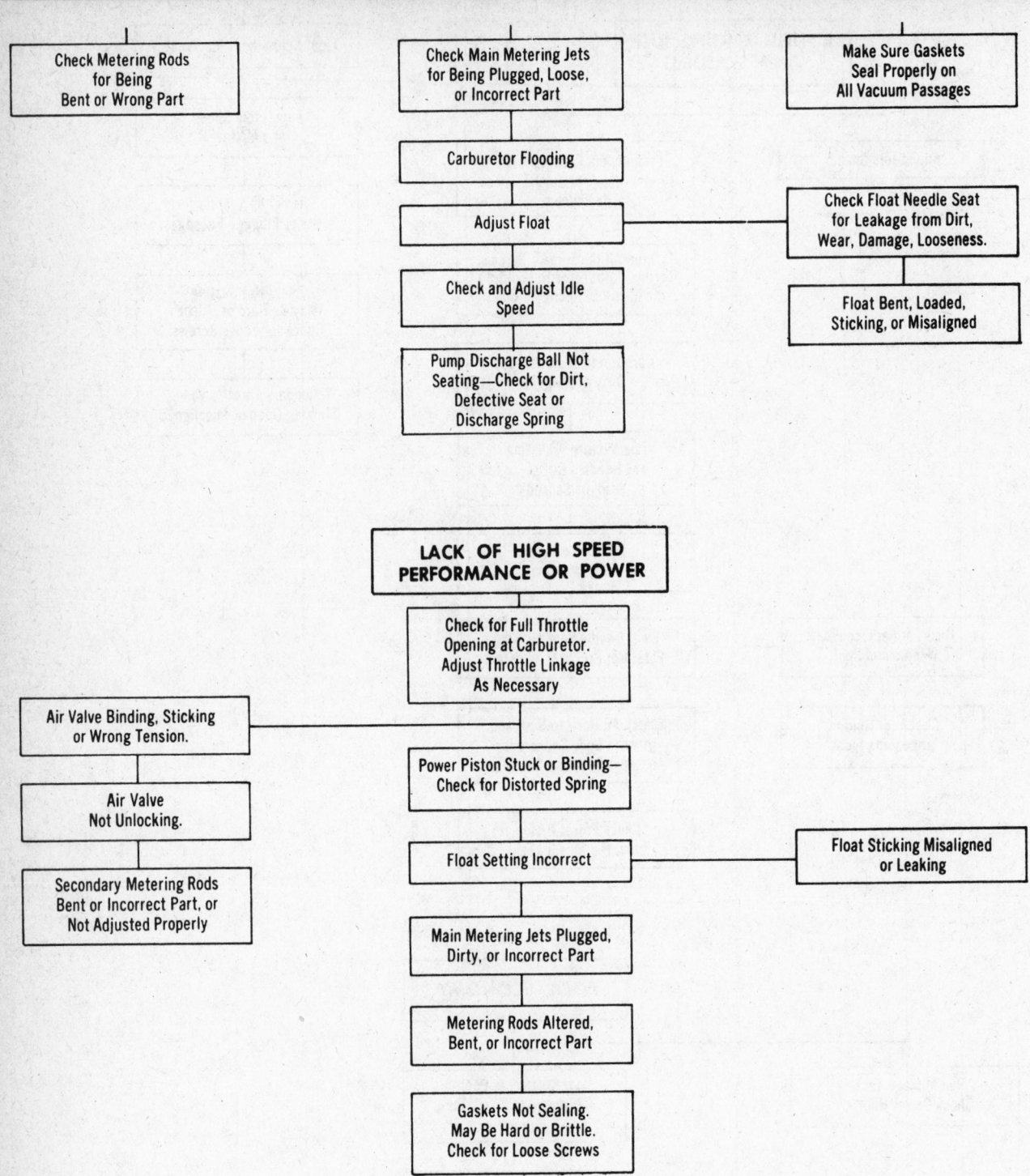

Check Metering Rods for Being Bent or Wrong Part

Check Main Metering Jets for Being Plugged, Loose, or Incorrect Part

Make Sure Gaskets Seal Properly on All Vacuum Passages

Carburetor Flooding

Adjust Float

Check Float Needle Seat for Leakage from Dirt, Wear, Damage, Looseness.

Check and Adjust Idle Speed

Float Bent, Loaded, Sticking, or Misaligned

Pump Discharge Ball Not Seating—Check for Dirt, Defective Seat or Discharge Spring

LACK OF HIGH SPEED PERFORMANCE OR POWER

Check for Full Throttle Opening at Carburetor. Adjust Throttle Linkage As Necessary

Air Valve Binding, Sticking or Wrong Tension.

Power Piston Stuck or Binding— Check for Distorted Spring

Air Valve Not Unlocking.

Float Setting Incorrect

Float Sticking Misaligned or Leaking

Secondary Metering Rods Bent or Incorrect Part, or Not Adjusted Properly

Main Metering Jets Plugged, Dirty, or Incorrect Part

Metering Rods Altered, Bent, or Incorrect Part

Gaskets Not Sealing. May Be Hard or Brittle. Check for Loose Screws

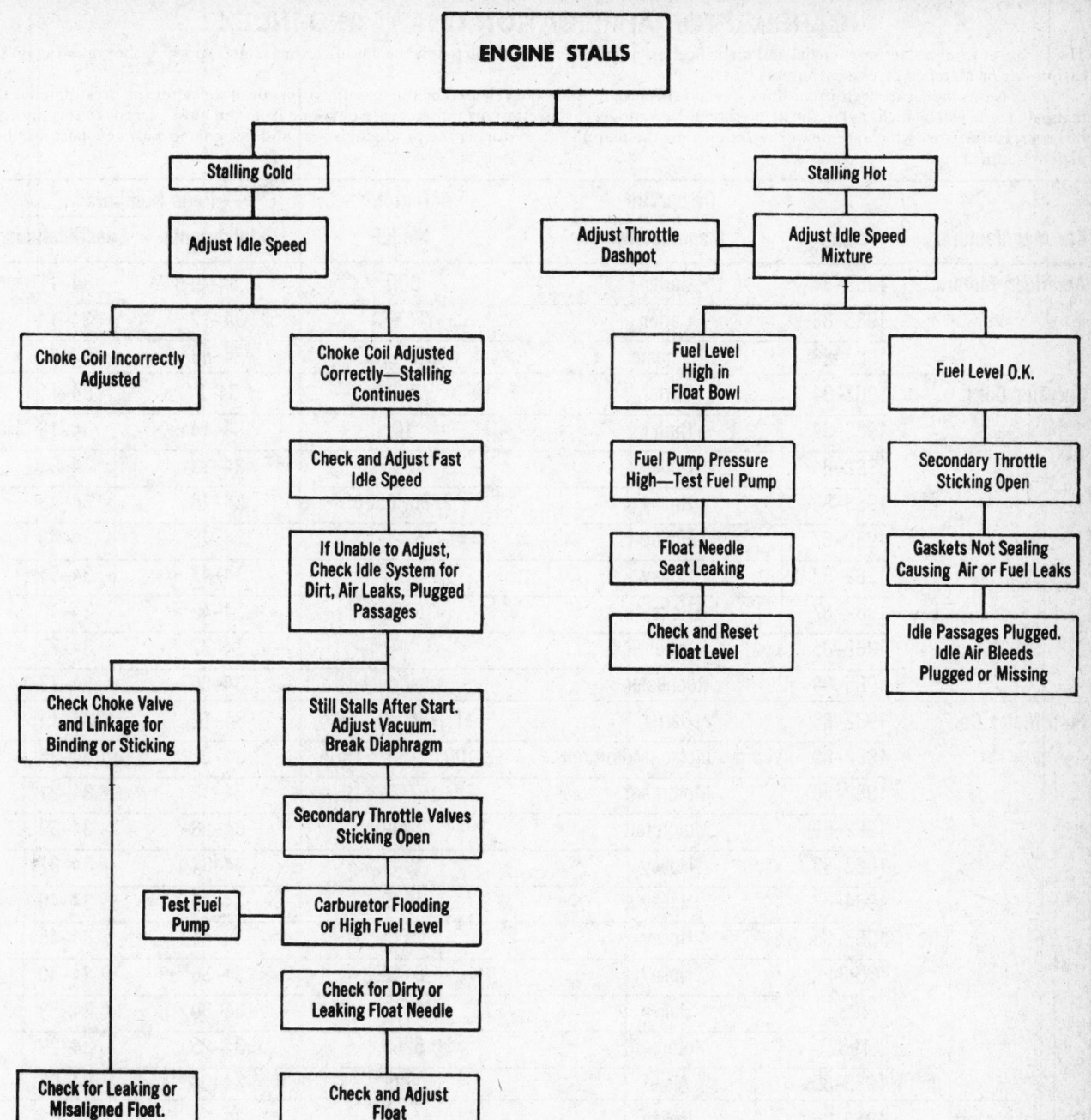

ENGINE STALLS

Stalling Cold

Adjust Idle Speed

Choke Coil Incorrectly Adjusted

Choke Coil Adjusted Correctly—Stalling Continues

Check and Adjust Fast Idle Speed

If Unable to Adjust, Check Idle System for Dirt, Air Leaks, Plugged Passages

Check Choke Valve and Linkage for Binding or Sticking

Still Stalls After Start. Adjust Vacuum. Break Diaphragm

Secondary Throttle Valves Sticking Open

Test Fuel Pump

Carburetor Flooding or High Fuel Level

Check for Dirty or Leaking Float Needle

Check for Leaking or Misaligned Float.

Check and Adjust Float

Stalling Hot

Adjust Throttle Dashpot

Adjust Idle Speed Mixture

Fuel Level High in Float Bowl

Fuel Pump Pressure High—Test Fuel Pump

Float Needle Seat Leaking

Check and Reset Float Level

Fuel Level O.K.

Secondary Throttle Sticking Open

Gaskets Not Sealing Causing Air or Fuel Leaks

Idle Passages Plugged. Idle Air Bleeds Plugged or Missing

CARBURETOR APPLICATION CHART AND INDEX

The carburetor manufacturer, model and identification numbers which are listed in the specifications chart, appear either on a tag on the carburetor or stamped on the carburetor body.

NOTE: New model carburetor part numbers and specifications are not released by the manufacturers until well after the press date for this manual. These will be included in the next edition. New model carburetor part numbers are obtained from the most current factory sources, however, carburetors which are new or redesigned by the manufacturer during the production year and designated with new part numbers may not appear.

Car Manufacturer	Year	Carburetor Manufacturer	Carburetor Model	Page Numbers	
				Adjustments	Specifications
American Motors	1982–84	Carter	BBD	34–2	34–11
	1983–88	Carter	YF, YFA	34–12	34–14
	1982–86	Rochester	2SE, E2SE	34–53	34–60
Chrysler Corp.	1982–84	Carter	BBD	34–2	34–11
	1982–84	Carter	TQ	34–14	34–18
	1982–84	Holley	1945	34–33	34–35
	1985–89	Holley	2280, 6280	34–40	34–43
	1982–87	Holley	5220	34–45	34–48
	1982–83	Holley	6145	34–47	34–51
	1982–87	Holley	6520	34–45	34–48
	1982–85	Mikuni	NA	34–72	34–72
	1985–89	Rochester	Quadrajet	34–66	34–73
Ford Motor Co.	1982–86	Carter	YF, YFA, YFA-FB	34–12	34–14
	1982–85	Ford, Autolite, Motorcraft	2100, 2150, 2150A	34–22	34–25
	1982–86	Motorcarft	740	34–18	34–21
	1982–89	Motorcraft	7200VV	34–28	34–32
	1982–83	Holley	1946	34–34	34–37
	1984–87	Holley	1949	34–36	34–40
	1983–85	Holley	4180C	34–41	34–45
	1984	Holley	6149	34–36	34–40
	1982	Holley	6500	34–50	34–53
	1982	Motorcraft	5200	34–25	34–29
	1985–89	Aisan	2bbl	34–90	34–90
General Motors	1982–86	Holley	6510C	34–50	34–53
	1982–87	Holley	5210C	34–44	34–47
	1982–86	Rochester	2SE, E2SE	34–53	34–60
	1982–87	Rochester E2ME, E2MC	2MC, M2MC, M2ME,	34–58	34–68
	1982–89	Rochester	Quadrajet	34–66	34–73
	1985–89	Nippon Kikaki	2bbl	34–85	34–85
	1985–89	Hitachi	2bbl	34–89	34–89
	1985–89	Aisan	2bbl	34–90	34–90

ing screw on top of the piston. If it is disturbed, reset the gap at the top of the piston to 0.035–0.040 in.

3. Back off the curb idle adjustment until the throttle valves are completely closed. Count the number of turns so that the screw can later be returned to the original position. Then turn the idle screw in 1 full turn on AMC products only.

4. Fully depress the step-up piston while holding moderate pressure on the rod lifter tab and loosen and tighten the rod lifter lockscrew.

5. Release the piston and rod lifter; return the curb idle screw to its original position.

6. Replace the dust cover, unless the accelerator pump is to be adjusted.

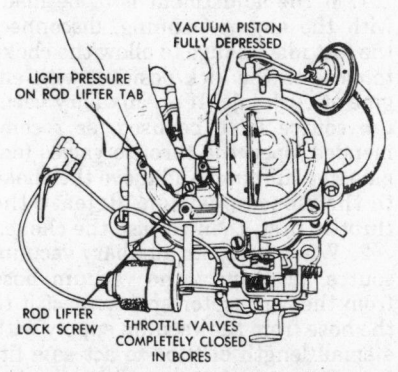

BBD vacuum step-up piston adjustment

ACCELERATOR PUMP STROKE ADJUSTMENT

1. Back off the idle adjusting screw. Open the choke valve so that the fast idle cam allows the throttle valves to close. Be sure that the accelerator pump "S" link is in the outer hole of the pump arm if there are 2 holes.

2. Turn the idle adjusting screw in 2 complete turns after it contacts the stop.

3. Remove the dust cover. With the throttle valves closed tightly, measure the distance between the top of the air horn and the top of the pump plunger shaft. If the dimension is not as specified, loosen the pump arm adjusting lockscrew (near the plunger shaft) and rotate the sleeve to obtain the correct dimension.

FAST IDLE CAM POSITION ADJUSTMENT

1. With the fast idle speed adjusting screw contacting the **SECOND HIGHEST** step on the fast idle cam, move the choke valve toward the closed position with light pressure on the choke shaft lever. On AMC, loosen the choke cover and turn ¼ turn rich.

2. Insert the specified drill (refer to Specifications), between the top of the choke valve and the wall of the air

horn. An adjustment will be necessary if a slight drag is not obtained as the drill is being removed.

3. If an adjustment is required, bend the fast idle connector rod at the angle.

4. Reset the choke cover to specification.

ACCELERATOR PUMP AND BOWL VENT

Chrysler Models

1. The accelerator pump stroke adjustment and the curb idle speed must be adjusted first.

2. Remove the air cleaner, step-up piston cover and the gasket.

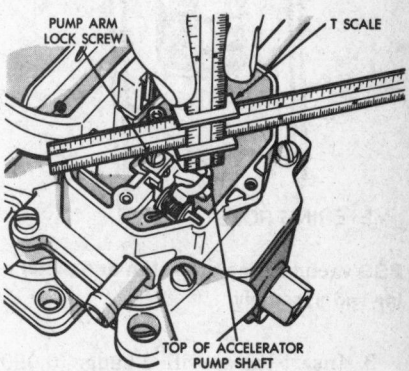

BBD accelerator pump stroke adjustment

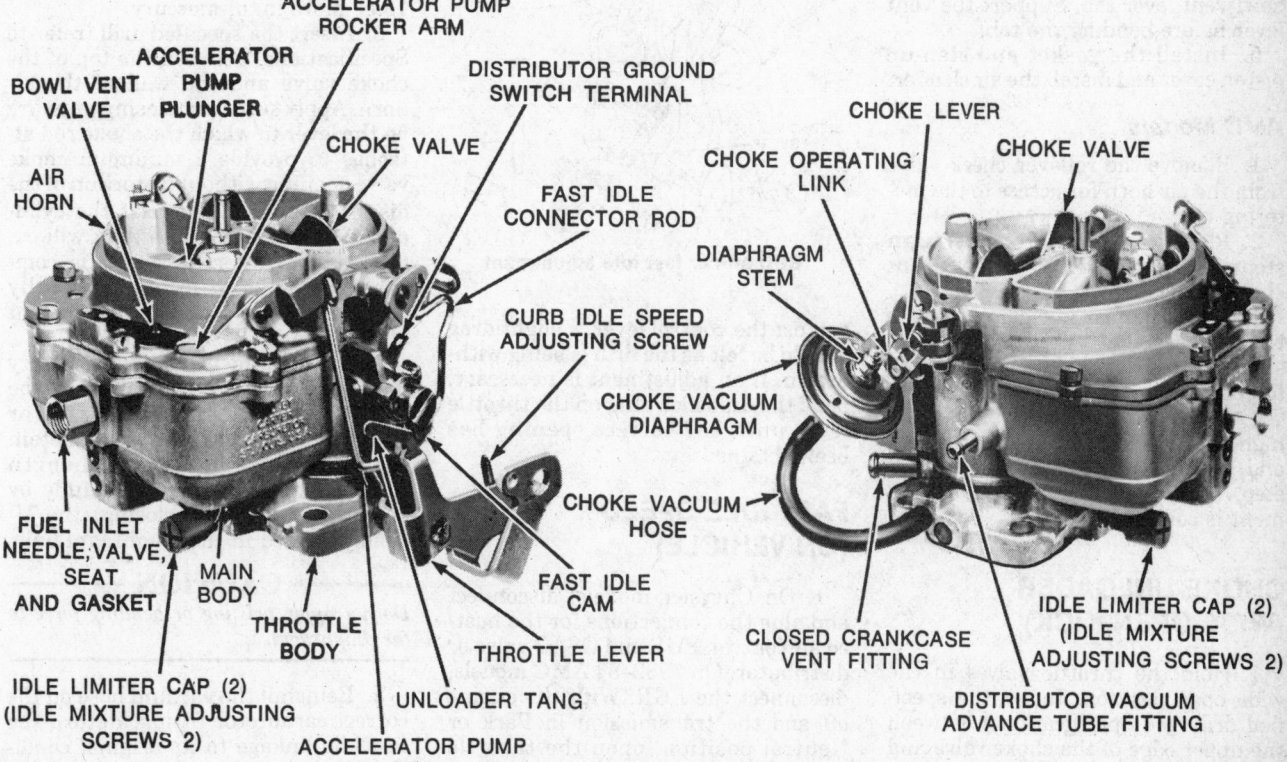

BBD carburetor assembly—typical

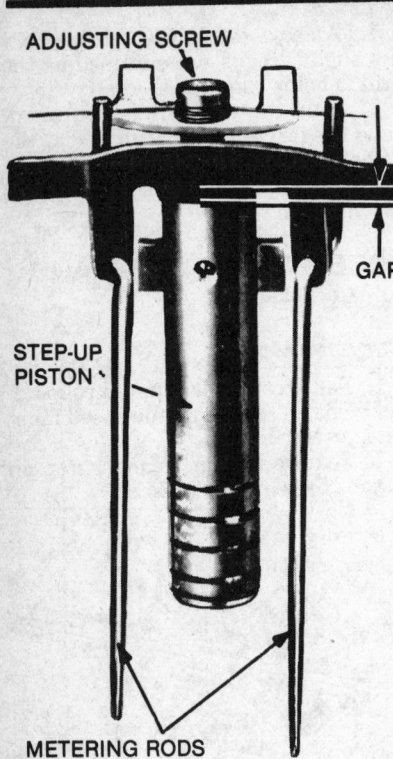

ADJUSTING SCREW

GAP

STEP-UP
PISTON

METERING RODS

BBD vacuum step-up piston and metering rod assembly

3. Insert the specified gauge (0.080 in.) between the top of the bowl vent valve and the seat.

4. If adjustment is needed, bend the bowl vent lever tab. Support the vent lever before bending the tab.

5. Install the gasket and step-up piston cover and install the air cleaner.

AMC Models

1. Remove the rollover check valve from the air horn for access to the metering rod.

2. Place the throttle on the **high** step of the fast idle cam. The bowl vent should be closed.

3. Move the fast idle cam until the throttle screw drops to the second step. The vent should be just starting to open.

4. If the vent is not closed on the high, fourth and third steps of the cam and starting to open on the second step, bend the tab until the adjustment is correct.

CHOKE UNLOADER (WIDE OPEN KICK)

1. Hold the throttle valves in the wide open position. Insert the specified drill (see Specifications) between the upper edge of the choke valve and the inner wall of the air horn.

2. With a finger lightly pressing

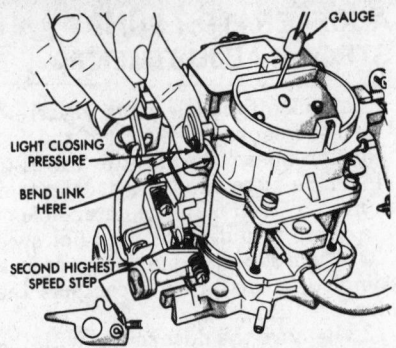

GAUGE

LIGHT CLOSING PRESSURE

BEND LINK HERE

SECOND HIGHEST SPEED STEP

BBD fast idle cam position adjustment

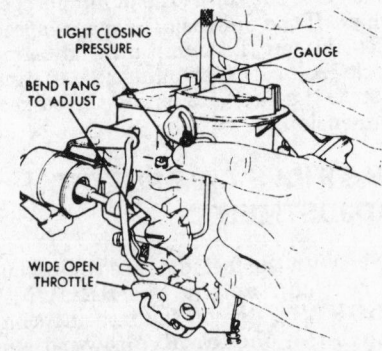

LIGHT CLOSING PRESSURE

BEND TANG TO ADJUST

GAUGE

WIDE OPEN THROTTLE

BBD choke unloader (wide open kick) adjustment

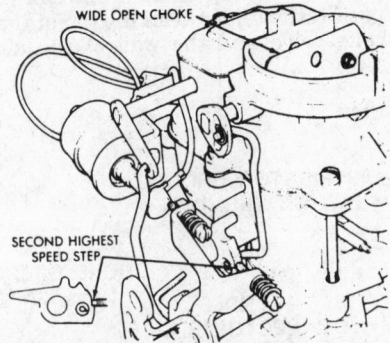

WIDE OPEN CHOKE

SECOND HIGHEST SPEED STEP

BBD on-car fast idle adjustment

against the control lever, a slight drag should be felt as the drill is being withdrawn. If an adjustment is necessary, bend the unloader tang on the throttle lever until the correct opening has been obtained.

FAST IDLE SPEED (ON VEHICLE)

1. On Chrysler models, disconnect and plug the connections for the heated air control. EGR and OSAC valve or distributor. On 1982–84 AMC models, disconnect the EGR. With the engine off and the transmission in Park or Neutral position, open the throttle slightly.

2. Close the choke valve until the

fast idle screw can be positioned on the **SECOND HIGHEST** step of the fast idle cam.

3. Start the engine and let the idle stabilize. Turn the fast idle speed screw in or out to obtain the specifed speed.

4. Stopping the engine between adjustments is not necessary. However, reposition the fast idle speed screw on the cam after each speed adjustment to provide the correct throttle closing torque.

VACUUM KICK (INITIAL CHOKE VALVE CLEARANCE) ADJUSTMENT

Chrysler Models

1. If the adjustment is to be made with the engine running, disconnect the fast idle linkage to allow the choke to close to the kick position with engine at curb idle. If an auxiliary vacuum source is to be used, as recommended, open the throttle valves (engine not running) and move the choke to the closed position. Release the throttle first, then release the choke.

2. When using an auxiliary vacuum source, disconnect the vacuum hose from the carburetor and connect it to the hose from the vacuum supply with a small length of tube to act as a fitting. Removal of the hose from the diaphragm may require sufficient force to damage the system. Apply a vacuum of 15 or more in. of mercury.

3. Insert the specified drill (refer to Specifications) between the top of the choke valve and the wall of the air horn. Apply sufficient closing pressure on the lever to which the choke rod attaches to provide a minimum choke valve opening without distortion of the diaphragm link. Note that the cylindrical stem of the diaphragm will extend as the internal spring is compressed. This spring must be fully compressed for proper measurement of the vacuum kick adjustment.

4. An adjustment will be necessary if a slight drag is not obtained as the drill is being removed. Shorten or lengthen the diaphragm link to obtain the correct choke opening. Length changes should be made carefully by bending (opening or closing) the U-bend provided in the diaphragm link.

— CAUTION —
Do not apply twisting or bending force to the diaphragm.

5. Reinstall the vacuum hose on the correct carburetor fitting. Return the fast idle linkage to its original condition if it was disturbed, as suggested in Step 1.

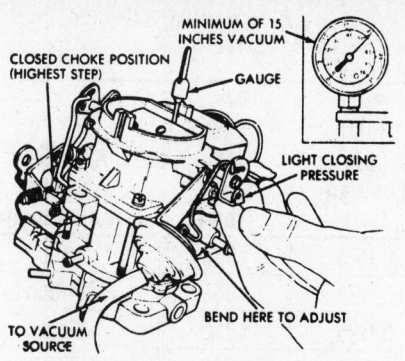

BBD vacuum kick adjustment

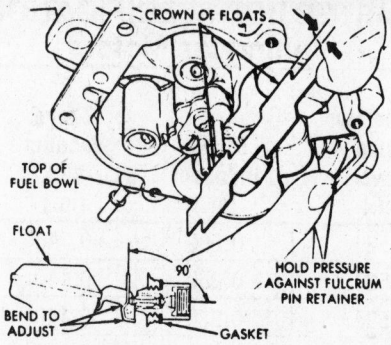

BBD float level adjustment

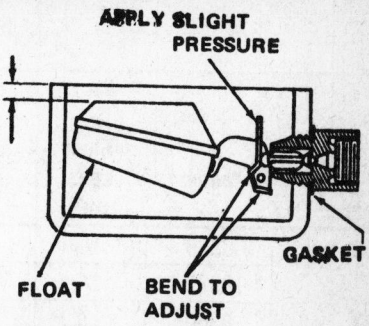

BBD float level adjustment for AMC products

6. Make the following check: with no vacuum applied to the diaphragm, the choke valve should move freely between the open and closed positions. If its movement is not free, examine the linkage for misalignment or interference caused by the bending operation. Repeat the adjustment if necessary to provide proper link operations.

AMC Models

This adjustment is called Initial Choke Valve Clearance Adjustment on AMC products.

1. Loosen the choke cover, turn the cover ¼ turn rich and tighten a cover screw.
2. Apply a vacuum of at least 19 in. Hg to pull the diaphragm in against the stop.
3. Open the throttle valve slightly to place the fast idle screw on the **high** step of the cam.
4. Measure the clearance between the choke plate upper edge and the air horn wall.

5. Adjust the clearance between the choke plate upper edge and the air horn wall by bending the diaphragm connector link at the angle. Reset the choke or replace the cover.

FLOAT LEVEL

Chrysler Models

1. Invert the carburetor so that the weight of the floats is the only force on the needle and seat.
2. Use a T-scale to check the float level. Measure from the surface of the fuel bowl to the crown of each float at center.
3. To adjust the float level, hold the floats on the bottom of the bowl and bend the float lip to give the specified dimension.

AMC Models

1. Remove the air horn.

2. Hold the float lip gently against the needle to raise the float.
3. Place a straightedge across the float bowl to measure the float level at the top of the float.
4. To adjust, bend the float lip, being careful not to exert pressure on the synthetic needle tip.

DASHPOT ADJUSTMENT

Chrysler Models

The dashpot is used on manual transmission models only.

1. Make sure that the curb idle speed is correctly adjusted.
2. Start the engine. Position the throttle lever so that the actuating tab is just contacting the dashpot plunger stem. Let the engine speed stabilize for 30 seconds.
3. The speed should be 2500 rpm.
4. Adjust the setting by loosening the locknut and moving the dashpot.

CARTER BBD SPECIFICATIONS
Chrysler Products

Year	Model ②	Float Level (in.)	Accelerator Pump Travel (in.)	Bowl Vent (in.)	Choke Unloader (in.)	Choke Vacuum Kick (in.)	Fast Idle Cam Position (in.)	Fast Idle Speed (rpm)	Automatic Choke Adjustment
'82	8290S	¼	0.500 ①	0.080	0.280	0.100	0.070	1600	Fixed
	8291S	¼	0.500 ①	0.080	0.280	0.130	0.070	1400	Fixed
	8292S	¼	0.500 ①	0.080	0.280	0.130	0.070	1600 ③	Fixed
'83	8290S	¼	0.470 ①	0.080	0.280	0.100	0.070	1600	Fixed
	8291S	¼	0.470 ①	0.080	0.280	0.130	0.070	1400	Fixed
	8369S	¼	0.500 ①	0.080	0.280	0.130	0.070	1500	Fixed
'84	8385S	¼	0.470 ①	0.080	0.280	0.130	0.070	1400	Fixed
	8369S	¼	0.500	0.080	0.280	0.130	0.070	1500	Fixed

① At idle
② Models numbers located on tag or casting
③ 1982: 1500 rpm

CARTER BBD SPECIFICATIONS
American Motors

Year	Model ①	Float Level (in.)	Accelerator Pump Travel (in.)	Choke Unloader (in.)	Choke Vacuum Kick (in.)	Fast Idle Cam Position (in.)	Fast Idle Speed (rpm)	Automatic Choke Adjustment
'82	8338	1/4	0.520	0.280	0.140	0.095	1850	1 Rich
	8339	1/4	0.520	0.280	0.140	0.095	1850	1 Rich
'83	8360	1/4	0.520	0.280	0.140	0.095	1850	Fixed
	8364	1/4	0.520	0.280	0.140	0.095	1700	Fixed
	8367	1/4	0.520	0.280	0.140	0.095	1700	Fixed
	8362	1/4	0.520	0.280	0.140	0.095	1850	Fixed
'84–'85	8383	1/4	0.520	0.280	0.140	0.095	1850	1/2–1 1/2 Rich
	8384	1/4	0.520	0.280	0.140	0.095	1700	1/2–1 1/2 Rich

① Model numbers located on the tag or casting

Model YF AND YFA

The YF and YFA carburetors are single barrel downdraft carburetors with a diaphragm type accelerator pump and diaphragm operated metering rods.

FLOAT ADJUSTMENT

1. Invert the air horn assembly and check the clearance from the top of the float to the surface of the air horn with a T-scale. The air horn should be held at eye level when gauging and the float arm should be resting on the needle pin.
2. Do not exert pressure on the needle valve when measuring or adjusting the float. Bend the float arm as necessary to adjust the float level.

—— CAUTION ——

Do not bend the tab at the end of the float arm as it prevents the float from striking the bottom of the fuel bowl when empty and keep the needle in place.

METERING ROD ADJUSTMENT

1. Remove the air horn. Back out the idle speed adjusting screw until the throttle plate is seated fully in its bore.
2. Press down on the upper end of the diaphragm shaft until the diaphragm bottoms in the vacuum chamber.
3. The metering rod should contact the bottom of the metering rod well. The lifter link at the outer end nearest the springs and at the supporting link should be bottomed.
4. On models not equipped with an adjusting screw, adjust by bending the lip of the metering rod is attached.
5. On models with an adjusting screw, turn the screw until the metering rod just bottoms in the body casting. For final adjustment, turn the screw an additional turn clockwise.

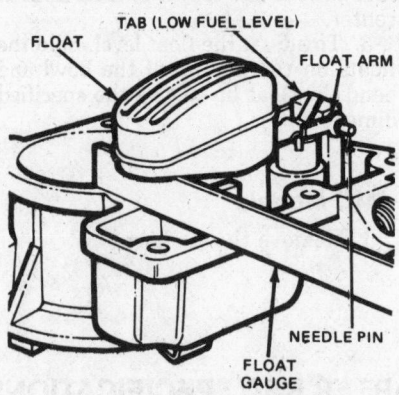

YFA float level adjustment

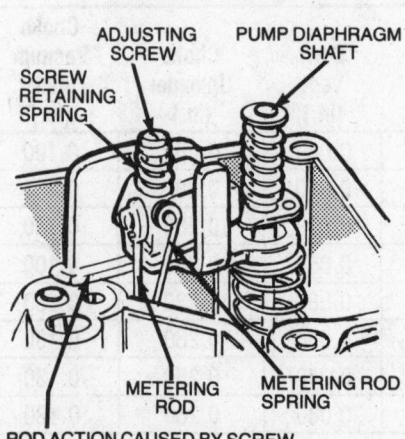

ROD ACTION CAUSED BY SCREW ACTING AS PIVOT POINT FOR LEVER

YFA metering rod adjustment

FAST IDLE CAM ADJUSTMENT

1. Put the fast idle screw on the **SECOND HIGHEST** step of the fast idle cam against the shoulder of the high step.
2. Adjust by bending the choke plate connecting rod to obtain the specified clearance between the lower edge of the choke plate and the air horn wall.

CHOKE UNLOADER ADJUSTMENT

With the throttle valve held wide open and the choke valve held in the closed position, bend the unloader tang on the throttle lever to obtain the specified clearance between the lower edge of the choke valve and the air horn wall.

AUTOMATIC CHOKE ADJUSTMENT

Loosen the choke cover retaining screws, then turn the choke cover so

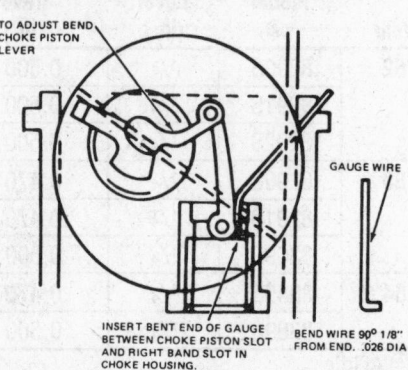

Choke plate pulldown—piston type choke—YFA

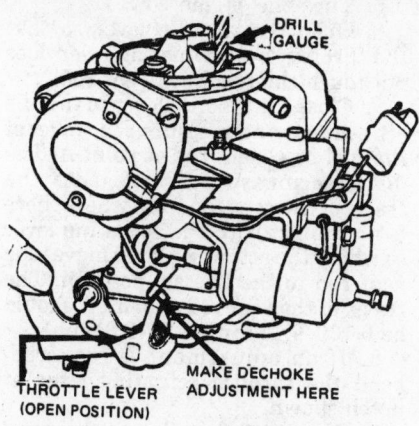

YFA choke unloader adjustment

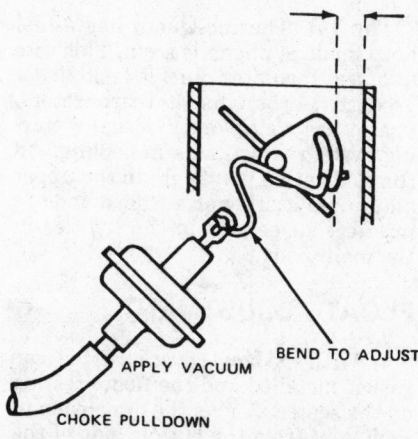

Choke plate pulldown—diaphragm type choke—YFA

that the index mark on the cover lines up with the specified mark on the choke housing.

CHOKE PLATE PULLDOWN ADJUSTMENT

1983–84 Piston Type Choke

NOTE: This adjustment requires that the thermostatic spring housing and gasket (choke cap) are removed.

1. Remove the air cleaner assembly, then the choke cap.
2. Bend a 0.026 in. diameter wire gauge at a 90 degree angle approximately ⅛ in. from the end. Insert the bent end of the gauge between the choke piston slot and the right hand slot in the choke housing. Rotate the choke piston lever counterclockwise until the gauge is shut in the piston slot.
3. Apply light pressure on the choke piston lever to hold the gauge in place, then measure the clearance between the lower edge of the choke plate and the carburetor bore using a drill with the diameter equal to the specified pulldown clearance.
4. Bend the choke piston lever to obtain the proper clearance.
5. Install the choke cap.

Diaphragm Type Choke

1. Activate the pulldown motor by applying an external vacuum source.
2. Close the choke plate as far as possible without forcing it.

3. Using a drill of the specified size, measure the clearance between the lower edge of the choke plate and the air horn wall.
4. If adjustment is necessary bend the choke diaphragm link as required.

CHOKE CAP REMOVAL

1983–84

NOTE: The automatic choke has 2 rivets and a screw retaining the choke cap in place. There is a locking and indexing plate to prevent misadjustment.

1. Remove the air cleaner assembly from the carburetor.
2. Check the choke cap retaining ring rivets to determine if the mandrel is well below the rivet head. If the mandrel appears to be at or within the rivet head thickness, drive it down or out with a ⅙ in. diameter punch.
3. Use a ⅛ in. diameter or No. 32 drill (.128 in. diameter) for drilling the rivet heads. Drill into the rivet head until the rivet head comes loose from the rivet body.
4. After the rivet head is removed, drive the remaining portion of the rivet out of the hole with a ⅛ in. diameter punch.

NOTE: This procedure must be followed to retain the hole size.

5. Repeat Steps 1–4 for the remaining rivet.
6. Remove the screw in the conventional manner.

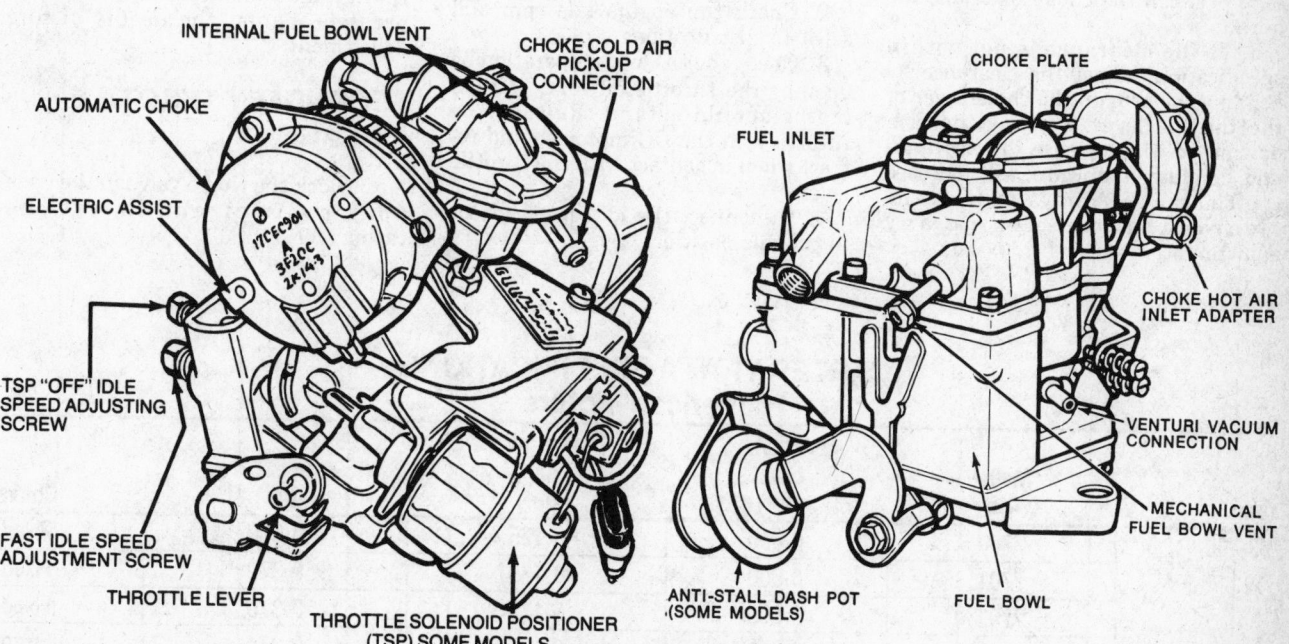

Carter YFA carburetor—typical

CHOKE CAP INSTALLATION

1. Install the choke cap gasket.
2. Install the locking and indexing plate.
3. Install the notched gasket.
4. Install the choke cap, making certain that the bimetal loop is positioned around the choke lever tang.
5. While holding the cap in place, actuate the choke plate to make certain that the bimetal loop is properly engaged with the lever tang. Set the retaining clamp over the choke cap and orient the clamp to match the holes in the casting (the holes are not equally spaced). Make sure the retaining clamp is not upside down.
6. Place a rivet in the rivet gun and trigger the gun lightly to retain the rivet (⅛ in. diameter × ½ in. long × ¼ in. diameter head).
7. Press the rivet fully into the casting after passing it through the retaining clamp and pop rivet (mandrel breaks off).
8. Repeat this step for the remaining rivet.
9. Install the screw in the conventional manner. Tighten 17–20 inch lbs.

CHOKER PLATE CLEARANCE (DECHOKE) ADJUSTMENT

1. Remove the air cleaner assembly.
2. Hold the throttle plate fully open and close the choke plate as far as possible without forcing it. Use a drill of the proper diameter to check the clearance between the choke plate and air horn.
3. If the clearance is not within specification, adjust the clearance by bending the arm on the choke lever of the throttle lever. Bending the arm downward will decrease the clearance and bending it upward will increase the clearance. Always recheck the clearance after making any adjustment.

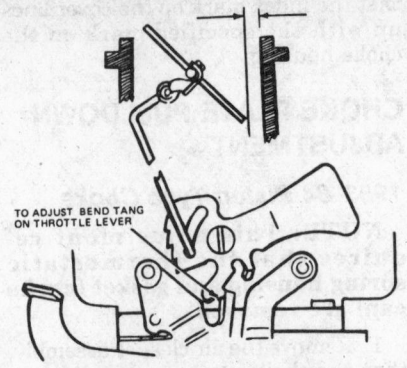

Dechoke adjustment—YFA

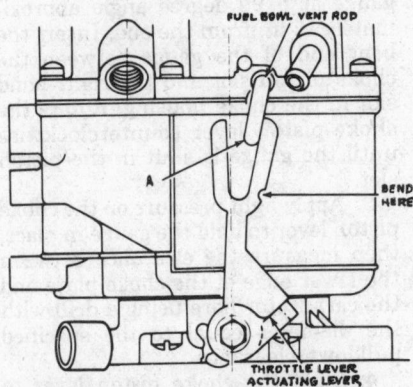

Mechanical fuel bowl vent adjustment—YFA

MECHANICAL FUEL BOWL VENT ADJUSTMENT

1. Start the engine and wait until it has reached normal operating temperature before proceeding.
2. Check the engine idle rpm and set it to specifications.
3. Check the DC motor operation by opening the throttle off idle. The DC motor should extend. Release the throttle and the DC motor should retract when in contact with the throttle lever.
4. Disconnect the idle speed motor in the idle position.

5. Turn the engine OFF.
6. Open the throttle lever so that the throttle lever actuating lever does not touch the fuel bowl vent rod.
7. Close the throttle lever to the idle set position and measure the travel of the fuel bowl vent rod at point A. The distance measured represents the travel of the vent rod from where there is no contact with the actuating lever to where the actuating lever moves the vent rod to the idle set position. The travel of the vent rod at point A should be 0.100–0.150 in. (2.54–3.81mm).
8. If an adjustment is required, bend the throttle actuating lever at notch shown.
9. Reconnect the idle speed control motor.

Model TQ

The TQ (Thermo-Quad) has a fuel bowl made of phenolic resin. This acts as a heat insulator. Fuel is kept 20 degrees cooler than in metal carburetors. It also has a suspended design metering system which aids in cooling. All the calibration points are in the upper aluminum casting or air horn and are in effect suspended in the cavities in the main body.

FLOAT ADJUSTMENT

1. With the bowl cover inverted, the gasket installed and the floats resting on the seated needle, the dimension of each float from the bottom side of the float to the cover gasket should be as shown in the specifications chart.
2. To adjust, bend the float lever. Do not allow the float lever lip to be pressed against the needle during adjustment.

SECONDARY THROTTLE LINKAGE

1. Block the choke valve in the wide open position and invert the carburetor.

CARTER YF, YFA SPECIFICATIONS
American Motors

Year	Model ①	Float Level (in.)	Fast Idle Cam (in.)	Unloader (in.)	Choke
'83–'85	7700	0.600	0.175	0.370	Fixed
	7701	0.600	0.175	0.370	Fixed
	7702	0.600	0.175	0.370	Fixed
	7703	0.600	0.175	0.370	Fixed

① Model numbers located on the tag or casting

CARTER YF, YFA, YFA-FB SPECIFICATIONS
Ford Motor Co.

Year	Model ①	Float Level (in.)	Fast Idle Cam (in.)	Choke Plate Pulldown (in.)	Unloader (in.)	Dechoke (in.)	Choke
'83	E3ZE-LA	0.650	0.140	0.260	—	0.220	—
	E3ZE-MA	0.650	0.140	0.260	—	0.220	—
	E3ZE-TB	0.650	0.140	0.240	—	0.220	—
	E3ZE-UA	0.650	0.140	0.240	—	0.220	—
	E3ZE-VA	0.650	0.140	0.260	—	0.220	—
	E3ZE-YA	0.650	0.140	0.260	—	0.220	—
	E3ZE-NB	0.650	0.160	0.260	—	0.220	—
	E3ZE-PB	0.650	0.160	0.260	—	0.220	—
	E3ZE-ASA	0.650	0.160	0.260	—	0.220	—
	E3ZE-APA	0.650	0.140	0.240	—	0.220	—
	E3ZE-ARA	0.650	0.140	0.240	—	0.220	—
	E3ZE-ADA	0.650	0.140	0.260	—	0.220	—
	E3ZE-AEA	0.650	0.140	0.260	—	0.220	—
	E3ZE-ACA	0.650	0.140	0.260	—	0.220	—
	E3ZE-ATA	0.650	0.160	0.260	—	0.220	—
	E3ZE-ABA	0.650	0.140	0.260	—	0.220	—
	E3ZE-UB	0.650	0.140	0.240	—	0.220	—
	E3ZE-TC	0.650	0.140	0.240	—	0.220	—
'84	E4ZE-HC,DB	0.650	0.140	0.260	—	0.270	—
	E4ZE-MA,NA	0.650	0.140	0.240	—	0.270	—
	E4ZE-PA,RA	0.650	0.140	0.260	—	0.270	—
'85	E5ZE-CA	0.650	0.140	0.260	—	0.270	—
	E5ZE-AA	0.650	0.140	0.260	—	0.270	—
'86	E5ZE-AA	0.650	0.140	0.260	—	0.270	—
	E5ZE-AB	0.650	0.140	0.260	—	0.270	—
	E5ZE-CA	0.650	0.140	0.260	—	0.270	—
	E5ZE-CB	0.650	0.140	0.260	—	0.270	—
	E6ZE-EA	0.650	0.140	0.260	—	0.270	—
	E6ZE-DA	0.650	0.140	0.260	—	0.270	—

① Model number located on the tag or casting

2. Slowly open the primary throttle valves until the secondary valves start to open. Measure between the lower edge of the primary valve and its bore. Open the throttle to the wide open position. The primary and secondary levers should contact the stops at the same time.

3. If it is necessary to adjust, bend the secondary throttle operating rod at the lower angle until the correct dimension is obtained.

SECONDARY AIR VALVE OPENING

1. With the air valve in the closed position, the opening along the air valve at its long side must be at its maximum and be parallel with the air horn gasket surface.

2. With the air valve wide open, the opening of the air valve at the short side and the air horn must match the dimensions in the Specifications

Charts. The corner of the air valve is notched for adjustment. Bend the corner with a pair of pliers to give proper opening.

ACCELERATOR PUMP STROKE ADJUSTMENT

1. Make sure the throttle connector rod is in the correct hole of the pump arm.

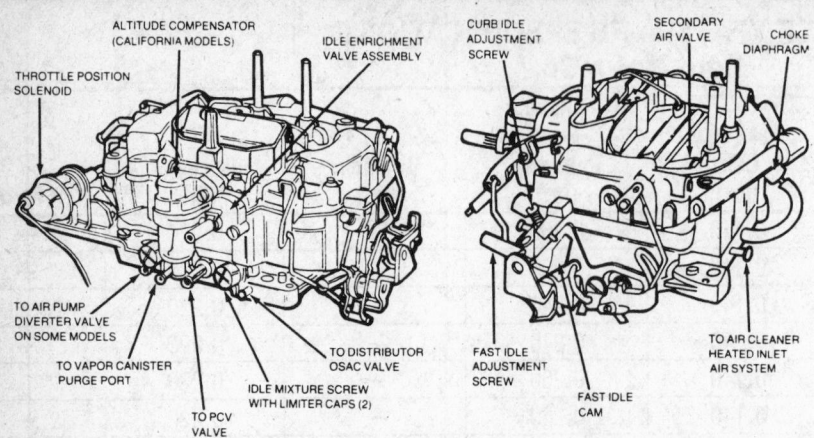

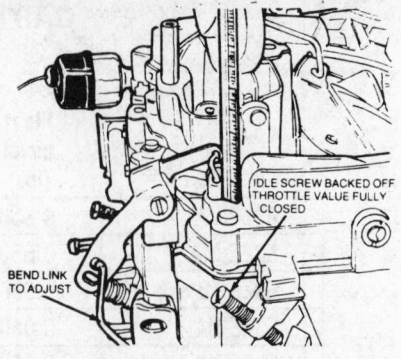

TQ carburetor assembly—typical

TQ accelerator pump adjustment

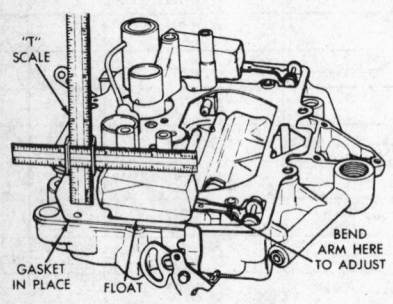

TQ float adjustment

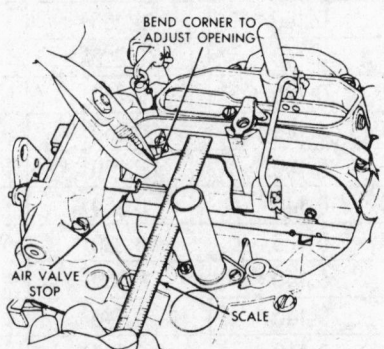

TQ secondary air valve adjustment

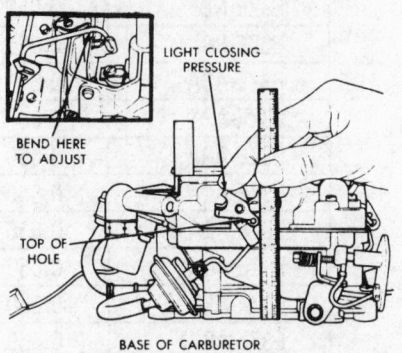

TQ choke control lever

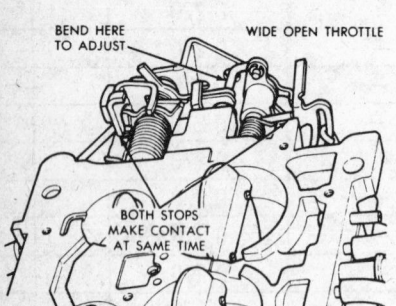

TQ secondary throttle adjustment

2. Measure the height of the accelerator pump plunger at curb idle. The ignition switch must be on if there is an idle stop solenoid.

3. Adjust the plunger height by bending the throttle connector rod.

NOTE: Carburetors with staged pump systems require a second height measurement at the throttle position related to a secondary throttle lockout.

First Stage

1. Make sure the throttle connector rod is in the correct pump arm slot.

2. Use a scale to measure the height of the accelerator pump plunger stem at curb idle.

3. Adjust the pump plunger height by bending the throttle connector rod.

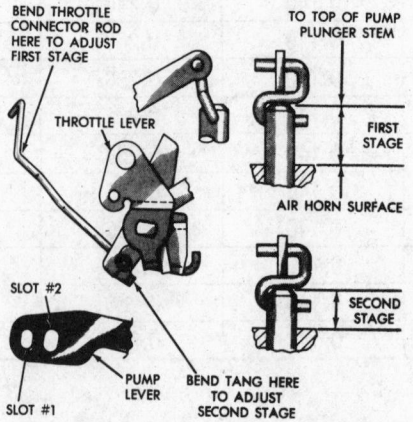

TQ accelerator pump stroke adjustment

Second Stage

1. Open the choke then open the throttle until the secondary lockout is just applied. The plunger downward travel stops at that point.

2. Use a scale to measure the accelerator pump plunger height.

3. Adjust by bending the tang.

CHOKE CONTROL LEVER

1. Disconnect the diaphragm rod.

2. Close the choke by pushing on

the choke lever with the throttle partly open.

3. Measure the vertical distance from the top of the rod hole in the control lever down to the carburetor base. The dimension should be as shown in the Specifications Chart.

4. To adjust, bend the link which connects the choke shafts. If an adjustment is needed, the vacuum kick, fast idle cam and choke unloader must be readjusted.

CHOKE VACUUM KICK ADJUSTMENT

NOTE: The test can be made on or off the vehicle.

1. If the adjustment is to be made with the engine running, back off the fast idle speed screw until the choke can be closed to the kick position with the engine at curb idle. Note the number of screw turns required so that the fast idle can be returned to the original adjustment.

2. If an auxiliary vacuum source is to be used, open the throttle valve (engine not running) and move the choke to the closed position. Release the throttle first, then release the choke. When using an auxiliary vacuum source, disconnect the vacuum hose from the carburetor and connect it to the hose from the vacuum supply with

a small length of tube to act as a fitting. Removal of the hose from the diaphragm may require sufficient force to bend the bracket. Apply a vacuum of 15 or more in. of mercury.

3. Insert the specified drill between the long side, lower edge, of the choke valve and the air horn wall.

4. Apply sufficient pressure on the choke control lever to provide a minimum choke valve opening. The spring connecting the control lever to the adjustment lever must be fully extended for proper adjustment.

5. Bend the tang to change the contact with the end of the diaphragm rod. Do not adjust the diaphragm rod. A slight drag should be felt as the drill is being removed.

FAST IDLE CAM LINKAGE

1. With the fast idle screw on the **second fastest** step of the cam against the shoulder of the first step, there should be 0.100 in. between the air horn wall and edge of the choke valve.

2. To adjust, bend the fast idle connector rod at the lower angle.

SECONDARY THROTTLE LOCKOUT

1. Move the choke control lever to the open choke position.

2. Measure the clearance between the lockout lever and the stop.

3. Bend the tang on the fast idle control lever to provide the proper clearance. Clearance should be 0.060–0.090 in.

BOWL VENT VALVE ADJUSTMENT

1. Remove the air cleaner. Disconnect the hose to the solenoid bowl vent diaphragm.

2. Connect an auxiliary vacuum source. With 15 in. Hg applied, the valve should move down. This can be observed down through the air horn vent tube.

3. Turn the ignition switch on and disconnect the auxiliary vacuum source. The valve should remain down. With the ignition off, the valve should move back up.

4. If the valve does not move down when vacuum is applied, the diaphragm is leaking and must be replaced. If the valve does not stay down with the ignition on and the vacuum removed, the solenoid or the wiring is defective.

FAST IDLE SPEED CAM

1. Disconnect and plug the heated air, EGR, OSAC valve, or distributor

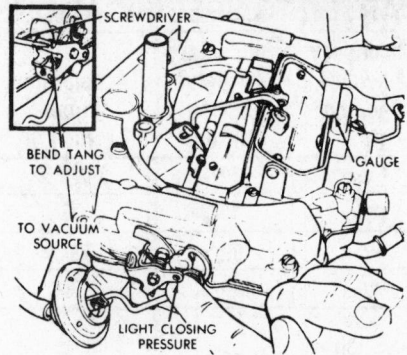

TQ vacuum kick adjustment

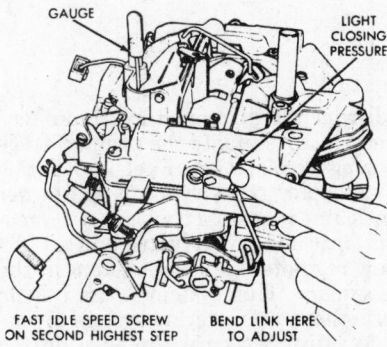

TQ fast idle cam linkage adjustment

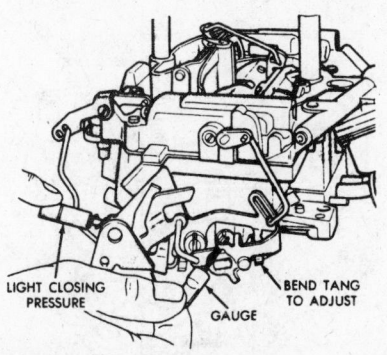

TQ secondary throttle lockout adjustment

connections. With lean burn, do not disconnect the spark control computer hose. Use a jumper wire to ground the carburetor idle stop switch. With the engine off and the transmission in Park or Neutral, open the throttle slightly.

2. Close the choke valve until the fast idle screw can be positioned on the **second** step of the cam against the shoulder of the first step.

3. Start the engine and adjust the screw to obtain the specified fast idle speed.

CHOKE UNLOADER ADJUSTMENT

1. Hold the throttle valves in the wide open position and insert the spec-

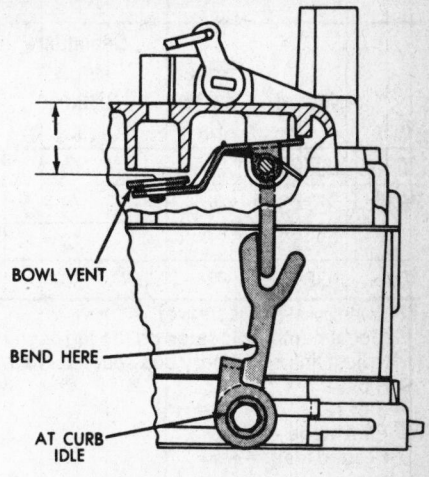

TQ bowl vent adjustment

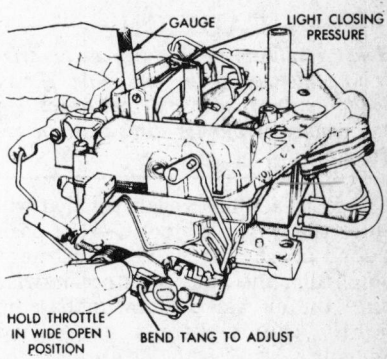

TQ choke unloader adjustment

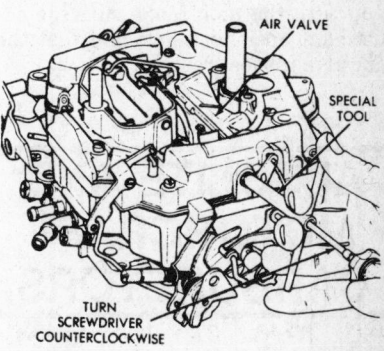

TQ air valve spring tension adjustment

ified drill between the bottom of the choke valve and inner wall of the air horn.

2. With a finger pressing lightly against the choke control lever, a slight drag should be felt as the drill is being withdrawn.

3. To adjust, bend the tang on the fast idle lever.

SECONDARY AIR VALVE SPRING TENSION

1. Loosen the air valve lock plug and allow the air valve to position itself in the wide open position.

CARTER TQ SPECIFICATIONS

Year	Model ①	Float Setting (in.)	Secondary Throttle Linkage (in.)	Secondary Air Valve Opening (in.)	Secondary Air Valve Spring (turns)	Accelerator Pump (in.)	Choke Control Lever (in.)	Choke Unloader (in.)	Vacuum Kick (in.)	Fast Idle Speed (rpm)
'82	9372S	29/32	②	13/32	1 3/4	33/64 ④	3 3/8	0.310	0.130	1400
'83	9374S	29/32	②	13/32	1 3/4	⑤	3 3/8	0.310	0.130	1400
	9385S	29/32	②	13/32	1 3/4	33/64 ④	3 3/8	0.310	0.130	1400
'84	93895	29/32	②	13/32	1 3/4	⑤	—	0.310	0.130	1400

NOTE: All choke settings are fixed.
① Model numbers located on the tag or on the casting
② Adjust link so primary and secondary stops both contact at same time
③ Slot #1
④ Slot #2
⑤ First stage—33/64
   Second stage—25/64

── CAUTION ──

Hold the adjustment plug with a screwdriver when loosening the lock plug. If you don't, the spring may snap out of position and require carburetor disassembly to retrieve it.

2. With a long screwdriver that will enter the center of tool C–4152 positioned on the air valve adjustment plug, turn the plug counterclockwise until the air valve contacts the stop lightly, then tighten the specified amount.

3. Hold the adjustment plug with the screwdriver and tighten the lock plug with the tool. Make sure the adjustment does not move and that the air valve moves freely.

AUTOLITE AND MOTORCRAFT CARBURETORS

Model 740

The model 740 has 5 basic systems: choke system, idle system, main metering system, acceleration system and power enrichment system. The choke system is used for cold starting and features a bi-metallic spring and an electric heater for fast cold starts and improved warm-up. The idle system is a separate and adjustable system for the correct air/fuel mixture for both idle and low speed performance.

The main metering system provides the correct air/fuel mixture for normal cruising speeds. A main metering system is provided for both primary and secondary stage operation. The accelerating system is mechanically operat-ed from the primary throttle linkage and provides fuel to the primary stage during acceleration. Fuel is provided by a diaphragm-type pump. The power enrichment system consists of a vacuum operated power valve and an airflow-regulated pullover system in the secondary. This system is used along with the main metering system to provide satisfactory performance during moderate to heavy acceleration. Distributor and EGR vacuum ports are lo-

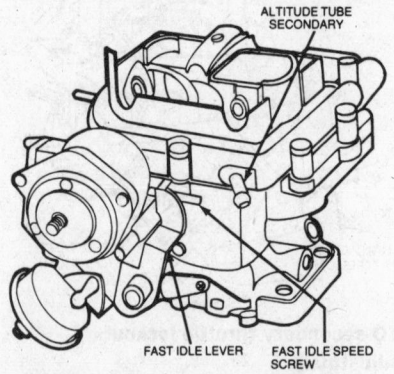

Model 740 carburetor—¾ front view

cated in the primary venturi area of the carburetor.

FAST IDLE CAM

1. Set the fast idle screw on the kickdown step of the cam against the shoulder of the **top** step.

2. Manually close the primary choke plate and measure the distance between the downstream side of the choke plate and the air horn wall.

3. Adjust the right fork of the choke bimetal shaft, which engages the fast idle cam, by bending the fork up and down to obtain the specified clearance.

FAST IDLE

1. Place the transmission in Neutral or Park.

2. Bring the engine to normal operating temperature.

3. Disconnect and plug the vacuum hose at the EGR and purge valves.

4. Identify the vacuum source to the air bypass section of the air supply control valve. If a vacuum hose is connected to the carburetor, disconnect

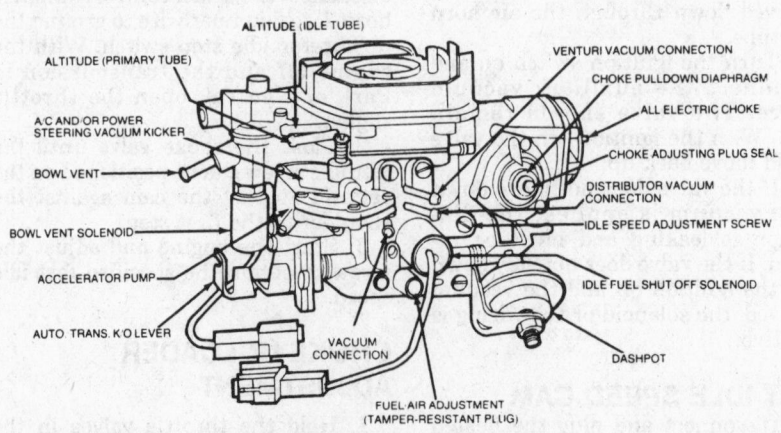

Model 740 carburetor—full rear

the hose and plug the hose at the air supply control valve.

5. Place the fast idle adjustment on the **second** step of the fast idle cam. Run the engine until the cooling fan comes on.

6. While the cooling fan is on, check the fast idle rpm. If an adjustment is necessary, loosen the locknut and adjust to the idle to the specification on the underhood decal.

7. Remove all plugs and reconnect the hoses to their original position.

DASHPOT

With the throttle set at the curb idle position, fully depress the dashpot stem and measure the distance between the stem and the throttle lever. Adjust by loosening the locknut and turning the dashpot.

CHOKE PLATE PULLDOWN ADJUSTMENT

NOTE: The following procedure requires the removal of the carburetor and also the choke cap which is retained by rivets.

1. On 1982–83 models only, remove the carburetor from the engine.
2. Remove the choke cap as follows:
   a. Check the rivets to determine if mandrel is well below the rivet head. If mandrel is within the rivet head thickness, drive it down or out with a $\frac{1}{16}$ in. diameter tip punch.
   b. With a $\frac{1}{8}$ in. diameter drill, drill into the rivet head until the rivet head comes loose from the rivet body. Use light pressure on the drill bit or the rivet will just spin in the hole.
   c. After drilling off the rivet head, drive the remaining rivet out of the hole with a $\frac{1}{8}$ in. diameter punch.
   d. Repeat Steps (a thru c) to remove the remaining rivet.
3. On 1982–83 models, connect a vacuum source to the vacuum passage adjacent to the primary throttle bore. On 1984 and later models connect a vacuum source to the vacuum tube on the choke pulldown cover.
4. Set the fast idle adjusting screw on the **high** step of the fast idle cam by temporarily opening the throttle lever and rotating the choke bimetal shaft lever counterclockwise until the choke plates are in the fully closed position.
5. While applying the external vacuum, lightly force the choke thermostat actuating lever counterclockwise.
6. Using the drill diameter specified in the carburetor specifications table at the end of this section, measure the clearance between the down-stream side of the choke plate and the air horn wall.

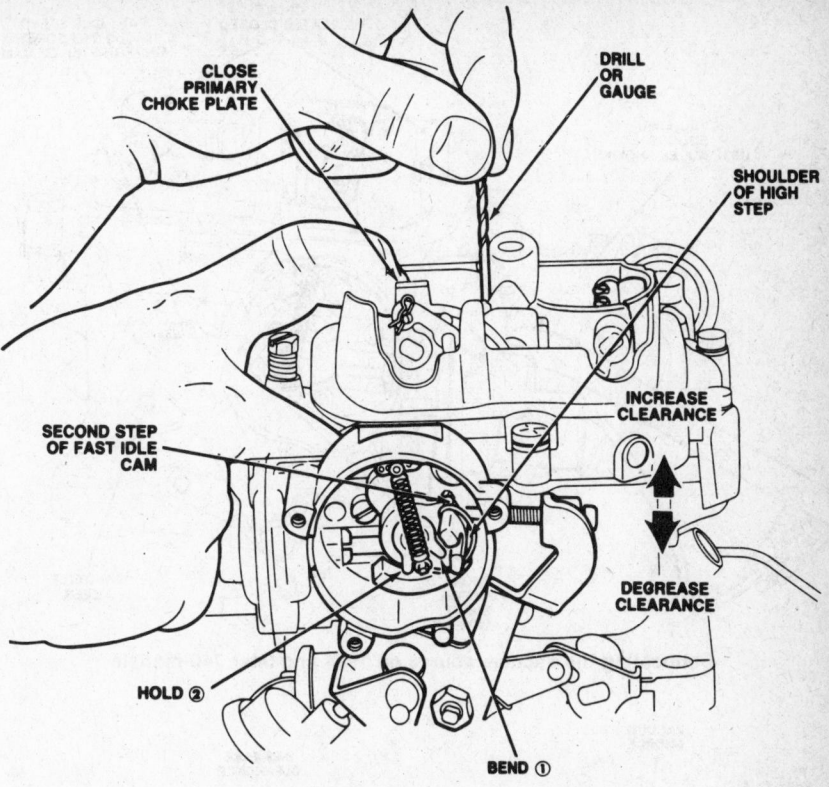

Fast idle cam adjustment—model 740

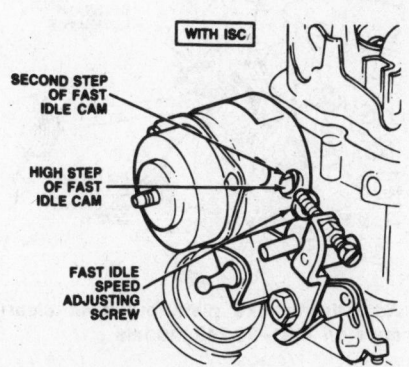

Fast idle speed adjusting screw and fast idle cam—model 740

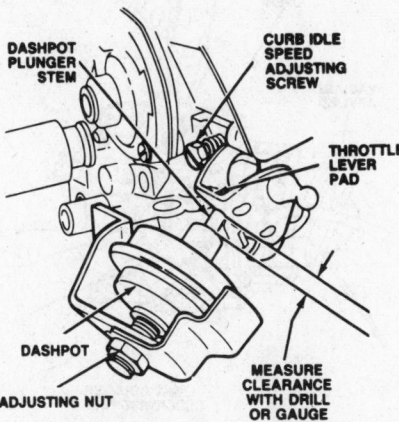

Dashpot assembly—model 740

7. If an adjustment is necessary, turn the vacuum diaphragm adjusting screw in or out as required.

NOTE: On 1984 and later models the choke pulldown adjustment screw is sealed with a limiting plug. Refer to the procedure which follows for removal.

CHOKE PULLDOWN LIMITING PLUG REMOVAL

1984 and Later Models Only

1. Remove the choke pulldown diaphragm cover.
2. Using pliers, grasp the back of the adjustment screw and turn it out of the cover.
3. Drive the plugs out of the cover, using a punch and a hammer.

——— **CAUTION** ———

Always wear eye protection when driving out plugs.

DRY FLOAT ADJUSTMENT

1. Place the air horn assembly upside down and at a 45 degree angle with the air horn gasket in place. The float tang should rest lightly on the inlet needle.

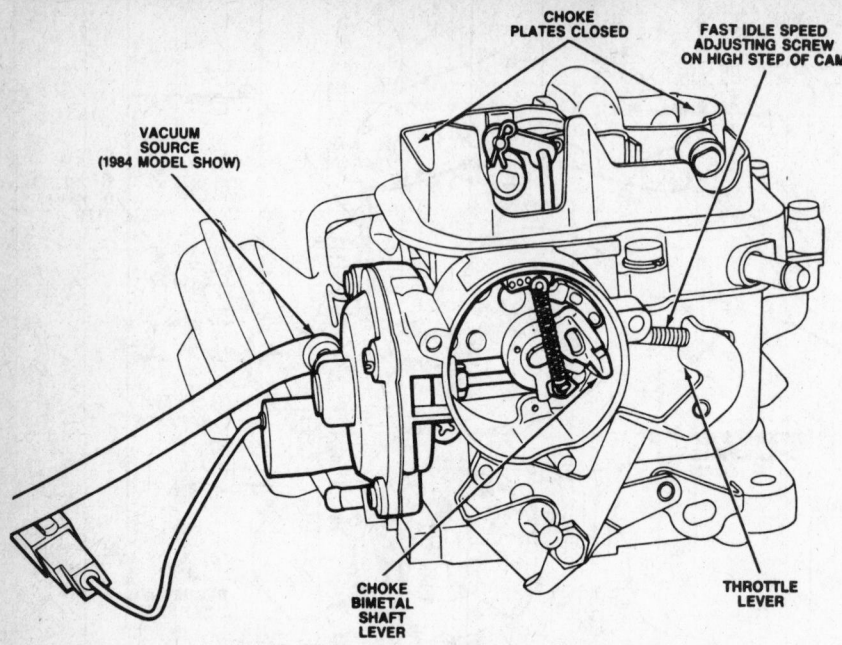

Connecting the vacuum source on 1984 and later 740 models

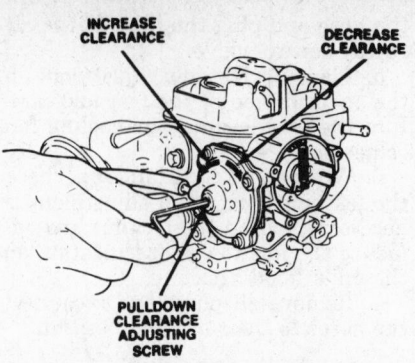

Adjusting choke plate pulldown clearance on 1984 and later 740 models

2. Measure the clearance with a suitable gauge at the extreme end or toe of the float.

3. Remove the float and adjust to specification by bending the float level adjusting tang up or down.

NOTE: Care must be taken not to scratch or damage the float tang while adjusting.

FLOAT DROP ADJUSTMENT

1. Suspend the air horn assembly in the normal position with the air horn gasket in position.

2. The distance from the air horn gasket to the bottom of the float should be 1.69 ± 0.31 in. (43 ± 8mm).

3. Remove the float and adjust to specification by bending the float drop tang.

WIDE OPEN THROTTLE (WOT) A/C CUT-OUT SWITCH

A visual inspection is required to ensure adequate pin and actuating arm overlap with the carburetor linkage in the WOT position.

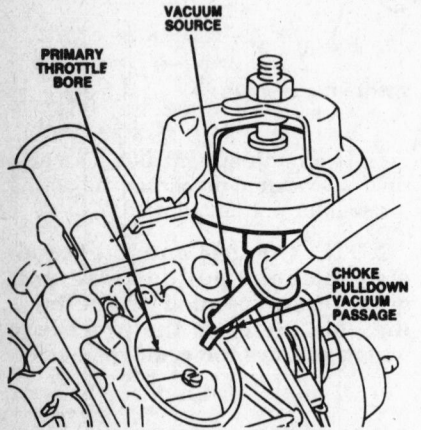

Connecting the vacuum source on 1981–83 740 models

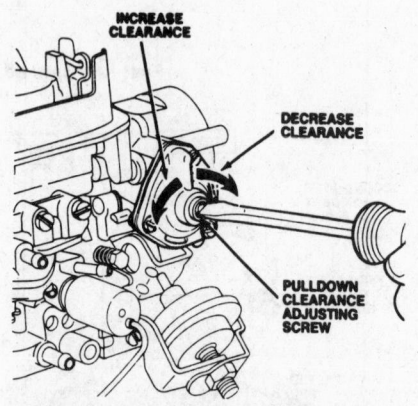

Adjusting choke plate pulldown clearance on 1981–83 740 models

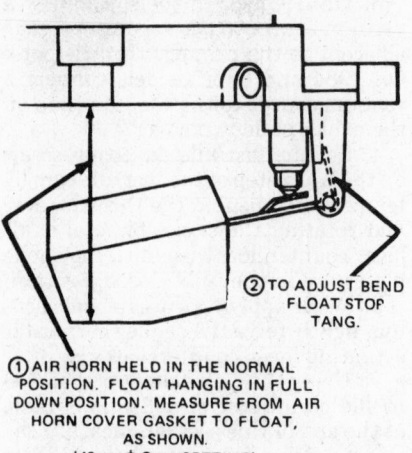

② TO ADJUST BEND FLOAT STOP TANG.

① AIR HORN HELD IN THE NORMAL POSITION. FLOAT HANGING IN FULL DOWN POSITION. MEASURE FROM AIR HORN COVER GASKET TO FLOAT, AS SHOWN. (43mm ± 8mm SETTING)

Float drop adjustment—Model 740

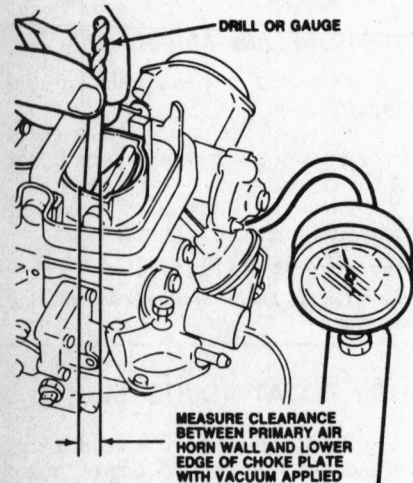

Measuring choke plate pulldown clearance on 1981–83 740 models

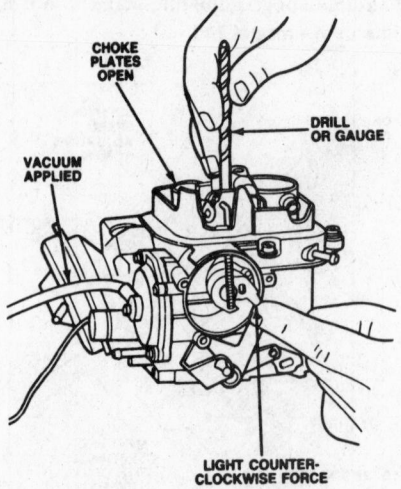

Measuring choke plate pulldown clearance on 1984 and later 740 models

MOTORCRAFT MODEL 740 SPECIFICATIONS
Escort, Lynx, Exp, Lynx

Year	(9510)* Carburetor Identification	Dry Float Level (in.)	Choke Plate Pulldown (in.)	Fast Idle Cam Linkage (in.)	Fast Idle (rpm)	Dechoke (in.)	Choke Setting	Dashpot (in.)
'82	E1GE-CA	0.250	0.120	0.080	2400	0.140	Index	0.140
	E1GE-DA	0.250	0.120	0.080	2400	0.140	Index	0.140
	E1EE-ALA	0.250	0.160	0.080	2400	0.140	1 Lean	0.160
	E1GE-GA	0.250	0.160	0.080	2400	0.140	1 Lean	0.160
	E1EE-APA	0.250	0.160	0.080	2400	0.140	1 Lean	0.160
	E1EE-NA	0.250	0.160	0.080	2400	0.140	1 Lean	0.160
	E1GE-EA	0.250	0.160	0.080	2400	0.140	1 Lean	0.160
	E1EE-ZA	0.250	0.160	0.080	2400	0.140	1 Lean	0.160
	E2EE-JA	0.250	0.138	0.080	2400	0.140	Index	0.060
	E2EE-GA	0.250	0.138	0.080	2200	0.140	Index	0.060
	E2EE-GC	0.250	0.138	0.080	2200	0.140	Index	0.140
	E2EE-EA	0.250	0.138	0.080	2400	0.140	Index	0.160
	E2EE-SA	0.250	0.138	0.080	2400	0.140	Index	0.060
	E2EE-LC	0.250	0.177	0.080	①	0.140	Index	0.160
	E2EE-LA	0.250	0.138	0.080	2400	0.140	Index	0.160
	E2EE-ZA	0.250	0.138	0.080	2400	0.140	2 Rich	0.160
	E2EE-NA	0.250	0.138	0.080	2400	0.140	Index	0.160
	E2EE-AAA	0.250	0.138	0.080	2400	0.140	2 Rich	0.160
	E2EE-PA	0.250	0.138	0.080	2400	0.140	Index	0.160
	E2EE-PC	0.250	0.177	0.080	2200	0.140	Index	0.160
	E2EE-NC	0.250	0.177	0.080	2200	0.140	Index	0.160
	E2EE-VA	0.250	0.138	0.080	2400	0.140	1 Lean	0.160
	E2EE-YA	0.250	0.138	0.080	2400	0.140	1 Lean	0.160
	E2EE-MC	0.250	0.177	0.080	2200	0.140	Index	0.160
	E2EE-MA	0.250	0.138	0.080	2400	0.140	Index	0.160
'83	E3EE-CA	0.300	0.320	0.080	①	0.140	NA	0.140
	E3EE-EA	0.300	0.320	0.080	①	0.140	NA	0.140
	E3EE-DA	0.300	0.340	0.080	①	0.140	NA	0.140
	E3EE-AA	0.300	0.140	0.080	①	0.140	NA	0.140
	E3EE-JA	0.300	0.140	0.080	①	0.140	NA	0.140
	E3EE-BA	0.300	0.140	0.080	①	0.140	NA	0.140
	E3EE-KA	0.300	0.140	0.080	①	0.140	NA	0.140
	E3EE-GB	0.300	0.312	0.080	①	0.140	NA	0.095
	E3EE-NA	0.300	0.140	0.080	①	0.140	NA	—
	E3EE-PA	0.300	0.140	0.080	①	0.140	NA	0.140
	E3GE-DA	0.300	0.170	0.080	①	0.140	NA	0.140
	E3GE-HA	0.300	0.170	0.080	①	0.140	NA	0.140
	E3GE-FA	0.300	0.170	0.080	①	0.140	NA	0.140
	E3GE-JA	0.300	0.170	0.080	①	0.140	NA	0.160
	E3GE-PA	0.300	0.260	0.080	①	0.140	NA	0.140
	E3GE-SA	0.300	0.260	0.080	①	0.140	NA	0.140
	E3GE-RA	0.300	0.260	0.080	①	0.140	NA	0.140

MOTORCRAFT MODEL 740 SPECIFICATIONS
Escort, Lynx, Exp, Lynx

Year	(9510)* Carburetor Identification	Dry Float Level (in.)	Choke Plate Pulldown (in.)	Fast Idle Cam Linkage (in.)	Fast Idle (rpm)	Dechoke (in.)	Choke Setting	Dashpot (in.)
'83	E3GE-MA	0.300	0.280	0.093	①	0.140	NA	0.160
	E3GE-UA	0.300	0.280	0.093	①	0.140	NA	0.160
	E3GE-NA	0.300	0.140	0.093	①	0.140	NA	0.160
	E3GE-KB	0.300	0.300	0.080	①	0.140	NA	0.160
	E3GE-KD	0.300	0.300	0.080	①	0.140	NA	0.160
	E3GE-LA	0.300	0.300	0.080	①	0.140	NA	0.160
	E3GE-LC	0.300	0.300	0.080	①	0.140	NA	0.160
	E3GE-DC	0.300	0.170	0.080	①	0.140	NA	—
	E3GE-FC	0.300	0.170	0.080	①	0.140	NA	—
	E3GE-JC	0.300	0.170	0.080	①	0.140	NA	—
'84–'85	E4EE-YA	0.300	0.320	0.110	①	0.140	NA	0.095
	E4EE-ACA	0.300	0.320	0.080	①	0.140	NA	0.080
	E4EE-ADA	0.300	0.260	0.080	①	0.140	NA	0.140
	E4EE-ABA	0.300	0.320	0.110	①	0.140	NA	0.095
	E4EE-AAA	0.300	0.320	0.095	①	0.140	NA	0.095
	E4EE-AFA	0.300	0.218	0.080	①	0.140	NA	—
	E4GE-LA	0.300	0.300	0.080	①	0.140	NA	0.160
	E4GE-KA	0.300	0.300	0.080	①	0.140	NA	0.160
	E4GE-SA	0.300	0.280	0.100	①	0.140	NA	0.160
	E4GE-MA	0.300	0.300	0.180	①	0.140	NA	0.160
	E4GE-UA	0.300	0.325	0.080	①	0.140	NA	—
	E4GE-TA	0.300	0.300	0.125	①	0.140	NA	—
	E4GE-RA	0.300	0.325	0.130	①	0.140	NA	—
	E4GE-ACA	0.300	0.140	0.080	①	0.140	NA	0.080
	E4GE-ZA	0.300	0.250	0.108	①	0.140	NA	—
'86	E5GE-AAA	0.300	0.300	0.110	①	0.140	NA	0.060
	E5GE-ADA	0.300	0.300	0.100	①	0.140	NA	0.020
	E5GE-ACA	0.300	0.300	0.100	①	0.140	NA	0.020
	E5GE-AEC	0.300	0.280	0.080	①	0.140	NA	0.080
	E5GE-AFC	0.300	0.280	0.080	①	0.140	NA	0.060

*Basic carburetor number for Ford Carburetors
NA—Not available
① See underhood decal.

Adjustments to the switch position are made by bending it's support bracket outboard. A 0.120 in. (3mm) minimum overlap is desired. Precaution is required to ensure adequate clearance between the tip of the carburetor fast idle lever and switch housing.

Models 2100 and 2150

The Model 2100 and 2150 2 barrel carburetor are basically the same in con-struction. Adjustments are performed in the same manner for both carburetors.

FLOAT LEVEL (DRY)

The dry float level measurement is a preliminary check and must be followed by a wet float level measurement with the carburetor mounted on the engine.

1. With the air horn removed, gently raise the float to seat the inlet nee-dle by applying light finger pressure at the float tab. Lower the float by reducing finger pressure until a light step is felt. Measure the distance between the main body gasket surface (gasket removed) and the top of the float. This measurement should be taken near the center of the float at a point ⅛ in. from the free-end of the float.

NOTE: 1983 and later carbure-tors are equipped with a spring loaded fuel inlet needle and the

ball must not be depressed when the fuel level check is being made.

2. If necessary, bend the float tab to obtain the correct level.

FLOAT LEVEL (WET)

1. Remove the screws that hold the air horn to the main body and break the seal between the air horn and main body. Leave the air horn and gasket loosely in place on top of the main body.

2. Start the engine and allow it to idle for at least 3 minutes.

3. After the engine has idled long enough to stabilize the fuel level, remove the air horn assembly.

4. With the engine idling, use a T-scale to measure the distance from the top of the fuel bowl machined surface to the surface of the fuel. The scale must be held at least ¼ in. away from any vertical surface to ensure proper measurement.

5. If any adjustment is required, stop the engine to avoid a fire from fuel spraying on the engine.

6. Bend the float tab upward to raise the level and downward to lower the level.

NOTE: Be sure to hold the fuel inlet needle off its seat when bending the float tab so as not to damage the Viton® tip.

7. Each time the float level is changed, the air horn must be temporarily positioned and the engine started to stabilize the fuel level before again checking it.

CHOKE PLATE PULLDOWN

Model 2100

1. Loosen the screws on the choke cover and rotate the cover ¼ turn counterclockwise (rich), then tighten the screws.

2. Operate the throttle to allow full closing of the choke plate.

3. Press down on the choke modulator arm until the choke modulator diaphragm is bottomed and then measure the distance from the lower edge of the choke plate to the inside air horn wall.

4. Adjustment is achieve by turning the diaphragm stop screw on the underside of the air horn.

5. Turn the screw clockwise to decrease clearance and counterclockwise to increase clearance.

NOTE: Do not reset the choke cover until the fast idle cam adjustment is made.

Model 2150

1. Remove the air cleaner assembly.

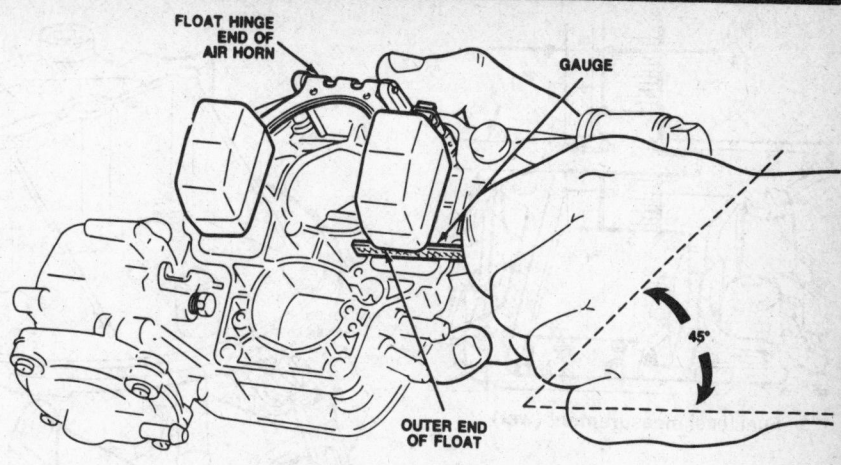

Measuring float clearance—model 740

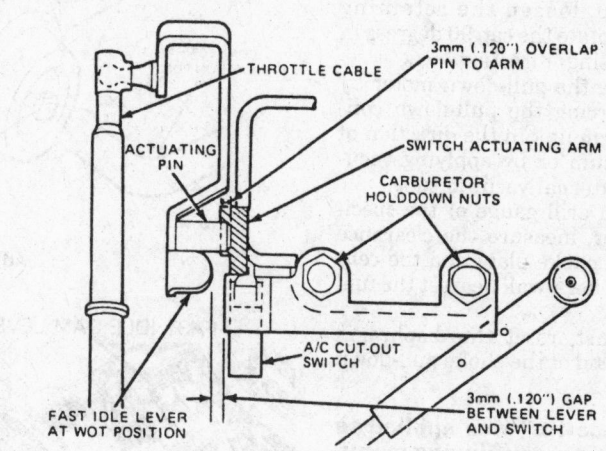

(WOT) A/C cut-off switch adjustment—Model 740

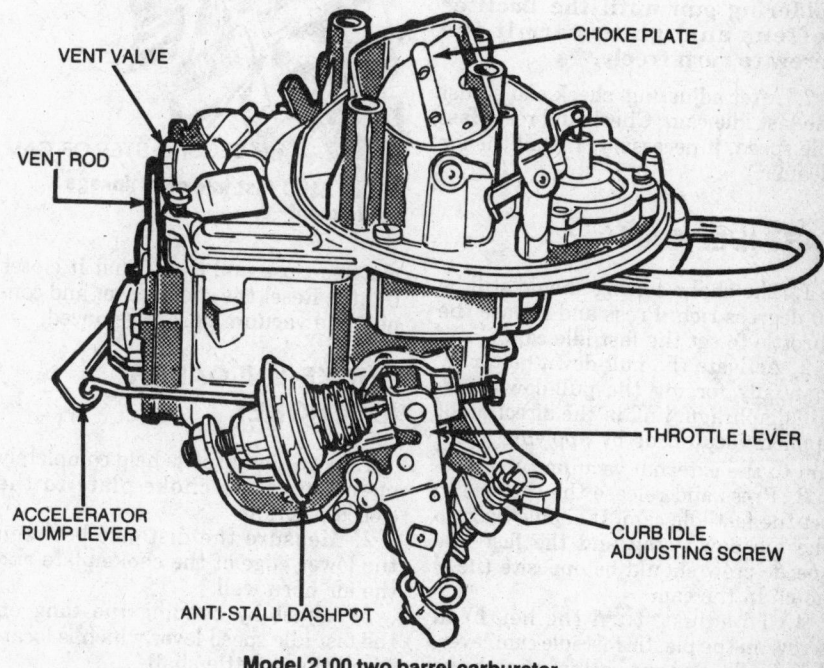

Model 2100 two barrel carburetor

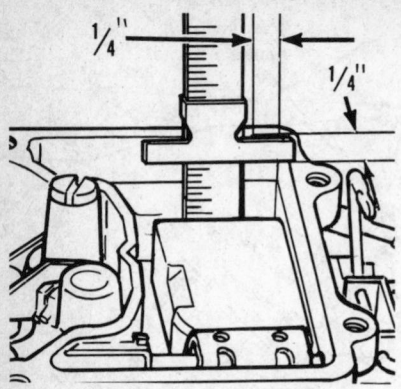

Fuel level measurement (wet)

2. Set the throttle on the **top** step of the fast idle cam.

3. Noting the position of the choke housing cap, loosen the retaining screws and rotate the cap 90 degrees in the rich (closing) direction.

4. Activate the pull-down motor by manually forcing the pull-down control diaphragm link in the direction of applied vacuum or by applying vacuum to the external vacuum tube.

5. Using a drill gauge of the specified diameter, measure the clearance between the choke plate and the center of the air horn wall nearest the fuel bowl.

6. To adjust, reset the diaphragm stop on the end of the choke pull-down diaphragm.

NOTE: Loctite® was applied to the adjusting screw during manufacture and this will have to be loosened before the adjustment can be made. Heat the area around the screw with an electric soldering gun until the Loctite® softens enough to permit the screw to turn freely.

7. After adjusting, check and adjust the fast idle cam. Check and reset fast idle speed, if necessary. Install the air cleaner.

FAST IDLE CAM

1. The choke setting should still be 90 degrees rich. Press and release the throttle to set the fast idle cam.

2. Activate the pull-down motor by manually forcing the pull-down control diaphragm link in the direction of applied vacuum or by applying vacuum to the external vacuum tube.

3. Press and release the throttle to set the fast idle cam. It should drop to the kickdown step and the fast idle speed screw should be opposite the V notch in the cam.

4. To adjust, turn the hex head screw on the plastic fast idle cam lever. After adjustment, allow the choke

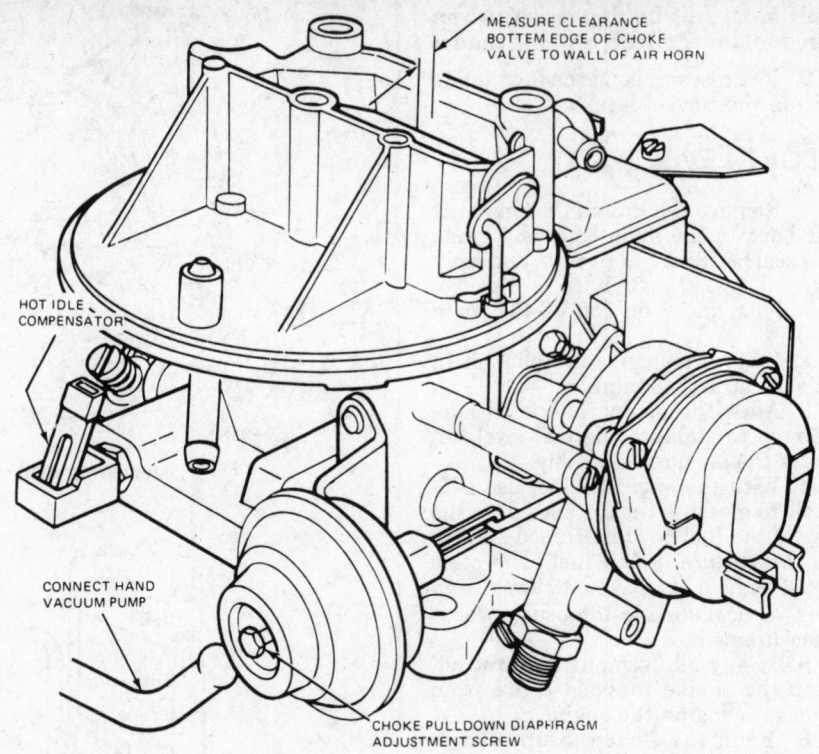

Adjusting choke plate pulldown

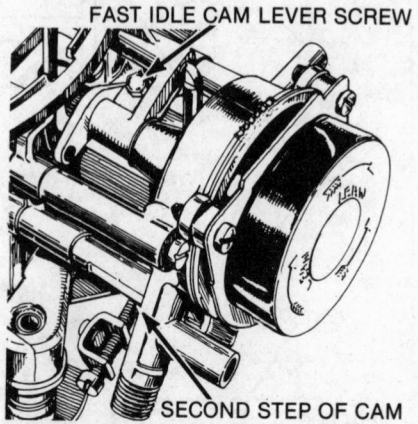

2100, 2150 fast idle cam linkage adjustment

plate to close and check that it closes tightly. Reset the choke cover and connect the vacuum hose if removed.

CHOKE UNLOADER (DECHOKE)

1. With the throttle held completely open, move the choke plate to the closed position.

2. Measure the distance between the lower edge of the choke plate and the air horn wall.

3. Adjust by bending the tang on the fast idle speed lever which is located on the throttle shaft.

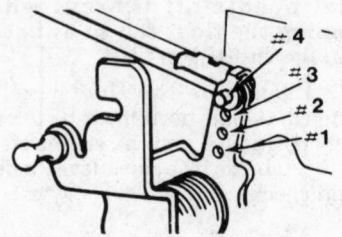

Accelerator pump stroke adjustment

NOTE: Final unloader adjustment must be performed on the car and the throttle should be opened by using the accelerator pedal of the car. This is to be sure that full throttle operation is achieved.

ACCELERATOR PUMP

The accelerator pump operating rod must be positioned in the proper holes of the accelerator pump lever and the throttle over-travel lever to assure correct pump travel. If adjustment is required, additional holes are provided in the throttle over-travel lever.

DASHPOT ADJUSTMENT

With the throttle set at the curb idle position, fully depress the dashpot stem and measure the distance between the stem and the throttle lever.

Adjust by loosening the locknut and turning the dashpot.

FAST IDLE

Adjust the fast idle with the engine at normal operating temperature. On AMC cars, plug the spark port on the carburetor and remove the EGR vacuum line at the valve and plug it. On Ford cars, if the engine is equipped with a spark delay valve, remove it and reroute the partial throttle vacuum signal line directly to the advance side of the distributor. If the distributor is a dual diaphragm type, leave the manifold vacuum line connected to the retard side of the distributor and remove and plug the line to the advance side.

If an EGR/PVS valve or cold weather modulator is located in the vacuum hose routing, disconnect and plug the hose at the EGR valve. If the engine does not have a cold weather modulator or an EGR/PVC valve, leave the EGR hose attaching. Trace the thermactor (air pump) dump valve

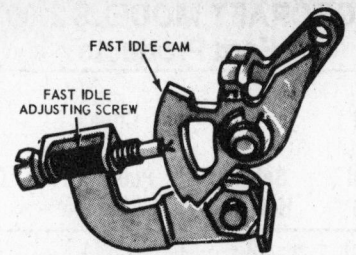

Fast idle adjustment

vacuum hose from the dump valve to the carburetor; disconnect the dump valve vacuum hose nearest the carburetor, plug the original vacuum source and connect the dump valve directly to manifold vacuum. The fast idle screw should be resting against the **SECOND** step of the fast idle cam on all models except Fords with the 302 engine, which have the screw set on the **HIGH** step of the cam. Adjust the fast idle speed by turning the fast idle screw.

Model 5200

The 5200 carburetor is a 2-stage, 2-venturi carburetor in which the secondary venturi is the larger and is mechanically operated.

FAST IDLE CAM

1982

1. Place the fast idle screw on the **second** step of the fast idle cam against the shoulder of the top step.

FORD, AUTOLITE, MOTORCRAFT MODELS 2100, 2150 SPECIFICATIONS
Ford Products

Year	(9510)* Carburetor Identification	Dry Float Level (in.)	Wet Float Level (in.)	Pump Setting Hole # ①	Choke Plate Pulldown (in.)	Fast Idle Cam Linkage Clearance (in.)	Fast Idle (rmp)	Dechoke (in)	Choke Setting
'82	E2BE-UA	7/16	0.810	2	0.110	②	2200	0.250	④
	E2BE-AAA	7/16	0.810	2	0.110	②	2200	0.250	④
	E2BE-VA	7/16	0.810	2	0.113	②	2200	0.250	④
	E2BE-ABA	7/16	0.810	2	0.113	②	2200	0.250	④
	E2BE-AGA	7/16	0.810	2	0.113 ⑤	②	2200	0.250	④
	E2BE-AHA	7/16	0.810	2	0.113	②	2200	0.250	④
	E2VE-CA	7/16	0.810	2	0.113	②	2200	0.250	④
	E24E-CA	7/16	0.810	2	0.110	②	1200	0.250	④
	E24E-DA	7/16	0.810	2	0.110	②	1200	0.250	④
	E24E-AA	7/16	0.810	2	0.110	②	2100	0.250	④
	E24E-BA	7/16	0.810	2	0.110	②	2100	0.250	④
	E24E-EA	7/16	0.810	2	0.110	②	③	0.250	④
	E24E-FA	7/16	0.810	2	0.110	②	③	0.250	④
	E2KE-AA	7/16	0.810	2	0.140	②	1500	0.250	④
	E2KE-BA	7/16	0.810	2	0.140	②	1500	0.250	④
	E2WE-EA	7/16	0.810	2	0.137	②	1500	0.250	④
	E2WE-FA	7/16	0.810	2	0.137	②	1500	0.250	④
	E2DE-JA	7/16	0.810	2	0.137	②	1600	0.250	④
	E2DE-KA	7/16	0.810	2	0.137	②	1600	0.250	④
	E2DE-LA	7/16	0.810	2	0.137	②	1700	0.250	④
	E2DE-MA	7/16	0.810	2	0.137	②	1700	0.250	④

34 CARBURETOR SERVICE

FORD, AUTOLITE, MOTORCRAFT MODELS 2100, 2150 SPECIFICATIONS
Ford Products

Year	(9510)* Carburetor Identification	Dry Float Level (in.)	Wet Float Level (in.)	Pump Setting Hole # ①	Choke Plate Pulldown (in.)	Fast Idle Cam Linkage Clearance (in.)	Fast Idle (rmp)	Dechoke (in)	Choke Setting
'82	E25E-DA	7/16	0.810	2	0.144	②	1500	0.250	④
	E2AE-SA	7/16	0.810	2	0.172	②	1550	0.250	④
	E25E-CA	7/16	0.810	2	0.137	②	1700	0.250	④
	E2ZE-BAA	13/32	0.780	2	0.172 ⑤	②	1400	0.250	④
	E2ZE-BBA	13/32	0.780	2	0.172 ⑤	②	1400	0.250	④
	E3CE-LA	7/16	0.810	3	0.103	②	2200	0.250	④
	E3CE-MA	7/16	0.810	3	0.103	②	2200	0.250	④
	E3CE-JA	7/16	0.810	3	0.103	②	2200	0.250	④
	E3CE-KA	7/16	0.810	3	0.103	②	2200	0.250	④
	E3CE-NA	7/16	0.810	3	0.120	②	2100	0.250	④
	E3CE-PA	7/16	0.810	3	0.120	②	2100	0.250	④
'83	E3CE-AA	7/16	0.810	3	0.103	②	2200	0.250	④
	E3CE-BA	7/16	0.810	3	0.103	②	2200	0.250	④
	E3CE-GA	7/16	0.810	3	0.103	②	2200	0.250	④
	E3CE-HA	7/16	0.810	3	0.103	②	2200	0.250	④
	E3CE-EA	7/16	0.810	3	0.113	②	2100	0.250	④
	E3CE-FA	7/16	0.810	3	0.113	②	2100	0.250	④
	E3SE-ATA	7/16	0.810	3	0.113	②	2200	0.250	④
	E3SE-AUA	7/16	0.810	3	0.113	②	2200	0.250	④
	E3SE-ALA	7/16	0.810	3	0.107	②	2200	0.250	④
	E3SE-AMA	7/16	0.810	3	0.107	②	2200	0.250	④
	E3SE-BDA	7/16	0.810	3	0.107	②	2200	0.250	④
	E3SE-BEA	7/16	0.810	3	0.107	②	2200	0.250	④
	E3SE-ANA	7/16	0.810	3	0.101	②	2200	0.250	④
	E3SE-APA	7/16	0.810	3	0.101	②	2200	0.250	④
	E3SE-AJA								
	E3SE-BFA	7/16	0.810	3	0.107	②	2200	0.250	④
	E3SE-BGA	7/16	0.810	3	0.107	②	2200	0.250	④
	E3SE-EA	7/16	0.810	3	0.113	②	2200	0.250	④
	E3SE-FA	7/16	0.810	3	0.113	②	2200	Dechoke	④
	E3SE-LA	7/16	0.810	3	0.107	②	2200	0.250	④
	E3SE-MA	7/16	0.810	3	0.107	②	2200	0.250	④
	E3SE-JA	7/16	0.810	3	0.101	②	2200	0.250	④
	E3SE-KA	7/16	0.810	3	0.101	②	2200	0.250	④
	E3SE-NA	7/16	0.810	3	0.107	②	2200	0.250	④
	E3SE-PA	7/16	0.810	3	0.107	②	2200	0.250	④
	E3SE-GA	7/16	0.810	3	0.120	②	2100	0.250	④
	E3SE-HA	7/16	0.810	3	0.120	②	2100	0.250	④
	E3AE-TA	7/16	0.810	3	0.103	②	2200	0.250	④
	E3AE-ADA	7/16	0.810	3	0.103	②	2200	0.250	④
	E3AE-UA	7/16	0.810	3	0.103	②	2200	0.250	④
	E3AE-AEA	7/16	0.810	3	0.103	②	2200	0.250	④

FORD, AUTOLITE, MOTORCRAFT MODELS 2100, 2150 SPECIFICATIONS
Ford Products

Year	(9510)* Carburetor Identification	Dry Float Level (in.)	Wet Float Level (in.)	Pump Setting Hole # ①	Choke Plate Pulldown (in.)	Fast Idle Cam Linkage Clearance (in.)	Fast Idle (rmp)	Dechoke (in)	Choke Setting
'83	E3AE-TA	7/16	0.810	3	0.103	②	2200	0.250	④
	E3AE-UA	7/16	0.810	3	0.103	②	2200	0.250	④
	E3AE-RA	7/16	0.810	3	0.103	②	2200	0.250	④
	E3AE-SA	7/16	0.810	3	0.103	②	2200	0.250	④
	E3AE-EA	7/16	0.810	2	—	②	1550	0.250	④
'84	E3EA-EA	7/16	0.810	2	—	②	1550	0.250	④
	E4CE-AA	7/16	0.810	3	0.103	②	2200	0.250	2NR
	E4CE-BA	7/16	0.810	3	0.103	②	2200	0.250	2NR
	E4SE-CA	7/16	0.810	3	0.103	②	2200	0.250	④
	E4SE-DA	7/16	0.810	3	0.103	②	2200	0.250	④
'85	E4SE-CA	3/32	0.810	3	0.103	—	③	0.250	4NR
	E4SE-DA	3/32	0.810	3	0.103	—	③	0.250	4NR
	E5SE-CA E3AE-EA(Alt)	7/16	0.810	2	—	④	③	0.250	④

*Basic carburetor number for Ford products
① With link in inboard hole of pump lever
② Opposite "V" notch; see text
③ See underhood decal
④ V-notch
⑤ ± .010″

2. Apply light pressure (downward) on the choke lever tang and using the proper size drill, measure the clearance between the lower edge of the choke plate and the air horn wall.

3. Bend the choke lever tang down to increase clearance and up to decrease the clearance.

NOTE: Ford recommends that if an adjustment is necessary, the choke lever should be replaced since the lever tang is hardened.

CHOKE PLATE PULLDOWN

1982

NOTE: The following procedure requires the removal of the carburetor and also the choke cap which is retained by rivets.

1. Remove the carburetor from the engine.
2. Remove the choke cap as follows:
   a. Check the rivets to determine if mandrel is well below the rivet head. If mandrel is within the rivet head thickness, drive it down or out with a 1/16 in. diameter tip punch.
   b. With a 1/8 in. diameter drill, drill into the rivet head until the rivet head comes loose from the rivet

body. Use light pressure on the drill bit or the rivet will just spin in the hole.

c. After drilling off the rivet head, drive the remaining rivet out of the hole with a 1/8 in. diameter punch.

d. Repeat Steps (a thru c) to remove the remaining rivet.

3. Remove the plastic dust cover.
4. Place the fast idle adjusting screw on the **high** step of the fast idle cam.
5. Attach a rubber band to remove the slack from the choke linkage. Push the diaphragm stem back against the stop screw.

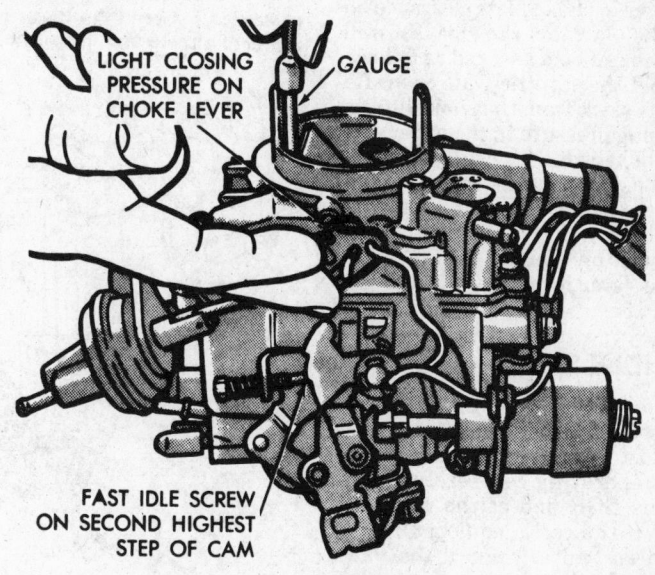

LIGHT CLOSING PRESSURE ON CHOKE LEVER

GAUGE

FAST IDLE SCREW ON SECOND HIGHEST STEP OF CAM

Fast idle cam adjustment—Holley 1945

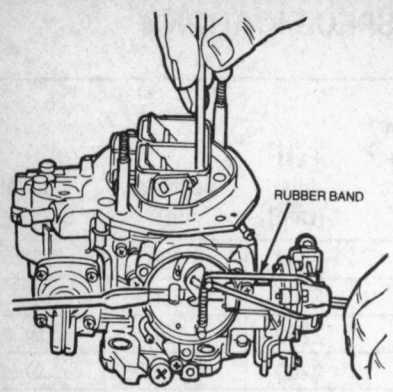

Choke plate pulldown adjustment

6. Using the specified diameter drill check the clearance between the lower edge of the choke plate and the air horn wall.

7. If an adjustment is necessary, obtain a replacement kit containing a new choke pulldown diaphragm cover, adjusting screw and cup plug.

8. After installing the adjusting screw in the cover, adjust the pulldown by turning the screw clockwise to decrease and counterclockwise to increase the setting.

9. After making the adjustment, install a new plug in the choke pulldown adjustment access opening.

10. Remove the rubber band and reinstall the choke cap using rivets (1/8 in. diameter x 1/2 in. long with a 1/4 in. diameter head).

DECHOKE (UNLOADER) ADJUSTMENT

Dechoke clearance adjustment is controlled by the fast idle cam adjustment. The figures in the specification chart refer to choke plate clearance between the plate and the air horn wall. Clearance can be measured as follows:

1. Hold the throttle wide open. Remove any slack from the choke linkage by applying pressure to the upper edge of the choke valve.

2. Measure the distance between the lower edge of the choke plate and the air horn wall.

3. Adjust by bending the tab on the fast idle lever where it touches the cam.

FAST IDLE SPEED

Set the fast idle speed with the fast idle screw positioned on the **second** step of the fast idle cam and with the engine at operating temperature. Remove the EGR line at the valve and plug it. If the car is equipped with a spark delay valve, remove the valve and route the distributor advance vacuum signal directly to the distributor

advance diaphragm. On all manual transmission models, remove and plug the vacuum line to the distributor. If the distributor also has a retard diaphragm, leave the hose connected to it alone. If the engine has a deceleration valve, remove this hose at the carburetor and plug it. Finally, if the car has air conditioning it must be off before adjusting the fast idle.

FLOAT LEVEL ADJUSTMENT

With the bowl cover held upside down and the float tang resting lightly on the spring loaded fuel inlet needle, measure the clearance between the edge of the float and the bowl cover. To adjust the level, bend the float tang up or down as required. Adjust both floats equally.

SECONDARY THROTTLE STOP SCREW

1. Turn the secondary throttle stop screw counterclockwise until the secondary throttle plate seats in its bore.

2. Turn the screw clockwise until it touches the tab on the secondary throttle lever.

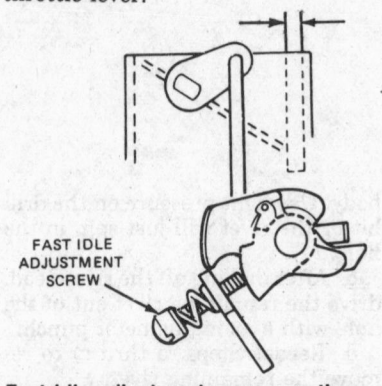

Fast idle adjustment—measure the clearance between the lower edge of the choke plate and the air horn wall

3. Add 1/4 turn clockwise for 4 cylinder engines.

7200 VV

Since the design of the 7200 VV (variable venturi) carburetor differs considerably from the other carburetors in the Ford lineup, an explanation in the theory and operation is presented here.

In exterior appearance, the variable venturi carburetor is similar to conventional carburetors and like a conventional carburetor, it uses a normal float and fuel bowl system. However, the similarity ends there. In place of a normal choke plate and fixed area venturis, the 7200VV carburetor has a pair of small oblong castings in the top of the upper carburetor body where you would normally expect to see the choke plate. These castings slide back and forth across the top of the carbu-

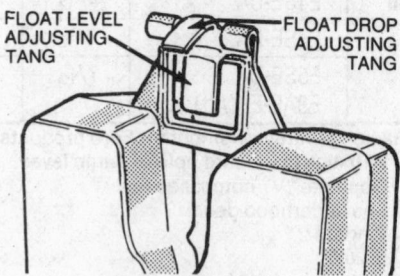

Float adjustment

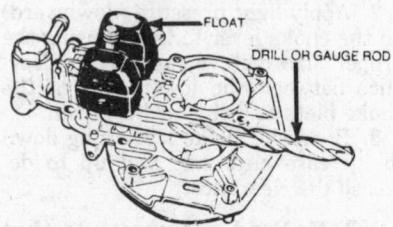

Checking the float level

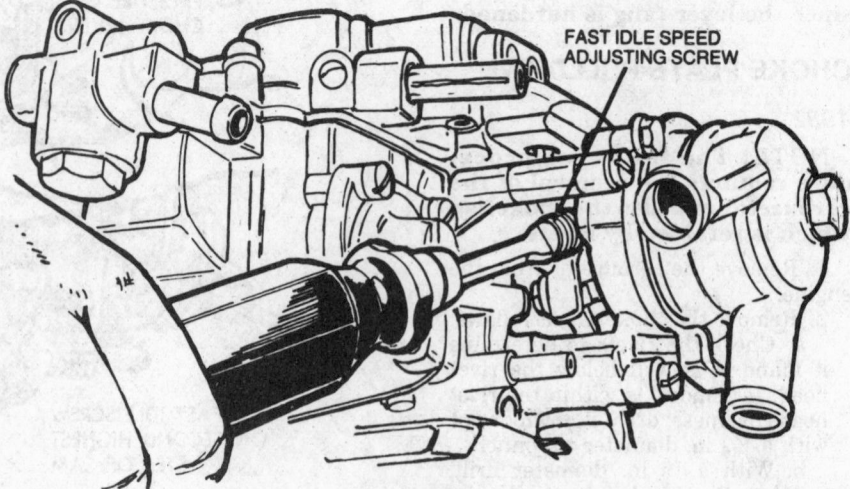

Fast idle adjustment

MOTORCRAFT MODEL 5200
Ford Products

Year	(9510)* Carburetor Identification ①	Dry Float Level (in.)	Pump Hole Setting	Choke Plate Pulldown (in.)	Fast Idle Cam Linkage (in.)	Fast Idle (rpm)	Dechoke (in.)	Choke Setting
'82	E1ZE-ADB	.41–.51	3	0.275	0.240	1600	0.393	—
	E1ZE-ACA	.41–.51	2	0.200	.080	1800	0.196	—
	E1BE-RA, GA	.41–.51	2	0.200	.080	1800	0.196	—
	E1ZE-YA	.41–.51	2	0.200	.080	2000	0.196	—
	E1ZE-VA	.41–.51	2	0.200	.080	2000	0.196	—
	E2ZE-AFA	.41–.51	2	0.236	0.118	1800	0.236	—
	E2ZE-AHA	.41–.51	2	0.236	0.118	2000	0.236	—
	E2ZE-ABA	.41–.51	2	0.236	0.118	2000	0.236	—
	E2ZE-AGA	.41–.51	2	0.236	0.118	2000	0.236	—
	E2ZE-AAA	.41–.51	2	0.236	0.118	2000	0.236	—

*Basic carburetor number
① Figure given is for all manual transmissions; for automatic trans. the figures are: (49 states) 2000 RPM; (Calif.) 1800 RPM.
② See underhood decal

retor in response to air/fuel demands. Their movement is controlled by a spring-loaded diaphragm valve regulated by a vacuum signal taken below the venturis in the throttle bores. As the throttle is opened, the strength of the vacuum signal increases, opening the venturis and allowing more air to enter the carburetor.

Fuel is admitted into the venturi area by means of tapered metering rods that fit into the main jets. These rods are attached to the venturis and the venturis open or close in response to air demand. The fuel needed to maintain the proper mixture increases or decreases as the metering rods slide in the jets. In comparison to a conventional carburetor with fixed venturis and a variable air supply, this system provides much more precise control of the fuel/air supply during all modes of operation. Because of the variable venturi principle, there are fewer fuel metering systems and fuel passages. The only auxiliary fuel metering systems required are an idle trim, accelerator pump (similar to a conventional carburetor), starting enrichment and cold running enrichment.

NOTE: Adjustment, assembly and disassembly of this carburetor require special tools for some of the operations. These tools are available (see the Tools and Equipment Section). Do not attempt any operations on this carburetor without first checking to see if you need the special tools for that particular operation. The adjustment and repair procedures given here mention when and if you will need the special tools.

FLOAT LEVEL ADJUSTMENT

1. Remove and invert the upper part of the carburetor, with the gasket in place.
2. Measure the vertical distance between the carburetor body, outside the gasket and the bottom of the float.
3. To adjust, bend the float operating lever that contacts the needle valve. Make sure that the float remains parallel to the gasket surface.

FLOAT DROP ADJUSTMENT

1. Remove and hold the upper part of the carburetor upright.
2. Measure the vertical distance between the carburetor body, outside the gasket and the bottom of the float.

3. Adjust by bending the stop tab on the float lever that contacts the hinge pin.

FAST IDLE SPEED ADJUSTMENT

1. With the engine warmed up and idling, place the fast idle lever on the step of the fast idle cam specified on the engine compartment sticker or in the specifications chart. Disconnect and plug the EGR vacuum line.
2. Make sure the high speed cam positioner lever is disengaged.
3. Turn the fast idle speed screw to adjust to the specified speed.

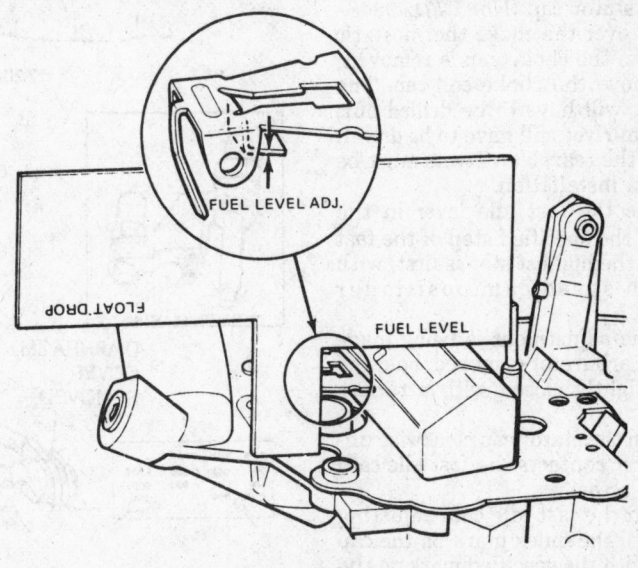

7200 VV float level adjustment

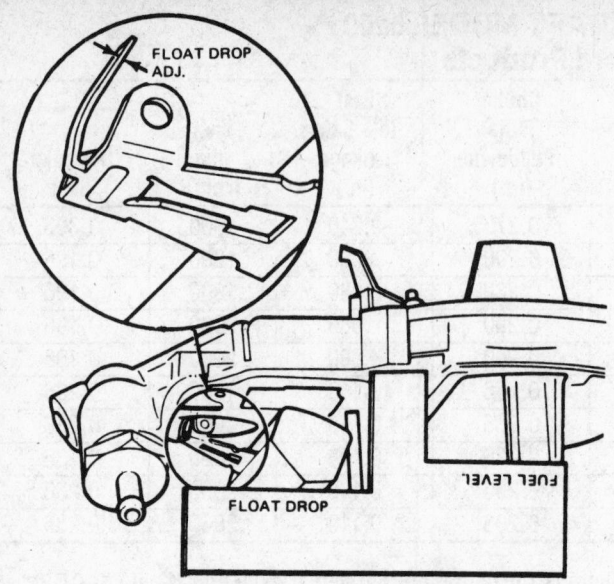

7200 VV float drop adjustment

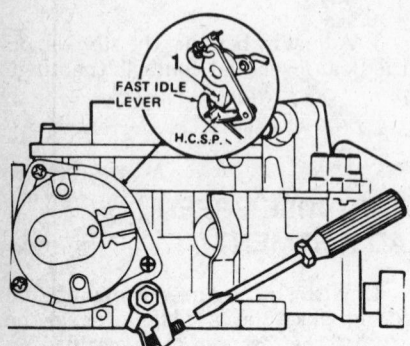

7200 VV fast idle speed adjustment

FAST IDLE CAM ADJUSTMENT

Special tool needed for this job; Ford calls it a stator cap (No. T77L–9848–A). It fits over the choke thermostatic lever when the choke cap is removed.

1. Remove the choke coil cap. The top rivets will have to be drilled out; the bottom rivet will have to be driven out from the rear. New rivets must be used upon installation.

2. Place the fast idle lever in the corner of the specified step of the fast idle cam (the highest step is first) with the high speed cam positioner retracted.

3. If the adjustment is being made with the carburetor removed, hold the throttle lightly closed with a rubber band.

4. Turn the stator cap clockwise until the lever contacts the fast idle cam adjusting screw.

5. Turn the fast idle cam adjusting screw until the index mark on the cap lines up with the specified mark on the casting.

6. Remove the stator cap. Install the choke coil cap and set to the specified housing mark.

COLD ENRICHMENT METERING ROD ADJUSTMENT

A dial indicator and the stator cap are required for this adjustment.

1. Remove the choke coil cap. The top rivets will have to be drilled out; the bottom rivet will have to be driven out from the rear. New rivets must be used upon installation.

2. Attach a weight to the choke coil mechanism to seat the cold enrichment rod.

3. Install and zero a dial indicator with the tip on top of the enrichment rod. Raise and release the weight to verify zero on the dial indicator.

4. With the stator cap at the index

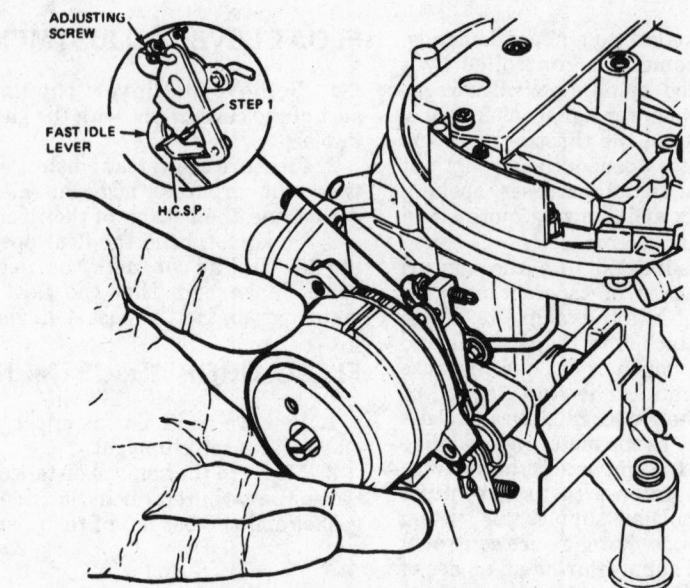

7200 VV fast idle cam adjustment

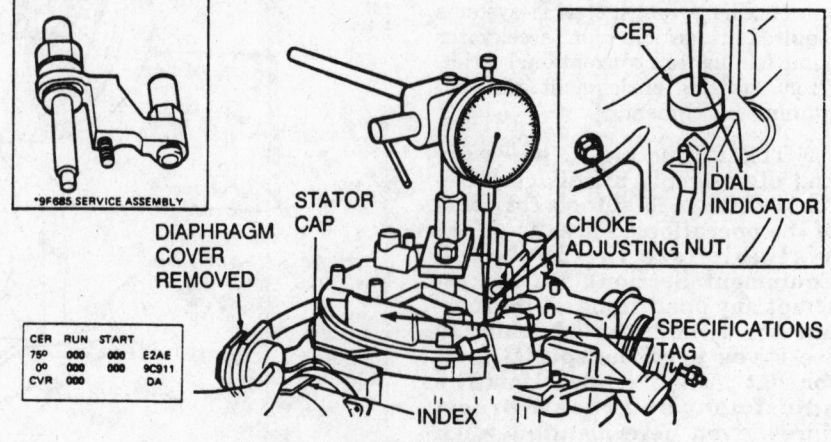

7200—Cold enrichment rod adjustment

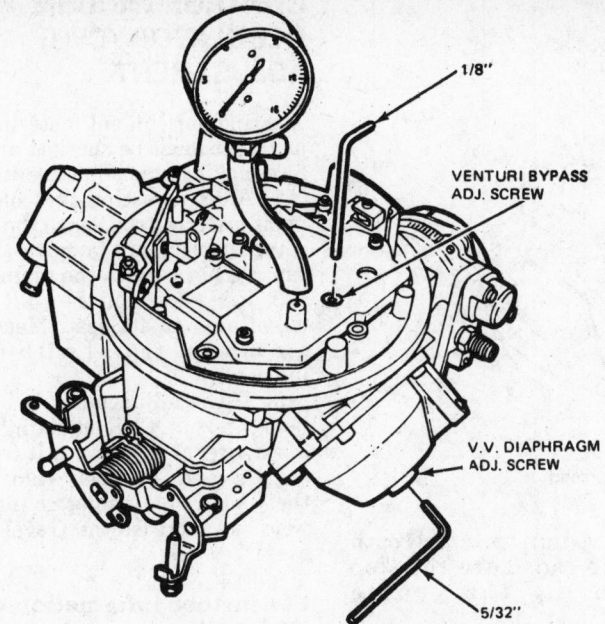

7200 VV control vacuum adjustment

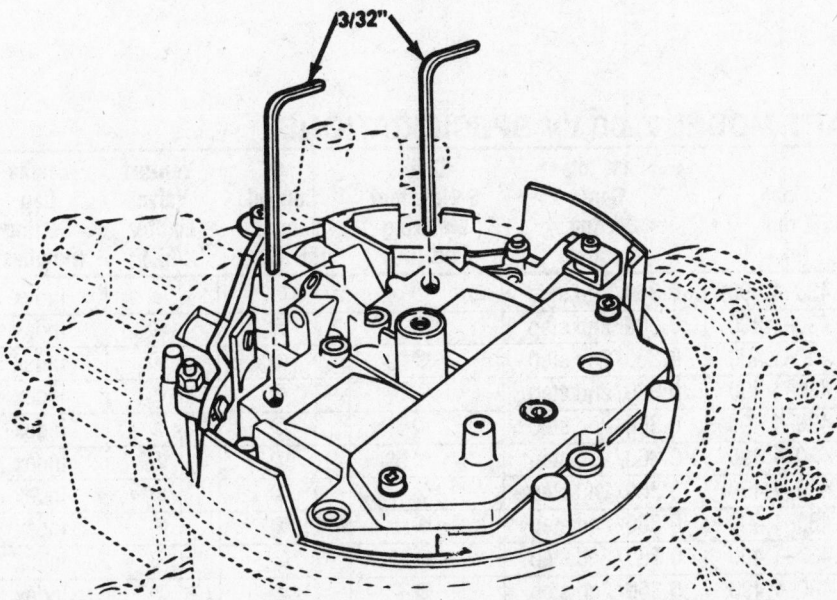

7200 VV idle mixture adjustment

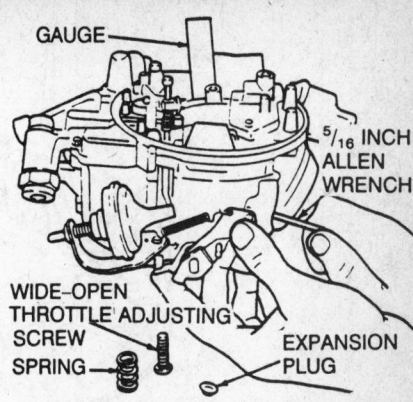

7200–Wide open throttle limiter adjustment

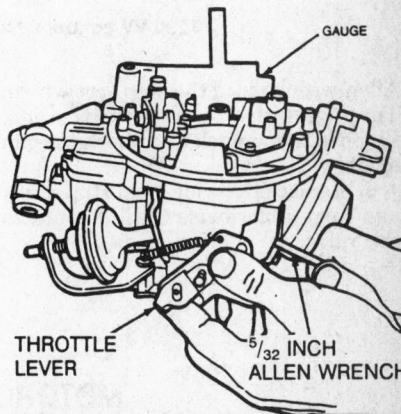

7200–Wide open throttle maximum opening

position, the dial indicator should read the specified dimension on the specification tag. If needed, turn the adjusting nut to correct.

5. Install the choke cap at the correct setting.

CONTROL VACUUM ADJUSTMENT

1982 Only

This adjustment is necessary only on non-feedback systems.

1. Remove the carburetor. Remove the venturi valve diaphragm plug with a centerpunch.

2. If the carburetor has a venturi valve bypass plug, remove it by removing the 2 cover retaining screws; invert and remove the bypass screw plug venturi valve bypass and diaphragm plugs.

VENTURI VALVE LIMITER ADJUSTMENT

1. Remove the carburetor. Take off

the venturi valve cover and the 2 rollers.

2. Use a center punch to loosen the expansion plug at the rear of the carburetor main body on the throttle side. from the cover with a drift. Install the cover.

3. Install the carburetor. Start the engine and allow it to reach normal operating temperature. Connect a vacuum gauge to the venturi valve cover. Set the idle speed to 500 rpm with the transmission in Drive.

4. Push and hold the venturi valve closed. Adjust the bypass screw to obtain a reading of 8 in. H_2O on the vacuum gauge. Make sure the idle speed remains constant. Open and close the throttle and check the idle speed.

5. With the engine idling, adjust the venturi valve diaphragm screw to obtain a reading of 6 in. H_2O. Set the curb idle to specification. Install new Remove it.

3. Use an Allen wrench to remove the venturi valve wide open stop screw.

4. Hold the throttle wide open.

5. Apply a light closing pressure on the venturi valve and check the gap between the valve and the air horn wall. To adjust, move the venturi valve to the wide open position and insert an

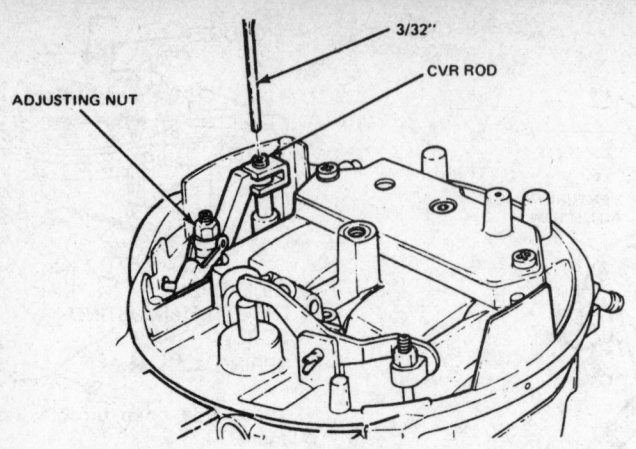

3/32''

CVR ROD

ADJUSTING NUT

7200 VV control vacuum regulator adjustment

CONTROL VACUUM REGULATOR (CVR) ADJUSTMENT

The cold enrichment metering rod adjustment must be checked and set before making this adjustment.

1. After adjusting the cold enrichment metering rod, leave the dial indicator in place but remove the stator cap. Do not re-zero the dial indicator.

2. Press down on the CVR rod until it bottoms on its seat. Measure this amount of travel with the dial indicator.

3. If the adjustment is incorrect, hold the ⅜ in. CVR adjusting nut with a box wrench to prevent it from turning. Use a $\frac{3}{32}$ in. Allen wrench to turn the CVR rod; turning counter-clockwise will increase the travel and vice versa.

For further information on feedback carburetors, please refer to *Chilton's Guide To Fuel Injection And Feedback Carburetors.*

Allen wrench into the stop screw hole. Turn clockwise to increase the gap. Remove the wrench and check the gap again.

6. Replace the wide open stop screw and turn it clockwise until it contacts the valve.

7. Push the venturi valve wide open and check the gap. Turn the stop screw to bring the gap to specifications.

8. Reassemble the carburetor with a new expansion plug.

MOTORCRAFT MODEL 7200 VV SPECIFICATIONS

Year	Model	Float Level (in.)	Float Drop (in.)	Fast Idle Cam Setting (notches)	Cold Enrichment Metering Rod (in.)	Control Vacuum (in. H₂O)	Venturi Valve Limiter (in.)	Choke Cap Setting (notches)
'82	E2AE-LB	1.010–1.070	1.430–1.490	0.360/2nd step	⑦	②	⑧	Index
	E2DE-NA	1.010–1.070	1.430–1.490	0.360/2nd step	⑦	②	⑧	Index
	E2AE-LC	1.010–1.070	1.430–1.490	0.360/2nd step	⑦	②	⑧	Index
	E25E-FA	1.010–1.070	1.430–1.490	0.360/2nd step	⑦	②	⑧	Index
	E25E-GB	1.010–1.070	1.430–1.490	0.360/2nd step	⑧	②	⑨	Index
	E2SE-GA	1.010–1.070	1.430–1.490	0.360/2nd step	⑦	②	⑧	Index
	E2AE-RA	1.010–1.070	1.430–1.490	0.360/2nd step	⑨	②	⑧	Index
	E1AE-ACA	1.010–1.070	1.430–1.490	0.360/2nd step	⑨	②	⑧	Index
	E2SE-DB	1.010–1.070	1.430–1.490	0.360/2nd step	⑩	②	⑧	Index
	E2SE-DA	1.010–1.070	1.430–1.490	0.360/2nd step	⑩	②	⑧	Index
	E1AE-SA	1.010–1.070	1.430–1.490	0.360/2nd step	⑪	②	⑫	1 Rich
	E2AE-MA	1.010–1.070	1.430–1.490	0.360/2nd step	⑪	②	⑫	1 Rich
	E2AE-MB	1.010–1.070	1.430–1.490	0.360/2nd step	⑪	②	⑫	1 Rich
	E2AE-TA	1.010–1.070	1.430–1.490	0.360/2nd step	⑪	②	⑫	Index
	E2AE-TB	1.010–1.070	1.430–1.490	0.360/2nd step	⑪	②	⑫	Index
	E25E-AC	1.010–1.070	1.430–1.490	0.360/2nd step	⑩	②	⑧	Index
	E1AE-AGA	1.010–1.070	1.430–1.490	0.360/2nd step	⑪	②	⑧	Index
	E2AE-NA	1.010–1.070	1.430–1.490	0.360/2nd step	⑪	②	⑧	Index
'83	E2AE-NA	1.010–1.070	1.430–1.490	0.360/2nd step	⑪	②	⑧	Index
	E2AE-AJA	1.010–1.070	1.430–1.490	0.360/2nd step	⑪	②	⑧	Index
	E2AE-APA	1.010–1.070	1.430–1.490	0.360/2nd step	⑪	②	⑧	Index
'84–'86	E2AE-AJA	1.010–1.070	1.430–1.490	0.360/2nd step	⑪	②	⑧	Index
	E2AE-APA	1.010–1.070	1.430–1.490	0.360/2nd step	⑪	②	⑧	Index

MOTORCRAFT MODEL 7200 VV SPECIFICATIONS

Year	Model	Float Level (in.)	Float Drop (in.)	Fast Idle Cam Setting (notches)	Cold Enrichment Metering Rod (in.)	Control Vacuum (in. H₂0)	Venturi Valve Limiter (in.)	Choke Cap Setting (notches)
'87	E2AE-AJA	1.010–1.070	1.430–1.490	0.360/2nd step	⑫	②	⑧	Index
	E2AE-APA	1.010–1.070	1.430–1.490	0.360/2nd step	⑫	②	⑧	Index
'88–'89	E7AE-AA	1.010–1.070	1.430–1.490	0.360/2nd step	⑫	②	⑧	Index
	E8AE-AA	1.010–1.070	1.430–1.490	0.360/2nd step	⑫	②	⑧	Index

① Not used
② See text
③ Opening gap: 0.99–1.01
   Closing gap: 0.39–0.41
④ Maximum opening: .99/1.01
   Wide open on throttle: .94/.98
⑤ Maximum opening: .99/1.01
   Wide open on throttle: .74/.76
⑥ 0°F—0.490 @ starting position
   75°F—0.475 @ starting position
⑦ 0°F—0.525 @ starting position
   75°F—0.445 @ starting position

⑧ Maximum opening: .99/1.01
   Wide open on throttle: .39/.41
⑨ 0°F—0.490 @ starting position
   75°F—0.445 @ starting position
⑩ 0°F—0.525 @ starting position
   75°F—0.475 @ starting position
⑪ 0°F—0.490 @ starting position
   75°F—0.460 @ starting position
⑫ Maximum opening: .99/1.01
   Wide open on throttle: .74/.76
⑬ Maximum opening: .99/1.01
   Wide open on throttle: .48/.52

HOLLEY CARBURETORS

Model 1945

The model 1945 carburetor is a concentric downdraft single barrel carburetor with an internal float bowl which completely surrounds the venturi. The unit uses dual nitrophyl floats which permit operation at extreme angles. It is used on Chrysler Corporation 6 cylinder engines.

FLOAT ADJUSTMENT

1. Remove the float bowl cover and invert the bowl. Hold the retaining spring in place.
2. Place a straight-edge across the surface of the bowl. The gasket should be in place. The straight-edge should just clear the toes of the floats by the specified measurement.
3. If the adjustment is necessary, bend the float tang to obtain the correct adjustment.

FAST IDLE ADJUSTMENT

1. Remove the air cleaner and disconnect the vacuum lines to the heated air control and the OSAC (Orifice Spark Advance Control) valve. If there is no OSAC valve, disconnect the hose to the distributor and the EGR hose. Cap all carburetor vacuum fittings.
2. With the engine off, transmission in Neutral and the parking brake set, open the throttle and close the choke.

3. Close the throttle. This will place the fast idle speed screw on the highest step.
4. Move the fast idle cam until the screw drops to the **SECOND HIGHEST** speed step.
5. Start the engine and stabilize the engine speed. Rotate the fast idle speed screw to obtain the specified setting. See Specifications Chart.

FAST IDLE CAM ADJUSTMENT

1. Place the fast idle speed adjusting screw on the **SECOND HIGHEST** step of the fast idle cam.
2. Place light pressure on the choke shaft lever to move the choke valve towards the close position.
3. Insert the specified gauge between the top of the choke and the air horn wall at the throttle lever side.
4. To adjust bend the fast idle connector rod at angle until the correct valve opening is obtained.

CHOKE UNLOADER ADJUSTMENT

1. Hold the throttle valves wide-open and insert the specified gauge between the upper edge of the choke valve and the inner wall of the air horn.
2. Place slight pressure against the control lever and attempt to remove the gauge. There should be a slight drag as the gauge is being withdrawn. If adjustment is necessary, bend the unloader tang on the throttle lever un-

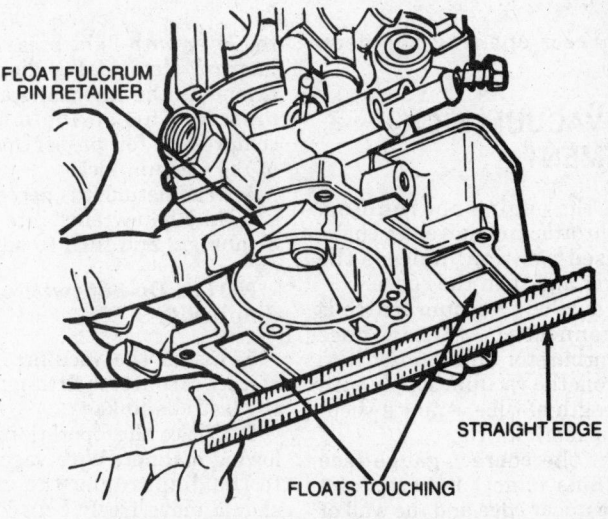

FLOAT FULCRUM PIN RETAINER

STRAIGHT EDGE

FLOATS TOUCHING

Checking the float adjustment—Holley 1945

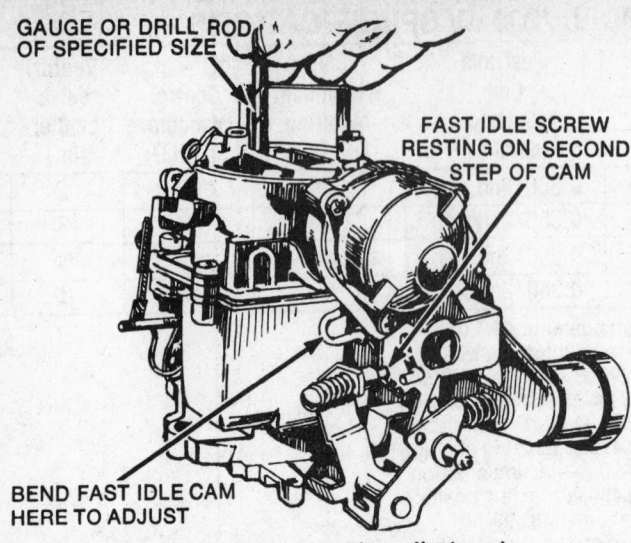

GAUGE OR DRILL ROD OF SPECIFIED SIZE

FAST IDLE SCREW RESTING ON SECOND STEP OF CAM

BEND FAST IDLE CAM HERE TO ADJUST

Fast idle cam position adjustment

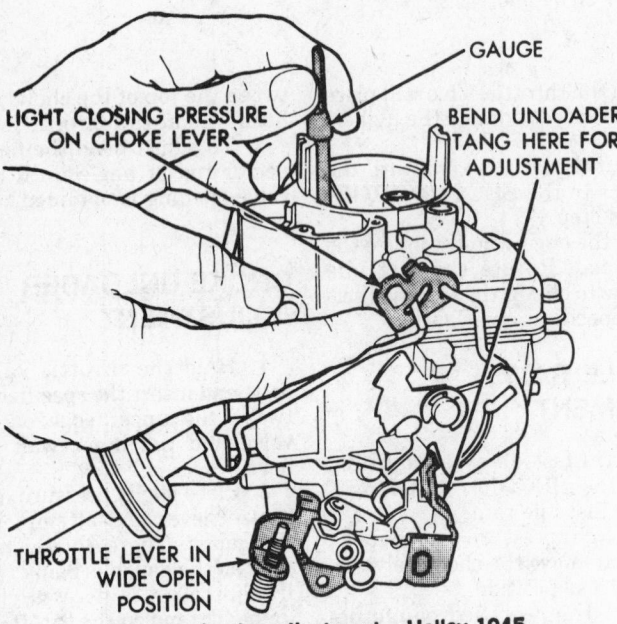

GAUGE

LIGHT CLOSING PRESSURE ON CHOKE LEVER

BEND UNLOADER TANG HERE FOR ADJUSTMENT

THROTTLE LEVER IN WIDE OPEN POSITION

Choke unloader adjustment—Holley 1945

til the correct opening has been obtained.

CHOKE VACUUM KICK ADJUSTMENT

1. With the engine not running, open the throttle and move the choke to the closed position. Release the throttle first and then the choke.

2. If an auxiliary vacuum source is used, disconnect the vacuum hose from the carburetor and connect it to the hose from the vacuum supply with an extra length of tube. Apply a vacuum of 15 or more in. Hg.

3. Insert the correct gauge (see Specifications chart) between the choke valve upper edge and the wall of the air horn. Close and hold the choke

rod lever with light pressure. The cylindrical stem of the diaphragm will extend as the internal spring is compressed. This spring must be fully compressed for proper measurement of the vacuum kick.

4. If adjustment is necessary, insert a $5/64$ in. Allen wrench into the vacuum diaphragm and turn to adjust.

NOTE: Do not twist or bend the diaphragm.

5. Install the vacuum hose on the correct carburetor fitting and connect the fast idle linkage.

6. Check the operation in the following manner. With vacuum applied to the diaphragm, the choke valve should move freely between the open and closed positions. If there is binding, examine the linkage for misalignment or interference caused by bending.

ACCELERATOR PUMP ADJUSTMENT

1. With the throttle in the curb idle position, measure the distance between the pump link pivot and the link connection to the throttle lever.

2. If the measurement is incorrect, the link may be bent at the "U" to adjust.

NOTE: If the pump link is adjusted, the "Bowl Vent Adjustment" must be checked and if necessary, reset.

BOWL VENT ADJUSTMENT

1. With the throttle set at curb idle speed, measure the distance from the cover support surface down to the flat on the bowl vent leer.

2. If adjustment is necessary, turn the bowl vent lever adjusting screw with a screwdriver.

3. Install the bowl vent spring and cover plate.

Model 1946

This unit is a 1–barrel, altitude compensating model used on Fairmont, Fairmont Futura, Zephyr, Mustang and Capri cars with the 200 cu. in., 6 cylinder engine and the 1982 Thunderbird, XR-7, Granada and Cougar cars with the 200 cu. in. 6 cylinder engine and automatic transmission.

FAST IDLE CAM POSITION ADJUSTMENT

1. Position the fast idle adjusting screw on the **SECOND HIGHEST** step of the fast idle cam.

2. Lightly move the choke plate toward the closed position.

3. Check the fast idle cam setting by placing the correct gauge (see specifications) between the upper edge of the choke plate and the air horn wall.

4. If the setting is not as specified, bend the fast idle cam link.

FAST IDLE ADJUSTMENT

1. Remove the spark delay valve, if so equipped and route the distributor vacuum hose directly to the advance side of the distributor.

2. Trace the EGR signal vacuum hose from the EGR valve to the carburetor, If an EGR/PVS valve or cold weather modulator is located in the hose, disconnect the EGR hose at the EGR valve and plug the hose. If not

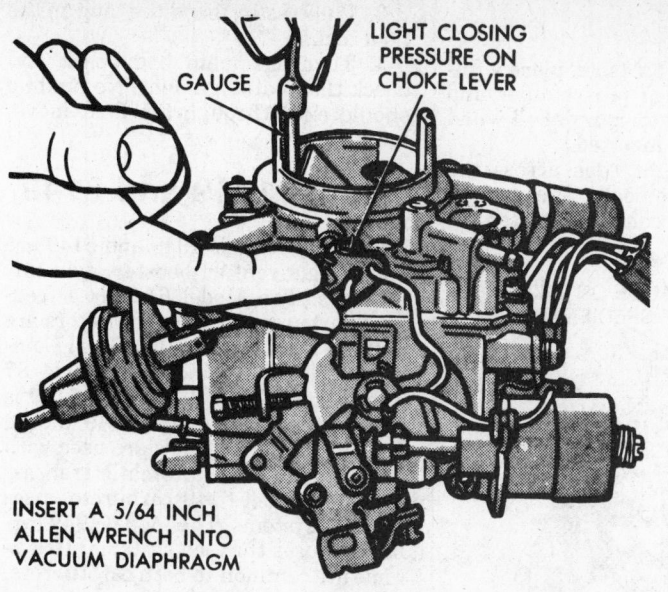

Choke vacuum kick adjustment, 1982—Holley 1945

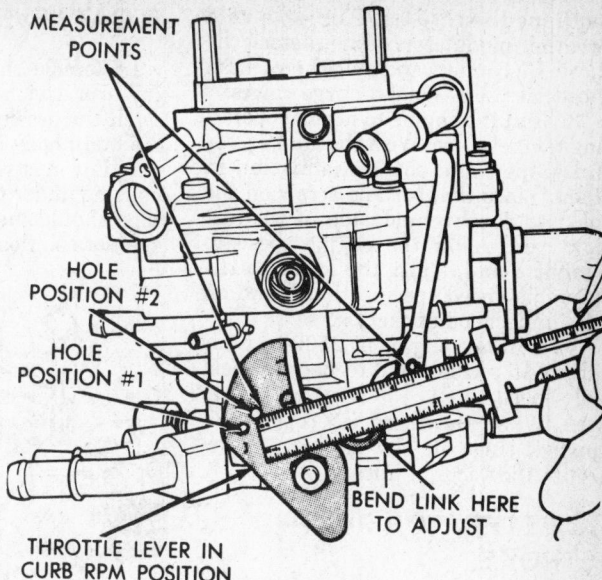

Accelerator pump adjustment

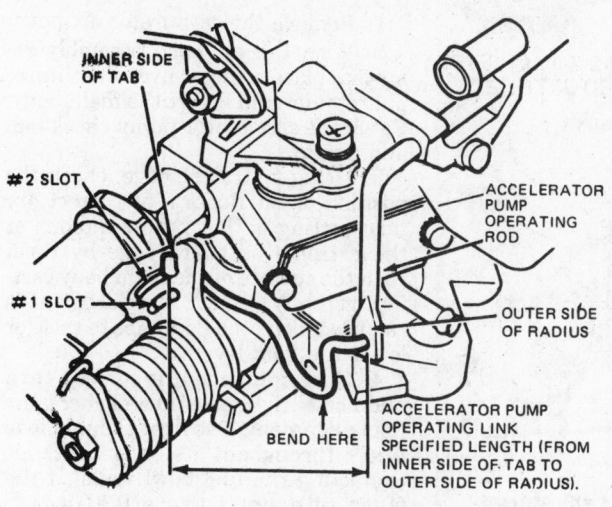

Accelerator pump adjustment

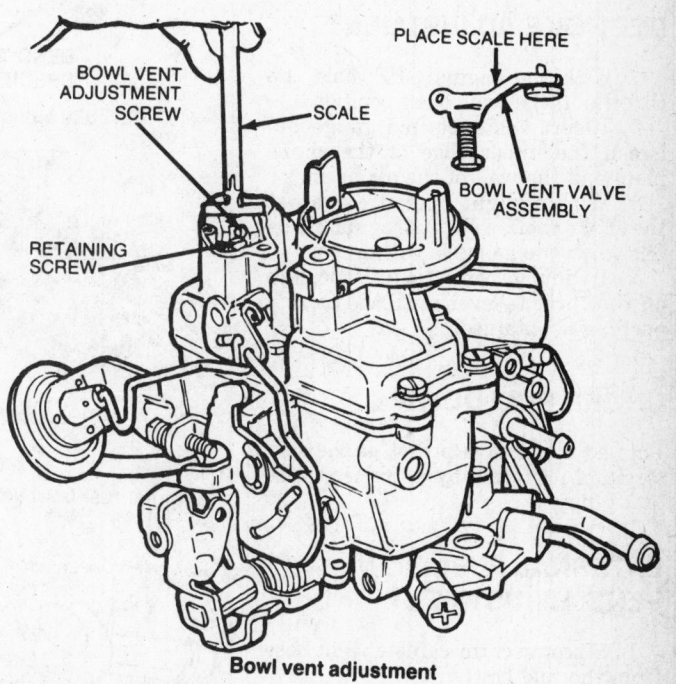

Bowl vent adjustment

HOLLEY MODEL 1945
Chrysler Corporation

Year	Carb. Part No. ①	Float Level (in.)	Accelerator Pump Adjustment (in.)	Bowl Vent Clearance (in.)	Fast Idle (rpm)	Choke Unloader Clearance (in.)	Vacuum Kick (in.)	Fast Idle Cam Position (in.)	Choke
'82	R-9627A	③	1.615 ②	—	1600	.250	.150	.090	Fixed
	R-9628A	③	1.615 ②	—	1800	.250	.150	.090	Fixed

① Located on a tag attached to the carburetor.
② Position #2
③ Flush with the top of the main body casting to 0.050″ above

equipped with EGR/PVS or a cold weather modulator, do not detach the hose. Disconnect and plug the vacuum hoses at the EGR and purge valves.

3. Run the engine to normal operating temperature. With the choke plate fully open and the transmission in Park, place the fast idle screw on the next to the **highest** step of the fast idle cam. Allow the engine speed to stabilize and adjust the speed to the fast idle speed specification found on the underhood sticker.

4. Run the engine at 2500 rpm for about 15 seconds and recheck the fast idle speed.

5. When the speed is properly adjusted, turn off the engine and reroute the vacuum lines.

ACCELERATOR PUMP STROKE

The accelerator pump stroke is preset at the factory and should not be adjusted to improve driveability.

DECHOKE ADJUSTMENT

1. With the engine OFF, hold the throttle in the wide open position.

2. Insert the specified gauge between the upper edge of the choke plate and the wall of the air horn.

3. With a slight pressure against the choke shaft, a slight drag should be felt when the gauge is withdrawn.

4. To adjust, bend the unloader tab on the throttle lever until the correct opening is obtained.

CHOKE PULLDOWN

This adjustment is preset at the factory and protected by a tamper resistant plug.

EXTERNAL FUEL BOWL VENT ADJUSTMENT

1. Disconnect the canister vent hose from the fuel bowl vent.

2. Attach a hand operated vacuum pump to the vent tube using a 3/8 in. adapter.

3. Remove the vent cover and gasket and vent spring.

4. The adjusting screw is located on the nylon arm. Turn it clockwise until no more than 1/8 in. of threads is visible above the vent arm.

5. Operate the hand vacuum pump and turn the screw 1/8 turn at a time counterclockwise, until vacuum is registered on the gauge. Release the vacuum and turn the screw 1/2 turn clockwise. Disconnect the pump and replace the vent cover.

FLOAT LEVEL

1. Remove the air horn, place a finger over the hinge pin retainer and catch the accelerator pump ball when the main body is inverted.

2. Lay a straight edge across the housing under the floats. The straight edge should just contact the step (or heel) of the float.

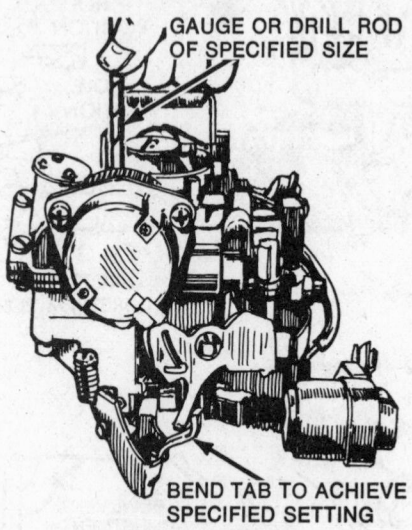

GAUGE OR DRILL ROD OF SPECIFIED SIZE

BEND TAB TO ACHIEVE SPECIFIED SETTING

Dechoke adjustment

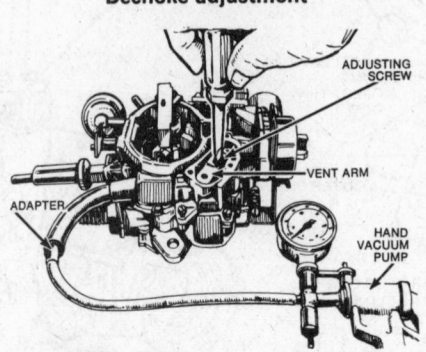

ADJUSTING SCREW

VENT ARM

ADAPTER

HAND VACUUM PUMP

External fuel bowl vent adjustment

3. If necessary, bend the tang on the float arm.

4. Turn the main body back and check the float alignment. No binding should exist through the float movement range.

Model 1949 and 6149

The Holley Models 1949 and 6149 are both single venturi booster style carburetors. The Model 6149 is a feedback carburetor. Both carburetors are used on the 2.3 liter High Swirl Combustion (HSC) engine, in the 1984–87 Tempo and Topaz. The Model 6149 is used in the USA and the 1949 is used in Canada. Both models are used with either manual or automatic transaxles. The Model 6149 carburetor uses 12 basic systems. The Model 1949 carburetor uses thirteen systems. 10 systems are common to both carburetors.

DRY FLOAT LEVEL ADJUSTMENT

1. Remove the carburetor air horn.

2. With the air horn assembly removed, place a finger over float hinge pin retainer and invert the main body. Catch the accelerator pump check ball and weight.

3. Using a straight edge, check the position of the floats. The correct dry float setting is that both pontoons at the extreme outboard edge by flush with the surface of the main body casting (without gasket). If adjustment is required, bend the float tabs to raise or lower the float level.

4. Once adjustment is correct, turn main body right side up and check the float alignment. The float should move freely throughout its range without contacting the fuel bowl walls. If the float pontoons are misaligned,

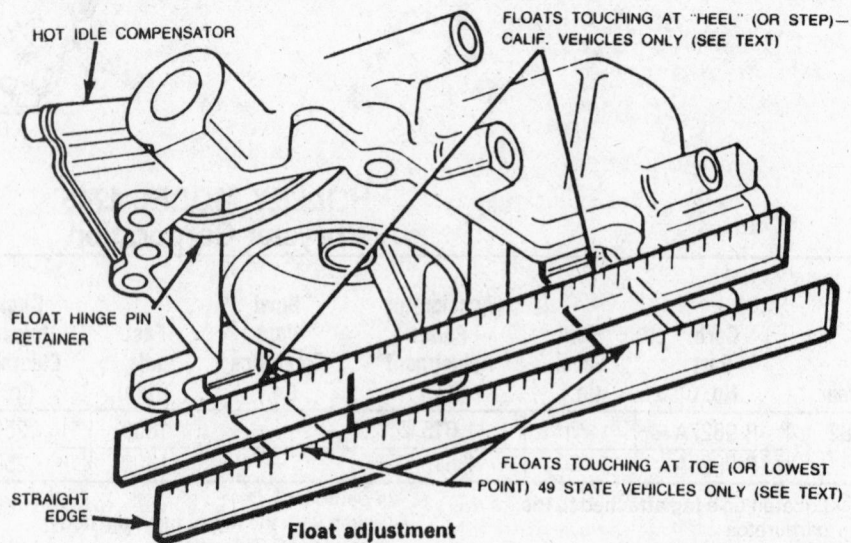

HOT IDLE COMPENSATOR

FLOATS TOUCHING AT "HEEL" (OR STEP)— CALIF. VEHICLES ONLY (SEE TEXT)

FLOAT HINGE PIN RETAINER

FLOATS TOUCHING AT TOE (OR LOWEST POINT) 49 STATE VEHICLES ONLY (SEE TEXT)

STRAIGHT EDGE

Float adjustment

HOLLEY MODEL 1946
Ford Motor Co.

Year	Part Number	Float Level (in.)	Choke Pulldown (in.)	Dechoke (in.)	Fast Idle Cam (in.)	Accelerator Pump Stroke Slot
'82	EIBE-AGA	.69	.120	.150	.086	#2
	E2BE-CA	.69	.110	.150	.078	#2
	E2BE-BA	.69	.110	.150	.078	#2
	E2BE-JA	.69	.110	.150	.078	#2
	E2BE-HA	.69	.110	.150	.078	#2
	E2BE-TA	.69	.110	.150	.078	#2
	E2BE-SA	.69	.110	.150	.078	#2
'83	E2BE-CA	.69	.110	.150	.078	#2
	E2BE-BA	.69	.110	.150	.078	#2
	E2BE-TA	.69	.110	.150	.078	#2
	E2BE-SA	.69	.110	.150	.078	#2
	E3SE-CA	.69	.105	.150	.078	#2
	E3SE-DA	.69	.105	.150	.078	#2
	E3SE-AA	.69	.095	.150	.078	#2
	E3SE-BA	.69	.095	.150	.078	#2

straighten them by bending the float arms. Recheck the float level adjustment.

5. During assembly, insert the check ball first and then the weight.

AUXILIARY MAIN JET/ PULLOVER VALVE ADJUSTMENT

The length of the auxiliary main jet/pullover valve adjustment screw which protrudes through the back side (side opposite the adjustment screw head) of the throttle pick-up lever must be 0.345 ± 0.010 in. (8.76mm). To adjust, turn screw in or out as required.

MECHANICAL FUEL BOWL VENT ADJUSTMENT (LEVER CLEARANCE)

Off Vehicle Adjustment

1. Secure the choke plate in the wide-open position.
2. Set the throttle at the TSP Off position.
3. Turn the TSP Off idle adjustment screw counterclockwise until the throttle plate is closed in the throttle bore.
4. Fuel bowl vent clearance: Dimension A should be within 0.120 ± 0.010 in. (3.05mm).
5. If the adjustment is out of specification, bend the bowl vent actuator lever at the adjustment point to obtain the required clearance.

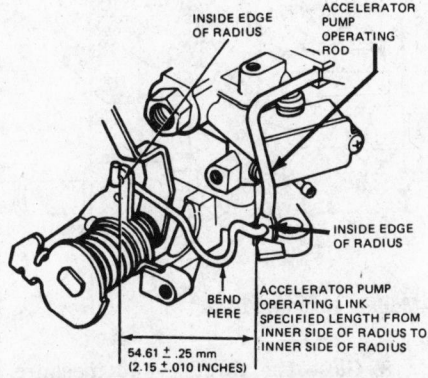

Auxiliary main jet/Pullover valve (timing adjustment)—Models 1949 and 6149

NOTE: Do not bend the fuel bowl vent arm and/or adjacent portion of the actuator lever. TSP Off rpm must be set after the carburetor installation.

On Vehicle Adjustment

NOTE: This adjustment must be performed after the curb idle speed has been set to the specification.

1. Secure the choke plate in the wide open position.
2. Turn the ignition key to the On position to activate the TSP (engine not running). Open the throttle so that the TSP plunger extends.
3. Verify that the throttle is in the idle set position (contacting the TSP plunger). Measure the clearance of the fuel bowl vent arm to the bowl vent actuating lever.

4. Fuel bowl vent clearance: Dimension A should be within 0.020–0.040 in.

NOTE: There is a difference in the on vehicle and off vehicle specification.

5. If the dimension is out of specification, bend the bowl vent actuator lever at the adjustment point to obtain the required clearance.

NOTE: Do not bend the fuel bowl vent arm and/or adjacent portion of the actuating lever.

ACCELERATOR PUMP STROKE ADJUSTMENT

1. Check the length of the accelerator pump operating link from its inside edge at the accelerator pump operating rod to its inside edge at the throttle lever hole. The dimension should be 2.15 ± .010 in. (54.61 ± .25 mm).
2. Adjust to the proper length by bending the loop in the operating link.

CHOKE PLATE PULLDOWN ADJUSTMENT

NOTE: This adjustment is preset at the factory and protected by a tamper resistant plug.

FAST IDLE CAM INDEX ADJUSTMENT

1. With the engine cool, position the

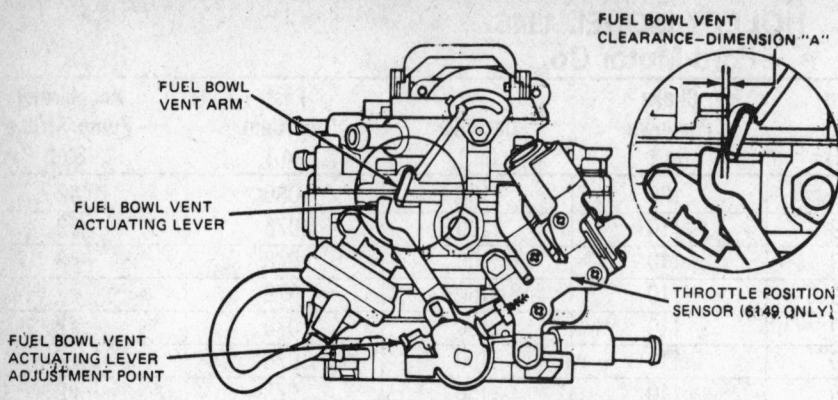

Mechanical fuel bowl vent adjustment—Models 1949 and 6149

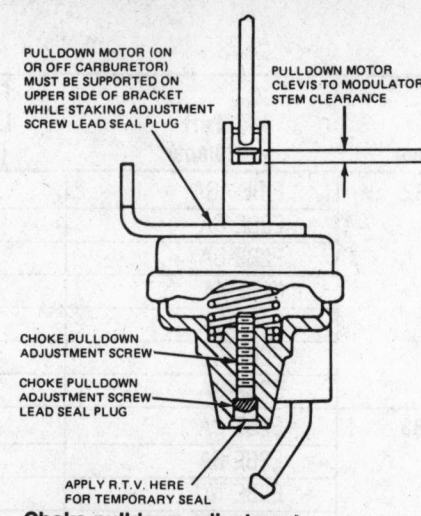

Choke pulldown adjustment—Models 1949 and 6149

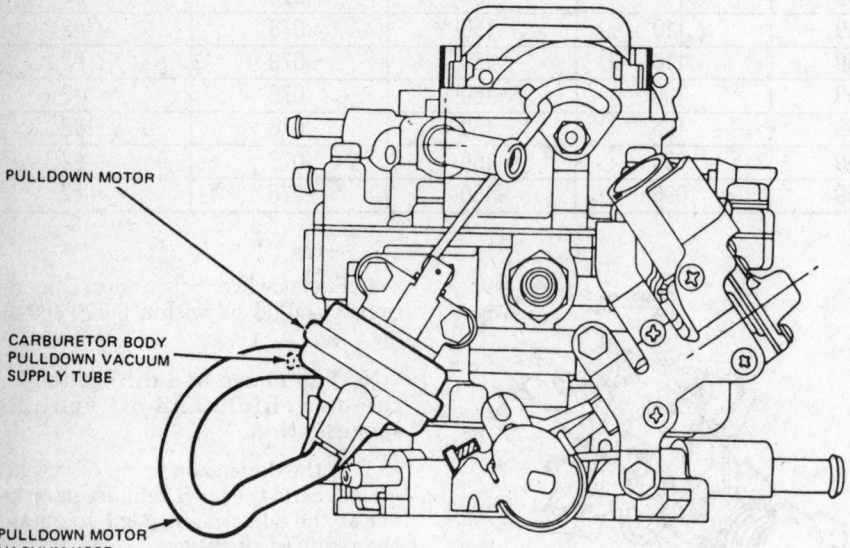

Choke plate pulldown motor—Models 1949 and 6149

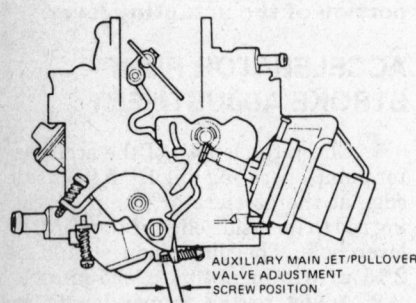

Accelerator pump stroke adjustment—Models 1949 and 6149

fast idle screw on the **high** step of the fast idle cam.

2. Activate the pulldown motor by applying an external vacuum source of 15–20 in. Hg.

3. Apply light pressure to the upper edge of the choke plate in the closing direction to remove clearance between the pulldown motor clevis and the modulator stem.

4. Open the throttle slightly and allow the fast idle cam to drop.

5. Close the throttle and measure the clearance between the top edge of the fast idle rpm adjusting screw and the shoulder of the fast idle cam **high** step (Dimension A is the fast idle cam index shown in the illustration). Refer to the specifications table.

6. Remove the light closing pressure from the upper edge of the choke plate.

7. Open the throttle to the wide open position and return slowly.

8. The fast idle adjustment screw must contact the lower end of the fast idle cam kickdown step by at least half of its diameter 4 carburetors with 4 step cams or must contact the **third** step by at least half of its diameter without contacting the second or fourth steps for carburetors with 5 step cams.

9. If Steps 5 and 8 are okay, the fast idle cam index is within specification. If adjustment is necessary, bend the fast idle cam link at the loop to obtain the correct specification at Dimension A (see the specifications table).

DECHOKE ADJUSTMENT

1. With the engine off and cool, hold the throttle in the wide open position.

2. Use a drill of the specified size and measure the clearance between the upper edge of the choke plate and the air horn wall.

3. With slight pressure against the choke shaft, a slight drag should be felt when the gauge is withdrawn.

4. To adjust, bend the tang on the throttle lever as required.

FEEDBACK SYSTEM DIAPHRAGM ADJUSTMENT
Model 6149

1. Remove the main system feedback diaphragm adjustment screw lead sealing disc from the air horn screw boss by drilling a $3/32$ in. diameter hole through the disc, then inserting a small punch to pry the disc out.

2. Turn the main system feedback adjustment screw as required to position the top of the screw 0.180 ± 0.010 in. (4.57mm) below the top of the air horn adjustment screw boss.

NOTE: For carburetors stamped with an "S" on the top of the air horn adjustment screw boss, adjust screw position to 0.250 ± 0.010 in. (6.35mm).

3. Install a new lead sealing disc and stake with a ¼ in. flat-ended punch.

4. Apply an external vacuum source (hand vacuum pump, 10 in. Hg maximum) and check for leaks, diaphragm should hold vacuum.

WOT A/C CUT-OFF SWITCH ADJUSTMENT
Model 1949

The WOT A/C cut-off switch is a

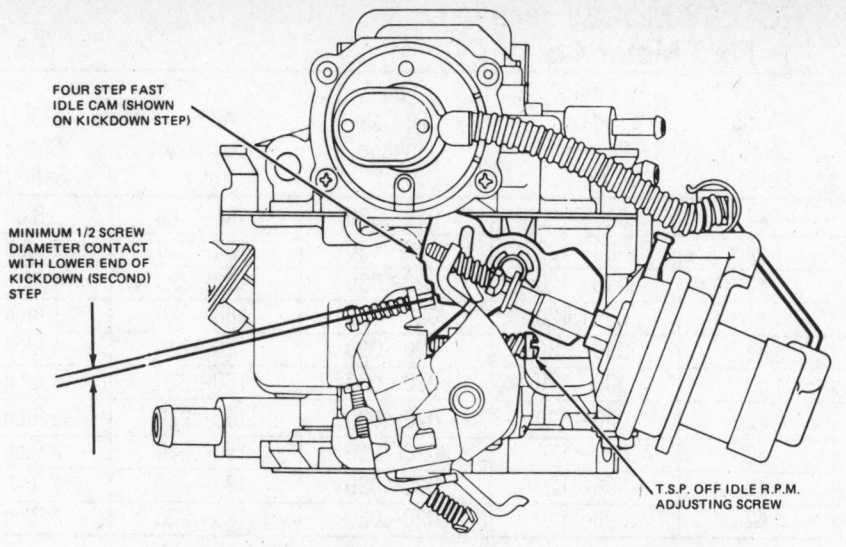

Fast idle cam index (four step idle cams)—Models 1949 and 6149

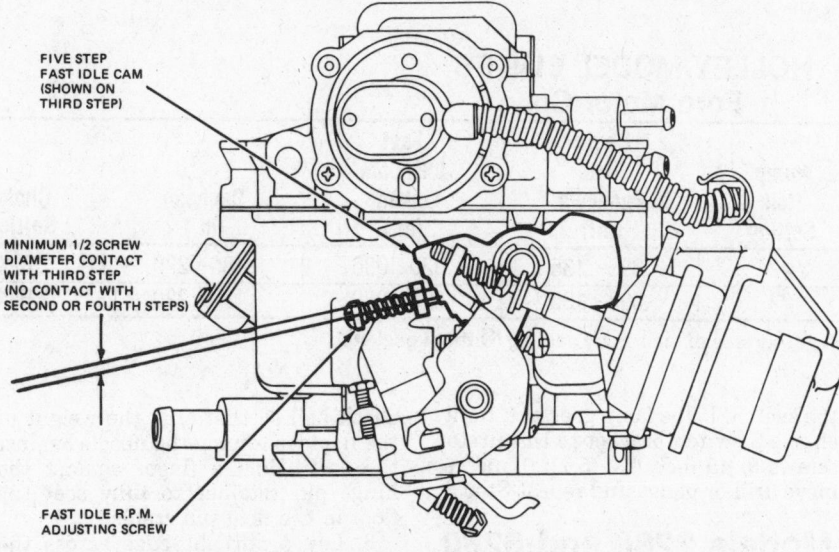

Fast idle cam index (five step cams)—Models 1949 and 6149

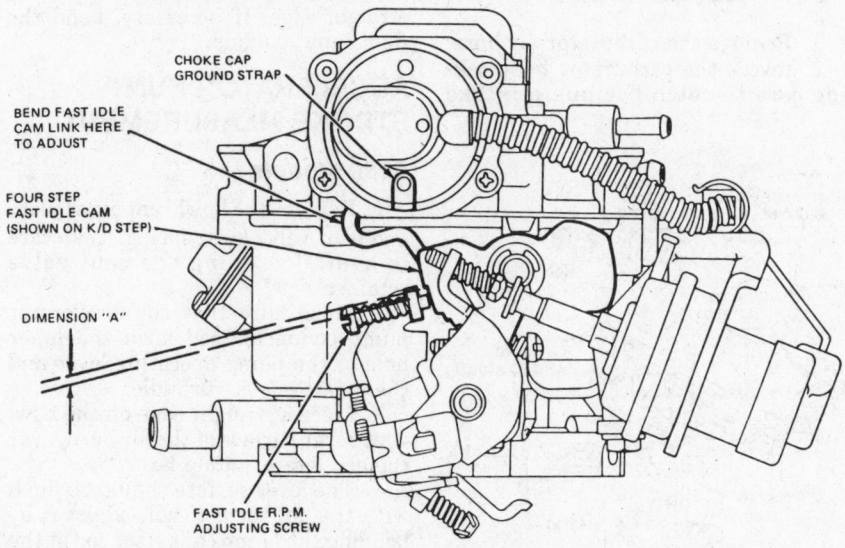

Fast idle cam index adjustment—Models 1949 and 6149

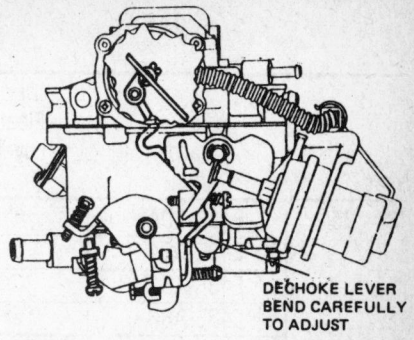

Dechoke adjustment—Models 1949 and 6149

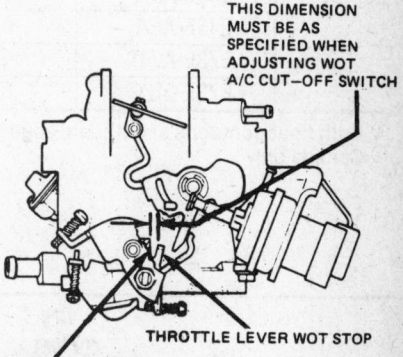

WOT A/C cut-off switch adjustment (clearance)—Model 1949

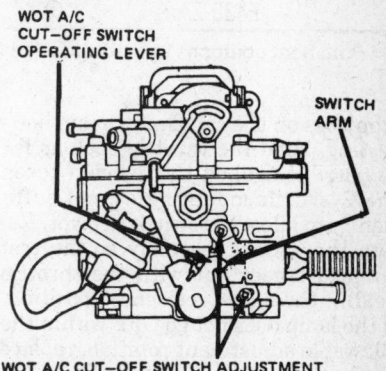

WOT A/C cut-off switch adjustment screws—Model 1949

normally closed switch (allowing current to flow at any throttle position other than wide-open throttle).

1. Disconnect the wiring harness at the switch connector.

2. Connect a 12 volt DC power supply and test lamp. With the throttle at curb idle, TSP off idle or fast idle position, the test light must be ON. If the test lamp does not light, replace the switch assembly.

3. Rotate the throttle to the wide-open position. The test lamp must go OFF, indicating an open circuit.

4. If the lamp remains ON, insert a 0.165 in. drill or gauge between the throttle lever WOT stop and the WOT

HOLLEY MODEL 1949
Ford Motor Co.

Year	Carb. Iden.	Dry Float Level (in.)	Pump Hole Setting	Choke Plate Pulldown (in.)	Fast Idle Cam Linkage (in.)	Dechoke (in.)	Choke Setting
'84–'85	E43E-ADA	①	#2	.080–.120	.020–.030	.180–.220	2 Rich
	E43E-AEA	①	#2	.080–.120	.020–.030	.180–.220	2 Rich
	E43E-ABA	①	#2	.090–.120	.020–.030	.180–.220	1 Rich
	E43E-ABB	①	#2	.090–.120	.020–.030	.180–.220	1 Rich
	E43E-ACA	①	#2	.090–.130	.020–.030	.180–.220	1 Rich
	E43E-ACB	①	#2	.090–.130	.020–.030	.180–.220	1 Rich
'86–'87	E43E-ADA	①	#2	.080–.120	.020–.030	.180–.220	2 Rich
	E43E-AEA	①	#2	.080–.120	.020–.030	.180–.220	2 Rich
	E73E-AV ②	①	#2	.090–.120	.020–.030	.180–.220	1 Rich
	E73E-BB ②	①	#2	.090–.120	.020–.030	.180–.220	1 Rich

① Both float pontoons at outboard edge flush with surface of main body casting (without gasket).
② Canada only

HOLLEY MODEL 6149-FB
Ford Motor Co.

Year	Carb. Iden.	Dry Float Level (in.)	Pump Hole Setting	Choke Plate Pulldown (in.)	Fast Idle Cam Linkage (in.)	Dechoke (in.)	Choke Setting
'84	E43E-VA	①	#2	.095–.135	.020–.030	.180–.220	2 Rich
	E43E-ZA	①	#2	.095–.135	.020–.030	.180–.220	2 Rich

① Both float pontoons at outboard edge flush with surface of main body casting (without gasket).

stop boss on the carburetor main body casting. Hold the throttle open as far as possible against the gauge. Loosen the 2 switch mounting screws sufficiently to allow the switch to pivot. Rotate the switch assembly so the test lamp just goes out with the throttle held in the above referenced position. If the lamp does not go OFF within the allowable adjustment rotation, replace the switch. If the lamp goes out, tighten the 2 switch bracket-to-carburetor screws to 45 inch lbs. (5 Nm) and remove drill or gauge and repeat Step 3.

Models 2280 and 6280
FLOAT ADJUSTMENT

1. Remove the carburetor air horn.
2. Invert the carburetor body taking care to catch the pump intake check ball so that only the weight of the floats is forcing the needle against the seat. Hold a finger against the hinge pin retainer to fully seat the float in the float pin cradle.
3. Lay a straight edge across the float bowl. The toe of each float should be as per specifications from the straight-edge. If necessary, bend the float tang to adjust.

ACCELERATOR PUMP STROKE MEASUREMENT

2280 Models

1. Remove the bowl vent cover plate and vent valve lever spring. Take care to avoid loosening the vent valve retainer.
2. Make sure that the accelerator pump connector rod is in the inner hole of the pump operating lever and the throttle is at curb idle.
3. Place a straight edge on the bowl vent cover surface of the air horn, over the accelerator pump lever.
4. The lever surface should be flush with the air horn. If not, adjust it by bending the pump connector rod at the 90 degree bend.

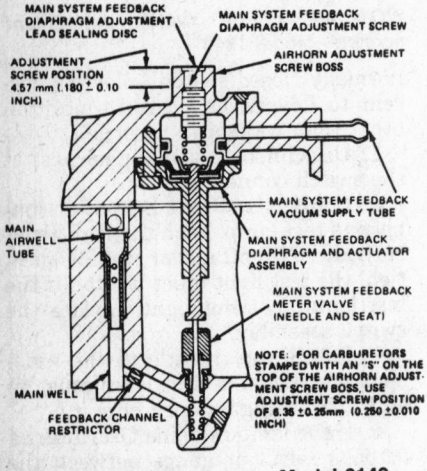

Diaphragm adjustment—Model 6149

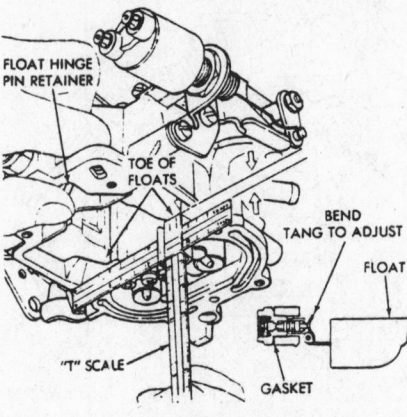

Float adjustment

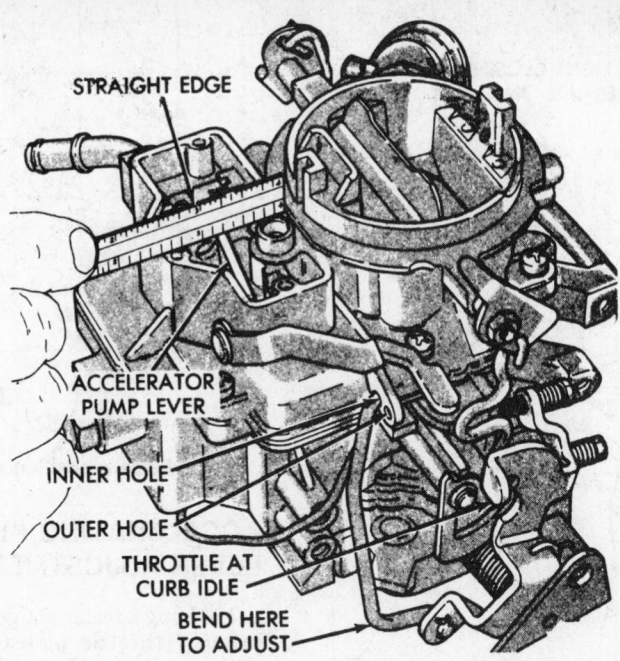

STRAIGHT EDGE

ACCELERATOR PUMP LEVER

INNER HOLE

OUTER HOLE

THROTTLE AT CURB IDLE

BEND HERE TO ADJUST

Accelerator pump stroke adjustment—model 2280

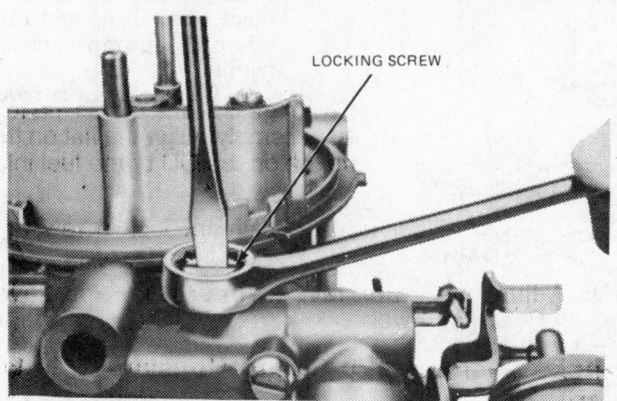

LOCKING SCREW

Fuel level adjustment—wet—Holley 4180C

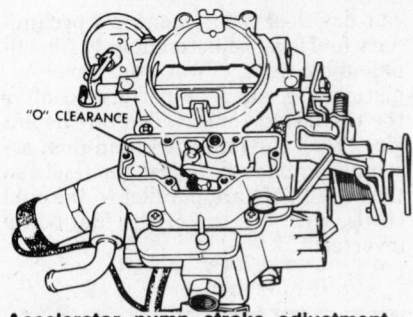

"O" CLEARANCE

Accelerator pump stroke adjustment—model 6280

NOTE: If this adjustment is changed, both the bowl vent and the mechanical power valve adjustments must be reset.

6280 Models

1. Remove the bowl vent cover plate and gasket.
2. With all pump links and levers installed, adjust the accelerator pump cap nut for zero clearance between the pump lever and the cap nut. Check that the wide open throttle can be reached without binding.
3. Install the gasket and the bowl vent cover plate.

CHOKE UNLOADER ADJUSTMENT

1. Hold the throttle valves in the wide open position.
2. Lightly press a finger against the control lever to move the choke valve toward the closed position.
3. Insert the specified gauge between the top of the choke valve and the air horn wall.
4. Adjust, if necessary, by bending the tang on the accelerator pump lever.

CHOKE VACUUM KICK ADJUSTMENT

1. Open the throttle, close the choke, then close the throttle to trap the fast idle cam at the closed choke position.
2. Disconnect the vacuum hose from the carburetor and connect it to an auxiliary vacuum source with a length of hose. Apply at least 15 in. Hg.
3. Completely compress the choke lever spring in the diaphragm stem without distorting the linkage.
4. Insert the specified gauge between the top of the choke valve and the air horn wall.
5. Adjust by bending the diaphragm link. Check for free movement. Replace the vacuum hose.

FAST IDLE CAM POSITION ADJUSTMENT

1. Position the adjusting screw on the **SECOND HIGHEST** step of the fast idle cam.
2. Move the choke towards the closed position with light finger pressure.
3. Insert the specified gauge between the choke valve and the air horn wall.
4. Adjust by opening or closing the U-bend in the fast idle connector link.

MECHANICAL POWER VALVE ADJUSTMENT

2280 Models Only

1. Remove the bowl vent cover plate, vent valve lever, spring and retainer. Remove the lever pivot pin.
2. Hold the throttle in the wide open position.
3. Using a $5/64$ in. Allen wrench, press the mechanical power valve adjustment screw down and release it to determine if clearance exists. Turn the screw clockwise until clear is zero.
4. Adjust by turning the screw 1 turn counterclockwise.
5. Install all parts.

Model 4180-C

The Holley 4180-C 4 bbl carburetor is a downdraft, 2-stage carburetor, It can be considered as 2 dual carburetors; the front half supplies an air/fuel mixture throughout the entire range of engine operation (primary stage) with the other functioning only when a greater quantity of air/fuel mixture is required (secondary stage).

The primary stage (front section of the carburetor contains a fuel bowl, metering block and an accelerating

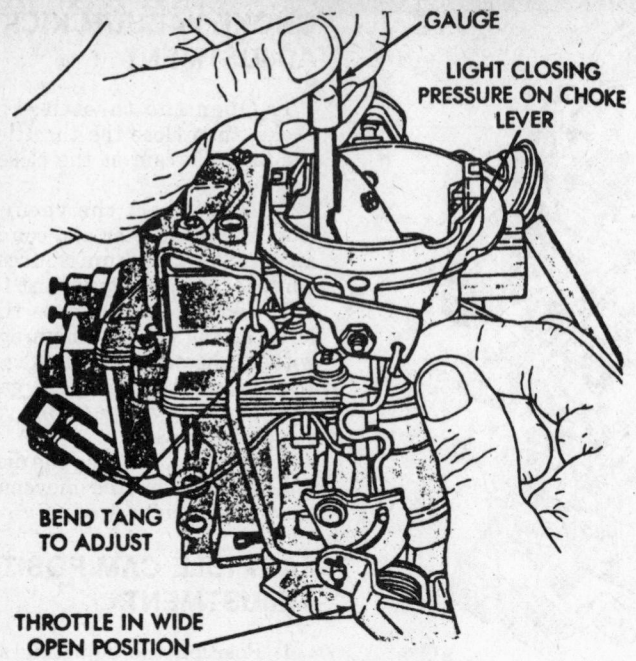

BEND TANG TO ADJUST

THROTTLE IN WIDE OPEN POSITION

GAUGE

LIGHT CLOSING PRESSURE ON CHOKE LEVER

Choke unloader adjustment

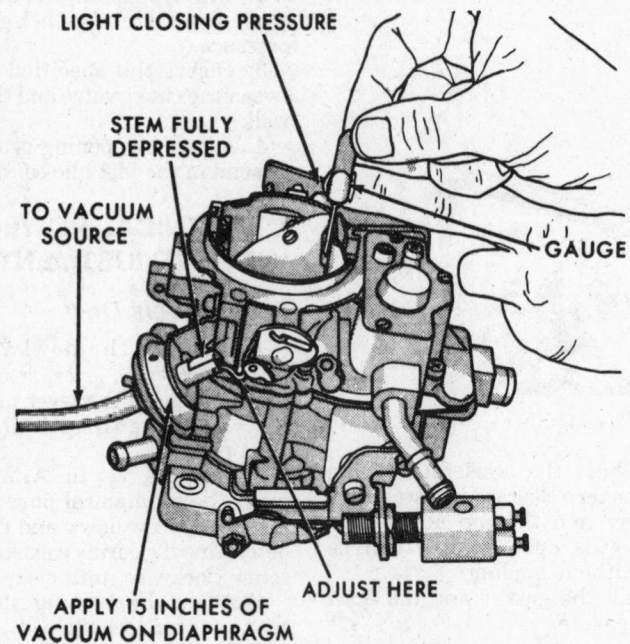

LIGHT CLOSING PRESSURE

STEM FULLY DEPRESSED

TO VACUUM SOURCE

GAUGE

APPLY 15 INCHES OF VACUUM ON DIAPHRAGM

ADJUST HERE

Choke vacuum kick adjustment

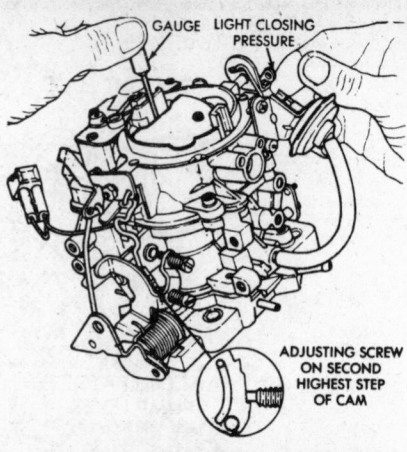

GAUGE LIGHT CLOSING PRESSURE

ADJUSTING SCREW ON SECOND HIGHEST STEP OF CAM

Fast idle cam position adjustment

ACCELERATING PUMP LEVER ADJUSTMENT

1. Using a feeler gauge and with the primary throttle plates in the wide open position, there should be the specified clearance between the accelerating pump operating lever adjustment screw head and the pump arm when the pump arm is depressed manually.

2. If adjustment is required, loosen and then hold the lock screw and turn the adjusting nut in to increase the clearance and out to decrease the clearance. One half turn of the adjusting nut is equal to approximately 0.015 in. (0.381mm). When the proper adjustment has been obtained, hold the adjustment in position with a wrench and tighten the nut.

DRY FUEL LEVEL FLOAT ADJUSTMENT

The dry float adjustment is a preliminary fuel level adjustment only. The final adjustment, ("Wet Fuel Level Adjustment"), must be performed after the carburetor is installed on the engine. With the fuel bowls and float assemblies removed, adjust the floats so that the floats are parallel to the fuel bowls, with the top of the fuel bowls inverted.

WET FUEL LEVEL ADJUSTMENT

The fuel pump pressure and volume must be to specifications prior to performing the following adjustments.

1. Operate the engine to normalize engine temperatures and place the vehicle on a flat surface, as near level as possible. Remove the air cleaner, if it was not previously removed.

2. Run the engine at 1000 rpm for

pump assembly. The primary barrels each contain a primary and booster venturi, main fuel discharge nozzle, throttle plate and idle fuel passage. The Model 4180-C uses an electric choke with hot air assist. The secondary stage, (rear section), of the carburetor contains a fuel bowl, metering body and secondary throttle operating diaphragm assembly.

Each secondary barrel contains a primary and booster venturi, idle fuel passages, main secondary fuel discharge nozzle, throttle plate and a transfer system fuel passage from the primary fuel bowl. A fuel inlet system for both the primary and the secondary stages for the carburetor provides the fuel metering systems with a constant supply of fuel. The 4180-C carburetor is used on the 1983 Ford Mustang with the 302 V8 engine.

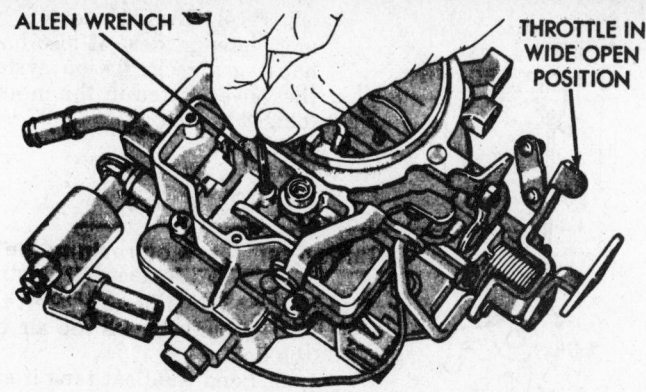

ALLEN WRENCH

THROTTLE IN WIDE OPEN POSITION

Mechanical power valve adjustment

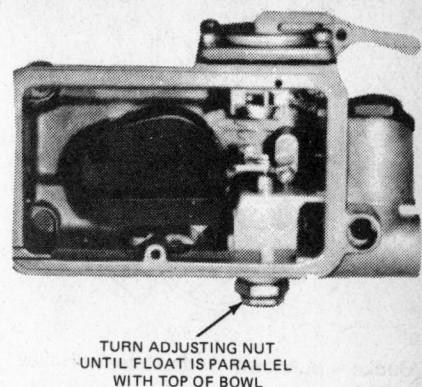

TURN ADJUSTING NUT UNTIL FLOAT IS PARALLEL WITH TOP OF BOWL (HOLDING BOWL UPSIDE DOWN)

Dry float adjustment—Holley 4180C

about 30 seconds to stabilize the fuel level.

3. Stop the engine and remove the sight plug on the side of the primary carburetor bowl.

4. Check the fuel level. It should be at bottom of sight plug hole. If fuel spills out when the sight plug is removed, lower the fuel level. If the fuel level is below the sight plug hole, raise the fuel level.

—— CAUTION ——

Do not loosen the lock screw or nut or attempt to adjust the fuel level with the sight plug removed or the engine running because the fuel may spray out creating a fire hazard.

5. Adjust the front level as necessary by loosening the lock screw and turning the adjusting nut clockwise to lower fuel level or counterclockwise to raise fuel level, ($\frac{1}{16}$ turn adjusting nut will change fuel level approximately $\frac{1}{32}$ in.). Tighten the lock screw and install the sight plug, using the old gas-

ket. Start engine and run at 1000 rpm for about 30 seconds to stabilize fuel level.

6. Stop the engine, remove the sight plug and check the fuel level. Repeat Step 5 until the fuel level is at the bottom of the sight plug hole. When the fuel level is at the bottom of the sight plug hole, install the sight plug using new adjusting plug gasket.

7. Repeat Steps 3–6 for the secondary fuel bowl.

NOTE: The secondary throttle must be used to stabilize the fuel level in the secondary fuel bowl.

SECONDARY THROTTLE PLATE ADJUSTMENT

1. With carburetor off the engine, hold the secondary throttle plates closed.

2. Turn the secondary throttle shaft lever adjusting screw (stop screw) out (counterclockwise) until

the secondary throttle plates seat in the throttle bores.

3. Turn the screw in clockwise until the screw JUST contacts the secondary lever, then turn screw in (clockwise) ¼ turn.

CHOKE PULLDOWN ADJUSTMENT

1. Remove the choke thermostat housing, gasket and retainer. See the choke cap removal and installation procedure below.

2. Insert a piece of wire into the choke piston bore to move the piston down against the stop screw. Maintain light closing pressure on the choke plate and measure the gap between the lower edge of the choke plate and the air horn wall.

3. To adjust, remove the putty covering the adjustment screw and turn the screw clockwise to decrease or counter-clockwise to increase the gap

HOLLEY MODEL 2280/6280
Chrysler Corporation

Year	Carb. Part No.	Float Level (in.)	Accelerator Pump Adjustment (in.)	Fast Idle (rpm)	Choke Unloader Clearance (in.)	Vacuum Kick (in.)	Fast Idle Cam Position (in.)	Choke
'85	R-40121-A	9/32	①	1700	.280	.130	.060	Fixed
	R-40157-A	9/32	①	1600	.200	.140	.052	Fixed
'86	R-40276A	9/32	.180	②	.280	.130	.060	Fixed
	R-40245A	9/32	.050	②	.200	.140	.052	Fixed
'87	R-40276A	9/32	.180	②	.280	.130	.060	Fixed
	R-40245A	9/32	.050	②	.200	.140	.052	Fixed
'88	R-40276A	9/32	.180	②	.280	.130	.060	Fixed
	R-40354A	9/32	.050	②	.200	.140	.052	Fixed
'89	R-40276A	9/32	.180	②	.280	.130	.060	Fixed
	R-40354A	9/32	.050	②	.200	.140	.052	Fixed

① Flush with top of bowl vent casting
② Refer to underhood sticker

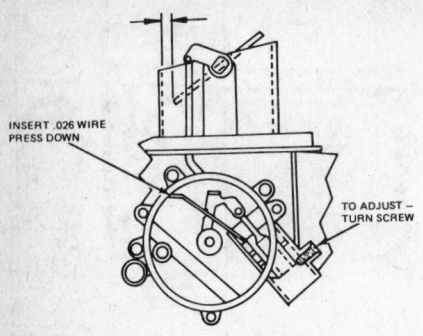

Choke pulldown adjustment—Holley 4180C

setting. Take care to close the choke plate during screw adjustment. The screw may be turned into the side of piston, resulting in damage to piston.

4. Reinstall the choke thermostatic housing, gasket and retainer.

DECHOKE ADJUSTMENT

1. Hold the throttle in the wide open position.
2. Apply light closing pressure to the choke plate and measure the gap between the lower edge of the choke plate and the air horn wall.
3. To adjust, bend the pawl on the fast idle lever.

CHOKE THERMOSTATIC SPRING HOUSING (CHOKE CAP)

Removal

1. Remove the carburetor from vehicle.
2. Using a hacksaw carefully cut a slot in the head of the breakaway screw. Using a proper sized straight blade screw driver, remove the breakaway screw in the conventional manner.
3. Repeat Step 2 for the remaining breakaway screw.
4. Remove the remaining standard screw. Remove the retaining ring, choke cap and gasket.

Installation

1. Install the choke cap gasket. Install the choke cap by engaging the bimetal loop on the choke thermostatic lever.
2. Install the retaining ring. Loosely install 2 new breakaway screws and 1 standard screw.
3. Align the choke cap to the proper index mark.
4. Tighten the breakaway screws until the heads break off. Tighten the remaining screw to 16–18 inch lbs. (1.8–2.0 Nm).

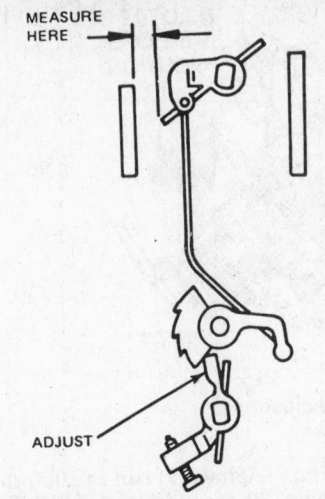

Dechoke adjustment—Holley 4180C

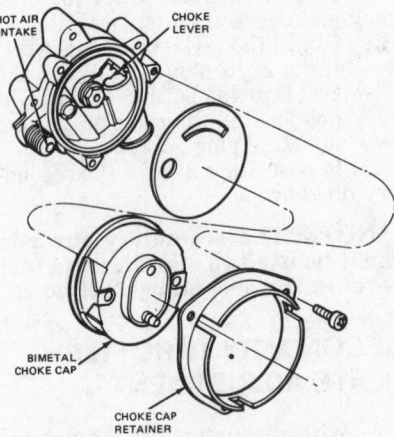

Automatic choke—Holley 4180C

5. Install the carburetor on the vehicle.

FAST IDLE CAM SET

1. Rotate the choke cap 45 degrees counterclockwise (rich) to close the choke plate. Tighten the attaching screw at the time.
2. Open and close the throttle to place the fast idle screw on the **top** step of the cam.
3. Place a pulldown gauge between the lower edge of the choke plate and the air horn wall, then open and close the throttle to allow the fast idle cam to drop.
4. Press upward on the fast idle cam. There should be little or no movement indicating that the fast idle screw is on the kickdown **second** step of the cam, against the first step.

Model 5210-C

The Holley 5210-C is a progressive 2 barrel carburetor with an automatic choke system which is activated by a water heated thermostatic coil. An electrically heated choke is used on most later models. It also has an exhaust gas recirculation system with the valve located in the intake manifold. It is used on 1982–87 Chevettes (Canada).

FLOAT LEVEL

1. With the carburetor air horn inverted and the float tang resting lightly on the inlet needle, insert the specified gauge between the air horn and the float.
2. Bend the float tang if an adjustment is needed.

FAST IDLE CAM ADJUSTMENT

1. Place the fast idle screw on the **second** step of the fast idle cam and against the shoulder of the high step.
2. Place the specified drill or gauge on the down side of the choke plate.
3. To adjust, bend the choke lever tang.

CHOKE PLATE PULLDOWN (VACUUM BREAK) ADJUSTMENT

1982–87 Models

1. Attach a hand vacuum pump to the vacuum break diaphragm; apply vacuum and seat the diaphragm.
2. Push the fast idle cam lever down to close the choke plate.
3. Take any slack out of the linkage in the open choke position.
4. Insert the specified gauge between the lower edge of the choke plate and the air horn wall.
5. If the clearance is incorrect, turn the vacuum break adjusting screw, located in the break housing, to adjust.

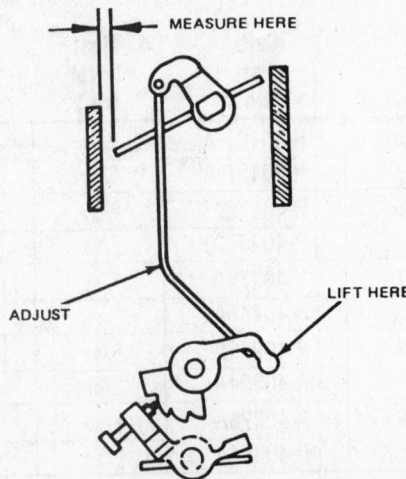

Fast idle cam set—Holley 4180C

HOLLEY MODEL 4180C
Ford Motor Company

Year	(9510)* Carburetor Identification	Dry Float Level (in.)	Wet Float Level (in.)	Pump Setting Hole	Choke Plate Pulldown (in.)	Fast Idle Cam Linkage Clearance (in.)	Fast Idle (rpm)	Dechoke (in)	Choke Setting
'83	E3ZE-AUA	②	①	#1	.195–.215	NA	③	.300	3 Rich
	E3ZE-BGA	②	①	#1	.195–.215	NA	③	.300	3 Rich
'84	E4ZE-SA	②	①	#1	.195–.215	NA	③	.300	1 Lean
'85	E5ZE-GA	—	①	#1	.168–.188	—	③	.300	2 Lean

NA—not available
① Bottom of sight plug
② See text
③ See Underhood sticker

CHOKE UNLOADER ADJUSTMENT

1. Position the throttle lever at the wide open position.
2. Insert a gauge of the size specified in the chart between the lower edge of the choke valve and the air horn wall.
3. Bend the unloader tang for adjustment.

FAST IDLE SPEED ADJUSTMENT

1. The engine must be at normal operating temperature with the air cleaner off.
2. With the engine running, position the fast idle screw on the **high** step of the cam for GM cars, or on the **second** step against the shoulder of the **high** step for AMC cars. Plug the EGR Port on the carburetor.
3. Adjust the speed by turning the fast idle screw.

Models 5220 and 6520

Both of these models are staged dual venturi carburetors. The model 6520 has the electronic feedback system. On the 6520 always check the condition of hoses and related wiring before making any carburetor adjustments.

For further information on feedback carburetors, please refer to *Chilton's Guide To Fuel Injection And Feedback Carburetors.*

FLOAT SETTING AND FLOAT DROP ADJUSTMENT

1. Remove and invert the air horn.

2. Insert a 0.480 in. gauge between the air horn and float.
3. If necessary, bend the tang on the float arm to adjust.
4. Turn the air horn right side up and allow the float to hang freely. Measure the float drop from the bottom of the air horn to the bottom of the float. It should be exactly 1⅞ in. Correct by bending the float tang.

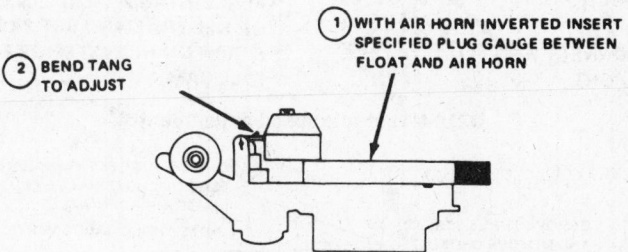

5210-C Float level adjustment

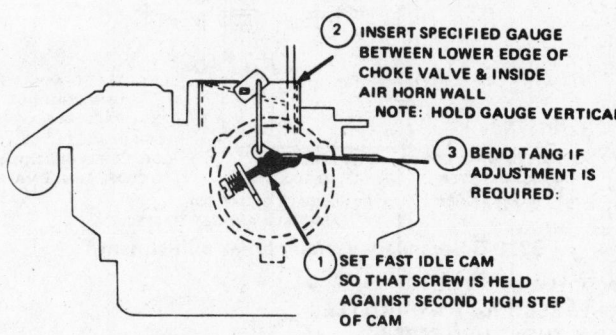

5210-C Fast idle cam adjustment

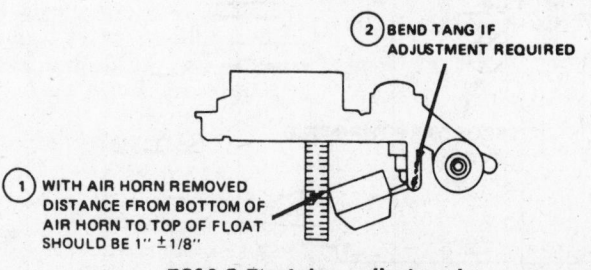

5210-C Float drop adjustment

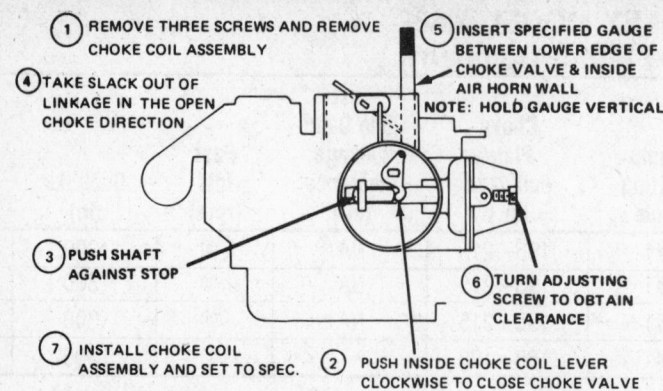

5210-C Vacuum break (choke plate pulldown) adjustment

- ① REMOVE THREE SCREWS AND REMOVE CHOKE COIL ASSEMBLY
- ④ TAKE SLACK OUT OF LINKAGE IN THE OPEN CHOKE DIRECTION
- ③ PUSH SHAFT AGAINST STOP
- ⑦ INSTALL CHOKE COIL ASSEMBLY AND SET TO SPEC.
- ⑤ INSERT SPECIFIED GAUGE BETWEEN LOWER EDGE OF CHOKE VALVE & INSIDE AIR HORN WALL NOTE: HOLD GAUGE VERTICAL
- ⑥ TURN ADJUSTING SCREW TO OBTAIN CLEARANCE
- ② PUSH INSIDE CHOKE COIL LEVER CLOCKWISE TO CLOSE CHOKE VALVE

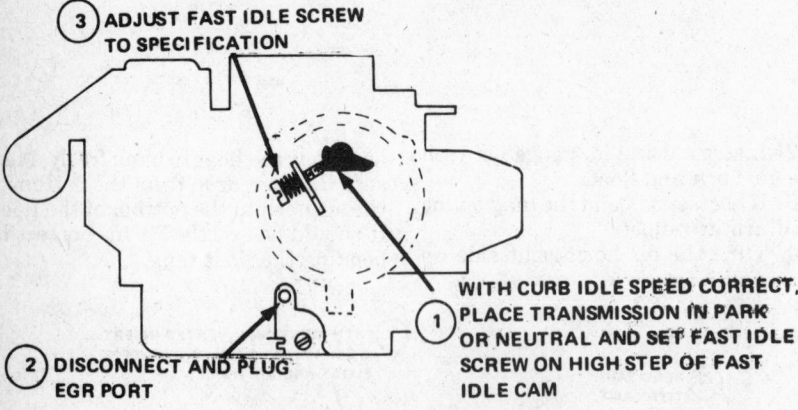

5210-C Fast idle speed adjustment

- ③ ADJUST FAST IDLE SCREW TO SPECIFICATION
- ② DISCONNECT AND PLUG EGR PORT
- ① WITH CURB IDLE SPEED CORRECT, PLACE TRANSMISSION IN PARK OR NEUTRAL AND SET FAST IDLE SCREW ON HIGH STEP OF FAST IDLE CAM

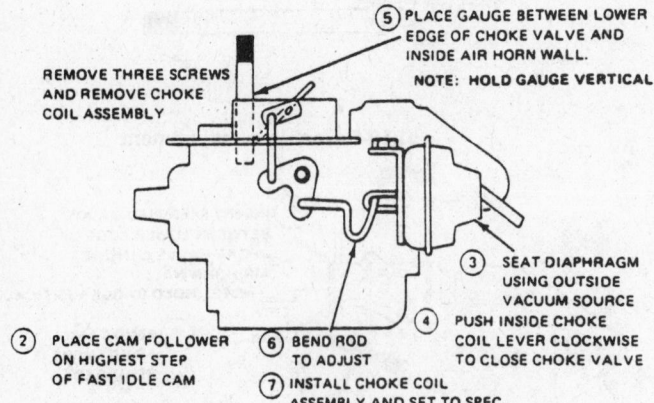

5210-C Secondary vacuum break adjustment

- REMOVE THREE SCREWS AND REMOVE CHOKE COIL ASSEMBLY
- ⑤ PLACE GAUGE BETWEEN LOWER EDGE OF CHOKE VALVE AND INSIDE AIR HORN WALL. NOTE: HOLD GAUGE VERTICAL
- ② PLACE CAM FOLLOWER ON HIGHEST STEP OF FAST IDLE CAM
- ⑥ BEND ROD TO ADJUST
- ⑦ INSTALL CHOKE COIL ASSEMBLY AND SET TO SPEC.
- ③ SEAT DIAPHRAGM USING OUTSIDE VACUUM SOURCE
- ④ PUSH INSIDE CHOKE COIL LEVER CLOCKWISE TO CLOSE CHOKE VALVE

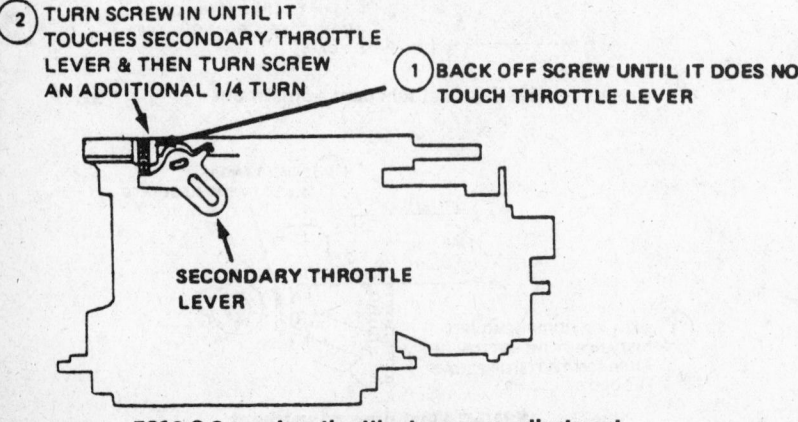

5210-C Secondary throttle stop screw adjustment

- ② TURN SCREW IN UNTIL IT TOUCHES SECONDARY THROTTLE LEVER & THEN TURN SCREW AN ADDITIONAL 1/4 TURN
- ① BACK OFF SCREW UNTIL IT DOES NOT TOUCH THROTTLE LEVER
- SECONDARY THROTTLE LEVER

- ② INSERT SPECIFIED GAUGE BETWEEN LOWER EDGE OF CHOKE VALVE & INSIDE AIR HORN WALL

  NOTE: HOLD GAUGE VERTICAL
- ③ BEND TANG AT EXISTING RADIUS TO ADJUST
- ① POSITION THROTTLE LEVER TO WIDE-OPEN

5210-C Choke unloader adjustment

VACUUM KICK ADJUSTMENT

1. Open the throttle, close the choke, then close the throttle to trap the fast idle system at the closed choke position.
2. Disconnect the vacuum hose to the carburetor and connect it to an auxiliary vacuum source.
3. Apply at least 15 in. Hg vacuum to the unit.
4. Apply sufficient force to close the choke valve without distorting the linkage.
5. Insert a gauge between the top of the choke plate and the air horn wall.
6. Set to specifications by rotating the Allen screw in the center diaphragm housing.
7. Replace the vacuum hose.

FAST IDLE SPEED ADJUSTMENT

1. Remove the air cleaner, disconnect and plug the EGR line, but DO NOT disconnect the spark control computer vacuum line. Turn the air conditioning off.
2. Disconnect the radiator fan electrical connector and use a jumper wire to complete the circuit at the fan. Do not short to ground, as this will damage the system.
3. With the parking brake set and the transmission in Neutral, (engine still off), open the throttle and place the fast idle screw on the **slowest** step of the cam.
4. Start the engine and check the idle speed. If it continues to rise slowly, the idle stop switch is not grounded properly.
5. Adjust the fast idle with the screw, moving the screw off the cam each time to adjust. Allow the screw to

HOLLEY MODEL 5210-C
Chevrolet Chevette

Year	Carb. Part No. ① ②	Float Level (Dry) (in.)	Fast Idle Cam (in.)	Secondary Vacuum Break (in.)	Fast Idle Setting (rpm)	Choke Unloader (in.)	Choke Setting
'82	14043392	0.50	0.110	0.120	2500	0.275	Fixed
	14043393	0.50	0.110	0.120	2500	0.350	Fixed
'83 (Canada)	All	0.50	0.090	③	④	0.275	Fixed
'84–'85 (Canada)	14076317	0.50	0.110	⑤	④	0.350	Fixed
	14076318	0.50	0.110	⑤	④	0.300	Fixed
	14076319	0.50	0.120	⑥	④	0.350	Fixed
'86 (Canada)	14076393	0.50	0.100	⑤	④	0.325	Fixed
	14076394	0.50	0.090	⑤	④	0.275	Fixed
'87 (Canada)	14076393	0.50	0.100	⑤	④	0.325	Fixed
	14076394	0.50	0.090	⑤	④	0.275	Fixed

① Located on tag attached to the carburetor, or on the casting or choke plate
② GM identification numbers are used in place of the Holley numbers
③ Hot: 0.280
   Cold: 0.100
④ See underhood sticker
⑤ Hot: 0.250
   Cold: 0.100
⑥ Hot: 0.290
   Cold: 0.110

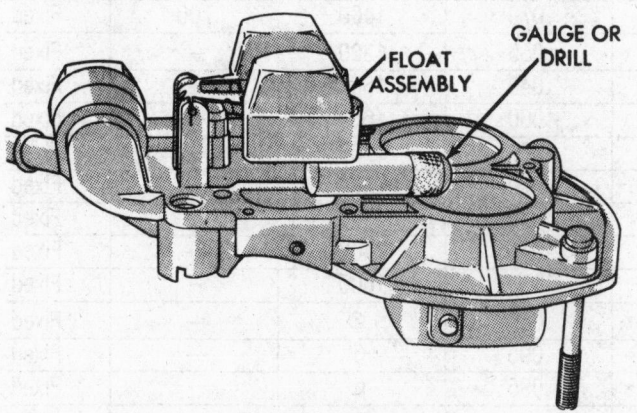

Float setting adjustment

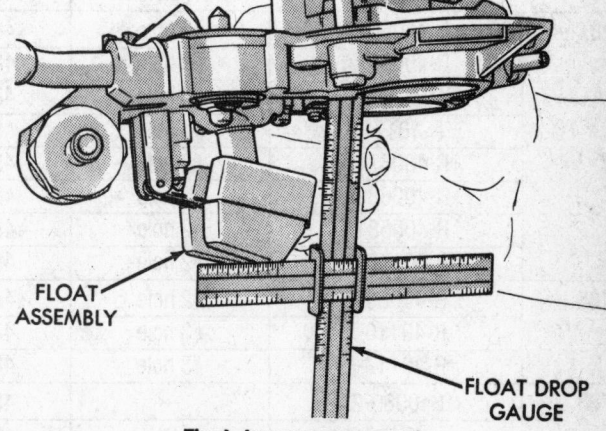

Float drop measurement

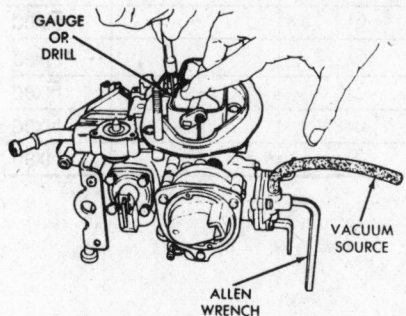

Vacuum kick adjustment

fall back against the cam and the speed to stabilize between each adjustment.

Model 6145

FLOAT ADJUSTMENT

1. With the gasket in place, invert

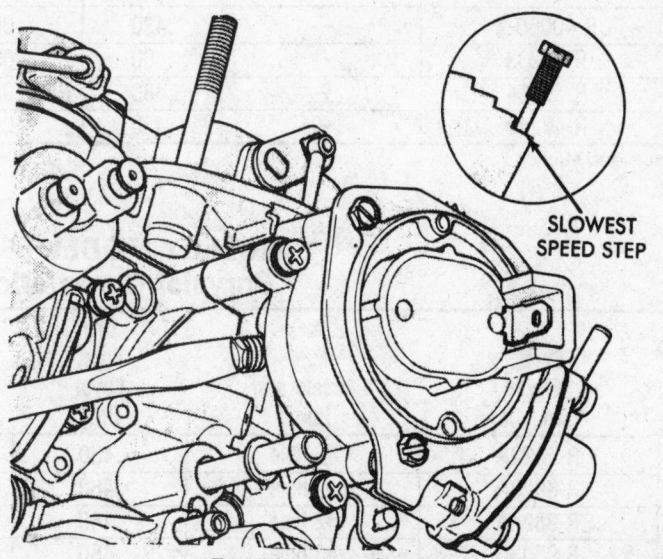

Fast idle speed adjustment

HOLLEY MODEL 5220
Chrysler Corporation

Year	Carb. Part No.	Accelerator Pump	Dry Float Level (in.)	Vacuum Kick (in.)	Fast Idle RPM (w/fan)	Throttle Stop Speed RPM	Choke
'82	R-9582A	#3 hole	.480	.060	1200	700	Fixed
	R-8583A	#3 hole	.480	.060	1200	—	Fixed
	R-9584A	#3 hole	.480	.060	1500	700	Fixed
	R-9585A	#3 hole	.480	.060	1500	700	Fixed
	R-9820A	#2 hole	.480	.080	1400	—	Fixed
	R-9513A	#2 hole	.480	.120	1400	—	Fixed
	R-9514A	#2 hole	.480	.120	1400	—	Fixed
	R-9499A	#2 hole	.480	.130	1400	700	Fixed
	R-9511A	#3 hole	.480	.130	1400	700	Fixed
	R-9512A	#2 hole	.480	.130	1400	—	Fixed
'83	R-40020A	#3 hole	.480	.055	1500	—	Fixed
	R-40022A	#3 hole	.480	.055	1500	—	Fixed
	R-40023A	#2 hole	.480	.070	1400	700	Fixed
	R-40024A	#2 hole	.480	.070	1400	700	Fixed
	R-40025A	#2 hole	.480	.070	1400	700	Fixed
	R-40026A	#7 hole	.480	.070	1400	700	Fixed
'84	R-400601A	#2 hole	.480	.055	1200	—	Fixed
	R-400851A	#2 hole	.480	.040	1500	—	Fixed
	R-40170A	#3 hole	.480	.060	1650	—	Fixed
	R-40171A	#3 hole	.480	.060	1700	—	Fixed
	R-400671A	#3 hole	.480	.070	1500	—	Fixed
	R-400681A	#3 hole	.480	.070	1700	—	Fixed
	R-400581A	#2 hole	.480	.070	1400	—	Fixed
	R-401071A	#2 hole	.480	.070	1600	—	Fixed
'85	R-40060-A	#2 hole	.480	.050	①	—	Fixed
	R-40116-A	#3 hole	.480	.095	①	—	Fixed
	R-40117-A	#3 hole	.480	.095	①	—	Fixed
'86	R-40060-2A	—	.480	.055	①	—	Fixed
	R-40116-A	—	.480	.095	①	—	Fixed
	R-40117-A	—	.480	.095	①	—	Fixed
'87	R-40060-2	—	.480	.055	①	—	Fixed
	R-40233	—	.480	.095	①	—	Fixed
	R-40234	—	.480	.095	①	—	Fixed
	R-40240	—	.480	.095	①	—	Fixed

① See underhood sticker

HOLLEY MODEL 6520
Chrysler Corporation

Year	Carb. Part No. ①	Accelerator Pump	Dry Float Level (in.)	Float Drop (in.)	Vacuum Kick (in.)	Fast Idle RPM
'82	R-9822A	#2 hole	.480	1.875	.080	1400
	R-9823A	#2 hole	.480	1.875	.080	1400
	R-9824A	#2 hole	.480	1.875	.065	1400
	R-9503A	#3 hole	.480	1.875	.085	1300

HOLLEY MODEL 6520
Chrysler Corporation

Year	Carb. Part No. ①	Accelerator Pump	Dry Float Level (in.)	Float Drop (in.)	Vacuum Kick (in.)	Fast Idle RPM
'82	R-9504A	#3 hole	.480	1.875	.085	1300
	R-9505A	#3 hole	.480	1.875	.100	1600
	R-9506A	#3 hole	.480	1.875	.100	1600
	R-9750A	#3 hole	.480	1.875	.085	1300
	R-9751A	#3 hole	.480	1.875	.085	1300
	R-9509A	#3 hole	.480	1.875	.085	1600
	R-9510A	#3 hole	.480	1.875	.085	1600
	R-9752A	#3 hole	.480	1.875	.100	1600
	R-9753A	#3 hole	.480	1.875	.100	1600
	R-9507A	#3 hole	.480	1.875	.085	1300
	R-9508A	#3 hole	.480	1.875	.085	1300
'83	R-40003A	#3 hole	.480	1.875	.070	1400
	R-40004A	#3 hole	.480	1.875	.080	1500
	R-40005A	#3 hole	.480	1.875	.080	1350
	R-40006A	#3 hole	.480	1.875	.080	1275
	R-40007A	#3 hole	.480	1.875	.070	1400
	R-40008A	#3 hole	.480	1.875	.070	1600
	R-40010A	#3 hole	.480	1.875	.080	1500
	R-40012A	#3 hole	.480	1.875	.070	1600
	R-40014A	#3 hole	.480	1.875	.080	1275
	R-40080A	#2 hole	.480	1.875	.045	1400
	R-40081A	#3 hole	.480	1.875	.045	1400
'84	R-400641A	#3 hole	.480	1.875	.080	1500
	R-400651A	#3 hole	.480	1.875	.080	1600
	R-400811A	#2 hole	.480	1.875	.080	1500
	R-400821A	#2 hole	.480	1.875	.080	1600
	R-40071A	#3 hole	.480	1.875	.080	1500
	R-40122A	#2 hole	.480	1.875	.080	1500
'85	R-40058A	#2 hole	.480	1.875	.070	1400
	R-40134A	#3 hole	.480	1.875	.075	1700
	R-40135A	#3 hole	.480	1.875	.075	1850
	R-40138A	#3 hole	.480	1.875	.075	1700
	R-40139A	#3 hole	.480	1.875	.075	1850
'86	R-40058-1A	—	.480	1.875	.070	①
	R-40134-A	—	.480	1.875	.075	①
	R-40135-1A	—	.480	1.875	.075	①
	R-40138-1A	—	.480	1.875	.075	①
	R-40139-1A	—	.480	1.875	.075	①
'87	R-40295A	—	.480	1.875	.075	①
	R-40296A	—	.480	1.875	.075	①

① Refer to underhood sticker

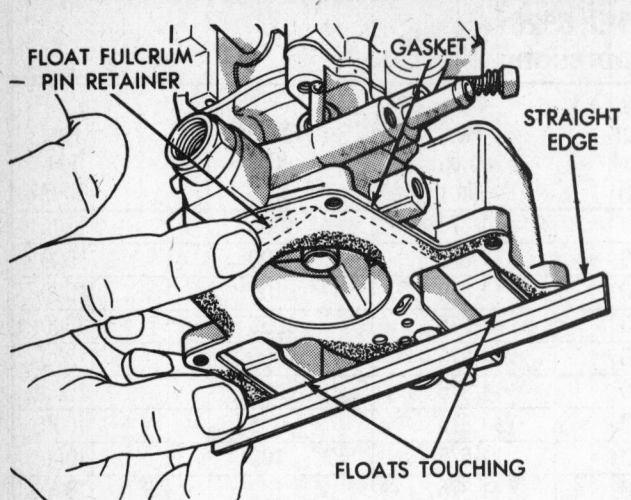

Float level adjustment—Holley 6145

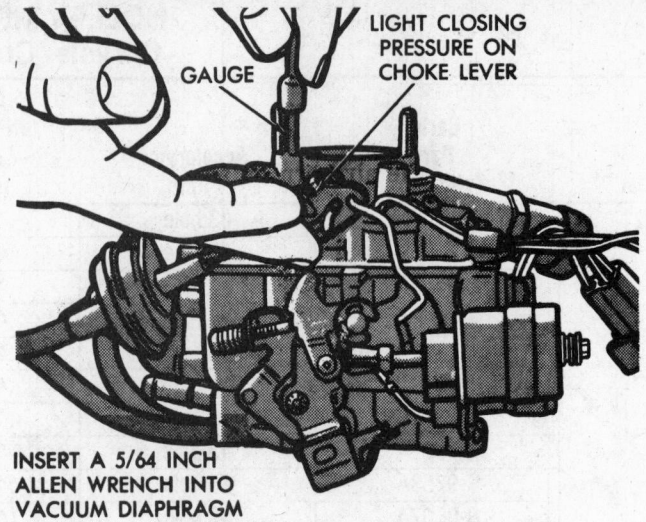

INSERT A 5/64 INCH
ALLEN WRENCH INTO
VACUUM DIAPHRAGM
TO ADJUST VACUUM KICK

Choke vacuum kick adjustment, 1982–83—Holley 6145

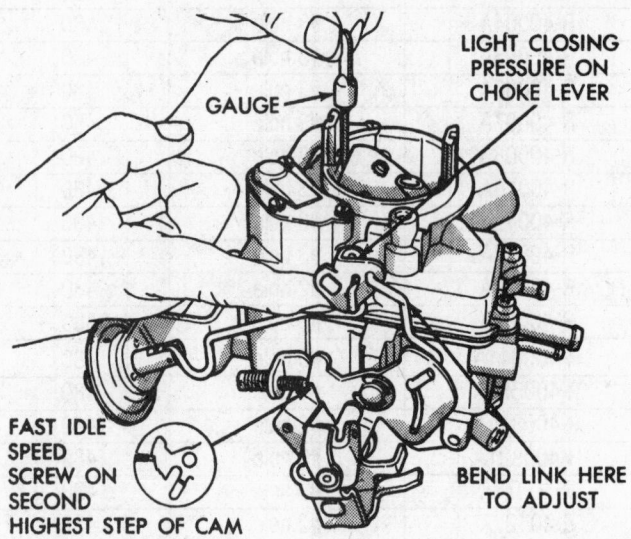

Fast idle cam adjustment, typical—Holley 6145

the bowl and place a straight edge across the gasket surface. The portion of the floats, farthest from the fuel inlet, should just touch the straight edge.

2. If adjustment is necessary, bend the float tang.

CHOKE VACUUM KICK ADJUSTMENT

1. Open the throttle and close the choke. Then close throttle so that the fast idle cam is at the closed position.

2. Disconnect the vacuum hose from the carburetor and connect it to a hose of an auxiliary vacuum source with an extra length of tube. Apply a vacuum of 15 or more in. of mercury.

3. Apply light pressure on the choke lever to close the choke and measure the distance between the choke valve and the air horn wall on the throttle lever side with the specified gauge.

4. Insert a $\frac{5}{64}$ in. Allen wrench into the choke diaphragm and turn to adjust the choke vacuum kick.

5. Reconnect the vacuum hose after adjustment.

FAST IDLE CAM ADJUSTMENT

1. Position the fast idle speed adjusting screw on the **SECOND HIGHEST** step of the fast idle cam.

2. Using light pressure on the choke shaft lever, move the choke towards the closed position.

3. Insert the specified gauge between the top of the choke valve and the air horn wall at the throttle lever side.

4. If an adjustment is necessary, bend the fast idle connecting rod at the angle until the correct valve opening is obtained.

CHOKE UNLOADER ADJUSTMENT

1. Hold the throttle valves in the wide open position.

2. Using light pressure on the control lever, move the choke valve towards the closed position.

3. Insert the specified gauge between the top of the choke valve and the air horn wall.

4. To adjust bend the tang on the throttle lever.

ACCELERATOR PUMP ADJUSTMENT

1. Place the throttle in the curb idle position with the accelerator pump operating link in the proper slot in the throttle lever.

2. Measure the pump operating link and bend the link if needed to specifications.

Models 6500 and 6510-C

The 6500 is a Holley-Weber Unit used on all 1982 models with the 2.3L engine equipped with the Feedback Electronic Engine Control System. With the exception of an externally variable fuel metering system in place of the fuel enrichment valve, it is identical to the model Motorcraft 5200. For all adjustments, refer to this listing in the Motorcraft section of Carburetor Unit Repair.

The 6510-C is used on the Chevette and T-1000. This is a staged, 2 barrel unit which incorporates a feedback air/fuel metering system.

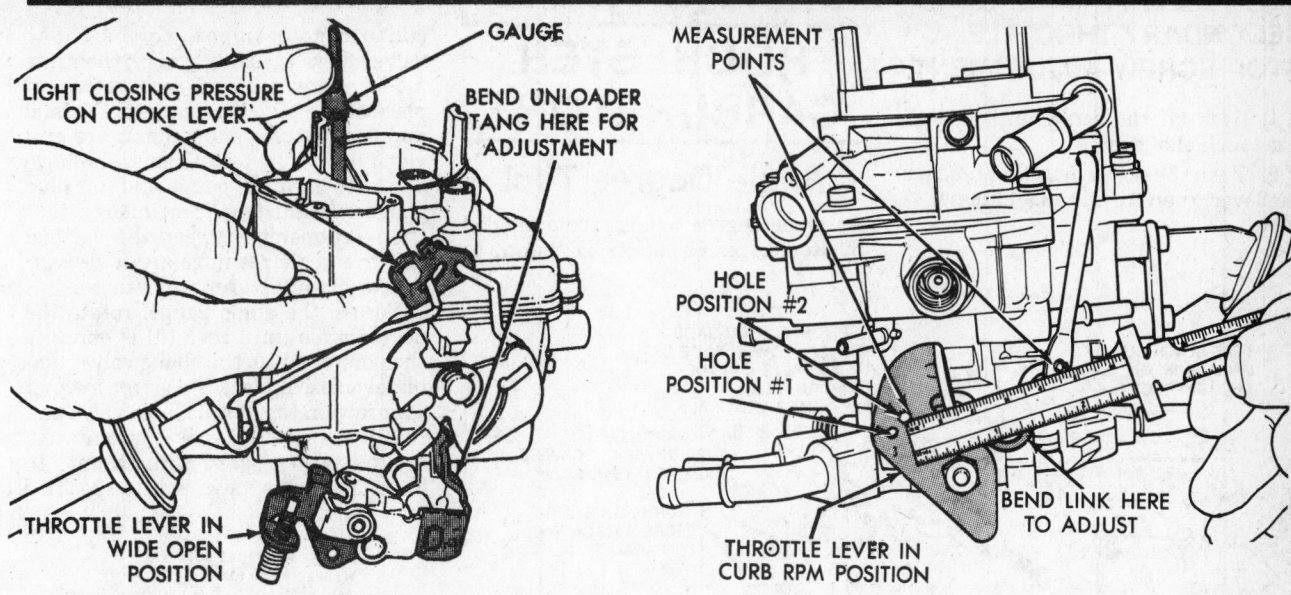

Choke unloader adjustment, typical—Holley 6145

Accelerator pump adjustment, typical—Holley 6145

For further information on feedback carburetors, please refer to *Chilton's Guide To Fuel Injection And Feedback Carburetors.*

VACUUM BREAK ADJUSTMENT

1982–83 Models

1. Attach a hand vacuum pump to the vacuum break diaphragm. Apply vacuum until the diaphragm is seated.
2. Push the fast idle cam lever down to close the choke plate.
3. Take the slack out of the linkage in the open choke position.
4. Insert the specified gauge between the lower edge of the choke plate and the air horn wall.
5. If the clearance is incorrect, turn the screw in the end of the diaphragm to adjust.

FAST IDLE CAM ADJUSTMENT

1. Set the fast idle cam so that the screw is on the **SECOND HIGHEST** step of the fast idle cam.
2. Insert the specified gauge between the lower edge of the choke valve and the air horn wall.
3. Bend the tang on the arm to adjust.

UNLOADER ADJUSTMENT

1. Place the throttle in the wide open position.
2. Insert a 0.350 in. gauge between the lower edge of the choke valve and the air horn wall.
3. Bend the tang on the choke arm to adjust.

FAST IDLE ADJUSTMENT

With the curb idle speed correct, place the fast idle screw on the **highest** cam step and adjust to the specified rpm.

NOTE: The EGR line must be disconnected and plugged.

FLOAT LEVEL ADJUSTMENT

1. Remove and invert the air horn.
2. Place the specified gauge between the air horn and the float.
3. If necessary, bend the float arm tang to adjust.

HOLLEY MODEL 6145
Chrysler Corporation

Year	Carb. Part No. ①	Float Level (in.)	Accelerator Pump Adjustment (in.)	Bowl Vent Clearance (in.)	Fast Idle (rpm)	Choke Unloader Clearance (in.)	Vacuum Kick (in.)	Fast Idle Cam Position (in.)	Choke
'82	R-9936A	②	1.616 ③	④	1950	.250	.150	.090	Fixed
	R-9695A	②	1.615 ③	④	1950 ⑤	.250	.150	.090	Fixed
'83	R-40042A	②	1.615 ③	④	2000	.250	.150	.090	Fixed

① Located on a tag attached to the carburetor
② Flush with the top of the main body casting to .050″ above
③ Position #2
④ Not Adjustable
⑤ Cordoba and Mirada—2000 rpm

SECONDARY THROTTLE STOP SCREW ADJUSTMENT

1. Back off the screw until it does not touch the lever.

2. Turn the screw in until it touches the lever, then turn it an additional ¼ turn.

ROCHESTER CARBURETORS

Angle Degree Tool

An angle degree tool is recommended by Rochester Products Division, to confirm adjustments to the choke valve and related linkages on their late model 2 and 4 barrel carburetors, in place of the plug type gauges. Decimal and degree conversion charts are provided for use by technicians who have access to an angle gauge and not plug gauges. It must be remembered that the relationship between the decimal and the angle readings are not exact, due to manufacturers tolerances.

To use the angle gauge, rotate the degree scale until zero (0) is opposite the pointer. With the choke valve completely closed, place the gauge magnet squarely on top of the choke valve and rotate the bubble until it is centered. Make the necessary adjustments to have the choke valve at the specified

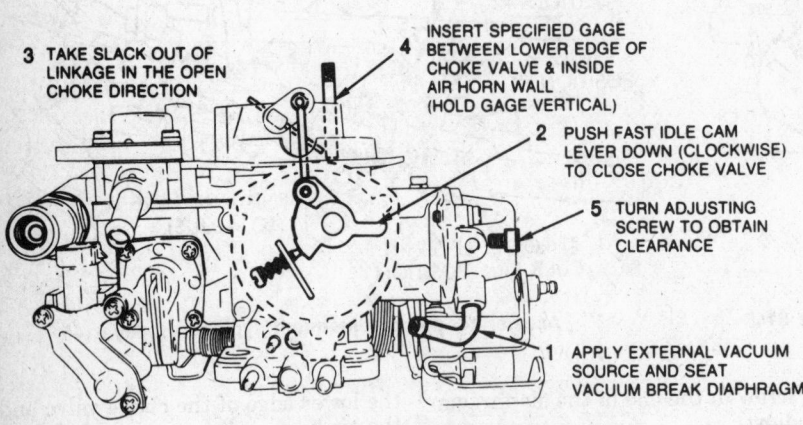

3 TAKE SLACK OUT OF LINKAGE IN THE OPEN CHOKE DIRECTION

4 INSERT SPECIFIED GAGE BETWEEN LOWER EDGE OF CHOKE VALVE & INSIDE AIR HORN WALL (HOLD GAGE VERTICAL)

2 PUSH FAST IDLE CAM LEVER DOWN (CLOCKWISE) TO CLOSE CHOKE VALVE

5 TURN ADJUSTING SCREW TO OBTAIN CLEARANCE

1 APPLY EXTERNAL VACUUM SOURCE AND SEAT VACUUM BREAK DIAPHRAGM

Vacuum break adjustment—Holley 6510C

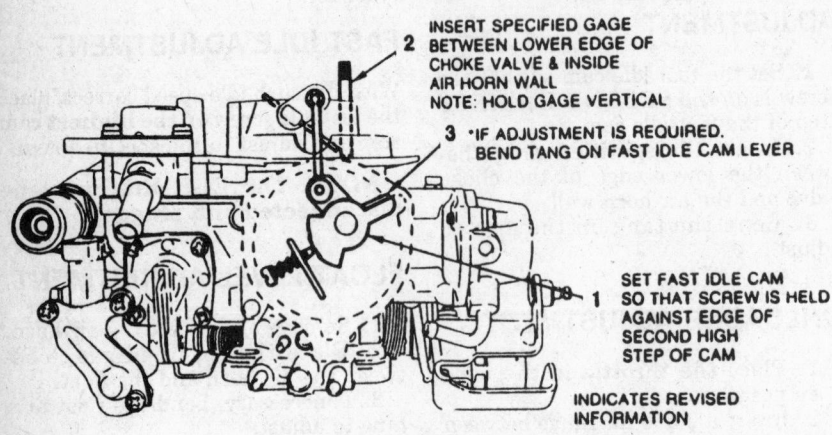

2 INSERT SPECIFIED GAGE BETWEEN LOWER EDGE OF CHOKE VALVE & INSIDE AIR HORN WALL NOTE: HOLD GAGE VERTICAL

3 *IF ADJUSTMENT IS REQUIRED, BEND TANG ON FAST IDLE CAM LEVER

1 SET FAST IDLE CAM SO THAT SCREW IS HELD AGAINST EDGE OF SECOND HIGH STEP OF CAM

* INDICATES REVISED INFORMATION

Fast idle cam adjustment—Holley 6510C

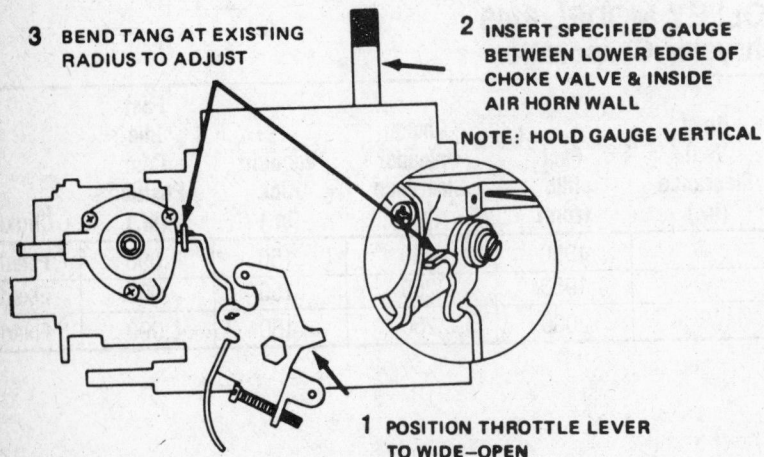

3 BEND TANG AT EXISTING RADIUS TO ADJUST

2 INSERT SPECIFIED GAUGE BETWEEN LOWER EDGE OF CHOKE VALVE & INSIDE AIR HORN WALL

NOTE: HOLD GAUGE VERTICAL

1 POSITION THROTTLE LEVER TO WIDE-OPEN

Choke unloader adjustment

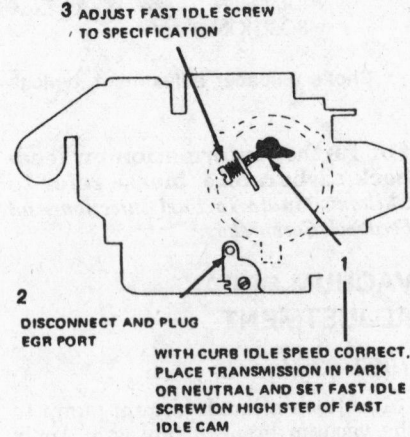

3 ADJUST FAST IDLE SCREW TO SPECIFICATION

2 DISCONNECT AND PLUG EGR PORT

WITH CURB IDLE SPEED CORRECT, PLACE TRANSMISSION IN PARK OR NEUTRAL AND SET FAST IDLE SCREW ON HIGH STEP OF FAST IDLE CAM

Fast idle speed adjustment

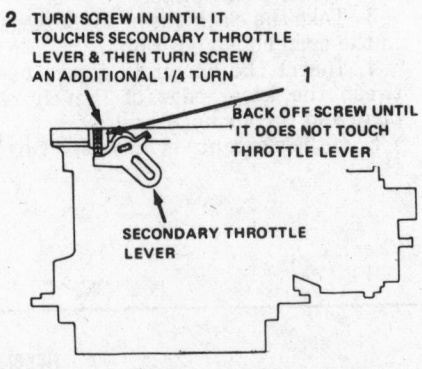

2 TURN SCREW IN UNTIL IT TOUCHES SECONDARY THROTTLE LEVER & THEN TURN SCREW AN ADDITIONAL 1/4 TURN

1 BACK OFF SCREW UNTIL IT DOES NOT TOUCH THROTTLE LEVER

SECONDARY THROTTLE LEVER

Secondary throttle stop screw adjustment

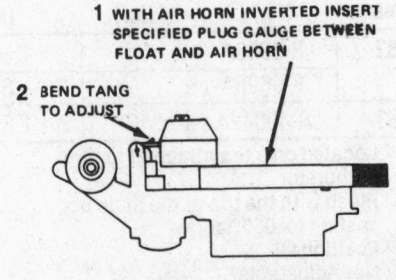

1 WITH AIR HORN INVERTED INSERT SPECIFIED PLUG GAUGE BETWEEN FLOAT AND AIR HORN

2 BEND TANG TO ADJUST

Float level adjustment

HOLLEY MODEL 6500
Ford Bobcat, Pinto, Mustang, Capri, Fairmont, Zephyr, Granada, Cougar

Year	Carburetor Identification	Dry Float Level (in.)	Pump Hole Setting	Choke Plate Pulldown (in.)	Fast Idle Cam Linkage (in.)	Dechoke (in.)	Choke Setting
'82	E2ZE-ARA	.41–.51	2	0.275	0.118	0.393	—
	E2ZE-APA	.41–.51	2	0.275	0.118	0.393	—
	E2ZE-VA	.41–.51	3	0.275	0.118	0.393	—
	E2ZE-ADA	.41–.51	3	0.275	0.118	0.393	—
	E2ZE-ACA	.41–.51	3	0.275	0.118	0.393	—
	E2ZE-UA	.41–.51	3	0.275	0.118	0.393	—

HOLLEY MODEL 6510-C
General Motors Corporation

Year	Part Number	Vacuum Break Adjustment (in.)	Fast Idle Cam Adjustment (in.)	Unloader Adjustment (in.)	Fast Idle Adjustment (rpm)	Float Level Adjustment (in.)	Choke Setting
'82	14032364	.270	.080	.350	①	.500	Fixed
	14032365	.270	.080	.350	①	.500	Fixed
	14032366	.270	.080	.350	①	.500	Fixed
	14032367	.270	.080	.350	①	.500	Fixed
	14032368	.270	.080	.350	①	.500	Fixed
	14032369	.270	.080	.350	①	.500	Fixed
	14032370	.270	.080	.350	①	.500	Fixed
	14032371	.270	.080	.350	①	.500	Fixed
	14033392	.270	.080	.350	①	.500	Fixed
	14033393	.270	.080	.350	①	.500	Fixed
	14047072	.270	.080	.350	①	.500	Fixed
'83	14048827	.270	.080	.350	①	.500	Fixed
	14048828	.300	.080	.350	①	.500	Fixed
	14048829	.270	.080	.350	①	.500	Fixed
'84–'86	14068690	.270	.080	.350	①	.500	Fixed
	14068691	.270	.080	.350	①	.500	Fixed
	14068692	.300	.080	.350	①	.500	Fixed
	14076363	.300	.080	.350	①	.500	Fixed

① See underhood decal

degree angle opening as read from the degree angle tool.

NOTE: The carburetor may be off the engine for adjustments. Be sure the carburetor is held firmly during the use of the angle gauge.

Model Identification

General Motors Rochester carburetors are identified by their model number. The first number indicates the number of barrels, while the last let-

ters indicates the type of choke used. These are V for the manifold mounted choke coil, C for the choke coil mounted on the carburetor and E for electric choke, also mounted on the carburetor. Model numbers ending in A indicate an altitude-compensating carburetor.

Models 2SE and E2SE

The Rochester 2SE and E2SE Varajet II carburetors are 2 barrel, 2 stage downdraft units. Most carburetor

components are aluminum. The E2SE is used both in conventional installations and in the Computer Controlled Catalytic Converter System. In that installation the E2SE is equipped with an electrically operated mixture control solenoid, controlled by the Electronic Control Module. The 2SE and E2SE are also used on the AMC 4 cylinder in 1982–83.

For further information on feedback carburetors, please refer to *Chilton's Guide To Fuel Injection And Feedback Carburetors.*

PLUGGING AIR BLEED HOLES

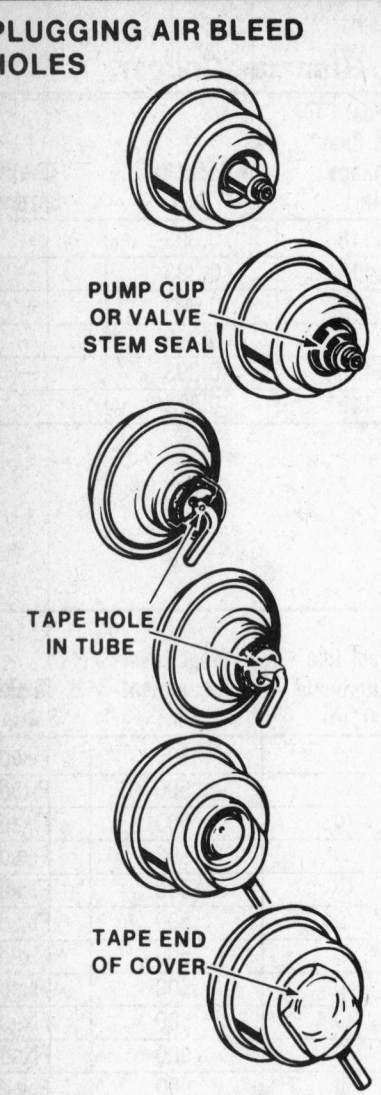

PUMP CUP OR VALVE STEM SEAL

TAPE HOLE IN TUBE

TAPE END OF COVER

Vacuum break information—E2SE

NOTE: Due to the presence of Ethyl Alcohol in some gasolines, the black rubber pump cup swells causing driveability complaints. In order to correct this problem, all "Varajet", "Dualjet" and "Quadrajet" carburetors with a "MW" designation (machined pump well) stamped on the carburetor next to the fuel inlet should use a Red Viton® pump cup when rebuilding the carburetor. The Red Viton® cup is NOT to be used on carburetors with tapered pump wells (no "MW" stamped on the fuel inlet). All "Monojet", "Dualjet" and "Quadrajet" carburetors with a tapered pump well should use a Blue Viton® pump and should be replaced as an assembly only. Because of differences in design, the Blue Viton® cup is NOT interchangable with the red cup.

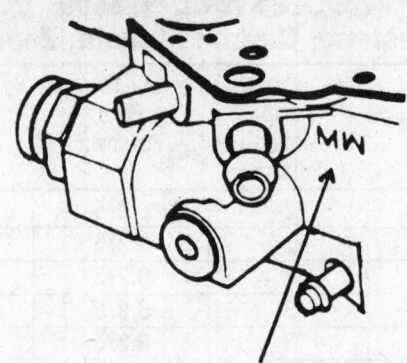

Machined pump well designation shown next to fuel inlet

FLOAT ADJUSTMENT

1. Remove the air horn from the throttle body.
2. Use your fingers to hold the retainer in place and to push the float down into light contact with the needle.
3. Measure the distance from the toe of the float (furtherest from the hinge) to the top of the carburetor (gasket removed).
4. To adjust, remove the float and gently bend the arm to specification. After adjustment, check the float alignment in the chamber.

NOTE: Some models have a float stabilizer spring. If used, remove the spring with float. Use care when removing.

PUMP ADJUSTMENT

No pump adjustment is required.

FAST IDLE ADJUSTMENT

1. Set the ignition timing and curb idle speed and disconnect and plug hoses as directed on the emission control decal.
2. Place the fast idle screw on the **highest** step of the cam.
3. Start the engine and adjust the engine speed to specification with the fast idle screw.

NOTE: On models using a clip to retain pump rod in pump lever, no pump adjustment is required. On models using the "CLIPLESS" pump rod, the pump rod adjustment should not be changed from the original factory setting unless gauging shows it to be out of specification. The pump lever is made from heavy duty, hardened steel making bending difficult. Do not remove pump lever for bending unless absolutely necessary.

CHOKE COIL LEVER ADJUSTMENT

1. Remove the 3 retaining screws and remove the choke cover and coil. On models with a riveted choke cover, drill out the 3 rivets and remove the cover and choke coil.

NOTE: A choke stat cover retainer kit is required for reassembly.

2. Place the fast idle screw on the **high** step of the cam.
3. Close the choke by pushing in on the intermediate choke lever. On front wheel drive models, the intermediate choke lever is behind the choke vacuum diaphragm.
4. Insert a drill or gauge of the specified size into the hole in the choke housing. The choke lever in the housing should be up against the side of the gauge.
5. If the lever does not just touch the gauge, bend the intermediate choke rod to adjust.

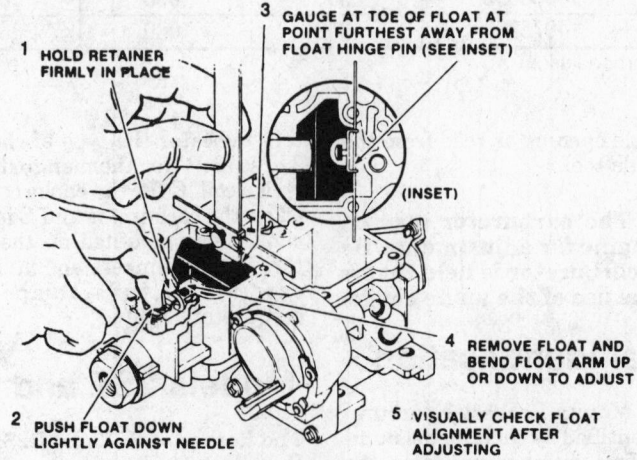

3 GAUGE AT TOE OF FLOAT AT POINT FURTHEST AWAY FROM FLOAT HINGE PIN (SEE INSET)

1 HOLD RETAINER FIRMLY IN PLACE

(INSET)

4 REMOVE FLOAT AND BEND FLOAT ARM UP OR DOWN TO ADJUST

2 PUSH FLOAT DOWN LIGHTLY AGAINST NEEDLE

5 VISUALLY CHECK FLOAT ALIGNMENT AFTER ADJUSTING

2SE, E2SE float adjustment

FAST IDLE CAM (CHOKE ROD) ADJUSTMENT

1982 Models

NOTE: A special angle gauge should be used.

1. Adjust the choke coil lever and fast idle first.
2. Rotate the degree scale until it is zeroed.
3. Close the choke and install the degree scale onto the choke plate. Center the leveling bubble.

4. Rotate the scale so that the specified degree is opposite the scale pointer.
5. Place the fast idle screw on the **second step** of the cam (against the high step). Close the choke by pushing in the intermediate lever.
6. Push on the vacuum break lever in the direction of opening choke until the lever is against the rear tang on the choke lever.
7. Bend the fast idle cam rod at the "U" to adjust the angle to specifications.

1983–84 Models

Refer to the illustration for the adjustment procedure on these models.

AIR VALVE ROD ADJUSTMENT

1982 Models

1. Align the 0 degree mark with the pointer on an angle gauge.
2. Close the air valve and place a magnet on top of it.
3. Rotate the bubble until it is centered.
4. Rotate the degree scale until the

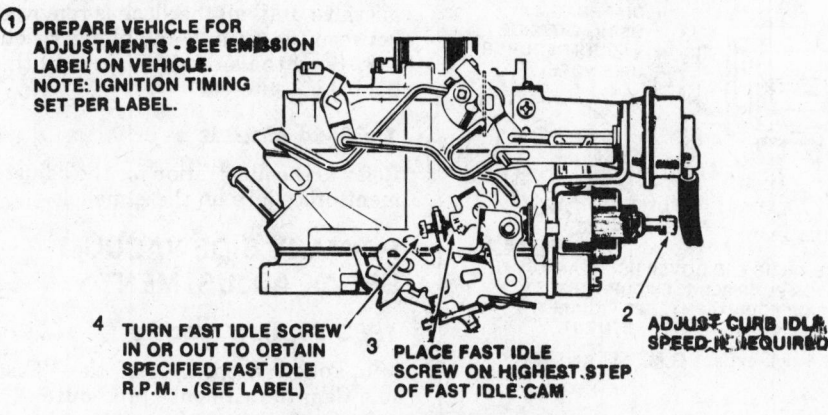

① PREPARE VEHICLE FOR ADJUSTMENTS - SEE EMISSION LABEL ON VEHICLE. NOTE: IGNITION TIMING SET PER LABEL.

4 TURN FAST IDLE SCREW IN OR OUT TO OBTAIN SPECIFIED FAST IDLE R.P.M. - (SEE LABEL)

3 PLACE FAST IDLE SCREW ON HIGHEST STEP OF FAST IDLE CAM

2 ADJUST CURB IDLE SPEED IF REQUIRED

2SE, E2SE fast idle adjustment

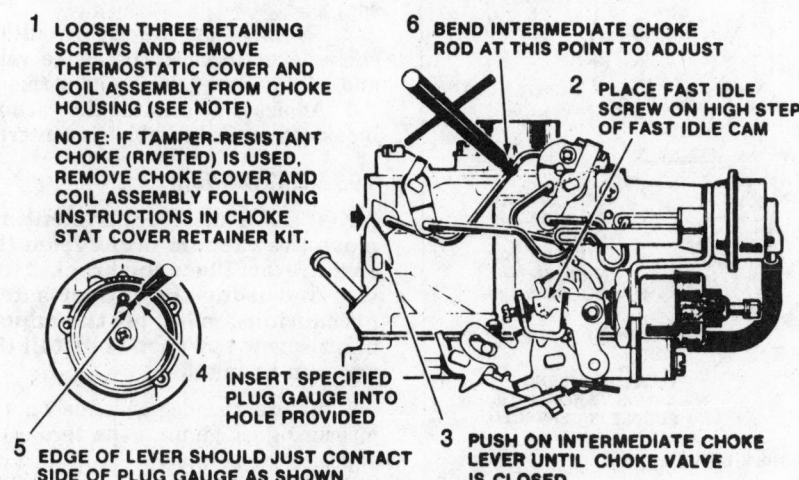

1 LOOSEN THREE RETAINING SCREWS AND REMOVE THERMOSTATIC COVER AND COIL ASSEMBLY FROM CHOKE HOUSING (SEE NOTE)

NOTE: IF TAMPER-RESISTANT CHOKE (RIVETED) IS USED, REMOVE CHOKE COVER AND COIL ASSEMBLY FOLLOWING INSTRUCTIONS IN CHOKE STAT COVER RETAINER KIT.

4 INSERT SPECIFIED PLUG GAUGE INTO HOLE PROVIDED

5 EDGE OF LEVER SHOULD JUST CONTACT SIDE OF PLUG GAUGE AS SHOWN

6 BEND INTERMEDIATE CHOKE ROD AT THIS POINT TO ADJUST

2 PLACE FAST IDLE SCREW ON HIGH STEP OF FAST IDLE CAM

3 PUSH ON INTERMEDIATE CHOKE LEVER UNTIL CHOKE VALVE IS CLOSED

2SE, E2SE choke coil lever adjustment

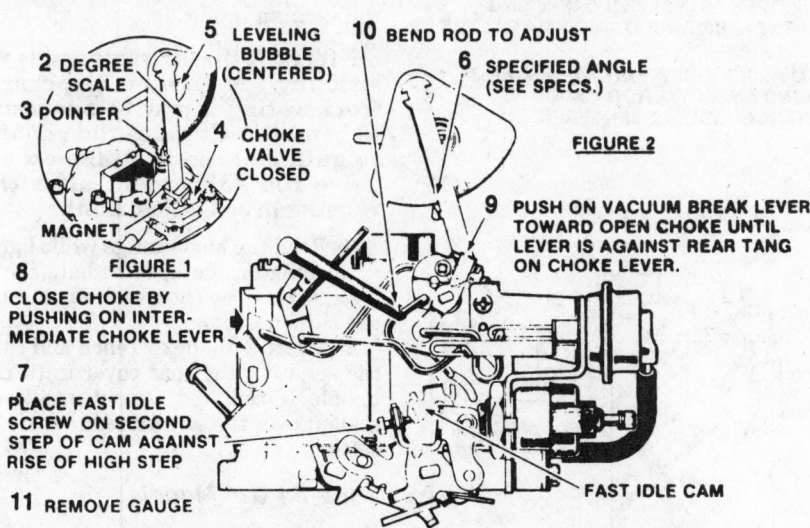

5 LEVELING BUBBLE (CENTERED)
2 DEGREE SCALE
3 POINTER
4 CHOKE VALVE CLOSED
MAGNET

10 BEND ROD TO ADJUST
6 SPECIFIED ANGLE (SEE SPECS.)

FIGURE 2

9 PUSH ON VACUUM BREAK LEVER TOWARD OPEN CHOKE UNTIL LEVER IS AGAINST REAR TANG ON CHOKE LEVER.

8 FIGURE 1
CLOSE CHOKE BY PUSHING ON INTERMEDIATE CHOKE LEVER

7 PLACE FAST IDLE SCREW ON SECOND STEP OF CAM AGAINST RISE OF HIGH STEP

11 REMOVE GAUGE

FAST IDLE CAM

2SE, E2SE fast idle cam adjustment—models through 1982

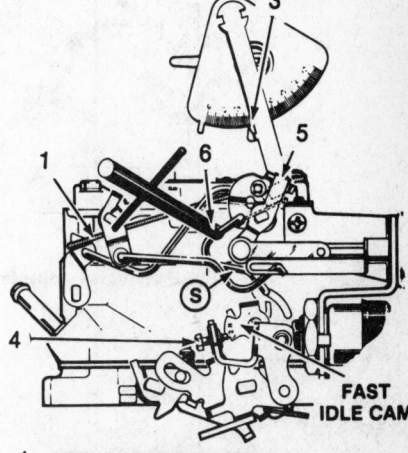

FAST IDLE CAM

1 ATTACH RUBBER BAND TO INTERMEDIATE CHOKE LEVER.

2 OPEN THROTTLE TO ALLOW CHOKE VALVE TO CLOSE.

3 SET UP ANGLE GAGE AND SET ANGLE TO SPECIFICATIONS.

4 PLACE FAST IDLE SCREW ON SECOND STEP OF CAM AGAINST RISE OF HIGH STEP.

5 PUSH ON CHOKE SHAFT LEVER TO OPEN CHOKE VALVE AND TO MAKE CONTACT WITH BLACK CLOSING TANG.

6 SUPPORT AT "S" AND ADJUST BY BENDING FAST IDLE CAM ROD UNTIL BUBBLE IS CENTERED.

E2SE fast idle cam (choke rod) adjustment—1983 and later

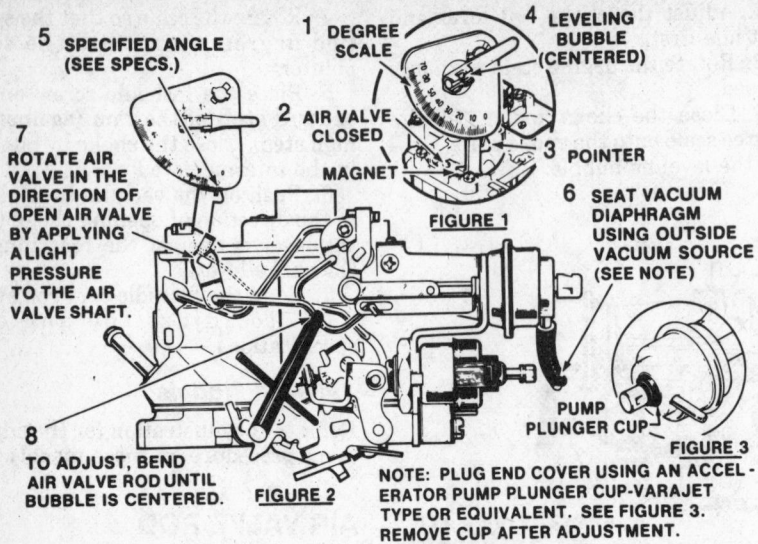

5 SPECIFIED ANGLE (SEE SPECS.)

1 DEGREE SCALE

4 LEVELING BUBBLE (CENTERED)

2 AIR VALVE CLOSED

MAGNET

3 POINTER

FIGURE 1

7 ROTATE AIR VALVE IN THE DIRECTION OF OPEN AIR VALVE BY APPLYING A LIGHT PRESSURE TO THE AIR VALVE SHAFT.

6 SEAT VACUUM DIAPHRAGM USING OUTSIDE VACUUM SOURCE (SEE NOTE)

PUMP PLUNGER CUP

FIGURE 3

8 TO ADJUST, BEND AIR VALVE ROD UNTIL BUBBLE IS CENTERED. FIGURE 2

NOTE: PLUG END COVER USING AN ACCELERATOR PUMP PLUNGER CUP-VARAJET TYPE OR EQUIVALENT. SEE FIGURE 3. REMOVE CUP AFTER ADJUSTMENT.

E2SE air valve adjustment—1981–82 4 cyl. except G.M. "J" series

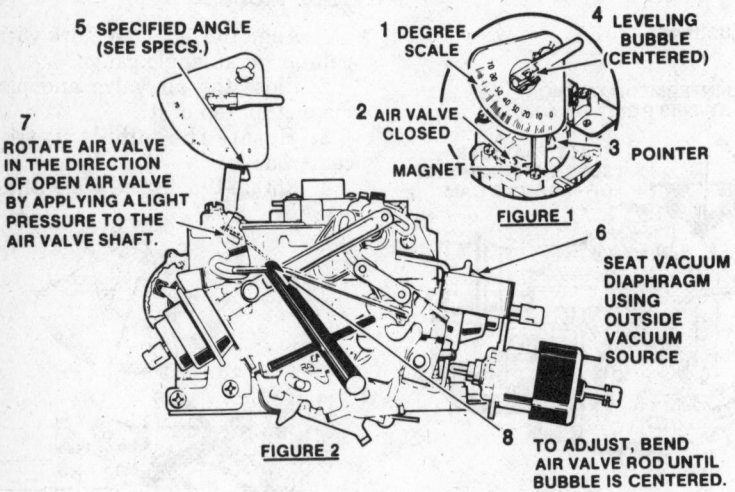

5 SPECIFIED ANGLE (SEE SPECS.)

1 DEGREE SCALE

4 LEVELING BUBBLE (CENTERED)

2 AIR VALVE CLOSED

MAGNET

3 POINTER

FIGURE 1

7 ROTATE AIR VALVE IN THE DIRECTION OF OPEN AIR VALVE BY APPLYING A LIGHT PRESSURE TO THE AIR VALVE SHAFT.

6 SEAT VACUUM DIAPHRAGM USING OUTSIDE VACUUM SOURCE

8 TO ADJUST, BEND AIR VALVE ROD UNTIL BUBBLE IS CENTERED.

FIGURE 2

E2SE air valve adjustment—1981–82 V6 engine

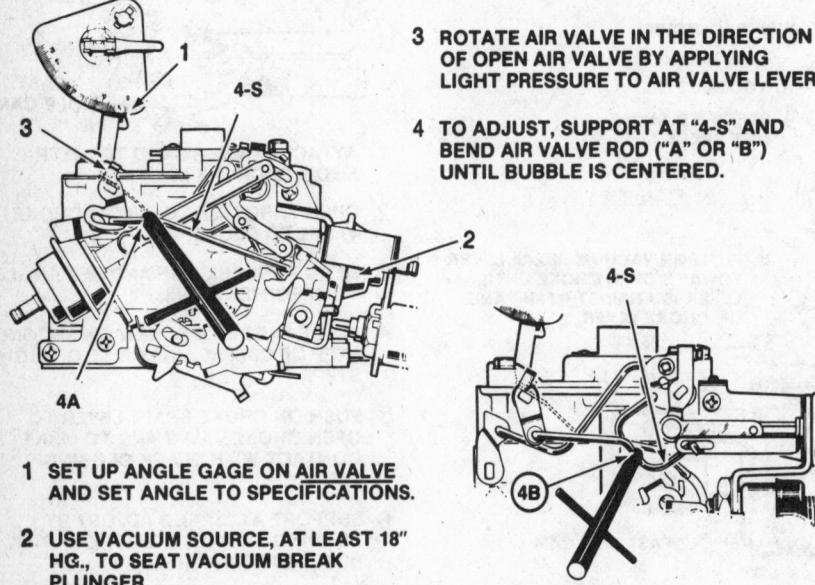

3 ROTATE AIR VALVE IN THE DIRECTION OF OPEN AIR VALVE BY APPLYING LIGHT PRESSURE TO AIR VALVE LEVER.

4 TO ADJUST, SUPPORT AT "4-S" AND BEND AIR VALVE ROD ("A" OR "B") UNTIL BUBBLE IS CENTERED.

1 SET UP ANGLE GAGE ON AIR VALVE AND SET ANGLE TO SPECIFICATIONS.

2 USE VACUUM SOURCE, AT LEAST 18" HG., TO SEAT VACUUM BREAK PLUNGER.

E2SE air valve rod adjustment—1983 and later

specified degree mark is aligned with the pointer.

5. Seat the vacuum diaphragm using an external vacuum source.

6. On 4 cylinder models plug the end cover. Unplug it after adjustment.

7. Apply light pressure to the air valve shaft in the direction to open the air valve until all the slack is removed between the air link and plunger slot.

8. Bend the air valve link until the bubble is centered.

1983–84 Models

Refer to the illustration for the adjustment procedure on these models.

PRIMARY SIDE VACUUM BREAK ADJUSTMENT

1982–83 AMC Models

1. Follow Steps 1–4 of the "Fast Idle Cam Adjustment" procedure.

2. Seat the choke vacuum diaphragm with an outside vacuum source.

3. Push in on the intermediate choke lever to close the choke valve and hold it closed during adjustment.

4. Adjust it by bending the vacuum break rod until the bubble is centered.

1982 GM Models

NOTE: Prior to adjustment, remove the vacuum break from the carburetor. Place the bracket in a vise and using the proper safety precautions, grind off the adjustment screw cap then reinstall the vacuum break.

1. Rotate the degree scale on the measuring gauge until the zero (0) is opposite the pointer.

2. Seat the choke vacuum diaphragm by applying an external vacuum source of over 5 in. Hg vacuum to the vacuum brake.

NOTE: If the air valve rod is restricting the vacuum diaphragm from seating it may be necessary to bend the air valve rod slightly to gain clearance. Make an air valve rod adjustment after the vacuum break adjustment.

3. Read the angle gauge while lightly pushing on the intermediate choke lever so that the choke valve is toward the close position.

4. Use a 1/8 in. hex wrench and turn the screw in the rear cover until the bubble is centered. Apply a silicone sealant over the screw head to seal the setting.

1983–84 GM Models

Refer to the illustration for the adjustment procedure on these models.

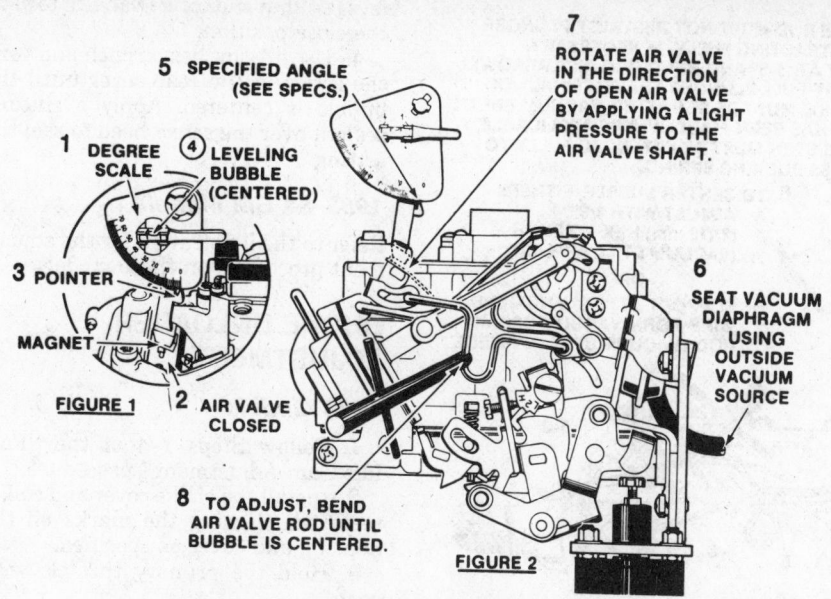

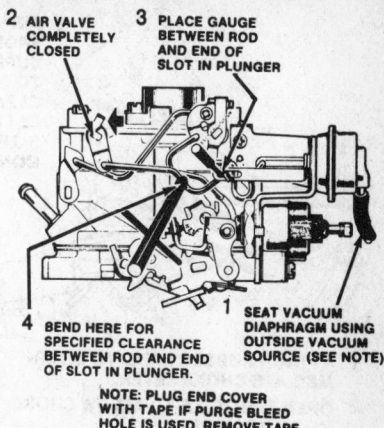

2SE and E2SE air valve rod adjustment—1980 G.M. models, 1980–82 American Motors

E2SE air valve adjustment—1982 G.M. J series

ELECTRIC CHOKE SETTING

This procedure is only for those carburetors with choke covers retained by screws. Riveted choke covers are preset and nonadjustable.

1. Loosen the 3 retaining screws.
2. Place the fast idle screw on the **high step** of the cam.
3. Rotate the choke cover to align the cover mark with the specified housing mark.

NOTE: The specification "index" which appears in the specification table refers to the mark between "1 notch lean" and "1 notch rich".

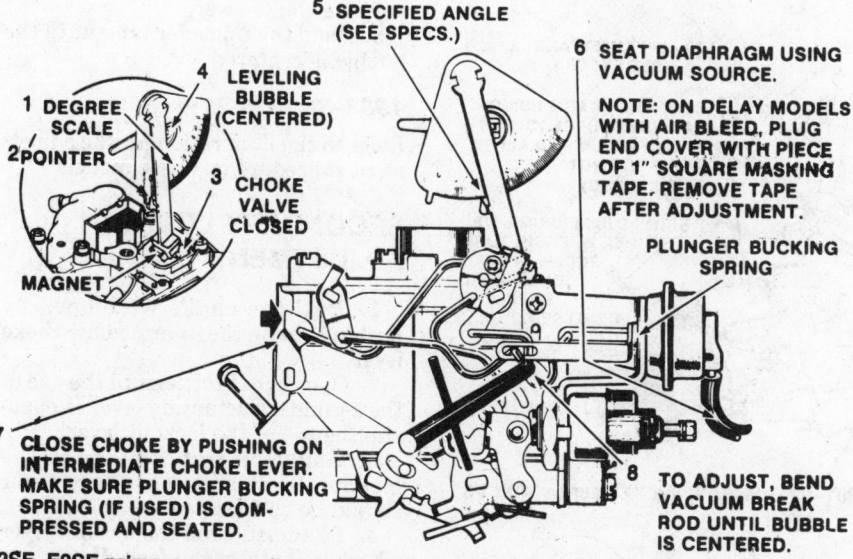

2SE, E2SE primary vacuum break adjustment—1980 G.M. and 1980–83 American Motors with 4 cyl. engines

SECONDARY VACUUM BREAK ADJUSTMENT

1982 GM Models

NOTE: Plug the end cover using an accelerator pump plunger cup or equivalent. Remove the cup after the adjustment (A and X series only).

1. Rotate the degree scale on the measuring gauge until the zero (0) is opposite the pointer.
2. Seat the choke vacuum diaphragm by applying an external vacuum source of over 5 in. vacuum to the vacuum break.

NOTE: If the air valve rod is restricting the vacuum diaphragm from seating it may be necessary to bend the air valve rod slightly to gain clearance. Make an air valve rod adjustment after the vacuum break adjustment.

3. Read the angle gauge while lightly pushing on the intermediate choke

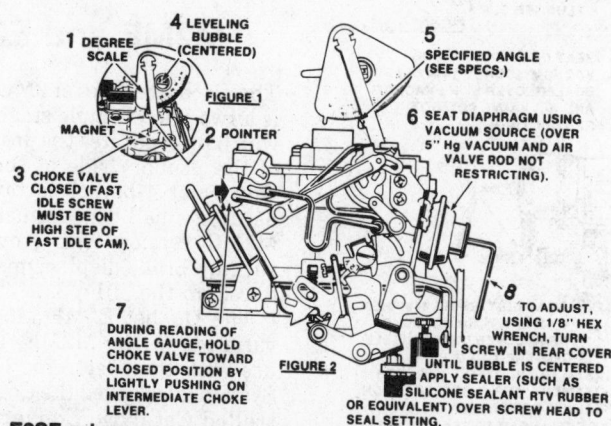

E2SE primary vacuum break adjustment—4 cyl.—1982 G.M. J series

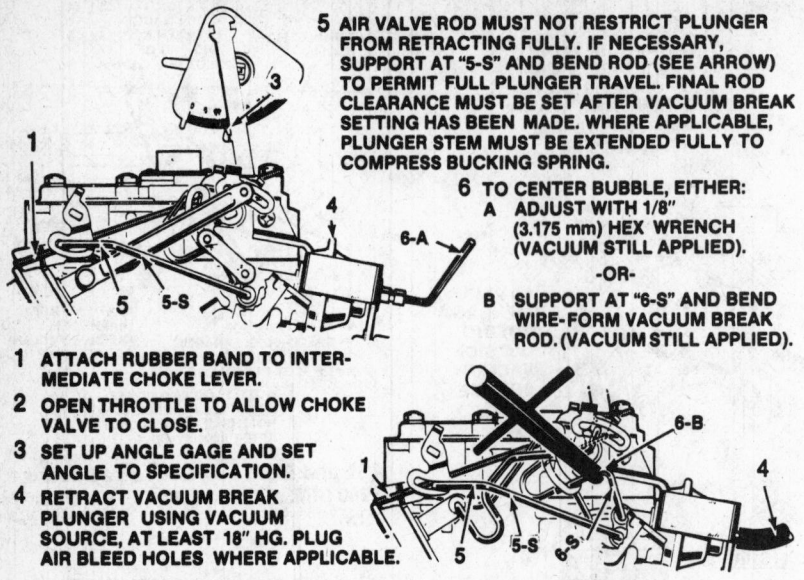

5 AIR VALVE ROD MUST NOT RESTRICT PLUNGER FROM RETRACTING FULLY. IF NECESSARY, SUPPORT AT "5-S" AND BEND ROD (SEE ARROW) TO PERMIT FULL PLUNGER TRAVEL. FINAL ROD CLEARANCE MUST BE SET AFTER VACUUM BREAK SETTING HAS BEEN MADE. WHERE APPLICABLE, PLUNGER STEM MUST BE EXTENDED FULLY TO COMPRESS BUCKING SPRING.

6 TO CENTER BUBBLE, EITHER:
A ADJUST WITH 1/8" (3.175 mm) HEX WRENCH (VACUUM STILL APPLIED).
-OR-
B SUPPORT AT "6-S" AND BEND WIRE-FORM VACUUM BREAK ROD. (VACUUM STILL APPLIED).

1 ATTACH RUBBER BAND TO INTER-MEDIATE CHOKE LEVER.
2 OPEN THROTTLE TO ALLOW CHOKE VALVE TO CLOSE.
3 SET UP ANGLE GAGE AND SET ANGLE TO SPECIFICATION.
4 RETRACT VACUUM BREAK PLUNGER USING VACUUM SOURCE, AT LEAST 18" HG. PLUG AIR BLEED HOLES WHERE APPLICABLE.

E2SE primary vacuum break adjustment—1983 and later

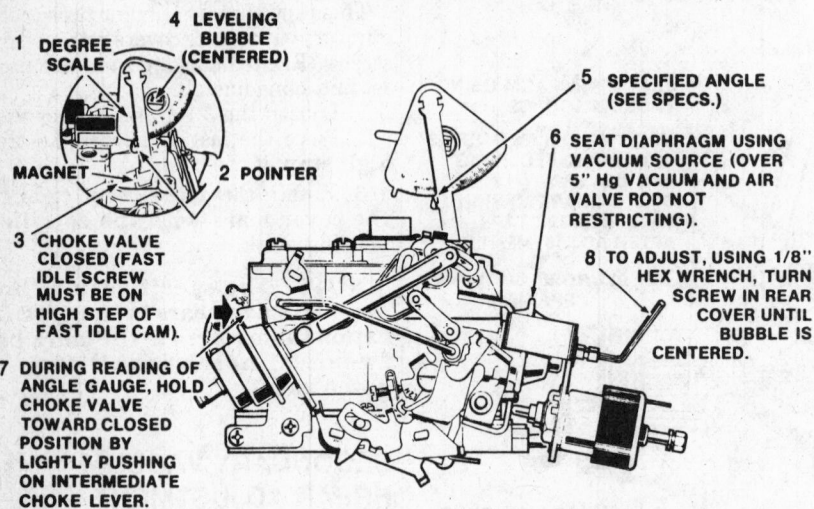

1 DEGREE SCALE
4 LEVELING BUBBLE (CENTERED)
MAGNET
2 POINTER
5 SPECIFIED ANGLE (SEE SPECS.)
6 SEAT DIAPHRAGM USING VACUUM SOURCE (OVER 5" Hg VACUUM AND AIR VALVE ROD NOT RESTRICTING).
8 TO ADJUST, USING 1/8" HEX WRENCH, TURN SCREW IN REAR COVER UNTIL BUBBLE IS CENTERED.

3 CHOKE VALVE CLOSED (FAST IDLE SCREW MUST BE ON HIGH STEP OF FAST IDLE CAM).
7 DURING READING OF ANGLE GAUGE, HOLD CHOKE VALVE TOWARD CLOSED POSITION BY LIGHTLY PUSHING ON INTERMEDIATE CHOKE LEVER.

E2SE primary vacuum break adjustment—1981–82 G.M. "A" and "X" series with V6 engine

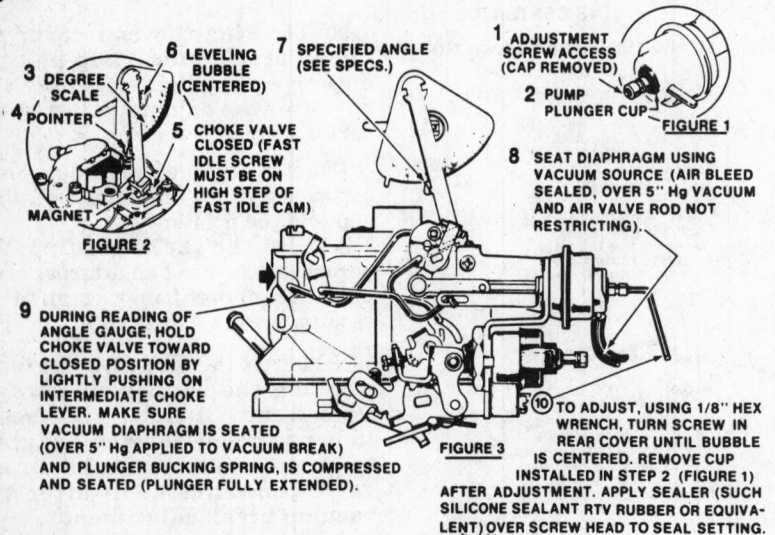

3 DEGREE SCALE
4 POINTER
6 LEVELING BUBBLE (CENTERED)
7 SPECIFIED ANGLE (SEE SPECS.)
1 ADJUSTMENT SCREW ACCESS (CAP REMOVED)
2 PUMP PLUNGER CUP
FIGURE 1

5 CHOKE VALVE CLOSED (FAST IDLE SCREW MUST BE ON HIGH STEP OF FAST IDLE CAM).
MAGNET
FIGURE 2

8 SEAT DIAPHRAGM USING VACUUM SOURCE (AIR BLEED SEALED, OVER 5" Hg VACUUM AND AIR VALVE ROD NOT RESTRICTING).

9 DURING READING OF ANGLE GAUGE, HOLD CHOKE VALVE TOWARD CLOSED POSITION BY LIGHTLY PUSHING ON INTERMEDIATE CHOKE LEVER. MAKE SURE VACUUM DIAPHRAGM IS SEATED (OVER 5" Hg APPLIED TO VACUUM BREAK) AND PLUNGER BUCKING SPRING, IS COMPRESSED AND SEATED (PLUNGER FULLY EXTENDED).
FIGURE 3

10 TO ADJUST, USING 1/8" HEX WRENCH, TURN SCREW IN REAR COVER UNTIL BUBBLE IS CENTERED. REMOVE CUP INSTALLED IN STEP 2 (FIGURE 1) AFTER ADJUSTMENT. APPLY SEALER (SUCH SILICONE SEALANT RTV RUBBER OR EQUIVA-LENT) OVER SCREW HEAD TO SEAL SETTING.

E2SE primary vacuum break adjustment—1981–82 G.M. "A" and "X" series with 4 cyl engine

lever so that the choke valve is toward the close position.

4. Use a 1/8 in. hex wrench and turn the screw in the rear cover until the bubble is centered. Apply a silicone sealant over the screw head to seal the setting.

1983–84 GM Models

Refer to the illustration for the adjustment procedure on these models.

CHOKE UNLOADER ADJUSTMENT

1982 Models

1. Follow Steps 1–4 of the "Fast Idle Cam Adjustment" procedure.
2. Install the choke cover and coil, if removed, aligning the marks on the housing and cover as specified.
3. Hold the primary throttle wide open.
4. If the engine is warm, close the choke valve by pushing in on the intermediate choke lever.
5. Bend the unloader tang until the bubble is centered.

1983–84 Models

Refer to the illustration for the adjustment procedure on these models.

SECONDARY LOCKOUT ADJUSTMENT

1. Pull the choke wide open by pushing out on the intermediate choke lever.
2. Open the throttle until the end of the secondary actuating lever is opposite the toe of the lockout lever.
3. Gauge clearance between the lockout lever and secondary lever should be as specified.
4. To adjust, bend the lockout lever where it contacts the fast idle cam.

Models 2MC, M2MC, M2ME and E2ME

The Rochester model 2MC carburetor is a two-barrel single stage carburetor which incorporates the design features of the primary side of the Rochester Quadrajet 4-barrel carburetor. It is used on small displacement V8s. The M2MC version with front and rear vacuum brake diaphragms, was introduced on the 301 V8.

The Dualjet E2ME Model 210 is a variation of the M2ME, modified for use with the Electronic Fuel Control System (also called the Computer Controlled Catalytic Converter, or C-4, System). An electrically operated mixture control solenoid is mounted in the

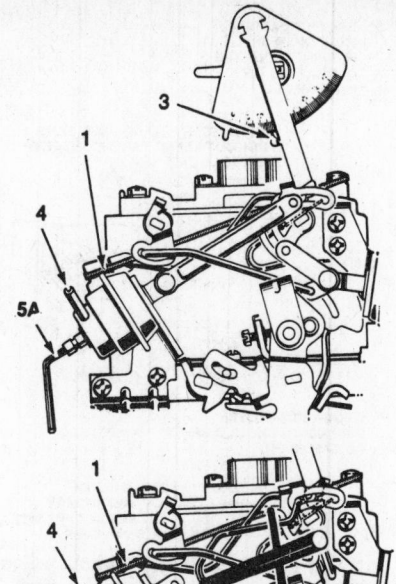

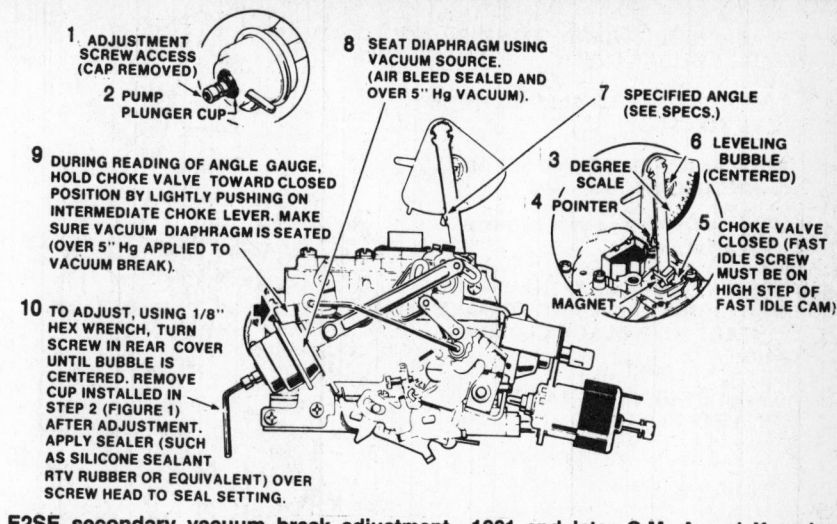

1 **ADJUSTMENT SCREW ACCESS (CAP REMOVED)**

2 **PUMP PLUNGER CUP**

8 **SEAT DIAPHRAGM USING VACUUM SOURCE. (AIR BLEED SEALED AND OVER 5" Hg VACUUM).**

7 **SPECIFIED ANGLE (SEE SPECS.)**

3 **DEGREE SCALE**

4 **POINTER**

6 **LEVELING BUBBLE (CENTERED)**

5 **CHOKE VALVE CLOSED (FAST IDLE SCREW MUST BE ON HIGH STEP OF FAST IDLE CAM)**

MAGNET

9 **DURING READING OF ANGLE GAUGE, HOLD CHOKE VALVE TOWARD CLOSED POSITION BY LIGHTLY PUSHING ON INTERMEDIATE CHOKE LEVER. MAKE SURE VACUUM DIAPHRAGM IS SEATED (OVER 5" Hg APPLIED TO VACUUM BREAK).**

10 **TO ADJUST, USING 1/8" HEX WRENCH, TURN SCREW IN REAR COVER UNTIL BUBBLE IS CENTERED. REMOVE CUP INSTALLED IN STEP 2 (FIGURE 1) AFTER ADJUSTMENT. APPLY SEALER (SUCH AS SILICONE SEALANT RTV RUBBER OR EQUIVALENT) OVER SCREW HEAD TO SEAL SETTING.**

E2SE secondary vacuum break adjustment—1981 and later G.M. A and X series

1 ATTACH RUBBER BAND TO INTER-MEDIATE CHOKE LEVER.

2 OPEN THROTTLE TO ALLOW CHOKE VALVE TO CLOSE.

3 SET UP ANGLE GAGE AND SET ANGLE TO SPECIFICATION.

4 RETRACT VACUUM BREAK PLUNGER USING VACUUM SOURCE, AT LEAST 18" HG. PLUG AIR BLEED HOLES WHERE APPLICABLE.

WHERE APPLICABLE, PLUNGER STEM MUST BE EXTENDED FULLY TO COM-PRESS PLUNGER BUCKING SPRING.

5 TO CENTER BUBBLE, EITHER:

A. ADJUST WITH 1/8" (3.175 mm) HEX WRENCH (VACUUM STILL APPLIED)

-OR-

B. SUPPORT AT "5-S", BEND WIRE-FORM VACUUM BREAK ROD (VACUUM STILL APPLIED)

E2SE secondary vacuum break adjust-ment—1983 and later

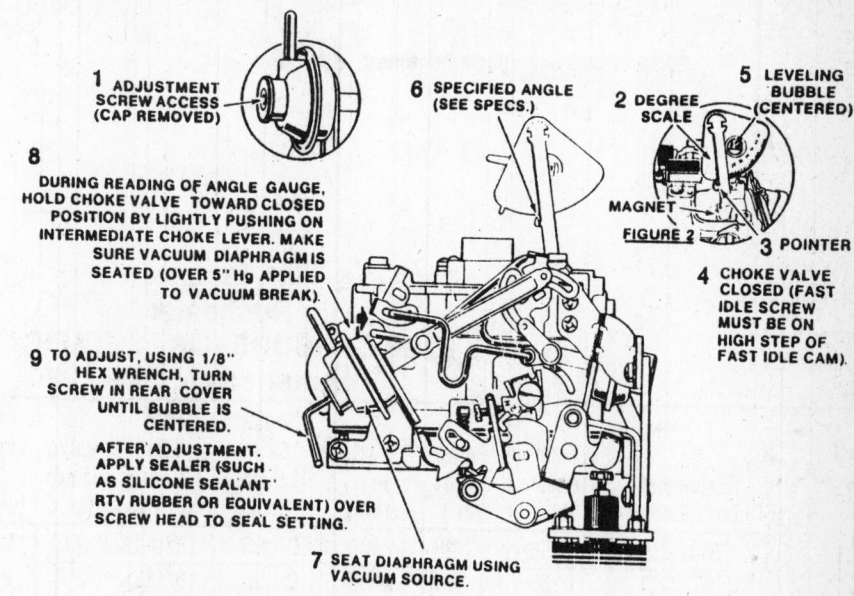

1 **ADJUSTMENT SCREW ACCESS (CAP REMOVED)**

8 **DURING READING OF ANGLE GAUGE, HOLD CHOKE VALVE TOWARD CLOSED POSITION BY LIGHTLY PUSHING ON INTERMEDIATE CHOKE LEVER. MAKE SURE VACUUM DIAPHRAGM IS SEATED (OVER 5" Hg APPLIED TO VACUUM BREAK).**

9 **TO ADJUST, USING 1/8" HEX WRENCH, TURN SCREW IN REAR COVER UNTIL BUBBLE IS CENTERED. AFTER ADJUSTMENT. APPLY SEALER (SUCH AS SILICONE SEALANT RTV RUBBER OR EQUIVALENT) OVER SCREW HEAD TO SEAL SETTING.**

7 **SEAT DIAPHRAGM USING VACUUM SOURCE.**

6 **SPECIFIED ANGLE (SEE SPECS.)**

2 **DEGREE SCALE**

5 **LEVELING BUBBLE (CENTERED)**

MAGNET

FIGURE 2

3 **POINTER**

4 **CHOKE VALVE CLOSED (FAST IDLE SCREW MUST BE ON HIGH STEP OF FAST IDLE CAM)**

E2SE secondary vacuum break adjustment—1982 G.M. J series

float bowl. Mixture is thus controlled by the Electronic Control Module, in response to signals from the oxygen sensor mounted in the exhaust system upstream of the catalytic converter.

For further information on feed-back carburetors, please refer to *Chilton's Guide To Fuel Injection And Feedback Carburetors.*

FLOAT LEVEL ADJUSTMENT

See the illustration for float level ad-justment for all carburetors. The E2ME procedure is the same except for adjustment (Step 4 in the figure). For the E2ME only, if the float level is too high, hold the retainer firmly in

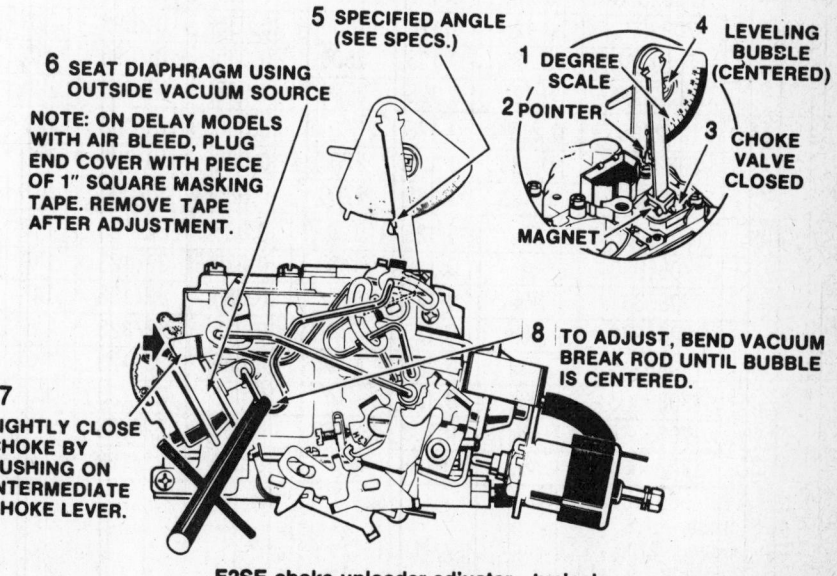

6 **SEAT DIAPHRAGM USING OUTSIDE VACUUM SOURCE**

NOTE: ON DELAY MODELS WITH AIR BLEED, PLUG END COVER WITH PIECE OF 1" SQUARE MASKING TAPE. REMOVE TAPE AFTER ADJUSTMENT.

5 **SPECIFIED ANGLE (SEE SPECS.)**

1 **DEGREE SCALE**

2 **POINTER**

4 **LEVELING BUBBLE (CENTERED)**

3 **CHOKE VALVE CLOSED**

MAGNET

8 **TO ADJUST, BEND VACUUM BREAK ROD UNTIL BUBBLE IS CENTERED.**

7 **LIGHTLY CLOSE CHOKE BY PUSHING ON INTERMEDIATE CHOKE LEVER.**

E2SE choke unloader adjuster—typical

1 **ATTACH RUBBER BAND TO INTERMEDIATE CHOKE LEVER.**

2 **OPEN THROTTLE TO ALLOW CHOKE VALVE TO CLOSE.**

3 **SET UP ANGLE GAGE AND SET ANGLE TO SPECIFICATIONS.**

4 **HOLD THROTTLE LEVER IN WIDE OPEN POSITION.**

5 **PUSH ON CHOKE SHAFT LEVER TO OPEN CHOKE VALVE AND TO MAKE CONTACT WITH BLACK CLOSING TANG.**

6 **ADJUST BY BENDING TANG UNTIL BUBBLE IS CENTERED.**

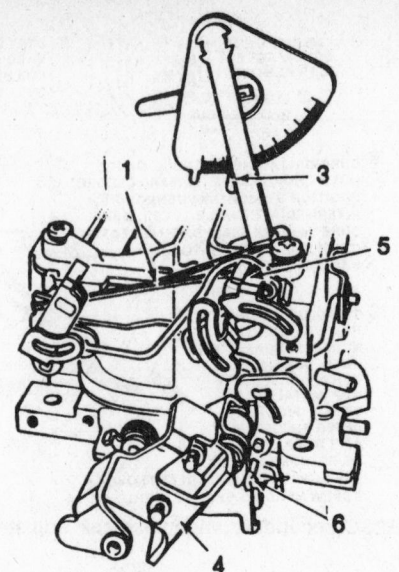

E2SE choke unloader adjustment—1983 and later

1 **HOLD CHOKE VALVE WIDE OPEN BY PUSHING COUNTER-CLOCKWISE ON INTERMEDIATE CHOKE LEVER.**

4 **IF NECESSARY TO ADJUST, BEND LOCKOUT LEVER TANG CONTACTING FAST IDLE CAM.**

3 **GAUGE CLEARANCE - DIMENSION SHOULD BE AS SPECIFIED.**

2 **OPEN THROTTLE LEVER UNTIL END OF SECONDARY ACTUATING LEVER IS OPPOSITE TOE OF LOCKOUT LEVER.**

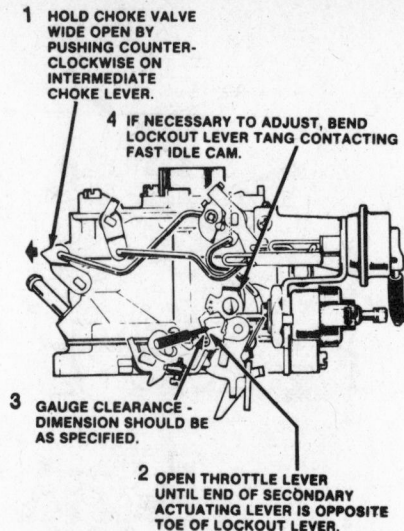

2SE and E2SE secondary lockout adjustment—typical

Rochester
2SE, E2SE CARBURETOR SPECIFICATIONS
American Motors

Year	Carburetor Identification	Float Level (in.)	Pump Rod (in.)	Fast Idle (rpm)	Choke Coil Lever (in.)	Fast Idle Cam (deg./in.)	Air Valve Rod (in.)	Primary Vacuum Break (deg./in.)	Choke Setting (notches)	Choke Unloader (deg./in.)	Secondary Lockout (in.)
'82	17082385	0.256	0.128	2400	0.085	18/.096	2①	21/.117	Fixed	34/.211	0.065
	17082383	0.256	0.128	2400	0.085	18/.096	2①	21/.117	Fixed	34/.211	0.065
	17082380	0.216	0.128	2400	0.085	18/.096	2①	21/.117	Fixed	34/.211	0.065
	17082386	0.125	0.128	2400	0.065	18/.096	2①	19/.103	Fixed	34/.211	0.065
	17082387	0.125	0.128	2600	0.085	18/.096	2①	19/.103	Fixed	34/.211	0.065
	17082388	0.125	0.128	2500	0.085	18/.096	2①	19/.103	Fixed	34/.211	0.065
	17082389	0.125	0.128	2500	0.085	18/.096	2①	19/.103	Fixed	34/.211	0.065
'83–'84	1982380	0.216②	0.128	2500③	0.085	18/.096	2①	21/.117	Fixed	34/.211	0.065
	1983384	0.138	0.128	2700	0.085	18/.096	2①	19/.103	Fixed	34/.211	0.065
	1983385	0.138	0.128	2700	0.085	18/.096	②①	19/.103	Fixed	34/.211	0.065
'85–'86	17085006	4/32	0.128	④	0.085	22/.123	1①	21/.117	Fixed	40/.260	0.025
	17085380	5/32	0.128	④	0.085	22/.123	1①	26/.149	Fixed	40/.260	0.025
	17085381	5/32	0.128	④	0.085	22/.123	1①	26/.149	Fixed	40/.260	0.025
	17085382	5/32	0.128	④	0.085	22/.123	1①	26/.149	Fixed	40/.260	0.025
	17085383	5/32	0.128	④	0.085	22/.123	1①	26/.149	Fixed	40/.260	0.025
	17085385	5/32	0.128	④	0.085	22/.123	1①	26/.149	Fixed	40/.260	0.025
	17085388	4/32	0.128	④	0.085	22/.123	1①	21/.117	Fixed	30/.179	0.025
	17086081	4/32	0.128	④	0.085	22/.123	1①	25/.142	Fixed	30/.179	0.025

① Degrees—see procedure
② Auto. trans.—.138
③ Auto. trans.—2700
④ See underhood decal

Rochester
2SE, E2SE CARBURETOR SPECIFICATIONS
General Motors—U.S.A.

Year	Carburetor Identification	Float Level (in.)	Pump Rod (in.)	Fast Idle (rpm)	Choke Coil Lever (in.)	Fast Idle Cam (deg./in.)	Air Valve Rod (in.)	Primary Vacuum Break (deg./in.)	Choke Setting (notches)	Secondary Vacuum Break (deg./in.)	Choke Unloader (deg./in.)	Secondary Lockout (in.)
'82	17081600	5/16	Fixed	①	③	24/.136	1 ②	20/.110	Fixed	27/.157	35/.220	③
	17081601	5/16	Fixed	①	③	24/1.36	1 ②	20/.110	Fixed	27/.157	35/.220	③
	17081607	5/16	Fixed	①	③	24/.136	1 ②	20/.110	Fixed	27/.157	35/.220	③
	17081700	5/16	Fixed	①	③	24/.136	1 ②	20/.110	Fixed	27/.157	35/.220	③
	17081701	5/16	Fixed	①	③	24/.136	1 ②	20/.110	Fixed	27/.157	35/.220	③
	17082196	5/16	Fixed	①	.085	18/.096	1 ②	21/.117	Fixed	19/.103	27/157	③
	17082316	1/4	Fixed	2600	.085	17/.090	1 ②	30/.179	Fixed	34/.211	45/.304	③
	17082317	1/4	Fixed	2600	.085	17/.090	1 ②	30/.179	Fixed	35/.220	45/.304	③
	17082320	1/4	Fixed	2800	.085	25/.142	1 ②	30/.179	Fixed	35/.220	45/.304	③
	17082321	1/4	Fixed	2600	.085	25/.142	1 ②	30/.179	Fixed	35/.220	45/.304	③
	17082390	13/32	Fixed	2500	.085	17/.090	1 ②	26/.149	Fixed	34/.211	35/.220	.011-.040
	17082391	13/32	Fixed	2600	.085	25/.142	1 ②	29/.171	Fixed	35/.220	35/.220	.011-.040
	17082490	13/32	Fixed	2500	.085	17/.090	1 ②	26/.149	Fixed	34/.211	35/.220	.011-.040
	17082491	13/32	Fixed	2600	.085	25/.142	1 ②	29/.171	Fixed	35/.220	35/.220	.011-.040
	17082640	1/4	Fixed	2600	.085	17/.090	1 ②	30/.179	Fixed	34/.211	45/.304	③
	17082641	1/4	Fixed	2400	.085	17/.090	1 ②	30/.179	Fixed	35/.220	45/.304	③
	17082642	1/4	Fixed	2800	.085	25/.142	1 ②	30/.179	Fixed	35/.220	45/.304	③
'83	17083356	13/32	Fixed	①	.085	22/.123	1 ②	25/.142	Fixed	35/.220	30/.179	.025
	17083357	13/32	Fixed	①	.085	22/.123	1 ②	25/.142	Fixed	35/.220	30/.179	.025
	17083358	13/32	Fixed	①	.085	22/.123	1 ②	25/.142	Fixed	35/.220	30/.179	.025
	17083359	13/32	Fixed	①	.085	22/.123	1 ②	25/.142	Fixed	35/.220	30/.179	.025
	17083368	13/32	Fixed	①	.085	22/.123	1 ②	25/.142	Fixed	35/.220	30/.179	.025
	17083369	13/32	Fixed	①	.085	22/.123	1 ②	25/.142	Fixed	35/.220	30/.179	.025
	17083370	13/32	Fixed	①	.085	22/.123	1 ②	25/.142	Fixed	35/.220	30/.179	.025
	17083391	13/32	Fixed	①	.085	28/.164	1 ②	30/.179	Fixed	35/.220	38/.243	.025
	17083392	13/32	Fixed	①	.085	28/.164	1 ②	30/.179	Fixed	35/.220	38/.243	.025
	17083393	13/32	Fixed	①	.085	28/.164	1 ②	30/.179	Fixed	35/.220	38/.243	.025
	17083394	13/32	Fixed	①	.085	28/.164	1 ②	30/.179	Fixed	35/.220	38/.243	.025
	17083395	13/32	Fixed	①	.085	28/.164	1 ②	30/.179	Fixed	35/.220	38/.243	.025
	17083396	13/32	Fixed	①	.085	28/.164	1 ②	30/.179	Fixed	35/.220	38/.243	.025
	17083397	13/32	Fixed	①	.085	28/.164	1 ②	30/.179	Fixed	35/.220	38/.243	.025
	17083450	1/4	Fixed	Fixed	.085	28/.164	1 ②	27/.157	Fixed	35/.220	45/.304	.025
	17083451	1/4	Fixed	①	.085	28/.164	1 ②	27/.157	Fixed	35/.220	45/.304	.025
	17083452	1/4	Fixed	①	.085	28/.164	1 ②	27/.157	Fixed	35/.220	45/.304	.025
	17083453	1/4	Fixed	①	.085	28/.164	1 ②	27/.157	Fixed	35/.220	45/.304	.025
	17083454	1/4	Fixed	①	.085	28/.164	1 ②	27/.157	Fixed	35/.220	45/.304	.025
	17083455	1/4	Fixed	①	.085	28/.164	1 ②	27/.157	Fixed	35/.220	45/.304	.025
	17083456	1/4	Fixed	①	.085	28/.164	1 ②	27/.157	Fixed	35/.220	45/.304	.025
	17083630	1/4	Fixed	①	.085	28/.164	1 ②	27/.157	Fixed	35/.220	45/.304	.025
	17083631	1/4	Fixed	①	.085	28/.164	1 ②	27/.157	Fixed	35/.220	45/.304	.025
	17083632	1/4	Fixed	①	.085	28/.164	1 ②	27/.157	Fixed	35/.220	45/.304	.025
	17083633	1/4	Fixed	①	.085	28/.164	1 ②	27/.157	Fixed	35/.220	45/.304	.025
	17083634	1/4	Fixed	①	.085	28/.164	1 ②	27/.157	Fixed	35/.220	45/.304	.025
	17083635	1/4	Fixed	①	.085	28/.164	1 ②	27/.157	Fixed	35/.220	45/.304	.025
	17083636	1/4	Fixed	①	.085	28/.164	1 ②	27/.157	Fixed	35/.220	45/.304	.025

Rochester
2SE, E2SE CARBURETOR SPECIFICATIONS
General Motors—U.S.A.

Year	Carburetor Identification	Float Level (in.)	Pump Rod (in.)	Fast Idle (rpm)	Choke Coil Lever (in.)	Fast Idle Cam (deg./in.)	Air Valve Rod (in.)	Primary Vacuum Break (deg./in.)	Choke Setting (notches)	Secondary Vacuum Break (deg./in.)	Choke Unloader (deg./in.)	Secondary Lockout (in.)
'84	17072683	9/32	Fixed	①	.085	28/.164	1 ②	25/.142	Fixed	35/.220	45/.304	.025
	17074812	9/32	Fixed	①	.085	28/.164	1 ②	25/.142	Fixed	35/.220	45/.304	.025
	17084356	9/32	Fixed	①	.085	22/.123	1 ②	25/.142	Fixed	30/.179	30/.179	.025
	17084357	9/32	Fixed	①	.085	22/.123	1 ②	25/.142	Fixed	30/.179	30/.179	.025
	17084358	9/32	Fixed	①	.085	22/.123	1 ②	25/.142	Fixed	30/.179	30/.179	.025
	17084359	9/32	Fixed	①	.085	22/.123	1 ②	25/.142	Fixed	30/.179	30/.179	.025
	17084368	1/8	Fixed	①	.085	22/.123	1 ②	25/.142	Fixed	30/.179	30/.179	.025
	17084370	1/8	Fixed	①	.085	22/.123	1 ②	25/.142	Fixed	30/.179	30/.179	.025
	17084430	11/32	Fixed	①	.085	15/.077	1 ②	26/.149	Fixed	30/.179	30/.179	.025
	17084431	11/32	Fixed	①	.085	15/.077	1 ②	26/.149	Fixed	38/.243	42/.277	.025
	17084434	11/32	Fixed	①	.085	15/.077	1 ②	26/.149	Fixed	38/.243	42/.277	.025
	17084435	11/32	Fixed	①	.085	15/.077	1 ②	26/.149	Fixed	38/.243	42/.277	.025
	17084452	5/32	Fixed	①	.085	28/.164	1 ②	25/.142	Fixed	38/.243	42/.377	.025
	17084453	5/32	Fixed	①	.085	28/.164	1 ②	25/.142	Fixed	35/.220	45/.304	.025
	17084455	5/32	Fixed	①	.085	28/.164	1 ②	25/.142	Fixed	35/.220	45/.304	.025
	17084456	5/32	Fixed	①	.085	28/.164	1 ②	25/.142	Fixed	35/.220	45/.304	.025
	17084458	5/32	Fixed	①	.085	28/.164	1 ②	25/.142	Fixed	35/.220	45/.304	.025
	17084532	5/32	Fixed	①	.085	28/.164	1 ②	25/.142	Fixed	35/.220	45/.304	.025
	17084534	5/32	Fixed	①	.085	28/.164	1 ②	25/.142	Fixed	35/.220	45/.304	.025
	17084535	5/32	Fixed	①	.085	28/.164	1 ②	25/.142	Fixed	35/.220	45/.304	.025
	17084537	5/32	Fixed	①	.085	28/.164	1 ②	25/.142	Fixed	35/.220	45/.304	.025
	17084538	5/32	Fixed	①	.085	28/.164	1 ②	25/.142	Fixed	35/.220	45/.304	.025
	17084540	5/32	Fixed	①	.085	28/.164	1 ②	25/.142	Fixed	35/.220	45/.304	.025
	17084542	1/8	Fixed	①	.085	28/.164	1 ②	25/.142	Fixed	35/.220	45/.304	.025
	17084632	9/32	Fixed	①	.085	28/.164	1 ②	25/.142	Fixed	35/.220	45/.304	.025
	17084633	9/32	Fixed	①	.085	28/.164	1 ②	25/.142	Fixed	35/.220	45/.304	.025
	17084635	9/32	Fixed	①	.085	28/.164	1 ②	25/.142	Fixed	35/.220	45/.304	.025
	17084636	9/32	Fixed	①	.085	28/.164	1 ②	25/.142	Fixed	35/.220	45/.304	.025
'85	17084534	5/32	Fixed	①	.085	28/.164	1 ②	25/.142	Fixed	35/.220	45/.304	—
	17084535	5/32	Fixed	①	.085	28/.164	1 ②	25/.142	Fixed	35/.220	45/.304	—
	17084540	5/32	Fixed	①	.085	28/.164	1 ②	25/.142	Fixed	35/.220	45/.304	—
	17084542	4/32	Fixed	①	.085	28/.164	1 ②	25/.142	Fixed	35/.220	45/.304	—
	17085356	9/32	Fixed	①	.085	22/.123	1 ②	25/.142	Fixed	30/.179	30/.179	—
	17085357	9/32	Fixed	①	.085	22/.123	1 ②	25/.142	Fixed	30/.179	30/.179	—
	17085358	9/32	Fixed	①	.085	22/.123	1 ②	25/.142	Fixed	30/.179	30/.179	—
	17085359	9/32	Fixed	①	.085	22/.123	1 ②	25/.142	Fixed	30/.179	30/.179	—
	17085368	4/32	Fixed	①	.085	22/.123	1 ②	25/.142	Fixed	30/.179	30/.179	—
	17085369	9/32	Fixed	①	.085	22/.123	1 ②	25/.142	Fixed	30/.179	30/.179	—
	17085370	4/32	Fixed	①	.085	22/.123	1 ②	25/.142	Fixed	30/.179	30/.179	—
	17085371	9/32	Fixed	①	.085	22/.123	1 ②	25/.142	Fixed	30/.179	30/.179	—
	17085452	5/32	Fixed	①	.085	28/.164	1 ②	25/.142	Fixed	35/.220	45/.304	—
	17085453	5/32	Fixed	①	.085	28/.164	1 ②	25/.142	Fixed	35/.220	45/.304	—
	17085458	5/32	Fixed	①	.085	28/.164	1 ②	25/.142	Fixed	35/.220	45/.304	—

Rochester
2SE, E2SE CARBURETOR SPECIFICATIONS
General Motors—U.S.A.

Year	Carburetor Identification	Float Level (in.)	Pump Rod (in.)	Fast Idle (rpm)	Choke Coil Lever (in.)	Fast Idle Cam (deg./in.)	Air Valve Rod (in.)	Primary Vacuum Break (deg./in.)	Choke Setting (notches)	Secondary Vacuum Break (deg./in.)	Choke Unloader (deg./in.)	Secondary Lockout (in.)
'86	17084534	5/32	Fixed	①	.085	28/.164	1 ②	25/.142	Fixed	35/.220	45/.304	—
	17084535	5/32	Fixed	①	.085	28/.164	1 ②	25/.142	Fixed	35/.220	45/.304	—
	17084540	5/32	Fixed	①	.085	28/.164	1 ②	25/.142	Fixed	35/.220	45/.304	—
	17084542	5/32	Fixed	①	.085	28/.164	1 ②	25/.142	Fixed	35/.220	45/.304	—

① See underhood decal
② Measurement in degrees
③ Not available

Rochester
2SE, E2SE CARBURETOR SPECIFICATIONS
General Motors—Canada

Year	Carburetor Identification	Float Level (in.)	Pump Rod (in.)	Fast Idle (rpm)	Choke Coil Lever (in.)	Fast Idle Cam (deg./in.)	Air Valve Rod (in.)	Primary Vacuum Break (deg./in.)	Choke Setting (notches)	Secondary Vacuum Break (deg./in.)	Choke Unloader (deg./in.)	Secondary Lockout (in.)
'82	17082440	1/4	19/32	①	.085	24/.136	1	30/.179	Fixed	32/.195	45/.304	②
	17082441	1/4	19/32	①	.085	24/.136	1	30/.179	Fixed	32/.195	45/.304	②
	17082443	1/4	19/32	①	.085	24/.136	1	30/.179	Fixed	32/.195	45/.304	②
	17082460	1/4	19/32	①	.085	18/.096	1	21/.117	Fixed	—	36/.227	②
	17082461	1/4	19/32	①	.085	18/.096	1	21/.117	Fixed	—	36/.227	②
	17082462	1/4	19/32	①	.085	18/.096	1	21/.117	Fixed	—	36/.227	②
	17082464	1/8	19/32	①	.085	18/.096	1	21/.117	Fixed	—	36/.227	②
	17082465	1/8	19/32	①	.085	18/.096	1	21/.117	Fixed	—	36/.227	②
	17082466	1/8	19/32	①	.085	18/.096	1	21/.117	Fixed	—	36/.227	②
	17082620	7/16	19/32	①	.085	24/.136	1	30/.179	Fixed	32/.195	45/.304	②
	17082621	7/16	19/32	①	.085	24/.136	1	30/.179	Fixed	32/.195	45/.304	②
	17082622	7/16	19/32	①	.085	24/.136	1	30/.179	Fixed	32/.195	45/.304	②
	17082623	7/16	19/32	①	.085	24/.136	1	30/.179	Fixed	32/.195	45/.304	②
'83	17083311	5/16	Fixed	①	.085	24/.136	1	18/.096	Fixed	20/.110	35/.220	.025
	17083314	5/16	Fixed	①	.085	24/.136	1	16/.083	Fixed	20/.110	35/.220	.025
	17083401	5/16	Fixed	①	.085	24/.136	1	18/.096	Fixed	20/.110	35/.220	.025
	17083440	1/4	19/32	①	.085	24/.136	1	28/.164	Fixed	32/.195	40/.260	.025
	17083441	1/4	19/32	①	.085	24/.136	1	28/.164	Fixed	32/.195	40/.260	.025
	17083442	1/4	19/32	①	.085	24/.136	1	28/.164	Fixed	32/.195	40/.260	.025
	17083443	1/4	19/32	①	.085	24/.136	1	28/.164	Fixed	32/.195	40/.260	.025
	17083444	1/4	19/32	①	.085	24/.136	1	28/.164	Fixed	32/.195	40/.260	.025
	17083445	1/4	19/32	①	.085	24/.136	1	28/.164	Fixed	32/.195	40/.260	.025
	17083460	1/4	19/32	①	.085	18/.096	1	19/.103	Fixed	—	36/.227	.025
	17083461	1/4	19/32	①	.085	18/.096	1	18/.096	Fixed	—	36/.227	.025
	17083462	1/4	19/32	①	.085	18/.096	1	19/.103	Fixed	—	36/.227	.025
	17083464	1/8	19/32	①	.085	18/.096	1	19/.103	Fixed	—	36/.227	.025
	17083465	1/8	19/32	①	.085	18/.096	1	20/.110	Fixed	—	36/.227	.025
	17083466	1/8	19/32	①	.085	18/.096	1	19/.103	Fixed	—	36/.227	.025
	17083620	7/16	19/32	①	.085	24/.136	1	28/.164	Fixed	32/.195	40/.260	.025
	17083621	7/16	19/32	①	.085	24/.136	1	28/.164	Fixed	32/.195	40/.260	.025
	17083622	7/16	19/32	①	.085	24/.136	1	28/.164	Fixed	34/.195	40/.260	.025
	17083623	7/16	19/32	①	.085	24/.136	1	28/.164	Fixed	32/.195	40/.260	.025

Rochester
2SE, E2SE CARBURETOR SPECIFICATIONS
General Motors—Canada

Year	Carburetor Identification	Float Level (in.)	Pump Rod (in.)	Fast Idle (rpm)	Choke Coil Lever (in.)	Fast Idle Cam (deg./in.)	Air Valve Rod (in.)	Primary Vacuum Break (deg./in.)	Choke Setting (notches)	Secondary Vacuum Break (deg./in.)	Choke Unloader (deg./in.)	Secondary Lockout (in.)
'84	17084312	5/16	Fixed	①	.085	24/.136	1	18/.096	Fixed	20/.110	35/.220	.025
	17084314	5/16	Fixed	①	.085	29/.171	1	16/.083	Fixed	20/.110	30/.179	.025
	17084480	1/4	Fixed	①	.085	24/.136	1	28/.164	Fixed	32/.195	45/.304	.025
	17084481	1/4	Fixed	①	.085	24/.136	1	28/.164	Fixed	32/.195	45/.304	.025
	17084482	1/4	Fixed	①	.085	24/.136	1	28/.164	Fixed	32/.195	45/.304	.025
	17084483	1/4	Fixed	①	.085	24/.136	1	28/.164	Fixed	32/.195	45/.304	.025
	17084484	1/4	Fixed	①	.085	24/.136	1	28/.164	Fixed	32/.195	45/.304	.025
	17084485	1/4	Fixed	①	.085	24/.136	1	28/.164	Fixed	32/.195	45/.304	.025
	17084486	1/4	Fixed	①	.085	24/.136	1	28/.164	Fixed	32/.195	45/.304	.025
	17084487	1/4	Fixed	①	.085	24/.136	1	28/.164	Fixed	32/.195	45/.304	.025
	17084620	7/16	Fixed	①	.085	24/.136	1	26/.149	Fixed	32/.195	45/.304	.025
	17084621	7/16	Fixed	①	.085	24/.136	1	26/.149	Fixed	32/.195	45/.304	.025
	17084622	7/16	Fixed	①	.085	24/.136	1	26/.149	Fixed	32/.195	45/.304	.025
	17084623	7/16	Fixed	①	.085	24/.136	1	26/.149	Fixed	32/.195	45/.304	.025
'85	17084312	5/16	Fixed	①	.085	—	1	18/.096	Fixed	20/.110	35/.220	—
	17084314	5/16	Fixed	①	.085	—	1	16/.083	Fixed	20/.110	30/.179	—
	17085484	12/32	Fixed	①	.085	—	1	28/.164	Fixed	32/.195	45/.304	—
	17085485	12/32	Fixed	①	.085	—	1	28/.164	Fixed	32/.195	45/.304	—
	17085482	12/32	Fixed	①	.085	—	1	28/.164	Fixed	32/.195	45/.304	—
	17085483	12/32	Fixed	①	.085	—	1	28/.164	Fixed	32/.195	45/.304	—
	17085484	12/32	Fixed	①	.085	—	1	28/.164	Fixed	32/.195	45/.304	—
	17085485	12/32	Fixed	①	.085	—	1	28/.164	Fixed	32/.195	45/.304	—
	17085486	12/32	Fixed	①	.085	—	1	28/.164	Fixed	32/.195	45/.304	—
	17085487	12/32	Fixed	①	.085	—	1	28/.164	Fixed	32/.195	45/.304	—
'86	17086484	12/32	Fixed	①	.085	—	1	28/.164	Fixed	32/.195	45/.304	—
	17086485	12/32	Fixed	①	.085	—	1	28/.164	Fixed	32/.195	45/.304	—
	17086486	4/32	Fixed	①	.085	—	1	28/.164	Fixed	32/.195	45/.304	—
	17086487	4/32	Fixed	①	.085	—	1	28/.164	Fixed	32/.195	45/.304	—
'87	17084312	5/16	Fixed	①	.085	—	1	18/.096	Fixed	20/.110	35/.220	—
	17084314	5/16	Fixed	①	.085	—	1	16/.083	Fixed	20/.110	30/.179	—
	17085482	3/8	Fixed	①	.085	—	1	28/.164	Fixed	32/.195	45/.304	—
	17085483	3/8	Fixed	①	.085	—	1	28/.164	Fixed	32/.195	45/.304	—
	17085484	3/8	Fixed	①	.085	—	1	28/.164	Fixed	32/.195	45/.304	—
	17085485	3/8	Fixed	①	.085	—	1	28/.164	Fixed	32/.195	45/.304	—

① See underhood decal
② Not available

place and push down on the center of the float to adjust.

If the float level is too low on the E2ME, lift out the metering rods. Remove the solenoid connector screws. Turn the lean mixture solenoid screw in clockwise, counting the exact number of turns until the screw is lightly bottomed in the bowl. Then turn the screw out counterclockwise and remove it. Lift out the solenoid and connector. Remove the float and bend the

arm up to adjust. Install the parts, installing the mixture solenoid screw in until it is lightly bottomed, then turning it out the exact number of turns counted earlier.

FAST IDLE SPEED

1. Place the fast idle lever on the high step of the fast idle cam.
2. Turn the fast idle screw out until the throttle valves are closed.

3. Turn the screw in to contact the lever, then turn it in the number of turns listed in the specifications. Check this preliminary setting against the sticker figure.

FAST IDLE CAM (CHOKE ROD) ADJUSTMENT

1. Adjust the fast idle speed.
2. Place the cam follower lever on the **second** step of the fast idle cam,

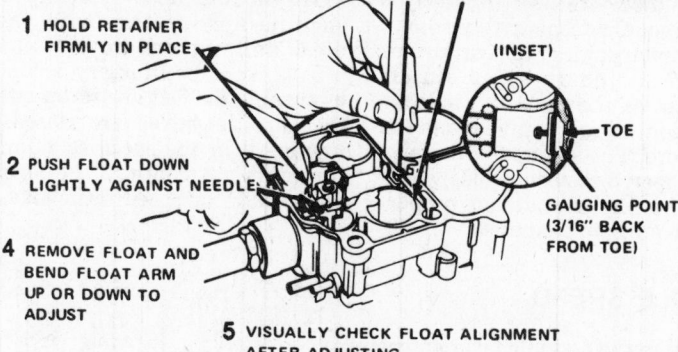

2MC, M2MC, M2ME, E2ME float level adjustment—typical

1 HOLD RETAINER FIRMLY IN PLACE

2 PUSH FLOAT DOWN LIGHTLY AGAINST NEEDLE

3 GAUGE FROM TOP OF CASTING TO TOP OF FLOAT – GAUGING POINT 3/16" BACK FROM END OF FLOAT AT TOE (SEE INSET)

4 REMOVE FLOAT AND BEND FLOAT ARM UP OR DOWN TO ADJUST

5 VISUALLY CHECK FLOAT ALIGNMENT AFTER ADJUSTING

(INSET) TOE — GAUGING POINT (3/16" BACK FROM TOE)

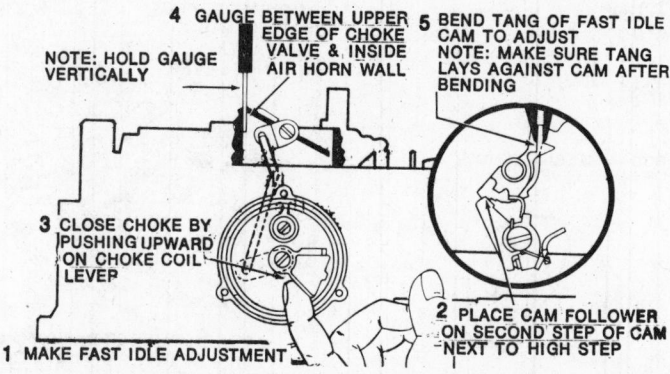

2MC, M2MC, M2ME, E2ME fast idle cam adjustment—typical

NOTE: HOLD GAUGE VERTICALLY

4 GAUGE BETWEEN UPPER EDGE OF CHOKE VALVE & INSIDE AIR HORN WALL

5 BEND TANG OF FAST IDLE CAM TO ADJUST NOTE: MAKE SURE TANG LAYS AGAINST CAM AFTER BENDING

3 CLOSE CHOKE BY PUSHING UPWARD ON CHOKE COIL LEVER

2 PLACE CAM FOLLOWER ON SECOND STEP OF CAM NEXT TO HIGH STEP

1 MAKE FAST IDLE ADJUSTMENT

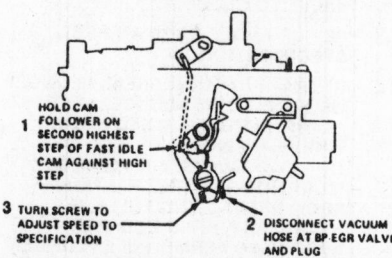

1 HOLD CAM FOLLOWER ON SECOND HIGHEST STEP OF FAST IDLE CAM AGAINST HIGH STEP

3 TURN SCREW TO ADJUST SPEED TO SPECIFICATION

2 DISCONNECT VACUUM HOSE AT BP EGR VALVE AND PLUG

M2MC and E2ME fast idle speed adjustment—typical

holding it firmly against the rise of the high step.

3. Close the choke valve by pushing upward on the choke coil lever inside the choke housing, or by pushing up on the vacuum break lever tang.

4. Gauge between the upper edge of the choke valve and the inside of the air horn wall.

5. Bend the tang on the fast idle cam to adjust.

PUMP ADJUSTMENT

This adjustment is not required on E2ME carburetors used in conjunction with the computer controlled systems.

1. With the fast idle cam follower off the steps of the fast idle cam, back out the idle speed screw until the throttle valves are completely closed.

2. Place the pump rod in the proper hole of the lever.

3. Measure from the top of the choke valve wall, next to the vent stack, to the top of the pump stem.

4. Bend the pump lever to adjust.

CHOKE COIL LEVER ADJUSTMENT

1. Remove the choke cover and thermostatic coil from the choke housing. On models with a fixed choke cover, drill out the rivets and remove the cover. A stat cover kit will be required for assembly.

2. Push up on the coil tang (counterclockwise) until the choke valve is closed. The top of the choke rod should be at the bottom of the slot in the choke valve lever. Place the fast idle cam follower on the **high** step of the cam.

3. Insert a 0.120 in. plug gauge in the hole in the choke housing.

4. The lower edge of the choke coil lever should just contact the side of the plug gauge.

5. Bend the choke rod to adjust.

2MC LEAN/RICH VACUUM BRAKE ADJUSTMENT

1. Place the cam follower on the **highest** step of the fast idle cam.

2. Seat the vacuum break diaphragm by using an outside vacuum source. Tape over the bleed hole, if any, under the rubber cover on the diaphragm.

3. Remove the choke cover and thermostatic coil and push up on the coil lever inside the choke housing until the tang on the vacuum break lever contacts the tang on the vacuum break plunger stem. Do not compress the bucking spring for lean adjustment. Compress the bucking spring for rich adjustment.

4. With the choke rod in the bottom of the slot in the choke lever, gauge between the upper edge of the choke valve and the inside wall of the air horn.

5. Bend the link rod at the vacuum break plunger stem to adjust the rich setting. Bend the link rod at the opposite end from the diaphragm to adjust the lean setting.

FRONT/REAR VACUUM BRAKE ADJUSTMENT

1982–84 Models

On these models a choke valve measuring gauge J–26701 or equivalent is used to measure angle (degrees instead of inches). See illustration for procedure.

UNLOADER ADJUSTMENT

1. With the choke valve completely closed, hold the throttle valves wide open.

2. Measure between the upper edge of the choke valve and air horn wall.

3. Bend the tang on the fast idle lever to obtain the proper measurement.

AIR CONDITIONING IDLE SPEED-UP SOLENOID ADJUSTMENT

1. With the engine at normal operating temperature and the air conditioning turned on but the compressor clutch lead disconnected, the solenoid should be electrically energized (plunger stem extended). Open the throttle slightly to allow the solenoid plunger to fully extend.

2. Adjust the plunger screw to obtain the specified idle speed.

3. Turn off the air conditioner. The solenoid plunger should move away from the tang on the throttle lever.

4. Adjust the curb idle speed with the idle speed screw, if necessary.

NOTE: Do not adjust if carburetor is computer controlled.

Quadrajet

The Rochester Quadrajet carburetor is a 2 stage, 4-barrel downdraft carburetor. It has been built in many variations designated as 4MC, 4MV, M4MC, M4MCA, M4ME, M4MEA, E4MC and E4ME. See the beginning of the Rochester section for an explanation of these designations.

The primary side of the carburetor is equipped with 2 primary bores and a triple venturi with plain tube nozzles. During off idle and part throttle operation, the fuel is metered through tapered metering rods operating in specially designed jets positioned by a manifold vacuum responsive piston.

The secondary side of the carburetor contains 2 secondary bores. An air valve is used on the secondary side for metering control and supplements the primary bore. The secondary air valve operates tapered metering rods which regulate the fuel in constant proportion to the air being supplied.

FAST IDLE SPEED

1. Position the fast idle lever on the **high** step of the fast idle cam.

2. Be sure that the choke is wide open and the engine warm. Plug the EGR vacuum hose. Disconnect the vacuum hose to the front vacuum break unit, if there are two.

3. Make a preliminary adjustment by turning the fast idle screw out until the throttle valves are closed, then turning it in the specified number of turns after it contacts the lever (see the carburetor specifications).

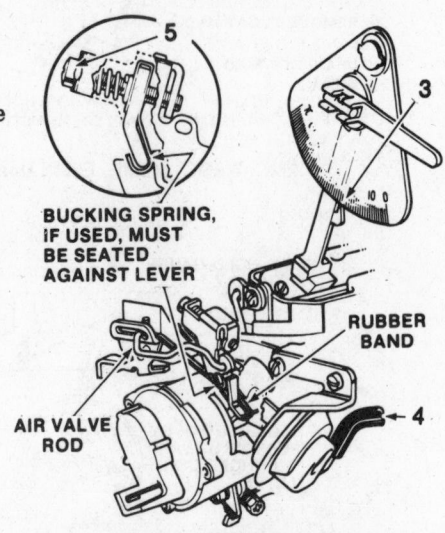

1 ATTACH RUBBER BAND TO GREEN TANG OF INTERMEDIATE CHOKE SHAFT

2 OPEN THROTTLE TO ALLOW CHOKE VALVE TO CLOSE

3 SET UP ANGLE GAGE AND SET TO SPECIFICATION

4 RETRACT VACUUM BREAK PLUNGER USING VACUUM SOURCE, AT LEAST 18" HG. PLUG AIR BLEED HOLES WHERE APPLICABLE ON QUADRAJETS, AIR VALVE ROD MUST NOT RESTRICT PLUNGER FROM RETRACTING FULLY. IF NECESSARY, BEND ROD (SEE ARROW) TO PERMIT FULL PLUNGER TRAVEL. FINAL ROD CLEARANCE MUST BE SET AFTER VACUUM BREAK SETTING HAS BEEN MADE.

5 WITH AT LEAST 18" HG STILL APPLIED, ADJUST SCREW TO CENTER BUBBLE

E2ME front vacuum break adjustment—1983 and later

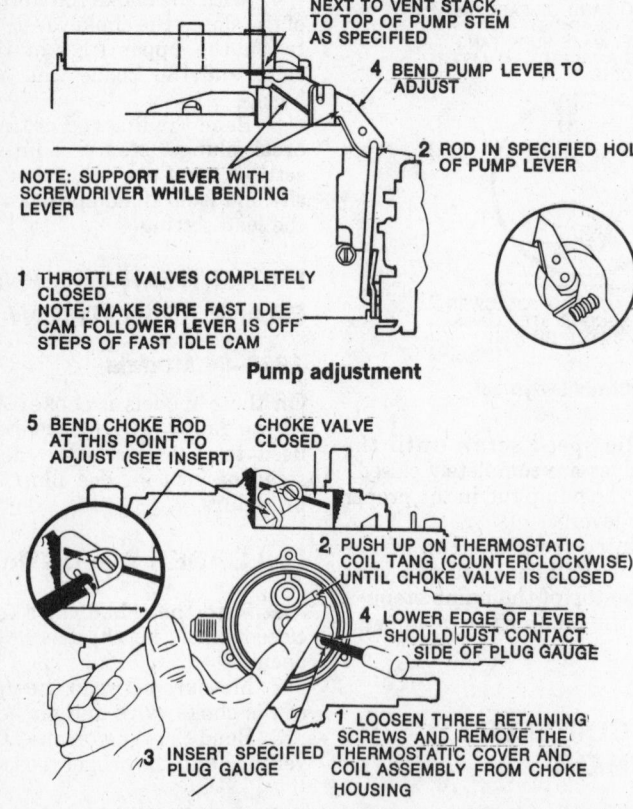

3 GAUGE FROM TOP OF CHOKE VALVE WALL NEXT TO VENT STACK, TO TOP OF PUMP STEM AS SPECIFIED

4 BEND PUMP LEVER TO ADJUST

2 ROD IN SPECIFIED HOLE OF PUMP LEVER

NOTE: SUPPORT LEVER WITH SCREWDRIVER WHILE BENDING LEVER

1 THROTTLE VALVES COMPLETELY CLOSED
NOTE: MAKE SURE FAST IDLE CAM FOLLOWER LEVER IS OFF STEPS OF FAST IDLE CAM

Pump adjustment

5 BEND CHOKE ROD AT THIS POINT TO ADJUST (SEE INSERT)

CHOKE VALVE CLOSED

2 PUSH UP ON THERMOSTATIC COIL TANG (COUNTERCLOCKWISE) UNTIL CHOKE VALVE IS CLOSED

4 LOWER EDGE OF LEVER SHOULD JUST CONTACT SIDE OF PLUG GAUGE

3 INSERT SPECIFIED PLUG GAUGE

1 LOOSEN THREE RETAINING SCREWS AND REMOVE THE THERMOSTATIC COVER AND COIL ASSEMBLY FROM CHOKE HOUSING

2MC, M2MC, M2ME, E2MC choke coil lever adjustment—typical

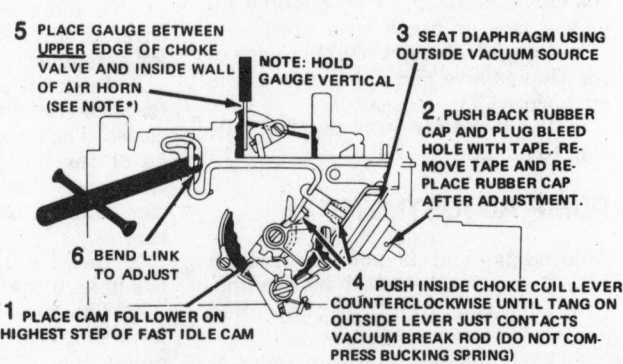

5 PLACE GAUGE BETWEEN UPPER EDGE OF CHOKE VALVE AND INSIDE WALL OF AIR HORN (SEE NOTE*)

NOTE: HOLD GAUGE VERTICAL

SEAT DIAPHRAGM USING OUTSIDE VACUUM SOURCE

6 BEND LOWER END OF ROD TO ADJUST

2 PUSH BACK RUBBER CAP AND PLUG BLEED HOLE WITH TAPE. REMOVE TAPE AND REPLACE RUBBER CAP AFTER ADJUSTMENT.

1 PLACE CAM FOLLOWER ON HIGHEST STEP OF FAST IDLE CAM

4 PUSH INSIDE CHOKE COIL LEVER COUNTERCLOCKWISE UNTIL TANG ON OUTSIDE LEVER CONTACTS VACUUM BREAK ROD AND BUCKING SPRING IS COMPRESSED

2MC rich vacuum break setting

5 PLACE GAUGE BETWEEN UPPER EDGE OF CHOKE VALVE AND INSIDE WALL OF AIR HORN (SEE NOTE*)

NOTE: HOLD GAUGE VERTICAL

3 SEAT DIAPHRAGM USING OUTSIDE VACUUM SOURCE

2 PUSH BACK RUBBER CAP AND PLUG BLEED HOLE WITH TAPE. REMOVE TAPE AND REPLACE RUBBER CAP AFTER ADJUSTMENT.

6 BEND LINK TO ADJUST

1 PLACE CAM FOLLOWER ON HIGHEST STEP OF FAST IDLE CAM

4 PUSH INSIDE CHOKE COIL LEVER COUNTERCLOCKWISE UNTIL TANG ON OUTSIDE LEVER JUST CONTACTS VACUUM BREAK ROD (DO NOT COMPRESS BUCKING SPRING)

2MC lean vacuum break setting

1 ATTACH RUBBER BAND TO GREEN TANG OF INTERMEDIATE CHOKE SHAFT.

2 OPEN THROTTLE TO ALLOW CHOKE VALVE TO CLOSE.

3 SET UP ANGLE GAGE AND SET ANGLE TO SPECIFICATION.

4 RETRACT VACUUM BREAK PLUNGER, USING VACUUM SOURCE, AT LEAST 18" HG. PLUG AIR BLEED HOLES WHERE APPLICABLE.

4A ON QUADRAJETS, AIR VALVE ROD MUST NOT RESTRICT PLUNGER FROM RETRACTING FULLY. IF NECESSARY, BEND ROD HERE TO PERMIT FULL PLUNGER TRAVEL. WHERE APPLICABLE, PLUNGER STEM MUST BE EXTENDED FULLY TO COMPRESS PLUNGER BUCKING SPRING.

5 TO CENTER BUBBLE, EITHER:
A. ADJUST WITH 1/8" HEX WRENCH (VACUUM STILL APPLIED)

-OR-

B. SUPPORT AT "S" AND BEND VACUUM BREAK ROD (VACUUM STILL APPLIED)

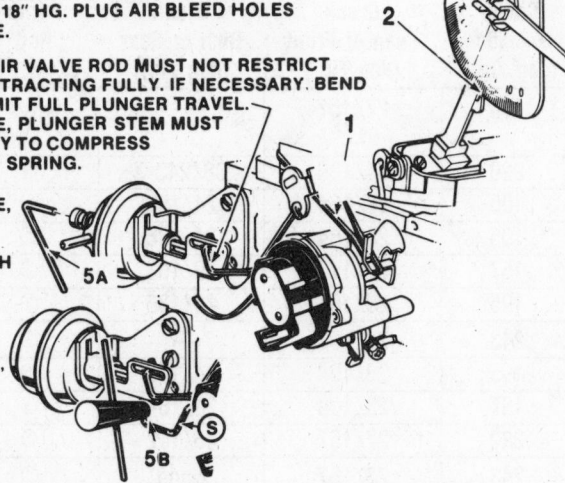

E2ME rear vacuum break adjustment— 1983 and later

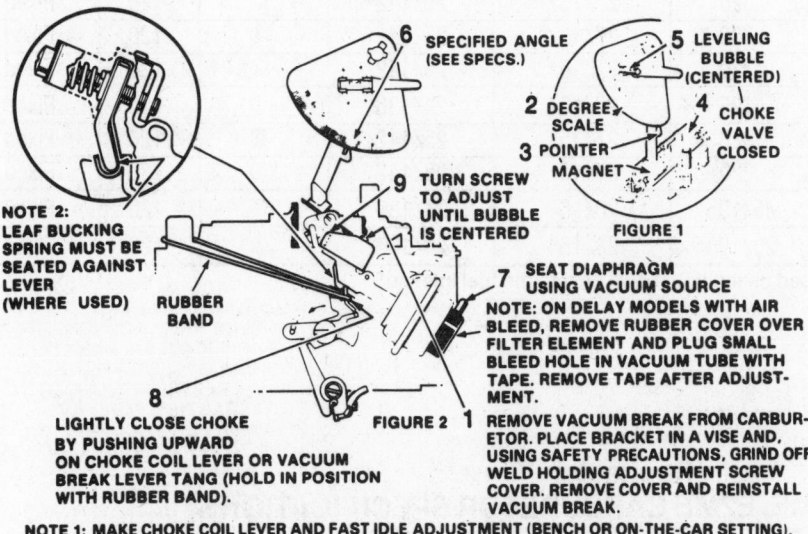

NOTE 2: LEAF BUCKING SPRING MUST BE SEATED AGAINST LEVER (WHERE USED)

RUBBER BAND

6 SPECIFIED ANGLE (SEE SPECS.)

2 DEGREE SCALE
3 POINTER
MAGNET

5 LEVELING BUBBLE (CENTERED)

4 CHOKE VALVE CLOSED

9 TURN SCREW TO ADJUST UNTIL BUBBLE IS CENTERED

FIGURE 1

7 SEAT DIAPHRAGM USING VACUUM SOURCE
NOTE: ON DELAY MODELS WITH AIR BLEED, REMOVE RUBBER COVER OVER FILTER ELEMENT AND PLUG SMALL BLEED HOLE IN VACUUM TUBE WITH TAPE. REMOVE TAPE AFTER ADJUSTMENT.

8 LIGHTLY CLOSE CHOKE BY PUSHING UPWARD ON CHOKE COIL LEVER OR VACUUM BREAK LEVER TANG (HOLD IN POSITION WITH RUBBER BAND).

FIGURE 2

1 REMOVE VACUUM BREAK FROM CARBURETOR. PLACE BRACKET IN A VISE AND, USING SAFETY PRECAUTIONS, GRIND OFF WELD HOLDING ADJUSTMENT SCREW COVER. REMOVE COVER AND REINSTALL VACUUM BREAK.

NOTE 1: MAKE CHOKE COIL LEVER AND FAST IDLE ADJUSTMENT (BENCH OR ON-THE-CAR SETTING). DO NOT REMOVE RIVETS AND CHOKE COVER TO PERFORM THIS ADJUSTMENT. USE RUBBER BAND ON VACUUM BREAK LEVER TANG TO HOLD CHOKE VALVE CLOSED (STEP 8).

E2ME front vacuum break adjustment—1981–82

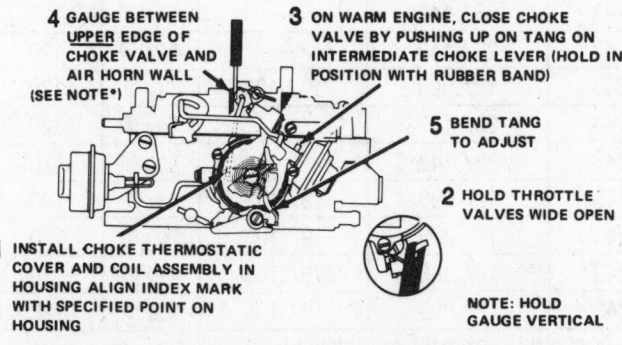

4 GAUGE BETWEEN UPPER EDGE OF CHOKE VALVE AND AIR HORN WALL (SEE NOTE*)

3 ON WARM ENGINE, CLOSE CHOKE VALVE BY PUSHING UP ON TANG ON INTERMEDIATE CHOKE LEVER (HOLD IN POSITION WITH RUBBER BAND)

5 BEND TANG TO ADJUST

2 HOLD THROTTLE VALVES WIDE OPEN

1 INSTALL CHOKE THERMOSTATIC COVER AND COIL ASSEMBLY IN HOUSING ALIGN INDEX MARK WITH SPECIFIED POINT ON HOUSING

NOTE: HOLD GAUGE VERTICAL

2MC, M2MC, M2ME, E2ME unloader adjustment—typical

4. Use the fast idle screw to adjust the fast idle to the speed and under the conditions, specified on the engine compartment sticker or in the specifications chart.

CHOKE ROD (FAST IDLE CAM)

1. Adjust the fast idle and place the cam follower on the **second** step of the fast idle cam against the shoulder of the high step.
2. Close the choke valve by exerting counterclockwise pressure on the external choke lever. Remove the coil assembly from the choke housing and push upon the choke coil lever. On models with a fixed (riveted) choke cover, push up on the vacuum brake lever tang and hold in position with a rubber band.
3. Insert a gauge of the proper size between the upper edge of the choke valve and the inside air horn wall.
4. To adjust the valve, bend the tang on the fast idle cam. Be sure that the tang rests against the cam after bending.

PRIMARY (FRONT) VACUUM BREAK

A choke valve measuring gauge J–26701 or equivalent is used to measure angle (degrees instead of inches). See illustration for procedures.

SECONDARY (REAR) VACUUM BRAKE ADJUSTMENT

A choke valve measuring gauge J–26701 or equivalent is used to measure the angle (degrees instead of inches). See illustrations for procedure.

CHOKE LINK

See the illustration for E4MC fast idle cam adjustment.

CHOKE UNLOADER

1. Push up on the vacuum break lever to close the choke valve and fully open the throttle valves.
2. Measure the distance from the upper edge of the choke valve to the air horn wall.
3. To adjust, bend the tang on the fast idle lever.

4MV CHOKE COIL ROD

1. Close the choke valve by rotating the choke coil lever counter-clockwise.

Rochester
2MC, M2MC, M2ME, E2ME CARBURETOR SPECIFICATIONS
General Motors—U.S.A.

Year	Carburetor Identification ①	Float Level (in.)	Choke Rod (in.)	Choke Unloader (deg./in.)	Vacuum Break Lean or Front (deg./in.)	Vacuum Break Rich or Rear (deg./in.)	Pump Rod (in.)	Choke Coil Lever (in.)	Automatic Choke (notches)
'82	17082130, 132, 138, 140	3/8	.110	.164	27/.157	—	③	③	Fixed
	17082150	13/32	.071	.220	24/.136	38/.243 ④	③	③	Fixed
	17082182, 184	5/16	.096	.195	28/.164	24/.136	③	③	Fixed
	17082192, 194	5/16	.096	.195	28/.164	24/.136	③	③	Fixed
	17082196	5/16	.096	.157	21/.117	19/.103	③	③	Fixed
	17082497	5/16	.113	.195	28/.164	24/.136	③	.120	Fixed
'83	17082130, 132	3/8	.110	.243	27/.157	—	③	.120	Fixed
	17083190, 192	5/16	.096	.195	28/.164	24/.136	③	.120	Fixed
	17083193	5/16	.090	.157	23/.129	28/.164	③	.120	Fixed
	17083194	5/16	.090	.220	27/.157	25/.142	③	.120	Fixed
'84	17082130	3/8	.110	.243	27/.157	None	③	.120	Fixed
	17082132	3/8	.110	.243	27/.157	None	③	.120	Fixed
	17084191	5/16	.096	.195	28/.164	24/.136	③	.120	Fixed
	17084193	5/16	.090	.220	27/.157	25/.142	③	.120	Fixed
	17084194	5/16	.090	.220	27/.157	25/.142	③	.120	Fixed
	17084195	5/16	.090	.220	27/.157	25/.142	③	.120	Fixed
'85	17085190	10/32	.096	.195	28/.164	24/.136	③	.120	Fixed
	17085192	11/32	.090	.220	27/.157	25/.142	③	.120	Fixed
	17085194	11/32	.090	.220	27/.157	25/.142	③	.120	Fixed
'86	17086190	10/32	.096	35/.195	28/.164	24/.136	③	.120	Fixed
'87	17086190	10/32	.096	35/.195	28/.164	24/.136	③	.120	Fixed

① The carburetor identification number is stamped on the float bowl, next to the fuel inlet nut.
② Inner hole
③ Not Adjustable
④ High altitude—0.206

Rochester
2MC, M2MC, M2ME, E2ME CARBURETOR SPECIFICATIONS
General Motors—Canada

Year	Carburetor Identification ①	Float Level (in.)	Choke Rod (in.)	Choke Unloader (in.)	Vacuum Break Lean or Front (deg./in.)	Vacuum Break Rich or Rear (deg./in.)	Pump Rod (in.)	Choke Coil Lever (in.)	Automatic Choke (notches)
'82	17082174	9/32	.110	.243	25/.142	—	5/16 ②	.120	Fixed
	17082175	9/32	.110	.243	25/.142	—	5/16 ②	.120	Fixed
	17082492	9/32	.139	.243	17/.090	19/.103	1/4 ②	.120	Fixed
	17082172	9/32	.110	.243	25/.142	—	5/16 ②	.120	Fixed
	17082173	9/32	.110	.243	25/.142	—	5/16 ②	.120	Fixed
'83-'84	17083172	9/32	.139	.243	17/.090	19/.103	1/4 ②	.120	Fixed
'85	17085170	9/32	.139	.243	17/.090	19/.103	9/32 ②	.120	Fixed
'86	17086170	9/32	.139	.243	17/.090	19/.103	9/32 ②	.120	Fixed
'87	17087170	9/32	.139	.243	17/.090	19/.103	9/32 ②	.120	Fixed

① The carburetor identification number is stamped on the float bowl, next to the fuel inlet nut.
② Inner hole

2. Disconnect the thermostatic coil rod from the upper lever.

3. Push down on the rod until it contacts the bracket of the coil.

4. The rod must fit in the notch of the upper lever.

5. If it does not, it must be bent on the curved portion just below the upper lever.

1 REMOVE VACUUM BREAK FROM CARBURETOR. PLACE BRACKET IN A VISE AND, USING SAFETY PRECAUTIONS, GRIND OFF ADJUSTMENT SCREW CAP. REINSTALL VACUUM BREAK.

9 TO ADJUST, USING 1/8" HEX WRENCH TURN SCREW IN REAR COVER UNTIL BUBBLE IS CENTERED. APPLY SEALER (SUCH AS SILICONE SEALANT RTV RUBBER OR EQUIVALENT) OVER SCREW HEAD TO SEAL SETTING.

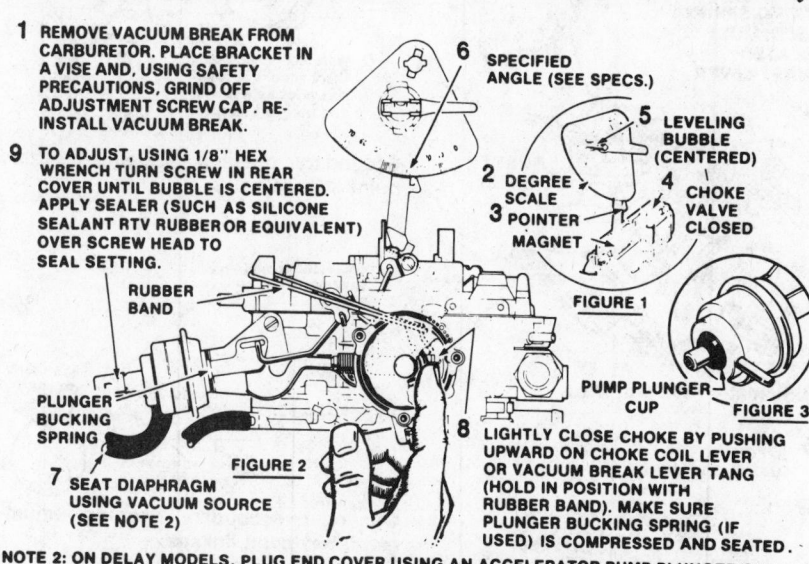

FIGURE 2

RUBBER BAND

PLUNGER BUCKING SPRING

7 SEAT DIAPHRAGM USING VACUUM SOURCE (SEE NOTE 2)

6 SPECIFIED ANGLE (SEE SPECS.)

5 LEVELING BUBBLE (CENTERED)

2 DEGREE SCALE

4 CHOKE VALVE CLOSED

3 POINTER MAGNET

FIGURE 1

PUMP PLUNGER CUP FIGURE 3

8 LIGHTLY CLOSE CHOKE BY PUSHING UPWARD ON CHOKE COIL LEVER OR VACUUM BREAK LEVER TANG (HOLD IN POSITION WITH RUBBER BAND). MAKE SURE PLUNGER BUCKING SPRING (IF USED) IS COMPRESSED AND SEATED.

NOTE 2: ON DELAY MODELS, PLUG END COVER USING AN ACCELERATOR PUMP PLUNGER CUP - 2G TYPE (FIGURE 3) OR EQUIVALENT. SEAT VACUUM DIAPHRAGM MAKING SURE VACUUM IS ABOVE 5" Hg WHEN READING GAUGE (STEP 9). REMOVE CUP AFTER ADJUSTMENT.

NOTE 1: MAKE CHOKE COIL LEVER ADJUSTMENT AND FAST IDLE ADJUSTMENT. DO NOT REMOVE RIVETS AND CHOKE COVER TO PERFORM THIS ADJUSTMENT. USE RUBBER BAND ON VACUUM BREAK LEVER TANG TO HOLD CHOKE VALVE CLOSED (STEP 8).

E2ME rear vacuum break adjustment—1981–82

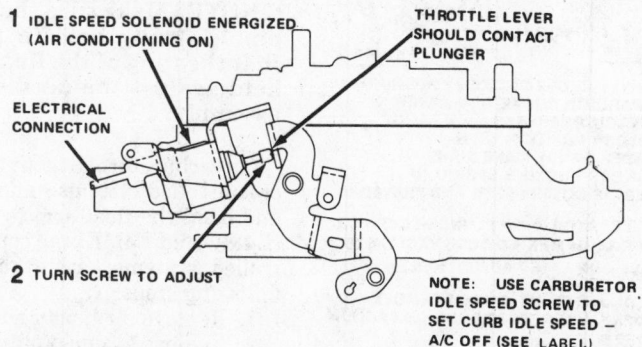

1 IDLE SPEED SOLENOID ENERGIZED (AIR CONDITIONING ON)

THROTTLE LEVER SHOULD CONTACT PLUNGER

ELECTRICAL CONNECTION

2 TURN SCREW TO ADJUST

NOTE: USE CARBURETOR IDLE SPEED SCREW TO SET CURB IDLE SPEED — A/C OFF (SEE LABEL)

2MC, M2MC air conditioning idle speed-up solenoid adjustment

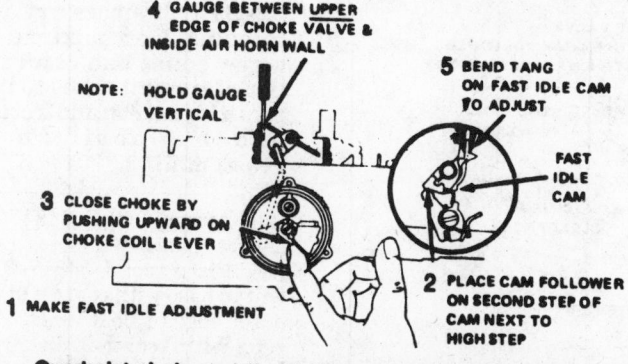

4 GAUGE BETWEEN UPPER EDGE OF CHOKE VALVE & INSIDE AIR HORN WALL

NOTE: HOLD GAUGE VERTICAL

5 BEND TANG ON FAST IDLE CAM TO ADJUST

FAST IDLE CAM

3 CLOSE CHOKE BY PUSHING UPWARD ON CHOKE COIL LEVER

1 MAKE FAST IDLE ADJUSTMENT

2 PLACE CAM FOLLOWER ON SECOND STEP OF CAM NEXT TO HIGH STEP

Quadrajet choke rod (fast idle cam) adjustment—typical

MC AND ME CHOKE COIL LEVER ADJUSTMENT

1. Remove the choke cover and thermostatic coil from the choke housing. On models with a fixed (riveted) choke cover, the rivets must be drilled out. A choke stat kit is necessary for assembly. Place the fast idle cam follower on the high step.

2. Push up on the coil tang (counter-clockwise) until the choke valve is closed. The top of the choke rod should be at the bottom of the slot in the choke valve lever.

3. Insert a 0.120 in. drill bit in the hole in the choke housing.

4. The lower edge of the choke coil lever should just contact the side of the plug gauge.

5. Bend the choke rod at the top angle to adjust.

SECONDARY CLOSING ADJUSTMENT

This adjustment assures proper closing of the secondary throttle plates.

1. Set the slow idle as per instructions in the appropriate car section. Make sure that the fast idle cam follower is not resting on the fast idle cam and the choke valve is wide open.

2. There should be 0.020 in. clearance between the secondary throttle actuating rod and the front of the slot on the secondary throttle lever with the closing tang on the throttle lever resting against the actuating lever.

3. Bend the secondary closing tang on the primary throttle actuating rod or lever to adjust.

SECONDARY OPENING ADJUSTMENT

1. Open the primary throttle valves until the actuating link contacts the upper tang on the secondary lever.

2. With the 2 point linkage, the bottom of the link should be in the center of the secondary lever slot.

3. With the 3 point linkage, there should be 0.070 in. clearance between the link and the middle tang.

4. Bend the upper tang on the secondary lever to adjust as necessary.

FLOAT LEVEL

With the air horn assembly removed, measure the distance from the air

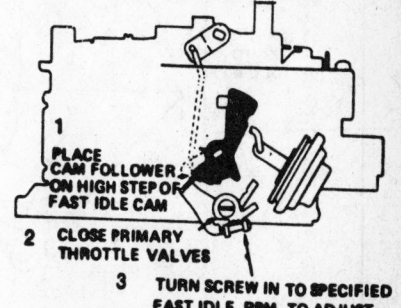

1 PLACE CAM FOLLOWER ON HIGH STEP OF FAST IDLE CAM

2 CLOSE PRIMARY THROTTLE VALVES

3 TURN SCREW IN TO SPECIFIED FAST IDLE RPM TO ADJUST

Quadrajet fast idle adjustment

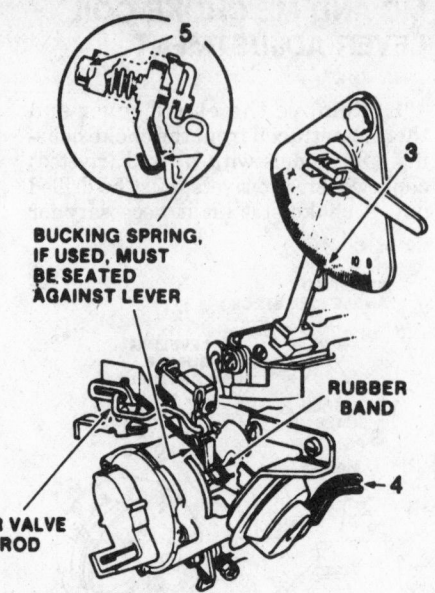

1 ATTACH RUBBER BAND TO GREEN TANG OF INTERMEDIATE CHOKE SHAFT

2 OPEN THROTTLE TO ALLOW CHOKE VALVE TO CLOSE

3 SET UP ANGLE GAGE AND SET TO SPECIFICATION

4 RETRACT VACUUM BREAK PLUNGER USING VACUUM SOURCE, AT LEAST 18" HG. PLUG AIR BLEED HOLES WHERE APPLICABLE.

ON QUADRAJETS, AIR VALVE ROD MUST NOT RESTRICT PLUNGER FROM RETRACTING FULLY. IF NECESSARY, BEND ROD (SEE ARROW) TO PERMIT FULL PLUNGER TRAVEL. FINAL ROD CLEARANCE MUST BE SET AFTER VACUUM BREAK SETTING HAS BEEN MADE.

5 WITH AT LEAST 18" HG STILL APPLIED, ADJUST SCREW TO CENTER BUBBLE

BUCKING SPRING, IF USED, MUST BE SEATED AGAINST LEVER

RUBBER BAND

AIR VALVE ROD

Quadrajet front vacuum break adjustment—1982 and later

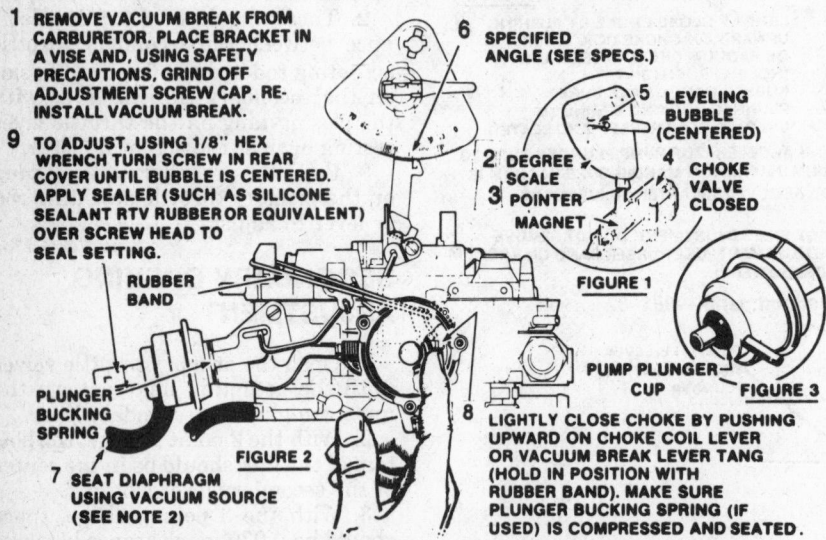

1 REMOVE VACUUM BREAK FROM CARBURETOR. PLACE BRACKET IN A VISE AND, USING SAFETY PRECAUTIONS, GRIND OFF ADJUSTMENT SCREW CAP. REINSTALL VACUUM BREAK.

9 TO ADJUST, USING 1/8" HEX WRENCH TURN SCREW IN REAR COVER UNTIL BUBBLE IS CENTERED. APPLY SEALER (SUCH AS SILICONE SEALANT RTV RUBBER OR EQUIVALENT) OVER SCREW HEAD TO SEAL SETTING.

RUBBER BAND

PLUNGER BUCKING SPRING

7 SEAT DIAPHRAGM USING VACUUM SOURCE (SEE NOTE 2)

FIGURE 2

6 SPECIFIED ANGLE (SEE SPECS.)

2 DEGREE SCALE

3 POINTER MAGNET

5 LEVELING BUBBLE (CENTERED)

4 CHOKE VALVE CLOSED

FIGURE 1

PUMP PLUNGER CUP   FIGURE 3

8 LIGHTLY CLOSE CHOKE BY PUSHING UPWARD ON CHOKE COIL LEVER OR VACUUM BREAK LEVER TANG (HOLD IN POSITION WITH RUBBER BAND). MAKE SURE PLUNGER BUCKING SPRING (IF USED) IS COMPRESSED AND SEATED.

NOTE 2: ON DELAY MODELS, PLUG END COVER USING AN ACCELERATOR PUMP PLUNGER CUP - 2G TYPE (FIGURE 3) OR EQUIVALENT. SEAT VACUUM DIAPHRAGM MAKING SURE VACUUM IS ABOVE 5" Hg WHEN READING GAUGE (STEP 9). REMOVE CUP AFTER ADJUSTMENT.

NOTE 1: MAKE CHOKE COIL LEVER ADJUSTMENT AND FAST IDLE ADJUSTMENT. DO NOT REMOVE RIVETS AND CHOKE COVER TO PERFORM THIS ADJUSTMENT. USE RUBBER BAND ON VACUUM BREAK LEVER TANG TO HOLD CHOKE VALVE CLOSED (STEP 8).

Quadrajet rear vacuum break adjustment—1981-82

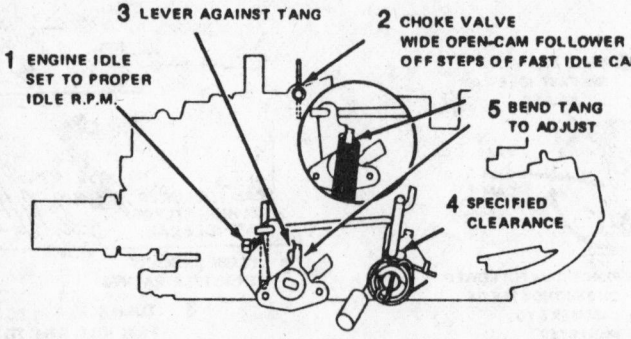

3 LEVER AGAINST TANG

2 CHOKE VALVE WIDE OPEN-CAM FOLLOWER OFF STEPS OF FAST IDLE CAM

1 ENGINE IDLE SET TO PROPER IDLE R.P.M.

5 BEND TANG TO ADJUST

4 SPECIFIED CLEARANCE

Quadrajet Secondary Closing Adjustment

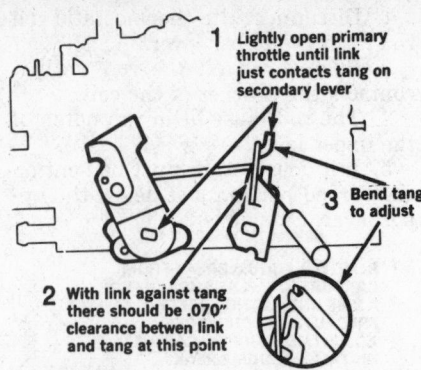

1 Lightly open primary throttle until link just contacts tang on secondary lever

3 Bend tang to adjust

2 With link against tang there should be .070" clearance betwen link and tang at this point

Secondary opening adjustment—three point linkage

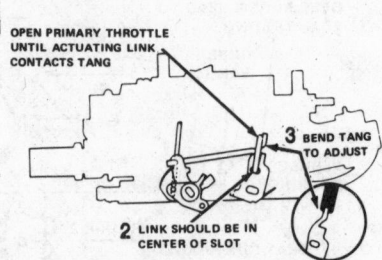

1 OPEN PRIMARY THROTTLE UNTIL ACTUATING LINK CONTACTS TANG

3 BEND TANG TO ADJUST

2 LINK SHOULD BE IN CENTER OF SLOT

Quadrajet secondary opening adjustment, two point linkage

horn gasket surface (gasket removed) to the top of the float at the toe ($\frac{3}{16}$ in. back from the toe).

NOTE: Make sure the retaining pin is firmly held in place and that the tang of the float is lightly held against the needle and seat assembly.

On carburetors without the computer controlled systems remove the float and bend the float arm to adjust. For (E4MC and E4ME) the computer controlled systems carburetors use the following steps:

1. Remove air horn and gasket.
2. Remove solenoid plunger, metering rods and float bowl insert.

NOTE: If necessary to remove solenoid lean mixture adjusting screw count and record the number of turns it takes to lightly bottom the screw and return to the exact position when reassembling.

3. Attach tool J–34817 or equivalent to float bowl.
4. Place tool J–34817–3 or equivalent in base with contact pin resting on outer edge of float lever.
5. With tool J–9789–90 or equivalent, measure the distance from the

1. ATTACH RUBBER BAND TO GREEN TANG OF INTERMEDIATE CHOKE SHAFT.

2. OPEN THROTTLE TO ALLOW CHOKE VALVE TO CLOSE.

3. SET UP ANGLE GAGE AND SET ANGLE TO SPECIFICATION.

   RETRACT VACUUM BREAK PLUNGER, USING VACUUM SOURCE, AT LEAST 18" HG. PLUG AIR BLEED HOLES WHERE APPLICABLE.

4A. ON QUADRAJETS, AIR VALVE ROD MUST NOT RESTRICT PLUNGER FROM RETRACTING FULLY. IF NECESSARY, BEND ROD HERE TO PERMIT FULL PLUNGER TRAVEL. WHERE APPLICABLE, PLUNGER STEM MUST BE EXTENDED FULLY TO COMPRESS PLUNGER BUCKING SPRING.

5. TO CENTER BUBBLE, EITHER:
   A. ADJUST WITH 1/8" HEX WRENCH (VACUUM STILL APPLIED)

   -OR-

   B. SUPPORT AT "S" AND BEND VACUUM BREAK ROD (VACUUM STILL APPLIED)

Quadrajet rear vacuum break adjustment—typical 1983 and later

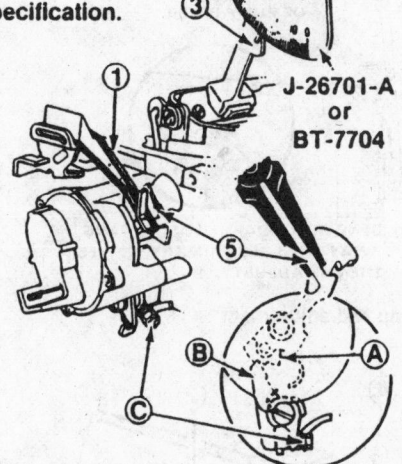

① Attach rubber band to Vacuum Break Lever of Intermediate Choke Shaft.

② Open Throttle to allow Choke Valve to close.

③ Set up Angle Gage and set to specification.

④ Place Fast Idle Cam Ⓐ on second step against Cam Follower Lever Ⓑ, with Lever contacting rise of High Step. If Lever does not contact Cam, turn Fast Idle Adjusting Screw Ⓒ in additional turn(s).

⑤ Adjust, if bubble is not recentered, by bending Fast Idle Cam Kick Lever with pliers.

Feedback Quadrajet–Fast idle cam adjustment

J-26701-A or BT-7704

top of casting to top of float, at a point 3/16 from large end of float.

6. If more than 2/32 from specification, use tool J-34817-15 or equivalent to bend lever up or down.

7. Recheck float alignment.

8. Install the parts, turning the mixture solenoid screw in until it is lightly bottomed, then unscrewing it the exact number of turns counted earlier.

ACCELERATOR PUMP

The accelerator pump is not adjustable on computer controlled carburetors (E4MC and E4ME).

1. Close the primary throttle valves by backing out the slow idle screw and making sure that the fast idle cam follower is off the steps of the fast idle cam.

2. Bend the secondary throttle closing tang away from the primary throttle lever, if necessary, to insure that the primary throttle valves are fully closed.

3. With the pump in the appropriate hole in the pump lever, measure from the top of the choke valve wall to the top of the pump stem.

4. To adjust, bend the pump lever.

5. After adjusting, readjust the secondary throttle tang and the slow idle screw.

AIR VALVE SPRING ADJUSTMENT

To adjust the air valve spring windup, loosen the Allen head lockscrew and turn the adjusting screw counterclockwise to remove all spring tension. With the air valve closed, turn the adjusting screw clockwise the specified number of turns after the torsion spring contacts the pin on the shaft. Hold the adjusting screw in this position and tighten the lockscrew.

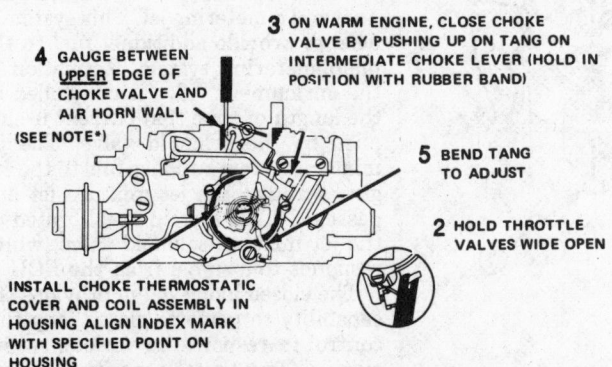

4 GAUGE BETWEEN UPPER EDGE OF CHOKE VALVE AND AIR HORN WALL (SEE NOTE*)

3 ON WARM ENGINE, CLOSE CHOKE VALVE BY PUSHING UP ON TANG ON INTERMEDIATE CHOKE LEVER (HOLD IN POSITION WITH RUBBER BAND)

5 BEND TANG TO ADJUST

2 HOLD THROTTLE VALVES WIDE OPEN

1 INSTALL CHOKE THERMOSTATIC COVER AND COIL ASSEMBLY IN HOUSING ALIGN INDEX MARK WITH SPECIFIED POINT ON HOUSING

Quadrajet unloader adjustment—typical

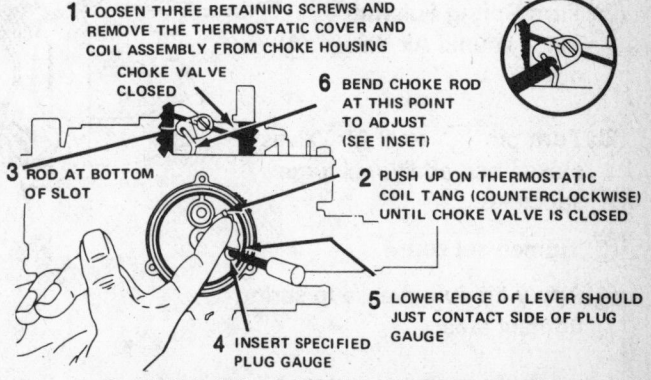

1 LOOSEN THREE RETAINING SCREWS AND REMOVE THE THERMOSTATIC COVER AND COIL ASSEMBLY FROM CHOKE HOUSING

CHOKE VALVE CLOSED

6 BEND CHOKE ROD AT THIS POINT TO ADJUST (SEE INSET)

2 PUSH UP ON THERMOSTATIC COIL TANG (COUNTERCLOCKWISE) UNTIL CHOKE VALVE IS CLOSED

3 ROD AT BOTTOM OF SLOT

4 INSERT SPECIFIED PLUG GAUGE

5 LOWER EDGE OF LEVER SHOULD JUST CONTACT SIDE OF PLUG GAUGE

Quadrajet choke coil lever adjustment—typical

1. REMOVE AIR HORN & GASKET.

2. REMOVE SOLENOID PLUNGER, METERING RODS, FLOAT BOWL INSERT. IF NECESSARY TO REMOVE SOLENOID (LEAN MIXTURE) ADJUSTING SCREW, COUNT AND MAKE RECORD OF NUMBER OF TURNS IT TAKES TO LIGHTLY BOTTOM SCREW, USING J-28696-10 OR BT-7928. (RETURN TO EXACT POSITION WHEN REASSEMBLING.)

3. ATTACH J-34817-1 OR BT-8227A-1 TO FLOAT BOWL.

4. PLACE J-34817-3 OR BT-8227A IN BASE WITH CONTACT PIN RESTING ON OUTER EDGE OF FLOAT LEVER.

5. MEASURE DISTANCE FROM TOP OF CASTING TO TOP OF FLOAT, AT POINT 3/16" FROM LARGE END OF FLOAT. USE J-9789-90 OR BT-8037.

6. IF MORE THAN ±2/32" FROM SPECIFICATION, USE J-34817-15 OR BT-8233 TO BEND LEVER UP OR DOWN. REMOVE BENDING TOOL AND MEASURE, REPEATING UNTIL WITHIN SPECIFICATION.

7. CHECK FLOAT ALIGNMENT.

8. REASSEMBLE CARBURETOR.

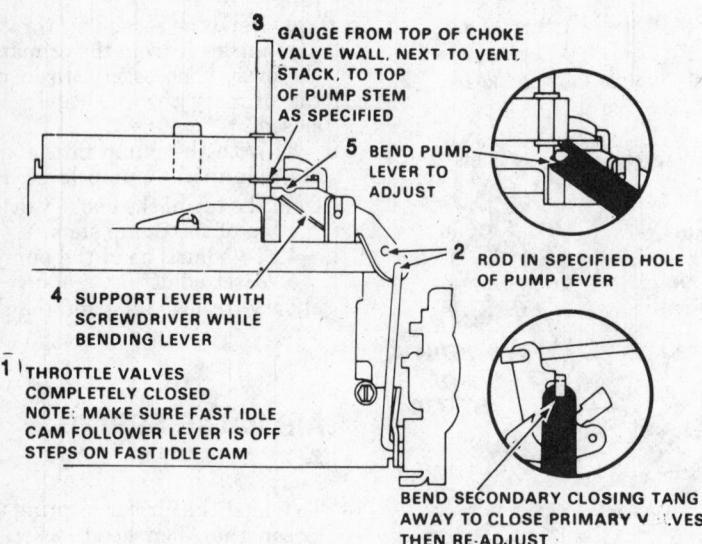

Feedback Quadrajet–Float adjustment

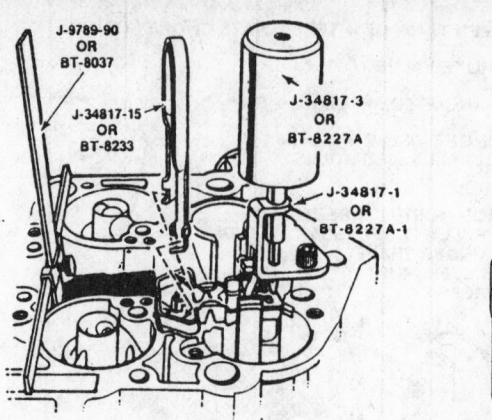

Typical air horn screw location and tightening sequence

3 GAUGE FROM TOP OF CHOKE VALVE WALL, NEXT TO VENT STACK, TO TOP OF PUMP STEM AS SPECIFIED

5 BEND PUMP LEVER TO ADJUST

2 ROD IN SPECIFIED HOLE OF PUMP LEVER

4 SUPPORT LEVER WITH SCREWDRIVER WHILE BENDING LEVER

1 THROTTLE VALVES COMPLETELY CLOSED NOTE: MAKE SURE FAST IDLE CAM FOLLOWER LEVER IS OFF STEPS ON FAST IDLE CAM

BEND SECONDARY CLOSING TANG AWAY TO CLOSE PRIMARY VALVES, THEN RE-ADJUST

Quadrajet accelerator pump rod adjustment

① Loosen set screw .

②a Turn Spring Fulcrum Pin ↻ until Air Valves Ⓐ open.

②b Turn pin ↺ until Air Valves close, then additional turns specified.

③ Tighten set screw.

④ Apply Lithium grease to spring contact area.

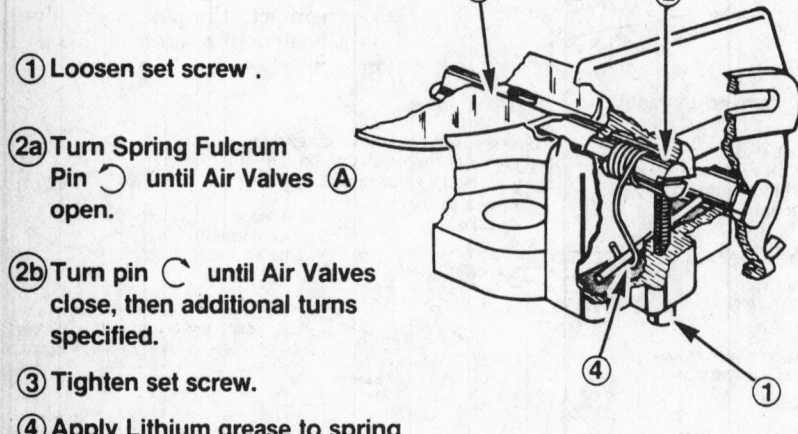

Typical E4MC air valve return spring adjustment

MIKUNI CARBURETORS

2.6L Feedback Carburetor

All Federal and California 2.6L Mitsubishi engines are equipped with a 2 barrel downdraft carburetor designed for electronic fuel control and closed loop operation. With the closed loop system of mixture control, this carburetor includes the special feature to provide optimum air/fuel control during all ranges of engine operation. Fuel metering is accomplished through the use of 3 solenoid valves which reduce or add fuel to the engine.

There are 8 basic systems in the feedback carburetor: fuel inlet, primary metering, secondary metering, accelerator pump, choke, jet mixture, enrichment and fuel cut-off. The first 5 systems are basically the same between standard and feedback carburetors. The remaining 3 are unique to feedback carburetors. The enrichment system consists of an enrichment solenoid and a metering jet. This system is used to provide additional fuel to the main metering system. Activation of the enrichment valve is controlled by the length of time that current is supplied by the solenoid valve. The jet mixture system supplies fuel to the engine through the jet mixture jet and passages. This system is calibrated by the jet mixture solenoid valve, which responds to a signal from the ECU.

The closed loop system provides the capability to perform closed loop fuel control in response to various sensor signals. The throttle position sensor (TPS) provides angle information to

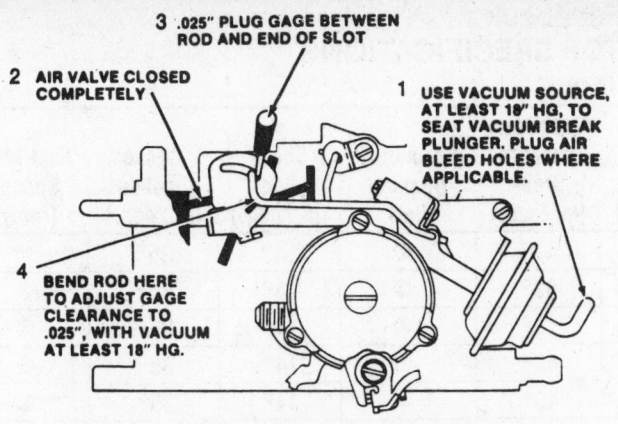

Air valve rod adjustment, Front—E4ME, E4MC

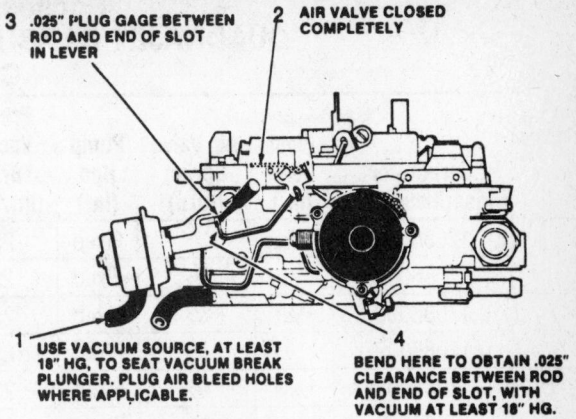

Air valve rod adjustment, Rear—E4ME, E4MC

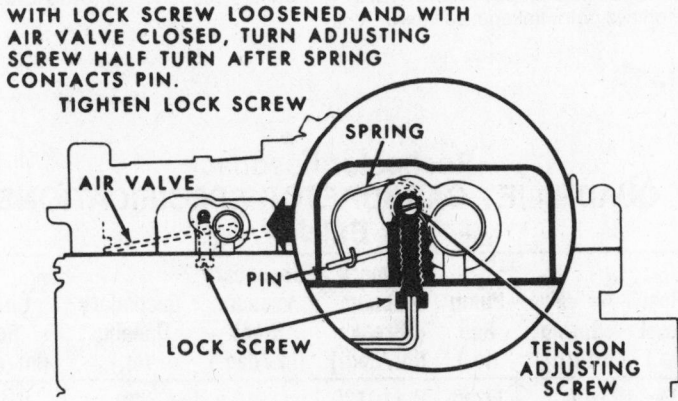

Quadrajet air valve spring setting—typical

Rochester
QUADRAJET CARBURETOR SPECIFICATIONS
Chrysler Products

Year	Carburetor Identification ①	Float Level (in.)	Air Valve Spring (turn)	Pump Rod (in.)	Primary Vacuum Break (in./deg.)	Secondary Vacuum Break (in./deg.)	Secondary Opening (in.)	Choke Rod (in.)	Choke Unloader (in.)	Fast Idle Speed ④ (rpm)
'85	17085407	14/32	7/8	—	.193/25°	—	—	—	.250	1450
'86–'89	17085433	14/32	7/8	—	.140/25	—	—	.120	.179 ②	①

① Refer to the underhood sticker
② Angel Method 30°

Rochester Feedback
QUADRAJET CARBURETOR SPECIFICATIONS
Cadillac

Year	Carburetor Identification ①	Float Level (in.)	Air Valve Spring (turn)	Pump Rod (in.)	Primary Vacuum Break (in./deg.)	Secondary Vacuum Break (in./deg.)	Secondary Opening (in.)	Choke Rod (in./deg.)	Choke Unloader (in./deg.)	Fast Idle Speed (rpm)
'82	17082246	3/8	5/8	Fixed	0.149/26	0.149/26	②	0.139	0.195	③
	17082247	13/32	5/8	Fixed	0.164/28	0.136/24	②	0.139	0.243	③
'83	17082266	3/8	5/8	Fixed	0.149/26	0.149/26	②	0.071	0.195	③
	17082267	3/8	5/8	Fixed	0.149/26	0.149/26	②	0.071	0.195	③

Rochester Feedback
QUADRAJET CARBURETOR SPECIFICATIONS
Cadillac

Year	Carburetor Identification ①	Float Level (in.)	Air Valve Spring (turn)	Pump Rod (in.)	Primary Vacuum Break (in./deg.)	Secondary Vacuum Break (in./deg.)	Secondary Opening (in.)	Choke Rod (in./deg.)	Choke Unloader (in./deg.)	Fast Idle Speed (rpm)
'86	17086008	11/32	1/2	Fixed	25°	43°	②	14°	35°	③
	17086009	14/32	1/2	Fixed	25°	43°	②	14°	35°	③
'87	17086008	11/32	1/2	Fixed	25°	43°	②	14°	35°	③
	17086009	14/32	1/2	Fixed	25°	43°	②	14°	35°	③
'88–'89	17086008	11/32	1/2	Fixed	25°	43°	②	14°	35°	③
	17086009	14/32	1/2	Fixed	25°	43°	②	14°	35°	③
	17088115	11/32	1/2	Fixed	25°	43°	②	14°	35°	③

① The carburetor identification number is stamped on the float bowl, near the secondary throttle lever.
② No measurement necessary on two point linkage; see text.
③ See underhood decal.

Rochester Feedback
QUADRAJET CARBURETOR SPECIFICATIONS
Buick

Year	Carburetor Identification ①	Float Level (in.)	Air Valve Spring (turn)	Pump Rod (in.)	Primary Vacuum Break (in./deg.)	Secondary Vacuum Break (in./deg.)	Secondary Opening (in.)	Choke Rod (in./deg.)	Choke Unloader (in/deg.)	Fast Idle Speed (rpm)
'82	17082202	11/32	7/8	Fixed	0.110/20	—	②	0.110	0.243	④
	17082204	11/32	3/8	Fixed	0.110/20	—	②	0.110	0.243	④
	17082244	7/16	9/16	Fixed	0.117/21	0.083/16	②	0.139	0.195	④
	17082245	3/8	5/8	Fixed	0.149/26	0.149/26	②	0.139	0.195	④
	17082246	3/8	5/8	Fixed	0.149/26	0.149/26	②	0.139	0.195	④
	17082247	13/32	5/8	Fixed	0.164/28	0.136/24	②	0.139	0.243	④
	17082248	13/32	5/8	Fixed	0.164/28	0.136/24	②	0.139	0.243	④
	17082251	15/32	1/2	Fixed	0.142/25	0.304/45	②	0.071	0.220	④
	17082253	15/32	1/2	Fixed	0.142/25	0.227/36	②	0.071	0.220	④
	17082264	7/16	9/16	Fixed	0.117/20	0.083/16	②	0.139	0.195	④
	17082265	3/8	5/8	Fixed	0.149/26	0.149/26	②	0.139	0.195	④
	17082266	3/8	5/8	Fixed	0.149/26	0.149/26	②	0.139	0.195	④
	17082267	3/8	5/8	Fixed	0.164/28	0.136/24	②	0.139	0.243	④
	17082268	13/32	5/8	Fixed	0.164/28	0.136/24	②	0.139	0.243	④
'83	17082265	3/8	5/8	Fixed	0.149/26	0.149/26	②	0.139	0.195	③
	17082266	3/8	5/8	Fixed	0.149/26	0.149/26	②	0.139	0.195	③
	17082267	3/8	5/8	Fixed	0.149/26	0.149/26	②	0.096	0.195	③
	17082268	3/8	5/8	Fixed	0.149/26	0.149/26	②	0.096	0.195	③
	17083242	9/32	9/16	Fixed	0.110/20	—	②	0.139	0.243	③
	17083244	1/4	9/16	Fixed	0.117/21	0.083/16	②	0.139	0.195	③
	17083248	3/8	5/8	Fixed	0.149/26	0.149/26	②	0.139	0.195	③
	17083250	7/16	1/2	Fixed	0.157/27	0.271/42	②	0.071	0.220	③
	17083253	7/16	1/2	Fixed	0.157/27	0.269/41	②	0.071	0.220	③
	17083553	7/16	1/2	Fixed	0.157/27	0.269/41	②	0.071	0.220	③

Rochester Feedback
QUADRAJET CARBURETOR SPECIFICATIONS
Buick

Year	Carburetor Identification ①	Float Level (in.)	Air Valve Spring (turn)	Pump Rod (in.)	Primary Vacuum Break (in./deg.)	Secondary Vacuum Break (in./deg.)	Secondary Opening (in.)	Choke Rod (in./deg.)	Choke Unloader (in/deg.)	Fast Idle Speed (rpm)
'84	17084201	11/32	7/8	Fixed	0.157/27	—	②	0.110	0.243	③
	17084205	11/32	7/8	Fixed	0.157/27	—	②	0.243	0.243	③
	17084208	11/32	7/8	Fixed	0.157/27	—	②	0.110	0.243	③
	17084209	11/32	7/8	Fixed	0.157/27	—	②	0.243	0.243	③
	17084210	11/32	7/8	Fixed	0.157/27	—	②	0.110	0.243	③
	17084240	5/16	1	Fixed	0.136/24	—	②	—	0.195	③
	17084244	5/16	1	Fixed	0.136/24	—	②	—	0.195	③
	17084246	5/16	1	Fixed	0.123/22	0.136/24	②	—	0.195	③
	17084248	5/16	1	Fixed	0.136/24	—	②	—	0.195	③
	17084252	7/16	1/2	Fixed	0.157/27	0.269/41	②	—	0.220	③
	17084254	7/16	1/2	Fixed	0.157/27	0.269/41	②	—	0.220	③
'85	17085202	11/32	7/8	Fixed	0.157/27	—	②	—	38°	③
	17085203	11/32	7/8	Fixed	0.157/27	—	②	—	38°	③
	17085204	11/32	7/8	Fixed	0.157/27	—	②	—	38°	③
	17085208	11/32	7/8	Fixed	0.157/27	—	②	—	38°	③
	17085218	11/32	7/8	Fixed	0.157/27	—	②	—	38°	③
	17085282	11/32	1/2	Fixed	0.142/25	0.273/43	②	—	35°	③
	17085502	14/32	7/8	Fixed	0.149/26	0.227/36	②	—	39°	③
	17085503	14/32	7/8	Fixed	0.149/26	0.227/36	②	—	39°	③
	17085506	14/32	1	Fixed	0.157/27	0.227/36	②	—	36°	③
	17085508	14/32	1	Fixed	0.157/27	0.227/36	②	—	36°	③
	17085524	14/32	1	Fixed	0.142/25	0.227/36	②	—	36°	③
	17085526	14/32	1	Fixed	0.142/25	0.227/36	②	—	36°	③
	17085554	14/32	1/2	Fixed	0.157/27	0.269/41	②	—	35°	③
'86	17086008	11/32	1/2	Fixed	25°	43°	②	14°	35°	③
'87	17086008	11/32	1/2	Fixed	25°	43°	②	14°	35°	③
'88–'89	17086008	11/32	1/2	Fixed	25°	43°	②	14°	35°	③
	17088115	11/32	1/2	Fixed	25°	43°	②	14°	35°	③

① The carburetor identification number is stamped on the float bowl, near the secondary throttle lever.
② No measurement necessary on two point linkage; see text
③ See underhood decal
④ 3 turns after contacting lever for preliminary setting

Rochester Feedback
QUADRAJET CARBURETOR SPECIFICATIONS
Chevrolet

Year	Carburetor Identification ①	Float Level (in.)	Air Valve Spring (turn)	Pump Rod (in.)	Primary Vacuum (deg./in.)	Secondary Vacuum (deg./in.)	Secondary Opening (in.)	Choke Rod (deg./in.)	Choke Unloader (deg./in.)	Fast Idle Speed (rpm)
'82	17082202	11/32	7/8	Fixed	0.157	—	②	0.110	0.243	④
	17082204	11/32	7/8	Fixed	0.157	—	②	0.110	0.243	④
	17082203	11/32	7/8	Fixed	0.157	—	②	0.243	0.243	④
	17082207	11/32	7/8	Fixed	0.157	—	②	0.243	0.243	④

Rochester Feedback
QUADRAJET CARBURETOR SPECIFICATIONS
Chevrolet

Year	Carburetor Identification ①	Float Level (in.)	Air Valve Spring (turn)	Pump Rod (in.)	Primary Vacuum (deg./in.)	Secondary Vacuum (deg./in.)	Secondary Opening (in.)	Choke Rod (deg./in.)	Choke Unloader (deg./in.)	Fast Idle Speed (rpm)
'83	17083202	11/32	7/8	Fixed	—	27/.157	②	0.110	0.243	③
	17083203	11/32	7/8	Fixed	—	27/.157	②	0.243	0.243	③
	17083204	11/32	7/8	Fixed	—	27/.157	②	0.110	0.243	③
	17083207	11/32	7/8	Fixed	—	27/.157	②	0.243	0.243	③
	17083216	11/32	7/8	Fixed	—	27/.157	②	0.110	0.243	③
	17083218	11/32	7/8	Fixed	—	27/.157	②	0.110	0.243	③
	17083236	11/32	7/8	Fixed	—	27/.157	②	0.110	0.243	③
	17083506	7/16	7/8	Fixed	27/.157	36/.227	②	0.110	0.227	③
	17083508	7/16	7/8	Fixed	27/.157	36/.227	②	0.110	0.227	③
	17083524	7/16	7/8	Fixed	25/.142	36/.227	②	0.110	0.227	③
	17083526	7/16	7/8	Fixed	25/.142	36/.227	②	0.110	0.227	③
'84	17084201	11/32	7/8	Fixed	.157/27	—	②	0.110	0.243	③
	17084205	11/32	7/8	Fixed	.157/27	—	②	0.243	0.243	③
	17084208	11/32	7/8	Fixed	.157/27	—	②	0.110	0.243	③
	17084209	11/32	7/8	Fixed	.157/27	—	②	0.243	0.243	③
	17084210	11/32	7/8	Fixed	.157/27	—	②	0.110	0.243	③
	17084507	7/16	1	Fixed	.157/27	.227/36	②	0.110	0.227	③
	17084509	7/16	1	Fixed	.157/27	.227/36	②	0.110	0.227	③
	17084525	7/16	1	Fixed	.142/25	.227/36	②	0.110	0.227	③
	17084527	7/16	1	Fixed	.142/25	.227/36	②	0.110	0.227	③
'85	17085202	11/32	7/8	Fixed	.157/27	—	②	0.110	0.243/38°	③
	17085203	11/32	7/8	Fixed	.157/27	—	②	⑧	0.243/38°	③
	17085204	11/32	7/8	Fixed	.157/27	—	②	0.110	0.243/38°	③
	17085207	11/32	7/8	Fixed	.157/27	—	②	0.243	0.243/38°	③
	17085218	11/32	7/8	Fixed	.157/27	—	②	0.110	0.243/38°	③
	17085282	11/32	1/2	Fixed	.142/25	0.273/43	②	0.110	0.220/35°	③
	17085502	14/32	7/8	Fixed	.149/26	0.227/36	②	0.110	0.251/39°	③
	17085503	14/32	7/8	Fixed	.149/26	0.227/36	②	0.110	0.251/39°	③
	17085506	14/32	1	Fixed	.157/27	0.227/36	②	0.110	0.227/36°	③
	17085508	14/32	1	Fixed	.157/27	0.227/36	②	0.110	0.227/36°	③
	17085524	14/32	1	Fixed	.142/25	0.227/36	②	0.110	0.227/36°	③
	17085526	14/32	1	Fixed	.142/25	0.227/36	②	0.110	0.227/36°	③
	17085554	14/32	1/2	Fixed	.157/27	0.269/41	②	0.071	0.220/35°	③
'86	17086003	11/32	7/8	Fixed	.157/27	—	②	—	0.243/38°	③
	17086004	11/32	7/8	Fixed	.157/27	—	②	—	0.243/38°	③
	17086005	11/32	7/8	Fixed	.157/27	—	②	—	0.243/38°	③
	17086006	11/32	7/8	Fixed	.157/27	—	②	—	0.243/38°	③
'87	17086008	11/32	7/8	Fixed	.157/27	—	②	—	0.243/35°	③
	17087129	11/32	7/8	Fixed	.157/27	—	②	—	0.243/38°	③
	17087130	11/32	7/8	Fixed	.157/27	—	②	—	0.243/38°	③
	17087132	11/32	7/8	Fixed	.157/27	—	②	—	0.243/38°	③

Rochester Feedback
QUADRAJET CARBURETOR SPECIFICATIONS
Chevrolet

Year	Carburetor Identification ①	Float Level (in.)	Air Valve Spring (turn)	Pump Rod (in.)	Primary Vacuum (deg./in.)	Secondary Vacuum (deg./in.)	Secondary Opening (in.)	Choke Rod (deg./in.)	Choke Unloader (deg./in.)	Fast Idle Speed (rpm)
'88–'89	17087306	11/32	7/8	Fixed	27°	—	②	20°	32°	③
	17087129	11/32	7/8	Fixed	27°	—	②	20°	32°	③
	17087132	11/32	7/8	Fixed	27°	—	②	20°	32°	③

① The carburetor identification number is stamped on the float bowl, near the secondary throttle lever.
② No measurement necessary on two point linkage; see text.
③ See underhood decal.
④ 3⅛ turns after contacting lever for preliminary setting

QUADRAJET FEEDBACK CARBURETOR SPECIFICATIONS
Oldsmobile

Year	Carburetor Identification ①	Float Level (in.)	Air Valve Spring (turn)	Pump Rod (in.)	Primary Vacuum Break (in./deg.)	Secondary Vacuum Break (in./deg.)	Secondary Opening (in.)	Choke Rod (in./deg.)	Choke Unloader (in./deg.)	Fast Idle Speed (rpm)
'82	17082202	11/32	7/8	Fixed	0.110/20	—	②	0.110	0.243	④
	17082204	11/32	3/8	Fixed	0.110/20	—	②	0.110	0.243	④
	17082244	7/16	9/16	Fixed	0.117/21	0.083/16	②	0.139	0.195	④
	17082245	3/8	5/8	Fixed	0.149/26	0.149/26	②	0.139	0.195	④
	17082246	3/8	5/8	Fixed	0.149/26	0.149/26	②	0.139	0.195	④
	17082247	13/32	5/8	Fixed	0.164/28	0.136/24	②	0.139	0.243	④
	17082248	13/32	5/8	Fixed	0.164/28	0.136/24	②	0.139	0.243	④
	17082251	15/32	1/2	Fixed	0.142/25	0.304/45	②	0.071	0.220	④
	17082253	15/32	1/2	Fixed	0.142/25	0.227/36	②	0.071	0.220	④
	17082264	7/16	9/16	Fixed	0.117/20	0.083/16	②	0.139	0.195	④
	17082265	3/8	5/8	Fixed	0.149/26	0.149/26	②	0.139	0.195	④
	17082266	3/8	5/8	Fixed	0.149/26	0.149/26	②	0.139	0.195	④
	17082267	3/8	5/8	Fixed	0.164/28	0.136/24	②	0.139	0.243	④
	17082268	13/32	5/8	Fixed	0.164/28	0.136/24	②	0.139	0.243	④
'83	17082265	3/8	5/8	Fixed	0.149/26	0.149/26	②	0.139	0.195	③
	17082266	3/8	5/8	Fixed	0.149/26	0.149/26	②	0.139	0.195	③
	17082267	3/8	5/8	Fixed	0.149/26	0.149/26	②	0.096	0.195	③
	17082268	3/8	5/8	Fixed	0.149/26	0.149/26	②	0.096	0.195	③
	17083242	9/32	9/16	Fixed	0.110/20	—	②	0.139	0.243	③
	17083244	1/4	9/16	Fixed	0.117/21	0.083/16	②	0.139	0.195	③
	17083248	3/8	5/8	Fixed	0.149/26	0.149/26	②	0.139	0.195	③
	17083250	7/16	1/2	Fixed	0.157/27	0.271/42	②	0.071	0.220	③
	17083253	7/16	1/2	Fixed	0.157/27	0.269/41	②	0.071	0.220	③
	17083553	7/16	1/2	Fixed	0.157/27	0.269/41	②	0.071	0.220	③
'84	17084201	11/32	7/8	Fixed	0.157/27	—	②	0.110	0.243	③
	17084205	11/32	7/8	Fixed	0.157/27	—	②	0.243	0.243	③
	17084208	11/32	7/8	Fixed	0.157/27	—	②	0.110	0.243	③
	17084209	11/32	7/8	Fixed	0.157/27	—	②	0.243	0.243	③
	17084210	11/32	7/8	Fixed	0.157/27	—	②	0.110	0.243	③
	17084240	5/16	1	Fixed	0.136/24	—	②	—	0.195	③
	17084244	5/16	1	Fixed	0.136/24	—	②	—	0.195	③
	17084246	5/16	1	Fixed	0.123/22	0.136/24	②	—	0.195	③
	17084248	5/16	1	Fixed	0.136/24	—	②	—	0.195	③
	17084252	7/16	1/2	Fixed	0.157/27	0.269/41	②	—	0.220/35°	③
	17084254	7/16	1/2	Fixed	0.157/27	0.269/41	②	—	0.220/35°	③
'85	17084282	11/32	1/2	Fixed	0.142/25	0.278/43	②	0.110	0.220/35°	③
	17085554	14/32	1/2	Fixed	0.157/27	0.269/41	②	0.110	0.220/35°	③

QUADRAJET FEEDBACK CARBURETOR SPECIFICATIONS
Oldsmobile

Year	Carburetor Identification ①	Float Level (in.)	Air Valve Spring (turn)	Pump Rod (in.)	Primary Vacuum Break (in./deg.)	Secondary Vacuum Break (in./deg.)	Secondary Opening (in.)	Choke Rod (in./deg.)	Choke Unloader (in./deg.)	Fast Idle Speed (rpm)
'86	17086008	11/32	1/2	Fixed	0.142/25	0.287/43	②	0.171/14°	0.220/35°	③
	17086009	14/32	1/2	Fixed	0.142/25	0.287/43	②	0.171/14°	0.220/35°	③
'87	17086008	11/32	1/2	Fixed	0.142/25	0.287/43	②	0.171/14°	0.220/35°	③
	17086009	14/32	1/2	Fixed	0.142/25	0.287/43	②	0.171/14°	0.220/35°	③
'88–'89	17086008	11/32	1/2	Fixed	25°	43°	②	14°	35°	③
	17088115	11/32	1/2	Fixed	25°	43°	②	14°	35°	③

① The carburetor identification number is stamped on the float bowl, next to the secondary throttle lever.
② No measurement necessary on two point linkage; see text.
③ See underhood decal.
④ 3 turns after contacting lever for preliminary setting.

QUADRAJET FEEDBACK CARBURETOR SPECIFICATIONS
Pontiac

Year	Carburetor Identification ①	Float Level (in.)	Air Valve Spring (turn)	Pump Rod (in.)	Primary Vacuum Break (in./deg.)	Secondary Vacuum Break (in./deg.)	Secondary Opening (in.)	Choke Rod (in./deg.)	Choke Unloader (in./deg.)	Fast Idle Speed (rpm)
'82	17082202	11/32	7/8	Fixed	0.110/20 ⑦	—	②	0.110	0.243	④⑤
	17082204	11/32	3/8 ⑧	Fixed	0.110/20 ⑦	—	②	0.110	0.243	④⑤
	17082203	11/32	7/8	Fixed	0.157/27	—	②	0.243	0.243	⑤
	17082207	11/32	7/8	Fixed	0.157/27	—	②	0.243	0.243	⑤
	17082244	7/16	9/16	Fixed	0.117/21	0.083/16	②	0.139	0.195	④
	17082245	3/8	5/8	Fixed	0.149/26	0.149/26	②	0.139	0.195	④
	17082246	3/8	5/8	Fixed	0.149/26	0.149/26	②	0.139	0.195	④
	17082247	13/32	5/8	Fixed	0.164/28	0.136/24	②	0.139	0.243	④
	17082248	13/32	5/8	Fixed	0.164/28	0.136/24	②	0.139	0.243	④
	17082251	15/32	1/2	Fixed	0.142/25	0.304/45	②	0.071	0.220	④
	17082253	15/32	1/2	Fixed	0.142/25	0.227/36	②	0.071	0.220	④
	17082264	7/16	9/16	Fixed	0.117/20	0.083/16	②	0.139	0.195	④
	17082265	3/8	5/8	Fixed	0.149/26	0.149/26	②	0.139	0.195	④
	17082266	3/8	5/8	Fixed	0.149/26	0.149/26	②	0.139	0.195	④
	17082267	3/8	5/8	Fixed	0.164/28	0.136/24	②	0.139	0.243	④
	17082268	13/32	5/8	Fixed	0.164/28	0.136/24	②	0.139	0.243	④
'83	17082265	3/8	5/8	Fixed	0.149/26	0.149/26	②	0.139	0.195	③
	17082266	3/8	5/8	Fixed	0.149/26	0.149/26	②	0.139	0.195	③
	17082267	3/8	5/8	Fixed	0.149/26	0.149/26	②	0.096	0.195	③
	17082268	3/8	5/8	Fixed	0.149/26	0.149/26	②	0.096	0.195	③
	17083242	9/32	9/16	Fixed	0.110/20	—	②	0.139	0.243	③
	17083244	1/4	9/16	Fixed	0.117/21	0.083/16	②	0.139	0.195	③
	17083248	3/8	5/8	Fixed	0.149/26	0.149/26	②	0.139	0.195	③
	17083250	7/16	1/2	Fixed	0.157/27	0.271/42	②	0.071	0.220	③
	17083253	7/16	1/2	Fixed	0.157/27	0.269/41	②	0.071	0.220	③
	17083553	7/16	1/2	Fixed	0.157/27	0.269/41	②	0.071	0.220	③
'84	17084201	11/32	7/8	Fixed	0.157/27	—	②	0.110	0.243	③
	17084205	11/32	7/8	Fixed	0.157/27	—	②	0.243	0.243	③
	17084208	11/32	7/8	Fixed	0.157/27	—	②	0.110	0.243	③
	17084209	11/32	7/8	Fixed	0.157/27	—	②	0.243	0.243	③
	17084210	11/32	7/8	Fixed	0.157/27	—	②	0.110	0.243	③
	17084240	5/16	1	Fixed	0.136/24	—	②	—	0.195	③
	17084244	5/16	1	Fixed	0.136/24	—	②	—	0.195	③
	17084246	5/16	1	Fixed	0.123/22	0.136/24	②	—	0.195	③
	17084248	5/16	1	Fixed	0.136/24	—	②	—	0.195	③
	17084252	7/16	1/2	Fixed	0.157/27	0.269/41	②	—	0.220	③
	17084254	7/16	1/2	Fixed	0.157/27	0.269/41	②	—	0.220	③

QUADRAJET FEEDBACK CARBURETOR SPECIFICATIONS
Pontiac

Year	Carburetor Identification ①	Float Level (in.)	Air Valve Spring (turn)	Pump Rod (in.)	Primary Vacuum Break (in./deg.)	Secondary Vacuum Break (in./deg.)	Secondary Opening (in.)	Choke Rod (in./deg.)	Choke Unloader (in./deg.)	Fast Idle Speed (rpm)
'85	17085202	11/32	7/8	Fixed	0.157/27	—	②	0.110	0.243/38	③
	17085203	11/32	7/8	Fixed	0.157/27	—	②	⑧	0.243/38	③
	17085204	11/32	7/8	Fixed	0.157/27	—	②	0.110	0.243/38	③
	17085207	11/32	7/8	Fixed	0.157/27	—	②	0.243	0.243/38	③
	17085218	11/32	7/8	Fixed	0.157/27	—	②	0.110	0.243/38	③
	17085282	11/32	1/2	Fixed	0.142/25	0.273/43	②	0.110	0.220/35	③
	17085502	14/32	7/8	Fixed	0.149/26	0.227/36	②	0.110	0.251/39	③
	17085503	14/32	7/8	Fixed	0.149/26	0.227/36	②	0.110	0.251/39	③
	17085506	14/32	1	Fixed	0.157/27	0.227/36	②	0.110	0.227/36	③
	17085508	14/32	1	Fixed	0.157/27	0.227/36	②	0.110	0.227/36	③
	17085524	14/32	1	Fixed	0.142/25	0.227/36	②	0.110	0.227/36	③
	17085526	14/32	1	Fixed	0.142/25	0.227/36	②	0.110	0.227/36	③
	17085554	14/32	1/2	Fixed	0.157/27	0.269/41	②	0.071	0.220/35	③
'86	17086003	11/32	7/8	Fixed	0.157/27	—	②	0.110	0.243/38	③
	17086004	11/32	7/8	Fixed	0.157/27	—	②	0.110	0.243/38	③
	17086005	11/32	7/8	Fixed	0.157/27	—	②	0.243	0.243/38	③
	17086006	11/32	7/8	Fixed	0.157/27	—	②	0.110	0.243/38	③
	17086007	11/32	1/2	Fixed	0.142/25	0.287/43	②	0.071	0.220/35	③
	17086008	11/32	1/2	Fixed	0.142/25	0.287/43	②	0.071	0.220/35	③
	17086040	11/32	7/8	Fixed	0.157/27	—	②	0.110	0.243/38	③
'87	17087130	11/32	7/8	Fixed	0.157/27	—	②	0.110	0.243/38	③
	17087131	11/32	7/8	Fixed	0.157/27	—	②	0.110	0.243/38	③
	17087133	11/32	7/8	Fixed	0.157/27	—	②	0.110	0.243/38	③
	17086008	11/32	1/2	Fixed	0.142/25	0.287/43	②	0.071	0.220/35	③
'88-'89	17086008	11/32	1/2	Fixed	25°	43°	—	14°	35°	
	17088115	11/32	1/2	Fixed	25°	43°	—	14°	35°	

① The carburetor identification number is stamped on the float bowl, near the secondary throttle lever.
② No measurement necessary on two point linkage; see text.
③ See underhood decal.
④ 3 turns after contacting lever for preliminary setting.
⑤ Firebird—3⅛ turns after contacting lever for preliminary setting.
⑥ Firebird—⅞
⑦ Firebird—0.157 in./27°
⑧ 3 step cam: 0.110, 2 step cam: 0.243

QUADRAJET CARBURETOR SPECIFICATIONS
All Canadian Models

Year	Carburetor Identification ①	Float Level (in.)	Air Valve Spring (turn)	Pump Rod (in.)	Primary Vacuum Break (deg./in.)	Secondary Vacuum Break (deg./in.)	Secondary Opening (deg./in.)	Choke Rod (deg./in.)	Choke Unloader (deg./in.)	Fast Idle Speed ② (rpm)
'82	17082280	3/8	7/8	9/32 ②	25/0.142	—	④	0.110	0.243	⑤
	17082281	3/8	7/8	9/32 ②	25/0.142	—	④	0.110	0.243	⑤
	17082282	3/8	7/8	9/32 ②	25/0.142	—	④	0.110	0.243	⑤
	17082283	3/8	7/8	9/32 ②	25/0.142	—	④	0.110	0.243	⑤
	17082286	13/32	1/2	9/32 ②	22/0.123	34/0.211	④	0.077	0.243	⑤
	17082287	13/32	1/2	9/32 ②	22/0.123	34/0.211	④	0.077	0.243	⑤
	17082288	3/8	7/8	9/32 ②	25/0.142	—	④	0.110	0.243	⑤
	17082289	3/8	7/8	9/32 ②	25/0.142	—	④	0.110	0.243	⑤
	17082296	1/2	7/8	9/32 ②	25/0.142	—	④	0.110	0.243	⑤
	17082297	1/2	7/8	9/32 ②	25/0.142	—	④	0.110	0.243	⑤

QUADRAJET CARBURETOR SPECIFICATIONS
All Canadian Models

Year	Carburetor Identi- fication ①	Float Level (in.)	Air Valve Spring (turn)	Pump Rod (in.)	Primary Vacuum Break (deg./in.)	Secondary Vacuum Break (deg./in.)	Secondary Opening (deg./in.)	Choke Rod (deg./in.)	Choke Unloader (deg./in.)	Fast Idle Speed ② (rpm)
'83	17080213	3/8	1	9/32	23/.129	30/.179	④	0.234	0.260	⑤
	17082213	9/32	1	9/32	23/.129	30/.179	④	0.234	0.260	⑤
	17082282	3/8	7/8	9/32	25/.142	—	④	0.110	0.243	⑤
	17082283	3/8	7/8	9/32	25/.142	—	④	0.110	0.243	⑤
	17082286	13/32	1/2	9/32	23/.129	34/.211	④	0.107	0.220	⑤
	17082287	13/32	1/2	9/32	23/.129	34/.211	④	0.107	0.220	⑤
	17082296	1/2	7/8	9/32	25/.142	—	④	0.110	0.243	⑤
	17082297	1/2	7/8	9/32	25/.142	—	④	0.110	0.243	⑤
	17083280	3/8	7/8	9/32	25/.142	—	④	0.110	0.243	⑤
	17083281	3/8	7/8	9/32	25/.142	—	④	0.110	0.243	⑤
	17083282	3/8	7/8	9/32	25/.142	—	④	0.110	0.243	⑤
	17083283	3/8	7/8	9/32	25/.142	—	④	0.110	0.243	⑤
	17083290	13/32	7/8	9/32	—	24/.136	④	0.314	0.251	⑤
	17083292	13/32	7/8	9/32	—	24/.136	④	0.314	0.251	⑤
	17083298	3/8	1	9/32	23/.129	30/.179	④	0.234	0.260	⑤
'84	17084280	3/8	7/8	9/32 ②	23/.129	—	④	0.110	0.243	⑤
	17084281	3/8	7/8	9/32 ②	23/.129	—	④	0.110	0.243	⑤
	17084282	3/8	7/8	9/32 ②	23/.129	—	④	0.110	0.243	⑤
	17084283	3/8	7/8	9/32 ②	23/.129	—	④	0.110	0.243	⑤
	17084284	3/8	7/8	9/32 ②	23/.129	—	④	0.110	0.243	⑤
	17084285	3/8	7/8	9/32 ②	23/.129	—	④	0.110	0.243	⑤
	17084286	13/32	1/2	9/32 ②	23/.129	34/.211	④	0.107	0.220	⑤
	17084287	13/32	1/2	9/32 ②	23/.129	34/.211	④	0.107	0.220	⑤
	17084288	3/8	7/8	9/32 ②	23/.129	—	④	0.110	0.243	⑤
	17084289	3/8	7/8	9/32 ②	23/.129	—	④	0.110	0.243	⑤
	17084296	1/2	7/8	9/32 ②	23/.129	—	④	0.110	0.243	⑤
	17084297	1/2	7/8	9/32 ②	23/.129	—	④	0.110	0.243	⑤
'85	17080213	3/8	1	9/32 ②	23/.129	30/0.179	④	0.234	40/0.260	⑤
	17080298	3/8	1	9/32 ②	23/.129	30/0.179	④	0.234	40/0.260	⑤
	17082213	3/8	1	9/32 ②	23/.129	30/0.179	④	0.234	40/0.260	⑤
	17083298	3/8	1	9/32 ②	23/.129	30/0.179	④	0.234	40/0.260	⑤
	17085247	13/32	7/8	9/32 ②	20/0.110	—	④	0.096	30/0.179	⑤
	17085246	13/32	7/8	9/32 ②	20/0.110	—	④	0.096	30/0.179	⑤
	17085249	13/32	7/8	9/32 ②	20/0.110	—	④	0.096	30/0.179	⑤
	17085248	13/32	7/8	9/32 ②	20/0.110	—	④	0.096	30/0.179	⑤
	17085580	3/8	7/8	9/32 ②	21/0.117	—	④	0.077	30/0.179	⑤
	17085582	3/8	7/8	9/32 ②	21/0.117	—	④	0.077	30/0.179	⑤
	17085581	3/8	7/8	9/32 ②	21/0.117	—	④	0.077	30/0.179	⑤
	17085583	3/8	7/8	9/32 ②	21/0.117	—	④	0.077	30/0.179	⑤
	17085584	3/8	7/8	9/32 ②	21/0.117	—	④	0.077	30/0.179	⑤
	17085586	3/8	7/8	9/32 ②	21/0.117	—	④	0.077	30/0.179	⑤
	17085592	13/32	1/2	9/32 ②	21/0.117	34/.211	④	0.077	35/0.220	⑤

QUADRAJET CARBURETOR SPECIFICATIONS
All Canadian Models

Year	Carburetor Identi-fication ①	Float Level (in.)	Air Valve Spring (turn)	Pump Rod (in.)	Primary Vacuum Break (deg./in.)	Secondary Vacuum Break (deg./in.)	Secondary Opening (deg./in.)	Choke Rod (deg./in.)	Choke Unloader (deg./in.)	Fast Idle Speed ② (rpm)
	17085594	13/32	1/2	9/32 ②	21/0.117	34/.211	④	0.077	28/0.164	⑤
	17085588	3/8	7/8	9/32 ②	21/0.117	—	④	0.077	30/0.179	⑤
	17085590	3/8	7/8	9/32 ②	21/0.117	—	④	0.077	30/0.179	⑤
	17085596	1/2	7/8	9/32 ②	23/0.129	—	④	0.077	38/0.243	⑤
	17085598	1/2	7/8	9/32 ②	23/0.129	—	④	0.077	38/0.243	⑤
'86	17086246	13/32	7/8	9/32 ②	20/0.110	—	④	0.096	30/0.179	⑤
	17086247	13/32	7/8	9/32 ②	20/0.110	—	④	0.096	30/0.179	⑤
	17086248	13/32	7/8	9/32 ②	20/0.110	—	④	0.096	30/0.179	⑤
	17086249	13/32	7/8	9/32 ②	20/0.110	—	④	0.096	30/0.179	⑤
	17086580	3/8	7/8	9/32 ②	21/0.117	—	④	0.077	30/0.179	⑤
	17086581	3/8	7/8	9/32 ②	21/0.117	—	④	0.077	30/0.179	⑤
	17086582	3/8	7/8	9/32 ②	21/0.117	—	④	0.077	30/0.179	⑤
	17086583	3/8	7/8	9/32 ②	21/0.117	—	④	0.077	30/0.179	⑤
	17086584	3/8	7/8	9/32 ②	21/0.117	—	④	0.077	30/0.179	⑤
	17086586	3/8	7/8	9/32 ②	21/0.117	—	④	0.077	30/0.179	⑤
	17086588	3/8	7/8	9/32 ②	21/0.117	—	④	0.077	30/0.179	⑤
	17086590	3/8	7/8	9/32 ②	21/0.117	—	④	0.077	30/0.179	⑤
	17086596	1/2	7/8	9/32 ②	21/0.117	—	④	0.077	30/0.179	⑤
	17086598	1/2	7/8	9/32 ②	21/0.117	—	④	0.077	30/0.179	⑤
'87	17087117	1/2	7/8	9/32	23/.129	—	④	0.077	26/.149	⑤
	17087118	1/2	7/8	9/32	23/.129	—	④	0.077	26/.149	⑤
	17087119	1/2	7/8	9/32	23/.129	—	④	0.077	26/.149	⑤
	17087120	1/2	7/8	9/32	23/.129	—	④	0.077	26/.149	⑤
	17087123	1/2	7/8	9/32	23/.129	—	④	0.077	26/.149	⑤
	17087124	1/2	7/8	9/32	23/.129	—	④	0.077	26/.149	⑤
	17087125	1/2	7/8	9/32	25/.142	—	④	0.077	26/.149	⑤
	17087126	1/2	7/8	9/32	25/.142	—	④	0.077	26/.149	⑤
	17087207	13/32	1/2	9/32	21/.117	—	④	0.077	28/.164	⑤
	17087211	13/32	1/2	9/32	21/.117	—	④	0.077	28/.164	⑤
'88-'89	17086008	11/32	1/2	Fixed	25/.142	43°	④	14°	35°	⑤
	17088115	11/32	1/2	Fixed	25/.142	43°	④	14°	35°	⑤
	17087211	11/32	1/2	9/32	21/.117	—	④	14°	28/.164	⑤

① The carburetor identification number is stamped on the float bowl, near the secondary throttle lever.
② Inner hole
③ Outer hole
④ No measurement necessary on two point linkage; see text.
⑤ See underhood decal

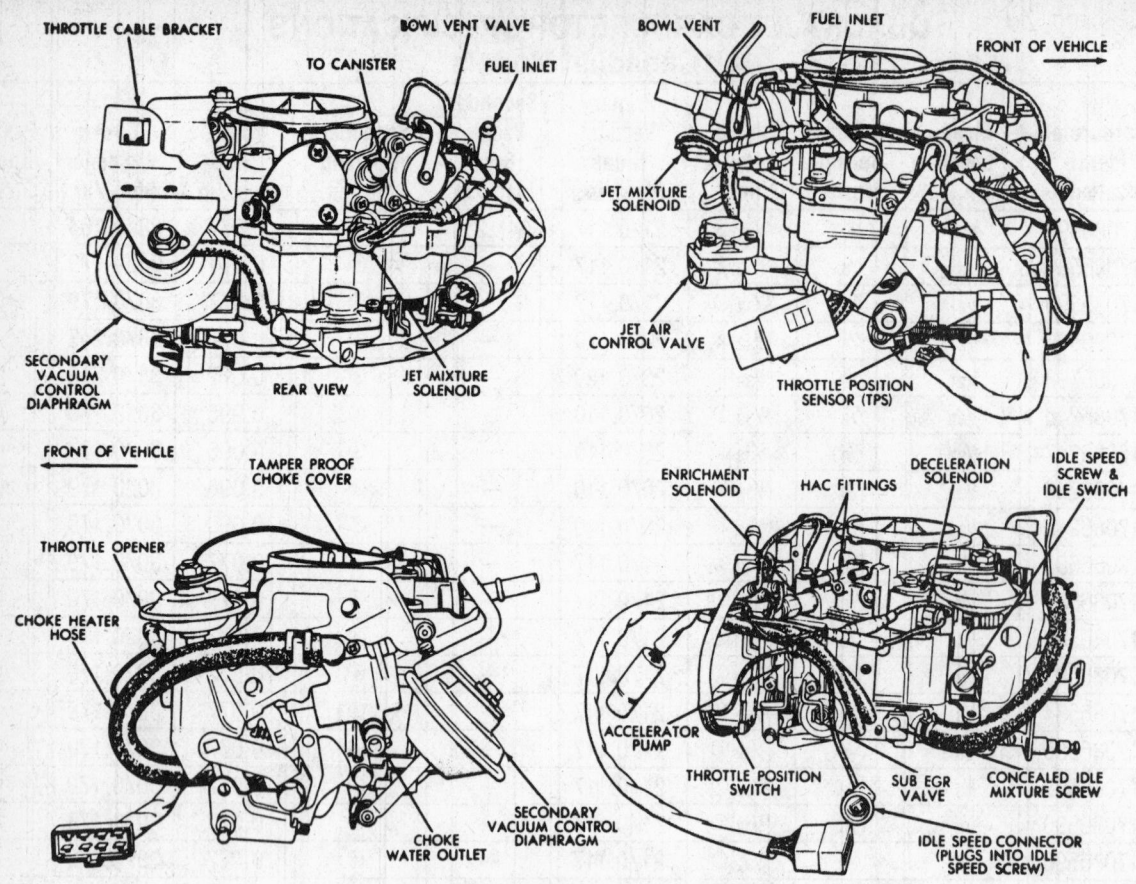

THROTTLE CABLE BRACKET
BOWL VENT VALVE
TO CANISTER
FUEL INLET
BOWL VENT
FUEL INLET
FRONT OF VEHICLE
JET MIXTURE SOLENOID
JET AIR CONTROL VALVE
SECONDARY VACUUM CONTROL DIAPHRAGM
REAR VIEW
JET MIXTURE SOLENOID
THROTTLE POSITION SENSOR (TPS)

FRONT OF VEHICLE
TAMPER PROOF CHOKE COVER
THROTTLE OPENER
CHOKE HEATER HOSE
ENRICHMENT SOLENOID
HAC FITTINGS
DECELERATION SOLENOID
IDLE SPEED SCREW & IDLE SWITCH
ACCELERATOR PUMP
THROTTLE POSITION SWITCH
SUB EGR VALVE
CONCEALED IDLE MIXTURE SCREW
CHOKE WATER OUTLET
SECONDARY VACUUM CONTROL DIAPHRAGM
IDLE SPEED CONNECTOR (PLUGS INTO IDLE SPEED SCREW)

Mikuni feedback carburetor assembly

the ECU. The (TPS) is mounted on the carburetor. The idle position switch is installed on the carburetor and is **ON** when the throttle plate is at the closed or idle position. It provides information to the ECU and is used to adjust idle speed.

Standard Carburetor

All front wheel drive models (USA and Canadian), with the 2.6L (156 cubic inch) Mitsubishi engine are equipped with a conventional downdraft 2 barrel compound type carburetor. The automatic choke is a thermowax type which is controlled by engine coolant temperature. This carburetor also features a diaphragm type accelerator pump, bowl vent, fuel cut-off solenoid, air switching valve (ASV), sub EGR valve, coasting air valve (CAV), jet air control valve (JACV) and a high altitude compensation (HAC) system (California only). The air switching valve system is activated by ported carburetor vacuum and supplies additional air to the low speed passage by cutting off fuel flow to the bypass holes and pilot outlet.

DISASSEMBLY

1. Compress the clamps and remove

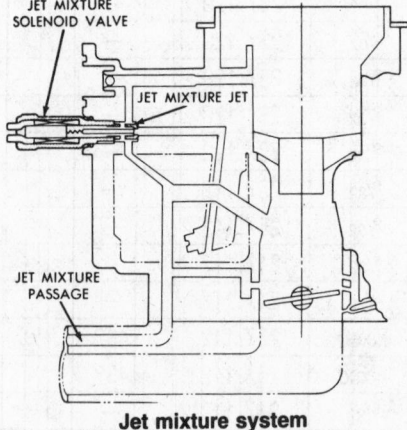

JET MIXTURE SOLENOID VALVE
JET MIXTURE JET
JET MIXTURE PASSAGE

Jet mixture system

the water hose from the choke assembly.

2. Drill out the staked portions of the staked cover screws.

3. Using a small hammer and a pointed punch, gently tap the edge of the remaining screw counterclockwise until the screw is removed. Remove the choke cover.

4. Note the relationship between the punched mark and the scribed line on the choke pinion plate. During reassembly the line and punch mark must be aligned to this position.

5. Remove the E-clip from the throttle opener link. Remove the throttle opener screws and set the opener aside.

6. Remove the ground wire from the fuel cut-off solenoid (if equipped), then remove the mounting screw and set the solenoid aside.

7. Remove the throttle return spring and the damper spring.

8. Remove the "E" clips and the choke unloader link from carburetor.

9. Disconnect the vacuum hose and link from the vacuum chamber, remove the mounting screws and set the chamber aside.

10. On feedback models, remove the screws securing the throttle position sensor and set the sensor aside. Remove the vacuum connector hoses from the carburetor on all models.

11. Disconnect the accelerator linkage.

12. Remove the 6 airhorn mounting screws and seperate the air horn from the carburetor body.

13. Slide out the float pivot pin and remove the float assembly.

14. Unscrew the retainer and remove the needle seat and the screen assembly. Do not lose the shim from under the needle seat assembly.

15. On feedback models, disconnect

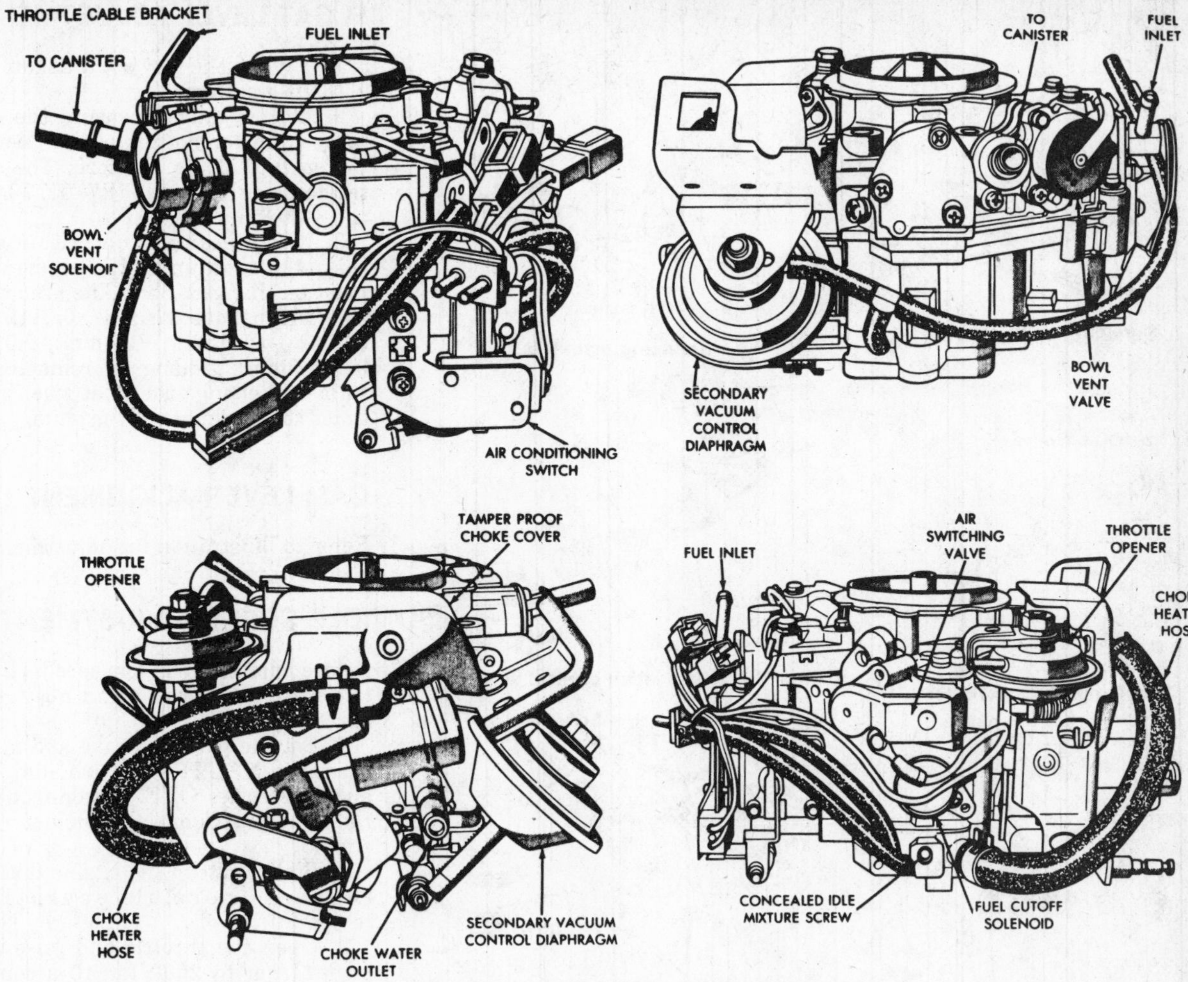

THROTTLE CABLE BRACKET
FUEL INLET
TO CANISTER
BOWL VENT SOLENOID
AIR CONDITIONING SWITCH

TO CANISTER
FUEL INLET
SECONDARY VACUUM CONTROL DIAPHRAGM
BOWL VENT VALVE

THROTTLE OPENER
TAMPER PROOF CHOKE COVER
AIR SWITCHING VALVE
THROTTLE OPENER
FUEL INLET
CHOKE HEATER HOSE
CHOKE HEATER HOSE
CHOKE WATER OUTLET
SECONDARY VACUUM CONTROL DIAPHRAGM
CONCEALED IDLE MIXTURE SCREW
FUEL CUTOFF SOLENOID

Mikuni non—feedback carburetor assembly

CHOKE COVER ATTACHING SCREWS

Feedback model choke cover screws

THROTTLE SENSOR

Servicing throttle position sensor

CAM LEVER
PAINTED PUNCH MARK
SCRIBED LINES
PINION PLATE

Pinion plate alignment

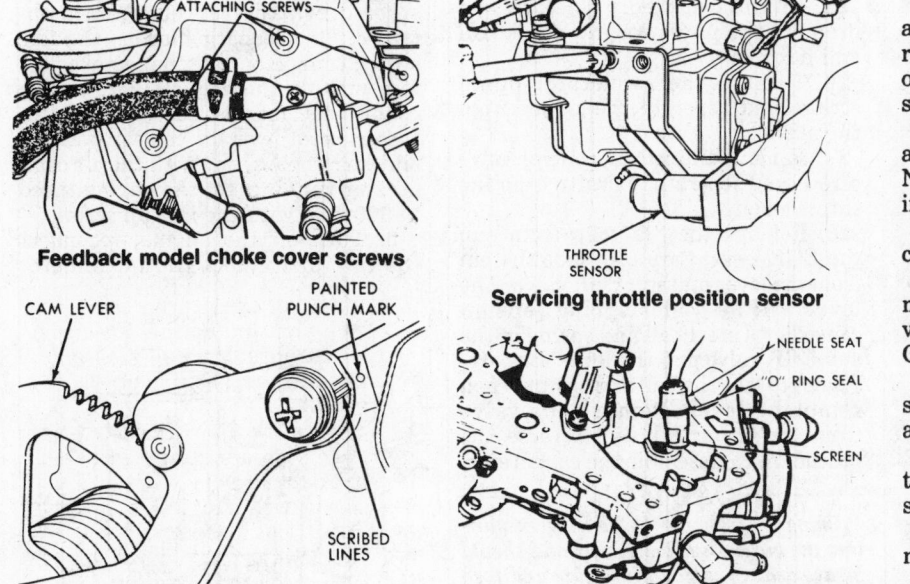

NEEDLE SEAT
"O" RING SEAL
SCREEN
NEEDLE SEAT RETAINER

Servicing needle seat assembly

the solenoid wiring and unscrew the solenoid from the air horn.

16. Remove the venturi retainers and both venturis. Discard the O-rings. Mark both the primary and secondary venturi so they can be reinstalled in their proper positions.

17. Remove the primary and secondary main jets from their pedestals. Note the jet numbers for proper installation.

18. Remove the pedestals and discard the gaskets.

19. Remove the bowl vent solenoid mounting screws, seperate the bowl vent from the air horn and discard the O-ring and seal.

20. Remove the enrichment valve screws and seperate the valve from the air horn. Remove the jet.

21. On non feedback models, remove the air switching valve screws and seperate the valve from the air horn.

22. Remove the screw, lock and primary jet set.

23. Remove the screw, lock and secondary jet set.

24. Remove the primary and secondary air bleed jets from top of the air

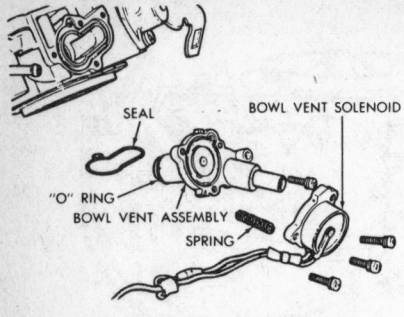

Servicing bowl vent

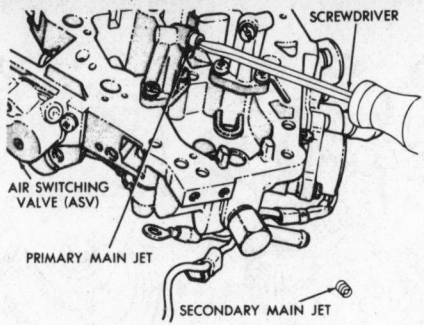

Servicing main jets

FLOAT LEVEL ADJUSTMENT

1. Invert the air horn assembly without a gasket.

2. With a gauge, measure the distance from the bottom of the float to the surface of the air horn. The distance should be 0.0787–0.779 in. (17.8–20.8mm).

3. If the reading is not within this range the shim under the needle seat must be changed. Shim kits are available which have 3 shims: 0.0118 in. (0.3mm), 0.0157 in. (0.4mm), 0.0196 in. (0.5mm). Adding or removing a shim will change the float level by 3 times the thickness of the shim.

CAM LEVER ALIGNMENT

Refer to illustration for adjustment.

IDLE SPEED ADJUSTMENT

Before adjusting the idle speed, check the ignition timing and adjust if necessary.

1. Set the parking brake and place the car in **NEUTRAL**. Turn all lights and accessories **OFF**. Disconnect the radiator fan. Connect tachometer to engine.

2. Start and run the engine until it reaches normal operating temperature.

3. Open the throttle and raise the engine rpm to 2500 for 10 seconds, then return the engine to idle.

4. Wait 2 minutes and note the rpm indicated on the tachometer. If rpm is different from that specified on the underhood sticker, turn the adjusting screw until the correct rpm is obtained. On feedback models, the idle switch connector must be removed before making this adjustment. On air conditioned models, set the temperature control lever to coldest position and turn the A/C on. With the air compressor running, set the engine speed to 900 rpm with the idle up screw.

5. Turn off the engine, reconnect the fan, disconnect the tachometer

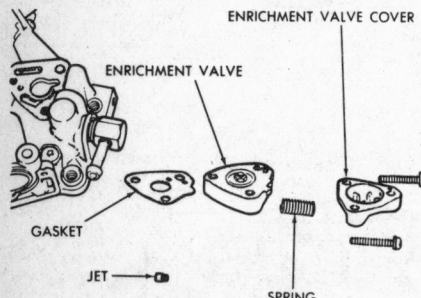

Servicing enrichment jet

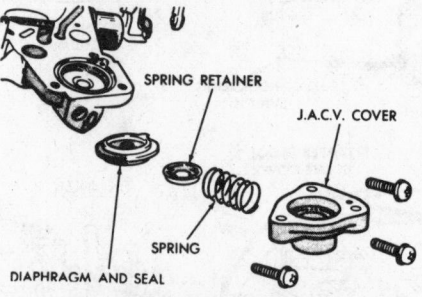

Servicing jet air control valve

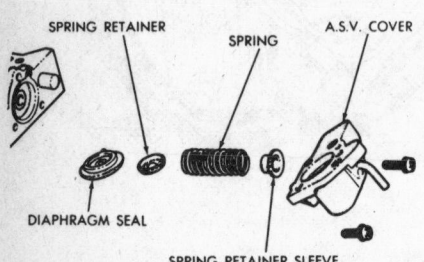

Servicing air switching valve

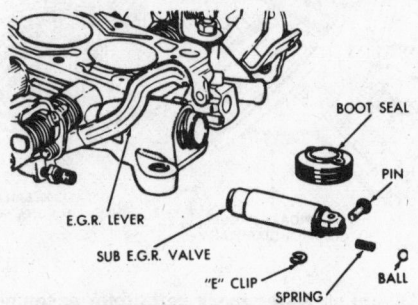

Servicing sub EGR assembly

horn. Note the sizes for proper reinstallation.

25. Invert the air horn carefully and drop out the pump weight, check ball and hex nut.

26. Remove the accelerator pump screws and seperate the pump from the air horn.

27. Remove the jet air control valve screws and seperate the valve from the throttle body.

28. Remove the "E" clip from sub the EGR lever. Carefully slide the pin from the lever and sub EGR valve. The lever will be under spring tension caused by a steel ball and spring in the sub EGR valve and the lever. Be careful not to lose the ball and spring when removing lever. Remove the valve from the throttle boby. Reverse the procedure to Assemble the carburetor.

—— CAUTION ——

Priming a carburetor by pouring gasoline into the air horn is dangerous and should be avoided. Cranking the engine and then depressing the accelerator several times is the recommended way to prime the carburetor.

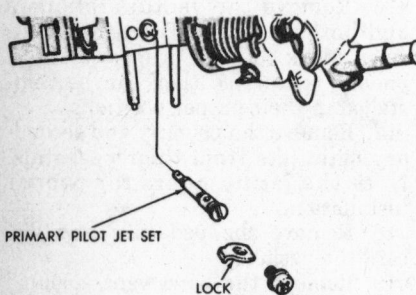

Servicing primary jet set

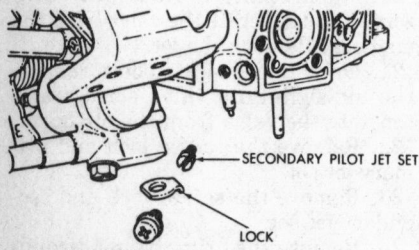

Servicing secondary jet set

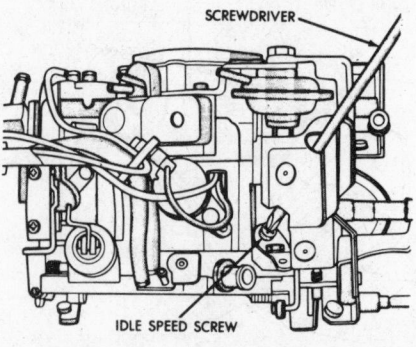

Idle speed adjustment

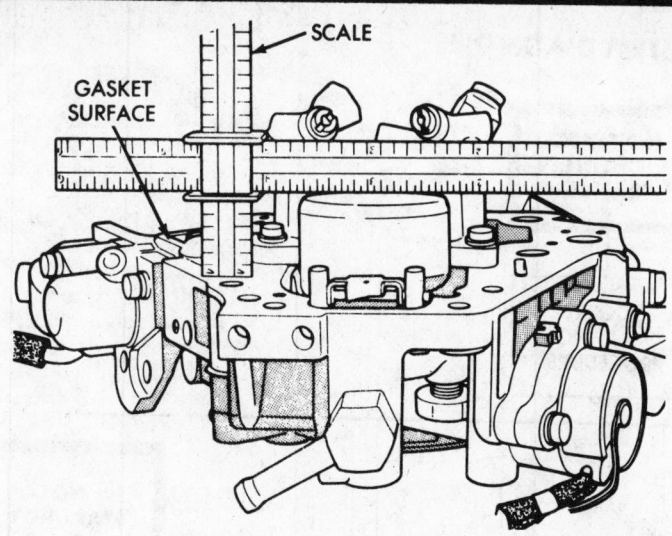

Checking the dry float level

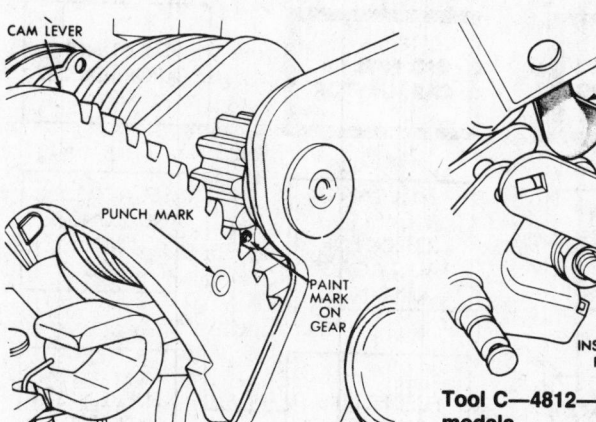

Cam lever alignment

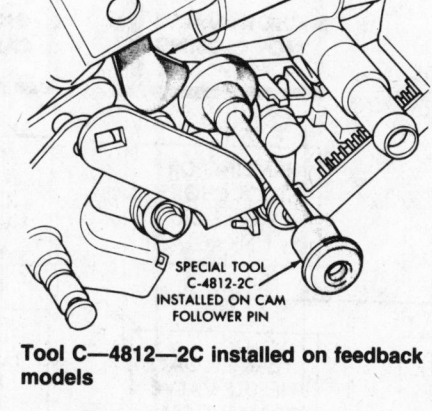

Tool C—4812—2C installed on feedback models

and reconnect the idle switch connector.

FAST IDLE SPEED ADJUSTMENT

1. Set the parking brake and place the car in Neutral. Turn off all lights and accessories. Disconnect the radiator fan. Connect tachometer to engine.
2. Start and run the engine until it reaches normal operating temperature.
3. Disconnect and plug the vacuum advance hose at the distributor. Disconnect the radiator fan.
4. Open the throttle slightly and install tool C–4812–2C on the choke cam follower pin.
5. Release the throttle lever and adjust the fast idle speed to the specification on the underhood sticker.
6. Remove the tool, turn off the engine, reconnect the fan, unplug and reconnect the vacuum advance hose and remove the tachometer.

NIPPON KIKAKI CARBURETORS

Spectrum cv 2 Barrel Carburetor

PRIMARY THROTTLE VALVE OPENING (FULL OPENING)

1. Inspect the angle of the primary throttle valve when the throttle valve has been fully opened. The valve angle should be 90 degrees from the horizontal plane.
2. If adjustment is needed, bend the throttle adjust arm.

SECONDARY THROTTLE VALVE OPENING

1. Open the throttle lever, fully open the secondary throttle valve and inspect the angle. The valve angle should be 87 degrees from the horizontal plane.
2. If needed bend the secondary shaft lever to adjust.

CHOKE VALVE ADJUSTMENT (THIRD STAGE)

Check the choke valve in the third stage of the fast idle cam.

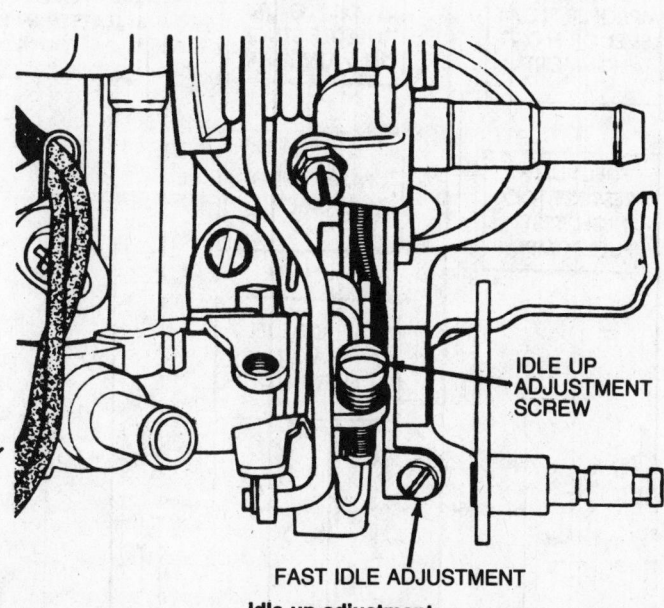

FAST IDLE ADJUSTMENT

Idle up adjustment

FUEL SYSTEM DIAGNOSIS

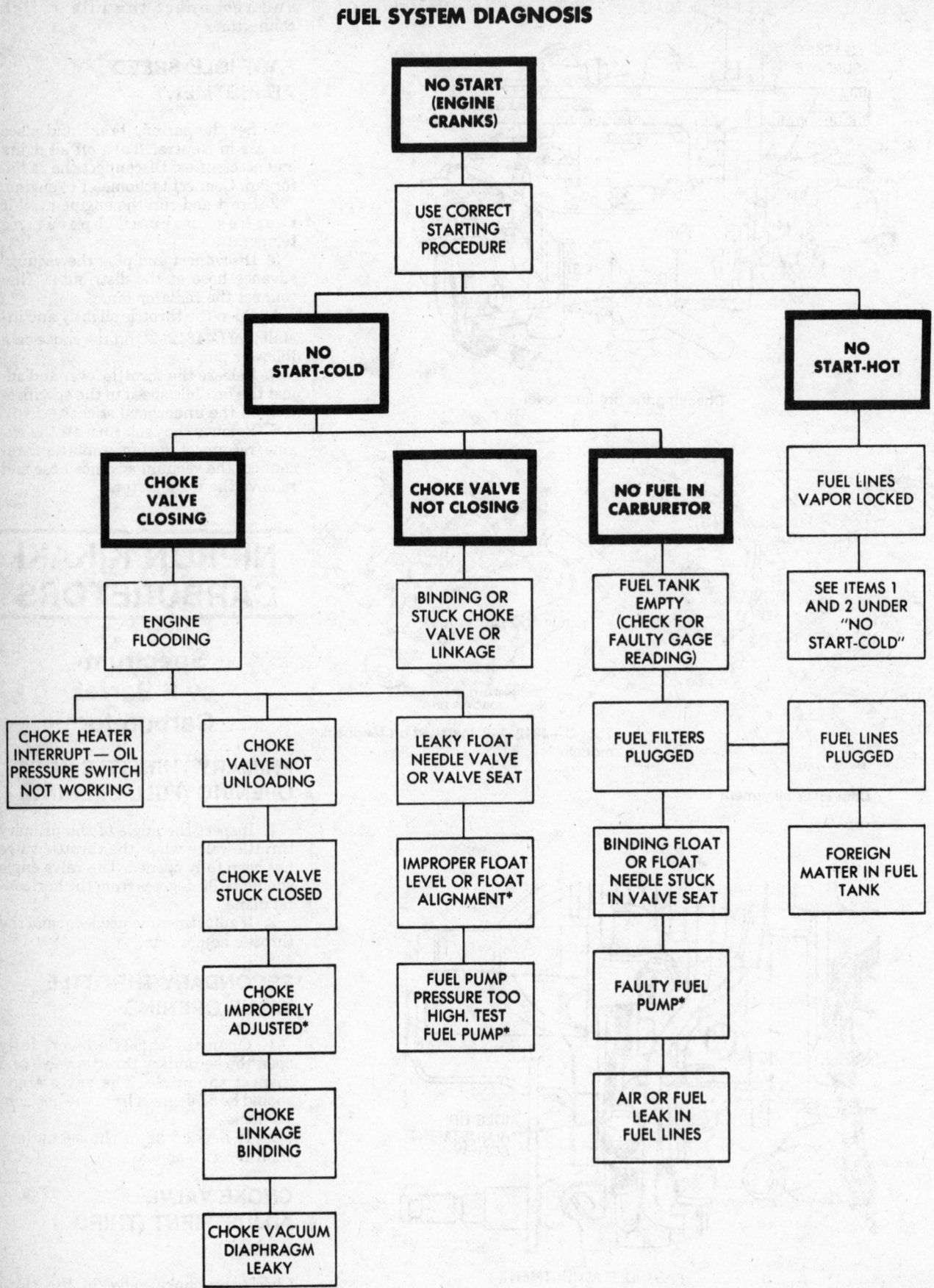

NO START (ENGINE CRANKS)

USE CORRECT STARTING PROCEDURE

NO START-COLD

NO START-HOT

CHOKE VALVE CLOSING

CHOKE VALVE NOT CLOSING

NO FUEL IN CARBURETOR

FUEL LINES VAPOR LOCKED

ENGINE FLOODING

BINDING OR STUCK CHOKE VALVE OR LINKAGE

FUEL TANK EMPTY (CHECK FOR FAULTY GAGE READING)

SEE ITEMS 1 AND 2 UNDER "NO START-COLD"

CHOKE HEATER INTERRUPT — OIL PRESSURE SWITCH NOT WORKING

CHOKE VALVE NOT UNLOADING

LEAKY FLOAT NEEDLE VALVE OR VALVE SEAT

FUEL FILTERS PLUGGED

FUEL LINES PLUGGED

CHOKE VALVE STUCK CLOSED

IMPROPER FLOAT LEVEL OR FLOAT ALIGNMENT*

BINDING FLOAT OR FLOAT NEEDLE STUCK IN VALVE SEAT

FOREIGN MATTER IN FUEL TANK

CHOKE IMPROPERLY ADJUSTED*

FUEL PUMP PRESSURE TOO HIGH. TEST FUEL PUMP*

FAULTY FUEL PUMP*

CHOKE LINKAGE BINDING

AIR OR FUEL LEAK IN FUEL LINES

CHOKE VACUUM DIAPHRAGM LEAKY

1.Set the choke valve to full open.

2.Slowly open the throttle lever while lightly pushing the choke valve in the closing direction with your fingers and set the choke valve to the third stage of the fast idle cam.

3.The choke valve clearance should be 0.093 in.

d.If adjustment is needed, remove the rivet of the automatic choke and adjust by bending the choke lever in the housing. Reinstall the choke lever by riveting.

PRIMARY THROTTLE VALVE OPENING (SECOND STAGE)

Check the clearance of the primary throttle valve in the second stage of the fast idle cam.

1.Set the choke valve to full open.

2.Open the throttle valve slowly while pushing the choke valve lightly in the closing direction with your fingers and set the choke valve to the second stage of the fast idle cam.

3.The primary throttle valve clearance should be: A/T-0.692 in., M/T-0.543 in.

4.Adjustment is made with the fast idle screw.

UNLOADER ADJUSTMENT

1. Check the clearance of the choke valve when the primary throttle valve has been fully opened. The clearance should be 0.071 in.

2. If adjustment is needed remove the rivet of the automatic choke and adjust it by bending the choke lever in the housing. Reinstall the choke lever by riveting.

CHOKE BREAKER ADJUSTMENT

1. Apply a vacuum of about 400mm Hg to the choke breaker diaphragm unit.

2. Lightly push the choke valve to the closing side. The clearance should be 1985: 0.053 in., 1986–89: 0.057 in.

3. Adjust by bending the choke lever.

THROTTLE POSITION SENSOR (TPS) TEST AND ADJUSTMENT

NOTE: After the connection of the ohmmeter is made to the TPS, this test should be performed in as short of time as possible.

1. Check that the TPS bracket screws are tight.

2. Check that there is no play in the TPS arm and primary throttle valve arm.

3. Connect an ohmmeter to the green and black leads of the TPS.

4. Open the throttle lever about one-third (no continuity in this case) and then gradually close the lever and check that there is continuity when the primary slot valve reaches the the prescribed clearance of .015(A/T), .011(M/T).

5. Adjust by loosening the TPS

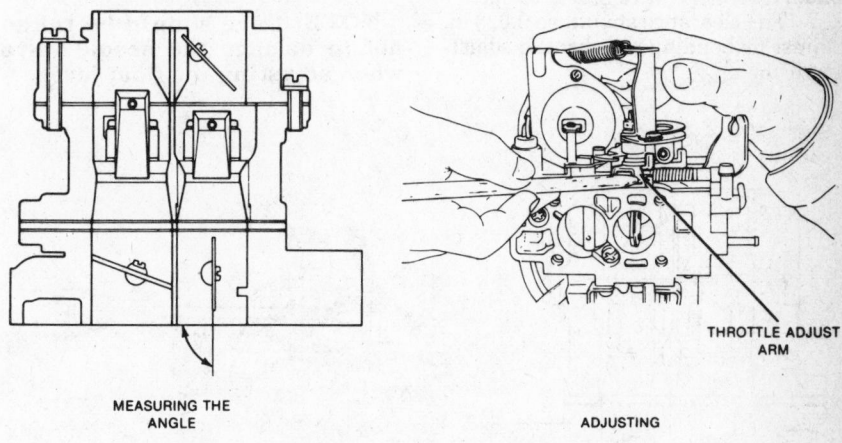

MEASURING THE ANGLE

ADJUSTING

THROTTLE ADJUST ARM

Primary throttle valve angle (full open) — Spectrum

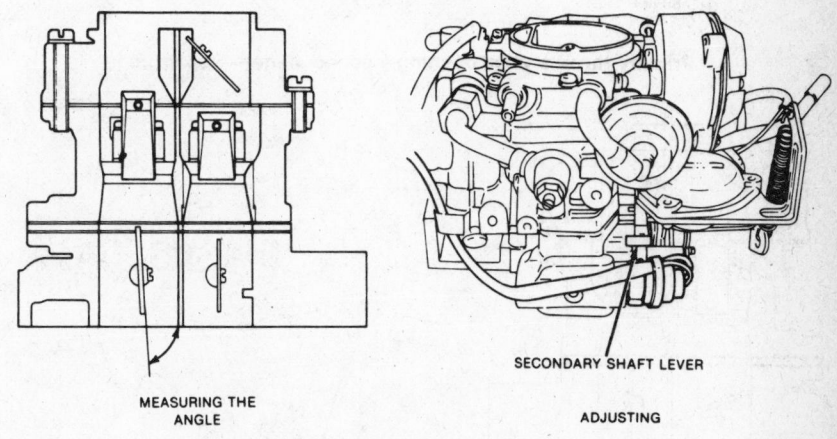

MEASURING THE ANGLE

ADJUSTING

SECONDARY SHAFT LEVER

Secondary throttle valve opening — Spectrum

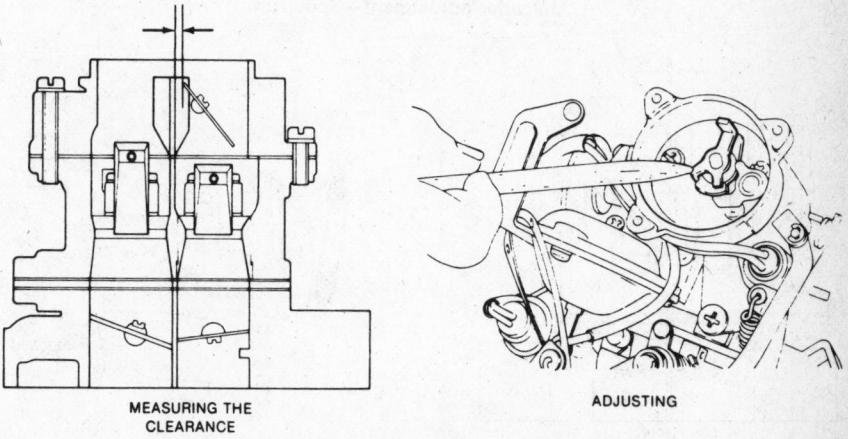

MEASURING THE CLEARANCE

ADJUSTING

Choke valve adjustment (third stage) — Spectrum

screws. After adjustment check the clearance as in Step 4.

SECONDARY TOUCH ANGLE

1. Measure the primary throttle valve opening at the same time the secondary throttle valve starts to open.
2. The clearance should be 0.023 in. Adjust by bending the throttle adjusting arm.

FLOAT LEVEL ADJUSTMENT

1. Measure the clearance between the float top and gasket when the float is in the raised position. The clearance should be 0.059 in.
2. Bend tab (A) to adjust.

NOTE: Care should be taken not to damage the needle valve when adjusting the float level.

3. Measure the clearance between the float bottom and gasket at the lowered position of the float. the clearance should be 1.7 in. Adjust by bending (B) shown in the illustration.

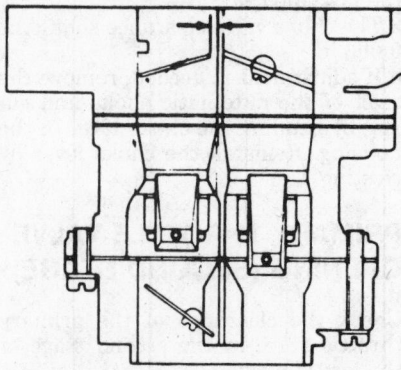

Throttle position sensor adjustment—Spectrum

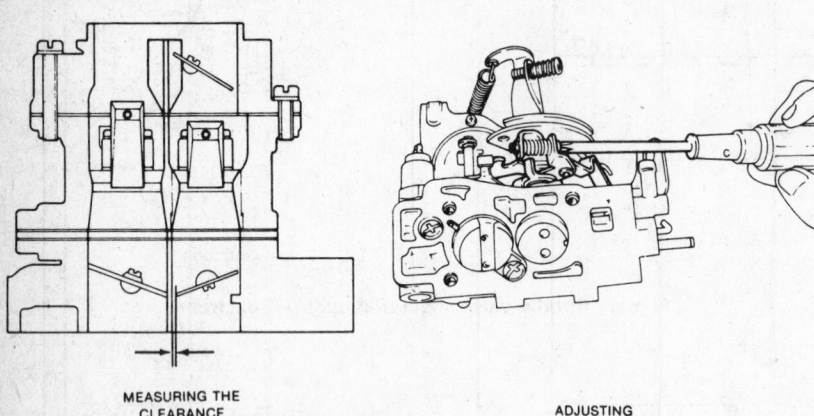

MEASURING THE CLEARANCE

ADJUSTING

Primary throttle valve opening (second stage)—Spectrum

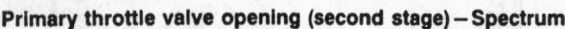

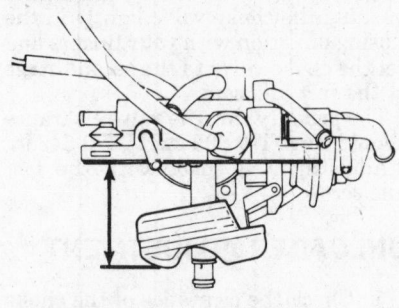

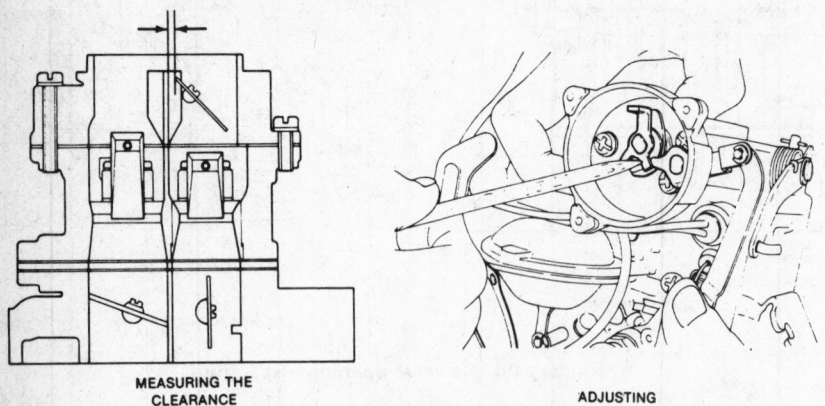

MEASURING THE CLEARANCE

ADJUSTING

Unloader adjustment—Spectrum

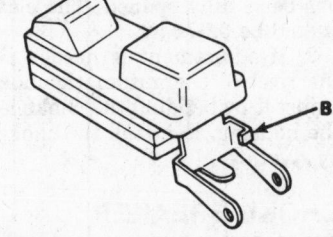

Bend tab (B) to adjust the lower float level—Spectrum

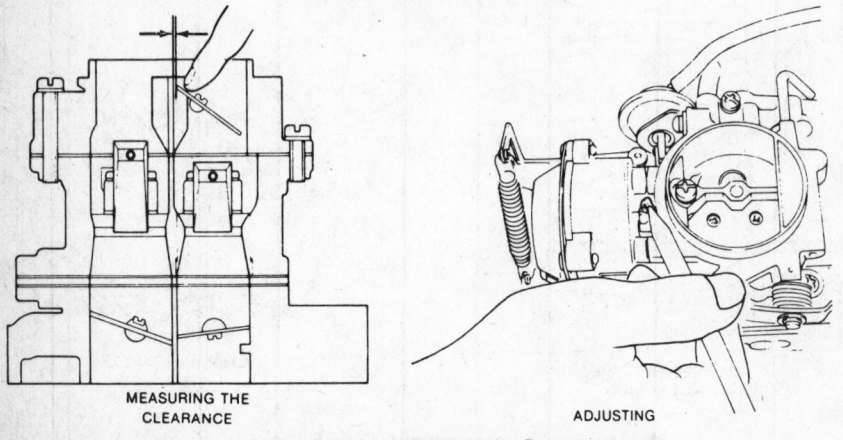

MEASURING THE CLEARANCE

ADJUSTING

Choke breaker adjustment—Spectrum

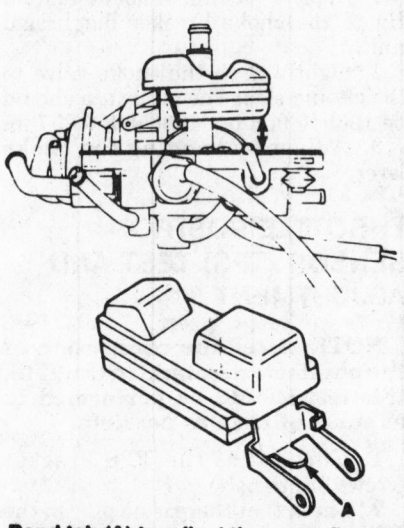

Bend tab (A) to adjust the upper float level—Spectrum

HITACHI CARBURETORS

Sprint 2 Barrel Carburetor MRO8

FLOAT LEVEL ADJUSTMENT

The fuel level in the float chamber should be within the round mark at the center of the level gauge. If it is not, check and adjust the float level as follows:

1. Remove and invert the air horn.
2. Measure the distance between the float and the gasketed surface of the choke chamber. The measured distance is the float level and it should be 0.21–0.24 in. The measurement should be made without the gasket on the air horn.
3. Adjustment is made by bending the tongue up and down.

IDLE-UP ADJUSTMENT

The idle-up actuator operates even when the cooling fan is running. Therefore the idle-up adjustment must be performed when the cooling fan is not running.

Manual Transmission Models

1. Warm up the engine to normal operating temperature.
2. After warming up, run the engine at idle speed.
3. Check to make sure that the idle-up adjusting screw moves down (indicating that the idle-up is at work) when the lights are turned ON.
4. With the lights turned ON, check the engine rpm (idle-up speed). Be sure that the heater fan, rear defogger (if equipped), engine cooling fan and air conditioner (if equipped) are all turned OFF. The idle-up speed should be 750–850 rpm. Adjust by turning the adjusting screw.
5. After making the idle-up adjustment, make sure the idle-up adjusting screw moves as in Step 3 when only the heater fan is operated and then only the rear defogger or engine cooling fan is operated (lights should be off).

Automatic Transmission Models

1. Warm up the engine to normal operating temperature.
2. After warming up, run the engine at idle speed.

3. Apply the parking brake and block the drive wheels.
4. Turn all accessories **OFF**.
5. With the brake pedal depressed, shift the selector lever to **Drive** range. Check to make sure that the idle-up adjusting screw moves down (indicating that the idle-up is at work).
6. Check the idle-up speed (do not depress the accelerator pedal). The Idle-up speed should be between 700–800 rpm. Adjustment is made by turning the adjusting screw.

CHOKE ADJUSTMENT

Perform the following check and ad-

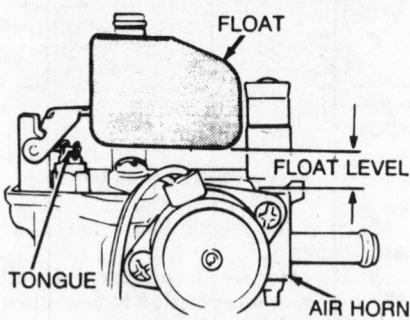

Float level adjustment — Sprint

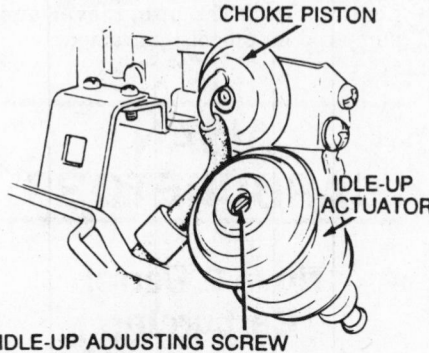

Idle-up adjusting screw — Sprint

Ambient temperature	Clearance
25°C (77°F)	0.1—0.5 mm 0.004—0.019 in
35°C (95°F)	0.7—1.7 mm 0.03—0.06 in

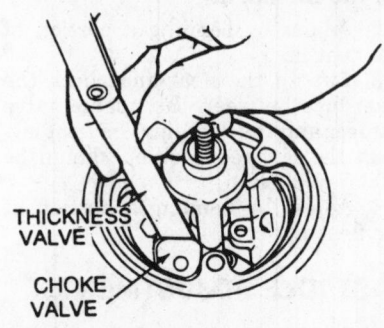

Choke valve to bore clearance — Sprint

justments with the air cleaner top removed and the engine cold.

Choke Valve

1. Check the choke valve for smooth movement by pushing it with a finger.
2. Make sure that the choke valve is closed almost completely when ambient temperature is below 77°F and the engine is cold.
3. Check to see that the choke valve to carburetor bore clearance is within specifications when the ambient temperature is above 77°F and the engine is cool.
4. If clearance is found to be excessively large or small in the above check, remove the air cleaner case and check the strangler spring, choke piston and each link in the choke system for smooth operation. Lubricate the choke valve shaft and each link with a spray lubricant if necessary. Do not remove the riveted choke lever guide.
5. If after lubrication the clearance is still out of specification, remove the carburetor from the intake manifold and remove the idle-up actuator from the carburetor. Turn the fast idle cam counterclockwise and insert an available pin into the holes on the cam and bracket to lock the cam. In this state, bend the choke lever up or down with pliers. Bending up causes the choke valve to close and vice versa.

Choke Piston

1. Disconnect the choke piston hose at the throttle chamber.
2. While lightly pushing down on the choke valve to the closing position with your finger, apply vacuum to the choke piston hose and check to make sure that the choke valve to the carburetor bore clearance is 0.09–0.10 in.
3. With vacuum applied as in Step 2, move the choke piston rod with a small tool and check to see that the choke valve to carburetor bore clearance is within 0.16–0.18 1n.

FAST IDLE CAM ADJUSTMENT

NOTE: Ambient temperature must be between 72°F–82°F before performing this check.

1. Drain the cooling system when the engine is cold and remove the carburetor from the intake manifold.
2. Leave the carburetor in a place where the ambient temperature is between 72–82°F for an hour.
3. After an hour, make sure that the mark on the cam and the center of the cam follower are in alignment.

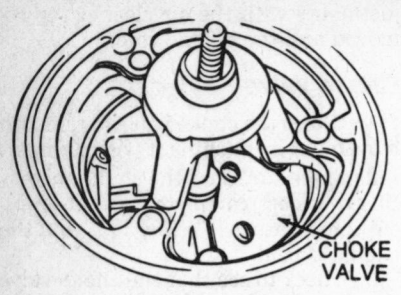

Choke valve – Sprint

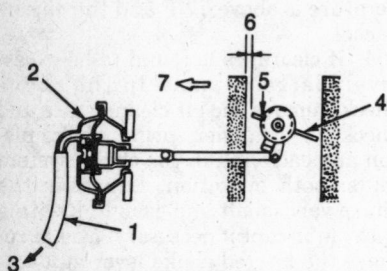

1. Choke piston hose
2. Choke piston
3. Vacuum
4. Choke valve
5. Push here lightly
6. Choke valve to bore clearance
7. Forward

Checking choke piston – Sprint

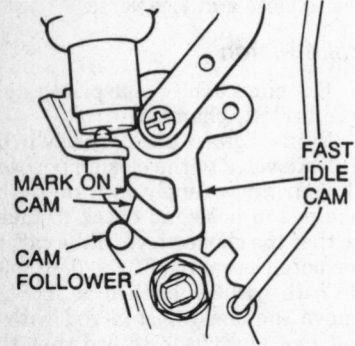

Mark on cam and cam follower

UNLOADER ADJUSTMENT

NOTE: Perform this check and adjustment when the engine is cool.

1. Remove the air cleaner cover.
2. Make sure that the choke valve is closed.
3. Fully open the throttle valve and check the choke valve to carburetor bore clearance is within 0.10–0.12 in.
4. If the clearance is out of specification adjust by bending the unloader arm.

PUMP STROKE ADJUSTMENT

1. Warm up the engine to normal operating temperature.

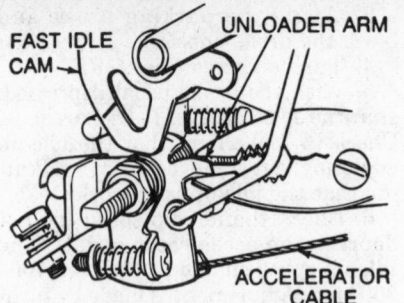

Unloader level arm – Sprint

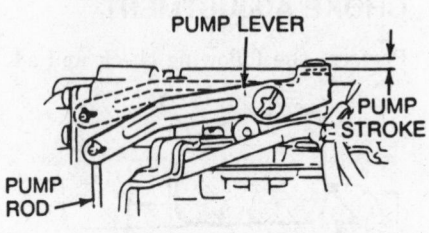

Pump stroke – Sprint

2. Stop the engine and remove the air cleaner.
3. Depress the accelerator pedal all the way from idle position to wide open throttle and take the measurement of the pump stroke. The pump stroke should be 0.16–0.18 in. If out of specification check the pump lever and pump rod for smooth movement.

AISAN CARBURETORS

Nova 2 Barrel Carburetor

FLOAT ADJUSTMENT

1. Allow the float the hang down by its own weight. Check the clearance between the float tip and air horn. The float level should be 0.075 in.

NOTE: This measurement should be made without a gasket on the air horn.

2. Adjust by bending a portion of the float lip.
3. Lift up the float and check the clearance between the needle valve plunger and the float lip. The float level in the lowered position should be 0.0657–0.0783 in.
4. Adjust by bending a portion of the float lip.

FAST IDLE ADJUSTMENT

1. Stop the engine and remove the air cleaner.

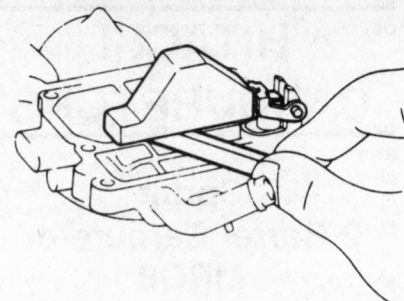

Checking the float level in the upper position – Nova

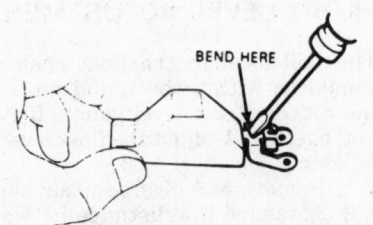

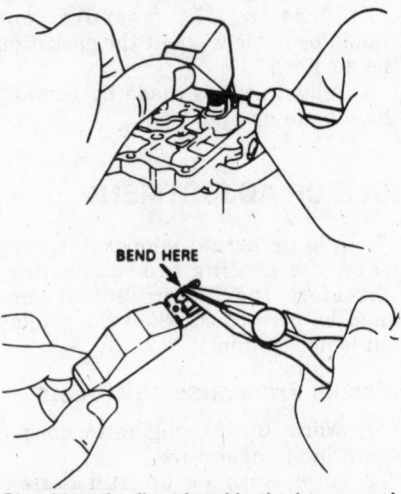

Checking the float level in the lower position – Nova

2. Disconnect and plug the hot idle compensator hose to prevent rough idle.
3. Shut off the choke opener and EGR systems by disconnecting the hose from the Thermo Vacuum Switching Valve M and plugging the M port.
4. Hold the throttle slightly open, push the choke valve closed and hold it closed while releasing the throttle valve.
5. Start the engine but do NOT depress the accelerator pedal.
6. Set the fast idle speed by turning the fast idle screw.
7. Fast idle speed should be: 3000rpm.

THROTTLE VALVE OPENING

1. Check the full opening angle of the primary throttle valve, with a T

scale. The standard angle should be 90 degrees from the horizontal plane.

2. Adjust by bending the 1st throttle lever stopper.

3. Check the full opening clearance between the secondary throttle valve and the body. The standard clearance should be 0.500 in.

4. Adjust by bending the secondary throttle lever stopper.

KICK-UP ADJUSTMENT

1. With the primary throttle valve fully opened, check the clearance between the secondary throttle valve and the body. The clearance should be 0.006 in.

2. Adjust by bending the secondary throttle lever.

SECONDARY TOUCH ADJUSTMENT

1. Check the primary throttle valve opening clearance at the same time the 1st kick lever just touches the 2nd kick lever. The clearance should be 1985: 0.170 in., 1986–89: 0.230 in.

2. Adjust by bending the 1st kick lever.

UNLOADER ADJUSTMENT

1. With the primary throttle valve fully opened, check that the choke valve clearance is 0.120 in.

2. Adjust by bending the fast idle lever.

CHOKE BREAKER ADJUSTMENT

1. Set the idle cam. While holding the throttle slightly open, push the choke valve closed and hold it closed as you release the throttle valve.

2. Apply vacuum to the choke breaker 1st diaphragm.

3. Check the choke valve clearance. It should be 0.095 in.

4. Adjust by bending the relief lever.

5. Apply vacuum to choke diaphragms 1st and 2nd.

6. Check the choke valve clearance. It should be 0.245 in.

7. Adjust by turning the diaphragm adjusting screw.

PUMP STROKE ADJUSTMENT

1. With the choke fully opened, measure the length of the stroke. 1985: 0.157 in., 1986–89: 0.079 in.

2. Adjust the pump stroke by bending the connecting link.

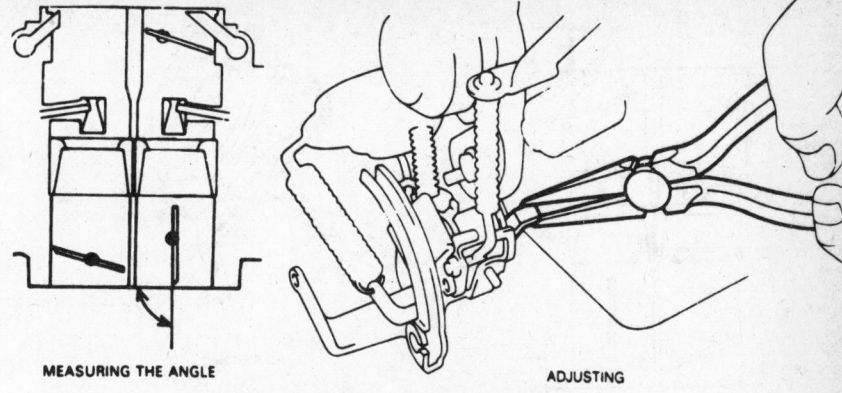

Primary throttle valve adjustment – Nova

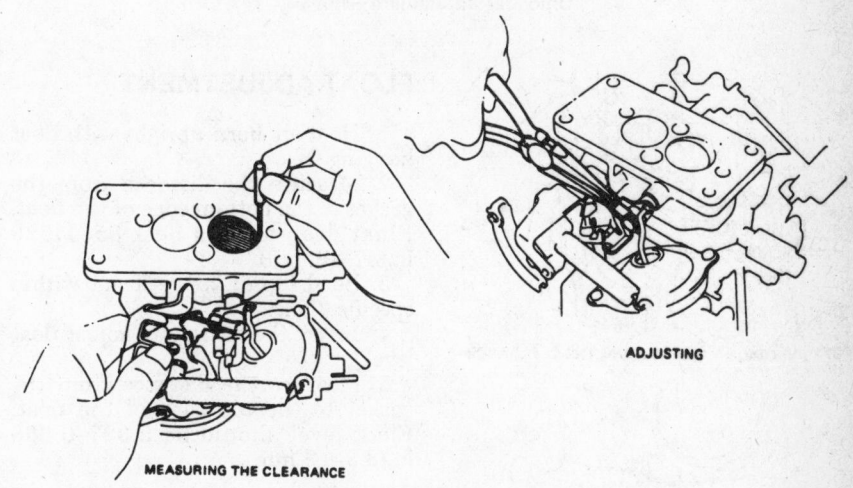

Kick-up adjustment – Nova

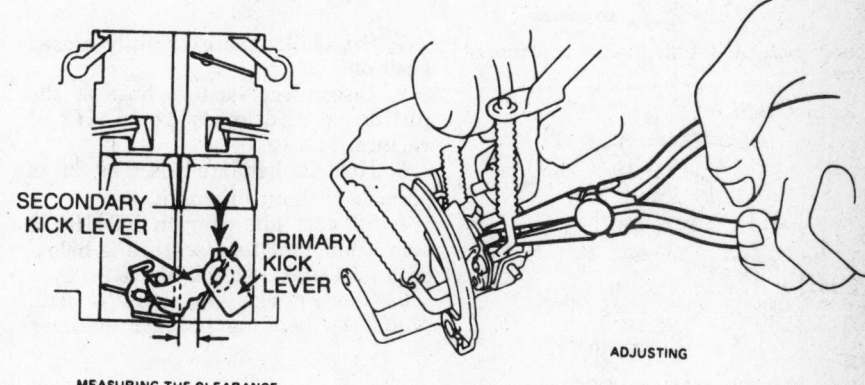

Secondary touch adjustment – Nova

Festiva 2–V Carburetor

The Festiva uses a 2 barrel electronically controlled feedback carburetor made by Aisan. To set the idle mixture on this vehicle requires the use of an exhaust gas analyzer. Before condemning this carburetor, make certain fuel pressure is correct. All ignition and electronic controls and must also be functioning properly. If removing the base plate note the location of the hollow attaching screw, the hole provides vacuum to the power valve. The following adjustments can be made with the carburetor on the vehicle except the throttle plate adjustments.

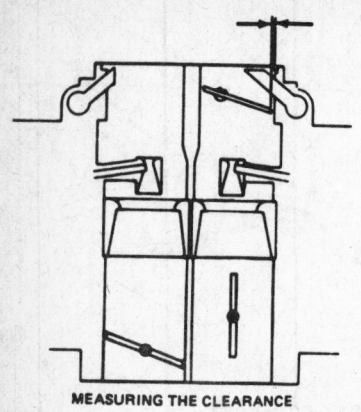

MEASURING THE CLEARANCE

Unloader adjustment—Nova

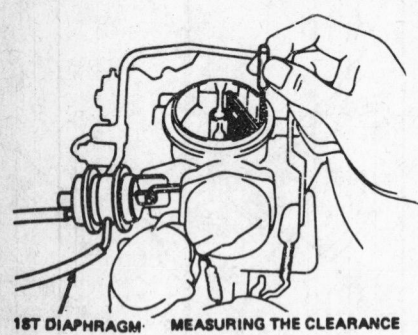

1ST DIAPHRAGM   MEASURING THE CLEARANCE

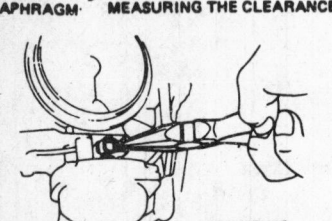

ADJUSTING

Choke breaker 1st diaphragm adjustment Nova

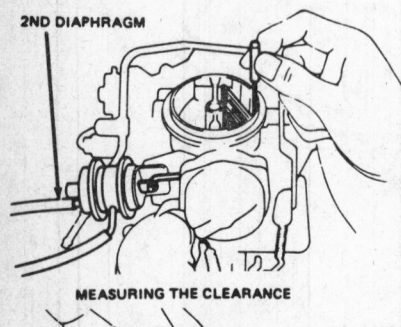

2ND DIAPHRAGM

MEASURING THE CLEARANCE

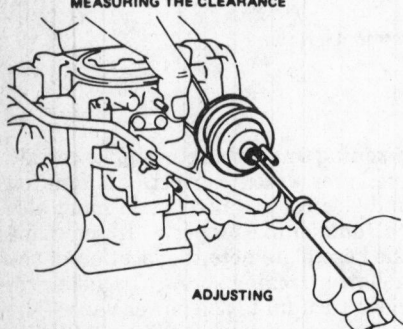

ADJUSTING

Choke breaker 1st and 2nd diaphragm adjustment—Nova

ADJUSTING

FLOAT ADJUSTMENT

1. Hold air horn upright with float hanging free.
2. Measure the distance from the gasket to the bottom edge of the float. Float drop should be 1.85-1.929 in.(47-49 mm).
3. Bend tap on hinge if not within specifications.
4. Invert the airhorn to adjust float level.
5. Measure the distance from the gasket to the top edge of the float. Float level should be 0.327-0.366 in.(8.3-9.3 mm).

CHOKE BREAKER ADJUSTMENT

1. Set choke plate to fully closed position.
2. Disconnect vacuum hose at the pulldown and apply 16 in. Hg of vacuum.
3. Hold choke plate closed as far as possible without forcing it.
4. Set fast idle cam on **FOURTH** step if ambient temperature is below 86°F or **THIRD** step if above 86°F.
5. Check choke gap with $5/16$ drill. Adjust by bending breaker adjuster tab.

CHOKE UNLOADER

1. Hold choke plate closed as far as possible without forcing it.
2. Distance between choke plate and air horn should be .059-.076 in.(drill size $1/16$) while holding throttle wide open.
3. Adjust clearance by bending rod.

CHOKE PLATE CLEARANCE

1. Set fast idle on **THRID** step of cam.
2. Distance between choke plate

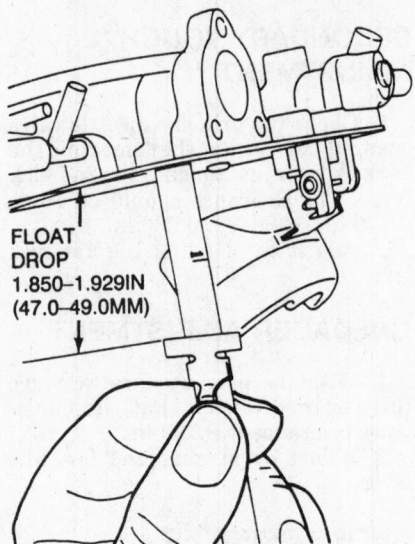

THROTTLE BODY

THROTTLE BODY SCREW

HOLLOW SCREW

Festiva base screw locations

FLOAT DROP 1.850-1.929IN (47.0-49.0MM)

Festiva float drop

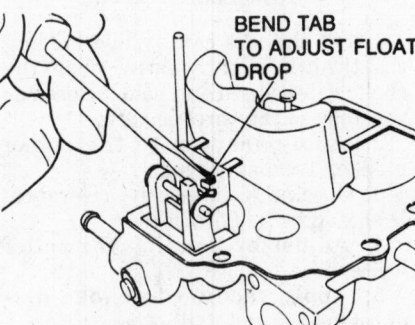

BEND TAB TO ADJUST FLOAT DROP

Festiva float drop adjustment

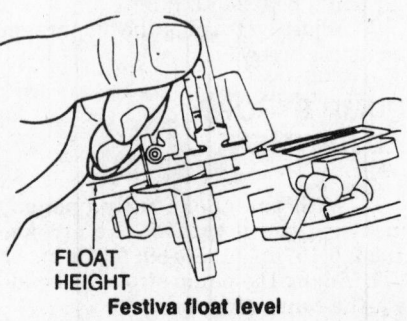

FLOAT HEIGHT

Festiva float level

and air horn should be .024–.037 in.(drill size $\frac{1}{32}$).

3. Adjust clearance by bending the tap.

SECONDARY THROTTLE PLATE

1. With carburetor assembly re-

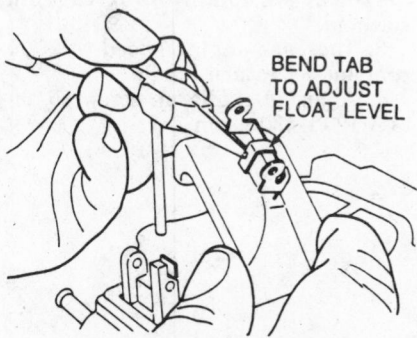

Festiva float level adjustment

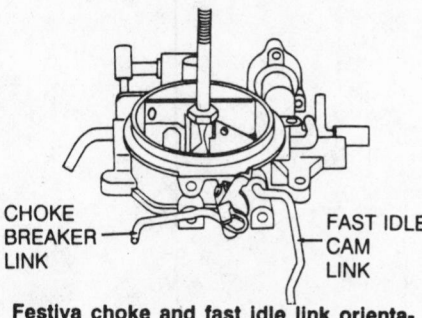

Festiva choke and fast idle link orientation

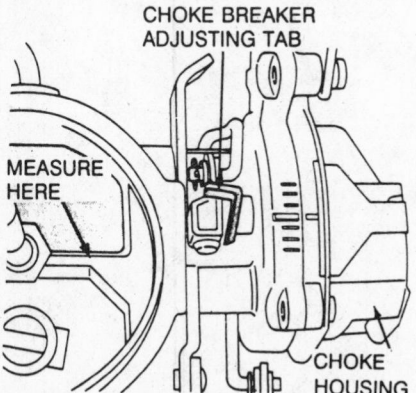

Festiva choke breaker diaphragm adjustment

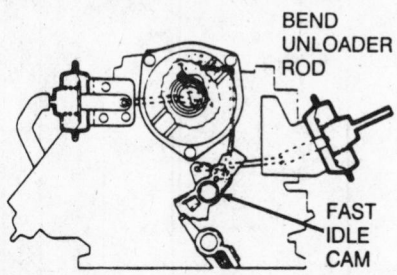

Festiva choke unloader adjustment

moved from engine, slowly open throttle while watching the secondary plate.

2. When the secondary plate just starts to open the clearance to the throttle wall should be .0372 in. (⅜ drill size).

3. Adjust clearance by bending tap at secondary shaft.

THROTTLE OPENING

1. With carburetor assembly removed from engine, position idle cam against the **THRID step.**

2. The distance between the throttle and venturi wall should be .009–.014 in.(.25–.36 mm).

3. Adjust to specifications using the fast idle cam screw.

IDLE MIXTURE

1. Run engine to reach normal temperature.

2. Insert probe into the secondary air hose and plug hose to prevent leaking past the probe lead.

3. Adjust mixture screw until analyzer shows CO concentration of 1.5–2.5%.

CURB IDLE

1. Run engine to reach normal temperature, place transmission in **NEUTRAL** and set parking brake.

2. Adjust idle to 700–760 RPM using idle adjusting screw.

FAST IDLE BREAKER

1. Run engine to reach normal temperature.

2. Set fast idle cam on **SECOND step.**

3. Turn fast idle cam breaker adjusting screw to obtain an engine speed of 1650–2150 RPM.

FAST IDLE ADJUSTMENT

1. Disconnect and plug vacuum hose at the fast idle cam servo.

2. Set fast idle cam on **THIRD** step.

3. Adjust engine speed to 1650–2150 RPM using fast idle screw.

ELECTRICAL LOAD IDLE-UP ADJUSTMENT

1. Run engine to reach normal temperature.

2. Disconnect brown electrical connector at electrical vacuum solenoid.

3. Increase engine speed to 2000 rpm and let return to idle.

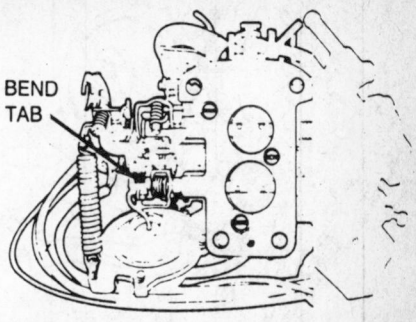

Festiva secondary throttle plate adjustment

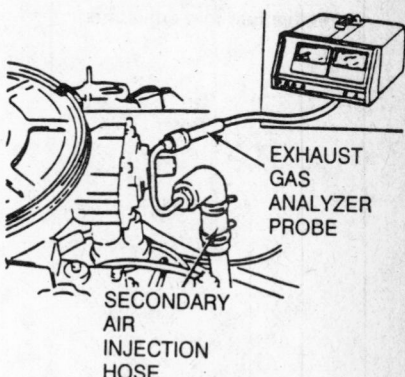

Festiva exhaust gas analyzer probe connection

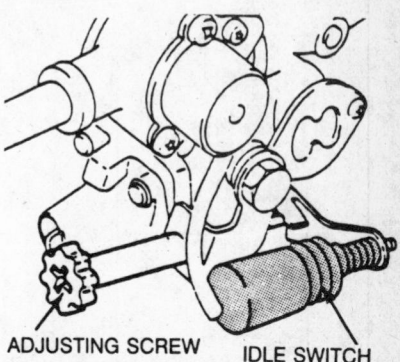

Festiva curb idle speed adjustment

Festiva fast idle cam adjustment

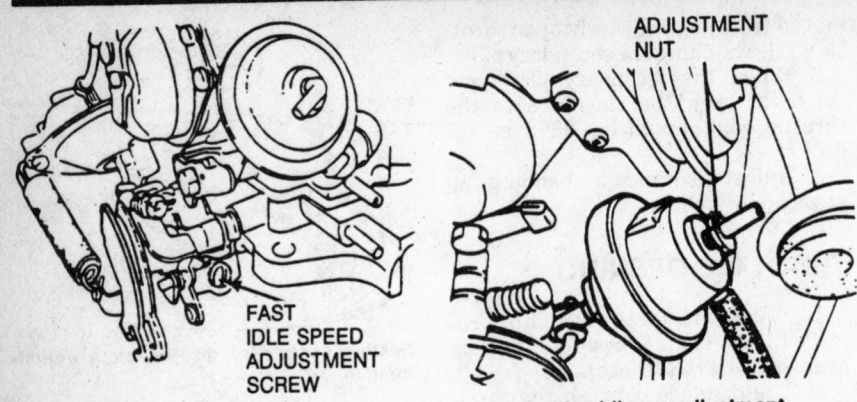

FAST IDLE SPEED ADJUSTMENT SCREW

Festiva fast idle adjustment

ADJUSTMENT NUT

Festiva idle–up adjustment

4. Adjust servo nut to obtain at idle of 750–850 rpm.

AIR CONDITIONING IDLE-UP

1. Run engine to reach normal temperature.
2. Disconnect orange electrical connector at air conditioning vacuum solenoid.
3. Increase engine speed to 2000 rpm and let return to idle.
4. Adjust A/C idle–up screw to obtain 1200–1300 rpm.

Turbocharging 35

Theory

The internal combustion engine can be thought of as an air pump. The action of the pistons moving down or up in their cylinders when the intake or exhaust valves are open alternately draws air and fuel into the engine or expels burnt gases into the atmosphere. The amount of air and fuel pulled into the engine (known as an engine's volumetric efficiency) is governed by the drawing efficiency of the piston as it descends in its cylinder, and by the scavenging effect of the exiting exhaust gases, which act to pull additional air/fuel mixture in through the open intake valves during valve overlap periods. The more air and fuel each cylinder pulls in, the more power the engine will produce.

Theoretically, a normally aspirated engine should be able to draw in an amount of air and fuel equal to its displacement (e.g. a 350 cu in. engine should draw in 350 cu in. of air and fuel). In practice, however, only about 80% of the displacement capacity is drawn through because of flow restrictions, the slight pressure drop through the carburetor, and the inability of the exhaust stroke to drive out all of the burnt gases.

There are several ways to increase an engine's drawing power (volumetric efficiency). These include increasing valve overlap, increasing engine bore and/or stroke, supercharging the engine, or (the most popular approach) turbocharging.

In effect, the turbocharger is an air pump which crams more air/fuel mixture into the cylinders than they could possibly draw in by themselves.

In doing so, the turbocharger increases the engine's volumetric efficiency past its normal 80%, which proportionately increases engine horsepower and torque output.

Perhaps the most advantageous aspect of the turbocharger is that it does not require usable engine horsepower to operate. By comparison, say a car is climbing a steep hill and the driver decides to turn on the air conditioner. The moment the air conditioner is turned on, a power drain on the engine can usually be felt. That's because some of the power that was being used to drive the car up the hill is now being used to turn the air conditioner compressor. A turbocharger, on the other hand, does not drain power from the engine to operate because it uses the free energy of the exhaust gases as they are blown out of the en-

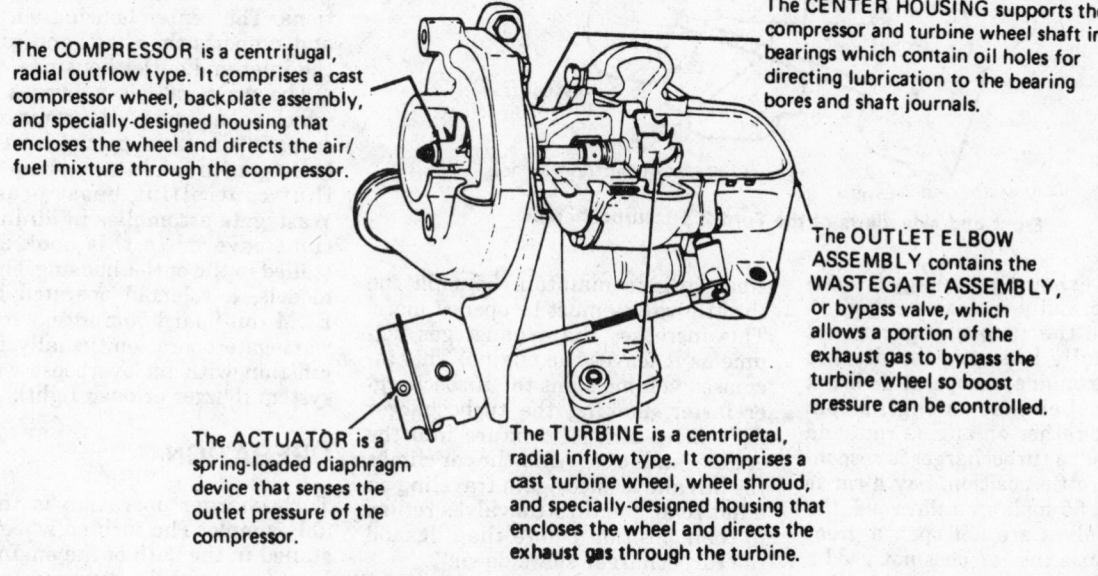

The CENTER HOUSING supports the compressor and turbine wheel shaft in bearings which contain oil holes for directing lubrication to the bearing bores and shaft journals.

The COMPRESSOR is a centrifugal, radial outflow type. It comprises a cast compressor wheel, backplate assembly, and specially-designed housing that encloses the wheel and directs the air/fuel mixture through the compressor.

The OUTLET ELBOW ASSEMBLY contains the WASTEGATE ASSEMBLY, or bypass valve, which allows a portion of the exhaust gas to bypass the turbine wheel so boost pressure can be controlled.

The ACTUATOR is a spring-loaded diaphragm device that senses the outlet pressure of the compressor.

The TURBINE is a centripetal, radial inflow type. It comprises a cast turbine wheel, wheel shroud, and specially-designed housing that encloses the wheel and directs the exhaust gas through the turbine.

Turbocharger components, typical of all models

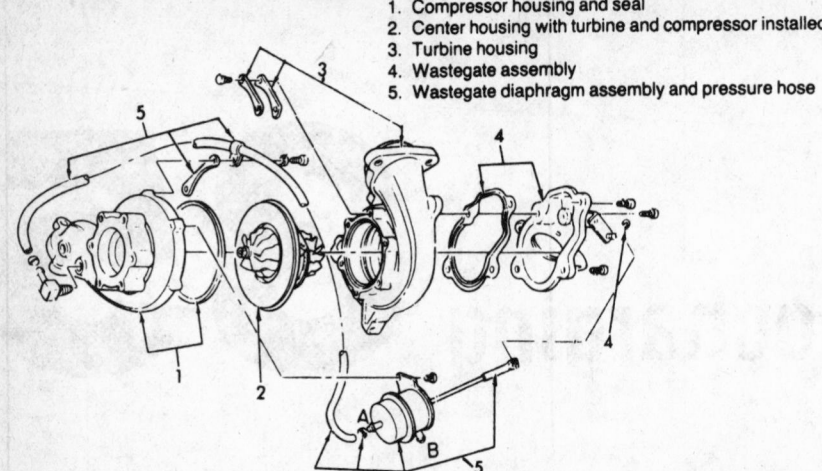

1. Compressor housing and seal
2. Center housing with turbine and compressor installed
3. Turbine housing
4. Wastegate assembly
5. Wastegate diaphragm assembly and pressure hose

Typical GM 3.8L (231 cu In.) engine turbocharger. "A" Is pressure side of wastegate diaphragm, "B" Is vacuum side

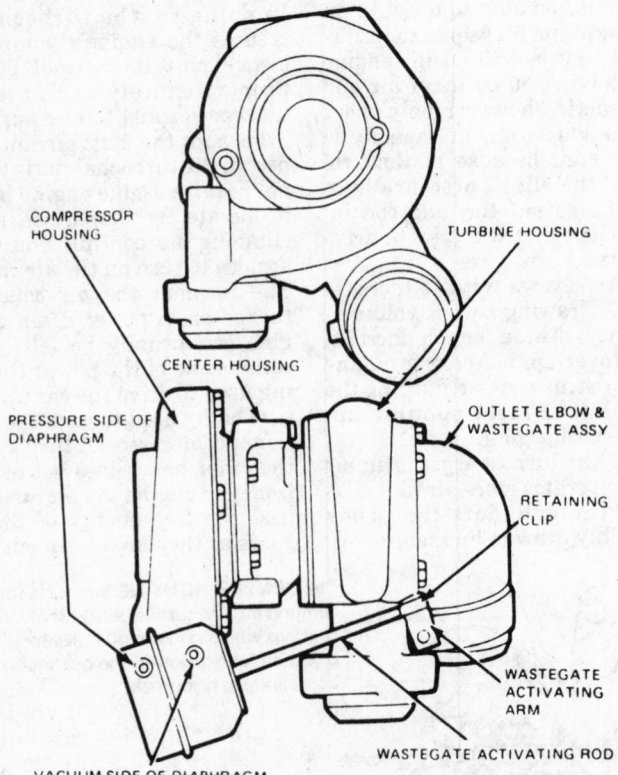

Front and side views of the Ford 2.3 L turbocharger

gine. This exhaust gas energy is wasted on a normally aspirated engine.

Because the turbocharger is not mechanically linked to the driving part of the engine, its operation is not directly dependent on engine rpm alone, but rather on engine rpm and engine load: a turbocharger is responsive to throttle position. Say a car is driving at 55 mph on a flat road: the throttle valves are not open a great deal, because the car does not need a great deal of energy to travel at this speed. Soon the car starts to climb a steep hill: to maintain 55 mph the throttle valves must be opened more. This increases the exhaust gas volume as it leaves the engine. This increased volume spins the turbocharger faster, making the turbocharger force more air/fuel mixture into the engine, and so on. After the car climbs the hill and is once again traveling on a flat road, the throttle valves return to their position before the hill, and the turbocharger slows down.

An adequate supply of clean engine oil is essential for cooling and lubrica-

tion and to maintain the turbocharger bearing assembly. The turbocharger wheels routinely operate at 130,000–140,000 rpm during boost and any interruption in the oil supply to the bearing assembly can result in major turbocharger damage. Contamination of the engine oil can also cause serious damage. Any time a basic engine bearing (main, connecting rod or camshaft) is replaced due to damage, the oil and oil filter must be changed and the turbocharger flushed with clean engine oil to remove any contamination. In addition, any time the turbocharger is removed for service or as part of another procedure, the oil and oil filter should be changed. When first starting the engine after removing the turbocharger, fill the turbocharger oil passage with clean engine oil and crank the engine a few times to allow oil pressure to build up. It's also a good idea to allow the engine to idle for one minute before shutting it off, especially when running at freeway speeds for long periods of time, to prevent the possibility of turbocharger bearing damage due to sudden oil starvation.

COMPONENTS

The turbocharger unit consists of two vaned wheels (compressor and turbine) connected by a common axle (shaft), and a housing which can be sub-divided into three sections: inlet (or compressor), center, and outlet (or turbine). The inlet housing surrounds the compressor wheel, and connects to the air intake and the intake manifold. The outlet housing surrounds the turbine wheel, and connects to the exhaust system; it also houses the wastegate assembly in many installations. The center housing surrounds and supports the shaft, and connects the inlet and outlet housings.

The wastegate is a bypass valve, which opens at a predetermined pressure. It shunts a portion of the exhaust gas around the turbine wheel, thus controlling boost pressure. Wastegate assemblies in all installations covered in this book are installed in the outlet housing. On some models, a solenoid operated by the ECM (on-board computer) controls wastegate operation, usually in conjunction with an overboost warning system (buzzer or dash light).

OPERATION

Turbocharger operation is remarkably simple. The turbine wheel is installed in the path of the engine's exhaust gas, and the compressor wheel is installed in the intake path. Exhaust gas is directed through the turbine housing, causing the turbine wheel to spin. This spinning motion is transferred by the connecting shaft to the compressor wheel. As the compressor wheel spins, it packs the intake charge into a dense mass, which is fed into the engine. Combustion converts the charge into exhaust. The exhaust charge is directed through the turbine housing, where it spins the turbine wheel, and then out through the turbine housing discharge into the exhaust system.

Thus, turbocharger operation is self-perpetuating. However, unchecked turbocharger operation will increase compressor pressure (called boost pressure) beyond the design limits of the engine, and will seriously damage internal engine components. Boost pressure is controlled by the wastegate. When boost pressure rises to a predetermined value, the wastegate opens, bypassing exhaust flow around the turbine.

Greater volumetric efficiency is a benefit of the turbocharging process, but increased cylinder pressure is a drawback, because it raises the engine's octane requirement. The two are inseparable, so a method must be devised to compensate for the increased octane requirement to avoid detonation (spark knock). Water injection, alcohol injection, low boost pressures, charge intercoolers, ignition spark retardation, and alcohol fuels have all been used to control detonation, with varying degrees of success.

Ford controls detonation by limiting boost and by spark retardation. Wastegate operation begins at five psi, and enough exhaust gas is routed around the turbine to limit boost to a maximum of six psi. The electronic ignition system has been modified in the turbocharged engine to include two spark retardation points. When boost pressure reaches approximately one-half to one psi, a switch in the intake manifold sends a signal to the ignition module, which retards ignition timing six degrees. A second manifold switch sends its signal when boost reaches four psi, resulting in an additional six degrees of retard.

The General Motors system of detonation control is slightly different. Boost is limited to a maximum of approximately six psi. In addition, a detonation sensor is installed in the engine block (V6) or intake manifold (V8). Vibrations caused by detonation are transmitted to the sensor, which sends a signal to the Electronic Spark Control (ESC) module. The module processes this signal, and sends a command signal to the HEI distribu-

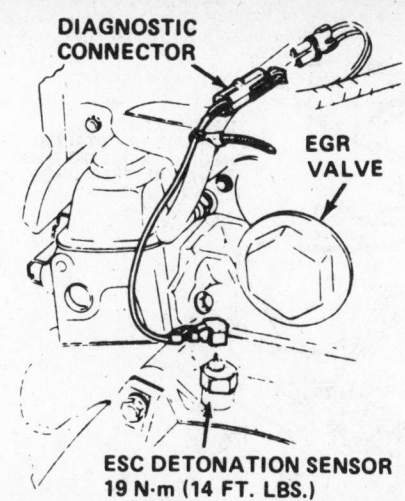

ESC DETONATION SENSOR 19 N·m (14 FT. LBS.)

Buick 231 V6 (3.8 L) detonation sensor installation

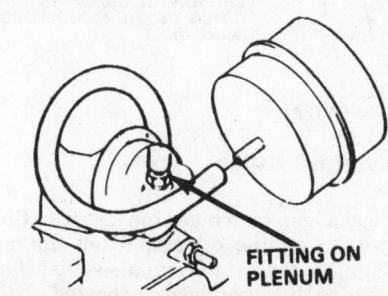

New type GM wastegate diaphragm uses plenum vacuum only—1981 and later Buick Regal unit shown

Pontiac turbocharged V8 detonation sensor location

tor to retard timing. Timing retard ranges up to 22° on V6s, or 15° on V8s.

LUBRICATION

The turbocharger shaft spins in bearings lubricated by engine oil. Turbine

speeds routinely reach 120,000–140,000 rpm, making an adequate and well-filtered oil supply critical for proper operation. Any interruption or contamination of the oil supply will result in engine damage as well. Ford cautions that accelerating the engine to top rpm immediately after starting can result in engine and turbocharger damage (due to the lack of oil pressure). Immediately shutting down the engine after it has been operated at high rpm for an extended period can also result in turbocharger damage, since oil pressure will be shut off, but the turbine will continue to spin for a few moments. Shutting the throttle abruptly when the engine is at high speed can also cause extensive damage, but for a different reason: sudden closed throttle operation causes the mixture to become very lean, resulting in detonation, high engine temperature, and consequent damage.

General Motors recommends the following procedure before starting the engine when changing the oil and filter, or performing any operation which results in oil drainage or loss:

1. Disconnect the ignition switch connector (pink wire) from the HEI distributor module.

2. Crank the engine several times until the oil light goes out. Do not crank the engine for more than thirty seconds at a time to avoid starter damage.

3. Reconnect the pink wire. Start the engine.

Turbocharger Maintenance

Proper maintenance is important, particularly regarding air and oil filtration, to maximize the service life and performance of the turbocharger. Experience has shown that the main cause of turbocharger failure is due to oil lag, restriction or lack of oil flow and dirt in the oil. The second principle cause of failure is foreign objects entering the compressor and/or turbine wheels.

AIR INTAKE SYSTEM

Dust or sand entering the turbocharger compressor housing from a leaky air inlet system can seriously erode the compressor wheel blades and will result in deterioration of turbocharger and engine performance. The wearing away of the blades, if uneven, can induce shaft motion which will pound out the turbocharger shaft bearings. Ingestion of sand or dust will also cause excessive wear on engine parts, such as pistons, rings, valves, etc.

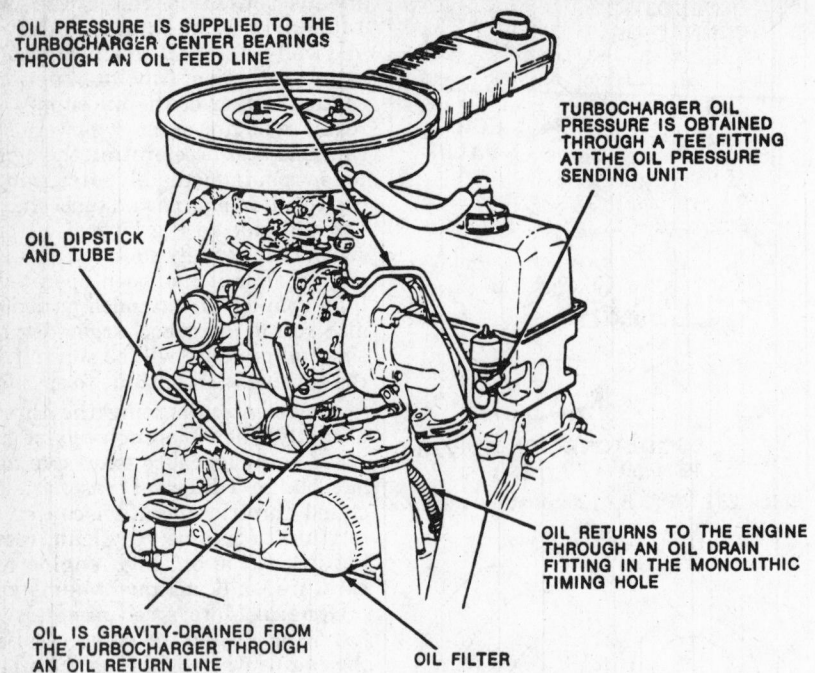

OIL PRESSURE IS SUPPLIED TO THE TURBOCHARGER CENTER BEARINGS THROUGH AN OIL FEED LINE

TURBOCHARGER OIL PRESSURE IS OBTAINED THROUGH A TEE FITTING AT THE OIL PRESSURE SENDING UNIT

OIL DIPSTICK AND TUBE

OIL RETURNS TO THE ENGINE THROUGH AN OIL DRAIN FITTING IN THE MONOLITHIC TIMING HOLE

OIL IS GRAVITY-DRAINED FROM THE TURBOCHARGER THROUGH AN OIL RETURN LINE

OIL FILTER

Ford 2.3 L turbocharger lubrication

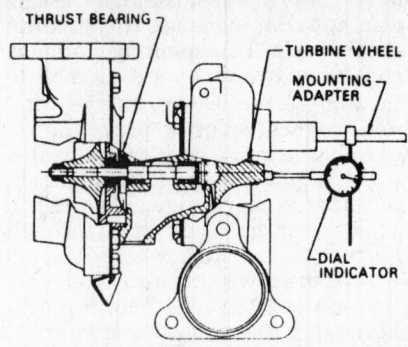

THRUST BEARING — TURBINE WHEEL — MOUNTING ADAPTER — DIAL INDICATOR

Thrust bearing clearance measurement

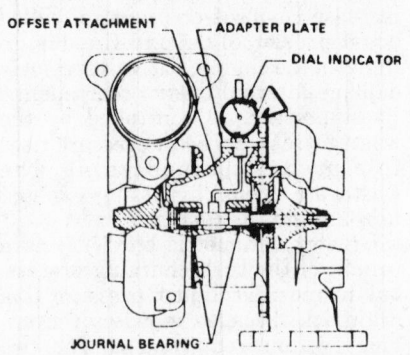

OFFSET ATTACHMENT — ADAPTER PLATE — DIAL INDICATOR — JOURNAL BEARING

Journal bearing clearance measurement

Plugged or restricted air cleaner systems (due to neglected air filter changes) will reduce air pressure and volume at the compressor air inlet and cause the turbocharger to lose performance. The restricted air cleaner and the resultant air pressure drop between cleaner and turbocharger can, during engine idle periods, cause oil pullover at the compressor end of the turbocharger and result in an oil leak at the seal.

LUBRICATION SYSTEM

Dirt or foreign material, when introduced into the turbocharger bearing system by the lube oil, causes wear on the center housing bearing bore surfaces. Contaminents act as abrasives and will eventually cause the shaft hub and either or both wheels to rub on the housings, causing the rotating assembly to turn slower. Engine power loss, excessive smoke, excessive noise and appearance of oil at either or both ends of the turbocharger could be noted. Contaminated and dirty oil problems can be eliminated by regular oil and filter changes.

A turbocharger should never be operated under engine load conditions with less than 30 psi oil pressure. The turbocharger is much more sensitive to a limited oil supply than an engine, due to the high rotational speed of the shaft and relatively small area of the bearing surfaces. Oil pressure and flow lag during engine starting can have a detrimental effect on the tur-

bocharger bearings, most critical after an engine oil and filter change. Similar conditions can also exist if an engine has not been operated for a long period of time, since engine lube systems tend to bleed down. Before allowing the engine to start, it should be cranked over a few times until a steady oil pressure reading is observed. Turbocharger bearing damage can occur if the oil delay is in excess of 30 seconds and much sooner if the engine is allowed to accelerate much beyond low idle rpm.

Turbocharger Troubleshooting

A turbocharger does not basically change the operating characteristics of an engine. The turbocharger's only function is to supply a greater volume of compressed air to the engine so that more fuel can be burned to produce more power. It cannot overcome such things as malfunctions in the engine fuel system, ignition timing, plugged air cleaner elements, etc. If a turbocharged engine system has malfunctioned and the turbocharger has been inspected and determined to be functioning normally, proceed with troubleshooting as though the engine were naturally aspirated (non-turbocharged). Simply replacing a good turbocharger with another will not correct engine deficiencies. Always inspect and asses turbocharger condi-

tion before removing it from the engine as follows:

1. Remove the inlet and exhaust ducts from the turbocharger.
2. Inspect both turbocharger wheels for blade damage caused by foreign material entering the turbocharger. The wheels can be visually checked by simply looking through the compressor housing inlet opening while holding the the throttle blade open. A light is necessary when examining the turbine wheel blade tips since they are positioned inside the turbine housing. Look between the turbine wheel blades from the exhaust outlet end of the turbine housing.
3. Inspect the outer blade tip edges on both wheels adjacent to their respective housing bores and check for wheel rub.
4. Rotate the shaft wheel assembly by hand and feel for drag or binding conditions. Push the shaft to one side, rotate it and feel for rub. It should turn smoothly.
5. Lift both ends of the shaft up and down at the same time and feel for excessive journal bearing clearance. If clearance is normal, very little shaft movement will be detected. Actual shaft end play can be measured with a dial indicator without removing the turbocharger from the engine.
6. If the shaft assembly rotates

freely and no wheel damage, binding or rub has been noted, it can be assumed that the turbocharger is not in need of service.

—— CAUTION ——

Operation of the turbocharger without all normally installed inlet ducts and filters connected can result in personal injury and equipment damage from foreign objects entering the turbocharger.

TESTING WASTEGATE OPERATION

As noted before, the wastegate is a safety valve for the engine. If the wastegate sticks shut, boost pressure will build until the air/fuel mixture charge becomes too powerful for the mechanical components (pistons, bearings, etc.) and causes engine damage.

If the wastegate sticks open, little or no boost will be received from the turbocharger, which translates into mediocre engine performance. The simplest wastegate test is to remove the pressure hose at the wastegate diaphragm unit, connect a pressure pump (such as the type used for cooling system testing) and apply pressure. At the specified opening pressure (7 psi for Ford, 8.5–9.5 for GM), the link between the wastegate and its diaphragm unit will just move (about .015 in). The movement is not great, but it should be easy to see.

If the wastegate does not move, try to operate the linkage by hand. It should move under moderate hand pressure. If it moves, the problem is probably in the diaphragm unit (broken diaphragm). To test the diaphragm, remove the vacuum hose from the diaphragm, hook up a manual vacuum pump and apply 25 in. Hg of vacuum to the diaphragm unit. If the vacuum drops below 18 in. Hg within one minute, replace the diaphragm unit.

NOTE: Some 1981 and later GM turbos have a new type of diaphragm which opens the wastegate during idle and part throttle, when there's no boost, to reduce engine backpressure and improve fuel economy. To test this type of unit, apply about 20 in. Hg of vacuum to the diaphragm unit: the wastegate link should move slightly. This unit operates solely with plenum vacuum and can be identified by the absence of a boost pressure signal line on the diaphragm unit.

TESTING OPERATION OF GM DETONATION SENSOR

Connect a tachometer and timing light to the engine, run the engine at 1800–2500 rpm and tap on the intake manifold next to the detonation sensor.

NOTE: Be careful to keep all wires, clothing and tools away from moving engine parts.

Rap continuously, quickly and moderately hard. This should trigger the detonation sensor. When it triggers, engine speed should drop at least 200 rpm and timing should retard at least 4°, probably more.

TURBOCHARGER TROUBLESHOOTING

Problem	Cause	How To Check	Solution
No boost	Gasket leak, hole in exhaust system	Temporarily block tailpipe with engine running. Any exhaust leaks in the system will be heard.	Repair leaks (usually at gasket surfaces)
	Dirty air filter	Remove air filter and check	Replace or clean filter
	Blocked air intake	Visually inspect for blockage	Clear intake
	Worn valves or rings	Compression test engine	Repair
	Throttle valves not opening completely	Manually operate throttle linkage, check valve movement	Adjust linkage, repair carburetor
	Exhaust blockage	Check catalytic converter for melted and blocked catalyst, check muffler and exhaust pipes for debris	Replace catalytic converter, repair exhaust system
	Wastegate stuck open	Test wastegate operation	Repair or replace wastegate assembly
Fuel odor under boost	Leak at compressor or intake manifold	Look for fuel stains at fittings	Tighten fittings or replace gaskets
Ignition miss at high speed, under load	Spark plug gap too large	Remove spark plugs, measure gap	Reduce gap
	Faulty coil	Test Coil	Replace
Ignition miss (often)	Excessive resistance in ignition cables	Check cable resistance (see Tune-Up Unit Repair section)	Replace cables as necessary
Oil leaks into turbine	Blocked oil return hose	Remove hose and check for blockage or crimps	Repair or replace hose

TURBOCHARGER TROUBLESHOOTING

Problem	Cause	How To Check	Solution
Detonation	Fuel octane rating too low	Check octane rating of fuel used against that recommended by manufacturer (consult owner's manual)	Switch to higher octane unleaded fuel
	Faulty sensor	Check G.M. as instructed here; have Ford system checked by qualified technician	Replace as necessary
	Faulty ignition retard unit	Refer to qualified technician	Repair or replace as necessary
	Engine overheating	Check coolant level, debris clogged radiator, no coolant circulation, blocked thermostat	Repair or replace as necessary
Poor idle	Air leak between compressor and carburetor	Listen at joints for hissing sound while the engine idles	Repair

EMISSION CONTROLS

Emission control devices are designed to eliminate the chemical compounds that escape from the engine crankcase, from the exhaust and from evaporation of fuel out of the tank and carburetor. With the growing use of onboard computers, it has become possible for car manufacturers to meet strict Federal emission standards by using electronic engine controls to monitor operating conditions and adjust engine calibrations for the best possible performance and economy with minimum emissions.

Engine calibration has a big effect on emissions out the tailpipe. The calibration consists of spark timing, fuel mixture, choke setting, idle speed and spark plug gap. Calibrations are not a service problem as long as the engine is adjusted to the factory specifications, which are found on a sticker in the engine compartment. Engines must be adjusted to these factory specifications or emissions will be high. Additionally, emission control systems have become such an integral part of the overall engine design that best engine performance is dependent on best emission control system performance. This is especially true for computer controlled systems.

NOTE: Any attempt to disconnect or bypass any OEM emission device is a violation of federal law.

The latest emission control systems use electronic instead of vacuum devices and are much more sensitive to malfunctions in any component. Following is a description of each group of controls and how they work to reduce emissions. Due to the complex nature of modern electronic engine control systems, comprehensive diagnosis and testing procedures fall outside the confines of this repair manual. For complete information on diagnosis, testing and repair procedures concerning all modern engine and emission control systems, please refer to *Chilton's Guide To Electronic Engine Controls.*

Emission Service Indicators

RESET PROCEDURES

Indicator lights or flags will periodically appear on or near instrument cluster to alert the driver that various emission control components need to be serviced or replaced. Most of the reminder lights are triggered at preset mileages programmed into either mechanical or electronic counter or odometer switches. The mechanical counter switches are normally operated by the speedometer cable, while the electronic counter switches are pulsed by a speed sensor usually located in the speedometer assembly. After servicing the indicated emission system (EGR valve, Oxygen sensor, etc.), the service indicator device will have to be reset to eliminate the light or flag. Follow the appropriate procedure outlined below for each year and model listed.

American Motors

The reset switch is located under the hood on the left side of the firewall, between the upper and lower speedometer cables. There is a rest screw on the unit that must be rotated one-quarter turn to the detent position.

Chrysler Corporation

1980 MODELS

Chrysler models use either electronic or mechanical service counters. The electronic switch is located under the instrument panel somewhere near the lower left instrument cluster. It is usually covered with a green plastic case.

To reset the mechanical switch, remove it from the mounting bracket and then remove the plastic case. Insert a small screwdriver or rod into the hole in the switch body to close the contacts and turn off the indicator light. To reset the mechanical switch, first locate the unit between the upper and lower speedometer cables. Turn the screw on the upper side of the switch to reset.

General Motors

1980 CADILLAC

To reset the switch, remove the lower steering column cover and locate the reset cable at the lower left side of the speedometer cluster. Pull the cable lightly to reset the switch, then replace the column cover. Do not pull hard on the cable or damage to the cable and switch will occur.

1980 AND LATER MODELS

An emission indicator flag will appear in the odometer window when service is necessary on some 1980 and later GM models. The flags are marked SENSOR, EMISSION, or

FLAG WINDOW IN SPEEDOMETER FACE

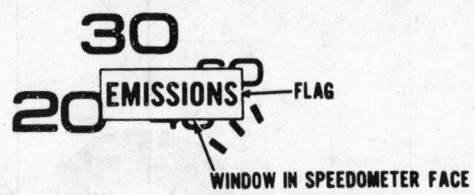

RESETTING FLAG WITH DOWNWARD MOVEMENT

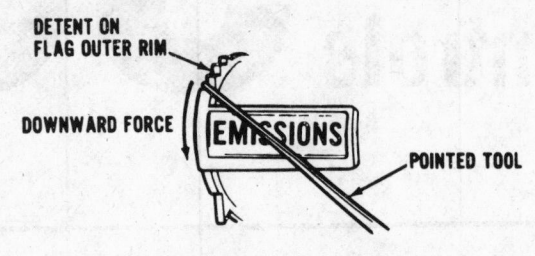

FLAG IN RESET POSITION

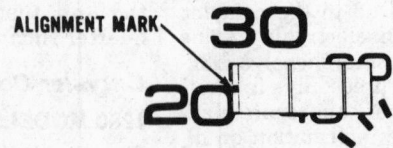

Resetting Emissions flag on 1980 GM models—typical

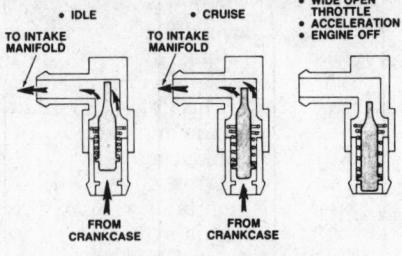

PCV valve operation

CATALYST, depending on the device that is schedule for regular maintenance. To reset the flag, first remove the instrument panel trim plate and instrument cluster cover lens. There are reset notches on the driver's side of the indicator flag.

Insert a long, pointed probe diagonally into the detents on the upper left side and rotate the flag downward until an alignment mark becomes visible in the left side of the odometer window. Once the flag has been lowered, replace the cluster lens and trim plate.

CRANKCASE CONTROLS

PCV System

Ventilation of a crankcase is necessary because of the compression blow-by past and piston rings. This blow-by is mostly unburned gasoline. If allowed to stay in the crankcase, it dilutes the oil and increases engine wear. The PCV system uses engine vacuum to draw out the crankcase fumes. The crankcase or the rocker arm cover is connected by a hose to engine vacuum at the intake manifold or carburetor. When the engine is running, the crankcase fumes are drawn into the engine and burned in the combustion chamber. Fresh air enters the crankcase through the oil filler cap on the open system. When the oil filler cap is connected to the air cleaner, it is known as a closed system.

At wide open throttle, there is little vacuum in the engine, so the PCV system doesn't pull any fumes out of the crankcase. Because the hose connection from the crankcase to the intake manifold acts like a vacuum leak, there has to to be some kind of control to limit the air flow. The PCV valve is the control. It can be an actual valve, with an internal plunger, or a simple orifice without any moving parts. In the plunger types, a spring moves the plunger against engine vacuum, allowing less flow at high vacuum and more flow at low vacuum. In the event of a backfire, the plunger moves to close the PCV valve and prevent a possible crankcase explosion.

Fresh air enters the air cleaner and goes through a hose to the crankcase or rocker cover. The fumes exit the crankcase and enter the intake manifold, either through a hose or some other type of connection, usually with a PCV valve controlling the flow. Most systems use some kind of PCV filter, usually mounted at the end of the hose in the air cleaner. The filter keeps dust from entering the crankcase and also prevents oil fumes from ruining the air cleaner element.

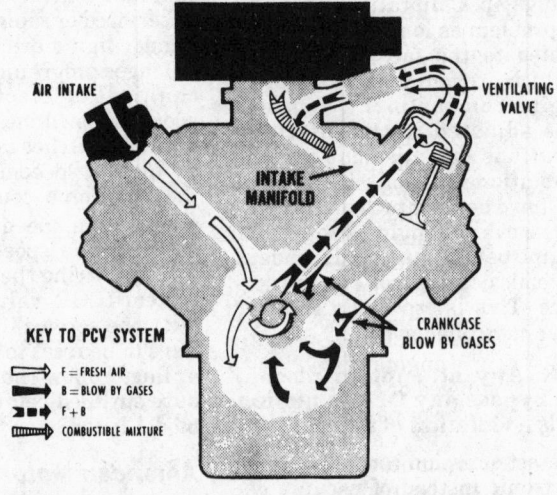

Typical open crankcase ventilation system

GM diesel V8 engines are equipped with one of two different crankcase ventilation systems. The first system uses a crankcase vacuum regulator valve to meter the flow of crankcase gases back into the engine. The regulator limits crankcase vacuum as the gases are drawn from the valve covers through the regulator, and into the air crossover. This sytem is used on 1981 and later non-California models. Other models use a crankcase flow control valve to meter the blow-by gases back into the engine. On these models, a ventilation hose runs from each valve cover and connects the flow control valve, which is screwed into the back of the air crossover.

TESTING PCV SYSTEMS

NOTE: Do not attempt to test the crankcase controls on GM V8 diesels. Instead, clean the valve cover filter assemblies and vent pipes and check rubber fittings every 15,000 miles, and replace or clean the breather cap assembly and ventilation regulator valve (if equipped) every 30,000 miles.

Checking crankcase vacuum is the most effective way to test any PCV sytem. If there is a vacuum in the crankcase, then the major part of the system has to be working. Inspect the system to find out where the fresh air enters the engine. This is usually through a hose attached to the air cleaner, but is may be through the oil filler cap on some models. If the fresh air entry is separate from the oil filler cap, simply remove the cap.

On all models, use a piece of paper or a PCV tester to measure the crankcase vacuum at the oil filler cap, with the cap removed and the engine idling in Park or Neutral. It may take a few seconds for the vacuum to build up enough to suck the piece of paper against the oil filler hole. If the vacuum does not build up, check to be sure you have plugged the fresh air entry. An alternate method on some cars is to use the piece of paper or PCV tester on the end of the fresh air entry hose. When you do it that way, the oil filler cap must be the solid type and you must leave it in place.

If there is no crankcase vacuum, pull the PCV valve from the crankcase and hold your finger over the end of it. You should feel full manifold vacuum with the engine idling. If not, the valve is plugged or there is an obstruction in a hose or passageway. On some designs the valve may be screwed into its mounting, with a hose leading to the rocker cover or crankcase. If the valve has good suc-

tion, but there is no crankcase vacuum, check the hose to be sure it is open. PCV valves that are restricted or plugged must be replaced, unless they are the type that will come apart for cleaning. Lack of crankcase vacuum can also be caused by vacuum leaks at rocker cover, oil pan, or other engine gaskets. Usually, tightening the bolts will stop the leak.

In some extreme cases, usually on high mileage engines, the PCV system is in good shape, but the blow-by past the rings is so much that the system can't handle it, and the engine will blow smoke out the oil filler hole. Switching to a PCV valve with a higher flow may temporarily correct the problem. But the only good solution is to overhaul the engine. If the motor oil is contaminated with gasoline, the PCV system will pick up the unburned vapors, add them to the intake mixture and cause the engine to run excessively rich. After checking crankcase vacuum, always check the condition of the fresh air filter and hose, to be sure they are clean and not clogged.

NOTE: The PCV system operation is not computer controlled, but if inoperative it will directly affect the operation of any computerized emission system. If poor performance is a problem, check the PCV system first.

running, a hose to the intake manifold or carburetor base allows engine vacuum to pull fresh air through the canister, drawing the vapors into the engine where they are burned. Fresh air enters the canister through a filter, which keeps the charcoal clean.

When the engine is running, air must enter the tank to replace the fuel that is used up and prevent a vacuum. On all makes of canister storage models, air enters the tank through the filter in the canister, but air can also enter the tank through the pressure-vacuum tank cap.

All evaporation control systems use some sort of vapor separator at the fuel tank to prevent liquid fuel from traveling along the vent line to the canister. The early models had very elaborate separators mounted separately from the tank, but now they are simpler and usually attached to the top of the tank. The only periodic servicing required on evaporation controls is replacement of the canister filter on those models on which it is replaceable.

NOTE: If the vent lines become blocked, it is possible for some evaporation control systems to pull liquid fuel from the tank into the charcoal canister. If any charcoal canister is found to be fuel-soaked it should be replaced and all hoses checked for obstructions.

FUEL EVAPORATION CONTROLS

Charcoal Canister Vapor System

Evaporation controls are made up of hoses which allow the tank and carburetor vapors to go to a canister filled with charcoal. When the engine is

EXHAUST CONTROLS

Thermostatic Air Cleaner (TAC)

Fresh air supplied to the air cleaner comes either from the normal snorkle, or from a tube connected to an exhaust manifold stove. A door in the snorkle regulates the source of incoming air so that a warm engine always

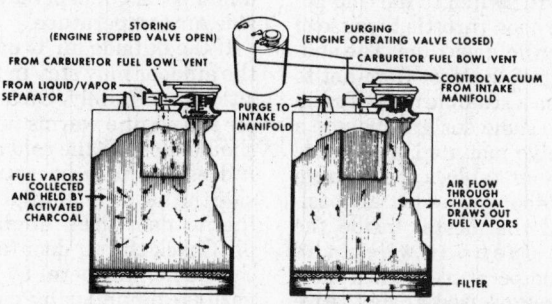

Vapor storage canister operation—typical

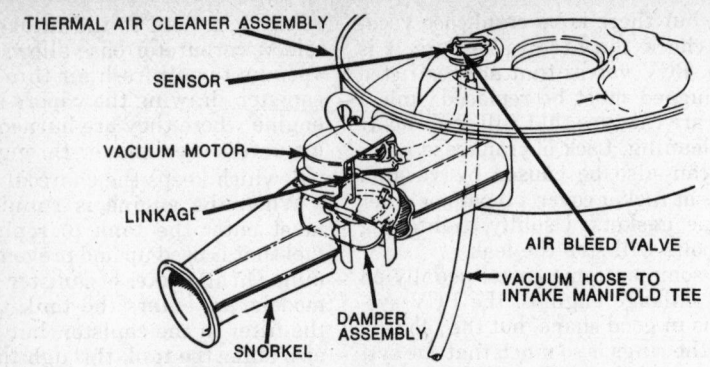

THERMAL AIR CLEANER ASSEMBLY

SENSOR

VACUUM MOTOR

LINKAGE

AIR BLEED VALVE

VACUUM HOSE TO INTAKE MANIFOLD TEE

DAMPER ASSEMBLY

SNORKEL

Vacuum controlled thermostatic air cleaner.

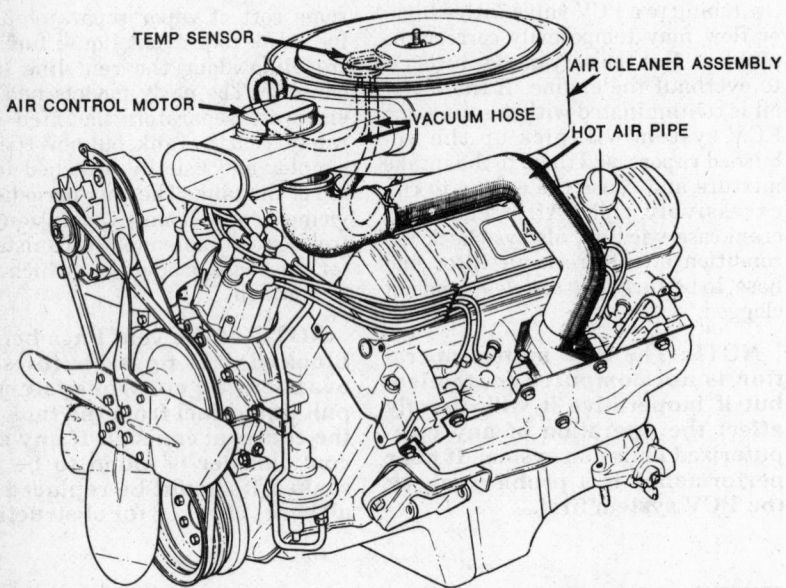

TEMP SENSOR

AIR CONTROL MOTOR

VACUUM HOSE

AIR CLEANER ASSEMBLY

HOT AIR PIPE

A typical heated air cleaner system, with the hot air pipe connected to the left exhaust manifold

takes in warm air, approximately 100°F. The snorkel door may be controlled in any number of ways, but most are vacuum operated. The vacuum operated designs use a thermostatic bimetal switch inside the air cleaner that bleeds off vacuum as the engine warms up and regulates the position of the air door.

Vacuum operated air doors are all designed so that the air cleaner takes in cold air when there is no vacuum. This means that an air door in the hot air position will switch to the cold position at wide open throttle because of the loss of manifold vacuum. The sudden switching of the door from hot to cold may cause a stumble or misfire in the engine, so some designs include a modulator valve mounted on the side of the air cleaner to block the vacuum and hold the door in the hot air position. A small thermostat inside the modulator opens it when the underhood temperatures reach normal. Other designs used a delay valve that allows the air door to move to the

cold position slowly, to prevent stumble.

TESTING TAC OPERATION

To test the vacuum type of heated air cleaner, inspect the air door with the engine off. It should be in the cold air position. Start the engine. If the engine is cold, the air door should move to the hot air position. As the engine warms up, the air door should move to a mid position, depending on the outside air temperature.

If the outside air is extremely cold, the air door may stay in the hot air position indefinitely. On a warm day, after the engine warms up, the air door should move to the cold air position. If it doesn't, the temperature sensor inside the air cleaner might be faulty, or the air door itself might be hanging up. Check the air door (a small mirror can be helpful here) by using a hand vacuum pump, or by running a hose from manifold vacuum to the vacuum

motor. Connect and disconnect the hose to see if the air door moves freely. If the air door is free, check out the hoses for leaks or blockage. If the hoses are okay, the trouble must be in the temperature sensor, and it should be replaced.

Both General Motors and Ford use a modulator in the air cleaner vacuum line on some engines. The modulator mounts on the side of the air cleaner and has two hose connections, one to the air cleaner temperature sensor, and the other to the vacuum motor. Below 50-80°F. the modulator is a one-way check valve, which allows vacuum to move the air door to the hot air position, but traps the vacuum so the door will not jump back to the cold air position during acceleration. This prevent a stumble.

After the module warms up the check valve unseats so that the vacuum can pass freely in either direction, and the air door then operates normally. The connections from the modulator are important. The connection in the center (usually the larger diameter) goes to the vacuum motor, and the connection on the edge goes to the vacuum source, which is the temperature sensor.

To test the modulator on a cold engine, apply enough vacuum to the edge port to move the air door to the hot position. Then remove the hose from the port, and the air door should stay in the hot position. Make the same test when the engine is warmed up, and the air door should move to the cold position when you pull off the hose.

Exhaust Gas Recirculation (EGR)

Gasoline Engines

NOx (oxides of nitrogen) is a tailpipe emission caused by the oxidation of nitrogen in the combustion chamber. When the peak combustion temperatures go over 2500°F, NOx is formed in excessive amounts. To keep the combustion temperatures down, exhaust gas is recirculated by allowing intake manifold vacuum to draw exhaust gas into the intake manifold. The lower combustion temperatures also help control spark knock (ping).

An EGR valve is used to control the flow of exhaust gas into the intake manifold. All EGR valves look similar and are operated by vacuum. When the vacuum is off, the valve is closed. Several different types of controls are used to turn the vacuum to the EGR valve on and off. Most of them have to do with engine temperature, as de-

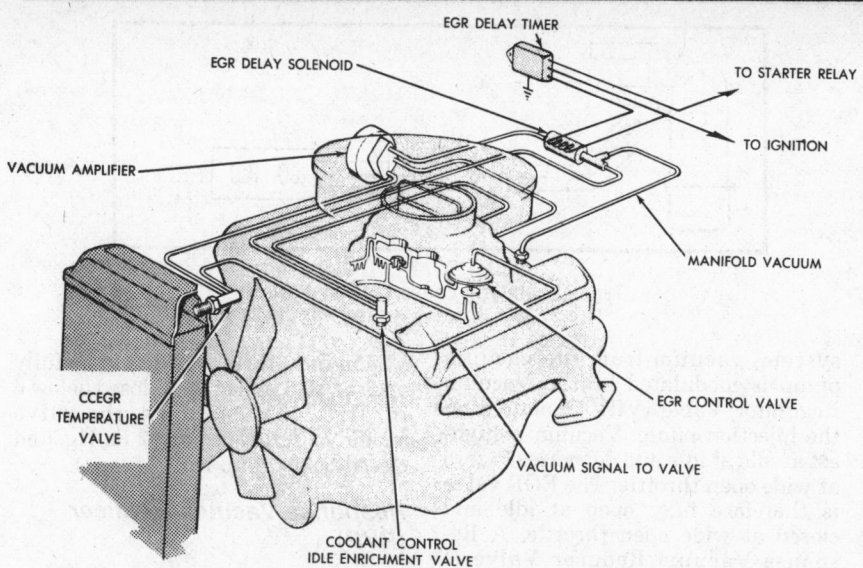

VENTURI VACUUM EXHAUST GAS RECIRCULATION

EGR DELAY TIMER
EGR DELAY SOLENOID
TO STARTER RELAY
VACUUM AMPLIFIER
TO IGNITION
MANIFOLD VACUUM
CCEGR TEMPERATURE VALVE
EGR CONTROL VALVE
VACUUM SIGNAL TO VALVE
COOLANT CONTROL IDLE ENRICHMENT VALVE

Venturi vacuum exhaust gas recirculation

scribed later. On computerized control systems, EGR operation is regulated by the electronic control unit.

NOTE: **All EGR systems are designed to cut off exhaust recirculation when the engine is cold, at idle, or under hard acceleration. If the EGR valve is stuck open, the engine won't idle.**

TESTING EGR SYSTEM

--- CAUTION ---

The EGR valve gets hot during normal operation. Take normal precautions to avoid accidental burns.

Testing of EGR systems should verify that when the engine is at normal operating temperature the EGR valve is closed at idle, open above idle, and that the exhaust gas is actually recirculating. If the EGR valve sticks open at idle, the engine will run very rough, or may not even start. If this happens the valve should be removed and cleaned or replaced. To check for valve operating above idle, check with a mirror to see if the diaphragm or stem moves when the engine is at fast idle in Park or Neutral. If the diaphragm does not move when the throttle is opened, there is either a problem with vacuum, or the valve is stuck closed. With a vacuum gauge hooked up to the EGR port, you should see vacuum on the gauge when the throttle is opened. EGR valves should not leak when tested with a hand vacuum pump. If they do they must be replaced.

NOTE: **The EGR valve should open when about 3–5 in. Hg. is ap-**

plied with a hand vacuum pump. Back pressure operated EGR valves cannot be vacuum tested.

To find out if the exhaust gas is actually recirculating, use a hand vacuum pump to open the EGR valve with the engine idling. If the engine runs rough or dies, the exhaust gas is recir-

culating. If the engine does not run rough, make a second test of 2500 rpm. Opening the EGR valve at that rpm should cause a change in engine speed. If it does, the exhaust gas is recirculating. To make the 2500 rpm test, remove and plug the hose from the EGR port. Attach the suction hose to the EGR valve before running the engine at 2500 rpm. Simply pulling off the EGR hose at 2500 rpm is not a valid test, because the extra air entering the engine through the hose could cause a speed change by itself.

If the exhaust is not recirculating, it means that a passageway or the valve itself is clogged up. The only way to fix it is to clean out the clogging as best you can, replace the clogged part, or replace the EGR valve. Many EGR valves have a back pressure sensor built into the valve. This sensor is a pressure operated bleed that disables the EGR valve and keeps it closed when there is no exhaust pressure. This type of valve cannot be tested with a hand vacuum pump with the engine off because the bleed is open. The only practical way to test these new valves is by substitution of a known good valve. If a valve is not available, the suspect valve can be removed, and the mounting holes temporarily taped shut. If this cor-

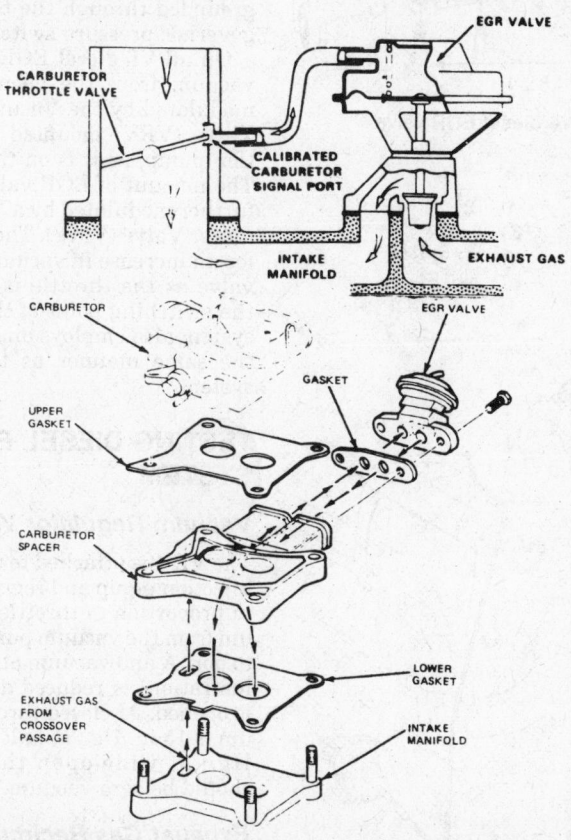

CARBURETOR THROTTLE VALVE
EGR VALVE
CALIBRATED CARBURETOR SIGNAL PORT
INTAKE MANIFOLD
EXHAUST GAS
CARBURETOR
EGR VALVE
GASKET
UPPER GASKET
CARBURETOR SPACER
LOWER GASKET
EXHAUST GAS FROM CROSSOVER PASSAGE
INTAKE MANIFOLD

Most cars use an EGR system with a valve and a ported vacuum signal, as shown here. Some cars use the venturi vacuum with a separate amplifier to operate the valve.

rects the problem, then a new valve should be installed.

Diesel EGR Systems

GM V6 and V8 Engines

GM has equipped its V8 and V6 diesel engines with EGR systems. The diesel EGR systems work in the same basic manner as gasoline engine EGR systems: exhaust gases are introduced into the combustion chambers to reduce combustion temperatures, and thus lower the formation of nitrogen oxides (NOx). There are two systems used on the V8 diesels. One is used on the B (large body) type station wagons, and one system is used on all other cars.

On the B–body station wagon EGR

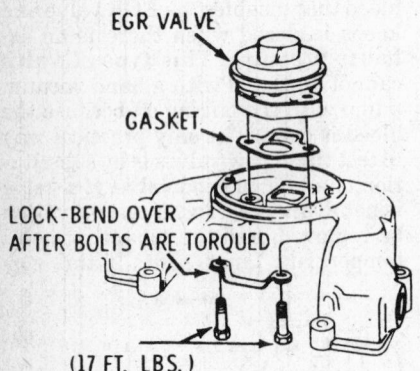

GM V6 diesel EGR valve

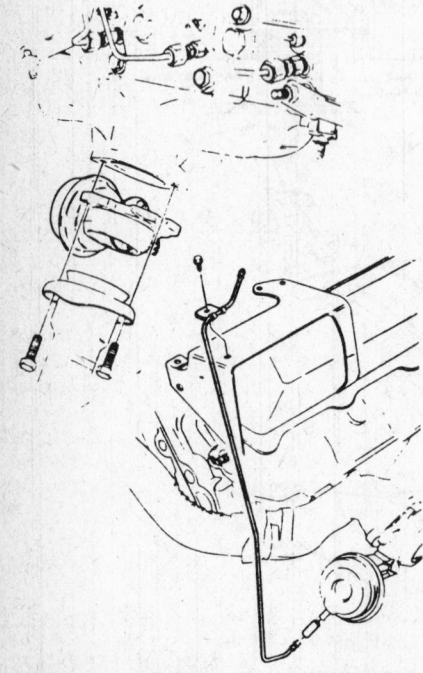

GM V6 diesel Exhaust Pressure Regulator Valve (EPR)

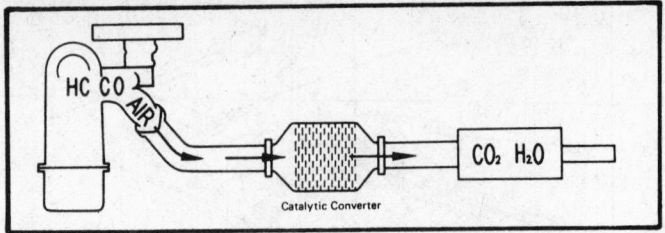

Typical catalytic converter installation

system, vacuum from the vacuum pump is modulated by the Vacuum Regulator Valve (VRV) mounted on the injection pump. Vacuum is highest at idle at idle and decreases to zero at wide open throttle. The EGR valve is therefore fully open at idle and closed at wide open throttle. A Response Vacuum Reducer Valve is used between the VRV and the EGR valve to allow the EGR valve to change position quickly as throttle position is changed.

On all other V8 diesel engines, the EGR system is the same as used on the B-body wagon, except a solenoid is added to the system that shuts off vacuum to the EGR valve when the Torque Converter Clutch is engaged. This solenoid is fed 12V from the TCC switch portion of the VRV and is grounded through the transmission's governor pressure switch.

On all V6 diesel EGR systems, the vacuum from the vacuum pump is modulated by the Vacuum Regulator Valve (VRV) mounted on the injection pump, as it is on the V8 diesels. The amount of EGR valve opening is further modulated by a Vacuum Modulator Valve (VMV). The VMV allows for an increase in vacuum to the EGR valve as the throttle is closed, up to the switching point of the VMV. The system also employs an VRV valve in the same manner as the V8 diesel system.

TESTING DIESEL EGR SYSTEM

Vacuum Regulator Valve (VRV)

The VRV is attached to the side of the injection pump and regulates vacuum in proportion to throttle angle. Vacuum from the vacuum pump is supplied to port A and vacuum at port B (see illustration) is reduced as the throttle is opened. At closed throttle the vacuum is 15 in. Hg.; at half throttle, 6 in. Hg.; at wide open throttle there should be zero vacuum.

Exhaust Gas Recirculation (EGR) VALVE

Apply vacuum to the vacuum port. On

V8 engines, the valve should be fully open at 10.5 in. Hg. and closed below 6 in. Hg. On V6 engines, the valve should be fully open at 12 in. Hg. and closed below 6 in. Hg.

Response Vacuum Reducer (RVR)

Connect a vacuum gauge to the port marked "To EGR valve or TCC solenoid". Connect a hand operated vacuum pump to the VRV port. Draw 15 in. of vacuum on the pump and the reading on the vacuum gauge should be .75 in. Hg. lower than the vacuum pump reading on all except High Altitude V8 engines. On High Altitude V8 engines ONLY, the reading should be 2.5 in. Hg. lower.

Exhaust Pressure Regulator Valve (V6 Diesels)

Apply vacuum to the vacuum port of the valve. The valve should be fully closed at 12 in. Hg. and open below 6 in. Hg.

Vacuum Modulator Valve (VMV)

To test the VMV, block the drive wheels, and apply the parking brake. With the shift lever in Park, start the engine and run at a slow idle. Connect a vacuum gauge to the hose that connects to the port marked "MAN". There should be at least 14 in. Hg. of vacuum. If not, check the vacuum pump, VRV, RVR, solenoid, and all connecting hoses. Reconnect the hose to the "MAN" port. Connect a vacuum gauge to the "DIST" port on the VMV. The vacuum reading should be 12 in. Hg. except on High Altitude cars, which should be 9 in. Hg.

Catalytic Converters

Two main types of converters are used on today's vehicles. The first is an oxidation type converter containing two precious (noble) metals, platinum and palladium to effectively catalyze the oxidation of the hydrocarbons (HC) and carbon monoxide (CO). The second type converter used is considered a three-way catalyst, containing plat-

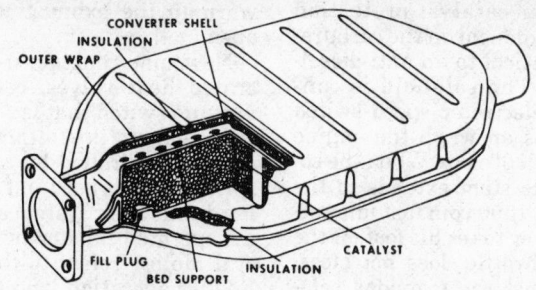

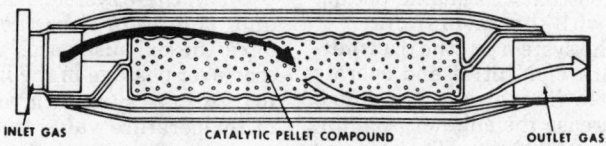

Pellet type catalytic converter

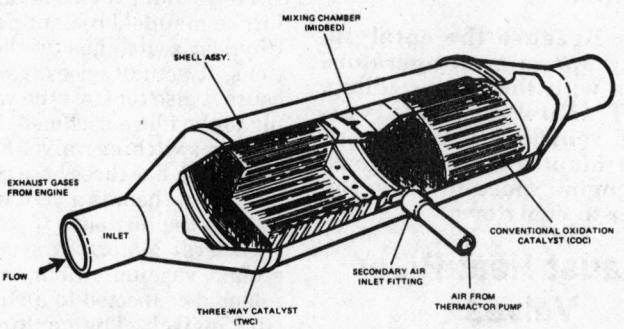

Sectional view of three-way catalytic converter

inum and rhoduim in the front part of the converter to reduce the oxides of nitrogen (NOx), while platinum and palladium are used in the rear section to oxidize the hydrocarbons (HC) and carbon monoxide (CO), as was done in the two-way converters.

Oxidizing Catalytic Converters

These converters do not operate unless there is sufficient oxygen in the exhaust stream. It is extremely important that the proper amount of oxygen is supplied at all times. This is accomplished by a secondary air source, provided by either an air pump system or a pulse air type system. The catalytic converter system is protected by several devices that block out the secondary air supply when the engine is laboring under any abnormal hot or cold operating situation, preventing converter overheating and burnout. Converter temperatures are normally between 900 and 1500°F, with peak temperatures around 1800°F, so the converterss must be hot to properly perform their functions. Should the converter be

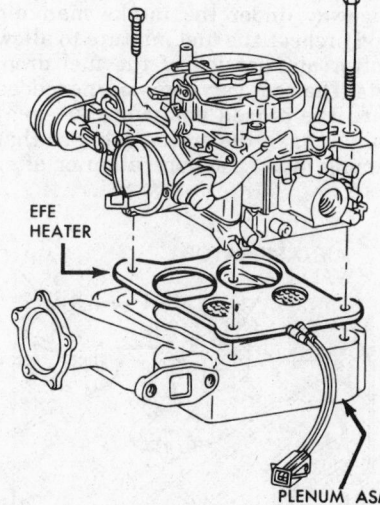

1981 G.M. electric early fuel evaporative heater

supplied too rich a mixture of hydrocarbons (HC), such as would result from a misfiring spark plug or stuck choke valve, along with an oversupply of fresh air, the converter temperature would increase sharply, causing a burnout of the catalyst material.

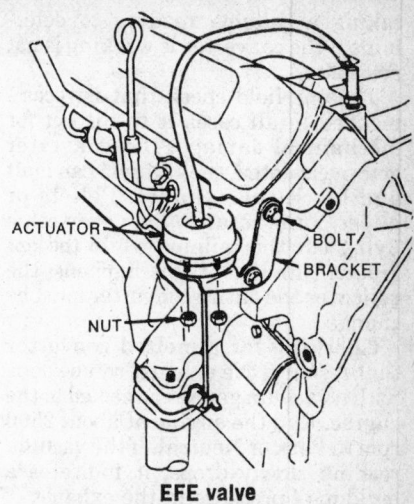

EFE valve

NOTE: Some computer controlled systems use an air management valve to increase converter efficiency by routing air to the exhaust system under certain conditions.

Three-Way Catalytic Converters

The three-way catalytic converters use a combination of catalysts which produce two different chemical reactions, oxidation and reduction. By adding fresh air to the unburned hydrocarbons (HC) and carbon monoxide (CO) within the converter, the oxidizing or combustion process takes place.

Just the reverse process is required to lower the oxides of nitrogen (NOx) emissions. The oxides of nitrogen (NOx) already contains excessive oxygen and the process of separating the excess oxygen from the nitrogen is called a reducing reaction. This reducing or reduction process is done in the front section of the converter while the oxidizing process is accomplished in the rear section. A fresh air connector is located on the center of the converter shell to add fresh air from the air system as required.

To enable the three-way converter to operate properly, the engine air/fuel ratio must be held within a tight range, called a "Stoichiometric" range. This is accomplished with the use of the closed loop, feedback fuel management systems incorporating the latest electronic controls.

TESTING

There is no way to test a catalytic converter in the field to see if it is actually working. Tailpipe readings may be used to set carburetor idle mixtures, when the car maker requires it, but taking a tailpipe reading to determine if the converter is working is not possible.

The one field check that is recommended in all cases is to inspect for mechanical damage. If a converter gets overheated, the catalyst can melt and block the exhaust. Pellets or pieces of the catalyst may even come flying out the tailpipe while the engine is running. If this happens, the pellets or the entire converter must be changed.

Checking for a melted converter that restricts the exhaust can be done with a vacuum gauge connected to the engine. Run the engine at about 2500 rpm in Park or Neutral. If the vacuum reading slowly drops, it indicates a buildup of pressure in the exhaust.

The use of leaded fuel will slowly destroy the efficiency of the catalyst. If used long enough, leaded fuel can even cause catalyst plugging to the point where the engine will not run. If you know that a car has been run on several tanks or leaded fuel, then you can be sure that the catalyst is ruined. The only thing you can do is change the catalyst or install a new converter.

NOTE: Do not change the catalyst if the car has been run on only one tank or less of leaded fuel. Switching back to unleaded will allow the catalyst to recover and be almost as efficient as it was.

CONVERTER OVERHEAT PROTECTION

Some cars have overheat protection systems for the converter. Ford Motor Co. sometimes uses a heat sensitive switch mounted in the floorpan above the converter. The switch turns a vacuum to the air pump bypass valve. When the vacuum is shut off the bypass valve dumps the pump air into the atmosphere, diverting the air away from the exhaust system. Without the air in the exhaust, the converter's catalytic heat reaction slows and the system cools down.

Chrysler Corporation cars use an overheat protection system that holds the throttle open to prevent high speed closed throttle deceleration. Any engine decelerating on closed throttle is usually running rich, because the high vacuum pulls so much fuel out of the carburetor bowl through the idle circuit. This rich mixture can cause the catalytic reaction to speed up, increasing the heat generated to dangerous levels. Holding the throttle open slightly while decelerating allows more air into the engine and eliminates the problem.

The Chrysler catalyst protection system uses a solenoid on the carburetor that is identical to an anti-dieseling solenoid. The solenoid is controlled by an electronic speed switch and only comes on when the engine speed is above 2000 rpm. When the solenoid is on, its stem extends to the equivalent of a 1500 rpm fast idle setting. If the driver takes his foot off the throttle, the throttle does not close, but rests against the extended solenoid stem. The solenoid goes off below 2000 rpm so that the engine doesn't run away with the car in traffic.

To test the system put the transmission in Park or Neutral and operate the throttle from under the hood. Slowly increase the engine speed until it is above 2000 rpm. The solenoid stem should extend. As the speed drops below 2000 rpm, the stem should retract

NOTE: Because the catalytic converter operating temperature increases with the engine idling, DO NOT allow any catalyst-equipped vehicle to idle for more than five minutes without increasing the engine speed to allow the converter to cool down.

Exhaust Heat Riser Valves

Exhaust heat riser valves have been used for many years to force part of the engine exhaust through a passageway under the intake manifold and preheat the fuel mixture to allow better atomization of the fuel droplets. The heat valve was spring loaded into the closed position, but heat would make the spring relax so that during high speed operation or after

warmup the exhaust would push it open.

Now, many engines use vacuum-operated heat valves, controlled by a vacuum switch that is sensitive to engine temperature (although the above system, controlled by a thermostatic spring, is still used in some engines). Ford calls their system simply a vacuum operated exhaust heat valve. General Motors refers to theirs as Early Fuel Evaporation, and Chrysler calls theirs a Power Heat Control Valve.

On all these systems, manifold vacuum is used to close the valve, and force the exhaust gases through the crossover passage in the intake manifold. All the systems have some kind of temperature valve that shuts the vacuum off when the engine warms up. Both Chrysler and Ford products use a simple coolant temperature-sensitive vacuum switch mounted on the intake manifold coolant passage. The Chyrsler switch has two hose connections. It actually does triple duty because it also controls the vacuum supply to the idle enrichment system and the air switching valve. Ford's vacuum switch has three hose connections, but one of them is a vent with a filter to keep the dirt out.

General Motors cars use either a coolant vacuum switch, or a vacuum solenoid connected to an oil temperature switch. The coolant vacuum switch has two hose connections and a vent when it controls the heat valve only. When it is tied into other emission control systems, it can have as many as five hose connections, and a vent. Many General Motors cars also have a check valve in the hose so that vacuum will be trapped in the heat valve actuator when the engine is accelerated. This keeps the heat valve

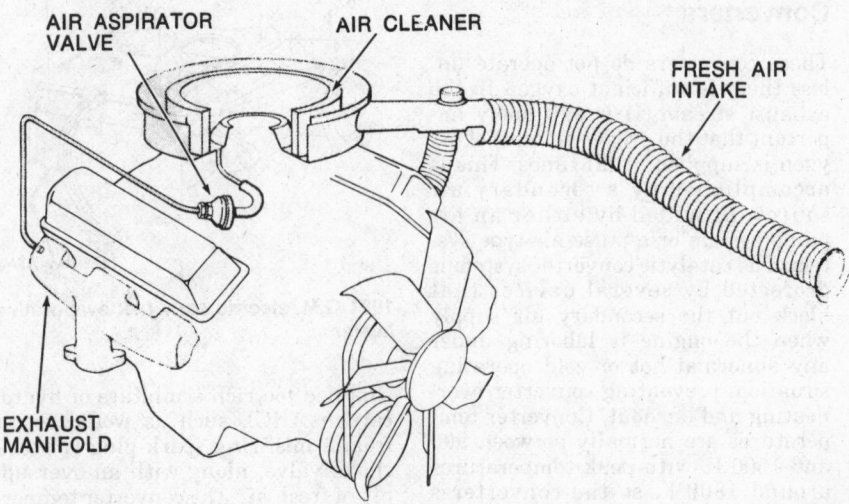

Chrysler Air Aspirator system

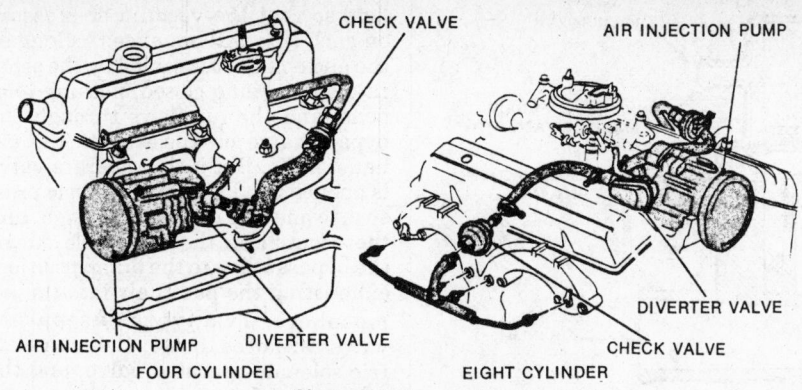

Chevrolet air pump system

CHECK VALVE
AIR INJECTION PUMP
AIR INJECTION PUMP
DIVERTER VALVE
DIVERTER VALVE
CHECK VALVE
FOUR CYLINDER
EIGHT CYLINDER

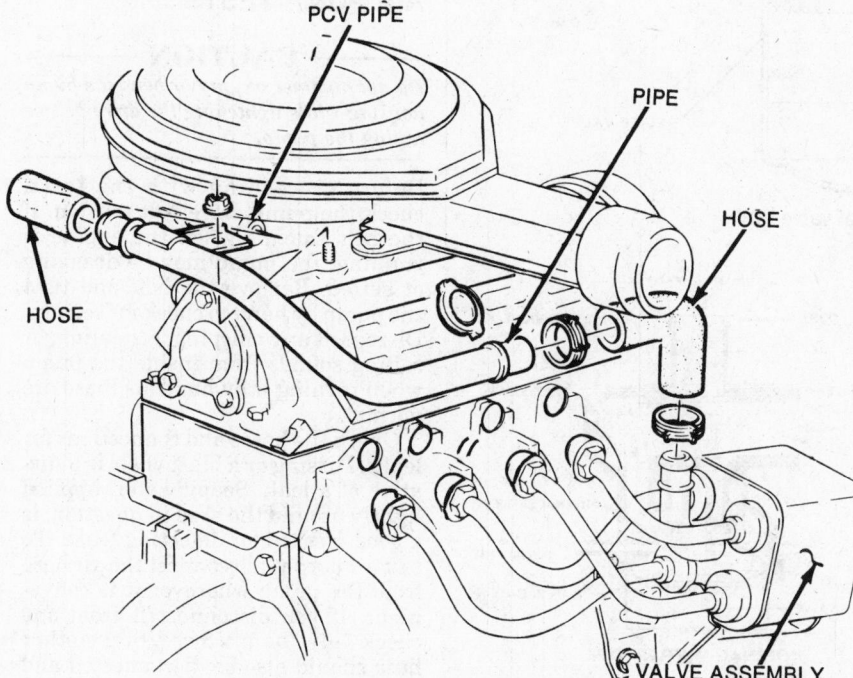

Chevette Pulse Air pipe and hose

PCV PIPE
PIPE
HOSE
HOSE
HOSE
VALVE ASSEMBLY

TESTING EFE HEATER

To check the resistance of the heater, turn the ignition OFF, disconnect the heater electrical connector, using a ohmmeter, measure the resistance across the two terminals of the heater connector. If resistance is under 2 ohms, the heater is good. If not, replace the heater.

Air Injection Systems

On these systems, a belt-driven air pump supplies air to small tubes positioned in the exhaust port near each exhaust valve. The air mixes with any unburned hydrocarbons in the exhaust and the hydrocarbons burn up in the exhaust system. On late model engines, air may not be pumped to every exhaust port, and some engines have only a single air injection fitting on the exhaust pipe near its connection to the exhaust manifold. Air injection systems are frequently used on engines with catalytic converters so that the converter gets enough air to keep the reaction going.

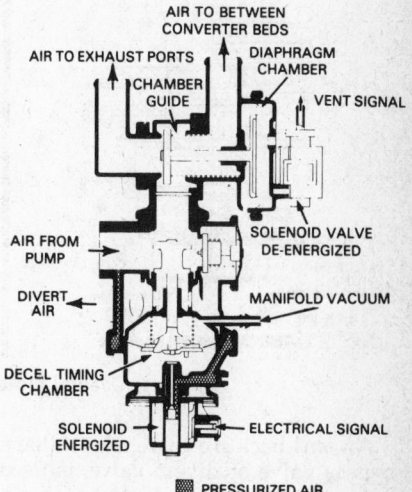

AIR TO BETWEEN CONVERTER BEDS
AIR TO EXHAUST PORTS
DIAPHRAGM CHAMBER
CHAMBER GUIDE
VENT SIGNAL
AIR FROM PUMP
SOLENOID VALVE DE-ENERGIZED
DIVERT AIR
MANIFOLD VACUUM
DECEL TIMING CHAMBER
SOLENOID ENERGIZED
ELECTRICAL SIGNAL
■ PRESSURIZED AIR

AIR SWITCHING VALVE CROSS SECTION
(AIR TO CONVERTER OPERATION)

Typical GM air switching valve (ASV) assembly

Plumbing on air injection systems varies considerably. At first, all the plumbing was external, with individual tubes inserted into each exhaust port either through the cylinder head or the exhaust manifold. Now many engines have internal passageways to duct the air to the exhaust port. A check valve is used between the pump and the exhaust port nozzle to keep hot exhaust gases from traveling up the plumbing and destroying the pump. Some V8 and V6 engines use two check valves.

in the closed position and prevents a rattle.

TESTING

Testing the vacuum operated heat riser valve is a matter of making sure it closes and opens freely. You can move it by hand to see if it works, on a warm engine. On a cold engine, the valve should be closed, and disconnecting the hose should allow it to open (engine idling). On a cold engine, there should be vacuum at the vacuum actuator, and on a warm engine the vacuum should be shut off.

GM Early Fuel Evaporation (EFE) System

The electrically operated EFE system

used on some 1981 and later GM engines performs the same function as the vacuum operated heat riser on other engines, which is to preheat the engine induction system during cold driveway. Rapid heating is desirable because it provides quick fuel evaporation and more uniform fuel distribution to aid cold driveability.

The electrically heated EFE system has a ceramic heater grid located underneath the primary bore(s) of the carburetor which is part of the carburetor insulator. When the ignition is turned on and engine coolant temperature is low, voltage is applied to the EFE relay, which in turn transfers the voltage to the EFE heater in the ceramic grid. When temperature increases, a thermal valve switch de-energizes the relay and the heater is turned off.

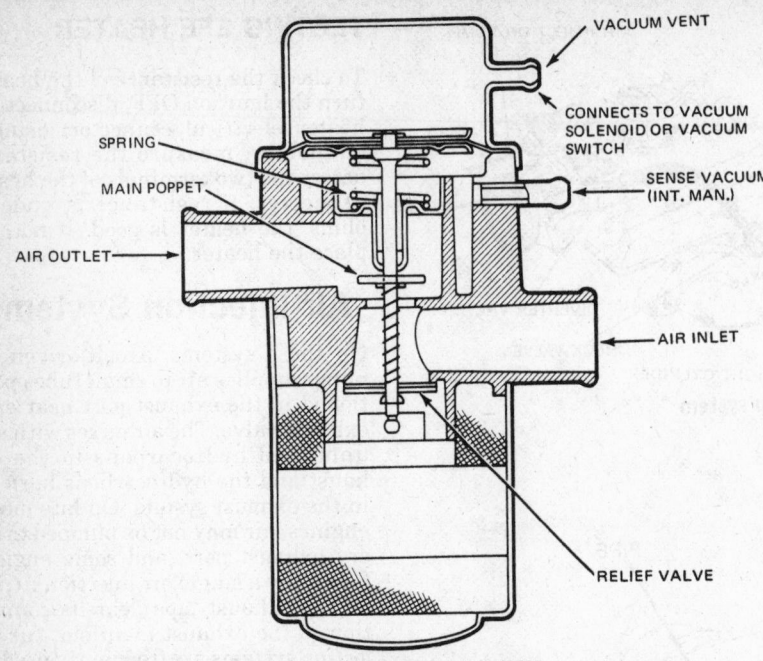

Vacuum differential valve-VDV

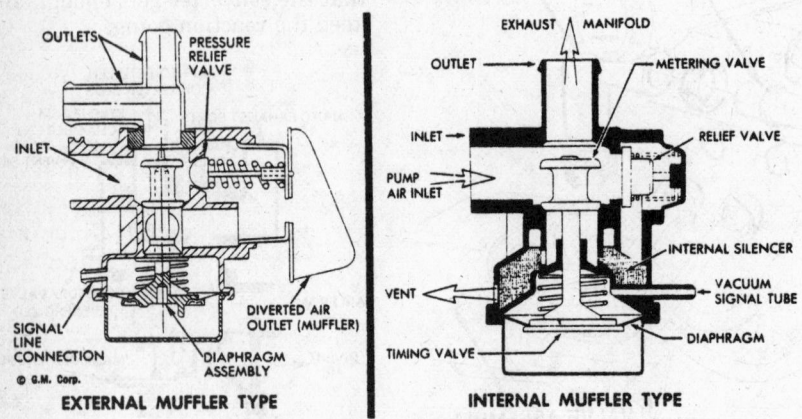

General Motors Diverter Valves

An anti-backfire valve, also called a bypass valve or divert valve, is used between the pump and the check valve. Usually, the diverter valve is mounted on the pump or near it. A small sensing hose connects the diverter valve to intake manifold vacuum. When the vacuum rises during deceleration, the diverter valve opens and vents the pump air into the atmosphere. This prevents an over-rich fuel mixture in the exhaust system from exploding or backfiring out the tailpipe. Some systems have a delay valve, similar to a spark delay valve, in the sensing hose. This delays for a few seconds the drop in vacuum when the throttle closes, so that the air is not dumped every time the driver takes his foot off the throttle in traffic.

Temperature controls are also used in the sensing hose hookup. Usually, the temperature valve shuts the vacuum off when the engine is cold, so that the pump air doesn't go to the engine exhaust ports until the engine warms up. Some cars have a temperature sensor mounted under the car above the catalytic converter. If the converter overheats, the sensor turns off a solenoid which shuts off the air to the diverter valve. The diverter valve then goes to the dump position, shutting off the air to the exhaust to keep the converter from melting or burning up.

Ford Motor Company 4-cylinder, V6, and some inline 6 engines use a unique air bypass valve, with two small sensing hoes connected to it. Each of the hoses connects to one side of a diaphragm in the valve. The hose on the body of the valve connects to manifold vacuum, and the hose closer to the end connects to a separate on-off valve. The diaphragm has a small

hole so that the vacuum or pressure on each side will equalize. As long as the end chamber is sealed by the separate valve being closed, nothing happens, and the air flows through the bypass valve on the way to the exhaust ports. But if the separate valve is opened it admits atmospheric pressure to one side of the diaphragm, and the vacuum on the other side moves the bypass valve to the dump position, exhausting the pump air into the atmosphere. Two types of separate valves are used, one of them an electric solenoid operated valve, and the other a vacuum-operated valve.

AIR PUMP TESTS

—— CAUTION ——
Do not hammer on, pry or bend the pump housing while tightening the drive belt or testing the pump.

Before proceeding with the tests, check the pump drive belt tension. If the belt squeals when the engine is running, the pump may be dragging or seized. Remove the belt and turn the pump by hand to check for seizure. Disregard any chirping, squealing, or rolling sounds from inside the pump when turning it by hand, as these are normal.

Check the hoses and connections for leaks. Hissing or a blast of air is indicative of a leak. Soapy water, applied lightly around the area in question, is a good method for detecting leaks. To test air output, disconnect the air hose from the pump wherever it is convenient. If you disconnect it from one check valve on a V8 or V6, the other hose should also be disconnected and plugged for the test. Run the engine at idle and feel the blast of air from the hose with your hand. Increase the engine speed to 1500 rpm and feel the blast of air again. If the blast increases and is steady, the pump is okay.

Pump Noise Diagnosis

The air pump is normally noisy. As engine speed increases, the noise of the pump will rise in pitch. The rolling sound the pump bearings make is normal. However, if this sound becomes objectionable at certain speeds, the pump is defective and will have to be replaced. A continual hissing sound from the air pump pressure relief valve at idle indicates a defective valve. Replace the relief valve.

If the pump rear bearing fails, a continual knocking sound will be hard. Since the rear bearing is not separately replaceable, the pump will have to be replaced as an assembly.

DIVERTER (ANTI-BACKFIRE) VALVE TEST

Detach the hose, which runs from the bypass valve to the check valve. Connect a tachometer to the engine. With the engine running at normal idle speed, check to see that air is flowing from the bypass valve hose connection. Increase the engine speed to 1500-2000 rpm and allow the throttle to snap shut. The flow of air from the bypass valve at the check valve hose connection should stop momentarily and air should then flow from the exhaust port on the valve body or the silencer assembly.

Let the throttle snap shut several times. If the flow of air is not diverted into the atmosphere from the valve exhaust port or if it fails to stop flowing from the hose connection, check the vacuum lines and connections. If these are tight, either the bypass valve or one of the accessory valves in the small sensing hose is defective and must be replaced. A leaking diaphragm will cause the air to flow out both the hose connection and the exhaust port at the same time. If this happens, replace the valve.

NOTE: Late model systems should stop flowing at idle, as described earlier. If not, the bypass valve or accessory valve is defective.

CHECK VALVE TEST

Remove the hose from the check valve. With the engine running at 1500 rpm in Park or Neutral, hold the back of your hand near the check valve to test for exhaust gas leakage. If the valve leaks, it must be replaced.

NOTE: Vibration and flutter of the valve at idle is a normal condition caused by exhaust pulsations. It does not mean that the valve is defective.

VACUUM DIFFERENTIAL VALVE TEST

Disconnect the small sensing hose at the bypass valve and connect a vacuum gauge to the hose. With the engine idling in Park or Neutral, the gauge should read full manifold vacuum. Run the engine at a steady 2500 rpm in Park or Neutral, and release the throttle. As the engine decelerates, the vacuum gauge should drop close to zero, then return to full manifold vacuum as the engine speed drops to idle. If not, the VDV is defective and must be replaced.

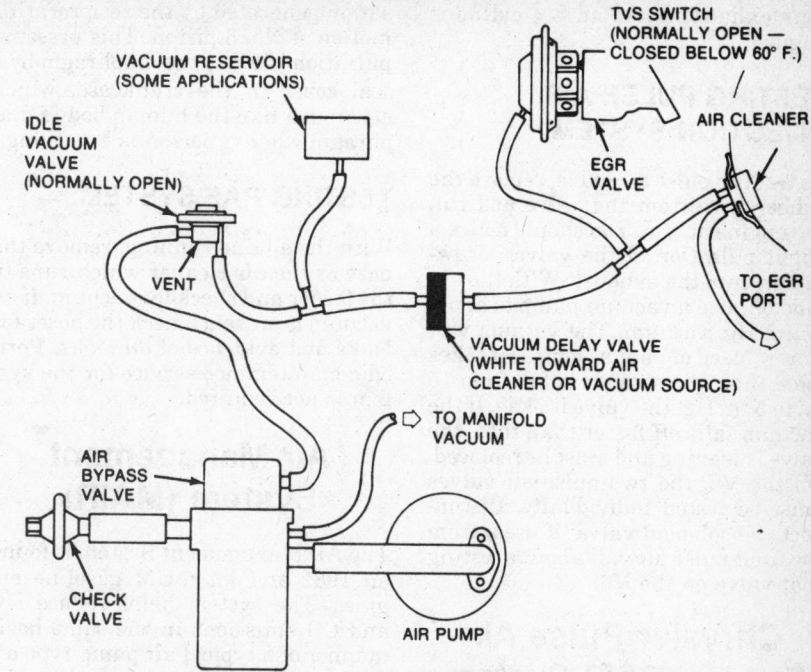

Air pump system using a timed air by-pass valve vacuum vent

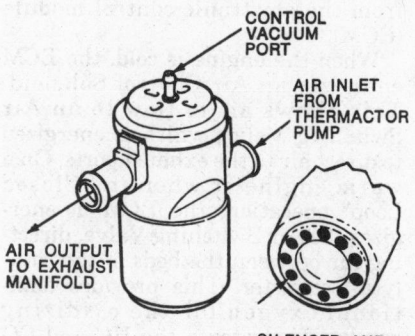

Catalyst cars use a different air bypass valve, with small hose connecting to the end.

NOTE: The small hose nozzle should be connected to manifold vacuum.

Chrysler Air Aspirator System (AAS)

Chrysler Corporation cars which use this system have done away with the air pump. The complete air aspirator system consists of a hose from the clean side of the air cleaner, the aspirator valve mounted on top of the engine, and a tube connecting the valve with the exhaust manifold. The suction in the exhaust draws in air through the air cleaner and this extra air helps the catalytic converter burn up the pollutants. The aspirator valve is similar to the check valve used with all air pump systems. It keeps the exhaust from flowing back into the air cleaner, but allows clean air to go into the exhaust.

TESTING AAS VALVE

Testing the air aspirator valve is done by disconnecting the hose from the air cleaner and checking for slight suction at idle with a piece of paper over the end of the valve. Speeding the engine up slightly will show if the valve is leaking. Exhaust should not come out of the valve. Vibration of the valve diaphragm is normal due to exhaust impulses.

GM Pulse Air Injection System

This system is similar to Chrysler's Air Aspirator. A hose from the clean side of the air cleaner connects to the pulse air valve. Tubes connect the pulse air valve to each cylinder's exhaust port. Suction in the exhaust draws fresh air from the air cleaner into the exhaust, and the air helps the catalytic converter burn up the pollutants. The pulse air valve consists of four or six check valves built into a housing. It allows each exhaust port to suck in fresh air independently of the other ports. The check valves only open when there is suction in the exhaust. If there is any back pressure, the check valves close to prevent exhaust flow back into the air cleaner. On some applications the pulse air valve is connected to only three of the four exhaust ports on a 4-cylinder engine.

TESTING PULSE AIR INJECTION SYSTEM

To test the pulse air valve, remove the rubber hose from the valve and run the engine at idle. You should notice a slight pulsation of the valves, drawing air into the exhaust. With the engine off, use a vacuum pump to apply 15 in. Hg. vacuum. The vacuum will slowly bleed off, but as long as it takes more than two seconds to fall from 15 in. to 5 in. Hg. the valve is okay. If the vacuum falls off faster than that, the valve is leaking and must be replaced. On the V6, the two pulse air valves must be tested individually. Disconnect the solenoid valve (if used) from the front pulse air valve before testing that valve on the V6.

Chrysler Pulse Air Feeder (PAF) System

The PAF system supplies secondary air into the exhaust system between the front and rear catalytic converters, which promotes oxidation of exhaust emissions in the rear catalytic converter. The system consists of a pulse air feeder, which contains two reed valve assemblies, a hose which links the pulse air feeder to the air cleaner, and a tube which runs from the feeder to the exhaust system. At the bottom of the feeder there are two tubes, one which runs into the oil sump and one which connects to No. 3 cylinder crankcase above the oil level. The main reed valve is actuated by a diaphragm in the feeder which, in turn, is activated by the pressure pulsation generated by the reciprocating motion of No. 3 piston. This pressure pulsation is fed to the diaphragm by a seal cover in the crankcase, which acts much like the human body's diaphragm when a person is breathing.

TESTING PAF SYSTEM

With the engine running, remove the hose at the air cleaner which runs to the feeder and check for vacuum. If no vacuum is present, check the hoses for leaks and evidence of oil leaks. Periodic maintenance service for the system is not required.

Air Management System (MAIR)

The Air Management System is found on 1981 and later GM gasoline engines. The system helps reduce HC and CO emissions in the same basic manner of a typical air pump-type air injection system, except that the MAIR system is controlled by signals from the electronic control module (ECM).

When the engine is cold, the ECM energizes an Air Control Solenoid. This allows air to flow to an Air Switching Valve, which is energized to direct air to the exhaust ports. On a warm engine or when in "Closed Loop" operation, the ECM de-energizes the Air Switching Valve, directing air between the beds of the catalytic converter. This provides additional oxygen for the oxidizing catalyst to decrease the HC and CO levels. If the Air Control Valve detects a rapid increase in manifold vacuum (deceleration, etc.), certain operating modes (wide open throttle, etc.), or the ECM self-diagnostic system detects any problem in the MAIR system as a whole, air is diverted (divert mode) to the air cleaner or directly into the atmosphere.

The air flow and control hoses transmit pressurized air to the catalytic converter or to the exhaust ports through internal (intake manifold) passages or external piping. The check valves prevent backflow of exhaust gas into the air distribution system. The valve prevents backflow when the air pump "bypasses" at high speed and loads, or in case the air pump malfunctions.

NOTE: Due to the complex nature of modern electronic engine control systems, comprehensive diagnosis and testing procedures fall outside the confines of this repair manual. For complete information on diagnosis, testing and repair procedures concerning all modern engine and emission control systems, please refer to *Chilton's Guide To Electronic Engine Controls*.

Ford Pulse Air (Thermactor II) System

Some Ford engines are equipped with an air injection system which does not use an air pump. Instead, natural pulses present in the exhaust system are used to pull the air into the system through the pulse air valves. The pulse valve is connected to the exhaust manifold by a tube and to the air cleaner or silencer with a hose. Make sure air can flow freely through the air cleaner or silencer to the check valve.

Electronic Engine Controls 37

ENGINE ELECTRONICS

In the ladder part of the 1960's, Robert Bosch introduce the first true electronically controlled engine with an on-board computer. Today, almost every car produced has some kind of electronic control. The once mechanically controlled engine functions are all but extinct.

The first system, Bosch D-Jetronic, is comprised of electrically energized fuel injectors in which the injection time is controlled by an electronic control unit (ECU). The early system delivered a basic quantity of fuel and varied from this point depending upon engine load, engine speed and engine temperature.

Since the early days of ECU, the controls have become more complex, with a much greater amount of computer memory and even the ability to learn.

In this section the topics will include different types of electronically controlled fuel induction, spark control, the sensors and switches that provide the ECU with information, other non-engine related controls that the ECU might supply and some ECU self-diagnostics.

The most common fuel induction system with an ECU is electronic fuel injection. In this system fuel can be delivered many different ways. One of which is the single point injection (SPI) were one or two injectors are mounted on a throttle body assembly. Fuel is delivered constantly through the injector(s), but in varying quanti-

ties. The SPI system very much resembles a carbureted system. SPI is more commonly known as throttle body injection (TBI). Another fuel injection system is multi-point injection (MPI). This system supplies one injector for each cylinder, usually positioned in the intake manifold, just above the intake valve. In MPI, fuel can be injected in two ways. One is to energize a group of injectors, thus atomizing fuel in the intake manifold and storing it for a short time until the intake valve opens. The second way is to sequentially energize each cylinder's injector as the intake valve is opened. This injection is the more efficient, effective and more complex system.

Another fuel induction system utilizing an ECU is the feedback carburetor (FBC). A conventional carburetor is still used but it has a more precise air/fuel mixture control which is achieved through an integral mixture control solenoid. The solenoid is energized on and off by the ECU to maintain mixture demand. The ECU calculates air/fuel mixture demand changes by the data it receives through remote sensors. The most important sensor (and makes the system possible) is an oxygen (O_2) sensor (which will be discussed later in this section). The ECU monitors the exhaust gases for rich/lean conditions by way of the O_2 sensor and, in turn, controls the air/fuel mixture by increasing or decreasing the duty cycles (on and off) to the mixture control solenoid for an optimum 14.7:1 air/fuel ratio.

ECU Self-Diagnostics

The ECU can detect a malfuction or

abnornality in the sensors or in the ECU itself and display a warning light on the instrument panel when it does. When this occurs, the ECU stores a trouble code for future system diagnosis. If the problem is sever enough to where it inhibits closed loop operation, the ECU will assume a backup system. This fail-safe circuit is pre-programmed into the ECU for minimal driveability operation so the vehicle can be driven to a nearby service facility. The trouble codes are usually a two digit numbers identified by the number of diagnostic LED or check engine light flashes. The trouble codes assist the service technician in isolating a faulty circuit or component within the system.

Electronic Data Sensors

The engine control system consists of various data sensors. Although data sensor names and applications vary from system to system, the most common input sensors/switches are:
- oxygen (O_2) sensor
- coolant temperature sensor
- manifold air pressure (MAP) sensor
- vehicle speed sensor (VSS)
- throttle position sensor (TPS)
- engine speed reference or distributor reference (rpm)
- air flow sensor
- air intake temperature sensor
- crankshaft sensor
- detonation (knock) sensor
- throttle body temperature sensor
- throttle idle switch
- transmission or drive switch
- a/c compressor clutch switch

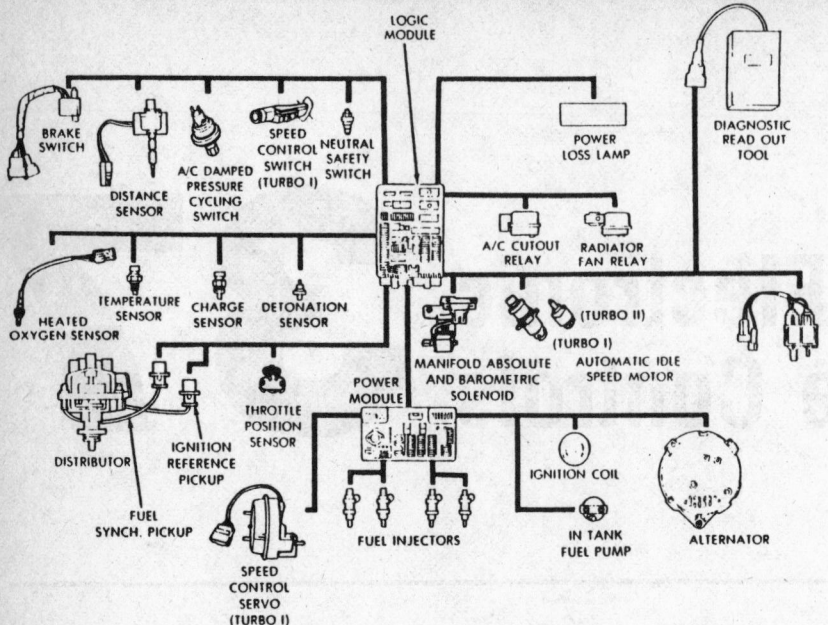

Electronic engine control components

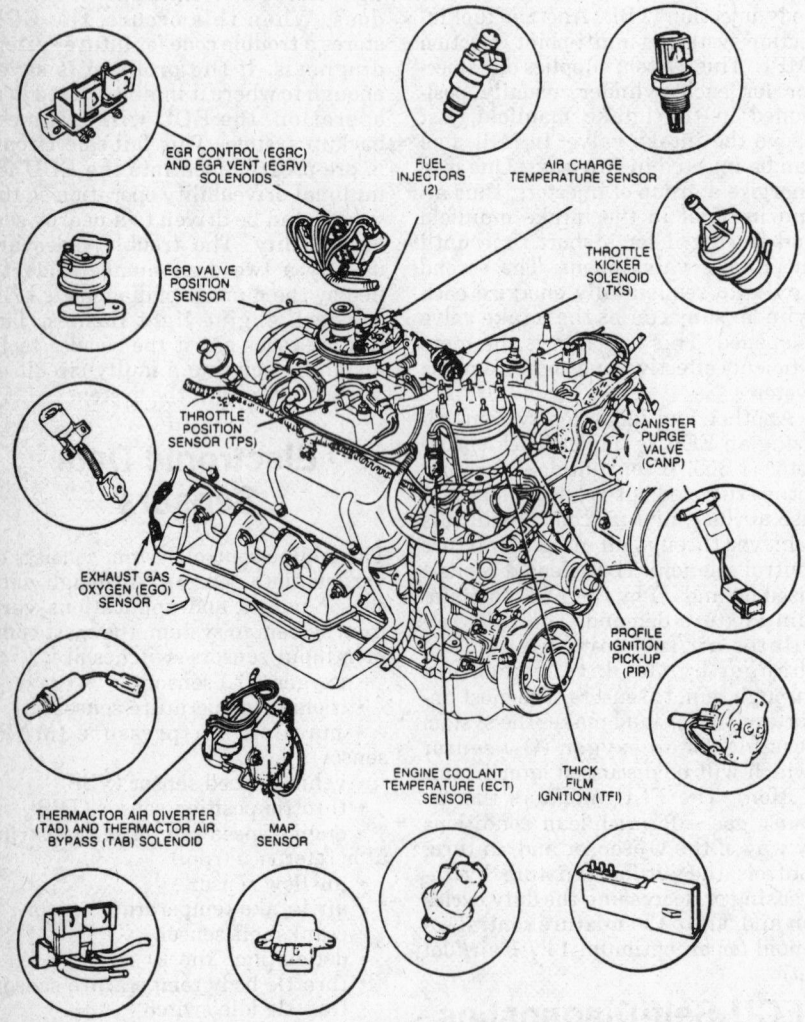

Electronic engine control component locations

- power steering pump switch
- altitude or barometric pressure sensor
- wide open throttle switch

Electronically Controlled Devices

Some of the output devices that the ECU may control vary from system to system, but the most common output or ECU controlled devices are:

- fuel injector(s)
- air/fuel mixture solenoid
- fuel pump relay
- a/c compressor clutch relay
- idle air control (IAC) valve
- idle speed control (ISC) motor
- ignition spark/timing
- canister purge solenoid
- torque converter clutch solenoid (automatic transmission)
- air management system (air induction)
- idle-up or throttle kicker solenoid
- alternator field control (charging system)
- turbocharger boost wastegate
- cooling fan relay

Component Description

THROTTLE BODY

The throttle body, in most fuel injected systems, is usually an alumunum housing that consists of one or two throttle blades which are attached to a throttle shaft. The housing has a throttle position sensor (TPS) sensor, idle air control motor and, in some cases, throttle body temperature sensor. On SPI systems, the housing also has an injector(s) and (in some cases) a fuel pressure regulator. The throttle body throttle blade controls the amount of air that enters the engine as well as the amount of vacuum.

ELECTRONIC CONTROL UNIT (ECU)

The ECU monitors and controls all engine control functions. The ECU consists of input and output devices, a central processing unit, a power supply and various memory banks. The input and output devices of the ECU convert electrical signals received by the data sensors and switches to the digital signal that are used by the central processing unit. The central processing unit receives digital signals that are used to perform all mathematical computations and logic

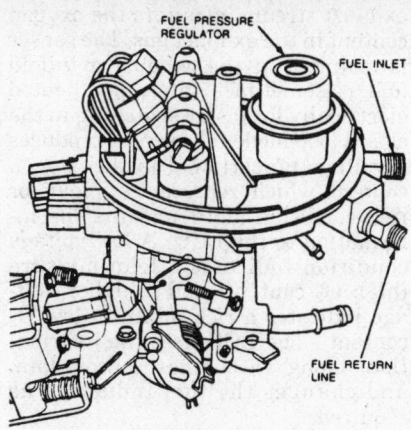

Throttle body – TBI

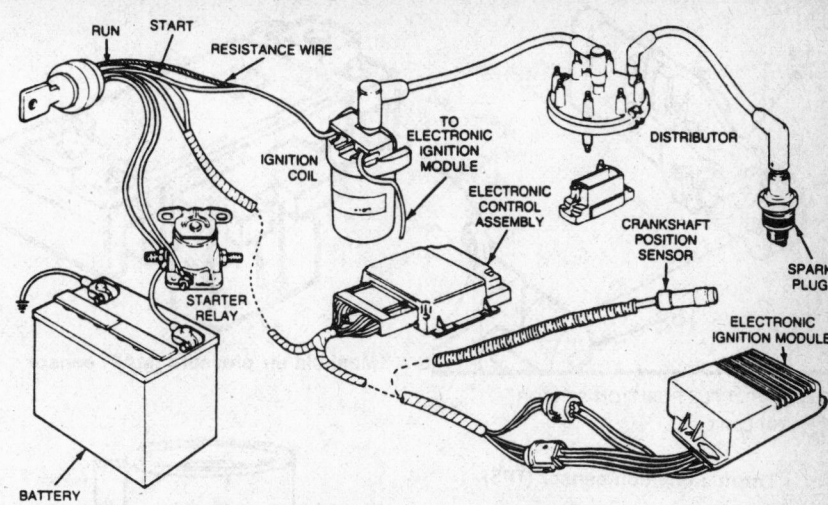

Electronic ignition system using ECU

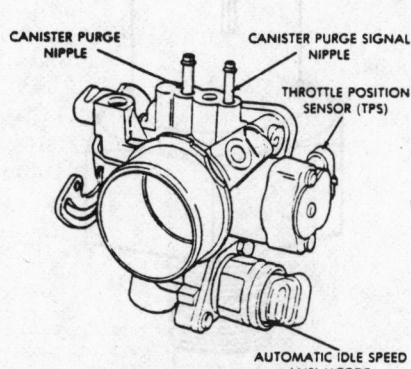

Throttle body – MFI

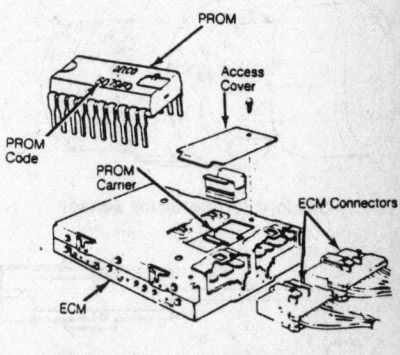

Electronic control unit prom

functions necessary to deliver proper air/fuel mixture. The central processing unit is also responsible for calculating spark timing information. The main source of power that allows the ECU to function is generated from the battery of the vehicle and transported through the ignition system. The memory bank of the ECU is programmed with exact information that is used by the ECU during the open loop mode. This data is also used when a sensor of other component fails, allowing the vehicle to be driven to a repair facility.

CALIBRATION ASSSEMBLY OR PROM (PROGRAMMABLE READ ONLY MEMORY)

Some vehicle manufactures use one ECU for several different model vehicles. This interchangeable ECU is possible through the use of a calibration assembly or prom. Information about the vehicle's engine, transmission, body and drive axle ratio are programmed and permanently stored into the assembly. If the battery supply should become disconnected from the ECU, the data stored into the assembly is not lost.

ELECTRONIC SPARK CONTROL (ESC)

The vehicles equipped with an ESC have the ability to change the ignition timing under any and all operating conditions. Data from various remote sensors (coolant temperature, throttle position, rpm, etc.) is transmitted to the ESC. The ESC computes the information and triggers the ignition spark at precisely the right instant. Some ESC systems (ie.,turbocharged engines) use a detonation (knock) sensor which senses pre-ignition and

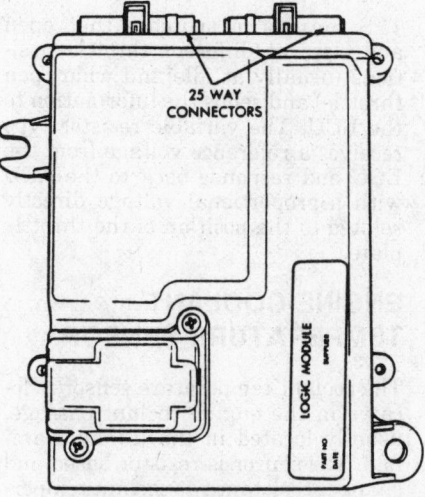

Electronic control unit

transmits the information to the ESC. The ESC modifies spark advance and boost pressure in order to eliminate knock.

MASS AIR FLOW SENSOR

The mass air flow (MAF) sensor is

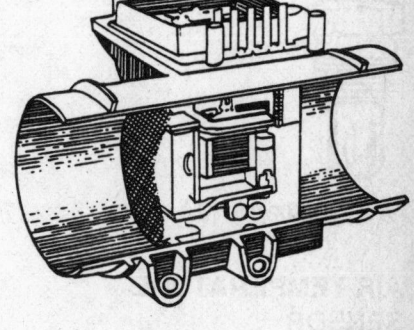

Mass air flow (MAF) sensor

only incorporated in some Multi-point fuel injection systems. The MAF sensor is a very complex device which measures the air mass of the engine intake. Because the air mass is always changing with temperature, humidity and altitude, the fuel delivery rate must be adjusted to compensate for these changes so that a precise fuel mixture can be maintained.

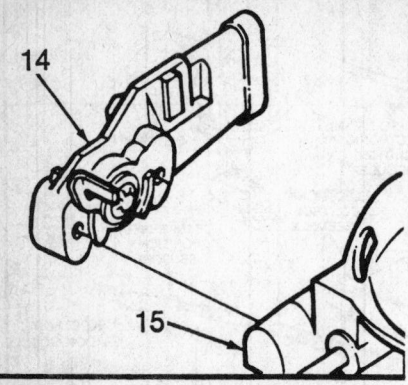

14 THROTTLE POSITION SENSOR
15 TBI UNIT

Throttle position sensor (TPS)

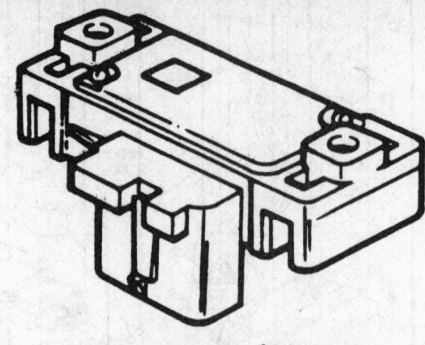

Manifold air pressure (MAP) sensor

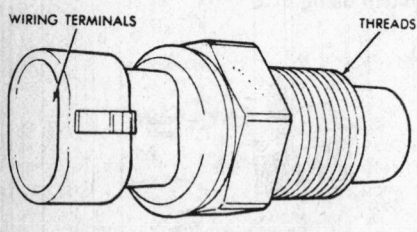

WIRING TERMINALS   THREADS

Coolant temperature sensor

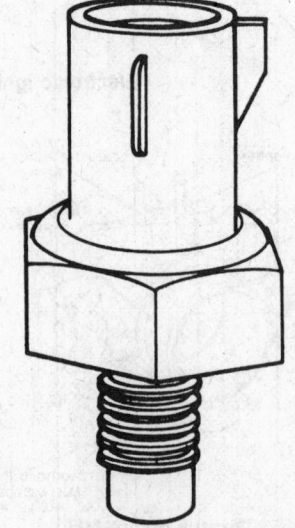

Detonation (knock) sensor

Oxygen (O₂) sensor

AIR TEMPERATURE SENSOR

The air temperature sensor is located in the air stream of the air flow meter. The sensor supplies incoming air temperature information to the ECU. The ECU uses this data, along with other data, to regulate fuel injection rate.

THROTTLE POSITION SENSOR (TPS)

The TPS can be either a switch (or a combination of switches) or a variable resistor which is much more accurate in throttle position. The switch type

TPS consists of switches that open and close at different throttle positions (usually at idle and wide open throttle) and sends the information to the ECU. The variable resistor type receives a reference voltage from the ECU and responds back to the ECU with a proportional voltage directly related to the position of the throttle plate.

ENGINE COOLANT TEMPERATURE SENSOR

The coolant temperature sensor is located in the engine coolant passage, usually located in the intake manifold. The sensor is resistor based and changes resistance as coolant temperature changes. The sensor uses a reference voltage and the output voltage is sent to the ECU. The ECU calculates engine warm up and provides an optimum fuel enrichment when the engine is cold.

OXYGEN (O₂) SENSOR

The O₂ sensor, which is placed in the

exhaust stream, monitors the oxygen content in the exhaust gas. The sensor is mounted in the exhaust manifold and is sometimes internally heated electrically for faster switching to the closed loop mode. The sensor produces a voltage proportional to the oxygen content which represents a lean or rich condition and transmits the information to the ECU. A low voltage condition indicates a lean mixture (high O_2 content) and a higher voltage indicates a rich mixture (low O_2 content). The ECU uses the information, along with other sensor data, and changes the fuel induction as required.

CYLINDER HEAD TEMPERATURE SENSOR

The cylinder head temperature sensor monitors the temperature of the cylinder head and transmits the information to the ECU. The sensor is located in the cylinder head and is a temperature sensitive resistive unit known as a thermistor.

VEHICLE SPEED SENSOR (VSS)

The VSS provides vehicle speed data to the ECU in the form of pulse signals. There are many different types of VSS, some using a reed switch installed in the speed meter unit and others using a optical type. In the optical type a light emitting diode (LED) is used to transmit light and photo diode receives the light. A shutter device, which is usually in-line with the speedometer cable, allows the LED light to reach the photo diode in vehicle speed related pulses. The reed switch type relies on a reed switch that opens and closes by way of a rotating magnet. The magnet rotates proportionally with the vehicle speed.

MANIFOLD AIR PRESSURE (MAP) SENSOR

The MAP sensor is a device that monitors manifold absolute pressure. The sensor is mounted remotely and senses vacuum through a connecting hose. The MAP sensor has a reference voltage from the ECU and transmits remaining voltage to the ECU to calculate engine load. The ECU uses this data along with other data to determine fuel demands.

DETONATION (KNOCK) SENSOR

The detonation sensor generates a

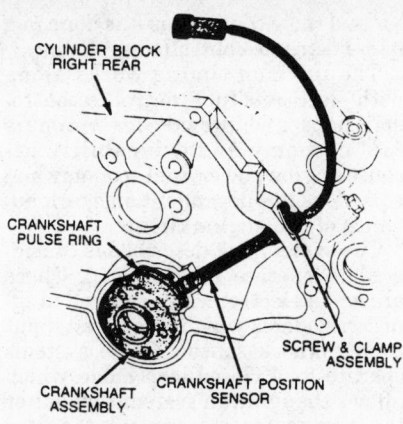

Crankshaft position sensor

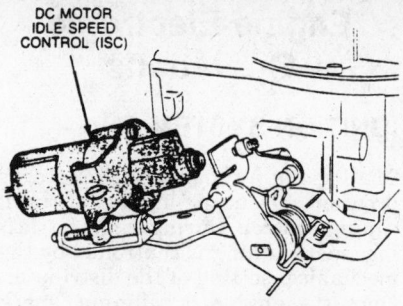

Idle speed control (ISC) motor

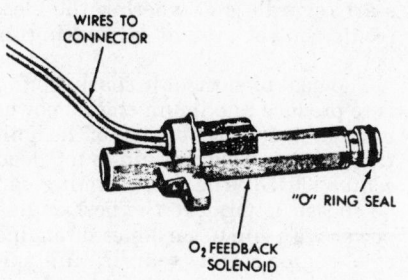

Air/fuel mixture solenoid

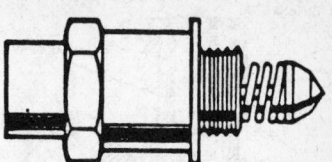

DUAL TAPER VALVE

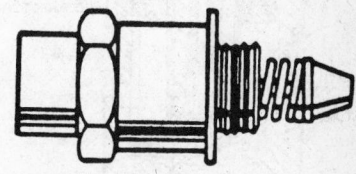

BLUNT PINTLE

Idle air control (IAC) valves

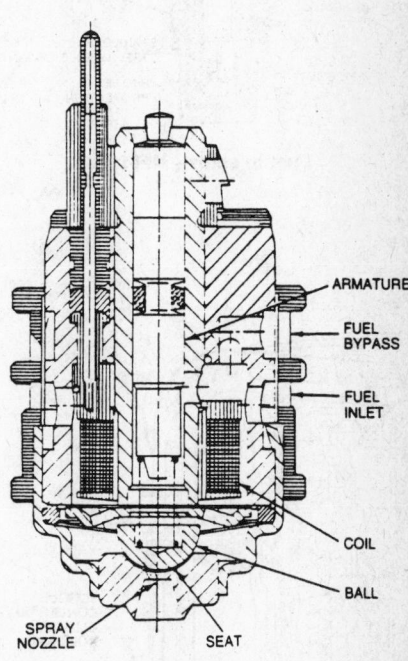

Fuel injector — TBI type

signal when pre-ignition (knock) occurs in one or more combustion chambers. The sensor is made of a material that is sensitive to oscillation that the engine knock produces and sends signals to the ECU. The ECU, in turn, delays the ignition signal which retards the ignition timing and continues to do this until the engine knock ceases.

CRANKSHAFT (REFERENCE MARK) SENSOR

The crankshaft sensor may be located at either the rear of the engine, at the flywheel or at the front of the engine, near the crankshaft pulley. The sensor detects crankshaft position in relation to top dead center and transmits the signals to ECU.

IDLE SPEED CONTROL (ISC) MOTOR

The ISC is sometimes included on a feedback carburetor system and mounted to the side of the carburetor. The motor driven ISC would maintain a steady idle by way of the ECU. When an added load is put on the engine (air conditioning or when vehicle is in drive) the ECU could increase the idle via the ISC by extending a plunger which would open the throttle valve.

AIR/FUEL MIXTURE SOLENOID

The air/fuel mixture solenoid on feedback carburetor operates in conjunction with the fixed metering jets and/or the manually adjustable idle speed mixture screw. The ECU energizes and de-energizes the solenoid in the closed loop mode. The solenoid usually controls a fixed air bleed and/or fuel discharge port.

IDLE AIR CONTROL (IAC)

The IAC in a fuel injection system controls the air flow around the throttle plate by extending and retracting a bypass valve in the bypass port. The ECU controls the valve by sending voltage pulses called counts or steps to increase or decrease the bypass air flow, thus increasing and decreasing the idle speed.

FUEL INJECTOR

Throttle Body Type

The fuel injector is an electric solenoid controlled by the ECU. The ECU controls the injector by varying voltage pulse widths. When electrical current is supplied to the injector a spring loaded ball is lifted from its seat. This allows fuel to flow through spray orifices and deflects off the sharp edge of the injector nozzle. This action causes the fuel to form a 45° cone shaped spray pattern before entering the air stream in the throttle body.

Multiport Type

The fuel injector is an electric solenoid controlled by the ECU. The ECU controls the injector by varying voltage pulse widths. When electrical current is supplied to the injector, the armature and pintle move a short distance against a spring, opening a small orifice. Fuel is supplied to the inlet of the injector by the fuel pump, then passes through the injector, around the pintle and out the orifice. Since the fuel is under high pressure, a fine spray is developed in the shape of a hollow cone. The injector, through this spraying action, atomizes the fuel and distributes it into the air entering the combustion chamber.

TORQUE CONVERTER CLUTCH (TCC) SOLENOID

The TCC solenoid is used on some automatic transmission, which allows for better fuel economy. When certain engine and vehicle speeds have been met, the ECU energizes the solenoid. This allows transmission fluid to flow into passages in the torque converter,

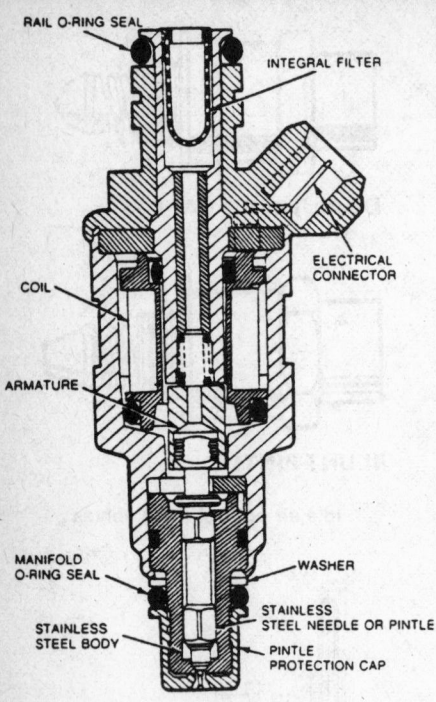

Fuel Injector — MFI type

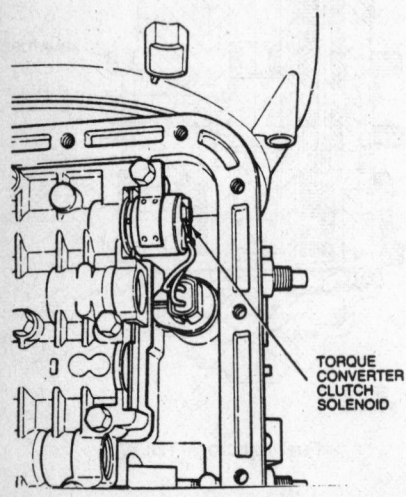

Torque converter clutch (TCC) solenoid

which causes the converter to lock up. This lockup is similar to a direct connection made possible in a manual transmission.

FUEL PUMP RELAY

The fuel is supplied under pressure, usually by an electric fuel pump. The ECU controls the fuel pump relay, which controls the fuel pump operation. When the ignition is switch ON, the fuel pump relay is energized and the fuel pump is activated. The pump primes the fuel system with fuel to a pre-determined pressure.

Engine Electronic Operations

IGNITION SYSTEM

The logic in a computerized system's program selects the method of spark timing control. During engine starting, spark timing is controlled by the mechanical setting of the distributor. Once the engine is running, spark timing is turned over to the ECU. This scheme ensures that the car will start regardless of whether the electronic control system is working or not.

The goal of electronic spark timing is to produce maximum engine power by adjustment the advance of the ignition firing in relationship to top dead center (TDC). The spark timing can be chosen to produce the best engine power with input variables of engine rpm, engine coolant temperature, initial and operating manifold or barometric pressure.

The total spark advance is determined by computing the information received from the various engine sensors which affect spark timing. The processor will then adjust the timing according to information that has been calibrated in it. The processor has programmed into it specific information on:

Warm-Up Spark Advance – this is used when the engine is cold, since a greater amount of advance is required while the engine warms up.

Special Spark Advance – to improve fuel economy during steady driving conditions.

Spark Advance Due to Barometric Pressure – this is used when barometric pressure exceeds a preset calibrated amount.

All of this information is then added together and the initial mechanical advance (if equipped) is subtracted to determine the final spark advance.

The processor receives a timing pulse from a sensor which indicates crankshaft position for top dead center and engines rpm. The processor makes a decision based upon this information and the information that was calibrated into it. at that time, the computer sends a pulse to the ignition actuator circuit which opens the ignition coil primary circuit to generate a secondary voltage pulse to fire the spark plugs. In some cases, the circuitry to open the primary of the coil may be in the computerized controller. The spark selection is performed mechanically by the distribu-

tor and rotor contacts as it is done in a non-electronic controlled system.

The ignition timing works along with electronic fuel control to control emissions and provide for optimum fuel economy and driveability because engine power, fuel economy and emissions are dependent on spark advance of the engine timing.

The system just described is considered to operate in open-loop. There are some electronically controlled ignition systems which receive an input from a knock sensor. These systems operate in a closed-loop mode which allows the ignition system to monitor the engine for mechanical changes, such as engine knock.

Engine knock is a condition where the air/fuel mixture in the cylinder does not burn normally. the pressure rise during this burning is so rapid compared to normal combustion that it is accompanied by an audible "knock".

Through some low level knock is acceptable, it is important to avoid excessive knock. To control engine knock, a knock sensor is installed in the engine or intake manifold. This helps to detect excessive engine knock.

The knock sensor is a tuned accelerometer and produces an output voltage depending on the amount of engine vibration occurring in a certain frequency band. When the processor receives a signal from the knock sensor, it retards the spark advance until the knocking stops and then starts increasing it again. This cycle is repeated as long as engine knock occurs.

FUEL CONTROL

In order for the processor to control fuel, it requires a sensor or sensors to monitor the state of the engine, and one or more actuators to do the actual controlling. The sensors measure: exhaust gas oxygen, manifold or barometric absolute pressure, engine rpm and speed, inlet air and coolant temperatures. Actuators are energized to control the air/fuel ratio.

The primary purpose of this control system is to maintain air/fuel ratio at or near 14.7:1 ratio. This is accomplished in two modes (during normal engine operation) open and closed loop. The electronic fuel control system can operate in closed loop only when certain conditions are satisfied. Open loop mode is employed whenever these conditions are not satisfied. However, for either mode, the exhaust emissions will satisfy federal requirements if the average air/fuel ratio is held within the tolerance limits.

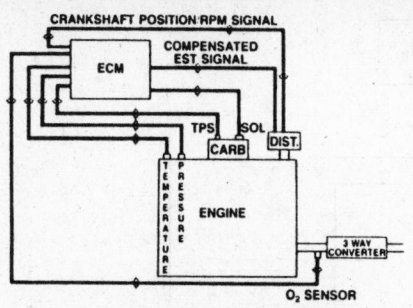

Electronic spark timing system

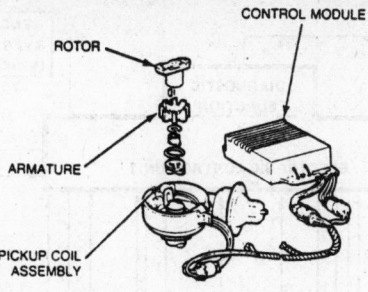

Solid state ignition system

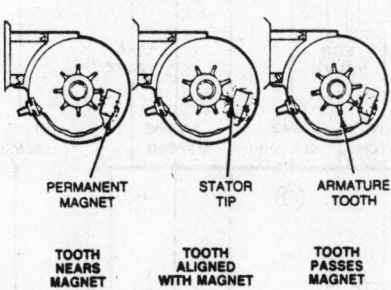

Distributor pick-up coil and armature assembly

In addition to open and closed loop control modes, a practical fuel control system has other operating modes depending on engine conditions. These handle such conditions as starting, rapid acceleration or heavy load, sudden deceleration, idling, etc.

An automotive engine has various operating modes as the operating conditions change. Preprogrammed into the processor, control logic determines the operating mode from the engine conditions that exist. From these engine conditions, the system determines which operating modes are to be performed.

There are seven different engine operating modes which affect fuel control: engine crank, engine warmup, open loop, closed loop control, hard acceleration, deceleration and idle. The program for mode control logic determines the engine operating mode by reading various sensors.

When the ignition switch is initially switched on, the mode control logic automatically selects an engine-start control scheme which provides the low air/fuel ratio required for starting the engine. Once the engine rpm rises above the cranking value, the controller identifies the engine-started mode and passes control to the program for the engine warm-up mode. This operating mode keeps the air/fuel ratio low to prevent engine stall during cool weather until engine coolant temperature rises above a preset value.

When the coolant temperature rises, the mode control logic directs the system to operate in the open loop control mode until a certain time has elapsed and the exhaust gas sensor warms up enough to provide accurate readings. This condition is detected by monitoring the exhaust gas sensor's output for voltage readings above a certain minimum air/fuel mixture voltage set point. when the sensor has indicated a rich mixture a certain number of times (depending on calibration), and after the engine has been in open loop for a specific time, the control mode logic selects the closed loop mode for the system.

The engine remains in the closed loop mode until either the exhaust gas sensor cools and fails to switch (from rich to lean) for a certain length of time, or a hard acceleration or deceleration occurs. If the sensor cools, the control mode logic selects the open loop mode again.

During hard acceleration of heavy engine loads, the control mode logic chooses a scheme which provides a rich air/fuel mixture for the duration of the acceleration or heavy load. This scheme provides maximum power, but poor emissions control and poor fuel economy. After the need for enrichment has passed, control is returned to either open or closed loop depending on the control mode logic selection conditions that exist at that time.

During periods of deceleration, the air/fuel ratio is increased to reduce emissions of HC and CO due to unburned fuel. When idle conditions are present, control mode logic passes system control to the idle speed control mode. In this mode, the engine speed is controlled to reduce engine roughness and stalling which might occur because the idle load has changed due to air conditioner compressor operation, alternator operation, or gearshift positioning from PARK or NEUTRAL to DRIVE.

Engine Crank

While the engine is being cranked,

the fuel control system must provide an intake air/fuel ratio anywhere from 2:1 to 12:1, depending on engine temperature. Low temperatures affect the carburetor's ability to atomize or mix the incoming air and fuel. At low temperature, the fuel tends to form into large droplets. The larger fuel droplets tend to increase the apparent air/fuel ratio because the amount of usable fuel in the air is reduced, therefore, the system must provide a decreased air/fuel ratio to provide the engine with a more combustible air/fuel mixture. The engine temperature is read by the processor through an analog to digital converter from a temperature sensor in the engine water coolant passage. The processor's calibration determines what the proper air/fuel ratio must be at that temperature. The air/fuel is determined and controlled as in the open loop mode.

Engine Warm-up

While the engine is warming up, an enriched air/fuel ratio is still needed to keep it running smoothly, but the required air/fuel ratio changes as the temperature increases. Therefore, the fuel control system will stay in the open loop mode, but the air/fuel ratio commands continue to be altered due to the temperature changes. The emphasis in this control mode is on rapid and smooth engine warm-up. Fuel economy and emission control are still a secondary concern. The controller determines the warm-up time period based on the coolant temperature when the warm-up mode was selected. Naturally, an initially cold engine requires a longer warm-up time than a warm engine. The time allowed by the controller timer is chosen according to the calibration of the processor.

OPEN LOOP CONTROL

Open loop fuel control is used when the engine has not reached a preset operating condition. This condition is sensed by various sensors located in and around the engine, and include engine coolant temperature, air charge temperature, engine time on, etc. After all these preset conditions are met, the system will go into closed loop. During certain operating conditions, such as a wide open throttle condition the system will go back into open loop.

CLOSED LOOP CONTROL

Closed loop fuel control is selected when the engine is warm and the exhaust gas oxygen sensor exceeds its minimum operating temperature. The intake air/fuel ratio is controlled in a closed loop by measuring the ex-

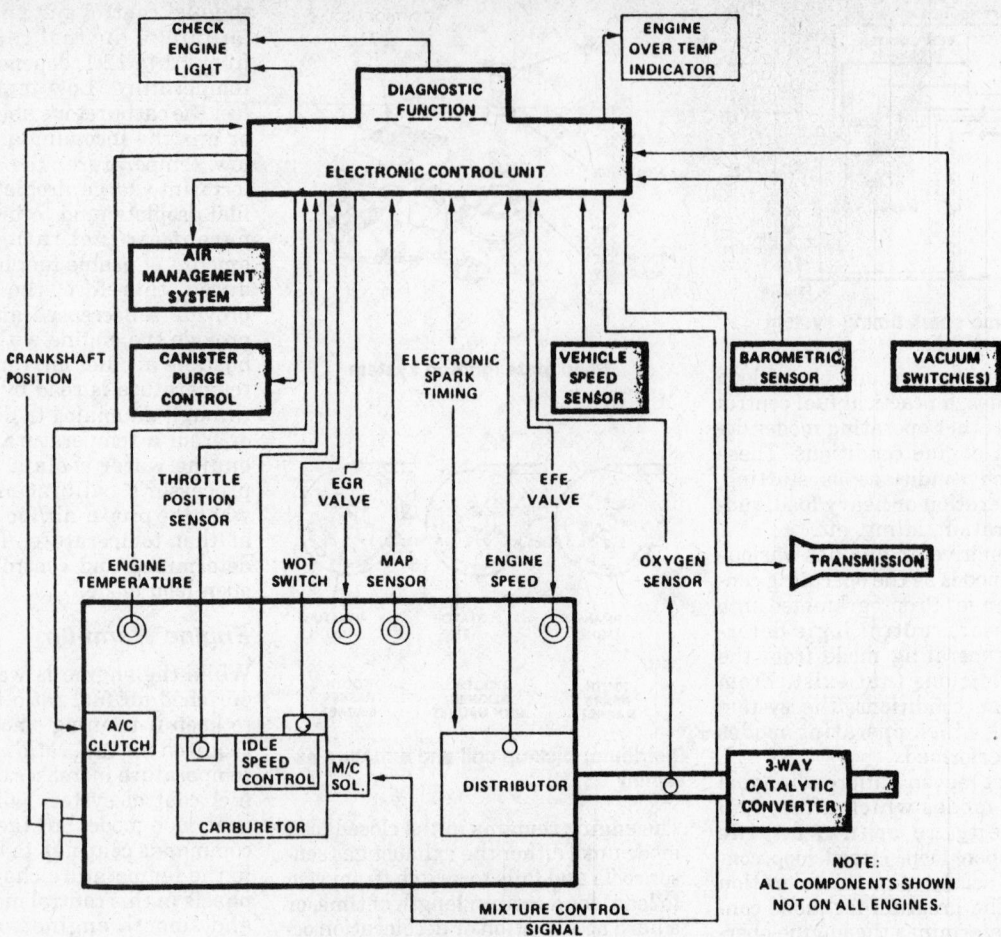

Typical electronic feedback carburetor system

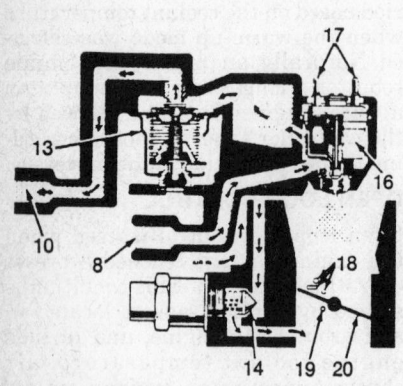

8 **FUEL SUPPLY**
10 **FUEL RETURN**
13 **PRESSURE REGULATOR (PART OF FUEL METER COVER)**
14 **IDLE AIR CONTROL (IAC) VALVE (SHOWN OPEN)**
16 **FUEL INJECTOR**
17 **FUEL INJECTOR TERMINALS**
18 **PORTED VACUUM SOURCES***
19 **MANIFOLD VACUUM SOURCE***
20 **THROTTLE VALVE**

*May Be Different on some Models.

Throttle body injection air and fuel flow

haust gas at the exhaust manifold and altering the input fuel flow rate or the air entering the main metering systems (depending on the type of fuel system used).

ACCELERATION ENRICHMENT (OPEN LOOP)

During periods of heavy engine load, such as wide open acceleration, fuel control is adjusted to provide an enriched ratio to maximize engine power while neglecting fuel economy and emission.

The computer detects this condition by reading the throttle position sensor voltage or the MAP sensor. Low intake manifold vacuum or throttle position corresponds to heavy engine loads. The fuel control system controller responds by increasing the amount of fuel to enter the intake manifold or to decrease the amount of air n the main metering system. This enrichment allows the engine to operate with a power greater than that allowed when emissions and fuel economy are controlled within specifications.

DECELERATION AND IDLE SPEED CONTROL (OPEN LOOP)

During periods of light engine load and high rpm, such as during closed throttle deceleration, coasting or engine idle, the engine requires a very lean air/fuel ratio to reduce excess emissions of HC and CO. Deceleration is indicated by a sudden increase in manifold vacuum and throttle position, indicating a closed throttle. When these conditions are detected by the processor, it computes a change in the amount of fuel required or amount of air entering the main or idle speed passages (depending on type of fuel system used). On certain engine engine applications which electronic fuel injection, the fuel may even be turned completely off during closed throttle deceleration.

Idle speed control is used to prevent engine stall during idle. The goal is to allow the engine to idle at as low an rpm as possible, yet keep the engine from running rough and stalling when power takeoff accessories such as air conditioning compressors are turned on.

Engine Rebuilding 38

This section describes, in detail, the procedures involved in rebuilding a typical engine. The procedures are basically identical to those used in rebuilding engines of nearly all design and configurations.

The section is divided into two parts. The first, Cylinder Head Reconditioning, assumes that the cylinder head is removed from the engine, all manifolds are removed, and the cylinder head is on a workbench. The camshaft should be removed from overhead cam cylinder heads. The second section, Cylinder Block Reconditioning, covers the block, pistons, connecting rods and crankshaft. It is assumed that the engine is mounted on a work stand, and the cylinder head and all accessories are removed.

Procedures are identified as follows:

Unmarked—Basic procedures that must be performed in order to successfully complete the rebuilding process.

Starred (*)—Procedures that should be performed to ensure maximum performance and engine life.

Double starred (**)—Procedures that may be performed to increase engine performance and reliability.

In many cases, a choice of methods is also provided. Methods are identified in the same manner as procedures. The choice of method for a procedure is at the discretion of the user.

The tools required for the basic rebuilding procedure should, with minor exceptions, be those included in a mechanic's tool kit. An accurate torque wrench, and a dial indicator (reading in thousandths) mounted on a universal base should be available. Special tools, where required, all are readily available from the major tool suppliers. The services of a competent automotive machine shop must also be readily available.

When assembling the engine, any parts that will be in frictional contact must be prelubricated, to provide protection on initial start-up. Any product specifically formulated for this purpose may be used. NOTE: *Do not use engine oil.* Where semi-permanent (locked but removable) installation of bolts or nuts is desired, threads should be cleaned and coated with Loctite® or a similar product (non-hardening).

Aluminum has become increasingly popular for use in engines, due to its low weight and excellent heat transfer characteristics. The following precautions must be observed when handling aluminum engine parts:

—Never hot-tank aluminum parts.

—Remove all aluminum parts (identification tags, etc.) from engine parts before hot-tanking (otherwise they will be removed during the process).

—Always coat threads lightly with engine oil or anti-seize compounds before installation, to prevent seizure.

—Never over-torque bolts or spark plugs in aluminum threads. Should stripping occur, threads can be restored using any of a number of thread repair kits available (see next section).

Magnaflux and Zyglo are inspection techniques used to locate material flaws, such as stress cracks. Magnafluxing coats the part with fine magnetic particles, and subjects the part to a magnetic field. Cracks cause breaks in the magnetic field, which are outlined by the particles. Since Magnaflux is a magnetic process, it is applicable only to ferrous materials. The Zyglo process coats the material with a fluorescent dye penetrant, and then subjects it to blacklight inspection, under which cracks glow brightly. Parts made of any material may be tested using Zyglo. While Magnaflux and Zyglo are excellent for general inspection, and locating hidden defects, specific checks of suspected cracks may be made at lower cost and more readily using spot check dye. The dye is sprayed onto the suspected area, wiped off, and the area is then sprayed with a developer. Cracks then will show up brightly. Spot check dyes will only indicate surface cracks; therefore, structural cracks below the surface may escape detection. When questionable, the part should be tested using Magnaflux or Zyglo.

REPAIRING DAMAGED THREADS

Several methods of repairing damaged threads are available. Heli-Coil® (shown here), Keenserts® and Microdot® are among the most widely used. All involve basically

the same principle—drilling out stripped threads, tapping the hole and installing a prewound insert— making welding, plugging and oversize fasteners unnecessary.

Two types of thread repair inserts are usually supplied—a standard type for most Inch Coarse, Inch Fine, Metric Coarse and Metric Fine thread sizes and a spark plug type to fit most spark plug port sizes. Consult the individual manufacturer's catalog to determine exact applications. Typical thread repair kits will contain a selection of prewound threaded inserts, a tap (corresponding to the outside diameter threads of the insert) and an installation tool. Most manufacturers also supply blister-packed thread repair inserts separately and a master kit with a variety of taps and inserts plus installation tools.

Before effecting a repair to a threaded hole, remove any snapped, broken or damaged bolts or studs. Penetrating oil can be used to free frozen threads; the offending item can be removed with locking pliers or with a screw or stud extractor. After the hole is clear, the thread can be repaired as follows.

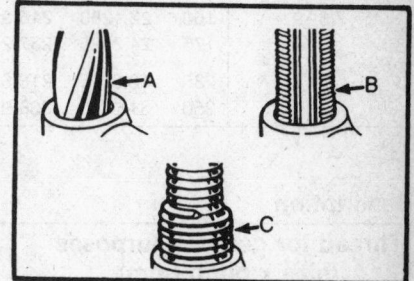

A. Drill out the damaged threads with the specified drill. Drill completely through the hole or to the bottom of a blind hole.

B. With the tap supplied tap the hole to receive the threaded insert. Keep the tap well oiled and back it out frequently to avoid clogging the threads.

C. Screw the threaded insert onto the installation tool until the tang engages the slot. Screw the insert into the tapped hole until it is ¼–½ turn below the top surface. After installation, break the tang off with a hammer and punch.

STANDARD TORQUE SPECIFICATIONS AND CAPSCREW MARKINGS

Newton-Meter has been designated as the world standard for measuring torque and will gradually replace the foot-pound and kilogram-meter torque measuring standard. Torquing tools are still being manufactured with foot-pounds and kilogram-meter scales, along with the new Newton-Meter standard. To assist the repairman, foot-pounds, kilogram-meter and Newton-Meter are listed in the following charts, and should be followed as applicable.

U.S. BOLTS

SAE Grade Number	1 or 2			5			6 or 7			8		
Capscrew Head Markings: Manufacturer's marks may vary. Three-line markings on heads below indicate SAE Grade 5.							(cross mark)			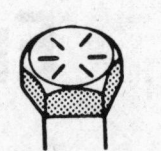		
Usage	Used Frequently			Used Frequently			Used at Times			Used at Times		
Quality of Material	Indeterminate			Minimum Commercial			Medium Commercial			Best Commercial		
Capacity Body Size	Torque			Torque			Torque			Torque		
(inches) – (thread)	Ft-Lb	kgm	Nm	Ft-Lb	kgm	Nm	Ft-Lb	kgm	Nm	Ft-Lb	kgm	Nm
1/4–20	5	0.6915	6.7791	8	1.1064	10.8465	10	1.3630	13.5582	12	1.6596	16.2698
–28	6	0.8298	8.1349	10	1.3830	13.5582				14	1.9362	18.9815
5/16–18	11	1.5213	14.9140	17	2.3511	23.0489	19	2.6277	25.7605	24	3.3192	32.5396
–24	13	1.7979	17.6256	19	2.6277	25.7605				27	3.7341	36.6071
3/8–16	18	2.4894	24.4047	31	4.2873	42.0304	34	4.7022	46.0978	44	6.0852	59.6560
–24	20	2.7660	27.1164	35	4.8405	47.4536				49	6.7767	66.4351
7/16–14	28	3.8132	37.9629	49	6.7767	66.4351	55	7.6065	74.5700	70	9.6810	94.9073
–20	30	4.1490	40.6745	55	7.6065	74.5700				78	10.7874	105.7538
1/2–13	39	5.3937	52.8769	75	10.3725	101.6863	85	11.7555	115.2445	105	14.5215	142.3609
–20	41	5.6703	55.5885	85	11.7555	115.2445				120	16.5860	162.6960
9/16–12	51	7.0533	69.1467	110	15.2130	149.1380	120	16.5960	162.6960	155	21.4365	210.1490
–18	55	7.6065	74.5700	120	16.5960	162.6960				170	23.5110	230.4860
5/8–11	83	11.4789	112.5329	150	20.7450	203.3700	167	23.0961	226.4186	210	29.0430	284.7180
–18	95	13.1385	128.8027	170	23.5110	230.4860				240	33.1920	325.3920
3/4–10	105	14.5215	142.3609	270	37.3410	366.0660	280	38.7240	379.6240	375	51.8625	508.4250
–16	115	15.9045	155.9170	295	40.7985	399.9610				420	58.0860	568.4360
7/8–9	160	22.1280	216.9280	395	54.6285	535.5410	440	60.8520	596.5520	605	83.6715	820.2590
–14	175	24.2025	237.2650	435	60.1605	589.7730				675	93.3525	915.1650
1–8	236	32.5005	318.6130	590	81.5970	799.9220	660	91.2780	894.8280	910	125.8530	1233.7780
–14	250	34.5750	338.9500	660	91.2780	849.8280				990	136.9170	1342.2420

METRIC BOLTS

Description	Torque ft-lbs. (Nm)			
Thread for general purposes (size x pitch (mm))	Head Mark 4		Head Mark 7	
6 x 1.0	2.2 to 2.9	(3.0 to 3.9)	3.6 to 5.8	(4.9 to 7.8)
8 x 1.25	5.8 to 8.7	(7.9 to 12)	9.4 to 14	(13 to 19)
10 x 1.25	12 to 17	(16 to 23)	20 to 29	(27 to 39)
12 x 1.25	21 to 32	(29 to 43)	35 to 53	(47 to 72)
14 x 1.5	35 to 52	(48 to 70)	57 to 85	(77 to 110)
16 x 1.5	51 to 77	(67 to 100)	90 to 120	(130 to 160)
18 x 1.5	74 tc 110	(100 to 150)	130 to 170	(180 to 230)
20 x 1.5	110 to 140	(150 to 190)	190 to 240	(160 to 320)
22 x 1.5	150 to 190	(200 to 260)	250 to 320	(340 to 430)
24 x 1.5	190 to 240	(260 to 320)	310 to 410	(420 to 550)

CAUTION: Bolts threaded into aluminum require much less torque

NOTE: This engine rebuilding section is a guide to accepted rebuilding procedures. Typical examples of standard rebuilding procedures are illustrated.

CYLINDER HEAD RECONDITIONING

Procedure	Method
Identify the valves:	Invert the cylinder head, and number the valve faces front to rear, using a permanent felt-tip marker.
Remove the rocker arms (OHV engines only):	Remove the rocker arms with shaft(s) or balls and nuts. Wire the sets of rockers, balls and nuts together, and identify according to the corresponding valve.
Remove the camshaft (OHC engines only):	See the engine service procedures earlier in this book for details concerning specific engines.
Remove the valves and springs:	Using an appropriate valve spring compressor (depending on the configuration of the cylinder head), compress the valve springs. Lift out the keepers with needlenose pliers, release the compressor, and remove the valve, spring, and spring retainer.
Remove glow plugs and fuel injectors (Diesel engines only):	Label and remove all fuel injectors and glow plugs from the head. Glow plugs unscrew. See the appropriate car section for injector removal. Inspect glow plugs for bulges, cracks or signs of melting. Clean injector tips with a steel brush, then inspect for evidence of melting.
**Remove pre-combustion chamber inserts (Diesel engines only):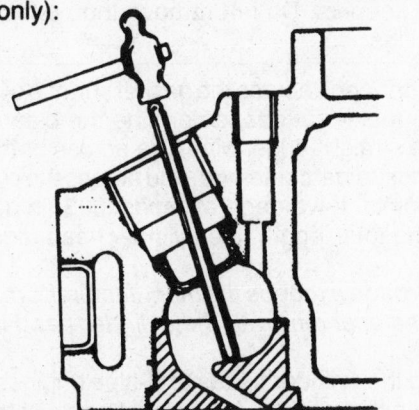	**Remove the pre-combustion chambers using a hammer and a thin, blunt brass drift, inserted through the injector hole (or glow plug hole, whichever is more convenient). If chamber is to be reused, carefully remove all carbon from it. NOTE: *Remove chamber only if being replaced, if a glow plug tip has broken off and must be removed, or if chamber is obviously damaged or loose.*

Removing pre-combustion chamber with a drift (© G.M. Corp.)

Check the valve stem-to-guide clearance: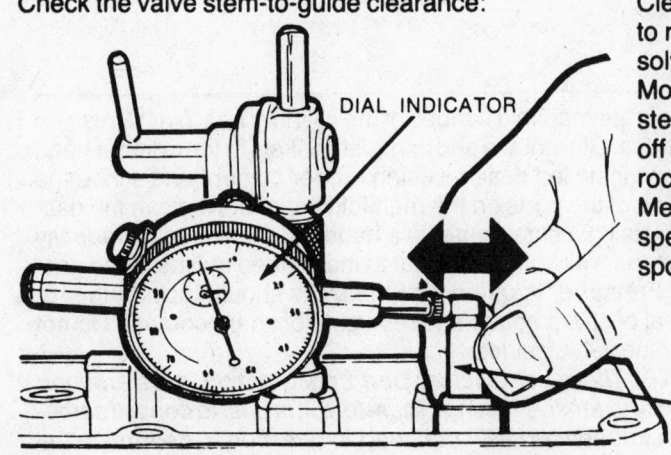	Clean the valve stem with lacquer thinner or a similar solvent to remove all gum and varnish. Clean the valve guides using solvent and an expanding wire-type valve guide cleaner. Mount a dial indicator so that the stem is at 90° to the valve stem, as close to the valve guide as possible. Move the valve off its seat, and measure the valve guide-to-stem clearance by rocking the stem back and forth to actuate the dial indicator. Measure the valve stems using a micrometer, and compare to specifications, to determine whether stem or guide wear is responsible for excessive clearance.

DIAL INDICATOR

VALVE STEM

Checking the valve stem-to-guide clearance

CYLINDER HEAD RECONDITIONING

Procedure	Method

De-carbon the cylinder head and valves:

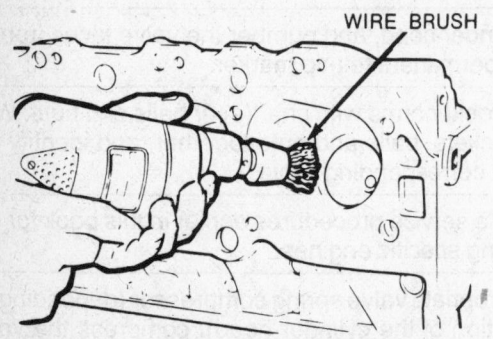

WIRE BRUSH

Removing carbon from the cylinder head

Chip carbon away from the valve heads, combustion chambers, and ports, using a chisel made of hardwood. Remove the remaining deposits with a stiff wire brush.
NOTE: *Ensure that the deposits are actually removed, rather than burnished.*

Hot-tank the cylinder head (cast iron heads only):
CAUTION: *Do not hot-tank aluminum parts.*

Have the cylinder head hot-tanked to remove grease, corrosion, and scale from the water passages.
NOTE: *In the case of overhead cam cylinder heads, consult the operator to determine whether the camshaft bearings will be damaged by the caustic solution.*

Degrease the remaining cylinder head parts:

Using solvent (i.e., Gunk), clean the rockers, rocker shaft(s) (where applicable), rocker balls and nuts, springs, spring retainers, and keepers. Do not remove the protective coating from the springs.

Check the cylinder head for warpage:

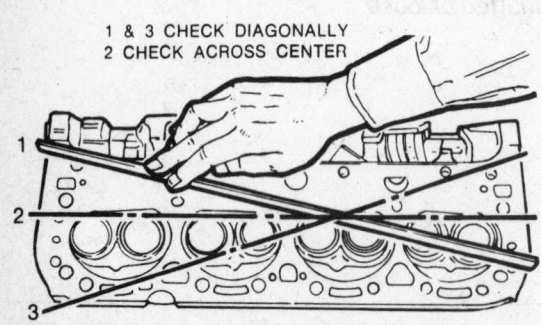

1 & 3 CHECK DIAGONALLY
2 CHECK ACROSS CENTER

Checking cylinder head for warpage

Place a straight-edge across the gasket surface of the cylinder head. Using feeler gauges, determine the clearance at the center of the straight-edge. Measure across both diagonals, along the longitudinal centerline, and across the cylinder head at several points. If warpage exceeds .003′ in a 6′ span, or .006′ over the total length, the cylinder head must be resurfaced.
NOTE: *If warpage exceeds the manufacturer's maximum tolerance for material removal, the cylinder head must be replaced.*
When milling the cylinder heads of V-type engines, the intake manifold mounting position is altered, and must be corrected by milling the manifold flange a proportionate amount.

**Porting and gasket matching:

****Coat the manifold flanges of the cylinder head with Prussian blue dye. Glue intake and exhaust gaskets to the cylinder head in their installed position using rubber cement and scribe the outline of the ports on the manifold flanges. Remove the gaskets. Using a small cutter in a hand-held power tool gradually taper the walls of the port out to the scribed outline of the gasket. Further enlargement of the ports should include the removal of sharp edges and radiusing of sharp corners. Do not alter the valve guides.
NOTE: *The most efficient port configuration is determined only by extensive testing. Therefore, it is best to consult someone experienced with the head in question to determine the optimum alterations.*

CYLINDER HEAD RECONDITIONING

Procedure	Method

*Knurling the valve guides:

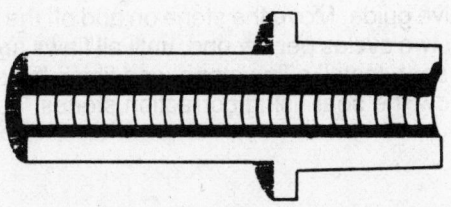

Cut-away view of a knurled valve guide

*Valve guides which are not excessively worn or distorted may, in some cases, be knurled rather than replaced. Knurling is a process in which metal is displaced and raised, thereby reducing clearance. Knurling also provides excellent oil control. The possibility of knurling rather than replacing valve guides should be discussed with a machinist.

Replacing the valve guides:
NOTE: *Valve guides should only be replaced if damaged or if an oversize valve stem is not available.*

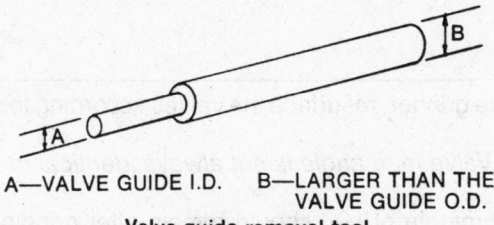

A—VALVE GUIDE I.D.   B—LARGER THAN THE VALVE GUIDE O.D.
Valve guide removal tool

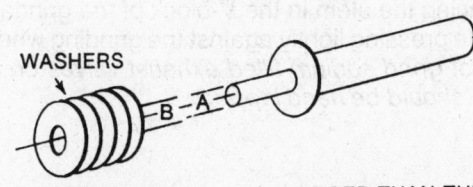

WASHERS

A—VALVE GUIDE I.D.   B—LARGER THAN THE VALVE GUIDE O.D.

Valve guide installation tool (with washers used for installation)

Depending on the type of cylinder head, valve guides may be pressed, hammered, or shrunk in. In cases where the guides are shrunk into the head, replacement should be left to an equipped machine shop. In other cases, the guides are replaced as follows: Press or tap the valve guides out of the head using a stepped drift (see illustration). Determine the height above the boss that the guide must extend, and obtain a stack of washers, their I.D. similar to the guide's O.D., of that height. Place the stack of washers on the guide, and insert the guide into the boss.
NOTE: *Valve guides are often tapered or beveled for installation.*
Using the stepped installation tool (see illustration), press or tap the guides into position. Ream the guides according to the size of the valve stem.

Replacing valve seat inserts:

Replacement of valve seat inserts which are worn beyond resurfacing or broken, if feasible, must be done by a machine shop.

Resurfacing the valve seats using reamers:

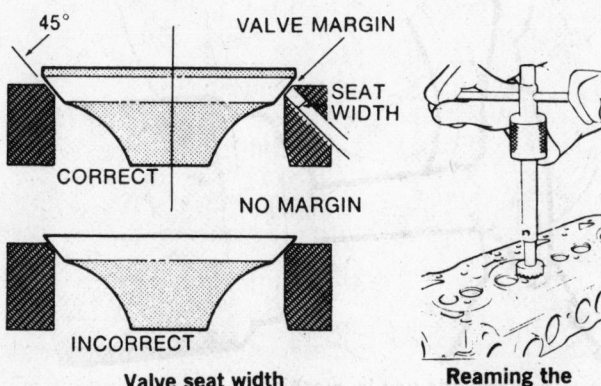

45°   VALVE MARGIN
SEAT WIDTH
CORRECT
NO MARGIN
INCORRECT

Valve seat width and centering

Reaming the valve seat

Select a reamer of the correct seat angle, slightly larger than the diameter of the valve seat, and assemble it with a pilot of the correct size. Install the pilot into the valve guide, and using steady pressure, turn the reamer clockwise.
CAUTION: *Do not turn the reamer counterclockwise.*
Remove only as much material as necessary to clean the seat. Check the concentricity of the seat (see below). If the dye method is not used, coat the valve face with Prussian blue dye, install and rotate it on the valve seat. Using the dye marked area as a centering guide, center and narrow the valve seat to specifications with correction cutters.
NOTE: *When no specifications are available, minimum seat width for exhaust valves should be 5/64", intake valves 1/16".*
After making correction cuts, check the position of the valve seat on the valve face using Prussian blue dye.
NOTE: *Do not cut induction hardened seats; they must be ground.*

CYLINDER HEAD RECONDITIONING

Procedure	Method

*Resurfacing the valve seats using a grinder:

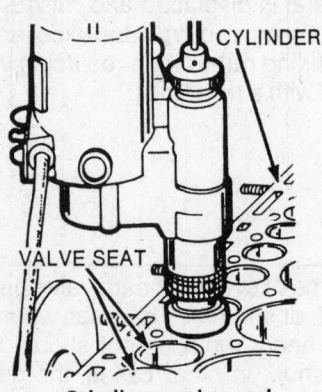

CYLINDER

VALVE SEAT

Grinding a valve seat

*Select a pilot of the correct size, and a coarse stone of the correct seat angle. Lubricate the pilot if necessary, and install the tool in the valve guide. Move the stone on and off the seat at approximately two cycles per second, until all flaws are removed from the seat. Install a fine stone, and finish the seat. Center and narrow the seat using correction stones, as described above.

Resurfacing (grinding) the valve face:

FOR DIMENSIONS, REFER TO SPECIFICATIONS

CHECK FOR BENT STEM

DIAMETER

VALVE FACE ANGLE

1/32" MINIMUM

THIS LINE PARALLEL WITH VALVE HEAD

Critical valve dimensions

Using a valve grinder, resurface the valves according to specifications.
CAUTION: *Valve face angle is not always identical to valve seat angle.*
A minimum margin of 1/32" should remain after grinding the valve. The valve stem top should also be squared and resurfaced, by placing the stem in the V-block of the grinder, and turning it while pressing lightly against the grinding wheel.
NOTE: *Do not grind sodium filled exhaust valves on a machine. These should be hand lapped.*

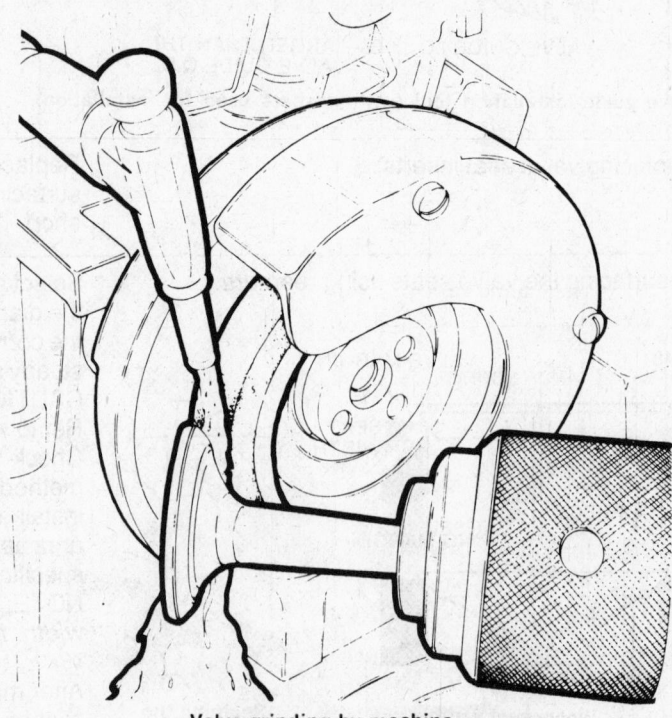

Valve grinding by machine

CYLINDER HEAD RECONDITIONING

Procedure	Method

Checking the valve seat concentricity:

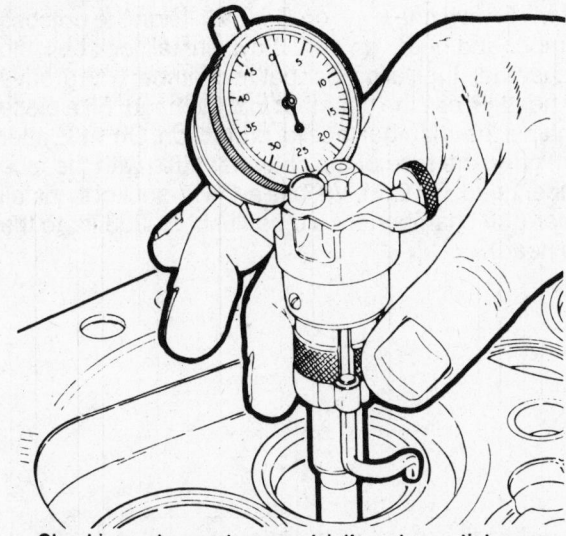

Checking valve seat concentricity using a dial gauge

Coat the valve face with Prussian blue dye, install the valve, and rotate it on the valve seat. If the entire seat becomes coated, and the valve is known to be concentric, the seat is concentric.
*Install the dial gauge pilot into the guide, and rest the arm on the valve seat. Zero the gauge, and rotate the arm around the seat. Run-out should not exceed .002".

---

*Lapping the valves:
NOTE: *Valve lapping is done to ensure efficient sealing of resurfaced valves and seats.*

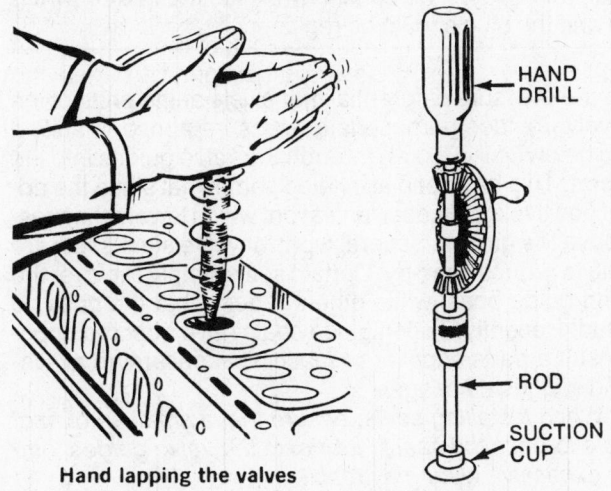

HAND DRILL

ROD

SUCTION CUP

Home made mechanical valve lapping tool

Hand lapping the valves

*Invert the cylinder head, lightly lubricate the valve stems, and install the valves in the head as numbered. Coat valve seats with fine grinding compound, and attach the lapping tool suction cup to a valve head.
NOTE: *Moisten the suction cup.*
Rotate the tool between the palms, changing position and lifting the tool often to prevent grooving. Lap the valve until a smooth, polished seat is evident. Remove the valve and tool, and rinse away all traces of grinding compound.
**Fasten a suction cup to a piece of drill rod, and mount the rod in a hand drill. Proceed as above, using the hand drill as a lapping tool.
CAUTION: *Due to the higher speeds involved when using the hand drill, care must be exercised to avoid grooving the seat.* Lift the tool and change direction of rotation often.

Check the valve springs:

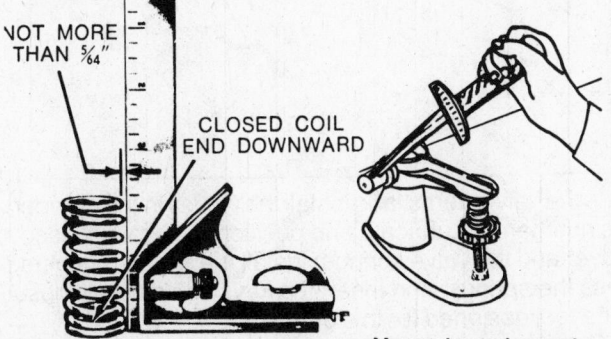

NOT MORE THAN $\frac{5}{64}$"

CLOSED COIL END DOWNWARD

Checking valve spring free length and squareness

Measuring valve spring test pressure

Place the spring on a flat surface next to a square. Measure the height of the spring, and rotate it against the edge of the square to measure distortion. If spring height varies (by comparison) by more than $\frac{1}{16}$" or if distortion exceeds $\frac{1}{16}$", replace the spring.
**In addition to evaluating the spring as above, test the spring pressure at the installed and compressed (installed height minus valve lift) height using a valve spring tester. Springs used on small displacement engines (up to 3 liters) should be ∓ 1 lb. of all other springs in either position. A tolerance of ∓ 5 lbs. is permissible on larger engines.

CYLINDER HEAD RECONDITIONING

Procedure	Method

Install pre-combustion chambers (Diesel engines only)

Pre-combustion chambers are press-fit into the head. The chambers will fit only one way: on G.M. V8, align the notches in the chamber and head; on 1.8L 4 cyl., install lock ball into groove in chamber, then align lock ball in chamber with groove in cylinder head. Press the chamber into the head. Fit a piece of metal against the chamber face for protection. On 1.8L, after installation, grind the face of the chamber flush with the face of the cylinder head. On G.M. V8, use a 1¼ in. socket to install the chamber (the chamber should be flush ± .003 in. to the face of the head).

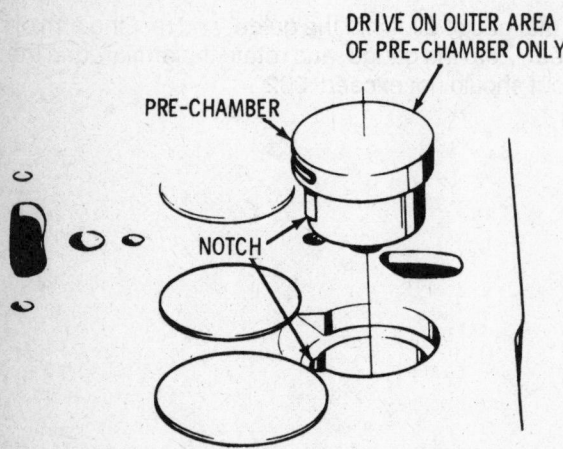

DRIVE ON OUTER AREA OF PRE-CHAMBER ONLY

PRE-CHAMBER

NOTCH

Align the notches to install the pre-combustion chamber (© G.M. Corp.)

Install fuel injectors and glow plugs (Diesel engines)

Before installing glow plugs, check for continuity across plug terminals and body. If no continuity exists, the heater wire is broken and the plug should be replaced.

---

*Install valve stem seals:

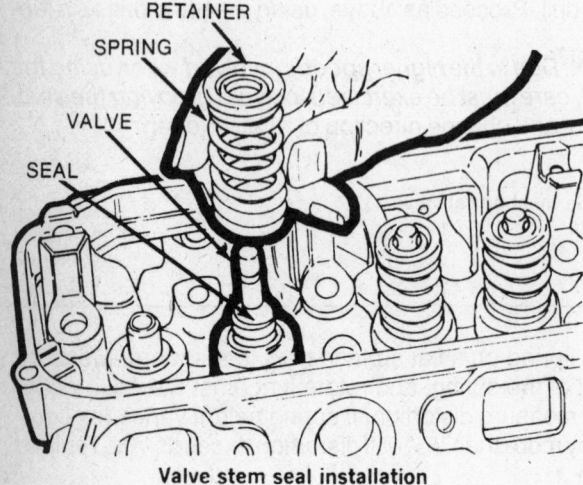

RETAINER

SPRING

VALVE

SEAL

Valve stem seal installation

*Due to the pressure differential that exists at the ends of the intake valve guides (atmospheric pressure above, manifold vacuum below), oil is drawn through the valve guides into the intake port. This has been alleviated somewhat since the addition of positive crankcase ventilation, which lowers the pressure above the guides. Several types of valve stem seals are available to reduce blow-by. Certain seals simply slip over the stem and guide boss, while others require that the boss be machined. Recently, Teflon guide seals have become popular. Consult a parts supplier or machinist concerning availability and suggested usages.
NOTE: *When installing seals, ensure that a small amount of oil is able to pass the seal to lubricate the valve guides; otherwise, excessive wear may result.*

Install the valves:

Lubricate the valve stems, and install the valves in the cylinder head as numbered. Lubricate and position the seals (if used, see above) and the valve springs. Install the spring retainers, compress the springs, and insert the keys using needlenose pliers or a tool designed for this purpose.
NOTE: *Retain the keys with wheel bearing grease during installation.*

CYLINDER HEAD RECONDITIONING

Procedure	Method

Check valve spring installed height:

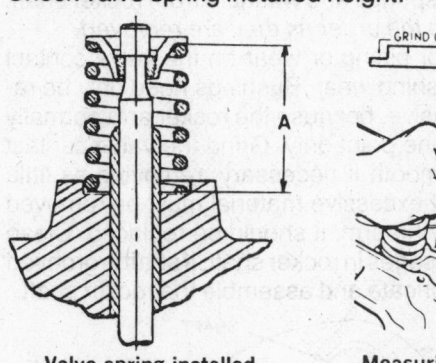

GRIND OUT THIS PORTION

Valve spring installed
height dimension

Measuring valve spring
installed height

Measure the distance between the spring pad and the lower edge of the spring retainer, and compare to specifications. If the installed height is incorrect, add shim washers between the spring pad and the spring.
CAUTION: *Use only washers designed for this purpose.*

Install the camshaft (OHC engines only) and check end play:

See the engine service procedures earlier in this book for details concerning specific engines.

Inspect the rocker arms, balls, studs, and nuts (OHV engines only):

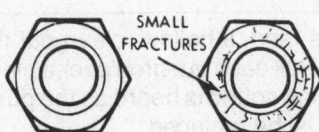

SMALL
FRACTURES

Stress cracks in the rocker nuts

Visually inspect the rocker arms, balls, studs, and nuts for cracks, galling, burning, scoring or wear. If all parts are intact, liberally lubricate the rocker arms and balls, and install them on the cylinder head. If wear is noted on a rocker arm at the point of valve contact, grind it smooth and square, removing as little material as possible. Replace the rocker arm if excessively worn. If a rocker stud shows signs of wear, it must be replaced (see below). If a rocker nut shows stress cracks, replace it. If an exhaust ball is galled or burned, substitute the intake ball from the same cylinder (if it is intact), and install a new intake ball.
NOTE: *Avoid using new rocker balls on exhaust valves.*

Replacing rocker studs (OHV engines only):

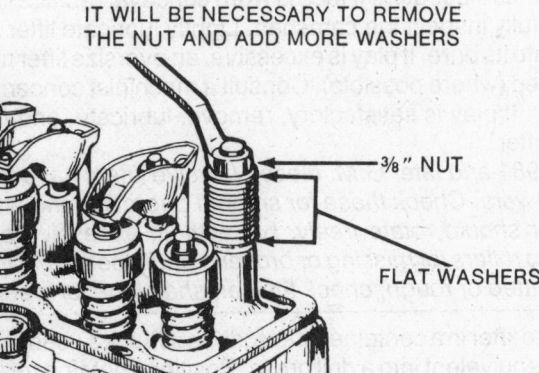

AS STUB BEGINS TO PULL UP,
IT WILL BE NECESSARY TO REMOVE
THE NUT AND ADD MORE WASHERS

⅜″ NUT

FLAT WASHERS

Extracting a pressed-in rocker stud

In order to remove a threaded stud, lock two nuts on the stud, and unscrew the stud using the lower nut. Coat the lower threads of the new stud with Loctite®, and install.
Two alternative methods are available for replacing pressed in studs. Remove the damaged stud using a stack of washers and a nut (see illustration). In the first, the boss is reamed .005–.006″ oversize, and an oversize stud pressed in. Control the stud extension over the boss using washers, in the same manner as valve guides. Before installing the stud, coat it with white lead and grease. To retain the stud more positively drill a hole through the stud and boss, and install a roll pin. In the second method, the boss is tapped, and a threaded stud installed. Retain the stud using Loctite® Stud and Bearing Mount.

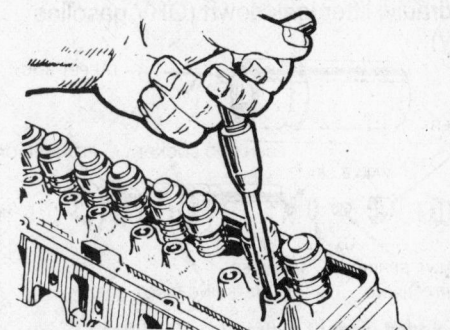

Reaming the stud bore for oversize rocker studs

CYLINDER HEAD RECONDITIONING

Procedure	Method

Inspect the rocker shaft(s) and rocker arms (OHV engines only):

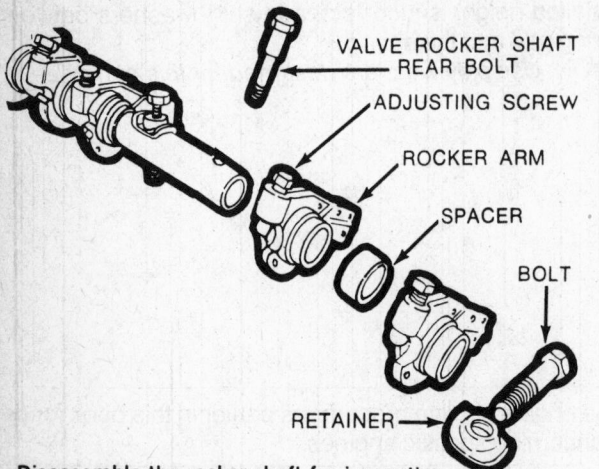

VALVE ROCKER SHAFT REAR BOLT
ADJUSTING SCREW
ROCKER ARM
SPACER
BOLT
RETAINER

Disassemble the rocker shaft for inspection

Remove rocker arms, springs and washers from rocker shaft. NOTE: *Lay out parts in the order as they are removed.*
Inspect rocker arms for pitting or wear on the valve contact point, or excessive bushing wear. Bushings need only be replaced if wear is excessive, because the rocker arm normally contacts the shaft at one point only. Grind the valve contact point of rocker arm smooth if necessary, removing as little material as possible. If excessive material must be removed to smooth and square the arm, it should be replaced. Clean out all oil holes and passages in rocker shaft. If shaft is grooved or worn, replace it. Lubricate and assemble the rocker shaft.

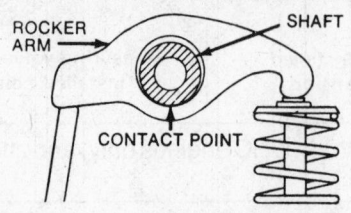

ROCKER ARM   SHAFT
CONTACT POINT

Rocker arm-to-rocker shaft contact area

Inspect the camshaft bushings and the camshaft (OHC engines):

See next section.

Inspect the pushrods (OHV engines only):

Remove the pushrods, and, if hollow, clean out the oil passages using fine wire. Roll each pushrod over a piece of clean glass. If a distinct clicking sound is heard as the pushrod rolls, the rod is bent, and must be replaced.

*The length of all pushrods must be equal. Measure the length of the pushrods, compare to specifications, and replace as necessary.

Inspect the valve lifters (OHV engines only):

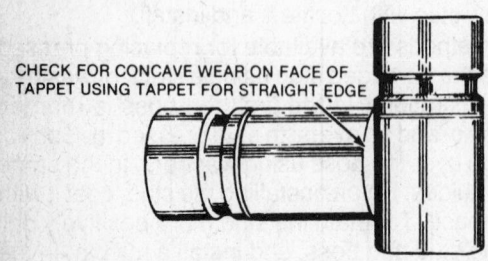

CHECK FOR CONCAVE WEAR ON FACE OF TAPPET USING TAPPET FOR STRAIGHT EDGE

Checking the lifter face

Remove lifters from their bores, and remove gum and varnish, using solvent. Clean walls of lifter bores. Check lifters for concave wear as illustrated. If face is worn concave, replace lifter, and carefully inspect the camshaft. Lightly lubricate lifter and insert it into its bore. If play is excessive, an oversize lifter must be installed (where possible). Consult a machinist concerning feasibility. If play is satisfactory, remove, lubricate, and reinstall the lifter.
NOTE: *1981 and later G.M. diesel V8 valve lifters have roller cam followers. Check these for smooth operation and wear. The roller should rotate freely, but without excessive play. Check the rollers for missing or broken needle bearings. If the roller is pitted or rough, check the camshaft lobe for wear.*

---

*Testing hydraulic lifter leak down (OHV gasoline engines only):

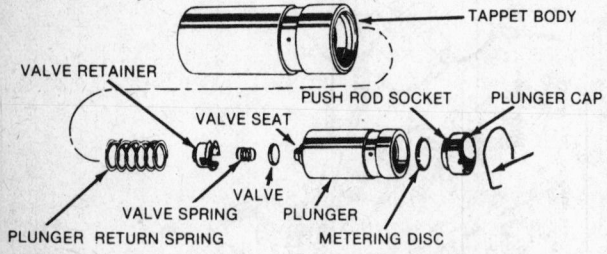

TAPPET BODY
VALVE RETAINER
PUSH ROD SOCKET   PLUNGER CAP
VALVE SEAT
VALVE
VALVE SPRING   PLUNGER
PLUNGER RETURN SPRING   METERING DISC

Typical exploded view of hydraulic valve lifter

Submerge lifter in a container of kerosene. Chuck a used pushrod or its equivalent into a drill press. Position container of kerosene so pushrod acts on the lifter plunger. Pump lifter with the drill press, until resistance increases. Pump several more times to bleed any air out of lifter. Apply very firm, constant pressure to the lifter, and observe rate at which fluid bleeds out of lifter. If the fluid bleeds very quickly (less than 15 seconds), lifter is defective. If the time exceeds 60 seconds, lifter is sticking. In either case, recondition or replace lifter. If lifter is operating properly (leak down time 15–60 seconds), lubricate and install it.

CYLINDER HEAD RECONDITIONING

Procedure	Method
Bleed the hydraulic lifters (diesel engines only):	After the cylinder heads are installed on G.M. V8 diesels, the valve lifters must be bled down before the crankshaft is turned. Failure to bleed down the lifters will cause damage to the valve train. See diesel engine rocker arm replacement procedure in Oldsmobile 88, 98, etc. car section for procedures. NOTE: *When installing new lifters, prime by working the lifter plunger while submerged in clean kerosene or diesel fuel.*

CYLINDER BLOCK RECONDITIONING

Procedure	Method
Checking the main bearing clearance: 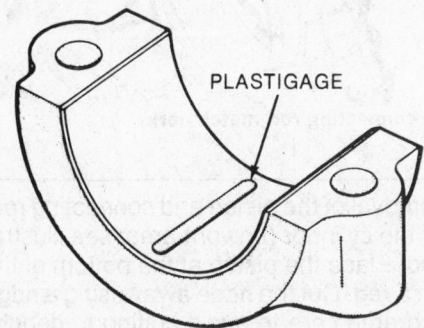 Plastigage® installed on the lower bearing shell 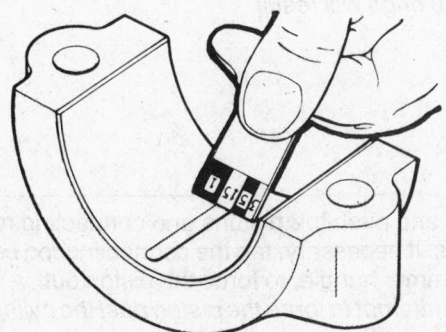 Measuring Plastigage® to determine bearing clearance	Invert engine, and remove cap from the bearing to be checked. Using a clean, dry rag, thoroughly clean all oil from crankshaft journal and bearing insert. NOTE: *Plastigage is soluble in oil; therefore, oil on the journal or bearing could result in erroneous readings.* Place a piece of Plastigage along the full length of journal, reinstall cap, and torque to specifications. Remove bearing cap, and determine bearing clearance by comparing width of Plastigage to the scale on Plastigage envelope. Journal taper is determined by comparing width of the Plastigage strip near its ends. Rotate crankshaft 90° and retest, to determine journal eccentricity. NOTE: *Do not rotate crankshaft with Plastigage installed.* If bearing insert and journal appear intact, and are within tolerances, no further main bearing service is required. If bearing or journal appear defective, cause of failure should be determined before replacement. *Remove crankshaft from block (see below). Measure the main bearing journals at each end twice (90° apart) using a micrometer, to determine diameter, journal taper and eccentricity. If journals are within tolerances, reinstall bearing caps at their specified torque. Using a telescope gauge and micrometer, measure bearing I.D. parallel to piston axis and at 30° on each side of piston axis. Subtract journal O.D. from bearing I.D. to determine oil clearance. If crankshaft journals appear defective, or do no meet tolerances, there is no need to measure bearings; for the crankshaft will require grinding and/or undersize bearings will be required. If bearing appears defective, cause for failure should be determined prior to replacement.
Checking the connecting rod bearing clearance:	Connecting rod bearing clearance is checked in the same manner as main bearing clearance, using Plastigage. Before removing the crankshaft, connecting rod side clearance also should be measured and recorded. *Checking connecting rod bearing clearance, using a micrometer, is identical to checking main bearing clearance. If no other service is required, the piston and rod assemblies need not be removed.

CYLINDER BLOCK RECONDITIONING

Procedure	Method
Removing the crankshaft:	Using a punch, mark the corresponding main bearing caps and saddles according to position (i.e., one punch on the front main cap and saddle, two on the second, three on the third, etc.). Using number stamps, identify the corresponding connecting rods and caps, according to cylinder (if no numbers are present). Remove the main and connecting rod caps, and place sleeves of plastic tubing over the connecting rod bolts, to protect the journals as the crankshaft is removed. Lift the crankshaft out of the block.

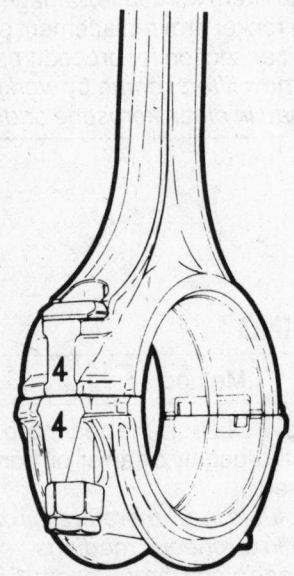

Connecting rod matched to cylinder with a number stamp

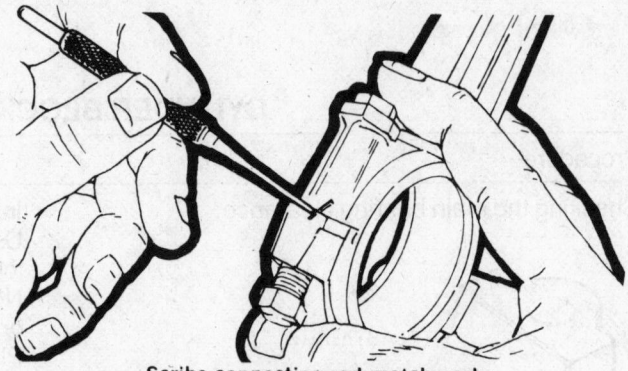

Scribe connecting rod matchmarks

Procedure	Method
Remove the ridge from the top of the cylinder:	In order to facilitate removal of the piston and connecting rod, the ridge at the top of the cylinder (unworn area; see illustration) must be removed. Place the piston at the bottom of the bore, and cover it with a rag. Cut the ridge away using a ridge reamer, exercising extreme care to avoid cutting to deeply. Remove the rag, and remove cuttings that remain on the piston. CAUTION: *If the ridge is not removed, and new rings are installed, damage to rings will result.*

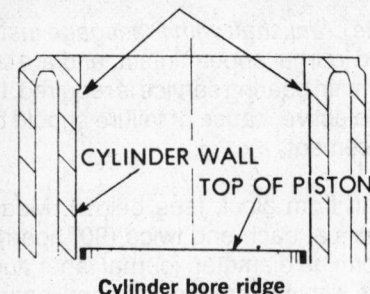

RIDGE CAUSED BY CYLINDER WEAR

CYLINDER WALL

TOP OF PISTON

Cylinder bore ridge

Procedure	Method
Removing the piston and connecting rod:	Invert the engine, and push the pistons and connecting rods out of the cylinders. If necessary, tap the connecting rod boss with a wooden hammer handle, to force the piston out. CAUTION: *Do not attempt to force the piston past the cylinder ridge* (see above).

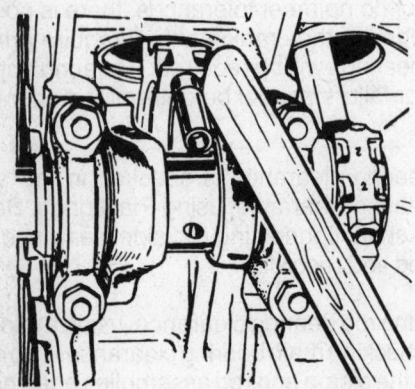

Removing the piston

CYLINDER BLOCK RECONDITIONING

Procedure	Method
Service the crankshaft:	Ensure that all oil holes and passages in the crankshaft are open and free of sludge. If necessary, have the crankshaft ground to the largest possible undersize. **Have the crankshaft Magnafluxed, to locate stress cracks. Consult a machinist concerning additional service procedures, such as surface hardening (e.g., nitriding, Tuftriding) to improve wear characteristics, cross drilling and chamfering the oil holes to improve lubrication, and balancing.
Removing freeze plugs:	Drill a small hole in the middle of the freeze plugs. Thread a large sheet metal screw into the hole and remove the plug with a slide hammer.
Remove the oil gallery plugs:	Threaded plugs should be removed using an appropriate (usually square) wrench. To remove soft, pressed in plugs, drill a hole in the plug, and thread in a sheet metal screw. Pull the plug out by the screw using pliers.
Hot-tank the block: NOTE: *Do not hot-tank aluminum parts.*	Have the block hot-tanked to remove grease, corrosion, and scale from the water jackets. NOTE: *Consult the operator to determine whether the camshaft bearings will be damaged during the hot-tank process.*

Check the block for cracks:	Visually inspect the block for cracks or chips. The most common locations are as follows:
	    Adjacent to freeze plugs.
	    Between the cylinders and water jackets.
	    Adjacent to the main bearing saddles.
	    At the extreme bottom of the cylinders.
	Check only suspected cracks using spot check dye (see introduction). If a crack is located, consult a machinist concerning possible repairs.
	
	**Magnaflux the block to locate hidden cracks. If cracks are located, consult a machinist about feasibility of repair.

Install the oil gallery plugs and freeze plugs:	Coat freeze plugs with sealer and tap into position using a piece of pipe, slightly smaller than the plug, as a driver. To ensure retention, stake the edges of the plugs. Coat threaded oil gallery plugs with sealer and install. Drive replacement soft plugs into block using a large drift as a driver. *Rather than reinstalling lead plugs, drill and tap the holes, and install threaded plugs.
*Check the deck height:	*The deck height is the distance from the crankshaft centerline to the block deck. To measure, invert the engine, and install the crankshaft, retaining it with the center main cap. Measure the distance from the crankshaft journal to the block deck, parallel to the cylinder centerline. Measure the diameter of the end (front and rear) main journals, parallel to the centerline of the cylinders, divide the diameter in half, and subtract it from the previous measurement. The results of the front and rear measurements should be identical. If the difference exceeds .005″, the deck height should be corrected. NOTE: *Block deck height and warpage should be corrected at the same time.*

CYLINDER BLOCK RECONDITIONING

Procedure	Method

Check the block deck for warpage:

Using a straightedge and feeler gauges, check the block deck for warpage in the same manner that the cylinder head is checked (see Cylinder Head Reconditioning). If warpage exceeds specifications, have the deck resurfaced.

NOTE: *In certain cases a specification for total material removal (Cylinder head and block deck) is provided. This specification must not be exceeded.*

Check the bore diameter and surface:

Measuring the cylinder bore with a dial gauge

Visually inspect the cylinder bores for roughness, scoring, or scuffing. If evident, the cylinder bore must be bored or honed oversize to eliminate imperfections, and the smallest possible oversize piston used. The new pistons should be given to the machinist with the block, so that the cylinders can be bored or honed exactly to the piston size (plus clearance). If no flaws are evident, measure the bore diameter using a telescope gauge and micrometer, or dial guage, parallel and perpendicular to the engine centerline, at the top (below the ridge) and bottom of the bore. Subtract the bottom measurements from the top to determine taper, and the parallel to the centerline measurements from the perpendicular measurements to determine eccentricity. If the measurements are not within specifications, the cylinder must be bored or honed, and an oversize piston installed. If the measurements are within specifications the cylinder may be used as is, with only finish honing (see below).

NOTE: *Prior to boring, check the block deck warpage, height and bearing alignment.*

CAUTION: *The 4 cyl. 140 G.M. engine cylinder walls are impregnated with silicone. Boring or honing can be done only by a shop with the proper equipment.*

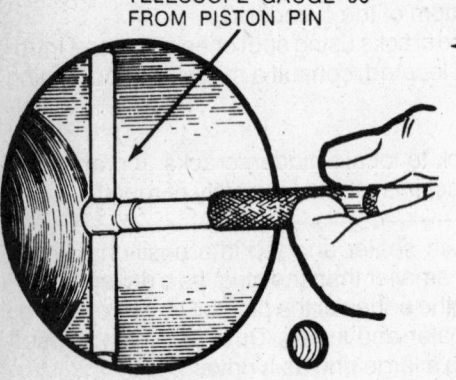

TELESCOPE GAUGE 90°
FROM PISTON PIN

Measuring cylinder bore with a telescope gauge

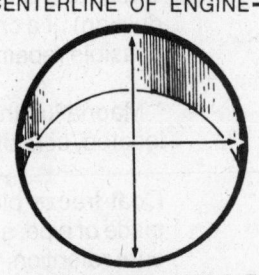

← CENTERLINE OF ENGINE →

A—AT RIGHT ANGLE TO
CENTERLINE OF ENGINE
B—PARALLEL TO
CENTERLINE OF ENGINE
Cylinder bore measuring points

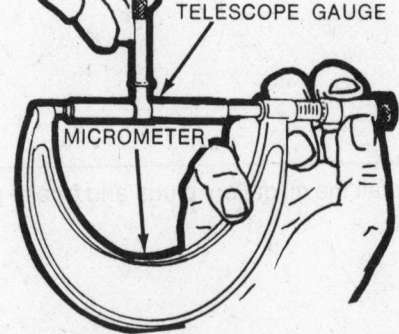

TELESCOPE GAUGE

MICROMETER

Determining cylinder bore by measuring telescope gauge with a micrometer

Check the cylinder block bearing alignment:

Checking main bearing saddle alignment

Remove the upper bearing inserts. Place a straightedge in the bearing saddles along the centerline of the crankshaft. If clearance exists between the straightedge and the center saddle, the block must be alignbored.

CYLINDER BLOCK RECONDITIONING

Procedure

Method

Clean and inspect the pistons and connecting rods:

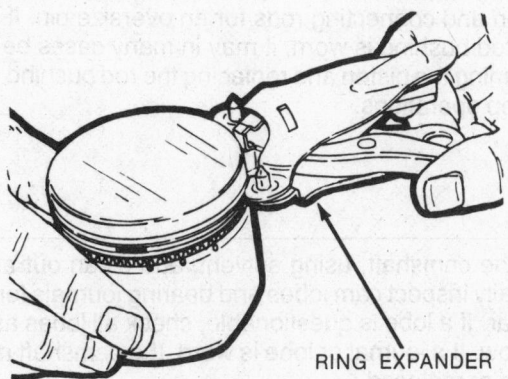

RING EXPANDER

Removing the piston rings

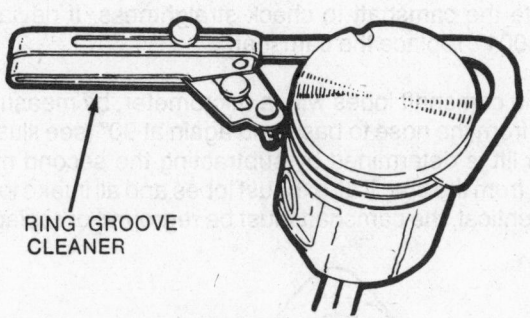

RING GROOVE
CLEANER

Cleaning the piston ring grooves

Using a ring expander, remove the rings from the piston. Remove the retaining rings (if so equipped) and remove piston pin.

NOTE: *If the piston pin must be pressed out, determine the proper method and use the proper tools; otherwise the piston will distort.*

Clean the ring grooves using an appropriate tool, exercising care to avoid cutting too deeply. Thoroughly clean all carbon and varnish from the piston with solvent.

CAUTION: *Do not use a wire brush or caustic solvent on pistons.*

Inspect the pistons for scuffing, scoring, cracks, pitting, or excessive ring groove wear. If wear is evident, the piston must be replaced. Check the connecting rod length by measuring the rod from the inside of the large end to the inside of the small end using calipers (see illustration). All connecting rods should be equal length. Replace any rod that differs from the others in the engine.

*Have the connecting rod alignment checked in an alignment fixture by a machinist. Replace any twisted or bent rods.

*Magnaflux the connecting rods to locate stress cracks. If cracks are found, replace the connecting rod.

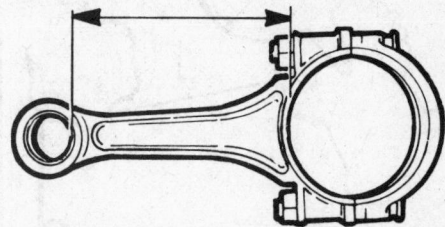

Check the connecting rod length (arrow)

Fit the pistons to the cylinders:

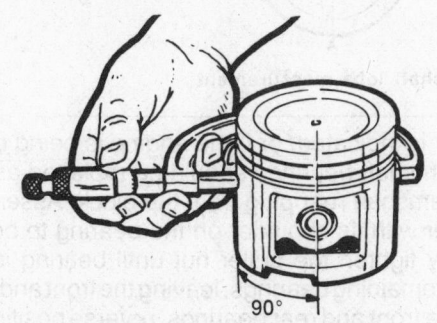

90°

Measuring the piston prior to fitting

Using a telescope gauge and micrometer, or a dial gauge, measure the cylinder bore diameter perpendicular to the piston pin, 2½° below the deck. Measure the piston perpendicular to its pin on the skirt. The difference between the two measurements is the piston clearance. If the clearance is within specifications or slightly below (after boring or honing), finish honing is all that is required. If the clearance is excessive, try to obtain a slightly larger piston to bring clearance within specifications. Where this is not possible, obtain the first oversize piston, and hone (or if necessary, bore) the cylinder to size.

Assemble the pistons and connecting rods:

Inspect piston pin, connecting rod small end bushing, and piston bore for galling, scoring, or excessive wear. If evident, replace defective part(s). Measure the I.D. of the piston boss and connecting rod small end, and the O.D. of the piston pin. If within specifications, assemble piston pin and rod.

CAUTION: *If piston pin must be pressed in, determine the proper method and use the proper tools; otherwise the piston will distort.*

CYLINDER BLOCK RECONDITIONING

Procedure	Method

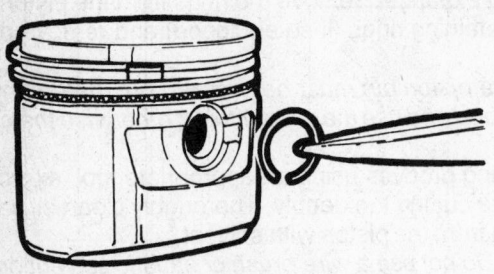

Installing piston pin lock rings

Install the lock rings; ensure that they seat properly. If the parts are not within specifications, determine the service method for the type of engine. In some cases, piston and pin are serviced as an assembly when either is defective. Others specify reaming the piston and connecting rods for an oversize pin. If the connecting rod bushing is worn, it may in many cases be replaced. Reaming the piston and replacing the rod bushing are machine shop operations.

Clean and inspect the camshaft:

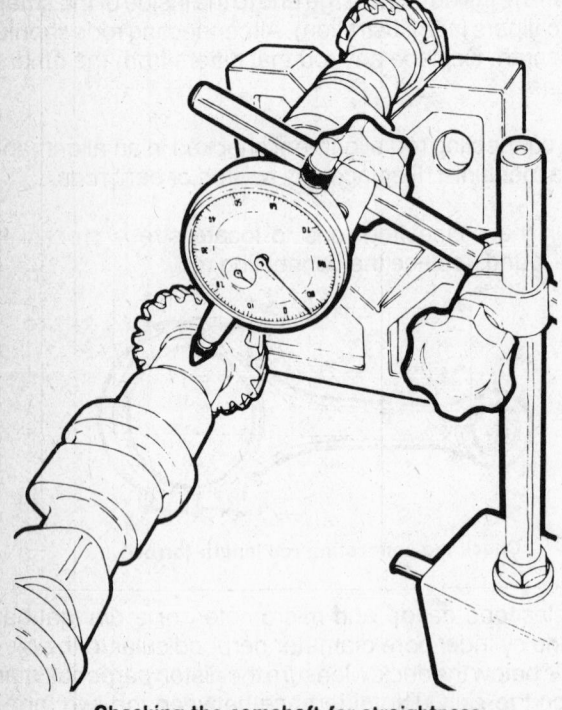

Checking the camshaft for straightness

Degrease the camshaft, using solvent, and clean out all oil holes. Visually inspect cam lobes and bearing journals for excessive wear. If a lobe is questionable, check all lobes as indicated below. If a journal or lobe is worn, the camshaft must be reground or replaced.
NOTE: *If a journal is worn, there is a good chance that the bushings are worn.*
If lobes and journals appear intact, place the front and rear journals in V-blocks, and rest a dial indicator on the center journal. Rotate the camshaft to check straightness. If deviation exceeds .001°, replace the camshaft.

*Check the camshaft lobes with a micrometer, by measuring the lobes from the nose to base and again at 90° (see illustration). The lift is determined by subtracting the second measurement from the first. If all exhaust lobes and all intake lobes are not identical, the camshaft must be reground or replaced.

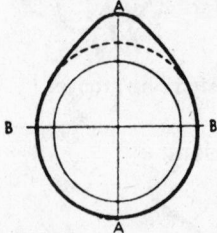

Camshaft lobe measurement

Replace the camshaft bearings (OHV engines only):

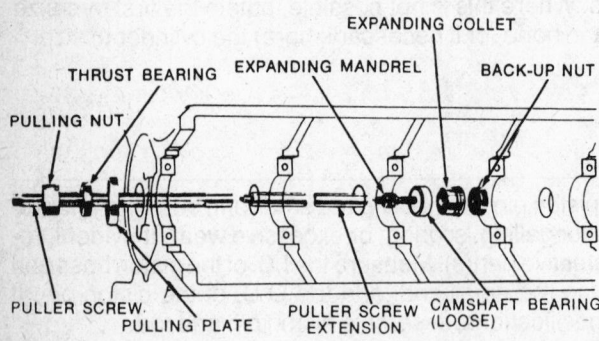

Camshaft removal and installation tool (typical)

If excessive wear is indicated, or if the engine is being completely rebuilt, camshaft bearings should be replaced as follows: Drive the camshaft rear plug from the block. Assemble the removal puller with its shoulder on the bearing to be removed. Gradually tighten the puller nut until bearing is removed. Remove remaining bearings, leaving the front and rear for last. To remove front and rear bearings, reverse position of the tool, so as to pull the bearings in toward the center of the block. Leave the tool in this position, pilot the new front and rear bearings on the installer, and pull them into position: Return the tool to its original position and pull remaining bearings into postion.
NOTE: *Ensure that oil holes align when installing bearings.*
Replace camshaft rear plug, and stake it into position to aid retention.

CYLINDER BLOCK RECONDITIONING

Procedure	Method

Finish hone the cylinders:

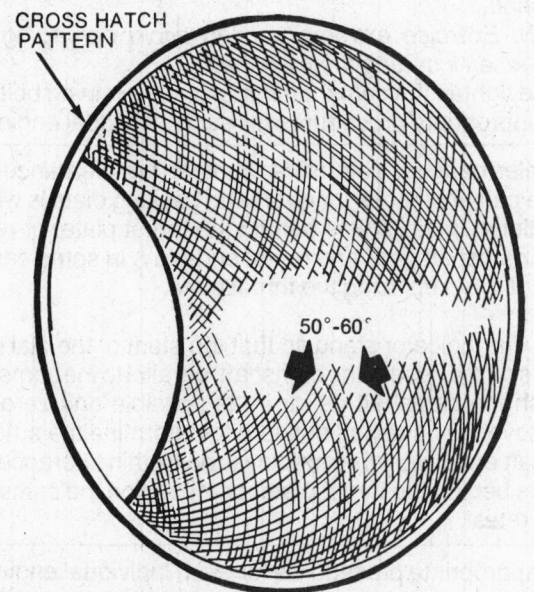

CROSS HATCH PATTERN

50°-60°

Chuck a flexible drive hone into a power drill, and insert it into the cylinder. Start the hone, and move it up and down the cylinder at a rate which will produce approximately a 60° cross-hatch pattern (see illustration).
NOTE: *Do not extend the hone below the cylinder bore.*
After developing the pattern, remove the hone and recheck piston fit. Wash the cylinders with a detergent and water solution to remove abrasive dust, dry, and wipe several times with a rag soaked in engine oil.

Check piston ring end-gap:

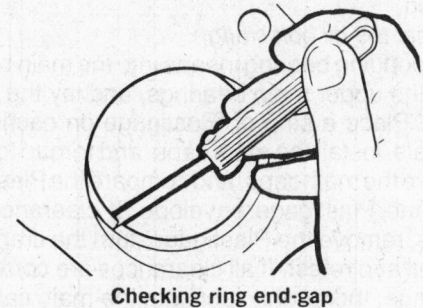

Checking ring end-gap

Compress the piston rings to be used in a cylinder, one at a time, into that cylinder, and press them approximately 1″ below the deck with an inverted piston. Using feeler gauges, measure the ring end-gap, and compare to specifications. Pull the ring out of the cylinder and file the ends with a fine file to obtain proper clearance.
CAUTION: *If inadequate ring end-gap is utilized, ring breakage will result.*

Install the piston rings:

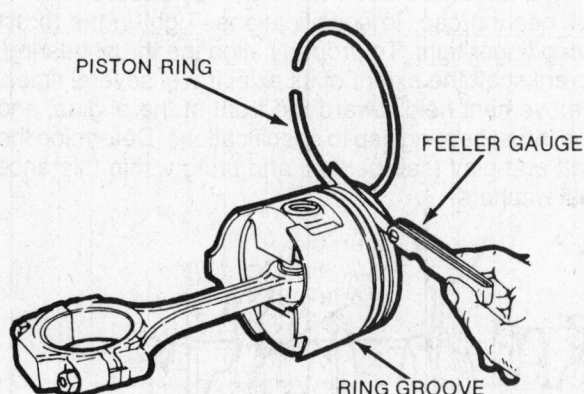

PISTON RING

FEELER GAUGE

RING GROOVE

Checking ring side clearance

Inspect the ring grooves in the piston for excessive wear or taper. If necessary, recut the groove(s) for use with an overwidth ring or a standard ring and spacer. If the groove is worn uniformly, overwidth rings, or standard rings and spacers may be installed without recutting. Roll the outside of the ring around the groove to check for burrs or deposits. If any are found, remove with a fine file. Hold the ring in the groove, and measure side clearance. If necessary, correct as indicated above.
NOTE: *Always install any additional spacers above the piston ring.*
The ring groove must be deep enough to allow the ring to seat below the lands (see illustration). In many cases, a "go-no-go" depth gauge will be provided with the piston rings. Shallow grooves may be corrected by recutting, while deep grooves require some type of filler or expander behind the piston. Consult the piston ring supplier concerning the suggested method. Install the rings on the piston, lowest ring first, using a ring expander.
NOTE: *Position the ring markings as specified by the manufacturer (see car section).*

CYLINDER BLOCK RECONDITIONING

Procedure	Method
Install the camshaft (OHV engines only):	Liberally lubricate the camshaft lobes and journals, and install the camshaft. CAUTION: *Exercise extreme care to avoid damaging the bearings when inserting the camshaft.* Install and tighten the camshaft thrust plate retaining bolts. See the appropriate procedures for each individual engine.
Check camshaft end-play (OHV engines only): 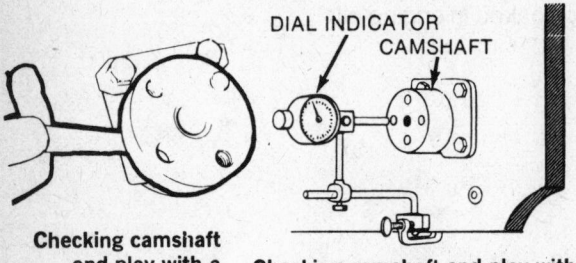 **Checking camshaft end-play with a feeler gauge** **Checking camshaft end-play with a dial indicator**	Using feeler gauges, determine whether the clearance between the camshaft boss (or gear) and backing plate is within specifications. Install shims behind the thrust plate, or reposition the camshaft gear and retest end-play. In some cases, adjustment is by replacing the thrust plate. *Mount a dial indicator stand so that the stem of the dial indicator rests on the nose of the camshaft, parallel to the camshaft axis. Push the camshaft as far in as possible and zero the gauge. Move the camshaft outward to determine the amount of camshaft endplay. If the endplay is not within tolerance, install shims behind the thrust plate, or reposition the camshaft gear and retest.
Install the rear main seal (where applicable):	See the appropriate procedures for each individual engine.
Install the crankshaft: 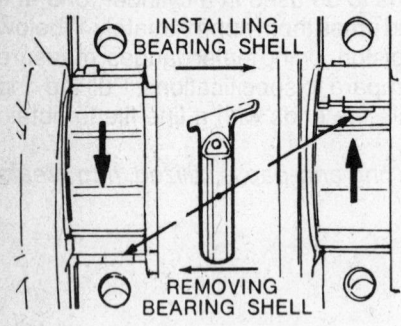 **Removal and installation of upper bearing insert using a roll-out pin** 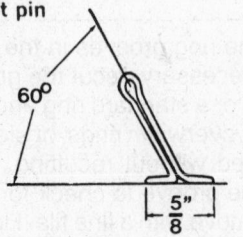 **Home-made bearing roll-out pin**	Thoroughly clean the main bearing saddles and caps. Place the upper halves of the bearing inserts on the saddles and press into position. NOTE: *Ensure that the oil holes align.* Press the corresponding bearing inserts into the main bearing caps. Lubricate the upper main bearings, and lay the crankshaft in position. Place a strip of Plastigage on each of the crankshaft journals, install the main caps, and torque to specifications. Remove the main caps, and compare the Plastigage to the scale on the Plastigage envelope. If clearances are within tolerances, remove the Plastigage, turn the crankshaft 90°, wipe off all oil and retest. If all clearances are correct, remove all Plastigage, thoroughly lubricate the main caps and bearing journals, and install the main caps. If clearances are not within tolerance, the upper bearing inserts may be removed, without removing the crankshaft, using a bearing roll out pin (see illustration). Roll in a bearing that will provide proper clearance, and retest. Torque all main caps, excluding the thrust bearing cap, to specifications. Tighten the thrust bearing cap finger tight. To properly align the thrust bearing, pry the crankshaft the extent of its axial travel several times, the last movement held toward the front of the engine, and torque the thrust bearing cap to specifications. Determine the crankshaft end-play (see below), and bring within tolerance with thrust washers.

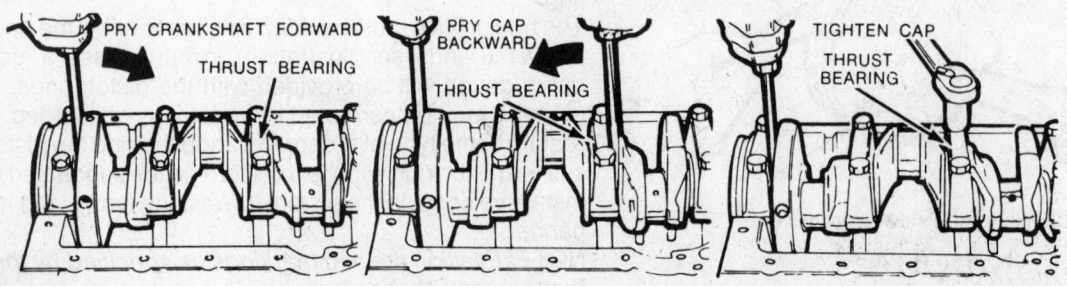

Aligning the thrust bearing

CYLINDER BLOCK RECONDITIONING

Procedure

Method

Measure crankshaft end-play:

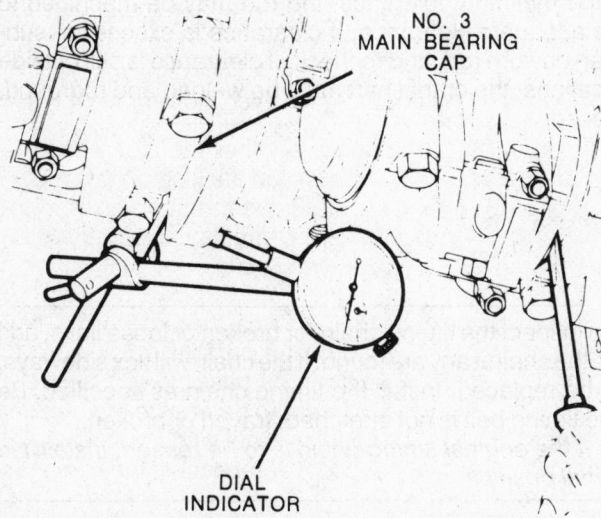

NO. 3
MAIN BEARING
CAP

DIAL
INDICATOR

Checking crankshaft end-play with a dial indicator

Mount a dial indicator stand on the front of the block, with the dial indicator stem resting on the nose of the crankshaft, parallel to the crankshaft axis. Pry the crankshaft the extent of its travel rearward, and zero the indicator. Pry the crankshaft forward and record crankshaft end-play.

NOTE: *Crankshaft end-play also may be measured at the thrust bearing, using feeler gauges* (see illustration).

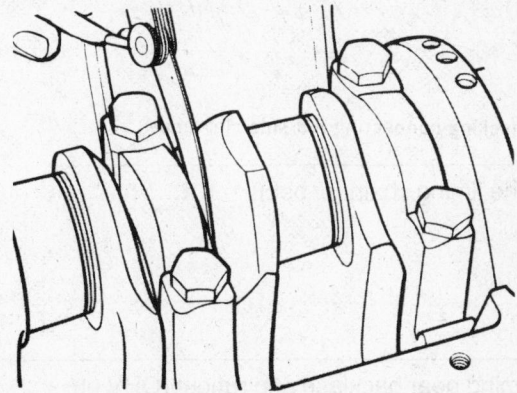

Checking crankshaft end-play with a feeler gauge

Install the pistons:

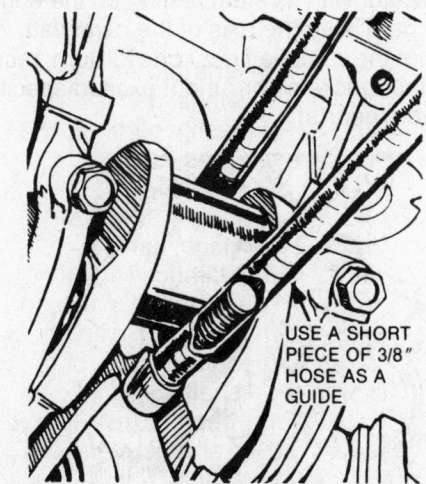

USE A SHORT
PIECE OF 3/8″
HOSE AS A
GUIDE

Tubing used to protect crankshaft journals and cylinder walls during piston installation

Press the upper connecting rod bearing halves into the connecting rods, and the lower halves into the connecting rod caps. Position the piston ring gaps according to specifications (see car section), and lubricate the pistons. Install a ring compressor on a piston, and press two long (8″) pieces of plastic tubing over the rod bolts. Using the tubes as a guide, press the pistons into the bores and onto the crankshaft with a wooden hammer handle. After seating the rod on the crankshaft journal, remove the tubes and install the cap finger tight. Install the remaining pistons in the same manner. Invert the engine and check the bearing clearance at two points (90° apart) on each journal with Plastigage.

NOTE: *Do not turn the crankshaft with Plastigage installed.* If clearance is within tolerances, remove *all* Plastigage, thoroughly lubricate the journals, and torque the rod caps to specifications. If clearance is not within specifications, install different thickness bearing inserts and recheck.

CAUTION: *Never shim or file the connecting rods or caps.* Always install plastic tube sleeves over the rod bolts when the caps are not installed, to protect the crankshaft journals.

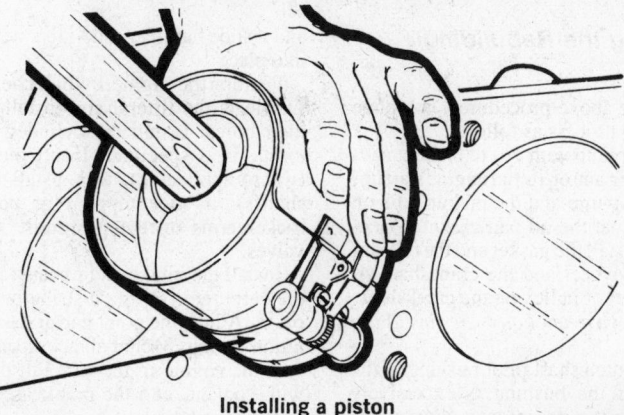

RING COMPRESSOR

Installing a piston

CYLINDER BLOCK RECONDITIONING

Procedure	Method
Check connecting rod side clearance: 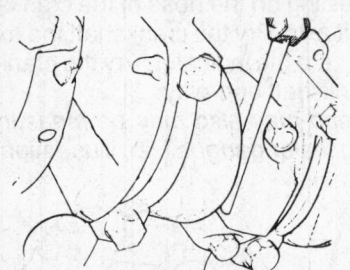 Checking connecting rod side clearance	Determine the clearance between the sides of the connecting rods and the crankshaft, using feeler gauges. If clearance is below the minimum tolerance, the rod may be machined to provide adequate clearance. If clearance is excessive, substitute an unworn rod, and recheck. If clearance is still outside specifications, the crankshaft must be welded and reground, or replaced.
Inspect the timing chain (or belt):	Visually inspect the timing chain for broken or loose links, and replace the chain if any are found. If the chain will flex sideways, it must be replaced. Install the timing chain as specified. Be sure the timing belt is not stretched, frayed or broken. NOTE: *If the original timing chain is to be reused, install it in its original position.*
Check timing gear backlash and runout (OHV engines): 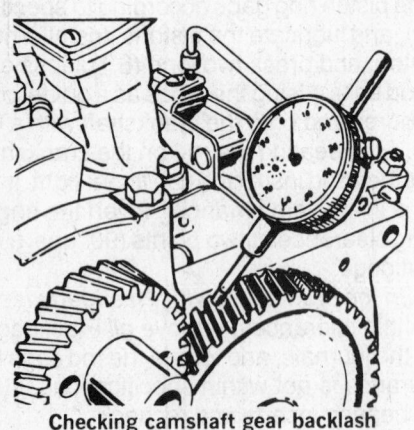 Checking camshaft gear backlash	Mount a dial indicator with its stem resting on a tooth of the camshaft gear (as illustrated). Rotate the gear until all slack is removed, and zero the indicator. Rotate the gear in the opposite direction until slack is removed, and record gear backlash. Mount the indicator with its stem resting on the edge of the camshaft gear, parallel to the axis of the camshaft. Zero the indicator, and turn the camshaft gear one full turn, recording the runout. If either backlash or runout exceed specifications, replace the worn gear(s). 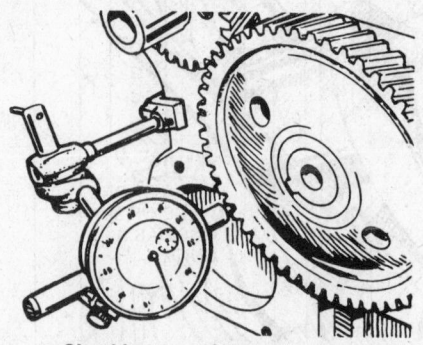 Checking camshaft gear runout

Completing the Rebuilding Process

Following the above procedures, complete the rebuilding process as follows:

Fill the oil pump with oil, to prevent cavitating (sucking air) on initial engine start up. Install the oil pump and the pickup tube on the engine. Coat the oil pan gasket as necessary, and install the gasket and the oil pan. Mount the flywheel and the crankshaft vibration damper or pulley on the crankshaft. NOTE: *Always use new bolts when installing the flywheel.*

Inspect the clutch shaft pilot bushing in the crankshaft. If the bushing is excessively worn, remove it with an expanding puller and a slide hammer, and tap a new bushing into place.

Position the engine, cylinder head side up. Lubricate the lifters, and install them into their bores. Install the cylinder head, and torque it as specified. Insert the pushrods (where applicable), and install the rocker shaft(s) (if so equipped) or position the rocker arms on the pushrods. Adjust the valves.

Install the intake and exhaust manifolds, the carburetor(s), the distributor and spark plugs. Adjust the point gap and the static ignition timing. Mount all accessories and install the engine in the car. Fill the radiator with coolant, and the crankcase with high quality engine oil.

Break-in Procedure

Start the engine, and allow it to run at low speed for a few minutes, while checking for leaks. Stop the engine, check the oil level, and fill as necessary. Restart the engine, and fill the cooling system to capacity. Check the point dwell angle and adjust the ignition timing and the valves. Run the engine at low to medium speed (800–2500 rpm) for approximately ½ hour, and retorque the cylinder head bolts. Road test the car, and check again for leaks.

Follow the manufacturer's recommended engine break-in procedure and maintenance schedule for new engines.

Automatic Transmission **39**

AUTOMATIC TRANSMISSION APPLICATION CHART

| Make | Vehicle | | | Transmission | | |
	Year	Model		Model	Speeds	Page
AMC/Chrysler	1982–89	AMC, Chrysler RWD		A904, A998, A999, 727	3	39–4
Ford	1982–89	Continental, Town Car, Crown Victoria, Cougar, XR7, LTD, Marquis, Thunderbird, Mark VI, Mark VII, Mustang, Capri		AOD	4	39–9
	1982–89	Capri, Cougar, XR7, Fairmont, Granada, Mustang, Thunderbird, Zephyr, LTD, Marquis		C3	3	39–11
				AOD	4	39–9
	1982–89	Capri, Mustang, Fairmont, Cougar, XR7, Zephyr, LTD, Marquis, Thunderbird		C5	3	39–13
				C6	3	39–14
				A4LD	3	39–16
	1984½-85	Mark VII, Continental with Diesel Engines		ZF 4HP-22	3	39–15
General Motors	1982–87	Chevette, Pontiac 1000		THM 180C	3	39–19
	1982–89	Caprice, Camaro, Century, Chevette, Chevette Diesel, Cutlass, Electra, El Camino, Grand Prix Impala, LeSabre, Malibu, Monte Carlo, Regal, Regal Diesel		THM 200C	3	39–19
	1982–89	Brougham, Deville, Deville Diesel		THM 200-4R	4	39–21
	1982–89	Electra, Electra Diesel, LeSabre, Regal Turbo		THM 200-4R	4	39–21
	1983–85	88, 98, Hurst Olds 88, 98 Diesel, Parisienne Diesel		THM 200-4R	4	39–21
	1983–85	Impala, LeSabre, Regal Caprice, Malibu, Monte Carlo, Delta 88, Cutlass, Bonneville, Grand Prix		THM 250C	4	39–21

AUTOMATIC TRANSMISSION APPLICATION CHART

| Make | Vehicle | | Transmission | | |
	Year	Model	Model	Speeds	Page
	1982–84	Bonneville, Grand Prix,	THM 350C	3	39–23
		LeSabre, Parisienne	THM 400	3	39–25
	1983–85	Caprice, Impala, Malibu, Monte Carlo, Delta 88, Cutlass	THM 350C	3	39–23
	1983–89	Camaro, Caprice, Corvette, Firebird, Impala	THM 700-R4	4	39–25

AUTOMATIC TRANSAXLE APPLICATION CHART

| Make | Vehicle | | Transmission | | |
	Year	Model	Model	Speeds	Page
Chrysler	1982–89	FWD	A-404, A-413, A-415, A-470	3	39–8
Ford	1982–89	Escort, EXP, Lynx, LN7, Tempo, Topaz	ATX	3	39–17
	1986–89	Taurus, Sable	AXOD	4	39–18
General Motors	1982–89	A-Body, X-Body, J-Body, N-Body	THM 125C	3	39–26
	1981–85	E-Body, K-Body	THM 325-4L	4	39–27
	1984–89	C-Body, N-Body	THM 440-T4	3	39–28
	1985–89	S-Body (Nova)	A131L	3	39–28
			A240E	4	39–28
	1985–89	R-Body (Spectrum)	KF100	3	39–28

TRANSMISSION IDENTIFICATION BY PAN GASKET

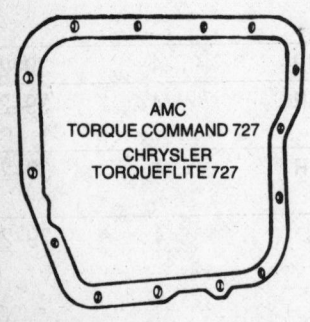

AMC
TORQUE COMMAND 727
CHRYSLER
TORQUEFLITE 727

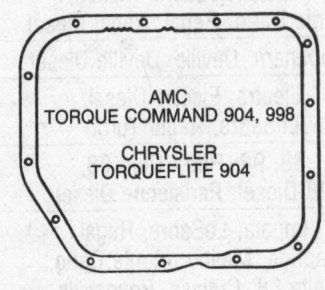

AMC
TORQUE COMMAND 904, 998
CHRYSLER
TORQUEFLITE 904

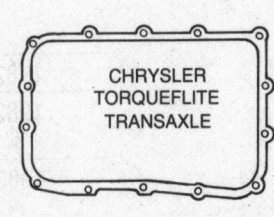

CHRYSLER
TORQUEFLITE
TRANSAXLE

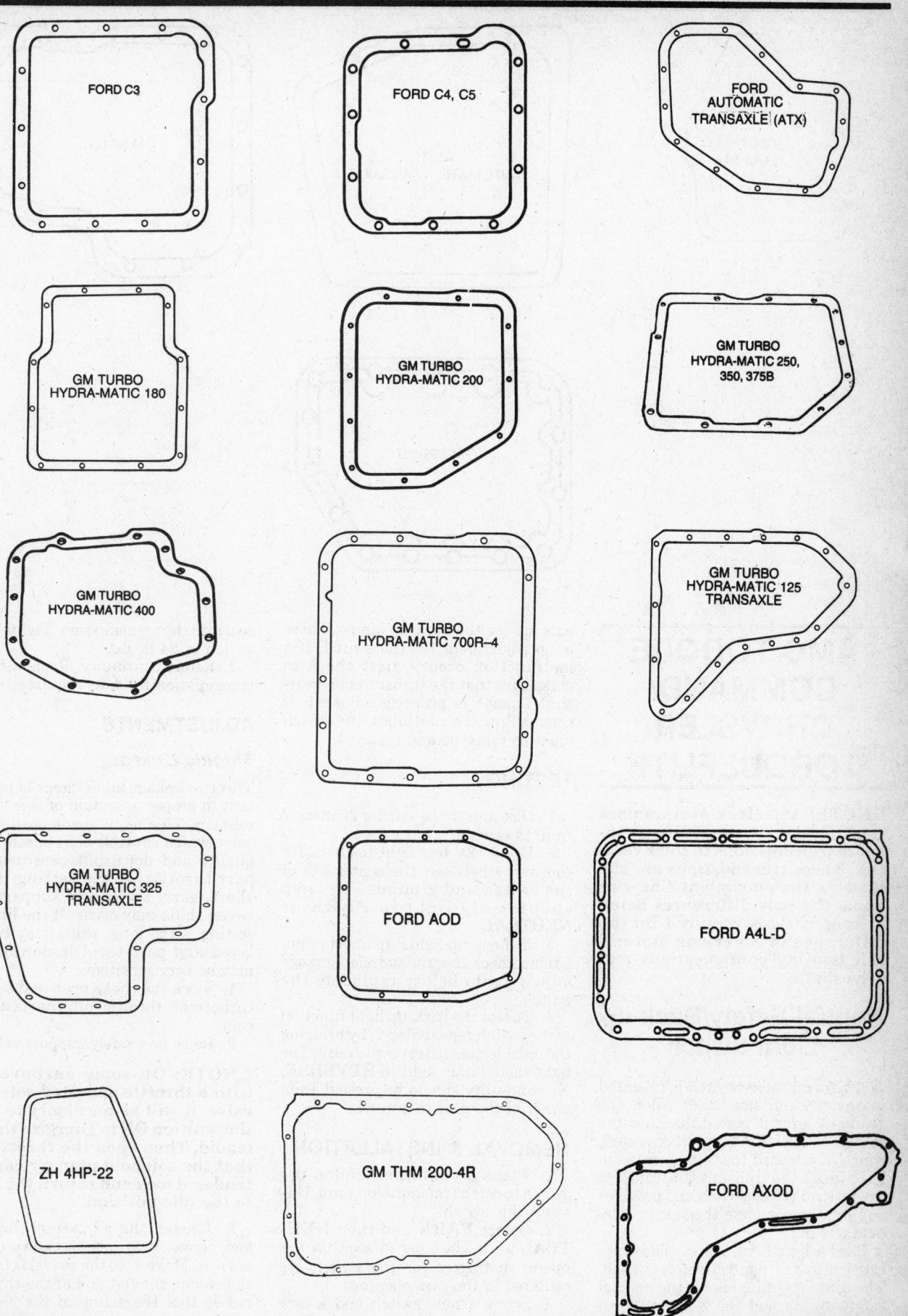

FORD C3

FORD C4, C5

FORD AUTOMATIC TRANSAXLE (ATX)

GM TURBO HYDRA-MATIC 180

GM TURBO HYDRA-MATIC 200

GM TURBO HYDRA-MATIC 250, 350, 375B

GM TURBO HYDRA-MATIC 400

GM TURBO HYDRA-MATIC 700R–4

GM TURBO HYDRA-MATIC 125 TRANSAXLE

GM TURBO HYDRA-MATIC 325 TRANSAXLE

FORD AOD

FORD A4L-D

ZH 4HP-22

GM THM 200-4R

FORD AXOD

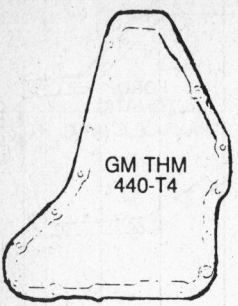

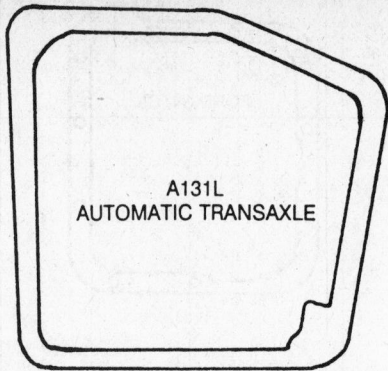

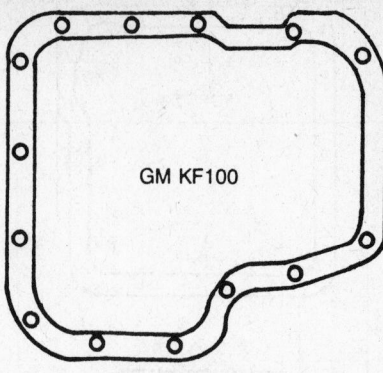

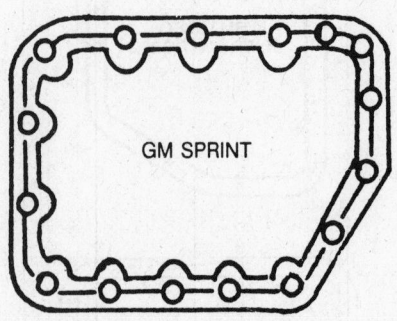

AMC TORQUE COMMAND/ CHRYSLER TORQUEFLITE

NOTE: American Motors uses the Chrysler TorqueFlite automatic transmissions in their vehicles. These transmissions are the same as the equivalent Chrysler units, the only differences being in case designs required by the difference in American Motors' bell housing configurations and driveshafts.

Neutral Safety/Back-up Light Switch

The Neutral safety switch is mounted in the transmission case. When the gearshift lever is placed in either the **PARK** or **NEUTRAL** position a cam, which is attached to the transmission lever inside the transmission, contacts the neutral safety switch and provides a ground to complete the starter solenoid circuit.

The back-up lamp switch is incorporated into the neutral safety switch. The center terminal is for the neutral safety switch and the 2 outer termi-

nals are for the back-up lamps. There is no adjustment for the switch. If a malfunction occurs, first check to make sure that the transmission gearshift linkage is properly adjusted. If the malfunction continues, the switch must be removed and replaced.

TESTING

1. Disconnect the wiring connector from the switch.
2. Use a 12V test light to check for continuity between the center pin of the switch and ground. The lamp should only light in **PARK** or **NEUTRAL**.
3. If the lamp lights up in other positions, check the transmission linkage adjustments before replacing the switch.
4. To test the back-up light function of the switch repeat Step 2, by bridging the outside pins to test continuity. The light should only light in **REVERSE**. No continuity should be present from either of the pins to ground.

REMOVAL & INSTALLATION

1. Place a container under the switch to catch transmission fluid. Unscrew the switch.
2. Select **PARK** and then **NEUTRAL** while checking to see that the operation fingers for the switch are centered in the case opening.
3. Screw a new switch and a new

seal into the transmission. Tighten the switch to 24 ft. lbs.
4. Retest continuity. Replenish the transmission fluid, as required.

ADJUSTMENTS

Throttle Linkage

Throttle linkage adjustment is important to proper operation of this transmission. This adjustment positions a valve which controls shift speed, shift quality and downshift sensitivity at part throttle. If the setting is too short, early shifts and slippage between shifts may occur. If the linkage setting is too long, shifts may be delayed and part throttle downshifts may be very sensitive.

1. Block the choke open and set the carburetor throttle off the fast idle cam.
2. Raise and safely support vehicle.

NOTE: On some carburetors with a throttle operated solenoid valve, it will be necessary to turn the ignition ON to energize the solenoid. Then open the throttle so that the solenoid plunger can extend and lock and return the carb to the idle position.

3. Loosen the adjustment swivel lock screw. It is not necessary to remove it. Make sure the swivel is free to slide along the flat end of the throttle rod so that the action of the preload

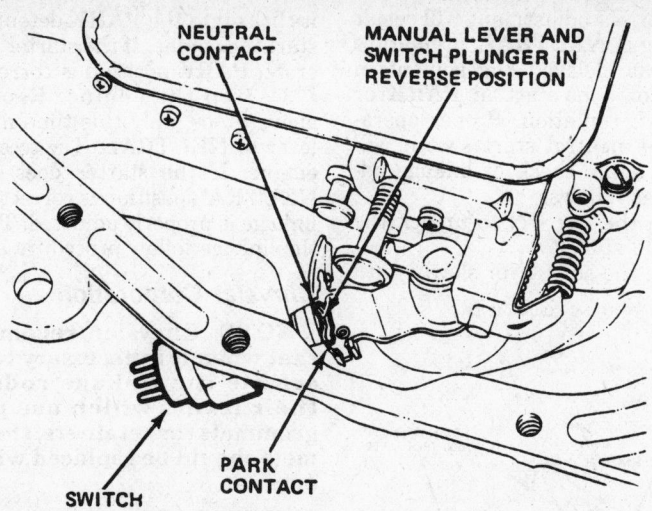

Torque-Command and TorqueFlite neutral start and backup light switch; pan removed, looking up

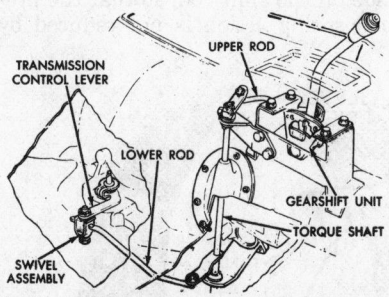

Typical automatic console shift linkage

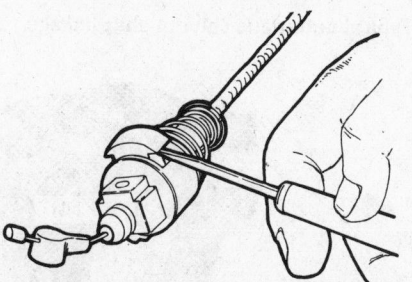

Throttle cable used with the AMC 151 engine. The snap-lock is shown in the raised (unlocked) position.

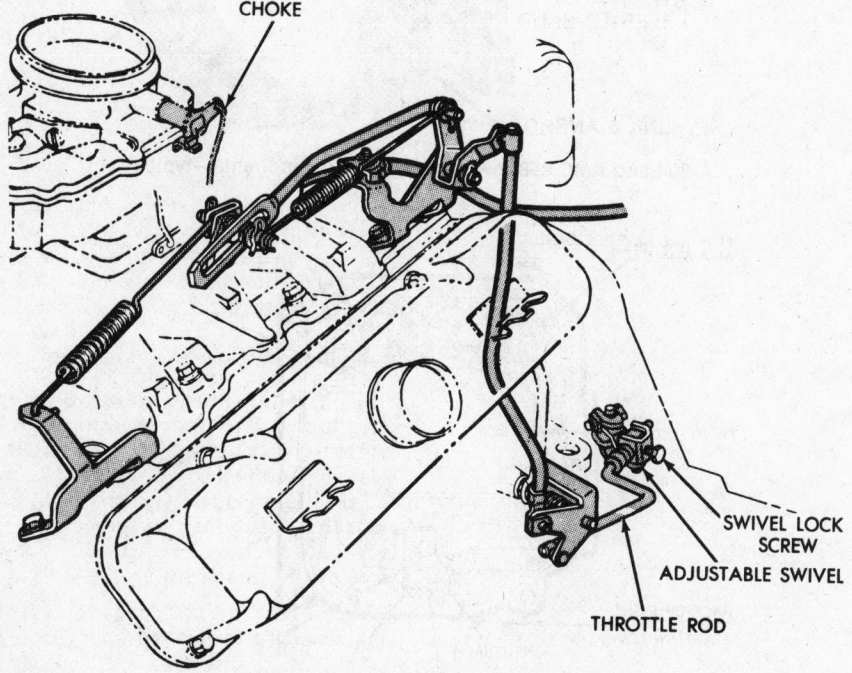

V8 throttle rod adjustment—6 cyl. similar

spring is in no way restricted. If necessary, disassemble and clean parts in solvent so action is free.

NOTE: Make sure to note proper assembly sequence as you take the mechanism apart, as improper assembly could prove dangerous.

4. Hold the transmission lever forward against its internal stop, then tighten the lock screw. If possible, use an inch pound torque wrench and torque to 100 inch lbs.

5. Restore freedom to the choke linkage if it has been blocked. Test the freedom of operation of the linkage by moving the throttle rod rearward and then slowly releasing it. Confirm that it will return fully forward.

Throttle Cable

1982–85 4 CYLINDER ENGINE

1. Remove the air cleaner assembly.
2. Remove the spark plug wire separator from the throttle cable bracket and move the separator and wires aside.
3. Raise and safely support the vehicle.
4. Remove the strut rod bushing heat shield to gain access to the transmission throttle control lever.
5. Hold the throttle lever rearward against its stop. Use the spare spring to hold the lever. Hook one end of spring to the lever and hook the opposite end of the spring to a convenient attachment point.
6. Lower the vehicle.
7. Block the choke open and set the carburetor linkage completely off the fast idle cam.
8. On 4 cylinder vehicles without air conditioning; turn the ignition key to the **ON** position to energize the throttle stop solenoid.
9. Unlock the throttle control cable by releasing the T-shaped cable adjuster clamp. Release the clamp by lifting upward with a small screwdriver.
10. Grasp the cable outer sheath and move the cable and sheath forward to remove any cable load on the throttle bellcrank.

NOTE: The bell crank is part of the carburetor throttle linkage.

11. Adjust the cable by moving the cable and sheath rearward until there is 0 lash between the plastic cable end and the bellcrank ball.
12. When 0 lash between the cable end and bellcrank is achieved, lock the cable by pressing the T-shaped cable adjuster clamp downward until the clamp snaps into place.
13. Turn the ignition **OFF**. Install the spark plug wires and separator,

connect the throttle stop solenoid on air conditioned vehicles and install the air cleaner.

14. Remove the holding spring from the transmission throttle control lever. Install the strut rod bushing heat shield and lower the vehicle.

15. Road test the vehicle and check the transmission operation. Readjust the throttle cable if necessary.

NOTE: Some V8 cars use a slightly different arrangement, in that the adjusting link is pushed instead of pulled to remove the slack. However, the end result should be the same, and no slack or lash should be permitted. Many Chrysler Corp. vehicles use a lower bellcrank with a short throttle rod and adjustable swivel to hook up to the transmission throttle lever. In these cases, make sure the swivel is free to slide along the throttle rod so that the small preload spring action is not impaired. If necessary, clean and lightly lubricate. Again, the throttle lever must be held firmly forward against its internal stop. In this case, the linkage slack, or backlash was automatically removed by the small preload spring.

1986–89 4 CYLINDER ENGINE

1. Either run the engine until it is hot and verify that the fast idle cam has no effect on idle speed or disconnect the choke mechanism so the throttle will be at the normal hot idle position.

2. Loosen the locking screw that fastens the cable mounting bracket in place. Position the bracket so that both of its alignment tabs touch the case surface of the transaxle. Hold it in this position and then torque the mounting screw to 104 inch lbs.

3. Release the cross lock on the cable housing by pulling it upward. Make sure the cable is free to slide all the way toward the engine against its stop. Then, move the transaxle throttle lever all the way clockwise so it is against its internal stop, and then press the cross-lock downward into the locked position.

4. Reconnect the choke, if it was disconnected. Test the freedom of operation of the cable as follows: Move the transaxle throttle lever forward and then slowly release it. It should return fully rearward. Do not lubricate any parts of the mechanism.

Gear Shift Linkage

The gear shift linkage adjustment is important because the linkage positions the manual valve in the valve body. Incorrect adjustment will result in creeping in **NEUTRAL**, premature clutch wear, delayed engagement in any gear or a no-start in **PARK** or **NEUTRAL** condition. Proper operation of the neutral start switch will provide a quick check of linkage adjustment as follows:

1. Turn the key **ON** to unlock the column and shift lever.

2. Move the shift lever slowly until

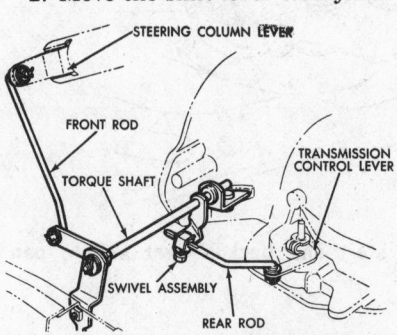

Typical automatic column shift linkage

it clicks into the **PARK** detent. Try to start the engine. If the starter does operate, **PARK** position is correct.

3. Stop the engine. Repeat the above Steps, only this time move the lever to **NEUTRAL**. Try to start the engine. If the starter does operate, **NEUTRAL** position is correct and the linkage is properly adjusted. To adjust the linkage follow procedure below.

Chrysler Corporation

NOTE: Chrysler recommends that when it is necessary to disassemble the linkage rods from their levers which use plastic grommets for retainers, the grommets should be replaced with new ones.

COLUMN SHIFT

1. Make sure all of the linkage moves freely, especially the adjustable slide on the shift rod, so that the preload spring action is not reduced by

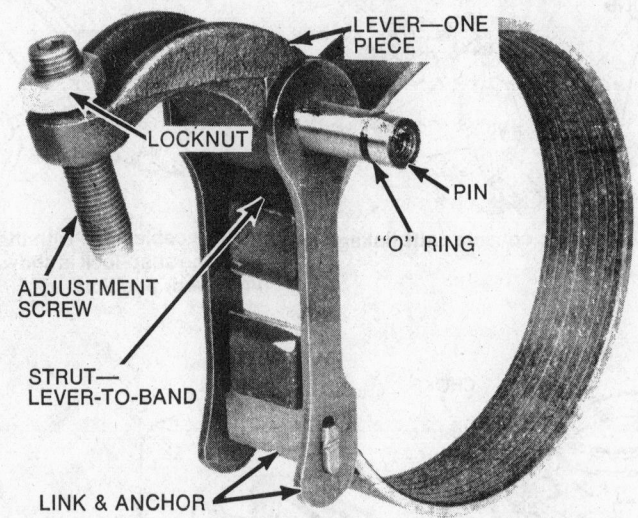

A-904 and AMC 998 low-reverse band components—typical

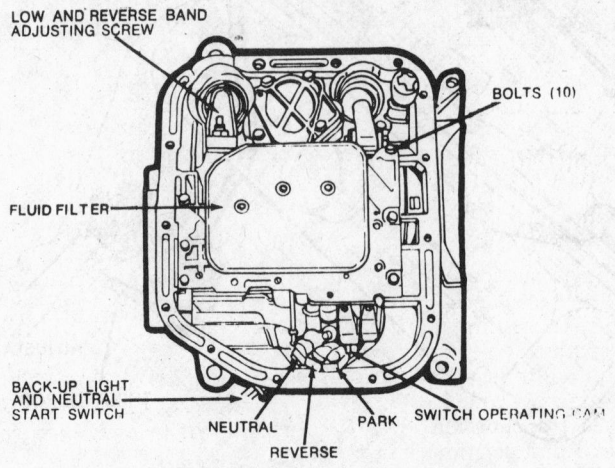

Low and reverse band adjusting screw location

BAND ADJUSTMENT SPECIFICATIONS
AMC Torque Command

Year	Band	Engine and Transmission Models				
		2.0L/904	2.5L/904	232 cid/904	258 cid/Std. 904	304 cid/998
1982–89	Front Band①	–	2.5	–	2.5	2.5
	Rear Band①	–	7②	–	7	4

NOTE: Numbers represent back-off turns from specified torque. Torque locknut to 35 ft. lbs. when adjustment is completed
① Backed off from 72 inch lbs.
② Backed off from 41 inch lbs.

BAND ADJUSTMENT SPECIFICATIONS
Chrysler Corporation TorqueFlite

		Engine and Transmission Numbers						
		A904		A904-LA				A727
					360-2 bbl		360-2 bbl	
Year	Band	225	225	318	360-4 bbl	318	360-4 bbl	360 HP
1982-89	Front Band①	2.5③	–	2.5③	–	2.5	–	–
	Rear Band	7②③	–	4③	–	2	–	–

NOTE: Numbers represent back-off turns from specified torque. Torque lock-nut to 35 ft. lbs. when adjustment is completed
① Backed off from 72 inch lbs. torque
② Backed off from 41 inch lbs. torque
③ With wideration gears

friction. Disassemble, clean and lube if necessary.

2. Put the shift lever in **PARK**.

3. With the adjustable swivel loose, move the shift lever all the way to the rear-most detent position, which is **PARK**.

4. Tighten the swivel lock bolt. Torque it to 90 inch lbs.

5. Verify that the vehicle will only start in **PARK** or **NEUTRAL**.

CONSOLE SHIFT

1. Adjustment is similar to above, but no preload spring is used. Make sure that with the shift handle in **PARK**, the transmission lever is in the rear-most detent position, which is **PARK**.

2. Tighten the swivel lock bolt with no load applied in either direction on the linkage.

3. Verify that the vehicle will only start in **PARK** or **NEUTRAL**.

American Motors

1. From under car, loosen the nuts on the trunnions (swivels).

2. Disengage the trunnion and shift rod at the bellcrank.

3. Place the shift lever in **PARK** and lock the steering column.

4. Move the transmission lever to the rear-most detent position, which is **PARK**.

5. Eliminate the backlash by pulling downward on the shiftrod and pressing upward on the outer bellcrank.

6. Adjust the trunnion on the shift rod to be a free fit into bellcrank arm, then tighten the jamnuts, making sure that the shift rod does not turn while tightening nuts.

7. Verify that the vehicle will only start in **PARK** or **NEUTRAL**.

ADJUSTMENTS

Bands

KICKDOWN (FRONT) BAND

The kickdown band adjusting screw is located on the left side of the transmission case above the throttle and shift linkage levers. On 4wd AMC models, it may be necessary to remove the front axle driveshaft to gain proper access to the adjusting screw and locknut.

1. Raise and safely support the front of the vehicle. Loosen the locknut and back off about 5 turns. Be sure the adjusting screw is free in the case.

2. Use a torque wrench and 5/16 inch square socket, to tighten the adjusting screw to exactly 72 inch lbs.

3. Back off the adjusting screw exactly to specification. Hold the adjusting screw so that it does not turn and tighten the locknut to 35 ft. lbs.

REAR BAND

The rear band adjustment is an inside adjustment so the pan must be removed.

1. Raise and safely support the vehicle.

2. Remove the oil pan and drain the fluid.

3. Look carefully at the fluid, filter and pan bottom for a heavy accumulation of friction material or metal particles. A little accumulation can be considered normal, but a heavy concentration indicates damaged or worn parts.

4. Adjust the band by loosening the locknut, then tightening adjusting screw to the specified torque, using a small torque wrench and a ¼ in. hex head socket.

5. Back off the adjusting screw to the specified amount of turns. Refer to the specification chart.

6. Install the locknut, tighten to 35 ft. lbs. making sure adjusting screw does not turn.

NOTE: Install a new transmission filter. Torque the 3 screws to 35 inch lbs.

7. Using a new gasket on the pan, install and torque bolts evenly to 150 inch lbs.

8. Lower the vehicle and fill the transmission with the specified amount of Dexron® II type fluid.

Oil Pan

REMOVAL & INSTALLATION

No fluid or filter changes are required for the life of the car if it is used in normal service. Severe service (trailer towing, commercial use, police or taxi use) requires a fluid and filter change every 15,000 miles for Chrysler cars, or every 25,000 miles for AMC cars (refer to your owners manual). Band adjustments should be performed at the same intervals for cars used in severe service.

1. Drive the car until the transmission fluid is at normal operating temperature. Raise and safely support the vehicle.

2. Unbolt the pan. Be ready with a large container to catch the fluid.

NOTE: If the fluid smells burnt or is discolored, serious transmission troubles should be suspected.

3. When the fluid is drained, remove the pan.

4. Unscrew and discard the filter.

5. Install a new filter. The proper torque is 28 inch lbs. for AMC, or 35 inch lbs. for Chrysler.

6. Clean out the pan, being extremely careful not to leave any lint from rags inside.

7. Replace the pan gasket. Tighten the pan bolts to 10–12 ft. lbs. in a criss-cross pattern.

8. It is a good idea to measure the amount of fluid drained from the transmission, because some fluid will remain inside. Initially pour 3 quarts of Dexron® II automatic transmission fluid through the dipstick tube.

9. Start the engine in **NEUTRAL** and allow it to idle for 2 minutes. Do not race the engine. Set the parking brake and shift through each position slowly, then move the lever to **PARK**. Add fluid as necessary until correct level is reached.

CHRYSLER CORPORATION

NOTE: Chrysler recommends that when it is necessary to disassemble the linkage rods from their levers which use plastic grommets for retainers, the grommets should be replaced with new ones.

A–404 Automatic Transaxle

ADJUSTMENTS

Gear Shift Linkage

CONSOLE SHIFT

1. Put the gearshift into the **PARK** position.

2. Loosen the clamp bolt on the gearshift cable bracket. Then, pull the shift lever all the way to the front detent position. Tighten the lock bolt to 90 inch lbs.

3. Check the adjustment by making sure that: the detent positions for **NEUTRAL** and drive correspond with the stops for the lever gate; and that the starter will operate only with the shift lever in **PARK** and **NEUTRAL** positions.

Band

KICKDOWN (FRONT) BAND

The kickdown band (front band) has its adjusting screw located on the top front (left side) of the transaxle case. Adjustment is as follows:

1. Loosen the locknut and back off about 5 turns.

2. Tighten the adjusting screw to 72 inch lbs..

3. Back off adjusting screw 3 turns for 1982–89 models, from the 72 inch lbs. torque, then hold this position and tighten the lock nut to 35 ft. lbs.

LOW-REVERSE (REAR) BAND

The low-reverse band (rear band) is not adjustable in this unit. The band lining itself needs to be inspected to determine the need for replacement. The grooves must be no less than 0.008 in. (0.2mm) deep at any point to still be usable. With a 100 pound force applied to band around drum, the end gap must not be less than 0.020 in. (0.5mm).

Torqueflite Automatic Transaxle A–413, A–415 and A–470

ADJUSTMENTS

Gear Shift Linkage

CONSOLE SHIFT

1. Put the gearshift into the **PARK** position.

2. Loosen the clamp bolt on the gearshift cable bracket. Then, pull the shift lever all the way to the front detent position. Tighten the lock bolt to 90 inch lbs.

3. Check the adjustment by making sure that: the detent positions for **NEUTRAL** and drive correspond with the stops for the lever gate; and that the starter will operate only with the shift lever in **PARK** and **NEUTRAL** positions.

Throttle Cable

Bring engine to operating temperature and be sure the carburetor is off fast idle. Check idle speed with tachometer. Disconnect choke if necessary to keep carburetor off fast idle.

1. Loosen the adjustment bracket lock screw. The bracket must be free to slide on its slot. If necessary, disassemble and clean or repair. Lube with a good quality light grease.

2. Hold the transaxle throttle lever firmly rearward against its internal stop, and then tighten the adjusting lock screw to 105 inch lbs. (12 Nm). This automatically removes cable backlash.

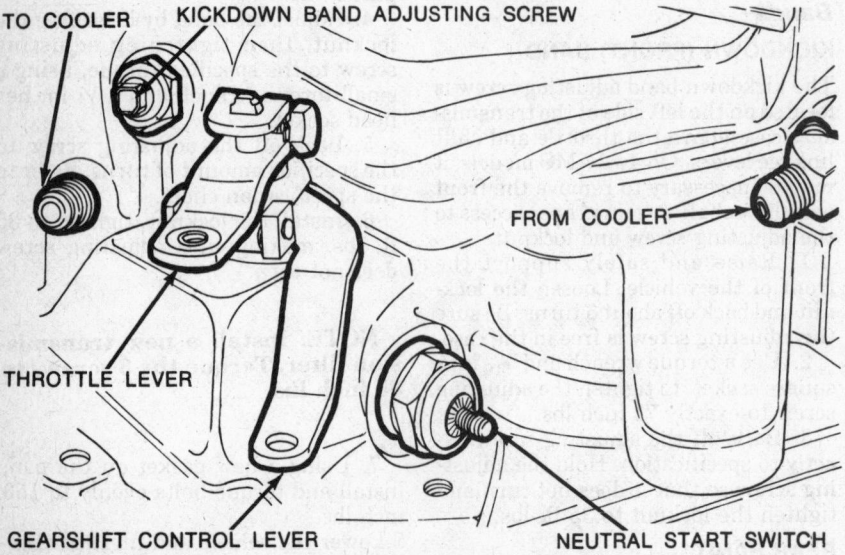

Torque-Command and TorqueFlite external adjustments and controls

BAND ADJUSTMENT SPECIFICATIONS
Chrysler Corporation Transaxle

| | | Engine and Transmission Models | | | | |
| | | A-404 | | | A-413, A-470 | |
Year	Band	1.7L	2.2L	2.6L	2.2L	2.6L
1982-83	Front Band	3.0②	3.0②	3.0②	2.0②	2.0②
	Rear Band	①	①	①	3.5③	3.5③
1984-89	Front Band	—	—	—	2.5②④	2.5②④
	Rear Band	—	—	—	3.5③④	3.5③④

① Not adjustable
② Backed off form 72 inch lbs. torque
③ Backed off form 41 inch lbs. torque
④ 1.6L engine with A415 — 3.0 Rear band — non-adjustable

3. Connect choke if it was disconnected. Test for freedom of movement by pushing the lever forward and slowly release it to confirm that it will return fully rearward.

Band Adjustment

A–415

The kickdown (front) band has its adjusting screw located on the top front (left side) of the transaxle case. Adjustment is as follows:
1. Loosen the lock nut and back off about 5 turns.
2. Tighten the adjusting screw to 72 inch lbs.
3. Back off adjusting screw 3 turns from the 72 inch lbs. torque, then hold this position and tighten the lock nut to 35 ft. lbs.

The low/reverse band (rear) band is not adjustable in this unit. The band lining itself needs to be inspected to determine the need for replacement. The grooves must be no less than 0.008 in (0.2mm) deep at any point to still be usable. With the oil pan down and 30 psi shop air applied to the low/reverse servo, the gap at the band endsmust not be less than 0.080 in. (2mm).

A–413 AND A–470

The kickdown band (front) band has its adjusting screw located on the front left top of the transaxle case, in the same location as the A–415 transaxle. The adjustment is as follows:
1. Loosen the locknut and back off approximately 5 turns.
2. Tighten the band adjusting screw to 72 inch lbs. (8 Nm).
3. Back off the adjusting screw 2½ turns.
4. Hold this position on the adjusting screw and tighten the lock nut to 35 ft. lbs. (47 Nm).

The low/reverse band (rear) is adjustable with the bottom oil pan off. Before attempting the band adjustment, the low/reverse band should be checked for proper end gap as follows:

1. Remove the lower oil pan and pressurize the low/reverse servo with 30 psi shop air pressure.
2. Measure the gap between the band ends. If the gap is less than 0.080 in (2.0mm), the band is worn excessively and should be replaced.

To adjust the low/reverse band, proceed as follows:
1. Loosen the back off the locknut approximately 5 turns.
2. Tighten the adjusting screw to 41 inch lbs. (5 Nm) true torque.
3. Back off the adjusting screw 3½ turns, hold adjusting screw position and tighten the locknut to 10 ft. lbs. (l4 Nm).
4. Reinstall oil pan and fill unit with correct type fluid.

Neutral Safety Switch

The neutral safety switch used on this transaxle includes provision for the backup lamp switch function. The neutral start circuit is through the center pin on the 3 terminal/switch. It provides a ground for the starter solenoid circuit through the center pin when in **PARK** or **NEUTRAL**. The 2 outside terminals of the neutral switch are for the circuit feeding the backup lamps.

Oil Pan

REMOVAL & INSTALLATION

1. Raise vehicle and support safely. Loosen, but do not remove the pan bolts. Gently pull one corner down so fluid will drain into a container with a large opening. If transmission is hot, be careful of the oil.
2. When drained, remove the bolts and pan.
3. Carefully inspect the filter and pan bottom for a heavy concentration of friction material or metal particles. A little accumulation can be considered normal, but a heady build-up indicates damaged or worn parts.

NOTE: Filter replacement is recommended whenever oil pan is removed. A special Torx® drive bit will be required. Torque screws to 35 inch lbs.

4. Check pan carefully for distortion, straightening the edges with a block of wood and a mallet if necessary. Clean pan well.
5. Apply a bead of RTV sealant on pan and install. Torque bolts to 150 inch lbs. (16 Nm).
6. Refill with 4 quarts Dexron®. Idle engine for 2 minutes, moving selector through each position, ending in **PARK**. Check fluid and add if necessary.
7. Make sure dipstick rubber seal is firmly seated to keep out water and dirt.

FORD MOTOR COMPANY

Automatic Overdrive (AOD)

ADJUSTMENTS

Throttle Valve (T.V.) Control Linkage System

The throttle valve (T.V.) control linkage system consists of the linkage lever on the carburetor, the transmission control rod assembly and the external T.V. control lever on the transmission.

The T.V. control linkage is set to its proper length during initial assembly using the sliding trunnion block at the transmission end of the T.V. control rod assembly. Under normal circumstances, it should not be necessary to alter this adjustment. Any required adjustment of the T.V. control linkage can normally be accomplished using the adjustment screw on the linkage lever at the carburetor. Major linkage adjustment (sliding trunnion on rod) may only be required after maintenance involving the removal and/or replacement of the carburetor, T.V. control rod assembly or the transmission. Minor linkage adjustment (adjustment screw on linkage lever) may be required after idle speed adjustments greater than 50 rpm and to correct complaints of poor transmission shift quality.

When the linkage is properly adjusted, the T.V. control lever on the transmission will be at its internal idle stop position (lever up as far as it will trav-

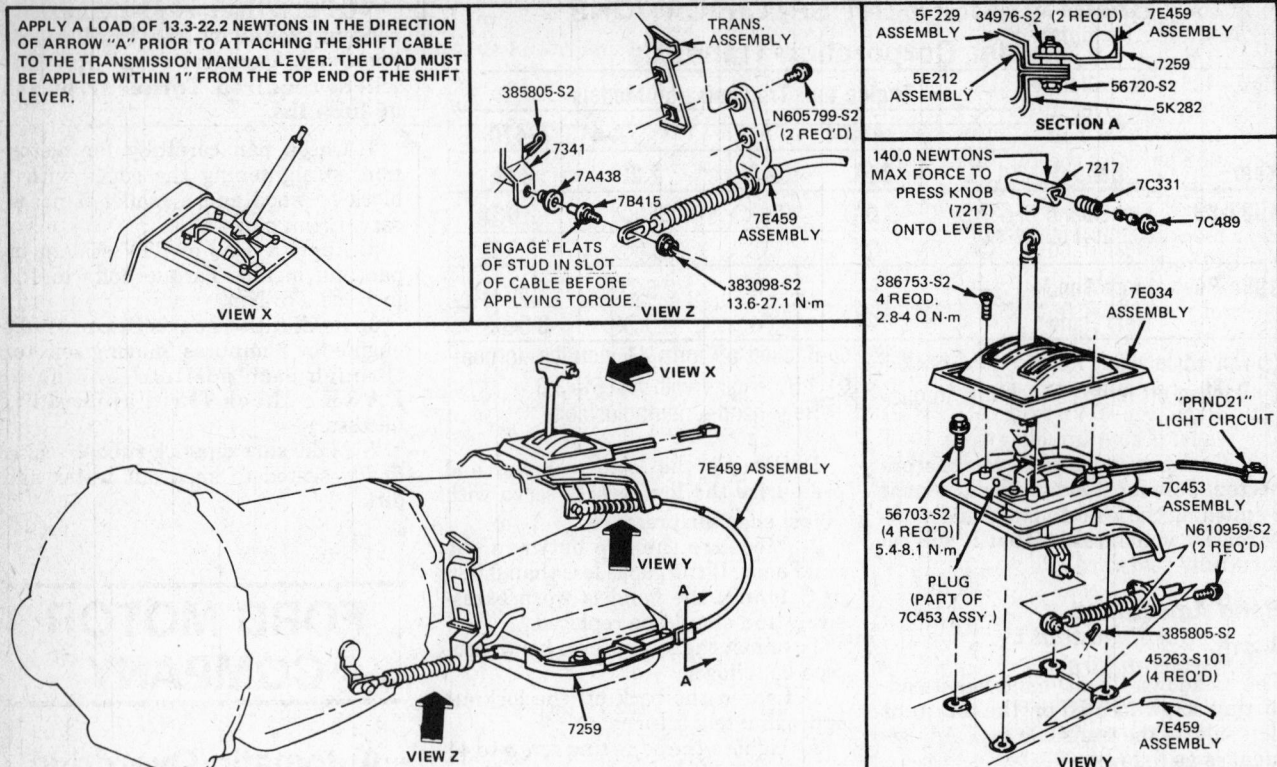

APPLY A LOAD OF 13.3-22.2 NEWTONS IN THE DIRECTION OF ARROW "A" PRIOR TO ATTACHING THE SHIFT CABLE TO THE TRANSMISSION MANUAL LEVER. THE LOAD MUST BE APPLIED WITHIN 1" FROM THE TOP END OF THE SHIFT LEVER.

VIEW X

385805-S2
7341
7A438
7B415
ENGAGE FLATS OF STUD IN SLOT OF CABLE BEFORE APPLYING TORQUE.
TRANS. ASSEMBLY
N605799-S2 (2 REQ'D)
7E459 ASSEMBLY
383098-S2 13.6-27.1 N·m
VIEW Z

5F229 ASSEMBLY
34976-S2 (2 REQ'D)
7E459 ASSEMBLY
5E212 ASSEMBLY
7259
56720-S2
5K282
SECTION A

140.0 NEWTONS MAX FORCE TO PRESS KNOB (7217) ONTO LEVER
7217
7C331
7C489
386753-S2 4 REQD. 2.8-4 Q N·m
7E034 ASSEMBLY
"PRND21" LIGHT CIRCUIT
7C453 ASSEMBLY
56703-S2 (4 REQ'D) 5.4-8.1 N·m
N610959-S2 (2 REQ'D)
PLUG (PART OF 7C453 ASSY.)
385805-S2
45263-S101 (4 REQ'D)
7E459 ASSEMBLY
VIEW Y

VIEW X
7E459 ASSEMBLY
VIEW Y
7259
VIEW Z
A

Typical cable-type floor shift mechanism

To retract the idle Speed Control Solenoid plunger, jumper, the Self-Test Input Connector and the signal return ground of the Self-Test Connector

SELF-TEST INPUT CONNECTOR
SELF TEST CONNECTOR SIGNAL RETURN (GROUND)

el) when the carburetor is at its hot idle stop with the engine off. There will be a light contact force between the throttle lever and end of the linkage lever adjustment screw. Due to flexibility in the linkage system, the linkage lever adjustment screw would have to be backed out approximately 3 turns before a gap between the screw and throttle lever could be detected.

At wide open throttle, the T.V. control lever on the transmission may or may not be at its wide open stop. The wide open throttle position must not be used as the reference point in adjusting the linkage.

Linkage Adjustment at Carburetor

The T.V. control linkage may be ad-

justed at the carburetor using the following procedure.

1. Remove the fast idle cam on the carburetor so that the throttle lever is at its idle stop. Place the shift lever in **NEUTRAL** not **PARK** and set the parking brake. Turn the engine **OFF**. On models other than 1985–89 cars with the 3.8 liter engine, skip to Step 3.

2. On 1985–89 models, the 3.8 liter engine has a DC motor idle speed control. The plunger on this control must be retracted before adjusting the T.V. linkage; you cannot perform the adjustment by merely turning the ignition **OFF**. Locate the Self-Test Connector and Self-Test Input Connector in the engine compartment, near the right side fender apron. Connect a jumper wire between the Self-Test Input Connector and signal return ground on the Self-Test Connector. Turn the ignition switch to the **RUN** position without starting the engine, and leave it on for a full 10 seconds, to give the plunger time to retract fully. Then, turn off the ignition switch and remove the jumper wire.

3. Back out the linkage lever adjusting screw all the way (screw end is flush with lever face).

4. Turn in the adjusting screw until a thin shim (0.005 in. max) or piece of writing paper fits snug between the end of the screw and the throttle lever.

To eliminate the effect of friction, push the linkage lever forward (tending to close gap). Release it before checking clearance between the end of the screw and the throttle lever. Do not apply any load on the levers with tools or hands while checking the gap.

5. Turn in the adjusting screw an additional 3 turns. (3 turns are preferred. 1 turn minimum is permissible if screw travel is limited).

6. If it is not possible to turn in adjusting screw at least one additional turn or if there was insufficient screw adjusting capacity to obtain an initial gap in Step 2, refer to "Linkage Adjustment at Transmission."

Linkage Adjustment at Transmission

The linkage lever adjustment screw has a limited adjustment capability. If it is not possible to adjust the T.V. linkage using this screw, the length of the T.V. control rod assembly must be readjusted using the following procedure. This procedure must also be followed whenever a new T.V. control rod assembly is installed.

1. Set the engine curb idle speed to specification.

2. With the engine **OFF**, de-cam the fast idle cam on the carburetor so that the throttle lever is against the idle stop. Place the shift lever in **NEUTRAL** and set the parking brake.

3. Set the linkage lever adjustment screw at approximately mid-range.

4. If a new T.V. control rod assembly is being installed, connect the rod to the linkage lever at the carburetor.

5. Loosen the bolt on the sliding trunnion block on the T.V. control rod assembly. Remove any corrosion from the control rod and free-up the trunnion block so that it slides freely on the control rod.

6. Push up on the lower end of the control rod to insure that the linkage lever at carburetor is firmly against the throttle lever. Release force on the rod. The rod must stay up.

7. Push the T.V. control lever on the transmission up against its internal stop with a firm force (approximately 5 pounds) and tighten the bolt on the trunnion block. Do not relax the force on the lever until the bolt is tightened.

Linkage Adjustment Using T.V. Control Pressure

The following procedure may be used to check and/or adjust the T.V. control linkage using T.V. control pressure.

1. Place the shift selector lever in **NEUTRAL** and disconnect the idle kicker solenoid. Set the parking brake.

2. Attach a 0–100 psi pressure gauge to the T.V. Port on the transmission. It's best to use a gauge with 8 feet of hose so you can read it while the engine is running. You may have to rig a piping elbow to keep the hose away from the exhaust system.

3. Operate the engine until normal operating temperature is reached and the throttle lever is off fast idle. Leave the engine running.

4. Verify that the throttle lever is at its idle stop. Follow the specified procedure below, depending on the model year of the car:

1982–83

a. Observing the pressure gauge, pull back slowly on the Throttle Valve rod at the carburetor. Watch for the pressure to increase suddenly approximately 15–30 psi with only a slight motion of the T.V. rod. This is the "breakpoint". It, ideally, should occur when the gap is $5/32$–$7/32$ in. The maximum specification is $1/16$–$5/16$ in. An effective means of measuring the gap is to insert standard size drills into the gap between the linkage lever adjustment screw and the throttle lever. If the breakpoint occurs at less than $1/16$ in., the T.V. linkages is set too long; if it occurs at greater than a $5/16$ in. gap, the linkage is set too short. Adjust the linkage as described in Step 6.

1984–89

a. Fabricate a block 0.397 plus or minus 0.007 in. thick, or use a Letter X drill or 10mm or $25/32$ in. drill. Insert the gauge block or drill shank between the throttle lever and adjusting screw on the transmission linkage lever. Then, note the transmission pressure. It must be 30–40 psi. Proceed to the next step to adjust.

Correct a long setting or low pressure by backing out the linkage lever adjustment screw. Turn in the adjusting screw for a short rod or high pressure condition. If insufficient adjusting capacity is available, the T.V. control rod length must be reset using the procedure described in "Linkage Adjustment at Transmission". On 1984–89 models only: Remove the gauge block or drill, and recheck the pressure. It must be less then 5 psi. If necessary, back out the adjusting screw until pressure just drops below 5 psi. Reinstall the gauge block and verify that the pressure is still 30–40 psi.

If the limits specified cannot be obtained, diagnosis of the transmission control pressure system is required.

Gear Shift Linkage

1. Loosen the linkage adjustment screw located in the engine compartment of Ford/Mercury full size and Lincoln/Mark VI, and under the car on Cougar/Thunderbird models.

2. Move the shift selector firmly against the overdrive gate stop. Hang a weight on the lever to hold it in place.

3. Locate the overdrive detent in the transmission, third from the front.

4. Tighten the adjustment screw. Recheck the adjustment before driving the vehicle.

Neutral Safety Switch

The neutral safety switch in the transmission is merely an on-off switch actuated by the manual linkage detent mechanism within the transmission. The switch is replaceable if defective, but is non-adjustable.

Oil Pan

REMOVAL & INSTALLATION

It is not necessary, under normal operating conditions, to periodically change the transmission fluid. Only under severe conditions (police or taxi) or in the case of a major overhaul is it recommended that the fluid be changed.

When the reason for a fluid change is internal transmission damage, it is necessary to also flush the transmission cooler and cooler lines to remove any traces of abrasive matter from the system.

NOTE: When flushing torque converters, use only professional equipment designed for this purpose. Traces of solvent in the converter could cause severe transmission damage in the future.

1. Raise and safely support the vehicle on jackstands.

2. Place a drain pan under transmission.

3. Loosen the transmission pan attaching bolts to drain fluid above pan level.

4. When the fluid has drained to the level of the pan mounting flange, remove the attaching bolts beginning at the rear of the pan. Gradually drop the pan and drain slowly.

5. After draining the fluid, remove and thoroughly clean the transmission pan. Discard the filter, valve body to filter gasket, and transmission pan gasket.

6. Install new filter and filter to valve body gasket. Do not attempt to clean and reuse the old filter.

7. Using a new gasket, install the pan on the transmission.

8. Add 3 quarts of the specified fluid Ford CJ or Dexron® II, through the fill tube.

9. Check and adjust the fluid level as necessary.

C3 Transmission

ADJUSTMENTS

Vacuum Diaphragm

The vacuum diaphragms used in production are nonadjustable. Adjustable type units are available for installation in the transmission, allowing changes in the control pressures.

An adjusting screw is located in the vacuum nipple of the diaphragm and is accessible after removing the vacuum supply line from the diaphragm. Using a small screwdriver and turning the screw clockwise will increase the control pressure, while turning the screw counter-clockwise will decrease the control pressure. One complete turn of the adjusting screw will change the control pressure approximately 2–3 psi.

NOTE: The diaphragm should not be adjusted to provide pressures below the specified ranges to change shift engagement feel, as soft or slipping shift points could result and damage to the transmission could occur.

Throttle Linkage

Throttle pressure control linkage is not used on the C3 automatic transmission. A vacuum-operated diaphragm assembly is used to control and modulate the throttle pressure in proportion to the road speed, throttle opening and internal oil pressures.

A downshift control rod is used and is connected to the carburetor control linkage. Both linkages must be properly adjusted to actuate the downshift system.

Accelerator and Downshift Linkage

1. With the engine **OFF**, fully depress the accelerator pedal and hold in place. Inspect the carburetor for wide open throttle plates and full accelerator linkage travel. Adjust as necessary.

2. With the accelerator fully depressed and adjusted, push the downshift control rod downward to its fully depressed position (downshift valve in the transmission fully depressed).

3. A clearance of 0.010–0.080 in. between the tip of the kickdown adjusting screw and the throttle lever should exist. Adjust the screw as necessary.

4. Release the accelerator linkage. The linkage and the downshift control rod must return to their closed position by return spring tension.

Band Adjustment

NOTE: The intermediate band is the only adjustment needed during normal operation. The reverse band is adjusted internally during assembly or at times of overhaul.

1. Locate the adjusting screw on the left side of the transmission case, in front of the manual control lever.

2. Remove the downshift control rod from the downshift control lever to gain access to the adjusting screw and locknut.

3. Clean the dirt and foreign material from the locknut area. Loosen, remove and discard the locknut from the adjusting screw.

4. Install a new locknut on the adjusting screw.

5. Tighten the adjusting screw to 10 ft. lbs. of torque.

NOTE: A special wrench with a present click or overrun can be used to tighten the adjusting screw.

6. Back the adjusting screw off exactly 1½ turns; 2 turns for 1984–89 models.

7. Hold the adjustment and tighten the locknut to 35–45 ft. lbs. torque.

8. Install the downshift control rod to the downshift control lever.

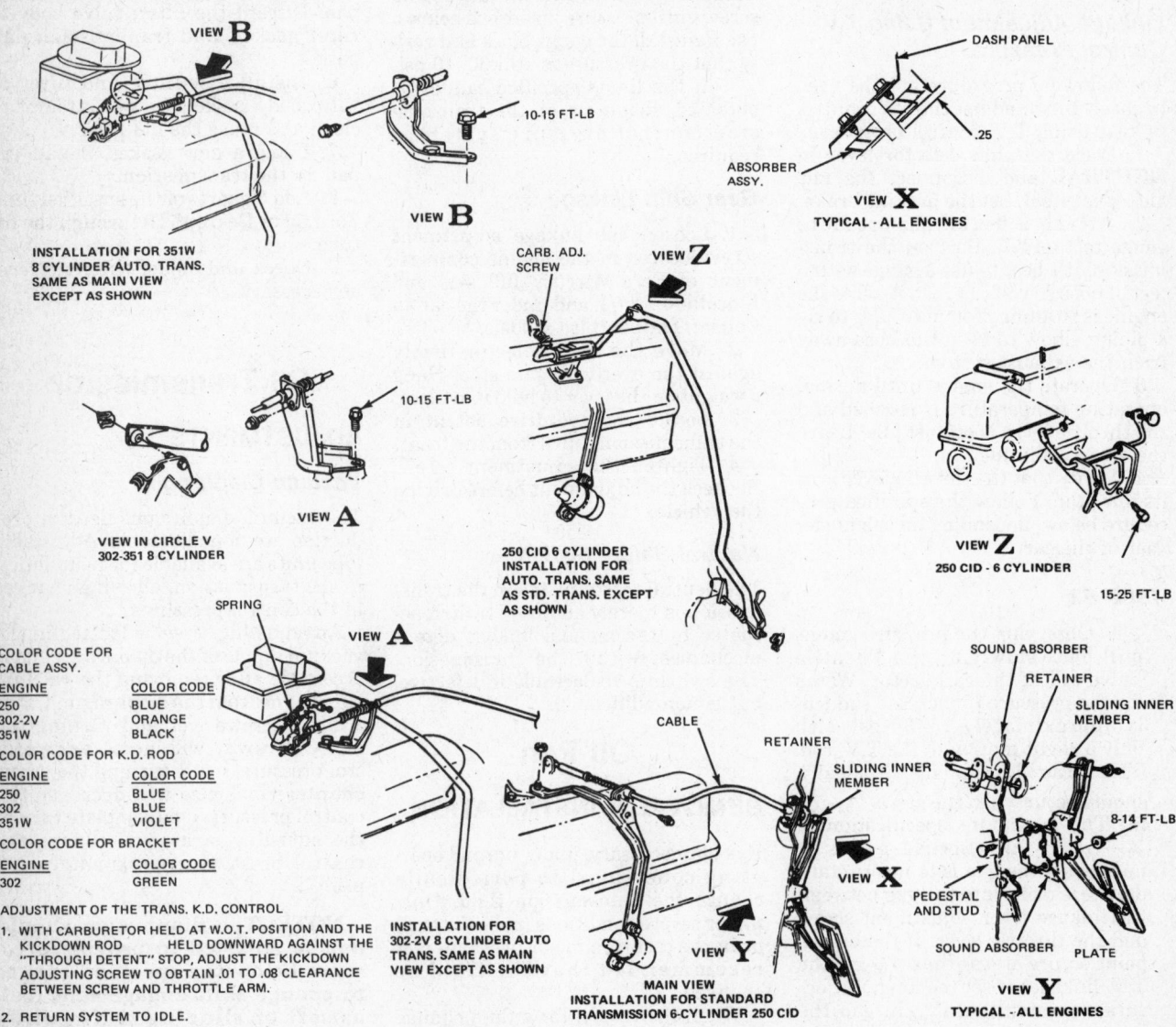

Typical throttle and downshift linkage—except ATX

Gear Shift Linkage

COLUMN SHIFT

1. Place the selector lever in the **D** position against the **D** stop of the shift gate.

NOTE: The selector lever should be held by hand or by a weight, against the D stop of the shift gate during any adjustments.

2. Loosen the shift rod adjusting nut.

3. Position the transmission lever in the **D** detent, which is third from the front.

NOTE: The control rod may have to be disconnected at the adjusting nut and bolt to properly engage the transmission detent.

4. Recheck the selector lever so that it is against the **D** stop of the shift gate. Tighten the shift rod adjusting nut securely.

NOTE: Engage the flats of the stud in the control rod slot before tightening the nut, if equipped.

5. Operate the gear selector through the detents and check for proper alignment of the lever indicator to the shift detents. Readjust as necessary.

CONSOLE OR FLOOR SHIFT

1. Place the selector lever in the **D** position and against the rearward **D** stop of the shift gate. Hold in position while any adjustments are made.

2. Loosen the shift linkage adjusting nut and move the selector lever to the **D** position on the transmission (third position from the front).

3. With the selector lever and the manual lever in the **D** positions respectively, tighten the shift linkage adjusting nut to 10–15 ft. lbs.

Neutral Safety Switch

NOTE: The C3 automatic transmission has a screwtype neutral start switch, located above the manual control lever on the transmission case. The internal shift detent operates the switch contacts to allow the engine to start in either PARK or NEUTRAL positions and to operate the back-up lights when the transmission is in the REVERSE position.

REMOVAL & INSTALLATION

1. Raise the vehicle, support safely. Disconnect the wire connector from the switch.

2. Use a thin wall socket and unscrew the switch from the transmission case.

NOTE: Use only a thin wall socket and not a wrench to avoid crushing the switch during removal or installation.

3. Install a new O-ring on the switch and install the unit into the transmission case. Torque the switch 12–15 ft. lbs.

4. Install the wire connector to the switch.

5. Check the operation of the switch in each detent position. The engine should start in **NEUTRAL** and **PARK** positions only, and the back-up lights should be on when the transmission is in reverse.

Oil Pan

REMOVAL & INSTALLATION

1. Raise the vehicle and support safely.

2. Position a drain pan beneath the transmission pan and starting at the rear, loosen, but do not remove the pan bolts.

3. Loosen the pan from the transmission case allow the fluid to drain gradually.

4. Remove all pan bolts except 2 at the front of the pan and allow the fluid to continue draining.

5. Remove the pan; clean the old gasket from the pan and transmission case.

6. Install a new gasket on the pan and install it to the transmission case.

7. Install all pan bolts and torque to 12–17 ft. lbs.

8. Install 3 quarts of Dexron® II or "CJ" type transmission fluid into the filler tube (converter not drained). When refilling a dry transmission and converter, install 5 quarts of fluid into the transmission.

9. Start the engine and operate the engine at idle speed for approximately 2 minutes. Then raise the engine speed to approximately 1200 rpm until the engine/transmission assembly reaches normal operating temperature.

NOTE: Do not race the engine during warmup.

10. Check the fluid level after moving the gear selector through all ranges. Correct the fluid level as necessary.

Vacuum Diaphragm

REMOVAL & INSTALLATION

1. Raise the vehicle and support safely. Disconnect the vacuum hoses(s) from the diaphragm unit.

2. Remove the retaining bracket and bolt holding the diaphragm unit to the transmission case.

NOTE: Do not pry or bend the retainer bracket.

3. Pull the vacuum diaphragm, the actuating pin and the throttle valve from the transmission case. Remove the O-ring from the assembly.

4. Install a new O-ring on the diaphragm unit.

5. Install the throttle valve, the actuating pin and the vacuum diaphragm tubes towards the transmission case and install the assembly into the case.

6. Install the retaining bracket and bolt and torque to 15–23 inch lbs.

C5 Transmission

ADJUSTMENTS

Gear Shift Linkage

1. Loosen the nut or screw at the slotted rod in the linkage.

2. Put the selector in the **D** position, firmly against the shift gate stop.

3. Shift the manual lever on the transmission to the **D** position which is 3 detents away from **PARK**.

4. Tighten the nut or screw securely in the slotted rod of the linkage.

5. Repeat the linkage check with the shift lever and the shift gate stop. Readjust as required.

Downshift Linkage

1. Hold the throttle wide open against its stop.

2. Push the rod down to force the downshift valve to bottom in the valve body.

3. Measure the clearance between the tip of the adjusting screw and the throttle lever. The clearance should be 0.050–0.070 in.

4. Turn the adjusting screw to obtain the proper clearance.

Band Adjustment

1. Remove the adjusting screw locknut and discard.

2. Install a new locknut on the adjusting screw, loosely.

3. Tighten the adjusting screw to 10 ft. lbs. torque, or until the adjusting tool overruns and clicks.

4. Back the adjusting screw off exactly the specified number of turns: Intermediate band 4¼ turns: Low-Reverse band 3 turns.

5. Hold the adjustment screw at the specified back-off turns and tighten the new locknuts to 35–45 ft. lbs.

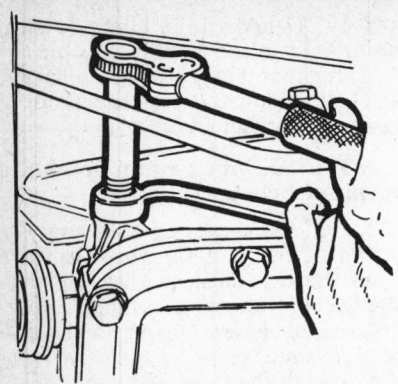

C5 low-reverse band adjustment

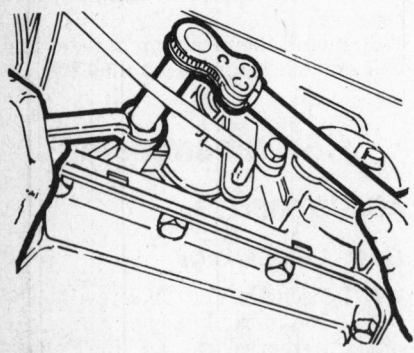

C5 and C6 intermediate band adjustment

Neutral Start Switch

1. Place the selector in the **NEUTRAL** position and hold.
2. Loosen the switch bolts and insert a ³/₃₂ in. gauge pin or drill through the hole in the switch.
3. Wiggle the switch until the drill seats in the case.
4. Tighten the switch bolts to 55–75 inch lbs. torque and remove the drill.

Vacuum Diaphragm

Adjustment of the vacuum diaphragm is controlled by the installation of longer or shorter throttle valve rods to obtain the proper line pressure. 5 selective rods are used.

NOTE: The following procedure will determine if a change in the length of the rod is required.

1. Attach a tachometer to the engine.
2. Attach a hand vacuum pump to the transmission vacuum diaphragm unit.
3. Attach a hydraulic pressure gauge to the control pressure outlet on the transmission.
4. Firmly apply the parking brake. On vehicles equipped with a vacuum brake release, apply the service brakes. Otherwise the parking brake will release when the selector is moved to Drive.

LINE PRESSURE CHART

Transmission Model	Range	10″ Vacuum
PEN-C,G,J,K	D	#90–101
PEM-AL,AM	2,1	123–136
	R	151–168
PEP-E,F,G,H,P,N	D	#87–97
	2,1	119–132
	R	145–162
PEP-B,D	D	#86–99
	2,1	120–132
	R	143–165

NOTE: Refer to the ID tag for the transmission model.

5. Start the engine, allow it to reach normal operating temperature.
6. Set the engine idle speed to the specified rpm.
7. Adjust engine speed to 1000 rpm and apply 10 inches of vacuum to vacuum diaphragm unit. Read and record the control pressure in all selector positions.
8. Compare the pressure readings from Step 7 to the specified pressure in the line Pressure chart and Proceed as follows: Pressure within specification no change required. Pressure below specification use the next longest rod. Pressure above specification use the next shortest rod. If the length of the rod is not known, it should be measured with a micrometer.

Oil Pan

REMOVAL & INSTALLATION

1. Raise the vehicle and support safely.
2. Loosen the oil pan retaining bolts, removing only enough bolts to tilt the oil pan and drain the fluid.
3. Carefully remove the remaining bolts and the oil pan from the transmission. Pour out the remaining fluid from the oil pan.

NOTE: Discard the nylon shipping plug found in the bottom of the oil pan.

4. Thoroughly clean and remove all gasket material from the oil pan and the pan mounting surface of the transmission case.
5. Install new gasket and mount the pan to the transmission case.
6. Install the pan retaining bolts and torque to 12–16 ft. lbs.
7. Lower the vehicle and fill the transmission with fluid. Type "H" only. Start the engine and recheck the fluid level. Correct as required.

C6 Transmission

ADJUSTMENTS

Throttle Linkage

1. Position the carburetor in the wide open throttle position (WOT).
2. Hold the kickdown rod downward with a 4½ lb. weight against the through detent stop.
3. Adjust the kickdown adjusting screw to obtain 0.010–0.080 in. clearance between the screw and the throttle arm.
4. Return the system to idle.

Band Adjustment

NOTE: The only adjustment that is needed on the C6 automatic transmission is the intermediate band adjustment.

1. Raise the vehicle and support on jackstands.
2. Clean all the grease and dirt away from the band adjusting screw area. Remove and discard the locknut.
3. Install a new locknut and torque the adjusting screw to 10 ft. lbs. Back off the adjusting screw 1½ turns.
4. Hold the adjusting screw, so that it does not turn, and torque the locknut to 40 ft. lbs.
5. Lower the vehicle. Road test and correct as necessary.

Gear Shift Linkage
COLUMN SHIFT

1. Place the transmission selector level in the **DRIVE** position. Make sure that the lever is tight against the Drive stop.

NOTE: If necessary a 10–15 lb. weight should be hung on the transmission shift lever to be sure that the lever remains against the Drive stop during the adjusting procedure.

2. Loosen the shift rod adjusting nut. On vehicles equipped with a shift cable, remove the nut, and remove the cable from the transmission lever stud.
3. Shift the transmission lever into the **DRIVE** position.
4. On vehicles equipped with a shift cable, place the cable end on the transmission lever stud, using care to align the flats on the stud with the flats on the shift cable. Start the adjustment nut.
5. Make sure that the transmission lever has not moved from the Drive stop. Torque the adjusting nut to 15 ft. lbs.
6. Check the transmission operation for all selector lever detent positions.

FLOOR SHIFT

1. Position the transmission selector lever in the **DRIVE** position against the rearward Drive stop.

2. Raise the vehicle and loosen the manual lever shift rod retaining nut. Move the transmission manual lever to the **DRIVE** position.

3. With the transmission selector lever and the manual lever in the **DRIVE** position, torque the attaching nut to 15 ft. lbs.

4. Check the operation of the transmission in each selector lever position. Lower the vehicle.

Neutral Safety Switch

ALL MODELS

1. With the transmission manual lever properly adjusted, loosen the 2 neutral safety switch bolts.

2. With the transmission manual lever in **NEUTRAL**, rotate the switch and insert the gauge pin (No. 43 drill bit) into the gauge pin holes of the neutral safety switch.

NOTE: The gauge pin has to be inserted to a full $^{31}/_{64}$ inch into the 3 holes of the neutral safety switch.

3. Torque the neutral safety switch bolts to 55–75 ft. lbs. Remove the gauge pin from the neutral safety switch.

4. Check the operation of the neutral safety switch.

NOTE: The engine should start with the transmission selector lever in (P) PARK or (N) NEUTRAL only.

Oil Pan

REMOVAL & INSTALLATION

1. Raise the vehicle and support on jackstands. Place a drain pan under the transmission.

2. Loosen the automatic transmission oil pan bolts and drain the automatic transmission fluid from the unit.

3. When the transmission fluid has drained to the level of the oil pan flange, remove the rest of the transmission oil pan bolts working from the rear and both sides of the pan to allow the transmission pan to drop and the fluid to drain slowly.

4. When the fluid has drained to the level of the pan flange, remove the rest of the pan bolts. Work from the rear and both sides of the pan to allow it to drop and drain slowly.

5. Install a new transmission pan gasket on the transmission pan and place it against the transmission case.

6. Install all the transmission oil pan bolts. Torque the bolts to 12–17 ft. lbs.

7. Install 3 quarts of automatic transmission fluid (converter not drained). Be sure to use the proper grade and type transmission fluid; failure
to do this could result in serious internal transmission damage. Use "CJ" or Dexron® II fluid.

8. When refilling a dry transmission and torque converter install 5 quarts of the proper grade and type automatic transmission fluid into the transmission.

9. Start the engine and operate the engine at idle speed for approximately 2 minutes and then raise the engine speed to approximately 1200 rpm until the engine/transmission assembly reaches normal operating temperature.

NOTE: Do not race the engine during warm-up.

10. Check the fluid level after moving the gear selector through all ranges. Correct the fluid level as necessary.

Vacuum Diaphragm

REMOVAL & INSTALLATION

1. Raise the vehicle and support on jackstands.

2. Disconnect the vacuum diaphragm hoses.

3. Remove the vacuum unit retaining bracket and bolt. Pull the vacuum diaphragm from the transmission case.

NOTE: Do not pry or bend this bracket, as damage to the bracket could result.

4. Remove the vacuum unit control rod from the transmission case.

5. Place the vacuum control rod in the transmission case.

6. Install the vacuum diaphragm unit into the transmission case. Secure the unit with the retaining bracket and bolt. Torque the bolt 12–16 ft. lbs.

7. Reinstall the vacuum hoses to their proper places on the diaphragm unit.

8. Lower the vehicle and road test as required.

NOTE: Some models use an adjustable vacuum diaphragm (modulator). To adjust insert a small screwdriver into the nipple end and turn adjusting screw. One complete turn of screw
should change the pressure 2–3 psi.

ZF Transmission

ADJUSTMENTS

Gear Shift Linkage

1. Put the selector lever in the **OVERDRIVE** position, tight against the stop and retain it with a weight. With a floorshift model, block the lever rearward.

2. Disconnect the linkage at the lever on the transmission or bellcrank.

3. Shift the lever fully counterclockwise; then shift back 3 detents (to the Overdrive position). The ZF transmission has an extra detent which is not used, do not be confused.

4. Connect the linkage. Check that the gear selector is still in the **OVERDRIVE** position and tighten the nut securely.

Kickdown Cable

1. Set the injector pump top lever at the full throttle position.

2. Loosen the front adjusting nut. Tighten the rear adjusting nut on the threaded barrel until a gap of 1.54–1.57 in. exists between the edge of the crimped bead on the cable closest to the barrel and the end of the threaded barrel.

3. Tighten the forward adjusting nut to lock the cable assembly to the bracket and recheck the adjustment gap.

Oil Pan

REMOVAL & INSTALLATION

1. Raise and support the vehicle safely on jackstands.

2. Remove the drain plug and catch the fluid in a suitable container.

3. Remove the bolt that attaches the filler stub tube to the converter housing and disconnect the tube from the oil pan.

4. Remove the bolts and clamps that secure the pan to the transmission.

5. Use a Torx® bit No. 27 to remove the 3 bolts that attach the oil screen to the valve body.

6. Install a new O-ring on the screen and install.

7. Position a new gasket on the cleaned oil pan and install with edge clamps in position. Connect the filler tube. Add quats of Dexron®II fluid, run the engine and fill the transmission to the correct level.

A4LD Automatic Transmission

ADJUSTMENTS

Gear Shift Linkage
CONSOLE SHIFT

1. Place the shift lever in the **OVERDRIVE** position.
2. Raise the vehicle and support it safely. Then loosen the adjusting screw on the shift cable and remove the end fitting from the manual lever ball stud.
3. Move the shift lever all the way rearward, then move it 3 detents forward.
4. Connect the cable end fitting to the lever.

NOTE: Too much pressure on the arm can move the shifter to the DRIVE position. Apply pressure only until the pressure resistance of the detent nib is felt.

5. Tighten the adjusting screw to 45–60 inch lbs.
6. After the adjustment has been made, check the **PARK** engagement. The shift lever must move to the right when engaged in the **PARK** detent.
7. With the engine operating and the brakes locked, move the shift lever in all detents to ensure correct engagement. Readjust if necessary.

Kickdown Cable

The self adjusting kickdown cable has the self adjuster mechanism located in the engine compartment at the inlet for the cable into the dash area and is self adjusting over a tolerance of 1.0 in.

To adjust the cable to begin the self adjusting procedure, reset the cable by depressing the semi-circular metal tab on the self adjuster mechanism and pull the cable towards the front of the vehicle removing all the slack from cable.

This will automatically readjust the cable to its proper length when kicked down.

NOTE: The cable must be readjusted whenever it is removed or replaced.

Vacuum Modulator

A vacuum modulator is used to tailor the transmission shifting to the engine operation, with no adjustments available.

Neutral Safety Switch

The neutral safety switch is a non-adjustable unit that must be replaced if a malfunction occurs.

With the brakes applied, the operation of the switch can be checked with the engine being able to start in only the **N** or **P** positions.

If the switch must be replaced, tighten the new switch to only 7–10 ft. lbs.

NOTE: Ford Motor Company recommends the use of a special socket, part number T74P–77247–A or its equivalent, to avoid crushing the switch side wall.

Band Adjustment
OVERDRIVE AND INTERMEDIATE BANDS

NOTE: The adjustment procedure is the same for both the overdrive and intermediate bands.

1. Loosen and remove the band locknut on the adjusting screw. A new locknut must be installed on the adjusting screw for proper adjusting screw retention.
2. Install the new locknut loosely and with band adjusting tool, No. T71P–77370–A or its equivalent, tighten the adjusting screw until the tool handle clicks at a preset 10 ft. lbs.
3. Back off the adjusting screw 2 full turns.
4. Hold the adjusting screw and tighten the new locknut to 35–45 ft. lbs.

LOW/REVERSE BAND

1. Drain the fluid and remove the pan and the screen/filter.
2. Remove the low/reverse servo cover. Remove the servo piston and install a servo piston checking spring, No. D4ZZ7D031–A or its equivalent. Re-install the servo piston.
3. With the cover gasket in place, assemble band checking tool, No. T74P–77190–A or its equivalent, to the servo cover bolt area. Tighten the 3 attaching bolts.
4. With a torque wrench, tighten the servo checking tool adjusting bolt to 35 inch lbs.
5. Install dial indicator tool, No. 4201–C or its equivalent, with bracket installed to the transmission case and position the dial indicator on the piston pad. Zero the dial indicator needle.
6. Carefully back the servo tool adjusting screw out until the piston bottoms on the tool. Record the distance the servo piston traveled as registered on the dial indicator.
7. If the piston travel is between 0.120–0.220 in., it is within specifications.
8. If the piston travel is more than 0.220 in., install a longer rod.
9. If the piston travel is less than 0.120 in., install a shorter rod.
10. After installing the new piston

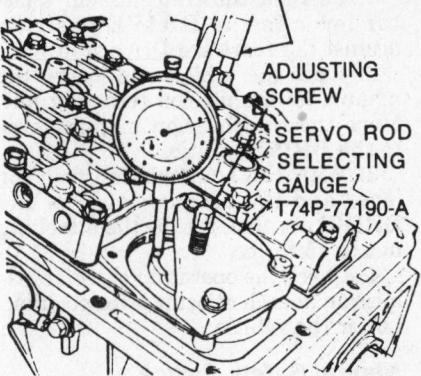

DIAL INDICATOR WITH BRACKETRY TOOL 4201-C
ADJUSTING SCREW
SERVO ROD SELECTING GAUGE T74P-77190-A

A4LD automatic transmission band adjustment

and rod, recheck the piston travel to make sure the travel is within specifications.
11. Remove the servo adjusting tool, dial indicator and the servo checking spring.
12. Complete the assembly of the servo cover, screen/filter, pan and filling of the transmission with fluid.

Oil Pan

REMOVAL & INSTALLATION

The oil pan must be loosened and removed to drain the transmission fluid and service the fluid filter/screen. A new gasket is necessary before the oil pan is installed.

1. Loosen the pan attaching bolts to drain the fluid from the pan.

— **CAUTION** —

Extreme care must be exercised during the fluid draining, to prevent skin burns from hot fluid.

2. When the fluid has drained to its level in the pan, carefully remove the pan and finish draining the fluid into a container.
3. Remove and clean the filter/screen. Discard the old gasket.

NOTE: The oil filter screen has been changed in the 1986–89.

4. Place a new gasket on the pan and install the pan in place on the transmission. Torque the bolts to 5–10 ft. lbs.
5. Add approximately 3 quarts of fluid to the unit, start the engine and warm to normal operating temperature.
6. Inspect the fluid level with the dipstick and correct the fluid level as necessary.

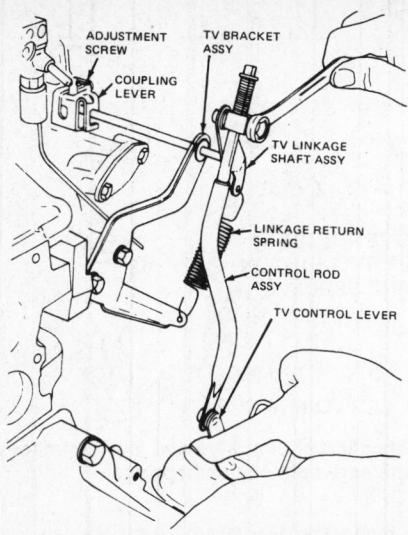

Throttle linkage adjustment—all models with an ATX

Automatic Transaxle (ATX)

ADJUSTMENTS

Gear Shift Linkage

NOTE: This is a critical adjustment. Be sure the D detent in the transaxle corresponds exactly with the stop in the console.

1. Raise and support the vehicle safely on jackstands. Position the selector lever in the **DRIVE** position, against the rearward stop. Hold in position while the adjustment is being done.

2. Loosen the lever to control cable retaining nut and move the transmission lever to the **DRIVE** position, second detent from the most rearward position.

3. Having both the transaxle detent and the shift stop in the console correspond, tighten the retaining nut 10–15 ft. lbs.

4. Lower the vehicle and verify the adjustment. Be sure the park mechanism and the neutral start switch function properly.

Throttle Linkage

MANUAL

NOTE: The T.V. control linkage must be adjusted at the T.V. control rod assembly sliding trunnion block using the following procedure.

1. Set the engine curb idle speed to specification.

2. After the curb idle check, turn the engine **OFF** and insure that the carburetor throttle lever is against the hot engine curb idle stop. The choke must be off.

NOTE: The linkage cannot be properly set if the choke is allowed to cool and the throttle lever allowed to be on the choke fast idle cam.

3. Set the coupling lever adjustment screw at its approximate mid-range. Insure that the T.V. linkage shaft assembly is fully seated upward into the coupling lever.

4. Loosen the bolt on the sliding trunnion block on the T.V. control rod assembly one turn minimum.

5. Free-up the trunnion block so that it slides freely on the control rod.

6. Rotate the transaxle T.V. control lever up using one finger and a light force, approximately 5 pounds, to insure that the T.V. control lever is against its internal idle stop. Without relaxing the force on the T.V. control lever, tighten the bolt on the trunnion block to specification (7–11 ft. lbs.).

7. Verify that the carburetor throttle lever is still against the hot engine curb idle stop.

USING LINE PRESSURE

NOTE: The following procedure may be used to check and/or adjust the T.V. control linkage using a line pressure gauge.

1. Place the shift selector lever in the **PARK** position.

2. Apply the emergency brake.

3. Attach a 0–300 psi pressure gauge to the line press port on the transaxle with sufficient flexible hose to make gauge accessible while operating engine.

4. Operate the engine until normal operating temperature is reached and the throttle lever is against the hot engine curb idle stop (with A/C off, if so equipped).

5. Verify that the coupling lever adjusting screw is in contact with the T.V. linkage shaft assembly. If not, then the linkage must first be readjusted.

6. Verify that the carburetor throttle lever is against its hot engine curb idle stop. With the engine operating at idle and in **PARK**, line pressure must be 43–59 psi. If line pressure is greater than 59 psi, the T.V. control linkage is set too long.

7. Place a 4mm drill (a $\frac{5}{32}$ in. drill or 0.157 gauge pin) between the coupling lever adjustment screw and the T.V. linkage shaft. With the engine operating at idle and in **PARK**, the line pressure must be 72–88 psi. A low reading indicates linkage is set short. A high reading indicates linkage is set too long.

8. Correct a long setting by backing out (counterclockwise) the coupling lever adjustment screw. Turn in (clockwise) the adjustment screw for a short rod condition. This adjusting screw will change line pressure by approximately 2 psi per turn. If insufficient adjusting capacity is available, the T.V. control rod length must be reset.

LINE PRESSURE①

Range	Pressure (At Idle)	Pressure (WOT Stall)
D-2-1	43–5 psi	105–127 psi
R	70–105 psi	230–285 psi
P-N	43–58 psi	②

①Governor pressure is at zero (vehicle stationary). Transaxle is at operating temperature.

②Not available.

Neutral Safety Switch

1. Loosen the 2 switch retaining bolts and place the lever in the **NEUTRAL** position.

2. Insert a $\frac{3}{32}$ in. drill bit through the hole in the neutral start switch.

3. Move the neutral switch until the drill seats in the case.

4. Torque the neutral start switch retaining bolts to 7–9 ft. lbs.

5. Remove the drill from the switch.

Band Adjustment

NOTE: The band adjustment is done during a transaxle overhaul with the use of special tools. Selective sized servo pistons are used to correctly position the band for its application.

Oil Pan

REMOVAL & INSTALLATION

1. Raise the vehicle and support on jackstands.

2. Place a drain pan under the transaxle.

3. Loosen the pan attaching bolts and drain the fluid from transaxle.

4. When the fluid has drained to the level of the pan flange, remove the rest of the pan bolts. Work from the rear and both sides of the to allow it to drop and drain slowly.

5. When all of the fluid has drained from the transaxle, remove and thoroughly clean the pan. Discard the gasket.

6. Remove the 3 retaining bolts and remove the filter. Discard the seal.

7. Install a new oil filter and seal. Tighten the bolts 7–9 ft. lbs.

8. Place a new gasket on the oil pan and install the oil pan on the transaxle

case. Tighten the retaining bolts to 15–19 ft. lbs.

9. Fill the transaxle to the correct level with Dexron® II automatic transmission fluid.

Neutral Start Switch

REMOVAL & INSTALLATION

1. Disconnect the negative battery cable.

2. Remove the 2 managed air valve supply rear hoses and all vacuum lines from the managed air valve.

3. Remove the managed air valve supply hose band to intermediate shift control bracket attaching screw.

4. Remove the air cleaner.

5. Disconnect the neutral start switch connector.

6. Remove the two neutral start switch attaching bolts.

7. Remove the neutral start switch.

8. Install the neutral start switch on the manual shaft.

9. Loosely install the 2 neutral start switch attaching bolts and washers.

10. Using a No. 43 drill (0.089 in.), set the neutral start switch.

11. Tighten the attaching bolts to 7–9 ft. lbs.

12. Connect the neutral start switch connector.

13. Install the managed air valve supply hose band to intermediate shift control bracket attaching screw.

14. Connect the 2 managed air valve supply rear hoses and all vacuum hoses to the managed air valve.

15. Install the air cleaner.

16. Connect the battery.

17. Start the engine in both **PARK** and **NEUTRAL**.

Automatic Transaxle (AXOD)

NOTE: The fluid used in the AXOD transaxle unit must be Motorcraft Type H, XT–4–H or their equivalent.

ADJUSTMENTS

Throttle Valve (T.V.) Cable

The throttle valve cable normally does not need adjustment. The only time the cable should have to be adjusted is if one of the following components are replaced.

1. Main control assembly.

2. Throttle valve cable.

3. Throttle valve cable engine mounting bracket.

4. Throttle control lever link or lever assembly.

5. Engine throttle body.

6. Transaxle assembly.

Adjustment

1. Connect the T.V. cable eye to the throttle control lever link and attach the cable boot to the chain cover.

2. With the T.V. cable mounted in the engine bracket, make sure the threaded shank is fully retracted. The retract the shank, hold the spring rest and wiggle the top of the thread shank while pressing the shank towards the spring.

3. Attach the end of the T.V. cable to the throttle body.

4. Rotate the throttle lever the WOT position and release.

NOTE: The threaded shank must show movement or rachet out of the grip jaws. If no movement is observed, inspect the cable system for broken or disconnected components and repeat the procedure.

Floor/Column Shift

1. Position the selector lever in the **OVERDRIVE** position against the rearward stop. The shift lever must be held in the rearward position while the linkage is being adjusted.

2. Loosen the manual lever to control cable retaining nut.

3. Move the transaxle manual lever to the **OVERDRIVE** position, second detent from the most rearward position.

4. Tighten the attaching nut to 10–15 ft. lbs. (14–20 Nm).

5. Check the operation of the transaxle in each selector lever position. Make sure that **PARK** or **NEUTRAL** start switch is functioning properly.

Neutral Start Switch

1. With the manual shift in the **NEUTRAL** detent, align the switch, using a No. 43 (0.089 in.) drill bit or its equivalent.

2. Tighten the retaining bolts 7–9 ft. lbs.(9–12 Nm).

NOTE: The neutral start switch is located on the side of the transaxle.

Band Adjustments

Both the overdrive and the low/intermediate bands have special measurements that must be taken with special measuring tools that will measure the servo travel.

OVERDRIVE SERVO MEASUREMENT

0.070–0.149 in. (1.8–3.8mm).

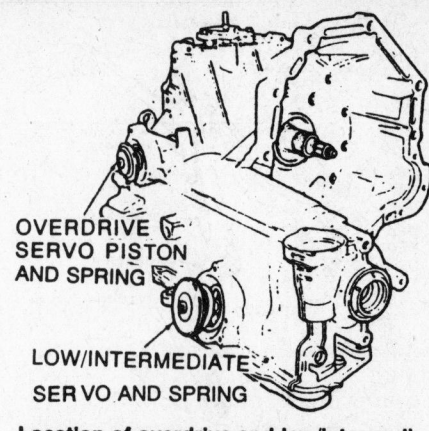

OVERDRIVE SERVO PISTON AND SPRING

LOW/INTERMEDIATE SERVO AND SPRING

Location of overdrive and low/intermediate servo pistons and springs

LOW/INTERMEDIATE SERVO MEASUREMENT

0.216–0.255 in (5.5–6.5mm).

NOTE: If a new low/intermediate band is installed, the measurement should be 0.196–0.236 in. (5.0–6.0mm).

Oil Pan

REMOVAL & INSTALLATION

1. Raise the vehicle and support safely.

2. Place a wide mouthed drain pan under the transaxle assembly.

3. Loosen the side pump and valve body pan bolts and allow the fluid to drain.

4. Loosen the lower pan bolts and with the pan loose from the transaxle, allow the fluid to drain to the level of the pan flange.

5. When the fluid has drained, remove the remaining pan bolts and remove both pans from the transaxle.

—— CAUTION ——

NOTE:

Fluid will be remaining in the lower pan until it is removed from the transaxle case. If the fluid is hot, be extremely careful of skin burns.

6. Install new gaskets on the oil pans and install the pans on the transaxle. Tighten the pan bolts to 10–12 ft. lbs.

7. Lower the vehicle and fill the transaxle with correct fluid.

8. Start the vehicle and recheck the fluid level.

NOTE: The fill capacity of a completely empty transaxle is 10.4 U.S. quarts.

GENERAL MOTORS CORPORATION

THM 180C Automatic Transmission

NOTE: Only automatic transmission fluid marked Dexron® II is to be used in the THM 180C automatic transmission.

ADJUSTMENTS

Detent (Downshift) Cable

1. The detent cable runs from the right hand hook up on the transmission, through a support on the cam cover to the carburetor. A "snaplock", device holds the cable to the support. To adjust the detent cable, first disengage the "snaplock". The cable should be free to slide through this lock.
2. Move the carburetor lever to the wide open throttle position.
3. Push the "snaplock" flush and return the carburetor to the closed position.

Low Band

1. Raise the vehicle and support safely.
2. Remove the oil pan and valve body from the transmission.
3. Loosen the locknut and tighten the servo adjusting bolt to 40 inch lbs.
4. Back the adjusting bolt off exactly 5 turns and tighten the locknut while holding the adjusting bolt to prevent turning.
5. Reinstall the valve body and oil pan. Fill the transmission with fluid to specifications. Start the engine and recheck the level. Check for leakage. Lower the vehicle and roadtest.

Vacuum Modulator

REMOVAL & INSTALLATION

1. The vacuum modulator threads into the case from the rear, just above the transmission oil pan flange.
2. When removing the modulator, be careful of the plunger. Always install a new O-ring when changing modulators. Lube the O-ring with petroleum jelly or Dexron® II.
3. Due to the shape of the modulator, it will be difficult to use a torque wrench. However, torque should be 35–40 ft. lbs.

Oil Pan

REMOVAL & INSTALLATION

1. To remove the oil pan, first raise and safely support vehicle.
2. Remove the oil pan bolts from the front and side of the pan, allowing the oil to drain into a pan.
3. Remove the remaining bolts and tap pan loose.
4. Clean pan well. Debris in the pan should be investigated as part of transmission diagnosis.
5. Remove the bolts holding the screen to the valve body; remove the screen. Discard gasket and thoroughly clean the screen in solvent and dry with compressed air.
6. Install screen with new gasket and torque bolts to 13–15 ft. lbs.
7. Install pan with new gasket and torque bolts to 7–10 ft. lbs.
8. Lower car and refill with 3 quarts Dexron® II.
9. Allow engine to idle in **PARK**, move selector through each range and end up in **PARK**.
10. Add fluid if necessary.

NOTE: There is no provision for draining the converter.

THM 200C Automatic Transmission

NOTE: The torque converter is a welded unit and cannot be disassembled for service. Any internal malfunctions require the replacement of converter assembly. The replacement converter must be matched to the model transmission through parts identification. No specific identification is available for matching the converter to the transmission for the average repair shop.

Vehicles equipped with diesel engines use a different torque converter. To identify these units, examine the weld nuts. Most gas engine converters have their weld nuts spot welded onto the converter housing, usually in 2 spots. The diesel converters have the weld nuts completely welded around their entire circumference.

Vehicles equipped with turbocharged V6 engines use a different torque converter. These units have a high stall speed converter, allowing a

1. Retainer
2. Washer
3. Lever
4. Park sleeve
5. Detent cable assembly
6. Cable seal
7. Cable retainer
8. Screw (M6.3 × 16 × 9.8)
9. Indicator lamp housing
10. Screw (M4.2 × 1.41 × 10)
11. Nut
12. Pointer
13. Shifter assembly
14. Washer
15. Bushing
16. Nut
17. Handle assembly
18. Nut
19. Back-up lamp switch
20. Shaft housing assembly
21. Shifter lever
22. Rod adjusting link
23. Shift selector rod assembly
24. Nut (M10 × 1.5)
25. Shift selector rod clevis pin
26. Shift selector rod clevis

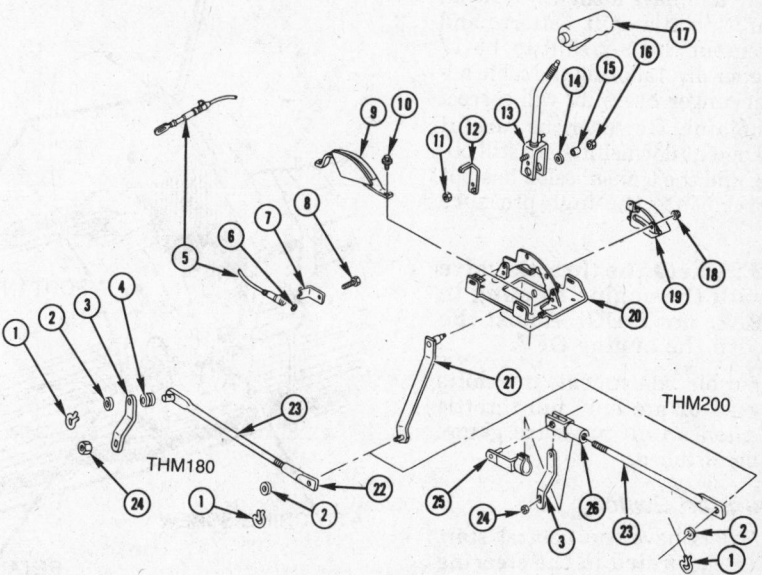

Chevette and T1000 floor shift linkage. Note the difference between the THM180 and THM200 linkage

stall speed of about 2800 rpm. These converters must not be replaced with a standard converter, otherwise performance will be sluggish and unsatisfactory. When ordering replacements for the turbo-charged units, make certain to specify that the vehicle has turbocharging in order to obtain the proper replacement.

Use only Dexron® II automatic transmission fluid or its equivalent to fill, refill or correct the fluid level.

ADJUSTMENTS

Throttle Valve Cable

1. Check transmission oil level and correct as required.
2. Make sure the engine is in a reasonable state of tune.
3. If possible, doublecheck a parts catalog source to insure that the proper cable has been installed on the vehicle.
4. Check that the T.V. cable is connected at both ends.
5. Adjust cable as follows.
   a. Unlock the "snap lock" on the T.V. cable.
   b. With the engine **OFF**, move the carburetor lever to the wide open position.
   c. Hold the lever and push the "snap lock" flush to hold the cable housing securely.
   d. Release carburetor lever.
   e. Check cable for sticking and binding.

----- CAUTION -----

If the cable is adjusted and locked properly, the cable housing will extend through the cable snap lock assembly from $^1/_{16}$–$^5/_{16}$ in.

After adjustment, some transmissions may still have a slightly delayed minimum throttle shift pattern, and even drag out the 1–2 shift to 14–17 mph. Generally, tailoring the cable adjustment longer by ⅛ in. will correct the complaint. However, be careful that the detent downshifts are still obtainable, and the transmission has not been forced into the high pressure mode.

NOTE: Check the throttle valve cable with the engine running in NEUTRAL, not PARK. Adjust the cable with the engine OFF.

If, after cable adjustment, the shifts are delayed or are only full throttle shifts, then an oil pressure gauge should be installed.

Neutral Start Switch

Some models have the neutral start switch incorporated in the steering column linkage and are not found in the normal position and in combination with the backup lamp switch. A mechanical block on the automatic transmission gear selector prevents the engine from starting except in the **NEUTRAL** or **PARK** positions.

Intermediate Band

The intermediate band is adjusted by a selective intermediate servo apply pin. Because of possible inaccessiblity to the intermediate servo piston assembly on the transmission/vehicle application, due to the clearance restrictions, the special tools needed for the pin selection cannot be installed and used. Should the band adjustment be necessary and the adjusting clearance is not available, the transmission would have to be removed from the vehicle.

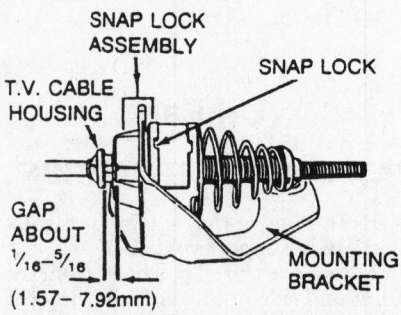

Throttle valve cable snap lock assembly

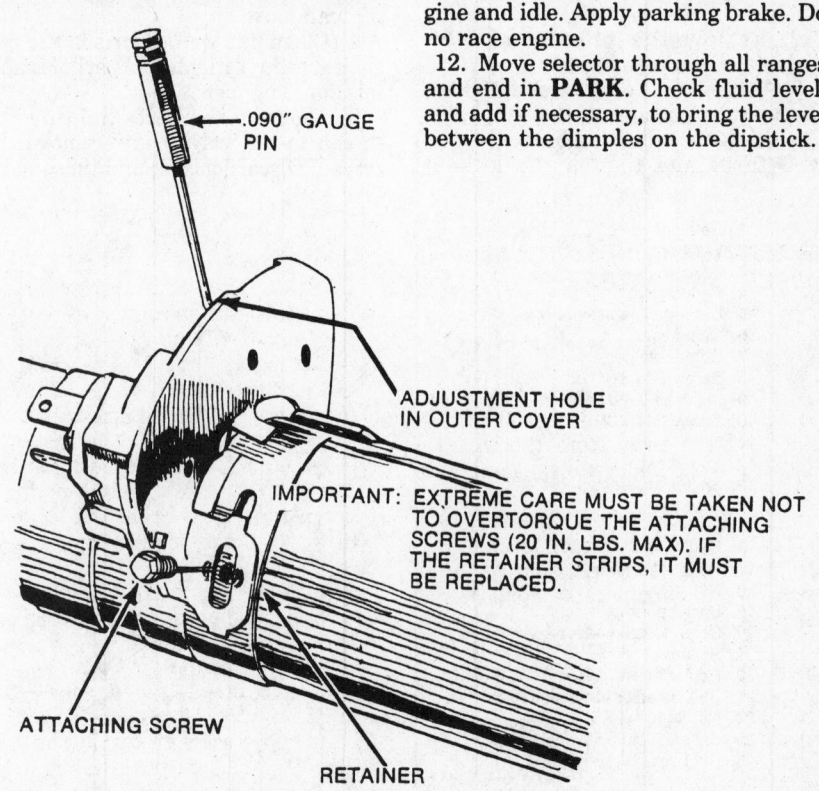

Neutral safety switch adjustment—column shift

Oil Pan

REMOVAL & INSTALLATION

1. Raise and safely support car.
2. Place drain pan under transmission oil pan. Remove the oil pan attaching bolts from the front and side of the pan.
3. Loosen, but do not remove the rear pan bolts, then bump the pan loose and allow fluid to drain.
4. Remove the remaining bolts and remove pan.
5. Clean pan in solvent and dry with compressed air.
6. Remove the 2 bolts holding the filter screen to the valve body. Discard gasket.
7. Clean screen in solvent and blow dry.
8. Install screen with new gasket; torque bolts to 6–10 ft. lbs.

NOTE: On some of the THM-200 a self aligning pan gasket is used. These gaskets have 3–4 smaller bolt holes in the corner of the gaskets. The purpose of these holes is to align the gasket to the oil pan and hold the bolts in place while the pan is being installed.

9. Install new gasket on pan and torque bolts to 10–13 ft. lbs.
10. Lower car and add 3 quarts of Dexron® II.
11. With selector in **PARK** start engine and idle. Apply parking brake. Do no race engine.
12. Move selector through all ranges and end in **PARK**. Check fluid level, and add if necessary, to bring the level between the dimples on the dipstick.

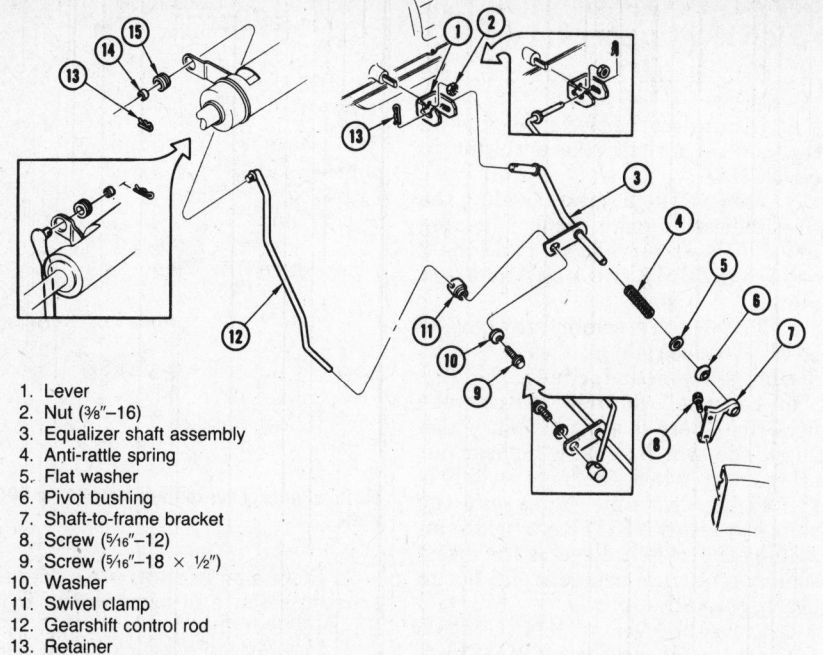

1. Lever
2. Nut (3/8″–16)
3. Equalizer shaft assembly
4. Anti-rattle spring
5. Flat washer
6. Pivot bushing
7. Shaft-to-frame bracket
8. Screw (5/16″–12)
9. Screw (5/16″–18 × 1/2″)
10. Washer
11. Swivel clamp
12. Gearshift control rod
13. Retainer
14. Control rod sleeve
15. Bushing

Typical rear wheel drive column shift linkage. Note that the location of the swivel clamp (11) may differ slightly between models.

THM 200–4R Automatic Transmission

ADJUSTMENTS

NOTE: Use only Dexron® II automatic transmission or its equivalent to fill, refill or correct the fluid level.

T.V. Cable

GASOLINE ENGINES WITH SELF-ADJUSTING CABLE

1. Be sure engine is stopped. Do not attempt to adjust with the engine running.
2. Depress the adjusting tab. Move the slider back through the fitting in the direction away from the throttle body until the slider stops against the fitting.
3. Release the adjusting tab.
4. Open the carburetor lever to the "full throttle stop" position to automatically adjust the cable. Release the carburetor lever.
5. Check the cable for binding and road test the vehicle. The adjustment is correct if the shifting is normal.
6. If the shift is delayed or only at full throttle, the oil pan will have to be removed and the internal linkage and valve body inspected for binding or distortion.

CABLES USED WITH DIESEL ENGINES

1. With the engine stopped, disconnect the cruise control rod, if equipped.
2. Disconnect the transmission T.V. or detent cable terminal from the throttel assembly.
3. Loosen the locknut on the pump rod and shorten by several turns.
4. Rotate the lever assembly to the full throttle position and hold.
5. Lenghten the pump rod until the injection pump lever contacts the full throttle stop.
6. Release the lever assembly and tighten the pump rod locknut.
7. Remove the pump rod from the lever assembly.
8. Reconnect the T.V. or detent cable terminal to the throttle assembly.
9. Depress and hold the metal readjustment tab on the cable upper end. Move the slider through the fitting in the direction away from the lever assembly until the slider stops against the fitting.
10. Release the tab, rotate the lever assembly to the full throttle stop and release the lever assembly.
11. Reconnect the pump rod and cruise control rod, if equipped.
12. If equipped with cruise control, adjust the servo throttle rod to a minumum slack and put the clip in the first free hole nearest the bellcrank, but within the servo bail.

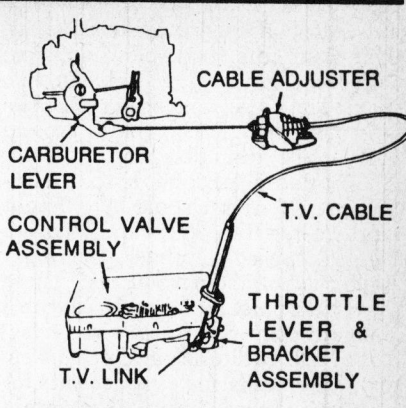

Throttle valve cable and linkage

Intermediate Band

The intermediate band is adjusted by selective sized apply pins, determined with the use of special measuring tools. This operation is normally performed during overhaul.

Oil Pan

REMOVAL & INSTALLATION

1. Raise the vehicle and support safely.
2. With a drain pan under the oil pan, remove the retaining bolts from the front and sides of the oil pan.
3. Loosen the rear bolts approximately 4 turns and carefully pry the oil pan loose from the transmission case.
4. Allow the fluid to drain into the drain pan and remove the retaining bolts from the rear of the oil pan and remove the pan and gasket.

NOTE: Various transmission models may have RTV sealant used in place of gaskets.

5. Using either the RTV or gasket on a clean oil pan, install the pan to the transmission case and tighten the retaining bolts to 10–13 ft. lbs. torque.

NOTE: Do no use the RTV sealant on oil pans that have raised stiffening ribs on the pan flange.

6. Lower the vehicle and add the proper amount of fluid to the transmission. Start engine and correct the fluid level as necessary.

THM 250C Automatic Transmission

NOTE: The torque converter is of welded construction and if damaged or contaminated, it should be replaced.

Vehicles equipped with diesel engine use a different torque converter. To identify these units, examine the weld nuts. Most gas engine converters have their weld nuts spot welded onto the converter housing, usually in two spots. The diesel converters have the weld nuts completely welded around their entire circumference.

Vehicles equipped with turbocharged V6 engines use a different torque converter. These units have a high stall speed converter, allowing a stall speed of about 2800 rpm. These converters must not be replaced with a standard converter, otherwise performance will be sluggish and unsatisfactory. When ordering replacements for the turbo-charged units, make certain to specify that the vehicle has turbocharging in order to obtain the proper replacement.

There are a number of differences between the standard version of this transmission and the lock-up torque converter version. The lock-up converter versions use a different case, an additional (auxiliary) valve body, and electrical solenoid, a governor pressure switch, and a different pump assembly and gasket, as well as a different input shaft. There are a few other components added to control the system, depending on the vehicle.

Use only automatic transmission fluids having the designations Dexron® II.

ADJUSTMENTS

Throttle Linkage (Control Cable)

1. With a small screwdriver, pry gently on the bottom of the snaplock to release the detent cable.
2. Push the carburetor lever to the wide open throttle position (engine off) and hold. Push the snaplock tab downward until flush with the cable.

Band Adjustment

The Turbo Hydramatic 250 is unique among the Hydramatic family in that it has an external band adjustment. The intermediate band adjustment should be performed every 60,000 miles along with a change of transmission fluid or sooner, if slippage is indicated. To adjust the band:
1. Place the gear selector in NEUTRAL and raise vehicle.
2. Hold the adjusting screw by means of an allen socket and loosen the locknut.
3. With a torque wrench on the socket, tighten the adjuster screw to 30 inch lbs. (3.5 Nm) then back off 3 complete turns. Hold the adjuster in position and tighten the locknut to 15 ft. lbs.

Neutral Start Switch
FLOOR SHIFT MODELS

1. Remove the 2 screws that hold the console.
2. Disconnect the electrical plugs on the neutral switch. Place shifter in NEUTRAL.
3. Remove the 2 screws holding the shift indication plate, 2 more holding the shift lever curved cover and the 2 others holding the neutral start switch.
4. The switch assembly may have to be tilted to the right as it is removed to disengage the actuator tang.
5. To install the new switch, take note that there is a plastic pin which aligns the switch. This will shear out of the way when the new switch is shifted the first time. Make sure the shift lever is in NEUTRAL before installing the switch. Reverse the disassembly sequence, being careful not to over-tighten the screws.
6. Move the lever out of NEUTRAL to shear the plastic locating pin. Check that the electrical connectors are firmly in place.
7. Apply brakes and check that vehicle will start in PARK and NEUTRAL only, and that the back-up lamps work properly.

If the switch is not being replaced, only adjusted, first obtain a piece of wire or other pin 0.090 in. in diameter. Then insert it in the service adjustment hole to hold the switch in NEUTRAL. Tighten the screws, remove pin and assemble console.

Vacuum Modulator
REMOVAL & INSTALLATION

1. Remove the vacuum hose from vacuum modulator. Inspect the hose for signs of transmission fluid that would indicate a leaky modulator.
2. Remove the modulator hold-down bolt and bracket.
3. Pull the modulator straight back from the case. If the modulator is to be reused, be sure to change the O-ring.
4. The modulator valve can be removed if necessary.
5. Installation is the reversal of the above sequence. Remember to renew the O-ring, coat it with petroleum jelly or Dexron® II. Check the vacuum hose for cracks and be sure to check and adjust the fluid level.

Oil Pan
REMOVAL & INSTALLATION

1. Raise and safely support vehicle. On some vehicles, the transmission may have to be supported and the crossmember removed for access.

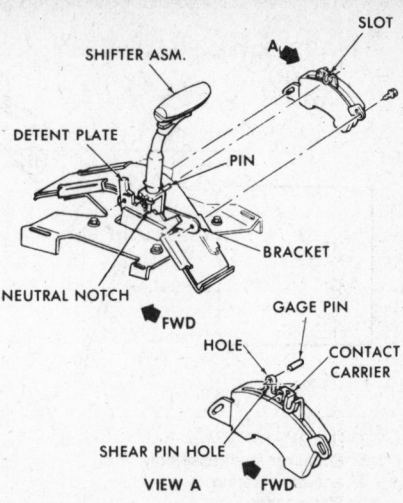

Neutral safety switch adjustment—floorshift

2. Place a large drain pan under the transmission and remove the front and side bolts on the pan.
3. Loosen but do not remove the rear pan bolts. Carefully bump the pan with a rubber mallet to free the pan. If the pan is pried loose instead, be very careful not to damage the gasket surfaces. Allow fluid to drain.
4. Remove the remaining screws, remove the pan and discard the gasket. Remove the 2 screws holding the strainer to the valve body, remove the strainer and its gasket.
5. Thoroughly clean the strainer with solvent and compressed air. If it cannot be cleaned well, replace it.
6. Make sure the pan is clean and that the gasket surfaces are clean and straight.
7. Using a new gasket, install the strainer and its 2 screws. Put a new gasket on the oil pan and carefully install the pan. Torque the pan bolts to 12 ft. lbs. (16 Nm).
8. Lower the vehicle and add approximately 5 pints of Dexron® II. With selector in PARK, apply brakes, start engine and allow to idle. **Do not race engine.** Make sure carburetor comes off fast idle. Move the selector through each range, end in PARK and check fluid level. Since the transmission is not yet to operating temperature, the proper level would be ¼ in. below "ADD". Do not overfill.

NOTE: There is no provision for draining the torque converter. In cases of transmission overhaul when the converter will be dry, approximately 20 pints will be required total. Do not overfill. Begin by adding 8 pints, and then continue to add while the engine is running, transmission in PARK, until the proper level is reached.

THM 350C Automatic Transmission

NOTE: The torque converter is of a welded construction and cannot be disassembled for repairs. Any internal malfunctions require the replacement of the complete converter assembly. The diameter of the converters vary from 11–13 in., depending upon the engine application in the vehicle. Converter replacement should be confined to the converter matching the transmission model and engine size. Do no attempt to interchange converters by diameter size only, as poor vehicle speed or operation can result.

Vehicles equipped with diesel engines use a different torque converter. To identify these units, examine the weld nuts. Most gas engine converters have their weld nuts spot welded onto the converter housing, usually in 2 spots. The diesel converters have the weld nuts completely welded around their entire circumference.

Vehicles eqipped with turbocharged V6 engines use a different torque converter. These units have a high stall speed converter, allowing a stall speed of about 2800 rpm. These converters must not be replaced with a standard converter, otherwise performance will be sluggish and unsatisfactory. When ordering replacements for the turbocharged units, make certain to specify that the vehicle has turbocharging in order to obtain the proper replacement.

Torrington bearings are used in various torque converter models in place of thrust spacers and should be considered when diagnosing bearing failure noises.

Converter clutch units are different for V6 or V8 engine applications and should not be interchanged. Poor engine and/or transmission operation will occur.

Use only Dexron® II automatic transmission fluid or its equivalent.

ADJUSTMENTS

Throttle Linkage

If the shift linkage and related parts do not appear to be at fault or out of adjustment, then the Detent Control Cable should be checked. The following procedure is suggested.

1. With a small prybar or equivalent, pry gently on the snaplock retainer to release the detent cable.
2. Push the carburetor lever to the wide open throttle position (engine off) and hold.

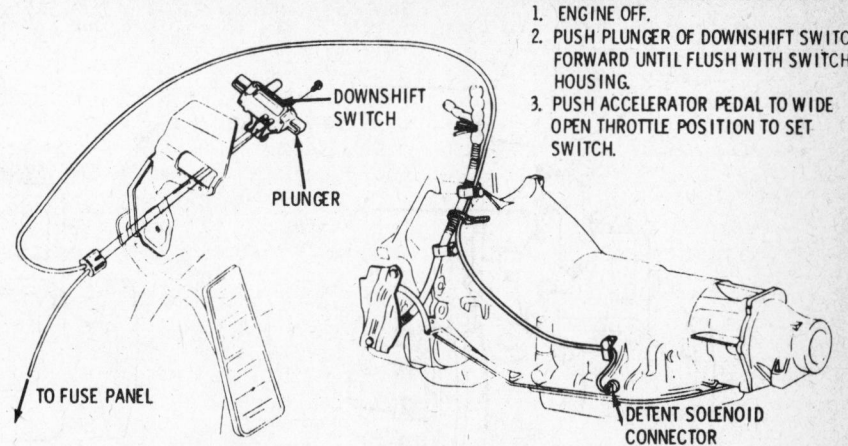

DOWNSHIFT SWITCH ADJUSTMENT
1. ENGINE OFF.
2. PUSH PLUNGER OF DOWNSHIFT SWITCH FORWARD UNTIL FLUSH WITH SWITCH HOUSING.
3. PUSH ACCELERATOR PEDAL TO WIDE OPEN THROTTLE POSITION TO SET SWITCH.

Detent (downshift) switch adjustment—except Cadillac

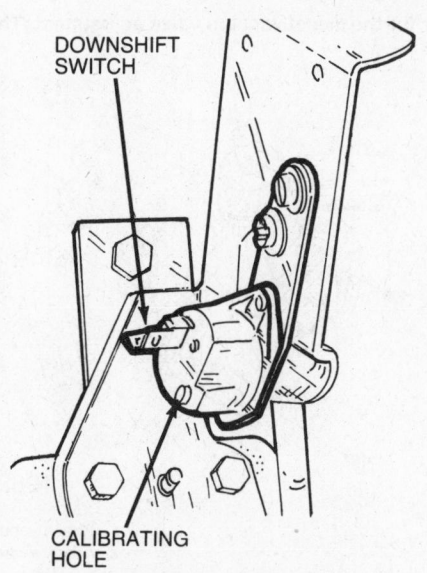

Cadillac accelerator pedal-mounted detent (downshift) switch

3. Push the snaplock downward until flush with the cable.

If none of the adjustments have cured the problem, and assuming that the engine is in at least a reasonable state of tune, then improper adjustment and incorrect fluid level can be ruled out. This leaves only hydraulic malfunctions or mechanical malfunctions. Therefore, to help pinpoint the problem, an oil pressure check should be made.

Band Adjustment

The intermediate overrun band has no external adjusting provision. A selective pin is used to control the servo piston travel during the application of the band. The valve body must be removed for this operation and a special pin selection tool must be used to determine the length pin needed.

Mechanical Neutral Start System

This system relies on a mechanical block, rather than the starter safety switch to prevent starting the engine in other than **PARK** or **NEUTRAL**.

The mechanical block is achieved by a cast in finger added to the switch actuator rack, which interferes with the bowl plate in all shift positions except **NEUTRAL** or **PARK**. This interference prevents rotation of the lock cylinder into the START position.

In either **P** or **N**, this finger passes through the bowl plate slots, allowing the lock cylinder full rotational travel into the Start position.

Vacuum Valve

DIESEL ENGINES

1. Remove the air cleaner assembly.
2. Remove the air intake crossover from the intake manifold. Cover the intake manifold passages to prevent foreign material from entering the engine.
3. Disconnect the throttle rod from the injection pump throttle lever.
4. Loosen the transmission vacuum valve-to-injection pump bolts.
5. Mark and disconnect the vacuum lines from the vacuum valve.
6. Attach a carburetor angle gauge adapter (Kent-Moore tool J–26701–15 or its eqvalent) to the injection pump throttle lever. Attach an angle gauge (J26701 or its eqvalent) to the gauge adapter.

NOTE: To service the V6 diesel, it may be necessary to file the gauge adapter in order for it to fit the thicker throttle lever of the V6 injection pump.

7. Turn thr throttle lever to the wide open throttle position. Set the angle gauge to zero degrees.

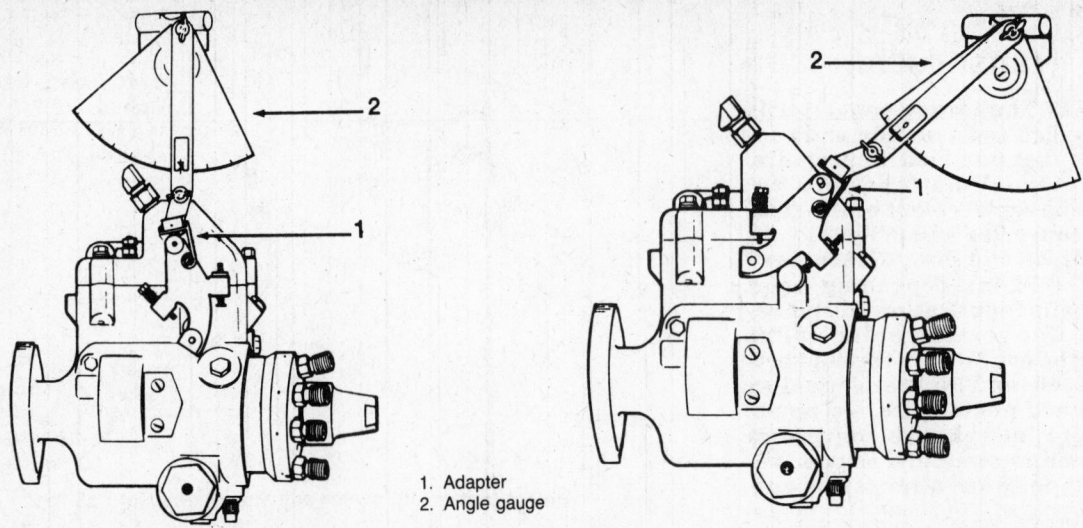

1. Adapter
2. Angle gauge

Installation of an angle gauge and an adapter for the diesel vacuum valve adjustment. The gauge is positioned differently, depending upon the type of throttle lever which is used.

Year	Engine	Setting
1982–88	V8	58°

Year	Engine	Setting	In. Hg.
1982–88	V8	58°	10½

8. Center the bubble in the gauge level.

9. Set the angle gauge to one of the following settings, according to the year and type of engine.

10. Attach a vacuum gauge to Port 2 and a vacuum source (hand-held vacuum pump) to Port 1 of the vacuum valve.

11. Apply 18–22 in. of vacuum to the valve. Slowly rotate the vacuum valve until the vacuum reading drops to one of the following values.

12. Tighten the vacuum valve retaining bolts.

13. Reconnect the origional vacuum lines in the vacuum valve.

14. Remove the angle gauge and adapter.

15. Connect the throttle rod to the throttle lever.

16. Install the air intake crossover, using new gaskets.

17. Install the air cleaner assembly.

Vacuum Modulator

REMOVAL & INSTALLATION

1. Remove the vacuum hose from the modulator. Inspect the hose for signs of transmission fluid that would indicate a leaky modulator.

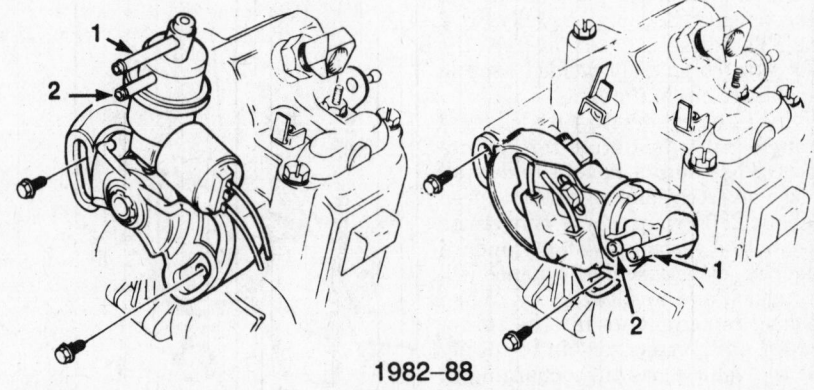

1982–88

1. Attach vacuum source here
2. Attach vacuum gauge here

Transmission vacuum valve adjustment— diesel models

2. Remove the modulator hold-down bolt and bracket.

3. Pull the modulator straight back from the case. If the modulator is to be reused, be sure to change the O-ring seal.

4. The modulator valve can be removed from the case for cleaning or inspection is necessary.

5. Installation is the reverse of the above sequence. Renew the O-ring, coat it with petroleum jelly or Dexron® II. The attaching bolt is torqued to 130 inch lbs.

6. When re-installing the vacuum hose be sure to check for cracks. The transmission fluid level should also be checked and adjusted if necessary.

Oil Pan

REMOVAL & INSTALLATION

1. Raise and safely support vehicle.

On some vehicles, the transmission may have to be jacked up slightly and supported and the crossmember removed for access.

2. Place a large drain pan under the transmission and remove the front and side bolts on the pan.

3. Loosen but do not remove the rear pan bolts. Allow the fluid to drain.

4. Remove the remaining screws, remove the pan and discard the gasket. Remove the 2 screws that hold the oil filter to the valve body and discard the filter and its gasket.

5. Thoroughly clean the oil pan and check that the gasket surface is flat and not distorted.

6. Using a new gasket, install a new filter and tighten the screws. Place a new gasket on the oil pan and carefully install the pan. Torque the pan bolts to 13 ft. lbs., being careful not to overtighten.

7. Lower the vehicle and add approximately 6 pints of Dexron® II.

With the selector in **PARK**, apply brakes, start engine and allow to idle. Do not race engine. Make sure the carburetor comes off fast idle. Move the selector through each range, end in **PARK** and check fluid level.

NOTE: There is no provision for draining the torque converter. In cases of transmission overhaul, when the converter will be empty, approximately 20 pints will be the required total. In cases where just the pan has been removed and drained, 8 pints should be sufficient. In any case, always check the dipstick rather than rely on a specific number of pints of fluid. Add while the engine is running, transmission in PARK, until the proper level is reached. Do not overfill.

THM 400 Automatic Transmission

NOTE: Use only automatic transmission fluids having the designations Dexron® II.

ADJUSTMENTS

Vacuum Modulator

Original equipment type modulators are not usually adjustable except on some older vehicles. Aftermarket type units often have a setscrew that can be adjusted to "fine tune" the shift speeds of the transmission. In practice, most rebuilders change the modulator with each unit that they rebuild since the modulator is sealed and it is difficult to determine a good one from a marginal one.

BAND

There is no external band adjustment on this unit. Band adjustment is only possible after the unit has been disassembled. A special tool is available for checking the pin length of the servo apply pin. These pins are changed if any adjustment is required. Generally, the band apply pins will not have to be changed unless the case is replaced.

Neutral Safety Switch

Most vehicles have a mechanical neutral start device enclosed in the steering column. This works in conjunction with the steering lock.

Oil Pan

REMOVAL & INSTALLATION

1. Raise and safely support vehicle. On some vehicles, the transmission

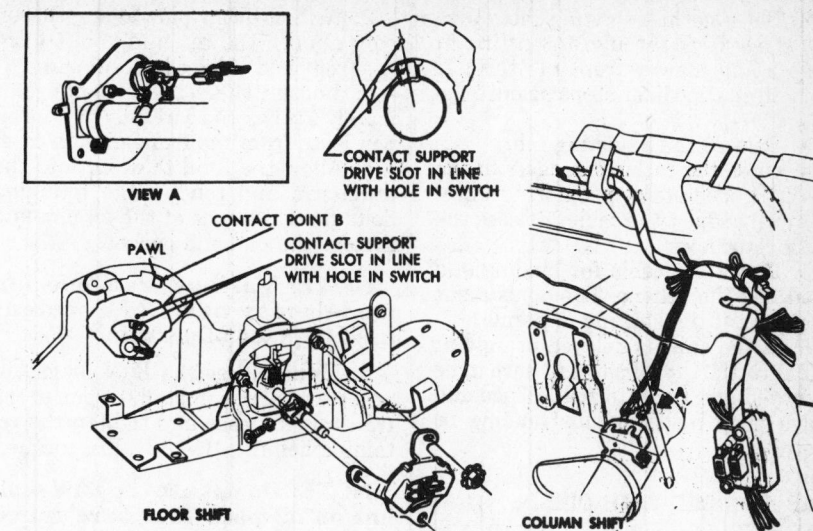

Typical neutral safety switch installation

may have to be supported and the crossmember removed for access.

2. Place a large drain pan under the transmission and remove the front and side bolts from the pan.

3. Loosen but do not remove the rear pan bolts. Carefully bump the pan with a rubber mallet to free the pan. If the pan is pried loose instead be very careful not to damage the gasket surfaces. Allow the fluid to drain.

4. Remove the remaining screws. Remove the pan and discard the gasket. Remove the attaching screw from the filter and remove the filter and pipe assembly.

5. Remove the pump intake pipe from the filter and discard the filter.

6. Remove and discard the intake pipe O-ring.

7. Thoroughly clean the oil pan and dry with compressed air. Make sure that all traces of the old gasket have been removed. Check the gasket surfaces of the pan for distortion, particularly around the bolt holes which are often dished in due to overtorque. If distorted, they can be straighten with a mallet and a block of wood.

8. Install a new O-ring onto the intake pipe and install the pipe into the filter.

9. Install the filter and pipe assembly into the transmission and install the retaining bolt.

10. Install a new gasket on the oil pan, making sure that all traces of the old gasket have been removed. Torque the pan bolts evenly to a torque of 12 ft. lbs.

11. Lower the vehicle and refill the transmission with approximately 4 quarts of Dexron® II since the filter has been replaced. If only the pan had been removed and the filter assembly was not disturbed, then less fluid will

be required; usually approximately 2–3 quarts will fill it depending on the model of the transmission.

Vacuum Modulator

REMOVAL & INSTALLATION

1. Raise and safely support vehicle.

2. Locate and remove the modulator retaining bolt. Disconnect the vacuum line.

3. Pull the modulator straight back from the case.

4. Discard the O-ring. The modulator valve can be removed from the case for cleaning if desired.

5. Install a new O-ring on the modulator body. Lube with petroleum jelly or transmission fluid.

6. Install the modulator valve if it was removed. Install the vacuum unit into the case.

7. Install the retainer and bolt. Torque to 20 ft. lbs. Connect the vacuum line.

THM 700–R4 Automatic Transmission

NOTE: Use only automatic transmission fluid having the designation of Dexron® II or its equivalent.

ADJUSTMENTS

T.V. Cable

GASOLINE ENGINES WITH SELF–ADJUSTING CABLE

1. Be sure engine is stopped. Do no attempt to adjust with the engine running.

2. Depress the adjusting tab. Move the slider back through the fitting in the direction away from the throttle body until the slider stops against the fitting.

3. Release the adjusting tab.

4. Open the carburetor lever to the "full throttle stop" position to automatically adjust the cable. Release the carburetor lever.

5. Check the cable for binding and road test the vehicle. The adjustment is correct if the shifting is normal.

6. If the shift is delayed or only at full throttle, the oil pan will have to be removed and the internal linkage and valve body inspected for binding or distortion.

CABLES USED WITH DIESEL ENGINES

1. With the engine stopped, disconnect the cruise control rod, if equpped.

2. Disconnect the transmission T.V. or detent cable terminal from the throttle assembly.

3. Loosen the locknut on the pump rod and shorten by several turns.

4. Rotate the lever assembly to the full throttle position and hold.

5. Lengthen the pump rod until the injection pump lever contacts the full throttle stop.

6. Release the lever assembly and tighten the pump rod locknut.

7. Remove the pump rod from the lever assembly.

8. Reconnect the T.V. or detent cable terminal to the throttle assembly.

9. Depress and hold the metal readjustment tab on the cable upper end. Move the slider through the fitting in the direction away from the lever assembly until the slider stops against the fitting.

10. Release the tab, rotate the lever assembly to the full throttle stop and release the lever assembly.

11. Reconnect the pump rod and cruise control rod, if equipped.

12. If equipped with cruise control, adjust the servo throttle rod to a minumum slack and put the clip in the first free hole nearest the bellcrank, but with the servo bail.

2–4 Band

The 2–4 band is adjusted by selective sized apply pins, determined with the use of special measuring tools. This operation is normally performed during overhaul.

Oil Pan

REMOVAL & INSTALLATION

1. Raise the vehicle and support safely.

2. With a drain pan under the oil pan, remove the retaining bolts from the front and sides of the oil pan.

3. Loosen the rear bolts approximately 4 turns and carefully pry the oil pan loose from the transmission case.

4. Allow the fluid to drain into the drain pan and remove the retaining bolts from the rear of the oil pan and remove the pan and gasket.

NOTE: Various transmission models may have RTV sealant used in place of gaskets.

5. Using either the RTV or gasket on a clean oil pan, install the pan to the transmission case and tighten the retaining bolts to 10–13 ft. lbs. torque.

NOTE: Do not use the RTV sealant on oil pans that have raised stiffening ribs on the pan flange.

6. Lower the vehicle and add the proper amount of fluid to the transmission. Start engine and correct the fluid level as necessary.

GENERAL MOTORS AUTOMATIC TRANSAXLE

Automatic Transaxle THM 125C

NOTE: Only automatic transmission fluid marked Dexron® II is to be used in the THM 125C transaxles.

ADJUSTMENTS

NOTE: To identify the transmission/transaxle used in your vehicle, refer to the transmission/transaxle oil pan outlines at the beginning of this section.

THROTTLE LINKAGE

The cable should be checked for freeness by pulling out on the upper end of the cable. The cable should travel a short distance with slight spring resistance. This light resistance is caused by the small coiled return spring on the T.V. lever and bracket that returns the lever to zero T.V., or closed throttle position. Pulling the cable farther out moves the lever to contact the T.V. plunger which compresses the T.V. cable, it should return to the zero T.V. position. This test checks the cable in

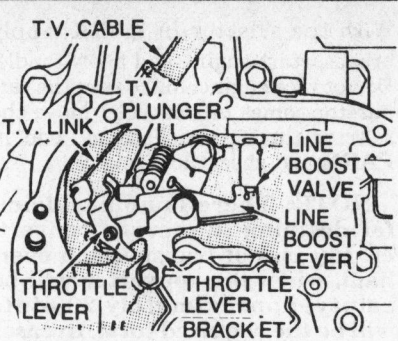

Throttle lever and bracket assembly

its housing, the T.V. lever and bracket, and the throttle valve plunger in its bushing for freeness. To check on the adjustment and verify that it is correct, use the following procedure.

1. Install line pressure gauge. Adjust engine speed to 1000 rpm with the selector in **PARK**, and check line pressure.

2. Check line pressure in **NEUTRAL** at 1000 rpm. Pressure should be in the same as or no more than 10 psi higher than in **PARK**.

3. Adjust engine speed to 1400 rpm and make sure that there is an increase in line pressure.

Readjustment

If readjustment is necessary, the following procedure is suggested:

1. Depress and hold the metal lock tab that will be found on the cable adjuster by the idler lever.

2. Move the slider through the fitting away from the idler lever until the slider stops against the fitting.

3. Release the metal lock tab.

4. As a double check, repeat the adjustment.

Intermediate Band

Selective sizes of the intermediate band apply pin are the only adjustment provided for the intermediate band. Special measuring tools are needed in conjunction with an inch pound torque wrench. To check for the proper intermediate band apply pin, the following procedure should be used.

1. Remove the lower cover pan and intermediate servo assembly.

2. Install the special indicator measuring tool and hold in place with 2 intermediate servo cover bolts.

3. Remove the band apply pin from the intermediate servo assembly and install the special measuring pin over the band apply pin.

4. Install the pin assembly into the previously attached indicator measuring gauge.

5. Apply 100 inch lbs. torque to the special indicator measuring tool to compress the band.

6. Should the indicator tool not register on its predetermined line, the apply pin would have to be changed and the procedure repeated.

7. Should the use of the selective pins not give the proper reading, the transaxle would have to be removed and disassembled and the band or components replaced.

Oil Pan

REMOVAL & INSTALLATION

1. Raise car and suitably support.
2. Place drain pan under transaxle oil pan.
3. Remove oil pan bolts from the front and side only.
4. Loosen rear oil pan bolts 4 Turns.
5. Lightly tap oil pan with rubber mallet to allow the fluid to drain.
6. To install reverse thr removal procedures. Torque pan bolts to 133 inch lbs.

Automatic Transaxle THM 325–4L

NOTE: Dexron® II automatic transmission fluid or its equivalent is the only recommended automatic transmission fluid to be used in this unit.

ADJUSTMENTS

Throttle Valve Linkage

1. Check transmission oil level and correct as required.
2. Be sure engine is operating properly and brakes are not dragging.
3. Check for correct cable.
4. Check that the cable is connected at both ends.

Adjusting Cable (Diesel Engine Only)

1. Stop engine.
2. Remove cruise control rod (if so equipped).
3. Disconnect transmission detent cable terminal from throttle assembly.
4. Loosen locknut on pump rod and shorten several turns.
5. Rotate the lever assembly to the full throttle position and hold.
6. Lengthen pump rod until the injection pump lever contacts the full throttle stop.
7. Release the lever assembly and tighten pump rod locknut.
8. Remove the pump rod from the lever assembly.
9. Reconnect the transmission detent cable terminal to throttle assembly.
10. Depress and hold the metal re-

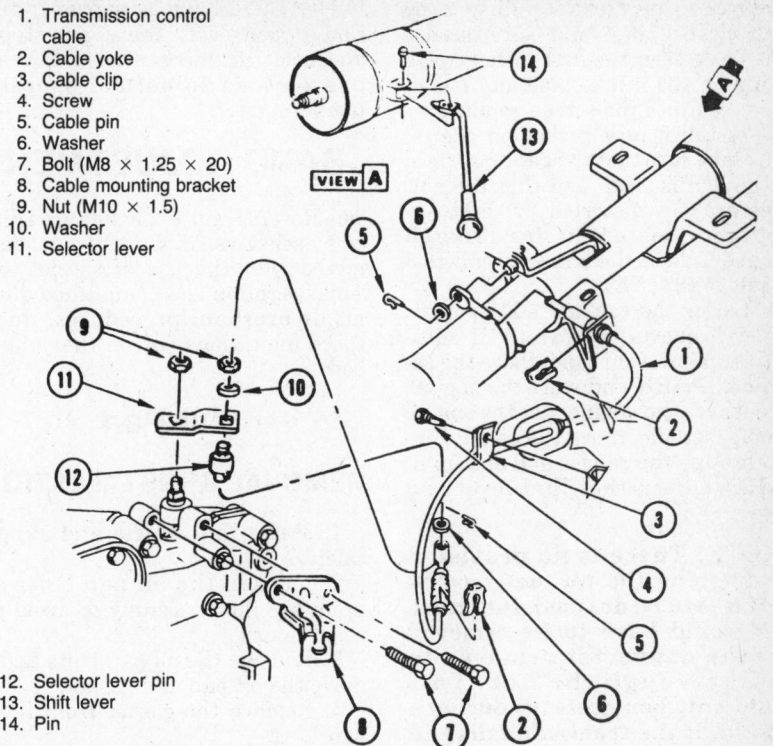

1. Transmission control cable
2. Cable yoke
3. Cable clip
4. Screw
5. Cable pin
6. Washer
7. Bolt (M8 × 1.25 × 20)
8. Cable mounting bracket
9. Nut (M10 × 1.5)
10. Washer
11. Selector lever
12. Selector lever pin
13. Shift lever
14. Pin

VIEW A

Typical front wheel drive column shift cable and related components—except Eldorado, Riviera, Seville, and Toronado. Note that the cable attachment at the transaxle is the same for floor shift models.

adjust tab on the cable upper end. Move the slider through the fitting in the direction away from the lever assembly until the slider stops against the fitting.
11. Release the re-adjust tab, rotate the lever assembly to the full throttle stop and release the lever assembly.
12. Reconnect the pump rod (and cruise control throttle rod if so equipped).
13. If equipped with cruise control, adjust the servo throttle rod to minimum slack (engine off) then put clip in first free hole closest to the bellcrank but within the servo bail.

Adjusting Type Cable (Gasoline Engine)

1. Stop engine.
2. Depress re-adjust tab. Move slider back through fitting in direction away from throttle body until slider stops against fitting.
3. Release re-adjust tab.
4. Open throttle valve lever to "full throttle stop" position to automatically adjust cable. Release throttle valve lever.
5. Check cable for sticking and binding.

BAND ADJUSTMENT

The THM 325–4L automatic transaxle

uses an intermediate band and intermediate servo assembly with a selective band apply pin. The use of special tools are needed to select the proper length apply pin and because of the transaxle location in the vehicle body, only the servo cover and piston assembly removal should be attempted. Band apply pin measurements should be accomplished with the transaxle removed from the vehicle.

Oil Pan

REMOVAL & INSTALLATION

1. Remove the oil pan by first raising and safely supporting the vehicle.
2. Place a large drain pan under the transaxle and remove the bolts from just 3 sides and loosen the bolts on the fourth side just enough to allow the pan to hang down and drain.
3. Remove the remaining bolts and the pan. Discard the gasket.
4. The pan should be cleaned with solvent and blown dry with compressed air.
5. If the filter is to be serviced, remove it and discard the O-ring that makes the seal at the intake pipe.
6. Thoroughly clean the screen in solvent and blow dry with compressed air. If, for some reason, contaminates

have made the screen too dirty to be easily cleaned, it should be replaced.

7. To reassemble, first install a new O-ring on the intake pipe and install the screen into the screen retainer.

8. Install a new gasket on the oil pan. Make sure that the gasket surface on the pan is clean and that the bolt holes are not distorted or dished-in from over-torqued bolts. Install the oil pan and tighten the screws evenly to a torque of 12 ft. lbs.

9. Lower the car and add approximately 5 quarts of Dexron® II automatic transmission fluid. Place the selector in **PARK** and start the engine. Do not race the engine. Let the engine idle off fast idle, move the selector lever through the ranges and end up in **PARK**. Check the fluid level and correct.

NOTE: There is no provision for draining the torque converter. If it is to be drained, the transaxle would have to be removed and the converter removed to drain through the hub. This would only be necessary during a rebuild. If the transaxle fails and metal particles and debris have been spread throughout the system, the converter should be replaced.

Automatic Transaxle THM 440–T4

NOTE: Dexron® II automatic transmission fluid or its equivalent is the only recommended automatic transmission fluid to be used in this unit. The use of any other grade of fluid can lead to unsatisfactory performance or complete unit failure.

ADJUSTMENTS

T.V. Cable

1. After the installation of the cable to the transaxle, engine bracket and cable actuating lever, be sure the cable slider is in its fully re-adusted position.

2. Rotate the cable actuating lever to its full travel position.

3. The slider must move (or rachet) towards the lever when the lever is in its rotated position.

Re–adjustment

1. Be sure the engine is stopped.

2. Depress and hold the metal re-adjust tab at the engine end of the T.V. cable.

3. Move the slider until it stops against the fitting.

4. Release the re-adjustment tab.

5. Check to be sure the cable moves freely. The cable may appear to function properly with the engine stopped and cold. Re-check after the vehicle has warmed to normal operating temperature.

BAND ADJUSTMENT

The Reverse and 1–2 bands are adjusted by selective sized apply pins, determined with the use of special tools. This operation is accomplished during major overhaul procedures, due to space limitations within the vehicle's body.

Oil Pan

REMOVAL & INSTALLATION

1. Raise the vehicle and support safely.

2. Loosen the oil pan bolts and drain the fluid carefully to avoid personal injury.

3. Remove the oil pan bolts and remove the oil pan and gasket.

4. Remove the gasket from the oil pan.

5. Install the oil pan and gasket.

6. Install the oil pan retaining bolts and torque to 10 ft. lbs.

7. Fill the transaxle with specified automatic transmission fluid, start the engine and recheck fluid level.

Vacuum Modulator

REMOVAL & INSTALLATION

1. Depending upon vehicle model, either raise and support safely or work from the top of the engine compartment Remove the vacuum line at the modulator.

2. Remove the modulator retaining screw and clamp at the base of the unit.

3. Remove the modulator and O-ring from the transaxle assembly.

4. Carefully install the modulator into the transaxle case. Do not damage the modulator valve.

5. Install the clamp and screw to hold the modulator to the case. Torque to 20 ft. lbs.

6. Install the vacuum hose to the modulator and complete assembly as required.

Automatic Transaxle A131L and A240E

NOTE: The A240E 4 speed transaxle, also called Electronic Controlled Transaxle (ECT), differs from the oil pressure control type transaxle A131L 3 speed in that it is controlled by a micro-computer. On the A131L the drain and refill capacity is 2.4 U.S. quarts and the dry fill capacity is 5.8 U.S. quarts. On the A240E the drain and refill capacity is 3.3 U.S. quarts and the dry fill capacity is 7.6 U.S. quarts. The correct fluid specification is the use of Dexron® II automatic transmission fluid, or its equivalent.

ADJUSTMENTS

Throttle Cable

1. Depress the accelerator pedal completely and check that the throttle valve opens fully. If the throttle valve does not open fully, adjust the accelerator link

2. Fully depress the accelerator

3. Loosen the adjustment nuts.

4. Adjust the throttle cable housing so that the distance between the end of the boot and the stopper on the cable is correct. The distance must be 0.04 in. (0.1mm).

5. Tighten the adjusting nuts and recheck the adjustment.

Transaxle Shift Control

1. Loosen the swivel nut on the lever.

2. Push the manual lever fully towards the right side of the vehicle.

3. Return the lever 2 notches to the **N** position.

4. Set the shift lever in the **N** position.

5. While holding the lever lightly towards the **R** position, tighten the swivel nut.

Neutral Start Switch

NOTE: If the engine will start with the shift selector in any range other than N or P positions, adjustment is required.

1. Loosen the neutral start switch bolts and set the shift lever in the **N** position.

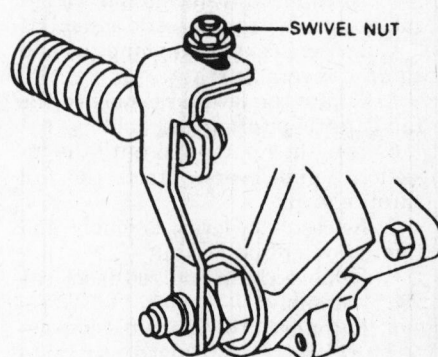

Shift cable adjustment – A131L transaxle

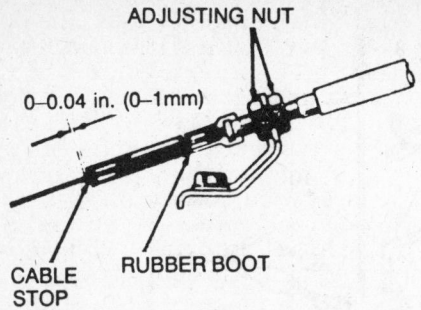

Throttle cable adjustment location

2. Disconnect the neutral start switch connector.
3. Connect an ohmmeter between the terminals.
4. Adjust the switch to the point where there is continuity between terminals.
5. Connect the neutral switch connector.
6. Torque the switch bolts to 48 inch lbs. (5.4 Nm).
7. Recheck the switch operation.

Oil Pan

REMOVAL & INSTALLATION

1. Raise the vehicle and support safely. Drain the transaxle fluid
2. Remove the oil pan retaining bolts, tap the oil pan lightly to remove.
3. Remove the oil pan gasket material and clean the surfaces thoroughly.
4. When installing the oil pan, be sure to use a new gasket.
5. Install a new filter or pick-up screen and replace the magnet into the oil cleaner.
6. Install the oil pan and fill the transaxle with the correct type of fluid and to the proper level.

Automatic Transaxle KF 100

NOTE: Dexron® II automatic transmission fluid or its equivalent is the only recommended automatic transmission fluid to be used in this unit. The use of any other grade of fluid can lead to unsatisfactory performance or complete unit failure.

ADJUSTMENTS

Shift Linkage/Cable

1. Loosen the two adjusting nuts at the control rod link and connect the shift cable to the link on the transaxle.
2. Shift the transaxle into the **NEUTRAL** detent.
3. Place the shifter lever into the

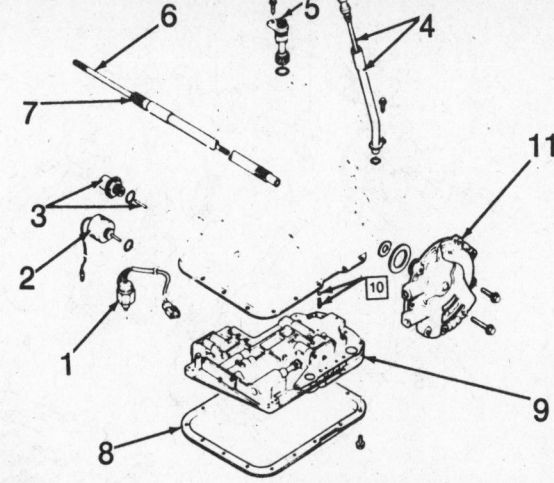

1. INHIBITOR SWITCH
2. KICKDOWN SOLENOID
3. VACUUM DIAPHRAGM AND DIAPHRAGM ROD
4. OIL LEVEL GAUGE AND TUBE
5. SPEEDOMETER DRIVEN GEAR
6. OIL PUMP SHAFT
7. TURBINE SHAFT
8. OIL PAN
9. CONTROL VALVE
10. STEEL BALL AND SPRING
11. OIL PUMP

External components—KF 100 transaxle

NEUTRAL position.
4. Rotate the link assembly clockwise to remove slack in the cable.
5. Tighten the rear adjusting nut until it makes contact with the link. Tighten the front adjusting nut until it makes contact with the link and tighten the adjusting nuts.

Oil Pan

REMOVAL & INSTALLATION

1. Jack up the front end of the car and support it safely.
2. Remove the drain plug located at the lower part of the differential.
3. Remove the oil pan and discard the gasket.
4. Clean all gasket material from the mating surface.
5. Using a new gasket, install the gasket and pan to the transaxle.
6. Install and tighten the drain plug.
7. Fill the transaxle through the filler tube using Dexron® ll Automatic Transmission Fluid.

Vacuum Modulator

REMOVAL & INSTALLATION

1. Disconnect the negative battery cable.
2. Disconnect the kickdown solenoid wire connector located at the left fender.
3. Raise the vehicle and suppot it safely.
4. Remove the kickdown solenoid at the transaxle.
5. Remove the vacuum modulator.
6. Installation is the reverse of the

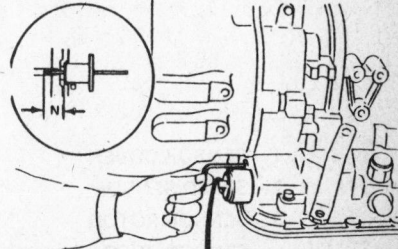

Size N	Diaphragm Rod Used
Under 26.9 mm (Under 1.06 in)	31.5 mm (1.24 in)
Over 25.4 mm (Over 1.00 in)	29.5 mm (1.160 in)
25.4 – 25.9 mm (1.00 – 1.02 in)	30.0 mm (1.180 in)
25.9 – 26.4 mm (1.02 – 1.04 in)	30.5 mm (1.200 in)
26.4 – 26.9 mm (1.04 – 1.06 in)	31.0 mm (1.220 in)

Measuring the vacuum diaphragm rod

removal procedure. If a new modulator is to be installed, use the following illustration to determine the proper vacuum diaphragm rod length.

Automatic Transaxle (Sprint)

NOTE: Dexron® II automatic transmission fluid or its equivalent is the only recommended automatic transmission fluid to be used in this unit. The use of any other grade of fluid can lead to unsatisfactory performance or complete unit failure.

Oil Pan

REMOVAL & INSTALLATION

1. Raise the vehicle and support it safely.

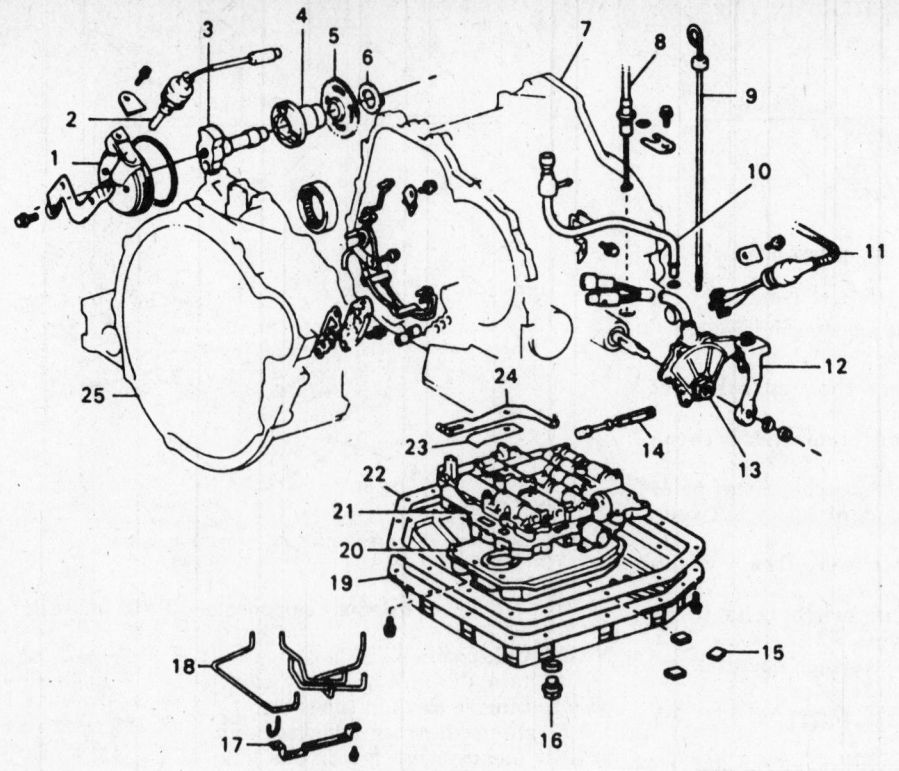

1	SENSOR COVER	10	OIL FILLER TUBE	19	OIL PAN
2	SPEED SENSOR	11	SOLENOID WIRE	20	OIL STRAINER
3	SENSOR ROTOR	12	MANUAL SHIFT LEVER	21	VALVE BODY ASSEMBLY
4	SENSOR ROTOR ADAPTOR	13	NEUTRAL START SWITCH	22	GASKET
5	GOVERNOR DRIVEN GEAR	14	MANUAL VALVE	23	SPRING PLATE
6	THRUST WASHER	15	MAGNET	24	MANUAL DETENT SPRING
7	TRANSAXLE CASE	16	DRAIN PLUG	25	TRANSAXLE HOUSING
8	THROTTLE CABLE	17	OIL TUBE BRACKET		
9	OIL LEVEL INDICATOR	18	OIL TUBE		

Transaxle components – A240E transaxle

2. Drain the transaxle fluid.
3. Remove the stabilizer shaft mounting bolts.
4. Remove the transaxle mounting member.
5. Remove the oil pan bolts.
6. Tap around the oil pan with a plastic hammer, and remove the oil pan.

NOTE: Do not force the oil pan off by prying with a flat tip screwdriver, as it may cause damage to the gasket mating surfaces.

7. Throughly remove all gasket material from the mating surface.
8. Clean the inside of the oil pan and install a new gasket.
9. Installation is the reverse of the removal procedure.

U-Joint, CV-Joint Overhaul 40

UNIVERSAL JOINTS

U-Joint is mechanic's jargon for universal joint. U-Joints should not be confused with U-bolts, which are U-shaped bolts used to connect U-joints to the differential pinion flange.

Universal joints provide flexibility between the driveshaft and axle housing to accommodate changes in the angle between them. Changes of length are accommodated by the sliding splined yoke between the driveshaft and transmission. The engine and transmission are mounted rigidly on the car frame. The angles between the transmission, driveshaft and axle change constantly as the car responds to various road conditions.

To give flexibility and still transmit power as smoothly as possible, several types of universal joints are used. The most common type of universal joint is the cross and yoke type. Yokes are used on the ends of the driveshaft with the yoke arms opposite each other. Another yoke is used opposite the driveshaft and when placed together, both yokes engage a center member, or cross, with four arms spaced 90° apart. The U-joint cross is alternately referred to as a spider, and the arms are called trunnions. A bearing cup (or cap) is used on each arm of the cross to accommodate movement as the driveshaft rotates. The bearings used are needle bearings.

A conventional universal joint will cause the driveshaft to speed up and slow down through each revolution and cause a corresponding change in the velocity of drive shaft. This change in speed causes natural vibrations to occur through the driveline, necessitating a third type of universal joint: The constant velocity joint. A rolling ball moves in a curved groove, located between two yoke-and-cross universal joints, connected to each other by a coupling yoke. The result is a uniform motion as the driveshaft rotates, avoiding the fluctuations in driveshaft speed. This type of joint is found in cars with sharp driveline angles, or where the extra measure of isolation is desirable.

Cross And Yoke U-Joint

OVERHAUL

There are two types of cross and yoke U-joints. One type retains the cross within the yoke with C-shaped snap rings. This type is found on all American Motors, Chrysler, and Ford Cars. GM cars generally use the second type of joint, which is held together by injection molded plastic retainer rings. The second type cannot be reassembled with the same parts, once disassembled. However, repair kits are available.

Snapring Type

1. Remove the driveshaft. For the correct procedure, see the car section for the model you are working on.

2. If the front yoke is to be disassembled, matchmark the driveshaft and sliding splined yoke (transmission yoke) so that driveline balance is preserved upon reassembly. Remove the snap rings which retain the bearing caps.

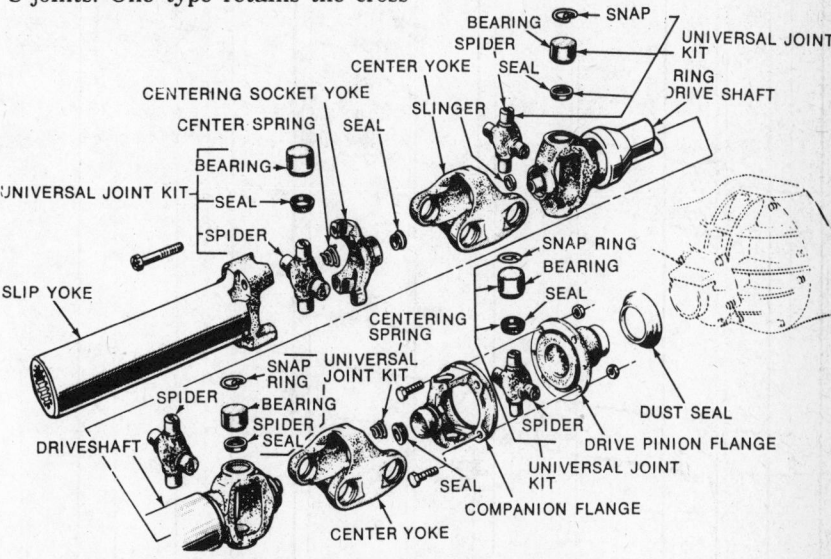

Typical driveshaft with cardan type U–joints

40–1

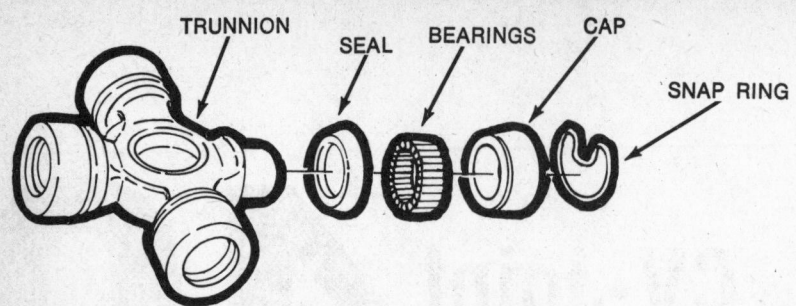

TRUNNION   SEAL   BEARINGS   CAP   SNAP RING

Snap ring type universal joint

3. Select two sockets, one small enough to pass through the yoke holes for the bearing caps, the other large enough to receive the bearing cap.

4. Using a vise or a press, position the small and large sockets on either side of the U-joint. Press in on the smaller socket so that it presses the opposite bearing cap out of the yoke and into the larger socket. If the cap does not come all the way out, grasp it with a pair of pliers and work it out.

5. Reverse the position of the sockets so that the smaller socket presses on the cross. Press the other bearing cap out of the yoke.

6. Repeat the procedure on the other bearings.

7. To install, grease the bearing caps and needles throughly if they are not pregreased. Start a new bearing cap into one side of the yoke. Position the cross in the yoke.

8. Select two sockets small enough to pass through the yoke holes. Put the sockets against the cross and the cap, and press the bearing cap $\frac{1}{4}$ inch below the surface of the yoke. If there is a sudden increase in the force needed to press the cap into place, or if the cross starts to bind, the bearings are

cocked, They must be removed and restarted in the yoke. Failure to do so will greatly reduce the life of the bearing.

9. Install a new snap ring.

10. Start a new bearing into the opposite side. Place a socket on it and press in until the opposite bearing contacts the snap ring.

11. Install a new snap ring. It may be necessary to grind the facing surface of the snap ring slightly to permit easier installation.

12. Install the other bearings in the same manner.

13. Check the joint for free movement. If binding exists, smack the yoke ears with a brass or plastic faced hammer to seat the bearing needles. Do not strike the bearings, and support the shaft firmly. Do not install the driveshaft until free movement exists at all joints.

Plastic Retainer Type

Remove and install the bearing caps

and trunnion (cross) as described for the snap-ring type universal joints. On an original universal joint, however, the bearing caps will be secured in the yokes with injected plastic. The plastic will shear when the bearing caps are pressed. Service snap-rings are installed in the groove on the inside (of yoke) of the installed caps.

NOTE: The plastic which retains the bearing will be sheared when the bearing cup is pressed out. Be sure to remove the remains of the plastic retainer from the ears of the yoke. It is easier to remove the remains if a small pin or punch is first driven through the injection holes in the yoke. Failure to remove all of the plastic remains may prevent the bearing cups from being pressed into place and the bearing retainers from being properly seated.

BEARING FOR
SNAP RING RETAINER

NYLON
RETAINER

SNAP
RING

BEARING FOR NYLON
RETAINER

GROOVE FOR
SNAP RING

U-joint locking methods

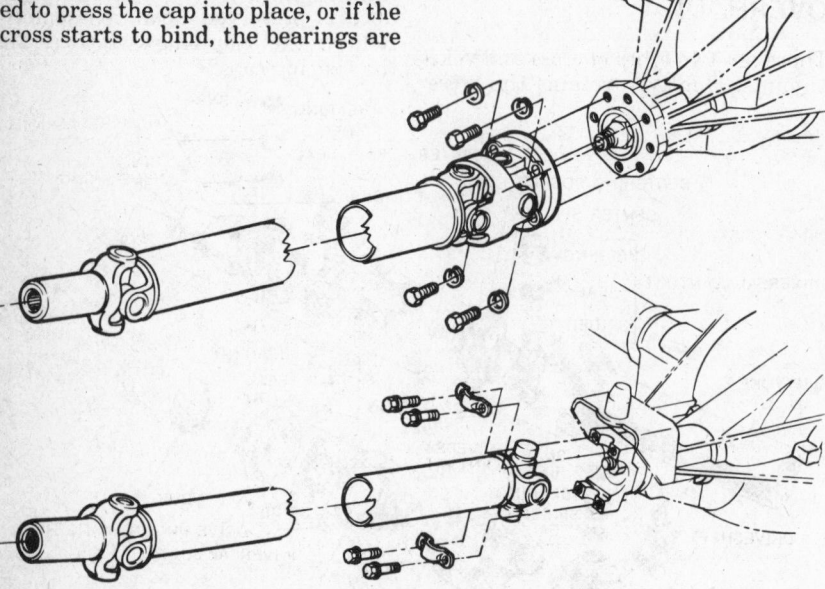

The driveshaft may be retained to the differential pinion by a flange (top) or by U-bolts or straps (bottom)

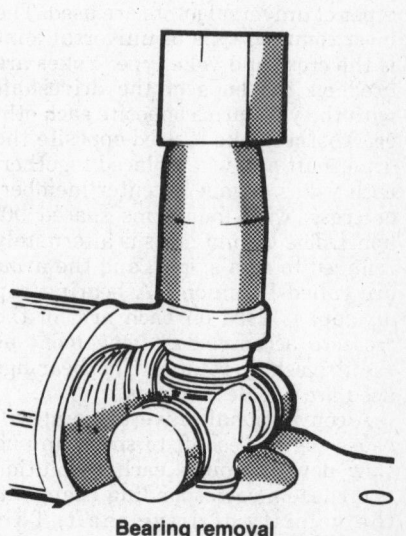

Bearing removal

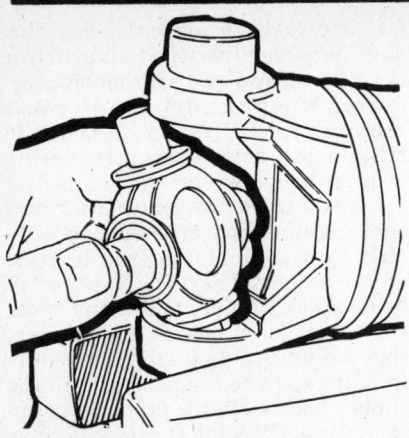

Press a bearing cap into the yoke, then install the cross

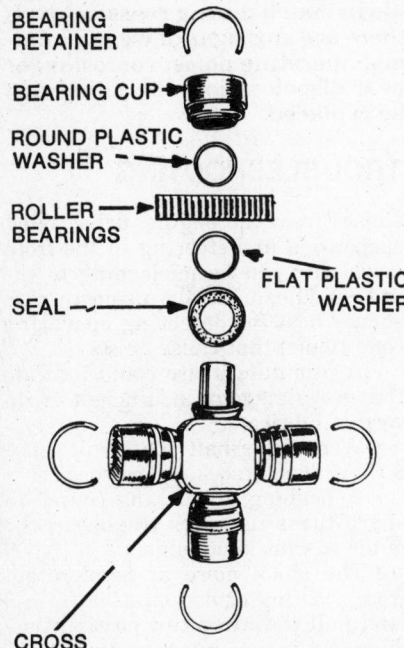

BEARING RETAINER

BEARING CUP

ROUND PLASTIC WASHER

ROLLER BEARINGS

FLAT PLASTIC WASHER

SEAL

CROSS

Plastic retainer U-joint repair kit components

Cardan Type U-Joint

OVERHAUL

Ford and Chrysler products with Cardan type U-joints use snap rings to retain the bearing cups in the yokes. Most GM cars have plastic retainers. Be sure to obtain the correct rebuilding kit.

1. Use a punch to mark the coupling yoke and the adjoining yokes before disassembly, to ensure proper reassembly and driveline balance.

2. It is easiest to remove the bearings from the coupling yoke first. Follow the order indicated in the illustration.

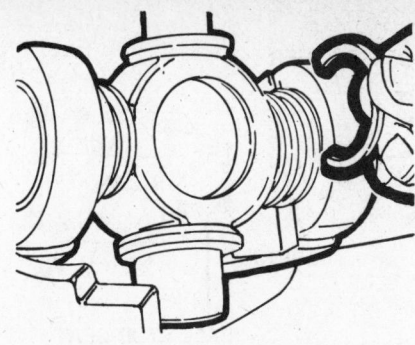

Service snap rings are installed inside the yoke

3. Support the driveshaft horizontally on a press stand, or on the workbench if a vise is being used.

4. If snap rings are used to retain the bearing cups, remove them. Place the rear ear of the coupling yoke over a socket large enough to receive the cup. Place a smaller socket, or a cross press made for the purpose, over the opposite cup. Press the bearing cup out of the coupling yoke ear. If the cup is not completely removed, insert a spacer and complete the operation, or grasp the cup with a pair of slip joint pliers and work it out. If the cups are retained by plastic, this will shear the retainers. Remove any bits of plastic.

5. Rotate the driveshaft and repeat the operation on the opposite cup.

6. Disengage the trunnions of the spider, still attached to the flanged yoke, from the coupling yoke, and pull the flanged yoke and spider from the center ball on the ball support tube yoke.

NOTE: The joint between the shaft and coupling yoke can be

serviced without disassembly of the joint between the coupling yoke and flanged yoke.

7. Pry the seal from the ball cavity, remove the washers, spring and three seats. Examine the ball stud seat and the ball stud for scores or wear. Worn parts can be replaced with a kit. Clean the ball seat cavity and fill it with grease. Install the spring, washer, ball seats, and spacer (washer) over the ball.

8. To assemble, insert one bearing cup part way into one ear of the ball support tube yoke and turn this cup to the bottom.

9. Insert the spider (cross) into the tube so that the trunnion (arm) seats freely in the cup.

10. Install the opposite cup part way, making sure that both cups are straight.

11. Press the cups into position, making sure that both cups squarely engage the spider. Back off if there is a sudden increase in resistance, indicating that a cup is cocked or a needle bearing is out of place.

12. As soon as one bearing retainer groove clears the yoke, stop and install the retainer (plastic retainer models). On models with snap rings, press the cups into place, then install the snap rings over the cups.

13. If difficulty is encountered installing the plastic retainers or the snap rings, smack the yoke sharply with a hammer to spring the ears slightly.

14. Install one bearing cup part way into the ear of the coupling yoke, Make sure that the alignment marks are matched, then engaged the coupling yoke over the spider and press

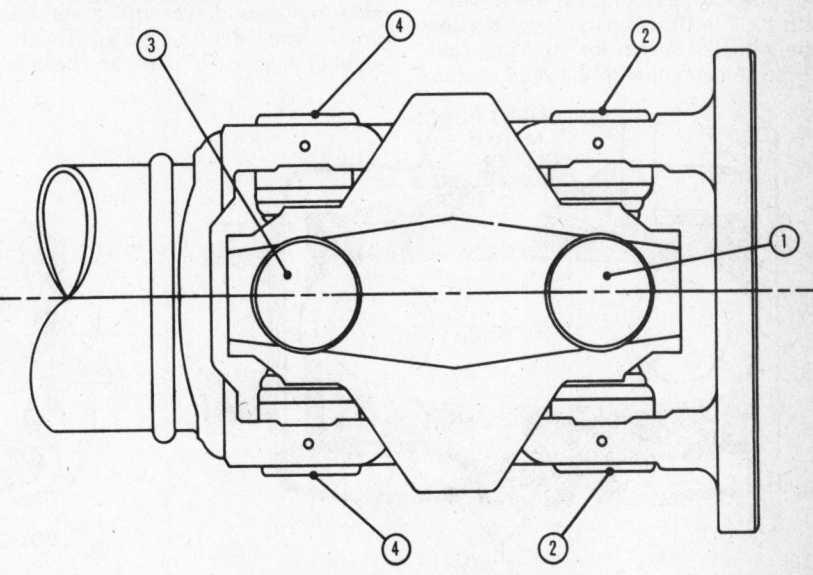

Cardan joint disassembly sequence

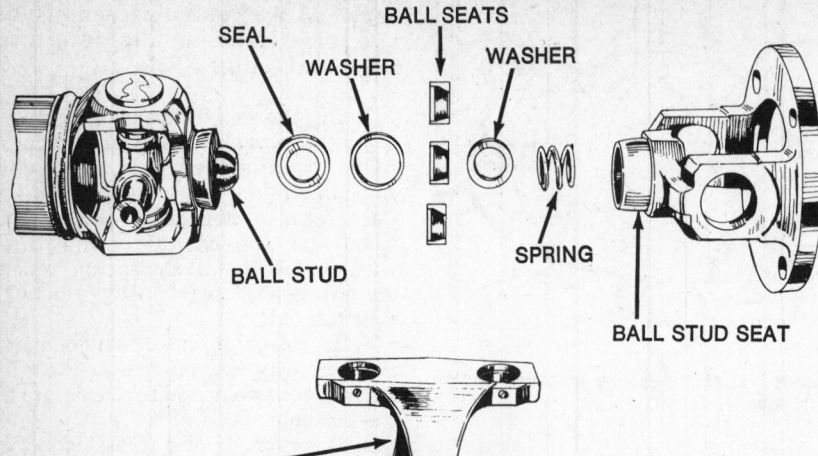

Cardan type joint

SEAL
WASHER
BALL SEATS
WASHER
BALL STUD
SPRING
BALL STUD SEAT
COUPLING YOKE

in the cups, installing the retainers or snap rings as before.

15. Install the cups and spider into the flanged yoke as with the previous yoke.

NOTE: The flange yoke should snap over center to the right or left and up or down by the pressure of the ball seat spring.

CONSTANT VELOCITY JOINTS

Front wheel drive vehicles present several unique problems to engineers because the driveshaft must do three things, simultaneously. It must allow the wheels to turn for steering, telescope to compensate for road surface

vibrations, and it must transmit torque continuously without vibration.

To compensate for these three factors a two-joint driveshaft allows the front wheels to perform these functions. This driveshaft mates disc type straight groove ball joint design with the bell type Rzeppa CV universal joint.

The Rzeppa joint on the outboard end of each driveshaft provides steering ability by allowing drive wheels to steer up to 43° while transmitting all available torque to the wheels. The inboard joint allows telescoping (up to $1\frac{1}{2}$ in.) through the rolling actions of balls in straight grooves and operates at angles up to 20°. The combined action of these two ball type U-joints eliminates vibration.

The typical front wheel drive vehicle uses two driveshaft assemblies-one to each driving wheel. Each assembly has a CV-joint at the wheel

end is called the inboard joint. This joint may be either the ball or tripot type. It allows the slip motion required when the driveshaft must shorten or lengthen in response to suspension action when traveling over an irregular surface.

Constant velocity joints are precision machined parts that have difficult jobs to perform in a hostile enviornment. They are exposed to heat, shock, torque, and many thousands of miles of service. For this reason, the lubricants used are specially formulated to be compatible with the rubber boot and give proper lubrication. Most CV-joint repair kits have this special lubricant included.

NOTE: Wear patterns in a used ball or tripot CV-joint are impossible to match during reassembly. If there are any signs of wear, abnormal operating noise, corrosion, or heat discoloration, the joint must be replaced.

TROUBLESHOOTING

Noises from the engine, drive axles, suspension and steering in the front drive cars can be misleading to the untrained ear. Ideally a smooth road serves best for detecting operating condition(s) that cause noise.

• A humming noise could indicate that early stage of insufficient or incorrect lubricant.

• Worn driveshaft joints will cause a continuous knock at low speeds.

• A popping or clicking sound on sharp turns indicates trouble in the outer or wheel end joint.

• The cluck noise at acceleration from coasting or deceleration from a load pull indicated two possibilities-damaged inner or transaxle joint or differential problem(s).

• An inner joint will create a vibra-

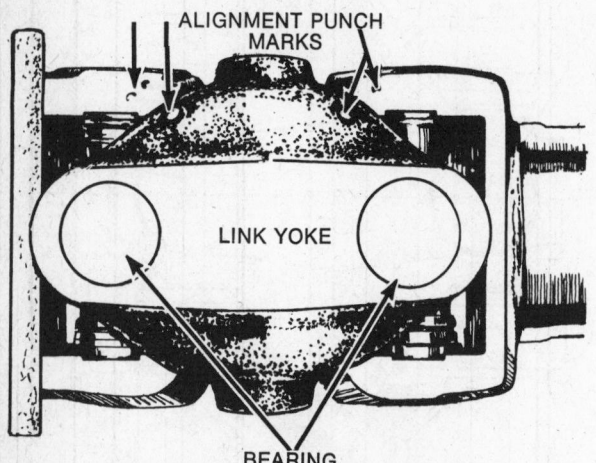

ALIGNMENT PUNCH MARKS
LINK YOKE
BEARING

Match marks for double cardan joint

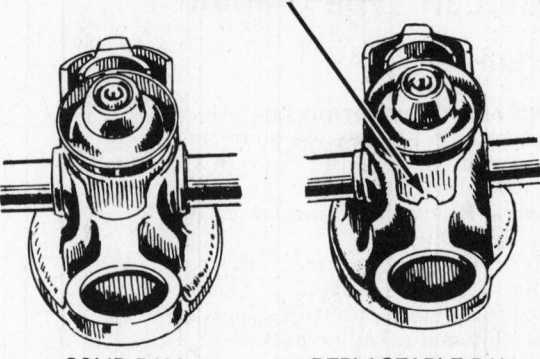

THIS NOTCH IDENTIFIES DRIVE SHAFT WITH REPLACEABLE BALL

SOLID BALL
REPLACEABLE BALL

Solid and replaceable U-Joint balls

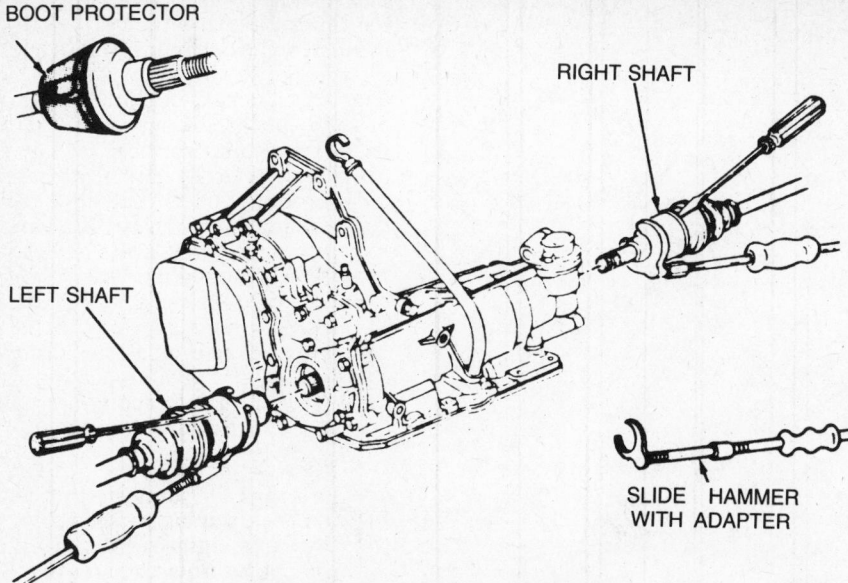

BOOT PROTECTOR
RIGHT SHAFT
LEFT SHAFT
SLIDE HAMMER
WITH ADAPTER
Removing axle shafts on GM models

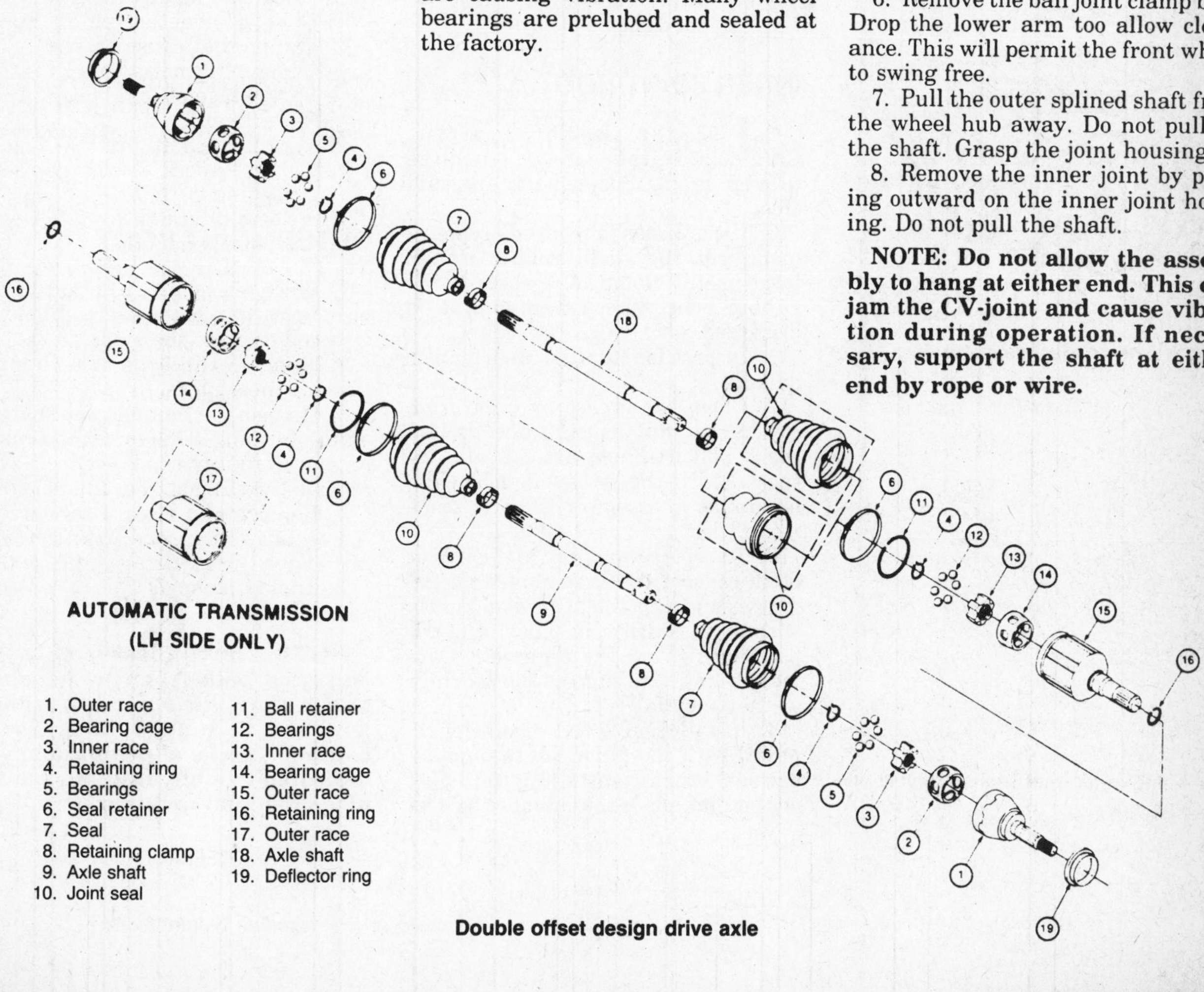

tion during acceleration due to plunging action hanging up and releasing repeatedly. Probable cause would be foreign particles or lack of lubrication, or improper assembly.

Remember that tires, suspension, engine, and exhaust system are all up front to add their noises.

• Make a check with front wheels elevated off ground. Spin the wheels by hand to determine if wheel bearing could be noisy or if out of round tires are causing vibration. Many wheel bearings are prelubed and sealed at the factory.

CAUTION

Personal injury can occur from spinning wheels by engine power. Spinning a wheel at excess speed may cause damage to CV-joints that could be operating at angles too steep when wheels are allowed to hang. Overspeeding might also cause damage to tires and the differential.

SHAFT REMOVAL

1. Remove the hub nut and discard it.
2. Drain the lubricant from the transaxle. Remove the differential cover (Chrysler only).
3. The speedometer pinion gear assembly must be removed before the right driveshaft can be removed (automatic transaxles only).
4. Rotate the driveshaft to view the circlip.
5. Compress the circlip tangs with needle nose pliers as you pry into the side gear. This compresses the circlip in position for shaft removal later. Keep an awl between the differential pinion shaft and the end face of the shaft to prevent circlip reentry to the groove.

NOTE: This applies to Chrysler cars only.

6. Remove the ball joint clamp bolt. Drop the lower arm too allow clearance. This will permit the front wheel to swing free.
7. Pull the outer splined shaft from the wheel hub away. Do not pull on the shaft. Grasp the joint housing.
8. Remove the inner joint by pulling outward on the inner joint housing. Do not pull the shaft.

NOTE: Do not allow the assembly to hang at either end. This can jam the CV-joint and cause vibration during operation. If necessary, support the shaft at either end by rope or wire.

AUTOMATIC TRANSMISSION
(LH SIDE ONLY)

1. Outer race
2. Bearing cage
3. Inner race
4. Retaining ring
5. Bearings
6. Seal retainer
7. Seal
8. Retaining clamp
9. Axle shaft
10. Joint seal
11. Ball retainer
12. Bearings
13. Inner race
14. Bearing cage
15. Outer race
16. Retaining ring
17. Outer race
18. Axle shaft
19. Deflector ring

Double offset design drive axle

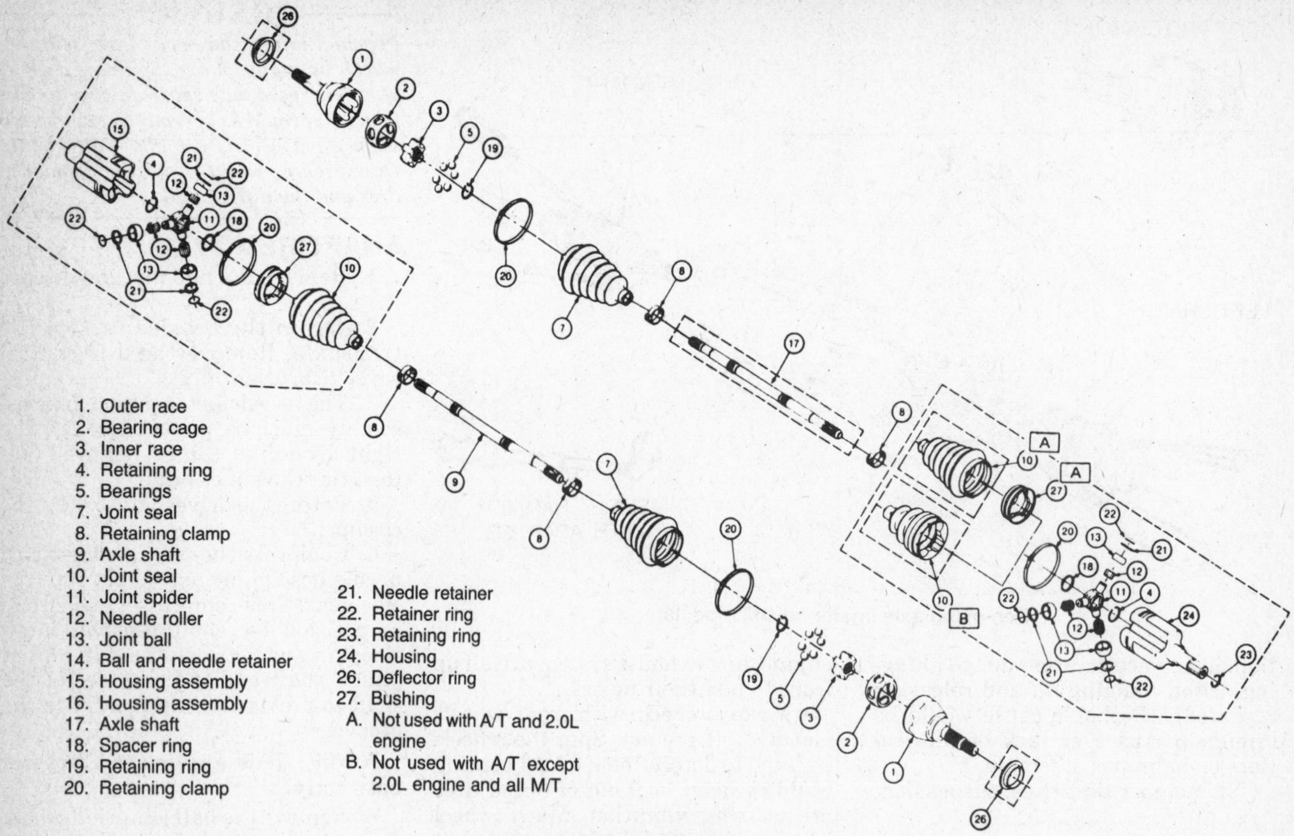

1. Outer race
2. Bearing cage
3. Inner race
4. Retaining ring
5. Bearings
7. Joint seal
8. Retaining clamp
9. Axle shaft
10. Joint seal
11. Joint spider
12. Needle roller
13. Joint ball
14. Ball and needle retainer
15. Housing assembly
16. Housing assembly
17. Axle shaft
18. Spacer ring
19. Retaining ring
20. Retaining clamp

21. Needle retainer
22. Retainer ring
23. Retaining ring
24. Housing
26. Deflector ring
27. Bushing
A. Not used with A/T and 2.0L engine
B. Not used with A/T except 2.0L engine and all M/T

Tri-pot design drive axle

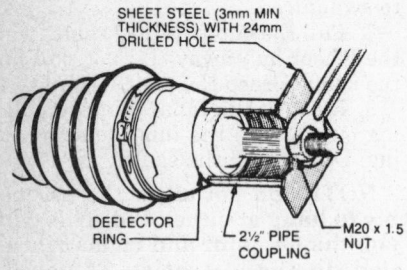

Installing steel deflector ring

SHEET STEEL (3mm MIN THICKNESS) WITH 24mm DRILLED HOLE

DEFLECTOR RING

2½" PIPE COUPLING

M20 x 1.5 NUT

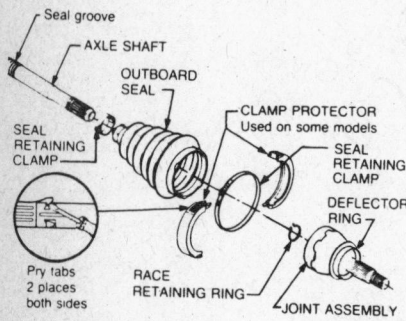

Removing outer joint seal on double offset type axle

Seal groove
AXLE SHAFT
OUTBOARD SEAL
SEAL RETAINING CLAMP
CLAMP PROTECTOR Used on some models
SEAL RETAINING CLAMP
DEFLECTOR RING
Pry tabs 2 places both sides
RACE RETAINING RING
JOINT ASSEMBLY

INNER JOINT/BOOT

9. Place the assembly in a vise. Care must be taken not to crush the tubular shafts. Some shafts are solid steel.

10. If the inner joint needs replacement, cut the small rubber clamp, large metal clamp, and remove the rubber boot. These items must be discarded.

11. Inspect for internal wear and/or damage.

12. Clean the grease by hand from inside the joint housing and around the 3 ball trunnion assembly to inspect. Mark the tri-pot and housing for proper reassembly, If it is to be reinstalled.

13. To replace the boot, CV-joint, or both, remove the snap ring from the groove and tap the trunnion lightly with a brass drift pin. Leave the tripot bearings on the trunnion. Care must be taken to support the bearings as they may fall off.

14. Installation is the reverse of removal with the following recommendations. When reinstalling the tripot on the shaft place the chamber face to-

ward the retainer groove. The grease provided with the repair kit must be used. It can not be substituted with any other type grease.

OUTER JOINT/BOOT

1. Place the shaft in a soft-jawed vise. Be careful not to overtighten the vise and damage the shaft.

2. Remove the boot and clamps. Discard these parts.

3. Using a soft hammer rap sharply on the housing. This forces the inner race over the internal circlip. Never remove the slinger from the housing.

4. Remove and discard the circlip. A new one is included with the boot kit. Leave the lock ring in place.

5. Installation is the reverse of removal.

NOTE: Never disassemble the cage and balls from the housing. Reuse the joint assembly with a new boot kit, unless the grease is contaminated and prior diagnosis indicated trouble. In that case replace the joint and boot.

Strut Overhaul 41

STRUT SERVICE AND REPAIR

MacPherson struts are appearing on the front (and rear) wheels of more and more cars. The strut design takes up less room in the engine compartment, compared to a conventional upper and lower arm with shock absorber arrangement. The trend toward smaller, lighter and more efficient packaging mandates the use of a strut suspension to permit more room for engine accessories and front wheel drive components.

Strut Suspension Design

In a conventional front suspension, the wheel is attached to a spindle, which is in turn, connected to upper and lower control arms through upper and lower ball joints. A coil spring between the control arms (sometimes on top of the upper arm) supports the weight of the vehicle and a shock absorber controls rebound and dampens oscillations.

In a strut type suspension, the strut performs a shock dampening function, like a shock absorber, but unlike a conventional shock absorber, the strut is a structural part of the vehicle's suspension.

The strut assembly usually contains a spring seat to retain the coil spring that supports the vehicle's weight. The shock absorber is built into the body of the strut housing. The strut is normally attached at the bottom to the lower control arm and at the top to the car body. The upper mount usually features a bearing that permits the

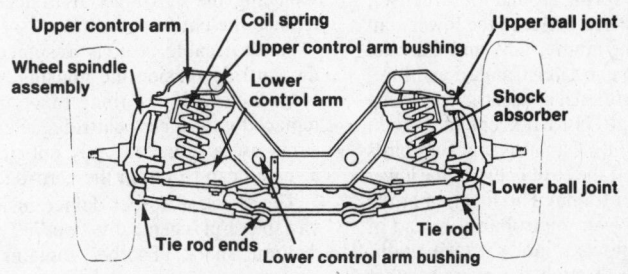

Conventional upper and lower arm suspension

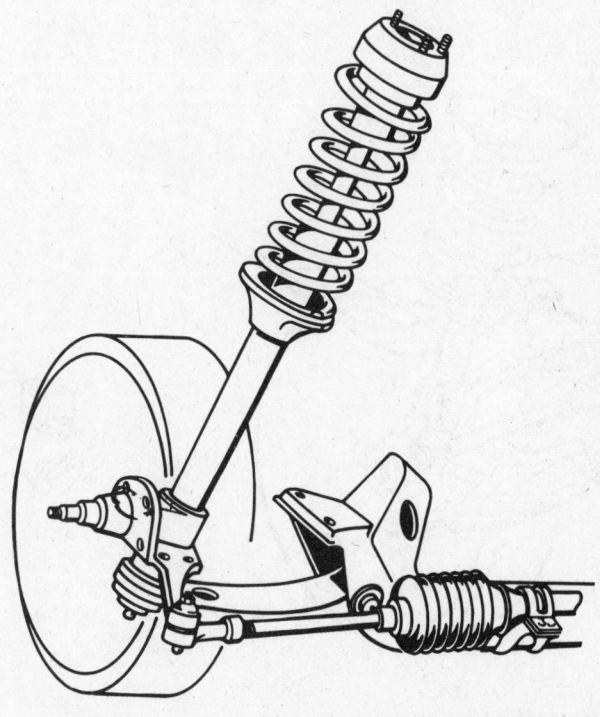

Strut with concentric coil spring (rear wheel drive)

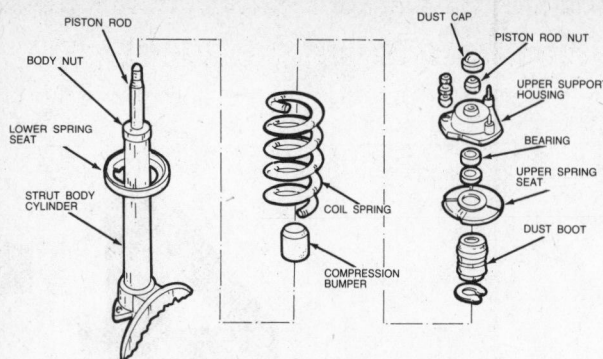

Exploded view of a typical strut

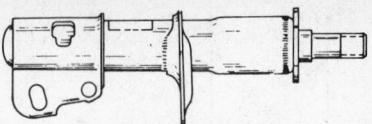

A sealed strut has no body nut and is serviceable by replacement

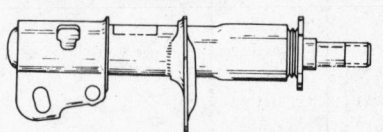

Serviceable struts have a removeable body nut to allow replacement of the strut cartridge

coil spring to rotate as the wheels turn for smoother steering. The entire design eliminates the need for the upper control arm, upper ball joint and many of the conventional suspension bushings. The lower ball joint is no longer a load carrying unit, because it is isolated from the weight of the vehicle.

Domestic struts have taken 2 forms—a concentric coil spring around the strut itself and a spring located between the lower control arm and the frame. GM and Chrysler (except for '82 and later Camaro and Firebird) use the traditional concentric coil spring around the strut. Ford (except the Escort and Lynx) and '82 Camaros and Fire-birds use the spring off the strut between the lower control arm and frame. The location of the spring on the lower control arm instead of on the strut, allows minor road vibrations to be absorbed through the chassis rather than be fed back to the driver through the steering system.

Serviceability

Struts fall into 2 broad categories—serviceable and sealed units. A sealed strut is designed so that the top closure of the strut assembly is permanently sealed. There is no access to the shock absorber cartridge inside the strut housing and no means of replacing the cartridge. It is necessary to replace the entire strut unit.

A serviceable strut is designed so that the cartridge inside the housing, that provides the shock absorbing function, can be replaced with a new cartridge. Serviceable struts use a threaded body nut in place of a sealed cap to retain the cartridge.

The shock absorber device inside a serviceable strut is generally "wet". This means that the shock absorber contains oil that contacts and lubricates the inner wall of the strut body. The oil is sealed inside the strut by the body nut, O-ring and piston rod seal.

Servicing a "wet" strut with the equivalent components involves a thorough cleaning of the inside of the strut body, absolute cleanliness and great care in reassembly.

Cartridge inserts were developed to simplify servicing "wet" struts. The insert is a factory sealed replacement for the strut shock absorber. The replacement cartridge is simply substituted for the original shock absorber cartridge and retained with the body nut, avoiding the near laboratory-like conditions required to service a "wet" strut with "wet" service components.

Most OEM domestic struts are serviced by replacement of the entire unit. There is no strut cartridge to replace. Exceptions to this general rule are the struts used on GM front wheel drive J-cars and A-cars, which feature an internally threaded housing, accessible by removing the OEM cap from the housing. Once the old cartridge is removed, a new cartridge can be threaded

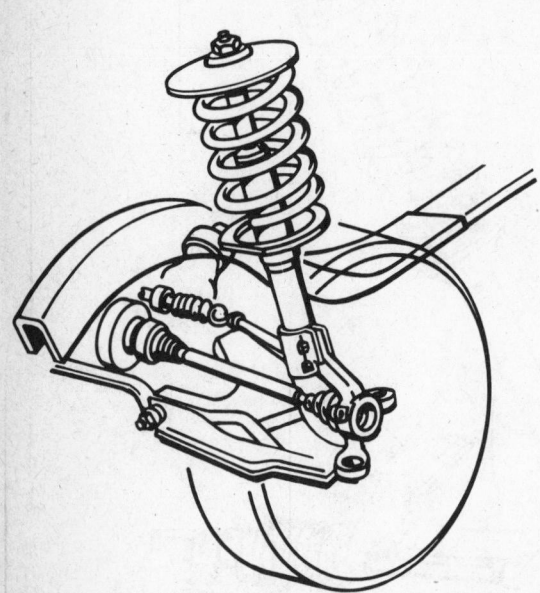

Strut with concentric coil spring (front wheel drive)

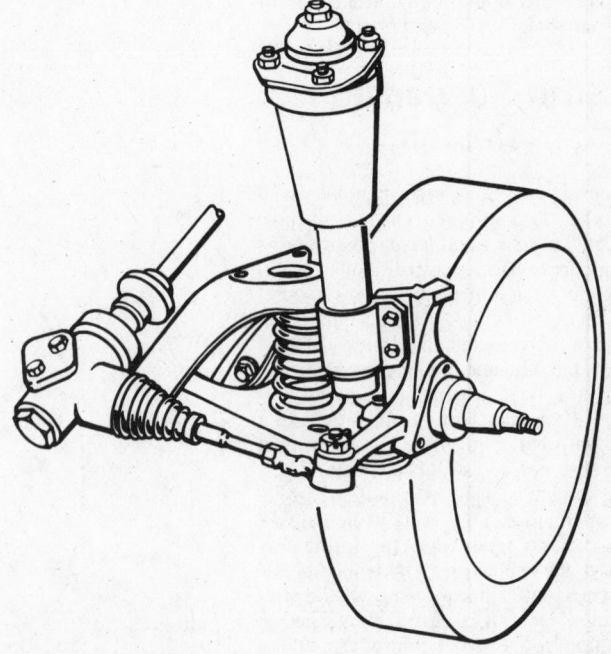

Modified MacPherson strut design with coil spring on the lower arm

into the housing.

Sealed, OEM units can also be serviced by replacement with an aftermarket unit, that will permit future servicing by cartridge replacement.

WHEEL ALIGNMENT

It is not always necessary to re-align the wheels after struts are serviced. If care is taken matchmarking affected components and in reassembling, alignment may be unaffected. However, if wheels were not in proper alignment prior to service, or if the entire strut assembly was replaced, a wheel alignment check should be made. Generally, only camber is adjustable, and then only within a narrow range.

Do not attempt to bend components to correct wheel alignment.

Since the majority of OEM struts are serviced by replacement, most manufacturers recommend wheel alignment following strut replacement.

Tools

Without the right tools, a strut job will take longer than necessary and can be dangerous.

A normal selection of hand tools such as open end and box wrenches, sockets, pliers, screwdrivers and hammers are necessary to work on struts. Extensions and universal joints will help reach tight spots. Be sure to have both metric and inch-sized wrenches on hand. Two big time-savers are "crowsfeet" and ratcheting box wrenches in assorted sizes. Torx fasteners are also showing up more and more in chassis fasteners.

In addition to the normal handtools, some sort of spanner is necessary to remove the body nut on serviceable struts. Sometimes a pipe wrench can be used successfully.

Strut and cartridge replacement requires a spring compressor.

Makeshift tools for compressing coil springs—threaded rod, chains, wire or other methods—should never be used. The coil spring is under tremendous compression and can fly off causing personal injury and damage to equipment. Use only a good quality spring compressor such as described below.

Economy, or manual, spring compressors are the least expensive but more time consuming to use. Angle hooks grasp the spring coils and must be compressed with a wrench. For those who service struts infrequently, this is probably the wisest investment for purchase.

Other manual spring compressors (jaws type) are faster to operate, have a more positive gripping action and can be used on or off the car. These types are probably not cost effective for the do-it-yourselfer, but can be rented from auto supply stores for single-time use.

For volume work, compressors that are pneumatically or hydraulically operated are

MAINTAINING WHEEL ALIGNMENT

The location and method of adjusting wheel alignment determines the components that must be match-marked to maintain wheel alignment. There are 4 basic methods of adjusting wheel alignment. Almost all cars use one of these or a slight variation.

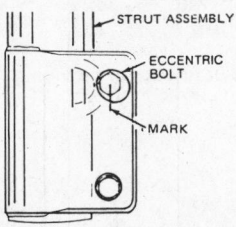

Mark the eccentric (camber adjusting bolt) relative to the clevis mounting bracket.

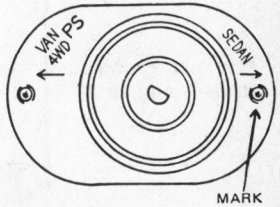

Mark the mounting stud that faces the front of the vehicle. This type of bracket is reversible for varying applications.

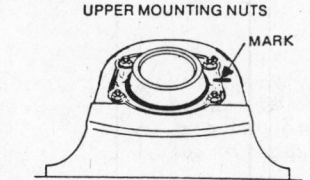

Mark the upper support housing relative to the inner fender before removing the strut from the upper mount.

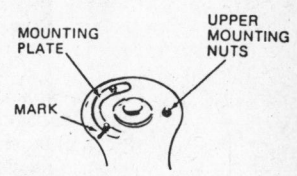

Mark the location of the mounting plate relative to the location on the inner fender.

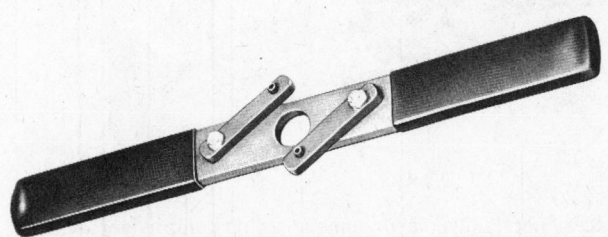

A simple spanner wrench designed for use with body nuts equipped with recessed lugs. A pipe wrench is a frequent substitute

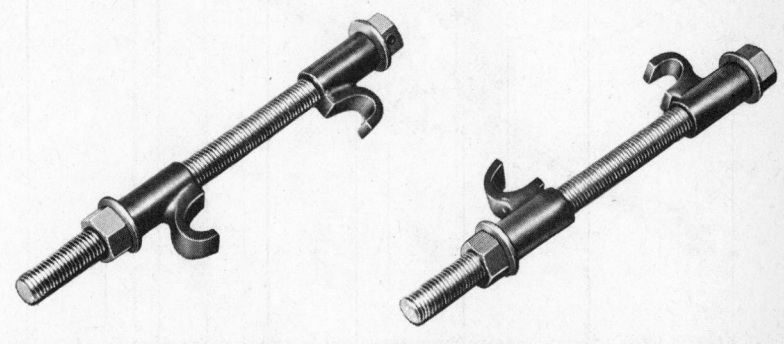

An economical manual spring compressor

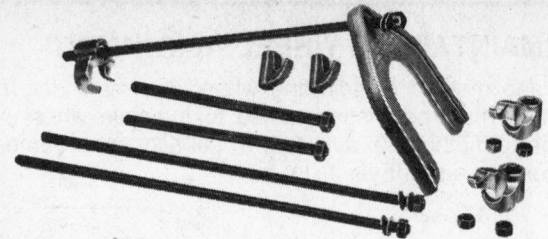

A manual spring compressor with plates or hooks for servicing virtually any strut

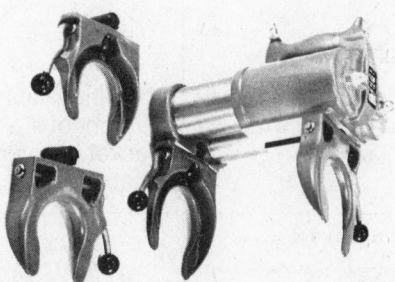

Lightweight, air operated, portable spring compressor can be used on or off the vehicle. Extra shoes are available to handle all strut applications

Stationary, universal pneumatic spring compressor

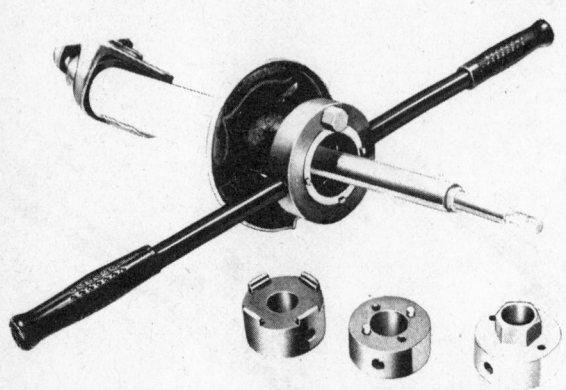

Spanner wrench with adaptor inserts for various applications of body nuts. This type of spanner can be used with a torque wrench for retorqueing the body nut

best. Air operated compressors are suitable for all types of struts (through use of adaptors), are lightweight and can be used on or off the vehicle. Bench mounted hydraulically operated units are probably the safest, but are also the most expensive and require that the strut be removed from the vehicle, which means separating brake lines and other connections which can be time consuming.

There are also universal kits that fit all struts in either the manual or air operated types.

Regardless of what type of spring compressor you're using, GM front wheel drive A-, J-, and X-cars as well as Chrysler Corp. Omni, Horizon and K-cars, require the use of a special spring compressor with self-leveling plates to grasp the spring seats as the spring is compressed. Likewise, the portable, pneumatic units have extra wide shoe sets suitable for these cars. The shoes are also epoxy coated to avoid scratching the coated springs on these models.

GM front wheel drive A-, J- and X-cars also make use of a camber assist tool, that makes camber adjustment a one man job.

A tube cutter is necessary on GM J-cars to cut the welded top from the strut housing for cartridge replacement.

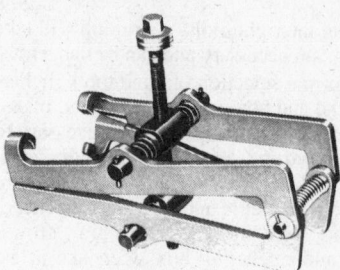

"Jaws" type spring compressor

Spring compressor for GM and Chrysler product applications

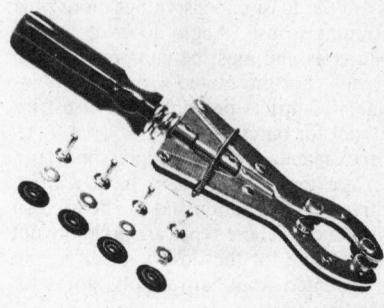

A tube cutter allows opening of the GM J-car struts for cartridge replacement

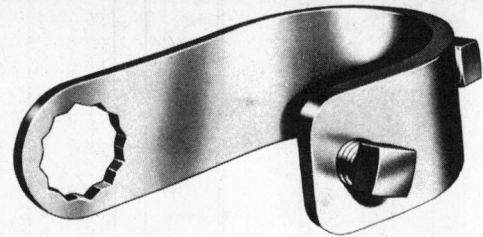

A camber assist tool makes GM cars a one-man job

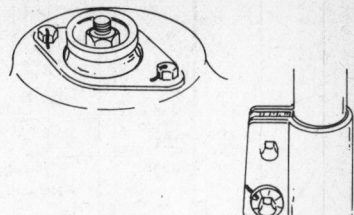

Mark the position of the attachments that control wheel alignment. See Maintaining Wheel Alignment earlier in this section

Repair Tips

1. Make sure you have all the tools you'll need. NEVER IMPROVISE A SPRING COMPRESSOR.

2. Normally both front struts should be repaired or replaced at the same time.

3. The easiest way to work on most struts is to remove the entire unit from the vehicle, unless you have access to an air operated spring compressor. Some struts, however, can, and should, be repaired while installed on the vehicle.

4. Always read the instructions packaged with any replacement parts. In partic-ular, note whether the body nut is supplied new or re-used.

5. Mark the position(s) of any bearing plate nuts or cam bolts to assure proper alignment after installation.

6. Be sure to protect the rubber boot on the drive axle of front wheel drive cars.

7. If necessary to remove the brake cal-iper, do not let the caliper hang by the brake hose. Suspend the caliper from a wire hook or rope.

8. Be careful in clamping a strut in a vise. Special fixtures are available to hold struts in a vise, but are not necessary if care is used to be sure the housing is not crushed or dented. A block of soft wood on either side of the housing will prevent most damage.

9. Use a spring compressor to relieve tension from the spring. Be sure to clean and lubricate the screw threads, particularly on hand operated (manual) spring compressors.

Some springs have a special coating that should not be scuffed.

10. If you are replacing the strut cartridge, clean the inside of the strut housing and the body nut threads before replacing the oil and installing a new cartridge.

11. Be sure to use OEM quality fasteners any time a fastener is replaced.

STRUT OVERHAUL (OFF-CAR)

Following is a typical overhaul procedure of a serviceable MacPherson strut, after having removed the strut from the vehicle. The vehicle should be firmly supported. If it is necessary, to separate the brake line from the strut for strut removal, the brakes will have to be bled after reinstallation. See the manufacturer's car section for specific MacPherson strut removal and installation procedures.

Photos Courtesy Gabriel Div., Maremont Corp.

Step 1. Examine the strut assembly for damage, dented strut body, spring seat, broken or missing strut mounting parts. Any of these will require replacement of the complete assembly. Also inspect other suspension components for wear or damage

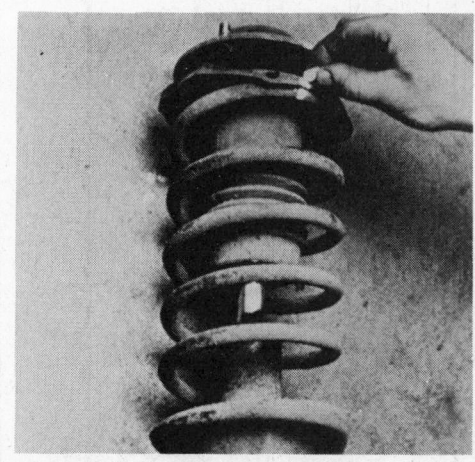

Step 2. Matchmark the upper end of the coil spring and bearing plate to avoid confusion during reassembly

Step 3. To make servicing easier, clamp the strut in a strut vise. The strut vise is designed to clamp the strut tight without damage to strut cylinder. It is very handy for strut work and can be used in your shop vise or mounted to any bench

Step 4. Before using the manual spring compressor, lubricate both sides of the thrust washers and the threads with a light coat of grease

Step 5. Install the compressor hooks on opposite sides of the coil spring with the hooks attached to the upper-most and lower-most spring coils. To avoid possible slippage, use tape or small hose clamps on either side of the compressor hooks

Step 6. Alternately tighten the bolts a few turns at a time until all tension is removed from the spring seat

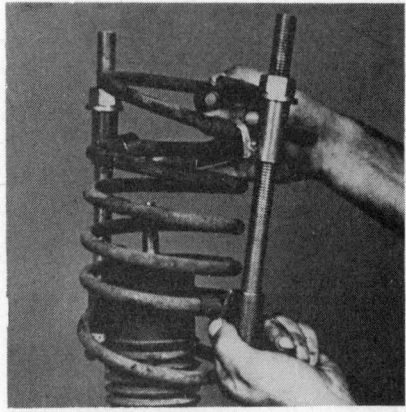

Step 7. Remove the piston rod nut and disassemble the upper mounting parts, keeping them in order for reassembly. Remove the coil spring. There is no need to remove the compressor from the coil spring

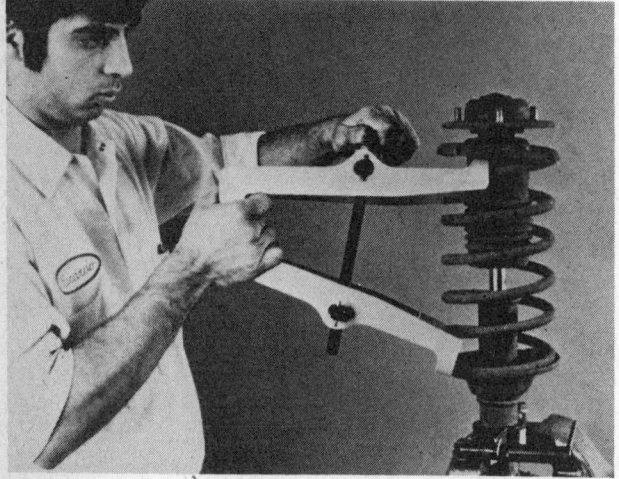

Step 8. An alternative to the manual compressor is the "jaws" type. Turn the load screw to open or close the compressor until the maximum number of spring coils can be engaged

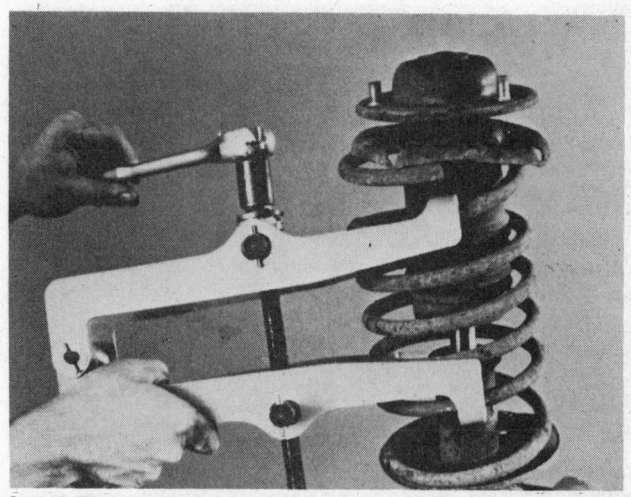

Step 9. Tighten the load screw until the coil spring is loose from the spring seats. There is no need to compress the spring any further

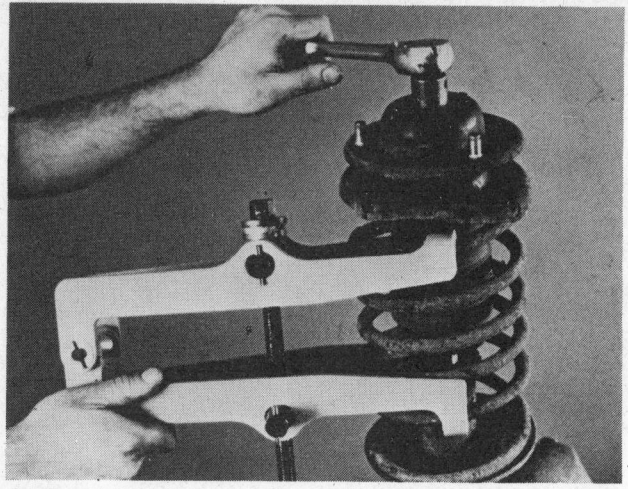

Step 10. Remove the piston rod nut and disassemble the upper mounting parts

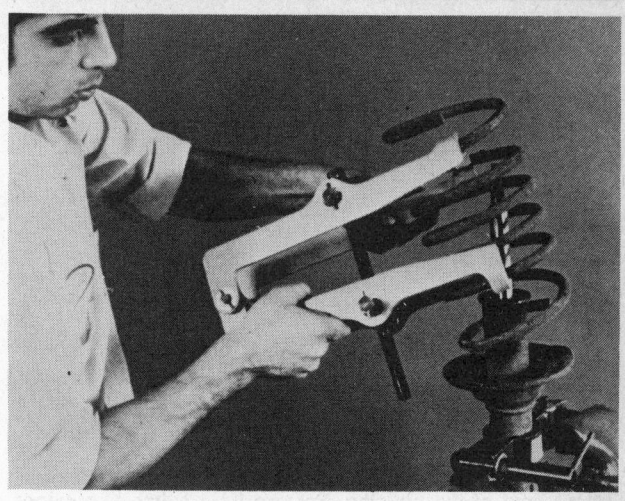

Step 11. Like the manual compressor, there is no need to remove the compressor from the coil spring. Remove the coil spring and compressor

Step 12. Keep the upper mounting parts in order of their removal. They'll be re–assembled in reverse order

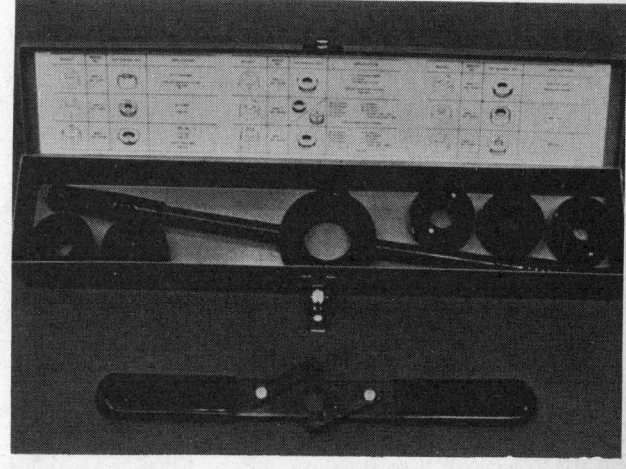

Step 13. A spanner wrench is necessary to remove body nuts, although a pipe wrench will do the job

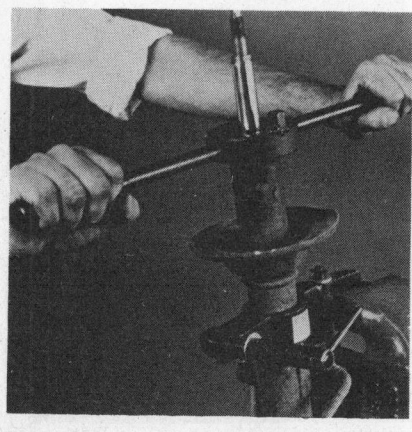

Step 14. Use the spanner wrench or pipe wrench to loosen the body nut

Step 15. Remove the body nut and discard if a new body nut came with the replacement cartridge. If not, save the body nut

Step 16. Use a scribe or suitable tool to remove the O-ring from the top of the housing

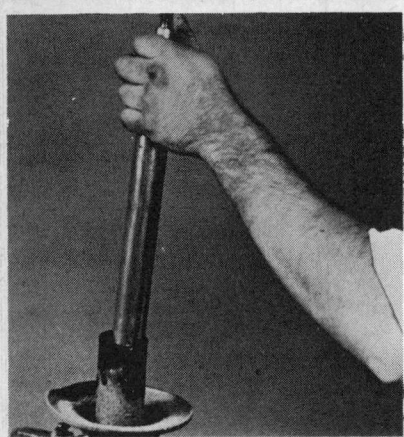

Step 17. Grasp the piston rod and pull cartridge out of the housing. Remove it slowly to avoid splashing oil. Be sure all pieces come out of the housing

Step 18. Pour all of the strut fluid into a suitable container, clean the inside of the strut cylinder, and inspect the cylinder for dents and to insure that all loose parts have been removed from inside of strut body

Step 19. Refill the cylinder with one ounce (a shot glass) of the original oil or fresh oil. The oil helps dissipate internal cartridge heat during operation and results in a cooler running, longer lasting unit. Do not put too much oil in—otherwise the oil may leak at the body nut after it expands when heated

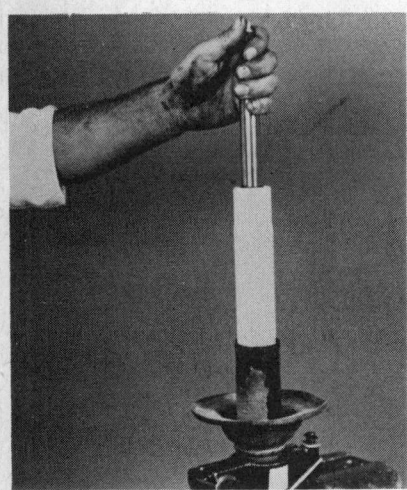

Step 20. Insert the new replacement cartridge into the strut body

Step 21. Push the piston rod *all* the way down, to avoid damage to the piston rod if the spaner wrench slips, and start the body nut by hand. Be sure it is not cross-threaded

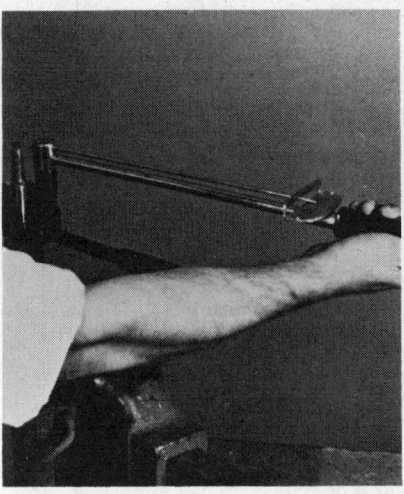

Step 22. Tighten the body nut securely

Step 23. Inspect the loose parts prior to re-assembly. Note the chalk mark location for proper seating of the upper spring seat

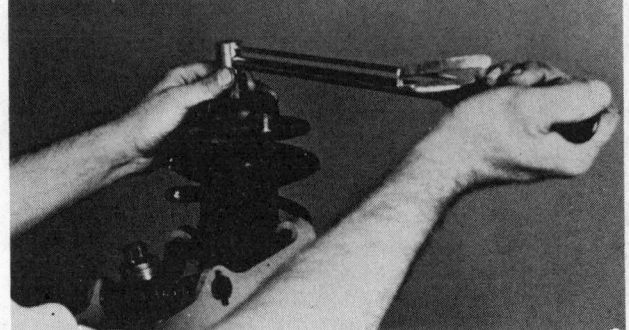

Step 24. Re-assemble the coil spring and upper mounting parts in reverse order. Tighten the piston rod nut and remove the spring compressor. Install the dust cap. Install the strut in the vehicle. See the car section for details

STRUT OVERHAUL

Most domestic car OEM MacPherson struts are sealed units and not repairable. The exceptions are GM front wheel drive A- and J-cars, which use replaceable cartridges. All other cars must use aftermarket struts to be serviceable at a future date. The following procedures cover disassembly of the strut, installation of a serviceable strut, reassembly and cartridge replacement on GM front wheel drive A- and J-models. Consult the applicable manufacturer's car section for removal and installation procedures.

Photos Courtesy Gabriel Div., Maremont Corp.

Step 1. **Most domestic cars are serviced initially by replacing the entire strut rather than by using a replacement cartridge. This is necessary because the original equipment struts are sealed shut and cannot be serviced with a replacement cartridge. After-market struts are designed with serviceable threaded body nuts which means they can be serviced in the future by installing a replacement cartridge, using normal cartridge service methods, rather than by replacing the entire strut**

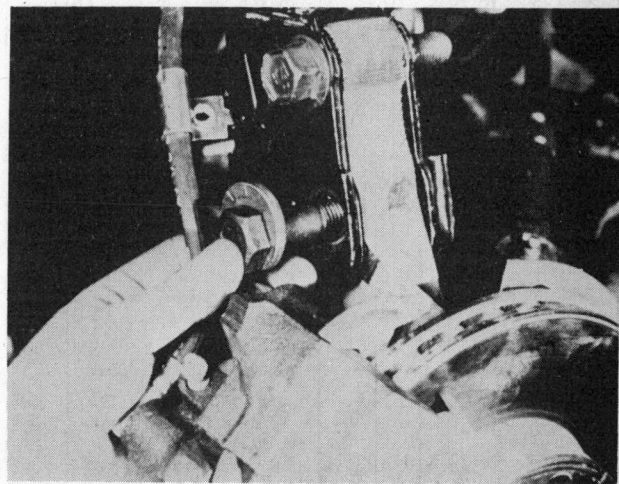

Step 2. **An X-car is shown, but the lower mount on the Citation is typical of many vehicles. They all have two bolt clevis mounts and the position of the strut determines the camber adjustment. This means that if you are replacing a sealed strut, front end alignment is necessary because the original alignment is eliminated when you change the strut. If the car has a serviceable strut, you can retain the alignment by marking the position of the mounting bolt relative to the strut. GM has made a running change on the lower mount of their X-Car. The earlier type had an eccentric bolt for camber adjustment. Camber on the latest type is adjusted by pushing or pulling on the wheel with the bolts loosened slightly, but the eccentric can be installed on later cars**

Step 3. **A special type spring compressor is required for the GM cars and Chrysler K and L cars. A compressor should be used that does not damage the protective coating on the coil spring. Virtually any compressor can be used on other car lines/models**

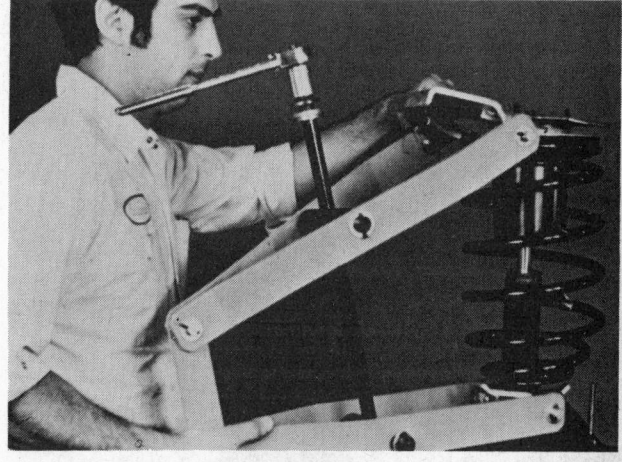

Step 4. **Secure the strut in the strut vise; turn the load screw counter-clockwise until the lower plate can be fitted under the lower spring seat and the upper plate can be fitted between the upper spring seat and support housing**

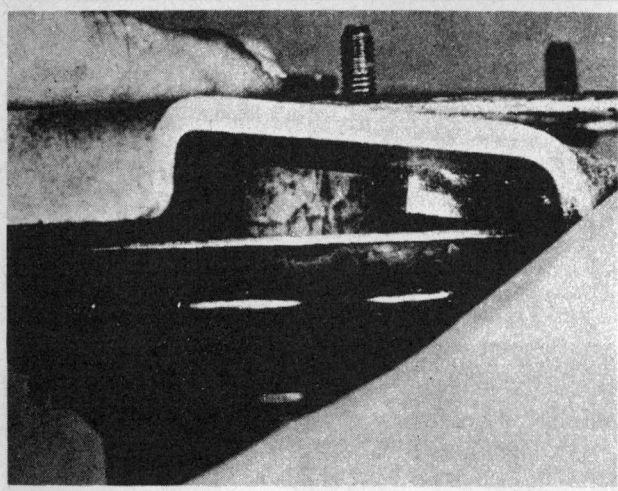

Step 5. Make sure that the crescent shaped bars on the upper compression plate are located inside the upper spring seat

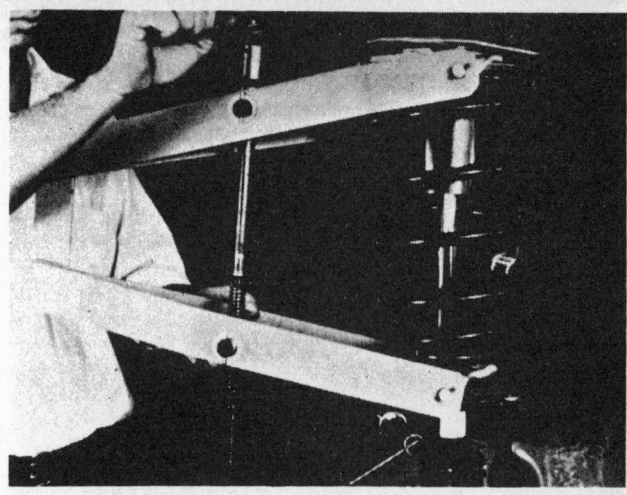

Step 6. Turn the load screw clockwise enough to tighten the compression plates on the spring seats. Stop and make sure that the coil spring will not arch, and that the pivot points are aligned with the center-line of the coil spring

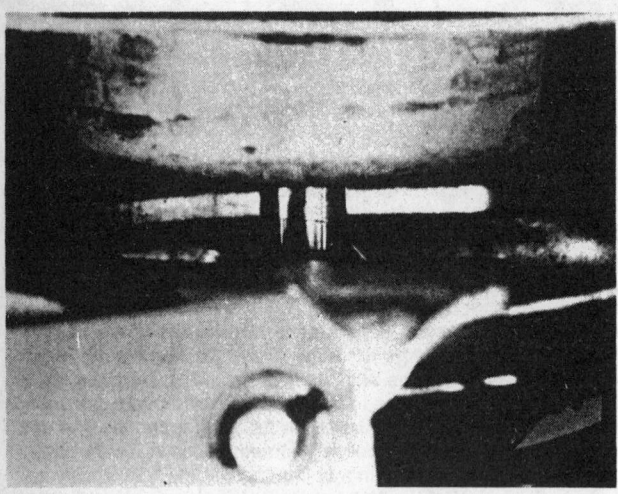

Step 7. Continue to tighten the load screw until the upper support housing can be pulled up to expose about ½ inch of piston rod. This assures that the spring load has been removed from upper spring seat

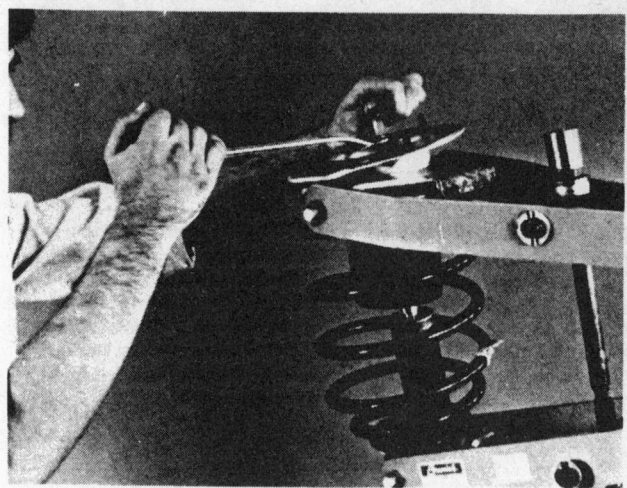

Step 8. Remove the piston rod nut with the aid of a wrench to keep the piston rod from turning and remove upper support housing

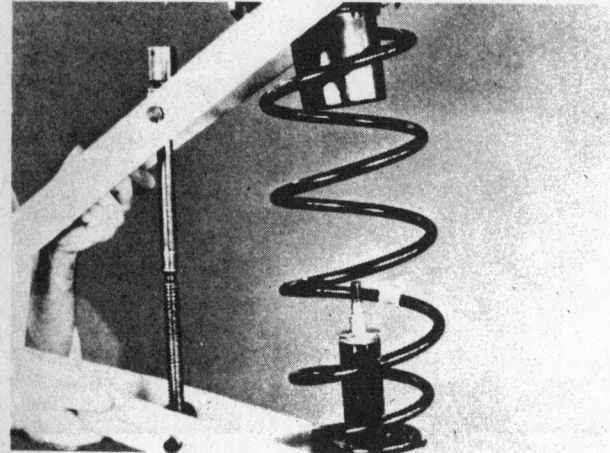

Step 9. Turn the load screw counter-clockwise until the spring tension is completely relieved. Remove the compressor, coil spring and upper support housing from the strut.

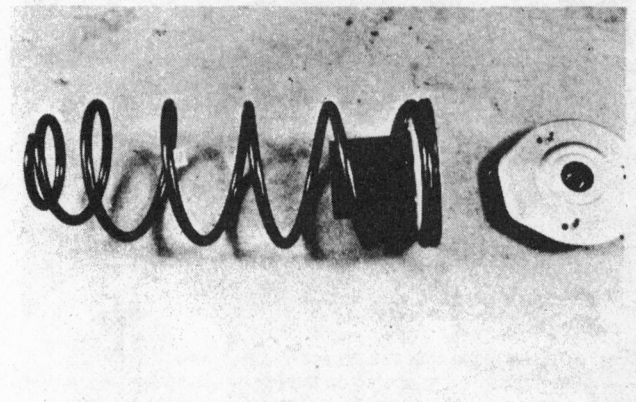

Step 10 Assemble the upper mounting parts in order of their removal. They'll be re-assembled in reverse order

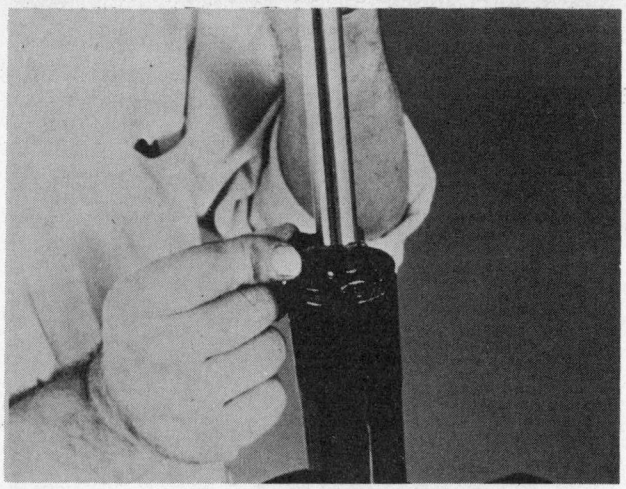

Step 11. Place the new strut in the vise and extend piston rod fully and install clip (spring type clothes pin will do) as shown. This keeps the piston rod extended while assembling the spring and upper mounting parts.

Step 12. Install the coil spring and upper spring seat on the new strut

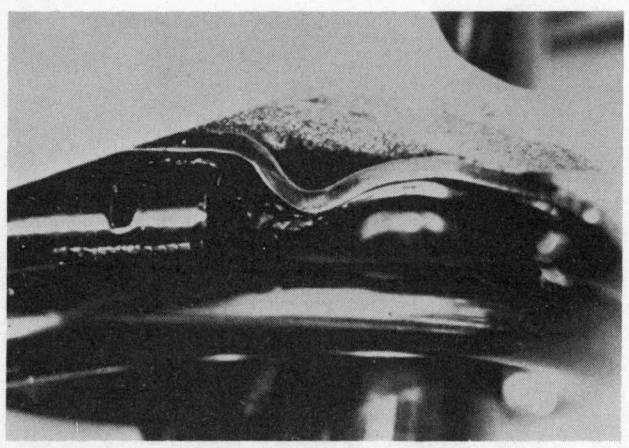

Step 13. Make sure that the spring helix is aligned with the lower spring seat

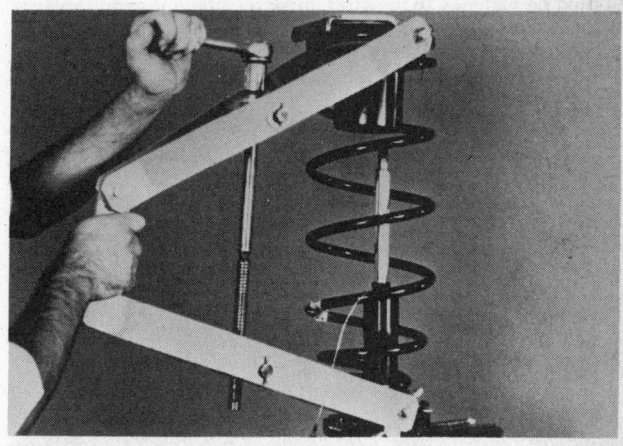

Step 14. Locate upper and lower compression plates on spring seat

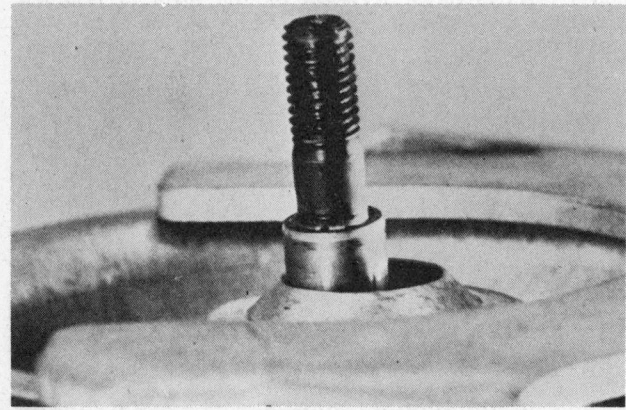

Step 15. Make sure that the crescent shaped bars on the upper compression plate are located on the upper spring seat as shown. Turn the load screw clockwise enough to tighten the compression plates on the upper and lower spring seats. Stop. Again, to assure that the coil spring will not arch, make sure that the pivot points are aligned with the centerline of the coil spring. Then continue turning the load screw clockwise until about 1½ inches of piston rod is showing above the upper spring seat

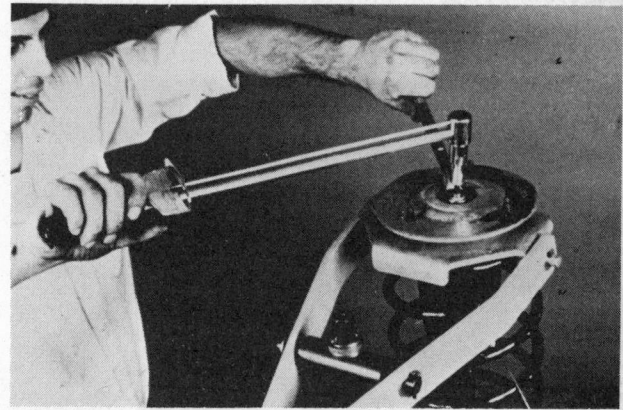

Step 16. Install upper support housing on piston rod. Tighten the piston rod nut and remove the compressor from the strut and the strut from the vise. Install the strut. See the car section for details

GM J- AND A-CARS ONLY

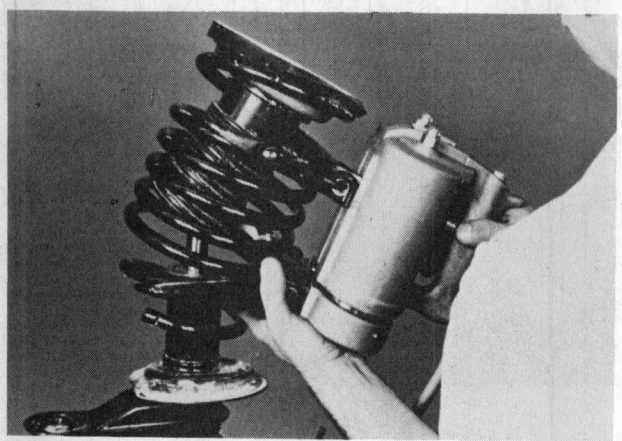

Step 1. Place the strut assembly in a vise, and compress the coil spring. Remove the piston rod, upper support housing, spring seat and coil spring. If the universal pneumatic spring compressor is used, an adaptor provided with the compressor should be fastened to the strut under the steering arm. The ears of the adaptor should be aligned with steering arm. The adaptor provides a square seating surface for the strut while it is being compressed

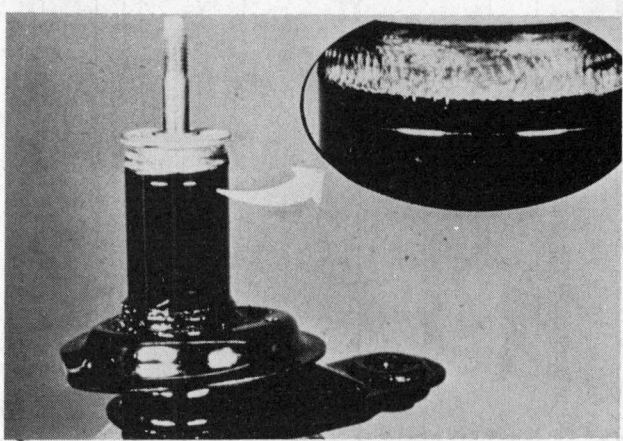

Step 2. J and A–car struts have a welded upper closure, but the strut is designed so the damping mechanism can be replaced with a cartridge insert. Just below the spin weld there is a cut-line scribed in the strut body

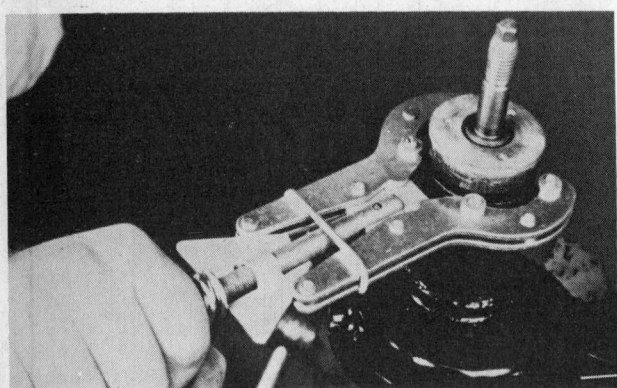

Step 3. Using a pipe cutter, cut open the strut body at the scribed line. (Note: *It is important that the cut be made on the cut-line)*

Step 4. Remove the cartridge and oil from the strut. Note the threads on the inside of the strut. Deburr the top of the strut body if necessary

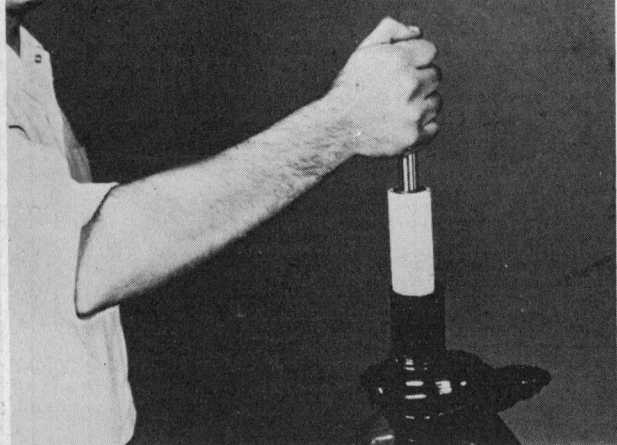

Step 5. Pour about one ounce of oil into the strut body and insert the replacement cartridge. Push the piston rod down and start the body nut by hand. Tighten the nut securely

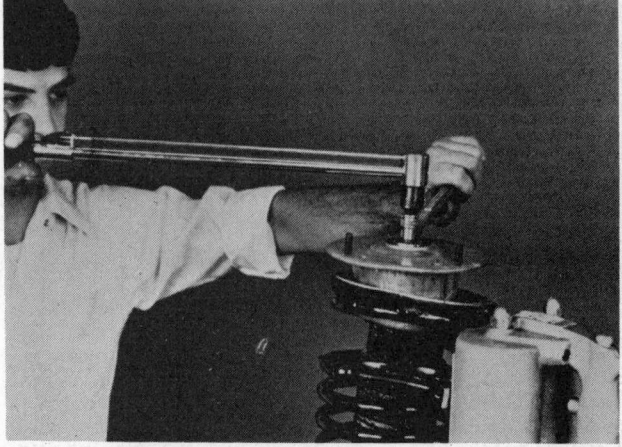

Step 6. Assemble spring, upper spring seat, and upper support housing on the strut, and tighten the new piston rod nut. The renewed strut is now ready to install on the vehicle. Release the spring tension

— MACPHERSON STRUT PROBLEM DIAGNOSIS —

Problems with MacPherson struts generally fall into 3 main categories: suspension, tire wear and steering. In general, the symptoms encountered are not significantly different from those encountered on conventional suspensions.

Suspension

Sag

Vehicle "sag" is a visible tilt of the car from one side to the other or one end to the other while parked on a level surface.

Weak or damaged strut springs could cause this condition and should be repaired immediately.

Sag will also cause steering and tire wear problems to be more pronounced and vehicle instability on rough roads. Front wheel alignment will not solve the problem.

Weak strut springs increase vehicle sag. See "Tire Cupping".

Cartridge Leaks

Strut cartridge leaks (not seepage) indicate the need for cartridge or strut replacement. Be sure the leakage is coming from the strut, and not from elsewhere on the vehicle.

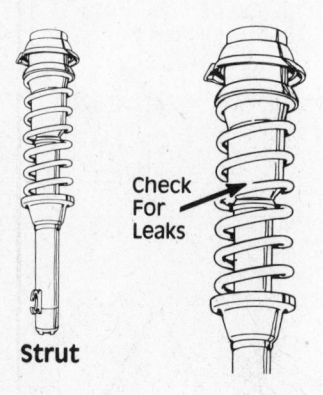

Check For Leaks

Strut

Abnormal Tire Wear

Wear on One Side

One sided tire wear indicates incorrect camber. Check the causes in the accompanying illustration and be sure the wheel alignment is correct.

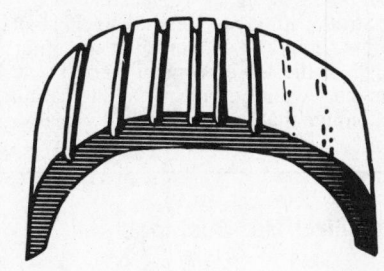

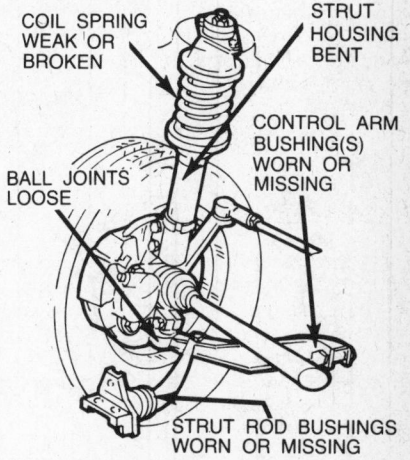

COIL SPRING WEAK OR BROKEN

STRUT HOUSING BENT

CONTROL ARM BUSHING(S) WORN OR MISSING

BALL JOINTS LOOSE

STRUT ROD BUSHINGS WORN OR MISSING

Tire "Cupping"

Cupped tires indicate any or all of the following problems.

1. A weak strut cartridge can be verified by bouncing each corner of the car vigorously and letting go. The car should not bounce more than once, if the shock absorber cartridges are good.

2. Weak strut springs allow sag to increase with only a slight amount of downward pressure. A visual inspection will reveal any broken springs or shiny spots.

3. Check for loose or worn wheel bearings with the weight of the car off of the wheel.

4. Check the wheel balance.

Tread Edge Wear

Wear along tread edges (feathering) indicates a suspension or steering system problem.

1. Strut rod bushings are worn or missing.

2. Tie rod end wear can be determined by grabbing the tie rod end firmly and forcing it up, down or sideways to check for lost motion.

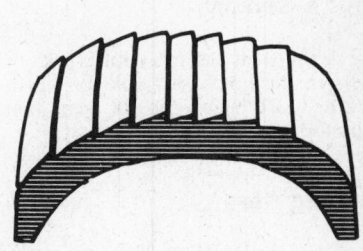

MACPHERSON STRUT PROBLEM DIAGNOSIS

Problems with MacPherson struts generally fall into 3 main categories: suspension, tire wear and steering. In general, the symptoms encountered are not significantly different from those encountered on conventional suspensions.

Steering

Tires

Both front tires should match and both rear tires should match. Be sure air pressure is correct.

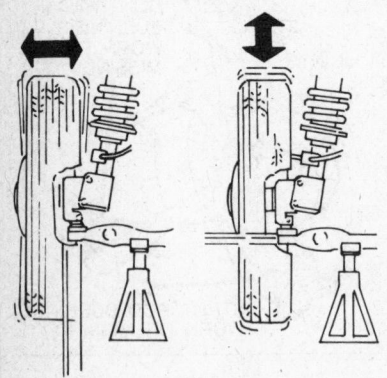

Strut Rod Bushings

Grasp the strut rod and shake it. Any noticeable play indicates excessive wear and need for parts replacement.

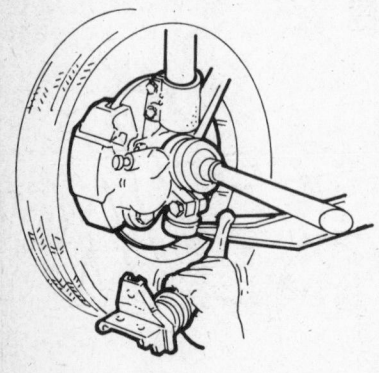

Ball Joints

Support the car under the frame or crossmember so that the jack does not interfere with the control arm. Rock the tire in and out and up and down. Excessive movement means that both ball joints should be replaced.

Struts with lower weight-carrying ball joints should be supported at the outer edge of the lower control arm. These vehicles usually have wear indicating ball joints that can be checked visually.

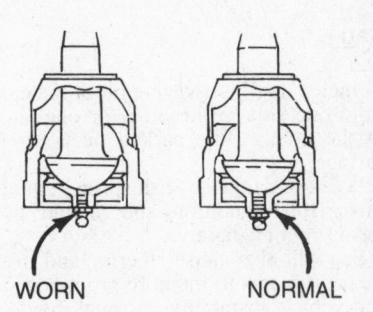

WORN   NORMAL

Stabilizer Bar Bushings

Check for worn bushings or lost motion with the vehicle level and the weight evenly distributed on all wheels.

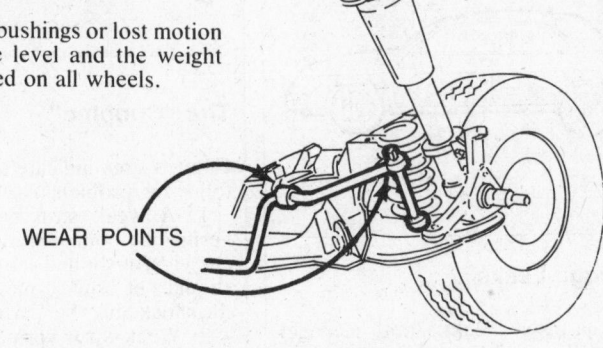

WEAR POINTS

Control Arm Bushings

Support the car under the frame or body and remove the weight from the wheel and control arm. Check for free-play in the bushings at the pivot point, using a pry bar.

NOTE: Some control arm bushings are serviceable only by replacing the entire arm.

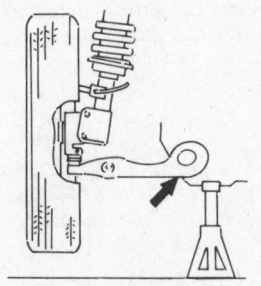

Strut Assembly

Check the strut assembly for cracks or dents in the housing. Look for worn, bent or loose piston rods or dents that will inhibit piston rod movement.

Steering Gear

Check for worn steering gear or loose or worn mounting bolts and bushings.

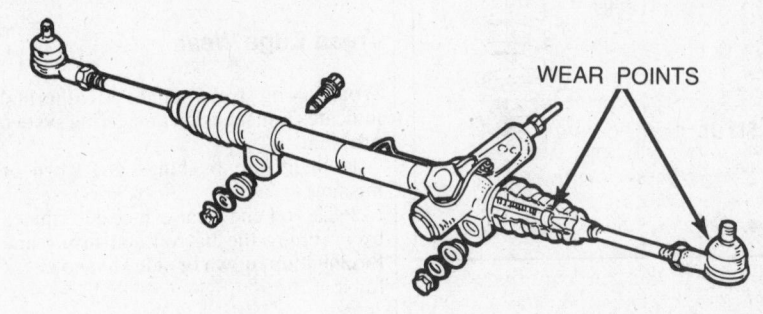

WEAR POINTS

BRAKES

Hydraulic Brake Component Service

BASIC OPERATING PRINCIPLES

The hydraulic brake system transports the power required to force the frictional surfaces of the braking system together from the pedal to the individual brake units at each wheel. A hydraulic system is used for 2 reasons. First, fluid under pressure can be carried to all parts of an automobile by small hoses (some of which are flexible) without taking up a significant amount of room or posing routing problems. Second, a great mechanical advantage can be given to the brake pedal end of the system and the foot pressure required to actuate the brakes can be reduced by making the surface area of the master cylinder pistons smaller than that of any of the pistons in the wheel cylinders or calipers.

The master cylinder consists of a double reservoir and piston assembly as well as other springs, fittings, etc. Double (dual) master cylinders are designed to separate the wheels from the others into a pair of hydraulic systems. The standard approach has been have separate circuits for the front and rear wheels. Newer models may have a diagonally split system; i.e. a front wheel and the opposite side rear wheel are in a separate circuit from the other front and rear wheel.

Steel lines carry the brake fluid to a point on the vehicles frame near each wheel. A flexible hose usually carries the fluid to the disc caliper or wheel cylinder. The flexible line allows for suspension and steering movement.

The rear wheel cylinders contain 2 pistons, 1 at either end, which push outward in opposite directions. Most brake calipers contain a single piston, however in some cases they may contain more.

All pistons employ some type of seal, usually made of rubber, to minimize fluid leakage. A rubber dust boot seals the outer end of the cylinder against dust and dirt. The boot fits around the outer end of the piston on disc brake calipers and around the brake actuating rod on the wheel cylinders.

The hydraulic system operates as follows: When at rest, the entire system, from the piston(s) in the master cylinder to those in the wheel cylinders or calipers, is full of brake fluid. Upon application of the brake pedal, fluid trapped in front of the master cylinder piston(s) is forced through the lines to the wheel cylinders and calipers. Here, it forces the pistons outward, in the case of drum brakes and inward toward the disc, in the case of disc brakes. The motion of the pistons is opposed by return springs mounted outside the cylinders in drum brakes and by internal springs or spring seals, in disc brakes.

Upon release of the brake pedal, a spring located inside the master cylinder immediately returns the master cylinder pistons to the normal position. The pistons contain check valves and the master cylinder has compensating ports drilled in it. These are uncovered as the pistons reach their normal position. The piston check valves

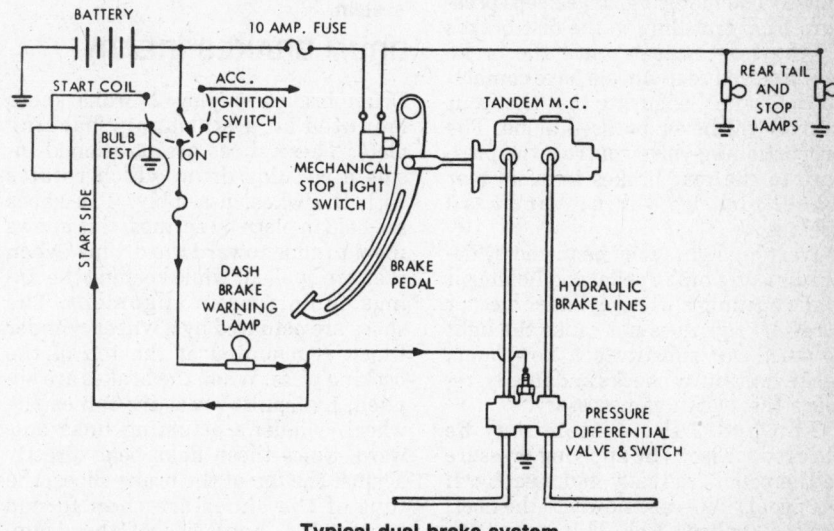

Typical dual brake system

allow fluid to flow toward the wheel cylinders or calipers as the pistons withdraw. Then, as the rubber boot/seal or return springs force the brake pads or shoes into the released position, the excess fluid returns to the reservoir through the compensating ports.

The dual master cylinder has 2 pistons, located 1 behind the other. The primary piston is actuated directly by mechanical linkage from the brake pedal. The secondary piston is actuated by fluid trapped between the 2 pistons. If a leak develops in front of the secondary piston, it moves forward until it bottoms against the front of the master cylinder. The fluid trapped between the pistons will operate opposite sides of the split system. If the other side of the system develops a leak, the primary piston will move forward until direct contact with the secondary piston takes place and it will force the secondary piston to actuate the other side of the split system. In either case the brake pedal drops closer to the floor board and less braking power is available.

The brake system uses a switch to warn the driver when only half of the brake system is operational. This switch is usually located in a valve body which is mounted on the firewall or the frame below the master cylinder. A hydraulic piston receives pressure from both circuits, each circuit's pressure being applied to opposite end of the piston. When the pressures are in balance, the piston remains stationary. When a circuit has a leak, however, the greater pressure in that circuit during brake application will push the piston to 1 side, closing the switch and activating the brake warning light.

In disc brake systems, this valve body contains a metering valve and, in some cases, a proportioning valve or valves. The metering valve keeps pressure from traveling to the disc brakes on the front wheels until the brake shoes on the rear wheels have contacted the drums, ensuring that the front brakes will never be used alone. The proportioning valve controls the pressure to the rear brakes to avoid rear wheel lock-up during very hard braking.

Warning lights may be tested by depressing the brake pedal and holding it while opening a wheel cylinder bleeder screw. If this does not cause the light to turn On, substitute a new lamp, make continuity checks and finally, replace the switch as necessary.

The hydraulic system may be checked for leaks by applying pressure to the pedal gradually and steadily. If the pedal sinks very slowly to the floor, the system has a leak. This is not to be confused with a springy or spongy feel due to the compression of air within the lines. If the system leaks, there will be a gradual change in the position of the pedal when a constant pressure is applied.

Check for leaks along all lines and at wheel cylinders or calipers. If no external leaks are apparent, the problem is inside the master cylinder.

DISC BRAKES

Disc brake systems utilize a disc (rotor) with brake pads positioned on either side of it. Braking effect is achieved in a manner similar to the way you would squeeze a spinning phonograph record between your fingers. The disc (rotor) is a casting which may be equipped with cooling fins between the 2 braking surfaces. The fins (if equipped) enable air to circulate between the braking surfaces making them less sensitive to heat buildup and more resistant to fade. Dirt and water do not affect braking action since contaminants are thrown off by the centrifugal action of the rotor or scraped off by the pads. Also, the equal clamping action of the brake pads tends to ensure uniform, straightline stops. Disc brakes are inherently self-adjusting.

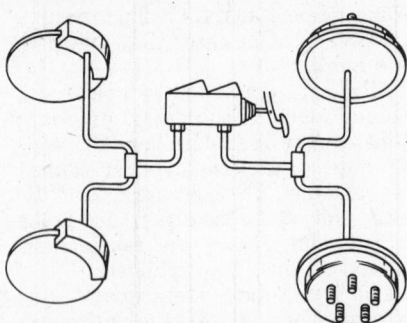

Typical front/rear split hydraulic brake system

DRUM BRAKES (REAR)

Drum brakes employ 2 brake shoes mounted on a stationary backing plate. These shoes are positioned inside a circular drum which rotates with the wheel assembly. The shoes are held in place by springs, this allows them to slide toward the drums (when they are applied) while keeping the linings and drums in alignment. The shoes are actuated by a wheel cylinder which is mounted at the top of the backing plate. When the brakes are applied, hydraulic pressure forces the wheel cylinder's actuating links outward. Since these links bear directly against the top of the brake shoes, the tops of the shoes are then forced against the inner side of the drum.

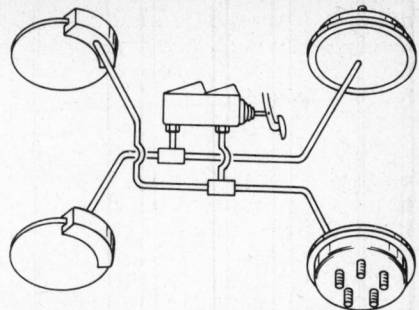

Typical diagonally split hydraulic brake system

This action forces the bottoms of the 2 shoes to contact the brake drum by rotating the entire assembly slightly (known as servo action). When pressure within the wheel cylinder is relaxed, return springs pull the shoes back away from the drum.

Rear drum brakes are (in most cases) designed to self-adjust themselves during application. Motion causes both shoes to rotate very slightly with the drum, rocking an adjusting lever, thereby causing rotation of the adjusting screw or lever.

POWER BRAKE SYSTEM

Power brakes operate just as standard brake systems except in the actuation of the master cylinder pistons. A vacuum diaphragm is located on the front of the master cylinder and assists the driver in applying the brakes, reducing both the effort and travel he must put into moving the brake pedal.

The vacuum diaphragm housing is connected to the intake manifold by a vacuum hose. A check valve is placed at the point where the hose enters the diaphragm housing, so that during periods of low manifold vacuum brake assist vacuum will not be lost.

Depressing the brake pedal closes off the vacuum source and allows atmospheric pressure to enter on 1 side of the diaphragm. This causes the master cylinder pistons to move and apply the brakes. When the brake pedal is released, vacuum is applied to both sides of the diaphragm and the return springs return the diaphragm and the master cylinder pistons to the released position. If the vacuum fails, the brake pedal rod will butt against the end of the master cylinder actuating rod and direct mechanical application will occur as the pedal is depressed.

MASTER CYLINDERS

———— CAUTION ————

The master cylinder unit is a highly calibrated unit specifically designed for the vehicle it is on. Although cylinders may look alike there are many differences in calibration. If replacement is necessary, make sure the replacement unit is the correct cylinder for the vehicle.

NOTE: Some GM vehicles are equipped with "Quick Take-Up" master cylinders which provide a large volume of fluid to the brakes at low pressure when the brake pedal is initially applied. This large volume of fluid is needed because self retracting piston seals are used on the caliper pistons. The piston seals pull the pistons into the calipers after the brakes are released, thereby preventing the brake pads from causing a drag on the rotors.

The "Quick Take-Up" master cylinder has a hydraulically operated brake warning light switch incorporated in the master cylinder body. The piston is accessible by removing the large plug at the front of the master cylinder body. Only remove the plug when overhauling the cylinder, as brake fluid will escape.

Overhaul procedures on these master cylinders are basically the same as those on conventional master cylinders.

Servicing Master Cylinders

NOTE: Plastic reservoirs need to be removed only for the following reasons: Reservoir is damaged or the rubber grommet(s) between the reservoir and bore is leaking. Removal of stop pin from Chrysler style plastic reservoir master cylinder to allow removal of pistons. Pin is located underneath front reservoir nipple. Service "Quick Take-up" valve on GM quick take-up master cylinders. The reservoir should be removed by first clamping the cylinder flange in a vice. Next remove the reservoir for the Chrysler style. Grasp the reservoir base on the end and pull away from the body. GM reservoirs must be removed by prying between the reservoir and casting with a pry bar.

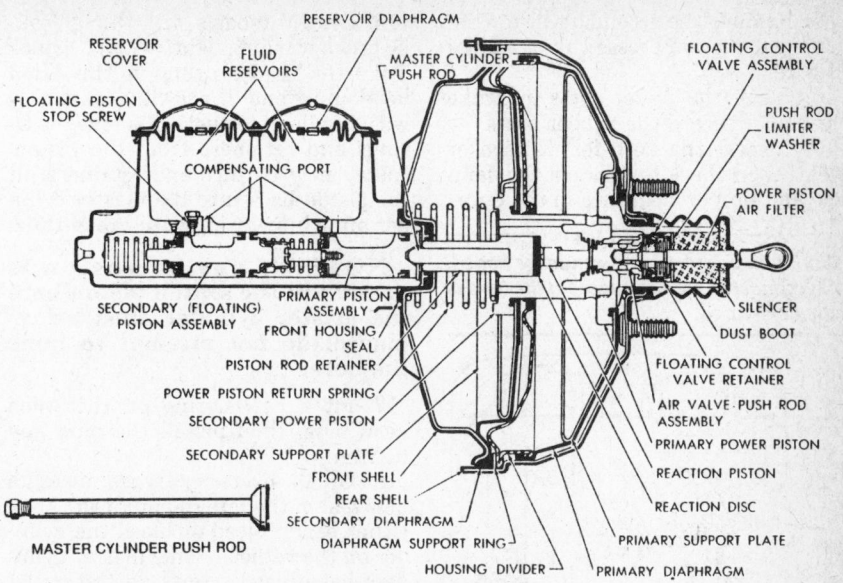

Typical dual master cylinder

Grommets can be reused if they are in good condition. Whether or not the reservoir is removed, it and the cover or caps should be thoroughly cleaned.

1. Remove the cylinder from the vehicle and drain the brake fluid.
2. Mount the cylinder in a vise so that the outlets are up and remove the rubber boot seal from the hub.
3. Remove the stop pin or screw from the bottom of the front reservoir, if present.
4. Remove the snapring from the front of the bore and the primary piston assembly.

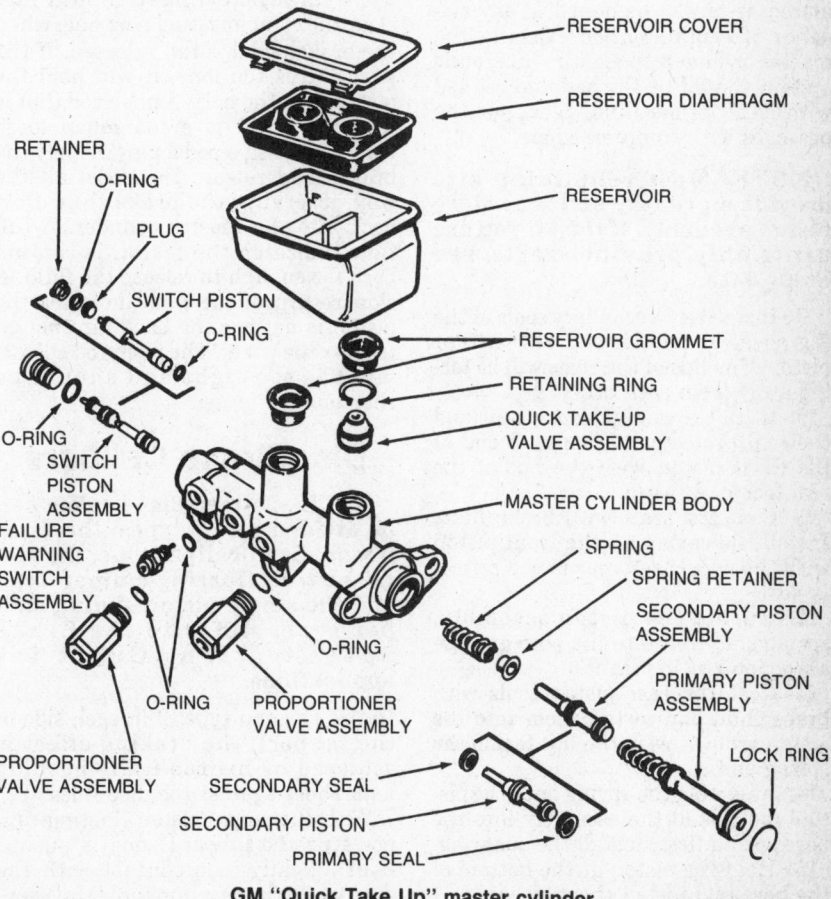

GM "Quick Take Up" master cylinder

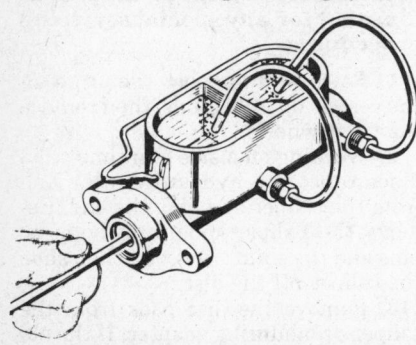

Pre-bleeding master cylinder

5. Remove the secondary piston assembly using compressed air or a piece of wire.

6. Clean the metal parts in brake fluid and discard the rubber parts.

7. Inspect the bore for damage or wear, then check the pistons for damage and proper clearance in the bore.

--- **CAUTION** ---

Aluminum cylinder bores cannot be honed. The cylinder must be replaced if the bore is pitted or scored.

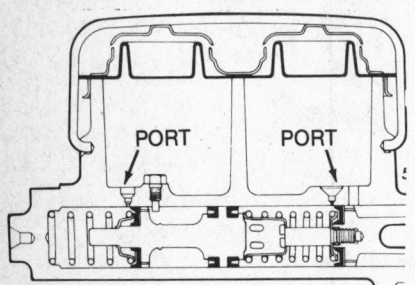

Feed and return ports

8. If the bore is only slightly scored or pitted it may be honed. (See CAUTION). Always use hones that are in good condition and completely clean the cylinder with brake fluid when the honing is completed. If any sign of wear or corrosion is apparent on "Quick Take-Up" master cylinder bores, the master cylinder must be replaced; it cannot be honed. If any evidence of contamination exists in the master cylinder the entire hydraulic system should be flushed and refilled with clean brake fluid. Blow out the passages with compressed air.

NOTE: Most rebuilding kits provide a primary and secondary piston assembly. If the kit you are using only provides seals, see Steps 9–13.

9. Install new secondary seals in the 2 grooves in the flat end of the front piston. The lips of the seals will be facing away from each other.

10. Install a new primary seal and the seal protector on opposite end of the front piston with the lips of the seal facing outward.

11. Coat the seals with brake fluid. Install the spring on the front piston with the spring retainer in the primary seal.

12. Insert the piston assembly, spring end first, into the bore and use a wooden rod to seat it.

13. Coat the rear piston seals with brake fluid and install them into the piston grooves with the lips facing the spring end.

14. Assemble the spring onto the piston and install the assembly into the bore spring first. Install the snapring.

15. Hold the piston at the bottom of the bore and install the stop screw.

16. On GM models with the hydraulic brake warning light switch ("Quick Take-Up" units), remove the Allen head plug and the switch assembly with needle nose pliers. Remove the O-rings and retainers from the piston. Install new O-rings and retainers, fit the piston back into the master cylinder after lubricating with brake fluid.

NOTE: If any corrosion is present in the switch piston bore the master cylinder must be replaced: do not attempt to hone the bore.

17. Fit a new O-ring on the Allen head plug, then install the plug and tighten.

18. On all master cylinders, install a new seal in the hub (if equipped), then either bench bleed or bleed the cylinder on the vehicle. Some master cylinders have bleed screws on the outlet flanges and may be bled without disturbing the wheel cylinders or calipers.

Master Cylinder Push Rod Adjustment

MODELS EQUIPPED WITH ADJUSTABLE PUSH ROD

After assembly of the master cylinder to the power section, the piston cup in the hydraulic cylinder should just clear the compensating port hole when the brake pedal is full released. If the push rod is too long, it will hold the piston over the port. A push rod that is too short, will give too much loose travel (excessive pedal play). Apply the brakes and release the pedal all the way observing the brake fluid flow back into the master cylinder. A full flow indicates the piston is coming back far enough to release the fluid. A slow return of the fluid indicates the piston is not coming back far enough to clear the ports. The push rod adjustment is too tight and should be shortened.

Disc Brake Calipers

NOTE: Caliper disc brakes can be divided into 3 types: the four-piston, fixed-caliper type; the single-piston, floating-caliper type and the single-piston sliding-caliper type. Refer to the Brake Specifications Chart for applications.

In the 4 piston type (2 in each side of the caliper), the braking effect is achieved by hydraulically pushing both shoes against the disc sides.

With the single piston floating-caliper type the inboard shoe is pushed hydraulically into contact with the disc, while the reaction force thus gen-

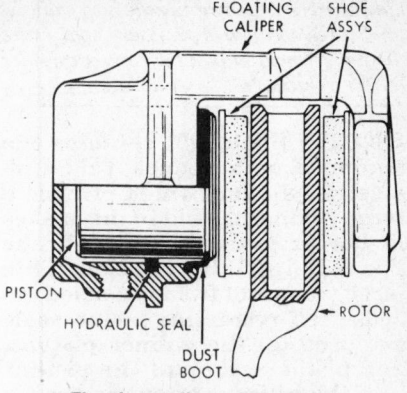

Floating caliper disc brake

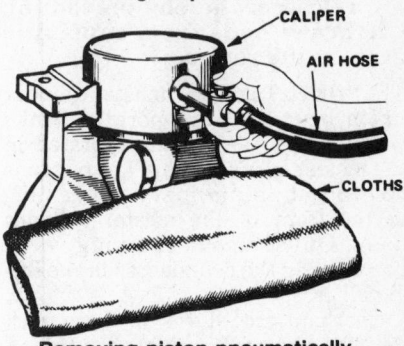

Removing piston pneumatically

erated is used to pull the outboard shoe into frictional contact (made possible by letting the caliper move slightly along the axle centerline).

In the sliding caliper (single piston) type, the caliper assembly slides along the machined surfaces of the anchor plate. A steel key located between the machined surfaces of the caliper and the machines surfaces of the anchor plate is held in place with either a retaining screw or a pair of cotter pins. The caliper is held in place against the anchor plate with 1 or 2 support springs.

SERVICING THE CALIPER ASSEMBLY

NOTE: The following is a general caliper service procedure. Before proceeding, check under the individual disc brake section for your vehicle (Delco Moraine, Bendix, etc.) for any special servicing procedures.

1. Raise and support the front of the vehicle on jackstands, then remove the front wheels.

2. Working on a side at a time only, disconnect the hydraulic inlet line from the caliper and plug the end. Remove the caliper mounting bolts or pins and the shims (if used), then slide the caliper off the disc.

3. Remove the disc pads from the caliper or mounting adapter. If the old ones are to be reused, make them so

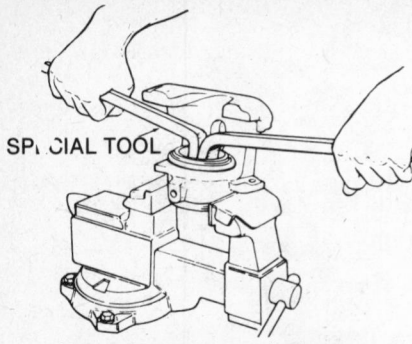

Removing hollow end piston

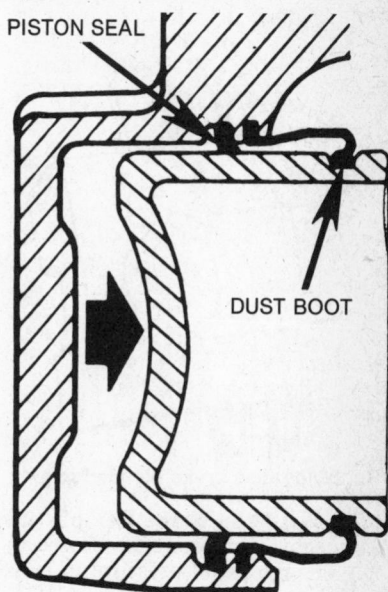

Removing pistons

that they can be reinstalled in their original positions.

4. Open the caliper bleed screw and drain the fluid. Clean the outside of the caliper and mount it in a vise with padded jaws.

CAUTION

When cleaning any brake components, use only brake fluid or denatured (Isopropyl) alcohol. Never use a mineral-based solvent, such as gasoline or paint thinner, since it will swell and quickly deteriorate the rubber parts. Alcohol must NOT be allowed to remain in any component that will hold brake fluid, this would lower the boiling point of the brake fluid.

---

5. Remove the bridge bolts (fixed type), separate the caliper halves and remove the 2 O-ring seals from the transfer holes.

6. Pry the lip on (each) piston dust boot from its groove, then remove the piston assemblies and spring(s) from the bore(s). If necessary, air pressure may be used to force the pistons(s) out of the bore(s), using care to prevent the piston from popping out of control.

7. Remove the boot(s) and seal(s) from the piston(s), then clean the piston(s) in brake fluid. Blow out the caliper passages with an air hose.

8. Inspect the cylinder bore(s) for scoring, pitting or corrosion. Corrosion is a pitted or rough condition not to be confused with staining. Light rough spots may be removed by rotat-

ing crocus cloth, using finger pressure, in the bores. DO NOT polish with an in and out motion or use any other abrasive.

9. If the piston(s) are pitted, scored or worn, they must be replaced. A corroded or deeply scored caliper should also be replaced.

10. Check the clearance of the piston(s) in the bores using a feeler gauge. Clearance should be 0.002–0.006 in. If there is excessive clearance the caliper must be replaced.

11. Replace all rubber parts and lubricate with brake fluid. Install the seals (or square cut rings) and boots in the grooves in each piston. The seal should be installed in the groove closest to the closed end of the piston with the seal lips facing the closed end. The lip on the boot should be facing the seal.

12. Lubricate the piston and bore with brake fluid. Position the piston return spring (if equipped), large coil first, in the piston bore.

13. Install the piston in the bore, taking great care to avoid damaging the seal lip as it passes the edge of the cylinder bore.

14. Compress the lip on the dust boot into the groove in the caliper. Be sure the boot is full seated in the groove, as poor sealing will allow contaminants to ruin the bore.

15. On fixed calipers: Position the O-rings in the cavities around the caliper transfer holes and fit the caliper halves together. Install the bridge bolts (lubricated with brake fluid) and be sure to torque to specification.

16. Install the disc pads in the caliper or adapter and remount the caliper on the hub. Connect the brake line to the caliper and bleed the brakes. Replace the wheels. Recheck the brake fluid level, check the brake pedal travel and road test the vehicle.

OVERHAUL TIPS

Field reports indicate that 2 factors determine whether to replace or rebuild calipers: Can the piston or pistons be removed? Will the bleed screw break off when removal is attempted? (Rebuilders will not accept a caliper with a broken bleed screw.) Since there is no way to predict how a bleed screw will react, follow this procedure to attempt removal.

1. Insert a drill shank into the bleed screw hole (snug fit).

2. Tap the screw on all sides.

3. Using a 6-point wrench, apply pressure gently while working the drill up and down slightly.

4. If the drill starts to bind, the screw is beginning to collapse and cannot be removed intact.

5. Heating the caliper is another successful, but time consuming, bleed screw removal technique. Remove the caliper from the vehicle. Heat the caliper. Shrink the bleed screw by applying dry ice and attempt to remove.

DISC BRAKE BLEEDER SCREW REPLACEMENT

1. Using the existing hole in bleed screw for a pilot, drill a ¼ in. hole completely through existing bleeder.

2. Increase the hole size to $\frac{7}{16}$ in.

3. Tap the hole using a ¼ in. (18-national pipe thread) ½ in. deep (full thread).

4. Install the bleeder repair kit.

5. Test for leaks and full brake pedal pressure.

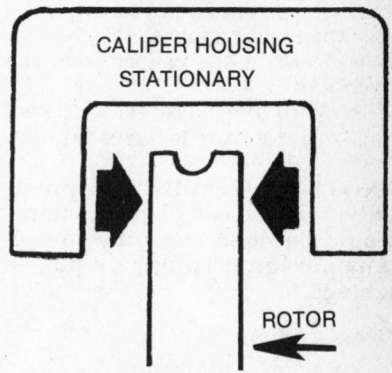

Brake applied

Fixed caliper type

FROZEN PISTONS

Sliding or Floating Caliper

1. Hydraulic removal:
   a. Remove the caliper assembly from the rotor.
   b. Remove brake pads and dust seal.

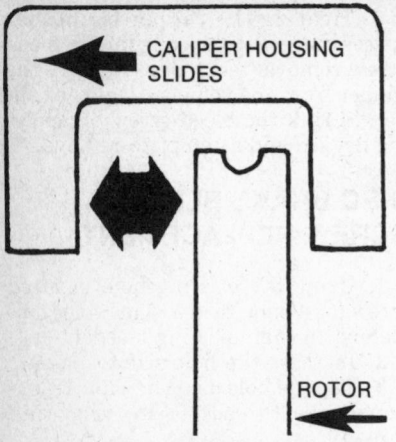

Floating (or sliding) caliper type

Replacing disc brake bleeder screw

CALIPER CLEANING

NOTE: Castinge s may be cleaned with any type cleaning fluid after all the rubber seals have been removed.

It is important that all traces of cleaning fluid be completely removed from the caliper casting. Rubber components are compatible with alcohol and/or brake fluid. Use a lint free wiping cloth to clean the caliper and parts. Black stains on the pistons or walls, caused by the seals, will not do harm; however, extreme cleanliness is essential. Blow out the passages with compressed air. A fine grade of crocus cloth may be used to correct minor imperfections in the cylinder bore. Slide crocus cloth with finger pressure in a circular rather than a lengthwise motion. DO NOT use any form of abrasive on a plated piston. Discard a piston which is pitted or has signs of plating wear.

REBUILDING CALIPERS

NOTE: If a fine stone honing of a caliper bore is necessary it should be done with skill and caution. Some vehicles can develop 800 psi hydraulic pressure on severe application so the honing must never exceed 0.003 in. Also the dust seal groove must be free of rust or nicks so that a perfect mating surface is possible on the piston and casting.

Installing Stroking Type Seals and Boots

Stretch the boot and seal over the piston and seat them. The seal lip on the Bendix and Delco styles, faces toward hydraulic pressure; boot lips face toward the brake shoe. Locate the return spring (if used) in the cylinder and carefully start the piston into the cylinder to avoid nicking the seal. Alignment tools are available for inserting the lip cup seals. Fully depress the piston into the bore in order to fasten the boot lip to the caliper housing. On the Delco types, use a wooden drift or a special seating tool to seat the boot ring in the caliper counterbore. It must be flush or below the caliper machined surface.

Installing Fixed Position (Rectangular Ring) Seals and Boots

Insert a rectangular ring seal into bore and at any location, push the ring into the seal groove. From this area, with a finger, gently work around the bore until the ring is seated in this channel. Be sure the ring does not twist or roll

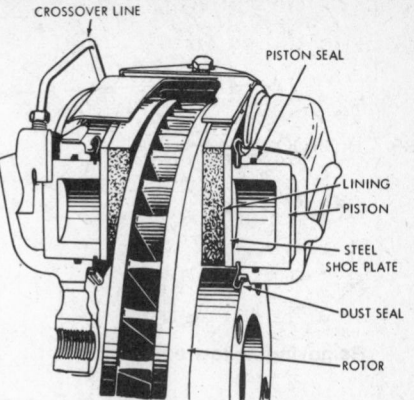

Fixed caliper disc brake

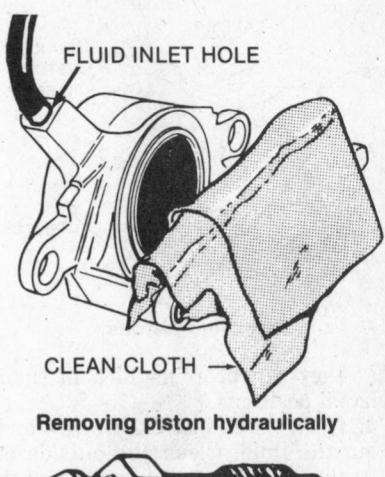

Removing piston hydraulically

Bleed screw

c. With the brake flexible line connected and bleed screw closed apply enough pedal pressure to move the piston most of the way out of the bore (brake fluid will begin to ooze past the piston inner seal).

2. Pneumatic removal:

a. Remove the caliper from the vehicle.

b. With the bleed screw closed, apply air pressure to force the piston out.

NOTE: Hydraulic and pneumatic methods of piston removal should be done carefully to prevent personal injury or piston damage.

Fixed Caliper

NOTE: The hydraulic or pneumatic methods which apply to the single piston type caliper will not work on the multiple piston typbrake caliper.

1. Remove the caliper from the vehicle with the 2 halves separated.

2. Mount in a vise and use a piston puller (many types available) to remove the pistons.

in the groove. When the boot lip is retained inside the cylinder bore, insert the boot in the same manner. Then work the inside of the boot over the pressure end of the piston, stretching the boot with a small plastic tool and pressing the piston through the seal, straight in, until it bottoms. The inside of the boot should slide on the piston and come to rest in the boot groove. If the boot lip is retained outside of the cylinder bore, first stretch boot over the piston and seat it in its groove, then press the piston through the seal. Fully depress the piston to 50–100 lbs. in order to fasten the boot lip in place. On the Delco-Moraine types, use a wooden drift or a special seating tool to seat the metal boot ring in the caliper counterbore below the face of the caliper.

Installing Fixed-Caliper Bridge Bolts

If the caliper contains internal fluid crossover passages, be sure to install new O-ring seals at the joints. Mate the caliper halves and install high ten-

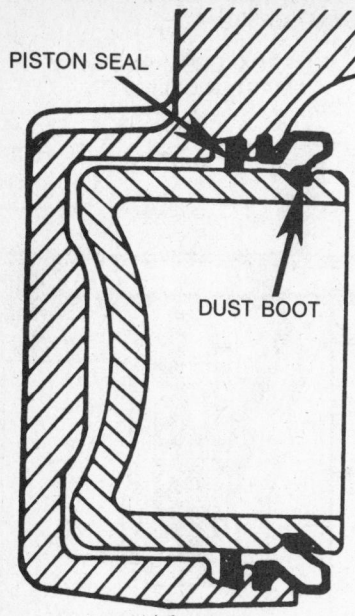

PISTON SEAL

DUST BOOT

Brake released

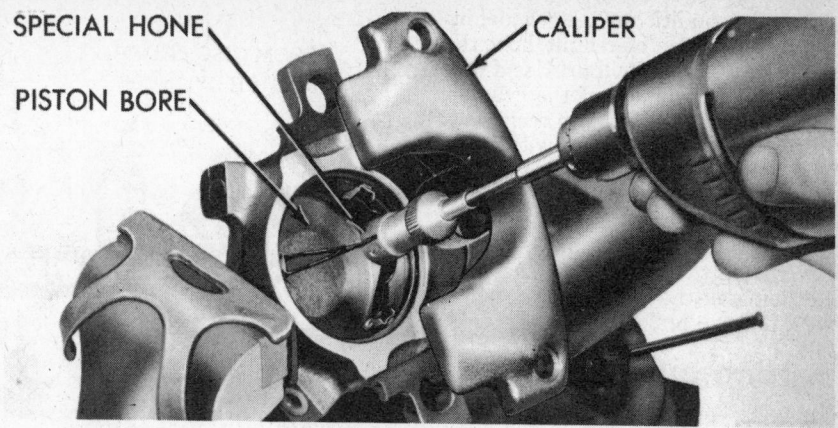

SPECIAL HONE

PISTON BORE

CALIPER

Honing cylinder bore

sile strength bridge bolts. Never replace the bridge bolts with ordinary standard hardware bolts.

Wheel Cylinders

Wheel cylinders contain a pair of opposed pistons fitted with rubber cups, compression spring and sometimes expander washers to keep the cups tight against the pistons.

SERVICING

1. Raise and support the vehicle on jackstands. Remove the wheel and drum assemblies from the side to be serviced.

2. Remove the brake shoes, then clean the backing plate and the wheel cylinder. Rebuilding can be done on the vehicle, depending on the design of the brake backing plate. If the backing plate is recessed to the point that it is impossible to get a hone into the cylinder, the cylinder has to be removed.

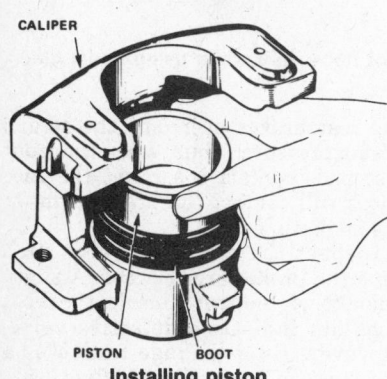

CALIPER

PISTON   BOOT

Installing piston

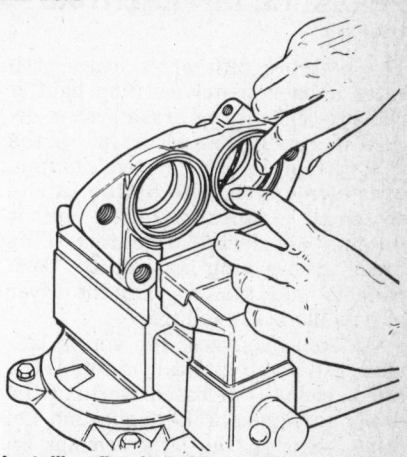

Installing fixed position rectangular ring seal (seal lip toward pressure side)

3. To remove the cylinder; disconnect the brake line from the rear of the cylinder, remove the mounting bolts or retainers and the cylinders.

NOTE: On some models, the wheel cylinder is contained by a retaining ring. In order to remove the rear wheel cylinders, remove the wheel cylinder retainer. Insert 2 pin punches or equivalent tools into the access slots and bend both tabs at the same time thereby releasing the cylinder. Use a new retainer when reinstalling the wheel cylinder. The new retainer can be driven on using a $1\frac{1}{8}$ in. socket with an extension bar.

4. Remove the rubber boots (dust covers) from the ends of the cylinder. Remove the pistons, the piston cups (expanders, if equipped) and the spring from the inside of the cylinder. Remove the bleeder screw and make sure it is not clogged.

5. Discard all of the parts that the rebuilding kit will replace.

6. Examine the inside of the cylinder. If it is severely rusted, pitted or scratched install a new or rebuilt cylinder.

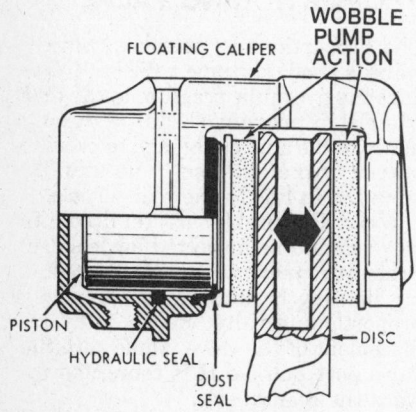

PISTON

BOOT

Assembling boot on piston

WOBBLE PUMP ACTION

FLOATING CALIPER

PISTON
HYDRAULIC SEAL
DUST SEAL
DISC

Wobble pump action

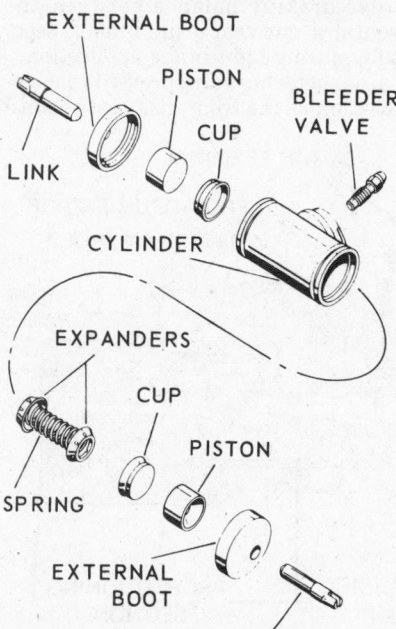

EXTERNAL BOOT
PISTON
CUP
BLEEDER VALVE
LINK
CYLINDER
EXPANDERS
CUP
PISTON
SPRING
EXTERNAL BOOT
LINK

Wheel cylinder components

7. If the condition of the cylinder indicates that it can be rebuilt, hone the bore. Light honing will provide a new surface on the inside of the cylinder which promotes better cup sealing.

8. Wash out the cylinder with brake fluid after honing. Reassemble the cylinder using the new parts provided in the kit. When assembling the cylinder dip all parts in brake fluid.

9. Install the cylinder on the vehicle. Reinstall the brakes, drum/wheel and bleed the brake system.

Hydraulic Control Valves

PRESSURE DIFFERENTIAL VALVE

The pressure differential valve activates a dash panel warning light if pressure loss in the brake system occurs. If pressure loss occurs in ½ of the split system the other system's normal pressure causes the piston in the switch to compress a spring until it touches an electrical contact. This turns the warning lamp on the dash panel to light, thus warning the driver of possible brake failure.

On some vehicles, the spring balance piston automatically resets as the brake pedal is released warning the driver only upon brake application. On other vehicles, the light remains on until manually cancelled.

Valves may be located separately, as part of a combination valve, or incorporated into the master cylinder.

Resetting Valves

On some vehicles, the valve piston(s) remain off center after failure until necessary repairs are made. The valve will automatically reset itself (after repairs) when pressure is equal on both sides of the system.

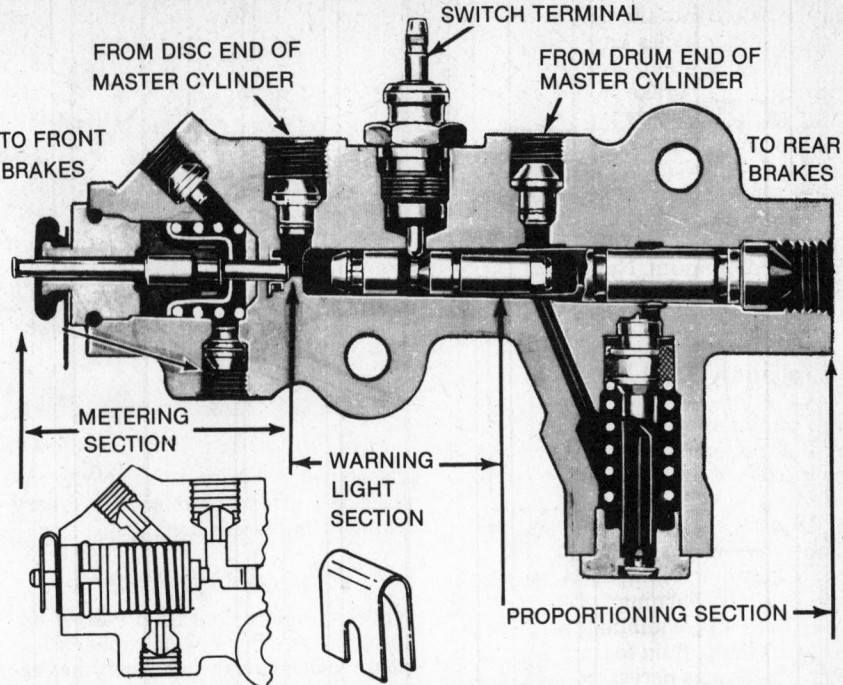

Hold valve out .060 in pressure bleed only-not necessary when using pedal bleed method

If the light does not go out, bleed the brake system that is opposite the failed system. If front brakes failed, bleed the rear brakes, this should force the light control piston toward center.

If this fails, remove the terminal switch. If brake fluid is present in the electrical area, the seals are gone, replace the complete valve assembly.

METERING VALVE

The metering valve's function is to improve braking balance between the front disc and rear drum brakes, especially during light brake application.

The metering valve prevents the application of the front disc brakes until the rear brakes overcome the return spring pressure. Thus, when the front disc pads contact the rotor, the rear shoes will contact the brake drum at the same time.

Inspect the metering valve each time the brakes are serviced. A slight amount of moisture inside the boot does not indicate a defective valve, however, fluid leakage indicates a damaged or worn valve. If fluid leakage is present the valve must be replaced.

The metering valve can be checked very simply. With the vehicle stopped, gently apply the brakes. At about 1 in. of travel a very small change in pedal effort (like a small bump) will be felt if the valve is operating properly. Metering valves are not serviceable and must be replaced (if defective).

PROPORTIONING VALVE

The proportioning (pressure control) valve is used, on some vehicles, to reduce the hydraulic pressure to the rear wheels to prevent skidding during heavy brake application and to provide better brake balance. It is usually mounted in line to the rear wheels.

When the brakes are serviced the valve should be inspected for leakage. Premature rear brake application during lighting braking can mean a bad proportioning valve. Repair is by replacement of the valve. Make sure the valve port marked **R** is connected toward the rear wheels.

On GM "Quick Take-Up" master cylinders, the proportioning valve(s) is

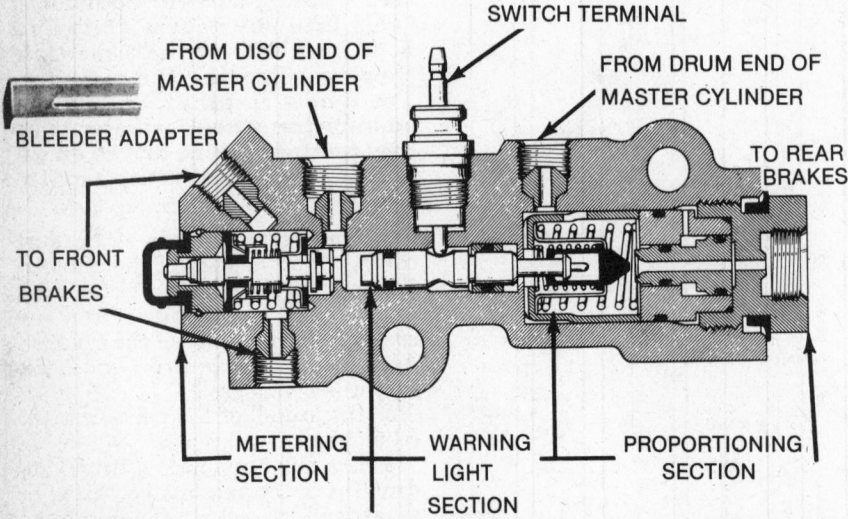

Push valve in when pressure bleeding-not necessary when using pedal bleed method

(are) screwed into the master cylinder. Since these vehicles have a diagonally split brake system, 2 valves are required. 1 rear brake line screws into each valve. The early type valves (GM front wheel drive) were steel and silver colored, an occasional "clunking" noise was encountered on some early models, but does not affect brake efficiency. Replacement valves are now made of aluminum. Never mix an aluminum valve with a steel valve, always use 2 aluminum valves.

COMBINATION VALVE

The combination valve may perform 2 or 3 functions. They are: metering, proportioning and brake failure warning.

Variations of the two-way combination valve are: proportioning and brake failure warning or metering and brake failure warning.

A three-way combination valve directs the brake fluid to the appropriate wheel, performs necessary valving and contains a brake failure warning.

The combination valve is usually mounted under the hood close to the master cylinder, where the brake lines can easily be connected and routed to the front or rear wheels.

The combination valve is non-serviceable and must be replaced if malfunctioning.

Brake Bleeding

The hydraulic brake system must be free of air to operate properly. Air can enter the system when hydraulic parts are disconnected for servicing or replacement, or when the fluid level in the master cylinder reservoirs is very low. Air in the system will give the brake pedal a spongy feeling upon application.

The quickest and easiest of the 2 ways for system bleeding is the pressure method but special equipment is needed to externally pressurize the hydraulic system. The other, more commonly used method of brake bleeding is done manually.

BLEEDING SEQUENCE

Bleeding may be required at only 1 or 2 wheels or at the master cylinder, depending upon what point the system was opened to air. If after bleeding the cylinder caliper that was rebuilt or replaced and the pedal still has a spongy feeling upon application, it will be necessary to bleed the entire system. Bleed the system in the following order:

1. **Master cylinder**: If the cylinder is not equipped with bleeder screws,

open the brake line(s) to the wheels slightly while pressure is applied to the brake pedal. Be sure to tighten the line before the brake pedal is released. The procedure for bench bleeding the master cylinder is in the following section.

2. **Power Brake Booster**: If the unit is equipped with bleeder screws, it should be bled after the master cylinder. The vehicle's engine should be off and the brake pedal applied several times to exhaust any vacuum in the booster. If the unit is equipped with 2 bleeder screws, always bleed the higher bleeder screw first.

3. **Combination Valve**: If equipped with a bleeder screw.

4. **Front/Back Split Systems**: Start with the wheel farthest away from the master cylinder, usually the right-rear wheel. Bleed the other rear wheel then the right-front and left-front.

NOTE: If you are unsuccessful in bleeding the front wheels, it may be necessary to deactivate the metering valve. This is accomplished by either pushing in, or pulling out a button or stem on the valve. The valve may be held by hand, with a special tool or taped, it should remain deactivated while the front brakes are bled.

5. **Diagonally Split System**: Start with the right-rear then the left-front. The left-rear then the right-front.

6. **Rear Disc Brakes**: If the vehicle is equipped with rear disc brakes and the calipers have 2 bleeder screws, bleed the inner first then the outer.

NOTE: DO NOT allow brake fluid to spill on the vehicles finish, it will remove the paint. Flush the area with water.

MANUAL BLEEDING

1. Clean the bleed screw at each wheel.

2. Start with the wheel farthest from the master cylinder (right-rear).

3. Attach a small rubber hose to the bleed screw and place the end in a clear container of brake fluid.

4. Fill the master cylinder with brake fluid. (Check often during bleeding). Have an assistant slowly pump up the brake pedal and hold pressure.

5. Open the bleed screw about one-quarter turn, press the brake pedal to the floor, close the bleed screw and slowly release the pedal. Continue until no more air bubbles are forced from the cylinder on application of the brake pedal.

6. Repeat procedure on remaining wheel cylinders and calipers, still

working from cylinder/caliper farthest from the master cylinder.

NOTE: Master cylinders equipped with bleed screws may be bled independently. When bleeding the Bendix-type dual master cylinder it is necessary to solidly cap 1 reservoir section while bleeding the other to prevent pressure loss through the cap vent hole.

— CAUTION —

The bleeder valve at the wheel cylinder must be closed at the end of each stroke and before the brake pedal is released, to insure that no air can enter the system. It is also important that the brake pedal be returned to the full up position so the piston in the master cylinder moves back enough to clear the bypass outlets.

PRESSURE BLEEDING DISC BRAKES

Pressure bleeding disc brakes will close the metering valve and the front brakes will not bleed. For this reason it is necessary to manually hold the metering valve open during pressure bleeding. Never use a block or clamp to hold the valve open and never force the valve stem beyond its normal position. Of the 2 different types of valves used, the most common type requires the valve stem to be held in while bleeding the brakes, while the second type requires the valve stem to be held out (0.060 in. minimum travel). Determine the type of visual inspection.

— CAUTION —

Special adapters are required when pressure bleeding cylinders with plastic reservoirs. Pressure bleeding equipment should be diaphragm type; placing a diaphragm between the pressurized air supply and the brake fluid. This prevents moisture and other contaminants from entering the hydraulic system.

NOTE: Front disc/rear drum equipped vehicles use a metering valve which closes off pressure to the front brakes under certain conditions. These systems contain manual release actuators, which must be engaged to pressure bleed the front brakes.

1. Connect the tank hydraulic hose and adapter to the master cylinder.

2. Close the hydraulic valve on the bleeder equipment.

3. Apply air pressure to the bleeder equipment following the equipment manufacturer's recommendations for correct air pressure.

4. Open the valve to bleed air out of

the pressure hose to the master cylinder. Never bleed this system using the secondary piston stopscrew on the bottom of many master cylinders.

5. Open the hydraulic valve and bleed each wheel cylinder or caliper. Bleed the rear brake system first when bleeding both front and rear systems.

FLUSHING HYDRAULIC BRAKE SYSTEMS

Hydraulic brake systems must be totally flushed if the fluid becomes contaminated with water, dirt or other corrosive chemicals. To flush, simply bleed the entire system until all of the fluid has been replaced with the correct type of new fluid.

BENCH BLEEDING MASTER CYLINDER

Bench bleeding the master cylinder before installing it on the vehicle reduces the possibility of getting air into the lines.

1. Connect 2 short pieces of brake line to the outlet fittings, bend them until the free end is below the fluid level in the master cylinder reservoirs.

2. Fill the reservoirs with fresh brake fluid. Pump the piston until no more air bubbles appear in the reservoir(s).

3. Disconnect the 2 short lines, refill the master cylinder and securely install the cylinder cap(s).

4. Install the master cylinder on the vehicle. Attach the lines but do not completely tighten them. Force any air that might have been trapped in the connection by slowly depressing the brake pedal. Tighten the lines before releasing the brake pedal.

GM QUICK TAKE-UP SYSTEM BLEEDING

Bleed the master cylinder as follows: disconnect the left-front brake line from the master cylinder. Fill the cylinder with fluid until it flows from the opened port. Connect the line and tighten the fitting. Apply the brake pedal slowly 1 time and keep it applied. Loosen the same brake line fitting to allow any air to escape. Retighten the fitting and release the brake pedal slowly. Wait 15 seconds and repeat the procedure until all of the air is expelled. Bleed the right-front connection in the same manner. Bleed the cylinders and calipers after you are sure all the air is out of the master cylinder.

─── **CAUTION** ───

Rapid pumping will move the secondary piston down the bore and make it difficult to bleed the system. Always apply slow pedal pressure.

Power Brakes
VACUUM OPERATED BOOSTER

Power brakes operate just as standard brake systems except in the actuation of the master cylinder pistons. A vacuum diaphragm is located on the front of the master cylinder to assist in applying the brakes, reducing both the effort and travel needed to move the brake pedal.

The vacuum diaphragm housing is connected to the intake manifold by a vacuum hose. A check valve is placed at the point where the hose enters the diaphragm housing, so that during periods of low manifold vacuum brake assist vacuum will not be lost.

Depressing the brake pedal closes off the vacuum source and allows atmospheric pressure to enter on 1 side of the diaphragm. This causes the master cylinder pistons to move and apply the brakes. When the brake pedal is released, vacuum is applied to both sides of the diaphragm, the return springs return the diaphragm and master cylinder pistons to the released position. If the vacuum fails, the brake pedal rod will butt against the end of the master cylinder actuating rod and direct mechanical application will occur as the pedal is depressed.

The hydraulic and mechanical problems that apply to conventional brake systems also apply to power brakes should be checked if the tests and chart below do not reveal the problem. Tests for a system vacuum leak as described below:

1. Operate the engine at idle with the transmission in Neutral without touching the brake pedal for at least 1 minute.

2. Turn **Off** the engine and wait 1 minute.

3. Test for the presence of assist vacuum by depressing the brake pedal and releasing it several times. Light application will produce less and less pedal travel, if vacuum was present. If there is no vacuum, air is leaking into the system somewhere.

4. Test the system operation as follows:

a. Pump the brake pedal (with engine off) until the supply vacuum is entirely gone.

b. Put light, steady pressure on the pedal. Start the engine and operate it at idle with the transmission in Neutral.

c. If the system is operating, the brake pedal should fall toward the floor when constant pressure is maintained on the pedal.

NOTE: **Power brake systems may be tested for hydraulic leaks just as ordinary systems are tested, except that the engine should be idling with the transmission in Neutral throughout the test.**

POWER BRAKE BOOSTER TROUBLESHOOTING

NOTE: **The following items are in addition to those listed in the "General Troubleshooting" section. Check those items first.**

Hard Pedal

1. Faulty vacuum check valve
2. Vacuum hose kinked, collapsed, plugged leaky or improperly connected
3. Internal leak in unit
4. Damaged vacuum cylinder
5. Damaged valve plunger
6. Broken or faulty springs
7. Broken plunger stem

Grabbing Brakes

1. Damaged vacuum cylinder
2. Faulty vacuum check valve
3. Vacuum hose leaky or improperly connected
4. Broken plunger stem

Pedal Goes to Floor

Generally, when this problem occurs, it is not caused by the power brake booster. In rare cases, a broken plunger stem may be at fault.

OVERHAUL

Most power brake boosters are serviced by replacement only. In many cases, repair parts are not available. A good many special tools are required for rebuilding these units. For these reasons, it would be most practical to replace a failed booster with a new or remanufactured unit.

Hydro-Boost Hydro-Boost II

Hydro-Boost differs from conventional power brake systems, in that it operates from the power steering pump fluid pressure rather than intake manifold vacuum.

The Hydro-Boost unit contains a spool valve with an open center which controls the strength of pump pressure when braking occurs. A lever assembly controls the valve's position. A boost piston provides the force necessary to operate the conventional master cylinder on the front of the booster.

A reserve of at least 2 assisted brake applications is supplied by an accumulator which is spring loaded on earlier and pneumatic on later models. The accumulator is an integral part of the Hydro-Boost II unit. The brakes can be applied manually if the reserve system is depleted.

All system checks, tests and troubleshooting procedure are the same for the 2 systems.

HYDRO-BOOST SYSTEM CHECKS

1. A defective Hydro-Boost cannot cause any of the following conditions: Noisy brakes, fading pedal or pulling brakes. If any of these occur, check elsewhere in the brake system.

2. Check the fluid level in the master cylinder. It should be within ¼ in. of the top; if not, add only DOT-3 or DOT-4 brake fluid until the correct level is reached.

3. Check the fluid level in the power steering pump. The engines should be at normal running temperature and stopped. The level should register on the pump dipstick. Add power steering fluid to bring the reservoir level up to the correct level. Low fluid level will result in both poor steering and stopping ability.

—————— CAUTION ——————

The brake hydraulic system uses brake fluid only, while the power steering and Hydro-Boost systems use power steering fluid only. Don't mix the two.

4. Check the power steering pump belt tension and inspect all of the power steering/Hydro-Boost hoses for kinks or leaks.

5. Check and adjust the engine idle speed, as necessary.

6. Check the power steering pump fluid for bubbles. If air bubbles are present in the fluid, bleed the system. Fill the power steering pump reservoir to specifications with the engine at normal operating temperature. With the engine running, rotate the steering wheel through its normal travel 3–4 times, without holding the wheel against the stops. Check the fluid level again.

7. If the problem still exists, go on to the Hydro-Boost test sections and troubleshooting chart.

HYDRO-BOOST TESTS

Functional Test

1. Check the brake system for leaks or low fluid level. Correct as necessary.

2. Place the transmission in Neutral and stop the engine. Apply the brakes 4–5 times to empty the accumulator.

3. Keep the pedal depressed with moderate (25–40 lbs.) pressure and start the engine.

4. The brake pedal should fall slightly and then push back up against your foot. If no movement is felt, the Hydro-Boost system is not working.

Accumulator Leak Test

1. Run the engine at normal idle. Turn the steering wheel against either stop; hold it there for no longer than 5 seconds. Center the steering wheel and stop the engine.

2. Keep applying the brakes until a ''hard'' pedal is obtained. There should be a minimum of 2 power (1 on Hydro-Boost II) assisted brake applications when pedal pressure of 20–25 lbs. is applied.

3. Start the engine and allow it to idle. Rotate the steering wheel against the stop. Listen for a light "hissing" sound; this is the accumulator being charged. Center the steering wheel and stop the engine.

4. Wait 1 hour and apply the brakes without starting the engine. As in Step 2, there should be at least 2 (1 on Hydro-Boost II) stops with power assist. If not, the accumulator is defective and must be replaced.

Hydro-Boost System Bleeding

NOTE: The system should be bled whenever the booster is removed and installed.

1. Fill the power steering pump until the fluid level is at the base of the pump reservoir neck. Disconnect the battery lead from the distributor.

NOTE: On diesel engines remove the electrical lead to the fuel solenoid terminal on the injection pump before cranking the engine.

2. Raise the front of the vehicle, turn the wheels all the way to the left and crank the engine for a few seconds.

3. Check the steering pump fluid level. If necessary, add fluid to the **ADD** mark on the dipstick.

4. Lower the vehicle, connect the battery lead and start the engine. Check the fluid level and add fluid to the **ADD** mark if necessary. With the engine running, turn the wheels from side-to-side to bleed air from the system. Make sure that the fluid level stays above the internal pump casting.

5. The Hydro-Boost system should now be fully bled. If the fluid is foaming after bleeding, stop the engine, let the system set for 1 hour. Add fluid to the **ADD** mark if necessary, then with the engine running, turn the wheels from side-to-side to bleed air from the system. Repeat this step if necessary.

6. The preceding procedures should be effective in removing excess air from the system, however, sometimes air may still remain trapped. When this happens the booster may make a "gulping" noise when the brake is applied. Lightly pumping the brake pedal with the engine running should cause this noise to disappear. After the noise stops, check the pump fluid level and add as necessary.

HYDRO-BOOST TROUBLESHOOTING

High Pedal and Steering Effort (Idle)

1. Loose/broken power steering pump belt
2. Low power steering fluid level
3. Leaking hoses or fittings
4. Low idle speed
5. Hose restriction
6. Defective power steering pump

High Pedal Effort (Idle)

1. Binding pedal/linkage
2. Fluid contamination
3. Defective Hydro-Boost unit

Poor Pedal Return

1. Binding pedal linkage
2. Restricted booster return line
3. Internal return system restriction

Pedal Chatter/Pulsation

1. Power steering/pump drivebelt slipping
2. Low power steering fluid level
3. Defective power steering pump
4. Defective Hydro-Boost unit

Brakes Oversensitive

1. Binding pedal/linkage
2. Defective Hydro-Boost unit

Noise

1. Low power steering fluid level
2. Air in the power steering fluid
3. Loose power steering pump drivebelt
4. Hose restrictions

OVERHAUL

Ford Motor Company services the Hydro-Boost unit with a replacement new or rebuilt unit only. No provisions are made for overhaul of the unit. GM Hydro-Boost units may be overhauled by qualified mechanics.

—————— CAUTION ——————

DO NOT attempt to interchange the parts between the Hydro-Boost units of different makes of vehicles, because of pressure differentials and differences of the tolerances of the internal parts. Pressure could exceed the normal accumulator release pressure of 1400 psi and injury or damage could result.

Disc Brake Rotors

RUNOUT

Manufacturers differ widely on permissible runout but too much can sometimes be felt as a pulsation at the brake pedal. A wobble pump effect is created when a rotor is not perfectly smooth and the pad hits the high spots forcing fluid back into the master cylinder. This alternating pressure causes a pulsating feeling which can be felt at the pedal when the brakes are applied.

To check the actual runout of the rotor, perform the following procedures:

1. Tighten the wheel spindle nut to a snug bearing adjustment, end-play removed.

2. Fasten a dial indicator on the suspension at a convenient place so that the indicator stylus contacts the rotor face approximately 1 in. from its outer edge.

3. Set the dial at zero. Check the total indicator reading while turning the rotor 1 full revolution. If the rotor is warped beyond the runout specifica-

tion, it is likely that it can be successfully remachined.

Lateral Runout: A wobbly movement of the rotor from side-to-side as it rotates. Excessive lateral runout causes the rotor faces to knock back the disc pads and can result in chatter, excessive pedal travel, pumping or fighting pedal and vibration during the braking action.

Parallelism (lack of): Refers to the amount of variation in the thickness of the rotor. Excessive variation can cause pedal vibration or fight, front end vibrations and possible "grab" during the braking action; a condition comparable to an "out-of-round brake drum." Check parallelism with a micrometer. "Mike" the thickness at 8 or more equally spaced points, equally distant from the outer edge of the rotor, preferably at midpoints of the braking surface. Parallelism then is the amount of variation between maximum and minimum measurements.

Surface or Micro-inch finish, flatness, smoothness: Different from parallelism, these terms refer to the degree of perfection of the flat surface on each side of the rotor; that is, the minute hills, valleys and swirls inherent in machining the surface. In a visual inspection, the remachined sur-

face should have a find ground polish with, at most, only a faint trace of non-directional swirls.

SERVICING THE DISC ROTOR
Disc Replacement

1. Raise and support the vehicle on jackstands, then remove the wheel/tire assembly.

2. Remove the caliper. Secure the caliper out of the way suspended by wire, DO NOT allow the caliper to hang by the brake hose.

3. Remove the wheel bearing nut from the spindle and the outer wheel bearing from the hub.

4. Remove the hub and disc assembly from the spindle.

5. To install, reverse the removal procedures.

NOTE: The disc is removable from the hub on the Eldorado, Toronado and Corvette (rear only). To separate the rear disc and hub on a (1982-87) Corvette the 3 hub-to-disc attaching rivets must be drilled out. This can be done with the hub and rotor mounted on the vehicle. It is not necessary to install new rivets when the disc is installed.

DISC BRAKE APPLICATION AND SPECIFICATIONS CHART

Car Manufacturer, Year & Model	Text Reference Type	Caliper Style	Brake Manufacturer	Anchor Bolt (ft. lbs.)	Brige, Pin or Key Bolts (ft. lbs.)	Wheel Lugs (ft. lbs.)	Normal Std.	Minimum Thickness Machine To	Discard At	Rotor Parallel Variation	Max. Runout
AMC/EAGLE											
1988-89 Premier	35	Floating	—	70	18.5	63	0.866	—	0.807	—	.003
1988-89 Medallion	35	Floating	—	48	18	67	0.775	—	0.697	—	.002
1982-89 Eagle	1	Sliding	Bendix	100	30	75	.880	.815	.810	.0005	.003
1982-83 Concord, Spirit	1	Sliding	Bendix	85	30	75	.880	.815	.810	.0005	.003
CHRYSLER CORP. — FRONT WHEEL DRIVE											
1988-89 Dynasty, New Yorker											
Front w/o H.D.	12	Floating	ATE	130-190	18–35	95	.935	.912	.882	.0005	.005
Front with H.D.	14	Floating	K/H	130-190	25-35	95	.345	.321	.291	.0005	.005
Rear	33	Folating	ATE	130-190	18-35	95	.350	—	.339	.0005	.003
1988-89 Daytona, Chrysler TC											
Front w/o H.D.	12	Floating	ATE	130-190	18–26	95	.935	.912	.882	.0005	.005
Front with H.D.	14	Floating	K/H	130-190	25-35	95	.935	.912	.882	.0005	.005
Rear	34	Floating	ATE	130-190	18-26	95	.345	.312	.291	.0005	.003
1987-89 Omni, Horizon	14	Floating	K/H	130-190	25-35	95	.500	.461	.431	.0005	.005
1987-89 Sundance, Shadow											
w/o H.D.	12	Floating	ATE	130-190	18-26	95	.935	..912	.882	.0005	.005
with H.D.	14	Floating	K/H	130-190	25-35	95	.935	.912	.882	.0005	.005

DISC BRAKE APPLICATION AND SPECIFICATIONS CHART

Car Manufacturer, Year & Model	Text Reference Type	Caliper Style	Brake Manufacturer	Anchor Bolt (ft. lbs.)	Brige, Pin or Key Bolts (ft. lbs.)	Wheel Lugs (ft. lbs.)	Normal Std.	Minimum Thickness Machine To	Discard At	Rotor Parallel Variation	Max. Run-out
1983-89 Aries, Reliant, LeBaron, Dodge 400 ('83), 600 (w/o H.D. brakes)	12	Floating	ATE	70-100	18-22	80	.935	912	.882	.0005	.004
1987 Charger, Turismo	14	Floating	K/H	130-190	25-35	95	.935	.912	.882	.0005	.005
1983-6 Charger, Omni, Horizon, Turismo	14	Floating	K/H	70-100	24-40	80	.500	.461	.431	.0005	.004
1983-89 with H.D. brakes	14	Floating	K/H	70-100	25-35	80	.935	.912	.882	.0005	.004
1983-89 E Class, New Yorker, Town & Country, Daytona, Laser	12 or 14	Floating	ATE or K/H	70-100	ATE: 18-22 K/H: 25-35	80	.935	.912	.882	.0005	.004
1982-88 Horizon, Charger, Turismo	11	Floating	K/H	70-100	25-40	80	.500	.461	.431	.0005	.004
1982 Aries, Reliant, LeBaron, Dodge 400	12	Floating	ATE	70-100	18-22	85	.935	.912	.882	.0005	.004
CHRYSLER CORP. — REAR WHEEL DRIVE											
1982-89 Cordoba, Diplomat, Gran Fury, Mirada, Imperial, New Yorker	6	Sliding	Chrysler	95-125	15-20	85	1.010	.955	.940	.0005	.004
FORD MOTOR CO. — FRONT WHEEL DRIVE											
1988-89 Festiva	30	Sliding	Ford	—	29-36	65-87	—	.463	.433	.0006	.003
1988-89 Tracer Front	30	Sliding	Ford	—	20-36	65-87	.710	.660	.630	.001	.004
Rear	31	Sliding	Ford	—	29-36	65-87	.390	.380	.350	.001	.004
1988-89 Lincoln Continental Front	10	Sliding	Ford	—	18-25	80-105	1.02	—	.974	.0004	.002
Rear	32	Sliding	Ford	—	23-36	80-105	1.02	—	.974	.0005	.002
1988-89 Taurus, Sable	10	Sliding	Ford	—	24-34	80-105	1.024	—	.974	.0005	.003
1988-89 Escort, Tempo, Topaz	10	Sliding	Ford	—	18-25	80-105	.945	.896	.882	.0004	.002
1986-87 Taurus, Sable	10	Sliding	Ford	—	18-25	80-105	.945	.896	.882	.0005	.003
1984-87 Escort, Lynx, LN7, EXP, Tempo, Topaz	10	Sliding	Ford	—	18-25	80-105	.945	.896	.882	.0004	.002
1982-83 Escort, Lynx, LN7, EXP	10	Sliding	Ford	—	18-25	80-105	.945	.896	.882	.0005	.002
FORD MOTOR CO. — REAR WHEEL DRIVE											
1988-89 Mark VII Front	13	Sliding	Ford	—	45-65	80-105	1.030	—	.972	.0005	.003
Rear	7	Sliding	K/H	80-110	29-37	80-105	.945	—	.895	.0005	.004
1988-89 Cougar, Mustang exc. 5.0L Thunderbird exc. Turbo	13	Sliding	Ford	—	45-65	80-105	.870	—	.810	.0005	.003
1987-89 Mustang 5.0L, Thunderbird Turbo Front	13	Sliding	Ford	—	45-65	80-105	1.030	—	.972	.0005	.003
Rear	32	Sliding	Ford	—	23-26	80-105	1.02	—	.974	.0005	.002

DISC BRAKE APPLICATION AND SPECIFICATIONS CHART

Car Manufacturer, Year & Model	Text Reference Type	Caliper Style	Brake Manufacturer	Anchor Bolt (ft. lbs.)	Brige, Pin or Key Bolts (ft. lbs.)	Wheel Lugs (ft. lbs.)	Normal Std.	Minimum Thickness Machine To	Discard At	Rotor Parallel Variation	Max. Run-out
1982-87 Lincoln Continental, Mark VII											
Front	13	Sliding	Ford	—	40-60	80-105	1.030	—	.972	.0005	.003
Rear	7	Sliding	K/H	85-115	15-20	80-105	.945	—	.895	.0004	.004
1983-89 Lincoln Town Car, Crown Victoria, Grand Marquis	13	Sliding	Ford	—	40-60	80-105	1.030	—	.972	.0005	.003
1982 Ford, Mercury, Lincoln	13	Sliding	Ford	—	40-60	80-105	1.030	—	.972	.0005	.003
1982-87 All Models except noted	13	Sliding	Ford	—	30-40	80-105	.870	—	.810	.0005	.003
1982 Rear Disc Brakes	7	Sliding	K/H	65-115	15-20	80-105	.945	—	.895	.0004	.003
GENERAL MOTORS—BUICK											
1988-89 Regal											
Front	24	Floating	Delco	79	—	100	1.040	1.019	.972	.0005	.003
Rear	25	Floating	Delco	79	—	100	.492	.476	.429	.0005	.003
1986-89 Riviera											
Front	26	Floating	Delco	83	63	100	1.943	.971	.956	.0005	.004
Rear	27	Floating	Delco	83	63	100	.494	.444	.429	.0005	.003
1985-89 Electra Limited, Park Avenue FWD	2	Floating	Delco	—	35	70	1.043	.972	.957	.0005	.004
1982-89 Electra, Estate Wagon RWD	2	Floating	Delco	—	35	80①	1.037	.980	.965	.0005	.004
1982-85 Riviera											
Front	2	Floating	Delco	—	35	100	1.037	.980	.965	.0005	.004
Rear	9	Floating	Delco	35	30	100	—	.980	.965	.0005	.004
1983-89 Century											
With H.D.	2	Floating	Delco	—	28	100	1.043	.972	.957	.0005	.004
w/o H.D.	2	Floating	Delco	—	28	100	.885	.830	.815	.0005	.004
1982-89 Skyhawk With vented disc	2	Floating	Delco	—	28	100	.885	.830	.815	.0005	.004
1982 Skyhawk With solid disc	2	Floating	Delco	—	28	100	—	.444	.429	.0005	.004
1982-87 Regal, 1985 LeSabre	2	Floating	Delco	—	35	70-80	1.043	.980	.965	.0005	.004
1982-89 Skylark	2	Floating	Delco	—	21-35	102	.885	.830	.815	.0005	.004
GENERAL MOTORS—CADILLAC											
1987-89 Allante											
Front	26	Floating	Delco	83	63	100	1.035	.971	.956	.0005	.004
Rear	27	Floating	Delco	83	63	100	.494	.444	.429	.0005	.003
1986-89 Eldorado											
Front	26	Floating	Delco	83	63	100	1.035	.971	.956	.0005	.004
Rear	27	Floating	Delco	83	63	100	.494	.444	.429	.0005	.003
1982-89 Cimaron	19	Floating	Delco	—	28	100	.885	.830	.815	.0005	.004
1985 Fleetwood, DeVille FWD	2	Floating	Delco	—	35	70	1.043	.972	.957	.0005	.004
1982-89 Brougham, Fleetwood, DeVille RWD											
Front	2	Floating	Delco	—	30	100	1.037④	.980	.965	.0005	.004
Rear	9	Floating	Delco	35	30	100	1.250	.910	.905	.0005	.004
1982-89 CC, Limousine	2	Floating	Delco	—	30	100	1.250	1.230	1.215	.0005	.004

DISC BRAKE APPLICATION AND SPECIFICATIONS CHART

Car Manufacturer, Year & Model	Text Reference Type	Caliper Style	Brake Manufacturer	Anchor Bolt (ft. lbs.)	Brige, Pin or Key Bolts (ft. lbs.)	Wheel Lugs (ft. lbs.)	Normal Std.	Minimum Thickness Machine To	Discard At	Rotor Parallel Variation	Max. Run-out
1982-89 Eldorado, Seville											
Front	2	Floating	Delco	—	28	100	1.035	.965	.957	.0005	.004
Rear	9	Floating	Delco	35	30	100	1.035	.965	.957	.0005	.004
GENERAL MOTORS — CHEVROLET											
1988-89 Nova											
Front	5	Floating	Delco	65	18	76	.531	.507	.472	.0005	.006
Rear	23	Floating	Delco	34	14	76	.354	—	.315	—	.006
1988-89 Corvette											
Front w/o H.D.	21	Floating	—	137	⑤	100	.795	.744	.724	.0005	.006
Front with H.D.	21	Floating	—	137	⑤	100	1.110	1.059	1.039	.0005	.006
Rear	22	Floating	—	70	⑤	100	.795	.744	.724	.0005	.006
1982-89 Full Size	2	Floating	Delco	—	35	80②	1.030	.980	.965	.0005	.004
1982-89 Malibu, Monte Carlo	2	Floating	Delco	—	35	80③	1.030	.960	.965	.0005	.004
1982-89 Camaro											
Front	2	Floating	Delco	—	21-35	80	1.030	.980	.965	.0005	.004
Rear	9	Floating	Delco	—	30-45	80	1.030	.980	.965	.0005	.004
1982 Corvette											
Front	4	Fixed	Delco	70	130	70④	1.285	1.230	1.215	.0005	.004
Rear	4	Fixed	Delco	70	60	70④	1.285	1.230	1.215	.0005	.004
1984-87 Corvette											
Front	16	Floating	Girlock	70	24	100	.780	.739	.724	.0005	.006
Rear	16	Floating	Girlock	44	24	100	.780	.739	.724	.0005	.006
1982-89 Celbrity, Cavalier	19	Floating	Delco	—	28	100		Vented		.0005	.004
1982-85 Citation	19	Floating	Delco	—	28	102	.885	.830	.815	.0005	.003
1985-87 Nova	5	Floating	—	65	18	76	.531	.507	.472	.0005	.006
1985-89 Spectrum	17	Floating	—	40	36	65	.433	.393	.378	.0005	.006
1985-89 Sprint	18	Floating	—	—	26	50	.394	.330	.315	.0005	.003
1982 Chevette	8	Floating	Delco	70	28	70	.440	.390	.374	.0005	.005
1983-87 Chevette	19	Floating	Delco	—	21-25	70	—	.390	.374	.0005	.005
1987-89 Corsica, Beretta	19	Floating	Delco	—	38	100	.880	.830	.815	.0005	.005
GENERAL MOTORS — OLDSMOBILE											
1986-89 Toronado											
Front	26	Floating	Delco	83	63	100	1.035	.971	.956	.0005	.004
Rear	27	Floating	Delco	83	63	100	.494	.444	.429	.0005	.003
1988-89 Cutlass Supreme											
Front	24	Floating	Delco	79	—	100	1.040	1.019	.972	.0005	.003
Rear	25	Floating	Delco	79	—	100	.492	.476	.429	.0005	.003
1988-89 Cutlass RWD	2	Floating	Delco	—	35	100	1.040	.980	.965	.0005	.004
1988-89 Delta 88	2	Floating	Delco	—	38	100	1.043	.972	.957	.0005	.004
1985-89 98 Regency, Brougham FWD	2	Floating	Delco	—	35	70	1.0443	.972	.957	.0005	.004
1982-89 Full Size	2	Floating	Delco	—	35	80①	1.040	.960	.965	.0005	.005
1982-85 Toronado											
Front	2	Floating	Delco	—	35	100	1.040	.980	.965	.0005	.004
Rear	9	Floating	Delco	32	30	100	1.040	.980	.965	.0005	.004
1982-89 Cutlass, Cutlass Supreme	2	Floating	Delco	—	35	80	1.040	.980	.965	.0005	.005
1982-89 Ciera, Firenza	2	Floating	Delco	—	28	100	1.043	.972	.957	.0005	.004
1982-84 Omega	2	Floating	Delco	—	28	103	.885	.830	.815	.0005	.003

DISC BRAKE APPLICATION AND SPECIFICATIONS CHART

Car Manufacturer, Year & Model	Text Reference Type	Caliper Style	Brake Manufacturer	Anchor Bolt (ft. lbs.)	Brige, Pin or Key Bolts (ft. lbs.)	Wheel Lugs (ft. lbs.)	Normal Std.	Minimum Thickness Machine To	Discard At	Rotor Parallel Variation	Max. Run-out
GENERAL MOTORS — PONTIAC											
1988-89 Fiero											
Front	28	Floating	–	74	74	100	.756	.702	.681	.0005	.003
Rear	29	Floating	–	74	74	100	.756	.702	.681	.0005	.003
1988-89 Grand Prix											
Front	24	Floating	–	79	–	100	1.040	1.019	.972	.0005	.003
Rear	25	Floating	–	79	–	100	.492	.476	.429	.0005	.003
1987-89 6000											
Front w/rear drum	2	Floating	Delco	–	38	100	–	.830	.815	.0005	.004
Front w/rear disc	2	Floating	Delco	–	38	100	1.043	.972	.957	.0005	.004
Rear	15	Floating	Delco	–	38	100	–	–	.444	.429	.0005	.004
1988-89 Grand Am	2	Floating	Delco	–	35	100	1.030	.980	.965	.0005	.004
1987-89 Bonneville	2	Floating	Delco	–	38	80	1.043	.972	.957	.0005	.004
1987-89 Firebird	2	Floating	Delco	–	21-35	80	1.043	.980	.965	.0005	.005
1982-85 Full Size	2	Floating	Delco	–	35	80①	1.040	.980	.965	.0005	.004
1982-89 Grand Prix Grand Am, Lemans	2	Floating	Delco	–	35	80	1.030	.980	.965	.0005	.004
1988-89 Lemans Daewoo	20	Floating	–	–	–	65	.500	.460	.420	.0004	.004
1982-88 Firebird											
Front	2	Floating	Delco	–	21-35	80	1.030	.980	.965	.0005	.004
Rear	9	Floating	Delco	–	30-45	80	1.030	.980	.965	.0005	.004
1982-86 6000, J2000	2	Floating	Delco	–	28	100	–	–	–	.0005	.004
1982-85 Phoenix, Ventura	2	Floating	Delco	–	28	103	.885	.830	.815	.0005	.003
1982 T1000	8	Floating	Delco	70	28	70	.440	.390	.374	.0005	.005
1983-87 T1000	2	Floating	Delco	–	21-25	70	.440	.390	.374	.0005	.005
1984-87 Fiero											
Front	2	Floating	Delco	–	35	81	–	.444	.390	.0005	.004
Rear	15	Floating	Delco	–	35	81	–	.444	.390	.0005	.004

① 100 with 1/2 in studs
② 100 on s/w
③ 90 with aluminum wheels
④ 80 with aluminum wheels

DISC BRAKE SERVICE

——— CAUTION ———

The asbestos dust thrown off from the brake linings or disc pads may be dangerous to your health if inhaled. Never use compressed air or your own breath to blow the dust from the brake assembly. Use an aerosol brake cleaner, damp rag or a vacuum cleaner with an approved asbestos filter. Dispose of the rag or cleaner bag properly. Do not move a vehicle until a firm brake pedal is obtained.

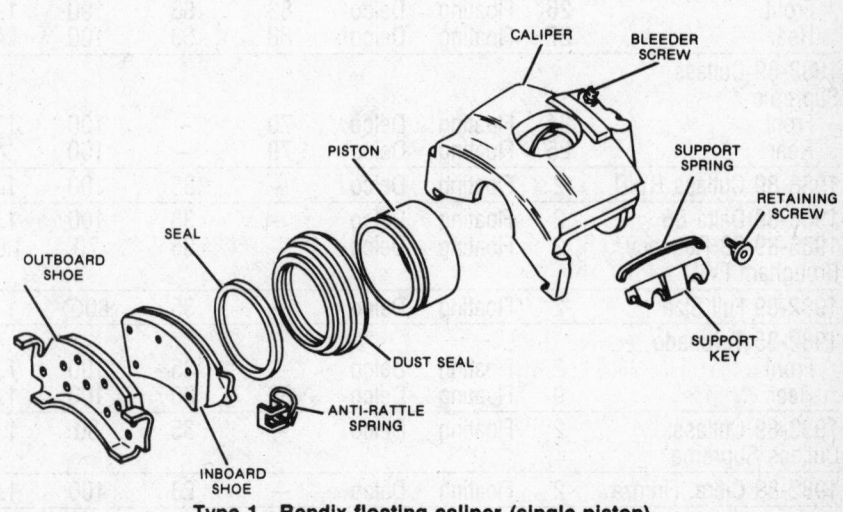

Type 1 — Bendix floating caliper (single piston)

INSPECTION

Disc pads (lining and shoe assemblies) should be replaced in axle sets (both wheels) when the lining on any pad is worn to $\frac{1}{16}$ in. at any point. If the lining is allowed to wear past $\frac{1}{16}$ in. minimum thickness, severe damage to the disc may result. However, State Inspection specifications take precedence over these general recommendations. Note that disc pads in floating caliper type brakes may wear at an angle and measurement should be made at the narrow end of the taper. Tapered linings should be replaced if the taper exceeds $\frac{1}{8}$ in. from end-to-end (the difference between the thickest and thinnest points).

NOTE: When replacing the pads, the piston is depressed and fluid is forced back to the reservoir. To prevent costly paint damage, remove some brake fluid (don't reuse) from the and install the reservoir cover before replacing the disc pads. Always work on 1 brake assembly at a time to reduce the risk of the oppsite piston leaving the caliper. When the caliper is unbolted from the hub, DO NOT let it dangle by the brake hose; it can be rested on a suspension member or wired onto the frame. All disc brake systems are self-adjusting and have no provision for manual adjustment.

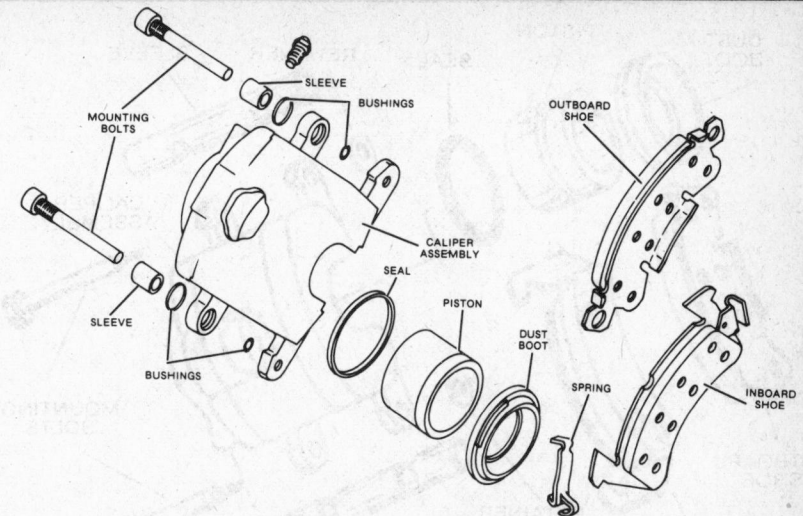

Type 2 — Delco floating caliper (single piston)

TYPE 1

Kelsey-Hayes or Bendix Sliding Caliper Disc Brakes (Single Piston)

PAD REPLACEMENT

1. Remove half of the brake fluid from the master cylinder.
2. Remove the retaining screw holding the caliper support key.
3. Using a hammer and a drift punch, drive the caliper retaining key and support spring from the anchor plate.
4. Lift the caliper from of the rotor.
5. Support caliper so it doesn't hang by the brake hose.
6. Using a large C-clamp, push the piston back into its bore, being careful not to scratch the piston or bore and being careful not to cut or tear the dust boot.

7. Remove the inboard pad and anti-rattle spring from the caliper support adapter.
8. Remove the outboard pad from the caliper. Check the condition of the rotor. If the rotor run out exceeds the manufacturer's specifications or has deep scratches, have the rotor resurfaced.
9. Clean all sliding surfaces on the adapter and caliper.

To Install:

10. Position the inboard brake pad and anti-rattle spring in the caliper support adapter.
11. Position the outboard brake pad in the caliper. Bend the ears (if necessary) to provide a slight interference fit on the caliper.
12. Position the caliper over the rotor; take care not to damage the caliper piston dust boot.
13. Position the caliper support spring and support key into the slot and drive them into the opening between the lower end of the caliper and the lower anchor plate abutment.
14. Install and tighten the key retaining screw.
15. Fill the master cylinder with brake fluid. Bleed the system (if necessary).

TYPE 2

Delco Floating Caliper (Single Piston)

PAD REPLACEMENT

1. Remove ½ of the brake fluid from the master cylinder.

2. Position a large C-clamp over the caliper with the screw end against the outboard brake pad. Tighten the clamp until the caliper is pushed out enough to bottom the piston.
3. Remove the C-clamp. Remove the 2 caliper guide pin mounts and lift the caliper from the rotor.
4. Support the caliper so there is no strain on the brake hose.
5. Press the outboard pad inward, then lift it from the caliper.
6. Press the inboard pad outward, then lift it from the caliper.
7. Remove and discard the 4 O-ring bushings and steel sleeves if new ones are to be installed. Check the condition of the rotor. If the rotor run out exceeds manufacturer's specifications or has deep scratches, re-machine the rotor.

To Install:

8. Lubricate and install the 4 O-ring bushings, install the sleeves, pressing them through the O-rings until the sleeve end on the pad side is flush with caliper ear. Position the inboard pad so the pad contacts the piston and the 2 support spring ends. Note that the inboard and outboard pads are similar but not interchangeable.
9. Press down on the ears at the top of the inboard pad until the pad lies flat and the spring ends are just inside the lower edge of the pad.
10. Position the outboard pad with the ears toward the positioning pin holes and the tab on the inner edge of the pad resting in the notch in the edge of the caliper. Bend the ears if necessary to provide slight interference fit on the caliper.
11. Press the outboard pad tightly into position and use a pair of pliers to clinch the ears of the outboard pad over the outboard caliper half.
12. Position the caliper over the rotor.

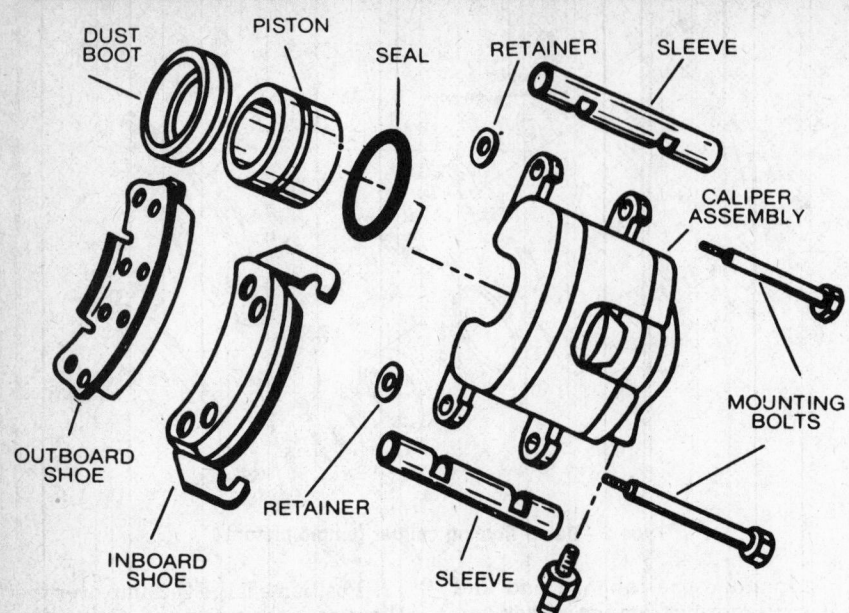

Type 3 – Delco sleeve type floating caliper (single piston)

3. Push the pistons back into their bores (being careful to push both pistons at once so as not to force the other out of its bore) and lift out 1 pad by tipping it down at the rear and up at the front.

4. Hold the rear piston in and slide the rear end of the new pad into place, being careful not to force out the front piston.

5. Check the condition of the rotor. If rotor run out exceeds 0.003 in. or has deep scratches, re-machine the rotor.

6. Push the front piston back into its bore and slide the front of the new pad into position.

7. Change the other pad in the same manner.

8. Reinstall the retaining pin through the caliper holes and through the holes in the pads.

9. Fill the master cylinder with fresh brake fluid.

---

13. Install the caliper mounting bolts and tighten to specification.

14. Fill the master cylinder with brake fluid.

TYPE 3

Delco Floating Caliper (Sleeve Type)

PAD REPLACEMENT

1. Remove ½ of the brake fluid from the master cylinder.

2. Remove 2 stamped nuts from the mounting pins and pins.

3. Lift the caliper from the rotor.

4. Support the caliper so there is no strain on the brake hose.

5. Using a large C-clamp, push the piston back into its bore, being careful not to cut or tear the dust boot.

6. Slide the pads past the mounting sleeve openings, then remove the pads, sleeves and bushing assemblies.

7. Check the condition of the rotor. If rotor run out exceeds manufacturer's specifications or has deep scratches, re-machine the rotor.

To Install:

8. Install the sleeves with shouldered ends of bushings to outside of vehicle.

9. Install the pads on the caliper with the ears over the sleeves.

10. Position the caliper on the rotor.

11. Install the mounting pins.

12. Install the stamped nuts on the mounting pins using a small socket to press them on as far as possible.

---

13. Fill the master cylinder with fluid.

TYPE 4

Delco Fixed Caliper (4 Pistons)

PAD REPLACEMENT

1. Remove ½ of the brake fluid from the master cylinder.

2. Remove the brake pad retaining pins.

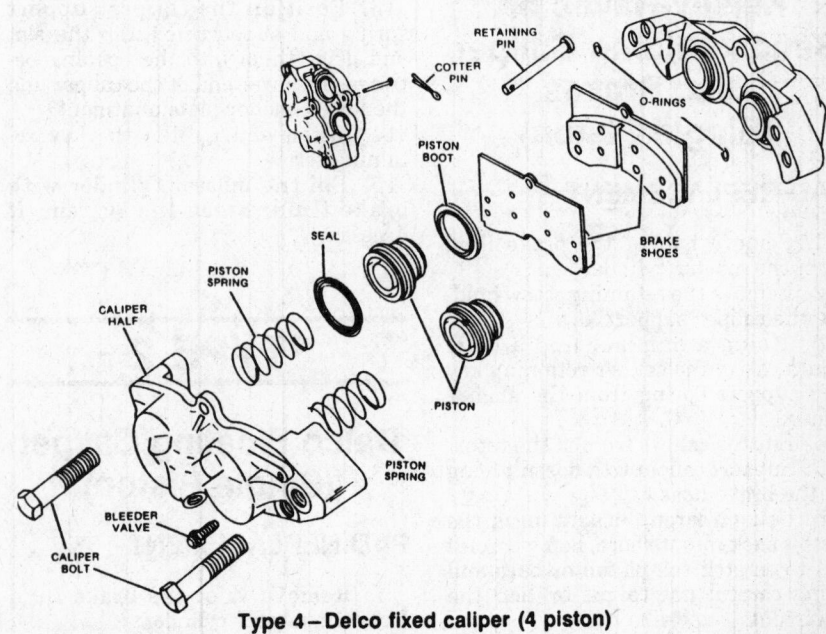

Type 4 – Delco fixed caliper (4 piston)

TYPE 5

Chevrolet Nova

PAD REPLACEMENT

1. Remove ⅔ of the brake fluid from the master cylinder.

2. Raise and support the front of the vehicle on jackstands. Mark the relationship of the wheel to the axle hub. Remove the front wheel; install 2 wheel lug nuts to retain the rotor.

3. Remove the caliper-to-mounting bracket pins.

4. Lift the caliper from the mounting bracket. Using a wire, support the

caliper so there is no strain on the brake hose.

5. Using a small pry bar or a C-clamp, force the piston back into the bore, being careful not to scratch the piston and/or bore. Be careful not to cut or tear the dust boots.

6. From the caliper, remove the brake pads, the wear indicator plates, the anti-squeal shims and the 4 support plates.

7. Check the rotor thickness and runout.

NOTE: If the rotor runout exceeds the manufacturer's specifications or has deep scratches, machine or replace it.

To Install:

8. Clean and lubricate (using silicone grease) the caliper guide pins and guide surfaces.

9. Install new support plates to the mounting bracket and new pad wear indicator plates to each pad.

NOTE: When installing the pad wear indicators, be sure the arrow on the indicator is facing in the direction of rotation.

10. Install a new anti-squeal shim to the backside of each pad.

11. Position the new pads on the mounting bracket.

NOTE: The inboard and outboard pads are identical and interchangeable.

12. Position the caliper on the mounting bracket.

13. Align the guide pin holes of the adapter and the caliper. Torque the mounting bracket-to-steering knuckle bolts to 65 ft. lbs. and guide pins to 18 ft. lbs.

14. Align and install the wheel to the axle hub, then lower the vehicle.

15. Refill the master cylinder to the proper level. If necessary, bleed the brake system.

1. Mounting bolt
2. Dust Boot
3. Collar
4. Slide bushing
5. Caliper housing
6. Piston
7. Piston seal
8. Boot
9. Set ring
10. Cap
11. Bleeder screw
12. Anti-squeal shim
13. Pad
14. Pad support plate
15. Pad wear indicator plate
16. Mounting bracket

Exploded view of the caliper assembly—GM Nova

5. Use a large C-clamp to force the piston back into its bore, being careful not to scratch the piston or bore and not to cut or tear the dust boot.

6. Pry the outboard pad from caliper.

7. Remove inboard pad from the adapter.

8. Check the condition of the rotor. If rotor run out exceeds the manufacturer's specifications or has deep scratches, re-machine the rotor.

To Install:

9. Adjust the ears of outboard pad to provide a tight fit and install the pad in the caliper recess.

10. Install the inboard pad with the flanges inserted in the adapter "ways."

11. Position the caliper on the rotor with the caliper engaging the adapter "ways."

12. Install the anti-rattle springs and the caliper retaining clips, then torque retaining screws to 180 inch lbs. (15 ft. lbs.).

13. Fill the master cylinder with brake fluid.

TYPE 7

Ford Rear Sliding Caliper

PAD REMOVAL

Except Mark VII Continental

1. Raise and support the rear of the vehicle on jackstands.

TYPE 6

Kelsey-Hayes/Chrysler Sliding Caliper

PAD REPLACEMENT

1. Remove ½ of the brake fluid from the master cylinder.

2. Remove caliper retaining clips and anti-rattle springs.

3. Lift the caliper from the rotor.

4. Support the caliper so there is no strain on the brake hose.

HOUSING
SCREW
BOOT & SEAL
SHOE AND LINING
PISTON

Type 6—Kelsey Hayes sliding caliper

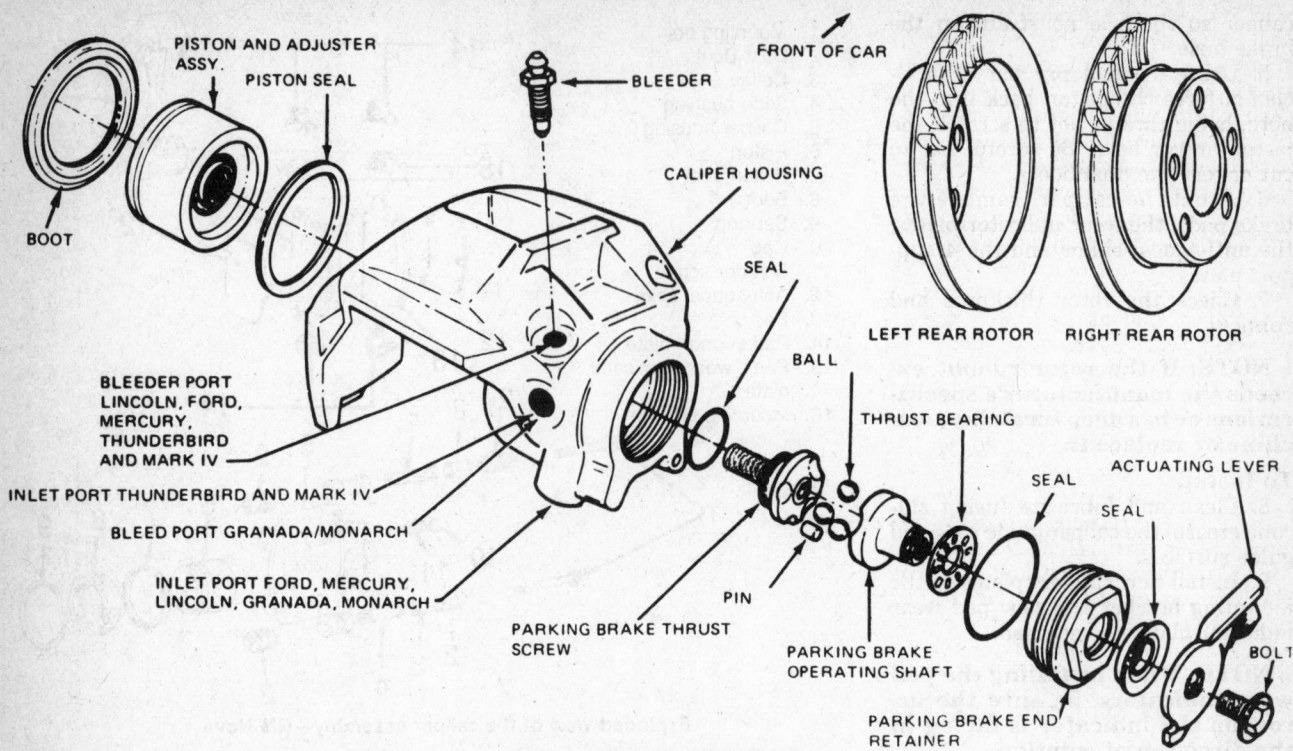

Type 7 — Ford rear disc brakes

2. Remove the wheel and tire assembly.

3. Remove the screw retaining the brake hose bracket to the shock absorber bracket.

4. Remove the retaining clip from the parking brake cable at the caliper. Remove the cable end from the parking brake.

5. Hold the slider pin hex heads with an open end wrench. Remove the upper pinch bolt. Loosen, but do not remove the lower pinch bolt.

6. Rotate the caliper away from the rotor.

7. Remove the inner and outer brake shoes and the anti-rattle clips (springs) from the anchor plate.

1. Caliper housing
2. Mounting bolt
3. Bracket
4. Spring
5. Parking brake lever
6. Nut
7. Boot and seal
8. Sleeve
9. Bushing
10. Bleeder valve
11. Fitting
12. Spring
13. Brake pads
14. Actuator assembly
15. Assembly screw
16. Spring

Mark VII Continental

1. Raise and support the vehicle on jackstands, then lock both front wheels.

2. Remove the wheel assemblies.

3. Disconnect the parking brake cable from the lever and bracket. Use care to avoid kinking or cutting the cable or return spring.

4. Remove the caliper locating pins.

5. Lift the caliper assembly away from the anchor plate by pushing the caliper upward toward the anchor plate, then rotate the lower end out of the anchor plate.

6. If insufficient clearance between the caliper, the shoe and the lining assemblies prevents removal of the cali-

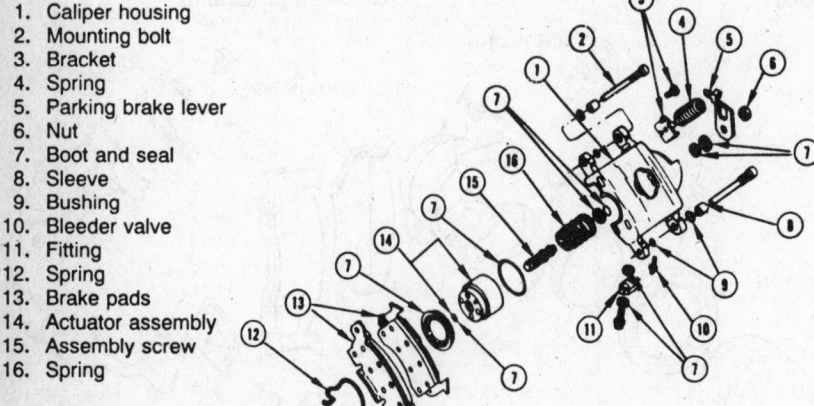

Type 7 — Ford rear disc brakes

per, it is necessary to loosen the caliper end retaining ½ turn, maximum, to allow the piston to be forced back into its bore. To loosen the end retainer, remove the parking brake lever, than ½ turn, the seal between the thrust screw and the housing may be broken and the brake fluid may leak into the parking brake mechanism chamber. In this case, the end retainer must be removed, then the internal parts cleaned andhen mark or scribe the end retainer and caliper housing to be sure that the end retainer is not loosened more than ½ turn. Force the piston back in its bore and remove the caliper.

——— CAUTION ———

If the retainer must be loosened more than ½ turn, the seal between the thrust screw and the housing may be broken and the brake fluid may leak into the parking brake mechanism chamber. In this case, the end retainer must be removed, then the internal parts cleaned and lubricated.

7. Remove the outer shoe and lining assembly from the anchor plate.

8. Remove the 2 rotor retainer nuts and the rotor from the axle shaft.

9. Remove the inner brake shoe and the lining assembly from the anchor plate. Remove anti-rattle clip from the anchor plate.

NOTE: If no further service than pad replacement is required, the brake hose removal is not necessary. DO NOT support the caliper by the brake hose.

10. Remove the flexible hose from the caliper by removing the hollow retaining bolt that connects the hose fitting to the caliper.

11. Clean the caliper, the anchor plate and the rotor assemblies, then inspect for signs of brake fluid leakage, excessive ear or damage. The caliper must be inspected for leakage both in the piston boot area and at the operating shaft seal area. Lightly sand or wire brush any rust or corrosion from the caliper and anchor plate sliding surfaces as well as the outer and inner brake shoe abutment surfaces. Inspect the brake shoes for wear. If either lining is worn to within ⅛ in. of the shoe surface, both the shoe and the lining assemblies must be replaced using the shoe and lining removal procedures.

12. If the end retainer has been loosened only ½ turn, reinstall the caliper in the anchor plate without the shoe and lining assemblies. Tighten the end retainer to 75–96 ft. lbs.

PAD INSTALLATION
Except Mark VII, Continental and Mustang SVO

1. The recommended procedure for this operation calls for removing the rotor from the vehicle and mounting the caliper in position in the anchor plate with the key only.

2. While holding the shaft, rotate the tool handle counterclockwise, until the tool is seated firmly against the piston.

NOTE: A special tool is needed to screw the piston back into its bore.

3. Now loosen the handle about a quarter turn. While holding the handle, rotate the tool shaft clockwise until the piston is fully bottomed in its bore.

4. Once the piston is bottomed, remove the caliper from the mounting plate and the tool from the caliper.

5. Reinstall the rotor.

6. Install the new pads. Make sure that the brake pad anti-rattle clip is in place in the lower inner brake pad support on the anchor plate, with the loop of the clip toward the inside of the anchor plate. Place the inboard pad on the anchor plate.

7. Install the outer brake pad with the lower flange ends against the caliper leg abutments and the brake pad upper flanges over the shoulders on the caliper legs.

The parking brake lever is attached to the operating shaft by a nylon-patch screw. When the parking brake is applied, the cable rotates the lever and operating shaft. The 3 steel balls, located in pockets on the opposing heads of the operating shaft and thrust screw, roll between ramps formed in these ball pockets. The balls force the thrust screw away from the operating shaft, driving the piston and pad against the rotor, creating the parking brake force.

Mark VII Continental

1. If the end retainer has been loosened only ½ turn, reinstall the caliper in the anchor plate without the shoe and lining assemblies. Tighten the end retainer to 75–96 ft. lbs.

2. Install the parking brake lever on its keyed spline; the lever arm must point down and rearward. The parking brake cable will then pass freely under the axle. Tighten the retainer screw to 16–22 ft. lbs. The parking brake lever must rotate freely after tightening the retainer screw. Remove the caliper from the anchor plate.

3. If new shoe and lining assemblies are to be installed, the piston must be screwed back into the caliper bore, using Tool No. T5P-2588-B or equivalent, to provide installation clearance. Remove the rotor and install the caliper, less the shoe and the lining assemblies, in the anchor plate. While holding the handle, rotate the tool shaft clockwise until the piston is fully bottomed in its bore; the piston will continue to turn even after it is bottomed. When there is no further inward movement of the piston and the tool handle is rotated until there is firm seating force, the piston is bottomed. Remove the tool and the caliper from the anchor plate.

4. Lubricate the anchor plate sliding ways with D7AE-019590-A or equivalent grease. Use only specified grease because a lower temperature type of lubricant may melt and contaminate the brake pads. Use care to prevent any lubricant from getting on the braking surface. Install the anti-rattle clip on the lower rail of the anchor plate.

5. Install the inner brake shoe and the lining assembly on the anchor plate with the lining toward the rotor. Be sure shoes are installed in their original positions as marked for identification before removal. Install the rotor and the 2 retainer nuts.

6. Install the correct hand outer brake shoe and lining assembly on the anchor plate with the lining toward the rotor and wear indicator toward the upper portion of the brake.

7. Install the flexible hose by placing a new washer on each side of the fitting outlet and inserting the attaching bolt through the washers and fitting, then torque to 20–30 ft. lbs.

8. Position the upper tab of the caliper housing on the anchor plate upper abutment surface.

9. Rotate the caliper housing until it is completely over the rotor. Use care so that the piston dust boot is not damaged.

10. Piston Position Adjustment: Pull the caliper outboard until the inner shoe and lining is firmly seated against the rotor, then measure the clearance between the outer shoe and caliper; the clearance must be ¹⁄₃₂–³⁄₃₂ in. If not, remove the caliper and readjust the piston to obtain required gap. Follow the procedure given in Step 14, then rotate the shaft counterclockwise to narrow the gap and clockwise to widen the gap (¼ turn of the piston moves it approximately ¹⁄₁₆ in.).

— CAUTION —

A clearance greater than ³⁄₃₂ in. may allow the adjuster to be pulled out of the piston when the service brake is applied. This will cause the parking brake mechanism to fail to adjust. It is then necessary to replace the piston/adjuster assembly.

11. Lubricate the locating pins and the inside of insulator with D7AZ-19A331-A or equivalent silicone grease. Add 1 drop of Locite® EOAC-19554-A or equivalent, to locating pin threads.

12. Install the locating pins through the caliper insulators and into the anchor plate; the pins must be hand inserted and hand started. Torque to 29–37 ft. lbs.

13. Connect the parking brake cable to the bracket and the lever on the caliper.

14. Bleed the brake system. Replace rubber bleed screw cap after bleeding.

15. Fill master cylinder as required to within ⅛ in. of the top of the reservoir.

16. Caliper Adjustment: With the engine running, pump the service brake lightly (approximately 14 lbs. pedal effort) about 40 times. Allow at least 1 second between pedal applications. As an alternative, with the engine Off, pump the service brake lightly (approximately 87 lbs. pedal effort) about 30 times. Now check the parking brake for excessive travel or very light effort. In either case, repeat the pumping the service brake or (if necessary) check the parking brake cable for proper tension. The caliper levers must return to the Off position when the parking brake is released.

17. Install the wheel/tire assembly and torque the wheel lug nuts to specification. Install the wheel cover. Remove the safety stands and lower the vehicle.

18. Be sure a firm brake pedal application is obtained and then road test for proper brake operation, including parking brakes.

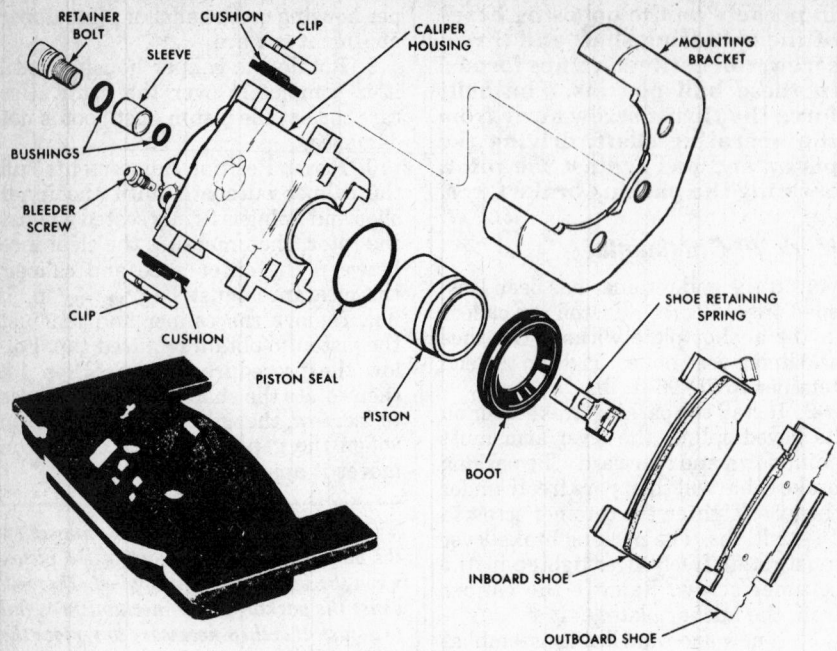

RETAINER BOLT • CUSHION • CLIP • CALIPER HOUSING • MOUNTING BRACKET • SLEEVE • BUSHINGS • BLEEDER SCREW • CLIP • CUSHION • PISTON SEAL • PISTON • BOOT • SHOE RETAINING SPRING • INBOARD SHOE • OUTBOARD SHOE

Type 8 – Chevette/T1000

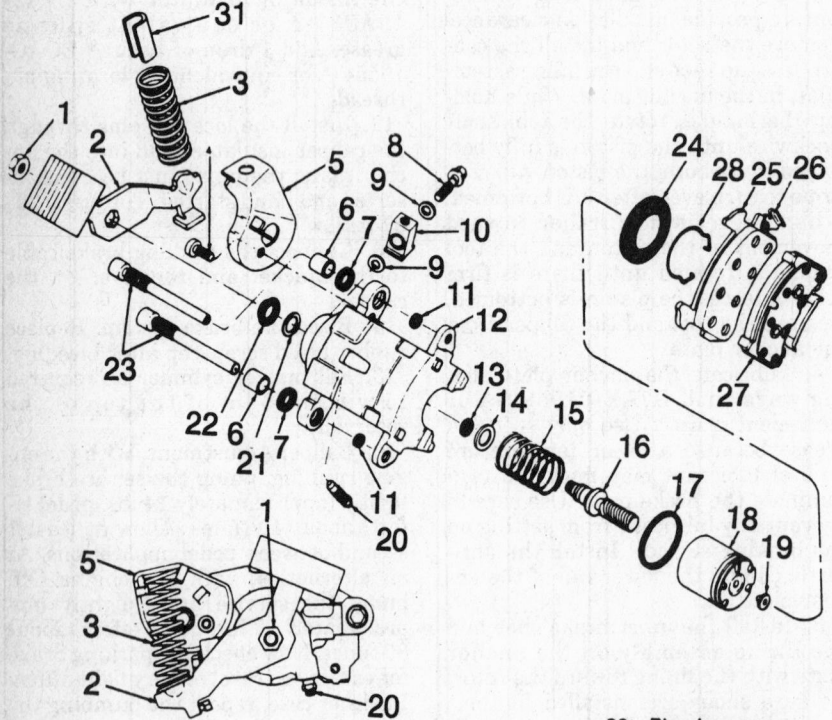

1. Nut
2. Lever
3. Return spring
4. Bolt
5. Bracket
6. Sleeve
7. Bushing
8. Bolt
9. Washer
10. Fitting
11. Bushing
12. Caliper housing
13. Shaft seal
14. Thrust washer
15. Balance spring
16. Actuator screw
17. Piston seal
18. Piston assembly
19. Two-way check valve
20. Bleeder screw
21. Anti-friction washer
22. Lever seal
23. Mounting bolt
24. Boot
25. Inboard shoe and lining
26. Wear sensor
27. Outboard shoe and lining
28. Shoe dampening spring
31. Damper

Type 9 – GM rear disc brake assembly

TYPE 8

Chevette/T1000

PAD REPLACEMENT

1. Remove ½ of the brake fluid from the master cylinder.

2. Using a large C-clamp, force the piston back into its bore, being careful not to scratch the piston or bore and being careful not to cut or tear the dust boot.

3. Remove the caliper mounting bracket-to-steering knuckle bolts.

4. Support the caliper so there is no strain on the brake hose.

NOTE: DO NOT remove the socket head retainer bolt.

5. Remove the old shoe and lining assemblies. If the retaining spring does not come out with the inboard shoe, remove the spring from the piston.

6. Check the condition of the rotor. If rotor run out exceeds the manufacturer's specifications or has deep scratches, re-machine the rotor.

To Install:

7. Before installing the inboard shoe, make sure that the shoe retaining spring is properly installed. Push the tab on the single-leg end of the spring down into the shoe hole, then snap the other 2 legs over the edge of the shoe notch.

8. Position the caliper over the rotor, align the bracket mounting holes and install the mounting bolts.

9. Clinch the outboard shoe to the caliper. After clinching, radial and end play of the outboard shoe should be 0–0.005 in. (0–0.127mm).

TYPE 9

GM Rear

PAD REPLACEMENT

NOTE: Calipers must be removed to replace linings.

1. Remove ⅔ of the fluid in the front master cylinder.

2. Remove the wheel/tire assembly and reinstall 1 wheel mounting nut, flat side toward rotor, to prevent rotor from falling when caliper is removed.

3. Loosen the tension on the parking brake cable at the equalizer and remove the cable from the parking brake lever at the caliper.

4. Remove the return spring, the lock nut, the lever, the lever seal and the anti-friction washer. The lever must be held in place while removing nut.

To install:

5. Using a C-clamp with the solid end of the lever stop and the screw end of the back of the outboard lining assembly, tighten the clamp until the piston bottoms in the caliper.

NOTE: DO NOT position C-clamp on the actuator screw.

6. Before removing the clamp, lube the caliper housing surface (under the lever seal) with silicone grease.

7. Install a new anti-friction washer, a new lever seal and the lever. Be certain to install lever on hex with the arm pointing downward.

8. Rotate lever toward the front of the vehicle; while holding it in this position install the nut and torque it to 25 ft. lbs. Rotate the lever back to the stop.

9. Install the lever return spring and remove C-clamp. The springs are color coded: Red for the right-side of the caliper and black for the left-side.

10. Remove the brake line from the caliper and plug the openings to retain the fluid.

NOTE: If the brake line nut is seized, the brass bolt and block on the caliper can be removed with the brake line attached by removing the bolt and block the copper washers after removing the caliper mounting bolts.

11. Remove the caliper mounting bolts, the caliper and the brake shoes.

12. Remove the 2 caliper mounting sleeves and the 4 bushings, then install new parts using a silicone lubricant (the sleeves are installed in the inner bushings).

13. Position the new inboard shoe assembly on the piston. The "D" shaped tab must fit in the indentation provided in the piston.

14. Install the new outboard shoe assembly.

15. To reinstall the caliper, replace any corroded caliper mounting bolts with new parts. Wire brushing or sanding will damage the bolt plating.

16. If the brass bolt and the block were removed with a brass pipe, unplug the fittings, then install the bolt and the block using 2 new copper gaskets. Torque to 30 ft. lbs. Be sure that the sleeves and pins are well lubricated with silicone (the mounting bolt should go under the inboard shoe ears).

17. Install the brake line tube nut into the caliper and pump the brake pedal to seat the lining against the rotor.

18. Clinch the upper ear of the outboard shoe by positioning a pair of pliers with 1 jaw on top of the upper ear and the other jaw in the notch or bottom of shoe, opposite the upper ear. After clinching, there should be no radial clearance between the shoe ears and the caliper housing. Repeat the clinching procedure (if necessary).

19. Connect and adjust the parking brake cables and bleed the rear brake system.

20. Install the wheel and the assembly. Torque the steel mounting nuts to 130 ft. lbs.

TYPE 10

Ford Front Drive Sliding Caliper

PAD REPLACEMENT

1. Remove the master cylinder cap and check the fluid level in the reservoirs. Remove the brake fluid until each reservoir is ½ full. Discard the removed fluid.

2. Remove the wheel/tire assembly from the rotor mounting face. Use care to avoid damage or interference with the caliper splash shield or the bleeder screw fitting.

3. Remove the brake caliper anti-rattle spring by applying upward pressure to the center portion of the spring until the spring tabs are free of the caliper holes.

4. Back out the caliper locating pins. DO NOT remove the pins completely unless the new bushings are to be installed. Reinstalling the pins after complete removal can be difficult.

5. Lift the caliper assembly from the integral knuckle, the anchor plate and the rotor. Remove the outer shoe and the lining assembly from the caliper assembly.

6. Remove the inner shoe and the lining assembly, then inspect both rotor braking surfaces. Minor scoring or build-up of the lining material does not require machining or replacement of the rotor.

7. Suspend the caliper inside the fender housing. Use care not to damage the caliper or stretch the brake hose.

To Install:

8. Use a 4 in. C-clamp and a block of wood $2\frac{3}{4} \times 1$ in. (approximately $\frac{3}{4}$ in. thick) to seat the caliper hydraulic piston in its bore. This must be done to provide clearance for the caliper assembly to fit over the rotor during installation. Extra care must be taken during this procedure to prevent damage to the aluminum piston. Metal or sharp objects cannot come into direct contact with the piston surface or damage will result.

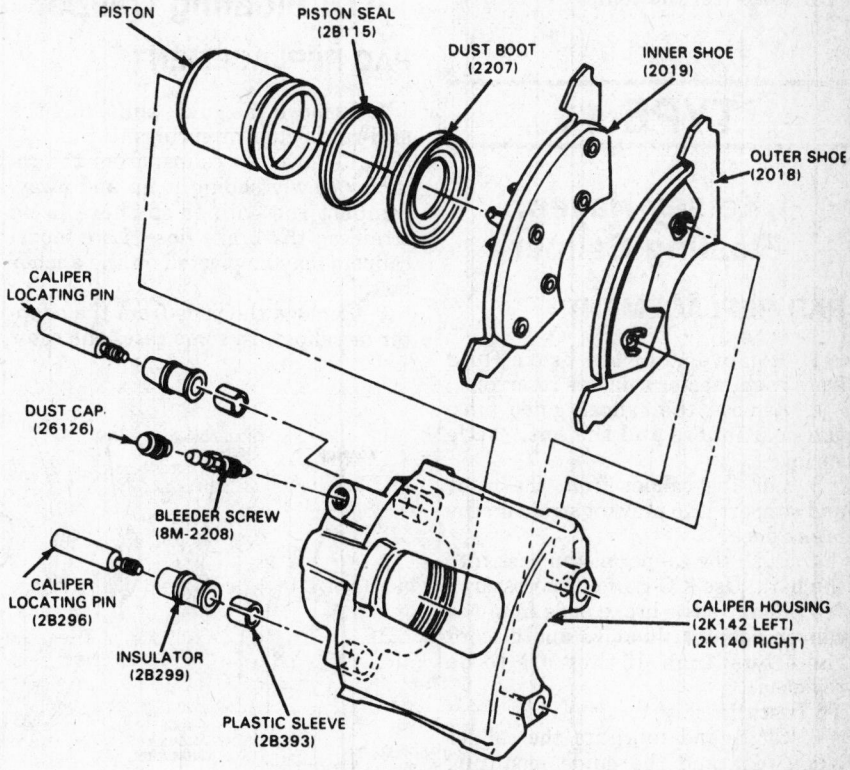

Type 10—Ford (FWD) floating caliper

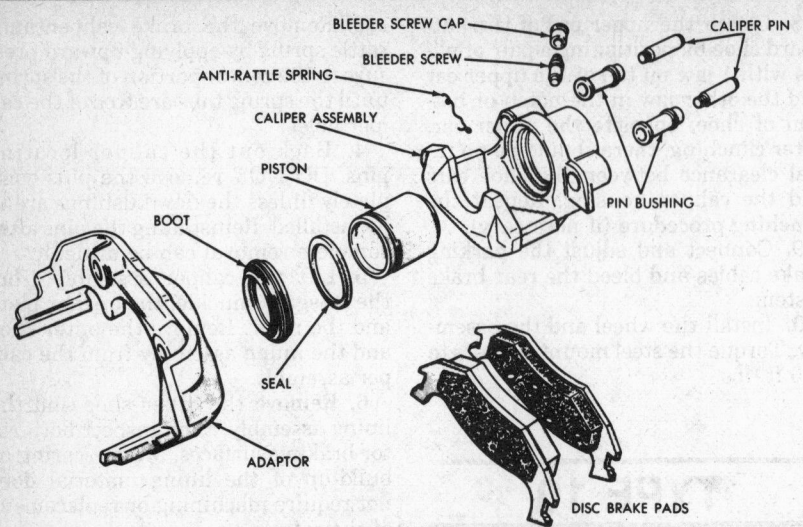

Type 11–Kelsey-Hayes floating caliper

9. Install the inner pad on the caliper piston. DO NOT bend the shoe clips during installation in the piston or distortion and rattles can occur.

10. Install the correct outer pad making sure the clips are properly seated. Replace the caliper anti-rattle spring. Refill the master cylinder to at least ¼ in. from the top in both reservoirs.

11. Install the wheel/tire assembly, then torque the wheel nuts to 80–105 ft. lbs.

12. Pump the brake pedal prior to moving the vehicle to position the brake pads.

13. Road test the vehicle.

TYPE 11

Kelsey-Hayes Floating Caliper

PAD REPLACEMENT

1. Remove ½ of the brake fluid from each master cylinder reservoir.

2. Remove the caliper guide pins, the positioners and the anti-rattle spring.

3. Lift the caliper from the rotor and support it to prevent strain on the brake hose.

4. Push the caliper piston back into the bore. Use a C-clamp if necessary.

5. Remove the brake pads from the caliper adaptor. Remove and discard the 4 bushings, if they are to be replaced.

To Install:

6. Clean and lubricate the caliper guide pins and the guide mounting surfaces. Install new guide bushings.

7. Position the new brake pads in the caliper adaptor.

8. Carefully lower the caliper over the adaptor. Install the guide pins and the anti-rattle spring. The anti-rattle spring is installed with the end loop inboard on the caliper lug.

9. Fill the master cylinder with new fluid. Bleed the brakes if necessary.

TYPE 12

ATE Floating Caliper

PAD REPLACEMENT

1. Remove the guide pin(s) and the anti-rattle clips or springs.

2. Remove the caliper from the rotor by slowly sliding it up and away. Support the caliper so there is no strain on the brake hose. Late model calipers may be pivoted on the anchor bolt.

3. Remove the pads from the adaptor or caliper. In some cases the rotor

must be removed to replace the inboard pad.

4. Push the caliper piston back into its bore.

To Install:

5. Install the pads and hardware into the adapter or caliper.

6. Position the caliper over the rotor, then install the guide pin(s), the anti-rattle springs or clips. Fill the master cylinder with new brake fluid. Bleed the brake system if necessary.

TYPE 13

Ford Sliding Caliper

PAD REPLACEMENT

1. Remove ½ of the brake fluid from the master cylinder reservoirs.

2. Remove the caliper guide pins.

3. Lift the caliper assembly from the rotor. Support the caliper so there is no strain on the brake hose.

4. Remove the outboard pad from the caliper. Remove the inboard pad from the piston.

NOTE: Step 6 can now be accomplished by using a C-clamp against the inboard pad.

5. Remove the insulators and inserts from the guide pin holes, if they are to be replaced.

6. Push the caliper piston back into its bore.

To Install:

7. Install the new guide bushings and insulators, if they are to be replaced.

8. Install the inboard pad into the piston. Install the outboard pad making sure the buttons are seated into the caliper body. The wear indicator faces toward the front of the vehicle.

9. Lower the caliper assembly onto the anchor plate and slide the guide pins through the holes in the caliper.

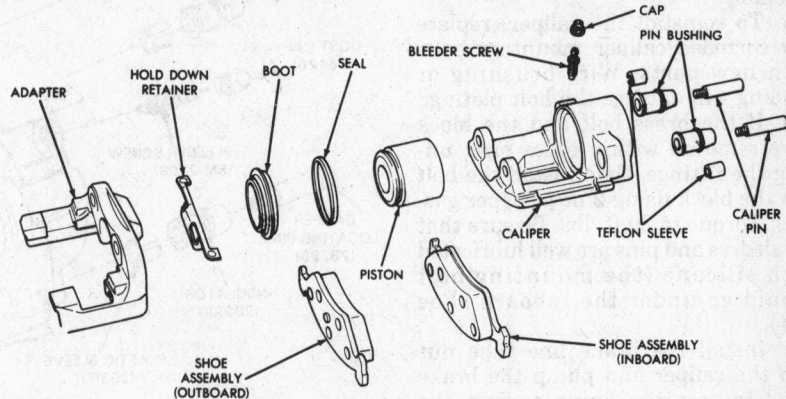

Type 12–ATE floating caliper

When the guide pins reach the rubber insulators, they will require more pressure. After the pins bottom thread them into the hole.

—— CAUTION ——
Take care not to cross thread the guide pins.

10. Refill the master cylinder with new brake fluid. Bleed the brake system if necessary.

TYPE 14

Kelsey-Hayes Floating Caliper

PAD REPLACEMENT

1. Remove ½ of the brake fluid from the master cylinder reservoir.
2. Remove the caliper guide pin, then slide the caliper up and way from the rotor. Secure the caliper out of the way with a wire. Avoid strain on the brake hose.
3. Remove the outboard pad from the caliper adapter.

NOTE: There are 3 retaining springs used. 1 spring is located at the top of the outboard caliper adapter and another at the bottom of the outboard pad and the last on the top of the inboard pad. Pay attention to the shape and location of these springs.

4. Remove the disc brake rotor by sliding it from the hub. Remove the inboard pad.
5. Push the caliper piston back into the caliper bore.
To Install:
6. Slide the inboard pad into position with the spring installed on the adapter.

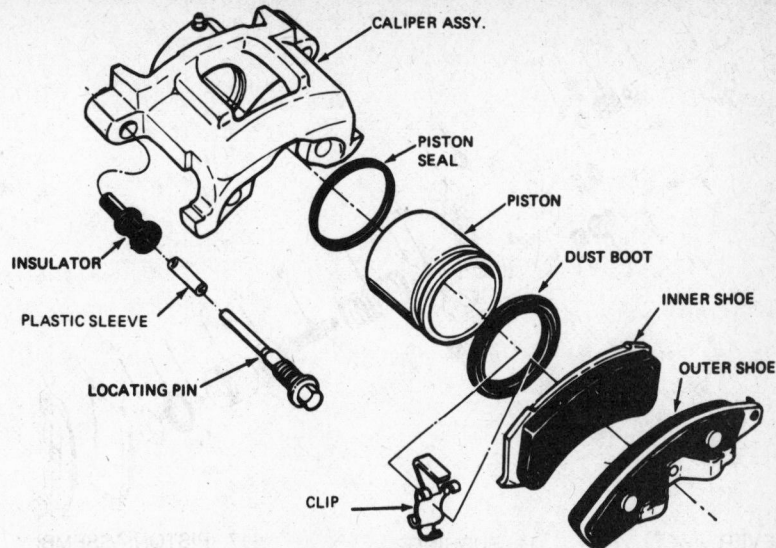

Type 13—Ford sliding caliper

7. Install the disc brake rotor. Slide the outboard pad and springs into position.
8. Lower the caliper down over the rotor and the pad adapter.
9. Install the guide pin by pressing in and turning to engage the threads.
10. Refill the master cylinder with new fluid. Pump the brake pedal several times to position the pads. Bleed the system if necessary.

TYPE 15

Delco Floating Rear Brake Caliper

PAD REPLACEMENT

1. Remove ⅔ of the brake fluid from the master cylinder.
2. Loosen the rear wheel lugs. Raise

and support the rear of the vehicle on jackstands.
3. Mark the wheel and axle lug for the same reinstallment location (to maintain factory balancing) and remove the wheel assemblies.
4. Reinstall 2 lug nuts to retain the brake rotor.
5. Loosen the tension on the parking brake cable by backing off the equalizer.
6. After the cable tension has been released, remove the cable end from the apply lever at the caliper.
7. Hold the apply lever in position and remove the retaining nut.
8. Remove the lever, the lever seal and the anti-friction washer.

NOTE: If the parking brake levers are not disconnected from the caliper during pad removal and installation, damage to the piston assembly will occur when it is moved back into the caliper bore.

9. Position a C-clamp over the caliper and tighten it until the piston bottoms in the caliper bore. Take care not to allow the C-clamp to contact the actuator screw on the caliper. Reinstall the anti-friction washer, the seal and the lever.
10. If caliper service is required, disconnect the brake line. Plug all of the openings.
11. Remove the caliper mounting bolts using a ³⁄₈ in. Allen head socket or wrench.
12. Remove the caliper by lifting it Up and Off the rotor. DO NOT permit the caliper to be suspended by the brake hose.
13. Remove the pads from the caliper. A suitable tool is required to pry the outboard pad from the caliper since it is retained by a spring button.

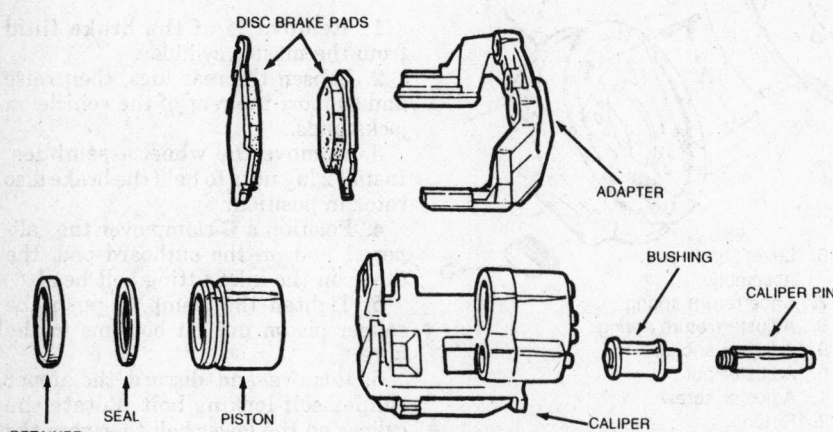

Type 14—Kelsey-Hayes floating caliper

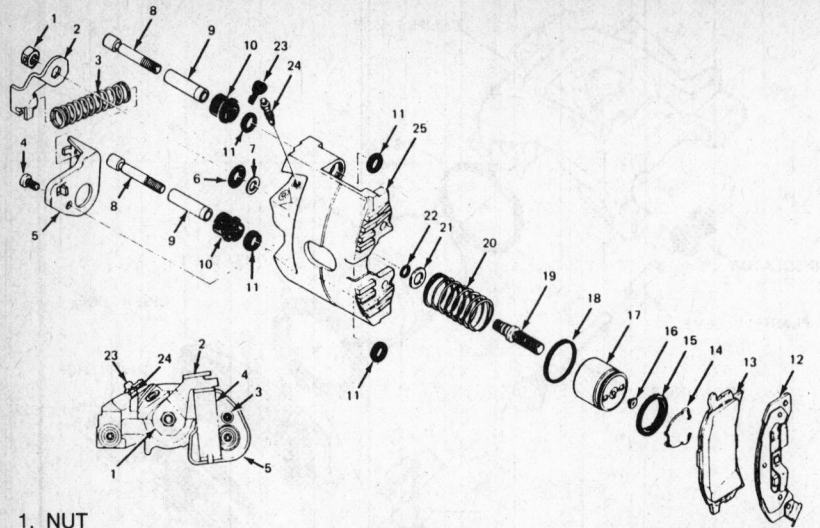

1. NUT
2. LEVER
3. RETURN SPRING
4. BOLT
5. BRACKET
6. LEVER SEAL
7. ANTI-FRICTION WASHER
8. MOUNTING BOLT
9. SLEEVE
10. BOLT BOOT

11. BUSHING
12. OUTBOARD SHOE & LINING
13. INBOARD SHOE & LINING
14. SHOE DAMPENING SPRING
15. CALIPER BOOT
16. TWO WAY CHECK VALVE

17. PISTON ASSEMBLY
18. PISTON SEAL
19. ACTUATOR SCREW
20. BALANCE SPRING
21. THRUST WASHER
22. SHAFT SEAL
23. PROTECTOR
24. BLEEDER VALVE
25. CALIPER HOUSING
26. WEAR SENSOR

Type 15—Delco floating rear caliper

1. Housing
2. Mounting bracket
3. Guide pin boot
4. Self-locking bolt
5. Piston seal
6. Piston
7. Piston boot
8. Outboard shoe & lining assembly
9. Inboard shoe & lining assembly
10. Guide pin
11. Bleeder screw
12. Cap

Type 16—Girlock front and rear caliper

14. Remove the pin bushings and sleeves from the caliper ears.

To Install:

15. Install new sleeves and bushings after lubricating them. Insure that the sleeve is flush with the pad side of the caliper ear.

16. Install the inboard pad. Make sure that the D-shaped retainer on the pad engages the D-shaped slot in the caliper piston. Turn piston (if necessary) for correct alignment.

17. Be sure that the wear indicator is mounted on the leading edge of the pad for forward rotation of the wheel.

18. Slide the edge of the metal shoe under the ends of the dampening spring and snap the pad into position flat against the caliper piston.

19. Mount the outboard pad in position. Be sure it snaps into the caliper recess.

20. Install the caliper over the disc rotor in the reverse order of removal. Apply the brakes several times to seat the linings, after filling the master cylinder. Bleed the brakes if necessary.

TYPE 16

Girlock Floating Front and Rear Calipers

PAD REPLACEMENT

1. Remove ⅔ of the brake fluid from the master cylinder.

2. Loosen the rear lugs, then raise and support the rear of the vehicle on jackstands.

3. Remove the wheel assemblies. Install 2 lug nuts to hold the brake disc rotor in position.

4. Position a C-clamp over the caliper, 1 end on the outboard pad, the other on the inlet fitting bolt head.

5. Tighten the clamp to push the caliper piston until it bottoms in the bore.

6. Remove and discard the upper caliper self-locking bolt. Rotate the caliper on the lower bolt to expose the brake pads.

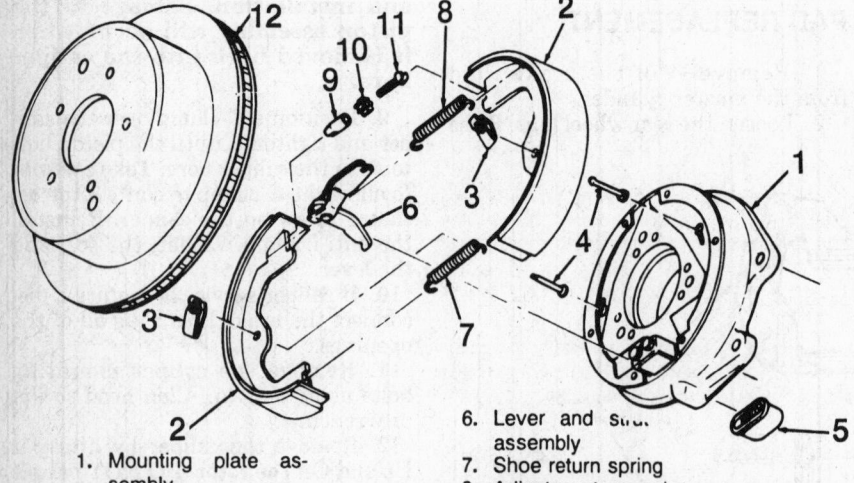

1. Mounting plate assembly
2. Shoe and lining
3. Hold-down spring
4. Hold-down pin
5. Boot

6. Lever and strut assembly
7. Shoe return spring
8. Adjuster return spring
9. Adjuster socket
10. Adjuster nut
11. Adjuster screw
12. Rotor

Exploded view of the parking brake assembly—GM Corvette

7. Remove the inner and outer pads from the caliper.

8. Clean the pad mounting frame on the caliper. Inspect the caliper for signs of fluid leakage. Remove and service the caliper if necessary.

To Install:

9. Install the new inner and outer pad into position on the caliper.

10. Rotate the caliper back into position over the disc brake rotor.

11. Install a new self-locking bolt and tighten to 22–25 ft. lbs.

12. Install the wheel assemblies and lower the vehicle.

13. Fill the master cylinder and pump the brake pedal several times to seat the pads. Bleed the brakes if necessary.

PARKING BRAKE SHOES REPLACEMENT

1. Remove the rear brake calipers and pads.

2. Remove the caliper support-to-axle hub bolts and the caliper support. Remove the rotor from the axle hub.

3. Spread the brake shoes and remove the star wheel adjuster (inspect the threads) and the star wheel adjuster spring.

4. Remove the hold down springs and pins from the shoes.

5. Using a pair of pliers, remove the shoe return springs.

6. Remove the primary/secondary shoes and the lining assemblies.

7. Clean and inspect the wear bracket, the shims, the springs and the rubber boots, replace the parts as necessary.

8. Using GM 5450032 or equivalent grease, lubricate the wear shims and the wear bracket.

9. To install, use new brake shoes and reverse the removal procedures. Adjust the parking brake shoes.

TYPE 17

Chevrolet Spectrum Front Disc Brake

PAD REPLACEMENT

1. Remove ⅔ of the brake fluid from the master cylinder.

2. Loosen the wheel lugs, then raise and support the front of the vehicle on jackstands.

3. Remove the front wheel assemblies. Install 2 lug nuts to hold the brake rotor in position.

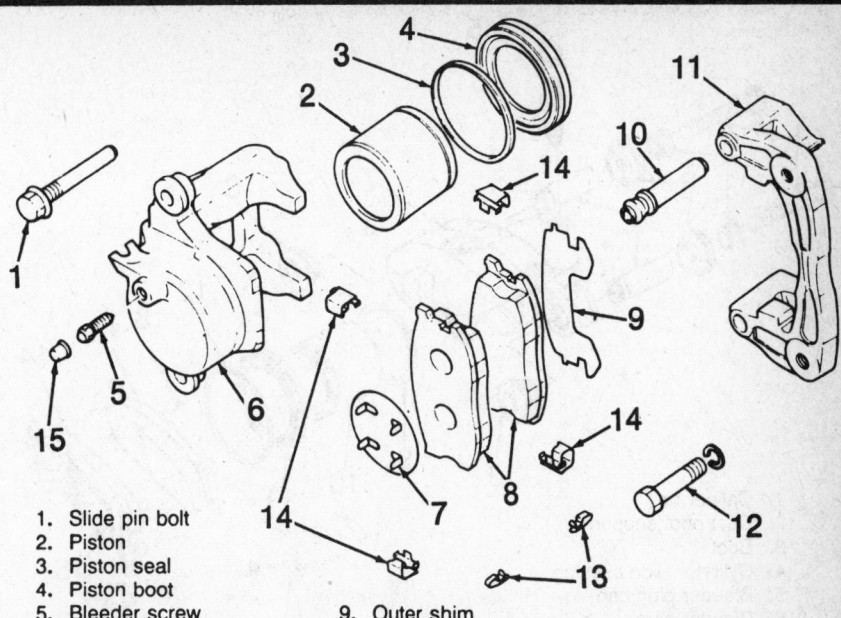

1. Slide pin bolt
2. Piston
3. Piston seal
4. Piston boot
5. Bleeder screw
6. Caliper body
7. Inner shim
8. Pads
9. Outer shim
10. Slide pin boot
11. Bracket
12. Bolt
13. Wear indicator
14. Retainer
15. Cap

Type 17–GM Spectrum front caliper (single piston)

4. Position a C-clamp over the caliper, 1 end on the outboard pad, the other on the inlet fitting bolt head.

5. Tighten the clamp to push the caliper piston to the bottom of the bore.

6. Remove the caliper-to-mounting bracket bolts and lift the caliper from the steering knuckle.

NOTE: When removing the caliper, DO NOT disconnect the brake hose from the caliper.

7. Using a wire, support the caliper from the vehicle.

8. From the caliper, remove the inner/outer pads, the pad wear indicators, the anti-squeal shims and the retainers.

9. Clean the pad mounting frame on the caliper. Inspect the caliper for signs of fluid leakage, then the rotor thickness and runout.

To Install:

10. Install grease inside of the slide pin bushing and the new inner/outer pads in position on the caliper.

11. Install new pad wear indicator plates to each pad.

NOTE: When installing the pad wear indicator plates, be sure the arrow on the pad wear indicator is facing the rotating direction of the rotor.

12. On the backside of each pad, install a new anti-squeal shim.

13. Install the new pads onto the mounting bracket.

14. Install the caliper assembly. Torque the mounting bracket-to-

steering knuckle bolts to 40 ft. lbs. and the caliper to mounting bracket bolts to 36 ft. lbs.

15. Install the wheel assemblies and lower the vehicle.

16. Refill the master cylinder and pump the brake pedal several times to seat the pads. Bleed the brakes if necessary.

TYPE 18

Chevrolet Sprint Front Disc Brake

PAD REPLACEMENT

1. Remove ⅔ of the brake fluid from the master cylinder.

2. Loosen the wheel lugs, then raise and support the front of the vehicle on jackstands.

3. Remove the front wheel assemblies. Install 2 lug nuts to hold the brake rotor in position.

4. Position a C-clamp over the caliper, 1 end on the outboard pad, the other on the inlet fitting bolt head.

5. Tighten the clamp to push the caliper piston to the bottom of the bore.

6. Remove the caliper-to-steering knuckle bolts and lift the caliper from the steering knuckle.

NOTE: When removing the caliper, DO NOT disconnect the brake hose from the caliper.

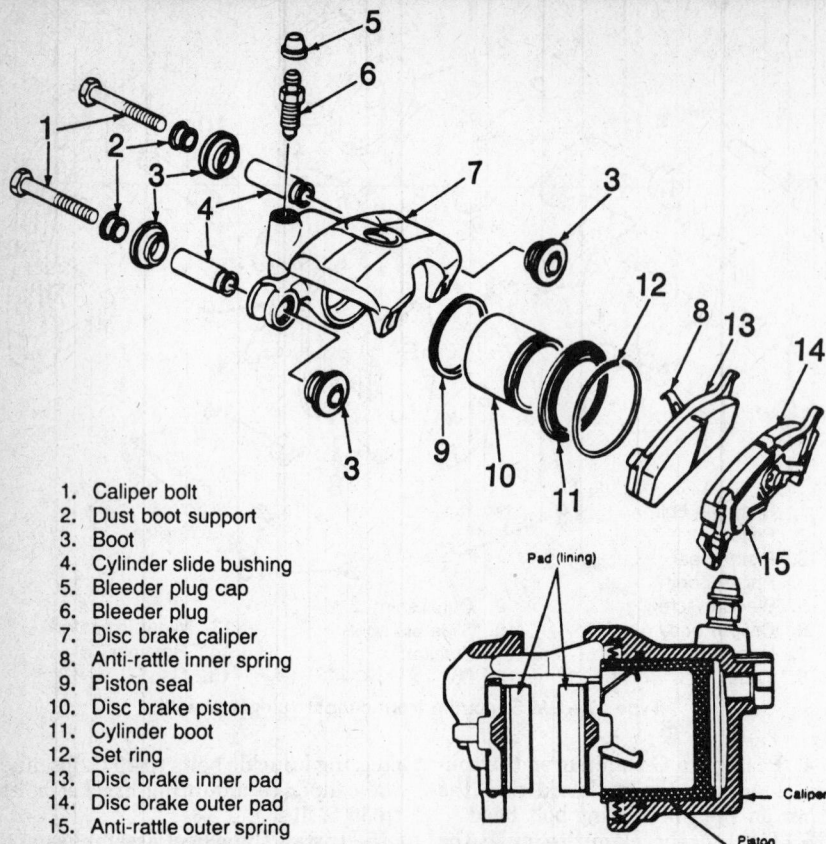

1. Caliper bolt
2. Dust boot support
3. Boot
4. Cylinder slide bushing
5. Bleeder plug cap
6. Bleeder plug
7. Disc brake caliper
8. Anti-rattle inner spring
9. Piston seal
10. Disc brake piston
11. Cylinder boot
12. Set ring
13. Disc brake inner pad
14. Disc brake outer pad
15. Anti-rattle outer spring

Type 18 – GM Sprint front caliper (single piston)

7. Using a wire, support the caliper from the vehicle.
8. From the caliper, remove the inner/outer pads and the anti-squeal shims.
9. Clean the pad mounting frame on the caliper. Inspect the caliper for signs of fluid leakage, the rotor thickness and runnout. Remove and service the caliper if necessary.

To Install:
10. Install new inner/outer pads into position on the caliper.
11. On the backside of each pad, install a new anti-squeal shim.

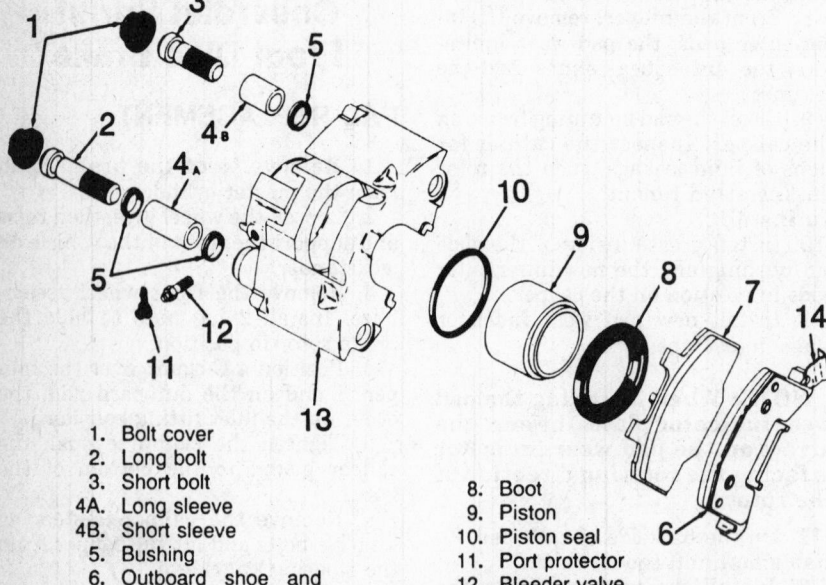

1. Bolt cover
2. Long bolt
3. Short bolt
4A. Long sleeve
4B. Short sleeve
5. Bushing
6. Outboard shoe and lining
7. Inboard shoe and lining
8. Boot
9. Piston
10. Piston seal
11. Port protector
12. Bleeder valve
13. Caliper housing
14. Wear sensor

Exploded view of the caliper assembly—GM Chevette

12. Install the new outside pad onto the mounting bracket.
13. Install the new inside pad onto the caliper.
14. Install the caliper assembly onto the mounting bracket and the springs onto the caliper. Torque the caliper-to-mounting bracket bolts to 17–26 ft. lbs.
15. Install the wheel assemblies and lower the vehicle.
16. Refill the master cylinder and pump the brake pedal several times to seat the pads. Bleed the brakes if necessary.

TYPE 19

Chevrolet Chevette, Corsica and Beretta Front Disc Brake

PAD REPLACEMENT

1. Remove ⅔ of the brake fluid from the master cylinder.
2. Loosen the wheel lugs, then raise and support the front of the vehicle on jackstands.
3. Remove the front wheel assemblies. Install 2 lug nuts to hold the brake rotor in position.
4. Remove the caliper-to-mounting bracket covers and the bolts.
5. Position a C-clamp over the caliper, 1 end on the outboard pad, the other on the inlet fitting bolt head.
6. Tighten the clamp to push the caliper piston to the bottom of the bore.
7. Lift the caliper from the steering knuckle.

NOTE: When removing the caliper, DO NOT disconnect the brake hose from the caliper.

8. Using a wire, support the caliper from the vehicle.
9. Using 12 in. pliers straighten the bent over tabs on the brake shoes (if necessary). Then, remove the inner/outer pads and the anti-squeal shims from the caliper.
10. Clean the pad mounting frame on the caliper. Inspect the caliper for signs of fluid leakage, the rotor thickness and runnout. Remove and service the caliper (if necessary).

To Install:
11. Using silicone grease, fill the caliper housing bushing cavities and install the bushing sleeves.
12. Install new inner/outer pads in position on the caliper.

13. Install the caliper assembly onto the mounting bracket. Torque the caliper-to-mounting bracket bolts to 30–45 ft. lbs.

14. Install the wheel assemblies and lower the vehicle.

15. Refill the master cylinder and pump the brake pedal several times to seat the pads.

16. Using an 8 oz. ball-peen hammer and a 16 oz. brass hammer, position the ball-peen hammer on the outboard pad tabs, then strike the ball-peen hammer with the brass hammer to bend the pad tabs at 45 degrees to the caliper; this clinches the outboard pad to the caliper. Bleed the brake system, if necessary.

TYPE 20

Pontiac LeMans Daewoo Front Disc Brake

PAD REPLACEMENT

1. Remove ⅔ of brake fluid from the master cylinder.

2. Raise the vehicle and support it safely on jack stands.

3. Mark the position of the front

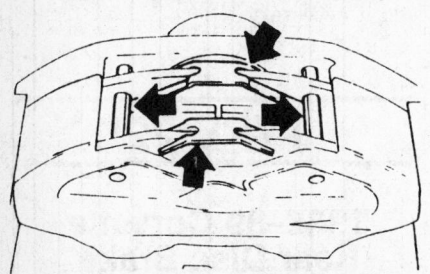

Type 20 – Capilper pin and clip placement

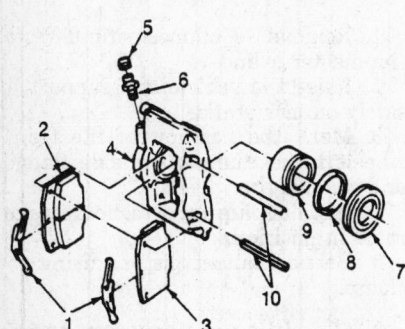

1. Anti-rattle clip
2. Shoe and lining
3. Shoe and lining
4. Caliper housing
5. Dust cap
6. Bleeder valve
7. Boot
8. Piston seal
9. Piston
10. Guide pins

Type 20 – Pontiac LeMans Daewoo

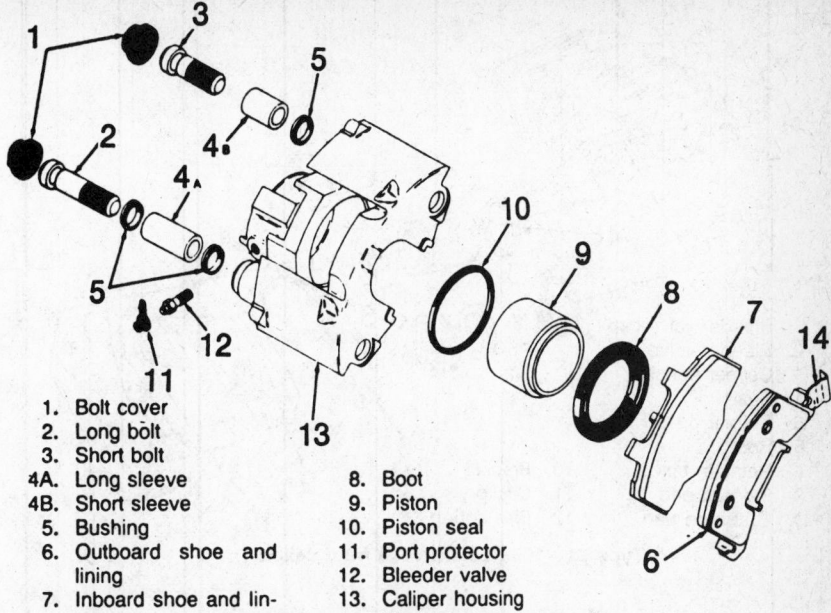

1. Bolt cover
2. Long bolt
3. Short bolt
4A. Long sleeve
4B. Short sleeve
5. Bushing
6. Outboard shoe and lining
7. Inboard shoe and lining
8. Boot
9. Piston
10. Piston seal
11. Port protector
12. Bleeder valve
13. Caliper housing
14. Wear sensor

Type 19 – GM Chevette, Corsica and Beretta

wheels in relation to the wheel hubs and remove the wheels.

NOTE: Caliper removal is not required to replace the pads or service the rotor.

4. Using a brass drift and hammer and working from the inner side of the caliper, drive out the pad and lining retaining pins.

— CAUTION —
The expanding springs in the caliper are held under tension from the retaining pins. Exercise caution when removing the pins.

5. Position a C-clamp over the caliper, 1 end on the outboard pad, the other on the inlet fitting bolt head.

6. Tighten the clamp to push the caliper piston to the bottom of the bore.

7. Remove the brake pads.

To Install:

8. Install new inner/outer pads and wear sensor in position on the caliper. Check that the pads and linings can be moved slightly backwards and forwards in the caliper.

9. Install the expanding springs.

10. Working from the outer side of the caliper, install the retaining pins so that the openings align.

11. Install the wheels and tires, aligning the previous marks.

12. Torque the lug nuts to 65 ft. lbs.

13. Lower the vehicle. Depress the brake pedal repeatedly to bring the brake pads and lingings in contact with the rotor.

14. Check the brake fluid level and add if necessary.

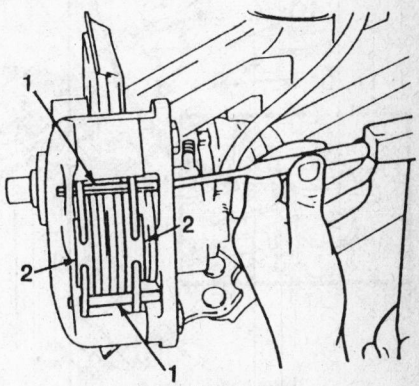

1. Retaining pins
2. Shoe and lining

Type 20 – Removing the retaining pins

TYPE 21

1988–89 Corvette Front Disc Brake

PAD REPLACEMENT

1. Remove ⅔ of brake fluid from the master cylinder.

2. Raise the vehicle and support it safely on jack stands.

3. Mark the position of the front wheels in relation to the wheel hubs and remove the wheels.

4. Install 2 lug nuts to hold brake rotor in position.

5. Remove circlip from inside of retaining pin.

6. Remove caliper retaining pins.

7. Place caliper on upper control to avoid damaging the brake hose.

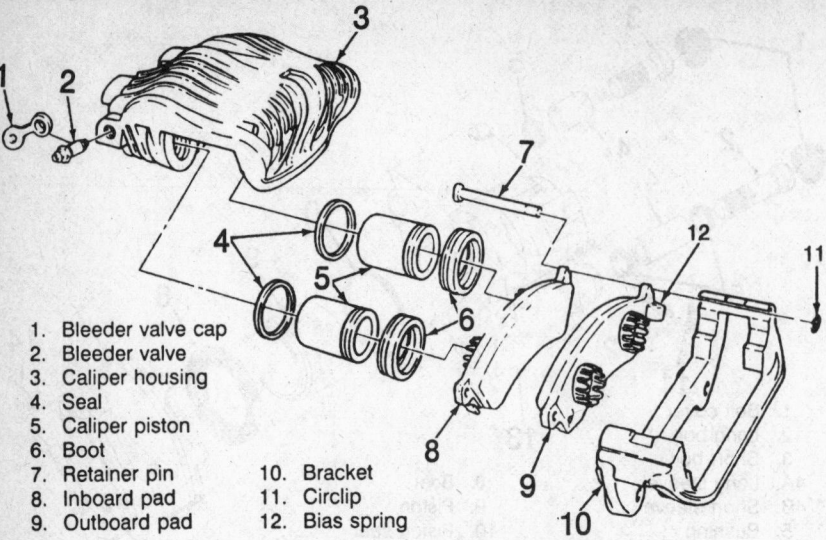

1. Bleeder valve cap
2. Bleeder valve
3. Caliper housing
4. Seal
5. Caliper piston
6. Boot
7. Retainer pin
8. Inboard pad
9. Outboard pad
10. Bracket
11. Circlip
12. Bias spring

Type 21 – 1988–89 Corvette front caliper

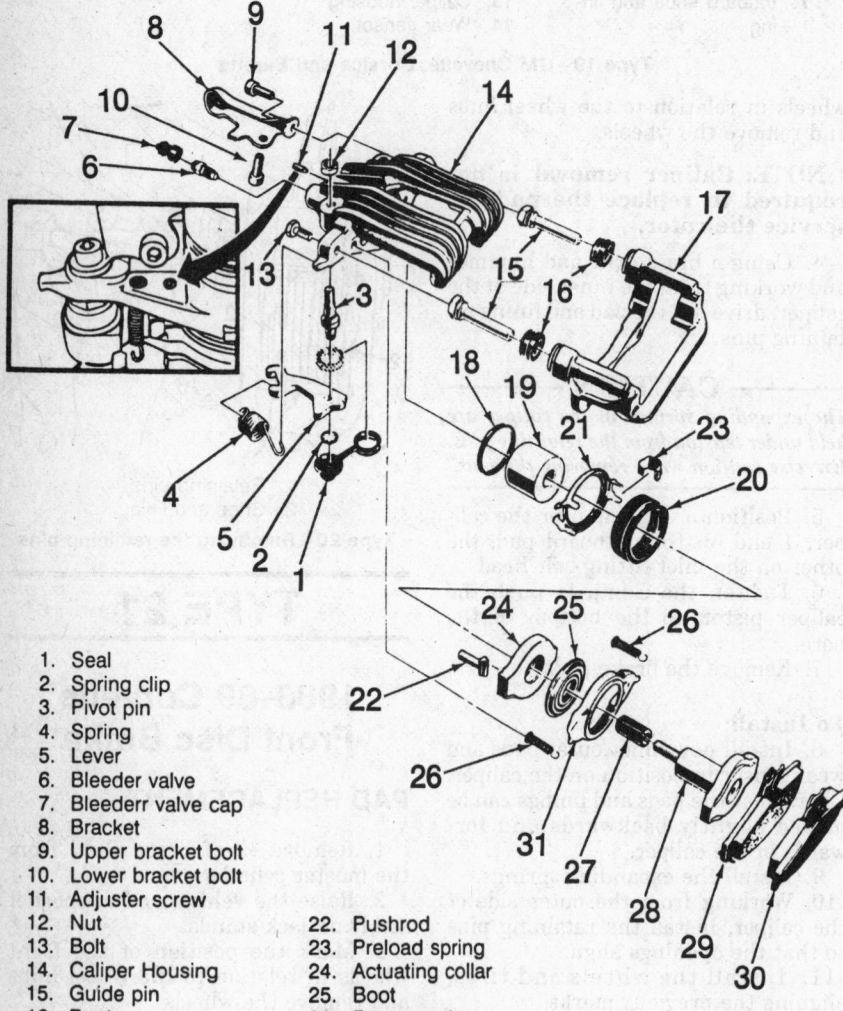

1. Seal
2. Spring clip
3. Pivot pin
4. Spring
5. Lever
6. Bleeder valve
7. Bleederr valve cap
8. Bracket
9. Upper bracket bolt
10. Lower bracket bolt
11. Adjuster screw
12. Nut
13. Bolt
14. Caliper Housing
15. Guide pin
16. Boot
17. Bracket
18. Seal
19. Piston
20. Boot
21. Retainer
22. Pushrod
23. Preload spring
24. Actuating collar
25. Boot
26. Return spring
27. Bushing
28. Clamp rod
29. Inboard pad
30. Outboard pad
31. Retainer

Type 22 – 1988–89 Corvette rear caliper

8. Bottom caliper pistons using C-clamp or pliers.

NOTE: The C-clamp or pliers must be placed at the center of the brake pad to press both pistons evenly.

9. Remove the brake pads.
To Install:
10. Install new inner/outer pads.

NOTE: Outboard pad with insulator is installed in the caliper housing, the inboard shoe and lining with wear sensor is presed into the caliper pistons.

11. Replace caliper over the rotor.
12. Install 1 new retainer pin and circlip.

NOTE: There are 2 types of replacement retainer pins. The circlip grooves are cut in different positions for standard and heavy duty calipers.

13. Press caliper housing down to compress bias springs and install second retainer pin and circlip.
14. Remove lug nuts holding rotor in place.
15. Install wheels and tires aligning the previous marks.
16. Torque lug nuts to 100 ft. lbs.
17. Lower the vehicle. With engine running pump brake pedal slowly several times to bring the pads in contact with the rotors.
18. Check the brake fluid level and add if necessary.

TYPE 22

1988–89 Corvette Rear Disc Brake

PAD REPLACEMENT

1. Remove ⅔ of brake fluid from the master cylinder.
2. Raise the vehicle and support it safely on jack stands.
3. Mark the position of the front wheels in relation to the axle flange and remove the wheels.
4. Install 2 lug nuts to hold brake rotor in position.
5. Bottom caliper pistons using C-clamp.

NOTE: It is not necessary to remove the parking brake caliper lever return spring. The end of the C-clamp must be placed on the inlet fitting bolt and the other end against the center of the outboard brake pad.

6. Remove upper caliper guide bolt.

NOTE: New guide bolt should be used.

7. Rotate the caliper housing on the lower caliper bolt.

8. Remove the brake pads.

To Install:

9. Install new inner/outer pads.

NOTE: Outboard pad with insulator is installed in the caliper housing, the inboard shoe and lining with wear sensor is presed into the caliper piston. The wear sensor must be in the trailing position with forward wheel rotation. Springs on outboard pad must not stick through the inspection hole in the caliper housing.

10. Rotate caliper over the rotor.

11. Install new caliper guide bolt.

12. Tighten caliper guide bolts to proper torque.

13. Remove lug nuts holding rotor in place.

14. Install wheels and tires aligning the previous marks.

15. Torque lug nuts to 100 ft. lbs.

16. Lower the vehicle. With engine running pump brake pedal slowly several times to bring the pads in contact with the rotors.

17. Check the brake fluid level and add if necessary.

TYPE 23

Nova
Rear Disc Brake

PAD REPLACEMENT

1. Remove ⅔ of brake fluid from the master cylinder.

2. Raise the vehicle and support it safely on jack stands.

3. Mark the position of the front wheels in relation to the axle hub and remove the wheels.

4. Remove the 2 caliper mounting bolts from the mounting bracket.

NOTE: It is not necessary to remove the caliper hose. Remove and support the caliper.

5. Remove the brake pads.

To Install:

6. Install new inner/outer pads.

7. Install new wear sensors.

NOTE: Be sure the arrow on the pad wear indicator is pointing in the rotating direction of the disc.

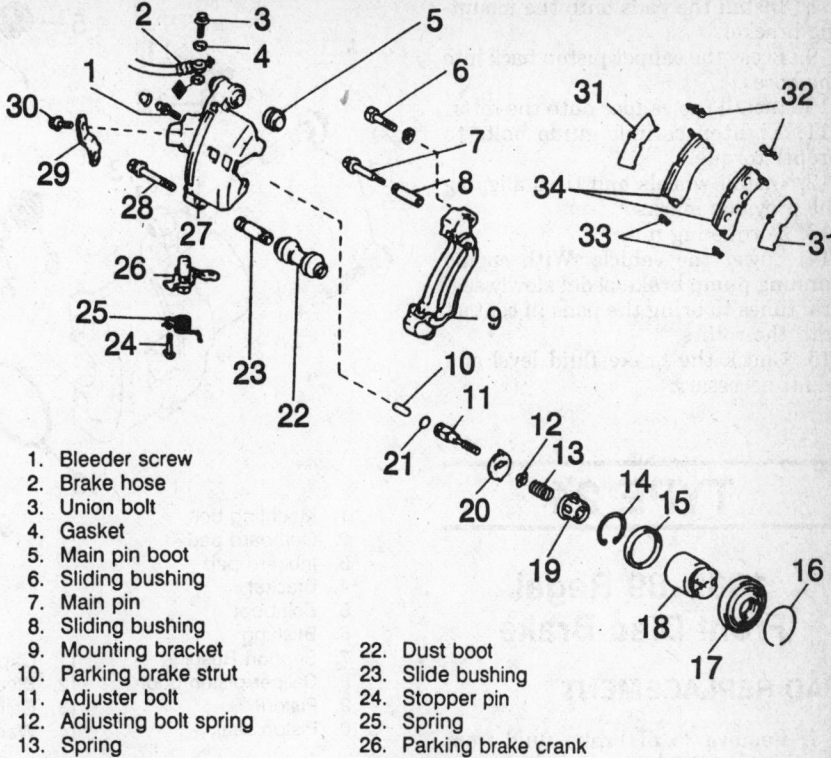

1. Bleeder screw
2. Brake hose
3. Union bolt
4. Gasket
5. Main pin boot
6. Sliding bushing
7. Main pin
8. Sliding bushing
9. Mounting bracket
10. Parking brake strut
11. Adjuster bolt
12. Adjusting bolt spring
13. Spring
14. Snap ring
15. Piston seal
16. Set ring
17. Boot
18. Piston
19. Adjusting bolt spring retainer
20. Adjusting bolt stopper
21. O-ring
22. Dust boot
23. Slide bushing
24. Stopper pin
25. Spring
26. Parking brake crank
27. Caliper housing
28. Mounting bolt
29. Cable support bracket
30. Cable support bracket bolt
31. Anti-squeal shim
32. Anti-rattle spring
33. Pad support plate
34. Pad

Type 23 – Nova rear caliper

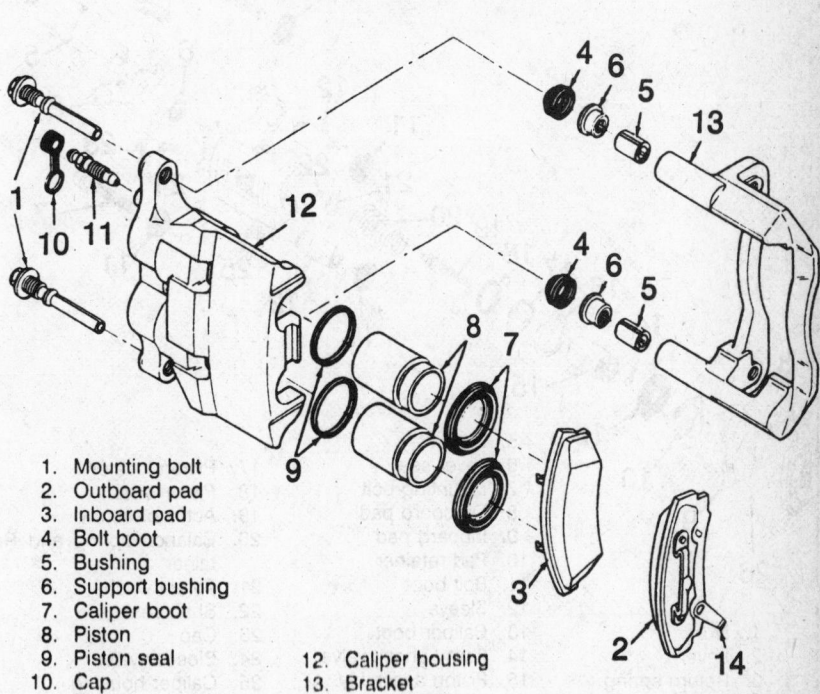

1. Mounting bolt
2. Outboard pad
3. Inboard pad
4. Bolt boot
5. Bushing
6. Support bushing
7. Caliper boot
8. Piston
9. Piston seal
10. Cap
11. Bleeder valve
12. Caliper housing
13. Bracket
14. Wear sensor

Type 24 – GM W-Body front caliper

8. Install the pads onto the mounting bracket.

9. Press the caliper piston back into the bore.

10. Install the caliper onto the rotor.

11. Tighten caliper guide bolts to proper torque.

12. Install wheels and tires aligning the previous marks.

13. Torque lug nuts.

14. Lower the vehicle. With engine running pump brake pedal slowly several times to bring the pads in contact with the rotors.

15. Check the brake fluid level and add if necessary.

TYPE 24

1988–89 Regal Front Disc Brake

PAD REPLACEMENT

1. Remove ⅔ of brake fluid from the master cylinder.

2. Raise the vehicle and support it safely on jack stands.

3. Mark the position of the front wheels in relation to the axle flange and remove the wheels.

4. Install 2 lug nuts to hold brake rotor in position.

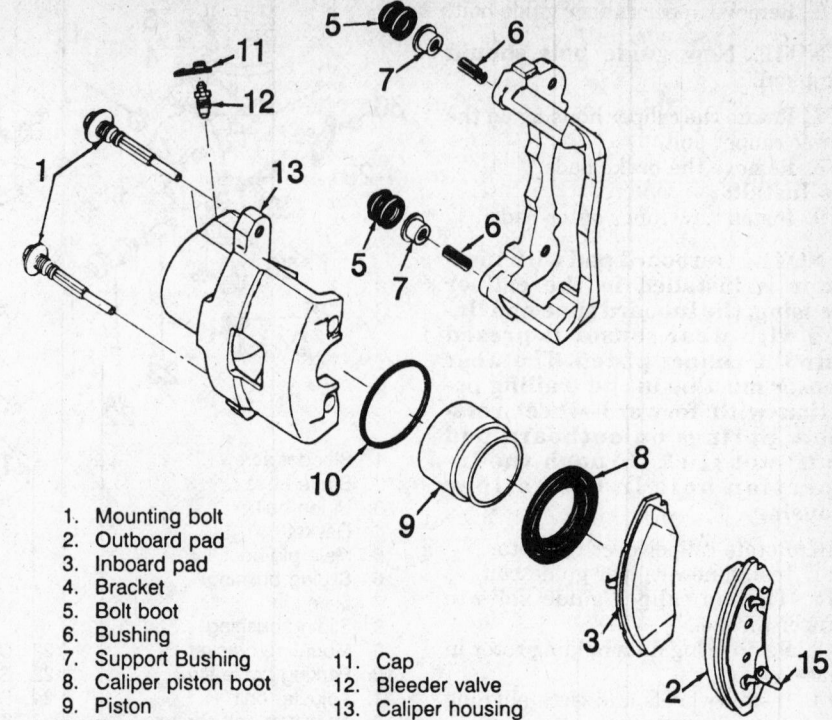

1. Mounting bolt
2. Outboard pad
3. Inboard pad
4. Bracket
5. Bolt boot
6. Bushing
7. Support Bushing
8. Caliper piston boot
9. Piston
10. Piston seal
11. Cap
12. Bleeder valve
13. Caliper housing
14. Wear sensor

Type 26 – Cadillac Allante and 1986–89 GM E-Body front caliper

5. Remove the 2 caliper mounting bolts from the mounting bracket.

NOTE: It is not necessary to remove the caliper hose. Remove and support the caliper.

6. Remove the brake pads.

To Install:

7. Install new inner/outer pads.

8. Install new wear sensors.

NOTE: Be sure the arrow on the pad wear indicator is pointing in the rotating direction of the disc.

9. Press the caliper piston back into the bore.

10. Install the pads onto the mounting bracket.

11. Install the caliper onto the rotor.

12. Tighten caliper guide bolts to proper torque.

13. Install wheels and tires aligning the previous marks.

14. Torque lug nuts.

15. Lower the vehicle. With engine running pump brake pedal slowly several times to bring the pads in contact with the rotors.

16. Check the brake fluid level and add if necessary.

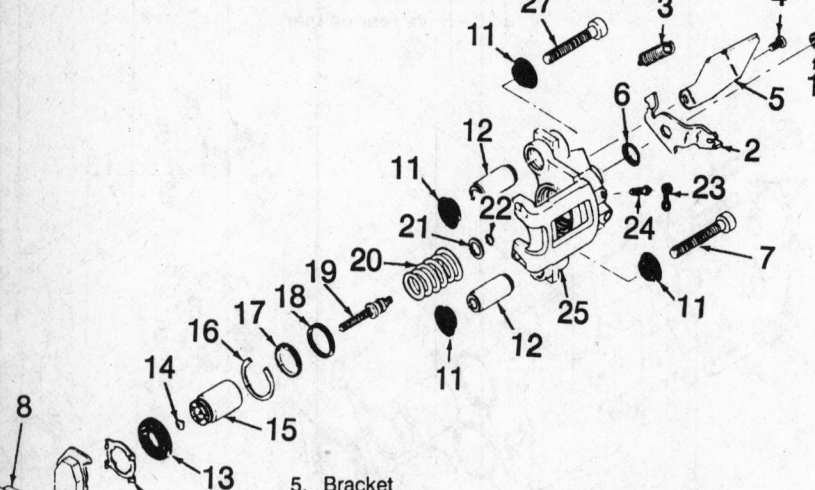

5. Bracket
6. Lever seal
7. Mounting bolt
8. Outboard pad
9. Inboard pad
10. Pad retainer
11. Bolt boot
12. Sleeve
13. Caliper boot
14. 2-way check valve
15. Piston assembly
16. Retainer
17. Piston locator
18. Piston seal
19. Actuator screw
20. Balance spring and Retainer
21. Thrust washer
22. Shaft seal
23. Cap
24. Bleeder valve
25. Caliper housing
26. Wear sensor

1. Nut
2. Lever
3. Return spring
4. Bolt

Type 25 – GM W-Body rear caliper

TYPE 25

1988–89 Regal Rear Disc Brake

PAD REPLACEMENT

1. Remove ⅔ of brake fluid from the master cylinder.

2. Raise the vehicle and support it safely on jack stands.

3. Mark the position of the front wheels in relation to the axle flange and remove the wheels.

4. Install 2 lug nuts to hold brake rotor in position.

5. Loosen tension on parking brake cable at equalizer.

6. Remove cable and return spring from lever.

7. Remove lock nut, lever and seal.

8. Remove parking cable bracket to allow access to upper mounting bolt.

9. Remove mounting bolds, using GM torque wrench adapter J–36581 or equivalent.

10. Remove caliper from rotor, disconnect brake hose support bracket and suspend with wire.

11. Use a screwdriver and disengage buttons on pad from holes in caliper and remove outboard pad.

12. From open side of caliper, press in on edge on inboard pad and tilt outward to release pad from retainer. Remove pad.

13. Remove 2 way valve from piston end.

To Install:

14. Press piston back into bore using 12 in. pliers.

NOTE: DO NOT allow pliers to contact actuator screw. Protect piston so as mot to damage surface.

15. Lubricate new two–way check valve and install into piston end.

16. Install the pads onto caliper.

NOTE: Piston must be properly aligned with 1 of the D–shaped notches is nearest the bridge of the caliper. Turn the piston with spanner wrench J–7624 or equivalent, if necessary.

17. Install the caliper onto the rotor.

NOTE: Take care not to bang bolts against boots. This could tear the boots.

18. Tighten caliper guide bolts to proper torque.

19. Install parking cable bracket.

20. Lubricate and install seal with bead against caliper housing.

21. Install level, nut and return spring.

NOTE: Hold lever against stop on caliper while tightening nut to prevent accidentail application of the parking brake.

22. Install parking brake cables. Parking brake levers should be against the lever stops on the caliper housing. Tighten cable at adjuster until either right or left lever begins to move off the stop; then loosen adjustment until lever is barely touching the stop.

23. Install wheels and tires aligning the previous marks.

24. Torque lug nuts.

25. Lower the vehicle. With engine running pump brake pedal slowly several times to bring the pads in contact with the rotors.

26. Check the brake fluid level and add if necessary.

TYPE 26

1986–89 GM E & V Body Front Disc Brake

PAD REPLACEMENT

1. Remove ⅔ of brake fluid from the master cylinder.

2. Raise the vehicle and support it safely on jack stands.

3. Mark the position of the front wheels in relation to the axle flange and remove the wheels.

4. Install 2 lug nuts to hold brake rotor in position.

5. Remove the 2 caliper mounting bolts from the mounting bracket.

NOTE: It is not necessary to remove the caliper hose. Remove and support the caliper.

6. Remove the brake pads.

To Install:

7. Press the caliper piston back into the bore.

8. Install new wear sensors.

NOTE: Wear sensor should be at trailing edge of pad during forward wheel rotation.

9. Install new inner/outer pads.

10. Install the caliper onto the rotor.

11. Tighten caliper guide bolts to proper torque.

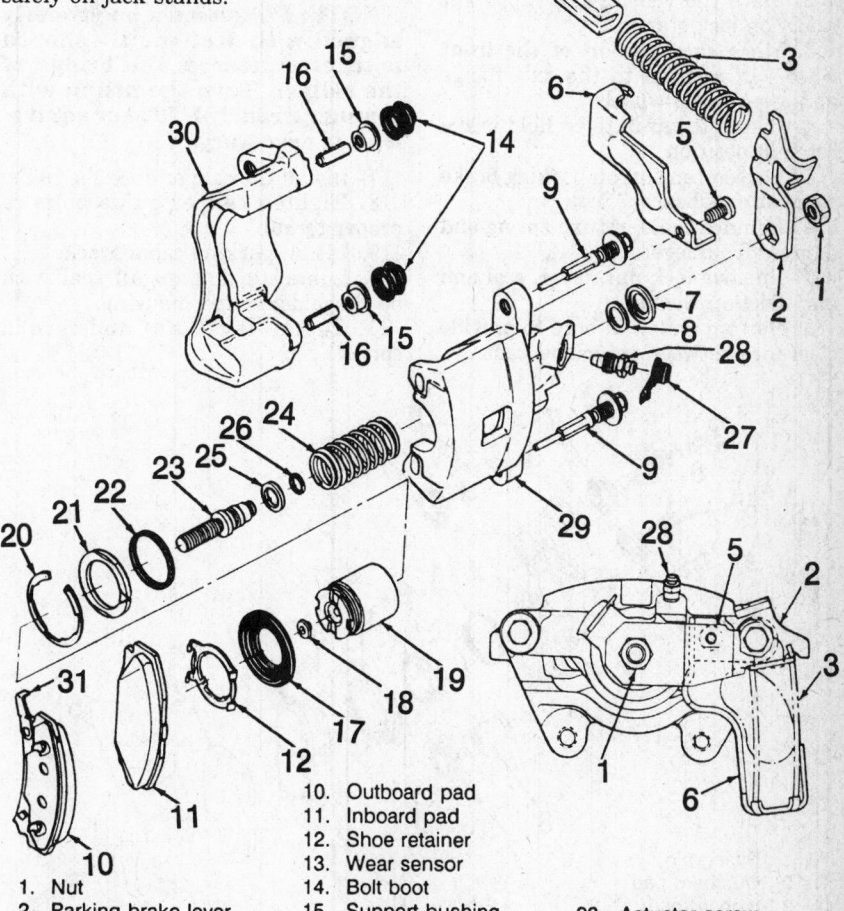

1. Nut	10. Outboard pad	23. Actuator screw
2. Parking brake lever	11. Inboard pad	24. Balance spring retainer
3. Return spring	12. Shoe retainer	25. Thrust washer
4. Damper	13. Wear sensor	26. Shaft seal
5. Bolt	14. Bolt boot	27. Cap
6. Bracket	15. Support bushing	28. Bleeder valve
7. Lever seal	16. Bushing	29. Caliper housing
8. Anti-Friction washer	17. Caliper piston boot	30. Bracket
9. Mounting bolt	18. 2-way check valve	
	19. Piston assembly	
	20. Retainer	
	21. Piston locator	
	22. Piston seal	

Type 27 – Cadillac Allante and 1986–89 GM E-Body rear caliper

12. Install wheels and tires aligning the previous marks.

13. Torque lug nuts.

14. Lower the vehicle. With engine running pump brake pedal slowly several times to bring the pads in contact with the rotors.

15. Check the brake fluid level and add if necessary.

TYPE 27

1986–89 GM E & V Body Rear Disc Brake

PAD REPLACEMENT

1. Remove ⅔ of brake fluid from the master cylinder.

2. Raise the vehicle and support it safely on jack stands.

3. Mark the position of the front wheels in relation to the axle flange and remove the wheels.

4. Install 2 lug nuts to hold brake rotor in position.

5. Loosen tension on parking brake cable at equalizer.

6. Remove cable, return spring and damper from lever.

7. Remove lock nut, lever, seal and anti-friction washer.

8. Bottom piston in bore to provide clearance between rotor and pads.

9. Remove mounting bolds.

10. Remove caliper from rotor and suspend with wire.

11. Use a screwdriver and disengage buttons on pad from holes in caliper and remove outboard pad.

12. From open side of caliper, press in on edge on inboard pad and tilt outward to release pad from retainer. Remove pad.

13. Remove two-way valve from piston end.

To Install:

14. Press piston back into bore using 12 in. pliers.

NOTE: DO NOT allow pliers to contact actuator screw. Protect piston so as not to damage surface.

15. Lubricate new 2 way check valve and install into piston end.

16. Install the pads onto caliper. Wear sensor should be at trailing end of pad during forward wheel rotation.

NOTE: Piston must be properly aligned with 1 of the D–shaped notches is nearest the bridge of the caliper. Turn the piston with spanner wrench J–7624 or equivalent, if necessary.

17. Install the caliper onto the rotor.

18. Tighten caliper guide bolts to proper torque.

19. Install parking cable bracket.

20. Lubricate and install seal with bead against caliper housing.

21. Install level, nut and return spring.

NOTE: Hold lever against stop on caliper while tightening nut to prevent accidentail application of the parking brake.

22. Install parking brake cables. Parking brake levers should be against the lever stops on the caliper housing. Tighten cable at adjuster until either right or left lever begins to move off the stop; then loosen adjustment until lever is barely touching the stop.

23. Install wheels and tires aligning the previous marks.

24. Torque lug nuts.

25. Lower the vehicle. With engine running pump brake pedal slowly several times to bring the pads in contact with the rotors.

26. Check the brake fluid level and add if necessary.

TYPE 28

1988–89 Fiero Front Disc Brake

PAD REPLACEMENT

1. Remove ⅔ of brake fluid from the master cylinder.

2. Raise the vehicle and support it safely on jack stands.

3. Mark the position of the front wheels in relation to the axle flange and remove the wheels.

4. Install 2 lug nuts to hold brake rotor in position.

5. Remove the 2 caliper mounting pins using tools J–36620 and J–6125–1b or equivalent. Insert J–36620 slide hammer though pin and install tool J–6125–1b on the end. Thrust weight away from caliper to pull pins out.

— **CAUTION** —

Be prepared to catch springs when removing spring pins. Springs may fly out causing injury.

6. Remove Spings from pad flanges.

7. Remove brake pads.

To Install:

8. Press the caliper piston back into the bore.

9. Install new wear sensors.

NOTE: Wear sensor should be at trailing edge of pad during forward wheel rotation.

10. Install new inner/outer pads.

11. Install the caliper onto the rotor.

12. Align 1 spring pin with pads and caliper. Tap in pin with soft brass drift until end of pin just emerges from inboard face of caliper.

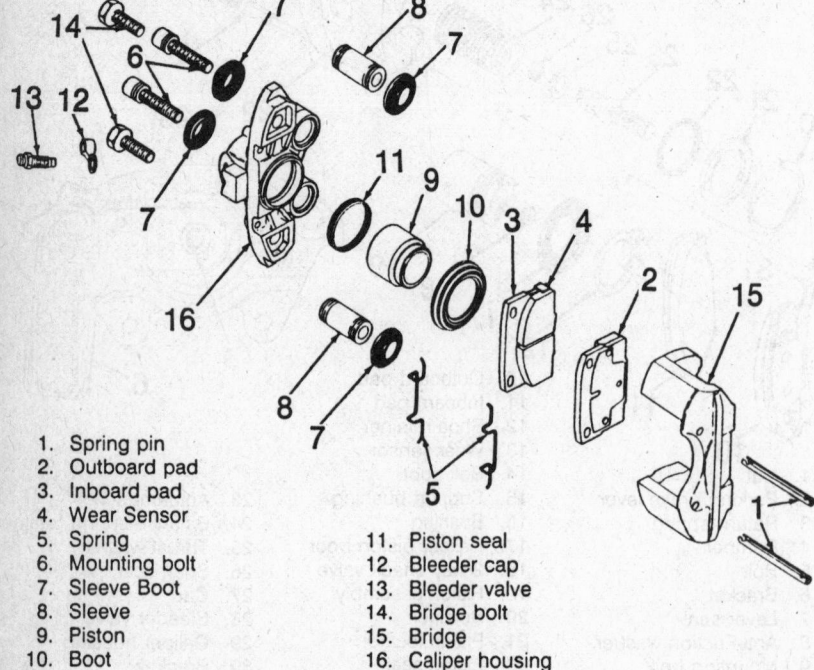

1. Spring pin
2. Outboard pad
3. Inboard pad
4. Wear Sensor
5. Spring
6. Mounting bolt
7. Sleeve Boot
8. Sleeve
9. Piston
10. Boot
11. Piston seal
12. Bleeder cap
13. Bleeder valve
14. Bridge bolt
15. Bridge
16. Caliper housing

Type 28 – 1988–89 Pontiac Fiero front caliper

13. Install springs 1 at a time. Hook end of spring under pin with center of spring over shoe flange.

14. Press down on other end of spring and install second pin through caliper and pad far enough to hold spring. Install second spring following the same procedure and finish tapping pin through caliper.

15. Install wheels and tires aligning the previous marks.

16. Torque lug nuts.

17. Lower the vehicle. With engine running pump brake pedal slowly several times to bring the pads in contact with the rotors.

18. Check the brake fluid level and add if necessary.

TYPE 29

1988–89 Fiero Rear Disc Brake

PAD REPLACEMENT

1. Remove ⅔ of brake fluid from the master cylinder.

2. Raise the vehicle and support it safely on jack stands.

3. Mark the position of the front wheels in relation to the axle flange and remove the wheels.

4. Install 2 lug nuts to hold brake rotor in position.

5. Remove the 2 caliper mounting pins using tools J–36620 and J–6125–1b or equivalent. Insert J–36620 slide hammer though pin and install tool J–6125–1b on the end. Thrust weight away from caliper to pull pins out.

--- CAUTION ---

Be prepared to catch springs when removing spring pins. Springs may fly out causing injury.

6. Remove Spings from pad flanges.

7. Remove brake pads.

To Install:

8. Bottom piston in bore using tool J–36621 or equivalent to turn piston. Turn right caliper piston clockwise and left caliper piston counterclockwise to move piston back.

9. Install new wear sensors.

NOTE: Wear sensor should be at trailing edge of pad during forward wheel rotation.

10. Install new inner/outer pads.

11. Install the caliper onto the rotor.

12. Align 1 spring pin with pads and caliper. Tap in pin with soft brass drift until end of pin just emerges from inboard face of caliper.

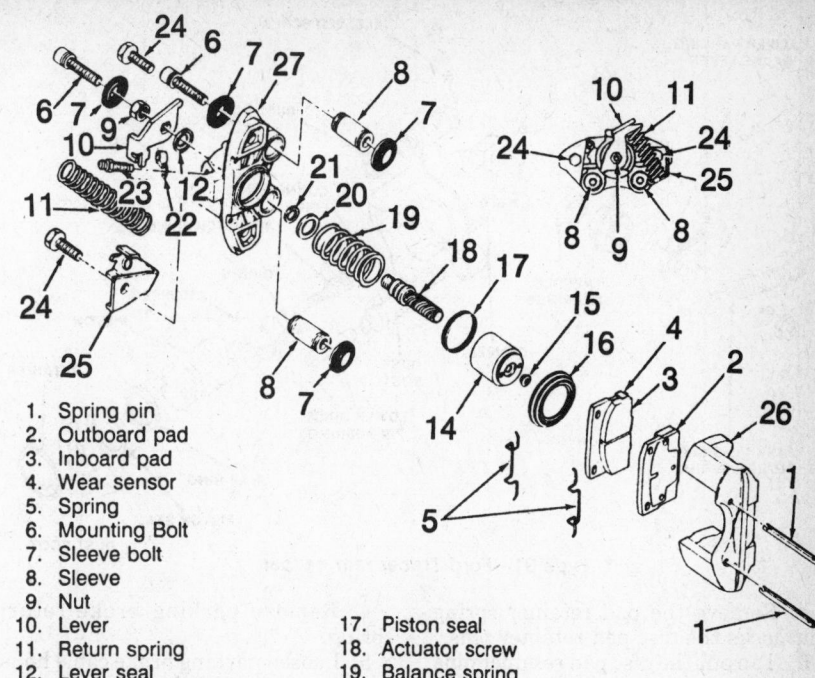

1. Spring pin	
2. Outboard pad	
3. Inboard pad	
4. Wear sensor	
5. Spring	
6. Mounting Bolt	
7. Sleeve bolt	
8. Sleeve	
9. Nut	
10. Lever	17. Piston seal
11. Return spring	18. Actuator screw
12. Lever seal	19. Balance spring
13. Caliper housing	20. Thrust washer
14. Piston assembly	21. Shart seal
15. 2-way check valve	22. Bleeder cap
16. Boot	23. Bleeder valve
	24. Bridge bolt
	25. Bracket
	26. Bridge

Type 29–1988–89 Pontiac Fiero rear caliper

13. Install springs 1 at a time. Hook end of spring under pin with center of spring over shoe flange.

14. Press down on other end of spring and install second pin through caliper and pad far enough to hold spring. Install second spring following the same procedure and finish tapping pin through caliper.

15. Install wheels and tires aligning the previous marks.

16. Torque lug nuts.

17. Lower the vehicle. With engine running pump brake pedal slowly several times to bring the pads in contact with the rotors.

18. Check the brake fluid level and add if necessary.

TYPE 30

Festiva and Tracer Front Disc Brake

PAD REPLACEMENT

1. Remove ⅔ of brake fluid from the master cylinder.

2. Raise the vehicle and support it safely on jack stands.

3. Remove the wheels.

NOTE: Caliper removal is not required to replace the pads.

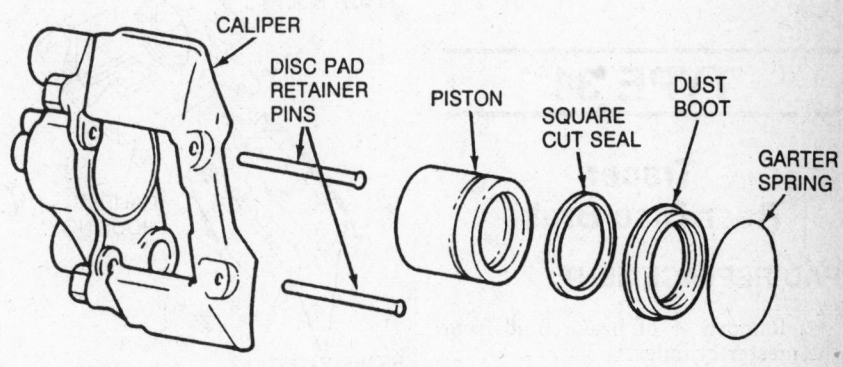

Type 30 – Ford Festiva and Tracer front caliper

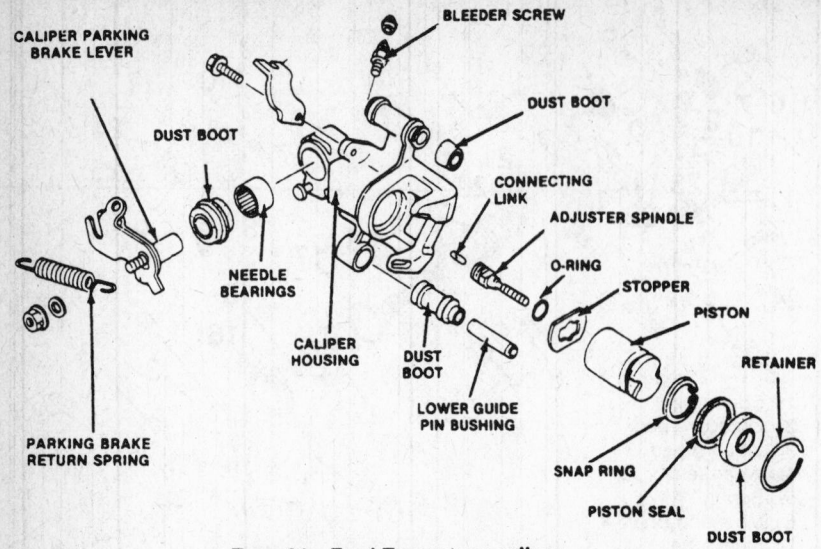

Type 31 – Ford Tracer rear caliper

4. Remove the pad retainer spring that locks the disc pad retainer pins.

5. Tap out the disc pad retainer pins using a hammer and pin punch.

6. Pry the caliper outboard and remove the outboard pad and shim. Mark the shims so they can be installed in thier original position.

7. Push the caliper inboard and remove the inboard pad and shim.

8. Remove the anchor plate clips and label them top and bottom.

To Install:

9. Install anchor plate clips in original locations.

10. Push caliper inboard and Install new inner pad and shim.

11. Pry caliper outboard and Install the outer pad and shim.

12. Install pad retaining pins.

13. Install pin retaining springs.

14. Install the wheels and tires.

15. Torque the lug nuts.

16. Lower the vehicle. Depress the brake pedal repeatedly to bring the brake pads and lingings in contact with the rotor.

17. Check the brake fluid level and add if necessary.

TYPE 31

Tracer
Rear Disc Brake

PAD REPLACEMENT

1. Remove ⅔ of brake fluid from the master cylinder.

2. Raise the vehicle and support it safely on jack stands.

3. Remove the wheels.

4. Remove parking brake return spring.

5. Loosen parking brake cable housing adjusting nut and remove the cable housing from the bracket on thr rear lower control arm.

6. Loosen the bolt connecting the parking brake cable bracket to the rear caliper.

NOTE: Caliper removal is not required to replace the pads.

7. Remove the parking brake cable from the rear caliper.

8. Loosen the lower caliper bolt and pivot the caliper upward.

9. Remove the pad retaining springs.

---

10. Remove the brake pads and shims.

11. Remove the anchor plate clips and label them top and bottom.

To Install:

12. Install anchor plate clips in original locations.

13. Install shims onto the back of the pads and install brake pads.

14. Pivot caliper over rotor and pads. Rotate disc brake piston if necessary.

15. Install lower caliper bolt and torque.

16. Install parking brake cable in the caliper parking brake lever.

17. Position the parking brake bracket against the rear caliper and install the attaching bolt.

18. Install the wheels and tires.

19. Torque the lug nuts.

20. Lower the vehicle. Depress the brake pedal repeatedly to bring the brake pads and lingings in contact with the rotor.

21. Check the brake fluid level and add if necessary.

TYPE 32

Continental (FWD)
and Thunderbird
Rear Disc Brake

PAD REPLACEMENT

1. Remove ⅔ of brake fluid from the master cylinder.

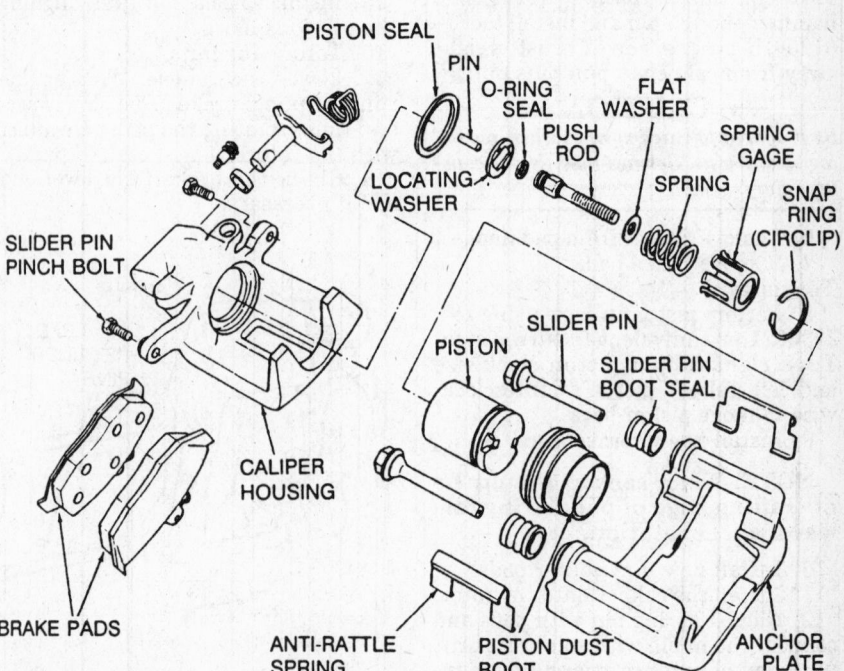

Type 32 – Lincoln Continental(FWD) and Thunderbird Turbo Coupe rear caliper

2. Raise the vehicle and support it safely on jack stands.

3. Remove the wheels.

4. Remove brake hose bracket from shock absorber bracket.

5. Remove retaining clip from parking brake cable at caliper and remove cable from brake lever.

NOTE: Caliper removal is not required to replace the pads.

6. Hold slider pin with open-end wrench and remove upper pinch bolt.

7. Hold slider pin with open-end wrench and loosen, but do not remove lower pinch bolt.

8. Rotate caliper away from rotor.

9. Remove brake pads and anti-rattle clips from anchor plate.

To Install:

10. Using tool T87P-2588-A or equivalent rotote piston clockwise until it is fully seated.

NOTE: Ensure that 1 of the 2 slots in piston face is positioned so it will engage nib on brake pad.

11. Install anti-rattle clips and pads on anchor plate.

12. Pivot caliper over rotor and pads. Rotate disc brake piston if necessary.

13. Apply threadlock or equivalent to pinch bolts.

14. Install pinch bolts and torque.

15. Install parking brake cable in the caliper parking brake lever.

16. Install the wheels and tires.

17. Torque the lug nuts.

18. Lower the vehicle. Depress the brake pedal repeatedly to bring the brake pads and lingings in contact with the rotor.

19. Check the brake fluid level and add if necessary.

TYPE 33

Chrysler Dynasty and New Yorker Rear Disc Brake

PAD REPLACEMENT

1. Remove ⅔ of brake fluid from the master cylinder.

2. Raise the vehicle and support it safely on jack stands.

3. Remove Wheels and tires.

NOTE: Caliper removal is not required to replace the pads or service the rotor.

4. Using a brass drift and hammer and working from the inner side of the

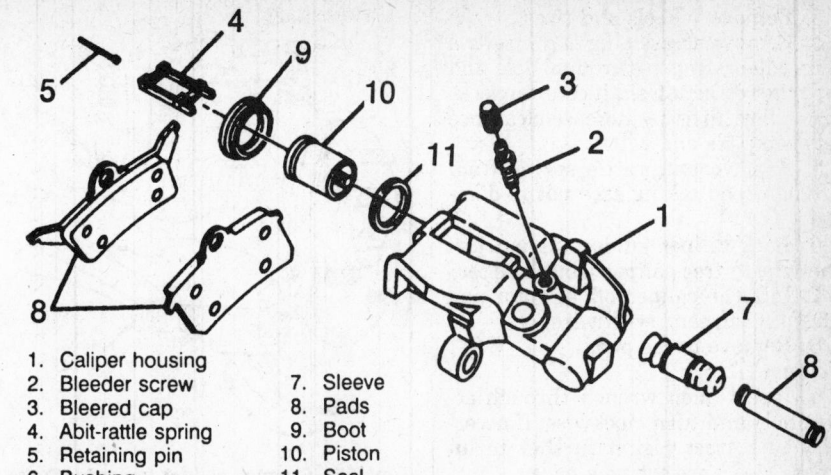

1. Caliper housing
2. Bleeder screw
3. Bleered cap
4. Abit-rattle spring
5. Retaining pin
6. Bushing
7. Sleeve
8. Pads
9. Boot
10. Piston
11. Seal

Type 33—Chrysler Dynasty and New Yorker rear caliper

caliper, drive out the pad and lining retaining pin.

5. Remove the 2 caliper mounting bolts.

6. Lift the caliper off of rotor and carefully suspend with wire to prevent damage to ABS sensor wire, brake hose and parking cable.

7. Remove the brake pads.

To Install:

8. Bottom the caliper piston in the bore.

9. Install new inner/outer pads.

10. Install the anti-rattle clips over pads.

11. Rest caliper on adapter plate and insert anti-rattle clip through opening in the caliper, the lower portion must be placed in position first and then release. The clip should fall into the correct position on the brake pads.

12. Install brake shoe retainer pin through pads and caliper.

13. Push down on upper portion of caliper, align and install upper mounting bolt.

14. Push down on lower portion of caliper, align and install lower mounting bolt.

15. Torque mounting bolts.

16. Install the wheels and tires.

17. Tighten lugs in proper sequence until all nuts are torqued to half specifications. Then repeat to full torque specifications.

18. Lower the vehicle. Depress the brake pedal repeatedly to bring the brake pads in contact with the rotor.

19. Check the brake fluid level and add if necessary.

TYPE 34

Chrysler Except Dynasty & New Yorker Rear Disc Brake

PAD REPLACEMENT

1. Remove ⅔ of brake fluid from the master cylinder.

2. Raise the vehicle and support it safely on jack stands.

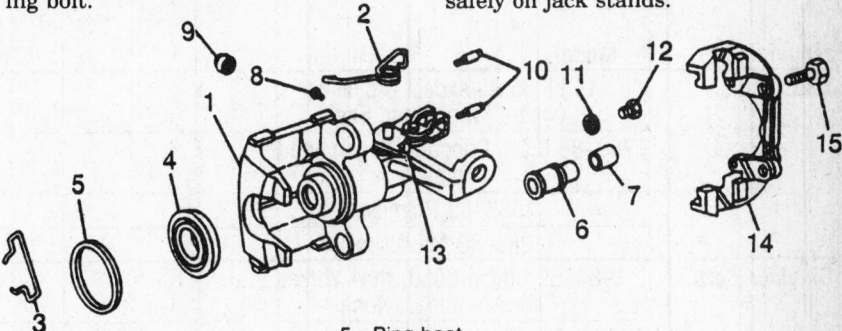

1. Caliper housing
2. Lever return spring
3. Anti-rattle clip
4. Boot
5. Ring boot
6. Busing
7. Sleeve
8. Bleeder screw
9. Bleeder cap
10. Retaining pins
11. Ring seal
12. Adjuster Screw cap
13. Stop roll-pin
14. Adapter
15. Adapter mounting bolt

Type 34—Chrysler TC and Daytona rear caliper

3. Remove Wheels and tires.

4. Remove access plug and insertr a 4mm allen wrench through hole and turn the retraction shaft counterclockwise a few turns ro increase clearance between pads and rotor.

5. Remove anti–rattle spring from outboard pad taking care not to damage it.

6. Back caliper guide pins out just enought to free caliper from adapter.

7. Lift the caliper off of rotor and carefully suspend with wire.

8. Remove brake pads.

To Install:

9. Insert allen wrench through access hole and turn clockwise, if necessary to retract piston further to increase clearance for new pads.

10. Install new inner/outer pads.

NOTE: The outboard pads are marked for right and left hand sides and must be properly installed.

11. Lower caliper over rotor and pads.

12. Install guide pins and tighten to proper torque.

13. Insert allen wrench through the access hole and turn clockwise until snug, (no clearance between pads and rotors) and back off ⅓ turn to obtain proper clearance.

14. Install the wheels and tires.

15. Tighten lugs in proper sequence until all nuts are torqued to half specifications. Then repeat to full torque specifications.

16. Lower the vehicle. Depress the brake pedal repeatedly to bring the brake pads in contact with the rotor.

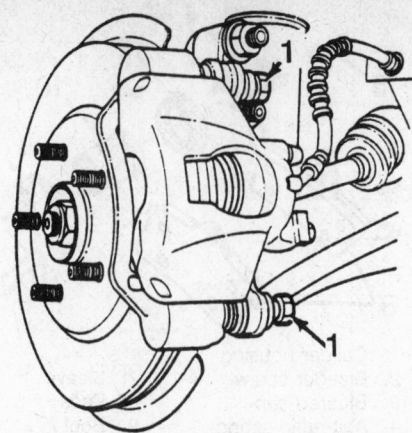

Type 35 – Premier caliper mounting bolts

17. Check the brake fluid level and add if necessary.

TYPE 35

AMC/Eagle: Premier & Medallion Front Disc Brake

PAD REPLACEMENT

1. Remove ⅔ of brake fluid from the master cylinder.

2. Raise the vehicle and support it safely on jack stands.

3. Remove wheels and tires.

4. Force piston back into the bore to allow clearance between pads and rotor.

5. On the Medallion remove just the lower caliper bolt using T40 torx head tool, on the Premier remove both caliper bolts.

6. On the Medallion rotate caliper up on the upper bolt to clear the rotor, on the Premier lift the caliper off of rotor and carefully suspend with wire.

7. Remove brake pads.

NOTE: Rotors must not be resurfaced, if rotor does not meet specifications it must be replaced.

To Install:

8. Press piston back into bore using piston installer or equivalent tool.

9. Install new inner/outer pads and anit–rattle clips.

NOTE: The anti–rattle clips must be located at the bottom of each disc brake pad. Caliper bolts should be lubricated before installing them.

10. Install caliper over rotor and pads.

11. Install caliper bolts and tighten to proper torque.

12. Install the wheels and tires.

13. Tighten lugs to proper torque specifications.

14. Lower the vehicle. Depress the brake pedal repeatedly to bring the brake pads in contact with the rotor.

15. Check the brake fluid level and add if necessary.

DRUM BRAKE SPECIFICATIONS

Manufacturer	Model		Brake Shoe Minimum Lining Thickness	Brake Drum Diameter Standard Size	Brake Drum Diameter Machine To	Wheel Lugs or Nuts Torque (ft. lbs.)
AMC-Eagle	1982–85 All except 6 cylinder Concord Wagon and Eagle		.030	9.000	9.060	75
	1982–88 6 cyl. Concord Wagon and Eagle		.030	10.000	10.060	75
	1988–89 Premier		.132	8.858	8.917	63
	1988–89 Medallion		.098	9.000	9.030	67
Chrysler Corp.	1984–89 Dodge 6000, New Yorker, Caravelle and Daytona		.030	8.861	8.920	95
	1982–88 LeBaron, Dodge 400, Horizon & Omni, 1982–83 Daytona and Lancer and 1982–86 Laser		.030	7.870	7.900	95
	1988–89 Dynasty, New Yorker, Aries,	Std.	.030	7.870	7.90	95
	Reliant, LeBaron & TC	H.D.	.030	8.861	8.920	95
	1982–85 Aries, Reliant		.030	7.870	7.900	85

DRUM BRAKE SPECIFICATIONS

Manufacturer	Model		Brake Shoe Minimum Lining Thickness	Brake Drum Diameter Standard Size	Brake Drum Diameter Machine To	Wheel Lugs or Nuts Torque (ft. lbs.)
Chrysler Corp.	1982–89 Caravelle, Cordoba, Diplomat,	w/10″ rear brakes	.030	10.000	10.060	85
	Gran Fury, Imperial, LeBaron, Mirada, New Yorker & Newport	w/11″ rear brakes	.030	11.000	11.060	85
	1986–89 Shadow & Sundance		①	7.835	7.935	95
Ford Motor Co.	1982–86 Thunderbird, Cougar	w/9″ rear brakes	.030	9.000	9.060	80-105
	and Mustang	w/10″ rear brake	.030	10.000	10.060	80-105
	1982–83 Granada	w/9″ rear brake	.030	9.000	9.060	80-105
		w/10″ rear brake	.030	10.000	10.060	80-105
	1982–88 Escort, Tempo & Topaz	w/7″ rear brake	.030	7.000	7.060	80-105
	and 1987 Lynx	w/8″ rear brake	.030	8.000	8.060	80-105
	1982–86 Capri & Fairmont and	w/9″ rear brake	.030	9.000	9.060	80-105
	1982–83 Zephyr	w/10″ rear brake	.030	10.000	10.060	80-105
	1982–89 Lincoln LTD, Mark VI,	w/10″ rear brake	.030	10.000	10.060	80-105
	Mark VII, Marquis & Town Car	w/11″ rear brake	.030	11.000	11.060	80-105
	1986–87 Taurus & Sable	Sedan, rear	①	8.850	8.909	80-105
		Wagon, rear	①	9.840	9.899	80-105
	1988–89 Taurus & Sable	Sedan	.030	8.858	8.918	80-105
		Wagon	.030	9.842	9.902	80-105
	1988–89 Tracer		.040	7.870	8.910	65-87
	1988–89 Festiva		.040	6.690	6.750	65-87
	1987–89 Cougar, Mustang and Thunderbird		.030	9.000	9.060	70-115
General Motors Buick	1982–89 Century & Skyhawk		①	7.880	7.899	100
	1982–88 LeSabre & Regal		①	9.500	9.560	80③
	1982–85 Riviera		①	9.500	9.560	100
	1982–84 Electra & Estate Wagon		①	11.000	11.060	100
	1982–87 Skylark & Regal (FWD)		①	7.880	7.899	103
	1982–89 Century, Electra & LeSabre		①	8.858	8.880	100
Cadillac	1982–89 Cimarron		.030	7.880	7.899	100
	1982–89 Fleetwood		.030	11.000	11.060	100
	1982–87 Fleetwood Limo, Com. Chassis			12.000	12.060	100
Chevrolet	1982–89 Celebrity, Cavalier		①	7.880	7.899	100
	1982–89 Camaro		①	9.500	9.560	80
	1986–89 Sprint		.110	7.090	—	29–50
	1986–89 Spectrum		.039	7.090	—	65
	1985–89 Nova		.039	7.913	—	76
	1982–89 Malibu and 1982–83 Monte Carlo		①	9.500	9.560	80
	1982–85 Citation		①	7.880	7.889	103
	1982–89 Impala & Caprice	w/9½″ rear brake	①	9.500	9.560	80
		w/11″ rear brake	①	11.000	11.060	100
	1982–87 Chevette		①	7.874	7.899	70
	1987–89 Beretta & Corsica		①	7.870	7.895	100
Oldsmobile	1982–89 Calais & Firenza		①	7.880	7.899	100
	1982–89 Cutlass Supreme & 88		①	9.500	9.560	100⑤
	1982–84 Omega		①	7.880	7.899	103
	1982–88 Toronado		①	9.500	9.560	100

DRUM BRAKE SPECIFICATIONS

Manufacturer	Model		Brake Shoe Minimum Lining Thickness	Brake Drum Diameter Standard Size	Brake Drum Diameter Machine To	Wheel Lugs or Nuts Torque (ft. lbs.)
Oldsmobile	1982–88 Custom Cruiser,	w/9.5″ rear brake	①	9.500	9.560	100
	88 (w/403) & 98	w/11″ rear brake	①	11.000	11.060	100
	1983–89 Cutlass Ciera		①	8.858	8.880	100
	1988–89 Delta 88		①	8.860	8.880	100
Pontiac	1982–89 A6000, J2000		①	7.880	7.899	100
	1982–88 Firebird	w/rear drum brake	①	9.500	9.560	80④
	1982–87 T1000 & 1000		①	7.874	7.899	70
	1982–84 Phoenix (FWD)		–	7.880	7.899	103
	1982–84 Bonneville, Catalina,	w/9.5″ rear brake	①	9.500	9.560	–
	Grand Am, Grand Prix & LeMans	w/11″ rear brake	①	11.000	11.060	80②
	1988–89 LeMans Daewoo		①	7.870	7.900	65
	1988–89 Grand Am		①	7.880	7.899	100
	1987–89 Bonneville		①	8.860	8.880	100

① .030 in. over rivet head, if bonded lining use .062 in.
② With ½ in. stud 100 ft. lbs.
③ With Aluminum wheels
LeSabre – 90 ft. lbs.
Regal – 100 ft. lbs.

④ Aluminum wheels
Corvette – 80
Camaro – 105
Others – 90
⑤ 88 with $7/16$ in. stud; 80 ft/lbs.

DRUM BRAKES

── CAUTION ──

The asbestos dust thrown off from the brake linings or disc pads may be dangerous to your health if inhaled. Never use compressed air or your own breath to blow the dust from the brake assembly. Use an aerosol brake cleaner, damp rag or a vacuum cleaner with an approved asbestos filter. Dispose of the rag or cleaner bag properly. Do not move a vehicle until a firm brake pedal is obtained.

Brake Drums
BRAKE DRUM TYPES

The FULL-CAST drum has a cast iron web (back) of $3/16$–$1/4$ in. thickness (passenger vehicle sizes) whereas the COMPOSITE drum has a steel web approximately ⅛ in. thick. These 2 types of drums, with few exceptions are not interchangeable.

BRAKE DRUM DEPTH

Rest a straight edge across the drum diameter on the open side. The actual drum depth then is the measurement at a right angle from the straight edge to that part of the web which mates against the hub mounting flange.

LOOK HERE FOR TURNED DRUM TOOL MARK RIDGE

0.60″

Oversize drum

ALUMINUM DRUMS

When replaced by other types, aluminum drums must be replaced in pairs.

METALLIC BRAKES

Drums designed for use with standard brake linings should not be used with metallic brakes.

REMOVING TIGHT DRUMS

Difficulty removing a brake drum can be caused by shoes which are expanded beyond the drum's inner diameter or shoes which have cut into and ridged the drum. In either case back off the adjuster to obtain sufficient clearance for removal.

BRAKE DRUM INSPECTION

The condition of the brake drum surface is just as important as the surface to the brake lining. All drum surfaces should be clean, smooth, free from hard spots, heat checks, score marks and foreign matter imbedded in the drum surface. They should not be out of round, bell-mouthed or barrel shaped. It is recommended that all drums be first checked with a drum micrometer to see if they are within oversize limits. If the drum is within safe limits, even though the surface appears smooth, it should be turned not only to assure a true drum surface but also to remove any possible contamination in the surface from previ-

DRUM

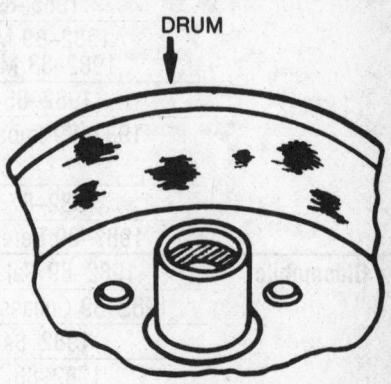

Hard or Chill Spots

ous brake linings, road dusts, etc. Too much metal removed from a drum is unsafe and may result in:

1. Brake fade due to the thin drum being unable to absorb the heat generated.

2. Poor and erratic brake due to distortion of drums.

3. Noise due to possible vibration caused by thin drums.

4. A cracked or broken drum on a severe or very hard brake application.

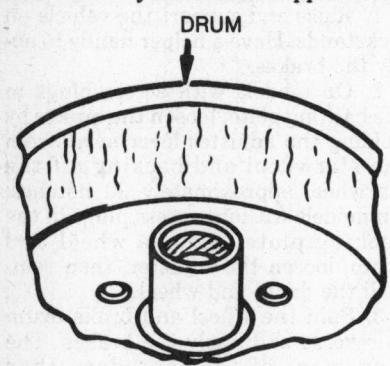

Heat checks

Sanding brake drums

NOTE: Brake drum run-out should not exceed 0.005 in. Drums turned to more than 0.060 in. oversize are unsafe and should be replaced with new drums, except for some heavy ribbed drums which have an 0.080 in. limit. It is recommended that the diameters of the left and right drums on every axle be within 0.010 in. of each other. In order to avoid erratic brake action when replacing drums, it is always good to replace the drums on both wheels at the same time. If the drums are true, smooth up any slight scores by polishing with fine emery cloth. If deep scores or grooves are present, which cannot be removed by this method, then the drum must be turned.

Duo-Servo Brakes

In the Duo-Servo design, the force which the wheel cylinder applies to the shoes is supplemented by the tendency

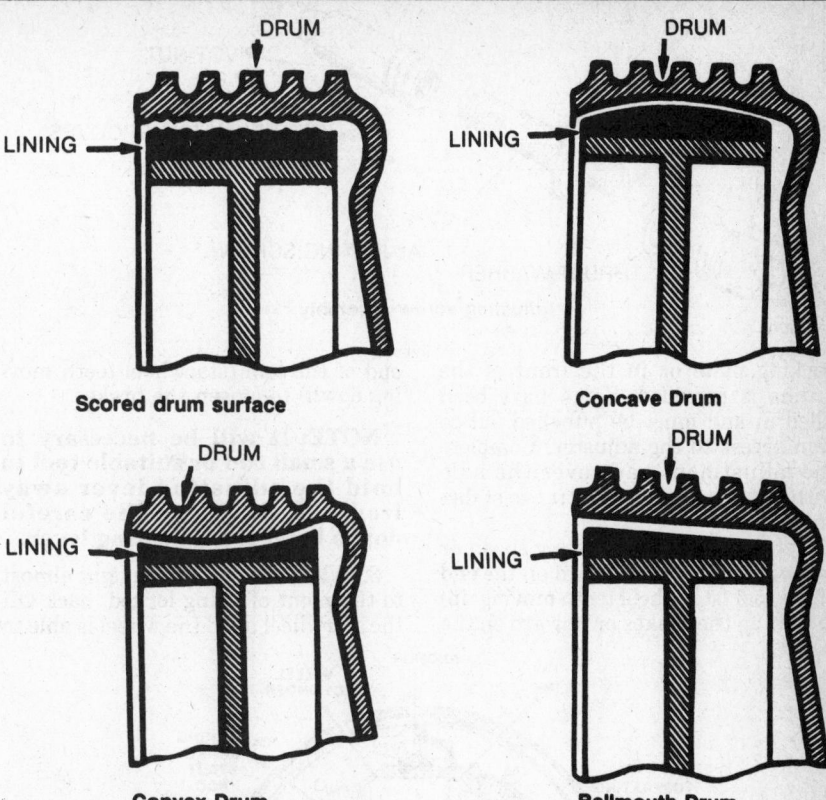

Scored drum surface

Concave Drum

Convex Drum

Bellmouth Drum

of the shoes to wrap or twist into the drum during braking. Thus 2 braking forces are applied at each drum every time the brakes are activated.

ADJUSTMENT

The duo-servo brake, with star and screw type self-adjusters, is used on most late model American vehicles. The same basic brake unit has been used on all vehicles. General Motors vehicles use a rod-operated lever to turn the star-wheel, while all others use a cable-operated lever. This is the only difference, other than size, among units used on different models. The drum brakes, used on today's vehicles, are usually self-adjusting. They require manual adjustment only when

the shoes have been replaced or when the star and screw adjuster has been disturbed.

NOTE: The drum brakes on most vehicles can be initially adjusted by removing the brake drum, measuring its internal diameter, then adjusting the shoes to that measurement and installing the drum. Use a vernier gauge to make the measurements. This method can be used on all models and may be preferable to punching out the covering over the access hole in the backing plate or brake drum edge.

1. Remove the access slot plug from the backing plate or front of drum. On some vehicles no access slot in the

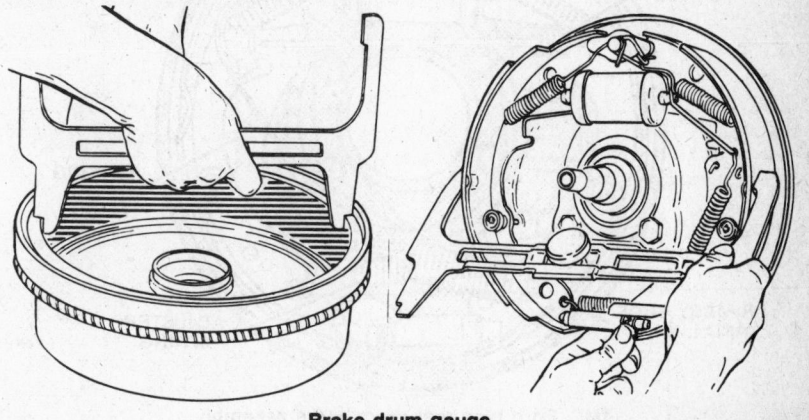

Brake drum gauge

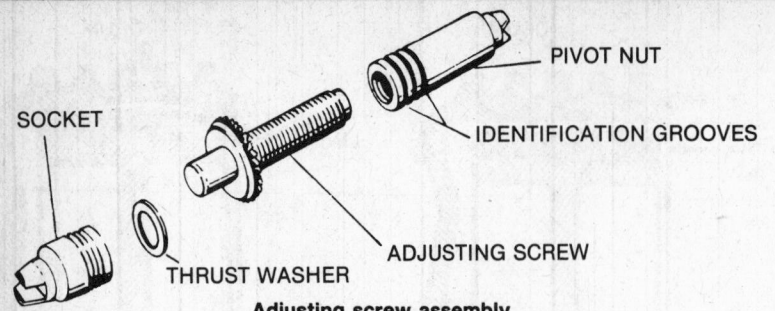

Adjusting screw assembly

backing plate or in the front of the drums is provided. Some have been filled in and must be punched out to gain access to the adjuster. Complete the adjustment and cover the hole with a plug to prevent entrance of dirt and water.

2. Using a brake adjusting spoon or screwdriver, pry downward on the end of the tool (starwheel teeth moving up) to tighten the brakes or upward on the end of the tool (starwheel teeth moving down) to loosen the brakes.

NOTE: It will be necessary to use a small rod or suitable tool to hold the adjusting lever away from the starwheel. Be careful not to bend the adjusting lever.

3. When the brakes are tight almost to the point of being locked, back Off the starwheel until the wheel is able to

rotate freely. The starwheel on each set of brakes (front or rear) must be backed off the same number of turns to prevent brake pull from side-to-side.

4. After adjustment, check brake pedal travel and then make several stops, while backing the vehicle up, to equalize both wheel systems.

TESTING ADJUSTER

1. Raise and support the vehicle on jackstands. Have a helper handy to apply the brakes.

2. On models with access plugs in the backing plate, loosen the brakes by holding the adjuster lever away from the starwheel and backing off the starwheel approximately 30 notches. On models without access plugs in the backing plate, remove wheel and drum, loosen the adjuster, then reinstall the drum and wheel.

3. Spin the wheel and brake drum in reverse and apply the brakes. The movement of the secondary shoe should pull the adjuster lever up and when the brakes are released the lever should snap down and turn the starwheel.

4. If the automatic adjuster doesn't work, the drum must be removed and the adjuster components inspected carefully for breakage, wear or improper installation.

BRAKE SHOE REMOVAL

NOTE: If you are not thoroughly familiar with the procedures involved in brake replacement, disassemble and assemble a side at a time, leaving the other wheel intact, as a reference.

1. Remove the brake drum.

2. Place the hollow end of a brake spring service tool on the brake shoe anchor pin and twist it to disengage 1 of the brake shoe return springs. Repeat this operation to remove the other return spring.

——— CAUTION ———

Be careful that the springs do not slip off the tool during removal, as the spring could break loose and cause personal injury.

3. Reach behind the brake backing plate and place a finger on the end of 1 of the brake hold-down mounting pins. Using a pair of pliers or special brake pin retainer tool, grasp the washer on the top of the hold-down spring that corresponds to the pin that you are holding. Push down on the pliers and turn them 90° to align the slot in the washer with the head on the spring mounting pin. Remove the spring and washer, then repeat this operation on

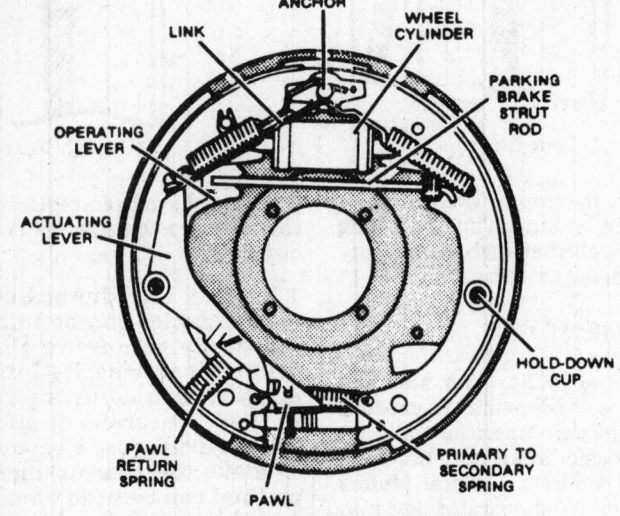

GM type rear drum brake assembly

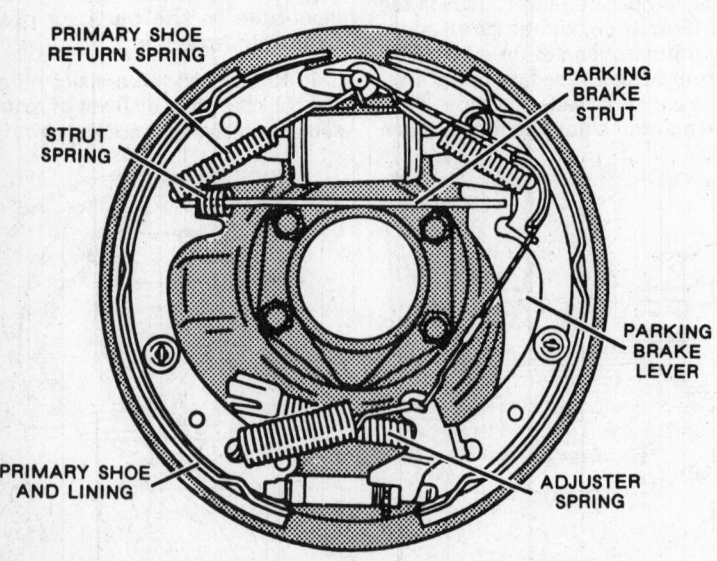

AMC, Ford type rear drum brake assembly

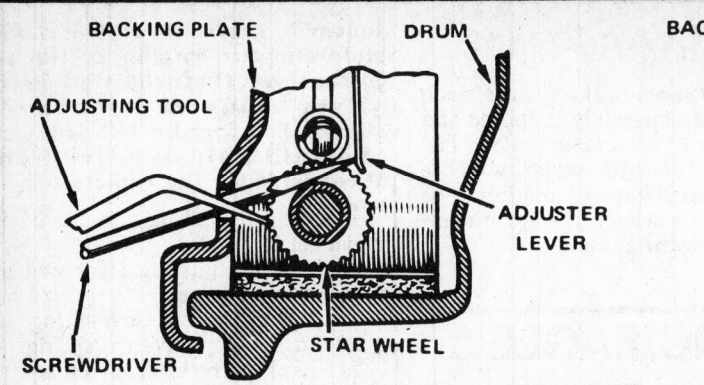

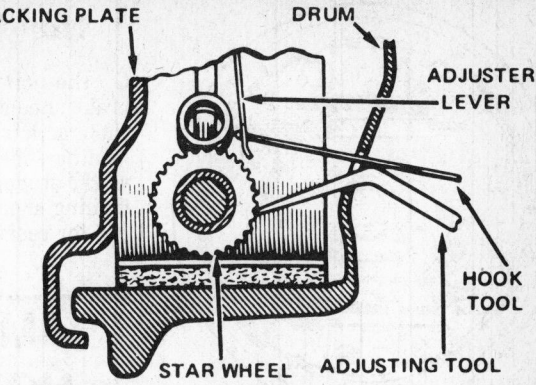

All cars except Chrysler and GM "H" body (Chevette)

Chrysler type

the hold-down spring of the other brake shoe.

4. Step 4 varies according to the manufacturer: On Ford and American Motors vehicles, place the tip of a screwdriver on the top of the brake adjusting screw and move the screwdriver upward to lift up on the brake adjusting lever. When there is enough slack in the automatic adjuster cable, disconnect the loop on the top of the cable from the anchor. Back off the adjusting screw while holding the adjustment lever away from the screw. Grasp the top of each brake shoe and move them outward to disengage from the wheel cylinder and parking brake link. When the brake shoes are clear, lift them from the backing plate. Twist the shoes slightly and the automatic adjuster assembly will disassemble itself.

5. On GM vehicles, remove the automatic adjuster link. Remove the automatic adjuster lever, the pivot and the override spring from the secondary spring as an assembly. Move the top of each brake shoe outward to clear the wheel cylinder pins and the parking brake link. Lift the brakes from the backing plate and remove the adjusting screw.

6. On Chrysler vehicles, (except some front wheel drive models), slide

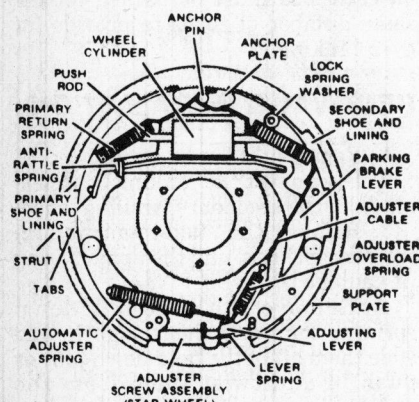

Chrysler type rear drum brake assembly

the automatic adjuster cable from the anchor pin and disengage it from the adjusting leer. Remove the cable, the overload spring and the cable guide. Disconnect the automatic adjuster lever return spring, then remove the spring and lever. Move the top of the brake shoes outward to clear the wheel cylinder pins and the parking brake link. Lift the brakes from the backing plate and remove the adjusting screw.

7. Grasp the end of the brake cable spring with a pair of pliers and, using the brake lever as a fulcrum, pull the end of the spring away from the lever. Disengage the cable from the brake lever.

BRAKE SHOE INSTALLATION

8. The brake cable must be connected to the secondary brake shoe before the shoe is installed on the backing plate. To do this, transfer the parking brake lever from the old secondary shoe to the new one. This is accomplished by spreading the bottom of the horseshoe clip and disengaging the lever. Position the lever on the new secondary shoe, then install the spring washer and the horseshoe clip. Close the bottom of the clip after installing it. Grasp the metal tip of the parking brake cable with a pair of pliers. Position a pair of side cutters on the end of the cable coil spring and using the pliers as a fulcrum, pull the coil spring back with the side cutters. Position the cable in the parking brake lever.

9. Apply a light coating of high temperature grease to the brake shoe contact points on the backing plate. Position the primary brake shoe on the front of the backing plate, then install the hold-down spring and washer over the mounting pin. Install the secondary shoe on the rear of the backing plate.

10. If working on rear brakes, install the parking brake link between the primary brake shoe and the secondary brake shoe.

11. Step 4 varies according to the manufacturer.

12. On Ford and American Motors vehicles, install the automatic adjuster cable loop end on the anchor pin. Make sure that the crimped side of the loop faces the backing plate.

13. On GM vehicles, assemble the automatic adjuster lever, the pivot and the override spring, then install to the secondary springs as an assembly.

14. On Chrysler, (except some front wheel drive models) install the automatic adjuster lever and the return spring. Install the adjuster overload spring and cable. The end of the cable engages with the adjusting lever while the other slips over the anchor pin underneath the primary and secondary return springs.

15. Install the return spring in the primary brake shoe and using the tapered end of a brake spring service tool, slide the top of the spring onto the anchor pin.

CAUTION

Be careful to make sure that the spring does not slip off the tool during installation, as the spring could break loose and cause personal injury.

16. Install the automatic adjuster cable guide in the secondary brake shoe, making sure that the flared hole in the cable guide is inside the hole in the brake shoe. Fit the cable into the groove in the top of the cable guide.

17. Install the secondary shoe return return spring through the hole in the cable guide and the brake shoe. Using the brake spring tool, slide the top of the spring onto the anchor pin.

18. Clean the threads on the adjusting screw and apply a light coating of high-temperature grease to the threads. Screw the adjuster closed, then open it ½ turn.

19. Install the adjusting screw between the brake shoes with the star wheel nearest to the secondary shoe. Make sure that the star wheel is in a position that is accessible from the adjusting slot in the backing plate.

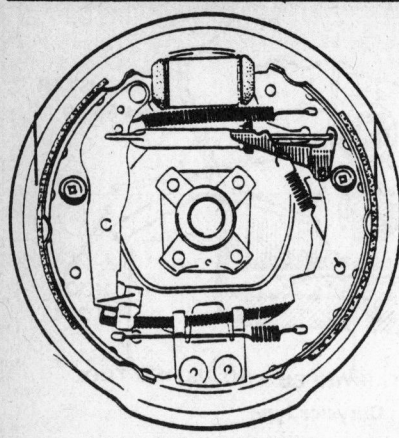

AMC/Eagle Medallion

20. Install the short, hooked end of the automatic adjuster spring in the proper hole in the primary brake shoe.

21. Connect the hooked end of the automatic adjuster cable and the free end of the automatic adjuster spring in the slot in the top of the automatic adjuster lever.

22. Pull the automatic adjuster lever (the lever will pull the cable and spring with it) downward and to the left and engage the pivot hook of the lever in the hole in the secondary brake shoe.

23. Check the entire brake assembly to make sure everything is installed properly. Make sure that the shoes engage the wheel cylinder properly and are flush on the anchor pin. Make sure that the automatic adjuster cable is flush on the anchor pin and in the slot on the block of cable guide. Make sure that the adjusting lever rests on the adjusting screw star wheel. Pull upward on the adjusting cable until the adjusting lever is free of the star wheel, then release the cable. The adjusting lever should snap back into place on the adjusting screw star wheel and turn the wheel 1 tooth.

24. Expand the brake adjusting screw until the brake drum will just fit over the brake shoes. Install the wheel and drum and adjust the brakes.

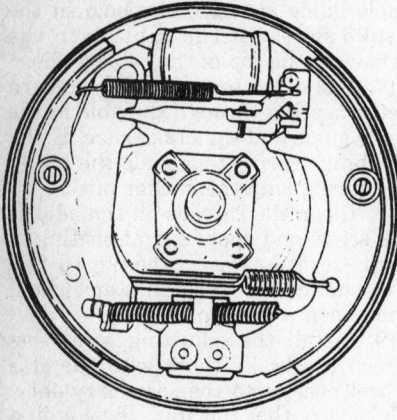

AMC/Eagle Premier

Non-Servo Brakes

On the non-servo brake system, each brake shoe is separately anchored and their action is not compounded. The leading shoe does the majority of the work, stopping forward motion. The trailing shoe works in the same manner for rearward motion.

AMC/EAGLE NON-SERVO BRAKES

REMOVAL & INSTALLATION

1. Remove the brake drum.

NOTE: The brake components are different for right and left sides, so it is important not to interchange them.

2. Remove upper return spring.
3. Remove lower return spring.
4. Remove adjuster lever spring and adjuster lever.
5. Remove parking brake cable from lever.
6. Remove the shoe holddown springs; compress them slightly and slide them off of the hold-down pins or push in and twist them from the mount pin.
7. Remove the adjuster screw assembly by spreading the shoes apart.
8. Remove brake shoes.
9. Remove parking brake lever from rear brake shoe if not included with new shoes.

To Install:

10. Inspect the brakes.
11. Lubricate the shoe contact areas on the brake backing plate and the web end of the brake shoe which contacts the anchor plate. Use a brake component lubricant or a high temperature brake grease made for the purpose. Lightly lubricate the self–adjusters threads.
12. If the hub was removed; clean, check and repack the rear wheel bearings. Make sure to properly torque the axle nut when reinstalling the hub, if removed.
13. Install old parking brake lever on trailing shoe if not included with new brake shoes.
14. Install trailing shoe and hold down spring.
15. Install parking brake cable onto the parking brake lever.
16. Install adjuster screw.

NOTE: On Premier be sure the larger of the 2 notches on the adjuster is installed to the brake shoe and the smaller to the adjuster lever. On the Medallion the silver adjuster (righthand threads) is for the left side and the gold adjuster (lefthand threads) is for the right side.

17. Install leading shoe and hold down spring.
18. Install adjusting lever and adjusting lever spring.
19. Install lower return spring.
20. Install upper return spring.
21. Replace the brake drum and retaining nuts/screws, if the hub was removed properly torque the axle nut.
22. Install wheels and tires, properly torque lug nuts.
23. Adjust brakes. On Medallion, press down on brake pedal several time to center and adjust brakes. On Premier, using adjusting tool through access hole rotate screw until drum has a heavy drag, then using small screwdriver through access hole push adjuster lever away from star and back off 1 full turn.

CHRYSLER NON-SERVO BRAKES

The rear brakes on the 1982 models are manually adjusted; the 1983-89 models are equipped with self-adjusters.

1. Remove the access slot plug from the upper part of the backing plate.
2. Using a thin brake adjusting spoon pry downward (left-side) or upward (right-side) on the end of the tool (starwheel teeth moving up) to tighten the brakes. The opposite applies to loosen the brakes.
3. When the brakes are tight almost to the point of being locked, back off on the starwheel 10 clicks. The starwheel on each side must be backed off the same number of turns to provide for even braking.

REMOVAL & INSTALLATION

1. Remove the brake drum.
2. Disconnect the parking brake cable from the secondary (trailing) shoe.
3. Remove the shoe-to-anchor retracting spring(s) and the upper spring (if equipped).
4. Remove the shoe holddown springs; compress them slightly and slide them off of the hold-down pins or push in and twist them from the mount pin.
5. Remove the adjuster screw assembly by spreading the shoes apart.

Disconnect the adjuster spring from the trailing shoes on self-adjuster models. The adjuster nut must be fully backed off.

6. Raise the parking brake lever. Pull the secondary (trailing) shoe away from the backing plate so pull-back spring tension is released.

7. Remove the secondary (trailing) shoe and disengage the spring end from the backing plate.

8. Raise the primary (leading) shoe to release spring tension. Remove the shoe and disengage the spring end from the backing plate.

To Install:

9. Inspect the brakes.

10. Lubricate the 6 shoe contact areas on the brake backing plate and the web end of the brake shoe which contacts the anchor plate. Use a multi-purpose lubricant or a high temperature brake grease made for the purpose.

11. Chrysler recommends that the rear wheel bearings be cleaned and re-packed whenever the brakes are re-newed. Be sure to install a new bearing seal.

12. With the leading shoe return spring in position on the shoe, install the shoe at the same time as you engage the return spring in the end support.

13. Position the end of the shoe under the anchor.

14. With the trailing shoe return spring in position, install the shoe at the same time as you engage the spring in the support (backing plate).

15. Position the end of the shoe under the anchor.

16. Spread the shoes and install the adjuster screw assembly making sure that the forked end that enters the shoe is curved down.

INSTALLATION PROCEDURE

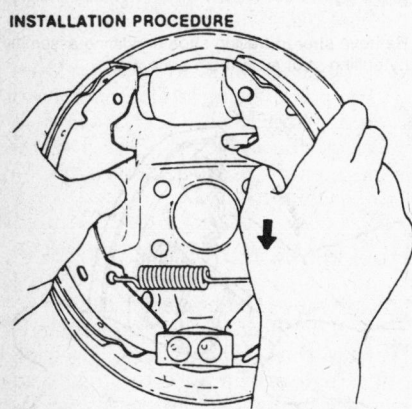

STEP 1

a. Assemble parking brake cable to trailing shoe and parking brake lever.

b. Install lower retracting spring to leading-trailing shoes.

c. Install this assembly to backing plate.

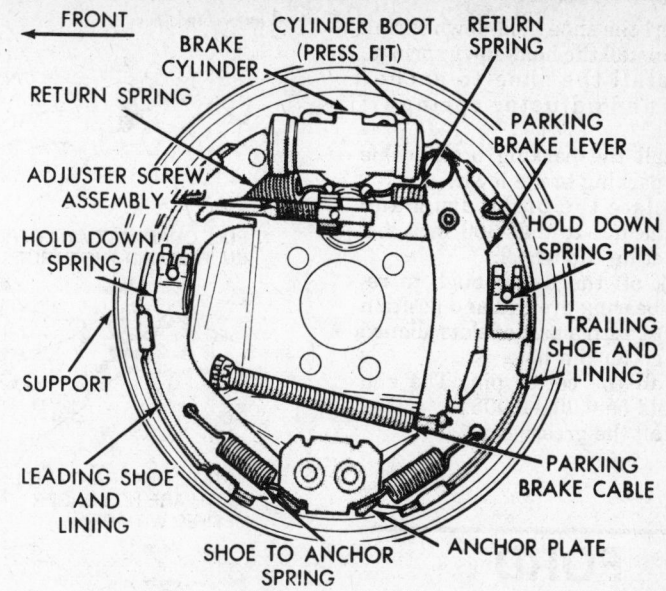

Chrysler non-servo rear brakes (non-self- adjusting)

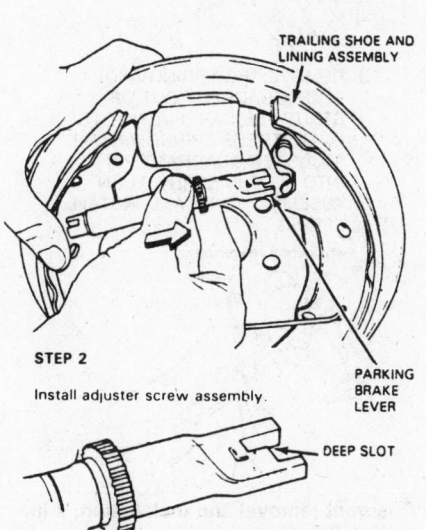

STEP 2

Install adjuster screw assembly.

NOTE: Socket Blade marked R and L. Install letter in upright position to insure proper slot engagement to parking brake lever.

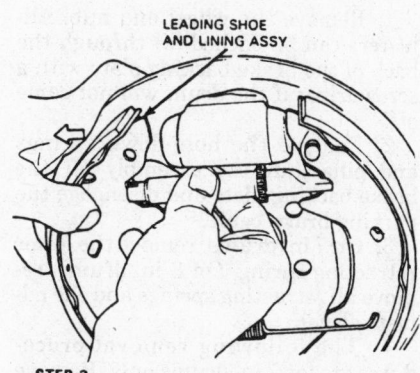

STEP 3

Install adjuster screw to leading shoe and lining assembly.

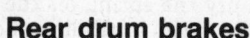

Rear drum brakes

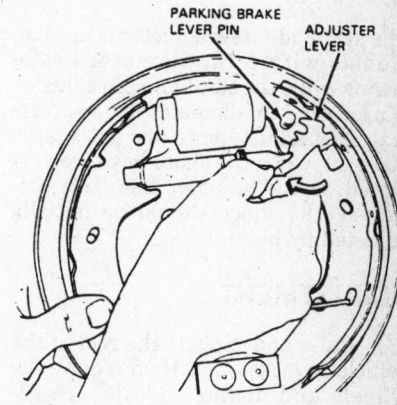

STEP 4

Install the adjuster lever in groove of parking brake lever pin.

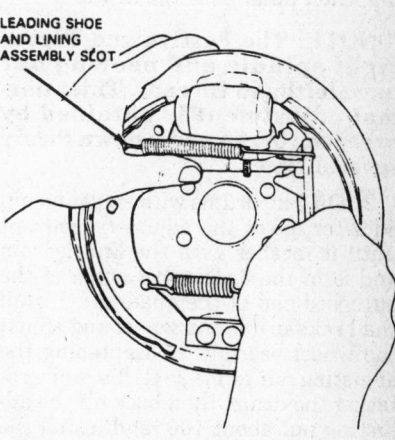

STEP 5

a. Install shoe holddown springs and pins.

b. Install upper retracting spring to leading shoe slot — stretch spring to install to trailing shoe. If adjuster lever does not contact star wheel after spring installation check adjuster socket installation.

17. Insert the shoe hold-down spring pins and install the hold-down springs.

18. Install the shoe-to-anchor springs and adjuster spring (if equipped).

19. Install the parking brake cable onto the parking brake lever.

20. Replace the brake drum and tighten the nut to 240–300 inch lbs. while rotating the wheel.

21. Back off the nut enough to release the bearing preload and position the locknut with a pair of slots aligned with the cotter pin hole.

22. Install the cotter pin. The end play should be 0.001–0.003 in.

23. Install the grease cap.

FORD NON-SERVO

The star and screw adjuster is used on models with 8 in. diameter brake drums while the strut and pin adjuster is used on 7 in. diameter drums. Normal shoe adjustments are automatic, however, when the shoes have been replaced or the adjuster has been disturbed, the shoes should be initially adjusted by hand.

ADJUSTMENT

1. Raise and support the rear of the vehicle on jackstands, then remove the wheels and drums. Drums are removed by releasing the parking brake, removing the dust cap, the cotter pin, the adjusting nut and the wheel bearing, then pulling off the drum.

NOTE: The Festiva and Tracer right spindle and bearing nut have lefthand threads. Thier normal adjustment is obtained by press the brake pedal down firmly several times.

2. On 7 in. drums with strut and pin adjuster, pivot the adjuster quadrant until it meshes with the knurled pin and is in the 3rd or 4th notch of the outboard end of the quadrant. Install the brake drum and wheel and adjust the wheel bearings by tightening the adjusting nut to 17–25 ft. lbs. while rotating the drum, then back off the adjusting nut about 100° and install the nut retainer and cotter pin.

3. The 8 in. drums are adjusted in the same manner as the star and screw adjuster drums described under "Duo-Servo" brakes, above. See that section for procedure.

4. Complete adjustment by applying the brakes several times.

REMOVAL PROCEDURE

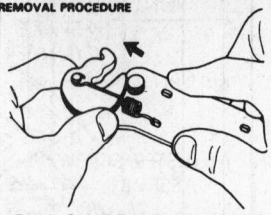

1. PULL QUADRANT AWAY FROM KNURLED PIN THE STRUT

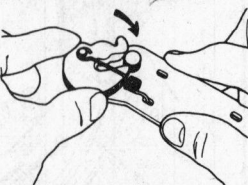

2. ROTATE QUADRANT UNTIL TEETH ARE NO LONGER MESHED WITH PIN.

3. REMOVE THE SPRING AND SLIDE QUADRANT OUT OF STRUT—BE CAREFUL NOT TO OVERSTRESS SPRING. INSTALL ADJUSTER QUADRANT PIN INTO SLOT IN STRUT. TURN ASSEMBLY OVER AND INSTALL SPRING

INSTALLATION PROCEDURE

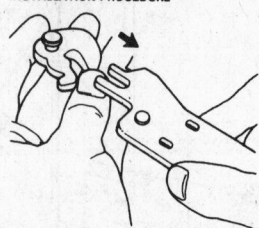

Quadrant removal and installation; 7 in. Ford non-servo brakes

REMOVAL & INSTALLATION

Except Tracer and Festiva

1. Remove the wheel and hub. Adjusters can be backed off through the back of the brake backing plate with a screwdriver if the drum will not come off.

2. Remove the hold-down springs and pins. Lift the assembly off the brake backing plate and disengage the parking brake cable.

3. On 7 in. drums, remove the lower retracting spring. On 8 in. drums, remove all retracting springs and the adjuster lever.

4. The following removal procedures are for 7 in. drums only. Remove the leading shoe retracting spring by rotating shoe to release spring tension. DO NOT pry the spring off the shoe. Remove the strut to trailing shoe as-

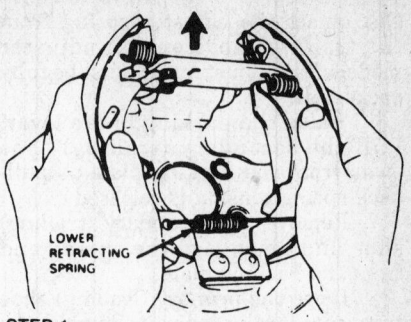

LOWER RETRACTING SPRING

STEP 1
a. Remove holddown springs and pins.
b. Lift assembly off backing plate.
c. Disengage parking brake cable.
d. Remove lower retracting spring.

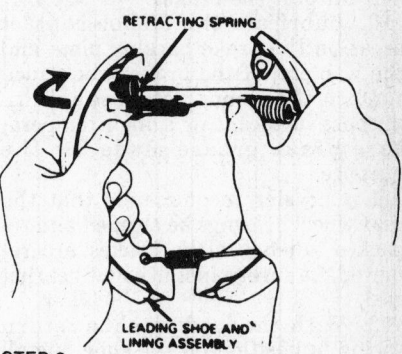

RETRACTING SPRING

LEADING SHOE AND LINING ASSEMBLY

STEP 2
Remove leading shoe retracting spring by rotating shoe as shown to release spring tension. Do not pry spring off shoe.

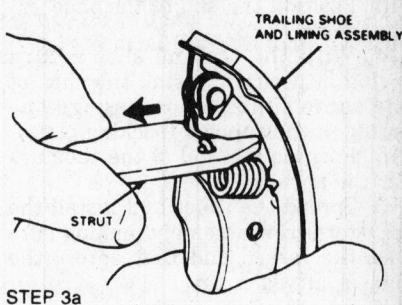

TRAILING SHOE AND LINING ASSEMBLY

STRUT

STEP 3a

Remove strut to trailing shoe and lining assembly by pulling strut away from shoe and . . .

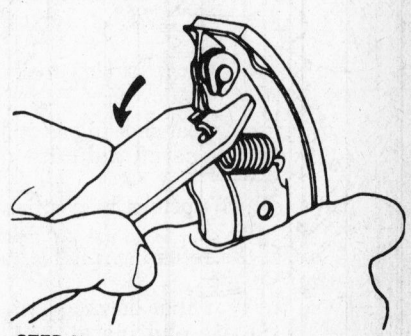

STEP 3b . . . twisting strut downward

STEP 3c

. . . toward technician until spring tension is released. Remove spring from slots.

Non-servo; 7 in. Ford rear brakes

sembly by pulling the strut away from the shoe and twisting the shoe downward until spring tension is released. Remove the spring from the slots.

5. To install, reverse the removal procedures. See adjustment procedure, above, for special information on initial adjustment techniques. Wheel bearings on 8 in. drums are adjusted in the same manner as 7 in. drums.

Tracer and Festiva

1. Remove wheel and tire assembly.
2. To remove drum; carefully raise staked portion or the locknut using a small cape chisel, remove nut, bearings and drum.

NOTE: The Festiva and Tracer right spindle and bearing nut have lefthand threads. Thier normal adjustment is obtained by press the brake pedal down firmly several times.

3. Remove hold down springs.
4. Pull front shoe away from backing plate and disconnect from springs.
5. Remove return springs from the rear shoe.
6. Disconnect the anti–rattle spring from the parking brake strut and the rear shoe.

NOTE: Unless broken leave the parking brake strut, adjuster mechanism and adjuster spring in place.

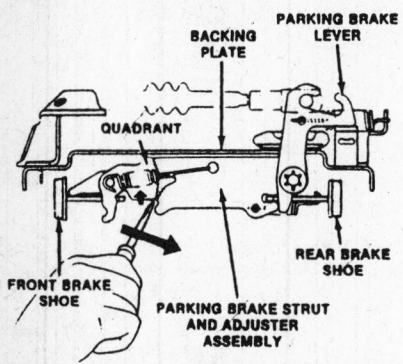

Ford Festiva and Tracer parking brake and adjuster assembly

7. Position new rear shoe in parking brake strut and install hold down spring.
8. Hook return springs in position on the rear shoe.
9. Connect the return springs onto the front shoe.
10. Push the rear shoe down against the backing plate and install hold down spring.
11. Insert a screwdriver between the knurled quadrant and the parking brake strut and twist until the quadrant just touches the backing plate.
12. Install the drum and tighten the bearing nut to a slight bearing preload.

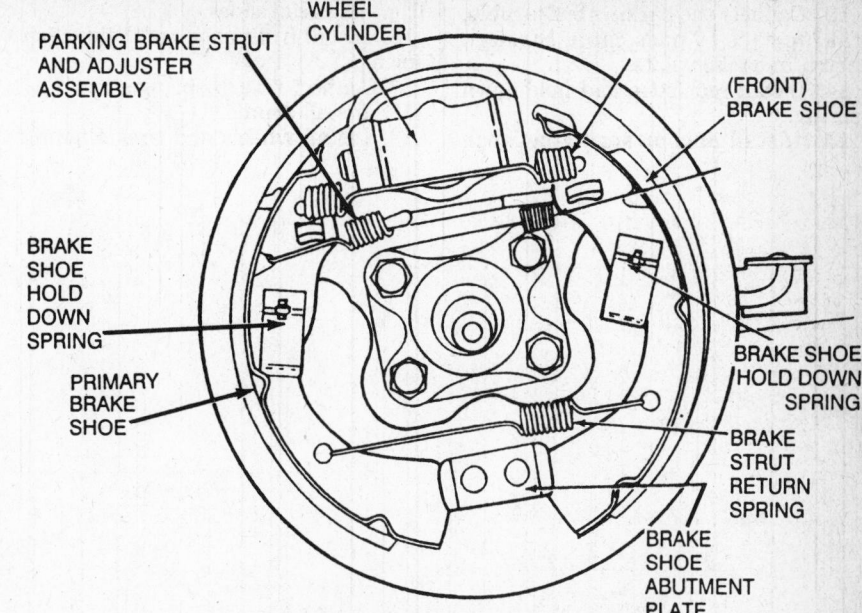

Ford Festiva and Tracer non-servo brakes

With a torque wrench on the lug nut at the 12 o'clock, measure the amount of force needed to rotate the drum. The proper specification are a drum drag of 1.3 to 4.3 inch lbs. not including seal drag.

13. Mount wheel and tire assembly and torque lug nuts.
14. Press the brake pedal down firmly several times to adjust and center the brakes.

GENERAL MOTORS NON-SERVO BRAKES

REMOVAL & INSTALLATION

1. Mark the relationship of the wheel to axle.
2. Remove rear wheels.
3. Remove the brake drum.

NOTE: The brake components are different for right and left sides, so it is important not to interchange them.

2. Remove front shoe hold down spring.
3. Remove anchor (lower) spring.
4. Remove rear shoe hold down spring.
5. Disconnect the parking brake cable from the anchor plate.

6. Disconnect the parking brake cable from teh lever and remove rear shoe and strut together.
7. Remove the adjuster screw assembly by spreading the shoes apart.
8. Remove adjuster from shoe, taking care not to damage C–clip or shim.
To Install:
9. Inspect the brakes.
10. Lubricate the shoe contact areas on the brake backing plate and the web end of the brake shoe which contacts the anchor plate. Use a brake component lubricant or a high temperature brake grease made for the purpose. Lightly lubricate the self–adjusters threads.
11. Install parking brake lever, shim and C–clip on rear shoe, check that the clearance between shoe and lever is .0138 in., if not re–shim.
12. Install strut and adjuster spring on rear shoe.

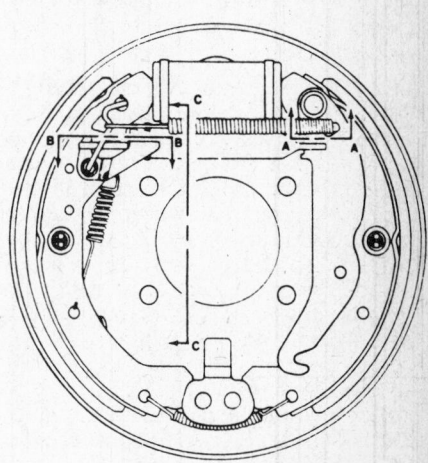

GM non-servo brakes

13. Connect the parking brake cable, taking care to pass cable through notch in anchor plate.

14. Install rear shoe and hold down spring.

15. Install anchor spring between front and rear shoes.

16. Install front shoe and hold down spring.

17 Connect return spring.

18. Install drums.

19. Install wheels and tires aligning the previous marks.

20. Adjust brakes using brake tool through access hole until drums have slight drag. Apply parking brake serveral times and re-check adjustment.

Transfer Case 43

43 TRANSFER CASES

AMC Eagle

Two different models of transfer cases have been used in 4WD American Motors passenger cars. All 1980-81 vehicles use the model 119 transfer case; later vehicles use the model 129 unit with the Select Drive 4WD system. Pars usage and operation are basically the same for both units, though the 129 is equipped for use in the 2WD mode. Minor differences between the two transfer cases will be noted as necessary throughout the section.

NOTE: Refer to the AMC car section for services not listed here.

LUBRICATION

The lubricant capacities and types are as follows:

    1980 model 119 — 3 pints of 10W-30 engine oil

    1981 model 119 — 4 pints of 10W-30 engine oil

    1982 and later model 129 — 7 pints of Dextron® II

NOTE: Lubricant capacities for 1982 and later transfer cases were increased from 6 to 7 pints as per an AMC service bulletin dated 5-84.

——— CAUTION ———

DO NOT use any type of lubricant additive in AMC transfer cases, as their use could cause transfer case damage

TROUBLESHOOTING

Vehicle Wanders or Pulls From a Straight-Ahead Position

1. Check the tire pressures (tires cold). The pressures must be within specification and must not vary more than 1 psi between sides.

2. Check that the tires are all of the same size and type. Replace the tire(s) if necessary until all are matched properly.

3. Check that the lubricant in the transfer case is of the correct type. Drain and refill the transfer case with the correct lubricant, if necessary.

Severe Low Speed Shudder

1. Low level of viscous silicone fluid in the viscous coupling. First, perform the in-car Torque Bias Test as outlined later. Follow the instructions with that procedure to remedy the problem. Check the transfer case fluid; if it is contaminated with viscous fluid, the transfer case must be completely disassembled for inspection. While the unit is disassembled, check for a cracked viscous coupling and/or damaged seal. Replace damaged parts as required.

2. Check that the front and rear axles are of the same gear ratio. Mismatched differential ratios can cause failure of the viscous coupling. Replace one of the gear sets in order to match the other.

Noisy Operation

NOTE: Do not compare the noise of a 4WD vehicle to that of a 2WD vehicle, as 4WD is inherently noisier due to the use of additional drive line components.

1. Check that the lubricant in the transfer case is of the correct type and quantity. Drain and refill, or add fluid as required. Check for fluid leakage.

2. Check the tire pressures, sizes, and styles as mentioned previously. Adjust the tire pressures or replace the tires as required.

In-Vehicle Services

LUBRICANT CHANGE

1. Raise the vehicle and support it safely with jackstands.

2. Place a drain an beneath the transfer case.

3. Remove both the drain and fill plugs and allow the lubricant to drain completely.

4. Install the drain plug and tighten it to 18 ft. lbs.

5. Fill the transfer case with the correct type of lubricant (10W-30 engine oil—119 unit: Dextron® II automatic transmission fluid—129 unit). The lubricant level should be up to the lower edge of the fill plug hole. Install the fill plug.

6. Drive the vehicle 8-10 miles to circulate the fluid throughout the transfer case.

7. Remove the fill plug and top off transfer case to the bottom edge of the fill plughole.

8. Install the fill plug and tighten it to 18 ft. lbs. (1980–81), 25 ft. lbs. (1982 and later).

9. Remove the drain pan from beneath the vehicle.

10. Remove the jackstands and lower the vehicle.

TORQUE BIAS TEST

This test may be performed to determine the condition of the viscous coupling, which is the "heart" of the AMC transfer case. Note that if a malfunction in the coupling is observed, the coupling cannot be repaired in any way—it must be replaced if defective. The following procedure is an in-vehicle test. If the transfer case is to be disassembled, test the coupling as outlined within the overhaul procedure (bench test).

1. Drive the vehicle onto a level surface, turn the engine OFF, and place the transmission shift lever in Neutral. On 1982 and later models, place the Select Drive lever in the 4WD position.

2. Raise one of the front wheels off of the floor, then remove the wheel cover from the raised wheel.

3. Attach a socket (of the same size as the lug nuts) to a torque wrench to any one of the lug nuts of the raised wheel.

4. Rotate the wheel with the torque wrench, and note the amount of torque required to turn the wheel.

5. A reading of 45 ft. lbs. minimum should be obtained. If a reading of less than 45 ft. lbs. was obtained, the transfer case must be disassembled, and the bench test of the coupling should be performed. If the reading was 45 ft. lbs. or more, the coupling is operating properly.

6. Remove the torque wrench and socket, then install the wheel cover and lower the vehicle.

PARTS REPLACEMENT

The following parts of the transfer case may be serviced while the unit is installed in the vehicle:
    a. Front and rear yokes
    b. Yoke seals
    c. Rear bearing and retainer
    d. Speedometer gear
The combined procedure which follows covers the replacement of these items.

1. Raise the vehicle and support it safely with jackstands.

2. Remove the transfer case skid plate.

3. Matchmark the propeller shafts and their respective yokes so that these parts may be properly aligned during assembly.

4. Disconnect the propeller shafts from the yokes, then tie the shafts out of the way.

5. Remove the speedometer cable and adapter from the rear retainer.

  NOTE: Discard the adapter seal. Use a NEW seal during assembly.

6. Support the engine and transmission using a small hydraulic jack with a block of wood placed between the jack and the transmission.

7. Remove the rear crossmember attaching nuts. Carefully lower the transfer case, just enough to gain access to the rear bearing retainer bolts.

8. Matchmark the retainer and the case so that the retainer may be properly reinstalled. Remove the rear yoke nut and seal washer.

9. Remove the rear yoke.

NOTE: If necessary, the front yoke may be removed in the same manner as the rear yoke.

10. Remove the rear retainer bolts. Tap the retainer lightly to loosen and remove it.

11. Remove the differential shim(s) and the speedometer gear from the rear output shaft.

12. If so equipped, remove the output bearing snap-ring. Remove the output bearing from the retainer.

13. Remove the yoke seal from the retainer. Clean the retainer thoroughly and remove the old sealant from the retainer and case mating surfaces.
Assemble the components in the following manner.

1. Install the output bearing into the retainer, making sure that the shielded side of the bearing faces the interior of the transfer case.

2. If so equipped, install the bearing retaining snap-ring.

3. Install a new yoke seal (or both seals, if removed), using Kent-Moore tool J-29162 or its equivalent.

4. Install the speedometer gear and differential shim(s).

5. Coat the mating surface of the retainer and the retainer bolt threads with sealer (Loctite 515 is recommended) and install the retainer. Be sure to align the matchmarks made during disassembly to locate the retainer.

6. Install and tighten the retainer bolts to 23 ft. lbs.

7. Install the yoke(s), new sealing washer(s), and new yoke nut(s). Torque the yoke nut(s) to 120 ft. lbs.

— **CAUTION** —
NEVER reuse the old yoke nuts.

8. Align the front propeller shaft and yoke matchmarks (which were made during disassembly) and attach the propeller shaft to the yoke. Torque the clamp strap bolts to 15 ft. lbs.

9. Install the transfer case drain plug and add the proper amount and type of lubricant to the transfer case.

10. Install the fill plug. Both of the plugs should be torqued to 18 ft. lbs.

11. Raise the transmission, transfer case, and rear crossmember enough to install the crossmember attaching nuts.

12. Install the crossmember attaching nuts and torque them to 30 ft. lbs.

13. Remove the hydraulic jack and wood block.

14. Align the matchmarks, then attach the rear propeller shaft to the yoke. Torque the clamp bolts to 15 ft. lbs.

15. Install a new O-ring seal on the speedometer adapter. Do not reuse the old seal. Install the adapter and cable into the rear retainer.

16. Install the transfer case skid plate.

17. Lower the vehicle.

TRANSFER CASE DISASSEMBLY

1. Remove the transfer case as outlined in the appropriate car section.

2. Remove the drain plug and drain the lubricant from the transfer case.

3. On 1982 and later models only, remove the nut and bolt which attaches the shift motor bracket to the transfer case. Remove the motor and bracket as an assembly.

4. Remove the nuts which attach the yokes. Discard the sealing washers. Remove the yokes.

5. Mount the transfer case on wood blocks which have V-notches cut into them to clear the front transfer case mounting studs.

6. Mark the relationship between the rear retainer and the case. Remove the retainer attaching bolts.

7. Pry the retainer off of the case using two screwdrivers placed into the two slots provided in the retainer for this purpose.

8. Remove the differential shim(s) and the speedometer gear from the rear output shaft.

9. Remove the front case-to-rear case bolts, then pry the cases apart with two screwdrivers.

— **CAUTION** —
Screwdriver slots are provided at each end of the rear case for this purpose.
DO NOT attempt to wedge the two halves apart.

10. Remove the thrust bearing and races from the front output shaft. Note their relationships so that these parts may be reinstalled properly.

11. Remove the oil pump from the rear output shaft, noting its position for reassembly.

12. Remove the rear output shaft from the viscous coupling.

13. Remove the pilot bearing rollers from the shaft coupling. Set the rollers aside in a group.

14. Remove the mainshaft O-ring from the end of the shaft.

15. Remove the viscous coupling from the mainshaft and side gear.

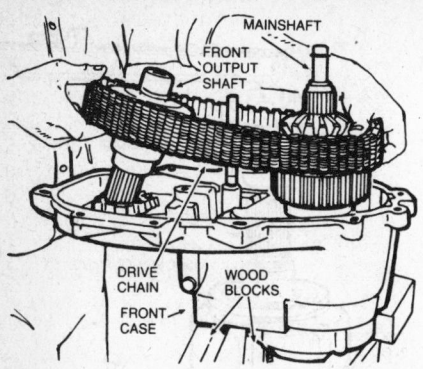

Removing the front output shaft, driven sprocket, and drive chain

16. Lift the front output shaft, sprocket, and chain upward, then tilt the front output shaft toward the mainshaft. Slide the chain off of the mainshaft drive sprocket and remove the assembly.

17. Remove the front thrust bearing assembly. The bearing will be positioned on either the front output shaft or the case.

18. Remove the drive chain from the front output shaft and sprocket.

19. Remove the driven sprocket-to-front output shaft snap-ring. Mark the sprocket and shaft so they may be reassembled properly, then remove the sprocket from the shaft.

20. Remove the mainshaft, side gear, clutch gear, drive sprocket and spline gear as an assembly. Set the assembly aside until disassembly of the front case has been completed.

21. Remove the range fork, rail and clutch sleeve as an assembly. Mark the sleeve and fork so that they be reassembled properly, then remove the sleeve from the fork.

22. On model 119 units, slide the rail out of the fork guide, On model 129 units, remove the pin to separate the fork and the rail, if necessary.

23. Inspect the rail, bracket, and fork for excessive wear, scoring, distortion, etc. Replace any part which is damaged.

24. Slide the rail through the range fork, and on 129 units, install the retaining pin. Set the assembly aside until transfer case assembly.

25. Remove the mainshaft thrust washer from the input gear, then remove the input gear, thrust bearing and race.

26. Remove the detent ball, spring and bolt.

27. Remove the retaining nut and washers from the range sector shaft. Tap the sector shaft with a plastic mallet to remove it from the case.

28. Remove the O-ring seal and seal retainer from the sector shaft bore in the case. The following Steps (29-35)

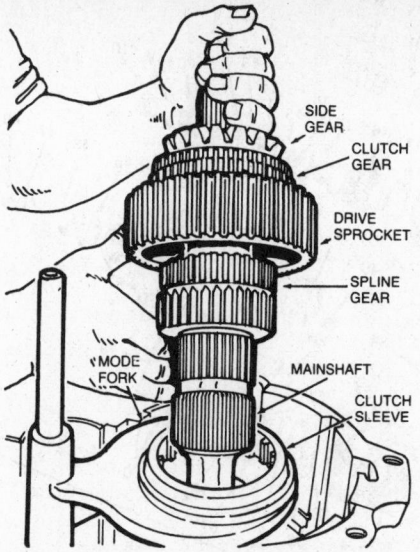

Removing the mainshaft and related components as an assembly

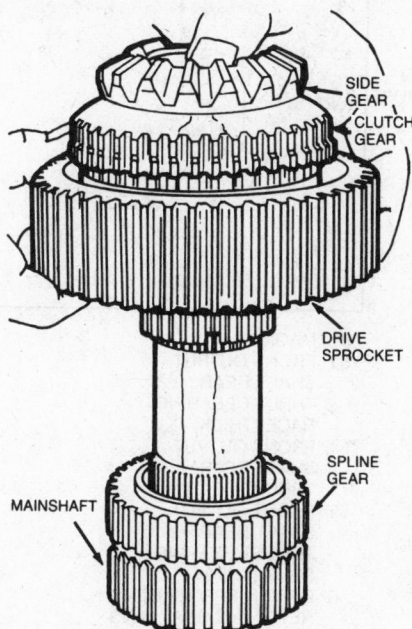

Removing the drive sprocket, clutch gear, side gear, and sprocket carrier

are used to disassemble the mainshaft and gears.

29. Pull the drive sprocket, clutch gear and side gear upward and off of the mainshaft.

30. Remove the needle bearings (82) and two bearing spacers from the mainshaft. Note the position of the spacers so that they may be reinstalled properly.

31. Remove the spline gear and thrust washer from the mainshaft.

32. Remove the side gear, clutch gear and thrust washer from the sprocket carrier and sprocket.

33. Remove the clutch gear and thrust washer from the side gear.

34. Remove the sprocket carrier snap-ring, then remove the drive sprocket from the carrier. Mark the sprocket and the carrier so that they may be reassembled in their proper relationship.

35. Remove the bearing spacers (3) and the sprocket carrier needle bearings (120) from the carrier.

——— **CAUTION** ———

DO NOT intermix the mainshaft needle bearings (Step 30) with the sprocket carrier needle bearings, as they are of different sizes.

36. Remove the rear output bearing and rear yoke seal from the rear retainer. Note that one side of the bearing is shielded—the bearing must be reinstalled in the same directions.

37. Remove the input gear and yoke seals from the front case.

CLEANING

All parts must be thoroughly washed with clean solvent. Be sure that all of the old lubricant and foreign matter has been removed from all transfer case parts. Verify that the oil feed ports and channels of both case halves are clear by flowing compressed air through them. Inspect all components according to the accompanying Transfer Case Inspection chart.

BEARING, BUSHING, AND SEAL REPLACEMENT
——— **CAUTION** ———

All bearings must be correctly positioned in the transfer case to avoid oil feed hole blockage. Always be sure that the feed holes are not blocked after any bearing has been replaced.

Front Output Shaft/Front Bearing

This bearing may be removed and installed with a bearing driver. Be sure that the driver contacts the bearings squarely, then check that the oil feed hole is not blocked after the bearing is in place.

Front Output Shaft/Rear Bearing

Replacement is performed in the same manner as the "Front Output Shaft - Front Bearing." Be sure that the bearing is seated flush with the edge of the bore in the case to allow room for the thrust bearing.

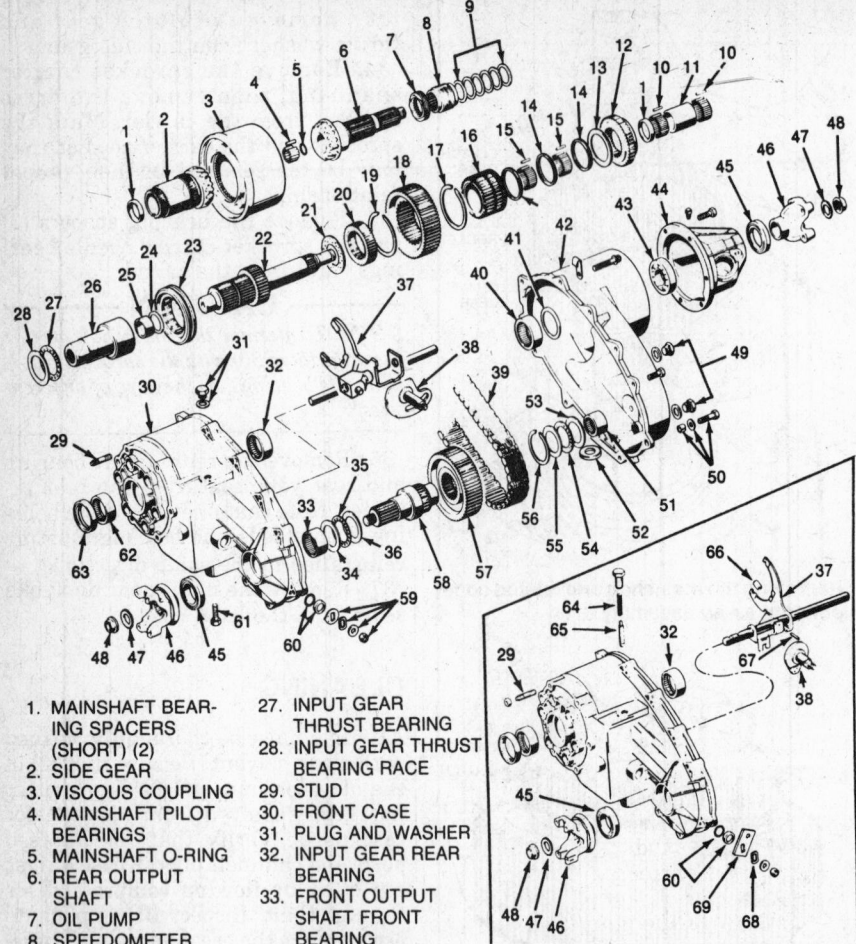

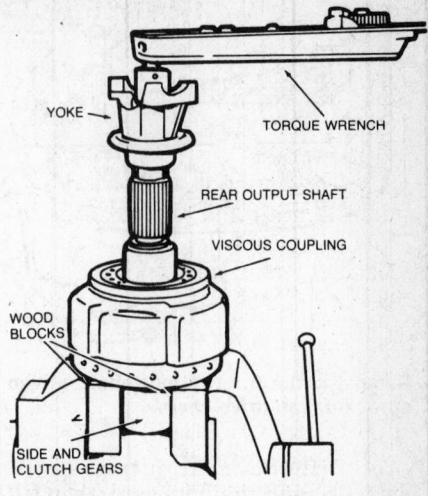

Bench-testing the torque bias of the viscous coupling

1. MAINSHAFT BEARING SPACERS (SHORT) (2)
2. SIDE GEAR
3. VISCOUS COUPLING
4. MAINSHAFT PILOT BEARINGS
5. MAINSHAFT O-RING
6. REAR OUTPUT SHAFT
7. OIL PUMP
8. SPEEDOMETER DRIVE GEAR
9. DIFFERENTIAL SHIMS
10. MAINSHAFT NEEDLE BEARINGS (82)
11. MAINSHAFT NEEDLE BEARING SPACER (LONG) (1)
12. CLUTCH GEAR
13. CLUTCH GEAR THRUST WASHER
14. SPROCKET CARRIER NEEDLE BEARING SPACER (3)
15. SPROCKET CARRIER NEEDLE BEARINGS (120)
16. SPROCKET CARRIER
17. SPROCKET CARRIER SNAP RING
18. DRIVE SPROCKET
19. SPROCKET CARRIER SNAP RING
20. SPLINE GEAR
21. MAINSHAFT THRUST WASHER
22. MAINSHAFT
23. CLUTCH SLEEVE
24. MAINSHAFT THRUST WASHER
25. MAINSHAFT BUSHING
26. INPUT GEAR
27. INPUT GEAR THRUST BEARING
28. INPUT GEAR THRUST BEARING RACE
29. STUD
30. FRONT CASE
31. PLUG AND WASHER
32. INPUT GEAR REAR BEARING
33. FRONT OUTPUT SHAFT FRONT BEARING
34. FRONT OUTPUT SHAFT FRONT THRUST BEARING RACE (THICK)
35. FRONT OUTPUT SHAFT FRONT THRUST BEARING
36. FRONT OUTPUT SHAFT FRONT THRUST BEARING RACE (THIN)
37. RANGE FORK AND RAIL
38. RANGE SECTOR
39. DRIVE CHAIN
40. REAR OUTPUT SHAFT BEARING
41. REAR OUTPUT SHAFT BEARING SEAL
42. REAR CASE
43. REAR OUTPUT BEARING
44. REAR RETAINER
45. YOKE SEAL
46. YOKE
47. SEAL WASHER
48. YOKE NUT
49. FILL AND DRAIN PLUGS
50. ALIGNMENT DOWEL, WASHER AND BOLT
51. FRONT OUTPUT SHAFT REAR BEARING
52. MAGNET
53. FRONT OUTPUT SHAFT REAR THRUST BEARING RACE (THICK)
54. FRONT OUTPUT SHAFT REAR THRUST BEARING
55. FRONT OUTPUT SHAFT REAR THRUST BEARING RACE (THIN)
56. DRIVEN SPROCKET RETAINING SNAP RING
57. DRIVEN SPROCKET
58. FRONT OUTPUT SHAFT
59. RANGE SECTOR SHAFT RETAINING LOCKNUT AND WASHERS
60. RANGE SECTOR SHAFT SEAL AND RETAINER
61. POSITIVE LOCK DETENT BOLT
62. INPUT GEAR FRONT BEARING
63. INPUT GEAR SEAL
64. SPRING
65. PLUNGER
66. SHIFT FORK PAD
67. PIN
68. RANGE LEVER COLLAR
69. RANGE LEVER

Exploded view of the AMC 4WD transfer case. Note the minor differences in parts usage for the model 129 unit (shown in inset).

Input Gear Front and Rear Bearings

1. Drive both bearings out at the same time, using an appropriate bearing driver.

2. Drive the new bearings into place one at a time (rear bearing first).

3. After installation, check that the oil feed holes are not blocked, and that the bearings are flush with the case bore surface.

4. Carefully drive a new oil seal into place.

Rear Output Shaft Bearing Race

1. Pull the race from the transfer case bore using a slide hammer and an appropriate adapter.

2. Using a small screwdriver, carefully pry out the rear output lip seal.

3. Install a new output lip seal.

4. Carefully drive a new bearing race into place, using a bearing driver.

5. Remove the tool, then check to make sure that the oil feed hole is clear.

Mainshaft Pilot Bushing

1. Position the input gear on an opened vise (bushing facing downward). The vise must be opened enough for the bushing to be clear of the vise jaws when pulled downward.

2. Using a slide hammer-type bushing puller, remove the bushing.

3. Drive the new bushing into place, making sure that the oil feed hole is properly aligned.

Rear Retainer Bearing and Seal

1. Remove the bearing using a brass drift and a hammer. The seal is removed in the same manner.

TRANSFER CASE INSPECTION

Inspect the:	For the following conditions:
Gear teeth	1,2
Gear splines	1,2,3,4
Snap-rings and thrust washers	1,2,5
Case halves and rear retainer	5,6,7,8,9
Viscous coupling	10,11,12
Needle, roller, ball, and thrust bearings	1,2,6,13,14
Bearing bores	1,2,5,6

1. Excessive wear
2. Damage
3. Burrs
4. Nicks (minor scratches may be smoothed with an oil-stone)
5. Distortion
6. Cracks
7. Porosity
8. Damaged mating surfaces
9. Stripped bolt threads
10. Perform bench-test of torque-bias
11. Damaged pinions and/or carrier
12. Fluid leakage
13. Note that the front output shaft thrust bearing surfaces are heat-treated—a brown or blue discoloration should be considered NORMAL.
14. Rotational roughness

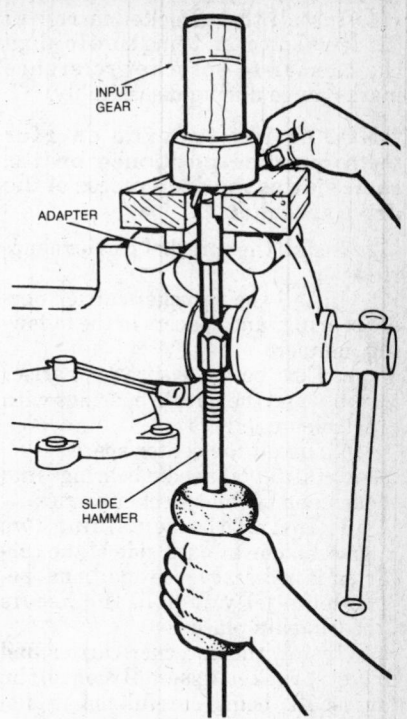

Removing the mainshaft pilot bushing

2. Drive the new bearing into place, making sure that the shielded side of the bearing faces the interior of the transfer case.

3. Carefully drive a new seal into the retainer.

BENCH-TESTING THE VISCOUS COUPLING

This torque bias test should be performed while the transfer case is disassembled for any reason, as the viscous coupling is the key to the operation of the AMC 4WD system. If a viscous coupling problem was previously diagnosed by the in-vehicle torque bias test, the coupling should again be tested according to the following procedure, for fault verification purposes.

1. Install the clutch gear onto the side gear.
2. Install the clutch gear/side gear assembly into the viscous coupling.
3. Mount the coupling and gear assembly in a vise, with wood blocks between the side gear and the vise jaws. Clamp the side gear firmly.
4. Make sure that the clutch gear is firmly engaged in the coupling, then install the rear output shaft in the viscous coupling.
5. Install the yoke on the rear output shaft and attach with the retaining nut.
6. Attach a socket (of the same size as the yoke nut) to a torque wrench. With the socket engaged to the yoke nut, rotate the rear output shaft and note the torque reading obtained with the torque wrench. The minimum acceptable rotational torque reading is 25 ft. lbs. If the reading is at or above 25 ft. lbs., the coupling is okay. If a lower torque reading is obtained, the coupling is defective and must be replaced.

7. Remove the yoke nut and yoke from the rear output shaft, then remove the coupling assembly from the vise.

TRANSFER CASE ASSEMBLY

NOTE: All parts should be lubricated prior to assembly, with either the specified lubricant (10W-30 engine oil for the model 119 unit; Dexron® II automatic transmission fluid for the 129), or petroleum jelly if stated within the procedure. DO NOT use any type of heavy grease (e.g. chassis lubricant) during assembly of the transfer case as lubricant of this nature can block the oil passages.

1. Install new yoke oil seals.
2. Install a new O-ring and retainer into the range sector shaft bore of the case.
3. Install the range sector. On model 119 units, install the washers and locknut on the sector shaft. On model 129 units, install the O-ring seal, retainer, range lever, washer, and locknut on the sector shaft.
4. Torque the sector shaft locknut to 17 ft. lbs.
5. Install the thrust bearing and race on the input gear. Install the gear into the front of the case.
6. Install the mainshaft thrust washer into the input gear.
7. Assemble the range fork, rail and clutch sleeve, then install the assembly into the case. Make sure that the rail is fully seated in the case bore.

NOTE: The rail bore of the front case must be perfectly dry. A small amount of oil in the bore will prevent proper sealing of the rail.

8. Install a thrust washer and a new O-ring on the mainshaft.
9. Coat the mainshaft needle bearing surface with petroleum jelly, then install the needle bearings and spacers in the following order.
   a. Install the short bearing spacer on the shaft.
   b. Install the first 41 needle bearings.
   c. Install the long bearing spacer.
   d. Install the remaining 41 needle bearings.
   e. Install the remaining short spacer.

NOTE: When installing the spacers, be careful not to disturb the needle bearings. If necessary, use additional petroleum jelly to hold the bearings in place.

10. Install the splined gear on the mainshaft, being careful not to disturb the bearings.

11. Install the sprocket carrier in the drive sprocket, being sure to align the carrier-to-sprocket reference marks made during disassembly.

NOTE: The tapered carrier teeth must be positioned on the same side as the deep recess of the drive sprocket.

12. Install the sprocket carrier snap-rings.
13. Install the sprocket carrier needle bearings and spacers in the following manner.

    a. Coat both the sprocket carrier recess and the needle bearings with petroleum jelly.

    b. Install the center spacer.

    c. Install 60 needle bearings into each end of the sprocket carrier.

    d. Install the remaining two spacers, one at each side of the carrier. If necessary, use additional petroleum jelly to hold the needle bearings in place.

14. Install the sprocket carrier and drive sprocket assembly onto the mainshaft, being careful not to disturb the bearings. Note that the recessed side of the drive sprocket must face upward.
15. Position the clutch gear thrust washer on the thrust surface of the sprocket carrier.
16. Install the clutch gear on the gear side, with the tapered edge of the clutch gear facing the side gear teeth.
17. Install the side gear and clutch gear assembly onto the mainshaft, being careful not to disturb the bearings. The side gear must be fully seated in the sprocket carrier.
18. Install the mainshaft and gear assembly into the case, being sure that the mainshaft is fully seated in the input gear.
19. Install the driven sprocket on the front output shaft, being sure to align the sprocket-to-shaft reference marks which were made during disassembly. Install the sprocket snap-ring.
20. Install the thick front thrust bearing race into the case, followed by the bearing, then the thin race.
21. Install the drive chain on the driven sprocket.
22. Raise and tilt the driven sprocket and chain in order to attach the opposite end of the chain to the drive sprocket.
23. Align the front output shaft with the bore of the case, then install the shaft. Make sure that the front shaft thrust bearing assembly is fully seated in the case.
24. Install the thin race of the front output shaft rear thrust bearing, fol-

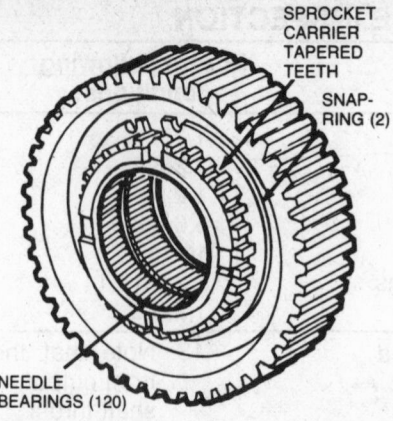

SPROCKET CARRIER TAPERED TEETH

SNAP-RING (2)

NEEDLE BEARINGS (120)

Sprocket carrier and drive sprocket assembly

lowed by the bearing, then the thick rear thrust bearing race.

25. Install the viscous coupling on the side gear and clutch gear. The coupling must be fully seated on the clutch gear, the clutch gear must be flush with the coupling, and the gear teeth should not be visible.
26. Coat the pilot bearing surface of the mainshaft and all of the pilot roller bearings with petroleum jelly. Install the pilot roller bearings on the shaft, using additional petroleum jelly to hold the bearings in place, if necessary.
27. Install the rear output shaft on the mainshaft, then into the viscous coupling. Be careful not to disturb the bearings during shaft installation. The shaft must be fully seated in the coupling; if necessary, tap the shaft with the plastic mallet to seat it.
28. Install the oil pump on the rear output shaft.
29. Install a new rear output shaft bearing oil seal.
30. Apply a bead of sealer (Loctite® 515 is recommended) to the mating surface of the rear case. If removed, reinstall the case magnet.
31. Install the front case to the rear case, being sure to align the dowels at the front case with the bolt holes of the rear case. Seat the rear case onto the front case.

NOTE: If the rear case will not seat completely into the front case, check for the following conditions:

    a. Oil present in the range fork rail bore.

    b. Rear thrust bearing assembly of the front output shaft is not aligned with the rear case.

    c. Mainshaft not completely seated.

    d. Rear case not aligned with the oil pump.

32. Install the rear case-to-front case bolts. Be sure to use flat washers on the bolts at the case ends where the alignment dowels are located. Torque the bolts to 23 ft. lbs.
33. Install the speedometer drive gear and the differential shims on the rear output shaft.
34. Align and temporarily install the rear retainer. Tighten, but do not "final-torque" the bolts.
35. Install the front and rear output shaft yokes. Install the original yoke nuts, then finger-tighten them only.
36. Mount a dial indicator on the rear retainer so that the indicator stylus contacts the rear yoke nut. The stylus must be in line with the rear output shaft.
37. Rotate the front output shaft 10–12 revolutions. Zero the dial indicator and rotate the front shaft one more full revolution. Note the dial indicator reading, which should be 0.002–0.010 in. If the end-play is okay, proceed to the next step. If the end-play is not within specifications, remove the rear retainer and add or subtract differential shims as required. Reinstall the rear retainer, yoke, and nut, the recheck the end play. Repeat if necessary until the end play is correct.
38. Remove the front and rear yokes, then discard the original yoke nuts.
39. Remove the rear retainer. Apply sealer (Loctite® 515 is recommended) to the retainer mating surface and all of the retainer bolt threads. Install the retainer and the bolts. Torque the retainer bolts to 23 ft. lbs.
40. Install the front and rear yokes, using new sealing washers and yoke nuts. Tighten the yoke nuts to 120 ft. lbs.
41. Install the detent ball, spring, and bolt. Apply sealer to the bolt threads and tighten the bolt to 23 ft. lbs.
42. Install the drain plug and washer.
43. Fill the transfer case with the proper types and amount of lubricant (see "Lubrication" at the beginning of this section).
44. Install the fill plug and washer, then tighten both the drain and fill plugs to 18 ft. lbs. (1980–81) 25 ft. lbs. (1982 and later).
45. If removed, install the plug and washer in the front case. Tighten to 18 ft. lbs.
46. On 1982 and later models, install the shift motor and bracket.
47. Reinstall the transfer case according to the procedure in the appropriate car section.

GENERAL CONVERSION TABLE

Multiply By	To Convert	To	
		Length	—
2.54	Inches	Centimeters	.3937
25.4	Inches	Millimeters	.03937
30.48	Feet	Centimeters	.0328
.304	Feet	Meters	3.28
.914	Yards	Meters	1.094
1.609	Miles	Kilometers	.621
		Volume	
.473	Pints	Liters	2.11
.946	Quarts	Liters	1.06
3.785	Gallons	Liters	.264
.016	Cubic inches	Liters	61.02
16.39	Cubic inches	Cubic cms.	.061
28.3	Cubic feet	Liters	.0353
		Mass (Weight)	
28.35	Ounces	Grams	.035
.4536	Pounds	Kilograms	2.20
		Area	
.645	Square inches	Square cms.	.155
.836	Square yds.	Square meters	1.196
		Force	
4.448	Pounds	Newtons	.225
.138	Ft./lbs.	Kilogram/meters	7.23
1.36	Ft./lbs.	Newton-meters	.737
.112	In./lbs.	Newton-meters	8.844
		Pressure	
.068	Psi	Atmospheres	14.7
6.89	Psi	Kilopascals	.145
		Other	
1.104	Horsepower (DIN)	Horsepower (SAE)	.9861
.746	Horsepower (SAE)	Kilowatts (KW)	1.34
1.60	Mph	Km/h	.625
.425	Mpg	Km/1	2.35
—	To obtain	From	Multiply by

TAP DRILL SIZES

NATIONAL COARSE OR U.S.S.						NATIONAL FINE OR S.A.E.					
Screw & Tap Size	Threads Per Inch	Use Drill Number	Screw & Tap Size	Threads Per Inch	Use Drill Number	Screw & Tap Size	Threads Per Inch	Use Drill Number	Screw & Tap Size	Threads Per Inch	Use Drill Number
No. 5	40	39	1/2	13	27/64	No. 5	44	37	1/2	20	29/64
No. 6	32	36	9/16	12	31/64	No. 6	40	33	9/16	18	33/64
No. 8	32	29	5/8	11	17/32	No. 8	36	29	5/8	18	37/64
No. 10	24	25	3/4	10	21/32	No. 10	32	21	3/4	16	11/16
No. 12	24	17	7/8	9	49/64	No. 12	28	15	7/8	14	13/16
1/4	20	8	1	8	7/8	1/4	28	3	1 1/8	12	1 3/64
5/16	18	F	1 1/8	7	63/64	5/16	24	1	1 1/4	12	1 11/64
3/8	16	5/16	1 1/4	7	1 7/64	3/8	24	Q	1 1/2	12	1 27/64
7/16	14	U	1 1/2	6	1 11/32	7/16	20	W			

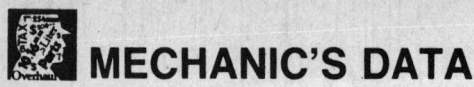
DRILL SIZES IN DECIMAL EQUIVALENTS

Inch	Decimal	Wire	mm	Inch	Decimal	Wire	mm	Inch	Decimal	Wire	mm	Inch	Decimal	Wire & Letter	mm	Inch	Decimal	Letter	mm	Inch	Decimal	mm
1/64	.0156		.39		.0610		1.55		.1285	30			.2090	4			.3160	O			.5315	13.5
	.0157		.4	1/16	.0625		1.59		.1299		3.3		.2126		5.4		.3189		8.1	35/64	.5469	13.89
	.0160	78			.0630		1.6		.1339		3.4		.2130	3			.3228		8.2		.5512	14.0
	.0165		.42		.0635	52			.1360	29			.2165		5.5		.3230	P		9/16	.5625	14.28
	.0173		.44		.0650		1.65		.1378		3.5	7/32	.2188		5.55		.3248		8.25		.5709	14.5
	.0177		.45		.0669		1.7		.1405	28			.2205		5.6		.3268		8.3	37/64	.5781	14.68
	.0180	77			.0670	51		9/64	.1406		3.57		.2210	2		21/64	.3281		8.33		.5906	15.0
	.0181		.46		.0689		1.75		.1417		3.6		.2244		5.7		.3307		8.4	19/32	.5938	15.08
	.0189		.48		.0700	50			.1440	27			.2264		5.75		.3320	Q		39/64	.6094	15.47
	.0197		.5		.0709		1.8		.1457		3.7		.2280	1			.3346		8.5		.6102	15.5
	.0200	76			.0728		1.85		.1470	26			.2283		5.8		.3386		8.6	5/8	.6250	15.87
	.0210	75			.0730	49			.1476		3.75		.2323		5.9		.3390	R			.6299	16.0
	.0217		.55		.0748		1.9		.1495	25			.2340	A			.3425		8.7	41/64	.6406	16.27
	.0225	74			.0760	48			.1496		3.8	15/64	.2344		5.95	11/32	.3438		8.73		.6496	16.5
	.0236		.6		.0768		1.95		.1520	24			.2362		6.0		.3445		8.75	21/32	.6562	16.66
	.0240	73		5/64	.0781		1.98		.1535		3.9		.2380	B			.3465		8.8		.6693	17.0
	.0250	72			.0785	47			.1540	23			.2402		6.1		.3480	S		43/64	.6719	17.06
	.0256		.65		.0787		2.0	5/32	.1562		3.96		.2420	C			.3504		8.9	11/16	.6875	17.46
	.0260	71			.0807		2.05		.1570	22			.2441		6.2		.3543		9.0		.6890	17.5
	.0276		.7		.0810	46			.1575		4.0		.2460	D			.3580	T		45/64	.7031	17.85
	.0280	70			.0820	45			.1590	21			.2461		6.25		.3583		9.1		.7087	18.0
	.0292	69			.0827		2.1		.1610	20			.2480		6.3	23/64	.3594		9.12	23/32	.7188	18.25
	.0295		.75		.0846		2.15		.1614		4.1	1/4	.2500	E	6.35		.3622		9.2		.7283	18.5
	.0310	68			.0860	44			.1654		4.2		.2520		6.4		.3642		9.25	47/64	.7344	18.65
1/32	.0312		.79		.0866		2.2		.1660	19			.2559		6.5		.3661		9.3		.7480	19.0
	.0315		.8		.0886		2.25		.1673		4.25		.2570	F			.3680	U		3/4	.7500	19.05
	.0320	67			.0890	43			.1693		4.3		.2598		6.6		.3701		9.4	49/64	.7656	19.44
	.0330	66			.0906		2.3		.1695	18			.2610	G			.3740		9.5		.7677	19.5
	.0335		.85		.0925		2.35	11/64	.1719		4.36		.2638		6.7	3/8	.3750		9.52	25/32	.7812	19.84
	.0350	65			.0935	42			.1730	17		17/64	.2656		6.74		.3770	V			.7874	20.0
	.0354		.9	3/32	.0938		2.38		.1732		4.4		.2657		6.75		.3780		9.6	51/64	.7969	20.24
	.0360	64			.0945		2.4		.1770	16			.2660	H			.3819		9.7		.8071	20.5
	.0370	63			.0960	41			.1772		4.5		.2677		6.8		.3839		9.75	13/16	.8125	20.63
	.0374		.95		.0965		2.45		.1800	15			.2717		6.9		.3858		9.8		.8268	21.0
	.0380	62			.0980	40			.1811		4.6		.2720	I			.3860	W		53/64	.8281	21.03
	.0390	61			.0981		2.5		.1820	14			.2756		7.0		.3898		9.9	27/32	.8438	21.43
	.0394		1.0		.0995	39			.1850	13			.2770	J		25/64	.3906		9.92		.8465	21.5
	.0400	60			.1015	38			.1850		4.7		.2795		7.1		.3937		10.0	55/64	.8594	21.82
	.0410	59			.1024		2.6		.1870		4.75		.2810	K			.3970	X			.8661	22.0
	.0413		1.05		.1040	37		3/16	.1875		4.76	9/32	.2812		7.14		.4040	Y		7/8	.8750	22.22
	.0420	58			.1063		2.7		.1890		4.8		.2835		7.2	13/32	.4062		10.31		.8858	22.5
	.0430	57			.1065	36			.1890	12			.2854		7.25		.4130	Z		57/64	.8906	22.62
	.0433		1.1		.1083		2.75		.1910	11			.2874		7.3		.4134		10.5		.9055	23.0
	.0453		1.15	7/64	.1094		2.77		.1929		4.9		.2900	L		27/64	.4219		10.71	29/32	.9062	23.01
	.0465	56			.1100	35			.1935	10			.2913		7.4		.4331		11.0	59/64	.9219	23.41
3/64	.0469		1.19		.1102		2.8		.1960	9			.2950	M		7/16	.4375		11.11		.9252	23.5
	.0472		1.2		.1110	34			.1969		5.0		.2953		7.5		.4528		11.5	15/16	.9375	23.81
	.0492		1.25		.1130	33			.1990	8		19/64	.2969		7.54	29/64	.4531		11.51		.9449	24.0
	.0512		1.3		.1142		2.9		.2008		5.1		.2992		7.6	15/32	.4688		11.90	61/64	.9531	24.2
	.0520	55			.1160	32			.2010	7			.3020	N			.4724		12.0		.9646	24.5
	.0531		1.35		.1181		3.0	13/64	.2031		5.16		.3031		7.7	31/64	.4844		12.30	31/32	.9688	24.6
	.0550	54			.1200	31			.2040	6			.3051		7.75		.4921		12.5		.9843	25.0
	.0551		1.4		.1220		3.1		.2047		5.2		.3071		7.8	1/2	.5000		12.70	63/64	.9844	25.0
	.0571		1.45	1/8	.1250		3.17		.2055	5			.3110		7.9		.5118		13.0	1	1.0000	25.4
	.0591		1.5		.1260		3.2		.2067		5.25	5/16	.3125		7.93	33/64	.5156		13.09			
	.0595	53			.1280		3.25		.2087		5.3		.3150		8.0	17/32	.5312		13.49			